PETERSON'S PRIVATE SECONDARY SCHOOLS

2010

PETERSON'S
A nelnet COMPANY

PETERSON'S
A nelnet COMPANY

About Peterson's
To succeed on your lifelong educational journey, you will need accurate, dependable, and practical tools and resources. That is why Peterson's is everywhere education happens. Because whenever and however you need education content delivered, you can rely on Peterson's to provide the information, know-how, and guidance to help you reach your goals. Tools to match the right students with the right school. It's here. Personalized resources and expert guidance. It's here. Comprehensive and dependable education content—delivered whenever and however you need it. It's all here.

For more information, contact Peterson's, 2000 Lenox Drive, Lawrenceville, NJ 08648; 800-338-3282; or find us on the World Wide Web at www.petersons.com/about.

Previous editions under the title *Peterson's Guide to Independent Secondary Schools* © 1980, 1981, 1982, 1983, 1984, 1985, 1986, 1987, 1988, 1989, 1990, 1991, 1992 and *Peterson's Private Secondary Schools* 1993, 1994, 1995, 1996, 1997, 1998, 1999, 2000, 2001, 2002, 2003, 2004, 2005, 2006, 2007, 2008

Stephen Clemente, President; Bernadette Webster, Director of Publishing; Roger S. Williams, Sales and Marketing; Jill C. Schwartz, Editor; Dan Margolin, Research Project Manager; Cathleen Fee, Courtney Foust, Matthew Gazda, James Ranish, Research Associates; Phyllis Johnson, Programmer; Ray Golaszewski, Manufacturing Manager; Linda M. Williams, Composition Manager; Janet Garwo, Mimi Kaufman, Karen D. Mount, Danielle Vreeland, Client Relations Representatives

ISSN 1066-5366
ISBN 13: 978-0-7689-2700-9
ISBN 10: 0-7689-2700-5

Printed in the United States of America

10 9 8 7 6 5 4 3 2 1 11 10 09

Thirtieth Edition

By producing this book on recycled paper (40% post consumer waste) 162 trees were saved.

Contents

INDEX

A Note from the Peterson's Editors

Peterson's Private Secondary Schools 2010 is the authoritative source of information for parents and students who are exploring the alternative of privately provided education. In this edition, you will find information for more than 1,400 schools worldwide. The data published in this guide are obtained directly from the schools themselves to help you make a fully informed decision.

If you've decided to look into private schooling for your son or daughter but aren't sure how to begin, relax. You won't have to go it alone. **What You Should Know About Private Education** can help you plan your search and demystify the admission process. In the articles that follow, you'll find valuable advice from admission experts about applying to private secondary schools and choosing the school that's right for your child.

Schools will be pleased to know that Peterson's helped you in your private secondary school selection.

In "Why Choose an Independent School?" Patrick F. Bassett, President of the National Association of Independent Schools (NAIS), describes the reasons why an increasing number of families are considering private schooling.

If you want a private education for your child but are hesitant about sending him or her away to a boarding school, read "Another Option: Independent Day Schools" where Lila Lohr, former Head of School at Princeton Day School in Princeton, New Jersey, discusses the benefits of day schools.

From Howard and Matthew Greenes' "The Contemporary Boarding School: Change and Adaptability" to The Association of Boarding Schools' (TABS) "Study Confirms Benefits of Boarding School"—if you are having doubts about boarding schools, you'll want to check out these articles!

Mark Braun, Head of School at the Outdoor Academy, offers "Semester Schools: Great Opportunities," which explores various options for students to spend an exciting semester in a new "school-away-from-school."

If you are considering a special needs or therapeutic school for your child, you will want to read "Why a Therapeutic or Special Needs School?" by Diederik van Renesse, an educational consultant who specializes in this area.

To help you compare private schools and make the best choice for your child, check out "Finding the Perfect Match" by Helene Reynolds, a former educational planning and placement counselor.

"Plan a Successful School Search" gives you an overview of the admission process.

If the admission application forms have you baffled and confused, read "Understanding the Admission Application Form," by Gregg W. M. Maloberti, Dean of Admission at The Lawrenceville School.

For the lowdown on standardized testing, Heather Hoerle, Vice President of Member Relations at NAIS, describes the two tests most often required by private schools and the role that tests play in admission decisions in "About Standardized Tests."

In "Paying for a Private Education," Mark Mitchell, Vice President, School Information Services at NAIS, shares some thoughts on financing options.

Then, find out how "Searching for Private Schools Online" can simplify your efforts. Finally, "How to Use This Guide" gives you all the information you need on how to make *Peterson's Private Secondary Schools* work for you!

Next up, the **Quick-Reference Chart,** "Private Secondary Schools At-a-Glance," lists schools by state, U.S. territory, or country and provides essential information about a school's students, range of grade levels, enrollment figures, faculty, and special offerings.

The **School Profiles and Announcements** follow, and it's here you can learn more about particular schools. *Peterson's Private Secondary Schools* contains three **School Profiles and Announcements** sections—one for traditional college-preparatory and general academic schools, one for special needs schools that serve students with a variety of special learning and social needs, and one for junior boarding schools that serve students in middle school grades.

Close-Ups follow each **School Profiles and Announcements** section and feature expanded two-page school descriptions written exclusively for this guide. There is a reference at the end of a profile directing you to that school's **Close-Up.**

The **Specialized Directories** are generated from responses to Peterson's annual school survey. These directories group schools by the categories considered most important when choosing a private school, including type, entrance requirements, curricula, financial aid data, and special programs.

Finally, in the **Index** you'll find the "Alphabetical Listing of Schools" for the page references of schools that have already piqued your interest.

Peterson's publishes a full line of resources to help guide you and your family through the private secondary school admission process. Peterson's publications can be found at your local bookstore, library, and high school guidance office, and you can access us online at www.petersons.com.

We welcome any comments or suggestions you may have about this publication and invite you to complete our online survey at **www.petersons.com/booksurvey.** Or you can fill out the survey at the back of this book, tear it out, and mail it to us at:

Publishing Department
Peterson's, a Nelnet company
2000 Lenox Drive
Lawrenceville, NJ 08648

Your feedback will help us make your educational dreams possible.

Schools will be pleased to know that Peterson's helped you in your private secondary school selection. Admission staff members are more than happy to answer questions, address specific problems, and help in any way they can. The editors at Peterson's wish you great success in your search!

What You Should Know About Private Education

Why Choose an Independent School?

Patrick F. Bassett
President of the National Association of Independent Schools (NAIS)

Why do families choose independent private schools for their children? Many cite the intimate school size and setting, individualized attention, and high academic standards.

Recent research highlights the success of independent school graduates, who outperform graduates from all other types of schools in a whole host of categories, reflecting exceptional preparation for academic and civic life.

Although nearly all independent school graduates go on to attend college, *The Freshman Survey Trends Report*, a study conducted by the Higher Education Research Institute, found that 85 percent of students who attended independent schools that belong to the National Association of Independent Schools (NAIS) went on to attend "very high" or "highly selective" colleges and universities. This "persistence factor" is largely attributable to attending a school with high expectations for all students and a culture that reinforces achievement. The ethos of independent schools contributes to this equation, since everybody is expected to work hard and succeed academically.

NAIS school graduates were also more engaged with their communities than students from other types of schools. Forty-one percent of NAIS graduates said they expected to participate in volunteer or community activities in college, compared to just 24 percent of the whole group. NAIS graduates were also far more inclined to consider "keeping up-to-date with political affairs" essential (46 percent NAIS, 31 percent all).

Another study, the *National Educational Longitudinal Study* (conducted by the U.S. Department of Education) tracked students from public schools, parochial schools, NAIS independent schools, and other private schools from the time they were eighth graders in 1988 until the year 2000. Nearly all of the NAIS students in the NELS study had pursued postsecondary education by their mid-20s. More than three quarters had graduated from a college or university, including 8 percent who completed master's degrees, and 1.5 percent who achieved a Ph.D. or professional degree (e.g., M.D. or LL.B.) by their mid-20s.

With independent schools, you have the opportunity to choose a school with a philosophy, values, and approach to teaching that is the right fit for your child.

Perhaps the most significant factor that distinguished NAIS graduates from graduates of other types of schools was the strength of their commitment to community service and active civic participation. While slightly more than 1 out of 5 survey participants reported volunteering for civic events, nearly one third of NAIS school graduates said that they regularly participated in voluntary activities in their communities. NAIS students were also nearly twice as likely to volunteer to work for political campaigns and political causes. And NAIS students were committed to exercising their civic duty as voters. Whereas slightly more than half of all NELS participants voted in the presidential election before the study, more than 75 percent of NAIS school graduates registered their voices.

Another factor that contributes to the success of students in independent schools is the partnership with families. This coalescing of parental and school voices helps children prosper because the key adults in their lives reinforce a common set of values and speak with a common voice. Indeed, the great achievement of American education is that it offers families many choices of schooling so that they can find a school with a voice and vision to match their own.

Each independent school has a unique mission, culture, and personality. There are day schools, boarding schools, and combination day-boarding. Some independent schools have a few dozen students; others have several thousand. Some are coed; others are single-sex. Some independent schools have a religious affiliation; some are nonsectarian. Most serve students of average to exceptional academic ability, but some serve exclusively those with learning differences, and others serve highly gifted students. The vast majority of independent schools are college-prep.

With independent schools, you have the opportunity to choose a school with a philosophy, values, and approach to teaching that is the right fit for your child.

Make the choice of a lifetime. Choose an independent school.

Another Option: Independent Day Schools

Lila Lohr

For those of us who are fortunate enough to be able to send our children to an independent day school, it seems to offer the best of both worlds. Our children are able to reap the enormous benefits of an independent school education and we, as parents, are able to continue to play a vital, daily role in the education of our children. Parents enjoy being seen as partners with day schools in educating their children.

As more and more independent day schools have sprung up in communities across the country, more and more parents are choosing to send their children to them, even when it might involve a lengthy daily commute. Contrary to some old stereotypes, parents of independent school students are not all cut from the same mold, living in the same neighborhood with identical dreams and aspirations for their children. Independent school parents represent a wide range of interests, attitudes, and parenting styles.

They also have several things in common. Most parents send their children to independent day schools because they think their children will get a better education in a safe, value-laden environment. Many parents are willing to pay substantial annual tuition because they believe their children will be held to certain standards, challenged academically, and thoroughly prepared for college.

This willingness to make what are, for many, substantial financial sacrifices reflects the recognition that much of one's character is formed in school. Concerned parents want their children to go to schools where values are discussed and reinforced. They seek schools that have clear expectations and limits. The nonpublic status allows independent schools to establish specific standards of behavior and performance and to suspend or expel students who don't conform to those expectations.

Understanding the power of adolescent peer pressure, parents are eager to have their children go to school with other teens who are academically ambitious and required to behave. They seek an environment where it is "cool" to be smart, to work hard, and to be involved in the school community. In independent day schools, students spend their evenings doing homework, expect to be called on in class, and participate in sports or clubs.

Successful independent schools, whether elementary or high school, large or small, single-sex or coed, recognize the importance of a school-parent partnership in educating each child. Experienced faculty members and administrators readily acknowledge that, while they are experts on education, parents are the experts on their own children. Gone are the days when parents simply dropped their children off in the morning, picked them up at the end of the day, and assumed the school would do the educating. Clearly, children benefit enormously when their parents and teachers work together, sharing their observations and concerns openly and frequently.

Most independent schools welcome and encourage parental involvement and support.

Independent schools encourage this two-way give-and-take and are committed to taking it well beyond the public school model. Annual back-to-school nights are attended by more than 90 percent of parents. Teacher-parent and student-teacher-parent conferences, extensive written comments as part of the report cards, and adviser systems that encourage close faculty-student relationships are all structures that facilitate this parent-school partnership. Although more and more independent school parents work full-time, they make time for these critical opportunities to sit down and discuss their children's progress.

Most independent schools welcome and encourage parental involvement and support. Although the individual structures vary from school to school, most include opportunities beyond making cookies and chaperoning dances. Many parents enjoy being involved in community service projects, working on school fund raisers, participating in admission activities, sharing their expertise in appropriate academic classes, and even offering student internships. Most schools have made a concerted effort to structure specific opportunities for working parents to participate in the life of the school.

Independent day schools recognize the benefits of parent volunteers and of extending themselves so that parents feel that they are an important part of the school family. Buddy systems that pair new parents with families who have been at the school for several years help ease the transition for families who are new to the independent school sector.

Independent schools have also responded to increased parental interest in programs focusing on parenting skills. Recognizing the inherent difficulties of raising children, independent day schools have provided forums for discussing and learning about drugs, depression, stress management, peer pressure, and the like. Book groups, panel discussions, and workshops provide important opportunities for parents to share their concerns and to get to know the parents of their children's classmates. Schools recognize that this parent-to-parent communication and networking strengthens the entire school community.

Many current day school parents would contend that when you choose an independent day school for your child you are really choosing a school for the entire family. The students become so involved in their academic and extracurricular activities and the parents spend so much time at school supporting those activities that it does become the entire family's school.

Lila Lohr is a former Head of School at Princeton Day School in Princeton, New Jersey, and the Friends School of Baltimore in Baltimore, Maryland. She has been a teacher and an administrator in independent day schools for more than thirty years and is the mother of 3 independent day school graduates.

The Contemporary Boarding School: Change and Adaptability

Howard Greene
Matthew Greene

One of the most telling characteristics of the independent schools since their inception has been their ability to adapt to the significant social, political, and economic movements that have defined the evolutionary unfolding of an extraordinary nation. Those boarding schools that have survived and flourished over time have done so by adapting their curricula, the composition of their student bodies, and their facilities and resources to continue their role in training future leaders, regardless of their social, religious, and economic backgrounds.

How does this continuous state of adaptation and development translate to contemporary boarding school programs and populations? What do these schools stand for? How do they accomplish their primary goals? Here are the key features you should take note of as you consider this unique form of education.

Diversity

The American boarding school is viewed worldwide as an outstanding venue for students to obtain a first-rate education while they interact with a broad mix of other people. The resources and facilities are unmatched in any other country. Currently, more than 11,000 of the enrolled students in NAIS boarding schools are foreign nationals. Some of the larger, internationally recognized American schools enroll a large number of geographically diverse students.

The modern boarding school is, in fact, far more diverse than the local public schools that the majority of American students attend. Significant socioeconomic and continuing racial and ethnic segregation has resulted in homogeneous student bodies in many public school districts across the country. By contrast, boarding schools have a commitment to enroll outstanding students of all economic and social circumstances.

A Sense of Community

School leaders, when asked what defines their particular school, often refer to the power of community that envelops students, teachers, deans and administrators, coaches, and staff members. How valuable this is to all parties, especially to young men and women caught up in today's frenzied, competitive, and disjointed culture where it is easy to feel overwhelmed and uncertain. The desire to be in an environment where peers and adults are engaged with one another in a caring and supportive culture is a driving force for many who feel disconnected from, or simply not fully engaged with, the people and programs in their current school.

A Beacon of Educational Standards

Boarding schools have always set their own standards of educational attainment and pedagogy. Since they are not regulated by state educational bodies or influenced by the agendas of individual or party politics, the school professionals can design an academic and nonacademic curriculum that reflects the standards and goals they have set for their students.

Building Character

While all boarding schools have as their historic mission preparing students for university entrance and a successful academic experience, most have loftier goals in mind. Character is as important as acquired information and credits. Schools emphasize the development of critical thinking and analytical skills, an open mind to new and different ideas and opinions, excellent writing and oral skills, and an ability to think in mathematical and scientific terms. Most boarding schools look beyond these critical intellectual skills to the emotional, social, moral, and intellectual components of the education of the students in their charge. The residential community becomes a vital and active force in developing and honing these crucial skills. Every day, an individual might be called upon to make a decision in the classroom, on the playing field, or in the dormitory or dining hall that can have either a negative or positive impact on another student or the larger community.

The ultimate goal of the boarding school is not to create privileged adolescents who think and act alike but rather to consider the whole child at a critical stage in his or her moral and social development. There is a powerful force of stated ideals in the community at large that can be drawn on to help guide a young woman or man who has to decide how to behave in social situations, the classroom, the playing field, the dormitory, or even at home.

Boarding Schools as a Partnership

The Board of Trustees' Role

The members of the Board of Trustees are committed volunteers who have been elected to work as a cohesive group in overseeing the well-being of the school. The board is a legal entity charged with the responsibility of making certain the school is in sound fiscal and administrative condition and is fulfilling its stated mission. The board oversees the work of the head of school in the broadest sense and determines if he or she is responsibly managing the school. Typically, board members are recent and older graduates, parents of past and current students, or professional experts, all of whom work together to ensure that the school functions soundly on both an educational and financial basis. Boards generally choose their own members on the basis of a commitment to that institution's mission and purposes.

An independent school that is functioning well is, in large measure, the result of a healthy working relationship between the board and the senior management of the school. Together they review the annual operating budget, consider current and long-term strategic planning, and oversee fund-raising—in particular, capital campaigns to enlarge the school's endowment and physical facilities.

A number of schools include students in board meetings and specific committees. Typically, this includes the president of the student council who attends the general board meetings and student leaders who are active members of the student life committee. Their voices play a helpful role in determining school policies, rules, activities, and programs. In addition to the value added to the school community, these students gain a significant learning experience from such a deliberative process.

The School Head's Role

The head of school, reporting to the Board of Trustees, is the chief executive officer and is responsible for the operation of the school. It is his or her responsibility to execute the broad range of academic and noncurricular programs with the assistance of the faculty and other senior administrators, to hire and fire, to lead the faculty, to maintain a sound fiscal operation, to raise money from outside sources, and to serve as the educational visionary for the institution. A successfully run boarding school is a reflection of the mutual respect and effective working relationship between the head and the trustees.

In reviewing the merits of any boarding school for your child, be certain to learn about the relationship between the school head and the board, as well as the composition of the board. The days of a head staying at a school for twenty or thirty years are long gone, though some sitting heads have been in their position for close to that length of time. The norm these days is closer to the decade mark for a successful head running a well-managed school. A long-established or new head is not necessarily a sign either of school strength or weakness. Look beyond a head's tenure to seek out his or her experience level, accomplishments, energy, philosophy, and personal impact on a school.

The Faculty's Role

The opportunity to teach, counsel, and coach students in an intimate setting is what attracts most teachers to boarding schools. It is common practice for a faculty member in her role as dormitory parent, adviser, classroom teacher, coach, or administrator to seek out students whom she identifies as needing her help through the daily interaction that is part and parcel of the boarding life.

Boarding school teachers play an active and respected role in the affairs of their school. They serve on committees that set academic programs, grading standards, requirements for graduation, and standards of behavior. Faculty members work through academic departments to be certain that students are gaining a comprehensive and coherent education.

It is not happenstance that the great majority of boarding school teachers are graduates of strong liberal arts colleges and, most frequently, have graduate degrees in their particular discipline. A great many also played a sport at the intercollegiate level or were actively engaged in campus governance or the arts. The boarding school offers the teacher who loves her academic subject and has other talents the opportunity to share her enthusiasm with her students. The independent status of the school encourages the dedicated teacher to create and deliver a stimulating, effective curriculum that is usually free of topics, content, or lesson plans mandated by outside sources and without an end goal of preparation for standardized testing.

The Students' Role

Despite its traditions and culture, a school can, and often in large part does, reinvent itself every four years as new classes of students enter the school, gradually assume leadership responsibilities, and graduate, making room for new students to take their places. What an individual school "is" represents a shifting target because of the constant influx and egress of students. For prospective students, who those students are when they arrive constitutes one of the most significant influences on the boarding school experience and whether or not it is a good one.

Students in boarding schools today sit in on board meetings, judge fellow students on disciplinary committees, edit papers and yearbooks, serve as proctors or resident advisers in dormitories, and captain sports teams. They also conduct independent study projects, work with faculty as teaching assistants, guide tours on campus, talk with accreditation committees, and babysit faculty members' children. Students are active in community service projects on campus, in town, and around the world. They start new clubs, raise money for capital campaigns, and publish scientific research. They protest, vote, and serve as peer mediators and advisers. They sit around seminar tables discussing advanced literature and historical topics. They speak their minds, challenging faculty and administrators to improve courses, revise standards, and maintain their composure. Students at boarding schools are clearly not passive recipients; rather they are active participants in all aspects of school and community life.

The Parents' Role

One of the major changes in the boarding school partnership in recent years is the more active role that parents play. In past generations when the schools were more homogeneous in their student composition, parents were basically expected to leave the care and education of their children to the school's head and faculty. They were reassured that the moral, spiritual, and intellectual training of their offspring would be seen to. This is a far cry from the relationship contemporary parents, school administrators, and teachers understand as a partnership. Parents expect regular communications from their child's teachers and house advisers regarding student progress or any personal or academic difficulties. Heads of school and deans acknowledge that there is a regular flow of telephone calls and e-mails from the concerned parent. There is greater communication with parents regarding campus events and specific information about their child's engagement and performance.

One of the major changes in the boarding school partnership in recent years is the more active role that parents play.

Parenting a boarding school student involves a balancing act between being overly involved and too distant. Parents should neither assume that boarding schools will take over all parental and educational responsibilities for their children nor seek to insinuate themselves into every aspect of a student's school life. Parents should be watchful, involved, supportive, and attuned to the messages both the school and student are sending regarding the most appropriate and desirable level of engagement.

Schools also acknowledge that past and current parents are a major source of the financial support that enables them to carry on their stated purposes at the highest level of quality. Parents play a significant role in supporting fund-raising efforts and sponsoring events for current and prospective students and their parents. Most boarding schools have established parent committees that help to keep an open line of communication with the school's administrative leaders regarding parental concerns and recommendations for effective support of the students.

The Student Experience

Rather than interpreting discipline strictly as a punitive concept, schools use discipline as a teaching and learning tool. The community of faculty, deans, and students works together to establish agreeable rules of behavior. Each student must abide by this community ethos and, in the process of doing so, learns much about the interests and needs of others, the responsibility of an individual toward the common good, and the self-discipline and restraint that make this possible. The rewards are ample: a sense of responsibility and empowerment and the freedom to carry on one's daily life of activities and studies and time for friends. Those who break the rules find there is a response from the community and that appropriate action is taken.

Students play a major role in the smooth running of their school. Any school head will quickly confirm that his or her students are never shy or reluctant to make their voices heard on issues that affect their lives. Boarding students take it as fact that articulating their opinions to their teachers and administrators is a fundamental right.

Howard R. Greene, M.A., M.Ed., and Matthew W. Greene, Ph.D., have been providing personalized admissions counseling to guide students to the right secondary school, college, or graduate school for more than 35 years. They are the hosts of two PBS specials on college admission and have written numerous books, including the ***Greenes' Guides to Educational Planning Series.***

Originally published in a slightly different form in ***The Greenes' Guide to Boarding Schools*** *(Princeton: Peterson's, 2006), 9-19. Reprinted by permission of the authors.*

Study Confirms Benefits of Boarding School

Many people have long sung the praises of the boarding school experience. The high-level academics, the friendships, and the life lessons learned are without rival at private day or public schools, they say.

Now, a study released by The Association of Boarding Schools (TABS), a nonprofit organization of independent, college-preparatory schools, validates these claims. Not only do boarding school students spend more time studying (and less time watching TV), they are also better prepared for college and progress more quickly in their careers than their counterparts who attended private day or public schools.

The survey, which was conducted by the Baltimore-based research firm the Art & Science Group, involved interviews with 1,000 students and alumni from boarding schools, 1,100 from public schools, and 600 from private day schools (including independent day and parochial schools).

The results not only affirm the benefits enjoyed by boarding school graduates but those bestowed upon current boarding school students as well. "The study helps us better understand how the opportunities for interaction and learning beyond the classroom found at boarding schools impact a student's life at school and into adulthood," explains Steve Ruzicka, TABS executive director. Ruzicka says the survey also will provide boarding school alumni with empirical data to help when considering their children's educational options.

Rigorous Academics Prevail

Why do students apply to boarding schools? The TABS study found that the primary motivation for both applicants and their parents is the promise of a better education. And, happily, the vast majority of current and past students surveyed reported that their schools deliver on this promise. Current students indicated significantly higher levels of satisfaction with their academic experience at boarding schools than their peers at public and private day schools by more than ten percentage points (54 percent of boarding students versus 42 percent of private day students and 40 percent of public school students). Boarders reported in greater relative percentages that they find their schools academically challenging, that their peers are more motivated, and the quality of teaching is very high.

But the boarding environment is valued just as much for the opportunities for interaction and learning beyond the classroom. Interactions in the dining room, the dormitory, and on the playing field both complement and supplement academics, exposing students to a broad geographic and socioeconomic spectrum, challenging their boundaries, and broadening their vision of the world.

The Boarding School Boost

The 24/7 life at boarding schools also gives students a significant leg up when they attend college, the survey documents.

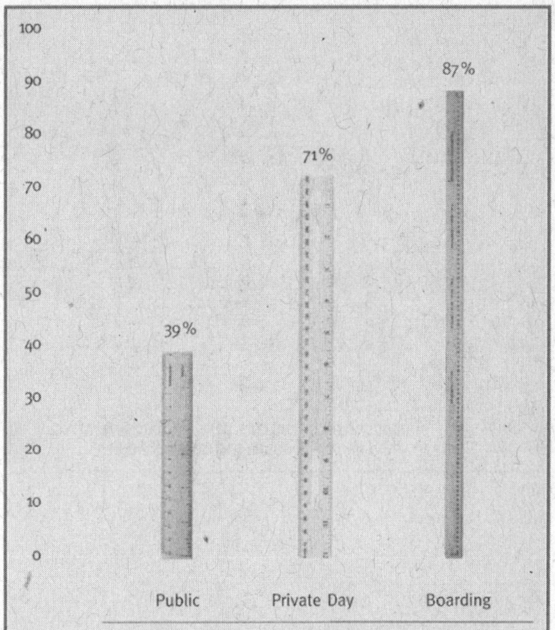

PERCENT OF GRADUATES WHO REPORT BEING VERY WELL PREPARED ACADEMICALLY FOR COLLEGE

Some 87 percent of boarding school graduates said they were very well prepared academically for college, with only 71 percent of private day and just 39 percent of public school alumni saying the same. And 78 percent of boarders reported that their schools also helped better prepare them to face the nonacademic aspects of college life, such as independence, social life, and time management. Only 36 percent of private day graduates and 23 percent of public school graduates said the same. The TABS survey also documented that a larger percentage of boarding school graduates go on to earn advanced degrees once they finish college: 50 percent, versus 36 percent of private day and 21 percent of public school alumni.

Beyond college, boarding school graduates also reap greater benefits from their on-campus experiences, advancing faster and further in their careers comparatively. The study scrutinized former boarders versus private day and public school graduates in terms of achieving positions in top management and found that by midcareer, 44 percent of boarding school graduates had reached positions in top management versus 33 percent of private day school graduates and 27 percent of public school graduates.

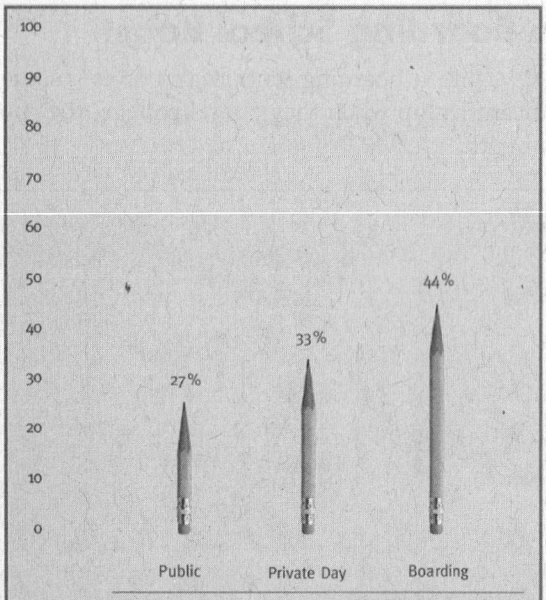

PERCENT OF GRADUATES WHO ACHIEVE POSITIONS IN TOP MANAGEMENT BY MID-CAREER

By late in their careers, more than half of the surveyed boarding school sample, 52 percent, held positions in top management as opposed to 39 percent of private day and 27 percent of public school graduates.

But perhaps the most compelling statistic that the study produced is the extremely high percentage—some 90 percent—of boarding school alumni who say they would, if given the opportunity, repeat their boarding school experience. This alone is a strong argument that validates the enduring value of the boarding school model. It is hoped that the study will help dispel many of the myths and stereotypes that have dogged the image of boarding schools over the last century and spread the good news that boarding schools today are diverse, exciting places for bright, well-adjusted students who are looking for success in their academic lives—and beyond.

For more information on TABS visit the Web site at www.schools.com.

Used by permission of The Association of Boarding Schools.

Semester Schools: Great Opportunities

Mark Braun
Head of School
The Outdoor Academy

Over the last twenty years, there has been tremendous growth in the range of educational opportunities available to young Americans. The advent of semester schools has played no small part in this trend. Similar in many ways to semester-abroad programs, semester schools provide secondary school students the opportunity to leave their home school for half an academic year to have a very different kind of experience—the experience of living and learning within a small community, among diverse students, and in a new and different place. The curricula of such schools tend to be thematic, interdisciplinary, rigorous, and experiential.

At semester schools, students have a full-immersion experience in a tightly knit learning community.

What Are the Benefits?

As a starting point for their programs, semester schools have embraced many of the qualities typical of independent schools. In fact, a number of semester schools were developed as extension programs by existing independent schools, providing unusual opportunities to their own students and those from other schools. Other semester schools have grown from independent educational organizations or foundations that bring their own educational interests and expertise to their semester programs. In both cases, semester schools provide the kind of challenging environment for which independent schools are known.

Across the board, semester school programs provide students with exceptional opportunities for contact with their teachers. Individual instruction and intimate classes are common, as is contact with teachers outside the classroom. At semester schools, students have a full-immersion experience in a tightly knit learning community. In such a setting, teachers are able to challenge each student in his or her own area of need, mentoring students to both academic and personal fulfillment.

Semester schools have developed around specialized curricular interests, often involving unique offerings or nontraditional subjects. In almost every case, these specialized curricula are related to the school's location. Indeed, place-based learning is a common thread in semester school education. Whether in New York City or the Appalachian Mountains, semester schools enable students to cultivate a sense of place and develop greater sensitivity to their surroundings. This is often accomplished through a combination of experiential education and traditional instruction. Students develop academic knowledge and practical skills in tandem through active participation in intellectual discourse, creative projects, hands-on exercises, and service learning opportunities. Throughout, emphasis is placed on the importance of combining intellectual exploration with thoughtful self-reflection, often facilitated by journaling exercises or group processing activities.

At semester schools, students inevitably learn their most important lessons through their membership in the school community. Living closely with peers and teachers and working together for the benefit of the group enables students to develop extraordinary communication skills and high levels of interpersonal accountability. Through this experience, students gain invaluable leadership and cooperation skills.

Ultimately, semester schools seek to impart translatable skills to their students. The common goal is for students to return to their schools and families with greater motivation, empathy, self-knowledge, and self-determination. These skills help to prepare students for the college experience and beyond. In addition, semester school participants report that their experiences helped to distinguish them in the college application process. Semester school programs are certainly not for everybody, but they serve an important role for students who are seeking something beyond the ordinary—

students who wish to know themselves and the world in a profound way. All of the following semester school programs manifest these same values in their own distinctive way.

CITYterm

Now in its thirteenth year, CITYterm is an interdisciplinary, experience-based program that takes 30 juniors and seniors from across the country and engages them in a semester-long study of New York City. CITYterm students typically spend three days a week in the classroom, reading, writing, and thinking about New York City, and three days a week in the city working on projects, studying diverse neighborhoods, or meeting with politicians, urban historians, authors, artists, actors, and various city experts. Much of the excitement of CITYterm comes from experiencing firsthand in the city what has been studied in the classroom. Many of the projects are done in collaborative teams where the groups engage not only in formal academic research at the city's libraries but also use the resources of New York City's residents and institutions to gather the information necessary for presentations. Students come to see themselves as the active creators of their own learning both in the classroom and in the world. Learn more about CITYterm by visiting www.cityterm.org.

The Island School

The Island School, founded in 1999 by The Lawrenceville School, is an independent academic program in the Bahamas for high school sophomores or juniors. The fourteen-week academic course of study includes honors classes in science, field research (a laboratory science), history, math, art, English literature, and physical/outdoor education and a weekly community service component. All courses are place-based and explicitly linked, taking advantage of the school's surroundings to both deepen understandings of complex academic and social issues and to make those understandings lasting by connecting course content with experience. Students apply their investigative, interpretive, and problem-solving skills during four- and eight-day kayaking expeditions, SCUBA diving opportunities, teaching environmental issues to local students, and in daily life at the school. In addition to traditional classroom assessments, students conduct research on mangrove communities, coastal management, artificial reefs, permaculture, and marine protected areas. These projects support national research and are conducted under the auspices of the

Bahamian government. At the conclusion of the semester, students present their work to a panel of visiting scientists and educators, including local and national government officials from the Bahamas. The opportunity to interact with the local community through research, outreach, and the rigorous physical and academic schedule creates a transformative experience for students. The admissions process is competitive, and selected students demonstrate solid academic performance, leadership potential, and a high degree of self-motivation. Contact The Island School for more information at www.islandschool.org.

The Maine Coast Semester

The Maine Coast Semester (MCS) offers a small group of eleventh-grade students the chance to live and work on a 400-acre saltwater peninsula with the goal of exploring the natural world through courses in natural science, environmental issues, literature and writing, art, history, mathematics, and foreign language. Since 1988, MCS has welcomed nearly 1,300 students from more than 230 public and private schools across the country and in Canada. The MCS community is small—39 students and 20 faculty members—and the application process is competitive. In addition to their studies, students work for several hours each afternoon on an organic farm, in a wood lot, or on maintenance and construction projects. Students who attend MCS are highly motivated, capable, and willing to take the risk of leaving friends and family for a portion of their high school career. They enjoy hard work, both intellectual and physical, and they demonstrate a tangible desire to contribute to the world. MCS students return to their schools with self-confidence, an appreciation for the struggles and rewards of community living, and an increased sense of ownership of their education. For information on The Maine Coast Semester, go to www.chewonki.org.

The Mountain School

The Mountain School of Milton Academy, founded in 1984, hosts 45 high school juniors from private and public schools throughout the United States who have chosen to spend four months on a working organic farm in Vermont. Courses provide a demanding and integrated learning experience, taking full advantage of the school's small size and mountain campus. Students and adults develop a social contract of mutual trust that expects individual and communal responsibility, models the values of simplicity and sustainability, and challenges teenagers to engage in meaningful work. Students live with teachers in small houses and help make important decisions concerning how to live together and manage the farm. Courses offered include English, environmental science, U.S. history, and all levels of math, physics, chemistry, Spanish, French, Latin, studio art, and humanities. To learn more about The Mountain School, please visit the Web site at www.mountainschool.org.

The Rocky Mountain Semester

The Rocky Mountain Semester (RMS) at the High Mountain Institute is an opportunity for high school juniors and seniors to examine the human relationship to the natural world through a combination of rigorous academics and extended wilderness expeditions. During the 110-day program, up to 38 students spend five weeks backpacking, skiing, and studying throughout the wilderness of Colorado and Utah. The remainder of the semester is spent on campus near Leadville, Colorado, where students pursue a rigorous course of study and learn how to live successfully in a small community environment. While at the RMS, most students take five or six classes—the only required elective is Practices and Principles: Ethics of the Natural World. It is in this class that students are taught the theoretical foundations for all that is done in the field, examine the human relationship to the natural world, and learn the skills necessary to travel safely and comfortably in remote settings. Students may also take literature of the natural world, natural science, U.S. history or AP U.S. history, Spanish or French, and mathematics. Interested parties can learn more about The Rocky Mountain Semester at www.hminet.org/RockyMountainSemester.

The Outdoor Academy of the Southern Appalachians

The Outdoor Academy offers tenth-grade and select eleventh-grade students from across the country a semester away in the mountains of North Carolina. Arising from more than eighty years of experiential education at Eagle's Nest Foundation, this school-away-from-school provides a college-preparatory curriculum along with special offerings in environmental education, outdoor leadership, the arts, and community service. Each semester, up to 35 students embrace the Southern Appalachians as a unique ecological, historical, and cultural American region. In this setting, students and teachers live as a close-knit community, and lessons of cooperation and responsibility abound. Students develop a healthy work ethic as course work and projects are pursued both in and out of the classroom. Courses in English, mathematics, science, history, foreign language, visual and performing arts, and music emphasize hands-on and cooperative learning. Classes often meet outside on the 180-acre wooded campus or in nearby national wilderness areas, where the natural world enhances intellectual pursuits. On weekends and extended trips, the outdoor leadership program teaches hiking, backpacking, caving, canoeing, and rock-climbing skills. The Outdoor Academy is open to students from both public and private secondary schools and is accredited by the Southern Association of Colleges and Schools. Learn more about The Outdoor Academy at www.enf.org/oa/index.html.

The Oxbow School

The Oxbow School in Napa, California, is a one-semester visual arts program for high school juniors and seniors from public and private schools nationwide. Oxbow offers students a unique educational experience focused on in-depth study in sculpture, printmaking, drawing and painting, and photography and digital media, including animation. The interdisciplinary, project-based curriculum emphasizes experiential learning, critical thinking, and the development of research skills as a means of focused artistic inquiry. Each semester, 2 Visiting Artists are invited to work collaboratively with students and teachers. By engaging students in the creative process, Oxbow fosters a deep appreciation for creativity in all areas of life beyond the classroom. Since its founding in 1998, students who have spent a semester at The Oxbow School have matriculated to leading universities, colleges, and independent colleges of art and design around the country. Learn more at www.oxbowschool.org.

The Woolman Semester

The Woolman Semester is a community-based, interdisciplinary program for high school juniors and seniors and first-year postgraduates. The mission of the school is to weave together peace, sustainability, and social action into an intensely rigorous academic experience. The school is located at the Sierra Friends Center in Nevada City, California, on a 230-acre campus complete with forests, fields, gardens, and livestock to use as a living laboratory, as well as for the wood chopping and lettuce harvesting of daily life! Classes generally meet in the morning, while labs, study groups, and farm work take place in the afternoon. Students and faculty members also participate in a two-week service project and a one-week wilderness trip. Get all the information on The Woolman Semester program at www.woolman.org.

The author wishes to acknowledge and thank all the semester school programs for contributing their school profiles and collaborating in order to spread the word about semester school education.

Why a Therapeutic or Special Needs School?

Diederik van Renesse

Families contact me when a son or daughter is experiencing increased difficulties in school or has shown a real change in attitude at home. Upon further discussion, parents often share the fact that they have spoken with their child's teachers and have held meetings to establish support systems in the school and at home. Evaluations, medications, therapists, and motivational counseling are but a few of the multiple approaches that parents and educators take—yet in some cases, the downward spiral continues. Anxiety builds in the student and family members; school avoidance and increased family turmoil reach a point where the situation is intolerable, and alternatives must be explored—be it a special needs school, a therapeutic school, or a combination of both.

Some families seek the help of an independent education consultant to identify the most appropriate setting.

But should that school be a day or residential school, and how do parents decide which will best meet their child's needs? Resources such as *Peterson's Private Secondary Schools*, the Internet, guidance/school counselors, and therapists are valuable; however, the subtle nuances involved in determining the environment that will best serve the child are difficult to ascertain. Some families seek the help of an independent education consultant to identify the most appropriate setting. Many independent education consultants specialize in working with children who have special needs such as learning differences, anxiety disorders, emotional issues, ADHD, opposition, defiance, school phobia, drug or alcohol abuse, Asperger Syndrome, autism, and more. Consultants have frequent contact with the schools, and they work closely with parents during the enrollment process.

Given the broad spectrum of needs presented by individual students, many parents question whether there is indeed a day school that can meet the needs of their child. The answer often depends on location, space availability, willingness to relocate, and appropriateness of the options. While there are many day school options throughout the United States, there are even more residential or boarding options. Clearly the decision to have your child attend a residential school is not made easily. As a family you may feel as though you do not have a choice—but you should undertake a thorough assessment of all the day options and how they might meet the majority of your child's needs.

When the primary concerns are learning differences, many local options (though often small and issue-specific) are available to families. Local counselors are often valuable resources as are local chapters of national LD organizations. If you come up with a variety of options, carefully compare them by visiting the schools and meeting with the specialists at each school—those individuals who will work directly with your child.

With the day options, it is important to keep the following factors in mind: program and staff credentials, transportation time to and from the school, availability of additional resources (support services) in or outside the school setting, sports and extracurricular offerings, facilities and accessibility, and your child's potential peer group. You will also need to assess many of these factors when considering residential schools, although most residential schools are more self-contained than day schools. Also significant is whether the school has been approved by and accepts funding from its state and/or school district.

For families who cannot avail themselves of local day options or whose child is best served in a residential setting, an even greater spectrum of options is available. These range from traditional boarding schools with built-in academic support services to therapeutic boarding schools, wilderness or outdoor therapeutic programs, emotional growth or behavior modification schools, transitional or independent living programs, and even residential treatment centers, hospitals, or other health facilities.

Given the breadth of the residential schools or programs, most families are best served by a team that includes not only the parents (and at times the student), but also the professionals who have taught, counseled, and worked closely with the child. Together, the team can identify the specific needs, deficits, or behavioral issues that must be addressed, and they can work together to match those with the appropriate schools. As with day schools, you should arrange to visit the facilities so that you are well-informed about each option and will be comfortable with your final decision. These visits are not only opportunities for you to meet the staff and students, but also for you and your child to begin a relationship that will continue when your child is enrolled.

There is no question that seeking alternative options, whether they are special needs or therapeutic, is a daunting task. However, with the help of expert resources and reliable professionals, the right school can make a significant and lasting impact on your child's health and well-being.

Diederik van Renesse is a Senior Partner at Steinbrecher & Partners Educational Consulting Services in Westport, Connecticut. A former teacher, admission director, and private school counselor, he now specializes in helping families throughout the United States and abroad with youngsters who require special needs or alternative schools or who need interventions and therapeutic settings.

Finding the Perfect Match

Helene Reynolds

One of the real benefits of independent education is that it allows you to deliberately seek out and choose a school community for your child. If you are like most parents, you want your child's school years to reflect an appropriate balance of academic challenge, social development, and exploration into athletics and the arts. You hope that through exposure to new ideas and sound mentoring your child will develop an awareness of individual social responsibility, as well as the study skills and work ethic to make a contribution to his or her world. It is every parent's fondest wish to have the school experience spark those areas of competence that can be pursued toward excellence and distinction.

An increasing number of parents realize that this ideal education is found outside their public school system, that shrinking budgets, divisive school boards, and overcrowded classrooms have resulted in schools where other agendas vie with education for attention and money. In this environment there is less time and energy for teachers to focus on individual needs.

The decision to choose a private school can be made for as many different reasons as there are families making the choice. Perhaps your child would benefit from smaller classes or accelerated instruction. Perhaps your child has needs or abilities that can be more appropriately addressed in a specialized environment. Perhaps you are concerned about the academic quality of your local public school and the impact it may have on your child's academic future. Or perhaps you feel that a private school education is a gift you can give your child to guide him or her toward a more successful future.

Every child is an individual, and this makes school choice a process unique to each family. The fact that your father attended a top-flight Eastern boarding school to prepare for the Ivy League does not necessarily make this educational course suitable for all of his grandchildren. In addition to determining the school's overall quality, you must explore the appropriateness of philosophy, curriculum, level of academic difficulty, and style before making your selection. The right school is the school where your child will thrive, and a famous name and a hallowed reputation are not necessarily the factors that define the right environment. The challenge is in discovering what the factors are that make the match between your child and his or her school the right one.

No matter how good its quality and reputation, a single school is unlikely to be able to meet the needs of all children. The question remains: How do families begin their search with confidence so they will find what they are looking for? How do they make the right connection?

As a parent, there are a number of steps you can follow to establish a reasoned and objective course of information gathering that will lead to a subjective discussion of this information and the way it applies to the student in question. This can only occur if the first step is done thoroughly and in an orderly manner. Ultimately, targeting a small group of schools, any of which could be an excellent choice, is only possible after information gathering and discussion have taken place. With work and a little luck, the result of this process is a school with an academically sound and challenging program based on an educational philosophy that is an extension of the family's views and which will provide an emotionally and socially supportive milieu for the child.

Step 1: Identify Student Needs

Often the decision to change schools seems to come out of the blue, but, in retrospect, it can be seen as a decision the family has been leading up to for some time. I would urge parents to decide on their own goals for the search first and to make sure, if possible, that they can work in concert toward meeting these goals before introducing the idea to their child. These goals are as different as the parents who hold them. For one parent, finding a school with a state-of-the-art computer program is a high priority. For another, finding a school with a full dance and music program is important. Others will be most concerned about finding a school that has the best record of college acceptances and highest SAT or ACT scores.

Once you have decided your own goals for the search, bring the child into the discussion. I often say to parents that the decision to explore is *not* the decision to change schools but only the decision to gather information and consider options. It is important to be aware that everyone has an individual style of decision making and that the decision to make a change is loaded with concerns, many of which will not be discovered until the process has begun.

If you have already made the decision to change your child's school, it is important to let your child know that this aspect of the decision is open to discussion but not to negotiation. It is equally important that you let your child know that he or she will have responsibility in choosing the specific school. Without that knowledge, your son or daughter may feel that he or she has no control over the course of his or her own life.

If you have already made the decision to change your child's school, it is important to let your child know that this aspect of the decision is open to discussion but not to negotiation.

Some students are responsible enough to take the lead in the exploration; some are too young to do so. But in all cases, children need reassurance about their future and clarity about the reasons for considering other school settings. Sometimes the situation is fraught with disparate opinions that can turn school choice into a family battleground, one in which the child is the ultimate casualty. It is always important to keep in mind that the welfare of the child is the primary goal.

The knowledge that each individual has his or her own agenda and way of making decisions should be warning enough to pursue some preliminary discussion so that you, as parents, can avoid the pitfall of conflicting goals and maintain a united front and a reasonably directed course of action. The family discussion should be energetic, and differences of opinion should be encouraged as healthy and necessary and expressed in a climate of trust and respect.

There are many reasons why you may, at this point, decide to involve a professional educational consultant. Often this choice is made to provide a neutral ground where you and your child can both speak and be heard. Another reason is to make sure that you have established a sound course of exploration that takes both your own and your child's needs into consideration. Consultants who are up-to-date on school information, who have visited each campus, and who are familiar with the situations of their clients can add immeasurably to the process. They can provide a reality check, reinforcement of personal impressions, and experience-based information support for people who are doing a search of this type for the first time. All the research in the world cannot replace the experience and industry knowledge of a seasoned professional. In addition, if the specific circumstances of the placement are delicate, the educational consultant is in a position to advocate for your child during the placement process. There are also situations in which a family in crisis doesn't have the time or the ability to approach school choice in a deliberate and objective manner.

These are some of the many reasons to engage the services of a consultant, but it is the family guidance aspect that most families overlook at the start of the process and value most highly after they have completed it. A good consultant provides neutral ground and information backup that are invaluable.

Step 2: Evaluate Your Child's Academic Profile

If your child's academic profile raises questions about his or her ability, learning style, or emotional profile, get a professional evaluation to make sure that your expectations for your child are congruent with the child's actual abilities and needs.

Start gathering information about your child from the current school. Ask guidance counselors and teachers for their observations, and request a formal meeting to review the standardized testing that virtually every school administers. Question their views of your child's behavior, attentiveness, and areas of strength and weakness. Make sure you fully understand the reasons behind their recommendations. Do not feel shy about calling back to ask questions at a later date, after you have had time to think and consider this important information. Your child's future may depend on the decisions you are making; don't hesitate to keep asking until you have the information you need.

If a picture of concern emerges, ask the guidance counselor, other parents, or your pediatrician for suggestions regarding learning specialists or psychologists in the community who work with children and can provide an evaluation of their academic ability, academic achievement, and learning style. The evaluation should be reviewed in-depth with the specialist, who should be asked about specific recommendations for changes in the youngster's schooling.

Remember, as the parent, it is ultimately your responsibility to weigh the ideas of others and to decide if the difficulty lies with your child or the environment, either of which could indicate a need for a change of school.

Step 3: Review the Goals of Placement

Discuss your differences of opinion about making a change. Identify a list of schools that creates a ballpark of educational possibilities. (An educational consultant can also be helpful at this stage.)

It is important that both you and your child take the time to consider what characteristics, large and small, you would like in the new school and which you would like to avoid. As you each make lists of priorities and discuss them, the process of school choice enters the subjective arena. The impersonal descriptions of school environments transform into very personal visualizations of the ways you and your child view the child in a new setting.

A chance to play ice hockey, a series of courses in Mandarin Chinese, the opportunity to take private flute lessons, or a desire to meet others from all over the world may sound like a bizarre mix of criteria, but the desire to explore and find all of these options in a single environment expresses the expansiveness of the student's mind and the areas he or she wants to perfect, try out, or explore. Don't expect perfectly logical thinking from your child as he or she considers options; don't take everything he or she says literally or too seriously. Open and respectful discussion will allow a child to embrace a new possibility one day and reject it the next—this is part of the process of decision making and affirmation and part of the fun of exploration.

Step 4: Set an Itinerary

Set an itinerary for visits and interviews so that you and your child can compare campuses and test your preconceived ideas of the schools you have researched against the reality of the campus community; forward standardized testing scores and transcripts to the schools prior to visits so that the admission office has pertinent information in advance of your meeting.

In order to allow your child the freedom to form opinions about the schools you visit, you may want to keep these pointers in mind:

- Parents should allow their child to be front and center during the visits and interviews—allow your child to answer questions, even if they leave out details you think are important.
- Parents should stay in the background and have confidence that the admission officers know how to engage kids in conversation.
- This may be the first time your child has been treated by a school as an individual and responsible person—enjoy watching him or her adjust to this as an observer, not as a protector or participant.
- Don't let your own anxiety ruin your child's experience.
- Discuss dress in advance so it doesn't become the issue and focus of the trip.

Keep your ideas and impressions to yourself and allow your child first shot at verbalizing opinions. Remember that immediate reactions are not final decisions; often the first response is only an attempt to process the experience.

Step 5: Use the Application Process for Personal Guidance

Make sure your child uses the application process not only to satisfy the school's need for information but also to continue the personal guidance process of working through and truly understanding his or her goals and expectations.

Application questions demand your child's personal insight and exploration. Addressing questions about significant experiences, people who have influenced his or her life, or selecting four words that best describe him or her are ways of coming to grips with who your child is and what he or she wants to accomplish both at the new school and in life. Although parents want their children to complete seamless and perfect applications, it is important to remember that the application must be the work of the child and that the parent has an excellent opportunity to discuss the questions and answers to help guide the student in a positive and objective self-review.

It is more important that the application essays accurately reflect the personality and values of the student than that they be technically flawless. Since the school is basing part of its acceptance decision on the contents of the application, the school needs to meet the real student in the application. The child's own determination of what it is important for the school to know about them is crucial to this process. That being said, parents can play an important role in helping the child understand the difference between unnecessarily brutal honesty and putting his or her best foot forward.

Step 6: Trust Your Observations

Although the process of school exploration depends on objectivity, it is rare that a family will embrace a school solely because of its computer labs, endowment, library, SAT or ACT scores, or football team. These objective criteria frame the search, but it tends to be the intangibles that determine the decision. It is the subjective—instinctive responses to events on campus, people met, quality of interview, unfathomable vibes—that makes the match.

It is important to review what aspects of the school environment made you feel at home. These questions apply equally to parent and child. Did you like the people you met on campus? Was the tour informational but informal, with students stopping to greet you or the tour guide? Was the tone of the campus (austere or homey, modern or traditional) consistent with the kind of educational atmosphere you are looking for? Are the sports facilities beyond your wildest expectation? Does the college-sending record give you confidence that your child will find an intellectually comfortable peer group? How long do the teachers tend to stay with the school, and do they send their own children there? If it is a boarding school, do teachers live on campus? How homey is the dorm setup?

The most fundamental questions are: Do people in the school community like where they are, trust each other, have respect for each other, and feel comfortable there? Is it a family you would care to join? These subjective responses will help you recognize which schools will make your child feel he or she is part of the community, where he or she will fit in and be respected for who he or she is and wants to become.

Helene Reynolds is a former educational consultant from Princeton, New Jersey.

Plan a Successful School Search

Application deadlines, entrance exams, interviews, and acceptance or rejection letters—these are some of the challenges you can expect to encounter when applying to private schools. The school search may seem daunting, but it doesn't have to be. Here are some tips to help get you on your way.

The first step is to gather information, preferably in the spring before you plan on applying. *Peterson's Private Secondary Schools*, with vital statistics on more than 1,400 leading private schools in the U.S. and abroad, can help you evaluate schools, clarify your choices, and hone your search.

If you're considering boarding schools, you may also want to obtain a free copy of the *Boarding Schools Directory* from The Association of Boarding Schools (TABS) by calling 202-965-8982 or visiting TABS's Web site (www.schools.com).

Visiting Schools

The next step is to start a list of schools that pique your or your child's interest. You'll want to call, fax, e-mail, or write to admission offices for catalogs and applications. At this stage, don't let cost rule out choices. You'll learn more about the school later—the financing resources it makes available to students and its policies of awarding aid.

With school brochures and catalogs in hand, start planning fall visits and interviews. Review your school calendar, noting Saturdays, holidays, and vacations. Try to plan interviews for these days off. Each interview could last about 3 hours, as campus tours and other activities are often included.

Once you have determined which schools you want to see, where they are, and in what order you want to see them, call each school to set the interview date and time.

Keep in mind that there is no "magic number" of schools to see. Some students interview at and apply to only one school, feeling that if they are not accepted, they will stay at their current school. Some students interview at many, thinking that considering a large number and a variety of schools will help them focus on real needs and desires.

After you've made an appointment to visit the school, reread the school's catalog and, if possible, its description in this guide, and check out its Web site so that facts about the school will be fresh in your mind when you visit.

The Application Process

Once the fact-finding is completed, your child will need to work on applications. Most schools have January or February deadlines, so it pays to begin filling out forms in November.

Applications may ask for all or some of the following: school records, references from teachers, a student statement, a writing sample or essay, an application fee, and medical history form.

If you are working with a hard-copy form, make photocopies of all application pages before your child begins to complete them. That way, he or she will have at least one copy for use as a rough draft. Also make copies of each completed application for your records.

References are usually written on specific school forms and are considered confidential. To ensure confidentiality, people providing references mail their comments directly to the school. A school may require four or five references—three academic references, usually from an English teacher, a math teacher, and one other teacher, and one or two references from other evaluators who know your child's strengths in areas other than academics. Ask these people in advance if they will write on your child's behalf. Give reference-writers appropriate forms with any special instructions and stamped envelopes addressed to the school; be sure to provide as much lead time before the deadline as possible.

Most schools have January or February deadlines, so it pays to begin filling out forms in November.

The student application is completed on a special form and consists of factual family information, as well as some long or short essay questions. As tempting as it may be to help, let your child do the writing. The schools need to see the student's style, mechanical skills, and the way he or she looks at life and education. Some schools require a corrected writing sample from an English assignment. In this case, have your child ask his or her English teacher to help choose his or her best work.

For additional information on applications, including the common application forms, check out "Understanding the Admission Application Form" on page 25.

Once the applications are mailed or submitted online, the hard part is done. Ask admission officers when you can expect to hear their decisions. Most schools will let you know in early March. While you wait, you may want to remind your son or daughter that being turned down by a school is not a statement about his or her worth. Schools have many different objectives in putting a class together. And that's a lesson that will come in handy when you face the college application process.

Understanding the Admission Application Form

Gregg W. M. Maloberti
Dean of Admission
The Lawrenceville School
Lawrenceville, New Jersey

Students applying to independent schools are presented with a myriad of options when it comes time to choose the method of completing the application process. Where once each school issued and required its own paper application, many schools now accept common applications such as the Secondary Schools Application from SSAT (Secondary School Admission Test), the Admission Application Form from TABS (The Association of Boarding Schools), or various other online application forms sponsored by individual schools and placement programs. With so many options, many applicants and parents are perplexed as to which method to employ, and others worry that the choice of one method over another may have a negative effect on their chances of admission. Understanding more about why these changes came about and how they save applicants and schools time and money may help applicants and their parents make an informed choice about which method to use.

The recent developments and innovations in independent school applications mirror the changes that have occurred at the college level. The College Board's Common Application is accepted at over 300 colleges and is available online. The Internet has accelerated the interest in online applications. At the same time, students are much more accustomed to writing on a computer than they once were with pen and paper. Concerns about the financial and environmental costs of a paper-based application that travels from the printer to the school, to the candidate, to the candidate's school, and back to the admission office by mail or courier contribute to the idea that the time of an online commonly accepted application has come.

The current version of the Secondary Schools Application is available on the SSAT Web site at http://www.ssat.org/publicsite.nsf/ssat/info/Application+Service, and the Admission Application Form is available in the TABS Boarding Schools Directory and in electronic form from the TABS Web site: http://www.schools.com/apply/forms.html.

There are a few schools that accept only the recommendation forms from the Admission Application Form. It's best to check with each school to find out which forms are preferred. The list of schools accepting the Secondary Schools Application from SSAT is available at this SSAT website: http://www.ssat.org/publicsite.nsf/ssat/info/Application+Service. The Admission Application Form is available at this TABS Web site: http://www.schools.com/forms/school_list.pdf.

Common Applications Make Sense

Anxious parents' lingering doubts about the use of one of the common application forms are hard to ignore: Will the substitution of the common application for the individual school's application cause the admission committee to be offended and compromise my child's chances for admission? Parents should rest assured that schools agreeing to accept the common application forms believe that a fair and effective admission decision can be made on the basis of the common form and that its use in no way erodes the quality of their selection process.

How Does the Common Application Differ?

All applications begin with a biographical sketch of the candidate: name, address, birth date, mailing address, parents' names, and schools attended. Information regarding sibling or legacy relationships, interest in financial aid, citizenship, language spoken, and even racial and ethnic diversity is collected as well. Except for the order in which these questions appear, there is little variation in these question types from one school's application to another. The common application forms certainly relieve candidates of the burden of providing the very same biographical information over and over again.

The second section of an application generally reveals a candidate's accomplishments and ambitions. Often, the applicants are asked to catalog their interests and activities in list or narrative form. Schools want to know what the candidate has done, for how long, with whom, and to what distinction, if any. In a few cases, some schools ask for a series of short answers to a combination of questions or look for the applicant to complete a sentence. There are generally no "right" answers to these questions—but honest answers can help the school begin to characterize the applicant's curiosity, maturity, ambition, and self-esteem. Here again, great similarity exists in the manner and style with which this information is gathered. While the common application forms ask these question types in a more direct manner, they are no less effective than the individual school's application, and their use affords a candidate a genuine measure of efficiency without compromising individuality.

Schools that advocate the use of their own applications over that of the common application forms often bitterly defend the third and final portion of their applications since it generally includes essay questions. With few exceptions, these questions, while occasionally posed in a unique or original manner, seek to probe much the same territory covered by the three choices listed in the essay section of the common application forms:

1. Describe a person you admire or who has influenced you a great deal.
2. What makes you the interesting person that you are?
3. Explain the impact of an event or activity that has created a change in your life or in your way of thinking.

Many schools that use the common applications require a supplement that affords an opportunity for candidates to provide information that is not requested by the common applications.

While the candidate's ability to write well is certainly under review in the essay question, the exercise investigates a candidate's values and explores the individual experiences that have shaped his or her character. These questions give candidates a chance to reveal such qualities as independence, self-reliance, creativity, originality, humility, generosity, curiosity, and genius. Viewed in this light, answering these questions becomes a tall order. The best advice may be to just answer them. In addition, candidates should recognize that although the content of their essays is always of interest, grammar, spelling, punctuation, organization, and the inclusion of evidence or examples are of equal importance.

Candidates who come from disadvantaged backgrounds often find this section of the application the most challenging and occasionally exclusionary. Some schools assume that all applicants have access to opportunities such as summer camps, music instruction, and periodicals and newspapers. Whatever the case, the common application forms attempt to be more inclusive of a broader set of experiences. In fact, many outreach agencies who seek to identify and place disadvantaged students in independent schools have either used one of the existing common application forms or have developed their own applications in lieu of individual school application forms.

If a student fears that using one of thc common applications will somehow fail to convey a unique aspect of his or her individuality or that the essay question answers will not speak to the unique qualities of why a particular school might be a good match, he or she may want to think about including an extra essay. Just because a candidate uses a common application does not mean that he or she must use a common approach to completing it. Imagine how welcome a splash of creativity might be to an individual reader or committee of admission officers who may read hundreds or even thousands of applications each admission season. An application that parrots the list of school courses, sports, and activities offers little insight into the candidate. A well-written application will be as unique as the individual who wrote it.

Applicants and their parents are not the only winners when a common application form is used. The teachers who dutifully complete countless recommendation forms enjoy the convenience of having to complete only one form for each of their students applying to independent schools. Practically speaking, if there is ever a time that a student wants to be in good favor with his or her teacher, it is the moment at which a reference is being given. Using a common application makes the process of applying to multiple schools a much more manageable endeavor. When there is only one form to complete, most teachers will provide longer and more informative answers that are far more helpful to admission officers. Common applications are a great remedy for the

Using a common application makes the process of applying to multiple schools a much more manageable endeavor.

fatigue and frustration endured by teachers who have been overwhelmed by a barrage of recommendation forms. Currently, there are even more schools accepting common recommendation forms than there are schools accepting the entire Secondary School Application or the Admission Application Form. Before discounting the benefits of a common application, be sure to consider at least the use of the recommendation forms.

Counselors and Consultants Speak Out

Lee Cary, Director of Admissions, Shore Country Day School in Beverly, Massachusetts, has been advising eighth-graders for many years and finds the workload associated with the application process unreasonable for most of her students. "It is inconceivable to expect a 14-year-old student to write upwards of eight individual essays, all of top quality. From taking time for school visits, making up missed schoolwork, organizing forms, completing paperwork, and polishing writing, the act of applying to secondary school becomes a whole second job for eighth-and ninth-grade students." Considering that the average application includes up to ten documents, some of which must pass between the applicant, the sending school, and back to the applicant or the receiving school, an eighth grader and his or her parents are now looking at completing more than eighty documents! On top of the testing process and applying for financial aid, this amounts to an enormous administrative challenge.

Karl Koenigsbauer, Director of Secondary School Placement, Eaglebrook School in Deerfield, Massachusetts, agrees that the common application forms make the process more efficient, but he worries about how they might erode the process as well. "My goal is to help students find the school that will be the best match for their abilities and interests. The essay questions from some schools really help the candidate to understand more about what qualities of mind and spirit a school values. When a candidate comes to me and says a particular question is too difficult, too simplistic, or just plain confusing, it gives me an opportunity to help him or her see how that question represents the identity of that particular school and why it may or may not be a good match. I worry that the common application forms will homogenize the application process to the point where I lose this opportunity to fine-tune the placement process."

Faith Howland, an independent educational consultant in Boston, Massachusetts, and a member of the Independent Educational Consultants Association (IECA), works with families to find the right school and is also often contacted for help when a student's first round of applications has not been successful. "The application process can be near overwhelming for 13- and 14-year-olds. To write as many as eight different applications, each with different essays, just when you are expected to get great grades and continue your sports commitments and other extracurricular activities—not to mention working to prepare for entrance tests. This is high stress! Use of a common application form would be supportive to students and would be extremely helpful in streamlining the teacher recommendations. For those kids who need to submit a second round of applications, the common application forms could be invaluable. These youngsters are coping with disappointment while needing to research new possibilities. If schools were willing to share the common application forms, it's conceivable that many more students who might simply give up if not successful on their first applications could be placed."

Many Schools, One Application

Increased acceptance of the Secondary Schools Application and the Admission Application Form could lead to a marked increase in applications. Common applications are especially helpful to the candidate who fails to earn any acceptance letters at the end of the application process. Traditionally, if a candidate wants to apply to a new list of schools, he or she must start from scratch and complete a new set of forms. Common applications certainly speed up this process, and in the case of the Secondary School Application from SSAT, sending an application to an additional school is as easy as sending the test scores. Candidates simply sign in to their accounts and select another school.

More than half of the candidates who apply to independent schools come from public schools and may not enjoy the benefit of placement counselors at their schools nor do they seek the advice of independent counselors. Regardless, most candidates are well served in using one of the common application forms when applying to multiple schools. One strategy may be to complete a few individual applications and then submit one of the common application forms to a few other schools—identifying some additional options and increasing the likelihood of having meaningful choices after the decision letters are mailed. Many candidates find it much easier to figure out which school they want once they know which school wants them.

Few schools realize how difficult the application process can be for families who are applying to more than one school. Common application forms make the process of applying to multiple schools a much more manageable endeavor. The use of a common application form affords families much more time and energy to devote to other aspects of the application and interview process. By reducing the duplicated paperwork of recommendations and the need to complete so many essays, applicants and their parents are granted a greater opportunity to discuss the real issues surrounding school selection, such as the compatibility of curriculum, style of teaching, and program offerings. Rather than creating folders for each school and chasing down multiple letters of recommendation, applicants and their parents can focus on just a few essays and remove the stress associated with sorting and tracking multiple documents.

Candidates and their families can be assured of the professionalism of admission officers and feel free to use one of the common applications. The Secondary School Application and the Admission Application Form represent the efforts of the very best admission officers who have put the interests of the applicant at the fore—shifting the focus away from the school and back to the candidate. Candidates can be confident that either common application form will more than adequately allow them to make a strong case for their own admission at any school accepting the form.

About Standardized Tests

Heather Hoerle

Vice President, Member Relations
National Association of Independent Schools (NAIS)

Mention the word "testing" to even the most capable student and he or she is likely to freeze in fear. It's no wonder, then, that standardized testing in the independent school admission process causes nail-biting among students and parents alike.

You may be wondering why private schools test prospective students in the first place. In most cases, standardized testing is used to evaluate a student's ability to perform outside of the classroom. Often, testing helps schools to understand whether they have an appropriate program for applicants. In some cases, private schools find they are best equipped to serve students with test results that fit within a specific range or percentile. Note that standardized testing is also used to place accepted students into appropriate classes in their new school.

> ***Often, testing helps schools to understand whether they have an appropriate program for applicants.***

Years ago, I took the Secondary School Admission Test (SSAT) as part of the admission process to a boarding school. After my scores came back, my grim-faced mother called the boarding school's admission director to discuss the results. Much to her relief and surprise, I was accepted by the school in spite of mediocre quantitative testing. Indeed, the strength of my application assured school officials that I was ready for their academic challenge, despite the "average" test results. The SSAT, while an important part of my application, did not tell admission officials about my motivation, nor did it yield any information about my academic and creative achievements.

While it is true that some schools assign a great deal of importance to standardized testing, it is just as true that many schools regard testing as only one part of the application process. Many private schools place equal value on the applicant's campus interview, the student's record of achievement, teacher recommendations, and student/parent written statements. In short, test scores cannot tell an individual's full story, and admission officials recognize this limitation, even as they require standardized testing.

The tests that are most frequently used by private secondary schools are the Secondary School Admission Test Board's SSAT and the Educational Records Bureau's Independent School Entrance Exam (ISEE).

Taking the SSAT

The SSAT, which is used to evaluate applicants for admission to grades 5–11, is a multiple-choice test that measures students' abilities in math and verbal areas and enables counselors to compare students' scores with those of private school applicants and the national school population. The SSAT takes more than 2 hours to complete. Two levels are administered. The lower level exam is taken by students in grades 5–7. The upper level is administered to students in grades 8–11. Students' scores are compared only to students in the same grade. The exam contains multiple-choice questions and a writing sample.

The SSAT is given nationally at more than 600 test sites in all fifty states on selected Saturdays during the school year (in October, November, December, January, February, March, April, and June). It is also given internationally in November, December, January, March, and April.

Applicants can arrange to have SSAT scores sent to several different schools. Registration forms and details about specific test sites, dates, and fees are available at www.ssat.org or by calling 609-683-4440. You can download a free copy of the *SSAT Student Guide* from the Web site. The Secondary School Admission Test Board also sells *Preparing and Applying for Independent School Admission and the SSAT,* a sample test booklet that contains an actual test form for student practice, for a small fee.

Taking the ISEE

The ISEE is used to assess the math and verbal abilities and achievement of students entering grades 5 through 12. The test is administered at three levels: a lower level for students applying to grades 5 and 6; a middle level for those students applying to grades 7 and 8; and an upper level for students applying to grades 9 through 12. Students' scores are compared only to students in the same grade.

The test, which takes about 3 hours to complete, has two components—a multiple-choice segment and a 30-minute essay. The essay, although not scored, gives schools a chance to see a student's writing on an informal topic. The turnaround time for score reporting is seven to ten business days.

The ISEE is administered at sites across the U.S. and abroad on dates chosen by the schools. Families can obtain test dates and locations by requesting a free student guide from the Educational Records Bureau online at www.erbtest.org. The Educational Records Bureau also publishes *What to Expect on the ISEE,* a sample test booklet that contains half-length practice tests.

How Important Are the Tests?

Parents may want to assure their child that his or her fate does not rely solely on test performance. According to admission counselors, test results are only one part of the admission process. Test scores may not directly relate to the grades a student is capable of achieving in school, and tests cannot measure motivation. Because admission representatives know that a student can contribute to the life of the school community in many different ways, they are careful to keep all of an applicant's talents, abilities, and achievements in mind when evaluating his or her potential for success.

Attention Students: Worried About Taking the SSAT or ISEE?

Here are a few tips to help ban the testing blues.

- Get plenty of rest the day before the test. You will need all of your concentration on the test date, and fatigue can wreak havoc on your ability to focus.
- Eat a meal before you take the test. Your brain needs the energy that food provides!
- Carefully read the materials provided by the sponsoring test group several days before testing is scheduled. Often a "practice test" is included in your registration materials and can be helpful in preparing you for the upcoming test.
- Be well prepared. Advance registration materials offer plenty of guidance on what you will need to bring to the test, such as your registration ticket and No. 2 pencils.
- Allow plenty of time to get to your test site. Be sure that you have directions to the test center, and arrive ahead of the test administration time in order to register on-site, find a bathroom, and get acclimated to the setting.
- As you are taking the test, do not get hung up on hard questions. Skip them and move on. If you have time at the end of each test section, return to unanswered questions and try again.
- Don't forget personal "comfort" items. If you have a cold, be sure to bring tissues and cough drops along. Have extra money on hand, since you may want something to drink during the break. Wear layers, just in case you get too hot or too cold while taking the test.
- Finally, relax! While it is important to do your best work on standardized tests, your future does not depend solely on your test results.

Paying for a Private Education

Mark J. Mitchell
Vice President, School Information Services National Association of Independent Schools (NAIS)

Imagine asking a car dealer to sell you a $15,000 sedan for $5000 because that is all you can afford. When you buy a car, you know that you will be paying more than it cost to design, build, ship, and sell the car. The sales staff will not offer you a price based on your income. At best, you may receive discounts, rebates, or other incentives that allow you to pay the lowest price the dealer is willing to accept. As a buyer, you even accept the notion that the car's value will depreciate as soon as you drive it off the lot. No matter how you look at it, you pay more than the car cost to make and ultimately more than it's worth.

Tuition at many private schools can easily approach the cost of a new car; however, paying for a private school education is not the same as buying a car. One difference is the availability of financial aid at thousands of schools in the United States and abroad to help offset the tuition. Imagine asking a school to accept $5000 for a $15,000 tuition because that is all you can afford to pay. That is exactly what private schools that provide need-based financial aid programs accomplish. Learning about the financing options and procedures available at private schools can make this imagined scenario a reality for many families.

Need-Based Financial Aid

Many private schools offer assistance to families who demonstrate financial need. In fact, for academic year 2007–08, schools that belong to the National Association of Independent Schools (NAIS) provided more than $1 trillion in need-based financial aid to nearly 18 percent of their students. The average grant for boarding school students was $20,818 and the average grant for day school students was $10,436. These need-based grants do not need to be repaid and are used to offset the school's tuition. Schools make this substantial commitment as one way of ensuring a socioeconomically diverse student body and to help ensure that every student qualified for admission has the best chance to enroll, regardless of his or her financial circumstances.

How Financial Need Is Determined

Many schools use a process of determining financial need that requires the completion of applications and the submission of tax forms and other documentation to help them decide how much help each family needs. Currently, more than 2,400 schools nationwide ask families to complete The School and Student Service (SSS) Parents' Financial Statement (PFS) online at www.nais.org to determine eligibility for aid. The PFS gathers information about family size, income and expenses, parents' assets and indebtedness, and the child's assets. From this and other information, schools are provided with an estimate of the amount of discretionary income (after several allowances are made for basic necessities) available for education costs. Schools review each case individually and use this estimate, along with such supporting documentation as most recent income tax forms, to make a final decision on your need for a financial aid grant. For more information, please visit www.nais.org/go/parents.

The amount of a need-based financial aid award varies from person to person and school to school. Just as individuals have different financial resources and obligations that dictate their need for assistance, schools have different resources and policies that dictate their ability to meet your financial need. Tuition costs, endowment incomes, and the school's philosophy about financial aid are a few of the things that can affect how much aid a school can offer. If your decision to send your child to a private school depends heavily on getting financial help, you would benefit from applying for aid at more than one school.

Merit-Based Awards

While the majority of aid offered is based on a family's financial situation, not everyone who receives financial assistance must demonstrate financial need. Private schools offer millions of dollars in merit-based scholarships to thousands of students. In the 2007–08 academic year, 299 NAIS-member schools awarded an average annual merit award worth $4151 to students, totaling more than $32.3 million. Even with this level of commitment, such awards are rare (just 5.2 percent of all enrolled students receive this type of aid) and, therefore; highly competitive. They may serve to reward demonstrated talents or achievements in areas ranging from academics to athletics to the arts.

Some additional resources may be available from organizations and agencies in your community. Civic and religious groups, foundations, and even your employer may sponsor scholarships for students at private schools. Unfortunately, these options tend to be few and far between, limited in number and size of award. Be sure to ask a financial aid officer at the school(s) in which you are interested if he or she is aware of such organizations and opportunities.

Whether it is offered by the school or a local organization, be sure to understand the requirements or conditions on which a merit-based scholarship is based. Ask if the award is renewable and, if so, under what conditions. Often, certain criteria must be met (such as minimum GPA, community service, or participation in activities) to ensure renewal of the award in subsequent years. (Some merit awards are available for just one year.)

The financial aid officer at the school is the best source of information about your options.

Tuition Financing Options

Whether or not you qualify for grants or scholarships, another way to get financial help involves finding ways to make tuition payments easier on your family's monthly budget. One common option is the tuition payment plan. These plans allow you to spread tuition payments (less any forms of financial aid you receive) over a period of eight to ten months. In most cases, payments start before the school year begins, but this method can be more feasible than coming up with one or two lump sum payments before the beginning of the school year. Payment plans may be administered by the schools themselves or by a private company approved by the school. They do not normally require credit checks or charge interest; however, they typically charge an application or service fee, which may include tuition insurance.

Since a high-quality education is one of the best investments they can make in their child's future, many parents finance the cost just as they would any other important expense. A number of schools, banks, and other agencies offer tuition loan programs specifically for elementary and secondary school expenses. While such loans are subject to credit checks and must be repaid with interest, they tend to offer rates and terms that are more favorable than those of other consumer loans. It pays to compare the details of more than one type of loan program to find the best one for your needs. Although they should always be regarded as an option of last resort, tuition loan programs can be helpful. Of course, every family must consider both the short- and long-term costs of borrowing and make its decision part of a larger plan for education financing.

A Final Word

Although the primary responsibility to pay for school costs rests with the family, there are options available if you need help. As you can see, financing a private school education can result in a partnership between the family, the school, and sometimes outside agencies or companies, with each making an effort to provide ways to meet the costs. The financial aid officer at the school is the best source of information about your options and is willing to help you in every way he or she can. Always go to the financial aid officer at a school in which you are interested whenever you have any questions or concerns about programs or the application process. Understanding your responsibilities, meeting deadlines, and learning about the full range of options is your best strategy for obtaining assistance. Although there are no guarantees, with proper planning and by asking the right questions, your family just might get the high-quality private education for less.

Searching for Private Schools Online

The Internet can be a great tool for parents gathering information about private secondary schools. The majority of private schools maintain their own Web sites, which often devote a large space to admissions information for prospective students and their parents. There are also many worthwhile third-party sites that are ready to help guide you through the various aspects of the selection process, including Petersons.com.

How Petersons.com Can Help

A great place to start your search is at Peterson's K–12 Planner at www.petersons.com/highschool. The Planner is a comprehensive tool that will help you make sense of the private school admission process. With a variety of options for finding a day or boarding school, www.petersons.com/highschool is your entry point to a wide range of valuable resources.

Peterson's K–12 Planner is organized into various sectors that make it easy for you to find the information you need.

Find a Private School

Peterson's K–12 Planner is organized into various sectors that make it easy for you to find the information you need. You can browse private schools by name or keyword, for starters, or do a detailed search on the following criteria:

- Location (enter a zip code or click on the state's name)
- All-girls schools
- All-boys schools
- Coed schools (boys and girls)
- Military schools
- Boarding schools
- Day schools
- Schools with a postgraduate year
- Junior boarding schools
- Special needs schools

You can enter a school's name in the box under Private Schools Name Search, and you can also do an alphabetical search.

If the schools you are interested in have provided Peterson's with a **Close-Up,** you can do a keyword search on that description. Within the **Close-Up,** schools are given the opportunity to communicate unique features of their programs to prospective students.

Once you have found the school of your choice, simply click on it to get information about the institution, including academic programs and facilities, faculty, student enrollment, applying, athletics, tuition, college acceptance, and graduation requirements.

School Web Site

For institutions that have provided information about their Web site, simply click the Visit School Site link to go directly to the institution's Web site. After you arrive at a school's Web site, look around and get a feel for the place. Often, schools offer virtual tours of the campus, complete with photos and commentary; many schools now offer video tours as well. Look at the admission section to find out what qualities they are looking for in prospective students and what important deadlines must be met. If you have any questions about the admission process or about the school in general, a visit to their Web site often yields an answer.

Get Free Info

If, after looking at the information provided on both Petersons.com and the school's Web site, you still have questions, you will want to use the "Get Free Info" feature to request more information and/or an application directly from the schools that interest you most. Just click on the "Get Free Info" link and send your message. In most instances, if you keep your questions short and to the point, you will receive an answer in no time at all.

Add to My Saved Schools

The My Saved Schools feature is designed to help you with your private school planning. Here you can save the list of schools you're interested in and then revisit at any time, access all the features of the site, and be reminded of important dates.

Prepare for Tests

At Peterson's, we understand that the private school admission process can be stressful. With the stakes so high and the competition getting tighter every year, it's easy to feel overwhelmed. Fortunately, preparing for the private schools' standardized tests can help to exert some control over the options available. By maximizing your test scores you can maximize your options.

At Petersons.com, two timed-full-length practice tests are online (for a small fee) for both the SSAT and the ISEE, the two most common private school admission exams. You can find these practice tests—as well as test information, sample questions, and important dates and deadlines—when you click on "Prepare for Tests" on the K–12 Planner page. Here you will also find test-prep information, a quick quiz, and practice tests for two exams used by private Catholic schools—the Cooperative Entrance Examination (COOP) and the High School Placement Test (HSPT). Practice tests and test-prep information are also available for New York City's Specialized High Schools Admission Test (SHSAT). In addition, on the "Prepare for Tests" page, you'll find Peterson's Advice Center, with such helpful articles as "Does Your Vocabulary Matter? Yes!" and "Beat Test Stress."

Putting It All Together

Choosing a private school is an involved and complicated process. The tools available to you on the Internet can help you to be more productive in this process. Put the information you receive from the schools together with the information you've gathered on the Internet, then use what you've learned to narrow your search to a manageable number of choices.

So, what are you waiting for? Turn on the computer; your child's future alma mater may be just a click away.

How to Use This Guide

Quick-Reference Chart

"Private Secondary Schools At-a-Glance" presents data listed in alphabetical order by state and U.S. territories; schools in Canada and other countries follow state listings. If your search is limited to a specific state, turn to the appropriate section and scan the chart for quick information about each school in that state: Are students boarding, day, or both? Is it coeducational? What grade levels are offered? How many students are enrolled? What is the student/faculty ratio? How many sports are offered? Does the school offer Advanced Placement test preparation?

School Profiles and Announcements

The **School Profiles and Announcements** contain basic information about the schools and are listed alphabetically in each section. An outline of a **School Profile** follows. The items of information found under each section heading are defined and displayed. Any item discussed below that is omitted from a **School Profile** either does not apply to that particular school or is one for which no information was supplied.

Heading Name and address of school, along with the name of the Head of School.

General Information Type (boys', girls', coeducational, boarding/day, distance learning) and academic emphasis, religious affiliation, grades, founding date, campus setting, nearest major city, housing, campus size, total number of buildings, accreditation and memberships, languages of instruction, endowment, enrollment, upper school average class size, and upper school faculty-student ratio.

Upper School Student Profile Breakdown by grade, gender, boarding/day, geography, and religion.

Faculty Total number; breakdown by gender, number with advanced degrees, and number who reside on campus.

Subjects Offered Academic and general subjects.

Graduation Requirements Subjects and other requirements, including community service.

Special Academic Programs Honors and Advanced Placement courses, accelerated programs, study at local college for college credit, study abroad, independent study, ESL programs, programs for gifted/remedial students and students with learning disabilities.

College Admission Counseling Number of recent graduates, representative list of colleges attended. May include mean or median SAT/ACT scores and percentage of students scoring over 600 on each section of the SAT, over 1800 on the combined SAT, or over 26 on the composite ACT.

Student Life Dress code, student council, discipline, and religious service attendance requirements.

Summer Programs Programs offered and focus; location; open to boys, girls, or both and availability to students from other schools; usual enrollment; program dates and application deadlines.

Tuition and Aid Costs, available financial aid.

Admissions New-student figures, admissions requirements, application deadlines, fees.

Athletics Sports, levels, and gender; number of PE instructors, coaches, and athletic trainers.

Computers List of classes that use computers, campus technology, and availability of student e-mail accounts, online student grades, and a published electronic and media policy.

Contact Person to whom inquiries should be addressed.

Announcements, written by school administrators, present information designed to complement the data already appearing in the **School Profile.**

Close-Ups

Close-Ups, written expressly for Peterson's by school administrators, provide in-depth information about the schools that have chosen to submit them. These descriptions are all in the same format to provide maximum comparability. **Close-Ups** follow each **School Profile** section; there is a page reference at the end of a **School Profile** directing you to that school's **Close-Up.** Schools are listed alphabetically in each section.

Special Needs Schools

One of the great strengths of private schools is their variety. This section is dedicated to the belief that there is an appropriate school setting for every child, one in which he or she will thrive academically, socially, and emotionally. The task for parents, counselors, and educators is to know the child's needs and the schools' resources well enough to make the right match.

Schools in this section serve those students who may have special challenges, including learning differences, dyslexia, language delay, attention deficit disorders, social maladjustment to family and surroundings, or emotional disturbances; these students may need individual attention or are underachieving for some other reason. Parents of children who lag significantly behind their grade level in basic academic skills or who have little or no motivation for schoolwork will also want to consult this section. (For easy reference, schools that offer extra help for students are identified in two directories: "Schools Reporting Programs for Students with Special Needs" and "Schools Reporting That They Accommodate Underachievers.") The schools included here chose to be in this section because they consider special needs education to be their primary focus. It is the mission of these schools, whose curricula and methodologies vary widely, to uncover a student's strengths and, with appropriate academic, social, and psychological counseling, enable him or her to succeed.

Junior Boarding Schools

As parents know, the early adolescent years are ones of tremendous physical and emotional change. Junior boarding schools specialize in this crucial period by taking advantage of children's natural curiosity, zest for learning, and growing self-awareness. While junior boarding schools enroll students with a wide range of academic abilities and levels of emoitional self-assurance, their goal is to meet each youngster's individual needs within a supportive community. They accomplish this through low student-teacher ratios and enrollment numbers deliverately kept low.

The boarding schools featured in this section serve students in the middle school grades (6–9); some offer primary programs as well. For more information about junior boarding schools, parents can visit the Junior Boarding Schools Association Web site at www.jbsa.org.

Specialized Directories

These directories are compiled from the information gathered in *Peterson's Annual Survey of Private Secondary Schools.* The schools that did not return a survey or provided incomplete data are not fully represented in these directories. For ease of reference, the directories are grouped by category: type, curricula, financial data, special programs, and special needs.

Index

The "Alphabetical Listing of Schools" shows page numbers for School Profiles in regular type, page numbers for School Profiles accompanied by Announcements in italic type, and page numbers for Close-Ups in boldface type.

Data Collection Procedures

The data contained in *Peterson's Private Secondary Schools* **School Profiles, Quick-Reference Chart, Specialized Directories,** and **Index** were collected through *Peterson's Annual Survey of Private Secondary Schools* during fall and winter 2008–09. Questionnaires were posted online. With minor exceptions, data for those schools that responded to the questionnaire were submitted by officials at the schools themselves. All usable information received in time for publication has been included. The omission of a particular item from a **School Profile** means that it is either not applicable to that school or not available or usable. Because of the extensive system of checks performed on the data collected by Peterson's, we believe that the information presented in this guide is accurate. Nonetheless, errors and omissions are possible in a data collection and processing endeavor of this scope. Therefore, students and parents should check with a specific school at the time of application to verify all pertinent information.

Criteria for Inclusion in This Book

Most schools in this book have curricula that are primarily college preparatory. If a school is accredited or is a candidate for accreditation by a regional accrediting group, including the European Council of International Schools, and/or is approved by a state Department of Education, and/or is a member of the National Association of Independent Schools or the European Council of International Schools, then such accreditation, approval, or membership is stated. Schools appearing in the **Special Needs Schools** section may not have such accreditation or approval.

Quick-Reference Chart

Private Secondary Schools At-a-Glance

	Students Accepted: Boarding Boys	Students Accepted: Boarding Girls	Students Accepted: Day Boys	Students Accepted: Day Girls	Grades: Lower	Grades: Middle	Grades: Upper	Student/Faculty: Total	Student/Faculty: Upper	Student/Faculty Ratio	School Offerings: Advanced Placement Preparation	School Offerings: Sports
UNITED STATES												
Alabama												
Alabama Christian Academy, Montgomery			X	X	K4–5		6–12	1,037	631		X	15
The Altamont School, Birmingham			X	X		5–8	9–12	347	219	5:1	X	18
American Christian Academy, Tuscaloosa			X	X	K–6	7–9	10–12	900	165	12:1	X	35
Briarwood Christian High School, Birmingham			X	X	K–6	7–8	9–12	1,945	568	23:1	X	18
Indian Springs School, Indian Springs	X	X	X	X			8–12	297	297	8:1	X	18
Lyman Ward Military Academy, Camp Hill	X				6–8		9–12	95	60	12:1	X	32
Madison Academy, Madison			X	X	PS–6		7–12	800	400	15:1		7
Marion Academy, Marion			X	X	K4–3	4–6	7–12	82	33	8:1		7
Mars Hill Bible School, Florence			X	X	K–4	5–8	9–12	611	211	14:1	X	14
Randolph School, Huntsville			X	X	K–6	7–8	9–12	904	278	12:1	X	16
St. Paul's Episcopal School, Mobile			X	X	PK–4	5–8	9–12	1,491	558	12:1	X	16
Shades Mountain Christian School, Hoover			X	X	K4–6	7–8	9–12	463	141	22:1	X	15
Trinity Presbyterian School, Montgomery			X	X	K–6	7–8	9–12	980	305	15:1	X	17
Westminster Christian Academy, Huntsville			X	X	K4–5	6–8	9–12	629	215	12:1	X	18
Alaska												
Grace Christian School, Anchorage			X	X	K–6	7–8	9–12	686	264	15:1	X	8
Arizona												
Blueprint Education, Glendale												
Brophy College Preparatory, Phoenix			X				9–12	1,253	1,253	15:1	X	44
Green Fields Country Day School, Tucson			X	X	K–5	6–8	9–12	187	66	4:1	X	14
Lourdes Catholic High School, Nogales			X	X	K–5	6–8	9–12	331	76	10:1		3
New Way Learning Academy, Scottsdale			X	X	K–6	7–8	9–12	119	41	7:1		3
Oak Creek Ranch School, West Sedona	X	X				6–8	9–12	83	73	8:1		55
The Orme School, Mayer	X	X	X	X	1–5	6–8	9–PG	152	130	7:1	X	40
Phoenix Christian Unified Schools, Phoenix			X	X	PS–6	7–8	9–12	732	315	20:1	X	17
Phoenix Country Day School, Paradise Valley			X	X	PK–4	5–8	9–12	728	252	9:1	X	23
St. Gregory College Preparatory School, Tucson			X	X		6–8	9–PG	310	164	10:1	X	23
Saint Mary's High School, Phoenix			X	X			9–12	774	774	17:1	X	19
Salpointe Catholic High School, Tucson			X	X				1,196	1,196	14:1	X	22
Seton Catholic High School, Chandler			X	X			9–12	544	544	14:1	X	15
Southwestern Academy, Rimrock	X	X	X	X			9–PG	32	32	3:1	X	37
Spring Ridge Academy, Spring Valley		X					9–12	70	70	8:1		21
Valley Lutheran High School, Phoenix			X	X			9–12	170	170	8:1		21
Verde Valley School, Sedona	X	X	X	X			9–12	116	116	6:1		43
Xavier College Preparatory, Phoenix				X			9–12	1,198	1,198	22:1	X	29
Arkansas												
Episcopal Collegiate School, Little Rock			X	X		6–8	9–12	376	206	10:1	X	16
Harding Academy, Searcy	X	X	X	X	K–6		7–12	589	288	11:1	X	10
Pulaski Academy, Little Rock			X	X	PK–4	5–8	9–12	1,313	374	13:1	X	21
Subiaco Academy, Subiaco	X		X			8–8	9–12	175	161	9:1	X	41
California												
Academy of Our Lady of Peace, San Diego				X			9–12	731	731	15:1	X	12
Alma Heights Christian Academy, Pacifica			X	X	K–4	5–8	9–12	269	91	6:1		7
Antelope Valley Christian School, Lancaster	X	X	X	X	K–6	7–8	9–12	257	69	11:1	X	11
Archbishop Mitty High School, San Jose			X	X			9–12	1,503	1,503	17:1	X	23
Archbishop Riordan High School, San Francisco			X				9–12	620	620	14:1	X	23
The Archer School for Girls, Los Angeles				X		6–8	9–12	495	283	7:1	X	9
Armona Union Academy, Armona			X	X	K–4	5–8	9–12	120	52	10:1		11
Army and Navy Academy, Carlsbad	X		X			7–8	9–12	269	233	9:1	X	35
The Athenian School, Danville	X	X	X	X		6–8	9–12	453	300	10:1	X	15
Bakersfield Christian High School, Bakersfield			X	X			9–12	506	506	17:1	X	12
Bellarmine-Jefferson High School, Burbank			X	X							X	3
Besant Hill School, Ojai	X	X	X	X			9–12	100	100	4:1	X	36
Bishop Alemany High School, Mission Hills			X	X			9–12	1,460	1,460	18:1	X	16
Bishop Conaty-Our Lady of Loretto High School, Los Angeles				X			9–12	338	338	16:1	X	6
Bishop Garcia Diego High School, Santa Barbara			X	X			9–12	307	307	12:1	X	22
Bishop Montgomery High School, Torrance			X	X			9–12	1,208	1,208	17:1	X	16
Bishop Mora Salesian High School, Los Angeles			X						387	15:1	X	20
The Branson School, Ross			X	X			9–12	320	320	9:1	X	14
Brentwood School, Los Angeles			X	X	K–6	7–8	9–12	984	457	8:1	X	41
Brethren Christian Junior and Senior High Schools, Huntington Beach			X	X		7–8	9–12	368	292	12:1	X	11
Bridgemont High School, San Francisco			X	X		8–8	9–12	54	46	5:1		12
Bridges Academy, Studio City			X	X		6–8	9–12	100	62	9:1		2
The Buckley School, Sherman Oaks			X	X	K–5	6–8	9–12	750	310	8:1	X	9
Campbell Hall (Episcopal), North Hollywood			X	X	K–6	7–8	9–12	1,094	535	8:1	X	20

Private Secondary Schools At-a-Glance

	STUDENTS ACCEPTED				GRADES			STUDENT/FACULTY			SCHOOL OFFERINGS	
	Boarding		Day									
	Boys	Girls	Boys	Girls	Lower	Middle	Upper	Total	Upper	Student/Faculty Ratio	Advanced Placement Preparation	Sports
Capistrano Valley Christian Schools, San Juan Capistrano			X	X	PS–6	7–8	9–12	475	200	13:1	X	13
Cardinal Newman High School, Santa Rosa			X				9–12	436	436	15:1	X	18
Carondelet High School, Concord				X			9–12	800	800	25:1	X	22
Castilleja School, Palo Alto				X		6–8	9–12	415	235	7:1	X	14
Cate School, Carpinteria	X	X	X	X			9–12	265	265	5:1	X	34
Central Catholic High School, Modesto			X	X			9–12	420	420	17:1	X	14
Central Valley Christian Academy, Ceres			X	X	K–5	6–8	9–12	240	94	10:1		14
Chadwick School, Palos Verdes Peninsula			X	X	K–6	7–8	9–12	831	362	6.3:1	X	19
Chaminade College Preparatory, West Hills			X	X			9–12	1,227	1,227	14:1	X	26
Children's Creative and Performing Arts Academy—Capa Division, San Diego	X	X	X	X	K–6	7–8	9–12	265	115	15:1	X	29
Chinese Christian Schools, San Leandro			X	X	K–5	6–8	9–12	908	226	12:1	X	11
Christian Junior–Senior High School, El Cajon			X	X		7–8	9–12	634	451	14:1	X	13
Christian School of the Desert, Bermuda Dunes			X	X	K–5	6–8	9–12	362	95	18:1	X	9
The College Preparatory School, Oakland			X	X			9–12	353	353	6:1	X	11
Cornelia Connelly School, Anaheim				X			9–12	299	299	9:1	X	11
Crespi Carmelite High School, Encino			X				9–12	589	589	23:1	X	15
Crossroads School for Arts & Sciences, Santa Monica			X	X	K–5	6–8	9–12	1,125	492	8:1		21
Crystal Springs Uplands School, Hillsborough			X	X		6–8	9–12	358	250	9:1	X	15
De La Salle High School, Concord			X				9–12	1,048	1,048	28:1	X	19
Drew School, San Francisco			X	X			9–12	245	245	8:1	X	24
Dunn School, Los Olivos	X	X	X	X		6–8	9–12	256	180	7:1	X	39
Eastside College Preparatory School, East Palo Alto	X	X	X	X		6–8	9–12	222	164	8:1	X	5
Emerson Honors High Schools, Orange	X	X	X	X	K–6		7–12	180	110	18:1	X	10
Escondido Adventist Academy, Escondido			X	X	K–5	6–8	9–12	215	105	10:1	X	4
Faith Christian High School, Yuba City			X	X			9–12	114	114	12:1	X	7
Flintridge Sacred Heart Academy, La Canada Flintridge		X		X			9–12	406	406	10:1	X	21
The Frostig School, Pasadena			X	X	1–5	6–8	9–12	120	48	6:1		4
Garces Memorial High School, Bakersfield			X	X			9–12	706	706	28:1	X	15
Grace Brethren School, Simi Valley			X	X	K–6	7–8	9–12	896	261	7:1	X	7
The Grauer School, Encinitas			X	X		6–8	9–12	150	88	7:1	X	30
Halstrom High School, Vista			X	X		7–8	9–12	28	27	1:1		
Halstrom High School—San Diego, San Diego			X	X		7–8	9–12	38	35	4:1	X	
The Harker School, San Jose			X	X	K–5	6–8	9–12	1,720	680	10:1	X	21
Harvard-Westlake School, North Hollywood			X	X		7–9	10–12	1,593	867	8:1	X	21
Head-Royce School, Oakland			X	X	K–5	6–8	9–12	798	341	9:1	X	20
Hebrew Academy, Huntington Beach					N–3	4–6		285		4:1	X	14
Highland Hall, A Waldorf School, Northridge			X	X	N–6	7–8	9–12	390	98	6:1		6
Hillcrest Christian School, Thousand Oaks			X	X	K–6	7–8	9–12	335	52	9:1	X	7
Holy Names High School, Oakland				X			9–12	300	300	11:1	X	13
Idyllwild Arts Academy, Idyllwild	X	X	X	X			9–PG	261	261	12:1	X	31
Immaculate Heart High School, Los Angeles				X		6–8	9–12	521	521			
International High School, San Francisco			X	X	PK–5	6–8	9–12	944	327	10:1		24
Jesuit High School, Carmichael			X				9–12	1,088	1,088	18:1	X	16
Junipero Serra High School, San Mateo			X				9–12	975	975	27:1	X	22
Kings Christian School, Lemoore			X	X	PK–6	7–8	9–12	313	109	15:1	X	17
La Cheim School, Antioch			X	X	4–5	6–8	9–12	20	10	4:1		2
Laurel Springs School, Ojai					1–5	6–8	9–12	1,633	913			
Le Lycee Francais de Los Angeles, Los Angeles			X	X	PS–5	6–8	9–12	732	129	15:1	X	8
Linfield Christian School, Temecula			X	X	K–5	6–8	9–12	855	368	19:1	X	11
Los Angeles Baptist Junior/Senior High School, North Hills			X	X		6–8	9–12	858	597	22:1	X	11
Los Angeles Lutheran High School, Sylmar			X	X		6–8	9–12	212	138	16:1	X	11
Louisville High School, Woodland Hills				X			9–12	454	454	25:1	X	12
Loyola High School, Jesuit College Preparatory, Los Angeles			X				9–12	1,212	1,212	15:1	X	14
Lutheran High School of San Diego, San Diego			X	X			9–12	92	92	12:1	X	7
Marin Academy, San Rafael			X	X			9–12	406	406	9:1	X	33
Marlborough School, Los Angeles				X		7–9	10–12	537	277	5:1	X	13
Marymount High School, Los Angeles				X			9–12	402	402	8:1	X	20
Menlo School, Atherton			X	X		6–8	9–12	750	530	10:1	X	16
Mercy High School, Red Bluff			X	X			9–12	104	104	10:1	X	15
Mercy High School College Preparatory, San Francisco				X			9–12	509	509	15:1	X	10
Mesa Grande Seventh-Day Academy, Calimesa			X	X	K–6	7–8	9–12	281	132	10:1		8
Midland School, Los Olivos	X	X	X	X			9–12	91	91	5:1	X	19
Mid-Peninsula High School, Menlo Park			X	X			9–12	109	109	5:1		7
Milken Community High School of Stephen S. Wise Temple, Los Angeles			X	X		7–8	9–12	790	585	7:1	X	16
Modesto Christian School, Modesto			X	X	K–5	6–8	9–12	650	309	9:1	X	13
Moreau Catholic High School, Hayward			X	X			9–12	930	930	18:1	X	21
Newbury Park Adventist Academy, Newbury Park			X	X						25:1		13
Notre Dame Academy, Los Angeles				X			9–12	470	470	12:1	X	9
Notre Dame High School, Belmont				X			9–12	580	580	16:1	X	16

Private Secondary Schools At-a-Glance

	STUDENTS ACCEPTED				GRADES			STUDENT/FACULTY			SCHOOL OFFERINGS	
	Boarding		Day									
	Boys	Girls	Boys	Girls	Lower	Middle	Upper	Total	Upper	Student/Faculty Ratio	Advanced Placement Preparation	Sports
Oak Grove School, Ojai	X	X	X	X	PK–6	7–8	9–12	200	42	7:1	X	17
Oakwood School, North Hollywood			X	X	K–6		7–12	764	476	7:1	X	44
Ojai Valley School, Ojai	X	X	X	X	PK–5	6–8	9–12	328	125	6:1	X	37
Orangewood Adventist Academy, Garden Grove			X	X	PK–5	6–8	9–12	251	85	10:1	X	7
Orinda Academy, Orinda			X	X		7–8	9–12	104	97	9:1	X	4
Oxford School, Rowland Heights			X	X		7–8	9–12	76	75	11:1	X	6
Pacific Academy, Encinitas			X	X		7–8	9–12	30	27	5:1	X	
Pacific Hills School, West Hollywood			X	X		6–8	9–12	245	194	15:1	X	12
Pacific Lutheran High School, Torrance							9–12	83	83	10:1	X	14
Palma High School, Salinas			X			7–8	9–12	625	444	15:1	X	13
Paradise Adventist Academy, Paradise			X	X	K–4	5–8	9–12	211	77	10:1		3
Polytechnic School, Pasadena			X	X	K–5	6–8	9–12	857	376	17:1		16
Providence High School, Burbank			X	X			9–12	518	518	15:1	X	14
Redwood Christian Schools, Castro Valley			X	X	K–6	7–8	9–12	702	253	24:1	X	8
Ripon Christian Schools, Ripon			X	X	K–5	6–8	9–12	703	264	18:1	X	12
Rolling Hills Preparatory School, San Pedro			X	X		6–8	9–12	240	140	9:1	X	18
Sacramento Adventist Academy, Carmichael			X	X	K–6	7–8	9–12	291	122	12:1		6
Sacramento Country Day School, Sacramento			X	X	PK–5	6–8	9–12	512	149	9:1	X	12
Sacramento Waldorf School, Fair Oaks			X	X	PK–8		9–12	433	155	7:1		31
Sage Hill School, Newport Coast			X	X			9–12	454	454	14:1	X	27
St. Augustine High School, San Diego			X				9–12	700	700	28:1	X	16
St. Catherine's Military Academy, Anaheim	X		X		K–6	7–8		134	81	8:1		24
Saint Elizabeth High School, Oakland			X	X			9–12	225	225	15:1	X	7
Saint Francis High School, Mountain View			X	X			9–12	1,666	1,666	29:1	X	35
Saint John Bosco High School, Bellflower			X				9–12	956	956	16:1	X	16
St. Joseph High School, Santa Maria			X	X			9–12	599	599	18:1		15
St. Margaret's Episcopal School, San Juan Capistrano			X	X	PS–5	6–8	9–12	1,227	404	6:1	X	26
Saint Mary's College High School, Berkeley			X	X			9–12	620	620	16:1	X	11
Saint Matthias High School, Downey				X				271	271	21:1	X	14
St. Michael's Preparatory School of the Norbertine Fathers, Silverado	X						9–12	64	64	3:1	X	11
Saint Monica's High School, Santa Monica			X	X			9–12	625	625	14:1	X	14
Saint Patrick—Saint Vincent High School, Vallejo			X	X			9–12	642	642	30:1	X	13
Salesian High School, Richmond			X	X			9–12	580	580	25:1	X	12
San Diego Academy, National City			X	X	K–6	7–8	9–12			12:1		3
San Diego Jewish Academy, San Diego			X	X	K–5	6–8	9–12	622	181	18:1	X	25
San Domenico School, San Anselmo		X	X	X	PK–5	6–8	9–12	529	135	8:1	X	6
San Francisco University High School, San Francisco			X	X			9–12	395	395	8:1	X	22
San Francisco Waldorf High School, San Francisco			X	X			9–12	148	148	15:1		17
Santa Margarita Catholic High School, Rancho Santa Margarita			X	X			9–12	1,650	1,650	16:1	X	51
Southwestern Academy, San Marino	X	X	X	X		6–8	9–PG	123	107	6:1	X	22
Squaw Valley Academy, Olympic Valley	X	X	X	X		6–8	9–12	84	76	7:1	X	68
Stanbridge Academy, San Mateo			X	X	K–6	7–8	9–12	104	51	8:1		23
Stevenson School, Pebble Beach	X	X	X	X	PK–5	6–8	9–12	756	548	10:1	X	34
Summerfield Waldorf School, Santa Rosa			X	X	K–6	7–8	9–12	380	96	7:1	X	5
The Thacher School, Ojai	X	X	X	X			9–12	249	249	5:1	X	40
Tri-City Christian Schools, Vista			X	X	PK–6	7–8	9–12	1,132	304	12:1	X	18
The Urban School of San Francisco, San Francisco			X	X			9–12	344	344	9:1	X	34
Ursuline High School, Santa Rosa				X			9–12	296	296	14:1	X	12
Valley Christian High School, Dublin			X	X		7–8	9–12	450	290	13:1		9
Valley Christian School, San Jose			X	X	K–5	6–8	9–12	2,285	1,239	17:1	X	20
Victor Valley Christian School, Victorville			X	X	K–6	7–8	9–12	419	165	15:1	X	10
Viewpoint School, Calabasas			X	X	K–5	6–8	9–12	1,210	485	10:1	X	27
Villanova Preparatory School, Ojai	X	X	X	X			9–12	315	315	10:1	X	17
The Waverly School, Pasadena			X	X	PK–6	7–8	9–12	327	101	8:1	X	12
The Webb Schools, Claremont	X	X	X	X			9–12	391	391	7:1	X	30
Western Christian Schools, Covina			X	X		7–8	9–12	483	430		X	10
Westridge School, Pasadena				X	4–6	7–8	9–12	502	288	9:1	X	15
Windward School, Los Angeles			X	X		7–8	9–12	477	328	7:1	X	6
Woodside Priory School, Portola Valley	X	X	X	X		6–8	9–12	352	257	10:1	X	20
Colorado												
Accelerated Schools, Denver	X	X	X	X	K–5	6–8	9–12	52	39	7:1	X	22
Alexander Dawson School, Lafayette			X	X	K–4	5–8	9–12	420	175	7:1	X	33
Bridge School, Boulder			X	X		6–8	9–12	55	32	7:1		5
Colorado Academy, Denver			X	X	PK–5	6–8	9–12	894	342	8:1	X	24
The Colorado Rocky Mountain School, Carbondale	X	X	X	X			9–12	156	156	5:1	X	30
The Colorado Springs School, Colorado Springs			X	X	PK–5	6–8	9–12	402	136	12:1	X	14
Denver Academy, Denver			X	X	1–6	7–8	9–12	439	250	6:1		28
Denver Christian High School, Denver			X	X			9–12	224	224	18:1		7
Denver Lutheran High School, Denver			X	X			9–12	210	210	17:1	X	15
Fountain Valley School of Colorado, Colorado Springs	X	X	X	X			9–12	250	250	6:1	X	37
Front Range Christian High School, Littleton			X	X	K–6	7–8	9–12	475	182	16:1	X	10
Humanex Academy, Englewood	X	X	X	X		7–8	9–12	63	56	7:1		16

Private Secondary Schools At-a-Glance

	Students Accepted: Boarding		Students Accepted: Day		Grades			Student/Faculty			School Offerings	
	Boys	Girls	Boys	Girls	Lower	Middle	Upper	Total	Upper	Student/Faculty Ratio	Advanced Placement Preparation	Sports
Kent Denver School, Englewood			X	X		6–8	9–12	659	438	7:1	X	27
The Lowell Whiteman School, Steamboat Springs	X	X	X	X			9–12	96	96	7:1	X	61
St. Mary's Academy, Englewood			X	X	K–5	6–8	9–12	738	269	10:1	X	17
St. Mary's High School, Colorado Springs			X	X			9–12	389	362	11:1	X	14
Telluride Mountain School, Telluride			X	X	PK–4	5–8	9–12	85	10	5:1		24
Connecticut												
Academy of Our Lady of Mercy, Milford				X			9–12	443	443	12:1		17
Avon Old Farms School, Avon	X		X				9–PG	405	405	7:1	X	50
Brunswick School, Greenwich			X		PK–4	5–8	9–12	894	333	6:1	X	18
Canterbury School, New Milford	X	X	X	X			9–PG	347	347	6:1	X	28
Chase Collegiate School, Waterbury			X	X	PK–5	6–8	9–12	514	190	6:1	X	24
Cheshire Academy, Cheshire	X	X	X	X		6–8	9–PG	372	324	7:1	X	23
Choate Rosemary Hall, Wallingford	X	X	X	X			9–12	850	850	6:1	X	44
Christian Heritage School, Trumbull			X	X	K–6	7–8	9–12	527	184	9:1	X	11
Convent of the Sacred Heart, Greenwich				X	PS–4	5–8	9–12	748	268	5:1	X	18
Eagle Hill School, Greenwich	X	X			1–6		7–9	230	115	4:1		33
Eagle Hill-Southport, Southport			X	X				112	17	4:1		9
East Catholic High School, Manchester			X	X			9–12	739	739	13:1	X	20
The Ethel Walker School, Simsbury		X		X		6–8	9–12	280	210	4:1	X	40
Fairfield College Preparatory School, Fairfield			X				9–12	917	917	15:1	X	29
The Forman School, Litchfield	X	X	X	X			9–12	182	182	3:1	X	32
Franklin Academy, East Haddam	X	X	X	X			9–PG	81	81	3:1		30
The Glenholme School, Washington	X	X	X	X				105		12:1		46
Greens Farms Academy, Greens Farms			X	X	K–5	6–8	9–12	650	278	6:1	X	38
Greenwich Academy, Greenwich				X	PK–4	5–8	9–12	791	320	6:1	X	30
Grove School, Madison	X	X	X	X		7–8	9–13	99	94	3:1		51
The Gunnery, Washington	X	X	X	X			9–PG	298	298	7:1	X	21
Hamden Hall Country Day School, Hamden			X	X	PK–6	7–8	9–12	565	268	8:1	X	18
Hopkins School, New Haven			X	X		7–8	9–12	670	520	6:1	X	40
The Hotchkiss School, Lakeville	X	X	X	X			9–PG	584	584	6:1	X	46
Hyde School, Woodstock	X	X	X	X			9–12	173	173	12:1	X	19
Immaculate High School, Danbury			X	X			9–12	436	436	10:1		26
Indian Mountain School, Lakeville	X	X	X	X	PK–4	5–6	7–9	258	145	4:1		19
Kent School, Kent	X	X	X	X			9–PG	574	574	8:1	X	37
King Low Heywood Thomas, Stamford			X	X	PK–5	6–8	9–12	655	271	7:1	X	25
Kingswood-Oxford School, West Hartford			X	X		6–8	9–12	570	399	8:1	X	19
The Loomis Chaffee School, Windsor	X	X	X	X			9–PG	714	714	5:1	X	49
Marianapolis Preparatory School, Thompson	X	X	X	X			9–PG	315	315	10:1	X	35
The Marvelwood School, Kent	X	X	X	X			9–12	165	165	4:1	X	31
The Master's School, West Simsbury			X	X	K–6	7–8	9–12	275	126	7:1	X	21
Mercy High School, Middletown				X			9–12	697	697	14:1	X	15
Miss Porter's School, Farmington		X		X			9–12	330	330	8:1	X	40
Northwest Catholic High School, West Hartford			X	X			9–12	620	620	12:1	X	33
The Norwich Free Academy, Norwich			X	X						22:1	X	27
The Oxford Academy, Westbrook	X						9–PG	38	38	1:1	X	13
Pomfret School, Pomfret	X	X	X	X			9–PG	355	355	6:1	X	31
The Rectory School, Pomfret	X	X	X	X	K–4	5–9		240	160	4:1		48
Rumsey Hall School, Washington Depot	X	X	X	X	K–5	6–9		309	202	8:1		46
St. Joseph High School, Trumbull			X	X			9–12	848	848	14:1	X	17
Saint Thomas More School, Oakdale	X					8	9–PG	210	194	7:1		40
Salisbury School, Salisbury	X		X				9–PG	295	295	6:1	X	20
South Kent School, South Kent	X		X				9–PG	145	145	4:1	X	25
Suffield Academy, Suffield	X	X	X	X			9–PG	405	405	5:1	X	28
The Taft School, Watertown	X	X	X	X			9–PG	577	577	6:1	X	46
Watkinson School, Hartford			X	X		6–8	9–PG	284	194	4:1		25
Westminster School, Simsbury	X	X	X	X			9–PG	385	385	5:1	X	30
Westover School, Middlebury		X		X			9–12	200	200	8:1	X	43
The Williams School, New London			X	X		7–8	9–12	315	247	6:1	X	15
The Woodhall School, Bethlehem	X		X				9–PG	42	42	4:1	X	34
Wooster School, Danbury			X	X	PK–5	6–8	9–12	350	147	10:1	X	16
Delaware												
Archmere Academy, Claymont			X	X			9–12	513	513	10:1	X	20
Salesianum School, Wilmington			X				9–12	1,019	1,019	12:1	X	21
Sanford School, Hockessin			X	X	PK–4	5–8	9–12	665	240		X	13
The Tatnall School, Wilmington			X	X	N–4	5–8	9–12	688	270	8:1	X	18
Tower Hill School, Wilmington			X	X	PK–4	5–8	9–12	725	210	7:1	X	22
Ursuline Academy, Wilmington			X	X	PK–6	7–8	9–12	638	224	14:1	X	17
Wilmington Friends School, Wilmington			X	X	PS–5	6–8	9–12	836	259	9:1	X	12
District of Columbia												
The Field School, Washington			X	X		7–8	9–12	320	260	6:1	X	20
Georgetown Day School, Washington			X	X	PK–5	6–8	9–12	1,031	458	7:1	X	8
Georgetown Visitation Preparatory School, Washington				X			9–12	479	479	10:1	X	18
Gonzaga College High School, Washington			X				9–12	942	942	10:1	X	28

Private Secondary Schools At-a-Glance

	STUDENTS ACCEPTED				GRADES			STUDENT/FACULTY			SCHOOL OFFERINGS	
	Boarding		Day									
	Boys	Girls	Boys	Girls	Lower	Middle	Upper	Total	Upper	Student/Faculty Ratio	Advanced Placement Preparation	Sports
Maret School, Washington			X	X	K–4	5–8	9–12	600	292	6:1	X	21
National Cathedral School, Washington				X	4–6	7–8	9–12	582	304	7:1	X	43
St. Albans School, Washington	X		X		4–8		9–12	578	317	7:1	X	33
St. Anselm's Abbey School, Washington			X			6–8	9–12	238	143	5:1	X	17
St. John's College High School, Washington			X	X			9–12	1,056	1,056	13:1	X	40
Washington International School, Washington			X	X	PK–5	6–8	9–12	894	254	7:1		10
Florida												
Academy of the Holy Names, Tampa			X	X	PK–4	5–8	9–12	852	313	15:1	X	19
Allison Academy, North Miami Beach			X	X		6–8	9–12	78	53	10:1	X	17
American Academy, Plantation			X	X	1–6	7–8	9–12	403	195	12:1		21
American Heritage School, Plantation			X	X	PK–6		7–12	2,189	1,379	13:1	X	17
Archbishop Edward A. McCarthy High School, Fort Lauderdale			X	X			9–12	1,400	1,400			
Argo Academy, Sarasota	X	X					12	38	38	4:1		7
The Benjamin School, North Palm Beach			X	X	PK–5	6–8	9–12	1,250	423	7:1	X	20
Berkeley Preparatory School, Tampa			X	X	PK–5	6–8	9–12	1,200	500	7:1	X	27
Bishop Kenny High School, Jacksonville			X	X			9–12	1,440	1,440		X	18
Bishop Verot High School, Fort Myers			X	X			9–12	728	728	18:1	X	18
The Bolles School, Jacksonville	X	X	X	X	PK–5	6–8	9–12	1,732	792	10:1	X	18
Canterbury School, Fort Myers			X	X	PK–5	6–8	9–12	685	215	10:1	X	13
The Canterbury School of Florida, St. Petersburg			X	X	PK–4	5–8	9–12	427	109	4:1	X	29
Cardinal Mooney High School, Sarasota			X	X			9–12	556	556	20:1	X	19
Cardinal Newman High School, West Palm Beach			X	X			9–12	782	782	25:1	X	18
Carrollton School of the Sacred Heart, Miami				X	PK–3	4–6	7–12	775	423	9:1	X	14
Chaminade-Madonna College Preparatory, Hollywood			X	X			9–12	704	704	19:1	X	23
Christian Home and Bible School, Mount Dora			X	X	K–5	6–8	9–12	601	220	15:1	X	12
The Community School of Naples, Naples			X	X	PK–5	6–8	9–12	803	285	12:1	X	18
Donna Klein Jewish Academy, Boca Raton			X	X	K–4	5–8	9–12	708	84	4:1	X	14
Episcopal High School of Jacksonville, Jacksonville			X	X		6–8	9–12	900	600	10:1	X	22
Father Lopez High School, Daytona Beach			X	X			9–12	275	275	20:1	X	15
The First Academy, Orlando			X	X	K–5	6–8	9–12	982	308	10:1	X	21
Forest Lake Academy, Apopka	X	X	X	X			9–12	344	344	16:1		11
Fort Lauderdale Preparatory School, Fort Lauderdale			X	X	PK–6		7–12	220	120	9:1	X	
Foundation Academy, Winter Garden			X	X	1–5	6–8	9–12	607	97	21:1	X	11
The Geneva School, Winter Park			X	X	K4–6	7–8	9–12	470	100	9:1	X	9
Glades Day School, Belle Glade			X	X	PK–6	7–8	9–12	540	252	15:1	X	13
Gulliver Preparatory School, Miami			X	X	PK–4	5–8	9–12	1,834	754	8:1	X	38
Jesuit High School of Tampa, Tampa			X				9–12	675	675	12:1	X	16
John Paul II Catholic High School, Tallahassee			X	X			9–12	129	129	8:1	X	9
Kaplan College Preparatory School, Hollywood			X	X		6–8	9–12	260	233		X	
La Salle High School, Miami			X	X			9–12	733	733	15:1	X	23
Miami Country Day School, Miami			X	X	PK–5	6–8	9–12	990	380	9:1	X	24
Montverde Academy, Montverde	X	X	X	X	PK–5	6–8	9–PG	665	329	12:1	X	32
The North Broward Preparatory Upper School, Coconut Creek	X	X	X	X	PK–5	6–8	9–12	1,583	698	12:1	X	30
Northside Christian School, St. Petersburg			X	X	PS–5	6–8	9–12	877	221	11:1	X	15
Out-Of-Door-Academy, Sarasota			X	X	PK–6	7–8	9–12	621	225	8:1	X	20
Pensacola Catholic High School, Pensacola			X	X			9–12	599	599	18:1	X	
Pine Crest School, Fort Lauderdale			X	X	PK–5	6–8	9–12	1,715	813	9:1	X	23
Rabbi Alexander S. Gross Hebrew Academy, Miami Beach			X	X	N–5	6–8	9–12	499	197	4:1	X	4
Ransom Everglades School, Miami			X	X		6–8	9–12	1,054	593	14:1	X	22
Saint Andrew's School, Boca Raton	X	X	X	X	JK–5	6–8	9–12	1,288	604	9:1	X	19
St. Brendan High School, Miami			X	X			9–12	1,187	1,187	15:1	X	11
Saint Edward's School, Vero Beach			X	X	PK–5	6–8	9–12	819	271	9:1	X	17
St. Joseph Academy, St. Augustine			X	X			9–12	335	335	13:1	X	16
Saint Stephen's Episcopal School, Bradenton			X	X	PK–6	7–8	9–12	725	247	10:1	X	27
St. Thomas Aquinas High School, Fort Lauderdale			X	X			9–12	2,152	2,152	18:1	X	21
The Samuel Scheck Hillel Community Day School, North Miami Beach			X	X	PK–5	6–8	9–12	1,053	295		X	11
Shorecrest Preparatory School, Saint Petersburg			X	X	PK–4	5–8	9–12	968	275	12:1	X	14
Tampa Preparatory School, Tampa			X	X		6–8	9–12	643	455	10:1	X	27
Trinity Preparatory School, Winter Park			X	X		6–8	9–12	827	487	12:1	X	22
University School of Nova Southeastern University, Fort Lauderdale			X	X	PK–5	6–8	9–12	1,851	648	11:1	X	18
The Vanguard School, Lake Wales	X	X	X	X		6–8	9–PG	130	118	10:1		27
Westminster Christian School, Miami			X	X	PK–5	6–8	9–12	1,162	447	11:1	X	13
Windermere Preparatory School, Windermere			X	X	PK–5	6–8	9–12	817	136	17:1	X	19
World Hope Academy, Miami					PK–5	6–8	9–12	305	300	20:1	X	
Georgia												
Advanced Academy of Georgia, Carrollton	X	X					10–12	71	71	14:1		7
Athens Academy, Athens			X	X	N–4	5–8	9–12	908	307	8:1	X	11
Atlanta International School, Atlanta			X	X	PK–5	6–8	9–12	934	277	7:1		11
Augusta Christian School (I), Martinez			X	X	K–5	6–8	9–12	544	259	14:1	X	13
Augusta Preparatory Day School, Martinez			X	X	PS–4	5–8	9–12	566	203	9:1		11

Private Secondary Schools At-a-Glance

	STUDENTS ACCEPTED				GRADES			STUDENT/FACULTY			SCHOOL OFFERINGS	
	Boarding		Day									
	Boys	Girls	Boys	Girls	Lower	Middle	Upper	Total	Upper	Student/Faculty Ratio	Advanced Placement Preparation	Sports
Benedictine Military School, Savannah			X				9–12	309	309	11:1	X	21
Ben Franklin Academy, Atlanta			X	X			9–12	130	130	3:1	X	4
Blessed Trinity High School, Roswell			X	X			9–12			12:1		17
Brenau Academy, Gainesville		X		X			9–PG	70	70	8:1		15
Brentwood School, Sandersville			X	X	PK–6	7–8	9–12	401	112	11:1	X	10
Brookstone School, Columbus			X	X	PK–5	6–8	9–12	826	273	10:1	X	12
Bulloch Academy, Statesboro			X	X	PK–5	6–8	9–12	460	100	16:1	X	17
Chatham Academy, Savannah			X	X	1–5	6–8	9–12	99	45	10:1		17
Darlington School, Rome	X	X	X	X	PK–5	6–8	9–PG	898	506	13:1	X	40
Deerfield-Windsor School, Albany			X	X	PK–5	6–8	9–12	848	250	18:1	X	12
Excel Christian Academy, Cartersville			X	X	K–5	6–8	9–12	373	110	18:1	X	8
First Presbyterian Day School, Macon			X	X	PK–5	6–8	9–12	982	362	12:1	X	16
Flint River Academy, Woodbury			X	X		6–8	9–12	382	104	14:1	X	15
Gables Academy, Stone Mountain	X	X	X	X	4–5	6–8	9–12	12	9	6:1		45
Georgia Military College High School, Milledgeville			X	X		6–8	9–12	500	250		X	10
Greater Atlanta Christian Schools, Norcross			X	X	P4–5	6–8	9–12	1,965	663	13:1	X	23
The Heritage School, Newnan			X	X	PK–4	5–8	9–12	401	140	7:1	X	28
Hidden Lake Academy, Dahlonega	X	X					7–PG	130	60	9:1		52
Holy Innocents' Episcopal School, Atlanta			X	X	PS–5	6–8	9–12	1,418	420	10:1	X	17
Horizons School, Atlanta	X	X	X	X	K–5	6–7	8–PG	100	60	10:1	X	1
King's Ridge Christian School, Alpharetta			X	X	K–5	6–8	9–12	625	77	8:1	X	16
Lakeview Academy, Gainesville			X	X	PK–5	6–8	9–12	598	138	5:1	X	15
The Lovett School, Atlanta			X	X	K–5	6–8	9–12	1,550	595	7:1	X	45
Marist School, Atlanta			X	X			7–12	1,070	1,070	11:1	X	19
National High School, Atlanta							9–12	91	91	12:1	X	
North Cobb Christian School, Kennesaw			X	X	PK–5	6–8	9–12	878	241	6:1	X	20
Oak Mountain Academy, Carrollton			X	X	K4–5	6–8	9–12	258	70	5:1	X	11
Pace Academy, Atlanta			X	X	K–5	6–8	9–12	996	385	7:1	X	20
The Paideia School, Atlanta			X	X	PK–6	7–8	9–12	923	389	9:1	X	21
Piedmont Academy, Monticello			X	X	PK–5	6–8	9–12	399	116	13:1		16
Rabun Gap-Nacoochee School, Rabun Gap	X	X	X	X		6–8	9–12	357	265	8:1	X	36
Riverside Military Academy, Gainesville	X		X			7–8	9–PG	358	300	10:1	X	48
St. Andrew's on the Marsh School, Savannah			X	X	PK–3	4–8	9–12	482	164	9:1	X	16
St. Francis School, Alpharetta			X	X	P3–5	6–8	9–12	827	287	14:1		16
St. Pius X Catholic High School, Atlanta			X	X			9–12	1,000	1,000	15:1	X	21
Savannah Christian Preparatory School, Savannah			X	X	PK–5	6–8	9–12	1,492	463	14:1	X	13
The Savannah Country Day School, Savannah			X	X	PK–5	6–8	9–12	1,002	292	10:1	X	27
Stratford Academy, Macon			X	X	PK–5	6–8	9–12	888	280	13:1	X	14
Tallulah Falls School, Tallulah Falls	X	X	X	X		6–8	9–12	137	93	10:1	X	31
Valwood School, Hahira			X	X	PK–5	6–8	9–12	381	95	6:1	X	11
The Walker School, Marietta			X	X	PK–5	6–8	9–12	1,066	369	14:1	X	30
The Westminster Schools, Atlanta			X	X	K–5	6–8	9–12	1,819	793	15:1	X	36
Westminster Schools of Augusta, Augusta			X	X	PK–5	6–8	9–12	535	153	8:1	X	10
Whitefield Academy, Mableton			X	X	PK–5	6–8	9–12	691	251	8:1	X	16
Woodward Academy, College Park			X	X	PK–6	7–8	9–12	2,924	1,073		X	20
Hawaii												
ASSETS School, Honolulu			X	X	K–8		9–12	357	100	7:1		33
Hanalani Schools, Mililani			X	X	PK–6		7–12	703	283	12:1	X	20
Hawaiian Mission Academy, Honolulu	X	X	X	X			9–12	113	113	15:1		2
Hawaii Baptist Academy, Honolulu			X	X	K–6	7–8	9–12	1,076	437	11:1	X	22
Hawai'i Preparatory Academy, Kamuela	X	X	X	X	K–5	6–8	9–12	575	336	9:1	X	25
Iolani School, Honolulu			X	X	K–6		7–12	1,842	1,299	12:1	X	27
Island School, Lihue			X	X	PK–5	6–8	9–12	336	108	11:1		18
La Pietra–Hawaii School for Girls, Honolulu				X		6–8	9–12	247	143	10:1	X	24
Lutheran High School of Hawaii, Honolulu			X	X			9–12	123	123	10:1	X	9
Maryknoll School, Honolulu			X	X	PK–5	6–8	9–12	1,372	563	11:1	X	32
Mid-Pacific Institute, Honolulu			X	X	K–5	6–8	9–12	1,515	836	19:1	X	31
The Parker School, Kamuela			X	X	K–5	6–8	9–12	296	120	8:1	X	11
Punahou School, Honolulu			X	X	K–5	6–8	9–12	3,754	1,729	12:1	X	23
St. Andrew's Priory School, Honolulu				X	K–5	6–8	9–12	491	188	8:1	X	34
St. Anthony's Junior-Senior High School, Wailuku			X	X		7–8	9–12	242	162	10:1	X	26
Saint Francis School, Honolulu			X	X	K–6	7–8	9–12	353	239	20:1	X	23
Seabury Hall, Makawao			X	X		6–8	9–12	421	288	10:1	X	15
Idaho												
Bishop Kelly High School, Boise			X	X			9–12	640	640	17:1	X	18
Cherry Gulch, Emmett	X					5–9		25	21	4:1		51
Cole Valley Christian High School, Meridian			X	X	K–6	7–8	9–12	715	234	9:1	X	10
The Community School, Sun Valley			X	X	K–5	6–8	9–12	307	109	8:1	X	37
Greenleaf Academy, Greenleaf			X	X	K–5	6–8	9–12	221	92	16:1		13
Northwest Academy, Naples	X	X					11–12	25	25	3:1		31
Riverstone International School, Boise			X	X	K–5	6–8	9–12	316	105	5:1		17
Illinois												
Aurora Central High School, Aurora			X	X			9–12	483	483	16:1	X	29
Bishop McNamara High School, Kankakee			X	X			9–12	438	438	23:1	X	23

Private Secondary Schools At-a-Glance

	STUDENTS ACCEPTED				GRADES			STUDENT/FACULTY			SCHOOL OFFERINGS	
	Boarding		Day									
	Boys	Girls	Boys	Girls	Lower	Middle	Upper	Total	Upper	Student/Faculty Ratio	Advanced Placement Preparation	Sports
Boylan Central Catholic High School, Rockford			X	X			9–12	1,263	1,263	14:1	X	29
Brehm Preparatory School, Carbondale	X	X	X	X		6–8	9–PG	97	88	4:1		15
The Chicago Academy for the Arts, Chicago			X	X			9–12	164	164	14:1	X	
Elgin Academy, Elgin			X	X	PS–4	5–8	9–12	445	130	7:1	X	13
Fox River Country Day School, Elgin	X	X	X	X	PK–5	6–8		204	28	13:1		25
Fox Valley Lutheran Academy, Elgin			X	X			9–12	23	23	3:1		3
Gordon Technical High School, Chicago			X	X			9–12	585	585	15:1	X	28
The Governor French Academy, Belleville	X	X	X	X	1–8		9–12	205	55	6:1	X	24
Guerin College Preparatory High School, River Grove			X	X			9–12	651	651	17:1	X	19
Holy Trinity High School, Chicago			X	X			9–12	400	400	13:1	X	10
Illiana Christian High School, Lansing			X	X			9–12	675	675	18:1	X	13
Immaculate Conception School, Elmhurst			X	X			9–12	254	254	12:1	X	17
Keith Country Day School, Rockford			X	X	PK–5	6–8	9–12	329	111	5:1	X	7
Lake Forest Academy, Lake Forest	X	X	X	X			9–12	391	391	6:1	X	26
Luther High School North, Chicago			X	X			9–12	224	224	16:1	X	14
Luther High School South, Chicago			X	X		6–8	9–12		131	11:1	X	12
Marian Central Catholic High School, Woodstock			X	X			9–12	758	758	14:1	X	16
Marist High School, Chicago			X	X			9–12	1,810	1,810	16:1	X	25
Marmion Academy, Aurora			X				9–12	520	520	11:1	X	21
Metro-East Lutheran High School, Edwardsville			X	X			9–12			15:1		15
Morgan Park Academy, Chicago			X	X	PK–5	6–8	9–12	474	157	5:1	X	18
Mother McAuley High School, Chicago				X			9–12	1,393	1,393	15:1	X	16
Nazareth Academy, LaGrange Park			X	X			9–12	787	787	17:1	X	15
North Shore Country Day School, Winnetka			X	X	PK–5	6–8	9–12	493	187	8:1	X	15
Queen of Peace High School, Burbank				X						16:1		
Regina Dominican High School, Wilmette				X			9–12	400	400	12:1	X	16
Roycemore School, Evanston			X	X	PK–4	5–8	9–12	249	84	9:1	X	4
Saint Anthony High School, Effingham			X	X			9–12	214	214	10:1	X	12
St. Gregory's High School, Chicago			X	X			9–12	331	331			8
Saint Joseph High School, Westchester			X	X			9–12	827	827	17:1	X	19
Saint Patrick High School, Chicago			X				9–12	915	915	25:1	X	15
Saint Viator High School, Arlington Heights			X	X			9–12	1,040	1,040	12:1		19
Schlarman High School, Danville			X	X			9–12	183	183	17:1	X	19
Timothy Christian High School, Elmhurst			X	X	K–6	7–8	9–12	1,036	398	13:1	X	12
Trinity High School, River Forest				X			9–12	521	521	14:1		11
University of Chicago Laboratory Schools, Chicago			X	X	N–4	5–8	9–12	1,774	498	10:1	X	14
Wheaton Academy, West Chicago			X	X			9–12	647	647	14:1	X	33
The Willows Academy, Des Plaines				X		6–8	9–12	229	154	10:1	X	9
Woodlands Academy of the Sacred Heart, Lake Forest		X		X			9–12	166	166	9:1	X	6
Indiana												
Bishop Luers High School, Fort Wayne			X	X			9–12	548	548	18:1	X	21
Cathedral High School, Indianapolis			X	X			9–12	1,288	1,288	13:1	X	32
The Culver Academies, Culver	X	X	X	X			9–PG	795	795	9:1	X	75
Evansville Day School, Evansville			X	X	PK–4	5–8	9–12	326	69	10:1	X	11
Howe Military School, Howe	X	X	X	X	5–8		9–12	153	115	9:1	X	15
Lakeland Christian Academy, Winona Lake			X	X		7–8	9–12	153	105	15:1		8
La Lumiere School, La Porte	X	X	X	X			9–PG	179	179	7:1	X	44
Lutheran High School, Indianapolis			X	X			9–12	279	279	14:1	X	14
Marian High School, Mishawaka			X	X			9–12	730	730	20:1	X	30
Mater Dei High School, Evansville			X	X			9–12	560	560	15:1	X	16
New Horizon Youth Ministries, Marion	X	X	X	X		7–8	9–12	26	26	4:1		34
Oldenburg Academy, Oldenburg			X	X			9–12	205	205	12:1	X	5
Park Tudor School, Indianapolis			X	X	PK–5	6–8	9–12	982	426	9:1	X	17
Reitz Memorial High School, Evansville			X	X			9–12	791	791	16:1	X	19
Roncalli High School, Indianapolis			X	X			9–12	1,142	1,142	14:1	X	32
Iowa												
Columbus High School, Waterloo			X	X			9–12	294	294	15:1	X	9
Dowling Catholic High School, West Des Moines			X	X			9–12	1,234	1,234	16:1	X	21
Maharishi School of the Age of Enlightenment, Fairfield			X	X	PS–6	7–9	10–12	204	62	10:1		31
Rivermont Collegiate, Bettendorf			X	X	PS–5	6–8	9–12	195	31	4:1	X	12
Scattergood Friends School, West Branch	X	X	X	X			9–PG	45	45	2:1		29
Kansas												
Hayden High School, Topeka			X	X			9–12	517	517	15:1	X	20
Hyman Brand Hebrew Academy of Greater Kansas City, Overland Park			X	X	K–5	6–8	9–12	227	58	5:1	X	8
Immaculata High School, Leavenworth			X	X			9–12	113	113	9:1		10
Independent School, Wichita			X	X	PK–5	6–8	9–12	719	259	10:1	X	16
Maur Hill-Mount Academy, Atchison	X	X	X	X			9–12	198	198	9:1		35
Saint Thomas Aquinas High School, Overland Park			X	X			9–12	1,092	1,092	15:1	X	18
Wichita Collegiate School, Wichita			X	X	PS–4	5–8	9–12	1,018	226	10:1	X	13

Private Secondary Schools At-a-Glance

	STUDENTS ACCEPTED				GRADES			STUDENT/FACULTY			SCHOOL OFFERINGS	
	Boarding		Day									
	Boys	Girls	Boys	Girls	Lower	Middle	Upper	Total	Upper	Student/Faculty Ratio	Advanced Placement Preparation	Sports
Kentucky												
Assumption High School, Louisville				X			9–12	969	969	10:1	X	21
Beth Haven Christian School, Louisville			X	X	K4–5	6–8	9–12	278	98	13:1	X	7
Calvary Christian Academy, Covington			X	X	K4–6	7–8	9–12	636	197	14:1	X	18
Community Christian Academy, Independence			X	X	PS–6	7–8	9–12	201	42	20:1		4
Kentucky Country Day School, Louisville			X	X	JK–4	5–8	9–12	902	269	8:1	X	20
Lexington Catholic High School, Lexington			X	X			9–12	860	860	14:1	X	23
Louisville Collegiate School, Louisville			X	X	JK–5	6–8	9–12	638	207	8:1	X	16
Oneida Baptist Institute, Oneida	X	X	X	X		6–8	9–12	300	225	11:1	X	10
St. Francis High School, Louisville			X	X			9–12	126	126	7:1	X	24
Saint Patrick's School, Maysville			X	X	K–5	6–8	9–12	290	110	13:1		10
Saint Xavier High School, Louisville			X				9–12	1,402	1,402	12:1	X	38
Sayre School, Lexington			X	X	PK–5	6–8	9–12	628	230	9:1	X	13
Trinity High School, Louisville			X				9–12	1,351	1,351	13:1	X	45
Louisiana												
Academy of the Sacred Heart, New Orleans				X	N–4	5–8	9–12	768	224	16:1	X	21
Archbishop Rummel High School, Metairie			X				8–12	1,150	1,000	10:1	X	20
Brother Martin High School, New Orleans			X			8	9–12	1,190	991	23:1	X	13
Hanson Memorial High School, Franklin			X	X		6–8	9–12	260	160	13:1		12
Holy Savior Menard Catholic High School, Alexandria			X	X		7–8	9–12	498	322	14:1	X	13
Isidore Newman School, New Orleans			X	X	PK–5	6–8	9–12	976	351	18:1	X	15
Metairie Park Country Day School, Metairie			X	X	PK–5	6–8	9–12	685	226	7:1	X	14
Notre Dame High School, Crowley			X	X			9–12	500	500	25:1		14
Ridgewood Preparatory School, Metairie			X	X	PK–4	5–8	9–12	280	149	25:1		7
St. Joseph's Academy, Baton Rouge				X			9–12	877	877	14:1	X	15
St. Martin's Episcopal School, Metairie			X	X	PK–5	6–8	9–12	613	226	9:1	X	15
St. Mary's Dominican High School, New Orleans				X			8–12	927	927	13:1	X	18
Teurlings Catholic High School, Lafayette			X	X			9–12	662	662	21:1	X	23
University Christian Preparatory School, Shreveport			X	X	K–5	6–8	9–12	127	51	14:1		24
Vandebilt Catholic High School, Houma			X	X			8–12	921	921	25:1		12
Xavier University Preparatory School, New Orleans				X		7–8	9–12	324	280	11:1		9
Maine												
Berwick Academy, South Berwick			X	X	K–4	5–8	9–12	593	251	12:1	X	10
Carrabassett Valley Academy, Carrabassett Valley	X	X	X	X	8–9		10–13	115	85	6:1		33
Cheverus High School, Portland			X	X			9–12	544	544	12:1	X	25
Deck House School, Edgecomb	X						10–12	12	12	2:1		
Elan School, Poland	X	X				8–8	9–12	62	62	6:1		46
Foxcroft Academy, Dover-Foxcroft	X	X	X	X			9–12	439	439	16:1	X	20
Fryeburg Academy, Fryeburg	X	X	X	X			9–PG	681	681	10:1	X	63
George Stevens Academy, Blue Hill	X	X	X	X			9–12	308	308	10:1	X	37
Gould Academy, Bethel	X	X	X	X			9–PG	249	249	6:1	X	12
Hebron Academy, Hebron	X	X	X	X		6–8	9–PG	260	219	7:1	X	14
Hyde School, Bath	X	X	X	X			9–12	129	129	5:1		27
John Bapst Memorial High School, Bangor			X	X			9–12	467	467	12:1	X	20
Kents Hill School, Kents Hill	X	X	X	X			9–PG	226	226	5:1	X	37
Lee Academy, Lee	X	X	X	X			9–PG	272	272	10:1	X	60
Maine Central Institute, Pittsfield	X	X	X	X			9–PG	485	485	15:1	X	25
Maine School of Science and Mathematics, Limestone	X	X					10–12	120	120	13:1	X	9
North Yarmouth Academy, Yarmouth			X	X		6–8	9–12	330	197	8:1	X	14
Saint Dominic Regional High School, Auburn			X	X			9–12	276	276	12:1	X	13
Washington Academy, East Machias	X	X	X	X			9–12	438	438	11:1	X	21
Waynflete School, Portland			X	X	PK–5	6–8	9–12	568	233	13:1		29
Maryland												
Academy of the Holy Cross, Kensington				X			9–12	626	626	14:1	X	19
Archbishop Curley High School, Baltimore			X				9–12	581	581	14:1	X	20
Archbishop Spalding High School, Severn			X	X			9–12	1,182	1,182	15:1	X	40
The Baltimore Actors' Theatre Conservatory, Baltimore			X	X	3–5	7–8	9–12	23	11	3:1	X	
The Barrie School, Silver Spring			X	X	N–5	6–8	9–12	395	111	7:1	X	15
Bishop Walsh Middle High School, Cumberland			X	X	PK–5	6–8	9–12	428	198	15:1	X	9
The Boys' Latin School of Maryland, Baltimore			X		K–5	6–8	9–12	650	291	8:1	X	18
The Bryn Mawr School for Girls, Baltimore			X	X	K–5	6–8	9–12	764	312	7:1	X	41
Calvert Hall College High School, Baltimore			X				9–12	1,254	1,254	13:1	X	29
The Calverton School, Huntingtown			X	X	PS–5	6–8	9–12	428	162	11:1	X	7
The Catholic High School of Baltimore, Baltimore				X			9–12	326	326	12:1	X	16
Chelsea School, Silver Spring			X	X		5–8	9–12	76	62	8:1		5
Connelly School of the Holy Child, Potomac				X		6–8	9–12	324	228	15:1	X	51
DeMatha Catholic High School, Hyattsville			X				9–12	996	996	13:1	X	23
Elizabeth Seton High School, Bladensburg				X			9–12	640	640	11:1	X	40
Garrison Forest School, Owings Mills		X	X	X	N–5	6–8	9–12	701	268	8:1	X	22
Georgetown Preparatory School, North Bethesda	X		X				9–12	466	466	8:1	X	53

Private Secondary Schools At-a-Glance

Private Secondary Schools At-a-Glance	STUDENTS ACCEPTED				GRADES			STUDENT/FACULTY			SCHOOL OFFERINGS	
	Boarding		Day									
	Boys	Girls	Boys	Girls	Lower	Middle	Upper	Total	Upper	Student/Faculty Ratio	Advanced Placement Preparation	Sports
Gilman School, Baltimore			X		P1–5	6–8	9–12	988	442	8:1	X	29
Glenelg Country School, Ellicott City			X	X	PK–5	6–8	9–12	825	280	6:1	X	26
Griggs University and International Academy, Silver Spring			X	X	PK–6	7–8	9–12	1,214	775			
Gunston Day School, Centreville			X	X			9–12	152	152	6:1	X	20
The Holton-Arms School, Bethesda				X	3–6	7–8	9–12	644	326	7:1	X	21
The Key School, Annapolis			X	X	PK–4	5–8	9–12	700	192	8:1	X	26
Landon School, Bethesda			X		3–5	6–8	9–12	679	343	8:1	X	28
Loyola-Blakefield, Baltimore			X			6–8	9–12	1,009	766	11:1	X	26
Maryvale Preparatory School, Brooklandville				X		6–8	9–12	392	304	9:1	X	14
McDonogh School, Owings Mills	X	X	X	X	K–4	5–8	9–12	1,293	569	9:1	X	25
The Nora School, Silver Spring			X	X			9–12	60	60	5:1		24
Notre Dame Preparatory School, Towson				X		6–8	9–12	756	572	9:1	X	23
Oldfields School, Glencoe		X		X			8–12	164	164	6:1	X	41
Queen Anne School, Upper Marlboro			X	X			6–12	155	155	7:1	X	18
Roland Park Country School, Baltimore				X	K–5	6–8	9–12	710	285	7:1	X	23
St. Andrew's Episcopal School, Potomac			X	X		6–8	9–12	455	324	7:1	X	16
Saint James School, St. James	X	X	X	X		8	9–12	225	201	7:1	X	23
St. John's Catholic Prep, Frederick			X	X			9–12	283	283	11:1	X	22
Saint Mary's High School, Annapolis			X	X			9–12	520	520	17:1	X	21
St. Paul's School, Brooklandville			X	X	K–4	5–8	9–12	851	340	8.5:1	X	27
St. Paul's School for Girls, Brooklandville				X		5–8	9–12	465	283	7:1	X	23
Saints Peter and Paul High School, Easton			X	X			9–12	201	201	8:1	X	11
St. Timothy's School, Stevenson		X		X			9–12	155	155	5:1		23
Sandy Spring Friends School, Sandy Spring	X	X	X	X	PK–5	6–8	9–12	571	251	8:1	X	20
Thornton Friends School, Silver Spring			X	X		6–8	9–12	58	46	6:1		17
Washington Waldorf School, Bethesda			X	X	PS–4	5–8	9–12	290	74	7:1	X	5
West Nottingham Academy, Colora	X	X	X	X			9–PG	123	123	6:1	X	19
Worcester Preparatory School, Berlin			X	X	PK–5	6–8	9–12	618	213	9:1	X	12
Massachusetts												
The Academy at Charlemont, Charlemont	X	X	X	X		7–8	9–PG	105	68	7:1		22
Academy at Swift River, Cummington	X	X					9–12	100	100	8:1		57
Austin Preparatory School, Reading			X	X		6–8		210		15:1	X	13
Bancroft School, Worcester			X	X	K–5	6–8	9–12	575	231	8:1	X	16
Beaver Country Day School, Chestnut Hill			X	X		6–8	9–12	428	307	8:1		27
Belmont Hill School, Belmont	X		X			7–9	10–12	445	241	6:1	X	21
The Bement School, Deerfield	X	X	X	X	K–5		6–9	240	114	6:1		33
Berkshire School, Sheffield	X	X	X	X			9–PG	371	371	6:1	X	33
Bishop Connolly High School, Fall River			X	X			9–12	414	414	16:1	X	17
Bishop Feehan High School, Attleboro			X	X			9–12	1,032	1,032	13:1	X	20
Bishop Stang High School, North Dartmouth			X	X			9–12	816	816	14:1	X	37
Boston College High School, Boston			X			7–8	9–12	1,543	1,305	13:1	X	21
Boston Trinity Academy, Boston			X	X		6–8	9–12	202	148	9:1		8
Boston University Academy, Boston			X	X			9–12	156	156	9:1		10
Brimmer and May School, Chestnut Hill			X	X	PK–5	6–8	9–12	407	135	5:1	X	16
Brooks School, North Andover	X	X	X	X			9–12	359	359	5:1	X	18
Buckingham Browne & Nichols School, Cambridge			X	X	PK–6	7–8	9–12	968	473	7:1	X	26
Buxton School, Williamstown	X	X	X	X			9–12	95	95	5:1		22
The Cambridge School of Weston, Weston	X	X	X	X			9–PG	333	333	6:1	X	47
Cape Cod Academy, Osterville			X	X	K–5	6–8	9–12	347	158	7:1	X	13
Catholic Memorial, West Roxbury			X			7–8	9–12	809	608	13:1	X	16
Central Catholic High School, Lawrence			X	X			9–12	1,350	1,350			25
Chapel Hill–Chauncy Hall School, Waltham	X	X	X	X			9–12	174	174	6:1	X	23
Commonwealth School, Boston			X	X			9–12	154	154	5:1	X	16
Concord Academy, Concord	X	X	X	X			9–12	367	367	6:1		34
Cushing Academy, Ashburnham	X	X	X	X			9–PG	441	441	8:1	X	37
Dana Hall School, Wellesley		X		X		6–8	9–12	500	370	9:1	X	44
Deerfield Academy, Deerfield	X	X	X	X			9–PG	600	600	5:1	X	40
Eaglebrook School, Deerfield	X		X			6–9		282	258	4:1		64
Eagle Hill School, Hardwick	X	X	X	X		8	9–12	158	148	4:1		36
Ecole Internationale de Boston / International School of Boston, Cambridge			X	X	PK–5	6–8	9–12	567	71	6:1		7
Falmouth Academy, Falmouth			X	X		7–8	9–12	213	144	4:1	X	3
Fay School, Southborough	X	X	X	X	1–5	6–9		380	217	6:1		36
The Fessenden School, West Newton	X		X		K–4	5–6	7–9	482	206	7:1		24
Fontbonne Academy, Milton				X			9–12	400	400	11:1	X	27
Gann Academy (The New Jewish High School of Greater Boston), Waltham			X	X			9–12	330	330	6:1	X	13
The Governor's Academy (formerly Governor Dummer Academy), Byfield	X	X	X	X			9–12	376	376	5:1	X	21
Groton School, Groton	X	X	X	X		8	9–12	356	331	3:1	X	38
Hillside School, Marlborough	X		X		5–6	7–9		139	106	6:1		46
The John Dewey Academy, Great Barrington	X	X					10–PG	30	30	3:1		
Landmark School, Prides Crossing	X	X	X	X	1–5	6–7	8–12	446	299	3:1		16
Lawrence Academy, Groton	X	X	X	X			9–12	396	396	8:1	X	26

Private Secondary Schools At-a-Glance

	STUDENTS ACCEPTED: Boarding		STUDENTS ACCEPTED: Day		GRADES			STUDENT/FACULTY			SCHOOL OFFERINGS	
	Boys	Girls	Boys	Girls	Lower	Middle	Upper	Total	Upper	Student/Faculty Ratio	Advanced Placement Preparation	Sports
Lexington Christian Academy, Lexington			X	X		6–8	9–12	333	234	11:1	X	26
Linden Hill School, Northfield	X		X					30	5	3:1		33
The MacDuffie School, Springfield	X	X	X	X		6–8	9–12	232	186	7:1	X	27
Matignon High School, Cambridge			X	X			9–12	350	350	15:1	X	21
Middlesex School, Concord	X	X	X	X			9–12	342	342	5:1	X	22
Milton Academy, Milton	X	X	X	X	K–5	6–8	9–12	964	669	5:1	X	29
Miss Hall's School, Pittsfield		X		X			9–12	195	195	6:1	X	31
Montrose School, Medfield				X		6–8	9–12	140	75	10:1	X	5
The Newman School, Boston			X	X			9–PG	230	230	14:1	X	19
Noble and Greenough School, Dedham	X	X	X	X		7–8	9–12	569	455	7:1	X	8
Northfield Mount Hermon School, Mount Hermon	X	X	X	X			9–PG	620	620	7:1	X	27
Notre Dame Academy, Hingham				X			9–12	595	595	10:1	X	24
Notre Dame Academy, Worcester				X			9–12	285	285	11:1	X	23
The Penikese Island School, Woods Hole	X							9	9	2:1		27
Phillips Academy (Andover), Andover	X	X	X	X			9–PG	1,090	1,090	5:1	X	48
Pioneer Valley Christian School, Springfield			X	X	PS–5	6–8	9–12	320	130	7:1	X	12
The Rivers School, Weston			X	X		6–8	9–12	440	332	8:1	X	18
Riverview School, East Sandwich	X	X	X	X		6–8	9–12	95	82	8:1		18
The Roxbury Latin School, West Roxbury			X				7–12	291	291	7:1	X	10
St. John's Preparatory School, Danvers			X				9–12	1,200	1,200	12:1	X	47
Saint Mark's School, Southborough	X	X	X	X			9–12	336	336	5:1	X	24
St. Sebastian's School, Needham			X			7–8	9–12	355	257	7:1	X	18
Stoneleigh–Burnham School, Greenfield		X		X		7–8	9–PG	127	98	6:1	X	21
The Sudbury Valley School, Framingham			X	X				180		16:1		
Tabor Academy, Marion	X	X	X	X			9–12	500	500	6:1	X	21
Trinity Catholic High School, Newton			X	X					234	13:1	X	19
Ursuline Academy, Dedham				X		7–8	9–12	388	288	9:1	X	16
Valley View School, North Brookfield	X					5–8	9–12	56	30	6:1		42
Waldorf High School of Massachusetts Bay, Belmont			X	X			9–12	58	58	6:1		3
Walnut Hill School, Natick	X	X	X	X			9–12	298	298	6:1	X	11
Waring School, Beverly			X	X		6–8	9–12	149	89	8:1	X	9
The Williston Northampton School, Easthampton	X	X	X	X		7–8	9–PG	536	450	7:1	X	38
Willow Hill School, Sudbury			X	X		6–8	9–12	60	35	4:1		24
The Winchendon School, Winchendon	X	X	X	X			8–PG	240	240	8:1	X	46
The Winsor School, Boston				X		5–8	9–12	425	233	7:1	X	13
Worcester Academy, Worcester	X	X	X	X		6–8	9–PG	657	496	7:1	X	23
Xaverian Brothers High School, Westwood			X				9–12	973	973	22:1	X	29
Michigan												
Academy of the Sacred Heart, Bloomfield Hills			X	X	N–4	5–8	9–12	563	148	7:1	X	11
Brother Rice High School, Bloomfield Hills			X				9–12	705	705	13:1	X	25
Cardinal Mooney Catholic College Preparatory High School, Marine City			X	X			9–12	198	198	10:1	X	11
Catholic Central High School, Novi			X				9–12	1,052	1,052	14:1	X	18
Detroit Country Day School, Beverly Hills	X	X	X	X	PK–5	6–8	9–12	1,600	661	8:1	X	29
Gabriel Richard High School, Riverview			X	X			9–12	443	443	15:1	X	16
Greenhills School, Ann Arbor			X	X		6–8	9–12	538	340	7:1	X	15
Heritage Christian Academy, North Branch			X	X	PK–6	7–8	9–12	80	9	4:1		5
Interlochen Arts Academy, Interlochen	X	X	X	X			9–PG	455	455	6:1	X	40
Ladywood High School, Livonia				X			9–12	410	410	13:1	X	23
Lansing Christian School, Lansing			X	X	PK–5	6–8	9–12	618	191	12:1	X	3
Lutheran High School Northwest, Rochester Hills			X	X			9–12	308	308	16:1	X	18
Marian High School, Bloomfield Hills				X			9–12	580	580	11:1	X	17
Powers Catholic High School, Flint			X	X			9–12	641	641	16:1	X	30
The Roeper School, Bloomfield Hills			X	X	PK–5	6–8	9–12	625	198	6:1	X	10
St. Mary's Preparatory School, Orchard Lake	X		X				9–12	500	500	10:1	X	43
Southfield Christian High School, Southfield			X	X	K–5	6–8	9–12	578	216	20:1	X	19
University Liggett School, Grosse Pointe Woods			X	X	PK–5	6–8	9–12	538	228	8:1	X	16
Valley Lutheran High School, Saginaw			X	X			9–12	354	354	17:1	X	6
The Valley School, Flint			X	X	PK–4	5–8	9–12	41	15	8:1		4
West Catholic High School, Grand Rapids			X	X			9–12	640	640	23:1	X	22
Minnesota												
Benilde–St. Margaret's School, St. Louis Park			X	X		7–8	9–12	1,171	888	12:1	X	25
The Blake School, Hopkins			X	X	PK–5	6–8	9–12	1,390	512	8:1	X	15
Breck School, Minneapolis			X	X	PK–4	5–8	9–12	1,199	409	11:1	X	19
Convent of the Visitation School, Mendota Heights			X	X	PK–5	6–8	9–12	582	328	10:1	X	18
Cotter Schools, Winona	X	X	X	X		7–8	9–12	419	314	16:1		24
Cretin-Derham Hall, Saint Paul			X	X			9–12	1,321	1,321	15:1	X	25
Marshall School, Duluth			X	X		5–8	9–12	432	267	11:1	X	18
Mounds Park Academy, St. Paul			X	X	PK–4	5–8	9–12	625	250	9:1	X	19
St. Croix Lutheran High School, West St. Paul	X	X	X	X		6–8	9–12	430	410	15:1	X	7
Saint John's Preparatory School, Collegeville	X	X	X	X		7–8	9–PG	338	259	10:1	X	50
St. Paul Academy and Summit School, St. Paul			X	X	K–5	6–8	9–12	862	345	7:1		25
Saint Thomas Academy, Mendota Heights			X			7–8	9–12	694	542	10:1	X	30
Shattuck-St. Mary's School, Faribault	X	X	X	X		6–8	9–12	434	381	9:1	X	22

Private Secondary Schools At-a-Glance

	Students Accepted: Boarding		Students Accepted: Day		Grades			Student/Faculty			School Offerings	
	Boys	Girls	Boys	Girls	Lower	Middle	Upper	Total	Upper	Student/Faculty Ratio	Advanced Placement Preparation	Sports
Mississippi												
Bass Memorial Academy, Lumberton	X	X	X	X					101	12:1		8
Chamberlain-Hunt Academy, Port Gibson	X		X	X		7–8	9–12	110	66	5:1	X	40
The Education Center, Jackson			X	X	1–6	7–8	9–12	170	125	9:1	X	
Jackson Academy, Jackson			X	X	PK–6	7–9	10–12	1,373	267	15:1	X	13
Jackson Preparatory School, Jackson			X	X		6–9	10–12	800	360	11:1	X	15
Madison-Ridgeland Academy, Madison			X	X	K–5	6–8	9–12	953	244	13:1	X	13
New Summit School, Jackson			X	X	K–5	6–8	9–12	94	36	10:1		15
Our Lady Academy, Bay St. Louis				X		7–8	9–12	269	159	13:1	X	12
Parklane Academy, McComb			X	X	PK–3	4–6	7–12	976	425	16:1	X	11
St. Andrew's Episcopal School, Ridgeland			X	X	PK–4	5–8	9–12	1,217	345	9:1	X	20
St. Stanislaus College, Bay St. Louis	X		X			6–8	9–12	427	309	23:1	X	15
Starkville Academy, Starkville			X	X	K–6		7–12	795	351	14:1	X	13
Washington County Day School, Greenville			X	X	PK–5	6–8	9–12	753	256	20:1		11
Missouri												
The Barstow School, Kansas City			X	X	PS–5	6–8	9–12	651	204	8:1	X	12
Chaminade College Preparatory School, St. Louis	X		X			6–8	9–12	850	552	10:1	X	21
Crossroads College Preparatory School, St. Louis			X	X		7–8	9–12	228	145	9:1	X	22
De Smet Jesuit High School, Creve Coeur			X							14:1	X	30
Greenwood Laboratory School, Springfield			X	X	K–6	7–8	9–12	339	94	28:1	X	8
John Burroughs School, St. Louis			X	X				600	404	7:1	X	29
Logos School, St. Louis			X	X		6–8	9–12	151	129	6:1		4
Lutheran High School, Kansas City			X	X			9–12	113	113	12:1		14
Lutheran High School North, St. Louis			X	X			9–12	384	384	13:1	X	12
Missouri Military Academy, Mexico	X					6–8	9–PG	270	210	11:1	X	45
Nerinx Hall, Webster Groves				X			9–12	620	620	10:1		13
New Covenant Academy, Springfield			X	X	JK–6	7–8	9–12	405	132	10:1		3
Saint Paul Lutheran High School, Concordia	X	X	X	X			9–12	186	186	11:1		19
Saint Teresa's Academy, Kansas City				X			9–12	533	533	12:1		24
Thomas Jefferson School, St. Louis	X	X	X	X		7–8	9–PG	78	61	7:1	X	11
Valle Catholic High School, Ste. Genevieve			X	X			9–12	152	152	8:1	X	13
Vianney High School, St. Louis			X				9–12	622	622	12:1	X	29
Villa Duchesne/Oak Hill School, St. Louis			X	X	JK–6		7–12	760	450	9:1	X	13
Visitation Academy of St. Louis County, St. Louis			X	X	PK–6		7–12	623	420	9:1	X	14
Montana												
Butte Central High School, Butte			X	X			9–12	121	121	10:1	X	11
Elk Mountain Academy, Heron	X						9–12	25	25	8:1		34
Headwaters Academy, Bozeman			X	X		6–8		24		5:1		48
Lustre Christian High School, Lustre	X	X	X	X			9–12	22	22	3:1		4
Montana Academy, Marion	X	X						70	70	2:1	X	43
Summit Preparatory School, Kalispell	X	X					9–12	50	50	5:1		54
Nebraska												
Brownell-Talbot School, Omaha			X	X	PK–4	5–8	9–12	462	128	9:1		16
Central Catholic Mid-High School, Grand Island			X	X		6–8	9–12	305	185	15:1	X	14
Mercy High School, Omaha				X			9–12	365	365	12:1	X	25
Mount Michael Benedictine School, Elkhorn	X		X				9–12	172	172	9:1	X	21
Nebraska Christian Schools, Central City	X	X	X	X	K–6	7–8	9–12	181	90	10:1		6
Pius X High School, Lincoln			X	X			9–12	1,024	1,024	14:1	X	17
Saint Cecilia High School, Hastings			X	X		6–8	9–12	296	183	8:1	X	21
Scotus Central Catholic High School, Columbus			X	X		7–8	9–12	359	218	12:1	X	13
Nevada												
Bishop Gorman High School, Las Vegas			X	X			9–12	1,141	1,141	25:1	X	21
Faith Lutheran High School, Las Vegas			X	X		6–8	9–12	1,282	704	17:1	X	18
The Meadows School, Las Vegas			X	X	PK–5	6–8	9–12	910	263	11:1	X	15
Sage Ridge School, Reno			X	X		5–8	9–12	234	82	8:1		15
New Hampshire												
Bishop Brady High School, Concord			X	X			9–12	446	446	15:1	X	29
Bishop Guertin High School, Nashua			X	X			9–12	900	900		X	34
Brewster Academy, Wolfeboro	X	X	X	X			9–PG	358	358	6:1	X	31
Cardigan Mountain School, Canaan	X		X			6–9		205	180	4:1		35
Coe-Brown Northwood Academy, Northwood			X	X			9–12	687	687	12:1	X	12
Community School, South Tamworth			X	X		7–8	9–12	30	27	6:1		21
Crotched Mountain Rehabilitation Center School, Greenfield	X	X	X	X					123			2
The Derryfield School, Manchester			X	X		6–8	9–12	385	262	8:1	X	23
Dublin Christian Academy, Dublin	X	X	X	X	K–6	7–8	9–12	116	71	8:1	X	11
Dublin School, Dublin	X	X	X	X			9–12	123	123	5:1	X	32
Hampshire Country School, Rindge	X				3–6		7–12	22	17	4:1		28
High Mowing School, Wilton	X	X	X	X			9–12	112	112	5:1	X	40
Holderness School, Plymouth	X	X	X	X			9–PG	281	281	6:1	X	48
Kimball Union Academy, Meriden	X	X	X	X			9–PG	355	355	6:1	X	37
Maharishi Academy of Total Knowledge, Antrim	X		X				9–12					27

Private Secondary Schools At-a-Glance

	STUDENTS ACCEPTED				GRADES			STUDENT/FACULTY			SCHOOL OFFERINGS	
	Boarding		Day									
	Boys	Girls	Boys	Girls	Lower	Middle	Upper	Total	Upper	Student/Faculty Ratio	Advanced Placement Preparation	Sports
New Hampton School, New Hampton	X	X	X	X			9–PG	321	321	5:1	X	42
Phillips Exeter Academy, Exeter	X	X	X	X			9–PG	1,045	1,045	5:1	X	43
Portsmouth Christian Academy, Dover			X	X	PK–5	6–8	9–12	797	244	11:1	X	12
St. Paul's School, Concord	X	X					9–12	533	533	5:1	X	32
St. Thomas Aquinas High School, Dover			X	X			9–12	719	719	15:1	X	18
Tilton School, Tilton	X	X	X	X			9–PG	256	256	5:1	X	27
Trinity High School, Manchester			X	X			9–12	442	442	16:1	X	22
Wediko School and Treatment Program, Windsor	X		X					40		2:1		40
The White Mountain School, Bethlehem	X	X	X	X			9–PG	95	95	5:1	X	41
New Jersey												
Academy of the Holy Angels, Demarest				X			9–12	567	567	11:1	X	17
The American Boychoir School, Princeton	X		X		4–5	6–8		48	22	3:1		19
Baptist High School, Haddon Heights			X	X	K–6	7–8	9–12	253	135	10:1	X	11
Barnstable Academy, Oakland			X	X		5–8	9–12	120	90	8:1	X	16
Bishop Eustace Preparatory School, Pennsauken			X	X			9–12	792	792	13:1	X	20
Bishop George Ahr High School, Edison			X	X			9–12	945	945	16:1	X	17
Blair Academy, Blairstown	X	X	X	X			9–PG	445	445	7:1	X	42
Christian Brothers Academy, Lincroft			X				9–12	935	935	14:1	X	15
Community High School, Teaneck			X	X				185	185			7
The Craig School, Mountain Lakes			X	X	3–8		9–12	153	46	6:1		3
Delbarton School, Morristown			X			7–8	9–12	538	476	10:1	X	28
DePaul Catholic High School, Wayne			X	X						19:1	X	31
Dwight-Englewood School, Englewood			X	X	PK–5	6–8	9–12	959	447	9:1	X	16
Eastern Christian High School, North Haledon			X	X	PK–4	5–8	9–12	827	351	10:1	X	30
Gill St. Bernard's School, Gladstone			X	X	PK–4	5–8	9–12	689	252	7:1	X	16
Hawthorne Christian Academy, Hawthorne			X	X	PS–5	6–8	9–12	462	161	7:1		9
The Hudson School, Hoboken			X	X		5–8	9–12	189	76	10:1	X	10
The Hun School of Princeton, Princeton	X	X	X	X		6–8	9–PG	595	504	8:1	X	36
Immaculate Conception High School, Lodi				X			9–12	172	172	11:1	X	16
Kent Place School, Summit			X	X	N–5	6–8	9–12	647	263	7:1	X	17
The King's Christian High School, Cherry Hill			X	X	P3–5	6–8	9–12	363	138	7:1	X	8
The Lawrenceville School, Lawrenceville	X	X	X	X			9–PG	795	795	8:1		51
Ma'ayanot Yeshiva High School for Girls of Bergan County, Teaneck				X			9–12	246	246	5:1	X	6
Marist High School, Bayonne			X	X				510	510	25:1	X	12
Mary Help of Christians Academy, North Haledon				X			9–12	230	230	8:1	X	8
Marylawn of the Oranges, South Orange				X			9–12	156	156	15:1	X	10
Monmouth Academy, Howell			X	X	K–4	5–8	9–12	98	37	8:1	X	9
Monsignor Donovan High School, Toms River			X	X			9–12	957	957	14:1	X	21
Moorestown Friends School, Moorestown			X	X	PS–4	5–8	9–12	725	289	9:1	X	17
Morristown-Beard School, Morristown			X	X		6–8	9–12	529	390	7:1	X	23
Mt. Saint Dominic Academy, Caldwell				X			9–12	330	330	10:1	X	20
Newark Academy, Livingston			X	X		6–8	9–12	559	398	12:1	X	32
Notre Dame High School, Lawrenceville			X	X			9–12	1,277	1,277	24:1	X	30
Oak Knoll School of the Holy Child, Summit			X	X	K–6		7–12	556	313	8:1	X	16
Our Lady of Mercy Academy, Newfield				X			9–12	203	203	11:1		22
Peddie School, Hightstown	X	X	X	X			9–PG	527	527	6:1	X	24
The Pennington School, Pennington	X	X	X	X		6–8	9–12	478	378	8:1	X	21
The Pingry School, Martinsville			X	X	K–5	6–8	9–12	1,055	529	8:1	X	22
Pope John XXIII Regional High School, Sparta			X	X			9–12	965	965	13:1		17
Purnell School, Pottersville		X		X			9–12	123	123	8:1		24
Ranney School, Tinton Falls			X	X	N–5	6–8	9–12	815	241		X	16
Rutgers Preparatory School, Somerset			X	X	PK–4	5–8	9–12	702	332	6:1	X	12
Saddle River Day School, Saddle River			X	X	K–5	6–8	9–12	276	137	7:1	X	17
Saint Augustine Preparatory School, Richland			X				9–12	647	647	13:1	X	24
St. Benedict's Preparatory School, Newark			X		7–8		9–12	550	483	11:1		21
Saint Dominic Academy, Jersey City				X			9–12	527	527	12:1	X	12
Saint Joseph Regional High School, Montvale			X				9–12	501	501	12:1	X	18
Saint Mary High School, Rutherford			X	X			9–12	342	342	10:1	X	11
St. Mary's Hall–Doane Academy, Burlington			X	X	PK–6		7–12	197	110	5:1	X	14
St. Peter's Preparatory School, Jersey City			X				9–12	919	919	12:1	X	29
Stuart Country Day School of the Sacred Heart, Princeton			X	X	PS–5	6–8	9–12	507	144	12:1	X	10
Villa Walsh Academy, Morristown				X		7–8	9–12	245	218	8:1	X	11
The Wardlaw-Hartridge School, Edison			X	X	PK–5	6–8	9–12	429	148	4:1	X	18
New Mexico												
Albuquerque Academy, Albuquerque			X	X		6–8	9–12	1,095	656	8:1	X	28
Chamisa Mesa High School, Taos			X	X			9–12	27	27	5:1		
McCurdy School, Espanola			X	X	PK–6	7–8	9–12	342	144	14:1	X	13
Menaul School, Albuquerque			X	X		6–8	9–12	154	80	9:1	X	11
Navajo Preparatory School, Inc., Farmington	X	X	X	X					183	15:1		8
New Mexico Military Institute, Roswell	X	X					9–12	380	380	15:1		43
Sandia Preparatory School, Albuquerque			X	X		6–8	9–12	664	383	10:1		27
Santa Fe Preparatory School, Santa Fe			X	X		7–8	9–12	350	230	10:1	X	16
The United World College—USA, Montezuma	X	X					11–12	200	200	8:1		50

Private Secondary Schools At-a-Glance

	STUDENTS ACCEPTED				GRADES			STUDENT/FACULTY			SCHOOL OFFERINGS	
	Boarding		Day									
	Boys	Girls	Boys	Girls	Lower	Middle	Upper	Total	Upper	Student/Faculty Ratio	Advanced Placement Preparation	Sports
New York												
Academy of Mount Saint Ursula, Bronx				X			9–12	400	400	17:1	X	9
Academy of Our Lady of Good Counsel High School, White Plains				X			9–12	303	303	11:1		8
Allendale Columbia School, Rochester			X	X	N–5	6–8	9–12	415	124	5:1	X	12
The Beekman School, New York			X	X			9–PG	80	80	8:1	X	
The Birch Wathen Lenox School, New York			X	X	K–5	6–8	9–12	550	170	12:1	X	23
The Brearley School, New York				X	K–4	5–8	9–12	690	212	6:1	X	26
The Browning School, New York			X		K–4	5–8	9–12	389	113	19:1	X	9
Buffalo Seminary, Buffalo				X			9–12	161	161	10:1	X	28
The Calhoun School, New York			X	X	N–4	5–8	9–12	734	185	5:1		16
Cascadilla School, Ithaca	X	X	X	X			9–PG	52	52	6:1	X	47
Cathedral High School, New York				X			9–12	684	684		X	5
The Chapin School, New York				X	K–3	4–7	8–12	673	240	4:1	X	59
Christian Brothers Academy, Albany			X			6–8	9–12	407	304	13:1	X	25
Christian Brothers Academy, Syracuse			X	X			7–12	750	750		X	17
Christian Central Academy, Williamsville			X	X	K–5	6–8	9–12	436	130	6:1	X	9
Columbia Grammar and Preparatory School, New York			X	X	PK–6		7–12	1,125	547	7:1	X	26
Convent of the Sacred Heart, New York				X	PK–4	5–7	8–12	684	259	16:1	X	23
The Dalton School, New York			X	X	K–3	4–8	9–12	1,275	432	7:1	X	16
Darrow School, New Lebanon	X	X	X	X			9–PG	98	98	4:1		24
Doane Stuart School, Albany			X	X	N–4	5–8	9–12	266	122	7:1	X	19
The Dominican Academy of the City of New York, New York				X			9–12	224	224	8:1	X	10
Emma Willard School, Troy		X		X			9–PG	311	311	5:1	X	35
The Family Foundation School, Hancock	X	X				6–8	9–12	245	242	8:1		27
Fontbonne Hall Academy, Brooklyn				X			9–12	536	536	12:1	X	17
Fordham Preparatory School, Bronx			X				9–12	953	953	10:1	X	22
French-American School of New York, Mamaroneck			X	X	N–5	6–8	9–12	824	127	7:1	X	9
Garden School, Jackson Heights			X	X	N–6		7–12	350		11:1	X	7
The Gow School, South Wales	X					7–9	10–PG	142	95	4:1		61
Green Meadow Waldorf School, Chestnut Ridge			X	X	N–8		9–12	375	80	9:1		8
Hackley School, Tarrytown	X	X	X	X	K–4	5–8	9–12	836	382	6:1	X	27
The Harley School, Rochester			X	X	N–4	5–8	9–12	501	170	7:1	X	15
The Harvey School, Katonah	X	X	X	X		6–8	9–12	340	235	7:1	X	21
Hebrew Academy-the Five Towns, Cedarhurst			X	X			9–12	488	488		X	7
Holy Trinity Diocesan High School, Hicksville			X	X			9–12	1,496	1,496		X	19
Hoosac School, Hoosick	X	X	X	X			8–PG	125	125	5:1	X	26
The Horace Mann School, Bronx			X	X	N–5	6–8	9–12	1,756	715	9:1	X	39
Houghton Academy, Houghton	X	X	X	X		6–8	9–PG	177	148	15:1		17
The Karafin School, Mount Kisco			X	X			9–12	82	75	6:1		36
Kildonan School, Amenia	X	X	X	X	2–6	7–9	10–PG	108	46	6:1		36
The Knox School, St. James	X	X	X	X		6–8	9–12	109	97	5:1	X	18
La Salle Institute, Troy			X			6–8	9–12	440	340	10:1	X	26
Little Red School House and Elisabeth Irwin High School, New York			X	X	N–4	5–8	9–12	565	177	7:1		16
Loyola School, New York			X	X			9–12	208	208	8:1	X	16
Lycee Français de New York, New York			X	X	N–5	6–9	10–12	1,376	284	9:1	X	34
Manlius Pebble Hill School, DeWitt			X	X	PK–5	6–8	9–12	582	261	6:1	X	25
Maplebrook School, Amenia	X	X	X	X				77	62	8:1		41
Martin Luther High School, Maspeth			X	X			9–12	316	316	15:1	X	19
The Mary Louis Academy, Jamaica Estates				X			9–12	962	962	13:1	X	22
Marymount School, New York			X	X	N–3	4–7	8–12	572	230	6:1	X	22
The Masters School, Dobbs Ferry	X	X	X	X		5–8	9–12	580	415	6:1	X	30
McQuaid Jesuit, Rochester			X			7–8	9–12	870	646	15:1	X	50
Millbrook School, Millbrook	X	X	X	X			9–12	258	258	5:1	X	28
Mother Cabrini High School, New York				X			9–12	350	350	13:1	X	6
National Sports Academy at Lake Placid, Lake Placid	X	X	X	X		8	9–PG	79	74	7:1	X	24
New York Military Academy, Cornwall-on-Hudson	X	X	X	X		7–8	9–12	146	123	10:1	X	17
The Nichols School, Buffalo			X	X		5–8	9–12	585	400	8:1	X	20
North Country School, Lake Placid	X	X	X	X		4–9		88	68	3:1		39
Northwood School, Lake Placid	X	X	X	X			9–12	174	174	6:1	X	49
Notre Dame- Bishop Gibbons School, Schenectady			X	X		6–8	9–12	316	197	11:1	X	15
Oakwood Friends School, Poughkeepsie	X	X	X	X		6–8	9–12	179	158	5:1	X	26
Our Lady of Mercy High School, Rochester				X		7–8	9–12	645	495	14:1	X	17
Our Saviour Lutheran School, Bronx			X	X	PK–3	4–6	7–12	348	151	13:1	X	6
The Packer Collegiate Institute, Brooklyn			X	X	PK–4	5–8	9–12	941	306	7:1	X	4
The Park School of Buffalo, Snyder			X	X	N–4	5–8	9–12	239	105	9:1	X	9
Poly Prep Country Day School, Brooklyn			X	X	N–4	5–8	9–12	1,010	481	7:1	X	28
Portledge School, Locust Valley			X	X	N–5	6–8	9–12	407	172	6:1	X	11
Poughkeepsie Day School, Poughkeepsie			X	X	PK–4	5–8	9–12	320	93	6:1	X	25
Preston High School, Bronx				X			9–12	611	611	15:1	X	9
Professional Children's School, New York			X	X		6–8	9–12	181	147	8:1		
Rambam Mesivta, Lawrence			X				9–12	156	156	3:1	X	9

Private Secondary Schools At-a-Glance

	STUDENTS ACCEPTED				GRADES			STUDENT/FACULTY			SCHOOL OFFERINGS	
	Boarding		Day									
	Boys	Girls	Boys	Girls	Lower	Middle	Upper	Total	Upper	Student/Faculty Ratio	Advanced Placement Preparation	Sports
Redemption Christian Academy, Troy	X	X	X	X	K–5	6–8	9–PG			10:1		3
Regis High School, New York			X				9–12	536	536	15:1	X	10
Rice High School, New York			X				9–12	276	276	15:1		10
Riverdale Country School, Riverdale			X	X	PK–5	6–8	9–12	1,084	456	8:1	X	22
Robert Louis Stevenson School, New York			X	X			8–PG	81	81	5:1		27
Rockland Country Day School, Congers			X	X	PK–5	6–8	9–12	145	65	6:1	X	18
Ross School, East Hampton	X	X	X	X	1–4	5–8	9–12	580	220			11
Rye Country Day School, Rye			X	X	PK–4	5–8	9–12	871	383	7:1	X	27
Saint Edmund High School, Brooklyn			X	X						15:1	X	13
St. Thomas Choir School, New York	X				3–6		7–8	36	21	5:1		21
Salesian High School, New Rochelle			X				9–12	500	500	11:1	X	21
School for Young Performers, New York			X	X	K–5	6–8	9–12			1:1	X	
School of the Holy Child, Rye				X		5–8	9–12	344	237	7:1	X	20
Seton Catholic Central High School, Binghamton			X	X			9–12	350	350	23:1	X	19
Smith School, New York			X	X		7–8	9–12	55	47	4:1		12
Soundview Preparatory School, Yorktown Heights			X	X		6–8	9–PG	65	55	5:1	X	10
The Spence School, New York				X	K–4	5–8	9–12	658	198	7:1	X	10
Staten Island Academy, Staten Island			X	X	PK–4	5–8	9–12	400	144	10:1	X	12
Stella Maris High School, Rockaway Park				X			9–12	299	299	8:1	X	11
The Stony Brook School, Stony Brook	X	X	X	X		7–8	9–12	337	253	8:1	X	15
Storm King School, Cornwall-on-Hudson	X	X	X	X		8–8	9–12	143	134	6:1	X	55
Trinity-Pawling School, Pawling	X		X			7–8	9–PG	320	290	8:1	X	39
Trinity School, New York			X	X	K–4	5–8	9–12	976	440	7:1	X	15
United Nations International School, New York			X	X	K–4	5–8	9–12	1,541	464	10:1		47
The Ursuline School, New Rochelle				X		6–8	9–12	823	659	18:1	X	15
The Waldorf School of Garden City, Garden City			X	X	N–5	6–8	9–12	349	88	7:1	X	14
The Windsor School, Flushing			X	X		6–8	9–13	147	138	14:1	X	11
Winston Preparatory School, New York			X	X		6–8	9–12	240	142	3:1		10
York Preparatory School, New York			X	X		6–8	9–12	336	238	5:1	X	26
North Carolina												
Arthur Morgan School, Burnsville	X	X	X	X		7–9		20	26	3:1		26
Asheville School, Asheville	X	X	X	X			9–12	260	260	7:1	X	44
Auldern Academy, Siler City		X					9–12	45	45	6:1	X	25
Bishop McGuinness Catholic High School, Kernersville			X	X			9–12	565	565	13:1	X	14
Camelot Academy, Durham			X	X	K–6		7–12	90	43	10:1	X	6
Cannon School, Concord			X	X	PK–4	5–8	9–12	915	340	9:1	X	27
Cape Fear Academy, Wilmington			X	X	PK–5	6–8	9–12	672	232	8:1	X	12
Cardinal Gibbons High School, Raleigh			X	X			9–12	1,132	1,132	24:1	X	20
Carolina Day School, Asheville			X	X	PK–5	6–8	9–12	651	175	9:1	X	13
Cary Academy, Cary			X	X		6–8	9–12	710	408	14:1	X	49
Charlotte Catholic High School, Charlotte			X	X			9–12	1,416	1,416		X	25
Charlotte Christian School, Charlotte			X	X	JK–5	6–8	9–12	1,078	392	11:1	X	21
Charlotte Country Day School, Charlotte			X	X	PK–4	5–8	9–12	1,633	475	12:1	X	21
Charlotte Latin School, Charlotte			X	X	K–5	6–8	9–12	1,378	481	8:1	X	29
Christ School, Arden	X		X			8–8	9–12	225	210	6:1	X	43
Durham Academy, Durham			X	X	PK–4	5–8	9–12	1,145	392	12:1	X	22
Fayetteville Academy, Fayetteville			X	X	PK–5	6–8	9–12	432	152	15:1	X	14
Forsyth Country Day School, Lewisville			X	X	PK–4	5–8	9–12	938	392	12:1	X	18
Gaston Day School, Gastonia			X	X	PS–4	5–8	9–12	513	143	8:1	X	24
Greenfield School, Wilson			X	X	PS–4	5–8	9–12	331	68	3:1	X	7
Greensboro Day School, Greensboro			X	X		6–8	9–12	903	340	13:1	X	18
Guilford Day School, Greensboro			X	X	1–5	6–8	9–12	136	55	8:1		8
Harrells Christian Academy, Harrells			X	X	K–5	6–8	9–12	494	140	10:1	X	8
The Hill Center, Durham Academy, Durham			X	X	K–5	6–8	9–12	164	79	4:1		
Kerr-Vance Academy, Henderson			X	X	PK–6	7–8	9–12	472	132	10:1	X	13
Oak Ridge Military Academy, Oak Ridge	X	X	X	X		6–8	9–12	160	130	11:1		24
The Oakwood School, Greenville			X	X	PK–3	4–7	8–12	334	62	8:1	X	10
The O'Neal School, Southern Pines			X	X	PK–4	5–8	9–12	440	163	10:1	X	11
Providence Day School, Charlotte			X	X	PK–5	6–8	9–12	1,528	509	7:1	X	23
Ravenscroft School, Raleigh			X	X	PK–5	6–8	9–12	1,229	446	8:1	X	22
Ridgecroft School, Ahoskie			X	X	PK–5	6–8	9–12	331	85	11:1	X	12
Rocky Mount Academy, Rocky Mount			X	X	PK–5	6–8	9–12	447	159	8:1	X	14
St. David's School, Raleigh			X	X	K–4	5–8	9–12	558	205	10:1	X	16
Saint Mary's School, Raleigh		X		X			9–12	297	297	8:1	X	16
Salem Academy, Winston-Salem		X		X			9–12	175	175	7:1	X	21
Salem Baptist Christian School, Winston Salem			X	X	P3–4	5–8	9–12	391	132	10:1	X	6
Stone Mountain School, Black Mountain	X					6–8	9–12	58	39	4:1		37
Wayne Country Day School, Goldsboro			X	X	PK–6		7–12	253	124	15:1	X	10
Westchester Country Day School, High Point			X	X	K–5	6–8	9–12	419	123	6:1	X	11
North Dakota												
Dickinson Trinity, Dickinson			X	X			7–12	254	254	11:1		18
Minot Bishop Ryan, Minot			X	X		7–8	9–12	420	280	17:1		14
Oak Grove Lutheran School, Fargo			X	X	K–5	6–8	9–12	505	193	12:1	X	15

Private Secondary Schools At-a-Glance

	STUDENTS ACCEPTED				GRADES			STUDENT/FACULTY			SCHOOL OFFERINGS	
	Boarding		Day									
	Boys	Girls	Boys	Girls	Lower	Middle	Upper	Total	Upper	Student/Faculty Ratio	Advanced Placement Preparation	Sports
Ohio												
Andrews Osborne Academy, Willoughby	X	X	X	X	PK–4	5–8	9–12	304	106	5:1	X	14
Archbishop Hoban High School, Akron			X	X			9–12	891	891	13:1		23
Archbishop McNicholas High School, Cincinnati			X	X			9–12	738	738	11:1	X	18
Benedictine High School, Cleveland			X				9–12	399	399	11:1	X	22
Bishop Fenwick High School, Franklin			X	X			9–12	550	550	16:1	X	18
Central Catholic High School, Canton			X	X			9–12	485	485	16:1	X	13
Central Catholic High School, Toledo			X	X								
Cincinnati Country Day School, Cincinnati			X	X	PK–5	6–8	9–12	800	253	9:1	X	14
The Columbus Academy, Gahanna			X	X	PK–4	5–8	9–12	1,057	361	8:1	X	14
Delphos Saint John's High School, Delphos			X	X			9–12	285	285	14:1		13
Elyria Catholic High School, Elyria			X	X			9–12	547	547	14:1	X	16
Excel Academy, Inc., Newark			X	X	K–5	6–8	9–12	150	49	3:1		5
Gilmour Academy, Gates Mills	X	X	X	X	PK–6	7–8	9–12	725	425	10:1	X	38
The Grand River Academy, Austinburg	X						9–12	111	111	6:1	X	62
Hathaway Brown School, Shaker Heights			X	X	PS–4	5–8	9–12	860	339	8:1	X	12
Hawken School, Gates Mills			X	X	PS–5	6–8	9–12	910	429	9:1	X	16
Lake Ridge Academy, North Ridgeville			X	X	K–5	6–8	9–12	357	154	8:1	X	23
Lawrence School, Sagamore Hills			X	X	1–6	7–8	9–12	299	134	11:1	X	27
Lehman High School, Sidney			X	X			9–12	234	234	15:1	X	16
Lutheran High School West, Rocky River			X	X			9–12	460	460	14:1	X	15
Magnificat High School, Rocky River				X			9–12	830	830	12:1	X	14
Maumee Valley Country Day School, Toledo			X	X	P3–6	7–8	9–12	479	187	10:1	X	13
Notre Dame-Cathedral Latin School, Chardon			X	X			9–12	749	749	15:1	X	17
Olney Friends School, Barnesville	X	X	X	X			9–12	62	62	5:1	X	26
Padua Franciscan High School, Parma			X	X			9–12	958	958	18:1	X	39
Regina High School, South Euclid				X			9–12	232	232	12:1	X	12
St. Francis de Sales High School, Toledo			X				9–12	617	617	14:1	X	17
Saint Joseph Central Catholic High School, Fremont			X	X			9–12	243	243	15:1	X	15
Saint Xavier High School, Cincinnati			X				9–12	1,560	1,560	15:1	X	17
The Seven Hills School, Cincinnati			X	X	PK–5	6–8	9–12	1,040	300	9:1	X	13
Stephen T. Badin High School, Hamilton			X	X			9–12	575	575	18:1	X	2
The Summit Country Day School, Cincinnati			X	X	PK–4	5–8	9–12	1,100	375	9:1	X	18
Trinity High School, Garfield Heights			X	X			9–12	367	367	10:1	X	16
The Wellington School, Columbus			X	X	PK–4	5–8	9–12	616	210	12:1	X	13
Western Reserve Academy, Hudson	X	X	X	X			9–12	370	370	6:1	X	44
Oklahoma												
Bishop McGuinness Catholic High School, Oklahoma City			X	X	9–10		11–12	693	314	14:1	X	17
Cascia Hall Preparatory School, Tulsa			X	X		6–8	9–12	588	379	12:1	X	17
Heritage Hall, Oklahoma City			X	X	PS–4	5–8	9–12	860	343	16:1	X	19
Holland Hall, Tulsa			X	X	PK–3	4–8	9–12	993	340	9:1	X	16
Oregon												
The Academy at Sisters, Bend		X				7–8	9–12			12:1		29
Academy for Global Exploration, Ashland	X	X					9–12	8	8	3:1		50
Blanchet School, Salem			X	X		7–8	9–12	392	253	18:1	X	12
Canyonville Christian Academy, Canyonville	X	X	X	X						15:1	X	11
The Catlin Gabel School, Portland			X	X	PS–5	6–8	9–12	733	290	7:1		46
CrossRoads, Medford			X	X						6:1		
Hosanna Christian School, Klamath Falls			X	X	PK–5	6–8	9–12	274	66	15:1		6
Lifegate School, Eugene	X	X	X	X		6–8	9–12	44	30	10:1	X	4
Mount Bachelor Academy, Prineville	X	X						101		4:1		17
The Northwest Academy, Portland			X	X		6–8	9–12	120	66	15:1		9
Oregon Episcopal School, Portland	X	X	X	X	PK–5	6–8	9–12	845	310	7:1	X	14
Pacific Crest Community School, Portland			X	X		7–8	9–12	85	70	9:1		11
Portland Lutheran School, Portland	X	X	X	X	PK–5	6–8	9–12	240	80	15:1	X	17
St. Mary's School, Medford			X	X		6–8	9–12	432	286	11:1	X	20
Santiam Christian School, Corvallis			X	X	PS–6	7–8	9–12	831	306	17:1	X	12
Pennsylvania												
Abington Friends School, Jenkintown			X	X	PK–5	6–8	9–12	640	258	7:1	X	11
Academy of Notre Dame de Namur, Villanova				X		6–8	9–12	526	381	8:1		17
Academy of the New Church Boys' School, Bryn Athyn	X		X				9–12	115	115	8:1	X	5
Academy of the New Church Girls' School, Bryn Athyn		X		X				113	113	8:1	X	8
The Agnes Irwin School, Rosemont				X	PK–4	5–8	9–12	681	244	7:1	X	29
The Baldwin School, Bryn Mawr				X	PK–5	6–8	9–12	587	206	7:1	X	17
Bishop Carroll High School, Ebensburg			X	X			9–12	236	236	12:1		12
Blue Mountain Academy, Hamburg	X	X	X	X			9–12	226	226	9:1	X	6
Carson Long Military Institute, New Bloomfield	X					6–8	9–12	135	112	11:1		21
Central Catholic High School, Pittsburgh			X				9–12	842	842	15:1	X	22
CFS, The School at Church Farm, Exton	X		X			7–8	9–12	180	138	7:1	X	17
Chestnut Hill Academy, Philadelphia			X		PK–5	6–8	9–12	570	222	7:1	X	18

Private Secondary Schools At-a-Glance

	STUDENTS ACCEPTED				GRADES			STUDENT/FACULTY			SCHOOL OFFERINGS	
	Boarding		Day									
	Boys	Girls	Boys	Girls	Lower	Middle	Upper	Total	Upper	Student/Faculty Ratio	Advanced Placement Preparation	Sports
Christopher Dock Mennonite High School, Lansdale			X	X			9–12	400	400	12:1	X	12
The Concept School, Westtown			X	X		4–8	9–12	40	25	8:1		11
Country Day School of the Sacred Heart, Bryn Mawr				X	PK–4	5–8	9–12	353	188	10:1	X	9
Delaware Valley Friends School, Paoli			X	X		7–8	9–12	205	165	5:1		14
Devon Preparatory School, Devon			X			6–8	9–12	298	230	10:1	X	11
The Ellis School, Pittsburgh				X	PK–4	5–8	9–12	486	166	7:1	X	10
Father Judge High School, Philadelphia			X				9–12	1,258	1,258	28:1		23
Friends' Central School, Wynnewood			X	X	PK–4	5–8	9–12	1,001	390	9:1		11
George School, Newtown	X	X	X	X			9–12	520	520	7:1	X	34
Germantown Academy, Fort Washington			X	X	PK–5	6–8	9–12	1,116	482	8:1	X	21
Germantown Friends School, Philadelphia			X	X	K–5	6–8	9–12	894	362	9:1		16
Girard College, Philadelphia	X	X			1–5	6–8	9–12	749	233	16:1	X	21
Gwynedd Mercy Academy, Gwynedd Valley				X			9–12	411	411	10:1	X	14
The Harrisburg Academy, Wormleysburg			X	X	N–4	5–8	9–12	453	128	8:1	X	9
The Haverford School, Haverford			X		PK–5	6–8	9–12	971	383	7:1		24
The Hill School, Pottstown	X	X	X	X			9–PG	489	489	7:1	X	25
The Hill Top Preparatory School, Rosemont			X	X		6–8	9–12	79	61	4:1		37
Holy Name High School, Reading			X	X			9–12	456	456	12:1	X	16
Jack M. Barrack Hebrew Academy (formerly Akiba Hebrew Academy), Bryn Mawr			X	X		6–8	9–12	309	223	8:1	X	12
The Janus School, Mount Joy			X	X	1–8		9–12	64	34	4:1		
Kimberton Waldorf School, Kimberton			X	X	PK–8		9–12	306	88	6:1		10
Lancaster Country Day School, Lancaster			X	X	PS–5	6–8	9–12	535	157	6:1	X	16
Lancaster Mennonite High School, Lancaster	X	X	X	X	PK–5	6–8	9–12	1,501	650	15:1	X	10
Lansdale Catholic High School, Lansdale			X	X			9–12	820	820		X	24
Lehigh Valley Christian High School, Allentown			X	X			9–12	167	167	12:1	X	8
Linden Hall, Lititz		X		X		6–8	9–PG	173	118	8:1	X	20
Mercersburg Academy, Mercersburg	X	X	X	X			9–PG	437	437	5:1	X	48
Mercyhurst Preparatory School, Erie			X	X			9–12	600	600	13:1		20
Mercy Vocational High School, Philadelphia			X	X						16:1		
MMI Preparatory School, Freeland			X	X		6–8	9–12	251	151	9.3:1	X	12
Moravian Academy, Bethlehem			X	X	PK–5	6–8	9–12	814	288	7:1	X	10
Mount Saint Joseph Academy, Flourtown				X			9–12	570	570	10:1	X	15
Notre Dame Junior/Senior High School, East Stroudsburg			X	X			9–12	259	259	15:1	X	14
The Oakland School, Pittsburgh			X	X			8–12	60	60	6:1		32
Perkiomen School, Pennsburg	X	X	X	X		5–8	9–PG	281	233	7:1	X	18
The Phelps School, Malvern	X		X				7–PG	142	142	5:1	X	29
Quigley Catholic High School, Baden			X	X			9–12	215	215	12:1	X	15
Saint Basil Academy, Jenkintown				X			9–12	410	410	13:1	X	11
Saint Joseph High School, Natrona Heights			X	X			9–12	180	180	14:1		11
St. Joseph's Preparatory School, Philadelphia			X				9–12	976	976	16:1	X	25
Sewickley Academy, Sewickley			X	X	PK–5	6–8	9–12	775	305	8:1	X	14
Shady Side Academy, Pittsburgh	X	X	X	X	PK–5	6–8	9–12	960	505	8:1	X	24
The Shipley School, Bryn Mawr			X	X	PK–5	6–8	9–12	882	343	7:1	X	25
Solebury School, New Hope	X	X	X	X		7–8	9–12	220	194	5:1	X	26
Valley Forge Military Academy & College, Wayne	X		X			7–8	9–PG	319	295	13:1	X	34
Villa Joseph Marie High School, Holland				X			9–12	381	381	14:1	X	13
Villa Maria Academy, Erie			X	X			9–12	295	295	9:1	X	14
Westtown School, Westtown	X	X	X	X	PK–5	6–8	9–12	789	410	8:1	X	39
William Penn Charter School, Philadelphia			X	X	PK–5	6–8	9–12	929	415	9:1	X	17
Winchester Thurston School, Pittsburgh			X	X	PK–5	6–8	9–12	627	203	7:1	X	23
Wyoming Seminary, Kingston	X	X	X	X	PK–8		9–PG	782	445	10:1	X	39
York Country Day School, York			X	X	PS–5	6–8	9–12	212	56	4:1	X	10
Puerto Rico												
Baldwin School of Puerto Rico, Inc., Bayamón			X	X	PK–6	7–8	9–12	781	195	10:1	X	12
The Caribbean School, Ponce			X	X	PK–6	7–8	9–12	570		7:1	X	
Colegio Puertorriqueno de Ninas, Guaynabo				X	PK–6	7–8	9–12	592	171	11:1	X	14
Commonwealth Parkville School, San Juan			X	X	PK–6	7–8	9–12	729	163	8:1	X	25
Fowlers Academy, Guaynabo			X	X		7–8	9–12	68	49	8:1		7
Guamani Private School, Guayama			X	X	1–6	7–8	9–12	606	164	13:1	X	6
Wesleyan Academy, Guaynabo			X	X	PK–6		7–12	922	332	23:1	X	11
Rhode Island												
Bishop Hendricken High School, Warwick			X				9–12	982	982	14:1	X	27
La Salle Academy, Providence			X	X		7–8	9–12	1,460	1,375	12:1	X	24
Lincoln School, Providence			X	X	N–5	6–8	9–12	388	167	4:1	X	10
Moses Brown School, Providence			X	X	N–5	6–8	9–12	787	394	8:1	X	22
Mount Saint Charles Academy, Woonsocket			X	X			7–12	993	993	14:1	X	24
Portsmouth Abbey School, Portsmouth	X	X	X	X			9–12	340	340	7:1	X	22
The Prout School, Wakefield			X	X			9–12	657	657	18:1		27
Providence Country Day School, East Providence			X	X		5–8	9–12	275	206	6:1	X	18
Rocky Hill School, East Greenwich			X	X	PS–5	6–8	9–12	352	164	7:1	X	18
St. Andrew's School, Barrington	X	X	X	X	3–5	6–8	9–12	223	165	5:1	X	32
St. George's School, Middletown	X	X	X	X			9–12	357	357	5:1	X	20
The Wheeler School, Providence			X	X	N–5	6–8	9–12	795	330	13:1	X	20

Private Secondary Schools At-a-Glance

	Students Accepted: Boarding		Students Accepted: Day		Grades			Student/Faculty			School Offerings	
	Boys	Girls	Boys	Girls	Lower	Middle	Upper	Total	Upper	Student/Faculty Ratio	Advanced Placement Preparation	Sports
South Carolina												
The Byrnes Schools, Florence			X	X	PK–6	7–8	9–12	259	84	9:1	X	13
Camden Military Academy, Camden	X					7–8	9–12	305	236	12:1	X	7
Cardinal Newman School, Columbia			X	X		7–8	9–12	483	309	10:1	X	15
Cherokee Creek Boys School, Westminster	X					5–9		36	34	6:1		34
Hammond School, Columbia			X	X	PK–4	5–8	9–12	980	264	9:1	X	42
Hilton Head Preparatory School, Hilton Head Island			X	X	K–5	6–8	9–12	439	180	12:1	X	15
Pinewood Preparatory School, Summerville			X	X						11:1	X	10
Porter-Gaud School, Charleston			X	X	1–5	6–8	9–12	921	326	12:1	X	25
St. Joseph's Catholic School, Greenville			X	X		6–8	9–12	540	284	13:1	X	14
Shannon Forest Christian School, Greenville			X	X	PK–5		6–12	568	312	17:1	X	10
Trident Academy, Mt. Pleasant	X	X	X	X	K–5	6–8	9–12	90	25	4:1		12
Westminster Catawba Christian, Rock Hill			X	X	PK–6	7–8	9–12	633	152		X	10
Wilson Hall, Sumter			X	X	PS–5	6–8	9–12	854	242	13:1	X	29
South Dakota												
Freeman Academy, Freeman	X	X	X	X	5–8		9–12	80	53	8:1		7
Sioux Falls Christian High School, Sioux Falls			X	X	K–5	6–8	9–12	764	208	19:1	X	8
Sky Ranch for Boys, Inc., Sky Ranch	X							32	17	6:1		21
Tennessee												
Battle Ground Academy, Franklin			X	X	K–4	5–8	9–12	968	392	11:1	X	30
Baylor School, Chattanooga	X	X	X	X		6–8	9–12	1,069	712	8:1	X	50
Boyd-Buchanan School, Chattanooga			X	X	K4–5	6–8	9–12	878	280	14:1	X	12
Columbia Academy, Columbia			X	X	K–6		7–12	617	269	13:1	X	14
Currey Ingram Academy, Brentwood			X	X	K–4	5–8	9–12	319	82	4:1		8
David Lipscomb High School, Nashville			X	X	PK–4	5–8	9–12	1,386	538	15:1	X	13
Donelson Christian Academy, Nashville			X	X	K–5	6–8	9–12	823	292	16:1	X	17
Evangelical Christian School, Cordova			X	X	K4–5	6–8	9–12	1,444	508	11:1	X	15
Ezell-Harding Christian School, Antioch			X	X	K–4	5–8	9–12	800	262	12:1	X	15
Father Ryan High School, Nashville			X	X			9–12	873	873	12:1	X	27
Franklin Road Academy, Nashville			X	X	PK–4	5–8	9–12	945	266	8:1	X	24
Girls Preparatory School, Chattanooga				X		6–8	9–12	660	391	6:1	X	42
Grace Baptist Academy, Chattanooga			X	X	K4–5	6–8	9–12	800	209	20:1		15
Harding Academy, Nashville			X	X	K–5	6–8		508	108			16
Hutchison School, Memphis				X	PK–4	5–8	9–12	931	233	16:1	X	13
Jackson Christian School, Jackson			X	X	JK–5	6–8	9–12	909	323	19:1		10
The King's Academy, Seymour	X	X	X	X	K4–5	6–8	9–12	377	145	14:1	X	22
Knoxville Catholic High School, Knoxville			X	X			9–12	624	624	13:1	X	21
Lausanne Collegiate School, Memphis			X	X	PK–4	5–8	9–12	745	252	9:1	X	42
The McCallie School, Chattanooga	X		X			6–8	9–12	919	653	8:1	X	62
Memphis University School, Memphis			X		7–8		9–12	650	416	10:1	X	13
Montgomery Bell Academy, Nashville			X			7–8	9–12	700	470	7:1	X	17
Notre Dame High School, Chattanooga			X	X			9–12	509	509	10:1	X	41
St. Andrew's–Sewanee School, Sewanee	X	X	X	X		6–8	9–12	262	186	7:1		32
St. Benedict at Auburndale, Cordova			X	X			9–12	941	941	13:1	X	23
St. Cecilia Academy, Nashville				X			9–12	239	239	9:1	X	20
St. George's Independent School, Collierville			X	X	PK–5	6–8	9–12	1,235	369	9:1	X	17
St. Mary's Episcopal School, Memphis				X	PK–4	5–8	9–12	866	229	13:1	X	12
University School of Jackson, Jackson			X	X	PK–5	6–8	9–12	1,221	351	11:1	X	15
The Webb School, Bell Buckle	X	X	X	X		6–8	9–PG	303	218	7:1	X	40
Webb School of Knoxville, Knoxville			X	X	K–5	6–8	9–12	1,049	475	10:1	X	20
Texas												
The Alexander School, Dallas			X	X		8–8	9–12	43	40	5:1	X	11
Allen Academy, Bryan			X	X	PK–5	6–8	9–12	284	80	10:1	X	14
All Saints' Episcopal School of Fort Worth, Fort Worth			X	X	K–6	7–8	9–12	805	270	9:1	X	25
The Awty International School, Houston			X	X	PK–5	6–8	9–12	1,200	350	18:1		15
Bishop Lynch Catholic High School, Dallas			X	X			9–12	1,038	1,038	12:1	X	28
Cistercian Preparatory School, Irving			X			5–8	9–12	345	173	7:1	X	12
Dallas Academy, Dallas			X	X	1–6	7–8	9–12	177	92	6:1		10
Dallas Christian School, Mesquite			X	X	PK–5	6–8	9–12	697	222	15:1		13
Duchesne Academy of the Sacred Heart, Houston				X	PK–4	5–8	9–12	685	263		X	14
The Emery Weiner School, Houston			X	X		6–8	9–12	460	255	8:1	X	13
Episcopal High School, Bellaire			X	X			9–12	659	659	9:1	X	19
The Episcopal School of Dallas, Dallas			X	X	PK–4	5–8	9–12	1,142	400	8:1	X	18
Fairhill School, Dallas			X	X	1–5	6–8	9–12	240	89	12:1		8
First Baptist Academy, Dallas			X	X	K–4	5–8	9–12	615	257	11:1	X	14
Fort Worth Country Day School, Fort Worth			X	X	K–4	5–8	9–12	1,115	393	10:1	X	21
Gateway School, Arlington			X	X		5–8	9–12	34	24	8:1		8
Greenhill School, Addison			X	X	PK–4	5–8	9–12	1,243	432	18:1	X	32
Hillcrest School, Midland			X	X	1–5	6–8	9–12	39	21	10:1		14
The Hockaday School, Dallas		X		X	PK–4	5–8	9–12	1,046	457	14:1	X	55
Huntington-Surrey School, Austin			X	X			9–12	61	61	4:1		
Jesuit College Preparatory School, Dallas			X				9–12	1,040	1,040	11:1	X	22

Private Secondary Schools At-a-Glance

	STUDENTS ACCEPTED				GRADES			STUDENT/FACULTY			SCHOOL OFFERINGS	
	Boarding		Day									
	Boys	Girls	Boys	Girls	Lower	Middle	Upper	Total	Upper	Student/Faculty Ratio	Advanced Placement Preparation	Sports
The John Cooper School, The Woodlands			X	X	PK–5	6–8	9–12	949	323	12:1	X	10
Lakehill Preparatory School, Dallas			X	X	K–4	5–8	9–12	400	106	12:1	X	14
Loretto Academy, El Paso			X	X	PK–5	6–8	9–12	707	396	20:1	X	13
Lutheran High North, Houston			X	X			9–12	295	295	22:1	X	19
Lydia Patterson Institute, El Paso			X	X		8	9–12	440	258	20:1	X	9
Memorial Hall School, Houston			X	X	4–5	6–8	9–12	110	85	14:1		7
The Oakridge School, Arlington			X	X	PS–4	5–8	9–12	891	291	10:1	X	15
Parish Episcopal School, Dallas			X	X	PK–4	5–8	9–12	1,101	278			16
Prestonwood Christian Academy, Plano			X	X	PK–4	5–8	9–12	1,443	460	9:1	X	13
Providence High School, San Antonio				X		6–8	9–12	340	231	10:1	X	12
St. Agnes Academy, Houston				X			9–12	861	861	15:1	X	17
St. Anthony Catholic High School, San Antonio	X	X	X	X			9–12	453	453	22:1	X	16
St. Augustine High School, Laredo			X	X		6–8	9–12	650	467	20:1	X	9
St. Mark's School of Texas, Dallas			X		1–4	5–8	9–12	841	364	8:1	X	41
Saint Mary's Hall, San Antonio			X	X	PK–5	6–8	9–PG	964	331	6:1	X	19
St. Stephen's Episcopal School, Austin	X	X	X	X		6–8	9–12	646	452	7:1	X	34
St. Thomas High School, Houston			X				9–12	711	711	13:1	X	10
San Marcos Baptist Academy, San Marcos	X	X	X	X		7–8	9–12	262	213	5:1	X	26
Second Baptist School, Houston			X	X	PK–4	5–8	9–12				X	9
Shelton School and Evaluation Center, Dallas			X	X	PS–4	5–8	9–12	862	238	8:1		10
Still Creek Christian School, Bryan	X	X	X	X	K–5	6–8	9–12	47	17	6:1		
Strake Jesuit College Preparatory, Houston			X				9–12	899	899	11:1	X	10
The Tenney School, Houston			X	X		6–8	9–12	42	31		X	
TMI—The Episcopal School of Texas, San Antonio	X	X	X	X		6–8	9–12	400	267	8:1	X	20
Trinity Christian Academy, Addison			X	X	K–4	5–8	9–12	1,515	482	10:1	X	19
Trinity School of Midland, Midland			X	X	PK–4	5–8	9–12	512	157	8:1	X	20
Trinity Valley School, Fort Worth			X	X	K–4	5–8	9–12	971	344	8:1	X	11
The Ursuline Academy of Dallas, Dallas				X			9–12	800	800	10:1	X	14
Vanguard Preparatory School, Dallas			X	X						6:1		
Westbury Christian School, Houston			X	X	PK–6	7–8	9–12	553	253	11:1	X	14
The Winston School, Dallas			X	X	1–6	7–8	9–12	205	110	5:1		19
The Winston School San Antonio, San Antonio			X	X	K–6	7–8	9–12	203	82	10:1		14
Utah												
Alpine Academy, Erda		X				7–8	9–12	50	42	4:1		25
Cedar Ridge Academy, Roosevelt	X	X					9–12	50	50	9:1		5
Cross Creek Programs, LaVerkin	X	X				7–8	9–12	200	170	15:1		21
New Haven, Spanish Fork		X				8–9	10–12	64	54	5:1		28
Rowland Hall-St. Mark's School, Salt Lake City			X	X	PK–5	6–8	9–12	996	271	8:1	X	36
Salt Lake Lutheran High School, Salt Lake City			X	X			9–12	82	82	7:1		13
Sorenson's Ranch School, Koosharem	X	X					7–12	75	75	7:1		46
Sunrise Academy, Hurricane		X						32		10:1		18
Wasatch Academy, Mt. Pleasant	X	X	X	X					208	10:1	X	69
The Waterford School, Sandy			X	X	PK–5	6–8	9–12	992	268	5:1	X	27
Vermont												
Bromley Brook School, Manchester Center		X					9–12	80	80	6:1		21
Burke Mountain Academy, East Burke	X	X	X	X			7–PG	64	64	7:1	X	7
Burr and Burton Academy, Manchester	X	X	X	X			9–12	686	686	12:1	X	21
The Greenwood School, Putney	X							46		2:1		27
King George School, Sutton	X	X						60		3:1		41
Lyndon Institute, Lyndon Center	X	X	X	X		8–8	9–12	626	626	10:1	X	27
Pine Ridge School, Williston	X	X	X	X				98	24	2:1		38
The Putney School, Putney	X	X	X	X			9–12	226	226	7:1	X	60
Rock Point School, Burlington	X	X	X	X			9–12	37	37	5:1		32
St. Johnsbury Academy, St. Johnsbury	X	X	X	X			9–PG	1,005	1,005		X	42
Stratton Mountain School, Stratton Mountain	X	X	X	X		7–8	9–PG	130	115	6:1		13
Virgin Islands												
Kingshill School, St. Croix			X	X		7–8	9–PG	26	15	4:1		24
St. Croix Country Day School, Kingshill			X	X	N–6	7–8	9–12	478	169	12:1	X	12
Virginia												
Benedictine High School, Richmond			X				9–12	268	268	9:1	X	25
Bishop Denis J. O'Connell High School, Arlington			X	X				1,360	1,360	12:1	X	20
Bishop Ireton High School, Alexandria			X	X			9–12	797	797	14:1	X	25
The Blue Ridge School, St. George	X						9–12	195	195	6:1		41
Cape Henry Collegiate School, Virginia Beach			X	X	PK–5	6–8	9–12	1,020	329	10:1	X	45
Carlisle School, Axton	X	X	X	X	PK–5	6–8	9–12	484	155	10:1	X	16
Christchurch School, Christchurch	X		X	X			8–PG	212	212	6:1	X	27
The Collegiate School, Richmond			X	X	K–4	5–8	9–12	1,555	499	15:1	X	24
Crawford Day School, Portsmouth			X	X	K–5	6–8	9–12	25	15	4:1		
Eastern Mennonite High School, Harrisonburg			X	X	K–5	6–8	9–12	381	204	10:1	X	11
Episcopal High School, Alexandria	X	X					9–12	435	435	6:1	X	39
Fishburne Military School, Waynesboro	X		X			8	9–12	180	165	9:1	X	23
Flint Hill School, Oakton			X	X	JK–4	5–8	9–12	1,099	491	10:1	X	31
Foxcroft School, Middleburg		X		X			9–12	185	185	6:1	X	24

Private Secondary Schools At-a-Glance

	STUDENTS ACCEPTED				GRADES			STUDENT/FACULTY			SCHOOL OFFERINGS	
	Boarding		Day									
	Boys	Girls	Boys	Girls	Lower	Middle	Upper	Total	Upper	Student/Faculty Ratio	Advanced Placement Preparation	Sports
Fuqua School, Farmville			X	X	PK–5	6–8	9–12	507	146	16:1	X	12
Hargrave Military Academy, Chatham	X		X			7–9	10–PG	365	300	12:1	X	48
Highland School, Warrenton			X	X	PK–4	5–8	9–12	540	225	6:1	X	34
Little Keswick School, Keswick	X							33		4:1		16
Massanutten Military Academy, Woodstock	X	X	X	X		7–8	9–PG	194	169	8:1	X	66
Miller School, Charlottesville	X	X	X	X		8–8	9–12	145	137	6:1	X	36
Norfolk Academy, Norfolk			X	X	1–6	7–9	10–12	1,233	349	10:1	X	26
Norfolk Christian School, Norfolk			X	X	PK–5	6–8	9–12	759	227	15:1	X	13
Norfolk Collegiate School, Norfolk			X	X	K–5	6–8	9–12	896	333	10:1	X	16
North Cross School, Roanoke			X	X	JK–5	6–8	9–12	521		6:1	X	13
Notre Dame Academy, Middleburg			X	X			9–12	250	250	9:1	X	18
Oak Hill Academy, Mouth of Wilson	X	X	X	X			8–12	137	137	10:1		34
Oakland School, Keswick	X	X	X	X						5:1		32
The Potomac School, McLean			X	X	K–3	4–8	9–12	956	374	6:1	X	25
Randolph-Macon Academy, Front Royal	X	X	X	X		6–8	9–PG	373	300	9:1	X	28
Roanoke Catholic School, Roanoke			X	X	PK–7		8–12	595			X	9
St. Anne's–Belfield School, Charlottesville	X	X	X	X	PK–4	5–8	9–12	841	333	7:1	X	21
St. Catherine's School, Richmond				X	PK–4	5–8	9–12	878	236	5:1	X	36
St. Christopher's School, Richmond			X		JK–5	6–8	9–12	955	309	7:1	X	23
Saint Gertrude High School, Richmond				X			9–12	273	273	9:1	X	13
St. Margaret's School, Tappahannock		X		X			8–12	152	152	6:1	X	26
St. Stephen's & St. Agnes School, Alexandria			X	X	JK–5	6–8	9–12	1,124	449	9:1	X	27
Shenandoah Valley Academy, New Market	X	X	X	X			9–12	221	221	14:1	X	17
Tandem Friends School, Charlottesville			X	X		5–8	9–12	237	132	8:1	X	10
Timber Ridge School, Cross Junction	X					6–8	9–12	85	64	10:1		4
Trinity Episcopal School, Richmond			X	X			8–12	441	441	10:1	X	35
Virginia Beach Friends School, Virginia Beach			X	X	1–5	6–8	9–12	210	55	5:1	X	10
Virginia Episcopal School, Lynchburg	X	X	X	X			9–12	262	262	8:1	X	32
Wakefield School, The Plains			X	X	PS–5	6–8	9–12	461	141	12:1	X	17
Washington												
Annie Wright School, Tacoma		X	X	X	PS–5	6–8	9–12	477	139	7:1		5
Bellevue Christian School, Clyde Hill			X	X	PK–6	7–8	9–12	1,300	360	21:1	X	21
Bishop Blanchet High School, Seattle			X	X			9–12	1,036	1,036	14:1	X	20
The Bush School, Seattle			X	X	K–5	6–8	9–12	578	238	6:1	X	28
Chrysalis School, Woodinville			X	X	K–6	7–8	9–12	257	198			
Eastside Catholic School, Sammamish			X	X		6–8	9–12	850	613	14:1	X	19
Explorations Academy, Bellingham			X	X				20	18	5:1	X	
King's High School, Seattle			X	X	PK–6	7–8	9–12	1,160	443	17:1	X	13
King's West School, Bremerton			X	X	K–6		7–12	380	201	10:1		8
Lakeside School, Seattle			X	X		5–8	9–12	776	518	10:1		15
The Northwest School, Seattle	X	X	X	X		6–8	9–12	477	346	9:1		13
Northwest Yeshiva High School, Mercer Island			X	X			9–12	92	92	4:1		6
O'Dea High School, Seattle			X				9–12	466	466	13:1	X	17
The Overlake School, Redmond			X	X		5–8	9–12	499	290	9:1	X	23
St. Christopher Academy, Seattle			X	X			9–12	20	20			
Saint George's School, Spokane			X	X	K–5	6–8	9–12	398	144	7:1	X	9
Seattle Academy of Arts and Sciences, Seattle			X	X		6–8	9–12	592	351	8:1		23
Seattle Christian Schools, Seattle			X	X	K–6	7–8	9–12	662	265	22:1	X	21
Seattle Lutheran High School, Seattle			X	X			9–12	186	186	9:1	X	18
Shoreline Christian, Shoreline			X	X	PS–6	7–8	9–12	270	90	7:1		8
University Prep, Seattle			X	X		6–8	9–12	484	287	9:1	X	19
West Virginia												
The Linsly School, Wheeling	X	X	X	X	5–8		9–12	443	287	10:1	X	47
Wisconsin												
Conserve School, Land O' Lakes	X	X					9–12	149	149	8:1	X	61
Fox Valley Lutheran High School, Appleton			X	X			9–12	640	640	14:1		13
Marquette University High School, Milwaukee			X				9–12	1,046	1,046	14:1	X	29
The Prairie School, Racine			X	X	PK–4	5–8	9–12	723	276	17:1	X	10
Saint Joan Antida High School, Milwaukee				X			9–12	346	346	14:1	X	7
St. John's Northwestern Military Academy, Delafield	X		X			7–8	9–12	300	225	12:1		14
Saint Joseph High School, Kenosha			X	X		7–8	9–12	461	306	20:1	X	8
St. Lawrence Seminary, Mount Calvary	X						9–12	200	200	10:1		25
University Lake School, Hartland			X	X	PK–5	6–8	9–12	325	88	9:1	X	13
University School of Milwaukee, Milwaukee			X	X	PK–4	5–8	9–12	1,082	366	9:1	X	15
Wisconsin Academy, Columbus	X	X	X	X			9–12	108	108	6:1		7
Wyoming												
Noah Webster Christian School, Cheyenne			X	X	K–6	7–8	9–12	89	10	15:1		
CANADA												
Academie Sainte Cecile International School, Windsor, ON	X	X	X	X	1–8		9–12	247	140	15:1	X	25

Private Secondary Schools At-a-Glance

	STUDENTS ACCEPTED				GRADES			STUDENT/FACULTY			SCHOOL OFFERINGS	
	Boarding		Day									
	Boys	Girls	Boys	Girls	Lower	Middle	Upper	Total	Upper	Student/Faculty Ratio	Advanced Placement Preparation	Sports
The Academy for Gifted Children (PACE), Richmond Hill, ON			X	X	1–3	4–7	8–12	288	130	15:1	X	37
Airdrie Koinonia Christian School, Airdrie, AB			X	X	K–6		7–12	277	116	14:1		15
Albert College, Belleville, ON	X	X	X	X	JK–6	7–8	9–PG	324	163	8:1	X	66
Alternative Learning Program, Edmonton, AB			X	X	1–6		7–9			10:1		
Arrowsmith School, Toronto, ON			X	X				75	20	8:1		
Ashbury College, Ottawa, ON	X	X	X	X	4–8		9–12	670	516	9:1		44
Austin Christian Academy, Austin, MB			X	X	K–3	4–8	9–12	43	9	12:1		
Balmoral Hall School, Winnipeg, MB		X		X	N–5	6–8	9–12	452	199	7:1	X	67
Bearspaw Christian School, Calgary, AB			X	X	1–6	7–9	10–12	482	114	20:1		11
The Bishop Strachan School, Toronto, ON		X		X	PK–6	7–8	9–12	891	461	9:1	X	52
Bodwell High School, North Vancouver, BC	X	X	X	X		8–9	10–12	365	265	15:1	X	43
Brentwood College School, Mill Bay, BC	X	X	X	X			9–12	435	435	9:1	X	43
Bronte College of Canada, Mississauga, ON	X	X	X	X			9–12	318	318	11:1	X	3
Calgary Academy, Calgary, AB			X	X	2–6		7–12	630	450	8:1		46
Centennial Academy, Montreal, QC			X	X			7–11	260	260	10:1		23
Century High School, Vancouver, BC			X	X			8–12	200	200	20:1		
Columbia International College of Canada, Hamilton, ON	X	X	X	X		7–8	9–12	1,134	1,120	20:1	X	42
Concordia Continuing Education High School, Edmonton, AB			X	X		7–9	10–12	150	125	14:1		4
Concordia High School, Edmonton, AB	X	X	X	X				133		10:1		14
The Country Day School, King City, ON			X	X	JK–6	7–8	9–12	720	320	10:1	X	25
Covenant Canadian Reformed School, Neerlandia, AB			X	X	K–6	7–9	10–12	170	25	10:1		16
Crawford Adventist Academy, Willowdale, ON			X	X	JK–6	7–8	9–12	468	159	16:1		10
Crestwood Preparatory College, Toronto, ON			X	X		7–8	9–12	525		16:1	X	15
Crofton House School, Vancouver, BC				X	1–6		7–12	723	455	10:1	X	27
De La Salle College, Toronto, ON			X	X	5–6	7–8	9–12	592	431	15:1	X	16
Eastside Christian Academy, Calgary, AB	X	X	X	X	K–6	7–9	10–12	100	30	25:1		6
Edison School, Okotoks, AB			X	X	K–4	5–8	9–12	198	48	12:1	X	7
Elmwood School, Ottawa, ON				X	JK–5	6–8	9–12	340	110	8:1		33
Elves Child Development Centre, Edmonton, AB	X	X	X	X	K–1	4–8	9–12	123	15	3:1		
Fieldstone Day School, Toronto, ON			X	X	JK–6		7–12	300	100	16:1	X	29
Foothills Academy, Calgary, AB			X	X	1–6	7–8	9–12	195	100	12:1		40
Fraser Academy, Vancouver, BC			X	X	1–7		8–12	199	119	3:1		25
Glen Eden School, Vancouver, BC			X	X						5:1		
Great Lakes Christian High School, Beamsville, ON	X	X	X	X			9–12	91	91	9:1		15
Hamilton District Christian High, Ancaster, ON			X	X			9–12	500	500	19:1	X	23
Havergal College, Toronto, ON		X		X	JK–6	7–8	9–12	915	468	9:1	X	76
Heritage Christian Academy, Calgary, AB			X	X	K–5	6–9	10–12	509	93	9:1		46
Heritage Christian School, Jordan, ON			X	X	K–8		9–12	568	164	15:1		5
Hope Christian School, Champion, AB			X	X	1–6	7–9	10–12	19	5	5:1		
Immanuel Christian High School, Lethbridge, AB			X	X		7–9	10–12	261	156	18:1		9
Imperial College of Toronto, Etobicoke, ON	X	X					11–12	202	202	22:1		
King's-Edgehill School, Windsor, NS	X	X	X	X		6–9	10–12	365	255	10:1		33
Kingsway College, Oshawa, ON	X	X	X	X			9–12	191	191	11:1		18
Koinonia Christian School, Red Deer, AB			X	X	K–5	6–8	9–12	189	61	12:1		6
Lakefield College School, Lakefield, ON	X	X	X	X			7–12	366	366	7:1	X	31
Landmark East School, Wolfville, NS	X	X	X	X		6–9	10–12	65	41	2:1		34
The Laureate Academy, Winnipeg, MB			X	X	1–5	6–8	9–12	95	45	5:1		32
Laurel View Academy, Barrie, ON			X	X						10:1		12
Lester B. Pearson United World College of the Pacific, Victoria, BC	X	X	X	X								
The Linden School, Toronto, ON				X	1–6	7–8	9–12	141	53	3:1	X	37
Luther College High School, Regina, SK	X	X	X	X			9–12	463	463	16:1		18
Lycee Claudel, Ottawa, ON			X	X			10–12	154	154	15:1	X	13
MacLachlan College, Oakville, ON			X	X	PK–8		9–12	344	133	10:1	X	39
Meadowridge School, Maple Ridge, BC			X	X	JK–5		6–12	500	199	9:1	X	12
Mennonite Collegiate Institute, Gretna, MB	X	X	X	X			9–12	153	153	11:1	X	11
Mentor College, Mississauga, ON			X	X	JK–4	5–8	9–12	1,580	640	14:1	X	32
Miss Edgar's and Miss Cramp's School, Montreal, QC				X	K–5	6–8	9–11	345	128	9:1	X	21
Mississauga Private School, Toronto, ON			X	X	JK–6	7–8	9–12	320	130	13:1		27
Nancy Campbell Collegiate Institute, London, ON	X	X	X	X	JK–6	7–8	9–12	219	162	9:1	X	16
New Tribes Mission Academy, Durham, ON			X	X	K–4	5–8	9–12	28	5	3:1		11
Niagara Christian Community of Schools, Fort Erie, ON	X	X	X	X	JK–6	7–8	9–12	379	255	17:1	X	28
Okanagan Adventist Academy, Kelowna, BC			X	X	K–7		8–12	104	49	11:1		16
Peoples Christian Academy, Toronto, ON			X	X	JK–6		7–12	695	325	10:1		9
Pic River Private High School, Heron Bay, ON			X	X						10:1		
Pinehurst School, St. Catharines, ON	X	X			7–8	9–10	11–12	30	16	10:1		66
Queen Margaret's School, Duncan, BC		X	X	X	JK–7		8–12	321	156	7:1		37
Queensway Christian College, Etobicoke, ON			X	X	JK–5	6–8	9–12	106	40	7:1		21
Quinte Christian High School, Belleville, ON			X	X			9–12	157	157	15:1		8
Richmond Christian School, Richmond, BC			X	X	K–7		8–12	286	286	16:1	X	6
Ridley College, St. Catharines, ON	X	X	X	X	1–4	5–8	9–PG	607	468	9:1	X	64

Private Secondary Schools At-a-Glance

	STUDENTS ACCEPTED				GRADES			STUDENT/FACULTY			SCHOOL OFFERINGS	
	Boarding		Day									
	Boys	Girls	Boys	Girls	Lower	Middle	Upper	Total	Upper	Student/Faculty Ratio	Advanced Placement Preparation	Sports
Ron Pettigrew Christian School, Dawson Creek, BC			X	X	JK–6	7–8	9–12	88	25	5:1		
Rosseau Lake College, Rosseau, ON	X	X	X	X		7–8	9–12	141	113	7:1		82
Rothesay Netherwood School, Rothesay, NB	X	X	X	X		6–8	9–12	250	200	8:1		46
Royal Canadian College, Vancouver, BC			X	X		8–10	11–12	56	38	15:1		5
Rundle College, Calgary, AB			X	X	PK–6	7–9	10–12	771	250	14:1		22
Sacred Heart School of Halifax, Halifax, NS			X	X	K–6		7–12	480	254	15:1	X	17
St. Andrew's College, Aurora, ON	X		X			6–8	9–12	560	433	9:1	X	62
St. Clement School, Ottawa, ON			X	X		7–8	9–12	33	20	5:1		10
St. Clement's School, Toronto, ON				X	1–6	7–9	10–12	448	177	9:1	X	40
St. George's School, Vancouver, BC	X		X		1–7		8–12	1,157	761	10:1	X	33
St. George's School of Montreal, Montreal, QC			X	X	K–6		7–11	503	316	17:1	X	24
St. John's International, Vancouver, BC			X	X		8–10	11–12	76	31	10:1		
St. John's-Ravenscourt School, Winnipeg, MB	X	X	X	X	1–5	6–8	9–12	806	350	9:1	X	31
St. Jude's School, Waterloo, ON			X	X	1–6	7–9	10–12	30	10	5:1		13
St. Margaret's School, Victoria, BC		X		X	JK–6		7–12	346	226	8:1	X	62
St. Michael's College School, Toronto, ON			X			7–8	9–12	1,083	881	16:1	X	23
St. Patrick High School, Yellowknife, NT			X	X			9–12	525	525			
St. Patrick's Regional Secondary, Vancouver, BC			X	X				500			X	
St. Paul's High School, Winnipeg, MB			X				9–12	586	586	14:1	X	20
Scarborough Christian School, North York, ON			X	X	JK–8			120	45	7:1		5
Sedbergh School, Montebello, QC	X	X	X	X		7–8	9–12	60	50	5:1		53
Selwyn House School, Westmount, QC			X		K–6	7–8	9–11	555	189	8:1		19
Sheila Morrison School, Utopia, ON	X	X	X	X	4–6	7–8	9–12	26	21	3:1		53
Smithville District Christian High School, Smithville, ON			X	X			9–12	225	225	11:1		10
Solomon Learning Institute, Ltd., Edmonton, AB			X	X					40	10:1		
Southridge School, Surrey, BC			X	X	K–3	4–7	8–12	662	328	10:1	X	36
Strathcona-Tweedsmuir School, Okotoks, AB			X	X	1–6	7–9	10–12	690	241	20:1		15
The Study School, Westmount, QC				X	K–3	4–6	7–11	387	175	8:1		32
Toronto District Christian High School, Woodbridge, ON			X	X			9–12	454	454	14:1		8
Toronto Waldorf School, Thornhill, ON			X	X	1–8		9–12	294	95	5:1		26
Town Centre Private High School, Markham, ON			X	X	1–6	7–8	9–12	1,400	200	15:1	X	21
Trafalgar Castle School, Whitby, ON		X		X				216	201	9:1	X	28
Trinity College School, Port Hope, ON	X	X	X	X		5–8	9–12	608	510	8:1	X	39
United Mennonite Educational Institute, Leamington, ON			X	X			9–12	80	80	15:1		13
University of Toronto Schools, Toronto, ON			X	X		7–8	9–12	640		12:1	X	44
West Island College, Calgary, AB			X	X		7–9	10–12	473	218	17:1	X	35
Willow Wood School, Don Mills, ON			X	X	1–6	7–8	9–12	216	125	7:1		28
INTERNATIONAL												
Aruba												
International School of Aruba, Oranjenstad			X	X	PK–5	6–8	9–12	158	45	8:1	X	8
Australia												
Mercedes College, Springfield			X	X	1–5	6–9	10–12	1,201	457	12:1		26
SCECGS Redlands, Cremorne			X	X	PK–5	6–8	9–12	1,550				19
Austria												
The American International School, Vienna			X	X	PK–5	6–8	9–PG	787	283	6:1		18
Bangladesh												
American International School, Dhaka, Dhaka			X	X	PK–5	6–8	9–12	691	207	15:1		7
Bermuda												
The Bermuda High School for Girls, Pembroke				X	1–6		7–13	746	392	12:1		33
Saltus Grammar School, Hamilton HMJX			X	X	K–5	6–8	9–12	1,083	258	13:1	X	16
Brazil												
Chapel School, Sao Paulo			X	X	PK–6		7–12	649	248	7:1		6
Escola Americana de Campinas, Campinas-SP			X	X	PK–5	6–8	9–12	487	94	7:1	X	27
Colombia												
Colegio Bolivar, Cali			X	X	PK–5	6–8	9–12	1,260	346	9:1	X	13
Colegio Nueva Granada, Bogota			X	X	PK–5	6–8	9–12	1,775	467	22:1	X	8
Costa Rica												
Marian Baker School, San Jose			X	X	PK–5	6–8	9–12	201	44	12:1	X	3
Denmark												
Copenhagen International School, 2900 Hellerup			X	X	PK–5		6–12	602	308	7:1		7
Ecuador												
Academia Cotopaxi, Quito			X	X	PK–8		9–12	439	135	7:1		5
Alliance Academy, Quito	X	X	X	X	PK–6		7–12	424	222	6:1	X	21

Private Secondary Schools At-a-Glance

	STUDENTS ACCEPTED				GRADES			STUDENT/FACULTY			SCHOOL OFFERINGS	
	Boarding		Day									
	Boys	Girls	Boys	Girls	Lower	Middle	Upper	Total	Upper	Student/Faculty Ratio	Advanced Placement Preparation	Sports
France												
American School of Paris, Saint Cloud			X	X	PK–5	6–8	9–13	800	351	7:1	X	12
The International School of Paris, 75016 Paris			X	X	K–5	6–8		303		8:1		17
The Lycee International, American Section, Saint-Germain-en-Laye Cedex			X	X	PK–5	6–9	10–12	689	189	18:1	X	13
Germany												
Bavarian International School, Haimhausen			X	X	PK–5	6–9	10–12	767	209	7:1		41
International School Hamburg, Hamburg			X	X	PK–5	6–8	9–12	690	190	7:1		3
Munich International School, Starnberg			X	X	PK–4	5–8	9–12	1,264	420	8:1		25
Greece												
American Community Schools of Athens, Athens			X	X	JK–5	6–8	9–12	774	305	17:1	X	11
International School of Athens, Kifissia—Athens			X	X	PK–6	7–9	10–12	378	125	9:1		9
Pinewood—The International School of Thessaloniki, Greece, Thessaloniki	X	X	X	X	PK–5	6–9	10–12	188	46	5:1		13
India												
Woodstock School, Uttarakhand	X	X	X	X	N–5	6–8	9–12	475	273	15:1	X	17
Italy												
American School of Milan, Noverasco di Opera, Milan			X	X	N–5	6–8	9–12	525	163	7:1		15
International School of Milan, 20146 Milan			X	X	K–5	6–9	10–13	1,300	240	7:1		23
Marymount International School, Rome			X	X	PK–5	6–8	9–12	715	224	15:1	X	7
St. Stephen's School, Rome, Rome	X	X	X	X			9–PG	229	229	7:1	X	9
Japan												
Canadian Academy, Kobe	X	X	X	X	PK–5	6–8	9–13	755	230	11:1	X	9
Columbia International School, Tokorozawa, Saitama	X	X	X	X	1–6	7–9	10–12	273	86	12:1	X	45
Hokkaido International School, Sapporo	X	X	X	X	PK–6	7–9	10–12	198	45	10:1	X	11
St. Mary's International School, Tokyo			X		K–6	7–8	9–12	923	298	10:1		21
Saint Maur International School, Yokohama			X	X	PK–5	6–8	9–12	468	138	5:1	X	7
Seisen International School, Tokyo			X	X	K–6	7–8	9–12	711	172	4:1		19
Yokohama International School, Yokohama			X	X	N–5	6–8	9–12	724	233	5:1		22
Jordan												
Ahliyyah School for Girls, Amman				X	1–6	7–10	11–12	1,018	148	4:1		37
Malta												
Verdala International School, Pembroke	X	X	X	X	PK–5	6–8	9–12	315	115	7:1		6
Mexico												
The American School Foundation, Mexico City, D.F.			X	X	PK–5	6–8	9–12	2,502	639	10:1	X	9
The American School of Puerto Vallarta, Puerto Vallarta, Jalisco			X	X	N–6	7–9	10–12	366	74	7:1	X	5
Netherlands												
American International School Rotterdam, Rotterdam			X	X	PK–5	6–8	9–12	213	39	6:1		7
The American School of The Hague, Wassenaar			X	X	PK–4	5–8	9–12	1,100	390	8:1	X	11
International School Eerde, Ommen	X	X	X	X								12
International School of Amsterdam, Amstelveen			X	X	PS–5	6–8	9–12	933	225	6:1		32
Rotterdam International Secondary School, Wolfert van Borselen, Rotterdam			X	X	6–8	9–10	11–12	175	67	10:1		8
Pakistan												
Karachi American School, Karachi			X	X	PS–5	6–8	9–12	331	114	6:1	X	21
Peru												
Colegio Franklin D. Roosevelt, Lima 12			X	X	N–5	6–8	9–12	1,405	382	11:1		23
Philippines												
International School Manila, 1634 Taguig City			X	X	PK–5	6–8	9–12	1,880	710	9:1	X	19
Portugal												
Carlucci American International School of Lisbon, Linhó, Sintra			X	X	PK–5	6–8	9–12	541	134	7.7:1		6
St. Dominic's International School, Portugal, Sao Domingos de Rana			X	X	1–6	7–11	12–13	654	101	3:1		15
Republic of Korea												
Seoul Foreign School, Seoul			X	X	PK–5	6–8	9–12	1,462	425	9:1	X	11
Romania												
American International School of Bucharest, Bucharest			X	X	PK–5	6–8	9–12	715	180	9:1		13

Private Secondary Schools At-a-Glance

	STUDENTS ACCEPTED				GRADES			STUDENT/FACULTY			SCHOOL OFFERINGS	
	Boarding		Day									
	Boys	Girls	Boys	Girls	Lower	Middle	Upper	Total	Upper	Student/Faculty Ratio	Advanced Placement Preparation	Sports
South Africa												
International School of South Africa, Mafikeng	X	X	X	X	7–9	10–11	12–13	418	50			12
Spain												
The American School of Madrid, Madrid			X	X	PK–5	6–8	9–12	867	254	9:1		8
International College Spain, Madrid			X	X	PK–5	6–8	9–12	680	221	10:1		25
Switzerland												
Aiglon College, Chesières-Villars	X	X	X	X	4–7	8–10	11–12	377	126	6:1		45
College du Leman International School, Versoix	X	X	X	X	K–5	6–8	9–13	1,754	656	7:1	X	44
Ecole d'Humanité, CH 6085 Hasliberg Goldern	X	X	X	X						5:1	X	35
International School of Berne, Guemligen 3073			X	X	PK–5		6–12	277	163	5:1		13
The International School of Geneva, Geneva			X	X	PK–6		7–13	4,010	2,330	11:1		16
International School of Lausanne, Le Mont-sur-Lausanne			X	X	PK–5	6–8	9–12	617	200	7:1		29
Neuchatel Junior College, 2002 NeuchÔtel	X	X					12	97	97	10:1	X	18
TASIS, The American School in Switzerland, Montagnola-Lugano	X	X	X	X	1–6	7–8	9–PG	581	341	5:1	X	35
Zurich International School, Wõdenswil			X	X	PS–5	6–8	9–13	1,313	440	7:1	X	26
Thailand												
International School Bangkok, Pakkret			X	X	PK–5	6–8	9–12	1,879	733	10:1	X	15
United Arab Emirates												
Dubai American Academy, Dubai			X	X	PK–5	6–8	9–12	2,308	551	12:1		39
United Kingdom												
ACS Cobham International School, Cobham, Surrey	X	X	X	X	N–4	5–8	9–12	1,308	430	9:1	X	15
ACS Egham International School, Surrey			X	X	N–5	6–8	9–12	584	168	9:1		14
ACS Hillingdon International School, Hillingdon, Middlesex			X	X	PK–4	5–8	9–12	589	229	9:1	X	10
The American School in London, London			X	X	PK–4	5–8	9–12	1,324	455	10:1	X	16
Brockwood Park School, Alresford	X	X						65	65	7:1		
The International School of Aberdeen, Aberdeen			X	X	PK–5	6–8	9–12	476	125	3:1		18
The International School of London, London W3 8LG			X	X	K–6	7–10	11–13	350	60	8:1		7
Marymount International School, Surrey		X		X		6–8	9–12	247	190	7:1		16
Merchiston Castle School, Edinburgh	X		X						196	9:1		26
St Leonards School and Sixth Form College, Fife, Scotland	X	X	X	X	1–7	8–11	12–13	453	126	7:1		53
TASIS The American School in England, Thorpe, Surrey	X	X	X	X	N–5	6–8	9–13	750	370	7:1	X	45

Traditional Day and Boarding Schools

ABINGTON FRIENDS SCHOOL

575 Washington Lane
Jenkintown, Pennsylvania 19046

Head of School: Mr. Richard F. Nourie

General Information Coeducational day college-preparatory, arts, and technology school, affiliated with Society of Friends. Grades PK–12. Founded: 1697. Setting: suburban. Nearest major city is Philadelphia. 37-acre campus. 5 buildings on campus. Approved or accredited by Middle States Association of Colleges and Schools and Pennsylvania Association of Independent Schools. Member of National Association of Independent Schools and Secondary School Admission Test Board. Endowment: $3.5 million. Total enrollment: 640. Upper school average class size: 14. Upper school faculty-student ratio: 1:7.

Upper School Student Profile Grade 9: 61 students (31 boys, 30 girls); Grade 10: 65 students (33 boys, 32 girls); Grade 11: 67 students (35 boys, 32 girls); Grade 12: 65 students (34 boys, 31 girls). 8% of students are members of Society of Friends.

Faculty School total: 84. In upper school: 19 men, 16 women; 16 have advanced degrees.

Subjects Offered Algebra, American history, American literature, art, biology, calculus, chemistry, community service, computer math, computer science, creative writing, drama, earth science, economics, English, English literature, environmental science, European history, fine arts, French, geometry, grammar, Greek, health, history, Latin, mathematics, music, physical education, physics, pre-calculus, religion, science, social studies, Spanish, theater, world history, world literature, writing.

Graduation Requirements Arts and fine arts (art, music, dance, drama), English, foreign language, mathematics, physical education (includes health), religion (includes Bible studies and theology), science, social studies (includes history), technology, participation in one sport in 9th through 12th grades, Quakerism course in 9th grade (one quarter). Community service is required.

Special Academic Programs Advanced Placement exam preparation; honors section; independent study; term-away projects.

College Admission Counseling 81 students graduated in 2008; all went to college, including Boston University; Penn State University Park; Temple University; The George Washington University. Median SAT critical reading: 630, median SAT math: 600, median composite ACT: 26. 59% scored over 600 on SAT critical reading, 52% scored over 600 on SAT math, 57% scored over 26 on composite ACT.

Student Life Upper grades have specified standards of dress, student council, honor system. Discipline rests primarily with faculty. Attendance at religious services is required.

Tuition and Aid Day student tuition: $23,600. Tuition installment plan (Insured Tuition Payment Plan, Academic Management Services Plan, 2-installment plan). Need-based scholarship grants, merit-based scholarship/grants (some need required) available. In 2008–09, 38% of upper-school students received aid. Total amount of financial aid awarded in 2008–09: $894,900.

Admissions Traditional secondary-level entrance grade is 9. For fall 2008, 85 students applied for upper-level admission, 45 were accepted, 23 enrolled. ISEE, SSAT or Wechsler Intelligence Scale for Children III required. Deadline for receipt of application materials: none. Application fee required: $40. On-campus interview required.

Athletics Interscholastic: baseball (boys), basketball (b,g), cross-country running (b,g), lacrosse (g), soccer (b,g), softball (g), tennis (b,g), track and field (b,g), wrestling (b); coed interscholastic: golf, ultimate Frisbee. 4 PE instructors, 10 coaches, 1 athletic trainer.

Computers Computers are regularly used in English, graphic design, mathematics, music, science, technology, Web site design classes. Computer network features include on-campus library services, Internet access, wireless campus network, family e-mail accounts. Computer access in designated common areas is available to students. The school has a published electronic and media policy.

Contact Vikki Toomer, Director of Admissions and Tuition Assistance. 215-576-3068. Fax: 215-886-9143. E-mail: vtoomer@abingtonfriends.net. Web site: www.abingtonfriends.net.

ACADEMIA COTOPAXI

De Las Higuerillas y Alondras
Monteserrin
PO Box 17-11-6510
Quito, Ecuador

Head of School: William Johnston, EdD

General Information Coeducational day college-preparatory, International Baccalaureate, and Ecuadorian Diploma school. Grades PK–12. Founded: 1959. Setting: suburban. 17-acre campus. 4 buildings on campus. Approved or accredited by Association of American Schools in South America, Ecuadorean Ministry of Education, International Baccalaureate Organization, and Southern Association of Colleges and Schools. Member of Secondary School Admission Test Board. Language of instruction: English. Total enrollment: 439. Upper school average class size: 15. Upper school faculty-student ratio: 1:7.

Upper School Student Profile Grade 9: 39 students (16 boys, 23 girls); Grade 10: 36 students (20 boys, 16 girls); Grade 11: 28 students (15 boys, 13 girls); Grade 12: 26 students (13 boys, 13 girls).

Faculty School total: 67. In upper school: 18 men, 49 women; 35 have advanced degrees.

Subjects Offered Algebra, American history, American literature, art, band, biology, calculus, chemistry, choir, computer literacy, computer programming, computer science, creative writing, drama, English, English literature, ESL, European history, French, geography, geometry, government/civics, history, international relations, journalism, mathematics, music, orchestra, physical education, physical science, physics, psychology, science, social studies, Spanish, swimming, theater, theory of knowledge, world history, world literature, writing, yearbook.

Graduation Requirements Arts and fine arts (art, music, dance, drama), computer science, English, foreign language, mathematics, physical education (includes health), science, social studies (includes history). Community service is required.

Special Academic Programs International Baccalaureate program; honors section; academic accommodation for the gifted, the musically talented, and the artistically talented; remedial reading and/or remedial writing; remedial math; programs in English, mathematics, general development for dyslexic students; special instructional classes for learning disabled students, students with Attention Deficit Disorder and dyslexia; ESL (16 students enrolled).

College Admission Counseling 29 students graduated in 2008; 26 went to college, including Boston College; Chapman University; Harvard University; The University of Texas at Austin; University of Florida; University of Pennsylvania. Other: 1 entered military service, 2 had other specific plans. Median SAT critical reading: 560, median SAT math: 530, median SAT writing: 520. 36% scored over 600 on SAT critical reading, 18% scored over 600 on SAT math, 36% scored over 600 on SAT writing.

Student Life Upper grades have specified standards of dress, student council, honor system. Discipline rests primarily with faculty.

Tuition and Aid Day student tuition: $14,023. Tuition installment plan (monthly payment plans). Merit scholarship grants, need-based scholarship grants, discounts for advance payment available. In 2008–09, 2% of upper-school students received aid; total upper-school merit-scholarship money awarded: $9000. Total amount of financial aid awarded in 2008–09: $12,000.

Admissions For fall 2008, 27 students applied for upper-level admission, 23 were accepted, 17 enrolled. Any standardized test, MAT 7 Metropolitan Achievement Test, Woodcock-Johnson/Reading Inventory, Woodcock-Munoz in English/Reading Comprehension or writing sample required. Deadline for receipt of application materials: none. Application fee required: $300. Interview required.

Athletics Interscholastic: basketball (boys, girls), soccer (b,g), swimming and diving (b,g), volleyball (b,g); intramural: weight training (b); coed intramural: swimming and diving. 2 PE instructors, 2 coaches.

Computers Computers are regularly used in business, design, graphic arts classes. Computer network features include on-campus library services, Internet access, wireless campus network, Internet filtering or blocking technology. Student e-mail accounts and computer access in designated common areas are available to students. Students grades are available online. The school has a published electronic and media policy.

Contact Paola Pereira, Director of Admissions and Outreach. 593-2 246-7411 Ext. 1106. Fax: 593-2 244-5195. E-mail: ppereira@cotopaxi.k12.ec. Web site: www.cotopaxi.k12.ec.

ACADEMIE SAINTE CECILE INTERNATIONAL SCHOOL

925 Cousineau Road
Windsor, Ontario N9G 1V8, Canada

Head of School: Mlle. Thérèse H. Gadoury

General Information Coeducational boarding and day college-preparatory, arts, and bilingual studies school, affiliated with Roman Catholic Church. Boarding grades 7–12, day grades 1–12. Founded: 1993. Setting: suburban. Nearest major city is Toronto, Canada. Students are housed in single-sex by floor dormitories. 30-acre campus. 1 building on campus. Approved or accredited by Canadian Association of Independent Schools, International Baccalaureate Organization, The Association of Boarding Schools, and Ontario Department of Education. Languages of instruction: English and French. Total enrollment: 247. Upper school average class size: 15. Upper school faculty-student ratio: 1:15.

Upper School Student Profile 60% of students are boarding students. 40% are province residents. 60% are international students. International students from Bermuda, Hong Kong, Jamaica, Mexico, Republic of Korea, and Taiwan; 7 other countries represented in student body. 70% of students are Roman Catholic.

Faculty School total: 50. In upper school: 13 men, 11 women; 10 have advanced degrees; 4 reside on campus.

Subjects Offered Accounting, advanced chemistry, advanced computer applications, advanced math, algebra, art, art education, art history, audio visual/media, ballet, basketball, biology, business technology, calculus, campus ministry, career education, careers, Catholic belief and practice, chemistry, choir, choral music, civics, classical music, computer information systems, computer keyboarding, computer programming, computer science, concert band, concert bell choir, concert choir, creative dance, creative drama, creative thinking, creative writing, critical thinking, critical writing, dance, dance performance, decision making skills, desktop publishing, desktop publishing, ESL, discrete mathematics, drama performance, drama workshop, dramatic arts, drawing, drawing and design, driver education, earth science, economics, English, English literature, environmental studies, ethics, expository writing, family living, French, French studies, geography, geometry, German, golf, handbells, health and wellness, health education, history, history of dance, history of music, history of religion, history of the Catholic Church, honors algebra, honors English, honors geometry, honors world history, instrumental music, International Baccalaureate courses, Internet, Internet research, intro to computers, Italian, jazz band, jazz dance, journalism, Latin, leadership skills, library skills, Life of Christ, literature, literature and composition-AP, mathematics, media studies, music, music appreciation, music composition, music history, music performance, music theory, organ, painting, philosophy, photography, physical education, physics, piano, poetry, prayer/spirituality, pre-algebra, pre-calculus, probability and statistics, public speaking, reading, reading/study skills, religion, religions, research skills, research techniques, SAT preparation, science, sculpture, Shakespeare, social studies, softball, Spanish, stage and body movement, stained glass, strings, student government, swimming, tennis, TOEFL preparation, track and field, values and decisions, visual arts, vocal ensemble, voice, volleyball, wind ensemble, wind instruments, world religions, writing skills, yearbook.

Graduation Requirements Ontario Ministry of Education requirements.

Special Academic Programs International Baccalaureate program; Advanced Placement exam preparation; honors section; accelerated programs; academic accommodation for the gifted, the musically talented, and the artistically talented; remedial reading and/or remedial writing; remedial math; ESL (60 students enrolled).

College Admission Counseling 30 students graduated in 2008; all went to college, including McMaster University; The University of British Columbia; The University of Western Ontario; University of Toronto; University of Waterloo; University of Windsor. Median SAT critical reading: 370, median SAT math: 620. 60% scored over 600 on SAT math.

Student Life Upper grades have uniform requirement, student council, honor system. Discipline rests primarily with faculty.

Summer Programs Remediation, enrichment, advancement, ESL, art/fine arts programs offered; session focuses on ESL; held on campus; accepts boys and girls; open to students from other schools. 25 students usually enrolled. 2009 schedule: June 29 to August 29. Application deadline: May 30.

Tuition and Aid Day student tuition: CAN$13,500; 7-day tuition and room/board: CAN$36,000. Tuition installment plan (Insured Tuition Payment Plan). Tuition reduction for siblings, merit scholarship grants available. In 2008–09, 5% of upper-school students received aid; total upper-school merit-scholarship money awarded: CAN$4500. Total amount of financial aid awarded in 2008–09: CAN$15,000.

Admissions Traditional secondary-level entrance grade is 9. Deadline for receipt of application materials: February 15. Application fee required: CAN$300. Interview recommended.

Athletics Interscholastic: aquatics (boys, girls), badminton (b,g), basketball (b,g), equestrian sports (b,g), golf (b,g), horseback riding (b,g), ice hockey (g), independent competitive sports (b,g), modern dance (b,g), physical fitness (b,g), soccer (b,g), softball (b,g), swimming and diving (b,g), tennis (b,g), volleyball (b,g); intramural: aquatics (b,g), badminton (b,g), ballet (g), basketball (b,g), bowling (b,g), cross-country running (b,g), dance (b,g), dressage (b,g), equestrian sports (b,g), golf (b,g), horseback riding (b,g), paddle tennis (b,g), soccer (b,g), softball (b,g), swimming and diving (b,g), table tennis (b,g), tennis (b,g), volleyball (b,g); coed interscholastic: aquatics, badminton, basketball, dressage, equestrian sports, fitness, golf, horseback riding, indoor track & field, modern dance, physical fitness, soccer, softball, swimming and diving, tennis, volleyball; coed intramural: aquatics, badminton, basketball, bowling, cross-country running, dance, dressage, equestrian sports, floor hockey, golf, horseback riding, modern dance, soccer, softball, swimming and diving, tennis, volleyball. 2 PE instructors, 8 coaches.

Computers Computers are regularly used in accounting, business, desktop publishing, ESL, information technology, mathematics classes. Computer network features include Internet access.

Contact Ms. Gwen A. Gatt, Admissions Clerk. 519-969-1291. Fax: 519-969-7953. E-mail: info@stececile.ca. Web site: www.stececile.ca.

THE ACADEMY AT CHARLEMONT

1359 Route 2
The Mohawk Trail
Charlemont, Massachusetts 01339

Head of School: Mr. Todd A. Sumner

General Information Coeducational boarding and day college-preparatory school. Boarding grades 9–PG, day grades 7–PG. Founded: 1981. Setting: rural. Nearest major city is Springfield. Students are housed in local homes. 52-acre campus. 3 buildings on campus. Approved or accredited by New England Association of Schools and Colleges and Massachusetts Department of Education. Member of National Association of Independent Schools. Endowment: $200,000. Total enrollment: 105. Upper school average class size: 17. Upper school faculty-student ratio: 1:7.

Upper School Student Profile Grade 9: 16 students (9 boys, 7 girls); Grade 10: 17 students (6 boys, 11 girls); Grade 11: 17 students (7 boys, 10 girls); Grade 12: 18 students (8 boys, 10 girls). 2% of students are boarding students. 90% are state residents. 3 states are represented in upper school student body. 2% are international students. International students from France and Slovakia.

Faculty School total: 18. In upper school: 9 men, 9 women; 6 have advanced degrees.

Subjects Offered Algebra, American legal systems, American literature, art, art history, biology, calculus, chemistry, computer science, creative writing, drama, earth science, ecology, English, English literature, environmental science, ethics, European history, expository writing, fine arts, French, geography, geometry, government/civics, grammar, health, history, Latin, mathematics, music, philosophy, photography, physical education, physics, religion, Russian, science, social studies, Spanish, speech, theater, trigonometry, world history, world literature.

Graduation Requirements Algebra, American government, American literature, American studies, arts and fine arts (art, music, dance, drama), biology, calculus, chemistry, civics, classical language, computer literacy, English, foreign language, four units of summer reading, geography, geometry, Latin, mathematics, physics, pre-calculus, science, senior project, social studies (includes history).

Special Academic Programs Independent study; study abroad.

College Admission Counseling 20 students graduated in 2008; all went to college, including Beloit College; Carleton College; Drew University; Earlham College; Rochester Institute of Technology; University of Chicago. Median SAT critical reading: 660, median SAT math: 610, median SAT writing: 660, median combined SAT: 1900, median composite ACT: 27.

Student Life Upper grades have specified standards of dress, student council, honor system. Discipline rests primarily with faculty.

Summer Programs Sports, art/fine arts programs offered; session focuses on Drama and soccer; held on campus; accepts boys and girls; open to students from other schools.

Tuition and Aid Day student tuition: $18,800; 7-day tuition and room/board: $28,000. Tuition installment plan (monthly payment plans, individually arranged payment plans). Need-based scholarship grants available. In 2008–09, 60% of upper-school students received aid. Total amount of financial aid awarded in 2008–09: $555,000.

Admissions Traditional secondary-level entrance grade is 9. For fall 2008, 25 students applied for upper-level admission, 14 were accepted, 10 enrolled. School's own test and writing sample required. Deadline for receipt of application materials: February 15. Application fee required: $30. On-campus interview recommended.

Athletics Interscholastic: alpine skiing (boys, girls), basketball (b,g), cross-country running (b,g), lacrosse (b,g), skiing (downhill) (b,g), soccer (b,g), ultimate Frisbee (b,g); intramural: indoor soccer (b,g); coed interscholastic: basketball; coed intramural: aerobics/dance, alpine skiing, basketball, bicycling, bocce, canoeing/kayaking, cooperative games, croquet, hiking/backpacking, kayaking, outdoor activities, outdoor recreation, rafting, skiing (cross-country), skiing (downhill), soccer, tennis, ultimate Frisbee, yoga. 7 coaches.

Computers Computers are regularly used in English, foreign language, history, mathematics, science classes. Computer network features include on-campus library services, Internet access, wireless campus network, Internet filtering or blocking technology, school Website for schedules and other administrative information. Student e-mail accounts and computer access in designated common areas are available to students. Students grades are available online. The school has a published electronic and media policy.

Contact Sandy Warren, Director of Admissions. 413-339-4912. Fax: 413-339-4324. E-mail: swarren@charlemont.org. Web site: www.charlemont.org.

THE ACADEMY AT SISTERS

Bend, Oregon

See Special Needs Schools section.

ACADEMY AT SWIFT RIVER

Cummington, Massachusetts

See Special Needs Schools section.

THE ACADEMY FOR GIFTED CHILDREN (PACE)

12 Bond Crescent
Richmond Hill, Ontario L4E 3K2, Canada

Head of School: Barbara Rosenberg

General Information Coeducational day college-preparatory and intellectually gifted school. Grades 1–12. Founded: 1993. Setting: suburban. Nearest major city is Toronto, Canada. 3-acre campus. 2 buildings on campus. Approved or accredited by Ontario Department of Education. Language of instruction: English. Total enrollment: 288. Upper school average class size: 17. Upper school faculty-student ratio: 1:15.

Upper School Student Profile Grade 8: 36 students (19 boys, 17 girls); Grade 9: 34 students (19 boys, 15 girls); Grade 10: 25 students (15 boys, 10 girls); Grade 11: 20 students (13 boys, 7 girls); Grade 12: 15 students (8 boys, 7 girls).

Faculty School total: 29. In upper school: 6 men, 8 women; 5 have advanced degrees.

Subjects Offered 20th century world history, Advanced Placement courses, algebra, analytic geometry, biology, calculus, calculus-AP, Canadian geography, Canadian history, Canadian law, career education, chemistry, chemistry-AP, civics, computer information systems, computer programming, computer science, computer science-AP, dramatic arts, English, finite math, French, French as a second language, geometry, health education, information technology, language, law, literature, math-

ematics, modern Western civilization, music, philosophy, physical education, physics, science, sociology, visual arts, world civilizations, writing skills.
Graduation Requirements Advanced chemistry, advanced math, algebra, analytic geometry, biology, calculus, Canadian geography, Canadian history, Canadian literature, career education, chemistry, civics, drawing, English literature, French as a second language, healthful living, law, music, philosophy, pre-algebra, pre-calculus, science, senior humanities, social sciences, sociology, theater arts, visual arts, minimum of 40 hours of community service, OSSLT.
Special Academic Programs Advanced Placement exam preparation; honors section; academic accommodation for the gifted.
College Admission Counseling 18 students graduated in 2008; all went to college, including Harvard University; Massachusetts Institute of Technology; Queen's University at Kingston; The University of Western Ontario; University of Pennsylvania; University of Toronto. Median SAT critical reading: 780, median SAT math: 800, median SAT writing: 780, median combined SAT: 2360. 100% scored over 600 on SAT critical reading, 100% scored over 600 on SAT math, 100% scored over 600 on SAT writing, 100% scored over 1800 on combined SAT.
Student Life Upper grades have specified standards of dress, student council, honor system. Discipline rests primarily with faculty.
Tuition and Aid Day student tuition: CAN$10,500. Tuition installment plan (monthly payment plans).
Admissions Traditional secondary-level entrance grade is 8. For fall 2008, 25 students applied for upper-level admission, 6 were accepted, 6 enrolled. Psychoeducational evaluation, Wechsler Individual Achievement Test and WISC III or other aptitude measures; standardized achievement test required. Deadline for receipt of application materials: none. No application fee required. On-campus interview required.
Athletics Interscholastic: badminton (boys, girls), ball hockey (b), baseball (b,g), basketball (b,g), flag football (b), floor hockey (b), golf (b,g), independent competitive sports (b,g), indoor soccer (b,g), soccer (b,g), softball (b,g), track and field (b,g), volleyball (b,g), winter soccer (b,g); intramural: badminton (b,g), basketball (b,g), soccer (b,g), softball (b,g); coed interscholastic: badminton, baseball, bowling, cross-country running, flag football, Frisbee, indoor soccer, ultimate Frisbee; coed intramural: alpine skiing, badminton, ball hockey, basketball, cross-country running, curling, floor hockey, handball, ice skating, indoor soccer, jogging, jump rope, life saving, martial arts, outdoor activities, outdoor education, outdoor skills, physical fitness, ropes courses, scuba diving, skiing (downhill), snowboarding, snowshoeing, ultimate Frisbee, volleyball, wall climbing, yoga. 1 PE instructor, 10 coaches.
Computers Computers are regularly used in career exploration, desktop publishing, digital applications, English, information technology, keyboarding, news writing, newspaper, photography, programming, science, technology, theater, writing, yearbook classes. Computer network features include Internet access, wireless campus network. Computer access in designated common areas is available to students. The school has a published electronic and media policy.
Contact Barbara Rosenberg, Director. 905-773-3997. Fax: 905-773-4722. Web site: www.pace.on.ca.

ACADEMY FOR GLOBAL EXPLORATION

PO Box 712
Ashland, Oregon 97520
Head of School: Mr. Greg Guevara
General Information Coeducational boarding college-preparatory, cultural studies, and outdoor education school. Grades 9–12. Founded: 2002. Setting: small town. Nearest major city is Portland. Students are housed in coed dormitories. 81-acre campus. 1 building on campus. Approved or accredited by Northwest Association of Accredited Schools and Oregon Department of Education. Total enrollment: 8. Upper school average class size: 4. Upper school faculty-student ratio: 1:3.
Upper School Student Profile Grade 10: 2 students (2 boys); Grade 11: 3 students (3 girls); Grade 12: 3 students (2 boys, 1 girl); Postgraduate: 2 students (2 boys). 100% of students are boarding students. 10% are state residents. 7 states are represented in upper school student body.
Faculty School total: 6. In upper school: 2 men, 2 women; 2 have advanced degrees; 4 reside on campus.
Subjects Offered Algebra, biology, chemistry, computer skills, cultural geography, earth science, English, environmental studies, foreign language, geometry, health, mathematics, photography, physical education, science, social studies, space and physical sciences, U.S. history, world history.
Graduation Requirements Cultural geography, electives, English, foreign language, mathematics, outdoor education, physical education (includes health), science, social studies (includes history), cultural studies, outdoor adventure.
Special Academic Programs Honors section; accelerated programs; independent study; study abroad; academic accommodation for the gifted; remedial reading and/or remedial writing; remedial math.
College Admission Counseling 2 students graduated in 2008.
Student Life Upper grades have student council, honor system. Discipline rests primarily with faculty.
Summer Programs Remediation, enrichment, advancement, sports, rigorous outdoor training programs offered; session focuses on outdoor adventure, cultural studies; held both on and off campus; held at various domestic venues and Nicaragua, Greece, Argentina; accepts boys and girls; open to students from other schools. 15 students usually enrolled. 2009 schedule: June 23 to July 15. Application deadline: none.
Tuition and Aid 7-day tuition and room/board: $27,540. Guaranteed tuition plan. Tuition installment plan (monthly payment plans, individually arranged payment plans, semester payment plan). Tuition reduction for siblings, merit scholarship grants, need-based scholarship grants available.
Admissions Traditional secondary-level entrance grade is 11. Deadline for receipt of application materials: none. Application fee required: $50. Interview required.
Athletics Coed Intramural: alpine skiing, backpacking, bicycling, canoeing/kayaking, climbing, combined training, cross-country running, fishing, fitness, fitness walking, fly fishing, Frisbee, hiking/backpacking, independent competitive sports, indoor soccer, jogging, kayaking, life saving, mountain biking, mountaineering, nordic skiing, outdoor activities, outdoor adventure, outdoor education, paddling, physical fitness, physical training, project adventure, rafting, rappelling, rock climbing, running, scuba diving, skateboarding, skiing (cross-country), skiing (downhill), skydiving, snowboarding, snowshoeing, soccer, speleology, surfing, telemark skiing, ultimate Frisbee, wall climbing, wilderness, wilderness survival, wildernessways, windsurfing, winter walking. 3 PE instructors.
Computers Computers are regularly used in all classes. Computer resources include Internet access, wireless campus network. Student e-mail accounts are available to students.
Contact Mr. Greg Guevara, Head of School. 541-913-0660. E-mail: admissions@agexplore.org. Web site: www.AGExplore.org.

ACADEMY OF MOUNT SAINT URSULA

330 Bedford Park Boulevard
Bronx, New York 10458-2493
Head of School: Dr. Joseph S Fusco, PhD
General Information Girls' day college-preparatory, arts, business, religious studies, and technology school, affiliated with Roman Catholic Church. Grades 9–12. Founded: 1855. Setting: urban. Nearest major city is New York. 12-acre campus. 1 building on campus. Approved or accredited by Middle States Association of Colleges and Schools, National Catholic Education Association, and New York State Board of Regents. Total enrollment: 400. Upper school average class size: 25. Upper school faculty-student ratio: 1:17.
Upper School Student Profile Grade 9: 116 students (116 girls); Grade 10: 99 students (99 girls); Grade 11: 90 students (90 girls); Grade 12: 95 students (95 girls). 64% of students are Roman Catholic.
Faculty School total: 34. In upper school: 9 men, 25 women; 30 have advanced degrees.
Subjects Offered Accounting, algebra, American history, American literature, anatomy, anthropology, art, Bible studies, biology, biology-AP, business law, calculus-AP, chemistry, community service, composition, computer math, computer programming, computer science, creative writing, driver education, earth science, economics, English, English literature, English-AP, European history, fine arts, French, general science, geometry, government/civics, health, history, history-AP, Italian, Latin, mathematics, music, physical education, physics, pre-calculus, religion, science, Shakespeare, social studies, sociology, Spanish, Spanish language-AP, Spanish literature-AP, speech, trigonometry, women's literature, word processing, world history, world literature, writing.
Graduation Requirements Arts and fine arts (art, music, dance, drama), business skills (includes word processing), computer science, English, foreign language, mathematics, physical education (includes health), religion (includes Bible studies and theology), science, social studies (includes history). Community service is required.
Special Academic Programs Advanced Placement exam preparation; honors section; academic accommodation for the musically talented and the artistically talented; remedial reading and/or remedial writing; remedial math.
College Admission Counseling 101 students graduated in 2008; 100 went to college, including City College of the City University of New York; Fordham University; Hunter College of the City University of New York; Manhattanville College; New York Institute of Technology; New York University. Other: 1 went to work.
Student Life Upper grades have uniform requirement, student council. Discipline rests primarily with faculty. Attendance at religious services is required.
Summer Programs Remediation programs offered; session focuses on high school prep in math and language arts for new 9th graders; held on campus; accepts girls; not open to students from other schools. 20 students usually enrolled. 2009 schedule: June 30 to July 17.
Tuition and Aid Day student tuition: $6000. Tuition installment plan (monthly payment plans, semester payment plan, prepayment discount plan). Merit scholarship grants, need-based scholarship grants, archdiocese program available. In 2008–09, 40% of upper-school students received aid; total upper-school merit-scholarship money awarded: $165,500. Total amount of financial aid awarded in 2008–09: $249,220.
Admissions Traditional secondary-level entrance grade is 9. For fall 2008, 535 students applied for upper-level admission, 350 were accepted, 116 enrolled. New York Archdiocesan Cooperative Entrance Examination required. Deadline for receipt of application materials: September 30. Application fee required: $100. Interview recommended.

Athletics Interscholastic: basketball, cheering, soccer, softball, swimming and diving, track and field, volleyball; intramural: basketball, dance, swimming and diving, tennis, track and field, volleyball. 2 PE instructors, 3 coaches.
Computers Computers are regularly used in accounting, English, foreign language, mathematics, science, social studies classes. Computer network features include on-campus library services, Internet access, wireless campus network, Internet filtering or blocking technology, science labs. Student e-mail accounts and computer access in designated common areas are available to students. The school has a published electronic and media policy.
Contact Ms. Kate Ostrander, Director of Admissions and Recruitment. 718-364-5353 Ext. 231. Fax: 718-364-2354. E-mail: kostrander@amsu.org. Web site: www.amsu.org.

ACADEMY OF NOTRE DAME DE NAMUR

560 Sproul Road
Villanova, Pennsylvania 19085-1220

Head of School: Mrs. Veronica Collins Harrington

General Information Girls' day college-preparatory school, affiliated with Roman Catholic Church. Grades 6–12. Founded: 1856. Setting: suburban. Nearest major city is Philadelphia. 38-acre campus. 9 buildings on campus. Approved or accredited by Middle States Association of Colleges and Schools, National Catholic Education Association, and Pennsylvania Department of Education. Member of National Association of Independent Schools. Endowment: $3.4 million. Total enrollment: 526. Upper school average class size: 13. Upper school faculty-student ratio: 1:8.
Upper School Student Profile Grade 9: 103 students (103 girls); Grade 10: 95 students (95 girls); Grade 11: 96 students (96 girls); Grade 12: 87 students (87 girls). 87.3% of students are Roman Catholic.
Faculty School total: 58. In upper school: 6 men, 42 women; 43 have advanced degrees.
Subjects Offered Bible, calculus, calculus-AP, Central and Eastern European history, ceramics, chemistry, chemistry-AP, choral music, Christian and Hebrew scripture, Christian ethics, comparative government and politics-AP, contemporary history, dance, economics, English, English literature, English literature and composition-AP, environmental science, European history, French, French language-AP, geometry, government and politics-AP, health, health education, Hebrew scripture, instrumental music, journalism, Latin, Latin-AP, literature, mathematics, multimedia design, music, music composition, music theory, music theory-AP, physics-AP, pre-algebra, pre-calculus, SAT/ACT preparation, Spanish, Spanish language-AP, U.S. government and politics-AP.
Graduation Requirements Art, dance, English, foreign language, guidance, mathematics, music, physical education (includes health), religion (includes Bible studies and theology), science, social studies (includes history), trigonometry, 40 hours of social service.
Special Academic Programs Honors section; independent study; study at local college for college credit.
College Admission Counseling 87 students graduated in 2008; all went to college, including Georgetown University; New York University; Penn State University Park; University of Notre Dame; University of Pennsylvania; Villanova University. Median SAT critical reading: 590, median SAT math: 580, median SAT writing: 600, median combined SAT: 1770. 48% scored over 600 on SAT critical reading, 46% scored over 600 on SAT math, 51% scored over 600 on SAT writing, 50% scored over 1800 on combined SAT.
Student Life Upper grades have uniform requirement, student council, honor system. Discipline rests primarily with faculty. Attendance at religious services is required.
Summer Programs Enrichment, advancement, sports, art/fine arts, computer instruction programs offered; session focuses on academic enrichment; held on campus; accepts boys and girls; open to students from other schools. 100 students usually enrolled. 2009 schedule: June 15 to July 24.
Tuition and Aid Day student tuition: $14,760–$16,660. Tuition installment plan (monthly payment plans, quarterly and semi-annual payment plans). Merit scholarship grants, need-based scholarship grants available. In 2008–09, 31% of upper-school students received aid; total upper-school merit-scholarship money awarded: $377,060. Total amount of financial aid awarded in 2008–09: $467,900.
Admissions Traditional secondary-level entrance grade is 9. For fall 2008, 238 students applied for upper-level admission, 197 were accepted, 62 enrolled. High School Placement Test required. Deadline for receipt of application materials: December 14. Application fee required: $30. Interview recommended.
Athletics Interscholastic: basketball, crew, cross-country running, diving, field hockey, golf, lacrosse, soccer, softball, swimming and diving, tennis, track and field, volleyball, winter (indoor) track; intramural: dance, kickball, modern dance. 4 PE instructors, 36 coaches, 1 athletic trainer.
Computers Computers are regularly used in all classes. Computer network features include on-campus library services, online commercial services, Internet access, Internet filtering or blocking technology, Smart Boards in classrooms. Student e-mail accounts are available to students. Students grades are available online. The school has a published electronic and media policy.
Contact Mrs. Diane Sander, Director of Admissions. 610-971-0498. Fax: 610-687-1912. E-mail: dsander@ndapa.org. Web site: www.ndapa.org.

ACADEMY OF OUR LADY OF GOOD COUNSEL HIGH SCHOOL

52 North Broadway
White Plains, New York 10603

Head of School: Sr. Carol Peterson

General Information Girls' day college-preparatory school, affiliated with Roman Catholic Church. Grades 9–12. Founded: 1922. Setting: suburban. 15-acre campus. 4 buildings on campus. Approved or accredited by Middle States Association of Colleges and Schools, National Catholic Education Association, New York Department of Education, and New York State Board of Regents. Total enrollment: 303. Upper school average class size: 24. Upper school faculty-student ratio: 1:11.
Upper School Student Profile Grade 9: 70 students (70 girls); Grade 10: 75 students (75 girls); Grade 11: 81 students (81 girls); Grade 12: 77 students (77 girls). 80% of students are Roman Catholic.
Faculty School total: 29. In upper school: 4 men, 24 women; 19 have advanced degrees.
Subjects Offered Advanced Placement courses, advertising design, algebra, American government, American history, American history-AP, anatomy and physiology, biology, biology-AP, British literature, British literature-AP, calculus-AP, communications, CPR, criminology, earth science, economics, European history-AP, French, geometry, global studies, government, guidance, health, Latin, painting, peace and justice, physics, pre-calculus, religion, Spanish, studio art, U.S. history, writing workshop.
Graduation Requirements Community Service at each grade level.
Special Academic Programs Honors section; study at local college for college credit.
College Admission Counseling 85 students graduated in 2008; all went to college, including Fordham University; Iona College; John Jay College of Criminal Justice of the City University of New York; Pace University; Westchester Community College. Mean SAT critical reading: 532, mean SAT math: 519, mean SAT writing: 544. 22% scored over 600 on SAT critical reading, 20% scored over 600 on SAT math, 28% scored over 600 on SAT writing.
Student Life Upper grades have uniform requirement, student council. Discipline rests primarily with faculty. Attendance at religious services is required.
Tuition and Aid Day student tuition: $7250. Tuition installment plan (monthly payment plans, quarterly payment plan, semiannual payment plan, annual payment plan). Tuition reduction for siblings, merit scholarship grants, need-based scholarship grants available. In 2008–09, 8% of upper-school students received aid; total upper-school merit-scholarship money awarded: $209,000. Total amount of financial aid awarded in 2008–09: $242,000.
Admissions Traditional secondary-level entrance grade is 9. For fall 2008, 420 students applied for upper-level admission, 300 were accepted, 70 enrolled. Application fee required: $55.
Athletics Interscholastic: basketball, cheering, soccer, softball, swimming and diving, tennis, track and field, volleyball. 3 PE instructors.
Computers Computer network features include on-campus library services. Computer access in designated common areas is available to students. The school has a published electronic and media policy.
Contact Mary Anne Polistina, Director of Admissions. 914-949-0178 Ext. 30. Fax: 914-682-3531. E-mail: admissions@goodcounselacademyhs.org. Web site: www.goodcounselacademyhs.org.

ACADEMY OF OUR LADY OF MERCY

200 High Street
Milford, Connecticut 06460

Head of School: Mrs. Barbara C. Griffin

General Information Girls' day college-preparatory, arts, religious studies, and technology school, affiliated with Roman Catholic Church. Grades 9–12. Founded: 1905. Setting: suburban. Nearest major city is New Haven. 30-acre campus. 5 buildings on campus. Approved or accredited by New England Association of Schools and Colleges and Connecticut Department of Education. Total enrollment: 443. Upper school average class size: 18. Upper school faculty-student ratio: 1:12.
Upper School Student Profile Grade 9: 128 students (128 girls); Grade 10: 91 students (91 girls); Grade 11: 103 students (103 girls); Grade 12: 121 students (121 girls). 82% of students are Roman Catholic.
Faculty School total: 47. In upper school: 2 men, 45 women; 39 have advanced degrees.
Subjects Offered Algebra, American history, American literature, anatomy, art, biology, business, calculus, chemistry, computer math, computer programming, English, English literature, environmental science, European history, fine arts, French, geometry, government/civics, health, history, journalism, Latin, mathematics, music, physical education, physics, physiology, religion, science, social studies, Spanish, trigonometry, world history, writing.
Graduation Requirements Arts and fine arts (art, music, dance, drama), English, foreign language, mathematics, physical education (includes health), religion (includes Bible studies and theology), science, social studies (includes history). Community service is required.
Special Academic Programs Honors section.

College Admission Counseling 105 students graduated in 2008; all went to college, including Boston College; College of the Holy Cross; Fairfield University; Loyola College in Maryland; Quinnipiac University; University of Connecticut. Mean SAT critical reading: 549, mean SAT math: 551, mean SAT writing: 568.
Student Life Upper grades have uniform requirement, student council, honor system. Discipline rests primarily with faculty. Attendance at religious services is required.
Tuition and Aid Day student tuition: $12,800. Tuition installment plan (FACTS Tuition Payment Plan, 1- and 2-payment plans). Tuition reduction for siblings, merit scholarship grants, need-based scholarship grants available. In 2008–09, 20% of upper-school students received aid; total upper-school merit-scholarship money awarded: $24,000. Total amount of financial aid awarded in 2008–09: $285,000.
Admissions Traditional secondary-level entrance grade is 9. For fall 2008, 300 students applied for upper-level admission, 212 were accepted, 128 enrolled. High School Placement Test required. Deadline for receipt of application materials: none. Application fee required: $50.
Athletics Interscholastic: basketball, cheering, cross-country running, diving, field hockey, golf, gymnastics, indoor track, lacrosse, running, skiing (downhill), soccer, softball, swimming and diving, tennis, track and field, volleyball; intramural: basketball. 1 PE instructor, 27 coaches, 1 athletic trainer.
Computers Computers are regularly used in mathematics classes. Computer network features include on-campus library services, online commercial services, Internet access, wireless campus network, Internet filtering or blocking technology. Campus intranet and student e-mail accounts are available to students.
Contact Mrs. Kathleen O. Shine, Director of Admissions and Financial Aid. 203-877-2786 Ext. 125. Fax: 203-876-9760. E-mail: kshine@lauraltonhall.org. Web site: www.lauraltonhall.org.

ACADEMY OF OUR LADY OF PEACE

4860 Oregon Street
San Diego, California 92116-1393

Head of School: Sr. Dolores Anchondo

General Information Girls' day college-preparatory, arts, and religious studies school, affiliated with Roman Catholic Church. Grades 9–12. Founded: 1882. Setting: urban. 20-acre campus. 7 buildings on campus. Approved or accredited by Western Association of Schools and Colleges, Western Catholic Education Association, and California Department of Education. Endowment: $250,000. Total enrollment: 731. Upper school average class size: 28. Upper school faculty-student ratio: 1:15.
Upper School Student Profile Grade 9: 210 students (210 girls); Grade 10: 185 students (185 girls); Grade 11: 163 students (163 girls); Grade 12: 173 students (173 girls). 91% of students are Roman Catholic.
Faculty School total: 53. In upper school: 13 men, 40 women; 41 have advanced degrees.
Subjects Offered Algebra, American literature, art, astronomy, Bible studies, biology, biology-AP, British literature, calculus, ceramics, chemistry, chemistry-AP, creative writing, dance, drama, economics, English, English-AP, ethics, fitness, French, French-AP, genetics, geometry, government, graphic arts, health, integrated science, marine biology, mathematics-AP, music appreciation, music theory-AP, oceanography, painting, physical education, physics, pre-calculus, psychology, Spanish, Spanish-AP, speech, studio art-AP, study skills, trigonometry, U.S. government-AP, U.S. history, U.S. history-AP, Western civilization, yearbook, yoga.
Graduation Requirements Arts and fine arts (art, music, dance, drama), English, foreign language, mathematics, physical education (includes health), religion (includes Bible studies and theology), science, social science, social studies (includes history), speech, 75 hours of community service, 9-11 reflection paper required for seniors.
Special Academic Programs Advanced Placement exam preparation; honors section.
College Admission Counseling 187 students graduated in 2008; 186 went to college, including California State University, San Marcos; Creighton University; Loyola Marymount University; San Diego State University; University of California, San Diego; University of San Diego. Other: 1 went to work. Median SAT critical reading: 560, median SAT math: 520, median SAT writing: 560, median combined SAT: 1640. 42.6% scored over 600 on SAT critical reading, 26.7% scored over 600 on SAT math, 45.5% scored over 600 on SAT writing, 40% scored over 26 on composite ACT.
Student Life Upper grades have uniform requirement, student council, honor system. Discipline rests equally with students and faculty. Attendance at religious services is required.
Summer Programs Remediation, enrichment, advancement, sports, art/fine arts, computer instruction programs offered; session focuses on remedial work and increased course selection coverage during regular school session; held on campus; accepts boys and girls; open to students from other schools. 250 students usually enrolled. 2009 schedule: June 15 to July 24. Application deadline: June 15.
Tuition and Aid Day student tuition: $10,420. Tuition installment plan (FACTS Tuition Payment Plan). Need-based scholarship grants available. In 2008–09, 25% of upper-school students received aid. Total amount of financial aid awarded in 2008–09: $990,000.
Admissions Traditional secondary-level entrance grade is 9. For fall 2008, 248 students applied for upper-level admission, 223 were accepted, 210 enrolled. High School Placement Test required. Deadline for receipt of application materials: none. Application fee required: $50. On-campus interview required.
Athletics Interscholastic: basketball, cheering, cross-country running, golf, gymnastics, independent competitive sports, soccer, softball, swimming and diving, tennis, track and field, volleyball. 4 PE instructors, 13 coaches.
Computers Computers are regularly used in computer applications, Web site design, word processing classes. Computer network features include on-campus library services, online commercial services, Internet access, wireless campus network, Internet filtering or blocking technology. Campus intranet and computer access in designated common areas are available to students. Students grades are available online. The school has a published electronic and media policy.
Contact Mrs. Sue De Winter, Administrative Assistant/Registrar. 619-725-9118. Fax: 619-297-2473. E mail: admissions@aolp.org. Web site: www.aolp.org.

ACADEMY OF THE HOLY ANGELS

315 Hillside Avenue
Demarest, New Jersey 07627-2799

Head of School: Sister Virginia Bobrowski, SSND

General Information Girls' day college-preparatory, arts, religious studies, bilingual studies, and technology school, affiliated with Roman Catholic Church. Grades 9–12. Founded: 1879. Setting: suburban. Nearest major city is New York, NY. 25-acre campus. 1 building on campus. Approved or accredited by Middle States Association of Colleges and Schools and National Catholic Education Association. Total enrollment: 567. Upper school average class size: 20. Upper school faculty-student ratio: 1:11.
Upper School Student Profile Grade 9: 144 students (144 girls); Grade 10: 138 students (138 girls); Grade 11: 129 students (129 girls); Grade 12: 156 students (156 girls). 80% of students are Roman Catholic.
Faculty School total: 80. In upper school: 8 men, 47 women; 37 have advanced degrees.
Subjects Offered Accounting, algebra, American history, American literature, anatomy, art, art history, biology, business law, business skills, calculus, chemistry, chorus, communications, community service, computer science, creative writing, design, drama, economics, English, English literature, European history, expository writing, film, fine arts, French, geometry, German, government/civics, grammar, graphic arts, health, history, humanities, instrumental music, Italian, journalism, Latin, mathematics, music, musical productions, photography, physical education, physics, physiology, psychology, religion, science, social studies, sociology, Spanish, theater, trigonometry, world history, world literature.
Graduation Requirements Arts and fine arts (art, music, dance, drama), business skills (includes word processing), computer science, English, foreign language, mathematics, physical education (includes health), religion (includes Bible studies and theology), science, social studies (includes history), 20 hours of community service.
Special Academic Programs Advanced Placement exam preparation; honors section; independent study; study at local college for college credit; academic accommodation for the gifted, the musically talented, and the artistically talented.
College Admission Counseling 153 students graduated in 2008; all went to college, including Boston College; College of the Holy Cross; Cornell University; Harvard University; New York University; Stanford University. Mean SAT critical reading: 594, mean SAT math: 570, mean SAT writing: 617, mean combined SAT: 1781.
Student Life Upper grades have uniform requirement, student council, honor system. Discipline rests primarily with faculty. Attendance at religious services is required.
Tuition and Aid Day student tuition: $10,900. Tuition installment plan (FACTS Tuition Payment Plan, individually arranged payment plans, single payment plan (with $150 discount)). Merit scholarship grants, need-based scholarship grants, Parents' Scholarship Fund Program (insures continuance of education in event of parental death) available. In 2008–09, 20% of upper-school students received aid; total upper-school merit-scholarship money awarded: $125,650. Total amount of financial aid awarded in 2008–09: $162,140.
Admissions Traditional secondary-level entrance grade is 9. For fall 2008, 630 students applied for upper-level admission, 240 were accepted, 147 enrolled. CTB/McGraw-Hill/Macmillan Co-op Test and Newark or Paterson Diocesan Test required. Deadline for receipt of application materials: November 30. Application fee required: $20.
Athletics Interscholastic: basketball, bowling, crew, cross-country running, dance team, fencing, indoor track & field, lacrosse, pom squad, soccer, softball, tennis, track and field, volleyball, winter (indoor) track; intramural: equestrian sports, fencing, martial arts. 3 PE instructors, 15 coaches, 1 athletic trainer.
Computers Computers are regularly used in all classes. Computer network features include on-campus library services, online commercial services, Internet access, wireless campus network, Internet filtering or blocking technology. Student e-mail accounts are available to students. Students grades are available online.
Contact Jennifer Moran, Principal. 201-768-7822 Ext. 202. Fax: 201-768-6933. E-mail: info@holyangels.org. Web site: www.holyangels.org.

ACADEMY OF THE HOLY CROSS

4920 Strathmore Avenue
Kensington, Maryland 20895-1299
Head of School: Dr. Claire M. Helm, PhD

General Information Girls' day college-preparatory, arts, and religious studies school, affiliated with Roman Catholic Church. Grades 9–12. Founded: 1868. Setting: suburban. Nearest major city is Rockville. 28-acre campus. 2 buildings on campus. Approved or accredited by Association of Independent Schools of Greater Washington, Middle States Association of Colleges and Schools, National Catholic Education Association, and Maryland Department of Education. Total enrollment: 626. Upper school average class size: 20. Upper school faculty-student ratio: 1:14.
Upper School Student Profile Grade 9: 153 students (153 girls); Grade 10: 160 students (160 girls); Grade 11: 153 students (153 girls); Grade 12: 160 students (160 girls). 89% of students are Roman Catholic.
Faculty School total: 59. In upper school: 14 men, 45 women.
Subjects Offered Acting, Advanced Placement courses, African studies, algebra, American history, American literature, Arabic, art, art history-AP, Asian studies, biology, biology-AP, calculus, calculus-AP, ceramics, chemistry, chemistry-AP, Christian scripture, computer science, concert choir, creative writing, design, drama, drawing, earth science, economics, English, English language and composition-AP, English literature, English literature and composition-AP, environmental science, ethnic studies, expository writing, fine arts, forensic science, French, genetics, geography, geometry, government/civics, grammar, health, Hebrew scripture, history, history of the Catholic Church, honors English, honors geometry, humanities, instrumental music, jazz dance, Latin, Latin American studies, madrigals, mathematics, moral theology, music, music appreciation, musical theater, musical theater dance, painting, peace studies, personal finance, photography, physical education, physical science, physics, physiology, pre-calculus, psychology, public speaking, religion, religious studies, science, sculpture, Shakespeare, social science, social studies, Spanish, sports medicine, statistics, studio art, studio art-AP, tap dance, technology, theater, theater design and production, theology, trigonometry, U.S. government, U.S. government-AP, U.S. history, U.S. history-AP, Web site design, world history, world studies.
Graduation Requirements Art, electives, English, foreign language, mathematics, performing arts, physical education (includes health), science, senior project, social science, social studies (includes history), theology, Christian service commitment.
Special Academic Programs Advanced Placement exam preparation; honors section; independent study; academic accommodation for the gifted and the artistically talented.
College Admission Counseling 162 students graduated in 2008; 158 went to college, including Salisbury University; The Catholic University of America; Towson University; University of Maryland, College Park; University of South Carolina; Virginia Polytechnic Institute and State University. Other: 3 went to work, 1 had other specific plans. Mean SAT critical reading: 564, mean SAT math: 542, mean SAT writing: 584, mean combined SAT: 1691, mean composite ACT: 24.
Student Life Upper grades have uniform requirement, student council, honor system. Discipline rests equally with students and faculty. Attendance at religious services is required.
Summer Programs Enrichment, advancement, sports, art/fine arts, computer instruction programs offered; session focuses on enrichment and athletic skill-building; held on campus; accepts girls; open to students from other schools. 200 students usually enrolled. 2009 schedule: June 15 to July 10. Application deadline: May 31.
Tuition and Aid Day student tuition: $15,550. Tuition installment plan (individually arranged payment plans). Tuition reduction for siblings, merit scholarship grants, need-based scholarship grants, alumnae stipends available. In 2008–09, 38% of upper-school students received aid.
Admissions Traditional secondary-level entrance grade is 9. For fall 2008, 344 students applied for upper-level admission, 271 were accepted, 153 enrolled. High School Placement Test required. Deadline for receipt of application materials: December 15. Application fee required: $50. On-campus interview required.
Athletics Interscholastic: archery, basketball, crew, cross-country running, diving, equestrian sports, field hockey, golf, lacrosse, soccer, softball, swimming and diving, tennis, track and field, volleyball; intramural: basketball, dance, dance team, drill team, golf, kayaking, lacrosse, soccer. 3 PE instructors, 35 coaches, 1 athletic trainer.
Computers Computers are regularly used in art, foreign language, mathematics, science, social science classes. Computer network features include on-campus library services, online commercial services, Internet access, wireless campus network, Internet filtering or blocking technology. Students grades are available online. The school has a published electronic and media policy.
Contact Mrs. Louise Hendon, Director of Admissions. 301-929-6442. Fax: 301-929-6440. E-mail: admissions@academyoftheholycross.org. Web site: www.academyoftheholycross.org.

ANNOUNCEMENT FROM THE SCHOOL The Academy of the Holy Cross, a Catholic college-preparatory school, is dedicated to educating young women in a Christ-centered community that values diversity. The Academy is committed to developing women of courage, compassion, and scholarship who responsibly embrace the social, spiritual, and intellectual challenges of the world.

ACADEMY OF THE HOLY NAMES

3319 Bayshore Boulevard
Tampa, Florida 33629-8899
Head of School: Jacqueline L. Landry

General Information Coeducational day (boys' only in lower grades) college-preparatory, arts, and religious studies school, affiliated with Roman Catholic Church. Boys grades PK–8, girls grades PK–12. Founded: 1881. Setting: urban. 19-acre campus. 6 buildings on campus. Approved or accredited by Association of Christian Schools International, Florida Council of Independent Schools, National Catholic Education Association, Southern Association of Colleges and Schools, and Florida Department of Education. Endowment: $4 million. Total enrollment: 852. Upper school average class size: 18. Upper school faculty-student ratio: 1:15.
Upper School Student Profile Grade 9: 82 students (82 girls); Grade 10: 81 students (81 girls); Grade 11: 74 students (74 girls); Grade 12: 76 students (76 girls). 72% of students are Roman Catholic.
Faculty School total: 95. In upper school: 2 men, 37 women; 24 have advanced degrees.
Subjects Offered 20th century history, accounting, algebra, American government-AP, American history, American history-AP, anatomy and physiology, art history-AP, biology, biology-AP, calculus, calculus-AP, ceramics, chemistry, chemistry-AP, Christian and Hebrew scripture, communications, computer applications, computer science, contemporary history, economics, English, English literature and composition-AP, environmental science-AP, ethics, French, French-AP, geometry, government, government-AP, honors algebra, honors English, honors geometry, honors U.S. history, honors world history, journalism, Latin, Latin-AP, law studies, marine biology, marketing, media, music, physical education, physics, physics-AP, psychology, religious education, social justice, Spanish, Spanish-AP, speech, statistics, world history, world religions.
Graduation Requirements 100 community service hours.
Special Academic Programs Advanced Placement exam preparation; honors section.
College Admission Counseling 87 students graduated in 2008; all went to college, including Boston College; College of Charleston; Florida State University; University of Florida; Vanderbilt University; Wake Forest University. Mean SAT critical reading: 572, mean SAT math: 558, mean SAT writing: 574, mean composite ACT: 25.
Student Life Upper grades have uniform requirement, student council, honor system. Discipline rests primarily with faculty. Attendance at religious services is required.
Summer Programs Enrichment, sports, art/fine arts programs offered; session focuses on enrichment; held on campus; accepts boys and girls; open to students from other schools. 2009 schedule: June to August.
Tuition and Aid Day student tuition: $13,660. Tuition installment plan (The Tuition Plan, monthly payment plans). Merit scholarship grants, need-based scholarship grants, paying campus jobs available. In 2008–09, 29% of upper-school students received aid; total upper-school merit-scholarship money awarded: $40,320. Total amount of financial aid awarded in 2008–09: $515,525.
Admissions Traditional secondary-level entrance grade is 9. Deadline for receipt of application materials: none. Application fee required: $30. On-campus interview required.
Athletics Interscholastic: aerobics/dance, aquatics, basketball, cheering, crew, cross-country running, dance, dance squad, dance team, diving, golf, physical fitness, softball, swimming and diving, tennis, track and field, volleyball, winter soccer; coed interscholastic: soccer. 3 PE instructors, 10 coaches, 1 athletic trainer.
Computers Computer network features include on-campus library services, Internet access, Internet filtering or blocking technology. Student e-mail accounts are available to students. Students grades are available online. The school has a published electronic and media policy.
Contact Admission Assistant. 813-839-5371 Ext. 307. Fax: 813-839-1486. E-mail: sgibbons@holynamestpa.org. Web site: www.holynamestpa.org.

ACADEMY OF THE NEW CHURCH BOYS' SCHOOL

2815 Benade Circle
Box 707
Bryn Athyn, Pennsylvania 19009
Head of School: Mr. R. Scott Daum

General Information Boys' boarding and day college-preparatory, arts, and religious studies school, affiliated with Christian faith. Grades 9–12. Founded: 1887. Setting: suburban. Nearest major city is Philadelphia. Students are housed in single-sex dormitories. 200-acre campus. 8 buildings on campus. Approved or accredited by Middle States Association of Colleges and Schools and Pennsylvania Department of Education. Endowment: $359.5 million. Total enrollment: 115. Upper school average class size: 15. Upper school faculty-student ratio: 1:8.
Upper School Student Profile Grade 9: 25 students (25 boys); Grade 10: 28 students (28 boys); Grade 11: 32 students (32 boys); Grade 12: 30 students (30 boys). 30% of students are boarding students. 70% are state residents. 22 states are represented in upper school student body. 6% are international students. International students from Canada, China, and Republic of Korea. 95% of students are Christian.
Faculty School total: 40. In upper school: 20 men, 20 women; 35 have advanced degrees; 10 reside on campus.

Subjects Offered Advanced chemistry, Advanced Placement courses, African-American literature, algebra, American history, American history-AP, American literature, American literature-AP, anatomy, ancient world history, art, art history, Bible studies, biology, British literature, calculus, calculus-AP, ceramics, chemistry, civics, computer programming, computer science, creative writing, dance, drama, ecology, English, English literature, English literature-AP, environmental science, European history, expository writing, fine arts, French, geometry, German, government/civics, grammar, health, history, honors U.S. history, industrial arts, journalism, Latin, mathematics, music, music theater, musical theater, philosophy, photography, physical education, physical science, physics, physiology, physiology-anatomy, portfolio art, pre-calculus, printmaking, probability and statistics, religion, religious education, religious studies, science, sculpture, senior project, social science, social studies, sociology, Spanish, speech, statistics, studio art, theater, theater arts, theater design and production, theater production, theology, trigonometry, U.S. history-AP, vocal ensemble, vocal music, women in literature, world history, world literature.

Graduation Requirements Arts and fine arts (art, music, dance, drama), English, foreign language, mathematics, physical education (includes health), religion (includes Bible studies and theology), science, social science, social studies (includes history).

Special Academic Programs Advanced Placement exam preparation; honors section; independent study; study at local college for college credit; academic accommodation for the gifted, the musically talented, and the artistically talented; remedial reading and/or remedial writing; remedial math; programs in English, mathematics, general development for dyslexic students.

College Admission Counseling 33 students graduated in 2008; 32 went to college, including Bryn Athyn College of the New Church; Penn State University Park; The George Washington University; University of Pennsylvania; University of Richmond; Virginia Polytechnic Institute and State University. Other: 1 went to work. Median SAT critical reading: 560, median SAT math: 610, median SAT writing: 540, median combined SAT: 1710. 40% scored over 600 on SAT critical reading, 53% scored over 600 on SAT math, 36% scored over 600 on SAT writing, 40% scored over 1800 on combined SAT.

Student Life Upper grades have specified standards of dress, student council. Discipline rests primarily with faculty. Attendance at religious services is required.

Summer Programs Enrichment, advancement, art/fine arts, computer instruction programs offered; session focuses on enrichment; held on campus; accepts boys and girls; open to students from other schools. 110 students usually enrolled. 2009 schedule: July 5 to July 26. Application deadline: June 1.

Tuition and Aid Day student tuition: $11,348; 7-day tuition and room/board: $16,256. Tuition installment plan (monthly payment plans, individually arranged payment plans, term payment plan). Need-based scholarship grants, middle-income loans available. In 2008–09, 56% of upper-school students received aid. Total amount of financial aid awarded in 2008–09: $495,747.

Admissions Traditional secondary-level entrance grade is 9. For fall 2008, 86 students applied for upper-level admission, 20 were accepted, 18 enrolled. Iowa Subtests, PSAT, SAT or SSAT required. Deadline for receipt of application materials: none. Application fee required: $50. Interview required.

Athletics Interscholastic: baseball, basketball, football, ice hockey, lacrosse. 1 PE instructor, 6 coaches, 1 athletic trainer.

Computers Computers are regularly used in English, foreign language, history, mathematics, science classes. Computer network features include on-campus library services, online commercial services, Internet access, wireless campus network, Internet filtering or blocking technology. Campus intranet and student e-mail accounts are available to students.

Contact Rev. Charles E. Blair, Admissions Officer. 267-502-2539. Fax: 267-502-2617. E-mail: charles.blair@ancss.org. Web site: www.ancss.org.

ACADEMY OF THE NEW CHURCH GIRLS' SCHOOL

2815 Benade Circle
Bryn Athyn, Pennsylvania 19009

Head of School: Susan O Odhner

General Information Girls' boarding and day college-preparatory, general academic, arts, and religious studies school, affiliated with Church of the New Jerusalem, Christian faith. Grades 9–12. Founded: 1884. Setting: suburban. Nearest major city is Philadelphia. Students are housed in single-sex dormitories. 200-acre campus. 8 buildings on campus. Approved or accredited by Middle States Association of Colleges and Schools and Pennsylvania Department of Education. Endowment: $359.5 million. Total enrollment: 113. Upper school average class size: 15. Upper school faculty-student ratio: 1:8.

Upper School Student Profile Grade 9: 15 students (15 girls); Grade 10: 28 students (28 girls); Grade 11: 40 students (40 girls); Grade 12: 30 students (30 girls). 32% of students are boarding students. 70% are state residents. 22 states are represented in upper school student body. 6% are international students. International students from Canada, China, and Republic of Korea. 95% of students are Church of the New Jerusalem, Christian.

Faculty School total: 40. In upper school: 20 men, 20 women; 35 have advanced degrees; 10 reside on campus.

Subjects Offered Advanced chemistry, Advanced Placement courses, African-American literature, algebra, American history, American history-AP, American literature, anatomy, ancient history, ancient world history, art, art history, Bible studies, biology, British literature, calculus, calculus-AP, chemistry, civics, computer science, creative writing, drafting, drama, dramatic arts, drawing, ecology, ecology, environmental systems, economics, English, English literature, English literature-AP, English-AP, European history, expository writing, film studies, fine arts, French, geometry, government/civics, grammar, health, history, honors algebra, honors English, honors geometry, honors U.S. history, human anatomy, Latin, mathematics, medieval history, music, painting, philosophy, photography, physical education, physical science, physics, physiology, pre-calculus, printmaking, religion, science, sculpture, senior project, social science, social studies, Spanish, speech, stained glass, statistics-AP, theater, theology, trigonometry, women in literature, world history, world literature.

Graduation Requirements Arts and fine arts (art, music, dance, drama), English, foreign language, mathematics, physical education (includes health), religion (includes Bible studies and theology), science, social science, social studies (includes history).

Special Academic Programs Advanced Placement exam preparation; honors section; independent study; study at local college for college credit; academic accommodation for the gifted, the musically talented, and the artistically talented; remedial reading and/or remedial writing; remedial math; special instructional classes for Attention Deficit Disorder and learning-disabled children; ESL (6 students enrolled).

College Admission Counseling 38 students graduated in 2008; 34 went to college, including Bryn Athyn College of the New Church; Penn State University Park; The George Washington University; University of Pennsylvania; University of Richmond; Virginia Polytechnic Institute and State University. Other: 1 went to work, 2 entered a postgraduate year, 1 had other specific plans. Median SAT critical reading: 580, median SAT math: 570, median SAT writing: 580, median combined SAT: 1730. 47% scored over 600 on SAT critical reading, 41% scored over 600 on SAT math, 44% scored over 600 on SAT writing, 47% scored over 1800 on combined SAT.

Student Life Upper grades have uniform requirement, student council. Discipline rests primarily with faculty. Attendance at religious services is required.

Summer Programs Enrichment, advancement, art/fine arts, computer instruction programs offered; session focuses on enrichment; held on campus; accepts boys and girls; open to students from other schools. 130 students usually enrolled. 2009 schedule: July 5 to August 3. Application deadline: June 1.

Tuition and Aid Day student tuition: $11,348; 7-day tuition and room/board: $16,256. Tuition installment plan (monthly payment plans, individually arranged payment plans, term payment plan). Need-based scholarship grants, need-based loans, middle-income loans available. In 2008–09, 51% of upper-school students received aid. Total amount of financial aid awarded in 2008–09: $375,723.

Admissions Traditional secondary-level entrance grade is 9. For fall 2008, 86 students applied for upper-level admission, 20 were accepted, 18 enrolled. Iowa Subtests, PSAT, SAT or SSAT required. Deadline for receipt of application materials: none. Application fee required: $50. Interview required.

Athletics Interscholastic: basketball, dance team, field hockey, lacrosse, soccer, softball, tennis, volleyball. 1 PE instructor, 6 coaches, 1 athletic trainer.

Computers Computers are regularly used in English, foreign language, history, mathematics, science classes. Computer network features include on-campus library services, online commercial services, Internet access, wireless campus network, Internet filtering or blocking technology. Campus intranet and student e-mail accounts are available to students.

Contact Rev. Charles E Blair, Director of Admissions. 267-502-2439. Fax: 267-502-2617. E-mail: charles.blair@ancss.org.

ACADEMY OF THE SACRED HEART

4521 St. Charles Avenue
New Orleans, Louisiana 70115-4831

Head of School: Dr. Timothy Matthew Burns, PhD

General Information Girls' day college-preparatory, arts, religious studies, bilingual studies, and technology school, affiliated with Roman Catholic Church. Grades N–12. Founded: 1887. Setting: urban. 7-acre campus. 2 buildings on campus. Approved or accredited by Independent Schools Association of the Southwest, National Catholic Education Association, Network of Sacred Heart Schools, Southern Association of Colleges and Schools, and Louisiana Department of Education. Endowment: $7.3 million. Total enrollment: 768. Upper school average class size: 18. Upper school faculty-student ratio: 1:16.

Upper School Student Profile Grade 9: 45 students (45 girls); Grade 10: 65 students (65 girls); Grade 11: 61 students (61 girls); Grade 12: 53 students (53 girls). 88% of students are Roman Catholic.

Faculty School total: 104. In upper school: 6 men, 24 women; 22 have advanced degrees.

Subjects Offered Advanced chemistry, algebra, American government, American government-AP, American history, American history-AP, American literature, American literature-AP, anatomy and physiology, art, astronomy, athletics, basketball, biology, biology-AP, calculus, calculus-AP, campus ministry, Catholic belief and practice, ceramics, cheerleading, chemistry, chemistry-AP, clayworking, college admission preparation, college awareness, college counseling, college planning, computer applications, computer education, computer processing, computer resources, computer science, computer skills, computer studies, creative writing, drawing, electives, English, English literature, English literature-AP, English-AP, foreign language, French, French-AP, geometry, government, government-AP, guidance, history of the Catholic Church, honors algebra, honors English, honors geometry, honors U.S. history, honors world history, painting, peer counseling, pre-calculus, religions, robotics, social justice, Spanish, Spanish-AP, U.S. government, U.S. government-AP, U.S. history, U.S. history-AP, video communication, Web site design, world history, world history-AP, world religions, zoology.

Graduation Requirements Advanced Placement courses, algebra, American government, American literature, arts and fine arts (art, music, dance, drama), athletics, Basic programming, British literature, calculus, career/college preparation, computer applications, computer literacy, electives, English, foreign language, geometry, guidance, moral theology, peer counseling, physical education (includes health), physics, religions, robotics, science, scripture, social justice, social studies (includes history), U.S. government, yearbook, senior speech, 50 hours of required community service.

Special Academic Programs Advanced Placement exam preparation; honors section.

College Admission Counseling 62 students graduated in 2008; all went to college, including College of Charleston; Louisiana State University and Agricultural and Mechanical College; Rhodes College; The University of Alabama; Tulane University; University of Georgia.

Student Life Upper grades have uniform requirement, student council, honor system. Discipline rests equally with students and faculty. Attendance at religious services is required.

Summer Programs Sports programs offered; session focuses on strength and conditioning; held both on and off campus; held at area tracks; accepts girls; not open to students from other schools. 12 students usually enrolled. 2009 schedule: June to August.

Tuition and Aid Day student tuition: $12,650. Tuition installment plan (The Tuition Plan, individually arranged payment plans, bank loan). Need-based scholarship grants available. In 2008–09, 20% of upper-school students received aid.

Admissions Traditional secondary-level entrance grade is 9. Admissions testing, ERB, OLSAT/Stanford or SAT required. Deadline for receipt of application materials: none. Application fee required: $50. Interview required.

Athletics Interscholastic: baseball, basketball, cheering, cross-country running, fitness, golf, indoor track & field, sailing, soccer, softball, strength & conditioning, swimming and diving, tennis, track and field, volleyball; intramural: aerobics, cooperative games, fitness, jogging, outdoor activities, outdoor recreation, physical fitness. 5 PE instructors, 14 coaches, 1 athletic trainer.

Computers Computers are regularly used in all classes. Computer network features include on-campus library services, online commercial services, Internet access, wireless campus network, Internet filtering or blocking technology. Campus intranet, student e-mail accounts, and computer access in designated common areas are available to students. Students grades are available online. The school has a published electronic and media policy.

Contact Ms. Christy Sevante, Admission Director. 504-269-1214. Fax: 504-896-7880. E-mail: csevante@ashrosary.org. Web site: www.ashrosary.org.

ACADEMY OF THE SACRED HEART

1250 Kensington Road
Bloomfield Hills, Michigan 48304-3029

Head of School: Bridget Bearss, RSCJ

General Information Coeducational day (boys' only in lower grades) college-preparatory, arts, religious studies, technology, experiential learning, and community service school, affiliated with Roman Catholic Church. Boys grades N–8, girls grades N–12. Founded: 1851. Setting: suburban. Nearest major city is Detroit. 45-acre campus. 1 building on campus. Approved or accredited by Independent Schools Association of the Central States, Network of Sacred Heart Schools, and Michigan Department of Education. Endowment: $3.8 million. Total enrollment: 563. Upper school average class size: 12. Upper school faculty-student ratio: 1:7.

Upper School Student Profile Grade 9: 33 students (33 girls); Grade 10: 37 students (37 girls); Grade 11: 39 students (39 girls); Grade 12: 39 students (39 girls). 68% of students are Roman Catholic.

Faculty School total: 85. In upper school: 6 men, 21 women; 17 have advanced degrees.

Subjects Offered 20th century history, Advanced Placement courses, algebra, American literature, art, art history, biology, calculus, calculus-AP, chemistry, child development, clayworking, community service, computer applications, computer graphics, concert band, concert choir, crafts, creative writing, earth science, economics, English literature, English literature-AP, English-AP, environmental science, European history, European history-AP, forensics, French, genetics, geometry, global studies, government/civics, health, health and wellness, honors algebra, honors geometry, interior design, jewelry making, Latin, literature, mathematics, photography, physical education, physical science, physics, pre-calculus, psychology, publications, social studies, sociology, Spanish, theater, theology, U.S. history, U.S. history-AP, video, Web site design, world history, world literature.

Graduation Requirements Arts and fine arts (art, music, dance, drama), computer applications, foreign language, government, health and wellness, literature, mathematics, physical education (includes health), science, social studies (includes history), theology, U.S. government, U.S. history, world history, world literature, Project Term, First Year Experience (arts lab). Community service is required.

Special Academic Programs Advanced Placement exam preparation; honors section; independent study; term-away projects; domestic exchange program (with Network of Sacred Heart Schools); academic accommodation for the gifted, the musically talented, and the artistically talented.

College Admission Counseling 38 students graduated in 2008; all went to college, including Central Michigan University; Colorado State University; John Carroll University; Michigan State University; Northwestern University; University of Michigan. Mean SAT critical reading: 585, mean SAT math: 584, mean SAT writing: 589, mean composite ACT: 25.

Student Life Upper grades have uniform requirement, student council, honor system. Discipline rests primarily with faculty. Attendance at religious services is required.

Summer Programs Enrichment, sports, art/fine arts, computer instruction programs offered; session focuses on enrichment/day camp; held on campus; accepts boys and girls; open to students from other schools. 338 students usually enrolled. 2009 schedule: June 22 to July 31. Application deadline: none.

Tuition and Aid Day student tuition: $18,600. Tuition installment plan (Academic Management Services Plan). Merit scholarship grants, need-based scholarship grants available. In 2008–09, 38% of upper-school students received aid; total upper-school merit-scholarship money awarded: $4000. Total amount of financial aid awarded in 2008–09: $669,220.

Admissions Traditional secondary-level entrance grade is 9. For fall 2008, 21 students applied for upper-level admission, 21 were accepted, 12 enrolled. Scholastic Testing Service High School Placement Test or Stanford Achievement Test required. Deadline for receipt of application materials: none. Application fee required: $50. On-campus interview required.

Athletics Interscholastic: basketball (girls), dance team (g), equestrian sports (g), field hockey (g), figure skating (g), golf (g), lacrosse (g), skiing (downhill) (g), softball (g), tennis (g), volleyball (g). 1 PE instructor, 11 coaches.

Computers Computers are regularly used in all academic classes. Computer network features include on-campus library services, online commercial services, Internet access, wireless campus network, Internet filtering or blocking technology, tablet PC/laptop program with wireless network and print services, classroom multimedia services, computer in each classroom. Campus intranet, student e-mail accounts, and computer access in designated common areas are available to students. Students grades are available online. The school has a published electronic and media policy.

Contact Barbara Lopiccolo, Director of Admissions. 248-646-8900 Ext. 129. Fax: 248-646-4143. E-mail: blopiccolo@ashmi.org. Web site: www.ashmi.org.

ANNOUNCEMENT FROM THE SCHOOL The Academy of the Sacred Heart (www.ashmi.org), a member of the Network of Sacred Heart Schools (www.sofie.org), was founded in 1851 and is Michigan's oldest independent school. Located in Bloomfield Hills, it is a Catholic, college-preparatory school for girls (age 3 through grade 12) and boys (age 3 through grade 8) of many cultures and faiths.

ACCELERATED SCHOOLS

2160 South Cook Street
Denver, Colorado 80210

Head of School: John Klieforth

General Information Coeducational boarding and day college-preparatory and bilingual studies school; primarily serves underachievers, students with learning disabilities, individuals with Attention Deficit Disorder, individuals with emotional and behavioral problems, dyslexic students, and bipolar disorders. Boarding boys grades 7–12, boarding girls grades 8–12, day boys grades K–12, day girls grades K–12. Founded: 1920. Setting: urban. Students are housed in host family homes. 4-acre campus. 3 buildings on campus. Approved or accredited by North Central Association of Colleges and Schools and Colorado Department of Education. Languages of instruction: English, Spanish, and French. Total enrollment: 52. Upper school average class size: 7. Upper school faculty-student ratio: 1:7.

Upper School Student Profile 5% of students are boarding students. 85% are state residents. 3 states are represented in upper school student body. International students from Japan, Republic of Korea, and Spain.

Faculty School total: 15. In upper school: 4 men, 4 women; 4 have advanced degrees.

Subjects Offered ACT preparation, algebra, American history, American literature, art, art history, biology, business, business skills, calculus, chemistry, computer math, computer science, creative writing, earth science, economics, English, English literature, French, geography, geology, geometry, government/civics, grammar, history, human biology, mathematics, philosophy, photography, physical education, physics, psychology, reading, science, social studies, sociology, Spanish, TOEFL preparation, trigonometry, world history, zoology.

Graduation Requirements Business skills (includes word processing), computer science, English, foreign language, mathematics, physical education (includes health), science, social studies (includes history).

Special Academic Programs Advanced Placement exam preparation; honors section; accelerated programs; study at local college for college credit; academic accommodation for the gifted; remedial reading and/or remedial writing; remedial math; programs in English, mathematics, general development for dyslexic students;

special instructional classes for students with Attention Deficit Disorder, learning disabilities, and dyslexia; ESL (5 students enrolled).
College Admission Counseling Colleges students went to include Arapahoe Community College; Colorado State University; Metropolitan State College of Denver; University of Denver; University of Northern Colorado.
Student Life Upper grades have specified standards of dress. Discipline rests primarily with faculty.
Tuition and Aid Day student tuition: $21,750; 7-day tuition and room/board: $28,950. Guaranteed tuition plan. Tuition installment plan (Key Tuition Payment Plan, monthly payment plans, individually arranged payment plans, Sallie Mae, Wells Fargo plan). Tuition reduction for siblings available. In 2007–08, 10% of upper-school students received aid. Total amount of financial aid awarded in 2007–08: $90,000.
Admissions Traditional secondary-level entrance grade is 10. For fall 2007, 75 students applied for upper-level admission, 50 were accepted, 40 enrolled. CTBS or ERB, Iowa Test of Educational Development or Iowa Tests of Basic Skills required. Deadline for receipt of application materials: none. No application fee required. Interview recommended.
Athletics Intramural: bowling (boys, girls); coed intramural: aerobics, aerobics/dance, alpine skiing, aquatics, archery, backpacking, badminton, baseball, basketball, bicycling, billiards, bowling, croquet, dance, fishing, flag football, Frisbee, golf, hiking/backpacking, horseback riding, ice skating, jogging. 2 PE instructors.
Computers Computers are regularly used in English, mathematics classes. Computer resources include Internet access, wireless campus network.
Contact Jane T. Queen, Associate Director. 303-758-2003. Fax: 303-757-4336. E-mail: queenjbqueen@aol.com. Web site: www.acceleratedschools.org.

See Close-Up on page 656.

ACS COBHAM INTERNATIONAL SCHOOL

Heywood, Portsmouth Road
Cobham, Surrey KT11 1BL, United Kingdom

Head of School: Tom Lehman

General Information Coeducational boarding and day college-preparatory, International Baccalaureate, and Advanced Placement school. Boarding grades 7–12, day grades N–12. Founded: 1967. Setting: suburban. Nearest major city is London, United Kingdom. Students are housed in single-sex dormitories. 128-acre campus. 4 buildings on campus. Approved or accredited by Independent Schools Council (UK), International Baccalaureate Organization, and New England Association of Schools and Colleges. Member of European Council of International Schools. Language of instruction: English. Total enrollment: 1,308. Upper school average class size: 18. Upper school faculty-student ratio: 1:9.
Upper School Student Profile Grade 9: 96 students (61 boys, 35 girls); Grade 10: 102 students (57 boys, 45 girls); Grade 11: 118 students (65 boys, 53 girls); Grade 12: 114 students (59 boys, 55 girls). 20% of students are boarding students. 86% are international students. International students from Canada, Denmark, Netherlands, Norway, Sweden, and United States; 43 other countries represented in student body.
Faculty School total: 140. In upper school: 19 men, 26 women; 20 have advanced degrees; 16 reside on campus.
Subjects Offered Algebra, American history, American literature, art, art history, biology, calculus, ceramics, chemistry, computer programming, computer science, drama, Dutch, economics, English, ESL, European history, fine arts, French, geometry, German, Japanese, journalism, mathematics, music, Norwegian, photography, physical education, physics, psychology, science, social studies, Spanish, speech, Swedish, theater, theory of knowledge, trigonometry, typing, world history, world literature, writing.
Graduation Requirements Arts and fine arts (art, music, dance, drama), English, foreign language, mathematics, physical education (includes health), science, social studies (includes history).
Special Academic Programs International Baccalaureate program; Advanced Placement exam preparation; honors section; academic accommodation for the gifted; ESL (25 students enrolled).
College Admission Counseling 124 students graduated in 2008; 88 went to college, including Harvard University; Harvey Mudd College; New York University; Northwestern University; Penn State University Park; The University of Texas at Austin. Other: 1 entered military service, 10 had other specific plans. Mean SAT critical reading: 548, mean SAT math: 572, mean SAT writing: 547, mean combined SAT: 1666.
Student Life Upper grades have specified standards of dress, student council, honor system. Discipline rests primarily with faculty.
Summer Programs Session focuses on British Studies Program, an integrated instruction and academic challenge; held on campus; accepts boys and girls; open to students from other schools. 20 students usually enrolled.
Tuition and Aid Day student tuition: £18,280; 5-day tuition and room/board: £28,330; 7-day tuition and room/board: £32,040. Tuition installment plan (quarterly installment plan). Bursaries available. In 2008–09, 1% of upper-school students received aid. Total amount of financial aid awarded in 2008–09: £41,320.
Admissions Traditional secondary-level entrance grade is 9. English for Non-native Speakers required. Deadline for receipt of application materials: none. Application fee required: £95. Interview recommended.
Athletics Interscholastic: baseball (boys), basketball (b,g), cheering (g), cross-country running (b,g), dance team (g), rugby (b), soccer (b,g), softball (g), tennis (b,g), track and field (b,g), volleyball (b,g); intramural: soccer (b,g), water polo (b); coed interscholastic: golf; coed intramural: horseback riding, weight training. 2 PE instructors.
Computers Computers are regularly used in all academic classes. Computer network features include on-campus library services, online commercial services, Internet access. The school has a published electronic and media policy.
Contact Heidi Ayoub, Dean of Admissions. 44-01932 867 251. Fax: 44-01932 869 789. E-mail: hayoub@acs-england.co.uk. Web site: www.acs-england.co.uk.

See Close-Up on page 658.

ACS EGHAM INTERNATIONAL SCHOOL

Woodlee, London Road (A30)
Surrey TW20 0HS, United Kingdom

Head of School: Ms. Moyra Hadley

General Information Coeducational day college-preparatory and International Baccalaureate school. Grades N–12. Founded: 1967. Setting: suburban. Nearest major city is London, United Kingdom. 20-acre campus. 5 buildings on campus. Approved or accredited by Independent Schools Council (UK), International Baccalaureate Organization, and New England Association of Schools and Colleges. Member of European Council of International Schools. Language of instruction: English. Total enrollment: 584. Upper school average class size: 15. Upper school faculty-student ratio: 1:9.
Upper School Student Profile Grade 9: 54 students (27 boys, 27 girls); Grade 10: 51 students (28 boys, 23 girls); Grade 11: 42 students (26 boys, 16 girls); Grade 12: 26 students (14 boys, 12 girls).
Faculty School total: 68. In upper school: 9 men, 12 women; 10 have advanced degrees.
Subjects Offered Algebra, art, band, biology, chemistry, choir, college counseling, community service, computer science, computer skills, drama, economics, English, environmental systems, European history, forensics, French, geometry, history, information technology, integrated mathematics, International Baccalaureate courses, mathematics, music, physical education, physics, psychology, Spanish, theater arts, theory of knowledge, visual arts, world studies.
Graduation Requirements Arts and fine arts (art, music, dance, drama), English, foreign language, mathematics, physical education (includes health), science, social studies (includes history).
Special Academic Programs International Baccalaureate program; academic accommodation for the gifted; ESL (55 students enrolled).
College Admission Counseling 26 students graduated in 2008; 19 went to college, including Boston University; James Madison University; Lewis & Clark College; New York University; University of Vermont; Washington and Lee University. Other: 1 entered military service. Mean SAT critical reading: 580, mean SAT math: 570, mean SAT writing: 562, mean combined SAT: 1712.
Student Life Upper grades have specified standards of dress, student council, honor system. Discipline rests primarily with faculty.
Summer Programs Session focuses on British Studies Program—integrated instruction/academic challenge; held off campus; held at ACS Cobham International School Campus and Cobham, Surrey, UK; accepts boys and girls; open to students from other schools. 15 students usually enrolled. 2009 schedule: July to July.
Tuition and Aid Day student tuition: £16,280–£16,330. Tuition installment plan (quarterly payment plan). Bursaries available. In 2008–09, 3% of upper-school students received aid. Total amount of financial aid awarded in 2008–09: £11,426.
Admissions Traditional secondary-level entrance grade is 9. English for Non-native Speakers required. Deadline for receipt of application materials: none. Application fee required: £95. Interview recommended.
Athletics Interscholastic: baseball (boys), cheering (g), rugby (b), softball (g), track and field (b,g), volleyball (g); intramural: dance (g); coed interscholastic: basketball, cross-country running, indoor track & field, soccer, tennis; coed intramural: fencing, golf, soccer. 4 PE instructors, 4 coaches.
Computers Computers are regularly used in all classes. Computer network features include on-campus library services, online commercial services, Internet access, wireless campus network, Internet filtering or blocking technology. Student e-mail accounts are available to students.
Contact Ms. Julia Love, Dean of Admissions. 44-01784 430611. Fax: 44-01784-430626. E-mail: eghamadmission@acs-england.co.uk. Web site: www.acs-england.co.uk/schools/egham/index.htm.

ACS HILLINGDON INTERNATIONAL SCHOOL

Hillingdon Court
108 Vine Lane
Hillingdon, Middlesex UB10 0BE, United Kingdom

Head of School: Mrs. Ginger G. Apple

General Information Coeducational day college-preparatory, International Baccalaureate, and Advanced Placement school. Grades PK–12. Founded: 1967. Setting: suburban. Nearest major city is London, United Kingdom. 11-acre campus. 1 building on campus. Approved or accredited by Independent Schools Council (UK), International Baccalaureate Organization, and New England Association of Schools and Colleges. Member of European Council of International Schools. Language of instruction: English. Total enrollment: 589. Upper school average class size: 15. Upper school faculty-student ratio: 1:9.

Upper School Student Profile Grade 9: 62 students (29 boys, 33 girls); Grade 10: 60 students (25 boys, 35 girls); Grade 11: 59 students (29 boys, 30 girls); Grade 12: 48 students (27 boys, 21 girls).

Faculty School total: 70. In upper school: 11 men, 15 women; 12 have advanced degrees.

Subjects Offered Advanced Placement courses, algebra, art, art-AP, biology, calculus, chemistry, chemistry-AP, computer graphics, computer science, Dutch, economics, English, English language-AP, English literature and composition-AP, English literature-AP, environmental science, ESL, French, geography, geometry, health, information technology, integrated science, Japanese, macro/microeconomics-AP, math methods, music theory-AP, physical education, physics, physics-AP, psychology, psychology-AP, Spanish, theory of knowledge, U.S. history-AP, Web site design, world history.

Graduation Requirements Arts and fine arts (art, music, dance, drama), English, foreign language, mathematics, physical education (includes health), science, social studies (includes history).

Special Academic Programs International Baccalaureate program; Advanced Placement exam preparation; honors section; academic accommodation for the gifted; ESL.

College Admission Counseling 70 students graduated in 2008; 51 went to college, including Baylor University; Bowdoin College; Furman University; The University of Kansas; University of Central Florida; Wheaton College. Other: 1 entered military service, 6 had other specific plans. Mean SAT critical reading: 548, mean SAT math: 564, mean composite ACT: 25.

Student Life Upper grades have specified standards of dress, student council, honor system. Discipline rests primarily with faculty.

Summer Programs Session focuses on British Studies Program, an integrated instruction and academic challenge; held off campus; held at ACS Cobham International School Campus; accepts boys and girls; open to students from other schools. 20 students usually enrolled. 2009 schedule: July to July. Application deadline: none.

Tuition and Aid Day student tuition: £8310–£17,410. Tuition installment plan (quarterly installment plan). Bursaries available. In 2008–09, 8% of upper-school students received aid. Total amount of financial aid awarded in 2008–09: £48,000.

Admissions Traditional secondary-level entrance grade is 9. English for Non-native Speakers required. Deadline for receipt of application materials: none. Application fee required: £95. Interview recommended.

Athletics Interscholastic: baseball (boys), basketball (b,g), cross-country running (b,g), rugby (b), soccer (b,g), softball (g), swimming and diving (b,g), tennis (b,g), track and field (b,g), volleyball (b,g). 4 PE instructors, 20 coaches.

Computers Computers are regularly used in all academic classes. Computer network features include on-campus library services, Internet access, Internet filtering or blocking technology. The school has a published electronic and media policy.

Contact Ms. Rudianne Soltis, Dean of Admissions. 44-01895-818402. Fax: 44-01895-818404. E-mail: rsoltis@acs-england.co.uk. Web site: www.acs-england.co.uk.

ADELPHI ACADEMY

8515 Ridge Boulevard
Brooklyn, New York 11209

ANNOUNCEMENT FROM THE SCHOOL As the oldest private, independent, continuing, coeducational, college-preparatory day school in Brooklyn, Adelphi Academy has effectively prepared young people for college, careers, and life for 145 years. Founded in 1863 and located in the historic Bay Ridge section of Brooklyn, Adelphi enrolls students from Pre-Kindergarten through 12th grade. A strong emphasis is placed on small class size, critical thinking, and challenging hands-on learning within a small, nurturing, and caring environment through Adelphi's founding principles of pride, tradition, spirit, and excellence. The student-teacher ratio is 8 to 1. Adelphi features Project Succeed, a special needs program for college-bound students with learning disabilities. Before- and after-school care, financial aid, summer school, and summer day camp programs are available.

ADVANCED ACADEMY OF GEORGIA

Honors House
University of West Georgia
Carrollton, Georgia 30118

Head of School: Dr. Michael Hester

General Information Coeducational boarding college-preparatory, arts, business, technology, and mathematics, science, and humanities school. Grades 10–12. Founded: 1995. Setting: small town. Nearest major city is Atlanta. Students are housed in coed dormitories. 394-acre campus. 89 buildings on campus. Approved or accredited by Southern Association of Colleges and Schools and Georgia Department of Education. Total enrollment: 71. Upper school average class size: 14. Upper school faculty-student ratio: 1:14.

Upper School Student Profile 100% of students are boarding students. 86% are state residents. 4 states are represented in upper school student body. 8% are international students. International students from Russian Federation and Spain.

Faculty School total: 270. In upper school: 149 men, 121 women; all have advanced degrees.

Subjects Offered 20th century American writers, 20th century history, 20th century physics, 20th century world history, accounting, acting, advanced chemistry, advanced computer applications, advanced math, advanced studio art-AP, African American history, African American studies, African-American literature, algebra, American biography, American Civil War, American culture, American democracy, American foreign policy, American government, American history, American legal systems, American literature, American sign language, analysis, analysis and differential calculus, analysis of data, analytic geometry, anatomy, ancient world history, ancient/medieval philosophy, animal behavior, anthropology, archaeology, art, art and culture, art appreciation, art education, art history, Asian history, Asian literature, Asian studies, astronomy, astrophysics, athletics, band, banking, Bible as literature, biochemistry, bioethics, DNA and culture, biology, biotechnology, Black history, British history, British literature, British literature (honors), British National Curriculum, business applications, business communications, business education, business law, business mathematics, business skills, business studies, business technology, calculus, cell biology, chemistry, child development, Chinese, Chinese history, Chinese literature, Chinese studies, choir, cinematography, civics/free enterprise, civil rights, Civil War, civil war history, classical civilization, classical Greek literature, classical language, classical music, classical studies, communications, comparative government and politics, comparative politics, computer animation, computer applications, computer art, computer education, computer graphics, computer information systems, computer math, computer multimedia, computer music, computer processing, computer programming, computer science, computer technologies, constitutional history of U.S., constitutional law, consumer economics, critical thinking, critical writing, data analysis, debate, democracy in America, desktop publishing, discrete math, discrete mathematics, DNA, DNA research, DNA science lab, drama, drawing, drawing and design, early childhood, earth and space science, earth science, earth systems analysis, East Asian history, East European studies, Eastern religion and philosophy, Eastern world civilizations, ecology, economics, economics and history, education, English, English composition, English literature, ensembles, entrepreneurship, environmental geography, environmental science, environmental systems, ethics, ethnic literature, ethnic studies, European civilization, European history, film appreciation, film studies, first aid, fitness, forensic science, forensics, French, gender issues, genetics, geography, geology, geometry, German, German literature, global issues, global science, global studies, golf, government/civics, graphic arts, graphic design, graphics, Greek, Greek culture, Holocaust and other genocides, Holocaust legacy, Holocaust seminar, Holocaust studies, honors algebra, honors English, honors geometry, honors U.S. history, honors world history, human anatomy, human sexuality, intro to computers, Japanese, jazz, jazz band, Jewish history, Jewish studies, language arts, Latin, law, law and the legal system, law studies, library, library research, life saving, linear algebra, literature by women, literature seminar, logic, logic, rhetoric, and debate, management information systems, marching band, marine biology, marketing, math analysis, math applications, mathematical modeling, media communications, methods of research, microbiology, microeconomics, Middle East, military history, minority studies, model United Nations, modeling, modern Chinese history, modern civilization, modern European history, modern political theory, modern politics, modern problems, modern Western civilization, modern world history, money management, music, music appreciation, music composition, Native American history, Native American studies, natural history, newspaper, North American literature, oceanography, organic chemistry, painting, parent/child development, performing arts, personal and social education, personal development, personal finance, personal fitness, philosophy, philosophy of government, photography, photojournalism, physical education, physical fitness, physical science, physics, physiology, piano, political economics, political economy, political science, political systems, political thought, post-calculus, pre-calculus, printmaking, probability, probability and statistics, psychology, public policy, public speaking, publications, publishing, radio broadcasting, religion and culture, religious education, religious studies, Roman civilization, Roman culture, ROTC, Russian, Russian history, Russian literature, Russian studies, science and technology, science fiction, Shakespeare, Shakespearean histories, social education, social justice, social psychology, social science, social sciences, social studies, society, society and culture, society challenge and change, society, politics and law, sociology, South African history, Southern literature, Spanish, Spanish literature, speech and debate, speech and oral interpretations, speech communications, sports medicine, sports nutrition, state government, state history, statistics, stock market, student teaching, studio art, technical arts, technical drawing, technical education, technical skills, technical studies, technical theater, technical writing, technology, telecommunications, telecommunications and the Internet, television, The 20th Century, the Presidency, the Sixties, traditional camping, U.S. constitutional history, U.S. government, U.S. government and politics, U.S. history, U.S. literature, U.S. Presidents, United Nations and international issues, Vietnam War, visual and performing arts, visual arts, visual literacy, visual reality, water color painting, weight training, Western civilization,

Western literature, Western philosophy, western religions, Western religions, women in literature, women in society, women in the classical world, women in world history, women spirituality and faith, women's health, women's literature, women's studies, world civilizations, world cultures, world geography, world governments, world history, world issues, world literature, world religions, world studies, World War I, World War II, World-Wide-Web publishing, writing.
Graduation Requirements Students must complete Georgia high school requirements which are satisfied through equivalent college courses offered by the university.
Special Academic Programs Honors section; independent study; study at local college for college credit; study abroad; academic accommodation for the gifted, the musically talented, and the artistically talented.
College Admission Counseling 32 students graduated in 2008; all went to college, including Agnes Scott College; Brown University; Georgia Institute of Technology; Georgia State University; Savannah College of Art and Design; University of Georgia. Mean SAT critical reading: 648, mean SAT math: 645. 79% scored over 600 on SAT critical reading, 75% scored over 600 on SAT math.
Student Life Upper grades have student council, honor system. Discipline rests equally with students and faculty.
Summer Programs Advancement, art/fine arts programs offered; session focuses on arts and humanities, mathematics and science; held on campus; accepts boys and girls; open to students from other schools. 2009 schedule: July 11 to July 24. Application deadline: June 1.
Tuition and Aid 5-day tuition and room/board: $5200; 7-day tuition and room/board: $5200. Merit scholarship grants, need-based scholarship grants, need-based loans, middle-income loans, paying campus jobs available. In 2008–09, 65% of upper-school students received aid; total upper-school merit-scholarship money awarded: $24,000. Total amount of financial aid awarded in 2008–09: $83,700.
Admissions Traditional secondary-level entrance grade is 10. ACT or SAT required. Deadline for receipt of application materials: July 1. Application fee required: $30. Interview required.
Athletics Coed Intramural: basketball, flag football, Frisbee, paint ball, soccer, softball, ultimate Frisbee.
Computers Computers are regularly used in all classes. Computer network features include on-campus library services, online commercial services, Internet access, wireless campus network, Internet filtering or blocking technology. Student e-mail accounts are available to students. Students grades are available online. The school has a published electronic and media policy.
Contact Ms. Anneliesa Finch, Program Specialist. 678-839-6249. Fax: 678-839-0636. E-mail: afinch@westga.edu. Web site: www.advancedacademy.org.

THE AGNES IRWIN SCHOOL

Ithan Avenue and Conestoga Road
Rosemont, Pennsylvania 19010

Head of School: Ms. Helen Rowland Marter

General Information Girls' day college-preparatory school. Grades PK–12. Founded: 1869. Setting: suburban. Nearest major city is Philadelphia. 18-acre campus. 5 buildings on campus. Approved or accredited by Middle States Association of Colleges and Schools, National Independent Private Schools Association, Pennsylvania Association of Independent Schools, Western Catholic Education Association, and Pennsylvania Department of Education. Member of National Association of Independent Schools, Secondary School Admission Test Board, and National Coalition of Girls' Schools. Endowment: $22.4 million. Total enrollment: 681. Upper school average class size: 15. Upper school faculty-student ratio: 1:7.
Upper School Student Profile Grade 9: 65 students (65 girls); Grade 10: 61 students (61 girls); Grade 11: 51 students (51 girls); Grade 12: 67 students (67 girls).
Faculty School total: 94. In upper school: 16 men, 34 women; 36 have advanced degrees.
Subjects Offered 20th century world history, advanced studio art-AP, algebra, American history, American history-AP, American literature, American literature-AP, Asian studies, bioethics, bioethics, DNA and culture, biology, biology-AP, calculus, calculus-AP, chemistry, chemistry-AP, computer applications, dance, drama, economics, English, English language-AP, English literature, English literature and composition-AP, environmental science-AP, European history, European history-AP, finite math, French, French-AP, geometry, Greek, health, history, Japanese history, Latin, Latin-AP, media studies, Middle East, Middle Eastern history, music theory, photo shop, photography, physical education, physics, physics-AP, pre-calculus, public speaking, robotics, Spanish, Spanish-AP, statistics, studio art, theater arts, trigonometry.
Graduation Requirements Arts and fine arts (art, music, dance, drama), English, foreign language, history, mathematics, physical education (includes health), science, Senior Assembly given by each girl before graduation. Community service is required.
Special Academic Programs Advanced Placement exam preparation; honors section; independent study; term-away projects; study abroad; academic accommodation for the gifted.
College Admission Counseling 62 students graduated in 2008; all went to college, including Boston University; Dartmouth College; Franklin & Marshall College; Georgetown University; Tulane University; University of Pennsylvania. 77% scored over 600 on SAT critical reading, 86% scored over 600 on SAT math, 91% scored over 600 on SAT writing.
Student Life Upper grades have uniform requirement, student council, honor system. Discipline rests equally with students and faculty.
Summer Programs Remediation, enrichment, advancement, sports, art/fine arts, computer instruction programs offered; session focuses on arts, academics, athletics; held on campus; accepts boys and girls; open to students from other schools. 1,000 students usually enrolled. 2009 schedule: June 15 to July 31. Application deadline: none.
Tuition and Aid Day student tuition: $25,200. Tuition installment plan (monthly payment plans). Need-based scholarship grants available. In 2008–09, 17% of upper-school students received aid.
Admissions Traditional secondary-level entrance grade is 9. For fall 2008, 67 students applied for upper-level admission, 29 were accepted, 17 enrolled. ISEE, SSAT or WISC-R or WISC-III required. Deadline for receipt of application materials: January 12. Application fee required: $50. Interview required.
Athletics Interscholastic: basketball, crew, cross-country running, diving, field hockey, golf, independent competitive sports, lacrosse, running, soccer, softball, squash, strength & conditioning, swimming and diving, tennis, track and field, volleyball, weight training; intramural: aerobics, aerobics/Nautilus, ballet, dance, drill team, fencing, fitness, modern dance, Nautilus, physical fitness, physical training, strength & conditioning, weight training. 7 PE instructors, 34 coaches, 1 athletic trainer.
Computers Computers are regularly used in art, English, foreign language, history, mathematics, media arts, photography, science, yearbook classes. Computer network features include on-campus library services, online commercial services, Internet access, wireless campus network, Blackboard, digital video editing, audio recording studio, online databases. Campus intranet and computer access in designated common areas are available to students. The school has a published electronic and media policy.
Contact Mrs. Sally B. Keidel, Director of Enrollment Management. 610-525-8400. Fax: 610-525-8908. E-mail: skeidel@agnesirwin.org. Web site: www.agnesirwin.org.

See Close-Up on page 660.

AHLIYYAH SCHOOL FOR GIRLS

PO Box 2035
Amman 11181, Jordan

Head of School: Mrs. Haifa Hajjar Najjar

General Information Girls' day college-preparatory, general academic, arts, business, bilingual studies, and technology school, affiliated with Christian faith, Muslim faith; primarily serves students with learning disabilities, individuals with Attention Deficit Disorder, individuals with emotional and behavioral problems, and dyslexic students. Grades 1–12. Founded: 1926. Setting: urban. 1-hectare campus. 4 buildings on campus. Approved or accredited by International Baccalaureate Organization and National Association of Episcopal Schools. Member of European Council of International Schools. Languages of instruction: English and Arabic. Endowment: 2 million Jordanian dinars. Total enrollment: 1,018. Upper school average class size: 15. Upper school faculty-student ratio: 1:4.
Upper School Student Profile Grade 11: 70 students (70 girls); Grade 12: 78 students (78 girls). 100% of students are Christian, Muslim.
Faculty School total: 155. In upper school: 9 men, 28 women; 14 have advanced degrees.
Subjects Offered Accounting, Arabic, art, art appreciation, art history, biology, business, chemistry, Chinese, choir, civics, computers, drama, economics, English, French, geology, history, information technology, literature, management information systems, mathematics, music, physical education, physics, religion, social studies, statistics, theater arts, theory of knowledge, visual arts.
Graduation Requirements Jordanian Secondary School Certificate Examination / Ministry of Education, International Baccalaureate Diploma Examination (non-IB students must complete CAS program).
Special Academic Programs International Baccalaureate program; domestic exchange program; academic accommodation for the gifted and the artistically talented; programs in English, mathematics, general development for dyslexic students; special instructional classes for deaf students, students with mild to moderate learning disabilities, Attention Deficit Disorder, and dyslexia.
College Admission Counseling 70 students graduated in 2008; all went to college, including Iowa State University of Science and Technology; McGill University; Ottawa University; The American University in Cairo; University of Toronto.
Student Life Upper grades have uniform requirement, student council. Discipline rests equally with students and faculty.
Tuition and Aid Day student tuition: 2000 Jordanian dinars–5000 Jordanian dinars. Tuition installment plan (Insured Tuition Payment Plan, monthly payment plans, individually arranged payment plans). Tuition reduction for siblings, bursaries, need-based scholarship grants, support from the Anglican Community available. In 2008–09, 17% of upper-school students received aid. Total amount of financial aid awarded in 2008–09: 28,000 Jordanian dinars.
Admissions Traditional secondary-level entrance grade is 11. For fall 2008, 10 students applied for upper-level admission, 3 were accepted, 3 enrolled. Admissions testing required. Deadline for receipt of application materials: June 15. Application fee required: 20 Jordanian dinars. On-campus interview required.
Athletics Interscholastic: basketball (girls), combined training (g), cooperative games (g), cross-country running (g), fitness (g), fitness walking (g), gymnastics (g),

handball (g), independent competitive sports (g), indoor soccer (g), indoor track (g), jogging (g), outdoor adventure (g), outdoor recreation (g), outdoor skills (g), physical fitness (g), physical training (g), rhythmic gymnastics (g), running (g), self defense (g), swimming and diving (g), team handball (g), tennis (g), track and field (g), volleyball (g), walking (g); intramural: ballet (g), basketball (g), climbing (g), combined training (g), cooperative games (g), cross-country running (g), fitness (g), fitness walking (g), football (g), gymnastics (g), handball (g), hiking/backpacking (g), horseback riding (g), independent competitive sports (g), jogging (g), jump rope (g), modern dance (g), outdoor adventure (g), outdoor recreation (g), outdoor skills (g), paint ball (g), physical fitness (g), physical training (g), rhythmic gymnastics (g), rock climbing (g), ropes courses (g), rugby (g), running (g), self defense (g), team handball (g), track and field (g), volleyball (g), walking (g). 1 PE instructor, 2 coaches, 3 athletic trainers.

Computers Computers are regularly used in all academic classes. Computer network features include on-campus library services, Internet access, wireless campus network, Internet filtering or blocking technology. Campus intranet, student e-mail accounts, and computer access in designated common areas are available to students. Students grades are available online.

Contact Mrs. Alice Abboud, Head of Secondary School/Associate Head. 962-6-4624872 Ext. 111. Fax: 962-6-4621594. E-mail: a.abboud@asg.edu.jo. Web site: www.asg.edu.jo.

AIGLON COLLEGE

rue Centrale
Chesières-Villars 1885, Switzerland

Head of School: Peter Armstrong

General Information Coeducational boarding and day and distance learning college-preparatory, general academic, and bilingual studies school. Grades 4–PG. Distance learning grade X. Founded: 1949. Setting: rural. Nearest major city is Montreux, Switzerland. Students are housed in single-sex dormitories. 14-acre campus. 15 buildings on campus. Approved or accredited by New England Association of Schools and Colleges. Member of European Council of International Schools. Language of instruction: English. Total enrollment: 377. Upper school average class size: 8. Upper school faculty-student ratio: 1:6.

Upper School Student Profile Grade 6: 26 students (17 boys, 9 girls); Grade 7: 34 students (21 boys, 13 girls); Grade 8: 55 students (30 boys, 25 girls); Grade 9: 56 students (29 boys, 27 girls); Grade 10: 55 students (33 boys, 22 girls); Grade 11: 57 students (30 boys, 27 girls). 90% of students are boarding students. 90% are international students. International students from Afghanistan, India, Russian Federation, Spain, United Kingdom, and United States; 45 other countries represented in student body.

Faculty School total: 70. In upper school: 31 men, 30 women; 25 have advanced degrees; 24 reside on campus.

Subjects Offered Art, biology, business studies, chemistry, computer science, drama, economics, English, English literature, European history, French, geography, German, history, mathematics, media studies, music, philosophy, physical education, physics, psychology, science, Spanish.

Graduation Requirements General Certificate of Secondary Education, A-level exams.

Special Academic Programs Academic accommodation for the gifted, the musically talented, and the artistically talented; remedial reading and/or remedial writing; programs in general development for dyslexic students; ESL (60 students enrolled).

College Admission Counseling 55 students graduated in 2008; 53 went to college, including Bentley University; Emerson College; McGill University; Northeastern University. Other: 2 had other specific plans.

Student Life Upper grades have uniform requirement, student council, honor system. Discipline rests primarily with faculty.

Summer Programs ESL, sports programs offered; session focuses on language and outdoor activities; held both on and off campus; held at local area sites; accepts boys and girls; open to students from other schools. 200 students usually enrolled. 2009 schedule: July 1 to August 23. Application deadline: none.

Tuition and Aid Day student tuition: 51,300 Swiss francs; 7-day tuition and room/board: 73,300 Swiss francs. Bursaries, need-based scholarship grants available. In 2008–09, 2% of upper-school students received aid. Total amount of financial aid awarded in 2008–09: 245,000 Swiss francs.

Admissions For fall 2008, 100 students applied for upper-level admission, 30 were accepted, 29 enrolled. Achievement tests and admissions testing required. Deadline for receipt of application materials: none. Application fee required: 500 Swiss francs. Interview required.

Athletics Interscholastic: alpine skiing (boys, girls), aquatics (b,g), badminton (b,g), ballet (g), basketball (b,g), climbing (b,g), cricket (b,g), cross-country running (b,g), dance (g), fitness (b,g), football (b,g), freestyle skiing (b,g), golf (b,g), gymnastics (b,g), hockey (b,g), horseback riding (b,g), ice skating (b,g), indoor hockey (b,g), indoor soccer (b,g), jogging (b,g), life saving (b,g), mountain biking (b,g), mountaineering (b,g), nordic skiing (b,g), outdoor activities (b,g), physical fitness (b,g), physical training (b,g), rock climbing (b,g), ropes courses (b,g), rounders (b,g), rugby (b,g), running (b,g), skiing (cross-country) (b,g), skiing (downhill) (b,g), snowboarding (b,g), snowshoeing (b,g), soccer (b,g), squash (b,g), strength & conditioning (b,g), swimming and diving (b,g), tennis (b,g), track and field (b,g), volleyball (b,g), weight training (b,g), yoga (b,g); intramural: alpine skiing (b,g), aquatics (b,g), badminton (b,g), ballet (g), basketball (b,g), climbing (b,g), cricket (b,g), cross-country running (b,g), dance (g), fitness (b,g), football (b,g), freestyle skiing (b,g), golf (b,g), gymnastics (b,g), hockey (b,g), horseback riding (b,g), ice skating (b,g), indoor hockey (b,g), indoor soccer (b,g), jogging (b,g), life saving (b,g), mountain biking (b,g), mountaineering (b,g), nordic skiing (b,g), outdoor activities (b,g), physical fitness (b,g), physical training (b,g), rock climbing (b,g), ropes courses (b,g), rounders (b,g), rugby (b,g), running (b,g), skiing (cross-country) (b,g), skiing (downhill) (b,g), snowboarding (b,g), snowshoeing (b,g), soccer (b,g), squash (b,g), strength & conditioning (b,g), swimming and diving (b,g), tennis (b,g), track and field (b,g), volleyball (b,g), weight training (b,g), yoga (b,g). 8 PE instructors.

Computers Computers are regularly used in all classes. Computer network features include on-campus library services, Internet access, wireless campus network, Internet filtering or blocking technology, over 220 networked computers. Campus intranet and student e-mail accounts are available to students. The school has a published electronic and media policy.

Contact Mary Sidebottom, Director of Admissions. 41-24-4966161. Fax: 41-24-4966162. E-mail: admissions@aiglon.ch. Web site: www.aiglon.ch.

AIRDRIE KOINONIA CHRISTIAN SCHOOL

2104 Big Hill Springs Road
Airdrie, Alberta T4B 2A3, Canada

Head of School: Mr. Earl Driedger

General Information Coeducational day and distance learning college-preparatory, general academic, and religious studies school, affiliated with Christian faith, Evangelical/Fundamental faith. Grades K–12. Distance learning grades 10–12. Founded: 1987. Setting: rural. Nearest major city is Calgary, Canada. 5-acre campus. 1 building on campus. Approved or accredited by Association of Christian Schools International and Alberta Department of Education. Language of instruction: English. Total enrollment: 277. Upper school average class size: 19. Upper school faculty-student ratio: 1:14.

Upper School Student Profile Grade 7: 21 students (14 boys, 7 girls); Grade 8: 25 students (13 boys, 12 girls); Grade 9: 19 students (7 boys, 12 girls); Grade 10: 16 students (5 boys, 11 girls); Grade 11: 13 students (8 boys, 5 girls); Grade 12: 22 students (11 boys, 11 girls). 100% of students are Christian faith, Evangelical/Fundamental faith.

Faculty School total: 9. In upper school: 3 men, 3 women; 2 have advanced degrees.

Subjects Offered Art, biology, career and personal planning, chemistry, Christian doctrine, Christian ethics, Christian scripture, computer information systems, computer keyboarding, computer processing, concert bell choir, drama, English, ethics, family life, French, general math, health education, law studies, mathematics, physics, pre-algebra, science, world religions.

Graduation Requirements Career planning, career technology, Christian studies, English, science, social studies (includes history), 75 hours of community service.

Special Academic Programs Independent study; academic accommodation for the gifted; remedial math; special instructional classes for students with learning disabilities and Attention Deficit Disorder.

College Admission Counseling 15 students graduated in 2008; 4 went to college, including University of Calgary. Other: 11 went to work.

Student Life Upper grades have specified standards of dress, student council, honor system. Discipline rests primarily with faculty. Attendance at religious services is required.

Tuition and Aid Day student tuition: CAN$4368. Tuition installment plan (monthly payment plans, individually arranged payment plans). Tuition reduction for siblings, need-based scholarship grants available. In 2008–09, 5% of upper-school students received aid. Total amount of financial aid awarded in 2008–09: CAN$15,000.

Admissions For fall 2008, 5 students applied for upper-level admission, 5 were accepted, 5 enrolled. Deadline for receipt of application materials: none. Application fee required: CAN$25. On-campus interview required.

Athletics Interscholastic: badminton (boys, girls), basketball (b,g), cross-country running (b,g), track and field (b,g), volleyball (b,g); coed interscholastic: badminton, physical fitness, soccer; coed intramural: floor hockey, mountain biking, outdoor adventure, outdoor education, rock climbing, skiing (downhill), snowboarding, soccer, softball. 1 PE instructor.

Computers Computer network features include on-campus library services, Internet access, Internet filtering or blocking technology. Computer access in designated common areas is available to students. Students grades are available online.

Contact Mrs. Mardelle Zieman, Office Manager. 403-948-5100. Fax: 403-948-5563. E-mail: officemanager@akcs.com. Web site: www.akcs.com.

ALABAMA CHRISTIAN ACADEMY

4700 Wares Ferry Road
Montgomery, Alabama 36109

Head of School: Mr. Ronnie C. Sewell

General Information Coeducational day college-preparatory, general academic, arts, religious studies, bilingual studies, and technology school, affiliated with Church of Christ. Grades K4–12. Founded: 1942. Setting: urban. 23-acre campus. 3 buildings on campus. Approved or accredited by Southern Association of Colleges and Schools and Alabama Department of Education. Total enrollment: 1,037. Upper school average class size: 21.

Upper School Student Profile 46% of students are members of Church of Christ.

Faculty School total: 64. In upper school: 18 men, 24 women.

Subjects Offered Algebra, American government, American literature, Bible, biology, British literature, business mathematics, calculus, chemistry, composition, computer applications, English, finite math, geography, geometry, grammar, health, honors English, physical education, physical science, physics, physiology, pre-algebra, pre-calculus, Spanish, trigonometry, U.S. history, world history.

Graduation Requirements American government, Bible, computer applications, economics, English, geography, mathematics, physical education (includes health), science, U.S. history, world history.

Special Academic Programs Advanced Placement exam preparation; honors section.

College Admission Counseling Colleges students went to include Auburn University; Auburn University Montgomery; Freed-Hardeman University; Harding University; Lipscomb University; The University of Alabama.

Student Life Upper grades have uniform requirement, student council, honor system. Discipline rests primarily with faculty.

Summer Programs Sports programs offered; session focuses on weight training; held on campus; accepts boys and girls; not open to students from other schools. 80 students usually enrolled. 2009 schedule: June 2 to August 1.

Tuition and Aid Day student tuition: $4914. Guaranteed tuition plan. Tuition installment plan (monthly payment plans). Tuition reduction for siblings, contact school for financial aid available. In 2008–09, 7% of upper-school students received aid. Total amount of financial aid awarded in 2008–09: $60,000.

Admissions Traditional secondary-level entrance grade is 9. Any standardized test required. Deadline for receipt of application materials: none. Application fee required: $240. On-campus interview required.

Athletics Interscholastic: baseball (boys), basketball (b,g), cheering (g), cross-country running (b,g), football (b), golf (b), physical training (b,g), running (b,g), soccer (b), softball (g), strength & conditioning (b,g), track and field (b,g), volleyball (g), weight training (b,g); coed interscholastic: jump rope, track and field. 2 PE instructors.

Computers Computers are regularly used in basic skills, business applications, career technology, reading, technology classes. Computer network features include on-campus library services, Internet access. The school has a published electronic and media policy.

Contact Mrs. Harriett Parker, Admissions. 334-277-1985 Ext. 227. Fax: 334-279-0604. E-mail: hparker@alabamachristian.com. Web site: www.alabamachristian.com.

ALBERT COLLEGE

160 Dundas Street West
Belleville, Ontario K8P 1A6, Canada

Head of School: Mr. Keith Stansfield

General Information Coeducational boarding and day college-preparatory, arts, and technology school, affiliated with United Church of Canada. Boarding grades 7–PG, day grades JK–PG. Founded: 1857. Setting: small town. Nearest major city is Toronto, Canada. Students are housed in single-sex dormitories. 25-acre campus. 7 buildings on campus. Approved or accredited by Canadian Association of Independent Schools, Canadian Educational Standards Institute, Conference of Independent Schools of Ontario, and Ontario Ministry of Education. Affiliate member of National Association of Independent Schools; member of Secondary School Admission Test Board. Language of instruction: English. Endowment: CAN$1.4 million. Total enrollment: 324. Upper school average class size: 15. Upper school faculty-student ratio: 1:8.

Upper School Student Profile Grade 9: 21 students (12 boys, 9 girls); Grade 10: 41 students (24 boys, 17 girls); Grade 11: 54 students (32 boys, 22 girls); Grade 12: 42 students (25 boys, 17 girls); Postgraduate: 7 students (7 boys). 63% of students are boarding students. 65% are province residents. 6 provinces are represented in upper school student body. 34% are international students. International students from Barbados, Bermuda, Hong Kong, Mexico, Republic of Korea, and Spain; 20 other countries represented in student body.

Faculty School total: 34. In upper school: 15 men, 14 women; 4 have advanced degrees; 14 reside on campus.

Subjects Offered Algebra, ancient history, art, art history, biology, business, calculus, Canadian geography, Canadian history, chemistry, computer science, drama, economics, English, English literature, English-AP, environmental science, ESL, European history, family studies, fine arts, finite math, French, French-AP, geography, history, law, mathematics, music, physical education, physics, science, social science, social studies, society challenge and change, world history.

Graduation Requirements Arts and fine arts (art, music, dance, drama), business skills (includes word processing), English, foreign language, mathematics, physical education (includes health), science, social science, social studies (includes history).

Special Academic Programs Advanced Placement exam preparation; accelerated programs; independent study; academic accommodation for the gifted, the musically talented, and the artistically talented; ESL (28 students enrolled).

College Admission Counseling 55 students graduated in 2008; 52 went to college, including Carleton University; McGill University; Queen's University at Kingston; The University of Western Ontario; University of Ottawa. Other: 1 went to work, 2 had other specific plans.

Student Life Upper grades have uniform requirement, student council, honor system. Discipline rests equally with students and faculty. Attendance at religious services is required.

Summer Programs ESL programs offered; session focuses on ESL, math, English; held on campus; accepts boys and girls; open to students from other schools. 20 students usually enrolled. 2009 schedule: August 1 to August 31. Application deadline: June 30.

Tuition and Aid Day student tuition: CAN$14,500–CAN$19,200; 5-day tuition and room/board: CAN$30,800; 7-day tuition and room/board: CAN$35,500–CAN$40,500. Tuition installment plan (Insured Tuition Payment Plan, monthly payment plans, individually arranged payment plans, 3-payment plan). Tuition reduction for siblings, bursaries, merit scholarship grants, need-based scholarship grants available. In 2008–09, 30% of upper-school students received aid; total upper-school merit-scholarship money awarded: CAN$90,551. Total amount of financial aid awarded in 2008–09: CAN$195,000.

Admissions Traditional secondary-level entrance grade is 9. For fall 2008, 109 students applied for upper-level admission, 87 were accepted, 63 enrolled. Gates MacGinite Reading Tests, Nelson-Denny Reading Test or SSAT required. Deadline for receipt of application materials: none. Application fee required: CAN$100. Interview required.

Athletics Interscholastic: alpine skiing (boys, girls), aquatics (b,g), badminton (b,g), basketball (b,g), cross-country running (b,g), field hockey (g), golf (b,g), ice hockey (b), lacrosse (g), rugby (b), running (b,g), skiing (cross-country) (b,g), skiing (downhill) (b,g), soccer (b,g), squash (b,g), tennis (b,g), track and field (b,g), volleyball (b,g); intramural: aerobics (g), aerobics/Nautilus (b,g), ball hockey (b), basketball (b,g), cross-country running (b,g), field hockey (g), floor hockey (b,g), golf (b), hockey (b), ice skating (b), indoor soccer (b,g), kayaking (b,g), lacrosse (g), rowing (b,g), rugby (b), running (b,g), soccer (b,g), tennis (b,g), track and field (b,g), volleyball (b,g), weight training (b); coed interscholastic: aquatics, nordic skiing, sailing, swimming and diving, tennis; coed intramural: aerobics, aerobics/dance, alpine skiing, aquatics, backpacking, bicycling, canoeing/kayaking, climbing, dance, fitness, flag football, Frisbee, gymnastics, hiking/backpacking, jogging, modern dance, mountain biking, nordic skiing, outdoor activities, outdoor recreation, outdoors, paddle tennis, paint ball, physical fitness, physical training, rafting, rappelling, rock climbing, roller blading, ropes courses, sailing, skateboarding, skiing (cross-country), skiing (downhill), snowboarding, squash, swimming and diving, table tennis, triathlon, ultimate Frisbee, wall climbing, wilderness, winter soccer, yoga. 4 PE instructors, 2 coaches.

Computers Computers are regularly used in English, mathematics, science classes. Computer network features include on-campus library services, Internet access, wireless campus network, Internet filtering or blocking technology. Student e-mail accounts are available to students. The school has a published electronic and media policy.

Contact Mrs. Heather Kidd, Director of Admission. 800-952-5237 Ext. 2204. Fax: 613-968-9651. E-mail: hkidd@albertc.on.ca. Web site: www.albertc.on.ca.

ALBUQUERQUE ACADEMY

6400 Wyoming Boulevard NE
Albuquerque, New Mexico 87109

Head of School: Andrew Watson

General Information Coeducational day college-preparatory, arts, and technology school. Grades 6–12. Founded: 1955. Setting: suburban. 312-acre campus. 10 buildings on campus. Approved or accredited by Independent Schools Association of the Southwest and New Mexico Department of Education. Member of National Association of Independent Schools and Secondary School Admission Test Board. Endowment: $24.2 million. Total enrollment: 1,095. Upper school average class size: 15. Upper school faculty-student ratio: 1:8.

Upper School Student Profile Grade 9: 169 students (90 boys, 79 girls); Grade 10: 163 students (80 boys, 83 girls); Grade 11: 160 students (79 boys, 81 girls); Grade 12: 164 students (83 boys, 81 girls).

Faculty School total: 180. In upper school: 72 men, 52 women; 97 have advanced degrees.

Subjects Offered Advanced Placement courses, algebra, American history, anatomy, Arabic, art, art history, astronomy, band, biochemistry, biology, calculus, chemistry, chemistry-AP, computer science, creative writing, dance, drama, drawing, earth science, economics, electronics, English, English-AP, European history, fine arts, French, French language-AP, genetics, geometry, German, government/civics, Hindi, history, history-AP, horticulture, Japanese, jazz, Latin American history, law, library studies, Mandarin, mathematics, media, music, outdoor education, painting, philosophy, photography, physical education, physics, physiology, printmaking, psychology, religion, robotics, Russian, science, social studies, Spanish, speech, swimming, theater, trigonometry, weight training, women's studies, world history, writing.

Graduation Requirements English, experiential education, foreign language, mathematics, physical education (includes health), science, social studies (includes history), experiential education (environmental and outdoor activities).

Special Academic Programs 18 Advanced Placement exams for which test preparation is offered; independent study; term-away projects; domestic exchange program (with The Catlin Gabel School, Charlotte Latin School, Cincinnati Country Day School, Hamden Hall Country Day School); study abroad.
College Admission Counseling 156 students graduated in 2008; all went to college, including Arizona State University; New Mexico State University; Santa Clara University; Tulane University; University of New Mexico; University of Southern California. Mean SAT critical reading: 665, mean SAT math: 655, mean SAT writing: 646, mean combined SAT: 1808, mean composite ACT: 30. 88% scored over 600 on SAT critical reading, 81% scored over 600 on SAT math, 79% scored over 600 on SAT writing, 92% scored over 1800 on combined SAT, 92% scored over 26 on composite ACT.
Student Life Upper grades have specified standards of dress, student council, honor system. Discipline rests primarily with faculty.
Summer Programs Remediation, enrichment, advancement, sports, art/fine arts, computer instruction programs offered; session focuses on enrichment; held on campus; open to students from other schools. 2,300 students usually enrolled. 2009 schedule: June 1 to July 11. Application deadline: May 29.
Tuition and Aid Day student tuition: $16,189. Tuition installment plan (FACTS Tuition Payment Plan, monthly payment plans, individually arranged payment plans, 1- and 2-payment plans). Need-based scholarship grants available. In 2008–09, 25% of upper-school students received aid. Total amount of financial aid awarded in 2008–09: $1,951,829.
Admissions Traditional secondary-level entrance grade is 9. For fall 2008, 111 students applied for upper-level admission, 49 were accepted, 41 enrolled. ISEE, school's own exam or SSAT required. Deadline for receipt of application materials: February 15. Application fee required: $50. On-campus interview required.
Athletics Interscholastic: baseball (boys), basketball (b,g), bowling (b,g), cross-country running (b,g), dance (b,g), diving (b,g), football (b), golf (b,g), hiking/backpacking (b,g), life saving (b,g), modern dance (b,g), outdoor education (b,g), outdoor skills (b,g), physical training (b,g), rafting (b,g), rappelling (b,g), rock climbing (b,g), soccer (b,g), softball (g), swimming and diving (b,g), tennis (b,g), track and field (b,g), volleyball (g), wrestling (b,g); coed intramural: ballet, basketball, canoeing/kayaking, wilderness, wilderness survival. 9 PE instructors, 84 coaches, 3 athletic trainers.
Computers Computers are regularly used in foreign language, history, library science, mathematics classes. Computer network features include on-campus library services, Internet access. The school has a published electronic and media policy.
Contact Judy Hudenko, Director of Admission. 505-828-3208. Fax: 505-828-3128. E-mail: hudenko@aa.edu. Web site: www.aa.edu.

ANNOUNCEMENT FROM THE SCHOOL Attracting some of the finest students and teachers in the country, Albuquerque Academy commits its resources to a mission comprising accessibility, affordability, excellence, caring, and outreach. The geography and culture of the Academy's Southwest home serve to enrich educational programs and foster creativity, personal balance, and a connection to the natural world.

ALEXANDER DAWSON SCHOOL

10455 Dawson Drive
Lafayette, Colorado 80026
Head of School: Mr. Brian Johnson

General Information Coeducational day college-preparatory, arts, and technology school. Grades K–12. Founded: 1970. Setting: rural. Nearest major city is Boulder. 95-acre campus. 11 buildings on campus. Approved or accredited by Association of Colorado Independent Schools and Colorado Department of Education. Member of National Association of Independent Schools and Secondary School Admission Test Board. Total enrollment: 420. Upper school average class size: 15. Upper school faculty-student ratio: 1:7.
Upper School Student Profile Grade 9: 40 students (25 boys, 15 girls); Grade 10: 47 students (27 boys, 20 girls); Grade 11: 46 students (19 boys, 27 girls); Grade 12: 42 students (25 boys, 17 girls).
Faculty School total: 53. In upper school: 17 men, 12 women; 12 have advanced degrees.
Subjects Offered Algebra, American history, American literature, art, art history, biology, calculus, ceramics, chemistry, Chinese, computer math, computer multimedia, computer programming, computer science, creative writing, dance, drafting, drama, earth science, economics, English, English literature, European history, expository writing, fine arts, French, geography, geometry, government-AP, government/civics, grammar, health, history, industrial arts, journalism, Latin, mathematics, mechanical drawing, music, photography, physical education, physics, science, social science, social studies, Spanish, speech, theater, trigonometry, world history, world literature, writing.
Graduation Requirements Arts and fine arts (art, music, dance, drama), computer science, English, foreign language, history, mathematics, science.
Special Academic Programs Advanced Placement exam preparation; honors section; independent study; term-away projects; study at local college for college credit; study abroad; academic accommodation for the gifted, the musically talented, and the artistically talented; special instructional classes for deaf students.
College Admission Counseling 50 students graduated in 2008; all went to college, including Pomona College; University of Denver; Wellesley College. Mean SAT critical reading: 616, mean SAT math: 620, mean composite ACT: 27.
Student Life Upper grades have specified standards of dress, student council, honor system. Discipline rests equally with students and faculty.
Summer Programs Enrichment, sports, art/fine arts, computer instruction programs offered; session focuses on athletics, foreign language (grades 4-10); held on campus; accepts boys and girls; open to students from other schools. 1,200 students usually enrolled. 2009 schedule: June 15 to August 5. Application deadline: none.
Tuition and Aid Day student tuition: $17,800. Tuition installment plan (Insured Tuition Payment Plan, monthly payment plans, individually arranged payment plans). Need-based scholarship grants, need-based loans available. In 2008–09, 15% of upper-school students received aid. Total amount of financial aid awarded in 2008–09: $720,000.
Admissions Traditional secondary-level entrance grade is 9. ERB required. Deadline for receipt of application materials: none. Application fee required: $100. Interview required.
Athletics Interscholastic: baseball (boys), basketball (b,g), lacrosse (b), soccer (b,g), softball (g), swimming and diving (b,g), synchronized swimming (g), tennis (b,g), volleyball (g); intramural: lacrosse (b); coed interscholastic: alpine skiing, canoeing/kayaking, cross-country running, equestrian sports, golf, kayaking, martial arts, paddling, skiing (downhill), Special Olympics, track and field; coed intramural: aerobics, backpacking, climbing, equestrian sports, fitness, flag football, football, Frisbee, golf, hiking/backpacking, indoor soccer, martial arts, outdoor activities, physical fitness, rafting, weight lifting. 3 PE instructors, 22 coaches, 1 athletic trainer.
Computers Computers are regularly used in art, mathematics, science classes. Computer network features include on-campus library services, online commercial services, Internet access, wireless campus network, Internet filtering or blocking technology. Students grades are available online. The school has a published electronic and media policy.
Contact Ms. Denise LaRusch, Assistant to the Director of Admissions. 303-665-6679. Fax: 303-381-0415. E-mail: dlarusch@dawsonschool.org. Web site: www.dawsonschool.org.

THE ALEXANDER SCHOOL

409 International Parkway
Dallas, Texas 75081
Head of School: Mr. David B. Bowlin

General Information Coeducational day college-preparatory, arts, and technology school. Grades 8–12. Founded: 1975. Setting: suburban. 2-acre campus. 1 building on campus. Approved or accredited by Southern Association of Colleges and Schools, Texas Education Agency, and The College Board. Languages of instruction: English and Spanish. Endowment: $1 million. Total enrollment: 43. Upper school average class size: 5. Upper school faculty-student ratio: 1:5.
Upper School Student Profile Grade 8: 3 students (3 boys); Grade 9: 6 students (3 boys, 3 girls); Grade 10: 6 students (3 boys, 3 girls); Grade 11: 14 students (7 boys, 7 girls); Grade 12: 14 students (8 boys, 6 girls).
Faculty School total: 7. In upper school: 4 men, 3 women; 5 have advanced degrees.
Subjects Offered 20th century physics, advanced chemistry, advanced math, African American history, algebra, alternative physical education, American Civil War, American history-AP, analysis and differential calculus, anatomy and physiology, ancient history, ancient world history, art, biology, biology-AP, British literature, British literature (honors), British literature-AP, business applications, calculus, calculus-AP, chemistry, chemistry-AP, civics/free enterprise, Civil War, composition, computer applications, computer keyboarding, computer literacy, consumer mathematics, critical studies in film, ecology, environmental systems, economics, English composition, English language and composition-AP, English literature, English literature and composition-AP, environmental science, ethics, European history-AP, general business, geography, geometry, government, grammar, health, history, honors algebra, honors English, honors geometry, honors U.S. history, honors world history, human anatomy, Japanese, Latin, martial arts, math review, mathematical modeling, music appreciation, music theory, personal fitness, philosophy, photography, photojournalism, physical education, physics, physics-AP, pre-algebra, pre-calculus, psychology, public speaking, science fiction, Shakespeare, Spanish, Spanish language-AP, U.S. government, U.S. history, U.S. history-AP, U.S. literature, weight training, yearbook.
Graduation Requirements Algebra, American government, American history, American literature, arts and fine arts (art, music, dance, drama), biology, British literature, chemistry, computer literacy, economics, electives, English, foreign language, geometry, health, physical fitness, physics, public speaking, world geography, world history.
Special Academic Programs Advanced Placement exam preparation; honors section; accelerated programs; independent study; study at local college for college credit; academic accommodation for the gifted.
College Admission Counseling 16 students graduated in 2008; 15 went to college, including Pace University; Southern Methodist University. Other: 1 went to work. Median SAT critical reading: 615, median SAT math: 540, median SAT writing: 620, median combined SAT: 1155, median composite ACT: 21. 75% scored over 600 on SAT critical reading, 25% scored over 600 on SAT math, 75% scored over 600 on SAT writing, 50% scored over 1800 on combined SAT.

Student Life Upper grades have specified standards of dress, student council, honor system. Discipline rests primarily with faculty.
Summer Programs Remediation, enrichment, advancement, computer instruction programs offered; session focuses on make-up/advancement; held on campus; accepts boys and girls; open to students from other schools. 25 students usually enrolled. 2009 schedule: June 8 to July 31. Application deadline: May 19.
Tuition and Aid Day student tuition: $18,000. Tuition installment plan (Key Tuition Payment Plan). Tuition reduction for siblings, need-based scholarship grants, paying campus jobs available. In 2008–09, 10% of upper-school students received aid. Total amount of financial aid awarded in 2008–09: $36,000.
Admissions Traditional secondary-level entrance grade is 10. For fall 2008, 30 students applied for upper-level admission, 15 were accepted, 15 enrolled. California Achievement Test required. Deadline for receipt of application materials: none. No application fee required. On-campus interview required.
Athletics Interscholastic: cross-country running (boys, girls), golf (b,g), independent competitive sports (b,g), tennis (b,g), track and field (b,g); intramural: basketball (b,g), flag football (b), martial arts (b,g); coed interscholastic: physical fitness; coed intramural: basketball, strength & conditioning, weight training. 1 PE instructor.
Computers Computers are regularly used in English, geography, history, keyboarding, photography, photojournalism, yearbook classes. Computer network features include Internet access, wireless campus network, Internet filtering or blocking technology. Students grades are available online.
Contact Ms. Kimberly V. Walker, Administration. 972-690-9210. Fax: 972-690-9284. E-mail: kim@alexanderschool.com. Web site: www.alexanderschool.com.

ALLEN ACADEMY

3201 Boonville Road
Bryan, Texas 77802

Head of School: Mr. Mark Bloom

General Information Coeducational day college-preparatory and ESL school. Grades PK–12. Founded: 1886. Setting: small town. Nearest major city is Houston. 40-acre campus. 3 buildings on campus. Approved or accredited by Southern Association of Colleges and Schools, Texas Education Agency, and The College Board. Total enrollment: 284. Upper school average class size: 18. Upper school faculty-student ratio: 1:10.
Upper School Student Profile Grade 9: 22 students (10 boys, 12 girls); Grade 10: 27 students (15 boys, 12 girls); Grade 11: 17 students (6 boys, 11 girls); Grade 12: 14 students (7 boys, 7 girls).
Faculty School total: 45. In upper school: 8 men, 8 women; 6 have advanced degrees.
Subjects Offered Algebra, American history, American history-AP, American literature, art, band, biology, biology-AP, calculus, calculus-AP, chemistry, choir, drama, drawing, English language-AP, English literature, English literature and composition-AP, English literature-AP, ESL, European history, European history-AP, French, French-AP, geometry, honors English, keyboarding/computer, multimedia, painting, physical education, physics-AP, pre-calculus, Spanish, Spanish-AP, world history, yearbook.
Graduation Requirements Algebra, American history, American literature, arts and fine arts (art, music, dance, drama), biology, chemistry, English composition, English literature, European history, geometry, physics, pre-calculus, world history.
Special Academic Programs Advanced Placement exam preparation; honors section; study at local college for college credit; ESL (34 students enrolled).
College Admission Counseling 14 students graduated in 2008; all went to college, including Baylor University; Carnegie Mellon University; Sam Houston State University; Texas A&M University; The University of Texas at Austin; Trinity University. Mean SAT critical reading: 588, mean SAT math: 620, mean SAT writing: 555, mean combined SAT: 1660.
Student Life Upper grades have uniform requirement, student council, honor system. Discipline rests equally with students and faculty.
Summer Programs Enrichment, ESL programs offered; session focuses on ESL and academics; held on campus; accepts boys and girls; open to students from other schools. 6 students usually enrolled. 2009 schedule: June 1 to June 30. Application deadline: May 1.
Tuition and Aid Day student tuition: $4425–$9710. Tuition installment plan (FACTS Tuition Payment Plan, semester payment plan). Need-based scholarship grants available. In 2008–09, 15% of upper-school students received aid. Total amount of financial aid awarded in 2008–09: $96,000.
Admissions Traditional secondary-level entrance grade is 9. For fall 2008, 15 students applied for upper-level admission, 12 were accepted, 12 enrolled. PSAT required. Deadline for receipt of application materials: none. Application fee required: $200. Interview recommended.
Athletics Interscholastic: baseball (boys), basketball (b,g), cheering (g), cross-country running (b,g), football (b), golf (b,g), softball (g), strength & conditioning (b), tennis (b,g), track and field (b,g), volleyball (g), winter soccer (b); coed intramural: basketball, combined training, weight training. 2 PE instructors, 4 coaches.
Computers Computers are regularly used in keyboarding, multimedia classes. Computer network features include Internet access, wireless campus network, Internet filtering or blocking technology. The school has a published electronic and media policy.
Contact Ms. Janet Harrison, Assistant Director of Admissions. 979-776-0731. E-mail: jharrison@allenacademy.org. Web site: www.allenacademy.org.

ANNOUNCEMENT FROM THE SCHOOL Allen Academy honors the integrity and worth of each student within a diverse school community. The school provides rigorous and dynamic programs in academics, fine and performing arts, and athletics. At Allen Academy, the teachers challenge students' intellectual, creative, and physical abilities. Allen Academy is a vibrant community that seeks to develop a sense of responsibility that helps young people make wise and ethical choices. The Academy builds the values of respect, compassion, and service to others—within the school community and in the larger community as well. Allen Academy believes that with intellectual curiosity, self-reliance, and a commitment to others, its students will make a difference in a changing world.

ALLENDALE COLUMBIA SCHOOL

519 Allens Creek Road
Rochester, New York 14618-3405

Head of School: Charles Hertrick

General Information Coeducational day college-preparatory school. Grades N–12. Founded: 1890. Setting: suburban. 30-acre campus. 5 buildings on campus. Approved or accredited by New York State Association of Independent Schools. Member of National Association of Independent Schools. Endowment: $16 million. Total enrollment: 415. Upper school average class size: 7. Upper school faculty-student ratio: 1:5.
Upper School Student Profile Grade 9: 31 students (15 boys, 16 girls); Grade 10: 24 students (14 boys, 10 girls); Grade 11: 45 students (18 boys, 27 girls); Grade 12: 24 students (13 boys, 11 girls).
Faculty School total: 64. In upper school: 13 men, 14 women; 23 have advanced degrees.
Subjects Offered Algebra, American history, American literature, art, biology, calculus, chemistry, computer science, earth science, English, English literature, European history, expository writing, French, geology, geometry, government/civics, grammar, health, history, Latin, mathematics, music, physical education, physics, science, social studies, Spanish, world history, writing.
Graduation Requirements Art, arts, computer science, English, foreign language, history, mathematics, physical education (includes health), science, participation in team sports.
Special Academic Programs 16 Advanced Placement exams for which test preparation is offered; independent study.
College Admission Counseling 52 students graduated in 2008; 51 went to college, including Cornell University; Duke University; Nazareth College of Rochester; Princeton University; Rochester Institute of Technology; University of Chicago. Other: 1 entered a postgraduate year. Mean SAT critical reading: 619, mean SAT math: 635, mean SAT writing: 623. 56% scored over 600 on SAT critical reading, 68% scored over 600 on SAT math, 56% scored over 600 on SAT writing.
Student Life Upper grades have specified standards of dress, student council. Discipline rests primarily with faculty.
Summer Programs Enrichment, sports, art/fine arts programs offered; session focuses on athletics and arts; held on campus; accepts boys and girls; open to students from other schools. 800 students usually enrolled. 2009 schedule: June 15 to August 7. Application deadline: none.
Tuition and Aid Day student tuition: $6200–$17,800. Tuition installment plan (FACTS Tuition Payment Plan). Need-based scholarship grants available. In 2008–09, 35% of upper-school students received aid. Total amount of financial aid awarded in 2008–09: $526,475.
Admissions Traditional secondary-level entrance grade is 9. For fall 2008, 53 students applied for upper-level admission, 18 were accepted, 14 enrolled. ERB—verbal abilities, reading comprehension, quantitative abilities (level F, form 1), ERB Reading and Math, essay, math and English placement tests, school's own exam or writing sample required. Deadline for receipt of application materials: none. Application fee required: $25. On-campus interview required.
Athletics Interscholastic: baseball (boys), basketball (b,g), cross-country running (b,g), soccer (b,g), softball (g), tennis (b,g), track and field (b,g), volleyball (g); coed interscholastic: bowling, golf, running, swimming and diving. 4 PE instructors.
Computers Computers are regularly used in all academic classes. Computer network features include on-campus library services, Internet access, wireless campus network, Internet filtering or blocking technology, county-wide library services. The school has a published electronic and media policy.
Contact Alan Carroll, Director of Admissions. 585-381-4560. Fax: 585-249-0230. E-mail: acarroll@allendalecolumbia.org. Web site: www.allendalecolumbia.org.

ALLIANCE ACADEMY

Casilla 17-11-06186
Quito, Ecuador

Head of School: Dr. David Wells

General Information Coeducational boarding and day and distance learning college-preparatory, arts, and religious studies school, affiliated with Christian faith. Boarding grades 7–12, day grades PK–12. Distance learning grades 10–12. Founded:

1929. Setting: urban. Students are housed in mission agency dormitories. 8-acre campus. 6 buildings on campus. Approved or accredited by Association of American Schools in South America, Association of Christian Schools International, and Southern Association of Colleges and Schools. Language of instruction: English. Total enrollment: 424. Upper school average class size: 20. Upper school faculty-student ratio: 1:6.

Upper School Student Profile Grade 7: 35 students (13 boys, 22 girls); Grade 8: 32 students (12 boys, 20 girls); Grade 9: 36 students (17 boys, 19 girls); Grade 10: 39 students (18 boys, 21 girls); Grade 11: 40 students (21 boys, 19 girls); Grade 12: 36 students (16 boys, 20 girls). 3% of students are boarding students. 68% are international students. International students from Canada, China, Japan, Republic of Korea, Taiwan, and United States; 9 other countries represented in student body. 70% of students are Christian faith.

Faculty School total: 57. In upper school: 19 men, 22 women; 14 have advanced degrees.

Subjects Offered Algebra, American history, American history-AP, American literature, art, auto mechanics, band, Bible, Bible as literature, Bible studies, biology, biology-AP, business, calculus, calculus-AP, chemistry, choir, Christian doctrine, Christian ethics, Christian studies, church history, computer applications, computer art, computer math, computer programming, computer science, computer science-AP, concert band, creative writing, debate, desktop publishing, drama, earth science, economics, English, English as a foreign language, English language-AP, English literature, English literature-AP, ESL, family and consumer science, fine arts, French, French as a second language, geography, geometry, government/civics, grammar, health, health education, history, home economics, industrial arts, jazz band, journalism, keyboarding, Life of Christ, marching band, mathematics, music, novel, photography, physical education, physics, piano, pre-algebra, pre-calculus, public speaking, religion, religion and culture, science, senior seminar, small engine repair, social science, social studies, Spanish, Spanish literature, Spanish literature-AP, speech, speech and debate, theater, trigonometry, U.S. history-AP, video communication, vocal ensemble, woodworking, world geography, world history, world religions, writing, yearbook.

Graduation Requirements 1½ elective credits, algebra, arts and fine arts (art, music, dance, drama), comparative government and politics, computer applications, English, foreign language, mathematics, physical education (includes health), religion (includes Bible studies and theology), science, social science, social studies (includes history), U.S. government and politics, U.S. history.

Special Academic Programs 12 Advanced Placement exams for which test preparation is offered; independent study; remedial reading and/or remedial writing; remedial math; programs in English, mathematics, general development for dyslexic students; special instructional classes for students with developmental and/or learning disabilities; ESL (24 students enrolled).

College Admission Counseling 36 students graduated in 2008; 33 went to college, including Azusa Pacific University; John Brown University; Simpson University; Worcester Polytechnic Institute. Other: 1 went to work, 2 entered military service. Median SAT critical reading: 520, median SAT math: 480, median SAT writing: 510, median combined SAT: 1510, median composite ACT: 21. 36% scored over 600 on SAT critical reading, 29% scored over 600 on SAT math, 30% scored over 600 on SAT writing, 32% scored over 1800 on combined SAT, 26% scored over 26 on composite ACT.

Student Life Upper grades have specified standards of dress, student council, honor system. Discipline rests primarily with faculty. Attendance at religious services is required.

Summer Programs Remediation, ESL programs offered; session focuses on ESL; held on campus; accepts boys and girls; not open to students from other schools. 12 students usually enrolled. 2009 schedule: July 6 to July 31. Application deadline: June 12.

Tuition and Aid Day student tuition: $7516. Tuition installment plan (monthly payment plans, individually arranged payment plans). Tuition reduction for siblings, need-based scholarship grants, tuition reduction for children of missionaries, two full scholarships for children of Ecuadorian military personnel available. In 2008–09, 5% of upper-school students received aid. Total amount of financial aid awarded in 2008–09: $200,000.

Admissions Traditional secondary-level entrance grade is 7. For fall 2008, 48 students applied for upper-level admission, 42 were accepted, 39 enrolled. English entrance exam, English proficiency, WRAT or writing sample required. Deadline for receipt of application materials: none. Application fee required: $100. On-campus interview required.

Athletics Interscholastic: basketball (boys, girls), soccer (b,g), volleyball (b,g); intramural: badminton (b,g), ball hockey (b), horseshoes (b), in-line hockey (b), modern dance (g), table tennis (b,g); coed intramural: backpacking, basketball, climbing, flag football, football, hiking/backpacking, indoor soccer, martial arts, outdoor adventure, paddle tennis, soccer, softball, strength & conditioning, table tennis, volleyball, wall climbing. 2 PE instructors, 1 coach.

Computers Computers are regularly used in basic skills, business education, career exploration, college planning, computer applications, design, desktop publishing, desktop publishing, ESL, digital applications, graphic design, independent study, information technology, introduction to technology, keyboarding, lab/keyboard, language development, media arts, media production, media services, photography, photojournalism, programming, publications, technology, video film production, word processing, writing fundamentals, yearbook classes. Computer network features include on-campus library services, online commercial services, Internet access, Internet filtering or blocking technology. Campus intranet is available to students. The school has a published electronic and media policy.

Contact Mrs. Alexandra Chavez, Director of Admissions. 593-2-226-6985. Fax: 593-2-226-4350. E-mail: achavez@alliance.k12.ec. Web site: www.alliance.k12.ec.

ALLISON ACADEMY

1881 Northeast 164th Street
North Miami Beach, Florida 33162

Head of School: Dr. Sarah F. Allison

General Information Coeducational day college-preparatory, general academic, arts, business, and English for Speakers of Other Languages school; primarily serves students with learning disabilities, individuals with Attention Deficit Disorder, and dyslexic students. Grades 6–12. Founded: 1983. Setting: urban. Nearest major city is Miami. 1-acre campus. 2 buildings on campus. Approved or accredited by Association of Independent Schools of Florida, CITA (Commission on International and Trans-Regional Accreditation), National Council for Private School Accreditation, Southern Association of Colleges and Schools, and Florida Department of Education. Upper school average class size: 15. Upper school faculty-student ratio: 1:10.

Upper School Student Profile Grade 6: 7 students (7 boys); Grade 7: 8 students (6 boys, 2 girls); Grade 8: 9 students (3 boys, 6 girls); Grade 9: 9 students (7 boys, 2 girls); Grade 10: 15 students (8 boys, 7 girls); Grade 11: 20 students (11 boys, 9 girls); Grade 12: 11 students (9 boys, 2 girls).

Faculty School total: 12. In upper school: 3 men, 8 women; 6 have advanced degrees.

Subjects Offered Algebra, American government, American history, anatomy, art history, arts, biology, chemistry, chorus, computer science, consumer mathematics, creative drama, drama, drawing, ecology, environmental systems, economics, economics and history, English, English literature, environmental science, ESL, film studies, fine arts, French, French language-AP, general math, geography, geometry, health education, history, humanities, life management skills, life skills, mathematics, painting, peer counseling, photography, physical education, physical science, physics, pre-calculus, psychology, reading, reading/study skills, SAT/ACT preparation, science, social science, social studies, Spanish, Spanish language-AP, sports, trigonometry, world culture, writing, yearbook.

Graduation Requirements Algebra, American government, arts and fine arts (art, music, dance, drama), business skills (includes word processing), chemistry, computer science, creative writing, drama, earth and space science, economics, English, English literature, foreign language, mathematics, physical education (includes health), science, social science, social studies (includes history), U.S. history, 75 hours of community service.

Special Academic Programs 1 Advanced Placement exam for which test preparation is offered; honors section; accelerated programs; study at local college for college credit; academic accommodation for the gifted and the artistically talented; remedial reading and/or remedial writing; remedial math; programs in English, mathematics, general development for dyslexic students; special instructional classes for students with learning disabilities, dyslexia, and Attention Deficit Disorder; ESL (1 student enrolled).

College Admission Counseling 22 students graduated in 2008; 18 went to college, including Broward Community College; Evangel University; Florida International University; Miami Dade College; Nova Southeastern University; St. Thomas University. Other: 1 went to work, 1 entered a postgraduate year, 2 had other specific plans. Median SAT critical reading: 500, median SAT math: 510, median composite ACT: 21. 5% scored over 600 on SAT critical reading, 10% scored over 600 on SAT math, 13% scored over 26 on composite ACT.

Student Life Upper grades have uniform requirement, student council. Discipline rests primarily with faculty.

Summer Programs Remediation, enrichment, advancement programs offered; held on campus; accepts boys and girls; open to students from other schools. 2009 schedule: June 15 to July 30. Application deadline: June 5.

Tuition and Aid Day student tuition: $12,000. Tuition installment plan (monthly payment plans, individually arranged payment plans). Tuition reduction for siblings, merit scholarship grants, need-based scholarship grants available. In 2008–09, 20% of upper-school students received aid; total upper-school merit-scholarship money awarded: $42,000. Total amount of financial aid awarded in 2008–09: $50,000.

Admissions Traditional secondary-level entrance grade is 9. For fall 2008, 34 students applied for upper-level admission, 29 were accepted, 28 enrolled. Admissions testing, CAT, CTBS (or similar from their school), Woodcock-Johnson or Woodcock-Johnson Revised Achievement Test required. Deadline for receipt of application materials: none. Application fee required: $400. Interview required.

Athletics Interscholastic: basketball (boys), cheering (g), swimming and diving (b), tennis (b,g), walking (g), weight training (b); intramural: basketball (b,g), cheering (g), golf (b), martial arts (b,g), soccer (b,g), softball (b,g), swimming and diving (b,g), table tennis (b,g), tennis (b,g), walking (g); coed interscholastic: bowling, flag football, kickball, physical fitness, tennis; coed intramural: badminton, martial arts, physical fitness, soccer, softball, swimming and diving, table tennis, tennis, volleyball. 2 PE instructors, 2 coaches.

Computers Computers are regularly used in art, business applications, computer applications, current events, drawing and design, English, foreign language, geography, health, history, keyboarding, life skills, mathematics, psychology, reading, SAT preparation, science, Spanish, video film production, word processing classes.

Computer resources include on-campus library services, online commercial services, Internet access. Student e-mail accounts and computer access in designated common areas are available to students. The school has a published electronic and media policy.
Contact Margaret Sheriff, Administrator. 305-940-3922. Fax: 305-940-1820. E-mail: msheriff@allisonacademy.com. Web site: www.allisonacademy.com.

ANNOUNCEMENT FROM THE SCHOOL Allison Academy continues its commitment to personalized education in which students' needs and strengths are addressed to guide the students in maximizing their academic, social, and physical development. Along with a highly structured academic program, students are offered an array of electives, including guitar, art, film studies, drama, tennis, and basketball.

ALL SAINTS' EPISCOPAL SCHOOL OF FORT WORTH

9700 Saints Circle
Fort Worth, Texas 76108

Head of School: Dr. Thaddeus B. Bird

General Information Coeducational day college-preparatory, arts, and religious studies school, affiliated with Episcopal Church. Grades K–12. Founded: 1951. Setting: suburban. 103-acre campus. 4 buildings on campus. Approved or accredited by Independent Schools Association of the Southwest, National Association of Episcopal Schools, Southwest Association of Episcopal Schools, and Texas Department of Education. Member of National Association of Independent Schools. Endowment: $5 million. Total enrollment: 805. Upper school average class size: 12. Upper school faculty-student ratio: 1:9.
Upper School Student Profile Grade 9: 72 students (36 boys, 36 girls); Grade 10: 67 students (43 boys, 24 girls); Grade 11: 68 students (33 boys, 35 girls); Grade 12: 63 students (40 boys, 23 girls). 21% of students are members of Episcopal Church.
Faculty School total: 83. In upper school: 15 men, 21 women; 17 have advanced degrees.
Subjects Offered Advanced math, algebra, anatomy and physiology, art, ballet, Bible studies, biology, biology-AP, calculus-AP, chemistry, chemistry-AP, choral music, classical civilization, classical studies, classics, college admission preparation, college planning, college writing, computer science-AP, computers, dance, digital photography, drama, ecology, environmental systems, economics, English, English language and composition-AP, English literature and composition-AP, environmental science, environmental studies, ethics, forensics, geometry, honors algebra, honors English, honors geometry, honors U.S. history, honors world history, Latin, Latin-AP, musical productions, physics, physics-AP, pre-calculus, publications, Spanish, Spanish language-AP, Spanish-AP, speech, studio art-AP, U.S. government-AP, U.S. history, U.S. history-AP, Western civilization, writing.
Graduation Requirements Arts and fine arts (art, music, dance, drama), computer science, English, foreign language, mathematics, religion (includes Bible studies and theology), science, social studies (includes history), speech. Community service is required.
Special Academic Programs Advanced Placement exam preparation; honors section.
College Admission Counseling 63 students graduated in 2008; all went to college, including Baylor University; Texas A&M University; Texas Christian University; Texas Tech University; The University of Texas at Austin; University of Mississippi. Mean SAT critical reading: 564, mean SAT math: 550, mean SAT writing: 570, mean combined SAT: 1684.
Student Life Upper grades have uniform requirement, student council, honor system. Discipline rests equally with students and faculty. Attendance at religious services is required.
Summer Programs Enrichment, sports, art/fine arts, rigorous outdoor training, computer instruction programs offered; session focuses on enrichment; held both on and off campus; held at out of state trips and area sporting venues; accepts boys and girls; open to students from other schools. 350 students usually enrolled. 2009 schedule: June to August.
Tuition and Aid Day student tuition: $13,900. Tuition installment plan (Insured Tuition Payment Plan, monthly payment plans). Merit scholarship grants, need-based scholarship grants available. In 2008–09, 20% of upper-school students received aid; total upper-school merit-scholarship money awarded: $78,710. Total amount of financial aid awarded in 2008–09: $260,930.
Admissions Traditional secondary-level entrance grade is 9. For fall 2008, 50 students applied for upper-level admission, 30 were accepted, 22 enrolled. ERB or ISEE required. Deadline for receipt of application materials: none. Application fee required: $75. Interview required.
Athletics Interscholastic: ballet (boys, girls), baseball (b), basketball (b,g), cheering (g), combined training (b,g), cross-country running (b,g), dance team (g), field hockey (g), football (b), golf (b,g), rodeo (b,g), soccer (b,g), softball (g), swimming and diving (b,g), tennis (b,g), track and field (b,g), volleyball (g), winter soccer (b,g), wrestling (g); intramural: outdoor adventure (b,g), physical training (b,g), weight lifting (b,g), weight training (b,g); coed intramural: cooperative games, strength & conditioning. 10 PE instructors, 15 coaches, 1 athletic trainer.
Computers Computers are regularly used in college planning, data processing, drawing and design, foreign language, library, newspaper, science, yearbook classes. Computer network features include on-campus library services, online commercial services, Internet access, wireless campus network, Internet filtering or blocking technology. Computer access in designated common areas is available to students. The school has a published electronic and media policy.
Contact Robyn Rutkowski, Admissions Assistant. 817-560-5746 Ext. 330. Fax: 817-560-5720. E-mail: robynrutkowski@aseschool.org. Web site: www.asesftw.org.

ALMA HEIGHTS CHRISTIAN ACADEMY

1030 Linda Mar Boulevard
Pacifica, California 94044

Head of School: David Welling

General Information Coeducational day college-preparatory and general academic school, affiliated with Christian faith; primarily serves individuals with Attention Deficit Disorder and dyslexic students. Grades K–12. Founded: 1955. Setting: suburban. Nearest major city is San Francisco. 40-acre campus. 5 buildings on campus. Approved or accredited by Association of Christian Schools International, Western Association of Schools and Colleges, and California Department of Education. Upper school average class size: 22. Upper school faculty-student ratio: 1:6.
Upper School Student Profile 65% of students are Christian faith.
Faculty School total: 30. In upper school: 9 men, 5 women; 4 have advanced degrees.
Student Life Upper grades have uniform requirement, student council, honor system. Discipline rests primarily with faculty. Attendance at religious services is required.
Tuition and Aid Day student tuition: $9015. Tuition reduction for siblings, merit scholarship grants, need-based scholarship grants, paying campus jobs available. In 2008–09, 2% of upper-school students received aid. Total amount of financial aid awarded in 2008–09: $5500.
Admissions Placement test required. Deadline for receipt of application materials: none. Application fee required: $75. Interview required.
Athletics Interscholastic: baseball (boys), basketball (b,g), soccer (b), softball (g), volleyball (b,g); intramural: flag football (b), indoor soccer (b); coed interscholastic: soccer. 3 PE instructors.
Computers Computer resources include online commercial services, Internet access, wireless campus network, Internet filtering or blocking technology. Campus intranet and student e-mail accounts are available to students. Students grades are available online.
Contact 650-355-1935. Fax: 650-355-3488. Web site: www.almaheights.org.

ALPINE ACADEMY

Erda, Utah

See Special Needs Schools section.

THE ALTAMONT SCHOOL

4801 Altamont Road
Birmingham, Alabama 35222

Head of School: Mrs. Sarah W. Whiteside

General Information Coeducational day college-preparatory, arts, and technology school. Grades 5–12. Founded: 1922. Setting: urban. 40-acre campus. 4 buildings on campus. Approved or accredited by National Independent Private Schools Association, Southern Association of Colleges and Schools, Southern Association of Independent Schools, The College Board, and Alabama Department of Education. Member of National Association of Independent Schools. Endowment: $8 million. Total enrollment: 347. Upper school average class size: 15. Upper school faculty-student ratio: 1:5.
Faculty School total: 56. In upper school: 19 men, 24 women; 32 have advanced degrees.
Subjects Offered 20th century American writers, acting, advanced chemistry, advanced computer applications, algebra, American history, American literature, anatomy and physiology, art, art history, astronomy, biology, calculus, chemistry, Chinese, Chinese history, Chinese literature, Chinese studies, computer keyboarding, computer programming, computer science, concert choir, creative drama, creative writing, earth science, ecology, economics and history, English, English literature, European history, film and new technologies, finite math, French, geography, geometry, government/civics, health, history, independent study, instruments, Internet research, jazz band, journalism, Latin, mathematics, music, orchestra, photography, physical education, physics, pre-calculus, science, social studies, Spanish, speech, speech and debate, statistics, theater, theater arts, track and field, travel, trigonometry, U.S. government, U.S. history, video film production, visual and performing arts, vocal music, weight training, world history, world literature, writing.
Graduation Requirements American history, computer applications, English, foreign language, health and wellness, history, mathematics, physical education (includes health), science, speech.
Special Academic Programs Advanced Placement exam preparation; honors section; independent study; study at local college for college credit; study abroad.
College Admission Counseling 65 students graduated in 2008; 64 went to college, including Birmingham-Southern College; Sewanee: The University of the South; The University of Alabama; Trinity University; Vanderbilt University; Washington University in St. Louis. Other: 1 had other specific plans. Median SAT critical reading:

650, median SAT math: 645, median SAT writing: 640, median combined SAT: 1940, median composite ACT: 30. 80% scored over 600 on SAT critical reading, 82% scored over 600 on SAT math, 80% scored over 600 on SAT writing, 82% scored over 1800 on combined SAT, 88% scored over 26 on composite ACT.

Student Life Upper grades have specified standards of dress, student council, honor system. Discipline rests equally with students and faculty.

Summer Programs Remediation, enrichment, advancement, sports, art/fine arts, rigorous outdoor training, computer instruction programs offered; session focuses on academic credit and fun; held on campus; accepts boys and girls; open to students from other schools. 300 students usually enrolled. 2009 schedule: June 2 to July 10. Application deadline: none.

Tuition and Aid Day student tuition: $11,999–$15,696. Tuition reduction for siblings, merit scholarship grants, need-based scholarship grants, paying campus jobs available. In 2008–09, 19% of upper-school students received aid; total upper-school merit-scholarship money awarded: $87,439. Total amount of financial aid awarded in 2008–09: $568,684.

Admissions Traditional secondary-level entrance grade is 9. For fall 2008, 37 students applied for upper-level admission, 29 were accepted, 19 enrolled. ISEE required. Deadline for receipt of application materials: none. Application fee required: $50. On-campus interview required.

Athletics Interscholastic: baseball (boys), basketball (b,g), combined training (b,g), cross-country running (b,g), indoor track & field (b,g), physical training (b,g), running (b,g), soccer (b,g), softball (g), strength & conditioning (b,g), swimming and diving (b,g), tennis (b,g), track and field (b,g), volleyball (g), weight training (b,g), winter (indoor) track (b,g); coed interscholastic: golf, running; coed intramural: ultimate Frisbee. 4 PE instructors, 6 coaches, 1 athletic trainer.

Computers Computers are regularly used in all academic, basic skills, multimedia classes. Computer network features include on-campus library services, online commercial services, Internet access, Internet filtering or blocking technology. Student e-mail accounts and computer access in designated common areas are available to students. Students grades are available online. The school has a published electronic and media policy.

Contact Mr. James M. Wiygul, Director of Admissions. 205-445-1232. Fax: 205-871-5666. E-mail: admissions@altamontschool.org. Web site: www.altamontschool.org.

ANNOUNCEMENT FROM THE SCHOOL Picture a school where it's cool to be smart; where a top runner might star in a play; a science whiz might tutor a younger peer in English, or a once-shy student might become the class president; where passionate teachers go the extra mile for every student every day; where the arts are as important as athletics; where students of different backgrounds and cultures share in the process of discovery; where reading is revered; where multiple language offerings include Latin, Greek, and Mandarin Chinese; where upholding the Honor Code is a source of real pride. Picture The Altamont School, a place devoted to educating New Renaissance Students, future leaders armed with multiple skills, broad perspectives, and a love of learning. Altamont helps students ask good questions, while discovering their hidden talents. Core competencies prepare students for entering a world of change, where they will face problems that are as yet unimaginable. At Altamont, students are not simply prepared to enter a "good" college, although the School's college attendance list stacks up with those of the best independent schools in the U.S. Rather, students are helped to reach deep within themselves to become masters of their own lifelong journeys of discovery. At the end of the day, The Altamont School is about preparing each student to live a more meaningful life and shape a more livable world.

ALTERNATIVE LEARNING PROGRAM

#101, 10010 105th Street
Edmonton, Alberta T5J 1C7, Canada

Head of School: Ms. Rachel Posch

General Information Coeducational day college-preparatory, general academic, and vocational school; primarily serves underachievers, students with learning disabilities, individuals with Attention Deficit Disorder, and dyslexic students. Grades 1–9. Founded: 1994. Setting: urban. 1 building on campus. Approved or accredited by Alberta Department of Education. Language of instruction: English. Upper school average class size: 10. Upper school faculty-student ratio: 1:10.

Faculty School total: 2. In upper school: 1 man, 1 woman; all have advanced degrees.

Subjects Offered Career education, career experience, career exploration, career planning, career/college preparation, careers, college admission preparation, college planning, computer literacy, computer skills, creative writing, language arts, life skills, literacy, mathematics.

Special Academic Programs Programs in English, mathematics, general development for dyslexic students.

Student Life Discipline rests equally with students and faculty.

Admissions Admissions testing, math and English placement tests, placement test, school placement exam, school's own exam and writing sample required. Deadline for receipt of application materials: none. No application fee required. On-campus interview required.

Computers Computer network features include Internet access.

Contact Mrs. Michelle Weeks, Student Intake Officer. 780-428-7590 Ext. 5122. Fax: 780-420-0805. E-mail: mweeks@johnhoward.org.

AMERICAN ACADEMY

Plantation, Florida

See Special Needs Schools section.

THE AMERICAN BOYCHOIR SCHOOL

Princeton, New Jersey

See Junior Boarding Schools section.

AMERICAN CHRISTIAN ACADEMY

2300 Veterans Memorial Parkway
Tuscaloosa, Alabama 35404

Head of School: Dr. Dan Carden

General Information Coeducational day college-preparatory, religious studies, and technology school, affiliated with Christian faith; primarily serves individuals with Attention Deficit Disorder. Grades K–12. Founded: 1979. Setting: small town. 20-acre campus. 6 buildings on campus. Approved or accredited by Association of Christian Schools International and Southern Association of Colleges and Schools. Endowment: $100,000. Total enrollment: 900. Upper school average class size: 20. Upper school faculty-student ratio: 1:12.

Upper School Student Profile Grade 10: 114 students (32 boys, 82 girls); Grade 11: 65 students (37 boys, 28 girls); Grade 12: 40 students (19 boys, 21 girls). 75% of students are Christian.

Faculty School total: 55. In upper school: 14 men, 37 women; 15 have advanced degrees.

Subjects Offered Algebra, anatomy, Bible, biology, calculus, chemistry, computers, earth science, economics, English, English-AP, fine arts, geography, geology, government, health, history, life science, marine biology, mathematics, physical education, physics, reading, science, Southern literature, Spanish, typing, world history.

Graduation Requirements Arts and fine arts (art, music, dance, drama), business skills (includes word processing), computer science, English, foreign language, mathematics, physical education (includes health), religion (includes Bible studies and theology), science, social science, social studies (includes history), accelerated reading is required in all grades. Community service is required.

Special Academic Programs Advanced Placement exam preparation; honors section; accelerated programs; independent study; study at local college for college credit; study abroad; special instructional classes for deaf students.

College Admission Counseling 49 students graduated in 2008; 48 went to college, including Auburn University; Birmingham-Southern College; Samford University; Shelton State Community College; The University of Alabama; University of South Alabama. Other: 1 entered military service. Median composite ACT: 25. 42% scored over 26 on composite ACT.

Student Life Upper grades have specified standards of dress, student council, honor system. Discipline rests primarily with faculty. Attendance at religious services is required.

Tuition and Aid Day student tuition: $4800. Tuition installment plan (monthly payment plans, individually arranged payment plans). Tuition reduction for siblings, need-based scholarship grants, paying campus jobs available. In 2008–09, 12% of upper-school students received aid. Total amount of financial aid awarded in 2008–09: $65,000.

Admissions Traditional secondary-level entrance grade is 10. For fall 2008, 61 students applied for upper-level admission, 45 were accepted, 41 enrolled. Scholastic Achievement Test required. Deadline for receipt of application materials: none. Application fee required: $125. Interview required.

Athletics Interscholastic: baseball (boys), basketball (b,g), cheering (g), cross-country running (b,g), dance squad (g), dance team (g), danceline (g), flag football (b), football (b), golf (b,g), indoor track (b,g), indoor track & field (b,g), power lifting (b), soccer (b,g), softball (g), strength & conditioning (b,g), swimming and diving (b,g), tennis (b,g), track and field (b,g), volleyball (g), weight lifting (b,g), weight training (b,g), wrestling (b); intramural: aerobics (g), aerobics/dance (g), basketball (b,g), cheering (g), dance squad (g), dance team (g), danceline (g), flagball (b,g), gymnastics (g), in-line skating (b,g), outdoor activities (b,g), paint ball (b), physical training (b,g), roller blading (b,g), softball (g), strength & conditioning (b,g), swimming and diving (b,g), touch football (b,g); coed intramural: flagball, outdoor activities, physical fitness, running. 3 PE instructors, 12 coaches, 1 athletic trainer.

Computers Computers are regularly used in computer applications, foreign language, mathematics, typing, video film production classes. Computer network features include on-campus library services, Internet access, wireless campus network, Internet filtering or blocking technology. Campus intranet, student e-mail accounts, and computer access in designated common areas are available to students. Students grades are available online.

Contact Nancy Hastings, Director of Admissions. 205-553-5963 Ext. 12. Fax: 205-553-5942. E-mail: nhastings@acacademy.com. Web site: www.acacademy.com.

AMERICAN COMMUNITY SCHOOLS OF ATHENS

129 Aghias Paraskevis Street
Halandri
Athens 152 34, Greece

Head of School: Dr. Stefanos Gialamas

General Information Coeducational day college-preparatory, arts, and technology school; primarily serves students with learning disabilities and mild learning disabilities. Grades JK–12. Founded: 1945. Setting: suburban. 3-hectare campus. 4 buildings on campus. Approved or accredited by CITA (Commission on International and Trans-Regional Accreditation), European Council of International Schools, and Middle States Association of Colleges and Schools. Language of instruction: English. Total enrollment: 774. Upper school average class size: 17. Upper school faculty-student ratio: 1:17.

Upper School Student Profile Grade 9: 65 students (30 boys, 35 girls); Grade 10: 85 students (44 boys, 41 girls); Grade 11: 90 students (39 boys, 51 girls); Grade 12: 65 students (36 boys, 29 girls).

Faculty School total: 88. In upper school: 11 men, 20 women; 26 have advanced degrees.

Subjects Offered Algebra, American history, American literature, analysis, Arabic, art, art history, band, biology, business skills, calculus, chemistry, Chinese, computer programming, computer science, dance, drama, earth science, economics, English, English literature, environmental science, ESL, European history, expository writing, fine arts, French, geometry, German, government/civics, grammar, Greek, history, humanities, information technology, journalism, mathematics, music, peer counseling, photography, physical education, physical science, physics, psychology, science, social science, social studies, sociology, Spanish, speech, statistics, theater, theory of knowledge, trigonometry, writing.

Graduation Requirements Arts and fine arts (art, music, dance, drama), computer science, English, foreign language, mathematics, physical education (includes health), science, social science, social studies (includes history).

Special Academic Programs International Baccalaureate program; Advanced Placement exam preparation; honors section; accelerated programs; independent study; study at local college for college credit; academic accommodation for the gifted; remedial reading and/or remedial writing; remedial math; programs in English, mathematics, general development for dyslexic students; special instructional classes for deaf students, blind students, students with mild special needs; ESL (17 students enrolled).

College Admission Counseling 88 students graduated in 2008; all went to college, including Boston College; Boston University; California Institute of Technology; Northwestern University; The Johns Hopkins University; University of Pennsylvania. Mean SAT critical reading: 523, mean SAT math: 550, mean SAT writing: 531. 25% scored over 600 on SAT critical reading, 23% scored over 600 on SAT math, 25% scored over 600 on SAT writing.

Student Life Upper grades have specified standards of dress, student council. Discipline rests primarily with faculty.

Summer Programs Enrichment, advancement, ESL, sports, art/fine arts, computer instruction programs offered; session focuses on recreational and international leadership, creative thinking through mathematical thinking; held both on and off campus; held at various museums and historical sites (for the leadership program); accepts boys and girls; open to students from other schools. 150 students usually enrolled. 2009 schedule: June 22 to July 11. Application deadline: April 15.

Tuition and Aid Day student tuition: €7840–€15,830. Tuition installment plan (individually arranged payment plans, semester and quarterly payment plans). Tuition reduction for siblings, need-based scholarship grants available. In 2008–09, 1% of upper-school students received aid. Total amount of financial aid awarded in 2008–09: €60,000.

Admissions Traditional secondary-level entrance grade is 9. For fall 2008, 85 students applied for upper-level admission, 80 were accepted, 78 enrolled. English for Non-native Speakers or math and English placement tests required. Deadline for receipt of application materials: none. No application fee required. Interview required.

Athletics Interscholastic: basketball (boys, girls), cross-country running (b,g), soccer (b,g), softball (b,g), swimming and diving (b,g), tennis (b,g), track and field (b,g), volleyball (b,g), wrestling (b); coed interscholastic: gymnastics; coed intramural: martial arts. 2 PE instructors, 3 coaches.

Computers Computers are regularly used in all academic classes. Computer network features include Internet access.

Contact John G. Papadakis, Director of Enrollment Management, Community and Public Affairs. 30-210-639-3200. Fax: 30-210-639-0051. E-mail: papadakisj@acs.gr. Web site: www.acs.gr.

AMERICAN HERITAGE SCHOOL

12200 West Broward Boulevard
Plantation, Florida 33325

Head of School: William R. Laurie

General Information Coeducational day college-preparatory, arts, and pre-medical, pre-law, pre-engineering school. Grades PK–12. Founded: 1969. Setting: suburban. Nearest major city is Fort Lauderdale. 40-acre campus. 5 buildings on campus. Approved or accredited by Association of Independent Schools of Florida, CITA (Commission on International and Trans-Regional Accreditation), Southern Association of Colleges and Schools, and Florida Department of Education. Total enrollment: 2,189. Upper school average class size: 17. Upper school faculty-student ratio: 1:13.

Upper School Student Profile Grade 7: 180 students (78 boys, 102 girls); Grade 8: 185 students (87 boys, 98 girls); Grade 9: 264 students (141 boys, 123 girls); Grade 10: 263 students (134 boys, 129 girls); Grade 11: 260 students (131 boys, 129 girls); Grade 12: 227 students (124 boys, 103 girls).

Faculty School total: 188. In upper school: 34 men, 72 women; 56 have advanced degrees.

Subjects Offered Algebra, American government, American government-AP, American history, American history-AP, American legal systems, American literature, American literature-AP, anatomy and physiology, architectural drawing, art, band, biology, biology-AP, calculus-AP, ceramics, chemistry, chemistry-AP, Chinese, chorus, community service, computer graphics, computer science, costumes and make-up, creative writing, dance, drama, drawing, economics, economics-AP, English, English language and composition-AP, English literature, English literature and composition-AP, environmental science, environmental science-AP, ESL, fine arts, French, French-AP, geometry, graphic design, guitar, honors algebra, honors English, honors geometry, honors U.S. history, honors world history, journalism, law studies, mathematics, music theory-AP, oceanography, orchestra, painting, photography, physical education, physics, physics-AP, portfolio art, pre-algebra, pre-calculus, probability and statistics, psychology, SAT/ACT preparation, science, sculpture, set design, Spanish, Spanish-AP, sports medicine, stagecraft, studio art, theater, vocal music, Web site design, weight training, word processing, world history, world literature, world religions, writing, yearbook.

Graduation Requirements Arts and fine arts (art, music, dance, drama), English, foreign language, mathematics, physical education (includes health), science, social studies (includes history), acceptance to a 4-year college. Community service is required.

Special Academic Programs Advanced Placement exam preparation; honors section; academic accommodation for the gifted, the musically talented, and the artistically talented; ESL (30 students enrolled).

College Admission Counseling 212 students graduated in 2008; all went to college, including Florida Atlantic University; Florida Gulf Coast University; Florida State University; Nova Southeastern University; University of Central Florida; University of Florida. Median SAT critical reading: 560, median SAT math: 580, median SAT writing: 550. 40% scored over 600 on SAT critical reading, 45% scored over 600 on SAT math, 35% scored over 600 on SAT writing.

Student Life Upper grades have uniform requirement, student council. Discipline rests primarily with faculty.

Summer Programs Remediation, enrichment, advancement, ESL, art/fine arts, computer instruction programs offered; session focuses on academics; held on campus; accepts boys and girls; open to students from other schools. 600 students usually enrolled. 2009 schedule: June 8 to August 7. Application deadline: none.

Tuition and Aid Day student tuition: $15,794–$19,879. Tuition installment plan (monthly payment plans, semester payment plan). Tuition reduction for siblings, merit scholarship grants, need-based scholarship grants, need-based loans available. In 2008–09, 22% of upper-school students received aid; total upper-school merit-scholarship money awarded: $3,622,481. Total amount of financial aid awarded in 2008–09: $4,800,000.

Admissions Traditional secondary-level entrance grade is 9. Slossen Intelligence and Stanford Achievement Test required. Deadline for receipt of application materials: none. Application fee required: $100. On-campus interview required.

Athletics Interscholastic: baseball (boys), basketball (b,g), cross-country running (b,g), diving (b,g), football (b), golf (b,g), soccer (b,g), softball (g), swimming and diving (b,g), tennis (b,g), track and field (b,g), volleyball (b,g), weight training (b,g), winter soccer (b,g), wrestling (b); coed interscholastic: cheering, physical fitness. 7 PE instructors, 4 coaches.

Computers Computers are regularly used in computer applications, desktop publishing, digital applications, drafting, drawing and design, economics, engineering, English, ESL, French, geography, graphic design, history, keyboarding, library, literary magazine, mathematics, media arts, media production, multimedia, music, music technology, newspaper, photography, programming, psychology, reading, SAT preparation, social sciences, Spanish, speech, Web site design, writing, yearbook classes. Computer network features include on-campus library services, online commercial services, Internet access, wireless campus network, Internet filtering or blocking technology, Questia. Computer access in designated common areas is available to students. Students grades are available online. The school has a published electronic and media policy.

Contact William R. Laurie, President. 954-472-0022 Ext. 3062. Fax: 954-472-3088. E-mail: admission@ahschool.com. Web site: www.ahschool.com.

See Close-Up on page 662.

THE AMERICAN INTERNATIONAL SCHOOL

Salmannsdorfer Strasse 47
Vienna A-1190, Austria

Head of School: Mrs. Ellen Deitsch Stern

General Information Coeducational day college-preparatory, International Baccalaureate, and US High School Diploma school. Grades PK–12. Founded: 1959.

Setting: suburban. 15-acre campus. 1 building on campus. Approved or accredited by Middle States Association of Colleges and Schools. Affiliate member of National Association of Independent Schools; member of European Council of International Schools. Language of instruction: English. Total enrollment: 787. Upper school average class size: 20. Upper school faculty-student ratio: 1:6.

Upper School Student Profile Grade 9: 70 students (32 boys, 38 girls); Grade 10: 55 students (25 boys, 30 girls); Grade 11: 65 students (35 boys, 30 girls); Grade 12: 63 students (29 boys, 34 girls); Postgraduate: 2 students (1 boy, 1 girl).

Faculty School total: 94. In upper school: 19 men, 18 women; 22 have advanced degrees.

Subjects Offered Algebra, American history, American literature, band, biology, ceramics, chemistry, computer science, computers, drama, economics, English, English literature, European history, fine arts, French, geometry, German, health, history, mathematics, music, physical education, physical science, physics, programming, psychology, science, social science, social studies, Spanish, statistics, strings, studio art, theory of knowledge, visual arts, world history, yearbook.

Graduation Requirements Arts and fine arts (art, music, dance, drama), English, foreign language, mathematics, physical education (includes health), science, social studies (includes history).

Special Academic Programs International Baccalaureate program; independent study; ESL.

College Admission Counseling 54 students graduated in 2008; 52 went to college, including Brown University; Harvard University; McGill University; Ohio Wesleyan University; Stanford University; University of Pennsylvania. Other: 1 entered military service, 1 had other specific plans.

Student Life Upper grades have student council, honor system. Discipline rests equally with students and faculty.

Tuition and Aid Day student tuition: €16,850–€17,100. Tuition installment plan (individually arranged payment plans). Need-based scholarship grants available.

Admissions Deadline for receipt of application materials: none. Application fee required: €165. On-campus interview recommended.

Athletics Interscholastic: baseball (boys), basketball (b,g), cross-country running (b,g), soccer (b,g), softball (g), swimming and diving (b,g), tennis (b,g), track and field (b,g), volleyball (b,g); intramural: ballet (g), weight lifting (b,g); coed interscholastic: aquatics; coed intramural: aerobics/dance, badminton, basketball, dance, golf, gymnastics, martial arts, soccer, softball. 2 PE instructors, 19 coaches.

Computers Computers are regularly used in English, ESL, French, mathematics, science, Spanish, yearbook classes. Computer network features include on-campus library services, Internet access, wireless campus network, Internet filtering or blocking technology. Campus intranet, student e-mail accounts, and computer access in designated common areas are available to students. Students grades are available online. The school has a published electronic and media policy.

Contact Jennifer Wallner, Director of Admissions. +43-1-40132 Ext. 218. Fax: +43-1-40132-5. E-mail: J.Wallner@ais.at. Web site: www.ais.at.

AMERICAN INTERNATIONAL SCHOOL, DHAKA

PO Box 6106
Gulshan
Dhaka, Bangladesh

Head of School: Mr. Walter Plotkin

General Information Coeducational day college-preparatory school. Grades PK–12. Founded: 1972. Setting: suburban. 4-acre campus. 1 building on campus. Approved or accredited by European Council of International Schools and New England Association of Schools and Colleges. Language of instruction: English. Total enrollment: 691. Upper school average class size: 18. Upper school faculty-student ratio: 1:15.

Upper School Student Profile Grade 9: 50 students (25 boys, 25 girls); Grade 10: 57 students (38 boys, 19 girls); Grade 11: 56 students (31 boys, 25 girls); Grade 12: 44 students (27 boys, 17 girls).

Faculty School total: 95. In upper school: 20 men, 14 women; 24 have advanced degrees.

Subjects Offered Algebra, American literature, art, biology, chemistry, choir, choral music, computer science, concert band, creative writing, critical writing, digital photography, drawing, economics, electives, English, English literature, environmental science, ESL, fine arts, fitness, French, geography, geometry, language arts, mathematics, media arts, model United Nations, modern languages, modern world history, music, music theory, painting, physical education, physics, printmaking, psychology, science, sculpture, senior project, social studies, Spanish, speech, sports, study skills, symphonic band, theater arts, theory of knowledge, trigonometry, visual arts, women in literature, yearbook.

Special Academic Programs International Baccalaureate program; ESL.

College Admission Counseling 41 students graduated in 2008; all went to college, including Franklin & Marshall College; McGill University; The George Washington University; University of Toronto; Wellesley College. Mean SAT critical reading: 519, mean SAT math: 573, mean SAT writing: 516, mean combined SAT: 1608, mean composite ACT: 22. 27% scored over 600 on SAT critical reading, 42% scored over 600 on SAT math, 19% scored over 600 on SAT writing, 19% scored over 1800 on combined SAT, 18% scored over 26 on composite ACT.

Student Life Upper grades have student council, honor system. Discipline rests primarily with faculty.

Tuition and Aid Day student tuition: $17,940.

Admissions For fall 2008, 65 students applied for upper-level admission, 54 were accepted, 54 enrolled. Math and English placement tests required. Deadline for receipt of application materials: none. Application fee required: $50. On-campus interview required.

Athletics Interscholastic: basketball (boys, girls), cricket (b), soccer (b,g), swimming and diving (b,g), tennis (b,g), track and field (b,g), volleyball (b,g); intramural: basketball (b,g), soccer (b,g), swimming and diving (b,g), volleyball (b,g).

Computers Computers are regularly used in all academic classes. Computer network features include on-campus library services, online commercial services, Internet access, wireless campus network. Student e-mail accounts are available to students. Students grades are available online. The school has a published electronic and media policy.

Contact Mrs. Kanwal Bhagat, Registrar. 882 2452 Ext. 139. Fax: 882 3175. E-mail: admissions@ais-dhaka.net. Web site: www.ais-dhaka.net.

AMERICAN INTERNATIONAL SCHOOL OF BUCHAREST

Sos. Pipera-Tunari 196
Commune Voluntari-Pipera
Bucharest, Romania

Head of School: Dr. David Ottaviano

General Information Coeducational day college-preparatory and International Baccalaureate school. Grades PK–12. Founded: 1962. Setting: suburban. 10-hectare campus. 4 buildings on campus. Approved or accredited by European Council of International Schools, International Baccalaureate Organization, and New England Association of Schools and Colleges. Language of instruction: English. Total enrollment: 715. Upper school average class size: 17. Upper school faculty-student ratio: 1:9.

Upper School Student Profile Grade 9: 50 students (22 boys, 28 girls); Grade 10: 44 students (21 boys, 23 girls); Grade 11: 45 students (22 boys, 23 girls); Grade 12: 41 students (19 boys, 22 girls).

Faculty School total: 93. In upper school: 20 men, 28 women; 12 have advanced degrees.

Subjects Offered Advanced math, art, arts, athletics, band, biology, chemistry, choir, chorus, computer graphics, computers, design, desktop publishing, drama, economics, English, ESL, filmmaking, French, global issues, history, integrated mathematics, language, literature, mathematics, music, physical education, physics, Spanish, technology, theory of knowledge, world cultures.

Graduation Requirements Art, biology, chemistry, computer literacy, economics and history, English, foreign language, history, International Baccalaureate courses, life skills, mathematics, physical education (includes health), 25 hours of community service each year of high school.

Special Academic Programs International Baccalaureate program; independent study; ESL (175 students enrolled).

College Admission Counseling 40 students graduated in 2008; 37 went to college, including Bates College; Columbia College; Pomona College; University of Chicago; University of Pennsylvania; Vassar College. Other: 2 entered military service, 1 had other specific plans.

Student Life Upper grades have specified standards of dress, student council. Discipline rests primarily with faculty.

Tuition and Aid Day student tuition: €15,150. Tuition installment plan (individually arranged payment plans, 3-payment installment plan). Need-based scholarship grants available. In 2008–09, 2% of upper-school students received aid. Total amount of financial aid awarded in 2008–09: $5000.

Admissions Traditional secondary-level entrance grade is 9. For fall 2008, 53 students applied for upper-level admission, 44 were accepted, 42 enrolled. English entrance exam, Math Placement Exam, Secondary Level English Proficiency or writing sample required. Deadline for receipt of application materials: none. Application fee required: €800. On-campus interview recommended.

Athletics Interscholastic: basketball (boys, girls), cross-country running (b,g), soccer (b,g), softball (b,g), swimming and diving (b,g), tennis (b,g), volleyball (b,g); intramural: basketball (b,g), indoor hockey (b,g), indoor soccer (b,g); coed intramural: outdoor adventure, outdoor education, physical fitness, sailing, soccer, softball. 5 PE instructors, 4 coaches, 1 athletic trainer.

Computers Computers are regularly used in desktop publishing, graphics, information technology, video film production, yearbook classes. Computer network features include on-campus library services, online commercial services, Internet access, wireless campus network, Internet filtering or blocking technology. Student e-mail accounts and computer access in designated common areas are available to students. Students grades are available online. The school has a published electronic and media policy.

Contact Ms. Catalina Pieptea, Admission Officer. 40-21-204-4368. Fax: 40-21-204-4384. E-mail: admiss@aisb.ro. Web site: www.aisb.ro.

AMERICAN INTERNATIONAL SCHOOL ROTTERDAM

Verhulstlann 21
Rotterdam 3055 WJ, Netherlands

Head of School: Mr. Brian D. Atkins

General Information Coeducational day college-preparatory school. Grades PK–12. Founded: 1959. Setting: suburban. 5-acre campus. 1 building on campus. Approved or accredited by European Council of International Schools, International Baccalaureate Organization, and New England Association of Schools and Colleges. Language of instruction: English. Total enrollment: 213. Upper school average class size: 12. Upper school faculty-student ratio: 1:6.

Upper School Student Profile Grade 6: 12 students (6 boys, 6 girls); Grade 7: 8 students (5 boys, 3 girls); Grade 8: 11 students (8 boys, 3 girls); Grade 9: 5 students (2 boys, 3 girls); Grade 10: 11 students (6 boys, 5 girls); Grade 11: 15 students (10 boys, 5 girls); Grade 12: 8 students (4 boys, 4 girls).

Faculty School total: 40. In upper school: 11 men, 13 women; 17 have advanced degrees.

Subjects Offered Algebra, American history, American literature, art, biology, British literature, chemistry, computer applications, concert band, current history, digital photography, drama, Dutch, earth science, ecology, environmental systems, English literature, ESL, European history, fine arts, French, geography, geometry, global issues, health, history, instrumental music, integrated physics, International Baccalaureate courses, journalism, library assistant, math applications, photography, physical education, physical science, physics, Spanish, sports, trigonometry, yearbook.

Special Academic Programs International Baccalaureate program; independent study; remedial reading and/or remedial writing; remedial math; programs in English, mathematics, general development for dyslexic students; ESL (12 students enrolled).

College Admission Counseling 14 students graduated in 2008; all went to college, including The University of North Carolina at Asheville; The University of Texas at Austin; United States Air Force Academy; University of Florida.

Student Life Upper grades have specified standards of dress, student council, honor system. Discipline rests primarily with faculty.

Tuition and Aid Day student tuition: €16,950. Tuition installment plan (individually arranged payment plans). Financial aid available to upper-school students. In 2008–09, 2% of upper-school students received aid. Total amount of financial aid awarded in 2008–09: €15,000.

Admissions Admissions testing, English entrance exam and mathematics proficiency exam required. Deadline for receipt of application materials: none. No application fee required. On-campus interview required.

Athletics Interscholastic: basketball (boys, girls), soccer (b,g), volleyball (g); coed interscholastic: softball, swimming and diving, tennis, track and field. 2 PE instructors, 4 coaches.

Computers Computers are regularly used in all classes. Computer network features include on-campus library services, online commercial services, Internet access, wireless campus network. Campus intranet and student e-mail accounts are available to students. The school has a published electronic and media policy.

Contact Mrs. Aurora George-Kelso, Admissions Contact. 31-(10)422-5351. Fax: 31-(10)422-4075. E-mail: a.george-kelso@aisr.nl. Web site: www.aisr.nl.

THE AMERICAN SCHOOL FOUNDATION

Bondojito 215
Colonia Las Americas
Mexico City, D.F. 01120, Mexico

Head of School: Mr. Paul Williams

General Information Coeducational day college-preparatory, arts, bilingual studies, and technology school. Grades PK–12. Founded: 1888. Setting: urban. 17-acre campus. 4 buildings on campus. Approved or accredited by International Baccalaureate Organization and Southern Association of Colleges and Schools. Affiliate member of National Association of Independent Schools. Languages of instruction: English and Spanish. Endowment: 36 million Mexican pesos. Total enrollment: 2,502. Upper school average class size: 18. Upper school faculty-student ratio: 1:10.

Upper School Student Profile Grade 9: 156 students (82 boys, 74 girls); Grade 10: 168 students (85 boys, 83 girls); Grade 11: 161 students (85 boys, 76 girls); Grade 12: 156 students (80 boys, 76 girls).

Faculty School total: 252. In upper school: 27 men, 39 women; 37 have advanced degrees.

Subjects Offered Advanced Placement courses, algebra, American history, American literature, anatomy, anthropology, art, art history, biology, business skills, calculus, ceramics, chemistry, community service, computer programming, computer science, drafting, drama, driver education, earth science, ecology, economics, English, English literature, European history, expository writing, film, fine arts, French, geography, geometry, government/civics, grammar, health, history, humanities, Italian, journalism, mathematics, mechanical drawing, Mexican history, music, personal development, philosophy, photography, physical education, physics, physiology, psychology, religion, science, social science, social studies, Spanish, speech, statistics, theater, trigonometry, typing, world history, world literature, writing, zoology.

Graduation Requirements Arts and fine arts (art, music, dance, drama), computer science, English, foreign language, foreign policy, mathematics, physical education (includes health), science, social science, social studies (includes history). Community service is required.

Special Academic Programs International Baccalaureate program; 15 Advanced Placement exams for which test preparation is offered; honors section; remedial reading and/or remedial writing; remedial math; programs in English, mathematics, general development for dyslexic students; special instructional classes for students with learning disabilities (through the Learning Skills Center), Attention Deficit Disorder, and dyslexia; ESL (20 students enrolled).

College Admission Counseling 159 students graduated in 2008; 140 went to college, including American University; Babson College; Boston University; Bryn Mawr College; New York University; University of Pennsylvania. Other: 19 had other specific plans. Median SAT critical reading: 553, median SAT math: 560, median SAT writing: 550, median composite ACT: 26.

Student Life Upper grades have specified standards of dress, student council. Discipline rests primarily with faculty.

Summer Programs Remediation, enrichment, advancement, ESL, art/fine arts, computer instruction programs offered; session focuses on remediation and enrichment; held on campus; accepts boys and girls; open to students from other schools. 781 students usually enrolled. 2009 schedule: June 22 to July 31. Application deadline: none.

Tuition and Aid Day student tuition: 13,600 Mexican pesos. Merit scholarship grants, need-based scholarship grants available. In 2008–09, 13% of upper-school students received aid; total upper-school merit-scholarship money awarded: 750,000 Mexican pesos. Total amount of financial aid awarded in 2008–09: 4,500,000 Mexican pesos.

Admissions Traditional secondary-level entrance grade is 10. For fall 2008, 82 students applied for upper-level admission, 68 were accepted, 66 enrolled. Gates MacGinite Reading Tests required. Deadline for receipt of application materials: none. Application fee required: 700 Mexican pesos. On-campus interview required.

Athletics Interscholastic: basketball (boys, girls), football (b), soccer (b,g), softball (g), swimming and diving (b,g), volleyball (b,g); intramural: basketball (b,g), football (b), soccer (b), softball (g); coed interscholastic: gymnastics, tennis, track and field; coed intramural: swimming and diving, tennis, track and field, volleyball. 8 PE instructors, 24 coaches.

Computers Computers are regularly used in all academic classes. Computer network features include on-campus library services, online commercial services, Internet access, wireless campus network, Internet filtering or blocking technology. Student e-mail accounts and computer access in designated common areas are available to students. Students grades are available online. The school has a published electronic and media policy.

Contact Julie Hellmund, Director of Admission. 52-555-227-4900. Fax: 52-55273-4357. E-mail: hellmundj@asf.edu.mx. Web site: www.asf.edu.mx.

THE AMERICAN SCHOOL IN LONDON

One Waverley Place
London NW8 0NP, United Kingdom

Head of School: Coreen R. Hester

General Information Coeducational day college-preparatory school. Grades PK–12. Founded: 1951. Setting: urban. 3-acre campus. 1 building on campus. Approved or accredited by European Council of International Schools and Middle States Association of Colleges and Schools. Affiliate member of National Association of Independent Schools; member of Secondary School Admission Test Board. Language of instruction: English. Endowment: £500,000. Total enrollment: 1,324. Upper school average class size: 15. Upper school faculty-student ratio: 1:10.

Upper School Student Profile Grade 9: 108 students (61 boys, 47 girls); Grade 10: 117 students (49 boys, 68 girls); Grade 11: 110 students (54 boys, 56 girls); Grade 12: 120 students (51 boys, 69 girls).

Faculty School total: 162. In upper school: 26 men, 29 women; 50 have advanced degrees.

Subjects Offered Acting, African studies, algebra, American literature, anatomy and physiology, Arabic, architectural drawing, art, art history-AP, Asian literature, astronomy, biology, biology-AP, British literature, calculus, calculus-AP, chemistry, chemistry-AP, Chinese, Chinese studies, comparative cultures, computer animation, computer applications, computer science-AP, concert band, concert choir, dance, digital art, digital imaging, digital music, digital photography, drawing, ecology, economics, economics-AP, environmental science, environmental studies, European history, European literature, film, French, French language-AP, French literature-AP, genetics, geometry, German, German-AP, guitar, health, human geography—AP, independent study, Japanese, jazz band, journalism, Latin, Middle East, modern European history-AP, music theory-AP, mythology, orchestra, painting, photography, physical education, physics-AP, play production, poetry, pre-calculus, printmaking, psychology, Russian, Russian literature, Russian studies, Shakespeare, Spanish, Spanish language-AP, Spanish literature-AP, Spanish-AP, statistics-AP, studio art—AP, trigonometry, U.S. history, U.S. history-AP, video and animation, video film production, Web site design, Western civilization, woodworking, world geography, world literature, writing, yearbook.

Graduation Requirements Arts and fine arts (art, music, dance, drama), computer science, English, foreign language, mathematics, physical education (includes health), science, social studies (includes history).

Special Academic Programs Advanced Placement exam preparation; independent study; programs in general development for dyslexic students; ESL.

College Admission Counseling 117 students graduated in 2008; 116 went to college, including Georgetown University; Hamilton College; Middlebury College; New York University; The George Washington University; University of Pennsylvania. Other: 1 had other specific plans. Mean SAT critical reading: 641, mean SAT math: 649, mean SAT writing: 654.

Student Life Upper grades have student council, honor system. Discipline rests primarily with faculty.

Tuition and Aid Day student tuition: £20,000. Tuition installment plan (monthly payment plans, individually arranged payment plans). Need-based scholarship grants available. In 2008–09, 2% of upper-school students received aid.

Admissions Any standardized test, ERB or ISEE required. Deadline for receipt of application materials: none. Application fee required: £100. On-campus interview recommended.

Athletics Interscholastic: baseball (boys), basketball (b,g), cheering (g), crew (b,g), cross-country running (b,g), dance (g), field hockey (g), rugby (b), soccer (b,g), softball (g), swimming and diving (b,g), tennis (b,g), track and field (b,g), volleyball (b,g); coed intramural: badminton, kickball, soccer, swimming and diving, tennis. 5 PE instructors, 58 coaches.

Computers Computers are regularly used in animation, English, foreign language, journalism, mathematics, media arts, media production, science, social studies, video film production, Web site design, yearbook classes. Computer network features include on-campus library services, Internet access, wireless campus network. Student e-mail accounts are available to students.

Contact Jodi Coats, Dean of Admissions. 44-20-7449-1221. Fax: 44-20-7449-1350. E-mail: admissions@asl.org. Web site: www.asl.org.

ANNOUNCEMENT FROM THE SCHOOL The American School in London provides an educational program designed to meet the individual needs of an academically motivated student body. The program emphasizes academic excellence, and intellectual growth is linked with social, moral, and physical development. The School takes full advantage of the unique offerings presented by its location in the United Kingdom, its proximity to continental Europe, and its international student body.

See Close-Up on page 664.

THE AMERICAN SCHOOL OF MADRID

Ctra. de Aravaca a Húmera, km. 2
Madrid 28023, Spain

Head of School: Mr. William D. O'Hale

General Information Coeducational day college-preparatory, arts, and technology school. Grades PK–12. Founded: 1961. Setting: suburban. 4-hectare campus. 5 buildings on campus. Approved or accredited by International Baccalaureate Organization and Middle States Association of Colleges and Schools. Affiliate member of National Association of Independent Schools; member of European Council of International Schools. Language of instruction: English. Total enrollment: 867. Upper school average class size: 20. Upper school faculty-student ratio: 1:9.

Upper School Student Profile Grade 9: 62 students (32 boys, 30 girls); Grade 10: 80 students (32 boys, 48 girls); Grade 11: 55 students (22 boys, 33 girls); Grade 12: 57 students (26 boys, 31 girls).

Faculty School total: 96. In upper school: 15 men, 16 women; 30 have advanced degrees.

Subjects Offered 3-dimensional art, algebra, American history, American literature, art, biology, business studies, calculus, chemistry, choir, computer math, computer science, computer skills, computer-aided design, creative writing, debate, earth science, English, English literature, environmental science, European history, expository writing, French, geography, geometry, government/civics, health, history, instrumental music, jazz band, journalism, mathematics, music, orchestra, philosophy, physical education, physics, psychology, science, social studies, Spanish, speech, U.S. history, world history, world literature, world wide web design, yearbook.

Graduation Requirements Electives, English, foreign language, information technology, mathematics, physical education (includes health), science, social studies (includes history).

Special Academic Programs International Baccalaureate program; independent study; ESL (50 students enrolled).

College Admission Counseling 49 students graduated in 2008; 45 went to college, including Boston University; Georgetown University; New York University; Penn State University Park; Saint Louis University; University of Miami. Other: 1 entered a postgraduate year, 3 had other specific plans. Mean SAT math: 580, mean SAT writing: 570.

Student Life Upper grades have specified standards of dress, student council, honor system. Discipline rests equally with students and faculty.

Summer Programs ESL, sports, art/fine arts, computer instruction programs offered; session focuses on ESL, soccer; held on campus; accepts boys and girls; open to students from other schools. 275 students usually enrolled. 2009 schedule: July 1 to July 31. Application deadline: June.

Tuition and Aid Day student tuition: €17,320. Tuition installment plan (monthly payment plans, individually arranged payment plans, semester payment plan). Tuition reduction for siblings, need-based scholarship grants, scholarships for children of employees available. In 2008–09, 5% of upper-school students received aid.

Admissions Traditional secondary-level entrance grade is 11. For fall 2008, 77 students applied for upper-level admission, 40 were accepted, 40 enrolled. Achievement/Aptitude/Writing, Comprehensive Test of Basic Skills, ERB, independent norms, Iowa Tests of Basic Skills, PSAT or TAP required. Deadline for receipt of application materials: none. Application fee required: €130. On-campus interview required.

Athletics Interscholastic: basketball (boys, girls), soccer (b,g), volleyball (b,g); coed interscholastic: golf, gymnastics, martial arts, tennis; coed intramural: weight lifting. 1 PE instructor, 7 coaches.

Computers Computers are regularly used in all classes. Computer network features include on-campus library services, Internet access, wireless campus network, Internet filtering or blocking technology. Campus intranet is available to students. The school has a published electronic and media policy.

Contact Ms. Sholeh Farpour, Admissions Head. 34-91 740 19 04. Fax: 34-91 357 2678. E-mail: admissions@asmadrid.org. Web site: www.asmadrid.org.

ANNOUNCEMENT FROM THE SCHOOL Founded in 1961, this college-preparatory coeducational day school enrolls approximately 865 students from more than fifty nations in grade K1 (3 years old) through grade 12. Its primary objective is to provide a traditional US curriculum consistent with that of the best American schools. In addition, students may opt to complete the Spanish *Programa Oficial* and the International Baccalaureate (IB) diploma. Classes are taught in English; Spanish and French are offered as second and third languages. The "Experience Spain" program allows students from other schools in grades 10–12 to attend ASM for a semester or a year while living with host families. Headmaster: William O'Hale. The American School of Madrid is accredited by the Middle States Association, the Spanish Ministry of Education, and the International Baccalaureate Organization.

AMERICAN SCHOOL OF MILAN

Villaggio Mirasole
Noverasco di Opera, Milan 20090, Italy

Head of School: Dr. Alan Austen

General Information Coeducational day college-preparatory, bilingual studies, and International Baccalaureate school. Grades N–12. Founded: 1962. Setting: suburban. Nearest major city is Milan, Italy. 8-acre campus. 1 building on campus. Approved or accredited by Department of Defense Dependents Schools, International Baccalaureate Organization, Middle States Association of Colleges and Schools, and US Department of State. Affiliate member of National Association of Independent Schools; member of European Council of International Schools. Language of instruction: English. Total enrollment: 525. Upper school average class size: 20. Upper school faculty-student ratio: 1:7.

Upper School Student Profile Grade 6: 45 students (27 boys, 18 girls); Grade 7: 43 students (19 boys, 24 girls); Grade 8: 40 students (25 boys, 15 girls); Grade 9: 40 students (18 boys, 22 girls); Grade 10: 45 students (17 boys, 28 girls); Grade 11: 51 students (24 boys, 27 girls); Grade 12: 41 students (21 boys, 20 girls).

Faculty School total: 74. In upper school: 7 men, 18 women; 19 have advanced degrees.

Subjects Offered Algebra, American literature, art, biology, calculus, chemistry, community service, computer programming, computer science, creative writing, ecology, English, English literature, ESL, European history, expository writing, fine arts, French, geology, geometry, grammar, history, Italian, mathematics, music, physical education, physics, psychology, science, social science, social studies, theory of knowledge, trigonometry, world history, world literature, writing.

Graduation Requirements Arts and fine arts (art, music, dance, drama), computer science, English, foreign language, mathematics, physical education (includes health), science, social science, social studies (includes history), 100 hours of CAS (Creativity, Action, Service) each year.

Special Academic Programs International Baccalaureate program; independent study; remedial reading and/or remedial writing; remedial math; ESL (30 students enrolled).

College Admission Counseling 23 students graduated in 2008; all went to college. Median SAT critical reading: 603, median SAT math: 607, median SAT writing: 588.

Student Life Upper grades have specified standards of dress, student council, honor system. Discipline rests primarily with faculty.

Tuition and Aid Day student tuition: €11,450–€15,670. Tuition installment plan (individually arranged payment plans).

Admissions Traditional secondary-level entrance grade is 9. For fall 2008, 132 students applied for upper-level admission, 102 were accepted, 98 enrolled. English for Non-native Speakers required. Deadline for receipt of application materials: none. Application fee required: €250. On-campus interview recommended.

Athletics Interscholastic: aerobics (boys, girls), basketball (b,g), cross-country running (b,g), dance team (g), soccer (b,g), tennis (b,g), track and field (b,g), volleyball (b,g); intramural: golf (b,g); coed intramural: aerobics/dance, ballet, basketball, martial arts, soccer, softball, swimming and diving, table tennis, tennis, volleyball. 3 PE instructors, 4 coaches.
Computers Computers are regularly used in college planning, desktop publishing, ESL, English, ESL, history, humanities, journalism, library, library skills, literary magazine, mathematics, media arts, research skills, science, technology, writing, yearbook classes. Computer network features include on-campus library services, online commercial services, Internet access, wireless campus network, Internet filtering or blocking technology. Student e-mail accounts and computer access in designated common areas are available to students. Students grades are available online. The school has a published electronic and media policy.
Contact Ms. Linda Kavanagh, Director of Admissions. 39-02-53000015. Fax: 39-02-93660932. E-mail: admissions@asmilan.org. Web site: www.asmilan.org.

AMERICAN SCHOOL OF PARIS

41 rue Pasteur
BP 82
Saint Cloud 92210, France
Head of School: Dr. Jack Davis

General Information Coeducational day college-preparatory school. Grades PK–13. Founded: 1946. Setting: suburban. Nearest major city is Paris, France. 12-acre campus. 7 buildings on campus. Approved or accredited by European Council of International Schools and Middle States Association of Colleges and Schools. Affiliate member of National Association of Independent Schools; member of Secondary School Admission Test Board. Language of instruction: English. Total enrollment: 800. Upper school average class size: 15. Upper school faculty-student ratio: 1:7.
Upper School Student Profile Grade 9: 85 students (52 boys, 33 girls); Grade 10: 92 students (52 boys, 40 girls); Grade 11: 85 students (44 boys, 41 girls); Grade 12: 89 students (46 boys, 43 girls); Grade 13: 2 students (2 girls).
Faculty School total: 107. In upper school: 25 men, 26 women; 35 have advanced degrees.
Subjects Offered Algebra, American history, American literature, art, band, biology, calculus, ceramics, chemistry, choir, computer graphics, computer programming, computer science, drawing, economics, English, English literature, environmental science, European history, film and new technologies, filmmaking, French, geometry, global issues, global studies, graphic arts, health, humanities, information technology, music, music technology, painting, photography, physical education, physics, pre-calculus, psychology, science, sculpture, social studies, Spanish, theater, theory of knowledge, trigonometry, Web site design, world history, world literature, writing.
Graduation Requirements Arts and fine arts (art, music, dance, drama), computer science, English, foreign language, mathematics, performing arts, physical education (includes health), science, social studies (includes history).
Special Academic Programs International Baccalaureate program; Advanced Placement exam preparation; honors section; independent study; academic accommodation for the gifted, the musically talented, and the artistically talented; remedial reading and/or remedial writing; remedial math; programs in English, mathematics, general development for dyslexic students; ESL (4 students enrolled).
College Admission Counseling 88 students graduated in 2008; 80 went to college, including Boston University; Northeastern University; The American University of Paris; Tufts University. Other: 1 entered military service, 1 entered a postgraduate year, 6 had other specific plans. Mean SAT critical reading: 604, mean SAT math: 639, mean SAT writing: 614.
Student Life Upper grades have specified standards of dress, student council. Discipline rests primarily with faculty.
Summer Programs Enrichment, ESL, sports, art/fine arts, computer instruction programs offered; session focuses on English and French as a Second Language; held on campus; accepts boys and girls; open to students from other schools. 900 students usually enrolled. 2009 schedule: June 22 to July 24. Application deadline: none.
Tuition and Aid Day student tuition: €23,500. Tuition installment plan (monthly payment plans, individually arranged payment plans). Need-based scholarship grants available. In 2008–09, 3% of upper-school students received aid. Total amount of financial aid awarded in 2008–09: €24,600.
Admissions Traditional secondary-level entrance grade is 9. For fall 2008, 165 students applied for upper-level admission, 157 were accepted, 142 enrolled. Deadline for receipt of application materials: none. Application fee required: €800. On-campus interview recommended.
Athletics Interscholastic: baseball (boys), basketball (b,g), cross-country running (b,g), dance team (g), golf (b,g), soccer (b,g), softball (g), swimming and diving (b,g), tennis (b,g), track and field (b,g), volleyball (b,g); coed interscholastic: golf; coed intramural: basketball, climbing, soccer, softball, track and field. 4 PE instructors, 6 coaches.
Computers Computers are regularly used in English, foreign language, graphic arts, information technology, mathematics, music, science classes. Computer network features include on-campus library services, online commercial services, Internet access, wireless campus network, on-line learning platform. Campus intranet, student e-mail accounts, and computer access in designated common areas are available to students. Students grades are available online.
Contact Mrs. Philipa Lane, Admissions Assistant. 331-41.12.86.55. Fax: 331-41.12.82.47. E-mail: admissions@asparis.fr. Web site: www.asparis.org.

THE AMERICAN SCHOOL OF PUERTO VALLARTA

Albatros # 29
Marina Vallarta
Puerto Vallarta, Jalisco 48354, Mexico
Head of School: Mr. Gerald Selitzer

General Information Coeducational day college-preparatory, arts, bilingual studies, and technology school. Grades N–12. Founded: 1986. Setting: small town. Nearest major city is Puerto Vallarta, Mexico. 7-acre campus. 2 buildings on campus. Approved or accredited by Southern Association of Colleges and Schools, US Department of State, and state department of education. Languages of instruction: English and Spanish. Endowment: 2 million Mexican pesos. Total enrollment: 366. Upper school average class size: 25. Upper school faculty-student ratio: 1:7.
Upper School Student Profile Grade 10: 21 students (14 boys, 7 girls); Grade 11: 24 students (14 boys, 10 girls); Grade 12: 29 students (20 boys, 9 girls).
Faculty School total: 43. In upper school: 10 have advanced degrees.
Subjects Offered Advanced Placement courses, algebra, American literature, art, biology, British literature, calculus, calculus-AP, chemistry, chorus, civics, computer science, computers, conceptual physics, earth science, economics-AP, English, English literature, English literature and composition-AP, etymology, geography, journalism, law, life science, literature, literature and composition-AP, mathematics, Mexican history, Mexican literature, philosophy, physical science, physics, pre-algebra, pre-calculus, robotics, Spanish, Spanish language-AP, Spanish literature, Spanish literature-AP, trigonometry, U.S. history, U.S. history-AP, world history.
Graduation Requirements Art, British literature, calculus, computer education, conceptual physics, economics, English literature, mathematics, Mexican history, Mexican literature, physical education (includes health), Spanish, Spanish literature, U.S. history.
Special Academic Programs Advanced Placement exam preparation; independent study; remedial reading and/or remedial writing; remedial math.
College Admission Counseling 25 students graduated in 2008; 20 went to college, including Austin College; Beloit College; Cornell University; Haverford College; Rochester Institute of Technology; The University of British Columbia. Other: 2 went to work, 3 had other specific plans.
Student Life Upper grades have uniform requirement, student council, honor system. Discipline rests primarily with faculty.
Summer Programs Remediation, ESL, sports programs offered; session focuses on remediation and make-up; held on campus; accepts boys and girls; open to students from other schools. 10 students usually enrolled. 2009 schedule: July 8 to August 15. Application deadline: none.
Tuition and Aid Day student tuition: $5348–$8424. Tuition installment plan (monthly payment plans, individually arranged payment plans). Tuition reduction for siblings, need-based scholarship grants available. In 2008–09, 10% of upper-school students received aid.
Admissions Traditional secondary-level entrance grade is 10. For fall 2008, 19 students applied for upper-level admission, 6 were accepted, 2 enrolled. Achievement tests, admissions testing, English language and math, reading, and mental ability tests required. Deadline for receipt of application materials: none. No application fee required. Interview required.
Athletics Interscholastic: basketball (boys, girls), golf (b,g), soccer (b,g), tennis (b,g); intramural: basketball (b,g), jump rope (g). 3 PE instructors, 4 coaches, 3 athletic trainers.
Computers Computers are regularly used in computer applications, history, keyboarding, lab/keyboard, science, social studies, Spanish, technology, yearbook classes. Computer network features include on-campus library services, Internet access, wireless campus network, Internet filtering or blocking technology. Campus intranet and computer access in designated common areas are available to students. Students grades are available online. The school has a published electronic and media policy.
Contact Mrs. Elise Langley, Admissions Coordinator. 52-322 226 7672. Fax: 52-322 226 7677. E-mail: llangley@aspv.edu.mx. Web site: www.aspv.edu.mx.

THE AMERICAN SCHOOL OF THE HAGUE

Rijksstraatweg 200
Wassenaar 2241 BX, Netherlands
Head of School: Richard Spradling

General Information Coeducational day college-preparatory, arts, technology, and applied and performing arts school. Grades PK–12. Founded: 1953. Setting: suburban. Nearest major city is The Hague, Netherlands. 11-acre campus. 1 building on campus. Approved or accredited by European Council of International Schools, International Baccalaureate Organization, Middle States Association of Colleges and Schools, and The College Board. Language of instruction: English. Total enrollment: 1,100. Upper school average class size: 18. Upper school faculty-student ratio: 1:8.

Upper School Student Profile Grade 9: 103 students (48 boys, 55 girls); Grade 10: 101 students (59 boys, 42 girls); Grade 11: 96 students (53 boys, 43 girls); Grade 12: 90 students (37 boys, 53 girls).

Faculty School total: 142. In upper school: 24 men, 27 women; 40 have advanced degrees.

Subjects Offered 3-dimensional design, advanced chemistry, advertising design, algebra, American literature, art history, art-AP, band, biology, biology-AP, calculus, calculus-AP, ceramics, chemistry, chemistry-AP, choir, comparative government and politics, computer applications, computer multimedia, computer music, computer science, computer-aided design, creative writing, current events, dance, debate, dramatic arts, drawing, Dutch, earth science, economics, economics-AP, English, English literature, English-AP, environmental systems, ESL, European history, French, French-AP, geometry, German, German-AP, global studies, guidance, health and wellness, history of the Americas, honors algebra, honors geometry, human geography—AP, information technology, instrumental music, international affairs, International Baccalaureate courses, jazz band, math analysis, math methods, mathematics-AP, multimedia, music composition, music technology, music theory-AP, music-AP, orchestra, peer counseling, photography, physical education, physics, physics-AP, pre-calculus, programming, psychology, public speaking, sculpture, senior composition, sociology, Spanish, Spanish-AP, speech and debate, stagecraft, statistics-AP, student publications, studio art, theater arts, theater design and production, theory of knowledge, trigonometry, U.S. history, U.S. history-AP, video film production, Web site design, Western civilization, world history, writing, yearbook.

Graduation Requirements Arts, computer information systems, English, health and wellness, mathematics, modern languages, physical education (includes health), science, service learning/internship, social studies (includes history).

Special Academic Programs International Baccalaureate program; Advanced Placement exam preparation; honors section; independent study; academic accommodation for the gifted, the musically talented, and the artistically talented; remedial reading and/or remedial writing; ESL (20 students enrolled).

College Admission Counseling 99 students graduated in 2008; 92 went to college, including Harvard University; McGill University; Michigan State University; University of California, Berkeley; University of Edinburgh; Virginia Polytechnic Institute and State University. Other: 1 entered military service, 3 entered a postgraduate year, 3 had other specific plans. Mean SAT critical reading: 574, mean SAT math: 591, mean SAT writing: 575, mean combined SAT: 1740.

Student Life Upper grades have specified standards of dress, student council, honor system. Discipline rests primarily with faculty.

Tuition and Aid Day student tuition: €16,200. Tuition installment plan (individually arranged payment plans).

Admissions For fall 2008, 88 students applied for upper-level admission, 85 were accepted, 76 enrolled. Deadline for receipt of application materials: none. No application fee required. Interview required.

Athletics Interscholastic: baseball (boys), basketball (b,g), cross-country running (b,g), soccer (b,g), softball (g), swimming and diving (b,g), tennis (b,g), track and field (b,g), volleyball (b,g); intramural: baseball (b), basketball (b,g), dance team (g), soccer (b,g), softball (g), volleyball (b,g); coed interscholastic: cheering. 2 PE instructors, 9 coaches.

Computers Computers are regularly used in all classes. Computer network features include on-campus library services, online commercial services, Internet access, wireless campus network, Internet filtering or blocking technology. Campus intranet and student e-mail accounts are available to students. Students grades are available online. The school has a published electronic and media policy.

Contact Laura Romains, Admissions Director. 31-70-512-1080. Fax: 31-70-512-1076. E-mail: admissions@ash.nl. Web site: www.ash.nl.

ANNOUNCEMENT FROM THE SCHOOL The American School of The Hague (ASH) serves the educational needs of the American and international corporate and diplomatic communities in the Netherlands. Students represent sixty cultures; half are from North America. While ASH reflects the American educational philosophy, the diverse backgrounds of the students foster teaching and learning in the context of international understanding and global citizenship. ASH is a school with a rigorous academic program. The High School curriculum emphasizes preparation for university studies in all countries of the world. Graduates earn a U.S. high school diploma. In addition, students have the opportunity to earn an International Baccalaureate Diploma or to specialize in Advanced Placement subjects. ASH students move with confidence to new schools throughout the world, and more than 98% of each graduating class enters university. The academic program includes a wide range of fine and applied arts courses, with a curriculum that is technologically competitive throughout the disciplines. A full sports program and extracurricular activities are an important part of student life. The Hague International Model United Nations, a major event for many ASH High School students, is sponsored by the School each January for more than 3,000 international participants. The arts program offers individual and group instruction in vocal and instrumental music, and the ASH Jazz Band is well known throughout Europe. Athletic teams in ten sports travel throughout Europe competing with other international schools. The 11-acre contemporary campus has spacious classrooms, specialized teaching areas, and multiple science and multimedia labs in separate academic wings for the Elementary School, Middle School, and High School. Facilities include three libraries, holding a total of 50,000 volumes; two cafeterias; high-quality facilities for music and theater; and four gymnasia plus a double sport hall. The grounds include outdoor areas for all age groups, basketball courts, and soccer and baseball fields.

ANDREWS OSBORNE ACADEMY

38588 Mentor Avenue
Willoughby, Ohio 44094
Head of School: Dr. David N. Rath

General Information Coeducational boarding and day college-preparatory and arts school. Boarding grades 7–12, day grades PK–12. Founded: 1910. Setting: suburban. Nearest major city is Cleveland. Students are housed in single-sex dormitories. 300-acre campus. 12 buildings on campus. Approved or accredited by Independent Schools Association of the Central States, Midwest Association of Boarding Schools, Ohio Association of Independent Schools, The Association of Boarding Schools, and Ohio Department of Education. Member of National Association of Independent Schools and Secondary School Admission Test Board. Endowment: $12 million. Total enrollment: 304. Upper school average class size: 10. Upper school faculty-student ratio: 1:5.

Upper School Student Profile Grade 9: 19 students (19 girls); Grade 10: 32 students (32 girls); Grade 11: 31 students (31 girls); Grade 12: 24 students (24 girls). 10 states are represented in upper school student body.

Faculty School total: 25. In upper school: 7 men, 18 women; 18 have advanced degrees; 10 reside on campus.

Subjects Offered Algebra, American government, American literature, art, astronomy, biology, biology-AP, calculus, calculus-AP, ceramics, chemistry, chemistry-AP, choir, choral music, community service, CPR, drama, economics, English, English composition, English language-AP, English literature, English literature and composition-AP, environmental science, equine studies, ESL, ethics, film history, fine arts, first aid, French, French language-AP, geometry with art applications, government, grammar, health science, history, honors algebra, honors English, honors geometry, independent study, instrumental music, Mandarin, mathematics, music, painting, physical education, physics, portfolio art, pre-calculus, probability and statistics, science, social studies, Spanish, Spanish language-AP, speech, studio art, textiles, theater, TOEFL preparation, U.S. history, U.S. history-AP, women in literature, world history.

Graduation Requirements Algebra, arts and fine arts (art, music, dance, drama), biology, computer literacy, CPR, English, foreign language, geometry, mathematics, physical education (includes health), science, social studies (includes history), speech, acceptance into at least one U.S. college or university. Community service is required.

Special Academic Programs Advanced Placement exam preparation; honors section; independent study; study at local college for college credit; academic accommodation for the gifted, the musically talented, and the artistically talented; ESL (35 students enrolled).

College Admission Counseling 29 students graduated in 2007; all went to college, including DePaul University; Emory University; John Carroll University; Mercyhurst College; The Ohio State University. Mean SAT critical reading: 561, mean SAT math: 548, mean SAT writing: 537, mean combined SAT: 1646, mean composite ACT: 24.

Student Life Upper grades have specified standards of dress, student council, honor system. Discipline rests primarily with faculty.

Tuition and Aid Day student tuition: $16,050; 5-day tuition and room/board: $23,100; 7-day tuition and room/board: $28,350. Tuition installment plan (monthly payment plans, individually arranged payment plans). Merit scholarship grants, need-based scholarship grants available. In 2007–08, 50% of upper-school students received aid; total upper-school merit-scholarship money awarded: $87,190. Total amount of financial aid awarded in 2007–08: $401,000.

Admissions Traditional secondary-level entrance grade is 9. ISEE, SSAT, TOEFL or SLEP or writing sample required. Deadline for receipt of application materials: none. Application fee required: $40. On-campus interview required.

Athletics Interscholastic: baseball (boys), basketball (b,g), lacrosse (b,g), soccer (b,g), softball (g), tennis (b,g), volleyball (g); intramural: flag football (g), table tennis (g); coed interscholastic: equestrian sports, horseback riding; coed intramural: alpine skiing, equestrian sports, horseback riding, skiing (downhill), snowboarding. 1 PE instructor, 1 coach, 1 athletic trainer.

Computers Computers are regularly used in art, English, foreign language, history, mathematics, music, science classes. Computer network features include on-campus

library services, online commercial services, Internet access, Internet filtering or blocking technology. Student e-mail accounts and computer access in designated common areas are available to students. Students grades are available online. The school has a published electronic and media policy.
Contact Mr. Doug Goodman, Director of Admission. 440-942-3600 Ext. 226. Fax: 440-954-5020. E-mail: dgoodman@AndrewsOsborne.org. Web site: www.AndrewsOsborne.org.

See Close-Up on page 666.

ANNIE WRIGHT SCHOOL

827 North Tacoma Avenue
Tacoma, Washington 98403
Head of School: Rick Clarke

General Information Girls' boarding and coeducational day college-preparatory, arts, technology, and mathematics, science and music school, affiliated with Episcopal Church. Boarding girls grades 9–12, day boys grades PS–8, day girls grades PS–12. Founded: 1884. Setting: suburban. Nearest major city is Seattle. Students are housed in single-sex dormitories. 10-acre campus. 2 buildings on campus. Approved or accredited by National Association of Episcopal Schools, National Independent Private Schools Association, Northwest Association of Schools and Colleges, Pacific Northwest Association of Independent Schools, The Association of Boarding Schools, and Washington Department of Education. Member of National Association of Independent Schools and Secondary School Admission Test Board. Endowment: $15 million. Total enrollment: 477. Upper school average class size: 11. Upper school faculty-student ratio: 1:7.
Upper School Student Profile Grade 9: 30 students (30 girls); Grade 10: 31 students (31 girls); Grade 11: 40 students (40 girls); Grade 12: 38 students (38 girls). 50% of students are boarding students. 64% are state residents. 7 states are represented in upper school student body. 31% are international students. International students from Bermuda, China, Republic of Korea, Taiwan, United Republic of Tanzania, and Venezuela; 3 other countries represented in student body. 10% of students are members of Episcopal Church.
Faculty School total: 75. In upper school: 12 men, 17 women; 15 have advanced degrees; 9 reside on campus.
Subjects Offered Algebra, American history, American literature, anatomy, art, art history, biology, calculus, ceramics, chemistry, computer programming, computer science, creative writing, dance, drama, earth science, economics, English, English literature, ESL, fine arts, French, geometry, government/civics, health, history, Japanese, mathematics, music, music history, physical education, physics, religion, science, social studies, Spanish, theater, world history, world literature.
Graduation Requirements Arts and fine arts (art, music, dance, drama), computer science, English, foreign language, mathematics, physical education (includes health), religion (includes Bible studies and theology), science, social studies (includes history), swim safety test.
Special Academic Programs Independent study; term-away projects; study abroad.
College Admission Counseling 16 students graduated in 2008; 15 went to college, including Babson College; Dartmouth College; Middlebury College; New York University; The George Washington University; University of Washington. Other: 1 had other specific plans.
Student Life Upper grades have uniform requirement, student council, honor system. Discipline rests equally with students and faculty.
Tuition and Aid Day student tuition: $17,100; 7-day tuition and room/board: $34,000. Tuition installment plan (monthly payment plans, individually arranged payment plans). Merit scholarship grants, need-based scholarship grants available. In 2008–09, 43% of upper-school students received aid; total upper-school merit-scholarship money awarded: $300,000. Total amount of financial aid awarded in 2008–09: $300,000.
Admissions Traditional secondary-level entrance grade is 9. SSAT and TOEFL required. Deadline for receipt of application materials: March 3. Application fee required: $75. Interview required.
Athletics Interscholastic: basketball, crew, cross-country running, golf, soccer. 5 PE instructors, 10 coaches, 1 athletic trainer.
Computers Computers are regularly used in all classes.
Contact Jesse W. Fortney, Director of Admissions and Financial Aid. 253-284-8601. Fax: 253-572-3616. E-mail: admission@aw.org. Web site: www.aw.org.

ANTELOPE VALLEY CHRISTIAN SCHOOL

3700 West Avenue L
Lancaster, California 93536
Head of School: Mr. Douglas McKenzie

General Information Coeducational boarding and day college-preparatory school, affiliated with Assemblies of God. Boarding grades 6–12, day grades K–12. Founded: 1987. Setting: suburban. Nearest major city is Los Angeles. Students are housed in single-sex by floor dormitories. 35-acre campus. 8 buildings on campus. Approved or accredited by Association of Christian Schools International, Western Association of Schools and Colleges, and California Department of Education. Total enrollment: 257. Upper school average class size: 24. Upper school faculty-student ratio: 1:11.
Upper School Student Profile Grade 6: 15 students (11 boys, 4 girls); Grade 7: 15 students (2 boys, 13 girls); Grade 8: 25 students (10 boys, 15 girls); Grade 9: 18 students (8 boys, 10 girls); Grade 10: 25 students (18 boys, 7 girls); Grade 11: 10 students (5 boys, 5 girls); Grade 12: 13 students (8 boys, 5 girls). 40% of students are boarding students. 60% are state residents. 1 state is represented in upper school student body. 40% are international students. International students from Cambodia, China, Hong Kong, and Republic of Korea. 70% of students are Assemblies of God.
Faculty School total: 28. In upper school: 7 men, 8 women; 3 have advanced degrees; 4 reside on campus.
Subjects Offered Acting, advanced math, advanced TOEFL/grammar, American government-AP, American history-AP, American literature, American literature-AP, analytic geometry, athletics, Bible, biology-AP, business, calculus, cheerleading, chemistry, computer programming, computers, consumer economics, consumer mathematics, design, drama, drawing, earth science, economics, electives, English, English as a foreign language, English language and composition-AP, English language-AP, English literature and composition-AP, English-AP, fine arts, foreign language, geography, geometry, government, government/civics, health, health education, history, history-AP, journalism, leadership and service, mathematics, music, newspaper, physical education, physics, SAT preparation, science, TOEFL preparation, trigonometry, typing, U.S. government, U.S. history, weight training, weightlifting, world geography, world history, world literature, writing, yearbook.
Special Academic Programs 4 Advanced Placement exams for which test preparation is offered; ESL (20 students enrolled).
College Admission Counseling 18 students graduated in 2008; 16 went to college. Other: 1 went to work, 1 had other specific plans.
Student Life Upper grades have specified standards of dress, student council, honor system. Discipline rests primarily with faculty. Attendance at religious services is required.
Summer Programs Remediation, advancement, ESL programs offered; session focuses on remediation/make-up, advancement; held on campus; accepts boys and girls; open to students from other schools. 50 students usually enrolled. 2009 schedule: June 15 to July 24. Application deadline: May 15.
Tuition and Aid Tuition reduction for siblings, need-based scholarship grants available. In 2008–09, 2% of upper-school students received aid.
Admissions Traditional secondary-level entrance grade is 9. Deadline for receipt of application materials: none. Application fee required: $100. Interview recommended.
Athletics Interscholastic: baseball (boys), basketball (b,g), cheering (g), flag football (b,g), football (b), physical fitness (b,g), physical training (b), softball (g), volleyball (g), weight training (b); coed interscholastic: physical fitness, soccer, volleyball. 2 PE instructors, 5 coaches.
Computers Computers are regularly used in construction classes. Computer network features include Internet access, wireless campus network, Internet filtering or blocking technology. Student e-mail accounts are available to students. Students grades are available online. The school has a published electronic and media policy.
Contact Mrs. Christina M. Clark, Director of International Programs. 661-943-0044 Ext. 122. Fax: 661-943-6774. E-mail: cclark@avcs.edu. Web site: www.avcs.edu.

ARCHBISHOP CURLEY HIGH SCHOOL

3701 Sinclair Lane
Baltimore, Maryland 21213
Head of School: Fr. Michael T. Martin

General Information Boys' day college-preparatory school, affiliated with Roman Catholic Church. Grades 9–12. Founded: 1961. Setting: urban. 33-acre campus. 2 buildings on campus. Approved or accredited by Middle States Association of Colleges and Schools and Maryland Department of Education. Endowment: $3.2 million. Total enrollment: 581. Upper school average class size: 22. Upper school faculty-student ratio: 1:14.
Upper School Student Profile Grade 9: 147 students (147 boys); Grade 10: 150 students (150 boys); Grade 11: 141 students (141 boys); Grade 12: 143 students (143 boys). 70% of students are Roman Catholic.
Faculty School total: 51. In upper school: 41 men, 10 women; 24 have advanced degrees.
Subjects Offered 20th century world history, 3-dimensional design, accounting, advanced chemistry, advanced computer applications, advanced math, algebra, American government, American government-AP, American history, American history-AP, American literature, analytic geometry, art, art appreciation, astronomy, band, Basic programming, biology, biology-AP, British literature, British literature (honors), business law, business mathematics, calculus, calculus-AP, campus ministry, Catholic belief and practice, chemistry, chemistry-AP, choral music, Christian and Hebrew scripture, Christian doctrine, Christian ethics, computer applications, computer keyboarding, computer studies, concert band, consumer law, consumer mathematics, earth science, English, English literature and composition-AP, environmental science, ethical decision making, European history, fine arts, French, freshman seminar, geography, geometry, government, government-AP, health, history of the Catholic Church, HTML design, instrumental music, jazz band, journalism, Latin, Life of Christ, music theory, photography, physical science, physics, physics-AP, pre-algebra, pre-calculus, probability and statistics, psychology, psychology-AP, reading/study skills, SAT/ACT preparation, Spanish, Spanish language-AP.

Graduation Requirements Algebra, American government, American history, art appreciation, biology, British literature, chemistry, church history, computer applications, computer keyboarding, English, foreign language, geometry, Life of Christ, physical fitness, physics, world history, world religions, 30 hours of community service with a written paper.
Special Academic Programs Advanced Placement exam preparation; honors section; independent study; study at local college for college credit; remedial reading and/or remedial writing; remedial math; programs in English, mathematics for dyslexic students.
College Admission Counseling 149 students graduated in 2008; they went to Loyola College in Maryland; Towson University; University of Maryland, Baltimore County; University of Maryland, College Park.
Student Life Upper grades have specified standards of dress, student council, honor system. Discipline rests primarily with faculty. Attendance at religious services is required.
Summer Programs Remediation, enrichment, advancement, sports, art/fine arts programs offered; held on campus; accepts boys and girls; open to students from other schools. 2009 schedule: June 15 to August 20. Application deadline: June 15.
Tuition and Aid Day student tuition: $10,100. Tuition installment plan (Academic Management Services Plan, monthly payment plans, individually arranged payment plans). Tuition reduction for siblings, merit scholarship grants, need-based scholarship grants, paying campus jobs available.
Admissions Traditional secondary-level entrance grade is 9. For fall 2008, 304 students applied for upper-level admission, 159 enrolled. High School Placement Test (closed version) from Scholastic Testing Service required. Deadline for receipt of application materials: January 4. Application fee required: $10. Interview required.
Athletics Interscholastic: baseball, basketball, cross-country running, football, golf, ice hockey, indoor track & field, lacrosse, soccer, swimming and diving, tennis, track and field, volleyball, wrestling; intramural: basketball, bowling, golf, martial arts, tennis, touch football, volleyball, weight lifting, weight training, whiffle ball, wrestling. 2 PE instructors, 32 coaches, 1 athletic trainer.
Computers Computers are regularly used in English, graphic arts, journalism, library, photography, SAT preparation, science, technology classes. Computer network features include on-campus library services, Internet access.
Contact Mr. John Tucker, Admissions Director. 410-485-5000 Ext. 289. Fax: 410-485-1090. E-mail: jtucker@archbishopcurley.org. Web site: www.archbishopcurley.org.

ARCHBISHOP EDWARD A. MCCARTHY HIGH SCHOOL

5451 South Flamingo Road
Fort Lauderdale, Florida 33330

Head of School: Dr. Richard Perhla

General Information Coeducational day college-preparatory, arts, business, religious studies, bilingual studies, and technology school, affiliated with Roman Catholic Church. Grades 9–12. Founded: 1998. Setting: suburban. 8 buildings on campus. Approved or accredited by Southern Association of Colleges and Schools and Florida Department of Education. Total enrollment: 1,400. Upper school average class size: 25.
Student Life Upper grades have uniform requirement, student council, honor system. Discipline rests primarily with faculty.
Tuition and Aid Tuition installment plan (FACTS Tuition Payment Plan). Tuition reduction for siblings available.
Admissions High School Placement Test required. Deadline for receipt of application materials: January 27. Application fee required.
Contact Ms. Kathy Manning, Director of Admissions. 954-434-8820. Fax: 954-680-4835. E-mail: kmanning@mccarthyhigh.org.

ARCHBISHOP HOBAN HIGH SCHOOL

1 Holy Cross Boulevard
Akron, Ohio 44306

Head of School: Br. Kenneth Haders, CSC

General Information Coeducational day college-preparatory, arts, business, religious studies, technology, and family and consumer sciences school, affiliated with Roman Catholic Church. Grades 9–12. Founded: 1953. Setting: urban. 55-acre campus. 3 buildings on campus. Approved or accredited by National Christian School Association, North Central Association of Colleges and Schools, Ohio Catholic Schools Accreditation Association (OCSAA), and Ohio Department of Education. Endowment: $6 million. Total enrollment: 891. Upper school average class size: 23. Upper school faculty-student ratio: 1:13.
Upper School Student Profile Grade 9: 239 students (103 boys, 136 girls); Grade 10: 209 students (104 boys, 105 girls); Grade 11: 235 students (120 boys, 115 girls); Grade 12: 208 students (118 boys, 90 girls). 80% of students are Roman Catholic.
Faculty School total: 71. In upper school: 40 men, 30 women; 46 have advanced degrees.
Subjects Offered Accounting, Advanced Placement courses, advanced studio art-AP, algebra, American literature, anatomy and physiology, art, astronomy, Basic programming, biology, biology-AP, British literature, calculus-AP, Catholic belief and practice, chemistry, chemistry-AP, child development, choir, Christian and Hebrew scripture, church history, computer applications, computer graphics, computer technologies, conceptual physics, concert band, concert choir, creative arts, digital imaging, drama, drawing and design, earth science, economics, electronic music, engineering, English, English literature and composition-AP, environmental science, European history-AP, fine arts, food and nutrition, French, geometry, health education, history of the Catholic Church, honors algebra, honors English, honors geometry, honors world history, Italian, Latin, learning strategies, marching band, music theory, painting, peer counseling, physical education, physics, pre-algebra, pre-calculus, social justice, Spanish, statistics-AP, studio art, trigonometry, U.S. government, U.S. history, U.S. history-AP, values and decisions, Web site design, world affairs, world cultures, world literature, yearbook.
Graduation Requirements Algebra, American literature, arts and fine arts (art, music, dance, drama), biology, British literature, Catholic belief and practice, Christian and Hebrew scripture, church history, economics, electives, English, geometry, health education, moral theology, physical education (includes health), religious studies, U.S. government, U.S. history, world cultures, world literature, Christian Service totaling 75 hours over four years.
Special Academic Programs Honors section; academic accommodation for the gifted; remedial reading and/or remedial writing; remedial math.
College Admission Counseling 218 students graduated in 2008; 210 went to college, including Kent State University; Ohio University; The Ohio State University; The University of Akron; The University of Toledo; University of Dayton. Other: 4 went to work, 3 entered military service, 1 had other specific plans. Median SAT critical reading: 550, median SAT math: 550, median SAT writing: 550, median composite ACT: 24. 26% scored over 600 on SAT critical reading, 34% scored over 600 on SAT math, 25% scored over 600 on SAT writing, 25% scored over 1800 on combined SAT, 37% scored over 26 on composite ACT.
Student Life Upper grades have specified standards of dress, student council, honor system. Discipline rests primarily with faculty. Attendance at religious services is required.
Tuition and Aid Day student tuition: $7800. Tuition installment plan (FACTS Tuition Payment Plan, individually arranged payment plans). Tuition reduction for siblings, merit scholarship grants, need-based scholarship grants, paying campus jobs available. In 2008–09, 56% of upper-school students received aid; total upper-school merit-scholarship money awarded: $264,600. Total amount of financial aid awarded in 2008–09: $1,504,618.
Admissions Traditional secondary-level entrance grade is 9. For fall 2008, 305 students applied for upper-level admission, 250 were accepted, 240 enrolled. High School Placement Test required. Deadline for receipt of application materials: none. No application fee required. Interview recommended.
Athletics Interscholastic: baseball (boys), basketball (b,g), bowling (b,g), cross-country running (b,g), dance team (g), football (b), golf (b,g), gymnastics (g), ice hockey (b), indoor track & field (b), lacrosse (b), soccer (b,g), softball (g), swimming and diving (b,g), tennis (b,g), track and field (b,g), volleyball (b,g), wrestling (b); intramural: flag football (g); coed interscholastic: cheering; coed intramural: basketball, strength & conditioning, ultimate Frisbee, weight training. 1 PE instructor, 1 athletic trainer.
Computers Computers are regularly used in all classes. Computer network features include on-campus library services, Internet access, wireless campus network, Internet filtering or blocking technology. Computer access in designated common areas is available to students. Students grades are available online. The school has a published electronic and media policy.
Contact Mrs. Katy Karg, Admissions Counselor. 330-773-6658 Ext. 215. Fax: 330-773-9100. E-mail: kargk@hoban.org. Web site: www.hoban.org.

ARCHBISHOP MCNICHOLAS HIGH SCHOOL

6536 Beechmont Avenue
Cincinnati, Ohio 45230-2098

Head of School: Mr. Brian D. Pendergest

General Information Coeducational day college-preparatory, general academic, arts, business, technology, and Services for the Learning Disabled school, affiliated with Roman Catholic Church. Grades 9–12. Founded: 1951. Setting: suburban. 48-acre campus. 3 buildings on campus. Approved or accredited by National Catholic Education Association, North Central Association of Colleges and Schools, Ohio Catholic Schools Accreditation Association (OCSAA), The College Board, and Ohio Department of Education. Total enrollment: 738. Upper school average class size: 18. Upper school faculty-student ratio: 1:11.
Upper School Student Profile Grade 9: 178 students (91 boys, 87 girls); Grade 10: 189 students (91 boys, 98 girls); Grade 11: 184 students (90 boys, 94 girls); Grade 12: 187 students (101 boys, 86 girls). 92% of students are Roman Catholic.
Faculty School total: 52. In upper school: 19 men, 33 women; 26 have advanced degrees.
Subjects Offered Accounting, advanced computer applications, advanced math, Advanced Placement courses, advanced studio art-AP, algebra, American history, American history-AP, American legal systems, American literature, anatomy and physiology, architectural drawing, band, Basic programming, biology, biology-AP, British literature, business applications, calculus-AP, Catholic belief and practice, ceramics, chemistry, choir, church history, civics, communication skills, computer art, computer processing, computer programming, computer programming-AP, computer

technologies, computer-aided design, concert band, concert choir, creative writing, design, developmental math, digital photography, directing, drama, drawing and design, English, English literature and composition-AP, European history-AP, French, government and politics-AP, guitar, health, honors algebra, honors English, honors geometry, integrated science, intro to computers, journalism, Latin, Latin-AP, Life of Christ, marching band, moral theology, music appreciation, music theory-AP, Native American studies, photography, physical education, physical science, physics, physics-AP, portfolio art, pottery, pre-algebra, pre-calculus, reading, reading/study skills, skills for success, Spanish, Spanish language-AP, Spanish literature-AP, speech and debate, street law, studio art, studio art-AP, theater, U.S. government and politics-AP, video film production, Web site design, world history, world religions, writing.

Graduation Requirements Algebra, American government, American history, American literature, arts and fine arts (art, music, dance, drama), biology, British literature, Catholic belief and practice, civics, communication skills, computer applications, English, foreign language, geometry, mathematics, religion (includes Bible studies and theology), science, social justice, world history, senior-year retreat, a minimum of 40 hours of community service.

Special Academic Programs Advanced Placement exam preparation; honors section; academic accommodation for the gifted, the musically talented, and the artistically talented; remedial reading and/or remedial writing; remedial math; programs in English, mathematics, general development for dyslexic students.

College Admission Counseling 206 students graduated in 2008; 196 went to college, including Miami University; Northern Kentucky University; Ohio University; University of Cincinnati; University of Dayton; Xavier University. Other: 10 went to work. 24% scored over 26 on composite ACT.

Student Life Upper grades have uniform requirement, student council. Discipline rests primarily with faculty. Attendance at religious services is required.

Summer Programs Remediation programs offered; session focuses on remediation of failed courses or new PE credit; held on campus; accepts boys and girls; not open to students from other schools. 40 students usually enrolled. 2009 schedule: June 15 to July 19. Application deadline: June 9.

Tuition and Aid Day student tuition: $7500. Tuition installment plan (FACTS Tuition Payment Plan, individually arranged payment plans, Sallie Mae). Tuition reduction for siblings, merit scholarship grants, need-based scholarship grants available. In 2008–09, 11% of upper-school students received aid; total upper-school merit-scholarship money awarded: $199,550. Total amount of financial aid awarded in 2008–09: $326,450.

Admissions Traditional secondary-level entrance grade is 9. High School Placement Test (closed version) from Scholastic Testing Service required. Deadline for receipt of application materials: December 12. No application fee required.

Athletics Interscholastic: baseball (boys), basketball (b,g), bowling (b,g), cheering (g), dance team (g), football (b), golf (b,g), soccer (b,g), softball (g), track and field (b,g), volleyball (b,g), wrestling (b); coed interscholastic: cross-country running, swimming and diving, track and field; coed intramural: bicycling, flag football, skiing (downhill), snowboarding. 44 coaches, 3 athletic trainers.

Computers Computers are regularly used in computer applications, data processing, English, foreign language, French, graphic design, history, journalism, mathematics, multimedia, photography, programming, publications, reading, religion, science, Spanish, video film production, Web site design, writing classes. Computer network features include on-campus library services, Internet access, Internet filtering or blocking technology, student files, Edline. Students grades are available online. The school has a published electronic and media policy.

Contact Mrs. Catherine H Sherrick, Director of Recruitment and Retention. 513-231-3500 Ext. 5817. Fax: 513-231-1351. E-mail: csherrick@mcnhs.org. Web site: www.mcnhs.org.

ARCHBISHOP MITTY HIGH SCHOOL

5000 Mitty Avenue
San Jose, California 95129

Head of School: Mr. Tim Brosnan

General Information Coeducational day college-preparatory, arts, religious studies, and technology school, affiliated with Roman Catholic Church. Grades 9–12. Founded: 1964. Setting: suburban. 24-acre campus. 11 buildings on campus. Approved or accredited by Western Association of Schools and Colleges, Western Catholic Education Association, and California Department of Education. Endowment: $6.5 million. Total enrollment: 1,503. Upper school average class size: 27. Upper school faculty-student ratio: 1:17.

Upper School Student Profile Grade 9: 418 students (195 boys, 223 girls); Grade 10: 413 students (191 boys, 222 girls); Grade 11: 425 students (179 boys, 246 girls); Grade 12: 375 students (167 boys, 208 girls). 75% of students are Roman Catholic.

Faculty School total: 110. In upper school: 55 men, 55 women; 65 have advanced degrees.

Subjects Offered 3-dimensional art, acting, American government-AP, American history-AP, American literature-AP, ancient world history, art, biology, biology-AP, British literature, calculus, calculus-AP, Catholic belief and practice, chemistry, chemistry-AP, choral music, chorus, church history, college placement, college writing, community service, computer graphics, computer multimedia, concert band, concert choir, drawing, economics and history, English, English language and composition-AP, English literature, English literature-AP, French, French language-AP, French literature-AP, French studies, French-AP, geometry, history-AP, honors algebra, honors English, honors geometry, honors U.S. history, honors world history, music, music appreciation, music theory-AP, philosophy, physics, physics-AP, political science, religion, social sciences, Spanish, Spanish language-AP, Spanish literature, Spanish literature-AP, student government, theater arts, U.S. government and politics, U.S. government and politics-AP, U.S. history, U.S. history-AP, U.S. literature, visual and performing arts, visual arts, world history.

Graduation Requirements Art, English, foreign language, mathematics, philosophy, physical education (includes health), religious studies, science, social sciences, 100 hours of Christian service.

Special Academic Programs 17 Advanced Placement exams for which test preparation is offered; honors section; study at local college for college credit.

College Admission Counseling 400 students graduated in 2008; 399 went to college, including Georgetown University; Harvard University; New York University; Santa Clara University; Stanford University; University of Notre Dame. Other: 1 entered military service. Mean SAT critical reading: 650, mean SAT math: 680, mean SAT writing: 670.

Student Life Upper grades have specified standards of dress, student council, honor system. Discipline rests primarily with faculty. Attendance at religious services is required.

Summer Programs Remediation, enrichment, advancement, sports, art/fine arts, computer instruction programs offered; session focuses on academics and athletics; held on campus; accepts boys and girls; open to students from other schools. 250 students usually enrolled. 2009 schedule: June 15 to July 24. Application deadline: May 31.

Tuition and Aid Day student tuition: $12,900. Tuition installment plan (FACTS Tuition Payment Plan). Need-based scholarship grants, middle-income loans, paying campus jobs available. In 2008–09, 14% of upper-school students received aid. Total amount of financial aid awarded in 2008–09: $1,600,000.

Admissions Traditional secondary-level entrance grade is 9. For fall 2008, 1,200 students applied for upper-level admission, 425 were accepted, 425 enrolled. High School Placement Test required. Deadline for receipt of application materials: December 15. Application fee required: $65.

Athletics Interscholastic: aquatics (boys, girls), badminton (b,g), baseball (b), basketball (b,g), cross-country running (b,g), dance team (g), diving (b,g), field hockey (g), football (b), lacrosse (b), softball (g), swimming and diving (b,g), tennis (b,g), track and field (b,g), volleyball (b,g), water polo (b,g), weight training (b,g), winter soccer (b,g); coed interscholastic: golf, strength & conditioning, wrestling; coed intramural: in-line hockey, in-line skating. 4 PE instructors, 110 coaches, 2 athletic trainers.

Computers Computers are regularly used in design classes. Computer network features include on-campus library services, online commercial services, Internet access, wireless campus network, Internet filtering or blocking technology. Campus intranet, student e-mail accounts, and computer access in designated common areas are available to students. Students grades are available online. The school has a published electronic and media policy.

Contact Mrs. Lori Robowski, Assistant for Admissions. 408-342-4300. Fax: 408-342-4308. E-mail: admissions@mitty.com. Web site: www.mitty.com/.

ARCHBISHOP RIORDAN HIGH SCHOOL

175 Phelan Avenue
San Francisco, California 94112

Head of School: Mr. Kevin R. Asbra

General Information Boys' day college-preparatory school, affiliated with Roman Catholic Church; primarily serves students with learning disabilities. Grades 9–12. Founded: 1949. Setting: urban. 10-acre campus. 4 buildings on campus. Approved or accredited by National Catholic Education Association, Western Association of Schools and Colleges, and California Department of Education. Endowment: $3 million. Total enrollment: 620. Upper school average class size: 26. Upper school faculty-student ratio: 1:14.

Upper School Student Profile Grade 9: 196 students (196 boys); Grade 10: 173 students (173 boys); Grade 11: 175 students (175 boys); Grade 12: 173 students (173 boys). 81% of students are Roman Catholic.

Faculty School total: 59. In upper school: 39 men, 20 women; 35 have advanced degrees.

Subjects Offered 20th century American writers, algebra, American history, American literature, anatomy, art, art appreciation, biology, broadcasting, business, calculus, chemistry, community service, computer science, creative writing, drama, earth science, economics, English, English literature, ethics, European history, expository writing, fine arts, geography, geometry, government/civics, grammar, health, history, mathematics, music, physical education, physics, physiology, religion, science, social studies, Spanish, statistics, theater, theology, trigonometry, world history, world literature, writing.

Graduation Requirements Arts and fine arts (art, music, dance, drama), computer science, English, foreign language, mathematics, physical education (includes health), religion (includes Bible studies and theology), science, social science, social studies (includes history). Community service is required.

Special Academic Programs Advanced Placement exam preparation; honors section; study at local college for college credit; programs in English, mathematics, general development for dyslexic students.

College Admission Counseling 160 students graduated in 2008; 158 went to college, including City College of San Francisco; San Francisco State University; San Jose State University; Santa Clara University; University of California, Berkeley. Other: 2 had other specific plans.
Student Life Upper grades have specified standards of dress, student council, honor system. Discipline rests primarily with faculty. Attendance at religious services is required.
Summer Programs Remediation programs offered; held on campus; accepts boys; not open to students from other schools. 2009 schedule: June 8 to July 10.
Tuition and Aid Day student tuition: $13,000. Tuition installment plan (monthly payment plans). Need-based scholarship grants available. In 2008–09, 20% of upper-school students received aid. Total amount of financial aid awarded in 2008–09: $750,000.
Admissions High School Placement Test required. Deadline for receipt of application materials: December 12. Application fee required: $100.
Athletics Interscholastic: baseball, basketball, cross-country running, football, golf, soccer, tennis, track and field, wrestling; intramural: basketball, bowling, cheering, flag football, floor hockey, indoor hockey, indoor soccer, martial arts, physical fitness, physical training, soccer, speedball, strength & conditioning, table tennis, volleyball, weight lifting. 4 coaches, 1 athletic trainer.
Computers Computers are regularly used in computer applications, desktop publishing, English, foreign language, humanities, journalism, mathematics, newspaper, religion, science, social studies, Web site design, word processing, writing, writing fundamentals, yearbook classes. Computer network features include on-campus library services, online commercial services, Internet access, wireless campus network, Internet filtering or blocking technology. Students grades are available online.
Contact Ms. Rose Aragon, Admission Secretary. 415-586-1256. Fax: 415-587-1310. E-mail: raragon@riordanhs.org. Web site: www.riordanhs.org.

ARCHBISHOP RUMMEL HIGH SCHOOL

1901 Severn Avenue
Metairie, Louisiana 70001-2893

Head of School: Mr. Michael J. Begg

General Information Boys' day college-preparatory, arts, religious studies, and technology school, affiliated with Roman Catholic Church; primarily serves students with learning disabilities and individuals with Attention Deficit Disorder. Grades 8–12. Founded: 1962. Setting: suburban. Nearest major city is New Orleans. 20-acre campus. 10 buildings on campus. Approved or accredited by Association for Experiential Education, National Catholic Education Association, Southern Association of Colleges and Schools, and Louisiana Department of Education. Total enrollment: 1,150. Upper school average class size: 27. Upper school faculty-student ratio: 1:10.
Upper School Student Profile Grade 8: 150 students (150 boys); Grade 9: 253 students (253 boys); Grade 10: 256 students (256 boys); Grade 11: 230 students (230 boys); Grade 12: 261 students (261 boys). 90% of students are Roman Catholic.
Faculty School total: 95. In upper school: 50 men, 25 women; 45 have advanced degrees.
Subjects Offered ACT preparation, advanced biology, advanced chemistry, advanced computer applications, advanced math, advanced studio art-AP, algebra, American government, American government-AP, American history, American history-AP, American literature, American literature-AP, anatomy, anatomy and physiology, ancient world history, art, art appreciation, art-AP, band, biology, British literature, British literature (honors), British literature-AP, calculus, calculus-AP, campus ministry, Catholic belief and practice, ceramics, chemistry, chemistry-AP, civics, computer applications, computer literacy, computer science, creative writing, economics, English, English language and composition-AP, English literature, English literature and composition-AP, environmental science, European history, European literature, fine arts, French, geography, geometry, government-AP, health education, history of the Catholic Church, honors algebra, honors English, honors geometry, honors U.S. history, honors world history, human anatomy, instrumental music, language arts, Latin, moral theology, physics, psychology, reading, sociology, Spanish, Spanish literature, speech, statistics-AP, street law, studio art, studio art—AP, studio art-AP, U.S. government-AP, U.S. history, U.S. history-AP, U.S. literature, United States government-AP, Web site design, Western civilization, Western civilization-AP, world geography.
Graduation Requirements ACT preparation, advanced math, American history, art appreciation, biology, Catholic belief and practice, chemistry, civics, computer applications, computer literacy, computer science, English, environmental science, foreign language, geography, health education, history of the Catholic Church, physical education (includes health), physical science, physics, reading, U.S. history, Western civilization, world geography.
Special Academic Programs Advanced Placement exam preparation; honors section; programs in general development for dyslexic students.
College Admission Counseling 230 students graduated in 2008; 200 went to college, including Louisiana State University and Agricultural and Mechanical College; Loyola University New Orleans; University of New Orleans. Other: 10 went to work, 20 entered military service.
Student Life Upper grades have uniform requirement, student council, honor system. Discipline rests primarily with faculty. Attendance at religious services is required.
Summer Programs Remediation, enrichment, advancement, sports, art/fine arts, rigorous outdoor training, computer instruction programs offered; session focuses on student involvement and fun; held on campus; accepts boys and girls; open to students from other schools. 200 students usually enrolled. 2009 schedule: June 2 to July 18.
Tuition and Aid Day student tuition: $5670. Tuition installment plan (monthly payment plans). Merit scholarship grants, need-based scholarship grants, paying campus jobs available. In 2008–09, 20% of upper-school students received aid.
Admissions Traditional secondary-level entrance grade is 8. High School Placement Test required. Deadline for receipt of application materials: January 12. Application fee required: $20. Interview required.
Athletics Interscholastic: baseball, basketball, bowling, cheering, cross-country running, field hockey, football, Frisbee, golf, hockey, jogging, rugby, soccer, strength & conditioning, swimming and diving, tennis, track and field, whiffle ball, wrestling; intramural: flag football. 10 PE instructors, 25 coaches, 2 athletic trainers.
Computers Computers are regularly used in computer applications, creative writing, English, multimedia, programming, reading, science classes. Computer resources include on-campus library services, Internet access, Internet filtering or blocking technology. Students grades are available online. The school has a published electronic and media policy.
Contact Joseph A. Serio, Director of Communications. 504-834-5592 Ext. 263. Fax: 504-833-2232. E-mail: jserio@rummelraiders.com. Web site: www.rummelraiders.com.

ARCHBISHOP SPALDING HIGH SCHOOL

8080 New Cut Road
Severn, Maryland 21144

Head of School: Mrs. Kathleen Mahar

General Information Coeducational day college-preparatory, arts, business, religious studies, and technology school, affiliated with Roman Catholic Church. Grades 9–12. Founded: 1965. Setting: suburban. Nearest major city is Baltimore. 52-acre campus. 1 building on campus. Approved or accredited by Association of Independent Maryland Schools, Middle States Association of Colleges and Schools, National Catholic Education Association, and Maryland Department of Education. Endowment: $1 million. Total enrollment: 1,182. Upper school average class size: 23. Upper school faculty-student ratio: 1:15.
Upper School Student Profile Grade 9: 304 students (150 boys, 154 girls); Grade 10: 295 students (145 boys, 150 girls); Grade 11: 314 students (149 boys, 165 girls); Grade 12: 269 students (130 boys, 139 girls). 79.5% of students are Roman Catholic.
Faculty School total: 81. In upper school: 24 men, 57 women; 48 have advanced degrees.
Subjects Offered 20th century American writers, 20th century history, 3-dimensional art, accounting, advanced biology, advanced chemistry, advanced computer applications, advanced math, Advanced Placement courses, advanced studio art-AP, advertising design, aerobics, algebra, American government, American government-AP, American history, American literature, American literature-AP, anatomy, anatomy and physiology, applied arts, applied music, art, art history, astronomy, band, Basic programming, biology, botany, business, business law, calculus, calculus-AP, campus ministry, Catholic belief and practice, ceramics, chemistry, chemistry-AP, chorus, Christian and Hebrew scripture, college counseling, college placement, college writing, communication skills, community service, comparative religion, computer animation, computer applications, computer art, computer education, computer graphics, computer information systems, computer keyboarding, computer literacy, computer multimedia, computer processing, computer programming, computer programming-AP, computer resources, computer science, computer science-AP, computer skills, computer studies, computer technologies, computer technology certification, computer tools, computer-aided design, computers, conceptual physics, CPR, creative writing, drama, drawing and design, earth science, ecology, environmental systems, economics, English, English language and composition-AP, English literature, English literature and composition-AP, ethics, European history, European history-AP, film, film and new technologies, film appreciation, film history, film series, film studies, filmmaking, fine arts, French, geology, geometry, grammar, guitar, health education, honors algebra, honors English, honors geometry, honors U.S. history, honors world history, jazz band, Latin, Latin-AP, law, literary magazine, marine biology, music, music theory, painting, photography, physical education, physics, pre-calculus, psychology, religion, science, social studies, sociology, Spanish, Spanish-AP, sports medicine, statistics-AP, strings, student government, studio art-AP, symphonic band, theater, theology, trigonometry, U.S. government and politics-AP, U.S. history, U.S. history-AP, visual and performing arts, visual arts, vocal ensemble, vocal jazz, vocal music, voice, Web site design, weight fitness, weight training, weightlifting, Western civilization, wind ensemble, work-study, world history, world literature, world religions, writing, yearbook, zoology.
Graduation Requirements Arts and fine arts (art, music, dance, drama), computer science, CPR, English, foreign language, mathematics, physical education (includes health), religion (includes Bible studies and theology), science, social science, Religious retreat in senior year, CPR Certification, Technology/Computer requirement. Community service is required.
Special Academic Programs Advanced Placement exam preparation; honors section; accelerated programs; independent study; study at local college for college credit; academic accommodation for the gifted, the musically talented, and the

artistically talented; remedial reading and/or remedial writing; remedial math; programs in English, mathematics for dyslexic students; special instructional classes for students with mild learning differences (additional cost).

College Admission Counseling 239 students graduated in 2008; 237 went to college, including Anne Arundel Community College; Salisbury University; Towson University; University of Maryland, Baltimore County; University of Maryland, College Park; York College of Pennsylvania. Other: 2 went to work. Mean SAT critical reading: 551, mean SAT math: 558, mean SAT writing: 554.

Student Life Upper grades have uniform requirement, student council, honor system. Discipline rests primarily with faculty. Attendance at religious services is required.

Summer Programs Session focuses on study skills and SAT prep; held on campus; accepts boys and girls; not open to students from other schools. 160 students usually enrolled. 2009 schedule: June 15 to August 28. Application deadline: May 25.

Tuition and Aid Day student tuition: $10,655. Tuition installment plan (The Tuition Plan, monthly payment plans, one-time, semiannual, quarterly payment plans, monthly with Tuition Management). Merit scholarship grants, need-based scholarship grants, paying campus jobs available. In 2008–09, 20% of upper-school students received aid; total upper-school merit-scholarship money awarded: $418,286. Total amount of financial aid awarded in 2008–09: $792,049.

Admissions Traditional secondary-level entrance grade is 9. For fall 2008, 587 students applied for upper-level admission, 403 were accepted, 303 enrolled. High School Placement Test (closed version) from Scholastic Testing Service required. Deadline for receipt of application materials: January 4. Application fee required: $100. On-campus interview recommended.

Athletics Interscholastic: aerobics/dance (girls), baseball (b), basketball (b,g), cheering (g), cross-country running (b,g), dance team (g), field hockey (g), football (b), hockey (b,g), ice hockey (b,g), indoor track & field (b,g), lacrosse (b,g), rugby (b), soccer (b,g), softball (g), swimming and diving (b,g), track and field (b,g), volleyball (b,g), winter (indoor) track (b,g), wrestling (b); intramural: flag football (g), triathlon (b); coed interscholastic: golf, tennis; coed intramural: backpacking, bicycling, canoeing/kayaking, climbing, equestrian sports, hiking/backpacking, kayaking, outdoor adventure, outdoor skills, sailboarding, sailing, skiing (downhill), snowboarding, ultimate Frisbee, weight training, yoga. 3 PE instructors, 82 coaches, 2 athletic trainers.

Computers Computers are regularly used in accounting, art, business, career exploration, computer applications, economics, English, foreign language, graphic design, keyboarding, literary magazine, mathematics, music, newspaper, programming, religion, religious studies, science, social studies, study skills, technology, Web site design, word processing, writing, yearbook classes. Computer network features include on-campus library services, online commercial services, Internet access, wireless campus network, Internet filtering or blocking technology. Computer access in designated common areas is available to students. Students grades are available online. The school has a published electronic and media policy.

Contact Mr. Thomas Miller, Director of Admissions. 410-969-9105 Ext. 233. Fax: 410-969-1026. E-mail: millert@archbishopspalding.org. Web site: www.archbishopspalding.org.

THE ARCHER SCHOOL FOR GIRLS

11725 Sunset Boulevard
Los Angeles, California 90049

Head of School: Elizabeth English

General Information Girls' day college-preparatory school. Grades 6–12. Founded: 1995. Setting: suburban. 6-acre campus. 1 building on campus. Approved or accredited by California Association of Independent Schools, The College Board, Western Association of Schools and Colleges, and California Department of Education. Endowment: $1.9 million. Total enrollment: 495. Upper school average class size: 16. Upper school faculty-student ratio: 1:7.

Upper School Student Profile Grade 9: 75 students (75 girls); Grade 10: 68 students (68 girls); Grade 11: 70 students (70 girls); Grade 12: 70 students (70 girls).

Faculty School total: 79. In upper school: 17 men, 62 women; 45 have advanced degrees.

Subjects Offered 20th century history, acting, advanced chemistry, advanced math, algebra, American literature, ancient history, archaeology, architectural drawing, art, art appreciation, art history, art history-AP, biology, biology-AP, calculus, calculus-AP, career/college preparation, ceramics, chemistry, chemistry-AP, Chinese, choir, classical studies, college admission preparation, college counseling, community service, computer applications, computer graphics, computer literacy, critical studies in film, debate, digital imaging, drama, drawing and design, earth and space science, English, English composition, English language-AP, English literature, English literature-AP, environmental science-AP, experiential education, film appreciation, fitness, French, French language-AP, geometry, history, honors U.S. history, human development, human geography—AP, independent study, intro to computers, journalism, Latin, law studies, literary magazine, marine biology, marine ecology, media literacy, modern world history, music, orchestra, performing arts, photography, physics, portfolio art, pre-algebra, pre-calculus, psychology, robotics, Roman civilization, self-defense, senior seminar, Spanish, Spanish language-AP, speech and debate, statistics-AP, student government, student publications, theater, theater arts, U.S. history, U.S. history-AP, wilderness experience, yearbook.

Graduation Requirements Arts and fine arts (art, music, dance, drama), English, foreign language, history, mathematics, performing arts, physical education (includes health), science, service learning/internship, annual participation in Arrow Week (experiential education program).

Special Academic Programs Advanced Placement exam preparation; honors section.

College Admission Counseling 71 students graduated in 2008; 69 went to college, including American University; The George Washington University; University of California, Santa Barbara; University of Southern California. Other: 1 went to work, 1 had other specific plans. Median SAT critical reading: 600, median SAT math: 575, median SAT writing: 645, median combined SAT: 1820.

Student Life Upper grades have uniform requirement, student council. Discipline rests primarily with faculty.

Tuition and Aid Day student tuition: $28,150. Tuition installment plan (FACTS Tuition Payment Plan). Need-based scholarship grants available. In 2008–09, 17% of upper-school students received aid. Total amount of financial aid awarded in 2008–09: $1,900,125.

Admissions Traditional secondary-level entrance grade is 9. For fall 2008, 66 students applied for upper-level admission, 46 were accepted, 13 enrolled. ISEE required. Deadline for receipt of application materials: January 16. Application fee required: $100. On-campus interview required.

Athletics Interscholastic: basketball, cross-country running, equestrian sports, soccer, softball, swimming and diving, tennis, track and field, volleyball. 5 PE instructors, 16 coaches.

Computers Computers are regularly used in all academic classes. Computer network features include on-campus library services, online commercial services, Internet access, wireless campus network. Student e-mail accounts are available to students. The school has a published electronic and media policy.

Contact Molly Arnason, Director of Admissions. 310-873-7037. Fax: 310-873-7052. E-mail: marnason@archer.org. Web site: www.archer.org/.

ARCHMERE ACADEMY

3600 Philadelphia Pike
Box 130
Claymont, Delaware 19703

Head of School: Rev. Joseph McLaughlin, OPRAEM

General Information Coeducational day college-preparatory, arts, religious studies, and technology school, affiliated with Roman Catholic Church. Grades 9–12. Founded: 1932. Setting: suburban. Nearest major city is Wilmington. 38-acre campus. 8 buildings on campus. Approved or accredited by Middle States Association of Colleges and Schools, National Catholic Education Association, and Delaware Department of Education. Member of National Association of Independent Schools. Endowment: $8.4 million. Total enrollment: 513. Upper school average class size: 16. Upper school faculty-student ratio: 1:10.

Upper School Student Profile Grade 9: 135 students (72 boys, 63 girls); Grade 10: 128 students (61 boys, 67 girls); Grade 11: 129 students (58 boys, 71 girls); Grade 12: 121 students (58 boys, 63 girls). 74% of students are Roman Catholic.

Faculty School total: 59. In upper school: 31 men, 25 women; 51 have advanced degrees.

Subjects Offered Algebra, American history, American literature, architecture, art, art history, Bible studies, biology, calculus, chemistry, Chinese, computer programming, computer science, creative writing, drama, driver education, ecology, economics, English, English literature, environmental science, ethics, European history, expository writing, French, geometry, German, government/civics, grammar, health, history, mathematics, music, philosophy, physical education, physics, psychology, reading, religion, science, social studies, Spanish, speech, statistics, theater, theology, trigonometry, world history, writing.

Graduation Requirements Computer science, English, foreign language, mathematics, physical education (includes health), religion (includes Bible studies and theology), science, social studies (includes history), speech.

Special Academic Programs Advanced Placement exam preparation; honors section; independent study; study abroad; academic accommodation for the gifted, the musically talented, and the artistically talented; programs in English, mathematics for dyslexic students.

College Admission Counseling 118 students graduated in 2007; all went to college, including Boston University; Hofstra University; Penn State University Park; Saint Joseph's University; University of Delaware; University of Maryland, College Park. Median SAT critical reading: 595, median SAT math: 600, median SAT writing: 615. 48% scored over 600 on SAT critical reading, 48% scored over 600 on SAT math, 52% scored over 600 on SAT writing.

Student Life Upper grades have uniform requirement, student council, honor system. Discipline rests primarily with faculty. Attendance at religious services is required.

Tuition and Aid Day student tuition: $17,100. Tuition installment plan (10-Month Automatic Debit Plan). Merit scholarship grants, need-based scholarship grants, grants for children of faculty and staff, minority scholarships/grants available. In 2007–08, 45% of upper-school students received aid; total upper-school merit-scholarship money awarded: $174,000. Total amount of financial aid awarded in 2007–08: $1,020,000.

Admissions Traditional secondary-level entrance grade is 9. For fall 2007, 270 students applied for upper-level admission, 187 were accepted, 135 enrolled. Deadline for receipt of application materials: none. Application fee required: $35. On-campus interview required.

Athletics Interscholastic: baseball (boys), basketball (b,g), cheering (g), cross-country running (b,g), field hockey (g), football (b), golf (b,g), ice hockey (b,g), indoor track (b,g), lacrosse (b,g), soccer (b,g), softball (g), swimming and diving (b,g), tennis (b,g), track and field (b,g), volleyball (g), wrestling (b); coed interscholastic: winter (indoor) track; coed intramural: basketball, bowling, fencing. 1 PE instructor, 16 coaches, 2 athletic trainers.

Computers Computers are regularly used in art, English, foreign language, history, mathematics, multimedia, science classes. Computer network features include on-campus library services, online commercial services, Internet access, wireless campus network. Student e-mail accounts are available to students. The school has a published electronic and media policy.

Contact Dr. William J. Doyle, PhD, Academic Dean. 302-798-6632 Ext. 705. E-mail: wdoyle@archmereacademy.org. Web site: www.archmereacademy.com.

ANNOUNCEMENT FROM THE SCHOOL Archmere Academy is a Roman Catholic, independent, college-preparatory school inspired by the Norbertine tradition and a heritage of committed faculty, alumni, families, and friends. Through dedication to academic excellence, social development, community service, and faith reflection, Archmere focuses on the education of the whole student.

ARGO ACADEMY

PO Box 5477
Sarasota, Florida 34277

Head of School: Mr. Michael Meighan

General Information Coeducational boarding college-preparatory, vocational, marine science, nautical science, experiential education, and student leadership, community service school. Grade 12. Founded: 1999. Students are housed in 88-foot or 112-foot schooner. Approved or accredited by Florida Department of Education. Total enrollment: 38. Upper school average class size: 18. Upper school faculty-student ratio: 1:4.

Upper School Student Profile 100% of students are boarding students. 19 states are represented in upper school student body. 10% are international students. International students from Canada.

Faculty School total: 10. In upper school: 5 men, 5 women; 4 have advanced degrees; all reside on campus.

Subjects Offered Boating, communications, community service, CPR, first aid, independent study, leadership, marine biology, navigation, oceanography, personal development, scuba diving.

Special Academic Programs Independent study; study at local college for college credit; study abroad.

College Admission Counseling Colleges students went to include University of Colorado at Boulder; University of Vermont.

Student Life Upper grades have specified standards of dress, student council. Discipline rests primarily with faculty.

Tuition and Aid 7-day tuition and room/board: $18,000. Tuition reduction for siblings, Student Loan Xpress available.

Admissions Traditional secondary-level entrance grade is 12. Deadline for receipt of application materials: none. Application fee required: $500. Interview required.

Athletics Coed Intramural: fishing, hiking/backpacking, outdoor activities, sailing, scuba diving, swimming and diving, windsurfing.

Contact Mrs. Gina Barnaba, Director of Admissions. 941-924-6789. Fax: 941-924-6075. E-mail: info@seamester.com. Web site: www.seamester.com.

ARMBRAE ACADEMY

1400 Oxford Street
Halifax, Nova Scotia B3H 3Y8, Canada

ANNOUNCEMENT FROM THE SCHOOL Armbrae Academy is the technology leader in Nova Scotia. Armbrae aims to provide a first-class university-preparatory program while maintaining the small classes and personal atmosphere that bring students to the Academy and keep them there. In the past five years, 99% of Armbrae graduates have entered their university of choice.

ARMONA UNION ACADEMY

14435 Locust Street
PO Box 397
Armona, California 93202

Head of School: Mr. Erik Borges

General Information Coeducational day college-preparatory, general academic, and religious studies school, affiliated with Seventh-day Adventists. Grades K–12. Founded: 1904. Setting: small town. Nearest major city is Fresno. 20-acre campus. 5 buildings on campus. Approved or accredited by Western Association of Schools and Colleges and California Department of Education. Member of Secondary School Admission Test Board. Endowment: $98,000. Total enrollment: 120. Upper school average class size: 15. Upper school faculty-student ratio: 1:10.

Upper School Student Profile Grade 9: 12 students (5 boys, 7 girls); Grade 10: 14 students (6 boys, 8 girls); Grade 11: 14 students (4 boys, 10 girls); Grade 12: 12 students (5 boys, 7 girls). 85% of students are Seventh-day Adventists.

Faculty School total: 13. In upper school: 5 men, 1 woman; 3 have advanced degrees.

Subjects Offered Algebra, American history, American literature, art, Bible studies, biology, business, chemistry, choir, communications, community service, computer science, drama, economics, English, English literature, fine arts, geometry, government, mathematics, physical education, physical science, physics, religion, science, social science, Spanish, world history, world literature, yearbook.

Graduation Requirements Arts and fine arts (art, music, dance, drama), business skills (includes word processing), computer science, English, foreign language, mathematics, physical education (includes health), religion (includes Bible studies and theology), science, social science, social studies (includes history). Community service is required.

Special Academic Programs Study at local college for college credit.

College Admission Counseling 6 students graduated in 2008; 5 went to college, including Pacific Union College; Southern Adventist University. Other: 1 went to work.

Student Life Upper grades have specified standards of dress, student council. Discipline rests primarily with faculty. Attendance at religious services is required.

Tuition and Aid Day student tuition: $5140. Guaranteed tuition plan. Tuition installment plan (monthly payment plans, individually arranged payment plans). Tuition reduction for siblings, need-based scholarship grants available. In 2008–09, 60% of upper-school students received aid. Total amount of financial aid awarded in 2008–09: $50,000.

Admissions Traditional secondary-level entrance grade is 9. For fall 2008, 12 students applied for upper-level admission, 7 were accepted, 7 enrolled. Deadline for receipt of application materials: August 15. Application fee required: $75. Interview required.

Athletics Interscholastic: basketball (boys, girls), flag football (b,g), football (b,g), volleyball (b,g); intramural: basketball (b,g), flag football (b,g); coed interscholastic: baseball, outdoor education, soccer, softball, track and field; coed intramural: baseball, outdoor education, paddle tennis, soccer, softball, table tennis, track and field, volleyball.

Computers Computers are regularly used in English, history, mathematics, science, yearbook classes. Computer network features include on-campus library services, online commercial services, Internet access, Internet filtering or blocking technology. Students grades are available online. The school has a published electronic and media policy.

Contact Mrs. Aniesha Kleinhammer, Registrar. 559-582-4468 Ext. 10. Fax: 559-582-6609. E-mail: anieshask@yahoo.com. Web site: www.auaweb.com.

ARMY AND NAVY ACADEMY

2605 Carlsbad Boulevard
PO Box 3000
Carlsbad, California 92018-3000

Head of School: Brig. Gen. Stephen M. Bliss, Retd.

General Information Boys' boarding and day college-preparatory, Junior ROTC, and military school. Grades 7–12. Founded: 1910. Setting: small town. Nearest major city is San Diego. Students are housed in single-sex dormitories. 16-acre campus. 34 buildings on campus. Approved or accredited by California Association of Independent Schools and Western Association of Schools and Colleges. Member of National Association of Independent Schools and Secondary School Admission Test Board. Endowment: $402,816. Total enrollment: 269. Upper school average class size: 11. Upper school faculty-student ratio: 1:9.

Upper School Student Profile Grade 9: 47 students (47 boys); Grade 10: 63 students (63 boys); Grade 11: 65 students (65 boys); Grade 12: 58 students (58 boys). 93% of students are boarding students. 69% are state residents. 17 states are represented in upper school student body. 11% are international students. International students from China, Mexico, Republic of Korea, Russian Federation, Singapore, and Taiwan; 4 other countries represented in student body.

Faculty School total: 31. In upper school: 17 men, 14 women; 15 have advanced degrees; 5 reside on campus.

Subjects Offered Algebra, art, biology, biology-AP, calculus-AP, chemistry, chemistry-AP, drama, economics, English, English-AP, ESL, French, geography, geometry, guitar, honors algebra, honors English, honors geometry, journalism, marching band, music appreciation, music technology, photography, physical education, physics, physics-AP, pre-calculus, psychology-AP, Spanish, Spanish-AP, studio art-AP, study skills, U.S. government, U.S. history, U.S. history-AP, world history, yearbook.

Graduation Requirements Arts and fine arts (art, music, dance, drama), electives, English, foreign language, lab science, leadership education training, mathematics, physical education (includes health), SAT preparation, social studies (includes history).

Special Academic Programs 9 Advanced Placement exams for which test preparation is offered; honors section; remedial reading and/or remedial writing; special instructional classes for students with Attention Deficit Disorder and learning disabilities; ESL (10 students enrolled).
College Admission Counseling 55 students graduated in 2008; 49 went to college, including San Francisco State University; The University of Arizona; University of California, Davis; University of California, Irvine; University of California, Santa Barbara; University of San Diego. Other: 2 went to work, 2 entered military service, 2 had other specific plans. Median SAT critical reading: 500, median SAT math: 525, median SAT writing: 520. 9% scored over 600 on SAT critical reading, 14% scored over 600 on SAT math, 9% scored over 600 on SAT writing.
Student Life Upper grades have uniform requirement, student council, honor system. Discipline rests primarily with faculty.
Summer Programs Remediation, enrichment, ESL, art/fine arts, computer instruction programs offered; session focuses on enrichment and remediation; held on campus; accepts boys and girls; open to students from other schools. 185 students usually enrolled. 2009 schedule: June 30 to August 2. Application deadline: none.
Tuition and Aid Day student tuition: $18,300; 7-day tuition and room/board: $29,995. Tuition installment plan (individually arranged payment plans). Tuition reduction for siblings, need-based scholarship grants available. In 2008–09, 19% of upper-school students received aid. Total amount of financial aid awarded in 2008–09: $323,475.
Admissions Traditional secondary-level entrance grade is 9. For fall 2008, 257 students applied for upper-level admission, 142 were accepted, 118 enrolled. Any standardized test, Otis-Lennon School Ability Test or TOEFL required. Deadline for receipt of application materials: none. Application fee required: $100. Interview required.
Athletics Interscholastic: aquatics, baseball, basketball, cross-country running, drill team, flag football, football, golf, in-line hockey, marksmanship, riflery, roller hockey, ropes courses, soccer, surfing, swimming and diving, tennis, track and field, water polo, weight lifting, wrestling; intramural: aquatics, bicycling, billiards, combined training, fitness, hockey, independent competitive sports, JROTC drill, outdoor activities, outdoor recreation, physical fitness, physical training, roller hockey, skateboarding, strength & conditioning, surfing, volleyball. 15 coaches, 1 athletic trainer.
Computers Computers are regularly used in journalism, music technology, yearbook classes. Computer network features include on-campus library services, Internet access, wireless campus network, Internet filtering or blocking technology. Student e-mail accounts and computer access in designated common areas are available to students. Students grades are available online. The school has a published electronic and media policy.
Contact Candice Heidenrich, Director of Admissions. 888-762-2338. Fax: 760-434-5948. E-mail: admissions@armyandnavyacademy.org. Web site: www.armyandnavyacademy.org.

ARROWSMITH SCHOOL

Toronto, Ontario, Canada
See Special Needs Schools section.

ARTHUR MORGAN SCHOOL

Burnsville, North Carolina
See Special Needs Schools section.

ASHBURY COLLEGE

362 Mariposa Avenue
Ottawa, Ontario K1M 0T3, Canada
Head of School: Mr. Tam Matthews

General Information Coeducational boarding and day college-preparatory, bilingual studies, and International Baccalaureate school, affiliated with Anglican Church of Canada. Boarding boys grades 9–12, boarding girls grades 9–12, day boys grades 4–12, day girls grades 9–12. Founded: 1891. Setting: urban. Students are housed in single-sex dormitories. 13-acre campus. 3 buildings on campus. Approved or accredited by Canadian Association of Independent Schools, Canadian Educational Standards Institute, Conference of Independent Schools of Ontario, International Baccalaureate Organization, Ontario Ministry of Education, and The Association of Boarding Schools. Affiliate member of National Association of Independent Schools. Languages of instruction: English and French. Endowment: CAN$6.5 million. Total enrollment: 670. Upper school average class size: 17. Upper school faculty-student ratio: 1:9.
Upper School Student Profile Grade 6: 35 students (35 boys); Grade 7: 50 students (50 boys); Grade 8: 55 students (55 boys); Grade 9: 120 students (64 boys, 56 girls); Grade 10: 126 students (72 boys, 54 girls); Grade 11: 121 students (64 boys, 57 girls); Grade 12: 119 students (64 boys, 55 girls). 20% of students are boarding students. 75% are province residents. 7 provinces are represented in upper school student body. 15% are international students. International students from Germany, Hong Kong, Japan, Mexico, Republic of Korea, and United States; 24 other countries represented in student body.
Faculty School total: 60. In upper school: 30 men, 30 women; 45 have advanced degrees; 15 reside on campus.
Subjects Offered Accounting, advanced chemistry, advanced math, algebra, American history, art, art history, biology, business, business skills, calculus, Canadian geography, Canadian history, chemistry, computer applications, computer programming, computer science, creative writing, drama, driver education, economics, English, English literature, environmental science, ESL, European history, fine arts, French, geography, geometry, health, history, mathematics, music, physical education, physics, science, social studies, sociology, Spanish, theater, theory of knowledge, world history, world literature.
Graduation Requirements English, mathematics, science. Community service is required.
Special Academic Programs International Baccalaureate program; independent study; term-away projects; study abroad; ESL (22 students enrolled).
College Admission Counseling 122 students graduated in 2008; all went to college, including Dalhousie University; McGill University; Queen's University at Kingston; The University of Western Ontario; University of Ottawa; University of Toronto. Mean SAT critical reading: 600, mean SAT math: 644, mean SAT writing: 591.
Student Life Upper grades have uniform requirement, student council, honor system. Discipline rests primarily with faculty. Attendance at religious services is required.
Summer Programs Remediation, enrichment, advancement, ESL, sports, computer instruction programs offered; session focuses on academics; held on campus; accepts boys and girls; open to students from other schools. 85 students usually enrolled. 2009 schedule: July 1 to August 31. Application deadline: June 20.
Tuition and Aid Day student tuition: CAN$17,650; 7-day tuition and room/board: CAN$38,850. Tuition installment plan (monthly payment plans, individually arranged payment plans). Tuition reduction for siblings, bursaries, merit scholarship grants available. In 2008–09, 20% of upper-school students received aid; total upper-school merit-scholarship money awarded: CAN$55,000. Total amount of financial aid awarded in 2008–09: CAN$470,000.
Admissions Traditional secondary-level entrance grade is 9. For fall 2008, 350 students applied for upper-level admission, 266 were accepted, 123 enrolled. Canadian Standardized Test, SLEP or TOEFL required. Deadline for receipt of application materials: none. Application fee required: CAN$100. Interview required.
Athletics Interscholastic: alpine skiing (boys, girls), badminton (b,g), basketball (b,g), cross-country running (b,g), field hockey (g), football (b), golf (b,g), hockey (b), ice hockey (b), independent competitive sports (b,g), rowing (b,g), rugby (b,g), skiing (downhill) (b,g), soccer (b,g), tennis (b,g), track and field (b,g), volleyball (b,g); intramural: badminton (b,g), ball hockey (b,g), basketball (b,g), ice hockey (b), modern dance (b), outdoor education (b,g), rugby (b,g); coed interscholastic: baseball, running; coed intramural: alpine skiing, basketball, canoeing/kayaking, climbing, cooperative games, fitness, flag football, Frisbee, hiking/backpacking, indoor soccer, life saving, martial arts, Nautilus, nordic skiing, outdoor activities, physical fitness, physical training, skiing (cross-country), skiing (downhill), snowboarding, soccer, softball, strength & conditioning, tennis, track and field, ultimate Frisbee, volleyball, weight training, yoga. 5 PE instructors, 10 coaches.
Computers Computers are regularly used in art, business applications, business education, data processing, economics, geography, graphic arts, humanities, information technology, mathematics, music, science, yearbook classes. Computer network features include on-campus library services, Internet access, wireless campus network, Internet filtering or blocking technology. Campus intranet, student e-mail accounts, and computer access in designated common areas are available to students. Students grades are available online. The school has a published electronic and media policy.
Contact Mrs. Padme Raina, Manager of International Admissions. 613-749-5954 Ext. 368. Fax: 613-749-9724. E-mail: praina@ashbury.ca. Web site: www.ashbury.ca.

ASHEVILLE SCHOOL

360 Asheville School Road
Asheville, North Carolina 28806
Head of School: Archibald R. Montgomery, IV

General Information Coeducational boarding and day college-preparatory, arts, and technology school, affiliated with Christian faith. Grades 9–12. Founded: 1900. Setting: suburban. Students are housed in single-sex by floor dormitories. 300-acre campus. 19 buildings on campus. Approved or accredited by North Carolina Association of Independent Schools, Southern Association of Colleges and Schools, Southern Association of Independent Schools, The Association of Boarding Schools, and North Carolina Department of Education. Member of National Association of Independent Schools and Secondary School Admission Test Board. Endowment: $30 million. Total enrollment: 260. Upper school average class size: 13. Upper school faculty-student ratio: 1:7.
Upper School Student Profile Grade 9: 61 students (26 boys, 35 girls); Grade 10: 75 students (34 boys, 41 girls); Grade 11: 67 students (30 boys, 37 girls); Grade 12: 57 students (29 boys, 28 girls). 75% of students are boarding students. 50% are state residents. 22 states are represented in upper school student body. 14% are international students. International students from Bahamas, China, Republic of Korea, Saudi Arabia, Taiwan, and Thailand; 6 other countries represented in student body. 75% of students are Christian faith.
Faculty School total: 36. In upper school: 21 men, 15 women; 25 have advanced degrees; 28 reside on campus.

Subjects Offered Algebra, American history, American literature, ancient history, art, biology, calculus, chemistry, Chinese, creative writing, English, English literature, European history, finite math, French, geometry, grammar, humanities, Latin, literature, mathematics, medieval/Renaissance history, music, physics, pre-calculus, science, social studies, Spanish, studio art, Western civilization, world history, world literature, writing.
Graduation Requirements Arts and fine arts (art, music, dance, drama), English, foreign language, history, mathematics, music, science, Senior Demonstration (series of research papers and oral defense of work), three-day camping trip, Senior Chapel Talk (public speaking).
Special Academic Programs 17 Advanced Placement exams for which test preparation is offered; honors section; academic accommodation for the gifted.
College Admission Counseling 60 students graduated in 2008; 59 went to college, including Cornell University; Harvard University; New York University; Sewanee: The University of the South; The University of North Carolina at Chapel Hill. Other: 1 had other specific plans.
Student Life Upper grades have specified standards of dress, student council, honor system. Discipline rests equally with students and faculty. Attendance at religious services is required.
Summer Programs Enrichment, ESL, art/fine arts, rigorous outdoor training, computer instruction programs offered; session focuses on leadership, problem solving, mountaineering, art and film; held on campus; accepts boys and girls; open to students from other schools. 80 students usually enrolled. 2009 schedule: June 21 to July 11. Application deadline: May 1.
Tuition and Aid Day student tuition: $22,420; 7-day tuition and room/board: $38,720. Tuition installment plan (monthly payment plans, individually arranged payment plans). Merit scholarship grants, need-based scholarship grants, tuition remission for children of faculty available. In 2008–09, 25% of upper-school students received aid; total upper-school merit-scholarship money awarded: $5000. Total amount of financial aid awarded in 2008–09: $1,803,000.
Admissions Traditional secondary-level entrance grade is 9. For fall 2008, 300 students applied for upper-level admission, 150 were accepted, 108 enrolled. PSAT or SAT for applicants to grade 11 and 12, SSAT or TOEFL required. Deadline for receipt of application materials: February 1. Application fee required: $50. On-campus interview required.
Athletics Interscholastic: baseball (boys), basketball (b,g), cross-country running (b,g), field hockey (g), football (b), running (b,g), soccer (b,g), swimming and diving (b,g), tennis (b,g), track and field (b,g), volleyball (g), wrestling (b); intramural: alpine skiing (b,g), dance (g), lacrosse (b); coed interscholastic: equestrian sports, golf, horseback riding; coed intramural: backpacking, canoeing/kayaking, climbing, dance, equestrian sports, fitness, fly fishing, Frisbee, hiking/backpacking, horseback riding, kayaking, life saving, modern dance, mountain biking, mountaineering, Nautilus, outdoor activities, physical fitness, rock climbing, ropes courses, skateboarding, skiing (downhill), snowboarding, strength & conditioning, table tennis, wall climbing, weight lifting, wilderness, yoga. 3 coaches, 1 athletic trainer.
Computers Computers are regularly used in French, humanities, Latin, mathematics, science, Spanish classes. Computer network features include on-campus library services, online commercial services, Internet access, Internet filtering or blocking technology. Campus intranet, student e-mail accounts, and computer access in designated common areas are available to students. Students grades are available online. The school has a published electronic and media policy.
Contact Cyndi Madden, Admission Coordinator. 828-254-6345 Ext. 4022. Fax: 828-210-6109. E-mail: admission@ashevilleschool.org. Web site: www.ashevilleschool.org.

ANNOUNCEMENT FROM THE SCHOOL Asheville's summer program, Summer Academic Adventures, offers academically talented and high-achieving students entering grades 6–11 the chance to learn through experience and find motivation for the regular school year while having fun. Outdoor adventure supplements academic enrichment courses such as The Game of Life (math in the real world), Roller Coaster Physics, Film Production (students film and produce a documentary), Wilderness Adventure, and many others. Students may attend one or both three-week sessions.

See Close-Up on page 668.

ASSETS SCHOOL

Honolulu, Hawaii
See Special Needs Schools section.

ASSUMPTION HIGH SCHOOL

2170 Tyler Lane
Louisville, Kentucky 40205
Head of School: Mrs. Elaine Salvo

General Information Girls' day college-preparatory, arts, business, religious studies, and technology school, affiliated with Roman Catholic Church. Grades 9–12. Founded: 1955. Setting: suburban. 5-acre campus. 3 buildings on campus. Approved or accredited by National Catholic Education Association, Southern Association of Colleges and Schools, and Kentucky Department of Education. Endowment: $672,000. Total enrollment: 969. Upper school average class size: 19. Upper school faculty-student ratio: 1:10.
Upper School Student Profile Grade 9: 228 students (228 girls); Grade 10: 209 students (209 girls); Grade 11: 292 students (292 girls); Grade 12: 240 students (240 girls). 86% of students are Roman Catholic.
Faculty School total: 87. In upper school: 13 men, 74 women; 82 have advanced degrees.
Subjects Offered 3-dimensional art, accounting, acting, advanced chemistry, advanced math, Advanced Placement courses, algebra, American government-AP, American history, American history-AP, American literature, anatomy, art, art history-AP, astronomy, biology, biology-AP, broadcast journalism, business, business law, calculus, calculus-AP, ceramics, chemistry, chemistry-AP, child development, choral music, chorus, community service, computer applications, computer graphics, computer information systems, computer programming, computer science, crafts, creative writing, death and loss, drama, economics, English, English literature, English literature and composition-AP, environmental science, European history, family living, fine arts, finite math, fitness, forensics, French, French language-AP, geography, geometry, government/civics, health, health education, history, home economics, humanities, Internet, journalism, leadership, marine biology, mathematics, music, personal development, physical education, physical science, physics, physiology, pre-calculus, psychology, psychology-AP, public speaking, religion, SAT/ACT preparation, science, social studies, sociology, Spanish, Spanish language-AP, speech, studio art-AP, theater, theology, U.S. government and politics-AP, word processing, world history, world literature.
Graduation Requirements Arts and fine arts (art, music, dance, drama), English, foreign language, humanities, mathematics, personal development, physical education (includes health), public speaking, religion (includes Bible studies and theology), science, social studies (includes history). Community service is required.
Special Academic Programs 20 Advanced Placement exams for which test preparation is offered; honors section; study at local college for college credit; academic accommodation for the gifted; programs in English, mathematics, general development for dyslexic students; special instructional classes for learning difference students.
College Admission Counseling 245 students graduated in 2008; 242 went to college, including Bellarmine University; Jefferson Community and Technical College; Morehead State University; University of Kentucky; University of Louisville; Western Kentucky University. Other: 3 had other specific plans. Mean combined SAT: 1725, mean composite ACT: 24.
Student Life Upper grades have uniform requirement, student council, honor system. Discipline rests primarily with faculty. Attendance at religious services is required.
Summer Programs Sports, art/fine arts, computer instruction programs offered; session focuses on academics and sports camps; held on campus; accepts girls; open to students from other schools. 200 students usually enrolled. 2009 schedule: June 6 to August 2. Application deadline: June 15.
Tuition and Aid Day student tuition: $9100. Tuition installment plan (FACTS Tuition Payment Plan). Merit scholarship grants, need-based scholarship grants available. In 2008–09, 16% of upper-school students received aid; total upper-school merit-scholarship money awarded: $21,950. Total amount of financial aid awarded in 2008–09: $360,000.
Admissions Traditional secondary-level entrance grade is 9. Scholastic Testing Service and STS required. Deadline for receipt of application materials: none. Application fee required: $200. On-campus interview required.
Athletics Interscholastic: basketball, cheering, cross-country running, dance team, field hockey, golf, ice hockey, lacrosse, rowing, soccer, softball, swimming and diving, tennis, track and field, volleyball; intramural: basketball, bowling, hiking/backpacking, ice skating, kickball, table tennis, volleyball, walking. 2 PE instructors, 35 coaches.
Computers Computers are regularly used in all academic classes. Computer network features include on-campus library services, online commercial services, Internet access, wireless campus network, Internet filtering or blocking technology. Campus intranet, student e-mail accounts, and computer access in designated common areas are available to students. Students grades are available online. The school has a published electronic and media policy.
Contact Mrs. Becky Henle, Principal. 502-458-9551. Fax: 502-454-8411. E-mail: becky.henle@ahsrockets.org. Web site: www.ahsrockets.org.

THE ATHENIAN SCHOOL

2100 Mount Diablo Scenic Boulevard
Danville, California 94506
Head of School: Eleanor Dase

General Information Coeducational boarding and day college-preparatory school. Boarding grades 9–12, day grades 6–12. Founded: 1965. Setting: suburban. Nearest major city is San Francisco. Students are housed in single-sex dormitories. 75-acre campus. 24 buildings on campus. Approved or accredited by California Association of Independent Schools, The Association of Boarding Schools, The College Board, Western Association of Schools and Colleges, and California Department of Education. Member of National Association of Independent Schools and Secondary School Admission Test Board. Endowment: $400,000. Total enrollment: 453. Upper school average class size: 15. Upper school faculty-student ratio: 1:10.

Upper School Student Profile Grade 9: 71 students (41 boys, 30 girls); Grade 10: 79 students (38 boys, 41 girls); Grade 11: 78 students (39 boys, 39 girls); Grade 12: 72 students (39 boys, 33 girls). 14% of students are boarding students. 90% are state residents. 2 states are represented in upper school student body. 10% are international students. International students from China, Hong Kong, Japan, Republic of Korea, Taiwan, and Thailand; 5 other countries represented in student body.
Faculty School total: 53. In upper school: 20 men, 23 women; 31 have advanced degrees; 25 reside on campus.
Subjects Offered African-American studies, algebra, American history, American literature, American literature-AP, anatomy, art, art history, Asian history, Asian literature, biology, calculus-AP, ceramics, chemistry, classical studies, college writing, community service, comparative cultures, comparative religion, computer programming, computer science, computer skills, contemporary history, creative writing, dance, dance performance, debate, drama, drama performance, drama workshop, drawing, earth science, ecology, economics, economics and history, English, English as a foreign language, English literature, English-AP, environmental studies, ESL, ethics, European history, European history-AP, expository writing, fencing, fine arts, French, French-AP, geography, geology, geometry, government/civics, graphic design, health, history, humanities, introduction to technology, jazz band, jewelry making, literary magazine, literature seminar, literature-AP, mathematics, modern European history-AP, music, music history, music performance, musical theater, painting, philosophy, photography, physical education, physics, science, science project, sculpture, sociology, Spanish, Spanish literature-AP, Spanish-AP, stained glass, statistics, statistics-AP, theater, theater design and production, trigonometry, U.S. history-AP, wilderness experience, world cultures, world history, world literature, writing, yearbook, yoga.
Graduation Requirements American history, arts and fine arts (art, music, dance, drama), English, foreign language, history, literature, mathematics, physical education (includes health), science, wilderness experience, world history. Community service is required.
Special Academic Programs Advanced Placement exam preparation; honors section; independent study; term-away projects; study at local college for college credit; domestic exchange program; study abroad; ESL (8 students enrolled).
College Admission Counseling 71 students graduated in 2008; all went to college, including California Polytechnic State University, San Luis Obispo; Syracuse University; University of California, Berkeley; University of California, Santa Cruz; University of Colorado at Boulder; University of Southern California. Median combined SAT: 1930. 56% scored over 1800 on combined SAT.
Student Life Upper grades have specified standards of dress, student council. Discipline rests equally with students and faculty.
Summer Programs Enrichment, advancement, ESL, sports, art/fine arts, computer instruction programs offered; session focuses on academic enrichment, sports, and ESL; held on campus; accepts boys and girls; open to students from other schools. 200 students usually enrolled. 2009 schedule: June 13 to August 10. Application deadline: none.
Tuition and Aid Day student tuition: $27,520; 5-day tuition and room/board: $42,250; 7-day tuition and room/board: $42,250. Tuition installment plan (Insured Tuition Payment Plan, monthly payment plans). Need-based scholarship grants available. In 2008–09, 20% of upper-school students received aid. Total amount of financial aid awarded in 2008–09: $1,730,000.
Admissions Traditional secondary-level entrance grade is 9. For fall 2008, 399 students applied for upper-level admission, 105 were accepted, 45 enrolled. International English Language Test, ISEE, SLEP, SSAT or TOEFL required. Deadline for receipt of application materials: January 15. Application fee required: $75. Interview required.
Athletics Interscholastic: baseball (boys), basketball (b,g), cross-country running (b,g), golf (b), soccer (b,g), softball (g), swimming and diving (b,g), tennis (b,g); coed interscholastic: volleyball, wrestling; coed intramural: basketball, climbing, cross-country running, dance, fencing, weight training, yoga. 12 coaches.
Computers Computers are regularly used in English, foreign language, graphic design, history, humanities, information technology, library science, literary magazine, mathematics, publications, science, yearbook classes. Computer network features include on-campus library services, online commercial services, Internet access, wireless campus network, Internet filtering or blocking technology. Student e-mail accounts are available to students. Students grades are available online. The school has a published electronic and media policy.
Contact Beverly Gomer, Associate Director of Admission. 925-362-7223. Fax: 925-362-7228. E-mail: bgomer@athenian.org. Web site: www.athenian.org.

ANNOUNCEMENT FROM THE SCHOOL The San Francisco Bay Area's only nonsectarian day and boarding school, Athenian prepares students for lives of purpose and personal fulfillment as citizens of the world. At Athenian, learning is meaningful, interesting, and motivating. Distinctive programs include town meetings, the Athenian Wilderness Experience, international exchanges, robotics, airplane construction, and community service. Virtually 100 percent of the students gain admission to outstanding four-year colleges. Athenian equips graduates with a deep understanding of themselves, extraordinary skills for achievement, and the compassion to make a positive difference in the world.

See Close-Up on page 670.

ATHENS ACADEMY

1281 Spartan Lane
PO Box 6548
Athens, Georgia 30604

Head of School: J. Robert Chambers Jr.

General Information Coeducational day college-preparatory and technology school. Grades N–12. Founded: 1967. Setting: suburban. Nearest major city is Atlanta. 105-acre campus. 11 buildings on campus. Approved or accredited by Georgia Independent School Association, Southern Association of Colleges and Schools, Southern Association of Independent Schools, and Georgia Department of Education. Member of National Association of Independent Schools. Endowment: $4.9 million. Total enrollment: 908. Upper school average class size: 18. Upper school faculty-student ratio: 1:8.
Upper School Student Profile Grade 9: 84 students (42 boys, 42 girls); Grade 10: 83 students (44 boys, 39 girls); Grade 11: 74 students (37 boys, 37 girls); Grade 12: 66 students (33 boys, 33 girls).
Faculty School total: 102. In upper school: 22 men, 20 women; 31 have advanced degrees.
Subjects Offered Algebra, American history, American literature, anatomy, art, art history, biology, calculus, chemistry, chemistry-AP, computer math, creative writing, drama, ecology, economics, English, English literature, European history, expository writing, fine arts, French, geography, geometry, government/civics, grammar, health, history, Latin, mathematics, music, photography, physical education, physical science, physics, physiology, science, social studies, Spanish, statistics, theater, trigonometry, world history, world literature.
Graduation Requirements Arts and fine arts (art, music, dance, drama), English, foreign language, mathematics, physical education (includes health), science, social studies (includes history).
Special Academic Programs 13 Advanced Placement exams for which test preparation is offered; honors section.
College Admission Counseling 80 students graduated in 2008; all went to college, including Georgia Institute of Technology; University of Georgia. Median SAT critical reading: 623, median SAT math: 629, median SAT writing: 606, median combined SAT: 1858, median composite ACT: 27.
Student Life Upper grades have specified standards of dress, student council, honor system. Discipline rests primarily with faculty.
Summer Programs Remediation, enrichment, computer instruction programs offered; session focuses on enrichment and review; held on campus; accepts boys and girls; open to students from other schools. 80 students usually enrolled. 2009 schedule: June 15 to August 13. Application deadline: none.
Tuition and Aid Day student tuition: $12,665. Tuition installment plan (Insured Tuition Payment Plan, monthly payment plans). Tuition reduction for siblings, need-based scholarship grants available. In 2008–09, 20% of upper-school students received aid. Total amount of financial aid awarded in 2008–09: $400,000.
Admissions Traditional secondary-level entrance grade is 9. For fall 2008, 48 students applied for upper-level admission, 31 enrolled. CTP III and Otis-Lennon School Ability Test, ERB CPT III required. Deadline for receipt of application materials: February 12. Application fee required: $85. On-campus interview required.
Athletics Interscholastic: baseball (boys), basketball (b,g), cheering (g), cross-country running (b,g), football (b), soccer (b,g), swimming and diving (b,g), tennis (b,g), track and field (b,g), volleyball (g); coed interscholastic: cross-country running, golf, swimming and diving, tennis, track and field. 6 PE instructors, 5 coaches.
Computers Computers are regularly used in English, French, history, Latin, mathematics, science, Spanish classes. Computer network features include on-campus library services, online commercial services, Internet access, wireless campus network. Student e-mail accounts are available to students. The school has a published electronic and media policy.
Contact Stuart A. Todd, Director of Admissions. 706-549-9225. Fax: 706-354-3775. E-mail: stodd@athensacademy.org. Web site: www.athensacademy.org.

ATLANTA INTERNATIONAL SCHOOL

2890 North Fulton Drive
Atlanta, Georgia 30305

Head of School: Dr. Robert Brindley

General Information Coeducational day college-preparatory, bilingual studies, and International Baccalaureate school. Grades PK–12. Founded: 1984. Setting: urban. 10-acre campus. 3 buildings on campus. Approved or accredited by European Council of International Schools, French Ministry of Education, Georgia Independent School Association, International Baccalaureate Organization, National Independent Private Schools Association, Southern Association of Colleges and Schools, Southern Association of Independent Schools, and Georgia Department of Education. Member of National Association of Independent Schools. Endowment: $7.3 million. Total enrollment: 934. Upper school average class size: 15. Upper school faculty-student ratio: 1:7.
Upper School Student Profile Grade 9: 66 students (42 boys, 24 girls); Grade 10: 70 students (33 boys, 37 girls); Grade 11: 76 students (39 boys, 37 girls); Grade 12: 65 students (24 boys, 41 girls).
Faculty School total: 134. In upper school: 24 men, 43 women; 23 have advanced degrees.

Subjects Offered American history, art, biology, chemistry, Chinese, choir, chorus, computer science, contemporary issues, English, English literature, ESL, fine arts, French, French as a second language, geography, German, health, integrated mathematics, International Baccalaureate courses, jazz band, lab/keyboard, Latin, math methods, mathematics, model United Nations, physical education, physics, SAT preparation, science, science and technology, social studies, Spanish, theater, theater arts, theory of knowledge, world history, yearbook.

Graduation Requirements Arts and fine arts (art, music, dance, drama), English, foreign language, mathematics, physical education (includes health), science, social studies (includes history), theory of knowledge, extended essay/research project. Community service is required.

Special Academic Programs International Baccalaureate program; independent study; term-away projects; study abroad; ESL (45 students enrolled).

College Admission Counseling 55 students graduated in 2008; all went to college, including Georgia Institute of Technology; Northeastern University; The George Washington University; University of Pennsylvania; Vanderbilt University; Wake Forest University. 62% scored over 600 on SAT critical reading, 61% scored over 600 on SAT math, 65% scored over 600 on SAT writing.

Student Life Upper grades have specified standards of dress, student council. Discipline rests primarily with faculty.

Summer Programs Remediation, enrichment, advancement, ESL, sports, art/fine arts, computer instruction programs offered; session focuses on Language acquisition (French, Spanish, German, Chinese, ESL), day camps, sport camps, theater, robotics, chess; held on campus; accepts boys and girls; open to students from other schools. 150 students usually enrolled. 2009 schedule: June 15 to July 31. Application deadline: May 1.

Tuition and Aid Day student tuition: $15,510–$17,830. Tuition installment plan (Insured Tuition Payment Plan). Need-based scholarship grants available.

Admissions Traditional secondary-level entrance grade is 9. For fall 2008, 57 students applied for upper-level admission, 47 were accepted, 31 enrolled. Deadline for receipt of application materials: none. Application fee required: $100. Interview recommended.

Athletics Interscholastic: baseball (boys), basketball (b,g), cross-country running (b,g), soccer (b,g), swimming and diving (b,g), tennis (b,g), track and field (b,g), volleyball (g); intramural: strength & conditioning (b,g), track and field (b,g); coed intramural: basketball, fitness, jogging, volleyball. 9 PE instructors, 7 coaches, 3 athletic trainers.

Computers Computers are regularly used in all academic classes. Computer network features include Internet access, Internet filtering or blocking technology, server space for file storage, online classroom, multi-user learning software. Student e-mail accounts and computer access in designated common areas are available to students. Students grades are available online. The school has a published electronic and media policy.

Contact Ms. Pattie Webb, Assistant to Director of Admissions. 404-841-3891. Fax: 404-841-3873. E-mail: pwebb@aischool.org. Web site: www.aischool.org.

AUGUSTA CHRISTIAN SCHOOL (I)

313 Baston Road
Martinez, Georgia 30907

Head of School: Dr. John B. Bartlett

General Information Coeducational day college-preparatory, arts, religious studies, and technology school. Grades K–12. Founded: 1958. Setting: suburban. Nearest major city is Augusta. 26-acre campus. 10 buildings on campus. Approved or accredited by Association of Christian Schools International, Southern Association of Colleges and Schools, and Georgia Department of Education. Total enrollment: 544. Upper school average class size: 18. Upper school faculty-student ratio: 1:14.

Upper School Student Profile Grade 9: 78 students (48 boys, 30 girls); Grade 10: 63 students (23 boys, 40 girls); Grade 11: 62 students (36 boys, 26 girls); Grade 12: 56 students (30 boys, 26 girls).

Faculty School total: 54. In upper school: 10 men, 13 women; 3 have advanced degrees.

Subjects Offered Advanced chemistry, advanced computer applications, advanced math, Advanced Placement courses, algebra, American government, American history, American history-AP, American literature, anatomy and physiology, art, athletic training, athletics, band, baseball, basketball, Bible, biology, biology-AP, British literature, British literature-AP, calculus-AP, ceramics, cheerleading, chemistry, choir, choral music, chorus, Christian education, Christian studies, college counseling, comparative religion, computer education, computer keyboarding, computer skills, drama, drama performance, earth science, ecology, economics and history, electives, English, English composition, English literature, English literature-AP, English-AP, European history, French, general science, geography, geometry, government, grammar, health, history, instrumental music, keyboarding, life skills, mathematics, mathematics-AP, music appreciation, musical productions, New Testament, physics, piano, pre-algebra, pre-calculus, public speaking, reading, remedial/makeup course work, SAT preparation, science, social studies, Spanish, speech, sports, state history, student government, swimming, U.S. government, U.S. history, U.S. history-AP, U.S. literature, volleyball, weight training, weightlifting, world history, wrestling, yearbook.

Graduation Requirements Computers, early childhood, electives, English, foreign language, mathematics, physical education (includes health), science, social studies (includes history), speech.

Special Academic Programs Advanced Placement exam preparation; honors section.

College Admission Counseling Colleges students went to include Augusta State University; Georgia Southern University; University of Georgia.

Student Life Upper grades have specified standards of dress, student council. Discipline rests primarily with faculty. Attendance at religious services is required.

Summer Programs Remediation programs offered; session focuses on academics; held on campus; accepts boys and girls; open to students from other schools.

Tuition and Aid Day student tuition: $5610–$7856. Tuition installment plan (Insured Tuition Payment Plan, monthly payment plans, individually arranged payment plans). Tuition reduction for siblings, need-based scholarship grants available.

Admissions Traditional secondary-level entrance grade is 9. Stanford Achievement Test required. Deadline for receipt of application materials: none. Application fee required: $600. Interview required.

Athletics Interscholastic: baseball (boys), basketball (b,g), cheering (g), cross-country running (b,g), football (b), golf (b), soccer (b,g), softball (g), swimming and diving (b,g), tennis (b,g), track and field (b,g), volleyball (g), wrestling (b). 4 PE instructors.

Computers Computers are regularly used in computer applications, keyboarding, yearbook classes. Computer network features include on-campus library services, Internet access, Internet filtering or blocking technology. Campus intranet is available to students. Students grades are available online. The school has a published electronic and media policy.

Contact Mrs. Lauren Banks, Director of Admissions. 706-863-2905 Ext. 144. Fax: 706-860-6618. E-mail: laurenbanks@augustachristian.org.

AUGUSTA PREPARATORY DAY SCHOOL

285 Flowing Wells Road
Martinez, Georgia 30907

Head of School: Jack R. Hall

General Information Coeducational day college-preparatory school. Grades PS–12. Founded: 1960. Setting: suburban. Nearest major city is Augusta. 52-acre campus. 6 buildings on campus. Approved or accredited by Georgia Independent School Association, Southern Association of Colleges and Schools, and Southern Association of Independent Schools. Member of National Association of Independent Schools and Secondary School Admission Test Board. Endowment: $1.4 million. Total enrollment: 566. Upper school average class size: 11. Upper school faculty-student ratio: 1:9.

Upper School Student Profile Grade 9: 48 students (16 boys, 32 girls); Grade 10: 54 students (25 boys, 29 girls); Grade 11: 53 students (26 boys, 27 girls); Grade 12: 48 students (22 boys, 26 girls).

Faculty School total: 65. In upper school: 15 men, 10 women; 18 have advanced degrees.

Subjects Offered 20th century world history, Advanced Placement courses, advanced studio art-AP, algebra, American history, American literature, art, biology, biology-AP, calculus, calculus-AP, chemistry, chemistry-AP, computer programming, debate, drama, ecology, economics, English, English literature, English literature-AP, European history-AP, French, French-AP, geometry, government, government/civics, grammar, Latin, Latin-AP, marine science, physics, pre-calculus, senior project, Spanish, Spanish-AP, statistics-AP, studio art-AP, theater design and production, U.S. history-AP, world history.

Graduation Requirements Arts and fine arts (art, music, dance, drama), English, foreign language, mathematics, science, social studies (includes history), Senior Speech, Senior Project.

Special Academic Programs Honors section; independent study; term-away projects; academic accommodation for the gifted.

College Admission Counseling 41 students graduated in 2008; all went to college, including College of Charleston; Emory University; Furman University; Mercer University; University of Georgia; Washington University in St. Louis. Median SAT critical reading: 630, median SAT math: 610, median SAT writing: 630, median combined SAT: 1880, median composite ACT: 27. 56% scored over 600 on SAT critical reading, 51% scored over 600 on SAT math, 61% scored over 600 on SAT writing, 63% scored over 1800 on combined SAT, 58% scored over 26 on composite ACT.

Student Life Upper grades have specified standards of dress, student council, honor system. Discipline rests equally with students and faculty.

Summer Programs Enrichment, sports, art/fine arts, computer instruction programs offered; session focuses on Enrichment; held on campus; accepts boys and girls; open to students from other schools. 2009 schedule: June 8 to August 1.

Tuition and Aid Day student tuition: $5100–$11,820. Tuition installment plan (monthly payment plans). Tuition reduction for siblings, need-based scholarship grants, Community Enrichment Scholarship Program, merit & need-based available. In 2008–09, 20% of upper-school students received aid.

Admissions Traditional secondary-level entrance grade is 9. For fall 2008, 26 students applied for upper-level admission, 24 were accepted, 22 enrolled. ERB CTP III required. Deadline for receipt of application materials: none. Application fee required: $75. On-campus interview required.

Athletics Interscholastic: baseball (boys), basketball (b,g), cheering (g), cross-country running (b,g), football (b), golf (b), soccer (b,g), swimming and diving (b,g), tennis (b,g), volleyball (g), weight training (b,g). 3 PE instructors, 1 athletic trainer.
Computers Computers are regularly used in all classes. Computer network features include on-campus library services, online commercial services, Internet access, wireless campus network, Internet filtering or blocking technology. Campus intranet and computer access in designated common areas are available to students. The school has a published electronic and media policy.
Contact Rosie Herrmann, Director of Admission. 706-863-1906 Ext. 201. Fax: 706-863-6198. E-mail: admissions@augustaprep.org. Web site: www.augustaprep.org.

AULDERN ACADEMY

990 Glovers Grove Church Road
Siler City, North Carolina 27344

Head of School: Ms. Jane Samuel

General Information Girls' boarding college-preparatory and arts school; primarily serves students with learning disabilities and individuals with Attention Deficit Disorder. Grades 9–12. Founded: 2001. Setting: rural. Nearest major city is Chapel Hill. Students are housed in single-sex dormitories. 86-acre campus. 4 buildings on campus. Approved or accredited by National Independent Private Schools Association and North Carolina Department of Education. Candidate for accreditation by Southern Association of Colleges and Schools. Total enrollment: 45. Upper school average class size: 8. Upper school faculty-student ratio: 1:6.
Upper School Student Profile Grade 9: 4 students (4 girls); Grade 10: 10 students (10 girls); Grade 11: 10 students (10 girls); Grade 12: 21 students (21 girls). 100% of students are boarding students. International students from France and United Kingdom.
Faculty School total: 7. In upper school: 5 men, 2 women; 3 have advanced degrees; 3 reside on campus.
Subjects Offered 3-dimensional design, adolescent issues, advanced chemistry, advanced math, algebra, American government-AP, American literature, anatomy and physiology, art, art history, biology, biology-AP, British literature, calculus, calculus-AP, career/college preparation, chemistry, chemistry-AP, computer education, current history, economics, economics-AP, English language and composition-AP, foreign language, geology, geometry, health education, photo shop, physical education, physical fitness, physics, physics-AP, pre-calculus, science, Spanish, Spanish language-AP, study skills, U.S. government, U.S. history, values and decisions, world history.
Graduation Requirements Electives, English, foreign language, mathematics, physical education (includes health), science, social studies (includes history).
Special Academic Programs Advanced Placement exam preparation; independent study; special instructional classes for students with mild learning disabilities, mild Attention Deficit Disorder, and mild behavioral and/or emotional problems (anxiety, depression).
College Admission Counseling 13 students graduated in 2008; 12 went to college, including Austin College; Georgia College & State University; Peace College; Saint Mary's College of California; University of Denver. Mean SAT critical reading: 580, mean SAT math: 550.
Student Life Upper grades have specified standards of dress, student council, honor system. Discipline rests equally with students and faculty.
Summer Programs Remediation, advancement, art/fine arts, computer instruction programs offered; session focuses on academics; held on campus; accepts girls; not open to students from other schools. 39 students usually enrolled. 2009 schedule: June 8 to August 6.
Tuition and Aid 7-day tuition and room/board: $40,000. Guaranteed tuition plan. Tuition installment plan (Key Tuition Payment Plan, monthly payment plans, individually arranged payment plans). Need-based scholarship grants available.
Admissions Comprehensive educational evaluation and psychoeducational evaluation required. Deadline for receipt of application materials: none. No application fee required. Interview required.
Athletics Intramural: aerobics, aerobics/dance, basketball, bicycling, combined training, cooperative games, dance, fitness, fitness walking, horseback riding, indoor soccer, jogging, mountain biking, outdoor activities, physical fitness, running, soccer, strength & conditioning, table tennis, tennis, triathlon, volleyball, walking, weight lifting, weight training. 1 PE instructor.
Computers Computer network features include on-campus library services, Internet access, Internet filtering or blocking technology.
Contact Ms. Jane Samuel, Admissions Director. 919-837-2336 Ext. 200. Fax: 919-837-5284. E-mail: jane.samuel@threesprings.com. Web site: www.auldern.com.

ANNOUNCEMENT FROM THE SCHOOL Auldern Academy is a college-preparatory boarding school offering a traditional boarding school environment, challenging and supportive academics, and a personal growth plan to prepare young women for transition to college and independence. Auldern serves academically capable young women, grades 9–12, who have successfully completed a previous therapeutic placement and would benefit from more structure and support than a typical boarding school provides.

AURORA CENTRAL HIGH SCHOOL

1255 North Edgelawn Drive
Aurora, Illinois 60506-1673

Head of School: Very Rev. F. William Etheredge

General Information Coeducational day college-preparatory school, affiliated with Roman Catholic Church. Grades 9–12. Founded: 1968. Setting: urban. 47-acre campus. 1 building on campus. Approved or accredited by National Catholic Education Association, North Central Association of Colleges and Schools, and Illinois Department of Education. Endowment: $8.1 million. Total enrollment: 483. Upper school average class size: 25. Upper school faculty-student ratio: 1:16.
Upper School Student Profile Grade 9: 124 students (60 boys, 64 girls); Grade 10: 150 students (74 boys, 76 girls); Grade 11: 118 students (58 boys, 60 girls); Grade 12: 91 students (46 boys, 45 girls). 87% of students are Roman Catholic.
Faculty School total: 35. In upper school: 18 men, 17 women; 31 have advanced degrees.
Subjects Offered American government-AP, American history, American literature-AP, art, athletics, band, Bible, biology, biology-AP, calculus-AP, campus ministry, chemistry, chemistry-AP, civil war history, comparative religion, computer skills, constitutional history of U.S., consumer economics, contemporary history, CPR, creative writing, earth science, ecology, environmental systems, electives, engineering, English, English composition, English literature, English literature-AP, environmental science, ethics, fine arts, foreign language, French, French-AP, geometry, health, history, home economics, honors algebra, honors English, honors geometry, honors U.S. history, honors world history, instrumental music, Internet, journalism, keyboarding/computer, Latin, math applications, mathematics, medieval history, moral theology, music, newspaper, oral communications, physical education, political science, pre-algebra, pre-calculus, psychology, reading/study skills, science, Shakespeare, social justice, Spanish, Spanish-AP, theology, U.S. government and politics, U.S. government and politics-AP, U.S. history-AP, Western civilization, world history, World War II, yearbook.
Graduation Requirements Algebra, biology, Catholic belief and practice, Christian and Hebrew scripture, constitutional history of U.S., consumer economics, English, English literature, geometry, history, keyboarding/computer, language and composition, moral theology, physical education (includes health), religion (includes Bible studies and theology), science, scripture, U.S. government, U.S. history, retreat programs. Community service is required.
Special Academic Programs 6 Advanced Placement exams for which test preparation is offered; honors section; independent study; study at local college for college credit; academic accommodation for the gifted; remedial reading and/or remedial writing; remedial math.
College Admission Counseling 93 students graduated in 2008; 90 went to college, including Benedictine University; Illinois State University; Loyola University Chicago; Marquette University; Northern Illinois University; University of Illinois at Urbana–Champaign. Other: 1 went to work, 2 entered military service. Median composite ACT: 19.
Student Life Upper grades have uniform requirement, student council, honor system. Discipline rests primarily with faculty. Attendance at religious services is required.
Summer Programs Enrichment, sports, art/fine arts programs offered; session focuses on skill development; held both on and off campus; held at golf course and park district facilities; accepts boys and girls; open to students from other schools. 150 students usually enrolled. 2009 schedule: June 7 to August 7. Application deadline: June 7.
Tuition and Aid Day student tuition: $4200. Tuition installment plan (monthly payment plans). Tuition reduction for siblings, merit scholarship grants, need-based scholarship grants, need-based loans available. In 2008–09, 15% of upper-school students received aid; total upper-school merit-scholarship money awarded: $20,000. Total amount of financial aid awarded in 2008–09: $100,000.
Admissions Traditional secondary-level entrance grade is 9. High School Placement Test required. Deadline for receipt of application materials: none. Application fee required: $50. Interview recommended.
Athletics Interscholastic: aerobics/dance (girls), baseball (b,g), basketball (b,g), cheering (g), cross-country running (b,g), dance (g), dance squad (g), dance team (g), football (b), golf (b,g), indoor track (b,g), indoor track & field (b,g), pom squad (g), soccer (b,g), softball (g), tennis (b,g), volleyball (g), wrestling (b); intramural: aerobics/dance (g), baseball (b,g), basketball (b,g), flag football (b), floor hockey (g), football (b), indoor track (b,g), indoor track & field (b,g), jogging (b,g), physical fitness (b,g), physical training (b,g), power lifting (b,g), soccer (b,g), softball (b,g), volleyball (b,g), weight lifting (b,g), weight training (b,g), winter (indoor) track (b,g), wrestling (b); coed intramural: modern dance, physical fitness, physical training, power lifting, soccer, swimming and diving, volleyball, weight lifting, weight training, winter (indoor) track. 3 PE instructors, 51 coaches, 2 athletic trainers.
Computers Computers are regularly used in drafting, engineering, English, French, history, Spanish, technology classes. Computer network features include on-campus library services, online commercial services, Internet access, Internet filtering or blocking technology. The school has a published electronic and media policy.
Contact Mr. Brian Casey, Development Assistant. 630-907-0095 Ext. 21. Fax: 630-907-1076. E-mail: bcasey@auroracentral.com. Web site: www.auroracentral.com.

AUSTIN CHRISTIAN ACADEMY

Box 460
Austin, Manitoba R0H 0C0, Canada

Head of School: Adm. James Zurbriggen, EdD

General Information Coeducational day college-preparatory and general academic school, affiliated with Christian faith. Grades K–12. Founded: 1983. Setting: rural. Nearest major city is Portage la Prairie, Canada. 3-acre campus. 1 building on campus. Approved or accredited by Association of Christian Schools International and Manitoba Department of Education. Language of instruction: English. Total enrollment: 43. Upper school average class size: 8. Upper school faculty-student ratio: 1:12.

Upper School Student Profile Grade 9: 5 students (2 boys, 3 girls); Grade 11: 5 students (2 boys, 3 girls); Grade 12: 1 student (1 boy). 100% of students are Christian.

Faculty School total: 3. In upper school: 1 man, 2 women.

Graduation Requirements Manitoba Department of Education requirements.

College Admission Counseling Colleges students went to include The University of Winnipeg.

Student Life Upper grades have uniform requirement. Discipline rests primarily with faculty. Attendance at religious services is required.

Tuition and Aid Day student tuition: CAN$2300. Tuition installment plan (monthly payment plans).

Admissions Deadline for receipt of application materials: May 19. No application fee required. On-campus interview required.

Computers Computers are regularly used in career education, career exploration, creative writing, French as a second language, mathematics, reading classes. Computer resources include Internet access.

Contact Becky Zurbriggen, Secretary. 204-637-2303. Fax: 204-637-3127. E-mail: ausaca@xplornet.com.

AUSTIN PREPARATORY SCHOOL

101 Willow Street
Reading, Massachusetts 01867

Head of School: Mr. Paul J. Moran

General Information Coeducational day college-preparatory and religious studies school, affiliated with Roman Catholic Church. Grades 6–12. Founded: 1961. Setting: suburban. Nearest major city is Boston. 42-acre campus. 2 buildings on campus. Approved or accredited by Association of Independent Schools in New England, National Catholic Education Association, National Independent Private Schools Association, New England Association of Schools and Colleges, and Massachusetts Department of Education. Member of National Association of Independent Schools. Upper school average class size: 14. Upper school faculty-student ratio: 1:15.

Upper School Student Profile 84% of students are Roman Catholic.

Faculty School total: 64. In upper school: 25 men, 15 women.

Subjects Offered Algebra, American history, American literature, anatomy, Bible studies, biology, botany, business, calculus, chemistry, computer math, computer programming, computer science, creative writing, earth science, economics, English, English literature, environmental science, French, geography, geology, geometry, government/civics, grammar, history, Latin, marine biology, mathematics, oceanography, physics, physiology, religion, Russian, science, social studies, sociology, Spanish, statistics, trigonometry, writing.

Graduation Requirements English, foreign language, mathematics, religion (includes Bible studies and theology), science, social studies (includes history).

Special Academic Programs Advanced Placement exam preparation; honors section; study at local college for college credit.

College Admission Counseling 78 students graduated in 2008; all went to college, including Assumption College; Boston College; Boston University; Merrimack College; Northeastern University; University of Massachusetts Lowell. 30% scored over 600 on SAT critical reading, 30% scored over 600 on SAT math.

Student Life Upper grades have uniform requirement, student council. Discipline rests primarily with faculty.

Tuition and Aid Day student tuition: $11,400. Tuition installment plan (Academic Management Services Plan, monthly payment plans, see school Website for full description). Tuition reduction for siblings, merit scholarship grants, need-based scholarship grants available. Total amount of financial aid awarded in 2008–09: $293,004.

Admissions For fall 2008, 170 students applied for upper-level admission, 130 were accepted. Archdiocese of Boston High School entrance exam provided by STS required. Deadline for receipt of application materials: December 31. No application fee required.

Athletics Interscholastic: baseball (boys), basketball (b,g), cross-country running (b,g), football (b), golf (b,g), ice hockey (b), lacrosse (b), skiing (downhill) (b,g), soccer (b,g), softball (g), swimming and diving (b,g), tennis (b,g), track and field (b,g); intramural: basketball (b,g), skiing (downhill) (b,g), softball (b,g); coed interscholastic: golf, skiing (downhill), swimming and diving; coed intramural: basketball, skiing (downhill), softball. 52 coaches, 1 athletic trainer.

Computers Computers are regularly used in English, foreign language, mathematics, science classes. Computer network features include on-campus library services, Internet access.

Contact Mrs. Terese M. Glionna, Headmaster's Administrative Assistant/Office Mgr. 781-944-4900 Ext. 822. Fax: 781-942-4593. E-mail: tglionna@austinprepschool.org. Web site: www.austinprepschool.org.

AVON OLD FARMS SCHOOL

500 Old Farms Road
Avon, Connecticut 06001

Head of School: Kenneth H. LaRocque

General Information Boys' boarding and day college-preparatory school. Boarding grades 9–PG, day grades 9–12. Founded: 1927. Setting: suburban. Nearest major city is Hartford. Students are housed in single-sex dormitories. 990-acre campus. 39 buildings on campus. Approved or accredited by Connecticut Association of Independent Schools, New England Association of Schools and Colleges, The Association of Boarding Schools, and Connecticut Department of Education. Member of National Association of Independent Schools and Secondary School Admission Test Board. Endowment: $33 million. Total enrollment: 405. Upper school average class size: 13. Upper school faculty-student ratio: 1:7.

Upper School Student Profile Grade 9: 76 students (76 boys); Grade 10: 97 students (97 boys); Grade 11: 111 students (111 boys); Grade 12: 105 students (105 boys); Postgraduate: 16 students (16 boys). 74% of students are boarding students. 47% are state residents. 24 states are represented in upper school student body. 10% are international students. International students from Canada, China, Panama, Republic of Korea, Spain, and United Kingdom; 10 other countries represented in student body.

Faculty School total: 57. In upper school: 39 men, 18 women; 32 have advanced degrees; 49 reside on campus.

Subjects Offered Advanced math, advanced studio art-AP, algebra, American Civil War, American government-AP, American history-AP, American legal systems, American literature, ancient history, architectural drawing, architecture, art, art-AP, Basic programming, biology, biology-AP, calculus, calculus-AP, ceramics, chamber groups, chemistry, chorus, computer programming, concert band, design, digital photography, economics, economics-AP, English, English language and composition-AP, English literature, English literature and composition-AP, English literature-AP, environmental science, environmental science-AP, European history, fine arts, foundations of civilization, French, French language-AP, geology, geometry, government-AP, guitar, honors algebra, honors English, honors geometry, human sexuality, jazz band, Latin, macro/microeconomics-AP, model United Nations, modern history, moral reasoning, music theory, photography, physics, physics-AP, pre-calculus, probability and statistics, public speaking, Spanish, Spanish language-AP, statistics-AP, studio art-AP, trigonometry, U.S. government, U.S. government-AP, woodworking, world history, World War I, World War II.

Graduation Requirements Algebra, American literature, arts and fine arts (art, music, dance, drama), biology, computer applications, computer keyboarding, English, English composition, foreign language, geometry, mathematics, science, social science, U.S. history.

Special Academic Programs Advanced Placement exam preparation; honors section; independent study; academic accommodation for the gifted and the artistically talented.

College Admission Counseling 127 students graduated in 2008; 124 went to college, including Boston College; Cornell University; Hamilton College; United States Military Academy; Wake Forest University; Yale University. Other: 2 entered a postgraduate year, 1 had other specific plans. Median SAT critical reading: 560, median SAT math: 660, median SAT writing: 556, median combined SAT: 1780. 34% scored over 600 on SAT critical reading, 52% scored over 600 on SAT math, 36% scored over 600 on SAT writing, 41% scored over 1800 on combined SAT.

Student Life Upper grades have specified standards of dress, student council. Discipline rests primarily with faculty.

Tuition and Aid Day student tuition: $31,100; 5-day tuition and room/board: $40,850; 7-day tuition and room/board: $40,850. Tuition installment plan (Insured Tuition Payment Plan, monthly payment plans, individually arranged payment plans). Merit scholarship grants, need-based scholarship grants, need-based loans available. In 2008–09, 28% of upper-school students received aid; total upper-school merit-scholarship money awarded: $61,500. Total amount of financial aid awarded in 2008–09: $2,970,000.

Admissions Traditional secondary-level entrance grade is 9. For fall 2008, 525 students applied for upper-level admission, 253 were accepted, 148 enrolled. PSAT, SAT, SSAT or TOEFL required. Deadline for receipt of application materials: February 1. Application fee required: $50. On-campus interview required.

Athletics Interscholastic: alpine skiing (boys), baseball (b), basketball (b), cross-country running (b), football (b), golf (b), hockey (b), ice hockey (b), indoor hockey (b), lacrosse (b), riflery (b), running (b), skiing (downhill) (b), soccer (b), squash (b), swimming and diving (b), tennis (b), track and field (b), wrestling (b); intramural: alpine skiing (b), ball hockey (b), basketball (b), bicycling (b), combined training (b), cross-country running (b), fishing (b), fitness (b), flag football (b), floor hockey (b), fly fishing (b), freestyle skiing (b), Frisbee (b), golf (b), hockey (b), ice hockey (b), indoor hockey (b), jogging (b), mountain biking (b), Nautilus (b), nordic skiing (b), outdoor activities (b), physical training (b), roller blading (b), ropes courses (b), rugby (b), running (b), scuba diving (b), skateboarding (b), skiing (cross-country) (b), skiing (downhill) (b), snowboarding (b), squash (b), street hockey (b), strength & condi-

tioning (b), swimming and diving (b), table tennis (b), tennis (b), touch football (b), ultimate Frisbee (b), water polo (b), weight lifting (b), weight training (b). 2 coaches, 1 athletic trainer.
Computers Computers are regularly used in English, foreign language, history, mathematics, science classes. Computer network features include on-campus library services, online commercial services, Internet access, Internet filtering or blocking technology, Blackboard, SmartBoards. Student e-mail accounts are available to students. The school has a published electronic and media policy.
Contact Mr. Brendon A. Welker, Director of Admissions. 800-464-2866. Fax: 860-675-6051. E-mail: welkerb@avonoldfarms.com. Web site: www.avonoldfarms.com.

See Close Up on page 672.

THE AWTY INTERNATIONAL SCHOOL

7455 Awty School Lane
Houston, Texas 77055
Head of School: Dr. David Watson

General Information Coeducational day college-preparatory and bilingual studies school. Grades PK–12. Founded: 1956. Setting: urban. 25-acre campus. 15 buildings on campus. Approved or accredited by French Ministry of Education, Independent Schools Association of the Southwest, International Baccalaureate Organization, and Texas Department of Education. Member of National Association of Independent Schools, Secondary School Admission Test Board, and European Council of International Schools. Languages of instruction: English, Spanish, and French. Endowment: $2.8 million. Total enrollment: 1,200. Upper school average class size: 18. Upper school faculty-student ratio: 1:18.
Upper School Student Profile Grade 9: 95 students (41 boys, 54 girls); Grade 10: 86 students (36 boys, 50 girls); Grade 11: 90 students (38 boys, 52 girls); Grade 12: 79 students (30 boys, 49 girls).
Faculty School total: 145. In upper school: 31 men, 52 women; 39 have advanced degrees.
Subjects Offered Algebra, American history, Arabic, art, biology, calculus, chemistry, community service, computer programming, computer science, computer studies, drama, Dutch, English, ESL, fine arts, French, geography, geometry, German, grammar, history, Italian, Mandarin, mathematics, music, Norwegian, philosophy, physical education, physics, science, social science, social studies, Spanish, theater, theory of knowledge, trigonometry, world history, world literature, writing.
Graduation Requirements Arts and fine arts (art, music, dance, drama), computer science, English, foreign language, mathematics, physical education (includes health), science, social science, social studies (includes history), 4000-word extended essay. Community service is required.
Special Academic Programs International Baccalaureate program; ESL (20 students enrolled).
College Admission Counseling 82 students graduated in 2008; all went to college, including Carnegie Mellon University; McGill University; Rice University; The University of Texas at Austin; University of Houston; Vanderbilt University. Median SAT critical reading: 600, median SAT math: 620, median composite ACT: 25. 59% scored over 600 on SAT critical reading, 74% scored over 600 on SAT math, 45% scored over 26 on composite ACT.
Student Life Upper grades have uniform requirement, student council, honor system. Discipline rests primarily with faculty.
Tuition and Aid Day student tuition: $17,310. Tuition installment plan (monthly payment plans, semiannual payment plan, Dewar Tuition Refund Plan). Need-based scholarship grants available. In 2008–09, 6% of upper-school students received aid. Total amount of financial aid awarded in 2008–09: $271,700.
Admissions Traditional secondary-level entrance grade is 9. For fall 2008, 140 students applied for upper-level admission, 63 were accepted, 37 enrolled. ISEE, OLSAT, ERB or writing sample required. Deadline for receipt of application materials: none. Application fee required: $100. On-campus interview required.
Athletics Interscholastic: basketball (boys, girls), cheering (g), cross-country running (b,g), soccer (b,g), tennis (b,g), track and field (b,g), volleyball (g), winter soccer (g); intramural: dance (g), dance squad (g), dance team (g), flag football (b); coed interscholastic: golf, swimming and diving; coed intramural: badminton. 5 PE instructors, 20 coaches.
Computers Computers are regularly used in foreign language, science classes. Computer network features include on-campus library services, Internet access. The school has a published electronic and media policy.
Contact Erika Benavente, Acting Director of Admissions. 713-686-4850. Fax: 713-579-0003. E-mail: ebenavente@awty.org. Web site: www.awty.org.

BAKERSFIELD CHRISTIAN HIGH SCHOOL

12775 Stockdale Highway
Bakersfield, California 93314
Head of School: Mr. Daniel H. Cole

General Information Coeducational day college-preparatory and religious studies school, affiliated with Christian faith. Grades 9–12. Founded: 1979. Setting: suburban. 47-acre campus. 9 buildings on campus. Approved or accredited by Association of Christian Schools International, Western Association of Schools and Colleges, and California Department of Education. Endowment: $500,000. Total enrollment: 506. Upper school average class size: 22. Upper school faculty-student ratio: 1:17.
Faculty School total: 44. In upper school: 21 men, 23 women; 7 have advanced degrees.
Subjects Offered Advanced Placement courses, advanced studio art-AP, agriculture, American literature, American literature-AP, Bible, biology, biology-AP, British literature, British literature-AP, calculus, calculus-AP, chemistry, chemistry-AP, choir, Christian ethics, comparative religion, computer animation, contemporary issues, digital photography, drama, economics, economics-AP, English, English literature, English literature-AP, English-AP, European history, European history-AP, foreign language, forensics, French, history-AP, human anatomy, introduction to literature, jazz band, performing arts, photography, physical science, physics, physics AP, pre-calculus, Spanish, Spanish-AP, statistics, statistics-AP, studio art, studio art-AP, U.S. history, U.S. history-AP, video and animation, world history, world literature.
Graduation Requirements 40 hours community service.
Special Academic Programs Advanced Placement exam preparation; independent study.
Student Life Upper grades have specified standards of dress, student council, honor system. Discipline rests primarily with faculty. Attendance at religious services is required.
Tuition and Aid Day student tuition: $8025. Tuition installment plan (FACTS Tuition Payment Plan, monthly payment plans, individually arranged payment plans). Tuition reduction for siblings, need-based financial aid available. In 2008–09, 26% of upper-school students received aid.
Admissions Traditional secondary-level entrance grade is 9. Application fee required: $50. On-campus interview required.
Athletics Interscholastic: baseball (boys), basketball (b,g), cheering (g), football (b), softball (g), tennis (b,g), volleyball (g), wrestling (b); coed interscholastic: cross-country running, golf, swimming and diving, track and field. 10 coaches, 1 athletic trainer.
Computers Computer network features include on-campus library services, Internet access, Internet filtering or blocking technology. Computer access in designated common areas is available to students. Students grades are available online. The school has a published electronic and media policy.
Contact Mrs. Debbie Camp, Director of Admissions. 661-410-7000. Fax: 661-410-7007. E-mail: dcamp@bakersfieldchristian.com. Web site: www.bakersfieldchristian.com.

THE BALDWIN SCHOOL

701 West Montgomery Avenue
Bryn Mawr, Pennsylvania 19010
Head of School: Mrs. Sally M. Powell

General Information Girls' day college-preparatory, arts, technology, and athletics school. Grades PK–12. Founded: 1888. Setting: suburban. Nearest major city is Philadelphia. 25-acre campus. 5 buildings on campus. Approved or accredited by Middle States Association of Colleges and Schools and Pennsylvania Association of Independent Schools. Member of National Association of Independent Schools and Secondary School Admission Test Board. Endowment: $7.7 million. Total enrollment: 587. Upper school average class size: 16. Upper school faculty-student ratio: 1:7.
Upper School Student Profile Grade 9: 47 students (47 girls); Grade 10: 61 students (61 girls); Grade 11: 49 students (49 girls); Grade 12: 49 students (49 girls).
Faculty School total: 90. In upper school: 9 men, 31 women; 34 have advanced degrees.
Subjects Offered Advanced Placement courses, algebra, American history, American literature, anthropology, architecture, art, art history, athletics, basketball, bell choir, biology, biology-AP, calculus, calculus-AP, ceramics, chemistry, chemistry-AP, chorus, classical Greek literature, community service, computer science, contemporary issues, creative writing, dance, drama, earth science, English, English literature, environmental studies, ethics, European history, fine arts, French, French literature-AP, geometry, health, history, human development, Latin, mathematics, music, photography, physical education, physics, physics-AP, science, senior internship, social studies, softball, Spanish, speech, swimming, tennis, theater, trigonometry, U.S. history, U.S. history-AP, vocal ensemble, volleyball, world history, world literature.
Graduation Requirements Arts, English, foreign language, history, life skills, mathematics, science, U.S. history.
Special Academic Programs Advanced Placement exam preparation; honors section; independent study; academic accommodation for the gifted, the musically talented, and the artistically talented.
College Admission Counseling 53 students graduated in 2008; 52 went to college, including Franklin & Marshall College; Princeton University; The George Washington University; University of Pennsylvania. Other: 1 had other specific plans.
Student Life Upper grades have uniform requirement, student council, honor system. Discipline rests equally with students and faculty.
Tuition and Aid Day student tuition: $24,775. Tuition installment plan (monthly payment plans, individually arranged payment plans). Need-based scholarship grants available. In 2008–09, 27% of upper-school students received aid. Total amount of financial aid awarded in 2008–09: $865,226.
Admissions Traditional secondary-level entrance grade is 9. For fall 2008, 42 students applied for upper-level admission, 26 were accepted, 9 enrolled. ISEE, SSAT,

Wechsler Intelligence Scale for Children or writing sample required. Deadline for receipt of application materials: February 1. Application fee required: $50. On-campus interview required.
Athletics Interscholastic: basketball, crew, cross-country running, dance, field hockey, golf, independent competitive sports, lacrosse, rowing, running, soccer, softball, squash, swimming and diving, tennis, volleyball, winter (indoor) track. 7 PE instructors, 40 coaches, 1 athletic trainer.
Computers Computers are regularly used in all academic classes. Computer network features include on-campus library services, Internet access. Campus intranet, student e-mail accounts, and computer access in designated common areas are available to students. The school has a published electronic and media policy.
Contact Sarah J. Goebel, Director of Admissions and Financial Aid. 610-525-2700 Ext. 251. Fax: 610-581-7231. E-mail: sgoebel@baldwinschool.org. Web site: www.baldwinschool.org.

ANNOUNCEMENT FROM THE SCHOOL The Baldwin School provides a rigorous intellectual experience within a respectful and diverse community. Exceptional and competitive opportunities exist both in and out of the classroom in academics, the arts, and athletics. Committed, caring, and innovative faculty members supported by strong school leadership and extensive technology resources make the learning experience an engaging one.

See Close-Up on page 674.

BALDWIN SCHOOL OF PUERTO RICO, INC.

PO Box 1827
Bayamón, Puerto Rico 00960-1827
Head of School: Dr. Günther Brandt

General Information Coeducational day college-preparatory school. Grades PK–12. Founded: 1968. Setting: suburban. Nearest major city is San Juan. 23-acre campus. 6 buildings on campus. Approved or accredited by Middle States Association of Colleges and Schools and Puerto Rico Department of Education. Member of National Association of Independent Schools. Languages of instruction: English and Spanish. Total enrollment: 781. Upper school average class size: 20. Upper school faculty-student ratio: 1:10.
Upper School Student Profile Grade 9: 52 students (29 boys, 23 girls); Grade 10: 44 students (28 boys, 16 girls); Grade 11: 55 students (31 boys, 24 girls); Grade 12: 44 students (15 boys, 29 girls).
Faculty School total: 74. In upper school: 6 men, 30 women; 23 have advanced degrees.
Subjects Offered Algebra, American history, American literature, art, biology, biology-AP, British literature, calculus, calculus-AP, chemistry, chemistry-AP, computer information systems, computer literacy, computer programming, computer science, computers, English, English literature, English literature-AP, environmental science, ESL, European history-AP, fine arts, French, French-AP, geography, geometry, grammar, history, mathematics, music, physical education, physics, pre-calculus, psychology, Puerto Rican history, science, social studies, Spanish, Spanish language-AP, Spanish literature-AP, study skills, visual arts, vocal music, world literature, writing.
Graduation Requirements Algebra, American history, American literature, arts and fine arts (art, music, dance, drama), biology, British literature, chemistry, computer science, English, English literature, geometry, mathematics, physical education (includes health), Puerto Rican history, science, social studies (includes history), Spanish, U.S. history, Western civilization.
Special Academic Programs Advanced Placement exam preparation; honors section.
College Admission Counseling 51 students graduated in 2008; all went to college, including Boston College; Boston University; Purdue University; The George Washington University; Tufts University; University of Puerto Rico, Río Piedras. Median SAT critical reading: 565, median SAT math: 589, median SAT writing: 592.
Student Life Upper grades have uniform requirement, student council, honor system. Discipline rests equally with students and faculty.
Summer Programs Remediation, enrichment, ESL, computer instruction programs offered; session focuses on remediation; held on campus; accepts boys and girls; open to students from other schools. 163 students usually enrolled. 2009 schedule: June 1 to June 26. Application deadline: May 13.
Tuition and Aid Day student tuition: $10,395–$10,995. Guaranteed tuition plan. Tuition installment plan (biannual payment plan). Tuition reduction for siblings, need-based scholarship grants, tuition reduction for children of staff, full-scholarship program for eligible students available. In 2008–09, 1% of upper-school students received aid. Total amount of financial aid awarded in 2008–09: $12,000.
Admissions Traditional secondary-level entrance grade is 9. For fall 2008, 20 students applied for upper-level admission, 13 were accepted, 13 enrolled. Stanford Achievement Test, Otis-Lennon required. Deadline for receipt of application materials: none. Application fee required: $150. On-campus interview required.
Athletics Interscholastic: baseball (boys), basketball (b,g), cheering (g), indoor soccer (b,g), soccer (b,g), swimming and diving (b,g), tennis (b,g), volleyball (b,g); intramural: flag football (b,g), touch football (b,g); coed interscholastic: golf, physical fitness. 6 PE instructors, 17 coaches, 1 athletic trainer.
Computers Computers are regularly used in English, history, mathematics, science, Spanish, technology classes. Computer network features include on-campus library services, Internet access, wireless campus network, Internet filtering or blocking technology. Computer access in designated common areas is available to students. Students grades are available online.
Contact Mrs. Ely Mejías, Director of Admissions. 787-720-2421 Ext. 239. Fax: 787-790-0619. E-mail: emejias@baldwin-school.org. Web site: www.baldwin-school.org.

BALMORAL HALL SCHOOL

630 Westminster Avenue
Winnipeg, Manitoba R3C 3S1, Canada
Head of School: Mrs. Donna Alexander

General Information Girls' boarding and day college-preparatory, arts, technology, and athletics—Prep hockey school. Boarding grades 6–12, day grades N–12. Founded: 1901. Setting: urban. Students are housed in apartment-style residence. 12-acre campus. 2 buildings on campus. Approved or accredited by Canadian Association of Independent Schools, Canadian Educational Standards Institute, International Baccalaureate Organization, The Association of Boarding Schools, and Manitoba Department of Education. Affiliate member of National Association of Independent Schools; member of Secondary School Admission Test Board. Language of instruction: English. Endowment: CAN$550,000. Total enrollment: 452. Upper school average class size: 18. Upper school faculty-student ratio: 1:7.
Upper School Student Profile Grade 9: 30 students (30 girls); Grade 10: 53 students (53 girls); Grade 11: 69 students (69 girls); Grade 12: 47 students (47 girls). 19% of students are boarding students. 81% are province residents. 3 provinces are represented in upper school student body. 18% are international students. International students from China, Hong Kong, Japan, Mexico, Republic of Korea, and Taiwan; 3 other countries represented in student body.
Faculty School total: 69. In upper school: 10 men, 16 women; 6 have advanced degrees; 5 reside on campus.
Subjects Offered Acting, advanced math, Advanced Placement courses, advanced studio art-AP, advanced TOEFL/grammar, aerobics, art, art-AP, biology, biology-AP, business, calculus, calculus-AP, career and personal planning, career/college preparation, chemistry, chemistry-AP, choir, college planning, communications, community service, computer science, computer science-AP, consumer mathematics, dance performance, debate, desktop publishing, digital art, digital photography, drama, driver education, English, English language and composition-AP, English literature, English literature and composition-AP, English literature-AP, English/composition-AP, ESL, ethics, European history, French, French language-AP, French literature-AP, general science, geography, health, history, history-AP, jazz ensemble, journalism, mathematics, mathematics-AP, media arts, modern Western civilization, multimedia, music, musical theater, performing arts, personal development, physical education, physics, physics-AP, pre-calculus, psychology-AP, SAT/ACT preparation, science, social studies, Spanish, Spanish-AP, studio art—AP, technology, vocal ensemble, world affairs, world history.
Graduation Requirements Minimum of 10 hours per year of Service Learning participation in grades 9 through 12.
Special Academic Programs Advanced Placement exam preparation; honors section; accelerated programs; study at local college for college credit; academic accommodation for the gifted; ESL (30 students enrolled).
College Admission Counseling 49 students graduated in 2008; all went to college, including McGill University; Queen's University at Kingston; The University of Western Ontario; The University of Winnipeg; University of Manitoba; University of Toronto.
Student Life Upper grades have uniform requirement, student council, honor system. Discipline rests primarily with faculty.
Summer Programs Enrichment, ESL programs offered; session focuses on ESL and Canadian experience for boarding; held on campus; accepts girls; open to students from other schools. 15 students usually enrolled. 2009 schedule: July 30 to August 24. Application deadline: none.
Tuition and Aid 7-day tuition and room/board: CAN$36,200. Tuition installment plan (monthly payment plans, international students must pay in full prior to official letter of acceptance). Tuition reduction for siblings, bursaries, merit scholarship grants available. In 2008–09, 30% of upper-school students received aid; total upper-school merit-scholarship money awarded: CAN$100,000. Total amount of financial aid awarded in 2008–09: CAN$250,000.
Admissions Traditional secondary-level entrance grade is 9. School's own exam required. Deadline for receipt of application materials: none. Application fee required: CAN$150. Interview recommended.
Athletics Interscholastic: badminton, basketball, cross-country running, curling, Frisbee, golf, ice hockey, indoor track & field, outdoor skills, running, soccer, speedskating, track and field, ultimate Frisbee, volleyball; intramural: aerobics, aerobics/dance, aerobics/Nautilus, alpine skiing, backpacking, badminton, ballet, baseball, basketball, bicycling, bowling, broomball, cooperative games, Cosom hockey, cross-country running, curling, dance, dance team, fencing, field hockey, figure skating, fitness, fitness walking, flag football, floor hockey, Frisbee, golf, gymnastics, handball, hiking/backpacking, hockey, ice hockey, ice skating, in-line skating, indoor hockey, indoor track & field, jogging, jump rope, modern dance, netball, outdoor activities, outdoor education, outdoor skills, physical fitness, physical

training, roller blading, rowing, rugby, running, skiing (cross-country), skiing (downhill), snowboarding, snowshoeing, soccer, softball, speedskating, strength & conditioning, swimming and diving, table tennis, tennis, track and field, ultimate Frisbee, volleyball, walking, wall climbing, weight training, yoga. 2 PE instructors, 4 coaches.

Computers Computers are regularly used in all classes. Computer network features include on-campus library services, Internet access, wireless campus network, Internet filtering or blocking technology. Campus intranet, student e-mail accounts, and computer access in designated common areas are available to students. Students grades are available online. The school has a published electronic and media policy.

Contact Pamela K. McGhie, Director of Admissions. 204-784-1621. Fax: 204-774-5534. E-mail: admissions@balmoralhall.com. Web site: www.balmoralhall.com.

THE BALTIMORE ACTORS' THEATRE CONSERVATORY

The Dumbarton House
300 Dumbarton Road
Baltimore, Maryland 21212-1532

Head of School: Walter E. Anderson

General Information Coeducational day and distance learning college-preparatory and arts school. Grades K–12. Distance learning grades 9–12. Founded: 1979. Setting: suburban. 35-acre campus. 3 buildings on campus. Approved or accredited by Association of Independent Maryland Schools, Middle States Association of Colleges and Schools, and Maryland Department of Education. Endowment: $200,000. Total enrollment: 23. Upper school average class size: 6. Upper school faculty-student ratio: 1:3.

Upper School Student Profile Grade 9: 4 students (2 boys, 2 girls); Grade 10: 4 students (2 boys, 2 girls); Grade 11: 2 students (2 girls); Grade 12: 1 student (1 girl).

Faculty School total: 11. In upper school: 1 man, 8 women; 9 have advanced degrees.

Subjects Offered Acting, algebra, American history-AP, ballet, biology-AP, British literature, chemistry, English language-AP, French, geometry, health science, music history, music theory-AP, novels, physics, pre-calculus, psychology, sociology, theater history, trigonometry, world history, world history-AP.

Graduation Requirements Algebra, American history, ballet, chemistry, English, French, geometry, modern dance, music history, music theory, physical science, psychology, sociology, theater history, Western civilization-AP, world history, Students are required to complete graduation requirements in the three performing arts areas of music, drama, and dance.

Special Academic Programs Advanced Placement exam preparation; honors section; accelerated programs; independent study; study at local college for college credit; academic accommodation for the gifted, the musically talented, and the artistically talented.

College Admission Counseling 2 students graduated in 2008. Median SAT critical reading: 600, median SAT math: 570, median composite ACT: 26.

Student Life Upper grades have uniform requirement, student council, honor system. Discipline rests primarily with faculty.

Summer Programs Remediation, art/fine arts programs offered; session focuses on music, drama, dance, and art; held off campus; held at theatre in Oregon Ridge Park, Hunt Valley, Maryland; accepts boys and girls; open to students from other schools. 30 students usually enrolled. 2009 schedule: July 24 to August 8. Application deadline: none.

Tuition and Aid Day student tuition: $10,000. Tuition installment plan (SMART Tuition Payment Plan, FACTS Tuition Payment Plan). Need-based scholarship grants, PLATO Loans, prepGATE Loans available. In 2008–09, 10% of upper-school students received aid. Total amount of financial aid awarded in 2008–09: $12,000.

Admissions Traditional secondary-level entrance grade is 9. Any standardized test, English, French, and math proficiency and writing sample required. Deadline for receipt of application materials: April 3. Application fee required: $50. On-campus interview required.

Computers Computers are regularly used in college planning, creative writing, dance, desktop publishing, English, historical foundations for arts, history, independent study, introduction to technology, keyboarding, music, music technology, psychology, senior seminar, theater, theater arts, word processing, writing classes. Computer network features include Internet access, wireless campus network, Internet filtering or blocking technology. Student e-mail accounts are available to students. The school has a published electronic and media policy.

Contact Mr. Walter E. Anderson, Headmaster. 410-337-8519. Fax: 410-337-8582. E-mail: batpro@baltimoreactorstheatre.org. Web site: www.baltimoreactorstheatre.org.

BANCROFT SCHOOL

110 Shore Drive
Worcester, Massachusetts 01605

Head of School: Mr. Scott R. Reisinger

General Information Coeducational day college-preparatory school. Grades K–12. Founded: 1900. Setting: suburban. Nearest major city is Boston. 30-acre campus. 7 buildings on campus. Approved or accredited by Association of Independent Schools in New England, New England Association of Schools and Colleges, and Massachusetts Department of Education. Member of National Association of Independent Schools and Secondary School Admission Test Board. Endowment: $20 million. Total enrollment: 575. Upper school average class size: 12. Upper school faculty-student ratio: 1:8.

Upper School Student Profile Grade 9: 67 students (30 boys, 37 girls); Grade 10: 57 students (23 boys, 34 girls); Grade 11: 58 students (19 boys, 39 girls); Grade 12: 49 students (21 boys, 28 girls).

Faculty School total: 75. In upper school: 20 men, 15 women; 28 have advanced degrees.

Subjects Offered Acting, Advanced Placement courses, advanced studio art-AP, algebra, American history, American history-AP, American literature, art, art history, art history-AP, biology, biology AP, biotechnology, calculus, calculus-AP, ceramics, chamber groups, chemistry, chemistry-AP, chorus, community service, computer graphics, computer science, DNA, drama, dramatic arts, English, English language and composition-AP, English literature, English literature and composition-AP, ethics, European history, European history-AP, French, French-AP, geometry, health, history, jazz band, Latin, Latin-AP, literature by women, marine biology, music, music appreciation, photography, physical education, physics, pre-calculus, psychology, science, senior project, Shakespeare, Spanish, Spanish-AP, theater, theater production, trigonometry, U.S. history-AP, women in world history, world history.

Graduation Requirements Arts and fine arts (art, music, dance, drama), English, foreign language, mathematics, physical education (includes health), science, senior project, social studies (includes history), Senior Thesis and Spring Senior Project. Community service is required.

Special Academic Programs Advanced Placement exam preparation; honors section; independent study; study at local college for college credit; study abroad.

College Admission Counseling 56 students graduated in 2008; all went to college, including Connecticut College; Harvard University; Rensselaer Polytechnic Institute; The George Washington University; Tufts University; University of Pennsylvania. Median SAT critical reading: 650, median SAT math: 650.

Student Life Upper grades have specified standards of dress, student council, honor system. Discipline rests primarily with faculty.

Summer Programs Enrichment, advancement, sports, art/fine arts, computer instruction programs offered; session focuses on community outreach; held on campus; accepts boys and girls; open to students from other schools. 300 students usually enrolled. 2009 schedule: June 21 to August 6. Application deadline: none.

Tuition and Aid Day student tuition: $22,900. Tuition installment plan (Insured Tuition Payment Plan, individually arranged payment plans, 10-month school payment plan). Merit scholarship grants, need-based scholarship grants, scholarship for Worcester residents, merit scholarships available. In 2008–09, 30% of upper-school students received aid; total upper-school merit-scholarship money awarded: $16,000. Total amount of financial aid awarded in 2008–09: $80,000.

Admissions Traditional secondary-level entrance grade is 9. ISEE, SSAT or Wechsler Intelligence Scale for Children required. Deadline for receipt of application materials: February 1. Application fee required: $50. On-campus interview required.

Athletics Interscholastic: alpine skiing (boys, girls), baseball (b), basketball (b,g), crew (b,g), cross-country running (b,g), field hockey (g), lacrosse (b,g), soccer (b,g), softball (g), tennis (b,g), volleyball (g), wrestling (b); coed interscholastic: golf, skiing (downhill); coed intramural: dance, track and field. 5 PE instructors, 9 coaches, 1 athletic trainer.

Computers Computers are regularly used in all classes. Computer network features include on-campus library services, online commercial services, Internet access, wireless campus network, Internet filtering or blocking technology. Student e-mail accounts and computer access in designated common areas are available to students. Students grades are available online. The school has a published electronic and media policy.

Contact Mrs. Debbie Lamir, Admission Office Assistant. 508-853-2640 Ext. 206. Fax: 508-853-7824. E-mail: dlamir@bancroftschool.org. Web site: www.bancroftschool.org.

ANNOUNCEMENT FROM THE SCHOOL "Bancroft School is a vital, stimulating, and nurturing community of learners. A challenging academic program, a commitment to educating the whole child, and a friendly, supportive environment define the School. From achieving academic excellence and supporting division-winning teams to embracing the arts and encouraging service to others, Bancroft empowers students in grades K through 12, inspires their success, and celebrates the diverse, global community." Scott R. Reisinger, Headmaster of Bancroft School.

BAPTIST HIGH SCHOOL

300 Station Avenue
Haddon Heights, New Jersey 08035

Head of School: Mrs. Lynn L. Conahan

General Information Coeducational day college-preparatory, general academic, arts, business, religious studies, and technology school, affiliated with General Association of Regular Baptist Churches. Grades K–12. Founded: 1972. Setting: small town. Nearest major city is Philadelphia, PA. 1 building on campus. Approved or accredited by Association of Christian Schools International, Middle States Association of Colleges and Schools, and New Jersey Department of Education. Total enrollment: 253. Upper school average class size: 25. Upper school faculty-student ratio: 1:10.

Upper School Student Profile Grade 9: 24 students (13 boys, 11 girls); Grade 10: 36 students (16 boys, 20 girls); Grade 11: 31 students (13 boys, 18 girls); Grade 12: 42 students (20 boys, 22 girls). 80% of students are General Association of Regular Baptist Churches.

Faculty School total: 21. In upper school: 8 men, 13 women; 6 have advanced degrees.

Subjects Offered Accounting, advanced chemistry, advanced computer applications, advanced math, algebra, American government, American history-AP, American literature-AP, analytic geometry, anatomy and physiology, applied music, art, art and culture, art appreciation, arts, Basic programming, Bible studies, biology, business mathematics, calculus, calculus-AP, chemistry, choir, church history, civics, communication skills, computer applications, computer programming, creative writing, desktop publishing, dramatic arts, economics, English composition, English literature, English literature and composition-AP, ethics, foreign language, French, general math, general science, geometry, grammar, health, history, jazz band, keyboarding, physics, pre-algebra, pre-calculus, SAT preparation, Spanish, speech, Western civilization, women's health, world history, world history-AP, yearbook.

Graduation Requirements 20th century history, 20th century world history, algebra, American government, American literature, arts appreciation, Bible, biology, British literature, chemistry, computer science, economics, electives, English composition, English literature, ethics, geometry, health, Holocaust studies, lab/keyboard, physical science.

Special Academic Programs Advanced Placement exam preparation; honors section; remedial reading and/or remedial writing; remedial math; ESL (10 students enrolled).

College Admission Counseling 43 students graduated in 2008; all went to college, including Cedarville University; Liberty University; Rutgers, The State University of New Jersey, Rutgers College. Mean SAT critical reading: 570, mean SAT math: 530, mean SAT writing: 560. 32% scored over 600 on SAT critical reading, 38% scored over 600 on SAT math, 27% scored over 600 on SAT writing.

Student Life Upper grades have specified standards of dress, student council, honor system. Discipline rests primarily with faculty. Attendance at religious services is required.

Summer Programs Sports, computer instruction programs offered; session focuses on Skill Building; held on campus; accepts boys and girls; open to students from other schools. 50 students usually enrolled. 2009 schedule: June 18 to August 31.

Tuition and Aid Day student tuition: $7000. Tuition installment plan (SMART Tuition Payment Plan). Tuition reduction for siblings, need-based scholarship grants available. In 2008–09, 8% of upper-school students received aid. Total amount of financial aid awarded in 2008–09: $60,000.

Admissions Traditional secondary-level entrance grade is 9. Gates MacGinite Reading Tests and WRAT required. Deadline for receipt of application materials: none. Application fee required: $100. Interview required.

Athletics Interscholastic: baseball (boys), basketball (b,g), cheering (g), soccer (b,g), softball (g); intramural: floor hockey (b), indoor hockey (b,g); coed interscholastic: cross-country running, golf, track and field; coed intramural: volleyball. 2 PE instructors, 11 coaches.

Computers Computers are regularly used in accounting, business applications, mathematics classes. Computer network features include on-campus library services, Internet access, Internet filtering or blocking technology. The school has a published electronic and media policy.

Contact Mrs. Wendy Mayo, Administrative Assistant. 856-547-2996 Ext. 228. Fax: 856-547-6584. E-mail: bhs@baptistregional.org. Web site: www.baptistregional.org.

BARNSTABLE ACADEMY

8 Wright Way
Oakland, New Jersey 07436

Head of School: Ms. Lizanne M. Coyne

General Information Coeducational day college-preparatory, general academic, arts, and technology school. Grades 5–12. Founded: 1978. Setting: suburban. Nearest major city is New York, NY. 4-acre campus. 1 building on campus. Approved or accredited by Middle States Association of Colleges and Schools, National Independent Private Schools Association, and New Jersey Department of Education. Total enrollment: 120. Upper school average class size: 10. Upper school faculty-student ratio: 1:8.

Upper School Student Profile Grade 6: 8 students (5 boys, 3 girls); Grade 7: 10 students (8 boys, 2 girls); Grade 8: 12 students (9 boys, 3 girls); Grade 9: 19 students (12 boys, 7 girls); Grade 10: 26 students (17 boys, 9 girls); Grade 11: 26 students (17 boys, 9 girls); Grade 12: 19 students (13 boys, 6 girls).

Faculty School total: 20. In upper school: 6 men, 11 women; 12 have advanced degrees.

Subjects Offered Advanced math, algebra, American culture, American government, American legal systems, biology, business mathematics, chemistry, computer applications, contemporary issues, earth and space science, economics, English literature, English-AP, French, geometry, Latin, physical education, physics, psychology, Spanish, U.S. history, world history.

Special Academic Programs Advanced Placement exam preparation; honors section; accelerated programs; independent study; study at local college for college credit; academic accommodation for the gifted, the musically talented, and the artistically talented; remedial reading and/or remedial writing; remedial math; programs in English, general development for dyslexic students; special instructional classes for students with learning disabilities and Attention Deficit Disorder, the fragile emotionally disturbed; ESL (8 students enrolled).

College Admission Counseling 31 students graduated in 2008; 29 went to college, including Drew University; Drexel University; University at Albany, State University of New York; Villanova University. Other: 1 went to work, 1 had other specific plans. Median SAT critical reading: 520, median SAT math: 530. 25% scored over 600 on SAT critical reading, 25% scored over 600 on SAT math, 25% scored over 600 on SAT writing, 25% scored over 1800 on combined SAT.

Student Life Upper grades have specified standards of dress, student council. Discipline rests primarily with faculty.

Summer Programs Remediation, enrichment, advancement programs offered; held on campus; accepts boys and girls; open to students from other schools. 25 students usually enrolled. 2009 schedule: June 29 to July 31. Application deadline: June 28.

Tuition and Aid Day student tuition: $20,500–$25,750. Tuition installment plan (monthly payment plans, individually arranged payment plans). Tuition reduction for siblings, merit scholarship grants, need-based scholarship grants available. In 2008–09, 30% of upper-school students received aid; total upper-school merit-scholarship money awarded: $150,000. Total amount of financial aid awarded in 2008–09: $300,000.

Admissions Traditional secondary-level entrance grade is 9. For fall 2008, 168 students applied for upper-level admission, 87 were accepted, 52 enrolled. Deadline for receipt of application materials: none. No application fee required. On-campus interview required.

Athletics Interscholastic: baseball (boys), cheering (g), softball (g); coed interscholastic: aerobics/Nautilus, basketball, bowling, dance, horseback riding, Nautilus, physical training, soccer, tennis, walking; coed intramural: aerobics, aerobics/dance, aerobics/Nautilus, alpine skiing. 2 PE instructors, 3 coaches.

Computers Computer network features include Internet access, Internet filtering or blocking technology. Campus intranet is available to students.

Contact Mr. Robert S. Wolk, Director. 201-651-0200. Fax: 201-337-9797. E-mail: barnstableadmin@gmail.com. Web site: www.barnstableacademy.com.

THE BARRIE SCHOOL

13500 Layhill Road
Silver Spring, Maryland 20906

Head of School: Mr. Michael Kennedy

General Information Coeducational day college-preparatory, arts, Humanities, and Science school. Grades N–12. Founded: 1932. Setting: suburban. Nearest major city is Washington, DC. 45-acre campus. 7 buildings on campus. Approved or accredited by Association of Independent Maryland Schools, Association of Independent Schools of Greater Washington, Middle States Association of Colleges and Schools, and Maryland Department of Education. Member of National Association of Independent Schools. Endowment: $1 million. Total enrollment: 395. Upper school average class size: 15. Upper school faculty-student ratio: 1:7.

Upper School Student Profile Grade 9: 31 students (16 boys, 15 girls); Grade 10: 20 students (8 boys, 12 girls); Grade 11: 36 students (26 boys, 10 girls); Grade 12: 24 students (10 boys, 14 girls).

Faculty School total: 60. In upper school: 6 men, 5 women; 11 have advanced degrees.

Subjects Offered Acting, Advanced Placement courses, algebra, American history, American literature, art, art history, athletics, biology, calculus, chemistry, chorus, community service, creative writing, drama, earth science, electives, English, English literature, environmental science, European history, experiential education, expository writing, fine arts, French, geometry, government/civics, health, history, humanities, Latin, mathematics, music, physical education, physics, science, social studies, Spanish, theater, world history, world literature, writing.

Graduation Requirements Arts and fine arts (art, music, dance, drama), English, foreign language, humanities, mathematics, physical education (includes health), science, 80 hours of community service.

Special Academic Programs Advanced Placement exam preparation.

College Admission Counseling 24 students graduated in 2008; 22 went to college, including Babson College; University of Maryland, College Park; Wittenberg University. Other: 2 had other specific plans. Median SAT critical reading: 640, median SAT math: 620, median SAT writing: 610, median combined SAT: 1870, median composite ACT: 24.

Student Life Upper grades have specified standards of dress, student council, honor system. Discipline rests primarily with faculty.

Tuition and Aid Day student tuition: $23,150. Tuition installment plan (Key Tuition Payment Plan, monthly payment plans, The Tuition Refund Plan). Need based financial aid grants available. In 2008–09, 23% of upper-school students received aid. Total amount of financial aid awarded in 2008–09: $196,860.

Admissions Traditional secondary-level entrance grade is 9. For fall 2008, 37 students applied for upper-level admission, 21 were accepted, 13 enrolled. Admissions testing, ISEE, SSAT, TOEFL and Wechsler Intelligence Scale for Children required. Deadline for receipt of application materials: January 16. Application fee required: $100. On-campus interview required.

Athletics Interscholastic: baseball (boys), basketball (b,g), lacrosse (b,g), soccer (b,g), volleyball (g); coed interscholastic: cross-country running, equestrian sports, golf, horseback riding, outdoor activities, physical fitness, running, tennis, track and field, wrestling. 2 PE instructors, 31 coaches, 1 athletic trainer.

Computers Computers are regularly used in all academic classes. Computer network features include on-campus library services, Internet access, wireless campus network, Internet filtering or blocking technology. Campus intranet is available to students. The school has a published electronic and media policy.

Contact Ms. Diane Clem, Admission Assistant. 301-576-2800. Fax: 301-576-2803. E-mail: dclem@barrie.org. Web site: www.barrie.org.

THE BARSTOW SCHOOL

11511 State Line Road
Kansas City, Missouri 64114

Head of School: Shane A. Foster

General Information Coeducational day college-preparatory school. Grades PS–12. Founded: 1884. Setting: suburban. 40-acre campus. 1 building on campus. Approved or accredited by Independent Schools Association of the Central States and Missouri Independent School Association. Member of National Association of Independent Schools. Endowment: $7.9 million. Total enrollment: 651. Upper school average class size: 15. Upper school faculty-student ratio: 1:8.

Upper School Student Profile Grade 9: 61 students (30 boys, 31 girls); Grade 10: 52 students (25 boys, 27 girls); Grade 11: 43 students (26 boys, 17 girls); Grade 12: 48 students (26 boys, 22 girls).

Faculty School total: 70. In upper school: 14 men, 11 women; 20 have advanced degrees.

Subjects Offered Acting, advanced chemistry, advanced math, Advanced Placement courses, algebra, American history, American literature, ancient history, art, art history, Asian history, astronomy, biology, biology-AP, calculus, calculus-AP, ceramics, chemistry, chemistry-AP, Chinese, choir, community service, computer programming, computer science, computer science-AP, creative writing, debate, drawing, English, English language-AP, English literature, English literature-AP, ethics, European history, European history-AP, fine arts, French, French language-AP, French literature-AP, geography, geology, geometry, Japanese, journalism, mathematics, music, photography, physical education, physics, science, social studies, Spanish, Spanish language-AP, speech, statistics, statistics-AP, trigonometry, U.S. government, U.S. history-AP, world history, writing.

Graduation Requirements Arts and fine arts (art, music, dance, drama), computer literacy, English, foreign language, mathematics, physical education (includes health), science, social studies (includes history), Service hour requirement. Community service is required.

Special Academic Programs Advanced Placement exam preparation; honors section; independent study; study at local college for college credit.

College Admission Counseling 41 students graduated in 2008; 40 went to college, including Drake University; Emory University; Kansas State University; The University of Kansas; University of Pennsylvania; Washington University in St. Louis. Other: 1 had other specific plans. Mean SAT critical reading: 582, mean SAT math: 602, mean composite ACT: 28. 65% scored over 600 on SAT critical reading, 50% scored over 600 on SAT math.

Student Life Upper grades have specified standards of dress, student council, honor system. Discipline rests equally with students and faculty.

Summer Programs Enrichment, advancement, sports, art/fine arts, computer instruction programs offered; session focuses on enrichment; held on campus; accepts boys and girls; open to students from other schools. 950 students usually enrolled. 2009 schedule: June 1 to August 7. Application deadline: none.

Tuition and Aid Day student tuition: $11,125–$16,480. Tuition installment plan (SMART Tuition Payment Plan). Merit scholarship grants, need-based scholarship grants, need-based loans available. In 2008–09, 17% of upper-school students received aid; total upper-school merit-scholarship money awarded: $40,500. Total amount of financial aid awarded in 2008–09: $349,386.

Admissions Traditional secondary-level entrance grade is 9. For fall 2008, 210 students applied for upper-level admission, 162 were accepted, 119 enrolled. ERB, Otis-Lennon Mental Ability Test and writing sample required. Deadline for receipt of application materials: May 2. Application fee required: $45. On-campus interview recommended.

Athletics Interscholastic: aquatics (boys, girls), baseball (b), basketball (b,g), cheering (g), cross-country running (b,g), dance team (g), golf (b,g), soccer (b,g), softball (g), tennis (b,g), track and field (b,g), volleyball (g). 3 PE instructors, 15 coaches.

Computers Computers are regularly used in all academic classes. Computer network features include on-campus library services, online commercial services, Internet access, wireless campus network, Internet filtering or blocking technology. Campus intranet and student e-mail accounts are available to students. Students grades are available online. The school has a published electronic and media policy.

Contact Ms. Catherine Shurtleff, Admissions Coordinator. 816-942-3255. Fax: 816-942-3227. E-mail: Cshurtleff@barstowschool.org. Web site: www.barstowschool.org.

BASS MEMORIAL ACADEMY

6433 US Highway 11
Lumberton, Mississippi 39455

Head of School: William Craig Ziesmer

General Information Coeducational boarding and day college-preparatory, general academic, and religious studies school, affiliated with Seventh-day Adventists. Grades 9–12. Founded: 1961. Setting: rural. Nearest major city is Hattiesburg. Students are housed in single-sex dormitories. 350-acre campus. 10 buildings on campus. Approved or accredited by National Council for Private School Accreditation and Southern Association of Colleges and Schools. Upper school average class size: 28. Upper school faculty-student ratio: 1:12.

Upper School Student Profile Grade 9: 28 students (12 boys, 16 girls); Grade 10: 27 students (12 boys, 15 girls); Grade 11: 18 students (12 boys, 6 girls); Grade 12: 28 students (12 boys, 16 girls). 93% of students are boarding students. 46% are state residents. 7 states are represented in upper school student body. International students from Liberia and Mexico; 1 other country represented in student body. 95% of students are Seventh-day Adventists.

Faculty School total: 11. In upper school: 6 men, 5 women; 6 have advanced degrees; 8 reside on campus.

Subjects Offered Algebra, anatomy, biology, chemistry, community service, computer science, concert band, drama, economics, English, English literature, fine arts, geometry, government/civics, grammar, health, history, journalism, mathematics, music, physical education, physics, religion, Spanish, world history, writing.

Graduation Requirements Arts and fine arts (art, music, dance, drama), business skills (includes word processing), computer science, English, foreign language, mathematics, physical education (includes health), religion (includes Bible studies and theology), science, social studies (includes history). Community service is required.

Special Academic Programs Accelerated programs; independent study; study at local college for college credit; academic accommodation for the gifted and the musically talented; remedial reading and/or remedial writing; remedial math.

College Admission Counseling 37 students graduated in 2008; 35 went to college, including Florida Hospital College of Health Sciences; Southern Adventist University; Southwestern Adventist University. Other: 2 went to work. Mean composite ACT: 20.

Student Life Upper grades have specified standards of dress, student council. Discipline rests equally with students and faculty. Attendance at religious services is required.

Tuition and Aid Day student tuition: $7250; 7-day tuition and room/board: $12,650. Tuition installment plan (individually arranged payment plans). Tuition reduction for siblings, merit scholarship grants, need-based scholarship grants, paying campus jobs, matching scholarships paid by donors, alumni, and churches available. In 2008–09, 75% of upper-school students received aid.

Admissions Traditional secondary-level entrance grade is 9. Deadline for receipt of application materials: none. Application fee required. Interview recommended.

Athletics Interscholastic: basketball (boys, girls); intramural: basketball (b,g), flag football (b,g), floor hockey (b,g), soccer (b,g), softball (b,g); coed intramural: gymnastics, tennis, volleyball. 1 PE instructor.

Computers Computers are regularly used in foreign language, history, mathematics, science, yearbook classes. Computer network features include on-campus library services, Internet access, Internet filtering or blocking technology. Student e-mail accounts are available to students. Students grades are available online. The school has a published electronic and media policy.

Contact Cathy Barker, Registrar. 601-794-8561. Fax: 601-794-8881. E-mail: cbark123@aol.com.

BATTLE GROUND ACADEMY

PO Box 1889
Franklin, Tennessee 37065-1889

Head of School: Dr. William R. Mott

General Information Coeducational day college-preparatory, arts, and technology school. Grades K–12. Founded: 1889. Setting: suburban. Nearest major city is Nashville. 55-acre campus. 10 buildings on campus. Approved or accredited by Southern Association of Colleges and Schools, Southern Association of Independent Schools, Tennessee Association of Independent Schools, and Tennessee Department of Education. Member of National Association of Independent Schools. Endowment: $8 million. Total enrollment: 968. Upper school average class size: 16. Upper school faculty-student ratio: 1:11.

Faculty School total: 110. In upper school: 26 men, 20 women; 27 have advanced degrees.

Subjects Offered Accounting, algebra, American history, American literature, art, art history, biology, calculus, chemistry, chorus, computer applications, computer programming, computer science, drama, early childhood, economics, English, English literature, English literature and composition-AP, European history, fine arts, French, French-AP, geography, geometry, government/civics, grammar, health, history, Latin, mathematics, modern European history-AP, music, music history, physical education, physics, science, social studies, Spanish, speech, technical theater, theater, trigonometry, U.S. history, U.S. history-AP, world history, world history-AP, world literature, writing.

Graduation Requirements Arts and fine arts (art, music, dance, drama), computer science, English, foreign language, mathematics, physical education (includes health), science, social studies (includes history). Community service is required.

Special Academic Programs Advanced Placement exam preparation; honors section.

College Admission Counseling 86 students graduated in 2008; all went to college. Median combined SAT: 1200, median composite ACT: 25.

Student Life Upper grades have uniform requirement, student council, honor system. Discipline rests primarily with faculty.

Summer Programs Remediation, enrichment, sports, art/fine arts, computer instruction programs offered; session focuses on remediation, enrichment, and sports; held both on and off campus; held at local farm; accepts boys and girls; open to students from other schools. 350 students usually enrolled. 2009 schedule: June 5 to August 4. Application deadline: none.

Tuition and Aid Day student tuition: $15,135. Tuition installment plan (The Tuition Plan, FACTS Tuition Payment Plan, monthly payment plans, individually arranged payment plans). Merit scholarship grants, need-based scholarship grants, paying campus jobs available. In 2008–09, 15% of upper-school students received aid; total upper-school merit-scholarship money awarded: $750,000. Total amount of financial aid awarded in 2008–09: $750,000.

Admissions Traditional secondary-level entrance grade is 9. ISEE required. Deadline for receipt of application materials: none. Application fee required: $50. Interview recommended.

Athletics Interscholastic: baseball (boys), basketball (b,g), cheering (g), cross-country running (b,g), dance team (g), fitness (b,g), football (b), golf (b,g), physical fitness (b,g), physical training (b,g), soccer (b,g), softball (g), strength & conditioning (b,g), swimming and diving (b,g), tennis (b,g), track and field (b,g), volleyball (g), weight training (b,g), wrestling (b); intramural: baseball (b,g), basketball (b,g), fitness (b,g), football (b), softball (g); coed interscholastic: bowling, fitness, hockey, ice hockey, marksmanship, riflery, trap and skeet; coed intramural: fitness, hiking/backpacking, mountain biking, outdoor activities, physical training, rock climbing, ropes courses, soccer. 4 PE instructors, 2 coaches, 1 athletic trainer.

Computers Computers are regularly used in art, college planning, desktop publishing, English, foreign language, geography, history, library, literary magazine, mathematics, newspaper, photography, SAT preparation, science, social studies, Spanish, study skills, technology, theater, writing classes. Computer network features include on-campus library services, online commercial services, Internet access, wireless campus network, Internet filtering or blocking technology. Computer access in designated common areas is available to students. Students grades are available online. The school has a published electronic and media policy.

Contact Ms. Cathy Irwin, Director of Admissions. 615-567-9014. E-mail: cathyi@battlegroundacademy.org. Web site: www.battlegroundacademy.org.

BAVARIAN INTERNATIONAL SCHOOL

Schloss Haimhausen
Hauptstrasse 1
Haimhausen D-85778, Germany

Head of School: Bryan Nixon

General Information Coeducational day college-preparatory, general academic, arts, business, bilingual studies, technology, and physical education school. Grades PK–12. Founded: 1991. Setting: small town. Nearest major city is Munich, Germany. 10-acre campus. 5 buildings on campus. Approved or accredited by European Council of International Schools and New England Association of Schools and Colleges. Language of instruction: English. Total enrollment: 767. Upper school average class size: 19. Upper school faculty-student ratio: 1:7.

Upper School Student Profile Grade 9: 51 students (27 boys, 24 girls); Grade 10: 55 students (29 boys, 26 girls); Grade 11: 55 students (28 boys, 27 girls); Grade 12: 46 students (18 boys, 28 girls).

Faculty School total: 35. In upper school: 9 men, 26 women; 24 have advanced degrees.

Subjects Offered Art, chemistry, community service, computer science, English, fine arts, French, French language-AP, geography, German, history, Japanese, mathematics, music, physical education, physics, science, social studies, theater.

Special Academic Programs International Baccalaureate program; independent study; remedial reading and/or remedial writing; remedial math; programs in English, mathematics, general development for dyslexic students; special instructional classes for students with learning disabilities and dyslexia; ESL (40 students enrolled).

College Admission Counseling 42 students graduated in 2008; 35 went to college, including University of South Carolina. Other: 1 went to work, 1 entered military service, 1 entered a postgraduate year, 4 had other specific plans.

Student Life Upper grades have specified standards of dress, student council, honor system. Discipline rests primarily with faculty.

Summer Programs Enrichment, ESL, sports, art/fine arts, computer instruction programs offered; session focuses on English as an additional language; held on campus; accepts boys and girls; open to students from other schools. 2009 schedule: July 1 to July 31. Application deadline: none.

Tuition and Aid Day student tuition: €13,950–€18,450. Tuition installment plan (yearly payment plan, 2-payment plan). Tuition reduction for siblings available.

Admissions English proficiency or mathematics proficiency exam required. Deadline for receipt of application materials: none. No application fee required. On-campus interview required.

Athletics Interscholastic: cheering (girls); coed interscholastic: aerobics, aerobics/dance, alpine skiing, badminton, ball hockey, ballet, baseball, basketball, climbing, combined training, cooperative games, cricket, cross-country running, dance, field hockey, football, golf, gymnastics, handball, indoor hockey, indoor soccer, indoor track & field, jogging, judo, netball, outdoor activities, outdoors, physical training, rock climbing, rugby, running, skiing (downhill), snowboarding, soccer, softball, swimming and diving, tennis, track and field, volleyball, winter soccer. 3 PE instructors, 6 coaches.

Computers Computers are regularly used in art, business, English, ESL, information technology, photography, science, typing, video film production, writing, yearbook classes. Computer network features include on-campus library services, online commercial services, Internet access, wireless campus network, Internet filtering or blocking technology. Campus intranet, student e-mail accounts, and computer access in designated common areas are available to students. The school has a published electronic and media policy.

Contact Katharina Lippacher, Registrar. 49-8133-917 Ext. 121. Fax: 49-8133-917 Ext. 182. E-mail: k.lippacher@bis-school.com. Web site: www.bis-school.com.

ANNOUNCEMENT FROM THE SCHOOL The Bavarian International School e.V. was established in 1990 to offer an English language education to children from the international community in the north of Munich. The School's 2008–09 enrolment of 770 students from Pre-Reception (age 4) through grade 12 represents forty-four nationalities. BIS has been authorized to administer the IB Diploma Programme since 1995, and it strongly encourages and supports all Upper School students who possess the necessary aptitude and motivation to complete the requirements of the Diploma Programme in Grades 11–12. More than 95% of all BIS graduates go on to continue their education at leading colleges and universities around the world. The teaching faculty is made up of 74 full-time teachers and 5 part-time teachers, from fourteen different nations. All teachers are university graduates, with ten years of teaching experience, on average. The School offers teachers regular professional development opportunities in Germany and abroad to support their ongoing quest for excellence. Set in a green and peaceful park-like environment, the impressive and historic mansion, known as Schloss Haimhausen, houses Upper School classrooms and offices. Adjacent modern, purpose-built buildings house Middle and Lower School classrooms. Science rooms, music rooms, libraries, computer suites, a sports hall with an adjoining track and field, cafeterias, and a Performing Arts Centre enhance the facility, which opens onto a vista of field and forest. The wide range of extracurricular activities includes Model United Nations, Yearbook, Middle School Newspaper, Chinese, Art Club, Drama Club, Fashion Club, Theatre Production, Ballet, Irish Dancing, Drumming, Judo, Karate, Touch Rugby, Field Hockey, and Cheerleading. The athletics programme includes basketball, cross-country, golf, skiing, soccer, softball, swimming, tennis, track and field, and volleyball. A well-developed bus transportation system provides access for students from the greater Munich area, as well as from neighboring cities such as Ingolstadt and Landshut.

BAYLOR SCHOOL

PO Box 1337
Chattanooga, Tennessee 37401

Head of School: Dr. Bill Stacy

General Information Coeducational boarding and day college-preparatory school. Boarding grades 9–12, day grades 6–12. Founded: 1893. Setting: suburban. Nearest major city is Atlanta, GA. Students are housed in single-sex dormitories. 670-acre campus. 27 buildings on campus. Approved or accredited by Southern Association of Colleges and Schools, Southern Association of Independent Schools, Tennessee Association of Independent Schools, The Association of Boarding Schools, and Tennessee Department of Education. Member of National Association of Independent Schools and Secondary School Admission Test Board. Endowment: $70 million. Total enrollment: 1,069. Upper school average class size: 14. Upper school faculty-student ratio: 1:8.

Upper School Student Profile Grade 9: 171 students (91 boys, 80 girls); Grade 10: 163 students (86 boys, 77 girls); Grade 11: 184 students (83 boys, 101 girls); Grade 12: 194 students (104 boys, 90 girls). 30% of students are boarding students. 81% are state residents. 21 states are represented in upper school student body. 8% are international students. International students from Bahamas, China, Finland, Germany, Republic of Korea, and Taiwan; 11 other countries represented in student body.

Faculty School total: 125. In upper school: 75 men, 50 women; 76 have advanced degrees; 40 reside on campus.

Subjects Offered Algebra, American history, American literature, anthropology, art, art history, art history-AP, art-AP, astronomy, biology, biology-AP, calculus-AP, ceramics, chemistry, chemistry-AP, computer math, computer science, computer science-AP, creative writing, dance, drama, driver education, economics, English, English language-AP, English literature, English literature-AP, environmental science, environmental science-AP, ethics, European history, European history-AP, film, fine arts, finite math, forensic science, French, French-AP, genetics, geography, geometry, German, German-AP, government/civics, history, human geography—AP, Latin, Latin-AP, mathematics, music, photography, physical education, physics, physics-AP, religion, science, social studies, Spanish, Spanish-AP, speech, statistics, statistics-AP, theater, trigonometry, U.S. history-AP, video, world history, world literature.

Graduation Requirements Arts and fine arts (art, music, dance, drama), English, foreign language, mathematics, physical education (includes health), science, social studies (includes history), Leadership Baylor, summer reading.

Special Academic Programs 22 Advanced Placement exams for which test preparation is offered; honors section; academic accommodation for the gifted, the musically talented, and the artistically talented; special instructional classes for deaf students.

College Admission Counseling 190 students graduated in 2008; 188 went to college, including Boston University; Georgia Institute of Technology; The University of North Carolina at Chapel Hill; The University of Tennessee; University of Pennsylvania; Wake Forest University. Other: 1 entered military service, 1 had other specific plans.

Student Life Upper grades have specified standards of dress, student council, honor system. Discipline rests primarily with faculty.

Summer Programs Enrichment, sports, art/fine arts, rigorous outdoor training, computer instruction programs offered; session focuses on sports, arts, wilderness activities; held both on and off campus; held at locations near Chattanooga and various locations throughout the U.S. for adventure travel trips; accepts boys and girls; open to students from other schools. 500 students usually enrolled. 2009 schedule: June 10 to July 27. Application deadline: none.

Tuition and Aid Day student tuition: $19,152; 7-day tuition and room/board: $38,991. Tuition installment plan (The Tuition Plan, Insured Tuition Payment Plan, Key Tuition Payment Plan, monthly payment plans, individually arranged payment plans). Merit scholarship grants, need-based scholarship grants available. In 2008–09, 40% of upper-school students received aid; total upper-school merit-scholarship money awarded: $350,000. Total amount of financial aid awarded in 2008–09: $2,000,000.

Admissions Traditional secondary-level entrance grade is 9. For fall 2008, 305 students applied for upper-level admission, 185 were accepted, 119 enrolled. ISEE, SSAT or TOEFL required. Deadline for receipt of application materials: none. Application fee required: $75. Interview required.

Athletics Interscholastic: aquatics (boys, girls), baseball (b), basketball (b,g), bowling (b,g), cheering (g), crew (b,g), cross-country running (b,g), dance (g), dance team (g), diving (b,g), fencing (b,g), football (b), golf (b,g), lacrosse (b,g), modern dance (g), soccer (b,g), softball (g), swimming and diving (b,g), tennis (b,g), track and field (b,g), volleyball (g), wrestling (b); intramural: ballet (g), dance (g), weight lifting (b,g); coed interscholastic: aerobics/dance, rowing, running, strength & conditioning; coed intramural: backpacking, bicycling, canoeing/kayaking, climbing, fitness, fly fishing, Frisbee, hiking/backpacking, kayaking, mountain biking, mountaineering, ocean paddling, outdoor activities, outdoor adventure, outdoor education, physical fitness, rafting, rock climbing, scuba diving, ultimate Frisbee, wall climbing, wilderness survival. 4 PE instructors, 10 coaches, 2 athletic trainers.

Computers Computers are regularly used in art, English, history, mathematics, photography, publications, science, Spanish, technology, theater arts, writing, yearbook classes. Computer network features include on-campus library services, online commercial services, Internet access, wireless campus network, Internet filtering or blocking technology. Student e-mail accounts and computer access in designated common areas are available to students. Students grades are available online. The school has a published electronic and media policy.

Contact Mr. Jon Bloom, Associate Director of Admission. 423-267-8505 Ext. 804. Fax: 423-757-2525. E-mail: jbloom@baylorschool.org. Web site: www.baylorschool.org.

BEARSPAW CHRISTIAN SCHOOL

15001 69 Street NW
Calgary, Alberta T3R 1C5, Canada

Head of School: Mr. Kelly Blake

General Information Coeducational day and distance learning college-preparatory and religious studies school, affiliated with Christian faith. Grades 1–12. Distance learning grades 10–12. Founded: 1991. Setting: rural. 40-acre campus. 1 building on campus. Approved or accredited by Association of Christian Schools International, Association of Independent Schools and Colleges of Alberta, and Alberta Department of Education. Language of instruction: English. Total enrollment: 482. Upper school average class size: 21. Upper school faculty-student ratio: 1:20.

Upper School Student Profile Grade 10: 41 students (13 boys, 28 girls); Grade 11: 42 students (26 boys, 16 girls); Grade 12: 31 students (10 boys, 21 girls). 90% of students are Christian faith.

Faculty School total: 38. In upper school: 6 men, 14 women; 2 have advanced degrees.

Subjects Offered 20th century history, 20th century world history, advanced chemistry, advanced math, algebra, applied music, art, athletics, Bible studies, biology, calculus, Canadian history, career education, chemistry, Christian education, computer applications, English composition, French as a second language, general math, keyboarding/computer, physical education, science, social studies, wilderness experience, world history.

Graduation Requirements Bible, English, mathematics, science, social studies (includes history).

Special Academic Programs Special instructional classes for students with learning disabilities, Attention Deficit Disorder, emotional problems, and dyslexia.

College Admission Counseling 16 students graduated in 2008; 12 went to college, including University of Calgary. Other: 4 went to work.

Student Life Upper grades have uniform requirement. Discipline rests primarily with faculty. Attendance at religious services is required.

Tuition and Aid Day student tuition: CAN$4850. Tuition installment plan (monthly payment plans, individually arranged payment plans). Tuition reduction for siblings, need-based scholarship grants available. In 2008–09, 6% of upper-school students received aid. Total amount of financial aid awarded in 2008–09: CAN$16,725.

Admissions Traditional secondary-level entrance grade is 10. For fall 2008, 32 students applied for upper-level admission, 31 were accepted, 1 enrolled. WAIS, WICS required. Deadline for receipt of application materials: September 30. Application fee required: CAN$400. Interview required.

Athletics Interscholastic: badminton (boys, girls), basketball (b,g), cross-country running (b,g), curling (b,g), floor hockey (b,g), golf (b,g), track and field (b,g), volleyball (b,g); intramural: badminton (b,g), basketball (b,g), cross-country running (b,g), flag football (b,g), floor hockey (b,g), track and field (b,g), volleyball (b,g), wrestling (b); coed interscholastic: badminton, soccer; coed intramural: badminton, basketball, flag football, volleyball. 3 PE instructors.

Computers Computers are regularly used in all academic classes. Computer network features include Internet access, wireless campus network, Internet filtering or blocking technology. Student e-mail accounts and computer access in designated common areas are available to students. Students grades are available online. The school has a published electronic and media policy.

Contact Mrs. Karin Spoletini, Administrative Assistant. 403-295-2566 Ext. 221. Fax: 403-275-8170. E-mail: kspoletini@bearspawschool.com. Web site: www.bearspawschool.com.

BEAVER COUNTRY DAY SCHOOL

791 Hammond Street
Chestnut Hill, Massachusetts 02467

Head of School: Peter R. Hutton

General Information Coeducational day college-preparatory and arts school. Grades 6–12. Founded: 1920. Setting: suburban. Nearest major city is Boston. 17-acre campus. 2 buildings on campus. Approved or accredited by Association of Independent Schools in New England, New England Association of Schools and Colleges, The College Board, and Massachusetts Department of Education. Member of National Association of Independent Schools and Secondary School Admission Test Board. Endowment: $5.2 million. Total enrollment: 428. Upper school average class size: 15. Upper school faculty-student ratio: 1:8.

Upper School Student Profile Grade 9: 72 students (38 boys, 34 girls); Grade 10: 79 students (35 boys, 44 girls); Grade 11: 78 students (40 boys, 38 girls); Grade 12: 78 students (40 boys, 38 girls).

Faculty School total: 71. In upper school: 24 men, 34 women; 41 have advanced degrees.

Subjects Offered 20th century history, 3-dimensional art, 3-dimensional design, acting, advanced chemistry, advanced math, algebra, American history, American literature, anatomy and physiology, art, art history, astronomy, biology, calculus, ceramics, chamber groups, chemistry, child development, China/Japan history, Chinese history, chorus, civil rights, classical music, college counseling, college placement, college writing, community service, comparative civilizations, comparative cultures, comparative government and politics, comparative religion, computer graphics, computer math, computer programming, computer skills, contemporary history, costumes and make-up, creative writing, dance, decision making, diversity studies, drafting, drama, driver education, economics, English, English literature, ethical decision making, ethics, European civilization, European history, expository writing, fine arts, French, French as a second language, geography, geometry, government/civics, grammar, health, history, Holocaust studies, honors algebra, honors English, honors geometry, honors U.S. history, human biology, independent study, international affairs, jazz, jazz band, journalism, junior and senior seminars, Latin American history, Latin American studies, mathematics, Middle Eastern history, modern Chinese history, modern European history, music, musical theater, painting, peer counseling, philosophy, photography, physical education, physics, play production, poetry, pre-calculus, programming, psychology, science, Shakespeare, sign language, social justice, social studies, society, politics and law, Spanish, Spanish literature, squash, statistics, studio art, study skills, theater, trigonometry, typing, U.S. history, world history, writing.

Graduation Requirements Arts, English, foreign language, history, interdisciplinary studies, mathematics, physical education (includes health), science, 40 hours of community service.

Special Academic Programs Honors section; independent study.

College Admission Counseling 74 students graduated in 2008; all went to college, including Boston University; Bowdoin College; Brandeis University; Brown University; Syracuse University; The Colorado College.

Student Life Upper grades have student council, honor system. Discipline rests equally with students and faculty.
Tuition and Aid Day student tuition: $31,450. Tuition installment plan (Academic Management Services Plan, Key Tuition Payment Plan, monthly payment plans, individually arranged payment plans). Need-based scholarship grants available. In 2008–09, 25% of upper-school students received aid. Total amount of financial aid awarded in 2008–09: $2,200,000.
Admissions Traditional secondary-level entrance grade is 9. For fall 2008, 226 students applied for upper-level admission, 110 were accepted, 45 enrolled. ISEE or SSAT required. Deadline for receipt of application materials: January 15. Application fee required: $45. On-campus interview required.
Athletics Interscholastic: baseball (boys), basketball (b,g), cross-country running (b,g), field hockey (g), lacrosse (b,g), soccer (b,g), softball (g), tennis (b,g), volleyball (g), wrestling (b); coed interscholastic: baseball, bicycling, cross-country running, fencing, fitness, Frisbee, golf, martial arts, mountain biking, physical fitness, physical training, squash, strength & conditioning, ultimate Frisbee, yoga; coed intramural: aerobics, aerobics/dance, ballet, dance. 3 PE instructors, 15 coaches, 1 athletic trainer.
Computers Computers are regularly used in art, English, foreign language, history, mathematics, science classes. Computer network features include on-campus library services, online commercial services, Internet access, wireless campus network, Internet filtering or blocking technology. Student e-mail accounts are available to students. The school has a published electronic and media policy.
Contact Nedda Bonassera, Admission Office Manager. 617-738-2725. Fax: 617-738-2767. E-mail: admission@bcdschool.org. Web site: www.bcdschool.org.

ANNOUNCEMENT FROM THE SCHOOL Beaver Country Day School, just outside of Boston, offers a balanced college-preparatory curriculum in academics, arts, and athletics for grades 6–12. The diversity of its students (more than 25% are minorities) and faculty members (20% are minorities), together with a mission that emphasizes innovation in learning and teaching, provides a dynamic and challenging curriculum and community. With an average class size of 15, teachers provide attention and encouragement to all students. Included on the 22-acre campus are a professional biotechnology lab, a Visual and Performing Arts Center, a 39,000-square-foot athletic center, and an open and spacious library.

THE BEEKMAN SCHOOL

220 East 50th Street
New York, New York 10022

Head of School: George Higgins

General Information Coeducational day college-preparatory, general academic, arts, and technology school. Grades 9–PG. Founded: 1925. Setting: urban. 1 building on campus. Approved or accredited by New York State Board of Regents. Total enrollment: 80. Upper school average class size: 8. Upper school faculty-student ratio: 1:8.
Upper School Student Profile Grade 9: 15 students (8 boys, 7 girls); Grade 10: 19 students (11 boys, 8 girls); Grade 11: 21 students (12 boys, 9 girls); Grade 12: 25 students (13 boys, 12 girls); Postgraduate: 2 students (1 boy, 1 girl).
Faculty School total: 13. In upper school: 4 men, 9 women; 11 have advanced degrees.
Subjects Offered Advanced Placement courses, algebra, American history, ancient world history, art, astronomy, bioethics, biology, business mathematics, calculus, calculus-AP, chemistry, computer animation, computer art, computer science, conceptual physics, creative writing, drama, drawing, Eastern religion and philosophy, ecology, economics, electronics, English, environmental science, ESL, European history, film, French, geometry, government, health, journalism, modern politics, modern world history, photography, physical education, physical science, physics, poetry, pre-calculus, psychology, SAT preparation, sculpture, Spanish, TOEFL preparation, trigonometry, U.S. history, video film production, Web site design, Western philosophy.
Graduation Requirements Art, computer technologies, electives, English, foreign language, health education, mathematics, physical education (includes health), science, social studies (includes history).
Special Academic Programs Advanced Placement exam preparation; honors section; accelerated programs; independent study; academic accommodation for the gifted, the musically talented, and the artistically talented; remedial reading and/or remedial writing; remedial math; programs in English, mathematics, general development for dyslexic students; ESL (4 students enrolled).
College Admission Counseling 28 students graduated in 2008; 27 went to college, including Arizona State University; Boston University; Fordham University; New York University; Sarah Lawrence College; University of Vermont. Other: 1 had other specific plans. Mean SAT critical reading: 529, mean SAT math: 553, mean SAT writing: 535. 33% scored over 600 on SAT critical reading, 27% scored over 600 on SAT math, 30% scored over 600 on SAT writing.
Student Life Upper grades have honor system. Discipline rests primarily with faculty.
Summer Programs Remediation, enrichment, advancement, ESL programs offered; session focuses on academics; held on campus; accepts boys and girls; open to students from other schools. 35 students usually enrolled. 2009 schedule: July 6 to August 18. Application deadline: June 26.
Tuition and Aid Day student tuition: $26,000. Tuition installment plan (monthly payment plans, individually arranged payment plans).
Admissions Traditional secondary-level entrance grade is 9. For fall 2008, 39 students applied for upper-level admission, 38 were accepted, 33 enrolled. Deadline for receipt of application materials: none. No application fee required. On-campus interview required.
Athletics 1 PE instructor.
Computers Computer resources include online commercial services, Internet access.
Contact George Higgins, Headmaster. 212-755-6666. Fax: 212-888-6085. E-mail: georgeh@beekmanschool.org. Web site: www.BeekmanSchool.org.

ANNOUNCEMENT FROM THE SCHOOL The Beekman School/The Tutoring School provides a traditional academic education taught in a unique and intimate environment. The faculty encourages students to become actively involved in their education and to develop a sense of commitment, responsibility, and love of learning. The Beekman School has a strong tradition of successfully educating virtually all types of students. The School's success is due in part to maintaining small class sizes; flexible, individualized class scheduling; and careful guidance from a devoted staff.

See Close-Up on page 676.

BELLARMINE-JEFFERSON HIGH SCHOOL

465 East Olive Avenue
Burbank, California 91501-2176

General Information Coeducational day college-preparatory, arts, business, religious studies, and technology school, affiliated with Roman Catholic Church. Grades 9–12. Founded: 1940. Setting: urban. 4 buildings on campus. Approved or accredited by Western Association of Schools and Colleges and California Department of Education. Upper school average class size: 20.
Faculty In upper school: 30 have advanced degrees.
Special Academic Programs International Baccalaureate program; Advanced Placement exam preparation; honors section.
College Admission Counseling 91 students graduated in 2008.
Student Life Upper grades have uniform requirement, student council, honor system. Discipline rests primarily with faculty. Attendance at religious services is required.
Tuition and Aid Tuition installment plan (The Tuition Plan). Tuition reduction for siblings, merit scholarship grants, need-based scholarship grants available.
Admissions High School Placement Test required. Deadline for receipt of application materials: January 23. Application fee required: $50. Interview required.
Athletics Interscholastic: aerobics (girls), baseball (b); coed interscholastic: basketball.
Computers The school has a published electronic and media policy.
Contact 818-972-1400.

BELLEVUE CHRISTIAN SCHOOL

1601 98th Avenue NE
Clyde Hill, Washington 98004-3400

Head of School: Ron Taylor

General Information Coeducational day college-preparatory, general academic, arts, business, vocational, religious studies, and technology school. Grades PK–12. Founded: 1950. Setting: suburban. Nearest major city is Bellevue. 10-acre campus. 5 buildings on campus. Approved or accredited by Christian Schools International, Northwest Association of Accredited Schools, and Washington Department of Education. Endowment: $1 million. Total enrollment: 1,300. Upper school average class size: 20. Upper school faculty-student ratio: 1:21.
Faculty School total: 38. In upper school: 18 men, 20 women; 24 have advanced degrees.
Subjects Offered 20th century world history, accounting, advanced chemistry, Advanced Placement courses, algebra, art, athletics, band, Bible, biology, calculus-AP, chemistry, chemistry-AP, choral music, church history, community service, drama, economics, English, English-AP, ethics, fine arts, foreign language, geometry, German, jazz band, mathematics, physical education, physical science, physics, religion, social science, social studies, Spanish, Spanish language-AP, trigonometry, U.S. history-AP, yearbook.
Graduation Requirements Arts and fine arts (art, music, dance, drama), English, foreign language, mathematics, physical education (includes health), religion (includes Bible studies and theology), science, social science, social studies (includes history), technology. Community service is required.
Special Academic Programs Advanced Placement exam preparation; honors section; academic accommodation for the gifted, the musically talented, and the artistically talented; programs in English, mathematics for dyslexic students; ESL (7 students enrolled).

College Admission Counseling 82 students graduated in 2008; 78 went to college, including Seattle Pacific University; University of Washington; Washington State University; Western Washington University. Other: 1 went to work, 1 entered military service, 2 had other specific plans.
Student Life Upper grades have specified standards of dress, student council. Discipline rests primarily with faculty. Attendance at religious services is required.
Summer Programs Enrichment, advancement, sports, art/fine arts, computer instruction programs offered; session focuses on providing additional course offerings that might not fit in the schedule during the academic year; held on campus; accepts boys and girls; not open to students from other schools. 100 students usually enrolled. 2009 schedule: July to August. Application deadline: June.
Tuition and Aid Day student tuition: $10,390. Tuition installment plan (monthly payment plans). Tuition reduction for siblings, financial aid awarded on basis of report and ability to pay available. In 2008–09, 15% of upper-school students received aid. Total amount of financial aid awarded in 2008–09: $900,000.
Admissions Traditional secondary-level entrance grade is 9. Deadline for receipt of application materials: none. Application fee required: $75. Interview required.
Athletics Interscholastic: baseball (boys), basketball (b,g), cheering (g), combined training (b,g), cooperative games (b,g), cross-country running (b,g), fitness (b,g), golf (b,g), outdoor activities (b,g), outdoor education (b,g), physical fitness (b,g), physical training (b,g), running (b,g), soccer (b,g), softball (g), strength & conditioning (b,g), track and field (b,g), volleyball (g), weight lifting (b,g), weight training (b,g), wrestling (b).
Computers Computers are regularly used in art, Bible studies, computer applications, desktop publishing, drawing and design, keyboarding, library, newspaper, photography, video film production, Web site design, yearbook classes. Computer network features include on-campus library services, Internet access, Internet filtering or blocking technology. Student e-mail accounts are available to students. Students grades are available online. The school has a published electronic and media policy.
Contact Jaime Heise, Admissions Coordinator. 425-454-4402 Ext. 215. Fax: 425-454-4418. E-mail: jheise@bellevuechristian.org. Web site: www.bellevuechristian.org.

BELMONT HILL SCHOOL

350 Prospect Street
Belmont, Massachusetts 02478-2662
Head of School: Dr. Richard I. Melvoin

General Information Boys' boarding and day college-preparatory, arts, and technology school. Boarding grades 9–12, day grades 7–12. Founded: 1923. Setting: suburban. Nearest major city is Boston. Students are housed in single-sex dormitories. 34-acre campus. 14 buildings on campus. Approved or accredited by Association of Independent Schools in New England, Massachusetts Department of Education, and New England Association of Schools and Colleges. Member of National Association of Independent Schools and Secondary School Admission Test Board. Endowment: $61 million. Total enrollment: 445. Upper school average class size: 12. Upper school faculty-student ratio: 1:6.
Upper School Student Profile Grade 7: 56 students (56 boys); Grade 8: 69 students (69 boys); Grade 9: 79 students (79 boys); Grade 10: 85 students (85 boys); Grade 11: 83 students (83 boys); Grade 12: 73 students (73 boys). 1% of students are boarding students. 100% are state residents.
Faculty School total: 68. In upper school: 54 men, 14 women; 67 have advanced degrees; 6 reside on campus.
Subjects Offered Algebra, American history, American literature, architecture, art, art history, astronomy, biology, calculus, ceramics, chemistry, Chinese, computer math, computer programming, computer science, creative writing, drafting, drama, earth science, economics, engineering, English, English literature, ethics, European history, expository writing, fine arts, French, geography, geology, geometry, German, government/civics, grammar, health, history, industrial arts, journalism, Latin, mathematics, mechanical drawing, music, philosophy, photography, physical education, physics, psychology, science, social studies, Spanish, speech, statistics, theater, trigonometry, woodworking, world history, writing.
Graduation Requirements Arts and fine arts (art, music, dance, drama), computer science, English, foreign language, mathematics, physical education (includes health), science, social studies (includes history), senior wooden panel carving (a tradition since 1923).
Special Academic Programs Advanced Placement exam preparation; honors section; independent study; term-away projects; study at local college for college credit; study abroad.
College Admission Counseling 71 students graduated in 2008; all went to college, including Boston College; Brown University; Georgetown University; Harvard University; Trinity College; Tufts University. Mean SAT critical reading: 650, mean SAT math: 680, mean SAT writing: 660.
Student Life Upper grades have specified standards of dress, student council, honor system. Discipline rests equally with students and faculty.
Summer Programs Remediation, enrichment, advancement, sports, art/fine arts, computer instruction programs offered; session focuses on academics; held on campus; accepts boys and girls; open to students from other schools. 1,000 students usually enrolled. 2009 schedule: June to August. Application deadline: June 1.
Tuition and Aid Day student tuition: $31,000; 5-day tuition and room/board: $37,150. Tuition installment plan (Key Tuition Payment Plan, FACTS Tuition Payment Plan, monthly payment plans, individually arranged payment plans). Need-based scholarship grants, need-based loans, middle-income loans available. In 2008–09, 28% of upper-school students received aid. Total amount of financial aid awarded in 2008–09: $2,300,000.
Admissions Traditional secondary-level entrance grade is 10. For fall 2008, 362 students applied for upper-level admission, 127 were accepted, 85 enrolled. ISEE and SSAT required. Deadline for receipt of application materials: February 1. Application fee required: $40. On-campus interview required.
Athletics Interscholastic: alpine skiing, baseball, basketball, crew, cross-country running, football, golf, ice hockey, lacrosse, sailing, skiing (cross-country), skiing (downhill), soccer, squash, tennis, track and field, wrestling; intramural: basketball, bicycling, crew, cross-country running, football, ice hockey, skiing (cross-country), squash, strength & conditioning, tennis, touch football, weight lifting. 2 athletic trainers.
Computers Computers are regularly used in economics, foreign language, mathematics, science classes. Computer network features include on-campus library services, online commercial services, Internet access.
Contact Mr. Michael R. Grant, Director of Admission. 617-484-4410 Ext. 257. Fax: 617-484-4829. E-mail: grant@belmont-hill.org. Web site: www.belmont-hill.org.

ANNOUNCEMENT FROM THE SCHOOL Belmont Hill School, founded in 1923 and located in the suburbs of Boston, Massachusetts, is an independent boys' day and boarding school (five days) that provides a rigorous learning environment for grades 7–12. Small classes and a full schedule from 8 a.m. to 5 p.m. combine classical education with extensive opportunities in athletics, music, theater, visual arts, community service, and other activities. Though diverse in backgrounds and teaching styles, Belmont Hill faculty members share common core values: an insistence upon holding students to high standards; a concern for developing character and values; a recognition that life's lessons can be taught throughout the day, on athletic fields and in rehearsal halls as well as in classrooms; a concern for each student's total development, social and personal as well as academic; and a willingness to provide extra help, whenever and wherever necessary. Belmont Hill is what it is, in large measure, because of the School's single-sex status, which puts the focus on the total development of boys into men. The teachers know the developmental stages of boys and how boys learn best. Boys speak up and stay focused in class, unafraid to take risks and unconcerned about how they are perceived. They feel free to pursue theater, music, or visual arts. They feel free to tutor a child or brighten a senior citizen's day. They feel free, in sum, to develop their talents and to share their humanity, unfettered by juvenile notions of what it means to "be a man" and energized by the spirit of camaraderie that permeates the School. Belmont Hill is a boys' school, but what is more important is that it is a good school. "Goodness" is measured by the character of the students and the citizens they become. Belmont Hill strives to have its students leave with a love of learning and a willingness to work hard, take risks, take a stand, and make a difference.

THE BEMENT SCHOOL

Deerfield, Massachusetts
See Junior Boarding Schools section.

BENEDICTINE HIGH SCHOOL

2900 Martin Luther King, Jr. Drive
Cleveland, Ohio 44104
Head of School: Mr. Joe Gressock

General Information Boys' day college-preparatory and religious studies school, affiliated with Roman Catholic Church. Grades 9–12. Founded: 1927. Setting: urban. 13-acre campus. 3 buildings on campus. Approved or accredited by North Central Association of Colleges and Schools, Ohio Catholic Schools Accreditation Association (OCSAA), and Ohio Department of Education. Total enrollment: 399. Upper school average class size: 15. Upper school faculty-student ratio: 1:11.
Upper School Student Profile Grade 9: 123 students (123 boys); Grade 10: 104 students (104 boys); Grade 11: 90 students (90 boys); Grade 12: 82 students (82 boys). 85% of students are Roman Catholic.
Faculty School total: 34. In upper school: 31 men, 3 women; 31 have advanced degrees.
Subjects Offered Advanced chemistry, advanced math, Advanced Placement courses, aesthetics, algebra, American literature, American literature-AP, analysis and differential calculus, analytic geometry, Ancient Greek, ancient history, ancient world history, art, athletic training, band, Basic programming, Bible studies, biology, biology-AP, British literature-AP, business education, business law, calculus, calculus-AP, Catholic belief and practice, Central and Eastern European history, ceramics, chemistry, choir, chorus, church history, Civil War, civil war history, classical Greek literature, classical language, computer education, computer graphics, computer information systems, computer keyboarding, computer literacy, computer programming, computer skills, computer-aided design, concert band, concert choir, current events, drawing, drawing and design, economics, electives, English, English

literature and composition-AP, European history-AP, film studies, foreign language, French, geometry, German, government, government-AP, government/civics, government/civics-AP, graphic design, health, honors algebra, honors English, honors geometry, honors U.S. history, honors world history, human geography—AP, jazz band, journalism, keyboarding/computer, lab science, Latin, Latin-AP, Life of Christ, marching band, marketing, moral theology, music, music appreciation, New Testament, painting, physical education, pre-calculus, probability and statistics, psychology, Russian, Shakespeare.

Graduation Requirements 1½ elective credits, 20th century American writers, 20th century history, 20th century world history, algebra, American government, American history, American literature, ancient history, ancient world history, art, biology, British literature, chemistry, church history, computer applications, English, foreign language, geometry, physical education (includes health), physics, senior project, theology, U.S. history, world history, community service hours.

Special Academic Programs Advanced Placement exam preparation; honors section; remedial reading and/or remedial writing; remedial math.

College Admission Counseling 86 students graduated in 2008; 85 went to college, including Cleveland State University; John Carroll University; Mount Union College; The Ohio State University; The University of Akron; University of Dayton. Other: 1 went to work. Mean SAT critical reading: 551, mean SAT math: 528, mean SAT writing: 527, mean combined SAT: 1606, mean composite ACT: 22.

Student Life Upper grades have specified standards of dress, student council, honor system. Discipline rests primarily with faculty. Attendance at religious services is required.

Summer Programs Enrichment, sports, computer instruction programs offered; held on campus; accepts boys and girls; open to students from other schools. 150 students usually enrolled. 2009 schedule: June 8 to July 24. Application deadline: June 1.

Tuition and Aid Day student tuition: $7800. Tuition installment plan (monthly payment plans, individually arranged payment plans). Tuition reduction for siblings, merit scholarship grants, need-based scholarship grants, paying campus jobs available. In 2008–09, 60% of upper-school students received aid.

Admissions Traditional secondary-level entrance grade is 9. For fall 2008, 250 students applied for upper-level admission, 175 were accepted, 132 enrolled. High School Placement Test (closed version) from Scholastic Testing Service required. Deadline for receipt of application materials: none. Application fee required: $150. Interview recommended.

Athletics Interscholastic: baseball, basketball, bowling, cross-country running, football, golf, hockey, ice hockey, lacrosse, soccer, swimming and diving, track and field, wrestling; intramural: baseball, basketball, flag football, football, physical fitness, physical training, skiing (downhill), snowboarding, strength & conditioning, volleyball, weight lifting, weight training. 10 coaches, 2 athletic trainers.

Computers Computers are regularly used in computer applications, creative writing, current events, data processing, design, English, graphic design, history, independent study, information technology, library, mathematics, newspaper, technical drawing, yearbook classes. Computer network features include on-campus library services, online commercial services, Internet access, wireless campus network, Internet filtering or blocking technology. Student e-mail accounts are available to students. Students grades are available online. The school has a published electronic and media policy.

Contact Mr. Kieran Patton, Director of Admissions. 216-421-2080 Ext. 356. Fax: 216-421-1100. E-mail: kpatton@cbhs.net. Web site: www.cbhs.net.

BENEDICTINE HIGH SCHOOL

304 North Sheppard Street
Richmond, Virginia 23221

Head of School: John McGinty

General Information Boys' day college-preparatory, arts, religious studies, Junior ROTC, and military school, affiliated with Roman Catholic Church. Grades 9–12. Founded: 1911. Setting: urban. 28-acre campus. 4 buildings on campus. Approved or accredited by National Catholic Education Association, Southern Association of Colleges and Schools, Virginia Association of Independent Schools, and Virginia Department of Education. Member of National Association of Independent Schools. Endowment: $1.9 million. Total enrollment: 268. Upper school average class size: 17. Upper school faculty-student ratio: 1:9.

Upper School Student Profile Grade 9: 80 students (80 boys); Grade 10: 69 students (69 boys); Grade 11: 62 students (62 boys); Grade 12: 57 students (57 boys). 55% of students are Roman Catholic.

Faculty School total: 34. In upper school: 22 men, 12 women; 17 have advanced degrees.

Subjects Offered Algebra, American literature, anatomy and physiology, art, band, biology, biology-AP, calculus, calculus-AP, Catholic belief and practice, chemistry, communication arts, comparative government and politics-AP, computer applications, computer programming, creative writing, discrete math, economics, English, English literature, English literature and composition-AP, environmental science, French, geography, geometry, graphic arts, journalism, JROTC, Latin, Latin-AP, physical education, physics, pre-calculus, religion, robotics, Spanish, sports science, sports team management, statistics, U.S. and Virginia government, U.S. government, U.S. government and politics, U.S. government and politics-AP, U.S. government-AP, U.S. history, U.S. history-AP, world history, world literature, yearbook.

Graduation Requirements Arts and fine arts (art, music, dance, drama), electives, English, JROTC, lab science, language, mathematics, physical education (includes health), religion (includes Bible studies and theology), social studies (includes history).

Special Academic Programs Advanced Placement exam preparation; honors section; independent study; academic accommodation for the gifted and the artistically talented.

College Admission Counseling 74 students graduated in 2008; 71 went to college, including Hampden-Sydney College; James Madison University; Savannah College of Art and Design; Virginia Commonwealth University; Virginia Military Institute; Virginia Polytechnic Institute and State University. Other: 1 went to work, 1 entered military service, 1 entered a postgraduate year.

Student Life Upper grades have uniform requirement, student council, honor system. Discipline rests equally with students and faculty. Attendance at religious services is required.

Summer Programs Remediation programs offered; session focuses on remediation for incoming freshmen; held on campus; accepts boys and girls; open to students from other schools. 15 students usually enrolled. 2009 schedule: June 15 to July 16.

Tuition and Aid Day student tuition: $11,700. Tuition installment plan (FACTS Tuition Payment Plan). Merit scholarship grants, need-based scholarship grants available. In 2008–09, 38% of upper-school students received aid; total upper-school merit-scholarship money awarded: $167,000. Total amount of financial aid awarded in 2008–09: $495,000.

Admissions Traditional secondary-level entrance grade is 9. For fall 2008, 142 students applied for upper-level admission, 122 were accepted, 98 enrolled. SSAT required. Deadline for receipt of application materials: none. Application fee required: $50. Interview required.

Athletics Interscholastic: baseball, basketball, cross-country running, football, golf, indoor track & field, JROTC drill, lacrosse, marksmanship, outdoor skills, riflery, soccer, swimming and diving, tennis, track and field, winter (indoor) track, wrestling; intramural: outdoor adventure, outdoor education, rappelling, strength & conditioning, weight lifting, weight training, wilderness survival, wildernessways. 1 PE instructor, 15 coaches, 1 athletic trainer.

Computers Computers are regularly used in English, graphic arts, journalism, photojournalism, programming, yearbook classes. Computer resources include on-campus library services, Internet access. Student e-mail accounts are available to students. The school has a published electronic and media policy.

Contact Mrs. Sandy M. Carli, Associate Director of Admission. 804-342-1314. Fax: 804-342-1349. E-mail: scarli@benedictinehighschool.org. Web site: www.benedictinehighschool.org.

BENEDICTINE MILITARY SCHOOL

6502 Seawright Drive
Savannah, Georgia 31406

Head of School: Ms. Deborah Antosca, EdD

General Information Boys' day college-preparatory, arts, religious studies, technology, and military school, affiliated with Roman Catholic Church. Grades 9–12. Founded: 1902. Setting: suburban. 100-acre campus. 4 buildings on campus. Approved or accredited by Southern Association of Colleges and Schools and Georgia Department of Education. Endowment: $2.1 million. Total enrollment: 309. Upper school average class size: 15. Upper school faculty-student ratio: 1:11.

Upper School Student Profile Grade 9: 88 students (88 boys); Grade 10: 80 students (80 boys); Grade 11: 70 students (70 boys); Grade 12: 71 students (71 boys). 70% of students are Roman Catholic.

Faculty School total: 33. In upper school: 22 men, 10 women; 20 have advanced degrees.

Subjects Offered Algebra, American history, American literature, band, biology, calculus, calculus-AP, chemistry, chorus, Christian and Hebrew scripture, communications, comparative religion, computer programming, economics, English, English language and composition-AP, English literature, English literature and composition-AP, English-AP, environmental science-AP, European history-AP, French, geography, geometry, health, Hebrew scripture, honors English, honors geometry, JROTC, Latin, photography, physical education, physics, religion, robotics, Spanish, studio art, trigonometry, U.S. government, U.S. history, U.S. history-AP, weight training, world history, world wide web design.

Graduation Requirements English, foreign language, mathematics, physical education (includes health), religion (includes Bible studies and theology), science, social science, social studies (includes history), JROTC for students entering as freshmen and sophomores, 70 hour minimum community service.

Special Academic Programs 6 Advanced Placement exams for which test preparation is offered; honors section; independent study; academic accommodation for the gifted.

College Admission Counseling 91 students graduated in 2008; 87 went to college, including Armstrong Atlantic State University; Georgia Institute of Technology; Georgia Southern University; Kennesaw State University; University of Georgia. Other: 3 went to work, 1 entered military service. Mean SAT critical reading: 529, mean SAT math: 523, mean SAT writing: 498, mean combined SAT: 1550. 25% scored over 600 on SAT critical reading, 25% scored over 600 on SAT math, 25% scored over 600 on SAT writing, 25% scored over 1800 on combined SAT.

Student Life Upper grades have uniform requirement, student council, honor system. Discipline rests primarily with faculty. Attendance at religious services is required.
Summer Programs Remediation programs offered; session focuses on make-up credits for courses failed during the school year; held on campus; accepts boys; not open to students from other schools. 25 students usually enrolled. 2009 schedule: June 5 to July 8. Application deadline: June 1.
Tuition and Aid Day student tuition: $9200. Tuition installment plan (FACTS Tuition Payment Plan, monthly payment plans). Need-based scholarship grants, discount for children of employees (50%) available. In 2008–09, 34% of upper-school students received aid. Total amount of financial aid awarded in 2008–09: $380,000.
Admissions Traditional secondary-level entrance grade is 9. For fall 2008, 109 students applied for upper-level admission, 98 were accepted, 88 enrolled. Explore required. Deadline for receipt of application materials: none. Application fee required: $50. Interview required.
Athletics Interscholastic: baseball, basketball, cross-country running, drill team, football, golf, in-line hockey, JROTC drill, physical fitness, physical training, riflery, sailing, soccer, swimming and diving, tennis, track and field, weight lifting, wrestling; intramural: physical fitness, racquetball, strength & conditioning, weight training. 3 PE instructors, 14 coaches, 1 athletic trainer.
Computers Computers are regularly used in English, programming, SAT preparation, Web site design classes. Computer network features include on-campus library services, Internet access. Students grades are available online.
Contact Mr. Will Fleming, Director of Admissions. 912-644-7007. Fax: 912-356-3527. E-mail: will.fleming@bcsav.net.

BEN FRANKLIN ACADEMY

1585 Clifton Road
Atlanta, Georgia 30329

Head of School: Dr. Wood Smethurst

General Information Coeducational day college-preparatory school. Grades 9–12. Founded: 1987. Setting: urban. 3-acre campus. 2 buildings on campus. Approved or accredited by Georgia Independent School Association, Southern Association of Colleges and Schools, and Georgia Department of Education. Total enrollment: 130. Upper school average class size: 1. Upper school faculty-student ratio: 1:3.
Faculty School total: 29. In upper school: 12 men, 17 women; 15 have advanced degrees.
Special Academic Programs Advanced Placement exam preparation; honors section; accelerated programs.
College Admission Counseling 62 students graduated in 2008; all went to college.
Student Life Upper grades have specified standards of dress. Discipline rests primarily with faculty.
Tuition and Aid Day student tuition: $22,120. Need-based scholarship grants available.
Admissions Traditional secondary-level entrance grade is 10. Deadline for receipt of application materials: none. No application fee required. On-campus interview required.
Athletics Coed Interscholastic: basketball, cross-country running, golf, tennis.
Computers Computer resources include on-campus library services, Internet access, Internet filtering or blocking technology. Campus intranet and student e-mail accounts are available to students. The school has a published electronic and media policy.
Contact Dr. Martha B. Burdette, Dean of Studies. 404-633-7404. Fax: 404-321-0610. E-mail: bfa@benfranklinacademy.org. Web site: www.benfranklinacademy.org.

ANNOUNCEMENT FROM THE SCHOOL Ben Franklin Academy is a coeducational, college-preparatory high school, accredited by the Southern Association of Colleges and Schools (SACS), for students who are not thriving in traditional schools. The Academy offers individualized instruction to a wide range of students and develops a plan to meet each student's unique needs. For more information, students can visit the Academy's Web site at www.benfranklinacademy.org.

BENILDE–ST. MARGARET'S SCHOOL

2501 Highway 100 South
St. Louis Park, Minnesota 55416

Head of School: Robert Tift

General Information Coeducational day college-preparatory, general academic, religious studies, and technology school, affiliated with Roman Catholic Church. Grades 7–12. Founded: 1907. Setting: suburban. Nearest major city is Minneapolis. 33-acre campus. 3 buildings on campus. Approved or accredited by North Central Association of Colleges and Schools and Minnesota Department of Education. Endowment: $4.1 million. Total enrollment: 1,171. Upper school average class size: 21. Upper school faculty-student ratio: 1:12.
Upper School Student Profile Grade 9: 237 students (142 boys, 95 girls); Grade 10: 234 students (122 boys, 112 girls); Grade 11: 217 students (101 boys, 116 girls); Grade 12: 200 students (100 boys, 100 girls). 80% of students are Roman Catholic.
Faculty School total: 94. In upper school: 36 men, 58 women; 52 have advanced degrees.
Subjects Offered Accounting, acting, advanced computer applications, advanced math, Advanced Placement courses, algebra, American government-AP, American history, American history-AP, American literature, ancient history, applied music, art, art appreciation, astronomy, aviation, band, Bible studies, biology, biology-AP, British literature, business, calculus, calculus-AP, career/college preparation, Catholic belief and practice, ceramics, chemistry, choir, church history, civics, comparative government and politics-AP, comparative religion, competitive science projects, computer programming, computer science, creative writing, death and loss, debate, drama, drawing and design, driver education, earth science, ecology, economics, economics and history, English, English literature, English literature-AP, environmental science, European history, European history-AP, film, fine arts, French, French-AP, geography, geometry, government/civics, health, history, journalism, keyboarding, language-AP, Latin, mathematics, music, orchestra, painting, photography, physical education, physics, psychology, religion, science, social studies, Spanish, Spanish-AP, speech, statistics-AP, stock market, theater, theology, trigonometry, word processing, world history, world literature, world religions, writing.
Graduation Requirements Arts and fine arts (art, music, dance, drama), electives, English, foreign language, guidance, mathematics, physical education (includes health), religion (includes Bible studies and theology), science, social studies (includes history).
Special Academic Programs Advanced Placement exam preparation; honors section; independent study; study at local college for college credit.
College Admission Counseling 218 students graduated in 2008; 214 went to college, including College of Saint Benedict; Iowa State University of Science and Technology; St. Thomas University; University of Minnesota, Duluth; University of Minnesota, Twin Cities Campus; University of Wisconsin–Madison. Other: 4 had other specific plans. Mean SAT critical reading: 591, mean SAT math: 617, mean SAT writing: 582, mean composite ACT: 25. 52% scored over 600 on SAT critical reading, 64% scored over 600 on SAT math, 44% scored over 600 on SAT writing, 40% scored over 26 on composite ACT.
Student Life Upper grades have specified standards of dress, student council. Discipline rests primarily with faculty. Attendance at religious services is required.
Summer Programs Sports, art/fine arts programs offered; held on campus; accepts boys and girls; open to students from other schools. 600 students usually enrolled. 2009 schedule: June to August. Application deadline: May.
Tuition and Aid Day student tuition: $10,600. Tuition installment plan (monthly payment plans, individually arranged payment plans). Merit scholarship grants, need-based scholarship grants, paying campus jobs available. In 2008–09, 15% of upper-school students received aid; total upper-school merit-scholarship money awarded: $35,000. Total amount of financial aid awarded in 2008–09: $737,600.
Admissions Traditional secondary-level entrance grade is 9. ACT-Explore and any standardized test required. Deadline for receipt of application materials: January 20. No application fee required. On-campus interview recommended.
Athletics Interscholastic: alpine skiing (boys, girls), baseball (b), basketball (b,g), cheering (g), cross-country running (b,g), dance team (g), diving (b,g), football (b), golf (b,g), hockey (b,g), ice hockey (b,g), lacrosse (b,g), nordic skiing (b,g), sailing (b,g), skiing (cross-country) (b,g), skiing (downhill) (b,g), soccer (b,g), softball (g), swimming and diving (b,g), tennis (b,g), track and field (b,g), volleyball (g), weight training (b,g), wrestling (b); intramural: basketball (b,g); coed interscholastic: bowling. 3 PE instructors, 15 coaches, 1 athletic trainer.
Computers Computers are regularly used in all classes. Computer network features include on-campus library services, Internet access, wireless campus network, Internet filtering or blocking technology. Campus intranet and computer access in designated common areas are available to students. Students grades are available online. The school has a published electronic and media policy.
Contact Mary Periolat, Director of Admissions. 952-915-4345. Fax: 952-920-8889. E-mail: admissions@bsm-online.org. Web site: www.bsm-online.org.

ANNOUNCEMENT FROM THE SCHOOL Benilde–St. Margaret's (BSM) is a Catholic community for students in grades 7–12. BSM takes pride in an impressive academic reputation based on a challenging college-preparatory curriculum, which includes thirteen AP courses. Demonstrating a strong history of extracurricular programs, BSM was represented in thirteen state competitions during the 2007–08 school year and was recently ranked first in the state for having the highest percentage of students participating in extracurricular activities. With a full-time service-learning coordinator, BSM is one of two National Leader Schools in Minnesota for service-learning, a strategy that combines academics with community service. BSM also counts as strengths its modest class sizes, a caring atmosphere, and an award-winning pre-engineering program.

THE BENJAMIN SCHOOL

11000 Ellison Wilson Road
North Palm Beach, Florida 33408

Head of School: Mr. Robert S. Goldberg

General Information Coeducational day college-preparatory and arts school. Grades PK–12. Founded: 1960. Setting: suburban. Nearest major city is West Palm Beach. 50-acre campus. 5 buildings on campus. Approved or accredited by Florida Council of Independent Schools, Southern Association of Colleges and Schools, and

Florida Department of Education. Member of National Association of Independent Schools and Secondary School Admission Test Board. Endowment: $3 million. Total enrollment: 1,250. Upper school average class size: 16. Upper school faculty-student ratio: 1:7.

Upper School Student Profile Grade 9: 112 students (56 boys, 56 girls); Grade 10: 119 students (45 boys, 74 girls); Grade 11: 92 students (46 boys, 46 girls); Grade 12: 100 students (55 boys, 45 girls).

Faculty School total: 173. In upper school: 19 men, 25 women; 17 have advanced degrees.

Subjects Offered 3-dimensional art, acting, African studies, algebra, American history, anatomy and physiology, art, art history, Asian studies, band, Basic programming, biology, biology-AP, calculus, calculus-AP, Caribbean history, cartooning/animation, ceramics, chemistry, chemistry-AP, choral music, chorus, comparative government and politics-AP, comparative religion, composition-AP, computer animation, computer programming, computer science, computer science-AP, current events, dance, debate, drama, earth science, ecology, economics, economics-AP, English, English language and composition-AP, English literature, English literature and composition-AP, environmental science, European history, expository writing, film studies, French, French language-AP, genetics, geometry, government-AP, government/civics, grammar, honors English, honors geometry, literature and composition-AP, marine biology, modern European history-AP, mythology, physical education, physics, piano, pre-calculus, psychology, SAT preparation, Spanish, Spanish language-AP, Spanish literature-AP, speech, statistics-AP, theater, trigonometry, U.S. government, U.S. government and politics-AP, U.S. government-AP, U.S. history-AP, video film production, world history.

Graduation Requirements Arts and fine arts (art, music, dance, drama), computer science, English, foreign language, mathematics, physical education (includes health), science, social science, social studies (includes history), work program for seniors.

Special Academic Programs 17 Advanced Placement exams for which test preparation is offered; honors section; study at local college for college credit; academic accommodation for the gifted, the musically talented, and the artistically talented.

College Admission Counseling 95 students graduated in 2008; all went to college, including College of Charleston; Florida State University; Southern Methodist University; University of Central Florida; University of Florida; University of Miami. Mean SAT critical reading: 575, mean SAT math: 584, mean SAT writing: 590, mean composite ACT: 26.

Student Life Upper grades have uniform requirement, student council, honor system. Discipline rests primarily with faculty.

Summer Programs Enrichment, advancement, sports, computer instruction programs offered; session focuses on academic advancement; held on campus; accepts boys and girls; open to students from other schools. 40 students usually enrolled. 2009 schedule: June 1 to July 10. Application deadline: May 1.

Tuition and Aid Day student tuition: $21,525. Tuition installment plan (monthly payment plans, The Tuition Solution). Merit scholarship grants, need-based scholarship grants, need-based loans available. In 2008–09, 17% of upper-school students received aid; total upper-school merit-scholarship money awarded: $21,525. Total amount of financial aid awarded in 2008–09: $750,000.

Admissions Traditional secondary-level entrance grade is 9. For fall 2008, 94 students applied for upper-level admission, 85 were accepted, 57 enrolled. ERB or SSAT required. Deadline for receipt of application materials: February 1. Application fee required: $100. On-campus interview required.

Athletics Interscholastic: baseball (boys), basketball (b,g), cheering (g), cross-country running (b,g), dance (g), dance team (g), football (b), golf (b,g), lacrosse (b,g), soccer (b,g), softball (g), tennis (b,g), volleyball (g), wrestling (b); coed interscholastic: aerobics/dance, bowling, diving, swimming and diving, track and field; coed intramural: sailing. 2 PE instructors, 1 coach, 1 athletic trainer.

Computers Computers are regularly used in art, English, foreign language, history, mathematics, science classes. Computer network features include on-campus library services, Internet access, wireless campus network, Internet filtering or blocking technology, tablet laptop program for grades 9 to 12. Student e-mail accounts are available to students. The school has a published electronic and media policy.

Contact Mrs. Mary Lou Primm, Director of Admission. 561-472-3451. Fax: 561-472-3410. E-mail: mprimm@thebenjaminschool.org. Web site: www.thebenjaminschool.org.

BENTLEY SCHOOL

1 Hiller Drive
Oakland, California 94618

ANNOUNCEMENT FROM THE SCHOOL As a kindergarten through grade 12, coeducational, independent school, Bentley School inspires academic excellence, personal achievement, and character by engaging students' intellect and creativity and by encouraging them to embrace values that enrich themselves, the community, and the world. Bentley's motto is "Scire Desidero: I Desire to Know." As Bentley pursues its mission, it is guided by the values at the heart of a Bentley education. These core values define and sustain Bentley's traditions and illuminate future endeavors: Integrity: the upholding of honor, dignity, and compassion; Excellence: Bentley's comprehensive curriculum and academic program promote a lifelong pursuit and love of learning; Courage: Bentley provides an environment that allows students to take risks and to confront challenges in creative ways; Ingenuity: Bentley encourages students to explore their individual talents and discover a willingness to engage in critical thought; Inclusion: Bentley is a community that represents diverse backgrounds and experiences, always striving for respectful and compassionate relationships among students, teachers, and parents.

BERKELEY PREPARATORY SCHOOL

4811 Kelly Road
Tampa, Florida 33615

Head of School: Joseph A. Merluzzi

General Information Coeducational day college-preparatory, arts, religious studies, bilingual studies, and technology school, affiliated with Episcopal Church. Grades PK–12. Founded: 1960. Setting: suburban. 76-acre campus. 8 buildings on campus. Approved or accredited by Florida Council of Independent Schools, National Association of Episcopal Schools, Southern Association of Colleges and Schools, The College Board, and Florida Department of Education. Member of National Association of Independent Schools and Secondary School Admission Test Board. Total enrollment: 1,200. Upper school average class size: 15. Upper school faculty-student ratio: 1:7.

Faculty School total: 145. In upper school: 22 men, 27 women.

Subjects Offered African history, algebra, American government, American history, American literature, art, art history, biology, biology-AP, calculus, calculus-AP, ceramics, chemistry, chemistry-AP, China/Japan history, community service, computer math, computer programming, computer science, creative writing, dance, drama, drama performance, drama workshop, early childhood, economics, English, English literature, English-AP, environmental science-AP, etymology, European history, expository writing, fine arts, French, French-AP, freshman seminar, geography, geometry, government/civics, grammar, guitar, health, history, history of China and Japan, honors algebra, honors English, honors geometry, instruments, Latin, Latin American history, Latin-AP, logic, Mandarin, math analysis, mathematics, media arts, microbiology, modern European history, modern European history-AP, music, performing arts, philosophy, physical education, physics, physics-AP, pre-calculus, psychology, religious studies, SAT preparation, science, social studies, Spanish, Spanish-AP, speech, stage design, statistics, statistics-AP, technical theater, television, theater, theater production, U.S. history, U.S. history-AP, video, video film production, Western civilization, world history, world literature, writing.

Graduation Requirements Arts and fine arts (art, music, dance, drama), computer science, English, foreign language, mathematics, physical education (includes health), religious studies, science, social studies (includes history). Community service is required.

Special Academic Programs Advanced Placement exam preparation; honors section; independent study; study abroad.

College Admission Counseling 129 students graduated in 2008; all went to college, including Duke University; Georgetown University; Northwestern University; Southern Methodist University; University of Miami; University of Pennsylvania. Median SAT critical reading: 620, median SAT math: 630, median SAT writing: 620, median combined SAT: 1880, median composite ACT: 28. 58% scored over 600 on SAT critical reading, 61% scored over 600 on SAT math, 64% scored over 600 on SAT writing, 62% scored over 1800 on combined SAT, 63% scored over 26 on composite ACT.

Student Life Upper grades have specified standards of dress, student council, honor system. Discipline rests equally with students and faculty.

Summer Programs Remediation, enrichment, advancement, sports, art/fine arts, computer instruction programs offered; session focuses on setting a fun pace for excellence; held on campus; accepts boys and girls; open to students from other schools. 2,000 students usually enrolled. 2009 schedule: June 1 to July 24. Application deadline: none.

Tuition and Aid Day student tuition: $17,000. Tuition installment plan (5-installment plan). Need-based scholarship grants available.

Admissions Traditional secondary-level entrance grade is 9. Otis-Lennon Mental Ability Test and SSAT required. Deadline for receipt of application materials: January 30. Application fee required: $50. On-campus interview required.

Athletics Interscholastic: baseball (boys), basketball (b,g), cheering (g), crew (b,g), cross-country running (b,g), dance squad (g), dance team (g), diving (b,g), football (b), golf (b,g), lacrosse (b), rowing (b,g), soccer (b,g), softball (g), swimming and diving (b,g), tennis (b,g), track and field (b,g), volleyball (b,g); coed interscholastic: weight lifting, wrestling; coed intramural: physical fitness, physical training, power lifting, project adventure, strength & conditioning, wall climbing, weight training. 11 PE instructors, 50 coaches, 2 athletic trainers.

Computers Computers are regularly used in art, English, foreign language, history, mathematics, music, science classes. Computer network features include on-campus library services, online commercial services, Internet access, wireless campus network, Internet filtering or blocking technology. Student e-mail accounts are available to students. Students grades are available online. The school has a published electronic and media policy.

Contact Janie McIlvaine, Director of Admissions. 813-885-1673. Fax: 813-886-6933. E-mail: mcilvjan@berkeleyprep.org. Web site: www.berkeleyprep.org.

See Close-Up on page 678.

BERKSHIRE SCHOOL

245 North Undermountain Road
Sheffield, Massachusetts 01257

Head of School: Michael J. Maher

General Information Coeducational boarding and day college-preparatory, arts, and technology school. Grades 9–PG. Founded: 1907. Setting: rural. Nearest major city is Hartford, CT. Students are housed in single-sex dormitories. 550-acre campus. 36 buildings on campus. Approved or accredited by Association of Independent Schools in New England, New England Association of Schools and Colleges, and The Association of Boarding Schools. Member of National Association of Independent Schools and Secondary School Admission Test Board. Endowment: $83.5 million. Total enrollment: 371. Upper school average class size: 12. Upper school faculty-student ratio: 1:6.

Upper School Student Profile Grade 9: 65 students (39 boys, 26 girls); Grade 10: 93 students (55 boys, 38 girls); Grade 11: 106 students (58 boys, 48 girls); Grade 12: 91 students (53 boys, 38 girls); Postgraduate: 16 students (11 boys, 5 girls). 89% of students are boarding students. 20% are state residents. 28 states are represented in upper school student body. 19% are international students. International students from Canada, Germany, Hong Kong, Republic of Korea, Taiwan, and Viet Nam; 22 other countries represented in student body.

Faculty School total: 67. In upper school: 39 men, 28 women; 32 have advanced degrees; 52 reside on campus.

Subjects Offered 3-dimensional design, acting, Advanced Placement courses, algebra, American government, American history, American literature, anatomy, ancient history, animal behavior, art, art history, astronomy, biology, calculus, ceramics, chemistry, Chinese, choral music, chorus, comparative government and politics, comparative religion, composition, computer programming, computer science, constitutional law, creative writing, dance, digital art, drama, drawing and design, economics, English, English literature, environmental science, ESL, ethics, European history, expository writing, forensic science, French, genetics, geology, geometry, health, history, instrumental music, Latin, mathematics, music, music technology, painting, philosophy, photography, physics, physiology, pre-calculus, psychology, public speaking, science, Spanish, statistics, studio art, theater, trigonometry, writing.

Graduation Requirements Arts and fine arts (art, music, dance, drama), English, foreign language, history, introduction to technology, mathematics, science. Community service is required.

Special Academic Programs Advanced Placement exam preparation; honors section; independent study; study abroad; ESL (16 students enrolled).

College Admission Counseling 113 students graduated in 2008; 104 went to college, including Boston College; Cornell University; Dartmouth College; Northeastern University; St. Lawrence University; University of Vermont. Other: 3 entered a postgraduate year, 6 had other specific plans.

Student Life Upper grades have specified standards of dress, student council, honor system. Discipline rests equally with students and faculty.

Tuition and Aid Day student tuition: $32,700; 7-day tuition and room/board: $42,450. Tuition installment plan (Academic Management Services Plan, Key Tuition Payment Plan, monthly payment plans). Merit scholarship grants, need-based scholarship grants available. In 2008–09, 29% of upper-school students received aid; total upper-school merit-scholarship money awarded: $53,500. Total amount of financial aid awarded in 2008–09: $2,800,000.

Admissions Traditional secondary-level entrance grade is 9. For fall 2008, 925 students applied for upper-level admission, 335 were accepted, 150 enrolled. ACT, PSAT, SAT, SSAT or TOEFL required. Deadline for receipt of application materials: January 31. Application fee required: $50. Interview required.

Athletics Interscholastic: baseball (boys), basketball (b,g), crew (b,g), cross-country running (b,g), field hockey (g), football (b), ice hockey (b,g), lacrosse (b,g), soccer (b,g), softball (g), squash (b,g), tennis (b,g), track and field (b,g), volleyball (g); coed interscholastic: alpine skiing, golf, mountain biking; coed intramural: alpine skiing, climbing, dance, fly fishing, hiking/backpacking, modern dance, mountaineering, outdoor adventure, outdoor education, outdoor skills, rappelling, rock climbing, ropes courses, skiing (downhill), snowboarding, wilderness, wilderness survival. 2 athletic trainers.

Computers Computers are regularly used in art, mathematics, music, science, technology classes. Computer network features include on-campus library services, online commercial services, Internet access, wireless campus network, Internet filtering or blocking technology, network printing, interactive Polyvision white boards (smart boards). Campus intranet and student e-mail accounts are available to students. The school has a published electronic and media policy.

Contact Mr. Andrew L. Bogardus, Director of Admission. 413-229-1003. Fax: 413-229-1016. E-mail: admission@berkshireschool.org. Web site: www.berkshireschool.org.

See Close-Up on page 680.

THE BERMUDA HIGH SCHOOL FOR GIRLS

19 Richmond Road
Pembroke HM 08, Bermuda

Head of School: Mrs. Linda (Noble) Parker

General Information Girls' day college-preparatory, general academic, arts, and business school. Grades 1–13. Founded: 1894. Setting: small town. Nearest major city is Hamilton, Bermuda. 8-acre campus. 4 buildings on campus. Approved or accredited by state department of education. Affiliate member of National Association of Independent Schools; member of European Council of International Schools. Language of instruction: English. Endowment: 5 million Bermuda dollars. Total enrollment: 746. Upper school average class size: 16. Upper school faculty-student ratio: 1:12.

Upper School Student Profile Grade 10: 37 students (37 girls); Grade 11: 44 students (44 girls); Grade 12: 55 students (4 boys, 51 girls); Grade 13: 44 students (5 boys, 39 girls).

Faculty School total: 85. In upper school: 11 men, 44 women; 25 have advanced degrees.

Subjects Offered Accounting, algebra, art, arts, biology, business, business skills, business studies, calculus, chemistry, computer science, dance, drama, economics, English, English literature, European history, expository writing, fine arts, French, geography, geometry, grammar, health, history, keyboarding, Latin, mathematics, music, physical education, physics, science, social studies, Spanish, theater, trigonometry, world history.

Graduation Requirements Arts and fine arts (art, music, dance, drama), business skills (includes word processing), computer science, English, fitness, foreign language, geography, mathematics, physical education (includes health), science, social studies (includes history).

Special Academic Programs International Baccalaureate program; remedial reading and/or remedial writing.

College Admission Counseling 35 students graduated in 2008; 34 went to college, including Bentley University; Berklee College of Music; Queen's University at Kingston; Ryerson University; St. John's University; University of Toronto. Other: 1 went to work.

Student Life Upper grades have uniform requirement, student council. Discipline rests primarily with faculty.

Tuition and Aid Day student tuition: 15,730 Bermuda dollars–17,300 Bermuda dollars. Tuition installment plan (monthly payment plans, individually arranged payment plans). Bursaries, merit scholarship grants, need-based scholarship grants available. In 2008–09, 39% of upper-school students received aid. Total amount of financial aid awarded in 2008–09: 332,100 Bermuda dollars.

Admissions Traditional secondary-level entrance grade is 7. For fall 2008, 30 students applied for upper-level admission, 13 were accepted, 12 enrolled. School's own test required. Deadline for receipt of application materials: none. Application fee required: 50 Bermuda dollars. Interview recommended.

Athletics Interscholastic: aquatics (girls), basketball (g), cross-country running (g), field hockey (g), gymnastics (g), netball (g), soccer (g), swimming and diving (g), tennis (g), track and field (g), volleyball (g); intramural: aerobics (g), aerobics/dance (g), aerobics/Nautilus (g), backpacking (g), badminton (g), ball hockey (g), ballet (g), basketball (g), cooperative games (g), cross-country running (g), curling (g), dance (g), dressage (g), field hockey (g), fitness (g), fitness walking (g), floor hockey (g), gymnastics (g), jogging (g), Nautilus (g), netball (g), outdoor education (g), outdoor skills (g), physical fitness (g), soccer (g), softball (g), squash (g), track and field (g), volleyball (g), wall climbing (g). 3 PE instructors, 10 coaches.

Computers Computers are regularly used in business skills, business studies, English, foreign language, French, geography, history, introduction to technology, mathematics, research skills, Spanish, word processing, yearbook classes. Computer network features include on-campus library services, Internet access, Internet filtering or blocking technology. Campus intranet, student e-mail accounts, and computer access in designated common areas are available to students. Students grades are available online. The school has a published electronic and media policy.

Contact Mrs. Levyette Robinson, Head of Secondary Department. 441-295-6153. Fax: 441-278-3017. E-mail: lrobinson@bhs.bm. Web site: www.bhs.bm.

BERWICK ACADEMY

31 Academy Street
South Berwick, Maine 03908

Head of School: Gregory J. Schneider

General Information Coeducational day college-preparatory and arts school. Grades K–PG. Founded: 1791. Setting: small town. Nearest major city is Portsmouth, NH. 72-acre campus. 11 buildings on campus. Approved or accredited by New England Association of Schools and Colleges and Maine Department of Education. Member of National Association of Independent Schools and Secondary School Admission Test Board. Endowment: $18.5 million. Total enrollment: 593. Upper school average class size: 14. Upper school faculty-student ratio: 1:12.

Upper School Student Profile Grade 9: 60 students (37 boys, 23 girls); Grade 10: 71 students (35 boys, 36 girls); Grade 11: 64 students (32 boys, 32 girls); Grade 12: 55 students (24 boys, 31 girls); Postgraduate: 1 student (1 girl).

Faculty School total: 88. In upper school: 13 men, 17 women; 16 have advanced degrees.

Subjects Offered Algebra, American history, American literature, art, art history, biology, calculus, chemistry, computer math, computer programming, computer science, dance, English, ethics, European history, fine arts, French, geometry, government/civics, health, history, journalism, Latin, mathematics, metalworking, music, physical education, physics, science, social studies, Spanish, statistics, theater arts, trigonometry, world history.

Graduation Requirements Algebra, analysis, arts and fine arts (art, music, dance, drama), biology, chemistry, computer science, English, English literature, European civilization, foreign language, languages, mathematics, physical education (includes health), physics, science, social studies (includes history).

Special Academic Programs Advanced Placement exam preparation; honors section; independent study; term-away projects; study abroad; academic accommodation for the gifted, the musically talented, and the artistically talented.

College Admission Counseling 66 students graduated in 2008; 64 went to college, including Bowdoin College; Dartmouth College. Other: 1 entered a postgraduate year, 1 had other specific plans. 56% scored over 600 on SAT critical reading, 60% scored over 600 on SAT math, 61% scored over 600 on SAT writing.

Student Life Upper grades have specified standards of dress, student council, honor system. Discipline rests equally with students and faculty.

Summer Programs Session focuses on study skills; held on campus; accepts boys and girls; open to students from other schools. 48 students usually enrolled. 2009 schedule: August 1 to August 15. Application deadline: June 30.

Tuition and Aid Day student tuition: $22,400. Tuition installment plan (FACTS Tuition Payment Plan). Need-based scholarship grants, need-based loans available. In 2008–09, 33% of upper-school students received aid. Total amount of financial aid awarded in 2008–09: $1,450,000.

Admissions Traditional secondary-level entrance grade is 9. For fall 2008, 102 students applied for upper-level admission, 77 were accepted, 42 enrolled. ERB or SSAT or WISC III required. Deadline for receipt of application materials: January 31. Application fee required: $50. Interview required.

Athletics Interscholastic: alpine skiing (boys, girls), baseball (b), basketball (b,g), cross-country running (b,g), dance (b,g), golf (b,g), ice hockey (b,g), lacrosse (b,g); intramural: wilderness (g); coed intramural: bicycling, wilderness. 3 PE instructors, 4 coaches, 2 athletic trainers.

Computers Computers are regularly used in art, dance, English, foreign language, graphic design, history, humanities, independent study, library, mathematics, SAT preparation, science, social studies, theater arts, writing, yearbook classes. Computer network features include on-campus library services, Internet access, wireless campus network, Internet filtering or blocking technology. Student e-mail accounts are available to students. The school has a published electronic and media policy.

Contact Diane M. Field, Director of Admission and Financial Aid. 207-384-2164 Ext. 2301. Fax: 207-384-3332. E-mail: dfield@berwickacademy.org. Web site: www.berwickacademy.org.

BESANT HILL SCHOOL

8585 Highway 150
PO Box 850
Ojai, California 93024

Head of School: Mr. Paul Amadio

General Information Coeducational boarding and day college-preparatory and arts school; primarily serves students with learning disabilities. Grades 9–12. Founded: 1946. Setting: rural. Nearest major city is Los Angeles. Students are housed in single-sex dormitories. 500-acre campus. 14 buildings on campus. Approved or accredited by California Association of Independent Schools, The Association of Boarding Schools, Western Association of Schools and Colleges, and California Department of Education. Member of National Association of Independent Schools and Secondary School Admission Test Board. Languages of instruction: English and Spanish. Endowment: $1 million. Total enrollment: 100. Upper school average class size: 10. Upper school faculty-student ratio: 1:4.

Upper School Student Profile Grade 9: 20 students (10 boys, 10 girls); Grade 10: 24 students (12 boys, 12 girls); Grade 11: 26 students (13 boys, 13 girls); Grade 12: 28 students (14 boys, 14 girls); Postgraduate: 2 students (1 boy, 1 girl). 80% of students are boarding students. 50% are state residents. 17 states are represented in upper school student body. 23% are international students. International students from Cameroon, Canada, China, Japan, Mexico, and Taiwan; 5 other countries represented in student body.

Faculty School total: 25. In upper school: 12 men, 13 women; 13 have advanced degrees; 18 reside on campus.

Subjects Offered Acting, adolescent issues, algebra, American history, art, art history, astronomy, biology, calculus, calculus-AP, ceramics, chemistry, computer science, digital art, drama, driver education, English, English as a foreign language, English language and composition-AP, English literature, English-AP, environmental science, ESL, ethics, expository writing, film, fine arts, geography, geometry, government/civics, history, mathematics, music, music history, music theory, music theory-AP, philosophy, photography, physical education, physics, scene study, science, social science, social studies, Spanish, theater, world history.

Graduation Requirements Arts and fine arts (art, music, dance, drama), English, foreign language, mathematics, physical education (includes health), science, social science, social studies (includes history).

Special Academic Programs Advanced Placement exam preparation; honors section; independent study; study at local college for college credit; academic accommodation for the musically talented and the artistically talented; ESL (9 students enrolled).

College Admission Counseling 27 students graduated in 2007; all went to college, including Pitzer College; Sarah Lawrence College; The Evergreen State College; University of California, Santa Barbara; University of California, Santa Cruz; University of Puget Sound. Median SAT critical reading: 580, median SAT math: 550, median SAT writing: 500. 18% scored over 600 on SAT critical reading, 10% scored over 600 on SAT math, 15% scored over 600 on SAT writing.

Student Life Upper grades have student council, honor system. Discipline rests equally with students and faculty.

Tuition and Aid Day student tuition: $19,900; 7-day tuition and room/board: $37,700. Tuition installment plan (Academic Management Services Plan, Key Tuition Payment Plan). Tuition reduction for siblings, need-based scholarship grants, paying campus jobs available. In 2007–08, 22% of upper-school students received aid. Total amount of financial aid awarded in 2007–08: $325,000.

Admissions Traditional secondary-level entrance grade is 9. For fall 2007, 245 students applied for upper-level admission, 118 were accepted, 47 enrolled. Deadline for receipt of application materials: February 22. Application fee required: $50. On-campus interview required.

Athletics Interscholastic: basketball (boys); intramural: baseball (b), basketball (b), soccer (b,g), softball (b), volleyball (g), wrestling (b); coed interscholastic: aerobics, aerobics/dance, backpacking, cross-country running, dance, fitness, fitness walking, Frisbee, golf, hiking/backpacking, mountain biking, outdoor activities, outdoor education, outdoor skills, paddle tennis, physical training, ropes courses, skeet shooting, surfing, ultimate Frisbee, walking, yoga; coed intramural: bicycling, billiards, running, skiing (downhill), swimming and diving, table tennis, tennis, track and field. 2 coaches.

Computers Computers are regularly used in desktop publishing, graphic arts, graphic design, mathematics, media arts, publications, video film production classes. Computer network features include on-campus library services, online commercial services, Internet access, wireless campus network, Internet filtering or blocking technology. Student e-mail accounts are available to students.

Contact Randy Bertin, Director of Admission and Financial Aid. 805-646-4343 Ext. 422. Fax: 805-646-4371. E-mail: rbertin@besanthill.org. Web site: www.besanthill.org.

See Close-Up on page 682.

BETH HAVEN CHRISTIAN SCHOOL

5515 Johnsontown Road
Louisville, Kentucky 40272

Head of School: Mr. Kevin Sample

General Information Coeducational day college-preparatory and religious studies school, affiliated with Baptist Church. Grades K4–12. Founded: 1971. Setting: suburban. 2-acre campus. 1 building on campus. Approved or accredited by Association of Christian Schools International and Kentucky Department of Education. Total enrollment: 278. Upper school average class size: 18. Upper school faculty-student ratio: 1:13.

Upper School Student Profile Grade 9: 29 students (14 boys, 15 girls); Grade 10: 27 students (13 boys, 14 girls); Grade 11: 21 students (16 boys, 5 girls); Grade 12: 27 students (13 boys, 14 girls). 65% of students are Baptist.

Faculty School total: 25. In upper school: 6 men, 12 women; 7 have advanced degrees.

Subjects Offered ACT preparation, Advanced Placement courses, algebra, American history, American literature, analytic geometry, art appreciation, Bible studies, biology, British literature (honors), business mathematics, calculus-AP, chemistry, computer applications, computer keyboarding, drama, dramatic arts, earth science, economics, English, English composition, English language and composition-AP, health, honors algebra, honors English, honors geometry, honors U.S. history, honors world history, independent study, journalism, lab science, psychology, psychology-AP, senior seminar, Spanish, speech, trigonometry, U.S. government and politics-AP, world geography, world history, yearbook.

Graduation Requirements ACT preparation, algebra, American government, American history, American literature, analytic geometry, arts appreciation, Bible, biology, British literature, chemistry, earth science, economics, English, language, physical education (includes health), world geography, world history.

Special Academic Programs Advanced Placement exam preparation; honors section; independent study; study at local college for college credit.

College Admission Counseling 15 students graduated in 2008; 13 went to college, including Eastern Kentucky University; Indiana University Bloomington; Jefferson Community and Technical College; University of Louisville; Western Kentucky University. Other: 2 went to work. Median composite ACT: 22. 5% scored over 26 on composite ACT.

Student Life Upper grades have uniform requirement, honor system. Discipline rests primarily with faculty.

Summer Programs Remediation, sports programs offered; held on campus; accepts boys and girls; not open to students from other schools. 50 students usually enrolled. 2009 schedule: June 8 to June 19. Application deadline: June 8.

Tuition and Aid Day student tuition: $3600. Tuition installment plan (FACTS Tuition Payment Plan). Tuition reduction for siblings, two full-tuition memorial scholarships are awarded each year based on a combination of merit and need available. In 2008–09, 2% of upper-school students received aid. Total amount of financial aid awarded in 2008–09: $7600.
Admissions Traditional secondary-level entrance grade is 9. For fall 2008, 22 students applied for upper-level admission, 20 were accepted, 19 enrolled. Stanford Test of Academic Skills required. Deadline for receipt of application materials: none. Application fee required: $250. Interview required.
Athletics Interscholastic: baseball (boys), basketball (b,g), cheering (g), football (b), softball (g), volleyball (g); coed interscholastic: cross-country running. 1 PE instructor.
Computers Computers are regularly used in business applications, computer applications, English, journalism, yearbook classes. Computer network features include Internet access, Internet filtering or blocking technology. Computer access in designated common areas is available to students. Students grades are available online. The school has a published electronic and media policy.
Contact Ms. Lisa Vincent, Registrar. 502-937-3516. Fax: 502-937-3364. E-mail: lvincent@bethhaven.com.

THE BIRCH WATHEN LENOX SCHOOL

210 East 77th Street
New York, New York 10075
Head of School: Mr. Frank J. Carnabuci III

General Information Coeducational day college-preparatory school. Grades K–12. Founded: 1916. Setting: urban. 1 building on campus. Approved or accredited by New York State Association of Independent Schools and New York Department of Education. Member of National Association of Independent Schools. Endowment: $5.2 million. Total enrollment: 550. Upper school average class size: 15. Upper school faculty-student ratio: 1:12.
Upper School Student Profile Grade 9: 46 students (24 boys, 22 girls); Grade 10: 45 students (25 boys, 20 girls); Grade 11: 46 students (23 boys, 23 girls); Grade 12: 48 students (22 boys, 26 girls).
Faculty School total: 70. In upper school: 15 men, 25 women; 40 have advanced degrees.
Subjects Offered Algebra, American history, American history-AP, American literature, American literature-AP, art, art history, biology, calculus, ceramics, chemistry, community service, computer math, computer science, creative writing, dance, drama, driver education, economics, English, English literature, environmental science, European history, expository writing, fine arts, French, geography, geology, geometry, government/civics, grammar, industrial arts, Japanese, journalism, mathematics, music, philosophy, photography, physical education, physics, science, Shakespeare, social studies, Spanish, speech, swimming, theater, trigonometry, typing, world history, writing.
Graduation Requirements 20th century world history, arts and fine arts (art, music, dance, drama), computer science, English, foreign language, mathematics, physical education (includes health), science, social studies (includes history). Community service is required.
Special Academic Programs Advanced Placement exam preparation; honors section; independent study; study abroad; academic accommodation for the gifted.
College Admission Counseling 44 students graduated in 2008; all went to college, including Columbia University; Middlebury College; Princeton University; Trinity College; University of Pennsylvania; Vanderbilt University. Mean SAT critical reading: 640, mean SAT math: 630.
Student Life Upper grades have specified standards of dress, student council, honor system. Discipline rests equally with students and faculty.
Tuition and Aid Day student tuition: $31,646. Tuition installment plan (Key Tuition Payment Plan, monthly payment plans, individually arranged payment plans). Merit scholarship grants, need-based scholarship grants available. In 2008–09, 15% of upper-school students received aid; total upper-school merit-scholarship money awarded: $100,000. Total amount of financial aid awarded in 2008–09: $1,200,000.
Admissions Traditional secondary-level entrance grade is 9. For fall 2008, 100 students applied for upper-level admission, 30 were accepted, 20 enrolled. ERB, ISEE, Math Placement Exam or writing sample required. Deadline for receipt of application materials: none. Application fee required: $50. On-campus interview required.
Athletics Interscholastic: baseball (boys), basketball (b,g), cross-country running (b,g), field hockey (g), hockey (b), ice hockey (b), soccer (b,g), softball (g), swimming and diving (b,g), tennis (b,g), track and field (b,g), volleyball (b,g); intramural: aerobics (b,g), baseball (b), basketball (b,g), dance (b), ice hockey (b), indoor soccer (b), running (b,g), skiing (downhill) (b,g), soccer (b,g), softball (g), swimming and diving (b,g), tennis (b,g), track and field (b,g), volleyball (b,g); coed interscholastic: cross-country running, golf, indoor track & field, lacrosse; coed intramural: bicycling, dance, golf, gymnastics, indoor track & field, skiing (cross-country), skiing (downhill). 5 PE instructors, 8 coaches.
Computers Computers are regularly used in all academic classes. Computer network features include on-campus library services, Internet access, wireless campus network. Student e-mail accounts are available to students.
Contact Billie Williams, Admissions Coordinator. 212-861-0404. Fax: 212-879-3388. E-mail: bwilliams@bwl.org. Web site: www.bwl.org.

BISHOP ALEMANY HIGH SCHOOL

11111 North Alemany Drive
Mission Hills, California 91345
Head of School: Mr. Frank Ferry

General Information Coeducational day college-preparatory and religious studies school, affiliated with Roman Catholic Church. Grades 9–12. Founded: 1956. Setting: suburban. Nearest major city is Los Angeles. 22-acre campus. 5 buildings on campus. Approved or accredited by National Lutheran School Accreditation and Western Association of Schools and Colleges. Total enrollment: 1,460. Upper school average class size: 22. Upper school faculty-student ratio: 1:18.
Upper School Student Profile Grade 9: 492 students (251 boys, 241 girls); Grade 10: 410 students (203 boys, 207 girls); Grade 11: 366 students (171 boys, 195 girls); Grade 12: 322 students (154 boys, 168 girls). 88% of students are Roman Catholic.
Faculty School total: 85. In upper school: 41 men, 44 women; 51 have advanced degrees.
Subjects Offered Algebra, American history, American history-AP, American literature, anatomy, architecture, art, art history, athletics, Bible studies, biology, biology-AP, business, calculus, calculus-AP, ceramics, chemistry, chemistry-AP, computer programming, computer science, drafting, drama, earth science, economics, economics-AP, engineering, English, English literature, English-AP, ethics, European history, European history-AP, fine arts, French, geography, geometry, government-AP, government/civics, grammar, health, history, journalism, mathematics, music, philosophy, physical education, physics, physics-AP, physiology, psychology, religion, science, social studies, Spanish, Spanish language-AP, Spanish literature-AP, speech, theater, theology, trigonometry, typing, world history, world literature, writing.
Graduation Requirements Arts and fine arts (art, music, dance, drama), computer science, English, foreign language, mathematics, physical education (includes health), religion (includes Bible studies and theology), science, social studies (includes history).
Special Academic Programs Advanced Placement exam preparation; honors section; remedial reading and/or remedial writing; remedial math.
College Admission Counseling 383 students graduated in 2008; 360 went to college, including California State University, Northridge; Loyola Marymount University; University of California, Los Angeles; University of California, Santa Barbara. Other: 3 went to work, 5 entered military service, 15 had other specific plans.
Student Life Upper grades have uniform requirement, student council, honor system. Discipline rests primarily with faculty. Attendance at religious services is required.
Summer Programs Remediation, enrichment, advancement, sports, art/fine arts, computer instruction programs offered; held on campus; accepts boys and girls; not open to students from other schools. 800 students usually enrolled. 2009 schedule: June 16 to July 24. Application deadline: June 16.
Tuition and Aid Day student tuition: $6710. Tuition installment plan (FACTS Tuition Payment Plan). Tuition reduction for siblings, financial aid for Catholic students available. Total amount of financial aid awarded in 2008–09: $210,000.
Admissions Traditional secondary-level entrance grade is 9. For fall 2008, 600 students applied for upper-level admission, 505 were accepted, 500 enrolled. SAS, STS-HSPT required. Deadline for receipt of application materials: none. Application fee required: $60. Interview required.
Athletics Interscholastic: aquatics (boys, girls), baseball (b), basketball (b,g), cheering (b,g), cross-country running (b,g), drill team (g), football (b), golf (b,g), soccer (b,g), softball (g), swimming and diving (b,g), tennis (g), track and field (b,g), volleyball (b,g), water polo (b,g), wrestling (b); coed interscholastic: wrestling. 12 coaches, 1 athletic trainer.
Computers Computers are regularly used in newspaper, yearbook classes. Computer network features include on-campus library services, Internet access. Student e-mail accounts are available to students. Students grades are available online. The school has a published electronic and media policy.
Contact Mr. Bill Oates, Director Community Outreach. 818-365-3925 Ext. 5222. Fax: 818-837-5390. Web site: www.alemany.org.

BISHOP BLANCHET HIGH SCHOOL

8200 Wallingford Avenue North
Seattle, Washington 98103-4599
Head of School: Dr. Maureen O'Shaughnessy

General Information Coeducational day college-preparatory, arts, and religious studies school, affiliated with Roman Catholic Church. Grades 9–12. Founded: 1954. Setting: urban. 9-acre campus. 1 building on campus. Approved or accredited by National Catholic Education Association, Northwest Association of Schools and Colleges, and Washington Department of Education. Endowment: $5.5 million. Total enrollment: 1,036. Upper school average class size: 24. Upper school faculty-student ratio: 1:14.
Upper School Student Profile Grade 9: 259 students (133 boys, 126 girls); Grade 10: 237 students (139 boys, 98 girls); Grade 11: 270 students (112 boys, 158 girls); Grade 12: 268 students (148 boys, 120 girls). 79% of students are Roman Catholic.
Faculty School total: 64. In upper school: 31 men, 33 women; 45 have advanced degrees.
Subjects Offered 20th century American writers, 20th century world history, 3-dimensional design, advanced chemistry, American foreign policy, American history-AP, American literature, anatomy and physiology, applied arts, applied music,

art, arts and crafts, ASB Leadership, band, biology, bookkeeping, British literature, British literature (honors), business applications, business law, calculus, calculus-AP, Catholic belief and practice, ceramics, chamber groups, chemistry, chemistry-AP, choral music, comparative religion, contemporary history, desktop publishing, discrete mathematics, drama, drama performance, economics, English composition, English literature, ethics, ethnic literature, ethnic studies, European history, family living, French, German, government, guitar, health, history of rock and roll, history of the Catholic Church, instrumental music, Japanese, jazz band, language arts, Life of Christ, literature, marching band, math analysis, musical productions, performing arts, personal finance, philosophy, photography, physical education, physics, psychology, religion, scripture, set design, Spanish, U.S. history, vocal ensemble.

Graduation Requirements Art, business education, English, lab science, mathematics, physical education (includes health), religion (includes Bible studies and theology), social studies (includes history).

Special Academic Programs Advanced Placement exam preparation; honors section; study at local college for college credit; programs in general development for dyslexic students.

College Admission Counseling 254 students graduated in 2008; 251 went to college, including Gonzaga University; Seattle University; University of Portland; University of Washington; Washington State University; Western Washington University. Other: 2 went to work, 1 entered military service.

Student Life Upper grades have specified standards of dress, student council, honor system. Discipline rests primarily with faculty. Attendance at religious services is required.

Summer Programs Remediation programs offered; session focuses on students with learning needs; held on campus; accepts boys and girls; not open to students from other schools. 20 students usually enrolled. 2009 schedule: June 20 to July 22. Application deadline: May 6.

Tuition and Aid Day student tuition: $8976. Tuition installment plan (monthly payment plans, individually arranged payment plans). Tuition reduction for siblings, merit scholarship grants, need-based scholarship grants available. In 2008–09, 33% of upper-school students received aid; total upper-school merit-scholarship money awarded: $50,000. Total amount of financial aid awarded in 2008–09: $1,200,000.

Admissions Traditional secondary-level entrance grade is 9. ACT-Explore required. Deadline for receipt of application materials: January 15. Application fee required: $25.

Athletics Interscholastic: baseball (boys), basketball (b,g), cheering (g), cross-country running (b,g), football (b), golf (b,g), lacrosse (b), soccer (b,g), softball (g), volleyball (g), wrestling (b); intramural: dance team (g); coed interscholastic: swimming and diving, tennis, track and field; coed intramural: alpine skiing, basketball, bowling, golf, hiking/backpacking, skiing (downhill), snowboarding, soccer, softball, tennis, volleyball. 6 PE instructors, 1 athletic trainer.

Computers Computers are regularly used in accounting, business applications, business education, career exploration, college planning, computer applications, data processing, desktop publishing, foreign language, journalism, keyboarding, library skills, mathematics, newspaper, photography, science, video film production, word processing, yearbook classes. Computer network features include on-campus library services, online commercial services, Internet access, Internet filtering or blocking technology. Campus intranet, student e-mail accounts, and computer access in designated common areas are available to students. Students grades are available online. The school has a published electronic and media policy.

Contact Patrick J. Fennessy, Director of Admissions and Communications. 206-527-7741. Fax: 206-527-7712. E-mail: pfennessy@bishopblanchet.org. Web site: www.bishopblanchet.org.

BISHOP BRADY HIGH SCHOOL

25 Columbus Avenue
Concord, New Hampshire 03301

Head of School: Gregory Roberts

General Information Coeducational day college-preparatory school, affiliated with Roman Catholic Church. Grades 9–12. Founded: 1963. Setting: suburban. 8-acre campus. 1 building on campus. Approved or accredited by New England Association of Schools and Colleges and New Hampshire Department of Education. Total enrollment: 446. Upper school average class size: 17. Upper school faculty-student ratio: 1:15.

Upper School Student Profile Grade 9: 124 students (61 boys, 63 girls); Grade 10: 118 students (57 boys, 61 girls); Grade 11: 98 students (46 boys, 52 girls); Grade 12: 106 students (50 boys, 56 girls). 70% of students are Roman Catholic.

Faculty School total: 34. In upper school: 14 men, 20 women; 25 have advanced degrees.

Subjects Offered Advanced chemistry, advanced math, algebra, anatomy and physiology, art appreciation, arts, biology, biology-AP, calculus-AP, career/college preparation, chemistry, chemistry-AP, Christian scripture, college awareness, college counseling, computer education, conceptual physics, drama, English, English literature-AP, English-AP, film studies, French-AP, freshman seminar, geometry, guidance, health education, history, history-AP, honors English, Latin, moral theology, music appreciation, musical theater, physical education, physics-AP, pre-calculus, probability and statistics, psychology, religious studies, research and reference, SAT preparation, social justice, theology, trigonometry, U.S. history-AP, world religions, writing.

Graduation Requirements Algebra, American literature, arts and fine arts (art, music, dance, drama), biology, chemistry, computer education, English, geometry, languages, physical education (includes health), science, social studies (includes history), theology, 70 hours of community service.

Special Academic Programs Advanced Placement exam preparation; honors section; study at local college for college credit; academic accommodation for the gifted; ESL (12 students enrolled).

College Admission Counseling 90 students graduated in 2008; 85 went to college, including Clarkson University; College of the Holy Cross; Providence College; Saint Anselm College; University of New Hampshire. Other: 4 went to work, 1 entered military service. Mean SAT critical reading: 549, mean SAT math: 543, mean composite ACT: 28. 26% scored over 600 on SAT critical reading, 25% scored over 600 on SAT math.

Student Life Upper grades have specified standards of dress, student council, honor system. Discipline rests primarily with faculty. Attendance at religious services is required.

Summer Programs Remediation, sports programs offered; session focuses on football and conditioning, mathematics; held on campus; accepts boys and girls; not open to students from other schools. 60 students usually enrolled. 2009 schedule: June 20 to August 15.

Tuition and Aid Day student tuition: $7900. Tuition installment plan (Insured Tuition Payment Plan, monthly payment plans, individually arranged payment plans). Tuition reduction for siblings, merit scholarship grants, need-based scholarship grants available. In 2008–09, 15% of upper-school students received aid.

Admissions Traditional secondary-level entrance grade is 9. For fall 2008, 135 students applied for upper-level admission, 130 were accepted, 101 enrolled. ACT-Explore required. Deadline for receipt of application materials: August 15. Application fee required: $25. Interview required.

Athletics Interscholastic: alpine skiing (boys, girls), baseball (b), basketball (b,g), cheering (g), cross-country running (b,g), field hockey (g), football (b), golf (b,g), hockey (b), ice hockey (b), indoor track (b,g), lacrosse (b,g), skiing (downhill) (b,g), soccer (b,g), softball (g), tennis (b,g), track and field (b,g); intramural: basketball (b,g); coed interscholastic: equestrian sports, juggling, outdoor activities, outdoor adventure; coed intramural: basketball, indoor track, outdoor activities, outdoor adventure, rock climbing, skiing (cross-country), skiing (downhill), snowboarding, strength & conditioning, table tennis, volleyball, weight lifting, weight training. 1 PE instructor.

Computers Computers are regularly used in business applications, college planning, journalism, literary magazine, newspaper classes. Computer network features include online commercial services, Internet access, Internet filtering or blocking technology. Student e-mail accounts are available to students. Students grades are available online. The school has a published electronic and media policy.

Contact Mrs. Lonna J. Abbott, Director of Admissions. 603-224-7418 Ext. 224. Fax: 603-228-6664. E-mail: labbott@bishopbrady.edu. Web site: www.bishopbrady.edu.

BISHOP CARROLL HIGH SCHOOL

728 Ben Franklin Highway
Ebensburg, Pennsylvania 15931

Head of School: Mr. Kristie Wolfe

General Information Coeducational day college-preparatory, general academic, vocational, and religious studies school, affiliated with Roman Catholic Church. Grades 9–12. Founded: 1960. Setting: small town. Nearest major city is Johnstown. 1 building on campus. Approved or accredited by Middle States Association of Colleges and Schools and Pennsylvania Department of Education. Total enrollment: 236. Upper school average class size: 20. Upper school faculty-student ratio: 1:12.

Upper School Student Profile Grade 9: 59 students (27 boys, 32 girls); Grade 10: 59 students (38 boys, 21 girls); Grade 11: 60 students (27 boys, 33 girls); Grade 12: 58 students (32 boys, 26 girls). 97% of students are Roman Catholic.

Faculty School total: 25. In upper school: 9 men, 16 women; 12 have advanced degrees.

Subjects Offered Accounting, algebra, American government, anatomy and physiology, art, art appreciation, band, biology, calculus, Catholic belief and practice, chemistry, chorus, civics, computer applications, computer keyboarding, computer programming, earth science, ecology, English, European history, finance, French, government, health, history, home economics, Latin, music appreciation, personal finance, physical education, physics, psychology, public speaking, reading, religion, science, Spanish, trigonometry, U.S. government, U.S. history, Web site design, zoology.

Graduation Requirements Algebra, arts appreciation, biology, Catholic belief and practice, chemistry, civics, computer applications, computer keyboarding, English, geography, government, lab science, language, mathematics, music theory, physical education (includes health), reading, science, social science, U.S. history, world history, 20 hours of community service per year, .25 Accelerated Reader Credit per year.

Special Academic Programs Honors section; independent study; study at local college for college credit; remedial reading and/or remedial writing; special instructional classes for deaf students, blind students.

College Admission Counseling 64 students graduated in 2008; 47 went to college, including Indiana University of Pennsylvania; Penn State University Park; St. Francis College; University of Pittsburgh. Other: 5 went to work, 2 entered military service,

6 entered a postgraduate year, 4 had other specific plans. Mean SAT critical reading: 495, mean SAT math: 478, mean SAT writing: 488, mean composite ACT: 20.
Student Life Upper grades have uniform requirement. Discipline rests primarily with faculty. Attendance at religious services is required.
Tuition and Aid Day student tuition: $5150. Tuition installment plan (monthly payment plans, individually arranged payment plans). Need-based scholarship grants, paying campus jobs, 0% Payment Plans, alumni-funded scholarships available. In 2008–09, 84% of upper-school students received aid. Total amount of financial aid awarded in 2008–09: $462,210.
Admissions Traditional secondary-level entrance grade is 9. Diocesan Entrance Exam required. Deadline for receipt of application materials: none. No application fee required. Interview recommended.
Athletics Interscholastic: baseball (boys), basketball (b,g), cheering (g), football (b), golf (b,g), soccer (b,g), softball (g), swimming and diving (b,g), track and field (b,g), volleyball (g), wrestling (b); coed intramural: bowling. 2 PE instructors, 34 coaches, 1 athletic trainer.
Computers Computers are regularly used in computer applications, keyboarding, Web site design classes. Computer network features include on-campus library services, online commercial services, Internet access. Students grades are available online. The school has a published electronic and media policy.
Contact Mrs. Kristie Wolfe, Principal. 814-472-7500 Ext. 106. Fax: 814-472-8020. Web site: www.bishopcarroll.com.

BISHOP CONATY-OUR LADY OF LORETTO HIGH SCHOOL

2900 West Pico Boulevard
Los Angeles, California 90006
Head of School: Mr. Richard A. Spicer

General Information Girls' day college-preparatory, general academic, arts, religious studies, and technology school, affiliated with Roman Catholic Church. Grades 9–12. Founded: 1923. Setting: urban. 3-acre campus. 2 buildings on campus. Approved or accredited by National Catholic Education Association, The College Board, Western Association of Schools and Colleges, Western Catholic Education Association, and California Department of Education. Endowment: $644,800. Total enrollment: 338. Upper school average class size: 22. Upper school faculty-student ratio: 1:16.
Upper School Student Profile Grade 9: 87 students (87 girls); Grade 10: 77 students (77 girls); Grade 11: 80 students (80 girls); Grade 12: 94 students (94 girls). 91% of students are Roman Catholic.
Faculty School total: 21. In upper school: 8 men, 13 women; 20 have advanced degrees.
Subjects Offered Aerobics, algebra, American literature, anatomy and physiology, athletics, biology, British literature, Catholic belief and practice, ceramics, chemistry, Christian and Hebrew scripture, computers, dance performance, drama, drawing and design, economics, English, French, geometry, government, health, honors algebra, honors English, honors geometry, honors U.S. history, honors world history, integrated science, journalism, moral reasoning, music, painting, physical education, physics, physiology, pre-calculus, religion, social justice, Spanish, Spanish language-AP, Spanish literature-AP, trigonometry, U.S. history, video film production, visual arts, Web site design, world history, world literature, world religions, yearbook.
Graduation Requirements Arts and fine arts (art, music, dance, drama), computer science, English, foreign language, mathematics, religion (includes Bible studies and theology), science, social studies (includes history), 100 hours of community service.
Special Academic Programs Advanced Placement exam preparation; honors section; remedial reading and/or remedial writing; remedial math.
College Admission Counseling 82 students graduated in 2008; 76 went to college, including California State University, Dominguez Hills; California State University, Northridge; Mount St. Mary's College; Santa Monica College; University of California, Los Angeles; University of California, Riverside. Other: 3 entered a postgraduate year, 3 had other specific plans. Median SAT critical reading: 440, median SAT math: 410, median SAT writing: 440, median combined SAT: 1290, median composite ACT: 17. 6% scored over 600 on SAT critical reading, 8% scored over 600 on SAT math, 12% scored over 600 on SAT writing, 5% scored over 1800 on combined SAT, 6% scored over 26 on composite ACT.
Student Life Upper grades have uniform requirement, student council, honor system. Discipline rests primarily with faculty. Attendance at religious services is required.
Summer Programs Remediation, enrichment, advancement, art/fine arts, computer instruction programs offered; session focuses on make-up courses and strengthening incoming freshmen skills; held on campus; accepts girls; not open to students from other schools. 195 students usually enrolled. 2009 schedule: June 22 to July 24. Application deadline: June 1.
Tuition and Aid Day student tuition: $5555–$5955. Tuition installment plan (monthly payment plans, individually arranged payment plans). Need-based scholarship grants, paying campus jobs available. In 2008–09, 71% of upper-school students received aid. Total amount of financial aid awarded in 2008–09: $581,779.
Admissions Traditional secondary-level entrance grade is 9. For fall 2008, 101 students applied for upper-level admission, 100 were accepted, 87 enrolled. High School Placement Test required. Deadline for receipt of application materials: August 15. Application fee required: $25. On-campus interview required.
Athletics Interscholastic: basketball, cross-country running, dance, soccer, softball, volleyball. 3 coaches.
Computers Computers are regularly used in computer applications, video film production, Web site design, yearbook classes. Computer network features include on-campus library services, Internet access. The school has a published electronic and media policy.
Contact Sr. Harriet Stellern, Director of Admissions. 323-737-0012 Ext. 103. Fax: 323-737-1749. E-mail: hstellern@bishopconatyloretto.org. Web site: www.bishopconatyloretto.org.

BISHOP CONNOLLY HIGH SCHOOL

373 Elsbree Street
Fall River, Massachusetts 02720
Head of School: Mr. Michael Scanlan

General Information Coeducational day college-preparatory and religious studies school, affiliated with Roman Catholic Church. Grades 9–12. Founded: 1966. Setting: suburban. Nearest major city is Providence, RI. 72-acre campus. 1 building on campus. Approved or accredited by New England Association of Schools and Colleges and Massachusetts Department of Education. Total enrollment: 414. Upper school average class size: 18. Upper school faculty-student ratio: 1:16.
Upper School Student Profile 90% of students are Roman Catholic.
Faculty School total: 30. In upper school: 18 men, 12 women; 22 have advanced degrees.
Subjects Offered Advanced Placement courses, algebra, American literature, American studies, anatomy and physiology, art, art history, Bible studies, biology, biology-AP, British literature, British literature (honors), calculus, calculus-AP, campus ministry, chemistry, chemistry-AP, choir, chorus, community service, computer keyboarding, computer programming, creative writing, desktop publishing, drama, English, English literature, English-AP, environmental science, European history-AP, French, French-AP, geometry, health, history, honors algebra, honors English, honors geometry, honors U.S. history, honors world history, human biology, instrumental music, math analysis, mathematics, music, music history, music theory, physical education, physics, Portuguese, psychology, religion, science, social studies, Spanish, theology, trigonometry, U.S. history-AP, world history, world literature.
Graduation Requirements English, foreign language, mathematics, religion (includes Bible studies and theology), science, social studies (includes history). Community service is required.
Special Academic Programs Advanced Placement exam preparation; honors section; independent study; study at local college for college credit.
College Admission Counseling 108 students graduated in 2008; they went to Bridgewater State College; Northeastern University; Providence College; Quinnipiac University; University of Massachusetts Dartmouth; University of Rhode Island. Mean SAT critical reading: 525, mean SAT math: 471. 13% scored over 600 on SAT critical reading, 11% scored over 600 on SAT math.
Student Life Upper grades have uniform requirement, student council. Discipline rests primarily with faculty. Attendance at religious services is required.
Tuition and Aid Day student tuition: $7100. Tuition installment plan (FACTS Tuition Payment Plan, monthly payment plans). Merit scholarship grants, need-based scholarship grants available. In 2008–09, 33% of upper-school students received aid.
Admissions Traditional secondary-level entrance grade is 9. High School Placement Test required. Deadline for receipt of application materials: none. No application fee required. Interview recommended.
Athletics Interscholastic: baseball (boys), basketball (b,g), cheering (b,g), cross-country running (b,g), football (b), ice hockey (b), lacrosse (b), soccer (b,g), softball (g), tennis (b,g), track and field (b,g), volleyball (g), winter (indoor) track (b,g); intramural: field hockey (g); coed interscholastic: golf, indoor soccer, indoor track & field. 2 PE instructors, 32 coaches, 1 athletic trainer.
Computers Computers are regularly used in all classes. Computer network features include online commercial services, Internet access, wireless campus network, Internet filtering or blocking technology. Computer access in designated common areas is available to students. The school has a published electronic and media policy.
Contact Mr. Anthony C. Ciampanelli, Director of Admissions. 508-676-1071 Ext. 333. Fax: 508-676-8594. E-mail: aciampanelli@bishopconnolly.com. Web site: www.bishopconnolly.com.

BISHOP DENIS J. O'CONNELL HIGH SCHOOL

6600 Little Falls Road
Arlington, Virginia 22213
Head of School: Mr. Barry E. Breen

General Information Coeducational day college-preparatory, arts, business, religious studies, and technology school, affiliated with Roman Catholic Church. Grades 9–12. Founded: 1957. Setting: suburban. Nearest major city is Washington, DC. 28-acre campus. 1 building on campus. Approved or accredited by National Catholic Education Association, Southern Association of Colleges and Schools, Southern Association of Independent Schools, Virginia Association of Independent Schools, and Virginia Department of Education. Member of Secondary School Admission Test Board. Total enrollment: 1,360. Upper school average class size: 21. Upper school faculty-student ratio: 1:12.

Upper School Student Profile Grade 9: 289 students (141 boys, 148 girls); Grade 10: 357 students (192 boys, 165 girls); Grade 11: 350 students (180 boys, 170 girls); Grade 12: 364 students (187 boys, 177 girls). 90% of students are Roman Catholic.
Faculty School total: 116.
Subjects Offered Accounting, algebra, American history, American literature, analysis, art, art history, athletic training, Basic programming, Bible studies, biology, biology-AP, business, calculus, calculus-AP, chemistry, chemistry-AP, choir, choral music, chorus, comparative government and politics-AP, computer graphics, computer multimedia, computer programming, computer science, computer science-AP, computer skills, creative writing, digital art, dramatic arts, driver education, earth science, East Asian history, economics, English, English language-AP, English literature, English literature-AP, environmental science-AP, European history, European history-AP, fine arts, forensic science, French, French language-AP, geography, geometry, German, German-AP, government-AP, government/civics, guitar, health, history, honors English, honors geometry, honors U.S. history, honors world history, introduction to theater, Italian, jazz band, journalism, Latin, macroeconomics-AP, marketing, mathematics, media arts, microeconomics-AP, modern European history-AP, music, music theory-AP, nationalism and ethnic conflict, New Testament, physical education, physics, physics-AP, piano, psychology-AP, public speaking, religion, remedial study skills, science, social science, social studies, sociology, Spanish, Spanish language-AP, Spanish literature-AP, speech, sports conditioning, statistics-AP, studio art—AP, theology, trigonometry, U.S. and Virginia history, U.S. government, U.S. history, U.S. history-AP, United States government-AP, voice ensemble, Web site design, world history, world literature.
Graduation Requirements Arts and fine arts (art, music, dance, drama), computer science, English, foreign language, mathematics, physical education (includes health), religion (includes Bible studies and theology), science, social science, social studies (includes history), Community service program incorporated into graduation requirements.
Special Academic Programs Advanced Placement exam preparation; honors section; study at local college for college credit; academic accommodation for the gifted; remedial math.
College Admission Counseling 330 students graduated in 2008; 327 went to college, including George Mason University; James Madison University; The College of William and Mary; University of Mary Washington; University of Virginia; Virginia Polytechnic Institute and State University. Other: 1 went to work, 1 entered military service, 1 entered a postgraduate year. Median SAT critical reading: 574, median SAT math: 565, median SAT writing: 563.
Student Life Upper grades have uniform requirement, student council, honor system. Discipline rests primarily with faculty. Attendance at religious services is required.
Summer Programs Remediation, enrichment, advancement, computer instruction programs offered; held on campus; accepts boys and girls; open to students from other schools. 220 students usually enrolled. 2009 schedule: June 21 to July 23. Application deadline: none.
Tuition and Aid Day student tuition: $9020–$13,245. Tuition installment plan (FACTS Tuition Payment Plan). Tuition reduction for siblings, merit scholarship grants, need-based scholarship grants, scholarship competition only for eighth graders currently enrolled in a Diocese of Arlington Catholic school available. In 2008–09, 20% of upper-school students received aid. Total amount of financial aid awarded in 2008–09: $750,000.
Admissions High School Placement Test required. Deadline for receipt of application materials: January 23. Application fee required: $50.
Athletics Interscholastic: baseball (boys), basketball (b,g), crew (b,g), cross-country running (b,g), dance team (g), diving (b,g), football (b), ice hockey (b), lacrosse (b,g), soccer (b,g), softball (g), swimming and diving (b,g), tennis (b,g), track and field (b,g), volleyball (g), wrestling (b); intramural: basketball (b,g), weight lifting (b,g); coed interscholastic: golf; coed intramural: crew, flag football, softball, ultimate Frisbee, volleyball. 7 PE instructors, 7 coaches, 1 athletic trainer.
Computers Computers are regularly used in art, business, computer applications, English, foreign language, health, history, mathematics, science, social sciences classes. Computer network features include on-campus library services, online commercial services, Internet access, Internet filtering or blocking technology. Computer access in designated common areas is available to students. Students grades are available online. The school has a published electronic and media policy.
Contact Mrs. Mary McAlevy, Director of Admissions. 703-237-1433. Fax: 703-241-9066. E-mail: mmcalevy@bishopoconnell.org. Web site: www.bishopoconnell.org.

BISHOP EUSTACE PREPARATORY SCHOOL

5552 Route 70
Pennsauken, New Jersey 08109-4798
Head of School: Br. James Beamesderfer, SAC
General Information Coeducational day college-preparatory, arts, religious studies, and technology school, affiliated with Roman Catholic Church. Grades 9–12. Founded: 1954. Setting: suburban. Nearest major city is Philadelphia, PA. 32-acre campus. 7 buildings on campus. Approved or accredited by Middle States Association of Colleges and Schools and New Jersey Department of Education. Endowment: $3.3 million. Total enrollment: 792. Upper school average class size: 21. Upper school faculty-student ratio: 1:13.
Upper School Student Profile 88% of students are Roman Catholic.
Faculty School total: 58. In upper school: 29 men, 29 women; 43 have advanced degrees.
Subjects Offered Advanced chemistry, advanced computer applications, Advanced Placement courses, algebra, American history, American history-AP, American literature, anatomy, anatomy and physiology, applied music, art and culture, art history, band, Bible studies, biology, biology-AP, British literature, British literature (honors), calculus, calculus-AP, campus ministry, career education, career exploration, career/college preparation, chemistry, chemistry-AP, choir, Christian doctrine, Christian education, Christian ethics, Christian scripture, clinical chemistry, college counseling, college placement, college planning, comparative religion, computer education, computer science-AP, creative writing, discrete math, driver education, economics, economics and history, electives, English, English literature, English literature and composition-AP, environmental science, environmental science-AP, ethics, European history-AP, film, film and literature, fine arts, French, French as a second language, gender issues, genetics, geometry, German, government and politics-AP, government/civics, grammar, health, history, honors algebra, honors English, honors geometry, honors U.S. history, honors world history, instrumental music, journalism, Latin, law, law studies, macroeconomics-AP, mathematics, mathematics-AP, music, music composition, music history, music theory, music theory-AP, physical education, physical science, physics, physics-AP, physiology, pre-calculus, psychology, psychology-AP, science, sex education, social studies, sociology, Spanish, Spanish-AP, statistics-AP, theology, trigonometry, U.S. government and politics-AP, U.S. history, U.S. history-AP, vocal music, women's studies, world affairs, world history, world religions.
Graduation Requirements Arts and fine arts (art, music, dance, drama), career exploration, computer science, English, foreign language, mathematics, physical education (includes health), religion (includes Bible studies and theology), science, social studies (includes history). Community service is required.
Special Academic Programs 16 Advanced Placement exams for which test preparation is offered; honors section; independent study; study at local college for college credit; academic accommodation for the gifted and the musically talented.
College Admission Counseling 182 students graduated in 2008; 179 went to college, including Drexel University; La Salle University; Loyola College in Maryland; Saint Joseph's University; The Catholic University of America; Villanova University. Other: 1 went to work, 2 had other specific plans. 44% scored over 600 on SAT critical reading, 51% scored over 600 on SAT math, 46% scored over 600 on SAT writing.
Student Life Upper grades have uniform requirement, student council, honor system. Discipline rests primarily with faculty. Attendance at religious services is required.
Summer Programs Enrichment, advancement, sports programs offered; session focuses on student recruitment and enrichment; held on campus; accepts boys and girls; open to students from other schools. 150 students usually enrolled. 2009 schedule: June to August. Application deadline: May.
Tuition and Aid Day student tuition: $13,200. Tuition installment plan (FACTS Tuition Payment Plan). Merit scholarship grants, need-based scholarship grants available. In 2008–09, 35% of upper-school students received aid; total upper-school merit-scholarship money awarded: $237,600. Total amount of financial aid awarded in 2008–09: $600,000.
Admissions Traditional secondary-level entrance grade is 9. Common entrance examinations, math and English placement tests or placement test required. Deadline for receipt of application materials: none. Application fee required: $50.
Athletics Interscholastic: baseball (boys), basketball (b,g), bowling (b,g), cheering (g), crew (b,g), cross-country running (b,g), field hockey (g), football (b), ice hockey (b), indoor track & field (b,g), lacrosse (b,g), running (b,g), soccer (b,g), softball (g), swimming and diving (b,g), tennis (b,g), track and field (b,g); coed interscholastic: aquatics, diving, golf. 3 PE instructors, 61 coaches, 1 athletic trainer.
Computers Computers are regularly used in all academic classes. Computer network features include on-campus library services, online commercial services, Internet access, wireless campus network, Internet filtering or blocking technology. Campus intranet and computer access in designated common areas are available to students. Students grades are available online. The school has a published electronic and media policy.
Contact Mrs. Marylou Williams, Admissions Coordinator. 856-662-2160 Ext. 262. Fax: 856-665-2184. E-mail: mwilliams@eustace.org. Web site: www.eustace.org.

BISHOP FEEHAN HIGH SCHOOL

70 Holcott Drive
Attleboro, Massachusetts 02703
Head of School: Mr. Christopher E. Servant
General Information Coeducational day college-preparatory, arts, and religious studies school, affiliated with Roman Catholic Church. Grades 9–12. Founded: 1961. Setting: suburban. Nearest major city is Providence, RI. 25-acre campus. 3 buildings on campus. Approved or accredited by National Catholic Education Association, New England Association of Schools and Colleges, and Massachusetts Department of Education. Total enrollment: 1,032. Upper school average class size: 17. Upper school faculty-student ratio: 1:13.
Upper School Student Profile 90% of students are Roman Catholic.
Faculty School total: 95. In upper school: 35 men, 60 women; 52 have advanced degrees.

Subjects Offered Advanced chemistry, algebra, American literature, analytic geometry, anatomy and physiology, Arabic, art, art history, Bible studies, bioethics, biology, biology-AP, British literature, British literature (honors), business applications, business law, calculus, calculus-AP, campus ministry, Catholic belief and practice, chemistry, chemistry-AP, choir, choral music, chorus, Christian and Hebrew scripture, Christian doctrine, Christian education, Christian ethics, Christian studies, Christian testament, Christianity, college counseling, college planning, composition, computer animation, computer applications, computer graphics, computer keyboarding, computer programming, conceptual physics, concert band, concert choir, dance, drama, drama workshop, drawing, driver education, earth science, ecology, environmental systems, economics, English, English composition, English language and composition-AP, English literature and composition-AP, environmental science, European history, French, genetics, geometry, government and politics-AP, guidance, health and wellness, history of the Catholic Church, honors algebra, honors English, honors geometry, honors U.S. history, honors world history, integrated mathematics, jazz ensemble, lab science, Latin, Mandarin, music theory, mythology, oral communications, physical education, physics, pre-calculus, probability and statistics, psychology, psychology-AP, SAT preparation, Shakespeare, sign language, sociology, Spanish, Spanish language-AP, statistics, statistics-AP, studio art-AP, theater arts, theology, U.S. history, U.S. history-AP, Web site design, word processing, world religions.
Graduation Requirements Biology, career education, chemistry, electives, English, foreign language, mathematics, physics, research skills, SAT preparation, science, study skills, theology, U.S. history, word processing, world history.
Special Academic Programs Advanced Placement exam preparation; honors section.
College Admission Counseling 226 students graduated in 2008; 225 went to college, including Assumption College; Merrimack College; Providence College; Stonehill College; University of Massachusetts Amherst; University of Rhode Island. Other: 1 went to work. Mean SAT critical reading: 568, mean SAT math: 569, mean SAT writing: 573, mean composite ACT: 24.
Student Life Upper grades have uniform requirement, student council. Discipline rests primarily with faculty. Attendance at religious services is required.
Summer Programs Enrichment programs offered; session focuses on sports; held on campus; accepts boys and girls; not open to students from other schools. 300 students usually enrolled. 2009 schedule: July to August. Application deadline: May.
Tuition and Aid Day student tuition: $7900. Tuition installment plan (FACTS Tuition Payment Plan). Merit scholarship grants, need-based scholarship grants available. In 2008–09, 20% of upper-school students received aid; total upper-school merit-scholarship money awarded: $10,000. Total amount of financial aid awarded in 2008–09: $400,000.
Admissions Traditional secondary-level entrance grade is 10. For fall 2008, 535 students applied for upper-level admission, 300 were accepted, 280 enrolled. Scholastic Testing Service High School Placement Test required. Deadline for receipt of application materials: December 18. No application fee required. Interview required.
Athletics Interscholastic: baseball (boys), basketball (b,g), cheering (g), diving (b,g), football (b), indoor track & field (b,g), lacrosse (b,g), soccer (b,g), softball (g), swimming and diving (b,g), tennis (b,g), track and field (b,g), volleyball (g); intramural: ice skating (g); coed interscholastic: cross-country running, dance, dance squad, fencing, golf, ice hockey; coed intramural: fencing. 2 PE instructors, 30 coaches, 1 athletic trainer.
Computers Computers are regularly used in all classes. Computer network features include on-campus library services, Internet access, wireless campus network, Internet filtering or blocking technology. Campus intranet and computer access in designated common areas are available to students. Students grades are available online. The school has a published electronic and media policy.
Contact Lynn Gale, Admissions Assistant. 508-226-6223 Ext. 119. Fax: 508-226-7696. E-mail: lgale@bishopfeehan.com. Web site: www.bishopfeehan.com.

BISHOP FENWICK HIGH SCHOOL

4855 State Route 122
Franklin, Ohio 45005
Head of School: Mrs. Catherine Mulligan

General Information Coeducational day college-preparatory, arts, and religious studies school, affiliated with Roman Catholic Church. Grades 9–12. Founded: 1952. Setting: small town. Nearest major city is Cincinnati. 66-acre campus. 1 building on campus. Approved or accredited by National Catholic Education Association, North Central Association of Colleges and Schools, Ohio Catholic Schools Accreditation Association (OCSAA), and Ohio Department of Education. Upper school average class size: 24. Upper school faculty-student ratio: 1:16.
Upper School Student Profile Grade 9: 143 students (75 boys, 68 girls); Grade 10: 161 students (101 boys, 60 girls); Grade 11: 136 students (65 boys, 71 girls); Grade 12: 110 students (51 boys, 59 girls). 85% of students are Roman Catholic.
Faculty School total: 37. In upper school: 17 men, 17 women; 14 have advanced degrees.
Subjects Offered Accounting, algebra, American democracy, art, art-AP, athletic training, biology, botany, calculus-AP, cell biology, chemistry, chorus, computer graphics, computer programming, concert band, creative writing, economics, English, English-AP, ensembles, fine arts, French, functions, general business, geometry, government, government/civics-AP, health, honors algebra, honors English, honors geometry, integrated math, jazz band, Latin, Latin-AP, leadership skills, marching band, mathematics, multimedia, music appreciation, mythology, physical education, physical science, physics, physiology, portfolio art, pre-algebra, psychology, publications, religion, science, social studies, Spanish, statistics, study skills, technology, theater, theater arts, trigonometry, U.S. history, U.S. history-AP, Web site design, world geography, world history, writing, yearbook, zoology.
Graduation Requirements Arts and fine arts (art, music, dance, drama), English, foreign language, mathematics, religion (includes Bible studies and theology), science, social studies (includes history), community service, retreats, pass the Ohio Graduation Test.
Special Academic Programs Advanced Placement exam preparation; honors section; study at local college for college credit.
College Admission Counseling 116 students graduated in 2008; 113 went to college, including Miami University; Ohio University; The Ohio State University; University of Cincinnati; University of Dayton; Xavier University. Other: 3 went to work. Median composite ACT: 24. Mean SAT critical reading: 551, mean SAT math: 543, mean SAT writing: 541. 31% scored over 600 on SAT critical reading, 32% scored over 600 on SAT math, 26% scored over 600 on SAT writing, 26% scored over 26 on composite ACT.
Student Life Upper grades have uniform requirement, student council. Discipline rests primarily with faculty. Attendance at religious services is required.
Tuition and Aid Day student tuition: $6200. Tuition installment plan (TMS). Tuition reduction for siblings, merit scholarship grants, need-based scholarship grants available. In 2008–09, 10% of upper-school students received aid; total upper-school merit-scholarship money awarded: $2000. Total amount of financial aid awarded in 2008–09: $70,000.
Admissions Traditional secondary-level entrance grade is 9. High School Placement Test required. Deadline for receipt of application materials: none. No application fee required.
Athletics Interscholastic: baseball (boys), basketball (b,g), cheering (g), cross-country running (b,g), dance team (g), football (b), golf (b,g), lacrosse (b,g), soccer (b,g), softball (g), swimming and diving (b,g), tennis (b,g), track and field (b,g), volleyball (b,g), weight training (b,g), wrestling (b); intramural: basketball (b), in-line hockey (b), weight training (b,g); coed interscholastic: bowling. 2 PE instructors, 17 coaches, 1 athletic trainer.
Computers Computer network features include on-campus library services, Internet access, wireless campus network, Internet filtering or blocking technology. Campus intranet, student e-mail accounts, and computer access in designated common areas are available to students. Students grades are available online. The school has a published electronic and media policy.
Contact Mrs. Betty Turvy, Admissions Coordinator. 513-423-0723 Ext. 215. Fax: 513-420-8690. E-mail: c1_turvy@swoca.net. Web site: www.fenwickfalcons.org.

BISHOP GARCIA DIEGO HIGH SCHOOL

4000 La Colina Road
Santa Barbara, California 93110-1496
Head of School: Rev. Fr. Thomas J. Elewaut

General Information Coeducational day and distance learning college-preparatory, arts, religious studies, and technology school, affiliated with Roman Catholic Church; primarily serves students with learning disabilities, individuals with Attention Deficit Disorder, and dyslexic students. Grades 9–12. Distance learning grades 9–12. Founded: 1959. Setting: small town. Nearest major city is Los Angeles. 16-acre campus. 10 buildings on campus. Approved or accredited by California Association of Independent Schools, National Catholic Education Association, Western Association of Schools and Colleges, and California Department of Education. Endowment: $250,000. Total enrollment: 307. Upper school average class size: 18. Upper school faculty-student ratio: 1:12.
Upper School Student Profile Grade 9: 77 students (38 boys, 39 girls); Grade 10: 85 students (44 boys, 41 girls); Grade 11: 73 students (38 boys, 35 girls); Grade 12: 65 students (30 boys, 35 girls). 80% of students are Roman Catholic.
Faculty School total: 31. In upper school: 15 men, 16 women; 21 have advanced degrees.
Subjects Offered Algebra, American government-AP, American history-AP, American literature, anatomy, arts, band, biology, calculus, calculus-AP, ceramics, chemistry, chemistry-AP, chorus, community service, composition, computer science, dance, economics, English, English literature, English-AP, fine arts, fitness, French, French-AP, geometry, government-AP, history-AP, humanities, mathematics, music, physical education, physical science, physics, physics-AP, psychology, religion, science, Shakespeare, social science, social studies, Spanish, Spanish-AP, speech, statistics-AP, weight training, world history, world literature, yearbook.
Graduation Requirements Arts and fine arts (art, music, dance, drama), computer science, English, foreign language, mathematics, physical education (includes health), religion (includes Bible studies and theology), science, social science, social studies (includes history), CAP portfolio. Community service is required.
Special Academic Programs Advanced Placement exam preparation; honors section; independent study; study at local college for college credit; remedial reading and/or remedial writing; remedial math; programs in English, mathematics, general development for dyslexic students.

College Admission Counseling 62 students graduated in 2008; all went to college, including Loyola Marymount University; Santa Barbara City College; University of California, Santa Barbara; University of San Diego. 31% scored over 600 on SAT critical reading, 37% scored over 600 on SAT math, 28% scored over 600 on SAT writing, 36% scored over 26 on composite ACT.
Student Life Upper grades have specified standards of dress, student council. Discipline rests primarily with faculty. Attendance at religious services is required.
Summer Programs Remediation, enrichment, advancement, computer instruction programs offered; session focuses on high school preparation and make-up courses; held on campus; accepts boys and girls; open to students from other schools. 65 students usually enrolled. 2009 schedule: June 18 to July 31. Application deadline: June 18.
Tuition and Aid Day student tuition: $12,200. Guaranteed tuition plan. Tuition installment plan (FACTS Tuition Payment Plan, annual and semiannual payment plan). Need-based scholarship grants, paying campus jobs available. In 2008–09, 60% of upper-school students received aid. Total amount of financial aid awarded in 2008–09: $940,000.
Admissions Traditional secondary-level entrance grade is 9. For fall 2008, 131 students applied for upper-level admission, 105 were accepted, 77 enrolled. High School Placement Test or High School Placement Test (closed version) from Scholastic Testing Service required. Deadline for receipt of application materials: none. Application fee required: $50. On-campus interview recommended.
Athletics Interscholastic: baseball (boys), basketball (b,g), cheering (g), cross-country running (b,g), football (b), golf (b,g), soccer (b,g), softball (g), tennis (b,g), track and field (b,g), volleyball (b,g), wrestling (b); intramural: physical fitness (b,g), physical training (b,g), power lifting (b,g), weight lifting (b,g), weight training (b,g); coed intramural: bicycling, crew, martial arts, mountain biking, physical fitness, physical training, power lifting, ropes courses, weight lifting, weight training. 2 PE instructors, 25 coaches, 1 athletic trainer.
Computers Computers are regularly used in business applications, college planning, desktop publishing, ESL, graphic design, information technology, introduction to technology, keyboarding, library science, mathematics, media, media production, photography, programming, publications, science, technology, yearbook classes. Computer network features include on-campus library services, online commercial services, Internet access. The school has a published electronic and media policy.
Contact Mrs. Debbie Herrrera, Director of Admissions and Public Relations. 805-967-1266 Ext. 118. Fax: 805-964-3178. E-mail: dherrera@bishopdiego.org. Web site: www.bishopdiego.org.

BISHOP GEORGE AHR HIGH SCHOOL

1 Tingley Lane
Edison, New Jersey 08820

Head of School: Sr. Donna Marie Trukowski, CSSF

General Information Coeducational day and distance learning college-preparatory, arts, religious studies, and technology school, affiliated with Roman Catholic Church. Grades 9–12. Distance learning grades 9–12. Founded: 1969. Setting: suburban. 24-acre campus. 1 building on campus. Approved or accredited by Middle States Association of Colleges and Schools, National Catholic Education Association, and New Jersey Department of Education. Total enrollment: 945. Upper school average class size: 24. Upper school faculty-student ratio: 1:16.
Upper School Student Profile 85% of students are Roman Catholic.
Faculty School total: 59. In upper school: 22 men, 37 women; 35 have advanced degrees.
Special Academic Programs Advanced Placement exam preparation; honors section; study at local college for college credit.
College Admission Counseling 219 students graduated in 2008; 215 went to college. Other: 3 went to work, 1 entered military service.
Student Life Upper grades have uniform requirement, student council. Discipline rests primarily with faculty. Attendance at religious services is required.
Tuition and Aid Day student tuition: $8400. Tuition installment plan (The Tuition Plan, SMART Tuition Payment Plan, individually arranged payment plans). Merit scholarship grants, need-based scholarship grants available.
Admissions Traditional secondary-level entrance grade is 9. For fall 2008, 856 students applied for upper-level admission, 350 were accepted, 275 enrolled. High School Placement Test required. Deadline for receipt of application materials: none. Application fee required. Interview recommended.
Athletics Interscholastic: cheering (girls), dance (g), football (b), golf (b), gymnastics (g), softball (g), swimming and diving (g), volleyball (g), weight training (b), wrestling (b); coed interscholastic: aquatics, baseball, basketball, bowling, cross-country running, physical training, winter (indoor) track. 7 PE instructors, 35 coaches, 1 athletic trainer.
Computers Computer network features include on-campus library services, online commercial services, Internet access, wireless campus network. Campus intranet and computer access in designated common areas are available to students. Students grades are available online. The school has a published electronic and media policy.
Contact Mrs. Cora Medley, Counseling and Admissions Secretary. 732-549-1108 Ext. 616. Fax: 732-549-9050. E-mail: cmedley@bgahs.org. Web site: www.bgahs.org.

BISHOP GORMAN HIGH SCHOOL

5959 South Hualapai Way
Las Vegas, Nevada 89148

Head of School: Mrs. Aggie Evert

General Information Coeducational day college-preparatory and religious studies school, affiliated with Roman Catholic Church. Grades 9–12. Founded: 1954. Setting: suburban. 35-acre campus. 10 buildings on campus. Approved or accredited by Northwest Association of Accredited Schools, Northwest Association of Schools and Colleges, and Nevada Department of Education. Total enrollment: 1,141. Upper school average class size: 25. Upper school faculty-student ratio: 1:25.
Upper School Student Profile 80% of students are Roman Catholic.
Faculty School total: 65. In upper school: 29 men, 34 women; 50 have advanced degrees.
Subjects Offered Accounting, Advanced Placement courses, algebra, art, band, biology, biology-AP, calculus, campus ministry, chemistry, choral music, chorus, church history, college counseling, composition, computer applications, criminal justice, drama, driver education, economics, economics-AP, English language and composition-AP, English literature-AP, ethics, French, geometry, government-AP, government/civics, health education, honors algebra, honors English, honors geometry, honors U.S. history, honors world history, human anatomy, journalism, literature and composition-AP, literature-AP, macro/microeconomics-AP, marine biology, microeconomics-AP, music, New Testament, performing arts, photography, physical education, physics, physiology, physiology-anatomy, pottery, pre-calculus, probability and statistics, psychology, publications, religion, SAT/ACT preparation, sociology, Spanish, Spanish language-AP, Spanish-AP, speech, statistics-AP, student publications, theater, theater arts, theater design and production, theology, trigonometry, U.S. constitutional history, U.S. government, U.S. government-AP, U.S. history, U.S. history-AP, United States government-AP, world culture, world cultures, world geography, world history, world history-AP, world religions, world religions, writing workshop, yearbook.
Graduation Requirements American government, arts and fine arts (art, music, dance, drama), computer science, English, foreign language, lab science, mathematics, physical education (includes health), science, social studies (includes history), theology. Community service is required.
Special Academic Programs Advanced Placement exam preparation; honors section; academic accommodation for the gifted, the musically talented, and the artistically talented; remedial reading and/or remedial writing; remedial math.
College Admission Counseling 206 students graduated in 2008; 185 went to college, including Loyola Marymount University; Northern Arizona University; Santa Clara University; University of Nevada, Las Vegas; University of Nevada, Reno; University of San Diego. Other: 8 went to work, 5 entered military service, 8 had other specific plans. Median SAT critical reading: 542, median SAT math: 535, median SAT writing: 536, median combined SAT: 1610, median composite ACT: 23.
Student Life Upper grades have uniform requirement, student council, honor system. Discipline rests primarily with faculty. Attendance at religious services is required.
Summer Programs Remediation, enrichment, advancement, sports programs offered; session focuses on Enrichment; held on campus; accepts boys and girls; not open to students from other schools. 400 students usually enrolled. 2009 schedule: June 6 to August 1. Application deadline: June 1.
Tuition and Aid Day student tuition: $8500–$9950. Tuition installment plan (monthly payment plans, individually arranged payment plans, Tuition Management Systems). Merit scholarship grants, need-based scholarship grants available. Total upper-school merit-scholarship money awarded for 2008–09: $178,200.
Admissions Traditional secondary-level entrance grade is 9. High School Placement Test required. Deadline for receipt of application materials: none. Application fee required: $50. Interview recommended.
Athletics Interscholastic: baseball (boys), basketball (b,g), bowling (b,g), cheering (g), cross-country running (b,g), dance team (g), football (b), golf (b,g), lacrosse (b,g), soccer (b,g), softball (g), swimming and diving (b,g), tennis (b,g), volleyball (b,g), winter soccer (b,g), wrestling (b); coed interscholastic: strength & conditioning, track and field, weight lifting; coed intramural: equestrian sports, horseback riding. 50 coaches, 1 athletic trainer.
Computers Computers are regularly used in English, French, geography, journalism, library, mathematics, newspaper, religion, science, yearbook classes. Computer network features include on-campus library services, Internet access, wireless campus network, Internet filtering or blocking technology. Student e-mail accounts are available to students. Students grades are available online. The school has a published electronic and media policy.
Contact Mr. Tracy Goode, Assistant Principal of Admissions. 702-732-1945 Ext. 4011. Fax: 702-732-2856. E-mail: admissions@bishopgorman.org. Web site: www.bishopgorman.org.

BISHOP GUERTIN HIGH SCHOOL

194 Lund Road
Nashua, New Hampshire 03060-4398

Head of School: Br. Mark Hilton, SC

General Information Coeducational day college-preparatory, arts, religious studies, bilingual studies, and technology school, affiliated with Roman Catholic Church. Grades 9–12. Founded: 1963. Setting: suburban. Nearest major city is Boston, MA.

19-acre campus. 1 building on campus. Approved or accredited by New England Association of Schools and Colleges and New Hampshire Department of Education. Total enrollment: 900. Upper school average class size: 20.

Upper School Student Profile 80% of students are Roman Catholic.

Faculty School total: 67. In upper school: 35 men, 30 women; 55 have advanced degrees.

Subjects Offered 20th century history, acting, advanced chemistry, advanced computer applications, advanced math, algebra, American literature-AP, analysis and differential calculus, anatomy and physiology, art appreciation, art history, band, Bible studies, biology, biology-AP, British history, British literature, British literature (honors), business law, calculus, calculus-AP, campus ministry, career/college preparation, chemistry, chemistry-AP, chorus, Christian and Hebrew scripture, Christian doctrine, Christian education, Christian ethics, Christianity, church history, civics, college admission preparation, college counseling, college writing, community service, comparative government and politics, comparative government and politics-AP, comparative religion, computer applications, computer art, computer education, computer literacy, computer multimedia, computer processing, computer programming, computer programming-AP, computer science, computer technologies, computer-aided design, constitutional history of U.S., consumer economics, contemporary history, CPR, creative writing, death and loss, debate, desktop publishing, digital photography, discrete math, dramatic arts, drawing, driver education, economics, emergency medicine, English, English composition, English literature, English literature and composition-AP, English-AP, environmental science, ethics, European history, fine arts, foreign language, French, geography, geometry, government/civics, grammar, health, health and wellness, health education, history, honors geometry, honors U.S. history, honors world history, human anatomy, human biology, human sexuality, instrumental music, journalism, Latin, Latin-AP, law, literary magazine, marching band, mechanics of writing, moral reasoning, moral theology, music, philosophy, physical education, physics, pre-calculus, psychology, religion, religious studies, science, senior seminar, Shakespeare, social studies, Spanish, statistics, studio art, studio art-AP, The 20th Century, theater, trigonometry, U.S. government and politics, U.S. government and politics-AP, U.S. history, U.S. history-AP, U.S. literature, world history, world literature.

Graduation Requirements Arts and fine arts (art, music, dance, drama), computer science, physical education (includes health), religion (includes Bible studies and theology). Community service is required.

Special Academic Programs Advanced Placement exam preparation; honors section; independent study; study at local college for college credit; study abroad; academic accommodation for the gifted, the musically talented, and the artistically talented.

College Admission Counseling 212 students graduated in 2008; 210 went to college, including Boston University; Holy Cross College; Northeastern University; University of Connecticut; University of New Hampshire. Other: 1 entered military service, 1 entered a postgraduate year.

Student Life Upper grades have specified standards of dress, student council, honor system. Discipline rests primarily with faculty. Attendance at religious services is required.

Summer Programs Remediation, enrichment, sports, computer instruction programs offered; session focuses on remediation; held on campus; accepts boys and girls; not open to students from other schools. 40 students usually enrolled. 2009 schedule: July 5 to July 29. Application deadline: May 1.

Tuition and Aid Tuition installment plan (FACTS Tuition Payment Plan, individually arranged payment plans). Merit scholarship grants, need-based scholarship grants, paying campus jobs available. In 2008–09, 10% of upper-school students received aid.

Admissions Traditional secondary-level entrance grade is 9. Catholic High School Entrance Examination required. Deadline for receipt of application materials: January 9. Application fee required: $25.

Athletics Interscholastic: baseball (boys), basketball (b,g), cheering (b,g), cross-country running (b,g), football (b), gymnastics (g), hockey (b,g), ice hockey (b,g), lacrosse (b), skiing (downhill) (b,g), soccer (b,g), softball (g), swimming and diving (b,g), tennis (b,g), track and field (b,g), volleyball (g), wrestling (b); intramural: crew (b,g); coed interscholastic: aquatics, cheering, golf, ice hockey, indoor track, nordic skiing, paint ball, skiing (downhill); coed intramural: aerobics/dance, basketball, bowling, crew, dance, fishing, freestyle skiing, golf, mountain biking, outdoor education, strength & conditioning, swimming and diving, table tennis, tennis, volleyball, weight lifting, weight training. 4 PE instructors, 55 coaches, 2 athletic trainers.

Computers Computers are regularly used in career education, career exploration, career technology, college planning, data processing, desktop publishing, independent study, information technology, introduction to technology, library, library science, library skills, literary magazine, multimedia, music, news writing, newspaper, programming, publications, publishing, research skills, stock market, technology, Web site design, word processing, yearbook classes. Computer network features include on-campus library services, online commercial services, Internet access, wireless campus network, Internet filtering or blocking technology. Student e-mail accounts are available to students. The school has a published electronic and media policy.

Contact Ms. Jamie Gregoire, Director of Admissions. 603-889-4107 Ext. 4304. Fax: 603-889-0701. E-mail: admit@bghs.org. Web site: www.bghs.org.

BISHOP HENDRICKEN HIGH SCHOOL

2615 Warwick Avenue
Warwick, Rhode Island 02889

Head of School: Br. Thomas R. Leto

General Information Boys' day college-preparatory, arts, business, religious studies, and technology school, affiliated with Roman Catholic Church. Grades 9–12. Founded: 1959. Setting: suburban. Nearest major city is Providence. 34-acre campus. 1 building on campus. Approved or accredited by New England Association of Schools and Colleges and Rhode Island Department of Education. Total enrollment: 982. Upper school average class size: 22. Upper school faculty-student ratio: 1:14.

Upper School Student Profile Grade 9: 244 students (244 boys); Grade 10: 252 students (252 boys); Grade 11: 250 students (250 boys); Grade 12: 236 students (236 boys). 85% of students are Roman Catholic.

Faculty School total: 75. In upper school: 53 men, 22 women; 45 have advanced degrees.

Special Academic Programs 10 Advanced Placement exams for which test preparation is offered; honors section.

College Admission Counseling 245 students graduated in 2008; 241 went to college. Other: 2 entered a postgraduate year. Mean SAT critical reading: 532, mean SAT math: 543, mean SAT writing: 537.

Student Life Upper grades have specified standards of dress, student council, honor system. Discipline rests primarily with faculty. Attendance at religious services is required.

Tuition and Aid Day student tuition: $9875. Tuition installment plan (individually arranged payment plans). Merit scholarship grants, need-based scholarship grants available. In 2008–09, 33% of upper-school students received aid; total upper-school merit-scholarship money awarded: $160,000. Total amount of financial aid awarded in 2008–09: $500,000.

Admissions Traditional secondary-level entrance grade is 9. Catholic High School Entrance Examination required. Deadline for receipt of application materials: February. Application fee required: $25.

Athletics Interscholastic: baseball, basketball, cross-country running, diving, football, golf, ice hockey, indoor track, indoor track & field, lacrosse, rugby, sailing, soccer, swimming and diving, tennis, track and field, volleyball, winter (indoor) track, wrestling; intramural: archery, badminton, billiards, bocce, bowling, flag football, golf, handball, rugby, whiffle ball. 4 PE instructors, 1 athletic trainer.

Computers Computer resources include Internet access, wireless campus network, Internet filtering or blocking technology. Students grades are available online. The school has a published electronic and media policy.

Contact Mrs. Dianne M. O'Reilly, Director of Admissions. 401-739-3450 Ext. 163. Fax: 401-732-8261. E-mail: doreilly@hendricken.com. Web site: www.hendricken.com.

BISHOP IRETON HIGH SCHOOL

201 Cambridge Road
Alexandria, Virginia 22314-4899

Head of School: Mr. Timothy Hamer

General Information Coeducational day college-preparatory, arts, religious studies, and technology school, affiliated with Roman Catholic Church. Grades 9–12. Founded: 1964. Setting: suburban. 12-acre campus. 1 building on campus. Approved or accredited by National Catholic Education Association and Southern Association of Colleges and Schools. Endowment: $1 million. Total enrollment: 797. Upper school average class size: 24. Upper school faculty-student ratio: 1:14.

Upper School Student Profile Grade 9: 199 students (102 boys, 97 girls); Grade 10: 211 students (95 boys, 116 girls); Grade 11: 197 students (93 boys, 104 girls); Grade 12: 190 students (90 boys, 100 girls). 92% of students are Roman Catholic.

Faculty School total: 65. In upper school: 29 men, 34 women; 46 have advanced degrees.

Subjects Offered Advanced Placement courses, Catholic belief and practice, computer science, driver education, English, film, fine arts, foreign language, health, mathematics, physical education, religion, science, social studies.

Graduation Requirements Arts and fine arts (art, music, dance, drama), computer science, English, foreign language, mathematics, physical education (includes health), religion (includes Bible studies and theology), science, social studies (includes history), 60 hours of community service.

Special Academic Programs Advanced Placement exam preparation; honors section; academic accommodation for the musically talented; special instructional classes for students with Attention Deficit Disorder.

College Admission Counseling 196 students graduated in 2008; 195 went to college, including George Mason University; James Madison University; Old Dominion University; The College of William and Mary; University of Virginia; Virginia Polytechnic Institute and State University. Other: 1 entered military service. Mean SAT critical reading: 591, mean SAT math: 585, mean SAT writing: 597, mean combined SAT: 1773.

Student Life Upper grades have uniform requirement, honor system. Discipline rests primarily with faculty. Attendance at religious services is required.

Summer Programs Remediation, enrichment, computer instruction programs offered; session focuses on remediation; held on campus; accepts boys and girls; open to students from other schools. 25 students usually enrolled. 2009 schedule: June to July.

Tuition and Aid Day student tuition: $10,400–$14,950. Tuition installment plan (FACTS Tuition Payment Plan, monthly payment plans). Tuition reduction for siblings, merit scholarship grants, need-based scholarship grants available. In 2008–09, 9% of upper-school students received aid; total upper-school merit-scholarship money awarded: $100,000. Total amount of financial aid awarded in 2008–09: $350,000.

Admissions Traditional secondary-level entrance grade is 9. For fall 2008, 445 students applied for upper-level admission, 387 were accepted, 220 enrolled. High School Placement Test (closed version) from Scholastic Testing Service required. Deadline for receipt of application materials: January 23. Application fee required: $50.

Athletics Interscholastic: baseball (boys), basketball (b,g), football (b), lacrosse (b,g), soccer (b,g), softball (g), swimming and diving (b,g), tennis (b,g), track and field (b,g), volleyball (g), water polo (b), winter (indoor) track (b,g), wrestling (b); intramural: weight training (b,g); coed interscholastic: cheering, crew, cross-country running, diving, golf, ice hockey, indoor track, water polo, weight training; coed intramural: dance team, freestyle skiing, skiing (downhill), table tennis. 4 PE instructors, 3 coaches, 1 athletic trainer.

Computers Computers are regularly used in all academic classes. Computer network features include on-campus library services, online commercial services, Internet access, Internet filtering or blocking technology. Student e-mail accounts and computer access in designated common areas are available to students. The school has a published electronic and media policy.

Contact Mr. Peter J. Hamer, Director of Admissions. 703-212-5190. Fax: 703-212-8173. E-mail: hamerp@bishopireton.org. Web site: www.bishopireton.org.

BISHOP KELLY HIGH SCHOOL

7009 Franklin Road
Boise, Idaho 83709-0922

Head of School: Mr. Robert R. Wehde

General Information Coeducational day college-preparatory and religious studies school, affiliated with Roman Catholic Church. Grades 9–12. Founded: 1964. Setting: suburban. 70-acre campus. 2 buildings on campus. Approved or accredited by National Catholic Education Association, Northwest Association of Accredited Schools, and Idaho Department of Education. Endowment: $5.7 million. Total enrollment: 640. Upper school average class size: 22. Upper school faculty-student ratio: 1:17.

Upper School Student Profile Grade 9: 159 students (85 boys, 74 girls); Grade 10: 160 students (93 boys, 67 girls); Grade 11: 163 students (88 boys, 75 girls); Grade 12: 156 students (79 boys, 77 girls); Grade 13: 2 students (2 boys). 84% of students are Roman Catholic.

Faculty School total: 46. In upper school: 21 men, 25 women; 25 have advanced degrees.

Subjects Offered Advanced Placement courses, advanced studio art-AP, algebra, American government, American history-AP, art, art appreciation, art-AP, band, biology, biology-AP, calculus, calculus-AP, campus ministry, Catholic belief and practice, chemistry, chemistry-AP, choir, Christian and Hebrew scripture, Christianity, comparative religion, computer applications, computer programming, conceptual physics, creative writing, drama, earth science, ecology, economics, English, English literature and composition-AP, French, geology, geometry, health, history of the Catholic Church, horticulture, instrumental music, journalism, Latin, physical education, physics, physics-AP, pottery, pre-algebra, pre-calculus, psychology, reading/study skills, religious education, religious studies, Spanish, Spanish-AP, speech, speech and debate, sports medicine, statistics-AP, theater, theater arts, trigonometry, U.S. government, U.S. history, video film production, Western civilization, world civilizations, yearbook.

Graduation Requirements Computer science, English, foreign language, mathematics, physical education (includes health), religion (includes Bible studies and theology), science, social studies (includes history), 30 hours of community service.

Special Academic Programs Advanced Placement exam preparation; honors section; independent study; study at local college for college credit; remedial reading and/or remedial writing.

College Admission Counseling 144 students graduated in 2008; 138 went to college, including Boise State University; Carroll University; Gonzaga University; The College of Idaho; University of Idaho; University of Portland. Other: 3 went to work, 1 entered military service.

Student Life Upper grades have specified standards of dress, student council, honor system. Discipline rests primarily with faculty. Attendance at religious services is required.

Tuition and Aid Day student tuition: $6500. Guaranteed tuition plan. Tuition installment plan (The Tuition Plan, monthly payment plans, individually arranged payment plans). Need-based scholarship grants available. In 2008–09, 76% of upper-school students received aid. Total amount of financial aid awarded in 2008–09: $879,656.

Admissions Traditional secondary-level entrance grade is 9. Deadline for receipt of application materials: none. Application fee required: $205.

Athletics Interscholastic: baseball (boys), basketball (b,g), cheering (g), cross-country running (b,g), dance team (g), football (b), golf (b,g), lacrosse (b,g), skiing (downhill) (b,g), snowboarding (b,g), soccer (b,g), softball (g), swimming and diving (b,g), tennis (b,g), track and field (b,g), volleyball (g), weight lifting (b,g), wrestling (b). 2 PE instructors, 16 coaches, 2 athletic trainers.

Computers Computers are regularly used in art, economics, English, foreign language, history, journalism, mathematics, science classes. Computer network features include on-campus library services, Internet access, Internet filtering or blocking technology. Student e-mail accounts and computer access in designated common areas are available to students. Students grades are available online. The school has a published electronic and media policy.

Contact Ms. Brenda Iazzetta, Registrar. 208-375-6010. Fax: 208-375-3626. E-mail: biazzetta@bk.org. Web site: www.bk.org.

BISHOP KENNY HIGH SCHOOL

1055 Kingman Avenue
Jacksonville, Florida 32207

Head of School: Rev. Michael R. Houle

General Information Coeducational day college-preparatory school. Grades 9–12. Approved or accredited by Southern Association of Colleges and Schools. Total enrollment: 1,440. Upper school average class size: 22.

Upper School Student Profile Grade 9: 367 students (184 boys, 183 girls); Grade 10: 343 students (171 boys, 172 girls); Grade 11: 364 students (193 boys, 171 girls); Grade 12: 366 students (179 boys, 187 girls).

Graduation Requirements 20th century physics, electives, English, foreign language, mathematics, performing arts, personal fitness, practical arts, religion (includes Bible studies and theology), science, social studies (includes history), Service Hour Requirements.

Special Academic Programs Advanced Placement exam preparation; honors section.

College Admission Counseling 286 students graduated in 2008; 277 went to college, including Tallahassee Community College. Other: 3 entered military service, 2 entered a postgraduate year, 4 had other specific plans. 58% scored over 600 on SAT critical reading, 43% scored over 600 on SAT math, 48% scored over 600 on SAT writing, 45% scored over 1800 on combined SAT, 59% scored over 26 on composite ACT.

Summer Programs Remediation, advancement, sports programs offered; session focuses on academics; held on campus; accepts boys and girls; not open to students from other schools. 300 students usually enrolled. 2009 schedule: June 8 to July 16. Application deadline: June 11.

Tuition and Aid Day student tuition: $5880. Tuition installment plan (monthly payment plans, individually arranged payment plans). Tuition reduction for siblings, need-based loans available.

Admissions Traditional secondary-level entrance grade is 9. ACT-Explore or Explore required. Deadline for receipt of application materials: none. Application fee required: $300. On-campus interview required.

Athletics Interscholastic: baseball (boys), basketball (b,g), cheering (g), cross-country running (b,g), diving (b,g), drill team (g), football (b), golf (b,g), JROTC drill (b,g), riflery (b,g), soccer (b,g), softball (g), swimming and diving (b,g), tennis (b,g), track and field (b,g), volleyball (g), weight lifting (b), wrestling (b). 5 PE instructors, 5 coaches, 2 athletic trainers.

Computers Computers are regularly used in accounting, computer applications, desktop publishing, journalism, keyboarding, newspaper, technology, word processing, yearbook classes. Computer resources include on-campus library services, Internet access, Internet filtering or blocking technology, design software for Journalism and MultiMedia. The school has a published electronic and media policy.

Contact Mrs. Sheila W. Marovich, Director of Admissions. 904-398-7545. Fax: 904-398-5728. E-mail: development@bishopkenny.org. Web site: www.bishopkenny.org.

BISHOP LUERS HIGH SCHOOL

333 East Paulding Road
Fort Wayne, Indiana 46816

Head of School: Mrs. Mary T. Keefer

General Information Coeducational day college-preparatory and religious studies school, affiliated with Roman Catholic Church. Grades 9–12. Founded: 1958. Setting: urban. 5-acre campus. 1 building on campus. Approved or accredited by National Catholic Education Association, North Central Association of Colleges and Schools, and Indiana Department of Education. Total enrollment: 548. Upper school average class size: 25. Upper school faculty-student ratio: 1:18.

Upper School Student Profile Grade 9: 142 students (73 boys, 69 girls); Grade 10: 141 students (74 boys, 67 girls); Grade 11: 141 students (66 boys, 75 girls); Grade 12: 124 students (65 boys, 59 girls). 89% of students are Roman Catholic.

Faculty School total: 30. In upper school: 12 men, 18 women; 18 have advanced degrees.

Subjects Offered 3-dimensional art, accounting, algebra, Bible, biology, biology-AP, business, business law, calculus-AP, chamber groups, chemistry, chemistry-AP, chorus, church history, computer applications, computer programming, concert band, creative writing, drawing, economics, English, French, geometry, government, health education, honors algebra, honors English, honors geometry, honors U.S. history, honors world history, Latin, music appreciation, music theory, painting, physical education, physics, physiology, pre-calculus, psychology, sculpture, sociology, Spanish, speech communications, statistics and probability, student government, student publications, study skills, theater arts, theater production, theology, trigonometry, U.S. history, world civilizations, world geography, world history.

Graduation Requirements Computers, English, mathematics, physical education (includes health), religion (includes Bible studies and theology), science, social studies (includes history).

Special Academic Programs Advanced Placement exam preparation; honors section; study at local college for college credit; academic accommodation for the gifted and the musically talented; remedial reading and/or remedial writing; remedial math.

College Admission Counseling 122 students graduated in 2008; 117 went to college, including Indiana University–Purdue University Fort Wayne; Purdue University. Other: 3 went to work, 2 entered military service. Mean SAT critical reading: 513, mean SAT math: 507, mean SAT writing: 495.

Student Life Upper grades have specified standards of dress, student council. Discipline rests equally with students and faculty. Attendance at religious services is required.

Summer Programs Remediation, sports programs offered; session focuses on camps and enrichment; held on campus; accepts boys and girls; open to students from other schools. 250 students usually enrolled. 2009 schedule: June 15 to August 10. Application deadline: May 30.

Tuition and Aid Day student tuition: $3875. Tuition installment plan (FACTS Tuition Payment Plan). Tuition reduction for siblings, merit scholarship grants, need-based scholarship grants, paying campus jobs available. In 2008–09, 61% of upper-school students received aid.

Admissions Traditional secondary-level entrance grade is 9. For fall 2008, 160 students applied for upper-level admission, 157 were accepted, 146 enrolled. Deadline for receipt of application materials: none. Application fee required: $120.

Athletics Interscholastic: baseball (boys), basketball (b,g), bowling (b,g), cheering (g), cross-country running (b,g), dance (g), dance team (g), diving (b,g), football (b), golf (b,g), lacrosse (b), riflery (b,g), running (b,g), soccer (b,g), softball (g), swimming and diving (b,g), tennis (b,g), track and field (b,g), volleyball (g), wrestling (g); intramural: lacrosse (b,g); coed intramural: lacrosse, riflery, weight training. 2 PE instructors, 25 coaches, 2 athletic trainers.

Computers Computers are regularly used in all academic, business, yearbook classes. Computer network features include on-campus library services, Internet access, Internet filtering or blocking technology. Students grades are available online. The school has a published electronic and media policy.

Contact Mrs. Jennifer Andorfer, Co-Director of Admissions and Public Relations. 260-456-1261 Ext. 3141. Fax: 260-456-1262. E-mail: jandorfer@bishopluers.org. Web site: www.bishopluers.org/.

BISHOP LYNCH CATHOLIC HIGH SCHOOL

9750 Ferguson Road
Dallas, Texas 75228

Head of School: Edward E. Leyden

General Information Coeducational day college-preparatory, arts, religious studies, and technology school, affiliated with Roman Catholic Church. Grades 9–12. Founded: 1963. Setting: urban. 22-acre campus. 7 buildings on campus. Approved or accredited by Southern Association of Colleges and Schools, Texas Catholic Conference, and Texas Education Agency. Endowment: $2 million. Total enrollment: 1,038. Upper school average class size: 24. Upper school faculty-student ratio: 1:12.

Upper School Student Profile Grade 9: 266 students (114 boys, 152 girls); Grade 10: 276 students (131 boys, 145 girls); Grade 11: 255 students (106 boys, 149 girls); Grade 12: 242 students (106 boys, 136 girls). 79% of students are Roman Catholic.

Faculty School total: 95. In upper school: 40 men, 55 women; 56 have advanced degrees.

Subjects Offered 3-dimensional design, algebra, American government-AP, American history, American history-AP, American literature, art, Asian history, astronomy, band, Basic programming, biology, biology-AP, business, business law, calculus, calculus-AP, campus ministry, chemistry, chemistry-AP, choir, choreography, Christian and Hebrew scripture, Christian doctrine, Christian ethics, church history, community service, computer math, computer programming, computer science, concert band, creative writing, dance, design, drama, drawing, driver education, economics, English, English literature, English-AP, environmental science, film, fine arts, French, geometry, German, government, government-AP, health, history, Holocaust studies, honors algebra, honors English, honors geometry, honors U.S. history, honors world history, jazz band, keyboarding, Latin, Latin-AP, leadership and service, marching band, mathematics, media arts, media literacy, media production, medieval/Renaissance history, Mexican history, musical productions, painting, personal finance, photography, physical education, physical science, physics, physics-AP, pre-calculus, psychology, psychology-AP, publications, religion, SAT/ACT preparation, science, social studies, sociology, Spanish, speech, statistics, theater, theater arts, theater production, theology, world history, yearbook.

Graduation Requirements Arts and fine arts (art, music, dance, drama), computer science, English, foreign language, mathematics, physical education (includes health), religion (includes Bible studies and theology), science, social studies (includes history), speech, U.S. government, U.S. history, world history. Community service is required.

Special Academic Programs Advanced Placement exam preparation; honors section; study at local college for college credit; academic accommodation for the gifted; remedial reading and/or remedial writing; remedial math; programs in English, mathematics for dyslexic students.

College Admission Counseling 243 students graduated in 2008; 242 went to college, including Oklahoma State University; Texas A&M University; Texas Tech University; University of Arkansas; University of North Texas; University of Oklahoma. Other: 1 had other specific plans.

Student Life Upper grades have uniform requirement, student council, honor system. Discipline rests primarily with faculty. Attendance at religious services is required.

Summer Programs Remediation, enrichment, sports, art/fine arts programs offered; held both on and off campus; held at some Athletic Camps are held at the appropriate venue (Swimming, Tennis, etc.); accepts boys and girls; open to students from other schools. 200 students usually enrolled. 2009 schedule: June 8 to July 10.

Tuition and Aid Day student tuition: $11,000. Tuition installment plan (guaranteed bank loan plan). Tuition reduction for siblings, merit scholarship grants, need-based scholarship grants, paying campus jobs available. In 2008–09, 33% of upper-school students received aid; total upper-school merit-scholarship money awarded: $60,500. Total amount of financial aid awarded in 2008–09: $190,700.

Admissions Traditional secondary-level entrance grade is 9. For fall 2008, 598 students applied for upper-level admission, 400 were accepted, 264 enrolled. ISEE required. Deadline for receipt of application materials: none. Application fee required: $75. On-campus interview required.

Athletics Interscholastic: aquatics (boys, girls), baseball (b), basketball (b,g), cheering (g), cross-country running (b,g), dance team (g), drill team (g), football (b), golf (b,g), power lifting (b), soccer (b,g), softball (g); intramural: lacrosse (b,g); coed interscholastic: boxing, combined training, dance, diving, hockey, ice hockey; coed intramural: bicycling, bowling, climbing, crew, paddle tennis, paint ball, rock climbing, sailing, skateboarding. 2 PE instructors, 28 coaches, 1 athletic trainer.

Computers Computers are regularly used in economics, English, foreign language, literary magazine, mathematics, media arts, media production, newspaper, publications, science, yearbook classes. Computer network features include on-campus library services, Internet access, wireless campus network, Internet filtering or blocking technology. Student e-mail accounts and computer access in designated common areas are available to students. Students grades are available online. The school has a published electronic and media policy.

Contact Tricia Roos, Director of Admissions. 214-324-3607 Ext. 127. Fax: 214-324-3600. E-mail: tricia.roos@bishoplynch.org. Web site: www.bishoplynch.org.

BISHOP MCGUINNESS CATHOLIC HIGH SCHOOL

1725 NC Highway 66 South
Kernersville, North Carolina 27284

Head of School: Mr. George L. Repass

General Information Coeducational day college-preparatory, arts, and religious studies school, affiliated with Roman Catholic Church. Grades 9–12. Founded: 1959. Setting: suburban. Nearest major city is Winston-Salem. 2 buildings on campus. Approved or accredited by Northwest Association of Accredited Schools, Southern Association of Colleges and Schools, The College Board, and North Carolina Department of Education. Endowment: $100,000. Total enrollment: 565. Upper school average class size: 18. Upper school faculty-student ratio: 1:13.

Upper School Student Profile Grade 9: 153 students (75 boys, 78 girls); Grade 10: 134 students (70 boys, 64 girls); Grade 11: 144 students (78 boys, 66 girls); Grade 12: 134 students (71 boys, 63 girls). 75% of students are Roman Catholic.

Faculty School total: 39. In upper school: 20 men, 19 women; 31 have advanced degrees.

Subjects Offered Algebra, American history, anatomy, arts, biology, biology-AP, calculus, chemistry, chemistry-AP, community service, computer science, creative writing, earth science, English, English-AP, fine arts, French, French-AP, geometry, health, Latin, mathematics, music, photography, physical education, physical science, physics, political science, religion, science, social studies, Spanish, Spanish-AP, trigonometry, world history.

Graduation Requirements Arts and fine arts (art, music, dance, drama), English, foreign language, mathematics, physical education (includes health), religion (includes Bible studies and theology), science, social studies (includes history). Community service is required.

Special Academic Programs Advanced Placement exam preparation; honors section; independent study; term-away projects; study at local college for college credit.

College Admission Counseling 96 students graduated in 2008; all went to college, including Appalachian State University; North Carolina State University; The University of North Carolina at Asheville; The University of North Carolina at Chapel Hill; The University of North Carolina at Charlotte; The University of North Carolina Wilmington. Mean SAT critical reading: 544, mean SAT math: 528, mean SAT writing: 540, mean combined SAT: 1612, mean composite ACT: 22. 30% scored over 600 on SAT critical reading, 25% scored over 600 on SAT math, 30% scored over 600 on SAT writing, 28% scored over 1800 on combined SAT, 23% scored over 26 on composite ACT.

Student Life Upper grades have specified standards of dress, student council, honor system. Discipline rests primarily with faculty. Attendance at religious services is required.
Tuition and Aid Day student tuition: $6200–$8200. Tuition installment plan (monthly payment plans, yearly, semester and quarterly payment plans). Tuition reduction for siblings, need-based scholarship grants available. In 2008–09, 18% of upper-school students received aid. Total amount of financial aid awarded in 2008–09: $313,106.
Admissions Traditional secondary-level entrance grade is 9. For fall 2008, 210 students applied for upper-level admission, 183 were accepted, 172 enrolled. Achievement/Aptitude/Writing required. Deadline for receipt of application materials: none. Application fee required: $75. On-campus interview required.
Athletics Interscholastic: baseball (boys), basketball (b,g), cheering (g), football (b), lacrosse (b), soccer (b,g), softball (g), tennis (b,g), volleyball (g), wrestling (b); coed interscholastic: cross-country running, golf, swimming and diving, track and field. 1 PE instructor, 40 coaches, 2 athletic trainers.
Computers Computer resources include on-campus library services, Internet access, Internet filtering or blocking technology. Student e-mail accounts and computer access in designated common areas are available to students. Students grades are available online.
Contact Mr. Robert Belcher, Admissions Director. 336-564-1011. Fax: 336-564-1060. E-mail: rb@bmhs.us. Web site: www.bmhs.us.

BISHOP MCGUINNESS CATHOLIC HIGH SCHOOL

801 Northwest 50th Street
Oklahoma City, Oklahoma 73118-6001

Head of School: Mr. David L. Morton

General Information Coeducational day college-preparatory, arts, business, religious studies, bilingual studies, and technology school, affiliated with Roman Catholic Church. Grades 9–12. Founded: 1950. Setting: urban. 20-acre campus. 4 buildings on campus. Approved or accredited by North Central Association of Colleges and Schools and Oklahoma Department of Education. Endowment: $1.2 million. Total enrollment: 693. Upper school average class size: 17. Upper school faculty-student ratio: 1:14.
Upper School Student Profile Grade 11: 164 students (84 boys, 80 girls); Grade 12: 150 students (78 boys, 72 girls). 75% of students are Roman Catholic.
Faculty School total: 54. In upper school: 9 men, 14 women; 14 have advanced degrees.
Subjects Offered Algebra, American literature, American literature-AP, art, band, Bible studies, biology, biology-AP, business, calculus-AP, Catholic belief and practice, ceramics, chemistry, chorus, church history, computer technologies, creative writing, culinary arts, current events, dance, debate, design, drama, drawing, economics, electives, English, English literature, English literature-AP, ethics, French, geography, geometry, German, government, government-AP, health and wellness, history of the Catholic Church, honors algebra, honors English, honors geometry, HTML design, introduction to theater, Latin, leadership, learning lab, newspaper, orchestra, painting, personal finance, photography, physical education, physical science, physics, physics-AP, physiology, play production, practical arts, prayer/spirituality, pre-calculus, psychology, scripture, sociology, Spanish, speech, stagecraft, theater, U.S. history, U.S. history-AP, weight training, world history, world history-AP, world religions, writing workshop, yearbook.
Graduation Requirements Arts and fine arts (art, music, dance, drama), electives, English, foreign language, mathematics, physical education (includes health), practical arts, science, social studies (includes history), theology, 90 hours of Christian service.
Special Academic Programs 8 Advanced Placement exams for which test preparation is offered; honors section; academic accommodation for the gifted and the artistically talented; programs in English, mathematics for dyslexic students; special instructional classes for students with learning differences.
College Admission Counseling 172 students graduated in 2008; 167 went to college, including Colorado School of Mines; Oklahoma State University; University of Arkansas; University of Oklahoma; University of Tulsa. Other: 2 went to work, 1 entered a postgraduate year, 2 had other specific plans. Mean SAT critical reading: 583, mean SAT math: 558, mean SAT writing: 578, mean composite ACT: 24. 38% scored over 600 on SAT critical reading, 32% scored over 600 on SAT math, 34% scored over 600 on SAT writing.
Student Life Upper grades have uniform requirement, student council, honor system. Discipline rests primarily with faculty. Attendance at religious services is required.
Tuition and Aid Day student tuition: $6950. Tuition installment plan (FACTS Tuition Payment Plan). Need-based scholarship grants, paying campus jobs available. In 2008–09, 18% of upper-school students received aid. Total amount of financial aid awarded in 2008–09: $128,875.
Admissions Traditional secondary-level entrance grade is 11. For fall 2008, 12 students applied for upper-level admission, 12 were accepted, 12 enrolled. STS required. Deadline for receipt of application materials: May 1. Application fee required: $350. On-campus interview required.
Athletics Interscholastic: baseball (boys), basketball (b,g), bowling (b,g), cheering (g), cross-country running (b,g), dance team (b,g), football (b), golf (b,g), soccer (b,g), softball (g), swimming and diving (b,g), tennis (b,g), track and field (b,g), volleyball (g), weight training (b,g), winter (indoor) track (b,g), wrestling (b); coed interscholastic: bowling. 1 PE instructor.
Computers Computers are regularly used in all academic classes. Computer network features include on-campus library services, online commercial services, Internet access, wireless campus network, Internet filtering or blocking technology, laptop classroom computers, wireless printing, eBooks, and My Road. Student e-mail accounts and computer access in designated common areas are available to students. Students grades are available online. The school has a published electronic and media policy.
Contact Ms. Amy Hanson, 9th Grade Counselor. 405-842-6638 Ext. 225. Fax: 405-858-9550. E-mail: ahanson@bmchs.org. Web site: www.bmchs.org.

BISHOP MCNAMARA HIGH SCHOOL

550 West Brookmont Boulevard
Kankakee, Illinois 60901

Head of School: Mr. James R. Laurenti

General Information Coeducational day college-preparatory and vocational school, affiliated with Roman Catholic Church. Grades 9–12. Founded: 1924. Setting: suburban. Nearest major city is Joliet. 25-acre campus. 2 buildings on campus. Approved or accredited by Illinois Department of Education. Endowment: $2.4 million. Total enrollment: 438. Upper school average class size: 23. Upper school faculty-student ratio: 1:23.
Upper School Student Profile Grade 9: 130 students (70 boys, 60 girls); Grade 10: 96 students (50 boys, 46 girls); Grade 11: 115 students (60 boys, 55 girls); Grade 12: 97 students (53 boys, 44 girls). 80% of students are Roman Catholic.
Faculty School total: 35. In upper school: 14 men, 19 women; 19 have advanced degrees.
Subjects Offered Accounting, ACT preparation, algebra, American history, American history-AP, American literature, art, auto body, band, biology, business technology, calculus-AP, Catholic belief and practice, chemistry, chemistry-AP, computer technologies, computers, construction, design, drafting, English, English literature, English-AP, French, French-AP, geometry, health, honors geometry, metalworking, physical education, physical science, physics, physics-AP, physiology, pre-algebra, pre-calculus, psychology, psychology-AP, scripture, Spanish, Spanish-AP, studio art, trigonometry, welding, world geography, world history, world religions.
Graduation Requirements Art, electives, English, mathematics, modern languages, physical education (includes health), religion (includes Bible studies and theology), science, social studies (includes history), vocational arts.
Special Academic Programs Advanced Placement exam preparation; honors section; independent study; special instructional classes for students with Attention Deficit Disorder.
College Admission Counseling 106 students graduated in 2008; 97 went to college, including Eastern Illinois University; Illinois State University; Kankakee Community College; Northern Illinois University; University of Illinois at Urbana–Champaign. Other: 7 went to work, 2 entered military service. Median composite ACT: 25. 39% scored over 26 on composite ACT.
Student Life Upper grades have specified standards of dress, student council. Discipline rests primarily with faculty. Attendance at religious services is required.
Summer Programs Remediation, enrichment, sports programs offered; held on campus; accepts boys and girls; open to students from other schools. 100 students usually enrolled. 2009 schedule: June 11 to August 4. Application deadline: May 1.
Tuition and Aid Day student tuition: $5550. Tuition installment plan (FACTS Tuition Payment Plan). Tuition reduction for siblings, merit scholarship grants, need-based scholarship grants available. In 2008–09, 30% of upper-school students received aid; total upper-school merit-scholarship money awarded: $43,000. Total amount of financial aid awarded in 2008–09: $200,000.
Admissions Traditional secondary-level entrance grade is 9. For fall 2008, 153 students applied for upper-level admission, 146 were accepted, 130 enrolled. High School Placement Test or High School Placement Test (closed version) from Scholastic Testing Service required. Deadline for receipt of application materials: August 23. Application fee required: $30. Interview required.
Athletics Interscholastic: aerobics/dance (girls), baseball (b), basketball (b,g), cheering (g), cross-country running (b,g), dance (g), dance squad (g), dance team (g), flag football (b), football (b), golf (b), gymnastics (g), pom squad (g), soccer (b,g), softball (g), strength & conditioning (b,g), swimming and diving (b,g), tennis (b,g), track and field (b,g), volleyball (g), weight training (b,g), wrestling (b); intramural: basketball (b), bowling (b,g). 2 PE instructors, 8 coaches, 1 athletic trainer.
Computers Computers are regularly used in all academic classes. Computer network features include on-campus library services, Internet access, wireless campus network, Internet filtering or blocking technology. Student e-mail accounts are available to students. Students grades are available online. The school has a published electronic and media policy.
Contact Kurt F. Weigt, Principal. 815-932-7413 Ext. 225. Fax: 815-932-0926. E-mail: kweigt@bishop-mcnamara.org. Web site: www.bishopmac.com.

BISHOP MONTGOMERY HIGH SCHOOL

5430 Torrance Boulevard
Torrance, California 90503

Head of School: Ms. Rosemary Distaso-Libbon

General Information Coeducational day college-preparatory, arts, religious studies, and technology school, affiliated with Roman Catholic Church. Grades 9–12. Founded: 1957. Setting: suburban. Nearest major city is Los Angeles. 27-acre campus. 8 buildings on campus. Approved or accredited by National Catholic Education Association, Western Association of Schools and Colleges, Western Catholic Education Association, and California Department of Education. Total enrollment: 1,208. Upper school average class size: 26. Upper school faculty-student ratio: 1:17.
Upper School Student Profile Grade 9: 311 students (142 boys, 169 girls); Grade 10: 349 students (156 boys, 193 girls); Grade 11: 286 students (109 boys, 177 girls); Grade 12: 262 students (110 boys, 152 girls). 75% of students are Roman Catholic.
Faculty School total: 71. In upper school: 32 men, 39 women; 47 have advanced degrees.
Subjects Offered Algebra, American history, American history-AP, American literature, anatomy, art, band, Bible studies, biology, calculus, career exploration, chemistry, chorus, composition, computer science, consumer economics, drama, economics, English, English literature, English literature-AP, fine arts, French, geometry, government/civics, health, history, keyboarding, languages, life science, literature, mathematics, peer counseling, physical education, physics, physics-AP, physiology, religion, science, social studies, Spanish, statistics, theater, trigonometry, weight training, world history, yearbook.
Graduation Requirements Arts and fine arts (art, music, dance, drama), business skills (includes word processing), computer science, English, mathematics, physical education (includes health), religion (includes Bible studies and theology), science, social studies (includes history).
Special Academic Programs Advanced Placement exam preparation; honors section.
College Admission Counseling 280 students graduated in 2008; 276 went to college, including California State University, Long Beach; El Camino College; Loyola Marymount University; San Diego State University; University of California, Irvine; University of California, Los Angeles. Other: 1 went to work, 3 entered military service. 16% scored over 600 on SAT critical reading, 18% scored over 600 on SAT math, 15% scored over 26 on composite ACT.
Student Life Upper grades have uniform requirement, student council. Discipline rests primarily with faculty. Attendance at religious services is required.
Summer Programs Remediation, enrichment, advancement, sports, art/fine arts, computer instruction programs offered; session focuses on Academic enrichment/remediation & athletic conditioning; held on campus; accepts boys and girls; open to students from other schools. 900 students usually enrolled. 2009 schedule: June 22 to July 24. Application deadline: May 5.
Tuition and Aid Day student tuition: $6500. Tuition installment plan (monthly payment plans). Tuition reduction for siblings, financial need available. In 2008–09, 3% of upper-school students received aid. Total amount of financial aid awarded in 2008–09: $30,000.
Admissions Traditional secondary-level entrance grade is 9. For fall 2008, 480 students applied for upper-level admission, 340 were accepted, 328 enrolled. High School Placement Test and Stanford 9 required. Deadline for receipt of application materials: January 16. Application fee required: $75. On-campus interview required.
Athletics Interscholastic: baseball (boys), basketball (b,g), cross-country running (b,g), dance (b,g), football (b), golf (b,g), soccer (b,g), softball (g), strength & conditioning (b,g), tennis (b,g), volleyball (b,g); coed interscholastic: aerobics, dance squad, surfing, swimming and diving, track and field. 2 PE instructors, 32 coaches, 2 athletic trainers.
Computers Computers are regularly used in library, newspaper, programming, publications, technology, Web site design classes. Computer network features include on-campus library services, Internet access, wireless campus network. Students grades are available online. The school has a published electronic and media policy.
Contact Mrs. Helen Ingino, Admissions Assistant. 310-540-2021 Ext. 227. Fax: 310-792-1273. E-mail: hingino@bmhs-la.org. Web site: www.bmhs-la.org.

BISHOP MORA SALESIAN HIGH SCHOOL

960 South Soto Street
Los Angeles, California 90023

Head of School: Mr. Samuel Robles

General Information Boys' day college-preparatory, general academic, and religious studies school, affiliated with Roman Catholic Church. Grades 9–12. Founded: 1958. Setting: urban. 2 buildings on campus. Approved or accredited by Accrediting Commission for Schools, Western Association of Schools and Colleges, and California Department of Education. Upper school average class size: 28. Upper school faculty-student ratio: 1:15.
Upper School Student Profile Grade 9: 108 students (108 boys); Grade 10: 88 students (88 boys); Grade 11: 105 students (105 boys); Grade 12: 86 students (86 boys). 98% of students are Roman Catholic.
Faculty School total: 30. In upper school: 23 men, 7 women; 11 have advanced degrees.
Subjects Offered Advanced biology, advanced chemistry, advanced math, Advanced Placement courses, algebra, American government-AP, American history, American history-AP, American literature, anatomy and physiology, applied music, art, arts appreciation, athletic training, athletics, baseball, basketball, Bible studies, biology, biology-AP, British history, British literature, British literature (honors), business, calculus, calculus-AP, Catholic belief and practice, cheerleading, chemistry, chemistry-AP, Christianity, church history, cinematography, college admission preparation, college awareness, college counseling, college placement, college planning, computer applications, computer science, creative writing, drama, drawing, driver education, economics, economics-AP, English, English literature, English-AP, environmental science, ethics, European history, expository writing, fine arts, geometry, government/civics, grammar, health, health education, Hispanic literature, history, mathematics, music, physical education, physical science, physics, physics-AP, pre-algebra, pre-calculus, psychology, psychology-AP, religion, science, social studies, Spanish, Spanish-AP, speech and debate, theater, theology, trigonometry, volleyball, weight training, world history, world literature, writing.
Graduation Requirements Arts and fine arts (art, music, dance, drama), computer science, English, foreign language, mathematics, physical education (includes health), religion (includes Bible studies and theology), religious studies, science, social studies (includes history), Christian service program.
Special Academic Programs Advanced Placement exam preparation; independent study; academic accommodation for the musically talented and the artistically talented; remedial reading and/or remedial writing.
College Admission Counseling 80 students graduated in 2008; 79 went to college, including California State University, Los Angeles; Georgetown University; The Catholic University of America; University of California, Los Angeles; University of California, Riverside; Whittier College. Other: 1 went to work.
Student Life Upper grades have uniform requirement, student council, honor system. Discipline rests equally with students and faculty. Attendance at religious services is required.
Summer Programs Remediation, enrichment, advancement, sports, art/fine arts, rigorous outdoor training, computer instruction programs offered; held on campus; accepts boys and girls; open to students from other schools. 200 students usually enrolled. 2009 schedule: June 19 to July 31. Application deadline: May.
Tuition and Aid Day student tuition: $5000. Tuition installment plan (FACTS Tuition Payment Plan, monthly payment plans, individually arranged payment plans). Tuition reduction for siblings, merit scholarship grants, need-based scholarship grants available. In 2008–09, 55% of upper-school students received aid; total upper-school merit-scholarship money awarded: $2000. Total amount of financial aid awarded in 2008–09: $2000.
Admissions Traditional secondary-level entrance grade is 9. School's own exam required. Deadline for receipt of application materials: April 1. Application fee required: $50. On-campus interview required.
Athletics Interscholastic: baseball, basketball, bicycling, cross-country running, football, golf, physical fitness, physical training, running, soccer, swimming and diving, track and field, volleyball, weight training, wrestling; intramural: aerobics/Nautilus, basketball, cheering, dance squad, dance team, soccer, yoga.
Computers Computers are regularly used in English, mathematics classes.
Contact Mr. Mark Johnson, Vice Principal/Director of Curriculum. 213-261-7124. Fax: 213-261-9474. E-mail: heymrj@salesianmustangs.com.

BISHOP STANG HIGH SCHOOL

500 Slocum Road
North Dartmouth, Massachusetts 02747-2999

Head of School: Mrs. Theresa E. Dougall

General Information Coeducational day college-preparatory, arts, business, religious studies, and technology school, affiliated with Roman Catholic Church. Grades 9–12. Founded: 1959. Setting: suburban. Nearest major city is New Bedford. 8-acre campus. 1 building on campus. Approved or accredited by New England Association of Schools and Colleges and Massachusetts Department of Education. Endowment: $2 million. Total enrollment: 816. Upper school average class size: 25. Upper school faculty-student ratio: 1:14.
Upper School Student Profile Grade 9: 218 students (105 boys, 113 girls); Grade 10: 205 students (105 boys, 100 girls); Grade 11: 196 students (93 boys, 103 girls); Grade 12: 197 students (94 boys, 103 girls). 80% of students are Roman Catholic.
Faculty School total: 60. In upper school: 22 men, 38 women; 23 have advanced degrees.
Subjects Offered 3-dimensional design, advanced biology, algebra, American history, American literature, anatomy and physiology, art, biochemistry, bioethics, biology, biology-AP, calculus, calculus-AP, campus ministry, Catholic belief and practice, chemistry, chemistry-AP, chorus, church history, communications, community service, computer science, concert band, criminal justice, criminology, death and loss, driver education, ecology, English, English literature, English-AP, environmental science, fine arts, French, geometry, government/civics, health, history, history of the Catholic Church, instrumental music, introduction to theater, Latin, Life of Christ, marine biology, marketing, mathematics, mechanical drawing, media production, modern European history-AP, moral theology, music, oceanography, photography, physical education, physics, physics-AP, physiology, Portuguese, prayer/spirituality, psychology, psychology-AP, religion, religious studies, science, social

science, social studies, sociology, Spanish, study skills, technical drawing, theater arts, trigonometry, Web authoring, world history, world literature, writing, yearbook.
Graduation Requirements Arts and fine arts (art, music, dance, drama), business skills (includes word processing), computer science, English, foreign language, mathematics, physical education (includes health), religion (includes Bible studies and theology), science, social science, social studies (includes history). Community service is required.
Special Academic Programs Advanced Placement exam preparation; honors section; study at local college for college credit; remedial reading and/or remedial writing; remedial math; programs in English, mathematics, general development for dyslexic students.
College Admission Counseling 203 students graduated in 2008; 198 went to college, including Bridgewater State College; Northeastern University; Providence College; Suffolk University; University of Massachusetts Dartmouth; University of Rhode Island. Other: 5 went to work. Mean SAT critical reading: 562, mean SAT math: 535, mean SAT writing: 561, mean combined SAT: 1651.
Student Life Upper grades have uniform requirement, student council, honor system. Discipline rests equally with students and faculty. Attendance at religious services is required.
Summer Programs Enrichment, computer instruction programs offered; session focuses on computer and math enrichment; held on campus; accepts boys and girls; not open to students from other schools. 15 students usually enrolled. 2009 schedule: July to July.
Tuition and Aid Day student tuition: $7150. Tuition installment plan (FACTS Tuition Payment Plan, monthly payment plans). Merit scholarship grants, need-based scholarship grants available. In 2008–09, 25% of upper-school students received aid; total upper-school merit-scholarship money awarded: $12,500. Total amount of financial aid awarded in 2008–09: $504,000.
Admissions Traditional secondary-level entrance grade is 9. For fall 2008, 345 students applied for upper-level admission, 287 were accepted, 211 enrolled. SLEP; Woodcock Johnson Writing Sample and STS, Diocese Test required. Deadline for receipt of application materials: none. No application fee required. On-campus interview recommended.
Athletics Interscholastic: aquatics (boys, girls), baseball (b), basketball (b,g), cheering (g), cross-country running (b,g), diving (b,g), field hockey (g), football (b), golf (b,g), ice hockey (b), lacrosse (b,g), soccer (b,g), softball (g), swimming and diving (b,g), tennis (b,g), track and field (b,g), volleyball (g), winter (indoor) track (b,g); intramural: fitness (b,g); coed interscholastic: indoor track & field, sailing; coed intramural: backpacking, bicycling, canoeing/kayaking, climbing, hiking/backpacking, kayaking, outdoor activities, outdoor adventure, physical training, rock climbing, sailing, skiing (downhill), snowboarding, strength & conditioning, wall climbing, weight lifting, weight training. 10 coaches, 1 athletic trainer.
Computers Computer network features include on-campus library services, online commercial services, Internet access, wireless campus network, Internet filtering or blocking technology. Campus intranet and computer access in designated common areas are available to students. The school has a published electronic and media policy.
Contact Mrs. Christine Payette, Admissions Director. 508-996-5602 Ext. 424. Fax: 508-994-6756. E-mail: admits@bishopstang.com. Web site: www.bishopstang.com.

THE BISHOP STRACHAN SCHOOL

298 Lonsdale Road
Toronto, Ontario M4V 1X2, Canada

Head of School: Mrs. Kim Gordon

General Information Girls' boarding and day and distance learning college-preparatory, arts, business, religious studies, and technology school, affiliated with Anglican Church of Canada. Boarding grades 7–12, day grades PK–12. Distance learning grades 9–12. Founded: 1867. Setting: urban. Students are housed in single-sex dormitories. 7-acre campus. 1 building on campus. Approved or accredited by Canadian Association of Independent Schools, Canadian Educational Standards Institute, The Association of Boarding Schools, and Ontario Department of Education. Affiliate member of National Association of Independent Schools; member of Secondary School Admission Test Board. Language of instruction: English. Endowment: CAN$12 million. Total enrollment: 891. Upper school average class size: 20. Upper school faculty-student ratio: 1:9.
Upper School Student Profile Grade 6: 44 students (44 girls); Grade 7: 82 students (82 girls); Grade 8: 100 students (100 girls); Grade 9: 118 students (118 girls); Grade 10: 123 students (123 girls); Grade 11: 115 students (115 girls); Grade 12: 105 students (105 girls). 16% of students are boarding students. 90% are province residents. 6 provinces are represented in upper school student body. 10% are international students. International students from Bahamas, China, Ghana, Nepal, Republic of Korea, and United States; 14 other countries represented in student body. 30% of students are members of Anglican Church of Canada.
Faculty School total: 111. In upper school: 20 men, 61 women; 30 have advanced degrees; 5 reside on campus.
Subjects Offered Accounting, algebra, American history, aquatics, art, art history, biology, biology-AP, business, business skills, calculus, calculus-AP, Canadian geography, Canadian history, career and personal planning, career education, chemistry, chemistry-AP, computer programming, computer science, computer science-AP, creative writing, drama, earth science, ecology, economics, English, English language-AP, English literature, English literature-AP, environmental science, ESL, ethics, European history, expository writing, fine arts, French, French language-AP, geography, geometry, government/civics, graphic arts, health, history, Italian, Latin, macroeconomics-AP, Mandarin, mathematics, microeconomics-AP, music, philosophy, physical education, physics, religion, science, social science, social studies, Spanish, Spanish language-AP, statistics-AP, theater, trigonometry, U.S. history-AP, world history.
Graduation Requirements Arts, Canadian geography, Canadian history, career education, civics, English, French, mathematics, physical education (includes health), science, 40 hours of community service, completion of 30 credits from grade 9-12.
Special Academic Programs Advanced Placement exam preparation; honors section; accelerated programs; independent study; term-away projects; study abroad; academic accommodation for the gifted, the musically talented, and the artistically talented; ESL (12 students enrolled).
College Admission Counseling 122 students graduated in 2008; 121 went to college, including Cornell University; McGill University; Queen's University at Kingston; University of Southern California; University of Toronto; Yale University. Other: 1 had other specific plans. Mean SAT critical reading: 609, mean SAT math: 610, mean SAT writing: 599.
Student Life Upper grades have uniform requirement, student council, honor system. Discipline rests primarily with faculty. Attendance at religious services is required.
Summer Programs Enrichment, advancement, ESL, art/fine arts, rigorous outdoor training, computer instruction programs offered; session focuses on ESL, languages, science, math, economics, arts, geography; online courses are available through e-academy; held both on and off campus; held at France and worldwide; accepts boys and girls; open to students from other schools. 200 students usually enrolled. 2009 schedule: July 2 to July 29. Application deadline: June 15.
Tuition and Aid Day student tuition: CAN$22,450; 7-day tuition and room/board: CAN$41,200. Tuition installment plan (monthly payment plans, 3-installment plan). Bursaries, merit scholarship grants available. In 2008–09, 5% of upper-school students received aid; total upper-school merit-scholarship money awarded: CAN$95,000. Total amount of financial aid awarded in 2008–09: CAN$500,000.
Admissions Traditional secondary-level entrance grade is 9. For fall 2008, 351 students applied for upper-level admission, 159 were accepted, 115 enrolled. Admissions testing, SSAT or WISC III or TOEFL required. Deadline for receipt of application materials: none. Application fee required: CAN$150. Interview required.
Athletics Interscholastic: alpine skiing (girls), aquatics (g), archery (g), artistic gym (g), badminton (g), basketball (g), cross-country running (g), curling (g), field hockey (g), golf (g), gymnastics (g), hockey (g), ice hockey (g), nordic skiing (g), rhythmic gymnastics (g), skiing (downhill) (g), soccer (g), softball (g), swimming and diving (g), tennis (g), track and field (g), volleyball (g); intramural: aerobics (g), aerobics/dance (g), backpacking (g), ballet (g), canoeing/kayaking (g), climbing (g), cooperative games (g), crew (g), dance (g), fencing (g), fitness (g), hiking/backpacking (g), kayaking (g), life saving (g), modern dance (g), outdoor adventure (g), outdoor education (g), outdoor recreation (g), physical training (g), rappelling (g), rock climbing (g), ropes courses (g), rowing (g), running (g), self defense (g), synchronized swimming (g), wall climbing (g), weight training (g), wilderness survival (g), yoga (g). 11 PE instructors.
Computers Computers are regularly used in art, business studies, career education, career exploration, economics, English, foreign language, geography, history, mathematics, music, science classes. Computer network features include on-campus library services, Internet access, wireless campus network, Internet filtering or blocking technology, laptop program (grades 9-12). Campus intranet and student e-mail accounts are available to students.
Contact Ms. Suzanne Ranson, Admissions Assistant. 416-483-4325 Ext. 1220. Fax: 416-481-5632. E-mail: admissions@bss.on.ca. Web site: www.bss.on.ca.

See Close-Up on page 684.

BISHOP VEROT HIGH SCHOOL

5598 Sunrise Drive
Fort Myers, Florida 33919-1799

Head of School: Fr. J. Christian Beretta, OSFS

General Information Coeducational day college-preparatory, arts, religious studies, technology, Honors, and Advanced Placement school, affiliated with Roman Catholic Church. Grades 9–12. Founded: 1962. Setting: suburban. Nearest major city is Tampa. 20-acre campus. 8 buildings on campus. Approved or accredited by Southern Association of Colleges and Schools and Florida Department of Education. Endowment: $1.5 million. Total enrollment: 728. Upper school average class size: 26. Upper school faculty-student ratio: 1:18.
Upper School Student Profile Grade 9: 192 students (91 boys, 101 girls); Grade 10: 182 students (100 boys, 82 girls); Grade 11: 188 students (95 boys, 93 girls); Grade 12: 166 students (90 boys, 76 girls). 65% of students are Roman Catholic.
Faculty School total: 52. In upper school: 21 men, 31 women; 25 have advanced degrees.
Subjects Offered Acting, Advanced Placement courses, algebra, American government, American government-AP, American history, American history-AP, American literature, American sign language, art, athletic training, band, Bible studies, biology, biology-AP, British literature, British literature (honors), broadcast journalism, business, calculus-AP, ceramics, chemistry, chemistry-AP, choir, church history, comparative government and politics-AP, computer studies, creative writing,

drafting, drama, drawing, driver education, economics, electives, English, English literature and composition-AP, English literature-AP, environmental science, European history-AP, fine arts, foreign language, French, geometry, government, government-AP, health education, history, history of the Catholic Church, history-AP, honors algebra, honors English, honors geometry, honors U.S. history, honors world history, industrial arts, integrated mathematics, journalism, law studies, marine biology, mathematics, newspaper, painting, personal fitness, photography, physical education, physics, physics-AP, pottery, practical arts, pre-algebra, pre-calculus, probability and statistics, SAT preparation, Spanish, Spanish language-AP, speech, studio art, television, theater, U.S. history, U.S. history-AP, Web site design, weightlifting, world history, world history-AP, writing, yearbook.

Graduation Requirements Algebra, American government, arts and fine arts (art, music, dance, drama), biology, British literature, chemistry, economics, electives, English, English composition, foreign language, geometry, government, health education, mathematics, moral theology, personal fitness, physics, practical arts, psychology, religion (includes Bible studies and theology), science, sociology, U.S. history, world history, world literature.

Special Academic Programs Advanced Placement exam preparation; honors section; study at local college for college credit; remedial math.

College Admission Counseling 179 students graduated in 2008; 176 went to college, including Florida Gulf Coast University; Florida State University; University of Central Florida; University of Florida; University of Miami; University of Notre Dame. Other: 1 went to work, 2 entered military service. Mean SAT critical reading: 529, mean SAT math: 535, mean SAT writing: 511, mean combined SAT: 1575, mean composite ACT: 23. 21% scored over 600 on SAT critical reading, 26% scored over 600 on SAT math, 17% scored over 600 on SAT writing, 21% scored over 26 on composite ACT.

Student Life Upper grades have specified standards of dress, student council, honor system. Discipline rests primarily with faculty. Attendance at religious services is required.

Summer Programs Enrichment, sports, rigorous outdoor training programs offered; session focuses on elective credit, enrichment; held on campus; accepts boys and girls; not open to students from other schools. 100 students usually enrolled.

Tuition and Aid Day student tuition: $9225. Tuition installment plan (FACTS Tuition Payment Plan, monthly payment plans, individually arranged payment plans, quarterly payment plan). Merit scholarship grants, need-based scholarship grants, tuition reduction for contributing Catholic families available. In 2008–09, 25% of upper-school students received aid; total upper-school merit-scholarship money awarded: $86,000. Total amount of financial aid awarded in 2008–09: $1,057,000.

Admissions Traditional secondary-level entrance grade is 9. High School Placement Test required. Deadline for receipt of application materials: none. Application fee required: $50.

Athletics Interscholastic: baseball (boys), basketball (b,g), cheering (g), cross-country running (b,g), diving (b,g), football (b), golf (b,g), soccer (b,g), softball (g), swimming and diving (b,g), tennis (b,g), track and field (b,g), volleyball (g), weight lifting (b,g); intramural: ice hockey (b), weight training (b,g); coed interscholastic: lacrosse, strength & conditioning; coed intramural: lacrosse. 2 PE instructors, 20 coaches, 1 athletic trainer.

Computers Computers are regularly used in career exploration, college planning, drafting, information technology, library, media production, newspaper, photography, publications, SAT preparation, technology, vocational-technical courses, Web site design, yearbook classes. Computer network features include on-campus library services, Internet access, Internet filtering or blocking technology. Students grades are available online. The school has a published electronic and media policy.

Contact Ms. Deanna Custer, Director of Admission. 239-274-6760. Fax: 239-274-6795. E-mail: deanna.custer@bvhs.org. Web site: www.bvhs.org.

BISHOP WALSH MIDDLE HIGH SCHOOL

700 Bishop Walsh Road
Cumberland, Maryland 21502

Head of School: Mr. Samuel Torres

General Information Coeducational day college-preparatory school, affiliated with Roman Catholic Church. Grades PK–12. Founded: 1966. Setting: small town. 10-acre campus. 1 building on campus. Approved or accredited by National Catholic Education Association and Maryland Department of Education. Total enrollment: 428. Upper school average class size: 20. Upper school faculty-student ratio: 1:15.

Upper School Student Profile Grade 9: 46 students (13 boys, 33 girls); Grade 10: 58 students (28 boys, 30 girls); Grade 11: 47 students (25 boys, 22 girls); Grade 12: 47 students (25 boys, 22 girls). 70% of students are Roman Catholic.

Faculty School total: 45. In upper school: 8 men, 12 women; 15 have advanced degrees.

Special Academic Programs Advanced Placement exam preparation; honors section; remedial reading and/or remedial writing; programs in English, general development for dyslexic students.

College Admission Counseling 52 students graduated in 2008; all went to college, including Frostburg State University; West Virginia University.

Student Life Upper grades have uniform requirement, student council. Discipline rests primarily with faculty. Attendance at religious services is required.

Summer Programs Enrichment, advancement programs offered; session focuses on European History, Spanish, Math; held on campus; accepts boys and girls; not open to students from other schools. 40 students usually enrolled. 2009 schedule: June 15 to July 15. Application deadline: May 29.

Tuition and Aid Day student tuition: $4900. Tuition installment plan (FACTS Tuition Payment Plan, monthly payment plans). Need-based scholarship grants available. In 2008–09, 50% of upper-school students received aid. Total amount of financial aid awarded in 2008–09: $30,000.

Admissions Traditional secondary-level entrance grade is 9. Deadline for receipt of application materials: August 31. Application fee required: $30. Interview required.

Athletics Interscholastic: baseball (boys), basketball (b,g), bowling (b,g), cheering (g), football (b), golf (b), soccer (b,g), softball (g), volleyball (g). 1 PE instructor, 8 coaches, 1 athletic trainer.

Computers Computer network features include Internet access. Students grades are available online. The school has a published electronic and media policy.

Contact Mrs. Erin Dale, Administrative Assistant. 301-724-5360 Ext. 104. Fax: 301-722-0555. E-mail: edale@bishopwalsh.org. Web site: www.bishopwalsh.org.

BLAIR ACADEMY

2 Park Street
Blairstown, New Jersey 07825

Head of School: T. Chandler Hardwick III

General Information Coeducational boarding and day college-preparatory and arts school, affiliated with Presbyterian Church. Boarding grades 9–PG, day grades 9–12. Founded: 1848. Setting: rural. Nearest major city is New York, NY. Students are housed in single-sex dormitories. 423-acre campus. 42 buildings on campus. Approved or accredited by Middle States Association of Colleges and Schools, New Jersey Association of Independent Schools, The Association of Boarding Schools, and New Jersey Department of Education. Member of National Association of Independent Schools and Secondary School Admission Test Board. Endowment: $61.6 million. Total enrollment: 445. Upper school average class size: 10. Upper school faculty-student ratio: 1:7.

Upper School Student Profile Grade 9: 79 students (40 boys, 39 girls); Grade 10: 116 students (65 boys, 51 girls); Grade 11: 118 students (71 boys, 47 girls); Grade 12: 112 students (68 boys, 44 girls); Postgraduate: 18 students (15 boys, 3 girls). 77% of students are boarding students. 55% are state residents. 22 states are represented in upper school student body. 9% are international students. International students from Dominican Republic, Hong Kong, Japan, Republic of Korea, Taiwan, and Thailand; 16 other countries represented in student body.

Faculty School total: 86. In upper school: 39 men, 27 women; 49 have advanced degrees; 76 reside on campus.

Subjects Offered 3-dimensional art, 3-dimensional design, acting, advanced chemistry, advanced math, Advanced Placement courses, advanced studio art-AP, aerospace science, African history, algebra, American government, American history, American history-AP, American literature, anatomy, architectural drawing, architecture, art, art history, art history-AP, art-AP, Asian studies, astronomy, aviation, biochemistry, biology, biology-AP, biotechnology, calculus, calculus-AP, ceramics, chemistry, chemistry-AP, Chinese, Chinese history, comparative government and politics-AP, computer programming, computer science, computer science-AP, creative writing, dance, drafting, drama, dramatic arts, drawing, drawing and design, driver education, economics, economics and history, economics-AP, English, English language-AP, English literature, English literature-AP, environmental science, environmental science-AP, ethics, European history, European history-AP, expository writing, filmmaking, fine arts, French, French language-AP, geometry, government/civics, health, history, Japanese history, jazz band, jewelry making, Latin, marine biology, marine science, mathematics, mechanical drawing, music, music theory-AP, navigation, painting, philosophy, photography, physical education, physics, physiology, pre-calculus, psychology, religion, Russian studies, science, social studies, Spanish, Spanish language-AP, statistics-AP, theater, theology, world history, world literature, writing.

Graduation Requirements Arts and fine arts (art, music, dance, drama), English, foreign language, mathematics, physical education (includes health), religion (includes Bible studies and theology), science, social studies (includes history).

Special Academic Programs 21 Advanced Placement exams for which test preparation is offered; honors section; independent study; study abroad.

College Admission Counseling 140 students graduated in 2008; all went to college, including Boston University; Bowdoin College; Brown University; New York University; University of Michigan; Villanova University. Mean SAT critical reading: 610, mean SAT math: 620, mean SAT writing: 620.

Student Life Upper grades have specified standards of dress, student council, honor system. Discipline rests equally with students and faculty. Attendance at religious services is required.

Tuition and Aid Day student tuition: $30,000; 7-day tuition and room/board: $41,600. Tuition installment plan (Key Tuition Payment Plan, monthly payment plans). Need-based scholarship grants, need-based loans available. In 2008–09, 32% of upper-school students received aid. Total amount of financial aid awarded in 2008–09: $3,524,500.

Admissions Traditional secondary-level entrance grade is 9. For fall 2008, 659 students applied for upper-level admission, 268 were accepted, 146 enrolled. SSAT or TOEFL required. Deadline for receipt of application materials: February 1. Application fee required: $50. On-campus interview required.

Athletics Interscholastic: alpine skiing (boys, girls), baseball (b), basketball (b,g), crew (b,g), cross-country running (b,g), field hockey (g), football (b), golf (b,g), ice hockey (b), indoor track (b,g), lacrosse (b,g), rowing (b,g), running (b,g), skiing (downhill) (b,g), soccer (b,g), softball (g), squash (b,g), swimming and diving (b,g), tennis (b,g), track and field (b,g), winter (indoor) track (b,g), wrestling (b); intramural: basketball (b,g), crew (b,g), ice hockey (g), rowing (b,g); coed intramural: aerobics, aerobics/Nautilus, alpine skiing, bicycling, canoeing/kayaking, dance, equestrian sports, fitness, flag football, golf, horseback riding, kayaking, life saving, modern dance, mountain biking, outdoor skills, physical fitness, physical training, skiing (downhill), snowboarding, soccer, squash, swimming and diving, tennis, weight lifting, weight training, yoga. 3 athletic trainers.

Computers Computers are regularly used in English, graphic design, history, information technology, mathematics, media production, science, video film production classes. Computer network features include on-campus library services, online commercial services, Internet access, Internet filtering or blocking technology. Campus intranet, student e-mail accounts, and computer access in designated common areas are available to students. The school has a published electronic and media policy.

Contact Ryan M. Pagotto, Dean of Admissions. 800-462-5247. Fax: 908-362-7975. E-mail: admissions@blair.edu. Web site: www.blair.edu.

ANNOUNCEMENT FROM THE SCHOOL In its 161st year, Blair continues to offer a superior college-preparatory program while holding firmly to its tradition of being a supportive, family-oriented community with a dynamic classroom experience. In this environment, students build greater self-esteem, learn to advocate for themselves, and develop the leadership skills necessary for success in college and beyond. In the athletic and artistic arenas, Blair students enhance their potential and awaken new interests with the guidance and support of outstanding coaches, directors, and teachers. Traditional sports, plus golf, skiing, squash, ice hockey, and crew are offered. In addition, Blair boasts a notable fine and performing arts program featuring theatrical productions, instrumental and choral ensembles, dance, architecture, video production, and numerous other arts offerings. The Academy is located in the foothills of the Pocono Mountains, with easy access to New York City and Philadelphia. Blair's recent capital campaign provided funding for several major improvements to the physical plant, including a new turf field, track, and tennis house; an arts center; a technology center; a new library; a new girls' dormitory; and renovations to existing dorms. Currently, the school is building a student activities and athletic center to complement its existing facilities.

See Close-Up on page 686.

THE BLAKE SCHOOL

110 Blake Road South
Hopkins, Minnesota 55343

Head of School: John C. Gulla

General Information Coeducational day college-preparatory school. Grades PK–12. Founded: 1900. Setting: urban. Nearest major city is Minneapolis. 5-acre campus. 1 building on campus. Approved or accredited by Independent Schools Association of the Central States. Member of National Association of Independent Schools. Endowment: $50 million. Total enrollment: 1,390. Upper school average class size: 16. Upper school faculty-student ratio: 1:8.

Upper School Student Profile Grade 9: 132 students (58 boys, 74 girls); Grade 10: 125 students (68 boys, 57 girls); Grade 11: 130 students (61 boys, 69 girls); Grade 12: 125 students (58 boys, 67 girls).

Faculty School total: 136. In upper school: 26 men, 30 women; 36 have advanced degrees.

Subjects Offered Advanced chemistry, African-American literature, algebra, American history, American literature, art, Asian studies, astronomy, band, biology, biology-AP, calculus, calculus-AP, ceramics, chemistry, chemistry-AP, Chinese, choir, chorus, communication arts, communications, computer math, creative writing, debate, design, drama, drawing, economics, English, English literature, English-AP, ethics, European history, European history-AP, fine arts, French, French language-AP, French literature-AP, geology, geometry, German-AP, government/civics, history, instrumental music, jazz ensemble, journalism, Latin, mathematics, multicultural studies, music, painting, performing arts, photography, physical education, physics, physics-AP, policy and value, political science, printmaking, psychology, religion, science, sculpture, senior project, social psychology, social studies, Spanish, Spanish language-AP, speech, statistics, statistics-AP, studio art, studio art-AP, theater, theater arts, trigonometry, visual and performing arts, vocal ensemble, women's studies, world cultures, world history, world literature, writing.

Graduation Requirements Arts and fine arts (art, music, dance, drama), communications, English, foreign language, mathematics, physical education (includes health), science, social studies (includes history), assembly speech.

Special Academic Programs 14 Advanced Placement exams for which test preparation is offered; term-away projects; study at local college for college credit; study abroad.

College Admission Counseling 124 students graduated in 2008; 121 went to college, including Boston College; Carleton College; Columbia College; Georgetown University; University of Colorado at Boulder; University of Wisconsin–Madison. Other: 2 entered military service, 1 had other specific plans. Median SAT critical reading: 640, median SAT math: 650, median SAT writing: 640, median combined SAT: 1930, median composite ACT: 28. 71% scored over 600 on SAT critical reading, 76% scored over 600 on SAT math, 69% scored over 600 on SAT writing, 70% scored over 26 on composite ACT.

Student Life Upper grades have specified standards of dress, student council, honor system. Discipline rests primarily with faculty.

Summer Programs Remediation, enrichment, advancement, sports programs offered; session focuses on broad-based program including academics, arts, and sports; held both on and off campus; held at local lakes and beaches, museums, other locations; accepts boys and girls; open to students from other schools. 250 students usually enrolled. 2009 schedule: June 15 to August 1.

Tuition and Aid Day student tuition: $20,800. Tuition installment plan (local bank-arranged plan). Need-based scholarship grants, need-based loans, academic year low-interest loans, tuition remission for children of faculty available. In 2008–09, 22% of upper-school students received aid. Total amount of financial aid awarded in 2008–09: $1,741,745.

Admissions Traditional secondary-level entrance grade is 9. For fall 2008, 77 students applied for upper-level admission, 49 were accepted, 40 enrolled. ERB or WISC/Woodcock-Johnson required. Deadline for receipt of application materials: January 31. Application fee required: $100. On-campus interview required.

Athletics Interscholastic: alpine skiing (boys, girls), baseball (b), basketball (b,g), cross-country running (b,g), diving (b,g), football (b), golf (b,g), ice hockey (b,g), lacrosse (b,g), skiing (cross-country) (b,g), skiing (downhill) (b,g), soccer (b,g), softball (g), swimming and diving (b,g); coed interscholastic: fencing. 1 PE instructor, 45 coaches, 1 athletic trainer.

Computers Computers are regularly used in art, English, foreign language, history, language development, library, mathematics, media arts, music, newspaper, photography, science, social studies, writing, yearbook classes. Computer network features include on-campus library services, online commercial services, Internet access, wireless campus network, Internet filtering or blocking technology, laptops. Campus intranet, student e-mail accounts, and computer access in designated common areas are available to students. Students grades are available online. The school has a published electronic and media policy.

Contact Adaline Shinkle, Director of Admissions. 952-988-3420. Fax: 952-988-3455. E-mail: ashinkle@blakeschool.org. Web site: www.blakeschool.org.

BLANCHET SCHOOL

4373 Market Street NE
Salem, Oregon 97305

Head of School: Mr. Robert Weber

General Information Coeducational day college-preparatory, arts, and religious studies school, affiliated with Roman Catholic Church. Grades 7–12. Founded: 1995. Setting: suburban. 22-acre campus. 2 buildings on campus. Approved or accredited by National Catholic Education Association, Northwest Association of Schools and Colleges, and Oregon Department of Education. Endowment: $114,000. Total enrollment: 392. Upper school average class size: 18. Upper school faculty-student ratio: 1:18.

Upper School Student Profile Grade 9: 66 students (25 boys, 41 girls); Grade 10: 72 students (34 boys, 38 girls); Grade 11: 58 students (26 boys, 32 girls); Grade 12: 56 students (30 boys, 26 girls). 75% of students are Roman Catholic.

Faculty School total: 25. In upper school: 11 men, 13 women; 19 have advanced degrees.

Subjects Offered 1968, American history-AP, American literature, anatomy and physiology, art, band, Basic programming, biology, British literature, calculus, campus ministry, career and personal planning, Catholic belief and practice, chemistry, choir, civics, college counseling, college placement, comparative religion, composition, computer programming, CPR, critical thinking, critical writing, economics, economics and history, English, English literature, English literature and composition-AP, ESL, European history-AP, first aid, fitness, French, global science, global studies, government, health, health and safety, health and wellness, health education, history of the Catholic Church, history-AP, lab science, library studies, mathematics, music, physical fitness, physical science, physics, pre-algebra, pre-calculus, publications, religion, religion and culture, SAT/ACT preparation, Spanish, Spanish language-AP, U.S. government, U.S. history, weight training, world history, World War II, yearbook.

Graduation Requirements Applied arts, arts and fine arts (art, music, dance, drama), electives, English, foreign language, mathematics, physical education (includes health), religion (includes Bible studies and theology), science, social studies (includes history), 20 hours of community service for each year in attendance.

Special Academic Programs 2 Advanced Placement exams for which test preparation is offered; honors section; independent study; study at local college for college credit; special instructional classes for deaf students; ESL (6 students enrolled).

College Admission Counseling 52 students graduated in 2008; 49 went to college, including Chemeketa Community College; Oregon Institute of Technology; Oregon State University; University of Oregon; University of Portland; Willamette University. Other: 3 had other specific plans. Median SAT critical reading: 544, median SAT math: 588, median SAT writing: 554, median composite ACT: 26.

Student Life Upper grades have specified standards of dress, student council. Discipline rests equally with students and faculty. Attendance at religious services is required.
Summer Programs Remediation, enrichment, sports programs offered; session focuses on preparation for the next academic year, athletic training; held on campus; accepts boys and girls; open to students from other schools. 75 students usually enrolled. 2009 schedule: June 13 to August 17.
Tuition and Aid Day student tuition: $6490. Tuition installment plan (FACTS Tuition Payment Plan). Tuition reduction for siblings, merit scholarship grants, need-based scholarship grants, paying campus jobs available. In 2008–09, 33% of upper-school students received aid; total upper-school merit-scholarship money awarded: $21,000. Total amount of financial aid awarded in 2008–09: $235,000.
Admissions Traditional secondary-level entrance grade is 9. For fall 2008, 93 students applied for upper-level admission, 90 were accepted, 87 enrolled. Deadline for receipt of application materials: none. Application fee required: $100. Interview recommended.
Athletics Interscholastic: baseball (boys), basketball (b,g), cross-country running (b,g), football (b), golf (b,g), soccer (b,g), softball (g), swimming and diving (b,g), tennis (b,g), track and field (b,g), volleyball (g); intramural: weight training (b,g). 2 PE instructors.
Computers Computer resources include on-campus library services, online commercial services, Internet access, Internet filtering or blocking technology. The school has a published electronic and media policy.
Contact Mrs. Cathy McClaughry, Admissions Office. 503-391-2639. Fax: 503-399-1259. E-mail: cathy@blanchetcatholicschool.com. Web site: www.blanchetcatholicschool.com.

BLESSED TRINITY HIGH SCHOOL

11320 Woodstock Road
Roswell, Georgia 30075

Head of School: Mr. Frank Moore

General Information Coeducational day college-preparatory school, affiliated with Roman Catholic Church. Grades 9–12. Founded: 2000. Setting: suburban. Nearest major city is Atlanta. 68-acre campus. 2 buildings on campus. Approved or accredited by Georgia Independent School Association, Southern Association of Colleges and Schools, and Georgia Department of Education. Upper school average class size: 19. Upper school faculty-student ratio: 1:12.
Upper School Student Profile 87% of students are Roman Catholic.
Faculty School total: 67. In upper school: 28 men, 39 women; 36 have advanced degrees.
College Admission Counseling Colleges students went to include Auburn University; Georgia College & State University; Georgia Institute of Technology; University of Georgia.
Student Life Upper grades have uniform requirement, student council. Discipline rests primarily with faculty. Attendance at religious services is required.
Tuition and Aid Tuition installment plan (FACTS Tuition Payment Plan). Need-based scholarship grants available.
Admissions Traditional secondary-level entrance grade is 9. SSAT required. Deadline for receipt of application materials: January 30. Application fee required: $75.
Athletics Interscholastic: baseball (boys), basketball (b,g), cheering (g), cross-country running (b,g), dance (b,g), dance team (g), football (b), golf (b,g), lacrosse (b,g), soccer (b,g), softball (g), strength & conditioning (b,g), swimming and diving (b,g), tennis (b,g), track and field (b,g), volleyball (g), wrestling (b). 4 PE instructors, 1 athletic trainer.
Contact Mr. Brian Marks, Director of Admissions. 678-277-0983 Ext. 502. Fax: 678-277-9756. E-mail: bmarks@btcatholic.org. Web site: www.btcatholic.org.

BLUE MOUNTAIN ACADEMY

2363 Mountain Road
Hamburg, Pennsylvania 19526

Head of School: Mr. Rob S. Gettys

General Information Coeducational boarding and day college-preparatory, religious studies, leadership, and aviation school, affiliated with Seventh-day Adventists. Grades 9–12. Founded: 1955. Setting: rural. Students are housed in single-sex dormitories. 735-acre campus. 6 buildings on campus. Approved or accredited by Middle States Association of Colleges and Schools. Total enrollment: 226. Upper school average class size: 23. Upper school faculty-student ratio: 1:9.
Upper School Student Profile Grade 9: 37 students (19 boys, 18 girls); Grade 10: 54 students (18 boys, 36 girls); Grade 11: 69 students (37 boys, 32 girls); Grade 12: 72 students (31 boys, 41 girls). 76% of students are boarding students. 46% are state residents. 13 states are represented in upper school student body. 5% are international students. International students from Bermuda, Republic of Korea, and Saudi Arabia; 2 other countries represented in student body. 85% of students are Seventh-day Adventists.
Faculty School total: 23. In upper school: 15 men, 8 women; 14 have advanced degrees; 20 reside on campus.
Subjects Offered Accounting, Advanced Placement courses, algebra, anatomy and physiology, art, auto body, auto mechanics, band, bell choir, Bible, biology, business mathematics, chemistry, chemistry-AP, choir, computer applications, desktop publishing, digital photography, English, English literature and composition-AP, fiber arts, flight instruction, food and nutrition, French, geometry, golf, gymnastics, health, home economics, honors English, honors world history, leadership, life science, music appreciation, music theory, organ, physical education, physics, piano, pre-algebra, pre-calculus, psychology, sewing, Spanish, U.S. government, U.S. history, U.S. history-AP, weightlifting, Western civilization, world history.
Graduation Requirements Algebra, arts, Bible, biology, computer applications, electives, English, foreign language, mathematics, physical education (includes health), science, social science, U.S. government, U.S. history, work-study, work study credit per semester enrolled.
Special Academic Programs 3 Advanced Placement exams for which test preparation is offered; honors section; accelerated programs; study at local college for college credit; academic accommodation for the musically talented; remedial reading and/or remedial writing; remedial math; programs in English, mathematics, general development for dyslexic students.
College Admission Counseling 71 students graduated in 2008; 65 went to college, including Andrews University; Columbia Union College; La Sierra University; Pacific Union College; Southern Adventist University. Other: 5 went to work, 1 had other specific plans.
Student Life Upper grades have specified standards of dress, student council, honor system. Discipline rests primarily with faculty. Attendance at religious services is required.
Tuition and Aid Day student tuition: $10,180; 7-day tuition and room/board: $16,160. Tuition reduction for siblings, need-based scholarship grants, need-based loans, middle-income loans, paying campus jobs available. In 2008–09, 45% of upper-school students received aid. Total amount of financial aid awarded in 2008–09: $265,000.
Admissions Traditional secondary-level entrance grade is 9. Math Placement Exam required. Deadline for receipt of application materials: none. Application fee required: $15. Interview recommended.
Athletics Intramural: basketball (boys, girls), flag football (b,g), soccer (b,g), softball (b,g), volleyball (b,g); coed intramural: basketball, flag football, gymnastics, soccer, softball, volleyball. 1 PE instructor.
Computers Computers are regularly used in accounting, desktop publishing, history, keyboarding, mathematics, photography, psychology, religion, science, yearbook classes. Computer network features include on-campus library services, Internet access. Student e-mail accounts and computer access in designated common areas are available to students. Students grades are available online. The school has a published electronic and media policy.
Contact Mrs. Diana Engen, Registrar. 610-562-2291. Fax: 610-562-8050. E-mail: dianae@bma.us. Web site: www.bma.us.

BLUEPRINT EDUCATION

5651 W Talavi Boulevard
Ste 170
Glendale, Arizona 85306

Head of School: Beth Collins

General Information Distance learning only college-preparatory, general academic, technology, and distance learning school. Distance learning grades 7–12. Founded: 1969. Approved or accredited by Arizona Association of Independent Schools, CITA (Commission on International and Trans-Regional Accreditation), North Central Association of Colleges and Schools, and Arizona Department of Education.
Faculty School total: 9. In upper school: 3 men, 6 women; 8 have advanced degrees.
Subjects Offered Algebra, American government, American history, art, art appreciation, art history, auto mechanics, auto shop, biology, British literature, calculus, career and personal planning, career education, career experience, career exploration, career planning, careers, chemistry, child development, communication skills, communications, computer applications, computer education, computer literacy, computer science, consumer economics, decision making skills, drawing, driver education, earth science, economics, English, English composition, entrepreneurship, foreign language, general business, geometry, government, health and wellness, health education, human development, independent study, interpersonal skills, life management skills, mathematics, music theory, painting, parenting, personal development, physical education, physical fitness, physics, pre-algebra, psychology, reading, reading/study skills, short story, single survival, Spanish, speech, speech communications, statistics, study skills, travel, trigonometry, vocational skills, weight training, weightlifting, wellness, wilderness education, work experience, work-study, world geography, world history.
Graduation Requirements Arts and fine arts (art, music, dance, drama), computers, English, foreign language, geography, mathematics, science, social studies (includes history), speech.
Special Academic Programs Accelerated programs; independent study; academic accommodation for the musically talented and the artistically talented; remedial reading and/or remedial writing; remedial math.

College Admission Counseling Colleges students went to include Arizona State University; Northern Arizona University; Pima Community College; The University of Arizona.
Student Life Upper grades have honor system.
Summer Programs Remediation, advancement programs offered; session focuses on remediation and advancement; held off campus; held at various locations for independent study; accepts boys and girls; open to students from other schools.
Admissions Deadline for receipt of application materials: none. Application fee required: $39.
Computers Computers are regularly used in all academic classes. Computer resources include Internet access. Students grades are available online. The school has a published electronic and media policy.
Contact Jennifer Blackstone, Assistant Superintendent for Distance Learning. 800-426-4952 Ext. 4820. Fax: 602-943-9700. E-mail: jenniferb@blueprinteducation.org. Web site: www.blueprinteducation.org.

THE BLUE RIDGE SCHOOL

273 Mayo Drive
St. George, Virginia 22935
Head of School: Dr. David A. Bouton

General Information Boys' boarding college-preparatory, arts, and technology school, affiliated with Episcopal Church. Grades 9–12. Founded: 1909. Setting: rural. Nearest major city is Charlottesville. Students are housed in single-sex dormitories. 750-acre campus. 11 buildings on campus. Approved or accredited by National Association of Episcopal Schools, Southern Association of Colleges and Schools, The Association of Boarding Schools, Virginia Association of Independent Schools, and Virginia Department of Education. Member of National Association of Independent Schools and Secondary School Admission Test Board. Endowment: $12 million. Total enrollment: 195. Upper school average class size: 9. Upper school faculty-student ratio: 1:6.
Upper School Student Profile Grade 9: 38 students (38 boys); Grade 10: 53 students (53 boys); Grade 11: 51 students (51 boys); Grade 12: 53 students (53 boys). 100% of students are boarding students. 32% are state residents. 19 states are represented in upper school student body. 26% are international students. International students from China, Croatia, and Taiwan; 11 other countries represented in student body.
Faculty School total: 35. In upper school: 29 men, 6 women; 16 have advanced degrees; 27 reside on campus.
Subjects Offered Algebra, American history, American literature, anatomy, art, astronomy, biology, calculus, chemistry, choir, computer applications, computer programming, computer science, decision making skills, discrete mathematics, drama, driver education, English, environmental science, ESL, European history, French, geometry, guitar, health, honors English, honors geometry, honors U.S. history, integrated science, keyboarding, leadership training, mathematics, music, music history, outdoor education, physics, pre-algebra, pre-calculus, Spanish, trigonometry, U.S. history, world history, world literature, writing, yearbook.
Graduation Requirements Algebra, American history, American literature, biology, decision making skills, English, foreign language, geometry, leadership training, mathematics, physical education (includes health), science, social studies (includes history).
Special Academic Programs Honors section; remedial reading and/or remedial writing; special instructional classes for programs for students with learning disabilities, Attention Deficit Disorder and dyslexia; ESL (14 students enrolled).
College Admission Counseling 43 students graduated in 2008; all went to college, including Hampden-Sydney College; Lynchburg College; University of South Carolina; Virginia Polytechnic Institute and State University.
Student Life Upper grades have specified standards of dress, student council, honor system. Discipline rests primarily with faculty. Attendance at religious services is required.
Tuition and Aid 7-day tuition and room/board: $31,900. Tuition installment plan (Insured Tuition Payment Plan, Academic Management Services Plan). Merit scholarship grants, need-based scholarship grants, paying campus jobs available. In 2008–09, 37% of upper-school students received aid; total upper-school merit-scholarship money awarded: $92,000. Total amount of financial aid awarded in 2008–09: $1,195,505.
Admissions For fall 2008, 165 students applied for upper-level admission, 133 were accepted, 95 enrolled. Any standardized test required. Deadline for receipt of application materials: none. Application fee required: $50. On-campus interview required.
Athletics Interscholastic: baseball, basketball, cross-country running, football, golf, indoor soccer, indoor track, lacrosse, mountain biking, soccer, tennis, track and field, volleyball, wrestling; intramural: alpine skiing, backpacking, bicycling, canoeing/kayaking, climbing, cooperative games, fishing, fitness, hiking/backpacking, kayaking, life saving, mountain biking, mountaineering, outdoor activities, physical training, rafting, rappelling, rock climbing, ropes courses, skiing (downhill), snowboarding, strength & conditioning, ultimate Frisbee, wall climbing, weight lifting, weight training, wilderness, wilderness survival. 1 coach, 1 athletic trainer.
Computers Computers are regularly used in English, ESL, foreign language, mathematics, science, study skills, word processing, writing, yearbook classes. Computer network features include on-campus library services, online commercial services, Internet access, wireless campus network, Internet filtering or blocking technology. Student e-mail accounts are available to students. Students grades are available online. The school has a published electronic and media policy.
Contact Mr. James H. Miller III, Assistant Director of Admissions. 434-985-2811 Ext. 143. Fax: 434-992-0536. E-mail: jmiller@blueridgeschool.com. Web site: www.blueridgeschool.com.

ANNOUNCEMENT FROM THE SCHOOL Blue Ridge School will freeze tuition for families who pay their portion of the tuition in full prior to August 1 of each school year. The School also earmarks a portion of its financial aid budget for scholarships for middle-income families.

See Close-Up on page 688.

BODWELL HIGH SCHOOL

955 Harbourside Drive
North Vancouver, British Columbia V7P 3S4, Canada
Head of School: Mr. Stephen Smith

General Information Coeducational boarding and day college-preparatory, arts, business, and technology school. Grades 8–12. Founded: 1991. Setting: suburban. Students are housed in single-sex by floor dormitories. 2-acre campus. 2 buildings on campus. Approved or accredited by British Columbia Department of Education. Language of instruction: English. Endowment: CAN$18 million. Total enrollment: 365. Upper school average class size: 20. Upper school faculty-student ratio: 1:15.
Upper School Student Profile 30% of students are boarding students. 25% are province residents. 8 provinces are represented in upper school student body. 75% are international students. International students from Hong Kong, Japan, Mexico, Republic of Korea, Singapore, and Taiwan; 30 other countries represented in student body.
Faculty School total: 30. In upper school: 17 men, 13 women; 11 have advanced degrees; 2 reside on campus.
Subjects Offered 3-dimensional art, art, art-AP, band, biology, calculus, chemistry, choral music, communications, composition, computer applications, economics, English, entrepreneurship, geography, history, information technology, Japanese, Mandarin, mathematics, physical education, physics, psychology, social studies.
Graduation Requirements British Columbia Ministry of Education requirements.
Special Academic Programs Advanced Placement exam preparation; accelerated programs; academic accommodation for the gifted; ESL (90 students enrolled).
College Admission Counseling 130 students graduated in 2008; 120 went to college, including Simon Fraser University; The University of British Columbia; University of Alberta; University of Calgary; University of Toronto. Other: 10 had other specific plans.
Student Life Upper grades have uniform requirement, student council, honor system. Discipline rests primarily with faculty.
Summer Programs Advancement, ESL, sports, art/fine arts, computer instruction programs offered; session focuses on ESL and activities; held both on and off campus; held at University of British Columbia, University of Victoria, and Whistler; accepts boys and girls; open to students from other schools. 500 students usually enrolled. 2009 schedule: July 5 to August 15. Application deadline: May 15.
Tuition and Aid Day student tuition: CAN$11,200; 7-day tuition and room/board: CAN$26,800. Guaranteed tuition plan. Tuition installment plan (individually arranged payment plans). Merit scholarship grants available. In 2008–09, 2% of upper-school students received aid; total upper-school merit-scholarship money awarded: CAN$50,000.
Admissions Traditional secondary-level entrance grade is 10. For fall 2008, 170 students applied for upper-level admission, 130 were accepted, 130 enrolled. Deadline for receipt of application materials: none. Application fee required: CAN$200. Interview recommended.
Athletics Interscholastic: aquatics (boys, girls), baseball (b), basketball (b,g), cross-country running (b,g), soccer (b), swimming and diving (b,g), volleyball (g); intramural: aquatics (b,g), badminton (b,g), baseball (b,g), basketball (b,g), cheering (g), fitness (b,g), floor hockey (b,g), hiking/backpacking (b,g), ice skating (b,g), indoor soccer (b), kayaking (b), martial arts (b), mountain biking (b,g), outdoor activities (b,g), outdoor education (b,g), running (b,g), skateboarding (b,g), skiing (downhill) (b,g), snowboarding (b,g), snowshoeing (b,g), soccer (b), swimming and diving (b,g), table tennis (b,g), tennis (b,g), track and field (b,g), triathlon (b), volleyball (b,g), wilderness (b,g); coed interscholastic: aerobics/dance, aquatics, backpacking, badminton, ball hockey, bicycling, blading, bowling, canoeing/kayaking, fitness, floor hockey, swimming and diving; coed intramural: aquatics, badminton, bicycling, bowling, canoeing/kayaking, climbing, cross-country running, dance, fishing, fitness, floor hockey, fly fishing, golf, hiking/backpacking, ice skating, indoor soccer, kayaking, martial arts, mountain biking, outdoor activities, outdoor education, rock climbing, roller blading, running, skateboarding, skiing (downhill), snowboarding, snowshoeing, swimming and diving, table tennis, tennis, track and field, volleyball, wilderness. 2 PE instructors, 5 coaches.
Computers Computers are regularly used in all academic classes. Computer network features include on-campus library services, Internet access, wireless campus network, Internet filtering or blocking technology. Student e-mail accounts are available to students. The school has a published electronic and media policy.

Bodwell High School

Contact Ms. Jennifer Chen, Admissions Officer. 604-924-5066 Ext. 118. Fax: 604-924-5058. E-mail: office@bodwell.edu. Web site: www.bodwell.edu.

THE BOLLES SCHOOL

7400 San Jose Boulevard
Jacksonville, Florida 32217-3499

Head of School: John E. Trainer, Jr., PhD

General Information Coeducational boarding and day college-preparatory and arts school. Boarding grades 7–PG, day grades PK–PG. Founded: 1933. Setting: suburban. Students are housed in single-sex dormitories. 52-acre campus. 8 buildings on campus. Approved or accredited by Florida Council of Independent Schools, Southern Association of Colleges and Schools, Southern Association of Independent Schools, The Association of Boarding Schools, and Florida Department of Education. Member of National Association of Independent Schools and Secondary School Admission Test Board. Endowment: $11.4 million. Total enrollment: 1,732. Upper school average class size: 17. Upper school faculty-student ratio: 1:10.

Upper School Student Profile Grade 9: 186 students (93 boys, 93 girls); Grade 10: 202 students (117 boys, 85 girls); Grade 11: 203 students (115 boys, 88 girls); Grade 12: 201 students (104 boys, 97 girls). 10% of students are boarding students. 92% are state residents. 8 states are represented in upper school student body. 6% are international students. International students from China, Germany, Japan, Mexico, Republic of Korea, and Saudi Arabia; 9 other countries represented in student body.

Faculty School total: 175. In upper school: 38 men, 41 women; 49 have advanced degrees; 6 reside on campus.

Subjects Offered Acting, algebra, American Civil War, American government, American government-AP, American history, American literature, anatomy, art, art history, band, biology, biology-AP, British literature, calculus, calculus-AP, ceramics, chemistry, chemistry-AP, Chinese, chorus, comparative government and politics-AP, composition, computer applications, computer science, computer science-AP, contemporary history, creative writing, dance, data analysis, design, directing, drama, drawing, driver education, earth science, ecology, economics, English, environmental science, ESL, European history, fine arts, fitness, French, geography, geometry, German, government/civics, health, history, history-AP, humanities, Japanese, journalism, Latin, life management skills, life skills, literature, marine science, mathematics, Middle Eastern history, modern European history-AP, music, music theory, mythology, neurobiology, painting, performing arts, philosophy, photography, physical education, physics, physics-AP, portfolio art, pre-algebra, pre-calculus, programming, psychology, public speaking, publications, science, sculpture, social science, social studies, Spanish, statistics, statistics-AP, studio art, theater, visual arts, Web site design, weight training, Western civilization, world culture, world history.

Graduation Requirements Arts and fine arts (art, music, dance, drama), English, foreign language, mathematics, physical education (includes health), science, social studies (includes history).

Special Academic Programs Advanced Placement exam preparation; honors section; independent study; term-away projects; ESL (26 students enrolled).

College Admission Counseling 182 students graduated in 2008; all went to college, including Auburn University; Florida State University; The University of Alabama; University of Florida; University of Georgia; University of North Florida. 47% scored over 600 on SAT critical reading, 52% scored over 600 on SAT math, 51% scored over 600 on SAT writing, 48% scored over 1800 on combined SAT, 45% scored over 26 on composite ACT.

Student Life Upper grades have specified standards of dress, student council, honor system. Discipline rests primarily with faculty.

Summer Programs Enrichment, ESL, art/fine arts, computer instruction programs offered; held on campus; accepts boys and girls; open to students from other schools. 150 students usually enrolled. 2009 schedule: June 8 to July 24.

Tuition and Aid Day student tuition: $16,800; 7-day tuition and room/board: $36,000. Tuition installment plan (major increment payment plan, 10-month plan, June payment plan). Need-based scholarship grants, Faculty tuition remission available. In 2008–09, 12% of upper-school students received aid. Total amount of financial aid awarded in 2008–09: $1,763,724.

Admissions Traditional secondary-level entrance grade is 9. For fall 2008, 287 students applied for upper-level admission, 117 were accepted, 76 enrolled. ISEE required. Deadline for receipt of application materials: none. Application fee required: $45. Interview required.

Athletics Interscholastic: baseball (boys), basketball (b,g), cheering (g), crew (b,g), cross-country running (b,g), dance (b,g), diving (b,g), football (b), golf (b,g), lacrosse (b), soccer (b,g), softball (g), swimming and diving (b,g), tennis (b,g), track and field (b,g), volleyball (b,g), weight lifting (b), wrestling (b). 2 PE instructors, 5 coaches, 1 athletic trainer.

Computers Computers are regularly used in all academic classes. Computer network features include on-campus library services, online commercial services, Internet access, wireless campus network, Internet filtering or blocking technology. Computer access in designated common areas is available to students. Students grades are available online. The school has a published electronic and media policy.

Contact Mark I. Frampton, Director of Upper School and Boarding Admission. 904-256-5032. Fax: 904-739-9929. E-mail: framptonm@bolles.org. Web site: www.bolles.org.

See Close-Up on page 690.

BOSTON COLLEGE HIGH SCHOOL

150 Morrissey Boulevard
Boston, Massachusetts 02125

Head of School: Mr. William Kemeza

General Information Boys' day college-preparatory, arts, and religious studies school, affiliated with Roman Catholic Church. Grades 7–12. Founded: 1863. Setting: urban. 40-acre campus. 5 buildings on campus. Approved or accredited by Association of Independent Schools in New England, Jesuit Secondary Education Association, National Catholic Education Association, New England Association of Schools and Colleges, and Massachusetts Department of Education. Member of Secondary School Admission Test Board. Endowment: $40 million. Total enrollment: 1,543. Upper school average class size: 23. Upper school faculty-student ratio: 1:13.

Upper School Student Profile Grade 9: 306 students (306 boys); Grade 10: 313 students (313 boys); Grade 11: 357 students (357 boys); Grade 12: 329 students (329 boys). 85% of students are Roman Catholic.

Faculty School total: 143. In upper school: 69 men, 50 women; 87 have advanced degrees.

Subjects Offered Acting, Advanced Placement courses, algebra, American government-AP, American history, American history-AP, American literature, anatomy and physiology, Ancient Greek, art, art history, astronomy, band, Bible studies, biology, biology-AP, British literature, British literature (honors), calculus, calculus-AP, calligraphy, chemistry, chemistry-AP, Chinese, choir, Christian doctrine, composition-AP, computer math, computer programming, computer science, computer science-AP, creative writing, digital photography, drafting, drama, dramatic arts, driver education, ecology, economics, economics-AP, electronics, English, English language and composition-AP, English literature, English literature and composition-AP, environmental science, environmental science-AP, environmental studies, ethics, European history, European history-AP, film, fine arts, forensic science, French, French language-AP, French literature-AP, geometry, German, government and politics-AP, government/civics, grammar, graphic design, Greek, guitar, health, health and wellness, history, Homeric Greek, integrated science, Japanese, Latin, Latin-AP, marine biology, mathematics, modern world history, music, music theory-AP, physics, physics-AP, pre-calculus, printmaking, probability and statistics, psychology, religion, science, social justice, social studies, Spanish, Spanish language-AP, Spanish literature-AP, statistics-AP, trigonometry, U.S. history-AP, world history, world literature.

Graduation Requirements Arts and fine arts (art, music, dance, drama), English, foreign language, mathematics, religion (includes Bible studies and theology), science, social studies (includes history), 150+ hours of community service over 4 years.

Special Academic Programs 24 Advanced Placement exams for which test preparation is offered; honors section; independent study; term-away projects; study abroad; academic accommodation for the gifted; special instructional classes for blind students; ESL (10 students enrolled).

College Admission Counseling 269 students graduated in 2008; 256 went to college, including Bentley University; Boston College; College of the Holy Cross; Fordham University; Loyola College in Maryland. Other: 4 entered a postgraduate year. Mean SAT critical reading: 582, mean SAT math: 598, mean SAT writing: 591, mean combined SAT: 1771.

Student Life Upper grades have specified standards of dress, student council. Discipline rests primarily with faculty.

Summer Programs Remediation, enrichment, advancement, sports, art/fine arts, computer instruction programs offered; session focuses on Enrichment/Advancement in academics and athletics; held on campus; accepts boys and girls; open to students from other schools. 100 students usually enrolled. 2009 schedule: June 28 to July 30. Application deadline: none.

Tuition and Aid Day student tuition: $13,850. Tuition installment plan (monthly payment plans). Merit scholarship grants, need-based scholarship grants, need-based loans available. In 2008–09, 35% of upper-school students received aid; total upper-school merit-scholarship money awarded: $140,000. Total amount of financial aid awarded in 2008–09: $3,100,000.

Admissions Traditional secondary-level entrance grade is 9. For fall 2008, 750 students applied for upper-level admission, 529 were accepted, 315 enrolled. High School Placement Test or SSAT required. Deadline for receipt of application materials: December 21. No application fee required.

Athletics Interscholastic: baseball, basketball, cross-country running, football, golf, ice hockey, lacrosse, rugby, sailing, skiing (downhill), soccer, swimming and diving, tennis, track and field, volleyball, winter (indoor) track; intramural: basketball, bicycling, crew, flag football, Frisbee, hiking/backpacking, tennis. 42 coaches, 1 athletic trainer.

Computers Computers are regularly used in English, foreign language, mathematics, religious studies, science, social science classes. Computer network features include on-campus library services, online commercial services, Internet access, wireless campus network, Internet filtering or blocking technology. Student e-mail accounts and computer access in designated common areas are available to students. Students grades are available online.

Contact Mr. Michael Brennan, Director of Admissions. 617-474-5010. Fax: 617-474-5015. E-mail: brennan@bchigh.edu. Web site: www.bchigh.edu/.

BOSTON TRINITY ACADEMY

17 Hale Street
Boston, Massachusetts 02136

Head of School: Dr. Timothy P Wiens

General Information Coeducational day college-preparatory school, affiliated with Christian faith. Grades 6–12. Founded: 2002. Setting: urban. 5-acre campus. 1 building on campus. Approved or accredited by Association of Independent Schools in New England, New England Association of Schools and Colleges, and Massachusetts Department of Education. Total enrollment: 202. Upper school average class size: 16. Upper school faculty-student ratio: 1:9.

Upper School Student Profile Grade 6: 13 students (6 boys, 7 girls); Grade 7: 23 students (11 boys, 12 girls); Grade 8: 18 students (10 boys, 8 girls); Grade 9: 33 students (16 boys, 17 girls); Grade 10: 47 students (29 boys, 18 girls); Grade 11: 32 students (13 boys, 19 girls); Grade 12: 36 students (20 boys, 16 girls). 70% of students are Christian faith.

Faculty School total: 27. In upper school: 10 men, 15 women; 17 have advanced degrees.

Subjects Offered 20th century history, 20th century physics, 20th century world history, advanced biology, advanced math, African American studies, algebra, American history-AP, American literature-AP, anatomy and physiology, Ancient Greek, ancient history, art, art history, basketball, Bible, biology-AP, British literature-AP, calculus-AP, chemistry, choir, civil rights, drama performance, English, English language and composition-AP, European history-AP, French, geometry, Greek, New Testament, participation in sports, performing arts, physics, pre-algebra, pre-calculus, Spanish, transition mathematics, U.S. history-AP.

Graduation Requirements All students must take four advanced placement courses to graduate, All seniors write a thesis for Senior Synthesis: Christianity and Culture. They then defend in front of a panel of college professors.

Special Academic Programs Study at local college for college credit; ESL (6 students enrolled).

College Admission Counseling 17 students graduated in 2008; all went to college, including Dartmouth College; Gordon College; McGill University; Occidental College; The Johns Hopkins University; University of Pennsylvania.

Student Life Upper grades have uniform requirement, student council, honor system. Discipline rests primarily with faculty. Attendance at religious services is required.

Summer Programs Advancement programs offered; session focuses on math; held on campus; accepts boys and girls; open to students from other schools. 14 students usually enrolled. 2009 schedule: June 15 to July 5. Application deadline: none.

Tuition and Aid Day student tuition: $12,200. Tuition installment plan (FACTS Tuition Payment Plan). Need-based scholarship grants available. In 2008–09, 60% of upper-school students received aid. Total amount of financial aid awarded in 2008–09: $900,000.

Admissions Traditional secondary-level entrance grade is 9. For fall 2008, 82 students applied for upper-level admission, 40 were accepted, 26 enrolled. ISEE or SSAT required. Deadline for receipt of application materials: February 15. Application fee required: $50. Interview required.

Athletics Interscholastic: basketball (boys, girls), crew (b,g), cross-country running (b), lacrosse (b,g), soccer (b,g), tennis (g), ultimate Frisbee (b,g), wrestling (b). 1 coach.

Computers Computer network features include on-campus library services, Internet access, wireless campus network, Internet filtering or blocking technology. Campus intranet and computer access in designated common areas are available to students. Students grades are available online. The school has a published electronic and media policy.

Contact Mrs. Susan Yem, Assistant Director of Admission. 617-364-3700 Ext. 219. Fax: 617-364-3800. E-mail: syem@bostontrinity.org. Web site: www.bostontrinity.org.

BOSTON UNIVERSITY ACADEMY

One University Road
Boston, Massachusetts 02215

Head of School: Mr. James Berkman

General Information Coeducational day college-preparatory and arts school. Grades 9–12. Founded: 1993. Setting: urban. 132-acre campus. 1 building on campus. Approved or accredited by Association of Independent Schools in New England, New England Association of Schools and Colleges, and Massachusetts Department of Education. Member of National Association of Independent Schools and Secondary School Admission Test Board. Total enrollment: 156. Upper school average class size: 12. Upper school faculty-student ratio: 1:9.

Upper School Student Profile Grade 9: 42 students (24 boys, 18 girls); Grade 10: 40 students (19 boys, 21 girls); Grade 11: 35 students (22 boys, 13 girls); Grade 12: 39 students (18 boys, 21 girls).

Faculty School total: 19. In upper school: 11 men, 6 women; 14 have advanced degrees.

Subjects Offered Advanced math, algebra, American history, American literature, ancient history, art, art history, biology, calculus, chemistry, Chinese, classical studies, college counseling, community service, computer programming, drama, English, English literature, European history, French, geometry, German, Greek, Hebrew, history, Italian, Japanese, Latin, music, physical education, physics, robotics, Russian, sculpture, senior project, Spanish, statistics, theater, trigonometry, writing.

Graduation Requirements Arts and fine arts (art, music, dance, drama), chemistry, English, Greek, history, Latin, mathematics, physical education (includes health), physics, two-semester senior thesis project. Community service is required.

Special Academic Programs Honors section; accelerated programs; independent study; study at local college for college credit; academic accommodation for the gifted.

College Admission Counseling 33 students graduated in 2008; all went to college, including Boston University; Brandeis University; Case Western Reserve University; Massachusetts Institute of Technology; McGill University; Princeton University. 100% scored over 600 on SAT critical reading, 100% scored over 600 on SAT math, 100% scored over 600 on SAT writing.

Student Life Upper grades have student council, honor system. Discipline rests equally with students and faculty.

Tuition and Aid Day student tuition: $27,887. Tuition installment plan (Insured Tuition Payment Plan, Academic Management Services Plan, monthly payment plans). Merit scholarship grants, need-based scholarship grants available. In 2008–09, 29% of upper-school students received aid; total upper-school merit-scholarship money awarded: $24,500. Total amount of financial aid awarded in 2008–09: $773,507.

Admissions Traditional secondary-level entrance grade is 9. For fall 2008, 146 students applied for upper-level admission, 94 were accepted, 49 enrolled. PSAT or SSAT required. Deadline for receipt of application materials: January 31. Application fee required: $45. On-campus interview required.

Athletics Interscholastic: basketball (boys, girls), crew (b,g); coed interscholastic: cross-country running, fencing, sailing, soccer, tennis, ultimate Frisbee; coed intramural: dance, fitness. 10 PE instructors, 7 coaches.

Computers Computers are regularly used in art, English, foreign language, history, mathematics, science classes. Computer network features include on-campus library services, online commercial services, Internet access, Internet filtering or blocking technology, internal electronic bulletin board system. Student e-mail accounts are available to students. Students grades are available online. The school has a published electronic and media policy.

Contact Ms. Abby Walsh, Interim Assistant Director of Admission. 617-358-2493. Fax: 617-353-8999. E-mail: abby_walsh@buacademy.org. Web site: www.buacademy.org.

ANNOUNCEMENT FROM THE SCHOOL Boston University Academy provides an exceptional education for students with genuine intellectual curiosity, strong academic abilities, and a diversity of interests. Located on the Boston University campus, the Academy offers 155 students in grades 9 through 12 a "ceilingless" educational experience, one in which students' zeal for learning takes them as far as they are capable. Small class sizes and close relationships with faculty members allow Academy students to pursue their passions and nurture their talents. At the Academy, ambitious students find a community that supports and celebrates their growth, not only as thinkers, but also as individuals. A classically based core curriculum serves as a foundation for the critical thinking and inquiry skills needed for an in-depth study of the humanities and sciences. For the first two years, Academy students take courses in traditional disciplines—English, mathematics, science, history, the visual and performing arts, and physical education—in addition to studying either Latin or ancient Greek. Juniors and seniors continue to take courses offered by the Academy in addition to enrolling in courses at Boston University. Students regularly complete up to twelve courses (40 college credits) from the University's undergraduate curriculum prior to graduation; students take as many as two University classes a semester during their junior year and as many as four classes each semester as seniors. Each senior also has the opportunity to work alongside a university professor on a yearlong independent research project. The Academy specializes in giving students the intellectual stimulation they crave—along with the social, recreational, artistic, athletic, leadership, and personal growth opportunities they desire. Popular student groups include, but are not limited to, Art Club, Ballroom Dancing, Chamber Orchestra, Chorus, Drama Club, Environmental Club, Jazz Band, Literary Magazine, Math Club, Model UN, Robotics Team, Science Team, Student Council, Student Newspaper, and Yearbook.

BOYD-BUCHANAN SCHOOL

4626 Bonnieway Drive
Chattanooga, Tennessee 37411

Head of School: Lanny Witt

General Information Coeducational day college-preparatory and religious studies school, affiliated with Church of Christ. Grades K4–12. Founded: 1952. Setting: urban. 40-acre campus. 6 buildings on campus. Approved or accredited by National Christian School Association, Southern Association of Colleges and Schools, Tennessee Association of Independent Schools, and Tennessee Department of Education. Endowment: $3 million. Total enrollment: 878. Upper school average class size: 20. Upper school faculty-student ratio: 1:14.

Upper School Student Profile Grade 9: 74 students (31 boys, 43 girls); Grade 10: 61 students (27 boys, 34 girls); Grade 11: 83 students (52 boys, 31 girls); Grade 12: 62 students (27 boys, 35 girls). 40% of students are members of Church of Christ.
Faculty School total: 74. In upper school: 12 men, 34 women; 17 have advanced degrees.
Subjects Offered ACT preparation, Advanced Placement courses, algebra, American government, American history, American studies, art, band, Bible, biology, biology-AP, calculus, calculus-AP, chemistry, chemistry-AP, choir, choral music, chorus, computer applications, computer programming, concert choir, contemporary issues, contemporary problems, data processing, desktop publishing, ecology, economics, English, English composition, English language-AP, English literature, English literature and composition-AP, fitness, French, French-AP, geometry, government, health and wellness, honors algebra, honors English, honors geometry, integrated arts, jazz band, journalism, library assistant, music appreciation, music theory, physical science, physics, pre-algebra, pre-calculus, psychology, SAT/ACT preparation, sociology, Spanish, Spanish-AP, statistics and probability, theater arts, trigonometry, U.S. history, U.S. history-AP, Web site design, wellness, world geography, world history, yearbook.
Graduation Requirements Arts and fine arts (art, music, dance, drama), Bible, electives, English, foreign language, health and wellness, mathematics, physical education (includes health), science, social sciences.
Special Academic Programs 8 Advanced Placement exams for which test preparation is offered; honors section.
College Admission Counseling 95 students graduated in 2008; all went to college, including Chattanooga State Technical Community College; Lipscomb University; Middle Tennessee State University; Tennessee Technological University; The University of Tennessee; The University of Tennessee at Chattanooga.
Student Life Upper grades have uniform requirement, student council, honor system. Discipline rests primarily with faculty. Attendance at religious services is required.
Summer Programs Remediation, enrichment, sports programs offered; session focuses on Sports & Enrichment; held on campus; accepts boys and girls; open to students from other schools. 150 students usually enrolled. 2009 schedule: June 1 to July 31. Application deadline: June 1.
Tuition and Aid Day student tuition: $5804–$7990. Tuition installment plan (Tuition Bank). Tuition reduction for siblings, need-based scholarship grants, paying campus jobs available. In 2008–09, 4% of upper-school students received aid. Total amount of financial aid awarded in 2008–09: $80,000.
Admissions Traditional secondary-level entrance grade is 9. For fall 2008, 27 students applied for upper-level admission, 15 were accepted, 12 enrolled. Wide Range Achievement Test required. Deadline for receipt of application materials: none. Application fee required: $25. Interview required.
Athletics Interscholastic: baseball (boys), basketball (b,g), cheering (g), cross-country running (b,g), football (b), golf (b,g), soccer (b,g), softball (g), swimming and diving (b,g), tennis (b,g), volleyball (g), wrestling (b). 3 PE instructors, 18 coaches, 1 athletic trainer.
Computers Computers are regularly used in creative writing, data processing, desktop publishing, journalism, keyboarding, newspaper, programming, study skills, technology, Web site design, word processing, writing, yearbook classes. Computer network features include on-campus library services, online commercial services, Internet access, wireless campus network, Internet filtering or blocking technology. Campus intranet and computer access in designated common areas are available to students. Students grades are available online. The school has a published electronic and media policy.
Contact Charlotte H. White, Director of Admissions. 423-629-7610 Ext. 249. Fax: 423-508-2218. E-mail: cwhite@bbschool.org. Web site: www.bbschool.org.

BOYLAN CENTRAL CATHOLIC HIGH SCHOOL

4000 Saint Francis Drive
Rockford, Illinois 61103-1699

Head of School: Rev. Paul Lipinski

General Information Coeducational day and distance learning college-preparatory, general academic, arts, business, vocational, religious studies, bilingual studies, and technology school, affiliated with Roman Catholic Church. Grades 9–12. Distance learning grades 9–12. Founded: 1960. Setting: urban. Nearest major city is Chicago. 60-acre campus. 3 buildings on campus. Approved or accredited by National Catholic Education Association, North Central Association of Colleges and Schools, and Illinois Department of Education. Endowment: $3 million. Total enrollment: 1,263. Upper school average class size: 24. Upper school faculty-student ratio: 1:14.
Upper School Student Profile Grade 9: 346 students (171 boys, 175 girls); Grade 10: 331 students (168 boys, 163 girls); Grade 11: 273 students (140 boys, 133 girls); Grade 12: 313 students (141 boys, 172 girls). 87% of students are Roman Catholic.
Faculty School total: 91. In upper school: 34 men, 56 women; 60 have advanced degrees.
Subjects Offered 20th century history, 3-dimensional art, accounting, ACT preparation, acting, advanced computer applications, Advanced Placement courses, advanced studio art-AP, algebra, American history, American history-AP, American literature-AP, analysis and differential calculus, analytic geometry, anatomy and physiology, architectural drawing, architecture, art, art history, art history-AP, art-AP, athletics, auto mechanics, band, biology, bookkeeping, botany, British literature, British literature (honors), business, business education, business law, calculus, calculus-AP, career education, career exploration, career planning, Catholic belief and practice, cheerleading, chemistry, chemistry-AP, choir, chorus, Christian and Hebrew scripture, Christian doctrine, Christian ethics, church history, college counseling, communications, comparative religion, composition-AP, computer keyboarding, computer multimedia, computer-aided design, concert band, concert choir, consumer economics, consumer education, consumer law, consumer mathematics, contemporary history, contemporary issues, contemporary studies, creative writing, critical thinking, culinary arts, desktop publishing, drafting, drama, dramatic arts, earth science, English, English language-AP, English literature-AP, English/composition-AP, environmental science, European history, European history-AP, family and consumer science, family living, fashion, fiction, finite math, foods, French, French as a second language, French literature-AP, French AP, freshman foundations, general math, geography, geometry, German, graphics, guitar, health, health education, history of music, illustration, industrial technology, information processing, integrated science, jazz band, library assistant, marketing, music appreciation, music composition, music theory, physical science, physics, physics-AP, pre-algebra, pre-calculus, psychology, psychology-AP, religion, senior composition, Spanish, statistics, strings, studio art, swimming, trigonometry, U.S. history, Web authoring, Web site design, wood lab, woodworking, world geography, world history, world literature, writing, yearbook, zoology.
Graduation Requirements Consumer education, English, mathematics, physical education (includes health), religious studies, science, social studies (includes history), fine and applied arts, Community service.
Special Academic Programs 12 Advanced Placement exams for which test preparation is offered; honors section; independent study; study at local college for college credit; academic accommodation for the gifted, the musically talented, and the artistically talented; remedial reading and/or remedial writing; remedial math; programs in general development for dyslexic students; special instructional classes for deaf students, blind students.
College Admission Counseling 317 students graduated in 2008; 307 went to college, including Illinois State University; Loyola University Chicago; Marquette University; Northern Illinois University; The University of Iowa; University of Illinois at Urbana–Champaign. Other: 6 went to work, 4 entered military service.
Student Life Upper grades have uniform requirement, student council. Discipline rests primarily with faculty. Attendance at religious services is required.
Summer Programs Enrichment, sports, art/fine arts programs offered; session focuses on Enrichment; held on campus; accepts boys and girls; open to students from other schools. 150 students usually enrolled.
Tuition and Aid Day student tuition: $4800. Tuition installment plan (monthly payment plans, individually arranged payment plans, full-year or semester payment plan). Tuition reduction for siblings, need-based scholarship grants, paying campus jobs available. In 2008–09, 100% of upper-school students received aid. Total amount of financial aid awarded in 2008–09: $387,263.
Admissions Traditional secondary-level entrance grade is 9. For fall 2008, 346 students applied for upper-level admission, 346 were accepted, 346 enrolled. ETS HSPT (closed) required. Deadline for receipt of application materials: none. Application fee required: $75. Interview required.
Athletics Interscholastic: aerobics/dance (girls), baseball (b), basketball (b,g), bowling (b,g), cheering (g), cross-country running (b,g), dance team (g), diving (b,g), football (b), golf (b,g), ice hockey (b), soccer (b,g), softball (g), swimming and diving (b,g), tennis (b,g), track and field (b,g), volleyball (g), wrestling (b); intramural: aerobics (g), archery (b,g), fitness (b,g), golf (b,g), outdoor education (b,g), physical fitness (b,g), physical training (b,g), rowing (b,g), running (b,g), strength & conditioning (b,g), track and field (b,g), volleyball (b,g), weight training (b,g); coed intramural: dance. 6 PE instructors, 1 coach.
Computers Computers are regularly used in all academic, architecture, business applications, computer applications, desktop publishing, drawing and design, keyboarding, photography, publications, technical drawing, video film production, Web site design, word processing, yearbook classes. Computer resources include on-campus library services, Internet access, Internet filtering or blocking technology. Campus intranet and computer access in designated common areas are available to students. The school has a published electronic and media policy.
Contact Mr. Dennis Hiemenz, Assistant Principal. 815-877-0531 Ext. 227. Fax: 815-877-2544. E-mail: Dhiemenz@boylan.org. Web site: www.boylan.org.

THE BOYS' LATIN SCHOOL OF MARYLAND

822 West Lake Avenue
Baltimore, Maryland 21210

Head of School: Mr. Christopher J. Post

General Information Boys' day college-preparatory, arts, and technology school. Grades K–12. Founded: 1844. Setting: suburban. 41-acre campus. 4 buildings on campus. Approved or accredited by Association of Independent Maryland Schools and Maryland Department of Education. Member of National Association of Independent Schools. Endowment: $30 million. Total enrollment: 650. Upper school average class size: 15. Upper school faculty-student ratio: 1:8.
Upper School Student Profile Grade 9: 67 students (67 boys); Grade 10: 75 students (75 boys); Grade 11: 81 students (81 boys); Grade 12: 68 students (68 boys).
Faculty School total: 95. In upper school: 26 men, 13 women; 19 have advanced degrees.

Subjects Offered Advanced computer applications, Advanced Placement courses, African-American history, algebra, American history, American literature, art, art education, biology, calculus, calculus-AP, chemistry, chemistry-AP, community service, computer math, computer programming, computer science, drama, dramatic arts, ecology, economics, English, English language-AP, English literature, English literature-AP, environmental science, European history, European history-AP, expository writing, film, fine arts, French, geometry, government, government/civics, Greek culture, health education, history of mathematics, history-AP, honors algebra, honors English, honors geometry, honors U.S. history, honors world history, journalism, Latin, marine biology, mathematics, media studies, military history, music, music appreciation, physical education, physics, psychology, science, social studies, sociology, Spanish, theater, trigonometry, world history.

Graduation Requirements Arts and fine arts (art, music, dance, drama), computer science, English, foreign language, mathematics, physical education (includes health), science, social studies (includes history), study skills. Community service is required.

Special Academic Programs Advanced Placement exam preparation; honors section; independent study; term-away projects; academic accommodation for the gifted, the musically talented, and the artistically talented.

College Admission Counseling 60 students graduated in 2008; they went to Elon University; Loyola College in Maryland; Mount St. Mary's University; St. Mary's College of Maryland; University of Maryland, Baltimore County; Virginia Polytechnic Institute and State University. Median SAT critical reading: 520, median SAT math: 550, median SAT writing: 530, median combined SAT: 1590, median composite ACT: 18. 21% scored over 600 on SAT critical reading, 28% scored over 600 on SAT math, 19% scored over 600 on SAT writing, 21% scored over 1800 on combined SAT, 7% scored over 26 on composite ACT.

Student Life Upper grades have specified standards of dress, student council, honor system. Discipline rests primarily with faculty.

Summer Programs Remediation, enrichment, sports programs offered; held on campus; accepts boys and girls; open to students from other schools. 2009 schedule: June 16 to August 15. Application deadline: April 1.

Tuition and Aid Day student tuition: $18,200. Tuition installment plan (Academic Management Services Plan). Need-based scholarship grants, need-based grants available. In 2008–09, 28% of upper-school students received aid. Total amount of financial aid awarded in 2008–09: $1,215,100.

Admissions Traditional secondary-level entrance grade is 9. For fall 2008, 84 students applied for upper-level admission, 56 were accepted, 24 enrolled. ERB, ISEE or Otis-Lennon School Ability Test required. Deadline for receipt of application materials: none. Application fee required: $50. On-campus interview required.

Athletics Interscholastic: baseball, basketball, cross-country running, football, golf, ice hockey, lacrosse, outdoor adventure, outdoor education, physical fitness, physical training, soccer, squash, strength & conditioning, tennis, volleyball, wrestling; intramural: hiking/backpacking. 5 PE instructors, 9 coaches, 2 athletic trainers.

Computers Computers are regularly used in all academic classes. Computer network features include on-campus library services, online commercial services, Internet access, Internet filtering or blocking technology, intranet combining technology, curricular, and research capabilities. The school has a published electronic and media policy.

Contact Mr. James W. Currie Jr., Director of Middle and Upper School Admissions. 410-377-5192 Ext. 1139. Fax: 410-433-2571. E-mail: jcurrie@boyslatinmd.com. Web site: www.boyslatinmd.com.

THE BRANSON SCHOOL

39 Fernhill Avenue
PO Box 887
Ross, California 94957

Head of School: Mr. Thomas Woody Price, EdD

General Information Coeducational day college-preparatory, arts, and technology school. Grades 9–12. Founded: 1916. Setting: suburban. Nearest major city is San Francisco. 18-acre campus. 12 buildings on campus. Approved or accredited by California Association of Independent Schools and Western Association of Schools and Colleges. Member of National Association of Independent Schools and Secondary School Admission Test Board. Endowment: $14 million. Total enrollment: 320. Upper school average class size: 10. Upper school faculty-student ratio: 1:9.

Upper School Student Profile Grade 9: 78 students (39 boys, 39 girls); Grade 10: 83 students (48 boys, 35 girls); Grade 11: 80 students (43 boys, 37 girls); Grade 12: 79 students (49 boys, 30 girls).

Faculty School total: 52. In upper school: 24 men, 21 women; 27 have advanced degrees.

Subjects Offered Algebra, American history, American literature, art, art history, biology, calculus, ceramics, chemistry, community service, creative writing, dance, digital applications, drama, earth science, economics, English, English literature, English-AP, environmental science, European history, fine arts, geometry, government/civics, history, Latin, mathematics, mathematics-AP, music, outdoor education, philosophy, photography, physical education, physics, poetry, science, social science, social studies, Spanish, statistics, theater, trigonometry, world history, world literature.

Graduation Requirements Arts and fine arts (art, music, dance, drama), English, foreign language, mathematics, physical education (includes health), science, social science, social studies (includes history). Community service is required.

Special Academic Programs Advanced Placement exam preparation; honors section; independent study; study abroad.

College Admission Counseling 75 students graduated in 2008; all went to college, including New York University; Princeton University; Stanford University; University of California, Berkeley; University of California, Los Angeles; University of Southern California. Mean SAT critical reading: 646, mean SAT math: 664, mean SAT writing: 671, mean combined SAT: 1981, mean composite ACT: 27.

Student Life Upper grades have student council, honor system. Discipline rests equally with students and faculty.

Summer Programs Enrichment, advancement, art/fine arts, computer instruction programs offered; session focuses on enrichment; held on campus; accepts boys and girls; open to students from other schools. 250 students usually enrolled. 2009 schedule: June 15 to July 30. Application deadline: none.

Tuition and Aid Day student tuition: $31,315. Tuition installment plan (FACTS Tuition Payment Plan, individually arranged payment plans). Need-based scholarship grants available. In 2008–09, 18% of upper-school students received aid. Total amount of financial aid awarded in 2008–09: $1,400,000.

Admissions Traditional secondary-level entrance grade is 9. For fall 2008, 394 students applied for upper-level admission, 126 were accepted, 79 enrolled. ERB, ISEE, SSAT or Star-9 required. Deadline for receipt of application materials: January 15. Application fee required: $100. Interview required.

Athletics Interscholastic: baseball (boys), basketball (b,g), cross-country running (b,g), diving (b), equestrian sports (g), fencing (b,g), golf (b,g), lacrosse (b), sailing (b,g), soccer (b,g), softball (g), swimming and diving (b,g), tennis (b,g); coed interscholastic: crew. 3 PE instructors, 3 coaches.

Computers Computers are regularly used in English, mathematics, music, science classes. Computer network features include on-campus library services, Internet access, wireless campus network. Campus intranet and student e-mail accounts are available to students.

Contact Lisa Neumaier, Associate Director of Admission. 415-454-3612 Ext. 206. Fax: 415-454-4669. E-mail: lisa_neumaier@branson.org. Web site: www.branson.org.

THE BREARLEY SCHOOL

610 East 83rd Street
New York, New York 10028

Head of School: Dr. Stephanie J. Hull

General Information Girls' day college-preparatory school. Grades K–12. Founded: 1884. Setting: urban. 2 buildings on campus. Approved or accredited by New York State Association of Independent Schools. Member of National Association of Independent Schools. Endowment: $114 million. Total enrollment: 690. Upper school average class size: 12. Upper school faculty-student ratio: 1:6.

Upper School Student Profile Grade 9: 65 students (65 girls); Grade 10: 52 students (52 girls); Grade 11: 49 students (49 girls); Grade 12: 46 students (46 girls).

Faculty School total: 134. In upper school: 21 men, 53 women; 56 have advanced degrees.

Subjects Offered 20th century world history, acting, advanced biology, advanced chemistry, African history, African literature, algebra, American history, American literature, Ancient Greek, applied music, art, art history, astronomy, biology, calculus, calculus-AP, chamber groups, chemistry, computer science, contemporary women writers, drama, drawing, English, English literature, environmental science, expository writing, fiction, finite math, French, French language-AP, French literature-AP, geometry, history, history of China and Japan, independent study, Latin, Mandarin, mathematics, modern European history, multimedia design, music, oil painting, painting, physics, political thought, pre-calculus, senior project, Shakespeare, Spanish, statistics, trigonometry, vocal music, water color painting, Web site design, world history.

Graduation Requirements Arts and fine arts (art, music, dance, drama), English, foreign language, history, mathematics, physical education (includes health), science.

Special Academic Programs 16 Advanced Placement exams for which test preparation is offered; independent study; term-away projects; study abroad.

College Admission Counseling 55 students graduated in 2008; all went to college, including Georgetown University; Harvard University; Massachusetts Institute of Technology; Princeton University; Yale University. Median SAT critical reading: 720, median SAT math: 680. 97% scored over 600 on SAT critical reading, 99% scored over 600 on SAT math.

Student Life Upper grades have specified standards of dress, student council. Discipline rests equally with students and faculty.

Tuition and Aid Day student tuition: $33,025. Tuition installment plan (Key Tuition Payment Plan, individually arranged payment plans). Need-based scholarship grants, need-based loans available. In 2008–09, 25% of upper-school students received aid. Total amount of financial aid awarded in 2008–09: $1,344,940.

Admissions For fall 2008, 112 students applied for upper-level admission, 21 were accepted, 13 enrolled. ISEE and school's own exam required. Deadline for receipt of application materials: December 15. Application fee required: $60. On-campus interview required.

Athletics Interscholastic: aquatics, badminton, basketball, cross-country running, field hockey, gymnastics, lacrosse, soccer, softball, squash, swimming and diving, tennis, track and field, volleyball; intramural: aquatics, badminton, basketball, cooperative games, cricket, dance, dance team, field hockey, fitness, gymnastics, jogging, lacrosse, modern dance, physical fitness, soccer, softball, strength & conditioning, swimming and diving, tai chi, team handball, track and field, volleyball, yoga. 13 PE instructors, 3 coaches, 2 athletic trainers.
Computers Computers are regularly used in classics, English, foreign language, history, mathematics, multimedia, music, photography, science, theater arts, Web site design classes. Computer network features include on-campus library services, Internet access, wireless campus network, Britannica Online, EBSCO, SIRS Researcher, ProQuest, JSTOR, ArtStor, AtomicLearning.com (software tutorials), a file server. Student e-mail accounts and computer access in designated common areas are available to students. The school has a published electronic and media policy.
Contact Ms. Joan Kaplan, Director of Middle and Upper School Admission. 212-744-8582. Fax: 212-472-8020. E-mail: admission@brearley.org. Web site: www.brearley.org.

BRECK SCHOOL

123 Ottawa Avenue North
Minneapolis, Minnesota 55422
Head of School: Edward Kim

General Information Coeducational day college-preparatory, arts, and religious studies school, affiliated with Episcopal Church. Grades PK–12. Founded: 1886. Setting: suburban. 53-acre campus. 1 building on campus. Approved or accredited by Independent Schools Association of the Central States. Member of National Association of Independent Schools and Secondary School Admission Test Board. Endowment: $50.6 million. Total enrollment: 1,199. Upper school average class size: 17. Upper school faculty-student ratio: 1:11.
Upper School Student Profile Grade 9: 97 students (44 boys, 53 girls); Grade 10: 109 students (57 boys, 52 girls); Grade 11: 98 students (46 boys, 52 girls); Grade 12: 105 students (53 boys, 52 girls). 10% of students are members of Episcopal Church.
Faculty School total: 120. In upper school: 13 men, 15 women; 21 have advanced degrees.
Subjects Offered Algebra, American history, American literature, art, astronomy, biology, calculus, ceramics, chemistry, Chinese, chorus, community service, computer math, computer programming, creative writing, dance, drama, ecology, economics, English, English literature, environmental science, ethics, European history, expository writing, fine arts, French, geometry, health, history, mathematics, music, orchestra, physical education, physics, religion, science, social studies, Spanish, statistics, theater, theology, trigonometry, world history, world literature, writing.
Graduation Requirements Arts and fine arts (art, music, dance, drama), English, foreign language, mathematics, physical education (includes health), religion (includes Bible studies and theology), science, social studies (includes history), senior speech, May Program. Community service is required.
Special Academic Programs Advanced Placement exam preparation; honors section; independent study; term-away projects; academic accommodation for the gifted, the musically talented, and the artistically talented.
College Admission Counseling 100 students graduated in 2008; all went to college, including Boston College; Hamilton College; The Colorado College; The George Washington University; The University of Iowa; University of Chicago. Mean SAT critical reading: 612, mean SAT math: 603, mean SAT writing: 627, mean combined SAT: 1842, mean composite ACT: 27. 54% scored over 600 on SAT critical reading, 56% scored over 600 on SAT math, 63% scored over 600 on SAT writing, 54% scored over 1800 on combined SAT, 75% scored over 26 on composite ACT.
Student Life Upper grades have specified standards of dress, student council, honor system. Discipline rests equally with students and faculty. Attendance at religious services is required.
Tuition and Aid Day student tuition: $19,240. Tuition installment plan (Key Tuition Payment Plan). Need-based scholarship grants available. In 2008–09, 14% of upper-school students received aid. Total amount of financial aid awarded in 2008–09: $1,049,713.
Admissions Traditional secondary-level entrance grade is 9. For fall 2008, 100 students applied for upper-level admission, 49 were accepted, 32 enrolled. CTP III required. Deadline for receipt of application materials: February 1. Application fee required: $75. On-campus interview required.
Athletics Interscholastic: alpine skiing (boys, girls), baseball (b), basketball (b,g), cross-country running (b,g), diving (b,g), football (b), golf (b,g), gymnastics (g), ice hockey (b,g), lacrosse (b,g), nordic skiing (b,g), skiing (cross-country) (b,g), skiing (downhill) (b,g), soccer (b,g), softball (g), swimming and diving (b,g), tennis (b,g), track and field (b,g), volleyball (g). 6 PE instructors, 82 coaches, 1 athletic trainer.
Computers Computers are regularly used in all classes. Computer network features include on-campus library services, online commercial services, Internet access, wireless campus network, Internet filtering or blocking technology, multimedia imaging, video presentation, student laptop program. Campus intranet and student e-mail accounts are available to students. The school has a published electronic and media policy.
Contact Warner T. James Jr., Director of Admissions. 763-381-8200. Fax: 763-381-8288. E-mail: jim.james@breckschool.org. Web site: www.breckschool.org.

ANNOUNCEMENT FROM THE SCHOOL Breck School is an Episcopal, coeducational, college-preparatory day school enrolling boys and girls in preschool–grade 12. The School uses the cultural and educational resources of the Twin Cities metropolitan area to offer a vigorous college-preparatory curriculum. All divisions of the School have been honored by the U.S. Department of Education. The School was founded in 1886 and named for a pioneer missionary. Today it serves 1,200 students on a beautiful 50-acre campus just west of downtown Minneapolis. Breck believes that economic, religious, racial, and geographic diversity enrich the educational experience for all—a philosophy that is reflected in all educational and administrative policies, including admissions and financial aid. Breck students come from more than sixty communities throughout the Minneapolis–St. Paul metropolitan area. Curricular highlights include Breck's one-to-one laptop program for all students in grades 4–12, advanced research classes in science and history for Upper School students, Chinese or Spanish instruction beginning in kindergarten, and a fully integrated service learning program for all grades that culminates in the Upper School, where all students and faculty members travel to nearby service sites every Wednesday morning. The School's single campus encourages interaction among students at different grade levels, such as first grade/senior buddy pairings and Middle School and kindergarten "bio-buddies" who work together on science projects. Facilities include separate libraries, dining rooms, and commons areas for each division; natural wildlife ponds for year-round science study; and well-equipped spaces for the visual arts, performing arts, and athletics, such as sky-lit art studios, a 456-seat production theater, playing fields, running tracks, a swimming pool, and a large indoor fieldhouse, in addition to a detached ice arena. The spiritual and architectural focus of the campus is the Chapel of the Holy Spirit, which seats 1,300. Financial aid of more than $3 million supports approximately 17.5% of the student body, and the enrollment of students of color exceeds 25%. More than 75% of Breck faculty members hold advanced degrees.

BREHM PREPARATORY SCHOOL

Carbondale, Illinois
See Special Needs Schools section.

BRENAU ACADEMY

500 Washington Street SE
Gainesville, Georgia 30501
Head of School: Mr. Timothy A. Daniel

General Information Girls' boarding and day college-preparatory and arts school. Grades 9–PG. Founded: 1928. Setting: small town. Nearest major city is Atlanta. Students are housed in single-sex dormitories. 56-acre campus. 50 buildings on campus. Approved or accredited by Georgia Independent School Association, Southern Association of Colleges and Schools, Southern Association of Independent Schools, The Association of Boarding Schools, and Georgia Department of Education. Member of National Association of Independent Schools. Endowment: $50 million. Total enrollment: 70. Upper school average class size: 10. Upper school faculty-student ratio: 1:8.
Upper School Student Profile Grade 9: 10 students (10 girls); Grade 10: 20 students (20 girls); Grade 11: 25 students (25 girls); Grade 12: 15 students (15 girls). 80% of students are boarding students. 50% are state residents. 12 states are represented in upper school student body. 15% are international students. International students from Bermuda, China, Mexico, Republic of Korea, Saudi Arabia, and Taiwan; 10 other countries represented in student body.
Faculty School total: 12. In upper school: 3 men, 9 women; 8 have advanced degrees.
Subjects Offered Algebra, American government, American history, American literature, anatomy, ancient world history, art, biology, calculus, chemistry, chorus, civics, college counseling, composition, computer science, creative writing, dance, drama, driver education, economics, English, English composition, English literature, etymology, fine arts, French, geography, geometry, government, government/civics, grammar, health, history, honors English, human anatomy, journalism, mathematics, music, physical education, physics, poetry, pre-calculus, science, social science, social studies, Spanish, theater, trigonometry, world history.
Graduation Requirements Arts and fine arts (art, music, dance, drama), English, foreign language, mathematics, physical education (includes health), science, social science, social studies (includes history).
Special Academic Programs Honors section; accelerated programs; independent study; study at local college for college credit; academic accommodation for the gifted, the musically talented, and the artistically talented; programs in English, mathematics, general development for dyslexic students; special instructional classes for students with learning disabilities and Attention Deficit Disorder; ESL (6 students enrolled).
College Admission Counseling 15 students graduated in 2008; all went to college, including Auburn University; Boston College; Savannah College of Art and Design; The University of Texas at Austin; University of Georgia.
Student Life Upper grades have specified standards of dress, student council, honor system. Discipline rests primarily with faculty.

Summer Programs Enrichment, advancement, art/fine arts programs offered; session focuses on arts and communications; held on campus; accepts boys and girls; open to students from other schools. 200 students usually enrolled.
Tuition and Aid Day student tuition: $11,500; 7-day tuition and room/board: $25,400. Tuition installment plan (Academic Management Services Plan). Need-based scholarship grants available. In 2008–09, 10% of upper-school students received aid.
Admissions Traditional secondary-level entrance grade is 9. Deadline for receipt of application materials: none. Application fee required: $35. Interview required.
Athletics Interscholastic: basketball, cheering, cross-country running, dance, modern dance, outdoor activities, tennis, track and field, volleyball; intramural: basketball, billiards, bowling, flag football, hiking/backpacking, outdoor activities, soccer, softball, tennis, volleyball. 1 PE instructor, 3 coaches.
Computers Computers are regularly used in English, science classes. Computer network features include on-campus library services, online commercial services, Internet access.
Contact Laura Nicholson, Director of Admissions. 770-534-6140. Fax: 770-534-6298. E-mail: enroll@brenau.edu. Web site: www.brenauacademy.org.

ANNOUNCEMENT FROM THE SCHOOL Brenau Academy is a high school where girls grow into leaders, world citizens, and lifelong learners. A dedicated staff and faculty, small interactive classes, and a challenging, college-prep curriculum inspire students to set goals and reach them. Located on the thriving campus of Brenau Women's College, Academy students are able to take advantage of all the benefits that a college offers while still being in the protective environment of a high school. Brenau Academy graduates step onto college campuses confident in their ability to succeed. There is a future waiting at Brenau Academy. Come find your place with us.

See Close-Up on page 692.

BRENTWOOD COLLEGE SCHOOL

2735 Mount Baker Road
Mill Bay, British Columbia V0R 2P1, Canada

Head of School: Mrs. Andrea M. Pennells

General Information Coeducational boarding and day college-preparatory and fine arts, athletics, leadership, and citizenship school school. Grades 9–12. Founded: 1923. Setting: rural. Nearest major city is Victoria, Canada. Students are housed in single-sex dormitories. 40-acre campus. 15 buildings on campus. Approved or accredited by British Columbia Independent Schools Association, Canadian Association of Independent Schools, The Association of Boarding Schools, Western Boarding Schools Association, and British Columbia Department of Education. Affiliate member of National Association of Independent Schools. Language of instruction: English. Total enrollment: 435. Upper school average class size: 17. Upper school faculty-student ratio: 1:9.
Upper School Student Profile Grade 8: 41 students (25 boys, 16 girls); Grade 9: 67 students (39 boys, 28 girls); Grade 10: 102 students (51 boys, 51 girls); Grade 11: 111 students (58 boys, 53 girls); Grade 12: 114 students (58 boys, 56 girls). 81% of students are boarding students. 58% are province residents. 20 provinces are represented in upper school student body. 27% are international students. International students from Germany, Hong Kong, Mexico, Republic of Korea, Saudi Arabia, and United States; 12 other countries represented in student body.
Faculty School total: 50. In upper school: 24 men, 17 women; 12 have advanced degrees; 30 reside on campus.
Subjects Offered Advanced Placement courses, algebra, art history-AP, athletics, audio visual/media, band, basketball, biology, biology-AP, business, calculus, calculus-AP, Canadian geography, Canadian history, Canadian law, career and personal planning, ceramics, chemistry, chemistry-AP, choir, choreography, chorus, computer graphics, computer science, dance, dance performance, debate, design, drafting, drama, dramatic arts, drawing, economics, economics-AP, English, English literature, English literature-AP, French, French language-AP, geography, geometry, golf, government and politics-AP, health and wellness, history, information technology, instrumental music, international studies, jazz band, jazz ensemble, marketing, mathematics, music theater, musical productions, musical theater, orchestra, outdoor education, painting, photography, physics, physics-AP, pottery, psychology, psychology-AP, public speaking, science, sculpture, sex education, social studies, Spanish, Spanish-AP, stagecraft, technical theater, tennis, theater design and production, video film production, visual and performing arts, vocal jazz, volleyball, yearbook.
Graduation Requirements Arts and fine arts (art, music, dance, drama), career and personal planning, English, foreign language, mathematics, physical education (includes health), science, social studies (includes history).
Special Academic Programs Advanced Placement exam preparation.
College Admission Counseling 109 students graduated in 2008; all went to college, including Duke University; McGill University; Queen's University at Kingston; The University of British Columbia; University of California, Berkeley; University of California, Los Angeles.
Student Life Upper grades have uniform requirement, student council, honor system. Discipline rests primarily with faculty.
Tuition and Aid Day student tuition: CAN$18,250; 7-day tuition and room/board: CAN$34,200–CAN$43,600. Tuition reduction for siblings available.
Admissions Traditional secondary-level entrance grade is 9. Henmon-Nelson required. Deadline for receipt of application materials: none. Application fee required. Interview required.
Athletics Interscholastic: basketball (boys, girls), crew (b,g), cross-country running (b,g), field hockey (g), hockey (g), rowing (b,g), rugby (b,g), running (b,g), soccer (b,g), squash (b,g), tennis (b,g), volleyball (g); intramural: crew (b,g), cross-country running (b,g), field hockey (g), indoor hockey (g), soccer (b,g), squash (b,g), tennis (b,g), track and field (b,g), volleyball (g), weight training (g); coed interscholastic: badminton, ballet, canoeing/kayaking, fitness, golf, ice hockey, kayaking, martial arts, modern dance, ocean paddling, outdoor activities, rock climbing, sailing; coed intramural: aerobics, aerobics/dance, badminton, canoeing/kayaking, cooperative games, dance, fitness, floor hockey, hiking/backpacking, indoor soccer, kayaking, outdoor activities, physical fitness, physical training, rowing, rugby, running, skiing (downhill), snowboarding, strength & conditioning, table tennis, touch football, weight lifting, weight training. 6 PE instructors, 36 coaches.
Computers Computers are regularly used in photojournalism, video film production classes. Computer network features include on-campus library services, Internet access, wireless campus network. Campus intranet and student e-mail accounts are available to students.
Contact Mr. Clayton Johnston, Director of Admissions. 250-743-5521. Fax: 250-743-2911. E-mail: admissions@brentwood.bc.ca. Web site: www.brentwood.bc.ca.

ANNOUNCEMENT FROM THE SCHOOL Located in Mill Bay, British Columbia, Canada, Brentwood is a co-educational college-preparatory, boarding school for grades 9 through 12. Brentwood is home away from home for 350 boarders and 80 day students. Although most Brentonians hail from Western Canada and the American Pacific Northwest, more than twenty countries are typically represented in the student community. Combine timeless values with a challenging 21st-century academic curriculum supported by a dynamic sports programme and vibrant visual and performing arts electives that promote confidence and teamwork—that's Brentwood. Opportunities also abound for social time with friends, special events, and leadership through service. Brentwood's 40-acre oceanfront campus provides superb modern facilities for academics, athletics, and the arts, with comfortable accommodations in a pristine Vancouver Island setting.

See Close-Up on page 694.

BRENTWOOD SCHOOL

100 South Barrington Place
Los Angeles, California 90049

Head of School: Dr. Michael Pratt

General Information Coeducational day college-preparatory school. Grades K–12. Founded: 1972. Setting: suburban. 30-acre campus. 12 buildings on campus. Approved or accredited by California Association of Independent Schools and Western Association of Schools and Colleges. Member of National Association of Independent Schools and Secondary School Admission Test Board. Endowment: $7.8 million. Total enrollment: 984. Upper school average class size: 17. Upper school faculty-student ratio: 1:8.
Upper School Student Profile Grade 9: 115 students (54 boys, 61 girls); Grade 10: 123 students (62 boys, 61 girls); Grade 11: 111 students (61 boys, 50 girls); Grade 12: 108 students (56 boys, 52 girls).
Faculty School total: 100. In upper school: 45 men, 49 women; 70 have advanced degrees.
Subjects Offered Acting, Advanced Placement courses, advanced studio art-AP, algebra, American government-AP, American history, American literature, Ancient Greek, anthropology, art, art history, art history-AP, art-AP, astronomy, biology, biology-AP, calculus, calculus-AP, ceramics, chemistry, chemistry-AP, Chinese, choir, choral music, chorus, community service, comparative government and politics-AP, computer programming, computer programming-AP, computer science, computer science-AP, concert choir, creative writing, dance, digital photography, directing, drama, drawing, ecology, economics, economics-AP, English, English literature, environmental science-AP, European history, filmmaking, fine arts, French, French-AP, geometry, global studies, government and politics-AP, government-AP, history, honors algebra, honors English, honors geometry, human development, human geography—AP, Japanese, jazz band, jazz dance, journalism, language-AP, Latin, Latin-AP, literature-AP, math analysis, mathematics, music, music theater, music theory-AP, orchestra, organic chemistry, philosophy, photography, physical education, physics, physics-AP, probability and statistics, robotics, science, senior seminar, senior thesis, social science, social studies, Spanish, Spanish-AP, speech, speech and debate, stagecraft, stained glass, statistics-AP, studio art-AP, theater, U.S. government-AP, U.S. history-AP, video, word processing, world history, world literature.

Graduation Requirements Arts and fine arts (art, music, dance, drama), English, foreign language, mathematics, physical education (includes health), science, senior seminar, senior thesis, social science, social studies (includes history). Community service is required.

Special Academic Programs 26 Advanced Placement exams for which test preparation is offered; honors section; independent study; study at local college for college credit; academic accommodation for the gifted and the artistically talented.

College Admission Counseling 122 students graduated in 2008; 121 went to college, including Georgetown University; Stanford University; The Johns Hopkins University; University of Pennsylvania; University of Southern California. Other: 1 entered a postgraduate year. Mean SAT critical reading: 660, mean SAT math: 670, mean SAT writing: 680, mean combined SAT: 2010.

Student Life Upper grades have specified standards of dress, student council, honor system. Discipline rests primarily with faculty.

Summer Programs Remediation, enrichment, advancement, sports, art/fine arts, computer instruction programs offered; session focuses on academic enrichment and sports; held on campus; accepts boys and girls; open to students from other schools. 350 students usually enrolled. 2009 schedule: June 15 to July 31. Application deadline: none.

Tuition and Aid Day student tuition: $27,650. Tuition installment plan (Insured Tuition Payment Plan, monthly payment plans, individually arranged payment plans). Need-based scholarship grants available. In 2008–09, 15% of upper-school students received aid. Total amount of financial aid awarded in 2008–09: $3,100,000.

Admissions Traditional secondary-level entrance grade is 9. For fall 2008, 175 students applied for upper-level admission, 35 were accepted, 29 enrolled. ISEE required. Deadline for receipt of application materials: January 16. Application fee required: $100. On-campus interview required.

Athletics Interscholastic: baseball (boys), basketball (b,g), cheering (g), cross-country running (b,g), dance squad (g), dance team (g), football (b), independent competitive sports (b,g), lacrosse (b,g), soccer (b,g), softball (g), swimming and diving (b,g), tennis (b,g), track and field (b,g), volleyball (b,g), water polo (b), wrestling (b); intramural: modern dance (g), ultimate Frisbee (b); coed interscholastic: dance, diving, drill team, equestrian sports, fencing, football, golf, swimming and diving, water polo; coed intramural: bicycling, fitness, Frisbee, jogging, mountain biking, outdoor activities, physical fitness, physical training, running, sailing, surfing, table tennis, ultimate Frisbee, weight lifting, weight training, wilderness, yoga. 6 PE instructors, 40 coaches, 2 athletic trainers.

Computers Computers are regularly used in college planning, computer applications, desktop publishing, digital applications, foreign language, graphic design, introduction to technology, journalism, literary magazine, mathematics, media arts, media production, photojournalism, programming, publications, research skills, science, technical drawing, technology, video film production, Web site design classes. Computer network features include on-campus library services, online commercial services, Internet access, wireless campus network, Internet filtering or blocking technology. Campus intranet, student e-mail accounts, and computer access in designated common areas are available to students. Students grades are available online. The school has a published electronic and media policy.

Contact Ms. Judy Wray, Admissions Assistant. 310-889-2657. Fax: 310-476-4087. E-mail: jwray@bwscampus.com. Web site: www.bwscampus.com.

BRENTWOOD SCHOOL

PO Box 955
725 Linton Road
Sandersville, Georgia 31082

Head of School: Mrs. Jackie W. Holton

General Information Coeducational day college-preparatory school. Grades PK–12. Founded: 1969. Setting: rural. Nearest major city is Atlanta. 20-acre campus. 2 buildings on campus. Approved or accredited by Georgia Accrediting Commission and Southern Association of Colleges and Schools. Endowment: $1.4 million. Total enrollment: 401. Upper school average class size: 16. Upper school faculty-student ratio: 1:11.

Upper School Student Profile Grade 6: 29 students (17 boys, 12 girls); Grade 7: 44 students (29 boys, 15 girls); Grade 8: 24 students (9 boys, 15 girls); Grade 9: 29 students (16 boys, 13 girls); Grade 10: 19 students (8 boys, 11 girls); Grade 11: 34 students (18 boys, 16 girls); Grade 12: 30 students (16 boys, 14 girls).

Faculty School total: 31. In upper school: 2 men, 11 women; 9 have advanced degrees.

Subjects Offered Advanced Placement courses, algebra, American history, American literature, art, art history, biology, calculus, chemistry, computer science, creative writing, earth science, economics, English, English literature, environmental science, French, geography, geometry, government/civics, grammar, history, mathematics, music, music appreciation, physical education, physics, psychology, science, social studies, trigonometry, world history, world literature, writing.

Graduation Requirements Algebra, American government, American history, American literature, biology, British literature, chemistry, composition, computer applications, economics, electives, English, English composition, environmental science, foreign language, French, geography, geometry, mathematics, physical education (includes health), physical science, science, social studies (includes history), world history.

Special Academic Programs Advanced Placement exam preparation.

College Admission Counseling 19 students graduated in 2008; all went to college, including Georgia College & State University; Georgia Southern University; Middle Georgia College; University of Georgia; Valdosta State University. 25% scored over 600 on SAT critical reading, 20% scored over 600 on SAT math.

Student Life Upper grades have specified standards of dress, student council, honor system. Discipline rests primarily with faculty.

Tuition and Aid Day student tuition: $5800. Tuition installment plan (monthly payment plans). Tuition reduction for siblings, need-based scholarship grants available.

Admissions Traditional secondary-level entrance grade is 9. For fall 2008, 3 students applied for upper-level admission, 3 were accepted, 3 enrolled. Admissions testing required. Deadline for receipt of application materials: none. No application fee required. On-campus interview required.

Athletics Interscholastic: baseball (boys), basketball (b,g), cheering (g), cross-country running (b,g), dance team (g), football (b), golf (b,g), softball (g), tennis (b,g), track and field (b,g). 4 PE instructors, 4 coaches, 1 athletic trainer.

Computers Computers are regularly used in computer applications classes. Computer network features include on-campus library services, Internet access, Internet filtering or blocking technology. Campus intranet and computer access in designated common areas are available to students. The school has a published electronic and media policy.

Contact Mrs. Jackie W. Holton, Head of School. 912-552-5136. Fax: 912-552-2947. E-mail: jackie.holton@brentwoodschool.org. Web site: www.brentwoodschool.org.

BRETHREN CHRISTIAN JUNIOR AND SENIOR HIGH SCHOOLS

21141 Strathmoor Lane
Huntington Beach, California 92646

Head of School: Mr. Rick Niswonger

General Information Coeducational day college-preparatory, arts, and religious studies school, affiliated with Christian faith; primarily serves students with learning disabilities and individuals with Attention Deficit Disorder. Grades 7–12. Founded: 1947. Setting: suburban. 15-acre campus. 1 building on campus. Approved or accredited by Association of Christian Schools International, Western Association of Schools and Colleges, and California Department of Education. Endowment: $150,000. Total enrollment: 368. Upper school average class size: 22. Upper school faculty-student ratio: 1:12.

Upper School Student Profile Grade 9: 72 students (31 boys, 41 girls); Grade 10: 77 students (43 boys, 34 girls); Grade 11: 82 students (32 boys, 50 girls); Grade 12: 61 students (36 boys, 25 girls). 95% of students are Christian.

Faculty School total: 31. In upper school: 11 men, 15 women; 4 have advanced degrees.

Subjects Offered Advanced math, algebra, American government, American government-AP, American history-AP, American literature, anatomy and physiology, art, ASB Leadership, athletics, auto shop, band, basketball, Bible, biology, calculus-AP, cheerleading, chemistry, choir, Christian ethics, comedy, computer keyboarding, computer multimedia, concert band, consumer mathematics, drama, drama performance, drama workshop, earth science, economics, English literature, English literature and composition-AP, fitness, French, French language-AP, golf, government, jazz band, keyboarding/computer, math analysis, physical education, physics, pre-algebra, Spanish, Spanish language-AP, studio art, theater, U.S. history-AP, volleyball, weightlifting, world history-AP.

Graduation Requirements Algebra, American literature, arts and fine arts (art, music, dance, drama), Bible, biology, chemistry, computer applications, economics, English composition, English literature, geometry, physical education (includes health), U.S. government, U.S. history, world history.

Special Academic Programs Advanced Placement exam preparation; accelerated programs; academic accommodation for the gifted; remedial reading and/or remedial writing; remedial math; special instructional classes for deaf students, blind students.

College Admission Counseling 72 students graduated in 2008; 66 went to college, including Azusa Pacific University; Biola University; California State University, Long Beach; Chapman University; Point Loma Nazarene University; Vanguard University of Southern California. Other: 4 went to work, 1 entered military service, 1 had other specific plans. Median SAT critical reading: 553, median SAT math: 551, median SAT writing: 529.

Student Life Upper grades have specified standards of dress, student council. Discipline rests primarily with faculty. Attendance at religious services is required.

Summer Programs Remediation, advancement, sports, computer instruction programs offered; session focuses on remediation and advancement; held on campus; accepts boys and girls; not open to students from other schools. 30 students usually enrolled. 2009 schedule: June 16 to July 31. Application deadline: none.

Tuition and Aid Tuition installment plan (monthly payment plans, individually arranged payment plans, pre-payment discount). Need-based scholarship grants, need- and merit-based financial aid available. In 2008–09, 22% of upper-school students received aid. Total amount of financial aid awarded in 2008–09: $75,000.

Admissions Traditional secondary-level entrance grade is 9. For fall 2008, 66 students applied for upper-level admission, 57 were accepted, 56 enrolled.

Achievement tests and Math Placement Exam required. Deadline for receipt of application materials: none. Application fee required: $395. On-campus interview required.

Athletics Interscholastic: baseball (boys), basketball (b,g), cheering (g), cross-country running (b,g), football (b), golf (b), soccer (b,g), softball (g), tennis (b,g), track and field (b,g), volleyball (b,g). 2 PE instructors, 16 coaches.

Computers Computers are regularly used in computer applications, digital applications classes. Computer network features include on-campus library services, online commercial services, Internet access, wireless campus network, Internet filtering or blocking technology. Student e-mail accounts and computer access in designated common areas are available to students. Students grades are available online. The school has a published electronic and media policy.

Contact Mrs. June Helton, Records Secretary. 714-962-6617 Ext. 14. Fax: 714-962-3171. E-mail: jhelton@mail.bchs.net. Web site: www.bchs.net.

BREWSTER ACADEMY

80 Academy Drive
Wolfeboro, New Hampshire 03894

Head of School: Dr. Michael E. Cooper

General Information Coeducational boarding and day college-preparatory, arts, and technology school. Grades 9–PG. Founded: 1820. Setting: small town. Nearest major city is Boston, MA. Students are housed in single-sex dormitories. 80-acre campus. 39 buildings on campus. Approved or accredited by Independent Schools of Northern New England, New England Association of Schools and Colleges, and The Association of Boarding Schools. Member of National Association of Independent Schools and Secondary School Admission Test Board. Endowment: $15 million. Total enrollment: 358. Upper school average class size: 12. Upper school faculty-student ratio: 1:6.

Upper School Student Profile Grade 9: 57 students (30 boys, 27 girls); Grade 10: 95 students (49 boys, 46 girls); Grade 11: 101 students (53 boys, 48 girls); Grade 12: 92 students (57 boys, 35 girls); Postgraduate: 13 students (10 boys, 3 girls). 80% of students are boarding students. 29% are state residents. 25 states are represented in upper school student body. 17% are international students. International students from Canada, Germany, Japan, Republic of Korea, Taiwan, and Thailand; 10 other countries represented in student body.

Faculty School total: 60. In upper school: 33 men, 27 women; 24 have advanced degrees; 40 reside on campus.

Subjects Offered Algebra, art, art history, astronomy, biology, biology-AP, calculus, calculus-AP, chemistry, chorus, community service, computer graphics, creative writing, dance, dance performance, drama, driver education, ecology, environmental systems, economics, English, English language and composition-AP, English literature, English literature-AP, environmental science, ESL, French, geometry, jazz band, journalism, macroeconomics-AP, mathematics, music, photography, physics, physics-AP, pottery, science, Spanish, studio art, theater, U.S. history, U.S. history-AP, world history, writing.

Graduation Requirements English, foreign language, mathematics, science, social studies (includes history).

Special Academic Programs 8 Advanced Placement exams for which test preparation is offered; honors section; study abroad; programs in English, mathematics, general development for dyslexic students; ESL (19 students enrolled).

College Admission Counseling 104 students graduated in 2008; 102 went to college, including College of Charleston; Elon University; Rochester Institute of Technology; The George Washington University; University of New Hampshire; Worcester Polytechnic Institute. Other: 1 entered a postgraduate year, 1 had other specific plans. Median SAT critical reading: 500, median SAT math: 500, median SAT writing: 510, median combined SAT: 1530, median composite ACT: 18. 12% scored over 600 on SAT critical reading, 26% scored over 600 on SAT math, 12% scored over 600 on SAT writing, 18% scored over 1800 on combined SAT, 22% scored over 26 on composite ACT.

Student Life Upper grades have specified standards of dress, student council, honor system. Discipline rests primarily with faculty.

Summer Programs Enrichment, advancement, ESL, sports, art/fine arts, computer instruction programs offered; session focuses on humanities and math, study skills, technology in academics and the arts, outdoor adventure education; held on campus; accepts boys and girls; open to students from other schools. 50 students usually enrolled. 2009 schedule: June 26 to August 7. Application deadline: June 1.

Tuition and Aid Day student tuition: $24,450; 7-day tuition and room/board: $40,495. Tuition installment plan (monthly payment plans). Need-based scholarship grants, Sallie Mae Loans available. In 2008–09, 27% of upper-school students received aid. Total amount of financial aid awarded in 2008–09: $2,300,000.

Admissions Traditional secondary-level entrance grade is 9. For fall 2008, 561 students applied for upper-level admission, 251 were accepted, 134 enrolled. SSAT required. Deadline for receipt of application materials: February 1. Application fee required: $50. On-campus interview required.

Athletics Interscholastic: alpine skiing (boys, girls), baseball (b), basketball (b,g), crew (b,g), cross-country running (b,g), field hockey (g), ice hockey (b,g), lacrosse (b,g), nordic skiing (b,g), running (b,g), skiing (cross-country) (b,g), skiing (downhill) (b,g), soccer (b,g), softball (g), tennis (b,g); coed interscholastic: sailing, snowboarding; coed intramural: aerobics, alpine skiing, climbing, dance, equestrian sports, fitness, golf, outdoor skills, rock climbing, sailing, skiing (downhill), snowboarding, strength & conditioning, tennis, touch football, ultimate Frisbee, wall climbing, weight training, yoga. 2 athletic trainers.

Computers Computers are regularly used in all classes. Computer network features include on-campus library services, online commercial services, Internet access, Internet filtering or blocking technology. Campus intranet, student e-mail accounts, and computer access in designated common areas are available to students. Students grades are available online. The school has a published electronic and media policy.

Contact Mary Rohrbaugh, Admission Coordinator. 603-569-7200. Fax: 603-569-7272. E-mail: mary_rohrbaugh@brewsteracademy.org. Web site: www.brewsteracademy.org.

ANNOUNCEMENT FROM THE SCHOOL Brewster has become known worldwide for innovation and performance in secondary education. The Brewster program is designed to meet students at their current level of performance and accelerate them in their mastery of skills and knowledge, ensuring that Brewster graduates are prepared for the challenges of college and life after college.

See Close-Up on page 696.

BRIARWOOD CHRISTIAN HIGH SCHOOL

6255 Cahaba Valley Road
Birmingham, Alabama 35242

Head of School: Dr. Barrett Mosbacker

General Information Coeducational day college-preparatory, arts, and religious studies school, affiliated with Presbyterian Church in America. Grades K4–12. Founded: 1964. Setting: suburban. 85-acre campus. 5 buildings on campus. Approved or accredited by Association of Christian Schools International, Southern Association of Colleges and Schools, and Alabama Department of Education. Endowment: $500,000. Total enrollment: 1,945. Upper school average class size: 23. Upper school faculty-student ratio: 1:23.

Upper School Student Profile Grade 9: 147 students (77 boys, 70 girls); Grade 10: 143 students (73 boys, 70 girls); Grade 11: 136 students (68 boys, 68 girls); Grade 12: 141 students (71 boys, 70 girls). 40% of students are Presbyterian Church in America.

Faculty School total: 102. In upper school: 30 men, 25 women; 35 have advanced degrees.

Subjects Offered Accounting, algebra, American history, American literature, art, band, Bible studies, biology, calculus, chemistry, community service, computer science, creative writing, debate, drama, driver education, economics, English, English literature, ethics, European history, French, geometry, government, grammar, health, history, home economics, mathematics, music, philosophy, physical education, physics, psychology, religion, science, social science, social studies, Spanish, speech, trigonometry, world history, world literature.

Graduation Requirements 20th century history, business skills (includes word processing), computer science, English, foreign language, mathematics, physical education (includes health), religion (includes Bible studies and theology), science, social science, social studies (includes history). Community service is required.

Special Academic Programs Advanced Placement exam preparation; honors section; academic accommodation for the gifted; special instructional classes for students with learning disabilities, Attention Deficit Disorder.

College Admission Counseling 135 students graduated in 2008; 130 went to college, including Auburn University; Birmingham-Southern College; Samford University; The University of Alabama; Troy University; University of Mississippi. Other: 5 had other specific plans. Mean combined SAT: 1193, mean composite ACT: 25.

Student Life Upper grades have specified standards of dress, student council. Discipline rests primarily with faculty. Attendance at religious services is required.

Summer Programs Remediation, advancement programs offered; session focuses on social studies and mathematics; held on campus; accepts boys and girls; not open to students from other schools. 50 students usually enrolled. 2009 schedule: June to July.

Tuition and Aid Day student tuition: $5910. Tuition installment plan (monthly payment plans). Tuition reduction for siblings available.

Admissions Traditional secondary-level entrance grade is 9. For fall 2008, 83 students applied for upper-level admission, 42 were accepted, 41 enrolled. SSAT required. Deadline for receipt of application materials: none. Application fee required: $75. On-campus interview required.

Athletics Interscholastic: baseball (boys), basketball (b,g), cheering (g), cross-country running (b,g), dance team (g), football (b), golf (b,g), indoor track (b,g), indoor track & field (b,g), outdoor activities (b,g), physical fitness (b,g), soccer (b,g), softball (g), strength & conditioning (b), swimming and diving (b,g), tennis (b,g), track and field (b,g), volleyball (g). 5 PE instructors, 1 athletic trainer.

Computers Computers are regularly used in computer applications classes. Computer network features include on-campus library services, online commercial services, Internet access. Students grades are available online.

Contact Mrs. Kelly Mooney, Director of Admissions. 205-776-5812. Fax: 205-776-5816. E-mail: kmooney@briarwood.org. Web site: www.briarwoodchristianschool.org.

BRIDGEMONT HIGH SCHOOL

777 Brotherhood Way
San Francisco, California 94132

Head of School: Mr. Peter Tropper

General Information Coeducational day college-preparatory, arts, religious studies, and technology school, affiliated with Christian faith. Grades 8–12. Founded: 1975. Setting: urban. 5-acre campus. 4 buildings on campus. Approved or accredited by Association of Christian Schools International, CITA (Commission on International and Trans-Regional Accreditation), and Western Association of Schools and Colleges. Total enrollment: 54. Upper school average class size: 15. Upper school faculty-student ratio: 1:5.

Upper School Student Profile Grade 9: 11 students (6 boys, 5 girls); Grade 10: 13 students (5 boys, 8 girls); Grade 11: 7 students (4 boys, 3 girls); Grade 12: 15 students (10 boys, 5 girls). 50% of students are Christian faith.

Faculty School total: 12. In upper school: 6 men, 6 women; 5 have advanced degrees.

Subjects Offered Advanced math, Advanced Placement courses, algebra, American history, American literature, art, art history, arts, Bible studies, biology, calculus, chemistry, computer science, creative writing, drama, earth science, economics, English, English literature, environmental science, European history, expository writing, fine arts, French, French as a second language, geography, geometry, government/civics, grammar, health, history, mathematics, music, physical education, physics, religion, science, social science, social studies, Spanish, study skills, theater, trigonometry, U.S. history, world history, world literature, writing, yearbook.

Graduation Requirements Arts and fine arts (art, music, dance, drama), English, foreign language, mathematics, physical education (includes health), religion (includes Bible studies and theology), science, social science, social studies (includes history), field studies.

Special Academic Programs Honors section; accelerated programs; independent study.

College Admission Counseling 11 students graduated in 2008; all went to college, including California State University, Los Angeles; City College of San Francisco; San Francisco State University; San Jose State University; University of California, Davis; University of California, Irvine.

Student Life Upper grades have specified standards of dress, student council, honor system. Discipline rests primarily with faculty. Attendance at religious services is required.

Summer Programs Sports programs offered; session focuses on baseball and basketball; held both on and off campus; held at nearby gym and playing fields; accepts boys and girls; open to students from other schools. 25 students usually enrolled. 2009 schedule: June 26 to August 26. Application deadline: May 30.

Tuition and Aid Day student tuition: $9475. Tuition installment plan (FACTS Tuition Payment Plan, monthly payment plans, Tuition Management Systems Plan). Tuition reduction for siblings, need-based scholarship grants available. In 2008–09, 54% of upper-school students received aid. Total amount of financial aid awarded in 2008–09: $107,122.

Admissions Traditional secondary-level entrance grade is 9. For fall 2008, 16 students applied for upper-level admission, 16 were accepted, 15 enrolled. Essay, math and English placement tests and writing sample required. Deadline for receipt of application materials: none. Application fee required: $40. On-campus interview required.

Athletics Interscholastic: baseball (boys, girls), basketball (b), soccer (b), softball (g), volleyball (g); intramural: basketball (b,g), flag football (b,g), weight lifting (b); coed intramural: flag football, floor hockey, football, judo, jump rope, physical training, volleyball. 1 PE instructor, 4 coaches.

Computers Computers are regularly used in yearbook classes. Computer resources include Internet access, wireless campus network, Internet filtering or blocking technology, independent study courses through Acellus and NovelStar. Computer access in designated common areas is available to students. Students grades are available online.

Contact Mr. Paul S. Choy, Director of Student Development. 415-333-3888. Fax: 415-333-7603. E-mail: admissions@bridgemont.org. Web site: www.bridgemont.org.

BRIDGES ACADEMY

Studio City, California
See Special Needs Schools section.

BRIDGE SCHOOL

6717 South Boulder Road
Boulder, Colorado 80303-4319

Head of School: Mr. Richard Weeks

General Information Coeducational day college-preparatory, arts, and technology school. Grades 6–12. Founded: 1994. Setting: suburban. 5.5-acre campus. 1 building on campus. Approved or accredited by North Central Association of Colleges and Schools, The College Board, and Colorado Department of Education. Endowment: $20,000. Total enrollment: 55. Upper school average class size: 10. Upper school faculty-student ratio: 1:7.

Upper School Student Profile Grade 9: 8 students (3 boys, 5 girls); Grade 10: 8 students (7 boys, 1 girl); Grade 11: 8 students (4 boys, 4 girls); Grade 12: 8 students (5 boys, 3 girls).

Faculty School total: 14. In upper school: 2 men, 5 women; 6 have advanced degrees.

Subjects Offered Algebra, American culture, American democracy, American literature, ancient world history, applied arts, art, art education, British literature, chemistry, civics, comparative cultures, computers, contemporary history, digital art, English composition, ESL, European civilization, European history, foreign language, geometry, history, life science, mathematics, pre-algebra, science and technology, senior project, Shakespeare, U.S. government, volleyball, wilderness experience, world governments.

Graduation Requirements Art, arts and fine arts (art, music, dance, drama), computer literacy, English, foreign language, mathematics, social studies (includes history), May Term participation each year of attendance.

Special Academic Programs Independent study; term-away projects; ESL (6 students enrolled).

College Admission Counseling 15 went to college, including Colorado State University; Cornell College; Davidson College; St. Norbert College; University of Colorado at Boulder. Other: 1 had other specific plans.

Student Life Upper grades have specified standards of dress, student council, honor system. Discipline rests equally with students and faculty.

Tuition and Aid Day student tuition: $15,200. Tuition installment plan (individually arranged payment plans). Merit scholarship grants, need-based scholarship grants available. In 2008–09, 20% of upper-school students received aid; total upper-school merit-scholarship money awarded: $15,500. Total amount of financial aid awarded in 2008–09: $120,000.

Admissions Traditional secondary-level entrance grade is 9. For fall 2008, 35 students applied for upper-level admission, 25 were accepted, 20 enrolled. Achievement tests, school's own test and writing sample required. Deadline for receipt of application materials: none. Application fee required: $100. Interview required.

Athletics Interscholastic: basketball (boys), ultimate Frisbee (b,g), volleyball (g); coed interscholastic: Frisbee, soccer. 1 coach.

Computers Computers are regularly used in journalism, science, video film production, writing, yearbook classes. Computer network features include Internet access. Campus intranet is available to students. The school has a published electronic and media policy.

Contact Mrs. Leah Kahn, Director of Admissions and Marketing. 303-494-7551. Fax: 303-494-7558. E-mail: info@bridgeschoolboulder.org. Web site: www.bridgeschoolboulder.org.

BRIMMER AND MAY SCHOOL

69 Middlesex Road
Chestnut Hill, Massachusetts 02467

Head of School: Anne Reenstierna

General Information Coeducational day college-preparatory, arts, technology, and student-centered learning school. Grades PK–12. Founded: 1880. Setting: suburban. Nearest major city is Boston. 7-acre campus. 5 buildings on campus. Approved or accredited by Association of Independent Schools and Colleges of Alberta, Association of Independent Schools in New England, and New England Association of Schools and Colleges. Member of National Association of Independent Schools and Secondary School Admission Test Board. Endowment: $5.2 million. Total enrollment: 407. Upper school average class size: 14. Upper school faculty-student ratio: 1:5.

Upper School Student Profile Grade 9: 32 students (14 boys, 18 girls); Grade 10: 29 students (13 boys, 16 girls); Grade 11: 41 students (19 boys, 22 girls); Grade 12: 35 students (18 boys, 17 girls).

Faculty School total: 60. In upper school: 12 men, 21 women; 19 have advanced degrees.

Subjects Offered Acting, adolescent issues, Advanced Placement courses, advanced studio art-AP, algebra, American history, American literature, art, biology, biology-AP, calculus, ceramics, chamber groups, chemistry, chorus, college counseling, community service, computer education, computer programming, creative arts, creative writing, desktop publishing, drama, earth science, economics, economics-AP, electronic music, English, English as a foreign language, English literature, English literature-AP, ESL, European history, expository writing, fine arts, foreign policy, French, geometry, grammar, health, health education, history, Holocaust and other genocides, humanities, Internet research, life management skills, mathematics, music, music theory, newspaper, participation in sports, performing arts, photography, physical education, physical science, physics, psychology, social studies, Spanish, theater, trigonometry, typing, U.S. history, video film production, world history, world literature, writing, yearbook.

Graduation Requirements Arts and fine arts (art, music, dance, drama), computer science, English, foreign language, history, mathematics, physical education (includes health), science, senior independent project, portfolio projects. Community service is required.

Special Academic Programs Advanced Placement exam preparation; independent study; ESL (9 students enrolled).

College Admission Counseling 26 students graduated in 2008; 25 went to college, including Boston College; Bowdoin College; Connecticut College; Hamilton College; Wheaton College. Other: 1 entered military service.

Student Life Upper grades have specified standards of dress, student council, honor system. Discipline rests equally with students and faculty.
Tuition and Aid Day student tuition: $15,900–$28,100. Tuition installment plan (Academic Management Services Plan). Need-based scholarship grants available. In 2008–09, 37% of upper-school students received aid. Total amount of financial aid awarded in 2008–09: $1,141,575.
Admissions Traditional secondary-level entrance grade is 9. For fall 2008, 75 students applied for upper-level admission, 47 were accepted, 23 enrolled. ISEE, SSAT or TOEFL or SLEP required. Deadline for receipt of application materials: January 16. Application fee required: $45. On-campus interview required.
Athletics Interscholastic: baseball (boys), basketball (b,g), cross-country running (b,g), field hockey (g), lacrosse (b,g), soccer (b,g), softball (g), tennis (b,g); intramural: dance team (g); coed interscholastic: golf; coed intramural: fitness, outdoor education, physical fitness, skiing (downhill), strength & conditioning, tennis, weight training. 4 PE instructors, 2 coaches, 2 athletic trainers.
Computers Computers are regularly used in desktop publishing, graphic design, humanities, journalism, media production, typing, Web site design, yearbook classes. Computer network features include on-campus library services, online commercial services, Internet access, wireless campus network, Internet filtering or blocking technology. Student e-mail accounts are available to students.
Contact Barbara Shoolman, Director of Admissions. 617-738-8695. Fax: 617-734-5147. E-mail: admissions@brimmer.org. Web site: www.brimmerandmay.org.

BROCKWOOD PARK SCHOOL

Brockwood Park
Bramdean
Hampshire
Alresford SO24 0LQ, United Kingdom
Head of School: Mr. Bill Taylor

General Information Coeducational boarding college-preparatory, general academic, arts, business, vocational, religious studies, bilingual studies, and technology school. Ungraded, ages 14–19. Founded: 1969. Setting: rural. Nearest major city is Winchester, United Kingdom. Students are housed in individual rooms, single sex compound. 40-acre campus. 8 buildings on campus. Approved or accredited by Office for Standards in Education (OFSTED). Language of instruction: English. Total enrollment: 65. Upper school average class size: 7. Upper school faculty-student ratio: 1:7.
Upper School Student Profile 100% of students are boarding students. 75% are international students. International students from France, Germany, Italy, Netherlands, Spain, and United States; 10 other countries represented in student body.
Faculty School total: 30. In upper school: 12 men, 18 women; all have advanced degrees; all reside on campus.
Subjects Offered Area studies, art, band, biology, body human, bookbinding, business studies, career and personal planning, career education, carpentry, cartooning/animation, chamber groups, chemistry, choir, choral music, cinematography, classical music, communication skills, computers, design, desktop publishing, diversity studies, drama, drama performance, drama workshop, English, English literature, environmental education, ESL, ethics, ethics and responsibility, fabric arts, filmmaking, fine arts, folk dance, food and nutrition, French, gardening, gender issues, geography, graphic design, history, mathematics, music, physics, pottery, psychology, science, social studies, Spanish, statistics.
Graduation Requirements Graduation requirements determined individual basis.
Special Academic Programs Independent study; term-away projects; study abroad; academic accommodation for the gifted, the musically talented, and the artistically talented; remedial reading and/or remedial writing; remedial math; programs in English, mathematics, general development for dyslexic students; special instructional classes for deaf students, blind students; ESL (30 students enrolled).
College Admission Counseling 29 students graduated in 2008; 25 went to college, including University of London. Other: 2 went to work, 2 had other specific plans.
Student Life Upper grades have specified standards of dress, student council, honor system. Discipline rests equally with students and faculty.
Tuition and Aid 7-day tuition and room/board: £13,500. Tuition installment plan (individually arranged payment plans). Need-based scholarship grants available. In 2008–09, 10% of upper-school students received aid.
Admissions Traditional secondary-level entrance age is 14. 3-R Achievement Test, any standardized test or ESL required. Deadline for receipt of application materials: none. Application fee required: £20. On-campus interview required.
Athletics 1 coach, 2 athletic trainers.
Computers Computer network features include Internet access, Internet filtering or blocking technology.
Contact Mrs. Victoria Lewin, Admissions Officer. 44-1962 771744. Fax: 44-1962 771875. E-mail: enquiry@brockwood.org.uk. Web site: www.brockwood.org.uk.

BROMLEY BROOK SCHOOL

Manchester Center, Vermont
See Special Needs Schools section.

BRONTE COLLEGE OF CANADA

88 Bronte College Court
Mississauga, Ontario L5B 1M9, Canada
Head of School: Dr. Ahsing Chia-Looi

General Information Coeducational boarding and day college-preparatory, general academic, arts, business, technology, and Advanced Placement school. Grades 9–12. Founded: 1991. Setting: suburban. Nearest major city is Toronto, Canada. Students are housed in single-sex by floor dormitories. 4-acre campus. 1 building on campus. Approved or accredited by Ontario Department of Education. Language of instruction: English. Total enrollment: 318. Upper school average class size: 18. Upper school faculty-student ratio: 1:11.
Upper School Student Profile Grade 9: 15 students (10 boys, 5 girls); Grade 10: 41 students (23 boys, 18 girls); Grade 11: 81 students (48 boys, 33 girls); Grade 12: 181 students (102 boys, 79 girls). 75% of students are boarding students. 25% are province residents. 4 provinces are represented in upper school student body. 75% are international students. International students from China, Hong Kong, Indonesia, Mexico, Nigeria, and Viet Nam; 29 other countries represented in student body.
Faculty School total: 25. In upper school: 12 men, 13 women; 9 have advanced degrees; 2 reside on campus.
Subjects Offered Accounting, Advanced Placement courses, algebra, art, band, biology, biology-AP, business, business studies, calculus, calculus-AP, Canadian geography, Canadian history, Canadian law, career planning, careers, chemistry, chemistry-AP, civics, computer applications, computer science-AP, computer technologies, drama, dramatic arts, economics, economics-AP, English, English-AP, entrepreneurship, ESL, French, geography, geometry, healthful living, history, history-AP, mathematics, microeconomics, microeconomics-AP, music, philosophy, physical education, physics, physics-AP, psychology, psychology-AP, reading/study skills, science, studio art-AP, visual arts, writing skills.
Graduation Requirements Arts, business studies, career planning, civics, English, French, geography, history, mathematics, physical education (includes health), science, social science, technology.
Special Academic Programs Advanced Placement exam preparation; accelerated programs; independent study; study at local college for college credit; ESL (60 students enrolled).
College Admission Counseling 160 students graduated in 2008; 157 went to college, including McMaster University; Ryerson University; University of Toronto; University of Waterloo; York University. Other: 3 had other specific plans.
Student Life Upper grades have uniform requirement, student council, honor system. Discipline rests primarily with faculty.
Summer Programs Remediation, enrichment, advancement, ESL, computer instruction programs offered; session focuses on remediation; held on campus; accepts boys and girls; open to students from other schools. 100 students usually enrolled. 2009 schedule: July 6 to August 7. Application deadline: May 20.
Tuition and Aid Day student tuition: CAN$9000–CAN$10,200; 7-day tuition and room/board: CAN$11,040. Tuition installment plan (individually arranged payment plans, Canadian students (or Permanent Residents) semester payment plan).
Admissions Traditional secondary-level entrance grade is 9. For fall 2008, 300 students applied for upper-level admission, 206 were accepted, 176 enrolled. English proficiency, mathematics proficiency exam and SLEP required. Deadline for receipt of application materials: none. Application fee required: CAN$150. Interview required.
Athletics Interscholastic: basketball (boys, girls); intramural: badminton (b,g), basketball (b,g), soccer (b). 1 PE instructor, 2 coaches.
Computers Computers are regularly used in art, business, computer applications classes. Computer network features include Internet access, wireless campus network, Internet filtering or blocking technology. Computer access in designated common areas is available to students. Students grades are available online. The school has a published electronic and media policy.
Contact Ms. Barbara de Serres, Admissions Manager. 905-270-7788 Ext. 2025. Fax: 905-270-7828. E-mail: bdeserres@brontecollege.ca. Web site: www.brontecollege.ca.

BROOKS SCHOOL

1160 Great Pond Road
North Andover, Massachusetts 01845-1298
Head of School: Mr. John R. Packard

General Information Coeducational boarding and day college-preparatory school, affiliated with Episcopal Church. Grades 9–12. Founded: 1926. Setting: suburban. Nearest major city is Boston. Students are housed in single-sex dormitories. 251-acre campus. 39 buildings on campus. Approved or accredited by Association of Independent Schools in New England, New England Association of Schools and Colleges, The Association of Boarding Schools, and Massachusetts Department of Education. Member of National Association of Independent Schools and Secondary School Admission Test Board. Endowment: $73 million. Total enrollment: 359. Upper school average class size: 12. Upper school faculty-student ratio: 1:5.
Upper School Student Profile Grade 9: 74 students (39 boys, 35 girls); Grade 10: 90 students (51 boys, 39 girls); Grade 11: 96 students (51 boys, 45 girls); Grade 12: 99 students (59 boys, 40 girls). 70% of students are boarding students. 60% are state residents. 22 states are represented in upper school student body. 11% are international

students. International students from Canada, China, Hong Kong, Nigeria, Republic of Korea, and Thailand; 9 other countries represented in student body.

Faculty School total: 71. In upper school: 29 men, 42 women; 54 have advanced degrees; 47 reside on campus.

Subjects Offered Algebra, American government-AP, American history, American history-AP, American literature, art history, art history-AP, astronomy, Bible studies, biology, biology-AP, calculus, calculus-AP, ceramics, chemistry, chemistry-AP, Chinese, chorus, computer graphics, computer math, computer programming, computer science, creative writing, dance, drama, driver education, earth science, English, English literature, English-AP, environmental science-AP, ethics, etymology, European history, European history-AP, expository writing, film, fine arts, French, French language-AP, French literature-AP, French-AP, geology, geometry, government and politics-AP, grammar, Greek, health, history, history-AP, honors algebra, honors geometry, honors world history, integrated arts, Irish literature, Italian, journalism, Latin, Latin-AP, life skills, Mandarin, mathematics, Middle East, modern European history-AP, music, music theory, oceanography, ornithology, painting, philosophy, photography, physics, physics-AP, playwriting, poetry, psychology, public speaking, religion, rhetoric, robotics, senior project, senior seminar, Southern literature, Spanish, Spanish language-AP, Spanish literature, Spanish literature-AP, Spanish-AP, statistics, statistics-AP, studio art, theater, theater design and production, theology, trigonometry, visual arts, world history, world history-AP, world literature, writing.

Graduation Requirements Arts and fine arts (art, music, dance, drama), English, foreign language, health, history, mathematics, religion (includes Bible studies and theology), science. Community service is required.

Special Academic Programs 19 Advanced Placement exams for which test preparation is offered; honors section; independent study; term-away projects; study abroad.

College Admission Counseling 89 students graduated in 2008; all went to college, including Boston University; Colby College; Connecticut College; Cornell University; Trinity College; University of Pennsylvania. Median SAT critical reading: 597, median SAT math: 646, median SAT writing: 620, median combined SAT: 1840. 50% scored over 600 on SAT critical reading, 62% scored over 600 on SAT math, 55% scored over 600 on SAT writing, 54% scored over 1800 on combined SAT.

Student Life Upper grades have specified standards of dress, student council. Discipline rests primarily with faculty. Attendance at religious services is required.

Summer Programs Enrichment, advancement, sports, computer instruction programs offered; session focuses on English, mathematics, and SAT preparation; held on campus; accepts boys and girls; open to students from other schools. 70 students usually enrolled. 2009 schedule: June 28 to August 20. Application deadline: none.

Tuition and Aid Day student tuition: $31,710; 7-day tuition and room/board: $42,770. Tuition installment plan (Academic Management Services Plan, Key Tuition Payment Plan, individually arranged payment plans). Need-based scholarship grants available. In 2008–09, 21% of upper-school students received aid. Total amount of financial aid awarded in 2008–09: $2,007,000.

Admissions Traditional secondary-level entrance grade is 9. For fall 2008, 864 students applied for upper-level admission, 240 were accepted, 90 enrolled. ISEE or SSAT, ERB, PSAT, SAT, PLAN or ACT required. Deadline for receipt of application materials: February 1. Application fee required: $50. Interview required.

Athletics Interscholastic: baseball (boys), basketball (b,g), crew (b,g), cross-country running (b,g), field hockey (g), football (b), ice hockey (b,g), lacrosse (b,g), soccer (b,g), softball (g), squash (b,g), tennis (b,g), wrestling (b); intramural: ice hockey (b); coed intramural: fitness, golf, rugby, sailing, skiing (downhill). 1 athletic trainer.

Computers Computers are regularly used in all academic classes. Computer network features include on-campus library services, online commercial services, Internet access, wireless campus network, Internet filtering or blocking technology. Student e-mail accounts and computer access in designated common areas are available to students. The school has a published electronic and media policy.

Contact Judy Beams, Director of Admission. 978-725-6272. Fax: 978-725-6298. E-mail: admission@brooksschool.org. Web site: www.brooksschool.org.

ANNOUNCEMENT FROM THE SCHOOL At Brooks, small classes allow students to work closely with teachers, fostering relationships that are the core of the close-knit community. The challenging curriculum includes seventeen Advanced Placement (AP) courses. Arts are an integral part of school life. Numerous sports teams have won New England or league championships in recent years.

See Close-Up on page 698.

BROOKSTONE SCHOOL

440 Bradley Park Drive
Columbus, Georgia 31904-2989

Head of School: Scott A. Wilson

General Information Coeducational day college-preparatory school. Grades PK–12. Founded: 1951. Setting: suburban. Nearest major city is Atlanta. 112-acre campus. 11 buildings on campus. Approved or accredited by Georgia Independent School Association, Southern Association of Colleges and Schools, Southern Association of Independent Schools, and Georgia Department of Education. Member of National Association of Independent Schools. Endowment: $19.5 million. Total enrollment: 826. Upper school average class size: 14. Upper school faculty-student ratio: 1:10.

Upper School Student Profile Grade 9: 58 students (28 boys, 30 girls); Grade 10: 72 students (46 boys, 26 girls); Grade 11: 79 students (39 boys, 40 girls); Grade 12: 64 students (38 boys, 26 girls).

Faculty School total: 75. In upper school: 17 men, 17 women; 24 have advanced degrees.

Subjects Offered Advanced computer applications, Advanced Placement courses, algebra, American Civil War, American government, American government-AP, American history, American history-AP, American literature, anatomy and physiology, art, art-AP, band, biology, biology-AP, calculus, calculus-AP, chemistry, chemistry-AP, choral music, chorus, Civil War, communications, comparative government and politics-AP, comparative religion, computer applications, computer multimedia, computer programming, computer science, computer science-AP, computers, concert band, concert choir, constitutional law, creative writing, drama, ecology, economics, economics-AP, English, English composition, English literature, English literature and composition-AP, European history, European history-AP, fine arts, French, French language-AP, French-AP, geometry, government and politics-AP, graphic design, health, history-AP, honors algebra, honors English, honors geometry, human geography—AP, humanities, Latin, Latin-AP, law, literature and composition-AP, literature-AP, macro/microeconomics-AP, mathematics, mythology, neuroanatomy, ornithology, physical education, physics, pre-calculus, psychology, science, social science, social studies, Southern literature, Spanish, Spanish language-AP, Spanish-AP, statistics, statistics-AP, studio art-AP, theater, trigonometry, U.S. government, U.S. government and politics-AP, U.S. history, U.S. history-AP, weight training, world history, yearbook, zoology.

Graduation Requirements 3-dimensional design, algebra, American government, American history, arts and fine arts (art, music, dance, drama), biology, chemistry, computer science, economics, electives, English, foreign language, geometry, mathematics, physical education (includes health), science, social science, social studies (includes history), speech, world history, senior year speech.

Special Academic Programs Advanced Placement exam preparation; honors section.

College Admission Counseling 61 students graduated in 2008; all went to college, including Auburn University; Columbus State University; Georgia Institute of Technology; The University of Alabama; University of Georgia; University of Mississippi. Mean SAT critical reading: 577, mean SAT math: 570, mean SAT writing: 572, mean combined SAT: 1719. 44% scored over 600 on SAT critical reading, 42% scored over 600 on SAT math, 40% scored over 600 on SAT writing, 42% scored over 1800 on combined SAT.

Student Life Upper grades have specified standards of dress, student council, honor system. Discipline rests equally with students and faculty.

Tuition and Aid Day student tuition: $12,500. Tuition installment plan (monthly payment plans, individually arranged payment plans, 3 payments in months July, November, and February (no interest)). Tuition reduction for siblings, merit scholarship grants, need-based scholarship grants, need-based loans, middle-income loans available. In 2008–09, 16% of upper-school students received aid; total upper-school merit-scholarship money awarded: $336,000. Total amount of financial aid awarded in 2008–09: $633,400.

Admissions Traditional secondary-level entrance grade is 9. For fall 2008, 59 students applied for upper-level admission, 45 were accepted, 20 enrolled. SSAT, ERB, PSAT, SAT, PLAN or ACT required. Deadline for receipt of application materials: none. Application fee required: $50. On-campus interview required.

Athletics Interscholastic: baseball (boys), basketball (b,g), cheering (g), cross-country running (b,g), football (b), golf (b,g), soccer (b,g), softball (g), tennis (b,g), track and field (b,g), volleyball (g), wrestling (b); intramural: basketball (b,g). 6 PE instructors.

Computers Computers are regularly used in computer applications, creative writing, English, foreign language, French, graphic arts, history, information technology, mathematics, media production, Spanish, video film production, yearbook classes. Computer network features include on-campus library services, online commercial services, Internet access, wireless campus network, Internet filtering or blocking technology. Campus intranet and student e-mail accounts are available to students. Students grades are available online. The school has a published electronic and media policy.

Contact Mary S. Snyder, Enrollment Director. 706-324-1392. Fax: 706-571-0178. E-mail: msnyder@brookstoneschool.org. Web site: www.brookstoneschool.org.

ANNOUNCEMENT FROM THE SCHOOL Since 1951, Brookstone School has been committed to academic excellence. The Brookstone experience also provides the foundation for students to reach beyond the classroom and embrace the values of lifelong learning, integrity, personal responsibility, mutual respect, and service to others.

BROPHY COLLEGE PREPARATORY

4701 North Central Avenue
Phoenix, Arizona 85012-1797

Head of School: Rev. Ed Reese

General Information Boys' day college-preparatory, arts, religious studies, and technology school, affiliated with Roman Catholic Church (Jesuit order). Grades 9–12. Founded: 1928. Setting: urban. 38-acre campus. 8 buildings on campus. Approved or accredited by Jesuit Secondary Education Association, National Catholic Education Association, North Central Association of Colleges and Schools, and Western Catholic Education Association. Endowment: $19.1 million. Total enrollment: 1,253. Upper school average class size: 26. Upper school faculty-student ratio: 1:15.

Upper School Student Profile Grade 9: 342 students (342 boys); Grade 10: 306 students (306 boys); Grade 11: 324 students (324 boys); Grade 12: 281 students (281 boys). 64% of students are Roman Catholic Church (Jesuit order).

Faculty School total: 91. In upper school: 72 men, 19 women; 56 have advanced degrees.

Subjects Offered Advanced Placement courses, advanced studio art-AP, algebra, American history, American literature, anatomy, art, Bible studies, biology, business, calculus, chemistry, community service, computer math, computer programming, computer science, creative writing, drama, earth science, economics, engineering, English, English literature, ethics, European history, expository writing, fine arts, French, geography, geometry, government/civics, health, history, Latin, mathematics, mechanical drawing, music, physical education, physics, probability and statistics, psychology, religion, science, social science, social studies, sociology, Spanish, speech, theater, theology, trigonometry, video film production, world history, world literature.

Graduation Requirements Arts and fine arts (art, music, dance, drama), English, foreign language, mathematics, physical education (includes health), religion (includes Bible studies and theology), science, social studies (includes history). Community service is required.

Special Academic Programs Advanced Placement exam preparation; honors section; study at local college for college credit; study abroad.

College Admission Counseling 292 students graduated in 2008; all went to college, including Arizona State University; Boston College; Loyola Marymount University; Northern Arizona University; Santa Clara University; The University of Arizona. Median SAT critical reading: 575, median SAT math: 585, median SAT writing: 569, median combined SAT: 1729.

Student Life Upper grades have specified standards of dress, student council, honor system. Discipline rests primarily with faculty. Attendance at religious services is required.

Summer Programs Enrichment, advancement, sports, art/fine arts, computer instruction programs offered; session focuses on academic skills and sports; held both on and off campus; held at Manresa Retreat (Sedona, AZ) and Brophy East Campus; accepts boys and girls; open to students from other schools. 1,300 students usually enrolled. 2009 schedule: June 1 to July 2. Application deadline: May 30.

Tuition and Aid Day student tuition: $12,000. Tuition installment plan (The Tuition Plan, monthly payment plans, individually arranged payment plans). Need-based scholarship grants, paying campus jobs available. In 2008–09, 18% of upper-school students received aid. Total amount of financial aid awarded in 2008–09: $1,953,565.

Admissions Traditional secondary-level entrance grade is 9. For fall 2008, 581 students applied for upper-level admission, 375 were accepted, 335 enrolled. STS required. Deadline for receipt of application materials: January 31. Application fee required: $50. On-campus interview required.

Athletics Interscholastic: aquatics, baseball, basketball, cross-country running, diving, flagball, football, golf, ice hockey, lacrosse, soccer, swimming and diving, tennis, track and field, volleyball, wrestling; intramural: aquatics, badminton, baseball, basketball, bicycling, bowling, cheering, climbing, crew, cricket, fishing, fitness, flag football, Frisbee, golf, handball, hockey, ice hockey, lacrosse, mountain biking, outdoor activities, physical fitness, physical training, rock climbing, skiing (downhill), softball, strength & conditioning, table tennis, touch football, ultimate Frisbee, volleyball, wall climbing, water polo, weight lifting, weight training. 2 PE instructors, 15 coaches, 2 athletic trainers.

Computers Computers are regularly used in all academic classes. Computer network features include on-campus library services, online commercial services, Internet access, wireless campus network, Blackboard, computer tablets. Student e-mail accounts are available to students. Students grades are available online. The school has a published electronic and media policy.

Contact Ms. Alana Dorsey, Assistant to Director of Admissions. 602-264-5291 Ext. 6233. Fax: 602-234-1669. E-mail: adorsey@brophyprep.org. Web site: www.brophyprep.org/.

BROTHER MARTIN HIGH SCHOOL

4401 Elysian Fields Avenue
New Orleans, Louisiana 70122-3898

Head of School: Mr. Gregory Rando

General Information Boys' day college-preparatory school, affiliated with Roman Catholic Church. Grades 8–12. Founded: 1869. Setting: urban. 15-acre campus. 3 buildings on campus. Approved or accredited by National Catholic Education Association, Southern Association of Colleges and Schools, The College Board, and Louisiana Department of Education. Endowment: $2 million. Total enrollment: 1,190. Upper school average class size: 25. Upper school faculty-student ratio: 1:23.

Upper School Student Profile Grade 8: 199 students (199 boys); Grade 9: 255 students (255 boys); Grade 10: 252 students (252 boys); Grade 11: 226 students (226 boys); Grade 12: 258 students (258 boys). 88% of students are Roman Catholic.

Faculty School total: 101. In upper school: 65 men, 36 women; 54 have advanced degrees.

Subjects Offered Accounting, algebra, American history, art, band, biology, calculus, calculus-AP, chemistry, chorus, civics/free enterprise, computer programming, computer science, computer science-AP, creative writing, driver education, earth science, English, English-AP, French, geography, geometry, health, JROTC, Latin, mathematics, physical education, physical science, physics, physics-AP, religion, science, social science, social studies, Spanish, typing, world geography, world history.

Graduation Requirements Computer science, English, foreign language, mathematics, physical education (includes health), religion (includes Bible studies and theology), science, social science, social studies (includes history), honors students must have additional credits for graduation. Community service is required.

Special Academic Programs Advanced Placement exam preparation; honors section; study at local college for college credit; academic accommodation for the gifted, the musically talented, and the artistically talented.

College Admission Counseling 247 students graduated in 2008; 245 went to college, including Louisiana State University and Agricultural and Mechanical College; Loyola University New Orleans; The University of Alabama; Tulane University; University of New Orleans. Other: 2 went to work. Mean SAT math: 581, mean composite ACT: 24. 18% scored over 600 on SAT critical reading, 45% scored over 600 on SAT math, 40% scored over 26 on composite ACT.

Student Life Upper grades have uniform requirement, student council. Discipline rests primarily with faculty. Attendance at religious services is required.

Summer Programs Remediation, enrichment, advancement programs offered; session focuses on remediation and new course offerings; held on campus; accepts boys and girls; open to students from other schools. 150 students usually enrolled. 2009 schedule: June to July. Application deadline: June 1.

Tuition and Aid Day student tuition: $4090. Tuition installment plan (monthly payment plans). Merit scholarship grants, need-based scholarship grants, paying campus jobs available. In 2008–09, 12% of upper-school students received aid; total upper-school merit-scholarship money awarded: $45,000.

Admissions Deadline for receipt of application materials: June 1. No application fee required. On-campus interview required.

Athletics Interscholastic: baseball, basketball, bowling, cross-country running, football, golf, lacrosse, soccer, swimming and diving, tennis, track and field, wrestling; intramural: baseball, basketball, bowling, football, volleyball. 5 PE instructors, 21 coaches, 1 athletic trainer.

Computers Computers are regularly used in English, history, mathematics classes. Computer network features include on-campus library services, online commercial services, Internet access, Internet filtering or blocking technology. Campus intranet and student e-mail accounts are available to students. Students grades are available online.

Contact Gabrielle Macaluso, Director of Admissions. 504-283-1561. Fax: 504-286-8462.

BROTHER RICE HIGH SCHOOL

7101 Lahser Road
Bloomfield Hills, Michigan 48301

Head of School: Mr. John Birney

General Information Boys' day college-preparatory, arts, business, religious studies, and technology school, affiliated with Roman Catholic Church. Grades 9–12. Founded: 1960. Setting: suburban. Nearest major city is Detroit. 20-acre campus. 1 building on campus. Approved or accredited by North Central Association of Colleges and Schools and Michigan Department of Education. Total enrollment: 705. Upper school average class size: 22. Upper school faculty-student ratio: 1:13.

Upper School Student Profile Grade 9: 174 students (174 boys); Grade 10: 190 students (190 boys); Grade 11: 173 students (173 boys); Grade 12: 168 students (168 boys). 75% of students are Roman Catholic.

Faculty School total: 60. In upper school: 35 men, 11 women; 35 have advanced degrees.

Subjects Offered 20th century world history, accounting, algebra, American government, American government-AP, anatomy, anthropology, architectural drawing, art, band, biology, biology-AP, business law, calculus, calculus-AP, chemistry, choir, church history, computer science, computer science-AP, computers, concert band, creative writing, death and loss, debate, drama, earth science, economics, electronics, engineering, English, English composition, English language-AP, ensembles, European history, family living, forensics, French, French-AP, geometry, German, global science, health, jazz band, Latin, library science, literature, mathematics, mechanical drawing, music, music history, music theory, organic chemistry, photography, photojournalism, physical education, physics, physiology, pre-calculus, probability and statistics, psychology, social justice, Spanish, Spanish-AP, speech, studio art—AP, theology, trigonometry, U.S. history, U.S. history-AP, Western civilization, world geography, world religions.

Graduation Requirements Computer science, electives, English, foreign language, mathematics, physical education (includes health), science, social studies (includes history), speech, theology.
Special Academic Programs Advanced Placement exam preparation; honors section; remedial reading and/or remedial writing; remedial math.
College Admission Counseling 163 students graduated in 2008; all went to college, including Central Michigan University; Michigan State University; University of Michigan; Western Michigan University. Median SAT critical reading: 630, median SAT math: 670, median composite ACT: 25. 65% scored over 600 on SAT critical reading, 65% scored over 600 on SAT math, 55% scored over 26 on composite ACT.
Student Life Upper grades have specified standards of dress, student council, honor system. Discipline rests primarily with faculty. Attendance at religious services is required.
Summer Programs Remediation, enrichment, art/fine arts programs offered; session focuses on camps and enrichment; held on campus; accepts boys and girls; open to students from other schools. 400 students usually enrolled. 2009 schedule: June to August.
Tuition and Aid Day student tuition: $8790. Tuition installment plan (The Tuition Plan, monthly payment plans, individually arranged payment plans). Merit scholarship grants, need-based scholarship grants available. In 2008–09, 15% of upper-school students received aid; total upper-school merit-scholarship money awarded: $150,000. Total amount of financial aid awarded in 2008–09: $300,000.
Admissions Traditional secondary-level entrance grade is 9. For fall 2008, 438 students applied for upper-level admission, 250 were accepted, 174 enrolled. Gates MacGinite Reading/Key Math or SAS, STS-HSPT required. Deadline for receipt of application materials: July 31. No application fee required. Interview required.
Athletics Interscholastic: alpine skiing, baseball, basketball, bowling, cross-country running, diving, football, golf, hockey, ice hockey, lacrosse, skiing (downhill), soccer, swimming and diving, tennis, track and field, wrestling; intramural: basketball, bowling, fitness, football, golf, ice hockey, paint ball, rugby, skiing (downhill), snowboarding, strength & conditioning, touch football, ultimate Frisbee, winter (indoor) track. 50 coaches, 1 athletic trainer.
Computers Computer resources include online commercial services, Internet access. The school has a published electronic and media policy.
Contact Mr. David D. Sofran, Director of Admissions. 248-647-2526 Ext. 123. Fax: 248-647-2532. E-mail: sofran@brrice.edu.

BROWNELL-TALBOT SCHOOL

400 North Happy Hollow Boulevard
Omaha, Nebraska 68132
Head of School: Dianne Desler

General Information Coeducational day college-preparatory, arts, and technology school. Grades PS–12. Founded: 1863. Setting: suburban. 17-acre campus. 4 buildings on campus. Approved or accredited by Independent Schools Association of the Central States, North Central Association of Colleges and Schools, and Nebraska Department of Education. Member of National Association of Independent Schools and Educational Records Bureau. Endowment: $5.9 million. Total enrollment: 462. Upper school average class size: 15. Upper school faculty-student ratio: 1:9.
Upper School Student Profile Grade 9: 37 students (18 boys, 19 girls); Grade 10: 30 students (12 boys, 18 girls); Grade 11: 29 students (14 boys, 15 girls); Grade 12: 33 students (14 boys, 19 girls).
Faculty School total: 54. In upper school: 16 men, 13 women; 15 have advanced degrees.
Subjects Offered Advanced Placement courses, algebra, American history, American literature, art, biology, calculus, chemistry, college counseling, computer science, creative writing, dance, drama, economics, English, English literature, environmental science, European history, French, geometry, government/civics, history, journalism, Latin, law, mathematics, music, physical education, physics, robotics, Spanish, speech, sports, statistics, strings, swimming, technology, theater, trigonometry, weightlifting, world history, world literature, writing, yoga.
Graduation Requirements Arts and fine arts (art, music, dance, drama), English, foreign language, mathematics, physical education (includes health), science, social studies (includes history).
Special Academic Programs Study at local college for college credit; academic accommodation for the gifted.
College Admission Counseling 32 students graduated in 2008; all went to college, including Creighton University; Stanford University; University of Colorado at Boulder; University of Notre Dame; Washington University in St. Louis; Yale University. Mean SAT critical reading: 583, mean SAT math: 577, mean SAT writing: 587, mean combined SAT: 1747, mean composite ACT: 26. 44% scored over 600 on SAT critical reading, 52% scored over 600 on SAT math, 44% scored over 600 on SAT writing, 33% scored over 1800 on combined SAT, 73% scored over 26 on composite ACT.
Student Life Upper grades have uniform requirement, student council, honor system. Discipline rests primarily with faculty. Attendance at religious services is required.
Summer Programs Enrichment, sports programs offered; session focuses on robotics, sports; held on campus; accepts boys and girls; open to students from other schools. 100 students usually enrolled. 2009 schedule: June 12 to August 15. Application deadline: none.
Tuition and Aid Day student tuition: $13,100–$14,400. Tuition installment plan (FACTS Tuition Payment Plan, monthly payment plans, individually arranged payment plans, 2-payment plan). Need-based scholarship grants available. In 2008–09, 15% of upper-school students received aid. Total amount of financial aid awarded in 2008–09: $206,700.
Admissions Traditional secondary-level entrance grade is 9. For fall 2008, 39 students applied for upper-level admission, 11 were accepted, 11 enrolled. ERB (grade level), Otis-Lennon School Ability Test and Stanford Achievement Test required. Deadline for receipt of application materials: none. Application fee required: $50. On-campus interview required.
Athletics Interscholastic: baseball (boys), basketball (b,g), cheering (g), cross-country running (b,g), football (b), golf (b,g), soccer (b,g), swimming and diving (b,g), tennis (b,g), track and field (b,g), volleyball (g); intramural: weight lifting (b,g); coed interscholastic: modern dance; coed intramural: aerobics/dance, dance, yoga. 3 PE instructors, 5 coaches, 1 athletic trainer.
Computers Computers are regularly used in all academic classes. Computer network features include on-campus library services, Internet access, wireless campus network, Internet filtering or blocking technology, wireless laptop program (grades 9 to 12). Campus intranet, student e-mail accounts, and computer access in designated common areas are available to students. Students grades are available online. The school has a published electronic and media policy.
Contact Julie L. Adams, Director of Admissions. 402-556-3772 Ext. 116. Fax: 402-553-2994. E-mail: admissions@brownell.edu. Web site: www.brownell.edu.

THE BROWNING SCHOOL

52 East 62nd Street
New York, New York 10021
Head of School: Stephen M. Clement III

General Information Boys' day college-preparatory school. Grades K–12. Founded: 1888. Setting: urban. 2 buildings on campus. Approved or accredited by New York State Association of Independent Schools. Member of National Association of Independent Schools and Secondary School Admission Test Board. Endowment: $18 million. Total enrollment: 389. Upper school average class size: 15. Upper school faculty-student ratio: 1:19.
Upper School Student Profile Grade 9: 26 students (26 boys); Grade 10: 31 students (31 boys); Grade 11: 26 students (26 boys); Grade 12: 30 students (30 boys).
Faculty School total: 56. In upper school: 10 men, 12 women; 18 have advanced degrees.
Subjects Offered Algebra, American history, American literature, art, art history, biology, calculus, ceramics, chemistry, computer math, computer programming, computer science, drama, economics, English, English literature, environmental science, ethics, European history, fine arts, French, general science, geography, geometry, government/civics, grammar, health, history, Latin, mathematics, medieval/Renaissance history, music, philosophy, physical education, physics, political science, psychology, public speaking, science, social science, social studies, sociology, Spanish, speech, technology, theater, trigonometry.
Graduation Requirements Arts and fine arts (art, music, dance, drama), computer science, English, foreign language, mathematics, physical education (includes health), public speaking, science, social science, social studies (includes history), senior community service project.
Special Academic Programs Advanced Placement exam preparation; honors section; independent study; academic accommodation for the gifted.
College Admission Counseling 23 students graduated in 2007; all went to college, including Brown University; Claremont McKenna College; Lewis & Clark College; Middlebury College; University of Chicago; University of Michigan. 48% scored over 600 on SAT critical reading, 44% scored over 600 on SAT math.
Student Life Upper grades have specified standards of dress, student council, honor system. Discipline rests equally with students and faculty.
Tuition and Aid Day student tuition: $29,100. Tuition installment plan (Key Tuition Payment Plan). Need-based scholarship grants available. In 2007–08, 32% of upper-school students received aid. Total amount of financial aid awarded in 2007–08: $953,900.
Admissions Traditional secondary-level entrance grade is 9. For fall 2007, 72 students applied for upper-level admission, 26 were accepted, 9 enrolled. ERB, ISEE and SSAT required. Application fee required: $50. On-campus interview required.
Athletics Interscholastic: baseball, basketball, soccer, tennis; intramural: basketball, cross-country running, ice hockey, soccer, softball, tai chi; coed intramural: fencing. 4 PE instructors, 6 coaches.
Computers Computers are regularly used in English, foreign language, mathematics, science classes. Computer network features include on-campus library services, online commercial services, Internet access. Student e-mail accounts are available to students. The school has a published electronic and media policy.
Contact Liane Pei, Director of Admission. 212-838-6280. Fax: 212-355-5602. E-mail: lpei@browning.edu. Web site: www.browning.edu.

ANNOUNCEMENT FROM THE SCHOOL The Browning School was founded as a college-preparatory school for boys in 1888 by John A. Browning. A traditional curriculum helps support boys intellectually, physically, and emotionally from preprimary through grade 12. Located in the heart of New York

City, the Browning School utilizes the city for all of its vast resources. The 2008–09 school enrollment was 386 boys, with an average grade size of 30. The average class size is about 15 students. Browning is accredited by the New York State Association of Independent Schools (NYSAIS) and the National Association of Independent Schools (NAIS). Browning is a member of Interschool, a consortium of eight private New York City schools (Browning, Collegiate, Chapin, Brearley, Spence, Nightingale-Bamford, Trinity, and Dalton) that offers opportunities for academic sharing, extracurricular participation in the arts, and social activities for boys and girls. College guidance begins in 9th grade and continues throughout high school. In Form V and Form VI, the boys go on college trips and visit up to eight colleges each year. The Athletic Program includes intramural offerings, in addition to interscholastic competition in baseball, basketball, cross-country, soccer, tennis, and track. In high school, there are junior varsity and varsity teams. There is an afterschool program (Encore) for students in preprimary through grade 6. Student clubs and activities include the newspaper, yearbook, Student Council, community service, Computer Club, Drama Club, Model UN, Mock Trial, Investment Club, Multicultural Club, and Literary Magazine. Browning operates on a trimester system. Written reports are sent home to parents six times a year (at the midpoint and end of each trimester). Letter grades are given to students starting in grade 5. The final grades for each trimester are averaged to determine a final year grade, which becomes part of the student's permanent record. Effort and conduct ratings are also noted in the reports.

BRUNSWICK SCHOOL

100 Maher Avenue
Greenwich, Connecticut 06830

Head of School: Thomas W. Philip

General Information Boys' day college-preparatory school. Grades PK–12. Founded: 1902. Setting: suburban. Nearest major city is New York, NY. 118-acre campus. 4 buildings on campus. Approved or accredited by Connecticut Association of Independent Schools, New England Association of Schools and Colleges, and Connecticut Department of Education. Member of National Association of Independent Schools. Endowment: $93 million. Total enrollment: 894. Upper school average class size: 14. Upper school faculty-student ratio: 1:6.

Upper School Student Profile Grade 9: 84 students (84 boys); Grade 10: 83 students (83 boys); Grade 11: 86 students (86 boys); Grade 12: 80 students (80 boys).

Faculty School total: 171. In upper school: 40 men, 14 women; 45 have advanced degrees.

Subjects Offered 20th century history, 3-dimensional design, acting, advanced chemistry, African-American literature, algebra, American government-AP, American history, American history-AP, American literature, anthropology, Arabic, architecture, art, art history, art history-AP, astronomy, biology, biology-AP, calculus, calculus-AP, ceramics, chemistry, chemistry-AP, Chinese, choir, community service, computer graphics, computer programming, computer programming-AP, creative writing, digital art, digital music, drama, earth science, economics, economics-AP, English, environmental science-AP, ethics, European history, European history-AP, film and literature, fine arts, French, French language-AP, French literature-AP, geometry, government-AP, Greek, Greek culture, health, history, honors algebra, honors geometry, human geography—AP, Italian, Japanese history, jazz, jazz band, jazz ensemble, Latin, Latin American literature, Latin-AP, mathematics, media studies, microeconomics, military history, music, oceanography, philosophy, photography, physical education, physics, physics-AP, poetry, pre-calculus, psychology, psychology-AP, science, senior seminar, Shakespeare, short story, social studies, Spanish, Spanish language-AP, Spanish literature-AP, speech and debate, statistics-AP, studio art, studio art—AP, theater, trigonometry, U.S. government-AP, U.S. history-AP, world cultures, world history-AP, writing.

Graduation Requirements Arts and fine arts (art, music, dance, drama), English, foreign language, mathematics, physical education (includes health), science, social studies (includes history). Community service is required.

Special Academic Programs Advanced Placement exam preparation; honors section; independent study; term-away projects; academic accommodation for the gifted, the musically talented, and the artistically talented.

College Admission Counseling 79 students graduated in 2008; all went to college, including Brown University; Bucknell University; Dartmouth College; Georgetown University; Princeton University; University of Pennsylvania. Mean SAT critical reading: 660, mean SAT math: 660, mean SAT writing: 670. 75% scored over 600 on SAT critical reading, 80% scored over 600 on SAT math, 80% scored over 600 on SAT writing.

Student Life Upper grades have specified standards of dress, student council, honor system. Discipline rests equally with students and faculty.

Summer Programs Enrichment programs offered; session focuses on academic enrichment; held both on and off campus; held at integrated with summer programs abroad; accepts boys and girls; open to students from other schools. 2009 schedule: June 8 to July 3. Application deadline: April 1.

Tuition and Aid Day student tuition: $31,100. Tuition installment plan (Key Tuition Payment Plan, monthly payment plans). Need-based scholarship grants available. In 2008–09, 17% of upper-school students received aid. Total amount of financial aid awarded in 2008–09: $1,041,800.

Admissions Traditional secondary-level entrance grade is 9. For fall 2008, 137 students applied for upper-level admission, 28 were accepted, 22 enrolled. ISEE, PSAT or SSAT required. Deadline for receipt of application materials: December 15. Application fee required: $75. On-campus interview required.

Athletics Interscholastic: baseball, basketball, crew, cross-country running, fencing, fitness, football, golf, ice hockey, lacrosse, sailing, soccer, squash, tennis, track and field, wrestling; intramural: basketball, softball, squash, touch football. 4 PE instructors, 2 athletic trainers.

Computers Computers are regularly used in all classes. Computer network features include online commercial services, Internet access, wireless campus network, Internet filtering or blocking technology. Campus intranet and student e-mail accounts are available to students. The school has a published electronic and media policy.

Contact Jeffry Harris, Director of Admission. 203-625-5842. Fax: 203-625-5889. E-mail: jeffry_harris@brunswickschool.org. Web site: www.brunswickschool.org.

ANNOUNCEMENT FROM THE SCHOOL Brunswick School has coordinate classes and activities at the Upper School level with Greenwich Academy, the neighboring girls' school. The coed environment encompasses 80 percent of the classes and includes art, music, drama, community service, and social activities. Completed in 2008, the renovated Upper School campus features a new performing and visual arts center. In 2004, the Lower School moved to a new building on the 104-acre Edwards Campus where the Middle School has been located since 2000. In addition, that campus includes two athletic buildings with five basketball courts, a wrestling room, eight squash courts, a hockey rink, an artificial turf field, and five grass fields.

THE BRYN MAWR SCHOOL FOR GIRLS

109 West Melrose Avenue
Baltimore, Maryland 21210

Head of School: Maureen E. Walsh

General Information Coeducational day (boys' only in lower grades) college-preparatory school. Boys grade PK, girls grades PK–12. Founded: 1885. Setting: suburban. 26-acre campus. 9 buildings on campus. Approved or accredited by Association of Independent Maryland Schools and Maryland Department of Education. Member of National Association of Independent Schools. Endowment: $25.4 million. Total enrollment: 764. Upper school average class size: 15. Upper school faculty-student ratio: 1:7.

Upper School Student Profile Grade 9: 78 students (78 girls); Grade 10: 77 students (77 girls); Grade 11: 73 students (73 girls); Grade 12: 84 students (84 girls).

Faculty School total: 144. In upper school: 17 men, 40 women; 24 have advanced degrees.

Subjects Offered Accounting, algebra, American literature, anatomy, art, art history, astronomy, biology, calculus, ceramics, chemistry, Chinese, computer programming, computer science, creative writing, dance, drama, ecology, economics, emerging technology, English, English literature, ethics, European history, fine arts, French, geography, geometry, German, grammar, Greek, Latin, mathematics, moral theology, music, photography, physical education, physics, public speaking, Russian, science, social studies, Spanish, statistics, technology, theater, trigonometry, urban studies, world history, world literature, writing.

Graduation Requirements Arts and fine arts (art, music, dance, drama), emerging technology, English, foreign language, history, mathematics, physical education (includes health), public speaking, science, 50 hours of community service, convocation speech.

Special Academic Programs Advanced Placement exam preparation; honors section; independent study; term-away projects; study abroad; academic accommodation for the gifted, the musically talented, and the artistically talented.

College Admission Counseling 54 students graduated in 2008; all went to college, including Cornell University; Dartmouth College; Georgetown University; Tulane University; University of Maryland, College Park; Wellesley College. Mean SAT critical reading: 642, mean SAT math: 618, mean SAT writing: 663, mean combined SAT: 1923, mean composite ACT: 26.

Student Life Upper grades have uniform requirement, student council, honor system. Discipline rests equally with students and faculty.

Summer Programs Enrichment, sports, art/fine arts programs offered; session focuses on arts, crafts, language, culture, and sports; held on campus; accepts boys and girls; open to students from other schools. 900 students usually enrolled. 2009 schedule: June 15 to August 21. Application deadline: none.

Tuition and Aid Day student tuition: $21,990. Tuition installment plan (Insured Tuition Payment Plan, Academic Management Services Plan, Key Tuition Payment Plan, FACTS Tuition Payment Plan, monthly payment plans). Need-based scholarship grants, need-based loans, middle-income loans available. In 2008–09, 24% of upper-school students received aid. Total amount of financial aid awarded in 2008–09: $1,008,060.

Admissions Traditional secondary-level entrance grade is 9. For fall 2008, 82 students applied for upper-level admission, 58 were accepted, 28 enrolled. ISEE

required. Deadline for receipt of application materials: January 5. Application fee required: $60. On-campus interview required.
Athletics Interscholastic: badminton, ballet, basketball, crew, cross-country running, dance, field hockey, hockey, indoor soccer, indoor track & field, lacrosse, rowing, running, soccer, softball, squash, tennis, track and field, volleyball, winter (indoor) track, winter soccer; intramural: aerobics, aerobics/dance, aerobics/Nautilus, archery, badminton, ball hockey, basketball, bowling, cooperative games, croquet, cross-country running, dance, fitness, flag football, floor hockey, ice hockey, jogging, outdoor activities, physical training, pillo polo, ropes courses, running, strength & conditioning, tennis, touch football, weight training. 4 PE instructors, 45 coaches, 1 athletic trainer.
Computers Computers are regularly used in all academic, animation, art classes. Computer network features include on-campus library services, online commercial services, Internet access, off-campus e-mail. The school has a published electronic and media policy.
Contact Talia Titus, Director of Admission and Financial Aid. 410-323-8800 Ext. 1237. Fax: 410-435-4678. E-mail: titust@brynmawrschool.org. Web site: www.brynmawrschool.org.

BUCKINGHAM BROWNE & NICHOLS SCHOOL

80 Gerry's Landing Road
Cambridge, Massachusetts 02138-5512

Head of School: Rebecca T. Upham

General Information Coeducational day college-preparatory and arts school. Grades PK–12. Founded: 1883. Setting: urban. Nearest major city is Boston. 5-acre campus. 6 buildings on campus. Approved or accredited by Association of Independent Schools in New England, New England Association of Schools and Colleges, and Massachusetts Department of Education. Member of National Association of Independent Schools and Secondary School Admission Test Board. Endowment: $42 million. Total enrollment: 968. Upper school average class size: 13. Upper school faculty-student ratio: 1:7.
Upper School Student Profile Grade 9: 119 students (61 boys, 58 girls); Grade 10: 123 students (63 boys, 60 girls); Grade 11: 116 students (60 boys, 56 girls); Grade 12: 115 students (55 boys, 60 girls).
Faculty School total: 132. In upper school: 32 men, 31 women; 56 have advanced degrees.
Subjects Offered Advanced Placement courses, African-American studies, algebra, American history, American literature, ancient history, art, art history, art history-AP, biology, bivouac, calculus, ceramics, chemistry, Chinese, Chinese history, community service, computer science, dance, design, drama, economics, English, English literature, European history, film, fine arts, French, geometry, government/civics, history, Latin, mathematics, medieval history, music, photography, physical education, physics, physiology, psychology, Russian, science, social studies, Spanish, statistics, theater, trigonometry, video, woodworking.
Graduation Requirements Arts and fine arts (art, music, dance, drama), bivouac, English, foreign language, history, mathematics, science, senior spring project. Community service is required.
Special Academic Programs Advanced Placement exam preparation; honors section; independent study; term-away projects; study at local college for college credit; study abroad; academic accommodation for the gifted, the musically talented, and the artistically talented.
College Admission Counseling 114 students graduated in 2007; 113 went to college, including Harvard University; Middlebury College; New York University; University of Pennsylvania; Wesleyan University; Yale University. Mean SAT critical reading: 677, mean SAT math: 672. 85% scored over 600 on SAT critical reading, 84% scored over 600 on SAT math.
Student Life Upper grades have specified standards of dress, student council. Discipline rests equally with students and faculty.
Tuition and Aid Day student tuition: $31,440. Tuition installment plan (Insured Tuition Payment Plan, Key Tuition Payment Plan, monthly payment plans). Need-based scholarship grants available. In 2007–08, 23% of upper-school students received aid. Total amount of financial aid awarded in 2007–08: $2,334,090.
Admissions Traditional secondary-level entrance grade is 9. For fall 2007, 405 students applied for upper-level admission, 94 were accepted, 40 enrolled. ISEE or SSAT required. Deadline for receipt of application materials: January 15. Application fee required: $50. Interview required.
Athletics Interscholastic: baseball (boys), basketball (b,g), crew (b,g), cross-country running (b,g), fencing (b,g), field hockey (g), football (b), hockey (b,g), ice hockey (b,g), lacrosse (b,g), sailing (b,g), skiing (downhill) (b,g), soccer (b,g), softball (g), tennis (b,g), track and field (b,g), volleyball (g), wrestling (b); coed interscholastic: alpine skiing, golf; coed intramural: aerobics, aerobics/dance, aerobics/Nautilus, backpacking, fitness, physical fitness, sailing, tennis. 2 PE instructors, 20 coaches, 2 athletic trainers.
Computers Computers are regularly used in mathematics, programming, science, video film production classes. Computer network features include on-campus library services, online commercial services, Internet access. Student e-mail accounts are available to students. The school has a published electronic and media policy.
Contact Amy Pratt, Admission Assistant. 617-800-2136. Fax: 617-547-7696. E-mail: Amy_Pratt@bbns.org. Web site: www.bbns.org.

ANNOUNCEMENT FROM THE SCHOOL BB&N's proximity to the educational and cultural resources of Cambridge and Boston enriches its rigorous, broad curriculum and its vibrant, diverse community of learners. BB&N takes seriously its mission to prepare students for the challenges of an increasingly interdependent world and offers courses in Russian, French, Spanish, Latin, Mandarin Chinese, and Arabic. Strong programs in the humanities, sciences, mathematics, arts, and athletics prepare students for a wide range of selective colleges. Academic programs with schools in France, Italy, Russia, China, and Switzerland are available. The Nicholas Athletic Center includes a rink, fitness center, three basketball courts, and an indoor rowing tank. A new upper school wing with expanded space for classrooms and the arts opened in the fall of 2007.

THE BUCKLEY SCHOOL

3900 Stansbury Avenue
Sherman Oaks, California 91423

Head of School: Larry W. Dougherty, EdD

General Information Coeducational day college-preparatory, arts, and technology school. Grades K–12. Founded: 1933. Setting: suburban. Nearest major city is Los Angeles. 20-acre campus. 8 buildings on campus. Approved or accredited by California Association of Independent Schools, Western Association of Schools and Colleges, and California Department of Education. Member of National Association of Independent Schools. Endowment: $2.7 million. Total enrollment: 750. Upper school average class size: 14. Upper school faculty-student ratio: 1:8.
Upper School Student Profile Grade 9: 83 students (40 boys, 43 girls); Grade 10: 93 students (44 boys, 49 girls); Grade 11: 64 students (33 boys, 31 girls); Grade 12: 70 students (35 boys, 35 girls).
Faculty School total: 100. In upper school: 28 men, 27 women; 31 have advanced degrees.
Subjects Offered Algebra, American history, American literature, art history, biology, calculus, ceramics, chemistry, chorus, computer graphics, computer science, creative writing, dance, drama, ecology, English, English literature, fine arts, French, geology, geometry, government/civics, humanities, journalism, Latin, mathematics, music, music theory, orchestra, photography, physical education, physics, science, social science, Spanish, theater, trigonometry, world history, world literature, yoga.
Graduation Requirements Arts and fine arts (art, music, dance, drama), computer science, English, foreign language, humanities, mathematics, performing arts, physical education (includes health), science, social science. Community service is required.
Special Academic Programs Advanced Placement exam preparation; honors section; study abroad.
College Admission Counseling 75 students graduated in 2008; all went to college, including Columbia College; Loyola Marymount University; Rhode Island School of Design; University of California, Berkeley; University of Colorado at Boulder; University of Southern California.
Student Life Upper grades have uniform requirement, student council, honor system. Discipline rests equally with students and faculty.
Summer Programs Advancement, art/fine arts, computer instruction programs offered; session focuses on college preparatory courses and enrichment; held on campus; accepts boys and girls; open to students from other schools. 100 students usually enrolled.
Tuition and Aid Day student tuition: $24,775. Tuition installment plan (Academic Management Services Plan, Key Tuition Payment Plan). Need-based scholarship grants available. In 2008–09, 12% of upper-school students received aid. Total amount of financial aid awarded in 2008–09: $551,003.
Admissions Traditional secondary-level entrance grade is 9. ISEE required. Deadline for receipt of application materials: January 15. Application fee required: $100. On-campus interview required.
Athletics Interscholastic: baseball (boys), basketball (b,g), equestrian sports (b,g), soccer (b,g), softball (g), swimming and diving (b,g), tennis (b,g), volleyball (g); coed interscholastic: cross-country running. 12 PE instructors, 11 coaches, 2 athletic trainers.
Computers Computers are regularly used in art, English, graphic design, music, science, video film production classes. Computer network features include on-campus library services, online commercial services, Internet access, wireless campus network, Internet filtering or blocking technology, Web page design, online interaction with UCLA, online syllabi. Student e-mail accounts are available to students.
Contact Carinne M. Barker, Director of Admission and Financial Aid. 818-783-1610 Ext. 709. Fax: 818-461-6714. E-mail: admissions@buckleyla.org. Web site: www.buckleyla.org.

BUFFALO SEMINARY

205 Bidwell Parkway
Buffalo, New York 14222

Head of School: Jody Douglass

General Information Girls' day college-preparatory, arts, and technology school. Grades 9–12. Founded: 1851. Setting: urban. 1-acre campus. 1 building on campus. Approved or accredited by Middle States Association of Colleges and Schools, New York Department of Education, New York State Association of Independent Schools, and New York Department of Education. Member of National Association of Independent Schools. Total enrollment: 161. Upper school average class size: 11. Upper school faculty-student ratio: 1:10.

Upper School Student Profile Grade 9: 41 students (41 girls); Grade 10: 39 students (39 girls); Grade 11: 43 students (43 girls); Grade 12: 38 students (38 girls).

Faculty School total: 30. In upper school: 4 men, 26 women; 15 have advanced degrees.

Subjects Offered 20th century history, acting, advanced math, Advanced Placement courses, algebra, American biography, American government-AP, American history, American history-AP, American literature, American literature-AP, ancient history, applied arts, art, art appreciation, art history, art history-AP, astronomy, athletics, biology, biology-AP, British literature (honors), British literature-AP, calculus, chemistry, choral music, community service, composition-AP, computer science, conceptual physics, contemporary women writers, creative writing, dance, drama, drama workshop, dramatic arts, drawing, driver education, economics, English, English language and composition-AP, English language-AP, English literature, English literature and composition-AP, English literature-AP, English-AP, English/composition-AP, environmental science, European history, European history-AP, European literature, expository writing, fine arts, French, French language-AP, French literature-AP, geometry, grammar, honors English, honors U.S. history, honors world history, Latin, literature-AP, logic, mathematics, mathematics-AP, modern European history, modern European history-AP, music, photography, physical education, physics, science, social studies, Spanish, Spanish language-AP, Spanish literature-AP, statistics, theater, trigonometry, world history, world literature, writing.

Graduation Requirements Arts and fine arts (art, music, dance, drama), computer science, English, foreign language, health education, history, mathematics, physical education (includes health), science, Senior internship. Community service is required.

Special Academic Programs Advanced Placement exam preparation; honors section; independent study; academic accommodation for the gifted.

College Admission Counseling 51 students graduated in 2008; all went to college, including Boston College; Harvard University; University of Pittsburgh; University of Vermont. Mean SAT critical reading: 600, mean SAT math: 550. 71% scored over 600 on SAT critical reading, 65% scored over 600 on SAT math.

Student Life Upper grades have specified standards of dress, student council, honor system. Discipline rests primarily with faculty.

Tuition and Aid Day student tuition: $15,970; 7-day tuition and room/board: $32,500. Tuition installment plan (FACTS Tuition Payment Plan, monthly payment plans, individually arranged payment plans, 2-payment plan, prepayment discount plan). Merit scholarship grants, need-based scholarship grants available. In 2008–09, 42% of upper-school students received aid; total upper-school merit-scholarship money awarded: $30,000. Total amount of financial aid awarded in 2008–09: $400,000.

Admissions Traditional secondary-level entrance grade is 9. For fall 2008, 100 students applied for upper-level admission, 80 were accepted, 40 enrolled. School placement exam, school's own exam and writing sample required. Deadline for receipt of application materials: none. Application fee required: $25. On-campus interview required.

Athletics Interscholastic: basketball, crew, fencing, field hockey, golf, lacrosse, soccer, squash, swimming and diving, tennis; intramural: aerobics, aerobics/Nautilus, badminton, dance, drill team, fitness, fitness walking, indoor soccer, martial arts, Nautilus, physical fitness, physical training, self defense, skiing (downhill), strength & conditioning, tai chi, volleyball, yoga. 2 PE instructors, 20 coaches, 1 athletic trainer.

Computers Computers are regularly used in digital applications classes. Computer network features include on-campus library services, online commercial services, Internet access, wireless campus network, Internet filtering or blocking technology. Campus intranet, student e-mail accounts, and computer access in designated common areas are available to students. Students grades are available online. The school has a published electronic and media policy.

Contact Mrs. Carrie Auwarter, Director of Admission. 716-885-6780 Ext. 205. Fax: 716-885-6785. E-mail: cauwarter@buffaloseminary.org.

BULLOCH ACADEMY

873 Westside Road
Statesboro, Georgia 30458

Head of School: Dr. Brenda Shuman Riley

General Information Coeducational day college-preparatory and technology school, affiliated with Christian faith, Baptist Church. Grades PK–12. Founded: 1971. Setting: small town. Nearest major city is Savannah. 35-acre campus. 3 buildings on campus. Approved or accredited by Georgia Accrediting Commission, Georgia Independent School Association, Southern Association of Colleges and Schools, and Southern Association of Independent Schools. Total enrollment: 460. Upper school average class size: 16. Upper school faculty-student ratio: 1:16.

Upper School Student Profile Grade 9: 18 students (5 boys, 13 girls); Grade 10: 24 students (16 boys, 8 girls); Grade 11: 24 students (5 boys, 19 girls); Grade 12: 28 students (17 boys, 11 girls). 98% of students are Christian, Baptist.

Faculty School total: 27. In upper school: 4 men, 7 women; 3 have advanced degrees.

Subjects Offered Advanced Placement courses, American government, American government-AP, American history, art, art education, biology, calculus, chemistry, computer applications, computer science, earth science, economics, economics and history, English, ethics, geometry, government, government-AP, government/civics, health education, journalism, language and composition, language arts, literature-AP, mathematics-AP, music, performing arts, physical education, physics, physiology-anatomy, pre-algebra, pre-calculus, research skills, science, social science, Spanish, speech and debate, technology, U.S. history, Web site design, world geography, world history.

Graduation Requirements Computer science, English, foreign language, mathematics, physical education (includes health), science, social science, social studies (includes history).

Special Academic Programs 6 Advanced Placement exams for which test preparation is offered; honors section; independent study; study at local college for college credit; academic accommodation for the gifted, the musically talented, and the artistically talented.

College Admission Counseling 22 students graduated in 2008; all went to college, including Georgia College & State University; Georgia Southern University; Mercer University; Presbyterian College; University of Georgia. Median SAT critical reading: 584, median SAT math: 583, median SAT writing: 571, median combined SAT: 1738.

Student Life Upper grades have specified standards of dress, student council, honor system. Discipline rests primarily with faculty.

Summer Programs Enrichment, sports, art/fine arts, computer instruction programs offered; session focuses on week-long camps; held both on and off campus; held at college campuses; accepts boys and girls; open to students from other schools. 2009 schedule: May to August.

Tuition and Aid Day student tuition: $6082. Tuition installment plan (monthly payment plans, individually arranged payment plans). Tuition reduction for siblings, Tuition assistance available available.

Admissions Traditional secondary-level entrance grade is 9. For fall 2008, 5 students applied for upper-level admission, 5 were accepted, 5 enrolled. Any standardized test and Iowa Tests of Basic Skills required. Deadline for receipt of application materials: none. Application fee required: $350. Interview recommended.

Athletics Interscholastic: baseball (boys), basketball (b,g), cheering (g), cross-country running (b,g), dance team (g), football (b), golf (b,g), physical fitness (b,g), running (b,g), soccer (b,g), softball (g), strength & conditioning (b,g), tennis (b,g), track and field (b,g), weight lifting (b,g), weight training (b,g), wrestling (b); intramural: cheering (g), cross-country running (b,g), football (b), physical fitness (b,g); coed interscholastic: physical fitness; coed intramural: basketball, football, physical fitness. 3 PE instructors, 7 coaches, 2 athletic trainers.

Computers Computers are regularly used in art, career education, career exploration, computer applications, creative writing, desktop publishing, economics, geography, history, independent study, keyboarding, technology classes. Computer network features include on-campus library services, Internet access, Internet filtering or blocking technology. Student e-mail accounts are available to students. The school has a published electronic and media policy.

Contact Dr. Brenda Shuman Riley, Headmaster. 912-764-6297. Fax: 912-764-3165. E-mail: briley@bullochacademy.com. Web site: www.bullochacademy.com.

BURKE MOUNTAIN ACADEMY

PO Box 78
East Burke, Vermont 05832

Head of School: Kirk Dwyer

General Information Coeducational boarding and day college-preparatory school. Grades 7–PG. Founded: 1970. Setting: rural. Nearest major city is St. Johnsbury. Students are housed in coed dormitories. 33-acre campus. 9 buildings on campus. Approved or accredited by New England Association of Schools and Colleges and Vermont Department of Education. Member of National Association of Independent Schools. Total enrollment: 64. Upper school average class size: 15. Upper school faculty-student ratio: 1:7.

Upper School Student Profile Grade 7: 1 student (1 girl); Grade 8: 11 students (7 boys, 4 girls); Grade 9: 9 students (4 boys, 5 girls); Grade 10: 12 students (6 boys, 6 girls); Grade 11: 14 students (9 boys, 5 girls); Grade 12: 15 students (8 boys, 7 girls); Postgraduate: 3 students (3 girls). 7% of students are boarding students. 20% are state residents. 15 states are represented in upper school student body. 7% are international students. International students from Australia, Canada, and United Kingdom.

Faculty School total: 9. In upper school: 4 men, 5 women; 6 have advanced degrees; 3 reside on campus.

Subjects Offered Algebra, American history, American literature, art, biology, calculus, chemistry, creative writing, current events, English, English literature, European history, fine arts, French, geometry, history, mathematics, physical education, physics, science, social studies, world history, world literature, writing.

Graduation Requirements Arts and fine arts (art, music, dance, drama), English, foreign language, mathematics, physical education (includes health), science, social studies (includes history).

Special Academic Programs Advanced Placement exam preparation; independent study; term-away projects; study at local college for college credit; study abroad.

College Admission Counseling 12 students graduated in 2008; 9 went to college, including Middlebury College; St. Lawrence University; University of Vermont; Williams College. Other: 3 entered a postgraduate year.

Student Life Upper grades have honor system. Discipline rests equally with students and faculty.

Tuition and Aid Tuition installment plan (monthly payment plans, individually arranged payment plans). Need-based scholarship grants, need-based loans, paying campus jobs available.

Admissions SSAT required. Deadline for receipt of application materials: none. Application fee required: $100. Interview recommended.

Athletics Interscholastic: alpine skiing (boys, girls), golf (b,g), nordic skiing (b,g), skiing (cross-country) (b,g), skiing (downhill) (b,g), soccer (b,g); intramural: alpine skiing (b,g), nordic skiing (b,g), soccer (b,g); coed interscholastic: cross-country running. 6 coaches, 1 athletic trainer.

Computers Computers are regularly used in English, foreign language, mathematics, science classes. Computer resources include Internet access.

Contact Marcia Berry, Office Manager. 802-626-5607. Fax: 802-626-3784. E-mail: mberry@burkemtnacademy.org. Web site: www.burkemtnacademy.org.

BURR AND BURTON ACADEMY

57 Seminary Avenue
Manchester, Vermont 05254

Head of School: Mr. Mark Tashjian

General Information Coeducational boarding and day college-preparatory, general academic, arts, and technology school. Grades 9–12. Founded: 1829. Setting: small town. Nearest major city is Albany, NY. Students are housed in single-sex dormitories and homes of host families. 29-acre campus. 7 buildings on campus. Approved or accredited by New England Association of Schools and Colleges and Vermont Department of Education. Member of National Association of Independent Schools. Total enrollment: 686. Upper school average class size: 19. Upper school faculty-student ratio: 1:12.

Upper School Student Profile Grade 9: 172 students (96 boys, 76 girls); Grade 10: 155 students (67 boys, 88 girls); Grade 11: 226 students (106 boys, 120 girls); Grade 12: 179 students (95 boys, 84 girls). 1% are international students.

Faculty School total: 60. In upper school: 35 men, 25 women; 30 have advanced degrees.

Subjects Offered Algebra, American history, American literature, anatomy, art, art history, biology, business, calculus, chemistry, computer math, computer programming, computer science, drafting, drama, driver education, earth science, ecology, English, English literature, environmental science, expository writing, French, geometry, German, government/civics, health, history, industrial arts, mathematics, music, photography, physical education, physics, psychology, science, social studies, Spanish, theater, trigonometry, typing, world history, world literature.

Graduation Requirements Arts, computer literacy, English, mathematics, physical education (includes health), science, social studies (includes history). Community service is required.

Special Academic Programs Advanced Placement exam preparation; independent study; term-away projects; study abroad; remedial reading and/or remedial writing; remedial math; programs in English, mathematics, general development for dyslexic students; special instructional classes for deaf students, blind students; ESL (12 students enrolled).

College Admission Counseling 173 students graduated in 2008; 144 went to college, including Keene State College; Montana State University; Skidmore College; St. Lawrence University; University of Vermont. Other: 16 went to work, 5 entered military service, 1 entered a postgraduate year, 7 had other specific plans.

Student Life Upper grades have specified standards of dress, student council. Discipline rests primarily with faculty.

Tuition and Aid Day student tuition: $14,100; 7-day tuition and room/board: $31,500. Tuition installment plan (individually arranged payment plans).

Admissions Traditional secondary-level entrance grade is 9. School's own test and SLEP for foreign students required. Deadline for receipt of application materials: none. No application fee required. Interview recommended.

Athletics Interscholastic: alpine skiing (boys, girls), baseball (b), basketball (b,g), cross-country running (b,g), dance team (g), football (b), golf (b,g), ice hockey (b,g), lacrosse (b,g), nordic skiing (b,g), skiing (cross-country) (b,g), skiing (downhill) (b,g), soccer (b,g), softball (g), tennis (b,g), track and field (b,g); coed intramural: field hockey, floor hockey, outdoor adventure, outdoor education, volleyball. 3 PE instructors.

Computers Computers are regularly used in drafting, drawing and design, English, foreign language, graphic design, history, information technology, mathematics, science, video film production, Web site design, yearbook classes. Computer network features include on-campus library services, online commercial services, Internet access, Internet filtering or blocking technology.

Contact Mr. Philip G. Anton, Director of Admission and School Counseling. 802-362-1775 Ext. 125. Fax: 802-362-0574. E-mail: panton@burrburton.org. Web site: www.burrburton.org.

THE BUSH SCHOOL

3400 East Harrison Street
Seattle, Washington 98112

Head of School: Mr. Frank Magusin

General Information Coeducational day college-preparatory and experiential learning school. Grades K–12. Founded: 1924. Setting: urban. 6-acre campus. 2 buildings on campus. Approved or accredited by Northwest Association of Accredited Schools, Northwest Association of Schools and Colleges, Pacific Northwest Association of Independent Schools, and Washington Department of Education. Member of National Association of Independent Schools. Endowment: $10 million. Total enrollment: 578. Upper school average class size: 13. Upper school faculty-student ratio: 1:6.

Upper School Student Profile Grade 9: 70 students (32 boys, 38 girls); Grade 10: 62 students (35 boys, 27 girls); Grade 11: 50 students (22 boys, 28 girls); Grade 12: 56 students (33 boys, 23 girls).

Faculty School total: 80. In upper school: 18 men, 19 women; 28 have advanced degrees.

Subjects Offered Acting, advanced chemistry, advanced math, African American history, African American studies, algebra, American literature, anatomy and physiology, animal behavior, animal science, anthropology, art, art history, astronomy, Bible as literature, biology, biotechnology, calculus, career experience, cartooning/animation, ceramics, chemistry, civics, community service, comparative religion, composition, computer art, computer graphics, computer math, computer multimedia, computer programming, computer science, creative writing, critical writing, dance, digital art, directing, diversity studies, drama, drama workshop, drawing, drawing and design, earth science, ecology, English, English composition, English literature, ensembles, environmental science, environmental studies, ethics, ethics and responsibility, European civilization, European history, experiential education, expository writing, fiber arts, filmmaking, fine arts, fitness, foreign policy, French, genetics, geography, geology, geometry, glassblowing, golf, government/civics, health education, history, history of China and Japan, history of religion, human anatomy, improvisation, Indian studies, instrumental music, internship, Latin American literature, literary magazine, literature, literature by women, logic, marine science, mathematics, metalworking, microbiology, Middle East, music, music composition, music performance, music theater, music theory, musical productions, musical theater, newspaper, nuclear science, oceanography, oil painting, opera, outdoor education, painting, photography, physical education, physics, play production, playwriting and directing, poetry, pre-calculus, printmaking, probability and statistics, programming, psychology, public policy issues and action, religion and culture, Romantic period literature, Russia and contemporary Europe, Russian studies, science, sculpture, senior career experience, senior internship, senior project, service learning/internship, sewing, Shakespeare, short story, social studies, South African history, Spanish, Spanish literature, statistics, student publications, tennis, Thailand and Southeast Asia, theater, theater production, track and field, trigonometry, U.S. history, vocal ensemble, voice ensemble, volleyball, Western civilization, Western philosophy, wilderness camping, wilderness education, wilderness experience, wilderness studies, wilderness/outdoor program, women's literature, women's studies, woodworking, work experience, world cultures, world history, world literature, world religions, writing workshop, yearbook.

Graduation Requirements Arts and fine arts (art, music, dance, drama), computer science, English, foreign language, mathematics, physical education (includes health), physiology, science, social studies (includes history), experiential learning course every trimester. Community service is required.

Special Academic Programs Advanced Placement exam preparation; independent study; term-away projects; domestic exchange program (with The Network Program Schools); study abroad.

College Admission Counseling 56 students graduated in 2007; 45 went to college, including Lewis & Clark College; Mount Holyoke College; New York University; Pitzer College; The Colorado College; University of Washington.

Student Life Upper grades have student council, honor system. Discipline rests primarily with faculty.

Tuition and Aid Day student tuition: $22,200. Tuition installment plan (Insured Tuition Payment Plan, monthly payment plans, individually arranged payment plans, Dewar Tuition Refund Plan). Need-based scholarship grants available. In 2007–08, 15% of upper-school students received aid. Total amount of financial aid awarded in 2007–08: $495,178.

Admissions Traditional secondary-level entrance grade is 9. ISEE required. Deadline for receipt of application materials: January 17. Application fee required: $60. Interview required.

Athletics Interscholastic: baseball (boys), basketball (b,g), cross-country running (b,g), golf (b,g), running (b,g), skiing (cross-country) (b,g), soccer (b,g), tennis (b,g), track and field (b,g), ultimate Frisbee (b,g), volleyball (g); intramural: lacrosse (g); coed interscholastic: nordic skiing, skiing (cross-country), ultimate Frisbee; coed intramural: backpacking, climbing, curling, fencing, Frisbee, hiking/backpacking, outdoor activities, outdoor adventure, outdoor education, outdoor skills, rafting, rock climbing, skiing (downhill), ultimate Frisbee, weight training, wilderness. 3 PE instructors, 3 coaches.

Computers Computers are regularly used in art, English, foreign language, mathematics, multimedia, music, science, yearbook classes. Computer network features include on-campus library services, online commercial services, Internet access, wireless campus network, access to wide range of subscription databases with school password. Student e-mail accounts and computer access in designated common areas are available to students. The school has a published electronic and media policy.

Contact Ms. Johnica Hopkins, Admissions Assistant. 206-326-7736. Fax: 206-860-3876. E-mail: johnica.hopkins@bush.edu. Web site: www.bush.edu.

ANNOUNCEMENT FROM THE SCHOOL Founded in 1924, Bush School offers a K–12 educational program based on three foundations: 1) critical, independent, and creative thinking; 2) global citizenship and cultural competency; and 3) ethical thinking and action. Programs emphasize high academic standards and the development of the whole child within a "culture of kindness" that values diversity. Bush School enrolls 580 students; 25% are students of color, and 15% receive financial aid. The average class size is 15. Major entry grades are Kindergarten, sixth grade, and ninth grade.

BUTTE CENTRAL HIGH SCHOOL

9 South Idaho Street
Butte, Montana 59701

Head of School: Mr. Timothy Norbeck

General Information Coeducational day college-preparatory, arts, business, vocational, religious studies, and technology school, affiliated with Roman Catholic Church. Grades 9–12. Founded: 1892. Setting: small town. Nearest major city is Bozeman. 6-acre campus. 1 building on campus. Approved or accredited by National Catholic Education Association, Northwest Association of Accredited Schools, Northwest Association of Schools and Colleges, and Montana Department of Education. Endowment: $300,000. Total enrollment: 121. Upper school average class size: 15. Upper school faculty-student ratio: 1:10.

Upper School Student Profile Grade 9: 32 students (15 boys, 17 girls); Grade 10: 38 students (24 boys, 14 girls); Grade 11: 25 students (16 boys, 9 girls); Grade 12: 26 students (14 boys, 12 girls). 91% of students are Roman Catholic.

Faculty School total: 15. In upper school: 7 men, 7 women; 2 have advanced degrees.

Subjects Offered Accounting, ACT preparation, advanced math, Advanced Placement courses, algebra, American literature-AP, animal behavior, art, athletic training, biology, calculus, calculus-AP, career education, chemistry, choir, college counseling, college placement, college planning, college writing, community service, computer science, computers, debate, desktop publishing, drama, English, English literature and composition-AP, foreign language, French, French as a second language, geometry, government/civics, health, history, honors algebra, honors English, honors geometry, human biology, integrated mathematics, keyboarding, keyboarding/computer, mathematics, model United Nations, physical education, physics, pre-calculus, public speaking, reading, religion, SAT/ACT preparation, science, social studies, Spanish, sports medicine, student government, trigonometry, Web site design, weightlifting, world history, writing, yearbook.

Graduation Requirements American government, American history, arts and fine arts (art, music, dance, drama), electives, English, foreign language, global studies, health education, keyboarding/computer, mathematics, physical education (includes health), religion (includes Bible studies and theology), science, social studies (includes history), writing. Community service is required.

Special Academic Programs 2 Advanced Placement exams for which test preparation is offered; honors section; study at local college for college credit; remedial reading and/or remedial writing; remedial math.

College Admission Counseling 43 students graduated in 2008; 40 went to college, including Carroll University; Division of Technology of Montana Tech of The University of Montana; Gonzaga University; Montana State University; The University of Montana–Western. Other: 2 went to work, 1 had other specific plans. Median composite ACT: 20. 7% scored over 26 on composite ACT.

Student Life Upper grades have specified standards of dress, student council, honor system. Discipline rests primarily with faculty. Attendance at religious services is required.

Tuition and Aid Day student tuition: $4000–$6000. Guaranteed tuition plan. Tuition installment plan (FACTS Tuition Payment Plan, monthly payment plans, individually arranged payment plans). Tuition reduction for siblings, need-based scholarship grants available. In 2008–09, 25% of upper-school students received aid. Total amount of financial aid awarded in 2008–09: $68,000.

Admissions Traditional secondary-level entrance grade is 9. Admissions testing required. Deadline for receipt of application materials: none. Application fee required: $125. Interview required.

Athletics Interscholastic: basketball (boys, girls), cheering (g), cross-country running (b,g), football (b), golf (b,g), softball (g), strength & conditioning (b,g), tennis (b,g), track and field (b,g), volleyball (g), wrestling (b). 1 PE instructor, 30 coaches, 1 athletic trainer.

Computers Computers are regularly used in all academic classes. Computer network features include on-campus library services, Internet access, Internet filtering or blocking technology. The school has a published electronic and media policy.

Contact Mr. Timothy Norbeck, Principal. 406-782-6761. Fax: 406-723-3873. E-mail: tim.norbeck@buttecentralschools.org. Web site: www.buttecentralschools.org.

BUXTON SCHOOL

291 South Street
Williamstown, Massachusetts 01267

Head of School: C. William Bennett & Peter Smith

General Information Coeducational boarding and day college-preparatory and arts school. Grades 9–12. Founded: 1928. Setting: small town. Nearest major city is Boston. Students are housed in single-sex dormitories. 150-acre campus. 17 buildings on campus. Approved or accredited by Association of Independent Schools in New England, New England Association of Schools and Colleges, The Association of Boarding Schools, and Massachusetts Department of Education. Member of National Association of Independent Schools and Secondary School Admission Test Board. Endowment: $1.8 million. Total enrollment: 95. Upper school average class size: 9. Upper school faculty-student ratio: 1:5.

Upper School Student Profile Grade 9: 13 students (3 boys, 10 girls); Grade 10: 29 students (11 boys, 18 girls); Grade 11: 29 students (16 boys, 13 girls); Grade 12: 24 students (14 boys, 10 girls). 89% of students are boarding students. 16% are state residents. 17 states are represented in upper school student body. 11% are international students. International students from Bermuda, China, Ecuador, Japan, Mexico, and Republic of Korea; 2 other countries represented in student body.

Faculty School total: 21. In upper school: 12 men, 9 women; 5 have advanced degrees; 14 reside on campus.

Subjects Offered 20th century history, advanced math, African dance, African drumming, African studies, algebra, American history, American literature, American minority experience, anatomy and physiology, astronomy, biology, calculus, cell biology, ceramics, chemistry, costumes and make-up, creative writing, critical writing, dance performance, drama, drama performance, drawing, English, English literature, ensembles, environmental studies, ESL, European history, expository writing, fiction, French, gender issues, geology, geometry, global issues, grammar, improvisation, independent study, Indonesian, instruments, lab science, Latin American literature, linear algebra, literary genres, literature, marine biology, media literacy, metal-working, minority studies, multicultural studies, music, music composition, music performance, music theory, neuroscience, oceanography, painting, performing arts, philosophy, photography, physics, poetry, pre-calculus, printmaking, radio broadcasting, set design, social science, Spanish, studio art, technical theater, TOEFL preparation, video film production, voice, writing workshop.

Graduation Requirements American history, English, foreign language, lab science, mathematics, social science.

Special Academic Programs Honors section; academic accommodation for the gifted, the musically talented, and the artistically talented; ESL (7 students enrolled).

College Admission Counseling 24 students graduated in 2008; all went to college, including Bard College; Cornell University; Emory University; Mount Holyoke College; Oberlin College; Skidmore College.

Student Life Discipline rests primarily with faculty.

Tuition and Aid Day student tuition: $25,000; 7-day tuition and room/board: $39,500. Need-based scholarship grants, Need-based loans with limited in-house financing available. In 2008–09, 40% of upper-school students received aid. Total amount of financial aid awarded in 2008–09: $1,000,000.

Admissions Traditional secondary-level entrance grade is 9. For fall 2008, 80 students applied for upper-level admission, 52 were accepted, 40 enrolled. SSAT or TOEFL required. Deadline for receipt of application materials: February 1. Application fee required: $50. On-campus interview required.

Athletics Interscholastic: soccer (boys, girls); intramural: soccer (b,g); coed interscholastic: basketball; coed intramural: bicycling, dance, fitness, hiking/backpacking, horseback riding, indoor soccer, jogging, kayaking, martial arts, mountain biking, outdoor activities, physical training, running, skiing (downhill), snowboarding, soccer, table tennis, tennis, ultimate Frisbee, weight lifting, yoga.

Computers Computers are regularly used in history, mathematics, media production, multimedia, music, photography, science, video film production classes. Computer resources include Internet access, wireless campus network. Campus intranet and computer access in designated common areas are available to students. The school has a published electronic and media policy.

Contact Admissions Office. 413-458-3919. Fax: 413-458-9428. E-mail: Admissions@BuxtonSchool.org. Web site: www.BuxtonSchool.org.

ANNOUNCEMENT FROM THE SCHOOL Life at Buxton teaches the importance of a moral and active commitment to a small, diverse community. The sophisticated college-preparatory curriculum also includes art, music, and drama. The student-faculty ratio is 5:1. Individual attention and relationships with adults are emphasized. Work Program and the annual All-School Trip challenge students to meet demands collectively and creatively.

See Close-Up on page 700.

THE BYRNES SCHOOLS

1201 East Ashby Road
Florence, South Carolina 29506

Head of School: Mr. John W. Colby Jr.

General Information Coeducational day college-preparatory school. Grades PK–12. Founded: 1966. Setting: small town. 16-acre campus. 3 buildings on campus. Approved or accredited by South Carolina Independent School Association and Southern Association of Independent Schools. Candidate for accreditation by Southern Association of Colleges and Schools. Endowment: $25,000. Total enrollment: 259. Upper school average class size: 13. Upper school faculty-student ratio: 1:9.

Upper School Student Profile Grade 9: 15 students (4 boys, 11 girls); Grade 10: 13 students (10 boys, 3 girls); Grade 11: 23 students (15 boys, 8 girls); Grade 12: 33 students (20 boys, 13 girls).

Faculty School total: 31. In upper school: 7 men, 9 women; 10 have advanced degrees.

Subjects Offered Advanced Placement courses, algebra, American history, biology, biology-AP, calculus-AP, chemistry, chemistry-AP, computer science, earth science, economics, English, English-AP, environmental science, geography, geometry, government/civics, history-AP, mathematics, physical education, physics, science, social studies, Spanish, Spanish-AP, world history.

Graduation Requirements English, foreign language, mathematics, physical education (includes health), science, social studies (includes history).

Special Academic Programs Advanced Placement exam preparation; honors section; academic accommodation for the gifted.

College Admission Counseling 23 students graduated in 2008; all went to college, including Clemson University; Francis Marion University; Furman University; The Citadel, The Military College of South Carolina; University of South Carolina.

Student Life Upper grades have specified standards of dress, student council, honor system. Discipline rests primarily with faculty.

Summer Programs Remediation, advancement programs offered; session focuses on college prep; held on campus; accepts boys and girls; open to students from other schools. 15 students usually enrolled.

Tuition and Aid Day student tuition: $6500. Tuition installment plan (Insured Tuition Payment Plan). Tuition reduction for siblings, need-based scholarship grants available. In 2008–09, 5% of upper-school students received aid. Total amount of financial aid awarded in 2008–09: $12,000.

Admissions Traditional secondary-level entrance grade is 9. For fall 2008, 10 students applied for upper-level admission, 10 were accepted, 10 enrolled. Iowa Tests of Basic Skills, Metropolitan Achievement Test or Stanford Achievement Test required. Deadline for receipt of application materials: none. Application fee required: $50. On-campus interview required.

Athletics Interscholastic: baseball (boys), basketball (b,g), cheering (g), football (b), golf (b,g), soccer (b,g), softball (g), volleyball (g); intramural: aerobics/dance (g), strength & conditioning (b,g), weight lifting (b,g), weight training (b,g); coed intramural: tennis. 1 PE instructor, 1 athletic trainer.

Computers Computers are regularly used in mathematics, yearbook classes. Computer network features include Internet access. Students grades are available online. The school has a published electronic and media policy.

Contact Mrs. Brandis Winstead, Admissions Director. 843-622-0131 Ext. 153. Fax: 843-669-2466. E-mail: info@byrnesschools.org. Web site: www.byrnesschools.org.

CALGARY ACADEMY

9400-17 Avenue, SW
Calgary, Alberta T3H 4A6, Canada

Head of School: Mr. Peter E. Istvanffy

General Information Coeducational day college-preparatory, arts, and technology school; primarily serves underachievers and students with learning disabilities. Grades 2–12. Founded: 1981. Setting: urban. 17-acre campus. 3 buildings on campus. Approved or accredited by Association of Independent Schools and Colleges of Alberta and Alberta Department of Education. Language of instruction: English. Endowment: CAN$3 million. Total enrollment: 630. Upper school average class size: 16. Upper school faculty-student ratio: 1:8.

Faculty School total: 25. In upper school: 10 men, 15 women; 10 have advanced degrees.

Special Academic Programs Remedial reading and/or remedial writing; remedial math; programs in English, mathematics for dyslexic students; special instructional classes for deaf students.

College Admission Counseling 64 students graduated in 2008; 55 went to college. Other: 4 went to work, 4 had other specific plans.

Student Life Upper grades have specified standards of dress, student council, honor system. Discipline rests primarily with faculty.

Tuition and Aid Day student tuition: CAN$8600–CAN$15,000. Tuition installment plan (monthly payment plans, individually arranged payment plans). Bursaries available. In 2008–09, 5% of upper-school students received aid. Total amount of financial aid awarded in 2008–09: CAN$300,000.

Admissions For fall 2008, 200 students applied for upper-level admission, 150 were accepted, 150 enrolled. Achievement tests, Wechsler Individual Achievement Test and Wechsler Intelligence Scale for Children III required. Deadline for receipt of application materials: none. Application fee required: CAN$950. Interview required.

Athletics Interscholastic: badminton (boys, girls), ball hockey (b), basketball (b,g), cross-country running (b,g), golf (b,g), track and field (b,g), volleyball (b,g), wrestling (b,g); intramural: ice hockey (b,g), indoor soccer (b,g), racquetball (b,g), rock climbing (b,g), self defense (g), squash (b,g), weight training (b,g); coed interscholastic: curling; coed intramural: aerobics, aerobics/dance, aerobics/Nautilus, alpine skiing, aquatics, archery, badminton, ball hockey, baseball, bicycling, bowling, broomball, canoeing/kayaking, climbing, cooperative games, curling, dance, fitness, flag football, football, indoor soccer, modern dance, mountain biking, outdoor recreation, physical fitness, racquetball, sailing, scuba diving, skiing (cross-country), skiing (downhill), skydiving, snowboarding, swimming and diving, team handball, walking. 6 PE instructors, 45 coaches.

Computers Computers are regularly used in all academic classes. Computer network features include on-campus library services, Internet access, wireless campus network, Internet filtering or blocking technology. Campus intranet and computer access in designated common areas are available to students. Students grades are available online. The school has a published electronic and media policy.

Contact Ms. Joanne Endacott, Director of Admissions. 403-686-6444 Ext. 236. Fax: 403-686-3427. E-mail: jendacott@calgaryacademy.com. Web site: www.calgaryacademy.com.

THE CALHOUN SCHOOL

433 West End Avenue
New York, New York 10024

Head of School: Steven J. Nelson

General Information Coeducational day college-preparatory and arts school. Grades N–12. Founded: 1896. Setting: urban. 2 buildings on campus. Approved or accredited by New York State Association of Independent Schools and New York Department of Education. Member of National Association of Independent Schools. Endowment: $2.5 million. Total enrollment: 734. Upper school average class size: 15. Upper school faculty-student ratio: 1:5.

Upper School Student Profile Grade 9: 54 students (26 boys, 28 girls); Grade 10: 43 students (20 boys, 23 girls); Grade 11: 40 students (15 boys, 25 girls); Grade 12: 48 students (21 boys, 27 girls).

Faculty School total: 118. In upper school: 16 men, 18 women; 25 have advanced degrees.

Subjects Offered Acting, advanced biology, advanced chemistry, advanced computer applications, African-American literature, algebra, American history, American literature, anthropology, arts, biology, calculus, chemistry, child development, chorus, community service, computer math, computer programming, computer science, constitutional law, creative writing, English literature, English-AP, ethnic literature, French, geometry, healthful living, human sexuality, independent study, instrumental music, music history, peer counseling, photography, physical education, physics, pre-calculus, psychology, Shakespeare, Spanish, speech, studio art, theater, theater design and production, Web site design, world history, world literature.

Graduation Requirements Arts and fine arts (art, music, dance, drama), English, foreign language, mathematics, physical education (includes health), science, social studies (includes history), 9th grade Life Skills with peer leaders. Community service is required.

Special Academic Programs Independent study; domestic exchange program (with The Network Program Schools); academic accommodation for the gifted.

College Admission Counseling 48 students graduated in 2008; 44 went to college, including Bard College; Oberlin College; Syracuse University; University of Michigan; Wesleyan University; Wheaton College. Median SAT critical reading: 615, median SAT math: 572, median SAT writing: 604.

Student Life Upper grades have student council. Discipline rests primarily with faculty.

Summer Programs Art/fine arts programs offered; session focuses on Shakespeare production; held on campus; accepts boys and girls; open to students from other schools. 16 students usually enrolled. 2009 schedule: June 18 to July 27. Application deadline: March 1.

Tuition and Aid Day student tuition: $33,200. Tuition installment plan (Key Tuition Payment Plan, individually arranged payment plans, 60%/40% payment plan). Need-based scholarship grants, tuition reduction for faculty and staff available. In 2008–09, 21% of upper-school students received aid.

Admissions Traditional secondary-level entrance grade is 9. For fall 2008, 285 students applied for upper-level admission, 33 were accepted, 13 enrolled. ISEE required. Deadline for receipt of application materials: January 15. Application fee required: $50. On-campus interview required.

Athletics Interscholastic: baseball (boys, girls), basketball (b,g), cross-country running (b,g), track and field (b,g), volleyball (b,g); coed interscholastic: golf, soccer; coed intramural: aerobics, aerobics/Nautilus, basketball, fitness, golf, project adventure, sailing, soccer, strength & conditioning, tennis, weight training, yoga. 5 PE instructors, 2 coaches.

Computers Computers are regularly used in basic skills, mathematics, programming, video film production, Web site design classes. Computer network features include Internet access, MS Office, PowerPoint, Basic, Dreameaver, and Flash Software. Student e-mail accounts are available to students. The school has a published electronic and media policy.

Contact Jenny Eugenio, Associate Director of Admissions. 212-497-6510. Fax: 212-497-6531. E-mail: jenny.eugenio@calhoun.org. Web site: www.calhoun.org.

ANNOUNCEMENT FROM THE SCHOOL Calhoun's progressive program capitalizes on the intellectual curiosity and creative spirit inherent in every child. Classes are small and discussion based, learning is experiential and interdisciplinary, and the atmosphere is lively. In September 2004, Calhoun expanded its facilities with a new center for performing and studio arts, three science labs, and a regulation-size gymnasium.

CALVARY CHRISTIAN ACADEMY

5955 Taylor Mill Road
Covington, Kentucky 41015
Head of School: Dr. Don James

General Information Coeducational day college-preparatory, arts, religious studies, and technology school, affiliated with Baptist Church. Grades K4–12. Founded: 1974. Setting: suburban. Nearest major city is Cincinnati, OH. 72-acre campus. 1 building on campus. Approved or accredited by Association of Christian Schools International, CITA (Commission on International and Trans-Regional Accreditation), Southern Association of Colleges and Schools, and Kentucky Department of Education. Total enrollment: 636. Upper school average class size: 25. Upper school faculty-student ratio: 1:14.
Upper School Student Profile Grade 9: 46 students (22 boys, 24 girls); Grade 10: 53 students (27 boys, 26 girls); Grade 11: 50 students (30 boys, 20 girls); Grade 12: 48 students (16 boys, 32 girls). 65% of students are Baptist.
Faculty School total: 29. In upper school: 11 men, 9 women; 14 have advanced degrees.
Subjects Offered Advanced math, algebra, American literature-AP, ancient history, art, art appreciation, Bible, biology, biology-AP, calculus, chemistry, chemistry-AP, choir, chorus, Christian doctrine, Christian ethics, communication arts, computer applications, computer keyboarding, computer multimedia, computer science, concert band, concert choir, consumer mathematics, creative writing, cultural geography, drama, drama performance, earth science, English, English composition, English language and composition-AP, English language-AP, English literature, English literature and composition-AP, English literature-AP, English-AP, English/composition-AP, ethics, European history-AP, fitness, food and nutrition, general math, general science, geography, geometry, government-AP, grammar, health education, home economics, honors algebra, independent study, journalism, lab science, language arts, language-AP, library assistant, literature-AP, logic, music theory, newspaper, physical education, physical science, physics-AP, pre-algebra, pre-calculus, rhetoric, Spanish, Spanish-AP, speech and debate, student government, student publications, student teaching, U.S. government, U.S. government-AP, U.S. history, U.S. history-AP, world governments, world history, yearbook.
Graduation Requirements Algebra, art appreciation, Bible, biology, chemistry, Christian doctrine, church history, civics, English, English composition, English literature, European history, foreign language, geometry, health, physical science, U.S. government, U.S. history, world history.
Special Academic Programs Advanced Placement exam preparation; honors section; independent study; study at local college for college credit.
College Admission Counseling 48 students graduated in 2008; 46 went to college, including Cedarville University; Eastern Kentucky University; Northern Kentucky University; University of Cincinnati; University of Kentucky. Other: 2 went to work. Median composite ACT: 26. 25% scored over 26 on composite ACT.
Student Life Upper grades have uniform requirement, student council. Discipline rests primarily with faculty. Attendance at religious services is required.
Tuition and Aid Day student tuition: $4800. Tuition installment plan (FACTS Tuition Payment Plan, monthly payment plans, individually arranged payment plans). Tuition reduction for siblings, need-based scholarship grants, paying campus jobs available. In 2008–09, 8% of upper-school students received aid. Total amount of financial aid awarded in 2008–09: $25,000.
Admissions Traditional secondary-level entrance grade is 9. For fall 2008, 14 students applied for upper-level admission, 14 were accepted, 14 enrolled. Stanford Achievement Test required. Deadline for receipt of application materials: none. Application fee required: $285. Interview required.
Athletics Interscholastic: baseball (boys), basketball (b,g), bowling (b,g), cheering (g), cross-country running (b,g), diving (b,g), golf (b), horseback riding (b,g), physical fitness (b,g), soccer (b,g), softball (g), swimming and diving (b,g), volleyball (g); intramural: indoor soccer (b,g), strength & conditioning (b,g), weight training (b); coed intramural: bowling, gymnastics, physical fitness, running. 2 PE instructors, 15 coaches.
Computers Computers are regularly used in architecture, art, computer applications, design, desktop publishing, drafting, graphics, information technology, journalism, keyboarding, lab/keyboard, library, photography, photojournalism, science, Spanish, technical drawing, Web site design, yearbook classes. Computer network features include on-campus library services, Internet access, wireless campus network, Internet filtering or blocking technology. Campus intranet is available to students. Students grades are available online. The school has a published electronic and media policy.
Contact Mrs. Laurie Switzer, Registrar. 859-356-9201. Fax: 859-359-8962. E-mail: laurie.switzer@calvarychristianky.org. Web site: www.calvarychristianky.org.

CALVERT HALL COLLEGE HIGH SCHOOL

8102 LaSalle Road
Baltimore, Maryland 21286
Head of School: Br. Benedict Oliver, FSC

General Information Boys' day college-preparatory, arts, business, religious studies, and technology school, affiliated with Roman Catholic Church. Grades 9–12. Founded: 1845. Setting: suburban. 32-acre campus. 6 buildings on campus. Approved or accredited by Christian Brothers Association, Middle States Association of Colleges and Schools, National Catholic Education Association, The College Board, and Maryland Department of Education. Endowment: $4.3 million. Total enrollment: 1,254. Upper school average class size: 21. Upper school faculty-student ratio: 1:13.
Upper School Student Profile Grade 9: 325 students (325 boys); Grade 10: 325 students (325 boys); Grade 11: 283 students (283 boys); Grade 12: 321 students (321 boys). 72% of students are Roman Catholic.
Faculty School total: 100. In upper school: 72 men, 28 women; 62 have advanced degrees.
Subjects Offered Algebra, American history, American literature, art, art history, band, Bible studies, biology, business, business skills, calculus, chemistry, chorus, computer programming, computer science, creative writing, drama, earth science, economics, English, English literature, ethics, European history, fine arts, French, geography, geometry, German, government/civics, graphic arts, history, journalism, Latin, leadership skills, mathematics, music, painting, philosophy, physical education, physics, psychology, religion, science, sculpture, social science, social studies, Spanish, speech, statistics, theater, theology, typing, world history, world literature, writing.
Graduation Requirements Arts and fine arts (art, music, dance, drama), English, foreign language, mathematics, physical education (includes health), religion (includes Bible studies and theology), science, social science, social studies (includes history).
Special Academic Programs 21 Advanced Placement exams for which test preparation is offered; honors section; academic accommodation for the gifted, the musically talented, and the artistically talented; remedial reading and/or remedial writing; remedial math; programs in English, mathematics, general development for dyslexic students.
College Admission Counseling 260 students graduated in 2008; 257 went to college, including Frostburg State University; Salisbury University; Stevenson University; Towson University; University of Maryland, Baltimore County; University of Maryland, College Park. Other: 3 went to work.
Student Life Upper grades have specified standards of dress, student council. Discipline rests primarily with faculty. Attendance at religious services is required.
Summer Programs Remediation, enrichment, sports, art/fine arts, computer instruction programs offered; session focuses on remediation and make-up courses; held on campus; accepts boys and girls; open to students from other schools. 250 students usually enrolled. 2009 schedule: June 25 to July 27. Application deadline: June 15.
Tuition and Aid Day student tuition: $10,000. Tuition installment plan (monthly payment plans, individually arranged payment plans). Merit scholarship grants, need-based scholarship grants available. In 2008–09, 40% of upper-school students received aid; total upper-school merit-scholarship money awarded: $428,000. Total amount of financial aid awarded in 2008–09: $1,142,000.
Admissions Traditional secondary-level entrance grade is 9. STS required. Deadline for receipt of application materials: none. Application fee required: $20.
Athletics Interscholastic: aquatics, baseball, basketball, cross-country running, diving, football, golf, ice hockey, indoor track & field, lacrosse, rugby, soccer, swimming and diving, tennis, track and field, volleyball, water polo, winter (indoor) track, wrestling; intramural: basketball, bicycling, billiards, bocce, bowling, fitness, flag football, freestyle skiing, mountain biking, rugby, table tennis, weight lifting. 2 PE instructors, 12 coaches, 1 athletic trainer.
Computers Computers are regularly used in accounting, business, college planning, computer applications, digital applications, economics, English, foreign language, graphic design, history, independent study, journalism, keyboarding, library, literary magazine, mathematics, music, programming, religion, SAT preparation, science, social sciences, stock market, video film production, writing, yearbook classes. Computer network features include on-campus library services, Internet access, wireless campus network, Internet filtering or blocking technology. Campus intranet, student e-mail accounts, and computer access in designated common areas are available to students. Students grades are available online. The school has a published electronic and media policy.
Contact Chris Bengel, Director of Admissions. 410-825-4266 Ext. 126. Fax: 410-825-6826. E-mail: bengelc@calverthall.com. Web site: www.calverthall.com.

THE CALVERTON SCHOOL

300 Calverton School Road
Huntingtown, Maryland 20639
Head of School: Mr. Daniel Hildebrand

General Information Coeducational day college-preparatory, arts, and technology school. Grades PS–12. Founded: 1967. Setting: rural. Nearest major city is Annapolis. 159-acre campus. 3 buildings on campus. Approved or accredited by Association of Independent Maryland Schools, The College Board, and Maryland Department of

Education. Member of National Association of Independent Schools. Total enrollment: 428. Upper school average class size: 15. Upper school faculty-student ratio: 1:11.

Faculty School total: 49. In upper school: 9 men, 11 women; 16 have advanced degrees.

Subjects Offered Advanced Placement courses, algebra, American history, American literature, art, art history, biology, calculus, chemistry, Chesapeake Bay studies, chorus, creative writing, drama, economics, English, English literature, environmental science, European civilization, fine arts, French, French-AP, geometry, government/civics, health, humanities, journalism, literature, mathematics, physical education, physics, pre-calculus, public speaking, publications, SAT/ACT preparation, science, social studies, Spanish, Spanish-AP, studio art-AP, theater, trigonometry, U.S. history, U.S. history-AP, visual and performing arts, world civilizations, world history, world literature, yearbook.

Graduation Requirements Algebra, arts and fine arts (art, music, dance, drama), biology, chemistry, English, English composition, English literature, foreign language, geometry, mathematics, physical education (includes health), physics, science, social studies (includes history), trigonometry, U.S. history, world history.

Special Academic Programs Advanced Placement exam preparation; honors section; independent study.

College Admission Counseling 32 students graduated in 2008; all went to college. Median SAT critical reading: 562, median SAT math: 570, median SAT writing: 475, median combined SAT: 1600, median composite ACT: 25. 29% scored over 600 on SAT critical reading, 29% scored over 600 on SAT math, 22% scored over 600 on SAT writing, 14% scored over 1800 on combined SAT, 40% scored over 26 on composite ACT.

Student Life Upper grades have specified standards of dress, student council, honor system. Discipline rests equally with students and faculty.

Summer Programs Enrichment, advancement, sports, art/fine arts, computer instruction programs offered; session focuses on enrichment; held both on and off campus; held at various sites; accepts boys and girls; open to students from other schools. 125 students usually enrolled. 2009 schedule: June to August. Application deadline: none.

Tuition and Aid Day student tuition: $15,930. Tuition installment plan (Insured Tuition Payment Plan, monthly payment plans, individually arranged payment plans). Need-based scholarship grants available.

Admissions Traditional secondary-level entrance grade is 9. Admissions testing, Math Placement Exam, Otis-Lennon School Ability Test and writing sample required. Deadline for receipt of application materials: none. Application fee required: $35. On-campus interview required.

Athletics Interscholastic: basketball (boys, girls), cross-country running (b,g), lacrosse (b,g); coed interscholastic: field hockey, golf, soccer, tennis; coed intramural: basketball. 3 PE instructors, 10 coaches.

Computers Computers are regularly used in all academic classes. Computer network features include on-campus library services, online commercial services, Internet access, Internet filtering or blocking technology, research services and encyclopedia research programs. Student e-mail accounts are available to students.

Contact Mrs. Julie M. Simpson, Director of Admission. 888-678-0216 Ext. 108. Fax: 410-535-6934 Ext. 108. E-mail: jsimpson@CalvertonSchool.org. Web site: www.CalvertonSchool.org.

THE CAMBRIDGE SCHOOL OF WESTON

45 Georgian Road
Weston, Massachusetts 02493

Head of School: Jane Moulding

General Information Coeducational boarding and day college-preparatory and arts school. Grades 9–PG. Founded: 1886. Setting: suburban. Nearest major city is Boston. Students are housed in single-sex dormitories. 65-acre campus. 25 buildings on campus. Approved or accredited by Association of Independent Schools in New England, New England Association of Schools and Colleges, The Association of Boarding Schools, and The College Board. Member of National Association of Independent Schools and Secondary School Admission Test Board. Endowment: $5 million. Total enrollment: 333. Upper school average class size: 12. Upper school faculty-student ratio: 1:6.

Upper School Student Profile Grade 9: 71 students (26 boys, 45 girls); Grade 10: 92 students (44 boys, 48 girls); Grade 11: 77 students (34 boys, 43 girls); Grade 12: 93 students (36 boys, 57 girls). 24% of students are boarding students. 85% are state residents. 10 states are represented in upper school student body. 11% are international students. International students from Bermuda, Canada, Japan, Republic of Korea, Russian Federation, and Taiwan; 2 other countries represented in student body.

Faculty School total: 66. In upper school: 30 men, 33 women; 44 have advanced degrees; 21 reside on campus.

Subjects Offered 3-dimensional art, acting, Advanced Placement courses, aerospace science, African dance, African history, African literature, African studies, African-American history, African-American literature, African-American studies, algebra, American Civil War, American democracy, American history, American literature, American sign language, analytic geometry, anatomy, anatomy and physiology, animal behavior, animal science, art, art and culture, art history, Asian literature, athletics, backpacking, ballet, ballet technique, baseball, basketball, Bible studies, biology, Black history, botany, calculus, calculus-AP, cell biology, ceramics, chemistry, child development, Chinese history, choir, Civil War, collage and assemblage, community service, computer keyboarding, computer math, computer programming, computer science, computer skills, creative writing, dance, death and loss, digital art, digital photography, discrete math, drama, drama performance, drawing, driver education, earth science, ecology, economics, electronic music, English, English literature, English literature and composition-AP, environmental science, environmental systems, ethics, ethnic literature, European history, European literature, expository writing, fashion, film history, filmmaking, fine arts, foods, French, geography, geometry, government/civics, grammar, great books, Harlem Renaissance, health, health and wellness, history, history of ideas, history of music, history of science, independent study, interdisciplinary studies, jazz dance, jazz ensemble, journalism, Latin, Latin American literature, leadership education training, marine biology, mathematical modeling, mathematics, Middle East, model United Nations, music, ornithology, painting, philosophy, photography, physical education, physics, physiology, playwriting, poetry, Portuguese, psychology, religion, Roman civilization, science, sculpture, senior project, set design, Shakespeare, short story, social studies, sociology, Spanish, statistics, the Presidency, theater, trigonometry, U.S. constitutional history, weight training, wilderness experience, wilderness/outdoor program, world history, world literature, World War II, writing, yearbook, zoology.

Graduation Requirements Art history, arts and fine arts (art, music, dance, drama), computer literacy, English, foreign language, health education, history, mathematics, physical education (includes health), science, senior project. Community service is required.

Special Academic Programs Advanced Placement exam preparation; independent study; term-away projects; study abroad.

College Admission Counseling 86 students graduated in 2008; 84 went to college, including Bard College; Brown University; Hampshire College; Northeastern University; Smith College; Vassar College. Other: 2 had other specific plans. 71% scored over 600 on SAT critical reading, 62% scored over 600 on SAT math, 59% scored over 600 on SAT writing.

Student Life Upper grades have student council. Discipline rests equally with students and faculty.

Summer Programs Art/fine arts programs offered; session focuses on visual and performing arts; held on campus; accepts boys and girls; open to students from other schools. 100 students usually enrolled. 2009 schedule: June 23 to August 16. Application deadline: May 1.

Tuition and Aid Day student tuition: $32,500; 7-day tuition and room/board: $43,250. Tuition installment plan (Insured Tuition Payment Plan, Academic Management Services Plan, individually arranged payment plans, Academic Management Services Academic Credit Line, TuitionPay (administered by Sallie Mae)). Tuition reduction for siblings, need-based scholarship grants, paying campus jobs, AchieverLoans (Key Education Resources) available. In 2008–09, 23% of upper-school students received aid. Total amount of financial aid awarded in 2008–09: $1,700,000.

Admissions Traditional secondary-level entrance grade is 9. For fall 2008, 350 students applied for upper-level admission, 198 were accepted, 89 enrolled. ISEE, PSAT, SAT, SSAT or TOEFL required. Deadline for receipt of application materials: February 1. Application fee required: $45. Interview required.

Athletics Interscholastic: basketball (boys, girls), field hockey (g), lacrosse (g), soccer (b,g); coed interscholastic: baseball, cross-country running, Frisbee, running, tennis, ultimate Frisbee; coed intramural: aerobics, aerobics/dance, aerobics/Nautilus, alpine skiing, backpacking, ballet, bicycling, canoeing/kayaking, cheering, climbing, dance, dance team, fencing, fitness, Frisbee, golf, hiking/backpacking, indoor soccer, kayaking, martial arts, modern dance, nordic skiing, outdoor activities, physical fitness, physical training, rafting, rock climbing, roller blading, ropes courses, running, skateboarding, skiing (downhill), snowboarding, strength & conditioning, triathlon, ultimate Frisbee, volleyball, weight training, wilderness, yoga. 15 coaches, 1 athletic trainer.

Computers Computers are regularly used in art, college planning, English, ESL, ethics, French, graphic design, history, humanities, independent study, journalism, keyboarding, Latin, library, literary magazine, mathematics, music, newspaper, photography, programming, psychology, publications, science, Spanish, word processing, writing, yearbook classes. Computer network features include on-campus library services, online commercial services, Internet access, wireless campus network, Internet filtering or blocking technology, laptops available for use in-class. Student e-mail accounts and computer access in designated common areas are available to students.

Contact Trish Saunders, Director of Admissions. 781-642-8650. Fax: 781-398-8344. E-mail: admissions@csw.org. Web site: www.csw.org.

ANNOUNCEMENT FROM THE SCHOOL The Cambridge School of Weston (CSW) is a progressive, coeducational, day and boarding school for students in grades 9 through 12. CSW is a warm and spirited community that values intellectual challenge, artistic expression, and individual growth. CSW's unique and intensive academic program challenges students to be inquisitive, innovative, and proactive learners. Classes emphasize substantive exchange and debate. Students are encouraged to think for themselves, ask questions, and go beyond obvious answers. The Module System, a cornerstone of the School's academic approach for over thirty years, affords students the time and flexibility to dive into subjects in depth and to explore connections between disciplines. Classes are an hour-and-a-half long, and students concentrate intensely on three subjects at a time. Students are inspired to take intellectual and creative risks through a rich variety of 300 course offerings and to pursue both artistic and academic studies with equal passion and discipline. CSW places an emphasis on learning through experiences. Students are encouraged to participate in self-directed clubs and organizations and to feel empowered to make decisions about their academic and social lives. Diversity and community service also play a large role at CSW; students are inspired to seek opportunities to share each other's worlds, as well as celebrate differences of opinion, expression, and cultural background. At CSW, the core mission is to enable students to become thoughtful, creative, socially responsible, healthy adults. That, CSW believes, is the best preparation for college—and for life.

CAMDEN MILITARY ACADEMY

520 Highway 1 North
Camden, South Carolina 29020

Head of School: Col. Eric Boland

General Information Boys' boarding college-preparatory and military school; primarily serves students with learning disabilities, individuals with Attention Deficit Disorder, individuals with emotional and behavioral problems, and dyslexic students. Grades 7–PG. Founded: 1892. Setting: small town. Nearest major city is Columbia. Students are housed in single-sex dormitories. 50-acre campus. 15 buildings on campus. Approved or accredited by South Carolina Independent School Association and Southern Association of Colleges and Schools. Member of National Association of Independent Schools. Total enrollment: 305. Upper school average class size: 15. Upper school faculty-student ratio: 1:12.

Upper School Student Profile Grade 9: 54 students (54 boys); Grade 10: 58 students (58 boys); Grade 11: 60 students (60 boys); Grade 12: 64 students (64 boys). 100% of students are boarding students. 39% are state residents. 23 states are represented in upper school student body. International students from Bermuda, Cayman Islands, Ghana, Mexico, Republic of Korea, and Trinidad and Tobago.

Faculty School total: 49. In upper school: 35 men, 3 women; 23 have advanced degrees; 9 reside on campus.

Subjects Offered Algebra, American government, anatomy and physiology, band, biology, calculus, chemistry, computer applications, computer literacy, driver education, economics, English, French, geometry, humanities, physical science, physics, pre-calculus, psychology, sociology, Spanish, U.S. history, world geography, world history.

Graduation Requirements Computer literacy, English, foreign language, history, JROTC, mathematics, science.

Special Academic Programs Advanced Placement exam preparation; honors section; study at local college for college credit; remedial reading and/or remedial writing.

College Admission Counseling 67 students graduated in 2008; they went to University of South Carolina. Other: 1 went to work, 8 entered military service.

Student Life Upper grades have uniform requirement, student council, honor system. Discipline rests primarily with faculty.

Summer Programs Remediation, enrichment, advancement, ESL, sports, rigorous outdoor training programs offered; session focuses on academics and leadership; held both on and off campus; held at field studies and activities; accepts boys; open to students from other schools. 120 students usually enrolled. 2009 schedule: June 21 to July 31.

Admissions Traditional secondary-level entrance grade is 9. Deadline for receipt of application materials: none. Application fee required: $100. On-campus interview required.

Athletics Interscholastic: baseball, basketball, cross-country running, football, golf; intramural: aerobics, aquatics. 2 PE instructors, 15 coaches, 1 athletic trainer.

Computers Computers are regularly used in all academic classes. Computer resources include on-campus library services, Internet access. Student e-mail accounts are available to students.

Contact Mr. Casey Robinson, Director of Admissions. 803-432-6001. Fax: 803-425-1020. E-mail: admissions@camdenmilitary.com. Web site: www.camdenmilitary.com.

See Close-Up on page 702.

CAMELOT ACADEMY

809 Proctor Street
Durham, North Carolina 27707

Head of School: Thelma DeCarlo Glynn

General Information Coeducational day college-preparatory school. Grades K–12. Founded: 1982. Setting: small town. Nearest major city is Raleigh. 3-acre campus. 1 building on campus. Approved or accredited by National Independent Private Schools Association and North Carolina Department of Education. Total enrollment: 90. Upper school average class size: 10. Upper school faculty-student ratio: 1:10.

Faculty School total: 12. In upper school: 3 men, 4 women; 6 have advanced degrees.

Graduation Requirements Electives, foreign language, language arts, mathematics, physical education (includes health), science, social studies (includes history).

Special Academic Programs Advanced Placement exam preparation; honors section; accelerated programs; independent study; study at local college for college credit; academic accommodation for the gifted; remedial reading and/or remedial writing; remedial math.

College Admission Counseling 4 students graduated in 2008; all went to college, including Sarah Lawrence College; The University of North Carolina at Chapel Hill; Wofford College. Median SAT critical reading: 625, median SAT math: 645, median SAT writing: 595, median combined SAT: 1865. 75% scored over 600 on SAT critical reading, 75% scored over 600 on SAT math, 75% scored over 600 on SAT writing, 75% scored over 1800 on combined SAT.

Student Life Upper grades have specified standards of dress, honor system. Discipline rests primarily with faculty.

Summer Programs Remediation, enrichment, advancement programs offered; session focuses on language arts and mathematics for enrichment or remediation; held on campus; accepts boys and girls; open to students from other schools. 20 students usually enrolled. 2009 schedule: June 9 to August 2.

Tuition and Aid Day student tuition: $9250. Tuition installment plan (monthly payment plan through YourTuitionSolution.com). Tuition reduction for siblings, merit scholarship grants, need-based scholarship grants available. In 2008–09, 55% of upper-school students received aid; total upper-school merit-scholarship money awarded: $77,000. Total amount of financial aid awarded in 2008–09: $85,000.

Admissions Traditional secondary-level entrance grade is 9. ERB required. Deadline for receipt of application materials: none. Application fee required: $50. Interview required.

Athletics Interscholastic: basketball (boys); intramural: volleyball (g); coed interscholastic: soccer; coed intramural: aerobics, dance team, fitness. 1 PE instructor, 1 coach.

Computers Computer network features include Internet access. Computer access in designated common areas is available to students. The school has a published electronic and media policy.

Contact Ms. Wendy Morris, Office Manager. 919-688-3040. Fax: 919-682-4320. E-mail: wendy@camelotacademy.org. Web site: www.camelotacademy.org/.

CAMPBELL HALL (EPISCOPAL)

4533 Laurel Canyon Boulevard
North Hollywood, California 91607

Head of School: Rev. Julian Bull

General Information Coeducational day college-preparatory, arts, and technology school, affiliated with Episcopal Church. Grades K–12. Founded: 1944. Setting: suburban. Nearest major city is Los Angeles. 15-acre campus. 12 buildings on campus. Approved or accredited by California Association of Independent Schools, The College Board, Western Association of Schools and Colleges, and California Department of Education. Member of National Association of Independent Schools. Endowment: $5 million. Total enrollment: 1,094. Upper school average class size: 16. Upper school faculty-student ratio: 1:8.

Upper School Student Profile Grade 9: 136 students (67 boys, 69 girls); Grade 10: 132 students (69 boys, 63 girls); Grade 11: 140 students (74 boys, 66 girls); Grade 12: 127 students (64 boys, 63 girls). 7% of students are members of Episcopal Church.

Faculty School total: 112. In upper school: 23 men, 32 women; 30 have advanced degrees.

Subjects Offered Algebra, American history, American literature, American studies, ancient history, art, art history, astronomy, band, biology, calculus, ceramics, chemistry, community service, computer programming, computer science, creative writing, dance, drama, drawing, earth science, ecology, economics, English, English literature, environmental science, ethics, European history, fine arts, French, geography, geometry, government/civics, history, human development, humanities, instrumental music, Japanese, law, mathematics, music, orchestra, painting, philosophy, photography, physical education, physics, physiology, pre-calculus, printmaking, psychology, science, sculpture, senior seminar, social studies, sociology, Spanish, speech, statistics, theater, theater arts, trigonometry, voice, yearbook.

Graduation Requirements Arts and fine arts (art, music, dance, drama), computer science, English, foreign language, mathematics, physical education (includes health), science, social studies (includes history). Community service is required.

Special Academic Programs Advanced Placement exam preparation; honors section; independent study; study at local college for college credit.

College Admission Counseling 126 students graduated in 2008; all went to college, including Boston University; Brandeis University; New York University; University of California, Berkeley; University of California, Los Angeles; University of Southern California.

Student Life Upper grades have uniform requirement, student council, honor system. Discipline rests primarily with faculty. Attendance at religious services is required.

Summer Programs Enrichment, advancement, sports, art/fine arts, computer instruction programs offered; session focuses on creative arts & sports; held on campus; accepts boys and girls; open to students from other schools. 200 students usually enrolled. 2009 schedule: June 15 to July 31. Application deadline: June 1.

Tuition and Aid Day student tuition: $19,890–$24,910. Tuition installment plan (Insured Tuition Payment Plan, monthly payment plans, individually arranged payment plans). Tuition reduction for siblings, need-based scholarship grants, paying

campus jobs, Episcopal Credit Union tuition loans available. In 2008–09, 23% of upper-school students received aid. Total amount of financial aid awarded in 2008–09: $1,980,955.
Admissions Traditional secondary-level entrance grade is 9. ISEE required. Deadline for receipt of application materials: January 30. Application fee required: $100. On-campus interview required.
Athletics Interscholastic: aerobics/dance (boys, girls), ballet (b,g), baseball (b), basketball (b,g), cheering (b,g), cross-country running (b,g), dance (b,g), dance squad (b,g), equestrian sports (b,g), flag football (b,g), football (b), golf (b,g), horseback riding (b,g), modern dance (b,g), soccer (b,g), softball (g), tennis (b,g), track and field (b,g), volleyball (b,g); intramural: weight lifting (b,g); coed interscholastic: aerobics/dance, ballet, cheering, cross-country running, dance, dance squad, golf, horseback riding, modern dance, track and field. 5 PE instructors, 13 coaches, 2 athletic trainers.
Computers Computers are regularly used in art, English, foreign language, history, humanities, mathematics, science, theater arts classes. Computer network features include on-campus library services, online commercial services, Internet access, wireless campus network, Internet filtering or blocking technology. Campus intranet, student e-mail accounts, and computer access in designated common areas are available to students. The school has a published electronic and media policy.
Contact Ms. Alice Fleming, Director of Admissions. 818-980-7280. Fax: 818-762-3269. Web site: www.campbellhall.org.

See Close-Up on page 704.

CANADIAN ACADEMY

4-1 Koyo-cho Naka
Higashinada-ku
Kobe 658-0032, Japan
Head of School: Mr. Frederic Wesson

General Information Coeducational boarding and day college-preparatory school. Boarding grades 9–13, day grades PK–13. Founded: 1913. Setting: urban. Nearest major city is Osaka, Japan. Students are housed in single-sex dormitories. 3-hectare campus. 2 buildings on campus. Approved or accredited by International Baccalaureate Organization, Ministry of Education, Japan, The College Board, and Western Association of Schools and Colleges. Language of instruction: English. Total enrollment: 755. Upper school average class size: 15. Upper school faculty-student ratio: 1:11.
Upper School Student Profile Grade 9: 59 students (33 boys, 26 girls); Grade 10: 58 students (28 boys, 30 girls); Grade 11: 58 students (27 boys, 31 girls); Grade 12: 56 students (27 boys, 29 girls). 8% of students are boarding students. International students from China, India, Philippines, Republic of Korea, United Kingdom, and United States; 18 other countries represented in student body.
Faculty School total: 88. In upper school: 19 men, 15 women; 20 have advanced degrees; 19 reside on campus.
Subjects Offered Algebra, art, Asian history, biology, calculus, chemistry, choir, college writing, concert band, drama, economics, English, ESL, French, geometry, health, Japanese, Japanese history, jazz band, music, orchestra, physical education, physics, probability and statistics, publications, Spanish, theater arts, theory of knowledge, trigonometry, U.S. history, world literature.
Graduation Requirements Electives, English, mathematics, modern languages, performing arts, physical education (includes health), science, social studies (includes history), Senior Project.
Special Academic Programs International Baccalaureate program; Advanced Placement exam preparation; honors section; independent study; ESL (7 students enrolled).
College Admission Counseling 58 students graduated in 2008; 55 went to college, including Carnegie Mellon University; New York University; Penn State University Park; The University of Arizona; University of Washington. Other: 3 had other specific plans.
Student Life Upper grades have specified standards of dress, student council, honor system. Discipline rests primarily with faculty.
Summer Programs Enrichment, sports programs offered; session focuses on SAT preparation and tennis program; held on campus; accepts boys and girls; open to students from other schools. 2009 schedule: June 15 to July 10. Application deadline: May 25.
Tuition and Aid Day student tuition: ¥1,781,000; 7-day tuition and room/board: ¥2,716,000. Tuition installment plan (semester payment plan). Need-based scholarship grants available. In 2008–09, 5% of upper-school students received aid. Total amount of financial aid awarded in 2008–09: ¥3,966,000.
Admissions Traditional secondary-level entrance grade is 9. For fall 2008, 21 students applied for upper-level admission, 20 were accepted, 20 enrolled. English for Non-native Speakers, essay, math and English placement tests or SLEP for foreign students required. Deadline for receipt of application materials: none. Application fee required: ¥57,000. On-campus interview required.
Athletics Interscholastic: baseball (boys), basketball (b,g), soccer (b,g), softball (g), tennis (b,g), volleyball (b,g); intramural: baseball (b), basketball (b,g), soccer (b,g), softball (g), table tennis (b,g), volleyball (b,g), weight training (b,g); coed interscholastic: dance, tennis. 3 PE instructors.
Computers Computer network features include on-campus library services, online commercial services, Internet access, wireless campus network, Internet filtering or blocking technology, campus calendar. The school has a published electronic and media policy.
Contact Ms. Sandra Ota, Director of Admissions. 81-78-857-0100. Fax: 81-78-857-4095. E-mail: sandyo@mail.canacad.ac.jp. Web site: www.canacad.ac.jp.

CANNON SCHOOL

5801 Poplar Tent Road
Concord, North Carolina 28027
Head of School: Mr. Matthew Gossage

General Information Coeducational day college-preparatory school. Grades PK–12. Founded: 1969. Setting: suburban. Nearest major city is Charlotte. 65-acre campus. 3 buildings on campus. Approved or accredited by Southern Association of Colleges and Schools and North Carolina Department of Education. Endowment: $977,863. Total enrollment: 915. Upper school average class size: 17. Upper school faculty-student ratio: 1:9.
Faculty School total: 97. In upper school: 18 men, 28 women; 27 have advanced degrees.
Subjects Offered Acting, advanced math, algebra, American government-AP, American history, American history-AP, American literature, anatomy and physiology, biology, biology-AP, British literature, calculus-AP, character education, chemistry, chemistry-AP, Chinese, chorus, college counseling, computer programming-AP, creative writing, dance, directing, discrete mathematics, drawing, English, English language-AP, English literature-AP, environmental science-AP, ethics, film and literature, film history, finance, French, French-AP, functions, geometry, jazz band, Latin, law and the legal system, marine science, mathematical modeling, painting, physics, physics-AP, playwriting, poetry, pre-calculus, psychology-AP, publications, sculpture, senior project, Spanish, Spanish language-AP, statistics-AP, strings, studio art-AP, theater design and production, trigonometry, visual arts, weight training, wind ensemble, world history, world literature, world religions, yearbook.
Graduation Requirements Arts and fine arts (art, music, dance, drama), biology, chemistry, computer literacy, English, foreign language, history, mathematics, physical education (includes health), science, senior project, trigonometry, U.S. history. Community service is required.
Special Academic Programs Advanced Placement exam preparation; honors section; independent study.
College Admission Counseling 59 students graduated in 2008; 57 went to college, including Appalachian State University; Clemson University; Emory University; Furman University; North Carolina State University; The University of North Carolina at Chapel Hill. Other: 1 went to work, 1 entered military service. Mean SAT critical reading: 610, mean SAT math: 624, mean SAT writing: 623, mean combined SAT: 1857, mean composite ACT: 27.
Student Life Upper grades have specified standards of dress, student council, honor system. Discipline rests primarily with faculty.
Tuition and Aid Day student tuition: $16,100. Tuition installment plan (Insured Tuition Payment Plan, monthly payment plans). Need-based scholarship grants available. In 2008–09, 10% of upper-school students received aid. Total amount of financial aid awarded in 2008–09: $295,000.
Admissions Traditional secondary-level entrance grade is 9. For fall 2008, 79 students applied for upper-level admission, 33 were accepted, 24 enrolled. Admissions testing and ISEE required. Deadline for receipt of application materials: none. Application fee required: $90. On-campus interview required.
Athletics Interscholastic: baseball (boys), basketball (b,g), cheering (g), cross-country running (b,g), dance (g), dance team (g), football (b), indoor track (b,g), lacrosse (b), soccer (b,g), softball (g), swimming and diving (b,g), tennis (b,g), track and field (b,g), volleyball (g); intramural: ballet (g); coed interscholastic: golf, indoor track, weight training; coed intramural: blading, cheering, croquet, dance, Frisbee, independent competitive sports, jump rope, kickball, Newcombe ball, track and field, weight training, whiffle ball, yoga. 6 PE instructors, 28 coaches, 1 athletic trainer.
Computers Computers are regularly used in all academic, art, music classes. Computer network features include on-campus library services, online commercial services, Internet access, wireless campus network, Internet filtering or blocking technology, productivity software. Campus intranet, student e-mail accounts, and computer access in designated common areas are available to students. Students grades are available online. The school has a published electronic and media policy.
Contact Mr. William D. Diskin, Director of Admission. 704-721-7164. Fax: 704-788-7779. E-mail: wdiskin@cannonschool.org. Web site: www.cannonschool.org.

CANTERBURY SCHOOL

101 Aspetuck Avenue
New Milford, Connecticut 06776
Head of School: Thomas J. Sheehey III

General Information Coeducational boarding and day college-preparatory, arts, business, religious studies, bilingual studies, and technology school, affiliated with Roman Catholic Church. Grades 9–PG. Founded: 1915. Setting: small town. Nearest major city is Hartford. Students are housed in single-sex dormitories. 150-acre campus. 20 buildings on campus. Approved or accredited by New England Association of Schools and Colleges, The Association of Boarding Schools, and Connecticut Department of Education. Member of National Association of Independent Schools and Secondary School Admission Test Board. Languages of instruction: Spanish, French, and Italian. Endowment: $14 million. Total enrollment: 347. Upper school average class size: 11. Upper school faculty-student ratio: 1:6.

Upper School Student Profile Grade 9: 50 students (30 boys, 20 girls); Grade 10: 82 students (39 boys, 43 girls); Grade 11: 108 students (63 boys, 45 girls); Grade 12: 107 students (62 boys, 45 girls); Postgraduate: 21 students (19 boys, 2 girls). 65% of students are boarding students. 50% are state residents. 18 states are represented in upper school student body. 12% are international students. International students from Australia, China, Germany, Republic of Korea, Spain, and Taiwan; 12 other countries represented in student body. 65% of students are Roman Catholic.

Faculty School total: 76. In upper school: 40 men, 36 women; 45 have advanced degrees; 56 reside on campus.

Subjects Offered 1½ elective credits, adolescent issues, algebra, American history, American literature, anthropology, art, art history, astronomy, biochemistry, biology, calculus, ceramics, chemistry, civil rights, computer programming, computer science, creative writing, dance, drama, driver education, earth science, economics, English, English literature, environmental science, ethics, European history, expository writing, fine arts, French, geography, geology, geometry, grammar, history, Irish studies, Latin, marine biology, mathematics, microbiology, music, oceanography, philosophy, photography, physics, physiology, religion, science, social studies, Spanish, Spanish literature, speech, statistics, theater, theology, trigonometry, women's studies, world history, world literature, writing.

Graduation Requirements Arts and fine arts (art, music, dance, drama), computer science, English, foreign language, mathematics, New Testament, religion (includes Bible studies and theology), science, social studies (includes history).

Special Academic Programs Advanced Placement exam preparation; honors section; independent study; term-away projects; ESL (15 students enrolled).

College Admission Counseling 107 students graduated in 2007; 105 went to college, including Boston University; Hobart and William Smith Colleges; Sacred Heart University; University of Connecticut. Other: 2 had other specific plans. 25% scored over 600 on SAT critical reading, 35% scored over 600 on SAT math.

Student Life Upper grades have specified standards of dress, student council, honor system. Discipline rests primarily with faculty. Attendance at religious services is required.

Tuition and Aid Day student tuition: $29,000; 7-day tuition and room/board: $38,000. Tuition installment plan (Academic Management Services Plan, Key Tuition Payment Plan). Need-based scholarship grants, need-based loans, middle-income loans available. In 2007–08, 36% of upper-school students received aid. Total amount of financial aid awarded in 2007–08: $1,900,000.

Admissions Traditional secondary-level entrance grade is 9. For fall 2007, 597 students applied for upper-level admission, 273 were accepted, 122 enrolled. SLEP, SSAT, TOEFL and writing sample required. Deadline for receipt of application materials: January 31. Application fee required: $50. Interview required.

Athletics Interscholastic: baseball (boys), basketball (b,g), cross-country running (b,g), diving (b,g), field hockey (g), football (b), ice hockey (b,g), lacrosse (b,g), soccer (b,g), softball (g), squash (b,g), swimming and diving (b,g), tennis (b,g), track and field (b,g), volleyball (g); intramural: dance (g), equestrian sports (g), hockey (b,g), horseback riding (b,g); coed interscholastic: crew, golf, water polo, wrestling; coed intramural: fitness, softball, Special Olympics, strength & conditioning, weight lifting, weight training. 40 coaches, 2 athletic trainers.

Computers Computers are regularly used in accounting, English, mathematics, multimedia, science classes. Computer network features include on-campus library services, Internet access, wireless campus network, Internet filtering or blocking technology. Student e-mail accounts and computer access in designated common areas are available to students. Students grades are available online. The school has a published electronic and media policy.

Contact Keith R. Holton, Director of Admission. 860-210-3832. Fax: 860-350-1120. E-mail: admissions@cbury.org. Web site: www.cbury.org.

ANNOUNCEMENT FROM THE SCHOOL Canterbury prides itself on creating a value-based community where every student experiences a broad and challenging program in a small school setting. The School's educational environment fosters academic rigor, athletic development, artistic enrichment, and spiritual growth. The hallmark of a Canterbury education is the School's willingness to accept students as they are, support them when necessary, challenge them when appropriate, and inspire them to become moral leaders in a secular world.

See Close-Up on page 706.

CANTERBURY SCHOOL

8141 College Parkway
Fort Myers, Florida 33919

Head of School: Mr. John Anthony (Tony) Paulus II

General Information Coeducational day college-preparatory school. Grades PK–12. Founded: 1964. Setting: suburban. Nearest major city is Tampa. 32-acre campus. 8 buildings on campus. Approved or accredited by Florida Council of Independent Schools, Southern Association of Colleges and Schools, The College Board, and Florida Department of Education. Member of National Association of Independent Schools and Secondary School Admission Test Board. Endowment: $7.2 million. Total enrollment: 685. Upper school average class size: 16. Upper school faculty-student ratio: 1:10.

Upper School Student Profile Grade 9: 55 students (26 boys, 29 girls); Grade 10: 57 students (28 boys, 29 girls); Grade 11: 57 students (31 boys, 26 girls); Grade 12: 46 students (22 boys, 24 girls).

Faculty School total: 95. In upper school: 21 men, 19 women; 26 have advanced degrees.

Subjects Offered Advanced Placement courses, algebra, American government-AP, American history, American history-AP, American literature, anatomy, art, art history, biology, biology-AP, British literature, calculus, calculus-AP, ceramics, chemistry, chemistry-AP, comparative government and politics-AP, computer programming, constitutional law, creative writing, critical writing, drama, earth science, ecology, economics, English, English literature, English literature-AP, environmental science-AP, European history, fine arts, French, French language-AP, geography, geometry, government/civics, grammar, health, history, Latin, macroeconomics-AP, marine biology, mathematics, music, nationalism and ethnic conflict, photography, physical education, physics, physics-AP, physiology, SAT preparation, science, social studies, sociology, Spanish, Spanish language-AP, speech, statistics, theater, U.S. history, United Nations and international issues, world history, world literature, writing, yearbook.

Graduation Requirements Arts and fine arts (art, music, dance, drama), English, foreign language, mathematics, physical education (includes health), science, social studies (includes history), speech. Community service is required.

Special Academic Programs 14 Advanced Placement exams for which test preparation is offered; independent study; study at local college for college credit; study abroad.

College Admission Counseling 41 students graduated in 2008; all went to college, including Boston University; Emory University; Florida Gulf Coast University; Mercer University; University of Central Florida; Wake Forest University. Mean SAT critical reading: 600, mean SAT math: 610, mean SAT writing: 610, mean composite ACT: 27.

Student Life Upper grades have specified standards of dress, student council, honor system. Discipline rests primarily with faculty.

Summer Programs Remediation, enrichment, advancement, sports, art/fine arts programs offered; session focuses on academic enrichment; held on campus; accepts boys and girls; open to students from other schools. 125 students usually enrolled. 2009 schedule: June 15 to July 31.

Tuition and Aid Day student tuition: $13,445–$17,285. Tuition installment plan (monthly payment plans, quarterly payment plan). Merit scholarship grants, need-based scholarship grants available. In 2008–09, 64% of upper-school students received aid; total upper-school merit-scholarship money awarded: $178,045. Total amount of financial aid awarded in 2008–09: $712,703.

Admissions Traditional secondary-level entrance grade is 9. For fall 2008, 45 students applied for upper-level admission, 22 were accepted, 15 enrolled. ERB CTP IV required. Deadline for receipt of application materials: none. Application fee required: $75. Interview recommended.

Athletics Interscholastic: baseball (boys), basketball (b,g), cheering (b,g), cross-country running (b,g), lacrosse (b,g), soccer (b,g), softball (g), track and field (b,g), volleyball (g), winter soccer (b,g); intramural: basketball (b,g), cheering (b,g), cross-country running (b,g), soccer (b,g), volleyball (b,g), winter soccer (b,g); coed interscholastic: golf, swimming and diving, tennis; coed intramural: swimming and diving. 2 PE instructors, 2 coaches.

Computers Computers are regularly used in art, college planning, English, foreign language, French, history, independent study, journalism, Latin, library, mathematics, science, social sciences, Spanish, speech, theater arts, yearbook classes. Computer network features include on-campus library services, online commercial services, Internet access, wireless campus network, Internet filtering or blocking technology. Student e-mail accounts are available to students. The school has a published electronic and media policy.

Contact Ms. Julie A. Peters, Director of Admission. 239-415-8945. Fax: 239-481-8339. E-mail: jpeters@canterburyfortmyers.org. Web site: www.canterburyfortmyers.org.

ANNOUNCEMENT FROM THE SCHOOL Canterbury School, founded in 1964, is the only independent prekindergarten through grade 12, nonsectarian, coeducational, college-preparatory day school serving the rapidly growing Lee County area. The School's ten-building, 33-acre campus is adjacent to Edison Community College. A member of the National Association of Independent Schools, Canterbury is fully accredited by the Florida Council of Independent Schools and the Florida Kindergarten Council and is also a member of the Cum Laude Society. Canterbury's motto, "Education, Character, Leadership, Service," defines the focus of the School's program and underscores all that is done, in and out of the classroom. At all levels, the academic program emphasizes individual growth, skill development, a high caliber of instruction, collaboration, and high standards. Canterbury provides all students with an opportunity to challenge themselves and take risks in an atmosphere of mutual respect and partnership among students, parents, and teachers. Led by a talented and dedicated faculty, the School seeks to build a close-knit community of learners where the whole child is nurtured and can develop and where the model of a liberal arts education thrives. At Canterbury, the life of the mind is complemented by a strong athletics program, a commitment to the arts and creativity, and a fluency in technology. These elements unite in a secure and modern facility to instill in students a love of learning that prepares them for life. An honor code and required community service promote personal integrity and service in the Canterbury community; graduates are expected to be lifelong learners and responsible citizens well-prepared to help shape a changing world. All graduates continue their education. Graduates matriculate at universities and colleges around the country, including Davidson, Harvard, Johns Hopkins, Northwestern, Notre Dame, Princeton, U.S. Military Academy at West Point, U.S. Naval Academy, Wake Forest, and the Universities of Florida, Pennsylvania, and Miami.

THE CANTERBURY SCHOOL OF FLORIDA

990 62nd Avenue NE
St. Petersburg, Florida 33702

Head of School: Mr. Mac H. Hall

General Information Coeducational day college-preparatory, arts, and marine studies, international program school, affiliated with Episcopal Church. Grades PK–12. Founded: 1968. Setting: suburban. Nearest major city is Tampa. 20-acre campus. 5 buildings on campus. Approved or accredited by Florida Council of Independent Schools, National Association of Episcopal Schools, National Independent Private Schools Association, The College Board, and Florida Department of Education. Endowment: $115,000. Total enrollment: 427. Upper school average class size: 15. Upper school faculty-student ratio: 1:4.

Upper School Student Profile Grade 9: 32 students (12 boys, 20 girls); Grade 10: 28 students (12 boys, 16 girls); Grade 11: 26 students (13 boys, 13 girls); Grade 12: 23 students (11 boys, 12 girls). 5% of students are members of Episcopal Church.

Faculty School total: 60. In upper school: 15 men, 12 women; 18 have advanced degrees.

Subjects Offered 20th century world history, advanced computer applications, Advanced Placement courses, algebra, American government, American literature, anatomy, Ancient Greek, ancient world history, art, art history, art history-AP, astronomy, athletics, band, Basic programming, biology, biology-AP, British literature, British literature (honors), calculus, calculus-AP, career exploration, ceramics, character education, chemistry, chemistry-AP, choral music, chorus, classical language, classical studies, college counseling, college placement, community service, competitive science projects, computer keyboarding, computer multimedia, computer science, computer science-AP, computer skills, contemporary issues, creative writing, dance, dance performance, digital imaging, earth science, economics, English, English composition, English literature, English literature-AP, environmental science, environmental science-AP, environmental studies, ethics, European history, expository writing, film studies, fine arts, finite math, foreign language, French, French-AP, freshman seminar, geography, geometry, government/civics, grammar, Greek culture, guitar, health, history, history of music, history-AP, honors algebra, honors geometry, human geography—AP, independent living, interdisciplinary studies, journalism, keyboarding/computer, Latin, Latin-AP, leadership, leadership and service, library skills, life science, life skills, marine biology, marine ecology, marine science, marine studies, mathematics, mathematics-AP, mechanical drawing, mentorship program, modern world history, multimedia, music, musical productions, musical theater, oceanography, outdoor education, personal and social education, personal fitness, photojournalism, physical education, physical science, physics, physics-AP, play production, portfolio art, pottery, prayer/spirituality, pre-algebra, pre-calculus, pre-college orientation, psychology, psychology-AP, reading/study skills, robotics, SAT preparation, SAT/ACT preparation, science, senior composition, senior seminar, senior thesis, Shakespeare, social science, social studies, Spanish, Spanish language-AP, Spanish-AP, speech, speech and debate, sports conditioning, stagecraft, statistics-AP, student government, student publications, student teaching, studio art-AP, technical theater, theater arts, theater design and production, theater history, U.S. history, U.S. history-AP, values and decisions, visual and performing arts, weight fitness, weight training, Western philosophy, world history, world literature, world religions, yearbook.

Graduation Requirements Arts and fine arts (art, music, dance, drama), career/college preparation, electives, English, ethics, foreign language, history, mathematics, physical education (includes health), research, science, senior seminar, writing, research and writing, miniterms. Community service is required.

Special Academic Programs Advanced Placement exam preparation; honors section; independent study; term-away projects; study at local college for college credit; study abroad.

College Admission Counseling 24 students graduated in 2008; all went to college.

Student Life Upper grades have specified standards of dress, student council, honor system. Discipline rests equally with students and faculty. Attendance at religious services is required.

Summer Programs Remediation, enrichment, sports, art/fine arts, computer instruction programs offered; session focuses on multi-discipline skills and abilities; held on campus; accepts boys and girls; open to students from other schools. 50 students usually enrolled. 2009 schedule: June 8 to August 7. Application deadline: March 15.

Tuition and Aid Day student tuition: $12,500–$13,900. Tuition installment plan (Insured Tuition Payment Plan, monthly payment plans, individually arranged payment plans). Tuition reduction for siblings, need-based scholarship grants available. In 2008–09, 20% of upper-school students received aid. Total amount of financial aid awarded in 2008–09: $575,000.

Admissions Traditional secondary-level entrance grade is 9. For fall 2008, 21 students applied for upper-level admission, 19 were accepted, 18 enrolled. 3-R Achievement Test, any standardized test, ERB or TOEFL required. Deadline for receipt of application materials: none. Application fee required: $75. On-campus interview required.

Athletics Interscholastic: baseball (boys), basketball (b,g), cross-country running (b,g), diving (g), football (b), golf (b), soccer (b,g), softball (g), swimming and diving (g), tennis (b,g), volleyball (g); intramural: strength & conditioning (b); coed interscholastic: cheering, cross-country running, golf, soccer; coed intramural: canoeing/kayaking, dance, fitness, flag football, floor hockey, hiking/backpacking, indoor hockey, kayaking, modern dance, outdoor activities, outdoor education, paddle tennis, physical fitness, ropes courses, ultimate Frisbee, weight training. 4 PE instructors, 21 coaches, 1 athletic trainer.

Computers Computers are regularly used in all academic classes. Computer network features include on-campus library services, online commercial services, Internet access, wireless campus network, Internet filtering or blocking technology, remote access to second campus;. Computer access in designated common areas is available to students. Students grades are available online. The school has a published electronic and media policy.

Contact Ms. Daryl DeBerry, Director of Admissions and Communications. 727-521-5903. Fax: 727-521-5991. E-mail: ddeberry@canterbury-fl.org. Web site: www.canterbury-fl.org.

CANYONVILLE CHRISTIAN ACADEMY

PO Box 1100
Canyonville, Oregon 97417-1100

Head of School: Cathy Lovato

General Information Coeducational boarding and day college-preparatory, religious studies, and English for Speakers of Other Languages school, affiliated with Christian faith. Grades 9–12. Founded: 1924. Setting: rural. Nearest major city is Medford. Students are housed in single-sex dormitories. 10-acre campus. 11 buildings on campus. Approved or accredited by Association of Christian Schools International, Northwest Association of Schools and Colleges, The Association of Boarding Schools, and Oregon Department of Education. Upper school average class size: 20. Upper school faculty-student ratio: 1:15.

Upper School Student Profile 80% of students are boarding students. 20% are state residents. 10 states are represented in upper school student body. 65% are international students. International students from China, Republic of Korea, Spain, Taiwan, Ukraine, and Viet Nam; 10 other countries represented in student body. 70% of students are Christian faith.

Faculty School total: 20. In upper school: 5 men, 7 women; 5 have advanced degrees; 14 reside on campus.

Subjects Offered Advanced Placement courses, aerobics, algebra, American culture, American history, art, Bible, biology, calculus, calculus-AP, career/college preparation, chemistry, choir, Christian doctrine, composition, computer education, computer keyboarding, computer technologies, computers, consumer economics, culinary arts, desktop publishing, economics, English, English literature, ESL, foreign language, French as a second language, general science, government, grammar, health, integrative seminar, keyboarding, language and composition, library assistant, Life of Christ, mathematics, New Testament, orchestra, physical education, physical science, physics, pre-calculus, religious education, senior seminar, Spanish, speech and debate, theology, U.S. government, U.S. history, United States government-AP, world history.

Graduation Requirements 1½ elective credits, algebra, arts and fine arts (art, music, dance, drama), Bible, biology, economics, English, foreign language, government, health and wellness, mathematics, physical education (includes health), physical science, speech and debate, U.S. history, world history.

Special Academic Programs Advanced Placement exam preparation; honors section; accelerated programs; independent study; study at local college for college credit; remedial math; ESL (50 students enrolled).

College Admission Counseling 42 students graduated in 2008; 38 went to college, including Michigan State University; Oregon State University; University of Oregon; University of Washington; Vanguard University of Southern California; Washington State University. Median SAT critical reading: 486, median SAT math: 523, median SAT writing: 488. Mean combined SAT: 1643.

Student Life Upper grades have specified standards of dress, student council, honor system. Discipline rests primarily with faculty. Attendance at religious services is required.

Tuition and Aid Day student tuition: $4600; 7-day tuition and room/board: $19,500. Tuition installment plan (monthly payment plans, individually arranged payment plans). Tuition reduction for siblings, merit scholarship grants, need-based scholarship grants, paying campus jobs available. In 2008–09, 10% of upper-school students received aid; total upper-school merit-scholarship money awarded: $30,000. Total amount of financial aid awarded in 2008–09: $80,000.

Admissions Traditional secondary-level entrance grade is 9. TOEFL or SLEP required. Deadline for receipt of application materials: none. Application fee required: $100. Interview recommended.

Athletics Interscholastic: basketball (boys, girls), cheering (g), cross-country running (b,g), soccer (b), tennis (b,g), track and field (b,g), volleyball (g); intramural: aerobics (g), soccer (b); coed interscholastic: soccer, tennis; coed intramural: badminton, basketball, billiards, table tennis, tennis, volleyball. 3 PE instructors, 9 coaches.

Computers Computers are regularly used in business applications, keyboarding, technology, yearbook classes. Computer network features include Internet access, wireless campus network, Internet filtering or blocking technology. Student e-mail accounts and computer access in designated common areas are available to students. Students grades are available online.

Contact Noel Schaak, Asst. Headmaster. 541-839-4401. Fax: 541-839-6228. E-mail: cca@canyonville.net. Web site: www.canyonville.net.

CAPE COD ACADEMY

50 Osterville–West Barnstable Road
Osterville, Massachusetts 02655

Head of School: Clark J. Daggett

General Information Coeducational day college-preparatory, arts, and technology school. Grades K–12. Founded: 1976. Setting: small town. Nearest major city is Boston. 46-acre campus. 5 buildings on campus. Approved or accredited by Association of Independent Schools in New England and New England Association of Schools and Colleges. Member of National Association of Independent Schools and Secondary School Admission Test Board. Endowment: $2.2 million. Total enrollment: 347. Upper school average class size: 14. Upper school faculty-student ratio: 1:7.

Upper School Student Profile Grade 9: 32 students (18 boys, 14 girls); Grade 10: 41 students (20 boys, 21 girls); Grade 11: 45 students (29 boys, 16 girls); Grade 12: 38 students (22 boys, 16 girls).

Faculty School total: 60. In upper school: 19 men, 25 women; 34 have advanced degrees.

Subjects Offered Advanced biology, advanced chemistry, advanced math, Advanced Placement courses, advanced studio art-AP, algebra, American history, American literature, art, art history, art history-AP, art-AP, biology, calculus, calculus-AP, ceramics, chemistry, chemistry-AP, community service, computer math, computer programming, computer science, digital photography, drama, earth science, English, English literature, English-AP, environmental science, ethics, European history, expository writing, fine arts, French, French-AP, geography, geometry, health, history, history-AP, honors algebra, honors geometry, Latin, mathematics, music, music composition, music history, music theory, philosophy, photography, physical education, physics, SAT preparation, science, senior internship, social science, social studies, Spanish, Spanish-AP, statistics-AP, studio art-AP, theater, trigonometry, world history, world literature.

Graduation Requirements Arts and fine arts (art, music, dance, drama), computer science, English, foreign language, independent study, mathematics, physical education (includes health), science, social science, social studies (includes history). Community service is required.

Special Academic Programs Advanced Placement exam preparation; honors section; independent study; term-away projects; study abroad.

College Admission Counseling 57 students graduated in 2008; all went to college, including Boston College; Boston University; Brandeis University; Connecticut College; Middlebury College; University of Massachusetts Amherst. Mean SAT critical reading: 595, mean SAT math: 624.

Student Life Upper grades have specified standards of dress, student council, honor system. Discipline rests primarily with faculty.

Tuition and Aid Day student tuition: $18,320–$22,020. Tuition installment plan (Academic Management Services Plan, monthly payment plans). Need-based scholarship grants available. In 2008–09, 30% of upper-school students received aid. Total amount of financial aid awarded in 2008–09: $1,115,000.

Admissions Traditional secondary-level entrance grade is 9. For fall 2008, 32 students applied for upper-level admission, 24 were accepted, 16 enrolled. ISEE, Otis-Lennon School Ability Test or SSAT required. Deadline for receipt of application materials: February 1. Application fee required: $95. On-campus interview required.

Athletics Interscholastic: baseball (boys), basketball (b,g), lacrosse (b,g), soccer (b,g), tennis (b,g); coed interscholastic: cross-country running, golf; coed intramural: archery, ball hockey, basketball, combined training, fitness, floor hockey, soccer, weight training. 3 PE instructors, 9 coaches, 1 athletic trainer.

Computers Computers are regularly used in all classes. Computer network features include on-campus library services, online commercial services, Internet access, wireless campus network, Internet filtering or blocking technology. Campus intranet, student e-mail accounts, and computer access in designated common areas are available to students. Students grades are available online. The school has a published electronic and media policy.

Contact Mr. Stephen A. DiPaolo, Director of Admissions. 508-428-5400 Ext. 216. Fax: 508-428-0701. E-mail: admissions@capecodacademy.org. Web site: www.capecodacademy.org.

CAPE FEAR ACADEMY

3900 South College Road
Wilmington, North Carolina 28412

Head of School: Mr. John B. Meehl

General Information Coeducational day college-preparatory and arts school. Grades PK–12. Founded: 1967. Setting: suburban. 27-acre campus. 3 buildings on campus. Approved or accredited by Southern Association of Colleges and Schools, Southern Association of Independent Schools, and North Carolina Department of Education. Member of National Association of Independent Schools. Endowment: $562,250. Total enrollment: 672. Upper school average class size: 17. Upper school faculty-student ratio: 1:8.

Upper School Student Profile Grade 9: 59 students (24 boys, 35 girls); Grade 10: 61 students (32 boys, 29 girls); Grade 11: 57 students (34 boys, 23 girls); Grade 12: 55 students (30 boys, 25 girls).

Faculty School total: 81. In upper school: 9 men, 17 women; 12 have advanced degrees.

Subjects Offered Algebra, American government-AP, American history, American history-AP, American literature, American literature-AP, analysis, art, art history, band, biology, biology-AP, calculus-AP, chemistry, choral music, comparative government and politics-AP, computer science, drama, English, English language-AP, English literature, English literature-AP, environmental science, European history, finance, fine arts, geometry, government and politics-AP, government-AP, history, journalism, keyboarding/computer, language, literature, mathematics, music, music theory-AP, musical theater, newspaper, organizational studies, physical education, physics, pre-calculus, psychology, publications, science, social studies, Spanish, theater, world history.

Graduation Requirements Arts and fine arts (art, music, dance, drama), biology, English, foreign language, mathematics, physical education (includes health), science, social studies (includes history). Community service is required.

Special Academic Programs 11 Advanced Placement exams for which test preparation is offered; honors section; independent study; study at local college for college credit.

College Admission Counseling 49 students graduated in 2008; all went to college, including Davidson College; Duke University; East Carolina University; North Carolina State University; The University of North Carolina at Chapel Hill; The University of North Carolina Wilmington. Mean SAT critical reading: 588, mean SAT math: 581. 45% scored over 600 on SAT critical reading, 40% scored over 600 on SAT math.

Student Life Upper grades have specified standards of dress, student council, honor system. Discipline rests primarily with faculty.

Summer Programs Enrichment, sports, art/fine arts programs offered; session focuses on enrichment and sports; held on campus; accepts boys and girls; open to students from other schools. 250 students usually enrolled. 2009 schedule: June 15 to August 14. Application deadline: none.

Tuition and Aid Day student tuition: $11,920. Tuition installment plan (Insured Tuition Payment Plan, FACTS Tuition Payment Plan). Merit scholarship grants, need-based scholarship grants available. In 2008–09, 20% of upper-school students received aid; total upper-school merit-scholarship money awarded: $130,500. Total amount of financial aid awarded in 2008–09: $195,057.

Admissions Traditional secondary-level entrance grade is 9. For fall 2008, 58 students applied for upper-level admission, 19 were accepted, 19 enrolled. ERB, ISEE, PSAT or SAT or SSAT required. Deadline for receipt of application materials: none. Application fee required: $75. On-campus interview recommended.

Athletics Interscholastic: basketball (boys, girls), field hockey (g), lacrosse (b,g), soccer (b,g), softball (g), tennis (b,g), volleyball (g); coed interscholastic: cheering, cross-country running, golf, surfing, swimming and diving. 2 PE instructors, 11 coaches, 1 athletic trainer.

Computers Computers are regularly used in all academic classes. Computer network features include on-campus library services, online commercial services, Internet access, wireless campus network, Internet filtering or blocking technology. Campus intranet, student e-mail accounts, and computer access in designated common areas are available to students. Students grades are available online. The school has a published electronic and media policy.

Contact Mrs. Susan Mixon Harrell, Director of Admission. 910-791-0287 Ext. 1015. Fax: 910-791-0290. E-mail: sharrell@capefearacademy.org. Web site: www.capefearacademy.org.

CAPE HENRY COLLEGIATE SCHOOL

1320 Mill Dam Road
Virginia Beach, Virginia 23454-2306

Head of School: Dr. John P. Lewis

General Information Coeducational day college-preparatory, arts, technology, and Global Education school. Grades PK–12. Founded: 1924. Setting: suburban. 30-acre campus. 9 buildings on campus. Approved or accredited by Virginia Association of Independent Schools. Member of National Association of Independent Schools. Endowment: $6 million. Total enrollment: 1,020. Upper school average class size: 14. Upper school faculty-student ratio: 1:10.

Upper School Student Profile Grade 6: 80 students (38 boys, 42 girls); Grade 7: 97 students (50 boys, 47 girls); Grade 8: 98 students (51 boys, 47 girls); Grade 9: 81

students (43 boys, 38 girls); Grade 10: 83 students (42 boys, 41 girls); Grade 11: 85 students (48 boys, 37 girls); Grade 12: 80 students (44 boys, 36 girls).
Faculty School total: 135. In upper school: 21 men, 39 women; 34 have advanced degrees.
Subjects Offered Algebra, American history, American literature, art, art history, biology, botany, business skills, calculus, ceramics, chemistry, community service, computer programming, computer science, creative writing, drama, driver education, earth science, ecology, economics, English, English literature, environmental science, European history, expository writing, fine arts, French, geography, geology, geometry, government/civics, health, history, journalism, Latin, law, marine biology, mathematics, music, oceanography, photography, physical education, physics, science, social science, social studies, sociology, Spanish, speech, statistics, theater, trigonometry, world history, world literature, writing.
Graduation Requirements Arts and fine arts (art, music, dance, drama), computer science, English, foreign language, mathematics, physical education (includes health), science, social science, social studies (includes history), senior speech. Community service is required.
Special Academic Programs Advanced Placement exam preparation; honors section; independent study; academic accommodation for the gifted, the musically talented, and the artistically talented; ESL (25 students enrolled).
College Admission Counseling 84 students graduated in 2008; all went to college, including Hampden-Sydney College; James Madison University; The College of William and Mary; University of Virginia; Virginia Polytechnic Institute and State University; Washington and Lee University.
Student Life Upper grades have specified standards of dress, student council, honor system. Discipline rests equally with students and faculty.
Summer Programs Enrichment, advancement, ESL, sports, art/fine arts, computer instruction programs offered; session focuses on academics and enrichment; held on campus; accepts boys and girls; open to students from other schools. 1,200 students usually enrolled. 2009 schedule: June 8 to August 14. Application deadline: none.
Tuition and Aid Day student tuition: $13,185–$15,300. Tuition installment plan (The Tuition Plan, Insured Tuition Payment Plan, monthly payment plans, individually arranged payment plans, 3-payment plan). Merit scholarship grants, need-based scholarship grants available. In 2008–09, 16% of upper-school students received aid; total upper-school merit-scholarship money awarded: $70,000. Total amount of financial aid awarded in 2008–09: $375,000.
Admissions Traditional secondary-level entrance grade is 9. For fall 2008, 78 students applied for upper-level admission, 38 were accepted, 26 enrolled. ISEE or writing sample required. Deadline for receipt of application materials: February 15. Application fee required: $50. On-campus interview required.
Athletics Interscholastic: baseball (boys), basketball (b,g), crew (b,g), cross-country running (b,g), field hockey (g), golf (b,g), lacrosse (b,g), soccer (b,g), softball (g), tennis (b,g), volleyball (b,g), wrestling (b); intramural: baseball (b), basketball (b,g), crew (b,g), cross-country running (b,g), field hockey (g), floor hockey (b,g), wrestling (b); coed interscholastic: cheering, swimming and diving, track and field; coed intramural: aerobics, aerobics/dance, aerobics/Nautilus, archery, backpacking, badminton, ballet, cheering, dance, fishing, fitness, fitness walking, golf, hiking/backpacking, jogging, kayaking, lacrosse, modern dance, ocean paddling, outdoor activities, outdoor adventure, physical fitness, physical training, skiing (downhill), snowboarding, soccer, strength & conditioning, surfing, swimming and diving, table tennis, tennis, volleyball, weight lifting, weight training, wilderness, yoga. 5 PE instructors, 16 coaches, 1 athletic trainer.
Computers Computers are regularly used in computer applications, desktop publishing, graphic arts, information technology, literary magazine, newspaper, publications, technology, video film production, Web site design, word processing, yearbook classes. Computer network features include on-campus library services, online commercial services, Internet access, wireless campus network, Internet filtering or blocking technology. Student e-mail accounts and computer access in designated common areas are available to students. Students grades are available online. The school has a published electronic and media policy.
Contact Mrs. Julie Wiley Levine, Director of Admissions. 757-963-8244. Fax: 757-491-9111. E-mail: julielevine@capehenry.org. Web site: www.capehenrycollegiate.org.

ANNOUNCEMENT FROM THE SCHOOL Named for the nearby landing site of the nation's first settlers, Cape Henry Collegiate School prides itself on preparing leaders of the future. The coastal school has just over 1,000 students in Prekindergarten through grade 12. The core values of scholarship, integrity, opportunity, and community motivate students and faculty members to manifest excellence in a challenging college-preparatory curriculum.

CAPISTRANO VALLEY CHRISTIAN SCHOOLS

32032 Del Obispo Street
San Juan Capistrano, California 92675
Head of School: Dr. Dave Baker

General Information Coeducational day college-preparatory, arts, religious studies, bilingual studies, and technology school, affiliated with Christian faith. Grades JK–12. Founded: 1972. Setting: suburban. Nearest major city is Los Angeles. 8-acre campus. 2 buildings on campus. Approved or accredited by Western Association of Schools and Colleges and California Department of Education. Total enrollment: 475. Upper school average class size: 18. Upper school faculty-student ratio: 1:13.
Upper School Student Profile Grade 9: 56 students (28 boys, 28 girls); Grade 10: 50 students (26 boys, 24 girls); Grade 11: 61 students (34 boys, 27 girls); Grade 12: 53 students (24 boys, 29 girls). 80% of students are Christian.
Faculty School total: 42. In upper school: 8 men, 12 women; 9 have advanced degrees.
Subjects Offered Advanced math, algebra, American history, American literature, anatomy, art, Bible studies, biology, biology-AP, calculus-AP, career planning, chemistry, choir, college counseling, college placement, composition, composition-AP, computer animation, computer applications, computer education, computer information systems, computer keyboarding, computer literacy, computer multimedia, computer skills, computer technologies, desktop publishing, drama performance, ecology, economics, English, English literature-AP, English-AP, ESL, European history, freshman foundations, geometry, government, health, history, honors algebra, honors English, independent study, Internet, intro to computers, journalism, lab science, leadership, physical education, physical science, physics, public speaking, research skills, Spanish, Spanish-AP, student government, U.S. government-AP, U.S. history-AP, Web site design, world culture, yearbook.
Graduation Requirements Algebra, American government, American history, American literature, arts and fine arts (art, music, dance, drama), Bible, biology, composition, computer skills, economics, electives, English, European history, foreign language, freshman foundations, geometry, physical education (includes health), research skills, speech, our grad requirements meet UC and CSU entrance requirements.
Special Academic Programs Advanced Placement exam preparation; honors section; independent study; ESL (30 students enrolled).
College Admission Counseling 63 students graduated in 2008; 61 went to college. Other: 1 went to work, 1 entered military service. Median SAT critical reading: 510, median SAT math: 540. 22% scored over 600 on SAT critical reading, 25% scored over 600 on SAT math.
Student Life Upper grades have uniform requirement, student council, honor system. Discipline rests primarily with faculty.
Summer Programs Advancement, sports, art/fine arts programs offered; held on campus; accepts boys and girls; open to students from other schools. 35 students usually enrolled. 2009 schedule: June 20 to July 25. Application deadline: May 1.
Tuition and Aid Day student tuition: $10,270. Tuition installment plan (monthly payment plans). Tuition reduction for siblings, need-based scholarship grants available. In 2008–09, 5% of upper-school students received aid. Total amount of financial aid awarded in 2008–09: $225,000.
Admissions Traditional secondary-level entrance grade is 9. For fall 2008, 120 students applied for upper-level admission, 90 were accepted, 75 enrolled. ESOL English Proficiency Test, High School Placement Test, Stanford Test of Academic Skills or TOEFL required. Deadline for receipt of application materials: none. Application fee required: $100. On-campus interview required.
Athletics Interscholastic: baseball (boys), basketball (b,g), cheering (g), cross-country running (b,g), dance (g), football (b), golf (b,g), soccer (b,g), softball (g), tennis (b,g), volleyball (b,g), weight lifting (b); coed interscholastic: equestrian sports. 2 PE instructors, 53 coaches, 1 athletic trainer.
Computers Computers are regularly used in journalism, yearbook classes. Computer network features include on-campus library services, Internet access, wireless campus network. Campus intranet, student e-mail accounts, and computer access in designated common areas are available to students. Students grades are available online. The school has a published electronic and media policy.
Contact Jo Beveridge, Director of Admissions/Development. 949-493-5683 Ext. 109. Fax: 949-493-6057. E-mail: jbeveridge@cvcs.org. Web site: www.cvcs.org.

CARDIGAN MOUNTAIN SCHOOL

Canaan, New Hampshire
See Junior Boarding Schools section.

CARDINAL GIBBONS HIGH SCHOOL

1401 Edwards Mill Road
Raleigh, North Carolina 27607
Head of School: Mr. Jason Curtis

General Information Coeducational day college-preparatory, arts, business, religious studies, and technology school, affiliated with Roman Catholic Church. Grades 9–12. Founded: 1909. Setting: suburban. 36-acre campus. 1 building on campus. Approved or accredited by Southern Association of Colleges and Schools and Southern Association of Independent Schools. Endowment: $75,000. Total enrollment: 1,132. Upper school average class size: 24. Upper school faculty-student ratio: 1:24.
Upper School Student Profile Grade 9: 295 students (155 boys, 140 girls); Grade 10: 277 students (151 boys, 126 girls); Grade 11: 290 students (147 boys, 143 girls); Grade 12: 270 students (120 boys, 150 girls). 86% of students are Roman Catholic.
Faculty School total: 90. In upper school: 37 men, 52 women.
Special Academic Programs Advanced Placement exam preparation.

College Admission Counseling 270 students graduated in 2008; 269 went to college, including University of Notre Dame. Other: 1 had other specific plans.
Student Life Upper grades have uniform requirement, student council. Discipline rests primarily with faculty. Attendance at religious services is required.
Summer Programs Sports programs offered; session focuses on sports; held on campus; accepts boys and girls; open to students from other schools. 2009 schedule: June to August.
Tuition and Aid Day student tuition: $8100–$11,440. Tuition installment plan (FACTS Tuition Payment Plan). Need-based scholarship grants available.
Admissions Traditional secondary-level entrance grade is 9. Application fee required: $75. On-campus interview required.
Athletics Interscholastic: baseball (boys, girls), basketball (b,g), cheering (g), cross-country running (b,g), dance (g), dance squad (g), dance team (g), football (b), golf (b,g), lacrosse (b,g), outdoor education (b,g), roller hockey (b), soccer (b,g), softball (g), swimming and diving (b,g), tennis (b,g), track and field (b,g), volleyball (g), weight lifting (b,g), wrestling (b).
Contact Mrs. Marianne McCarty, Admissions Director. 919-834-1625 Ext. 209. Fax: 919-834-9771. E-mail: mmccarty@cghsnc.org. Web site: www.cghsnc.org.

CARDINAL MOONEY CATHOLIC COLLEGE PREPARATORY HIGH SCHOOL

660 South Water Street
Marine City, Michigan 48039
Head of School: Sr. Karen Lietz, OP

General Information Coeducational day college-preparatory school, affiliated with Roman Catholic Church. Grades 9–12. Founded: 1977. Setting: small town. Nearest major city is Mount Clemens. 1-acre campus. 1 building on campus. Approved or accredited by Michigan Association of Non-Public Schools, North Central Association of Colleges and Schools, and Michigan Department of Education. Total enrollment: 198. Upper school average class size: 22. Upper school faculty-student ratio: 1:10.
Upper School Student Profile Grade 9: 48 students (21 boys, 27 girls); Grade 10: 54 students (28 boys, 26 girls); Grade 11: 50 students (29 boys, 21 girls); Grade 12: 46 students (19 boys, 27 girls). 90% of students are Roman Catholic.
Faculty School total: 20. In upper school: 5 men, 15 women; 10 have advanced degrees.
Subjects Offered Advanced Placement courses, advanced studio art-AP, algebra, American literature, anatomy, art, biology, calculus, Catholic belief and practice, chemistry, choir, computer applications, computer skills, drama, economics, English, fiction, French, French language-AP, geography, geometry, government, government-AP, health, humanities, Italian, library science, moral and social development, mythology, physical education, physical science, physics, poetry, pre-calculus, Spanish, Spanish language-AP, statistics, study skills, U.S. history, U.S. history-AP, world history, world literature, yearbook.
Special Academic Programs Advanced Placement exam preparation; honors section.
College Admission Counseling 37 students graduated in 2008; all went to college, including Central Michigan University; Grand Valley State University; Michigan State University; Oakland University; University of Detroit Mercy; University of Michigan.
Student Life Upper grades have uniform requirement, student council, honor system. Discipline rests primarily with faculty. Attendance at religious services is required.
Tuition and Aid Tuition installment plan (monthly payment plans). Tuition reduction for siblings available.
Admissions Traditional secondary-level entrance grade is 9. For fall 2008, 51 students applied for upper-level admission, 51 were accepted, 51 enrolled. High School Placement Test required. Deadline for receipt of application materials: none. Application fee required: $250. Interview required.
Athletics Interscholastic: baseball (boys), basketball (b,g), bowling (b,g), cheering (g), cross-country running (b,g), equestrian sports (g), football (b), golf (b), soccer (b,g), softball (g), volleyball (g); coed interscholastic: cross-country running. 1 PE instructor, 6 coaches.
Computers Computers are regularly used in computer applications, data processing, desktop publishing, word processing classes. Computer network features include on-campus library services, Internet access, Internet filtering or blocking technology. Students grades are available online. The school has a published electronic and media policy.
Contact Sr. Karen Lietz, OP, Principal. 810-765-8825 Ext. 14. Fax: 810-765-7164. E-mail: klietz@cardinalmooneycatholic.com.

CARDINAL MOONEY HIGH SCHOOL

4171 Fruitville Road
Sarasota, Florida 34232
Head of School: Sr. Mary Lucia Haas, SND

General Information Coeducational day college-preparatory, arts, religious studies, and technology school, affiliated with Roman Catholic Church. Grades 9–12. Founded: 1959. Setting: suburban. Nearest major city is Tampa. 36-acre campus. 6 buildings on campus. Approved or accredited by Southern Association of Colleges and Schools and Southern Association of Independent Schools. Endowment: $1.8 million. Total enrollment: 556. Upper school average class size: 18. Upper school faculty-student ratio: 1:20.
Upper School Student Profile Grade 9: 162 students (74 boys, 88 girls); Grade 10: 121 students (74 boys, 47 girls); Grade 11: 125 students (76 boys, 49 girls); Grade 12: 148 students (67 boys, 81 girls). 80% of students are Roman Catholic.
Faculty School total: 45. In upper school: 20 men, 25 women; 25 have advanced degrees.
Subjects Offered Algebra, American government, American government-AP, American history, anatomy, art, biology, business, calculus, ceramics, chemistry, chorus, Christian and Hebrew scripture, community service, computer applications, computer graphics, computer keyboarding, contemporary history, creative writing, dance, drama, earth science, economics, economics and history, English, English literature, environmental science, fine arts, French, geometry, guitar, health, history, instrumental music, integrated math, journalism, learning strategies, marine biology, mathematics, music, physical education, physics, psychology, science, social justice, social studies, sociology, Spanish, speech, theology, trigonometry, world history, world literature, world religions.
Graduation Requirements Arts and fine arts (art, music, dance, drama), business skills (includes word processing), electives, English, foreign language, mathematics, musical theater, physical education (includes health), religion (includes Bible studies and theology), science, social science, social studies (includes history), 100 hours of community service.
Special Academic Programs Advanced Placement exam preparation; honors section; academic accommodation for the musically talented and the artistically talented.
College Admission Counseling 121 students graduated in 2008; 119 went to college, including Florida State University; University of Central Florida; University of Florida; University of South Florida. Other: 1 went to work, 1 entered military service. Median SAT critical reading: 540, median SAT math: 540, median composite ACT: 22. 34% scored over 600 on SAT critical reading, 31% scored over 600 on SAT math, 21% scored over 26 on composite ACT.
Student Life Upper grades have specified standards of dress, student council. Discipline rests primarily with faculty. Attendance at religious services is required.
Tuition and Aid Day student tuition: $5200–$6750. Tuition installment plan (monthly payment plans, semester payment plan). Tuition reduction for siblings, merit scholarship grants, need-based scholarship grants, paying campus jobs available. In 2008–09, 15% of upper-school students received aid; total upper-school merit-scholarship money awarded: $12,250. Total amount of financial aid awarded in 2008–09: $155,650.
Admissions Traditional secondary-level entrance grade is 9. For fall 2008, 180 students applied for upper-level admission, 180 were accepted, 162 enrolled. Placement test or STS required. Deadline for receipt of application materials: none. No application fee required. On-campus interview required.
Athletics Interscholastic: aerobics (boys, girls), aerobics/dance (g), baseball (b), basketball (b,g), cheering (b,g), cross-country running (b,g), dance (g), dance team (g), football (b), golf (b,g), modern dance (g), soccer (b,g), softball (g), strength & conditioning (b,g), swimming and diving (b,g), track and field (b,g), volleyball (g), weight lifting (b,g), weight training (b,g). 4 PE instructors, 66 coaches, 1 athletic trainer.
Computers Computers are regularly used in art, mathematics, science classes. Computer network features include on-campus library services, online commercial services, Internet access.
Contact Mrs. Joanne Mades, Registrar. 941-371-4917. Fax: 941-371-6924. E-mail: jmades@cmhs-sarasota.org. Web site: www.cmhs-sarasota.org.

CARDINAL NEWMAN HIGH SCHOOL

50 Ursuline Road
Santa Rosa, California 95403
Head of School: Mr. Graham Rutherford

General Information Boys' day college-preparatory and religious studies school, affiliated with Roman Catholic Church. Grades 9–12. Founded: 1964. Setting: suburban. Nearest major city is San Francisco. 40-acre campus. 16 buildings on campus. Approved or accredited by Western Association of Schools and Colleges, Western Catholic Education Association, and California Department of Education. Endowment: $4.3 million. Total enrollment: 436. Upper school average class size: 22. Upper school faculty-student ratio: 1:15.
Upper School Student Profile Grade 9: 121 students (121 boys); Grade 10: 124 students (124 boys); Grade 11: 88 students (88 boys); Grade 12: 99 students (99 boys). 66% of students are Roman Catholic.
Faculty School total: 34. In upper school: 23 men, 9 women; 20 have advanced degrees.
Subjects Offered Algebra, art appreciation, biology, calculus-AP, campus ministry, chemistry, chemistry-AP, computer science, creative writing, design, desktop publishing, drama, drawing, driver education, economics, English, English-AP, environmental science, ethics, fine arts, French, geometry, health, journalism, Latin, Latin-AP, performing arts, photography, physics-AP, psychology, social justice, Spanish, Spanish-AP, theology, trigonometry, U.S. government, U.S. history, U.S. history-AP, world history, yearbook.

Graduation Requirements Arts and fine arts (art, music, dance, drama), computer science, English, foreign language, mathematics, physical education (includes health), religion (includes Bible studies and theology), science, social studies (includes history), senior service project, 20 hours of community service work per year.
Special Academic Programs Advanced Placement exam preparation; honors section; study at local college for college credit.
College Admission Counseling 101 students graduated in 2008; all went to college, including California Polytechnic State University, San Luis Obispo; California State University; California State University, Chico; Santa Clara University; University of California, Davis; University of California, Santa Barbara. Mean SAT critical reading: 550, mean SAT math: 580, mean composite ACT: 24.
Student Life Upper grades have specified standards of dress, student council, honor system. Discipline rests equally with students and faculty. Attendance at religious services is required.
Summer Programs Remediation, enrichment, advancement, art/fine arts, computer instruction programs offered; session focuses on U.S. government, geometry, entry-level mathematics, and English; held on campus; accepts boys; open to students from other schools. 85 students usually enrolled. 2009 schedule: June 15 to July 20. Application deadline: May 1.
Tuition and Aid Day student tuition: $10,800. Tuition installment plan (individually arranged payment plans, monthly, quarterly, semester, and annual payment plans). Merit scholarship grants, need-based scholarship grants available. In 2008–09, 21% of upper-school students received aid. Total amount of financial aid awarded in 2008–09: $207,000.
Admissions For fall 2008, 159 students applied for upper-level admission, 126 were accepted, 121 enrolled. Scholastic Testing Service High School Placement Test and STS required. Deadline for receipt of application materials: January 9. Application fee required: $120. On-campus interview required.
Athletics Interscholastic: baseball, basketball, cheering (g), cross-country running, diving, football, golf, soccer, swimming and diving, tennis, track and field, water polo, wrestling; intramural: baseball, basketball, fencing, soccer, table tennis, touch football, ultimate Frisbee, volleyball; coed interscholastic: cross-country running. 1 PE instructor, 21 coaches, 2 athletic trainers.
Computers Computers are regularly used in art, Bible studies, college planning, desktop publishing, economics, English, French as a second language, geography, health, history, humanities, Latin, mathematics, music, photography, religious studies, SAT preparation, science, senior seminar, social sciences, social studies, Spanish, speech, theater arts, theology, video film production, writing, yearbook classes. Computer network features include on-campus library services, online commercial services, Internet access. The school has a published electronic and media policy.
Contact Mr. Pat Piehl, Director of Enrollment. 707-546-6470 Ext. 220. Fax: 707-544-8502. E-mail: piehl@cardinalnewman.org. Web site: www.cardinalnewman.org.

CARDINAL NEWMAN HIGH SCHOOL

512 Spencer Drive
West Palm Beach, Florida 33409-3699
Head of School: Fr. David W. Carr

General Information Coeducational day college-preparatory and IB Diploma school, affiliated with Roman Catholic Church. Grades 9–12. Founded: 1961. Setting: urban. Nearest major city is Miami. 50-acre campus. 5 buildings on campus. Approved or accredited by National Catholic Education Association, Southern Association of Colleges and Schools, and Florida Department of Education. Total enrollment: 782. Upper school average class size: 25. Upper school faculty-student ratio: 1:25.
Upper School Student Profile Grade 9: 176 students (80 boys, 96 girls); Grade 10: 211 students (111 boys, 100 girls); Grade 11: 188 students (100 boys, 88 girls); Grade 12: 207 students (107 boys, 100 girls). 80% of students are Roman Catholic.
Faculty School total: 60. In upper school: 23 men, 37 women; 38 have advanced degrees.
Subjects Offered Algebra, American government, American history, American literature, anatomy and physiology, art, band, Bible studies, biology, biology-AP, calculus, calculus-AP, chemistry, chorus, church history, college writing, computer applications, computer science, creative writing, desktop publishing, discrete math, drama, economics, English, English literature, English-AP, ethics, European history, fine arts, French, French-AP, geometry, government/civics, health, history, honors algebra, honors English, honors geometry, integrated science, International Baccalaureate courses, journalism, leadership training, marine biology, mathematics, music appreciation, newspaper, physical education, physics, political science, pre-calculus, probability and statistics, religion, social justice, social studies, Spanish, speech, world history, world literature, writing, yearbook.
Graduation Requirements Arts and fine arts (art, music, dance, drama), computer science, English, foreign language, mathematics, physical education (includes health), religion (includes Bible studies and theology), science, social studies (includes history), 100-hour community service requirement.
Special Academic Programs International Baccalaureate program; Advanced Placement exam preparation; honors section; study at local college for college credit; academic accommodation for the gifted; remedial reading and/or remedial writing; remedial math.
College Admission Counseling 222 students graduated in 2008; 221 went to college, including Florida Atlantic University; Florida State University; Palm Beach Community College; University of Central Florida; University of Florida; University of North Florida. Other: 1 entered military service.
Student Life Upper grades have uniform requirement, student council, honor system. Discipline rests primarily with faculty. Attendance at religious services is required.
Summer Programs Remediation, enrichment, sports programs offered; session focuses on freshman preparation; held on campus; accepts boys and girls; not open to students from other schools. 75 students usually enrolled. 2009 schedule: June 15 to June 30.
Tuition and Aid Day student tuition: $8200–$9300. Tuition installment plan (FACTS Tuition Payment Plan). Need-based scholarship grants available. In 2008–09, 18% of upper-school students received aid.
Admissions Traditional secondary-level entrance grade is 9. STS required. Deadline for receipt of application materials: none. Application fee required: $50. On-campus interview recommended.
Athletics Interscholastic: baseball (boys), basketball (b,g), bowling (b,g), cheering (g), cross-country running (b,g), dance team (g), diving (b,g), football (b), golf (b,g), lacrosse (b,g), physical fitness (b,g), soccer (b,g), softball (g), swimming and diving (b,g), tennis (b,g), track and field (b,g), volleyball (g), wrestling (b). 3 PE instructors, 1 athletic trainer.
Computers Computers are regularly used in all academic, Bible studies, yearbook classes. Computer resources include on-campus library services, online commercial services, Internet access, Internet filtering or blocking technology. Students grades are available online. The school has a published electronic and media policy.
Contact Mrs. Jan Joy, Admissions Coordinator. 561-242-2268. Fax: 561-683-7307. E-mail: jjoy@cardinalnewman.com. Web site: www.cardinalnewman.com.

ANNOUNCEMENT FROM THE SCHOOL Through academic, religious, service, athletic, and extracurricular programs, Cardinal Newman High School, an IB World School, educates the whole person and helps students to develop their God-given talents. The School produces individuals who are academically competitive and spiritually alive. Cardinal Newman places 99% of its graduating class in national colleges and universities.

CARDINAL NEWMAN SCHOOL

4701 Forest Drive
Columbia, South Carolina 29206-3108
Head of School: Mrs. Jacqualine Kasprowski

General Information Coeducational day college-preparatory, arts, religious studies, and technology school, affiliated with Roman Catholic Church. Grades 7–12. Founded: 1858. Setting: urban. 16-acre campus. 4 buildings on campus. Approved or accredited by National Catholic Education Association, South Carolina Independent School Association, Southern Association of Colleges and Schools, and South Carolina Department of Education. Total enrollment: 483. Upper school average class size: 20. Upper school faculty-student ratio: 1:10.
Upper School Student Profile Grade 9: 85 students (37 boys, 48 girls); Grade 10: 82 students (39 boys, 43 girls); Grade 11: 64 students (35 boys, 29 girls); Grade 12: 78 students (45 boys, 33 girls). 73% of students are Roman Catholic.
Faculty School total: 31. In upper school: 12 men, 19 women; 16 have advanced degrees.
Subjects Offered Algebra, American government, anatomy, art, biology, biology-AP, calculus, ceramics, chemistry, choral music, computer applications, drama, drawing, economics, English composition, English literature, French, geometry, government, honors algebra, honors English, honors geometry, honors U.S. history, journalism, Latin, painting, philosophy, physical education, physics, pre-calculus, psychology, public speaking, SAT preparation, Spanish, studio art, theology, U.S. history, world civilizations, yearbook.
Graduation Requirements Algebra, arts and fine arts (art, music, dance, drama), biology, chemistry, computer applications, economics, electives, English, foreign language, geometry, government, physical education (includes health), physics, theology, U.S. history, world civilizations, 40 hours of community service (seniors).
Special Academic Programs 1 Advanced Placement exam for which test preparation is offered; honors section; independent study; study at local college for college credit; programs in English, mathematics for dyslexic students; special instructional classes for deaf students, blind students.
College Admission Counseling 53 students graduated in 2008; all went to college, including Clemson University; College of Charleston; The University of Alabama; University of South Carolina; York University. Mean SAT critical reading: 586, mean SAT math: 566, mean combined SAT: 1152.
Student Life Upper grades have uniform requirement, student council, honor system. Discipline rests primarily with faculty. Attendance at religious services is required.
Tuition and Aid Day student tuition: $7536–$8556. Tuition installment plan (FACTS Tuition Payment Plan). Need-based scholarship grants, PSAS Financial Aid available.
Admissions Traditional secondary-level entrance grade is 9. For fall 2008, 55 students applied for upper-level admission, 54 were accepted, 54 enrolled. Deadline for receipt of application materials: none. Application fee required: $40. On-campus interview required.
Athletics Interscholastic: baseball (boys), basketball (b,g), cheering (g), cross-country running (b,g), football (b), golf (b,g), physical training (b,g), soccer (b,g),

softball (g), swimming and diving (b,g), tennis (b,g), volleyball (g), weight training (b,g), wrestling (b); coed interscholastic: outdoor adventure.

Computers Computers are regularly used in all academic classes. Computer network features include on-campus library services, Internet access, wireless campus network. Campus intranet and computer access in designated common areas are available to students. Students grades are available online.

Contact Ms. Theresa Harper, Admissions Coordinator/Registrar. 803-782-2814 Ext. 11. Fax: 803-782-9314. E-mail: tharper@cnhs.org. Web site: www.cnhs.org.

THE CARIBBEAN SCHOOL

1689 Calle Navarra
Urb. La Rambla
Ponce, Puerto Rico 00730-4043

Head of School: Mr. James E. DiSebastian

General Information Coeducational day college-preparatory school. Grades PK–12. Founded: 1954. Setting: suburban. 10-acre campus. 3 buildings on campus. Approved or accredited by Middle States Association of Colleges and Schools, The College Board, US Department of State, and Puerto Rico Department of Education. Member of European Council of International Schools. Total enrollment: 570. Upper school average class size: 20. Upper school faculty-student ratio: 1:7.

Faculty School total: 75. In upper school: 4 have advanced degrees.

Special Academic Programs Advanced Placement exam preparation; honors section; independent study.

College Admission Counseling 19 students graduated in 2008; all went to college.

Student Life Upper grades have uniform requirement, student council. Discipline rests primarily with faculty.

Admissions Application fee required: $25. Interview required.

Athletics 3 PE instructors.

Computers Computer resources include Internet access, Internet filtering or blocking technology. The school has a published electronic and media policy.

Contact Mrs. Mayra Bonilla, Administrative Manager. 787-843-2048 Ext. 2. Fax: 787-844-5626. E-mail: discovercs@gmail.com. Web site: www.caribbeanschool.org.

CARLISLE SCHOOL

300 Carlisle Road
Axton, Virginia 24054

Head of School: Mr. Simon A. Owen-Williams

General Information Coeducational boarding and day college-preparatory, International Baccalaureate (IB), and IB Middle Years Program school. Boarding grades 9–12, day grades PK–12. Founded: 1968. Setting: rural. Nearest major city is Danville. Students are housed in single-sex dormitories. 50-acre campus. 5 buildings on campus. Approved or accredited by Academy of Orton-Gillingham Practitioners and Educators, International Baccalaureate Organization, Southern Association of Colleges and Schools, Virginia Association of Independent Schools, and Virginia Department of Education. Member of National Association of Independent Schools. Endowment: $1.5 million. Total enrollment: 484. Upper school average class size: 16. Upper school faculty-student ratio: 1:10.

Upper School Student Profile Grade 9: 31 students (21 boys, 10 girls); Grade 10: 34 students (20 boys, 14 girls); Grade 11: 49 students (26 boys, 23 girls); Grade 12: 41 students (24 boys, 17 girls). 5% of students are boarding students. 70% are state residents. 2 states are represented in upper school student body. 19% are international students. International students from China, Nigeria, Republic of Korea, Taiwan, and Viet Nam.

Faculty School total: 59. In upper school: 1 man, 20 women; 9 have advanced degrees; 1 resides on campus.

Subjects Offered Advanced computer applications, advanced math, Advanced Placement courses, algebra, American government, American government-AP, American history, American history-AP, American literature, art, art history, arts, band, biology, biology-AP, calculus, calculus-AP, chemistry, chemistry-AP, choir, composition-AP, computer information systems, computer programming, computer science, computer science-AP, concert band, creative dance, creative drama, creative writing, dance, drama, earth science, economics, economics-AP, English, English language and composition-AP, English literature, English literature and composition-AP, English literature-AP, fine arts, geography, geometry, government, government/civics, grammar, health, health and wellness, history, history of the Americas, honors algebra, honors English, honors geometry, independent study, International Baccalaureate courses, intro to computers, jazz band, jazz ensemble, journalism, lab science, madrigals, mathematics, mathematics-AP, Microsoft, music, physical education, physics, physics-AP, play production, pre-algebra, pre-calculus, psychology, psychology-AP, publications, science, senior project, sex education, social studies, Spanish, Spanish literature, Spanish-AP, speech, statistics, statistics-AP, studio art, theater, theory of knowledge, U.S. government-AP, U.S. history-AP, wind ensemble, world civilizations, world history, world history-AP, World War I, World War II, world wide web design, yearbook.

Graduation Requirements Advanced math, algebra, arts and fine arts (art, music, dance, drama), computer science, electives, English, foreign language, mathematics, physical education (includes health), science, social studies (includes history), U.S. and Virginia history, U.S. government, Community and Service, Senior Project.

Special Academic Programs International Baccalaureate program; Advanced Placement exam preparation; honors section; independent study; term-away projects; study at local college for college credit; ESL (17 students enrolled).

College Admission Counseling 30 students graduated in 2008; all went to college, including Hampden-Sydney College; Penn State Erie, The Behrend College; The College of William and Mary; University of Virginia; Virginia Polytechnic Institute and State University; Wake Forest University. Median SAT critical reading: 546, median SAT math: 540, median SAT writing: 526. 33% scored over 600 on SAT critical reading, 37% scored over 600 on SAT math, 33% scored over 600 on SAT writing.

Student Life Upper grades have specified standards of dress, student council, honor system. Discipline rests equally with students and faculty.

Summer Programs Remediation, enrichment, advancement, ESL, sports, art/fine arts, computer instruction programs offered; session focuses on enrichment, academics, sports, fun; held on campus; accepts boys and girls; open to students from other schools. 60 students usually enrolled. 2009 schedule: June 15 to August 15. Application deadline: June 1.

Tuition and Aid Day student tuition: $8950. Tuition installment plan (Insured Tuition Payment Plan, FACTS Tuition Payment Plan). Need-based scholarship grants available. In 2008–09, 50% of upper-school students received aid. Total amount of financial aid awarded in 2008–09: $112,000.

Admissions Traditional secondary-level entrance grade is 9. For fall 2008, 145 students applied for upper-level admission, 111 were accepted, 98 enrolled. Nelson-Denny Reading Test, Woodcock-Johnson or writing sample required. Deadline for receipt of application materials: none. Application fee required: $50. On-campus interview required.

Athletics Interscholastic: basketball (boys, girls), cheering (g), field hockey (g), football (b), soccer (b,g), softball (g), tennis (b,g), volleyball (g); intramural: basketball (b,g), cheering (g), softball (g); coed interscholastic: baseball, cross-country running, dance, fencing, golf; coed intramural: aerobics/Nautilus, basketball, Frisbee, weight lifting. 2 PE instructors, 12 coaches.

Computers Computers are regularly used in all academic classes. Computer network features include on-campus library services, online commercial services, Internet access, wireless campus network, Internet filtering or blocking technology. Campus intranet is available to students. The school has a published electronic and media policy.

Contact Mrs. Marie Ferguson, Admissions Assistant. 276-632-7288 Ext. 221. Fax: 276-632-9545. E-mail: mferguson@carlisleschool.org. Web site: www.carlisleschool.org.

CARLUCCI AMERICAN INTERNATIONAL SCHOOL OF LISBON

Rua António dos Reis, 95
Linhó, Sintra 2710-301, Portugal

Head of School: Ms. Blannie M. Curtis

General Information Coeducational day college-preparatory and Portuguese Equivalência Program school. Grades PK–12. Founded: 1956. Setting: small town. Nearest major city is Lisbon, Portugal. 4-hectare campus. 4 buildings on campus. Approved or accredited by European Council of International Schools, International Baccalaureate Organization, New England Association of Schools and Colleges, US Department of State, and state department of education. Language of instruction: English. Total enrollment: 541. Upper school average class size: 15. Upper school faculty-student ratio: 1:8.

Upper School Student Profile Grade 9: 37 students (21 boys, 16 girls); Grade 10: 40 students (25 boys, 15 girls); Grade 11: 28 students (11 boys, 17 girls); Grade 12: 29 students (18 boys, 11 girls).

Faculty School total: 66. In upper school: 16 men, 19 women; 13 have advanced degrees.

Subjects Offered Algebra, art, biology, business studies, chemistry, choir, computer applications, computer art, economics, English, European history, French, geography, geometry, International Baccalaureate courses, model United Nations, modern civilization, music, physical education, physics, Portuguese, Portuguese literature, SAT preparation, Spanish, theory of knowledge, U.S. history, U.S. literature, writing workshop, yearbook.

Graduation Requirements Arts and fine arts (art, music, dance, drama), computer science, electives, English, foreign language, mathematics, physical education (includes health), science, social studies (includes history), Community service (for International Baccalaureate diploma candidates).

Special Academic Programs International Baccalaureate program; honors section; independent study; academic accommodation for the gifted; remedial reading and/or remedial writing; remedial math; programs in general development for dyslexic students; ESL (20 students enrolled).

College Admission Counseling 38 students graduated in 2008; 31 went to college, including Boston University; Ithaca College; Lynchburg College; The University of Texas at Arlington; University of California, Irvine; University of San Diego. Other: 1 went to work, 6 had other specific plans. Median SAT critical reading: 600, median SAT math: 570, median SAT writing: 610, median combined SAT: 1780. 72% scored over 600 on SAT critical reading, 28% scored over 600 on SAT math, 64% scored over 600 on SAT writing, 36% scored over 1800 on combined SAT.

Student Life Upper grades have specified standards of dress, student council. Discipline rests equally with students and faculty.
Tuition and Aid Day student tuition: €11,436–€15,688. Tuition installment plan (monthly payment plans, individually arranged payment plans, early payment discount, quarterly payment plan). Tuition reduction for siblings, merit scholarship grants, need-based scholarship grants, Merit based scholarships are available to students resident in Sintra, Portugal only available. In 2008–09, 5% of upper-school students received aid; total upper-school merit-scholarship money awarded: €110,746.
Admissions English for Non-native Speakers and Math Placement Exam required. Deadline for receipt of application materials: none. No application fee required. Interview recommended.
Athletics Interscholastic: basketball (boys, girls), cross-country running (b,g), soccer (b,g), track and field (b,g), volleyball (b,g); intramural: basketball (b,g), soccer (b,g); coed intramural: golf, volleyball. 4 PE instructors, 12 coaches.
Computers Computers are regularly used in art, economics, English, foreign language, graphic design, history, independent study, journalism, mathematics, science, technology, yearbook classes. Computer resources include on-campus library services, Internet access, wireless campus network, Internet filtering or blocking technology. Campus intranet and computer access in designated common areas are available to students. Students grades are available online.
Contact Ms. Elizabeth Halkon, Admissions Coordinator. 351-21-923-9800. Fax: 351-21-923-9809. E-mail: admissions@caislisbon.org. Web site: www.caislisbon.org.

CAROLINA DAY SCHOOL

1345 Hendersonville Road
Asheville, North Carolina 28803

Head of School: Beverly H. Sgro, PhD

General Information Coeducational day college-preparatory school; primarily serves dyslexic students. Grades PK–12. Founded: 1987. Setting: suburban. 60-acre campus. 2 buildings on campus. Approved or accredited by North Carolina Association of Independent Schools, Southern Association of Colleges and Schools, Southern Association of Independent Schools, and North Carolina Department of Education. Member of National Association of Independent Schools. Endowment: $3.6 million. Total enrollment: 651. Upper school average class size: 17. Upper school faculty-student ratio: 1:9.
Upper School Student Profile Grade 9: 55 students (23 boys, 32 girls); Grade 10: 37 students (15 boys, 22 girls); Grade 11: 44 students (19 boys, 25 girls); Grade 12: 39 students (22 boys, 17 girls).
Faculty School total: 89. In upper school: 11 men, 14 women; 17 have advanced degrees.
Subjects Offered Advanced chemistry, Advanced Placement courses, advanced studio art-AP, algebra, American literature, Arabic, art history, art history-AP, biology, biology-AP, calculus, calculus-AP, ceramics, chemistry, chemistry-AP, chorus, composition-AP, computer science, computer science-AP, conceptual physics, CPR, creative writing, debate, drama, drama performance, ecology, electronics, English, English language and composition-AP, English literature, environmental science-AP, European history-AP, fiction, foreign language, French, French studies, French-AP, functions, geometry, global studies, history, jewelry making, language and composition, linear algebra, linguistics, literature, literature and composition-AP, literature-AP, Mandarin, martial arts, music theory, music theory-AP, philosophy, photography, physical education, physics, physics-AP, pre-calculus, reading/study skills, research, robotics, science, senior project, Shakespeare, Spanish, Spanish-AP, speech, speech and debate, statistics-AP, studio art, theater, U.S. government-AP, U.S. history, U.S. history-AP, Western literature, world issues, world literature.
Graduation Requirements Algebra, arts and fine arts (art, music, dance, drama), biology, chemistry, electives, English, geometry, global studies, history, modern languages, physical education (includes health), public speaking, social studies (includes history), U.S. history, CPR/First Aid (non-credit class).
Special Academic Programs Advanced Placement exam preparation; honors section; independent study; programs in English, mathematics, general development for dyslexic students; special instructional classes for students with Attention Deficit Disorder and learning disabilities.
College Admission Counseling 48 students graduated in 2008; all went to college, including Colgate University; Davidson College; Duke University; Elon University; The University of North Carolina at Chapel Hill; The University of North Carolina Wilmington. Median SAT critical reading: 600, median SAT math: 605, median SAT writing: 620, median combined SAT: 1815. 48% scored over 600 on SAT critical reading, 50% scored over 600 on SAT math, 55% scored over 600 on SAT writing, 50% scored over 1800 on combined SAT.
Student Life Upper grades have specified standards of dress, student council, honor system. Discipline rests equally with students and faculty.
Summer Programs Enrichment, sports, art/fine arts, computer instruction programs offered; session focuses on recreation and enrichment; held on campus; accepts boys and girls; open to students from other schools. 94 students usually enrolled. 2009 schedule: June 15 to July 31. Application deadline: April 16.
Tuition and Aid Day student tuition: $16,050–$17,360. Tuition installment plan (Insured Tuition Payment Plan, FACTS Tuition Payment Plan, monthly payment plans, individually arranged payment plans, 1-payment plan or 2-installments plan (August and January)). Merit scholarship grants, need-based scholarship grants available. In 2008–09, 39% of upper-school students received aid; total upper-school merit-scholarship money awarded: $75,295. Total amount of financial aid awarded in 2008–09: $537,208.
Admissions Traditional secondary-level entrance grade is 9. For fall 2008, 39 students applied for upper-level admission, 28 were accepted, 23 enrolled. ERB, ISEE or SSAT required. Deadline for receipt of application materials: none. Application fee required: $100. On-campus interview required.
Athletics Interscholastic: baseball (boys), basketball (b,g), cross-country running (b,g), field hockey (g), martial arts (b,g), soccer (b,g), swimming and diving (b,g), tennis (b,g), track and field (b,g), volleyball (g); coed interscholastic: golf; coed intramural: basketball, kickball, soccer, touch football, volleyball. 1 PE instructor, 2 coaches, 1 athletic trainer.
Computers Computers are regularly used in all academic classes. Computer network features include on-campus library services, online commercial services, Internet access, wireless campus network, Internet filtering or blocking technology. Student e-mail accounts and computer access in designated common areas are available to students.
Contact Robin Goertz, Director of Admissions. 828-274-0757 Ext. 310. Fax: 828-274-0756. E-mail: admissions@cdschool.org. Web site: www.cdschool.org.

ANNOUNCEMENT FROM THE SCHOOL Carolina Day School is a comprehensive, college-preparatory, independent school in Asheville. The School discovers the promise, inspires the journey, and celebrates the achievement of every student. Working in partnership with parents, Carolina Day School challenges young people to pursue their quest for personal excellence by providing them with a rigorous college-preparatory program. The School is situated on 28 wooded acres adjacent to the Blue Ridge Parkway in the mountains of western North Carolina. The School carries on the traditions of academic excellence, social responsibility, and character development, which were strengthened by the 1987 merger of Asheville Country Day School (founded in 1936) and St. Genevieve/Gibbons Hall (founded in 1908). The School serves approximately 670 students in grades PK–12, with an approximate class size of 16. Carolina Day students respond to high expectations in a supportive learning environment, as evidenced by consistently high SAT scores and successful college placements. Satisfied parents voice their support for the School with high re-enrollment rates, citing the quality of teaching as the factor most responsible for their children's positive educational experiences. Distinctive features of the curriculum include fifteen Advanced Placement courses, a variety of athletic and arts offerings, outdoor and environmental education, leadership training, character education, a college guidance program, and a focus on community service. Successful capital campaigns during the last ten years have enabled the School to improve academic facilities, build a gymnasium/fitness center, establish a division for students with learning differences, and build an athletic complex on 32.5 newly acquired acres.

CARONDELET HIGH SCHOOL

1133 Winton Drive
Concord, California 94518

Head of School: Teresa Hurlbut, EdD

General Information Girls' day college-preparatory, arts, religious studies, and technology school, affiliated with Roman Catholic Church. Grades 9–12. Founded: 1965. Setting: suburban. Nearest major city is Oakland. 9-acre campus. 5 buildings on campus. Approved or accredited by Western Association of Schools and Colleges. Total enrollment: 800. Upper school average class size: 30. Upper school faculty-student ratio: 1:25.
Upper School Student Profile Grade 9: 200 students (200 girls); Grade 10: 200 students (200 girls); Grade 11: 200 students (200 girls); Grade 12: 200 students (200 girls). 90% of students are Roman Catholic.
Faculty School total: 61. In upper school: 13 men, 48 women; 30 have advanced degrees.
Subjects Offered Algebra, American studies, animation, architectural drawing, art, band, biology, calculus, calculus-AP, cartooning, chemistry, chorus, church history, civics, community service, computer applications, concert band, concert choir, creative writing, criminal justice, dance, design, drafting, drawing, economics, English, English-AP, ethics, finite math, fitness, French, geometry, government-AP, health, honors algebra, honors English, honors geometry, Italian, jazz band, journalism, Latin, marching band, marine biology, music history, music theory, musical theater, orchestra, painting, physical education, physics, physics-AP, physiology, pre-algebra, pre-calculus, psychology, psychology-AP, relationships, sculpture, Spanish, Spanish-AP, sports medicine, statistics, studio art-AP, technical drawing, transition mathematics, U.S. history, U.S. history-AP, water color painting, Web site design, women's health, world arts, world civilizations, world religions, writing, yearbook.
Graduation Requirements Computer literacy, English, mathematics, modern languages, physical education (includes health), religious studies, science, social studies (includes history), visual and performing arts.

Special Academic Programs 12 Advanced Placement exams for which test preparation is offered; honors section; independent study; academic accommodation for the gifted.
College Admission Counseling 200 students graduated in 2008; 198 went to college, including California Polytechnic State University, San Luis Obispo; California State University, Chico; University of California, Berkeley. Other: 2 went to work. Mean SAT critical reading: 548, mean SAT math: 538, mean SAT writing: 556, mean composite ACT: 24.
Student Life Upper grades have uniform requirement, honor system. Discipline rests primarily with faculty. Attendance at religious services is required.
Tuition and Aid Day student tuition: $12,250. Tuition installment plan (monthly payment plans, prepayment plan, semester or quarterly payment plans). Need-based scholarship grants, paying campus jobs available. In 2008–09, 17% of upper-school students received aid.
Admissions Traditional secondary-level entrance grade is 9. For fall 2008, 380 students applied for upper-level admission, 240 were accepted, 220 enrolled. High School Placement Test required. Deadline for receipt of application materials: December 8. Application fee required: $75. On-campus interview recommended.
Athletics Interscholastic: aquatics, basketball, cheering, combined training, cross-country running, dance squad, dance team, diving, golf, lacrosse, soccer, softball, swimming and diving, tennis, volleyball, water polo; intramural: badminton, basketball, broomball, flag football, physical fitness, physical training, touch football, volleyball. 3 PE instructors, 40 coaches, 1 athletic trainer.
Computers Computers are regularly used in computer applications classes. Computer resources include on-campus library services, Internet access, wireless campus network, Internet filtering or blocking technology. Student e-mail accounts are available to students. Students grades are available online. The school has a published electronic and media policy.
Contact Ms. Kathy Harris, Director of Admissions. 925-686-5353 Ext. 161. Fax: 925-671-9429. E-mail: kharris@carondeleths.org. Web site: www.carondelet.pvt.k12.ca.us/.

CARRABASSETT VALLEY ACADEMY

3197 Carrabassett Drive
Carrabassett Valley, Maine 04947
Head of School: Mr. John C. Ritzo

General Information Coeducational boarding and day college-preparatory and arts school. Grades 8–PG. Founded: 1982. Setting: rural. Nearest major city is Waterville. Students are housed in single-sex by floor dormitories. 8-acre campus. 3 buildings on campus. Approved or accredited by New England Association of Schools and Colleges and Maine Department of Education. Total enrollment: 115. Upper school average class size: 12. Upper school faculty-student ratio: 1:6.
Upper School Student Profile Grade 10: 20 students (16 boys, 4 girls); Grade 11: 42 students (26 boys, 16 girls); Grade 12: 23 students (14 boys, 9 girls). 60% of students are boarding students. 61% are state residents. 12 states are represented in upper school student body. 1% are international students. International students from Australia, Canada, Georgia, Republic of Korea, and Spain.
Faculty School total: 14. In upper school: 5 men, 8 women; 5 have advanced degrees; 8 reside on campus.
Subjects Offered Algebra, American history, American literature, biology, calculus, chemistry, earth science, English, European history, fine arts, French, geography, geometry, health, history, mathematics, music, physical education, physics, precalculus, publications, science, social studies, Spanish, sports conditioning, studio art, world history.
Graduation Requirements Algebra, American history, applied arts, arts and fine arts (art, music, dance, drama), athletic training, athletics, biology, chemistry, computer literacy, earth science, English, foreign language, geometry, health education, physical education (includes health), science, senior project, social studies (includes history), Western civilization, world cultures, participation and training in alpine racing, freestyle skiing, snowboarding, big mountain skiing and riding, Nordic skiing, or ski patrol.
Special Academic Programs Honors section; ESL (2 students enrolled).
College Admission Counseling 28 students graduated in 2008; 27 went to college, including Bates College; Middlebury College; Montana State University; Smith College; University of Maine; University of Vermont. Other: 1 went to work. Median SAT critical reading: 510, median SAT math: 535.
Student Life Upper grades have specified standards of dress, student council, honor system. Discipline rests primarily with faculty.
Summer Programs Advancement, sports programs offered; session focuses on ski and snowboard training, completing sections of sciences in advance of school year; held both on and off campus; held at Blackcomb, British Columbia, Mt. Hood, Oregon, and New Zealand; accepts boys and girls; open to students from other schools. 30 students usually enrolled. 2009 schedule: June 27 to August 18. Application deadline: May 1.
Tuition and Aid Day student tuition: $28,200; 7-day tuition and room/board: $37,300. Tuition installment plan (monthly payment plans). Need-based scholarship grants available.
Admissions Traditional secondary-level entrance grade is 10. Deadline for receipt of application materials: March 31. Application fee required: $40. Interview required.
Athletics Interscholastic: alpine skiing (boys, girls), freestyle skiing (b,g), skiing (downhill) (b,g), snowboarding (b,g), soccer (b,g); intramural: weight lifting (b,g), weight training (b,g); coed interscholastic: bicycling, mountain biking, skateboarding; coed intramural: aerobics/dance, backpacking, bicycling, canoeing/kayaking, climbing, combined training, fitness, golf, hiking/backpacking, in-line skating, kayaking, mountaineering, outdoor activities, physical fitness, physical training, rappelling, roller blading, running, Special Olympics, tennis, ultimate Frisbee, volleyball, wall climbing, wilderness. 17 coaches, 1 athletic trainer.
Computers Computers are regularly used in all classes. Computer network features include online commercial services, Internet access, wireless campus network, Internet filtering or blocking technology. Student e-mail accounts and computer access in designated common areas are available to students. Students grades are available online. The school has a published electronic and media policy.
Contact Mrs. Dawn Smith, Director of Admissions. 207-237-2250. Fax: 207-237-2213. E-mail: dsmith@gocva.com. Web site: www.gocva.com.

ANNOUNCEMENT FROM THE SCHOOL CVA is an independent, coeducational, boarding and day school for grades 8 through postgraduate. The intent and purpose of the Academy is to foster individual student development by providing the optimum balance of excellence in athletic training with a focus on competitive or big mountain skiing/snowboarding, college-preparatory academics, and responsible living. Carrabassett Valley Academy is located at Sugarloaf.

CARROLLTON SCHOOL OF THE SACRED HEART

3747 Main Highway
Miami, Florida 33133
Head of School: Sr. Suzanne Cooke

General Information Girls' day college-preparatory, arts, religious studies, bilingual studies, and technology school, affiliated with Roman Catholic Church. Grades PK–12. Founded: 1961. Setting: urban. 17-acre campus. 5 buildings on campus. Approved or accredited by Florida Council of Independent Schools, Network of Sacred Heart Schools, and Southern Association of Colleges and Schools. Endowment: $2 million. Total enrollment: 775. Upper school average class size: 15. Upper school faculty-student ratio: 1:9.
Upper School Student Profile Grade 6: 48 students (48 girls); Grade 7: 45 students (45 girls); Grade 8: 48 students (48 girls); Grade 9: 64 students (64 girls); Grade 10: 64 students (64 girls); Grade 11: 80 students (80 girls); Grade 12: 73 students (73 girls). 87% of students are Roman Catholic.
Faculty School total: 74. In upper school: 9 men, 24 women; 20 have advanced degrees.
Subjects Offered Algebra, American history, American literature, anatomy and physiology, art, art history, Bible studies, biology, British literature, calculus, chemistry, computer science, debate, drama, earth systems analysis, economics, English, English literature, environmental science, ethics, expository writing, fine arts, French, general science, geometry, government/civics, grammar, health, history, humanities, journalism, mathematics, music, photography, physical education, physical science, physics, pre-calculus, psychology, religion, science, scripture, social science, social studies, Spanish, speech, theater, trigonometry, vocal ensemble, world history, world literature.
Graduation Requirements Arts and fine arts (art, music, dance, drama), computer science, English, foreign language, mathematics, physical education (includes health), religion (includes Bible studies and theology), science, social studies (includes history). Community service is required.
Special Academic Programs International Baccalaureate program; Advanced Placement exam preparation; honors section; independent study; study at local college for college credit; domestic exchange program; study abroad.
College Admission Counseling 58 students graduated in 2008; all went to college, including Boston College; Northwestern University; University of Miami; Vanderbilt University. Median SAT critical reading: 580, median SAT math: 590, median composite ACT: 24. 51% scored over 600 on SAT critical reading, 47% scored over 600 on SAT math, 30% scored over 26 on composite ACT.
Student Life Upper grades have uniform requirement, student council, honor system. Discipline rests primarily with faculty. Attendance at religious services is required.
Tuition and Aid Day student tuition: $2120. Tuition installment plan (Insured Tuition Payment Plan, monthly payment plans). Merit scholarship grants, need-based scholarship grants available. In 2008–09, 15% of upper-school students received aid; total upper-school merit-scholarship money awarded: $45,000. Total amount of financial aid awarded in 2008–09: $920,000.
Admissions Traditional secondary-level entrance grade is 9. For fall 2008, 132 students applied for upper-level admission, 37 were accepted, 30 enrolled. Admissions testing required. Deadline for receipt of application materials: February 1. Application fee required: $100. On-campus interview required.
Athletics Interscholastic: aquatics, basketball, crew, cross-country running, golf, sailing, soccer, softball, swimming and diving, tennis, track and field, volleyball, water polo, winter soccer. 4 PE instructors, 8 coaches.
Computers Computers are regularly used in all academic classes. Computer network features include on-campus library services, online commercial services, Internet access, laptop program. The school has a published electronic and media policy.

Contact Ms. Ana J. Roye, Admissions Director. 305-446-5673 Ext. 1224. Fax: 305-446-4160. E-mail: aluna@carrollton.org. Web site: www.carrollton.org.

CARSON LONG MILITARY INSTITUTE

200 North Carlisle Street
New Bloomfield, Pennsylvania 17068-0098

Head of School: Col. Matthew J. Brown

General Information Boys' boarding college-preparatory, bilingual studies, Offer ESL (English as Second Language), and military school. Grades 6–12. Founded: 1836. Setting: small town. Nearest major city is Harrisburg. Students are housed in single-sex dormitories. 56-acre campus. 4 buildings on campus. Approved or accredited by Middle States Association of Colleges and Schools. Member of National Association of Independent Schools and Pennsylvania Association of Independent Schools. Endowment: $1.8 million. Total enrollment: 135. Upper school average class size: 12. Upper school faculty-student ratio: 1:11.

Upper School Student Profile Grade 9: 20 students (20 boys); Grade 10: 29 students (29 boys); Grade 11: 30 students (30 boys); Grade 12: 33 students (33 boys). 100% of students are boarding students. 11% are state residents. 21 states are represented in upper school student body. 11% are international students. International students from China, Dominican Republic, Mexico, Morocco, Republic of Korea, and Taiwan; 3 other countries represented in student body.

Faculty School total: 24. In upper school: 18 men, 6 women; 7 have advanced degrees; 13 reside on campus.

Subjects Offered Algebra, American history, American literature, art, biology, calculus, chemistry, choral music, computer science, earth science, economics, English, English literature, ESL, French, geography, geometry, government/civics, grammar, health, history, journalism, JROTC, mathematics, music, music appreciation, music theory, physical education, physics, science, social science, social studies, sociology, Spanish, speech, trigonometry, world history.

Graduation Requirements Computer science, English, foreign language, mathematics, physical education (includes health), science, social science, social studies (includes history), requirements for academic diploma differ.

Special Academic Programs Honors section; independent study; ESL (18 students enrolled).

College Admission Counseling 36 students graduated in 2008; 35 went to college, including John Jay College of Criminal Justice of the City University of New York; Norwich University; Penn State University Park; Stony Brook University, State University of New York; The Ohio State University; Virginia Commonwealth University. Other: 1 entered military service. Median SAT critical reading: 460, median SAT math: 480, median composite ACT: 24. 3% scored over 600 on SAT critical reading, 6% scored over 600 on SAT math.

Student Life Upper grades have uniform requirement, student council, honor system. Discipline rests equally with students and faculty. Attendance at religious services is required.

Tuition and Aid 7-day tuition and room/board: $15,900. Tuition installment plan (FACTS Tuition Payment Plan, individually arranged payment plans, PLEASE loans). Merit scholarship grants, merit-based scholarships for returning students only available. In 2008–09, 7% of upper-school students received aid; total upper-school merit-scholarship money awarded: $24,000.

Admissions Traditional secondary-level entrance grade is 10. For fall 2008, 120 students applied for upper-level admission, 91 were accepted, 67 enrolled. School's own exam required. Deadline for receipt of application materials: none. Application fee required: $65. On-campus interview required.

Athletics Interscholastic: baseball (boys), basketball (b), cross-country running (b), drill team (b), fencing (b), fitness (b), football (b), JROTC drill (b), marksmanship (b), pistol (b), riflery (b), skiing (downhill) (b), soccer (b), tennis (b), touch football (b), track and field (b), weight lifting (b), wrestling (b); intramural: baseball (b), basketball (b), fitness (b), flagball (b), football (b), Frisbee (b), indoor soccer (b), JROTC drill (b).

Computers Computers are regularly used in English, JROTC, library, mathematics, SAT preparation classes. Computer resources include on-campus library services, Internet access, Internet filtering or blocking technology. The school has a published electronic and media policy.

Contact Lt. Col. David M. Comolli, Dean of Admissions. 717-582-2121. Fax: 717-582-8763. E-mail: david.comolli@carsonlong.org. Web site: www.carsonlong.org.

CARY ACADEMY

1500 North Harrison Avenue
Cary, North Carolina 27513

Head of School: Mr. Donald S. Berger

General Information Coeducational day college-preparatory, arts, and technology school. Grades 6–12. Founded: 1996. Setting: suburban. Nearest major city is Raleigh. 52-acre campus. 6 buildings on campus. Approved or accredited by North Carolina Association of Independent Schools, Southern Association of Colleges and Schools, Southern Association of Independent Schools, and North Carolina Department of Education. Total enrollment: 710. Upper school average class size: 14. Upper school faculty-student ratio: 1:14.

Upper School Student Profile Grade 9: 104 students (54 boys, 50 girls); Grade 10: 106 students (61 boys, 45 girls); Grade 11: 100 students (52 boys, 48 girls); Grade 12: 98 students (45 boys, 53 girls).

Faculty School total: 77. In upper school: 29 men, 19 women; 38 have advanced degrees.

Subjects Offered Advanced Placement courses, algebra, American history, American history-AP, American literature, American literature-AP, anatomy and physiology, biology, biology-AP, calculus, calculus-AP, ceramics, chamber groups, chemistry, chemistry-AP, Chinese, computer programming, computer programming-AP, concert choir, debate, digital photography, drawing, economics, economics-AP, environmental science, environmental science-AP, film studies, forensic science, French language-AP, French literature-AP, French-AP, genetics, geometry, German, German literature, German-AP, health education, instruments, jazz band, journalism, modern European history-AP, multimedia design, music composition, music theory, music theory-AP, orchestra, painting, photography, physical education, physics, physics-AP, pre-calculus, programming, Spanish language-AP, Spanish literature, Spanish literature-AP, Spanish-AP, statistics and probability, statistics-AP, studio art, studio art-AP, technical theater, theater production, trigonometry, U.S. government-AP, video, voice, Web site design, wind ensemble, world arts, world history, world literature, yearbook.

Graduation Requirements Algebra, American history, American literature, biology, chemistry, foreign language, physical education (includes health), physics, world history, world literature.

Special Academic Programs Advanced Placement exam preparation; honors section; independent study; academic accommodation for the gifted, the musically talented, and the artistically talented.

College Admission Counseling 99 students graduated in 2008; all went to college, including Duke University; North Carolina State University; Princeton University; The University of North Carolina at Chapel Hill; The University of North Carolina Wilmington; University of Maryland, College Park. Mean SAT critical reading: 646, mean SAT math: 647, mean SAT writing: 639, mean combined SAT: 1932.

Student Life Upper grades have specified standards of dress, student council, honor system. Discipline rests equally with students and faculty.

Summer Programs Enrichment, sports, art/fine arts, computer instruction programs offered; session focuses on enrichment; held on campus; accepts boys and girls; open to students from other schools. 1,000 students usually enrolled. 2009 schedule: June 11 to July 27. Application deadline: none.

Tuition and Aid Day student tuition: $17,750. Tuition installment plan (Academic Management Services Plan, monthly payment plans). Merit scholarship grants, need-based loans available. In 2008–09, 15% of upper-school students received aid; total upper-school merit-scholarship money awarded: $10,000. Total amount of financial aid awarded in 2008–09: $647,020.

Admissions Traditional secondary-level entrance grade is 9. For fall 2008, 82 students applied for upper-level admission, 50 were accepted, 37 enrolled. Achievement/Aptitude/Writing, ERB CTP IV or ISEE required. Deadline for receipt of application materials: none. Application fee required: $110. Interview required.

Athletics Interscholastic: aquatics (boys, girls), baseball (b), basketball (b,g), cheering (b,g), cross-country running (b,g), field hockey (g), golf (b), lacrosse (b), soccer (b,g), softball (g), swimming and diving (b,g), tennis (b,g), track and field (b,g), volleyball (g), wrestling (g); intramural: baseball (b), basketball (b,g), cooperative games (b,g), dance (b,g), dance squad (g), fitness (b,g), fitness walking (b,g), Fives (b,g), floor hockey (b,g), indoor soccer (b,g), modern dance (g), soccer (b,g), softball (g), strength & conditioning (b,g), tennis (b,g), touch football (b,g), track and field (b,g), ultimate Frisbee (b,g), volleyball (b,g), walking (b,g), weight lifting (b,g), wrestling (b,g); coed intramural: aerobics, aerobics/dance, aerobics/Nautilus, badminton, basketball, billiards, bowling, cooperative games, dance, fitness, fitness walking, Fives, floor hockey, Frisbee, golf, gymnastics, handball, indoor soccer, jogging, jump rope, kickball, martial arts, modern dance, Newcombe ball, physical fitness, running, soccer, strength & conditioning, table tennis, tai chi, tennis, touch football, track and field, ultimate Frisbee, volleyball, walking, weight lifting, weight training, winter walking. 4 PE instructors, 40 coaches, 1 athletic trainer.

Computers Computers are regularly used in all academic, animation, desktop publishing, drawing and design, independent study, media arts, media production, music, theater arts, video film production, yearbook classes. Computer network features include on-campus library services, online commercial services, Internet access, wireless campus network, Internet filtering or blocking technology, each student is issued a free laptop computer. Campus intranet, student e-mail accounts, and computer access in designated common areas are available to students. Students grades are available online. The school has a published electronic and media policy.

Contact Ms. Denise Goodman, Director of Admissions. 919-228-4550. Fax: 919-677-4002. E-mail: denise_goodman@caryacademy.org. Web site: www.caryacademy.org.

CASCADILLA SCHOOL

116 Summit Street
Ithaca, New York 14850

Head of School: Patricia T. Kendall

General Information Coeducational boarding and day college-preparatory, arts, bilingual studies, and English/Language Arts-The Cascadilla Seminar/Cornell Univ school; primarily serves We are prepared to work with all students who may have special needs. Grades 9–PG. Founded: 1870. Setting: urban. Nearest major city is Syracuse. Students are housed in single-sex dormitories. 2-acre campus. 3 buildings on campus. Approved or accredited by Colombian Ministry of Education, Ministry of Education (Thailand), Ministry of Education, Japan, New York State Board of Regents, New York State University, The College Board, and US Department of State. Endowment: $1.2 million. Total enrollment: 52. Upper school average class size: 7. Upper school faculty-student ratio: 1:6.

Upper School Student Profile Grade 9: 16 students (8 boys, 8 girls); Grade 10: 10 students (5 boys, 5 girls); Grade 11: 16 students (8 boys, 8 girls); Grade 12: 10 students (5 boys, 5 girls). 15% of students are boarding students. 80% are state residents. 6 states are represented in upper school student body. 15% are international students. International students from Angola, Austria, China, Colombia, Republic of Korea, and Taiwan; 4 other countries represented in student body.

Faculty School total: 14. In upper school: 7 men, 7 women; 12 have advanced degrees; 4 reside on campus.

Subjects Offered Advanced chemistry, Advanced Placement courses, advanced TOEFL/grammar, African literature, algebra, American history, American literature, anatomy and physiology, art, biochemistry, biology, biology-AP, calculus, calculus-AP, career/college preparation, chemistry, chemistry-AP, college admission preparation, college awareness, college counseling, college placement, college planning, college writing, computer programming, computer science, creative writing, decision making, decision making skills, drama performance, driver education, earth science, economics, English, English as a foreign language, English composition, English literature, English literature and composition-AP, English literature-AP, environmental education, environmental science, ESL, ethics, European history, expository writing, fabric arts, French, French as a second language, geometry, government/civics, health, health and wellness, health education, history, honors algebra, honors English, honors geometry, honors U.S. history, honors world history, lab science, leadership skills, mathematics, philosophy, photography, physical education, physics, psychology, public speaking, reading, reading/study skills, SAT preparation, SAT/ACT preparation, science, Shakespeare, social studies, Spanish, trigonometry, typing, video film production, world history, world history-AP, world literature, writing.

Graduation Requirements Arts and fine arts (art, music, dance, drama), computer science, current events, debate, economics, English, foreign language, international affairs, mathematics, physical education (includes health), political science, public speaking, research, research and reference, science, social studies (includes history), English V -The Cascadilla Seminar (for college research preparation). Community service is required.

Special Academic Programs Advanced Placement exam preparation; honors section; accelerated programs; independent study; study at local college for college credit; academic accommodation for the gifted and the artistically talented; remedial reading and/or remedial writing; remedial math; programs in English, mathematics for dyslexic students; special instructional classes for students with learning disabilities and Attention Deficit Disorder; ESL (17 students enrolled).

College Admission Counseling 18 students graduated in 2008; 17 went to college, including Cornell University; Emory University; Syracuse University; University of Colorado at Boulder; University of Michigan. Other: 1 had other specific plans. Median SAT critical reading: 600, median SAT math: 650, median SAT writing: 550. 50% scored over 600 on SAT critical reading, 50% scored over 600 on SAT math, 15% scored over 600 on SAT writing.

Student Life Upper grades have specified standards of dress, student council, honor system. Discipline rests equally with students and faculty.

Summer Programs Remediation, enrichment, advancement, ESL, art/fine arts programs offered; session focuses on academics; held on campus; accepts boys and girls; open to students from other schools. 40 students usually enrolled. 2009 schedule: July 1 to August 17. Application deadline: June 30.

Tuition and Aid Day student tuition: $10,000; 7-day tuition and room/board: $30,000. Tuition installment plan (monthly payment plans, individually arranged payment plans). Tuition reduction for siblings, merit scholarship grants, need-based scholarship grants available. In 2008–09, 40% of upper-school students received aid; total upper-school merit-scholarship money awarded: $50,000. Total amount of financial aid awarded in 2008–09: $60,000.

Admissions Traditional secondary-level entrance grade is 10. For fall 2008, 50 students applied for upper-level admission, 15 were accepted, 15 enrolled. English Composition Test for ESL students, English entrance exam, English for Non-native Speakers, English language, English proficiency, High School Placement Test, math and English placement tests, mathematics proficiency exam, non-standardized placement tests, Reading for Understanding, school's own exam, skills for ESL students or writing sample required. Deadline for receipt of application materials: none. Application fee required: $50. Interview recommended.

Athletics Interscholastic: crew (boys, girls); intramural: crew (b,g), fencing (b), independent competitive sports (b,g), rowing (b,g), sailing (b,g), skiing (cross-country) (b,g), skiing (downhill) (b,g), soccer (b,g); coed interscholastic: aerobics, aerobics/Nautilus, alpine skiing, aquatics, backpacking, badminton, basketball, billiards, blading, bowling, climbing, combined training, fitness, fitness walking, Frisbee, hiking/backpacking, jogging, kayaking, nordic skiing, physical fitness, physical training, swimming and diving, table tennis, weight lifting, yoga; coed intramural: aerobics, aerobics/dance, badminton, basketball, blading, bowling, horseback riding, independent competitive sports, jogging, Nautilus, nordic skiing, outdoor activities, outdoor adventure, physical fitness, physical training, pillo polo, racquetball, rowing, sailboarding, skiing (cross-country), skiing (downhill), snowboarding, strength & conditioning, volleyball, walking, wall climbing, windsurfing. 2 PE instructors.

Computers Computers are regularly used in career exploration, college planning, creative writing, desktop publishing, desktop publishing, ESL, literary magazine, mathematics, media arts, newspaper, photography, publishing, research skills, SAT preparation, senior seminar, Spanish, stock market, theater, theater arts, video film production, Web site design, word processing, writing, writing, yearbook classes. Computer network features include on-campus library services, online commercial services, Internet access, Internet filtering or blocking technology. Student e-mail accounts are available to students. Students grades are available online.

Contact Donna W. Collins, Administrative Assistant. 607-272-3110. Fax: 607-272-0747. E-mail: admissions@cascadillaschool.org. Web site: www.cascadillaschool.org.

See Close-Up on page 708.

CASCIA HALL PREPARATORY SCHOOL

2520 South Yorktown Avenue
Tulsa, Oklahoma 74114-2803

Head of School: Rev. Bernard C. Scianna, OSA

General Information Coeducational day college-preparatory and liberal arts school, affiliated with Roman Catholic Church; primarily serves students with learning disabilities, individuals with Attention Deficit Disorder, and dyslexic students. Grades 6–12. Founded: 1926. Setting: urban. 40-acre campus. 10 buildings on campus. Approved or accredited by National Catholic Education Association, North Central Association of Colleges and Schools, and Oklahoma Department of Education. Endowment: $5 million. Total enrollment: 588. Upper school average class size: 18. Upper school faculty-student ratio: 1:12.

Upper School Student Profile Grade 9: 101 students (55 boys, 46 girls); Grade 10: 96 students (52 boys, 44 girls); Grade 11: 86 students (47 boys, 39 girls); Grade 12: 96 students (49 boys, 47 girls). 45% of students are Roman Catholic.

Faculty School total: 48. In upper school: 19 men, 20 women; 32 have advanced degrees.

Subjects Offered 20th century physics, Advanced Placement courses, algebra, American government-AP, ancient world history, art, art-AP, astronomy, Basic programming, Bible studies, biology, business, calculus, calculus-AP, career exploration, Catholic belief and practice, Central and Eastern European history, chemistry, chemistry-AP, Chinese, Chinese studies, chorus, Christian ethics, church history, composition, computer science, creative writing, driver education, English language and composition-AP, English literature and composition-AP, ethics, European history-AP, French, geography, geometry, German, government-AP, grammar, health, Holocaust studies, Latin, literature, philosophy, photography, physics, physics-AP, pre-calculus, psychology, Russian studies, SAT/ACT preparation, senior seminar, senior thesis, Spanish, Spanish language-AP, speech, speech and debate, statistics and probability, theater, theology, trigonometry, U.S. history, world history, yearbook.

Graduation Requirements Arts and fine arts (art, music, dance, drama), career exploration, computer science, English, foreign language, mathematics, religion (includes Bible studies and theology), science, senior seminar, social science, social studies (includes history), community service.

Special Academic Programs Advanced Placement exam preparation; honors section; independent study; study abroad; academic accommodation for the gifted.

College Admission Counseling 89 students graduated in 2008; all went to college, including Kansas State University; Oklahoma State University; Texas Christian University; The University of Kansas; University of Oklahoma; University of Tulsa. Median SAT critical reading: 580, median SAT math: 590, median SAT writing: 596, median composite ACT: 26. 51% scored over 600 on SAT critical reading, 44% scored over 600 on SAT math, 53% scored over 600 on SAT writing, 46% scored over 26 on composite ACT.

Student Life Upper grades have uniform requirement, student council. Discipline rests primarily with faculty. Attendance at religious services is required.

Summer Programs Sports, art/fine arts programs offered; session focuses on sports camp, driver's education, and fine arts; held on campus; accepts boys and girls; open to students from other schools. 500 students usually enrolled. 2009 schedule: June to August. Application deadline: May.

Tuition and Aid Day student tuition: $9975. Tuition installment plan (monthly payment plans). Tuition reduction for siblings, need-based scholarship grants available. In 2008–09, 20% of upper-school students received aid. Total amount of financial aid awarded in 2008–09: $228,571.

Admissions Traditional secondary-level entrance grade is 9. For fall 2008, 93 students applied for upper-level admission, 55 were accepted, 42 enrolled. 3-R Achievement Test and ACT-Explore required. Deadline for receipt of application materials: June. Application fee required: $25. On-campus interview required.

Athletics Interscholastic: baseball (boys), basketball (b,g), bowling (b,g), cheering (g), cross-country running (b,g), football (b), golf (b,g), power lifting (b,g), soccer (b,g), softball (g), strength & conditioning (b,g), tennis (b,g), track and field (b,g), volleyball (g), weight training (b,g), wrestling (b); coed intramural: ultimate Frisbee. 17 coaches, 1 athletic trainer.

Computers Computers are regularly used in all classes. Computer network features include on-campus library services, online commercial services, Internet access,

wireless campus network, Internet filtering or blocking technology, InfoTrac Search Bank, Internet access to local and state university library catalogues. Campus intranet, student e-mail accounts, and computer access in designated common areas are available to students. The school has a published electronic and media policy.

Contact Carol B. Bradley, Coordinator of Admissions and Communications. 918-746-2604. Fax: 918-746-2640. E-mail: cbradley@casciahall.org. Web site: www.casciahall.org.

CASTILLEJA SCHOOL

1310 Bryant Street
Palo Alto, California 94301

Head of School: Joan Z. Lonergan

General Information Girls' day college-preparatory, arts, and technology school. Grades 6–12. Founded: 1907. Setting: suburban. Nearest major city is San Francisco. 5-acre campus. 7 buildings on campus. Approved or accredited by California Association of Independent Schools, National Council for Private School Accreditation, and Western Association of Schools and Colleges. Member of National Association of Independent Schools and Secondary School Admission Test Board. Endowment: $35 million. Total enrollment: 415. Upper school average class size: 14. Upper school faculty-student ratio: 1:7.

Upper School Student Profile Grade 9: 60 students (60 girls); Grade 10: 58 students (58 girls); Grade 11: 57 students (57 girls); Grade 12: 60 students (60 girls).

Faculty School total: 65. In upper school: 12 men, 34 women; 40 have advanced degrees.

Subjects Offered Advanced Placement courses, African studies, algebra, American history, American literature, art, art history, biology, calculus, ceramics, chemistry, computer math, computer science, creative writing, drama, economics, English, English literature, environmental science, European history, expository writing, fine arts, French, geometry, global issues, government/civics, grammar, health, history, Japanese, journalism, Latin, marine biology, mathematics, music, philosophy, physical education, physics, psychology, Russian history, science, social studies, Spanish, speech, statistics, theater, trigonometry, world history, writing.

Graduation Requirements Arts and fine arts (art, music, dance, drama), English, foreign language, health and wellness, mathematics, science, social studies (includes history).

Special Academic Programs Advanced Placement exam preparation; honors section; independent study; academic accommodation for the gifted.

College Admission Counseling 57 students graduated in 2008; all went to college, including Harvard University; Santa Clara University; Scripps College; Stanford University; Tufts University; University of California, Berkeley. Mean SAT critical reading: 698, mean SAT math: 674, mean SAT writing: 704.

Student Life Upper grades have uniform requirement, student council, honor system. Discipline rests equally with students and faculty.

Tuition and Aid Day student tuition: $28,125. Tuition installment plan (monthly payment plans, individually arranged payment plans). Need-based scholarship grants available. In 2008–09, 18% of upper-school students received aid. Total amount of financial aid awarded in 2008–09: $900,000.

Admissions Traditional secondary-level entrance grade is 9. For fall 2008, 103 students applied for upper-level admission, 32 were accepted, 20 enrolled. ISEE, SSAT or TOEFL required. Deadline for receipt of application materials: January 15. Application fee required: $75. On-campus interview required.

Athletics Interscholastic: basketball, cross-country running, golf, lacrosse, soccer, softball, swimming and diving, tennis, track and field, volleyball, water polo; intramural: climbing, fitness, rock climbing. 6 PE instructors, 15 coaches, 1 athletic trainer.

Computers Computers are regularly used in art, English, foreign language, history, mathematics, science classes. Computer network features include on-campus library services, online commercial services, Internet access, wireless campus network, Internet filtering or blocking technology. Campus intranet and student e-mail accounts are available to students. The school has a published electronic and media policy.

Contact Jill V. W. Lee, Director of Admission. 650-470-7731. Fax: 650-326-8036. E-mail: jill_lee@castilleja.org. Web site: www.castilleja.org.

ANNOUNCEMENT FROM THE SCHOOL Castilleja School celebrated its centennial in 2007–08 and is a leading independent girls' school, known for academic excellence, comprehensive co-curricular activities (including athletics, performing arts, community service, and student-led clubs), and a global program promoting awareness, compassion, and engagement. Using pedagogical approaches drawn from research findings on the distinctive ways girls learn, a dedicated faculty serves a diverse enrollment of 415 students (grades 6–12), fostering lifelong learners and progressive leaders.

CATE SCHOOL

1960 Cate Mesa Road
Carpinteria, California 93013

Head of School: Benjamin D. Williams, IV

General Information Coeducational boarding and day college-preparatory school. Grades 9–12. Founded: 1910. Setting: small town. Nearest major city is Santa Barbara. Students are housed in single-sex dormitories. 150-acre campus. 18 buildings on campus. Approved or accredited by California Association of Independent Schools, The Association of Boarding Schools, and Western Association of Schools and Colleges. Member of National Association of Independent Schools and Secondary School Admission Test Board. Endowment: $60 million. Total enrollment: 265. Upper school average class size: 10. Upper school faculty-student ratio: 1:5.

Upper School Student Profile Grade 9: 55 students (27 boys, 28 girls); Grade 10: 70 students (35 boys, 35 girls); Grade 11: 70 students (35 boys, 35 girls); Grade 12: 70 students (35 boys, 35 girls). 83% of students are boarding students. 51% are state residents. 20 states are represented in upper school student body. 15% are international students. International students from Hong Kong, Jamaica, Saudi Arabia, Singapore, Thailand, and United Kingdom; 6 other countries represented in student body.

Faculty School total: 52. In upper school: 34 men, 18 women; 43 have advanced degrees; 51 reside on campus.

Subjects Offered Advanced studio art-AP, algebra, American government-AP, American history, American literature, art, art history-AP, Asian history, biology, biology-AP, calculus, ceramics, chemistry, chemistry-AP, Chinese, choir, computer programming, computer science, computer science-AP, creative writing, digital art, drama, drama performance, economics-AP, English, English literature, environmental science-AP, ethics, European history, finance, fine arts, French, French-AP, freshman seminar, genetics, geometry, government-AP, human development, international relations, Japanese, marine biology, multimedia, music, photography, physics, physics-AP, physiology-anatomy, pre-calculus, psychology, Spanish, Spanish-AP, statistics, statistics-AP, studio art—AP, the Sixties, theater, trigonometry, U.S. history-AP, world history, writing.

Graduation Requirements Arts and fine arts (art, music, dance, drama), English, foreign language, history, human development, mathematics, science, social science.

Special Academic Programs Advanced Placement exam preparation; honors section; independent study; term-away projects; study abroad; academic accommodation for the gifted, the musically talented, and the artistically talented; special instructional classes for deaf students.

College Admission Counseling 70 students graduated in 2007; all went to college, including Columbia College; New York University; University of California, Berkeley; University of California, San Diego; University of California, Santa Cruz; University of Southern California. Median SAT critical reading: 650, median SAT math: 660, median SAT writing: 680. 81% scored over 600 on SAT critical reading, 81% scored over 600 on SAT math, 83% scored over 600 on SAT writing.

Student Life Upper grades have specified standards of dress, student council, honor system. Discipline rests equally with students and faculty.

Tuition and Aid Day student tuition: $29,350; 7-day tuition and room/board: $38,100. Tuition installment plan (The Tuition Plan, Insured Tuition Payment Plan, Key Tuition Payment Plan, monthly payment plans). Need-based scholarship grants available. In 2007–08, 25% of upper-school students received aid. Total amount of financial aid awarded in 2007–08: $2,130,000.

Admissions Traditional secondary-level entrance grade is 9. For fall 2007, 500 students applied for upper-level admission, 125 were accepted, 76 enrolled. ISEE, PSAT and SAT for applicants to grade 11 and 12 or SSAT, ERB, PSAT, SAT, PLAN or ACT required. Deadline for receipt of application materials: January 15. Application fee required: $75. On-campus interview required.

Athletics Interscholastic: baseball (boys), basketball (b,g), cross-country running (b,g), football (b), lacrosse (b,g), soccer (b,g), softball (g), squash (b,g), tennis (b,g), track and field (b,g), volleyball (b,g), water polo (b,g); coed interscholastic: golf, swimming and diving; coed intramural: aerobics, aerobics/Nautilus, backpacking, bicycling, canoeing/kayaking, climbing, dance, fitness, hiking/backpacking, kayaking, modern dance, mountain biking, outdoor activities, outdoors, physical fitness, physical training, ropes courses, surfing, ultimate Frisbee, yoga. 3 coaches, 1 athletic trainer.

Computers Computers are regularly used in English, history, humanities, literary magazine, mathematics, media arts, media production, multimedia, music, newspaper, photography, science, yearbook classes. Computer network features include on-campus library services, online commercial services, Internet access, Internet filtering or blocking technology. Campus intranet, student e-mail accounts, and computer access in designated common areas are available to students. The school has a published electronic and media policy.

Contact Charlotte Brownlee, Director of Admission. 805-684-8409 Ext. 216. Fax: 805-684-2279. E-mail: charlotte_brownlee@cate.org. Web site: www.cate.org.

ANNOUNCEMENT FROM THE SCHOOL Cate School is a boarding school located outside Santa Barbara. The 265 students participate in a highly rigorous academic curriculum, featuring a combined thirty-eight AP and honors courses. All students are involved in an extracurricular program that includes athletics, drama, music, dance, community service, and an extensive outdoor program.

CATHEDRAL HIGH SCHOOL

5225 East 56th Street
Indianapolis, Indiana 46226

Head of School: Mr. Stephen J. Helmich

General Information Coeducational day college-preparatory, arts, religious studies, technology, International Baccalaureate, and AP/Honors school, affiliated with Roman Catholic Church; primarily serves students with learning disabilities. Grades 9–12. Founded: 1918. Setting: urban. 40-acre campus. 5 buildings on campus. Approved or accredited by Independent Schools Association of the Central States, National Catholic Education Association, North Central Association of Colleges and Schools, and Indiana Department of Education. Endowment: $30 million. Total enrollment: 1,288. Upper school average class size: 19. Upper school faculty-student ratio: 1:13.

Upper School Student Profile 80% of students are Roman Catholic.

Faculty School total: 105. In upper school: 47 men, 58 women; 54 have advanced degrees.

Subjects Offered Advanced biology, advanced chemistry, advanced math, Advanced Placement courses, algebra, American government-AP, American history, American history-AP, American literature-AP, American studies, anatomy, anatomy and physiology, art and culture, art history, arts, Bible, Bible studies, biology, botany, business, business communications, business education, business law, calculus, calculus-AP, career and personal planning, Catholic belief and practice, ceramics, chemistry, chemistry-AP, choir, choral music, chorus, Christianity, civics, civil war history, college counseling, composition-AP, computer science, debate, drama, driver education, earth science, economics, economics-AP, English, English literature, English literature and composition-AP, English literature-AP, English-AP, English/composition-AP, environmental science, fine arts, French, French language-AP, geography, geology, geometry, German, German-AP, government and politics-AP, government-AP, history, history-AP, independent study, journalism, lab science, language development, Latin, life science, macro/microeconomics-AP, mathematics, mathematics-AP, microbiology, music, music appreciation, news writing, newspaper, organic chemistry, photography, photojournalism, physical education, physical fitness, physics, physiology, psychology, religion, SAT/ACT preparation, science, social science, social studies, sociology, Spanish, speech, textiles, theater, theater design and production, theater production, theory of knowledge, trigonometry, U.S. government-AP, U.S. history, U.S. history-AP, vocal music, world history, world literature.

Graduation Requirements Arts and fine arts (art, music, dance, drama), biology, composition, economics, English, foreign language, government, mathematics, modern world history, physical education (includes health), religious studies, science, social studies (includes history), speech and debate, technology, 30 hours annually of community service.

Special Academic Programs International Baccalaureate program; Advanced Placement exam preparation; honors section; independent study; academic accommodation for the gifted, the musically talented, and the artistically talented; remedial reading and/or remedial writing; remedial math; programs in English, mathematics for dyslexic students; special instructional classes for deaf students, blind students, students with learning disabilities, Attention Deficit Disorder, and dyslexia.

College Admission Counseling 314 students graduated in 2008; 312 went to college, including Ball State University; Indiana University Bloomington; Loyola University Chicago; Purdue University; University of Dayton; Xavier University. Other: 2 had other specific plans. Median SAT critical reading: 558, median SAT math: 561, median SAT writing: 550, median combined SAT: 1669. Mean composite ACT: 25.

Student Life Upper grades have uniform requirement, student council. Discipline rests primarily with faculty. Attendance at religious services is required.

Summer Programs Remediation, enrichment, advancement, sports, art/fine arts, computer instruction programs offered; session focuses on advancement; held on campus; accepts boys and girls; not open to students from other schools. 500 students usually enrolled. 2009 schedule: June 8 to July 3. Application deadline: March 6.

Tuition and Aid Day student tuition: $10,100. Tuition installment plan (Key Tuition Payment Plan, monthly payment plans). Merit scholarship grants, need-based scholarship grants, paying campus jobs available. In 2008–09, 35% of upper-school students received aid; total upper-school merit-scholarship money awarded: $280,000. Total amount of financial aid awarded in 2008–09: $2,000,000.

Admissions Traditional secondary-level entrance grade is 9. For fall 2008, 552 students applied for upper-level admission, 432 were accepted, 352 enrolled. High School Placement Test and High School Placement Test (closed version) from Scholastic Testing Service required. Deadline for receipt of application materials: December 12. No application fee required. On-campus interview required.

Athletics Interscholastic: baseball (boys), basketball (b,g), bowling (b,g), cheering (g), cross-country running (b,g), diving (b,g), football (b), golf (b,g), soccer (b,g), softball (g), swimming and diving (b,g), tennis (b,g), track and field (b,g), volleyball (g), wrestling (b); intramural: curling (b), dance squad (g), dance team (g), field hockey (g), kickball (g), lacrosse (b,g), rugby (b,g), volleyball (b), weight lifting (b,g); coed interscholastic: ice hockey; coed intramural: badminton, bicycling, crew, fencing, Frisbee, martial arts, skiing (downhill), ultimate Frisbee. 6 PE instructors, 1 athletic trainer.

Computers Computers are regularly used in business, foreign language, information technology, mathematics, newspaper, photography, science, writing, yearbook classes. Computer network features include on-campus library services, online commercial services, Internet access, wireless campus network, Internet filtering or blocking technology. Student e-mail accounts are available to students. Students grades are available online. The school has a published electronic and media policy.

Contact Mrs. Diane Szymanski, Vice President for Enrollment Management. 317-542-1481. Fax: 317-542-1484. E-mail: dszymanski@cathedral-irish.org. Web site: www.cathedral-irish.org.

CATHEDRAL HIGH SCHOOL

350 East 56th Street
New York, New York 10022-4199

Head of School: Ms. Joan Close

General Information Girls' day college-preparatory, arts, business, religious studies, and technology school, affiliated with Roman Catholic Church. Grades 9–12. Founded: 1905. Setting: urban. 1 building on campus. Approved or accredited by Middle States Association of Colleges and Schools, National Catholic Education Association, New York Department of Education, New York State Board of Regents, and The College Board. Endowment: $1 million. Upper school average class size: 35.

Upper School Student Profile Grade 9: 149 students (149 girls); Grade 10: 191 students (191 girls); Grade 11: 172 students (172 girls); Grade 12: 172 students (172 girls). 75% of students are Roman Catholic.

Subjects Offered Advanced Placement courses, algebra, art, band, biology, biology-AP, business law, business skills, business studies, calculus, calculus-AP, campus ministry, career education internship, career exploration, Catholic belief and practice, chemistry, chemistry-AP, choir, chorus, Christian doctrine, college admission preparation, college counseling, computer education, computer graphics, computers, constitutional history of U.S., crafts, drama, earth science, economics, electives, English composition, English literature, English-AP, English/composition-AP, fashion, fitness, foreign language, French, general math, geometry, government, guidance, health, health education, honors algebra, honors English, honors geometry, honors U.S. history, honors world history, HTML design, integrated math, internship, lab science, law and the legal system, literature, mathematics-AP, physics, physics-AP, physiology, portfolio art, pre-algebra, pre-calculus, psychology, psychology-AP, religion, science, social education, sociology, Spanish language-AP, Spanish literature, Spanish-AP, studio art, U.S. government, U.S. history, U.S. history-AP, world history, world wide web design.

Graduation Requirements Art, electives, English, foreign language, mathematics, music, physical education (includes health), religion (includes Bible studies and theology), science, social studies (includes history).

Special Academic Programs 7 Advanced Placement exams for which test preparation is offered; honors section; remedial reading and/or remedial writing; remedial math.

College Admission Counseling 226 students graduated in 2008; 216 went to college, including City College of the City University of New York; Hunter College of the City University of New York; John Jay College of Criminal Justice of the City University of New York; Pace University; Queens College of the City University of New York; St. John's University. Other: 1 went to work, 1 entered military service, 6 entered a postgraduate year, 2 had other specific plans. Median SAT critical reading: 440, median SAT math: 420, median SAT writing: 440, median combined SAT: 1300. .9% scored over 600 on SAT critical reading, 1.3% scored over 600 on SAT math, .9% scored over 600 on SAT writing, 3.1% scored over 1800 on combined SAT.

Student Life Upper grades have uniform requirement, student council, honor system. Attendance at religious services is required.

Summer Programs Remediation programs offered; held on campus; accepts boys and girls; open to students from other schools. 2009 schedule: July to August. Application deadline: July.

Tuition and Aid Day student tuition: $6025. Tuition installment plan (monthly payment plans). Tuition reduction for siblings, merit scholarship grants, need-based scholarship grants available. Total upper-school merit-scholarship money awarded for 2008–09: $133,000. Total amount of financial aid awarded in 2008–09: $310,000.

Admissions Traditional secondary-level entrance grade is 9. For fall 2008, 800 students applied for upper-level admission, 400 were accepted, 150 enrolled. Catholic High School Entrance Examination required. Deadline for receipt of application materials: August. No application fee required.

Athletics Interscholastic: basketball, soccer, softball, volleyball; intramural: swimming and diving. 1 PE instructor, 4 coaches.

Computers Computers are regularly used in all academic classes. Computer network features include on-campus library services, Internet access, Internet filtering or blocking technology. Student e-mail accounts are available to students.

Contact Ms. Rosemary Eivers, Assistant Principal Academics. 212-688-1545 Ext. 219. Fax: 212-754-2024. E-mail: reivers@cathedralhs.org. Web site: www.cathedralhs.org.

CATHOLIC CENTRAL HIGH SCHOOL

27225 Wixom Road
Novi, Michigan 48374

Head of School: Fr. Richard Ranalletti, CSB

General Information Boys' day college-preparatory, arts, business, vocational, religious studies, and technology school, affiliated with Roman Catholic Church. Grades 9–12. Founded: 1928. Setting: suburban. Nearest major city is Detroit. 60-acre campus. 1 building on campus. Approved or accredited by North Central Association of Colleges and Schools and Michigan Department of Education. Endowment: $3 million. Total enrollment: 1,052. Upper school average class size: 24. Upper school faculty-student ratio: 1:14.

Upper School Student Profile Grade 9: 297 students (297 boys); Grade 10: 278 students (278 boys); Grade 11: 283 students (283 boys); Grade 12: 194 students (194 boys). 89% of students are Roman Catholic.

Faculty School total: 73. In upper school: 54 men, 19 women; 58 have advanced degrees.

Subjects Offered Algebra, American government, American government-AP, American history-AP, anatomy and physiology, art, art history, biology, biology-AP, chemistry, chemistry-AP, church history, computer science-AP, drawing, English, environmental science, European history-AP, French, geometry, health, history, journalism, keyboarding, keyboarding/computer, Latin, mathematics, microeconomics, painting, physics, pre-calculus, psychology, science, sculpture, social justice, sociology, Spanish, Spanish-AP, theology, trigonometry, U.S. history, Web site design, world history.

Special Academic Programs Advanced Placement exam preparation; honors section.

College Admission Counseling 249 students graduated in 2008; 234 went to college, including Central Michigan University; Eastern Michigan University; Michigan State University; Oakland University; University of Detroit Mercy; University of Michigan. Other: 2 entered military service. Mean SAT critical reading: 625, mean SAT math: 641, mean SAT writing: 613, mean composite ACT: 25.

Student Life Upper grades have specified standards of dress, student council, honor system. Discipline rests equally with students and faculty. Attendance at religious services is required.

Tuition and Aid Day student tuition: $9000. Tuition installment plan (monthly payment plans, individually arranged payment plans). Tuition reduction for siblings, merit scholarship grants, need-based scholarship grants available. In 2008–09, 30% of upper-school students received aid; total upper-school merit-scholarship money awarded: $50,000.

Admissions Traditional secondary-level entrance grade is 9. For fall 2008, 533 students applied for upper-level admission, 458 were accepted, 297 enrolled. STS required. Deadline for receipt of application materials: March 22. No application fee required. Interview recommended.

Athletics Interscholastic: alpine skiing, baseball, basketball, bowling, cross-country running, diving, ice hockey, lacrosse, physical fitness, physical training, skiing (downhill), soccer, swimming and diving, tennis, track and field, wrestling; intramural: basketball, cross-country running, flag football, ice hockey, touch football. 3 PE instructors, 54 coaches, 1 athletic trainer.

Computers Computer network features include on-campus library services, Internet access. The school has a published electronic and media policy.

Contact Mr. Aaron Babicz, Director of Admissions. 248-596-3874. Fax: 248-596-3839. E-mail: ababicz@catholiccentral.net. Web site: www.catholiccentral.net.

THE CATHOLIC HIGH SCHOOL OF BALTIMORE

2800 Edison Highway
Baltimore, Maryland 21213

Head of School: Dr. Barbara D. Nazelrod

General Information Girls' day college-preparatory, general academic, arts, business, religious studies, and technology school, affiliated with Roman Catholic Church. Grades 9–12. Founded: 1939. Setting: urban. 6-acre campus. 1 building on campus. Approved or accredited by Association of Independent Maryland Schools, Middle States Association of Colleges and Schools, National Catholic Education Association, and Maryland Department of Education. Endowment: $3 million. Total enrollment: 326. Upper school average class size: 17. Upper school faculty-student ratio: 1:12.

Upper School Student Profile Grade 9: 114 students (114 girls); Grade 10: 75 students (75 girls); Grade 11: 67 students (67 girls); Grade 12: 70 students (70 girls). 75% of students are Roman Catholic.

Faculty School total: 33. In upper school: 14 men, 17 women; 21 have advanced degrees.

Subjects Offered Algebra, American history, American literature, anatomy, art, band, biology, calculus, chemistry, community service, computer programming, computer science, creative writing, dance, drama, driver education, earth science, economics, English, English literature, expository writing, fine arts, French, geometry, government/civics, grammar, health, history, instrumental music, journalism, keyboarding, literature, mathematics, music, personal development, photography, physical education, physics, physiology, psychology, reading, religion, science, social studies, Spanish, speech, study skills, technology, theater, theology, world history, world literature.

Graduation Requirements Arts and fine arts (art, music, dance, drama), computer science, English, foreign language, mathematics, physical education (includes health), religion (includes Bible studies and theology), science, social studies (includes history). Community service is required.

Special Academic Programs Advanced Placement exam preparation; honors section; independent study; study at local college for college credit; remedial reading and/or remedial writing; remedial math; programs in English, mathematics, general development for dyslexic students.

College Admission Counseling 59 students graduated in 2008; 55 went to college, including Stevenson University; Towson University; University of Maryland, Baltimore County. Other: 4 went to work. Median SAT critical reading: 502, median SAT math: 468, median SAT writing: 500, median combined SAT: 1504, median composite ACT: 21. 9% scored over 600 on SAT critical reading, 9% scored over 600 on SAT math, 13% scored over 600 on SAT writing, 11% scored over 1800 on combined SAT, 18% scored over 26 on composite ACT.

Student Life Upper grades have uniform requirement, student council, honor system. Discipline rests primarily with faculty. Attendance at religious services is required.

Summer Programs Remediation, enrichment, sports, art/fine arts programs offered; session focuses on enrichment; held both on and off campus; held at sport fields; accepts girls; open to students from other schools. 30 students usually enrolled. 2009 schedule: June 19 to July 20. Application deadline: none.

Tuition and Aid Day student tuition: $9800. Tuition installment plan (Insured Tuition Payment Plan, FACTS Tuition Payment Plan, biannual payment plan, annual payment plan). Tuition reduction for siblings, merit scholarship grants, need-based scholarship grants available. In 2008–09, 29% of upper-school students received aid; total upper-school merit-scholarship money awarded: $214,450. Total amount of financial aid awarded in 2008–09: $385,000.

Admissions Traditional secondary-level entrance grade is 9. For fall 2008, 211 students applied for upper-level admission, 180 were accepted, 114 enrolled. High School Placement Test required. Deadline for receipt of application materials: none. Application fee required: $30. On-campus interview required.

Athletics Interscholastic: basketball, cheering, cross-country running, dance team, field hockey, indoor track & field, lacrosse, soccer, softball, swimming and diving, tennis, track and field, volleyball; intramural: aerobics, aerobics/dance, cooperative games. 1 PE instructor, 12 coaches, 1 athletic trainer.

Computers Computers are regularly used in art, English, foreign language, history, mathematics, music, science, theology classes. Computer network features include on-campus library services, online commercial services, Internet access. Students grades are available online. The school has a published electronic and media policy.

Contact Mrs. Barbara Czawlytko, Administrative Assistant. 410-732-6200 Ext. 213. Fax: 410-732-7639. E-mail: bczawlytko@thecatholichighschool.org. Web site: www.thecatholichighschool.org.

CATHOLIC MEMORIAL

235 Baker Street
West Roxbury, Massachusetts 02132

Head of School: Mr. Paul E. Sheff

General Information Boys' day college-preparatory, arts, religious studies, and technology school, affiliated with Roman Catholic Church. Grades 7–12. Founded: 1957. Setting: suburban. Nearest major city is Boston. 15-acre campus. 3 buildings on campus. Approved or accredited by Association of Independent Schools in New England, National Catholic Education Association, New England Association of Schools and Colleges, and Massachusetts Department of Education. Endowment: $2.5 million. Total enrollment: 809. Upper school average class size: 25. Upper school faculty-student ratio: 1:13.

Upper School Student Profile Grade 7: 80 students (80 boys); Grade 8: 100 students (100 boys); Grade 9: 167 students (167 boys); Grade 10: 171 students (171 boys); Grade 11: 129 students (129 boys); Grade 12: 141 students (141 boys). 90% of students are Roman Catholic.

Faculty School total: 66. In upper school: 50 men, 16 women; 50 have advanced degrees.

Subjects Offered Accounting, algebra, American history, American literature, anatomy, art, art history, Bible studies, biology, business skills, calculus, chemistry, Chinese, Chinese studies, computer math, computer programming, computer science, creative writing, driver education, earth science, economics, English, English literature, ethics, European history, expository writing, fine arts, French, geography, geometry, government/civics, grammar, health, history, Italian, journalism, Latin, mathematics, physical education, physics, physiology, psychology, public speaking, religion, science, social science, social studies, sociology, Spanish, trigonometry, typing, world geography, world history, world literature, writing.

Graduation Requirements Arts and fine arts (art, music, dance, drama), business skills (includes word processing), computer science, English, foreign language, mathematics, physical education (includes health), religion (includes Bible studies and theology), science, social science, social studies (includes history).

Special Academic Programs 12 Advanced Placement exams for which test preparation is offered; honors section; academic accommodation for the musically talented and the artistically talented; remedial reading and/or remedial writing; remedial math.

College Admission Counseling 165 students graduated in 2008; 148 went to college, including Boston College; Boston University; College of the Holy Cross; Northeastern University; Stonehill College; University of Massachusetts Amherst. Other: 5 went to work, 5 entered military service, 2 entered a postgraduate year.

Student Life Upper grades have uniform requirement, student council. Discipline rests primarily with faculty. Attendance at religious services is required.

Summer Programs Enrichment, advancement programs offered; session focuses on experiential learning; held both on and off campus; held at Boston Harbor, Mt.

Washington, Walden Pond, Cape Cod and Yankee Stadium; accepts boys and girls; open to students from other schools. 75 students usually enrolled. 2009 schedule: June 28 to August 1.

Tuition and Aid Day student tuition: $12,175. Tuition installment plan (FACTS Tuition Payment Plan). Merit scholarship grants, need-based scholarship grants available. In 2008–09, 27% of upper-school students received aid; total upper-school merit-scholarship money awarded: $130,000.

Admissions Traditional secondary-level entrance grade is 9. For fall 2008, 400 students applied for upper-level admission, 300 were accepted, 100 enrolled. Archdiocese of Boston High School entrance exam provided by STS required. Deadline for receipt of application materials: December 30. No application fee required. Interview recommended.

Athletics Interscholastic: baseball, basketball, cross-country running, football, golf, ice hockey, lacrosse, rugby, soccer, swimming and diving, tennis, track and field, volleyball, weight lifting, wrestling; intramural: baseball, basketball, football, softball, volleyball. 3 PE instructors, 32 coaches, 2 athletic trainers.

Computers Computers are regularly used in all classes. Computer network features include on-campus library services, Internet access, wireless campus network, Internet filtering or blocking technology. The school has a published electronic and media policy.

Contact Mr. John Mazza, Director of Admissions. 617-469-8034. Fax: 617-325-0888. Web site: www.catholicmemorial.org.

THE CATLIN GABEL SCHOOL

8825 Southwest Barnes Road
Portland, Oregon 97225

Head of School: Dr. Lark Palma

General Information Coeducational day college-preparatory, arts, technology, and sciences school. Grades PK–12. Founded: 1957. Setting: suburban. 54-acre campus. 13 buildings on campus. Approved or accredited by Northwest Association of Schools and Colleges and Pacific Northwest Association of Independent Schools. Member of National Association of Independent Schools and Secondary School Admission Test Board. Endowment: $19.5 million. Total enrollment: 733. Upper school average class size: 13. Upper school faculty-student ratio: 1:7.

Upper School Student Profile Grade 9: 69 students (32 boys, 37 girls); Grade 10: 75 students (38 boys, 37 girls); Grade 11: 69 students (36 boys, 33 girls); Grade 12: 77 students (35 boys, 42 girls).

Faculty School total: 87. In upper school: 28 men, 22 women; 34 have advanced degrees.

Subjects Offered 3-dimensional art, 3-dimensional design, acting, advanced chemistry, advanced computer applications, advanced math, African-American history, algebra, American democracy, American foreign policy, American history, American literature, ancient world history, applied music, art, art history, arts, astronomy, athletics, baseball, Basic programming, basketball, biology, bookbinding, bookmaking, bowling, calculus, calligraphy, ceramics, chemistry, Chinese, choir, college admission preparation, college counseling, comedy, communication skills, computer art, computer graphics, computer programming, computer resources, computer science, computer skills, computer studies, concert choir, creative writing, critical studies in film, critical thinking, debate, digital imaging, digital photography, drama, drama performance, dramatic arts, drawing and design, driver education, ecology, economics, English, English literature, ensembles, ethics and responsibility, European history, expository writing, fiber arts, film studies, fine arts, foreign language, foreign policy, French, geometry, golf, government/civics, graphic arts, graphic design, health, history, human sexuality, Islamic studies, Japanese, jazz band, mathematics, model United Nations, music, music theory, musical productions, ornithology, outdoor education, peer counseling, performing arts, photo shop, photography, physical education, physical fitness, physics, playwriting and directing, pre-calculus, robotics, science, set design, Shakespeare, social studies, Spanish, Spanish literature, speech and debate, stage design, stagecraft, statistics, statistics and probability, strings, studio art, study skills, technical theater, tennis, textiles, theater, theater arts, theater design and production, track and field, trigonometry, U.S. history, visual and performing arts, vocal ensemble, voice, voice ensemble, volleyball, weight fitness, weight training, wind instruments, woodworking, world affairs, world history, world literature, world wide web design, writing, writing workshop, yearbook.

Graduation Requirements Arts and fine arts (art, music, dance, drama), English, foreign language, mathematics, physical education (includes health), science, social studies (includes history). Community service is required.

Special Academic Programs Honors section; independent study; term-away projects; study at local college for college credit; domestic exchange program; study abroad; academic accommodation for the gifted, the musically talented, and the artistically talented.

College Admission Counseling 64 students graduated in 2008; all went to college, including Bard College; Boston College; Claremont McKenna College; Occidental College; Reed College; University of Puget Sound. Mean SAT critical reading: 660, mean SAT math: 668. 89% scored over 600 on SAT critical reading, 87% scored over 600 on SAT math, 80% scored over 600 on SAT writing, 86% scored over 1800 on combined SAT.

Student Life Upper grades have student council, honor system. Discipline rests equally with students and faculty.

Summer Programs Enrichment, art/fine arts, computer instruction programs offered; session focuses on Arts and Enrichment; held both on and off campus; held at various outdoor areas—hiking, climbing, etc.; accepts boys and girls; open to students from other schools. 85 students usually enrolled. 2009 schedule: June 29 to July 31.

Tuition and Aid Day student tuition: $21,840. Tuition installment plan (Insured Tuition Payment Plan, monthly payment plans, individually arranged payment plans). Need-based scholarship grants available. In 2008–09, 24% of upper-school students received aid. Total amount of financial aid awarded in 2008–09: $1,108,088.

Admissions Traditional secondary-level entrance grade is 9. For fall 2008, 64 students applied for upper-level admission, 50 were accepted, 29 enrolled. SSAT required. Deadline for receipt of application materials: February 9. Application fee required: $75. On-campus interview required.

Athletics Interscholastic: baseball (boys, girls), basketball (b,g), cross-country running (b,g), golf (b,g), racquetball (b,g), soccer (b,g), tennis (b,g), track and field (b,g), volleyball (g); coed interscholastic: racquetball; coed intramural: alpine skiing, backpacking, bicycling, bowling, canoeing/kayaking, climbing, fishing, fitness, Frisbee, hiking/backpacking, jogging, kayaking, mountain biking, mountaineering, nordic skiing, ocean paddling, outdoor activities, paddling, physical fitness, physical training, rafting, rock climbing, ropes courses, running, skiing (cross-country), skiing (downhill), snowshoeing, strength & conditioning, telemark skiing, ultimate Frisbee, walking, wall climbing, weight lifting, weight training, wilderness, wilderness survival, yoga. 6 PE instructors, 20 coaches.

Computers Computers are regularly used in animation, art, engineering, English, foreign language, graphic design, mathematics, science, theater, writing classes. Computer network features include on-campus library services, online commercial services, Internet access, wireless campus network, laptop requirement for all upper school students, videoconferencing, SmartBoards. Student e-mail accounts are available to students. The school has a published electronic and media policy.

Contact Ms. Marsha Trump, Assistant Director of Admission. 503-297-1894 Ext. 349. Fax: 503-297-0139. E-mail: trumpm@catlin.edu. Web site: www.catlin.edu.

CEDAR RIDGE ACADEMY

Roosevelt, Utah

See Special Needs Schools section.

CENTENNIAL ACADEMY

3641 Prud'homme Avenue
Montreal, Quebec H4A 3H6, Canada

Head of School: Mrs. Angela Burgos

General Information Coeducational day college-preparatory school; primarily serves students with learning disabilities, individuals with Attention Deficit Disorder, and dyslexic students. Grades 7–11. Founded: 1969. Setting: urban. 1 building on campus. Approved or accredited by Canadian Association of Independent Schools, Canadian Educational Standards Institute, Quebec Association of Independent Schools, and Quebec Department of Education. Language of instruction: English. Total enrollment: 260. Upper school average class size: 17. Upper school faculty-student ratio: 1:10.

Upper School Student Profile Grade 7: 31 students (24 boys, 7 girls); Grade 8: 38 students (31 boys, 7 girls); Grade 9: 60 students (52 boys, 8 girls); Grade 10: 60 students (45 boys, 15 girls); Grade 11: 71 students (51 boys, 20 girls).

Faculty School total: 30. In upper school: 12 men, 18 women; 18 have advanced degrees.

Subjects Offered Advanced chemistry, advanced math, art, art history, athletics, audio visual/media, band, basketball, biology, body human, bowling, Canadian geography, Canadian history, career and personal planning, career/college preparation, chemistry, competitive science projects, computer applications, computer multimedia, computer resources, computer science, creative writing, drama, economics, electives, English, fitness, French as a second language, general science, geography, golf, guidance, jazz band, lab science, language arts, leadership, library, mathematics, media studies, music, physical education, reading, science, sports, student government, swimming, tennis, volleyball, wrestling, yearbook.

Graduation Requirements Canadian history, English, French as a second language, general science, mathematics.

Special Academic Programs Independent study.

College Admission Counseling 66 students graduated in 2008.

Student Life Upper grades have uniform requirement, honor system. Discipline rests primarily with faculty.

Tuition and Aid Day student tuition: CAN$15,560–CAN$15,750. Tuition installment plan (monthly payment plans). Bursaries, merit scholarship grants available. In 2008–09, 6% of upper-school students received aid. Total amount of financial aid awarded in 2008–09: CAN$705,500.

Admissions Traditional secondary-level entrance grade is 7. For fall 2008, 136 students applied for upper-level admission, 90 were accepted, 55 enrolled. Canadian Standardized Test and Otis-Lennon School Ability Test required. Deadline for receipt of application materials: none. Application fee required: CAN$50. Interview required.

Athletics Interscholastic: basketball (boys, girls), soccer (b,g), touch football (g); coed interscholastic: cross-country running, curling, golf, running, swimming and

diving, track and field, wrestling; coed intramural: badminton, ball hockey, basketball, bowling, broomball, Cosom hockey, cross-country running, fitness, floor hockey, handball, hockey, ice hockey, Newcombe ball, running, soccer, softball, track and field, volleyball. 2 PE instructors.
Computers Computers are regularly used in all academic classes. Computer network features include on-campus library services, Internet access, wireless campus network, Internet filtering or blocking technology. Student e-mail accounts are available to students. The school has a published electronic and media policy.
Contact Ms. Debbie Haley, Coordinator of Admissions. 514-486-5533 Ext. 238. Fax: 514-486-1401. E-mail: dhaley@centennial.qc.ca. Web site: www.centennial.qc.ca.

CENTRAL CATHOLIC HIGH SCHOOL

200 South Carpenter Road
Modesto, California 95351
Head of School: Jim Pecchenino
General Information Coeducational day college-preparatory, arts, religious studies, bilingual studies, and technology school, affiliated with Roman Catholic Church. Grades 9–12. Founded: 1966. Setting: urban. Nearest major city is Sacramento. 21-acre campus. 13 buildings on campus. Approved or accredited by Western Association of Schools and Colleges and Western Catholic Education Association. Endowment: $1.1 million. Total enrollment: 420. Upper school average class size: 25. Upper school faculty-student ratio: 1:17.
Upper School Student Profile Grade 9: 106 students (57 boys, 49 girls); Grade 10: 120 students (67 boys, 53 girls); Grade 11: 106 students (59 boys, 47 girls); Grade 12: 88 students (47 boys, 41 girls). 81% of students are Roman Catholic.
Faculty School total: 27. In upper school: 10 men, 17 women; 11 have advanced degrees.
Subjects Offered Algebra, American history, American literature, art, Bible studies, biology, broadcast journalism, calculus, chemistry, choir, computer programming, computer science, creative writing, dance, drama, earth science, economics, English, English literature, environmental science, ethics, European history, expository writing, film appreciation, fine arts, geometry, government/civics, grammar, graphics, health, history, mathematics, music, music appreciation, philosophy, physical education, physics, pre-algebra, pre-calculus, psychology, psychology-AP, religion, science, social science, social studies, Spanish, speech, theater, theology, trigonometry, world history, world literature, writing, yearbook.
Graduation Requirements Arts and fine arts (art, music, dance, drama), computer science, English, mathematics, physical education (includes health), religion (includes Bible studies and theology), science, social science, social studies (includes history), speech, 80 Christian service hours. Community service is required.
Special Academic Programs Advanced Placement exam preparation; honors section; study at local college for college credit; academic accommodation for the gifted; remedial reading and/or remedial writing; remedial math; programs in English, mathematics, general development for dyslexic students.
College Admission Counseling 106 students graduated in 2008; all went to college, including California Polytechnic State University, San Luis Obispo; California State University, Stanislaus; Modesto Junior College; Saint Mary's College of California; University of California, Berkeley; University of Notre Dame. Mean SAT critical reading: 530, mean SAT math: 518, mean SAT writing: 518, mean combined SAT: 1566, mean composite ACT: 22.
Student Life Upper grades have specified standards of dress, student council, honor system. Discipline rests primarily with faculty. Attendance at religious services is required.
Summer Programs Remediation programs offered; session focuses on remediation; held on campus; accepts boys and girls; open to students from other schools. 50 students usually enrolled. 2009 schedule: June 8 to July 3. Application deadline: May 6.
Tuition and Aid Day student tuition: $8153–$8500. Guaranteed tuition plan. Tuition installment plan (monthly payment plans, Tuition Management Systems Plan, quarterly and semiannual payment plans). Tuition reduction for siblings, merit scholarship grants, need-based scholarship grants, paying campus jobs available. In 2008–09, 28% of upper-school students received aid; total upper-school merit-scholarship money awarded: $13,700. Total amount of financial aid awarded in 2008–09: $283,480.
Admissions Traditional secondary-level entrance grade is 9. For fall 2008, 136 students applied for upper-level admission, 106 were accepted, 106 enrolled. Cognitive Abilities Test, Iowa Test of Educational Development or USC/UC Math Diagnostic Test required. Deadline for receipt of application materials: none. Application fee required: $45. On-campus interview required.
Athletics Interscholastic: baseball (boys), basketball (b,g), cheering (g), football (b), golf (b,g), soccer (b,g), softball (g), track and field (b,g), volleyball (g), wrestling (b); coed interscholastic: cross-country running, dance, swimming and diving, tennis. 2 PE instructors, 84 coaches.
Computers Computers are regularly used in English, foreign language, graphic arts, literacy, mathematics, science, social studies, technology, Web site design, yearbook classes. Computer network features include on-campus library services, Internet access, Internet filtering or blocking technology. Student e-mail accounts and computer access in designated common areas are available to students. Students grades are available online. The school has a published electronic and media policy.
Contact Jodi Tybor, Admissions Coordinator/Registrar. 209-524-9611 Ext. 104. Fax: 209-524-4913. E-mail: tybor@cchsca.org. Web site: www.cchsca.org.

CENTRAL CATHOLIC HIGH SCHOOL

300 Hampshire Street
Lawrence, Massachusetts 01841
Head of School: Mr. David M. DeFillippo
General Information Coeducational day college-preparatory, arts, business, religious studies, and technology school, affiliated with Roman Catholic Church. Grades 9–12. Founded: 1935. Setting: urban. Nearest major city is Boston. 1 building on campus. Approved or accredited by Commission on Independent Schools, New England Association of Schools and Colleges, and Massachusetts Department of Education. Total enrollment: 1,350. Upper school average class size: 25.
Upper School Student Profile Grade 9: 364 students (182 boys, 182 girls); Grade 10: 338 students (157 boys, 181 girls); Grade 11: 327 students (163 boys, 164 girls); Grade 12: 321 students (153 boys, 168 girls). 80% of students are Roman Catholic.
Faculty School total: 93. In upper school: 50 men, 43 women; 72 have advanced degrees.
Subjects Offered Art, arts, computer science, English, fine arts, French, health, mathematics, physical education, religion, science, social studies, Spanish.
Graduation Requirements Arts and fine arts (art, music, dance, drama), computer science, English, foreign language, mathematics, religion (includes Bible studies and theology), science, social studies (includes history).
Student Life Upper grades have uniform requirement, student council, honor system. Discipline rests primarily with faculty. Attendance at religious services is required.
Tuition and Aid Tuition installment plan (FACTS Tuition Payment Plan, monthly payment plans). Tuition reduction for siblings, merit scholarship grants, need-based scholarship grants available.
Admissions Traditional secondary-level entrance grade is 9. Archdiocese of Boston High School entrance exam provided by STS and High School Placement Test required. Deadline for receipt of application materials: May 15. No application fee required. Interview required.
Athletics Interscholastic: baseball (boys), basketball (b,g), bowling (b,g), cheering (g), cross-country running (b,g), dance squad (b,g), equestrian sports (b,g), field hockey (g), figure skating (g), fishing (b,g), football (b), golf (b,g), gymnastics (g), hockey (b), ice hockey (b), indoor track (b,g), lacrosse (b,g), soccer (b,g), softball (g), swimming and diving (b,g), tennis (b,g), track and field (b,g), volleyball (b,g), wall climbing (b,g), wrestling (b). 3 PE instructors, 1 athletic trainer.
Computers Computer network features include on-campus library services, Internet access, wireless campus network, Internet filtering or blocking technology. Campus intranet, student e-mail accounts, and computer access in designated common areas are available to students. The school has a published electronic and media policy.
Contact Mrs. Kathleen Gerow, Director of Admissions. 978-682-0260. Fax: 978-685-2707. Web site: www.centralcatholic.net.

CENTRAL CATHOLIC HIGH SCHOOL

4824 Tuscarawas Street West
Canton, Ohio 44708-5198
Head of School: Rev. Robert W. Kaylor
General Information Coeducational day college-preparatory school, affiliated with Roman Catholic Church. Grades 9–12. Founded: 1905. Setting: suburban. 65-acre campus. 1 building on campus. Approved or accredited by North Central Association of Colleges and Schools, Ohio Catholic Schools Accreditation Association (OCSAA), and Ohio Department of Education. Total enrollment: 485. Upper school average class size: 25. Upper school faculty-student ratio: 1:16.
Upper School Student Profile Grade 9: 112 students (63 boys, 49 girls); Grade 10: 134 students (62 boys, 72 girls); Grade 11: 124 students (69 boys, 55 girls); Grade 12: 115 students (57 boys, 58 girls). 90% of students are Roman Catholic.
Faculty School total: 45. In upper school: 23 men, 22 women; 25 have advanced degrees.
Special Academic Programs Advanced Placement exam preparation.
College Admission Counseling 128 students graduated in 2008; 123 went to college, including Ohio University. Other: 4 went to work, 1 entered military service.
Student Life Upper grades have specified standards of dress, student council, honor system. Discipline rests equally with students and faculty. Attendance at religious services is required.
Tuition and Aid Day student tuition: $5525–$5925. Tuition installment plan (FACTS Tuition Payment Plan, monthly payment plans, individually arranged payment plans). Tuition reduction for siblings, merit scholarship grants, need-based scholarship grants available. In 2008–09, 35% of upper-school students received aid; total upper-school merit-scholarship money awarded: $20,000. Total amount of financial aid awarded in 2008–09: $125,000.
Admissions Deadline for receipt of application materials: May 15. Application fee required: $15.
Athletics Interscholastic: baseball (boys), basketball (b,g), bowling (b,g), cheering (g), cross-country running (b,g), football (b), golf (b,g), soccer (b,g), softball (g), swimming and diving (b,g), tennis (b,g), volleyball (g), wrestling (b).
Computers The school has a published electronic and media policy.

Contact 330-478-2131. Fax: 330-478-6086. Web site: www.cchsweb.com.

CENTRAL CATHOLIC HIGH SCHOOL

2550 Cherry Street
Toledo, Ohio 43608

Head of School: Rev. Dennis P. Hartigan

General Information Coeducational day college-preparatory school, affiliated with Roman Catholic Church. Grades 9–12. Founded: 1920. Setting: urban. 25-acre campus. 3 buildings on campus. Approved or accredited by Ohio Department of Education. Upper school average class size: 23.
Upper School Student Profile 75% of students are Roman Catholic.
Student Life Upper grades have uniform requirement, student council, honor system. Discipline rests primarily with faculty. Attendance at religious services is required.
Admissions No application fee required.
Computers The school has a published electronic and media policy.
Contact Mrs. Sandy Faunce, Registrar. 419-255-2280 Ext. 151. Fax: 419-259-2848. E-mail: sfaunce@centralcatholic.org. Web site: www.centralcatholic.org.

CENTRAL CATHOLIC HIGH SCHOOL

4720 Fifth Avenue
Pittsburgh, Pennsylvania 15213

Head of School: Br. Richard F. Grzeskiewicz, FSC

General Information Boys' day college-preparatory, arts, business, and religious studies school, affiliated with Roman Catholic Church. Grades 9–12. Founded: 1927. Setting: urban. 2 buildings on campus. Approved or accredited by Middle States Association of Colleges and Schools and Pennsylvania Department of Education. Endowment: $6 million. Total enrollment: 842. Upper school average class size: 21. Upper school faculty-student ratio: 1:15.
Upper School Student Profile Grade 9: 227 students (227 boys); Grade 10: 233 students (233 boys); Grade 11: 200 students (200 boys); Grade 12: 182 students (182 boys). 83% of students are Roman Catholic.
Faculty School total: 66. In upper school: 53 men, 13 women; 23 have advanced degrees.
Subjects Offered 1968, accounting, algebra, American foreign policy, American literature, art, biology, biology-AP, British literature, British literature (honors), business, business mathematics, calculus, calculus-AP, chemistry, chemistry-AP, computer science, computers, consumer education, debate, economics-AP, electives, English, English-AP, environmental science, European history-AP, foreign language, French, geometry, German, health, history, honors algebra, honors English, honors geometry, instrumental music, Italian, Latin, law, marketing, math analysis, mathematics, music, music theory, physical education, physics, physics-AP, pre-calculus, probability and statistics, programming, psychology, religion, science, social studies, sociology, Spanish, Spanish-AP, studio art, theater arts, trigonometry, U.S. history, U.S. history-AP, vocal music, world history, world literature, writing.
Special Academic Programs Advanced Placement exam preparation; honors section; study at local college for college credit; academic accommodation for the gifted.
College Admission Counseling 205 students graduated in 2008; 193 went to college, including Carnegie Mellon University; Duquesne University; Penn State University Park; University of Dayton; University of Pittsburgh; Villanova University. Other: 2 went to work, 2 entered military service, 1 entered a postgraduate year. Mean SAT critical reading: 552, mean SAT math: 553, mean SAT writing: 539, mean combined SAT: 1644. 35% scored over 600 on SAT critical reading, 35% scored over 600 on SAT math, 35% scored over 600 on SAT writing.
Student Life Upper grades have specified standards of dress, student council. Discipline rests primarily with faculty. Attendance at religious services is required.
Summer Programs Remediation programs offered; session focuses on make-up courses; held on campus; accepts boys; not open to students from other schools. 60 students usually enrolled. 2009 schedule: June to July.
Tuition and Aid Day student tuition: $7750. Tuition installment plan (SMART Tuition Payment Plan). Need-based scholarship grants available. In 2008–09, 35% of upper-school students received aid. Total amount of financial aid awarded in 2008–09: $650,000.
Admissions Traditional secondary-level entrance grade is 9. For fall 2008, 300 students applied for upper-level admission, 280 were accepted, 235 enrolled. Scholastic Testing Service High School Placement Test or STS Examination required. Deadline for receipt of application materials: February 1. No application fee required. Interview recommended.
Athletics Interscholastic: baseball, basketball, bowling, crew, cross-country running, fencing, football, golf, hockey, ice hockey, in-line hockey, lacrosse, soccer, squash, swimming and diving, tennis, track and field, volleyball, wrestling; intramural: basketball, flag football, football, Frisbee, touch football. 2 PE instructors, 27 coaches, 2 athletic trainers.
Computers Computers are regularly used in business applications, college planning, data processing, library skills, mathematics, newspaper, yearbook classes. Computer network features include on-campus library services, online commercial services, Internet access, wireless campus network, Internet filtering or blocking technology. Campus intranet, student e-mail accounts, and computer access in designated common areas are available to students. Students grades are available online. The school has a published electronic and media policy.
Contact Mr. Brian Miller, Director of Admissions. 412-621-7505. Fax: 412-208-0555. E-mail: bmiller@pittcentralcatholic.org. Web site: www.pittcentralcatholic.org.

CENTRAL CATHOLIC MID-HIGH SCHOOL

1200 Ruby Avenue
Grand Island, Nebraska 68803-3799

Head of School: Mr. John Golka

General Information Coeducational day college-preparatory and religious studies school, affiliated with Roman Catholic Church. Grades 6–12. Founded: 1956. Setting: suburban. 1 building on campus. Approved or accredited by National Catholic Education Association, North Central Association of Colleges and Schools, The College Board, and Nebraska Department of Education. Total enrollment: 305. Upper school average class size: 17. Upper school faculty-student ratio: 1:15.
Upper School Student Profile Grade 9: 54 students (22 boys, 32 girls); Grade 10: 38 students (18 boys, 20 girls); Grade 11: 44 students (24 boys, 20 girls); Grade 12: 38 students (21 boys, 17 girls). 98% of students are Roman Catholic.
Faculty School total: 38. In upper school: 8 men, 30 women; 13 have advanced degrees.
Subjects Offered ACT preparation, advanced chemistry, Advanced Placement courses, algebra, American government, American history, art, audio visual/media, basketball, biology, calculus-AP, career education, careers, Catholic belief and practice, cheerleading, chemistry, college writing, commercial art, computer applications, concert band, concert choir, contemporary problems, CPR, desktop publishing, drama, driver education, economics, English, English composition, English/composition-AP, environmental science, general science, golf, government, guidance, health, history, human biology, instrumental music, jazz band, journalism, marching band, mechanical drawing, music, music theory, newspaper, novels, physical education, physics, pre-algebra, pre-calculus, psychology, public speaking, religious studies, senior seminar, sociology, Spanish, speech, tennis, U.S. government, video film production, vocal music, volleyball, Web site design, weight training, world history, wrestling, yearbook.
Graduation Requirements American government, American history, American literature, biology, composition, computer applications, English, English composition, English literature, geography, government, history, mathematics, physical education (includes health), reading, religion (includes Bible studies and theology), science, senior seminar, world history, Community Service.
Special Academic Programs Advanced Placement exam preparation; study at local college for college credit.
College Admission Counseling 38 students graduated in 2008; 36 went to college, including Creighton University; University of Nebraska–Lincoln; University of Nebraska at Kearney; University of Nebraska at Omaha. Other: 1 went to work, 1 entered military service. Median composite ACT: 24. 29% scored over 26 on composite ACT.
Student Life Upper grades have uniform requirement, student council. Discipline rests primarily with faculty. Attendance at religious services is required.
Summer Programs Remediation programs offered; session focuses on English and math; held on campus; accepts boys and girls; not open to students from other schools. 10 students usually enrolled. 2009 schedule: June to July. Application deadline: May.
Tuition and Aid Tuition installment plan (monthly payment plans). Need-based scholarship grants, paying campus jobs available.
Admissions Traditional secondary-level entrance grade is 9. Deadline for receipt of application materials: none. Application fee required: $100.
Athletics Interscholastic: baseball (boys), basketball (b,g), cheering (g), cross-country running (b,g), dance team (g), football (b), golf (b,g), physical fitness (b,g), soccer (b,g), track and field (b,g), volleyball (g), weight training (b,g), wrestling (b); coed interscholastic: power lifting. 2 PE instructors.
Computers Computers are regularly used in computer applications, desktop publishing, drafting, English, journalism, keyboarding, Web site design, writing, yearbook classes. Computer network features include on-campus library services, Internet access, Internet filtering or blocking technology. Computer access in designated common areas is available to students. Students grades are available online. The school has a published electronic and media policy.
Contact Admissions. 308-384-2440. Fax: 308-389-3274. Web site: www.gicentralcatholic.org/.

CENTRAL VALLEY CHRISTIAN ACADEMY

2020 Academy Place
Ceres, California 95071

Head of School: Wayne Dunbar

General Information Coeducational day college-preparatory, arts, vocational, religious studies, and technology school, affiliated with Seventh-day Adventist Church. Grades K–12. Founded: 1910. Setting: suburban. 30-acre campus. 3 buildings on campus. Approved or accredited by Board of Regents, General Conference of

Seventh-day Adventists, Western Association of Schools and Colleges, and California Department of Education. Total enrollment: 240. Upper school average class size: 24. Upper school faculty-student ratio: 1:10.

Upper School Student Profile Grade 9: 20 students (13 boys, 7 girls); Grade 10: 19 students (10 boys, 9 girls); Grade 11: 30 students (16 boys, 14 girls); Grade 12: 25 students (11 boys, 14 girls); Postgraduate: 94 students (50 boys, 44 girls). 85% of students are Seventh-day Adventists.

Faculty School total: 20. In upper school: 4 men, 5 women; 3 have advanced degrees.

Subjects Offered Algebra, art, audio visual/media, auto shop, band, biology, broadcasting, chemistry, choir, community service, computer keyboarding, computer resources, drama, economics, English, geometry, gymnastics, health, home economics, music, physical education, physical science, physics, pre-algebra, religion, Spanish, U.S. government, U.S. history, world history.

Graduation Requirements Algebra, American government, American history, arts and fine arts (art, music, dance, drama), biology, career education, chemistry, computer literacy, earth science, electives, English, geometry, government/civics, keyboarding, physical education (includes health), physics, practical arts, religion (includes Bible studies and theology), science, Spanish, work experience. Community service is required.

Special Academic Programs Honors section; accelerated programs; independent study; study at local college for college credit.

College Admission Counseling 23 students graduated in 2008; 20 went to college, including Pacific Union College; Walla Walla University. Other: 2 went to work, 1 had other specific plans.

Student Life Upper grades have uniform requirement, student council, honor system. Discipline rests primarily with faculty. Attendance at religious services is required.

Tuition and Aid Day student tuition: $7100. Tuition installment plan (The Tuition Plan, monthly payment plans, individually arranged payment plans). Tuition reduction for siblings, need-based scholarship grants, paying campus jobs available. In 2008–09, 30% of upper-school students received aid.

Admissions Traditional secondary-level entrance grade is 9. TOEFL required. Deadline for receipt of application materials: none. No application fee required. Interview required.

Athletics Interscholastic: basketball (boys, girls), fitness (b,g), flag football (b,g), independent competitive sports (b,g), indoor track & field (b,g), soccer (b,g), softball (b,g), volleyball (b,g); intramural: baseball (g), basketball (b,g), fitness (b,g), flag football (b,g), gymnastics (b,g), indoor track & field (b,g), physical fitness (b,g), soccer (b,g), softball (b,g), tennis (b,g), track and field (b,g), ultimate Frisbee (b,g), volleyball (b,g); coed interscholastic: basketball, fitness, flag football, independent competitive sports, indoor track & field, soccer, softball, volleyball; coed intramural: basketball, fitness, flag football, gymnastics, indoor track & field, physical fitness, soccer, softball, tennis, track and field, ultimate Frisbee, volleyball. 1 PE instructor, 1 coach.

Computers Computers are regularly used in independent study, journalism, keyboarding, mathematics, media production, science, Spanish, video film production, yearbook classes. Computer resources include Internet access, wireless campus network, Internet filtering or blocking technology. Students grades are available online. The school has a published electronic and media policy.

Contact Lisa Nuss, Registrar. 209-537-4521. Fax: 209-538-0706. E-mail: nussl@cvcaonline.net.

CENTURY HIGH SCHOOL

300-1788 West Broadway
Vancouver, British Columbia V6J 1Y1, Canada

Head of School: Dr. Godwin S. Choy

General Information Coeducational day college-preparatory school. Grades 8–12. Founded: 1997. Setting: urban. 1 building on campus. Approved or accredited by British Columbia Department of Education. Language of instruction: English. Total enrollment: 200. Upper school average class size: 20. Upper school faculty-student ratio: 1:20.

Faculty School total: 9. In upper school: 4 men, 3 women; 3 have advanced degrees.

Subjects Offered Accounting, biology, calculus, Cantonese, career and personal planning, chemistry, creative arts, English, geography, Japanese, language arts, Mandarin, mathematics, physics, science, social studies.

Special Academic Programs ESL (6 students enrolled).

College Admission Counseling 100 students graduated in 2008; 90 went to college, including Dalhousie University; Queen's University at Kingston; Simon Fraser University; The University of British Columbia; University of Toronto; University of Victoria. Other: 10 went to work.

Student Life Discipline rests primarily with faculty.

Summer Programs Advancement programs offered; session focuses on English, math, social studies; held on campus; open to students from other schools. 2009 schedule: July 3 to August 15.

Tuition and Aid Day student tuition: CAN$12,000.

Admissions Traditional secondary-level entrance grade is 8. Deadline for receipt of application materials: none. Application fee required: CAN$200.

Computers Computers are regularly used in accounting classes. Computer resources include Internet access, Internet filtering or blocking technology. Student e-mail accounts are available to students.

Contact Ms. Noel P. Lee, Director of Admissions. 604-730-8138 Ext. 106. Fax: 604-731-9542. E-mail: noel@centuryhighschool.ca. Web site: www.centuryhighschool.ca.

CFS, THE SCHOOL AT CHURCH FARM

1001 E. Lincoln Highway
Exton, Pennsylvania 19341

Head of School: Thomas G. Rodd Jr.

General Information Boys' boarding and day college-preparatory and arts school, affiliated with Episcopal Church. Grades 7–12. Founded: 1918. Setting: suburban. Nearest major city is Philadelphia. Students are housed in single-sex dormitories. 200-acre campus. 19 buildings on campus. Approved or accredited by Middle States Association of Colleges and Schools, National Association of Episcopal Schools, The Association of Boarding Schools, and Pennsylvania Department of Education. Member of National Association of Independent Schools and Secondary School Admission Test Board. Endowment: $135 million. Total enrollment: 180. Upper school average class size: 10. Upper school faculty-student ratio: 1:7.

Upper School Student Profile Grade 9: 37 students (37 boys); Grade 10: 36 students (36 boys); Grade 11: 32 students (32 boys); Grade 12: 32 students (32 boys). 86% of students are boarding students. 47% are state residents. 12 states are represented in upper school student body. 22% are international students. International students from China, Kenya, Republic of Korea, and Thailand; 3 other countries represented in student body. 15% of students are members of Episcopal Church.

Faculty School total: 35. In upper school: 24 men, 11 women; 18 have advanced degrees; 26 reside on campus.

Subjects Offered 20th century history, 3-dimensional design, African-American history, algebra, American government, American history, American history-AP, American literature, American studies, anatomy and physiology, art, art history, biology, biology-AP, British literature, calculus-AP, ceramics, chemistry, chemistry-AP, choir, choral music, clayworking, college writing, composition, computer science, construction, creative writing, design, drama, driver education, earth science, ecology, economics, English, English-AP, environmental science, ethics, European history, expository writing, film and literature, fine arts, French, geometry, government/civics, grammar, health, history, history of jazz, industrial arts, instrumental music, journalism, leadership, mathematics, medieval history, music, music history, music technology, musicianship, mythology, photography, physical education, physics, physics-AP, poetry, pre-calculus, psychology, public speaking, Russian history, science, Shakespeare, Shakespearean histories, social studies, sociology, Spanish, speech, statistics, technology, theater, trigonometry, Vietnam history, Vietnam War, weaving, Web site design, woodworking, world history, world literature, world religions, World War II, writing.

Graduation Requirements Arts and fine arts (art, music, dance, drama), English, foreign language, mathematics, physical education (includes health), religion (includes Bible studies and theology), science, social studies (includes history), technology, Challenge of Required Experience (combination of community service and outdoor educational experience).

Special Academic Programs Advanced Placement exam preparation; honors section; independent study; academic accommodation for the gifted, the musically talented, and the artistically talented.

College Admission Counseling 30 students graduated in 2008; all went to college, including Babson College; Carnegie Mellon University; Cornell University; The Ohio State University; University of Illinois at Urbana–Champaign; University of Michigan. Median SAT critical reading: 535, median SAT math: 615, median SAT writing: 535, median combined SAT: 1745. 20% scored over 600 on SAT critical reading, 57% scored over 600 on SAT math, 33% scored over 600 on SAT writing, 40% scored over 1800 on combined SAT.

Student Life Upper grades have specified standards of dress, student council. Discipline rests primarily with faculty. Attendance at religious services is required.

Tuition and Aid Day student tuition: $4000–$12,500; 7-day tuition and room/board: $4000–$18,000. Guaranteed tuition plan. Tuition installment plan (monthly payment plans, individually arranged payment plans). Need-based scholarship grants, Scholarships from third-party agencies with which the school has established relationships. available. In 2008–09, 100% of upper-school students received aid. Total amount of financial aid awarded in 2008–09: $8,408,700.

Admissions Traditional secondary-level entrance grade is 9. For fall 2008, 225 students applied for upper-level admission, 66 were accepted, 59 enrolled. ISEE or SSAT required. Deadline for receipt of application materials: May 1. Application fee required: $25. Interview required.

Athletics Interscholastic: baseball, basketball, cross-country running, fencing, golf, indoor track, soccer, tennis, track and field, wrestling; intramural: fitness, floor hockey, indoor soccer, physical fitness, strength & conditioning, touch football, weight lifting. 10 coaches.

Computers Computers are regularly used in art, English, foreign language, history, industrial technology, mathematics, music, science classes. Computer network features include on-campus library services, online commercial services, Internet access, Internet filtering or blocking technology, each student receives a laptop computer. Campus intranet and student e-mail accounts are available to students. The school has a published electronic and media policy.

Contact Bart Bronk, Director of Admissions. 610-363-5346. Fax: 610-280-6746. E-mail: bbronk@gocfs.net. Web site: www.gocfs.net.

ANNOUNCEMENT FROM THE SCHOOL Located in Exton, Pennsylvania, just 35 miles west of Philadelphia, CFS is a small, all-boys college-preparatory boarding and day school. With 180 students in grades 7–12, CFS provides an intimate educational setting that allows academically talented students to thrive. With myriad honors and AP classes, advanced electives, and substantial co-curricular programming in music and the arts (including renowned choir, jazz, woodworking, and clay programs), CFS has a balanced, yet rigorous academic culture in which students are encouraged to find—and pursue—their passion. They do so in a technology-rich environment; each student gets his own laptop. Students enjoy meaningful faculty relationships with a 7:1 student-teacher ratio; the average faculty tenure is more than fifteen years. Over the past five years, 97% of CFS graduates went on to a college or university, including such schools as Carnegie Mellon, Columbia, Cornell, Dartmouth, Drexel, Duke, Emory, Johns Hopkins, Ohio State, Pepperdine, Swarthmore, and the Universities of Chicago, Illinois, Michigan, Pennsylvania, and Rhode Island. CFS boarding students, who in 2008–09 composed 87% of the student body, live in ten cottage-style dormitories with peers from their grade. Each dormitory is staffed by 2 full-time dormitory faculty members (separate from the academic faculty) who help the students learn the time-management and independent living skills, which are crucial to success at the collegiate level. Students can participate in ten interscholastic sports, including fencing and golf, and every student has the chance to play. CFS is further distinguished by its uncommon affordability. Thanks to one of the strongest endowment-per-student rates in the nation, CFS is able to assess tuition on a need-based sliding scale. CFS is committed to ensuring that every qualified student, regardless of his economic ability, can afford the promise of a CFS education. In 2008–09, 100% of CFS students received scholarship support totaling more than $9 million.

CHADWICK SCHOOL

26800 South Academy Drive
Palos Verdes Peninsula, California 90274

Head of School: Frederick T. Hill

General Information Coeducational day college-preparatory, arts, and technology school. Grades K–12. Founded: 1935. Setting: suburban. Nearest major city is Los Angeles. 45-acre campus. 5 buildings on campus. Approved or accredited by Association for Experiential Education, California Association of Independent Schools, The College Board, Western Association of Schools and Colleges, and California Department of Education. Member of National Association of Independent Schools. Endowment: $25 million. Total enrollment: 831. Upper school average class size: 16. Upper school faculty-student ratio: 1:6.

Upper School Student Profile Grade 9: 100 students (48 boys, 52 girls); Grade 10: 99 students (42 boys, 57 girls); Grade 11: 85 students (37 boys, 48 girls); Grade 12: 78 students (41 boys, 37 girls).

Faculty School total: 70. In upper school: 26 men, 31 women; 37 have advanced degrees.

Subjects Offered Advanced Placement courses, African history, algebra, American history, American literature, art, art history-AP, art-AP, Asian history, biology, calculus, calculus-AP, ceramics, chemistry, chemistry-AP, choral music, computer math, computer programming, computer science, creative writing, dance, drama, English, English literature, English literature-AP, European history, expository writing, fine arts, French, French-AP, geometry, grammar, health, history, history of science, honors algebra, honors geometry, instrumental music, Latin, Latin American history, life science, Mandarin, marine biology, mathematics, Middle East, Middle Eastern history, music, music theory-AP, outdoor education, photography, physical education, physics, pre-calculus, probability, robotics, science, social studies, South African history, Spanish, Spanish-AP, speech, statistics, theater, trigonometry, U.S. history-AP, wilderness/outdoor program, world history, world literature, writing, yearbook.

Graduation Requirements Arts and fine arts (art, music, dance, drama), English, foreign language, history, mathematics, outdoor education, physical education (includes health), science.

Special Academic Programs Advanced Placement exam preparation; honors section; independent study; term-away projects; study abroad; academic accommodation for the gifted, the musically talented, and the artistically talented.

College Admission Counseling 87 students graduated in 2008; all went to college, including Bucknell University; Dartmouth College; Loyola Marymount University; Stanford University; University of Southern California; Yale University. Mean SAT critical reading: 664, mean SAT math: 681, mean SAT writing: 677, mean combined SAT: 2022.

Student Life Upper grades have specified standards of dress, student council, honor system. Discipline rests equally with students and faculty.

Summer Programs Sports, art/fine arts, computer instruction programs offered; session focuses on fine and performing arts, academics, athletics, enrichment; held on campus; accepts boys and girls; open to students from other schools. 500 students usually enrolled. 2009 schedule: June 24 to July 26. Application deadline: April.

Tuition and Aid Day student tuition: $24,205. Tuition installment plan (Key Tuition Payment Plan, individually arranged payment plans). Need-based scholarship grants, paying campus jobs, Malone Scholarships (need/merit-based), MacFarlane Scholarship (need/merit-based) available. In 2008–09, 18% of upper-school students received aid. Total amount of financial aid awarded in 2008–09: $2,400,000.

Admissions Traditional secondary-level entrance grade is 9. ISEE required. Deadline for receipt of application materials: January 26. Application fee required: $125. On-campus interview required.

Athletics Interscholastic: baseball (boys), basketball (b,g), cheering (g), cross-country running (b,g), diving (b,g), football (b), golf (b,g), lacrosse (b,g), soccer (b,g), softball (g), swimming and diving (b,g), tennis (b,g), track and field (b,g), volleyball (b,g), water polo (b,g); intramural: aerobics/dance (g), dance (g), horseback riding (g); coed interscholastic: cheering, equestrian sports. 11 coaches, 1 athletic trainer.

Computers Computers are regularly used in art, computer applications, creative writing, drawing and design, English, foreign language, geography, graphic arts, health, history, humanities, mathematics, music, newspaper, photography, photojournalism, publications, science, social studies, Web site design, yearbook classes. Computer network features include on-campus library services, Internet access, wireless campus network, Internet filtering or blocking technology. Campus intranet, student e-mail accounts, and computer access in designated common areas are available to students. Students grades are available online. The school has a published electronic and media policy.

Contact Rita Mills, Admission Manager. 310-377-1543 Ext. 4025. Fax: 310-377-0380. E-mail: admissions@chadwickschool.org. Web site: www.chadwickschool.org.

ANNOUNCEMENT FROM THE SCHOOL Chadwick School, founded in 1935, is a nonprofit, nondenominational, coeducational day school (Grades K–12) that serves a culturally and economically diverse student body. Chadwick's mission encourages personal excellence; the mastery of academic, artistic, and athletic skills; and the development of social and individual responsibility. Chadwick School is located on 45 acres atop the beautiful Palos Verdes Peninsula, with approximately one third of the faculty living on campus. In the Village School (Grades K–6), the class size ranges from 18 to 20 students. Language arts, social studies, mathematics, and science are taught by the classroom teachers in a program coordinated with specialists in art, music, science, technology, foreign languages, and physical education. With an average-class-size of 17 students, the Middle and Upper Schools have a rigorous core curriculum that includes English, history, science, mathematics, foreign language, visual arts, performing arts, technology, and physical education and athletics. In the Upper School, a full range of honors and AP classes is available. Three counselors offer a comprehensive college-counseling program. Numerous extracurricular opportunities are available, including student government, literary magazine, newspaper, yearbook production, and special-interest clubs. Performing arts are housed in the Laverty Center, with comprehensive drama, dance, and vocal and instrumental programs. Twenty-four athletic teams compete at the varsity level. Technology is integrated into the curriculum and the School has five computer labs. The Leavenworth Library, with a total of 35,000 volumes, has separate sections for Grades K–6 and Grades 7–12. The community service program is part of the afternoon daily schedule; students have the opportunity to leave campus regularly and volunteer at local agencies and schools. Beginning in the third grade with a three-day trip and culminating in an eighteen-day senior trip just prior to graduation, the outdoor education program presents unique learning opportunities for all students. Because of Chadwick's global focus, students may participate in international study and community service programs. Transportation and need-based financial aid, including the need-merit Malone and MacFarlane Scholarships, are available.

CHAMBERLAIN-HUNT ACADEMY

124 McComb Avenue
Port Gibson, Mississippi 39150

Head of School: Col. Jack Gardner West

General Information Boys' boarding and coeducational day college-preparatory, arts, religious studies, bilingual studies, technology, Music, and military school, affiliated with Presbyterian Church, Reformed Church. Boarding boys grades 7–12, day boys grades 7–12, day girls grades 7–12. Founded: 1879. Setting: small town. Nearest major city is Vicksburg. Students are housed in single-sex dormitories. 120-acre campus. 11 buildings on campus. Approved or accredited by Assocaition of Classical Christian Schools, Association of Christian Schools International, Mississippi Private School Association, Southern Association of Colleges and Schools, and Mississippi Department of Education. Endowment: $29 million. Total enrollment: 110. Upper school average class size: 10. Upper school faculty-student ratio: 1:5.

Upper School Student Profile Grade 9: 15 students (14 boys, 1 girl); Grade 10: 17 students (17 boys); Grade 11: 14 students (13 boys, 1 girl); Grade 12: 20 students (19 boys, 1 girl). 90% of students are boarding students. 27% are state residents. 23 states are represented in upper school student body. 2% are international students. International students from China, Republic of Korea, and United Kingdom. 9% of students are Presbyterian, Reformed.

Faculty School total: 23. In upper school: 14 men, 4 women; 12 have advanced degrees; 14 reside on campus.

Subjects Offered ACT preparation, advanced math, Advanced Placement courses, algebra, American Civil War, American government, American history, American literature-AP, ancient history, art, Bible, biology, British literature, business, calculus, chemistry, choir, Christian doctrine, Christian ethics, church history, classical Greek literature, computer keyboarding, computer programming, computer skills, CPR, earth science, economics, English, English literature, English literature-AP, ethics, French, geometry, government, Latin, logic, men's studies, military history, physics, pre-algebra, rhetoric, Spanish, theology, U.S. government, U.S. history, vocal ensemble, wilderness experience, world history, world wide web design.
Graduation Requirements Algebra, American literature, anatomy and physiology, Bible, biology, British literature, chemistry, classical Greek literature, economics, electives, geometry, intro to computers, languages, medieval literature, rhetoric, state history, Talmud, U.S. government, U.S. history, world geography, world history, oral comprehensive exams, senior speech, worldview class.
Special Academic Programs International Baccalaureate program; Advanced Placement exam preparation; honors section; academic accommodation for the gifted, the musically talented, and the artistically talented; remedial reading and/or remedial writing; remedial math.
College Admission Counseling 15 students graduated in 2008; 10 went to college, including Harding University; Louisiana State University and Agricultural and Mechanical College; Mississippi College; Mississippi State University; Palm Beach Atlantic University; University of Mississippi. Other: 2 went to work, 3 entered military service.
Student Life Upper grades have uniform requirement, student council, honor system. Discipline rests primarily with faculty. Attendance at religious services is required.
Summer Programs Remediation, enrichment, advancement, sports, rigorous outdoor training programs offered; session focuses on remediation and advancement courses along with weekend activities such as rafting, paintball, and ropes course; held both on and off campus; held at weekend rafting trip, professional sporting events, and history trip (one week); accepts boys; open to students from other schools. 55 students usually enrolled. 2009 schedule: June 1 to June 28. Application deadline: May 21.
Tuition and Aid Day student tuition: $6000; 7-day tuition and room/board: $16,500. Tuition installment plan (monthly payment plans). Tuition reduction for siblings, need-based scholarship grants available. In 2008–09, 29% of upper-school students received aid. Total amount of financial aid awarded in 2008–09: $222,870.
Admissions Traditional secondary-level entrance grade is 9. For fall 2008, 69 students applied for upper-level admission, 66 were accepted, 66 enrolled. Deadline for receipt of application materials: none. Application fee required: $50. On-campus interview required.
Athletics Interscholastic: basketball (boys), cross-country running (b), soccer (b), track and field (b), winter soccer (b); intramural: aquatics (b), backpacking (b), baseball (b), basketball (b), canoeing/kayaking (b), climbing (b), cross-country running (b), fishing (b), fitness (b), flag football (b), hiking/backpacking (b), indoor soccer (b), jogging (b), life saving (b), marksmanship (b), outdoor activities (b), paint ball (b), physical fitness (b), physical training (b), riflery (b), rock climbing (b), ropes courses (b), running (b), skeet shooting (b), soccer (b), strength & conditioning (b), swimming and diving (b), table tennis (b), tennis (b), track and field (g), ultimate Frisbee (b), volleyball (b), wall climbing (b), water polo (b), weight lifting (b), weight training (b), wilderness (b), wilderness survival (b), wildernessways (b). 4 PE instructors, 1 coach, 1 athletic trainer.
Computers Computers are regularly used in library skills, programming, typing, Web site design classes. Computer resources include on-campus library services, online commercial services, Internet access, Internet filtering or blocking technology. The school has a published electronic and media policy.
Contact Maj. Christopher Michael Blackwell, Director of Admissions. 601-437-8855. Fax: 601-437-3212. E-mail: admissions@chamberlain-hunt.com. Web site: www.chamberlain-hunt.com/.

CHAMINADE COLLEGE PREPARATORY

7500 Chaminade Avenue
West Hills, California 91304

Head of School: Br. Thomas Fahy

General Information Coeducational day college-preparatory, arts, religious studies, and technology school, affiliated with Roman Catholic Church. Grades 9–12. Founded: 1952. Setting: suburban. Nearest major city is Los Angeles. 21-acre campus. 13 buildings on campus. Approved or accredited by Western Association of Schools and Colleges, Western Catholic Education Association, and California Department of Education. Endowment: $5 million. Total enrollment: 1,227. Upper school average class size: 26. Upper school faculty-student ratio: 1:14.
Upper School Student Profile Grade 9: 343 students (177 boys, 166 girls); Grade 10: 303 students (165 boys, 138 girls); Grade 11: 278 students (156 boys, 122 girls); Grade 12: 292 students (141 boys, 151 girls). 53% of students are Roman Catholic.
Faculty School total: 84. In upper school: 34 men, 50 women; 54 have advanced degrees.
Subjects Offered Algebra, American history, American literature, anatomy, art, art history, athletic training, band, baseball, basketball, biology, biology-AP, British literature, British literature (honors), calculus, calculus-AP, chemistry, chemistry-AP, Christian and Hebrew scripture, community service, comparative government and politics-AP, composition, computer programming, computer programming-AP, computer science, creative writing, dance, dance performance, debate, drama, drawing, driver education, economics, economics and history, English, English language-AP, English literature and composition-AP, environmental science-AP, ethics, European history, expository writing, film studies, finance, fine arts, finite math, French, French language-AP, French literature-AP, geography, geometry, government-AP, government/civics, guitar, jazz ensemble, journalism, Latin, Latin-AP, literature and composition-AP, macroeconomics-AP, marching band, mathematics, microeconomics-AP, modern European history-AP, music, music appreciation, music performance, physical education, physical science, physics, physics-AP, physiology, play/screen writing, psychology, psychology-AP, religion, science, science fiction, scripture, Shakespeare, social studies, Spanish, Spanish language-AP, Spanish literature-AP, speech, speech and debate, sports medicine, statistics and probability, statistics-AP, studio art, theater, trigonometry, U.S. government, U.S. history, U.S. history-AP, United States government-AP, visual and performing arts, visual arts, Western philosophy, Western religions, women's studies, world history, world history-AP, world literature, writing.
Graduation Requirements Arts and fine arts (art, music, dance, drama), college writing, computer science, English, foreign language, mathematics, physical education (includes health), religious studies, science, social studies (includes history), speech. Community service is required.
Special Academic Programs Advanced Placement exam preparation; honors section.
College Admission Counseling 277 students graduated in 2008; 275 went to college, including California State University, Northridge; University of California, Davis; University of California, Santa Barbara; University of California, Santa Cruz; University of Colorado at Boulder; University of Southern California. Other: 2 had other specific plans. Mean SAT critical reading: 587, mean SAT math: 585, mean SAT writing: 600, mean composite ACT: 26. 44% scored over 600 on SAT critical reading, 46% scored over 600 on SAT math, 51% scored over 600 on SAT writing, 48% scored over 26 on composite ACT.
Student Life Upper grades have uniform requirement, student council, honor system. Discipline rests primarily with faculty. Attendance at religious services is required.
Summer Programs Remediation, enrichment, advancement, sports, computer instruction programs offered; session focuses on remediation; held on campus; accepts boys and girls; open to students from other schools. 600 students usually enrolled. 2009 schedule: June 22 to July 31. Application deadline: none.
Tuition and Aid Day student tuition: $10,500. Tuition installment plan (monthly payment plans, 2-payment plan, discounted 1-payment plan). Merit scholarship grants, need-based scholarship grants available. In 2008–09, 15% of upper-school students received aid; total upper-school merit-scholarship money awarded: $20,000. Total amount of financial aid awarded in 2008–09: $955,760.
Admissions Traditional secondary-level entrance grade is 9. For fall 2008, 272 students applied for upper-level admission, 234 were accepted, 174 enrolled. Non-standardized placement tests required. Deadline for receipt of application materials: January 16. Application fee required: $100. On-campus interview required.
Athletics Interscholastic: aquatics (boys, girls), baseball (b), basketball (b,g), cross-country running (b,g), equestrian sports (b,g), fencing (b,g), field hockey (g), football (b), golf (b,g), lacrosse (b,g), soccer (b,g), softball (g), strength & conditioning (b,g), swimming and diving (b,g), tennis (b,g), track and field (b,g), volleyball (b,g), weight training (b,g), wrestling (b); coed interscholastic: cheering, equestrian sports, physical fitness, strength & conditioning, weight training; coed intramural: cheering, dance, dance team, fitness, hiking/backpacking, table tennis. 5 PE instructors, 82 coaches, 1 athletic trainer.
Computers Computers are regularly used in creative writing, data processing, information technology, introduction to technology, literary magazine, news writing, newspaper, photojournalism, writing, writing, yearbook classes. Computer network features include on-campus library services, online commercial services, Internet access, wireless campus network. Students grades are available online. The school has a published electronic and media policy.
Contact Ms. Cheryl Peugh, Assistant to Admissions and Registrar. 818-347-8300 Ext. 355. Fax: 818-348-8374. E-mail: cpeugh@chaminade.org. Web site: www.chaminade.org.

CHAMINADE COLLEGE PREPARATORY SCHOOL

425 South Lindbergh Boulevard
St. Louis, Missouri 63131-2799

Head of School: Rev. Ralph A. Siefert, SM

General Information Boys' boarding and day college-preparatory, arts, business, religious studies, bilingual studies, and technology school, affiliated with Roman Catholic Church. Grades 6–12. Founded: 1910. Setting: suburban. Students are housed in single-sex dormitories. 55-acre campus. 12 buildings on campus. Approved or accredited by Independent Schools Association of the Central States, Midwest Association of Boarding Schools, National Catholic Education Association, North Central Association of Colleges and Schools, The Association of Boarding Schools, and Missouri Department of Education. Member of National Association of Independent Schools and Secondary School Admission Test Board. Endowment: $6 million. Total enrollment: 850. Upper school average class size: 19. Upper school faculty-student ratio: 1:10.
Upper School Student Profile Grade 9: 140 students (140 boys); Grade 10: 130 students (130 boys); Grade 11: 141 students (141 boys); Grade 12: 141 students (141 boys). 9% of students are boarding students. 92% are state residents. 6 states are

represented in upper school student body. 7% are international students. International students from China, Hong Kong, Mexico, Republic of Korea, Rwanda, and Taiwan; 1 other country represented in student body. 80% of students are Roman Catholic.
Faculty School total: 93. In upper school: 68 men, 17 women; 60 have advanced degrees; 5 reside on campus.
Subjects Offered Accounting, algebra, American history, American history-AP, American literature, architecture, art, art history, band, Bible studies, biology, biology-AP, botany, business, business skills, calculus, calculus-AP, chemistry, chemistry-AP, community service, computer programming, computer programming-AP, computer science, creative writing, drama, earth science, ecology, economics, economics-AP, engineering, English, English literature, English literature-AP, English/composition-AP, European history, European history-AP, expository writing, fine arts, French, French-AP, geography, geology, geometry, government/civics, grammar, health, history, industrial arts, Japanese, keyboarding, Latin, Latin-AP, mathematics, music theory-AP, physical education, physics, physics-AP, psychology, psychology-AP, religion, science, social studies, sociology, Spanish, Spanish-AP, speech, statistics, statistics-AP, studio art-AP, theater, theology, trigonometry, weight training, world affairs, world history, world literature, writing.
Graduation Requirements Arts and fine arts (art, music, dance, drama), business skills (includes word processing), computer science, English, foreign language, mathematics, physical education (includes health), religion (includes Bible studies and theology), science, social studies (includes history). Community service is required.
Special Academic Programs Advanced Placement exam preparation; honors section; study at local college for college credit; academic accommodation for the gifted; ESL (30 students enrolled).
College Admission Counseling 141 students graduated in 2008; all went to college, including Saint Louis University; Truman State University; University of Dayton; University of Missouri–Columbia; University of Notre Dame; Vanderbilt University. Mean SAT critical reading: 580, mean SAT math: 590, mean composite ACT: 25. 45% scored over 600 on SAT critical reading, 48% scored over 600 on SAT math, 46% scored over 26 on composite ACT.
Student Life Upper grades have specified standards of dress, honor system. Discipline rests primarily with faculty. Attendance at religious services is required.
Summer Programs Enrichment, sports programs offered; held on campus; accepts boys and girls; open to students from other schools. 500 students usually enrolled. 2009 schedule: June to July.
Tuition and Aid Day student tuition: $13,150; 5-day tuition and room/board: $26,450; 7-day tuition and room/board: $27,450. Tuition installment plan (FACTS Tuition Payment Plan). Merit scholarship grants, need-based scholarship grants, need-based loans, paying campus jobs available. In 2008–09, 25% of upper-school students received aid; total upper-school merit-scholarship money awarded: $1,000,000. Total amount of financial aid awarded in 2008–09: $1,400,000.
Admissions Traditional secondary-level entrance grade is 9. For fall 2008, 46 students applied for upper-level admission, 35 were accepted, 30 enrolled. ISEE required. Deadline for receipt of application materials: none. Application fee required: $50. Interview required.
Athletics Interscholastic: baseball, basketball, bowling, cross-country running, diving, football, golf, ice hockey, lacrosse, racquetball, soccer, swimming and diving, tennis, track and field, volleyball, wrestling; intramural: in-line hockey, rugby, table tennis, ultimate Frisbee, weight training. 5 PE instructors, 30 coaches, 1 athletic trainer.
Computers Computers are regularly used in all academic classes. Computer network features include on-campus library services, online commercial services, Internet access, wireless campus network, Internet filtering or blocking technology. Campus intranet and student e-mail accounts are available to students. Students grades are available online. The school has a published electronic and media policy.
Contact Mr. J.B. Gorgen, Associate Director of Admissions. 314-692-6640. Fax: 314-993-5732. E-mail: jbgorgen@chaminade-stl.com. Web site: www.chaminade-stl.com.

CHAMINADE-MADONNA COLLEGE PREPARATORY

500 Chaminade Drive
Hollywood, Florida 33021-5800

Head of School: Fr. Larry Doersching, SM

General Information Coeducational day college-preparatory, arts, business, and religious studies school, affiliated with Roman Catholic Church; primarily serves students with learning disabilities, individuals with Attention Deficit Disorder, individuals with emotional and behavioral problems, and dyslexic students. Grades 9–12. Founded: 1960. Setting: suburban. Nearest major city is Fort Lauderdale. 13-acre campus. 10 buildings on campus. Approved or accredited by Southern Association of Colleges and Schools and Florida Department of Education. Total enrollment: 704. Upper school average class size: 26. Upper school faculty-student ratio: 1:19.
Upper School Student Profile Grade 9: 179 students (102 boys, 77 girls); Grade 10: 174 students (103 boys, 71 girls); Grade 11: 169 students (91 boys, 78 girls); Grade 12: 182 students (83 boys, 99 girls). 70% of students are Roman Catholic.
Faculty School total: 67. In upper school: 30 men, 37 women.
Subjects Offered Advanced chemistry, advanced computer applications, advanced math, advanced studio art-AP, algebra, American history, American literature, anatomy, art, art history, band, biology, business skills, calculus, ceramics, chemistry, choir, community service, computer applications, creative writing, design, directing, drama, economics, English, fine arts, French, geography, geometry, government/civics, health, history, international relations, journalism, keyboarding, law, marine biology, marketing, mathematics, meteorology, music, philosophy, physical education, physics, physiology, play production, practical arts, pre-calculus, psychology, reading, religion, science, Shakespeare, social studies, sociology, Spanish, speech, stagecraft, theater, trigonometry, word processing, world history, writing, yearbook.
Graduation Requirements Arts and fine arts (art, music, dance, drama), business skills (includes word processing), English, foreign language, mathematics, physical education (includes health), practical arts, religion (includes Bible studies and theology), science, social studies (includes history), 80 community service hours.
Special Academic Programs 10 Advanced Placement exams for which test preparation is offered; honors section; study at local college for college credit; academic accommodation for the gifted, the musically talented, and the artistically talented; remedial reading and/or remedial writing; remedial math; programs in general development for dyslexic students; special instructional classes for students with learning disabilities, Attention Deficit Disorder, and dyslexia.
College Admission Counseling 184 students graduated in 2008; all went to college, including Florida Atlantic University; Florida International University; Florida State University; University of Central Florida; University of Florida; University of Miami. Mean SAT critical reading: 512, mean SAT math: 504, mean composite ACT: 20.
Student Life Upper grades have uniform requirement, student council, honor system. Discipline rests primarily with faculty. Attendance at religious services is required.
Tuition and Aid Day student tuition: $8800. Tuition installment plan (monthly payment plans). Need-based scholarship grants available. In 2008–09, 33% of upper-school students received aid. Total amount of financial aid awarded in 2008–09: $400,000.
Admissions Traditional secondary-level entrance grade is 9. For fall 2008, 300 students applied for upper-level admission, 250 were accepted, 180 enrolled. High School Placement Test (closed version) from Scholastic Testing Service required. Deadline for receipt of application materials: January 21. Application fee required: $50. Interview required.
Athletics Interscholastic: baseball (boys), basketball (b,g), cheering (g), cross-country running (b,g), dance (g), dance team (g), flag football (g), football (b), golf (b,g), hockey (b,g), ice hockey (b,g), lacrosse (g), soccer (b,g), swimming and diving (b,g), track and field (b,g), volleyball (b,g), wrestling (b); intramural: aerobics/dance (g), danceline (g), football (b,g); coed intramural: blading, bowling, fishing, in-line hockey. 2 PE instructors, 1 athletic trainer.
Computers Computers are regularly used in English, mathematics, reading classes. Computer resources include on-campus library services, online commercial services, Internet access. The school has a published electronic and media policy.
Contact Mr. Tim Tyrrell, Director of Enrollment Management. 954-989-5150 Ext. 112. Fax: 954-983-4663. E-mail: ttyrrell@cmlions.org. Web site: www.cmlions.org.

CHAMISA MESA HIGH SCHOOL

PO Box 3560
Taos, New Mexico 87571

Head of School: Mr. Michael LaValley

General Information Coeducational day college-preparatory and arts school. Grades 9–12. Founded: 1990. Setting: small town. Nearest major city is Santa Fe. 2-acre campus. 4 buildings on campus. Approved or accredited by North Central Association of Colleges and Schools and New Mexico Department of Education. Total enrollment: 27. Upper school average class size: 10. Upper school faculty-student ratio: 1:5.
Upper School Student Profile Grade 9: 8 students (1 boy, 7 girls); Grade 10: 9 students (4 boys, 5 girls); Grade 11: 6 students (2 boys, 4 girls); Grade 12: 4 students (3 boys, 1 girl).
Faculty School total: 5. In upper school: 2 men, 3 women; 1 has an advanced degree.
Special Academic Programs Honors section.
College Admission Counseling 23 students graduated in 2008; 20 went to college, including Stanford University; University of New Mexico. Other: 2 went to work, 1 had other specific plans.
Student Life Upper grades have honor system. Discipline rests primarily with faculty.
Tuition and Aid Day student tuition: $6000. Tuition installment plan (monthly payment plans).
Admissions Traditional secondary-level entrance grade is 9. Deadline for receipt of application materials: none. No application fee required. Interview required.
Computers Computers are regularly used in foreign language classes. Computer network features include Internet access.
Contact Admissions. 575-751-0943. Fax: 575-751-3715. E-mail: clavalley@chamisamesa.net. Web site: www.chamisamesa.net.

CHAPEL HILL–CHAUNCY HALL SCHOOL

785 Beaver Street
Waltham, Massachusetts 02452

Head of School: Siri Akal Khalsa, EdD

General Information Coeducational boarding and day college-preparatory and arts school; primarily serves individuals with Attention Deficit Disorder and dyslexic students. Grades 9–PG. Founded: 1828. Setting: suburban. Nearest major city is Boston. Students are housed in single-sex dormitories. 37-acre campus. 11 buildings on campus. Approved or accredited by Association of Independent Schools in New England, New England Association of Schools and Colleges, The Association of Boarding Schools, and Massachusetts Department of Education. Member of National Association of Independent Schools and Secondary School Admission Test Board. Endowment: $1.6 million. Total enrollment: 174. Upper school average class size: 12. Upper school faculty-student ratio: 1:6.

Upper School Student Profile Grade 9: 28 students (18 boys, 10 girls); Grade 10: 51 students (31 boys, 20 girls); Grade 11: 52 students (26 boys, 26 girls); Grade 12: 41 students (22 boys, 19 girls); Postgraduate: 2 students (2 boys). 47% of students are boarding students. 70% are state residents. 7 states are represented in upper school student body. 23% are international students. International students from China, Japan, Republic of Korea, Spain, Taiwan, and Viet Nam; 6 other countries represented in student body.

Faculty School total: 31. In upper school: 15 men, 16 women; 12 have advanced degrees; 21 reside on campus.

Subjects Offered Acting, adolescent issues, advanced studio art-AP, algebra, American history, American literature, art, biology, calculus, ceramics, chemistry, comparative religion, creative writing, drama, economics, English, English literature, English-AP, ESL, European history, fine arts, geography, geometry, government/civics, grammar, health, history, journalism, mathematics, music, photography, physical education, physics, psychology, science, social studies, Spanish, theater, world history, world literature, writing.

Graduation Requirements Arts and fine arts (art, music, dance, drama), English, foreign language, mathematics, physical education (includes health), science, social studies (includes history), senior presentations, earn Charger Points for service. Community service is required.

Special Academic Programs Advanced Placement exam preparation; independent study; programs in general development for dyslexic students; special instructional classes for students with mild to moderate learning disabilities; ESL (12 students enrolled).

College Admission Counseling 44 students graduated in 2008; all went to college, including College of the Holy Cross; Connecticut College; Northeastern University; Oberlin College; Savannah College of Art and Design; School of the Art Institute of Chicago. Mean SAT critical reading: 513, mean SAT math: 527, mean SAT writing: 510. 6% scored over 600 on SAT critical reading, 28% scored over 600 on SAT math.

Student Life Upper grades have student council. Discipline rests equally with students and faculty.

Tuition and Aid Day student tuition: $31,900; 7-day tuition and room/board: $42,600. Tuition installment plan (Key Tuition Payment Plan, monthly payment plans, individually arranged payment plans). Need-based scholarship grants available. In 2008–09, 22% of upper-school students received aid. Total amount of financial aid awarded in 2008–09: $825,000.

Admissions Traditional secondary-level entrance grade is 9. For fall 2008, 190 students applied for upper-level admission, 121 were accepted, 56 enrolled. SSAT or WISC III, TOEFL or SLEP or WISC or WAIS required. Deadline for receipt of application materials: February 1. Application fee required: $50. Interview required.

Athletics Interscholastic: baseball (boys), basketball (b,g), field hockey (g), lacrosse (b,g), soccer (b,g), softball (g), volleyball (g), wrestling (b); coed interscholastic: climbing, combined training, cross-country running, fitness, Frisbee, golf, rock climbing, ropes courses, ultimate Frisbee; coed intramural: aerobics/dance, cooperative games, fitness, physical fitness, racquetball, rock climbing, ropes courses, swimming and diving, yoga. 1 PE instructor, 1 athletic trainer.

Computers Computers are regularly used in art, English, history, mathematics, multimedia, newspaper, yearbook classes. Computer network features include on-campus library services, Internet access, wireless campus network, Internet filtering or blocking technology. Student e-mail accounts and computer access in designated common areas are available to students. Students grades are available online. The school has a published electronic and media policy.

Contact Ms. Lisa Zannella, Director of Admissions. 781-314-0800. Fax: 781-894-5205. E-mail: lzannella@chch.org. Web site: www.chch.org.

CHAPEL SCHOOL

Escola Maria Imaculada
Rua Vigário João de Pontes, 537
Sao Paulo 04748-000, Brazil

Head of School: John Ciallelo

General Information Coeducational day college-preparatory, religious studies, Brazilian Studies, and International Baccalaureate Diploma school, affiliated with Roman Catholic Church. Grades PK–12. Founded: 1947. Setting: suburban. Nearest major city is São Paulo, Brazil. 3-hectare campus. 4 buildings on campus. Approved or accredited by Southern Association of Colleges and Schools. Languages of instruction: English and Portuguese. Total enrollment: 649. Upper school average class size: 23. Upper school faculty-student ratio: 1:7.

Upper School Student Profile Grade 10: 36 students (21 boys, 15 girls); Grade 11: 39 students (17 boys, 22 girls); Grade 12: 37 students (18 boys, 19 girls). 80% of students are Roman Catholic.

Faculty School total: 75. In upper school: 15 men, 25 women; 25 have advanced degrees.

Special Academic Programs International Baccalaureate program; independent study; ESL (15 students enrolled).

College Admission Counseling 38 students graduated in 2008; all went to college, including Babson College; Penn State University Park; The University of British Columbia; University of Notre Dame; Villanova University; Yale University. Median SAT critical reading: 559, median SAT math: 562, median SAT writing: 569.

Student Life Upper grades have specified standards of dress, student council, honor system. Discipline rests primarily with faculty. Attendance at religious services is required.

Tuition and Aid Day student tuition: 398,400 Brazilian reals. Financial aid available to upper-school students. In 2008–09, 8% of upper-school students received aid.

Admissions Traditional secondary-level entrance grade is 10. Admissions testing required. Deadline for receipt of application materials: none. No application fee required. Interview required.

Athletics Interscholastic: basketball (boys, girls), cheering (g), climbing (b,g), soccer (b,g), softball (b,g), volleyball (g). 3 PE instructors, 5 coaches.

Computers Computer network features include on-campus library services, Internet access, wireless campus network, Internet filtering or blocking technology. Students grades are available online. The school has a published electronic and media policy.

Contact Adriana Marques, Admissions Director. 55-11-2101-7400 Ext. 7412. Fax: 55-11-5521-7763. E-mail: admissions@chapelschool.com. Web site: www.chapelschool.com.

THE CHAPIN SCHOOL

100 East End Avenue
New York, New York 10028

Head of School: Dr. Patricia T. Hayot

General Information Girls' day college-preparatory school. Grades K–12. Founded: 1901. Setting: urban. 1 building on campus. Approved or accredited by New York State Association of Independent Schools and New York Department of Education. Member of National Association of Independent Schools. Endowment: $90.1 million. Total enrollment: 673. Upper school average class size: 16. Upper school faculty-student ratio: 1:4.

Upper School Student Profile Grade 8: 53 students (53 girls); Grade 9: 63 students (63 girls); Grade 10: 44 students (44 girls); Grade 11: 46 students (46 girls); Grade 12: 34 students (34 girls).

Faculty School total: 118. In upper school: 16 men, 45 women; 50 have advanced degrees.

Subjects Offered Advanced Placement courses, African drumming, African history, African-American history, algebra, American history, American literature, art, art history, Asian history, astronomy, biology, calculus, ceramics, chemistry, Chinese, comparative religion, computer math, computer science, creative writing, dance, design, digital imaging, DNA, drama, drawing, electronics, English, English literature, European history, expository writing, fine arts, French, geography, geometry, government/civics, grammar, Greek, health, history, Latin, Latin American literature, life skills, mathematics, multimedia, music, painting, philosophy, photography, physical education, physics, poetry, psychology, public speaking, religion, Russian literature, science, sculpture, social studies, Spanish, statistics, theater, trigonometry, video, writing.

Graduation Requirements Arts and fine arts (art, music, dance, drama), computer science, English, English literature and composition-AP, foreign language, mathematics, physical education (includes health), science, social studies (includes history).

Special Academic Programs Advanced Placement exam preparation; honors section; term-away projects; study abroad; special instructional classes for deaf students.

College Admission Counseling 51 students graduated in 2008; all went to college, including Amherst College; Columbia College; Georgetown University; Harvard University; Stanford University; Yale University.

Student Life Upper grades have uniform requirement, student council, honor system. Discipline rests primarily with faculty.

Tuition and Aid Day student tuition: $29,100. Need-based scholarship grants, Key Education Resources available. In 2008–09, 25% of upper-school students received aid. Total amount of financial aid awarded in 2008–09: $1,547,750.

Admissions Traditional secondary-level entrance grade is 9. For fall 2008, 78 students applied for upper-level admission, 34 were accepted, 14 enrolled. ISEE and math and English placement tests required. Deadline for receipt of application materials: December 15. Application fee required: $50. On-campus interview required.

Athletics Interscholastic: badminton, basketball, cross-country running, field hockey, gymnastics, independent competitive sports, lacrosse, soccer, softball, squash, swimming and diving, tennis, track and field, volleyball; intramural: aerobics, aerobics/dance, aerobics/Nautilus, aquatics, badminton, ball hockey, ballet, basketball, cooperative games, cross-country running, curling, dance, diving, fencing, field hockey, fitness, fitness walking, flag football, floor hockey, football, Frisbee, gymnastics, handball, indoor hockey, indoor soccer, indoor track & field, jogging, kickball, lacrosse, life saving, martial arts, modern dance, Nautilus, outdoor activities, physical fitness, physical training, project adventure, ropes courses, self defense, skiing (downhill), snowboarding, soccer, softball, squash, strength & conditioning, swimming and diving, tai chi, team handball, tennis, touch football, track and field, ultimate Frisbee, volleyball, walking, water polo, weight training, whiffle ball, yoga; coed interscholastic: fencing. 14 PE instructors, 6 coaches, 1 athletic trainer.

Computers Computers are regularly used in art, dance, English, foreign language, history, mathematics, music, science classes. Computer network features include on-campus library services, Internet access, wireless campus network, ProQuest, SIRS Knowledge Source. Campus intranet and student e-mail accounts are available to students. The school has a published electronic and media policy.

Contact Tina I. Herman, Director of Admissions. 212-744-2335. Fax: 212-628-2126. E-mail: admissions@chapin.edu. Web site: www.chapin.edu.

CHARLOTTE CATHOLIC HIGH SCHOOL

7702 Pineville Matthews Road
Charlotte, North Carolina 28226

Head of School: Mr. Gerald S. Healy

General Information Coeducational day college-preparatory, arts, and religious studies school, affiliated with Roman Catholic Church. Grades 9–12. Founded: 1955. Setting: urban. 1 building on campus. Approved or accredited by National Catholic Education Association, North Carolina Association of Independent Schools, and Southern Association of Colleges and Schools. Total enrollment: 1,416. Upper school average class size: 20.

Upper School Student Profile 92% of students are Roman Catholic.

Faculty School total: 105. In upper school: 33 men, 72 women.

Subjects Offered Accounting, algebra, American government-AP, American literature, American literature-AP, analysis, analysis and differential calculus, anatomy and physiology, applied arts, applied music, art, band, Basic programming, Bible studies, biology, biology-AP, British literature, British literature (honors), business, calculus, calculus-AP, campus ministry, Catholic belief and practice, chemistry, chemistry-AP, choir, chorus, Christian and Hebrew scripture, Christian ethics, Christian scripture, college counseling, college placement, computer applications, computer programming, computers, concert band, dance, dance performance, desktop publishing, drama, drama performance, earth science, economics, English, English language and composition-AP, English literature and composition-AP, environmental science, environmental science-AP, ethics and responsibility, European history-AP, fitness, French, geography, German, government, government-AP, guidance, guitar, health, history of the Catholic Church, honors algebra, honors English, honors U.S. history, honors world history, jazz band, Latin, Latin-AP, library, library assistant, Life of Christ, marching band, math analysis, model United Nations, musical productions, musical theater, newspaper, oceanography, painting, performing arts, physical education, physics, physics-AP, piano, play production, politics, psychology, public speaking, religion, remedial study skills, SAT preparation, social justice, Spanish, Spanish language-AP, statistics-AP, student government, theater, track and field, trigonometry, U.S. history, U.S. history-AP, Web site design, word processing, world geography, world history, world religions, wrestling, yearbook.

Graduation Requirements Algebra, biology, British literature, chemistry, economics, English, geometry, physical science, public service, religion (includes Bible studies and theology), trigonometry, U.S. government, U.S. history, world history.

Special Academic Programs Advanced Placement exam preparation; honors section.

College Admission Counseling 333 students graduated in 2008; 330 went to college, including Appalachian State University; East Carolina University; North Carolina State University; The University of North Carolina at Chapel Hill; The University of North Carolina at Charlotte; University of South Carolina. Other: 1 went to work, 2 entered military service.

Student Life Upper grades have specified standards of dress, student council, honor system. Discipline rests primarily with faculty. Attendance at religious services is required.

Tuition and Aid Day student tuition: $7500. Tuition installment plan (monthly payment plans). Need-based scholarship grants available.

Admissions High School Placement Test required. Deadline for receipt of application materials: none. Application fee required: $100. Interview required.

Athletics Interscholastic: baseball (boys), basketball (b,g), cheering (g), cross-country running (b,g), dance (g), dance team (g), diving (b,g), football (b), golf (b,g), lacrosse (b), running (b,g), soccer (b,g), softball (g), swimming and diving (b,g), tennis (b,g), volleyball (g), wrestling (b); intramural: dance (g), rugby (b); coed intramural: archery, backpacking, badminton, basketball, bowling, fitness, physical fitness, ultimate Frisbee. 4 PE instructors, 2 athletic trainers.

Computers Computers are regularly used in accounting, college planning, desktop publishing, yearbook classes. Computer network features include Internet access. The school has a published electronic and media policy.

Contact Mr. Steven H. Carpenter, Assistant Principal. 704-543-1127. Fax: 704-543-1217. E-mail: shcarpenter@charlottecatholic.com. Web site: www.gocougars.org.

CHARLOTTE CHRISTIAN SCHOOL

7301 Sardis Road
Charlotte, North Carolina 28270

Head of School: Dr. Leo Orsino

General Information Coeducational day college-preparatory school, affiliated with Christian faith. Grades JK–12. Founded: 1950. Setting: suburban. 55-acre campus. 4 buildings on campus. Approved or accredited by Association of Christian Schools International, North Carolina Association of Independent Schools, Southern Association of Colleges and Schools, Southern Association of Independent Schools, and North Carolina Department of Education. Total enrollment: 1,078. Upper school average class size: 20. Upper school faculty-student ratio: 1:11.

Upper School Student Profile Grade 6: 69 students (41 boys, 28 girls); Grade 7: 89 students (61 boys, 28 girls); Grade 8: 91 students (45 boys, 46 girls); Grade 9: 100 students (49 boys, 51 girls); Grade 10: 108 students (61 boys, 47 girls); Grade 11: 95 students (54 boys, 41 girls); Grade 12: 89 students (48 boys, 41 girls). 100% of students are Christian faith.

Faculty School total: 127. In upper school: 18 men, 18 women; 14 have advanced degrees.

Subjects Offered Accounting, acting, advanced studio art-AP, algebra, American culture, American government, American government-AP, American literature, anatomy and physiology, art, art history-AP, athletic training, band, biology, biology-AP, British literature, business, business law, calculus-AP, chamber groups, chemistry, choreography, Christian education, Christian ethics, church history, civil war history, computer applications, computer science-AP, computer-aided design, economics, English literature, environmental science-AP, European history-AP, French, French-AP, geometry, German, graphic arts, graphic design, health and wellness, language-AP, Latin, leadership, learning strategies, Life of Christ, literature and composition-AP, marketing, math applications, music composition, music theory-AP, newspaper, painting, photography, physical education, physical science, physics, physics-AP, pre-calculus, psychology, public speaking, research skills, SAT preparation, sign language, Spanish, Spanish-AP, speech and debate, sports medicine, stage design, statistics-AP, studio art—AP, theater, theater design and production, trigonometry, U.S. history, U.S. history-AP, video film production, voice, voice and diction, Web site design, weight training, wind ensemble, world civilizations, world literature, World War II, yearbook.

Graduation Requirements Bible studies, English, foreign language, mathematics, physical education (includes health), SAT preparation, science, social studies (includes history), speech, service hours, visual or performing arts.

Special Academic Programs Advanced Placement exam preparation; honors section; study at local college for college credit.

College Admission Counseling 93 students graduated in 2008; all went to college, including Appalachian State University; Furman University; Liberty University; North Carolina State University; The University of North Carolina at Chapel Hill; Wake Forest University. Mean composite ACT: 25.

Student Life Upper grades have specified standards of dress, student council, honor system. Discipline rests primarily with faculty. Attendance at religious services is required.

Summer Programs Enrichment, advancement, sports, art/fine arts, rigorous outdoor training, computer instruction programs offered; session focuses on enrichment; held on campus; accepts boys and girls; open to students from other schools. 300 students usually enrolled. 2009 schedule: June to August. Application deadline: none.

Tuition and Aid Day student tuition: $10,300–$14,700. Tuition installment plan (The Tuition Plan, Insured Tuition Payment Plan, monthly payment plans, individually arranged payment plans). Tuition reduction for siblings, need-based scholarship grants available. In 2008–09, 20% of upper-school students received aid. Total amount of financial aid awarded in 2008–09: $389,150.

Admissions Traditional secondary-level entrance grade is 9. Admissions testing or ISEE required. Deadline for receipt of application materials: none. Application fee required: $75. On-campus interview required.

Athletics Interscholastic: baseball (boys), basketball (b,g), cheering (g), cross-country running (b,g), dance (g), football (b), golf (b), indoor track (b,g), soccer (b,g), softball (g), swimming and diving (b,g), tennis (b,g), track and field (b,g), volleyball (g), wrestling (b); intramural: basketball (b,g), cheering (g), jogging (g); coed interscholastic: physical fitness, physical training, strength & conditioning, weight training; coed intramural: basketball, fencing, tennis, weight training. 2 PE instructors, 25 coaches, 1 athletic trainer.

Computers Computers are regularly used in all classes. Computer network features include on-campus library services, Internet access, wireless campus network, Internet filtering or blocking technology, NewsBank InfoWeb. Students grades are available online.

Contact Mrs. Cathie Broocks, Director of Admissions. 704-366-5657. Fax: 704-366-5678. E-mail: cathie.broocks@charchrist.com. Web site: www.charlottechristian.com.

CHARLOTTE COUNTRY DAY SCHOOL

1440 Carmel Road
Charlotte, North Carolina 28226

Head of School: Margaret E. Gragg

General Information Coeducational day college-preparatory school. Grades JK–12. Founded: 1941. Setting: suburban. 60-acre campus. 10 buildings on campus. Approved or accredited by North Carolina Association of Independent Schools, Southern Association of Colleges and Schools, Southern Association of Independent Schools, and North Carolina Department of Education. Member of National Association of Independent Schools and Secondary School Admission Test Board. Endowment: $18.6 million. Total enrollment: 1,633. Upper school average class size: 15. Upper school faculty-student ratio: 1:12.

Upper School Student Profile Grade 9: 122 students (72 boys, 50 girls); Grade 10: 124 students (54 boys, 70 girls); Grade 11: 114 students (65 boys, 49 girls); Grade 12: 116 students (61 boys, 55 girls).

Faculty School total: 205. In upper school: 35 men, 27 women; 36 have advanced degrees.

Subjects Offered Algebra, American history, American history-AP, anatomy, art, art history-AP, astronomy, biology, biology-AP, biotechnology, calculus-AP, ceramics, chemistry, chemistry-AP, Chinese, computer graphics, computer science, computer science-AP, creative writing, dance, debate, discrete math, drama, ecology, economics, English, English literature, English-AP, environmental science-AP, ESL, European history, European history-AP, French, French-AP, geography, geometry, German, German-AP, Japanese, journalism, Latin, Latin-AP, library studies, music, non-Western societies, novels, photography, physical education, physics, physics-AP, physiology, poetry, political science, pre-calculus, probability and statistics, psychology-AP, sculpture, Shakespeare, short story, Spanish, Spanish-AP, studio art-AP, theater, theory of knowledge, trigonometry, typing, visual arts, yearbook.

Graduation Requirements Arts and fine arts (art, music, dance, drama), computer science, English, foreign language, mathematics, physical education (includes health), science, social sciences, social studies (includes history). Community service is required.

Special Academic Programs International Baccalaureate program; Advanced Placement exam preparation; honors section; independent study; term-away projects; study abroad; academic accommodation for the gifted; ESL (9 students enrolled).

College Admission Counseling 116 students graduated in 2008; all went to college, including Duke University; The University of North Carolina at Chapel Hill; University of Georgia; University of South Carolina; University of Virginia; Washington and Lee University. Median SAT critical reading: 620, median SAT math: 650, median SAT writing: 630, median combined SAT: 1900, median composite ACT: 26. 61% scored over 600 on SAT critical reading, 76% scored over 600 on SAT math, 63% scored over 600 on SAT writing, 65% scored over 1800 on combined SAT, 56% scored over 26 on composite ACT.

Student Life Upper grades have specified standards of dress, student council, honor system. Discipline rests primarily with faculty.

Summer Programs Remediation, enrichment, advancement, ESL, sports, art/fine arts, computer instruction programs offered; session focuses on enrichment classes, academic courses, and sports camps; held on campus; accepts boys and girls; open to students from other schools. 200 students usually enrolled. 2009 schedule: June 15 to July 17. Application deadline: none.

Tuition and Aid Day student tuition: $19,500. Tuition installment plan (The Tuition Plan, Insured Tuition Payment Plan, monthly payment plans). Need-based scholarship grants available. In 2008–09, 18% of upper-school students received aid. Total amount of financial aid awarded in 2008–09: $1,395,838.

Admissions Traditional secondary-level entrance grade is 9. For fall 2008, 85 students applied for upper-level admission, 44 were accepted, 32 enrolled. CTP III, ERB or ISEE required. Deadline for receipt of application materials: January 15. Application fee required: $90. On-campus interview required.

Athletics Interscholastic: baseball (boys), basketball (b,g), cheering (g), crew (g), cross-country running (b,g), dance (g), dance team (g), field hockey (g), fitness (b,g), football (b), golf (b,g), lacrosse (b,g), soccer (b,g), softball (g), strength & conditioning (b,g), swimming and diving (b,g), tennis (b,g), track and field (b,g), volleyball (g), weight training (b,g), wrestling (b). 1 PE instructor, 34 coaches, 3 athletic trainers.

Computers Computers are regularly used in English, foreign language, mathematics, science classes. Computer network features include on-campus library services, Internet access, wireless campus network, Internet filtering or blocking technology. Campus intranet and student e-mail accounts are available to students. Students grades are available online. The school has a published electronic and media policy.

Contact Nancy R. Ehringhaus, Director of Admissions. 704-943-4530 Ext. 4531. Fax: 704-943-4536. E-mail: nancy.ehringhaus@charlottecountryday.org. Web site: www.charlottecountryday.org.

ANNOUNCEMENT FROM THE SCHOOL Charlotte Country Day School strives to be the benchmark of academic excellence in college-preparatory education through superior teaching of a rigorous curriculum. As one of the largest independent schools in the country, Charlotte Country Day blends the abilities of students, aspirations of parents, and skills of professional educators to create a culture of achievement, honor, and compassion. Students in Junior Kindergarten through grade 12 are offered a premier international studies program, state-of-the-art technology, an innovative lab-based science program, a strong fine arts curriculum, an International Baccalaureate program, more than sixty athletic teams, an award-winning physical education program, and a strong focus on community service.

CHARLOTTE LATIN SCHOOL

9502 Providence Road
Charlotte, North Carolina 28277-8695

Head of School: Mr. Arch N. McIntosh Jr.

General Information Coeducational day college-preparatory school. Grades K–12. Founded: 1970. Setting: suburban. 122-acre campus. 14 buildings on campus. Approved or accredited by North Carolina Association of Independent Schools, Southern Association of Colleges and Schools, Southern Association of Independent Schools, and North Carolina Department of Education. Member of National Association of Independent Schools and Secondary School Admission Test Board. Endowment: $24.8 million. Total enrollment: 1,378. Upper school average class size: 16. Upper school faculty-student ratio: 1:8.

Upper School Student Profile Grade 9: 124 students (64 boys, 60 girls); Grade 10: 119 students (64 boys, 55 girls); Grade 11: 125 students (62 boys, 63 girls); Grade 12: 113 students (53 boys, 60 girls).

Faculty School total: 149. In upper school: 32 men, 28 women; 41 have advanced degrees.

Subjects Offered 20th century American writers, 20th century history, 20th century physics, 20th century world history, 3-dimensional art, advanced chemistry, Advanced Placement courses, algebra, American culture, American government, American government-AP, American history, American history-AP, American literature, art, biology, biology-AP, British literature, calculus, calculus-AP, ceramics, chemistry, chemistry-AP, college counseling, computer math, computer programming, computer science, computer science-AP, creative writing, drama, driver education, earth science, ecology, economics, economics and history, engineering, English, English literature, English-AP, environmental science, European history, European history-AP, expository writing, finite math, French, French-AP, geography, geology, geometry, German, German-AP, government/civics, grammar, Greek, health, history, Holocaust and other genocides, international relations, international studies, journalism, Latin, Latin-AP, leadership and service, mathematics, music, music theory-AP, physical education, physics, physics-AP, psychology, science, social studies, Spanish, Spanish language-AP, Spanish-AP, speech, sports medicine, statistics-AP, theater, trigonometry, U.S. government and politics-AP, Web site design, world history, world literature, writing.

Graduation Requirements Electives, English, foreign language, history, mathematics, physical education (includes health), science.

Special Academic Programs Advanced Placement exam preparation; honors section; study abroad; academic accommodation for the gifted.

College Admission Counseling 117 students graduated in 2008; all went to college, including Davidson College; Duke University; Elon University; North Carolina State University; The University of North Carolina at Chapel Hill; University of South Carolina. Median SAT critical reading: 640, median SAT math: 650, median SAT writing: 650, median combined SAT: 1940. Mean composite ACT: 27. 60% scored over 600 on SAT critical reading, 73% scored over 600 on SAT math, 68% scored over 600 on SAT writing, 67% scored over 1800 on combined SAT.

Student Life Upper grades have specified standards of dress, student council, honor system. Discipline rests primarily with faculty.

Summer Programs Enrichment, sports, art/fine arts, computer instruction programs offered; session focuses on Enrichment, Sports Camps; held both on and off campus; held at while the summer camps program is based on campus, some camps include field trips off campus; accepts boys and girls; open to students from other schools. 850 students usually enrolled. 2009 schedule: June 15 to July 31. Application deadline: none.

Tuition and Aid Day student tuition: $18,000. Tuition installment plan (monthly payment plans, individually arranged payment plans). Merit scholarship grants, need-based scholarship grants available. In 2008–09, 13% of upper-school students received aid; total upper-school merit-scholarship money awarded: $201,200. Total amount of financial aid awarded in 2008–09: $501,500.

Admissions Traditional secondary-level entrance grade is 9. For fall 2008, 95 students applied for upper-level admission, 36 were accepted, 31 enrolled. ERB, ISEE, Wechsler Intelligence Scale for Children III or Woodcock-Johnson required. Deadline for receipt of application materials: none. Application fee required: $90. On-campus interview required.

Athletics Interscholastic: aquatics (boys, girls), baseball (b), basketball (b,g), cheering (g), cross-country running (b,g), dance team (g), field hockey (g), football (b), golf (b,g), independent competitive sports (b,g), indoor track (b,g), lacrosse (b,g), soccer (b,g), softball (g), swimming and diving (b,g), tennis (b,g), track and field (b,g), volleyball (g), wrestling (b); intramural: aerobics (g), badminton (b,g), basketball (b,g), dance (g), fencing (b), fitness (b,g), independent competitive sports (b,g), lacrosse (b,g), outdoor activities (b,g), physical fitness (b,g), physical training (b,g), strength & conditioning (b,g); coed interscholastic: ultimate Frisbee; coed intramural: badminton, fitness, outdoor activities, physical fitness, physical training, strength & conditioning, ultimate Frisbee. 8 PE instructors, 3 athletic trainers.

Computers Computers are regularly used in all academic classes. Computer network features include on-campus library services, online commercial services, Internet access, wireless campus network, Internet filtering or blocking technology. Computer access in designated common areas is available to students. The school has a published electronic and media policy.

Contact Ms. Kathryn B. Booe, Director of Admissions. 704-846-7207. Fax: 704-847-8776. E-mail: kbooe@charlottelatin.org. Web site: www.charlottelatin.org.

ANNOUNCEMENT FROM THE SCHOOL Charlotte Latin School provides a challenging yet nurturing atmosphere for its students. This balanced environment is fostered by the development of intellectual curiosity, a comprehensive athletic program, a solid commitment to the arts, an emphasis on character education, and an educational approach that is traditional in design but progressive in implementation. The School remains true to its founding parents' vision as a place where a stimulating learning environment is united with a vibrant family life, and where families from diverse backgrounds share the common value of respect for themselves and for others, as well as an enduring dedication to support their children's educational journey. As one of the nation's leading independent day schools, Charlotte Latin's numerous honors, including being the youngest school to receive a Cum Laude chapter, and three times being named a Blue Ribbon School of Excellence by the United States Department of Education, illustrate that from transitional kindergarten through grade 12, students thrive by all measurable standards. Students benefit from a college-preparatory curriculum. Younger students progress in developmentally appropriate steps, while Upper School students select from among sixteen Advanced Placement courses. Guided by an Honor Code, Charlotte Latin's students also are encouraged to participate in community service, special interest clubs, and international studies to prepare themselves better to understand and lead the world they shall inherit as adults. Each year, the students' SAT scores are at the top of the Charlotte region's scores (1294 average for the class of 2008). Charlotte Latin's seniors, who receive individual guidance from 2 full-time college counselors, are accepted by the nation's leading colleges and universities, including Ivy League schools. The School's campus, conveniently located in suburban Charlotte, encompasses fourteen major buildings and a complete athletics complex amid 122 acres of mature trees dotted with picturesque gardens and one-of-a-kind works of sculpture.

CHASE COLLEGIATE SCHOOL

565 Chase Parkway
Waterbury, Connecticut 06708-3394

Head of School: John D. Fixx

General Information Coeducational day college-preparatory and arts school. Grades PK–12. Founded: 1865. Setting: suburban. 47-acre campus. 8 buildings on campus. Approved or accredited by Connecticut Association of Independent Schools, New England Association of Schools and Colleges, and Connecticut Department of Education. Member of National Association of Independent Schools and Secondary School Admission Test Board. Endowment: $8.3 million. Total enrollment: 514. Upper school average class size: 11. Upper school faculty-student ratio: 1:6.

Upper School Student Profile Grade 9: 52 students (25 boys, 27 girls); Grade 10: 40 students (21 boys, 19 girls); Grade 11: 45 students (19 boys, 26 girls); Grade 12: 53 students (29 boys, 24 girls).

Faculty School total: 67. In upper school: 18 men, 13 women; 25 have advanced degrees.

Subjects Offered 20th century American writers, 20th century history, 3-dimensional art, acting, Advanced Placement courses, African-American literature, algebra, American foreign policy, American government-AP, ancient world history, animation, archaeology, art, art history-AP, astronomy, band, biology, biology-AP, calculus, calculus-AP, ceramics, chamber groups, chemistry, chemistry-AP, China/Japan history, chorus, classical Greek literature, classical language, college writing, computer animation, computer graphics, computer programming, computer science-AP, concert band, concert bell choir, current events, digital photography, directing, drama, drawing, ecology, economics, economics-AP, English, English language-AP, English literature and composition-AP, environmental science, environmental science-AP, ethics, film studies, filmmaking, fine arts, foreign policy, French, French language-AP, French literature-AP, freshman seminar, geometry, Greek, handbells, health and wellness, history of China and Japan, honors algebra, honors geometry, humanities, independent study, introduction to theater, jazz band, jazz ensemble, journalism, Latin, Latin-AP, macro/microeconomics-AP, model United Nations, modern European history, music, music technology, natural history, oceanography, oil painting, photography, physics, physics-AP, play production, playwriting and directing, pre-calculus, public speaking, sculpture, senior project, society and culture, socioeconomic problems, sociology, Spanish, Spanish literature-AP, Spanish-AP, statistics, statistics and probability, technical theater, technology, theater, U.S. history, U.S. history-AP, visual arts, water color painting, Web site design, woodworking, world cultures, world history-AP, yearbook.

Graduation Requirements Arts and fine arts (art, music, dance, drama), athletics, computer literacy, electives, English, ethics, foreign language, history, lab science, mathematics, music appreciation, psychology, public speaking, science, technology, theater arts, senior speech.

Special Academic Programs Advanced Placement exam preparation; honors section; accelerated programs; independent study; study abroad; academic accommodation for the gifted.

College Admission Counseling 42 students graduated in 2008; all went to college, including Brown University; Gettysburg College; Hampshire College; Quinnipiac University; The George Washington University; University of Rochester. Mean SAT critical reading: 582, mean SAT math: 580, mean SAT writing: 589.

Student Life Upper grades have specified standards of dress, student council, honor system. Discipline rests equally with students and faculty.

Summer Programs Enrichment, advancement, sports, art/fine arts, computer instruction programs offered; session focuses on enrichment and advancement; held on campus; accepts boys and girls; open to students from other schools. 500 students usually enrolled. 2009 schedule: June to July. Application deadline: none.

Tuition and Aid Day student tuition: $27,130. Tuition installment plan (Key Tuition Payment Plan, monthly payment plans). Merit scholarship grants, need-based scholarship grants, Founders' Scholarships (entering 9th grade) available. In 2008–09, 40% of upper-school students received aid; total upper-school merit-scholarship money awarded: $394,585. Total amount of financial aid awarded in 2008–09: $2,680,000.

Admissions Traditional secondary-level entrance grade is 9. For fall 2008, 73 students applied for upper-level admission, 60 were accepted, 34 enrolled. SSAT required. Deadline for receipt of application materials: none. Application fee required: $60. On-campus interview required.

Athletics Interscholastic: baseball (boys), basketball (b,g), cross-country running (b,g), lacrosse (b,g), soccer (b,g), softball (g), tennis (b,g), volleyball (g), wrestling (b,g); intramural: strength & conditioning (b,g); coed interscholastic: cross-country running, golf, independent competitive sports, swimming and diving, ultimate Frisbee, wrestling; coed intramural: aerobics/dance, aerobics/Nautilus, crew, dance, fitness, modern dance, outdoor education, skiing (downhill), snowboarding, weight training. 4 PE instructors, 12 coaches, 1 athletic trainer.

Computers Computers are regularly used in art, creative writing, English, foreign language, history, humanities, library, literary magazine, mathematics, music, newspaper, photography, research skills, SAT preparation, science, social science, study skills, technology, yearbook classes. Computer network features include on-campus library services, online commercial services, Internet access, wireless campus network, Internet filtering or blocking technology. Campus intranet, student e-mail accounts, and computer access in designated common areas are available to students. Students grades are available online. The school has a published electronic and media policy.

Contact Margy Foulk, Director of Admission. 203-236-9560. Fax: 203-236-9503. E-mail: mfoulk@chasemail.org. Web site: www.chasemail.org.

CHATHAM ACADEMY

Savannah, Georgia

See Special Needs Schools section.

CHELSEA SCHOOL

Silver Spring, Maryland

See Special Needs Schools section.

CHEROKEE CREEK BOYS SCHOOL

Westminster, South Carolina

See Special Needs Schools section.

CHERRY GULCH

Emmett, Idaho

See Special Needs Schools section.

CHESHIRE ACADEMY

10 Main Street
Cheshire, Connecticut 06410

Head of School: Douglas G. Rogers

General Information Coeducational boarding and day college-preparatory school. Boarding grades 9–PG, day grades 6–PG. Founded: 1794. Setting: small town. Nearest major city is New Haven. Students are housed in single-sex dormitories. 104-acre campus. 22 buildings on campus. Approved or accredited by Connecticut Association of Independent Schools, New England Association of Schools and Colleges, and The Association of Boarding Schools. Member of National Association of Independent Schools and Secondary School Admission Test Board. Endowment: $8 million. Total enrollment: 372. Upper school average class size: 12. Upper school faculty-student ratio: 1:7.

Upper School Student Profile Grade 9: 56 students (42 boys, 14 girls); Grade 10: 96 students (60 boys, 36 girls); Grade 11: 78 students (49 boys, 29 girls); Grade 12: 82 students (50 boys, 32 girls); Postgraduate: 12 students (12 boys). 60% of students

are boarding students. 63% are state residents. 12 states are represented in upper school student body. 30% are international students. International students from China, Japan, Republic of Korea, and Taiwan; 7 other countries represented in student body.
Faculty School total: 86. In upper school: 34 men, 42 women; 50 have advanced degrees; 27 reside on campus.
Subjects Offered Acting, Advanced Placement courses, algebra, American Civil War, American government, American history, American literature, anatomy, art, art history, Asian studies, biology, calculus, ceramics, chemistry, Chinese, community service, computer programming, computer science, creative writing, digital imaging, drama, earth science, ecology, economics, English, English literature, environmental science, ESL, European history, expository writing, fine arts, French, geography, geometry, government/civics, grammar, health, history, Latin American studies, mathematics, music, mythology, photography, physical education, physics, physiology, psychology, reading, science, social science, social studies, Spanish, speech, statistics, theater, Vietnam, world history, world literature, writing.
Graduation Requirements Arts and fine arts (art, music, dance, drama), computer science, electives, English, foreign language, mathematics, science, social science, social studies (includes history), senior speech, 10 hours of community service.
Special Academic Programs Advanced Placement exam preparation; honors section; accelerated programs; independent study; academic accommodation for the musically talented and the artistically talented; remedial reading and/or remedial writing; remedial math; programs in English, mathematics, general development for dyslexic students; ESL (30 students enrolled).
College Admission Counseling 95 students graduated in 2008; all went to college, including Carnegie Mellon University; Clark University; Fordham University; Ohio University; University of Michigan. Mean SAT critical reading: 523, mean SAT math: 618, mean SAT writing: 519, mean combined SAT: 1660, mean composite ACT: 23. 11% scored over 600 on SAT critical reading, 31% scored over 600 on SAT math, 13% scored over 600 on SAT writing, 19% scored over 1800 on combined SAT, 33% scored over 26 on composite ACT.
Student Life Upper grades have specified standards of dress, student council, honor system. Discipline rests primarily with faculty.
Summer Programs Sports programs offered; session focuses on athletics; held on campus; accepts boys and girls; open to students from other schools. 125 students usually enrolled. 2009 schedule: June 30 to August 5. Application deadline: May 31.
Tuition and Aid Day student tuition: $30,345; 7-day tuition and room/board: $41,470. Tuition installment plan (Key Tuition Payment Plan, monthly payment plans). Merit scholarship grants, need-based scholarship grants, need-based loans available. In 2008–09, 30% of upper-school students received aid; total upper-school merit-scholarship money awarded: $120,000. Total amount of financial aid awarded in 2008–09: $2,000,000.
Admissions Traditional secondary-level entrance grade is 9. For fall 2008, 450 students applied for upper-level admission, 225 were accepted, 139 enrolled. ACT, ISEE, PSAT, SAT, SSAT or TOEFL required. Deadline for receipt of application materials: February 1. Application fee required: $50. Interview required.
Athletics Interscholastic: baseball (boys), basketball (b,g), cross-country running (b,g), fencing (b,g), field hockey (g), football (b), golf (b), lacrosse (b,g), soccer (b,g), softball (g), swimming and diving (b,g), tennis (b,g), track and field (b,g), volleyball (g), wrestling (b); coed interscholastic: ultimate Frisbee; coed intramural: fitness, freestyle skiing, physical training, ropes courses, skiing (downhill), snowboarding, weight training. 1 PE instructor, 30 coaches, 1 athletic trainer.
Computers Computers are regularly used in art, foreign language, mathematics, science classes. Computer network features include on-campus library services, online commercial services, Internet access, wireless campus network, Internet filtering or blocking technology. Campus intranet, student e-mail accounts, and computer access in designated common areas are available to students. The school has a published electronic and media policy.
Contact Mona Brietrick, Office Manager. 203-272-5396 Ext. 277. Fax: 203-250-7209. E-mail: mona.brietrick@cheshireacademy.org. Web site: www.cheshireacademy.org.

ANNOUNCEMENT FROM THE SCHOOL Cheshire Academy has distinguished itself through a tradition of nurturing the unique talents, abilities, and interests of each student for more than 200 years. Through academics, arts, athletics, community service, and leadership opportunities, students are encouraged to find their voice, discern their potential, and claim their place in the world. Supported by the school's core values of *community, caring, diversity, respect,* and *intellectual and personal growth,* Cheshire Academy encourages its students to develop a global perspective that will help them become informed and capable leaders in an increasingly demanding world.

See Close-Up on page 710.

CHESTNUT HILL ACADEMY

500 West Willow Grove Avenue
Philadelphia, Pennsylvania 19118
Head of School: Mr. Francis P. Steel Jr.
General Information Boys' day college-preparatory, arts, technology, and Advanced Placement school. Grades PK–12. Founded: 1861. Setting: suburban. 25-acre campus. 6 buildings on campus. Approved or accredited by Middle States Association of Colleges and Schools, Pennsylvania Association of Independent Schools, and Pennsylvania Department of Education. Member of National Association of Independent Schools and Secondary School Admission Test Board. Endowment: $33 million. Total enrollment: 570. Upper school average class size: 16. Upper school faculty-student ratio: 1:7.
Upper School Student Profile Grade 9: 55 students (55 boys); Grade 10: 53 students (53 boys); Grade 11: 56 students (56 boys); Grade 12: 58 students (58 boys).
Faculty School total: 34. In upper school: 23 men, 11 women; 23 have advanced degrees.
Subjects Offered Algebra, American history, American literature, art, art history, biology, calculus, ceramics, chemistry, Chinese, college counseling, computer math, computer programming, computer science, creative writing, drama, earth science, engineering, English, English literature, environmental science, ethics, European history, expository writing, fine arts, French, geology, geometry, government/civics, grammar, health, history, Latin, mathematics, music, photography, physical education, physics, physiology, science, social studies, Spanish, theater, world history.
Graduation Requirements Arts and fine arts (art, music, dance, drama), athletics, computer science, English, foreign language, history, mathematics, music, physical education (includes health), science, speech, senior projects, senior speech. Community service is required.
Special Academic Programs Advanced Placement exam preparation; honors section; independent study; term-away projects; study abroad; academic accommodation for the gifted, the musically talented, and the artistically talented.
College Admission Counseling 48 students graduated in 2007; 47 went to college, including Franklin & Marshall College; Lehigh University; Moravian College; Penn State University Park; Skidmore College; University of Pennsylvania. Other: 1 entered a postgraduate year.
Student Life Upper grades have specified standards of dress, student council. Discipline rests equally with students and faculty.
Tuition and Aid Day student tuition: $20,400. Tuition installment plan (Insured Tuition Payment Plan, Academic Management Services Plan, monthly payment plans, individually arranged payment plans). Need-based scholarship grants, need-based loans available. In 2007–08, 24% of upper-school students received aid. Total amount of financial aid awarded in 2007–08: $1,082,450.
Admissions Traditional secondary-level entrance grade is 9. For fall 2007, 86 students applied for upper-level admission, 27 were accepted, 15 enrolled. ISEE or SSAT required. Deadline for receipt of application materials: none. Application fee required: $40. On-campus interview required.
Athletics Interscholastic: baseball, basketball, crew, cross-country running, football, golf, ice hockey, indoor track & field, lacrosse, soccer, squash, tennis, track and field, winter (indoor) track, wrestling; intramural: lacrosse, strength & conditioning, weight lifting, weight training. 2 PE instructors, 38 coaches, 2 athletic trainers.
Computers Computers are regularly used in all academic classes. Computer network features include on-campus library services, online commercial services, Internet access, wireless campus network, Internet filtering or blocking technology. Campus intranet, student e-mail accounts, and computer access in designated common areas are available to students. The school has a published electronic and media policy.
Contact Vincent Valenzuela, Director of Admissions. 215-247-4700 Ext. 1133. Fax: 215-247-8516. E-mail: vvalenzuela@chestnuthillacademy.org. Web site: www.chestnuthillacademy.org.

ANNOUNCEMENT FROM THE SCHOOL Chestnut Hill Academy (CHA), founded in 1861, is an all boys' school enrolling 558 boys in grades PreK through 12. Bordering on the Valley Green section of Fairmont Park in Philadelphia, CHA is housed in the historic Wissahickon Inn. The campus includes a state-of-the-art science facility and a newly expanded and renovated art department. An athletic complex for more than forty teams comprises squash and tennis courts; gymnasiums; baseball diamonds, football fields, soccer fields, and a new outdoor track. Golf matches are held at the adjacent Philadelphia Cricket Club, the crew team rows on the Schuylkill River. As a boys' school, the Lower School PreK–5 curricula emphasizes educational programs that challenge boys intellectually and excite their curiosity. Boys are also introduced to the core values of CHA: courage, honesty, integrity, loyalty, and sportsmanship. The Middle School gives boys the opportunity to gain confidence and skills oriented toward self-improvement. Active, rigorous learning in specific subject areas is supported in the Middle School by a focus on organizational, study, and collaborative skills. In the Upper School, where the average class size is 15, students have more than 100 course offerings, including college-preparatory, honors, and Advanced Placement options in every discipline. All CHA graduates continue their education in the finest and most selective colleges and universities. A unique aspect of the boys' education is the strategic partnership with Springside School for girls: a gradual introduction to coeducational learning. A field trip or two along with sharing grade-level performances are the foundation in the Lower School. In the Middle School, activities such as community service, drama, orchestra, and dances are coeducational. Finally, in the Upper School, boys have limited coeducational classes in 9th and 10th grades, with all classes fully co-ed integrated in their last two years. It is truly the best of both worlds.

CHEVERUS HIGH SCHOOL

267 Ocean Avenue
Portland, Maine 04103

Head of School: Mr. John H. R. Mullen

General Information Coeducational day college-preparatory, religious studies, technology, Honors, and AP Courses school, affiliated with Roman Catholic Church (Jesuit order). Grades 9–12. Founded: 1917. Setting: suburban. 32-acre campus. 2 buildings on campus. Approved or accredited by Independent Schools of Northern New England, Jesuit Secondary Education Association, New England Association of Schools and Colleges, and Maine Department of Education. Endowment: $3 million. Total enrollment: 544. Upper school average class size: 22. Upper school faculty-student ratio: 1:12.

Upper School Student Profile Grade 9: 148 students (91 boys, 57 girls); Grade 10: 138 students (81 boys, 57 girls); Grade 11: 139 students (68 boys, 71 girls); Grade 12: 119 students (69 boys, 50 girls). 65% of students are Roman Catholic Church (Jesuit order).

Faculty School total: 44. In upper school: 25 men, 19 women; 26 have advanced degrees.

Subjects Offered Advanced Placement courses, algebra, American history, art, biology, calculus, chemistry, college counseling, community service, economics, English, European history, fine arts, French, geography, geometry, government/civics, history, Latin, mathematics, music, physics, religion, science, social studies, Spanish, statistics, trigonometry, world history.

Graduation Requirements Arts and fine arts (art, music, dance, drama), computer science, English, foreign language, health, mathematics, science, social studies (includes history), theology. Community service is required.

Special Academic Programs Advanced Placement exam preparation; honors section; study at local college for college credit; programs in general development for dyslexic students.

College Admission Counseling 138 students graduated in 2008; 128 went to college, including College of the Holy Cross; Saint Anselm College; Saint Joseph's College of Maine; The Catholic University of America; University of Maine; University of Southern Maine. Other: 5 went to work, 3 entered a postgraduate year, 2 had other specific plans. Median SAT critical reading: 553, median SAT math: 570, median SAT writing: 554.

Student Life Upper grades have specified standards of dress, student council, honor system. Discipline rests primarily with faculty. Attendance at religious services is required.

Summer Programs Enrichment programs offered; session focuses on enrichment; held on campus; accepts boys and girls; open to students from other schools.

Tuition and Aid Day student tuition: $12,260. Tuition installment plan (FACTS Tuition Payment Plan, monthly payment plans, individually arranged payment plans). Tuition reduction for siblings, merit scholarship grants, need-based scholarship grants, paying campus jobs available. In 2008–09, 55% of upper-school students received aid; total upper-school merit-scholarship money awarded: $27,060. Total amount of financial aid awarded in 2008–09: $1,549,035.

Admissions Traditional secondary-level entrance grade is 9. For fall 2008, 340 students applied for upper-level admission, 173 were accepted, 151 enrolled. English language and Math Placement Exam required. Deadline for receipt of application materials: none. Application fee required: $50. On-campus interview required.

Athletics Interscholastic: baseball (boys), basketball (b,g), cross-country running (b,g), diving (b,g), field hockey (g), football (b), golf (b,g), ice hockey (b,g), indoor track & field (b,g), lacrosse (b,g), sailing (b,g), skiing (downhill) (b,g), soccer (b,g), softball (g), swimming and diving (b,g), tennis (b,g), track and field (b,g); intramural: basketball (b,g), flagball (b,g); coed interscholastic: alpine skiing, outdoor adventure; coed intramural: alpine skiing, backpacking, basketball, bicycling, flagball, hiking/backpacking, project adventure, volleyball. 82 coaches, 2 athletic trainers.

Computers Computers are regularly used in economics, history, information technology, mathematics, SAT preparation, science, word processing, yearbook classes. Computer network features include on-campus library services, online commercial services, Internet access. The school has a published electronic and media policy.

Contact Mr. Jack Dawson, Director of Admissions. 207-774-6238 Ext. 36. Fax: 207-321-0004. E-mail: dawson@cheverus.org. Web site: www.cheverus.org.

THE CHICAGO ACADEMY FOR THE ARTS

1010 West Chicago Avenue
Chicago, Illinois 60642

Head of School: Ms. Pamela Jordan

General Information Coeducational day college-preparatory and arts school. Grades 9–12. Founded: 1981. Setting: urban. 1-acre campus. 1 building on campus. Approved or accredited by Independent Schools Association of the Central States, North Central Association of Colleges and Schools, and Illinois Department of Education. Member of National Association of Independent Schools. Total enrollment: 164. Upper school average class size: 15. Upper school faculty-student ratio: 1:14.

Faculty School total: 41. In upper school: 24 men, 17 women; 19 have advanced degrees.

Subjects Offered Algebra, American history, anatomy, art history, arts, biology, calculus, chemistry, consumer law, creative writing, dance, drama, English, film, fine arts, French, geometry, historical foundations for arts, humanities, mathematics, music, physics, science, social science, Spanish, speech, theater.

Graduation Requirements Arts and fine arts (art, music, dance, drama), English, foreign language, mathematics, science, social science, U.S. history, requirements vary according to arts discipline.

Special Academic Programs Advanced Placement exam preparation; honors section; academic accommodation for the musically talented and the artistically talented; programs in general development for dyslexic students.

College Admission Counseling 44 students graduated in 2008; all went to college, including Columbia College; New York University; Purchase College, State University of New York; Rhode Island School of Design; School of the Art Institute of Chicago. Median composite ACT: 24.

Student Life Upper grades have student council. Discipline rests equally with students and faculty.

Tuition and Aid Day student tuition: $17,765. Need-based scholarship grants available. In 2008–09, 40% of upper-school students received aid.

Admissions Traditional secondary-level entrance grade is 9. For fall 2008, 120 students applied for upper-level admission, 84 were accepted, 61 enrolled. ISEE required. Deadline for receipt of application materials: January 15. Application fee required: $50. On-campus interview required.

Computers Computers are regularly used in English, historical foundations for arts classes. Computer resources include on-campus library services, online commercial services, Internet access, graphic design and production.

Contact Ms. Kaitlyn Myzwinski, Associate Director of Admissions. 312-421-0202 Ext. 21. Fax: 312-421-3816. E-mail: kmyzwinski@chicagoartsacademy.org. Web site: www.chicagoartsacademy.org.

CHILDREN'S CREATIVE AND PERFORMING ARTS ACADEMY—CAPA DIVISION

3051 El Cajon Blvd.
San Diego, California 92104

Head of School: Janet M. Cherif

General Information Coeducational boarding and day college-preparatory and arts school. Boarding grades 6–12, day grades K–12. Founded: 1981. Setting: urban. Students are housed in homestay families. 1-acre campus. 1 building on campus. Approved or accredited by Accreditation Commission of the Texas Association of Baptist Schools, Western Association of Schools and Colleges, and California Department of Education. Total enrollment: 265. Upper school average class size: 16. Upper school faculty-student ratio: 1:15.

Upper School Student Profile Grade 6: 15 students (8 boys, 7 girls); Grade 7: 15 students (8 boys, 7 girls); Grade 8: 15 students (9 boys, 6 girls); Grade 9: 31 students (11 boys, 20 girls); Grade 10: 28 students (12 boys, 16 girls); Grade 11: 28 students (13 boys, 15 girls); Grade 12: 28 students (15 boys, 13 girls). 15% of students are boarding students. 1 state is represented in upper school student body. 15% are international students. International students from China, Mexico, Republic of Korea, Singapore, Taiwan, and Thailand; 3 other countries represented in student body.

Faculty School total: 30. In upper school: 3 men, 14 women; 10 have advanced degrees.

Subjects Offered Accounting, algebra, American government, anatomy and physiology, art, art history-AP, art-AP, ballet, band, biology, business skills, calculus, ceramics, chamber groups, cheerleading, chemistry, Chinese, choreography, chorus, communications, community service, computer applications, computer literacy, computer programming-AP, concert choir, creative writing, dance performance, digital photography, drama, earth science, ecology, English, English-AP, ensembles, environmental science-AP, European history-AP, film, fitness, French, French language-AP, French literature-AP, geology, geometry, government and politics-AP, health, history-AP, honors world history, humanities, instrumental music, Japanese, jazz band, jazz dance, jazz ensemble, journalism, Latin, library studies, mathematics, mathematics-AP, modern dance, music history, music performance, music theory-AP, performing arts, physical education, physics, political science, portfolio art, pottery, pre-algebra, pre-calculus, psychology, reading/study skills, SAT preparation, science, senior seminar, social science, social studies, Spanish, Spanish language-AP, Spanish literature-AP, speech, statistics, studio art-AP, tap dance, trigonometry, U.S. history, vocal ensemble, vocal jazz, Web site design, Western civilization, writing, writing workshop, yearbook.

Graduation Requirements Arts, business skills (includes word processing), chorus, English, foreign language, mathematics, physical education (includes health), science, social science, visual and performing arts, senior recital or project. Community service is required.

Special Academic Programs 14 Advanced Placement exams for which test preparation is offered; honors section; accelerated programs; independent study; study at local college for college credit; academic accommodation for the gifted, the musically talented, and the artistically talented; remedial reading and/or remedial writing; remedial math; ESL (8 students enrolled).

College Admission Counseling 15 students graduated in 2008; all went to college, including The Boston Conservatory; University of California, Berkeley; University of California, Davis; University of California, San Diego; University of California, Santa

Barbara; University of Cincinnati. Median SAT critical reading: 627, median SAT math: 677, median SAT writing: 590, median combined SAT: 1894. 50% scored over 600 on SAT critical reading, 50% scored over 600 on SAT math, 45% scored over 600 on SAT writing, 45% scored over 1800 on combined SAT.

Student Life Upper grades have uniform requirement, student council, honor system. Discipline rests primarily with faculty.

Summer Programs Remediation, enrichment, advancement, ESL, art/fine arts, computer instruction programs offered; session focuses on advancement & ESL; held on campus; accepts boys and girls; open to students from other schools. 40 students usually enrolled. 2009 schedule: June 15 to August 21. Application deadline: none.

Tuition and Aid Day student tuition: $8500; 7-day tuition and room/board: $15,000. Tuition installment plan (monthly payment plans, individually arranged payment plans). Tuition reduction for siblings, merit scholarship grants, need-based scholarship grants, paying campus jobs available. In 2008–09, 20% of upper-school students received aid; total upper-school merit-scholarship money awarded: $10,000. Total amount of financial aid awarded in 2008–09: $25,000.

Admissions Traditional secondary-level entrance grade is 9. For fall 2008, 20 students applied for upper-level admission, 8 were accepted, 8 enrolled. Admissions testing, any standardized test, audition, math and English placement tests, Math Placement Exam or writing sample required. Deadline for receipt of application materials: none. Application fee required: $50. Interview recommended.

Athletics Interscholastic: artistic gym (girls), baseball (b,g), basketball (b,g), cross-country running (b,g), flag football (b), gymnastics (g), soccer (b,g), softball (g), track and field (b,g), volleyball (b,g); intramural: aerobics/dance (b,g), artistic gym (g), backpacking (b,g), badminton (b,g), ballet (b,g), baseball (b,g), basketball (b,g), bowling (b,g), cheering (g), dance (b,g), dance squad (b,g), dance team (b,g), fitness (b,g), flag football (b,g), gymnastics (b,g), hiking/backpacking (b,g), horseback riding (b,g), modern dance (b,g), outdoor activities (b,g), outdoor education (b,g), physical fitness (b,g), soccer (b,g), softball (b,g), surfing (b,g), swimming and diving (b,g), table tennis (b,g), track and field (b,g), volleyball (b,g); coed intramural: aerobics/dance, backpacking, badminton, ballet, baseball, bowling, dance, dance squad, dance team, fitness, flag football, hiking/backpacking, modern dance, outdoor activities, outdoor education, physical fitness, softball, surfing, swimming and diving, table tennis, track and field. 2 coaches.

Computers Computers are regularly used in architecture, business skills, creative writing, data processing, keyboarding, music, programming, SAT preparation, typing, video film production, Web site design, word processing, yearbook classes. Computer network features include Internet access, College credit classes on line.

Contact Karen Peterson, Admissions Department. 619-584-2454. Fax: 619-584-2422. E-mail: jmcherif@yahoo.com.

CHINESE CHRISTIAN SCHOOLS

750 Fargo Avenue
San Leandro, California 94579

Head of School: Mr. Robin S. Hom

General Information Coeducational day college-preparatory and religious studies school, affiliated with Bible Fellowship Church, Evangelical/Fundamental faith. Grades K–12. Founded: 1979. Setting: suburban. Nearest major city is Oakland. 10-acre campus. 7 buildings on campus. Approved or accredited by Association of Christian Schools International, The Hawaii Council of Private Schools, Western Association of Schools and Colleges, and California Department of Education. Languages of instruction: English and Mandarin. Endowment: $14,000. Total enrollment: 908. Upper school average class size: 20. Upper school faculty-student ratio: 1:12.

Upper School Student Profile Grade 9: 52 students (21 boys, 31 girls); Grade 10: 50 students (29 boys, 21 girls); Grade 11: 62 students (37 boys, 25 girls); Grade 12: 62 students (30 boys, 32 girls). 20% of students are Bible Fellowship Church, Evangelical/Fundamental faith.

Faculty School total: 40. In upper school: 15 men, 20 women; 12 have advanced degrees.

Subjects Offered Advanced computer applications, Advanced Placement courses, aerobics, algebra, American government, American government-AP, American history, American history-AP, American literature, American literature-AP, applied music, art, art-AP, audio visual/media, Basic programming, basketball, Bible, Bible studies, biology, biology-AP, British literature, calculus, calculus-AP, career/college preparation, chemistry, Chinese, Chinese studies, choir, choral music, Christian doctrine, Christian ethics, Christian studies, civics, civics/free enterprise, college counseling, college placement, college planning, communications, community service, comparative religion, computer applications, computer graphics, computer science, computer science-AP, CPR, debate, drama, driver education, economics, economics-AP, electives, English, English language-AP, English literature, English literature-AP, ESL, European history-AP, first aid, foreign language, general science, geometry, government, government and politics-AP, government-AP, graphic arts, honors English, intro to computers, language arts, leadership and service, learning strategies, library assistant, literature and composition-AP, literature-AP, macro/microeconomics-AP, macroeconomics-AP, Mandarin, marching band, marine science, martial arts, mathematics-AP, microeconomics, microeconomics-AP, music, newspaper, participation in sports, physical education, physics, physics-AP, pre-algebra, pre-calculus, probability and statistics, public speaking, religious education, religious studies, ROTC (for boys), SAT preparation, SAT/ACT preparation, science, science research, Spanish, speech, speech and debate, speech communications, sports, state history, statistics, student government, theater, theater arts, trigonometry, U.S. government, U.S. government and politics-AP, U.S. government-AP, U.S. history, U.S. history-AP, visual and performing arts, volleyball, Web authoring, world history, world wide web design, yearbook.

Graduation Requirements Algebra, American government, American history, Bible, Chinese, CPR, driver education, economics, English, first aid, foreign language, geometry, history, lab science, Life of Christ, mathematics, physical education (includes health), physics, pre-algebra, science, visual and performing arts, world history, Mandarin I or Chinese Culture class.

Special Academic Programs 13 Advanced Placement exams for which test preparation is offered; honors section; term-away projects; study at local college for college credit; academic accommodation for the gifted; remedial reading and/or remedial writing; ESL (9 students enrolled).

College Admission Counseling 49 students graduated in 2008; all went to college, including California State University, East Bay; University of California, Berkeley; University of California, Davis; University of California, Irvine; University of California, Los Angeles; University of California, San Diego. Mean SAT critical reading: 588, mean SAT math: 656, mean SAT writing: 583, mean combined SAT: 1827. 51% scored over 600 on SAT critical reading, 78% scored over 600 on SAT math, 49% scored over 600 on SAT writing, 54% scored over 1800 on combined SAT.

Student Life Upper grades have uniform requirement, student council. Discipline rests primarily with faculty. Attendance at religious services is required.

Summer Programs Remediation, enrichment, advancement, ESL, sports programs offered; session focuses on academic enrichment or remediation; held on campus; accepts boys and girls; open to students from other schools. 270 students usually enrolled. 2009 schedule: June 24 to August 24. Application deadline: May 15.

Tuition and Aid Day student tuition: $6075–$8350. Tuition installment plan (monthly payment plans, individually arranged payment plans, eTuition automatic electronic deposit). Tuition reduction for siblings, merit scholarship grants, need-based scholarship grants, paying campus jobs available. In 2008–09, 5% of upper-school students received aid; total upper-school merit-scholarship money awarded: $10,000. Total amount of financial aid awarded in 2008–09: $110,000.

Admissions Traditional secondary-level entrance grade is 9. For fall 2008, 60 students applied for upper-level admission, 57 were accepted, 57 enrolled. Achievement/Aptitude/Writing, admissions testing, California Achievement Test, CTBS (or similar from their school), Math Placement Exam, Stanford Achievement Test or writing sample required. Deadline for receipt of application materials: none. No application fee required. On-campus interview required.

Athletics Interscholastic: basketball (boys, girls), cross-country running (b,g), JROTC drill (b), soccer (b,g), tennis (b,g), track and field (b,g), volleyball (b,g); intramural: drill team (b), outdoor education (b,g), outdoor recreation (b,g); coed interscholastic: cross-country running, swimming and diving; coed intramural: outdoor education, outdoor recreation. 2 PE instructors, 1 coach.

Computers Computers are regularly used in lab/keyboard, library skills, programming, senior seminar, Web site design classes. Computer network features include on-campus library services, Internet access, wireless campus network, Internet filtering or blocking technology. Students grades are available online. The school has a published electronic and media policy.

Contact Mrs. Cindy Loh, Admissions Director. 510-351-4957 Ext. 210. Fax: 510-351-1789. E-mail: CindyLoh@ccs-rams.org. Web site: www.ccs-rams.org.

CHOATE ROSEMARY HALL

333 Christian Street
Wallingford, Connecticut 06492-3800

Head of School: Edward J. Shanahan, PhD

General Information Coeducational boarding and day college-preparatory school. Grades 9–PG. Founded: 1890. Setting: small town. Nearest major city is New Haven. Students are housed in single-sex dormitories. 450-acre campus. 119 buildings on campus. Approved or accredited by Connecticut Association of Independent Schools, New England Association of Schools and Colleges, The Association of Boarding Schools, and Connecticut Department of Education. Member of National Association of Independent Schools and Secondary School Admission Test Board. Endowment: $261 million. Total enrollment: 850. Upper school average class size: 12. Upper school faculty-student ratio: 1:6.

Upper School Student Profile Grade 9: 154 students (74 boys, 80 girls); Grade 10: 230 students (117 boys, 113 girls); Grade 11: 232 students (102 boys, 130 girls); Grade 12: 214 students (112 boys, 102 girls); Postgraduate: 20 students (17 boys, 3 girls). 72% of students are boarding students. 46% are state residents. 41 states are represented in upper school student body. 12% are international students. International students from Canada, China, Hong Kong, Republic of Korea, Singapore, and Thailand; 27 other countries represented in student body.

Faculty School total: 133. In upper school: 66 men, 53 women; 85 have advanced degrees; 108 reside on campus.

Subjects Offered 3-dimensional art, algebra, American history, American literature, anatomy, Arabic, architecture, art, astronomy, biology, British history, calculus, calculus-AP, ceramics, chemistry, chemistry-AP, child development, Chinese, computer math, computer programming, computer science, computer science-AP, creative writing, dance, drama, ecology, economics, electronics, English, English literature, environmental science, environmental science-AP, etymology, European history-AP, expository writing, fine arts, French, French language-AP, French studies, geometry, government and politics-AP, health, history, history-AP, Holocaust, interdisciplinary studies, international studies, Italian, language, Latin, Latin History, Latin-AP, linear algebra, logic, macroeconomics-AP, marine biology, mathematics, microbiology, microeconomics-AP, music, music appreciation, music composition, music history, music performance, music technology, music theater, music theory, music theory-AP, music-AP, musical productions, musical theater, musical theater dance, musicianship, philosophy, photography, physics, physics-AP, physiology, political science, psychology, psychology-AP, public speaking, religion, science, social studies, Spanish, Spanish language-AP, Spanish literature, Spanish literature-AP, Spanish-AP, statistics, statistics and probability, statistics-AP, studio art, theater, trigonometry, U.S. history, U.S. history-AP, visual arts, world history, world literature, writing.

Graduation Requirements Art, English, foreign language, global studies, history, mathematics, philosophy, physical education (includes health), science, 30 hours of community service.

Special Academic Programs Advanced Placement exam preparation; honors section; independent study; term-away projects; study abroad; academic accommodation for the gifted, the musically talented, and the artistically talented.

College Admission Counseling 237 students graduated in 2008; 229 went to college, including Brown University; Dartmouth College; Georgetown University; Princeton University; The George Washington University; Yale University. Other: 8 had other specific plans. Mean SAT critical reading: 664, mean SAT math: 682, mean SAT writing: 674, mean combined SAT: 2020, mean composite ACT: 27.

Student Life Upper grades have specified standards of dress, student council, honor system. Discipline rests primarily with faculty.

Summer Programs Enrichment, advancement, ESL, art/fine arts programs offered; session focuses on academic growth and enrichment; held both on and off campus; held at China, France, and Spain; accepts boys and girls; open to students from other schools. 500 students usually enrolled. 2009 schedule: June 28 to July 31. Application deadline: May 1.

Tuition and Aid Day student tuition: $31,310; 7-day tuition and room/board: $41,520. Tuition installment plan (Insured Tuition Payment Plan, Key Tuition Payment Plan, monthly payment plans). Need-based scholarship grants, need-based loans available. In 2008–09, 33% of upper-school students received aid. Total amount of financial aid awarded in 2008–09: $7,500,000.

Admissions Traditional secondary-level entrance grade is 9. For fall 2008, 1,651 students applied for upper-level admission, 461 were accepted, 279 enrolled. ACT, ISEE, PSAT or SAT for applicants to grade 11 and 12, SSAT or TOEFL required. Deadline for receipt of application materials: January 10. Application fee required: $50. Interview required.

Athletics Interscholastic: baseball (boys), basketball (b,g), crew (b,g), cross-country running (b,g), diving (b,g), field hockey (g), football (b), golf (b,g), ice hockey (b,g), lacrosse (b,g), soccer (b,g), softball (g), squash (b,g), swimming and diving (b,g), tennis (b,g), track and field (b,g), volleyball (b,g), water polo (b,g), wrestling (b); intramural: crew (b,g), squash (b,g); coed interscholastic: archery; coed intramural: aerobics, aerobics/dance, aerobics/Nautilus, ballet, basketball, dance, dance squad, fitness, Frisbee, martial arts, modern dance, Nautilus, outdoor activities, physical fitness, physical training, rock climbing, rowing, running, soccer, softball, strength & conditioning, swimming and diving, tennis, ultimate Frisbee, volleyball, wall climbing, weight lifting, weight training, winter (indoor) track, yoga. 10 coaches, 3 athletic trainers.

Computers Computers are regularly used in all academic, art, college planning, computer applications, desktop publishing, drawing and design, graphic design, information technology, library skills, literary magazine, media production, music, newspaper, photography, programming, stock market, study skills, theater arts, video film production, word processing, yearbook classes. Computer network features include on-campus library services, online commercial services, Internet access, wireless campus network, Internet filtering or blocking technology. Campus intranet, student e-mail accounts, and computer access in designated common areas are available to students. Students grades are available online. The school has a published electronic and media policy.

Contact Raymond M. Diffley III, Director of Admission. 203-697-2239. Fax: 203-697-2629. E-mail: admissions@choate.edu. Web site: www.choate.edu.

ANNOUNCEMENT FROM THE SCHOOL The Science Research Program provides a limited number of motivated students the opportunity to study recently published journal articles, familiarize themselves with research methods through pilot projects, and then spend the summer engaging in cutting-edge research in a university laboratory.

See Close-Up on page 712.

CHRISTCHURCH SCHOOL

49 Seahorse Lane
Christchurch, Virginia 23031

Head of School: Mr. John E. Byers

General Information Boys' boarding and coeducational day college-preparatory, arts, religious studies, technology, Marine and Environmental Sciences, and ESL school, affiliated with Episcopal Church, Roman Catholic Church; primarily serves individuals with Attention Deficit Disorder. Boarding boys grades 8–PG, day boys grades 8–PG, day girls grades 8–PG. Founded: 1921. Setting: rural. Nearest major city is Richmond. Students are housed in single-sex dormitories. 125-acre campus. 13 buildings on campus. Approved or accredited by National Association of Episcopal Schools, The Association of Boarding Schools, The College Board, Virginia Association of Independent Schools, and Virginia Department of Education. Member of National Association of Independent Schools and Secondary School Admission Test Board. Endowment: $2 million. Total enrollment: 212. Upper school average class size: 12. Upper school faculty-student ratio: 1:6.

Upper School Student Profile Grade 8: 8 students (8 boys); Grade 9: 40 students (34 boys, 6 girls); Grade 10: 44 students (38 boys, 6 girls); Grade 11: 66 students (54 boys, 12 girls); Grade 12: 54 students (42 boys, 12 girls). 60% of students are boarding students. 60% are state residents. 14 states are represented in upper school student body. 16% are international students. International students from Bermuda, China, Republic of Korea, and Spain; 4 other countries represented in student body. 38% of students are members of Episcopal Church, Roman Catholic.

Faculty School total: 36. In upper school: 23 men, 13 women; 24 have advanced degrees; 21 reside on campus.

Subjects Offered Adolescent issues, advanced chemistry, advanced math, algebra, American Civil War, American history, American history-AP, American literature, art, art history, biology, British literature-AP, calculus, calculus-AP, chemistry, chemistry-AP, comparative government and politics-AP, comparative political systems-AP, composition-AP, computer graphics, computer multimedia, computer science, conceptual physics, economics, English, English as a foreign language, English language-AP, English literature, English literature-AP, environmental science, environmental science-AP, ESL, ethics, fine arts, French, French-AP, geography, geometry, government and politics-AP, government/civics, health, health and wellness, health education, honors English, honors U.S. history, honors world history, marine biology, Native American history, physical education, physics, pre-calculus, religions, SAT preparation, SAT/ACT preparation, social justice, social studies, Spanish, Spanish-AP, statistics and probability, student government, technology, technology/design, theology, trigonometry, U.S. and Virginia government, U.S. and Virginia government-AP, U.S. and Virginia history, U.S. government and politics-AP, U.S. history-AP, United States government-AP, world history, world history-AP.

Graduation Requirements Arts and fine arts (art, music, dance, drama), English, foreign language, health and wellness, mathematics, physical education (includes health), religion (includes Bible studies and theology), science, social studies (includes history).

Special Academic Programs 11 Advanced Placement exams for which test preparation is offered; honors section; academic accommodation for the gifted; ESL (18 students enrolled).

College Admission Counseling 49 students graduated in 2008; all went to college, including East Carolina University; Hampden-Sydney College; James Madison University; Syracuse University; University of Mary Washington; Virginia Polytechnic Institute and State University. Mean SAT critical reading: 521, mean SAT math: 554, mean SAT writing: 516, mean combined SAT: 1591. 25% scored over 600 on SAT critical reading, 25% scored over 600 on SAT math.

Student Life Upper grades have specified standards of dress, student council, honor system. Discipline rests equally with students and faculty. Attendance at religious services is required.

Summer Programs Enrichment, sports programs offered; session focuses on marine and environmental science, sailing, crew, camping, fishing; held on campus; accepts boys and girls; open to students from other schools. 75 students usually enrolled. 2009 schedule: June 21 to July 25. Application deadline: none.

Tuition and Aid Day student tuition: $15,750; 7-day tuition and room/board: $37,250. Tuition installment plan (monthly payment plans, individually arranged payment plans, 10 month plan, 1st payment due 6/15, 4-payment plan, 1st payment due 6/16, 2-payment plan, 1st payment due 6/15). Merit scholarship grants, need-based scholarship grants available. In 2008–09, 34% of upper-school students received aid. Total amount of financial aid awarded in 2008–09: $1,242,400.

Admissions Traditional secondary-level entrance grade is 9. For fall 2008, 206 students applied for upper-level admission, 116 were accepted, 82 enrolled. PSAT or SAT, SSAT or TOEFL required. Deadline for receipt of application materials: none. Application fee required: $50. On-campus interview required.

Athletics Interscholastic: baseball (boys), basketball (b,g), crew (b,g), cross-country running (b,g), field hockey (g), football (b), golf (b), lacrosse (b), sailing (b,g), soccer (b,g), volleyball (g); intramural: basketball (b), weight training (b,g); coed interscholastic: cross-country running, golf, sailing; coed intramural: canoeing/kayaking, fishing, fitness, fly fishing, Frisbee, hiking/backpacking, indoor soccer, kayaking, outdoor education, physical training, sailing, snowboarding, soccer, strength & conditioning, tennis, winter soccer, yoga. 1 athletic trainer.

Computers Computers are regularly used in all academic classes. Computer network features include on-campus library services, online commercial services, Internet access, wireless campus network, Internet filtering or blocking technology. Campus intranet, student e-mail accounts, and computer access in designated common areas are available to students. Students grades are available online. The school has a published electronic and media policy.

Contact Ms. Nancy M. Nolan, Assistant Head for Admission and Marketing. 804-758-2306. Fax: 804-758-0721. E-mail: admission@christchurchschool.org. Web site: www.christchurchschool.org.

CHRISTIAN BROTHERS ACADEMY

850 Newman Springs Road
Lincroft, New Jersey 07738

Head of School: Br. James Butler, FSC

General Information Boys' day college-preparatory school, affiliated with Roman Catholic Church. Grades 9–12. Founded: 1959. Setting: suburban. Nearest major city is New York, NY. 157-acre campus. 3 buildings on campus. Approved or accredited by Middle States Association of Colleges and Schools. Endowment: $10.5 million. Total enrollment: 935. Upper school average class size: 18. Upper school faculty-student ratio: 1:14.

Upper School Student Profile Grade 9: 268 students (268 boys); Grade 10: 236 students (236 boys); Grade 11: 234 students (234 boys); Grade 12: 218 students (218 boys). 80% of students are Roman Catholic.

Faculty School total: 63. In upper school: 42 men, 17 women; 48 have advanced degrees.

Subjects Offered Algebra, American government, American history, anatomy and physiology, Bible studies, biology, business, business skills, calculus, chemistry, computer science, creative writing, driver education, economics, English, environmental science, European history, French, geometry, health, history, journalism, Latin, mathematics, physical education, physics, psychology, religion, science, social science, social studies, Spanish, theology, trigonometry, world history, world literature, writing.

Graduation Requirements Business skills (includes word processing), computer science, English, foreign language, mathematics, physical education (includes health), religion (includes Bible studies and theology), science, social science, social studies (includes history).

Special Academic Programs Advanced Placement exam preparation; honors section.

College Admission Counseling 209 students graduated in 2008; all went to college, including Fairfield University; La Salle University; Loyola College in Maryland; Providence College; Saint Joseph's University; Villanova University. Median SAT critical reading: 600, median SAT math: 610, median SAT writing: 610, median combined SAT: 1820.

Student Life Upper grades have specified standards of dress, student council. Discipline rests primarily with faculty. Attendance at religious services is required.

Tuition and Aid Day student tuition: $11,650. Tuition installment plan (Academic Management Services Plan, individually arranged payment plans). Merit scholarship grants, need-based scholarship grants available. In 2008–09, 10% of upper-school students received aid; total upper-school merit-scholarship money awarded: $123,200. Total amount of financial aid awarded in 2008–09: $770,650.

Admissions For fall 2008, 465 students applied for upper-level admission, 353 were accepted, 297 enrolled. School's own test required. Deadline for receipt of application materials: none. Application fee required: $75.

Athletics Interscholastic: baseball, basketball, bowling, cross-country running, golf, ice hockey, lacrosse, soccer, swimming and diving, tennis, track and field, winter (indoor) track, wrestling; intramural: baseball, basketball, bowling, Frisbee, soccer, tennis, volleyball. 3 PE instructors, 21 coaches, 1 athletic trainer.

Computers Computers are regularly used in mathematics, science classes. Computer network features include on-campus library services, Internet access.

Contact Br. James Butler, FSC, Principal. 732-747-1959 Ext. 100. Fax: 732-747-1643. Web site: www.cbalincroftnj.org.

CHRISTIAN BROTHERS ACADEMY

12 Airline Drive
Albany, New York 12205

Head of School: Mr. James P. Schlegel

General Information Boys' day college-preparatory, business, religious studies, Junior ROTC, and military school, affiliated with Roman Catholic Church. Grades 6–12. Founded: 1859. Setting: suburban. 120-acre campus. 1 building on campus. Approved or accredited by Middle States Association of Colleges and Schools and New York Department of Education. Endowment: $2.8 million. Total enrollment: 407. Upper school average class size: 18. Upper school faculty-student ratio: 1:13.

Upper School Student Profile Grade 9: 88 students (88 boys); Grade 10: 81 students (81 boys); Grade 11: 67 students (67 boys); Grade 12: 68 students (68 boys). 73% of students are Roman Catholic.

Faculty School total: 36. In upper school: 28 men, 6 women; 15 have advanced degrees.

Subjects Offered Accounting, advanced computer applications, algebra, American government, art, astronomy, band, biology, biology-AP, business law, calculus-AP, chemistry, chemistry-AP, computer technologies, creative writing, driver education, earth science, economics, English, English-AP, European history-AP, geology, geometry, global studies, health, life science, math analysis, mathematics, mechanical drawing, military science, music, physical education, physical science, physics, physics-AP, religion, science, sociology, Spanish, U.S. history, U.S. history-AP, Web site design.

Graduation Requirements Arts and fine arts (art, music, dance, drama), English, foreign language, health education, lab science, mathematics, military science, physical education (includes health), religion (includes Bible studies and theology), social studies (includes history), a service requirement.

Special Academic Programs 7 Advanced Placement exams for which test preparation is offered; honors section.

College Admission Counseling 104 students graduated in 2008; 102 went to college, including Clarkson University; Siena College; State University of New York at Binghamton; University at Albany, State University of New York. Other: 1 entered military service, 1 entered a postgraduate year. Mean SAT critical reading: 518, mean SAT math: 523, mean SAT writing: 508.

Student Life Upper grades have uniform requirement, student council, honor system. Discipline rests primarily with faculty. Attendance at religious services is required.

Summer Programs Sports programs offered; session focuses on youth basketball, youth lacrosse; held on campus; accepts boys; open to students from other schools. 50 students usually enrolled. 2009 schedule: July 6 to July 24.

Tuition and Aid Day student tuition: $10,200. Tuition installment plan (monthly payment plans, 3-payment plan). Merit scholarship grants, need-based scholarship grants available. In 2008–09, 52% of upper-school students received aid; total upper-school merit-scholarship money awarded: $426,900. Total amount of financial aid awarded in 2008–09: $483,070.

Admissions Traditional secondary-level entrance grade is 9. For fall 2008, 86 students applied for upper-level admission, 69 were accepted, 49 enrolled. Iowa Test of Educational Development required. Deadline for receipt of application materials: none. Application fee required: $200. Interview recommended.

Athletics Interscholastic: baseball, basketball, bowling, crew, cross-country running, football, golf, ice hockey, indoor track, indoor track & field, JROTC drill, lacrosse, marksmanship, riflery, skiing (downhill), soccer, tennis, track and field, wrestling; intramural: hiking/backpacking, outdoor activities, outdoor adventure, outdoor education, skiing (downhill), speleology, weight lifting. 3 PE instructors, 17 coaches, 1 athletic trainer.

Computers Computers are regularly used in all academic, career exploration, college planning, JROTC, keyboarding, Web site design, yearbook classes. Computer network features include on-campus library services, Internet access, wireless campus network, Internet filtering or blocking technology.

Contact Mr. Michael LaRose, AIA, Director of Admissions. 518-452-9809 Ext. 170. Fax: 518-452-9804. E-mail: laRose@cbaalbany.org. Web site: www.cbaalbany.org.

CHRISTIAN BROTHERS ACADEMY

6245 Randall Road
Syracuse, New York 13214

Head of School: Br. Thomas Zoppo, FSC

General Information Coeducational day college-preparatory and religious studies school, affiliated with Roman Catholic Church. Grades 7–12. Founded: 1900. Setting: suburban. 40-acre campus. 1 building on campus. Approved or accredited by Christian Brothers Association, Middle States Association of Colleges and Schools, and New York State Board of Regents. Endowment: $800,000. Total enrollment: 750. Upper school average class size: 25.

Upper School Student Profile 85% of students are Roman Catholic.

Faculty School total: 62. In upper school: 32 men, 30 women; 58 have advanced degrees.

Subjects Offered Advanced Placement courses, American history, American literature, art, biology, business, calculus, chemistry, chemistry-AP, earth science, economics, English, English literature, European history, expository writing, fine arts, French, government/civics, grammar, health, history, mathematics, music, physical education, physics, pre-calculus, psychology, religion, science, social science, social studies, Spanish, theology, world history, world literature.

Graduation Requirements Arts and fine arts (art, music, dance, drama), English, foreign language, mathematics, physical education (includes health), religion (includes Bible studies and theology), science, social science, social studies (includes history), community service for seniors.

Special Academic Programs Advanced Placement exam preparation; honors section.

College Admission Counseling 113 students graduated in 2008; all went to college, including Le Moyne College; Loyola College in Maryland; New York University; Saint Joseph's University; Syracuse University. Mean SAT critical reading: 579, mean SAT math: 581, mean composite ACT: 26.

Student Life Upper grades have specified standards of dress, student council. Discipline rests primarily with faculty. Attendance at religious services is required.

Tuition and Aid Day student tuition: $8000. Tuition installment plan (SMART Tuition Payment Plan, individually arranged payment plans). Merit scholarship grants, need-based scholarship grants available. In 2008–09, 95% of upper-school students received aid; total upper-school merit-scholarship money awarded: $650,000.

Admissions Traditional secondary-level entrance grade is 9. For fall 2008, 50 students applied for upper-level admission, 38 were accepted, 38 enrolled. Admissions testing required. Deadline for receipt of application materials: February 1. Application fee required: $40. Interview recommended.

Athletics Interscholastic: baseball (boys), basketball (b,g), cheering (g), cross-country running (b,g), diving (b,g), football (b), golf (b,g), gymnastics (b), ice hockey (b), lacrosse (b,g), soccer (b,g), softball (g), swimming and diving (b,g), tennis (b,g), track and field (b,g), volleyball (g); coed interscholastic: bowling. 3 PE instructors, 1 athletic trainer.

Computers Computer network features include on-campus library services, Internet access, Internet filtering or blocking technology. Students grades are available online. The school has a published electronic and media policy.

Contact Mr. Mark Person, Assistant Principal for Student Affairs. 315-446-5960 Ext. 1227. Fax: 315-446-3393. E-mail: mperson@cbasyracuse.org.

CHRISTIAN CENTRAL ACADEMY

39 Academy Street
Williamsville, New York 14221

Head of School: Nurline Lawrence

General Information Coeducational day college-preparatory, arts, and religious studies school, affiliated with Christian faith. Grades K–12. Founded: 1949. Setting: suburban. Nearest major city is Buffalo. 5-acre campus. 4 buildings on campus. Approved or accredited by Association of Christian Schools International and New York State Board of Regents. Endowment: $55,000. Total enrollment: 436. Upper school average class size: 20. Upper school faculty-student ratio: 1:6.

Upper School Student Profile Grade 9: 41 students (23 boys, 18 girls); Grade 10: 32 students (15 boys, 17 girls); Grade 11: 28 students (14 boys, 14 girls); Grade 12: 29 students (12 boys, 17 girls). 100% of students are Christian faith.

Faculty School total: 39. In upper school: 6 men, 15 women; 9 have advanced degrees.

Subjects Offered Advanced computer applications, advertising design, algebra, art, band, Bible, biology, calculus-AP, career/college preparation, chemistry, chorus, communications, computer skills, drawing, driver education, earth science, economics, English, English-AP, geometry, global studies, government, health, honors English, independent study, journalism, Latin, mathematics, music, music theory, orchestra, painting, physical education, physics, physics-AP, pre-calculus, Spanish, studio art, trigonometry, U.S. history, U.S. history-AP, yearbook.

Graduation Requirements Algebra, American government, American history, American literature, arts and fine arts (art, music, dance, drama), Bible, biology, chemistry, computer keyboarding, earth science, economics, English, geometry, global studies, physical education (includes health), physics, pre-calculus, Spanish, trigonometry, writing, Community service hours for all four years. Completion of standardized NYS Regents exams. Honors and High Honors diplomas have more rigorous req.

Special Academic Programs 4 Advanced Placement exams for which test preparation is offered; honors section; independent study.

College Admission Counseling 24 students graduated in 2008; all went to college, including Buffalo State College, State University of New York; Houghton College; University at Buffalo, the State University of New York; University of Notre Dame. Median SAT critical reading: 557, median SAT math: 533, median SAT writing: 545, median combined SAT: 1633. 25% scored over 600 on SAT critical reading, 30% scored over 600 on SAT math, 32% scored over 600 on SAT writing, 32% scored over 1800 on combined SAT.

Student Life Upper grades have specified standards of dress, student council, honor system. Discipline rests primarily with faculty. Attendance at religious services is required.

Summer Programs Sports programs offered; session focuses on basketball camp, soccer camp; held on campus; accepts boys and girls; open to students from other schools. 45 students usually enrolled. 2009 schedule: July to July.

Tuition and Aid Day student tuition: $6613. Tuition installment plan (FACTS Tuition Payment Plan, monthly payment plans, prepayment discount plans, multiple-student discounts, pastors/full-time Christian service discounts). Tuition reduction for siblings, merit scholarship grants, need-based scholarship grants available. In 2008–09, 29% of upper-school students received aid; total upper-school merit-scholarship money awarded: $7250. Total amount of financial aid awarded in 2008–09: $62,500.

Admissions Traditional secondary-level entrance grade is 9. For fall 2008, 21 students applied for upper-level admission, 17 were accepted, 16 enrolled. Admissions testing, Brigance Test of Basic Skills, essay, Iowa Subtests, school's own test or writing sample required. Deadline for receipt of application materials: none. Application fee required: $50. Interview recommended.

Athletics Interscholastic: baseball (boys), basketball (b,g), cross-country running (b,g), soccer (b,g), softball (g); intramural: basketball (b,g), cheering (g), soccer (b,g); coed interscholastic: soccer; coed intramural: basketball, skiing (downhill), snowboarding, volleyball. 2 PE instructors, 10 coaches.

Computers Computers are regularly used in college planning, computer applications, desktop publishing, drawing and design, English, journalism, yearbook classes. Computer resources include on-campus library services, Internet access, Internet filtering or blocking technology, Teacher-guided use of programs in various subject areas.

Contact Deborah L. White, Director of Admissions and Public Relations. 716-634-4821 Ext. 107. Fax: 716-634-5851. E-mail: ccaadmissions@roadrunner.com. Web site: www.christianca.com.

CHRISTIAN HERITAGE SCHOOL

575 White Plains Road
Trumbull, Connecticut 06611-4898

Head of School: Barry Giller

General Information Coeducational day college-preparatory, religious studies, and technology school. Grades K–12. Founded: 1977. Setting: suburban. Nearest major city is Bridgeport. 5-acre campus. 3 buildings on campus. Approved or accredited by Association of Christian Schools International, New England Association of Schools and Colleges, The College Board, and Connecticut Department of Education. Member of European Council of International Schools. Endowment: $470,000. Total enrollment: 527. Upper school average class size: 19. Upper school faculty-student ratio: 1:9.

Upper School Student Profile Grade 9: 40 students (19 boys, 21 girls); Grade 10: 47 students (23 boys, 24 girls); Grade 11: 35 students (19 boys, 16 girls); Grade 12: 44 students (28 boys, 16 girls).

Faculty School total: 57. In upper school: 18 men, 13 women; 16 have advanced degrees.

Subjects Offered 20th century American writers, 20th century history, 20th century physics, 20th century world history, advanced chemistry, advanced math, Advanced Placement courses, algebra, American democracy, American foreign policy, American government, American history, American history-AP, American literature, applied music, art, athletics, band, Basic programming, Bible, Bible studies, biology, biology-AP, British literature, business, calculus, calculus-AP, career and personal planning, career exploration, career/college preparation, chamber groups, chemistry, choir, choral music, chorus, Christian and Hebrew scripture, Christian doctrine, Christian education, Christian ethics, Christian scripture, Christian studies, Christian testament, Christianity, church history, classical Greek literature, classics, college admission preparation, college awareness, college counseling, college placement, college planning, college writing, communication skills, comparative government and politics, computer education, computer keyboarding, computer processing, computer programming, computer programming-AP, computer science, computer skills, computer technologies, concert band, concert choir, constitutional history of U.S., consumer mathematics, contemporary history, contemporary issues, contemporary issues in science, creative arts, current events, current history, data processing, desktop publishing, drama performance, drawing, earth science, English, English composition, English language-AP, English literature, English literature-AP, ensembles, ethics, ethics and responsibility, expository writing, French, functions, general science, geography, geometry, government/civics, grammar, health and wellness, health education, history, history-AP, honors algebra, honors English, honors geometry, honors U.S. history, human anatomy, human biology, inorganic chemistry, instrumental music, instruments, intro to computers, journalism, language and composition, life issues, Life of Christ, life science, literature, mathematics, mathematics-AP, moral and social development, moral reasoning, moral theology, music, music theory, musical productions, newspaper, novels, oral communications, painting, philosophy, physical education, physical science, physics, poetry, prayer/spirituality, pre-algebra, pre-calculus, public speaking, publications, reading/study skills, religion, religious education, science, science project, Shakespeare, social studies, Spanish, Spanish-AP, speech, statistics, student government, student publications, U.S. government, U.S. history-AP, vocal ensemble, vocal music, volleyball, work experience, world affairs, world history, writing, yearbook.

Graduation Requirements Electives, English, foreign language, mathematics, physical education (includes health), religion (includes Bible studies and theology), science, social studies (includes history).

Special Academic Programs Advanced Placement exam preparation; honors section; independent study.

College Admission Counseling 44 students graduated in 2008; all went to college, including Eastern University; LeTourneau University; University of Connecticut; Wheaton College. Median SAT critical reading: 579, median SAT math: 597, median SAT writing: 538, median combined SAT: 1695, median composite ACT: 25. 9% scored over 600 on SAT critical reading, 9% scored over 600 on SAT math, 8% scored over 600 on SAT writing, 10% scored over 1800 on combined SAT.

Student Life Upper grades have specified standards of dress, student council. Discipline rests primarily with faculty. Attendance at religious services is required.

Tuition and Aid Day student tuition: $9500–$13,500. Tuition installment plan (monthly payment plans, individually arranged payment plans, Tuition Management Systems). Need-based scholarship grants available. In 2008–09, 46% of upper-school students received aid. Total amount of financial aid awarded in 2008–09: $500,000.

Admissions Traditional secondary-level entrance grade is 9. For fall 2008, 28 students applied for upper-level admission, 12 were accepted, 12 enrolled. Admissions testing, Otis-Lennon School Ability Test and Stanford Achievement Test required. Deadline for receipt of application materials: none. Application fee required: $50. On-campus interview required.

Athletics Interscholastic: baseball (boys), basketball (b,g), soccer (b,g), tennis (b,g), volleyball (g); intramural: baseball (b), soccer (b,g), softball (g), weight lifting (b), weight training (b); coed interscholastic: cross-country running, golf; coed intramural: basketball, Frisbee. 4 PE instructors, 31 coaches.

Computers Computers are regularly used in business education, college planning, data processing, desktop publishing, journalism, keyboarding, mathematics, newspaper, programming, word processing, yearbook classes. Computer network features include on-campus library services, online commercial services, Internet access,

Internet filtering or blocking technology. Campus intranet and student e-mail accounts are available to students. Students grades are available online. The school has a published electronic and media policy.
Contact Mrs. Martha Olson, Director of Admissions. 203-261-6230 Ext. 555. Fax: 203-452-1531. E-mail: molson@kingsmen.org. Web site: www.kingsmen.org.

CHRISTIAN HOME AND BIBLE SCHOOL

301 West 13th Avenue
Mount Dora, Florida 32757
Head of School: Patrick Todd

General Information Coeducational day college-preparatory, general academic, arts, religious studies, and technology school, affiliated with Church of Christ. Grades K–12. Founded: 1945. Setting: small town. Nearest major city is Orlando. 70-acre campus. 9 buildings on campus. Approved or accredited by National Christian School Association, Southern Association of Colleges and Schools, and Florida Department of Education. Total enrollment: 601. Upper school average class size: 21. Upper school faculty-student ratio: 1:15.
Upper School Student Profile Grade 9: 55 students (32 boys, 23 girls); Grade 10: 62 students (36 boys, 26 girls); Grade 11: 48 students (24 boys, 24 girls); Grade 12: 51 students (26 boys, 25 girls). 25% of students are members of Church of Christ.
Faculty School total: 46. In upper school: 12 men, 12 women; 7 have advanced degrees.
Subjects Offered Algebra, American government, American history, anatomy and physiology, art, band, Bible, biology, calculus-AP, ceramics, chemistry, computer applications, computer skills, consumer mathematics, drama, drawing, economics, English, English literature-AP, European history, geography, geometry, government, health, honors algebra, honors English, honors geometry, honors world history, intro to computers, jazz band, journalism, life management skills, life skills, math applications, Microsoft, painting, personal fitness, photography, physical education, physical science, physics, pre-algebra, pre-calculus, psychology, sculpture, Spanish, state history, student publications, technology/design, television, theater, theater production, trigonometry, video communication, video film production, visual and performing arts, Web site design, weight training, word processing, world history.
Graduation Requirements Advanced math, algebra, American government, American history, arts and fine arts (art, music, dance, drama), Bible, economics, electives, English, foreign language, keyboarding/computer, lab science, life skills, physical education (includes health), physical science, world history, 80 Hours Community Service.
Special Academic Programs Advanced Placement exam preparation; honors section; independent study; study at local college for college credit.
College Admission Counseling 44 students graduated in 2008; all went to college, including Florida State University; Harding University; Sewanee: The University of the South; University of Central Florida; University of Florida; University of South Florida. Median SAT critical reading: 485, median SAT math: 480, median SAT writing: 470, median combined SAT: 1535, median composite ACT: 21. 25% scored over 600 on SAT critical reading, 8% scored over 600 on SAT math, 22% scored over 600 on SAT writing, 25% scored over 1800 on combined SAT, 18% scored over 26 on composite ACT.
Student Life Upper grades have specified standards of dress, student council. Discipline rests primarily with faculty. Attendance at religious services is required.
Tuition and Aid Day student tuition: $7092. Tuition installment plan (monthly payment plans). Tuition reduction for siblings, need-based scholarship grants, discount for members of the Churches of Christ available. In 2008–09, 10% of upper-school students received aid. Total amount of financial aid awarded in 2008–09: $40,000.
Admissions Traditional secondary-level entrance grade is 9. For fall 2008, 59 students applied for upper-level admission, 55 were accepted, 55 enrolled. Any standardized test required. Deadline for receipt of application materials: none. Application fee required: $100. On-campus interview required.
Athletics Interscholastic: baseball (boys), basketball (b,g), bowling (b,g), cheering (g), cross-country running (b,g), football (b), golf (b,g), softball (g), tennis (b,g), track and field (b,g), volleyball (g); coed interscholastic: soccer. 3 PE instructors.
Computers Computers are regularly used in independent study, journalism, library, mathematics, publications, reading, video film production, Web site design, yearbook classes. Computer network features include on-campus library services, Internet access, wireless campus network, Internet filtering or blocking technology, Net Classroom-communication for students and parents, Desk Top Monitoring and manage software, Accelerated Reader Access. Computer access in designated common areas is available to students. Students grades are available online. The school has a published electronic and media policy.
Contact Natalie Yawn, Admissions Director. 352-383-2155 Ext. 261. Fax: 352-383-0098. E-mail: natalie.yawn@chbs.org. Web site: www.chbs.org.

CHRISTIAN JUNIOR–SENIOR HIGH SCHOOL

2100 Greenfield Drive
El Cajon, California 92019
Head of School: Mr. Scottt Meadows

General Information Coeducational day college-preparatory, arts, religious studies, and ESL school, affiliated with Protestant Church. Grades 7–12. Founded: 1965. Setting: suburban. Nearest major city is San Diego. 13-acre campus. 10 buildings on campus. Approved or accredited by Association of Christian Schools International and Western Association of Schools and Colleges. Total enrollment: 634. Upper school average class size: 21. Upper school faculty-student ratio: 1:14.
Upper School Student Profile Grade 9: 121 students (66 boys, 55 girls); Grade 10: 111 students (53 boys, 58 girls); Grade 11: 118 students (64 boys, 54 girls); Grade 12: 101 students (55 boys, 46 girls). 80% of students are Protestant.
Faculty School total: 48. In upper school: 20 men, 23 women; 23 have advanced degrees.
Subjects Offered Advanced chemistry, Advanced Placement courses, algebra, American literature, anatomy and physiology, art, ASB Leadership, Bible studies, biology, British literature-AP, calculus, calculus-AP, ceramics, chemistry, chemistry-AP, comparative religion, computer applications, computer keyboarding, computer literacy, concert band, concert choir, drama, drama performance, economics, economics and history, English, English literature and composition-AP, English literature-AP, ensembles, ESL, film, food and nutrition, geometry, government, government and politics-AP, health, health education, home economics, honors algebra, honors English, honors geometry, interior design, journalism, leadership and service, library assistant, library science, Life of Christ, marching band, music, music theory, newspaper, physical education, physics, physics-AP, pre-algebra, pre-calculus, sewing, softball, Spanish, Spanish-AP, speech, speech and debate, sports conditioning, statistics, statistics and probability, swimming, symphonic band, theater arts, U.S. government, U.S. history, U.S. history-AP, visual and performing arts, visual arts, vocal ensemble, vocal music, volleyball, world history, world literature, yearbook.
Graduation Requirements Arts and fine arts (art, music, dance, drama), English, foreign language, health education, keyboarding/computer, mathematics, physical education (includes health), religion (includes Bible studies and theology), science, social studies (includes history), typing.
Special Academic Programs Advanced Placement exam preparation; honors section; ESL (102 students enrolled).
College Admission Counseling 95 students graduated in 2008; 94 went to college, including Azusa Pacific University; Point Loma Nazarene University; San Diego State University; University of California, Riverside; University of California, San Diego; Westmont College. Other: 1 went to work. Mean SAT critical reading: 528, mean SAT math: 548, mean SAT writing: 517, mean composite ACT: 23.
Student Life Upper grades have uniform requirement. Discipline rests primarily with faculty. Attendance at religious services is required.
Summer Programs Remediation, advancement programs offered; session focuses on academics (social science, foreign language); held on campus; accepts boys and girls; open to students from other schools. 40 students usually enrolled. 2009 schedule: June 18 to July 30. Application deadline: April 27.
Tuition and Aid Day student tuition: $13,000. Tuition installment plan (monthly payment plans). Tuition reduction for siblings, need-based scholarship grants available. In 2008–09, 20% of upper-school students received aid. Total amount of financial aid awarded in 2008–09: $400,000.
Admissions For fall 2008, 103 students applied for upper-level admission, 72 were accepted, 70 enrolled. Any standardized test, ESL, SCAT, Stanford Achievement Test or writing sample required. Deadline for receipt of application materials: none. Application fee required: $125. On-campus interview required.
Athletics Interscholastic: baseball (boys), basketball (b,g), cheering (g), football (b), golf (b,g), gymnastics (g), soccer (b,g), softball (g), tennis (b,g), volleyball (b,g); coed interscholastic: cross-country running, swimming and diving, track and field. 4 PE instructors, 45 coaches, 1 athletic trainer.
Computers Computers are regularly used in ESL, keyboarding, library science, mathematics, media production, newspaper, reading, research skills, science, social sciences, yearbook classes. Computer network features include on-campus library services, online commercial services, Internet access, Internet filtering or blocking technology, Blackboard, RenWeb. Students grades are available online.
Contact Karen Andrews, ESL Administrator. 619-440-1531. Fax: 619-590-1717. E-mail: karen.andrews@cussd.org. Web site: www.cussd.org.

CHRISTIAN SCHOOL OF THE DESERT

40-700 Yucca Lane
Bermuda Dunes, California 92203
Head of School: Mr. David E. Fulton

General Information Coeducational day college-preparatory, general academic, religious studies, and technology school. Grades K–12. Founded: 1976. Setting: rural. Nearest major city is La Quinta. 15-acre campus. 4 buildings on campus. Approved or accredited by Association of Christian Schools International, Western Association of Schools and Colleges, and California Department of Education. Total enrollment: 362. Upper school average class size: 18. Upper school faculty-student ratio: 1:18.
Upper School Student Profile Grade 9: 21 students (11 boys, 10 girls); Grade 10: 17 students (9 boys, 8 girls); Grade 11: 20 students (9 boys, 11 girls); Grade 12: 37 students (19 boys, 18 girls).
Faculty School total: 32. In upper school: 9 men, 5 women; 5 have advanced degrees.
Subjects Offered Algebra, American literature, art, art appreciation, Bible studies, biology, biology-AP, chemistry, computer science, creative writing, drama, English, English literature, English-AP, geography, geometry, health, history, history-AP,

journalism, keyboarding, mathematics, physical education, physical science, pre-calculus, reading, religion, science, social studies, Spanish, speech, values and decisions, yearbook.
Graduation Requirements Arts and fine arts (art, music, dance, drama), computer science, English, foreign language, mathematics, physical education (includes health), religion (includes Bible studies and theology), science, social science, social studies (includes history). Community service is required.
Special Academic Programs Advanced Placement exam preparation; honors section.
College Admission Counseling Colleges students went to include Azusa Pacific University; Biola University; California State University, Los Angeles; College of the Desert; University of California, San Diego.
Student Life Upper grades have specified standards of dress, student council, honor system. Discipline rests primarily with faculty. Attendance at religious services is required.
Tuition and Aid Tuition installment plan (FACTS Tuition Payment Plan). Tuition reduction for siblings, need-based scholarship grants available.
Admissions Traditional secondary-level entrance grade is 9. Scholastic Achievement Test required. Deadline for receipt of application materials: none. Application fee required: $225. Interview required.
Athletics Interscholastic: baseball (boys), basketball (b,g), cheering (g), cross-country running (b,g), football (b), golf (b,g), soccer (b,g), softball (g), walking (g); coed intramural: basketball. 3 PE instructors, 1 athletic trainer.
Computers Computers are regularly used in graphic design classes. Computer resources include Internet access. Computer access in designated common areas is available to students.
Contact Julie A Fulton, Office Manager. 760-345-2848 Ext. 203. Fax: 760-345-2848. E-mail: jfulton@csod.org. Web site: www.csod.org.

CHRISTOPHER DOCK MENNONITE HIGH SCHOOL

1000 Forty Foot Road
Lansdale, Pennsylvania 19446

Head of School: Elaine A. Moyer

General Information Coeducational day college-preparatory, general academic, arts, vocational, religious studies, and technology school, affiliated with Mennonite Church. Grades 9–12. Founded: 1954. Setting: suburban. Nearest major city is Philadelphia. 75-acre campus. 5 buildings on campus. Approved or accredited by Mennonite Education Agency, Mennonite Schools Council, Middle States Association of Colleges and Schools, and Pennsylvania Department of Education. Endowment: $1.3 million. Total enrollment: 400. Upper school average class size: 21. Upper school faculty-student ratio: 1:12.
Upper School Student Profile Grade 9: 109 students (55 boys, 54 girls); Grade 10: 99 students (43 boys, 56 girls); Grade 11: 97 students (54 boys, 43 girls); Grade 12: 95 students (46 boys, 49 girls). 62% of students are Mennonite.
Faculty School total: 33. In upper school: 17 men, 16 women; 22 have advanced degrees.
Subjects Offered Accounting, Advanced Placement courses, algebra, American history, American literature, anatomy, art, art history, Bible studies, biology, British literature, business, business skills, calculus, ceramics, chemistry, child development, communications, computer programming, computer science, creative writing, drama, driver education, earth science, economics, English, English literature, environmental science, European history, family and consumer sciences, fine arts, geography, geology, geometry, gerontology, government/civics, grammar, health, history, journalism, keyboarding, mathematics, music, photography, physical education, physics, religion, science, social science, social studies, Spanish, speech, statistics, theater, trigonometry, Web site design, word processing, world history, world literature.
Graduation Requirements Arts and fine arts (art, music, dance, drama), business skills (includes word processing), computer science, English, family and consumer sciences, mathematics, physical education (includes health), religion (includes Bible studies and theology), science, social science, social studies (includes history), three-day urban experience, senior independent study/service experience (one week), and a Senior Presentation.
Special Academic Programs Advanced Placement exam preparation; honors section; remedial reading and/or remedial writing; programs in English for dyslexic students.
College Admission Counseling 110 students graduated in 2008; 102 went to college, including Eastern Mennonite University; Eastern University; Goshen College; Messiah College; Montgomery County Community College. Other: 6 went to work, 2 had other specific plans. 23% scored over 600 on SAT critical reading, 29% scored over 600 on SAT math, 23% scored over 600 on SAT writing, 23% scored over 1800 on combined SAT.
Student Life Upper grades have specified standards of dress, student council, honor system. Discipline rests primarily with faculty. Attendance at religious services is required.
Tuition and Aid Day student tuition: $12,835. Tuition installment plan (monthly payment plans). Tuition reduction for siblings, need-based scholarship grants available. In 2008–09, 80% of upper-school students received aid. Total amount of financial aid awarded in 2008–09: $400,000.
Admissions Traditional secondary-level entrance grade is 9. For fall 2008, 155 students applied for upper-level admission, 125 were accepted, 123 enrolled. Deadline for receipt of application materials: none. Application fee required: $50. On-campus interview required.
Athletics Interscholastic: baseball (boys), basketball (b,g), bowling (b,g), cheering (g), cross-country running (b,g), field hockey (g), golf (b), soccer (b,g), softball (g), tennis (b,g), track and field (b,g), volleyball (b,g); coed interscholastic: bowling. 3 PE instructors, 32 coaches, 1 athletic trainer.
Computers Computers are regularly used in accounting, keyboarding, lab/keyboard, mathematics, music, programming, SAT preparation, science, Web site design, word processing, yearbook classes. Computer network features include on-campus library services, online commercial services, Internet access, wireless campus network, Internet filtering or blocking technology, PowerSchool, WinSNAP. Computer access in designated common areas is available to students. Students grades are available online.
Contact Lois Boaman, Director of Admissions. 215-362-2675. Fax: 215-362-2943. E-mail: laboaman@dockhs.org. Web site: www.dockhs.org.

CHRIST SCHOOL

500 Christ School Road
Arden, North Carolina 28704

Head of School: Mr. Paul Krieger

General Information Boys' boarding and day college-preparatory, arts, religious studies, and technology school, affiliated with Episcopal Church. Grades 8–12. Founded: 1900. Setting: rural. Nearest major city is Asheville. Students are housed in single-sex dormitories. 500-acre campus. 15 buildings on campus. Approved or accredited by National Association of Episcopal Schools, North Carolina Association of Independent Schools, Southern Association of Independent Schools, The Association of Boarding Schools, and North Carolina Department of Education. Member of National Association of Independent Schools and Secondary School Admission Test Board. Endowment: $10 million. Total enrollment: 225. Upper school average class size: 11. Upper school faculty-student ratio: 1:6.
Upper School Student Profile Grade 8: 15 students (15 boys); Grade 9: 45 students (45 boys); Grade 10: 56 students (56 boys); Grade 11: 58 students (58 boys); Grade 12: 51 students (51 boys). 75% of students are boarding students. 58% are state residents. 17 states are represented in upper school student body. 15% are international students. International students from Bahamas, Germany, Hong Kong, Jamaica, Republic of Korea, and Spain; 3 other countries represented in student body. 30% of students are members of Episcopal Church.
Faculty School total: 41. In upper school: 28 men, 9 women; 24 have advanced degrees; 30 reside on campus.
Subjects Offered Advanced Placement courses, African-American history, algebra, American history, American history-AP, American literature, anatomy and physiology, ancient history, art, art-AP, biology, calculus, calculus-AP, chemistry, computer programming, computer science-AP, drama, economics, English, English literature, English literature-AP, environmental science, ESL, European history, fine arts, French, geography, geometry, government, journalism, Latin, law, mathematics, medieval/Renaissance history, modern European history-AP, music, music theory, photography, physical science, physics, physics-AP, pre-calculus, religion, SAT/ACT preparation, science, social studies, Spanish, statistics, studio art, theater, TOEFL preparation, trigonometry, U.S. government, U.S. history, U.S. history-AP, Vietnam history, world geography, world history.
Graduation Requirements Arts and fine arts (art, music, dance, drama), computer literacy, English, foreign language, mathematics, physical education (includes health), religion (includes Bible studies and theology), science, social studies (includes history).
Special Academic Programs Advanced Placement exam preparation; honors section; independent study; academic accommodation for the gifted; ESL (13 students enrolled).
College Admission Counseling 44 students graduated in 2008; all went to college, including Duke University; Furman University; Hampden-Sydney College; The University of North Carolina at Chapel Hill; Wofford College.
Student Life Upper grades have specified standards of dress, student council, honor system. Discipline rests equally with students and faculty. Attendance at religious services is required.
Tuition and Aid Day student tuition: $18,630; 5-day tuition and room/board: $36,700; 7-day tuition and room/board: $36,700. Tuition installment plan (The Tuition Plan, Key Tuition Payment Plan, FACTS Tuition Payment Plan, monthly payment plans, 2-payment plan). Merit scholarship grants, need-based scholarship grants available. In 2008–09, 41% of upper-school students received aid; total upper-school merit-scholarship money awarded: $200,000. Total amount of financial aid awarded in 2008–09: $1,300,000.
Admissions Traditional secondary-level entrance grade is 9. For fall 2008, 170 students applied for upper-level admission, 110 were accepted, 84 enrolled. ACT, ISEE, PSAT, SAT, SSAT or Wechsler Intelligence Scale for Children III required. Deadline for receipt of application materials: none. Application fee required: $50. On-campus interview required.
Athletics Interscholastic: baseball, basketball, cross-country running, football, golf, lacrosse, soccer, swimming and diving, tennis, track and field, wrestling; intramural: alpine skiing, backpacking, bicycling, billiards, bowling, canoeing/kayaking,

climbing, fishing, flag football, Frisbee, hiking/backpacking, indoor soccer, kayaking, life saving, martial arts, mountain biking, mountaineering, outdoor activities, paint ball, racquetball, rappelling, rock climbing, running, skeet shooting, skiing (cross-country), skiing (downhill), strength & conditioning, table tennis, ultimate Frisbee, wallyball, weight lifting, weight training. 3 coaches, 1 athletic trainer.

Computers Computers are regularly used in all classes. Computer network features include on-campus library services, Internet access, wireless campus network, Internet filtering or blocking technology. Student e-mail accounts are available to students. Students grades are available online.

Contact Mr. Denis Stokes, Director of Admission. 828-684-6232 Ext. 118. Fax: 828-209-0003. E-mail: dstokes@christschool.org. Web site: www.christschool.org.

See Close-Up on page 714.

CHRYSALIS SCHOOL

14241 North East Woodinville-Duvall Road
PMB 243
Woodinville, Washington 98072

Head of School: Karen Fogle

General Information Coeducational day college-preparatory, general academic, arts, and technology school. Grades 1–12. Founded: 1983. Setting: suburban. Nearest major city is Seattle. 2 buildings on campus. Approved or accredited by Northwest Association of Accredited Schools, Northwest Association of Schools and Colleges, and Washington Department of Education. Total enrollment: 257. Upper school average class size: 8.

Upper School Student Profile Grade 9: 35 students (22 boys, 13 girls); Grade 10: 34 students (22 boys, 12 girls); Grade 11: 53 students (36 boys, 17 girls); Grade 12: 76 students (47 boys, 29 girls).

Faculty School total: 55. In upper school: 18 men, 23 women; 25 have advanced degrees.

Subjects Offered Career planning, computer technologies, English, filmmaking, French, geography, German, graphics, history, Japanese, mathematics, physical education, SAT preparation, science, social science, Spanish.

Graduation Requirements Computer literacy, English, foreign language, history, mathematics, physical education (includes health), science.

Special Academic Programs Honors section; accelerated programs; study at local college for college credit; academic accommodation for the gifted; remedial reading and/or remedial writing; remedial math; programs in English, mathematics, general development for dyslexic students; special instructional classes for students with learning disabilities.

College Admission Counseling 78 students graduated in 2008; 70 went to college, including Bellevue Community College; Central Washington University; University of Washington; Washington State University; Western Washington University. Other: 4 went to work, 2 entered military service, 2 had other specific plans.

Student Life Upper grades have specified standards of dress, honor system. Discipline rests primarily with faculty.

Tuition and Aid Tuition installment plan (monthly payment plans, individually arranged payment plans).

Admissions Traditional secondary-level entrance grade is 9. For fall 2008, 100 students applied for upper-level admission, 90 were accepted, 80 enrolled. Deadline for receipt of application materials: none. Application fee required: $450. On-campus interview required.

Computers Computers are regularly used in computer applications, English, foreign language, graphic arts, history, information technology, introduction to technology, keyboarding, mathematics, media, science, video film production, Web site design, word processing, yearbook classes. Computer resources include on-campus library services, online commercial services, Internet access.

Contact Wanda Metcalfe, Director of Student Services. 425-481-2228. Fax: 425-486-8107. E-mail: wanda@chrysalis-school.com. Web site: www.chrysalis-school.com.

CINCINNATI COUNTRY DAY SCHOOL

6905 Given Road
Cincinnati, Ohio 45243-2898

Head of School: Dr. Robert Macrae

General Information Coeducational day college-preparatory, arts, and technology school. Grades PK–12. Founded: 1926. Setting: suburban. 62-acre campus. 8 buildings on campus. Approved or accredited by Independent Schools Association of the Central States and Ohio Department of Education. Member of National Association of Independent Schools and Secondary School Admission Test Board. Endowment: $20 million. Total enrollment: 800. Upper school average class size: 15. Upper school faculty-student ratio: 1:9.

Upper School Student Profile Grade 9: 53 students (31 boys, 22 girls); Grade 10: 62 students (32 boys, 30 girls); Grade 11: 68 students (31 boys, 37 girls); Grade 12: 70 students (38 boys, 32 girls).

Faculty School total: 110. In upper school: 23 men, 15 women; 31 have advanced degrees.

Subjects Offered Acting, algebra, American history, American history-AP, American literature, analysis, art, art history, biology, biology-AP, calculus, calculus-AP, ceramics, chemistry, chemistry-AP, choir, computer graphics, computer programming, computer science, CPR, creative writing, dance, drama, earth science, English, English literature, European history, fine arts, French, French language-AP, French literature-AP, genetics, geometry, health, humanities, music, photography, physical education, physics, psychology, public speaking, Spanish, Spanish language-AP, Spanish literature-AP, speech, statistics, theater, trigonometry, world history.

Graduation Requirements Arts and fine arts (art, music, dance, drama), computer science, English, foreign language, history, mathematics, physical education (includes health), science, senior project. Community service is required.

Special Academic Programs Advanced Placement exam preparation; honors section; independent study; study abroad.

College Admission Counseling 68 students graduated in 2008; all went to college, including Boston University; Brown University; DePauw University; University of Michigan; Wake Forest University. Mean SAT critical reading: 620, mean SAT math: 640, mean SAT writing: 640, mean combined SAT: 1900.

Student Life Upper grades have specified standards of dress, student council, honor system. Discipline rests equally with students and faculty.

Summer Programs Remediation, enrichment, advancement, sports, art/fine arts, computer instruction programs offered; session focuses on camps and academic programs; held on campus; accepts boys and girls; open to students from other schools. 400 students usually enrolled. 2009 schedule: June 15 to August 8. Application deadline: May 30.

Tuition and Aid Day student tuition: $19,500. Tuition installment plan (Insured Tuition Payment Plan, FACTS Tuition Payment Plan, monthly payment plans). Merit scholarship grants, need-based scholarship grants, Parent Loans, Sallie Mae Loans available. In 2008–09, 17% of upper-school students received aid; total upper-school merit-scholarship money awarded: $27,500. Total amount of financial aid awarded in 2008–09: $750,000.

Admissions Traditional secondary-level entrance grade is 9. For fall 2008, 42 students applied for upper-level admission, 28 were accepted, 19 enrolled. ISEE, Otis-Lennon Ability or Stanford Achievement Test or SSAT, ERB, PSAT, SAT, PLAN or ACT required. Deadline for receipt of application materials: March 15. Application fee required: $50. Interview recommended.

Athletics Interscholastic: baseball (boys), basketball (b,g), crew (b,g), cross-country running (b,g), football (b), golf (b,g), gymnastics (g), lacrosse (b,g), softball (g), swimming and diving (b,g), tennis (b,g), track and field (b,g); intramural: dance team (g); coed interscholastic: crew, dance squad. 5 PE instructors, 1 athletic trainer.

Computers Computers are regularly used in all academic classes. Computer network features include on-campus library services, online commercial services, Internet access, wireless campus network, Internet filtering or blocking technology. Campus intranet and student e-mail accounts are available to students. Students grades are available online. The school has a published electronic and media policy.

Contact Aaron B. Kellenberger, Director of Admission. 513-979-0220. Fax: 513-527-7614. E-mail: kellenbea@countryday.net. Web site: www.countryday.net.

CISTERCIAN PREPARATORY SCHOOL

3660 Cistercian Road
Irving, Texas 75039

Head of School: Fr. Peter Verhalen

General Information Boys' day college-preparatory, arts, and religious studies school, affiliated with Roman Catholic Church. Grades 5–12. Founded: 1962. Setting: suburban. Nearest major city is Dallas. 80-acre campus. 7 buildings on campus. Approved or accredited by Independent Schools Association of the Southwest, Texas Catholic Conference, and Texas Department of Education. Member of National Association of Independent Schools. Endowment: $6.6 million. Total enrollment: 345. Upper school average class size: 22. Upper school faculty-student ratio: 1:7.

Upper School Student Profile Grade 9: 47 students (47 boys); Grade 10: 41 students (41 boys); Grade 11: 42 students (42 boys); Grade 12: 43 students (43 boys). 81% of students are Roman Catholic.

Faculty School total: 52. In upper school: 28 men, 8 women; 35 have advanced degrees.

Subjects Offered Advanced biology, advanced chemistry, algebra, American history, American literature, anatomy, art, athletics, baseball, basketball, biology, calculus, chemistry, computer science, creative writing, digital applications, drama, earth science, ecology, economics, English, English composition, English literature, epic literature, ethics, European history, expository writing, fine arts, French, geometry, government/civics, grammar, health, history, history of the Catholic Church, Latin, modern world history, music, performing arts, photography, physical education, physics, pre-algebra, pre-calculus, religion, science, senior project, social studies, Spanish, speech, studio art, swimming, tennis, Texas history, theology, trigonometry, world history, world literature.

Graduation Requirements Arts and fine arts (art, music, dance, drama), electives, English, foreign language, mathematics, physical education (includes health), science, senior project, social studies (includes history), theology, completion of an independent senior project during fourth quarter of senior year.

Special Academic Programs Advanced Placement exam preparation; independent study; study at local college for college credit.

College Admission Counseling 44 students graduated in 2008; all went to college, including Creighton University; Harvard University; Princeton University; Stanford University; Texas A&M University; The University of Texas at Austin. Median SAT critical reading: 730, median SAT math: 720, median SAT writing: 700, median combined SAT: 2170. 95% scored over 600 on SAT critical reading, 100% scored over 600 on SAT math, 100% scored over 600 on SAT writing, 100% scored over 1800 on combined SAT.

Student Life Upper grades have specified standards of dress, student council. Discipline rests primarily with faculty. Attendance at religious services is required.

Summer Programs Remediation, enrichment, sports, art/fine arts, computer instruction programs offered; session focuses on remediation and enrichment in mathematics and English, arts and fine arts, computers, and sports camp; held on campus; accepts boys; open to students from other schools. 125 students usually enrolled. 2009 schedule: June 1 to July 3. Application deadline: none.

Tuition and Aid Day student tuition: $14,100. Tuition installment plan (Tuition Management Systems Plan). Need-based scholarship grants available. In 2008–09, 24% of upper-school students received aid.

Admissions Traditional secondary-level entrance grade is 9. For fall 2008, 167 students applied for upper-level admission, 54 were accepted. English language, High School Placement Test, Iowa Tests of Basic Skills, ITBS achievement test, Kuhlmann-Anderson, mathematics proficiency exam or writing sample required. Deadline for receipt of application materials: January 30. Application fee required: $75.

Athletics Interscholastic: baseball, basketball, cross-country running, football, physical training, soccer, swimming and diving, tennis, track and field; intramural: basketball, physical training, soccer, strength & conditioning, ultimate Frisbee, volleyball. 2 coaches, 1 athletic trainer.

Computers Computers are regularly used in college planning, computer applications, digital applications, library, literary magazine, newspaper, photography, programming, publications, yearbook classes. Computer network features include on-campus library services, Internet access, online college applications, numerous online databases, reference sources. The school has a published electronic and media policy.

Contact Mrs. Sally L. Cook, Registrar. 469-499-5402. Fax: 469-499-5440. E-mail: scook@cistercian.org. Web site: www.cistercian.org.

ANNOUNCEMENT FROM THE SCHOOL At Cistercian, each class, or form, is assigned a Form Master, who accompanies his class from one year to the next. The Form Master is personally responsible for establishing the community within which each student can develop intellectually, emotionally, physically, and spiritually.

COE-BROWN NORTHWOOD ACADEMY

907 First New Hampshire Turnpike
Northwood, New Hampshire 03261

Head of School: Mr. David S. Smith

General Information Coeducational day college-preparatory, general academic, arts, business, vocational, bilingual studies, and technology school. Grades 9–12. Founded: 1867. Setting: rural. Nearest major city is Concord. 5 buildings on campus. Approved or accredited by New England Association of Schools and Colleges and New Hampshire Department of Education. Total enrollment: 687. Upper school average class size: 18. Upper school faculty-student ratio: 1:12.

Upper School Student Profile Grade 9: 179 students (88 boys, 91 girls); Grade 10: 178 students (89 boys, 89 girls); Grade 11: 171 students (80 boys, 91 girls); Grade 12: 159 students (81 boys, 78 girls).

Faculty School total: 66. In upper school: 32 men, 34 women.

Subjects Offered 3-dimensional art, 3-dimensional design, accounting, acting, advanced chemistry, advanced math, Advanced Placement courses, advanced studio art-AP, algebra, American government, American history, American history-AP, American literature, American literature-AP, American studies, analytic geometry, anatomy and physiology, animal science, architecture, art, art appreciation, arts and crafts, auto mechanics, band, Basic programming, biology, British literature, British literature (honors), business law, calculus, calculus-AP, chemistry, child development, chorus, computer applications, computer literacy, computer programming, contemporary problems, drama, drawing and design, earth science, economics, English, English literature-AP, environmental science, family life, film studies, French, freshman seminar, general math, geography, geology, geometry, health, honors algebra, honors English, honors geometry, honors U.S. history, horticulture, intro to computers, music theory, parent/child development, physical education, physics, piano, pre-algebra, psychology, senior project, Spanish, world history, zoology.

Graduation Requirements Algebra, art, biology, civics, economics, English, geometry, intro to computers, physical education (includes health), physical science, U.S. history, world cultures, senior portfolio project.

Special Academic Programs Advanced Placement exam preparation; honors section; independent study; remedial reading and/or remedial writing; remedial math; special instructional classes for deaf students, blind students.

College Admission Counseling 176 students graduated in 2008; 125 went to college, including Keene State College; Plymouth State University; University of New Hampshire. Other: 42 went to work, 5 entered military service. Mean SAT critical reading: 526, mean SAT math: 542, mean SAT writing: 518.

Student Life Upper grades have specified standards of dress, student council. Discipline rests primarily with faculty.

Summer Programs Remediation programs offered; session focuses on remediation; held on campus; accepts boys and girls; open to students from other schools. 30 students usually enrolled. 2009 schedule: June to August. Application deadline: June.

Tuition and Aid Day student tuition: $12,000.

Admissions Traditional secondary-level entrance grade is 9. For fall 2008, 196 students applied for upper-level admission, 184 were accepted, 179 enrolled. Deadline for receipt of application materials: January 9. No application fee required.

Athletics Interscholastic: baseball (boys), basketball (b,g), cheering (g), cross-country running (b,g), golf (b,g), soccer (b,g), softball (g), tennis (b,g), track and field (b,g), volleyball (b,g), winter (indoor) track (b,g); coed interscholastic: skiing (downhill). 3 PE instructors, 22 coaches.

Computers Computers are regularly used in accounting, architecture, art, basic skills, business, career exploration, economics, English, foreign language, journalism, keyboarding, library, literary magazine, photography, science, vocational-technical courses, Web site design, yearbook classes. Computer network features include on-campus library services, online commercial services, Internet access, wireless campus network, Internet filtering or blocking technology. Computer access in designated common areas is available to students. Students grades are available online. The school has a published electronic and media policy.

Contact Mrs. Cheri Wolf, Guidance Secretary. 603-942-5531. Fax: 603-942-7537. E-mail: cwolf@coebrownacademy.com.

COLEGIO BOLIVAR

Calle 5 # 122-21 Via a Pance
Cali, Colombia

Head of School: Mr. Joseph Nagy

General Information Coeducational day college-preparatory, bilingual studies, and technology school. Grades PK–12. Founded: 1947. Setting: suburban. 14-hectare campus. 7 buildings on campus. Approved or accredited by Association of American Schools in South America, Colombian Ministry of Education, and Southern Association of Colleges and Schools. Languages of instruction: English and Spanish. Total enrollment: 1,260. Upper school average class size: 17. Upper school faculty-student ratio: 1:9.

Upper School Student Profile Grade 9: 103 students (44 boys, 59 girls); Grade 10: 75 students (37 boys, 38 girls); Grade 11: 83 students (35 boys, 48 girls); Grade 12: 85 students (49 boys, 36 girls).

Faculty School total: 152. In upper school: 21 men, 15 women; 19 have advanced degrees.

Subjects Offered Advanced chemistry, Advanced Placement courses, algebra, American history, American literature, art, art history, biology, business, calculus, chemistry, computer science, dance, drama, English, English literature, environmental science, ESL, ethics, French, geology, government/civics, graphic design, history, journalism, mathematics, music, philosophy, photography, physical education, physics, programming, psychology, religion, robotics, social studies, Spanish, theater, trigonometry, world literature.

Graduation Requirements Algebra, American history, American literature, art, biology, calculus, chemistry, computer education, economics, electives, geography, geometry, history of the Americas, music, physical education (includes health), physics, political science, pre-calculus, senior project, Spanish, Spanish literature, trigonometry, world history, world literature, writing, social service hours.

Special Academic Programs Advanced Placement exam preparation; independent study; remedial reading and/or remedial writing; ESL.

College Admission Counseling 66 students graduated in 2008; 61 went to college, including Loras College; Purdue University; Trinity University; Tulane University; University of Virginia; Villanova University. Other: 5 had other specific plans. Mean SAT critical reading: 510, mean SAT math: 540, mean SAT writing: 510. 18% scored over 600 on SAT critical reading, 36% scored over 600 on SAT math, 12% scored over 600 on SAT writing.

Student Life Upper grades have specified standards of dress, student council, honor system. Discipline rests equally with students and faculty.

Tuition and Aid Day student tuition: 15,072,100 Colombian pesos–17,773,000 Colombian pesos. Tuition installment plan (monthly payment plans, annual payment plan). Need-based scholarship grants available. In 2008–09, 6% of upper-school students received aid.

Admissions Traditional secondary-level entrance grade is 9. For fall 2008, 23 students applied for upper-level admission, 4 enrolled. School's own exam required. Deadline for receipt of application materials: none. Application fee required: 80,000 Colombian pesos. On-campus interview required.

Athletics Interscholastic: aerobics/dance (girls), baseball (b), basketball (b,g), dance (g), equestrian sports (b,g), gymnastics (b,g), horseback riding (b,g), running (b,g), soccer (b,g), swimming and diving (b,g), track and field (b,g), volleyball (b,g); intramural: gymnastics (b,g), soccer (b,g), softball (b), swimming and diving (b,g), track and field (b,g), volleyball (b,g). 8 PE instructors, 23 coaches.

Computers Computers are regularly used in graphic design, photography, Web site design, yearbook classes. Computer network features include Internet access, Internet filtering or blocking technology. The school has a published electronic and media policy.

Contact Mrs. Patricia Nasser, Admissions Assistant. 57-2-555-2039 Ext. 274. Fax: 57-2-555-2041. E-mail: pnasser@colegiobolivar.edu.co. Web site: www.colegiobolivar.edu.co.

COLEGIO FRANKLIN D. ROOSEVELT

Av. Las Palmeras 325, Urbanizacion Camacho La Molina
Lima 12, Peru

Head of School: Dr. Carol Kluznik

General Information Coeducational day college-preparatory, general academic, arts, and technology school; primarily serves Mild LD. Grades N–12. Founded: 1946. Setting: suburban. Nearest major city is Lima, Peru. 23-acre campus. 5 buildings on campus. Approved or accredited by Southern Association of Colleges and Schools. Languages of instruction: English and Spanish. Total enrollment: 1,405. Upper school average class size: 20. Upper school faculty-student ratio: 1:11.

Upper School Student Profile Grade 9: 97 students (51 boys, 46 girls); Grade 10: 94 students (47 boys, 47 girls); Grade 11: 93 students (48 boys, 45 girls); Grade 12: 98 students (50 boys, 48 girls).

Faculty School total: 166. In upper school: 21 men, 26 women; 28 have advanced degrees.

Subjects Offered Advanced Placement courses, algebra, American history, American literature, art, biology, calculus, chemistry, computer programming, computer science, debate, digital photography, drama, drama performance, early childhood, earth science, economics, English, English literature, ESL, fine arts, French, French as a second language, geography, geometry, global issues, health, history, International Baccalaureate courses, journalism, keyboarding, mathematics, model United Nations, music, orchestra, photography, physical education, physical science, physics, psychology, science, social studies, Spanish, theater, theory of knowledge, trigonometry, U.S. history, world history, yearbook.

Graduation Requirements Arts and fine arts (art, music, dance, drama), English, foreign language, information technology, mathematics, physical education (includes health), science, social studies (includes history).

Special Academic Programs International Baccalaureate program; honors section; academic accommodation for the gifted, the musically talented, and the artistically talented; remedial reading and/or remedial writing; special instructional classes for students with mild learning disabilities; ESL (23 students enrolled).

College Admission Counseling 83 students graduated in 2008; all went to college, including Boston University; Cornell University; Princeton University; Purdue University; Stanford University; Vassar College. Mean SAT critical reading: 546, mean SAT math: 586, mean SAT writing: 532, mean composite ACT: 23.

Student Life Upper grades have uniform requirement, student council, honor system. Discipline rests primarily with faculty.

Tuition and Aid Day student tuition: $9200–$10,450. Tuition installment plan (monthly payment plans). Need-based scholarship grants available. In 2008–09, 0% of upper-school students received aid. Total amount of financial aid awarded in 2008–09: $4180.

Admissions Traditional secondary-level entrance grade is 9. For fall 2008, 59 students applied for upper-level admission, 57 were accepted, 57 enrolled. SAT or Stanford Achievement Test, Otis-Lennon School Ability Test required. Deadline for receipt of application materials: none. Application fee required: $200. On-campus interview required.

Athletics Interscholastic: aquatics (boys, girls), baseball (b), basketball (b,g), field hockey (b), in-line hockey (b), roller hockey (b), rugby (b), soccer (b,g), softball (b,g), surfing (b), swimming and diving (b,g), track and field (b,g), volleyball (b,g); intramural: basketball (b,g), rugby (b), soccer (b,g), softball (b,g), volleyball (b,g); coed intramural: aerobics, aerobics/Nautilus, climbing, fitness, floor hockey, in-line hockey, jogging, martial arts, outdoor adventure, surfing, volleyball, wall climbing, yoga. 4 PE instructors, 18 coaches.

Computers Computers are regularly used in art, English, history, mathematics, music, photography, science classes. Computer network features include on-campus library services, online commercial services, Internet access, wireless campus network, Internet filtering or blocking technology. Campus intranet and student e-mail accounts are available to students. Students grades are available online. The school has a published electronic and media policy.

Contact Nora Marquez, Director of Admissions. 51-1-435-0890 Ext. 4008. Fax: 51-1-7024500. E-mail: nmarquez@amersol.edu.pe. Web site: www.amersol.edu.pe.

COLEGIO NUEVA GRANADA

Carrera 2E #70-20
Bogota, Colombia

Head of School: Barry L. McCombs

General Information Coeducational day college-preparatory, Colombian Bachillerato, and Advanced Placement school. Grades PK–12. Founded: 1938. Setting: urban. 17-acre campus. 2 buildings on campus. Approved or accredited by Southern Association of Colleges and Schools. Languages of instruction: English and Spanish. Total enrollment: 1,775. Upper school average class size: 22. Upper school faculty-student ratio: 1:22.

Upper School Student Profile Grade 9: 126 students (67 boys, 59 girls); Grade 10: 118 students (66 boys, 52 girls); Grade 11: 118 students (62 boys, 56 girls); Grade 12: 105 students (66 boys, 39 girls).

Faculty School total: 221. In upper school: 22 men, 28 women; 20 have advanced degrees.

Subjects Offered Algebra, art, basketball, biology, biology-AP, calculus, calligraphy, chemistry, computer science, crafts, dance performance, drama, drawing, economics-AP, English, English-AP, ethics, European history-AP, French, geometry, government/civics, graphic design, human geography—AP, macroeconomics-AP, Mandarin, mathematics, model United Nations, music, philosophy, photography, physical education, physics, pre-calculus, religion, science, sex education, social studies, Spanish, Spanish language-AP, studio art-AP, theater, trigonometry, U.S. history, U.S. history-AP, volleyball, weight training, world history, world history-AP.

Graduation Requirements Arts and fine arts (art, music, dance, drama), computer education, electives, English, foreign language, mathematics, physical education (includes health), science, social science, social studies (includes history), senior independent project.

Special Academic Programs International Baccalaureate program; Advanced Placement exam preparation; honors section; independent study; academic accommodation for the gifted; programs in English, mathematics, general development for dyslexic students; special instructional classes for students with learning disabilities, students with emotional and behavioral problems, Attention Deficit Disorder; ESL (20 students enrolled).

College Admission Counseling 115 students graduated in 2008; 84 went to college, including American University; Boston University; Brandeis University; Cornell University; The George Washington University; University of Pennsylvania.

Student Life Upper grades have uniform requirement, student council, honor system. Discipline rests equally with students and faculty.

Tuition and Aid Tuition installment plan (5-installment plan). Need-based scholarship grants available. In 2008–09, 46% of upper-school students received aid. Total amount of financial aid awarded in 2008–09: 68,003,850 Colombian pesos.

Admissions Traditional secondary-level entrance grade is 10. For fall 2008, 39 students applied for upper-level admission, 36 were accepted, 31 enrolled. Academic Profile Tests and admissions testing required. Deadline for receipt of application materials: none. No application fee required. On-campus interview required.

Athletics Interscholastic: baseball (boys), basketball (b,g), gymnastics (g), soccer (b,g), table tennis (b,g), track and field (b,g), volleyball (b,g); intramural: basketball (b,g), soccer (b,g), table tennis (b,g), volleyball (b,g), weight training (b,g); coed interscholastic: track and field; coed intramural: basketball, soccer, table tennis, volleyball, weight training. 3 PE instructors, 11 coaches.

Computers Computers are regularly used in desktop publishing, introduction to technology, mathematics, science, technology, video film production, Web site design classes. Computer network features include on-campus library services, Internet access, wireless campus network, Internet filtering or blocking technology, Blackboard, SDS. Campus intranet, student e-mail accounts, and computer access in designated common areas are available to students. Students grades are available online.

Contact Katherine Ancizar, Director of Admissions. 57-1-321-1147. Fax: 57-1-211-3720. E-mail: kancizar@cng.edu. Web site: www.cng.edu.

COLEGIO PUERTORRIQUENO DE NINAS

Turquesa Street, Golden Gate
Guaynabo, Puerto Rico 00968

Head of School: Miss Ivette Nater

General Information Girls' day college-preparatory, arts, bilingual studies, and technology school. Grades PK–12. Founded: 1924. Setting: urban. Nearest major city is San Juan. 1 building on campus. Approved or accredited by Comisión Acreditadora de Instituciones Educativas, Middle States Association of Colleges and Schools, and Puerto Rico Department of Education. Languages of instruction: English, Spanish, and French. Total enrollment: 592. Upper school average class size: 25. Upper school faculty-student ratio: 1:11.

Upper School Student Profile Grade 9: 46 students (46 girls); Grade 10: 46 students (46 girls); Grade 11: 35 students (35 girls); Grade 12: 42 students (42 girls).

Faculty School total: 53. In upper school: 4 men, 21 women; 12 have advanced degrees.

Subjects Offered Algebra, American history, American literature, art, art history, biology, biology-AP, ceramics, chemistry, comparative government and politics-AP, computer programming, drama, ecology, English, English literature, French, geometry, grammar, health, history, home economics, mathematics, music, physical education, physics, science, social studies, Spanish, theater, typing, world history.

Graduation Requirements Computers, English, mathematics, science, social studies (includes history).

Special Academic Programs Advanced Placement exam preparation; honors section; ESL (170 students enrolled).

College Admission Counseling 42 students graduated in 2008; all went to college, including Babson College; Bentley University; Boston College; Georgetown University; Haverford College; Villanova University. Median SAT critical reading: 500, median SAT math: 463, median SAT writing: 520, median combined SAT: 1483. 5% scored over 600 on SAT critical reading, 3% scored over 600 on SAT math, 6% scored over 600 on SAT writing, 2% scored over 1800 on combined SAT.

Student Life Upper grades have uniform requirement, student council, honor system. Discipline rests equally with students and faculty.
Tuition and Aid Day student tuition: $6500. Tuition installment plan (monthly payment plans, individually arranged payment plans). Merit scholarship grants, need-based scholarship grants available. In 2008–09, 5% of upper-school students received aid; total upper-school merit-scholarship money awarded: $96,000. Total amount of financial aid awarded in 2008–09: $172,775.
Admissions Traditional secondary-level entrance grade is 9. For fall 2008, 12 students applied for upper-level admission, 7 were accepted, 5 enrolled. Learn Aid Aptitude Test required. Deadline for receipt of application materials: February 10. Application fee required: $30. On-campus interview required.
Athletics Interscholastic: bowling (girls), cross-country running (g), paddle tennis (g), soccer (g), softball (g), swimming and diving (g), table tennis (g), tennis (g), track and field (g), volleyball (g); intramural: ballet (g), basketball (g), bowling (g), cross-country running (g), jump rope (g), kickball (g), paddle tennis (g), soccer (g), track and field (g), volleyball (g). 2 PE instructors, 4 coaches, 1 athletic trainer.
Computers Computers are regularly used in basic skills, lab/keyboard classes. Computer network features include on-campus library services, Internet access, Internet filtering or blocking technology, ExPAN, Encarta. Campus intranet and computer access in designated common areas are available to students.
Contact Ritín Santaella, Registrar. 787-782-2618. Fax: 787-782-8370. Web site: www.cpnpr.org/.

COLE VALLEY CHRISTIAN HIGH SCHOOL

200 E. Carlton Avenue
Meridian, Idaho 83642
Head of School: Mr. Bradley Carr

General Information Coeducational day college-preparatory, general academic, arts, religious studies, and bilingual studies school, affiliated with Christian faith. Grades K–12. Founded: 1990. Setting: suburban. Nearest major city is Boise. 5-acre campus. 1 building on campus. Approved or accredited by Association of Christian Schools International, Northwest Association of Schools and Colleges, and Idaho Department of Education. Endowment: $17,000. Total enrollment: 715. Upper school average class size: 14. Upper school faculty-student ratio: 1:9.
Upper School Student Profile 100% of students are Christian.
Faculty School total: 16. In upper school: 11 men, 5 women; 5 have advanced degrees.
Subjects Offered 20th century history, algebra, American government, American literature, art, Bible, biology, British literature, calculus-AP, chemistry, choral music, computer literacy, ecology, economics, English, English literature, French, geometry, honors English, Latin, physical education, physical science, physics, pre-algebra, pre-calculus, Spanish, speech, U.S. history, world history, yearbook.
Graduation Requirements 20th century history, American government, economics, English, mathematics, physical education (includes health), religion (includes Bible studies and theology), science, social studies (includes history), speech.
Special Academic Programs Advanced Placement exam preparation; honors section; independent study.
College Admission Counseling 68 students graduated in 2008; 63 went to college, including Boise State University; Northwest Nazarene University; The College of Idaho. Other: 2 went to work, 1 entered military service.
Student Life Upper grades have specified standards of dress, student council, honor system. Discipline rests primarily with faculty. Attendance at religious services is required.
Tuition and Aid Day student tuition: $5249. Tuition installment plan (monthly payment plans, individually arranged payment plans). Tuition reduction for siblings, need-based scholarship grants available. In 2008–09, 20% of upper-school students received aid.
Admissions Traditional secondary-level entrance grade is 9. Deadline for receipt of application materials: none. Application fee required: $125. Interview required.
Athletics Interscholastic: basketball (boys, girls), cheering (g), cross-country running (b,g), football (b), track and field (b,g), volleyball (g), wrestling (b); intramural: skiing (cross-country) (b,g), skiing (downhill) (b,g), snowboarding (b,g). 3 PE instructors, 12 coaches.
Computers Computers are regularly used in all academic classes. Computer network features include on-campus library services, Internet access.
Contact Mrs. Robin Didriksen, Registrar/Assistant to the Principal. 208-898-9003. Fax: 208-898-9016. E-mail: rdidriksen@cvcsonline.org.

COLLEGE DU LEMAN INTERNATIONAL SCHOOL

74 route de Sauverny
Versoix CH-1290, Switzerland
Head of School: M. Paloma Marc

General Information Coeducational boarding and day college-preparatory, arts, business, and bilingual studies school. Boarding grades 6–13, day grades K–13. Founded: 1960. Setting: rural. Nearest major city is Geneva, Switzerland. Students are housed in single-sex dormitories. 18-acre campus. 14 buildings on campus. Approved or accredited by European Council of International Schools and New England Association of Schools and Colleges. Languages of instruction: English and French. Total enrollment: 1,754. Upper school average class size: 12. Upper school faculty-student ratio: 1:7.
Upper School Student Profile 30% of students are boarding students. 80% are international students. International students from China, France, Japan, Russian Federation, United Kingdom, and United States; 99 other countries represented in student body.
Faculty School total: 250. In upper school: 66 men, 40 women; 45 have advanced degrees; 17 reside on campus.
Subjects Offered Accounting, advanced chemistry, advanced computer applications, advanced math, Advanced Placement courses, American history, American history-AP, American literature-AP, analysis and differential calculus, analytic geometry, ancient history, Arabic, art, art education, art-AP, athletics, audio visual/media, baseball, basketball, biology-AP, British literature, business studies, calculus, calculus-AP, career/college preparation, chemistry, chemistry-AP, choir, college counseling, communication arts, computer applications, drama, earth science, economics-AP, English as a foreign language, English composition, English literature-AP, environmental science, ESL, European history, European history-AP, French, French language-AP, French literature-AP, geography, German, German-AP, health, health education, history, human biology, instrumental music, integrated mathematics, International Baccalaureate courses, international relations, languages, macro/microeconomics-AP, mechanics, model United Nations, music, orchestra, philosophy, photography, physical education, physics, physics-AP, piano, pre-calculus, probability and statistics, psychology, religion and culture, SAT preparation, science, sociology, softball, Spanish, Spanish language-AP, Spanish literature, Spanish literature-AP, tennis, volleyball, weight training, world cultures, yearbook.
Graduation Requirements English, foreign language, mathematics, physical education (includes health), science, social studies (includes history).
Special Academic Programs International Baccalaureate program; Advanced Placement exam preparation; honors section; academic accommodation for the gifted, the musically talented, and the artistically talented; remedial reading and/or remedial writing; programs in English for dyslexic students; special instructional classes for students with special needs; ESL.
College Admission Counseling 150 students graduated in 2008; 126 went to college, including London School of Economics and Political Science; Queen's University at Kingston; Stanford University; Tufts University; University of Cambridge; Yale University. Other: 24 had other specific plans.
Student Life Upper grades have specified standards of dress, student council, honor system. Discipline rests primarily with faculty.
Summer Programs Advancement, ESL, sports, art/fine arts, computer instruction programs offered; session focuses on language study (French, English and Spanish), sports, excursions; held on campus; accepts boys and girls; open to students from other schools. 250 students usually enrolled. 2009 schedule: July 3 to August 13. Application deadline: May 31.
Tuition and Aid Day student tuition: 20,600 Swiss francs–21,800 Swiss francs; 7-day tuition and room/board: 50,000 Swiss francs–52,000 Swiss francs. Tuition installment plan (monthly payment plans, individually arranged payment plans). Assistance consideration on an individual basis available.
Admissions Traditional secondary-level entrance grade is 9. For fall 2008, 560 students applied for upper-level admission, 491 were accepted, 491 enrolled. Any standardized test, English entrance exam and mathematics proficiency exam required. Deadline for receipt of application materials: none. Application fee required: 250 Swiss francs. Interview recommended.
Athletics Interscholastic: alpine skiing (boys, girls), badminton (b,g), basketball (b,g), cross-country running (b,g), floor hockey (b,g), golf (b,g), indoor hockey (b,g), indoor soccer (b,g), rugby (b), skiing (downhill) (b,g), snowboarding (b,g), soccer (b,g), swimming and diving (b,g), tennis (b,g), track and field (b,g), volleyball (b,g); intramural: aerobics (g), alpine skiing (b,g), badminton (b,g), baseball (b), basketball (b,g), cricket (b), cross-country running (b,g), dance squad (g), floor hockey (b,g), Frisbee (b,g), gymnastics (g), indoor hockey (b,g), indoor soccer (b,g), physical training (b,g), rugby (b), skiing (downhill) (b,g), snowboarding (b,g), soccer (b,g), softball (b,g), swimming and diving (b,g), table tennis (b,g), team handball (b,g), tennis (b,g), touch football (b), track and field (b,g), ultimate Frisbee (b,g), volleyball (b,g), walking (g), weight training (b); coed interscholastic: archery, baseball, indoor track & field, scooter football; coed intramural: aerobics, aerobics/dance, archery, bicycling, bowling, fitness, Frisbee, golf, horseback riding, jogging, judo, martial arts, physical fitness, physical training, running, softball, ultimate Frisbee, yoga. 8 PE instructors.
Computers Computers are regularly used in English, ESL, foreign language, mathematics, science classes. Computer network features include on-campus library services, online commercial services, Internet access, wireless campus network, Internet filtering or blocking technology. Students grades are available online. The school has a published electronic and media policy.
Contact Mr. Cédric Chaffois, Admission and External Relations Director. 41-22-775-5555. Fax: 41-22-775-5559. E-mail: admissions@cdl.ch. Web site: www.cdl.ch.

THE COLLEGE PREPARATORY SCHOOL

6100 Broadway
Oakland, California 94618

Head of School: Murray Cohen

General Information Coeducational day college-preparatory school. Grades 9–12. Founded: 1960. Setting: urban. Nearest major city is San Francisco. 6-acre campus. 14 buildings on campus. Approved or accredited by California Association of Independent Schools, Western Association of Schools and Colleges, and California Department of Education. Member of National Association of Independent Schools. Endowment: $11.1 million. Total enrollment: 353. Upper school average class size: 14. Upper school faculty-student ratio: 1:6.

Upper School Student Profile Grade 9: 92 students (40 boys, 52 girls); Grade 10: 88 students (39 boys, 49 girls); Grade 11: 87 students (43 boys, 44 girls); Grade 12: 86 students (42 boys, 44 girls).

Faculty School total: 55. In upper school: 19 men, 36 women; 43 have advanced degrees.

Subjects Offered 20th century American writers, 3-dimensional art, acting, advanced math, Advanced Placement courses, algebra, American government, American history, American literature, animal behavior, art, art-AP, astronomy, audio visual/media, biology, biology-AP, calculus, calculus-AP, chemistry, chemistry-AP, Chinese, Chinese literature, chorus, comparative religion, computer science, contemporary issues in science, creative writing, dance, dance performance, debate, digital applications, drama, drama performance, drawing and design, economics, English, English literature, environmental science-AP, European history, forensics, French, French literature-AP, French-AP, freshman foundations, genetics, geometry, health education, history, independent study, instruments, Japanese, jazz band, junior and senior seminars, language-AP, Latin, Latin American literature, Latin-AP, linguistics, mathematics, music, music theory-AP, orchestra, peer counseling, philosophy, photography, physical education, physical science, physics, physics-AP, poetry, psychology, science, Shakespeare, Spanish, Spanish-AP, stagecraft, statistics, statistics-AP, theater, theater design and production, U.S. government, vocal ensemble, Western civilization, women's studies, world civilizations, zoology.

Graduation Requirements Arts and fine arts (art, music, dance, drama), English, foreign language, freshman foundations, history, mathematics, physical education (includes health), science, sophomore health, Intraterm Program.

Special Academic Programs Advanced Placement exam preparation; honors section; independent study.

College Admission Counseling 81 students graduated in 2008; all went to college, including Columbia College; Middlebury College; Stanford University; University of California, Berkeley; University of Pennsylvania; Wesleyan University. Mean SAT critical reading: 721, mean SAT math: 722, mean SAT writing: 725, mean composite ACT: 30.

Student Life Upper grades have student council. Discipline rests equally with students and faculty.

Summer Programs Enrichment, advancement programs offered; session focuses on academic enrichment for under-represented middle-school students from Oakland public schools; held on campus; accepts boys and girls; open to students from other schools. 90 students usually enrolled. 2009 schedule: June 26 to July 24. Application deadline: March 2.

Tuition and Aid Day student tuition: $28,600. Tuition installment plan (FACTS Tuition Payment Plan, monthly payment plans). Need-based scholarship grants available. In 2008–09, 23% of upper-school students received aid. Total amount of financial aid awarded in 2008–09: $1,555,285.

Admissions Traditional secondary-level entrance grade is 9. For fall 2008, 325 students applied for upper-level admission, 129 were accepted, 92 enrolled. ISEE or SSAT required. Deadline for receipt of application materials: January 15. Application fee required: $75. On-campus interview required.

Athletics Interscholastic: baseball (boys), basketball (b,g), cross-country running (b,g), soccer (b,g), softball (g), swimming and diving (b,g), tennis (b,g), track and field (b,g), volleyball (b,g); coed interscholastic: golf; coed intramural: badminton, basketball, soccer, volleyball. 4 PE instructors, 21 coaches.

Computers Computers are regularly used in art, drawing and design, freshman foundations, mathematics, music, newspaper, science, theater arts, yearbook classes. Computer network features include on-campus library services, online commercial services, Internet access, wireless campus network, remote access to library services, Web publishing, remote file-server access, video recording and editing. Student e-mail accounts and computer access in designated common areas are available to students. The school has a published electronic and media policy.

Contact Jonathan Zucker, Director of Admission and Financial Aid. 510-652-4364. Fax: 510-652-7467. E-mail: jonathan@college-prep.org. Web site: www.college-prep.org.

THE COLLEGIATE SCHOOL

North Mooreland Road
Richmond, Virginia 23229

Head of School: Keith A. Evans

General Information Coeducational day college-preparatory, arts, and technology school. Grades K–12. Founded: 1915. Setting: suburban. 211-acre campus. 13 buildings on campus. Approved or accredited by Southern Association of Colleges and Schools, Virginia Association of Independent Schools, and Virginia Department of Education. Member of National Association of Independent Schools and Secondary School Admission Test Board. Endowment: $40.2 million. Total enrollment: 1,555. Upper school average class size: 15. Upper school faculty-student ratio: 1:15.

Upper School Student Profile Grade 9: 129 students (62 boys, 67 girls); Grade 10: 123 students (56 boys, 67 girls); Grade 11: 129 students (59 boys, 70 girls); Grade 12: 118 students (60 boys, 58 girls).

Faculty School total: 187. In upper school: 30 men, 34 women; 50 have advanced degrees.

Subjects Offered Acting, algebra, American history, American history-AP, American literature, art, biology, biology-AP, calculus-AP, ceramics, chemistry, chemistry-AP, community service, computer applications, creative writing, drama, driver education, earth science, economics, economics-AP, English, English literature, ethics, European history, fine arts, French, French-AP, geometry, government/civics, health, journalism, Latin, music, photography, physics, psychology, religion, robotics, senior seminar, Spanish, Spanish language-AP, statistics, theater, trigonometry, world history.

Graduation Requirements Arts and fine arts (art, music, dance, drama), English, ethics, foreign language, government, history, mathematics, physical education (includes health), religion (includes Bible studies and theology), science, sports, senior speech. Community service is required.

Special Academic Programs 11 Advanced Placement exams for which test preparation is offered; honors section; independent study; study at local college for college credit; programs in general development for dyslexic students.

College Admission Counseling 127 students graduated in 2008; all went to college, including Elon University; James Madison University; University of South Carolina; University of Virginia.

Student Life Upper grades have specified standards of dress, student council, honor system. Discipline rests equally with students and faculty.

Summer Programs Remediation, enrichment, advancement, sports, art/fine arts, computer instruction programs offered; session focuses on advancement, remediation, sports; held on campus; accepts boys and girls; open to students from other schools. 1,426 students usually enrolled. 2009 schedule: June 8 to July 31. Application deadline: none.

Tuition and Aid Day student tuition: $16,370. Tuition installment plan (Insured Tuition Payment Plan, monthly payment plans). Need-based scholarship grants available. In 2008–09, 12% of upper-school students received aid. Total amount of financial aid awarded in 2008–09: $638,522.

Admissions Traditional secondary-level entrance grade is 9. For fall 2008, 115 students applied for upper-level admission, 41 were accepted, 22 enrolled. PSAT and SAT for applicants to grade 11 and 12 or SSAT required. Deadline for receipt of application materials: none. Application fee required: $50. Interview required.

Athletics Interscholastic: baseball (boys), basketball (b,g), cross-country running (b,g), diving (b,g), field hockey (g), football (b), indoor track & field (b,g), lacrosse (b,g), soccer (b,g), softball (g), swimming and diving (b,g), tennis (b,g), track and field (b,g), volleyball (g), winter (indoor) track (b,g), wrestling (b); coed interscholastic: golf, indoor soccer; coed intramural: combined training, dance, dance squad, dance team, fitness, modern dance. 3 PE instructors, 31 coaches, 2 athletic trainers.

Computers Computers are regularly used in all academic classes. Computer network features include on-campus library services, Internet access, wireless campus network, Internet filtering or blocking technology. Student e-mail accounts are available to students. The school has a published electronic and media policy.

Contact Amanda L. Surgner, Director of Admission. 804-741-9722. Fax: 804-741-5472. E-mail: asurgner@collegiate-va.org. Web site: www.collegiate-va.org/.

COLORADO ACADEMY

3800 South Pierce Street
Denver, Colorado 80235

Head of School: Dr. Michael Davis

General Information Coeducational day college-preparatory, general academic, arts, and technology school. Grades PK–12. Founded: 1906. Setting: suburban. 94-acre campus. 12 buildings on campus. Approved or accredited by Association of Colorado Independent Schools and Colorado Department of Education. Member of National Association of Independent Schools and Secondary School Admission Test Board. Endowment: $18.5 million. Total enrollment: 894. Upper school average class size: 14. Upper school faculty-student ratio: 1:8.

Upper School Student Profile Grade 9: 88 students (44 boys, 44 girls); Grade 10: 86 students (38 boys, 48 girls); Grade 11: 82 students (44 boys, 38 girls); Grade 12: 86 students (47 boys, 39 girls).

Faculty School total: 113. In upper school: 20 men, 23 women; 36 have advanced degrees.

Subjects Offered Acting, advanced studio art-AP, African history, algebra, American history, American literature, art, bacteriology, biochemistry, biology, botany, calculus, chemistry, chorus, community service, computer science, creative writing, earth science, ecology, English, English literature, environmental science, European history, expository writing, fine arts, French, genetics, geography, geometry, grammar, health, history, humanities, international relations, marine biology, mathematics, microbiology, music, paleontology, philosophy, photography, physical education, physics, physiology, pre-calculus, psychology, rhetoric, science, social studies, Spanish, statistics, technical theater, theater, trigonometry, world literature, writing, zoology.

Graduation Requirements Arts and fine arts (art, music, dance, drama), computer skills, English, foreign language, mathematics, physical education (includes health), science, social studies (includes history), one-week experiential education program (Interim) required each year of upper school. Community service is required.
Special Academic Programs Advanced Placement exam preparation; honors section; independent study; term-away projects; academic accommodation for the gifted, the musically talented, and the artistically talented.
College Admission Counseling 83 students graduated in 2008; all went to college, including New York University; The Colorado College; University of Colorado at Boulder; University of Denver; University of Pennsylvania; University of Southern California. Mean SAT critical reading: 626, mean SAT math: 628, mean composite ACT: 27.
Student Life Upper grades have specified standards of dress, student council. Discipline rests equally with students and faculty.
Summer Programs Enrichment, sports, art/fine arts, rigorous outdoor training, computer instruction programs offered; session focuses on enrichment; held both on and off campus; held at regional and international locations; accepts boys and girls; open to students from other schools. 995 students usually enrolled. 2009 schedule: June 8 to August 8. Application deadline: none.
Tuition and Aid Day student tuition: $18,900. Tuition installment plan (monthly payment plans, individually arranged payment plans, 3-payment plan). Need-based scholarship grants available. In 2008–09, 15% of upper-school students received aid. Total amount of financial aid awarded in 2008–09: $2,029,000.
Admissions Traditional secondary-level entrance grade is 9. For fall 2008, 140 students applied for upper-level admission, 32 enrolled. ISEE or SSAT required. Deadline for receipt of application materials: February 1. Application fee required: $60. On-campus interview required.
Athletics Interscholastic: aquatics (girls), baseball (b), basketball (b,g), dance team (g), diving (g), field hockey (g), golf (b,g), ice hockey (b), independent competitive sports (b,g), lacrosse (b,g), soccer (b,g), swimming and diving (g), tennis (b,g), ultimate Frisbee (b,g), volleyball (g); intramural: aerobics/dance (g), dance (g); coed interscholastic: baseball, Circus, cross-country running, martial arts, racquetball, rock climbing, strength & conditioning, ultimate Frisbee, weight training. 5 PE instructors, 25 coaches, 1 athletic trainer.
Computers Computers are regularly used in English, foreign language, history, library, mathematics, music, photography, science, video film production, Web site design, yearbook classes. Computer network features include on-campus library services, online commercial services, Internet access, wireless campus network. Student e-mail accounts and computer access in designated common areas are available to students. Students grades are available online. The school has a published electronic and media policy.
Contact Linda Ozawa, Administrative Assistant, Admission Office. 303-914-2513. Fax: 303-914-2589. E-mail: linda.ozawa@coloradoacademy.org. Web site: www.coloradoacademy.org.

THE COLORADO ROCKY MOUNTAIN SCHOOL

1493 County Road 106
Carbondale, Colorado 81623
Head of School: Jeff Leahy

General Information Coeducational boarding and day college-preparatory and arts school. Grades 9–12. Founded: 1953. Setting: small town. Nearest major city is Denver. Students are housed in single-sex dormitories. 350-acre campus. 23 buildings on campus. Approved or accredited by Association for Experiential Education, Association of Colorado Independent Schools, The Association of Boarding Schools, and Colorado Department of Education. Member of National Association of Independent Schools and Secondary School Admission Test Board. Endowment: $13.8 million. Total enrollment: 156. Upper school average class size: 12. Upper school faculty-student ratio: 1:5.
Upper School Student Profile Grade 9: 32 students (21 boys, 11 girls); Grade 10: 38 students (20 boys, 18 girls); Grade 11: 53 students (33 boys, 20 girls); Grade 12: 33 students (16 boys, 17 girls). 60% of students are boarding students. 62% are state residents. 19 states are represented in upper school student body. 16% are international students. International students from China, Democratic People's Republic of Korea, Germany, India, Japan, and Venezuela; 4 other countries represented in student body.
Faculty School total: 42. In upper school: 21 men, 21 women; 21 have advanced degrees; 40 reside on campus.
Subjects Offered Advanced Placement courses, algebra, American literature, anthropology, art, art history, biology, botany, calculus, ceramics, chemistry, computer programming, computer science, creative writing, drama, earth science, ecology, English, English literature, environmental science, ESL, ethics, European history, expository writing, fine arts, French, gardening, geography, geology, geometry, geopolitics, government/civics, grammar, guitar, history, history of ideas, journalism, mathematics, music, philosophy, photography, physical education, physics, physiology, religion, science, Shakespeare, social studies, Spanish, theater, trigonometry, Western civilization, world history, world literature, writing.
Graduation Requirements Arts and fine arts (art, music, dance, drama), chemistry, English, foreign language, mathematics, science, senior project, social studies (includes history), participation in outdoor program. Community service is required.
Special Academic Programs Advanced Placement exam preparation; academic accommodation for the gifted, the musically talented, and the artistically talented; ESL (10 students enrolled).
College Admission Counseling 37 students graduated in 2007; all went to college, including Bates College; Dartmouth College; Lewis & Clark College; Middlebury College; The Colorado College; University of Vermont. Mean SAT critical reading: 577, mean SAT math: 564, mean SAT writing: 561, mean combined SAT: 1698, mean composite ACT: 23. 28% scored over 600 on SAT critical reading, 23% scored over 600 on SAT math, 25% scored over 600 on SAT writing, 25% scored over 1800 on combined SAT.
Student Life Upper grades have student council, honor system. Discipline rests equally with students and faculty.
Tuition and Aid Day student tuition: $22,200; 7-day tuition and room/board: $35,500. Tuition installment plan (monthly payment plans, individually arranged payment plans, 3rd party loan options). Merit scholarship grants, need-based scholarship grants, middle-income loans available. In 2007–08, 35% of upper-school students received aid; total upper-school merit-scholarship money awarded: $28,000. Total amount of financial aid awarded in 2007–08: $648,100.
Admissions Traditional secondary-level entrance grade is 9. For fall 2007, 143 students applied for upper-level admission, 108 were accepted, 66 enrolled. SLEP, SSAT or TOEFL required. Deadline for receipt of application materials: February 15. Application fee required: $50. Interview required.
Athletics Intramural: aerobics/dance (girls), basketball (b,g), dance (b,g), fly fishing (b,g), freestyle skiing (b,g), kayaking (b,g); coed interscholastic: alpine skiing, bicycling, canoeing/kayaking, climbing, cross-country running, independent competitive sports, kayaking, nordic skiing; coed intramural: alpine skiing, backpacking, basketball, bicycling, canoeing/kayaking, climbing, cross-country running, dance, equestrian sports, fishing, fitness, floor hockey, fly fishing, freestyle skiing, Frisbee, hiking/backpacking, horseshoes, jogging, kayaking, martial arts, mountain biking, mountaineering, nordic skiing, outdoor adventure, outdoor education, outdoor recreation, outdoor skills, outdoors. 4 coaches.
Computers Computers are regularly used in art, college planning, ESL, mathematics, science classes. Computer network features include on-campus library services, online commercial services, Internet access, wireless campus network, Internet filtering or blocking technology. Students grades are available online. The school has a published electronic and media policy.
Contact Heather Weymouth, Associate Director of Admission. 970-963-2562. Fax: 970-963-9865. E-mail: hweymouth@crms.org. Web site: www.crms.org.

ANNOUNCEMENT FROM THE SCHOOL Located in Carbondale, Colorado, the Colorado Rocky Mountain School (CRMS) is a boarding and day college-preparatory school for boys and girls in grades 9–12. Founded by John and Anne Holden in 1953, the School has always sustained the Holdens' vision that by nurturing civic courage, critical thought, an international scope of interest, and a responsibility to serve others, a CRMS education would produce citizens who could serve as protectors of democracy and peace. Today, the Colorado Rocky Mountain School continues to aspire to develop the unique potential of each student and believes that the study of Camus and Faulkner, organic chemistry and calculus, and history and photography share equal importance with mending fences, backpacking, kayaking, and other physical activities. CRMS offers a rigorous college-preparatory curriculum that encompasses a full range of academic courses, including selected Advanced Placement classes. The curriculum is designed to prepare students not only to attend college but also to find success there and to nurture a lifelong passion for learning. CRMS believes that the classroom must open onto the world, that learning is not easily contained, and that a scholar's life should encompass action as well as quiet study. In support of this belief, CRMS courses are balanced with a carefully constructed active curriculum, composed of outdoor education, sports, and work crew. The preeminent goal of Colorado Rocky Mountain School is to prepare students in mind, body, and spirit for the challenges they will face in college and beyond. By the time students graduate, they have been trained to think critically and write lucidly. CRMS graduates are well prepared to attend selective colleges and universities across the country. Ultimately, what makes CRMS so special is not its majestic setting at the foot of Mt. Sopris, its new classroom building, or its unparalleled outdoor program. Rather, it is the students and teachers who make up this community and call it home. The only way to feel that is to come and visit and see the School firsthand.

THE COLORADO SPRINGS SCHOOL

21 Broadmoor Avenue
Colorado Springs, Colorado 80906
Head of School: Mr. Kevin Reel

General Information Coeducational day college-preparatory, arts, and experiential learning school. Grades PK–12. Founded: 1962. Setting: suburban. 30-acre campus. 6 buildings on campus. Approved or accredited by Association of Colorado Independent Schools. Member of National Association of Independent Schools, Secondary School Admission Test Board, and National Association for College

Admission Counseling. Endowment: $3.1 million. Total enrollment: 402. Upper school average class size: 16. Upper school faculty-student ratio: 1:12.

Upper School Student Profile Grade 9: 30 students (14 boys, 16 girls); Grade 10: 30 students (11 boys, 19 girls); Grade 11: 40 students (21 boys, 19 girls); Grade 12: 36 students (24 boys, 12 girls).

Faculty School total: 55. In upper school: 12 men, 16 women; 18 have advanced degrees.

Subjects Offered 20th century history, acting, African history, African studies, algebra, American literature, anatomy and physiology, art history, band, biology, biology-AP, botany, calculus-AP, chemistry, choir, community service, composition, computer applications, directing, drama, drawing, economics, economics-AP, English, English literature-AP, environmental science, environmental science-AP, ethics, European history-AP, European literature, filmmaking, French, French language-AP, French literature-AP, functions, geography, geology, geometry, glass-blowing, global studies, government and politics-AP, grammar, history, Latin American history, literature, macro/microeconomics-AP, microeconomics, music, music appreciation, painting, philosophy, photography, physical education, physics, playwriting, pottery, pre-calculus, printmaking, SAT/ACT preparation, sculpture, Spanish, Spanish literature, Spanish literature-AP, speech, statistics, statistics-AP, studio art-AP, textiles, theater, trigonometry, U.S. history, U.S. history-AP, Western civilization, world geography, world history, world literature, writing, writing workshop, yearbook.

Graduation Requirements Arts and fine arts (art, music, dance, drama), athletics, college admission preparation, computer science, English, experiential education, foreign language, history, mathematics, science, social studies (includes history), speech and oral interpretations, Experience Centered Seminar each year, College Overview Course, 24 hours of community service per each year of high school.

Special Academic Programs Advanced Placement exam preparation; honors section; independent study; term-away projects; study abroad; academic accommodation for the gifted.

College Admission Counseling 36 students graduated in 2008; all went to college, including Colorado State University; The Colorado College; University of Denver; University of San Diego. Mean composite ACT: 27.

Student Life Upper grades have specified standards of dress, student council, honor system. Discipline rests equally with students and faculty.

Summer Programs Enrichment, advancement, sports, art/fine arts programs offered; held both on and off campus; held at various field trip locations; accepts boys and girls; open to students from other schools. 90 students usually enrolled. 2009 schedule: June 1 to July 3. Application deadline: April 15.

Tuition and Aid Day student tuition: $16,130. Tuition installment plan (Insured Tuition Payment Plan, monthly payment plans). Merit scholarship grants, need-based scholarship grants available. In 2008–09, 37% of upper-school students received aid; total upper-school merit-scholarship money awarded: $110,100. Total amount of financial aid awarded in 2008–09: $447,193.

Admissions Traditional secondary-level entrance grade is 9. For fall 2008, 32 students applied for upper-level admission, 13 were accepted, 10 enrolled. Deadline for receipt of application materials: none. Application fee required: $50. Interview required.

Athletics Interscholastic: basketball (boys, girls), cross-country running (b,g), golf (b), lacrosse (b), soccer (b,g), tennis (b,g), volleyball (g); intramural: physical fitness (b,g), physical training (b,g); coed intramural: mountaineering, outdoor education, rock climbing, skiing (cross-country), skiing (downhill). 2 PE instructors, 8 coaches.

Computers Computers are regularly used in all academic classes. Computer network features include on-campus library services, online commercial services, Internet access, wireless campus network, Internet filtering or blocking technology. Campus intranet, student e-mail accounts, and computer access in designated common areas are available to students. Students grades are available online. The school has a published electronic and media policy.

Contact Mrs. Eve Sckolnik, Director of Admission and Financial Aid. 719-475-9747 Ext. 512. Fax: 719-475-9864. E-mail: esckolnik@css.org. Web site: www.css.org.

ANNOUNCEMENT FROM THE SCHOOL CSS prepares students in Pre-Kindergarten through 12th grade to think independently and to meet the needs of a dynamic world as the School delivers strong academics, top college counseling, and learning specialists. The curriculum at CSS provides global perspectives, service learning, and character-building opportunities. The School creates a dynamic learning community and develops authentic relationships.

COLUMBIA ACADEMY

1101 West 7th Street
Columbia, Tennessee 38401

Head of School: Mr. Barry England

General Information Coeducational day college-preparatory, arts, business, religious studies, and technology school, affiliated with Church of Christ. Grades K–12. Founded: 1978. Setting: small town. Nearest major city is Nashville. 67-acre campus. 6 buildings on campus. Approved or accredited by National Christian School Association, Southern Association of Colleges and Schools, and Tennessee Department of Education. Total enrollment: 617. Upper school average class size: 18. Upper school faculty-student ratio: 1:13.

Upper School Student Profile Grade 7: 54 students (30 boys, 24 girls); Grade 8: 31 students (18 boys, 13 girls); Grade 9: 55 students (36 boys, 19 girls); Grade 10: 49 students (22 boys, 27 girls); Grade 11: 38 students (13 boys, 25 girls); Grade 12: 42 students (22 boys, 20 girls). 60% of students are members of Church of Christ.

Faculty School total: 64. In upper school: 15 men, 13 women; 16 have advanced degrees.

Subjects Offered Accounting, advanced math, algebra, American history, American literature, anatomy and physiology, art, band, Bible, biology, British literature, calculus, chemistry, chorus, composition, computer keyboarding, computer science, concert band, creative writing, economics, English, English literature and composition-AP, environmental science, fine arts, geography, geometry, government/civics, grammar, health, journalism, math review, music, physical education, physical science, physics, pre-calculus, psychology, religion, Spanish, speech, U.S. history-AP, world history.

Graduation Requirements Arts and fine arts (art, music, dance, drama), computer science, economics, electives, English, foreign language, mathematics, physical education (includes health), religion (includes Bible studies and theology), science, social science, social studies (includes history), speech, successfully pass the state Gateway Exams in Algebra I, English II and Biology, four hours of approved service required for each quarter enrolled.

Special Academic Programs Advanced Placement exam preparation; honors section; independent study; study at local college for college credit.

College Admission Counseling 42 students graduated in 2008; all went to college, including Columbia State Community College; Freed-Hardeman University; Harding University; Lipscomb University; Middle Tennessee State University; The University of Tennessee. Median composite ACT: 23. 26% scored over 26 on composite ACT.

Student Life Upper grades have specified standards of dress, student council, honor system. Discipline rests primarily with faculty.

Tuition and Aid Day student tuition: $5150. Tuition installment plan (monthly payment plans, individually arranged payment plans). Tuition reduction for siblings, need-based scholarship grants, paying campus jobs available. In 2008–09, 4% of upper-school students received aid.

Admissions Traditional secondary-level entrance grade is 9. For fall 2008, 26 students applied for upper-level admission, 25 were accepted, 21 enrolled. Otis-Lennon School Ability Test required. Deadline for receipt of application materials: none. Application fee required: $50. On-campus interview recommended.

Athletics Interscholastic: baseball (boys), basketball (b,g), bowling (b,g), cheering (g), football (b), golf (b,g), soccer (b,g), softball (g), strength & conditioning (b), tennis (b,g), trap and skeet (b,g), volleyball (g); intramural: flag football (g); coed interscholastic: cross-country running. 1 PE instructor.

Computers Computers are regularly used in accounting, computer applications, creative writing, journalism, keyboarding, library, yearbook classes. Computer network features include on-campus library services, Internet access. Students grades are available online. The school has a published electronic and media policy.

Contact Mrs. Benja White, Director of Admissions. 931-490-4302. Fax: 931-380-8506. E-mail: btwhite@colacademy.com. Web site: www.columbia-academy.net.

COLUMBIA GRAMMAR AND PREPARATORY SCHOOL

5 West 93rd Street
New York, New York 10025

Head of School: Dr. Richard J. Soghoian

General Information Coeducational day college-preparatory and arts school. Grades PK–12. Founded: 1764. Setting: urban. 3 buildings on campus. Approved or accredited by New York State Association of Independent Schools and New York Department of Education. Member of National Association of Independent Schools. Endowment: $20 million. Total enrollment: 1,125. Upper school average class size: 14. Upper school faculty-student ratio: 1:7.

Upper School Student Profile Grade 7: 86 students (40 boys, 46 girls); Grade 8: 77 students (36 boys, 41 girls); Grade 9: 101 students (54 boys, 47 girls); Grade 10: 100 students (54 boys, 46 girls); Grade 11: 112 students (60 boys, 52 girls); Grade 12: 98 students (46 boys, 52 girls).

Faculty School total: 218. In upper school: 36 men, 39 women; 62 have advanced degrees.

Subjects Offered 3-dimensional art, acting, advanced computer applications, Advanced Placement courses, American history, American literature, anatomy, anthropology, art, art history, biology, calculus, ceramics, chemistry, community service, comparative religion, computer programming, computer science, creative writing, drama, driver education, economics, English, English literature, environmental science, European history, expository writing, film, fine arts, French, genetics, geography, geology, government/civics, grammar, health, history, Japanese, journalism, Latin, mathematics, music, music history, philosophy, photography, physical education, physics, psychology, religion, science, social studies, sociology, Spanish, theater, world history, world literature, writing.

Graduation Requirements Arts and fine arts (art, music, dance, drama), computer science, English, foreign language, mathematics, physical education (includes health), science, social studies (includes history). Community service is required.

Special Academic Programs Advanced Placement exam preparation; honors section; independent study; academic accommodation for the gifted; remedial reading and/or remedial writing; remedial math; programs in English, mathematics, general development for dyslexic students.
College Admission Counseling 92 students graduated in 2008; all went to college, including Lehigh University; New York University; Oberlin College; University of Michigan; University of Pennsylvania; University of Rochester. Median SAT critical reading: 640, median SAT math: 630, median SAT writing: 670. 76% scored over 600 on SAT critical reading, 76% scored over 600 on SAT math, 75% scored over 600 on SAT writing.
Student Life Upper grades have specified standards of dress, student council. Discipline rests primarily with faculty.
Tuition and Aid Day student tuition: $32,540–$33,900. Tuition installment plan (monthly payment plans). Need-based scholarship grants available. In 2008–09, 23% of upper-school students received aid. Total amount of financial aid awarded in 2008–09: $2,445,655.
Admissions Traditional secondary-level entrance grade is 9. For fall 2008, 285 students applied for upper-level admission, 68 were accepted, 45 enrolled. ISEE required. Deadline for receipt of application materials: December 1. Application fee required: $60. On-campus interview required.
Athletics Interscholastic: baseball (boys), basketball (b,g), cross-country running (b,g), golf (b), ice skating (b), running (b,g), soccer (b,g), softball (g), swimming and diving (b), tennis (b,g), track and field (b,g), volleyball (g); coed interscholastic: ice hockey; coed intramural: aerobics, badminton, basketball, combined training, fitness, floor hockey, jogging, physical fitness, physical training, running, strength & conditioning, table tennis, touch football, ultimate Frisbee, volleyball, weight training. 5 PE instructors, 10 coaches.
Computers Computers are regularly used in desktop publishing, foreign language, graphics, science, typing, Web site design, writing fundamentals classes. Computer network features include on-campus library services, online commercial services, Internet access, wireless campus network, Internet filtering or blocking technology. Campus intranet, student e-mail accounts, and computer access in designated common areas are available to students. The school has a published electronic and media policy.
Contact Terry Centeno, Admissions Coordinator. 212-749-6200 Ext. 362. Fax: 212-961-3105. Web site: www.cgps.org.

See Close-Up on page 716.

COLUMBIA INTERNATIONAL COLLEGE OF CANADA

1003 Main Street West
Hamilton, Ontario L8S 4P3, Canada
Head of School: Mr. Ron Rambarran

General Information Coeducational boarding and day college-preparatory, general academic, arts, and business school. Grades 7–12. Founded: 1979. Setting: urban. Nearest major city is Toronto, Canada. Students are housed in single-sex by floor dormitories and single-sex dormitories. 20-acre campus. 3 buildings on campus. Approved or accredited by Ontario Ministry of Education and Ontario Department of Education. Language of instruction: English. Total enrollment: 1,134. Upper school average class size: 20. Upper school faculty-student ratio: 1:20.
Upper School Student Profile Grade 7: 4 students (1 boy, 3 girls); Grade 8: 10 students (5 boys, 5 girls); Grade 9: 61 students (45 boys, 16 girls); Grade 10: 77 students (55 boys, 22 girls); Grade 11: 160 students (73 boys, 87 girls); Grade 12: 822 students (458 boys, 364 girls). 80% of students are boarding students. 2% are province residents. 5 provinces are represented in upper school student body. 98% are international students. International students from China, Ghana, Mexico, Nigeria, Republic of Korea, and Russian Federation; 46 other countries represented in student body.
Faculty School total: 75. In upper school: 23 men, 30 women; 25 have advanced degrees.
Subjects Offered 20th century world history, accounting, advanced TOEFL/grammar, algebra, analysis and differential calculus, analytic geometry, art, art and culture, art appreciation, art education, biology, business, calculus, calculus-AP, Canadian geography, Canadian history, career education, chemistry, chemistry-AP, Chinese, civics, college counseling, computer education, computer programming, computer science, computer technologies, discrete mathematics, dramatic arts, economics, English, English composition, English literature, environmental education, ESL, French, French as a second language, general business, general math, general science, geography, geometry, history, intro to computers, kinesiology, lab science, language arts, law, leadership, leadership education training, leadership training, life management skills, life skills, Mandarin, math applications, math methods, mathematics, mathematics-AP, Mexican history, modern world history, music, outdoor education, physical education, physical fitness, physics, science, society challenge and change, Spanish, visual arts.
Graduation Requirements Arts, business, English, mathematics, science, social studies (includes history), Community Volunteer Hours, Ontario Secondary School Literacy Test.
Special Academic Programs Advanced Placement exam preparation; accelerated programs; study at local college for college credit; ESL (405 students enrolled).
College Admission Counseling 524 students graduated in 2008; all went to college, including Carleton University; McGill University; McMaster University; University of Toronto; University of Waterloo; York University.
Student Life Upper grades have uniform requirement, student council. Discipline rests primarily with faculty.
Summer Programs Remediation, advancement, ESL, sports, art/fine arts programs offered; session focuses on Academics, ESL and Leadership Education; held both on and off campus; held at Bark Lake Outdoor Education and Leadership Campus; accepts boys and girls; open to students from other schools. 700 students usually enrolled. 2009 schedule: June 29 to August 16. Application deadline: May 25.
Tuition and Aid Day student tuition: CAN$6750–CAN$16,820; 7-day tuition and room/board: CAN$11,000–CAN$27,020. Tuition reduction for siblings, merit scholarship grants available.
Admissions Traditional secondary-level entrance grade is 12. For fall 2008, 494 students applied for upper-level admission, 474 were accepted, 432 enrolled. Math and English placement tests required. Deadline for receipt of application materials: none. Application fee required: CAN$200. Interview recommended.
Athletics Interscholastic: badminton (boys, girls), basketball (b), indoor soccer (b), soccer (b); intramural: aerobics (g), aquatics (b,g), badminton (b,g), ball hockey (b,g), basketball (b,g), cheering (g), fishing (b), fitness (b,g), floor hockey (b), football (b), indoor soccer (b,g), outdoor activities (b,g), soccer (b,g), squash (b), strength & conditioning (b), swimming and diving (b,g), table tennis (b,g), tennis (b,g), volleyball (b,g), wallyball (b,g), weight training (b,g); coed interscholastic: badminton; coed intramural: badminton, ball hockey, canoeing/kayaking, cooperative games, cross-country running, fishing, floor hockey, golf, hiking/backpacking, ice skating, in-line skating, jogging, martial arts, outdoor activities, physical fitness, physical training, roller blading, ropes courses, running, self defense, skiing (cross-country), snowshoeing, squash, strength & conditioning, swimming and diving, table tennis, volleyball, wallyball, weight training, wilderness, wilderness survival, winter walking, yoga. 3 PE instructors, 4 coaches.
Computers Computers are regularly used in accounting, business, business applications, career education, economics, ESL, geography, music, science classes. Computer network features include Internet access, wireless campus network. Computer access in designated common areas is available to students. Students grades are available online.
Contact Ms. Marina Rosas, Admissions Officer. 905-572-7883 Ext. 2835. Fax: 905-572-9332. E-mail: admissions02@cic-totalcare.com. Web site: www.cic-TotalCare.com.

COLUMBIA INTERNATIONAL SCHOOL

153 Matsugo
Tokorozawa, Saitama 359-0027, Japan
Head of School: Mr. Barrie McCliggott

General Information Coeducational boarding and day college-preparatory, business, bilingual studies, and technology school. Boarding grades 7–12, day grades 1–12. Founded: 1988. Setting: suburban. Nearest major city is Tokyo, Japan. Students are housed in single-sex dormitories. 2-acre campus. 2 buildings on campus. Approved or accredited by Ontario Ministry of Education, Western Association of Schools and Colleges, and state department of education. Language of instruction: English. Endowment: ¥10 million. Total enrollment: 273. Upper school average class size: 14. Upper school faculty-student ratio: 1:12.
Upper School Student Profile Grade 10: 29 students (15 boys, 14 girls); Grade 11: 28 students (12 boys, 16 girls); Grade 12: 29 students (16 boys, 13 girls). 5% of students are boarding students. 10% are international students. International students from Canada, China, Philippines, Republic of Korea, United Kingdom, and United States; 10 other countries represented in student body.
Faculty School total: 32. In upper school: 18 men, 5 women; 7 have advanced degrees; 6 reside on campus.
Subjects Offered 1½ elective credits, 20th century world history, advanced TOEFL/grammar, algebra, ancient world history, art, Asian history, biology, business, calculus, Canadian geography, Canadian history, chemistry, communications, community service, computer keyboarding, computer science, computers, economics, English, ESL, foreign language, geography, geometry, global issues, history, Internet, keyboarding, literacy, mathematics, media studies, physical education, reading, TOEFL preparation, world issues, yearbook.
Graduation Requirements 20th century history, arts, Asian history, biology, chemistry, economics, English, geography, humanities, law, mathematics, physical education (includes health), science, social science, Ontario Literacy Test, 40 hours of community involvement activities.
Special Academic Programs Advanced Placement exam preparation; honors section; accelerated programs; independent study; study abroad; remedial reading and/or remedial writing; remedial math; ESL (70 students enrolled).
College Admission Counseling 25 students graduated in 2008; 21 went to college, including Queen's University at Kingston; Temple University; The University of British Columbia; University of Saskatchewan; University of Victoria; Western Michigan University. Other: 4 had other specific plans.
Student Life Upper grades have uniform requirement, student council, honor system. Discipline rests primarily with faculty.
Summer Programs Remediation, ESL, sports, art/fine arts, computer instruction programs offered; session focuses on ESL, computers, science, and art; held both on

and off campus; held at Tokyo, Japan, Edmonton, Canada, and Gold Coast, Australia; accepts boys and girls; open to students from other schools. 150 students usually enrolled. 2009 schedule: July 5 to August 9. Application deadline: June 30.
Tuition and Aid Day student tuition: ¥1,575,000; 7-day tuition and room/board: ¥2,805,000. Tuition installment plan (individually arranged payment plans, term payment plans). Tuition reduction for siblings, merit scholarship grants available. In 2008–09, 5% of upper-school students received aid; total upper-school merit-scholarship money awarded: ¥2,735,000. Total amount of financial aid awarded in 2008–09: ¥3,360,000.
Admissions Traditional secondary-level entrance grade is 10. For fall 2008, 67 students applied for upper-level admission, 32 were accepted, 28 enrolled. Any standardized test required. Deadline for receipt of application materials: none. Application fee required: ¥25,000. On-campus interview required.
Athletics Coed Intramural: aerobics, alpine skiing, artistic gym, badminton, ball hockey, baseball, basketball, bicycling, blading, bowling, climbing, cooperative games, dance, dance team, field hockey, floor hockey, football, freestyle skiing, Frisbee, hiking/backpacking, hockey, indoor hockey, indoor soccer, juggling, kickball, life saving, mountain biking, outdoor activities, physical fitness, power lifting, rock climbing, self defense, ski jumping, skiing (downhill), snowboarding, soccer, softball, table tennis, team handball, tennis, volleyball, wall climbing, weight lifting, weight training, yoga. 2 PE instructors.
Computers Computers are regularly used in wilderness education classes. Computer network features include Internet access, wireless campus network, Internet filtering or blocking technology, repair service. Campus intranet and student e-mail accounts are available to students. The school has a published electronic and media policy.
Contact Mr. Yoshitaka Matsumura, Administrator. +81-4-2946-1911. Fax: +81-4-2946-1955. E-mail: admissions@columbia-ca.co.jp. Web site: www.columbia-ca.co.jp.

ANNOUNCEMENT FROM THE SCHOOL CIS encourages personal growth, social awareness, and respect for achievement. The staff helps students develop powers of critical and creative thought, which prepare them for both the demands of postsecondary education and life as international citizens. Varied opportunities for achievement and personal fulfillment are provided through academic studies and extracurricular pursuits.

THE COLUMBUS ACADEMY

PO Box 30745
4300 Cherry Bottom Road
Gahanna, Ohio 43230

Head of School: John M. Mackenzie

General Information Coeducational day college-preparatory school. Grades PK–12. Founded: 1911. Setting: suburban. Nearest major city is Columbus. 233-acre campus. 16 buildings on campus. Approved or accredited by Independent Schools Association of the Central States, Ohio Association of Independent Schools, and Ohio Department of Education. Member of National Association of Independent Schools and Secondary School Admission Test Board. Endowment: $25.4 million. Total enrollment: 1,057. Upper school average class size: 15. Upper school faculty-student ratio: 1:8.
Upper School Student Profile Grade 9: 87 students (43 boys, 44 girls); Grade 10: 91 students (49 boys, 42 girls); Grade 11: 92 students (45 boys, 47 girls); Grade 12: 91 students (53 boys, 38 girls).
Faculty School total: 135. In upper school: 27 men, 22 women; 37 have advanced degrees.
Subjects Offered Advanced chemistry, advanced computer applications, advanced math, Advanced Placement courses, advanced studio art-AP, algebra, American government-AP, American history, American history-AP, American literature, analysis and differential calculus, art history, biology, biology-AP, British literature, calculus, calculus-AP, career/college preparation, ceramics, chemistry, chemistry-AP, China/Japan history, Chinese, choir, choral music, chorus, college counseling, comparative government and politics-AP, comparative political systems-AP, computer applications, computer education, computer programming-AP, computer science, computer science-AP, concert band, concert choir, creative writing, drawing and design, economics, economics-AP, English, European history, European history-AP, fine arts, French, French-AP, geology, geometry, government and politics-AP, government-AP, health education, history of China and Japan, instrumental music, integrated science, Latin, Latin-AP, military history, photography, physical education, physics, physics-AP, pre-calculus, Russian history, senior career experience, South African history, Spanish, Spanish language-AP, Spanish literature-AP, speech, strings, theater, trigonometry, U.S. government and politics, U.S. history-AP, weight training, world history, world religions.
Graduation Requirements Arts and fine arts (art, music, dance, drama), English, foreign language, mathematics, science, social studies (includes history), formal speech delivered to the students and faculty of the upper school during junior year, community service requirement.
Special Academic Programs Advanced Placement exam preparation; honors section; independent study; academic accommodation for the gifted.
College Admission Counseling 91 students graduated in 2008; 90 went to college, including Boston University; Kenyon College; Miami University; Northwestern University; Southern Methodist University; The Ohio State University. Other: 1 had other specific plans. Median SAT critical reading: 640, median SAT math: 670, median SAT writing: 650, median combined SAT: 1970, median composite ACT: 27. 74% scored over 600 on SAT critical reading, 78% scored over 600 on SAT math, 78% scored over 600 on SAT writing, 78% scored over 1800 on combined SAT, 74% scored over 26 on composite ACT.
Student Life Upper grades have specified standards of dress, student council. Discipline rests equally with students and faculty.
Summer Programs Remediation, enrichment, advancement, art/fine arts, computer instruction programs offered; session focuses on academic enrichment, fine arts, fun and games; held on campus; accepts boys and girls; open to students from other schools. 400 students usually enrolled. 2009 schedule: June 15 to August 22.
Tuition and Aid Day student tuition: $18,100. Tuition installment plan (The Tuition Plan, Academic Management Services Plan, Tuition Management Systems Plan). Need-based scholarship grants available. In 2008–09, 18% of upper-school students received aid. Total amount of financial aid awarded in 2008–09: $633,830.
Admissions Traditional secondary-level entrance grade is 9. For fall 2008, 66 students applied for upper-level admission, 33 were accepted, 25 enrolled. ISEE or SSAT required. Deadline for receipt of application materials: none. Application fee required: $50. On-campus interview required.
Athletics Interscholastic: baseball (boys), basketball (b,g), cross-country running (b,g), diving (b,g), field hockey (g), football (b), lacrosse (g), soccer (b,g), swimming and diving (b,g), tennis (b,g), track and field (b,g), volleyball (g), wrestling (b); coed intramural: bicycling. 3 PE instructors, 2 athletic trainers.
Computers Computers are regularly used in college planning, current events, economics, English, foreign language, humanities, journalism, Latin, learning cognition, library skills, mathematics, media production, multimedia, music, photography, publications, reading, remedial study skills, research skills, SAT preparation, science, technology, theater, writing classes. Computer network features include on-campus library services, online commercial services, Internet access, wireless campus network. Campus intranet, student e-mail accounts, and computer access in designated common areas are available to students. The school has a published electronic and media policy.
Contact John Wuorinen, Director of Admissions and Financial Aid. 614-337-4309. Fax: 614-475-0396. E-mail: wuorinen@columbusacademy.org. Web site: www.ColumbusAcademy.org.

ANNOUNCEMENT FROM THE SCHOOL Committed to its motto, "In Quest of the Best," the Columbus Academy is an academically rigorous school that emphasizes community service, diversity, and moral courage. Serving 1,050 girls and boys in grades preK–12, the Academy offers a comprehensive program in academics, athletics, the arts, and other cocurricular offerings. Learning takes place in impressive facilities on the 231-acre campus located 15 minutes from downtown Columbus.

COLUMBUS HIGH SCHOOL

3231 West 9th Street
Waterloo, Iowa 50702

Head of School: Mr. Tom Ulses

General Information Coeducational day college-preparatory and general academic school, affiliated with Roman Catholic Church. Grades 9–12. Founded: 1959. Setting: urban. 3-acre campus. 1 building on campus. Approved or accredited by National Catholic Education Association and Iowa Department of Education. Endowment: $1.3 million. Total enrollment: 294. Upper school average class size: 20. Upper school faculty-student ratio: 1:15.
Upper School Student Profile Grade 9: 80 students (50 boys, 30 girls); Grade 10: 71 students (41 boys, 30 girls); Grade 11: 82 students (43 boys, 39 girls); Grade 12: 61 students (32 boys, 29 girls). 90% of students are Roman Catholic.
Faculty School total: 21. In upper school: 11 men, 10 women; 8 have advanced degrees.
Subjects Offered Art, auto mechanics, business, computer programming, computer science, English, general science, home economics, industrial arts, instrumental music, mathematics, physical education, psychology, religion, science, social studies, Spanish, speech, vocal music, woodworking.
Graduation Requirements English, mathematics, physical education (includes health), religion (includes Bible studies and theology), science, social studies (includes history), speech.
Special Academic Programs Advanced Placement exam preparation; study at local college for college credit.
College Admission Counseling 79 students graduated in 2008; 78 went to college, including Hawkeye Community College; Iowa State University of Science and Technology; Loras College; The University of Iowa; University of Northern Iowa. Other: 1 entered a postgraduate year.
Student Life Upper grades have specified standards of dress, student council. Discipline rests primarily with faculty. Attendance at religious services is required.
Tuition and Aid Day student tuition: $3370–$5100. Tuition installment plan (FACTS Tuition Payment Plan, individually arranged payment plans). Need-based scholarship grants, paying campus jobs available.

Admissions Traditional secondary-level entrance grade is 9. For fall 2008, 80 students applied for upper-level admission, 80 were accepted, 80 enrolled. Deadline for receipt of application materials: none. Application fee required: $70. Interview required.
Athletics Interscholastic: baseball (boys), basketball (b,g), bowling (g), cheering (g), cross-country running (b,g), danceline (g), football (b), golf (b,g), hockey (b). 1 PE instructor, 1 athletic trainer.
Computers Computers are regularly used in English, science classes. Computer resources include on-campus library services, Internet access, Internet filtering or blocking technology. Students grades are available online. The school has a published electronic and media policy.
Contact Tom Ulses, Principal. 319-233-3358 Ext. 135. Fax: 319-235-0733 Ext. 319. E-mail: tulses@columbushigh.org.

COMMONWEALTH PARKVILLE SCHOOL

PO Box 70177
San Juan, Puerto Rico 00936-8177
Head of School: F. Richard Marracino

General Information Coeducational day college-preparatory, arts, and technology school. Grades PK–12. Founded: 1952. Setting: urban. Nearest major city is Hato Rey. 1-acre campus. 3 buildings on campus. Approved or accredited by Middle States Association of Colleges and Schools, The College Board, and Puerto Rico Department of Education. Endowment: $330,000. Total enrollment: 729. Upper school average class size: 13. Upper school faculty-student ratio: 1:8.
Upper School Student Profile Grade 9: 33 students (23 boys, 10 girls); Grade 10: 34 students (19 boys, 15 girls); Grade 11: 45 students (29 boys, 16 girls); Grade 12: 51 students (25 boys, 26 girls).
Faculty School total: 95. In upper school: 14 men, 20 women; 12 have advanced degrees.
Subjects Offered Advanced Placement courses, algebra, American history, American literature, anatomy and physiology, art, band, biology, biology-AP, business mathematics, calculus, ceramics, chemistry, chemistry-AP, civics, computer science, computer technologies, creative writing, dance, drama, drawing, earth science, ecology, English, English language and composition-AP, English literature, ethics, European history, forensics, French, geometry, health, jewelry making, journalism, mathematics, modern world history, music, music appreciation, music history, painting, physical education, physics, play production, pre-calculus, printmaking, psychology, sculpture, sociology, Spanish, Spanish-AP, stained glass, theater, trigonometry, U.S. history-AP, world history.
Graduation Requirements Computer science, English, ethics, foreign language, mathematics, physical education (includes health), Puerto Rican history, science, social studies (includes history), Spanish.
Special Academic Programs Advanced Placement exam preparation; honors section; independent study; domestic exchange program (with The Network Program Schools); programs in English, mathematics, general development for dyslexic students; special instructional classes for students with mild learning disabilities and Attention Deficit Disorder.
College Admission Counseling 52 students graduated in 2007; all went to college, including Boston University; Brown University; Franklin & Marshall College; Savannah College of Art and Design; University of Puerto Rico, Río Piedras; Villanova University. Mean SAT critical reading: 544, mean SAT math: 529, mean SAT writing: 534.
Student Life Upper grades have uniform requirement, student council, honor system. Discipline rests primarily with faculty.
Tuition and Aid Day student tuition: $8850–$10,950. Tuition installment plan (individually arranged payment plans, annual and semester payment plans). Tuition reduction for siblings, merit scholarship grants, need-based scholarship grants available. In 2007–08, 2% of upper-school students received aid; total upper-school merit-scholarship money awarded: $26,390. Total amount of financial aid awarded in 2007–08: $42,175.
Admissions Traditional secondary-level entrance grade is 9. For fall 2007, 13 students applied for upper-level admission, 9 were accepted, 8 enrolled. Stanford Achievement Test required. Deadline for receipt of application materials: none. Application fee required: $85. On-campus interview required.
Athletics Interscholastic: baseball (boys), basketball (b,g), cross-country running (b,g), football (b), indoor soccer (b,g), soccer (b,g), softball (g), track and field (b,g), volleyball (b,g); intramural: soccer (b,g), softball (b,g), volleyball (b,g); coed interscholastic: indoor soccer; coed intramural: badminton, basketball, cooperative games, field hockey, fitness, flag football, Frisbee, indoor soccer, jogging, outdoor activities, outdoor education, outdoor recreation, physical fitness, physical training, soccer, softball, strength & conditioning, table tennis, tennis, track and field, volleyball, walking. 3 PE instructors, 8 coaches, 1 athletic trainer.
Computers Computers are regularly used in English, mathematics, science, yearbook classes. Computer resources include on-campus library services, Internet access, wireless campus network, Internet filtering or blocking technology. Campus intranet is available to students. Students grades are available online. The school has a published electronic and media policy.
Contact Mrs. Jo-Ann Aranguren, Director of Admissions. 787-765-4411 Ext. 32. Fax: 787-764-3809. E-mail: jaranguren@cpspr.org. Web site: www.cpspr.org.

ANNOUNCEMENT FROM THE SCHOOL Unique characteristics include academic rigor, many activities and sports, close relationships among students and teachers, and emphasis on Puerto Rican culture. The Annual Giving Program has been earmarked to enhance facilities and technology initiatives. CPS has recently received an Edward E. Ford Foundation Matching Grant to support the Faculty Digital Training Initiative.

COMMONWEALTH SCHOOL

151 Commonwealth Avenue
Boston, Massachusetts 02116
Head of School: William D. Wharton

General Information Coeducational day college-preparatory, arts, and technology school. Grades 9–12. Founded: 1957. Setting: urban. 1 building on campus. Approved or accredited by Association of Independent Schools in New England, New England Association of Schools and Colleges, and Massachusetts Department of Education. Member of National Association of Independent Schools and Secondary School Admission Test Board. Endowment: $11.7 million. Total enrollment: 154. Upper school average class size: 12. Upper school faculty-student ratio: 1:5.
Upper School Student Profile Grade 9: 38 students (24 boys, 14 girls); Grade 10: 37 students (18 boys, 19 girls); Grade 11: 38 students (14 boys, 24 girls); Grade 12: 41 students (23 boys, 18 girls).
Faculty School total: 35. In upper school: 13 men, 22 women; 29 have advanced degrees.
Subjects Offered Advanced chemistry, advanced computer applications, advanced math, Advanced Placement courses, African American history, African-American literature, algebra, American history, analysis of data, ancient history, ancient world history, art, art history, biology, biology-AP, calculus, calculus-AP, ceramics, chamber groups, chemistry, choral music, chorus, classics, college counseling, community service, computer programming, computer science, current events, dance, drama, drawing, economics, English, English literature, European history, expository writing, film series, film studies, fine arts, French, geometry, Greek, history of the Americas, honors algebra, honors English, honors geometry, honors U.S. history, Japanese history, jazz, jazz band, jazz ensemble, jazz theory, Latin, Latin American history, mathematics, medieval history, medieval/Renaissance history, modern European history-AP, music, music theory, organic chemistry, philosophy, photography, physical education, physics, printmaking, probability and statistics, science, short story, Spanish, Spanish literature, theater, writing.
Graduation Requirements Algebra, ancient history, art, biology, calculus, chemistry, English, ethics, foreign language, geometry, medieval history, physical education (includes health), physics, U.S. history, City of Boston Course, completion of a one week project each year, Health and Community. Community service is required.
Special Academic Programs Advanced Placement exam preparation; honors section; independent study; study abroad; academic accommodation for the gifted, the musically talented, and the artistically talented.
College Admission Counseling 36 students graduated in 2008; all went to college, including Bates College; Boston College; Pomona College; Reed College; Smith College; Tufts University. Median SAT critical reading: 725, median SAT math: 720, median SAT writing: 735, median combined SAT: 2190.
Student Life Upper grades have honor system. Discipline rests primarily with faculty.
Tuition and Aid Day student tuition: $29,070. Tuition installment plan (Key Tuition Payment Plan). Need-based scholarship grants, need-based loans available. In 2008–09, 36% of upper-school students received aid. Total amount of financial aid awarded in 2008–09: $1,100,000.
Admissions Traditional secondary-level entrance grade is 9. For fall 2008, 175 students applied for upper-level admission, 60 were accepted, 44 enrolled. ISEE or SSAT required. Deadline for receipt of application materials: February 1. Application fee required: $45. On-campus interview required.
Athletics Interscholastic: basketball (boys, girls), independent competitive sports (b,g), soccer (b,g); coed interscholastic: baseball, fencing, squash, ultimate Frisbee; coed intramural: aerobics/Nautilus, ballet, cross-country running, dance, fencing, fitness, martial arts, sailing, squash, tai chi, yoga. 12 coaches.
Computers Computers are regularly used in photography, programming classes. Computer network features include on-campus library services, Internet access, wireless campus network, Internet filtering or blocking technology. Campus intranet, student e-mail accounts, and computer access in designated common areas are available to students. The school has a published electronic and media policy.
Contact Ms. Lihuan Li, Assistant Director of Admissions. 617-266-7525. Fax: 617-266-5769. E-mail: admissions@commschool.org. Web site: www.commschool.org.

See Close-Up on page 718.

COMMUNITY CHRISTIAN ACADEMY

11875 Taylor Mill Road
Independence, Kentucky 41051

Head of School: Tara Montez Bates

General Information Coeducational day college-preparatory and religious studies school, affiliated with Pentecostal Church. Grades PS–12. Founded: 1983. Setting: rural. Nearest major city is Cincinnati, OH. 107-acre campus. 2 buildings on campus. Approved or accredited by International Christian Accrediting Association and Kentucky Department of Education. Total enrollment: 201. Upper school average class size: 15. Upper school faculty-student ratio: 1:20.

Upper School Student Profile Grade 9: 14 students (9 boys, 5 girls); Grade 10: 8 students (4 boys, 4 girls); Grade 11: 10 students (5 boys, 5 girls); Grade 12: 10 students (7 boys, 3 girls). 50% of students are Pentecostal.

Faculty School total: 14. In upper school: 2 men, 4 women; 1 has an advanced degree.

Subjects Offered Advanced math, algebra, American history, art appreciation, Bible, biology, business skills, calculus, chemistry, choral music, computer applications, cultural geography, English, geography, health, integrated science, life skills, literature, pre-algebra, pre-calculus, Spanish.

Graduation Requirements Bible, electives, English, foreign language, mathematics, physical education (includes health), science, social studies (includes history), statistics, visual and performing arts.

College Admission Counseling 8 students graduated in 2008; all went to college, including Cincinnati State Technical and Community College; Northern Kentucky University. Mean composite ACT: 21.

Student Life Upper grades have specified standards of dress, student council, honor system. Discipline rests primarily with faculty. Attendance at religious services is required.

Tuition and Aid Day student tuition: $3200. Guaranteed tuition plan. Tuition installment plan (The Tuition Plan, monthly payment plans). Financial aid available to upper-school students. In 2008–09, 3% of upper-school students received aid. Total amount of financial aid awarded in 2008–09: $5000.

Admissions Traditional secondary-level entrance grade is 9. For fall 2008, 11 students applied for upper-level admission, 9 were accepted, 9 enrolled. Admissions testing required. Deadline for receipt of application materials: none. Application fee required: $50. Interview required.

Athletics Interscholastic: basketball (boys, girls), cheering (g), golf (b), volleyball (g). 1 PE instructor, 3 coaches.

Computers Computers are regularly used in foreign language classes. Computer network features include Internet access.

Contact Jackie Foote, Secretary. 859-356-7990 Ext. 112. Fax: 859-356-7991. E-mail: jackie.foote@ccaky.org. Web site: www.ccaky.org.

COMMUNITY HIGH SCHOOL

Teaneck, New Jersey
See Special Needs Schools section.

THE COMMUNITY SCHOOL

PO Box 2118
Sun Valley, Idaho 83353

Head of School: Andy Jones-Wilkins

General Information Coeducational day college-preparatory, arts, and technology school. Grades PK–12. Founded: 1973. Setting: rural. Nearest major city is Boise. 33-acre campus. 4 buildings on campus. Approved or accredited by Northwest Association of Schools and Colleges, Pacific Northwest Association of Independent Schools, and Idaho Department of Education. Member of National Association of Independent Schools, Secondary School Admission Test Board, and Council for the Advancement and Support of Education. Endowment: $3.1 million. Total enrollment: 307. Upper school average class size: 15. Upper school faculty-student ratio: 1:8.

Upper School Student Profile Grade 9: 29 students (14 boys, 15 girls); Grade 10: 26 students (11 boys, 15 girls); Grade 11: 27 students (13 boys, 14 girls); Grade 12: 27 students (16 boys, 11 girls).

Faculty School total: 52. In upper school: 10 men, 7 women; 11 have advanced degrees.

Subjects Offered Algebra, American history, American literature, art, biology, calculus, ceramics, chemistry, computer graphics, computer math, computer programming, computer science, constitutional law, creative writing, drama, earth science, ecology, economics, English, English literature, environmental science, ethics, European history, expository writing, fine arts, forensics, French, geography, geology, geometry, government/civics, history, human development, information technology, mathematics, music, musical productions, philosophy, photography, physical education, physics, science, social studies, Spanish, speech, statistics, theater, trigonometry, world history, world literature, writing.

Graduation Requirements Arts and fine arts (art, music, dance, drama), computer science, English, foreign language, mathematics, outdoor education, physical education (includes health), science, social studies (includes history), speech, senior thesis presentation, senior speech.

Special Academic Programs Advanced Placement exam preparation; honors section; independent study; term-away projects; academic accommodation for the gifted; programs in English, mathematics, general development for dyslexic students.

College Admission Counseling 26 students graduated in 2008; 24 went to college, including Dartmouth College; Duke University; Middlebury College; New York University; University of Colorado at Boulder; University of San Diego. Other: 2 had other specific plans. Mean SAT critical reading: 580, mean SAT math: 568, mean SAT writing: 596.

Student Life Upper grades have specified standards of dress, student council. Discipline rests primarily with faculty.

Summer Programs Enrichment, sports, art/fine arts, rigorous outdoor training, computer instruction programs offered; held both on and off campus; held at various sites for swimming, hiking, and exploring local mountains; accepts boys and girls; open to students from other schools. 100 students usually enrolled. 2009 schedule: June 15 to July 30. Application deadline: none.

Tuition and Aid Day student tuition: $22,400. Tuition installment plan (individually arranged payment plans). Merit scholarship grants, need-based scholarship grants available. In 2008–09, 27% of upper-school students received aid; total upper-school merit-scholarship money awarded: $10,700. Total amount of financial aid awarded in 2008–09: $497,150.

Admissions Traditional secondary-level entrance grade is 9. For fall 2008, 16 students applied for upper-level admission, 14 were accepted, 10 enrolled. SSAT and writing sample required. Deadline for receipt of application materials: February 23. Application fee required: $35. On-campus interview required.

Athletics Interscholastic: basketball (boys, girls), golf (b,g), ice hockey (b,g), ice skating (b,g), physical fitness (b,g), rock climbing (b,g), soccer (b,g), swimming and diving (g), tennis (b,g), volleyball (g); coed interscholastic: alpine skiing, backpacking, bicycling, canoeing/kayaking, climbing, cooperative games, cross-country running, equestrian sports, figure skating, fitness, flag football, freestyle skiing, hiking/backpacking, independent competitive sports, kayaking, mountain biking, mountaineering, nordic skiing, outdoor adventure, physical fitness, rafting, rock climbing, ropes courses, skiing (cross-country), skiing (downhill), snowboarding, snowshoeing, soccer, squash, telemark skiing, tennis. 2 PE instructors, 9 coaches.

Computers Computers are regularly used in English, foreign language, independent study, science, yearbook classes. Computer network features include on-campus library services, online commercial services, Internet access, wireless campus network. Student e-mail accounts are available to students. The school has a published electronic and media policy.

Contact Katie Raffetto, Director of Admission. 208-622-3960 Ext. 117. Fax: 208-622-3962. E-mail: kraffetto@communityschool.org. Web site: www.communityschool.org.

COMMUNITY SCHOOL

1164 Bunker Hill Road
South Tamworth, New Hampshire 03883-4181

Head of School: Jenny Rowe

General Information Coeducational day college-preparatory, arts, and environmental studies school. Grades 7–12. Founded: 1988. Setting: rural. Nearest major city is Conway. 310-acre campus. 2 buildings on campus. Approved or accredited by Association of Independent Schools in New England, New England Association of Schools and Colleges, and New Hampshire Department of Education. Endowment: $52,000. Total enrollment: 30. Upper school average class size: 6. Upper school faculty-student ratio: 1:6.

Upper School Student Profile Grade 7: 1 student (1 girl); Grade 8: 2 students (2 boys); Grade 9: 7 students (6 boys, 1 girl); Grade 10: 8 students (6 boys, 2 girls); Grade 11: 8 students (5 boys, 3 girls); Grade 12: 4 students (2 boys, 2 girls).

Faculty School total: 10. In upper school: 2 men, 8 women; 7 have advanced degrees.

Subjects Offered 20th century history, 20th century world history, advanced math, agriculture, agroecology, algebra, American culture, American democracy, American studies, ancient world history, applied skills, art and culture, art appreciation, biology, botany, calculus, career/college preparation, cell biology, chemistry, civics, civil rights, college planning, college writing, community garden, community service, composition, computer literacy, conflict resolution, consumer mathematics, CPR, creative thinking, creative writing, critical thinking, decision making skills, drama performance, earth science, ecology, environmental systems, English composition, English literature, environmental studies, ethics and responsibility, field ecology, first aid, food and nutrition, forestry, French, gardening, geography, geometry, global issues, high adventure outdoor program, human anatomy, human biology, independent study, integrated science, interdisciplinary studies, Internet research, land management, language arts, leadership training, literature, math applications, methods of research, modern European history, multicultural literature, music appreciation, natural resources management, navigation, novels, oceanography, organic gardening, philosophy, poetry, pre-algebra, pre-calculus, probability and statistics, reading/study skills, research techniques, senior project, sex education, short story, social studies, Spanish, trigonometry, U.S. government, U.S. history, U.S. literature, wilderness camping, wilderness education, wilderness/outdoor program, woodworking, world culture, world geography, writing fundamentals, writing workshop.

Graduation Requirements Art, computer education, English, foreign language, home economics, mathematics, physical education (includes health), science, senior project, social studies (includes history), technology, vocational arts, Senior project, Community service.

Special Academic Programs Independent study; term-away projects; study abroad; academic accommodation for the gifted and the artistically talented; remedial reading and/or remedial writing; remedial math.

College Admission Counseling 4 students graduated in 2008; 3 went to college, including Beloit College; University of Maine. Other: 1 went to work.

Student Life Upper grades have student council, honor system. Discipline rests equally with students and faculty.

Tuition and Aid Day student tuition: $12,900. Tuition installment plan (monthly payment plans, individually arranged payment plans). Tuition reduction for siblings, need-based scholarship grants, paying campus jobs available. In 2008–09, 65% of upper-school students received aid. Total amount of financial aid awarded in 2008–09: $108,000.

Admissions Traditional secondary-level entrance grade is 9. For fall 2008, 13 students applied for upper-level admission, 12 were accepted, 11 enrolled. Deadline for receipt of application materials: none. Application fee required: $25. Interview required.

Athletics Coed Interscholastic: aerobics, alpine skiing, aquatics, backpacking, cross-country running, fitness walking, hiking/backpacking, mountaineering, outdoor activities, outdoor education, outdoor skills, skiing (cross-country), skiing (downhill), snowboarding, snowshoeing, soccer, strength & conditioning, swimming and diving, tai chi, wilderness survival, winter walking.

Computers Computers are regularly used in accounting classes. Computer network features include on-campus library services, Internet access, wireless campus network. The school has a published electronic and media policy.

Contact Ms. Jenny Rowe, Admissions/Director. 603-323-7000. Fax: 603-323-8240. E-mail: jennyrowe@communityschoolnh.org. Web site: www.communityschoolnh.org.

THE COMMUNITY SCHOOL OF NAPLES

13275 Livingston Road
Naples, Florida 34109

Head of School: John E. Zeller Jr.

General Information Coeducational day college-preparatory, arts, and technology school. Grades PK–12. Founded: 1982. Setting: suburban. Nearest major city is Miami. 110-acre campus. 3 buildings on campus. Approved or accredited by Florida Council of Independent Schools and Florida Department of Education. Member of National Association of Independent Schools and Secondary School Admission Test Board. Endowment: $10 million. Total enrollment: 803. Upper school average class size: 12. Upper school faculty-student ratio: 1:12.

Upper School Student Profile Grade 9: 73 students (35 boys, 38 girls); Grade 10: 77 students (36 boys, 41 girls); Grade 11: 60 students (28 boys, 32 girls); Grade 12: 76 students (35 boys, 41 girls).

Faculty School total: 113. In upper school: 26 men, 25 women; 27 have advanced degrees.

Subjects Offered Algebra, American government, American government-AP, American history, American history-AP, American literature, American literature-AP, anatomy and physiology, art, art history-AP, band, biology, biology-AP, broadcasting, calculus, calculus-AP, chemistry, chemistry-AP, chorus, clayworking, comparative government and politics-AP, computer programming, computer science, computer science-AP, creative writing, digital photography, dramatic arts, drawing, economics, economics-AP, electives, English, English language and composition-AP, English language-AP, English literature and composition-AP, English literature-AP, English-AP, English/composition-AP, environmental science-AP, European history-AP, fine arts, French, French language-AP, French literature-AP, French-AP, geometry, German, government and politics-AP, government-AP, government/civics-AP, graphic design, health, history, history-AP, honors algebra, honors English, honors geometry, honors U.S. history, honors world history, Italian, jazz band, Latin, marine science, mathematics, mathematics-AP, music, music theory-AP, painting, performing arts, personal fitness, photography, physical education, physics, physics-AP, pre-calculus, psychology, science, Spanish, Spanish language-AP, Spanish literature-AP, Spanish-AP, statistics-AP, strings, studio art—AP, studio art-AP, theater, U.S. government and politics-AP, U.S. government-AP, U.S. history-AP, vocal music, Web site design, world history, world literature.

Graduation Requirements Arts and fine arts (art, music, dance, drama), computer science, electives, English, foreign language, history, mathematics, physical education (includes health), science, Community Service.

Special Academic Programs 23 Advanced Placement exams for which test preparation is offered; honors section; independent study; study at local college for college credit; study abroad.

College Admission Counseling 54 students graduated in 2008; all went to college, including Colgate University; Saint Louis University; University of Central Florida; University of Florida; University of Michigan; University of Notre Dame. Median SAT critical reading: 560, median SAT math: 630, median SAT writing: 580, median combined SAT: 1800, median composite ACT: 27. 37% scored over 600 on SAT critical reading, 55% scored over 600 on SAT math, 37% scored over 600 on SAT writing, 49% scored over 1800 on combined SAT, 56% scored over 26 on composite ACT.

Student Life Upper grades have specified standards of dress, student council, honor system. Discipline rests equally with students and faculty.

Summer Programs Enrichment programs offered; session focuses on Mathematics, English, and SAT preparation; held on campus; accepts boys and girls; not open to students from other schools. 40 students usually enrolled. 2009 schedule: June 8 to August 10. Application deadline: April 15.

Tuition and Aid Day student tuition: $21,700. Tuition installment plan (Insured Tuition Payment Plan, monthly payment plans, individually arranged payment plans). Need-based scholarship grants available. In 2008–09, 19% of upper-school students received aid. Total amount of financial aid awarded in 2008–09: $794,194.

Admissions Traditional secondary-level entrance grade is 9. School's own exam or SSAT required. Deadline for receipt of application materials: February 1. Application fee required: $100. On-campus interview required.

Athletics Interscholastic: baseball (boys), basketball (b,g), cheering (g), cross-country running (b,g), diving (b,g), golf (b,g), lacrosse (b), soccer (b,g), softball (g), swimming and diving (b,g), tennis (b,g), track and field (b,g), volleyball (g), winter soccer (b,g); intramural: cheering (g), cross-country running (g); coed intramural: indoor soccer, rock climbing, sailing, weight training. 5 PE instructors, 29 coaches, 1 athletic trainer.

Computers Computers are regularly used in art, computer applications, creative writing, design, desktop publishing, digital applications, English, foreign language, history, mathematics, music, science, Web site design, word processing, writing, writing, yearbook classes. Computer network features include on-campus library services, Internet access, Internet filtering or blocking technology. Student e-mail accounts and computer access in designated common areas are available to students. Students grades are available online. The school has a published electronic and media policy.

Contact Ms. Judy Evans, Director of Admissions. 239-597-7575 Ext. 205. Fax: 239-598-2973. E-mail: jevans@communityschoolnaples.org. Web site: www.communityschoolnaples.org.

ANNOUNCEMENT FROM THE SCHOOL Established in 1982, The Community School of Naples provides an independent, nondenominational, college-preparatory education to more than 800 students in prekindergarten through grade 12. CSN prioritizes academic excellence and character education, while emphasizing fine arts, athletics, and student activities. The School has received national recognition and proudly offers a financial aid program. John Zeller is Head of School.

THE CONCEPT SCHOOL

Route 926 & Westtown Road
Westtown, Pennsylvania 19395

Head of School: Mrs. Lauren Vangieri

General Information Coeducational day college-preparatory, general academic, arts, and technology school; primarily serves students with learning disabilities, individuals with Attention Deficit Disorder, and dyslexic students. Grades 4–12. Founded: 1972. Setting: suburban. Nearest major city is Philadelphia. 10-acre campus. 1 building on campus. Approved or accredited by Pennsylvania Department of Education. Endowment: $75,000. Total enrollment: 40. Upper school average class size: 8. Upper school faculty-student ratio: 1:8.

Upper School Student Profile Grade 9: 6 students (5 boys, 1 girl); Grade 10: 6 students (4 boys, 2 girls); Grade 11: 8 students (8 boys); Grade 12: 5 students (4 boys, 1 girl).

Faculty School total: 14. In upper school: 3 men, 4 women; 5 have advanced degrees.

Subjects Offered Algebra, American history, anthropology, art, art history, biology, chemistry, comparative religion, computer graphics, consumer mathematics, criminal justice, cultural arts, economics, English, environmental science, film, fine arts, foreign language, general science, geometry, government/civics, health, history, human development, independent study, keyboarding, language arts, Latin, mathematics, physical education, physics, physiology, pre-algebra, pre-calculus, psychology, science, social science, social studies, speech, trigonometry, U.S. government, visual arts.

Graduation Requirements Arts and fine arts (art, music, dance, drama), computer science, English, mathematics, physical education (includes health), science, social science, social studies (includes history).

Special Academic Programs Honors section; accelerated programs; independent study; study at local college for college credit; academic accommodation for the gifted and the artistically talented; remedial reading and/or remedial writing; remedial math; programs in English, mathematics, general development for dyslexic students; special instructional classes for deaf students, blind students, students with learning differences, Attention Deficit Disorder, Asperger's Syndrome, school phobia, dyslexia, Attention Deficit Hyperactivity Disorder, and Non-verbal Learning Disorder.

College Admission Counseling 8 students graduated in 2008; 6 went to college, including Pennsylvania State University System; Temple University; University of

Delaware; Villanova University; West Chester University of Pennsylvania; Widener University. Other: 2 went to work. Mean SAT critical reading: 520, mean SAT math: 490, mean SAT writing: 518.
Student Life Upper grades have specified standards of dress, honor system. Discipline rests equally with students and faculty.
Tuition and Aid Day student tuition: $16,900. Tuition installment plan (monthly payment plans). Tuition reduction for siblings available.
Admissions Traditional secondary-level entrance grade is 9. For fall 2008, 17 students applied for upper-level admission, 6 were accepted, 6 enrolled. Math and English placement tests and WISC/Woodcock-Johnson required. Deadline for receipt of application materials: none. Application fee required: $50. On-campus interview required.
Athletics Coed Intramural: aerobics, basketball, bowling, ice skating, in-line skating, physical fitness, physical training, roller skating, skiing (downhill), snowboarding, yoga. 1 PE instructor, 1 coach.
Computers Computers are regularly used in all academic, theater, theater arts classes. Computer network features include on-campus library services, Internet access, wireless campus network. Campus intranet and student e-mail accounts are available to students. The school has a published electronic and media policy.
Contact Mrs. Carol McAdam, School Secretary. 610-399-1135. Fax: 610-399-0767. E-mail: cmcadam@conceptschool.com. Web site: www.conceptschool.com.

ANNOUNCEMENT FROM THE SCHOOL The Concept School, a unique, small, educational environment, provides personalized learning for students with average or better academic and cognitive abilities. Teachers and the school psychologist work together to identify a student's learning profile, assess strengths, accommodate weaknesses, and address behaviors in a positive way. The structured college-prep program readies students for postsecondary placements; the courses capitalize on student strengths, broaden their knowledge, encourage critical-thinking skills, and solidify learning through application of skills rather than memorization. Seminar courses allow advanced study of topics leading to career choices.

CONCORD ACADEMY

166 Main Street
Concord, Massachusetts 01742
Head of School: Jacob A. Dresden

General Information Coeducational boarding and day college-preparatory and arts school. Grades 9–12. Founded: 1922. Setting: suburban. Nearest major city is Boston. Students are housed in single-sex dormitories. 39-acre campus. 29 buildings on campus. Approved or accredited by New England Association of Schools and Colleges, The Association of Boarding Schools, and Massachusetts Department of Education. Member of National Association of Independent Schools and Secondary School Admission Test Board. Endowment: $48 million. Total enrollment: 367. Upper school average class size: 12. Upper school faculty-student ratio: 1:6.
Upper School Student Profile Grade 9: 88 students (42 boys, 46 girls); Grade 10: 102 students (56 boys, 46 girls); Grade 11: 90 students (39 boys, 51 girls); Grade 12: 87 students (38 boys, 49 girls). 43% of students are boarding students. 74% are state residents. 20 states are represented in upper school student body. 8% are international students. International students from Canada, China, India, Republic of Korea, Taiwan, and Taiwan; 2 other countries represented in student body.
Faculty School total: 70. In upper school: 33 men, 37 women; 59 have advanced degrees; 25 reside on campus.
Subjects Offered 20th century American writers, 3-dimensional art, advanced chemistry, advanced math, African history, African-American literature, algebra, American history, American literature, ancient history, ancient world history, anthropology, applied music, architecture, art, art history, Asian history, astronomy, astrophysics, batik, Bible as literature, biochemistry, biology, bookmaking, British literature, calculus, ceramics, chamber groups, chemistry, Chinese history, choreography, chorus, classical civilization, classical Greek literature, classical language, computer multimedia, computer programming, computer science, computer studies, creative writing, critical studies in film, dance, dance performance, digital imaging, directing, drama, drama performance, drawing, earth science, economics, English, English literature, environmental science, environmental studies, European history, experimental science, expository writing, fiber arts, fiction, film, film history, filmmaking, forensic science, forensics, French, freshman seminar, geology, geometry, German, German literature, guitar, health and wellness, history, history of China and Japan, history of music, Holocaust, HTML design, improvisation, instruments, introduction to digital multitrack recording techniques, Irish literature, Islamic history, jazz ensemble, journalism, Latin, Latin American history, Latin American literature, life management skills, literature seminar, math analysis, mathematics, medieval/Renaissance history, Middle East, Middle Eastern history, model United Nations, modern dance, modern European history, modern languages, music, music composition, music history, music technology, music theory, musical productions, neuroscience, newspaper, novel, oceanography, orchestra, painting, performing arts, philosophy, photography, physical education, physics, piano, play/screen writing, poetry, post-calculus, pre-calculus, printmaking, Roman civilization, science, science fiction, sculpture, senior project, sex education, Shakespeare, Spanish, Spanish literature, statistics, statistics and probability, student publications, studio art, technical theater, theater, theater design and production, theater history, trigonometry, U.S. history, urban studies, visual arts, voice, Web site design, wind ensemble, writing.
Graduation Requirements Computer science, English, foreign language, history, mathematics, performing arts, physical education (includes health), science, visual arts.
Special Academic Programs Honors section; independent study; term-away projects; study abroad; academic accommodation for the gifted, the musically talented, and the artistically talented.
College Admission Counseling 96 students graduated in 2008; all went to college, including Amherst College; Brown University; Columbia College; Skidmore College; The Colorado College; Tufts University. Mean SAT critical reading: 686, mean SAT math: 668, mean SAT writing: 686, mean combined SAT: 2040.
Student Life Upper grades have student council, honor system. Discipline rests equally with students and faculty.
Tuition and Aid Day student tuition: $34,700; 7-day tuition and room/board: $42,910. Guaranteed tuition plan. Tuition installment plan (Key Tuition Payment Plan, monthly payment plans). Need-based scholarship grants, need-based loans available. In 2008–09, 20% of upper-school students received aid. Total amount of financial aid awarded in 2008–09: $2,329,142.
Admissions Traditional secondary-level entrance grade is 9. For fall 2008, 752 students applied for upper-level admission, 241 were accepted, 111 enrolled. ISEE, SSAT or TOEFL required. Deadline for receipt of application materials: January 15. Application fee required: $45. Interview recommended.
Athletics Interscholastic: baseball (boys), basketball (b,g), cross-country running (b,g), field hockey (g), lacrosse (b,g), skiing (downhill) (b,g), soccer (b,g), softball (g), squash (b,g), tennis (b,g), volleyball (g), wrestling (b); coed interscholastic: alpine skiing, golf, sailing, ultimate Frisbee; coed intramural: aerobics, aerobics/dance, ballet, canoeing/kayaking, combined training, cross-country running, dance, fencing, fitness, jogging, martial arts, modern dance, outdoor activities, physical fitness, physical training, self defense, skiing (downhill), strength & conditioning, ultimate Frisbee, weight training, yoga. 8 PE instructors, 35 coaches, 2 athletic trainers.
Computers Computers are regularly used in English, foreign language, history, library skills, mathematics, music, newspaper, science, social studies, technology, video film production, Web site design, yearbook classes. Computer network features include on-campus library services, online commercial services, Internet access, Internet filtering or blocking technology. Campus intranet and student e-mail accounts are available to students. The school has a published electronic and media policy.
Contact Pamela J. Safford, Associate Head for Enrollment and Planning. 978-402-2250. Fax: 978-402-2345. E-mail: admissions@concordacademy.org. Web site: www.concordacademy.org.

CONCORDIA CONTINUING EDUCATION HIGH SCHOOL

7128 Ada Boulevard
Edmonton, Alberta T5B 4E4, Canada
Head of School: Marilyn Westbury

General Information Coeducational day college-preparatory school, affiliated with Lutheran Church. Grades 7–12. Founded: 1921. Setting: urban. 10 buildings on campus. Approved or accredited by Alberta Department of Education. Language of instruction: English. Total enrollment: 150. Upper school faculty-student ratio: 1:14.
Upper School Student Profile 20% of students are Lutheran.
Faculty In upper school: 4 men, 7 women; 4 have advanced degrees.
Student Life Upper grades have specified standards of dress, student council, honor system. Discipline rests primarily with faculty.
Summer Programs Remediation programs offered; session focuses on academic; held on campus; accepts boys and girls; open to students from other schools. 30 students usually enrolled. 2009 schedule: July 2 to July 31.
Tuition and Aid Tuition installment plan (monthly payment plans). Bursaries available. In 2008–09, 10% of upper-school students received aid.
Admissions TOEFL or SLEP required. Deadline for receipt of application materials: none. No application fee required.
Athletics Interscholastic: badminton (boys, girls), basketball (b,g), hockey (b,g), soccer (b,g); intramural: badminton (b,g), basketball (b,g), hockey (b,g), soccer (b,g). 2 coaches.
Computers Computer network features include on-campus library services, Internet access, Internet filtering or blocking technology. Student e-mail accounts are available to students.
Contact Sandra Moffatt, Director, Academic Upgrading and Special Sessions. 780-413-7808. Fax: 780-466-9394. E-mail: sandra.moffatt@concordia.ab.ca.

CONCORDIA HIGH SCHOOL

7128 Ada Boulevard
Edmonton, Alberta T5B 4E4, Canada
Head of School: Mr. David Eifert

General Information Coeducational boarding and day college-preparatory, arts, and religious studies school, affiliated with Lutheran Church. Grades 10–12. Founded: 1921. Setting: urban. Students are housed in single-sex dormitories. 12-acre campus.

1 building on campus. Approved or accredited by Association of Independent Schools and Colleges of Alberta, Canadian Association of Independent Schools, and Alberta Department of Education. Languages of instruction: English and French. Total enrollment: 133. Upper school average class size: 16. Upper school faculty-student ratio: 1:10.

Upper School Student Profile 23% of students are boarding students. International students from Brazil, Hong Kong, Mexico, Republic of Korea, Thailand, and United States; 1 other country represented in student body. 20% of students are Lutheran.

Faculty School total: 15. In upper school: 5 men, 10 women; 7 have advanced degrees.

Subjects Offered Art, athletics, biology, career and personal planning, chemistry, choir, Christian education, drama, drama performance, English, French, information processing, mathematics, media arts, physical education, physics, religious studies, service learning/internship, social studies.

Graduation Requirements Advanced chemistry, advanced math, arts and fine arts (art, music, dance, drama), Christian education, French, language, religious studies.

Special Academic Programs Study at local college for college credit.

College Admission Counseling 39 students graduated in 2008; 36 went to college. Other: 3 went to work.

Student Life Upper grades have uniform requirement, student council. Discipline rests primarily with faculty. Attendance at religious services is required.

Admissions TOEFL or SLEP required. Deadline for receipt of application materials: none. Application fee required: CAN$150. Interview required.

Athletics Interscholastic: basketball (boys, girls); intramural: basketball (b,g), soccer (b,g), volleyball (b,g); coed interscholastic: badminton, fitness, lacrosse; coed intramural: alpine skiing, canoeing/kayaking, cheering, cross-country running, curling, golf, outdoor activities, physical fitness.

Computers Computers are regularly used in media arts classes.

Contact Mr. Keith Kruse, Assistant Principal. 780-479-9392. Fax: 780-479-5050. E-mail: keith.kruse@concordia.ab.ca. Web site: www.concordiahighschool.com.

CONNELLY SCHOOL OF THE HOLY CHILD

9029 Bradley Boulevard
Potomac, Maryland 20854

Head of School: Mrs. Maureen K. Appel

General Information Girls' day college-preparatory, arts, and religious studies school, affiliated with Roman Catholic Church. Grades 6–12. Founded: 1961. Setting: suburban. Nearest major city is Washington, DC. 9-acre campus. 2 buildings on campus. Approved or accredited by Association of Independent Maryland Schools, Association of Independent Schools of Greater Washington, Middle States Association of Colleges and Schools, National Catholic Education Association, The College Board, and Maryland Department of Education. Member of National Association of Independent Schools and Secondary School Admission Test Board. Endowment: $1 million. Total enrollment: 324. Upper school average class size: 15. Upper school faculty-student ratio: 1:15.

Upper School Student Profile Grade 6: 20 students (20 girls); Grade 7: 42 students (42 girls); Grade 8: 34 students (34 girls); Grade 9: 53 students (53 girls); Grade 10: 54 students (54 girls); Grade 11: 82 students (82 girls); Grade 12: 40 students (40 girls). 75% of students are Roman Catholic.

Faculty School total: 48. In upper school: 7 men, 28 women; 25 have advanced degrees.

Subjects Offered 20th century world history, Advanced Placement courses, algebra, American history, American literature, art, art history-AP, biology, biology-AP, calculus, calculus-AP, chemistry, community service, creative writing, drama, economics-AP, English, English language and composition-AP, English literature, English-AP, equestrian sports, fine arts, forensics, French, French language-AP, French literature-AP, French-AP, geometry, government/civics, health, history, human anatomy, humanities, instrumental music, literature, literature and composition-AP, mathematics, music, music theory, photography, physical education, physics, psychology-AP, religion, science, social studies, Spanish, Spanish-AP, speech, statistics-AP, theater, track and field, trigonometry, U.S. government-AP, U.S. history-AP, vocal jazz, volleyball, world history, world literature, writing.

Graduation Requirements Arts and fine arts (art, music, dance, drama), computer skills, English, foreign language, mathematics, physical education (includes health), religion (includes Bible studies and theology), science, social studies (includes history). Community service is required.

Special Academic Programs 13 Advanced Placement exams for which test preparation is offered; honors section; academic accommodation for the gifted, the musically talented, and the artistically talented.

College Admission Counseling 70 students graduated in 2008; all went to college, including Elon University; Fairfield University; Saint Joseph's University; The Catholic University of America; University of Maryland, Baltimore.

Student Life Upper grades have uniform requirement, student council, honor system. Discipline rests equally with students and faculty. Attendance at religious services is required.

Summer Programs Enrichment, sports, art/fine arts programs offered; session focuses on Enrichment; held on campus; accepts boys and girls; open to students from other schools. 30 students usually enrolled. 2009 schedule: June 15 to July 30. Application deadline: June.

Tuition and Aid Day student tuition: $20,580. Tuition installment plan (Insured Tuition Payment Plan, FACTS Tuition Payment Plan, monthly payment plans). Merit scholarship grants, need-based scholarship grants, middle-income loans available. In 2008–09, 20% of upper-school students received aid. Total amount of financial aid awarded in 2008–09: $500,000.

Admissions Traditional secondary-level entrance grade is 9. High School Placement Test, ISEE or SSAT required. Deadline for receipt of application materials: December 15. Application fee required: $50. Interview required.

Athletics Interscholastic: aerobics/dance (girls), basketball (g), cross-country running (g), dance (g), dance squad (g), dance team (g), diving (g), equestrian sports (g), field hockey (g), fitness (g), horseback riding (g), indoor track (g), lacrosse (g), modern dance (g), soccer (g), softball (g), swimming and diving (g), tennis (g), track and field (g), volleyball (g), winter (indoor) track (g); intramural: aerobics (g), aerobics/dance (g), archery (g), badminton (g), baseball (g), cooperative games (g), dance (g), deck hockey (g), fencing (g), field hockey (g), fitness (g), fitness walking (g), flag football (g), floor hockey (g), football (g), Frisbee (g), golf (g), independent competitive sports (g), indoor hockey (g), indoor soccer (g), indoor track & field (g), jogging (g), jump rope (g), kickball (g), lacrosse (g), physical fitness (g), running (g), self defense (g), soccer (g), softball (g), street hockey (g), strength & conditioning (g), touch football (g), track and field (g), ultimate Frisbee (g), walking (g), wall climbing (g), weight training (g). 3 PE instructors, 31 coaches, 1 athletic trainer.

Computers Computer network features include on-campus library services, online commercial services, Internet access, Internet filtering or blocking technology. Student e-mail accounts are available to students. The school has a published electronic and media policy.

Contact Mrs. Meg Mayo, Director of Admissions and Financial Aid. 301-365-0955 Ext. 2103. Fax: 301-365-0981. E-mail: admissions@holychild.org. Web site: www.holychild.org.

ANNOUNCEMENT FROM THE SCHOOL Connelly School of the Holy Child is a Catholic, college-preparatory, school, committed to the intellectual, spiritual, artistic, social, and physical development of young women in grades 6–12. The School emphasizes academic challenge, joy of learning, and the education of women of faith and action. In keeping with the philosophy of our founder, Cornelia Connelly, Holy Child values the uniqueness of each individual and fosters a life of service to others.

CONSERVE SCHOOL

5400 North Black Oak Lake Road
Land O' Lakes, Wisconsin 54540

Head of School: Mr. Stefan Anderson

General Information Coeducational boarding college-preparatory, arts, technology, and Environmental Science school. Grades 9–12. Founded: 2002. Setting: rural. Nearest major city is Green Bay. Students are housed in single-sex dormitories. 1,200-acre campus. 8 buildings on campus. Approved or accredited by Midwest Association of Boarding Schools. Candidate for accreditation by Independent Schools Association of the Central States. Endowment: $202 million. Total enrollment: 149. Upper school average class size: 15. Upper school faculty-student ratio: 1:8.

Upper School Student Profile Grade 9: 44 students (21 boys, 23 girls); Grade 10: 36 students (13 boys, 23 girls); Grade 11: 40 students (15 boys, 25 girls); Grade 12: 29 students (19 boys, 10 girls). 100% of students are boarding students. 49% are state residents. 15 states are represented in upper school student body. 27% are international students. International students from China, Germany, Republic of Korea, and Russian Federation; 7 other countries represented in student body.

Faculty School total: 23. In upper school: 10 men, 13 women; 19 have advanced degrees; 22 reside on campus.

Subjects Offered Algebra, American history, anatomy, band, biology, biology-AP, calculus, calculus-AP, ceramics, Chinese, choir, college placement, communication skills, computer technologies, creative writing, ecology, English literature, English-AP, environmental science, environmental science-AP, field ecology, fine arts, geology, geometry, government, health and wellness, history of science, integrated mathematics, journalism, music, orchestra, painting, photography, physics, physics-AP, pre-calculus, printmaking, research, Spanish, statistics, technology, U.S. government, U.S. history-AP, world history, world literature.

Graduation Requirements Arts and fine arts (art, music, dance, drama), English literature, history, mathematics, modern languages, science, wellness, independent research.

Special Academic Programs Advanced Placement exam preparation; honors section; academic accommodation for the gifted; ESL (8 students enrolled).

College Admission Counseling 38 students graduated in 2008; 37 went to college, including Brown University; Carleton College; Dartmouth College; The Colorado College; University of Wisconsin–Madison. Other: 1 went to work. Mean SAT critical reading: 606, mean SAT math: 626, mean SAT writing: 579, mean combined SAT: 1811, mean composite ACT: 27.

Student Life Upper grades have specified standards of dress, student council, honor system. Discipline rests equally with students and faculty.

Summer Programs Enrichment, ESL programs offered; session focuses on enrichment with environmental outdoor focus and ESL; held both on and off campus;

held at Northland College (Ashland, Wisconsin); accepts boys and girls; open to students from other schools. 45 students usually enrolled. 2009 schedule: June to August. Application deadline: May.

Tuition and Aid 7-day tuition and room/board: $30,000. Tuition installment plan (Key Tuition Payment Plan, monthly payment plans). Merit scholarship grants, need-based scholarship grants available. In 2008–09, 90% of upper-school students received aid; total upper-school merit-scholarship money awarded: $490,000. Total amount of financial aid awarded in 2008–09: $2,200,000.

Admissions Traditional secondary-level entrance grade is 9. For fall 2008, 139 students applied for upper-level admission, 84 were accepted, 67 enrolled. ISEE or SSAT, ERB, PSAT, SAT, PLAN or ACT required. Deadline for receipt of application materials: none. Application fee required: $35. Interview recommended.

Athletics Interscholastic: basketball (boys, girls), cross-country running (b,g), nordic skiing (b,g), skiing (cross-country) (b,g), soccer (b,g), track and field (b,g), volleyball (g); coed interscholastic: cheering, golf; coed intramural: aerobics, alpine skiing, archery, backpacking, badminton, biathlon, bicycling, canoeing/kayaking, climbing, cooperative games, dance, fishing, fitness, fitness walking, fly fishing, freestyle skiing, Frisbee, hiking/backpacking, ice skating, jogging, judo, juggling, kayaking, life saving, martial arts, modern dance, mountain biking, nordic skiing, outdoor activities, paint ball, physical fitness, physical training, racquetball, rock climbing, running, skiing (downhill), snowboarding, snowshoeing, strength & conditioning, swimming and diving, table tennis, telemark skiing, ultimate Frisbee, walking, wall climbing, wallyball, weight lifting, weight training, wilderness, wilderness survival, wilder-nessways, windsurfing, winter walking. 2 PE instructors, 5 coaches, 1 athletic trainer.

Computers Computers are regularly used in all academic classes. Computer network features include on-campus library services, online commercial services, Internet access, wireless campus network, Internet filtering or blocking technology. Campus intranet and student e-mail accounts are available to students. Students grades are available online. The school has a published electronic and media policy.

Contact Mrs. Linda LaChance, Associate Director of Admissions. 715-547-1301. Fax: 715-547-1390. E-mail: admissions@conserveschool.org. Web site: www.conserveschool.org.

See Close-Up on page 720.

CONVENT OF THE SACRED HEART

1177 King Street
Greenwich, Connecticut 06831

Head of School: Sr. Joan Magnetti, RSCJ

General Information Girls' day college-preparatory, arts, religious studies, and technology school, affiliated with Roman Catholic Church. Grades PS–12. Founded: 1848. Setting: suburban. Nearest major city is New York, NY. 110-acre campus. 10 buildings on campus. Approved or accredited by Connecticut Association of Independent Schools, Network of Sacred Heart Schools, New England Association of Schools and Colleges, and Connecticut Department of Education. Member of National Association of Independent Schools and Secondary School Admission Test Board. Endowment: $26.1 million. Total enrollment: 748. Upper school average class size: 13. Upper school faculty-student ratio: 1:5.

Upper School Student Profile Grade 9: 79 students (79 girls); Grade 10: 72 students (72 girls); Grade 11: 63 students (63 girls); Grade 12: 54 students (54 girls). 74% of students are Roman Catholic.

Faculty School total: 113. In upper school: 13 men, 37 women; 39 have advanced degrees.

Subjects Offered Advanced Placement courses, algebra, American history, American literature, American literature-AP, art, art history, astronomy, biology, biology-AP, broadcast journalism, calculus, ceramics, chemistry, choir, choral music, Christian education, Christian ethics, Christian scripture, Christian studies, Christian testament, Christianity, college counseling, college placement, community service, computer programming, computer science, creative writing, dance, dance perfor-mance, design, drama, earth science, ecology, English, English language and composition-AP, English literature, environmental science, ethics, European history, expository writing, fine arts, French, French-AP, geography, geometry, government/civics, grammar, health, history, journalism, Latin, logic, madrigals, mathematics, mathematics-AP, media production, moral and social development, music, photog-raphy, physical education, physics, pre-calculus, SAT/ACT preparation, science, social studies, Spanish, statistics, student publications, theater, theology, trigonometry, visual and performing arts, world history, world literature, writing, yearbook.

Graduation Requirements Arts and fine arts (art, music, dance, drama), electives, English, foreign language, mathematics, physical education (includes health), religion (includes Bible studies and theology), science, social studies (includes history). Community service is required.

Special Academic Programs Advanced Placement exam preparation; honors section; independent study; domestic exchange program (with Network of Sacred Heart Schools); study abroad; academic accommodation for the gifted.

College Admission Counseling 60 students graduated in 2007; all went to college, including Bucknell University; Georgetown University; Loyola College in Maryland; New York University; The George Washington University; Villanova University. Mean SAT critical reading: 627, mean SAT math: 623, mean SAT writing: 661.

Student Life Upper grades have uniform requirement, student council, honor system. Discipline rests primarily with faculty. Attendance at religious services is required.

Tuition and Aid Day student tuition: $28,500. Tuition installment plan (Academic Management Services Plan). Need-based scholarship grants available. In 2007–08, 22% of upper-school students received aid. Total amount of financial aid awarded in 2007–08: $1,205,750.

Admissions Traditional secondary-level entrance grade is 9. For fall 2007, 100 students applied for upper-level admission, 56 were accepted, 40 enrolled. ISEE or SSAT required. Deadline for receipt of application materials: February 1. Application fee required: $50. On-campus interview required.

Athletics Interscholastic: basketball, crew, cross-country running, diving, field hockey, golf, lacrosse, soccer, softball, squash, swimming and diving, tennis, volleyball; intramural: equestrian sports, fitness, independent competitive sports, physical training, strength & conditioning. 3 PE instructors, 34 coaches, 1 athletic trainer.

Computers Computers are regularly used in all academic classes. Computer network features include on-campus library services, online commercial services, Internet access, wireless campus network, Internet filtering or blocking technology, course selection online, laptops mandatory for students in grades 7-12. Campus intranet, student e-mail accounts, and computer access in designated common areas are available to students. Students grades are available online. The school has a published electronic and media policy.

Contact Katherine Machir, Director of Admission. 203-532-3534. Fax: 203-532-3301. E-mail: admission@cshgreenwich.org. Web site: www.cshgreenwich.org.

See Close-Up on page 722.

CONVENT OF THE SACRED HEART

1 East 91st Street
New York, New York 10128-0689

Head of School: Dr. Joseph J. Ciancaglini

General Information Girls' day college-preparatory, arts, religious studies, bilingual studies, and technology school, affiliated with Roman Catholic Church. Grades PK–12. Founded: 1881. Setting: urban. 2 buildings on campus. Approved or accredited by Network of Sacred Heart Schools, New York State Association of Independent Schools, and New York Department of Education. Member of National Association of Independent Schools and Secondary School Admission Test Board. Endowment: $33.8 million. Total enrollment: 684. Upper school average class size: 16. Upper school faculty-student ratio: 1:16.

Upper School Student Profile Grade 8: 51 students (51 girls); Grade 9: 59 students (59 girls); Grade 10: 50 students (50 girls); Grade 11: 49 students (49 girls); Grade 12: 50 students (50 girls). 66% of students are Roman Catholic.

Faculty School total: 110. In upper school: 10 men, 30 women; 38 have advanced degrees.

Subjects Offered Advanced studio art-AP, algebra, American history, American literature, art, audio visual/media, biology, biology-AP, calculus, calculus-AP, campus ministry, ceramics, chemistry, chemistry-AP, chorus, computer applications, computer multimedia, creative writing, dance, desktop publishing, digital photography, drama, earth science, East European studies, English, English literature, English literature-AP, environmental science, ethics, European history, expository writing, film history, fine arts, finite math, forensics, French, French-AP, functions, geography, geometry, government/civics, handbells, health, history, journalism, Latin, madrigals, math-ematics, model United Nations, multicultural literature, multimedia design, music, musical theater, performing arts, photography, physical education, physical science, physics, physics-AP, portfolio art, pottery, pre-calculus, religion, science, science research, social studies, Spanish, Spanish-AP, speech, statistics, statistics-AP, theater, theology, trigonometry, U.S. history-AP, visual arts, women's literature, world history, world issues, world literature, world religions, writing.

Graduation Requirements Arts and fine arts (art, music, dance, drama), computer science, English, foreign language, mathematics, physical education (includes health), religion (includes Bible studies and theology), science, social studies (includes history).

Special Academic Programs 15 Advanced Placement exams for which test preparation is offered; honors section; independent study; term-away projects; domestic exchange program (with Network of Sacred Heart Schools); study abroad.

College Admission Counseling 45 students graduated in 2008; all went to college, including Boston College; Georgetown University; Lehigh University; New York University; The George Washington University; University of Pennsylvania.

Student Life Upper grades have uniform requirement, student council. Discipline rests primarily with faculty. Attendance at religious services is required.

Summer Programs Sports, art/fine arts, computer instruction programs offered; session focuses on visual and performing arts; held on campus; accepts boys and girls; open to students from other schools. 200 students usually enrolled. 2009 schedule: June 30 to July 25. Application deadline: April 15.

Tuition and Aid Day student tuition: $30,970. Tuition installment plan (Key Tuition Payment Plan). Need-based scholarship grants, need-based loans available. In 2008–09, 37% of upper-school students received aid. Total amount of financial aid awarded in 2008–09: $1,800,000.

Admissions Traditional secondary-level entrance grade is 9. For fall 2008, 200 students applied for upper-level admission, 35 were accepted, 16 enrolled. ERB or ISEE required. Deadline for receipt of application materials: November 15. Application fee required: $65. On-campus interview required.

Athletics Interscholastic: basketball, cross-country running, indoor track & field, lacrosse, soccer, softball, swimming and diving, tennis, track and field, volleyball, winter (indoor) track; intramural: aerobics/dance, aquatics, ballet, basketball, dance, fitness, gymnastics, jogging, physical training, roller blading, running, soccer, softball, swimming and diving, tennis, volleyball, weight lifting, weight training. 8 PE instructors, 8 coaches, 1 athletic trainer.
Computers Computers are regularly used in all academic classes. Computer network features include on-campus library services, online commercial services, Internet access, wireless campus network, Internet filtering or blocking technology. Campus intranet, student e-mail accounts, and computer access in designated common areas are available to students. The school has a published electronic and media policy.
Contact Evin Watson, Admissions Office Coordinator. 212-722-4745 Ext. 105. Fax: 212-996-1784. E-mail: ewatson@cshnyc.org. Web site: www.cshnyc.org.

ANNOUNCEMENT FROM THE SCHOOL Chartered in 1881, Convent of the Sacred Heart is a member of the international Network of Sacred Heart Schools and the oldest independent girls' school in New York City. The beautiful facilities are located in two landmark buildings overlooking Central Park. The school is dedicated to the holistic development of young women, and committed to preparing students for the challenges of the modern world. The Lower School provides a strong learning foundation, and is designed to help students become inquisitive, original thinkers through intensive personal attention and small-group study. By the time students reach the Middle School, which comprises grades 5 through 7, they are ready for more abstract study in the basic subjects. The Upper School curriculum is rigorous. In addition to demanding college-preparatory courses, a wide variety of electives are offered, many highlighting the unique cultural advantages of New York City. Advanced Placement courses are offered in biology, calculus, chemistry, English literature, French language, French literature, government and politics, Latin literature, music theory, Spanish language, statistics, studio art, and U.S. history. In addition, religion courses are required of all Sacred Heart students. Co-curricular activities include student government; Model UN; literary, science, and foreign-language publications; theater; mock trial; forensics; Women of Proud Heritage; student council; hand bells; chorus; math team; Habitat for Humanity; and numerous other student-run clubs, while interscholastic athletic teams compete with other independent schools. Students may participate in an exchange program with other Sacred Heart schools in Europe and the United States. Service activities are expected of each student, exemplifying the commitment of Sacred Heart education to social justice and the support of the broader community.

CONVENT OF THE SACRED HEART HIGH SCHOOL

2222 Broadway
San Francisco, California 94115

ANNOUNCEMENT FROM THE SCHOOL Convent of the Sacred Heart High School is an independent, Catholic, college-preparatory high school for girls. Founded by the Religious of the Sacred Heart, Convent has provided excellence in education for young women since 1887. Convent is the only school to offer young women single sex education in a coed community.

CONVENT OF THE VISITATION SCHOOL

2455 Visitation Drive
Mendota Heights, Minnesota 55120-1696

Head of School: Dawn Nichols

General Information Coeducational day (boys' only in lower grades) college-preparatory, arts, religious studies, bilingual studies, and technology school, affiliated with Roman Catholic Church. Boys grades PK–6, girls grades PK–12. Founded: 1873. Setting: suburban. Nearest major city is St. Paul. 50-acre campus. 1 building on campus. Approved or accredited by Independent Schools Association of the Central States and Minnesota Department of Education. Member of National Association of Independent Schools and Secondary School Admission Test Board. Endowment: $13 million. Total enrollment: 582. Upper school average class size: 16. Upper school faculty-student ratio: 1:10.
Upper School Student Profile Grade 9: 85 students (85 girls); Grade 10: 79 students (79 girls); Grade 11: 77 students (77 girls); Grade 12: 87 students (87 girls). 85% of students are Roman Catholic.
Faculty School total: 59. In upper school: 7 men, 31 women; 31 have advanced degrees.
Subjects Offered Algebra, American history, American literature, anatomy, art, astronomy, ballet, biology, biology-AP, British literature, calculus, calculus-AP, ceramics, chamber groups, chemistry, Chinese, choir, choral music, Christian scripture, church history, composition, computer programming, computer science, creative writing, desktop publishing, drawing, economics, English, English literature, English literature-AP, European history, French, French-AP, genetics, geometry, government, graphic design, health, history, history-AP, honors algebra, Latin, literary genres, math analysis, mathematics, music, orchestra, painting, peer ministry, photography, physical education, physical science, physics, physiology, prayer/spirituality, psychology, religion, science, senior seminar, sociology, Spanish, Spanish-AP, speech, theater, U.S. government-AP, U.S. history, Web site design, women spirituality and faith, world culture, world history, world religions.
Graduation Requirements Arts and fine arts (art, music, dance, drama), computer science, English, foreign language, mathematics, physical education (includes health), religion (includes Bible studies and theology), science, social science, social studies (includes history), two-week senior year service project.
Special Academic Programs Advanced Placement exam preparation; honors section; independent study; study at local college for college credit.
College Admission Counseling 76 students graduated in 2008; all went to college, including College of Saint Benedict; Creighton University; Marquette University; Saint Mary's College; University of Minnesota, Twin Cities Campus; University of St. Thomas. Median SAT critical reading: 600, median SAT math: 570, median SAT writing: 600, median combined SAT: 1770, median composite ACT: 27. 53% scored over 600 on SAT critical reading, 45% scored over 600 on SAT math, 61% scored over 600 on SAT writing, 47% scored over 1800 on combined SAT, 56% scored over 26 on composite ACT.
Student Life Upper grades have uniform requirement, student council, honor system. Discipline rests primarily with faculty. Attendance at religious services is required.
Summer Programs Remediation, advancement programs offered; session focuses on Orton-Gillingham instruction method, ACT Prep; held on campus; accepts boys and girls; open to students from other schools. 175 students usually enrolled. 2009 schedule: June 8 to July 24. Application deadline: May 1.
Tuition and Aid Day student tuition: $16,767. Tuition installment plan (monthly payment plans, individually arranged payment plans, semiannual payment plan). Need-based scholarship grants, funds allocated from the Archdiocese available. In 2008–09, 27% of upper-school students received aid. Total amount of financial aid awarded in 2008–09: $832,155.
Admissions Traditional secondary-level entrance grade is 9. For fall 2008, 90 students applied for upper-level admission, 55 were accepted, 41 enrolled. ERB, Individual IQ and Iowa Tests of Basic Skills required. Deadline for receipt of application materials: January 16. Application fee required: $25. Interview required.
Athletics Interscholastic: alpine skiing, basketball, cross-country running, diving, golf, hockey, ice hockey, lacrosse, nordic skiing, skiing (cross-country), skiing (downhill), soccer, softball, swimming and diving, tennis, track and field, volleyball; intramural: ballet, basketball. 1 PE instructor, 30 coaches, 1 athletic trainer.
Computers Computers are regularly used in all classes. Computer network features include on-campus library services, online commercial services, Internet access, wireless campus network, Internet filtering or blocking technology. Students grades are available online. The school has a published electronic and media policy.
Contact Katie Owens, Director of Admissions. 651-683-1706. Fax: 651-454-7144. E-mail: kowens@vischool.org. Web site: www.visitation.net.

COPENHAGEN INTERNATIONAL SCHOOL

Hellerupvej 22
2900 Hellerup, Denmark

Head of School: Peter Wellby

General Information Coeducational day college-preparatory school. Grades 6–12. Founded: 1963. Setting: suburban. Nearest major city is Copenhagen, Denmark. 1-hectare campus. 2 buildings on campus. Approved or accredited by European Council of International Schools, International Baccalaureate Organization, and New England Association of Schools and Colleges. Language of instruction: English. Total enrollment: 602. Upper school average class size: 18. Upper school faculty-student ratio: 1:7.
Upper School Student Profile Grade 6: 41 students (22 boys, 19 girls); Grade 7: 46 students (19 boys, 27 girls); Grade 8: 39 students (20 boys, 19 girls); Grade 9: 44 students (21 boys, 23 girls); Grade 10: 44 students (21 boys, 23 girls); Grade 11: 54 students (31 boys, 23 girls); Grade 12: 40 students (21 boys, 19 girls).
Faculty School total: 88. In upper school: 27 men, 23 women; 50 have advanced degrees.
Subjects Offered Anthropology, art, biology, chemistry, computer programming, Danish, English, English literature, ESL, European history, French, German, history, International Baccalaureate courses, mathematics, music, physical education, physics, science, social science, social studies, theory of knowledge, world history.
Special Academic Programs International Baccalaureate program; special instructional classes for students with mild learning disabilities and dyslexia; ESL (54 students enrolled).
College Admission Counseling 34 students graduated in 2008; 33 went to college, including Harvard University; The University of North Carolina at Chapel Hill; Vanderbilt University. Other: 1 went to work.
Student Life Upper grades have student council, honor system. Discipline rests equally with students and faculty.
Summer Programs Remediation, ESL, sports, art/fine arts, computer instruction programs offered; held both on and off campus; held at Gentofte Stadium; accepts boys and girls; open to students from other schools. 60 students usually enrolled. 2009 schedule: June 25 to July 5. Application deadline: May 31.
Tuition and Aid Day student tuition: 114,000 Danish kroner. Tuition installment plan (monthly payment plans, individually arranged payment plans). Need-based schol-

arship grants available. In 2008–09, 15% of upper-school students received aid. Total amount of financial aid awarded in 2008–09: 4,000,000 Danish kroner.
Admissions Traditional secondary-level entrance grade is 10. For fall 2008, 59 students applied for upper-level admission, 57 were accepted, 56 enrolled. English for Non-native Speakers, math and English placement tests or writing sample required. Deadline for receipt of application materials: none. Application fee required: 25,000 Danish kroner. On-campus interview recommended.
Athletics Interscholastic: basketball (boys, girls), scooter football (b,g), soccer (b,g), softball (b,g), swimming and diving (b,g), tennis (b,g), volleyball (b,g). 3 PE instructors, 3 coaches.
Computers Computers are regularly used in English, geography, history, humanities, information technology, lab/keyboard, library, mathematics, media arts, programming, yearbook classes. Computer network features include on-campus library services, online commercial services, Internet access, wireless campus network, Internet filtering or blocking technology. Student e-mail accounts are available to students.
Contact Thomas Martin Nielsen, Admissions Officer. 45-39-46-33-00 Ext. 315. Fax: 45-39-61-22-30. E-mail: admission@cisdk.dk. Web site: www.cis-edu.dk.

CORNELIA CONNELLY SCHOOL

2323 West Broadway
Anaheim, California 92804

Head of School: Sr. Francine Gunther, SHCJ

General Information Girls' day college-preparatory, arts, and religious studies school, affiliated with Roman Catholic Church. Grades 9–12. Founded: 1961. Setting: urban. Nearest major city is Los Angeles. 6-acre campus. 9 buildings on campus. Approved or accredited by California Association of Independent Schools, National Catholic Education Association, Western Association of Schools and Colleges, and Western Catholic Education Association. Member of National Association of Independent Schools. Endowment: $50,280. Total enrollment: 299. Upper school average class size: 18. Upper school faculty-student ratio: 1:9.
Upper School Student Profile Grade 9: 80 students (80 girls); Grade 10: 76 students (76 girls); Grade 11: 65 students (65 girls); Grade 12: 78 students (78 girls). 80% of students are Roman Catholic.
Faculty School total: 31. In upper school: 9 men, 21 women; 21 have advanced degrees.
Subjects Offered Arts, chemistry, community service, English, fine arts, French, general science, Latin, mathematics, physical education, religion, science, social studies, Spanish.
Graduation Requirements Arts and fine arts (art, music, dance, drama), English, foreign language, mathematics, physical education (includes health), religion (includes Bible studies and theology), science, social studies (includes history). Community service is required.
Special Academic Programs International Baccalaureate program; Advanced Placement exam preparation; honors section; independent study; term-away projects.
College Admission Counseling 82 students graduated in 2008; all went to college, including California State University, Fullerton; California State University, Long Beach; Chapman University; Santa Clara University. Median SAT critical reading: 550, median SAT math: 500, median SAT writing: 560, median combined SAT: 1620, median composite ACT: 22. 28% scored over 600 on SAT critical reading, 21% scored over 600 on SAT math, 31% scored over 600 on SAT writing, 23% scored over 1800 on combined SAT, 24% scored over 26 on composite ACT.
Student Life Upper grades have uniform requirement, student council, honor system. Discipline rests primarily with faculty. Attendance at religious services is required.
Summer Programs Enrichment, advancement programs offered; held on campus; accepts boys and girls; open to students from other schools. 50 students usually enrolled. 2009 schedule: June 24 to July 31.
Tuition and Aid Day student tuition: $10,700. Tuition installment plan (Key Tuition Payment Plan, FACTS Tuition Payment Plan, 2-payment plan (July and December), 1-payment plan (July)). Merit scholarship grants, need-based scholarship grants available. In 2008–09, 7% of upper-school students received aid. Total amount of financial aid awarded in 2008–09: $162,800.
Admissions Traditional secondary-level entrance grade is 9. For fall 2008, 132 students applied for upper-level admission, 90 were accepted, 80 enrolled. High School Placement Test (closed version) from Scholastic Testing Service required. Deadline for receipt of application materials: January 30. Application fee required: $50. Interview required.
Athletics Interscholastic: basketball, cheering, cross-country running, golf, soccer, softball, swimming and diving, tennis, volleyball, water polo, winter soccer. 2 PE instructors, 7 coaches.
Computers Computers are regularly used in all academic, basic skills, college planning, library, publications, SAT preparation, yearbook classes. Computer network features include on-campus library services, Internet access, wireless campus network. Students grades are available online. The school has a published electronic and media policy.
Contact Ms. Abby Vanausdoll, Director of Admissions and Tuition Assistance. 714-776-1717 Ext. 234. Fax: 714-776-2534. E-mail: avanausdoll@connellyhs.org.

ANNOUNCEMENT FROM THE SCHOOL Cornelia Connelly High School is an independent, Catholic, fully accredited, college-preparatory high school for girls. Guided by trust, reverence, and respect, girls develop into self-confident, poised, and articulate women, empowered to transform our global society. Honors and Advanced Placement courses are available, as are numerous co-curricular activities including fine arts, athletics, and clubs.

COTTER SCHOOLS

1115 West Broadway
Winona, Minnesota 55987-1399

Head of School: Dr. Craig W. Junker, EdD

General Information Coeducational boarding and day college-preparatory, general academic, arts, religious studies, technology, and ESL school, affiliated with Roman Catholic Church. Boarding grades 9–12, day grades 7–12. Founded: 1911. Setting: small town. Nearest major city is Minneapolis. Students are housed in single-sex by floor dormitories. 75-acre campus. 7 buildings on campus. Approved or accredited by Midwest Association of Boarding Schools, National Catholic Education Association, North Central Association of Colleges and Schools, The Association of Boarding Schools, and Minnesota Department of Education. Total enrollment: 419. Upper school average class size: 16. Upper school faculty-student ratio: 1:16.
Upper School Student Profile Grade 7: 47 students (26 boys, 21 girls); Grade 8: 62 students (26 boys, 36 girls); Grade 9: 60 students (32 boys, 28 girls); Grade 10: 80 students (45 boys, 35 girls); Grade 11: 80 students (41 boys, 39 girls); Grade 12: 90 students (48 boys, 42 girls). 25% of students are boarding students. 65% are state residents. 3 states are represented in upper school student body. 24% are international students. International students from China, Japan, Mexico, Republic of Korea, Taiwan, and Viet Nam; 4 other countries represented in student body. 66% of students are Roman Catholic.
Faculty School total: 39. In upper school: 19 men, 20 women; 35 have advanced degrees; 2 reside on campus.
Subjects Offered Algebra, American history, anatomy, art, band, Bible, biology, calculus, calculus-AP, campus ministry, chemistry, chorus, Christian and Hebrew scripture, Christian ethics, community service, computer science, death and loss, economics, English, environmental science, ESL, German, health, Hebrew scripture, honors English, learning lab, linear algebra, literature and composition-AP, math analysis, mathematics, media, painting, physical education, physical science, physics, psychology, science, Spanish, statistics, U.S. history, U.S. history-AP, visual arts, world geography, world religions.
Graduation Requirements English, foreign language, mathematics, performing arts, physical education (includes health), religion (includes Bible studies and theology), science, social studies (includes history), visual arts, 80 hours of community service.
Special Academic Programs Honors section; accelerated programs; independent study; term-away projects; study at local college for college credit; study abroad; academic accommodation for the gifted, the musically talented, and the artistically talented; remedial reading and/or remedial writing; remedial math; programs in English, mathematics for dyslexic students; ESL (25 students enrolled).
College Admission Counseling 91 students graduated in 2008; all went to college, including Saint John's University; Saint Mary's University of Minnesota; University of Illinois at Urbana–Champaign; University of Minnesota, Twin Cities Campus; University of St. Thomas; University of Wisconsin–Madison. Median composite ACT: 24. 50% scored over 26 on composite ACT.
Student Life Upper grades have specified standards of dress, student council. Discipline rests primarily with faculty. Attendance at religious services is required.
Tuition and Aid Day student tuition: $5875; 5-day tuition and room/board: $22,050; 7-day tuition and room/board: $25,500. Tuition installment plan (monthly payment plans, individually arranged payment plans). Tuition reduction for siblings, need-based scholarship grants available. In 2008–09, 60% of upper-school students received aid.
Admissions Traditional secondary-level entrance grade is 9. For fall 2008, 56 students applied for upper-level admission, 36 were accepted, 31 enrolled. SLEP for foreign students or TOEFL required. Deadline for receipt of application materials: none. Application fee required: $50. Interview recommended.
Athletics Interscholastic: aerobics/dance (girls), baseball (b), basketball (b,g), cheering (g), cross-country running (b,g), dance (g), dance team (g), danceline (g), football (b), golf (b,g), gymnastics (g), hockey (b,g), ice hockey (b,g), skiing (cross-country) (b,g), soccer (b,g), softball (g), swimming and diving (b,g), tennis (b,g), track and field (b,g), volleyball (g), wrestling (b); intramural: basketball (b,g), indoor soccer (b); coed intramural: badminton, basketball, canoeing/kayaking, indoor soccer. 2 PE instructors, 66 coaches, 1 athletic trainer.
Computers Computers are regularly used in art, technology classes. Computer network features include on-campus library services, Internet access, Internet filtering or blocking technology. Campus intranet, student e-mail accounts, and computer access in designated common areas are available to students. The school has a published electronic and media policy.
Contact Mr. Will Gibson, Director of Admissions and International Programs. 507-453-5403. Fax: 507-453-5013. E-mail: wgibson@winonacotter.org. Web site: www.cotterschools.org.

THE COUNTRY DAY SCHOOL

13415 Dufferin Street
King City, Ontario L7B 1K5, Canada

Head of School: Mr. Paul C. Duckett

General Information Coeducational day college-preparatory, arts, business, and technology school. Grades JK–12. Founded: 1972. Setting: rural. Nearest major city is Toronto, Canada. 100-acre campus. 2 buildings on campus. Approved or accredited by Canadian Association of Independent Schools, Canadian Educational Standards Institute, Conference of Independent Schools of Ontario, and Ontario Department of Education. Language of instruction: English. Total enrollment: 720. Upper school average class size: 17. Upper school faculty-student ratio: 1:10.

Upper School Student Profile Grade 9: 80 students (40 boys, 40 girls); Grade 10: 80 students (40 boys, 40 girls); Grade 11: 80 students (40 boys, 40 girls); Grade 12: 80 students (40 boys, 40 girls).

Faculty School total: 79. In upper school: 28 men, 20 women.

Subjects Offered Advanced chemistry, advanced computer applications, advanced math, algebra, American history, anatomy and physiology, ancient history, ancient/medieval philosophy, art and culture, art history, athletics, band, biology, business studies, Canadian geography, Canadian history, Canadian literature, career education, career/college preparation, choir, comparative politics, computer programming, creative writing, English, environmental geography, European history, French, government/civics, history, languages, mathematics, modern Western civilization, performing arts, philosophy, physical education, physics, politics, science, society, world history.

Graduation Requirements Ministry Grade 10 Literacy Test (Government of Ontario).

Special Academic Programs Advanced Placement exam preparation; study abroad.

College Admission Counseling 79 students graduated in 2008; all went to college, including McGill University; McMaster University; Queen's University at Kingston; The University of Western Ontario; University of Guelph; University of Toronto.

Student Life Upper grades have uniform requirement, student council, honor system. Discipline rests primarily with faculty.

Summer Programs Advancement, art/fine arts programs offered; session focuses on advancement; held both on and off campus; held at Costa Rica, England, and Galapagos Islands; accepts boys and girls; open to students from other schools. 20 students usually enrolled. 2009 schedule: July 2 to July 31. Application deadline: March 1.

Tuition and Aid Day student tuition: CAN$20,630.

Admissions Traditional secondary-level entrance grade is 9. For fall 2008, 97 students applied for upper-level admission, 58 were accepted, 37 enrolled. CAT 5, SSAT or writing sample required. Deadline for receipt of application materials: none. Application fee required: CAN$100. On-campus interview required.

Athletics Interscholastic: baseball (girls), basketball (b,g), cross-country running (b,g), golf (b,g), hockey (b,g), ice hockey (b,g), rugby (b,g), running (b,g), soccer (b,g), softball (b,g), track and field (b,g), volleyball (b,g); intramural: badminton (b,g), basketball (b,g), bowling (b,g), ice hockey (b), ice skating (b,g), physical fitness (b,g), skiing (downhill) (b,g), snowboarding (b,g), soccer (b,g), softball (b,g), volleyball (b,g); coed intramural: curling, Frisbee, physical fitness, physical training, rock climbing, strength & conditioning, swimming and diving, table tennis. 5 PE instructors.

Computers Computers are regularly used in accounting, business, career education, English, geography, history, mathematics, media, music, writing, yearbook classes. Computer network features include on-campus library services, Internet access, wireless campus network, Internet filtering or blocking technology, access to online library resources from home, access to homework online via Blackboard Software. Campus intranet is available to students.

Contact Mr. David Huckvale, Director of Admission. 905-833-1220. Fax: 905-833-1350. E-mail: admissions@cds.on.ca. Web site: www.cds.on.ca/.

COUNTRY DAY SCHOOL OF THE SACRED HEART

480 Bryn Mawr Avenue
Bryn Mawr, Pennsylvania 19010

Head of School: Sr. Matthew Anita MacDonald, SSJ

General Information Girls' day college-preparatory, arts, religious studies, and technology school, affiliated with Roman Catholic Church. Grades PK–12. Founded: 1865. Setting: suburban. Nearest major city is Philadelphia. 16-acre campus. 3 buildings on campus. Approved or accredited by Middle States Association of Colleges and Schools, Network of Sacred Heart Schools, Pennsylvania Association of Independent Schools, and Pennsylvania Department of Education. Member of National Association of Independent Schools. Total enrollment: 353. Upper school average class size: 15. Upper school faculty-student ratio: 1:10.

Upper School Student Profile Grade 9: 50 students (50 girls); Grade 10: 46 students (46 girls); Grade 11: 50 students (50 girls); Grade 12: 42 students (42 girls). 75% of students are Roman Catholic.

Faculty School total: 44. In upper school: 4 men, 20 women; 19 have advanced degrees.

Subjects Offered Algebra, American history, American history-AP, American literature, art, arts, Bible studies, biology, calculus, chemistry, composition, computer science, economics, English, English literature, environmental science, ethics, European history, film, fine arts, French, geometry, government/civics, health, Latin, mathematics, media studies, physical education, physics, pre-calculus, religion, science, social science, social studies, Spanish, trigonometry, word processing, world history, world literature.

Graduation Requirements Arts and fine arts (art, music, dance, drama), English, foreign language, mathematics, physical education (includes health), religion (includes Bible studies and theology), science, social studies (includes history), two weeks of senior independent study with a working professional, 25 hours of community service per year.

Special Academic Programs Advanced Placement exam preparation; honors section; independent study; term-away projects; study at local college for college credit; domestic exchange program (with Network of Sacred Heart Schools); study abroad; academic accommodation for the musically talented.

College Admission Counseling 46 students graduated in 2008; all went to college, including Drexel University; Fordham University; Penn State University Park; Saint Joseph's University; The Catholic University of America; Villanova University. Mean SAT critical reading: 600, mean SAT math: 580, mean SAT writing: 610. 43% scored over 600 on SAT critical reading, 40% scored over 600 on SAT math, 49% scored over 600 on SAT writing.

Student Life Upper grades have uniform requirement, student council. Discipline rests equally with students and faculty. Attendance at religious services is required.

Tuition and Aid Day student tuition: $14,400. Tuition installment plan (SMART Tuition Payment Plan). Tuition reduction for siblings, merit scholarship grants, need-based scholarship grants available. In 2008–09, 59% of upper-school students received aid; total upper-school merit-scholarship money awarded: $320,500. Total amount of financial aid awarded in 2008–09: $423,000.

Admissions Traditional secondary-level entrance grade is 9. For fall 2008, 137 students applied for upper-level admission, 110 were accepted. High School Placement Test required. Deadline for receipt of application materials: none. Application fee required: $35. Interview required.

Athletics Interscholastic: basketball, crew, field hockey, golf, lacrosse, softball, tennis, track and field, volleyball. 2 PE instructors, 12 coaches, 1 athletic trainer.

Computers Computers are regularly used in English, foreign language, history, mathematics, science, technology classes. Computer network features include on-campus library services, online commercial services, Internet access. The school has a published electronic and media policy.

Contact Mrs. Laurie Nowlan, Director of Admissions. 610-527-3915 Ext. 214. Fax: 610-527-0942. E-mail: lnowlan@cdssh.org. Web site: www.cdssh.org.

COVENANT CANADIAN REFORMED SCHOOL

3030 TWP Road 615A
PO Box 67
Neerlandia, Alberta T0G 1R0, Canada

Head of School: Mr. Harry VanDelden

General Information Coeducational day college-preparatory, general academic, business, religious studies, and technology school, affiliated with Reformed Church. Grades K–12. Founded: 1977. Setting: rural. Nearest major city is Edmonton, Canada. 5-acre campus. 2 buildings on campus. Approved or accredited by Association of Independent Schools and Colleges of Alberta and Alberta Department of Education. Language of instruction: English. Total enrollment: 170. Upper school average class size: 10. Upper school faculty-student ratio: 1:10.

Upper School Student Profile Grade 10: 9 students (4 boys, 5 girls); Grade 11: 11 students (6 boys, 5 girls); Grade 12: 5 students (1 boy, 4 girls). 99% of students are Reformed.

Faculty School total: 12. In upper school: 6 men, 3 women; 1 has an advanced degree.

Subjects Offered Accounting, architectural drawing, Bible studies, biology, Canadian geography, career and personal planning, career technology, chemistry, child development, Christian education, computer information systems, computer keyboarding, computer skills, computer studies, consumer law, desktop publishing, digital photography, drawing and design, early childhood, electronic publishing, English, ESL, French as a second language, geology, health education, history, HTML design, information processing, intro to computers, introduction to technology, keyboarding/computer, mathematics, physical education, physics, prayer/spirituality, religious studies, science, sewing, social studies, theology and the arts, Web site design, Western religions, work experience, world geography, world religions, yearbook.

Graduation Requirements Student must pass religious studies courses offered, in grades 10, 11, and 12 for the years the student attended.

Special Academic Programs Independent study; remedial reading and/or remedial writing; remedial math.

College Admission Counseling 6 students graduated in 2008; 4 went to college, including University of Alberta. Other: 2 went to work.

Student Life Upper grades have specified standards of dress, student council. Discipline rests primarily with faculty.

Tuition and Aid Day student tuition: CAN$5100. Tuition installment plan (monthly payment plans, individually arranged payment plans).

Admissions Traditional secondary-level entrance grade is 10. Deadline for receipt of application materials: none. No application fee required. Interview required.

Covenant Canadian Reformed School

Athletics Interscholastic: volleyball (boys, girls); coed intramural: badminton, ball hockey, baseball, basketball, flag football, floor hockey, football, Frisbee, hockey, ice hockey, indoor hockey, indoor soccer, lacrosse, soccer, softball, volleyball.
Computers Computers are regularly used in all classes. Computer network features include on-campus library services, Internet access, Internet filtering or blocking technology. Computer access in designated common areas is available to students.
Contact Mr. Harry VanDelden, Principal. 780-674-4774. Fax: 780-401-3295. E-mail: hvd@xplornet.com.

THE CRAIG SCHOOL
Mountain Lakes, New Jersey
See Special Needs Schools section.

CRANBROOK SCHOOLS
39221 Woodward Avenue
PO Box 801
Bloomfield Hills, Michigan 48303-0801

See Close-Up on page 724.

CRAWFORD ADVENTIST ACADEMY
531 Finch Avenue West
Willowdale, Ontario M2R 3X2, Canada
Head of School: Mr. Norman Brown

General Information Coeducational day college-preparatory, arts, business, religious studies, bilingual studies, and technology school, affiliated with Seventh-day Adventist Church. Grades JK–12. Founded: 1954. Setting: urban. Nearest major city is Toronto, Canada. 5-acre campus. 1 building on campus. Approved or accredited by Ontario Ministry of Education and Ontario Department of Education. Language of instruction: English. Total enrollment: 468. Upper school average class size: 25. Upper school faculty-student ratio: 1:16.
Upper School Student Profile Grade 9: 47 students (24 boys, 23 girls); Grade 10: 44 students (22 boys, 22 girls); Grade 11: 38 students (12 boys, 26 girls); Grade 12: 30 students (13 boys, 17 girls). 90% of students are Seventh-day Adventists.
Faculty School total: 16. In upper school: 11 men, 4 women; 10 have advanced degrees.
Subjects Offered Advanced computer applications, band, Bible, biology, business, business technology, calculus, Canadian geography, Canadian history, chemistry, choir, civics, community service, computer applications, computer information systems, discrete mathematics, drama, dramatic arts, earth and space science, English, English composition, French, French as a second language, geography, guidance, independent study, information technology, marketing, mathematics, physical education, physics, religion, science, writing, yearbook.
Special Academic Programs Remedial reading and/or remedial writing; programs in English for dyslexic students; ESL (3 students enrolled).
College Admission Counseling 37 students graduated in 2008; 35 went to college, including Andrews University; Ryerson University; University of Toronto; University of Waterloo; York University. Other: 2 went to work. Median composite ACT: 20. 22% scored over 26 on composite ACT.
Student Life Upper grades have uniform requirement, student council, honor system. Discipline rests primarily with faculty.
Tuition and Aid Day student tuition: CAN$7600. Tuition installment plan (monthly payment plans). Tuition reduction for siblings, need-based scholarship grants, paying campus jobs available. In 2008–09, 10% of upper-school students received aid. Total amount of financial aid awarded in 2008–09: CAN$15,000.
Admissions Traditional secondary-level entrance grade is 9. For fall 2008, 27 students applied for upper-level admission, 25 were accepted, 25 enrolled. CAT 2 required. Deadline for receipt of application materials: none. Application fee required: CAN$25. On-campus interview required.
Athletics Interscholastic: basketball (boys, girls), cooperative games (b,g), flag football (b,g), softball (b,g), volleyball (b,g); intramural: basketball (b,g), flag football (b,g), floor hockey (b,g), indoor soccer (b,g), physical fitness (b,g), table tennis (b,g), volleyball (b,g); coed intramural: outdoor education, softball. 1 PE instructor, 1 coach.
Computers Computers are regularly used in accounting, business, computer applications, yearbook classes. Computer network features include Internet access, wireless campus network, Internet filtering or blocking technology. Student e-mail accounts and computer access in designated common areas are available to students. The school has a published electronic and media policy.
Contact Dr. Janice Patricia Maitland, Principal, 9-12. 416-633-0090 Ext. 223. Fax: 416-633-0467. E-mail: janypan@hotmail.com.

CRAWFORD DAY SCHOOL
Portsmouth, Virginia
See Special Needs Schools section.

CRESPI CARMELITE HIGH SCHOOL
5031 Alonzo Avenue
Encino, California 91316-3699
Head of School: Fr. Paul Henson, OCARM

General Information Boys' day college-preparatory, arts, and religious studies school, affiliated with Roman Catholic Church. Grades 9–12. Founded: 1959. Setting: suburban. Nearest major city is Los Angeles. 3-acre campus. 3 buildings on campus. Approved or accredited by Western Association of Schools and Colleges, Western Catholic Education Association, and California Department of Education. Total enrollment: 589. Upper school average class size: 23. Upper school faculty-student ratio: 1:23.
Upper School Student Profile Grade 9: 142 students (142 boys); Grade 10: 157 students (157 boys); Grade 11: 163 students (163 boys); Grade 12: 127 students (127 boys). 72% of students are Roman Catholic.
Faculty School total: 43. In upper school: 39 men, 4 women; 28 have advanced degrees.
Subjects Offered Advanced Placement courses, advanced studio art-AP, algebra, American history-AP, American literature-AP, anatomy and physiology, Ancient Greek, ancient world history, applied music, ASB Leadership, athletic training, audio visual/media, baseball, Basic programming, basketball, biology, biology-AP, British literature, British literature-AP, calculus, calculus-AP, chemistry, Christian scripture, church history, classical Greek literature, computer graphics, constitutional law, drama performance, driver education, earth science, economics and history, economics-AP, English composition, English literature and composition-AP, environmental science, ethics, European history-AP, film studies, geometry, golf, government, government and politics-AP, Greek, Greek culture, health, history of the Catholic Church, Holocaust, honors English, honors geometry, international studies, journalism, language and composition, Latin-AP, law, media arts, men's studies, model United Nations, moral and social development, music appreciation, music composition, photography, physical science, physics-AP, prayer/spirituality, pre-calculus, probability and statistics, psychology, social justice, Spanish language-AP, sports, sports conditioning, statistics-AP, student government, student publications, U.S. history, U.S. history-AP, video film production, Web site design, Western civilization, western religions, world cultures, world geography, world religions, yearbook, zoology.
Graduation Requirements Arts and fine arts (art, music, dance, drama), English, foreign language, mathematics, physical education (includes health), religion (includes Bible studies and theology), science, social science, social studies (includes history). Community service is required.
Special Academic Programs Advanced Placement exam preparation; honors section.
College Admission Counseling 136 students graduated in 2008; 133 went to college, including California Polytechnic State University, San Luis Obispo; California State University, Northridge; University of California, Los Angeles; University of California, Santa Barbara; University of San Diego. Other: 1 went to work, 2 entered military service. Median SAT critical reading: 519, median SAT math: 523, median SAT writing: 530, median composite ACT: 22. 27% scored over 600 on SAT critical reading, 24% scored over 600 on SAT math, 25% scored over 600 on SAT writing.
Student Life Upper grades have specified standards of dress, student council, honor system. Discipline rests primarily with faculty. Attendance at religious services is required.
Summer Programs Remediation, enrichment, advancement, sports, art/fine arts programs offered; session focuses on remediation and/or enrichment in math, science, language, and social studies; held on campus; accepts boys and girls; open to students from other schools. 250 students usually enrolled. 2009 schedule: June 29 to July 31. Application deadline: June 26.
Tuition and Aid Day student tuition: $10,950. Tuition installment plan (FACTS Tuition Payment Plan, Tuition Management Systems Plan). Merit scholarship grants, need-based scholarship grants available. In 2008–09, 18% of upper-school students received aid; total upper-school merit-scholarship money awarded: $59,500. Total amount of financial aid awarded in 2008–09: $512,600.
Admissions Traditional secondary-level entrance grade is 9. For fall 2008, 271 students applied for upper-level admission, 253 were accepted, 142 enrolled. High School Placement Test or High School Placement Test (closed version) from Scholastic Testing Service required. Deadline for receipt of application materials: February 6. Application fee required: $90. On-campus interview required.
Athletics Interscholastic: aquatics, baseball, basketball, cross-country running, football, golf, lacrosse, soccer, swimming and diving, tennis, track and field, volleyball, water polo, wrestling; intramural: basketball, table tennis. 4 PE instructors, 2 athletic trainers.
Computers Computers are regularly used in economics, English, foreign language, history, mathematics, media production, science, video film production, yearbook classes. Computer network features include on-campus library services, online commercial services, Internet access. The school has a published electronic and media policy.
Contact Mr. Robert Kodama, Director of Admissions. 818-345-1672 Ext. 310. Fax: 818-705-0209. E-mail: rkodama@crespi.org. Web site: www.crespi.org.

CRESTWOOD PREPARATORY COLLEGE

217 Brookbanks Drive
Toronto, Ontario M3A 2T7, Canada
Head of School: Mr. Vince Pagano

General Information Coeducational day college-preparatory school. Grades 7–12. Founded: 1980. Setting: urban. 1 building on campus. Approved or accredited by Ontario Department of Education. Language of instruction: English. Total enrollment: 525. Upper school average class size: 17. Upper school faculty-student ratio: 1:16.
Faculty School total: 52. In upper school: 27 men, 25 women.
Special Academic Programs Advanced Placement exam preparation.
Student Life Upper grades have uniform requirement, student council. Discipline rests primarily with faculty.
Tuition and Aid Day student tuition: CAN$18,600. Tuition installment plan (The Tuition Plan). Tuition reduction for siblings available.
Admissions Writing sample required. Deadline for receipt of application materials: February 2. Application fee required: CAN$100. Interview required.
Athletics Interscholastic: ball hockey (boys), baseball (b,g), basketball (b,g), golf (b), hockey (b,g), indoor track & field (b,g), running (b,g), softball (b,g), swimming and diving (b,g), volleyball (b,g); intramural: ball hockey (b), flag football (b), tai chi (b,g), ultimate Frisbee (b,g); coed intramural: Frisbee, scuba diving. 6 PE instructors.
Contact Mr. David Hecock. 416-391-1441 Ext. 23. Fax: 416-444-0949. E-mail: dhecock@crestwoodprepco.com. Web site: www.crestwoodprepco.com.

CRETIN-DERHAM HALL

550 South Albert Street
Saint Paul, Minnesota 55116
Head of School: Mr. Richard Engler

General Information Coeducational day college-preparatory, general academic, arts, business, religious studies, technology, and Junior ROTC school, affiliated with Roman Catholic Church. Grades 9–12. Founded: 1987. Setting: urban. Nearest major city is St. Paul. 15-acre campus. 5 buildings on campus. Approved or accredited by North Central Association of Colleges and Schools. Total enrollment: 1,321. Upper school average class size: 20. Upper school faculty-student ratio: 1:15.
Upper School Student Profile Grade 9: 330 students (168 boys, 162 girls); Grade 10: 333 students (171 boys, 162 girls); Grade 11: 326 students (159 boys, 167 girls); Grade 12: 332 students (176 boys, 156 girls). 93% of students are Roman Catholic.
Faculty School total: 119. In upper school: 57 men, 62 women; 61 have advanced degrees.
Subjects Offered 3-dimensional art, aerobics, algebra, American government-AP, American history, American literature, analysis, art history, arts, audio visual/media, biology, business, career exploration, chemistry, computer math, computer programming, computer science, drama, economics, English, environmental science, ethics, fine arts, French, geography, geometry, German, government/civics, history, JROTC, Latin, mathematics, music, physical education, physics, religion, science, social studies, Spanish, speech, theater, theology, trigonometry.
Graduation Requirements Arts and fine arts (art, music, dance, drama), English, foreign language, health science, mathematics, physical education (includes health), religion (includes Bible studies and theology), science, social studies (includes history).
Special Academic Programs Advanced Placement exam preparation; honors section; accelerated programs; independent study; study at local college for college credit; academic accommodation for the gifted; remedial reading and/or remedial writing; remedial math.
College Admission Counseling 310 students graduated in 2008; 306 went to college, including College of Saint Benedict; University of Minnesota, Twin Cities Campus; University of St. Thomas; University of Wisconsin–Madison. Other: 2 went to work, 2 had other specific plans.
Student Life Upper grades have uniform requirement, student council. Discipline rests primarily with faculty. Attendance at religious services is required.
Summer Programs Remediation, enrichment, sports, art/fine arts, computer instruction programs offered; session focuses on enrichment; held on campus; accepts boys and girls; open to students from other schools. 500 students usually enrolled. 2009 schedule: June to July. Application deadline: June 1.
Tuition and Aid Day student tuition: $9300. Tuition installment plan (monthly payment plans, individually arranged payment plans, 2- and 3-payment plans). Need-based scholarship grants, paying campus jobs available. In 2008–09, 44% of upper-school students received aid. Total amount of financial aid awarded in 2008–09: $1,500,000.
Admissions Traditional secondary-level entrance grade is 9. For fall 2008, 486 students applied for upper-level admission, 360 were accepted, 330 enrolled. STS required. Deadline for receipt of application materials: none. No application fee required.
Athletics Interscholastic: baseball (boys), basketball (b,g), cross-country running (b,g), dance team (g), diving (b,g), figure skating (g), football (b), golf (b,g), gymnastics (g), ice hockey (b,g), lacrosse (g), riflery (b,g), skiing (downhill) (b,g), soccer (b,g), softball (g), swimming and diving (b,g), tennis (b,g), track and field (b,g), ultimate Frisbee (b,g), volleyball (g); coed interscholastic: alpine skiing, badminton, cheering, fencing, JROTC drill; coed intramural: basketball, volleyball. 5 PE instructors, 1 athletic trainer.
Computers Computers are regularly used in all academic, data processing, publications, yearbook classes. Computer network features include on-campus library services, online commercial services, Internet access, Internet filtering or blocking technology, check assignments and contact faculty. Campus intranet and student e-mail accounts are available to students. Students grades are available online. The school has a published electronic and media policy.
Contact Mary Jo Groeller, Administrator of Admissions. 651-696-3302. Fax: 651-696-3394. E-mail: mjgroeller@c-dh.org. Web site: www.c-dh.org.

CROFTON HOUSE SCHOOL

3200 West 41st Avenue
Vancouver, British Columbia V6N 3E1, Canada
Head of School: Dr. Patricia J. Dawson

General Information Girls' day college-preparatory school. Grades 1–12. Founded: 1898. Setting: urban. 10-acre campus. 7 buildings on campus. Approved or accredited by California Association of Independent Schools and British Columbia Department of Education. Affiliate member of National Association of Independent Schools. Language of instruction: English. Endowment: CAN$2.7 million. Total enrollment: 723. Upper school average class size: 20. Upper school faculty-student ratio: 1:10.
Upper School Student Profile Grade 7: 40 students (40 girls); Grade 8: 93 students (93 girls); Grade 9: 87 students (87 girls); Grade 10: 100 students (100 girls); Grade 11: 93 students (93 girls); Grade 12: 82 students (82 girls).
Faculty School total: 76. In upper school: 11 men, 65 women; 16 have advanced degrees.
Subjects Offered Art, biology, calculus, chemistry, Chinese, computer science, drama, English, English literature, English literature-AP, fine arts, French, geography, history, home economics, mathematics, music, physical education, physics, science, social studies, Spanish, theater.
Graduation Requirements Arts and fine arts (art, music, dance, drama), athletics, career and personal planning, English, French, mathematics, science, social studies (includes history).
Special Academic Programs 9 Advanced Placement exams for which test preparation is offered; honors section.
College Admission Counseling 83 students graduated in 2008; all went to college, including McGill University; Queen's University at Kingston; The University of British Columbia; The University of Western Ontario; University of Toronto; University of Victoria.
Student Life Upper grades have uniform requirement, student council. Discipline rests primarily with faculty.
Tuition and Aid Day student tuition: CAN$14,607. Tuition installment plan (monthly payment plans, term payment plan (3 terms a year)). Tuition reduction for siblings, bursaries, merit scholarship grants available. In 2008–09, 4% of upper-school students received aid. Total amount of financial aid awarded in 2008–09: CAN$154,438.
Admissions Traditional secondary-level entrance grade is 8. For fall 2008, 226 students applied for upper-level admission, 133 were accepted, 114 enrolled. School's own exam or SSAT required. Deadline for receipt of application materials: December 1. Application fee required: CAN$250. On-campus interview required.
Athletics Interscholastic: badminton, basketball, cross-country running, field hockey, independent competitive sports, netball, soccer, tennis, track and field, volleyball; intramural: backpacking, badminton, baseball, basketball, bicycling, bowling, canoeing/kayaking, climbing, cooperative games, cross-country running, field hockey, fitness, flag football, floor hockey, hiking/backpacking, jogging, mountain biking, netball, outdoor activities, outdoor education, physical fitness, physical training, soccer, track and field, volleyball. 5 PE instructors, 25 coaches.
Computers Computers are regularly used in English, foreign language, mathematics, science, social studies, technology, video film production classes. Computer network features include on-campus library services, online commercial services, Internet access, Internet filtering or blocking technology. Campus intranet is available to students. The school has a published electronic and media policy.
Contact Ms. Andrea De Paoli, Admissions and Marketing Coordinator. 604-263-3255. Fax: 604-263-4941. E-mail: smacmillan@croftonhouse.ca. Web site: www.croftonhouse.ca.

CROSS CREEK PROGRAMS

LaVerkin, Utah
See Special Needs Schools section.

CROSSROADS

Medford, Oregon 97501
See Special Needs Schools section.

CROSSROADS COLLEGE PREPARATORY SCHOOL

500 DeBaliviere Avenue
St. Louis, Missouri 63112

Head of School: William B. Handmaker

General Information Coeducational day college-preparatory and arts school. Grades 7–12. Founded: 1974. Setting: urban. 20-acre campus. 1 building on campus. Approved or accredited by Independent Schools Association of the Central States and Missouri Department of Education. Member of National Association of Independent Schools and Secondary School Admission Test Board. Total enrollment: 228. Upper school average class size: 14. Upper school faculty-student ratio: 1:9.

Upper School Student Profile Grade 9: 40 students (17 boys, 23 girls); Grade 10: 28 students (10 boys, 18 girls); Grade 11: 40 students (21 boys, 19 girls); Grade 12: 33 students (14 boys, 19 girls).

Faculty School total: 28. In upper school: 11 men, 17 women; 17 have advanced degrees.

Subjects Offered 3-dimensional art, African American history, algebra, American literature, anatomy, art, art history, art history-AP, Asian history, biology, biology-AP, botany, calculus, calculus-AP, ceramics, chemistry, chemistry-AP, community service, comparative religion, computer applications, creative writing, drama, ecology, English, English literature, environmental science, environmental science-AP, European history, fine arts, French, geography, geology, geometry, history, journalism, keyboarding, Latin, literature and composition-AP, mathematics, music, music theater, photography, physical education, physics, psychology, social science, sociology, Spanish, speech, studio art-AP, theater, trigonometry, women's studies, word processing, world history, world literature.

Graduation Requirements American literature, arts and fine arts (art, music, dance, drama), biology, chemistry, classics, computer science, creative writing, earth science, electives, English composition, English literature, environmental science, foreign language, interdisciplinary studies, mathematics, non-Western literature, physical education (includes health), political science, practical arts, social science, social studies (includes history), U.S. government and politics, world cultures, one course taken at a local university or college during senior year.

Special Academic Programs Advanced Placement exam preparation; honors section; independent study; study at local college for college credit.

College Admission Counseling 26 students graduated in 2008; all went to college, including Boston University; Knox College; Oberlin College; Saint Louis University; Washington University in St. Louis; Wesleyan University. Mean SAT critical reading: 612, mean SAT math: 613, mean SAT writing: 644, mean composite ACT: 26.

Student Life Upper grades have specified standards of dress, student council, honor system. Discipline rests equally with students and faculty.

Summer Programs Enrichment, sports, art/fine arts programs offered; held on campus; accepts boys and girls; open to students from other schools.

Tuition and Aid Day student tuition: $15,550. Tuition installment plan (FACTS Tuition Payment Plan, monthly payment plans, individually arranged payment plans). Merit scholarship grants, need-based scholarship grants available. In 2008–09, 38% of upper-school students received aid.

Admissions Traditional secondary-level entrance grade is 9. For fall 2008, 25 students applied for upper-level admission, 15 were accepted, 10 enrolled. ISEE required. Deadline for receipt of application materials: January 15. Application fee required: $50. On-campus interview required.

Athletics Interscholastic: baseball (boys), basketball (b,g), indoor soccer (b,g), soccer (b,g), tennis (b,g), track and field (b,g), volleyball (g); intramural: soccer (b,g); coed interscholastic: bicycling, dance, fitness, physical fitness, physical training, weight lifting, weight training; coed intramural: aquatics, basketball, bicycling, dance team, drill team, fencing, indoor soccer, table tennis, touch football, volleyball, wall climbing, weight training, yoga. 5 PE instructors, 9 coaches.

Computers Computers are regularly used in computer applications, English, foreign language, history, journalism, mathematics, newspaper, programming, science, Web site design, word processing, writing, yearbook classes. Computer network features include on-campus library services, Internet access, wireless campus network, Internet filtering or blocking technology, SmartBoard usage in every academic classroom. Students grades are available online.

Contact Maggie Baisch, Director of Admission. 314-367-8101. Fax: 314-367-9711. E-mail: maggie@crossroadscollegeprep.org. Web site: www.crossroadscollegeprep.org.

CROSSROADS SCHOOL FOR ARTS & SCIENCES

1714 21st Street
Santa Monica, California 90404-3917

Head of School: Mr. Bob Riddle

General Information Coeducational day college-preparatory, arts, and technology school. Grades K–12. Founded: 1971. Setting: urban. Nearest major city is Los Angeles. 3-acre campus. 16 buildings on campus. Approved or accredited by California Association of Independent Schools, Western Association of Schools and Colleges, and California Department of Education. Member of National Association of Independent Schools. Endowment: $13 million. Total enrollment: 1,125. Upper school average class size: 17. Upper school faculty-student ratio: 1:8.

Upper School Student Profile Grade 9: 125 students (59 boys, 66 girls); Grade 10: 128 students (64 boys, 64 girls); Grade 11: 118 students (66 boys, 52 girls); Grade 12: 121 students (65 boys, 56 girls).

Faculty School total: 162. In upper school: 39 men, 35 women; 37 have advanced degrees.

Subjects Offered Algebra, American history, American studies, art history, biology, calculus, ceramics, chemistry, community service, computer programming, computer science, creative writing, critical studies in film, cultural arts, dance, earth and space science, English, environmental education, film studies, French, gender issues, geometry, graphic design, great books, Greek, human development, Japanese, jazz ensemble, jazz theory, journalism, Latin, marine biology, marine ecology, music appreciation, music theory, orchestra, photography, physical education, physics, physiology, pre-calculus, sculpture, Spanish, statistics, studio art, theater, trigonometry, video film production, world civilizations, yoga.

Graduation Requirements Arts and fine arts (art, music, dance, drama), English, foreign language, human development, mathematics, physical education (includes health), science, social studies (includes history). Community service is required.

Special Academic Programs Honors section; term-away projects; academic accommodation for the gifted, the musically talented, and the artistically talented.

College Admission Counseling 119 students graduated in 2008; all went to college, including Barnard College; Boston University; Eugene Lang College The New School for Liberal Arts; New York University; University of Southern California. Mean SAT critical reading: 632, mean SAT math: 612, mean SAT writing: 648, mean combined SAT: 1892, mean composite ACT: 26.

Student Life Upper grades have student council. Discipline rests primarily with faculty.

Summer Programs Remediation, enrichment, advancement, sports, art/fine arts, computer instruction programs offered; session focuses on enrichment; held on campus; accepts boys and girls; open to students from other schools. 1,100 students usually enrolled. 2009 schedule: June 22 to August 14. Application deadline: none.

Tuition and Aid Day student tuition: $27,200. Tuition installment plan (monthly payment plans, individually arranged payment plans). Merit scholarship grants, need-based loans, Tuition Reduction Fund available. In 2008–09, 18% of upper-school students received aid; total upper-school merit-scholarship money awarded: $50,000. Total amount of financial aid awarded in 2008–09: $1,959,000.

Admissions Traditional secondary-level entrance grade is 9. For fall 2008, 165 students applied for upper-level admission, 21 were accepted, 13 enrolled. ISEE required. Deadline for receipt of application materials: December 12. Application fee required: $125. On-campus interview required.

Athletics Interscholastic: baseball (boys), basketball (b,g), cross-country running (b,g), soccer (b,g), softball (g), tennis (b,g), track and field (b,g), volleyball (b,g); coed interscholastic: flag football, golf, swimming and diving; coed intramural: canoeing/kayaking, climbing, hiking/backpacking, kayaking, outdoor activities, outdoor education, rock climbing, ropes courses, snowshoeing, table tennis. 10 PE instructors, 29 coaches, 1 athletic trainer.

Computers Computers are regularly used in college planning, creative writing, foreign language, graphic design, journalism, Latin, mathematics, music, newspaper, programming, science classes. Computer network features include on-campus library services, online commercial services, Internet access, wireless campus network. Student e-mail accounts and computer access in designated common areas are available to students. The school has a published electronic and media policy.

Contact Celia Lee, Director of Admissions. 310-829-7391 Ext. 704. Fax: 310-392-9011. E-mail: clee@xrds.org. Web site: www.xrds.org.

CROTCHED MOUNTAIN REHABILITATION CENTER SCHOOL

Greenfield, New Hampshire

See Special Needs Schools section.

CRYSTAL SPRINGS UPLANDS SCHOOL

400 Uplands Drive
Hillsborough, California 94010

Head of School: Ms. Amy Richards

General Information Coeducational day college-preparatory school. Grades 6–12. Founded: 1952. Setting: suburban. Nearest major city is San Francisco. 10-acre campus. 4 buildings on campus. Approved or accredited by California Association of Independent Schools, Western Association of Schools and Colleges, and California Department of Education. Member of National Association of Independent Schools and Secondary School Admission Test Board. Endowment: $12 million. Total enrollment: 358. Upper school average class size: 14. Upper school faculty-student ratio: 1:9.

Upper School Student Profile Grade 9: 63 students (33 boys, 30 girls); Grade 10: 61 students (26 boys, 35 girls); Grade 11: 65 students (37 boys, 28 girls); Grade 12: 61 students (31 boys, 30 girls).

Faculty School total: 44. In upper school: 18 men, 26 women; 24 have advanced degrees.

Subjects Offered Acting, advanced computer applications, algebra, American government-AP, American history, American history-AP, American literature, art, art history-AP, art-AP, astronomy, biology, biology-AP, calculus, calculus-AP, ceramics, chamber groups, chemistry, chorus, comparative cultures, computer math, computer programming, computer science, concert bell choir, creative writing, dance, dance performance, drama, English, English literature, ensembles, environmental science-AP, European history, European history-AP, fine arts, French, French language-AP, French literature-AP, geometry, government and politics-AP, graphic design, health, history, mathematics, multicultural literature, music, music theory-AP, photography, physical education, physics, physics-AP, poetry, post-calculus, pre-calculus, science, Shakespeare, Spanish, Spanish language-AP, Spanish literature-AP, statistics, theater, video film production, wellness, world history, world literature, writing.

Graduation Requirements Arts and fine arts (art, music, dance, drama), English, foreign language, history, mathematics, physical education (includes health), science, senior project.

Special Academic Programs 16 Advanced Placement exams for which test preparation is offered; honors section; term-away projects; study abroad.

College Admission Counseling 58 students graduated in 2008; all went to college. Mean SAT critical reading: 669, mean SAT math: 688, mean SAT writing: 689.

Student Life Upper grades have specified standards of dress, student council, honor system. Discipline rests equally with students and faculty.

Tuition and Aid Day student tuition: $30,075. Tuition installment plan (Insured Tuition Payment Plan, monthly payment plans, Tuition Management Systems Plan). Need-based scholarship grants available. In 2008–09, 18% of upper-school students received aid. Total amount of financial aid awarded in 2008–09: $1,400,000.

Admissions Traditional secondary-level entrance grade is 9. ISEE or SSAT required. Deadline for receipt of application materials: January 15. Application fee required: $75. On-campus interview required.

Athletics Interscholastic: baseball (boys), basketball (b,g), cross-country running (b,g), football (b), soccer (b,g), swimming and diving (b,g), tennis (b,g), track and field (b,g), volleyball (b,g); coed interscholastic: badminton, golf; coed intramural: dance, fitness, outdoors, rock climbing. 3 PE instructors, 14 coaches, 1 athletic trainer.

Computers Computers are regularly used in all academic classes. Computer network features include on-campus library services, online commercial services, Internet access, wireless campus network, Internet filtering or blocking technology. Campus intranet, student e-mail accounts, and computer access in designated common areas are available to students. The school has a published electronic and media policy.

Contact Andrew Davis, Director of Admission. 650-342-4175 Ext. 1517. Fax: 650-342-7611. E-mail: admission@csus.org. Web site: www.csus.org.

ANNOUNCEMENT FROM THE SCHOOL The mission of CSUS is to stimulate intellectual and creative development within a community of trust, caring, and respect. The middle and high school programs are both vigorous and fun; students truly enjoy learning at CSUS. Because the classes are small, with an average of 14 students in a classroom, students develop close relationships with their teachers and coaches.

THE CULVER ACADEMIES

1300 Academy Road
Culver, Indiana 46511

Head of School: Mr. John N. Buxton

General Information Coeducational boarding and day college-preparatory and arts school. Grades 9–PG. Founded: 1894. Setting: small town. Nearest major city is South Bend. Students are housed in single-sex dormitories. 1,800-acre campus. 38 buildings on campus. Approved or accredited by Independent Schools Association of the Central States, North Central Association of Colleges and Schools, and Indiana Department of Education. Member of National Association of Independent Schools and Secondary School Admission Test Board. Endowment: $185 million. Total enrollment: 795. Upper school average class size: 14. Upper school faculty-student ratio: 1:9.

Upper School Student Profile Grade 9: 160 students (89 boys, 71 girls); Grade 10: 213 students (122 boys, 91 girls); Grade 11: 221 students (135 boys, 86 girls); Grade 12: 201 students (116 boys, 85 girls). 90% of students are boarding students. 30% are state residents. 41 states are represented in upper school student body. 19% are international students. International students from Canada, China, Mexico, Republic of Korea, Saudi Arabia, and Taiwan; 16 other countries represented in student body.

Faculty School total: 98. In upper school: 54 men, 44 women; 86 have advanced degrees; 4 reside on campus.

Subjects Offered Acting, advanced math, algebra, American government, American government-AP, American history, American history-AP, American literature, anatomy, art, art history, arts, astronomy, ballet, Basic programming, biology, biology-AP, calculus, calculus-AP, career/college preparation, ceramics, character education, chemistry, chemistry-AP, Chinese, choir, church history, college admission preparation, college placement, college planning, comparative religion, computer math, computer programming, computer science, computer science-AP, dance, drama, dramatic arts, driver education, economics, economics-AP, English, English language-AP, English literature, entrepreneurship, equestrian sports, equine science, equitation, ESL, ethics and responsibility, European history, film studies, fine arts, fitness, flight instruction, French, French-AP, freshman seminar, geology, geometry, German, German literature, German-AP, global studies, government, government-AP, government/civics, health and wellness, honors English, honors geometry, instrumental music, integrated math, integrated science, jazz band, Latin, Latin-AP, leadership training, library research, macro/microeconomics-AP, mathematics, mentorship program, music, music theory, music theory-AP, photography, physical education, physics, physics-AP, physiology, piano, play production, pottery, pre-algebra, pre-calculus, science, science research, Shakespeare, social studies, Spanish, Spanish language-AP, Spanish-AP, speech, statistics-AP, strings, theater, trigonometry, U.S. government and politics-AP, U.S. history-AP, world history, world religions.

Graduation Requirements Arts and fine arts (art, music, dance, drama), English, foreign language, health education, history, leadership training, mathematics, science, senior community service project.

Special Academic Programs 20 Advanced Placement exams for which test preparation is offered; honors section; academic accommodation for the gifted, the musically talented, and the artistically talented; ESL (16 students enrolled).

College Admission Counseling 210 students graduated in 2008; 199 went to college, including Bryn Mawr College; Indiana University Bloomington; Purdue University; Southern Methodist University; The University of North Carolina at Chapel Hill. Other: 1 entered a postgraduate year, 10 had other specific plans.

Student Life Upper grades have uniform requirement, student council, honor system. Discipline rests equally with students and faculty. Attendance at religious services is required.

Summer Programs Enrichment, advancement, ESL, sports, art/fine arts, computer instruction programs offered; session focuses on leadership training, citizenship, lifetime interests and skills development; held on campus; accepts boys and girls; open to students from other schools. 1,300 students usually enrolled. 2009 schedule: June 20 to August 9. Application deadline: May 1.

Tuition and Aid Day student tuition: $24,500; 7-day tuition and room/board: $34,000. Tuition installment plan (Key Tuition Payment Plan). Merit scholarship grants, need-based scholarship grants available. In 2008–09, 45% of upper-school students received aid; total upper-school merit-scholarship money awarded: $782,900. Total amount of financial aid awarded in 2008–09: $7,000,000.

Admissions Traditional secondary-level entrance grade is 9. For fall 2008, 2,500 students applied for upper-level admission, 528 were accepted, 268 enrolled. SCAT or SSAT required. Deadline for receipt of application materials: June 1. Application fee required: $30. Interview required.

Athletics Interscholastic: baseball (boys), basketball (b,g), cheering (g), crew (b,g), cross-country running (b,g), diving (b,g), equestrian sports (b,g), fencing (b,g), football (b), golf (b,g), horseback riding (b,g), ice hockey (b,g), indoor track & field (b,g), lacrosse (b,g), polo (b,g), soccer (b,g), softball (g), swimming and diving (b,g), tennis (b,g), track and field (b,g), volleyball (g), winter (indoor) track (b,g), wrestling (b); intramural: aerobics (b,g), ballet (g), basketball (b,g), dance (b,g), dance squad (g), dance team (g), danceline (g), drill team (b,g), ice hockey (b,g), indoor soccer (b,g), marksmanship (b,g), modern dance (g), paint ball (b,g), racquetball (b,g), rugby (b), soccer (b,g), touch football (b); coed interscholastic: dressage, sailing; coed intramural: aerobics, aerobics/dance, alpine skiing, aquatics, archery, backpacking, badminton, broomball, climbing, fitness, Frisbee, handball, hiking/backpacking, ice skating, independent competitive sports, indoor track & field, jogging, life saving, nordic skiing, outdoor adventure, physical fitness, physical training, power lifting, project adventure, ropes courses, rowing, running, scuba diving, skeet shooting, skiing (downhill), snowboarding, strength & conditioning, swimming and diving, table tennis, trap and skeet, ultimate Frisbee, wall climbing, weight training, yoga. 8 PE instructors, 4 athletic trainers.

Computers Computers are regularly used in all classes. Computer network features include on-campus library services, online commercial services, Internet access, wireless campus network, Internet filtering or blocking technology, each student is issued a laptop. Campus intranet and student e-mail accounts are available to students. Students grades are available online. The school has a published electronic and media policy.

Contact Mr. Michael Turnbull, Director of Admissions. 574-842-7100. Fax: 574-842-8066. E-mail: turnbul@culver.org. Web site: www.culver.org.

See Close-Up on page 726.

CURREY INGRAM ACADEMY

6544 Murray Lane
Brentwood, Tennessee 37027

Head of School: Ms. Kathleen G. Rayburn

General Information Coeducational day college-preparatory, arts, bilingual studies, technology, ethics and character education, and service learning school; primarily serves students with learning disabilities, individuals with Attention Deficit Disorder, dyslexic students, non-verbal learning disabilities, and speech and language disabilities. Grades K–12. Founded: 1968. Setting: rural. Nearest major city is Nashville. 83-acre campus. 7 buildings on campus. Approved or accredited by Council of Accreditation and School Improvement, Southern Association of Colleges and Schools, Southern Association of Independent Schools, Tennessee Association of Independent Schools, and Tennessee Department of Education. Endowment: $2.8 million. Total enrollment: 319. Upper school average class size: 7. Upper school faculty-student ratio: 1:4.

Upper School Student Profile Grade 9: 30 students (19 boys, 11 girls); Grade 10: 10 students (4 boys, 6 girls); Grade 11: 20 students (12 boys, 8 girls); Grade 12: 22 students (14 boys, 8 girls).
Faculty School total: 115. In upper school: 9 men, 13 women; 7 have advanced degrees.
Subjects Offered Algebra, American government, ancient world history, art, basic language skills, biology, British literature, character education, chemistry, cinematography, college admission preparation, college awareness, college counseling, college planning, community service, digital music, digital photography, drama performance, earth science, economics, electives, English composition, English literature, environmental science, ethics and responsibility, government, health, history, integrated technology fundamentals, learning strategies, life skills, literature, mentorship program, modern world history, music, newspaper, physical education, physics, pragmatics, pre-calculus, reading/study skills, social studies, sports, studio art, technology, video film production, vocal music, writing fundamentals, writing workshop, yearbook.
Graduation Requirements Arts and fine arts (art, music, dance, drama), electives, English, ethics, foreign language, mathematics, physical education (includes health), science, social studies (includes history), students who need remediation in reading/writing take Reading/Writing Workshop instead of foreign language, seniors must complete Service Learning credit plus 30 hours of community service.
Special Academic Programs Independent study; academic accommodation for the gifted, the musically talented, and the artistically talented; remedial reading and/or remedial writing; programs in English, mathematics, general development for dyslexic students.
College Admission Counseling 3 students graduated in 2008.
Student Life Upper grades have uniform requirement, student council, honor system. Discipline rests primarily with faculty.
Summer Programs Art/fine arts programs offered; session focuses on The Greater Nashville Rock and Roll Theatre Camp (open to grades 1-12); held on campus; accepts boys and girls; open to students from other schools. 2009 schedule: June.
Tuition and Aid Day student tuition: $30,468. Tuition installment plan (monthly payment plans). Need-based scholarship grants available. In 2008–09, 40% of upper-school students received aid. Total amount of financial aid awarded in 2008–09: $435,226.
Admissions Traditional secondary-level entrance grade is 9. For fall 2008, 11 students applied for upper-level admission, 9 were accepted, 6 enrolled. Psychoeducational evaluation required. Deadline for receipt of application materials: none. Application fee required: $250. Interview required.
Athletics Interscholastic: baseball (boys), basketball (b,g), cheering (g), cross-country running (b,g), football (b), softball (g), volleyball (g); coed interscholastic: soccer. 3 coaches, 1 athletic trainer.
Computers Computers are regularly used in all academic classes. Computer network features include on-campus library services, Internet access, wireless campus network, Internet filtering or blocking technology, iPods for instructional use. Students grades are available online. The school has a published electronic and media policy.
Contact Ms. Amber Mogg, Director of Admission. 615-507-3173 Ext. 244. Fax: 615-507-3170. E-mail: amber.mogg@curreyingram.org. Web site: www.curreyingram.org.

CUSHING ACADEMY

39 School Street
PO Box 8000
Ashburnham, Massachusetts 01430-8000
Head of School: Dr. James Tracey

General Information Coeducational boarding and day college-preparatory, arts, and technology school. Grades 9–PG. Founded: 1865. Setting: small town. Nearest major city is Boston. Students are housed in single-sex dormitories. 162-acre campus. 31 buildings on campus. Approved or accredited by New England Association of Schools and Colleges and Massachusetts Department of Education. Member of National Association of Independent Schools and Secondary School Admission Test Board. Endowment: $22.6 million. Total enrollment: 441. Upper school average class size: 12. Upper school faculty-student ratio: 1:8.
Upper School Student Profile Grade 9: 56 students (38 boys, 18 girls); Grade 10: 121 students (60 boys, 61 girls); Grade 11: 121 students (71 boys, 50 girls); Grade 12: 123 students (67 boys, 56 girls); Postgraduate: 21 students (20 boys, 1 girl). 86% of students are boarding students. 33% are state residents. 29 states are represented in upper school student body. 30% are international students. International students from Bermuda, China, Mexico, Republic of Korea, Spain, and Taiwan; 29 other countries represented in student body.
Faculty School total: 64. In upper school: 27 men, 37 women; 37 have advanced degrees; 47 reside on campus.
Subjects Offered Advanced Placement courses, aerobics, algebra, American government, American government-AP, American history, American literature, American literature-AP, anatomy, architectural drawing, art, biology, biology-AP, calculus, calculus-AP, chemistry, chemistry-AP, chorus, community service, computer programming, computer science, creative writing, dance, developmental language skills, digital photography, drafting, drama, drawing, driver education, ecology, economics, English, English literature, environmental science, ESL, ethics, European history, expository writing, fine arts, French, geometry, government/civics, grammar, health, history, Latin, Mandarin, marine biology, mathematics, mechanical drawing, music, music theory, photography, physics, physiology, pre-calculus, psychology, science, social studies, sociology, Spanish, speech, theater, trigonometry, world history, world literature, World-Wide-Web publishing, writing.
Graduation Requirements Arts and fine arts (art, music, dance, drama), computer science, English, foreign language, health and wellness, mathematics, science, social studies (includes history).
Special Academic Programs Advanced Placement exam preparation; honors section; independent study; term-away projects; academic accommodation for the gifted, the musically talented, and the artistically talented; remedial reading and/or remedial writing; remedial math; programs in English, mathematics, general development for dyslexic students; ESL (75 students enrolled).
College Admission Counseling 142 students graduated in 2008; 141 went to college, including Boston College; Cornell University; Purdue University; Saint Michael's College; The George Washington University; University of New Hampshire. Other: 1 entered a postgraduate year.
Student Life Upper grades have specified standards of dress, student council. Discipline rests primarily with faculty.
Summer Programs Remediation, enrichment, advancement, ESL, art/fine arts, computer instruction programs offered; session focuses on enrichment; held on campus; accepts boys and girls; open to students from other schools. 350 students usually enrolled. 2009 schedule: July 5 to August 7.
Tuition and Aid Day student tuition: $30,600; 7-day tuition and room/board: $42,000. Tuition installment plan (Academic Management Services Plan, FACTS Tuition Payment Plan, monthly payment plans). Merit scholarship grants, need-based scholarship grants available. In 2008–09, 23% of upper-school students received aid; total upper-school merit-scholarship money awarded: $150,000. Total amount of financial aid awarded in 2008–09: $2,500,000.
Admissions Traditional secondary-level entrance grade is 9. For fall 2008, 804 students applied for upper-level admission, 505 were accepted, 196 enrolled. ACT, PSAT, SAT, SLEP, SSAT or TOEFL required. Deadline for receipt of application materials: February 1. Application fee required: $50. Interview required.
Athletics Interscholastic: baseball (boys), basketball (b,g), field hockey (g), football (b), ice hockey (b,g), lacrosse (b,g), soccer (b,g), softball (g), tennis (b,g), track and field (b,g), volleyball (g); intramural: flag football (b); coed interscholastic: alpine skiing, cross-country running, golf, running; coed intramural: aerobics, aerobics/dance, alpine skiing, dance, equestrian sports, figure skating, fitness, horseback riding, ice hockey, ice skating, independent competitive sports, martial arts, modern dance, outdoor adventure, outdoor education, outdoor skills, physical training, ropes courses, skiing (downhill), snowboarding, strength & conditioning, wall climbing, weight training. 2 coaches, 2 athletic trainers.
Computers Computers are regularly used in art, English, history, mathematics, science classes. Computer network features include on-campus library services, Internet access, wireless campus network, Internet filtering or blocking technology, CushNet (on campus network). Campus intranet, student e-mail accounts, and computer access in designated common areas are available to students. The school has a published electronic and media policy.
Contact Mrs. Deborah Gustafson, Co-Director of Admission. 978-827-7300. Fax: 978-827-6253. E-mail: admission@cushing.org. Web site: www.cushing.org.

ANNOUNCEMENT FROM THE SCHOOL The hub of Cushing's academic program is the newly instituted Cushing Center for 21st Century Leadership. Designed to help high school students understand the world of today and tomorrow, meeting students at their academic level, the Center brings current issues into every classroom, drives curriculum, facilitates global travel experiences, and brings a range of speakers to campus in order to deliver the world to Cushing students. The Center also provides leadership and entrepreneurial opportunities on campus and coordinates the Cushing Scholars, an enrichment program for students selected on the basis of intellectual, athletic, and artistic promise, as well as leadership potential.

See Close-Up on page 728.

DALLAS ACADEMY

Dallas, Texas
See Special Needs Schools section.

DALLAS CHRISTIAN SCHOOL

1515 Republic Parkway
Mesquite, Texas 75150
Head of School: Mr. Terry A. Harlow

General Information Coeducational day college-preparatory and religious studies school, affiliated with Church of Christ. Grades PK–12. Founded: 1957. Setting: suburban. Nearest major city is Dallas. 60-acre campus. 7 buildings on campus. Approved or accredited by National Christian School Association, Southern Association of Colleges and Schools, and Texas Department of Education. Total enrollment: 697. Upper school average class size: 25. Upper school faculty-student ratio: 1:15.

Upper School Student Profile Grade 9: 50 students (22 boys, 28 girls); Grade 10: 52 students (32 boys, 20 girls); Grade 11: 54 students (26 boys, 28 girls); Grade 12: 53 students (26 boys, 27 girls). 36% of students are members of Church of Christ.

Faculty School total: 58. In upper school: 10 men, 12 women; 12 have advanced degrees.

Subjects Offered Algebra, American history, American literature, art, band, Bible studies, biology, calculus, cheerleading, chemistry, chorus, computer math, computer science, creative writing, drama, economics, English, English literature, fine arts, French, geography, geometry, government/civics, health, history, humanities, journalism, mathematics, newspaper, physical education, physics, religion, science, sign language, social studies, Spanish, speech, speech origins of English, theater, world history, world literature, yearbook.

Graduation Requirements Arts and fine arts (art, music, dance, drama), computer science, English, foreign language, mathematics, physical education (includes health), religion (includes Bible studies and theology), science, social studies (includes history), speech origins of English, seniors must take SAT or ACT.

Special Academic Programs Study at local college for college credit.

College Admission Counseling 68 students graduated in 2008; 67 went to college, including Abilene Christian University; Austin College; Baylor University; Dallas Baptist University; Pepperdine University; Texas A&M University. Other: 1 went to work. Mean combined SAT: 1550.

Student Life Upper grades have uniform requirement, student council, honor system. Discipline rests primarily with faculty. Attendance at religious services is required.

Tuition and Aid Day student tuition: $10,650. Tuition installment plan (FACTS Tuition Payment Plan). Tuition reduction for siblings, need-based scholarship grants available. In 2008–09, 6% of upper-school students received aid. Total amount of financial aid awarded in 2008–09: $182,101.

Admissions Traditional secondary-level entrance grade is 9. For fall 2008, 25 students applied for upper-level admission, 21 were accepted, 21 enrolled. Woodcock-Johnson Revised Achievement Test required. Deadline for receipt of application materials: none. No application fee required. On-campus interview required.

Athletics Interscholastic: baseball (boys), basketball (b,g), cheering (g), cross-country running (b,g), drill team (g), football (b), golf (b,g), soccer (b,g), softball (g), tennis (b,g), track and field (b,g), volleyball (g), wrestling (b). 2 PE instructors.

Computers Computers are regularly used in computer applications, newspaper, Web site design, yearbook classes. Computer network features include on-campus library services, Internet access, Internet filtering or blocking technology. Student e-mail accounts are available to students. Students grades are available online.

Contact Ms. Katie Neuroth, Admissions Counselor. 972-270-5495 Ext. 266. Fax: 972-686-9436. E-mail: kneuroth@dallaschristian.com. Web site: www.dallaschristian.com.

THE DALTON SCHOOL

108 East 89th Street
New York, New York 10128-1599

Head of School: Ellen C. Stein

General Information Coeducational day college-preparatory and arts school. Grades K–12. Founded: 1919. Setting: urban. 2 buildings on campus. Approved or accredited by New York State Association of Independent Schools. Member of National Association of Independent Schools and Secondary School Admission Test Board. Endowment: $65 million. Total enrollment: 1,275. Upper school average class size: 15. Upper school faculty-student ratio: 1:7.

Upper School Student Profile Grade 9: 118 students (58 boys, 60 girls); Grade 10: 110 students (53 boys, 57 girls); Grade 11: 104 students (53 boys, 51 girls); Grade 12: 100 students (50 boys, 50 girls).

Faculty School total: 203. In upper school: 60 men, 61 women; 58 have advanced degrees.

Subjects Offered Algebra, American history, American legal systems, American literature, architecture, art, art history, Asian literature, astronomy, biology, calculus, ceramics, chemistry, community service, computer programming, computer science, dance, earth science, ecology, economics, English, English literature, environmental science, ethics, European history, fine arts, French, geometry, government/civics, health, history, Latin, law, mathematics, music, philosophy, photography, physical education, physics, Russian literature, science, social studies, Spanish, theater, trigonometry, world history, world literature.

Graduation Requirements Arts and fine arts (art, music, dance, drama), computer science, English, foreign language, history, mathematics, physical education (includes health), science. Community service is required.

Special Academic Programs Advanced Placement exam preparation; honors section; study at local college for college credit.

College Admission Counseling 119 students graduated in 2008; all went to college, including Brown University; Columbia College; Princeton University; University of Pennsylvania; Wesleyan University; Yale University. Median SAT critical reading: 680, median SAT math: 680, median SAT writing: 715.

Student Life Upper grades have student council. Discipline rests equally with students and faculty.

Tuition and Aid Day student tuition: $33,100. Tuition installment plan (FACTS Tuition Payment Plan, 2-payment plan). Need-based scholarship grants available. In 2008–09, 22% of upper-school students received aid. Total amount of financial aid awarded in 2008–09: $2,687,955.

Admissions Traditional secondary-level entrance grade is 9. For fall 2008, 359 students applied for upper-level admission, 38 were accepted, 24 enrolled. ISEE or SSAT required. Deadline for receipt of application materials: November 21. Application fee required: $50. On-campus interview required.

Athletics Interscholastic: baseball (boys), basketball (b,g), lacrosse (b,g), soccer (b,g), softball (g), tennis (b,g), track and field (b,g), wrestling (b); intramural: baseball (b), basketball (b,g); coed interscholastic: cross-country running, football, swimming and diving, volleyball; coed intramural: cheering, dance, football, modern dance, ultimate Frisbee. 10 PE instructors, 14 coaches, 1 athletic trainer.

Computers Computers are regularly used in English, foreign language, mathematics, science classes. Computer network features include on-campus library services, online commercial services, Internet access, wireless campus network, Internet filtering or blocking technology. Student e-mail accounts and computer access in designated common areas are available to students.

Contact Eva Rado, Director, Middle and High School Admissions. 212-423-5262. Fax: 212-423-5259. E-mail: rado@dalton.org. Web site: www.dalton.org.

DANA HALL SCHOOL

45 Dana Road
Wellesley, Massachusetts 02482

Head of School: Caroline Erisman, JD

General Information Girls' boarding and day college-preparatory school. Boarding grades 9–12, day grades 6–12. Founded: 1881. Setting: suburban. Nearest major city is Boston. Students are housed in single-sex dormitories. 55-acre campus. 34 buildings on campus. Approved or accredited by Association of Independent Schools in New England, Massachusetts Department of Education, New England Association of Schools and Colleges, The Association of Boarding Schools, and Massachusetts Department of Education. Member of National Association of Independent Schools and Secondary School Admission Test Board. Endowment: $22 million. Total enrollment: 500. Upper school average class size: 12. Upper school faculty-student ratio: 1:9.

Upper School Student Profile Grade 9: 85 students (85 girls); Grade 10: 99 students (99 girls); Grade 11: 98 students (98 girls); Grade 12: 88 students (88 girls). 39% of students are boarding students. 75% are state residents. 11 states are represented in upper school student body. 12% are international students. International students from China, Japan, Mexico, Republic of Korea, Taiwan, and Thailand; 11 other countries represented in student body.

Faculty School total: 80. In upper school: 21 men, 45 women; 50 have advanced degrees; 33 reside on campus.

Subjects Offered African history, African studies, algebra, American history, American literature, architecture, art, art history, art-AP, astronomy, biology, calculus, ceramics, chemistry, chorus, community service, computer programming, computer science, creative writing, dance, dance performance, drama, drama workshop, drawing, East Asian history, economics, electives, English, English composition, English language and composition-AP, English/composition-AP, European history, European history-AP, fitness, French, French language-AP, French literature-AP, freshman foundations, geometry, government, government/civics, health, independent study, journalism, Latin, Latin American history, Latin-AP, leadership education training, library, Mandarin, marine biology, mathematics-AP, Middle Eastern history, music, music composition, music performance, music theory, musical theater, photography, physics, public speaking, Russian studies, scuba diving, Spanish, Spanish-AP, sports, statistics-AP, trigonometry, U.S. history-AP, U.S. literature, weight training, Western civilization, women in the classical world.

Graduation Requirements American history, area studies, computer science, English, fitness, foreign language, mathematics, performing arts, science, social studies (includes history), visual arts, 20 hours of community service.

Special Academic Programs 14 Advanced Placement exams for which test preparation is offered; honors section; independent study; term-away projects; study abroad.

College Admission Counseling 72 students graduated in 2008; all went to college, including Boston University; Brown University; Lehigh University; Smith College; The Colorado College; Tufts University. Mean SAT critical reading: 601, mean SAT math: 626, mean SAT writing: 627, mean combined SAT: 1854, mean composite ACT: 27. 47% scored over 600 on SAT critical reading, 65% scored over 600 on SAT math, 63% scored over 600 on SAT writing, 57% scored over 1800 on combined SAT, 70% scored over 26 on composite ACT.

Student Life Upper grades have specified standards of dress, student council, honor system. Discipline rests equally with students and faculty.

Summer Programs Enrichment, sports programs offered; session focuses on unique sporting experience, leadership training and confidence building for students ages 8-17; held both on and off campus; held at golf club, Sandwich, MA, and Hammond Pond Park; accepts boys and girls; open to students from other schools. 80 students usually enrolled. 2009 schedule: June 22 to July 31. Application deadline: May 31.

Tuition and Aid Day student tuition: $33,981; 7-day tuition and room/board: $44,904. Tuition installment plan (monthly payment plans, K-12 Family Education Loan, AchieverLoan). Merit scholarship grants, need-based scholarship grants,

need-based loans available. In 2008–09, 19% of upper-school students received aid; total upper-school merit-scholarship money awarded: $2500. Total amount of financial aid awarded in 2008–09: $2,378,827.
Admissions Traditional secondary-level entrance grade is 9. For fall 2008, 357 students applied for upper-level admission, 137 were accepted, 69 enrolled. ISEE, SSAT or TOEFL required. Deadline for receipt of application materials: February 1. Application fee required: $50. Interview required.
Athletics Interscholastic: basketball, cross-country running, equestrian sports, fencing, field hockey, golf, horseback riding, ice hockey, lacrosse, modern dance, soccer, softball, squash, swimming and diving, tennis, volleyball; intramural: aerobics, aerobics/dance, aquatics, ballet, climbing, crew, dance, fitness, Frisbee, golf, hiking/backpacking, horseback riding, ice hockey, indoor track, life saving, martial arts, modern dance, Nautilus, outdoor activities, physical fitness, physical training, rock climbing, scuba diving, self defense, skiing (downhill), squash, strength & conditioning, swimming and diving, tennis, touch football, track and field, ultimate Frisbee, weight lifting, weight training, yoga. 5 PE instructors, 20 coaches, 1 athletic trainer.
Computers Computers are regularly used in art, English, French, history, Latin, mathematics, science, Spanish, Web site design, yearbook classes. Computer network features include on-campus library services, online commercial services, Internet access, wireless campus network, Internet filtering or blocking technology. Campus intranet, student e-mail accounts, and computer access in designated common areas are available to students.
Contact Brenda Dowdell, Admission Office Manager. 781-235-3010 Ext. 2531. Fax: 781-239-1383. E-mail: admission@danahall.org. Web site: www.danahall.org.

See Close-Up on page 730.

DARLINGTON SCHOOL

1014 Cave Spring Road
Rome, Georgia 30161

Head of School: Thomas C. Whitworth III

General Information Coeducational boarding and day college-preparatory, arts, and technology school. Boarding grades 9–PG, day grades PK–PG. Founded: 1905. Setting: small town. Nearest major city is Atlanta. Students are housed in single-sex dormitories. 500-acre campus. 15 buildings on campus. Approved or accredited by Georgia Independent School Association, Southern Association of Colleges and Schools, Southern Association of Independent Schools, The Association of Boarding Schools, and Georgia Department of Education. Member of National Association of Independent Schools and Secondary School Admission Test Board. Endowment: $48 million. Total enrollment: 898. Upper school average class size: 14. Upper school faculty-student ratio: 1:13.
Upper School Student Profile Grade 6: 40 students (20 boys, 20 girls); Grade 7: 50 students (25 boys, 25 girls); Grade 8: 66 students (34 boys, 32 girls); Grade 9: 123 students (65 boys, 58 girls); Grade 10: 112 students (63 boys, 49 girls); Grade 11: 130 students (71 boys, 59 girls); Grade 12: 141 students (78 boys, 63 girls). 36% of students are boarding students. 84% are state residents. 19 states are represented in upper school student body. 16% are international students. International students from China, Germany, Jamaica, Republic of Korea, Taiwan, and Venezuela; 32 other countries represented in student body.
Faculty School total: 89. In upper school: 34 men, 19 women; 33 have advanced degrees; 55 reside on campus.
Subjects Offered Advanced biology, advanced chemistry, Advanced Placement courses, advanced studio art-AP, algebra, anatomy and physiology, ancient world history, art, art history, art history-AP, band, biology, biology-AP, calculus, calculus-AP, chemistry, chemistry-AP, choir, chorus, computer programming, computer science, computer science-AP, concert choir, creative writing, drama, drawing, economics, economics-AP, English, English language and composition-AP, English literature, English literature-AP, English-AP, ensembles, environmental science, environmental science-AP, ESL, European history-AP, fine arts, French, French-AP, geometry, government-AP, government/civics, graphic arts, graphic design, health, honors algebra, honors English, honors geometry, honors world history, humanities, jazz ensemble, journalism, lab science, macro/microeconomics-AP, macroeconomics-AP, modern European history-AP, music, music theory-AP, musical theater, newspaper, personal fitness, physical education, physics, physics-AP, pre-calculus, probability and statistics, psychology-AP, robotics, Spanish, Spanish language-AP, Spanish literature-AP, Spanish-AP, statistics-AP, studio art—AP, theater, trigonometry, U.S. history, U.S. history-AP, video, video film production, vocal ensemble, wind ensemble, world culture, world history, world history-AP, World-Wide-Web publishing, yearbook.
Graduation Requirements Arts and fine arts (art, music, dance, drama), English, foreign language, information technology, mathematics, physical education (includes health), science, social studies (includes history), Community Service/Servant Leadership Program, after school activity.
Special Academic Programs Advanced Placement exam preparation; honors section; ESL (8 students enrolled).
College Admission Counseling 114 students graduated in 2008; all went to college, including Auburn University; Georgia Institute of Technology; Mercer University; The University of Alabama; University of Georgia; University of Mississippi.
Student Life Upper grades have uniform requirement, student council, honor system. Discipline rests equally with students and faculty.
Summer Programs Enrichment, sports, art/fine arts, computer instruction programs offered; session focuses on academic enrichment and specialized sports camps for all ages; held on campus; accepts boys and girls; open to students from other schools. 2,000 students usually enrolled. 2009 schedule: June 7 to August 2. Application deadline: none.
Tuition and Aid Day student tuition: $15,800; 7-day tuition and room/board: $35,700. Tuition installment plan (monthly payment plans, individually arranged payment plans). Merit scholarship grants, need-based scholarship grants available. In 2008–09, 26% of upper-school students received aid; total upper-school merit-scholarship money awarded: $408,050. Total amount of financial aid awarded in 2008–09: $1,372,175.
Admissions Traditional secondary-level entrance grade is 9. For fall 2008, 271 students applied for upper-level admission, 175 were accepted, 118 enrolled. PSAT and SAT for applicants to grade 11 and 12, SSAT or WISC III or TOEFL required. Deadline for receipt of application materials: February 1. Application fee required: $50. Interview required.
Athletics Interscholastic: baseball (boys), basketball (b,g), cheering (g), crew (b,g), cross-country running (b,g), diving (b,g), football (b), golf (b,g), lacrosse (b,g), rowing (b,g), soccer (b,g), softball (g), swimming and diving (b,g), tennis (b,g), track and field (b,g), volleyball (g), wrestling (b); intramural: basketball (b,g), dance squad (g), fitness (b,g), flag football (b,g), flagball (b,g), indoor soccer (b), running (b,g), tennis (b,g), volleyball (b,g); coed intramural: aerobics, fishing, fly fishing, Frisbee, independent competitive sports, outdoor activities, outdoor education, outdoor recreation, physical fitness, physical training, skeet shooting, soccer, speleology, strength & conditioning, table tennis, ultimate Frisbee, weight lifting, weight training. 3 PE instructors, 6 coaches, 1 athletic trainer.
Computers Computers are regularly used in computer applications, English, foreign language, history, mathematics, science, Web site design classes. Computer network features include on-campus library services, Internet access, wireless campus network, Internet filtering or blocking technology. Campus intranet, student e-mail accounts, and computer access in designated common areas are available to students. Students grades are available online. The school has a published electronic and media policy.
Contact Mrs. Stormy S. Johnson, Director of Admission. 706-236-0426. Fax: 706-232-3600. E-mail: sjohnson@darlingtonschool.org. Web site: www.darlingtonschool.org.

See Close-Up on page 732.

DARROW SCHOOL

110 Darrow Road
New Lebanon, New York 12125

Head of School: Mrs. Nancy Wolf

General Information Coeducational boarding and day college-preparatory, arts, Hands-on Learning, and Sustainability school. Grades 9–PG. Founded: 1932. Setting: rural. Nearest major city is Pittsfield, MA. Students are housed in single-sex dormitories. 365-acre campus. 26 buildings on campus. Approved or accredited by Middle States Association of Colleges and Schools, New York State Association of Independent Schools, and The Association of Boarding Schools. Member of National Association of Independent Schools and Secondary School Admission Test Board. Endowment: $2.5 million. Total enrollment: 98. Upper school average class size: 9. Upper school faculty-student ratio: 1:4.
Upper School Student Profile Grade 9: 17 students (11 boys, 6 girls); Grade 10: 22 students (11 boys, 11 girls); Grade 11: 25 students (17 boys, 8 girls); Grade 12: 34 students (21 boys, 13 girls). 80% of students are boarding students. 45% are state residents. 13 states are represented in upper school student body. 16% are international students. International students from Angola, China, Gabon, Jamaica, Japan, and Republic of Korea; 1 other country represented in student body.
Faculty School total: 31. In upper school: 17 men, 14 women; 15 have advanced degrees; 30 reside on campus.
Subjects Offered 3-dimensional art, advanced math, African-American literature, algebra, American literature, art, art history, athletics, biology, calculus, ceramics, chemistry, civil rights, clayworking, computer graphics, creative writing, critical writing, culinary arts, design, digital art, drama, drawing, drawing and design, ecology, economics, English, English literature, ensembles, environmental education, environmental science, environmental studies, ESL, ethics, experiential education, fine arts, French, geometry, health and wellness, history, independent study, Latin American literature, leadership training, literature, mathematics, microeconomics, multicultural studies, music appreciation, music theory, oil painting, ornithology, photo shop, photography, physics, play production, poetry, portfolio art, pottery, pre-calculus, reading/study skills, Russian literature, science, social studies, Spanish, Spanish literature, sports, studio art, study skills, theater, U.S. history, Western civilization, women's literature, woodworking, writing, yearbook.
Graduation Requirements Arts, arts and fine arts (art, music, dance, drama), electives, English, foreign language, history, mathematics, physical education (includes health), science.
Special Academic Programs Independent study; academic accommodation for the musically talented and the artistically talented; ESL.

College Admission Counseling 39 students graduated in 2008; all went to college, including Colgate University; Fashion Institute of Technology; Hobart and William Smith Colleges; Howard University; The George Washington University; University of Vermont.

Student Life Upper grades have specified standards of dress, student council. Discipline rests equally with students and faculty.

Tuition and Aid Day student tuition: $23,600; 7-day tuition and room/board: $41,200. Tuition installment plan (Academic Management Services Plan, Key Tuition Payment Plan, individually arranged payment plans). Need-based scholarship grants available. In 2008–09, 38% of upper-school students received aid. Total amount of financial aid awarded in 2008–09: $941,850.

Admissions Traditional secondary-level entrance grade is 9. For fall 2008, 204 students applied for upper-level admission, 103 were accepted, 48 enrolled. SLEP for foreign students or TOEFL or SLEP required. Deadline for receipt of application materials: none. Application fee required: $50. On-campus interview required.

Athletics Interscholastic: baseball (boys), basketball (b,g), cross-country running (b,g), soccer (b,g), softball (g), tennis (b,g); coed interscholastic: cross-country running, Frisbee, lacrosse, tennis, ultimate Frisbee; coed intramural: alpine skiing, dance, fitness, freestyle skiing, hiking/backpacking, horseback riding, outdoor activities, outdoor education, physical fitness, rock climbing, skiing (cross-country), skiing (downhill), snowboarding, telemark skiing, weight lifting.

Computers Computers are regularly used in graphic design, photography classes. Computer network features include on-campus library services, Internet access, wireless campus network, Internet filtering or blocking technology. Campus intranet, student e-mail accounts, and computer access in designated common areas are available to students. The school has a published electronic and media policy.

Contact Ms. Jamie Hicks-Furgang, Director of Admission. 518-794-6008. Fax: 518-794-7065. E-mail: hicksj@darrowschool.org. Web site: www.darrowschool.org.

ANNOUNCEMENT FROM THE SCHOOL Living, working, learning in the classroom and beyond. These words have guided Darrow's educational philosophy for over 75 years. Hands-on learning, innovative teaching methods, and individual attention create an atmosphere that supports intellectual curiosity, individual creativity, and the power of hands-on learning. The new Joline Arts Center offers exceptional state-of-the-art spaces for all visual arts. "Darrow is more than a school; it is a home. Darrow has brought out the person in me who loves to learn." Zoe¨, '06.

See Close-Up on page 734.

DAVID LIPSCOMB HIGH SCHOOL

3901 Granny White Pike
Nashville, Tennessee 37204-3951

Head of School: Dr. Michael P. Hammond

General Information Coeducational day college-preparatory and religious studies school, affiliated with Church of Christ. Grades PK–12. Founded: 1891. Setting: suburban. 10-acre campus. 4 buildings on campus. Approved or accredited by National Christian School Association, Southern Association of Colleges and Schools, Southern Association of Independent Schools, Tennessee Association of Independent Schools, and Tennessee Department of Education. Endowment: $95,000. Total enrollment: 1,386. Upper school average class size: 20. Upper school faculty-student ratio: 1:15.

Upper School Student Profile Grade 9: 137 students (65 boys, 72 girls); Grade 10: 119 students (69 boys, 50 girls); Grade 11: 135 students (73 boys, 62 girls); Grade 12: 147 students (72 boys, 75 girls). 64% of students are members of Church of Christ.

Faculty School total: 35. In upper school: 16 men, 19 women; 25 have advanced degrees.

Subjects Offered Accounting, advanced computer applications, algebra, American government, American history, anatomy and physiology, art, band, biology, biology-AP, calculus-AP, chemistry, chemistry-AP, chorus, computer science, current history, drama, economics, English, French, geography, geometry, health, home economics, honors algebra, honors English, honors geometry, interior design, journalism, keyboarding, Latin, mathematics, modern history, painting, photography, physical education, physics, pre-algebra, psychology, religion, science, science research, social studies, Spanish, Spanish-AP, speech, statistics, trigonometry, visual arts, world history.

Graduation Requirements Economics, English, foreign language, mathematics, physical education (includes health), religion (includes Bible studies and theology), science, social studies (includes history), research paper, 60 hours of community service.

Special Academic Programs 4 Advanced Placement exams for which test preparation is offered; honors section; accelerated programs; study at local college for college credit; programs in general development for dyslexic students.

College Admission Counseling 132 students graduated in 2008; 131 went to college, including Belmont University; Harding University; Lipscomb University; Middle Tennessee State University; The University of Alabama; The University of Tennessee. Other: 1 entered military service. Mean composite ACT: 24.

Student Life Upper grades have uniform requirement, student council. Discipline rests primarily with faculty. Attendance at religious services is required.

Summer Programs Remediation, enrichment, sports, art/fine arts programs offered; session focuses on mathematics and English remediation; held on campus; accepts boys and girls; not open to students from other schools. 40 students usually enrolled. 2009 schedule: June 1 to July 31. Application deadline: May 15.

Tuition and Aid Day student tuition: $8445. Tuition installment plan (monthly payment plans, individually arranged payment plans). Tuition reduction for siblings, need-based scholarship grants available. In 2008–09, 1% of upper-school students received aid. Total amount of financial aid awarded in 2008–09: $46,840.

Admissions Traditional secondary-level entrance grade is 9. For fall 2008, 41 students applied for upper-level admission, 35 were accepted, 30 enrolled. TOEFL required. Deadline for receipt of application materials: none. Application fee required: $200. Interview required.

Athletics Interscholastic: baseball (boys), basketball (b,g), bowling (b,g), cheering (g), cross-country running (b,g), football (b), golf (b,g), soccer (b,g), softball (g), tennis (b,g), track and field (b,g), volleyball (g), wrestling (b); intramural: basketball (b,g); coed intramural: basketball. 2 PE instructors, 16 coaches, 1 athletic trainer.

Computers Computer network features include on-campus library services, online commercial services, Internet access, wireless campus network, Internet filtering or blocking technology. Student e-mail accounts and computer access in designated common areas are available to students. Students grades are available online. The school has a published electronic and media policy.

Contact Mrs. Kim Schow, Administrative Assistant. 615-966-6409. Fax: 615-966-7639. E-mail: kim.schow@lipscomb.edu. Web site: www.dlcs.lipscomb.edu.

DECK HOUSE SCHOOL

124 Deck House Road
Edgecomb, Maine 04556

Head of School: Mr. Thomas D. Blackford

General Information Boys' boarding college-preparatory and arts school. Grades 10–12. Founded: 1979. Setting: rural. Nearest major city is Portland. Students are housed in single-sex dormitories. 180-acre campus. 4 buildings on campus. Approved or accredited by Maine Department of Education. Candidate for accreditation by New England Association of Schools and Colleges. Endowment: $15,000. Total enrollment: 12. Upper school average class size: 3. Upper school faculty-student ratio: 1:2.

Upper School Student Profile Grade 10: 3 students (3 boys); Grade 11: 2 students (2 boys); Grade 12: 7 students (7 boys). 100% of students are boarding students. 16% are state residents. 9 states are represented in upper school student body.

Faculty School total: 7. In upper school: 3 men, 4 women; 3 have advanced degrees; 2 reside on campus.

Subjects Offered Accounting, advanced math, algebra, American literature, art, biology, business mathematics, calculus, chemistry, computer skills, consumer mathematics, creative writing, culinary arts, drama workshop, earth science, ecology, economics, economics and history, English, English composition, European history, foreign language, general math, geography, geometry, history, home economics, journalism, life science, literature, marine biology, modern European history, music, nutrition, photography, physical education, physical fitness, physical science, poetry, pre-calculus, Spanish, swimming, trigonometry, U.S. government, U.S. history, visual arts, Western civilization, world history.

Graduation Requirements Arts and fine arts (art, music, dance, drama), computer skills, electives, English, mathematics, physical education (includes health), science, social studies (includes history), state studies.

College Admission Counseling 3 students graduated in 2008; all went to college, including Academy of Art University.

Student Life Upper grades have honor system. Discipline rests equally with students and faculty.

Tuition and Aid 7-day tuition and room/board: $47,500. Guaranteed tuition plan. Tuition installment plan (monthly payment plans, individually arranged payment plans).

Admissions Traditional secondary-level entrance grade is 10. Deadline for receipt of application materials: none. No application fee required. Interview required.

Computers Computer network features include Internet access, Internet filtering or blocking technology. Campus intranet and computer access in designated common areas are available to students. The school has a published electronic and media policy.

Contact Mr. Thomas D. Blackford, Headmaster. 207-882-7055. Fax: 207-882-8151. E-mail: tom@deckhouseschool.org. Web site: www.deckhouseschool.org.

DEERFIELD ACADEMY

7 Boyden Lane
Deerfield, Massachusetts 01342

Head of School: Dr. Margarita O'Byrne Curtis

General Information Coeducational boarding and day college-preparatory school. Grades 9–PG. Founded: 1797. Setting: small town. Nearest major city is Hartford, CT. Students are housed in single-sex dormitories. 280-acre campus. 81 buildings on campus. Approved or accredited by Association of Independent Schools in New England, National Independent Private Schools Association, New England Association of Schools and Colleges, and Massachusetts Department of Education. Member of National Association of Independent Schools and Secondary School

Admission Test Board. Endowment: $363 million. Total enrollment: 600. Upper school average class size: 12. Upper school faculty-student ratio: 1:5.
Upper School Student Profile Grade 9: 101 students (51 boys, 50 girls); Grade 10: 158 students (81 boys, 77 girls); Grade 11: 167 students (80 boys, 87 girls); Grade 12: 150 students (74 boys, 76 girls); Postgraduate: 24 students (21 boys, 3 girls). 87% of students are boarding students. 25% are state residents. 34 states are represented in upper school student body. 11% are international students. International students from Bahamas, Canada, China, Jamaica, Republic of Korea, and United Kingdom; 18 other countries represented in student body.
Faculty School total: 118. In upper school: 69 men, 49 women; 83 have advanced degrees; 102 reside on campus.
Subjects Offered Advanced chemistry, advanced computer applications, advanced math, advanced studio art-AP, algebra, American government, American history-AP, American studies, analytic geometry, anatomy, applied arts, applied music, Arabic, architectural drawing, architecture, art, art history, art history-AP, Asian history, Asian literature, Asian studies, astronomy, Basic programming, biochemistry, biology, biology-AP, Black history, calculus, calculus-AP, ceramics, chemistry, chemistry-AP, Chinese, computer applications, computer math, computer programming, computer science, computer science-AP, concert band, creative writing, dance, dance performance, discrete math, drama, drama performance, drama workshop, drawing and design, earth science, Eastern religion and philosophy, ecology, economics, economics-AP, English, English literature, English literature-AP, English-AP, environmental science, ethics, European history, expository writing, fine arts, French, geology, geometry, Greek, health, health education, history, instrumental music, journalism, Latin, literature, mathematics, modern European history, music, philosophy, photography, physics, physics-AP, physiology, religion, science, social studies, Spanish, Spanish literature, statistics and probability, studio art, studio art-AP, theater, theater arts, trigonometry, U.S. history, U.S. literature, video, vocal music, Western civilization, world civilizations, world governments, world history, world literature, world religions, writing.
Graduation Requirements Arts and fine arts (art, music, dance, drama), English, foreign language, history, mathematics, philosophy, science.
Special Academic Programs Advanced Placement exam preparation; honors section; independent study; term-away projects; study abroad; academic accommodation for the gifted, the musically talented, and the artistically talented.
College Admission Counseling 198 students graduated in 2008; 182 went to college, including Brown University; Georgetown University; Harvard University; Middlebury College; Trinity College; Yale University. Other: 1 entered a postgraduate year, 15 had other specific plans. Median SAT critical reading: 650, median SAT math: 670, median SAT writing: 670.
Student Life Upper grades have specified standards of dress, student council, honor system. Discipline rests equally with students and faculty.
Tuition and Aid Day student tuition: $28,200; 7-day tuition and room/board: $39,275. Tuition installment plan (Academic Management Services Plan, Key Tuition Payment Plan). Need-based scholarship grants, need-based loans available. In 2008–09, 36% of upper-school students received aid. Total amount of financial aid awarded in 2008–09: $6,100,000.
Admissions Traditional secondary-level entrance grade is 9. For fall 2008, 1,883 students applied for upper-level admission, 357 were accepted, 227 enrolled. ACT, ISEE, SAT, SSAT or TOEFL required. Deadline for receipt of application materials: January 15. Application fee required: $40. Interview required.
Athletics Interscholastic: alpine skiing (boys, girls), baseball (b), basketball (b,g), crew (b,g), cross-country running (b,g), diving (b,g), field hockey (g), football (b), golf (b), ice hockey (b,g), lacrosse (b,g), skiing (downhill) (b,g), soccer (b,g), softball (g), squash (b,g), swimming and diving (b,g), tennis (b,g), track and field (b,g), volleyball (g), water polo (b,g), wrestling (b); intramural: dance (b,g), fitness (b,g), modern dance (b,g); coed interscholastic: bicycling, diving, golf, indoor track & field, swimming and diving; coed intramural: aerobics, aerobics/dance, aerobics/Nautilus, alpine skiing, aquatics, ballet, canoeing/kayaking, dance, fitness, hiking/backpacking, life saving, modern dance, outdoor skills, paddle tennis, sailing, skiing (downhill), snowboarding, soccer, squash, strength & conditioning, swimming and diving, tennis, volleyball, weight lifting. 1 coach, 2 athletic trainers.
Computers Computers are regularly used in architecture, mathematics, programming, science classes. Computer network features include on-campus library services, online commercial services, Internet access, wireless campus network. Campus intranet, student e-mail accounts, and computer access in designated common areas are available to students. Students grades are available online. The school has a published electronic and media policy.
Contact Patricia L. Gimbel, Dean of Admission and Financial Aid. 413-774-1400. Fax: 413-772-1100. E-mail: admission@deerfield.edu. Web site: www.deerfield.edu.

See Close-Up on page 736.

DEERFIELD-WINDSOR SCHOOL

2500 Nottingham Way
Albany, Georgia 31707

Head of School: W. T. Henry

General Information Coeducational day college-preparatory, arts, and technology school; primarily serves students with learning disabilities. Grades PK–12. Founded: 1964. Setting: suburban. Nearest major city is Atlanta. 24-acre campus. 1 building on campus. Approved or accredited by Southern Association of Colleges and Schools and Georgia Department of Education. Endowment: $1 million. Total enrollment: 848. Upper school average class size: 18. Upper school faculty-student ratio: 1:18.
Upper School Student Profile Grade 9: 67 students (33 boys, 34 girls); Grade 10: 58 students (29 boys, 29 girls); Grade 11: 56 students (24 boys, 32 girls); Grade 12: 69 students (31 boys, 38 girls).
Faculty School total: 56. In upper school: 9 men, 28 women; 22 have advanced degrees.
Subjects Offered Algebra, American history, American literature, art, art history, biology, calculus, chemistry, creative writing, drama, earth science, economics, English, English literature, environmental science, expository writing, French, geometry, government/civics, grammar, health, history, Latin, mathematics, music, physical education, physics, physiology, psychology, science, social science, social studies, Spanish, speech, theater, trigonometry, world history, world literature, writing.
Graduation Requirements 55 volunteer hours of community service.
Special Academic Programs 10 Advanced Placement exams for which test preparation is offered; honors section; independent study; study at local college for college credit; academic accommodation for the gifted and the artistically talented; programs in general development for dyslexic students.
College Admission Counseling 72 students graduated in 2008; all went to college, including Duke University; Samford University; Valdosta State University; Vanderbilt University. Mean SAT critical reading: 592, mean SAT math: 579, mean SAT writing: 599, mean combined SAT: 1770.
Student Life Upper grades have specified standards of dress, student council, honor system. Discipline rests primarily with faculty.
Tuition and Aid Day student tuition: $7000. Tuition installment plan (Insured Tuition Payment Plan, monthly payment plans, individually arranged payment plans, quarterly and semi-annual payment plans). Tuition reduction for siblings, merit scholarship grants, need-based tuition reduction available. In 2008–09, 7% of upper-school students received aid; total upper-school merit-scholarship money awarded: $20,000. Total amount of financial aid awarded in 2008–09: $20,000.
Admissions Traditional secondary-level entrance grade is 9. For fall 2008, 36 students applied for upper-level admission, 21 were accepted, 18 enrolled. ERB verbal, ERB math and Otis-Lennon Mental Ability Test required. Deadline for receipt of application materials: none. Application fee required: $30. On-campus interview required.
Athletics Interscholastic: baseball (boys), basketball (b,g), football (b), golf (b), soccer (b,g), softball (g), swimming and diving (b,g), tennis (b,g), track and field (b,g), wrestling (b); intramural: basketball (b,g), danceline (b,g), football (b), soccer (b,g); coed intramural: badminton. 4 PE instructors, 9 coaches, 1 athletic trainer.
Computers Computers are regularly used in mathematics, yearbook classes. Computer network features include on-campus library services, Internet access, wireless campus network.
Contact W. T. Henry, Headmaster. 912-435-1301. Fax: 912-888-6085. E-mail: wt.henry@deerfieldwindsor.com.

DE LA SALLE COLLEGE

131 Farnham Avenue
Toronto, Ontario M4V 1H7, Canada

Head of School: Br. Domenic Viggiani, FSC

General Information Coeducational day college-preparatory, arts, business, religious studies, bilingual studies, and technology school, affiliated with Roman Catholic Church. Grades 5–12. Founded: 1851. Setting: urban. 12-acre campus. 4 buildings on campus. Approved or accredited by Association of Independent Schools and Colleges of Alberta, Conference of Independent Schools of Ontario, and Ontario Department of Education. Language of instruction: English. Total enrollment: 592. Upper school average class size: 22. Upper school faculty-student ratio: 1:15.
Upper School Student Profile Grade 9: 101 students (38 boys, 63 girls); Grade 10: 124 students (62 boys, 62 girls); Grade 11: 102 students (51 boys, 51 girls); Grade 12: 97 students (50 boys, 47 girls). 90% of students are Roman Catholic.
Faculty School total: 44. In upper school: 30 men, 12 women.
Special Academic Programs Advanced Placement exam preparation; accelerated programs.
College Admission Counseling 100 students graduated in 2008; all went to college, including McGill University; McMaster University; Queen's University at Kingston; The University of Western Ontario; University of Toronto; York University.
Student Life Upper grades have uniform requirement, student council, honor system. Discipline rests primarily with faculty. Attendance at religious services is required.
Summer Programs Enrichment, advancement programs offered; held on campus; accepts boys and girls; open to students from other schools. 50 students usually enrolled.
Tuition and Aid Day student tuition: CAN$10,350. Tuition installment plan (monthly payment plans). Bursaries, merit scholarship grants, need-based scholarship grants available. In 2008–09, 10% of upper-school students received aid.
Admissions Traditional secondary-level entrance grade is 9. For fall 2008, 150 students applied for upper-level admission, 75 were accepted, 50 enrolled. SSAT required. Deadline for receipt of application materials: December 12. Application fee required: CAN$100. On-campus interview required.
Athletics Interscholastic: baseball (boys), basketball (b,g), field hockey (g), football (b), ice hockey (b,g), soccer (b,g), softball (g), volleyball (b,g); coed interscholastic:

alpine skiing, aquatics, badminton, cross-country running, golf, track and field; coed intramural: ball hockey, fencing. 4 PE instructors.
Computers Computer network features include Internet access, Internet filtering or blocking technology. Student e-mail accounts are available to students.
Contact Ms. Anna Di Benedetto, Admissions Secretary. 416-969-8771 Ext. 228. Fax: 416-969-9175. E-mail: adib@delasalleoaklands.org. Web site: www.delasalleoaklands.org.

DE LA SALLE HIGH SCHOOL

1130 Winton Drive
Concord, California 94518
Head of School: Br. Christopher Brady, FSC

General Information Boys' day college-preparatory, arts, and religious studies school, affiliated with Roman Catholic Church. Grades 9–12. Founded: 1965. Setting: suburban. Nearest major city is Oakland. 25-acre campus. 11 buildings on campus. Approved or accredited by Western Association of Schools and Colleges and Western Catholic Education Association. Endowment: $2.8 million. Total enrollment: 1,048. Upper school average class size: 30. Upper school faculty-student ratio: 1:28.
Upper School Student Profile Grade 9: 275 students (275 boys); Grade 10: 275 students (275 boys); Grade 11: 257 students (257 boys); Grade 12: 241 students (241 boys). 80% of students are Roman Catholic.
Faculty School total: 74. In upper school: 50 men, 24 women; 42 have advanced degrees.
Subjects Offered Algebra, American history, anatomy, art, band, Bible studies, biology, calculus, chemistry, chorus, design, drafting, drawing, economics, English, English-AP, ethics, fine arts, first aid, French, geometry, government/civics, health, history, Italian, jazz, Latin, literature, marine biology, mathematics, music theory, painting, physical education, physics, physiology, pre-calculus, psychology, religion, science, sculpture, social studies, Spanish, Spanish-AP, sports medicine, statistics, statistics-AP, trigonometry, world history, world religions, writing.
Graduation Requirements Arts and fine arts (art, music, dance, drama), English, foreign language, mathematics, physical education (includes health), religion (includes Bible studies and theology), science, social studies (includes history).
Special Academic Programs Advanced Placement exam preparation; honors section; independent study; remedial math.
College Admission Counseling 233 students graduated in 2008; 231 went to college, including California Polytechnic State University, San Luis Obispo; California State University, Chico; Saint Mary's College of California; Sonoma State University; The University of Arizona. Other: 1 entered military service, 1 entered a postgraduate year. Mean SAT critical reading: 556, mean SAT math: 583, mean SAT writing: 542, mean combined SAT: 1681, mean composite ACT: 25. 29% scored over 600 on SAT critical reading, 45% scored over 600 on SAT math, 22% scored over 600 on SAT writing, 31% scored over 1800 on combined SAT, 35% scored over 26 on composite ACT.
Student Life Upper grades have specified standards of dress, student council, honor system. Discipline rests primarily with faculty. Attendance at religious services is required.
Summer Programs Remediation programs offered; session focuses on remediation for incoming, conditionally accepted freshmen only; held on campus; accepts boys; not open to students from other schools. 30 students usually enrolled. 2009 schedule: June 15 to July 10. Application deadline: June 1.
Tuition and Aid Day student tuition: $13,500. Tuition installment plan (10-month, quarterly, semiannual, and annual payment plans). Need-based grants available. In 2008–09, 24% of upper-school students received aid. Total amount of financial aid awarded in 2008–09: $1,619,300.
Admissions Traditional secondary-level entrance grade is 9. For fall 2008, 451 students applied for upper-level admission, 297 were accepted, 275 enrolled. High School Placement Test required. Deadline for receipt of application materials: none. Application fee required: $75. On-campus interview required.
Athletics Interscholastic: baseball, basketball, bowling, cross-country running, diving, football, golf, lacrosse, rugby, soccer, swimming and diving, tennis, track and field, volleyball, water polo, wrestling; intramural: basketball, bowling, flag football, floor hockey, football, ultimate Frisbee. 2 PE instructors, 68 coaches, 2 athletic trainers.
Computers Computers are regularly used in animation, art, business applications, business education, business skills, business studies, career exploration, career technology, college planning, drawing and design, English, French, French as a second language, graphics, history, information technology, introduction to technology, language development, library, mathematics, media production, media services, music, newspaper, science, social studies, Spanish, technology, vocational-technical courses, yearbook classes. Computer network features include on-campus library services, Internet access, wireless campus network, Internet filtering or blocking technology. Student e-mail accounts and computer access in designated common areas are available to students. Students grades are available online. The school has a published electronic and media policy.
Contact Mr. Joseph Grantham, Director of Admissions. 925-288-8102. Fax: 925-686-3474. E-mail: granthamj@dlshs.org.

DELAWARE COUNTY CHRISTIAN SCHOOL

462 Malin Road
Newtown Square, Pennsylvania 19073-3499

ANNOUNCEMENT FROM THE SCHOOL Delaware County Christian School is the foremost independent Christian school in Philadelphia's Delaware Valley, with an enrollment of 875 students in grades PreK–12. The School, founded in 1950, provides a strong academic program within an evangelical Christian perspective. The Discovery Center provides both enrichment programs and educational support programs for students. Students are admitted on the basis of entrance tests, previous school records, and parental spiritual commitment.

DELAWARE VALLEY FRIENDS SCHOOL

Paoli, Pennsylvania
See Special Needs Schools section.

DELBARTON SCHOOL

230 Mendham Road
Morristown, New Jersey 07960
Head of School: Br. Paul Diveny, OSB

General Information Boys' day college-preparatory, arts, religious studies, and technology school, affiliated with Roman Catholic Church. Grades 7–12. Founded: 1939. Setting: suburban. Nearest major city is New York, NY. 400-acre campus. 7 buildings on campus. Approved or accredited by Middle States Association of Colleges and Schools, National Catholic Education Association, New Jersey Association of Independent Schools, and New Jersey Department of Education. Member of National Association of Independent Schools and Secondary School Admission Test Board. Endowment: $23.9 million. Total enrollment: 538. Upper school average class size: 15. Upper school faculty-student ratio: 1:10.
Upper School Student Profile Grade 9: 118 students (118 boys); Grade 10: 116 students (116 boys); Grade 11: 120 students (120 boys); Grade 12: 122 students (122 boys). 80% of students are Roman Catholic.
Faculty School total: 87. In upper school: 64 men, 14 women; 53 have advanced degrees.
Subjects Offered Accounting, advanced chemistry, algebra, American history, American literature, art, art history, astronomy, biology, calculus, chemistry, computer math, computer programming, computer science, creative writing, driver education, economics, English, English literature, environmental science, ethics, European history, fine arts, French, geography, geometry, German, grammar, health, history, international relations, Latin, mathematics, music, philosophy, physical education, physics, religion, Russian, social studies, Spanish, speech, trigonometry, world history.
Graduation Requirements Arts and fine arts (art, music, dance, drama), computer science, English, foreign language, mathematics, physical education (includes health), religion (includes Bible studies and theology), science, social studies (includes history), speech.
Special Academic Programs Advanced Placement exam preparation; independent study.
College Admission Counseling 114 students graduated in 2008; all went to college, including Colgate University; Cornell University; Georgetown University; Middlebury College; Princeton University; Villanova University.
Student Life Upper grades have specified standards of dress, student council, honor system. Discipline rests primarily with faculty. Attendance at religious services is required.
Summer Programs Enrichment, advancement, sports, computer instruction programs offered; session focuses on summer school (coed) and summer sports (boys); held on campus; accepts boys and girls; open to students from other schools. 1,000 students usually enrolled. 2009 schedule: June 24 to July 31. Application deadline: June 5.
Tuition and Aid Day student tuition: $24,975. Tuition installment plan (Key Tuition Payment Plan, monthly payment plans, individually arranged payment plans). Need-based scholarship grants available. In 2008–09, 15% of upper-school students received aid. Total amount of financial aid awarded in 2008–09: $1,200,000.
Admissions Traditional secondary-level entrance grade is 9. For fall 2008, 224 students applied for upper-level admission, 106 were accepted, 87 enrolled. Stanford Achievement Test, Otis-Lennon School Ability Test, school's own exam required. Deadline for receipt of application materials: November 29. Application fee required: $65. On-campus interview required.
Athletics Interscholastic: baseball, basketball, bowling, cross-country running, football, golf, ice hockey, indoor track, lacrosse, soccer, squash, swimming and diving, tennis, track and field, winter (indoor) track, wrestling; intramural: bicycling, combined training, fitness, flag football, Frisbee, independent competitive sports, mountain biking, skiing (downhill), strength & conditioning, ultimate Frisbee, weight lifting, weight training. 4 PE instructors.
Computers Computers are regularly used in music, science, word processing classes. Computer network features include on-campus library services, online commercial services, Internet access, wireless campus network. Student e-mail accounts are available to students. Students grades are available online.

Contact Mrs. Connie Curnow, Administrative Assistant—Office of Admissions. 973-538-3231 Ext. 3019. Fax: 973-538-8836. E-mail: ccurnow@delbarton.org. Web site: www.delbarton.org.

See Close-Up on page 738.

THE DELPHIAN SCHOOL

20950 Southwest Rock Creek Road
Sheridan, Oregon 97378

See Close-Up on page 740.

DELPHOS SAINT JOHN'S HIGH SCHOOL

515 East Second Street
Delphos, Ohio 45833

Head of School: Mr. Donald P. Huysman

General Information Coeducational day college-preparatory, general academic, arts, business, and religious studies school, affiliated with Roman Catholic Church; primarily serves underachievers. Grades 9–12. Founded: 1912. Setting: rural. Nearest major city is Lima. 2 buildings on campus. Approved or accredited by North Central Association of Colleges and Schools, Ohio Catholic Schools Accreditation Association (OCSAA), and Ohio Department of Education. Total enrollment: 285. Upper school average class size: 14. Upper school faculty-student ratio: 1:14.

Upper School Student Profile Grade 9: 79 students (42 boys, 37 girls); Grade 10: 73 students (38 boys, 35 girls); Grade 11: 66 students (27 boys, 39 girls); Grade 12: 67 students (31 boys, 36 girls). 96% of students are Roman Catholic.

Faculty School total: 25. In upper school: 10 men, 15 women; 7 have advanced degrees.

College Admission Counseling 101 students graduated in 2008; 60 went to college, including University of Dayton; Wright State University. Other: 5 went to work, 2 entered military service. Median composite ACT: 22. 12% scored over 26 on composite ACT.

Student Life Upper grades have uniform requirement. Discipline rests primarily with faculty. Attendance at religious services is required.

Tuition and Aid Day student tuition: $2300. Tuition installment plan (FACTS Tuition Payment Plan). Tuition reduction for siblings available. In 2008–09, 40% of upper-school students received aid.

Admissions Traditional secondary-level entrance grade is 9. Deadline for receipt of application materials: none. No application fee required. Interview required.

Athletics Interscholastic: basketball (boys, girls), cheering (g), cross-country running (b,g), football (b), golf (b,g), indoor track (b,g), soccer (g), strength & conditioning (b), volleyball (g), weight lifting (b,g), weight training (b,g), wrestling (b); intramural: baseball (b), basketball (b), strength & conditioning (b,g), volleyball (b,g). 12 coaches, 1 athletic trainer.

Computers Computers are regularly used in all academic classes. Computer network features include Internet access, Internet filtering or blocking technology.

Contact Mr. Alan Unterbrink, Guidance Counselor. 419-692-5371 Ext. 1135. Fax: 419-879-6874. E-mail: unterbrink@dsj.noacsc.org.

DEMATHA CATHOLIC HIGH SCHOOL

4313 Madison Street
Hyattsville, Maryland 20781

Head of School: Daniel J. McMahon, PhD

General Information Boys' day college-preparatory, arts, religious studies, and music (instrumental and choral) school, affiliated with Roman Catholic Church. Grades 9–12. Founded: 1946. Setting: suburban. Nearest major city is Washington, DC. 6-acre campus. 4 buildings on campus. Approved or accredited by Association of Independent Schools of Greater Washington, Middle States Association of Colleges and Schools, National Catholic Education Association, and Maryland Department of Education. Total enrollment: 996. Upper school average class size: 20. Upper school faculty-student ratio: 1:13.

Upper School Student Profile Grade 9: 266 students (266 boys); Grade 10: 269 students (269 boys); Grade 11: 236 students (236 boys); Grade 12: 225 students (225 boys). 63% of students are Roman Catholic.

Faculty School total: 90. In upper school: 66 men, 23 women; 56 have advanced degrees.

Subjects Offered Accounting, Advanced Placement courses, algebra, American government, American government-AP, American history, American history-AP, anatomy and physiology, art, art history, art-AP, astronomy, band, biology, biology-AP, British literature, British literature-AP, business, business law, calculus, calculus-AP, campus ministry, chemistry, chemistry-AP, choral music, chorus, Christian ethics, church history, college admission preparation, community service, computer applications, computer programming, computer science, computer science-AP, computer skills, computer studies, contemporary art, digital photography, English, English composition, English literature, environmental science, film studies, forensic science, French, French language-AP, geology, geometry, German, German-AP, government, government-AP, health, health education, history, history of religion, history of rock and roll, honors algebra, honors English, honors geometry, honors U.S. history, honors world history, instrumental music, jazz, journalism, Latin, Latin American studies, Latin-AP, literature-AP, mathematics, modern languages, music, music performance, mythology, newspaper, photography, photojournalism, physical education, physical science, physics, physics-AP, pre-calculus, psychology, SAT preparation, science, science research, social studies, Spanish, Spanish-AP, speech, sports medicine, statistics, studio art, studio art—AP, study skills, symphonic band, theology, trigonometry, U.S. government, U.S. history, U.S. literature, vocal music, world history, writing, yearbook.

Graduation Requirements Arts, computer science, English, foreign language, mathematics, physical education (includes health), science, social studies (includes history), theology, 55 hours of Christian service.

Special Academic Programs Advanced Placement exam preparation; honors section; independent study; academic accommodation for the gifted, the musically talented, and the artistically talented; remedial reading and/or remedial writing.

College Admission Counseling 233 students graduated in 2008; 228 went to college, including Anne Arundel Community College; Howard University; Salisbury University; St. Mary's College of Maryland; University of Maryland, Baltimore County; University of Maryland, College Park. Other: 2 went to work, 3 entered military service. Mean SAT critical reading: 532, mean SAT math: 545, mean SAT writing: 512, mean combined SAT: 1589. 26% scored over 600 on SAT critical reading, 29% scored over 600 on SAT math, 15% scored over 600 on SAT writing, 70% scored over 1800 on combined SAT.

Student Life Upper grades have uniform requirement, student council, honor system. Discipline rests primarily with faculty. Attendance at religious services is required.

Summer Programs Remediation, enrichment, sports, art/fine arts, computer instruction programs offered; session focuses on Remediation/Enrichment; held on campus; accepts boys and girls; open to students from other schools. 400 students usually enrolled. 2009 schedule: June 22 to July 24. Application deadline: June 12.

Tuition and Aid Day student tuition: $10,550. Tuition installment plan (FACTS Tuition Payment Plan). Tuition reduction for siblings, merit scholarship grants, need-based scholarship grants available. In 2008–09, 44% of upper-school students received aid; total upper-school merit-scholarship money awarded: $280,900. Total amount of financial aid awarded in 2008–09: $1,025,467.

Admissions Traditional secondary-level entrance grade is 9. For fall 2008, 700 students applied for upper-level admission, 394 were accepted, 275 enrolled. Archdiocese of Washington Entrance Exam, High School Placement Test or High School Placement Test (closed version) from Scholastic Testing Service required. Deadline for receipt of application materials: December 15. Application fee required: $50.

Athletics Interscholastic: baseball, basketball, crew, cross-country running, diving, football, golf, hockey, ice hockey, indoor track, indoor track & field, lacrosse, rugby, soccer, swimming and diving, tennis, track and field, ultimate Frisbee, water polo, winter (indoor) track, wrestling; intramural: basketball, bowling, strength & conditioning. 2 PE instructors, 1 coach, 2 athletic trainers.

Computers Computers are regularly used in computer applications, digital applications, independent study, lab/keyboard, library, newspaper, publishing, science, technology, Web site design, word processing, yearbook classes. Computer network features include on-campus library services, Internet access, wireless campus network, Internet filtering or blocking technology, ProQuest, SIRS, World Book. Computer access in designated common areas is available to students. The school has a published electronic and media policy.

Contact Mrs. Christine Thomas, Assistant Director of Admissions. 240-764-2210. Fax: 240-764-2277. E-mail: cthomas@dematha.org. Web site: www.dematha.org.

DENVER ACADEMY

Denver, Colorado

See Special Needs Schools section.

DENVER CHRISTIAN HIGH SCHOOL

2135 South Pearl Street
Denver, Colorado 80210

Head of School: Mr. Mark H. Swalley

General Information Coeducational day college-preparatory, general academic, arts, business, religious studies, bilingual studies, and technology school, affiliated with Christian Reformed Church. Grades 9–12. Founded: 1950. Setting: urban. 4-acre campus. 1 building on campus. Approved or accredited by Association of Christian Schools International, North Central Association of Colleges and Schools, and Colorado Department of Education. Endowment: $1.3 million. Total enrollment: 224. Upper school average class size: 15. Upper school faculty-student ratio: 1:18.

Upper School Student Profile Grade 9: 52 students (26 boys, 26 girls); Grade 10: 51 students (23 boys, 28 girls); Grade 11: 62 students (33 boys, 29 girls); Grade 12: 59 students (32 boys, 27 girls). 20% of students are members of Christian Reformed Church.

Faculty School total: 22. In upper school: 10 men, 12 women; 16 have advanced degrees.

Subjects Offered Acting, advanced chemistry, advanced computer applications, advanced math, algebra, American government, American history, American literature, art, band, Bible, biology, British literature, calculus, chamber groups,

chemistry, choir, Christian doctrine, Christian scripture, church history, composition, computer applications, computer keyboarding, concert band, concert choir, consumer economics, drama, driver education, earth science, European history, general math, government, grammar, health, introduction to literature, jazz band, keyboarding/computer, personal fitness, physical education, physical fitness, physics, poetry, pre-algebra, pre-calculus, psychology, research, senior seminar, Shakespeare, Spanish, speech, studio art, symphonic band, the Web, trigonometry, U.S. government, U.S. history, Web site design, weight fitness, Western civilization, world geography, world history, yearbook.
Special Academic Programs Honors section; independent study; special instructional classes for deaf students.
College Admission Counseling 81 students graduated in 2008; 78 went to college, including Azusa Pacific University; Calvin College; Colorado State University; University of Colorado at Boulder. Other: 3 went to work. Mean SAT critical reading: 560, mean SAT math: 545, mean composite ACT: 24.
Student Life Upper grades have specified standards of dress, student council. Discipline rests primarily with faculty. Attendance at religious services is required.
Tuition and Aid Day student tuition: $8500. Tuition installment plan (FACTS Tuition Payment Plan, monthly payment plans). Tuition reduction for siblings, merit scholarship grants, need-based scholarship grants available. In 2008–09, 30% of upper-school students received aid.
Admissions Traditional secondary-level entrance grade is 9. WISC-III and Woodcock-Johnson, WISC/Woodcock-Johnson or Woodcock-Johnson Educational Evaluation, WISC III required. Deadline for receipt of application materials: none. Application fee required: $260. Interview required.
Athletics Interscholastic: baseball (boys), basketball (b,g), cross-country running (b,g), dance team (g), football (b), golf (b,g), soccer (b,g). 1 PE instructor, 25 coaches.
Computers Computer network features include on-campus library services, Internet access, wireless campus network, Internet filtering or blocking technology. Student e-mail accounts are available to students. Students grades are available online. The school has a published electronic and media policy.
Contact Sheryl Vriesman, Admissions Secretary. 303-733-2421 Ext. 110. Fax: 303-733-7734. E-mail: sherylv@denver-christian.org.

DENVER LUTHERAN HIGH SCHOOL

3201 West Arizona Avenue
Denver, Colorado 80219
Head of School: Mr. Daniel Gehrke
General Information Coeducational day college-preparatory, general academic, arts, religious studies, and technology school, affiliated with Lutheran Church–Missouri Synod. Grades 9–12. Founded: 1955. Setting: urban. 12-acre campus. 1 building on campus. Approved or accredited by National Lutheran School Accreditation, North Central Association of Colleges and Schools, and Colorado Department of Education. Total enrollment: 210. Upper school average class size: 18. Upper school faculty-student ratio: 1:17.
Upper School Student Profile Grade 9: 49 students (22 boys, 27 girls); Grade 10: 56 students (33 boys, 23 girls); Grade 11: 53 students (21 boys, 32 girls); Grade 12: 52 students (23 boys, 29 girls). 70% of students are Lutheran Church–Missouri Synod.
Faculty School total: 18. In upper school: 13 men, 5 women; 5 have advanced degrees.
Subjects Offered 20th century history, algebra, art, band, biology, calculus, chemistry, chorus, computer programming, computer science, consumer mathematics, creative writing, English, fine arts, geography, geometry, literature, mathematics, physical education, physics, psychology, reading, religion, science, social science, social studies, Spanish, speech, trigonometry.
Graduation Requirements Algebra, American government, arts and fine arts (art, music, dance, drama), biology, chemistry, computer applications, electives, English, English composition, English literature, geography, mathematics, physical education (includes health), science, social science, social studies (includes history), religion class for each year enrolled.
Special Academic Programs Advanced Placement exam preparation; honors section; independent study; remedial reading and/or remedial writing; remedial math.
College Admission Counseling 51 students graduated in 2008; 49 went to college, including Colorado State University; Concordia University; Metropolitan State College of Denver; University of Colorado at Boulder; University of Northern Colorado. Other: 1 went to work, 1 had other specific plans. Mean composite ACT: 23.
Student Life Upper grades have specified standards of dress, student council, honor system. Discipline rests primarily with faculty. Attendance at religious services is required.
Tuition and Aid Day student tuition: $6850. Need-based scholarship grants available. In 2008–09, 30% of upper-school students received aid.
Admissions Traditional secondary-level entrance grade is 9. High School Placement Test required. Deadline for receipt of application materials: none. Application fee required: $100. On-campus interview required.
Athletics Interscholastic: baseball (boys), basketball (b,g), cross-country running (b,g), floor hockey (b), football (b), golf (b,g), roller hockey (b), soccer (b,g), softball (g), tennis (g), track and field (b,g), volleyball (g), weight training (b,g), wrestling (b); intramural: field hockey (b). 3 PE instructors, 6 coaches, 1 athletic trainer.
Computers Computers are regularly used in art, geography, graphic arts, theater arts, Web site design, yearbook classes. Computer network features include on-campus library services, online commercial services, Internet access. The school has a published electronic and media policy.
Contact Mrs. Tera Thomas, Admissions Director. 303-934-2345 Ext. 3306. Fax: 303-934-0455. Web site: www.denverlhs.org.

DEPAUL CATHOLIC HIGH SCHOOL

1512 Alps Road
Wayne, New Jersey 07470
Head of School: Mr. Bob Costello
General Information Coeducational day college-preparatory, arts, and religious studies school, affiliated with Roman Catholic Church. Grades 9–12. Founded: 1956. Setting: suburban. Nearest major city is New York, NY. 5-acre campus. 2 buildings on campus. Approved or accredited by National Catholic Education Association and New Jersey Department of Education. Upper school average class size: 24. Upper school faculty-student ratio: 1:19.
Upper School Student Profile 90% of students are Roman Catholic.
Faculty School total: 65. In upper school: 25 men, 40 women; 40 have advanced degrees.
Special Academic Programs International Baccalaureate program; Advanced Placement exam preparation; honors section; accelerated programs; remedial reading and/or remedial writing; remedial math; programs in general development for dyslexic students; special instructional classes for deaf students, blind students.
College Admission Counseling 195 students graduated in 2008; all went to college.
Student Life Upper grades have uniform requirement, student council, honor system. Discipline rests equally with students and faculty. Attendance at religious services is required.
Summer Programs Sports programs offered; held on campus; accepts boys and girls; open to students from other schools. 300 students usually enrolled. 2009 schedule: June 20 to July 31. Application deadline: June 21.
Tuition and Aid Day student tuition: $9490. Tuition installment plan (FACTS Tuition Payment Plan, monthly payment plans, individually arranged payment plans). Tuition reduction for siblings, merit scholarship grants, need-based scholarship grants available.
Admissions Cooperative Entrance Exam (McGraw-Hill) required. Deadline for receipt of application materials: December 1. No application fee required.
Athletics Interscholastic: baseball (boys), basketball (b,g), cheering (g), cross-country running (b,g), dance (g), dance squad (g), dance team (g), danceline (g), figure skating (g), football (b), indoor track (b,g), indoor track & field (b,g), lacrosse (b,g), modern dance (g), soccer (b,g), softball (b), swimming and diving (b,g), tennis (g), track and field (b,g), volleyball (b,g), weight lifting (b,g), weight training (b,g), winter (indoor) track (b,g), wrestling (b); intramural: equestrian sports (g), strength & conditioning (b,g); coed interscholastic: alpine skiing, bowling, golf, ice hockey, skiing (downhill). 5 PE instructors, 40 coaches, 1 athletic trainer.
Computers Computer network features include on-campus library services, Internet access, wireless campus network, Internet filtering or blocking technology. Campus intranet, student e-mail accounts, and computer access in designated common areas are available to students. Students grades are available online. The school has a published electronic and media policy.
Contact Mr. John W. Merritt, Director of Admissions. 973-694-3702 Ext. 410. Fax: 973-694-3525. E-mail: merrittj@dpchs.org. Web site: www.depaulcatholic.org.

THE DERRYFIELD SCHOOL

2108 River Road
Manchester, New Hampshire 03104-1396
Head of School: Mr. Craig Seller
General Information Coeducational day college-preparatory school. Grades 6–12. Founded: 1964. Setting: suburban. Nearest major city is Boston, MA. 84-acre campus. 3 buildings on campus. Approved or accredited by Association of Independent Schools in New England, Independent Schools of Northern New England, New England Association of Schools and Colleges, and New Hampshire Department of Education. Member of National Association of Independent Schools and Secondary School Admission Test Board. Endowment: $4.8 million. Total enrollment: 385. Upper school average class size: 14. Upper school faculty-student ratio: 1:8.
Upper School Student Profile Grade 9: 69 students (28 boys, 41 girls); Grade 10: 68 students (32 boys, 36 girls); Grade 11: 62 students (28 boys, 34 girls); Grade 12: 63 students (31 boys, 32 girls).
Faculty School total: 55. In upper school: 29 men, 26 women; 30 have advanced degrees.
Subjects Offered 3-dimensional art, African-American literature, algebra, American literature, anatomy and physiology, ancient world history, area studies, art, art history, biology, British literature, calculus, calculus-AP, chemistry, China/Japan history, Chinese, chorus, computer science, contemporary issues, creative writing, drafting, drama, driver education, earth science, economics, economics and history, engineering, English, English composition, English literature, English-AP, European history, expository writing, film, fine arts, French, French language-AP, French literature-AP, geography, geometry, global issues, government/civics, graphics,

Greek, health, history, Holocaust, independent study, Latin, Latin-AP, mathematics, media, music, music theory, mythology, organic chemistry, philosophy, physical education, physics, pre-calculus, public speaking, robotics, science, Shakespeare, social studies, Spanish, Spanish language-AP, Spanish literature-AP, speech, statistics, statistics-AP, studio art, theater, trigonometry, U.S. history-AP, Western civilization, world history, world literature, writing.

Graduation Requirements Arts and fine arts (art, music, dance, drama), athletics, English, foreign language, health and wellness, history, mathematics, science.

Special Academic Programs Advanced Placement exam preparation; honors section; independent study; term-away projects.

College Admission Counseling 53 students graduated in 2008; all went to college, including Bates College; Boston College; Lehigh University; Middlebury College; University of New Hampshire; Wellesley College. Mean SAT critical reading: 625, mean SAT math: 630, mean SAT writing: 637, mean combined SAT: 1888, mean composite ACT: 27.

Student Life Upper grades have specified standards of dress, student council. Discipline rests equally with students and faculty.

Summer Programs Art/fine arts programs offered; session focuses on theater camp; held on campus; accepts boys and girls; open to students from other schools. 50 students usually enrolled. 2009 schedule: July 6 to August 17. Application deadline: June.

Tuition and Aid Day student tuition: $22,750. Tuition installment plan (FACTS Tuition Payment Plan, monthly payment plans). Need-based scholarship grants available. In 2008–09, 16% of upper-school students received aid. Total amount of financial aid awarded in 2008–09: $1,069,506.

Admissions Traditional secondary-level entrance grade is 9. SSAT required. Deadline for receipt of application materials: February 2. Application fee required: $50. On-campus interview required.

Athletics Interscholastic: alpine skiing (boys, girls), baseball (b), basketball (b,g), crew (b,g), cross-country running (b,g), field hockey (g), independent competitive sports (b,g), lacrosse (b,g), skiing (cross-country) (b,g), skiing (downhill) (b,g), soccer (b,g), softball (g), tennis (b,g); coed interscholastic: golf, ice hockey, physical training; coed intramural: aerobics, ropes courses, snowboarding, swimming and diving, volleyball, weight training, yoga. 7 coaches, 1 athletic trainer.

Computers Computers are regularly used in geography, mathematics, media production, music, programming, science, Web site design classes. Computer network features include on-campus library services, online commercial services, Internet access, wireless campus network, online computer linked to New Hampshire State Library. Student e-mail accounts are available to students.

Contact Ms. Allison Price, Director of Admission. 603-669-4524 Ext. 153. Fax: 603-641-9521. E-mail: aprice@derryfield.org. Web site: www.derryfield.org.

See Close-Up on page 742.

DE SMET JESUIT HIGH SCHOOL

233 North New Ballas Road
Creve Coeur, Missouri 63141

Head of School: Dr. Gregory A. Densberger

General Information Boys' day college-preparatory, arts, and religious studies school, affiliated with Roman Catholic Church; primarily serves students with learning disabilities. Grades 9–12. Founded: 1967. Setting: suburban. Nearest major city is St. Louis. 30-acre campus. 3 buildings on campus. Approved or accredited by North Central Association of Colleges and Schools. Endowment: $3 million. Upper school average class size: 24. Upper school faculty-student ratio: 1:14.

Upper School Student Profile 94% of students are Roman Catholic.

Faculty School total: 89. In upper school: 78 men, 11 women; 57 have advanced degrees.

Subjects Offered Algebra, American history, American literature, art, biology, broadcasting, business, calculus, chemistry, computer math, computer programming, computer science, creative writing, dance, drafting, drama, driver education, earth science, economics, English, English literature, ethics, European history, expository writing, fine arts, French, geography, geometry, German, government/civics, grammar, history, journalism, Latin, mathematics, mechanical drawing, music, physical education, physics, psychology, religion, science, social science, social studies, sociology, Spanish, speech, theater, theology, trigonometry, typing, world history, writing.

Graduation Requirements Arts and fine arts (art, music, dance, drama), business skills (includes word processing), computer science, English, foreign language, mathematics, physical education (includes health), religion (includes Bible studies and theology), science, social science, social studies (includes history). Community service is required.

Special Academic Programs Advanced Placement exam preparation; honors section; study at local college for college credit.

College Admission Counseling 254 students graduated in 2008; 253 went to college, including Saint Louis University; St. Louis Community College at Meramec; Truman State University; University of Missouri–Columbia; University of Missouri–St. Louis. Other: 1 entered military service.

Student Life Upper grades have specified standards of dress, student council, honor system. Discipline rests primarily with faculty. Attendance at religious services is required.

Tuition and Aid Day student tuition: $9760. Tuition installment plan (monthly payment plans). Merit scholarship grants, need-based scholarship grants available. In 2008–09, 20% of upper-school students received aid.

Admissions Any standardized test or High School Placement Test required. Deadline for receipt of application materials: December 10. No application fee required. On-campus interview required.

Athletics Interscholastic: baseball, basketball, bowling, cross-country running, diving, football, golf, ice hockey, in-line hockey, lacrosse, racquetball, rugby, soccer, strength & conditioning, swimming and diving, team handball, tennis, track and field, volleyball, water polo, weight training, wrestling; intramural: floor hockey, Frisbee, in-line skating, outdoor recreation, paint ball, roller hockey, Special Olympics, ultimate Frisbee. 4 PE instructors, 25 coaches, 2 athletic trainers.

Computers Computers are regularly used in English, foreign language, history, mathematics, science classes. Computer network features include on-campus library services, online commercial services, Internet access. The school has a published electronic and media policy.

Contact Mrs. Anne G. Gibbons, Admissions Director. 314-567-3500 Ext. 247. Fax: 314-567-1519. E-mail: agibbons@desmet.org. Web site: www.desmet.org.

DETROIT COUNTRY DAY SCHOOL

22305 West Thirteen Mile Road
Beverly Hills, Michigan 48025-4435

Head of School: Glen P. Shilling

General Information Coeducational boarding and day college-preparatory and arts school. Boarding grades 7–12, day grades PK–12. Founded: 1914. Setting: suburban. Nearest major city is Detroit. Students are housed in on-campus homes. 100-acre campus. 4 buildings on campus. Approved or accredited by Independent Schools Association of the Central States and Michigan Department of Education. Member of National Association of Independent Schools. Endowment: $9 million. Total enrollment: 1,600. Upper school average class size: 15. Upper school faculty-student ratio: 1:8.

Upper School Student Profile Grade 9: 159 students (86 boys, 73 girls); Grade 10: 189 students (108 boys, 81 girls); Grade 11: 164 students (91 boys, 73 girls); Grade 12: 149 students (80 boys, 69 girls).

Faculty School total: 202. In upper school: 35 men, 37 women; 60 have advanced degrees.

Subjects Offered African-American studies, algebra, American history, American literature, American studies, anatomy, ancient history, art, astronomy, band, biology, botany, calculus, ceramics, chemistry, Chinese, chorus, college counseling, community service, composition, computer programming, computer science, current events, design, drama, drawing, ecology, economics, economics and history, English, English literature, environmental science, European history, fine arts, finite math, French, genetics, geometry, German, government/civics, grammar, graphic arts, health, history, humanities, Japanese, Latin, literature, mathematics, media, metalworking, microbiology, music, music history, music theory, natural history, orchestra, painting, photography, physical education, physical science, physics, physiology, poetry, pre-calculus, printmaking, science, sculpture, social studies, Spanish, speech, statistics, study skills, theater, theory of knowledge, Western civilization, world literature, zoology.

Graduation Requirements American history, arts and fine arts (art, music, dance, drama), college counseling, computer science, English, foreign language, mathematics, physical education (includes health), science, speech, athletic participation, skill-oriented activities, service-oriented activities.

Special Academic Programs International Baccalaureate program; Advanced Placement exam preparation; honors section; academic accommodation for the gifted, the musically talented, and the artistically talented.

College Admission Counseling 174 students graduated in 2008; 148 went to college, including Albion College; Michigan State University; University of Michigan. Mean SAT critical reading: 655, mean SAT math: 661, mean SAT writing: 632, mean combined SAT: 1948, mean composite ACT: 27.

Student Life Upper grades have uniform requirement, student council, honor system. Discipline rests primarily with faculty.

Summer Programs Enrichment, advancement, sports, art/fine arts, computer instruction programs offered; session focuses on academic enrichment and sports camps; held on campus; accepts boys and girls; open to students from other schools. 2009 schedule: June 18 to August 3.

Tuition and Aid Day student tuition: $24,240. Need-based scholarship grants, need-based loans available. In 2008–09, 10% of upper-school students received aid. Total amount of financial aid awarded in 2008–09: $2,500,000.

Admissions Traditional secondary-level entrance grade is 9. For fall 2008, 180 students applied for upper-level admission, 82 were accepted, 62 enrolled. ISEE and Otis-Lennon School Ability Test required. Deadline for receipt of application materials: none. Application fee required: $50. On-campus interview required.

Athletics Interscholastic: alpine skiing (boys, girls), ball hockey (g), baseball (b), basketball (b,g), bowling (b,g), cross-country running (b,g), dance squad (g), diving (b,g), field hockey (g), football (b), golf (b,g), hockey (b), ice hockey (b), lacrosse (b,g), skiing (downhill) (b,g), soccer (b,g), softball (g), swimming and diving (b,g), tennis (b,g), track and field (b,g), volleyball (g), wrestling (b); intramural: weight lifting (b,g); coed interscholastic: cheering, mountain biking, outdoor adventure,

snowboarding; coed intramural: basketball, project adventure, strength & conditioning. 4 coaches, 2 athletic trainers.
Computers Computers are regularly used in all classes. Computer network features include on-campus library services, online commercial services, Internet access, wireless campus network, Internet filtering or blocking technology. Campus intranet and student e-mail accounts are available to students. Students grades are available online. The school has a published electronic and media policy.
Contact Jorge Dante Hernandez Prosperi, Director of Admissions. 248-646-7717. Fax: 248-203-2184. E-mail: jprosperi@dcds.edu. Web site: www.dcds.edu.

DEVON PREPARATORY SCHOOL

363 Valley Forge Road
Devon, Pennsylvania 19333-1299

Head of School: Rev. James J. Shea, Sch.P

General Information Boys' day college-preparatory school, affiliated with Roman Catholic Church. Grades 6–12. Founded: 1956. Setting: suburban. Nearest major city is Philadelphia. 20-acre campus. 7 buildings on campus. Approved or accredited by Middle States Association of Colleges and Schools, Pennsylvania Association of Independent Schools, and Pennsylvania Department of Education. Endowment: $600,000. Total enrollment: 298. Upper school average class size: 15. Upper school faculty-student ratio: 1:10.
Upper School Student Profile Grade 9: 53 students (53 boys); Grade 10: 63 students (63 boys); Grade 11: 57 students (57 boys); Grade 12: 57 students (57 boys). 84% of students are Roman Catholic.
Faculty School total: 32. In upper school: 23 men, 9 women; 20 have advanced degrees.
Subjects Offered Accounting, Advanced Placement courses, algebra, American history, American literature, anatomy and physiology, art, biology, biology-AP, British literature, calculus, calculus-AP, chemistry, chemistry-AP, community service, computer science, computer science-AP, economics, English, European history, forensic science, forensics, French, French language-AP, geography, geometry, German, German-AP, health, language-AP, Latin, literature and composition-AP, mathematics, modern European history, music, performing arts, physical education, physics, physics-AP, political science, pre-calculus, religion, science, social studies, Spanish, Spanish-AP, trigonometry, U.S. history-AP, Vietnam War, world culture, world literature.
Graduation Requirements Computer science, English, foreign language, geography, Latin, mathematics, physical education (includes health), political science, religion (includes Bible studies and theology), science, social studies (includes history). Community service is required.
Special Academic Programs Advanced Placement exam preparation.
College Admission Counseling 49 students graduated in 2008; all went to college, including Fairfield University; Penn State University Park; Saint Joseph's University; University of Pennsylvania; Villanova University. Median SAT critical reading: 624, median SAT math: 634.
Student Life Upper grades have specified standards of dress, student council. Discipline rests primarily with faculty. Attendance at religious services is required.
Tuition and Aid Day student tuition: $15,900. Tuition installment plan (monthly payment plans). Tuition reduction for siblings, merit scholarship grants, need-based scholarship grants available. In 2008–09, 42% of upper-school students received aid; total upper-school merit-scholarship money awarded: $475,000. Total amount of financial aid awarded in 2008–09: $725,000.
Admissions Traditional secondary-level entrance grade is 9. For fall 2008, 200 students applied for upper-level admission, 150 were accepted, 50 enrolled. Math and English placement tests required. Deadline for receipt of application materials: none. Application fee required: $25. On-campus interview recommended.
Athletics Interscholastic: baseball, basketball, cross-country running, golf, indoor track & field, lacrosse, soccer, tennis, track and field; intramural: outdoor recreation, paint ball. 2 PE instructors, 8 coaches, 1 athletic trainer.
Computers Computers are regularly used in all academic, newspaper, technology, writing, yearbook classes. Computer network features include on-campus library services, Internet access. The school has a published electronic and media policy.
Contact Mr. Patrick Parsons, Director of Admissions. 610-688-7337 Ext. 129. Fax: 610-688-2409. E-mail: pparsons@devonprep.com. Web site: www.devonprep.com.

DICKINSON TRINITY

PO Box 1177
Dickinson, North Dakota 58601

Head of School: Sr. Dorothy Zeller

General Information Coeducational day college-preparatory, arts, business, religious studies, and technology school, affiliated with Roman Catholic Church; primarily serves students with learning disabilities. Grades 7–12. Founded: 1961. Setting: small town. Nearest major city is Bismarck. 18-acre campus. 1 building on campus. Approved or accredited by National Catholic Education Association, North Central Association of Colleges and Schools, and North Dakota Department of Education. Total enrollment: 254. Upper school average class size: 42. Upper school faculty-student ratio: 1:11.
Upper School Student Profile Grade 7: 39 students (17 boys, 22 girls); Grade 8: 47 students (29 boys, 18 girls); Grade 9: 47 students (21 boys, 26 girls); Grade 10: 36 students (16 boys, 20 girls); Grade 11: 40 students (18 boys, 22 girls); Grade 12: 45 students (22 boys, 23 girls). 97% of students are Roman Catholic.
Faculty School total: 22. In upper school: 8 men, 14 women.
Subjects Offered Accounting, advanced chemistry, algebra, American history, art, biology, business, business law, business skills, chemistry, communications, computer programming, computer science, English, geography, geometry, government/civics, health, instrumental music, journalism, keyboarding, mathematics, music, organic chemistry, physical education, physical science, physics, pre-calculus, psychology, religion, science, social science, social studies, Spanish, statistics, trigonometry, world history.
Graduation Requirements Business skills (includes word processing), English, mathematics, physical education (includes health), religion (includes Bible studies and theology), science, social science, social studies (includes history), community service hours for grade 11 and grade 12 students.
Special Academic Programs Independent study; study at local college for college credit; academic accommodation for the gifted; remedial reading and/or remedial writing; remedial math; special instructional classes for students with physical handicaps that do not preclude mobility.
College Admission Counseling 45 students graduated in 2008; they went to Dickinson State University; Minot State University; North Dakota State University; University of Mary; University of North Dakota; Valley City State University.
Student Life Upper grades have specified standards of dress, student council, honor system. Discipline rests primarily with faculty. Attendance at religious services is required.
Tuition and Aid Tuition installment plan (monthly payment plans, individually arranged payment plans, harvest season payments). Tuition reduction for siblings, need-based scholarship grants, paying campus jobs, partial tuition waver available.
Admissions Traditional secondary-level entrance grade is 9. For fall 2008, 6 students applied for upper-level admission, 6 were accepted, 6 enrolled. Deadline for receipt of application materials: none. No application fee required. On-campus interview required.
Athletics Interscholastic: baseball (boys), basketball (b,g), cheering (g), cross-country running (b,g), diving (b,g), football (b), golf (b,g), gymnastics (g), hockey (b,g), ice hockey (b,g), indoor track & field (b,g), softball (g), swimming and diving (b,g), track and field (b,g), volleyball (g), wrestling (b); coed intramural: archery, bowling, football. 2 PE instructors, 22 coaches.
Computers Computers are regularly used in business education, foreign language, mathematics classes. Computer resources include on-campus library services, Internet access, wireless campus network, Internet filtering or blocking technology. Campus intranet, student e-mail accounts, and computer access in designated common areas are available to students. Students grades are available online. The school has a published electronic and media policy.
Contact Rocklyn Cofer, Principal. 701-483-6081. Fax: 701-483-1450. E-mail: rocklyn.g.cofer@sendit.nodak.edu. Web site: www.trinityhighschool.com.

DOANE STUART SCHOOL

799 South Pearl Street
Albany, New York 12202

Head of School: Dr. Richard D. Enemark

General Information Coeducational day college-preparatory, arts, religious studies, Irish and Peace Studies, and Bioethics school, affiliated with Episcopal Church. Grades N–12. Founded: 1852. Setting: urban. 80-acre campus. 3 buildings on campus. Approved or accredited by National Association of Episcopal Schools, National Independent Private Schools Association, New York State Association of Independent Schools, and New York Department of Education. Member of National Association of Independent Schools and Secondary School Admission Test Board. Endowment: $1 million. Total enrollment: 266. Upper school average class size: 14. Upper school faculty-student ratio: 1:7.
Upper School Student Profile Grade 9: 32 students (22 boys, 10 girls); Grade 10: 29 students (14 boys, 15 girls); Grade 11: 24 students (10 boys, 14 girls); Grade 12: 37 students (18 boys, 19 girls). 10% of students are members of Episcopal Church.
Faculty School total: 50. In upper school: 10 men, 11 women; 12 have advanced degrees.
Subjects Offered Algebra, American history, American literature, art, biology, calculus, chemistry, community service, computer science, creative writing, earth science, economics, English, English literature, environmental science, ethics, fencing, fine arts, French, geometry, government/civics, health, history, mathematics, music, photography, physical education, physics, psychology, religion, science, social studies, Spanish, theater, trigonometry, world history, writing.
Special Academic Programs 30 Advanced Placement exams for which test preparation is offered; independent study; term-away projects; study at local college for college credit; domestic exchange program; study abroad; academic accommodation for the gifted, the musically talented, and the artistically talented.
College Admission Counseling 22 students graduated in 2008; all went to college, including Fordham University; New York University; Rensselaer Polytechnic Institute; The George Washington University; University at Albany, State University of New York; University of Vermont.

Student Life Upper grades have uniform requirement, student council. Discipline rests primarily with faculty. Attendance at religious services is required.
Tuition and Aid Day student tuition: $16,955–$18,850. Tuition installment plan (Academic Management Services Plan). Need-based scholarship grants available. In 2008–09, 40% of upper-school students received aid. Total amount of financial aid awarded in 2008–09: $421,122.
Admissions Traditional secondary-level entrance grade is 9. School's own test or SSAT required. Deadline for receipt of application materials: none. Application fee required: $75. On-campus interview required.
Athletics Interscholastic: baseball (boys), basketball (b,g), crew (b,g), fencing (b,g), softball (g), volleyball (g); intramural: backpacking (b,g); coed interscholastic: crew, cross-country running, fencing, independent competitive sports, physical fitness, strength & conditioning, tai chi, tennis, ultimate Frisbee, walking, yoga; coed intramural: backpacking, Frisbee, hiking/backpacking, independent competitive sports, jogging. 2 PE instructors, 8 coaches.
Computers Computers are regularly used in accounting, architecture, art, basic skills, business, career exploration, college planning, creative writing, current events, data processing, desktop publishing, drawing and design, economics, English, ethics, foreign language, freshman foundations, geography, graphic arts, graphic design, graphics, health, historical foundations for arts, history, humanities, independent study, introduction to technology, journalism, keyboarding, language development, learning cognition, library science, library skills, literary magazine, mathematics, media arts, media production, mentorship program, multimedia, music, music technology, news writing, newspaper, philosophy, photography, programming, psychology, publications, publishing, reading, religion, religious studies, remedial study skills, research skills, SAT preparation, science, senior seminar, social sciences, social studies, study skills, technology, theater, theater arts, video film production, Web site design, writing, writing fundamentals, yearbook classes. Computer resources include on-campus library services, online commercial services, Internet access, wireless campus network. Computer access in designated common areas is available to students. The school has a published electronic and media policy.
Contact Mr. Michael Green, Director of Admission. 518-465-5222 Ext. 241. Fax: 518-465-5230. E-mail: mgreen@doanestuart.org. Web site: www.doanestuart.org.

See Close-Up on page 744.

THE DOMINICAN ACADEMY OF THE CITY OF NEW YORK

44 East 68th Street
New York, New York 10065
Head of School: Sr. Joan Franks, OP

General Information Girls' day college-preparatory, arts, religious studies, and technology school, affiliated with Roman Catholic Church. Grades 9–12. Founded: 1897. Setting: urban. 1 building on campus. Approved or accredited by Middle States Association of Colleges and Schools, National Catholic Education Association, and New York State Board of Regents. Total enrollment: 224. Upper school average class size: 22. Upper school faculty-student ratio: 1:8.
Upper School Student Profile Grade 9: 70 students (70 girls); Grade 10: 51 students (51 girls); Grade 11: 52 students (52 girls); Grade 12: 51 students (51 girls). 90% of students are Roman Catholic.
Faculty School total: 29. In upper school: 6 men, 23 women; 24 have advanced degrees.
Subjects Offered Algebra, American history, American history-AP, American literature, art history-AP, biology, biology-AP, calculus, calculus-AP, chemistry, chemistry-AP, chorus, communications, computer science, creative writing, dance, debate, drama, economics, economics-AP, English, English literature, English-AP, European history-AP, forensic science, forensics, French, French-AP, geometry, global studies, government and politics-AP, government/civics, health, history, Latin, Latin-AP, library studies, logic, mathematics, music, music theory, physical education, physics, pre-calculus, psychology, religion, science, social studies, Spanish, Spanish-AP, world history.
Graduation Requirements Alternative physical education, arts and fine arts (art, music, dance, drama), English, foreign language, Latin, mathematics, religion (includes Bible studies and theology), science, social studies (includes history).
Special Academic Programs Advanced Placement exam preparation; study at local college for college credit.
College Admission Counseling 80 students graduated in 2008; all went to college, including Boston University; College of the Holy Cross; Columbia College; Fordham University; New York University; Tulane University.
Student Life Upper grades have uniform requirement, student council. Discipline rests primarily with faculty. Attendance at religious services is required.
Tuition and Aid Day student tuition: $9750. Tuition installment plan (FACTS Tuition Payment Plan, individually arranged payment plans, quarterly payment plan, semester payment plan). Tuition reduction for siblings, merit scholarship grants, need-based scholarship grants, paying campus jobs available. In 2008–09, 30% of upper-school students received aid; total upper-school merit-scholarship money awarded: $160,000. Total amount of financial aid awarded in 2008–09: $200,000.
Admissions Traditional secondary-level entrance grade is 9. For fall 2008, 360 students applied for upper-level admission, 200 were accepted, 70 enrolled. Catholic High School Entrance Examination required. Deadline for receipt of application materials: December 20. No application fee required.
Athletics Interscholastic: basketball, crew, cross-country running, soccer, softball, tennis, track and field, volleyball; intramural: billiards, dance, soccer, volleyball. 1 PE instructor, 2 coaches.
Computers Computers are regularly used in economics, history, library studies, mathematics, science, technology classes. Computer network features include on-campus library services, online commercial services, Internet access, wireless campus network, Internet filtering or blocking technology, T1 fiber optic network. Campus intranet, student e-mail accounts, and computer access in designated common areas are available to students. The school has a published electronic and media policy.
Contact Sr. Valerie Shaul, OP, Assistant Principal. 212-744-0195. Fax: 212-744-0375. E-mail: vshaul@dominicanacademy.org. Web site: www.dominicanacademy.org.

DONELSON CHRISTIAN ACADEMY

300 Danyacrest Drive
Nashville, Tennessee 37214
Head of School: Dr. Daniel W. Kellum Sr.

General Information Coeducational day college-preparatory, arts, religious studies, and technology school, affiliated with Christian faith. Grades K–12. Founded: 1971. Setting: suburban. 30-acre campus. 6 buildings on campus. Approved or accredited by Association of Christian Schools International, Southern Association of Colleges and Schools, Tennessee Association of Independent Schools, and Tennessee Department of Education. Endowment: $21,000. Total enrollment: 823. Upper school average class size: 18. Upper school faculty-student ratio: 1:16.
Upper School Student Profile Grade 9: 81 students (36 boys, 45 girls); Grade 10: 74 students (35 boys, 39 girls); Grade 11: 72 students (37 boys, 35 girls); Grade 12: 65 students (31 boys, 34 girls). 95% of students are Christian faith.
Faculty School total: 31. In upper school: 9 men, 19 women; 16 have advanced degrees.
Subjects Offered Algebra, American history, American literature, anatomy, art, Bible studies, biology, business, business skills, calculus, chemistry, community service, computer keyboarding, computer science, drama, earth science, ecology, economics, English, English literature, environmental science, fine arts, French, geography, geometry, government/civics, grammar, health, history, journalism, Latin, mathematics, music, physical education, physics, physiology, psychology, religion, science, social science, social studies, sociology, Spanish, speech, theater, world history, world literature.
Graduation Requirements Arts and fine arts (art, music, dance, drama), Bible, business skills (includes word processing), chemistry, computer science, electives, English, foreign language, mathematics, physical education (includes health), science, social science, social studies (includes history), speech, wellness, senior service (community service for senior high students).
Special Academic Programs Advanced Placement exam preparation; honors section; independent study; study at local college for college credit; academic accommodation for the gifted.
College Admission Counseling 74 students graduated in 2008; all went to college, including Lipscomb University; Middle Tennessee State University; Tennessee Technological University; The University of Tennessee System; Volunteer State Community College; Western Kentucky University. Mean composite ACT: 24. 28% scored over 26 on composite ACT.
Student Life Upper grades have uniform requirement, student council, honor system. Discipline rests primarily with faculty. Attendance at religious services is required.
Summer Programs Sports programs offered; session focuses on skill development; held on campus; accepts boys and girls; not open to students from other schools. 230 students usually enrolled. 2009 schedule: June 1 to August 1. Application deadline: none.
Tuition and Aid Day student tuition: $6995. Tuition installment plan (monthly payment plans). Need-based scholarship grants, paying campus jobs available. In 2008–09, 6% of upper-school students received aid. Total amount of financial aid awarded in 2008–09: $31,000.
Admissions Traditional secondary-level entrance grade is 9. For fall 2008, 18 students applied for upper-level admission, 18 were accepted, 18 enrolled. Achievement tests or Stanford Achievement Test required. Deadline for receipt of application materials: none. Application fee required: $40. On-campus interview required.
Athletics Interscholastic: baseball (boys), basketball (b,g), bowling (b,g), cheering (g), cross-country running (b,g), football (b), golf (b,g), soccer (b,g), softball (g), tennis (b,g), track and field (b,g), volleyball (g), wrestling (b); intramural: basketball (b,g); coed interscholastic: physical fitness, swimming and diving, weight training; coed intramural: fitness. 1 PE instructor, 2 coaches.
Computers Computers are regularly used in career exploration, college planning, creative writing, French, history, journalism, library, mathematics, newspaper, science, technology, yearbook classes. Computer network features include on-campus library services, Internet access, wireless campus network, Internet filtering or blocking technology. Campus intranet is available to students. Students grades are available online. The school has a published electronic and media policy.
Contact Mrs. Becky Rothman, Director of Admissions. 615-577-1216. Fax: 615-883-2998. E-mail: rrothman@dcanet.org. Web site: www.dcanet.org.

DONNA KLEIN JEWISH ACADEMY

21010 95th Avenue South
Boca Raton, Florida 33428-1524

Head of School: Stephen Thompson, PhD

General Information Coeducational day college-preparatory, religious studies, and bilingual studies school, affiliated with Jewish faith. Grades K–12. Founded: 1979. Setting: suburban. 32-acre campus. 2 buildings on campus. Approved or accredited by Association of Independent Schools of Florida, Florida Council of Independent Schools, French Ministry of Education, National Independent Private Schools Association, Southern Association of Colleges and Schools, and Florida Department of Education. Languages of instruction: English and Hebrew. Total enrollment: 708. Upper school average class size: 13. Upper school faculty-student ratio: 1:4.

Upper School Student Profile Grade 6: 70 students (33 boys, 37 girls); Grade 7: 59 students (28 boys, 31 girls); Grade 8: 49 students (24 boys, 25 girls); Grade 9: 29 students (12 boys, 17 girls); Grade 10: 12 students (8 boys, 4 girls); Grade 11: 21 students (11 boys, 10 girls); Grade 12: 22 students (9 boys, 13 girls). 100% of students are Jewish.

Faculty School total: 25. In upper school: 10 men, 10 women; 17 have advanced degrees.

Subjects Offered Advanced biology, advanced chemistry, advanced math, Advanced Placement courses, art, baseball, basketball, Bible studies, biology, calculus, chemistry, college counseling, computer programming, computer tools, debate, drama, economics, English, English language and composition-AP, English literature and composition-AP, environmental science, environmental science-AP, geometry, government, Hebrew, honors English, honors geometry, honors U.S. history, honors world history, Jewish history, Jewish studies, journalism, Judaic studies, literature and composition-AP, physical education, pre-calculus, SAT preparation, Spanish, statistics-AP, theater production, U.S. government and politics, U.S. history-AP, visual arts, world history, world history-AP, writing, yearbook.

Graduation Requirements Electives, English, foreign language, history, Judaic studies, mathematics, physical education (includes health), science, writing, Community Service hours that vary per grade.

Special Academic Programs 7 Advanced Placement exams for which test preparation is offered; study at local college for college credit.

College Admission Counseling 20 students graduated in 2008; all went to college, including Boston University; Florida State University; University of Central Florida; University of Florida.

Student Life Upper grades have specified standards of dress, student council, honor system. Discipline rests equally with students and faculty. Attendance at religious services is required.

Tuition and Aid Day student tuition: $15,980. Tuition installment plan (Key Tuition Payment Plan, FACTS Tuition Payment Plan, monthly payment plans, individually arranged payment plans). Need-based scholarship grants available. In 2008–09, 25% of upper-school students received aid.

Admissions Traditional secondary-level entrance grade is 9. For fall 2008, 15 students applied for upper-level admission, 4 were accepted, 4 enrolled. SSAT required. Deadline for receipt of application materials: none. Application fee required: $115. On-campus interview required.

Athletics Interscholastic: baseball (boys), basketball (b,g), cross-country running (b,g), soccer (b,g), tennis (b,g), volleyball (g); intramural: basketball (b,g), cheering (g), soccer (b,g); coed interscholastic: cross-country running, soccer, tennis; coed intramural: dance team, fitness, scuba diving, self defense, soccer, swimming and diving, tennis, weight lifting, weight training. 2 PE instructors, 2 coaches.

Computers Computers are regularly used in all classes. Computer network features include Internet access, wireless campus network. Students grades are available online. The school has a published electronic and media policy.

Contact Mrs. Jodi Orshan, Assistant Director of Admissions High School. 561-558-2583. Fax: 561-558-2581. E-mail: orshanj@dkja.org. Web site: www.dkja.org.

DOWLING CATHOLIC HIGH SCHOOL

1400 Buffalo Road
West Des Moines, Iowa 50265

Head of School: Dr. Jerry M. Deegan

General Information Coeducational day college-preparatory, general academic, arts, business, religious studies, bilingual studies, technology, Performing Arts, and Advanced Placement school, affiliated with Roman Catholic Church. Grades 9–12. Founded: 1918. Setting: suburban. 60-acre campus. 1 building on campus. Approved or accredited by North Central Association of Colleges and Schools and Iowa Department of Education. Endowment: $9 million. Total enrollment: 1,234. Upper school average class size: 20. Upper school faculty-student ratio: 1:16.

Upper School Student Profile 96% of students are Roman Catholic.

Faculty School total: 85. In upper school: 40 men, 45 women; 44 have advanced degrees.

Subjects Offered 20th century world history, accounting, ACT preparation, acting, advanced chemistry, advanced computer applications, advanced math, Advanced Placement courses, advertising design, algebra, American government, American government-AP, American history, American history-AP, American literature, American literature-AP, applied arts, aquatics, art, art history, athletics, band, baseball, Basic programming, biology, biology-AP, brass choir, British literature, business, business communications, business law, calculus, calculus-AP, career and personal planning, career planning, career/college preparation, ceramics, chamber groups, cheerleading, chemistry, chemistry-AP, choir, choral music, chorus, church history, college counseling, college planning, composition, composition-AP, computer applications, computer information systems, computer keyboarding, computer processing, computer programming, computers, concert band, concert choir, creative writing, digital photography, drama, economics, economics-AP, English, English composition, English language and composition-AP, English literature, environmental science, European history, European history-AP, finance, fine arts, foreign language, French, general business, general science, geography, geometry, German, government, government-AP, health, history, history-AP, honors algebra, honors English, honors geometry, honors U.S. history, honors world history, humanities, information processing, integrated math, jazz band, journalism, keyboarding, Latin, life saving, literature, literature-AP, marching band, metalworking, modern European history, newspaper, painting, personal finance, physical education, physics, physics-AP, play production, poetry, pottery, pre-algebra, pre-calculus, probability and statistics, programming, religion, SAT/ACT preparation, scuba diving, social justice, sociology, Spanish, Spanish language-AP, speech and debate, swimming, tennis, theater production, theology, U.S. government, U.S. government-AP, U.S. history, U.S. history-AP, visual arts, vocal jazz, weight training, world religions, yearbook.

Graduation Requirements Arts, business, electives, English, mathematics, reading, science, social studies (includes history), theology, Reading Across the Curriculum (RAC), 10 service hours per semester/20 per year, 10.5 credits of electives. Community service is required.

Special Academic Programs Advanced Placement exam preparation; honors section; accelerated programs; independent study; study at local college for college credit; academic accommodation for the gifted, the musically talented, and the artistically talented; remedial reading and/or remedial writing; remedial math; special instructional classes for blind students.

College Admission Counseling 295 students graduated in 2008; 290 went to college, including Creighton University; Iowa State University of Science and Technology; Loras College; The University of Iowa; University of Northern Iowa. Other: 2 went to work, 3 entered military service. Median SAT critical reading: 646, median SAT math: 653, median SAT writing: 631, median combined SAT: 643, median composite ACT: 24.

Student Life Upper grades have uniform requirement, student council, honor system. Discipline rests primarily with faculty. Attendance at religious services is required.

Summer Programs Enrichment, advancement, sports, art/fine arts, computer instruction programs offered; session focuses on advancement for the purpose of freeing up a slot in the schedule to take an elective; held on campus; accepts boys and girls; not open to students from other schools. 250 students usually enrolled. 2009 schedule: June 3 to July 1.

Tuition and Aid Day student tuition: $5374. Tuition installment plan (monthly payment plans, individually arranged payment plans). Need-based scholarship grants, paying campus jobs available. In 2008–09, 43% of upper-school students received aid. Total amount of financial aid awarded in 2008–09: $1,000,000.

Admissions Traditional secondary-level entrance grade is 9. Placement test required. Deadline for receipt of application materials: none. Application fee required: $85.

Athletics Interscholastic: aerobics/dance (girls), aquatics (b,g), baseball (b), basketball (b,g), bowling (b,g), cheering (g), cross-country running (b,g), dance team (b,g), diving (g), drill team (g), football (b), golf (b,g), hockey (b), soccer (b,g), softball (g), swimming and diving (b,g), tennis (b,g), track and field (b,g), volleyball (g), wrestling (b); coed interscholastic: cheering; coed intramural: ultimate Frisbee.

Computers Computers are regularly used in keyboarding classes. Computer network features include on-campus library services, Internet access, wireless campus network, Internet filtering or blocking technology. Computer access in designated common areas is available to students. Students grades are available online.

Contact Mrs. Tatia Eischeid, Admissions Assistant. 515-222-1047. Fax: 515-222-1056. E-mail: teischei@dowlingcatholic.org. Web site: www.dowlingcatholic.org.

DREW SCHOOL

2901 California Street
San Francisco, California 94115

Head of School: Mr. Samuel M. Cuddeback III

General Information Coeducational day college-preparatory, arts, and technology school. Grades 9–12. Founded: 1908. Setting: urban. 1-acre campus. 1 building on campus. Approved or accredited by California Association of Independent Schools, Western Association of Schools and Colleges, and California Department of Education. Member of National Association of Independent Schools and Secondary School Admission Test Board. Total enrollment: 245. Upper school average class size: 14. Upper school faculty-student ratio: 1:8.

Upper School Student Profile Grade 9: 57 students (25 boys, 32 girls); Grade 10: 58 students (31 boys, 27 girls); Grade 11: 66 students (28 boys, 38 girls); Grade 12: 64 students (31 boys, 33 girls).

Faculty School total: 32. In upper school: 17 men, 15 women; 20 have advanced degrees.

Subjects Offered Advanced chemistry, Advanced Placement courses, algebra, American literature, American sign language, analytic geometry, animation, anthropology, art, art history, arts, biology, calculus, cell biology, ceramics, chemistry,

chemistry-AP, computer animation, computer programming, computer science, computers, contemporary women writers, creative writing, drama, driver education, economics, English, ESL, fine arts, French, geometry, government/civics, mathematics, music, physical education, physics, science, social science, social studies, Spanish, studio art-AP, theater, world history, writing.
Graduation Requirements Arts and fine arts (art, music, dance, drama), English, foreign language, mathematics, physical education (includes health), science, social science, DEALL, senior project.
Special Academic Programs Advanced Placement exam preparation; honors section; independent study; study at local college for college credit; ESL (5 students enrolled).
College Admission Counseling 65 students graduated in 2007; 64 went to college, including The University of Arizona; University of California, Berkeley; University of California, Santa Barbara; University of California, Santa Cruz; University of Colorado at Boulder. Other: 1 had other specific plans.
Student Life Upper grades have student council, honor system. Discipline rests equally with students and faculty.
Tuition and Aid Day student tuition: $27,000. Tuition installment plan (Insured Tuition Payment Plan, Key Tuition Payment Plan, monthly payment plans, individually arranged payment plans, Key Education Resources). Need-based scholarship grants available. In 2007–08, 39% of upper-school students received aid. Total amount of financial aid awarded in 2007–08: $1,400,000.
Admissions Traditional secondary-level entrance grade is 9. For fall 2007, 342 students applied for upper-level admission, 77 enrolled. CTBS or ERB, ISEE or SSAT required. Deadline for receipt of application materials: January 10. Application fee required: $75. On-campus interview required.
Athletics Interscholastic: basketball (boys, girls), cross-country running (b,g), soccer (b,g), tennis (b,g), volleyball (b,g); coed interscholastic: baseball, independent competitive sports; coed intramural: baseball, basketball, bocce, bowling, climbing, cross-country running, dance, Frisbee, hiking/backpacking, indoor soccer, lacrosse, modern dance, outdoor adventure, outdoor education, physical fitness, rock climbing, soccer, table tennis, ultimate Frisbee, volleyball, weight training, yoga. 8 PE instructors, 4 coaches.
Computers Computers are regularly used in animation, graphic arts, media production, video film production classes. Computer network features include on-campus library services, online commercial services, Internet access, wireless campus network. Campus intranet and student e-mail accounts are available to students. Students grades are available online. The school has a published electronic and media policy.
Contact Ms. Elizabeth Tilden, Director of Marketing and Enrollment. 415-409-3739 Ext. 107. Fax: 415-346-0720. E-mail: et@drewschool.org. Web site: www.drewschool.org.

ANNOUNCEMENT FROM THE SCHOOL Founded in 1908 by the respected Bay Area educator John Sheehan Drew, the Drew School has grown from a one-student "coaching school" to a fully accredited coeducational college-preparatory school enrolling 250 students in grades 9 through 12. At Drew, the focus is on developing the whole student and cultivating each individual student's potential. Drew recognizes that it is not enough to prepare students for college. They must also be prepared for life, through citizenship, self-knowledge, and independent decision making. While pursuing a rigorous college-preparatory curriculum and constantly raising the bar of excellence, Drew students take part in integrative, hands-on, and experiential learning to connect what happens in the classroom with the world beyond the School. Drew's "education for life" sparks a keen desire to be an active participant in learning and personal growth, and the opportunities for self-discovery through academic and extracurricular involvement at Drew are nearly limitless. All students are encouraged to follow their passions beyond the classroom through unique programs like annual DEALL (Drew Education for Active Lifelong Learning) program, Friday Electives, and the three-week Senior Project. Drew's student to full-time faculty ratio is 8:1, and faculty members are both committed educators and caring people. They are strong allies in the learning process, and they teach beyond the curriculum—mentoring students individually and emphasizing character, values, self-confidence, and commitment to community. Every faculty member is an adviser and most coach a sports team or lead an extracurricular club. In Drew's environment of cooperation and participation, students can both develop existing gifts and explore emerging talents. The Drew faculty works together with students and parents to graduate individuals who are engaged learners, effective thinkers, skilled communicators, and morally developed citizens.

DUBAI AMERICAN ACADEMY

PO Box 32762
Dubai, United Arab Emirates

Head of School: Dr. Brian Matthews

General Information Coeducational day college-preparatory school. Grades PK–12. Founded: 1997. Setting: urban. 23-acre campus. 2 buildings on campus. Approved or accredited by European Council of International Schools, International Baccalaureate Organization, and New England Association of Schools and Colleges. Language of instruction: English. Total enrollment: 2,308. Upper school average class size: 20. Upper school faculty-student ratio: 1:12.
Faculty School total: 172. In upper school: 25 men, 24 women; 35 have advanced degrees.
Subjects Offered 20th century history, algebra, ancient world history, biology, business, chemistry, choir, computer science, digital photography, drama, economics, ESL, geometry, guidance, history, HTML design, International Baccalaureate courses, language arts, life skills, modern languages, music, physics, pre-algebra, pre-calculus, psychology, robotics, science, sociology, theory of knowledge, visual arts.
Special Academic Programs International Baccalaureate program.
College Admission Counseling 126 students graduated in 2008; 118 went to college. Other: 1 went to work, 7 had other specific plans.
Student Life Upper grades have uniform requirement, student council, honor system. Discipline rests primarily with faculty.
Tuition and Aid Day student tuition: 46,000 United Arab Emirates dirhams. Tuition installment plan (2-installment plan).
Admissions Traditional secondary-level entrance grade is 11. High School Placement Test required. Deadline for receipt of application materials: none. Application fee required: 350 United Arab Emirates dirhams.
Athletics Interscholastic: aerobics (boys, girls), aerobics/Nautilus (b,g), aquatics (b,g), badminton (b,g), ball hockey (b,g), baseball (b,g), basketball (b,g), bocce (b,g), cooperative games (b,g), cross-country running (b,g), fitness (b,g), flag football (b,g), floor hockey (b,g), Frisbee (b,g), indoor soccer (b,g), jogging (b,g), jump rope (b,g), kickball (b,g), lacrosse (b,g), life saving (b,g), Nautilus (b,g), Newcombe ball (b,g), physical fitness (b,g), physical training (b,g), rugby (b,g), running (b,g), soccer (b,g), softball (b,g), strength & conditioning (b,g), swimming and diving (b,g), touch football (b,g), track and field (b,g), ultimate Frisbee (b,g), volleyball (b,g), walking (b,g), water polo (b,g), water volleyball (b,g), weight lifting (b,g), weight training (b,g). 7 PE instructors.
Computers Computers are regularly used in all classes. Computer network features include on-campus library services, Internet access, wireless campus network, Internet filtering or blocking technology. Computer access in designated common areas is available to students. Students grades are available online.
Contact Mrs. Carla Fakhreddine, Registrar. 971-43479222. Fax: 971-43476070. E-mail: cfakhreddine@daa.sch.ae. Web site: www.gemsaa-dubai.com.

DUBLIN CHRISTIAN ACADEMY

106 Page Road
Box 521
Dublin, New Hampshire 03444

Head of School: Mr. Kevin E. Moody

General Information Coeducational boarding and day college-preparatory, arts, business, and religious studies school, affiliated with Christian faith, Baptist Church. Boarding grades 7–12, day grades K–12. Founded: 1964. Setting: rural. Nearest major city is Boston, MA. Students are housed in single-sex dormitories. 200-acre campus. 5 buildings on campus. Approved or accredited by New Hampshire Department of Education. Total enrollment: 116. Upper school average class size: 15. Upper school faculty-student ratio: 1:8.
Upper School Student Profile 41% of students are boarding students. 59% are state residents. 12 states are represented in upper school student body. 18% are international students. International students from China, Germany, and Republic of Korea. 80% of students are Christian faith, Baptist.
Faculty School total: 24. In upper school: 9 men, 11 women; 7 have advanced degrees; 17 reside on campus.
Subjects Offered Accounting, algebra, art, Bible studies, biology, business, calculus, ceramics, chemistry, chorus, computer literacy, consumer mathematics, economics, English, French, geometry, history, home economics, instrumental music, law, mathematics, music, physics, piano, religion, science, social studies, Spanish, speech, studio art, study skills, U.S. history, voice, word processing, world history.
Graduation Requirements English, foreign language, mathematics, religion (includes Bible studies and theology), science, social studies (includes history), speech.
Special Academic Programs Advanced Placement exam preparation; academic accommodation for the musically talented; remedial reading and/or remedial writing; remedial math.
College Admission Counseling 16 students graduated in 2008; 14 went to college, including Bob Jones University; Clearwater Christian College; Colorado Christian University; Liberty University; Montana State University; Texas Tech University. Other: 1 went to work, 1 entered a postgraduate year. Mean SAT critical reading: 620, mean SAT math: 560, mean composite ACT: 23.
Student Life Upper grades have uniform requirement, student council. Discipline rests primarily with faculty. Attendance at religious services is required.
Tuition and Aid Day student tuition: $6970; 7-day tuition and room/board: $13,200. Tuition installment plan (FACTS Tuition Payment Plan). Need-based scholarship grants available. In 2008–09, 20% of upper-school students received aid.
Admissions Deadline for receipt of application materials: June 15. Application fee required: $35. Interview recommended.

Athletics Interscholastic: basketball (boys, girls), soccer (b), volleyball (g); intramural: baseball (b), bicycling (b,g), cheering (g), flag football (b); coed intramural: alpine skiing, ice skating, snowboarding, softball.
Computers Computers are regularly used in accounting, business, English, foreign language, history, mathematics, music, science classes. Computer network features include on-campus library services, Internet access, Internet filtering or blocking technology.
Contact Mrs. Beth Fletcher, Admissions Secretary. 603-563-8505. Fax: 603-563-8008. E-mail: bfletcher@dublinchristian.org. Web site: www.dublinchristian.org.

DUBLIN SCHOOL

Box 522
18 Lehmann Way
Dublin, New Hampshire 03444-0522
Head of School: Richard Fox

General Information Coeducational boarding and day college-preparatory, arts, and technology school; primarily serves students with learning disabilities and individuals with Attention Deficit Disorder. Grades 9–12. Founded: 1935. Setting: rural. Nearest major city is Boston, MA. Students are housed in single-sex dormitories. 300-acre campus. 22 buildings on campus. Approved or accredited by Independent Schools of Northern New England, New England Association of Schools and Colleges, and The Association of Boarding Schools. Member of National Association of Independent Schools and Secondary School Admission Test Board. Endowment: $2.4 million. Total enrollment: 123. Upper school average class size: 10. Upper school faculty-student ratio: 1:5.
Upper School Student Profile Grade 9: 16 students (8 boys, 8 girls); Grade 10: 36 students (25 boys, 11 girls); Grade 11: 41 students (22 boys, 19 girls); Grade 12: 30 students (22 boys, 8 girls). 75% of students are boarding students. 31% are state residents. 20 states are represented in upper school student body. 25% are international students. International students from Chile, China, El Salvador, Hungary, Jamaica, and Republic of Korea; 6 other countries represented in student body.
Faculty School total: 27. In upper school: 15 men, 12 women; 18 have advanced degrees; 22 reside on campus.
Subjects Offered Acting, advanced math, African-American history, algebra, American foreign policy, American literature, anatomy and physiology, ancient world history, art, arts, biology, biology-AP, British literature, calculus, calculus-AP, carpentry, ceramics, chemistry, choir, chorus, college counseling, college placement, community service, computer education, computer literacy, computer programming, costumes and make-up, creative arts, creative dance, creative drama, cultural arts, dance performance, digital music, drama, drama performance, dramatic arts, drawing and design, electronic music, English, English composition, English literature, ESL, European civilization, European history, film history, fine arts, foreign policy, French, geology, geometry, guitar, honors U.S. history, instrumental music, Latin, library research, library skills, literature, marine biology, mathematics, modern dance, modern European history, music, music composition, music performance, music technology, music theory, musical productions, musical theater, musical theater dance, painting, personal and social education, personal development, philosophy, photography, physics, poetry, pre-algebra, pre-calculus, psychology, research, science, senior project, Shakespeare, social studies, Spanish, Spanish literature, stagecraft, statistics, student government, studio art, study skills, theater, theater arts, U.S. government and politics, U.S. history, U.S. history-AP, video film production, vocal ensemble, voice, weight training, world literature, writing, yearbook.
Graduation Requirements Art, arts, computer skills, English, general science, history, languages, mathematics, independent study in selected disciplines (for seniors), graduation requirements for honors diploma differ.
Special Academic Programs Advanced Placement exam preparation; honors section; independent study; term-away projects; domestic exchange program (with The Network Program Schools); academic accommodation for the artistically talented; programs in general development for dyslexic students; ESL (10 students enrolled).
College Admission Counseling 32 students graduated in 2007; all went to college, including Boston University; Cornell University; Indiana University Bloomington; New York University; Smith College; University of Vermont. Median SAT critical reading: 530, median SAT math: 495. 18% scored over 600 on SAT critical reading, 18% scored over 600 on SAT math.
Student Life Upper grades have specified standards of dress, student council. Discipline rests equally with students and faculty.
Tuition and Aid Day student tuition: $23,700; 7-day tuition and room/board: $39,000. Tuition installment plan (monthly payment plans). Need-based scholarship grants, need-based financial aid available. In 2007–08, 32% of upper-school students received aid. Total amount of financial aid awarded in 2007–08: $940,000.
Admissions Traditional secondary-level entrance grade is 9. For fall 2007, 169 students applied for upper-level admission, 108 were accepted, 43 enrolled. SSAT or TOEFL or SLEP required. Deadline for receipt of application materials: January 31. Application fee required: $50. Interview required.
Athletics Interscholastic: basketball (boys, girls), crew (b,g), lacrosse (b,g), snowboarding (b,g), soccer (b,g), tennis (b,g); coed interscholastic: aerobics/dance, alpine skiing, cross-country running, dance, dance squad, dance team, equestrian sports, modern dance, rowing, sailing; coed intramural: basketball, climbing, freestyle skiing, hiking/backpacking, indoor hockey, martial arts, nordic skiing, physical fitness, rock climbing, sailing, skiing (cross-country), skiing (downhill), squash, strength & conditioning, tennis, volleyball, wall climbing, weight lifting, weight training. 23 coaches, 1 athletic trainer.
Computers Computers are regularly used in all academic classes. Computer network features include on-campus library services, Internet access, wireless campus network, Internet filtering or blocking technology. Student e-mail accounts are available to students. The school has a published electronic and media policy.
Contact Sheila Bogan, Director of Admission and Financial Aid. 603-563-1233. Fax: 603-563-8671. E-mail: admission@dublinschool.org. Web site: www.dublinschool.org/.

ANNOUNCEMENT FROM THE SCHOOL Bradford D. Bates has been appointed the new Headmaster at Dublin School. Brad graduated from Belmont Hill School in 1987. He received a B.A. in history from Dartmouth College in 1991 and a master's degree in 1999. During his fourteen years at St. Andrews School (Delaware), he served as Dean of Students, Chair of the History Department, and Dorm Parent, and he also coached soccer and crew. Brad's father, Nathaniel Bates, graduated from Dublin School in 1953.

See Close-Up on page 746.

DUCHESNE ACADEMY OF THE SACRED HEART

10202 Memorial Drive
Houston, Texas 77024
Head of School: Sr. Jan Dunn, RSCJ

General Information Girls' day college-preparatory, arts, religious studies, and technology school, affiliated with Roman Catholic Church. Grades PK–12. Approved or accredited by Independent Schools Association of the Southwest, National Catholic Education Association, Texas Catholic Conference, and Texas Education Agency. Total enrollment: 685. Upper school average class size: 14.
Upper School Student Profile Grade 9: 76 students (76 girls); Grade 10: 63 students (63 girls); Grade 11: 70 students (70 girls); Grade 12: 54 students (54 girls).
Subjects Offered Algebra, American government-AP, American literature, art history, arts, band, Bible studies, bioethics, biology, British literature, calculus, calculus-AP, ceramics, chemistry, chemistry-AP, community service, composition, computer graphics, computer programming, creative writing, desktop publishing, drawing, economics, English, English literature, European history, fine arts, French, French-AP, geometry, government/civics, health, human sexuality, Internet, Latin, mathematics, music, photography, physical education, physical fitness, physics, prayer/spirituality, pre-calculus, psychology, religious studies, science, scripture, sexuality, Shakespeare, social justice, social studies, Spanish, Spanish-AP, speech, statistics, statistics-AP, studio art, theater, theater production, theology, U.S. history, U.S. history-AP, Western literature, women's studies, world history, world literature, world religions, writing.
Graduation Requirements Arts and fine arts (art, music, dance, drama), computer science, English, foreign language, history, mathematics, physical education (includes health), religion (includes Bible studies and theology), science, completion of social awareness program. Community service is required.
Special Academic Programs Advanced Placement exam preparation; honors section; independent study; domestic exchange program (with Network of Sacred Heart Schools); academic accommodation for the musically talented and the artistically talented.
College Admission Counseling 59 students graduated in 2008; 58 went to college, including Southern Methodist University; Texas A&M University; The University of Texas at Austin; University of Notre Dame; University of Southern California; Vanderbilt University. Other: 1 entered a postgraduate year. Median SAT critical reading: 650, median SAT math: 630, median SAT writing: 670, median combined SAT: 1950, median composite ACT: 28.
Summer Programs Enrichment, art/fine arts, computer instruction programs offered; session focuses on enrichment, high school credit, and math review; held on campus; accepts girls; open to students from other schools. 225 students usually enrolled. 2009 schedule: June 8 to July 24.
Tuition and Aid Day student tuition: $16,515. Tuition installment plan (monthly payment plans). Merit scholarship grants, need-based scholarship grants available. In 2008–09, 62% of upper-school students received aid; total upper-school merit-scholarship money awarded: $41,815. Total amount of financial aid awarded in 2008–09: $768,490.
Admissions Traditional secondary-level entrance grade is 9. For fall 2008, 118 students applied for upper-level admission, 75 were accepted, 33 enrolled. ISEE or Otis-Lennon School Ability Test required. Deadline for receipt of application materials: February 1. Application fee required: $80. On-campus interview required.
Athletics Interscholastic: basketball, combined training, cross-country running, dance team, diving, field hockey, golf, soccer, softball, swimming and diving, tennis, track and field, volleyball, winter soccer. 5 PE instructors, 25 coaches, 2 athletic trainers.
Computers Computers are regularly used in all academic classes. Computer network features include on-campus library services, online commercial services, Internet

access, wireless campus network, Internet filtering or blocking technology. The school has a published electronic and media policy.
Contact Mrs. Beth Speck, Director of Admission. 713-468-8211 Ext. 133. Fax: 713-465-9809. E-mail: beth.speck@duchesne.org. Web site: www.duchesne.org.

ANNOUNCEMENT FROM THE SCHOOL Facilities include a chapel; classroom buildings for Upper, Middle, and Lower Schools; a Fine Arts Building; a gymnasium; and two playing fields. The Academy boasts National Merit Finalists, Commended Scholars, Advanced Placement Scholars, and a National Achievement Scholarship Program. Duchesne offers an active sports program, as well as academic, fine arts, and technology competitions and a weekly community service commitment. Technology is integrated throughout the curriculum with state-of-the-art equipment, curriculum mapping, and laptops in grades 6–12. Duchesne Academy of the Sacred Heart is a member of the Network of Sacred Heart Schools. Contact via e-mail: admissions@duchesne.org, phone: 713-468-8211 Ext. 139, or visit the Web site at www.duchesne.org.

DUNN SCHOOL

PO Box 98
2555 West Highway 154
Los Olivos, California 93441
Head of School: Michael Beck

General Information Coeducational boarding and day college-preparatory and arts school. Boarding grades 9–12, day grades 6–12. Founded: 1957. Setting: small town. Nearest major city is Santa Barbara. Students are housed in single-sex dormitories. 57-acre campus. 15 buildings on campus. Approved or accredited by California Association of Independent Schools, National Association of Private Schools for Exceptional Children, National Independent Private Schools Association, The Association of Boarding Schools, Western Association of Schools and Colleges, and California Department of Education. Member of National Association of Independent Schools and Secondary School Admission Test Board. Endowment: $5 million. Total enrollment: 256. Upper school average class size: 14. Upper school faculty-student ratio: 1:7.
Upper School Student Profile Grade 9: 34 students (20 boys, 14 girls); Grade 10: 54 students (22 boys, 32 girls); Grade 11: 49 students (17 boys, 32 girls); Grade 12: 43 students (25 boys, 18 girls). 62% of students are boarding students. 69% are state residents. 14 states are represented in upper school student body. 22% are international students. International students from China, Ghana, Japan, Republic of Korea, Taiwan, and Thailand; 4 other countries represented in student body.
Faculty School total: 34. In upper school: 16 men, 18 women; 29 have advanced degrees; 26 reside on campus.
Subjects Offered African American studies, algebra, American history, American history-AP, art history, biology, biology-AP, calculus-AP, ceramics, chemistry, chemistry-AP, college counseling, conceptual physics, contemporary history, creative writing, economics, English, English language-AP, English literature-AP, environmental science, environmental science-AP, European history, experiential education, fine arts, French, French language-AP, guitar, human development, instrumental music, integrated math, microeconomics, music, outdoor education, photography, physics, science, social science, Spanish, Spanish language-AP, statistics and probability, statistics-AP, studio art, studio art-AP, world history.
Graduation Requirements Arts and fine arts (art, music, dance, drama), biology, chemistry, English, foreign language, history, lab science, mathematics, outdoor education, physics, science, U.S. government, U.S. history, world culture.
Special Academic Programs Advanced Placement exam preparation; honors section; independent study; special instructional classes for students with moderate to mild learning differences.
College Admission Counseling 35 students graduated in 2008; all went to college, including California Polytechnic State University, San Luis Obispo; Claremont McKenna College; University of California, Los Angeles; University of California, San Diego; University of Colorado at Boulder. Median SAT critical reading: 530, median SAT math: 585, median SAT writing: 555, median combined SAT: 1670.
Student Life Upper grades have specified standards of dress, student council, honor system. Discipline rests primarily with faculty.
Summer Programs Sports programs offered; session focuses on recreation; held on campus; accepts boys and girls; open to students from other schools. 200 students usually enrolled. 2009 schedule: June 25 to August 10.
Tuition and Aid Day student tuition: $18,650; 7-day tuition and room/board: $41,800. Tuition installment plan (Academic Management Services Plan, monthly payment plans, individually arranged payment plans, 2-payment plan). Need-based scholarship grants available. In 2008–09, 22% of upper-school students received aid. Total amount of financial aid awarded in 2008–09: $625,000.
Admissions Traditional secondary-level entrance grade is 9. For fall 2008, 140 students applied for upper-level admission, 78 were accepted, 48 enrolled. ISEE, SSAT or TOEFL required. Deadline for receipt of application materials: February 1. Application fee required: $50. Interview required.
Athletics Interscholastic: baseball (boys), basketball (b,g), football (b), lacrosse (b,g), soccer (b,g), tennis (b,g), volleyball (b,g); coed interscholastic: backpacking, canoeing/kayaking, climbing, cross-country running, dance, dance team, fitness, fitness walking, golf, kayaking, modern dance, outdoor education, physical fitness, physical training, rafting, rock climbing, strength & conditioning, swimming and diving, track and field, walking, weight lifting, weight training; coed intramural: equestrian sports, Frisbee, hiking/backpacking, horseback riding, horseshoes, indoor soccer, paddle tennis, rappelling, ropes courses, table tennis. 4 coaches, 1 athletic trainer.
Computers Computers are regularly used in art, college planning, English, history, mathematics, multimedia, music, publications, science, yearbook classes. Computer network features include on-campus library services, online commercial services, Internet access, wireless campus network, Internet filtering or blocking technology. Student e-mail accounts and computer access in designated common areas are available to students. The school has a published electronic and media policy.
Contact Ann E. Greenough, Director of Admission. 800-287-9197. Fax: 805-686-2078. E-mail: admissions@dunnschool.org. Web site: www.dunnschool.org.

ANNOUNCEMENT FROM THE SCHOOL Dunn School is an independent boarding and day school located in the Santa Ynez Valley, 30 miles northeast of Santa Barbara. The student body is composed of 110 boarding students and 78 day students. Dunn provides a personalized educational experience for students grounded in a rigorous college-preparatory curriculum. Students are assigned a faculty adviser with whom they meet four times a week. The adviser is responsible for monitoring each advisee in all academic and nonacademic areas, while remaining in close contact with parents. A personal approach to the college process is provided through the School's Personal Education Plan (PEP). The purpose of this plan is to create a curricular and co-curricular guide for the student, parents, adviser, and the college counselor as the student moves toward the goal of successful college placement. College planning involves individual appointments, group information sessions, a College Search Process class, meetings with college representatives, and preparation for the SAT and the TOEFL. All Dunn graduates are well prepared for the college of their choice. As a community, we are committed to the values of honesty, trust, and mutual respect, and leadership and character development are woven into all aspects of school life. Dunn's Outdoor Education Program provides an experiential approach to instilling these values. Students participate in class trips with the goal of fostering greater self-awareness through challenges and experiences in the outdoors. Dunn School has a Learning Skills (LS) Program that accommodates a select number of students with minimal, diagnosed language and learning difficulties. It is the goal of the LS Program to offer support and skills, building tools necessary for success in the Dunn School college-preparatory environment and beyond. LS students receive instruction in time management, organization, and study skills, and they do not receive accommodations that alter the content of course material.

DURHAM ACADEMY

3601 Ridge Road
Durham, North Carolina 27705
Head of School: Edward Costello

General Information Coeducational day college-preparatory school. Grades PK–12. Founded: 1933. Setting: suburban. 75-acre campus. 11 buildings on campus. Approved or accredited by North Carolina Association of Independent Schools, Southern Association of Colleges and Schools, Southern Association of Independent Schools, and North Carolina Department of Education. Member of National Association of Independent Schools and Secondary School Admission Test Board. Endowment: $9.6 million. Total enrollment: 1,145. Upper school average class size: 15. Upper school faculty-student ratio: 1:12.
Upper School Student Profile Grade 9: 98 students (47 boys, 51 girls); Grade 10: 96 students (49 boys, 47 girls); Grade 11: 98 students (49 boys, 49 girls); Grade 12: 100 students (48 boys, 52 girls).
Faculty School total: 156. In upper school: 26 men, 24 women; 39 have advanced degrees.
Subjects Offered Accounting, algebra, American history, American literature, Ancient Greek, art, art history, astronomy, biology, calculus, ceramics, chemistry, community service, computer graphics, computer programming, computer science, creative writing, dance, drama, ecology, economics, English, English literature, environmental science, fine arts, finite math, French, geometry, German, history, Latin, mathematics, music, outdoor education, physical education, physics, psychology, science, social studies, Spanish, statistics, theater.
Graduation Requirements Arts and fine arts (art, music, dance, drama), computer science, English, foreign language, mathematics, outdoor education, physical education (includes health), science, senior project, social studies (includes history), community service hours required for graduation.
Special Academic Programs Advanced Placement exam preparation; honors section; independent study; special instructional classes for students with learning disabilities and Attention Deficit Disorder.
College Admission Counseling 94 students graduated in 2008; 93 went to college, including Duke University; East Carolina University; Elon University; Harvard

University; North Carolina State University; The University of North Carolina at Chapel Hill. Other: 1 had other specific plans. Mean SAT critical reading: 636, mean SAT math: 644, mean SAT writing: 653.

Student Life Upper grades have specified standards of dress, student council, honor system. Discipline rests equally with students and faculty.

Summer Programs Enrichment, computer instruction programs offered; session focuses on academic enrichment, non-academic activities; held on campus; accepts boys and girls; open to students from other schools. 550 students usually enrolled. 2009 schedule: June 22 to July 31. Application deadline: none.

Tuition and Aid Day student tuition: $18,330. Tuition installment plan (Key Tuition Payment Plan, monthly payment plans). Need-based scholarship grants available. In 2008–09, 9% of upper-school students received aid. Total amount of financial aid awarded in 2008–09: $433,350.

Admissions Traditional secondary-level entrance grade is 9. For fall 2008, 87 students applied for upper-level admission, 42 were accepted, 32 enrolled. ISEE required. Deadline for receipt of application materials: January 16. Application fee required: $55. Interview required.

Athletics Interscholastic: baseball (boys), basketball (b,g), cross-country running (b,g), field hockey (g), golf (b), lacrosse (b,g), soccer (b,g), softball (g), swimming and diving (b,g), tennis (b,g), track and field (b,g), volleyball (g), weight training (b,g); intramural: dance team (g); coed interscholastic: golf, outdoor adventure, outdoor education, weight training; coed intramural: indoor soccer, martial arts, modern dance, physical fitness, physical training, winter soccer. 1 PE instructor, 3 coaches, 1 athletic trainer.

Computers Computers are regularly used in all classes. Computer network features include on-campus library services, online commercial services, Internet access, wireless campus network, Internet filtering or blocking technology. Student e-mail accounts and computer access in designated common areas are available to students. The school has a published electronic and media policy.

Contact Victoria Muradi, Director of Admission and Financial Aid. 919-493-5787. Fax: 919-489-4893. E-mail: admissions@da.org. Web site: www.da.org.

DWIGHT-ENGLEWOOD SCHOOL

315 East Palisade Avenue
Englewood, New Jersey 07631-0489

Head of School: Dr. Rodney V. De Jarnett

General Information Coeducational day college-preparatory, arts, and technology school. Grades PK–12. Founded: 1889. Setting: suburban. Nearest major city is New York, NY. 41-acre campus. 13 buildings on campus. Approved or accredited by Middle States Association of Colleges and Schools, New Jersey Association of Independent Schools, and New Jersey Department of Education. Member of National Association of Independent Schools and Secondary School Admission Test Board. Endowment: $10 million. Total enrollment: 959. Upper school average class size: 15. Upper school faculty-student ratio: 1:9.

Upper School Student Profile Grade 9: 116 students (54 boys, 62 girls); Grade 10: 114 students (62 boys, 52 girls); Grade 11: 111 students (61 boys, 50 girls); Grade 12: 106 students (54 boys, 52 girls).

Faculty School total: 130. In upper school: 32 men, 39 women; 48 have advanced degrees.

Subjects Offered Acting, advanced chemistry, advanced math, Advanced Placement courses, advanced studio art-AP, American government-AP, American history, American history-AP, American literature-AP, analysis, analysis and differential calculus, analysis of data, analytic geometry, ancient history, architecture, art, art history, art history-AP, bell choir, bioethics, bioethics, DNA and culture, biology, biology-AP, calculus-AP, ceramics, chemistry-AP, choir, chorus, community service, computer graphics, computer science-AP, concert bell choir, creative writing, critical thinking, data analysis, digital imaging, digital photography, drama, dramatic arts, drawing, drawing and design, economics and history, engineering, English, English language and composition-AP, English language-AP, English literature, English literature and composition-AP, English literature-AP, English-AP, environmental science, environmental science-AP, ethics, European history, evolution, fine arts, foreign language, fractal geometry, fractals, French, French language-AP, French literature-AP, French-AP, general science, genetics, geometry, government and politics-AP, government-AP, health, health education, history, history of jazz, independent study, Japanese, language-AP, Latin, law, literature and composition-AP, mathematics, orchestra, organic chemistry, painting, photography, physical education, physics-AP, printmaking, psychology, robotics, science, social studies, Spanish, statistics-AP, technology, world history.

Graduation Requirements Arts and fine arts (art, music, dance, drama), English, ethics, foreign language, mathematics, physical education (includes health), science, social studies (includes history), technology. Community service is required.

Special Academic Programs Advanced Placement exam preparation; honors section; independent study; study abroad.

College Admission Counseling 126 students graduated in 2008; all went to college, including Boston University; Columbia University; Cornell University; New York University; The George Washington University; University of Pennsylvania. Mean SAT critical reading: 652, mean SAT math: 648, mean SAT writing: 668. 44% scored over 600 on SAT critical reading, 54% scored over 600 on SAT math, 60% scored over 600 on SAT writing.

Student Life Upper grades have student council. Discipline rests primarily with faculty.

Summer Programs Remediation, enrichment, advancement, ESL, sports, art/fine arts, computer instruction programs offered; session focuses on academics and sports; held on campus; accepts boys and girls; open to students from other schools. 1,000 students usually enrolled. 2009 schedule: June to August. Application deadline: none.

Tuition and Aid Day student tuition: $25,303. Tuition installment plan (Key Tuition Payment Plan, monthly payment plans). Need-based scholarship grants, need-based loans, middle-income loans available. In 2008–09, 14% of upper-school students received aid. Total amount of financial aid awarded in 2008–09: $1,658,500.

Admissions Traditional secondary-level entrance grade is 9. For fall 2008, 206 students applied for upper-level admission, 113 were accepted, 61 enrolled. ISEE or SSAT required. Deadline for receipt of application materials: December 31. Application fee required: $65. On-campus interview required.

Athletics Interscholastic: baseball (boys), basketball (b,g), cross-country running (b,g), field hockey (g), football (b), golf (b,g), lacrosse (b,g), soccer (b,g), softball (g), tennis (b,g), track and field (b,g), volleyball (g), wrestling (b); intramural: cheering (g), fencing (b,g), hockey (b). 10 PE instructors, 15 coaches, 1 athletic trainer.

Computers Computers are regularly used in art, English, history, mathematics, science, technology classes. Computer network features include on-campus library services, online commercial services, Internet access, wireless campus network, Internet filtering or blocking technology, tablet PC program, Taub Tech Center. Student e-mail accounts and computer access in designated common areas are available to students. Students grades are available online. The school has a published electronic and media policy.

Contact Ms. Sherronda L. Oliver, Director of Enrollment and External Relations. 201-569-9500 Ext. 3500. Fax: 201-568-9451. E-mail: olives@d-e.org. Web site: www.d-e.org.

THE DWIGHT SCHOOL

291 Central Park West
New York, New York 10024

See Close-Up on page 748.

EAGLEBROOK SCHOOL

Deerfield, Massachusetts
See Junior Boarding Schools section.

EAGLE HILL SCHOOL

Greenwich, Connecticut
See Special Needs Schools section.

EAGLE HILL SCHOOL

Hardwick, Massachusetts
See Special Needs Schools section.

EAGLE HILL-SOUTHPORT

Southport, Connecticut
See Special Needs Schools section.

EAST CATHOLIC HIGH SCHOOL

115 New State Road
Manchester, Connecticut 06042-1898

Head of School: Mr. Christian Joseph Cashman

General Information Coeducational day college-preparatory, arts, and religious studies school, affiliated with Roman Catholic Church. Grades 9–12. Founded: 1961. Setting: suburban. Nearest major city is Hartford. 47-acre campus. 2 buildings on campus. Approved or accredited by Connecticut Association of Independent Schools, New England Association of Schools and Colleges, and Connecticut Department of Education. Total enrollment: 739. Upper school average class size: 19. Upper school faculty-student ratio: 1:13.

Upper School Student Profile Grade 9: 177 students (89 boys, 88 girls); Grade 10: 189 students (92 boys, 97 girls); Grade 11: 181 students (89 boys, 92 girls); Grade 12: 192 students (100 boys, 92 girls). 80% of students are Roman Catholic.

Faculty School total: 58. In upper school: 21 men, 37 women; 52 have advanced degrees.

Subjects Offered Algebra, American history, American history-AP, American literature, American literature-AP, anatomy, art, Bible studies, biology, biology-AP, business, calculus, calculus-AP, chemistry, chemistry-AP, computer programming, computer science, digital photography, economics, English, English literature, English literature-AP, environmental science, ethics, European history, expository writing, French, geography, geometry, government/civics, grammar, health, history, Latin, mathematics, music, music theory, music theory-AP, philosophy, physical education,

physics, physiology, psychology, religion, science, sculpture, social studies, sociology, Spanish, theology, trigonometry, world history, world literature, writing.
Graduation Requirements English, foreign language, health and wellness, mathematics, physical education (includes health), religion (includes Bible studies and theology), science, social studies (includes history), study skills.
Special Academic Programs Advanced Placement exam preparation; honors section.
College Admission Counseling 171 students graduated in 2008; 158 went to college, including Assumption College; Boston University; Central Connecticut State University; Eastern Connecticut State University; University of Connecticut; University of Hartford. Other: 1 went to work, 1 entered a postgraduate year, 1 had other specific plans.
Student Life Upper grades have uniform requirement, student council. Discipline rests primarily with faculty. Attendance at religious services is required.
Tuition and Aid Day student tuition: $9460. Tuition installment plan (FACTS Tuition Payment Plan, August prepayment discount plan). Tuition reduction for siblings, merit scholarship grants, need-based scholarship grants available.
Admissions Traditional secondary-level entrance grade is 9. High School Placement Test required. Deadline for receipt of application materials: none. Application fee required: $20.
Athletics Interscholastic: baseball (boys), basketball (b,g), cheering (g), cross-country running (b,g), dance team (g), football (b), golf (b,g), ice hockey (b), lacrosse (b,g), soccer (b,g), softball (g), swimming and diving (g), tennis (b,g), track and field (b,g), volleyball (g), weight lifting (b), winter (indoor) track (b,g), wrestling (b); intramural: volleyball (g); coed interscholastic: indoor track, table tennis. 2 PE instructors, 40 coaches, 1 athletic trainer.
Computers Computers are regularly used in all academic classes. Computer resources include on-campus library services, online commercial services, Internet access, wireless campus network, Internet filtering or blocking technology. The school has a published electronic and media policy.
Contact Ms. Jacqueline Gryphon, Director of Recruitment and Admissions. 860-649-5336 Ext. 238. Fax: 860-649-7191. E-mail: gryphonj@echs.com. Web site: www.echs.com.

EASTERN CHRISTIAN HIGH SCHOOL

50 Oakwood Avenue
North Haledon, New Jersey 07508

Head of School: Mr. Thomas Dykhouse

General Information Coeducational day college-preparatory, general academic, arts, and technology school, affiliated with Christian Reformed Church. Grades PK–12. Founded: 1892. Setting: suburban. Nearest major city is New York, NY. 27-acre campus. 1 building on campus. Approved or accredited by Association of Christian Schools International, Association of Independent Schools of Greater Washington, Christian Schools International, Middle States Association of Colleges and Schools, and New Jersey Department of Education. Endowment: $6 million. Total enrollment: 827. Upper school average class size: 20. Upper school faculty-student ratio: 1:10.
Upper School Student Profile Grade 9: 79 students (33 boys, 46 girls); Grade 10: 98 students (41 boys, 57 girls); Grade 11: 93 students (39 boys, 54 girls); Grade 12: 81 students (38 boys, 43 girls). 40% of students are members of Christian Reformed Church.
Faculty School total: 85. In upper school: 11 men, 22 women; 21 have advanced degrees.
Subjects Offered Accounting, advanced biology, algebra, American history, American legal systems, American literature, art, band, Bible studies, biology, business, business skills, calculus, chemistry, chorus, community service, composition, computer programming, computer science, computer-aided design, contemporary math, creative writing, driver education, English, English composition, English literature, entrepreneurship, ESL, European history, fine arts, French, geometry, government/civics, health, history, humanities, journalism, Latin, mathematics, music, orchestra, personal finance, physical education, physical science, physics, pre-calculus, psychology, science, social studies, sociology, Spanish, study skills, technical education, trigonometry, Web site design, world history, writing, writing workshop, yearbook.
Graduation Requirements Arts and fine arts (art, music, dance, drama), Bible, English, foreign language, lab science, leadership skills, mathematics, physical education (includes health), social studies (includes history), 50 hours of community service.
Special Academic Programs 1 Advanced Placement exam for which test preparation is offered; honors section; independent study; academic accommodation for the gifted, the musically talented, and the artistically talented; remedial reading and/or remedial writing; remedial math; programs in English, mathematics for dyslexic students; ESL (20 students enrolled).
College Admission Counseling 88 students graduated in 2008; 84 went to college, including Calvin College; Liberty University; Messiah College; Montclair State University; Palm Beach Atlantic University; William Paterson University of New Jersey. Other: 1 entered military service, 3 had other specific plans. Median SAT critical reading: 540, median SAT math: 510, median SAT writing: 510. Mean composite ACT: 20. 28% scored over 600 on SAT critical reading, 24% scored over 600 on SAT math, 25% scored over 600 on SAT writing.
Student Life Upper grades have specified standards of dress, student council. Discipline rests primarily with faculty. Attendance at religious services is required.
Tuition and Aid Day student tuition: $10,850. Tuition installment plan (SMART Tuition Payment Plan, monthly payment plans). Tuition reduction for siblings, need-based scholarship grants available.
Admissions Traditional secondary-level entrance grade is 9. For fall 2008, 73 students applied for upper-level admission, 45 were accepted, 44 enrolled. Deadline for receipt of application materials: none. Application fee required: $75. On-campus interview required.
Athletics Interscholastic: baseball (boys), basketball (b,g), bowling (b,g), cheering (g), cross-country running (b,g), golf (b,g), soccer (b,g), softball (g), tennis (b,g), track and field (b,g), volleyball (g); intramural: aerobics (b,g), badminton (b,g), basketball (b,g), fitness walking (b,g), flag football (b,g), flagball (b,g), football (b,g), Frisbee (b,g), golf (b,g), gymnastics (b,g), indoor soccer (b,g), lacrosse (b,g), paddle tennis (b,g), physical fitness (b,g), roller hockey (b,g), running (b,g), skateboarding (b,g), skiing (downhill) (b,g), soccer (b,g), softball (b,g), street hockey (b,g), table tennis (b,g), volleyball (b,g), weight lifting (b,g); coed intramural: aerobics, badminton, baseball, basketball, fitness walking, flag football, flagball, football, golf, gymnastics, indoor soccer, lacrosse, paddle tennis, physical fitness, roller hockey, running, skateboarding, skiing (downhill), soccer, softball, street hockey, table tennis, volleyball, weight lifting. 2 PE instructors, 18 coaches.
Computers Computers are regularly used in all academic classes. Computer network features include on-campus library services, Internet access, wireless campus network, Internet filtering or blocking technology, Microsoft Office, Microsoft Visual Studio, AutoCAD LT 2000, Adobe Photoshop, Adobe GoLive, Adobe Illustrator, Adobe LiveMotion, Macromedia Dreamweaver, Adobe Premiere, Lego Mindstorms NXT. Computer access in designated common areas is available to students. Students grades are available online. The school has a published electronic and media policy.
Contact Mr. G. Anthony Cantalupo, Admission Director. 973-427-6244 Ext. 207. Fax: 973-427-9775. E-mail: admissions@easternchristian.org. Web site: www.easternchristian.org.

EASTERN MENNONITE HIGH SCHOOL

801 Parkwood Drive
Harrisonburg, Virginia 22802

Head of School: Mr. Paul G. Leaman

General Information Coeducational day college-preparatory, general academic, arts, and religious studies school, affiliated with Mennonite Church. Grades K–12. Founded: 1917. Setting: small town. Nearest major city is Washington, DC. 24-acre campus. 1 building on campus. Approved or accredited by Southern Association of Colleges and Schools, Virginia Association of Independent Schools, and Virginia Department of Education. Endowment: $3 million. Total enrollment: 381. Upper school average class size: 20. Upper school faculty-student ratio: 1:10.
Upper School Student Profile Grade 9: 44 students (24 boys, 20 girls); Grade 10: 55 students (31 boys, 24 girls); Grade 11: 56 students (25 boys, 31 girls); Grade 12: 49 students (21 boys, 28 girls). 62% of students are Mennonite.
Faculty School total: 50. In upper school: 21 men, 14 women; 18 have advanced degrees.
Subjects Offered Acting, advanced math, algebra, American government, American history, American literature, analysis, applied music, art, art history, band, bell choir, Bible studies, biology, British literature, British literature (honors), business, business skills, ceramics, chemistry, Chinese, Chinese studies, choir, choral music, chorus, Christian and Hebrew scripture, Christian doctrine, Christian ethics, Christian studies, Christian testament, Christianity, church history, community service, computer education, computer science, concert choir, consumer mathematics, creative writing, desktop publishing, drama, drawing, driver education, earth science, economics, engineering, English, English composition, English literature, family and consumer sciences, fiction, fine arts, food and nutrition, food science, French, general science, geography, geometry, government, grammar, guitar, handbells, health, health education, history, home economics, honors English, human development, industrial arts, industrial technology, instrumental music, interior design, keyboarding/computer, Latin, mathematics, mechanical drawing, music, music composition, music theory, novel, oil painting, orchestra, outdoor education, painting, photography, physical education, physical science, physics, poetry, pottery, pre-algebra, religion, religious education, research skills, science, sculpture, sewing, shop, social science, social studies, sociology, Spanish, speech, speech communications, stained glass, study skills, theater, typing, U.S. government, U.S. history, vocal music, voice, water color painting, woodworking, world cultures, world history, writing.
Graduation Requirements Arts and fine arts (art, music, dance, drama), electives, English, foreign language, home economics, keyboarding/computer, mathematics, physical education (includes health), religion (includes Bible studies and theology), science, social studies (includes history), technical arts.
Special Academic Programs Advanced Placement exam preparation; independent study; study at local college for college credit; academic accommodation for the gifted; remedial reading and/or remedial writing; remedial math.
College Admission Counseling 49 students graduated in 2008; 44 went to college, including Eastern Mennonite University; James Madison University; New York University. Other: 2 went to work, 3 had other specific plans. Median SAT critical reading: 580, median SAT math: 590, median SAT writing: 560, median combined

SAT: 1710. 47% scored over 600 on SAT critical reading, 43% scored over 600 on SAT math, 35% scored over 600 on SAT writing, 37% scored over 1800 on combined SAT.
Student Life Upper grades have specified standards of dress, student council. Discipline rests primarily with faculty. Attendance at religious services is required.
Tuition and Aid Day student tuition: $5494–$11,787. Tuition installment plan (monthly payment plans, individually arranged payment plans). Need-based scholarship grants available. In 2008–09, 19% of upper-school students received aid. Total amount of financial aid awarded in 2008–09: $129,736.
Admissions Traditional secondary-level entrance grade is 9. For fall 2008, 33 students applied for upper-level admission, 30 were accepted, 27 enrolled. Any standardized test required. Deadline for receipt of application materials: none. Application fee required: $25. Interview recommended.
Athletics Interscholastic: basketball (boys, girls), cheering (g), cross-country running (b,g), golf (b), soccer (b,g), softball (g), tennis (b,g), track and field (b,g), volleyball (g); intramural: baseball (b), basketball (b,g), soccer (g), wrestling (b); coed interscholastic: baseball; coed intramural: volleyball. 3 PE instructors, 9 coaches, 2 athletic trainers.
Computers Computers are regularly used in business skills, foreign language, French, graphic design, industrial technology, library, literary magazine, mathematics, music, publications, research skills, science, social science, social studies, Web site design, word processing, yearbook classes. Computer resources include on-campus library services, Internet access. Computer access in designated common areas is available to students. Students grades are available online.
Contact Jean Smucker Fisher, Director of Admissions. 540-432-4521. Fax: 540-432-4528. E-mail: fisherj@emhs.net. Web site: www.emhs.net.

EASTSIDE CATHOLIC SCHOOL

232-228th Avenue SE
Sammamish, Washington 98074

Head of School: James Kubacki

General Information Coeducational day college-preparatory, arts, religious studies, and technology school, affiliated with Roman Catholic Church. Grades 6–12. Founded: 1980. Setting: suburban. 50-acre campus. 2 buildings on campus. Approved or accredited by National Catholic Education Association, Northwest Association of Schools and Colleges, Pacific Northwest Association of Independent Schools, and Washington Department of Education. Total enrollment: 850. Upper school average class size: 20. Upper school faculty-student ratio: 1:14.
Upper School Student Profile Grade 6: 87 students (49 boys, 38 girls); Grade 7: 75 students (39 boys, 36 girls); Grade 8: 75 students (44 boys, 31 girls); Grade 9: 184 students (100 boys, 84 girls); Grade 10: 163 students (92 boys, 71 girls); Grade 11: 128 students (70 boys, 58 girls); Grade 12: 141 students (77 boys, 64 girls). 65% of students are Roman Catholic.
Faculty School total: 59. In upper school: 25 men, 34 women; 37 have advanced degrees.
Subjects Offered Advanced Placement courses, algebra, American government, American history, American literature, anatomy and physiology, art, ASB Leadership, athletic training, band, biology, biology-AP, British literature, calculus, calculus-AP, calligraphy, campus ministry, Catholic belief and practice, ceramics, chemistry, chemistry-AP, choir, church history, community service, computers, contemporary issues, creative writing, debate, digital photography, drama, drawing, economics, English, English literature, French, French-AP, geometry, government and politics-AP, graphic design, health, history, honors algebra, honors English, honors geometry, honors U.S. history, honors world history, journalism, law, math analysis, music, painting, performing arts, physical education, physics, religious education, social justice, Spanish, Spanish-AP, speech and debate, studio art, theology, trigonometry, Web site design, world history, yearbook.
Graduation Requirements Arts and fine arts (art, music, dance, drama), business education, English, foreign language, mathematics, physical education (includes health), science, social science, theology, 100 hours of community service (over 4 years).
Special Academic Programs Advanced Placement exam preparation; honors section; study at local college for college credit.
College Admission Counseling 120 students graduated in 2008; 118 went to college, including Washington State University.
Student Life Upper grades have specified standards of dress, student council, honor system. Discipline rests primarily with faculty. Attendance at religious services is required.
Tuition and Aid Day student tuition: $15,252. Tuition installment plan (monthly payment plans). Need-based scholarship grants available. In 2008–09, 26% of upper-school students received aid. Total amount of financial aid awarded in 2008–09: $1,540,000.
Admissions Traditional secondary-level entrance grade is 9. Achievement/Aptitude/Writing or ISEE required. Deadline for receipt of application materials: January 15. Application fee required: $25. Interview required.
Athletics Interscholastic: baseball (boys), basketball (b,g), cheering (g), cross-country running (b,g), drill team (g), football (b), golf (b,g), lacrosse (b,g), soccer (b,g), softball (g), swimming and diving (b,g), tennis (b,g), track and field (b,g), volleyball (g), wrestling (b); coed interscholastic: Special Olympics; coed intramural: strength & conditioning, weight lifting, weight training. 2 PE instructors, 43 coaches, 2 athletic trainers.
Computers Computers are regularly used in business education, graphic design, technology, Web site design, yearbook classes. Computer network features include on-campus library services, online commercial services, Internet access, wireless campus network, Internet filtering or blocking technology. Students grades are available online.
Contact Helene Johnson, Director of Admission. 425-295-3014. Fax: 425-392-5160. E-mail: hjohnson@eastsidecatholic.org. Web site: www.eastsidecatholic.org.

EASTSIDE CHRISTIAN ACADEMY

1320 Abbeydale Drive SE
Calgary, Alberta T2A 7L8, Canada

Head of School: Dr. Frank Moody

General Information Coeducational boarding and day and distance learning college-preparatory, general academic, religious studies, and music school, affiliated with Christian faith. Grades K–12. Distance learning grades 10–12. Founded: 1999. Setting: urban. 4-acre campus. 1 building on campus. Approved or accredited by Association of Independent Schools and Colleges of Alberta, National Christian School Association, and Alberta Department of Education. Language of instruction: English. Total enrollment: 100. Upper school average class size: 30. Upper school faculty-student ratio: 1:25.
Upper School Student Profile 100% of students are Christian faith.
Faculty School total: 4. In upper school: 2 men, 2 women; 1 has an advanced degree.
Subjects Offered Algebra, art, Bible studies, biology, business, business mathematics, Canadian geography, Canadian history, career/college preparation, chemistry, church history, civics, computer literacy, economics, English, etymology, French, geometry, Greek, Life of Christ, literature, music, natural history, physical education, physical science, physics, Spanish, speech, typing, world geography, world history.
Graduation Requirements Algebra, Bible studies, biology, business education, Canadian geography, Canadian history, chemistry, Christian scripture, Christian testament, church history, concert band, data processing, economics, electives, English, etymology, French, geometry, German, mathematics, music, physical education (includes health), physical science, physics, religious education, social studies (includes history), Spanish, speech and debate, vocal music, volleyball, world geography, world history.
Special Academic Programs Honors section; accelerated programs; independent study; study at local college for college credit; academic accommodation for the gifted and the musically talented; remedial reading and/or remedial writing; remedial math.
College Admission Counseling 6 students graduated in 2008. Other: 6 went to work.
Student Life Upper grades have uniform requirement, student council, honor system. Discipline rests primarily with faculty. Attendance at religious services is required.
Summer Programs Remediation, advancement programs offered; session focuses on remediation/make-up; held on campus; accepts boys and girls; not open to students from other schools. 10 students usually enrolled. 2009 schedule: July 1 to August 15. Application deadline: May 15.
Tuition and Aid Day student tuition: CAN$3600. Tuition installment plan (monthly payment plans, individually arranged payment plans). Tuition reduction for siblings, bursaries, need-based scholarship grants available.
Admissions Traditional secondary-level entrance grade is 10. Traditional secondary-level entrance age is 16. For fall 2008, 21 students applied for upper-level admission, 21 were accepted, 21 enrolled. Cognitive Abilities Test, Diagnostic Achievement Battery-2 (for applicants from non-U.S. curriculum) and school placement exam required. Deadline for receipt of application materials: March 1. Application fee required: CAN$60. On-campus interview required.
Athletics Interscholastic: badminton (boys, girls), ball hockey (b,g), basketball (b,g), volleyball (b,g); coed interscholastic: soccer; coed intramural: badminton, ball hockey, basketball, floor hockey, volleyball. 1 PE instructor, 2 coaches.
Computers Computers are regularly used in career exploration, data processing, economics, English, French, geography, history, information technology, keyboarding, literacy, mathematics, media, reading, religion, religious studies, social studies, Spanish, speech, typing, word processing classes. Computer network features include Internet access, wireless campus network, Internet filtering or blocking technology. Computer access in designated common areas is available to students. Students grades are available online. The school has a published electronic and media policy.
Contact LaDawn Torgerson, Secretary. 403-569-1003 Ext. 200. Fax: 403-569-1023. E-mail: admin@ecaab.ca.

EASTSIDE COLLEGE PREPARATORY SCHOOL

1041 Myrtle Street
East Palo Alto, California 94303

Head of School: Chris Bischof

General Information Coeducational boarding and day college-preparatory school. Grades 6–12. Founded: 1996. Setting: suburban. Nearest major city is Oakland. Students are housed in single-sex dormitories. 6-acre campus. 7 buildings on campus. Approved or accredited by Western Association of Schools and Colleges and

California Department of Education. Total enrollment: 222. Upper school average class size: 18. Upper school faculty-student ratio: 1:8.
Upper School Student Profile Grade 9: 47 students (18 boys, 29 girls); Grade 10: 45 students (18 boys, 27 girls); Grade 11: 39 students (19 boys, 20 girls); Grade 12: 33 students (12 boys, 21 girls). 13% of students are boarding students. 100% are state residents. 1 state is represented in upper school student body.
Faculty School total: 30. In upper school: 8 men, 14 women; 20 have advanced degrees; 3 reside on campus.
Special Academic Programs Advanced Placement exam preparation.
Student Life Upper grades have specified standards of dress, student council, honor system. Discipline rests primarily with faculty.
Summer Programs Remediation, enrichment, advancement, sports, art/fine arts programs offered; session focuses on academic enrichment; held on campus; accepts boys and girls; not open to students from other schools. 80 students usually enrolled. 2009 schedule: June 16 to July 25. Application deadline: January 11.
Tuition and Aid Financial aid available to upper-school students. In 2008–09, 100% of upper-school students received aid. Total amount of financial aid awarded in 2008–09: $3,061,000.
Admissions Traditional secondary-level entrance grade is 9. For fall 2008, 130 students applied for upper-level admission, 30 were accepted, 27 enrolled. Deadline for receipt of application materials: January 11. No application fee required. Interview required.
Athletics Interscholastic: basketball (boys, girls), cross-country running (b), soccer (b,g), track and field (b,g), volleyball (b,g). 1 PE instructor, 3 coaches.
Computers Computer network features include Internet access, wireless campus network, Internet filtering or blocking technology. Student e-mail accounts are available to students. Students grades are available online.
Contact Helen Kim, Vice Principal. 650-688-0850 Ext. 109. Fax: 650-688-0859. E-mail: helenk@eastside.org. Web site: www.eastside.org.

ECOLE D'HUMANITÉ

CH 6085 Hasliberg Goldern, Switzerland

Head of School: Ms. Kathleen Hennessy

General Information Coeducational boarding and day college-preparatory, general academic, arts, vocational, and bilingual studies school. Grades 3–12. Founded: 1934. Setting: rural. Nearest major city is Lucerne, Switzerland. Students are housed in coed dormitories. 5-acre campus. 13 buildings on campus. Approved or accredited by CITA (Commission on International and Trans-Regional Accreditation), Department of Education of Bern, and Swiss Federation of Private Schools. Member of European Council of International Schools. Languages of instruction: English and German. Endowment: 1 million Swiss francs. Upper school average class size: 5. Upper school faculty-student ratio: 1:5.
Upper School Student Profile 93% of students are boarding students. 49% are international students. International students from Bhutan, Germany, Indonesia, Taiwan, United Kingdom, and United States; 13 other countries represented in student body.
Faculty School total: 42. In upper school: 15 men, 18 women; 9 have advanced degrees; 40 reside on campus.
Subjects Offered Algebra, American literature, art, art history, Asian history, band, batik, biology, bookmaking, calculus, career and personal planning, carpentry, ceramics, chemistry, choir, choreography, chorus, community service, computer programming, computer skills, costumes and make-up, creative dance, creative writing, culinary arts, cultural geography, current events, dance, dance performance, debate, drama, drama workshop, drawing, ecology, environmental systems, English, English as a foreign language, English composition, English literature, environmental science, ESL, European history, expository writing, fine arts, first aid, folk dance, French, French as a second language, gardening, geography, geometry, German, grammar, guitar, gymnastics, health, history, home economics, independent study, jazz ensemble, jewelry making, Latin, mathematics, modern dance, music, music appreciation, music performance, musical productions, musical theater, musical theater dance, outdoor education, peer counseling, philosophy, photo shop, photography, physical education, physics, piano, poetry, pottery, pre-calculus, psychology, radio broadcasting, religion, research skills, SAT preparation, science, sewing, Shakespeare, single survival, social science, social studies, studio art, swimming, theater, TOEFL preparation, trigonometry, U.S. history, vocal ensemble, voice, weaving, wind ensemble, women's studies, woodworking, world history, world literature, writing, yearbook, yoga.
Graduation Requirements English, foreign language, independent study, mathematics, physical education (includes health), research skills, SAT preparation, science, social science, social studies (includes history), 2x term paper methodology course, balance of courses in arts, sports, handcrafts. Community service is required.
Special Academic Programs Advanced Placement exam preparation; honors section; accelerated programs; independent study; term-away projects; academic accommodation for the gifted, the musically talented, and the artistically talented; remedial reading and/or remedial writing; remedial math; ESL (40 students enrolled).
College Admission Counseling 7 students graduated in 2008; 5 went to college, including Bard College; Dalhousie University; Middlebury College; Oberlin College; University of Chicago. Other: 1 went to work, 1 had other specific plans.
Student Life Upper grades have student council, honor system. Discipline rests equally with students and faculty.
Tuition and Aid Day student tuition: 19,000 Swiss francs; 7-day tuition and room/board: 43,000 Swiss francs–47,000 Swiss francs. Guaranteed tuition plan. Tuition installment plan (monthly payment plans, individually arranged payment plans). Need-based scholarship grants, need-based loans, middle-income loans available. In 2008–09, 20% of upper-school students received aid. Total amount of financial aid awarded in 2008–09: 180,000 Swiss francs.
Admissions Deadline for receipt of application materials: none. No application fee required. Interview recommended.
Athletics Intramural: basketball (boys, girls); coed intramural: aerobics, aerobics/dance, alpine skiing, archery, backpacking, badminton, ballet, baseball, basketball, bicycling, canoeing/kayaking, climbing, dance, freestyle skiing, Frisbee, gymnastics, hiking/backpacking, horseback riding, indoor soccer, juggling, kayaking, modern dance, rock climbing, skiing (downhill), snowboarding, snowshoeing, soccer, softball, strength & conditioning, swimming and diving, table tennis, tennis, ultimate Frisbee, volleyball, yoga. 5 athletic trainers.
Computers Computers are regularly used in career exploration, college planning, creative writing, data processing, English, graphic design, independent study, library, newspaper, photography, typing, yearbook classes. Computer resources include Internet access. Computer access in designated common areas is available to students.
Contact K. C. Hill, Dean of Admissions. 41-33-972-9272. Fax: 41-33-972-9272. E-mail: admissions@ecole.ch. Web site: www.ecole.ch.

ANNOUNCEMENT FROM THE SCHOOL The Ecole d'Humanité is a progressive, bilingual boarding school located in the heart of the Swiss Alps. Small, demanding classes; a familial atmosphere; an astonishing array of artistic courses; and close contact with the natural world encourage young people to "become who they are."

See Close-Up on page 750.

ECOLE INTERNATIONALE DE BOSTON / INTERNATIONAL SCHOOL OF BOSTON

45 Matignon Road
Cambridge, Massachusetts 02140

Head of School: Dr. John F. Larner

General Information Coeducational day college-preparatory, arts, and bilingual studies school. Grades PK–12. Founded: 1962. Setting: urban. Nearest major city is Boston. 5-acre campus. 2 buildings on campus. Approved or accredited by Association of Independent Schools in New England, European Council of International Schools, French Ministry of Education, International Baccalaureate Organization, New England Association of Schools and Colleges, and Massachusetts Department of Education. Member of National Association of Independent Schools. Languages of instruction: English and French. Endowment: $50,000. Total enrollment: 567. Upper school average class size: 10. Upper school faculty-student ratio: 1:6.
Upper School Student Profile Grade 9: 22 students (10 boys, 12 girls); Grade 10: 11 students (3 boys, 8 girls); Grade 11: 20 students (11 boys, 9 girls); Grade 12: 18 students (6 boys, 12 girls).
Faculty School total: 100. In upper school: 7 men, 20 women; 18 have advanced degrees.
Graduation Requirements French Baccalaureate requirements, International Baccalaureate requirements.
Special Academic Programs International Baccalaureate program; independent study; ESL (50 students enrolled).
College Admission Counseling 18 students graduated in 2008; all went to college, including Boston University.
Student Life Upper grades have specified standards of dress, student council. Discipline rests primarily with faculty.
Tuition and Aid Day student tuition: $20,710. Tuition installment plan (monthly payment plans). Bursaries, need-based scholarship grants available.
Admissions Traditional secondary-level entrance grade is 9. Placement test or PSAT or SAT required. Deadline for receipt of application materials: none. Application fee required: $75. Interview required.
Athletics Coed Intramural: basketball, fencing, handball, martial arts, outdoors, soccer, table tennis. 2 PE instructors.
Computers Computers are regularly used in science classes. Computer resources include on-campus library services, Internet access, Internet filtering or blocking technology. Students grades are available online. The school has a published electronic and media policy.
Contact Barbara Saran-Brunner, Director of Admissions. 617-499-1459. Fax: 617-234-0064. E-mail: bsaran@isbos.org. Web site: www.isbos.org.

EDISON SCHOOL

Box 2, Site 11, RR2
Okotoks, Alberta T1S 1A2, Canada

Head of School: Mrs. Beth Chernoff

General Information Coeducational day college-preparatory and general academic school. Grades K–12. Founded: 1993. Setting: small town. Nearest major city is Calgary, Canada. 5-acre campus. 3 buildings on campus. Approved or accredited by

Association of Independent Schools and Colleges of Alberta and Alberta Department of Education. Languages of instruction: English, Spanish, and French. Total enrollment: 198. Upper school average class size: 12. Upper school faculty-student ratio: 1:12.
Upper School Student Profile Grade 9: 12 students (6 boys, 6 girls); Grade 10: 12 students (6 boys, 6 girls); Grade 11: 12 students (6 boys, 6 girls); Grade 12: 12 students (6 boys, 6 girls).
Faculty School total: 18. In upper school: 5 men, 1 woman; 4 have advanced degrees.
Subjects Offered Advanced Placement courses, art, biology, chemistry, English, French, mathematics, physical education, physics, science, social studies, Spanish, standard curriculum.
Graduation Requirements Alberta Learning requirements.
Special Academic Programs Advanced Placement exam preparation; accelerated programs; independent study; study at local college for college credit; academic accommodation for the gifted.
College Admission Counseling 8 students graduated in 2008; 7 went to college, including The University of British Columbia; University of Alberta; University of Calgary; University of Waterloo. Other: 1 went to work. Median composite ACT: 26. 58% scored over 26 on composite ACT.
Student Life Upper grades have uniform requirement, student council, honor system. Discipline rests primarily with faculty.
Tuition and Aid Day student tuition: CAN$7000. Tuition installment plan (monthly payment plans). Tuition reduction for siblings available.
Admissions Traditional secondary-level entrance grade is 9. For fall 2008, 20 students applied for upper-level admission, 4 were accepted, 4 enrolled. Achievement tests or admissions testing required. Deadline for receipt of application materials: none. No application fee required. On-campus interview required.
Athletics Interscholastic: badminton (boys, girls), basketball (b,g), cross-country running (b,g), track and field (b,g), volleyball (b,g); intramural: badminton (b,g), basketball (b,g), cross-country running (b,g), volleyball (b,g); coed interscholastic: badminton, flag football; coed intramural: badminton, flag football, outdoor education. 1 PE instructor, 1 coach.
Computers Computers are regularly used in all classes. Computer resources include Internet access. Computer access in designated common areas is available to students.
Contact Mrs. Beth Chernoff, Head Mistress. 403-938-7670. Fax: 403-938-7224. E-mail: office@edisonschool.ca. Web site: www.edisonschool.ca.

THE EDUCATION CENTER

Jackson, Mississippi
See Special Needs Schools section.

ELAN SCHOOL

Poland, Maine
See Special Needs Schools section.

ELGIN ACADEMY

350 Park Street
Elgin, Illinois 60120

Head of School: Dr. John W. Cooper

General Information Coeducational day college-preparatory, arts, and technology school. Grades PS–12. Founded: 1839. Setting: suburban. Nearest major city is Chicago. 20-acre campus. 8 buildings on campus. Approved or accredited by Independent Schools Association of the Central States. Member of National Association of Independent Schools and Secondary School Admission Test Board. Endowment: $10 million. Total enrollment: 445. Upper school average class size: 12. Upper school faculty-student ratio: 1:7.
Upper School Student Profile Grade 9: 36 students (14 boys, 22 girls); Grade 10: 32 students (17 boys, 15 girls); Grade 11: 37 students (17 boys, 20 girls); Grade 12: 25 students (15 boys, 10 girls).
Faculty School total: 70. In upper school: 10 men, 13 women; 18 have advanced degrees.
Subjects Offered Algebra, American history, American literature, anatomy and physiology, art, art history, biology, calculus, ceramics, chemistry, computer programming, computer science, creative writing, drama, English, English literature, environmental science, European history, expository writing, fine arts, finite math, French, geometry, government/civics, grammar, history, Latin, Latin-AP, mathematics, music, painting, photography, physical education, psychology, psychology-AP, science, social studies, Spanish, statistics, theater, trigonometry, world history, world literature, writing.
Graduation Requirements Arts and fine arts (art, music, dance, drama), English, foreign language, mathematics, physical education (includes health), science, social studies (includes history).
Special Academic Programs 16 Advanced Placement exams for which test preparation is offered; honors section; independent study.
College Admission Counseling 25 students graduated in 2008; all went to college, including Lawrence University; New York University; Northwestern University; University of Notre Dame; Washington University in St. Louis; Wellesley College.
Student Life Upper grades have specified standards of dress, student council, honor system. Discipline rests primarily with faculty.
Tuition and Aid Day student tuition: $15,200. Tuition installment plan (FACTS Tuition Payment Plan, 10-month payment plan). Tuition reduction for siblings, merit scholarship grants, need-based scholarship grants available. In 2008–09, 25% of upper-school students received aid; total upper-school merit-scholarship money awarded: $120,000. Total amount of financial aid awarded in 2008–09: $1,100,000.
Admissions Traditional secondary-level entrance grade is 9. For fall 2008, 27 students applied for upper-level admission, 24 were accepted, 21 enrolled. ERB—verbal abilities, reading comprehension, quantitative abilities (level F, form 1) required. Deadline for receipt of application materials: none. Application fee required: $50. Interview required.
Athletics Interscholastic: baseball (boys), basketball (b,g), cross-country running (b,g), field hockey (g), soccer (b,g), softball (g), tennis (b,g), track and field (b,g); intramural: aerobics/dance (g); coed interscholastic: golf; coed intramural: aerobics, backpacking, canoeing/kayaking. 2 PE instructors, 3 coaches.
Computers Computers are regularly used in art, English, foreign language, mathematics, science, social studies classes. Computer network features include on-campus library services, online commercial services, Internet access, wireless campus network. Campus intranet is available to students. Students grades are available online. The school has a published electronic and media policy.
Contact Mr. Shannon D Howell, Director of Admission and Marketing. 847-695-0303. Fax: 847-695-5017. E-mail: showell@elginacademy.org. Web site: www.elginacademy.org.

ANNOUNCEMENT FROM THE SCHOOL Elgin Academy is celebrating its 170th year, making it the oldest college-preparatory school west of the Alleghenies. From its earliest days, the Academy has been both nonsectarian and coeducational. The campus is located 35 miles northwest of Chicago and serves the suburban communities of the greater Fox River Valley. The 18-acre campus, part of the historic district of Elgin, Illinois, houses the Lower, Middle, and Upper Schools and serves students in preschool through grade 12. The new Harold D. Rider Family Media, Science, and Fine Arts Center "green" building opened in October 2008. The total enrollment for the 2008–09 academic year was 439. The educational program is designed to give students a sound academic background in a broad range of the arts and sciences and the knowledge, skills, and attitudes necessary to become intellectually engaged and confident about their place in the world. The personal environment of the Academy encourages students to be active in the arts, co-curricular clubs, athletics, and community service. Team sports include baseball, basketball, cross-country, field hockey, golf, soccer, softball, tennis, track, and volleyball. Each year, Elgin graduates (all college bound) attend schools in all regions of the country, including Case Western Reserve, Columbia, Duke, Lawrence, Northwestern, Notre Dame, Washington (St. Louis), and Wellesley. The hallmarks of an Elgin Academy education include the following: a nationally recognized academic program, broad exposure to the arts, a close association with faculty as teachers and advisers, opportunities for personal growth and talent development, and complete preparation for successful college placement. The Academy offers selective admission and seeks students from social, economic, and ethnic diversity. Applicants are admitted for the fall semester on a rolling basis until available spaces in each grade level are filled. Late applicants who are admissible may be given wait-list status. The Academy's financial aid program assists 29% of the students who demonstrate financial need. For further information, please call the Office of Admission at 847-695-0303, e-mail: info@elginacademy.org, or visit the Web site at www.elginacademy.org.

ELIZABETH SETON HIGH SCHOOL

5715 Emerson Street
Bladensburg, Maryland 20710-1844

Head of School: Sr. Virginia Ann Brooks

General Information Girls' day college-preparatory, arts, business, religious studies, bilingual studies, and technology school, affiliated with Roman Catholic Church. Grades 9–12. Founded: 1959. Setting: suburban. Nearest major city is Washington, DC. 24-acre campus. 2 buildings on campus. Approved or accredited by Middle States Association of Colleges and Schools, National Catholic Education Association, and Maryland Department of Education. Total enrollment: 640. Upper school average class size: 18. Upper school faculty-student ratio: 1:11.
Upper School Student Profile Grade 9: 179 students (179 girls); Grade 10: 160 students (160 girls); Grade 11: 154 students (154 girls); Grade 12: 147 students (147 girls). 65% of students are Roman Catholic.
Faculty School total: 47. In upper school: 4 men, 43 women; 25 have advanced degrees.
Subjects Offered Accounting, advanced chemistry, advanced math, algebra, American government-AP, American history, American history-AP, American literature, analytic geometry, anatomy, art, art-AP, bioethics, biology, business, calculus, calculus-AP, ceramics, chemistry, choir, chorus, Christian and Hebrew scripture, Christianity, church history, community service, computer keyboarding, computer

multimedia, computer programming, computer science, desktop publishing, earth science, economics, English, English literature, English literature and composition-AP, English literature-AP, environmental science, ethics, European history, film and literature, fine arts, French, geography, geometry, government-AP, government/civics, grammar, health, history, home economics, honors algebra, honors English, honors geometry, journalism, Latin, mathematics, music, newspaper, philosophy, photography, physical education, physics, physiology, pre-calculus, probability and statistics, psychology, psychology-AP, religion, science, social studies, sociology, Spanish, speech, symphonic band, theology, trigonometry, Web site design, world history, world literature, writing.

Graduation Requirements 1½ elective credits, arts and fine arts (art, music, dance, drama), English, foreign language, health education, mathematics, physical education (includes health), religion (includes Bible studies and theology), science, social studies (includes history), technology. Community service is required.

Special Academic Programs Advanced Placement exam preparation; honors section; independent study; academic accommodation for the gifted, the musically talented, and the artistically talented; programs in general development for dyslexic students; special instructional classes for students with mild learning disabilities, organizational deficiencies, Attention Deficit Disorder, and dyslexia.

College Admission Counseling 141 students graduated in 2008; all went to college, including Frostburg State University; Temple University; The University of North Carolina Wilmington; Towson University; University of Maryland, Baltimore County; University of Maryland, College Park. Mean SAT critical reading: 565, mean SAT math: 543, mean SAT writing: 571.

Student Life Upper grades have uniform requirement, student council, honor system. Discipline rests equally with students and faculty. Attendance at religious services is required.

Summer Programs Remediation, enrichment, sports, art/fine arts programs offered; held on campus; accepts girls; open to students from other schools. 2009 schedule: June to August.

Tuition and Aid Day student tuition: $9500. Tuition installment plan (monthly payment plans, individually arranged payment plans, quarterly payment plan). Tuition reduction for siblings, merit scholarship grants, need-based scholarship grants, paying campus jobs available. In 2008–09, 50% of upper-school students received aid; total upper-school merit-scholarship money awarded: $165,000.

Admissions Traditional secondary-level entrance grade is 9. For fall 2008, 400 students applied for upper-level admission, 214 were accepted, 179 enrolled. High School Placement Test required. Deadline for receipt of application materials: December 8. Application fee required: $50. On-campus interview required.

Athletics Interscholastic: basketball, cheering, crew, cross-country running, dance squad, dance team, equestrian sports, field hockey, golf, horseback riding, indoor track, lacrosse, modern dance, pom squad, rowing, running, soccer, softball, swimming and diving, tennis, volleyball, winter (indoor) track; intramural: aerobics, aerobics/dance, aerobics/Nautilus, combined training, cooperative games, dance, dressage, equestrian sports, fitness, fitness walking, flag football, kickball, martial arts, ocean paddling, outdoor recreation, physical fitness, strength & conditioning, walking, weight training. 4 PE instructors, 32 coaches, 1 athletic trainer.

Computers Computers are regularly used in computer applications, desktop publishing, English, graphic design, independent study, keyboarding, lab/keyboard, literary magazine, multimedia, photojournalism, programming, research skills, science, typing, Web site design, word processing, yearbook classes. Computer network features include on-campus library services, online commercial services, Internet access, wireless campus network, Internet filtering or blocking technology. Student e-mail accounts are available to students. Students grades are available online. The school has a published electronic and media policy.

Contact Ms. Dawn Schiavone, Director of Admissions. 301-864-4532 Ext. 7115. Fax: 301-864-8946. E-mail: 520@setonhs.org. Web site: www.setonhs.org.

ELK MOUNTAIN ACADEMY

PO Box 330
Heron, Montana 59844

Head of School: Tina Stevens

General Information Boys' boarding college-preparatory, general academic, arts, and technology school; primarily serves students with learning disabilities, individuals with Attention Deficit Disorder, individuals with emotional and behavioral problems, dyslexic students, and drug/alcohol Addiction. Grades 9–12. Founded: 1994. Setting: rural. Nearest major city is Sandpoint, ID. Students are housed in single-sex dormitories. 90-acre campus. 1 building on campus. Approved or accredited by Northwest Association of Accredited Schools, Northwest Association of Schools and Colleges, and Montana Department of Education. Total enrollment: 25. Upper school average class size: 10. Upper school faculty-student ratio: 1:8.

Upper School Student Profile Grade 9: 3 students (3 boys); Grade 10: 6 students (6 boys); Grade 11: 8 students (8 boys); Grade 12: 8 students (8 boys). 100% of students are boarding students. 12 states are represented in upper school student body. 10% are international students. International students from Panama and United Kingdom.

Faculty School total: 4. In upper school: 2 men, 2 women; 2 have advanced degrees; 1 resides on campus.

Subjects Offered Algebra, American government, American history, American literature, anatomy and physiology, art, biology, British literature, chemistry, earth science, economics, English, English literature, geography, geometry, government, grammar, health, history, independent living, literature, pre-algebra, pre-calculus, psychology, science, speech, world history.

Special Academic Programs Accelerated programs; independent study; study at local college for college credit; remedial reading and/or remedial writing; remedial math; programs in English, mathematics for dyslexic students.

College Admission Counseling 8 students graduated in 2008; 3 went to college. Other: 3 went to work, 2 entered military service.

Student Life Upper grades have student council, honor system. Discipline rests equally with students and faculty.

Summer Programs Remediation, enrichment, advancement, art/fine arts programs offered; session focuses on General Academics; held on campus; accepts boys; not open to students from other schools. 25 students usually enrolled. 2009 schedule: June 15 to August 30. Application deadline: July 10.

Tuition and Aid Guaranteed tuition plan. Tuition installment plan (monthly payment plans). Tuition reduction for siblings, need-based scholarship grants, paying campus jobs available. In 2008–09, 10% of upper-school students received aid. Total amount of financial aid awarded in 2008–09: $100,000.

Admissions Traditional secondary-level entrance grade is 11. Deadline for receipt of application materials: none. No application fee required. Interview required.

Athletics Intramural: alpine skiing, backpacking, basketball, billiards, blading, bowling, canoeing/kayaking, climbing, cross-country running, fishing, fitness, fitness walking, fly fishing, freestyle skiing, Frisbee, hiking/backpacking, kayaking, lacrosse, outdoor activities, paint ball, physical training, racquetball, rafting, roller blading, snowboarding, snowshoeing, soccer, strength & conditioning, table tennis, ultimate Frisbee, weight lifting, wilderness, winter soccer, yoga. 4 PE instructors.

Computers Computers are regularly used in all classes. Computer network features include on-campus library services, Internet access, Internet filtering or blocking technology. Campus intranet and student e-mail accounts are available to students. The school has a published electronic and media policy.

Contact Loretta Olding, Director of Admissions. 406-847-4400. Fax: 406-847-0034. E-mail: lolding@elkmountainacademy.org. Web site: www.elkmountainacademy.org.

THE ELLIS SCHOOL

6425 Fifth Avenue
Pittsburgh, Pennsylvania 15206

Head of School: Dr. Mary H. Grant

General Information Girls' day college-preparatory school. Grades PK–12. Founded: 1916. Setting: urban. 8-acre campus. 9 buildings on campus. Approved or accredited by Pennsylvania Association of Independent Schools and Pennsylvania Department of Education. Member of National Association of Independent Schools. Endowment: $23.9 million. Total enrollment: 486. Upper school average class size: 10. Upper school faculty-student ratio: 1:7.

Upper School Student Profile Grade 9: 42 students (42 girls); Grade 10: 37 students (37 girls); Grade 11: 46 students (46 girls); Grade 12: 41 students (41 girls).

Faculty School total: 78. In upper school: 10 men, 25 women; 23 have advanced degrees.

Subjects Offered 20th century history, algebra, American history, American literature, anthropology, archaeology, art, art history, biology, calculus, ceramics, chemistry, computer science, creative writing, dance, drama, economics, English, English literature, European history, expository writing, fine arts, French, geometry, government/civics, health, history, journalism, Latin, linear algebra, mathematics, music, photography, physical education, physics, social studies, Spanish, speech, statistics, theater, trigonometry, world history, world literature, writing.

Graduation Requirements Arts and fine arts (art, music, dance, drama), computer literacy, English, first aid, foreign language, health education, mathematics, physical education (includes health), science, social studies (includes history), completion of three-week mini-course program (grades 9-11), senior projects.

Special Academic Programs Advanced Placement exam preparation; honors section; independent study; term-away projects.

College Admission Counseling 36 students graduated in 2008; all went to college, including American University; Carleton College; Carnegie Mellon University; Harvard University; Penn State University Park; University of Pittsburgh. Mean SAT critical reading: 634, mean SAT math: 642, mean SAT writing: 646, mean combined SAT: 1905. 61% scored over 600 on SAT critical reading, 75% scored over 600 on SAT math, 69% scored over 600 on SAT writing, 61% scored over 1800 on combined SAT, 54% scored over 26 on composite ACT.

Student Life Upper grades have uniform requirement, student council, honor system. Discipline rests primarily with faculty.

Tuition and Aid Day student tuition: $20,500. Tuition installment plan (Key Tuition Payment Plan, 10-month payment plan; two-payment plan). Need-based financial aid available. In 2008–09, 31% of upper-school students received aid. Total amount of financial aid awarded in 2008–09: $616,900.

Admissions Traditional secondary-level entrance grade is 9. For fall 2008, 44 students applied for upper-level admission, 31 were accepted, 15 enrolled. ISEE required. Deadline for receipt of application materials: none. Application fee required: $50. Interview required.

Athletics Interscholastic: basketball, crew, cross-country running, field hockey, gymnastics, lacrosse, soccer, softball, swimming and diving, tennis; intramural: crew, field hockey, lacrosse. 3 PE instructors, 6 coaches, 1 athletic trainer.

Computers Computers are regularly used in all classes. Computer network features include on-campus library services, online commercial services, Internet access. Student e-mail accounts are available to students. The school has a published electronic and media policy.

Contact Sara I. Leone, Director of Admissions. 412-661-4880. Fax: 412-661-7634. E-mail: admissions@theellisschool.org. Web site: www.theellisschool.org.

ELMWOOD SCHOOL

261 Buena Vista Road
Ottawa, Ontario K1M 0V9, Canada

Head of School: Ms. Cheryl Boughton

General Information Girls' day college-preparatory, arts, business, bilingual studies, and technology school. Grades JK–12. Founded: 1915. Setting: suburban. 2-acre campus. 1 building on campus. Approved or accredited by Canadian Association of Independent Schools, Canadian Educational Standards Institute, Conference of Independent Schools of Ontario, International Baccalaureate Organization, and Ontario Department of Education. Language of instruction: English. Total enrollment: 340. Upper school average class size: 10. Upper school faculty-student ratio: 1:8.

Faculty School total: 50. In upper school: 5 men, 25 women; 10 have advanced degrees.

Subjects Offered Algebra, art, art history, biology, business, calculus, Canadian geography, Canadian history, chemistry, communications, computer math, computer science, creative writing, drama, economics, English, English literature, environmental science, ESL, European history, fine arts, French, geography, geometry, German, grammar, health, history, Latin, mathematics, music, philosophy, physical education, physics, science, social studies, Spanish, theater, theory of knowledge, trigonometry, typing, world history, world literature.

Graduation Requirements Arts and fine arts (art, music, dance, drama), business skills (includes word processing), Canadian geography, Canadian history, English, foreign language, mathematics, physical education (includes health), science, social studies (includes history).

Special Academic Programs International Baccalaureate program; accelerated programs; independent study; term-away projects; study abroad; academic accommodation for the gifted; ESL.

College Admission Counseling 40 students graduated in 2008; all went to college, including McGill University; Queen's University at Kingston; The University of Western Ontario; University of Ottawa; University of Toronto; University of Waterloo.

Student Life Upper grades have uniform requirement, student council, honor system. Discipline rests primarily with faculty.

Tuition and Aid Day student tuition: CAN$13,900–CAN$17,175. Tuition installment plan (4-payment plan). Bursaries, merit scholarship grants available. In 2008–09, 5% of upper-school students received aid; total upper-school merit-scholarship money awarded: CAN$80,000. Total amount of financial aid awarded in 2008–09: CAN$200,000.

Admissions School's own exam required. Deadline for receipt of application materials: none. Application fee required: CAN$100. Interview required.

Athletics Interscholastic: aerobics, aerobics/dance, alpine skiing, aquatics, badminton, basketball, cheering, crew, cross-country running, field hockey, golf, handball, rugby, skiing (downhill), swimming and diving, team handball, tennis, touch football, ultimate Frisbee, volleyball, water polo; intramural: aerobics/Nautilus, badminton, ball hockey, ballet, basketball, dance, fitness walking, hiking/backpacking, ice hockey, outdoor adventure, ropes courses, snowboarding, wilderness, yoga. 4 PE instructors.

Computers Computers are regularly used in all classes. Computer network features include on-campus library services, Internet access, Internet filtering or blocking technology. Campus intranet, student e-mail accounts, and computer access in designated common areas are available to students.

Contact Ms. Donna Naufal Moffatt, Director of Admissions. 613-749-6761. Fax: 613-741-8210. E-mail: admissions@elmwood.on.ca. Web site: www.elmwood.ca.

ELVES CHILD DEVELOPMENT CENTRE

Edmonton, Alberta T5N 3Y7, Canada

See Special Needs Schools section.

ELYRIA CATHOLIC HIGH SCHOOL

725 Gulf Road
Elyria, Ohio 44035-3697

Head of School: Mr. Andrew Krakowiak

General Information Coeducational day college-preparatory, arts, business, and religious studies school, affiliated with Roman Catholic Church. Grades 9–12. Founded: 1948. Setting: suburban. Nearest major city is Cleveland. 16-acre campus. 1 building on campus. Approved or accredited by North Central Association of Colleges and Schools, Ohio Catholic Schools Accreditation Association (OCSAA), and Ohio Department of Education. Endowment: $3 million. Total enrollment: 547. Upper school average class size: 24. Upper school faculty-student ratio: 1:14.

Upper School Student Profile Grade 9: 122 students (74 boys, 48 girls); Grade 10: 149 students (69 boys, 80 girls); Grade 11: 154 students (83 boys, 71 girls); Grade 12: 122 students (69 boys, 53 girls). 90% of students are Roman Catholic.

Faculty School total: 40. In upper school: 18 men, 15 women; 19 have advanced degrees.

Subjects Offered Accounting, advanced math, algebra, American government, American history, American history-AP, analysis of data, anatomy and physiology, art, band, biology, business, calculus, calculus-AP, campus ministry, Catholic belief and practice, chamber groups, chemistry, child development, choir, Christian and Hebrew scripture, Christian doctrine, Christian ethics, church history, computer applications, concert band, concert choir, current events, data analysis, drama, drama performance, earth science, English, fine arts, food and nutrition, French, French language-AP, geometry, German, health, history, honors English, industrial arts, introduction to theater, journalism, leadership, life issues, marching band, music appreciation, parent/child development, peer ministry, physical fitness, physics, prayer/spirituality, pre-calculus, psychology, reading/study skills, social justice, Spanish, Spanish language-AP, theater, world religions, yearbook.

Graduation Requirements Arts and fine arts (art, music, dance, drama), computers, English, mathematics, physical education (includes health), religion (includes Bible studies and theology), science, social studies (includes history), school and community service hours, Ohio Proficiency Test.

Special Academic Programs Advanced Placement exam preparation; honors section; study at local college for college credit; remedial reading and/or remedial writing; remedial math; special instructional classes for students with learning disabilities and Attention Deficit Disorder.

College Admission Counseling 108 students graduated in 2008; 105 went to college, including Bowling Green State University; Kent State University; Ohio University; The Ohio State University; The University of Toledo; University of Dayton. Other: 2 went to work, 1 entered military service. Mean SAT critical reading: 570, mean SAT math: 557.

Student Life Upper grades have specified standards of dress, student council, honor system. Discipline rests primarily with faculty. Attendance at religious services is required.

Summer Programs Sports programs offered; session focuses on sports; held on campus; accepts boys and girls; open to students from other schools.

Tuition and Aid Day student tuition: $6300. Tuition installment plan (monthly payment plans). Tuition reduction for siblings, merit scholarship grants, need-based scholarship grants, paying campus jobs available. In 2008–09, 24% of upper-school students received aid; total upper-school merit-scholarship money awarded: $20,000. Total amount of financial aid awarded in 2008–09: $200,000.

Admissions Traditional secondary-level entrance grade is 9. High School Placement Test (closed version) from Scholastic Testing Service required. Deadline for receipt of application materials: January 23. No application fee required. Interview recommended.

Athletics Interscholastic: baseball (boys), basketball (b,g), cross-country running (b,g), football (b), golf (b), ice hockey (b), rugby (b), soccer (b,g), softball (g), tennis (b,g), volleyball (g), wrestling (b); coed interscholastic: bowling, cheering, swimming and diving, track and field. 2 PE instructors, 47 coaches, 1 athletic trainer.

Computers Computers are regularly used in business studies, journalism, newspaper, typing, word processing, yearbook classes. Computer network features include on-campus library services, Internet access, Internet filtering or blocking technology. Students grades are available online. The school has a published electronic and media policy.

Contact Mr. Michael Wisnor, Director of Admissions/Dean of Boys. 440-365-1821 Ext. 16. Fax: 440-365-7536. E-mail: wisnor@elyriacatholic.com. Web site: www.elyriacatholic.com.

EMERSON HONORS HIGH SCHOOLS

4100 East Walnut Street
Orange, California 92869

Head of School: Dr. Glory Ludwick

General Information Coeducational boarding and day college-preparatory, general academic, and arts school. Boarding grades 7–12, day grades K–12. Founded: 1958. Setting: suburban. Nearest major city is Los Angeles. Students are housed in homes of host families. 5-acre campus. 8 buildings on campus. Approved or accredited by Western Association of Schools and Colleges and California Department of Education. Total enrollment: 180. Upper school average class size: 18. Upper school faculty-student ratio: 1:18.

Upper School Student Profile Grade 7: 5 students (2 boys, 3 girls); Grade 8: 14 students (10 boys, 4 girls); Grade 9: 21 students (11 boys, 10 girls); Grade 10: 13 students (7 boys, 6 girls); Grade 11: 29 students (16 boys, 13 girls); Grade 12: 24 students (11 boys, 13 girls). 20% of students are boarding students. 80% are state residents. 3 states are represented in upper school student body. 20% are international students. International students from China, Japan, Republic of Korea, Taiwan, and Viet Nam; 5 other countries represented in student body.

Faculty School total: 25. In upper school: 7 men, 6 women; 11 have advanced degrees.

Subjects Offered Acting, advanced chemistry, advanced math, advanced TOEFL/grammar, algebra, American government, American government-AP, American history-AP, analysis and differential calculus, anatomy, ancient world history, applied arts, applied music, Arabic, art, art and culture, art appreciation, art education, art history, Basic programming, biology, biology-AP, calculus, calculus-AP, cell biology, ceramics, chemistry, chemistry-AP, Chinese, civil war history, classical civilization, classical Greek literature, classical music, classics, clayworking, computer keyboarding, computer processing, computer programming, computer skills, concert band, contemporary art, contemporary history, creative drama, creative writing, cultural geography, current events, current history, drama workshop, drawing, earth science, economics and history, Egyptian history, English, English literature, ESL, fine arts, gardening, general math, geography, geometry, grammar, jazz band, library skills, Mandarin, math analysis, physics, physics-AP, pre-algebra, pre-calculus, reading, SAT preparation, science, Shakespeare, Spanish, TOEFL preparation, U.S. history, world history.

Graduation Requirements Art, English, foreign language, mathematics, music, physical education (includes health), science, social studies (includes history). Community service is required.

Special Academic Programs Advanced Placement exam preparation; honors section; accelerated programs; independent study; study at local college for college credit; academic accommodation for the gifted, the musically talented, and the artistically talented; ESL (50 students enrolled).

College Admission Counseling 14 students graduated in 2008; 12 went to college, including California State University, Fullerton; Chapman University; Fashion Institute of Technology; New York University; University of California, Los Angeles. Other: 1 went to work, 1 entered military service.

Student Life Upper grades have specified standards of dress, honor system. Discipline rests equally with students and faculty.

Summer Programs Remediation, enrichment, advancement, ESL, sports, art/fine arts, computer instruction programs offered; session focuses on continuation of academic year program with additional electives; held on campus; accepts boys and girls; open to students from other schools. 100 students usually enrolled. 2009 schedule: June 29 to July 28. Application deadline: May 15.

Tuition and Aid Day student tuition: $12,150; 7-day tuition and room/board: $20,000–$30,000. Tuition installment plan (monthly payment plans, individually arranged payment plans). Tuition reduction for siblings, need-based scholarship grants available. In 2008–09, 10% of upper-school students received aid. Total amount of financial aid awarded in 2008–09: $50,000.

Admissions Traditional secondary-level entrance grade is 10. For fall 2008, 100 students applied for upper-level admission, 80 were accepted, 75 enrolled. Achievement tests or any standardized test required. Deadline for receipt of application materials: none. Application fee required: $250. Interview required.

Athletics Coed Interscholastic: baseball, basketball, cross-country running, fitness, flag football, handball, kickball, physical fitness, soccer, softball. 1 PE instructor, 1 coach.

Computers Computers are regularly used in desktop publishing, graphic design, keyboarding, Web site design, word processing, yearbook classes. Computer resources include Internet access, Internet filtering or blocking technology.

Contact Mrs. Cathie Peterson, Administration. 714-633-4774. E-mail: ryjeni@yahoo.com. Web site: www.eldorado-emerson.org.

THE EMERY WEINER SCHOOL

9825 Stella Link
Houston, Texas 77025

Head of School: Mr. Stuart J. Dow

General Information Coeducational day college-preparatory and religious studies school, affiliated with Jewish faith. Grades 6–12. Founded: 1978. Setting: urban. 12-acre campus. 2 buildings on campus. Approved or accredited by Independent Schools Association of the Southwest, Southern Association of Colleges and Schools, and Texas Department of Education. Endowment: $15 million. Total enrollment: 460. Upper school average class size: 13. Upper school faculty-student ratio: 1:8.

Upper School Student Profile Grade 9: 77 students (31 boys, 46 girls); Grade 10: 75 students (42 boys, 33 girls); Grade 11: 61 students (32 boys, 29 girls); Grade 12: 42 students (23 boys, 19 girls).

Faculty School total: 57. In upper school: 22 men, 17 women; 22 have advanced degrees.

Subjects Offered Acting, advanced chemistry, advanced math, algebra, art, biology, biology-AP, calculus, calculus-AP, ceramics, chemistry, chemistry-AP, civil war history, clayworking, composition, composition-AP, computer graphics, drama, drama performance, drawing, English, English-AP, foreign language, geometry, Hebrew, Hebrew scripture, history, history of religion, history-AP, honors English, honors U.S. history, Judaic studies, lab science, mathematics, mathematics-AP, newspaper, painting, physics, play production, play/screen writing, religion and culture, religious education, religious studies, Spanish, Spanish-AP, study skills, theater arts, theater design and production, U.S. history, U.S. history-AP, yearbook.

Graduation Requirements Arts, English, foreign language, history, Judaic studies, mathematics, physical education (includes health), science, one year Hebrew requirement for Upper School. Community service is required.

Special Academic Programs Advanced Placement exam preparation; honors section; independent study; academic accommodation for the gifted.

College Admission Counseling 44 students graduated in 2008; 42 went to college, including American University; Emory University; Indiana University Bloomington; The University of Texas at Austin; Trinity University; University of Michigan. Other: 2 entered a postgraduate year.

Student Life Upper grades have uniform requirement, student council, honor system. Discipline rests primarily with faculty. Attendance at religious services is required.

Tuition and Aid Day student tuition: $14,590. Tuition installment plan (monthly payment plans). Need-based scholarship grants available. In 2008–09, 18% of upper-school students received aid. Total amount of financial aid awarded in 2008–09: $590,000.

Admissions Traditional secondary-level entrance grade is 9. For fall 2008, 63 students applied for upper-level admission, 45 were accepted, 34 enrolled. ISEE required. Deadline for receipt of application materials: January 23. Application fee required: $100. On-campus interview required.

Athletics Interscholastic: baseball (boys), basketball (b,g), football (b), golf (b), soccer (b,g), softball (g), tennis (b,g), track and field (b,g), volleyball (g); intramural: aerobics/dance (g), dance (g), yoga (g); coed intramural: outdoor activities. 1 PE instructor, 14 coaches.

Computers Computers are regularly used in graphic design, Web site design classes. Computer network features include on-campus library services, online commercial services, Internet access, wireless campus network, Adobe Creative Suite, Microsoft Publisher, Word, Excel, PowerPoint. Student e-mail accounts and computer access in designated common areas are available to students. Students grades are available online. The school has a published electronic and media policy.

Contact Mrs. Rosiland Ivie, Registrar. 832-204-5900 Ext. 106. Fax: 832-204-5910. Web site: www.emeryweiner.org.

ANNOUNCEMENT FROM THE SCHOOL The Emery/Weiner School, a college-preparatory and Jewish community school, offers small class sizes, a strong advisory program, and highly qualified, caring faculty members. In addition to the challenging dual-studies curriculum (general and Judaic studies), Emery/Weiner provides a progressive, pluralistic environment that encourages students to take an active role in defining their community. Students also engage in experiential learning, including a two-week Interim Term (involving unique course offerings and outdoor education trips) and a one-week, culturally oriented spring trip for Upper School students.

EMMA WILLARD SCHOOL

285 Pawling Avenue
Troy, New York 12180

Head of School: Ms. Trudy E. Hall

General Information Girls' boarding and day college-preparatory and arts school. Grades 9–PG. Founded: 1814. Setting: suburban. Nearest major city is Albany. Students are housed in single-sex dormitories. 137-acre campus. 23 buildings on campus. Approved or accredited by New York State Association of Independent Schools, The Association of Boarding Schools, and New York Department of Education. Member of National Association of Independent Schools and Secondary School Admission Test Board. Endowment: $104 million. Total enrollment: 311. Upper school average class size: 11. Upper school faculty-student ratio: 1:5.

Upper School Student Profile Grade 9: 63 students (63 girls); Grade 10: 85 students (85 girls); Grade 11: 73 students (73 girls); Grade 12: 88 students (88 girls); Postgraduate: 2 students (2 girls). 70% of students are boarding students. 48% are state residents. 26 states are represented in upper school student body. 21% are international students. International students from China, Japan, Republic of Korea, Taiwan, United Kingdom, and Viet Nam; 21 other countries represented in student body.

Faculty School total: 69. In upper school: 16 men, 50 women; 51 have advanced degrees; 41 reside on campus.

Subjects Offered Advanced Placement courses, advanced studio art-AP, algebra, American history, American literature, ancient world history, art, art history, art history-AP, art-AP, ballet, bioethics, biology, biology-AP, calculus, calculus-AP, ceramics, chemistry, chemistry-AP, chorus, comparative government and politics-AP, computer programming, computer science, computer science-AP, conceptual physics, creative writing, dance, digital imaging, drama, drawing and design, driver education, economics, English, English literature, English literature and composition-AP, ESL, European history, expository writing, fiber arts, fine arts, forensic science, French, French language-AP, geometry, government and politics-AP, government-AP, government/civics, health and wellness, history, internship, Latin, Latin-AP, mathematics, medieval/Renaissance history, music, neuroscience, orchestra, photography, physical education, physics, physics-AP, poetry, practicum, pre-calculus, Russian, SAT preparation, science, social science, Spanish, Spanish language-AP, Spanish-AP, statistics, statistics-AP, studio art—AP, theater, trigonometry, U.S. history-AP, weaving, world history, world literature.

Graduation Requirements Arts and fine arts (art, music, dance, drama), computer science, English, foreign language, mathematics, physical education (includes health), science, social studies (includes history). Community service is required.

Special Academic Programs Advanced Placement exam preparation; independent study; term-away projects; study abroad; academic accommodation for the musically talented and the artistically talented; ESL (17 students enrolled).

College Admission Counseling 91 students graduated in 2008; 90 went to college, including Boston University; Carnegie Mellon University; Cornell University; Massachusetts Institute of Technology; Wellesley College; Yale University. Other: 1 had other specific plans. Median SAT critical reading: 650, median SAT math: 650, median SAT writing: 670, median combined SAT: 1906, median composite ACT: 28. 74% scored over 600 on SAT critical reading, 66% scored over 600 on SAT math, 76% scored over 600 on SAT writing, 59% scored over 1800 on combined SAT, 61% scored over 26 on composite ACT.
Student Life Upper grades have specified standards of dress, student council, honor system. Discipline rests equally with students and faculty.
Tuition and Aid Day student tuition: $25,000; 7-day tuition and room/board: $38,400. Tuition installment plan (Key Tuition Payment Plan, monthly payment plans). Merit scholarship grants, need-based scholarship grants, Davis Scholars Program, Day Student /Capital District Scholarships available. In 2008–09, 48% of upper-school students received aid. Total amount of financial aid awarded in 2008–09: $3,239,800.
Admissions Traditional secondary-level entrance grade is 9. For fall 2008, 363 students applied for upper-level admission, 192 were accepted, 107 enrolled. ERB, PSAT or SAT, SAT, SSAT or TOEFL required. Deadline for receipt of application materials: February 1. Application fee required: $50. Interview required.
Athletics Interscholastic: aquatics, basketball, crew, cross-country running, diving, field hockey, lacrosse, rowing, soccer, softball, swimming and diving, tennis, track and field, volleyball; intramural: aerobics, aerobics/dance, ballet, basketball, dance, fitness, fitness walking, floor hockey, hiking/backpacking, jogging, martial arts, modern dance, outdoor activities, physical fitness, physical training, running, skiing (downhill), snowboarding, soccer, softball, strength & conditioning, swimming and diving, tennis, ultimate Frisbee, volleyball, water polo, weight training. 3 PE instructors, 3 coaches, 1 athletic trainer.
Computers Computers are regularly used in all classes. Computer network features include on-campus library services, online commercial services, Internet access, wireless campus network, Internet filtering or blocking technology. Campus intranet, student e-mail accounts, and computer access in designated common areas are available to students. Students grades are available online. The school has a published electronic and media policy.
Contact Mrs. Christine Hoek, Director of Strategic Initiatives. 518-883-1362. Fax: 518-883-1805. E-mail: choek@emmawillard.org. Web site: www.emmawillard.org.

See Close-Up on page 752.

EPISCOPAL COLLEGIATE SCHOOL

1701 Cantrell Road
Little Rock, Arkansas 72201

Head of School: Mr. Steve Hickman

General Information Coeducational day college-preparatory, arts, and technology school, affiliated with Episcopal Church. Grades 6–12. Founded: 2000. Setting: suburban. Nearest major city is Dallas, TX. 30-acre campus. 3 buildings on campus. Approved or accredited by Southwest Association of Episcopal Schools. Endowment: $31 million. Total enrollment: 376. Upper school average class size: 15. Upper school faculty-student ratio: 1:10.
Upper School Student Profile Grade 9: 52 students (27 boys, 25 girls); Grade 10: 56 students (24 boys, 32 girls); Grade 11: 46 students (20 boys, 26 girls); Grade 12: 52 students (29 boys, 23 girls). 20% of students are members of Episcopal Church.
Faculty School total: 28. In upper school: 15 men, 13 women; 25 have advanced degrees.
Special Academic Programs 16 Advanced Placement exams for which test preparation is offered; honors section; independent study.
College Admission Counseling 49 students graduated in 2008; all went to college, including University of Arkansas.
Student Life Upper grades have uniform requirement, student council, honor system. Discipline rests primarily with faculty. Attendance at religious services is required.
Summer Programs Enrichment, sports, art/fine arts, computer instruction programs offered; session focuses on enrichment; accepts boys and girls; open to students from other schools. 150 students usually enrolled. 2009 schedule: June 1 to July 31. Application deadline: May 30.
Tuition and Aid Day student tuition: $8975. Tuition installment plan (monthly payment plans, individually arranged payment plans). Need-based scholarship grants available. In 2008–09, 25% of upper-school students received aid. Total amount of financial aid awarded in 2008–09: $525,000.
Admissions Traditional secondary-level entrance grade is 9. Stanford 9 required. Deadline for receipt of application materials: none. Application fee required: $50. Interview required.
Athletics Interscholastic: baseball (boys), basketball (b,g), cross-country running (b,g), fitness (b,g), football (b), golf (b,g), physical fitness (b,g), physical training (b,g), soccer (b,g), softball (g), tennis (b,g), track and field (b,g), volleyball (g), weight training (b,g), wrestling (b,g); coed interscholastic: cheering. 2 PE instructors, 8 coaches, 1 athletic trainer.
Computers Computer network features include on-campus library services, online commercial services, Internet access, Internet filtering or blocking technology. Students grades are available online. The school has a published electronic and media policy.
Contact Ms. Ashley Honeywell, Director of Admission. 501-372-1194 Ext. 406. Fax: 501-372-2160. E-mail: ahoneywell@episcopalcollegiate.org. Web site: www.episcopalcollegiate.org.

EPISCOPAL HIGH SCHOOL

4650 Bissonnet
Bellaire, Texas 77401

Head of School: Mr. C. Edward Smith

General Information Coeducational day college-preparatory, arts, religious studies, and technology school, affiliated with Episcopal Church. Grades 9–12. Founded: 1984. Setting: urban. Nearest major city is Houston. 35-acre campus. 7 buildings on campus. Approved or accredited by Independent Schools Association of the Southwest, National Association of Episcopal Schools, Texas Education Agency, and Texas Department of Education. Member of National Association of Independent Schools and Secondary School Admission Test Board. Total enrollment: 659. Upper school average class size: 18. Upper school faculty-student ratio: 1:9.
Upper School Student Profile Grade 9: 167 students (76 boys, 91 girls); Grade 10: 165 students (75 boys, 90 girls); Grade 11: 165 students (82 boys, 83 girls); Grade 12: 162 students (83 boys, 79 girls). 27.6% of students are members of Episcopal Church.
Faculty School total: 101. In upper school: 45 men, 56 women; 57 have advanced degrees.
Subjects Offered Acting, algebra, anatomy, ancient history, art appreciation, art history, band, Bible studies, biology, biology-AP, calculus-AP, ceramics, chemistry, choir, civil rights, dance, debate, design, drawing, English, English-AP, ethics, European history, French, French-AP, geography, geology, geometry, government, government-AP, graphic design, health, history of science, instrumental music, journalism, Latin, Latin American studies, music theory, newspaper, oceanography, orchestra, painting, photography, physical education, physics, physics-AP, physiology, pre-calculus, sculpture, Spanish, Spanish-AP, speech, stagecraft, statistics, theater, theology, U.S. history, U.S. history-AP, video film production, Vietnam War, world religions, World War II, writing, yearbook.
Graduation Requirements Arts and fine arts (art, music, dance, drama), English, foreign language, mathematics, physical education (includes health), religion (includes Bible studies and theology), religious studies, science, social studies (includes history).
Special Academic Programs Advanced Placement exam preparation; honors section; independent study; study at local college for college credit.
College Admission Counseling 135 students graduated in 2008; all went to college, including Baylor University; Southern Methodist University; Texas Christian University; The University of Texas at Austin; Vanderbilt University.
Student Life Upper grades have uniform requirement, student council, honor system. Discipline rests equally with students and faculty. Attendance at religious services is required.
Summer Programs Remediation, enrichment, advancement, art/fine arts programs offered; session focuses on remediation, advancement, enrichment; held on campus; accepts boys and girls; open to students from other schools. 225 students usually enrolled. 2009 schedule: June 4 to July 13. Application deadline: May 10.
Tuition and Aid Day student tuition: $19,260. Tuition installment plan (Insured Tuition Payment Plan, SMART Tuition Payment Plan, monthly payment plans). Need-based scholarship grants, middle-income loans available. In 2008–09, 16% of upper-school students received aid. Total amount of financial aid awarded in 2008–09: $1,700,000.
Admissions Traditional secondary-level entrance grade is 9. For fall 2008, 466 students applied for upper-level admission, 269 were accepted, 181 enrolled. ISEE and Otis-Lennon Ability or Stanford Achievement Test required. Deadline for receipt of application materials: January 5. Application fee required: $60. On-campus interview required.
Athletics Interscholastic: ballet (boys, girls), baseball (b), basketball (b,g), cheering (b,g), cross-country running (b,g), dance (b,g), field hockey (b,g), football (b), golf (b,g), lacrosse (b,g), physical fitness (b,g), running (b,g), softball (g), strength & conditioning (b,g), swimming and diving (b,g), tennis (b,g), track and field (b,g), volleyball (b,g), weight training (b,g). 7 PE instructors, 6 coaches, 1 athletic trainer.
Computers Computers are regularly used in art, English, foreign language, history, mathematics, music, religion, science classes. Computer network features include on-campus library services, online commercial services, Internet access, wireless campus network, CollegeView. The school has a published electronic and media policy.
Contact Audrey Koehler, Director of Admission. 713-512-3400. Fax: 713-512-3603. E-mail: kpiper@ehshouston.org. Web site: www.ehshouston.org/.

EPISCOPAL HIGH SCHOOL

1200 North Quaker Lane
Alexandria, Virginia 22302

Head of School: Mr. F. Robertson Hershey

General Information Coeducational boarding college-preparatory, arts, religious studies, and technology school, affiliated with Episcopal Church. Grades 9–12. Founded: 1839. Setting: urban. Nearest major city is Washington, DC. Students are housed in single-sex dormitories. 135-acre campus. 26 buildings on campus. Approved or accredited by Southern Association of Colleges and Schools, Virginia Association of Independent Schools, and Virginia Department of Education. Member of National Association of Independent Schools and Secondary School Admission Test Board. Endowment: $150 million. Total enrollment: 435. Upper school average class size: 12. Upper school faculty-student ratio: 1:6.

Upper School Student Profile Grade 9: 91 students (48 boys, 43 girls); Grade 10: 110 students (62 boys, 48 girls); Grade 11: 111 students (57 boys, 54 girls); Grade 12: 123 students (70 boys, 53 girls). 100% of students are boarding students. 35% are state residents. 30 states are represented in upper school student body. 8% are international students. International students from China, Jamaica, Republic of Korea, Saudi Arabia, Thailand, and Zimbabwe; 14 other countries represented in student body. 40% of students are members of Episcopal Church.

Faculty School total: 67. In upper school: 42 men, 25 women; 53 have advanced degrees; 57 reside on campus.

Subjects Offered Advanced chemistry, advanced math, advanced studio art-AP, algebra, American history, American literature, art, art history, art-AP, astronomy, biology, biology-AP, calculus, calculus-AP, ceramics, chemistry, chemistry-AP, Chinese, choir, composition-AP, computer programming, computer programming-AP, computer science, computer science-AP, creative writing, dance, drama, economics, economics-AP, English, English literature, English literature and composition-AP, English literature-AP, English-AP, English/composition-AP, environmental science, environmental science-AP, ethics, European history, European history-AP, fine arts, forensics, French, French language-AP, French literature-AP, geometry, German, German-AP, government-AP, government/civics, Greek, history, honors algebra, honors English, honors geometry, honors U.S. history, honors world history, international relations, international relations-AP, Latin, Latin-AP, mathematics, microeconomics-AP, Middle Eastern history, modern European history-AP, music, music theory-AP, photography, physical education, physics, physics-AP, pre-calculus, psychology-AP, religion, science, senior internship, Shakespeare, social science, social studies, Spanish, Spanish literature-AP, statistics-AP, theater, theology, trigonometry, U.S. history-AP, world history, world history-AP, writing.

Graduation Requirements Arts and fine arts (art, music, dance, drama), computer studies, English, foreign language, mathematics, physical education (includes health), science, social studies (includes history), theology.

Special Academic Programs Advanced Placement exam preparation; honors section; independent study; term-away projects; study abroad; academic accommodation for the gifted, the musically talented, and the artistically talented.

College Admission Counseling 107 students graduated in 2008; all went to college, including Princeton University; Sewanee: The University of the South; The University of North Carolina at Chapel Hill; Trinity College; University of Virginia; Washington and Lee University. 62% scored over 600 on SAT critical reading; 73% scored over 600 on SAT math.

Student Life Upper grades have specified standards of dress, student council, honor system. Discipline rests primarily with faculty. Attendance at religious services is required.

Tuition and Aid 7-day tuition and room/board: $40,875. Tuition installment plan (Insured Tuition Payment Plan, monthly payment plans). Merit scholarship grants, need-based scholarship grants, paying campus jobs available. In 2008–09, 30% of upper-school students received aid; total upper-school merit-scholarship money awarded: $127,000. Total amount of financial aid awarded in 2008–09: $3,300,000.

Admissions Traditional secondary-level entrance grade is 9. For fall 2008, 629 students applied for upper-level admission, 213 were accepted, 124 enrolled. ISEE, PSAT or SAT or SSAT required. Deadline for receipt of application materials: January 31. Application fee required: $50. Interview required.

Athletics Interscholastic: baseball (boys), basketball (b,g), crew (g), cross-country running (b,g), field hockey (g), football (b), golf (b), indoor soccer (g), indoor track & field (b,g), lacrosse (b,g), rowing (g), soccer (b,g), softball (g), squash (b,g), tennis (b,g), track and field (b,g), volleyball (g); intramural: soccer (b), strength & conditioning (b,g); coed interscholastic: aerobics, aerobics/dance, aerobics/Nautilus, backpacking, ballet, canoeing/kayaking, cheering, climbing, dance, fitness, hiking/backpacking, kayaking, rock climbing; coed intramural: ballet, fitness, modern dance, outdoor activities, physical fitness, physical training, power lifting, wall climbing, weight lifting, weight training. 4 coaches, 2 athletic trainers.

Computers Computers are regularly used in all academic classes. Computer network features include on-campus library services, online commercial services, Internet access, wireless campus network, Internet filtering or blocking technology. Campus intranet and student e-mail accounts are available to students. Students grades are available online. The school has a published electronic and media policy.

Contact Ms. Emily M. Atkinson, Director of Admission. 703-933-4062. Fax: 703-933-3016. E-mail: admissions@episcopalhighschool.org. Web site: www.episcopalhighschool.org.

ANNOUNCEMENT FROM THE SCHOOL Since 1839, Episcopal's unique program—fusing rigorous academics, character education, and spiritual life—has produced principled leaders in a variety of fields. Alumni include Senator John McCain (1954); Gaston Caperton (1959), President of the College Board; Todd Gray (1982) owner/chef of DC's Equinox Restaurant; and Julian Robertson (1951), financier.

See Close-Up on page 754.

EPISCOPAL HIGH SCHOOL OF JACKSONVILLE

4455 Atlantic Boulevard
Jacksonville, Florida 32207

Head of School: Dale D. Regan

General Information Coeducational day college-preparatory, arts, religious studies, and technology school, affiliated with Episcopal Church. Grades 6–12. Founded: 1966. Setting: urban. 88-acre campus. 25 buildings on campus. Approved or accredited by Florida Council of Independent Schools, National Association of Episcopal Schools, Southern Association of Colleges and Schools, and Southern Association of Independent Schools. Member of National Association of Independent Schools. Endowment: $6.8 million. Total enrollment: 900. Upper school average class size: 17. Upper school faculty-student ratio: 1:10.

Upper School Student Profile Grade 9: 162 students (88 boys, 74 girls); Grade 10: 139 students (67 boys, 72 girls); Grade 11: 153 students (70 boys, 83 girls); Grade 12: 149 students (82 boys, 67 girls). 25% of students are members of Episcopal Church.

Faculty School total: 90. In upper school: 34 men, 56 women; 58 have advanced degrees.

Subjects Offered Advanced studio art-AP, algebra, American government-AP, American history, American history-AP, American literature, ancient history, art, art history, art history-AP, band, Basic programming, biology, biology-AP, calculus, calculus-AP, ceramics, chemistry, chemistry-AP, computer programming, computer science, computer science-AP, dance, drama, earth science, economics, electronic publishing, English, English language and composition-AP, English literature and composition-AP, environmental science-AP, film appreciation, fine arts, French, French language-AP, geography, geometry, German, German-AP, government and politics-AP, government/civics, health, history, journalism, Latin, Latin-AP, marine biology, mathematics, music, music history, music theory, music theory-AP, photography, physical education, physics, public speaking, religion, religious studies, science, social studies, Spanish, Spanish language-AP, statistics, statistics-AP, studio art—AP, technical theater, theater, theology, trigonometry, U.S. government and politics-AP, world history, writing, yearbook.

Graduation Requirements Arts and fine arts (art, music, dance, drama), computer science, English, foreign language, leadership, library skills, mathematics, physical education (includes health), religion (includes Bible studies and theology), science, social studies (includes history). Community service is required.

Special Academic Programs Advanced Placement exam preparation; honors section; independent study; study abroad; academic accommodation for the gifted.

College Admission Counseling 147 students graduated in 2008; all went to college, including Florida State University; Sewanee: The University of the South; The University of Alabama; University of Central Florida; University of Florida. Mean SAT critical reading: 614, mean SAT math: 619, mean SAT writing: 605, mean composite ACT: 26. 59% scored over 600 on SAT critical reading, 58% scored over 600 on SAT math, 51% scored over 600 on SAT writing, 49% scored over 26 on composite ACT.

Student Life Upper grades have specified standards of dress, student council, honor system. Discipline rests equally with students and faculty. Attendance at religious services is required.

Summer Programs Remediation, enrichment, advancement, sports, art/fine arts, rigorous outdoor training, computer instruction programs offered; session focuses on academics, athletics, fine arts, specialty programs; held on campus; accepts boys and girls; open to students from other schools. 700 students usually enrolled. 2009 schedule: May 27 to August 5. Application deadline: May 26.

Tuition and Aid Day student tuition: $17,000. Tuition installment plan (Insured Tuition Payment Plan, monthly payment plans). Need-based scholarship grants available. In 2008–09, 19% of upper-school students received aid. Total amount of financial aid awarded in 2008–09: $1,395,000.

Admissions Traditional secondary-level entrance grade is 9. For fall 2008, 113 students applied for upper-level admission, 63 were accepted, 46 enrolled. 3-R Achievement Test required. Deadline for receipt of application materials: January 12. Application fee required: $50. On-campus interview required.

Athletics Interscholastic: baseball (boys), basketball (b,g), crew (b,g), cross-country running (b,g), football (b), golf (b,g), lacrosse (b,g), modern dance (b,g), soccer (b,g), softball (g), swimming and diving (b,g), tennis (b,g), track and field (b,g), volleyball (g), weight lifting (b), weight training (b), wrestling (b); intramural: dance (g); coed interscholastic: cheering, dance, dance squad, dance team; coed intramural: fencing. 7 PE instructors, 78 coaches, 3 athletic trainers.

Computers Computers are regularly used in all classes. Computer network features include on-campus library services, online commercial services, Internet access, wireless campus network, Internet filtering or blocking technology, Senior Systems' My BackPack online grading and student accounts. Campus intranet, student e-mail accounts, and computer access in designated common areas are available to students. Students grades are available online. The school has a published electronic and media policy.

Contact Peggy P. Fox, Director of Admissions. 904-396-7104. Fax: 904-396-0981. E-mail: foxp@episcopalhigh.org. Web site: www.episcopalhigh.org.

ANNOUNCEMENT FROM THE SCHOOL Offering a classic college-preparatory curriculum within a Christian context, Episcopal High School inspires students to pursue a diverse range of academic, athletic, arts, and community service interests. Small class size, talented faculty members, and state-of-the-art facilities on a riverfront campus make Episcopal High School a place where young people become young adults of integrity and perspective.

THE EPISCOPAL SCHOOL OF DALLAS

4100 Merrell Road
Dallas, Texas 75229

Head of School: Rev. Stephen B. Swann

General Information Coeducational day college-preparatory, arts, religious studies, and technology school, affiliated with Episcopal Church. Grades PK–12. Founded: 1974. Setting: suburban. 36-acre campus. 5 buildings on campus. Approved or accredited by Independent Schools Association of the Southwest, National Association of Episcopal Schools, National Independent Private Schools Association, Southwest Association of Episcopal Schools, Texas Education Agency, and Texas Department of Education. Member of National Association of Independent Schools and Secondary School Admission Test Board. Endowment: $25 million. Total enrollment: 1,142. Upper school average class size: 15. Upper school faculty-student ratio: 1:8.

Upper School Student Profile Grade 9: 100 students (47 boys, 53 girls); Grade 10: 103 students (45 boys, 58 girls); Grade 11: 101 students (53 boys, 48 girls); Grade 12: 96 students (45 boys, 51 girls). 38% of students are members of Episcopal Church.

Faculty School total: 154. In upper school: 36 men, 69 women; 69 have advanced degrees.

Subjects Offered Advanced Placement courses, algebra, American history, anatomy, art, art history, biology, calculus, chemistry, chorus, community service, computer math, computer science, creative writing, drama, earth science, ecology, economics, English, environmental science, ethics, European history, fine arts, French, geometry, government/civics, health, instrumental music, international relations, journalism, Latin, mathematics, Middle Eastern history, music, photography, physical education, physics, political science, pre-calculus, religion, science, social studies, Spanish, speech, theater, trigonometry, world history, world literature, writing.

Graduation Requirements Arts and fine arts (art, music, dance, drama), computer science, economics, English, foreign language, government, mathematics, physical education (includes health), religion (includes Bible studies and theology), science, social studies (includes history), participation in wilderness program. Community service is required.

Special Academic Programs Advanced Placement exam preparation; honors section; independent study.

College Admission Counseling 101 students graduated in 2008; all went to college, including Southern Methodist University; Texas A&M University; Texas Christian University; The University of Texas at Austin; University of Southern California; Vanderbilt University. 65% scored over 600 on SAT critical reading, 64% scored over 600 on SAT math, 68% scored over 600 on SAT writing, 63% scored over 26 on composite ACT.

Student Life Upper grades have uniform requirement, student council, honor system. Discipline rests equally with students and faculty. Attendance at religious services is required.

Summer Programs Enrichment, advancement, sports, art/fine arts, rigorous outdoor training, computer instruction programs offered; held both on and off campus; held at Wolf Run Outdoor Education Center; accepts boys and girls; open to students from other schools. 200 students usually enrolled. 2009 schedule: June 1 to August 12. Application deadline: May 29.

Tuition and Aid Day student tuition: $21,750. Tuition installment plan (Insured Tuition Payment Plan, FACTS Tuition Payment Plan, monthly payment plans). Need-based scholarship grants available. In 2008–09, 14% of upper-school students received aid. Total amount of financial aid awarded in 2008–09: $1,700,000.

Admissions Traditional secondary-level entrance grade is 9. For fall 2008, 107 students applied for upper-level admission, 57 were accepted, 25 enrolled. ISEE, SLEP for foreign students, SSAT or writing sample required. Deadline for receipt of application materials: January 30. Application fee required: $175. On-campus interview required.

Athletics Interscholastic: baseball (boys), basketball (b,g), cheering (g), crew (b,g), cross-country running (b,g), dance team (g), field hockey (g), football (b), golf (b,g), lacrosse (b,g), outdoor education (b,g), outdoor skills (b,g), rowing (b,g), soccer (b,g), softball (g), tennis (b,g), track and field (b,g), volleyball (g); coed interscholastic: crew. 2 PE instructors, 32 coaches, 2 athletic trainers.

Computers Computers are regularly used in English, journalism, mathematics, science classes. Computer network features include on-campus library services, online commercial services, Internet access. The school has a published electronic and media policy.

Contact Ruth Burke, Director of Admission and Financial Aid. 214-353-5827. Fax: 214-353-5872. E-mail: burker@esdallas.org. Web site: www.esdallas.org.

ANNOUNCEMENT FROM THE SCHOOL The Episcopal School of Dallas (ESD) is a faith-centered, coeducational, college-preparatory school whose mission is to educate young people having a variety of backgrounds and aptitudes. ESD provides a challenging, traditional curriculum along with community service, outdoor education, and a low student-teacher ratio. Activities include athletics, fine arts, publications, and special-interest clubs. The School's Headmaster is the Reverend Stephen B. Swann.

ESCOLA AMERICANA DE CAMPINAS

Rua Cajamar, 35
Chácara da Barra
Campinas-SP 13090-860, Brazil

Head of School: Stephen A. Herrera

General Information Coeducational day college-preparatory, arts, bilingual studies, and technology school. Grades PK–12. Founded: 1956. Setting: urban. Nearest major city is São Paulo, Brazil. 4-acre campus. 4 buildings on campus. Approved or accredited by Association of American Schools in South America and Southern Association of Colleges and Schools. Member of European Council of International Schools. Languages of instruction: English and Portuguese. Endowment: $350,000. Total enrollment: 487. Upper school average class size: 18. Upper school faculty-student ratio: 1:7.

Upper School Student Profile Grade 6: 34 students (16 boys, 18 girls); Grade 7: 37 students (21 boys, 16 girls); Grade 8: 34 students (20 boys, 14 girls); Grade 9: 27 students (8 boys, 19 girls); Grade 10: 24 students (16 boys, 8 girls); Grade 11: 26 students (10 boys, 16 girls); Grade 12: 17 students (8 boys, 9 girls).

Faculty School total: 58. In upper school: 8 men, 16 women; 20 have advanced degrees.

Subjects Offered Algebra, American history, American literature, art, biology, calculus, chemistry, computer science, creative writing, drama, economics, English, English literature, fine arts, geography, geometry, government/civics, grammar, history, journalism, mathematics, music, physical education, physics, Portuguese, psychology, science, social studies, speech, trigonometry, world history, world literature, writing.

Graduation Requirements Arts and fine arts (art, music, dance, drama), computer science, English, foreign language, mathematics, physical education (includes health), science, social studies (includes history). Community service is required.

Special Academic Programs Advanced Placement exam preparation; honors section; term-away projects; study at local college for college credit; study abroad; special instructional classes for students with mild learning differences; ESL (5 students enrolled).

College Admission Counseling 24 students graduated in 2008; 13 went to college, including School of the Art Institute of Chicago. Other: 1 went to work, 10 had other specific plans. Median SAT critical reading: 610, median SAT math: 640, median SAT writing: 540, median combined SAT: 1790.

Student Life Upper grades have student council, honor system. Discipline rests equally with students and faculty.

Tuition and Aid Day student tuition: 45,611 Brazilian reals. Tuition installment plan (monthly payment plans). Need-based scholarship grants available. In 2008–09, 10% of upper-school students received aid. Total amount of financial aid awarded in 2008–09: $51,000.

Admissions Traditional secondary-level entrance grade is 9. For fall 2008, 50 students applied for upper-level admission, 16 were accepted, 16 enrolled. Admissions testing, English Composition Test for ESL students, ERB CTP IV, Iowa Test, CTBS, or TAP, SAT and writing sample required. Deadline for receipt of application materials: September 3. No application fee required. On-campus interview required.

Athletics Interscholastic: basketball (boys, girls), canoeing/kayaking (g), cheering (g), indoor soccer (b,g), soccer (b,g), volleyball (g); intramural: ballet (g), basketball (b,g), canoeing/kayaking (g), cheering (g), climbing (b,g), indoor soccer (b,g), soccer (b,g); coed intramural: aerobics, baseball, basketball, climbing, cooperative games, fitness, flag football, Frisbee, gymnastics, handball, indoor soccer, jogging, judo, kickball, martial arts, physical fitness, self defense, soccer, softball, strength & conditioning, table tennis, track and field, ultimate Frisbee, volleyball. 6 PE instructors, 11 coaches.

Computers Computers are regularly used in art, English, history, independent study, mathematics, science, yearbook classes. Computer network features include on-campus library services, online commercial services, Internet access. Campus intranet is available to students.

Contact Davi Sanchez, High School Principal. 55-19-2102-1006. Fax: 55-19-2102-1016. E-mail: davi_sanchez@eac.com.br. Web site: www.eac.com.br.

ESCONDIDO ADVENTIST ACADEMY

1301 Deodar Road
Escondido, California 92026

Head of School: Kristine Fuentes

General Information Coeducational day college-preparatory and religious studies school, affiliated with Seventh-day Adventist Church. Grades K–12. Founded: 1903. Setting: suburban. Nearest major city is San Diego. 14-acre campus. 1 building on campus. Approved or accredited by Association of Christian Schools International, Board of Regents, General Conference of Seventh-day Adventists, Western Association of Schools and Colleges, and California Department of Education. Total enrollment: 215. Upper school average class size: 25. Upper school faculty-student ratio: 1:10.

Upper School Student Profile 85% of students are Seventh-day Adventists.

Faculty School total: 20. In upper school: 6 men, 5 women; 3 have advanced degrees.
Subjects Offered Algebra, anatomy, art, biology, biology-AP, calculus-AP, career education, chemistry, choir, computer literacy, economics, English, fine arts, geometry, health, keyboarding, life skills, orchestra, physical education, physical science, physics, physiology, pre-calculus, religion, SAT preparation, shop, Spanish, U.S. government, U.S. history, world history, yearbook.
Graduation Requirements Arts and fine arts (art, music, dance, drama), computer science, English, mathematics, physical education (includes health), religion (includes Bible studies and theology), science, social studies (includes history).
Special Academic Programs Advanced Placement exam preparation; honors section; accelerated programs; independent study.
College Admission Counseling 26 students graduated in 2008; 20 went to college, including California State University, San Marcos; La Sierra University; Pacific Union College; Palomar College. Other: 6 went to work.
Student Life Upper grades have specified standards of dress, student council, honor system. Discipline rests primarily with faculty. Attendance at religious services is required.
Tuition and Aid Day student tuition: $4830–$7430. Tuition installment plan (monthly payment plans, individually arranged payment plans). Tuition reduction for siblings, church scholarships available. In 2008–09, 15% of upper-school students received aid. Total amount of financial aid awarded in 2008–09: $30,000.
Admissions Traditional secondary-level entrance grade is 9. For fall 2008, 90 students applied for upper-level admission, 86 were accepted, 83 enrolled. Deadline for receipt of application materials: none. Application fee required: $175. On-campus interview required.
Athletics Interscholastic: basketball (boys, girls), softball (g), volleyball (b,g); intramural: basketball (b,g), football (b,g), softball (b). 2 PE instructors, 6 coaches.
Computers Computers are regularly used in computer applications classes. Computer network features include on-campus library services, Internet access, wireless campus network, Internet filtering or blocking technology. Students grades are available online. The school has a published electronic and media policy.
Contact Jane Nicola, Registrar. 760-746-1800. Fax: 760-743-3499. E-mail: registrar@eaaschool.org. Web site: www.eaaschool.org.

THE ETHEL WALKER SCHOOL

230 Bushy Hill Road
Simsbury, Connecticut 06070

Head of School: Mrs. Elizabeth Cromwell Speers

General Information Girls' boarding and day college-preparatory and arts school. Boarding grades 9–12, day grades 6–12. Founded: 1911. Setting: suburban. Nearest major city is Hartford. Students are housed in single-sex dormitories. 300-acre campus. 9 buildings on campus. Approved or accredited by Connecticut Association of Independent Schools, New England Association of Schools and Colleges, The Association of Boarding Schools, and Connecticut Department of Education. Member of National Association of Independent Schools and Secondary School Admission Test Board. Endowment: $16 million. Total enrollment: 280. Upper school average class size: 11. Upper school faculty-student ratio: 1:4.
Upper School Student Profile Grade 6: 15 students (15 girls); Grade 7: 24 students (24 girls); Grade 8: 28 students (28 girls); Grade 9: 36 students (36 girls); Grade 10: 69 students (69 girls); Grade 11: 60 students (60 girls); Grade 12: 48 students (48 girls). 50% of students are boarding students. 50% are state residents. 15 states are represented in upper school student body. 13% are international students. International students from Germany, Hong Kong, Mexico, Puerto Rico, Republic of Korea, and Spain; 4 other countries represented in student body.
Faculty School total: 65. In upper school: 11 men, 35 women; 15 have advanced degrees; 20 reside on campus.
Subjects Offered Acting, African drumming, algebra, American history, American literature, art, art history, Asian history, astronomy, ballet, bell choir, biology, calculus, calculus-AP, ceramics, chemistry, chemistry-AP, choir, choreography, college counseling, community service, computer science, computer science-AP, concert choir, creative writing, dance, dance performance, drama, drawing and design, driver education, earth science, English, English literature, English literature and composition-AP, environmental science, environmental science-AP, equestrian sports, ethics, ethics and responsibility, European history, fine arts, French, French language-AP, geography, geometry, health, history, history-AP, honors algebra, independent study, instrumental music, Latin, Latin American history, Latin-AP, mathematics, modern European history, music, music theory, musical theater, newspaper, peer counseling, personal fitness, photography, physical education, physics, poetry, pre-calculus, psychology-AP, SAT/ACT preparation, science, science project, science research, sculpture, senior project, set design, social science, Spanish, Spanish language-AP, Spanish literature-AP, Spanish-AP, student publications, studio art-AP, tap dance, the Web, trigonometry, U.S. history-AP, visual and performing arts, voice, women's health, world history, world literature, writing, yearbook.
Graduation Requirements Arts and fine arts (art, music, dance, drama), English, ethics, foreign language, history, leadership training, mathematics, physical education (includes health), science, women's health, junior/senior project. Community service is required.
Special Academic Programs Advanced Placement exam preparation; honors section; independent study; term-away projects; study at local college for college credit; study abroad; academic accommodation for the gifted, the musically talented, and the artistically talented.
College Admission Counseling 38 students graduated in 2008; all went to college, including American University; Bates College; Bentley University; Connecticut College; Georgetown University; Washington and Lee University. Mean SAT critical reading: 571, mean SAT math: 582.
Student Life Upper grades have specified standards of dress, student council, honor system. Discipline rests equally with students and faculty.
Tuition and Aid Day student tuition: $30,185; 7-day tuition and room/board: $41,675. Tuition installment plan (monthly payment plans, individually arranged payment plans, 1-, 2-, and 10-payment plans). Tuition reduction for siblings, merit scholarship grants, need-based scholarship grants available. In 2008–09, 40% of upper-school students received aid. Total amount of financial aid awarded in 2008–09: $2,000,000.
Admissions Traditional secondary-level entrance grade is 9. For fall 2008, 217 students applied for upper-level admission, 124 were accepted, 80 enrolled. SSAT required. Deadline for receipt of application materials: February 1. Application fee required: $60. Interview required.
Athletics Interscholastic: alpine skiing, basketball, biathlon, dance, dressage, equestrian sports, field hockey, golf, horseback riding, independent competitive sports, lacrosse, modern dance, nordic skiing, skiing (downhill), soccer, softball, tennis, volleyball; intramural: ballet, climbing, combined training, cross-country running, dance, dance team, equestrian sports, fitness, hiking/backpacking, jogging, kayaking, mountaineering, Nautilus, outdoor activities, physical fitness, physical training, rock climbing, ropes courses, running, strength & conditioning, wall climbing, weight lifting, weight training, yoga. 3 PE instructors, 15 coaches, 1 athletic trainer.
Computers Computers are regularly used in English, foreign language, graphic design, history, mathematics, photography, science classes. Computer network features include on-campus library services, online commercial services, Internet access, wireless campus network, Internet filtering or blocking technology, Apple Share, Local Talk/Ethernet. Student e-mail accounts are available to students. Students grades are available online. The school has a published electronic and media policy.
Contact Ms. Erin Corbett, Director of Admission. 860-408-4200. Fax: 860-408-4202. E-mail: erin_corbett@ethelwalker.org. Web site: www.ethelwalker.org.

EVANGELICAL CHRISTIAN SCHOOL

7600 Macon Road
PO Box 1030
Cordova, Tennessee 38088-1030

Head of School: Mr. Steve Collums

General Information Coeducational day college-preparatory, arts, business, religious studies, and technology school, affiliated with Christian faith. Grades JK–12. Founded: 1964. Setting: suburban. Nearest major city is Memphis. 40-acre campus. 12 buildings on campus. Approved or accredited by Association of Christian Schools International, Southern Association of Colleges and Schools, Southern Association of Independent Schools, Tennessee Association of Independent Schools, The College Board, and Tennessee Department of Education. Endowment: $400,000. Total enrollment: 1,444. Upper school average class size: 14. Upper school faculty-student ratio: 1:11.
Upper School Student Profile Grade 9: 118 students (60 boys, 58 girls); Grade 10: 128 students (67 boys, 61 girls); Grade 11: 122 students (60 boys, 62 girls); Grade 12: 140 students (72 boys, 68 girls). 100% of students are Christian faith.
Faculty School total: 168. In upper school: 20 men, 21 women; 18 have advanced degrees.
Subjects Offered Acting, Advanced Placement courses, algebra, American government, American government-AP, American history, American history-AP, anatomy, ancient history, art, art-AP, band, Bible studies, biology, business law, calculus, calculus-AP, chemistry, chorus, college placement, computer applications, computer science, concert choir, drama, economics, economics and history, English, English-AP, etymology, European history-AP, fine arts, French, general science, geometry, geometry with art applications, health, health and wellness, journalism, Latin, mathematics, newspaper, personal finance, physical education, physical fitness, physical science, physics, religion, science, social studies, Spanish, speech, speech communications, theater, theater arts, world civilizations, world history, yearbook.
Graduation Requirements Arts and fine arts (art, music, dance, drama), English, foreign language, mathematics, physical education (includes health), religion (includes Bible studies and theology), science, social studies (includes history), extracurricular activities.
Special Academic Programs Advanced Placement exam preparation; honors section; academic accommodation for the gifted, the musically talented, and the artistically talented; remedial reading and/or remedial writing; remedial math.
College Admission Counseling 114 students graduated in 2008; 112 went to college, including Auburn University; Samford University; The University of Alabama; The University of Tennessee; University of Memphis; University of Mississippi. Other: 1 entered military service, 1 had other specific plans. Mean SAT critical reading: 627, mean SAT math: 616, mean composite ACT: 26. 17% scored over 600 on SAT critical reading, 12% scored over 600 on SAT math, 32% scored over 26 on composite ACT.

Student Life Upper grades have uniform requirement, student council, honor system. Discipline rests primarily with faculty. Attendance at religious services is required.
Tuition and Aid Day student tuition: $10,285. Tuition installment plan (Insured Tuition Payment Plan, monthly payment plans, 2-payment plan (60% on June 1, 40% on December 1)). Need-based scholarship grants available. In 2008–09, 10% of upper-school students received aid. Total amount of financial aid awarded in 2008–09: $205,000.
Admissions Traditional secondary-level entrance grade is 9. For fall 2008, 36 students applied for upper-level admission, 30 were accepted, 28 enrolled. ISEE required. Deadline for receipt of application materials: none. Application fee required: $50. Interview required.
Athletics Interscholastic: baseball (boys), basketball (b,g), cheering (g), cross-country running (b,g), football (b), golf (b,g), physical fitness (b,g), soccer (b,g), softball (g), strength & conditioning (b,g), swimming and diving (b,g), tennis (b,g), track and field (b,g), volleyball (g), weight training (b,g). 3 PE instructors, 1 athletic trainer.
Computers Computers are regularly used in all classes. Computer network features include on-campus library services, online commercial services, Internet access, Internet filtering or blocking technology. Students grades are available online. The school has a published electronic and media policy.
Contact Mrs. Erin Dickson, Director of Admissions. 901-754-7217 Ext. 1101. Fax: 901-754-8123. E-mail: edickson@ecseagles.com. Web site: www.ecseagles.net.

EVANSVILLE DAY SCHOOL

3400 North Green River Road
Evansville, Indiana 47715

Head of School: Mr. Kendell Berry

General Information Coeducational day college-preparatory school. Grades PK–12. Founded: 1946. Setting: suburban. Nearest major city is St. Louis, MO. 55-acre campus. 1 building on campus. Approved or accredited by Independent Schools Association of the Central States and Indiana Department of Education. Member of National Association of Independent Schools. Endowment: $335,000. Total enrollment: 326. Upper school average class size: 15. Upper school faculty-student ratio: 1:10.
Upper School Student Profile Grade 9: 21 students (15 boys, 6 girls); Grade 10: 24 students (13 boys, 11 girls); Grade 11: 12 students (6 boys, 6 girls); Grade 12: 12 students (8 boys, 4 girls).
Faculty School total: 42. In upper school: 10 men, 6 women; 11 have advanced degrees.
Subjects Offered Advanced Placement courses, algebra, American history, American literature, art, biology, calculus, ceramics, chemistry, computer programming, computer science, creative writing, drama, economics, English, English literature, environmental science, expository writing, fine arts, French, geography, geometry, government/civics, grammar, health, history, journalism, mathematics, music, music theory, philosophy, physical education, physics, psychology, science, social science, social studies, sociology, Spanish, speech, theater, trigonometry, world history, world literature, world religions, writing, zoology.
Graduation Requirements Arts and fine arts (art, music, dance, drama), computer science, English, foreign language, mathematics, physical education (includes health), science, social science, social studies (includes history), speech.
Special Academic Programs Advanced Placement exam preparation; honors section; study at local college for college credit; academic accommodation for the gifted.
College Admission Counseling 14 students graduated in 2008; all went to college, including Emory University; Indiana University Bloomington; Purdue University; Smith College; University of Evansville; Wabash College. Median SAT critical reading: 560, median SAT math: 565, median SAT writing: 505, median composite ACT: 21. Mean combined SAT: 1661. 43% scored over 600 on SAT critical reading, 29% scored over 600 on SAT math, 21% scored over 600 on SAT writing, 35% scored over 1800 on combined SAT, 33% scored over 26 on composite ACT.
Student Life Upper grades have specified standards of dress, student council, honor system. Discipline rests primarily with faculty.
Summer Programs Enrichment, advancement, art/fine arts, computer instruction programs offered; session focuses on enrichment; held on campus; accepts boys and girls; open to students from other schools. 100 students usually enrolled. 2009 schedule: June 8 to June 20. Application deadline: May.
Tuition and Aid Day student tuition: $12,015. Tuition installment plan (Insured Tuition Payment Plan, monthly payment plans, pay in full: no fees, Pat semi-annually: no fees). Tuition reduction for siblings, merit scholarship grants, need-based scholarship grants, Professional Judgment scholarships available. In 2008–09, 20% of upper-school students received aid; total upper-school merit-scholarship money awarded: $112,000. Total amount of financial aid awarded in 2008–09: $183,000.
Admissions Traditional secondary-level entrance grade is 9. For fall 2008, 7 students applied for upper-level admission, 6 were accepted, 6 enrolled. English proficiency or ERB required. Deadline for receipt of application materials: none. Application fee required: $30. On-campus interview required.
Athletics Interscholastic: basketball (boys, girls), cheering (g), golf (b), outdoor adventure (b,g), physical fitness (b,g), pom squad (g), soccer (b,g), strength & conditioning (b,g), tennis (g), weight training (b); coed interscholastic: cheering, fitness walking. 3 PE instructors.
Computers Computers are regularly used in all academic, yearbook classes. Computer network features include on-campus library services, Internet access, Internet filtering or blocking technology. Student e-mail accounts and computer access in designated common areas are available to students. Students grades are available online. The school has a published electronic and media policy.
Contact Beth Baker, Director of Admission. 812-476-3039 Ext. 205. Fax: 812-476-4061. E-mail: bbaker@evansvilledayschool.org. Web site: www.evansvilledayschool.org.

EXCEL ACADEMY, INC.

Newark, Ohio

See Special Needs Schools section.

EXCEL CHRISTIAN ACADEMY

325 Old Mill Road
Cartersville, Georgia 30120

Head of School: Mr. Tommy Harris

General Information Coeducational day college-preparatory school, affiliated with Church of God. Grades K–12. Founded: 1993. Setting: suburban. 15-acre campus. 3 buildings on campus. Approved or accredited by Association of Christian Schools International, Southern Association of Colleges and Schools, and Georgia Department of Education. Total enrollment: 373. Upper school average class size: 20. Upper school faculty-student ratio: 1:18.
Upper School Student Profile Grade 6: 34 students (17 boys, 17 girls); Grade 7: 37 students (20 boys, 17 girls); Grade 8: 39 students (21 boys, 18 girls); Grade 9: 40 students (14 boys, 26 girls); Grade 10: 24 students (14 boys, 10 girls); Grade 11: 17 students (3 boys, 14 girls); Grade 12: 29 students (11 boys, 18 girls). 29% of students are Church of God.
Faculty School total: 33. In upper school: 6 men, 14 women; 5 have advanced degrees.
Graduation Requirements Advanced Placement courses, Bible, computer technologies, electives, English, foreign language, history, mathematics, physical education (includes health), science.
Special Academic Programs Advanced Placement exam preparation; honors section; study at local college for college credit.
College Admission Counseling 23 students graduated in 2008; 22 went to college, including Kennesaw State University; University of Georgia. Other: 1 went to work. Median SAT critical reading: 530, median SAT math: 530, median SAT writing: 540, median combined SAT: 1600. 35% scored over 600 on SAT critical reading, 22% scored over 600 on SAT math, 22% scored over 600 on SAT writing, 22% scored over 1800 on combined SAT.
Student Life Upper grades have uniform requirement, student council, honor system. Discipline rests primarily with faculty.
Tuition and Aid Day student tuition: $8520. Tuition installment plan (monthly payment plans). Need-based loans available. In 2008–09, 30% of upper-school students received aid.
Admissions Traditional secondary-level entrance grade is 10. For fall 2008, 21 students applied for upper-level admission, 21 were accepted, 17 enrolled. Any standardized test required. Deadline for receipt of application materials: March. Application fee required: $100. Interview required.
Athletics Interscholastic: baseball (boys), basketball (b,g), cheering (g), cross-country running (b,g), softball (g), tennis (b,g); intramural: football (b); coed interscholastic: weight training; coed intramural: cross-country running. 2 PE instructors, 2 coaches.
Computers Computers are regularly used in business education, desktop publishing, journalism, newspaper, SAT preparation classes. Computer resources include Internet access.
Contact Mrs. Krista K. Keefe, Counselor. 770-382-9488. Fax: 770-606-9884. E-mail: kkeefe@excelacademy.cc. Web site: www.excelacademy.cc.

EXPLORATIONS ACADEMY

PO Box 3014
Bellingham, Washington 98227

Head of School: Daniel Kirkpatrick

General Information Coeducational day college-preparatory, experiential education, and international field study expeditions school. Ungraded, ages 11–18. Founded: 1995. Setting: urban. Nearest major city is Vancouver, BC, Canada. 1-acre campus. 1 building on campus. Approved or accredited by Northwest Association of Accredited Schools, Northwest Association of Schools and Colleges, Pacific Northwest Association of Independent Schools, and Washington Department of Education. Languages of instruction: English and Spanish. Total enrollment: 20. Upper school average class size: 10. Upper school faculty-student ratio: 1:5.
Faculty School total: 7. In upper school: 3 men, 3 women; 4 have advanced degrees.
Subjects Offered Agriculture, American literature, anatomy and physiology, anthropology, archaeology, art, boat building, botany, calculus, carpentry, chemistry, computer graphics, computer programming, conflict resolution, construction, creative writing, desktop publishing, drawing, earth science, ecology, environmental science,

first aid, French, gardening, gender issues, geology, government, health, horticulture, human relations, journalism, Latin American studies, leadership training, marine biology, media, meteorology, microbiology, music, music history, painting, philosophy, photography, physical education, physics, poetry, political science, psychology, sculpture, sexuality, short story, Spanish, technology, theater design and production, video film production, world culture, world geography, world history, world literature, writing.

Graduation Requirements Arts and fine arts (art, music, dance, drama), computer science, English, foreign language, human relations, lab science, mathematics, occupational education, physical education (includes health), science, social science, social studies (includes history), Washington State and Northwest History, one term of self-designed interdisciplinary studies. Community service is required.

Special Academic Programs Advanced Placement exam preparation; honors section; accelerated programs; independent study; term-away projects; academic accommodation for the gifted.

College Admission Counseling 2 students graduated in 2008; all went to college, including The Evergreen State College; Western Washington University.

Student Life Upper grades have honor system. Discipline rests primarily with faculty.

Summer Programs Enrichment, advancement, art/fine arts, rigorous outdoor training programs offered; session focuses on experiential learning; held both on and off campus; held at local urban and wilderness areas; accepts boys and girls; open to students from other schools. 12 students usually enrolled. 2009 schedule: June 29 to August 21. Application deadline: none.

Tuition and Aid Day student tuition: $9200. Guaranteed tuition plan. Tuition installment plan (monthly payment plans, individually arranged payment plans, school's own payment plan). Tuition reduction for siblings, merit scholarship grants, need-based scholarship grants, need-based loans, low-interest loans with deferred payment available. In 2008–09, 40% of upper-school students received aid; total upper-school merit-scholarship money awarded: $35,000. Total amount of financial aid awarded in 2008–09: $74,000.

Admissions Traditional secondary-level entrance age is 14. Deadline for receipt of application materials: none. Application fee required: $50. Interview required.

Computers Computers are regularly used in animation, art, English, French, graphics, mathematics, media production, publications, SAT preparation, science, writing, yearbook classes. Computer network features include online commercial services, Internet access, wireless campus network. Computer access in designated common areas is available to students. The school has a published electronic and media policy.

Contact Betty McMahon, Registrar. 360-671-8085. Fax: 360-671-2521. E-mail: info@explorationsacademy.org. Web site: www.ExplorationsAcademy.org.

EZELL-HARDING CHRISTIAN SCHOOL

574 Bell Road
Antioch, Tennessee 37013

Head of School: Mr. Jackson Howell

General Information Coeducational day college-preparatory and religious studies school, affiliated with Church of Christ. Grades K–12. Founded: 1973. Setting: suburban. Nearest major city is Nashville. 30-acre campus. 1 building on campus. Approved or accredited by National Christian School Association, Southern Association of Colleges and Schools, and Tennessee Association of Independent Schools. Endowment: $100,000. Total enrollment: 800. Upper school average class size: 19. Upper school faculty-student ratio: 1:12.

Upper School Student Profile Grade 9: 65 students (35 boys, 30 girls); Grade 10: 70 students (44 boys, 26 girls); Grade 11: 76 students (30 boys, 46 girls); Grade 12: 51 students (21 boys, 30 girls). 40% of students are members of Church of Christ.

Faculty School total: 75. In upper school: 12 men, 16 women; 8 have advanced degrees.

Subjects Offered Advanced math, algebra, American history, anatomy and physiology, art, band, Bible, biology, calculus, chemistry, chorus, creative writing, economics, European history, fitness, French, geography, geometry, government, journalism, keyboarding, microcomputer technology applications, physical science, physics, psychology, sociology, Spanish, trigonometry, wellness, world history.

Graduation Requirements American history, Bible, computers, English, mathematics, physical education (includes health), science, wellness, economics or government, world history or European history.

Special Academic Programs Advanced Placement exam preparation; honors section.

College Admission Counseling 70 students graduated in 2008; 68 went to college, including Freed-Hardeman University; Harding University; Lipscomb University; Middle Tennessee State University; The University of Tennessee; Trevecca Nazarene University. Other: 1 went to work, 1 entered military service. Median composite ACT: 25. 20% scored over 26 on composite ACT.

Student Life Upper grades have specified standards of dress, student council. Discipline rests primarily with faculty.

Tuition and Aid Day student tuition: $6000. Tuition installment plan (The Tuition Plan, monthly payment plans). Need-based scholarship grants available.

Admissions Traditional secondary-level entrance grade is 9. For fall 2008, 30 students applied for upper-level admission, 25 were accepted, 25 enrolled. Deadline for receipt of application materials: none. Application fee required: $40. Interview recommended.

Athletics Interscholastic: baseball (boys), basketball (b,g), bowling (b,g), cheering (g), cross-country running (b,g), drill team (g), football (b), golf (b,g), hockey (b), soccer (b,g), softball (g), tennis (b,g), track and field (b,g), volleyball (g), weight training (b,g). 2 PE instructors, 6 coaches, 1 athletic trainer.

Computers Computer network features include on-campus library services, Internet access. Student e-mail accounts are available to students. Students grades are available online. The school has a published electronic and media policy.

Contact Mrs. Debbie S. Shaffer, Admissions Officer. 615-367-0532. Fax: 615-399-8747. E-mail: debbie.shaffer@ezellharding.com. Web site: www.ezellharding.com.

FAIRFIELD COLLEGE PREPARATORY SCHOOL

1073 North Benson Road
Fairfield, Connecticut 06824-5157

Head of School: Rev. John J. Hanwell, SJ

General Information Boys' day college-preparatory, arts, religious studies, and technology school, affiliated with Roman Catholic Church. Grades 9–12. Founded: 1942. Setting: suburban. Nearest major city is Bridgeport. 220-acre campus. 4 buildings on campus. Approved or accredited by Connecticut Association of Independent Schools, Jesuit Secondary Education Association, New England Association of Schools and Colleges, and Connecticut Department of Education. Member of National Association of Independent Schools. Endowment: $9 million. Total enrollment: 917. Upper school average class size: 21. Upper school faculty-student ratio: 1:15.

Upper School Student Profile Grade 9: 270 students (270 boys); Grade 10: 222 students (222 boys); Grade 11: 224 students (224 boys); Grade 12: 201 students (201 boys). 80% of students are Roman Catholic.

Faculty School total: 59. In upper school: 38 men, 21 women; 44 have advanced degrees.

Subjects Offered Algebra, American history, American literature, art, Asian studies, band, biology, calculus, career exploration, chemistry, chorus, community service, computer science, creative writing, drama, economics, English, English literature, European history, fine arts, French, geometry, history, journalism, Latin, mathematics, physics, religion, science, social studies, sociology, Spanish, theater, theology, trigonometry, world history, world literature.

Graduation Requirements Arts and fine arts (art, music, dance, drama), computer science, English, foreign language, mathematics, religion (includes Bible studies and theology), science, social studies (includes history), senior comprehensive exercises. Community service is required.

Special Academic Programs Advanced Placement exam preparation; honors section; study at local college for college credit.

College Admission Counseling 210 students graduated in 2008; 205 went to college, including Boston College; College of the Holy Cross; Fairfield University; Fordham University; Providence College; University of Connecticut. Other: 1 entered military service, 4 entered a postgraduate year. Mean SAT critical reading: 581, mean SAT math: 594, mean SAT writing: 588, mean combined SAT: 1763.

Student Life Upper grades have specified standards of dress, student council. Discipline rests primarily with faculty. Attendance at religious services is required.

Summer Programs Remediation, enrichment, sports, art/fine arts, computer instruction programs offered; session focuses on enrichment; held on campus; accepts boys; open to students from other schools. 160 students usually enrolled. 2009 schedule: June 30 to July 25.

Tuition and Aid Day student tuition: $14,285. Tuition installment plan (monthly payment plans). Need-based scholarship grants available. In 2008–09, 25% of upper-school students received aid. Total amount of financial aid awarded in 2008–09: $1,500,000.

Admissions Traditional secondary-level entrance grade is 9. For fall 2008, 510 students applied for upper-level admission, 320 were accepted, 272 enrolled. High School Placement Test required. Deadline for receipt of application materials: December 1. Application fee required: $60.

Athletics Interscholastic: alpine skiing, baseball, basketball, bowling, crew, cross-country running, diving, football, golf, ice hockey, indoor track & field, lacrosse, rugby, sailing, skiing (downhill), soccer, swimming and diving, tennis, track and field, winter (indoor) track, wrestling; intramural: basketball, bicycling, fitness, in-line skating, mountain biking, Nautilus, power lifting, skiing (downhill), strength & conditioning, weight lifting. 33 coaches, 2 athletic trainers.

Computers Computers are regularly used in art, English, foreign language, history, mathematics, science, technology, theology classes. Computer network features include on-campus library services, online commercial services, Internet access, Internet filtering or blocking technology. The school has a published electronic and media policy.

Contact Mrs. Colleen H. Adams, Director of Communications. 203-254-4200 Ext. 2487. Fax: 203-254-4071. E-mail: cadams@fairfieldprep.org. Web site: www.fairfieldprep.org.

FAIRHILL SCHOOL

Dallas, Texas

See Special Needs Schools section.

FAITH CHRISTIAN HIGH SCHOOL

3105 Colusa Highway
Yuba City, California 95993

Head of School: Mr. Stephen Finlay

General Information Coeducational day college-preparatory, arts, religious studies, and technology school, affiliated with Christian faith. Grades 9–12. Founded: 1975. Setting: rural. Nearest major city is Sacramento. 10-acre campus. 4 buildings on campus. Approved or accredited by Association of Christian Schools International, Western Association of Schools and Colleges, and California Department of Education. Total enrollment: 114. Upper school average class size: 25. Upper school faculty-student ratio: 1:12.

Upper School Student Profile Grade 9: 32 students (13 boys, 19 girls); Grade 10: 30 students (16 boys, 14 girls); Grade 11: 27 students (10 boys, 17 girls); Grade 12: 25 students (12 boys, 13 girls). 99% of students are Christian.

Faculty School total: 15. In upper school: 10 men, 5 women; 4 have advanced degrees.

Subjects Offered Algebra, arts, Bible, biology, biology-AP, British literature, calculus-AP, chemistry, civics, computer science, computer studies, concert band, drama, economics, English, English composition, English literature, English-AP, geography, geometry, government, health, honors English, physical education, physical science, pre-calculus, senior project, Spanish, trigonometry, U.S. history, world geography, world history, yearbook.

Graduation Requirements Algebra, Bible, biology, civics, economics, English, geometry, health, physical science, senior project, U.S. history, world geography, world history.

Special Academic Programs Advanced Placement exam preparation; study at local college for college credit.

College Admission Counseling 31 students graduated in 2008; 29 went to college, including Azusa Pacific University; Biola University; California State University, Chico; Point Loma Nazarene University; Simpson University; University of California, Davis. Other: 2 went to work. Median SAT critical reading: 510, median SAT math: 510, median SAT writing: 500, median combined SAT: 1520, median composite ACT: 22.

Student Life Upper grades have specified standards of dress, student council, honor system. Discipline rests primarily with faculty. Attendance at religious services is required.

Summer Programs Art/fine arts programs offered; session focuses on enrichment; held on campus; accepts boys and girls; open to students from other schools. 60 students usually enrolled. 2009 schedule: June 15 to July 12. Application deadline: May 30.

Tuition and Aid Day student tuition: $7245. Tuition installment plan (monthly payment plans). Tuition reduction for siblings, need-based scholarship grants available. In 2008–09, 10% of upper-school students received aid. Total amount of financial aid awarded in 2008–09: $50,000.

Admissions Traditional secondary-level entrance grade is 9. For fall 2008, 13 students applied for upper-level admission, 11 were accepted, 11 enrolled. Achievement tests required. Deadline for receipt of application materials: none. Application fee required: $50. Interview required.

Athletics Interscholastic: baseball (boys), basketball (b,g), cheering (g), cross-country running (b,g), soccer (b,g), volleyball (g); coed interscholastic: golf. 1 PE instructor, 8 coaches.

Computers Computers are regularly used in all academic classes. Computer network features include on-campus library services, Internet access, Internet filtering or blocking technology. Students grades are available online. The school has a published electronic and media policy.

Contact Mrs. Sue Shorey, Secretary. 530-674-5474. Fax: 530-674-0194. E-mail: sshorey@fcs-k12.org. Web site: www.fcs-k12.org.

FAITH LUTHERAN HIGH SCHOOL

2015 South Hualapai Way
Las Vegas, Nevada 89117-6949

Head of School: Mr. Kevin M. Dunning

General Information Coeducational day college-preparatory and religious studies school, affiliated with Lutheran Church–Missouri Synod, Evangelical Lutheran Church in America. Grades 6–12. Founded: 1979. Setting: suburban. 45-acre campus. 4 buildings on campus. Approved or accredited by Lutheran School Accreditation Commission, Northwest Association of Schools and Colleges, and Nevada Department of Education. Endowment: $1 million. Total enrollment: 1,282. Upper school average class size: 25. Upper school faculty-student ratio: 1:17.

Upper School Student Profile Grade 9: 178 students (69 boys, 109 girls); Grade 10: 186 students (88 boys, 98 girls); Grade 11: 184 students (90 boys, 94 girls); Grade 12: 156 students (71 boys, 85 girls). 23% of students are Lutheran Church–Missouri Synod, Evangelical Lutheran Church in America.

Faculty School total: 86. In upper school: 32 men, 54 women; 42 have advanced degrees.

Subjects Offered Algebra, American history, art, biology, chemistry, computer science, earth science, English, fine arts, fitness, geometry, German, health, mathematics, music, physical education, physical science, religion, SAT/ACT preparation, science, social studies, Spanish.

Graduation Requirements American history, arts and fine arts (art, music, dance, drama), computer science, English, foreign language, mathematics, physical education (includes health), religion (includes Bible studies and theology), science, social studies (includes history).

Special Academic Programs 7 Advanced Placement exams for which test preparation is offered; honors section; independent study; academic accommodation for the musically talented; remedial math.

College Admission Counseling 152 students graduated in 2008; 140 went to college, including Concordia University; University of Nevada, Las Vegas; University of Nevada, Reno. Other: 9 went to work, 3 entered military service. Median SAT critical reading: 560, median SAT math: 530, median SAT writing: 530, median combined SAT: 1620, median composite ACT: 24. 32% scored over 600 on SAT critical reading, 24% scored over 600 on SAT math, 25% scored over 600 on SAT writing, 25% scored over 1800 on combined SAT, 29% scored over 26 on composite ACT.

Student Life Upper grades have uniform requirement, student council. Discipline rests primarily with faculty. Attendance at religious services is required.

Tuition and Aid Day student tuition: $8400. Tuition installment plan (monthly payment plans, individually arranged payment plans). Tuition reduction for siblings, need-based scholarship grants available. In 2008–09, 10% of upper-school students received aid. Total amount of financial aid awarded in 2008–09: $220,000.

Admissions Traditional secondary-level entrance grade is 9. For fall 2008, 110 students applied for upper-level admission, 100 were accepted, 80 enrolled. High School Placement Test and Stanford 9 required. Deadline for receipt of application materials: none. Application fee required: $350. On-campus interview required.

Athletics Interscholastic: aerobics/dance (girls), aquatics (b,g), baseball (b), basketball (b,g), cheering (g), cross-country running (b,g), dance team (g), football (b), golf (b,g), lacrosse (b,g), soccer (b,g), softball (g), swimming and diving (b,g), tennis (b,g), track and field (b,g), volleyball (g); intramural: strength & conditioning (b,g); coed interscholastic: strength & conditioning; coed intramural: skiing (downhill). 7 PE instructors, 26 coaches.

Computers Computers are regularly used in keyboarding, yearbook classes. Computer network features include on-campus library services, online commercial services, Internet access, wireless campus network, Internet filtering or blocking technology. Student e-mail accounts and computer access in designated common areas are available to students. Students grades are available online. The school has a published electronic and media policy.

Contact Carol Neal, Registrar. 702-804-4400. Fax: 702-804-4488. E-mail: NealC@faithlutheranlv.org. Web site: www.faithlutheranlv.org.

FALMOUTH ACADEMY

7 Highfield Drive
Falmouth, Massachusetts 02540

Head of School: Mr. David C. Faus

General Information Coeducational day college-preparatory and arts school. Grades 7–12. Founded: 1976. Setting: small town. Nearest major city is Boston. 34-acre campus. 3 buildings on campus. Approved or accredited by Association of Independent Schools in New England and New England Association of Schools and Colleges. Member of National Association of Independent Schools and Secondary School Admission Test Board. Endowment: $3 million. Total enrollment: 213. Upper school average class size: 12. Upper school faculty-student ratio: 1:4.

Upper School Student Profile Grade 9: 34 students (16 boys, 18 girls); Grade 10: 38 students (16 boys, 22 girls); Grade 11: 38 students (15 boys, 23 girls); Grade 12: 38 students (18 boys, 20 girls).

Faculty School total: 35. In upper school: 14 men, 20 women; 24 have advanced degrees.

Subjects Offered Algebra, American history, American literature, art, biology, calculus, ceramics, chemistry, creative writing, drama, earth science, ecology, English, English literature, environmental science, European history, expository writing, fine arts, French, geography, geology, geometry, German, grammar, health, history, journalism, mathematics, music, photography, physical education, physics, science, sculpture, social studies, statistics, theater, trigonometry, woodworking, world history, world literature, writing.

Graduation Requirements Arts and fine arts (art, music, dance, drama), English, foreign language, history, mathematics, science.

Special Academic Programs Advanced Placement exam preparation; independent study; term-away projects; study abroad.

College Admission Counseling 28 students graduated in 2008; 25 went to college, including Brown University. Other: 3 had other specific plans. Mean SAT critical reading: 640, mean SAT math: 630, mean SAT writing: 640.

Student Life Upper grades have specified standards of dress, student council, honor system. Discipline rests primarily with faculty.

Tuition and Aid Day student tuition: $20,625. Merit scholarship grants, need-based scholarship grants, need-based loans, TERI Loans available. In 2008–09, 35% of

upper-school students received aid; total upper-school merit-scholarship money awarded: $2000. Total amount of financial aid awarded in 2008–09: $500,000.
Admissions Traditional secondary-level entrance grade is 9. For fall 2008, 20 students applied for upper-level admission, 15 were accepted, 5 enrolled. SSAT required. Deadline for receipt of application materials: March 1. Application fee required: $50. On-campus interview required.
Athletics Interscholastic: basketball (boys, girls), lacrosse (b,g), soccer (b,g). 1 PE instructor.
Computers Computers are regularly used in design, English, mathematics, science classes. Computer resources include on-campus library services, Internet access, Internet filtering or blocking technology. The school has a published electronic and media policy.
Contact Mr. Michael J. Earley, Director of Admissions. 508-457-9696 Ext. 224. Fax: 508-457-4112. E-mail: mearley@falmouthacademy.org. Web site: www.falmouthacademy.org.

ANNOUNCEMENT FROM THE SCHOOL Falmouth Academy is a deliberately small school with a traditional core curriculum that emphasizes reading and writing. In classes of 12–14 students gathered around oval tables, in the daily all-school meeting, and in extracurricular activities, students engage actively in the life of the community. FA conducts exchanges with schools in France and Germany.

THE FAMILY FOUNDATION SCHOOL

Hancock, New York

See Special Needs Schools section.

FATHER JUDGE HIGH SCHOOL

3301 Solly Avenue
Philadelphia, Pennsylvania 19136

Head of School: Dr. Kathleen Herpich

General Information Boys' day college-preparatory, arts, business, and religious studies school, affiliated with Roman Catholic Church; primarily serves students with learning disabilities. Grades 9–12. Founded: 1953. Setting: suburban. 3 buildings on campus. Approved or accredited by National Catholic Education Association and Pennsylvania Department of Education. Total enrollment: 1,258. Upper school average class size: 28. Upper school faculty-student ratio: 1:28.
Upper School Student Profile Grade 9: 277 students (277 boys); Grade 10: 341 students (341 boys); Grade 11: 291 students (291 boys); Grade 12: 349 students (349 boys). 98% of students are Roman Catholic.
Faculty School total: 68. In upper school: 41 men, 20 women.
Graduation Requirements 1½ elective credits, biology, English, foreign language, health education, mathematics, physical education (includes health), physical science, religion (includes Bible studies and theology), science, theology, U.S. government, world history.
College Admission Counseling 274 students graduated in 2008; 255 went to college, including Saint John's University; Temple University; The Catholic University of America; University of Delaware; University of Pennsylvania; West Chester University of Pennsylvania. Other: 10 went to work, 5 entered military service, 2 had other specific plans.
Student Life Upper grades have uniform requirement, student council, honor system. Discipline rests primarily with faculty. Attendance at religious services is required.
Tuition and Aid Tuition installment plan (monthly payment plans). Tuition reduction for siblings, need-based scholarship grants available. In 2008–09, 50% of upper-school students received aid.
Admissions Traditional secondary-level entrance grade is 10. Any standardized test or TerraNova required. Deadline for receipt of application materials: none. No application fee required.
Athletics Interscholastic: baseball, basketball, bowling, cheering (g), crew, cross-country running, dance (g), dance squad (g), dance team (g), danceline (g), golf, hockey, ice hockey, lacrosse, rugby, soccer, swimming and diving, tennis, track and field, winter (indoor) track, wrestling; intramural: flag football, touch football. 1 PE instructor, 30 coaches, 1 athletic trainer.
Computers Computers are regularly used in all classes. Computer network features include on-campus library services, Internet access, wireless campus network, Internet filtering or blocking technology. Students grades are available online. The school has a published electronic and media policy.
Contact Mr. Thomas Coyle, Admissions. 215-338-9494. Fax: 215-338-0250. E-mail: tcoyle@fatherjudge.com. Web site: www.fatherjudge.com.

FATHER LOPEZ HIGH SCHOOL

3918 LPGA Boulevard
Daytona Beach, Florida 32124

Head of School: Mr. George Pressey

General Information Coeducational day college-preparatory school, affiliated with Roman Catholic Church. Grades 9–12. Founded: 1959. Setting: urban. 90-acre campus. 7 buildings on campus. Approved or accredited by National Catholic Education Association, Southern Association of Colleges and Schools, and Florida Department of Education. Total enrollment: 275. Upper school average class size: 23. Upper school faculty-student ratio: 1:20.
Upper School Student Profile Grade 9: 74 students (30 boys, 44 girls); Grade 10: 60 students (26 boys, 34 girls); Grade 11: 64 students (33 boys, 31 girls); Grade 12: 68 students (27 boys, 41 girls). 80% of students are Roman Catholic.
Faculty School total: 26. In upper school: 13 men, 13 women; 14 have advanced degrees.
Subjects Offered Accounting, Advanced Placement courses, aerobics, algebra, American government, American government-AP, American history, American history-AP, American literature, anatomy and physiology, art, audio visual/media, biology, biology-AP, British literature, British literature-AP, calculus-AP, chemistry, computer applications, computer graphics, computer keyboarding, consumer mathematics, criminal justice, critical thinking, culinary arts, dance, digital photography, drama, drama performance, ecology, economics, English, English literature, English literature-AP, filmmaking, French, geography, geometry, government, government-AP, graphic design, health, health education, honors algebra, honors English, honors geometry, honors U.S. history, law, law studies, marine science, photography, physical education, pre-calculus, psychology, social justice, Spanish, theology, U.S. history, U.S. history-AP, Web site design, weight training, world geography, world history, writing.
Graduation Requirements Algebra, American government, American history, American literature, biology, British literature, cultural geography, economics, English, English literature, geometry, health and wellness, 100 hours of community service.
Special Academic Programs Advanced Placement exam preparation; honors section; study at local college for college credit.
College Admission Counseling 48 students graduated in 2008; 47 went to college, including Florida State University; University of Central Florida; University of Florida; University of Miami; University of North Florida. Other: 1 entered military service. Median combined SAT: 1034, median composite ACT: 22.
Student Life Upper grades have uniform requirement, student council, honor system. Discipline rests primarily with faculty. Attendance at religious services is required.
Tuition and Aid Day student tuition: $7400. Tuition installment plan (FACTS Tuition Payment Plan). Tuition subsidy for qualifying families available. In 2008–09, 25% of upper-school students received aid. Total amount of financial aid awarded in 2008–09: $100,000.
Admissions Traditional secondary-level entrance grade is 9. For fall 2008, 276 students applied for upper-level admission, 274 were accepted, 274 enrolled. High School Placement Test required. Deadline for receipt of application materials: none. No application fee required. Interview required.
Athletics Interscholastic: aerobics/dance (girls), baseball (b), basketball (b,g), cheering (g), cross-country running (b,g), dance team (g), football (b), golf (b,g), lacrosse (b), soccer (b,g), softball (g), swimming and diving (b,g), tennis (b,g), track and field (b,g), volleyball (g). 2 PE instructors, 10 coaches, 1 athletic trainer.
Computers Computers are regularly used in accounting, animation, computer applications, graphic design, keyboarding, media production, photography, video film production, yearbook classes. Computer network features include on-campus library services, Internet access, wireless campus network, Internet filtering or blocking technology. Student e-mail accounts and computer access in designated common areas are available to students. Students grades are available online. The school has a published electronic and media policy.
Contact Mr. George Pressey, Principal. 386-253-5213. Fax: 386-252-6101. E-mail: gpressey@fatherlopez.org. Web site: www.fatherlopez.org.

FATHER RYAN HIGH SCHOOL

700 Norwood Drive
Nashville, Tennessee 37204

Head of School: Mr. McIntyre Jim

General Information Coeducational day college-preparatory, arts, and religious studies school, affiliated with Roman Catholic Church. Grades 9–12. Founded: 1925. Setting: suburban. 40-acre campus. 5 buildings on campus. Approved or accredited by National Catholic Education Association, Southern Association of Colleges and Schools, Southern Association of Independent Schools, Tennessee Association of Independent Schools, and The College Board. Endowment: $5 million. Total enrollment: 873. Upper school average class size: 20. Upper school faculty-student ratio: 1:12.
Upper School Student Profile Grade 9: 215 students (120 boys, 95 girls); Grade 10: 213 students (122 boys, 91 girls); Grade 11: 213 students (109 boys, 104 girls); Grade 12: 232 students (122 boys, 110 girls). 90% of students are Roman Catholic.
Faculty School total: 77. In upper school: 37 men, 40 women; 46 have advanced degrees.
Subjects Offered 3-dimensional design, Advanced Placement courses, aerobics, algebra, American government, American government-AP, American history, American history-AP, American literature, anatomy, art, art history, art-AP, Bible studies, biology, British literature, calculus, calculus-AP, Catholic belief and practice, chemistry, chemistry-AP, chorus, church history, college counseling, college planning, college writing, computer programming, computer science, computer studies, dance, dance performance, drama, drama performance, driver education, economics, English,

English literature, English-AP, European history, European history-AP, film studies, French, French-AP, geography, geometry, government-AP, government/civics, grammar, health, history, honors geometry, honors U.S. history, journalism, Latin, mathematics, music, physical education, physics, physics-AP, physiology, psychology, psychology-AP, religion, SAT preparation, science, Shakespeare, social studies, Spanish, Spanish-AP, speech, statistics-AP, theater, theater production, theology, trigonometry, Web site design, wind ensemble, world history, world literature, world religions, writing.

Graduation Requirements Arts and fine arts (art, music, dance, drama), computer science, English, foreign language, health education, mathematics, physical education (includes health), religion (includes Bible studies and theology), science, social studies (includes history).

Special Academic Programs Advanced Placement exam preparation; honors section; academic accommodation for the gifted, the musically talented, and the artistically talented; programs in English, mathematics for dyslexic students.

College Admission Counseling 231 students graduated in 2008; 227 went to college, including Middle Tennessee State University; Saint Louis University; Tennessee Technological University; The University of Tennessee; University of Dayton; Western Kentucky University. Other: 2 went to work, 1 entered military service. Median SAT critical reading: 553, median SAT math: 524, median composite ACT: 24. 20% scored over 26 on composite ACT.

Student Life Upper grades have uniform requirement, student council. Discipline rests primarily with faculty. Attendance at religious services is required.

Summer Programs Remediation, enrichment, advancement, sports, art/fine arts, computer instruction programs offered; held on campus; accepts boys and girls; open to students from other schools. 200 students usually enrolled. 2009 schedule: June 1 to June 28. Application deadline: none.

Tuition and Aid Day student tuition: $8735. Tuition installment plan (FACTS Tuition Payment Plan, individually arranged payment plans). Tuition reduction for siblings, need-based scholarship grants available. In 2008–09, 13% of upper-school students received aid. Total amount of financial aid awarded in 2008–09: $300,000.

Admissions Traditional secondary-level entrance grade is 9. For fall 2008, 295 students applied for upper-level admission, 260 were accepted, 220 enrolled. High School Placement Test required. Deadline for receipt of application materials: none. Application fee required: $80. On-campus interview required.

Athletics Interscholastic: aquatics (boys, girls), baseball (b,g), basketball (b,g), bowling (b,g), cheering (g), cross-country running (b,g), dance (g), dance team (g), diving (b,g), football (b), golf (b,g), ice hockey (b), lacrosse (b), power lifting (b), soccer (b,g), softball (g), Special Olympics (b,g), strength & conditioning (b,g), swimming and diving (b,g), tennis (b,g), track and field (b,g), volleyball (g), weight lifting (b,g), wrestling (b); intramural: fishing (b,g), indoor soccer (b,g), physical fitness (b,g). 1 athletic trainer.

Computers Computers are regularly used in all classes. Computer network features include on-campus library services, online commercial services, Internet access, Internet filtering or blocking technology. Computer access in designated common areas is available to students. The school has a published electronic and media policy.

Contact Ms. Kate Goetzinger, Director of Admissions. 615-383-4200. Fax: 615-783-0264. E-mail: goetzinferk@fatherryan.org. Web site: www.fatherryan.org.

FAYETTEVILLE ACADEMY

3200 Cliffdale Road
Fayetteville, North Carolina 28303
Head of School: Mr. Richard D. Cameron

General Information Coeducational day college-preparatory, arts, and technology school. Grades PK–12. Founded: 1969. Setting: suburban. 30-acre campus. 10 buildings on campus. Approved or accredited by North Carolina Association of Independent Schools, Southern Association of Colleges and Schools, Southern Association of Independent Schools, The College Board, and North Carolina Department of Education. Endowment: $319,603. Total enrollment: 432. Upper school average class size: 15. Upper school faculty-student ratio: 1:15.

Upper School Student Profile Grade 9: 46 students (23 boys, 23 girls); Grade 10: 31 students (12 boys, 19 girls); Grade 11: 39 students (22 boys, 17 girls); Grade 12: 36 students (22 boys, 14 girls).

Faculty School total: 47. In upper school: 10 men, 15 women; 14 have advanced degrees.

Subjects Offered Algebra, American history, American literature, anatomy, art, band, biology, biology-AP, calculus, calculus-AP, chemistry, chemistry-AP, chorus, communications, ecology, English, English literature, English literature-AP, European history, European history-AP, geography, geometry, government/civics, history, honors geometry, mathematics, music, physical education, physics, physiology, pre-calculus, psychology, science, social studies, Spanish, Spanish-AP, trigonometry, typing, U.S. history-AP, weight training, world history, world history-AP, yearbook.

Graduation Requirements English, foreign language, history, lab science, mathematics, physical education (includes health), senior projects.

Special Academic Programs Advanced Placement exam preparation; honors section; study at local college for college credit.

College Admission Counseling 32 students graduated in 2008; all went to college, including East Carolina University; Meredith College; North Carolina State University; The University of North Carolina at Chapel Hill. Mean SAT critical reading: 573, mean SAT math: 566, mean SAT writing: 570, mean combined SAT: 1709, mean composite ACT: 25.

Student Life Upper grades have specified standards of dress, student council, honor system. Discipline rests primarily with faculty.

Summer Programs Enrichment, sports, art/fine arts, computer instruction programs offered; session focuses on enrichment; held on campus; accepts boys and girls; open to students from other schools. 350 students usually enrolled. 2009 schedule: June to August.

Tuition and Aid Day student tuition: $11,500. Tuition installment plan (monthly payment plans, payment in full, 3-payment plan). Need-based scholarship grants available. In 2008–09, 24% of upper-school students received aid. Total amount of financial aid awarded in 2008–09: $397,773.

Admissions Traditional secondary-level entrance grade is 9. For fall 2008, 36 students applied for upper-level admission, 30 were accepted, 22 enrolled. ERB and SSAT required. Deadline for receipt of application materials: none. Application fee required: $50. On-campus interview recommended.

Athletics Interscholastic: baseball (boys), basketball (b,g), cheering (g), cross-country running (b,g), golf (b), soccer (b,g), softball (g), tennis (b,g), track and field (b,g), volleyball (g), weight training (b,g); intramural: flag football (b), soccer (b,g), weight training (g); coed intramural: basketball, fitness, physical fitness, volleyball. 4 PE instructors, 10 coaches, 1 athletic trainer.

Computers Computers are regularly used in all classes. Computer network features include on-campus library services, online commercial services, Internet access. Students grades are available online.

Contact Ms. Barbara E. Lambert, Director of Admissions. 910-868-5131 Ext. 311. Fax: 910-868-7351. E-mail: blambert@fayettevilleacademy.com. Web site: www.fayettevilleacademy.com.

FAY SCHOOL

Southborough, Massachusetts
See Junior Boarding Schools section.

THE FESSENDEN SCHOOL

West Newton, Massachusetts
See Junior Boarding Schools section.

THE FIELD SCHOOL

2301 Foxhall Road NW
Washington, District of Columbia 20007
Head of School: Dale T. Johnson

General Information Coeducational day college-preparatory and arts school. Grades 7–12. Founded: 1972. Setting: urban. 10-acre campus. 4 buildings on campus. Approved or accredited by Association of Independent Schools of Greater Washington and Middle States Association of Colleges and Schools. Member of National Association of Independent Schools and Secondary School Admission Test Board. Total enrollment: 320. Upper school average class size: 11. Upper school faculty-student ratio: 1:6.

Upper School Student Profile Grade 7: 28 students (13 boys, 15 girls); Grade 8: 32 students (16 boys, 16 girls); Grade 9: 68 students (33 boys, 35 girls); Grade 10: 65 students (32 boys, 33 girls); Grade 11: 67 students (33 boys, 34 girls); Grade 12: 61 students (30 boys, 31 girls).

Faculty School total: 63. In upper school: 30 men, 33 women; 28 have advanced degrees.

Subjects Offered Algebra, American history, American literature, ancient history, art, art history, biology, calculus, ceramics, chemistry, computer math, creative writing, drama, earth science, English, English literature, environmental science, European history, expository writing, fine arts, French, geometry, government/civics, grammar, history, journalism, Latin, literature, mathematics, music, photography, physical education, physics, pre-calculus, science, social studies, space and physical sciences, Spanish, theater, trigonometry, typing, world history, world literature, writing.

Graduation Requirements Arts and fine arts (art, music, dance, drama), English, foreign language, mathematics, physical education (includes health), science, social studies (includes history), winter internship (2 weeks annually).

Special Academic Programs Advanced Placement exam preparation; accelerated programs; independent study; academic accommodation for the gifted, the musically talented, and the artistically talented; remedial math.

College Admission Counseling 71 students graduated in 2008; 69 went to college, including College of Charleston; Columbia College; Kenyon College; Oberlin College; University of Virginia; Wesleyan University. Other: 1 went to work, 1 had other specific plans.

Student Life Upper grades have student council, honor system. Discipline rests primarily with faculty.

Summer Programs Remediation, enrichment programs offered; session focuses on humanities and math; held on campus; accepts boys and girls; not open to students from other schools. 20 students usually enrolled. 2009 schedule: June 15 to July 15.

Tuition and Aid Day student tuition: $30,150. Tuition installment plan (Insured Tuition Payment Plan, Key Tuition Payment Plan, monthly payment plans). Need-based scholarship grants available. In 2008–09, 18% of upper-school students received aid. Total amount of financial aid awarded in 2008–09: $1,250,000.
Admissions Traditional secondary-level entrance grade is 9. For fall 2008, 195 students applied for upper-level admission, 77 were accepted, 44 enrolled. ISEE, SSAT or WISC-R or WISC-III required. Deadline for receipt of application materials: January 15. Application fee required: $80. On-campus interview required.
Athletics Interscholastic: baseball (boys), basketball (b,g), cross-country running (b,g), lacrosse (g), soccer (b,g), softball (g), swimming and diving (b,g), tennis (b,g), track and field (b,g), ultimate Frisbee (b,g), volleyball (g); intramural: basketball (b,g), bocce (b,g), bowling (b,g), fitness (b,g); coed interscholastic: Frisbee, swimming and diving; coed intramural: dance, fitness, Frisbee, indoor soccer, physical fitness, racquetball, ultimate Frisbee, volleyball, yoga.
Computers Computers are regularly used in English, foreign language, history, mathematics, media arts, science classes. Computer network features include on-campus library services, online commercial services, Internet access, Internet filtering or blocking technology. Campus intranet is available to students. The school has a published electronic and media policy.
Contact Maureen Miesmer, Associate Director of Admission. 202-295-5840. Fax: 202-295-5850. E-mail: admission@fieldschool.org. Web site: www.fieldschool.org.

FIELDSTONE DAY SCHOOL

2999 Dufferin Street
Toronto, Ontario M6B 3T4, Canada
Head of School: Jonathan Harris

General Information Coeducational day college-preparatory and general academic school. Grades JK–12. Founded: 1997. Setting: urban. 6-acre campus. 1 building on campus. Approved or accredited by Ontario Department of Education. Languages of instruction: English and French. Total enrollment: 300. Upper school average class size: 16. Upper school faculty-student ratio: 1:16.
Special Academic Programs Advanced Placement exam preparation; academic accommodation for the gifted, the musically talented, and the artistically talented; ESL (60 students enrolled).
College Admission Counseling 41 students graduated in 2008; all went to college, including York University.
Student Life Upper grades have uniform requirement, student council. Discipline rests equally with students and faculty.
Tuition and Aid Day student tuition: CAN$14,000.
Admissions Traditional secondary-level entrance grade is 9. Deadline for receipt of application materials: January 30. Application fee required: CAN$120. Interview required.
Athletics Interscholastic: badminton (boys, girls), baseball (b,g), cross-country running (b,g), football (b,g), hockey (b,g), ice hockey (b,g), independent competitive sports (b,g), soccer (b,g), softball (b,g); intramural: cross-country running (b,g), dance (b,g), independent competitive sports (b,g), jump rope (b,g), martial arts (b,g), mountain biking (b,g); coed interscholastic: ballet, basketball, cheering, cooperative games, Cosom hockey, cross-country running, freestyle skiing, Frisbee, gymnastics, hockey, ice skating, indoor soccer, modern dance, running, skiing (downhill); coed intramural: ball hockey, baseball, basketball, Cosom hockey, cross-country running, Frisbee, golf, hockey, rugby, running, soccer, softball. 2 PE instructors.
Computers Computers are regularly used in accounting classes. Computer network features include on-campus library services, Internet access. The school has a published electronic and media policy.
Contact Miss Le Luong, Director of Admissions. 416-486-4530. Fax: 416-487-8190. E-mail: admissions@fieldstonedayschool.org. Web site: www.fieldstonedayschool.org.

THE FIRST ACADEMY

2667 Bruton Boulevard
Orlando, Florida 32805
Head of School: Dr. Steve D. Whitaker

General Information Coeducational day college-preparatory, arts, religious studies, and technology school, affiliated with Baptist Church. Grades K–12. Founded: 1986. Setting: suburban. 140-acre campus. 3 buildings on campus. Approved or accredited by Association of Christian Schools International, Southern Association of Colleges and Schools, and Florida Department of Education. Endowment: $2.5 million. Total enrollment: 982. Upper school average class size: 17. Upper school faculty-student ratio: 1:10.
Upper School Student Profile 75% of students are Baptist.
Faculty School total: 85. In upper school: 15 men, 18 women; 12 have advanced degrees.
Subjects Offered Advanced chemistry, advanced computer applications, advanced math, Advanced Placement courses, advanced studio art-AP, algebra, American government, American government-AP, American history, American history-AP, American literature, American literature-AP, analytic geometry, anatomy, ancient world history, art, art-AP, athletics, audio visual/media, band, Bible, Bible studies, biology, biology-AP, British history, British literature, British literature (honors), British literature-AP, broadcasting, calculus, calculus-AP, chemistry, chemistry-AP, choir, Christian doctrine, Christian ethics, Christian testament, church history, comparative government and politics, composition, computer graphics, computer keyboarding, computer programming, computer science, creative writing, drama, economics, economics and history, electives, English, English composition, English literature, English literature-AP, English-AP, ethics, European history, European history-AP, expository writing, fine arts, finite math, forensics, genetics, geometry, government, grammar, health, history, history-AP, honors algebra, honors English, honors geometry, honors U.S. history, honors world history, integrated mathematics, journalism, Latin, Latin-AP, life management skills, life skills, literature, literature-AP, marine biology, mathematics, media communications, music, newspaper, philosophy, physical education, physical science, physics, physiology, politics, pottery, pre-algebra, pre-calculus, religion, SAT/ACT preparation, science, social science, social studies, sociology, Spanish, Spanish-AP, speech, speech and debate, theater, trigonometry, U.S. government, U.S. government-AP, world history, world history-AP, world literature, writing, yearbook.
Graduation Requirements Arts and fine arts (art, music, dance, drama), computer science, English, foreign language, mathematics, physical education (includes health), religion (includes Bible studies and theology), science, social science, social studies (includes history).
Special Academic Programs Advanced Placement exam preparation; honors section; independent study; academic accommodation for the gifted.
College Admission Counseling 74 students graduated in 2008; 73 went to college, including Auburn University; Clemson University; Florida State University; Samford University; University of Central Florida; University of Florida. Other: 1 had other specific plans.
Student Life Upper grades have uniform requirement, student council, honor system. Discipline rests primarily with faculty. Attendance at religious services is required.
Summer Programs Remediation, enrichment, sports, art/fine arts programs offered; session focuses on academics and athletic camps; held on campus; accepts boys and girls; open to students from other schools. 200 students usually enrolled. 2009 schedule: June 1 to July 3. Application deadline: March 1.
Tuition and Aid Day student tuition: $11,295–$11,595. Tuition installment plan (FACTS Tuition Payment Plan, monthly payment plans, individually arranged payment plans). Need-based scholarship grants available. In 2008–09, 25% of upper-school students received aid. Total amount of financial aid awarded in 2008–09: $250,000.
Admissions Traditional secondary-level entrance grade is 9. Otis-Lennon School Ability Test and Stanford Achievement Test required. Deadline for receipt of application materials: none. Application fee required: $100. On-campus interview required.
Athletics Interscholastic: baseball (boys), basketball (b,g), cheering (g), cross-country running (b,g), diving (b,g), flag football (b,g), football (b), golf (b,g), physical fitness (b,g), physical training (b,g), power lifting (b), running (b,g), soccer (b,g), softball (g), strength & conditioning (b,g), swimming and diving (b,g), tennis (b,g), track and field (b,g), volleyball (g), weight lifting (b), wrestling (b); coed intramural: basketball. 6 PE instructors, 18 coaches, 1 athletic trainer.
Computers Computers are regularly used in art, computer applications, English, foreign language, history, journalism, keyboarding, library, library skills, media production, science, yearbook classes. Computer network features include on-campus library services, Internet access, Internet filtering or blocking technology. Students grades are available online. The school has a published electronic and media policy.
Contact Mrs. Janie Weber, Admissions Assistant. 407-206-8602. Fax: 407-206-8700. E-mail: janieweber@thefirstacademy.org. Web site: www.TheFirstAcademy.org.

FIRST BAPTIST ACADEMY

PO Box 868
Dallas, Texas 75221
Head of School: Dr. Jake Walters

General Information Coeducational day college-preparatory, arts, religious studies, and technology school, affiliated with Baptist Church. Grades K–12. Founded: 1972. Setting: urban. 1 building on campus. Approved or accredited by Accreditation Commission of the Texas Association of Baptist Schools, Southern Association of Colleges and Schools, and Texas Department of Education. Endowment: $1 million. Total enrollment: 615. Upper school average class size: 22. Upper school faculty-student ratio: 1:11.
Upper School Student Profile 34% of students are Baptist.
Faculty School total: 69. In upper school: 16 men, 15 women; 11 have advanced degrees.
Subjects Offered Algebra, American history, biology, calculus, calculus-AP, chemistry, economics, English, English literature-AP, English-AP, fine arts, French, geometry, government-AP, history, Latin, math analysis, photography, physics, pre-calculus, Spanish, theater arts, world history.
Graduation Requirements Algebra, American history, arts and fine arts (art, music, dance, drama), Basic programming, Bible studies, biology, chemistry, economics, electives, English, French, government, history, keyboarding/computer, Latin, mathematics, physical education (includes health), physics, science, Spanish, U.S. history, world geography, government/economics. Community service is required.

Special Academic Programs Advanced Placement exam preparation; honors section.
College Admission Counseling 78 students graduated in 2008; all went to college, including Auburn University; Baylor University; Southern Methodist University; Texas Tech University; The University of Texas at Austin; University of Colorado at Boulder. Mean composite ACT: 23.
Student Life Upper grades have uniform requirement, student council, honor system. Discipline rests primarily with faculty. Attendance at religious services is required.
Tuition and Aid Day student tuition: $10,500. Tuition installment plan (FACTS Tuition Payment Plan). Need-based scholarship grants available. In 2008–09, 10% of upper-school students received aid.
Admissions Traditional secondary-level entrance grade is 9. ERB (grade level), ISEE or Stanford Achievement Test required. Deadline for receipt of application materials: none. Application fee required: $75. Interview required.
Athletics Interscholastic: aquatics (boys, girls), baseball (b), basketball (b,g), cheering (g), diving (b,g), football (b), golf (b,g), soccer (b,g), softball (g), swimming and diving (b,g), tennis (b,g), track and field (b,g), volleyball (g), wrestling (b). 2 PE instructors, 25 coaches.
Computers Computers are regularly used in desktop publishing classes. Computer resources include on-campus library services, Internet access. Student e-mail accounts are available to students. Students grades are available online. The school has a published electronic and media policy.
Contact Susan Money, Director of Admissions. 214-969-7861. Fax: 214-969-7797. E-mail: smoney@firstdallas.org.

FIRST PRESBYTERIAN DAY SCHOOL

5671 Calvin Drive
Macon, Georgia 31210

Head of School: Mr. Gregg E. Thompson

General Information Coeducational day college-preparatory, arts, and religious studies school, affiliated with Christian faith, Presbyterian Church in America. Grades PK–12. Founded: 1970. Setting: suburban. Nearest major city is Atlanta. 64-acre campus. 7 buildings on campus. Approved or accredited by Christian Schools International, Georgia Independent School Association, Southern Association of Colleges and Schools, Southern Association of Independent Schools, and Georgia Department of Education. Endowment: $3.1 million. Total enrollment: 982. Upper school average class size: 18. Upper school faculty-student ratio: 1:12.
Upper School Student Profile Grade 9: 91 students (43 boys, 48 girls); Grade 10: 89 students (47 boys, 42 girls); Grade 11: 90 students (44 boys, 46 girls); Grade 12: 92 students (47 boys, 45 girls). 96% of students are Christian, Presbyterian Church in America.
Faculty School total: 73. In upper school: 24 men, 26 women; 34 have advanced degrees.
Subjects Offered Accounting, advanced chemistry, Advanced Placement courses, algebra, American government-AP, American literature, anatomy and physiology, art, art appreciation, band, Bible, biology, biology-AP, British literature, calculus-AP, chemistry, chorus, comparative religion, computer applications, debate, economics, English, English language and composition-AP, English literature and composition-AP, family life, French, geometry, government, government-AP, honors algebra, honors English, honors geometry, journalism, Latin, Latin-AP, logic, model United Nations, modern European history, music appreciation, physical science, physics, pre-calculus, psychology, Spanish, statistics, studio art-AP, theater, U.S. history, U.S. history-AP, world history.
Graduation Requirements Arts and fine arts (art, music, dance, drama), Bible, computer skills, electives, English, foreign language, mathematics, physical education (includes health), science, social studies (includes history).
Special Academic Programs 9 Advanced Placement exams for which test preparation is offered; honors section.
College Admission Counseling 92 students graduated in 2008; all went to college, including Auburn University; Georgia Institute of Technology; Georgia Southern University; Mercer University; Samford University; University of Georgia. 29% scored over 600 on SAT critical reading, 28% scored over 600 on SAT math, 28% scored over 600 on SAT writing.
Student Life Upper grades have uniform requirement, student council, honor system. Discipline rests primarily with faculty. Attendance at religious services is required.
Summer Programs Remediation, enrichment, sports, art/fine arts programs offered; session focuses on reading and study skills, mathematics enrichment, science, sports; held on campus; accepts boys and girls; open to students from other schools. 200 students usually enrolled. 2009 schedule: June 10 to July 30. Application deadline: May 15.
Tuition and Aid Day student tuition: $9680. Tuition installment plan (monthly payment plans). Tuition reduction for siblings, merit scholarship grants, need-based scholarship grants available. In 2008–09, 21% of upper-school students received aid; total upper-school merit-scholarship money awarded: $4000. Total amount of financial aid awarded in 2008–09: $140,000.
Admissions Traditional secondary-level entrance grade is 9. CTP, Math Placement Exam, Stanford 9 or writing sample required. Deadline for receipt of application materials: February 1. Application fee required: $50. Interview recommended.
Athletics Interscholastic: baseball (boys), basketball (b,g), cheering (g), cross-country running (b,g), dance team (g), football (b), golf (b,g), soccer (b,g), softball (g), swimming and diving (b,g), tennis (b,g), track and field (b,g), wrestling (b,g); intramural: football (b), indoor soccer (b,g), soccer (b,g), strength & conditioning (b,g), weight training (b,g). 3 PE instructors, 5 coaches, 1 athletic trainer.
Computers Computers are regularly used in all classes. Computer network features include on-campus library services, online commercial services, Internet access, Internet filtering or blocking technology. Computer access in designated common areas is available to students. Students grades are available online. The school has a published electronic and media policy.
Contact Mr. Terrell Mitchell, Director of Admissions. 478-477-6505 Ext. 107. Fax: 478-477-2804. E-mail: tmitchell@fpdmacon.org. Web site: www.fpdmacon.org.

FISHBURNE MILITARY SCHOOL

225 South Wayne Avenue
Waynesboro, Virginia 22980

Head of School: Brig. Gen. William W. Alexander Jr.

General Information Boys' boarding and day college-preparatory, Army Junior ROTC, and military school. Grades 8–12. Founded: 1879. Setting: small town. Nearest major city is Washington, DC. Students are housed in single-sex dormitories. 10-acre campus. 4 buildings on campus. Approved or accredited by Southern Association of Colleges and Schools, Virginia Association of Independent Schools, and Virginia Department of Education. Endowment: $1.3 million. Total enrollment: 180. Upper school average class size: 9. Upper school faculty-student ratio: 1:9.
Upper School Student Profile Grade 9: 35 students (35 boys); Grade 10: 45 students (45 boys); Grade 11: 50 students (50 boys); Grade 12: 45 students (45 boys). 90% of students are boarding students. 17 states are represented in upper school student body. 5% are international students. International students from Aruba, Mexico, Republic of Korea, Russian Federation, Saudi Arabia, and Taiwan; 5 other countries represented in student body.
Faculty School total: 24. In upper school: 20 men, 4 women; 5 have advanced degrees; 6 reside on campus.
Subjects Offered Algebra, American history, American literature, biology, calculus, chemistry, computer programming, computer science, computer technologies, creative writing, driver education, earth science, English, English literature, environmental science, French, geography, geology, geometry, government/civics, grammar, health, history, JROTC, mathematics, military science, music, physical education, physics, science, social studies, Spanish, speech, trigonometry, world history.
Graduation Requirements Computer science, English, foreign language, JROTC, mathematics, physical education (includes health), science, social studies (includes history).
Special Academic Programs Advanced Placement exam preparation; honors section; study at local college for college credit; remedial reading and/or remedial writing; remedial math.
College Admission Counseling 47 students graduated in 2008; all went to college, including Miami University; Penn State University Park; United States Military Academy; University of Virginia; Virginia Military Institute; Virginia Polytechnic Institute and State University. Median SAT critical reading: 470, median SAT math: 530, median SAT writing: 540, median combined SAT: 1535. 4.5% scored over 600 on SAT critical reading, 11.4% scored over 600 on SAT math, 4.5% scored over 600 on SAT writing, 2.3% scored over 1800 on combined SAT.
Student Life Upper grades have uniform requirement, student council, honor system. Discipline rests equally with students and faculty.
Tuition and Aid Day student tuition: $9500; 7-day tuition and room/board: $23,400. Tuition installment plan (Key Tuition Payment Plan, monthly payment plans, individually arranged payment plans, Tuition Management Systems Plan). Tuition reduction for siblings, merit scholarship grants, need-based scholarship grants, band scholarships, tuition reduction for children of military personnel, PLATO Loans available. In 2008–09, 40% of upper-school students received aid. Total amount of financial aid awarded in 2008–09: $75,000.
Admissions Traditional secondary-level entrance grade is 10. For fall 2008, 200 students applied for upper-level admission, 180 were accepted, 65 enrolled. Deadline for receipt of application materials: none. Application fee required: $50. Interview required.
Athletics Interscholastic: baseball, basketball, canoeing/kayaking, cooperative games, cross-country running, drill team, football, golf, JROTC drill, lacrosse, marksmanship, outdoor adventure, paint ball, rappelling, riflery; intramural: baseball, basketball, billiards, bowling, fitness, Frisbee, martial arts, paint ball, rappelling, ropes courses, self defense, skiing (downhill). 1 PE instructor, 15 coaches, 1 athletic trainer.
Computers Computers are regularly used in English, foreign language, history, mathematics, science classes. Computer network features include on-campus library services, Internet access, Internet filtering or blocking technology. Campus intranet and student e-mail accounts are available to students. The school has a published electronic and media policy.
Contact Mr. Brock Selkow, Director of Admissions. 800-946-7773. Fax: 540-946-7738. E-mail: bselkow@fishburne.org. Web site: www.fishburne.org.

FLINT HILL SCHOOL

3320 Jermantown Road
Oakton, Virginia 22124

Head of School: Mr. John Thomas

General Information Coeducational day college-preparatory, arts, technology, and athletics, community service school. Grades JK–12. Founded: 1956. Setting: suburban. Nearest major city is Washington, DC. 50-acre campus. 1 building on campus. Approved or accredited by Virginia Association of Independent Schools and Virginia Department of Education. Member of National Association of Independent Schools and Secondary School Admission Test Board. Endowment: $1.2 million. Total enrollment: 1,099. Upper school average class size: 12. Upper school faculty-student ratio: 1:10.

Upper School Student Profile Grade 9: 114 students (67 boys, 47 girls); Grade 10: 125 students (66 boys, 59 girls); Grade 11: 122 students (65 boys, 57 girls); Grade 12: 130 students (67 boys, 63 girls).

Faculty School total: 141. In upper school: 21 men, 30 women; 36 have advanced degrees.

Subjects Offered 20th century history, advanced chemistry, algebra, art, ballet, biology, biology-AP, British literature, calculus, calculus-AP, ceramics, chemistry, chemistry-AP, choir, choral music, chorus, civil rights, community service, computer animation, computer graphics, computer programming, computer science-AP, concert band, concert choir, creative writing, digital imaging, discrete mathematics, drama, drawing, drawing and design, earth science, economics-AP, English, English literature, English literature and composition-AP, English-AP, environmental science, environmental science-AP, environmental studies, European civilization, European history, fine arts, French, French language-AP, French literature-AP, geometry, government-AP, history, history of music, honors English, improvisation, jazz band, jazz dance, Latin, Latin American studies, Latin-AP, macro/microeconomics-AP, marine science, modern European history-AP, music, music history, music theory, music theory-AP, orchestra, ornithology, photography, physical education, physics, physics-AP, playwriting, pre-calculus, psychology, psychology-AP, science, sculpture, senior project, Shakespeare, short story, Spanish, Spanish-AP, statistics-AP, studio art, study skills, symphonic band, theater, trigonometry, U.S. history, U.S. history-AP, world religions.

Graduation Requirements Arts and fine arts (art, music, dance, drama), athletics, English, foreign language, history, mathematics, physical education (includes health), science, Senior Project. Community service is required.

Special Academic Programs Advanced Placement exam preparation; honors section.

College Admission Counseling 114 students graduated in 2008; 113 went to college, including James Madison University; Radford University; Syracuse University; The College of William and Mary; University of Virginia; Virginia Polytechnic Institute and State University. Other: 1 had other specific plans. Median SAT critical reading: 610, median SAT math: 630, median SAT writing: 600, median combined SAT: 1850, median composite ACT: 26. 54% scored over 600 on SAT critical reading, 62% scored over 600 on SAT math, 54% scored over 600 on SAT writing, 60% scored over 1800 on combined SAT, 54% scored over 26 on composite ACT.

Student Life Upper grades have specified standards of dress, student council, honor system. Discipline rests primarily with faculty.

Summer Programs Remediation, enrichment, advancement, ESL, sports, art/fine arts, rigorous outdoor training, computer instruction programs offered; session focuses on academics, arts, enrichment, travel, and athletics; held both on and off campus; held at international venues and New Mexico; accepts boys and girls; open to students from other schools. 815 students usually enrolled. 2009 schedule: June 22 to July 31. Application deadline: none.

Tuition and Aid Day student tuition: $26,200. Tuition installment plan (Insured Tuition Payment Plan, FACTS Tuition Payment Plan, monthly payment plans, one payment, two payments or ten payments). Need-based scholarship grants available. In 2008–09, 16% of upper-school students received aid. Total amount of financial aid awarded in 2008–09: $1,500,000.

Admissions Traditional secondary-level entrance grade is 9. For fall 2008, 237 students applied for upper-level admission, 158 were accepted, 93 enrolled. SSAT required. Deadline for receipt of application materials: January 30. Application fee required: $75. On-campus interview required.

Athletics Interscholastic: baseball (boys), basketball (b,g), cross-country running (b,g), dance team (g), diving (b,g), football (b), golf (b), lacrosse (b,g), self defense (g), soccer (b,g), softball (g), swimming and diving (b,g), tennis (b,g), track and field (b,g), volleyball (g); coed interscholastic: independent competitive sports, physical fitness, running, strength & conditioning, yoga; coed intramural: aerobics/dance, canoeing/kayaking, climbing, dance, fitness, modern dance, mountaineering, outdoor education, physical fitness, physical training, strength & conditioning, wall climbing, weight training. 66 coaches, 2 athletic trainers.

Computers Computers are regularly used in animation, art, basic skills, college planning, English, foreign language, French, history, language development, library, mathematics, newspaper, science, Spanish, technology, writing, yearbook classes. Computer network features include on-campus library services, online commercial services, Internet access, wireless campus network, Internet filtering or blocking technology. Campus intranet, student e-mail accounts, and computer access in designated common areas are available to students. Students grades are available online. The school has a published electronic and media policy.

Contact Ms. Stacey Ahner, Director of Institutional Advancement and Admission. 703-584-2300. Fax: 703-242-0718. E-mail: admissions@flinthill.org. Web site: www.flinthill.org.

ANNOUNCEMENT FROM THE SCHOOL Flint Hill School, enrolling 1,099 students in JK–12, offers a rigorous college-preparatory program designed to maximize individual potential and transform that potential into success. The School is committed to developing individuals who seek excellence and embrace the "Driving Spirit" of Flint Hill School. Students are educated in an equitable, caring community—a diverse population of students, families, and faculty and staff members that welcomes and values individuals from all backgrounds. A strong Financial Aid program helps the School maintain the economic diversity of this vital community of learning and growth. Academic excellence is engendered within a value-centered community, where respect, responsibility, compassion, and honesty are fostered. Starting in the very early years, the School seeks to educate the whole child, offering social and emotional guidance as well as intellectual support so that each student may attain the best possible level of achievement. Class offerings at all levels, including AP and Honors programs, ensure student success. Two campuses on 50 acres house well-appointed library facilities, learning centers, and spacious science and computer labs. All faculty members work in fully networked classrooms, integrating multimedia and technology into the curriculum; an extensive experiential education program enhances classroom instruction. Athletic facilities include two full-size gymnasiums, eight tennis courts, a 400-meter track, a weight and fitness facility, and athletics fields—including one all-turf field—for all sports. League athletics complement the rigorous academic program, while fine arts programs feature hands-on learning with professionals in their field as well as master classes from visiting experts. The fine arts facilities include a 300-seat theater and art, dance, and music studios that are filled with natural light and encourage creative expression. The School also offers summer programs with a broad range of workshops, camps, and trips. Headmaster: John M. Thomas; Acting Director of Admission: Ms. Stacey Ahner.

FLINTRIDGE SACRED HEART ACADEMY

440 Saint Katherine Drive
La Canada Flintridge, California 91011

Head of School: Sr. Carolyn McCormack, OP

General Information Girls' boarding and day college-preparatory and arts school, affiliated with Roman Catholic Church. Grades 9–12. Founded: 1931. Setting: suburban. Nearest major city is Los Angeles. Students are housed in single-sex dormitories. 41-acre campus. 12 buildings on campus. Approved or accredited by California Association of Independent Schools, National Catholic Education Association, The Association of Boarding Schools, and Western Association of Schools and Colleges. Member of National Association of Independent Schools and Secondary School Admission Test Board. Languages of instruction: Spanish and French. Endowment: $6 million. Total enrollment: 406. Upper school average class size: 22. Upper school faculty-student ratio: 1:10.

Upper School Student Profile Grade 9: 99 students (99 girls); Grade 10: 100 students (100 girls); Grade 11: 112 students (112 girls); Grade 12: 95 students (95 girls). 12% of students are boarding students. 93% are state residents. 2 states are represented in upper school student body. 7% are international students. International students from Guatemala, Hong Kong, Japan, Republic of Korea, Taiwan, and Thailand; 9 other countries represented in student body. 70% of students are Roman Catholic.

Faculty School total: 37. In upper school: 11 men, 26 women; 23 have advanced degrees; 5 reside on campus.

Subjects Offered Algebra, American government, American government-AP, American history, American history-AP, American literature, American politics in film, analytic geometry, art, art history, art history-AP, ASB Leadership, astronomy, biology, biology-AP, calculus, calculus-AP, cell biology, chemistry, chorus, community service, computer applications, dance, drama, driver education, economics, English, English-AP, ensembles, ESL, ethics, French, French-AP, geology, geometry, government/civics, health, honors algebra, honors geometry, journalism, keyboarding, marine biology, oceanography, organic chemistry, physical education, physics, physiology-anatomy, piano, pre-calculus, psychology, religion, Spanish, Spanish-AP, stagecraft, studio art-AP, theater, theology, trigonometry, world history, yearbook.

Graduation Requirements Arts and fine arts (art, music, dance, drama), computer science, English, foreign language, mathematics, physical education (includes health), religion (includes Bible studies and theology), science, social studies (includes history). Community service is required.

Special Academic Programs 16 Advanced Placement exams for which test preparation is offered; honors section; ESL (5 students enrolled).

College Admission Counseling 97 students graduated in 2008; all went to college, including California Polytechnic State University, San Luis Obispo; University of California, Los Angeles; University of California, San Diego; University of California, Santa Cruz; University of San Diego; University of Southern California.

Student Life Upper grades have uniform requirement, student council. Discipline rests primarily with faculty. Attendance at religious services is required.

Summer Programs Enrichment, advancement, ESL, sports, art/fine arts, computer instruction programs offered; held on campus; accepts girls; not open to students from other schools. 75 students usually enrolled. 2009 schedule: June 28 to July 23. Application deadline: June 28.
Tuition and Aid Day student tuition: $17,950; 7-day tuition and room/board: $39,275. Tuition installment plan (The Tuition Plan, FACTS Tuition Payment Plan, 2-payment plan). Merit scholarship grants, need-based scholarship grants available. In 2008–09, 25% of upper-school students received aid; total upper-school merit-scholarship money awarded: $48,000. Total amount of financial aid awarded in 2008–09: $558,450.
Admissions Traditional secondary-level entrance grade is 9. For fall 2008, 191 students applied for upper-level admission, 152 were accepted, 99 enrolled. High School Placement Test, SSAT or TOEFL required. Deadline for receipt of application materials: January 12. Application fee required: $125. Interview required.
Athletics Interscholastic: aerobics/dance, aquatics, ballet, basketball, cross-country running, dance, diving, equestrian sports, golf, modern dance, outdoor activities, physical fitness, physical training, running, soccer, softball, swimming and diving, tennis, track and field, volleyball, water polo; intramural: aquatics, basketball, golf, soccer, softball, swimming and diving, volleyball. 2 PE instructors, 29 coaches.
Computers Computers are regularly used in college planning, creative writing, current events, economics, English, health, history, independent study, journalism, Latin, library, library skills, mathematics, media, newspaper, philosophy, photojournalism, psychology, religious studies, science, social sciences, social studies, Spanish, speech, study skills, technology, typing, yearbook classes. Computer network features include on-campus library services, online commercial services, Internet access, wireless campus network, Internet filtering or blocking technology, Parent net. Students grades are available online. The school has a published electronic and media policy.
Contact Annemarie Noltner, Admissions Assistant. 626-685-8333. Fax: 626-685-8520. E-mail: admissions@fsha.org. Web site: www.fsha.org.

FLINT RIVER ACADEMY

11556 East Highway 85
Woodbury, Georgia 30293

Head of School: Mr. Marlowe Hinson

General Information Coeducational day college-preparatory, arts, and technology school. Grades PK–12. Founded: 1967. Setting: rural. Nearest major city is Atlanta. 8-acre campus. 3 buildings on campus. Approved or accredited by Georgia Accrediting Commission and Southern Association of Colleges and Schools. Total enrollment: 382. Upper school average class size: 18. Upper school faculty-student ratio: 1:14.
Upper School Student Profile Grade 9: 25 students (11 boys, 14 girls); Grade 10: 35 students (18 boys, 17 girls); Grade 11: 24 students (8 boys, 16 girls); Grade 12: 20 students (11 boys, 9 girls).
Faculty School total: 45. In upper school: 2 men, 12 women; 10 have advanced degrees.
Subjects Offered Accounting, algebra, American history, American literature, art, biology, business, business skills, calculus, chemistry, computer math, computer science, creative writing, drama, earth science, economics, English, fine arts, geography, geometry, government/civics, grammar, health, history, mathematics, music, physical education, physics, physiology, science, social science, social studies, Spanish, Spanish-AP, speech, theater, trigonometry, typing, world history, world literature.
Graduation Requirements Arts and fine arts (art, music, dance, drama), business skills (includes word processing), computer science, English, foreign language, mathematics, physical education (includes health), science, social science, social studies (includes history).
Special Academic Programs Advanced Placement exam preparation; honors section; study at local college for college credit; academic accommodation for the musically talented and the artistically talented; remedial math.
College Admission Counseling 27 students graduated in 2008; 18 went to college, including Auburn University; Columbus State University; Georgia Southern University; University of Georgia; Valdosta State University. Other: 9 went to work. Median SAT critical reading: 506, median SAT math: 504, median SAT writing: 509, median combined SAT: 1521, median composite ACT: 20.
Student Life Upper grades have specified standards of dress, student council, honor system. Discipline rests primarily with faculty.
Tuition and Aid Day student tuition: $6190. Tuition installment plan (monthly payment plans). Tuition reduction for third sibling available.
Admissions Traditional secondary-level entrance grade is 9. For fall 2008, 10 students applied for upper-level admission, 10 were accepted, 10 enrolled. ACT-Explore required. Deadline for receipt of application materials: none. Application fee required: $50. On-campus interview required.
Athletics Interscholastic: baseball (boys), basketball (b,g), cheering (g), cross-country running (b,g), football (b), golf (b,g), softball (g), tennis (b,g), track and field (b,g); intramural: baseball (b), basketball (b,g), cheering (g), dance team (g), golf (g), soccer (b), softball (g), tennis (b,g), volleyball (b,g), weight lifting (b,g), weight training (b); coed intramural: ropes courses. 2 coaches.
Computers Computer network features include on-campus library services, Internet access.
Contact Ms. Peggy Wade, Guidance Counselor. 706-553-2541. Fax: 706-553-9777. E-mail: counselor@flintriveracademy.com. Web site: www.flintriveracademy.com.

FONTBONNE ACADEMY

930 Brook Road
Milton, Massachusetts 02186

Head of School: Dr. Anne Malone

General Information Girls' day college-preparatory, arts, religious studies, and technology school, affiliated with Roman Catholic Church. Grades 9–12. Founded: 1954. Setting: suburban. Nearest major city is Boston. 15-acre campus. 2 buildings on campus. Approved or accredited by Association of Independent Schools in New England, National Catholic Education Association, New England Association of Schools and Colleges, and Massachusetts Department of Education. Total enrollment: 400. Upper school average class size: 20. Upper school faculty-student ratio: 1:11.
Upper School Student Profile 80% of students are Roman Catholic.
Faculty School total: 46. In upper school: 8 men, 35 women; 34 have advanced degrees.
Subjects Offered 20th century American writers, advanced computer applications, algebra, American history, American history-AP, American literature, analytic geometry, applied music, art, art-AP, biology, biology-AP, British literature (honors), calculus-AP, career/college preparation, Catholic belief and practice, chemistry, choral music, chorus, church history, college admission preparation, college counseling, computer music, computer programming, conceptual physics, ecology, environmental systems, electronic music, English, English literature, English-AP, finance, fine arts, French, French-AP, freshman seminar, geometry, guidance, health, instrumental music, integrated mathematics, jazz ensemble, Latin, literature by women, media communications, physical education, physics, physiology, pre-calculus, research techniques, science, social justice, social studies, sociology, Spanish, Spanish-AP, theater production, theology, trigonometry, vocal jazz, women's literature, world history.
Graduation Requirements Arts and fine arts (art, music, dance, drama), biology, English, foreign language, mathematics, physical education (includes health), physical science, theology, U.S. history, U.S. literature, world history, 100 hours of community service.
Special Academic Programs Advanced Placement exam preparation; honors section; independent study.
College Admission Counseling 136 students graduated in 2008; 134 went to college, including Boston University; Providence College; Saint Anselm College; Suffolk University; University of Massachusetts Boston; University of New Hampshire. Other: 1 entered a postgraduate year, 1 had other specific plans.
Student Life Upper grades have uniform requirement, student council, honor system. Discipline rests primarily with faculty. Attendance at religious services is required.
Tuition and Aid Day student tuition: $12,000. Tuition installment plan (FACTS Tuition Payment Plan, 2-payment plan). Merit scholarship grants, need-based scholarship grants, tuition reduction for daughters of employees, work-study positions available.
Admissions Traditional secondary-level entrance grade is 9. For fall 2008, 570 students applied for upper-level admission, 310 were accepted, 100 enrolled. Archdiocese of Boston High School entrance exam provided by STS, High School Placement Test or standardized test scores required. Deadline for receipt of application materials: December 1. Application fee required: $30.
Athletics Interscholastic: alpine skiing, basketball, cheering, cross-country running, dance team, diving, golf, ice hockey, indoor track & field, lacrosse, skiing (downhill), soccer, softball, swimming and diving, tennis, track and field, volleyball, winter (indoor) track; intramural: basketball, dance, equestrian sports, flag football, floor hockey, horseback riding, lacrosse, Nautilus, physical fitness, physical training, strength & conditioning. 3 PE instructors, 26 coaches, 3 athletic trainers.
Computers Computers are regularly used in all classes. Computer network features include on-campus library services, online commercial services, Internet access, wireless campus network, Internet filtering or blocking technology. Student e-mail accounts are available to students. Students grades are available online. The school has a published electronic and media policy.
Contact Admissions. 617-696-3241. Fax: 617-696-7688. E-mail: bhiggins@fontbonneacademy.org. Web site: www.fontbonneacademy.org.

FONTBONNE HALL ACADEMY

9901 Shore Road
Brooklyn, New York 11209

Head of School: Sr. Dolores F. Crepeau, CSJ

General Information Girls' day college-preparatory, arts, religious studies, and technology school, affiliated with Roman Catholic Church. Grades 9–12. Founded: 1937. Nearest major city is New York. 5 buildings on campus. Approved or accredited by Middle States Association of Colleges and Schools and New York State Board of Regents. Endowment: $2 million. Total enrollment: 536. Upper school average class size: 20. Upper school faculty-student ratio: 1:12.
Upper School Student Profile Grade 9: 141 students (141 girls); Grade 10: 132 students (132 girls); Grade 11: 145 students (145 girls); Grade 12: 118 students (118 girls). 90% of students are Roman Catholic.

Faculty School total: 40. In upper school: 4 men, 36 women; 34 have advanced degrees.
Subjects Offered Advanced chemistry, algebra, anthropology, art, biology-AP, calculus, chemistry, chorus, computers, earth science, economics, English, forensics, government, health, history-AP, Italian, Latin, law, marine science, mathematics, music, photography, physical education, physics, religion, Spanish, U.S. history, world geography, world history.
Graduation Requirements Board of Regents requirements, 60 hours of service.
Special Academic Programs Advanced Placement exam preparation; honors section.
College Admission Counseling 131 students graduated in 2008; all went to college, including Boston University; Fordham University; Manhattan College; New York University; Saint Joseph's University; The Catholic University of America. Median SAT critical reading: 550, median SAT math: 550, median SAT writing: 600, median combined SAT: 1700.
Student Life Upper grades have uniform requirement, student council. Discipline rests primarily with faculty. Attendance at religious services is required.
Summer Programs Remediation, enrichment, sports programs offered; session focuses on preparation for Regents exams; held on campus; accepts girls; not open to students from other schools. 50 students usually enrolled. 2009 schedule: July 29 to August 10. Application deadline: June 25.
Tuition and Aid Day student tuition: $7400. Tuition installment plan (monthly payment plans, 3 payments per year). Tuition reduction for siblings, merit scholarship grants, need-based loans available. In 2008–09, 20% of upper-school students received aid; total upper-school merit-scholarship money awarded: $100,000. Total amount of financial aid awarded in 2008–09: $107,500.
Admissions Traditional secondary-level entrance grade is 9. For fall 2008, 372 students applied for upper-level admission, 254 were accepted, 141 enrolled. Diocesan Entrance Exam required. Deadline for receipt of application materials: January 6. Application fee required: $200. Interview required.
Athletics Interscholastic: aquatics, baseball, basketball, cheering, cross-country running, dance, dance squad, drill team, fishing, golf, running, soccer, softball, swimming and diving, tennis, track and field, volleyball. 2 PE instructors, 10 coaches, 2 athletic trainers.
Computers Computers are regularly used in all academic classes. Computer network features include on-campus library services, Internet access, wireless campus network, Internet filtering or blocking technology. The school has a published electronic and media policy.
Contact Sr. Dolores F. Crepeau, CSJ, Principal. 718-748-2244. Fax: 718-745-3841. E-mail: crepeau@fontbonne.org. Web site: www.fontbonne.org.

FOOTHILLS ACADEMY

Calgary, Alberta, Canada

See Special Needs Schools section.

FORDHAM PREPARATORY SCHOOL

East Fordham Road
Bronx, New York 10458-5175

Head of School: Rev. Kenneth J. Boller, SJ

General Information Boys' day college-preparatory school, affiliated with Roman Catholic Church. Grades 9–12. Founded: 1841. Setting: urban. Nearest major city is New York. 5-acre campus. 2 buildings on campus. Approved or accredited by Jesuit Secondary Education Association, Middle States Association of Colleges and Schools, National Catholic Education Association, New York State Association of Independent Schools, and New York Department of Education. Endowment: $1.3 million. Total enrollment: 953. Upper school average class size: 24. Upper school faculty-student ratio: 1:10.
Upper School Student Profile Grade 9: 271 students (271 boys); Grade 10: 229 students (229 boys); Grade 11: 211 students (211 boys); Grade 12: 242 students (242 boys). 80% of students are Roman Catholic.
Faculty School total: 91. In upper school: 65 men, 26 women; 79 have advanced degrees.
Subjects Offered Advanced chemistry, algebra, American Civil War, American history, American history-AP, American literature, Ancient Greek, architectural drawing, art history-AP, biochemistry, biology, biology-AP, British literature, calculus, calculus-AP, chemistry, chemistry-AP, Chinese, computer programming, computer programming-AP, constitutional history of U.S., creative writing, economics, emerging technology, English, English language and composition-AP, English literature-AP, European history-AP, finite math, forensic science, French, geometry, German, global studies, government and politics-AP, health, Italian, Latin, Latin-AP, macroeconomics-AP, media communications, modern history, modern world history, music, physical education, physics, physics-AP, poetry, pre-calculus, religious studies, science research, short story, Spanish, Spanish language-AP, Spanish literature-AP, statistics-AP, studio art, studio art-AP, trigonometry, world history-AP.
Graduation Requirements Arts and fine arts (art, music, dance, drama), English, foreign language, mathematics, physical education (includes health), religious studies, science, social studies (includes history), senior service project.
Special Academic Programs Advanced Placement exam preparation; honors section; study at local college for college credit.
College Admission Counseling 210 students graduated in 2008; 207 went to college, including College of the Holy Cross; Fordham University; Loyola College in Maryland; Penn State University Park; St. John's University; University at Albany, State University of New York. Other: 1 went to work, 1 entered military service, 1 entered a postgraduate year. Mean SAT critical reading: 601, mean SAT math: 605, mean SAT writing: 596.
Student Life Upper grades have specified standards of dress. Discipline rests primarily with faculty. Attendance at religious services is required.
Tuition and Aid Day student tuition: $12,560. Tuition installment plan (monthly payment plans). Merit scholarship grants, need based scholarship grants available. In 2008–09, 35% of upper-school students received aid; total upper-school merit-scholarship money awarded: $400,000. Total amount of financial aid awarded in 2008–09: $1,700,000.
Admissions Traditional secondary-level entrance grade is 9. For fall 2008, 1,139 students applied for upper-level admission, 642 were accepted, 271 enrolled. Cooperative Entrance Exam (McGraw-Hill), Diocesan Entrance Exam, ISEE, SSAT or STS required. Deadline for receipt of application materials: December 19. No application fee required. On-campus interview recommended.
Athletics Interscholastic: baseball, basketball, bowling, crew, cross-country running, diving, football, golf, ice hockey, indoor track, lacrosse, soccer, swimming and diving, tennis, track and field, volleyball, winter (indoor) track, wrestling; intramural: basketball, fitness, Frisbee, rock climbing, weight training. 2 PE instructors, 16 coaches.
Computers Computers are regularly used in English, foreign language, history, mathematics, science classes. Computer network features include on-campus library services, online commercial services, Internet access, wireless campus network, Internet filtering or blocking technology. Student e-mail accounts are available to students. The school has a published electronic and media policy.
Contact Christopher D. Lauber, Director of Admissions. 718-584-8367. Fax: 718-367-7598. E-mail: lauberc@fordhamprep.org. Web site: www.fordhamprep.org.

FOREST LAKE ACADEMY

500 Education Loop
Apopka, Florida 32703

Head of School: Gloria Becker

General Information Coeducational boarding and day and distance learning college-preparatory, arts, and religious studies school, affiliated with Seventh-day Adventists. Grades 9–12. Distance learning grades 9–12. Founded: 1918. Setting: suburban. Nearest major city is Orlando. Students are housed in single-sex dormitories. 200-acre campus. 9 buildings on campus. Approved or accredited by CITA (Commission on International and Trans-Regional Accreditation), National Council for Private School Accreditation, Southern Association of Colleges and Schools, and Florida Department of Education. Languages of instruction: English and Spanish. Total enrollment: 344. Upper school average class size: 22. Upper school faculty-student ratio: 1:16.
Upper School Student Profile Grade 9: 70 students (44 boys, 26 girls); Grade 10: 97 students (42 boys, 55 girls); Grade 11: 93 students (44 boys, 49 girls); Grade 12: 83 students (33 boys, 50 girls). 30% of students are boarding students. 83% are state residents. 8 states are represented in upper school student body. 10% are international students. International students from Cayman Islands, China, Honduras, Jamaica, Mexico, and Republic of Korea; 6 other countries represented in student body. 95% of students are Seventh-day Adventists.
Faculty School total: 21. In upper school: 13 men, 8 women; 15 have advanced degrees; 11 reside on campus.
Subjects Offered Algebra, American government, American literature, anatomy and physiology, art, Bible studies, biology, British literature, calculus, chemistry, composition, computer applications, concert band, concert choir, desktop publishing, economics, English, ensembles, geometry, health, honors algebra, honors English, honors geometry, honors world history, journalism, life management skills, music, photography, physical education, physics, pre-calculus, psychology, research skills, senior project, Spanish, statistics, U.S. government-AP, U.S. history, video communication, video film production, world history, world literature, yearbook.
Graduation Requirements Arts and fine arts (art, music, dance, drama), computer science, English, foreign language, mathematics, physical education (includes health), religion (includes Bible studies and theology), science, social science, social studies (includes history), 20 hours of community service activity for each year enrolled.
Special Academic Programs Honors section; study at local college for college credit.
College Admission Counseling 114 students graduated in 2008; 95 went to college, including Florida Hospital College of Health Sciences; Oakwood University; Southern Adventist University; Southwestern Adventist University; University of Central Florida; University of Florida. Other: 4 went to work. Median composite ACT: 21. 12% scored over 26 on composite ACT.
Student Life Upper grades have uniform requirement, honor system. Discipline rests primarily with faculty. Attendance at religious services is required.
Tuition and Aid Day student tuition: $8300; 7-day tuition and room/board: $15,075. Tuition installment plan (FACTS Tuition Payment Plan). Need-based scholarship

grants, paying campus jobs available. In 2008–09, 35% of upper-school students received aid. Total amount of financial aid awarded in 2008–09: $255,000.

Admissions Traditional secondary-level entrance grade is 9. ACT, Explore, PSAT or SAT required. Deadline for receipt of application materials: none. Application fee required: $60. Interview recommended.

Athletics Interscholastic: basketball (boys, girls), golf (b), volleyball (g); intramural: basketball (b); coed interscholastic: swimming and diving, track and field; coed intramural: canoeing/kayaking, flag football, outdoor activities, outdoor recreation, soccer, softball. 2 PE instructors, 11 coaches.

Computers Computers are regularly used in computer applications, desktop publishing, photography, Web site design, writing, yearbook classes. Computer network features include on-campus library services, Internet access, wireless campus network, Internet filtering or blocking technology, financial aid and grant search programs for college. Student e-mail accounts and computer access in designated common areas are available to students. Students grades are available online.

Contact Mrs. Claudia Dure C Osorio, Admissions Officer. 407-862-8411 Ext. 729. Fax: 407-862-7050. E-mail: osorioc@forestlake.org. Web site: www.forestlakeacademy.org.

THE FORMAN SCHOOL

Litchfield, Connecticut

See Special Needs Schools section.

FORSYTH COUNTRY DAY SCHOOL

5501 Shallowford Road
PO Box 549
Lewisville, North Carolina 27023-0549

Head of School: Mr. Henry M. Battle Jr.

General Information Coeducational day college-preparatory school. Grades PK–12. Founded: 1970. Setting: suburban. Nearest major city is Winston-Salem. 80-acre campus. 7 buildings on campus. Approved or accredited by North Carolina Association of Independent Schools, Southern Association of Colleges and Schools, Southern Association of Independent Schools, The College Board, and North Carolina Department of Education. Member of National Association of Independent Schools. Endowment: $16 million. Total enrollment: 938. Upper school average class size: 15. Upper school faculty-student ratio: 1:12.

Upper School Student Profile Grade 9: 92 students (56 boys, 36 girls); Grade 10: 98 students (60 boys, 38 girls); Grade 11: 107 students (61 boys, 46 girls); Grade 12: 95 students (48 boys, 47 girls).

Faculty School total: 175. In upper school: 18 men, 29 women; 24 have advanced degrees.

Subjects Offered Advanced Placement courses, advanced studio art-AP, algebra, American history, American history-AP, American literature, art, astronomy, biology, calculus, calculus-AP, ceramics, chemistry, Chinese studies, community service, computer math, computer programming, computer science, creative writing, digital art, drama, English, English literature, European history, fine arts, foreign policy, French, freshman seminar, geometry, grammar, health, history, history of science, humanities, international relations, Japanese studies, journalism, Latin, Mandarin, mathematics, Middle Eastern history, music, photography, physical education, physics, psychology, SAT/ACT preparation, science, social studies, Spanish, statistics-AP, theater, yearbook.

Graduation Requirements Arts and fine arts (art, music, dance, drama), English, foreign language, history, mathematics, physical education (includes health), physical fitness, science. Community service is required.

Special Academic Programs Advanced Placement exam preparation; honors section; academic accommodation for the gifted; programs in English, general development for dyslexic students; ESL (2 students enrolled).

College Admission Counseling 100 students graduated in 2008; 99 went to college, including Duke University; Elon University; North Carolina State University; The University of North Carolina at Chapel Hill; The University of North Carolina Wilmington; Wake Forest University. Other: 1 entered military service. Median SAT critical reading: 600, median SAT math: 610. 70% scored over 600 on SAT critical reading, 68% scored over 600 on SAT math.

Student Life Upper grades have specified standards of dress, student council, honor system. Discipline rests equally with students and faculty.

Summer Programs Enrichment programs offered; session focuses on leadership training; held both on and off campus; held at various businesses and offices throughout the community; accepts boys and girls; open to students from other schools. 50 students usually enrolled. 2009 schedule: June 15 to July 31.

Tuition and Aid Day student tuition: $16,500. Tuition installment plan (Insured Tuition Payment Plan, monthly payment plans, individually arranged payment plans). Need-based scholarship grants available. In 2008–09, 18% of upper-school students received aid. Total amount of financial aid awarded in 2008–09: $693,755.

Admissions Traditional secondary-level entrance grade is 9. For fall 2008, 74 students applied for upper-level admission, 65 were accepted, 49 enrolled. ERB CTP IV, WRAT and writing sample required. Deadline for receipt of application materials: none. Application fee required: $100. On-campus interview required.

Athletics Interscholastic: baseball (boys), basketball (b,g), cheering (g), cross-country running (b,g), dance team (g), field hockey (g), football (b), lacrosse (b), physical fitness (b,g), soccer (b,g), softball (g), tennis (b,g), track and field (b,g), volleyball (g), wrestling (b); coed interscholastic: golf, swimming and diving; coed intramural: sailing. 4 PE instructors, 4 coaches, 1 athletic trainer.

Computers Computers are regularly used in art, English, foreign language, history, mathematics, music, science classes. Computer network features include on-campus library services, online commercial services, Internet access, wireless campus network, Internet filtering or blocking technology. Student e-mail accounts are available to students. Students grades are available online. The school has a published electronic and media policy.

Contact Cindy C. Kluttz, Director of Admission. 336-945-3151 Ext. 340. Fax: 336-945-2907. E-mail: cindykluttz@fcds.org. Web site: www.fcds.org.

FORT LAUDERDALE PREPARATORY SCHOOL

3275 West Oakland Park Boulevard
Fort Lauderdale, Florida 33311

Head of School: Dr. Lawrence Berkowitz

General Information Coeducational day college-preparatory, general academic, arts, and technology school. Grades PK–12. Founded: 1986. Setting: urban. 5-acre campus. 1 building on campus. Approved or accredited by CITA (Commission on International and Trans-Regional Accreditation), Florida Council of Independent Schools, National Independent Private Schools Association, Southern Association of Colleges and Schools, and Florida Department of Education. Member of European Council of International Schools. Languages of instruction: English and Spanish. Upper school average class size: 16. Upper school faculty-student ratio: 1:9.

Upper School Student Profile Grade 6: 20 students (13 boys, 7 girls); Grade 7: 20 students (9 boys, 11 girls); Grade 8: 20 students (10 boys, 10 girls); Grade 9: 20 students (14 boys, 6 girls); Grade 10: 20 students (12 boys, 8 girls); Grade 11: 20 students (7 boys, 13 girls); Grade 12: 20 students (10 boys, 10 girls).

Faculty School total: 26. In upper school: 13 men, 11 women; 11 have advanced degrees.

Subjects Offered Accounting, ACT preparation, advanced chemistry, advanced computer applications, advanced math, Advanced Placement courses, advanced studio art-AP, advanced TOEFL/grammar, algebra, American government, American government-AP, American history, American history-AP, American literature, American literature-AP, art, art appreciation, art history, art history-AP, art-AP, automated accounting, Basic programming, biology, biology-AP, bookkeeping, British literature, British literature (honors), business applications, business education, business mathematics, calculus, calculus-AP, career education, career/college preparation, character education, chemistry, chemistry-AP.

Special Academic Programs International Baccalaureate program; Advanced Placement exam preparation; honors section; accelerated programs; independent study; study at local college for college credit; academic accommodation for the gifted; remedial reading and/or remedial writing; remedial math; programs in English, mathematics, general development for dyslexic students; ESL (17 students enrolled).

College Admission Counseling 20 students graduated in 2008; 18 went to college, including Florida Atlantic University; Florida State University; Hunter College of the City University of New York; University of Florida; University of Miami; University of South Florida. Other: 1 went to work, 1 entered military service.

Student Life Upper grades have uniform requirement, student council, honor system. Discipline rests primarily with faculty.

Summer Programs Remediation, enrichment, advancement, ESL, computer instruction programs offered; session focuses on academics; held on campus; accepts boys and girls; open to students from other schools. 100 students usually enrolled. 2009 schedule: June 18 to July 26.

Tuition and Aid Day student tuition: $11,150. Tuition installment plan (monthly payment plans, individually arranged payment plans). Tuition reduction for siblings, merit scholarship grants, need-based scholarship grants available. In 2008–09, 40% of upper-school students received aid; total upper-school merit-scholarship money awarded: $100,000. Total amount of financial aid awarded in 2008–09: $150,000.

Admissions Traditional secondary-level entrance grade is 7. For fall 2008, 100 students applied for upper-level admission, 70 were accepted, 60 enrolled. Admissions testing, High School Placement Test, math and English placement tests, Math Placement Exam, school's own exam, standardized test scores, Stanford Achievement Test, TOEFL or writing sample required. Deadline for receipt of application materials: none. Application fee required: $50. Interview recommended.

Athletics 2 PE instructors.

Computers Computers are regularly used in all academic classes. Computer network features include on-campus library services, Internet access, wireless campus network, Internet filtering or blocking technology. Campus intranet is available to students. The school has a published electronic and media policy.

Contact Jonathan A. Lonstein, Director of Admissions. 954-485-7500. Fax: 954-485-1732. E-mail: admissions@flps.com. Web site: www.flps.com/.

FORT WORTH COUNTRY DAY SCHOOL

4200 Country Day Lane
Fort Worth, Texas 76109-4299

Head of School: Evan D. Peterson

General Information Coeducational day college-preparatory and arts school. Grades K–12. Founded: 1962. Setting: suburban. 100-acre campus. 13 buildings on campus. Approved or accredited by Independent Schools Association of the Southwest. Member of National Association of Independent Schools. Endowment: $30 million. Total enrollment: 1,115. Upper school average class size: 14. Upper school faculty-student ratio: 1:10.

Upper School Student Profile Grade 9: 98 students (48 boys, 50 girls); Grade 10: 99 students (40 boys, 59 girls); Grade 11: 97 students (50 boys, 47 girls); Grade 12: 96 students (41 boys, 55 girls).

Faculty School total: 128. In upper school: 16 men, 21 women; 29 have advanced degrees.

Subjects Offered Algebra, American history, American literature, art, art history, biology, calculus, ceramics, chemistry, comparative religion, computer math, computer programming, computer science, computer technologies, creative writing, dance, drama, driver education, earth science, ecology, economics, English, English literature, European history, expository writing, fine arts, French, geography, geology, geometry, government/civics, grammar, health, history, journalism, Latin, mathematics, modern problems, music, music history, photography, physical education, physics, psychology, science, social studies, Spanish, speech, study skills, technology, theater, trigonometry, typing, word processing, world history, writing.

Graduation Requirements Algebra, American government, arts and fine arts (art, music, dance, drama), biology, English, foreign language, lab science, mathematics, physical education (includes health), science, social studies (includes history), participation in athletics. Community service is required.

Special Academic Programs 22 Advanced Placement exams for which test preparation is offered; honors section; independent study; term-away projects; study at local college for college credit; study abroad; academic accommodation for the gifted, the musically talented, and the artistically talented.

College Admission Counseling 92 students graduated in 2008; all went to college, including Texas A&M University; Texas Christian University; The University of Texas at Austin; University of Colorado at Boulder.

Student Life Upper grades have uniform requirement, student council, honor system. Discipline rests equally with students and faculty.

Summer Programs Remediation, enrichment, sports, art/fine arts programs offered; session focuses on athletics and enrichment; held both on and off campus; held at local golf course (for enrichment golf and golf team practice); accepts boys and girls; open to students from other schools. 300 students usually enrolled. 2009 schedule: June 1 to July 31. Application deadline: May 30.

Tuition and Aid Day student tuition: $15,700. Tuition installment plan (Key Tuition Payment Plan, monthly payment plans, individually arranged payment plans). Merit scholarship grants, need-based scholarship grants, Malone Scholars Program available. In 2008–09, 20% of upper-school students received aid; total upper-school merit-scholarship money awarded: $151,000. Total amount of financial aid awarded in 2008–09: $820,000.

Admissions Traditional secondary-level entrance grade is 9. For fall 2008, 84 students applied for upper-level admission, 43 were accepted, 33 enrolled. ERB or ISEE required. Deadline for receipt of application materials: March 7. Application fee required: $75. Interview required.

Athletics Interscholastic: baseball (boys), basketball (b,g), cheering (g), field hockey (g), football (b), lacrosse (b), swimming and diving (g), track and field (b,g), volleyball (b,g), winter soccer (b,g), wrestling (b); intramural: lacrosse (b); coed interscholastic: cross-country running, dance, dance team, fitness, golf, independent competitive sports, physical training, ropes courses, strength & conditioning, tennis. 12 PE instructors, 45 coaches, 2 athletic trainers.

Computers Computers are regularly used in architecture, college planning, computer applications, creative writing, desktop publishing, English, foreign language, history, humanities, introduction to technology, library skills, life skills, mathematics, music, newspaper, publications, reading, science, Web site design, writing, yearbook classes. Computer network features include on-campus library services, online commercial services, Internet access, wireless campus network, Internet filtering or blocking technology. Campus intranet, student e-mail accounts, and computer access in designated common areas are available to students. The school has a published electronic and media policy.

Contact Yolanda Espinoza, Admissions Associate. 817-302-3209. Fax: 817-377-3425. E-mail: yespinoza@fwcds.org. Web site: www.fwcds.org.

FOUNDATION ACADEMY

15304 Tilden Road
Winter Garden, Florida 34787

Head of School: Mr. Shawn Minks

General Information Coeducational day college-preparatory and general academic school, affiliated with Baptist Church; primarily serves students with learning disabilities, individuals with Attention Deficit Disorder, and dyslexic students. Grades 6–12. Founded: 1958. Setting: suburban. Nearest major city is Orlando. 75-acre campus. 3 buildings on campus. Approved or accredited by Association of Christian Schools International and Southern Association of Colleges and Schools. Total enrollment: 607. Upper school average class size: 24. Upper school faculty-student ratio: 1:21.

Upper School Student Profile Grade 6: 54 students (24 boys, 30 girls); Grade 7: 35 students (26 boys, 9 girls); Grade 8: 43 students (24 boys, 19 girls); Grade 9: 32 students (17 boys, 15 girls); Grade 10: 28 students (14 boys, 14 girls); Grade 11: 24 students (12 boys, 12 girls); Grade 12: 13 students (9 boys, 4 girls). 15% of students are Baptist.

Faculty School total: 25. In upper school: 6 men, 19 women; 5 have advanced degrees.

Subjects Offered Advanced Placement courses, anatomy and physiology, art, band, Bible, biology, biology-AP, business law, business mathematics, calculus, chemistry, college admission preparation, computer processing, drama, economics and history, English, English composition, English literature, English literature-AP, French, geometry, government, health education, history-AP, physical education, physical fitness, SAT preparation, science, science project, social psychology, Spanish, speech, sports conditioning, U.S. history, weight training.

Graduation Requirements Bible-4 credits.

Special Academic Programs Advanced Placement exam preparation; honors section; independent study; study at local college for college credit; remedial reading and/or remedial writing; remedial math; programs in English, mathematics for dyslexic students.

College Admission Counseling 26 students graduated in 2008; 25 went to college, including Florida Gulf Coast University; University of Central Florida; Valencia Community College. Other: 1 went to work.

Student Life Upper grades have uniform requirement, student council. Discipline rests primarily with faculty. Attendance at religious services is required.

Summer Programs Sports programs offered; session focuses on Sports Camps; held on campus; accepts boys and girls; open to students from other schools. 100 students usually enrolled. 2009 schedule: June 1 to July 31. Application deadline: June 15.

Tuition and Aid Day student tuition: $7800. Guaranteed tuition plan. Tuition installment plan (SMART Tuition Payment Plan). Need-based scholarship grants available. In 2008–09, 6% of upper-school students received aid.

Admissions For fall 2008, 49 students applied for upper-level admission, 30 were accepted, 28 enrolled. Any standardized test required. Deadline for receipt of application materials: none. Application fee required: $150. Interview required.

Athletics Interscholastic: baseball (boys), basketball (b,g), bordenball (b,g), cheering (g), cross-country running (b,g), football (b), golf (b), softball (g), tennis (b,g), track and field (b,g), volleyball (g). 2 PE instructors, 15 coaches.

Computers Computers are regularly used in computer applications, independent study, library skills, yearbook classes. Computer resources include on-campus library services, Internet access, Internet filtering or blocking technology. Campus intranet is available to students. Students grades are available online.

Contact Mrs. Melody Shiver, Student Advisor. 407-877-2744. Fax: 407-877-1985. E-mail: mshiver@foundationacademy.net. Web site: www.foundationacademy.net.

FOUNTAIN VALLEY SCHOOL OF COLORADO

6155 Fountain Valley School Road
Colorado Springs, Colorado 80911

Head of School: Craig W. Larimer Jr.

General Information Coeducational boarding and day college-preparatory, arts, and technology school. Grades 9–12. Founded: 1929. Setting: suburban. Students are housed in single-sex dormitories. 1,100-acre campus. 42 buildings on campus. Approved or accredited by Association of Colorado Independent Schools, The Association of Boarding Schools, and Colorado Department of Education. Member of National Association of Independent Schools and Secondary School Admission Test Board. Endowment: $34 million. Total enrollment: 250. Upper school average class size: 12. Upper school faculty-student ratio: 1:6.

Upper School Student Profile 62% of students are boarding students. 54% are state residents. 23 states are represented in upper school student body. 20% are international students. International students from China, Germany, Hong Kong, Republic of Korea, Saudi Arabia, and Taiwan; 7 other countries represented in student body.

Faculty School total: 42. In upper school: 25 men, 15 women; 26 have advanced degrees; 30 reside on campus.

Subjects Offered 20th century history, 20th century world history, 3-dimensional art, 3-dimensional design, acting, advanced chemistry, advanced computer applications, Advanced Placement courses, advanced studio art-AP, algebra, American history, American history-AP, American literature, American politics in film, biology, biology-AP, British literature, calculus, calculus-AP, ceramics, chamber groups, chemistry, chemistry-AP, college counseling, Colorado ecology, composition, computer applications, computer multimedia, computer programming, creative writing, desktop publishing, drama, English, English literature and composition-AP, environmental science-AP, ESL, European history, fiction, film and literature, film history, French, French language-AP, geology, geometry, honors algebra, honors English, honors geometry, instrumental music, jewelry making, literature, Mandarin, musical productions, outdoor education, philosophy, photography, physics, physics-AP, pre-calculus, senior project, senior seminar, Shakespeare, short story, South African history, Spanish, Spanish language-AP, statistics and probability, statistics-AP, strings, student government, student publications, studio art, studio art-AP, U.S. government and politics-AP, visual and performing arts, vocal ensemble, Western civilization, wilderness/outdoor program, wind ensemble, world history, world history-AP, world literature, writing.

Graduation Requirements Arts and fine arts (art, music, dance, drama), computer science, English, foreign language, history, mathematics, physical education (includes health), science, social studies (includes history), Community Service hours.

Special Academic Programs 19 Advanced Placement exams for which test preparation is offered; honors section; independent study; term-away projects; academic accommodation for the gifted, the musically talented, and the artistically talented; ESL (18 students enrolled).

College Admission Counseling 54 students graduated in 2008; 53 went to college, including University of San Francisco. Other: 1 had other specific plans. Mean SAT critical reading: 613, mean SAT math: 608, mean SAT writing: 607, mean composite ACT: 26.

Student Life Upper grades have specified standards of dress, student council, honor system. Discipline rests equally with students and faculty.

Summer Programs Sports, rigorous outdoor training programs offered; session focuses on outdoor education, natural sciences, leadership, sports camps; held both on and off campus; held at FVS' 40-acre Mountain Campus and surrounding Mount Princeton region; accepts boys and girls; open to students from other schools. 200 students usually enrolled. 2009 schedule: June 5 to August 15. Application deadline: none.

Tuition and Aid Day student tuition: $20,670; 7-day tuition and room/board: $38,100. Tuition installment plan (Key Tuition Payment Plan, monthly payment plans, individually arranged payment plans). Merit scholarship grants, need-based scholarship grants available. In 2008–09, 34% of upper-school students received aid; total upper-school merit-scholarship money awarded: $152,200. Total amount of financial aid awarded in 2008–09: $1,650,000.

Admissions Traditional secondary-level entrance grade is 9. For fall 2008, 211 students applied for upper-level admission, 131 were accepted, 90 enrolled. SSAT or TOEFL required. Deadline for receipt of application materials: February 1. Application fee required: $50. Interview required.

Athletics Interscholastic: basketball (boys, girls), cross-country running (b,g), diving (g), field hockey (g), hockey (b), ice hockey (b), lacrosse (b,g), soccer (b,g), swimming and diving (g), tennis (b,g), track and field (b,g), volleyball (b,g); coed interscholastic: climbing, equestrian sports, golf, horseback riding, independent competitive sports, Polocrosse, rock climbing, rodeo, skiing (downhill), snowboarding, squash, telemark skiing; coed intramural: aerobics/dance, alpine skiing, backpacking, climbing, dance, equestrian sports, fitness, golf, hiking/backpacking, horseback riding, modern dance, mountain biking, mountaineering, outdoor activities, physical fitness, Polocrosse, rock climbing, skiing (downhill), snowboarding, squash, strength & conditioning, telemark skiing, tennis, weight training. 2 coaches, 1 athletic trainer.

Computers Computers are regularly used in all academic, college planning, multimedia, news writing, newspaper, photography, publications, theater, Web site design, yearbook classes. Computer network features include on-campus library services, online commercial services, Internet access, wireless campus network, Internet filtering or blocking technology. Campus intranet, student e-mail accounts, and computer access in designated common areas are available to students. Students grades are available online. The school has a published electronic and media policy.

Contact Mr. Randy Roach, Director of Admission. 719-390-7035 Ext. 251. Fax: 719-390-7762. E-mail: admission@fvs.edu. Web site: www.fvs.edu.

See Close-Up on page 756.

FOWLERS ACADEMY

PO Box 921
Guaynabo, Puerto Rico 00970-0921

Head of School: Mrs. Carmen Tuominen

General Information Coeducational day college-preparatory school, affiliated with Christian faith; primarily serves underachievers. Grades 7–12. Founded: 1986. Setting: suburban. 2-acre campus. 2 buildings on campus. Approved or accredited by Comisión Acreditadora de Instituciones Educativas, Middle States Association of Colleges and Schools, The College Board, and Puerto Rico Department of Education. Languages of instruction: English and Spanish. Total enrollment: 68. Upper school average class size: 15. Upper school faculty-student ratio: 1:8.

Upper School Student Profile Grade 9: 13 students (12 boys, 1 girl); Grade 10: 13 students (9 boys, 4 girls); Grade 11: 12 students (11 boys, 1 girl); Grade 12: 12 students (9 boys, 3 girls).

Faculty School total: 9. In upper school: 3 men, 5 women; 2 have advanced degrees.

Subjects Offered Algebra, American literature, ancient world history, arts and crafts, Bible, career/college preparation, chemistry, Christian education, college counseling, computer literacy, earth science, English, film appreciation, geometry, keyboarding/computer, physical education, physics, pre-algebra, pre-college orientation, Puerto Rican history, Spanish, theater, U.S. history, world history.

Graduation Requirements Algebra, ancient world history, chemistry, Christian education, earth science, electives, English, geometry, physical education (includes health), physical science, physics, pre-college orientation, Puerto Rican history, Spanish, U.S. history, world history.

Special Academic Programs Accelerated programs; special instructional classes for students with ADD and LD.

College Admission Counseling 13 students graduated in 2008; 11 went to college, including University of Puerto Rico, Río Piedras. Other: 2 entered a postgraduate year.

Student Life Upper grades have uniform requirement, student council, honor system. Discipline rests primarily with faculty.

Summer Programs Remediation programs offered; session focuses on academic courses and remediation; held on campus; accepts boys and girls; open to students from other schools. 30 students usually enrolled. 2009 schedule: June 1 to June 26. Application deadline: May 31.

Tuition and Aid Day student tuition: $5900. Tuition installment plan (monthly payment plans). Tuition reduction for siblings, need-based scholarship grants available. In 2008–09, 3% of upper-school students received aid. Total amount of financial aid awarded in 2008–09: $4650.

Admissions Deadline for receipt of application materials: none. No application fee required. On-campus interview required.

Athletics Interscholastic: basketball (boys); intramural: basketball (b), volleyball (b,g); coed interscholastic: archery, fitness, physical fitness, soccer, volleyball; coed intramural: fitness, physical fitness, soccer, table tennis, volleyball. 1 PE instructor.

Computers Computers are regularly used in English, science, Spanish classes. Computer resources include Internet access, Internet filtering or blocking technology. Computer access in designated common areas is available to students.

Contact Mr. Lynette Montes, Registrar. 787-787-1350. Fax: 787-789-0055. E-mail: fowlers@coqui.net.

FOXCROFT ACADEMY

975 West Main Street
Dover-Foxcroft, Maine 04426

Head of School: Dr. Raymond Webb

General Information Coeducational boarding and day college-preparatory and technology school. Grades 9–12. Founded: 1823. Setting: small town. Nearest major city is Bangor. Students are housed in single-sex dormitories. 120-acre campus. 5 buildings on campus. Approved or accredited by Independent Schools of Northern New England, New England Association of Schools and Colleges, and Maine Department of Education. Endowment: $6 million. Total enrollment: 439. Upper school average class size: 16. Upper school faculty-student ratio: 1:16.

Upper School Student Profile Grade 9: 107 students (51 boys, 56 girls); Grade 10: 113 students (57 boys, 56 girls); Grade 11: 112 students (54 boys, 58 girls); Grade 12: 107 students (53 boys, 54 girls). 18% of students are boarding students. 82% are state residents. 2 states are represented in upper school student body. 18% are international students. International students from Austria, China, Germany, Japan, Republic of Korea, and Viet Nam; 7 other countries represented in student body.

Faculty School total: 36. In upper school: 19 men, 16 women; 24 have advanced degrees; 4 reside on campus.

Subjects Offered Advanced Placement courses, algebra, American literature, ancient history, art history, art-AP, auto mechanics, calculus-AP, career planning, cell biology, chemistry-AP, child development, Chinese, choral music, classical civilization, communication skills, computer art, computer programming, critical thinking, engineering, English, English-AP, ESL, ethics, family and consumer science, French, geometry, health, history-AP, home economics, honors algebra, honors English, honors U.S. history, jazz ensemble, Latin, literature-AP, mathematics-AP, model United Nations, modern history, multimedia, music, music composition, music theater, music theory, orchestra, parent/child development, peer counseling, personal fitness, physics-AP, poetry, political science, portfolio art, pre-calculus, SAT preparation, science project, Shakespeare, small engine repair, Spanish, statistics-AP, stock market, strings, student government, student publications, studio art—AP, swimming, technical drawing, theater arts, TOEFL preparation, U.S. government, U.S. history-AP, U.S. literature, video and animation, visual arts, vocal ensemble, Western civilization-AP, woodworking, work-study, world arts, world cultures, world geography, world history, world wide web design, writing, writing fundamentals, yearbook.

Graduation Requirements Advanced math, algebra, American government, American history, analytic geometry, art, arts and fine arts (art, music, dance, drama), biology, chemistry, classical language, college admission preparation, communication skills, composition, computer skills, computer technologies, desktop publishing, economics, English literature, ethics, family and consumer science, foreign language, human biology, languages, music, physical education (includes health), physics, pre-calculus, statistics, visual arts, Western civilization, world cultures, writing, writing skills, must meet performance standards in all core academic areas. Community service is required.

Special Academic Programs Advanced Placement exam preparation; honors section; independent study; academic accommodation for the gifted, the musically talented, and the artistically talented; remedial reading and/or remedial writing; remedial math; ESL (38 students enrolled).

College Admission Counseling 103 students graduated in 2008; 81 went to college, including Colby College; Cornell University; Michigan State University; New York University; Penn State University Park; University of Maine. Other: 8 went to work, 11 entered military service. Median SAT critical reading: 580, median SAT math: 710, median SAT writing: 525, median combined SAT: 1815.

Student Life Upper grades have specified standards of dress, student council, honor system. Discipline rests primarily with faculty.

Summer Programs Sports, art/fine arts programs offered; session focuses on art, music, and athletics; held on campus; accepts boys and girls; open to students from other schools. 120 students usually enrolled. 2009 schedule: June 15 to July 31. Application deadline: May 1.
Tuition and Aid Day student tuition: $10,900; 5-day tuition and room/board: $26,500; 7-day tuition and room/board: $31,800. Tuition installment plan (Key Tuition Payment Plan, monthly payment plans, individually arranged payment plans). Tuition reduction for siblings, merit scholarship grants, need-based scholarship grants available. In 2008–09, 10% of upper-school students received aid; total upper-school merit-scholarship money awarded: $13,000. Total amount of financial aid awarded in 2008–09: $56,000.
Admissions Traditional secondary-level entrance grade is 9. For fall 2008, 134 students applied for upper-level admission, 42 were accepted, 37 enrolled. TOEFL or SLEP or writing sample required. Deadline for receipt of application materials: none. Application fee required: $50. Interview required.
Athletics Interscholastic: baseball (boys), basketball (b,g), cheering (g), cross-country running (b,g), field hockey (g), football (b), golf (b,g), hockey (b), soccer (b,g), softball (g), tennis (b,g), winter (indoor) track (b,g), wrestling (b,g); coed interscholastic: aquatics, indoor track & field, swimming and diving, wrestling; coed intramural: fencing, floor hockey, outdoor activities, snowboarding. 2 PE instructors, 11 coaches.
Computers Computers are regularly used in all academic classes. Computer network features include on-campus library services, Internet access, wireless campus network. Student e-mail accounts and computer access in designated common areas are available to students. The school has a published electronic and media policy.
Contact Mrs. Hsi-Wen (Ruby Canning) YOU, Admissions Assistant. 207-564-8664. Fax: 207-564-8664. E-mail: ruby.canning@foxcroftacademy.org. Web site: www.foxcroftacademy.org.

See Close-Up on page 758.

FOXCROFT SCHOOL

PO Box 5555
Middleburg, Virginia 20118
Head of School: Mary Louise Leipheimer

General Information Girls' boarding and day college-preparatory school. Grades 9–12. Founded: 1914. Setting: rural. Nearest major city is Washington, DC. Students are housed in single-sex dormitories. 500-acre campus. 52 buildings on campus. Approved or accredited by The Association of Boarding Schools, Virginia Association of Independent Schools, and Virginia Department of Education. Member of National Association of Independent Schools and Secondary School Admission Test Board. Endowment: $27 million. Total enrollment: 185. Upper school average class size: 10. Upper school faculty-student ratio: 1:6.
Upper School Student Profile Grade 9: 32 students (32 girls); Grade 10: 52 students (52 girls); Grade 11: 57 students (57 girls); Grade 12: 44 students (44 girls). 79% of students are boarding students. 40% are state residents. 22 states are represented in upper school student body. 16% are international students. International students from Australia, China, France, Mexico, Republic of Korea, and Taiwan; 6 other countries represented in student body.
Faculty School total: 29. In upper school: 11 men, 18 women; 16 have advanced degrees; 24 reside on campus.
Subjects Offered 3-dimensional art, acting, advanced chemistry, algebra, American literature, analytic geometry, anatomy and physiology, ancient world history, architecture, art, art history, astronomy, ballet, biology, botany, British literature, calculus, calculus-AP, cell biology, ceramics, chemistry, chemistry-AP, choir, chorus, Civil War, college counseling, community service, comparative religion, computer graphics, computer science, conceptual physics, constitutional law, creative dance, creative drama, creative writing, current events, dance, debate, digital photography, discrete math, drama, drawing and design, ecology, economics, economics-AP, English, English composition, English literature, English literature-AP, environmental science, European civilization, European history, European literature, expository writing, fine arts, fitness, forensic science, French, French language-AP, general science, geology, geometry, grammar, health education, history, human anatomy, independent study, leadership training, library, macroeconomics-AP, mathematics, microbiology, music, music theory, music theory-AP, oceanography, painting, performing arts, photography, physical education, physics, piano, poetry, pottery, pre-calculus, printmaking, production, public speaking, Roman civilization, SAT preparation, sculpture, senior project, social studies, Spanish, Spanish language-AP, Spanish literature, Spanish literature-AP, statistics and probability, studio art, studio art—AP, technology, The 20th Century, trigonometry, U.S. history, U.S. history-AP, vocal ensemble, weight fitness, world cultures, world literature, writing, yearbook, yoga.
Graduation Requirements Arts and fine arts (art, music, dance, drama), English, foreign language, history, mathematics, physical education (includes health), science, Senior Project.
Special Academic Programs Advanced Placement exam preparation; honors section; independent study; term-away projects; study abroad; academic accommodation for the gifted, the musically talented, and the artistically talented.
College Admission Counseling 42 students graduated in 2008; all went to college, including College of Charleston; Duke University; The College of William and Mary; The Johns Hopkins University; University of Virginia; Wake Forest University. Mean SAT critical reading: 563, mean SAT math: 595, mean SAT writing: 571, mean combined SAT: 1729, mean composite ACT: 22.
Student Life Upper grades have specified standards of dress, student council. Discipline rests equally with students and faculty.
Tuition and Aid Day student tuition: $30,712; 7-day tuition and room/board: $40,950. Tuition installment plan (The Tuition Plan, Insured Tuition Payment Plan, Key Tuition Payment Plan, monthly payment plans, Tuition Management Systems Plan). Merit scholarship grants, need-based scholarship grants, need-based loans, middle-income loans available. In 2008–09, 24% of upper-school students received aid; total upper-school merit-scholarship money awarded: $115,878. Total amount of financial aid awarded in 2008–09: $1,142,075.
Admissions Traditional secondary-level entrance grade is 9. For fall 2008, 163 students applied for upper-level admission, 134 were accepted, 61 enrolled. SLEP for foreign students, SSAT and TOEFL required. Deadline for receipt of application materials: February 15. Application fee required: $50. Interview required.
Athletics Interscholastic: basketball, cross-country running, dressage, equestrian sports, field hockey, horseback riding, lacrosse, soccer, softball, swimming and diving, tennis, volleyball; intramural: aerobics/dance, combined training, dance, dance team, dressage, equestrian sports, field hockey, fitness, horseback riding, lacrosse, modern dance, physical fitness, physical training, rock climbing, strength & conditioning, weight training, yoga. 1 coach, 1 athletic trainer.
Computers Computers are regularly used in English, foreign language, graphic arts, graphic design, history, mathematics, music, science classes. Computer network features include on-campus library services, online commercial services, Internet access, wireless campus network, Internet filtering or blocking technology. Campus intranet and student e-mail accounts are available to students.
Contact Erica L. Ohanesian, Director of Admission. 540-687-4341. Fax: 540-687-3627. E-mail: eohanesian@foxcroft.org. Web site: www.foxcroft.org.

ANNOUNCEMENT FROM THE SCHOOL Foxcroft School does more than prepare young women for college and for life. It enables each student to find her unique voice. An academically demanding, wonderfully supportive school, Foxcroft is known for its exceptional faculty and its attention to the individual. Foxcroft provides its girls with a safe, secure place to learn, to grow, and to go beyond their own expectations of themselves.

See Close-Up on page 760.

FOX RIVER COUNTRY DAY SCHOOL

Elgin, Illinois
See Junior Boarding Schools section.

FOX VALLEY LUTHERAN ACADEMY

220 Division Street
Elgin, Illinois 60120
Head of School: Janet M. Burmeister

General Information Coeducational day college-preparatory and religious studies school, affiliated with Lutheran Church. Grades 9–12. Founded: 1974. Setting: suburban. Nearest major city is Chicago. 1 building on campus. Approved or accredited by National Lutheran School Accreditation, North Central Association of Colleges and Schools, and Illinois Department of Education. Total enrollment: 23. Upper school average class size: 7. Upper school faculty-student ratio: 1:3.
Upper School Student Profile Grade 9: 5 students (1 boy, 4 girls); Grade 10: 6 students (2 boys, 4 girls); Grade 11: 5 students (2 boys, 3 girls); Grade 12: 7 students (7 girls). 55% of students are Lutheran.
Faculty School total: 7. In upper school: 3 men, 4 women; 6 have advanced degrees.
Subjects Offered Algebra, American history, American literature, Bible studies, biology, chemistry, choir, computer science, earth science, economics, English, English literature, fine arts, geography, geometry, government/civics, health, mathematics, music, physical education, physics, psychology, religion, science, service learning/internship, social science, social studies, Spanish, speech, theology, trigonometry, typing, world history, world literature, writing.
Graduation Requirements Arts and fine arts (art, music, dance, drama), English, foreign language, mathematics, physical education (includes health), religion (includes Bible studies and theology), science, social science, social studies (includes history).
Special Academic Programs Independent study; study at local college for college credit.
College Admission Counseling 5 students graduated in 2008; all went to college, including Elgin Community College; Luther College; Valparaiso University.
Student Life Upper grades have specified standards of dress, student council. Discipline rests primarily with faculty. Attendance at religious services is required.
Tuition and Aid Day student tuition: $5875. Tuition installment plan (monthly payment plans, individually arranged payment plans, semiannual payment plan, annual payment plan). Merit scholarship grants, need-based scholarship grants

available. In 2008–09, 25% of upper-school students received aid; total upper-school merit-scholarship money awarded: $500. Total amount of financial aid awarded in 2008–09: $12,000.

Admissions Traditional secondary-level entrance grade is 9. For fall 2008, 1 student applied for upper-level admission, 1 was accepted, 1 enrolled. Deadline for receipt of application materials: none. Application fee required: $150. On-campus interview required.

Athletics Interscholastic: basketball (boys, girls), soccer (b), volleyball (g). 1 PE instructor, 2 coaches.

Computers Computers are regularly used in career education, college planning, computer applications, creative writing, English, health, independent study, keyboarding, senior seminar, Spanish, speech, study skills, word processing classes. Computer network features include Internet access, Internet filtering or blocking technology. Student e-mail accounts are available to students. The school has a published electronic and media policy.

Contact Jan Burmeister, Assistant Principal. 847-468-8207. Fax: 847-742-2930. E-mail: jburmeister@fvla.com. Web site: www.fvla.com.

FOX VALLEY LUTHERAN HIGH SCHOOL

5300 North Meade Street
Appleton, Wisconsin 54913-8383

Head of School: Mr. Paul Hartwig

General Information Coeducational day college-preparatory, general academic, arts, business, vocational, religious studies, and technology school, affiliated with Wisconsin Evangelical Lutheran Synod. Grades 9–12. Founded: 1953. Setting: suburban. 63-acre campus. 1 building on campus. Approved or accredited by Wisconsin Department of Education. Endowment: $2.5 million. Total enrollment: 640. Upper school average class size: 26. Upper school faculty-student ratio: 1:14.

Upper School Student Profile Grade 9: 155 students (82 boys, 73 girls); Grade 10: 139 students (73 boys, 66 girls); Grade 11: 168 students (84 boys, 84 girls); Grade 12: 156 students (81 boys, 75 girls); Grade 13: 178 students (90 boys, 88 girls). 85% of students are Wisconsin Evangelical Lutheran Synod.

Faculty School total: 44. In upper school: 32 men, 10 women; 18 have advanced degrees.

Subjects Offered Accounting, advanced chemistry, advanced computer applications, advanced math, algebra, American government, American history, American literature, art, athletics, band, basic language skills, Basic programming, Bible, Bible studies, biology, British literature, British literature (honors), British literature-AP, business, business law, calculus, calculus-AP, choir, Christian doctrine, church history, communication skills, comparative religion, composition, computer applications, computer keyboarding, computer programming, computer skills, computer-aided design, concert band, concert choir, construction, critical writing, digital photography, drama, earth science, economics, economics-AP, English, English composition, foods, general science, geometry, German, government, graphic arts, health and wellness, honors English, keyboarding/computer, language and composition, Latin, Life of Christ, modern Western civilization, modern world history, personal fitness, physical fitness, physics, piano, psychology, reading/study skills, religion, remedial/makeup course work, sewing, Spanish, statistics, symphonic band, woodworking, world geography, world history.

Graduation Requirements 1½ elective credits, arts and fine arts (art, music, dance, drama), English, mathematics, physical education (includes health), religion (includes Bible studies and theology), science.

Special Academic Programs Honors section; accelerated programs; study at local college for college credit; academic accommodation for the gifted; remedial reading and/or remedial writing; remedial math.

College Admission Counseling 153 students graduated in 2008; 141 went to college, including Martin Luther College; University of Wisconsin–Fox Valley; University of Wisconsin–Green Bay; University of Wisconsin–Milwaukee; University of Wisconsin–Oshkosh; University of Wisconsin–Stevens Point. Other: 2 went to work, 4 entered military service, 2 had other specific plans.

Student Life Upper grades have specified standards of dress, student council, honor system. Discipline rests primarily with faculty. Attendance at religious services is required.

Tuition and Aid Day student tuition: $4425–$6975. Tuition installment plan (FACTS Tuition Payment Plan). Tuition reduction for siblings, need-based scholarship grants available. In 2008–09, 25% of upper-school students received aid. Total amount of financial aid awarded in 2008–09: $290,000.

Admissions Traditional secondary-level entrance grade is 9. Explore required. Deadline for receipt of application materials: none. Application fee required: $25. Interview required.

Athletics Interscholastic: baseball (boys), basketball (b,g), cheering (g), cross-country running (b,g), dance team (g), football (b), golf (b,g), hockey (b), ice hockey (b), softball (g), track and field (b,g), volleyball (g), wrestling (b). 2 PE instructors, 1 athletic trainer.

Computers Computers are regularly used in business, current events, economics, English, graphic arts, keyboarding, science classes. Computer network features include on-campus library services, Internet access, Internet filtering or blocking technology. Campus intranet and student e-mail accounts are available to students. Students grades are available online. The school has a published electronic and media policy.

Contact Mrs. Gloria Knoll, Guidance Assistant. 920-739-4441. E-mail: gknoll@fvlhs.org. Web site: www.fvlhs.org.

FRANKLIN ACADEMY

East Haddam, Connecticut
See Special Needs Schools section.

FRANKLIN ROAD ACADEMY

4700 Franklin Road
Nashville, Tennessee 37220

Head of School: Dr. Margaret Wade

General Information Coeducational day college-preparatory, arts, religious studies, and technology school, affiliated with Christian faith; primarily serves students with learning disabilities and individuals with Attention Deficit Disorder. Grades PK–12. Founded: 1971. Setting: suburban. 57-acre campus. 5 buildings on campus. Approved or accredited by Southern Association of Colleges and Schools, Southern Association of Independent Schools, Tennessee Association of Independent Schools, and Tennessee Department of Education. Member of National Association of Independent Schools. Endowment: $2 million. Total enrollment: 945. Upper school average class size: 15. Upper school faculty-student ratio: 1:8.

Upper School Student Profile Grade 9: 70 students (35 boys, 35 girls); Grade 10: 70 students (35 boys, 35 girls); Grade 11: 65 students (30 boys, 35 girls); Grade 12: 61 students (30 boys, 31 girls). 90% of students are Christian faith.

Faculty School total: 100. In upper school: 21 men, 14 women; 20 have advanced degrees.

Subjects Offered Advanced chemistry, Advanced Placement courses, algebra, American history, American literature, art, art-AP, band, baseball, basketball, Bible, Bible studies, biology, biology-AP, calculus, calculus-AP, chemistry, chemistry-AP, choral music, Civil War, college counseling, computer education, computer music, computer programming, computer science, current events, dance, drama, dramatic arts, economics, economics and history, electronic music, English, English language-AP, English literature, English literature-AP, environmental science, European history, European history-AP, fine arts, French, French language-AP, French literature-AP, geometry, government/civics, grammar, history, history-AP, honors algebra, honors English, honors geometry, honors U.S. history, human anatomy, jazz band, keyboarding/computer, Latin, Latin-AP, Life of Christ, mathematics, mathematics-AP, model United Nations, music, music theory, personal development, physical education, physics, physics-AP, physiology-anatomy, pottery, pre-calculus, SAT preparation, SAT/ACT preparation, science, social science, social studies, Spanish, Spanish language-AP, Spanish literature-AP, speech, statistics, statistics-AP, student government, student publications, technical theater, theater, theater production, track and field, trigonometry, U.S. government, U.S. history, U.S. history-AP, vocal music, volleyball, weight training, world history, world literature, wrestling, writing.

Graduation Requirements Arts and fine arts (art, music, dance, drama), computer science, English, foreign language, mathematics, physical education (includes health), religion (includes Bible studies and theology), science, social studies (includes history). Community service is required.

Special Academic Programs Advanced Placement exam preparation; honors section; independent study; term-away projects; academic accommodation for the gifted, the musically talented, and the artistically talented.

College Admission Counseling 62 students graduated in 2008; all went to college, including Auburn University; Belmont University; Middle Tennessee State University; The University of Tennessee; University of Georgia. 40% scored over 600 on SAT critical reading, 50% scored over 600 on SAT math, 50% scored over 26 on composite ACT.

Student Life Upper grades have uniform requirement, student council, honor system. Discipline rests primarily with faculty.

Summer Programs Enrichment, sports, art/fine arts, computer instruction programs offered; session focuses on day camps, the arts, technology, and sports; held both on and off campus; held at Area swimming pool; accepts boys and girls; open to students from other schools. 400 students usually enrolled. 2009 schedule: May 26 to July 10.

Tuition and Aid Day student tuition: $14,850. Tuition installment plan (Insured Tuition Payment Plan, individually arranged payment plans). Need-based scholarship grants available. In 2008–09, 2% of upper-school students received aid. Total amount of financial aid awarded in 2008–09: $100,000.

Admissions Traditional secondary-level entrance grade is 9. For fall 2008, 104 students applied for upper-level admission, 65 were accepted, 23 enrolled. ISEE required. Deadline for receipt of application materials: none. Application fee required: $40. On-campus interview required.

Athletics Interscholastic: baseball (boys), basketball (b,g), bowling (b,g), cheering (g), cross-country running (b,g), dance (g), diving (b,g), football (b), golf (b,g), hockey (b), ice hockey (b), soccer (b,g), softball (g), swimming and diving (b,g), tennis (b,g), track and field (b,g), volleyball (g), wrestling (b); intramural: aerobics/dance (g), physical fitness (b,g), physical training (b,g), power lifting (b), strength & conditioning (b,g); coed intramural: aerobics/dance, riflery. 2 PE instructors, 2 coaches, 1 athletic trainer.

Computers Computers are regularly used in art, Bible studies, college planning, creative writing, economics, English, foreign language, French, history, journalism, keyboarding, Latin, library skills, literary magazine, mathematics, music, religious studies, science, social sciences, Spanish, technology, theater, theater arts, Web site design, writing, yearbook classes. Computer network features include on-campus library services, online commercial services, Internet access, wireless campus network, Internet filtering or blocking technology, networked instructional software. Student e-mail accounts are available to students. Students grades are available online. The school has a published electronic and media policy.
Contact Mrs. Jan Marshall, Associate Director of Admissions. 615-832-8845. Fax: 615-834-4137. E-mail: marshallj@franklinroadacademy.com. Web site: www.franklinroadacademy.com.

FRASER ACADEMY

Vancouver, British Columbia, Canada
See Special Needs Schools section.

FREDERICA ACADEMY

200 Hamilton Road
St. Simons Island, Georgia 31522

ANNOUNCEMENT FROM THE SCHOOL Frederica Academy is located on St. Simons Island in Southeast Georgia. In this unique and beautiful setting, there is a strong sense of community characterized by a supportive partnership among students, teachers, and parents. Each boy and girl is encouraged to maximize his or her potential as they develop in mind, body, and spirit. In a culture of learning, we cherish our environment; joyfully serve others; laugh heartily, and appreciate and encourage each other.

FREEMAN ACADEMY

748 South Main Street
PO Box 1000
Freeman, South Dakota 57029
Head of School: Ms. Pam Tieszen

General Information Coeducational boarding and day college-preparatory, arts, and religious studies school, affiliated with Mennonite Church. Boarding grades 9–12, day grades 5–12. Founded: 1900. Setting: rural. Nearest major city is Sioux Falls. Students are housed in coed dormitories and host family homes. 80-acre campus. 6 buildings on campus. Approved or accredited by Mennonite Schools Council, North Central Association of Colleges and Schools, and South Dakota Department of Education. Endowment: $953,000. Total enrollment: 80. Upper school average class size: 15. Upper school faculty-student ratio: 1:8.
Upper School Student Profile Grade 9: 7 students (2 boys, 5 girls); Grade 10: 13 students (5 boys, 8 girls); Grade 11: 11 students (4 boys, 7 girls); Grade 12: 22 students (10 boys, 12 girls). 13% of students are boarding students. 86% are state residents. 2 states are represented in upper school student body. 13% are international students. International students from China, Gambia, Taiwan, and Thailand. 80% of students are Mennonite.
Faculty School total: 12. In upper school: 5 men, 7 women; 2 have advanced degrees; 1 resides on campus.
Subjects Offered Computer science, English, fine arts, mathematics, religion, science, social science, social studies.
Graduation Requirements Arts and fine arts (art, music, dance, drama), computer science, English, foreign language, mathematics, religion (includes Bible studies and theology), science, social studies (includes history), Humanities.
Special Academic Programs Independent study; academic accommodation for the musically talented and the artistically talented.
College Admission Counseling 17 students graduated in 2008; all went to college, including Bethel College; Concordia College; South Dakota State University; The University of South Dakota. Median composite ACT: 24. 1% scored over 26 on composite ACT.
Student Life Upper grades have specified standards of dress, honor system. Discipline rests primarily with faculty. Attendance at religious services is required.
Tuition and Aid Day student tuition: $5358; 5-day tuition and room/board: $8188. Tuition installment plan (FACTS Tuition Payment Plan, monthly payment plans, semester payment plan). Tuition reduction for siblings, merit scholarship grants, need-based scholarship grants available. In 2008–09, 10% of upper-school students received aid; total upper-school merit-scholarship money awarded: $500. Total amount of financial aid awarded in 2008–09: $5000.
Admissions Traditional secondary-level entrance grade is 9. For fall 2008, 6 students applied for upper-level admission, 6 were accepted, 6 enrolled. Deadline for receipt of application materials: none. No application fee required. Interview recommended.
Athletics Interscholastic: basketball (boys, girls), cheering (g), cross-country running (b,g), golf (b,g), soccer (b,g), track and field (b,g), volleyball (g). 3 coaches.
Computers Computers are regularly used in English, keyboarding, mathematics, religion, science, social studies, speech, yearbook classes. Computer network features include on-campus library services, Internet access, wireless campus network, Internet filtering or blocking technology. Student e-mail accounts and computer access in designated common areas are available to students. Students grades are available online. The school has a published electronic and media policy.
Contact Ms. Bonnie Young, Enrollment Director. 605-925-4237 Ext. 225. Fax: 605-925-4271. E-mail: byoung@freemanacademy.org. Web site: www.freemanacademy.org.

FRENCH-AMERICAN SCHOOL OF NEW YORK

525 Fenimore Road
Mamaroneck, New York 10543
Head of School: Mr. Robert Leonhardt

General Information Coeducational day college-preparatory and bilingual studies school. Grades N–12. Founded: 1980. Setting: suburban. Nearest major city is White Plains. 1 building on campus. Approved or accredited by Middle States Association of Colleges and Schools, New York State Association of Independent Schools, and New York Department of Education. Languages of instruction: English and French. Total enrollment: 824. Upper school average class size: 18. Upper school faculty-student ratio: 1:7.
Upper School Student Profile Grade 9: 44 students (23 boys, 21 girls); Grade 10: 37 students (20 boys, 17 girls); Grade 11: 23 students (8 boys, 15 girls); Grade 12: 23 students (9 boys, 14 girls).
Faculty School total: 114. In upper school: 15 men, 36 women; 33 have advanced degrees.
Subjects Offered Algebra, American history, American literature, art, biology, choir, civics, computer applications, computer multimedia, current events, earth science, ecology, economics, English, ESL, European history, expository writing, French, French language-AP, French literature-AP, French studies, geometry, German, government, health, Latin, mathematics, multimedia, music, newspaper, philosophy, physical education, physics, public speaking, science, social studies, Spanish, Spanish language-AP, world history, world literature, writing, yearbook.
Special Academic Programs Advanced Placement exam preparation; honors section; ESL (34 students enrolled).
Student Life Upper grades have specified standards of dress, student council. Discipline rests primarily with faculty.
Tuition and Aid Day student tuition: $18,150–$21,400. Tuition installment plan (Academic Management Services Plan). Need-based scholarship grants available. In 2008–09, 5% of upper-school students received aid. Total amount of financial aid awarded in 2008–09: $65,168.
Admissions For fall 2008, 37 students applied for upper-level admission, 28 were accepted, 18 enrolled. English, French, and math proficiency required. Deadline for receipt of application materials: none. Application fee required: $80. Interview recommended.
Athletics Interscholastic: baseball (boys), basketball (b,g), cross-country running (b,g), rugby (b,g), soccer (b,g), softball (g), tennis (b,g); coed intramural: fencing, in-line hockey. 3 PE instructors, 3 coaches.
Computers Computers are regularly used in art, English, foreign language, French, history, mathematics, music, publications, science classes. Computer network features include on-campus library services, Internet access, Internet filtering or blocking technology, laptop use (in certain classes). Student e-mail accounts are available to students. The school has a published electronic and media policy.
Contact Mr. Antoine Agopian, Director of Admissions. 914-250-0400. Fax: 914-940-2214. E-mail: aagopian@fasny.org. Web site: www.fasny.org.

FRIENDS' CENTRAL SCHOOL

1101 City Avenue
Wynnewood, Pennsylvania 19096
Head of School: David Felsen

General Information Coeducational day college-preparatory school, affiliated with Society of Friends. Grades PK–12. Founded: 1845. Setting: suburban. Nearest major city is Philadelphia. 23-acre campus. 7 buildings on campus. Approved or accredited by Pennsylvania Association of Independent Schools and Pennsylvania Department of Education. Member of National Association of Independent Schools. Endowment: $16.5 million. Total enrollment: 1,001. Upper school average class size: 16. Upper school faculty-student ratio: 1:9.
Upper School Student Profile Grade 9: 105 students (56 boys, 49 girls); Grade 10: 93 students (43 boys, 50 girls); Grade 11: 98 students (43 boys, 55 girls); Grade 12: 94 students (49 boys, 45 girls). 4% of students are members of Society of Friends.
Faculty School total: 130. In upper school: 26 men, 26 women; 38 have advanced degrees.
Subjects Offered Advanced math, algebra, American history, American literature, Bible, biology, biology-AP, calculus, calculus-AP, ceramics, chemistry, chemistry-AP, chorus, computer applications, computer programming, conflict resolution, drama, English, French, French-AP, geometry, instrumental music, Latin, Latin-AP, life skills, media studies, modern European history, music history, music theory, philosophy, photography, physical education, physical science, physics, pre-calculus, psychology, sexuality, Spanish, Spanish-AP, statistics-AP, studio art, study skills, Western literature, women in world history, woodworking, world history, writing workshop.

Graduation Requirements Arts and fine arts (art, music, dance, drama), English, foreign language, history, mathematics, science, service learning/internship.

College Admission Counseling 93 students graduated in 2008; all went to college, including Drexel University; Franklin & Marshall College; Penn State University Park; Princeton University; Skidmore College; University of Pennsylvania. Mean SAT critical reading: 639, mean SAT math: 643.

Student Life Upper grades have specified standards of dress, student council. Discipline rests primarily with faculty. Attendance at religious services is required.

Tuition and Aid Day student tuition: $24,300. Tuition installment plan (monthly payment plans, Higher Education Service, Inc). Need-based scholarship grants available. In 2008–09, 26% of upper-school students received aid. Total amount of financial aid awarded in 2008–09: $1,664,425.

Admissions Traditional secondary-level entrance grade is 9. For fall 2008, 133 students applied for upper-level admission, 53 were accepted, 34 enrolled. ISEE, SSAT or Wechsler Intelligence Scale for Children III required. Deadline for receipt of application materials: January 15. Application fee required: $50. On-campus interview required.

Athletics Interscholastic: aquatics (boys, girls), baseball (b), basketball (b,g), cross-country running (b,g), field hockey (g); coed interscholastic: cheering, golf; coed intramural: aerobics/dance, aerobics/Nautilus, dance, fitness. 8 PE instructors, 10 coaches, 1 athletic trainer.

Computers Computers are regularly used in college planning, foreign language, French, health, information technology, introduction to technology, Latin, mathematics, publishing, science, Spanish, technology, Web site design, yearbook classes. Computer network features include on-campus library services, online commercial services, Internet access, wireless campus network, Internet filtering or blocking technology, intranet collaboration. Student e-mail accounts are available to students. The school has a published electronic and media policy.

Contact Barbara Behar, Director of Admission and Financial Aid. 610-645-5032. Fax: 610-649-5669. E-mail: admission@friendscentral.org. Web site: www.friendscentral.org.

FRONT RANGE CHRISTIAN HIGH SCHOOL

6637 West Ottawa Avenue
Littleton, Colorado 80128

Head of School: Pres. Brian Meek

General Information Coeducational day college-preparatory, general academic, arts, business, vocational, religious studies, bilingual studies, technology, and science, math, language arts, media school, affiliated with Christian faith. Grades K–12. Founded: 1994. Setting: suburban. Nearest major city is Denver. 20-acre campus. 3 buildings on campus. Approved or accredited by Association of Christian Schools International, North Central Association of Colleges and Schools, and Colorado Department of Education. Total enrollment: 475. Upper school average class size: 25. Upper school faculty-student ratio: 1:16.

Upper School Student Profile Grade 9: 50 students (17 boys, 33 girls); Grade 10: 40 students (19 boys, 21 girls); Grade 11: 55 students (31 boys, 24 girls); Grade 12: 37 students (12 boys, 25 girls). 100% of students are Christian faith.

Faculty School total: 35. In upper school: 10 men, 9 women; 10 have advanced degrees.

Special Academic Programs Advanced Placement exam preparation; honors section; academic accommodation for the gifted; remedial reading and/or remedial writing; remedial math; programs in English, mathematics, general development for dyslexic students; special instructional classes for deaf students, blind students.

College Admission Counseling 47 students graduated in 2008; 41 went to college, including Arapahoe Community College; Colorado State University; Metropolitan State College of Denver; Wheaton College. Other: 1 went to work, 5 had other specific plans. Mean SAT critical reading: 566, mean SAT math: 573, mean SAT writing: 576, mean combined SAT: 1144, mean composite ACT: 23.

Student Life Upper grades have specified standards of dress, student council, honor system. Discipline rests primarily with faculty. Attendance at religious services is required.

Tuition and Aid Day student tuition: $5955. Tuition installment plan (FACTS Tuition Payment Plan, monthly payment plans). Tuition reduction for siblings, need-based scholarship grants, paying campus jobs available. In 2008–09, 100% of upper-school students received aid. Total amount of financial aid awarded in 2008–09: $30,000.

Admissions Traditional secondary-level entrance grade is 9. For fall 2008, 20 students applied for upper-level admission, 15 were accepted, 14 enrolled. English proficiency, essay or Math Placement Exam required. Deadline for receipt of application materials: none. Application fee required: $50. Interview required.

Athletics Interscholastic: baseball (boys), basketball (b,g), cheering (g), cross-country running (g), dance (b,g), football (b), golf (b), physical fitness (b,g), soccer (g), volleyball (g); intramural: basketball (b,g), soccer (b), volleyball (g). 1 PE instructor, 28 coaches.

Computers Computers are regularly used in basic skills, computer applications, data processing, information technology, introduction to technology, keyboarding, media arts, multimedia, yearbook classes. Computer network features include on-campus library services, Internet access, Internet filtering or blocking technology, Renweb Parents access. Computer access in designated common areas is available to students. Students grades are available online. The school has a published electronic and media policy.

Contact Karen Kay, Admissions Coordinator. 303-531-4541. Fax: 720-922-3296. E-mail: kkay@frcs.org. Web site: www.frontrangechristian.org.

THE FROSTIG SCHOOL

Pasadena, California

See Special Needs Schools section.

FRYEBURG ACADEMY

745 Main Street
Fryeburg, Maine 04037-1329

Head of School: Mr. Daniel G. Lee Jr.

General Information Coeducational boarding and day college-preparatory, general academic, arts, and technology school. Grades 9–PG. Founded: 1792. Setting: small town. Nearest major city is Portland. Students are housed in single-sex dormitories. 34-acre campus. 16 buildings on campus. Approved or accredited by Association of Independent Schools in New England, Independent Schools of Northern New England, New England Association of Schools and Colleges, The Association of Boarding Schools, The College Board, and Maine Department of Education. Member of National Association of Independent Schools and Secondary School Admission Test Board. Endowment: $8 million. Total enrollment: 681. Upper school average class size: 15. Upper school faculty-student ratio: 1:10.

Upper School Student Profile Grade 9: 146 students (69 boys, 77 girls); Grade 10: 143 students (74 boys, 69 girls); Grade 11: 195 students (106 boys, 89 girls); Grade 12: 197 students (92 boys, 105 girls). 20% of students are boarding students. 83% are state residents. 9 states are represented in upper school student body. 14% are international students. International students from China, Democratic People's Republic of Korea, Germany, Spain, Taiwan, and Viet Nam; 15 other countries represented in student body.

Faculty School total: 67. In upper school: 35 men, 32 women; 25 have advanced degrees; 25 reside on campus.

Subjects Offered Algebra, American literature, anatomy, art, art history, biology, botany, business, calculus, chemistry, computer math, computer programming, computer science, creative writing, drafting, drama, driver education, earth science, ecology, economics, English, English literature, ethics, European history, expository writing, fine arts, French, geography, geometry, government/civics, grammar, health, history, industrial arts, journalism, Latin, linear algebra, marine biology, mathematics, mechanical drawing, music, photography, physical education, physics, physiology, psychology, science, social studies, sociology, Spanish, speech, theater, trigonometry, typing, world history, world literature, writing.

Graduation Requirements Arts and fine arts (art, music, dance, drama), computer science, English, foreign language, mathematics, physical education (includes health), science, social studies (includes history). Community service is required.

Special Academic Programs 14 Advanced Placement exams for which test preparation is offered; honors section; independent study; study at local college for college credit; academic accommodation for the musically talented; remedial reading and/or remedial writing; remedial math; programs in English, mathematics, general development for dyslexic students; special instructional classes for students with learning disabilities, Attention Deficit Disorder, and dyslexia; ESL (42 students enrolled).

College Admission Counseling 186 students graduated in 2008; 150 went to college, including Boston University; Colby College; Northeastern University; University of Illinois at Urbana–Champaign; University of Maine; University of New Hampshire. Other: 32 went to work, 4 entered military service.

Student Life Upper grades have specified standards of dress, student council. Discipline rests primarily with faculty.

Tuition and Aid Day student tuition: $17,750; 5-day tuition and room/board: $28,250; 7-day tuition and room/board: $35,500. Tuition installment plan (monthly payment plans, individually arranged payment plans). Need-based scholarship grants available. In 2008–09, 33% of upper-school students received aid. Total amount of financial aid awarded in 2008–09: $900,000.

Admissions Traditional secondary-level entrance grade is 10. For fall 2008, 208 students applied for upper-level admission, 175 were accepted, 66 enrolled. Writing sample required. Deadline for receipt of application materials: none. Application fee required: $50. Interview required.

Athletics Interscholastic: baseball (boys), basketball (b,g), cross-country running (b,g), field hockey (g), football (b), golf (b), hockey (b,g), ice hockey (b), lacrosse (b,g), skiing (cross-country) (b,g), skiing (downhill) (b,g), soccer (b,g), softball (g), tennis (b,g), track and field (b,g), wrestling (b); intramural: ice hockey (g), strength & conditioning (b,g), table tennis (b,g); coed interscholastic: alpine skiing, cheering, mountain biking, nordic skiing; coed intramural: alpine skiing, archery, backpacking, badminton, ball hockey, basketball, bicycling, billiards, bowling, canoeing/kayaking, climbing, figure skating, fishing, fitness, fitness walking, flag football, floor hockey, fly fishing, freestyle skiing, Frisbee, golf, hiking/backpacking, ice skating, jogging, kayaking, mountain biking, mountaineering, paint ball, physical fitness, physical training, pistol, rock climbing, roller blading, skiing (downhill), snowboarding, snowshoeing, swimming and diving, table tennis, tai chi, telemark skiing, tennis, ultimate Frisbee, volleyball, walking, wall climbing, weight lifting, whiffle ball, winter walking. 2 PE instructors, 3 coaches, 1 athletic trainer.

Computers Computers are regularly used in all classes. Computer network features include on-campus library services, Internet access, wireless campus network. Computer access in designated common areas is available to students. The school has a published electronic and media policy.

Contact Stephanie S. Morin, Director of Admission. 207-935-2013. Fax: 207-935-4292. E-mail: admissions@fryeburgacademy.org. Web site: www.fryeburgacademy.org.

See Close-Up on page 762.

FUQUA SCHOOL

605 Fuqua Drive
PO Drawer 328
Farmville, Virginia 23901

Head of School: Ms. Ruth S. Murphy

General Information Coeducational day college-preparatory, arts, business, and technology school. Grades PK–12. Founded: 1959. Setting: small town. Nearest major city is Richmond. 60-acre campus. 19 buildings on campus. Approved or accredited by Southern Association of Colleges and Schools, Virginia Association of Independent Schools, and Virginia Department of Education. Member of Secondary School Admission Test Board. Endowment: $6 million. Total enrollment: 507. Upper school average class size: 16. Upper school faculty-student ratio: 1:16.

Upper School Student Profile Grade 9: 41 students (18 boys, 23 girls); Grade 10: 38 students (9 boys, 29 girls); Grade 11: 41 students (19 boys, 22 girls); Grade 12: 35 students (17 boys, 18 girls).

Faculty School total: 58. In upper school: 6 men, 12 women; 6 have advanced degrees.

Subjects Offered Accounting, advanced computer applications, algebra, art, band, biology, biology-AP, business, calculus-AP, chemistry, communications, composition, computer information systems, consumer mathematics, current events, driver education, earth science, ecology, English, English-AP, environmental science, ethics, film studies, filmmaking, finance, fitness, genetics, geometry, government-AP, grammar, health, history-AP, journalism, newspaper, physics, pre-calculus, shop, Spanish, theater, U.S. government, U.S. history, world geography, yearbook, zoology.

Graduation Requirements Arts and fine arts (art, music, dance, drama), communications, composition, computer information systems, English, fitness, foreign language, grammar, health education, mathematics, physical education (includes health), science, social studies (includes history). Community service is required.

Special Academic Programs Advanced Placement exam preparation; honors section; accelerated programs; independent study; study at local college for college credit; academic accommodation for the gifted.

College Admission Counseling 39 students graduated in 2008; 38 went to college, including Christopher Newport University; Hampden-Sydney College; Radford University; Randolph-Macon College; University of Mary Washington; University of Virginia. Other: 1 had other specific plans. Median SAT critical reading: 517, median SAT math: 560, median SAT writing: 570, median composite ACT: 23. 20% scored over 600 on SAT critical reading, 33% scored over 600 on SAT math, 34% scored over 600 on SAT writing, 33% scored over 26 on composite ACT.

Student Life Upper grades have uniform requirement, student council, honor system. Discipline rests primarily with faculty.

Summer Programs Enrichment, sports programs offered; session focuses on sports and sport skills; held both on and off campus; held at Longwood University Golf Course; accepts boys and girls; open to students from other schools. 50 students usually enrolled. 2009 schedule: June 15 to July 31. Application deadline: May 15.

Tuition and Aid Day student tuition: $6790. Tuition installment plan (The Tuition Plan, Insured Tuition Payment Plan, monthly payment plans, individually arranged payment plans). Tuition reduction for siblings, merit scholarship grants, need-based scholarship grants available. In 2008–09, 48% of upper-school students received aid; total upper-school merit-scholarship money awarded: $8800. Total amount of financial aid awarded in 2008–09: $44,000.

Admissions Traditional secondary-level entrance grade is 9. For fall 2008, 13 students applied for upper-level admission, 11 were accepted, 10 enrolled. Placement test required. Deadline for receipt of application materials: none. Application fee required: $100. On-campus interview required.

Athletics Interscholastic: baseball (boys), basketball (b,g), cheering (g), football (b), softball (g), tennis (g), volleyball (g); coed interscholastic: cross-country running, golf, soccer, swimming and diving, track and field; coed intramural: basketball. 3 PE instructors, 38 coaches.

Computers Computers are regularly used in all classes. Computer network features include on-campus library services, online commercial services, Internet access, Internet filtering or blocking technology, video editing software, CD-ROM +RW and DVD +RW. Student e-mail accounts and computer access in designated common areas are available to students. The school has a published electronic and media policy.

Contact Mrs. Christy M. Murphy, Director of Admissions and Special Events. 434-392-4131 Ext. 273. Fax: 434-392-5062. E-mail: murphycm@fuquaschool.com. Web site: www.fuquaschool.com.

GABLES ACADEMY

Stone Mountain, Georgia

See Special Needs Schools section.

GABRIEL RICHARD HIGH SCHOOL

15325 Pennsylvania Road
Riverview, Michigan 48193

Head of School: Br. James Rottenbucher, CSC

General Information Coeducational day college-preparatory school, affiliated with Roman Catholic Church. Grades 9–12. Founded: 1965. Setting: suburban. Nearest major city is Detroit. 23-acre campus. 1 building on campus. Approved or accredited by Michigan Association of Non-Public Schools, North Central Association of Colleges and Schools, and Michigan Department of Education. Total enrollment: 443. Upper school average class size: 25. Upper school faculty-student ratio: 1:15.

Upper School Student Profile Grade 9: 96 students (57 boys, 39 girls); Grade 10: 116 students (53 boys, 63 girls); Grade 11: 115 students (65 boys, 50 girls); Grade 12: 116 students (58 boys, 58 girls). 90% of students are Roman Catholic.

Faculty School total: 30. In upper school: 11 men, 19 women; 17 have advanced degrees.

Subjects Offered 1½ elective credits, 20th century American writers, 20th century history, 20th century physics, 20th century world history, 3-dimensional art, accounting, acting, advanced chemistry, advanced math, Advanced Placement courses, advanced studio art-AP, algebra, American Civil War, American culture, American democracy, American foreign policy, American government, American government-AP, American history, American history-AP, American literature, American literature-AP, anatomy, anatomy and physiology, ancient history, ancient world history, animal science, art, band, basic language skills, biology, biology-AP, British literature (honors), business, business law, calculus, calculus-AP, campus ministry, Catholic belief and practice, ceramics, chemistry, chemistry-AP, child development, Christian doctrine, Christian education, Christian scripture, Christian testament, Christianity, church history, Civil War, civil war history, clayworking, college awareness, college counseling, college planning, communication skills, communications, comparative government and politics, comparative politics, comparative religion, computer information systems, computer keyboarding, constitutional history of U.S., constitutional law, desktop publishing, digital art, digital photography, drama, drawing, earth science, economics, English literature, English-AP, environmental science, European history-AP, family life, food and nutrition, foods, forensics, French, general business, general math, general science, geography, geometry, German, government, government-AP, graphic arts, health, history, history of the Catholic Church, history-AP, home economics, honors algebra, honors English, honors geometry, human anatomy, humanities, independent living, instrumental music, lab science, library assistant, logic, New Testament, participation in sports, peace and justice, peer ministry, photography, physical fitness, physics, physics-AP, portfolio art, pre-algebra, psychology-AP, publications, research, senior composition, sociology, Spanish, speech, sports, studio art-AP, theater arts, U.S. history, U.S. history-AP, United States government-AP, weight fitness, weight training, yearbook, zoology.

Graduation Requirements Arts and fine arts (art, music, dance, drama), English, mathematics, physical education (includes health), science, social studies (includes history), speech, theology.

Special Academic Programs Advanced Placement exam preparation; honors section; independent study; study at local college for college credit.

College Admission Counseling 103 students graduated in 2008; 102 went to college, including Central Michigan University; Grand Valley State University; Michigan State University; University of Michigan; University of Michigan–Dearborn; Wayne State University. Other: 1 went to work. Median composite ACT: 21. 15% scored over 26 on composite ACT.

Student Life Upper grades have uniform requirement, student council, honor system. Discipline rests primarily with faculty. Attendance at religious services is required.

Tuition and Aid Tuition installment plan (The Tuition Plan, Academic Management Services Plan). Tuition reduction for siblings, merit scholarship grants, need-based scholarship grants available.

Admissions Traditional secondary-level entrance grade is 9. For fall 2008, 115 students applied for upper-level admission, 115 were accepted, 115 enrolled. High School Placement Test required. Deadline for receipt of application materials: September 2. Application fee required: $100. Interview recommended.

Athletics Interscholastic: baseball (boys), basketball (b,g), bowling (b,g), cheering (g), cross-country running (b,g), dance squad (g), figure skating (b,g), football (b), golf (b), ice hockey (b), soccer (b,g), softball (g), tennis (b,g), track and field (b,g), volleyball (g), wrestling (b). 2 PE instructors.

Computers Computers are regularly used in desktop publishing, digital applications, keyboarding, research skills, speech classes. Computer network features include on-campus library services, Internet access. Computer access in designated common areas is available to students. Students grades are available online.

Contact Mrs. Joan Fitzgerald, Assistant Principal. 734-284-1875 Ext. 13. Fax: 734-284-9304. E-mail: jfitzgerald@grriverview.org. Web site: www.grriverview.org.

GANN ACADEMY (THE NEW JEWISH HIGH SCHOOL OF GREATER BOSTON)

333 Forest Street
Waltham, Massachusetts 02452

Head of School: Rabbi Marc A. Baker

General Information Coeducational day college-preparatory, arts, and religious studies school, affiliated with Jewish faith. Grades 9–12. Founded: 1997. Setting: suburban. Nearest major city is Boston. 20-acre campus. 2 buildings on campus. Approved or accredited by New England Association of Schools and Colleges and Massachusetts Department of Education. Total enrollment: 330. Upper school average class size: 14. Upper school faculty-student ratio: 1:6.

Upper School Student Profile Grade 9: 79 students (36 boys, 43 girls); Grade 10: 85 students (44 boys, 41 girls); Grade 11: 76 students (35 boys, 41 girls); Grade 12: 90 students (48 boys, 42 girls). 100% of students are Jewish.

Faculty School total: 73. In upper school: 30 men, 43 women; 57 have advanced degrees.

Subjects Offered Advanced Placement courses, algebra, American history-AP, American literature-AP, art history, arts, Bible as literature, biology, calculus, calculus-AP, chemistry, creative arts, creative writing, drama, English, geometry, health and wellness, Hebrew, history, Jewish history, Judaic studies, music, photography, physics, pre-calculus, Rabbinic literature, Spanish.

Graduation Requirements Arts, athletics, Bible as literature, English, health, Hebrew, history, mathematics, Rabbinic literature, science, Jewish Thought, Electives.

Special Academic Programs Advanced Placement exam preparation; study abroad.

College Admission Counseling 63 students graduated in 2008; 46 went to college, including Boston University; Brandeis University; Tufts University; University of Maryland, College Park; University of Rochester. Other: 1 went to work, 1 entered military service, 14 entered a postgraduate year, 1 had other specific plans. Median SAT critical reading: 630, median SAT math: 660, median SAT writing: 665, median combined SAT: 1965, median composite ACT: 26.

Student Life Upper grades have specified standards of dress, student council, honor system. Discipline rests primarily with faculty. Attendance at religious services is required.

Tuition and Aid Day student tuition: $26,250. Tuition installment plan (FACTS Tuition Payment Plan). Need-based scholarship grants available. In 2008–09, 27% of upper-school students received aid.

Admissions Traditional secondary-level entrance grade is 9. For fall 2008, 135 students applied for upper-level admission, 131 were accepted, 94 enrolled. SSAT required. Deadline for receipt of application materials: January 30. Application fee required: $100. On-campus interview required.

Athletics Interscholastic: baseball (boys), basketball (b,g), cross-country running (b,g), lacrosse (b,g), soccer (b,g), softball (g), tennis (b,g); intramural: basketball (b,g), tennis (b,g); coed interscholastic: ultimate Frisbee; coed intramural: fitness, golf, modern dance, table tennis, yoga. 26 coaches, 1 athletic trainer.

Computers Computer network features include on-campus library services, Internet access, Internet filtering or blocking technology, computer lab. Student e-mail accounts and computer access in designated common areas are available to students. The school has a published electronic and media policy.

Contact Orna Siegel, Director of Admissions. 781-642-6800 Ext. 101. Fax: 781-642-6805. E-mail: osiegel@gannacademy.org. Web site: www.gannacademy.org/.

GARCES MEMORIAL HIGH SCHOOL

2800 Loma Linda Drive
Bakersfield, California 93305

Head of School: Kathleen B. Bears

General Information Coeducational day college-preparatory school, affiliated with Roman Catholic Church. Grades 9–12. Founded: 1947. Setting: suburban. Nearest major city is Los Angeles. 32-acre campus. 16 buildings on campus. Approved or accredited by Western Association of Schools and Colleges and Western Catholic Education Association. Endowment: $460,000. Total enrollment: 706. Upper school average class size: 25. Upper school faculty-student ratio: 1:28.

Upper School Student Profile Grade 9: 188 students (95 boys, 93 girls); Grade 10: 165 students (89 boys, 76 girls); Grade 11: 196 students (106 boys, 90 girls); Grade 12: 157 students (81 boys, 76 girls). 75% of students are Roman Catholic.

Faculty School total: 49. In upper school: 22 men, 27 women; 25 have advanced degrees.

Subjects Offered Algebra, American history, American literature, anatomy, art, biology, calculus, chemistry, community service, computer science, creative writing, drama, driver education, economics, English, English literature, ethics, fine arts, French, geography, geometry, government/civics, graphic arts, health, history, journalism, mathematics, music, physical education, physics, physiology, psychology, religion, science, social studies, Spanish, theater, world history, world literature.

Graduation Requirements Arts and fine arts (art, music, dance, drama), English, foreign language, mathematics, physical education (includes health), religion (includes Bible studies and theology), science, social studies (includes history), 40 hours of community service.

Special Academic Programs Advanced Placement exam preparation; honors section; study at local college for college credit.

College Admission Counseling 170 students graduated in 2008; all went to college, including Bakersfield College; California Polytechnic State University, San Luis Obispo; California State University, Bakersfield; University of California, Davis; University of California, Irvine; University of California, Los Angeles. Mean SAT critical reading: 503, mean SAT math: 509, mean SAT writing: 507, mean composite ACT: 22. 15.3% scored over 600 on SAT critical reading, 16.9% scored over 600 on SAT math.

Student Life Upper grades have uniform requirement, student council. Discipline rests primarily with faculty. Attendance at religious services is required.

Summer Programs Remediation, enrichment, advancement, sports, art/fine arts, computer instruction programs offered; session focuses on mathematics and English; held on campus; accepts boys and girls; open to students from other schools. 800 students usually enrolled. 2009 schedule: June 8 to July 10. Application deadline: May 8.

Tuition and Aid Day student tuition: $6300–$6920. Tuition installment plan (monthly payment plans, individually arranged payment plans). Merit scholarship grants, need-based scholarship grants available. In 2008–09, 29% of upper-school students received aid; total upper-school merit-scholarship money awarded: $9035. Total amount of financial aid awarded in 2008–09: $296,265.

Admissions Traditional secondary-level entrance grade is 9. For fall 2008, 215 students applied for upper-level admission, 200 were accepted, 191 enrolled. CTBS/4 required. Deadline for receipt of application materials: January 11. Application fee required: $50. Interview required.

Athletics Interscholastic: baseball (boys), basketball (b,g), cheering (g), cross-country running (b,g), dance team (g), diving (b,g), football (b), golf (b,g), soccer (b,g), softball (g), swimming and diving (b,g), tennis (b,g), track and field (b,g), volleyball (g), weight training (b); intramural: baseball (b), basketball (b,g), volleyball (b,g); coed intramural: basketball, volleyball. 3 PE instructors, 28 coaches, 2 athletic trainers.

Computers Computers are regularly used in graphic arts, journalism, keyboarding classes. Computer resources include Internet access.

Contact Mrs. Joan M. Richardson, Registrar. 661-327-2578 Ext. 109. Fax: 661-327-5427. E-mail: jrichardson@garces.org. Web site: www.garces.org.

GARDEN SCHOOL

33-16 79th Street
Jackson Heights, New York 11372

Head of School: Dr. Richard Marotta

General Information Coeducational day college-preparatory school. Grades N–12. Founded: 1923. Setting: urban. Nearest major city is New York. 6-acre campus. 1 building on campus. Approved or accredited by Middle States Association of Colleges and Schools, New York State Association of Independent Schools, and New York Department of Education. Total enrollment: 350. Upper school average class size: 15. Upper school faculty-student ratio: 1:11.

Faculty School total: 36. In upper school: 10 men, 12 women; 17 have advanced degrees.

Subjects Offered Algebra, American history, American literature, art, bioethics, biology, calculus, chemistry, computer science, creative writing, economics, English, English literature, English literature-AP, ESL, European history, European history-AP, expository writing, forensics, French, French language-AP, geometry, grammar, history, mathematics, modern European history, modern European history-AP, music, physical education, physics, pre-algebra, pre-calculus, reading, science, Shakespeare, social studies, sociology, Spanish, Spanish language-AP, statistics, trigonometry, U.S. history, U.S. history-AP, world history, world literature, writing.

Graduation Requirements English, foreign language, mathematics, physical education (includes health), science, social studies (includes history).

Special Academic Programs 7 Advanced Placement exams for which test preparation is offered; honors section; independent study; ESL (10 students enrolled).

College Admission Counseling 32 students graduated in 2008; all went to college, including City College of the City University of New York; Fordham University; New York University; State University of New York at Binghamton.

Student Life Upper grades have specified standards of dress, student council. Discipline rests primarily with faculty.

Tuition and Aid Day student tuition: $15,500. Tuition installment plan (monthly payment plans, individually arranged payment plans, 3-part plan (no interest), 10-month plan (with interest)). Tuition reduction for siblings, merit scholarship grants, need-based scholarship grants, need-based loans available. In 2008–09, 15% of upper-school students received aid; total upper-school merit-scholarship money awarded: $280,865. Total amount of financial aid awarded in 2008–09: $306,920.

Admissions Traditional secondary-level entrance grade is 9. For fall 2008, 50 students applied for upper-level admission, 30 were accepted, 13 enrolled. School's own exam required. Deadline for receipt of application materials: none. Application fee required: $40. On-campus interview required.

Athletics Interscholastic: basketball (boys, girls), softball (b,g), volleyball (g); intramural: football (b), track and field (b,g); coed interscholastic: soccer, tennis. 2 PE instructors, 7 coaches.

Computers Computers are regularly used in computer applications classes. Computer resources include on-campus library services, Internet access, Internet filtering or blocking technology. Student e-mail accounts are available to students. The school has a published electronic and media policy.

Garden School

Contact Ms. Mary Petruso, Admissions Secretary. 718-335-6363. Fax: 718-565-1169. E-mail: mpetruso@gardenschool.org. Web site: www.gardenschool.org.

ANNOUNCEMENT FROM THE SCHOOL Garden School enrolls approximately 360 students, from 2 years old through the senior year of high school. The Garden School Plan rests upon a college-preparatory curriculum that combines traditional academics with an emphasis on the individual student. Garden School expects its students to pursue rigorous educational and community-directed goals.

GARRISON FOREST SCHOOL

300 Garrison Forest Road
Owings Mills, Maryland 21117

Head of School: Mr. G. Peter O'Neill Jr.

General Information Girls' boarding and day (coeducational in lower grades) college-preparatory, arts, and WISE school. Boarding girls grades 8–12, day boys grades N–K, day girls grades N–12. Founded: 1910. Setting: suburban. Nearest major city is Baltimore. Students are housed in single-sex dormitories. 110-acre campus. 18 buildings on campus. Approved or accredited by Association of Independent Maryland Schools, Middle States Association of Colleges and Schools, The Association of Boarding Schools, and Maryland Department of Education. Member of National Association of Independent Schools and Secondary School Admission Test Board. Endowment: $39 million. Total enrollment: 701. Upper school average class size: 14. Upper school faculty-student ratio: 1:8.

Upper School Student Profile Grade 6: 53 students (53 girls); Grade 7: 60 students (60 girls); Grade 8: 69 students (69 girls); Grade 9: 75 students (75 girls); Grade 10: 69 students (69 girls); Grade 11: 68 students (68 girls); Grade 12: 56 students (56 girls). 24% of students are boarding students. 11 states are represented in upper school student body. 5% are international students. International students from China, Mexico, Republic of Korea, Taiwan, and Thailand; 1 other country represented in student body.

Faculty School total: 109. In upper school: 11 men, 34 women; 40 have advanced degrees; 21 reside on campus.

Subjects Offered Algebra, American history, American literature, anatomy, animal behavior, art, art history, art history-AP, arts and crafts, biology, calculus, calculus-AP, ceramics, chemistry, chemistry-AP, child development, computer science, computer skills, creative writing, dance, decision making skills, design, drama, drawing, ecology, English, English literature, English-AP, ESL, ethics, fine arts, French, French-AP, geometry, history-AP, Latin, Latin-AP, life skills, mathematics, music, philosophy, photography, physical education, physics, physics-AP, portfolio art, public speaking, science, Spanish, Spanish-AP, statistics, theater, trigonometry, U.S. history-AP, world history.

Graduation Requirements Arts and fine arts (art, music, dance, drama), decision making skills, English, foreign language, mathematics, physical education (includes health), public speaking, science, social studies (includes history).

Special Academic Programs 13 Advanced Placement exams for which test preparation is offered; honors section; independent study; term-away projects; academic accommodation for the gifted, the musically talented, and the artistically talented; ESL (4 students enrolled).

College Admission Counseling 77 students graduated in 2008; all went to college, including College of Charleston; Cornell University; Denison University; Franklin & Marshall College; University of Maryland, College Park; University of Virginia. 50% scored over 600 on SAT critical reading, 50% scored over 600 on SAT math, 50% scored over 600 on SAT writing.

Student Life Upper grades have uniform requirement, student council, honor system. Discipline rests equally with students and faculty.

Summer Programs Sports, art/fine arts programs offered; held on campus; accepts boys and girls; open to students from other schools. 650 students usually enrolled. 2009 schedule: June 17 to August 1. Application deadline: June.

Tuition and Aid Day student tuition: $21,900; 7-day tuition and room/board: $38,500. Tuition installment plan (FACTS Tuition Payment Plan). Need-based scholarship grants, need-based loans available. In 2008–09, 29% of upper-school students received aid. Total amount of financial aid awarded in 2008–09: $2,153,805.

Admissions Traditional secondary-level entrance grade is 9. For fall 2008, 137 students applied for upper-level admission, 69 were accepted, 36 enrolled. ISEE and SSAT required. Deadline for receipt of application materials: January 7. Application fee required: $50. Interview required.

Athletics Interscholastic: badminton, basketball, cross-country running, equestrian sports, field hockey, golf, horseback riding, lacrosse, polo, soccer, softball, squash, tennis, winter soccer; intramural: aerobics, aerobics/dance, dance, fitness, modern dance, strength & conditioning, swimming and diving, yoga. 5 PE instructors, 12 coaches, 1 athletic trainer.

Computers Computers are regularly used in English, foreign language, history, mathematics, science classes. Computer network features include on-campus library services, Internet access, wireless campus network. Student e-mail accounts are available to students. The school has a published electronic and media policy.

Contact A. Randol Benedict, Director of Admission and Financial Aid. 410-363-1500. Fax: 410-363-8441. E-mail: gfsinfo@gfs.org. Web site: www.gfs.org.

ANNOUNCEMENT FROM THE SCHOOL Located 12 miles north of Baltimore, Maryland, Garrison Forest School's collegiate-style 110-acre campus features the finest in facilities, including a Fine and Performing Arts Center; an Equestrian Center for riding and polo, and collegiate-level athletic facilities that include two turf fields and a GREEN Middle School building. Garrison Forest is a boarding and day college-preparatory school for girls in grades PreFirst–12. The School's motto "To Be and Not To Seem" is lived out daily by each girl. Garrison Forest is deeply committed to equity, honesty, kindness, and respect as part of the educational experience. The School celebrates diversity both within its community and its curriculum and aspires to promote the understanding of all people. The Upper School's challenging curriculum offers numerous honors classes as well as thirteen Advanced Placement classes and unique academic programs that include Women in Science and Engineering (WISE), a partnership with The Johns Hopkins University that allows Garrison girls to work side-by-side with Hopkins researchers, and the Center for Public Purpose Partnerships with The Bloomberg School of Public Health and the University of Maryland where girls can focus on public-policy issues and financial literacy. Numerous Schoolwide community service efforts are held throughout the year with over 75% of the Upper School student body participating voluntarily. The School's Life Skills classes cultivate a system of ethical values based on honor and integrity. Garrison Forest's 2008–09 residential community is a "home away from home" for girls from eight states and seven countries. A wide range of extracurricular activities and the School's proximity to Baltimore and Washington, D.C., provide many cultural and recreational opportunities for both residential and day students. Garrison's "One School" philosophy promotes interdivisional programs, events, and activities where girls of all ages can interact and learn from each other.

GASTON DAY SCHOOL

2001 Gaston Day School Road
Gastonia, North Carolina 28056

Head of School: Dr. Richard E. Rankin

General Information Coeducational day college-preparatory and arts school. Grades PS–12. Founded: 1967. Setting: suburban. Nearest major city is Charlotte. 60-acre campus. 4 buildings on campus. Approved or accredited by North Carolina Association of Independent Schools, Southern Association of Colleges and Schools, Southern Association of Independent Schools, and North Carolina Department of Education. Member of National Association of Independent Schools. Endowment: $1.7 million. Total enrollment: 513. Upper school average class size: 15. Upper school faculty-student ratio: 1:8.

Upper School Student Profile Grade 9: 36 students (16 boys, 20 girls); Grade 10: 47 students (22 boys, 25 girls); Grade 11: 34 students (17 boys, 17 girls); Grade 12: 26 students (11 boys, 15 girls).

Faculty School total: 55. In upper school: 9 men, 15 women; 16 have advanced degrees.

Subjects Offered Advanced chemistry, Advanced Placement courses, advanced studio art-AP, algebra, American history-AP, art, biology, biology-AP, British literature, British literature (honors), calculus-AP, chemistry, chemistry-AP, chorus, creative writing, drama, English language and composition-AP, English literature and composition-AP, environmental science, environmental science-AP, film and literature, fine arts, French, general science, geometry, government/civics, honors algebra, honors English, honors geometry, honors U.S. history, honors world history, jazz band, learning lab, physics, pre-calculus, senior internship, Spanish, student government, studio art—AP, study skills, U.S. government, U.S. history, U.S. history-AP, United States government-AP, visual arts, weight training, world literature, yearbook.

Graduation Requirements Arts and fine arts (art, music, dance, drama), electives, English, foreign language, mathematics, physical education (includes health), science, social studies (includes history), 25 hours of community service per year, seniors must complete a senior project.

Special Academic Programs Advanced Placement exam preparation; honors section; independent study; academic accommodation for the gifted.

College Admission Counseling 29 students graduated in 2008; all went to college, including College of Charleston; Elon University; Middlebury College; Queens University of Charlotte; The University of North Carolina at Chapel Hill; University of Virginia. Mean SAT critical reading: 621, mean SAT math: 589.

Student Life Upper grades have specified standards of dress, student council, honor system. Discipline rests primarily with faculty.

Summer Programs Remediation, enrichment, advancement, sports programs offered; session focuses on academic enrichment, advancement in sports and arts; held on campus; accepts boys and girls; open to students from other schools. 200 students usually enrolled. 2009 schedule: June to August.

Tuition and Aid Day student tuition: $12,090. Tuition installment plan (monthly payment plans, individually arranged payment plans). Merit scholarship grants, need-based scholarship grants available. In 2008–09, 41% of upper-school students received aid; total upper-school merit-scholarship money awarded: $144,305. Total amount of financial aid awarded in 2008–09: $211,086.

Admissions Traditional secondary-level entrance grade is 9. For fall 2008, 27 students applied for upper-level admission, 23 were accepted, 13 enrolled. Battery of testing done through outside agency required. Deadline for receipt of application materials: none. Application fee required: $40. On-campus interview required.
Athletics Interscholastic: baseball (boys), basketball (b,g), bowling (b,g), cheering (g), cross-country running (b,g), soccer (b,g), softball (g), swimming and diving (b,g), tennis (b,g), track and field (b,g), volleyball (g); intramural: climbing (g), cooperative games (g), equestrian sports (g), fencing (b,g), floor hockey (b,g), physical fitness (b,g), physical training (b,g), strength & conditioning (b,g), ultimate Frisbee (b,g), weight lifting (b,g), weight training (b,g); coed interscholastic: golf; coed intramural: skeet shooting. 2 PE instructors, 24 coaches, 1 athletic trainer.
Computers Computers are regularly used in art, English, foreign language, history, journalism, mathematics, newspaper, science, yearbook classes. Computer network features include on-campus library services, online commercial services, Internet access, Internet filtering or blocking technology.
Contact Mrs. Martha Jayne Rhyne, Director of Admission. 704-864-7744 Ext. 174. Fax: 704-865-3813. E-mail: martha.rhyne@gastonday.org. Web site: www.gastonday.org.

GATEWAY SCHOOL

Arlington, Texas
See Special Needs Schools section.

THE GENEVA SCHOOL

2025 State Road 436
Winter Park, Florida 32792
Head of School: Rev. Robert Forrest Ingram

General Information Coeducational day college-preparatory, arts, and religious studies school, affiliated with Christian faith. Grades K4–12. Founded: 1993. Setting: suburban. Nearest major city is Orlando. 3-acre campus. 1 building on campus. Approved or accredited by Florida Council of Independent Schools. Total enrollment: 470. Upper school average class size: 18. Upper school faculty-student ratio: 1:9.
Upper School Student Profile Grade 9: 33 students (16 boys, 17 girls); Grade 10: 12 students (6 boys, 6 girls); Grade 11: 28 students (12 boys, 16 girls); Grade 12: 27 students (14 boys, 13 girls). 95% of students are Christian faith.
Faculty School total: 53. In upper school: 16 men, 11 women; 15 have advanced degrees.
Subjects Offered Advanced Placement courses, advanced studio art-AP, aesthetics, algebra, American government, anatomy and physiology, Ancient Greek, ancient world history, art, Bible, biology, British literature (honors), calculus, calculus-AP, chemistry, chemistry-AP, choir, choral music, Christian ethics, classical Greek literature, classics, comparative religion, critical thinking, critical writing, debate, drama, earth science, economics, English language and composition-AP, English literature and composition-AP, ethics, European history, foreign language, French, French-AP, history, honors algebra, honors English, honors geometry, honors U.S. history, honors world history, independent study, instrumental music, Irish literature, journalism, Latin, life management skills, mathematics, medieval literature, music appreciation, oral communications, philosophy, photography, photojournalism, physical education, physical fitness, physical science, physics, physics-AP, pre-algebra, pre-calculus, reading/study skills, rhetoric, science, senior thesis, Shakespeare, Spanish, speech and debate, studio art—AP, theater, theater arts, trigonometry, U.S. history, U.S. history-AP, world history, yearbook.
Graduation Requirements Arts and fine arts (art, music, dance, drama), athletics, Bible, electives, English, foreign language, history, mathematics, rhetoric, science.
Special Academic Programs 12 Advanced Placement exams for which test preparation is offered; honors section; independent study; study at local college for college credit; academic accommodation for the gifted and the musically talented.
College Admission Counseling 14 students graduated in 2008; all went to college, including Duke University; Furman University; Rollins College; Samford University; University of Central Florida; University of Florida. Median SAT critical reading: 610, median SAT math: 600, median SAT writing: 605, median combined SAT: 1750.
Student Life Upper grades have uniform requirement, student council, honor system. Discipline rests primarily with faculty. Attendance at religious services is required.
Summer Programs Enrichment, sports, art/fine arts programs offered; session focuses on sports; held both on and off campus; held at Winter Park; accepts boys and girls; open to students from other schools. 2009 schedule: June to August.
Tuition and Aid Day student tuition: $9130. Tuition installment plan (monthly payment plans). Need-based scholarship grants available. In 2008–09, 30% of upper-school students received aid.
Admissions Traditional secondary-level entrance grade is 9. For fall 2008, 45 students applied for upper-level admission, 25 were accepted, 24 enrolled. ISEE required. Deadline for receipt of application materials: none. Application fee required: $85. Interview required.
Athletics Interscholastic: baseball (boys), basketball (b,g), cross-country running (b,g), flag football (b), soccer (b,g), softball (g), tennis (b,g), volleyball (g); coed interscholastic: golf. 3 PE instructors, 10 coaches.
Computers Computers are regularly used in journalism, photography, yearbook classes. Computer network features include on-campus library services, Internet access, wireless campus network, Internet filtering or blocking technology. Students grades are available online.
Contact Mrs. Patti Rader, Director of Admission. 407-332-6363 Ext. 204. Fax: 407-332-1664. E-mail: pnrader@genevaschool.org. Web site: www.genevaschool.org.

GEORGE SCHOOL

1690 Newtown Langhorne Road
PO Box 4460
Newtown, Pennsylvania 18940
Head of School: Nancy O. Starmer

General Information Coeducational boarding and day college-preparatory, arts, religious studies, bilingual studies, and technology school, affiliated with Society of Friends. Grades 9–12. Founded: 1893. Setting: suburban. Nearest major city is Philadelphia. Students are housed in single-sex dormitories. 265-acre campus. 19 buildings on campus. Approved or accredited by Friends Council on Education, International Baccalaureate Organization, Middle States Association of Colleges and Schools, Pennsylvania Association of Independent Schools, The Association of Boarding Schools, The College Board, and Pennsylvania Department of Education. Member of National Association of Independent Schools and Secondary School Admission Test Board. Endowment: $7 million. Total enrollment: 520. Upper school average class size: 14. Upper school faculty-student ratio: 1:7.
Upper School Student Profile Grade 9: 117 students (61 boys, 56 girls); Grade 10: 137 students (63 boys, 74 girls); Grade 11: 136 students (59 boys, 77 girls); Grade 12: 130 students (61 boys, 69 girls). 53% of students are boarding students. 50% are state residents. 21 states are represented in upper school student body. 2% are international students. International students from Germany, Hong Kong, Japan, Republic of Korea, Taiwan, and United Kingdom; 23 other countries represented in student body. 15.8% of students are members of Society of Friends.
Faculty School total: 81. In upper school: 33 men, 41 women; 55 have advanced degrees; 48 reside on campus.
Subjects Offered African-American history, algebra, American history-AP, American literature, American literature-AP, art, Asian history, astronomy, athletics, Bible studies, biology, biology-AP, calculus, calculus-AP, ceramics, chemistry, chemistry-AP, Chinese, college counseling, community service, composition, computer programming, computer science, dance, desktop publishing, drama, drawing, driver education, English, English literature, English literature and composition-AP, English literature-AP, English-AP, environmental science, ESL, fine arts, French, French language-AP, geometry, global studies, health, history-AP, horticulture, hydrology, industrial arts, journalism, Latin, Latin American history, life science, literature, mathematics, Middle Eastern history, modern dance, modern European history, music theory, oceanography, orchestra, ornithology, painting, philosophy, photography, physical education, physics, physiology, pre-calculus, probability and statistics, religion, Russian history, science, science and technology, Spanish, Spanish language-AP, stagecraft, statistics-AP, theater, theory of knowledge, video film production, visual arts, vocal ensemble, woodworking, work camp program, world history, world literature.
Graduation Requirements Arts and fine arts (art, music, dance, drama), computer literacy, English, foreign language, mathematics, performing arts, physical education (includes health), religion (includes Bible studies and theology), science, social studies (includes history), word processing, 65 hours of community service.
Special Academic Programs International Baccalaureate program; Advanced Placement exam preparation; honors section; independent study; academic accommodation for the gifted; ESL (22 students enrolled).
College Admission Counseling 139 students graduated in 2008; 138 went to college, including Boston University; Connecticut College; Franklin & Marshall College; Guilford College; New York University; University of Pennsylvania.
Student Life Upper grades have specified standards of dress, student council, honor system. Discipline rests equally with students and faculty. Attendance at religious services is required.
Summer Programs Enrichment, advancement, ESL programs offered; session focuses on academic and social preparation; held on campus; accepts boys and girls; not open to students from other schools. 36 students usually enrolled.
Tuition and Aid Day student tuition: $29,300; 7-day tuition and room/board: $39,600. Tuition installment plan (monthly payment plans, individually arranged payment plans). Merit scholarship grants, need-based scholarship grants, need-based loans available. In 2008–09, 45% of upper-school students received aid; total upper-school merit-scholarship money awarded: $200,000. Total amount of financial aid awarded in 2008–09: $5,387,000.
Admissions Traditional secondary-level entrance grade is 9. For fall 2008, 609 students applied for upper-level admission, 323 were accepted, 172 enrolled. SSAT or TOEFL or SLEP required. Deadline for receipt of application materials: February 15. Application fee required: $50. Interview required.
Athletics Interscholastic: baseball (boys), basketball (b,g), cross-country running (b,g), field hockey (g), football (b), lacrosse (b,g), soccer (b,g), softball (g), swimming and diving (b,g), tennis (b,g), track and field (b,g), volleyball (g), wrestling (b,g); coed interscholastic: cheering, equestrian sports, golf, horseback riding, indoor track, winter

(indoor) track; coed intramural: aerobics/dance, aquatics, archery, badminton, basketball, dance, fitness, horseback riding, life saving, martial arts, modern dance, outdoor education, physical fitness, soccer, softball, strength & conditioning, swimming and diving, table tennis, volleyball, weight training, yoga. 5 PE instructors, 5 coaches, 1 athletic trainer.
Computers Computers are regularly used in English, ESL, foreign language, history, mathematics, newspaper, photography, science, yearbook classes. Computer network features include on-campus library services, online commercial services, Internet access, wireless campus network, Internet filtering or blocking technology. Campus intranet and student e-mail accounts are available to students.
Contact Jenna K. Davis, Director of Admission, Interim. 215-579-6547. Fax: 215-579-6549. E-mail: admission@georgeschool.org. Web site: www.georgeschool.org.

See Close-Up on page 764.

GEORGE STEVENS ACADEMY

23 Union Street
Blue Hill, Maine 04614

Head of School: Mr. John Greene

General Information Coeducational boarding and day college-preparatory, general academic, arts, vocational, and technology school. Grades 9–12. Founded: 1803. Setting: small town. Nearest major city is Bangor. Students are housed in single-sex dormitories and host family homes. 20-acre campus. 6 buildings on campus. Approved or accredited by Independent Schools of Northern New England, New England Association of Schools and Colleges, The College Board, and Maine Department of Education. Endowment: $1.2 million. Total enrollment: 308. Upper school average class size: 14. Upper school faculty-student ratio: 1:10.
Upper School Student Profile Grade 9: 66 students (26 boys, 40 girls); Grade 10: 82 students (34 boys, 48 girls); Grade 11: 88 students (43 boys, 45 girls); Grade 12: 72 students (31 boys, 41 girls). 6% of students are boarding students. 90% are state residents. 1 state is represented in upper school student body. 10% are international students. International students from China, Italy, Republic of Korea, Spain, Thailand, and Viet Nam; 1 other country represented in student body.
Faculty School total: 28. In upper school: 14 men, 14 women; 12 have advanced degrees.
Subjects Offered 20th century history, 3-dimensional design, advanced chemistry, advanced math, Advanced Placement courses, algebra, American literature, American literature-AP, art, art history, art-AP, arts and crafts, band, biology, British literature (honors), business mathematics, calculus-AP, carpentry, chamber groups, chemistry, computer applications, computer literacy, creative writing, critical thinking, desktop publishing, developmental language skills, drafting, drawing, driver education, earth science, electives, English, English-AP, environmental science, environmental science-AP, ESL, European history, fine arts, foreign language, forensics, French, general math, general science, geometry, German, health education, history, history-AP, honors algebra, honors English, honors geometry, honors U.S. history, human geography—AP, humanities, independent study, industrial arts, industrial technology, instrumental music, internship, jazz band, jazz ensemble, lab science, languages, Latin, literature, literature-AP, marine science, mathematics, mathematics-AP, mechanics, model United Nations, modern history, modern languages, modern problems, music, music theory, musical productions, mythology, personal fitness, photo shop, photography, physical education, physics, pre-algebra, pre-calculus, printmaking, psychology, reading/study skills, remedial study skills, science, senior project, shop, small engine repair, social issues, social science, Spanish, speech and debate, sports, statistics-AP, street law, student government, technology/design, TOEFL preparation, transportation technology, U.S. history, U.S. history-AP, Western civilization, wilderness/outdoor program, woodworking, work-study, World-Wide-Web publishing, writing.
Graduation Requirements Arts and fine arts (art, music, dance, drama), electives, English, foreign language, history, honors U.S. history, mathematics, physical education (includes health), science, social sciences, Maine Learning Results Requirements, Senior Debate.
Special Academic Programs Advanced Placement exam preparation; honors section; accelerated programs; independent study; term-away projects; academic accommodation for the gifted, the musically talented, and the artistically talented; remedial reading and/or remedial writing; remedial math; ESL (18 students enrolled).
College Admission Counseling 85 students graduated in 2008; 68 went to college, including University of Maine; University of Southern Maine; Wheaton College. Other: 16 went to work, 1 entered military service. Mean SAT critical reading: 510, mean SAT math: 479, mean SAT writing: 505, mean combined SAT: 1494. 20% scored over 600 on SAT critical reading, 17% scored over 600 on SAT math, 21% scored over 600 on SAT writing, 17% scored over 1800 on combined SAT.
Student Life Upper grades have student council. Discipline rests primarily with faculty.
Summer Programs Remediation, ESL, sports, art/fine arts programs offered; held on campus; accepts boys and girls; open to students from other schools. 2009 schedule: July.
Tuition and Aid 7-day tuition and room/board: $32,500. Tuition installment plan (monthly payment plans, individually arranged payment plans).
Admissions Traditional secondary-level entrance grade is 9. PSAT, SSAT or TOEFL or SLEP required. Deadline for receipt of application materials: April. Application fee required: $50. Interview required.
Athletics Interscholastic: baseball (boys), basketball (b,g), cheering (b,g), cross-country running (b,g), golf (b,g), independent competitive sports (b,g), indoor track & field (b,g), running (b,g), sailing (b,g), soccer (b,g), softball (g), swimming and diving (b,g), tennis (b,g), track and field (b,g), winter (indoor) track (b,g), wrestling (b,g); coed intramural: canoeing/kayaking, croquet, dance, dance team, fitness walking, flag football, floor hockey, hiking/backpacking, outdoor activities, physical fitness, physical training, skateboarding, skiing (cross-country), skiing (downhill), snowboarding, table tennis, ultimate Frisbee, volleyball, walking, weight training, wilderness. 2 PE instructors, 26 coaches.
Computers Computers are regularly used in all academic, computer applications, desktop publishing, Web site design classes. Computer network features include on-campus library services, Internet access, wireless campus network, Internet filtering or blocking technology. Computer access in designated common areas is available to students. Students grades are available online. The school has a published electronic and media policy.
Contact Ms. Sheryl Cole Stearns, International Program Director. 207-374-2808 Ext. 134. Fax: 207-374-2982. E-mail: s.stearns@georgestevens.org. Web site: www.georgestevensacademy.org.

See Close-Up on page 766.

GEORGETOWN DAY SCHOOL

4200 Davenport Street NW
Washington, District of Columbia 20016

Head of School: Peter M. Branch

General Information Coeducational day college-preparatory school. Grades PK–12. Founded: 1945. Setting: urban. 6-acre campus. 1 building on campus. Approved or accredited by Association of Independent Maryland Schools, Middle States Association of Colleges and Schools, and District of Columbia Department of Education. Member of National Association of Independent Schools and Secondary School Admission Test Board. Endowment: $7.5 million. Total enrollment: 1,031. Upper school average class size: 15. Upper school faculty-student ratio: 1:7.
Upper School Student Profile Grade 9: 114 students (55 boys, 59 girls); Grade 10: 117 students (63 boys, 54 girls); Grade 11: 114 students (56 boys, 58 girls); Grade 12: 113 students (56 boys, 57 girls).
Faculty School total: 160. In upper school: 30 men, 40 women; 49 have advanced degrees.
Subjects Offered Algebra, American history, American literature, anthropology, art, art history, astronomy, biology, calculus, ceramics, chemistry, community service, computer science, creative writing, dance, drama, driver education, economics, English, environmental science-AP, European history, fine arts, French, geometry, government/civics, history, Latin, law, linear algebra, mathematics, music, photography, physical education, physics, psychology, science, social studies, Spanish, statistics-AP, theater, trigonometry, world history.
Graduation Requirements Arts and fine arts (art, music, dance, drama), English, foreign language, literature, mathematics, physical education (includes health), science, social studies (includes history). Community service is required.
Special Academic Programs Advanced Placement exam preparation; honors section; independent study.
College Admission Counseling Colleges students went to include Brown University; Duke University; Harvard University; Oberlin College; Stanford University; Yale University.
Student Life Upper grades have student council, honor system. Discipline rests primarily with faculty.
Tuition and Aid Day student tuition: $22,620–$25,885. Tuition installment plan (Academic Management Services Plan, monthly payment plans). Need-based scholarship grants available. In 2007–08, 18% of upper-school students received aid. Total amount of financial aid awarded in 2007–08: $900,000.
Admissions Traditional secondary-level entrance grade is 9. For fall 2007, 242 students applied for upper-level admission, 84 were accepted, 54 enrolled. ISEE or SSAT required. Deadline for receipt of application materials: January 15. Application fee required: $65. On-campus interview required.
Athletics Interscholastic: baseball (boys), basketball (b,g), crew (b,g), cross-country running (b,g), lacrosse (b,g); intramural: indoor soccer (b,g); coed interscholastic: golf; coed intramural: flag football. 5 PE instructors, 6 coaches, 1 athletic trainer.
Computers Computers are regularly used in art, English, foreign language, history, mathematics, music, science classes. Computer network features include on-campus library services, online commercial services, Internet access, wireless campus network. Student e-mail accounts are available to students.
Contact Vincent W. Rowe Jr., Director of Enrollment Management and Financial Aid. 202-274-3210. Fax: 202-274-3211. E-mail: vrowe@gds.org. Web site: www.gds.org.

ANNOUNCEMENT FROM THE SCHOOL Georgetown Day School honors the integrity and worth of each individual within a diverse school community. The School is dedicated to providing a supportive educational atmosphere in which teachers challenge the intellectual, creative, and physical abilities of its students and foster strength of character and concern for others. Georgetown Day encourages its students to wonder, to inquire, and to be self-reliant, laying the foundation for a lifelong love of learning.

GEORGETOWN PREPARATORY SCHOOL

10900 Rockville Pike
North Bethesda, Maryland 20852-3299

Head of School: Mr. Jeff Jones

General Information Boys' boarding and day college-preparatory, arts, religious studies, and technology school, affiliated with Roman Catholic Church. Grades 9–12. Founded: 1789. Setting: suburban. Nearest major city is Washington, DC. Students are housed in single-sex dormitories. 92-acre campus. 8 buildings on campus. Approved or accredited by Middle States Association of Colleges and Schools, The Association of Boarding Schools, and Maryland Department of Education. Member of National Association of Independent Schools and Secondary School Admission Test Board. Endowment: $80 million. Total enrollment: 466. Upper school average class size: 15. Upper school faculty-student ratio: 1:8.

Upper School Student Profile Grade 9: 115 students (115 boys); Grade 10: 118 students (118 boys); Grade 11: 127 students (127 boys); Grade 12: 106 students (106 boys). 20% of students are boarding students. 60% are state residents. 17 states are represented in upper school student body. 10% are international students. International students from China, Indonesia, Mexico, Nigeria, Republic of Korea, and Taiwan; 13 other countries represented in student body. 75% of students are Roman Catholic.

Faculty School total: 55. In upper school: 37 men, 18 women; 47 have advanced degrees; 17 reside on campus.

Subjects Offered Algebra, American history, American literature, art, art history, Bible studies, biology, calculus, chemistry, computer programming, computer science, drama, driver education, economics, English, English literature, ESL, ethics, European history, fine arts, French, geometry, German, government/civics, history, journalism, Latin, mathematics, music, philosophy, physical education, physics, psychology, religion, science, social studies, Spanish, speech, stained glass, theater, theology, trigonometry, world history, world literature.

Graduation Requirements Arts and fine arts (art, music, dance, drama), classics, English, foreign language, mathematics, music theory, religion (includes Bible studies and theology), science, social studies (includes history), two years of Latin. Community service is required.

Special Academic Programs 24 Advanced Placement exams for which test preparation is offered; honors section; independent study; term-away projects; study abroad; academic accommodation for the gifted; ESL (10 students enrolled).

College Admission Counseling 108 students graduated in 2008; all went to college, including Boston College; Georgetown University; Princeton University; Stanford University; University of Pennsylvania; University of Virginia. 71% scored over 600 on SAT critical reading, 67% scored over 600 on SAT math.

Student Life Upper grades have specified standards of dress, student council. Discipline rests primarily with faculty. Attendance at religious services is required.

Summer Programs Remediation, enrichment, advancement, ESL, sports programs offered; session focuses on ESL; held on campus; accepts boys and girls; open to students from other schools. 75 students usually enrolled. 2009 schedule: June 28 to August 6. Application deadline: March 1.

Tuition and Aid Day student tuition: $24,200; 7-day tuition and room/board: $42,150. Tuition installment plan (FACTS Tuition Payment Plan). Need-based scholarship grants, middle-income loans available. In 2008–09, 25% of upper-school students received aid. Total amount of financial aid awarded in 2008–09: $1,800,000.

Admissions Traditional secondary-level entrance grade is 9. For fall 2008, 330 students applied for upper-level admission, 125 were accepted, 115 enrolled. SSAT required. Deadline for receipt of application materials: January 15. Application fee required: $100. Interview required.

Athletics Interscholastic: baseball, basketball, cross-country running, diving, fencing, football, golf, ice hockey, indoor soccer, indoor track & field, lacrosse, rugby, running, soccer, swimming and diving, tennis, track and field, winter (indoor) track, wrestling; intramural: basketball, bicycling, canoeing/kayaking, climbing, fitness, flag football, floor hockey, Frisbee, hiking/backpacking, ice skating, indoor hockey, kayaking, life saving, martial arts, mountain biking, Nautilus, ocean paddling, paddle tennis, paint ball, physical fitness, physical training, power lifting, racquetball, rappelling, rock climbing, ropes courses, scuba diving, skiing (downhill), snowboarding, soccer, softball, strength & conditioning, table tennis, tennis, ultimate Frisbee, volleyball, weight training. 16 coaches, 3 athletic trainers.

Computers Computers are regularly used in art, classics, data processing, English, French, history, Latin, mathematics, music, religious studies, science, Spanish, writing classes. Computer network features include on-campus library services, online commercial services, Internet access, wireless campus network, Internet filtering or blocking technology. Campus intranet, student e-mail accounts, and computer access in designated common areas are available to students. Students grades are available online. The school has a published electronic and media policy.

Contact Mr. Brian J. Gilbert, Dean of Admissions. 301-214-1215. Fax: 301-493-6128. E-mail: admissions@gprep.org. Web site: www.gprep.org.

GEORGETOWN VISITATION PREPARATORY SCHOOL

1524 35th Street NW
Washington, District of Columbia 20007

Head of School: Daniel M. Kerns Jr.

General Information Girls' day college-preparatory school, affiliated with Roman Catholic Church. Grades 9–12. Founded: 1799. Setting: urban. 23-acre campus. 7 buildings on campus. Approved or accredited by Association of Independent Schools of Greater Washington, Middle States Association of Colleges and Schools, National Independent Private Schools Association, and District of Columbia Department of Education. Member of National Association of Independent Schools. Endowment: $16.7 million. Total enrollment: 479. Upper school average class size: 15. Upper school faculty-student ratio: 1:10.

Upper School Student Profile Grade 9: 122 students (122 girls); Grade 10: 118 students (118 girls); Grade 11: 118 students (118 girls); Grade 12: 121 students (121 girls). 93% of students are Roman Catholic.

Faculty School total: 50. In upper school: 10 men, 40 women; 39 have advanced degrees.

Subjects Offered Advanced Placement courses, algebra, American history, American literature, anthropology, art, art history, Bible studies, biology, calculus, chemistry, computer programming, computer science, creative writing, dance, English, English literature, ethics, European history, expository writing, fine arts, French, geography, geometry, government-AP, government/civics, health, history, Latin, mathematics, music, philosophy, physical education, physics, psychology, religion, science, social science, social studies, Spanish, speech, theology, trigonometry, world history.

Graduation Requirements Arts and fine arts (art, music, dance, drama), English, foreign language, mathematics, physical education (includes health), religion (includes Bible studies and theology), science, social science, social studies (includes history), 80 hours of community service.

Special Academic Programs Advanced Placement exam preparation; honors section; independent study; study at local college for college credit.

College Admission Counseling 121 students graduated in 2008; all went to college, including Boston College; Georgetown University; Princeton University; University of Notre Dame; University of Virginia. Mean SAT critical reading: 651, mean SAT math: 626.

Student Life Upper grades have uniform requirement, student council, honor system. Discipline rests primarily with faculty. Attendance at religious services is required.

Summer Programs Enrichment, sports, art/fine arts, computer instruction programs offered; held on campus; accepts girls; not open to students from other schools. 100 students usually enrolled. 2009 schedule: June to July. Application deadline: April.

Tuition and Aid Day student tuition: $20,600. Tuition installment plan (FACTS Tuition Payment Plan, individually arranged payment plans). Merit scholarship grants, need-based scholarship grants available. In 2008–09, 25% of upper-school students received aid; total upper-school merit-scholarship money awarded: $55,000. Total amount of financial aid awarded in 2008–09: $1,250,000.

Admissions Traditional secondary-level entrance grade is 9. For fall 2008, 400 students applied for upper-level admission, 140 were accepted, 122 enrolled. High School Placement Test required. Deadline for receipt of application materials: December 5. Application fee required: $50. On-campus interview required.

Athletics Interscholastic: basketball, crew, cross-country running, dance, diving, field hockey, fitness, indoor track, lacrosse, soccer, softball, swimming and diving, tennis, track and field, volleyball; intramural: cheering, flag football, strength & conditioning. 4 PE instructors, 23 coaches, 1 athletic trainer.

Computers Computers are regularly used in art, English, French, history, mathematics, religion, science, Spanish classes. Computer network features include on-campus library services, online commercial services, Internet access, wireless campus network, Internet filtering or blocking technology. Student e-mail accounts are available to students.

Contact Janet Keller, Director of Admissions. 202-337-3350 Ext. 2241. Fax: 202-333-3522. E-mail: jkeller@visi.org. Web site: www.visi.org.

ANNOUNCEMENT FROM THE SCHOOL Since 1799, Georgetown Visitation has been educating women of faith, vision, and purpose. A dynamic, well-balanced Catholic education reaches a diverse community both intellectually and spiritually. Visitation's core curriculum, AP and honors courses, electives, Georgetown University Bridge Program, Language Consortium, extensive co-curriculars, eleven competitive sports, community service, traditions, and speaker forums make learning creative and challenging.

GEORGIA MILITARY COLLEGE HIGH SCHOOL

201 East Greene Street
Milledgeville, Georgia 31061

Head of School: Col. John Thornton

General Information Coeducational day college-preparatory and military school. Grades 6–12. Founded: 1879. Setting: small town. Nearest major city is Macon. 4 buildings on campus. Approved or accredited by Commission on Secondary and

Middle Schools, Southern Association of Colleges and Schools, and Georgia Department of Education. Total enrollment: 500. Upper school average class size: 20.
Upper School Student Profile Grade 9: 62 students (31 boys, 31 girls); Grade 10: 62 students (31 boys, 31 girls); Grade 11: 62 students (31 boys, 31 girls); Grade 12: 62 students (31 boys, 31 girls).
Faculty School total: 29. In upper school: 10 men, 8 women.
Subjects Offered Computer science, English, general science, health, JROTC, keyboarding, mathematics, physical education, social studies.
Special Academic Programs 2 Advanced Placement exams for which test preparation is offered; study at local college for college credit.
College Admission Counseling 57 students graduated in 2008; 54 went to college, including Armstrong Atlantic State University; Georgia College & State University; University of Georgia; Valdosta State University. Other: 3 entered military service.
Student Life Upper grades have uniform requirement, student council, honor system. Discipline rests equally with students and faculty.
Tuition and Aid Day student tuition: $4200. Need-based scholarship grants available.
Admissions Traditional secondary-level entrance grade is 9. Deadline for receipt of application materials: none. Application fee required: $35.
Athletics Interscholastic: baseball (boys), basketball (b,g), cheering (g), football (b), soccer (b,g), softball (g), tennis (b,g), track and field (b,g); coed interscholastic: golf, riflery.
Computers Computers are regularly used in computer applications, media production, SAT preparation, yearbook classes. The school has a published electronic and media policy.
Contact Mrs. Kim Mountain, Administrative Assistant. 478-445-2720. Fax: 478-445-4536. E-mail: kmountain@gmc.cc.ga.us.

GERMANTOWN ACADEMY

340 Morris Road
PO Box 287
Fort Washington, Pennsylvania 19034
Head of School: Mr. James W. Connor

General Information Coeducational day college-preparatory, arts, and technology school. Grades PK–12. Founded: 1759. Setting: suburban. Nearest major city is Philadelphia. 110-acre campus. 8 buildings on campus. Approved or accredited by Middle States Association of Colleges and Schools, Pennsylvania Association of Independent Schools, and Pennsylvania Department of Education. Member of National Association of Independent Schools. Endowment: $37 million. Total enrollment: 1,116. Upper school average class size: 15. Upper school faculty-student ratio: 1:8.
Upper School Student Profile Grade 9: 121 students (72 boys, 49 girls); Grade 10: 123 students (65 boys, 58 girls); Grade 11: 121 students (61 boys, 60 girls); Grade 12: 117 students (50 boys, 67 girls).
Faculty School total: 136. In upper school: 38 men, 25 women; 47 have advanced degrees.
Subjects Offered Acting, adolescent issues, African history, algebra, American history, American literature, art, art history, biology, botany, calculus, ceramics, chemistry, civil rights, computer math, computer science, creative writing, drama, economics, English, English literature, environmental science, European history, expository writing, film, fine arts, French, geography, geometry, government/civics, grammar, health, health education, history, Latin, marine biology, mathematics, medieval history, music, music history, music theory, philosophy, photography, physical education, physics, Russian, science, sculpture, social studies, society and culture, Spanish, speech, statistics, technology, trigonometry, women in world history, world history, writing.
Graduation Requirements Algebra, arts and fine arts (art, music, dance, drama), biology, chemistry, English, European history, foreign language, geometry, physical education (includes health), physics, U.S. history, ability to swim.
Special Academic Programs 19 Advanced Placement exams for which test preparation is offered; honors section; independent study.
College Admission Counseling 117 students graduated in 2008; 115 went to college, including Cornell University; New York University; Penn State University Park; The George Washington University; University of Pittsburgh; University of Virginia. Other: 1 went to work, 1 had other specific plans. Mean SAT critical reading: 618, mean SAT math: 631, mean SAT writing: 634, mean combined SAT: 1883, mean composite ACT: 26.
Student Life Upper grades have uniform requirement, student council, honor system. Discipline rests equally with students and faculty.
Summer Programs Enrichment, advancement, sports, art/fine arts, computer instruction programs offered; session focuses on challenging activities, fun and learning; held on campus; accepts boys and girls; open to students from other schools. 1,400 students usually enrolled. 2009 schedule: June 22 to July 31. Application deadline: none.
Tuition and Aid Day student tuition: $24,280. Tuition installment plan (Higher Education Service, Inc). Merit scholarship grants, need-based tuition assistance, need- and merit-based scholar programs available. In 2008–09, 16% of upper-school students received aid; total upper-school merit-scholarship money awarded: $8000. Total amount of financial aid awarded in 2008–09: $1,700,000.
Admissions Traditional secondary-level entrance grade is 9. For fall 2008, 143 students applied for upper-level admission, 60 were accepted, 40 enrolled. ISEE and SSAT required. Deadline for receipt of application materials: none. Application fee required: $40. On-campus interview required.
Athletics Interscholastic: baseball (boys), basketball (b,g), cheering (g), cross-country running (b,g), diving (b,g), field hockey (g), football (b), ice hockey (b), lacrosse (b,g), soccer (b,g), softball (g), swimming and diving (b,g), tennis (b,g), track and field (b,g), volleyball (g), water polo (b,g), wrestling (b); intramural: football (b,g), weight lifting (b,g); coed interscholastic: crew, golf, winter (indoor) track; coed intramural: crew. 7 PE instructors, 20 coaches, 2 athletic trainers.
Computers Computers are regularly used in English, foreign language, graphic arts, history, mathematics, photography, science classes. Computer network features include on-campus library services, online commercial services, Internet access, wireless campus network, Internet filtering or blocking technology. Student e-mail accounts are available to students.
Contact Admission Office. 215-643-1331. Fax: 215-646-1216. E-mail: admission@germantownacademy.org. Web site: www.germantownacademy.net.

GERMANTOWN FRIENDS SCHOOL

31 West Coulter Street
Philadelphia, Pennsylvania 19144
Head of School: Richard L. Wade

General Information Coeducational day college-preparatory, arts, and technology school, affiliated with Society of Friends. Grades K–12. Founded: 1845. Setting: urban. 21-acre campus. 20 buildings on campus. Approved or accredited by Friends Council on Education, Middle States Association of Colleges and Schools, and Pennsylvania Association of Independent Schools. Member of National Association of Independent Schools and Secondary School Admission Test Board. Endowment: $29.8 million. Total enrollment: 894. Upper school average class size: 18. Upper school faculty-student ratio: 1:9.
Upper School Student Profile Grade 9: 96 students (45 boys, 51 girls); Grade 10: 101 students (50 boys, 51 girls); Grade 11: 81 students (45 boys, 36 girls); Grade 12: 84 students (40 boys, 44 girls). 6.3% of students are members of Society of Friends.
Faculty School total: 144. In upper school: 31 men, 37 women; 44 have advanced degrees.
Subjects Offered 3-dimensional art, advanced chemistry, advanced math, algebra, American history, ancient history, art, art history, biology, calculus, chemistry, choir, chorus, comparative cultures, computer applications, computer programming, creative writing, drama, dramatic arts, drawing, English, environmental science, European history, French, geometry, graphic arts, Greek, health, human sexuality, independent study, instrumental music, jazz ensemble, Latin, Latin History, madrigals, mathematics, music, music theory, opera, orchestra, painting, philosophy, photography, physical education, physics, pre-calculus, science, social studies, Spanish, sports, stagecraft, statistics, studio art, theater, trigonometry, vocal music.
Graduation Requirements Arts and fine arts (art, music, dance, drama), English, foreign language, history, lab science, mathematics, music, physical education (includes health), month-long off-campus independent project.
Special Academic Programs Honors section; independent study; term-away projects; domestic exchange program (with The Network Program Schools, The Catlin Gabel School); study abroad; academic accommodation for the gifted, the musically talented, and the artistically talented; ESL (3 students enrolled).
College Admission Counseling 84 students graduated in 2008; 82 went to college, including New York University; Temple University; Trinity College; University of Pennsylvania; University of Pittsburgh; Yale University. Other: 2 had other specific plans. Mean SAT critical reading: 652, mean SAT math: 651, mean SAT writing: 665. 74% scored over 600 on SAT critical reading, 79% scored over 600 on SAT math, 81% scored over 600 on SAT writing.
Student Life Upper grades have student council. Discipline rests primarily with faculty. Attendance at religious services is required.
Tuition and Aid Day student tuition: $21,991–$22,377. Tuition installment plan (Academic Management Services Plan, Key Tuition Payment Plan, individually arranged payment plans). Need-based scholarship grants, need-based loans available. In 2008–09, 29% of upper-school students received aid. Total amount of financial aid awarded in 2008–09: $1,371,796.
Admissions Traditional secondary-level entrance grade is 9. For fall 2008, 83 students applied for upper-level admission, 43 were accepted, 22 enrolled. ISEE or SSAT required. Deadline for receipt of application materials: January 9. Application fee required: $40. On-campus interview required.
Athletics Interscholastic: baseball (boys), basketball (b,g), cross-country running (b,g), field hockey (g), indoor soccer (b,g), indoor track & field (b,g), lacrosse (g), soccer (b,g), softball (g), squash (b,g), tennis (b,g), track and field (b,g), wrestling (b); coed intramural: physical training, strength & conditioning, weight training. 5 PE instructors, 24 coaches, 1 athletic trainer.
Computers Computers are regularly used in art, English, foreign language, history, mathematics, music, photography, publications, science classes. Computer network features include on-campus library services, online commercial services, Internet access, wireless campus network, Internet filtering or blocking technology. Campus intranet, student e-mail accounts, and computer access in designated common areas are available to students.

Contact Laura Sharpless Myran, Director, Admissions and Financial Aid. 215-951-2346. Fax: 215-951-2370. E-mail: lauram@gfsnet.org. Web site: www.germantownfriends.org.

GILL ST. BERNARD'S SCHOOL

PO Box 604
St. Bernard's Road
Gladstone, New Jersey 07934

Head of School: Mr. S. A. Rowell

General Information Coeducational day college-preparatory school. Grades PK–12. Founded: 1900. Setting: small town. Nearest major city is New York, NY. 72-acre campus. 15 buildings on campus. Approved or accredited by Middle States Association of Colleges and Schools and New Jersey Association of Independent Schools. Member of National Association of Independent Schools and Secondary School Admission Test Board. Endowment: $5 million. Total enrollment: 689. Upper school average class size: 16. Upper school faculty-student ratio: 1:7.

Upper School Student Profile Grade 9: 70 students (37 boys, 33 girls); Grade 10: 73 students (36 boys, 37 girls); Grade 11: 50 students (25 boys, 25 girls); Grade 12: 59 students (27 boys, 32 girls).

Faculty School total: 98. In upper school: 20 men, 18 women; 30 have advanced degrees.

Subjects Offered 20th century world history, 3-dimensional art, advanced chemistry, advanced computer applications, advanced math, African-American studies, algebra, American democracy, American history, American history-AP, American literature, analysis and differential calculus, analytic geometry, art, astronomy, biology, biology-AP, British literature, British literature (honors), calculus, calculus-AP, chemistry, chemistry-AP, chorus, college counseling, comparative cultures, computer science, computer science-AP, contemporary issues, creative writing, earth science, economics, English, English literature, English literature-AP, environmental science, environmental science-AP, European history, European history-AP, fine arts, forensic science, French, gender issues, geography, geometry, government/civics, health, history, honors English, human geography—AP, independent study, international relations, Latin, Latin American literature, literature, mathematics, music, oceanography, philosophy, photography, physical education, physics, portfolio art, psychology, science, social studies, Spanish, Spanish-AP, technology, theater, U.S. government and politics-AP, woodworking, world history, world literature.

Graduation Requirements Arts and fine arts (art, music, dance, drama), English, foreign language, history, mathematics, science, The Unit: an intensive 2-week course each year of Upper School.

Special Academic Programs 14 Advanced Placement exams for which test preparation is offered; honors section; independent study; study abroad; academic accommodation for the gifted.

College Admission Counseling 54 students graduated in 2008; all went to college, including Bucknell University; Drew University; Franklin & Marshall College; Muhlenberg College; Princeton University; Syracuse University. 65% scored over 600 on SAT critical reading, 65% scored over 600 on SAT math, 70% scored over 600 on SAT writing.

Student Life Upper grades have specified standards of dress, student council, honor system. Discipline rests equally with students and faculty.

Summer Programs Enrichment, advancement, sports, art/fine arts programs offered; session focuses on academics, arts, sports, day and outdoor camping; held on campus; accepts boys and girls; open to students from other schools. 325 students usually enrolled. 2009 schedule: June 10 to August 20. Application deadline: none.

Tuition and Aid Day student tuition: $25,700. Tuition installment plan (Key Tuition Payment Plan). Merit scholarship grants, need-based scholarship grants available. In 2008–09, 9% of upper-school students received aid; total upper-school merit-scholarship money awarded: $104,000. Total amount of financial aid awarded in 2008–09: $944,000.

Admissions Traditional secondary-level entrance grade is 9. For fall 2008, 290 students applied for upper-level admission, 154 were accepted, 125 enrolled. ISEE or SSAT required. Deadline for receipt of application materials: February 15. Application fee required: $75. On-campus interview required.

Athletics Interscholastic: baseball (boys), basketball (b,g), cheering (g), cross-country running (b,g), fencing (b,g), ice hockey (b), indoor track & field (b,g), soccer (b,g), softball (g), tennis (b,g), track and field (b,g), winter (indoor) track (b,g); intramural: mountain biking (b,g), strength & conditioning (b,g); coed interscholastic: golf, swimming and diving. 6 PE instructors, 37 coaches, 1 athletic trainer.

Computers Computers are regularly used in art, computer applications, design, desktop publishing, graphic arts, graphic design, independent study, information technology, introduction to technology, journalism, library, library skills, literary magazine, multimedia, news writing, newspaper, photography, programming, research skills, science, technology, Web site design, yearbook classes. Computer network features include on-campus library services, online commercial services, Internet access, wireless campus network, Internet filtering or blocking technology. Campus intranet and computer access in designated common areas are available to students. The school has a published electronic and media policy.

Contact Mrs. Ann Marie Blackman, Admission Assistant. 908-234-1611 Ext. 245. Fax: 908-234-1712. E-mail: ablackman@gsbschool.org. Web site: www.gsbschool.org.

See Close-Up on page 768.

GILMAN SCHOOL

5407 Roland Avenue
Baltimore, Maryland 21210

Head of School: Mr. John E. Schmick

General Information Boys' day college-preparatory school. Grades P1–12. Founded: 1897. Setting: suburban. 68-acre campus. 5 buildings on campus. Approved or accredited by Association of Independent Maryland Schools, Middle States Association of Colleges and Schools, and Maryland Department of Education. Member of National Association of Independent Schools and Secondary School Admission Test Board. Endowment: $92 million. Total enrollment: 988. Upper school average class size: 16. Upper school faculty-student ratio: 1:8.

Upper School Student Profile Grade 9: 117 students (117 boys); Grade 10: 112 students (112 boys); Grade 11: 119 students (119 boys); Grade 12: 99 students (99 boys).

Faculty School total: 143. In upper school: 51 men, 10 women; 50 have advanced degrees.

Subjects Offered Algebra, American history, American literature, anatomy, Arabic, art, art history, biology, calculus, ceramics, chemistry, Chinese, community service, computer math, computer programming, computer science, creative writing, drafting, drama, driver education, ecology, economics, engineering, English, English literature, environmental science, European history, expository writing, fine arts, French, geometry, German, government/civics, grammar, Greek, history, industrial arts, Latin, mathematics, mechanical drawing, music, photography, physical education, physics, physiology, religion, Russian, science, social studies, Spanish, speech, statistics, theater, trigonometry, writing.

Graduation Requirements Art history, athletics, English, foreign language, history, mathematics, music appreciation, religions, science, senior project.

Special Academic Programs Advanced Placement exam preparation; honors section; independent study; term-away projects; academic accommodation for the gifted.

College Admission Counseling 112 students graduated in 2008; all went to college, including Brown University; Columbia College; Emory University; The George Washington University; University of Maryland, Baltimore; University of Pennsylvania. Mean SAT critical reading: 655, mean SAT math: 673, mean SAT writing: 626.

Student Life Upper grades have specified standards of dress, student council, honor system. Discipline rests primarily with faculty.

Summer Programs Remediation, enrichment, advancement, sports programs offered; session focuses on remediation; held on campus; accepts boys and girls; open to students from other schools. 200 students usually enrolled. 2009 schedule: June 19 to July 28. Application deadline: June 19.

Tuition and Aid Day student tuition: $21,690. Tuition installment plan (Insured Tuition Payment Plan, monthly payment plans, Gilman Monthly Payment Plan). Need-based scholarship grants, need-based loans available. In 2008–09, 23% of upper-school students received aid. Total amount of financial aid awarded in 2008–09: $140,000.

Admissions Traditional secondary-level entrance grade is 9. For fall 2008, 109 students applied for upper-level admission, 37 were accepted, 29 enrolled. ISEE required. Deadline for receipt of application materials: January 9. Application fee required: $50. On-campus interview required.

Athletics Interscholastic: baseball, basketball, cross-country running, diving, football, golf, ice hockey, indoor track, lacrosse, soccer, squash, swimming and diving, tennis, track and field, volleyball, water polo, winter (indoor) track, wrestling; intramural: basketball, bicycling, crew, cross-country running, fitness, flag football, Frisbee, golf, physical fitness, rugby, table tennis, tennis, touch football, weight lifting, winter soccer. 2 PE instructors, 2 athletic trainers.

Computers Computers are regularly used in computer applications, design, digital applications classes. Computer network features include on-campus library services, Internet access, wireless campus network. Campus intranet, student e-mail accounts, and computer access in designated common areas are available to students. The school has a published electronic and media policy.

Contact Allison Conner, Admissions Assistant. 410-323-7169. Fax: 410-864-2825. E-mail: aconner@gilman.edu. Web site: www.gilman.edu.

ANNOUNCEMENT FROM THE SCHOOL Founded in 1897 as the first country day school in the United States, Gilman is a college-preparatory school enrolling 983 boys in Kindergarten through twelfth grades. The School aims to provide thorough academic instruction, to promote physical vigor, and to develop sound character. The Upper School curriculum, which includes electives, Advanced Placement courses, and a coordinate program with nearby girls' schools, is enriched by many diverse extracurricular activities. A summer session is offered. Tuition for 2008–09 was $19,415–$21,690. John E. Schmick is

Gilman's Headmaster. Gilman is accredited by the Association of Independent Maryland Schools.

GILMOUR ACADEMY

34001 Cedar Road
Gates Mills, Ohio 44040-9356
Head of School: Br. Robert E. Lavelle, CSC

General Information Coeducational boarding and day college-preparatory, arts, religious studies, and technology school, affiliated with Roman Catholic Church. Boarding grades 7–12, day grades PK–12. Founded: 1946. Setting: suburban. Nearest major city is Cleveland. Students are housed in single-sex dormitories and boys' wing and girls' wing dormitory. 144-acre campus. 15 buildings on campus. Approved or accredited by Independent Schools Association of the Central States, Midwest Association of Boarding Schools, National Catholic Education Association, North Central Association of Colleges and Schools, Ohio Association of Independent Schools, The Association of Boarding Schools, and Ohio Department of Education. Member of National Association of Independent Schools and Secondary School Admission Test Board. Endowment: $41 million. Total enrollment: 725. Upper school average class size: 15. Upper school faculty-student ratio: 1:10.

Upper School Student Profile Grade 9: 110 students (52 boys, 58 girls); Grade 10: 109 students (51 boys, 58 girls); Grade 11: 104 students (52 boys, 52 girls); Grade 12: 112 students (54 boys, 58 girls); Postgraduate: 2 students (2 boys). 12% of students are boarding students. 88% are state residents. 15 states are represented in upper school student body. 3% are international students. International students from Canada, Republic of Korea, and Sweden. 80% of students are Roman Catholic.

Faculty School total: 92. In upper school: 36 men, 28 women; 47 have advanced degrees; 8 reside on campus.

Subjects Offered Advanced Placement courses, advanced studio art-AP, algebra, American government, American history, American literature, art, band, Bible, biology, biology-AP, British literature, broadcast journalism, calculus, calculus-AP, ceramics, chemistry, chemistry-AP, chorus, community service, computer programming, computer science, computer science-AP, creative writing, drama, drawing, economics, English, English literature, English-AP, ensembles, ESL, ethics, European history, European history-AP, fine arts, French, French language-AP, French-AP, geometry, geometry with art applications, government, government-AP, government/civics, health, history, history of rock and roll, independent study, jazz ensemble, journalism, Latin, Latin-AP, law, leadership, mathematics, mathematics-AP, model United Nations, modern European history-AP, music, musical productions, oil painting, painting, photography, physical education, physical fitness, physics, physics-AP, pre-algebra, pre-calculus, religion, religious studies, SAT/ACT preparation, science, social studies, Spanish, Spanish language-AP, speech, speech and debate, statistics-AP, student government, student publications, studio art, studio art-AP, swimming, theater, trigonometry, U.S. history, U.S. history-AP, weight training, work-study, world history, writing, writing workshop, yearbook.

Graduation Requirements Arts and fine arts (art, music, dance, drama), English, foreign language, mathematics, physical education (includes health), religion (includes Bible studies and theology), science, social studies (includes history), speech, Senior Project. Community service is required.

Special Academic Programs Advanced Placement exam preparation; accelerated programs; independent study; term-away projects; study at local college for college credit; academic accommodation for the gifted, the musically talented, and the artistically talented.

College Admission Counseling 100 students graduated in 2008; 98 went to college, including Boston College; Case Western Reserve University; John Carroll University; Loyola University Chicago; Miami University; University of Notre Dame. Other: 2 had other specific plans. Mean SAT critical reading: 560, mean SAT math: 570, mean SAT writing: 600, mean combined SAT: 1730, mean composite ACT: 25.

Student Life Upper grades have specified standards of dress, student council, honor system. Discipline rests equally with students and faculty. Attendance at religious services is required.

Summer Programs Sports programs offered; session focuses on athletics; held on campus; accepts boys and girls; open to students from other schools. 100 students usually enrolled. 2009 schedule: June to July. Application deadline: none.

Tuition and Aid Day student tuition: $9525–$23,045; 7-day tuition and room/board: $34,525. Tuition installment plan (SMART Tuition Payment Plan). Tuition reduction for siblings, merit scholarship grants, need-based scholarship grants, need-based loans, paying campus jobs, endowed scholarships with criteria specified by donors available. In 2008–09, 53% of upper-school students received aid; total upper-school merit-scholarship money awarded: $60,000. Total amount of financial aid awarded in 2008–09: $2,200,000.

Admissions Traditional secondary-level entrance grade is 9. For fall 2008, 200 students applied for upper-level admission, 170 were accepted, 98 enrolled. ACT, ISEE, PSAT, SAT, SSAT or TOEFL required. Deadline for receipt of application materials: none. Application fee required: $25. Interview required.

Athletics Interscholastic: baseball (boys), basketball (b,g), cross-country running (b,g), diving (b,g), football (b), gymnastics (g), hockey (b,g), ice hockey (b,g), lacrosse (b,g), running (b,g), soccer (b,g), softball (g), swimming and diving (b,g), tennis (b,g), track and field (b,g), volleyball (g), winter soccer (b,g); intramural: cheering (g), indoor soccer (b,g); coed interscholastic: figure skating, golf, indoor track, indoor track & field, winter (indoor) track; coed intramural: aerobics, alpine skiing, aquatics, basketball, bowling, broomball, figure skating, fitness, golf, ice skating, indoor track, paddle tennis, physical fitness, physical training, skiing (downhill), snowboarding, soccer, strength & conditioning, swimming and diving, tennis, volleyball, weight training, winter (indoor) track, winter soccer. 4 PE instructors, 5 coaches, 2 athletic trainers.

Computers Computers are regularly used in all academic classes. Computer network features include on-campus library services, online commercial services, Internet access, wireless campus network, Internet filtering or blocking technology, EXPAN (college guidance service). Campus intranet, student e-mail accounts, and computer access in designated common areas are available to students. Students grades are available online. The school has a published electronic and media policy.

Contact Mr. Steve M. Scheidt, Director of Middle and Upper School Admissions. 440-473-8050. Fax: 440-473-8010. E-mail: admissions@gilmour.org. Web site: www.gilmour.org.

ANNOUNCEMENT FROM THE SCHOOL Gilmour Academy students thrive in a student-centered, personalized academic environment where the education of the mind and heart takes center stage. The average class size is fewer than 15 students in Gilmour's people-intensive approach to learning. Dynamic student-teacher relationships, a highly focused student advisory program, and exceptional academic offerings enable students to achieve their personal best. As a Catholic independent school sponsored by the Congregation of Holy Cross, Gilmour emphasizes faith formation, inclusiveness, and spirituality. Students become people of great courage and learn to serve as competent moral leaders in their global community. Ninety-minute, discussion-based classes that meet on alternate days allow students to be active and engaged. The school's education goals focus on students being persons on a journey of faith; effective communicators; analytical, reflective, complex thinkers; problem-solvers; self-directed, lifelong learners; collaborative contributors; and morally responsible persons. Dedicated and supportive teachers, counselors, and other professionals serve to foster habits of the mind, habits of the heart, and habits of action. Students participate in local community service, mission trips across the United States, and service programs outside the country. Students perform authentic research through the science department's Catalyst Program, a semester-long externship in a variety of professional settings. Students work with experts in medicine, technology, and other fields at prominent area institutions. One hundred percent of graduates have strong college options at such fine schools as MIT, Princeton, the Universities of Notre Dame and Virginia, and many others. Gilmour's scenic 145-acre campus is home to a new 600-seat gymnasium and aquatic center. The school's facilities also include new science laboratories; art, music, and photography studios; a 550-seat Chapel; an 1,800-square-foot Digital Broadcast Media Center; two NHL-size hockey rinks; a fully equipped fitness center; a football stadium; an all-weather track; a golf practice range; eight tennis courts; and numerous other playing fields.

GIRARD COLLEGE

2101 South College Avenue
Box #121
Philadelphia, Pennsylvania 19121-4857
Head of School: Hon. Dominic Cermele

General Information Coeducational boarding college-preparatory and general academic school. Grades 1–12. Founded: 1848. Setting: urban. Students are housed in single-sex dormitories. 43-acre campus. 10 buildings on campus. Approved or accredited by Middle States Association of Colleges and Schools, The Association of Boarding Schools, and Pennsylvania Department of Education. Member of National Association of Independent Schools. Endowment: $355 million. Total enrollment: 749. Upper school average class size: 22. Upper school faculty-student ratio: 1:16.

Upper School Student Profile 100% of students are boarding students. 90% are state residents. 6 states are represented in upper school student body.

Faculty School total: 71. In upper school: 12 men, 9 women; 9 have advanced degrees; 1 resides on campus.

Subjects Offered Algebra, American history, American literature, anatomy, art, biology, calculus, chemistry, choir, college counseling, community service, computer literacy, earth science, English, English literature, European history, French, geometry, government/civics, health, honors algebra, honors English, honors geometry, honors U.S. history, instrumental music, jazz band, life management skills, mathematics, multicultural studies, music appreciation, physical education, physics, poetry, pre-calculus, SAT preparation, senior project, social studies, sociology, Spanish, video film production, world cultures.

Graduation Requirements College counseling, computer literacy, English, foreign language, mathematics, physical education (includes health), science, senior career experience, senior project, social science, social studies (includes history). Community service is required.

Special Academic Programs Advanced Placement exam preparation; honors section; study at local college for college credit; remedial reading and/or remedial writing; remedial math.

College Admission Counseling 41 students graduated in 2008; 40 went to college, including Columbia College; Howard University; Penn State University Park; Rutgers, The State University of New Jersey, New Brunswick; Temple University; Villanova University. Other: 1 had other specific plans. Mean SAT critical reading: 490, mean SAT math: 477.
Student Life Upper grades have uniform requirement, student council. Discipline rests primarily with faculty.
Tuition and Aid Full scholarships (if admission requirements met) available. In 2008–09, 100% of upper-school students received aid.
Admissions Traditional secondary-level entrance grade is 9. For fall 2008, 124 students applied for upper-level admission, 24 were accepted, 14 enrolled. Admissions testing and math, reading, and mental ability tests required. Deadline for receipt of application materials: none. No application fee required. On-campus interview required.
Athletics Interscholastic: baseball (boys), basketball (b,g), cross-country running (b,g), soccer (b,g), softball (g), tennis (g), track and field (b,g), winter (indoor) track (b,g), wrestling (b); intramural: strength & conditioning (b,g); coed interscholastic: cheering; coed intramural: aerobics, dance, flag football, life saving, martial arts, outdoor activities, outdoor adventure, physical fitness, swimming and diving, weight training. 1 PE instructor, 11 coaches.
Computers Computers are regularly used in college planning, English, foreign language, history, library, mathematics, newspaper, reading, research skills, SAT preparation, science, social studies, study skills, word processing, writing, yearbook classes. Computer network features include on-campus library services, online commercial services, Internet access, Internet filtering or blocking technology. Student e-mail accounts are available to students. The school has a published electronic and media policy.
Contact Admission Receptionist. 215-787-2620. Fax: 215-787-4402. E-mail: admissions@girardcollege.com. Web site: www.girardcollege.com.

GIRLS PREPARATORY SCHOOL

205 Island Avenue
Chattanooga, Tennessee 37405
Head of School: Mr. Stanley R. Tucker

General Information Girls' day college-preparatory, arts, and technology school. Grades 6–12. Founded: 1906. Setting: suburban. Nearest major city is Atlanta, GA. 55-acre campus. 8 buildings on campus. Approved or accredited by Southern Association of Colleges and Schools and Southern Association of Independent Schools. Member of National Association of Independent Schools. Endowment: $28.8 million. Total enrollment: 660. Upper school average class size: 15. Upper school faculty-student ratio: 1:6.
Upper School Student Profile Grade 9: 102 students (102 girls); Grade 10: 83 students (83 girls); Grade 11: 112 students (112 girls); Grade 12: 94 students (94 girls).
Faculty School total: 78. In upper school: 14 men, 30 women; 27 have advanced degrees.
Subjects Offered Algebra, American history, American literature, art, art history, Basic programming, Bible studies, biology, calculus, chemistry, computer science, dance, drama, economics, English, English literature, European history, fine arts, forensic science, French, geometry, government/civics, graphic design, history, Latin, mathematics, music, orchestra, physical education, physics, pottery, pre-calculus, religion, science, Spanish, statistics, trigonometry, world history.
Graduation Requirements Arts and fine arts (art, music, dance, drama), electives, English, foreign language, history, mathematics, physical education (includes health), religion (includes Bible studies and theology), science.
Special Academic Programs 21 Advanced Placement exams for which test preparation is offered; honors section; independent study.
College Admission Counseling 99 students graduated in 2008; all went to college, including Auburn University; Georgia Institute of Technology; The University of Alabama; The University of Tennessee; The University of Tennessee at Chattanooga; Wake Forest University. Median SAT critical reading: 610, median SAT math: 610, median SAT writing: 620, median combined SAT: 1850, median composite ACT: 27. 49% scored over 600 on SAT critical reading, 51% scored over 600 on SAT math, 57% scored over 600 on SAT writing, 57% scored over 1800 on combined SAT, 51% scored over 26 on composite ACT.
Student Life Upper grades have uniform requirement, student council, honor system. Discipline rests primarily with faculty.
Summer Programs Remediation, enrichment, advancement, sports, art/fine arts, computer instruction programs offered; session focuses on enrichment; held both on and off campus; held at field trips and Lupton Athletic fields; accepts boys and girls; open to students from other schools. 400 students usually enrolled. 2009 schedule: June 1 to July 17. Application deadline: none.
Tuition and Aid Day student tuition: $18,500. Tuition installment plan (Key Tuition Payment Plan, FACTS Tuition Payment Plan, monthly payment plans, individually arranged payment plans, 60%/40% and 100% payment plans). Need-based scholarship grants available. In 2008–09, 32% of upper-school students received aid. Total amount of financial aid awarded in 2008–09: $866,383.
Admissions Traditional secondary-level entrance grade is 9. For fall 2008, 50 students applied for upper-level admission, 33 were accepted, 17 enrolled. Admissions testing required. Deadline for receipt of application materials: none. Application fee required: $50. On-campus interview required.
Athletics Interscholastic: basketball, bowling, cheering, crew, cross-country running, diving, golf, lacrosse, rowing, soccer, softball, swimming and diving, tennis, track and field, volleyball; intramural: backpacking, bicycling, canoeing/kayaking, climbing, dance, dance squad, fitness, fitness walking, Frisbee, hiking/backpacking, jogging, kayaking, life saving, modern dance, mountain biking, outdoor activities, paddle tennis, physical fitness, rafting, rock climbing, running, self defense, strength & conditioning, ultimate Frisbee, walking, weight lifting, wilderness; coed interscholastic: cheering. 6 PE instructors, 24 coaches, 1 athletic trainer.
Computers Computers are regularly used in Bible studies, computer applications, dance, English, foreign language, history, mathematics, science classes. Computer network features include on-campus library services, online commercial services, Internet access, wireless campus network, Internet filtering or blocking technology, network printing. Student e-mail accounts and computer access in designated common areas are available to students. Students grades are available online. The school has a published electronic and media policy.
Contact Debbie Bonner Young, Director of Admissions. 423-634-7647. Fax: 423-634-7643. E-mail: dyoung@gps.edu.

ANNOUNCEMENT FROM THE SCHOOL One of the largest secondary girls' day schools in the United States, GPS enrolls more than 650 students in grades 6–12. GPS classrooms are incubators for educational innovation, where faculty members address the school's mission to "challenge girls to recognize their membership in the global community." Incorporating computer use in the classroom has been a priority since 1998, and today, few colleges and universities incorporate computer-based instruction into the classroom as much as GPS does. Honors classes and twenty-two AP offerings foster a solid academic preparation. Resources include fifty-one fine arts classes, fourteen competitive interscholastic sports, and more than sixty student organizations that provide leadership opportunities. Community service, a coordinate program with a local independent boys' school, and a nationally recognized character education program enrich the students' extracurricular lives.

GLADES DAY SCHOOL

400 Gator Boulevard
Belle Glade, Florida 33430
Head of School: Mr. James Teets

General Information Coeducational day college-preparatory and general academic school. Grades PK–12. Founded: 1965. Setting: small town. Nearest major city is West Palm Beach. 21-acre campus. 4 buildings on campus. Approved or accredited by Florida Council of Independent Schools. Total enrollment: 540. Upper school average class size: 20. Upper school faculty-student ratio: 1:15.
Upper School Student Profile Grade 9: 61 students (29 boys, 32 girls); Grade 10: 68 students (36 boys, 32 girls); Grade 11: 55 students (30 boys, 25 girls); Grade 12: 68 students (40 boys, 28 girls).
Faculty School total: 54. In upper school: 14 men, 18 women; 3 have advanced degrees.
Subjects Offered Advanced math, agriculture, algebra, American government, American history, American literature, anatomy, ancient history, art, Bible studies, biology, business education, calculus, chemistry, computer applications, computer keyboarding, computer skills, computer technologies, concert band, contemporary history, current events, earth science, economics, economics-AP, English, English literature, environmental science, European history, general math, geometry, grammar, health, health education, journalism, keyboarding, law studies, limnology, marching band, marine biology, microeconomics-AP, modern world history, physical education, physics, pre-calculus, SAT/ACT preparation, Spanish, trigonometry, U.S. history, weightlifting, Western civilization, world history, world history-AP, yearbook.
Graduation Requirements Algebra, American government, American literature, anatomy, ancient world history, arts and fine arts (art, music, dance, drama), biology, chemistry, computer applications, computer keyboarding, contemporary history, economics, English, English composition, English literature, foreign language, geometry, health education, macroeconomics-AP, marine biology, modern world history, physical education (includes health), physical fitness, physical science, physics, pre-calculus, Spanish, U.S. history, world history.
Special Academic Programs 2 Advanced Placement exams for which test preparation is offered; honors section; independent study; study at local college for college credit; programs in general development for dyslexic students.
College Admission Counseling 59 students graduated in 2008; 57 went to college, including Florida Atlantic University; Florida Gulf Coast University; Palm Beach Community College; Santa Fe Community College; Tallahassee Community College; University of Central Florida. Other: 2 went to work.
Student Life Upper grades have uniform requirement, student council, honor system. Discipline rests primarily with faculty.
Summer Programs Remediation programs offered; session focuses on remediation; held on campus; accepts boys and girls; not open to students from other schools. 20 students usually enrolled. 2009 schedule: June 7 to July 15. Application deadline: June 4.
Tuition and Aid Day student tuition: $4950–$6900. Tuition installment plan (FACTS Tuition Payment Plan, monthly payment plans, individually arranged payment plans).

Tuition reduction for siblings, need-based scholarship grants available. In 2008–09, 10% of upper-school students received aid.
Admissions Traditional secondary-level entrance grade is 9. For fall 2008, 75 students applied for upper-level admission, 70 were accepted, 68 enrolled. Deadline for receipt of application materials: none. Application fee required: $200. On-campus interview required.
Athletics Interscholastic: baseball (boys), basketball (b,g), cheering (g), cross-country running (b,g), football (b), golf (b), soccer (b,g), softball (g), track and field (b,g), volleyball (b,g); intramural: strength & conditioning (b,g), tennis (b,g), weight training (b,g). 3 PE instructors, 2 coaches, 1 athletic trainer.
Computers Computers are regularly used in current events, journalism, science, Web site design, word processing, yearbook classes. Computer network features include on-campus library services, Internet access, wireless campus network. Campus intranet and student e-mail accounts are available to students. Students grades are available online. The school has a published electronic and media policy.
Contact Mrs. Irene Tellechea, High School Secretary. 561-996-6769 Ext. 10. Fax: 561-992-9274. E-mail: admissions@gladesdayschool.com. Web site: www.gladesdayschool.com.

GLEN EDEN SCHOOL

Vancouver, British Columbia, Canada
See Special Needs Schools section.

GLENELG COUNTRY SCHOOL

12793 Folly Quarter Road
Ellicott City, Maryland 21042
Head of School: Gregory J. Ventre

General Information Coeducational day college-preparatory, arts, and technology school. Grades PK–12. Founded: 1954. Setting: suburban. Nearest major city is Baltimore. 87-acre campus. 1 building on campus. Approved or accredited by Association of Independent Maryland Schools, Middle States Association of Colleges and Schools, and Maryland Department of Education. Member of National Association of Independent Schools. Endowment: $800,000. Total enrollment: 825. Upper school average class size: 15. Upper school faculty-student ratio: 1:6.
Upper School Student Profile Grade 9: 69 students (40 boys, 29 girls); Grade 10: 69 students (34 boys, 35 girls); Grade 11: 68 students (39 boys, 29 girls); Grade 12: 73 students (36 boys, 37 girls).
Faculty School total: 123. In upper school: 25 men, 21 women; 30 have advanced degrees.
Subjects Offered Algebra, American history, American literature, art, art history, biology, biology-AP, calculus, calculus-AP, chemistry, chemistry-AP, Chinese, chorus, community service, computer science, creative writing, drama, English, English literature, English-AP, European history, expository writing, French, French-AP, geometry, history, humanities, integrative seminar, Latin, Latin-AP, mathematics, photography, physical education, physical science, physics, physics-AP, pre-calculus, psychology, publications, science, social studies, Spanish, Spanish-AP, statistics, studio art, theater, trigonometry, world affairs.
Graduation Requirements Civics, English, foreign language, integrative seminar, mathematics, physical education (includes health), science, social studies (includes history), participation in Civic Leadership Program, 25 hours of community service per year.
Special Academic Programs 18 Advanced Placement exams for which test preparation is offered; honors section; independent study; academic accommodation for the gifted.
College Admission Counseling 63 students graduated in 2008; all went to college, including American University; Cornell University; Elon University; Georgetown University; The Johns Hopkins University; University of Maryland, College Park. Median SAT critical reading: 608, median SAT math: 624. 52% scored over 600 on SAT critical reading, 56% scored over 600 on SAT math.
Student Life Upper grades have uniform requirement, student council, honor system. Discipline rests equally with students and faculty.
Summer Programs Remediation, enrichment, sports programs offered; session focuses on academics and athletics; held on campus; accepts boys and girls; open to students from other schools. 300 students usually enrolled. 2009 schedule: June 22 to July 31. Application deadline: May 31.
Tuition and Aid Day student tuition: $20,850. Tuition installment plan (monthly payment plans, individually arranged payment plans, 2-payment plan). Merit scholarship grants, need-based scholarship grants available. In 2008–09, 35% of upper-school students received aid; total upper-school merit-scholarship money awarded: $75,000. Total amount of financial aid awarded in 2008–09: $900,000.
Admissions Traditional secondary-level entrance grade is 9. For fall 2008, 58 students applied for upper-level admission, 47 were accepted, 25 enrolled. ISEE or SSAT required. Deadline for receipt of application materials: January 15. Application fee required: $75. On-campus interview required.
Athletics Interscholastic: baseball (boys), basketball (b,g), cross-country running (b,g), field hockey (g), golf (b,g), ice hockey (b), indoor soccer (g), lacrosse (b,g), soccer (b,g), tennis (b,g), volleyball (g), winter soccer (g), wrestling (b); coed interscholastic: golf, ice hockey; coed intramural: aerobics, aerobics/dance, dance, fitness, flag football, Frisbee, physical fitness, physical training, skiing (downhill), strength & conditioning, ultimate Frisbee, weight training, yoga. 5 PE instructors, 12 coaches, 1 athletic trainer.
Computers Computers are regularly used in all academic classes. Computer network features include on-campus library services, Internet access, wireless campus network. Campus intranet, student e-mail accounts, and computer access in designated common areas are available to students. Students grades are available online. The school has a published electronic and media policy.
Contact Mrs. Karen K. Wootton, Director of Admission and Financial Aid. 410-531-7346 Ext. 2203. Fax: 410-531-7363. E-mail: wootton@glenelg.org. Web site: www.glenelg.org.

ANNOUNCEMENT FROM THE SCHOOL Glenelg Country School was founded in 1954 by five Howard County families searching for an independent, coeducational, nonsectarian school that would provide small class sizes, excellent teachers, and a strong academic program. The School is located on 87 beautiful acres in the center of Howard County, accessible to both Baltimore and Washington. The Primary, Lower, Middle, and Upper Schools each have separate academic buildings. The Upper School, grades 9–12, opened an academic expansion and new athletic center in spring 2005. There are no boarding options available, and families are responsible for transportation to and from school. Seventy-five percent of the families live in Howard County. The mission of Glenelg Country School is to provide a challenging academic curriculum, enriching opportunities in the arts, and a vigorous athletic program in order to develop intellectual curiosity, personal integrity, compassion for others, and strong citizenship. In addition to strong academic offerings, including nineteen Advanced Placement courses, the Upper School offers opportunities in athletics (sixteen sports), fine and performing arts, special interest clubs, and community service. College preparation and selection are integral parts of the Upper School. A full-time college counselor and advisers and teachers provide guidance. The class of 2008 had a mean SAT of 1232; 88% took Advanced Placement courses; 83% were accepted by their first-choice college; 95% were accepted by their first- or second-choice college. The enrollment for 2008–09, from prekindergarten through grade 12, was 825 students. The Upper School enrolls 280 students (70 in the class of 2012), with enrollment predicted to reach 300 in the next few years. The male-female ratio is 1:1. The School is sensitive to ethnic diversity, with a minority population of 33%. A financial aid program allows for socioeconomic diversity, with 26% of students receiving need-based assistance.

THE GLENHOLME SCHOOL

Washington, Connecticut
See Special Needs Schools section.

GONZAGA COLLEGE HIGH SCHOOL

19 Eye Street NW
Washington, District of Columbia 20001
Head of School: Mr. Michael Pakenham

General Information Boys' day college-preparatory, arts, religious studies, and technology school, affiliated with Roman Catholic Church. Grades 9–12. Founded: 1821. Setting: urban. 1-acre campus: 7 buildings on campus. Approved or accredited by Association of Independent Schools of Greater Washington, Jesuit Secondary Education Association, Middle States Association of Colleges and Schools, and District of Columbia Department of Education. Endowment: $9.1 million. Total enrollment: 942. Upper school average class size: 24. Upper school faculty-student ratio: 1:10.
Upper School Student Profile Grade 9: 240 students (240 boys); Grade 10: 239 students (239 boys); Grade 11: 237 students (237 boys); Grade 12: 226 students (226 boys). 80% of students are Roman Catholic.
Faculty School total: 65. In upper school: 46 men, 19 women; 50 have advanced degrees.
Subjects Offered Advanced Placement courses, algebra, American history, American literature, American minority experience, art, biology, calculus, chemistry, choir, choral music, Christian ethics, Christian scripture, community service, computer math, computer programming, computer science, creative writing, drama, driver education, earth science, economics, economics-AP, English, English literature, English literature-AP, English-AP, ethics, European history, European history-AP, expository writing, film studies, fine arts, French, geometry, German, government/civics, grammar, Greek, health, history, Latin, mathematics, music, philosophy, photography, physical education, physics, political science, psychology, religion, Russian history, science, social justice, social science, social studies, Spanish, statistics, theology, trigonometry, world history, world literature.
Graduation Requirements Accounting, arts and fine arts (art, music, dance, drama), English, ethics, foreign language, mathematics, physical education (includes health), religion (includes Bible studies and theology), science, social justice, social science, social studies (includes history). Community service is required.

Special Academic Programs Advanced Placement exam preparation; honors section.

College Admission Counseling 234 students graduated in 2008; 232 went to college, including Boston College; Georgetown University; James Madison University; University of Maryland, College Park; University of Virginia; Virginia Polytechnic Institute and State University. Other: 2 entered a postgraduate year.

Student Life Upper grades have specified standards of dress, student council, honor system. Discipline rests primarily with faculty. Attendance at religious services is required.

Summer Programs Remediation, enrichment programs offered; session focuses on new student remediation, enrichment, and SAT preparation; held on campus; accepts boys and girls; open to students from other schools. 150 students usually enrolled. 2009 schedule: June 29 to July 24. Application deadline: June 17.

Tuition and Aid Day student tuition: $14,850. Tuition installment plan (Insured Tuition Payment Plan, monthly payment plans). Merit scholarship grants, need-based scholarship grants available. In 2008–09, 30% of upper-school students received aid; total upper-school merit-scholarship money awarded: $100,000. Total amount of financial aid awarded in 2008–09: $1,785,000.

Admissions Traditional secondary-level entrance grade is 9. For fall 2008, 750 students applied for upper-level admission, 310 were accepted, 240 enrolled. High School Placement Test (closed version) from Scholastic Testing Service required. Deadline for receipt of application materials: December 10. Application fee required: $35.

Athletics Interscholastic: baseball, basketball, crew, cross-country running, diving, fencing, football, golf, ice hockey, indoor track & field, lacrosse, rugby, soccer, squash, swimming and diving, tennis, track and field, water polo, winter (indoor) track, wrestling; intramural: basketball, bowling, football, martial arts, physical training, softball, table tennis, volleyball, weight lifting, whiffle ball. 2 PE instructors, 30 coaches, 2 athletic trainers.

Computers Computer network features include on-campus library services, Internet access. Student e-mail accounts are available to students.

Contact Mr. Andrew C. Battaile, Director of Admission. 202-336-7101. Fax: 202-454-1188. E-mail: abattaile@gonzaga.org. Web site: www.gonzaga.org.

GORDON TECHNICAL HIGH SCHOOL

3633 North California Avenue
Chicago, Illinois 60618

Head of School: Rev. Paul A. Sims, PhD

General Information Coeducational day college-preparatory, arts, business, vocational, religious studies, and technology school, affiliated with Roman Catholic Church; primarily serves students with learning disabilities. Grades 9–12. Founded: 1952. Setting: urban. 4-acre campus. 1 building on campus. Approved or accredited by North Central Association of Colleges and Schools and Illinois Department of Education. Endowment: $5 million. Total enrollment: 585. Upper school average class size: 25. Upper school faculty-student ratio: 1:15.

Upper School Student Profile Grade 9: 159 students (92 boys, 67 girls); Grade 10: 162 students (98 boys, 64 girls); Grade 11: 147 students (85 boys, 62 girls); Grade 12: 117 students (76 boys, 41 girls). 70% of students are Roman Catholic.

Faculty School total: 40. In upper school: 24 men, 12 women; 34 have advanced degrees.

Special Academic Programs 9 Advanced Placement exams for which test preparation is offered; honors section; academic accommodation for the gifted; remedial reading and/or remedial writing; remedial math.

College Admission Counseling Colleges students went to include DePaul University; Loyola University Chicago; Northeastern Illinois University; University of Illinois at Chicago; University of Illinois at Urbana–Champaign.

Student Life Upper grades have uniform requirement, student council, honor system. Discipline rests primarily with faculty. Attendance at religious services is required.

Summer Programs Remediation programs offered; held on campus; accepts boys and girls; not open to students from other schools. 100 students usually enrolled. 2009 schedule: June to July.

Tuition and Aid Day student tuition: $8250. Tuition installment plan (monthly payment plans). Tuition reduction for siblings, bursaries, merit scholarship grants, need-based scholarship grants, paying campus jobs available. In 2008–09, 60% of upper-school students received aid. Total amount of financial aid awarded in 2008–09: $550,000.

Admissions Traditional secondary-level entrance grade is 9. For fall 2008, 238 students applied for upper-level admission, 196 were accepted, 159 enrolled. Deadline for receipt of application materials: none. No application fee required. On-campus interview recommended.

Athletics Interscholastic: baseball (boys), basketball (b,g), cheering (g), cross-country running (b,g), dance team (g), football (b), indoor track (b,g), indoor track & field (b,g), pom squad (g), running (b,g), soccer (b,g), softball (g), volleyball (b,g), wrestling (b); intramural: baseball (b), basketball (b,g), power lifting (b), strength & conditioning (b,g), weight training (b,g); coed interscholastic: bowling; coed intramural: aerobics, aerobics/dance, aerobics/Nautilus, badminton, baseball, basketball, climbing, fitness, outdoor activities, outdoor adventure, physical fitness, track and field. 2 PE instructors, 1 coach.

Computers Computers are regularly used in all classes. Computer network features include on-campus library services, online commercial services, Internet access, wireless campus network. Students grades are available online. The school has a published electronic and media policy.

Contact Mr. Shay Boyle, Director of Admissions. 773-423-5014. Fax: 773-539-9158. E-mail: sboyle@gordontech.org. Web site: www.gordontech.org.

GOULD ACADEMY

PO Box 860
39 Church Street
Bethel, Maine 04217

Head of School: Daniel A. Kunkle

General Information Coeducational boarding and day college-preparatory, arts, and technology school. Grades 9–PG. Founded: 1836. Setting: small town. Nearest major city is Portland. Students are housed in single-sex dormitories. 456-acre campus. 30 buildings on campus. Approved or accredited by Association of Independent Schools in New England, Independent Schools of Northern New England, New England Association of Schools and Colleges, The Association of Boarding Schools, and Maine Department of Education. Member of National Association of Independent Schools and Secondary School Admission Test Board. Endowment: $9.5 million. Total enrollment: 249. Upper school average class size: 12. Upper school faculty-student ratio: 1:6.

Upper School Student Profile Grade 9: 52 students (33 boys, 19 girls); Grade 10: 59 students (34 boys, 25 girls); Grade 11: 70 students (48 boys, 22 girls); Grade 12: 65 students (38 boys, 27 girls); Postgraduate: 3 students (3 boys). 71% of students are boarding students. 42% are state residents. 22 states are represented in upper school student body. 20% are international students. International students from Afghanistan, China, Germany, Japan, Republic of Korea, and Taiwan; 5 other countries represented in student body.

Faculty School total: 44. In upper school: 23 men, 21 women; 25 have advanced degrees; 32 reside on campus.

Subjects Offered Acting, Advanced Placement courses, African-American literature, algebra, American foreign policy, American government-AP, American history, American literature, American literature-AP, analytic geometry, art, art history, athletic training, band, bioethics, DNA and culture, biology, biology-AP, British literature, British literature (honors), British literature-AP, calculus, calculus-AP, celestial navigation, ceramics, chemistry, chemistry-AP, chorus, Civil War, clay-working, college placement, computer information systems, computer music, computer programming, computer science, computers, conceptual physics, creative writing, debate, design, digital music, drama, drawing, earth science, Eastern religion and philosophy, ecology, economics, electives, electronic music, electronics, English, environmental science, environmental science-AP, ESL, European history, expository writing, foreign policy, French, geography, geometry, government and politics-AP, history, history-AP, honors algebra, honors English, honors world history, introduction to digital multitrack recording techniques, jazz band, jewelry making, Latin, learning strategies, literature by women, mathematics, music, music appreciation, music theory, musicianship, navigation, painting, philosophy, photography, physics, pottery, pre-calculus, printmaking, robotics, science, sculpture, Shakespeare, social studies, software design, Spanish, theater, U.S. government and politics-AP, video film production, women's literature, world history, writing.

Graduation Requirements English, foreign language, mathematics, physical education (includes health), science, social studies (includes history).

Special Academic Programs Advanced Placement exam preparation; honors section; independent study; term-away projects; study abroad; academic accommodation for the gifted, the musically talented, and the artistically talented; ESL (25 students enrolled).

College Admission Counseling 61 students graduated in 2008; all went to college, including Bentley University; Lewis & Clark College; Rochester Institute of Technology; Saint Michael's College; University of Illinois at Urbana–Champaign; University of Vermont.

Student Life Upper grades have specified standards of dress, student council, honor system. Discipline rests equally with students and faculty.

Tuition and Aid Day student tuition: $24,500; 7-day tuition and room/board: $41,500. Tuition installment plan (individually arranged payment plans, full-payment by August 15, 2/3 payment by August 12, 1/3 by December 1). Need-based scholarship grants, need-based loans available. In 2008–09, 38% of upper-school students received aid. Total amount of financial aid awarded in 2008–09: $1,355,000.

Admissions Traditional secondary-level entrance grade is 9. For fall 2008, 189 students applied for upper-level admission, 156 were accepted, 99 enrolled. SSAT required. Deadline for receipt of application materials: February 1. Application fee required: $30. Interview required.

Athletics Interscholastic: alpine skiing (boys, girls), baseball (b), basketball (b,g), bicycling (b,g), cross-country running (b,g), field hockey (g), freestyle skiing (b,g); coed interscholastic: climbing, dance, dressage, equestrian sports, golf; coed intramural: golf. 11 coaches, 1 athletic trainer.

Computers Computers are regularly used in English, foreign language, history, mathematics, music, science, technology classes. Computer network features include on-campus library services, Internet access, wireless campus network. Student e-mail accounts are available to students. Students grades are available online. The school has a published electronic and media policy.

Contact Todd Ormiston, Director of Admission. 207-824-7777. Fax: 207-824-2926. E-mail: todd.ormiston@gouldacademy.org. Web site: www.gouldacademy.org.

See Close-Up on page 770.

THE GOVERNOR FRENCH ACADEMY

219 West Main Street
Belleville, Illinois 62220-1537

Head of School: Mr. Phillip E. Paeltz

General Information Coeducational boarding and day college-preparatory, arts, bilingual studies, and technology school. Boarding grades 9–12, day grades K–12. Founded: 1983. Setting: small town. Nearest major city is St. Louis, MO. Students are housed in homes of local families. 3 buildings on campus. Approved or accredited by CITA (Commission on International and Trans-Regional Accreditation), North Central Association of Colleges and Schools, and Illinois Department of Education. Languages of instruction: English and Spanish. Endowment: $100,000. Total enrollment: 205. Upper school average class size: 15. Upper school faculty-student ratio: 1:6.

Upper School Student Profile Grade 9: 9 students (6 boys, 3 girls); Grade 10: 13 students (7 boys, 6 girls); Grade 11: 14 students (8 boys, 6 girls); Grade 12: 19 students (5 boys, 14 girls). 1% of students are boarding students. 98% are state residents. 2 states are represented in upper school student body. 1% are international students. International students from China, Japan, Pakistan, Republic of Korea, Saudi Arabia, and Taiwan; 5 other countries represented in student body.

Faculty School total: 14. In upper school: 6 men, 4 women; 6 have advanced degrees.

Subjects Offered Algebra, American history, American literature, art, biology, botany, calculus, chemistry, computer science, creative writing, earth science, ecology, economics, English, English literature, environmental science, European history, expository writing, geography, geometry, government/civics, grammar, history, history of ideas, mathematics, philosophy, physical education, physics, physiology, psychology, science, social science, social studies, sociology, Spanish, speech, statistics, theater arts, trigonometry, world history, world literature.

Graduation Requirements English, foreign language, mathematics, physical education (includes health), science, social science, vote of faculty.

Special Academic Programs 5 Advanced Placement exams for which test preparation is offered; accelerated programs; independent study; academic accommodation for the gifted, the musically talented, and the artistically talented; programs in English for dyslexic students; ESL (5 students enrolled).

College Admission Counseling 16 students graduated in 2008; all went to college, including Saint Louis University; Southern Illinois University Edwardsville; University of Illinois at Urbana–Champaign. Mean SAT critical reading: 601, mean SAT math: 638. 50% scored over 600 on SAT critical reading, 50% scored over 600 on SAT math.

Student Life Upper grades have uniform requirement, honor system. Discipline rests primarily with faculty.

Summer Programs Remediation, enrichment, advancement, art/fine arts, computer instruction programs offered; session focuses on academics; held on campus; accepts boys and girls; open to students from other schools. 85 students usually enrolled. 2009 schedule: June 22 to July 31. Application deadline: none.

Tuition and Aid Day student tuition: $5590; 7-day tuition and room/board: $22,200. Tuition installment plan (monthly payment plans). Tuition reduction for siblings available. In 2008–09, 5% of upper-school students received aid.

Admissions Traditional secondary-level entrance grade is 9. For fall 2008, 20 students applied for upper-level admission, 17 were accepted, 15 enrolled. Deadline for receipt of application materials: none. No application fee required. Interview required.

Athletics Interscholastic: basketball (boys, girls), volleyball (g); intramural: baseball (b), bowling (g), dance (g); coed interscholastic: bicycling, golf, soccer, tennis; coed intramural: climbing, fencing, fitness, golf, independent competitive sports, marksmanship, martial arts, Nautilus, rappelling, riflery, skateboarding, softball, swimming and diving, table tennis, track and field, wall climbing. 2 PE instructors, 2 coaches.

Computers Computers are regularly used in computer applications, science, yearbook classes. Computer network features include Internet access. The school has a published electronic and media policy.

Contact Ms. Carol Wilson, Director of Admissions. 618-233-7542. Fax: 618-233-0541. E-mail: admiss@governorfrench.com. Web site: www.governorfrench.com.

THE GOVERNOR'S ACADEMY (FORMERLY GOVERNOR DUMMER ACADEMY)

1 Elm Street
Byfield, Massachusetts 01922

Head of School: John Martin Doggett Jr.

General Information Coeducational boarding and day college-preparatory and arts school. Grades 9–12. Founded: 1763. Setting: rural. Nearest major city is Boston. Students are housed in single-sex dormitories. 450-acre campus. 40 buildings on campus. Approved or accredited by Association of Independent Schools in New England, New England Association of Schools and Colleges, and The Association of Boarding Schools. Member of National Association of Independent Schools and Secondary School Admission Test Board. Endowment: $82 million. Total enrollment: 376. Upper school average class size: 12. Upper school faculty-student ratio: 1:5.

Upper School Student Profile Grade 9: 84 students (45 boys, 39 girls); Grade 10: 94 students (56 boys, 38 girls); Grade 11: 101 students (55 boys, 46 girls); Grade 12: 97 students (50 boys, 47 girls). 65% of students are boarding students. 52% are state residents. 21 states are represented in upper school student body. 12% are international students. International students from Canada, Germany, Japan, Republic of Korea, Thailand, and United Kingdom; 7 other countries represented in student body.

Faculty In upper school: 35 men, 24 women; 40 have advanced degrees; 55 reside on campus.

Subjects Offered Advanced chemistry, algebra, American history, American history-AP, American literature, anatomy, art, band, biology, biology-AP, calculus-AP, ceramics, chemistry, Chinese, chorus, civics, computer graphics, computer math, computer programming, computer science, constitutional law, creative writing, dance, drama, driver education, ecology, economics, English literature, English literature and composition-AP, environmental science, ESL, European history, expository writing, filmmaking, fine arts, French, French-AP, geometry, German, health, history, Holocaust and other genocides, honors algebra, jazz band, Latin, marine biology, marine science, mathematics, Middle Eastern history, modern European history, modern European history-AP, music, music history, music theory, photography, physics, physics-AP, psychology, psychology-AP, religion, science, social studies, Spanish, Spanish-AP, statistics-AP, studio art—AP, theater, trigonometry, visual and performing arts, women's studies, writing.

Graduation Requirements Arts and fine arts (art, music, dance, drama), English, foreign language, history, mathematics, science, 50 hours of community service.

Special Academic Programs Advanced Placement exam preparation; honors section; independent study; study abroad; ESL (4 students enrolled).

College Admission Counseling 92 students graduated in 2008; all went to college, including Boston University; Colby College; Hobart and William Smith Colleges; Providence College; University of New Hampshire. Mean SAT critical reading: 577, mean SAT math: 612, mean SAT writing: 591, mean combined SAT: 1780. 37% scored over 600 on SAT critical reading, 50% scored over 600 on SAT math, 41% scored over 600 on SAT writing, 42% scored over 1800 on combined SAT.

Student Life Upper grades have specified standards of dress, student council, honor system. Discipline rests primarily with faculty.

Tuition and Aid Day student tuition: $32,600; 7-day tuition and room/board: $41,300. Tuition installment plan (The Tuition Plan, Academic Management Services Plan, monthly payment plans). Need-based scholarship grants available. In 2008–09, 27% of upper-school students received aid. Total amount of financial aid awarded in 2008–09: $2,200,000.

Admissions Traditional secondary-level entrance grade is 9. For fall 2008, 733 students applied for upper-level admission, 190 were accepted, 112 enrolled. ISEE, SSAT or TOEFL required. Deadline for receipt of application materials: January 31. Application fee required: $50. Interview required.

Athletics Interscholastic: baseball (boys), basketball (b,g), cross-country running (b,g), field hockey (g), football (b), ice hockey (b,g), lacrosse (b,g), soccer (b,g), softball (g), tennis (b,g), track and field (b,g), volleyball (g), wrestling (b); intramural: dance (g); coed interscholastic: golf; coed intramural: aerobics/dance, alpine skiing, dance, outdoor activities, outdoor recreation, skiing (downhill), yoga. 2 athletic trainers.

Computers Computers are regularly used in art, English, foreign language, history, mathematics, music, science classes. Computer network features include on-campus library services, online commercial services, Internet access, wireless campus network, Internet filtering or blocking technology, laptop sign-out in student center and library, Moodle Website for teachers and students to share course data, events, and discussions. Campus intranet, student e-mail accounts, and computer access in designated common areas are available to students. The school has a published electronic and media policy.

Contact Peter T. Bidstrup, Director of Admission. 978-499-3120. Fax: 978-462-1278. E-mail: admissions@thegovernorsacademy.org. Web site: www.thegovernorsacademy.org.

ANNOUNCEMENT FROM THE SCHOOL The Governor's Academy, located in Byfield, Massachusetts, on 500 acres of coastal farmland adjacent to the Great Atlantic salt marshes, was founded in 1763 by a bequest in the will of William Dummer, lieutenant governor and acting governor of the Massachusetts Bay Colony. The Governor's Academy combines centuries of tradition with a dedication to educational innovation. Students flourish in a diverse community distinguished by enduring relationships with teachers and defined by a commitment to learning and a thoughtful balance of academics, athletics, arts, and service to others. Academy graduates are lifelong learners who embrace their civic duty and global responsibility. The school's facilities include state-of-the-art science laboratories; a spacious student center with a snack bar, a book store, and wireless media center; a library with more than 37,000 books; nine dormitories; a performing arts center with practice rooms, a main stage, a black box theater, professional lighting and sound capabilities, and a full scene shop; some of the best playing fields in New England; a new hockey rink and turf field; and a campuswide computer network. Governor's Academy offers twenty

Advanced Placement courses distributed in all academic disciplines and five foreign languages: Chinese, French, German, Latin, and Spanish. Nearly 90 percent of the Academy's teachers live on campus in dormitories and other Academy housing. The Academy prides itself on a "triple threat" approach to a boarding education. Teachers are coaches and dorm parents, interacting with the Academy's students everyday in the classroom, on the fields and stages, and in the dormitories. The Governor's Academy is not just a school—it is a full-time community committed to the growth and development of young adults. There are approximately 375 students in grades 9 through 12, half girls and half boys. Two thirds of the students board; one third are day students from surrounding towns. Students come from twenty-one states and ten countries. One hundred percent of Governor's Academy graduates attend four-year colleges and universities.

THE GOW SCHOOL

South Wales, New York

See Special Needs Schools section.

GRACE BAPTIST ACADEMY

7815 Shallowford Road
Chattanooga, Tennessee 37421

Head of School: Mr. David Patrick

General Information Coeducational day college-preparatory and religious studies school, affiliated with Baptist Church. Grades K4–12. Founded: 1985. Setting: suburban. 2 buildings on campus. Approved or accredited by Association of Christian Schools International, Southern Association of Colleges and Schools, and Tennessee Department of Education. Total enrollment: 800. Upper school average class size: 22. Upper school faculty-student ratio: 1:20.

Upper School Student Profile Grade 9: 60 students (27 boys, 33 girls); Grade 10: 60 students (31 boys, 29 girls); Grade 11: 64 students (32 boys, 32 girls); Grade 12: 52 students (24 boys, 28 girls). 75% of students are Baptist.

Faculty School total: 47. In upper school: 10 men, 9 women; 5 have advanced degrees.

Subjects Offered Advanced computer applications, algebra, American government, American history, American literature, ancient world history, art, band, Bible, Bible studies, biology, biology-AP, calculus, chemistry, choir, Christian doctrine, Christian ethics, Christian testament, computer applications, drama performance, dramatic arts, economics, English, English composition, English literature, environmental studies, fitness, general math, general science, geometry, global studies, health, health and safety, honors English, honors world history, keyboarding, language arts, Life of Christ, mathematics, music, New Testament, physical education, physics, pre-algebra, pre-calculus, SAT/ACT preparation, Spanish, speech, state history, study skills, U.S. government and politics, U.S. history, weight training, weightlifting, world geography, yearbook.

Graduation Requirements Algebra, American history, Bible, biology, chemistry, computer applications, economics, English, English literature, geometry, global studies, government, physical education (includes health), Spanish, speech, U.S. history, visual and performing arts, 1/2 unit of speech.

Special Academic Programs Honors section; study at local college for college credit.

College Admission Counseling 58 students graduated in 2008; 54 went to college, including Chattanooga State Technical Community College; The University of Tennessee at Chattanooga. Other: 3 went to work, 1 entered a postgraduate year. Mean composite ACT: 22.

Student Life Upper grades have uniform requirement, student council, honor system. Discipline rests primarily with faculty. Attendance at religious services is required.

Summer Programs Remediation programs offered; held on campus; accepts boys and girls; open to students from other schools. 75 students usually enrolled. 2009 schedule: June 15 to July 17. Application deadline: June 5.

Tuition and Aid Tuition installment plan (monthly payment plans, bank draft). Tuition reduction for siblings, need-based scholarship grants available. In 2008–09, 5% of upper-school students received aid.

Admissions Traditional secondary-level entrance grade is 9. For fall 2008, 26 students applied for upper-level admission, 25 were accepted, 25 enrolled. Latest standardized score from previous school required. Deadline for receipt of application materials: none. Application fee required: $300. On-campus interview required.

Athletics Interscholastic: baseball (boys), basketball (b,g), cheering (g), cross-country running (b,g), football (b), soccer (b,g), softball (g), tennis (b,g), track and field (b,g), volleyball (g); intramural: physical training (b,g), strength & conditioning (b,g), weight lifting (b), weight training (b); coed interscholastic: golf. 2 PE instructors, 5 coaches, 1 athletic trainer.

Computers Computers are regularly used in computer applications, keyboarding classes. Computer resources include on-campus library services, Internet access, Internet filtering or blocking technology. Students grades are available online.

Contact Mrs. Janine McCurdy, Admissions Director. 423-892-8222 Ext. 115. Fax: 423-892-1194. E-mail: jmccurdy@gracechatt.org. Web site: www.gracechatt.org.

GRACE BRETHREN SCHOOL

1350 Cherry Avenue
Simi Valley, California 93065

Head of School: Mr. John Hynes

General Information Coeducational day college-preparatory, arts, vocational, and religious studies school, affiliated with Brethren Church, Christian faith. Grades PS–12. Founded: 1979. Setting: suburban. Nearest major city is Los Angeles. 12-acre campus. 9 buildings on campus. Approved or accredited by Association of Christian Schools International, Western Association of Schools and Colleges, and California Department of Education. Total enrollment: 896. Upper school average class size: 26. Upper school faculty-student ratio: 1:7.

Upper School Student Profile Grade 9: 84 students (47 boys, 37 girls); Grade 10: 60 students (38 boys, 22 girls); Grade 11: 68 students (28 boys, 40 girls); Grade 12: 49 students (26 boys, 23 girls). 95% of students are Brethren, Christian.

Faculty School total: 36. In upper school: 18 men, 18 women; 15 have advanced degrees.

Subjects Offered Accounting, Advanced Placement courses, algebra, American literature, American literature-AP, anatomy and physiology, ancient world history, art, ASB Leadership, athletic training, band, baseball, basketball, Bible, Bible studies, biology, British literature, British literature-AP, career/college preparation, cheerleading, chemistry, choir, college counseling, computer graphics, computer music, computer tools, concert choir, critical thinking, critical writing, digital photography, drama, drama performance, environmental science, film studies, forensic science, geometry, government and politics-AP, health, home economics, jazz band, jazz ensemble, New Testament, photography, physical education, physics, physics-AP, pre-algebra, pre-calculus, set design, softball, Spanish, Spanish language-AP, speech, stage design, statistics, statistics-AP, technical theater, U.S. government and politics, U.S. government and politics-AP, U.S. history, U.S. history-AP, visual and performing arts, volleyball, world cultures, world geography, world history, yearbook.

Graduation Requirements Bible studies, electives, English, foreign language, mathematics, physical education (includes health), science, social studies (includes history), visual and performing arts.

Special Academic Programs Advanced Placement exam preparation; honors section; independent study; study at local college for college credit; remedial math; special instructional classes for deaf students.

College Admission Counseling 47 students graduated in 2008; all went to college, including California State University, Northridge; Chapman University; Moorpark College; The Master's College and Seminary; University of California, San Diego; Westmont College. Median combined SAT: 1480. 15% scored over 1800 on combined SAT.

Student Life Upper grades have specified standards of dress, student council, honor system. Discipline rests primarily with faculty. Attendance at religious services is required.

Summer Programs Remediation, enrichment programs offered; session focuses on remediation; held on campus; accepts boys and girls; not open to students from other schools. 45 students usually enrolled. 2009 schedule: June 22 to July 31. Application deadline: June 19.

Tuition and Aid Day student tuition: $7584. Guaranteed tuition plan. Tuition installment plan (monthly payment plans). Tuition reduction for siblings available.

Admissions Traditional secondary-level entrance grade is 9. For fall 2008, 71 students applied for upper-level admission, 70 were accepted, 64 enrolled. Math Placement Exam, Stanford Achievement Test and writing sample required. Deadline for receipt of application materials: none. Application fee required: $350. On-campus interview required.

Athletics Interscholastic: baseball (boys), basketball (b,g), cheering (g), cross-country running (b,g), flag football (b), football (b), golf (b,g). 2 PE instructors, 16 coaches, 1 athletic trainer.

Computers Computers are regularly used in accounting, art, career exploration, college planning, foreign language, graphic arts, keyboarding, library, mathematics, photography, science, video film production, yearbook classes. Computer network features include on-campus library services, Internet access, wireless campus network, Internet filtering or blocking technology. Computer access in designated common areas is available to students. Students grades are available online. The school has a published electronic and media policy.

Contact Mrs. Kelley Windham, Registrar. 805-522-4667 Ext. 2033. Fax: 805-522-5617. E-mail: kwindham@gracebrethren.com. Web site: www.gracebrethren.com.

GRACE CHRISTIAN SCHOOL

12407 Pintail Street
Anchorage, Alaska 99516

Head of School: Nathan Davis

General Information Coeducational day college-preparatory, arts, religious studies, and technology school, affiliated with Christian faith; primarily serves students with learning disabilities, individuals with Attention Deficit Disorder, and dyslexic students. Grades K–12. Founded: 1980. Setting: urban. 7-acre campus. 3 buildings on campus. Approved or accredited by Association of Christian Schools International, Northwest Association of Accredited Schools, and Northwest Association of Schools and Colleges. Total enrollment: 686. Upper school average class size: 17. Upper school faculty-student ratio: 1:15.

Upper School Student Profile Grade 7: 61 students (36 boys, 25 girls); Grade 8: 63 students (38 boys, 25 girls); Grade 9: 70 students (32 boys, 38 girls); Grade 10: 75 students (36 boys, 39 girls); Grade 11: 61 students (24 boys, 37 girls); Grade 12: 58 students (31 boys, 27 girls). 99% of students are Christian faith.
Faculty School total: 51. In upper school: 12 men, 15 women; 7 have advanced degrees.
Subjects Offered Algebra, American government, American history, art, Bible, biology, biology-AP, calculus-AP, chemistry, chemistry-AP, choir, computer skills, computer technologies, creative writing, drama, economics, English, English language and composition-AP, English literature and composition-AP, English literature-AP, English/composition-AP, film, fine arts, French, geometry, health, literature, media, music theory-AP, physical education, physical science, physics, psychology, publications, science, social studies, Spanish, speech, trigonometry, U.S. history, weightlifting, world history, yearbook.
Graduation Requirements Algebra, American government, American literature, biology, British literature, consumer economics, electives, English composition, English literature, geometry, literary genres, literature, physical education (includes health), physical science, practical arts, U.S. history, world history, 1 Year of Bible for every year attending: 9th Grade—Old Testament Survey, 10th Grade—New Testament Survey, 11th Grade—Life & Times of Christ/Marriage & Family, 12th Grade—Defending Your Faith/Understanding the Times.
Special Academic Programs Advanced Placement exam preparation; remedial reading and/or remedial writing; programs in general development for dyslexic students.
College Admission Counseling 57 students graduated in 2008; 55 went to college, including Corban College; George Fox University; University of Alaska Anchorage; University of Alaska Fairbanks; University of Idaho; Westmont College. Other: 2 went to work. Mean SAT critical reading: 551, mean SAT math: 512, mean SAT writing: 532, mean composite ACT: 25. 33% scored over 600 on SAT critical reading, 33% scored over 600 on SAT math, 37% scored over 600 on SAT writing.
Student Life Upper grades have specified standards of dress, student council, honor system. Discipline rests primarily with faculty.
Summer Programs Enrichment programs offered; session focuses on Science/Forensics; held on campus; accepts boys and girls; open to students from other schools. 30 students usually enrolled. 2009 schedule: June 15 to June 30.
Tuition and Aid Day student tuition: $6300. Tuition installment plan (monthly payment plans, individually arranged payment plans). Tuition reduction for siblings, need-based scholarship grants available. In 2008–09, 12% of upper-school students received aid. Total amount of financial aid awarded in 2008–09: $170,000.
Admissions Traditional secondary-level entrance grade is 9. For fall 2008, 54 students applied for upper-level admission, 44 were accepted, 44 enrolled. Stanford Achievement Test required. Deadline for receipt of application materials: none. Application fee required: $50. Interview required.
Athletics Interscholastic: basketball (boys, girls), cheering (g), cross-country running (b,g), skiing (cross-country) (b,g), soccer (b,g), track and field (b,g), volleyball (g), wrestling (b). 2 PE instructors, 8 coaches.
Computers Computers are regularly used in career exploration, computer applications, French, media, publications, technology, yearbook classes. Computer network features include on-campus library services, online commercial services, Internet access.
Contact Darlene Kuiper, Admissions. 907-345-4814. Fax: 907-644-2260. E-mail: admissions@gracechristianalaska.org. Web site: www.gracechristianalaska.org.

THE GRAND RIVER ACADEMY

3042 College Street
Austinburg, Ohio 44010

Head of School: Randy Blum

General Information Boys' boarding college-preparatory, arts, and ESL school; primarily serves underachievers. Grades 9–PG. Founded: 1831. Setting: rural. Nearest major city is Cleveland. Students are housed in single-sex dormitories. 200-acre campus. 11 buildings on campus. Approved or accredited by Independent Schools Association of the Central States, Midwest Association of Boarding Schools, North Central Association of Colleges and Schools, The Association of Boarding Schools, and Ohio Department of Education. Member of National Association of Independent Schools. Endowment: $23 million. Total enrollment: 111. Upper school average class size: 7. Upper school faculty-student ratio: 1:6.
Upper School Student Profile Grade 9: 7 students (7 boys); Grade 10: 30 students (30 boys); Grade 11: 38 students (38 boys); Grade 12: 36 students (36 boys). 100% of students are boarding students. 30% are state residents. 18 states are represented in upper school student body. 16% are international students. International students from Canada, China, Guatemala, Republic of Korea, Spain, and Thailand.
Faculty School total: 24. In upper school: 17 men, 7 women; 12 have advanced degrees; 21 reside on campus.
Subjects Offered Advanced Placement courses, algebra, American history, American literature, art, biology, British literature (honors), calculus, calculus-AP, chemistry, civics, college writing, community service, computer applications, computer keyboarding, computer science, creative writing, digital photography, driver education, economics, English, English literature, environmental science, ESL, fine arts, French, geography, government, grammar, health, history, integrated science, lab science, mathematics, photography, physical education, physics, physics-AP, precalculus, psychology, public speaking, science, social studies, Spanish, speech, TOEFL preparation, Web site design, world history, world literature, writing.
Graduation Requirements Arts and fine arts (art, music, dance, drama), computer science, English, mathematics, physical education (includes health), science, social studies (includes history), acceptance at a college, passage of Ohio state-mandated proficiency tests. Community service is required.
Special Academic Programs Advanced Placement exam preparation; honors section; study at local college for college credit; remedial reading and/or remedial writing; special instructional classes for students with Attention Deficit Disorder; ESL (18 students enrolled).
College Admission Counseling 33 students graduated in 2008; all went to college, including Baldwin-Wallace College; Case Western Reserve University; Eastern Michigan University; John Carroll University; Penn State Erie, The Behrend College; Penn State University Park.
Student Life Upper grades have specified standards of dress, student council, honor system. Discipline rests primarily with faculty.
Summer Programs Remediation, enrichment, advancement, ESL, sports, art/fine arts, computer instruction programs offered; session focuses on ESL, enrichment, and remediation; held on campus; accepts boys and girls; open to students from other schools. 40 students usually enrolled. 2009 schedule: June 28 to August 8. Application deadline: June 22.
Tuition and Aid 5-day tuition and room/board: $29,250; 7-day tuition and room/board: $30,500. Tuition installment plan (Key Tuition Payment Plan). Merit scholarship grants, need-based scholarship grants, prepGATE Loans, PLATO Junior Loans available. In 2008–09, 10% of upper-school students received aid; total upper-school merit-scholarship money awarded: $49,000. Total amount of financial aid awarded in 2008–09: $110,000.
Admissions Traditional secondary-level entrance grade is 10. For fall 2008, 68 students applied for upper-level admission, 59 were accepted, 46 enrolled. Deadline for receipt of application materials: none. Application fee required: $35. On-campus interview required.
Athletics Interscholastic: baseball, basketball, cross-country running, golf, horseback riding, ice hockey, independent competitive sports, indoor soccer, soccer, swimming and diving, tennis, wrestling; intramural: backpacking, badminton, baseball, basketball, bicycling, billiards, bocce, bowling, canoeing/kayaking, equestrian sports, fishing, fitness, fitness walking, flag football, fly fishing, football, freestyle skiing, Frisbee, golf, hiking/backpacking, horseback riding, horseshoes, ice hockey, jogging, martial arts, mountain biking, Nautilus, outdoor activities, outdoor recreation, outdoor skills, paddle tennis, paint ball, physical fitness, physical training, power lifting, rafting, roller blading, roller skating, ropes courses, running, self defense, skateboarding, skiing (cross-country), skiing (downhill), snowboarding, soccer, softball, strength & conditioning, table tennis, tennis, touch football, ultimate Frisbee, volleyball, walking, weight lifting, weight training, whiffle ball, wrestling. 1 PE instructor.
Computers Computers are regularly used in English, ESL, foreign language, history, mathematics, science classes. Computer resources include on-campus library services, online commercial services, Internet access, wireless campus network, Internet filtering or blocking technology, mobile learning lab, classrooms linked to T-1, SmartBoards technology. Student e-mail accounts are available to students. Students grades are available online.
Contact Sam Corabi, Director of Admission. 440-275-2811 Ext. 25. Fax: 440-275-1825. E-mail: admissions@grandriver.org. Web site: www.grandriver.org.

THE GRAUER SCHOOL

1500 South El Camino Real
Encinitas, California 92024

Head of School: Dr. Stuart Robert Grauer, EdD

General Information Coeducational day and distance learning college-preparatory, arts, and technology school. Grades 6–12. Distance learning grades 9–12. Founded: 1991. Setting: suburban. Nearest major city is San Diego. 5-acre campus. 6 buildings on campus. Approved or accredited by California Association of Independent Schools, Western Association of Schools and Colleges, and California Department of Education. Endowment: $150,000. Total enrollment: 150. Upper school average class size: 12. Upper school faculty-student ratio: 1:7.
Upper School Student Profile Grade 6: 13 students (6 boys, 7 girls); Grade 7: 25 students (12 boys, 13 girls); Grade 8: 25 students (11 boys, 14 girls); Grade 9: 23 students (13 boys, 10 girls); Grade 10: 22 students (12 boys, 10 girls); Grade 11: 12 students (9 boys, 3 girls); Grade 12: 15 students (7 boys, 8 girls); Postgraduate: 2 students (1 boy, 1 girl).
Faculty School total: 30. In upper school: 13 men, 17 women; 6 have advanced degrees.
Subjects Offered ACT preparation, advanced biology, advanced chemistry, advanced math, advanced TOEFL/grammar, African dance, algebra, alternative physical education, American government, American history, anatomy and physiology, ancient history, applied music, art, art appreciation, art history, art history-AP, ASB Leadership, athletic training, audio visual/media, backpacking, baseball, basketball, bell choir, biology, business mathematics, calculus, character education, chemistry, Chinese, choir, civics, classical music, college admission preparation, college planning, community service, computer applications, computer education, computer keyboarding, computer multimedia, computers, creative writing, culinary

arts, drama, dramatic arts, earth and space science, economics, English literature, environmental education, ESL, ESL, experiential education, fencing, fitness, French, gardening, geography, geometry, global studies, health, high adventure outdoor program, honors algebra, honors English, honors geometry, honors U.S. history, honors world history, Japanese, Latin, leadership and service, marine science, multimedia, music, music appreciation, music performance, outdoor education, peace studies, personal fitness, photography, physical education, physics, pre-algebra, pre-calculus, religion, religion and culture, SAT preparation, Spanish, speech and debate, studio art, study skills, surfing, tennis, theater arts, trigonometry, U.S. government, U.S. history, U.S. literature, world geography, world history, world religions.

Graduation Requirements American history, art, biology, chemistry, college admission preparation, computer applications, computer skills, economics, English, experiential education, foreign language, French, geometry, life science, marine science, mathematics, non-Western literature, outdoor education, physical education (includes health), physical science, physics, pre-algebra, science, social studies (includes history), studio art, U.S. government, U.S. history, U.S. literature, Western civilization, Western literature, wilderness/outdoor program, world geography, world history, world literature, world religions, Expeditionary learning in the field and 50 hours community service.

Special Academic Programs Advanced Placement exam preparation; honors section; accelerated programs; independent study; study abroad; academic accommodation for the gifted, the musically talented, and the artistically talented; remedial math; special instructional classes for deaf students; ESL (2 students enrolled).

College Admission Counseling 16 students graduated in 2008; all went to college, including California Polytechnic State University, San Luis Obispo; University of California, Berkeley; University of California, Los Angeles; University of Minnesota, Twin Cities Campus; University of San Diego. Median SAT critical reading: 650, median SAT math: 500, median SAT writing: 600. 60% scored over 600 on SAT critical reading, 60% scored over 600 on SAT math.

Student Life Upper grades have specified standards of dress, student council, honor system. Discipline rests equally with students and faculty.

Summer Programs Remediation, enrichment, advancement, ESL, art/fine arts, computer instruction programs offered; session focuses on academics and enrichment; held on campus; accepts boys and girls; open to students from other schools. 60 students usually enrolled. 2009 schedule: June 23 to August 3. Application deadline: June 18.

Tuition and Aid Day student tuition: $18,000. Tuition installment plan (individually arranged payment plans, 3 payment plans). Tuition reduction for siblings, merit scholarship grants, need-based scholarship grants available. In 2008–09, 7% of upper-school students received aid. Total amount of financial aid awarded in 2008–09: $50,000.

Admissions Traditional secondary-level entrance grade is 9. For fall 2008, 103 students applied for upper-level admission, 26 were accepted, 15 enrolled. ISEE and Stanford 9 required. Deadline for receipt of application materials: February 15. Application fee required: $100. On-campus interview required.

Athletics Interscholastic: aerobics (boys, girls), aerobics/dance (b,g), badminton (b,g), baseball (b), basketball (b), fencing (b,g), fitness (b,g); intramural: equestrian sports (b,g), figure skating (b,g), flagball (b,g), ice hockey (b,g); coed interscholastic: cross-country running, soccer; coed intramural: aerobics, alpine skiing, backpacking, ball hockey, basketball, bocce, bowling, canoeing/kayaking, climbing, cross-country running, fitness, fitness walking, flag football, football, golf, hiking/backpacking, independent competitive sports, jogging, outdoor education, physical fitness, soccer, surfing. 4 PE instructors, 2 coaches, 1 athletic trainer.

Computers Computers are regularly used in ESL, foreign language, graphic arts, journalism, keyboarding, multimedia, SAT preparation, yearbook classes. Computer network features include Internet access, wireless campus network, Internet filtering or blocking technology. Campus intranet is available to students. Students grades are available online. The school has a published electronic and media policy.

Contact Mrs. Elizabeth Braymen, JD, Admissions Coordinator. 760-274-2116. Fax: 760-944-6784. E-mail: admissions@grauerschool.com. Web site: www.grauerschool.com.

GREATER ATLANTA CHRISTIAN SCHOOLS

1575 Indian Trail Road
Norcross, Georgia 30093

Head of School: Dr. David Fincher

General Information Coeducational day college-preparatory, arts, religious studies, and technology school. Grades P4–12. Founded: 1961. Setting: suburban. Nearest major city is Atlanta. 74-acre campus. 18 buildings on campus. Approved or accredited by Georgia Independent School Association, National Christian School Association, Southern Association of Colleges and Schools, Southern Association of Independent Schools, The College Board, and Georgia Department of Education. Endowment: $28.5 million. Total enrollment: 1,965. Upper school average class size: 16. Upper school faculty-student ratio: 1:13.

Upper School Student Profile Grade 9: 185 students (100 boys, 85 girls); Grade 10: 163 students (87 boys, 76 girls); Grade 11: 162 students (72 boys, 90 girls); Grade 12: 153 students (79 boys, 74 girls).

Faculty School total: 151. In upper school: 31 men, 28 women; 41 have advanced degrees.

Subjects Offered 3-dimensional art, accounting, Advanced Placement courses, algebra, American history-AP, American literature, analysis, anatomy, art appreciation, art history, art-AP, audio visual/media, band, Bible, biology-AP, British literature, business, calculus-AP, chemistry-AP, chorus, composition, computer applications, computer math, computer programming, computer science-AP, dramatic arts, economics-AP, English language and composition-AP, environmental science, ethics, European history, European history-AP, expository writing, French, geometry, government-AP, graphic design, home economics, honors English, journalism, language arts, Latin, music theory-AP, music-AP, newspaper, orchestra, painting, personal finance, philosophy, photography, physics-AP, physiology, pre-calculus, psychology-AP, religion, sculpture, sociology, Spanish, speech, speech communications, statistics, statistics-AP, studio art-AP, symphonic band, theology, trigonometry, U.S. history-AP, video film production, visual arts, Web site design, world history-AP, world literature, yearbook.

Graduation Requirements Computer science, English, foreign language, mathematics, physical education (includes health), religious studies, science, social science, social studies (includes history), one year of Bible for each year of attendance.

Special Academic Programs Advanced Placement exam preparation; honors section; study abroad; academic accommodation for the gifted, the musically talented, and the artistically talented.

College Admission Counseling 138 students graduated in 2008; all went to college, including Georgia Institute of Technology; Lipscomb University; The University of Alabama; University of Georgia; Valdosta State University. Median SAT critical reading: 584, median SAT math: 589, median SAT writing: 576, median combined SAT: 1749, median composite ACT: 25.

Student Life Upper grades have uniform requirement, student council, honor system. Discipline rests primarily with faculty. Attendance at religious services is required.

Tuition and Aid Day student tuition: $11,320–$12,950. Tuition installment plan (monthly payment plans, quarterly payment plan). Need-based scholarship grants available.

Admissions Traditional secondary-level entrance grade is 9. For fall 2008, 65 students applied for upper-level admission, 53 were accepted, 51 enrolled. CTBS/4 or SSAT required. Deadline for receipt of application materials: none. Application fee required: $160. On-campus interview required.

Athletics Interscholastic: baseball (boys), cheering (g), dance team (g), flag football (b), football (b), golf (b,g), lacrosse (b,g), soccer (b,g), softball (g), swimming and diving (b,g), tennis (b,g), volleyball (g), weight lifting (b), weight training (b), wrestling (b); intramural: aerobics (g), physical fitness (b,g), strength & conditioning (b,g); coed interscholastic: aquatics, basketball, cross-country running, diving, track and field. 5 PE instructors, 1 athletic trainer.

Computers Computers are regularly used in college planning classes. Computer network features include on-campus library services, online commercial services, Internet access, wireless campus network, Internet filtering or blocking technology. Students grades are available online. The school has a published electronic and media policy.

Contact Mrs. Linda Clovis, Director of Admissions. 770-243-2274. Fax: 770-243-2213. E-mail: lclovis@greateratlantachristian.org. Web site: www.greateratlantachristian.org.

GREAT LAKES CHRISTIAN HIGH SCHOOL

4875 King Street
Beamsville, Ontario L0R 1B6, Canada

Head of School: Mr. Don Rose

General Information Coeducational boarding and day college-preparatory, general academic, and religious studies school, affiliated with Church of Christ. Grades 9–12. Founded: 1952. Setting: small town. Nearest major city is Hamilton, Canada. Students are housed in single-sex dormitories. 15-acre campus. 6 buildings on campus. Approved or accredited by Ontario Ministry of Education and Ontario Department of Education. Endowment: CAN$500,000. Total enrollment: 91. Upper school average class size: 22. Upper school faculty-student ratio: 1:9.

Upper School Student Profile Grade 9: 22 students (9 boys, 13 girls); Grade 10: 23 students (13 boys, 10 girls); Grade 11: 22 students (10 boys, 12 girls); Grade 12: 25 students (13 boys, 12 girls). 55% of students are boarding students. 65% are province residents. 5 provinces are represented in upper school student body. 25% are international students. International students from China, Hong Kong, Japan, Republic of Korea, Taiwan, and United States. 40% of students are members of Church of Christ.

Faculty School total: 11. In upper school: 7 men, 4 women; 4 have advanced degrees; 3 reside on campus.

Subjects Offered 20th century world history, accounting, algebra, arts appreciation, Bible, biology, calculus, career and personal planning, chemistry, computer science, computer technologies, dramatic arts, economics, English, English composition, English language and composition-AP, English literature, English-AP, ESL, family studies, finite math, French, geography, history, mathematics, mathematics-AP, media, music, music composition, physical education, physics, society, technology, world issues.

Graduation Requirements 20th century history, advanced math, art, Bible, business, Canadian geography, Canadian history, Canadian literature, career planning, civics, computer information systems, conceptual physics, critical thinking, current events, economics, English, English composition, English literature, French as a

second language, geography, mathematics, physical education (includes health), science, society challenge and change, world geography, world history.
Special Academic Programs ESL (13 students enrolled).
College Admission Counseling 23 students graduated in 2008; 17 went to college, including Brock University; Carleton University; McMaster University; University of Toronto; Wilfrid Laurier University; York University. Other: 6 went to work.
Student Life Upper grades have uniform requirement, student council. Discipline rests primarily with faculty. Attendance at religious services is required.
Tuition and Aid Day student tuition: CAN$6800; 5-day tuition and room/board: CAN$11,700; 7-day tuition and room/board: CAN$13,300. Tuition installment plan (monthly payment plans, individually arranged payment plans). Tuition reduction for siblings, bursaries, merit scholarship grants, need-based scholarship grants, need-based loans, middle-income loans, paying campus jobs available. In 2008–09, 40% of upper-school students received aid; total upper-school merit-scholarship money awarded: CAN$12,000. Total amount of financial aid awarded in 2008–09: CAN$100,000.
Admissions Traditional secondary-level entrance grade is 9. SLEP required. Deadline for receipt of application materials: none. Application fee required: CAN$150. Interview recommended.
Athletics Interscholastic: badminton (boys, girls), basketball (b,g), cross-country running (b,g), golf (b), hockey (b,g), ice hockey (b,g), soccer (b,g), track and field (b,g), volleyball (b,g); intramural: aerobics (g), badminton (b,g), basketball (b,g), cooperative games (b,g), fitness (b,g), volleyball (b,g); coed interscholastic: badminton; coed intramural: badminton, ball hockey, baseball, basketball, cooperative games, floor hockey, hockey, volleyball. 2 PE instructors, 2 coaches.
Computers Computers are regularly used in accounting, business, music, technology, typing classes. Computer network features include Internet access, Internet filtering or blocking technology. Computer access in designated common areas is available to students.
Contact Mr. Tim E. Alexander, Director of Admissions. 905-563-5374 Ext. 212. Fax: 905-563-0818. E-mail: study@glchs.on.ca. Web site: www.glchs.on.ca.

GREENFIELD SCHOOL

PO Box 3525
Wilson, North Carolina 27895-3525

Head of School: Janet B. Beaman

General Information Coeducational day college-preparatory school. Grades PS–12. Founded: 1969. Setting: small town. Nearest major city is Raleigh. 61-acre campus. 9 buildings on campus. Approved or accredited by North Carolina Association of Independent Schools, Southern Association of Colleges and Schools, and North Carolina Department of Education. Member of National Association of Independent Schools. Total enrollment: 331. Upper school average class size: 17. Upper school faculty-student ratio: 1:3.
Upper School Student Profile Grade 9: 15 students (11 boys, 4 girls); Grade 10: 18 students (10 boys, 8 girls); Grade 11: 23 students (10 boys, 13 girls); Grade 12: 12 students (4 boys, 8 girls).
Faculty In upper school: 8 men, 16 women; 8 have advanced degrees.
Subjects Offered Advanced computer applications, advanced math, Advanced Placement courses, algebra, American history, American literature, ancient world history, anthropology, art, athletics, biology, British literature, calculus, calculus-AP, chemistry, chorus, college awareness, community service, computer applications, computer education, computer graphics, computer information systems, computer keyboarding, computer math, computer multimedia, computer processing, computer programming, computer programming-AP, computer science, computer skills, computer technologies, desktop publishing, drama, earth science, economics, electives, English, English literature, fine arts, foreign language, geography, geometry, government/civics, grammar, health, history, honors algebra, honors English, honors geometry, honors world history, keyboarding/computer, language arts, mathematics, music, physical education, physical science, physics, pre-algebra, pre-calculus, SAT preparation, science, social studies, sociology, Spanish, sports conditioning, trigonometry, Web site design, world geography, world history, writing, yearbook.
Graduation Requirements Arts and fine arts (art, music, dance, drama), computer science, English, foreign language, mathematics, physical education (includes health), science, social studies (includes history). Community service is required.
Special Academic Programs Advanced Placement exam preparation; honors section; independent study; study at local college for college credit; academic accommodation for the gifted; remedial reading and/or remedial writing; remedial math; programs in English, general development for dyslexic students.
College Admission Counseling 18 students graduated in 2008; all went to college, including College of Charleston; Hampden-Sydney College; North Carolina State University; Parsons The New School for Design; The University of North Carolina at Chapel Hill; The University of North Carolina Wilmington. Median SAT critical reading: 520, median SAT math: 590, median SAT writing: 550, median combined SAT: 1720, median composite ACT: 29. 21% scored over 600 on SAT critical reading, 37% scored over 600 on SAT math, 37% scored over 600 on SAT writing, 26% scored over 1800 on combined SAT, 80% scored over 26 on composite ACT.
Student Life Upper grades have specified standards of dress, student council, honor system. Discipline rests primarily with faculty.
Summer Programs Enrichment, sports, art/fine arts, computer instruction programs offered; session focuses on academic enrichment, athletic development, and relaxation; held on campus; accepts boys and girls; open to students from other schools. 300 students usually enrolled. 2009 schedule: June 1 to August 7. Application deadline: none.
Tuition and Aid Day student tuition: $7775. Tuition installment plan (monthly payment plans). Tuition reduction for siblings, merit scholarship grants, need-based scholarship grants available.
Admissions Traditional secondary-level entrance grade is 9. For fall 2008, 13 students applied for upper-level admission, 7 were accepted, 5 enrolled. Comprehensive Test of Basic Skills or CTP III required. Deadline for receipt of application materials: none. Application fee required: $100. On-campus interview required.
Athletics Interscholastic: baseball (boys), basketball (b,g), cheering (g), soccer (b,g), tennis (b,g), volleyball (g); coed interscholastic: golf. 3 PE instructors, 9 coaches.
Computers Computers are regularly used in all academic classes. Computer resources include on-campus library services, Internet access, Internet filtering or blocking technology. Computer access in designated common areas is available to students. The school has a published electronic and media policy.
Contact Diane Oliphant Hamilton, Director of Admissions/Community Relations. 252-237-8046. Fax: 252-237-1825. E-mail: hamiltond@greenfieldschool.org. Web site: www.greenfieldschool.org.

GREEN FIELDS COUNTRY DAY SCHOOL

6000 North Camino de la Tierra
Tucson, Arizona 85741

Head of School: Deac Etherington

General Information Coeducational day college-preparatory, arts, and technology school. Grades K–12. Founded: 1933. Setting: suburban. 22-acre campus. 15 buildings on campus. Approved or accredited by Arizona Association of Independent Schools, Missouri Independent School Association, and North Central Association of Colleges and Schools. Member of National Association of Independent Schools. Endowment: $1.2 million. Total enrollment: 187. Upper school average class size: 12. Upper school faculty-student ratio: 1:4.
Upper School Student Profile Grade 9: 16 students (8 boys, 8 girls); Grade 10: 23 students (11 boys, 12 girls); Grade 11: 15 students (6 boys, 9 girls); Grade 12: 12 students (7 boys, 5 girls).
Faculty School total: 29. In upper school: 9 men, 9 women; 12 have advanced degrees.
Subjects Offered 3-dimensional art, advanced chemistry, advanced computer applications, advanced math, Advanced Placement courses, advanced studio art-AP, algebra, American government, American government-AP, American history, American history-AP, American literature, anatomy and physiology, art, art-AP, Basic programming, biology, biology-AP, British literature (honors), British literature-AP, calculus, calculus-AP, ceramics, chemistry, chorus, college placement, computer programming, computer science, conceptual physics, drama, drama performance, English, environmental science-AP, European history, European history-AP, expository writing, fine arts, French, French language-AP, French literature-AP, French-AP, geography, geometry, government and politics-AP, government-AP, independent study, journalism, music theory, musical theater, newspaper, physical education, physics, political science, pre-calculus, probability and statistics, social studies, Spanish, Spanish-AP, studio art—AP, trigonometry, U.S. government and politics-AP, U.S. history-AP, Web site design, world history, writing, yearbook.
Graduation Requirements Advanced math, algebra, American history, American literature, arts and fine arts (art, music, dance, drama), biology, chemistry, computer skills, electives, English, English literature, foreign language, geometry, mathematics, physical education (includes health), science, social studies (includes history), world history, writing.
Special Academic Programs Advanced Placement exam preparation; independent study.
College Admission Counseling 12 students graduated in 2008; all went to college, including California Institute of Technology; Colgate University; Connecticut College; Grinnell College; Northern Arizona University; The University of Arizona. Median SAT critical reading: 630, median SAT math: 620. Mean composite ACT: 25.
Student Life Upper grades have specified standards of dress, student council, honor system. Discipline rests primarily with faculty.
Summer Programs Sports programs offered; session focuses on basketball and volleyball; held on campus; accepts boys and girls; open to students from other schools.
Tuition and Aid Day student tuition: $14,200. Tuition installment plan (FACTS Tuition Payment Plan, semester payment plan). Merit scholarship grants, need-based scholarship grants available. In 2008–09, 25% of upper-school students received aid; total upper-school merit-scholarship money awarded: $20,317. Total amount of financial aid awarded in 2008–09: $187,987.
Admissions Traditional secondary-level entrance grade is 9. Achievement tests or Achievement/Aptitude/Writing required. Deadline for receipt of application materials: none. Application fee required: $35. On-campus interview recommended.
Athletics Interscholastic: baseball (boys), basketball (b,g), softball (g), volleyball (g); coed interscholastic: physical fitness, physical training, soccer, track and field; coed intramural: climbing, outdoor adventure, outdoor skills, rock climbing, tennis, wall climbing. 2 PE instructors, 8 coaches.
Computers Computers are regularly used in English, mathematics, newspaper, science, yearbook classes. Computer resources include on-campus library services,

online commercial services, Internet access, Internet filtering or blocking technology. Computer access in designated common areas is available to students. The school has a published electronic and media policy.
Contact Carole Knapp, Director of Admission. 520-297-2288 Ext. 105. Fax: 520-297-2072. E-mail: admissions@greenfields.org. Web site: www.greenfields.org.

GREENHILL SCHOOL

4141 Spring Valley Road
Addison, Texas 75001
Head of School: Scott A. Griggs

General Information Coeducational day college-preparatory school. Grades PK–12. Founded: 1950. Setting: suburban. Nearest major city is Dallas. 78-acre campus. 8 buildings on campus. Approved or accredited by Independent Schools Association of the Southwest and Texas Department of Education. Member of National Association of Independent Schools and Secondary School Admission Test Board. Endowment: $22 million. Total enrollment: 1,243. Upper school average class size: 18. Upper school faculty-student ratio: 1:18.
Upper School Student Profile Grade 9: 114 students (57 boys, 57 girls); Grade 10: 108 students (52 boys, 56 girls); Grade 11: 104 students (45 boys, 59 girls); Grade 12: 106 students (49 boys, 57 girls).
Faculty School total: 138. In upper school: 29 men, 20 women.
Subjects Offered Algebra, American history, American literature, art, art history, biology, calculus, ceramics, chemistry, computer math, computer programming, computer science, creative writing, dance, drama, ecology, economics, English, English literature, European history, expository writing, fine arts, French, geometry, government/civics, grammar, health, history, journalism, Latin, Mandarin, mathematics, music, philosophy, photography, physical education, physics, science, social studies, Spanish, speech, theater, trigonometry, world history, world literature, writing.
Graduation Requirements Arts and fine arts (art, music, dance, drama), classical language, computer studies, English, history, mathematics, modern languages, physical education (includes health), science. Community service is required.
Special Academic Programs Advanced Placement exam preparation; honors section; independent study.
College Admission Counseling 107 students graduated in 2008; all went to college, including Columbia University; Southern Methodist University; Tufts University; University of Colorado at Boulder; University of Southern California; Yale University. Mean SAT critical reading: 636, mean SAT math: 648, mean SAT writing: 630.
Student Life Upper grades have specified standards of dress, student council, honor system. Discipline rests primarily with faculty.
Summer Programs Enrichment, sports, art/fine arts, computer instruction programs offered; session focuses on enrichment and sports; held on campus; accepts boys and girls; open to students from other schools. 1,230 students usually enrolled. 2009 schedule: June 8 to August 14. Application deadline: none.
Tuition and Aid Day student tuition: $21,050. Need-based scholarship grants available. In 2008–09, 17% of upper-school students received aid. Total amount of financial aid awarded in 2008–09: $1,036,200.
Admissions Traditional secondary-level entrance grade is 9. For fall 2008, 156 students applied for upper-level admission, 57 were accepted, 35 enrolled. ISEE required. Deadline for receipt of application materials: January 9. Application fee required: $175. Interview required.
Athletics Interscholastic: aquatics (boys, girls), baseball (b), basketball (b,g), cheering (g), field hockey (g), football (b), golf (b,g), lacrosse (b,g), rowing (b,g), running (b,g), soccer (b,g), softball (g), swimming and diving (b,g), tennis (b,g), track and field (b,g), ultimate Frisbee (b,g), volleyball (b,g), weight training (b,g), winter soccer (b,g); intramural: baseball (b), power lifting (b); coed interscholastic: cross-country running; coed intramural: aquatics, ballet, basketball, dance, fitness, Frisbee, physical fitness, strength & conditioning, table tennis, tai chi, ultimate Frisbee, water volleyball, weight lifting, weight training, yoga. 13 PE instructors, 14 coaches, 2 athletic trainers.
Computers Computers are regularly used in English, mathematics, science classes. Computer network features include on-campus library services, online commercial services, Internet access, wireless campus network, Internet filtering or blocking technology. Campus intranet, student e-mail accounts, and computer access in designated common areas are available to students. Students grades are available online. The school has a published electronic and media policy.
Contact Angela H. Woodson, Director of Admission. 972-628-5910. Fax: 972-404-8217. E-mail: admission@greenhill.org. Web site: www.greenhill.org.

GREENHILLS SCHOOL

850 Greenhills Drive
Ann Arbor, Michigan 48105
Head of School: Peter B. Fayroian

General Information Coeducational day college-preparatory and arts school. Grades 6–12. Founded: 1968. Setting: suburban. Nearest major city is Detroit. 30-acre campus. 1 building on campus. Approved or accredited by Independent Schools Association of the Central States and Michigan Department of Education. Member of National Association of Independent Schools and Secondary School Admission Test Board. Endowment: $8 million. Total enrollment: 538. Upper school average class size: 15. Upper school faculty-student ratio: 1:7.
Upper School Student Profile Grade 9: 84 students (30 boys, 54 girls); Grade 10: 83 students (32 boys, 51 girls); Grade 11: 85 students (41 boys, 44 girls); Grade 12: 88 students (44 boys, 44 girls).
Faculty School total: 70. In upper school: 17 men, 18 women; 35 have advanced degrees.
Subjects Offered 3-dimensional art, advanced chemistry, Advanced Placement courses, African-American literature, algebra, American history, American literature, ancient history, art, astronomy, biology, calculus, calculus-AP, ceramics, chemistry, Chinese, Chinese studies, chorus, community service, creative writing, discrete math, drama, drawing, economics, economics and history, English, English literature, ethics, European history, expository writing, fine arts, French, geometry, government, health, history, jazz, journalism, Latin, mathematics, music, orchestra, painting, photography, physical education, physical science, physics, science, social studies, Spanish, theater, trigonometry, world history, world literature, writing.
Graduation Requirements Arts and fine arts (art, music, dance, drama), English, foreign language, mathematics, physical education (includes health), science, social studies (includes history), Senior Project. Community service is required.
Special Academic Programs Advanced Placement exam preparation; honors section; independent study; academic accommodation for the gifted; programs in English, mathematics for dyslexic students; special instructional classes for blind students.
College Admission Counseling 68 students graduated in 2008; all went to college, including Pomona College; Princeton University; University of Michigan; Wesleyan University; Yale University. Median SAT critical reading: 655, median SAT math: 667, median combined SAT: 1322, median composite ACT: 29.
Student Life Upper grades have specified standards of dress, student council, honor system. Discipline rests equally with students and faculty.
Summer Programs Enrichment, sports, art/fine arts programs offered; session focuses on enrichment, academics, travel; held on campus; accepts boys and girls; open to students from other schools. 30 students usually enrolled. 2009 schedule: July 1 to July 30. Application deadline: none.
Tuition and Aid Day student tuition: $17,180. Tuition installment plan (FACTS Tuition Payment Plan). Need-based scholarship grants available. In 2008–09, 20% of upper-school students received aid. Total amount of financial aid awarded in 2008–09: $642,460.
Admissions Traditional secondary-level entrance grade is 9. For fall 2008, 82 students applied for upper-level admission, 36 were accepted, 30 enrolled. SSAT or TOEFL required. Deadline for receipt of application materials: January 25. Application fee required: $50. Interview required.
Athletics Interscholastic: baseball (boys), basketball (b,g), cross-country running (b,g), field hockey (g), golf (b,g), soccer (b,g), softball (g), tennis (b,g), track and field (b,g), volleyball (g); intramural: basketball (b,g), cross-country running (b,g), field hockey (g), soccer (b,g); coed interscholastic: equestrian sports, swimming and diving; coed intramural: hiking/backpacking, outdoor activities, outdoor education. 3 PE instructors, 1 athletic trainer.
Computers Computers are regularly used in all academic classes. Computer network features include on-campus library services, online commercial services, Internet access, Internet filtering or blocking technology. Campus intranet and computer access in designated common areas are available to students. Students grades are available online. The school has a published electronic and media policy.
Contact Betsy Ellsworth, Director of Admission and Financial Aid. 734-205-4061. Fax: 734-205-4056. E-mail: admission@greenhillsschool.org. Web site: www.greenhillsschool.org.

GREENLEAF ACADEMY

PO Box 368
Greenleaf, Idaho 83626
Head of School: Mr. Kenneth Sheldon

General Information Coeducational day college-preparatory, arts, religious studies, and technology school, affiliated with Evangelical Friends. Grades K–12. Founded: 1908. Setting: rural. Nearest major city is Boise. 15-acre campus. 1 building on campus. Approved or accredited by Association of Christian Schools International, Northwest Association of Schools and Colleges, and Idaho Department of Education. Endowment: $500,000. Total enrollment: 221. Upper school average class size: 20. Upper school faculty-student ratio: 1:16.
Upper School Student Profile Grade 9: 23 students (10 boys, 13 girls); Grade 10: 17 students (10 boys, 7 girls); Grade 11: 24 students (15 boys, 9 girls); Grade 12: 30 students (17 boys, 13 girls). 20% of students are Evangelical Friends.
Faculty School total: 22. In upper school: 5 men, 11 women; 3 have advanced degrees.
Subjects Offered Accounting, algebra, American history, art, band, Bible studies, biology, calculus, chemistry, chorus, computer science, economics, English, geography, geometry, government/civics, humanities, instrumental music, music, philosophy, physical education, physics, political science, Spanish, speech, trigonometry, weight training, word processing, world history, yearbook.
Graduation Requirements Arts and fine arts (art, music, dance, drama), business skills (includes word processing), computer science, English, foreign language,

mathematics, physical education (includes health), religion (includes Bible studies and theology), science, social science, social studies (includes history), speech. Community service is required.
Special Academic Programs Independent study; study at local college for college credit; programs in English, mathematics, general development for dyslexic students.
College Admission Counseling 25 students graduated in 2008; 22 went to college, including Boise State University; George Fox University; Northwest Nazarene University; The College of Idaho; Washington State University. Other: 3 went to work. Median SAT critical reading: 440, median SAT math: 390, median SAT writing: 300, median combined SAT: 980, median composite ACT: 20. 5% scored over 600 on SAT critical reading, 2% scored over 600 on SAT math, 5% scored over 600 on SAT writing.
Student Life Upper grades have specified standards of dress, student council, honor system. Discipline rests primarily with faculty. Attendance at religious services is required.
Summer Programs Sports programs offered; session focuses on summer basketball league; held on campus; accepts boys and girls; open to students from other schools. 20 students usually enrolled. 2009 schedule: June 1 to June 30. Application deadline: May 30.
Tuition and Aid Day student tuition: $4175. Tuition installment plan (monthly payment plans). Tuition reduction for siblings, need-based scholarship grants available. In 2008–09, 12% of upper-school students received aid. Total amount of financial aid awarded in 2008–09: $55,000.
Admissions Traditional secondary-level entrance grade is 9. For fall 2008, 15 students applied for upper-level admission, 15 were accepted, 15 enrolled. Deadline for receipt of application materials: none. Application fee required: $100. Interview required.
Athletics Interscholastic: baseball (boys), basketball (b,g), cheering (g), cross-country running (b,g), football (b), physical training (b,g), softball (g), strength & conditioning (b,g), track and field (b,g), volleyball (g), weight training (b,g); coed interscholastic: aerobics, fitness. 2 PE instructors, 5 coaches.
Computers Computers are regularly used in English, foreign language, history, mathematics, music, science classes. Computer network features include on-campus library services, online commercial services, Internet access, Internet filtering or blocking technology. Students grades are available online. The school has a published electronic and media policy.
Contact Mrs. Debbie Johnson, Office Manager/Secretary. 208-459-6346. Fax: 208-459-7700. E-mail: gfa@cableone.net. Web site: www.greenleafacademy.org.

GREEN MEADOW WALDORF SCHOOL

307 Hungry Hollow Road
Chestnut Ridge, New York 10977

Head of School: Kay Hoffman

General Information Coeducational day college-preparatory, general academic, and arts school. Grades N–12. Founded: 1950. Setting: suburban. Nearest major city is New York. 11-acre campus. 3 buildings on campus. Approved or accredited by Association of Waldorf Schools of North America, New York State Association of Independent Schools, and New York Department of Education. Total enrollment: 375. Upper school average class size: 28. Upper school faculty-student ratio: 1:9.
Upper School Student Profile Grade 9: 24 students (10 boys, 14 girls); Grade 10: 29 students (10 boys, 19 girls); Grade 11: 15 students (9 boys, 6 girls); Grade 12: 16 students (5 boys, 11 girls).
Faculty School total: 60. In upper school: 10 men, 9 women; 11 have advanced degrees.
Subjects Offered Algebra, American history, American literature, anatomy, architecture, art, art history, arts, batik, Bible studies, biology, botany, calculus, chemistry, computer math, computer science, creative writing, dance, drama, driver education, earth science, English, English literature, ethics, European history, expository writing, fine arts, French, geography, geology, geometry, German, government/civics, grammar, health, history, history of ideas, history of science, logic, marine biology, mathematics, music, orchestra, philosophy, physical education, physics, physiology, poetry, Russian literature, science, sculpture, social studies, Spanish, speech, theater, trigonometry, woodworking, world history, world literature, writing, zoology.
Graduation Requirements Arts and fine arts (art, music, dance, drama), English, foreign language, mathematics, physical education (includes health), science, social studies (includes history).
Special Academic Programs Honors section; independent study; term-away projects; study abroad; remedial reading and/or remedial writing; remedial math; programs in English for dyslexic students; ESL (7 students enrolled).
College Admission Counseling 29 students graduated in 2008; 27 went to college, including Bryn Mawr College; Loyola Marymount University; New York University; Parsons The New School for Design; The College of New Jersey; Trinity College. Other: 2 had other specific plans. 31% scored over 600 on SAT critical reading, 27% scored over 600 on SAT math.
Student Life Upper grades have specified standards of dress, student council. Discipline rests primarily with faculty.
Tuition and Aid Day student tuition: $16,900–$17,750. Guaranteed tuition plan. Tuition installment plan (Insured Tuition Payment Plan, monthly payment plans). Need-based scholarship grants available.
Admissions Traditional secondary-level entrance grade is 9. Deadline for receipt of application materials: none. Application fee required: $50. On-campus interview required.
Athletics Interscholastic: baseball (boys), basketball (b,g), softball (g), tennis (g), volleyball (g); intramural: basketball (b,g); coed interscholastic: Circus, cross-country running, horseback riding, tennis, volleyball; coed intramural: volleyball. 2 PE instructors, 5 coaches.
Computers Computers are regularly used in mathematics classes. Computer resources include Internet access, Internet filtering or blocking technology. Computer access in designated common areas is available to students. The school has a published electronic and media policy.
Contact Patricia Owens, Enrollment Coordinator. 845-356-2514 Ext. 302. Fax: 845-371-2358. E-mail: powens@gmws.org. Web site: www.gmws.org.

GREENSBORO DAY SCHOOL

5401 Lawndale Drive
Greensboro, North Carolina 27455

Head of School: Mr. Mark C. Hale

General Information Coeducational day college-preparatory, arts, and technology school. Grades K–12. Founded: 1970. Setting: suburban. 65-acre campus. 10 buildings on campus. Approved or accredited by Southern Association of Colleges and Schools. Member of National Association of Independent Schools. Total enrollment: 903. Upper school average class size: 16. Upper school faculty-student ratio: 1:13.
Faculty School total: 120.
Subjects Offered Algebra, American government, American history, American literature, art, art appreciation, biology, biology-AP, calculus, calculus-AP, chemistry, chorus, college admission preparation, college counseling, college placement, computer programming, computer science-AP, creative writing, drama, economics, English, English language-AP, English literature, ESL, European history, European history-AP, fine arts, French, French language-AP, French literature-AP, geometry, government/civics, health, history, journalism, Latin, Latin-AP, mathematics, music, photography, physical education, physics, physics-AP, psychology, SAT preparation, science, social studies, Spanish, Spanish language-AP, Spanish literature-AP, sports medicine, statistics-AP, theater, trigonometry, U.S. history-AP, world history, writing, yearbook.
Graduation Requirements Arts and fine arts (art, music, dance, drama), English, foreign language, mathematics, physical education (includes health), science, social studies (includes history), senior project (four-week internship).
Special Academic Programs Advanced Placement exam preparation; honors section; independent study; term-away projects; study abroad; academic accommodation for the gifted and the artistically talented; special instructional classes for students with learning disabilities and Attention Deficit Disorder; ESL (11 students enrolled).
College Admission Counseling 84 students graduated in 2008; all went to college, including Duke University; The University of North Carolina at Chapel Hill; The University of North Carolina at Charlotte; The University of North Carolina Wilmington; Wake Forest University. Median SAT critical reading: 600, median SAT math: 610, median SAT writing: 600.
Student Life Upper grades have specified standards of dress, student council, honor system. Discipline rests equally with students and faculty.
Summer Programs Remediation, enrichment, advancement, sports, art/fine arts, computer instruction programs offered; session focuses on enrichment and camps; held on campus; accepts boys and girls; open to students from other schools. 600 students usually enrolled.
Tuition and Aid Day student tuition: $7565–$17,420. Tuition installment plan (FACTS Tuition Payment Plan, monthly payment plans, individually arranged payment plans). Need-based scholarship grants available.
Admissions Traditional secondary-level entrance grade is 9. ERB (CTP-Verbal, Quantitative) required. Deadline for receipt of application materials: none. Application fee required: $50. On-campus interview required.
Athletics Interscholastic: baseball (boys), basketball (b,g), cheering (g), cross-country running (b,g), field hockey (g), golf (b), lacrosse (b,g), soccer (b,g), swimming and diving (b,g), tennis (b,g), track and field (b,g), volleyball (g), wrestling (b); intramural: weight lifting (b,g); coed interscholastic: aquatics; coed intramural: backpacking, badminton, basketball, ropes courses. 12 PE instructors, 20 coaches, 2 athletic trainers.
Computers Computers are regularly used in yearbook classes. Computer network features include on-campus library services, online commercial services, Internet access, wireless campus network, Internet filtering or blocking technology. Student e-mail accounts are available to students. Students grades are available online.
Contact Danette Morton, Director of Admission and Financial Aid. 336-288-8590 Ext. 223. Fax: 336-282-2905. E-mail: danettemorton@greensboroday.org. Web site: www.greensboroday.org.

ANNOUNCEMENT FROM THE SCHOOL Greensboro Day School is an independent, college-preparatory school offering a nurturing environment for more than 900 students in Transitional Kindergarten through grade 12. Outstanding attributes include a strong basic curriculum complemented by programs in athletics, performing and fine arts, computers, and foreign languages. GDS is a laptop school in grades 6–12.

GREENS FARMS ACADEMY

35 Beachside Avenue
PO Box 998
Greens Farms, Connecticut 06838-0998

Head of School: Janet M. Hartwell

General Information Coeducational day college-preparatory, arts, and technology school. Grades K–12. Founded: 1925. Setting: suburban. Nearest major city is New York, NY. 42-acre campus. 2 buildings on campus. Approved or accredited by Connecticut Association of Independent Schools, New England Association of Schools and Colleges, and Connecticut Department of Education. Member of National Association of Independent Schools and Secondary School Admission Test Board. Endowment: $23 million. Total enrollment: 650. Upper school average class size: 12. Upper school faculty-student ratio: 1:6.

Upper School Student Profile Grade 9: 69 students (31 boys, 38 girls); Grade 10: 73 students (35 boys, 38 girls); Grade 11: 69 students (38 boys, 31 girls); Grade 12: 67 students (35 boys, 32 girls).

Faculty School total: 89. In upper school: 23 men, 24 women; 25 have advanced degrees.

Subjects Offered Advanced studio art-AP, algebra, American government-AP, American history, American history-AP, American literature, American literature-AP, animation, architecture, art, art history, art-AP, biology, biology-AP, calculus, calculus-AP, chemistry, chemistry-AP, China/Japan history, Chinese, choral music, computer art, computer graphics, computer information systems, computer math, computer programming, computer science, concert choir, creative writing, digital art, digital music, digital photography, drama, earth science, ecology, economics, English, English literature, English literature-AP, English-AP, environmental science, environmental science-AP, European history, European history-AP, expository writing, fine arts, French, French-AP, geography, geology, geometry, government, government/civics, grammar, health, health and wellness, history, honors algebra, honors English, honors geometry, jazz ensemble, keyboarding, Latin, Latin-AP, life skills, literature-AP, Mandarin, mathematics, music, music theory, music theory-AP, newspaper, orchestra, philosophy, photography, physical education, physics, physics-AP, play production, pre-calculus, public speaking, science, senior project, senior seminar, social studies, Spanish, Spanish-AP, speech, squash, statistics-AP, studio art—AP, tennis, theater, theater design and production, theater history, trigonometry, U.S. government, U.S. history-AP, video film production, vocal ensemble, Web site design, weight training, wind ensemble, world history, world literature, world wide web design, wrestling, writing.

Graduation Requirements Algebra, arts and fine arts (art, music, dance, drama), athletics, biology, English, foreign language, geometry, history, mathematics, physical science, science.

Special Academic Programs Advanced Placement exam preparation; honors section; independent study; term-away projects; study abroad.

College Admission Counseling 58 students graduated in 2008; all went to college, including Boston University; Brown University; Columbia College; Cornell University; Georgetown University; University of Pennsylvania. Mean SAT critical reading: 634, mean SAT math: 626, mean SAT writing: 657, mean composite ACT: 27. 68% scored over 600 on SAT critical reading, 66% scored over 600 on SAT math, 79% scored over 600 on SAT writing.

Student Life Upper grades have specified standards of dress, student council, honor system. Discipline rests equally with students and faculty.

Summer Programs Remediation, enrichment, advancement, sports programs offered; session focuses on academics and athletics; held on campus; accepts boys and girls; open to students from other schools. 50 students usually enrolled. 2009 schedule: June 23 to August 1. Application deadline: April 30.

Tuition and Aid Day student tuition: $31,580. Tuition installment plan (Key Tuition Payment Plan). Need-based scholarship grants available. In 2008–09, 13% of upper-school students received aid. Total amount of financial aid awarded in 2008–09: $877,712.

Admissions Traditional secondary-level entrance grade is 9. For fall 2008, 127 students applied for upper-level admission, 72 were accepted, 41 enrolled. ISEE or SSAT required. Deadline for receipt of application materials: January 15. Application fee required: $75. On-campus interview required.

Athletics Interscholastic: baseball (boys), basketball (b,g), climbing (b,g), crew (b,g), cross-country running (b,g), field hockey (g), fitness (b,g), hockey (b), ice hockey (b), independent competitive sports (b,g), indoor hockey (b), lacrosse (b,g), physical fitness (b,g), physical training (b,g), running (b,g), soccer (b,g), softball (g), squash (b,g), tennis (b,g), volleyball (g), wrestling (b); intramural: aerobics/dance (g), dance (g); coed interscholastic: golf, independent competitive sports, rock climbing, rowing, running, sailing, wall climbing; coed intramural: climbing, fencing, figure skating, fitness, Frisbee, ice skating, Nautilus, physical fitness, physical training, rock climbing, strength & conditioning, ultimate Frisbee, weight lifting, weight training, yoga. 6 PE instructors, 12 coaches, 1 athletic trainer.

Computers Computers are regularly used in animation, art, English, foreign language, French, graphic arts, graphics, history, Latin, library, literary magazine, mathematics, music, newspaper, photography, science, Spanish, video film production, Web site design, yearbook classes. Computer network features include on-campus library services, online commercial services, Internet access, wireless campus network, Internet filtering or blocking technology. Student e-mail accounts and computer access in designated common areas are available to students. Students grades are available online. The school has a published electronic and media policy.

Contact Peggy Harwood, Admission Assistant. 203-256-7514. Fax: 203-256-7591. E-mail: admissions@gfacademy.org. Web site: www.gfacademy.org.

GREENWICH ACADEMY

200 North Maple Avenue
Greenwich, Connecticut 06830-4799

Head of School: Molly H. King

General Information Girls' day college-preparatory and arts school. Grades PK–12. Founded: 1827. Setting: suburban. Nearest major city is New York, NY. 39-acre campus. 6 buildings on campus. Approved or accredited by Connecticut Association of Independent Schools, New England Association of Schools and Colleges, and Connecticut Department of Education. Member of National Association of Independent Schools and Secondary School Admission Test Board. Endowment: $78.1 million. Total enrollment: 791. Upper school average class size: 13. Upper school faculty-student ratio: 1:6.

Upper School Student Profile Grade 9: 78 students (78 girls); Grade 10: 84 students (84 girls); Grade 11: 80 students (80 girls); Grade 12: 78 students (78 girls).

Faculty School total: 139. In upper school: 16 men, 33 women; 35 have advanced degrees.

Subjects Offered Advanced Placement courses, advanced studio art-AP, African-American literature, algebra, American history, American history-AP, American literature, ancient history, Arabic, architecture, art, art history, art history-AP, art-AP, astronomy, biochemistry, biology, biology-AP, calculus, calculus-AP, ceramics, chemistry, chemistry-AP, Chinese, classics, computer science, creative writing, dance, dance performance, drama, drama performance, earth science, ecology, economics, economics-AP, English, English literature, environmental science, European history, European history-AP, expository writing, film, film and literature, fine arts, foreign language, French, French language-AP, French literature-AP, French-AP, geology, geometry, government and politics-AP, government/civics, health, history, history-AP, honors algebra, honors geometry, independent study, Italian, Latin, Latin-AP, mathematics, mathematics-AP, medieval history, microeconomics, microeconomics-AP, music, music performance, music theory-AP, oceanography, physical education, physics, pre-calculus, psychology, science, senior project, Spanish, Spanish-AP, speech, statistics, studio art-AP, theater, trigonometry, world history, world literature.

Graduation Requirements Arts and fine arts (art, music, dance, drama), English, foreign language, mathematics, physical education (includes health), science, social studies (includes history). Community service is required.

Special Academic Programs Advanced Placement exam preparation; honors section; independent study; term-away projects; study abroad.

College Admission Counseling 78 students graduated in 2008; 77 went to college, including Brown University; Columbia College; Duke University; Elon University; Georgetown University; Williams College. Other: 1 entered a postgraduate year. Median SAT critical reading: 666, median SAT math: 667, median SAT writing: 695, median combined SAT: 2028, median composite ACT: 28. 81% scored over 600 on SAT critical reading, 79% scored over 600 on SAT math, 91% scored over 600 on SAT writing, 91% scored over 1800 on combined SAT, 86% scored over 26 on composite ACT.

Student Life Upper grades have uniform requirement, student council, honor system. Discipline rests equally with students and faculty.

Tuition and Aid Day student tuition: $31,100. Tuition installment plan (Key Tuition Payment Plan). Need-based scholarship grants, middle-income loans, PLITT Loans, tuition reduction for children of faculty and staff available. In 2008–09, 18% of upper-school students received aid. Total amount of financial aid awarded in 2008–09: $1,333,870.

Admissions Traditional secondary-level entrance grade is 9. For fall 2008, 128 students applied for upper-level admission, 51 were accepted, 38 enrolled. ERB, ISEE or SSAT required. Deadline for receipt of application materials: December 15. Application fee required: $75. On-campus interview required.

Athletics Interscholastic: basketball, crew, cross-country running, fencing, field hockey, golf, ice hockey, independent competitive sports, lacrosse, sailing, soccer, softball, squash, swimming and diving, tennis, volleyball; intramural: aerobics, aerobics/Nautilus, crew, dance, fitness, Frisbee, independent competitive sports, modern dance, Nautilus, physical fitness, physical training, running, self defense, strength & conditioning, tennis, weight lifting, yoga. 7 PE instructors, 54 coaches, 1 athletic trainer.

Computers Computers are regularly used in art, English, foreign language, history, humanities, mathematics, music, science classes. Computer network features include on-campus library services, online commercial services, Internet access, wireless campus network, Internet filtering or blocking technology. Campus intranet and student e-mail accounts are available to students. The school has a published electronic and media policy.

Contact Irene Mann, Admission Registrar. 203-625-8990. Fax: 203-625-8912. E-mail: imann@greenwichacademy.org. Web site: www.greenwichacademy.org.

ANNOUNCEMENT FROM THE SCHOOL Established in 1827, Greenwich Academy is located on a beautiful 39-acre campus. An independent, college-preparatory school for girls and women, grades PK–12, the Academy seeks to foster excellence. Its mission is to provide a challenging, comprehensive educational experience grounded in a rigorous liberal arts curriculum within an inclusive and diverse community. The school's motto, "Ad ingenium faciendum: Toward the Building of Character," reflects a focus on developing independent women of courage, integrity, and compassion. A challenging liberal arts curriculum offers opportunities for even the youngest girls to excel in mathematics, science, writing, technology, and the arts. Within the framework of tradition, Greenwich Academy integrates innovation and technology into all aspects of its program. Computer skills are developed throughout the Lower and Middle Schools. In grades 7–12, each student uses her own laptop in academic classes and for homework assignments. Foreign language instruction begins with conversational Spanish in grades PK–4, followed by Chinese, Latin, and a more formal study of Spanish or French in Middle School. The Lower and Middle Schools foster a love of reading, an understanding of mathematics, a foundation in world history and current events, and the principles of science. The Upper School focuses on liberal arts preparation for college in a wide variety of courses. All students at Greenwich Academy take 4 years of high school math and at least 3 years of high school science, including biology, chemistry, and physics. Twenty-six AP courses are offered. GA's coordinated program with Brunswick School for boys provides coed classes, including Chinese, Arabic, and Italian, as well as many joint music, drama, art, and community service projects. All students participate in intramural and interscholastic sports, dance, art, music, and community service, all of which help to develop team spirit, civic responsibility, and mutual respect. Two gymnasiums provide basketball courts, locker rooms, a fitness center, and five international squash courts that are adjacent to FieldTurf sports fields. Additional facilities include a performing arts center (with a 400-seat theater), a studio theater for dance and drama productions, acoustically correct choral and music rooms, a visual arts gallery, and a Middle/Upper School library. The PK–K classes are located on a 6.5-acre campus adjacent to soccer/sports fields.

GREENWOOD LABORATORY SCHOOL

901 South National Avenue
Springfield, Missouri 65897

Head of School: Dr. Janice Duncan

General Information Coeducational day college-preparatory, arts, and technology school. Grades K–12. Founded: 1908. Setting: urban. 3-acre campus. 1 building on campus. Approved or accredited by North Central Association of Colleges and Schools and Missouri Department of Education. Total enrollment: 339. Upper school average class size: 30. Upper school faculty-student ratio: 1:28.

Upper School Student Profile Grade 9: 30 students (15 boys, 15 girls); Grade 10: 19 students (15 boys, 4 girls); Grade 11: 26 students (12 boys, 14 girls); Grade 12: 19 students (9 boys, 10 girls).

Faculty School total: 32. In upper school: 10 men, 10 women; 19 have advanced degrees.

Subjects Offered English, fine arts, foreign language, health, instrumental music, mathematics, physical education, science, social studies, state government, vocal music.

Graduation Requirements Students have to pass a Graduation Exhibition and achieve Public Affairs Merits.

Special Academic Programs Advanced Placement exam preparation; study at local college for college credit; ESL (2 students enrolled).

College Admission Counseling 30 students graduated in 2008; all went to college, including University of Colorado at Boulder; University of Missouri–Columbia. Median composite ACT: 26. 47% scored over 26 on composite ACT.

Student Life Upper grades have student council. Discipline rests primarily with faculty.

Tuition and Aid Day student tuition: $4060. Tuition installment plan (individually arranged payment plans, single payment plan).

Admissions Traditional secondary-level entrance grade is 9. For fall 2008, 12 students applied for upper-level admission, 12 were accepted, 12 enrolled. Deadline for receipt of application materials: none. No application fee required. On-campus interview required.

Athletics Interscholastic: basketball (boys, girls), golf (b,g), soccer (b,g), swimming and diving (b,g), tennis (b,g); coed interscholastic: cross-country running, physical fitness, track and field. 3 PE instructors, 5 coaches.

Computers Computers are regularly used in word processing classes. Computer network features include on-campus library services, wireless campus network, Internet filtering or blocking technology. Student e-mail accounts and computer access in designated common areas are available to students. Students grades are available online. The school has a published electronic and media policy.

Contact Ms. Ruth Ann Johnson, Counselor. 417-836-7667. Fax: 417-836-8449. E-mail: RuthAnnJohnson@MissouriState.edu. Web site: www.education.missouristate.edu/greenwood.

THE GREENWOOD SCHOOL

Putney, Vermont

See Junior Boarding Schools section.

THE GRIER SCHOOL

PO Box 308
Tyrone, Pennsylvania 16686-0308

ANNOUNCEMENT FROM THE SCHOOL Located near Tyrone, Pennsylvania, the Grier School is an independent college-preparatory school for girls in grades 6–12. Founded in 1853, the School has always served young women by providing them with a blend of academics, athletics, and the arts. The School's motto, *Sana Mens in Corpore Sano* (A Sound Mind in a Sound Body), captures the spirit of the School. Grier School is 100% boarding, with more than 210 students. The students come from over twenty states and from fourteen other countries. Grier's residences are supervised by teams of full-time house mothers. Grier's 40 faculty members provide students with a very broad offering in all key disciplines. Most subject areas include classes taught at the AP level as well as Honors, A-Track, and B-Track. The typical class size at Grier is 9 students per teacher. 100% of Grier's graduates go on to four-year colleges or universities or to institutions specializing in the arts. Each weekend, at least five off-campus options provide students with the opportunity to shop, visit museums, see movies, dine out, experience outing club adventures, have dances at boys' schools, or participate in athletic events such as horse shows. Major off-campus trips to places like New York City or Washington, D.C., are offered once a month. The facilities at Grier combine old-fashioned charm with state-of-the-art contemporary construction. Since 2000, Grier has built four new large buildings and has completed extensive renovation of the older buildings. Among the projects are a new indoor equestrian center (2007), an expanded library (2006), a fitness center (2006), a performing arts center (2006), a science center (2003), and a Fine Arts Building (2001). In addition, Grier has five tennis courts, playing fields, an outdoor pool, a large gymnasium, and a sizeable stable. The School owns 320 acres of land. Grier's signature extracurricular programs are in dance, the arts, and horseback riding. The dance program involves 2 full-time teachers and has more than 80 students participating. Each year, the varsity dancers compete in competitions in major cities such as New York, Philadelphia, or Pittsburgh. The art program involves 5 full-time instructors who offer over twenty-five art classes each day. Each year, at least 5 Grier graduates plan to go to such competitive institutes of arts as Rhode Island School of Design, Pratt, Parsons, Maryland Institute College of Art, or the Fashion Institute of Technology. Grier's equestrian program includes 3 full-time teachers, an indoor riding ring, two outdoor rings, a network of trails, and over 45 horses. Varsity riders may participate in horse shows nearly every weekend, with the goal of going to the Equestrian Nationals at the end of the year.

GRIGGS UNIVERSITY AND INTERNATIONAL ACADEMY

12501 Old Columbia Pike
Silver Spring, Maryland 20904-6600

Head of School: Dr. Donald R. Sahly

General Information Coeducational day and distance learning college-preparatory, general academic, and religious studies school, affiliated with Seventh-day Adventist Church. Grades PK–PG. Distance learning grades K–12. Founded: 1909. Setting: suburban. Nearest major city is Washington, DC. 1 building on campus. Approved or accredited by Board of Regents, General Conference of Seventh-day Adventists, CITA (Commission on International and Trans-Regional Accreditation), Distance Education and Training Council, Middle States Association of Colleges and Schools, and Maryland Department of Education. Total enrollment: 1,214.

Upper School Student Profile 65% of students are Seventh-day Adventists.

Faculty School total: 32. In upper school: 13 men, 19 women; 17 have advanced degrees.

Subjects Offered Accounting, algebra, American government, American history, American literature, art appreciation, art history, arts, Bible studies, biology, business skills, chemistry, earth science, English, English literature, fine arts, food science, French, geography, geometry, government/civics, health, home economics, keyboarding, mathematics, music appreciation, physics, pre-algebra, science, social studies, Spanish, word processing, world history, writing.

Graduation Requirements Arts and fine arts (art, music, dance, drama), English, health, keyboarding/computer, language, mathematics, science, social studies (includes history), requirements for basic diploma differ. Community service is required.

Special Academic Programs Accelerated programs; independent study; study at local college for college credit.

College Admission Counseling 36 students graduated in 2008; they went to Andrews University; Columbia Union College; Loma Linda University; Southern Adventist University; Towson University; University of Maryland, Baltimore County.
Student Life Upper grades have honor system. Discipline rests primarily with faculty.
Summer Programs Remediation, enrichment programs offered; held on campus; accepts boys and girls; open to students from other schools.
Tuition and Aid Day student tuition: $1600–$1960. Tuition installment plan (monthly payment plans, individually arranged payment plans).
Admissions Deadline for receipt of application materials: none. Application fee required: $80.
Computers Computers are regularly used in word processing classes. Students grades are available online.
Contact Angie Deaver, Enrollment Services Director. 301-680-5170. Fax: 301-680-6577. E-mail: adeaver@griggs.edu. Web site: www.griggs.edu.

See Close-Up on page 772.

GROTON SCHOOL

Box 991
Farmers Row
Groton, Massachusetts 01450

Head of School: Richard B. Commons

General Information Coeducational boarding and day college-preparatory, arts, and religious studies school, affiliated with Episcopal Church. Grades 8–12. Founded: 1884. Setting: rural. Nearest major city is Boston. Students are housed in single-sex dormitories. 390-acre campus. 17 buildings on campus. Approved or accredited by Association of Independent Schools in New England, New England Association of Schools and Colleges, and The Association of Boarding Schools. Member of National Association of Independent Schools and Secondary School Admission Test Board. Endowment: $257 million. Total enrollment: 356. Upper school average class size: 13. Upper school faculty-student ratio: 1:3.
Upper School Student Profile Grade 9: 85 students (44 boys, 41 girls); Grade 10: 86 students (44 boys, 42 girls); Grade 11: 84 students (42 boys, 42 girls); Grade 12: 75 students (37 boys, 38 girls). 90% of students are boarding students. 31% are state residents. 31 states are represented in upper school student body. 9% are international students. International students from Canada, China, France, Italy, Republic of Korea, and United Kingdom; 10 other countries represented in student body.
Faculty School total: 84. In upper school: 49 men, 35 women; 60 have advanced degrees; 73 reside on campus.
Subjects Offered Advanced chemistry, advanced math, algebra, American literature, American literature-AP, analytic geometry, Ancient Greek, ancient world history, archaeology, art, art history, art history-AP, Bible studies, biology, biology-AP, botany, Buddhism, calculus, calculus-AP, cell biology, Central and Eastern European history, ceramics, chemistry, chemistry-AP, Chinese, choir, choral music, civil rights, Civil War, civil war history, classical Greek literature, classical language, classics, composition, composition-AP, creative writing, dance, discrete math, drawing, earth science, ecology, environmental systems, economics, English, English composition, English-AP, environmental science, environmental science-AP, environmental studies, ethics, European history, European history-AP, expository writing, fine arts, fractal geometry, fractals, French, French language-AP, French literature-AP, geography, geometry, government, grammar, Greek, health, history, Holocaust, honors algebra, honors English, honors geometry, honors U.S. history, honors world history, independent study, lab science, language-AP, Latin, Latin-AP, linear algebra, literature, literature and composition-AP, mathematics, mathematics-AP, modern European history, modern European history-AP, modern history, modern languages, modern world history, music, music history, music theory, organic biochemistry, painting, philosophy, photo shop, photography, physical science, physics, physics-AP, pre-algebra, pre-calculus, psychology, religion, religions, religious studies, science, Shakespeare, social science, Spanish, Spanish language-AP, Spanish literature, Spanish literature-AP, sports medicine, statistics, studio art, studio art-AP, theology, trigonometry, U.S. constitutional history, U.S. government, U.S. government and politics, U.S. government and politics-AP, U.S. history, U.S. history-AP, Western civilization, wood lab, woodworking, world history, world history-AP, writing.
Graduation Requirements Arts and fine arts (art, music, dance, drama), classical language, English, foreign language, mathematics, religious studies, science, social studies (includes history).
Special Academic Programs Advanced Placement exam preparation; honors section; independent study; study abroad; academic accommodation for the gifted, the musically talented, and the artistically talented.
College Admission Counseling 86 students graduated in 2008; all went to college, including Brown University; Carnegie Mellon University; Georgetown University; Harvard University; Tufts University. Median SAT critical reading: 690, median SAT math: 690, median SAT writing: 700.
Student Life Upper grades have specified standards of dress, student council, honor system. Discipline rests equally with students and faculty. Attendance at religious services is required.
Tuition and Aid Day student tuition: $33,260; 7-day tuition and room/board: $44,350. Tuition installment plan (Insured Tuition Payment Plan, Key Tuition Payment Plan, monthly payment plans, individually arranged payment plans). Need-based scholarship grants, need-based loans, Key Education Resources available. In 2008–09, 36% of upper-school students received aid. Total amount of financial aid awarded in 2008–09: $4,077,000.
Admissions Traditional secondary-level entrance grade is 9. For fall 2008, 863 students applied for upper-level admission, 144 were accepted, 77 enrolled. ISEE, SSAT or TOEFL required. Deadline for receipt of application materials: January 15. Application fee required: $50. Interview required.
Athletics Interscholastic: baseball (boys), basketball (b,g), crew (b,g), cross-country running (b,g), field hockey (g), Fives (b,g), football (b), hockey (b,g), ice hockey (b,g), lacrosse (b,g), rowing (b,g), soccer (b,g), squash (b,g), tennis (b,g); intramural: physical training (b,g), self defense (g), weight training (b,g); coed interscholastic: dance team; coed intramural: aerobics/dance, alpine skiing, dance, fitness, Fives, Frisbee, golf, ice skating, jogging, modern dance, nordic skiing, outdoor activities, skeet shooting, skiing (cross-country), skiing (downhill), soccer, strength & conditioning, swimming and diving, track and field, trap and skeet, ultimate Frisbee, yoga. 2 coaches, 1 athletic trainer.
Computers Computers are regularly used in English, history, mathematics, science classes. Computer network features include on-campus library services, Internet access, wireless campus network, Internet filtering or blocking technology, wireless environment in classrooms and library. Campus intranet and student e-mail accounts are available to students. The school has a published electronic and media policy.
Contact Mr. Ian Gracey, Director of Admission. 978-448-7510. Fax: 978-448-9623. E-mail: igracey@groton.org. Web site: www.groton.org.

See Close-Up on page 774.

GROVE SCHOOL

Madison, Connecticut
See Special Needs Schools section.

GUAMANI PRIVATE SCHOOL

PO Box 3000
Guayama, Puerto Rico 00785

Head of School: Mr. Eduardo Delgado

General Information Coeducational day college-preparatory and bilingual studies school. Grades 1–12. Founded: 1914. Setting: urban. Nearest major city is Caguas. 1-acre campus. 1 building on campus. Approved or accredited by Middle States Association of Colleges and Schools, National Catholic Education Association, and Puerto Rico Department of Education. Languages of instruction: English and Spanish. Total enrollment: 606. Upper school average class size: 20. Upper school faculty-student ratio: 1:13.
Faculty School total: 32. In upper school: 10 men, 10 women; 3 have advanced degrees.
Subjects Offered Advanced math, Advanced Placement courses, algebra, American government, American history, analysis and differential calculus, chemistry, civics, pre-algebra, pre-calculus, science project, science research, social sciences, social studies, sociology, Spanish, Spanish language-AP, U.S. literature, visual arts, world geography, world history.
Graduation Requirements Mathematics, science, social sciences, Spanish, acceptance into a college or university. Community service is required.
Special Academic Programs Advanced Placement exam preparation; honors section; independent study.
College Admission Counseling 23 students graduated in 2008; they went to Embry-Riddle Aeronautical University; Syracuse University; University of Puerto Rico, Cayey University College; University of Puerto Rico, Mayagüez Campus; University of Puerto Rico, Río Piedras. Other: 23 entered a postgraduate year.
Student Life Upper grades have uniform requirement, student council, honor system. Discipline rests primarily with faculty.
Summer Programs Remediation, ESL programs offered; held on campus; accepts boys and girls; open to students from other schools. 30 students usually enrolled. 2009 schedule: June 1 to June 30. Application deadline: May 27.
Admissions Traditional secondary-level entrance grade is 9. For fall 2008, 30 students applied for upper-level admission, 21 were accepted, 20 enrolled. School's own test or Test of Achievement and Proficiency required. Deadline for receipt of application materials: none. Application fee required: $30. Interview required.
Athletics Interscholastic: aerobics/dance (girls), basketball (b,g), cheering (g), dance squad (g), volleyball (b,g); coed interscholastic: dance team. 3 PE instructors, 2 coaches.
Computers Computers are regularly used in English, mathematics, science, social sciences, Spanish, word processing classes. Computer resources include on-campus library services, Internet access, wireless campus network, Internet filtering or blocking technology. The school has a published electronic and media policy.
Contact Mrs. Digna Torres, Secretary. 787-864-6880. Fax: 787-866-4947. Web site: www.guamani.com.

GUERIN COLLEGE PREPARATORY HIGH SCHOOL

8001 West Belmont
River Grove, Illinois 60171-1096

Head of School: Mrs. Elizabeth (Bonnie) Brown

General Information Coeducational day college-preparatory, arts, religious studies, and technology school, affiliated with Roman Catholic Church. Grades 9–12. Founded: 1962. Setting: suburban. Nearest major city is Chicago. 23-acre campus. 2 buildings on campus. Approved or accredited by National Catholic Education Association, North Central Association of Colleges and Schools, and Illinois Department of Education. Endowment: $2 million. Total enrollment: 651. Upper school average class size: 25. Upper school faculty-student ratio: 1:17.
Upper School Student Profile Grade 9: 166 students (91 boys, 75 girls); Grade 10: 156 students (72 boys, 84 girls); Grade 11: 173 students (67 boys, 106 girls); Grade 12: 156 students (64 boys, 92 girls). 92% of students are Roman Catholic.
Faculty School total: 58. In upper school: 17 men, 41 women; 26 have advanced degrees.
Graduation Requirements Arts and fine arts (art, music, dance, drama), computers, electives, English, mathematics, physical education (includes health), science, social science, speech, theology, theology and the arts, a minimum of four service-learning classes.
Special Academic Programs 11 Advanced Placement exams for which test preparation is offered; honors section; study at local college for college credit; ESL (1 student enrolled).
College Admission Counseling 140 students graduated in 2008; 134 went to college, including DePaul University; Dominican University; Eastern Illinois University; Illinois State University; Northeastern Illinois University; Northern Illinois University. Other: 1 went to work, 5 entered a postgraduate year. Median composite ACT: 21.
Student Life Upper grades have uniform requirement, student council. Discipline rests primarily with faculty. Attendance at religious services is required.
Summer Programs Remediation, enrichment, sports, art/fine arts, computer instruction programs offered; session focuses on summer camps, freshman experience, and computers; held on campus; accepts boys and girls; open to students from other schools. 200 students usually enrolled. 2009 schedule: June 13 to August 1.
Tuition and Aid Day student tuition: $7500. Tuition installment plan (monthly payment plans, individually arranged payment plans). Tuition reduction for siblings, merit scholarship grants, need-based scholarship grants, paying campus jobs available. In 2008–09, 40% of upper-school students received aid; total upper-school merit-scholarship money awarded: $100,000. Total amount of financial aid awarded in 2008–09: $380,000.
Admissions Traditional secondary-level entrance grade is 9. For fall 2008, 197 students applied for upper-level admission, 182 were accepted, 167 enrolled. Explore required. Deadline for receipt of application materials: none. Application fee required: $175.
Athletics Interscholastic: baseball (boys), basketball (b,g), dance (g), dance team (g), football (b), gymnastics (g), hockey (b), ice hockey (b), soccer (b,g), softball (g), strength & conditioning (b,g), volleyball (g), weight training (b,g); coed interscholastic: cheering, cross-country running, dance, golf, ice hockey, physical fitness, strength & conditioning, track and field, wrestling. 3 PE instructors, 30 coaches, 1 athletic trainer.
Computers Computers are regularly used in all academic, computer applications classes. Computer network features include Internet access, wireless campus network, Internet filtering or blocking technology, all 9th, 10th graders and 11th graders lease a laptop computer and bring to all classes. Student e-mail accounts and computer access in designated common areas are available to students. Students grades are available online. The school has a published electronic and media policy.
Contact Mrs. Valerie Reiss, Director of Admissions. 708-453-6233 Ext. 4732. Fax: 708-453-6296. E-mail: vreiss@guerinprep.org. Web site: www.guerinprep.org.

GUILFORD DAY SCHOOL

Greensboro, North Carolina
See Special Needs Schools section.

GULLIVER PREPARATORY SCHOOL

6575 North Kendall Drive
Miami, Florida 33156

Head of School: John W. Krutulis

General Information Coeducational day college-preparatory, arts, technology, International Baccalaureate, Architectural Design, and Pre-Engineering, Law & Litigation, Biomedical Sciences school. Grades PK–12. Founded: 1926. Setting: suburban. 14-acre campus. 3 buildings on campus. Approved or accredited by CITA (Commission on International and Trans-Regional Accreditation), Southern Association of Colleges and Schools, and Florida Department of Education. Member of Secondary School Admission Test Board. Total enrollment: 1,834. Upper school average class size: 14. Upper school faculty-student ratio: 1:8.
Faculty School total: 126. In upper school: 58 men, 68 women; 69 have advanced degrees.
Subjects Offered Algebra, American history, American literature, anatomy, architectural drawing, architecture, art, art history, biology, calculus, ceramics, chemistry, college admission preparation, college writing, computer animation, computer applications, computer keyboarding, computer processing, computer programming, computer programming-AP, computer science, computer science-AP, computer skills, computer studies, concert band, concert choir, creative writing, dance, desktop publishing, drafting, drama, economics, engineering, English, English literature, European history, fine arts, French, geometry, government/civics, history, Italian, Latin, marine biology, mathematics, mechanical drawing, music, newspaper, physical education, physics, psychology, science, social studies, Spanish, speech, statistics, theater, trigonometry, video, world history, world literature, yearbook, zoology.
Graduation Requirements Arts and fine arts (art, music, dance, drama), computer science, English, foreign language, mathematics, physical education (includes health), science, social studies (includes history). Community service is required.
Special Academic Programs International Baccalaureate program; Advanced Placement exam preparation; honors section; study at local college for college credit; academic accommodation for the gifted, the musically talented, and the artistically talented.
College Admission Counseling 180 students graduated in 2008; all went to college, including Boston University; Duke University; Florida International University; Florida State University; University of Florida; University of Miami. Mean SAT critical reading: 575, mean SAT math: 590, mean SAT writing: 578.
Student Life Upper grades have specified standards of dress, student council, honor system. Discipline rests primarily with faculty.
Summer Programs Remediation, enrichment, advancement, art/fine arts, rigorous outdoor training, computer instruction programs offered; session focuses on enrichment and reinforcement; held on campus; accepts boys and girls; not open to students from other schools. 175 students usually enrolled. 2009 schedule: June 8 to July 18. Application deadline: June 8.
Tuition and Aid Day student tuition: $8100–$23,380. Tuition installment plan (monthly payment plans, school's own tuition recovery plan). Tuition reduction for siblings, need-based scholarship grants, application and matriculation fee waived for children of alumni available.
Admissions Traditional secondary-level entrance grade is 9. For fall 2008, 340 students applied for upper-level admission, 242 were accepted, 134 enrolled. School's own exam and SSAT required. Deadline for receipt of application materials: February 20. Application fee required: $100. Interview recommended.
Athletics Interscholastic: aerobics/Nautilus (girls), baseball (b), basketball (b,g), cross-country running (b,g), dance (g), dance squad (g), dance team (g), diving (b,g), football (b), golf (b,g), gymnastics (b,g), lacrosse (b), physical training (b,g), running (b,g), soccer (b,g), softball (g), swimming and diving (b,g), tennis (b,g), track and field (b,g), volleyball (g), water polo (b,g); intramural: boxing (b,g), weight training (b,g); coed interscholastic: aerobics, bowling, cheering, modern dance, yoga; coed intramural: aerobics/dance, aerobics/Nautilus, badminton, dance, dance squad, dance team, fitness, flag football, Frisbee, kickball, modern dance, netball, physical fitness, running, strength & conditioning, touch football, yoga. 6 PE instructors, 55 coaches, 2 athletic trainers.
Computers Computers are regularly used in architecture, art, college planning, drafting, English, graphic arts, graphic design, keyboarding, newspaper, programming, science, technology, word processing, yearbook classes. Computer network features include on-campus library services, online commercial services, Internet access, wireless campus network, Internet filtering or blocking technology, modified laptop program, SMART Boards and Audio enhancement systems. Students grades are available online. The school has a published electronic and media policy.
Contact Carol A. Bowen, Director of Admission. 305-666-7937 Ext. 1408. Fax: 305-665-3791. E-mail: bowc@gulliverschools.org. Web site: www.gulliverschools.org.

THE GUNNERY

99 Green Hill Road
Washington, Connecticut 06793

Head of School: Susan G. Graham

General Information Coeducational boarding and day college-preparatory, arts, and technology school. Boarding grades 9–PG, day grades 9–12. Founded: 1850. Setting: rural. Nearest major city is Hartford. Students are housed in single-sex dormitories. 220-acre campus. 27 buildings on campus. Approved or accredited by Connecticut Association of Independent Schools, New England Association of Schools and Colleges, The Association of Boarding Schools, and Connecticut Department of Education. Member of National Association of Independent Schools and Secondary School Admission Test Board. Endowment: $21 million. Total enrollment: 298. Upper school average class size: 14. Upper school faculty-student ratio: 1:7.
Upper School Student Profile Grade 9: 49 students (29 boys, 20 girls); Grade 10: 67 students (44 boys, 23 girls); Grade 11: 90 students (60 boys, 30 girls); Grade 12: 95 students (74 boys, 21 girls); Postgraduate: 15 students (14 boys, 1 girl). 72% of students are boarding students. 50% are state residents. 26 states are represented in upper school student body. 15% are international students. International students from China, France, Germany, Japan, Republic of Korea, and Taiwan; 16 other countries represented in student body.
Faculty School total: 60. In upper school: 29 men, 26 women; 31 have advanced degrees.

Subjects Offered Advanced chemistry, algebra, American history, American history-AP, American literature, anatomy, art, art history, biology, calculus, ceramics, chemistry, computer graphics, computer math, computer programming, computer science, creative writing, drama, drawing, earth science, economics, economics-AP, English, English language-AP, English literature, English literature-AP, environmental science, environmental studies, ESL, ethics, ethics and responsibility, European history, European history-AP, expository writing, fine arts, French, geometry, government/civics, grammar, health, history, history of rock and roll, honors algebra, honors English, honors geometry, human development, instruments, marine biology, mathematics, modern European history-AP, music, music composition, mythology, painting, photography, physical education, physical science, physics, physics-AP, physiology, political science, pottery, pre-calculus, psychology, public speaking, science, social studies, sociology, Spanish, Spanish language-AP, Spanish literature-AP, speech, studio art, theater, trigonometry, U.S. history-AP, values and decisions, voice, world history, world literature, writing.

Graduation Requirements Arts and fine arts (art, music, dance, drama), English, ethics and responsibility, foreign language, history, human development, mathematics, physical education (includes health), public speaking, science, speech.

Special Academic Programs Advanced Placement exam preparation; honors section; independent study; term-away projects; study abroad; academic accommodation for the gifted, the musically talented, and the artistically talented; ESL (5 students enrolled).

College Admission Counseling 84 students graduated in 2008; 82 went to college, including Boston University; Hobart and William Smith Colleges; New York University; Northeastern University; United States Naval Academy; University of Wisconsin–Madison. Other: 2 had other specific plans.

Student Life Upper grades have uniform requirement, student council, honor system. Discipline rests equally with students and faculty.

Tuition and Aid Day student tuition: $31,400; 7-day tuition and room/board: $42,000. Tuition installment plan (Insured Tuition Payment Plan, Academic Management Services Plan, Key Tuition Payment Plan). Merit scholarship grants, need-based scholarship grants, need-based loans available. In 2008–09, 44% of upper-school students received aid. Total amount of financial aid awarded in 2008–09: $2,400,000.

Admissions Traditional secondary-level entrance grade is 9. For fall 2008, 575 students applied for upper-level admission, 330 were accepted, 109 enrolled. PSAT or SAT or SSAT required. Deadline for receipt of application materials: January 31. Application fee required: $50. On-campus interview required.

Athletics Interscholastic: baseball (boys), basketball (b,g), crew (b,g), cross-country running (b,g), field hockey (g), football (b), golf (b,g), ice hockey (b,g), lacrosse (b,g), soccer (b,g), softball (g), strength & conditioning (b,g), tennis (b,g), volleyball (g), wrestling (b); coed interscholastic: Frisbee; coed intramural: bicycling, fitness, outdoor adventure, outdoor education, yoga. 2 coaches, 1 athletic trainer.

Computers Computers are regularly used in art, English, foreign language, history, mathematics, music, science classes. Computer network features include on-campus library services, Internet access, wireless campus network. Campus intranet and student e-mail accounts are available to students.

Contact Shannon M. Baudo, Director of Admissions. 860-868-7334. Fax: 860-868-1614. E-mail: admissions@gunnery.org. Web site: www.gunnery.org.

See Close-Up on page 776.

GUNSTON DAY SCHOOL

911 Gunston Road
PO Box 200
Centreville, Maryland 21617

Head of School: Jeffrey Woodworth

General Information Coeducational day college-preparatory, arts, and technology school. Grades 9–12. Founded: 1911. Setting: rural. Nearest major city is Annapolis. 32-acre campus. 4 buildings on campus. Approved or accredited by Association of Independent Maryland Schools, Middle States Association of Colleges and Schools, and Maryland Department of Education. Member of National Association of Independent Schools and Secondary School Admission Test Board. Endowment: $1 million. Total enrollment: 152. Upper school average class size: 8. Upper school faculty-student ratio: 1:6.

Upper School Student Profile Grade 9: 36 students (14 boys, 22 girls); Grade 10: 44 students (20 boys, 24 girls); Grade 11: 32 students (18 boys, 14 girls); Grade 12: 40 students (23 boys, 17 girls).

Faculty School total: 27. In upper school: 16 men, 11 women; 14 have advanced degrees.

Subjects Offered Advanced Placement courses, advanced studio art-AP, African history, algebra, American government, American government-AP, American history, American literature, anatomy and physiology, art, art history-AP, biology, biology-AP, British literature (honors), calculus, calculus-AP, ceramics, chemistry, chemistry-AP, Chesapeake Bay studies, Chinese, Chinese history, college counseling, college placement, community service, computer applications, computer programming, computer science, digital photography, ecology, English, English literature, environmental science, ethics, film and literature, fine arts, French, French language-AP, French-AP, government/civics, health, history, history-AP, ideas, Japanese history, Latin, Latin American history, mathematics, music, music appreciation, performing arts, photography, physics, physics-AP, pottery, pre-calculus, pre-college orientation, printmaking, psychology, Russian history, SAT preparation, science, sculpture, senior thesis, silk screening, Spanish, statistics-AP, studio art, trigonometry, wellness, world history, world religions, world religions.

Graduation Requirements Arts and fine arts (art, music, dance, drama), athletics, computer science, English, foreign language, history, mathematics, science, social science. Community service is required.

Special Academic Programs Advanced Placement exam preparation; honors section; independent study; study at local college for college credit; academic accommodation for the gifted, the musically talented, and the artistically talented; ESL (12 students enrolled).

College Admission Counseling 41 students graduated in 2008; 40 went to college, including Davidson College; Dickinson College; Lehigh University; University of Maryland, College Park; University of Pennsylvania; Washington College. Other: 1 entered a postgraduate year.

Student Life Upper grades have specified standards of dress, student council, honor system. Discipline rests primarily with faculty.

Summer Programs Advancement programs offered; session focuses on Geometry; held on campus; accepts boys and girls; not open to students from other schools. 3 students usually enrolled. 2009 schedule: June 17 to July 22. Application deadline: none.

Tuition and Aid Day student tuition: $20,700. Tuition installment plan (Key Tuition Payment Plan, monthly payment plans). Merit scholarship grants, need-based scholarship grants available. In 2008–09, 33% of upper-school students received aid; total upper-school merit-scholarship money awarded: $31,050. Total amount of financial aid awarded in 2008–09: $500,000.

Admissions Traditional secondary-level entrance grade is 9. For fall 2008, 69 students applied for upper-level admission, 62 were accepted, 48 enrolled. ISEE or SSAT required. Deadline for receipt of application materials: February 1. Application fee required: $50. On-campus interview required.

Athletics Interscholastic: basketball (boys, girls), field hockey (g), lacrosse (b,g), soccer (b,g), swimming and diving (b,g), tennis (b,g); intramural: baseball (b), independent competitive sports (b,g), tennis (b,g); coed interscholastic: crew, equestrian sports, golf, horseback riding, sailing, swimming and diving, tennis; coed intramural: aerobics/dance, cross-country running, dance, fitness, independent competitive sports, modern dance, strength & conditioning, tennis, weight training. 4 coaches.

Computers Computers are regularly used in English, foreign language, history, mathematics, science classes. Computer network features include online commercial services, Internet access, wireless campus network, Internet filtering or blocking technology, JSTOR, Gale. Computer access in designated common areas is available to students.

Contact David Henry, Director of Admission. 410-758-0620. Fax: 410-758-0628. E-mail: dhenry@gunstondayschool.org. Web site: www.gunstondayschool.org/.

ANNOUNCEMENT FROM THE SCHOOL Gunston Day School is an independent, coeducational, college-preparatory school for motivated and capable students. Gunston fosters a supportive and challenging environment where the art of learning is practiced by encouraging critical thinking, creativity, stewardship, and self-discipline. The School community is committed to high standards of academic achievement, ethical behavior, and physical fitness.

GWYNEDD MERCY ACADEMY

1345 Sumneytown Pike
PO Box 902
Gwynedd Valley, Pennsylvania 19437-0902

Head of School: Sr. Kathleen Boyce, RSM

General Information Girls' day college-preparatory, arts, religious studies, and technology school, affiliated with Roman Catholic Church. Grades 9–12. Founded: 1861. Setting: suburban. Nearest major city is Philadelphia. 48-acre campus. 1 building on campus. Approved or accredited by Mercy Secondary Education Association, Middle States Association of Colleges and Schools, National Catholic Education Association, and Pennsylvania Department of Education. Total enrollment: 411. Upper school average class size: 18. Upper school faculty-student ratio: 1:10.

Upper School Student Profile Grade 9: 111 students (111 girls); Grade 10: 96 students (96 girls); Grade 11: 97 students (97 girls); Grade 12: 104 students (104 girls). 99% of students are Roman Catholic.

Faculty School total: 36. In upper school: 6 men, 30 women; 26 have advanced degrees.

Subjects Offered Accounting, Advanced Placement courses, algebra, American government-AP, American history, American history-AP, American literature, art, art appreciation, athletics, biology, business law, business skills, calculus, calculus-AP, chemistry, college counseling, computer science, computer skills, English, fine arts, French, geometry, health, health education, history, honors English, human development, Latin, library studies, mathematics, music, music theory, physical education, physical science, physics, piloting, post-calculus, pre-calculus, religion, social studies, Spanish, statistics-AP, study skills, theology, trigonometry, word processing, world culture, zoology.

Graduation Requirements English, foreign language, mathematics, physical education (includes health), religion (includes Bible studies and theology), science, social studies (includes history).
Special Academic Programs Advanced Placement exam preparation; honors section; study at local college for college credit; academic accommodation for the musically talented and the artistically talented.
College Admission Counseling 100 students graduated in 2008; 99 went to college, including Fordham University; Penn State University Park; Saint Joseph's University; Temple University; The University of Scranton. Other: 1 had other specific plans. Mean SAT critical reading: 569, mean SAT math: 547, mean SAT writing: 585, mean combined SAT: 1701, mean composite ACT: 28. 33% scored over 600 on SAT critical reading, 18% scored over 600 on SAT math, 37% scored over 600 on SAT writing, 29% scored over 1800 on combined SAT.
Student Life Upper grades have uniform requirement, student council, honor system. Discipline rests primarily with faculty. Attendance at religious services is required.
Summer Programs Sports programs offered; session focuses on Sports; held on campus; accepts girls; open to students from other schools. 85 students usually enrolled. 2009 schedule: June 10 to August 6.
Tuition and Aid Day student tuition: $12,300. Tuition installment plan (monthly payment plans, individually arranged payment plans, quarterly and semi-annual payment plans). Tuition reduction for siblings, merit scholarship grants, need-based scholarship grants available. In 2008–09, 5% of upper-school students received aid; total upper-school merit-scholarship money awarded: $22,000. Total amount of financial aid awarded in 2008–09: $82,000.
Admissions Traditional secondary-level entrance grade is 9. For fall 2008, 290 students applied for upper-level admission, 230 were accepted, 111 enrolled. Scholastic Testing Service High School Placement Test (open version) required. Deadline for receipt of application materials: November 11. Application fee required: $50.
Athletics Interscholastic: basketball, cross-country running, diving, field hockey, golf, indoor track, lacrosse, soccer, softball, swimming and diving, tennis, track and field, volleyball; intramural: dance. 2 PE instructors, 24 coaches, 1 athletic trainer.
Computers Computers are regularly used in art, business, English, foreign language, French, history, Latin, library skills, mathematics, music, newspaper, publications, religion, science, technology, word processing, writing, yearbook classes. Computer network features include on-campus library services, online commercial services, Internet access, Internet filtering or blocking technology. Student e-mail accounts are available to students. The school has a published electronic and media policy.
Contact Mrs. Kimberly Dunphy Scott, Director of Admissions. 215-646-8815 Ext. 329. Fax: 215-646-4361. E-mail: kscott@gmahs.org. Web site: www.gmahs.org.

HACKLEY SCHOOL

293 Benedict Avenue
Tarrytown, New York 10591
Head of School: Mr. Walter C. Johnson

General Information Coeducational boarding and day college-preparatory, arts, technology, and liberal arts; math & science school. Boarding grades 9–12, day grades K–12. Founded: 1899. Setting: suburban. Nearest major city is New York. Students are housed in single-sex dormitories. 285-acre campus. 15 buildings on campus. Approved or accredited by Middle States Association of Colleges and Schools, New York State Association of Independent Schools, New York State Board of Regents, and The Association of Boarding Schools. Member of National Association of Independent Schools and Secondary School Admission Test Board. Endowment: $31.2 million. Total enrollment: 836. Upper school average class size: 15. Upper school faculty-student ratio: 1:6.
Upper School Student Profile Grade 9: 92 students (49 boys, 43 girls); Grade 10: 97 students (47 boys, 50 girls); Grade 11: 98 students (44 boys, 54 girls); Grade 12: 95 students (46 boys, 49 girls). 7% of students are boarding students. 96% are state residents. 3 states are represented in upper school student body. 2% are international students. International students from Colombia, Ecuador, Japan, and Peru; 8 other countries represented in student body.
Faculty School total: 132. In upper school: 28 men, 35 women; 42 have advanced degrees; 50 reside on campus.
Subjects Offered 20th century world history, 3-dimensional art, algebra, American government-AP, American history, American history-AP, American literature, ancient history, anthropology, architectural drawing, art, art history-AP, biology, biology-AP, British literature, calculus-AP, ceramics, chemistry, chemistry-AP, Chinese, chorus, computer graphics, computer programming, computer science, computer science-AP, concert band, contemporary issues, creative writing, driver education, ecology, economics, electronic publishing, English, environmental science-AP, European history, fine arts, finite math, French, French language-AP, French literature-AP, geometry, Greek, history, Italian, Latin, Latin-AP, marine biology, mathematics, modern European history, music, music theory, music theory-AP, orchestra, organic chemistry, performing arts, photography, physical education, physics, physics-AP, pre-calculus, science, Spanish, Spanish language-AP, Spanish literature-AP, statistics-AP, studio art-AP, trigonometry, world history.
Graduation Requirements Arts and fine arts (art, music, dance, drama), English, foreign language, history, mathematics, physical education (includes health), science.
Special Academic Programs Advanced Placement exam preparation; honors section; independent study.
College Admission Counseling 90 students graduated in 2008; all went to college, including Colgate University; College of Charleston; Middlebury College; University of Pennsylvania; Vanderbilt University; Vassar College. 90% scored over 600 on SAT critical reading, 90% scored over 600 on SAT math.
Student Life Upper grades have specified standards of dress, student council. Discipline rests primarily with faculty.
Summer Programs Sports programs offered; session focuses on sports (football and basketball); held on campus; accepts boys and girls; open to students from other schools. 50 students usually enrolled. 2009 schedule: June to June.
Tuition and Aid Day student tuition: $28,700–$32,800; 5-day tuition and room/board: $42,900. Tuition installment plan (Insured Tuition Payment Plan, Academic Management Services Plan, Key Tuition Payment Plan, monthly payment plans). Need-based scholarship grants, need-based loans available. In 2008–09, 14% of upper-school students received aid. Total amount of financial aid awarded in 2008–09: $3,000,000.
Admissions Traditional secondary-level entrance grade is 9. For fall 2008, 216 students applied for upper-level admission, 68 were accepted, 38 enrolled. ERB, ISEE or SSAT required. Deadline for receipt of application materials: December 15. Application fee required: $55. On-campus interview required.
Athletics Interscholastic: baseball (boys), basketball (b,g), field hockey (g), football (b), golf (b,g), lacrosse (b,g), soccer (b,g), softball (g), squash (b,g), tennis (b,g), wrestling (b); intramural: squash (b,g); coed interscholastic: cross-country running, fencing, indoor track & field, strength & conditioning, swimming and diving, track and field; coed intramural: aerobics, aerobics/Nautilus, cooperative games, fitness, kayaking, physical fitness, physical training, ropes courses, weight training, yoga. 6 PE instructors, 9 coaches, 1 athletic trainer.
Computers Computers are regularly used in computer applications, desktop publishing, drawing and design, graphic arts, independent study, keyboarding, literary magazine, music, newspaper, photography, programming, Web site design, yearbook classes. Computer network features include on-campus library services, online commercial services, Internet access, wireless campus network, laptop loaner program. Campus intranet and computer access in designated common areas are available to students. Students grades are available online.
Contact Mrs. Lynn Hooley, Admissions Associate. 914-366-2642. Fax: 914-366-2636. E-mail: lhooley@hackleyschool.org. Web site: www.hackleyschool.org.

ANNOUNCEMENT FROM THE SCHOOL Hackley School is pleased to announce that during the summer of 2008, reconstruction and renovation began on Goodhue Memorial Hall and the two wings that once housed the technology department and several classrooms. The goal is to complete the project and move into the building by January 2010. The restored and renovated buildings will include the Middle and Upper School Library, a student lounge, history classrooms, and administrative offices, all of which will add 8,000 square feet to the Upper School facilities. In addition, Hackley School plans to renovate the Upper School classrooms and hallways. Throughout the school year, tours are conducted daily—fall tours take place from the second week of school in September to the Tuesday before Thanksgiving. In the summer, tours are only offered on Wednesdays. We look forward to walking with you through Hackley's refurbished facilities—come tour the school with us!

See Close-Up on page 778.

HALSTROM HIGH SCHOOL

380 South Melrose Drive
Suite 416
Vista, California 92081
Head of School: Ms. Gabe Azzaro

General Information Coeducational day and distance learning college-preparatory and general academic school; primarily serves dyslexic students. Grades 7–12. Distance learning grades 7–12. Founded: 1985. Setting: suburban. Nearest major city is San Diego. 1-acre campus. 1 building on campus. Approved or accredited by Western Association of Schools and Colleges and California Department of Education. Total enrollment: 28. Upper school average class size: 1. Upper school faculty-student ratio: 1:1.
Upper School Student Profile Grade 7: 1 student (1 boy); Grade 9: 1 student (1 girl); Grade 10: 6 students (3 boys, 3 girls); Grade 11: 8 students (5 boys, 3 girls); Grade 12: 12 students (8 boys, 4 girls).
Faculty School total: 13. In upper school: 1 man, 12 women; 4 have advanced degrees.
Subjects Offered Adolescent issues, advanced computer applications, algebra, American literature, anatomy and physiology, anthropology, art appreciation, astronomy, biology, calculus, chemistry, composition, creative writing, earth and space science, economics, English, English literature, French, geography, geometry, integrated mathematics, journalism, marine biology, math analysis, music appreciation, mythology, oceanography, physics, pre-calculus, printmaking, probability and statistics, psychology, reading, sociology, Spanish, theater, trigonometry, U.S. history, world history, world literature.

Graduation Requirements Arts and fine arts (art, music, dance, drama), English, foreign language, mathematics, personal development, practical arts, science, social science, 2 semesters of cultural geography, 1 semester of business math, 75 hours of volunteer service.
Special Academic Programs Accelerated programs; independent study; term-away projects; academic accommodation for the gifted, the musically talented, and the artistically talented; remedial reading and/or remedial writing; remedial math; programs in English, mathematics, general development for dyslexic students; special instructional classes for deaf students, blind students.
College Admission Counseling 6 students graduated in 2008; 4 went to college, including California State University, San Marcos; MiraCosta College; Palomar College; University of Southern California. Other: 2 went to work.
Student Life Upper grades have student council, honor system. Discipline rests primarily with faculty.
Summer Programs Remediation, enrichment, advancement, art/fine arts, computer instruction programs offered; session focuses on advancement; held on campus; accepts boys and girls; open to students from other schools. 125 students usually enrolled. 2009 schedule: June 15 to August 21. Application deadline: none.
Tuition and Aid Day student tuition: $7000–$10,000. Tuition installment plan (monthly payment plans, individually arranged payment plans). Tuition reduction for siblings, need-based scholarship grants, discount for teachers' sons/daughters available. In 2008–09, 5% of upper-school students received aid. Total amount of financial aid awarded in 2008–09: $10,000.
Admissions Traditional secondary-level entrance grade is 10. For fall 2008, 27 students applied for upper-level admission, 27 were accepted, 27 enrolled. Achievement/Aptitude/Writing required. Deadline for receipt of application materials: none. Application fee required: $150. On-campus interview required.
Computers Computers are regularly used in all academic, computer applications classes. Computer network features include Internet access, Internet filtering or blocking technology.
Contact Ms. Gabrielle Kathleen Azzaro, Director. 760-732-1200. Fax: 760-643-1849. E-mail: gabeazzaro@halstromhs.org. Web site: www.halstromhs.org.

HALSTROM HIGH SCHOOL—SAN DIEGO

5333 Mission Center Road
Suite 350
San Diego, California 92108-4340
Head of School: Mrs. Micaela Rall

General Information Coeducational day and distance learning college-preparatory, general academic, and vocational school; primarily serves underachievers and individuals with Attention Deficit Disorder. Grades 7–12. Distance learning grades 7–12. Founded: 1991. Setting: urban. 1 building on campus. Approved or accredited by Western Association of Schools and Colleges and California Department of Education. Total enrollment: 38. Upper school average class size: 1. Upper school faculty-student ratio: 1:4.
Upper School Student Profile Grade 7: 1 student (1 boy); Grade 8: 2 students (1 boy, 1 girl); Grade 9: 4 students (2 boys, 2 girls); Grade 10: 5 students (4 boys, 1 girl); Grade 11: 9 students (4 boys, 5 girls); Grade 12: 17 students (11 boys, 6 girls).
Faculty School total: 12. In upper school: 5 men, 7 women; 7 have advanced degrees.
Subjects Offered Algebra, American literature, anatomy and physiology, art appreciation, arts, biology, British literature, business mathematics, calculus, career/college preparation, chemistry, computer applications, contemporary issues, economics, English, fine arts, French, geometry, health, mathematics, physical education, physics, pre-calculus, social studies, Spanish, trigonometry, U.S. government, U.S. history, world history.
Graduation Requirements Arts and fine arts (art, music, dance, drama), computer applications, English, foreign language, mathematics, personal development, physical education (includes health), science, social studies (includes history), portfolio presentation, proficiency exams, volunteer credit hours. Community service is required.
Special Academic Programs Advanced Placement exam preparation; accelerated programs; term-away projects; study at local college for college credit; academic accommodation for the gifted, the musically talented, and the artistically talented; remedial reading and/or remedial writing; remedial math; special instructional classes for students with mild learning disabilities and Attention Deficit Disorder.
College Admission Counseling 12 students graduated in 2008; 10 went to college, including California State University, San Marcos; San Diego State University; University of California, Riverside; University of California, Santa Barbara. Other: 1 went to work, 1 had other specific plans.
Student Life Upper grades have honor system. Discipline rests primarily with faculty.
Summer Programs Remediation, enrichment, advancement, art/fine arts, computer instruction programs offered; session focuses on advancement and remedial academic work; held on campus; accepts boys and girls; open to students from other schools. 130 students usually enrolled. 2009 schedule: June 15 to August 21. Application deadline: June 1.
Tuition and Aid Day student tuition: $6120–$9180. Tuition installment plan (monthly payment plans, individually arranged payment plans). Tuition reduction for siblings, need-based scholarship grants available. In 2008–09, 5% of upper-school students received aid. Total amount of financial aid awarded in 2008–09: $6120.
Admissions Traditional secondary-level entrance grade is 10. For fall 2008, 35 students applied for upper-level admission, 35 were accepted, 35 enrolled. English language and Math Placement Exam required. Deadline for receipt of application materials: none. Application fee required: $150. On-campus interview required.
Computers Computers are regularly used in English, foreign language, history, mathematics, science classes. Computer network features include Internet access, wireless campus network, Internet filtering or blocking technology. Computer access in designated common areas is available to students. Students grades are available online. The school has a published electronic and media policy.
Contact Ashley Kowal, Administrative Assistant. 619-297-5311. Fax: 619-297-5313. E-mail: akowal@halstrom.org. Web site: www.halstrom.org.

HAMDEN HALL COUNTRY DAY SCHOOL

1108 Whitney Avenue
Hamden, Connecticut 06517
Head of School: Robert J. Izzo

General Information Coeducational day college-preparatory school. Grades PK–12. Founded: 1912. Setting: suburban. Nearest major city is New Haven. 42-acre campus. 8 buildings on campus. Approved or accredited by Connecticut Association of Independent Schools, New England Association of Schools and Colleges, and Connecticut Department of Education. Member of National Association of Independent Schools. Endowment: $4.6 million. Total enrollment: 565. Upper school average class size: 15. Upper school faculty-student ratio: 1:8.
Upper School Student Profile Grade 9: 74 students (40 boys, 34 girls); Grade 10: 67 students (38 boys, 29 girls); Grade 11: 68 students (41 boys, 27 girls); Grade 12: 59 students (35 boys, 24 girls).
Faculty School total: 81. In upper school: 23 men, 22 women; 29 have advanced degrees.
Subjects Offered African-American history, algebra, American literature, anatomy, art history, astronomy, biology, British literature, calculus, ceramics, chamber groups, chemistry, chorus, computer graphics, computer multimedia, computer programming, constitutional law, creative writing, digital photography, drama, drawing, electronics, English language and composition-AP, European history-AP, expository writing, French, genetics, geology, geometry, improvisation, independent study, jazz, Latin, life science, marine biology, meteorology, multimedia design, music appreciation, music history, music theory, oceanography, painting, peer counseling, performing arts, physiology, playwriting, poetry, printmaking, sculpture, Spanish, speech, statistics, theater, trigonometry, U.S. history, Western civilization, women in literature, world history, world literature, zoology.
Graduation Requirements Arts and fine arts (art, music, dance, drama), computer science, English, foreign language, mathematics, physical education (includes health), science, social studies (includes history), participation in 2 athletic seasons each year.
Special Academic Programs Advanced Placement exam preparation; honors section; independent study.
College Admission Counseling 61 students graduated in 2008; all went to college, including Skidmore College; Yale University. Median SAT critical reading: 600, median SAT math: 600, median SAT writing: 600, median combined SAT: 1800, median composite ACT: 26.
Student Life Upper grades have specified standards of dress, student council, honor system. Discipline rests equally with students and faculty.
Summer Programs Remediation, enrichment, advancement, sports, art/fine arts, computer instruction programs offered; held on campus; accepts boys and girls; open to students from other schools. 450 students usually enrolled. 2009 schedule: June 15 to August 7. Application deadline: none.
Tuition and Aid Day student tuition: $26,450. Tuition installment plan (Key Tuition Payment Plan). Need-based scholarship grants, need-based loans, paying campus jobs, Key Education Resources available. In 2008–09, 30% of upper-school students received aid.
Admissions Traditional secondary-level entrance grade is 9. For fall 2008, 160 students applied for upper-level admission, 118 were accepted, 52 enrolled. ISEE or SSAT required. Deadline for receipt of application materials: February 1. Application fee required: $50. Interview required.
Athletics Interscholastic: baseball (boys), basketball (b,g), field hockey (g), football (b), lacrosse (b,g), soccer (b,g), softball (g), tennis (b,g), volleyball (g), wrestling (b); coed interscholastic: cross-country running, golf, ice hockey, swimming and diving; coed intramural: outdoors, physical fitness, running, weight training. 3 PE instructors, 15 coaches, 1 athletic trainer.
Computers Computer network features include on-campus library services, Internet access, wireless campus network, Internet filtering or blocking technology. Student e-mail accounts are available to students. The school has a published electronic and media policy.
Contact Janet B. Izzo, Director of Admissions. 203-752-2610. Fax: 203-752-2611. E-mail: jizzo@hamdenhall.org. Web site: www.hamdenhall.org.

ANNOUNCEMENT FROM THE SCHOOL Hamden Hall Country Day School is a coeducational, college-preparatory school enrolling nearly 600 students in grades PK–12. It is set on 12 acres overlooking Lake Whitney in south-central Connecticut, just north of New Haven and Yale University, with an additional 30 acres of athletics fields. Hamden Hall was founded in 1912 as a day school for boys by Dr. John P. Cushing, its first headmaster. Coeducation was introduced in 1927 and, within seven years, the School was expanded to encompass grades 9–12. A comprehensive college-preparatory program was implemented in 1935. The mission of Hamden Hall is to provide a challenging education that fosters academic excellence while formulating a student's character, value system, and sense of independence. The faculty members, having earned 92 baccalaureate and 59 advanced degrees, including 7 doctorates, are well qualified in their areas of specialization. They serve as role models and mentors in the classroom, on the playing field, and in other areas of school life. With an 8:1 student-teacher ratio, the School aims to offer a nurturing environment in which young people can reach their full potential intellectually, physically, and socially. The program is specially structured for students making the transition from childhood to adolescence. The curriculum builds on the skills acquired in the early grades and combines them with new challenges and techniques designed to maximize learning. Students in the Upper School combine a demanding curriculum of interscholastic sports and a variety of clubs and extracurricular activities, including the Princeton Peer Leadership program. Advanced Placement and honors courses are offered in most major disciplines as is independent study. A full-time college counseling staff works with students and parents. In 2008, all of the 61 graduating students entered such colleges and universities as Brown, Dickinson, Gettysburg, Skidmore, Yale, and the University of Rochester.

HAMILTON DISTRICT CHRISTIAN HIGH

92 Glancaster Road
Ancaster, Ontario L9G 3K9, Canada
Head of School: Mr. George Van Kampen

General Information Coeducational day college-preparatory, general academic, arts, business, vocational, religious studies, and technology school, affiliated with Christian faith. Grades 9–12. Founded: 1956. Setting: suburban. Nearest major city is Hamilton, Canada. 22-acre campus. 1 building on campus. Approved or accredited by Christian Schools International and Ontario Ministry of Education. Language of instruction: English. Total enrollment: 500. Upper school average class size: 19. Upper school faculty-student ratio: 1:19.

Upper School Student Profile 100% of students are Christian faith.

Faculty School total: 36. In upper school: 21 men, 15 women; 8 have advanced degrees.

Subjects Offered 20th century history, 3-dimensional art, 3-dimensional design, accounting, acting, adolescent issues, advanced chemistry, advanced computer applications, advanced math, ancient history, ancient world history, applied arts, architectural drawing, art, art history, Bible, biology, business technology, calculus, Canadian geography, Canadian history, Canadian law, career experience, carpentry, chemistry, choir, civics, computer applications, computer keyboarding, computer multimedia, computer programming, computer technologies, computer-aided design, concert band, creative writing, drafting, drama, economics, English literature, environmental science, ESL, family and consumer sciences, finite math, food and nutrition, French, geometry, guidance, history, instrumental music, keyboarding/computer, leadership training, mathematics, media, modern Western civilization, music, peer counseling, personal finance, physical education, physics, religious studies, science, sociology, trigonometry, woodworking.

Graduation Requirements Art, Bible, Canadian geography, Canadian history, career education, civics, computer keyboarding, English, French, history, mathematics, science, 40 hours of community service.

Special Academic Programs 6 Advanced Placement exams for which test preparation is offered; independent study; term-away projects; academic accommodation for the musically talented and the artistically talented; remedial reading and/or remedial writing; remedial math; ESL (10 students enrolled).

College Admission Counseling 142 students graduated in 2008; 114 went to college, including McMaster University; Queen's University at Kingston; Redeemer University College; The University of Western Ontario; University of Waterloo; Wilfrid Laurier University. Other: 20 went to work, 8 had other specific plans. Median composite ACT: 23. 25% scored over 26 on composite ACT.

Student Life Upper grades have uniform requirement, student council. Discipline rests primarily with faculty.

Tuition and Aid Day student tuition: CAN$10,820. Tuition installment plan (monthly payment plans, individually arranged payment plans). Need-based scholarship grants, tuition assistance fund, family rate tuition; additional children at no extra charge, reduced rate for 2-school tuition families and home school families available. In 2008–09, 6% of upper-school students received aid. Total amount of financial aid awarded in 2008–09: CAN$72,000.

Admissions Traditional secondary-level entrance grade is 9. Deadline for receipt of application materials: none. No application fee required. Interview required.

Athletics Interscholastic: badminton (boys, girls), baseball (g), basketball (b,g), cross-country running (b,g), golf (b,g), hockey (b), ice hockey (b), lacrosse (b), running (b,g), soccer (b,g), softball (g), touch football (b), track and field (b,g), volleyball (b,g); intramural: ball hockey (b,g), basketball (b,g), flag football (b,g), floor hockey (b,g), volleyball (b,g), wallyball (b,g), whiffle ball (b,g); coed interscholastic: badminton, ultimate Frisbee; coed intramural: floor hockey, horseback riding, indoor soccer, mountain biking.

Computers Computers are regularly used in art, business studies, career education, career exploration, college planning, current events, desktop publishing, drafting, economics, English, ESL, ethics, geography, graphic arts, graphic design, history, independent study, keyboarding, library, literary magazine, mathematics, media production, music, news writing, newspaper, photography, religious studies, research skills, science, video film production, Web site design, writing, yearbook classes. Computer network features include on-campus library services, online commercial services, Internet access, wireless campus network, Internet filtering or blocking technology, course Web pages, course chat rooms. Campus intranet, student e-mail accounts, and computer access in designated common areas are available to students. Students grades are available online. The school has a published electronic and media policy.

Contact Ms. Janet Hagen, Office Manager. 905-648-6655 Ext. 103. Fax: 905-648-3139. E-mail: jhagen@hdch.org. Web site: www.hdch.org.

HAMMOND SCHOOL

854 Galway Lane
Columbia, South Carolina 29209
Head of School: Mr. Mike Collins

General Information Coeducational day college-preparatory, arts, and technology school. Grades PK–12. Founded: 1966. Setting: suburban. 108-acre campus. 20 buildings on campus. Approved or accredited by South Carolina Independent School Association and Southern Association of Colleges and Schools. Member of National Association of Independent Schools and Secondary School Admission Test Board. Endowment: $100,000. Total enrollment: 980. Upper school average class size: 15. Upper school faculty-student ratio: 1:9.

Upper School Student Profile Grade 9: 69 students (36 boys, 33 girls); Grade 10: 67 students (34 boys, 33 girls); Grade 11: 61 students (28 boys, 33 girls); Grade 12: 67 students (38 boys, 29 girls).

Faculty School total: 112. In upper school: 30 men, 30 women; 45 have advanced degrees.

Subjects Offered Advanced Placement courses, African American history, algebra, American government, American history, American literature, art, art history, biology, calculus, chemistry, choir, chorus, computer programming, computer science, creative writing, drama, earth science, economics, electives, English, English literature, European history, film studies, finite math, French, geometry, government/civics, history, journalism, Latin, mathematics, music, physical education, physics, science, social studies, Spanish, speech, trigonometry, world history, world literature.

Graduation Requirements Arts and fine arts (art, music, dance, drama), English, foreign language, mathematics, physical education (includes health), science, social studies (includes history).

Special Academic Programs Advanced Placement exam preparation; honors section; independent study; study abroad; academic accommodation for the gifted, the musically talented, and the artistically talented; remedial reading and/or remedial writing; programs in general development for dyslexic students.

College Admission Counseling 78 students graduated in 2008; all went to college, including Clemson University; The University of North Carolina at Chapel Hill; University of South Carolina; Washington and Lee University; Wofford College. 32% scored over 600 on SAT critical reading, 32% scored over 600 on SAT math, 32% scored over 600 on SAT writing.

Student Life Upper grades have uniform requirement, student council, honor system. Discipline rests primarily with faculty.

Tuition and Aid Day student tuition: $13,515. Tuition installment plan (Insured Tuition Payment Plan, local bank finance plan). Merit scholarship grants, need-based scholarship grants available. In 2008–09, 15% of upper-school students received aid. Total amount of financial aid awarded in 2008–09: $1,200,000.

Admissions Traditional secondary-level entrance grade is 9. For fall 2008, 52 students applied for upper-level admission, 28 were accepted, 24 enrolled. ACT, any standardized test, ISEE, PSAT or SSAT required. Deadline for receipt of application materials: none. Application fee required: $75. Interview required.

Athletics Interscholastic: aerobics/dance (girls), backpacking (b,g), ballet (b,g), baseball (b), basketball (b,g), canoeing/kayaking (b,g), cheering (b,g), climbing (b,g), combined training (b,g), cross-country running (b,g), dance squad (g), equestrian sports (b,g), fitness (b,g), football (b), Frisbee (b,g), golf (b,g), hiking/backpacking (b,g), horseback riding (b,g), kayaking (b,g), lacrosse (b), physical fitness (b,g), physical training (b,g), rafting (b,g), rappelling (b,g), rock climbing (b,g), ropes courses (b,g), skeet shooting (b,g), soccer (b,g), softball (g), strength & conditioning (b,g), swimming and diving (b,g), tennis (b,g), track and field (b,g), trap and skeet (b,g), ultimate Frisbee (b,g), volleyball (g), wall climbing (b,g), weight lifting (b,g), weight training (b,g), wilderness (b,g), wrestling (b); coed interscholastic: ballet, cheering, cross-country running, equestrian sports, Frisbee, golf, horseback riding, outdoor activities, skeet shooting, soccer, trap and skeet, ultimate Frisbee. 3 PE instructors, 1 coach, 1 athletic trainer.

Computers Computer network features include on-campus library services, online commercial services, Internet access, Internet filtering or blocking technology. Campus intranet and student e-mail accounts are available to students. Students grades are available online.

Contact Mr. Matt Radtke, Director of Admission. 803-776-0295. Fax: 803-776-0122. E-mail: mradtke@hammondschool.org. Web site: www.hammondschool.org.

ANNOUNCEMENT FROM THE SCHOOL Hammond School was founded in 1966 by a group of parents who were interested in developing an independent, college-preparatory school in Columbia, South Carolina. The School is located on a 108-acre campus in southeast Columbia. It is a coeducational school with 980 students attending preschool through grade 12. Hammond School has a reputation not only for academic excellence but also for its emphasis on character, honor, and service. An Honor Code dictates the high standards of behavior expected of Hammond students. The primary mission of the School is to provide a challenging academic program that prepares students to attend the finest colleges and universities in the nation. To that end, 112 faculty members teach in a small setting with a curriculum tailored to the individual. The educational plan focuses on skills. From the youngest to the oldest, students are expected to master foundational skills in the core curriculum areas of reading, writing, and computation. Advanced work is available in all disciplines and most students begin college with earned credits from Advanced Placement courses taken at Hammond. One hundred percent of Hammond graduates attend college. The average combined SAT score in 2007–08 was 1224. More Hammond graduates have received National Merit recognition than have graduates of any other area independent school. Hammond graduates attend Vanderbilt, Columbia, Clemson, Boston, Washington and Lee, Virginia, Tufts, UNC at Chapel Hill, Brigham Young, and Furman, among others. College counseling begins in grade 9 and culminates in the application and selection process in grade 12. Ninety-one percent of the class of 2008 earned academic scholarships to colleges and universities. Hammond offers a wide variety of extracurricular experiences for students. Beginning in grade 7, students may participate in interscholastic athletics in thirteen areas. Fine arts at Hammond are a major component of the program. Auditioned music students have performed at the Vatican twice and participated in a singing tour in the Czech Republic. Both visual arts and drama are equally recognized for their exhibitions and performances. In addition, an outdoor program offers nature and environmental study, as well as hiking, rock climbing, and white-water rafting. The global facet of the Hammond program includes the full-school study of a specific country each year and opportunities for international travel for upper school students and faculty members.

HAMPSHIRE COUNTRY SCHOOL

Rindge, New Hampshire

See Junior Boarding Schools section.

HANALANI SCHOOLS

94-294 Anania Drive
Mililani, Hawaii 96789

Head of School: Mr. Mark Y. Sugimoto

General Information Coeducational day college-preparatory, arts, religious studies, bilingual studies, and technology school, affiliated with Christian faith. Grades PK–12. Founded: 1952. Setting: suburban. 6-acre campus. 5 buildings on campus. Approved or accredited by The Hawaii Council of Private Schools, Western Association of Schools and Colleges, and Hawaii Department of Education. Total enrollment: 703. Upper school average class size: 20. Upper school faculty-student ratio: 1:12.

Upper School Student Profile Grade 7: 50 students (22 boys, 28 girls); Grade 8: 42 students (19 boys, 23 girls); Grade 9: 51 students (23 boys, 28 girls); Grade 10: 51 students (27 boys, 24 girls); Grade 11: 54 students (24 boys, 30 girls); Grade 12: 35 students (15 boys, 20 girls). 98% of students are Christian faith.

Faculty School total: 59. In upper school: 15 men, 10 women; 6 have advanced degrees.

Subjects Offered Advanced math, Advanced Placement courses, algebra, American government, American literature, art, band, basketball, Bible, Bible studies, biology, British literature, calculus, calculus-AP, cheerleading, chemistry, chemistry-AP, choir, chorus, Christian doctrine, Christian ethics, computer skills, concert band, consumer mathematics, drafting, drama, earth science, English composition, English literature, English-AP, ethics, geography, geometry, golf, grammar, handbells, intro to computers, Japanese, Japanese as Second Language, Japanese studies, journalism, keyboarding, language development, leadership training, Life of Christ, life science, music, paleontology, physical education, physical science, physics, piano, pre-algebra, pre-calculus, robotics, SAT preparation, sign language, Spanish, speech, student government, student publications, study skills, theology, transition mathematics, trigonometry, U.S. history, U.S. history-AP, video, voice, volleyball, world history, writing, yearbook.

Graduation Requirements Arts and fine arts (art, music, dance, drama), Bible, Bible studies, electives, English, foreign language, guidance, mathematics, physical education (includes health), science, social studies (includes history), technology. Community service is required.

Special Academic Programs Advanced Placement exam preparation; honors section; independent study; remedial reading and/or remedial writing; remedial math.

College Admission Counseling 32 students graduated in 2008; all went to college, including Chaminade University of Honolulu; Hawai'i Pacific University; Pacific University; University of California, Davis; University of California, Irvine; University of Hawaii at Manoa. Mean SAT critical reading: 522, mean SAT math: 512, mean SAT writing: 503, mean combined SAT: 1540. 25% scored over 600 on SAT critical reading, 10% scored over 600 on SAT math, 19% scored over 600 on SAT writing, 8% scored over 1800 on combined SAT.

Student Life Upper grades have uniform requirement, student council, honor system. Discipline rests primarily with faculty. Attendance at religious services is required.

Summer Programs Remediation, enrichment, advancement, sports, art/fine arts, computer instruction programs offered; session focuses on enrichment and advancement; held on campus; accepts boys and girls; open to students from other schools. 60 students usually enrolled. 2009 schedule: June 8 to July 17. Application deadline: June 6.

Tuition and Aid Day student tuition: $7995. Tuition installment plan (monthly payment plans, individually arranged payment plans, lump-sum payment). Tuition reduction for siblings, need-based scholarship grants, student referral credit available. In 2008–09, 9% of upper-school students received aid. Total amount of financial aid awarded in 2008–09: $78,363.

Admissions Traditional secondary-level entrance grade is 9. For fall 2008, 100 students applied for upper-level admission, 45 were accepted, 45 enrolled. School's own test and Stanford Achievement Test required. Deadline for receipt of application materials: none. Application fee required: $50. On-campus interview required.

Athletics Interscholastic: archery (boys), baseball (b), basketball (b,g), bowling (g), cheering (g), cross-country running (b), football (b), golf (b,g), soccer (b,g), track and field (b), volleyball (b,g); intramural: basketball (b,g), fitness (b,g), flag football (b,g), football (b,g), physical fitness (b,g), soccer (b,g), strength & conditioning (b,g), track and field (b,g), volleyball (b,g), weight lifting (b,g), weight training (b,g); coed intramural: indoor soccer, jump rope, kickball. 3 PE instructors, 2 coaches.

Computers Computers are regularly used in journalism, newspaper, science, social science, yearbook classes. Computer network features include on-campus library services, online commercial services, Internet access, wireless campus network, Internet filtering or blocking technology, desktop publishing applications, Ebsco, Moodle. Students grades are available online. The school has a published electronic and media policy.

Contact Ms. Nancy Jeanne Cowley, Admissions Director. 808-625-0737 Ext. 456. Fax: 808-625-0691. E-mail: admissions@hanalani.org. Web site: www.hanalani.org.

HANSON MEMORIAL HIGH SCHOOL

903 Anderson Street
Franklin, Louisiana 70538-0000

Head of School: Mr. Kenneth Edward Alfred

General Information Coeducational day and distance learning college-preparatory, general academic, arts, business, vocational, religious studies, and technology school, affiliated with Roman Catholic Church; primarily serves individuals with Attention Deficit Disorder and dyslexic students. Grades 6–12. Distance learning grades 9–12. Founded: 1925. Setting: rural. Nearest major city is Lafayette. 14-acre campus. 4 buildings on campus. Approved or accredited by National Catholic Education Association, Southern Association of Colleges and Schools, and Louisiana Department of Education. Total enrollment: 260. Upper school average class size: 23. Upper school faculty-student ratio: 1:13.

Upper School Student Profile 80% of students are Roman Catholic.

Faculty School total: 20. In upper school: 4 men, 16 women; 5 have advanced degrees.

Special Academic Programs Study at local college for college credit; programs in English, mathematics, general development for dyslexic students.

College Admission Counseling 38 students graduated in 2008; they went to Louisiana State University and Agricultural and Mechanical College.

Student Life Upper grades have uniform requirement, student council, honor system. Discipline rests primarily with faculty. Attendance at religious services is required.

Tuition and Aid Tuition installment plan (monthly payment plans). Tuition reduction for siblings, need-based scholarship grants available. In 2008–09, 10% of upper-school students received aid.

Admissions Deadline for receipt of application materials: February 28. No application fee required. On-campus interview required.

Athletics Interscholastic: baseball (boys), basketball (b,g), cheering (b,g), cross-country running (b,g), drill team (g), football (b), golf (b,g), gymnastics (b,g), softball (g), strength & conditioning (b,g), track and field (b,g), weight lifting (b,g); coed interscholastic: cheering, cross-country running, golf, gymnastics. 7 coaches.

Computers Computers are regularly used in all academic classes. Computer network features include on-campus library services, online commercial services, Internet access, wireless campus network, Internet filtering or blocking technology. Students grades are available online. The school has a published electronic and media policy.

Contact Mr. Kenneth E. Alfred, Principal. 337-828-3487. Fax: 337-828-0787. E-mail: kalfred@hansonmemorial.com. Web site: www.hansonmemorial.com.

HARDING ACADEMY

Box 10775, Harding University
1529 East Park Avenue
Searcy, Arkansas 72149

Head of School: Mark Benton

General Information Coeducational boarding and day college-preparatory, vocational, and religious studies school, affiliated with Church of Christ. Boarding grades 9–12, day grades K–12. Founded: 1924. Setting: small town. Nearest major city is Little Rock. Students are housed in single-sex dormitories. 15-acre campus. 1 building on campus. Approved or accredited by National Christian School Association, North Central Association of Colleges and Schools, and Arkansas Department of Education. Total enrollment: 589. Upper school average class size: 25. Upper school faculty-student ratio: 1:11.

Upper School Student Profile Grade 7: 53 students (28 boys, 25 girls); Grade 8: 48 students (20 boys, 28 girls); Grade 9: 39 students (16 boys, 23 girls); Grade 10: 44 students (22 boys, 22 girls); Grade 11: 48 students (26 boys, 22 girls); Grade 12: 55 students (30 boys, 25 girls). 9% of students are boarding students. 91% are state residents. 2 states are represented in upper school student body. 9% are international students. International students from China and Japan. 78% of students are members of Church of Christ.

Faculty School total: 55. In upper school: 16 men, 12 women; 21 have advanced degrees; 1 resides on campus.

Subjects Offered Accounting, ACT preparation, advanced math, algebra, American history, anatomy, art, Bible, Bible studies, biology, calculus-AP, chemistry, chorus, civics, computer applications, computer programming, consumer education, English, English-AP, family living, geography, geometry, health, history, history-AP, human anatomy, journalism, keyboarding/computer, life skills, mathematics, modern world history, music appreciation, physical education, physical science, physics-AP, pre-calculus, psychology, science, Spanish, speech, statistics, study skills, wellness.

Special Academic Programs Advanced Placement exam preparation; study at local college for college credit; academic accommodation for the gifted.

College Admission Counseling 46 students graduated in 2008; 44 went to college, including Arkansas State University; Harding University; Henderson State University.

Student Life Upper grades have specified standards of dress, student council, honor system. Discipline rests primarily with faculty. Attendance at religious services is required.

Tuition and Aid Day student tuition: $3250–$5250; 7-day tuition and room/board: $9500–$11,000. Tuition installment plan (monthly payment plans).

Admissions Traditional secondary-level entrance grade is 9. Any standardized test or TOEFL required. Deadline for receipt of application materials: none. Application fee required: $100. Interview recommended.

Athletics Interscholastic: baseball (boys), basketball (b,g), cheering (g), cross-country running (b,g), football (b), golf (b,g), softball (g), tennis (b,g), track and field (b,g), weight lifting (b). 4 PE instructors, 8 coaches.

Computers Computers are regularly used in all academic classes. Computer network features include on-campus library services, Internet access. Students grades are available online. The school has a published electronic and media policy.

Contact Darren Mathews, Dean of High School. 501-279-7201. Fax: 501-279-7213. E-mail: dmathews@harding.edu. Web site: www.harding.edu/hacademy/.

HARDING ACADEMY

170 Windsor Drive
Nashville, Tennessee 37205

Head of School: Ian Craig

General Information Coeducational day college-preparatory, general academic, arts, and technology school. Grades K–8. Founded: 1971. Setting: suburban. 7-acre campus. Approved or accredited by Southern Association of Colleges and Schools, Southern Association of Independent Schools, and Tennessee Department of Education. Endowment: $2.2 million. Total enrollment: 508.

Upper School Student Profile Grade 6: 57 students (26 boys, 31 girls); Grade 7: 53 students (26 boys, 27 girls); Grade 8: 55 students (23 boys, 32 girls).

Faculty School total: 61.

Subjects Offered Algebra, art, chorus, civics, computers, dance, drama, English, French, history, jazz band, lab science, library, mathematics, music, physical education, pre-algebra, science.

Student Life Upper grades have specified standards of dress, honor system. Discipline rests primarily with faculty.

Tuition and Aid Day student tuition: $13,045. Tuition installment plan (monthly payment plans). Need-based scholarship grants available.

Admissions Traditional secondary-level entrance grade is 7. Achievement/Aptitude/Writing, CTP III, ERB, Gates MacGinite (vocab) and Stanford Achievement Test (math), ISEE, Otis-Lennon School Ability Test or writing sample required. Deadline for receipt of application materials: none. Application fee required: $65.

Athletics Interscholastic: baseball (boys), basketball (b,g), cheering (g), soccer (b,g), softball (g), tennis (b,g), track and field (b,g), volleyball (g), wrestling (b); intramural: dance (g); coed interscholastic: cross-country running, golf; coed intramural: ballet, Frisbee, indoor soccer, modern dance. 4 PE instructors, 15 coaches.

Computers Computer resources include on-campus library services, online commercial services, Internet access, wireless campus network, Internet filtering or blocking technology. Campus intranet is available to students. Students grades are available online.

Contact Admission Department. 615-356-5510.

HARGRAVE MILITARY ACADEMY

200 Military Drive
Chatham, Virginia 24531

Head of School: Col. Wheeler Baker, USMC (Retired), PhD

General Information Boys' boarding and day college-preparatory, general academic, arts, religious studies, technology, academic post-graduate, leadership and ethics, and military school, affiliated with Baptist General Association of Virginia. Grades 7–PG. Founded: 1909. Setting: small town. Nearest major city is Danville. Students are housed in single-sex dormitories. 276-acre campus. 13 buildings on campus. Approved or accredited by Southern Association of Colleges and Schools, The Association of Boarding Schools, and Virginia Association of Independent Schools. Member of National Association of Independent Schools. Endowment: $4 million. Total enrollment: 365. Upper school average class size: 11. Upper school faculty-student ratio: 1:12.

Upper School Student Profile 95% of students are boarding students. 29% are state residents. 34 states are represented in upper school student body. 8% are international students. International students from China, Egypt, and Republic of Korea; 4 other countries represented in student body. 20% of students are Baptist General Association of Virginia.

Faculty School total: 52. In upper school: 35 men, 17 women; 30 have advanced degrees; 11 reside on campus.

Subjects Offered 3-dimensional design, advanced biology, advanced chemistry, advanced math, Advanced Placement courses, algebra, American government, American history, American literature, art, astronomy, Bible studies, biology, calculus, chemistry, creative writing, debate, drama, driver education, English, English literature, environmental science, ESL, French, geography, geometry, government/civics, health, history, journalism, leadership, leadership and service, leadership education training, leadership skills, leadership training, mathematics, media production, meteorology, physical education, physics, psychology, reading, religion, SAT/ACT preparation, science, social studies, sociology, Spanish, speech, study skills, TOEFL preparation, trigonometry.

Graduation Requirements Computer science, English, foreign language, mathematics, physical education (includes health), religion (includes Bible studies and theology), science, social studies (includes history).

Special Academic Programs Advanced Placement exam preparation; honors section; independent study; study at local college for college credit; remedial reading and/or remedial writing; remedial math; programs in general development for dyslexic students; special instructional classes for Students with Attention Deficit Disorder; ESL (8 students enrolled).

College Admission Counseling 76 students graduated in 2008; 74 went to college, including The University of North Carolina at Charlotte; United States Military Academy; United States Naval Academy; Virginia Military Institute; Virginia Polytechnic Institute and State University. Other: 1 entered military service, 1 entered a postgraduate year.

Student Life Upper grades have uniform requirement, student council, honor system. Discipline rests equally with students and faculty. Attendance at religious services is required.

Summer Programs Remediation, enrichment, advancement, ESL, sports, rigorous outdoor training, computer instruction programs offered; session focuses on academics/sports camps; held on campus; accepts boys; open to students from other schools. 150 students usually enrolled. 2009 schedule: June 28 to July 25. Application deadline: June 27.

Tuition and Aid Day student tuition: $13,500; 5-day tuition and room/board: $29,500; 7-day tuition and room/board: $29,500. Guaranteed tuition plan. Tuition installment plan (monthly payment plans, individually arranged payment plans). Tuition reduction for siblings, merit scholarship grants, need-based scholarship grants, need-based loans, Sallie Mae available. In 2008–09, 32% of upper-school students received aid; total upper-school merit-scholarship money awarded: $150,000. Total amount of financial aid awarded in 2008–09: $525,000.

Admissions Traditional secondary-level entrance grade is 10. Math and English placement tests required. Deadline for receipt of application materials: none. Application fee required: $75. Interview recommended.

Athletics Interscholastic: aquatics, baseball, basketball, cross-country running, diving, football, golf, lacrosse, marksmanship, riflery, soccer, swimming and diving, tennis, wrestling; intramural: aquatics, backpacking, billiards, canoeing/kayaking, climbing, cross-country running, drill team, fishing, fitness, fitness walking, hiking/backpacking, independent competitive sports, jogging, jump rope, kayaking, lacrosse, life saving, marksmanship, mountaineering, Nautilus, outdoor activities, paint ball, physical fitness, physical training, rappelling, riflery, rock climbing, ropes courses, running, scuba diving, skeet shooting, skiing (downhill), strength & conditioning, swimming and diving, table tennis, tennis, trap and skeet, walking, water polo, weight lifting, weight training. 2 PE instructors, 9 coaches, 1 athletic trainer.

Computers Computers are regularly used in all classes. Computer network features include on-campus library services, online commercial services, Internet access,

wireless campus network, Internet filtering or blocking technology. Campus intranet, student e-mail accounts, and computer access in designated common areas are available to students. Students grades are available online. The school has a published electronic and media policy.
Contact Mrs. Amy Walker, Director of Admissions. 434-432-2481 Ext. 2130. Fax: 434-432-3129. E-mail: admissions@hargrave.edu. Web site: www.hargrave.edu.

THE HARKER SCHOOL

500 Saratoga Avenue
San Jose, California 95129

Head of School: Christopher Nikoloff

General Information Coeducational day college-preparatory, arts, technology, and gifted students school. Grades K–12. Founded: 1893. Setting: urban. 16-acre campus. 7 buildings on campus. Approved or accredited by California Association of Independent Schools, Western Association of Schools and Colleges, and California Department of Education. Member of National Association of Independent Schools. Total enrollment: 1,720. Upper school average class size: 16. Upper school faculty-student ratio: 1:10.
Upper School Student Profile Grade 9: 175 students (100 boys, 75 girls); Grade 10: 166 students (81 boys, 85 girls); Grade 11: 168 students (83 boys, 85 girls); Grade 12: 173 students (83 boys, 90 girls).
Faculty In upper school: 39 men, 37 women; 59 have advanced degrees.
Subjects Offered Acting, advanced math, aerobics, algebra, American literature, architecture, art history-AP, Asian history, Asian literature, astronomy, baseball, basketball, biology, biology-AP, British literature, British literature (honors), calculus-AP, ceramics, chemistry, chemistry-AP, choir, college counseling, community service, computer programming, computer science-AP, contemporary women writers, dance, dance performance, debate, discrete mathematics, drawing, ecology, economics, electronics, engineering, English literature and composition-AP, environmental science-AP, ethics, European history-AP, evolution, expository writing, fencing, film and literature, fitness, French, French language-AP, French literature-AP, golf, graphic arts, honors algebra, honors geometry, instrumental music, international affairs, Japanese, Latin, Latin-AP, linear algebra, literary magazine, macro/microeconomics-AP, macroeconomics-AP, Mandarin, medieval literature, mentorship program, music, music theory-AP, newspaper, orchestra, organic chemistry, painting, physics, physics-AP, physiology-anatomy, play production, political thought, pre-calculus, psychology-AP, public policy, public speaking, radio broadcasting, robotics, scene study, sculpture, self-defense, Shakespeare, softball, Spanish, Spanish language-AP, Spanish literature-AP, statistics, stone carving, student government, studio art-AP, study skills, swimming, technical theater, tennis, theater arts, track and field, trigonometry, U.S. government and politics-AP, U.S. history, U.S. history-AP, video and animation, visual arts, vocal ensemble, volleyball, weight training, Western philosophy, women in world history, world history, wrestling, yearbook, yoga.
Graduation Requirements Algebra, arts and fine arts (art, music, dance, drama), biology, chemistry, computer science, English, foreign language, geometry, physical education (includes health), physics, public speaking, trigonometry, U.S. history, world history, 30 total hours of community service.
Special Academic Programs Advanced Placement exam preparation; honors section; independent study; academic accommodation for the gifted.
College Admission Counseling 154 students graduated in 2008; all went to college, including Harvard University; Stanford University; University of California, Berkeley; University of California, Los Angeles; University of California, San Diego; University of Southern California. Mean SAT critical reading: 688, mean SAT math: 712, mean SAT writing: 702.
Student Life Upper grades have specified standards of dress, student council, honor system. Discipline rests primarily with faculty.
Summer Programs Enrichment, advancement programs offered; session focuses on academics; held both on and off campus; held at venues abroad for upper school students; accepts boys and girls; open to students from other schools. 700 students usually enrolled. 2009 schedule: June 22 to August 14.
Tuition and Aid Day student tuition: $29,894. Need-based scholarship grants, need-based loans available. In 2008–09, 10% of upper-school students received aid.
Admissions Traditional secondary-level entrance grade is 9. ERB CTP IV, essay, ISEE or SSAT required. Deadline for receipt of application materials: January 15. Application fee required: $75. Interview required.
Athletics Interscholastic: baseball (boys), basketball (b,g), cross-country running (b,g), football (b), golf (b,g), lacrosse (g), soccer (b,g), softball (g), swimming and diving (b,g), tennis (b,g), track and field (b,g), volleyball (b,g), water polo (b,g), wrestling (b,g); coed interscholastic: cheering, football; coed intramural: aerobics/dance, dance, fencing, fitness, physical fitness, tennis, yoga. 6 PE instructors, 60 coaches, 1 athletic trainer.
Computers Computers are regularly used in all academic, graphic arts, newspaper, programming, yearbook classes. Computer network features include on-campus library services, online commercial services, Internet access, wireless campus network, Internet filtering or blocking technology, ProQuest, Gale Group, InfoTrac, Facts On File. Student e-mail accounts are available to students. The school has a published electronic and media policy.
Contact Ruth Tebo, Assistant to the Director of Admission. 408-249-2510. Fax: 408-984-2325. E-mail: rutht@harker.org. Web site: www.harker.org.

See Close-Up on page 780.

THE HARLEY SCHOOL

1981 Clover Street
Rochester, New York 14618

Head of School: Dr. Timothy Cottrell

General Information Coeducational day college-preparatory and arts school. Grades N–12. Founded: 1917. Setting: suburban. 25-acre campus. 3 buildings on campus. Approved or accredited by National Independent Private Schools Association and New York State Association of Independent Schools. Member of National Association of Independent Schools. Endowment: $113 million. Total enrollment: 501. Upper school average class size: 7. Upper school faculty-student ratio: 1:7.
Upper School Student Profile Grade 9: 41 students (20 boys, 21 girls); Grade 10: 45 students (18 boys, 27 girls); Grade 11: 43 students (23 boys, 20 girls); Grade 12: 41 students (23 boys, 18 girls).
Faculty School total: 80. In upper school: 14 men, 14 women; 24 have advanced degrees.
Subjects Offered Advanced Placement courses, algebra, American history, anthropology, art, art history, band, biology, calculus, ceramics, chamber groups, chemistry, choir, chorus, community service, computer graphics, computer math, computer programming, computer science, creative writing, desktop publishing, drama, drawing, driver education, English, English literature, environmental science, ethics, European history, expository writing, film, fine arts, foreign language, French, geometry, graphic arts, Greek, health, jazz band, Latin, mathematics, music, music theory, orchestra, photography, physical education, physics, psychology, science, Shakespeare, social studies, Spanish, speech, study skills, theater, voice, world history, writing.
Graduation Requirements Arts and fine arts (art, music, dance, drama), computer science, English, foreign language, internship, mathematics, physical education (includes health), science, social studies (includes history), participation in team sports. Community service is required.
Special Academic Programs 17 Advanced Placement exams for which test preparation is offered; honors section; independent study; study abroad.
College Admission Counseling 39 students graduated in 2008; all went to college, including Brandeis University; Lehigh University; Oberlin College; Rensselaer Polytechnic Institute; United States Naval Academy; Vassar College. Mean SAT critical reading: 600, mean SAT math: 570, mean SAT writing: 580.
Student Life Upper grades have student council, honor system. Discipline rests primarily with faculty.
Summer Programs Remediation, enrichment, sports, art/fine arts, computer instruction programs offered; session focuses on day camp, outdoor skills, swimming, tennis; held both on and off campus; held at field house, classrooms, grounds, field trips; accepts boys and girls; open to students from other schools. 200 students usually enrolled. 2009 schedule: June 8 to July 31. Application deadline: May.
Tuition and Aid Day student tuition: $15,180–$17,995. Tuition installment plan (Insured Tuition Payment Plan, Key Tuition Payment Plan, monthly payment plans, 2-payment plan, prepaid discount plan). Tuition reduction for siblings, need-based scholarship grants available. In 2008–09, 34% of upper-school students received aid.
Admissions Traditional secondary-level entrance grade is 9. For fall 2008, 27 students applied for upper-level admission, 21 were accepted, 19 enrolled. Essay and Math Placement Exam required. Deadline for receipt of application materials: none. Application fee required: $50. On-campus interview required.
Athletics Interscholastic: baseball (boys), basketball (b,g), bowling (b,g), golf (b), skiing (downhill) (b,g), soccer (b,g), softball (b,g), swimming and diving (b,g), tennis (b,g), track and field (b,g), volleyball (b,g); coed interscholastic: cross-country running, outdoor education, running, yoga. 3 PE instructors, 11 coaches.
Computers Computers are regularly used in all academic, art classes. Computer network features include Internet access, wireless campus network. The school has a published electronic and media policy.
Contact Ms. Valerie Myntti, Director of Admissions. 585-442-1770. Fax: 585-442-5758. E-mail: vmyntti@harleyschool.org.

ANNOUNCEMENT FROM THE SCHOOL Located in Rochester, New York, The Harley School is a coeducational, independent, college-preparatory school for students in Nursery thru grade 12. Since its founding in 1917, The Harley School has embraced the motto "Become what thou art." The School believes that joy in learning helps children discover their unique talents and passions. Today, The Harley School continues to involve students in a diverse and close-knit community. The School seeks to nurture individual strengths and strives to foster a desire for intellectual achievement, a creative imagination, a sense of the intrinsic excitement of learning, and an understanding of our varied roles in society. The Harley School values integrity, character, accountability, and mutual respect. Students are given clear expectations along with flexibility to pursue their social, academic, and personal interests in a structured, safe, and caring environment. The Harley School facilities include a new state-of-the-art Visual Arts center, science labs, a 575-seat theater, a glass studio, an indoor pool, a track, a field house, athletic fields, and tennis courts. In Lower School, the curriculum promotes the social, emotional, and aesthetic growth of the whole child. Commitment to global awareness starts early, as foreign language instruction begins in full-time Nursery. The Middle School academic program has strong roots in traditional education, where students need to learn and master basic skills to be successful in high school and beyond. Harley believes one of the most important aspects of Middle School is for students to have good, solid relationships with teachers they trust—in a community that provides a sense of belonging. The Upper School offers a diversified college-preparatory curriculum including seventeen AP courses. Special programs include Hospice, Glass Flame Work, Organic Gardening, and Scottish Studies, and there is a strong commitment to volunteerism. In addition, 100% of The Harley School graduates attend colleges or universities.

HARRELLS CHRISTIAN ACADEMY

360 Tomahawk Highway
PO Box 88
Harrells, North Carolina 28444

Head of School: Dr. Ronald L. Montgomery

General Information Coeducational day college-preparatory, arts, religious studies, and technology school, affiliated with Christian faith. Grades K–12. Founded: 1969. Setting: rural. Nearest major city is Wilmington. 32-acre campus. 7 buildings on campus. Approved or accredited by North Carolina Association of Independent Schools, Southern Association of Colleges and Schools, Southern Association of Independent Schools, and North Carolina Department of Education. Total enrollment: 494. Upper school average class size: 17. Upper school faculty-student ratio: 1:10.

Upper School Student Profile Grade 9: 43 students (26 boys, 17 girls); Grade 10: 30 students (15 boys, 15 girls); Grade 11: 39 students (21 boys, 18 girls); Grade 12: 28 students (14 boys, 14 girls). 96% of students are Christian.

Faculty School total: 15. In upper school: 2 men, 13 women; 5 have advanced degrees.

Subjects Offered Algebra, animal science, art, art education, biology, biotechnology, botany, British literature, calculus, ceramics, chemistry, computer art, earth science, English, English language and composition-AP, English literature, English literature and composition-AP, government/civics, history, history-AP, journalism, keyboarding/computer, Latin, mathematics, photography, physical education, physical science, physics, religion, social studies, Spanish, weightlifting, yearbook.

Graduation Requirements Biology, computer applications, electives, English, environmental science, foreign language, mathematics, physical education (includes health), physical science, religious studies, social studies (includes history). Community service is required.

Special Academic Programs 3 Advanced Placement exams for which test preparation is offered; honors section; independent study; study at local college for college credit; programs in English, mathematics, general development for dyslexic students.

College Admission Counseling 42 students graduated in 2008; 38 went to college, including Hampden-Sydney College; North Carolina State University; Peace College; The University of North Carolina Wilmington. Other: 1 went to work, 3 had other specific plans. Median combined SAT: 950, median composite ACT: 20. 15% scored over 26 on composite ACT.

Student Life Upper grades have specified standards of dress, student council, honor system. Discipline rests primarily with faculty. Attendance at religious services is required.

Tuition and Aid Day student tuition: $7110. Tuition installment plan (FACTS Tuition Payment Plan, individually arranged payment plans). Tuition reduction for siblings, need-based scholarship grants available. In 2008–09, 9% of upper-school students received aid. Total amount of financial aid awarded in 2008–09: $21,100.

Admissions Traditional secondary-level entrance grade is 10. For fall 2008, 25 students applied for upper-level admission, 21 were accepted, 17 enrolled. Admissions testing and Iowa Tests of Basic Skills required. Deadline for receipt of application materials: none. Application fee required: $35. On-campus interview required.

Athletics Interscholastic: baseball (boys), basketball (b,g), football (b), golf (b,g), soccer (b,g), softball (g), tennis (g), volleyball (g); coed intramural: basketball. 2 PE instructors, 3 coaches.

Computers Computers are regularly used in art, computer applications, English, journalism, keyboarding, yearbook classes. Computer resources include Internet access, Internet filtering or blocking technology.

Contact Mrs. Susan Frederick, Administrative Assistant. 910-532-4575 Ext. 221. Fax: 910-532-2958. E-mail: sfrederick@harrellsca.org. Web site: www.harrellschristianacademy.com.

THE HARRISBURG ACADEMY

10 Erford Road
Wormleysburg, Pennsylvania 17043

Head of School: Dr. James Newman

General Information Coeducational day college-preparatory and arts school. Grades N–12. Founded: 1784. Setting: suburban. Nearest major city is Harrisburg. 23-acre campus. 1 building on campus. Approved or accredited by International Baccalaureate Organization, Middle States Association of Colleges and Schools, Pennsylvania Association of Independent Schools, and Pennsylvania Department of Education. Member of National Association of Independent Schools. Endowment: $4 million. Total enrollment: 453. Upper school average class size: 9. Upper school faculty-student ratio: 1:8.

Upper School Student Profile Grade 9: 38 students (20 boys, 18 girls); Grade 10: 30 students (19 boys, 11 girls); Grade 11: 39 students (19 boys, 20 girls); Grade 12: 21 students (10 boys, 11 girls).

Faculty School total: 60. In upper school: 8 men, 13 women; 9 have advanced degrees.

Subjects Offered Advanced Placement courses, algebra, American history, American literature, art, biology, business skills, calculus, ceramics, chemistry, computer science, creative writing, drama, economics, English, English literature, environmental science, European history, expository writing, fine arts, French, geography, geometry, grammar, health, history, International Baccalaureate courses, Latin, mathematics, music, philosophy, physical education, physics, psychology, science, social studies, Spanish, speech, typing, world history, world literature, writing.

Graduation Requirements Arts and fine arts (art, music, dance, drama), business skills (includes word processing), college planning, English, foreign language, mathematics, physical education (includes health), public speaking, science, social studies (includes history). Community service is required.

Special Academic Programs International Baccalaureate program; Advanced Placement exam preparation; honors section; independent study; study at local college for college credit.

College Admission Counseling 36 students graduated in 2008; all went to college, including Arizona State University; Maryland Institute College of Art; Penn State University Park; University of Mississippi; University of Pennsylvania; Villanova University.

Student Life Upper grades have specified standards of dress, student council, honor system. Discipline rests primarily with faculty.

Tuition and Aid Day student tuition: $15,135. Tuition installment plan (Insured Tuition Payment Plan, monthly payment plans). Need-based scholarship grants, need-based loans available. In 2008–09, 8% of upper-school students received aid. Total amount of financial aid awarded in 2008–09: $450,811.

Admissions Traditional secondary-level entrance grade is 9. Admissions testing required. Deadline for receipt of application materials: none. Application fee required: $65. On-campus interview required.

Athletics Interscholastic: basketball (boys, girls), field hockey (g), golf (b), lacrosse (b), soccer (b,g), tennis (b,g); coed interscholastic: swimming and diving; coed intramural: cross-country running, skiing (downhill). 3 PE instructors, 18 coaches, 1 athletic trainer.

Computers Computers are regularly used in art, English, mathematics, music, science classes. Computer network features include on-campus library services, Internet access, wireless campus network, Internet filtering or blocking technology. Campus intranet and student e-mail accounts are available to students. Students grades are available online.

Contact Mrs. Jessica Warren, Director of Admissions. 717-763-7811 Ext. 313. Fax: 717-975-0894. E-mail: warren.j@harrisburgacademy.org. Web site: www.harrisburgacademy.org.

HARVARD-WESTLAKE SCHOOL

3700 Coldwater Canyon
North Hollywood, California 91604

Head of School: Thomas C. Hudnut

General Information Coeducational day college-preparatory school, affiliated with Episcopal Church. Grades 7–12. Founded: 1989. Setting: urban. Nearest major city is Los Angeles. 26-acre campus. 12 buildings on campus. Approved or accredited by California Association of Independent Schools and Western Association of Schools and Colleges. Member of National Association of Independent Schools. Endowment: $56.5 million. Total enrollment: 1,593. Upper school average class size: 16. Upper school faculty-student ratio: 1:8.

Upper School Student Profile Grade 10: 293 students (158 boys, 135 girls); Grade 11: 283 students (150 boys, 133 girls); Grade 12: 291 students (152 boys, 139 girls).

Faculty School total: 122. In upper school: 72 men, 50 women; 85 have advanced degrees.

Subjects Offered 3-dimensional art, advanced studio art-AP, algebra, American government-AP, American history, American literature, American literature-AP, anatomy, architecture, art, art history, art history-AP, Asian studies, astronomy, biology, biology-AP, calculus, calculus-AP, ceramics, chemistry, chemistry-AP, Chinese, choreography, chorus, classics, community service, computer animation, computer programming, computer science, computer science-AP, creative writing, dance, drama, drawing, economics, economics-AP, electronics, English, English language and composition-AP, English literature, English literature-AP, environmental science, environmental science-AP, European history, expository writing, film, film studies, fine arts, French, French language-AP, French literature-AP, geography, geology, geometry, government and politics-AP, government/civics, grammar, health, human development, Japanese, jazz, journalism, Latin, Latin-AP, logic, macro/microeconomics-AP, Mandarin, mathematics, music, music history, music theory-AP, oceanography, orchestra, painting, photography, physical education, physics,

physics-AP, physiology, political science, pre-calculus, psychology, Russian, science, senior project, Shakespeare, social studies, Spanish, Spanish language-AP, Spanish literature-AP, statistics, studio art-AP, technical theater, theater, trigonometry, U.S. history-AP, video, women's studies, world history, world literature, yearbook, zoology.

Graduation Requirements Arts and fine arts (art, music, dance, drama), English, foreign language, history, human development, mathematics, physical education (includes health), science. Community service is required.

Special Academic Programs Advanced Placement exam preparation; honors section; independent study; term-away projects; study at local college for college credit; study abroad; academic accommodation for the gifted, the musically talented, and the artistically talented.

College Admission Counseling 282 students graduated in 2008; 281 went to college, including Brown University; Columbia College; New York University; Princeton University; Stanford University; University of Southern California. Other: 1 had other specific plans. Mean SAT critical reading: 663, mean SAT math: 681, mean SAT writing: 676. 90% scored over 600 on SAT critical reading, 91% scored over 600 on SAT math.

Student Life Upper grades have specified standards of dress, student council, honor system. Discipline rests primarily with faculty.

Summer Programs Enrichment, sports, art/fine arts, rigorous outdoor training, computer instruction programs offered; session focuses on enrichment and sports; held both on and off campus; held at Mexico, China; accepts boys and girls; open to students from other schools. 500 students usually enrolled. 2009 schedule: June 23 to August 1. Application deadline: none.

Tuition and Aid Day student tuition: $26,250. Tuition installment plan (monthly payment plans, semiannual payment plan, triennial payment plan). Need-based scholarship grants, short-term loans (payable by end of year in which loan is made) available. In 2008–09, 15% of upper-school students received aid. Total amount of financial aid awarded in 2008–09: $3,000,850.

Admissions For fall 2008, 57 students applied for upper-level admission, 16 were accepted, 10 enrolled. ISEE required. Deadline for receipt of application materials: February 1. Application fee required: $125. On-campus interview required.

Athletics Interscholastic: baseball (boys), basketball (b,g), cross-country running (b,g), field hockey (g), football (b), golf (b,g), gymnastics (g), lacrosse (b), soccer (b,g), softball (g), swimming and diving (b,g), tennis (b,g), track and field (b,g), volleyball (b,g), water polo (b,g), wrestling (b); coed interscholastic: diving, equestrian sports, fencing, martial arts; coed intramural: badminton. 6 PE instructors, 32 coaches, 2 athletic trainers.

Computers Computers are regularly used in art, foreign language, history, mathematics, music, science classes. Computer resources include on-campus library services, Internet access, music composition and editing, foreign language lab. Student e-mail accounts are available to students.

Contact Elizabeth Gregory, Director of Admission. 310-274-7281. Fax: 310-288-3212. E-mail: egregory@hw.com. Web site: www.harvardwestlake.com.

ANNOUNCEMENT FROM THE SCHOOL Harvard-Westlake, a coeducational school enrolling 1,600 students, occupies two campuses in West Los Angeles: one for middle school students (grades 7–9) and one for high school students (grades 10–12). The curriculum and programs are designed for students who have the motivation and ability to pursue a rigorous college-preparatory course of study.

THE HARVEY SCHOOL

260 Jay Street
Katonah, New York 10536

Head of School: Mr. Barry W. Fenstermacher

General Information Coeducational boarding and day and distance learning college-preparatory school. Boarding grades 9–12, day grades 6–12. Distance learning grades 6–12. Founded: 1916. Setting: suburban. Students are housed in single-sex dormitories. 100-acre campus. 14 buildings on campus. Approved or accredited by New York State Association of Independent Schools and The Association of Boarding Schools. Member of National Association of Independent Schools. Endowment: $1.9 million. Total enrollment: 340. Upper school average class size: 12. Upper school faculty-student ratio: 1:7.

Upper School Student Profile Grade 9: 64 students (35 boys, 29 girls); Grade 10: 60 students (31 boys, 29 girls); Grade 11: 59 students (34 boys, 25 girls); Grade 12: 53 students (23 boys, 30 girls). 8% of students are boarding students. 85% are state residents. 3 states are represented in upper school student body.

Faculty School total: 64. In upper school: 21 men, 17 women; 26 have advanced degrees; 16 reside on campus.

Subjects Offered Algebra, American history, American literature, art, art history, biology, calculus, ceramics, chemistry, composition-AP, computer programming-AP, creative writing, drama, English, English literature, European history, expository writing, fine arts, French, general science, geology, geometry, government/civics, grammar, Greek, history, Japanese, Latin, mathematics, music, photography, physics, religion, science, social studies, Spanish, theater, trigonometry, world history, writing.

Graduation Requirements Arts and fine arts (art, music, dance, drama), English, foreign language, mathematics, science, social science, social studies (includes history).

Special Academic Programs Advanced Placement exam preparation; honors section; independent study.

College Admission Counseling 59 students graduated in 2008; all went to college, including Barnard College; Bentley University; Cornell University; University of Connecticut; Villanova University.

Student Life Upper grades have specified standards of dress, student council. Discipline rests primarily with faculty.

Summer Programs Remediation, advancement programs offered; session focuses on on-line academic course; held off campus; held at online program; accepts boys and girls; open to students from other schools. 20 students usually enrolled. 2009 schedule: June 20 to August. Application deadline: May.

Tuition and Aid Day student tuition: $28,900; 5-day tuition and room/board: $6000. Tuition installment plan (FACTS Tuition Payment Plan, individually arranged payment plans). Need-based scholarship grants available. In 2008–09, 20% of upper-school students received aid. Total amount of financial aid awarded in 2008–09: $1,150,000.

Admissions Traditional secondary-level entrance grade is 9. For fall 2008, 287 students applied for upper-level admission, 137 were accepted, 100 enrolled. Deadline for receipt of application materials: none. Application fee required: $50. Interview required.

Athletics Interscholastic: baseball (boys), basketball (b,g), dance team (g), football (b), ice hockey (b), lacrosse (b,g), rugby (b), soccer (b,g), softball (g), volleyball (g); coed interscholastic: baseball, cross-country running, dance, figure skating, fitness, golf, lacrosse, soccer, tennis, yoga; coed intramural: aerobics, fitness walking, Frisbee, mountain biking. 1 athletic trainer.

Computers Computers are regularly used in English, foreign language, history, mathematics, science classes. Computer resources include on-campus library services, online commercial services, Internet access. The school has a published electronic and media policy.

Contact Mr. William Porter, Director of Admissions. 914-232-3161 Ext. 113. Fax: 914-232-6034. E-mail: wporter@harveyschool.org. Web site: www.harveyschool.org.

ANNOUNCEMENT FROM THE SCHOOL Located on a wooded, 100-acre campus in Katonah, New York, The Harvey School is a coeducational college-preparatory school, enrolling students in grades 6 through 12. The School's mission is "to help students of varying abilities through a program of academic challenge, faculty support and out-of-class activities." Its warm, supportive, and challenging learning environment is further enhanced by a faculty that views education as a collaborative effort among students, parents, and teachers. Small class size (averaging 12 students) promotes academic achievement and personal growth. A vibrant After School Program helps students develop a positive self-image, reinforces self-esteem, emphasizes teamwork, and encourages friendship-building. The Upper School offers a diversified college-preparatory curriculum, including Advanced Placement courses in English, calculus, computer science, American history, European history, biology, chemistry, Latin, and Spanish. Students also experience academically rigorous art, drama, music, and creative writing programs. Middle School students are encouraged to develop their academic skills through an age-appropriate curriculum that stresses development in the arts, English, mathematics, history, natural science, and foreign languages, as well as wide-ranging extracurricular programming. Three Internet-accessible labs, the integration of computer technology into classes, and a distance learning program enhance the academic experience. The School is dedicated to the education of students in the visual and performing arts. A new art center gives students an opportunity to further hone their skills in music, dance, theater, digital photography, and ceramics. The interior includes a 3,320-square-foot black-box theater, dance studio, ceramic studio, choral music rooms, scene shop, art gallery, and digital art room. With a gymnasium, hockey rink, and acres of playing fields, the Interscholastic Athletic Program includes baseball, basketball, cross-country, dance, football, ice hockey, lacrosse, rugby, soccer, softball, tennis, and volleyball. The School offers an optional five-day residential program for ninth through twelfth grade students.

HATHAWAY BROWN SCHOOL

19600 North Park Boulevard
Shaker Heights, Ohio 44122

Head of School: H. William Christ

General Information Coeducational day (boys' only in lower grades) college-preparatory school. Boys grade PS, girls grades PS–12. Founded: 1876. Setting: suburban. Nearest major city is Cleveland. 18-acre campus. 1 building on campus. Approved or accredited by Independent Schools Association of the Central States and Ohio Association of Independent Schools. Member of National Association of Independent Schools. Endowment: $50 million. Total enrollment: 860. Upper school average class size: 13. Upper school faculty-student ratio: 1:8.

Upper School Student Profile Grade 9: 92 students (92 girls); Grade 10: 84 students (84 girls); Grade 11: 86 students (86 girls); Grade 12: 77 students (77 girls).
Faculty School total: 129. In upper school: 13 men, 41 women; 31 have advanced degrees.
Subjects Offered Advanced Placement courses, algebra, American history, American literature, anatomy, art, art history, biology, biology-AP, calculus, ceramics, chemistry, chemistry-AP, communications, community service, computer math, computer programming, computer science, creative writing, dance, drama, economics, engineering, English, English literature, environmental science, ethics, European history, expository writing, fine arts, French, geography, geometry, government/civics, graphic design, health, history, international relations, journalism, Latin, mathematics, microbiology, music, outdoor education, photography, physical education, physics, physics-AP, physiology, psychology, research seminar, science, social studies, Spanish, statistics, statistics-AP, theater, trigonometry, U.S. history, U.S. history-AP, woodworking, world history, writing.
Graduation Requirements Arts and fine arts (art, music, dance, drama), computer applications, computer science, English, foreign language, history, mathematics, physical education (includes health), science, senior speech, senior project.
Special Academic Programs Advanced Placement exam preparation; honors section; independent study; term-away projects; study at local college for college credit; study abroad; academic accommodation for the gifted and the musically talented.
College Admission Counseling 71 students graduated in 2007; all went to college, including Bates College; Brown University; Columbia College; Miami University; Yale University. Mean SAT critical reading: 633, mean SAT math: 631, mean SAT writing: 653, mean combined SAT: 1917.
Student Life Upper grades have specified standards of dress, student council, honor system. Discipline rests equally with students and faculty.
Tuition and Aid Day student tuition: $3530–$21,290. Tuition installment plan (Academic Management Services Plan, Key Tuition Payment Plan). Need-based scholarship grants available. In 2007–08, 32% of upper-school students received aid. Total amount of financial aid awarded in 2007–08: $1,721,000.
Admissions Traditional secondary-level entrance grade is 9. For fall 2007, 88 students applied for upper-level admission, 52 were accepted, 37 enrolled. ISEE required. Deadline for receipt of application materials: none. Application fee required: $30. On-campus interview required.
Athletics Interscholastic: basketball, cross-country running, diving, field hockey, golf, lacrosse, soccer, softball, swimming and diving, tennis, track and field; intramural: outdoor adventure. 6 PE instructors, 22 coaches, 1 athletic trainer.
Computers Computers are regularly used in all academic classes. Computer network features include on-campus library services, online commercial services, Internet access, wireless campus network, Internet filtering or blocking technology. Student e-mail accounts and computer access in designated common areas are available to students. The school has a published electronic and media policy.
Contact Ms. Denise Burks, Administrative Assistant. 216-932-4214 Ext. 244. Fax: 216-397-0992. E-mail: dburks@hb.edu. Web site: www.hb.edu.

ANNOUNCEMENT FROM THE SCHOOL Hathaway Brown School is Ohio's oldest independent preparatory school for girls in grades K–12. Hathaway Brown School also offers a coeducational early childhood program for boys and girls from 2 to 5 years of age. For more information, contact the Hathaway Brown Office of Admission at 216-320-8767.

THE HAVERFORD SCHOOL

450 Lancaster Avenue
Haverford, Pennsylvania 19041

Head of School: Dr. Joseph T. Cox

General Information Boys' day college-preparatory and arts school. Grades PK–12. Founded: 1884. Setting: suburban. Nearest major city is Philadelphia. 32-acre campus. 7 buildings on campus. Approved or accredited by Middle States Association of Colleges and Schools, Pennsylvania Association of Independent Schools, and Pennsylvania Department of Education. Member of National Association of Independent Schools and Secondary School Admission Test Board. Endowment: $34.4 million. Total enrollment: 971. Upper school average class size: 15. Upper school faculty-student ratio: 1:7.
Upper School Student Profile Grade 9: 96 students (96 boys); Grade 10: 102 students (102 boys); Grade 11: 97 students (97 boys); Grade 12: 88 students (88 boys).
Faculty School total: 130. In upper school: 34 men, 12 women; 31 have advanced degrees.
Subjects Offered Algebra, American history, American literature, animal behavior, art, astronomy, biology, calculus, ceramics, chemistry, Chinese, Chinese studies, drama, ecology, economics, economics and history, English, English literature, European history, fine arts, French, geology, geometry, German, government/civics, history, Latin, mathematics, music, photography, physical education, physics, physiology, science, social studies, Spanish, statistics, theater, trigonometry, world affairs, world history, world literature.
Graduation Requirements Arts and fine arts (art, music, dance, drama), English, foreign language, mathematics, physical education (includes health), science, social studies (includes history).
Special Academic Programs Honors section; independent study; term-away projects; academic accommodation for the gifted; remedial reading and/or remedial writing; remedial math.
College Admission Counseling 86 students graduated in 2008; 83 went to college, including Cornell University; Penn State University Park; Princeton University; The George Washington University; University of Pennsylvania; University of Richmond. Other: 1 entered a postgraduate year. Median SAT critical reading: 650, median SAT math: 660. Mean SAT writing: 640, mean combined SAT: 1930. 68% scored over 600 on SAT critical reading, 74% scored over 600 on SAT math, 27% scored over 600 on SAT writing.
Student Life Upper grades have specified standards of dress, student council, honor system. Discipline rests equally with students and faculty.
Tuition and Aid Day student tuition: $26,700. Tuition installment plan (Insured Tuition Payment Plan, monthly payment plans, individually arranged payment plans). Need-based scholarship grants available. In 2008–09, 27% of upper-school students received aid. Total amount of financial aid awarded in 2008–09: $1,531,588.
Admissions Traditional secondary-level entrance grade is 9. For fall 2008, 105 students applied for upper-level admission, 56 were accepted, 30 enrolled. ISEE or SSAT required. Deadline for receipt of application materials: none. Application fee required: $40. Interview required.
Athletics Interscholastic: aquatics, baseball, basketball, crew, cross-country running, football, golf, ice hockey, indoor track, lacrosse, rowing, soccer, squash, swimming and diving, tennis, track and field, water polo, winter (indoor) track, wrestling; intramural: fitness, physical fitness, physical training, soccer, strength & conditioning, weight training. 6 PE instructors, 2 coaches, 2 athletic trainers.
Computers Computers are regularly used in art, English, history, mathematics, music, science classes. Computer network features include on-campus library services, online commercial services, Internet access. Computer access in designated common areas is available to students. Students grades are available online. The school has a published electronic and media policy.
Contact Mr. Kevin P. Seits, Director of Admissions and Tuition Assistance. 610-642-3020 Ext. 1457. Fax: 610-642-8724. E-mail: kseits@haverford.org. Web site: www.haverford.org.

ANNOUNCEMENT FROM THE SCHOOL The Haverford School aspires to be the premier independent day school for boys, an institution whose graduates are recognized for their character and intellect. The junior kindergarten through grade 12 program provides a superior liberal arts education in a challenging and supportive environment that fosters integrity, leadership, friendship, school spirit, and a commitment to community. The School strives to prepare each student for life by emphasizing the joy of learning and the importance of self-knowledge and by developing his full intellectual, moral, social, artistic, athletic, and creative potential. The School understands boys' development and provides the support and challenge for 981 boys. The exclusively college-preparatory curriculum features advanced courses in English, American and European history, biology, chemistry, physics, math, French, Latin, Spanish, German, music, and fine arts. The state-of-the-art, campuswide network integrates technology into all aspects of the curriculum. Extracurricular activities include student council, newspaper, yearbook, chorus, community service, and a wide variety of clubs. Sixteen varsity sports are offered in upper school, and the School competes in the Inter-Academic League, the oldest such league in the country. From 2003 to 2007, the colleges matriculating the greatest number of Haverford alumni were Columbia, Cornell, Franklin & Marshall, George Washington, Penn State, Princeton, Villanova, and the Universities of Pennsylvania, Pittsburgh, and Richmond. SAT averages were Critical Reading 640, Math 650, and Writing 640. In 2003–07, 53% of students taking AP exams earned scores of 4 or 5. The School's recently renovated 32-acre suburban campus includes a new state-of-the-art athletic facility, a new Lower School designed to meet the educational needs of boys, a renovated Middle School facility, and a new Upper School opening in fall 2008. The campus includes seventy-one classrooms, a 650-seat auditorium, a 30,000-volume library, four computer labs, ten science labs, and ample art and music studio space. The endowment is more than $44.9 million. For more information, visit the School's Web site at www.haverford.org.

HAVERGAL COLLEGE

1451 Avenue Road
Toronto, Ontario M5N 2H9, Canada

Head of School: Dr. Susan R. Groesbeck

General Information Girls' boarding and day college-preparatory school, affiliated with Church of England (Anglican). Boarding grades 9–12, day grades JK–12. Founded: 1894. Setting: urban. Students are housed in single-sex dormitories. 22-acre campus. 4 buildings on campus. Approved or accredited by Canadian Association of Independent Schools, Canadian Educational Standards Institute, Conference of Independent Schools of Ontario, The Association of Boarding Schools, and Ontario Department of Education. Affiliate member of National Association of Independent Schools; member of Secondary School Admission Test Board. Language of instruction: English. Endowment: CAN$13.2 million. Total enrollment: 915. Upper school average class size: 20. Upper school faculty-student ratio: 1:9.

Upper School Student Profile Grade 9: 113 students (113 girls); Grade 10: 123 students (123 girls); Grade 11: 118 students (118 girls); Grade 12: 114 students (114 girls). 9% of students are boarding students. 93% are province residents. 3 provinces are represented in upper school student body. 7% are international students. International students from Bermuda, China, Germany, Mexico, and Republic of Korea; 9 other countries represented in student body. 20% of students are members of Church of England (Anglican).

Faculty School total: 107. In upper school: 12 men, 59 women; 23 have advanced degrees; 1 resides on campus.

Subjects Offered Algebra, American history, art, art history, biology, biology-AP, calculus, calculus-AP, career planning, chemistry, civics, computer science, creative writing, data processing, drama, economics, English, English literature, environmental geography, European history, French, French literature-AP, general science, geography, geometry, German, health, history, journalism, Latin, law, mathematics, media studies, music, philosophy, physical education, physics, politics, religious studies, social science, social studies, Spanish, Spanish-AP, trigonometry, writing.

Graduation Requirements Arts and fine arts (art, music, dance, drama), business skills (includes word processing), English, foreign language, mathematics, physical education (includes health), science, social science, technology, 40 hours of community service, provincial literacy test.

Special Academic Programs Advanced Placement exam preparation; honors section; accelerated programs; independent study; term-away projects; domestic exchange program; study abroad.

College Admission Counseling 119 students graduated in 2008; all went to college, including McGill University; McMaster University; Queen's University at Kingston; The University of British Columbia; The University of Western Ontario; University of Toronto.

Student Life Upper grades have uniform requirement, student council. Discipline rests primarily with faculty. Attendance at religious services is required.

Tuition and Aid Day student tuition: CAN$21,890; 7-day tuition and room/board: CAN$43,780. Tuition installment plan (monthly payment plans, individually arranged payment plans). Bursaries, merit scholarship grants available. In 2008–09, 4% of upper-school students received aid; total upper-school merit-scholarship money awarded: CAN$84,295. Total amount of financial aid awarded in 2008–09: CAN$319,585.

Admissions Traditional secondary-level entrance grade is 9. For fall 2008, 164 students applied for upper-level admission, 107 were accepted, 58 enrolled. SSAT required. Deadline for receipt of application materials: December 12. Application fee required: CAN$150. Interview required.

Athletics Interscholastic: alpine skiing, aquatics, badminton, basketball, crew, cross-country running, field hockey, hockey, ice hockey, indoor track & field, rowing, rugby, running, skiing (downhill), soccer, softball, swimming and diving, synchronized swimming, tennis, track and field, triathlon, ultimate Frisbee, volleyball; intramural: aerobics, aerobics/dance, aerobics/Nautilus, aquatics, badminton, ball hockey, basketball, bocce, bowling, broomball, climbing, cooperative games, cricket, cross-country running, curling, dance, field hockey, fitness, fitness walking, flag football, floor hockey, football, Frisbee, golf, handball, hiking/backpacking, hockey, ice skating, independent competitive sports, indoor soccer, indoor track & field, jogging, jump rope, kickball, lacrosse, life saving, martial arts, modern dance, netball, outdoor activities, paddle tennis, physical fitness, physical training, racquetball, rock climbing, ropes courses, rowing, rugby, running, self defense, skiing (downhill), snowboarding, snowshoeing, soccer, softball, speedball, squash, strength & conditioning, swimming and diving, synchronized swimming, table tennis, tennis, touch football, track and field, triathlon, ultimate Frisbee, volleyball, walking, wall climbing, water polo, weight lifting, whiffle ball, yoga. 6 PE instructors, 10 coaches, 1 athletic trainer.

Computers Computers are regularly used in English, foreign language, mathematics, science classes. Computer network features include on-campus library services, Internet access, wireless campus network, Internet filtering or blocking technology. Campus intranet and student e-mail accounts are available to students. The school has a published electronic and media policy.

Contact Ms. Pamela Newson, Upper School Admission Assistant. 416-482-4724. Fax: 416-483-9644. E-mail: pnewson@havergal.on.ca. Web site: www.havergal.on.ca.

HAWAIIAN MISSION ACADEMY

1438 Pensacola Street
Honolulu, Hawaii 96822

Head of School: Mr. Manuel Rodriguez

General Information Coeducational boarding and day college-preparatory, general academic, arts, business, religious studies, bilingual studies, and technology school, affiliated with Seventh-day Adventist Church. Grades 9–12. Founded: 1895. Setting: urban. Students are housed in single-sex by floor dormitories. 4-acre campus. 4 buildings on campus. Approved or accredited by The Hawaii Council of Private Schools, Western Association of Schools and Colleges, and Hawaii Department of Education. Total enrollment: 113. Upper school average class size: 25. Upper school faculty-student ratio: 1:15.

Upper School Student Profile Grade 9: 25 students (14 boys, 11 girls); Grade 10: 28 students (13 boys, 15 girls); Grade 11: 27 students (12 boys, 15 girls); Grade 12: 33 students (15 boys, 18 girls). 20% of students are boarding students. 46% are state residents. 2 states are represented in upper school student body. 50% are international students. International students from Hong Kong, Japan, Micronesia, Republic of Korea, and Taiwan. 80% of students are Seventh-day Adventists.

Faculty School total: 13. In upper school: 8 men, 5 women; 9 have advanced degrees; 2 reside on campus.

Subjects Offered Algebra, anatomy and physiology, art, Bible, biology, business, business education, business skills, calculus, chemistry, choir, Christianity, community service, computer keyboarding, computer literacy, computer science, conceptual physics, concert choir, desktop publishing, digital art, economics, electives, English, English literature, ESL, family and consumer science, family life, general science, geometry, grammar, Hawaiian history, health, independent living, interactive media, journalism, lab science, library, Microsoft, personal finance, physical education, pre-algebra, pre-calculus, Spanish, student government, student publications, U.S. government, U.S. history, video film production, weight training, work experience, work-study, world history, yearbook.

Graduation Requirements Algebra, arts and fine arts (art, music, dance, drama), biology, chemistry, computer keyboarding, computer literacy, English, foreign language, geometry, Hawaiian history, physical education (includes health), physics, practical arts, religion (includes Bible studies and theology), social studies (includes history), U.S. government, work experience, world history, 25 hours of community service per year, 100 hours of work experience throughout the 4 years combined.

Special Academic Programs Honors section; ESL (8 students enrolled).

College Admission Counseling 37 students graduated in 2008; all went to college, including Kapiolani Community College; La Sierra University; Pacific Union College; University of Hawaii at Manoa. Mean SAT critical reading: 505, mean SAT math: 535.

Student Life Upper grades have uniform requirement, student council. Discipline rests primarily with faculty.

Tuition and Aid Day student tuition: $11,800; 7-day tuition and room/board: $10,460. Tuition installment plan (Insured Tuition Payment Plan, monthly payment plans, individually arranged payment plans). Tuition reduction for siblings, need-based scholarship grants, paying campus jobs available. In 2008–09, 25% of upper-school students received aid.

Admissions Traditional secondary-level entrance grade is 9. SSAT required. Deadline for receipt of application materials: none. Application fee required: $25. Interview recommended.

Athletics Interscholastic: basketball (boys, girls), volleyball (b,g). 2 PE instructors, 6 coaches.

Computers Computers are regularly used in desktop publishing, economics, graphic arts, journalism, keyboarding, media production, newspaper, publications, video film production, word processing, yearbook classes. Computer network features include on-campus library services, Internet access. Students grades are available online.

Contact Mrs. Nenny Safotu, Registrar. 808-536-2207 Ext. 202. Fax: 808-524-3294. E-mail: registrar@hma4u.org. Web site: www.hma4u.org.

HAWAII BAPTIST ACADEMY

2429 Pali Highway
Honolulu, Hawaii 96817

Head of School: Richard Bento

General Information Coeducational day college-preparatory and Christian education school, affiliated with Southern Baptist Convention. Grades K–12. Founded: 1949. Setting: urban. 13-acre campus. 6 buildings on campus. Approved or accredited by Western Association of Schools and Colleges. Member of National Association of Independent Schools and Secondary School Admission Test Board. Endowment: $3.4 million. Total enrollment: 1,076. Upper school average class size: 20. Upper school faculty-student ratio: 1:11.

Upper School Student Profile Grade 9: 114 students (55 boys, 59 girls); Grade 10: 113 students (65 boys, 48 girls); Grade 11: 105 students (53 boys, 52 girls); Grade 12: 105 students (56 boys, 49 girls). 10% of students are Southern Baptist Convention.

Faculty School total: 80. In upper school: 15 men, 25 women; 18 have advanced degrees.

Subjects Offered Advanced Placement courses, algebra, American history, American history-AP, American literature, analytic geometry, anatomy and physiology, art, Asian history, astronomy, Basic programming, Bible studies, biology,

biology-AP, British literature, calculus-AP, ceramics, chemistry, chemistry-AP, Chinese, Christian education, Christian ethics, Christian studies, communication skills, comparative religion, computer applications, conceptual physics, concert band, creation science, creative writing, drama, drama performance, drawing, earth science, East European studies, economics, English, English language and composition-AP, English literature, English literature-AP, European history, European history-AP, fine arts, forensic science, French, geography, geometry, Hawaiian history, Japanese, journalism, marine biology, mathematics, mechanical drawing, music, music theory-AP, photography, physical education, physics, political science, psychology, religion, science, social studies, sociology, Spanish, speech, statistics, statistics-AP, trigonometry, world history, world literature, writing.

Graduation Requirements Algebra, arts and fine arts (art, music, dance, drama), Asian history, Bible studies, biology, communication skills, computer applications, conceptual physics, economics, English, foreign language, Hawaiian history, mathematics, physical education (includes health), political science, science, social studies (includes history).

Special Academic Programs Advanced Placement exam preparation; independent study.

College Admission Counseling 107 students graduated in 2008; 104 went to college, including Creighton University; Santa Clara University; Seattle University; University of California, Irvine; University of Hawaii at Manoa; University of Washington. Other: 3 had other specific plans. Mean SAT critical reading: 540, mean SAT math: 590, mean SAT writing: 541. 25% scored over 600 on SAT critical reading, 52% scored over 600 on SAT math, 25% scored over 600 on SAT writing.

Student Life Upper grades have uniform requirement, student council. Discipline rests primarily with faculty. Attendance at religious services is required.

Summer Programs Remediation, enrichment, sports, art/fine arts, computer instruction programs offered; session focuses on academic/social preparation for entrance to regular school, instruction/remediation, and personal growth; held both on and off campus; held at various recreation sites; accepts boys and girls; open to students from other schools. 315 students usually enrolled. 2009 schedule: June 15 to July 24. Application deadline: May 15.

Tuition and Aid Day student tuition: $10,725. Guaranteed tuition plan. Tuition installment plan (Insured Tuition Payment Plan, monthly payment plans). Need-based scholarship grants available. In 2008–09, 6% of upper-school students received aid. Total amount of financial aid awarded in 2008–09: $80,866.

Admissions Traditional secondary-level entrance grade is 9. For fall 2008, 74 students applied for upper-level admission, 21 were accepted, 12 enrolled. Achievement tests and SSAT required. Deadline for receipt of application materials: February 10. Application fee required: $60. On-campus interview required.

Athletics Interscholastic: aquatics (boys, girls), baseball (b), basketball (b,g), bowling (b,g), canoeing/kayaking (b,g), cheering (g), cross-country running (b,g), diving (b,g), football (b), golf (b,g), judo (b,g), kayaking (b,g), riflery (b,g), soccer (b,g), softball (g), swimming and diving (b,g), tennis (b,g), track and field (b,g), volleyball (b,g), water polo (b,g), wrestling (b,g); coed interscholastic: canoeing/kayaking, cheering, golf, sailing. 3 PE instructors, 30 coaches, 1 athletic trainer.

Computers Computers are regularly used in keyboarding, newspaper, programming, word processing, yearbook classes. Computer resources include Internet access, Internet filtering or blocking technology. The school has a published electronic and media policy.

Contact Mrs. Katherine Lee, Director of Admissions. 808-595-7585. Fax: 808-564-0332. E-mail: klee@hba.net. Web site: www.hba.net.

HAWAI'I PREPARATORY ACADEMY

65-1692 Kohala Mountain Road
Kamuela, Hawaii 96743-8476

Head of School: Mr. Lindsay Barnes Jr.

General Information Coeducational boarding and day college-preparatory school. Boarding grades 6–PG, day grades K–12. Founded: 1949. Setting: small town. Nearest major city is Kona. Students are housed in single-sex by floor dormitories and single-sex dormitories. 220-acre campus. 22 buildings on campus. Approved or accredited by The Association of Boarding Schools and Western Association of Schools and Colleges. Member of National Association of Independent Schools and Secondary School Admission Test Board. Endowment: $21.1 million. Total enrollment: 575. Upper school average class size: 12. Upper school faculty-student ratio: 1:9.

Upper School Student Profile Grade 9: 115 students (43 boys, 72 girls); Grade 10: 135 students (36 boys, 99 girls); Grade 11: 127 students (51 boys, 76 girls); Grade 12: 125 students (36 boys, 89 girls). 43% of students are boarding students. 71% are state residents. 16 states are represented in upper school student body. 16% are international students. International students from China, Democratic People's Republic of Korea, French Polynesia, Japan, Taiwan, and Thailand; 12 other countries represented in student body.

Faculty School total: 74. In upper school: 25 men, 20 women; 29 have advanced degrees; 21 reside on campus.

Subjects Offered 3-dimensional art, Advanced Placement courses, algebra, American literature, anatomy, anatomy and physiology, architectural drawing, architecture, art history, art history-AP, astronomy, band, Bible as literature, biology, biology-AP, calculus, calculus-AP, ceramics, chemistry, chemistry-AP, choir, composition, composition-AP, computer literacy, computer technologies, creative writing, digital photography, drama, drama performance, drawing, driver education, economics, English, environmental science, ESL, European history-AP, French, geology, geometry, graphic arts, Hawaiian history, health, honors algebra, honors world history, humanities, instrumental music, Japanese, literature-AP, marine biology, math applications, mathematics, music theory, nutrition, orchestra, painting, photography, photojournalism, physical education, physical science, physics, physics-AP, precalculus, probability and statistics, psychology, psychology-AP, science research, Shakespeare, Spanish, Spanish-AP, statistics-AP, strings, studio art, theater production, trigonometry, U.S. history, U.S. history-AP, video film production, visual arts, Web site design, wind instruments, world cultures, world history, world literature, world religions, yearbook.

Graduation Requirements Arts and fine arts (art, music, dance, drama), computer applications, electives, English, humanities, mathematics, modern languages, science, social studies (includes history), sports.

Special Academic Programs Advanced Placement exam preparation; honors section; independent study; ESL (15 students enrolled).

College Admission Counseling 80 students graduated in 2008; all went to college, including Boston University; Colorado State University; Northern Arizona University; Oregon State University; University of Hawaii at Manoa; University of Oregon. Mean SAT critical reading: 525, mean SAT math: 551, mean SAT writing: 532, mean combined SAT: 1608.

Student Life Upper grades have specified standards of dress, student council, honor system. Discipline rests equally with students and faculty.

Summer Programs Enrichment, ESL programs offered; session focuses on academic enrichment; held on campus; accepts boys and girls; open to students from other schools. 100 students usually enrolled. 2009 schedule: June 21 to July 17. Application deadline: April 15.

Tuition and Aid Day student tuition: $18,250; 7-day tuition and room/board: $36,150. Guaranteed tuition plan. Tuition installment plan (Key Tuition Payment Plan, monthly payment plans, prepayment plan, 2-payment plan). Need-based scholarship grants, Hawaii residential boarding grants available. In 2008–09, 28% of upper-school students received aid. Total amount of financial aid awarded in 2008–09: $1,600,000.

Admissions Traditional secondary-level entrance grade is 9. For fall 2008, 138 students applied for upper-level admission, 84 were accepted, 58 enrolled. Any standardized test, ISEE or SSAT required. Deadline for receipt of application materials: February 1. Application fee required: $75. Interview required.

Athletics Interscholastic: baseball (boys), basketball (b,g), cross-country running (b,g), ocean paddling (b,g), soccer (b,g), softball (g), swimming and diving (b,g), tennis (b,g), track and field (b,g), volleyball (b,g), water polo (g), wrestling (b,g); intramural: baseball (b); coed interscholastic: dressage, football, golf, horseback riding; coed intramural: badminton, basketball, dance, dressage, fencing, horseback riding, scuba diving, soccer, strength & conditioning, surfing, swimming and diving, tennis, ultimate Frisbee, volleyball, weight lifting, yoga. 1 athletic trainer.

Computers Computers are regularly used in computer applications, digital applications, graphic arts, science, video film production, yearbook classes. Computer network features include on-campus library services, online commercial services, Internet access, wireless campus network, Internet filtering or blocking technology. Campus intranet, student e-mail accounts, and computer access in designated common areas are available to students. Students grades are available online. The school has a published electronic and media policy.

Contact Mr. Joshua D. Clark, Director of Admission. 808-881-4321. Fax: 808-881-4003. E-mail: admissions@hpa.edu. Web site: www.hpa.edu/.

See Close-Up on page 782.

HAWKEN SCHOOL

12465 County Line Road
PO Box 8002
Gates Mills, Ohio 44040-8002

Head of School: D. Scott Looney

General Information Coeducational day college-preparatory, arts, and business school. Grades PS–12. Founded: 1915. Setting: suburban. Nearest major city is Cleveland. 325-acre campus. 5 buildings on campus. Approved or accredited by Independent Schools Association of the Central States and Ohio Department of Education. Member of National Association of Independent Schools. Endowment: $50.2 million. Total enrollment: 910. Upper school average class size: 15. Upper school faculty-student ratio: 1:9.

Upper School Student Profile Grade 9: 109 students (59 boys, 50 girls); Grade 10: 99 students (46 boys, 53 girls); Grade 11: 116 students (68 boys, 48 girls); Grade 12: 105 students (54 boys, 51 girls).

Faculty School total: 103. In upper school: 33 men, 19 women; 37 have advanced degrees.

Subjects Offered 20th century world history, accounting, acting, advanced chemistry, advanced math, Advanced Placement courses, advanced studio art-AP, African-American literature, algebra, American Civil War, American history, American history-AP, American literature, animal science, art, art appreciation, art history, band, Bible as literature, biology, botany, business, business mathematics, calculus, calculus-AP, ceramics, chemistry, chemistry-AP, Chinese, choir, choral music, chorus, Civil War, classical Greek literature, community service, computer applications, computer math, computer programming, computer science, computer science-AP, computer skills, concert band, creative dance, creative writing, dance, dance performance, drama, drawing, driver education, ecology, economics, economics and history, electronic music, English, English literature, English-AP, environmental science-AP, ethics, European history, field ecology, film, film studies, fine arts, first aid, French, French studies, French-AP, geography, geometry, government/civics, grammar, graphic design, health, history, history of jazz, history of rock and roll, Holocaust and other genocides, humanities, improvisation, Latin, Latin-AP, mathematics, mathematics-AP, music, music theory, outdoor education, painting, performing arts, philosophy, photography, physical education, physics, physics-AP, physiology, poetry, probability and statistics, qualitative analysis, science, science research, sculpture, senior project, social science, social studies, Spanish, Spanish literature-AP, speech, statistics-AP, strings, studio art—AP, swimming, theater, theater arts, theater design and production, theater production, trigonometry, U.S. history, U.S. history-AP, world history, world literature, World War I, World War II, writing.

Graduation Requirements Arts and fine arts (art, music, dance, drama), computer science, English, foreign language, history, mathematics, physical education (includes health), science. Community service is required.

Special Academic Programs Advanced Placement exam preparation; honors section; accelerated programs; independent study; term-away projects; study abroad; academic accommodation for the gifted and the musically talented.

College Admission Counseling 111 students graduated in 2008; all went to college, including Miami University; Oberlin College; Rochester Institute of Technology; Syracuse University; The Ohio State University; University of Rochester.

Student Life Upper grades have specified standards of dress, student council. Discipline rests equally with students and faculty.

Summer Programs Remediation, enrichment, advancement, computer instruction programs offered; session focuses on credit, review, preview and enrichment in English, math, computer studies, and health; held on campus; accepts boys and girls; open to students from other schools. 100 students usually enrolled. 2009 schedule: June 15 to July 24. Application deadline: none.

Tuition and Aid Day student tuition: $20,285–$21,940. Tuition installment plan (Key Tuition Payment Plan, installment payment plan (60 percent by 8/15 and 40 percent by 1/15), AchieverLoans (Key Education Resources)). Need-based scholarship grants, need-based loans available. In 2008–09, 33% of upper-school students received aid. Total amount of financial aid awarded in 2008–09: $2,137,466.

Admissions Traditional secondary-level entrance grade is 9. For fall 2008, 126 students applied for upper-level admission, 106 were accepted, 51 enrolled. ISEE required. Deadline for receipt of application materials: February 25. Application fee required: $25. On-campus interview required.

Athletics Interscholastic: baseball (boys), basketball (b,g), cross-country running (b,g), diving (b,g), field hockey (g), football (b), golf (b,g), lacrosse (b,g), soccer (b,g), softball (g), swimming and diving (b,g), tennis (b,g), track and field (b,g); intramural: basketball (b); coed intramural: dance, drill team, outdoor skills. 4 PE instructors, 31 coaches, 2 athletic trainers.

Computers Computers are regularly used in all classes. Computer network features include on-campus library services, Internet access, Internet filtering or blocking technology. Campus intranet and student e-mail accounts are available to students. The school has a published electronic and media policy.

Contact Heather Daly, Director of Admission and Financial Assistance. 440-423-2955. Fax: 440-423-2994. E-mail: hdaly@hawken.edu. Web site: www.hawken.edu/.

HAWTHORNE CHRISTIAN ACADEMY

2000 Route 208
Hawthorne, New Jersey 07506

Head of School: Mr. Donald J. Klingen

General Information Coeducational day college-preparatory, arts, religious studies, technology, music, and missions school, affiliated with Christian faith, Christian faith. Grades PS–12. Founded: 1981. Setting: suburban. Nearest major city is New York, NY. 22-acre campus. 4 buildings on campus. Approved or accredited by Association of Christian Schools International, Middle States Association of Colleges and Schools, and New Jersey Department of Education. Total enrollment: 462. Upper school average class size: 21. Upper school faculty-student ratio: 1:7.

Upper School Student Profile Grade 9: 37 students (14 boys, 23 girls); Grade 10: 33 students (23 boys, 10 girls); Grade 11: 46 students (27 boys, 19 girls); Grade 12: 45 students (23 boys, 22 girls). 100% of students are Christian faith, Christian.

Faculty School total: 60. In upper school: 10 men, 12 women; 6 have advanced degrees.

Subjects Offered Accounting, advanced computer applications, Advanced Placement courses, algebra, anatomy and physiology, art and culture, band, Basic programming, bell choir, Bible, biology, business applications, calculus, calculus-AP, chemistry, choir, choral music, chorus, composition, computer information systems, computer programming, computers, contemporary issues, creative writing, current events, drama, electives, English literature, English literature-AP, ensembles, foreign language, geometry, government, guidance, handbells, health, home economics, information technology, instrumental music, instruments, intro to computers, law, mathematics, music, music history, music theory, physical education, physical science, physics, politics, pre-calculus, psychology, Spanish, Spanish-AP, studio art, U.S. government, U.S. government and politics-AP, U.S. government-AP, U.S. history-AP, video, visual arts, voice, Web site design, world history, yearbook.

Graduation Requirements Algebra, Bible, biology, chemistry, English literature, English literature-AP, geometry, intro to computers, mathematics, physical education (includes health), physical science, pre-calculus, Spanish, U.S. government, U.S. history, U.S. history-AP, world history, Christian service hours, Apologetics and Current Issues, Specified number of Academic Elective Courses.

College Admission Counseling 34 students graduated in 2008; all went to college, including Cedarville University; Duke University; Gordon College; Liberty University; Wheaton College; William Paterson University of New Jersey. Mean combined SAT: 1134.

Student Life Upper grades have specified standards of dress, student council. Discipline rests primarily with faculty. Attendance at religious services is required.

Tuition and Aid Day student tuition: $9225. Tuition installment plan (monthly payment plans). Tuition reduction for siblings, merit scholarship grants, need-based scholarship grants, Pastoral Discounts, Teacher/Employee Discounts available. In 2008–09, 57% of upper-school students received aid; total upper-school merit-scholarship money awarded: $5500. Total amount of financial aid awarded in 2008–09: $125,467.

Admissions Traditional secondary-level entrance grade is 9. Admissions testing, Otis-Lennon School Ability Test or WRAT required. Deadline for receipt of application materials: none. Application fee required: $100. On-campus interview required.

Athletics Interscholastic: baseball (boys), basketball (b,g), cross-country running (b,g), golf (b,g), soccer (b,g), softball (g), strength & conditioning (b), track and field (b,g), volleyball (g); coed interscholastic: cross-country running, track and field. 2 PE instructors.

Computers Computers are regularly used in business applications, computer applications, information technology, introduction to technology, lab/keyboard, library, technology, Web site design, yearbook classes. Computer network features include on-campus library services, Internet access, Internet filtering or blocking technology. Campus intranet is available to students. Students grades are available online. The school has a published electronic and media policy.

Contact Mrs. Judith De Boer, Admissions Coordinator. 973-423-3331 Ext. 261. Fax: 973-238-1718. E-mail: jdeboer@hca.org.

HAYDEN HIGH SCHOOL

401 South West Gage
Topeka, Kansas 66606

Head of School: Mr. Richard L. Strecker

General Information Coeducational day college-preparatory, general academic, arts, business, religious studies, bilingual studies, and technology school, affiliated with Roman Catholic Church. Grades 9–12. Founded: 1911. Setting: suburban. 100-acre campus. 6 buildings on campus. Approved or accredited by North Central Association of Colleges and Schools and Kansas Department of Education. Endowment: $2 million. Total enrollment: 517. Upper school average class size: 18. Upper school faculty-student ratio: 1:15.

Upper School Student Profile Grade 9: 134 students (65 boys, 69 girls); Grade 10: 130 students (62 boys, 68 girls); Grade 11: 127 students (65 boys, 62 girls); Grade 12: 126 students (66 boys, 60 girls). 95% of students are Roman Catholic.

Faculty School total: 42. In upper school: 20 men, 18 women; 26 have advanced degrees.

Subjects Offered 20th century history, 20th century physics, 20th century world history, 3-dimensional art, 3-dimensional design, accounting, ACT preparation, acting, advanced chemistry, advanced computer applications, advanced math, algebra, alternative physical education, American Civil War, American democracy, American government-AP, American history-AP, American legal systems, American literature, analysis, analytic geometry, anatomy and physiology, applied arts, applied music, art, art appreciation, Basic programming, Bible, biology, biology-AP, bookkeeping, British literature, British literature (honors), broadcast journalism, business applications, business law, business mathematics, calculus, calculus-AP, campus ministry, career and personal planning, Catholic belief and practice, chemistry, chemistry-AP, child development, choir, choral music, choreography, Christian and Hebrew scripture, Christian doctrine, Christian ethics, Christianity, civics, classical language, comparative religion, competitive science projects, composition, computer applications, computer education, computer graphics, computer keyboarding, computer programming, computer skills, conceptual physics, concert band, constitutional history of U.S., creative writing, criminal justice, current events, dance, dance performance, death and loss, desktop publishing, digital photography, drama, drama performance, earth and space science, economics, English, English literature, English literature-AP, English-AP, fine arts, forensics, French, geometry, German, government, government-AP, health education, historiography, history, history of the Catholic Church, honors English, honors geometry, jazz band, keyboarding/computer, Latin, moral reasoning, moral theology, music, music performance, photography, physical education, physics, physics-AP, pre-algebra, pre-calculus, probability and statistics, psychology, reading, religion, science fiction, social justice, sociology, Spanish, speech and debate, studio art, theater, theology, trigonometry, U.S. government, U.S. history, vocal music.

Special Academic Programs 1 Advanced Placement exam for which test preparation is offered; honors section; independent study; study at local college for college credit; study abroad; academic accommodation for the gifted and the musically talented;

remedial reading and/or remedial writing; remedial math; special instructional classes for students with LD, ADD, dyslexia, emotional and behavioral problems.
College Admission Counseling 117 students graduated in 2008; 109 went to college, including Kansas State University; The University of Kansas; Washburn University. Other: 4 went to work, 1 entered military service, 3 had other specific plans. 62% scored over 26 on composite ACT.
Student Life Upper grades have uniform requirement, student council, honor system. Discipline rests primarily with faculty. Attendance at religious services is required.
Summer Programs Remediation, enrichment, advancement, sports, computer instruction programs offered; session focuses on advancement; held on campus; accepts boys and girls; not open to students from other schools. 20 students usually enrolled. 2009 schedule: June to July.
Tuition and Aid Day student tuition: $3850. Tuition installment plan (FACTS Tuition Payment Plan, monthly payment plans). Merit scholarship grants, need-based scholarship grants, paying campus jobs available. In 2008–09, 30% of upper-school students received aid; total upper-school merit-scholarship money awarded: $15,000. Total amount of financial aid awarded in 2008–09: $70,000.
Admissions Traditional secondary-level entrance grade is 9. For fall 2008, 150 students applied for upper-level admission, 148 were accepted, 134 enrolled. ACT, any standardized test or Explore required. Deadline for receipt of application materials: none. No application fee required. Interview recommended.
Athletics Interscholastic: aerobics/dance (girls), baseball (b), basketball (b,g), bowling (b,g), cheering (b,g), cross-country running (b,g), dance team (g), diving (b,g), drill team (g), football (b), golf (b,g), soccer (b,g), softball (g), strength & conditioning (b,g), swimming and diving (b,g), tennis (b,g), track and field (b,g), volleyball (g), weight training (b,g), wrestling (b); coed interscholastic: cheering. 3 PE instructors, 12 coaches, 2 athletic trainers.
Computers Computers are regularly used in all classes. Computer network features include on-campus library services, online commercial services, Internet access, Internet filtering or blocking technology. Student e-mail accounts are available to students. Students grades are available online. The school has a published electronic and media policy.
Contact Mr. Richard Strecker, President. 785-272-5210 Ext. 19. Fax: 785-272-2975. E-mail: streckerr@haydenhigh.org. Web site: www.haydenhigh.org.

HEAD-ROYCE SCHOOL

4315 Lincoln Avenue
Oakland, California 94602
Head of School: Paul Chapman

General Information Coeducational day college-preparatory, arts, and technology school. Grades K–12. Founded: 1887. Setting: urban. 14-acre campus. 8 buildings on campus. Approved or accredited by California Association of Independent Schools, Western Association of Schools and Colleges, and California Department of Education. Member of National Association of Independent Schools. Endowment: $20 million. Total enrollment: 798. Upper school average class size: 15. Upper school faculty-student ratio: 1:9.
Upper School Student Profile Grade 9: 85 students (39 boys, 46 girls); Grade 10: 89 students (37 boys, 52 girls); Grade 11: 86 students (43 boys, 43 girls); Grade 12: 81 students (37 boys, 44 girls).
Faculty School total: 95. In upper school: 24 men, 19 women; 29 have advanced degrees.
Subjects Offered Algebra, American history, American literature, art, art history, astronomy, biology, calculus, ceramics, chemistry, Chinese, community service, computer programming, computer science, creative writing, debate, drama, ecology, English, English literature, European history, expository writing, fine arts, French, geometry, graphic arts, health, history, journalism, Latin, marine biology, mathematics, music, neurobiology, photography, physical education, physics, psychology, science, social studies, Spanish, theater, trigonometry, typing, video, world history, world literature, writing.
Graduation Requirements Art history, arts and fine arts (art, music, dance, drama), computer science, English, foreign language, mathematics, physical education (includes health), science, social studies (includes history), 40 hours of community service.
Special Academic Programs Advanced Placement exam preparation; honors section; independent study; term-away projects; study at local college for college credit; study abroad; academic accommodation for the gifted, the musically talented, and the artistically talented.
College Admission Counseling 80 students graduated in 2008; all went to college, including New York University; Stanford University; University of California, Berkeley; University of California, Los Angeles; University of Pennsylvania; University of Southern California. Mean SAT critical reading: 664, mean SAT math: 660, mean SAT writing: 679.
Student Life Upper grades have specified standards of dress, student council, honor system. Discipline rests primarily with faculty.
Summer Programs Remediation, enrichment, advancement programs offered; session focuses on sports and enrichment; held on campus; accepts boys and girls; open to students from other schools. 600 students usually enrolled. 2009 schedule: June 22 to July 31. Application deadline: February.
Tuition and Aid Day student tuition: $27,000. Tuition installment plan (Academic Management Services Plan). Need-based scholarship grants, paying campus jobs, tuition remission for children of faculty and staff available. In 2008–09, 25% of upper-school students received aid. Total amount of financial aid awarded in 2008–09: $1,249,600.
Admissions Traditional secondary-level entrance grade is 9. For fall 2008, 160 students applied for upper-level admission, 92 were accepted, 30 enrolled. ISEE required. Deadline for receipt of application materials: January 15. Application fee required: $75. On-campus interview required.
Athletics Interscholastic: baseball (boys), basketball (b,g), cross-country running (b,g), dance squad (g), golf (b,g), lacrosse (b), modern dance (g), outdoor education (b,g), physical fitness (b,g), soccer (b,g), softball (g), strength & conditioning (b,g), swimming and diving (b,g), tennis (b,g), volleyball (b,g), weight lifting (b,g), weight training (b,g); coed interscholastic: cross-country running, golf, outdoor education, physical fitness, strength & conditioning, swimming and diving; coed intramural: bicycling, dance, ultimate Frisbee. 6 PE instructors, 39 coaches.
Computers Computers are regularly used in English, graphics, mathematics, science, yearbook classes. Computer network features include on-campus library services, online commercial services, Internet access, wireless campus network, laptop carts, smartboards. Student e-mail accounts are available to students. The school has a published electronic and media policy.
Contact Catherine Epstein, Director of Admissions. 510-531-1300. Fax: 510-530-8329. E-mail: cepstein@headroyce.org. Web site: www.headroyce.org.

ANNOUNCEMENT FROM THE SCHOOL Head-Royce offers a challenging program in the liberal arts and sciences. Students also participate in fine arts and physical education classes. A variety of student-led clubs and twenty-two athletic teams in ten sports enhance student life. Electives, senior projects, community service, and many Advanced Placement (AP) classes prepare students for outstanding colleges and universities.

HEADWATERS ACADEMY

418 West Garfield Street
Bozeman, Montana 59715
Head of School: Mr. Tim McWilliams

General Information Coeducational day college-preparatory, general academic, arts, and outdoor education school. Grades 6–8. Founded: 1990. Setting: small town. 1-acre campus. 2 buildings on campus. Candidate for accreditation by Pacific Northwest Association of Independent Schools. Total enrollment: 24. Upper school average class size: 12. Upper school faculty-student ratio: 1:5.
Faculty School total: 10. In upper school: 2 men, 7 women; 5 have advanced degrees.
Subjects Offered English, fine arts, general science, history, life science, mathematics, music, outdoor education, physics, social studies, Spanish, study skills.
Graduation Requirements Analysis of data, arts and fine arts (art, music, dance, drama), English, foreign language, history, mathematics, outdoor education, science, outdoor education. Community service is required.
Special Academic Programs Academic accommodation for the gifted, the musically talented, and the artistically talented.
College Admission Counseling 6 students graduated in 2008; all went to college, including Montana State University. Median SAT critical reading: 633, median SAT math: 592. 50% scored over 600 on SAT critical reading, 75% scored over 600 on SAT math.
Student Life Upper grades have specified standards of dress, student council, honor system. Discipline rests equally with students and faculty.
Tuition and Aid Day student tuition: $8400. Tuition installment plan (monthly payment plans, individually arranged payment plans). Tuition reduction for siblings, merit scholarship grants, need-based scholarship grants available. In 2008–09, 60% of upper-school students received aid; total upper-school merit-scholarship money awarded: $2000. Total amount of financial aid awarded in 2008–09: $100,000.
Admissions Deadline for receipt of application materials: April 30. Application fee required: $50. On-campus interview required.
Athletics Intramural: biathlon (boys, girls); coed intramural: aerobics, aerobics/dance, alpine skiing, backpacking, bicycling, bowling, boxing, canoeing/kayaking, climbing, cross-country running, fishing, fitness, flag football, fly fishing, Frisbee, golf, hiking/backpacking, ice skating, in-line skating, indoor track & field, kickball, mountain biking, mountaineering, nordic skiing, outdoor activities, physical fitness, rafting, rock climbing, roller blading, running, skiing (cross-country), skiing (downhill), snowboarding, snowshoeing, soccer, strength & conditioning, table tennis, tennis, touch football, ultimate Frisbee, volleyball, wall climbing, wilderness survival, wildernessways, winter (indoor) track, winter walking, yoga. 2 PE instructors.
Computers Computers are regularly used in English, foreign language, history, mathematics, science, study skills classes. Computer network features include on-campus library services, online commercial services, Internet access.
Contact Mr. Tim McWilliams, Headmaster. 406-585-9997. Fax: 406-585-9992. E-mail: admissions@headwatersacademy.com. Web site: www.headwatersacademy.com.

HEBREW ACADEMY

14401 Willow Lane
Huntington Beach, California 92647

Head of School: Mr. Ron Bank

General Information college-preparatory, general academic, religious studies, and technology school, affiliated with Jewish faith. Founded: 1969. Setting: suburban. 11-acre campus. 11 buildings on campus. Approved or accredited by Accrediting Commission for Schools, Association of Colorado Independent Schools, and Western Association of Schools and Colleges. Upper school average class size: 15. Upper school faculty-student ratio: 1:4.

Upper School Student Profile 100% of students are Jewish.

Faculty School total: 41. In upper school: 6 men, 12 women; 2 have advanced degrees.

Subjects Offered Algebra, American history, American literature, art history, biology, earth science, economics, English, English literature, geography, government/civics, grammar, Hebrew, history, mathematics, physical education, physics, physiology, psychology, religion, science, social science, social studies, theology, world culture, world history, writing.

Graduation Requirements Computer science, English, foreign language, mathematics, physical education (includes health), religion (includes Bible studies and theology), science, social science, social studies (includes history).

Special Academic Programs International Baccalaureate program; 5 Advanced Placement exams for which test preparation is offered; honors section; independent study; remedial reading and/or remedial writing; remedial math; programs in general development for dyslexic students.

College Admission Counseling 7 students graduated in 2008; 3 went to college.

Student Life Upper grades have uniform requirement, student council. Discipline rests primarily with faculty. Attendance at religious services is required.

Tuition and Aid Day student tuition: $13,000. Guaranteed tuition plan. Tuition installment plan (monthly payment plans, individually arranged payment plans). Tuition reduction for siblings, need-based scholarship grants available. In 2008–09, 30% of upper-school students received aid. Total amount of financial aid awarded in 2008–09: $30,000.

Admissions Deadline for receipt of application materials: none. Application fee required: $95. On-campus interview required.

Athletics Interscholastic: aerobics/dance (girls), aerobics/Nautilus (g), aquatics (b,g), archery (b,g), badminton (g), baseball (b,g), basketball (b,g), dance (g), jogging (b,g), physical fitness (b,g), soccer (b,g), softball (b,g), swimming and diving (b,g), volleyball (g). 1 PE instructor.

Computers Computers are regularly used in English, foreign language, science, technology classes. Computer network features include on-campus library services, online commercial services, Internet access, multimedia, including laser disks, digital cameras. Computer access in designated common areas is available to students.

Contact Mrs. Alex Greenberg, Director of Admissions. 714-898-0051 Ext. 284. Fax: 714-898-0633. E-mail: agreenberg@hebrewacademyhb.com.

HEBREW ACADEMY-THE FIVE TOWNS

635 Central Avenue
Cedarhurst, New York 11516

Head of School: Rabbi Zev Meir Friedman

General Information Coeducational day college-preparatory, arts, business, and religious studies school, affiliated with Jewish faith. Grades 9–12. Founded: 1978. Setting: suburban. Nearest major city is New York. 1 building on campus. Approved or accredited by Middle States Association of Colleges and Schools, The College Board, and New York Department of Education. Languages of instruction: English and Hebrew. Total enrollment: 488. Upper school average class size: 20.

Upper School Student Profile 100% of students are Jewish.

Faculty School total: 80.

Subjects Offered Advanced Placement courses, arts, English, fine arts, foreign language, Jewish studies, Judaic studies, mathematics, physical education, religion, science, social science, social studies.

Graduation Requirements Arts and fine arts (art, music, dance, drama), English, foreign language, Judaic studies, mathematics, physical education (includes health), religion (includes Bible studies and theology), science, social science, social studies (includes history).

Special Academic Programs Advanced Placement exam preparation; honors section; independent study; study abroad; academic accommodation for the artistically talented.

College Admission Counseling 158 students graduated in 2008; all went to college, including Columbia University; New York University; State University of New York at Binghamton; University of Maryland, College Park; University of Pennsylvania; Yeshiva University. Median SAT critical reading: 590, median SAT math: 610, median SAT writing: 570. 48% scored over 600 on SAT critical reading, 56% scored over 600 on SAT math, 41% scored over 600 on SAT writing.

Student Life Upper grades have specified standards of dress, student council, honor system. Discipline rests primarily with faculty. Attendance at religious services is required.

Tuition and Aid Tuition installment plan (monthly payment plans, individually arranged payment plans). Need-based scholarship grants available.

Admissions Traditional secondary-level entrance grade is 9. Board of Jewish Education Entrance Exam required. Deadline for receipt of application materials: March 15. Application fee required. On-campus interview required.

Athletics Interscholastic: baseball (boys, girls), basketball (b,g), field hockey (b), softball (b,g), tennis (b,g), volleyball (g); coed intramural: skiing (downhill). 2 PE instructors, 8 coaches.

Computers Computers are regularly used in computer applications classes. Computer resources include on-campus library services, online commercial services, Internet access, Internet filtering or blocking technology. Student e-mail accounts are available to students. The school has a published electronic and media policy.

Contact Mr. Stanley Blumenstein, Principal, General Studies. 516-569-3807. Fax: 516-374-5761.

HEBRON ACADEMY

PO Box 309
Hebron, Maine 04238

Head of School: Mr. John J. King

General Information Coeducational boarding and day college-preparatory, arts, business, religious studies, technology, Creative Writing, and Honors and AP Courses school. Boarding grades 9–PG, day grades 6–PG. Founded: 1804. Setting: rural. Nearest major city is Portland. Students are housed in single-sex dormitories. 1,500-acre campus. 22 buildings on campus. Approved or accredited by Independent Schools of Northern New England, New England Association of Schools and Colleges, The Association of Boarding Schools, and Maine Department of Education. Member of National Association of Independent Schools and Secondary School Admission Test Board. Endowment: $13 million. Total enrollment: 260. Upper school average class size: 12. Upper school faculty-student ratio: 1:7.

Upper School Student Profile Grade 9: 29 students (20 boys, 9 girls); Grade 10: 53 students (34 boys, 19 girls); Grade 11: 66 students (48 boys, 18 girls); Grade 12: 49 students (29 boys, 20 girls); Postgraduate: 11 students (11 boys). 65% of students are boarding students. 50% are state residents. 18 states are represented in upper school student body. 20% are international students. International students from Canada, China, Germany, Japan, Republic of Korea, and Spain; 5 other countries represented in student body.

Faculty School total: 39. In upper school: 19 men, 18 women; 14 have advanced degrees; 35 reside on campus.

Subjects Offered Algebra, art, art-AP, astronomy, biology, business studies, calculus, calculus-AP, chemistry, chemistry-AP, college counseling, composition, composition-AP, computer multimedia, computer programming, computer science, computer studies, current events, digital photography, drama, drawing, drawing and design, English, ESL, ethics, French, functions, geology, geometry, health and wellness, history, independent study, international relations, jazz, Latin, leadership training, music, music theory, painting, personal fitness, photography, physics, physiology-anatomy, piano, portfolio art, pottery, programming, psychology, sculpture, Spanish, studio art, trigonometry, U.S. history, wilderness education, world history, world religions.

Graduation Requirements Algebra, art, biology, chemistry, English, foreign language, geometry, U.S. history.

Special Academic Programs Advanced Placement exam preparation; honors section; independent study; academic accommodation for the gifted, the musically talented, and the artistically talented; ESL (12 students enrolled).

College Admission Counseling 79 students graduated in 2008; 75 went to college, including Bates College; Elmira College; University of Maine; University of New Hampshire; University of Pennsylvania. Other: 1 entered a postgraduate year, 3 had other specific plans. Median SAT critical reading: 500, median SAT math: 570. Mean SAT writing: 521, mean combined SAT: 1587. 17% scored over 600 on SAT critical reading, 30% scored over 600 on SAT math.

Student Life Upper grades have specified standards of dress, student council, honor system. Discipline rests primarily with faculty.

Tuition and Aid Day student tuition: $23,250; 7-day tuition and room/board: $41,975. Tuition installment plan (Insured Tuition Payment Plan, monthly payment plans). Merit scholarship grants, need-based scholarship grants, prepGATE Loans available. In 2008–09, 49% of upper-school students received aid; total upper-school merit-scholarship money awarded: $15,000. Total amount of financial aid awarded in 2008–09: $1,700,000.

Admissions Traditional secondary-level entrance grade is 9. For fall 2008, 377 students applied for upper-level admission, 272 were accepted, 120 enrolled. PSAT or SAT for applicants to grade 11 and 12, SSAT or TOEFL or SLEP required. Deadline for receipt of application materials: February 1. Application fee required: $50. Interview required.

Athletics Interscholastic: alpine skiing (boys, girls), baseball (b), basketball (b,g), cross-country running (b,g), field hockey (g), football (b), golf (b,g), ice hockey (b,g), lacrosse (b,g), mountain biking (b,g), outdoor education (b,g), outdoor skills (b,g), physical fitness (b,g); coed intramural: outdoor education, outdoor skills, roller hockey. 2 coaches, 2 athletic trainers.

Computers Computers are regularly used in art, graphic design, introduction to technology classes. Computer network features include on-campus library services, online commercial services, Internet access, wireless campus network, Internet filtering or blocking technology. Campus intranet, student e-mail accounts, and

computer access in designated common areas are available to students. Students grades are available online. The school has a published electronic and media policy.
Contact Mr. Joseph M. Hemmings, Director of Admission. 207-966-2100 Ext. 225. Fax: 207-966-1111. E-mail: admissions@hebronacademy.org. Web site: www.hebronacademy.org.

See Close-Up on page 784.

HERITAGE CHRISTIAN ACADEMY

6674 Rogers Drive
North Branch, Michigan 48461
Head of School: Mr. Matthew W. Byers

General Information Coeducational day college-preparatory and religious studies school, affiliated with Christian faith. Grades 7–12. Founded: 1976. Setting: rural. Nearest major city is Flint. 4-acre campus. 1 building on campus. Approved or accredited by Association of Christian Schools International and Michigan Department of Education. Total enrollment: 80. Upper school average class size: 9. Upper school faculty-student ratio: 1:4.
Upper School Student Profile Grade 9: 6 students (3 boys, 3 girls); Grade 11: 3 students (2 boys, 1 girl). 25% of students are Christian faith.
Faculty School total: 8. In upper school: 2 men, 3 women; 4 have advanced degrees.
Subjects Offered Algebra, American history, American literature, art, Bible studies, biology, calculus, chemistry, Christian doctrine, church history, concert choir, drama, economics, general math, geometry, history, Life of Christ, physical education, physical science, research techniques, Spanish, theology, world history.
College Admission Counseling 1 student graduated in 2008 and went to college.
Student Life Upper grades have uniform requirement, student council, honor system. Discipline rests primarily with faculty. Attendance at religious services is required.
Tuition and Aid Day student tuition: $4000. Tuition installment plan (FACTS Tuition Payment Plan). Tuition reduction for siblings, need-based scholarship grants available. In 2008–09, 50% of upper-school students received aid.
Admissions Traditional secondary-level entrance grade is 9. For fall 2008, 9 students applied for upper-level admission, 9 were accepted, 9 enrolled. Deadline for receipt of application materials: none. Application fee required: $50. Interview required.
Athletics Interscholastic: baseball (boys), basketball (b,g), football (b), softball (g), volleyball (g).
Computers Computer network features include Internet access. The school has a published electronic and media policy.
Contact Mrs. Mindy McInally, Administrative Assistant. 810-688-2575. Fax: 810-688-3635. E-mail: matthewbyers@yahoo.com. Web site: www.nbhca.org.

HERITAGE CHRISTIAN ACADEMY

2003 McKnight Boulevard NE
Calgary, Alberta T2E 6L2, Canada
Head of School: Mrs. LaVerne Pue

General Information Coeducational day college-preparatory, general academic, arts, religious studies, bilingual studies, and technology school, affiliated with Christian faith, Evangelical faith. Grades K–12. Founded: 1979. Setting: urban. 10-acre campus. 1 building on campus. Approved or accredited by Association of Christian Schools International, Association of Independent Schools and Colleges of Alberta, and Alberta Department of Education. Language of instruction: English. Total enrollment: 509. Upper school average class size: 27. Upper school faculty-student ratio: 1:9.
Upper School Student Profile Grade 10: 33 students (20 boys, 13 girls); Grade 11: 34 students (12 boys, 22 girls); Grade 12: 22 students (12 boys, 10 girls). 100% of students are Christian, members of Evangelical faith.
Faculty School total: 18. In upper school: 7 men, 4 women; 2 have advanced degrees.
Subjects Offered Advanced computer applications, art, band, Bible, biology, career and personal planning, chemistry, choir, choral music, Christian education, computer applications, computer multimedia, creative writing, English, essential learning systems, foods, French as a second language, health, language arts, mathematics, outdoor education, physical education, physics, religious studies, science, social studies, sports medicine, work experience.
Graduation Requirements English, mathematics, religious studies, science, social studies (includes history).
Special Academic Programs Independent study; remedial reading and/or remedial writing; remedial math; special instructional classes for deaf students, students with dyslexia addressed through IPPs and classroom accommodations.
College Admission Counseling 24 students graduated in 2008; 16 went to college, including McMaster University; University of Alberta; University of Calgary; University of Lethbridge. Other: 7 went to work, 1 had other specific plans.
Student Life Upper grades have uniform requirement, student council, honor system. Discipline rests primarily with faculty. Attendance at religious services is required.
Tuition and Aid Day student tuition: CAN$2490. Tuition installment plan (monthly payment plans, individually arranged payment plans). Tuition reduction for siblings available.
Admissions Traditional secondary-level entrance grade is 10. For fall 2008, 11 students applied for upper-level admission, 8 were accepted, 8 enrolled. CTBS (or similar from their school) required. Deadline for receipt of application materials: none. Application fee required: CAN$100. Interview required.
Athletics Interscholastic: badminton (boys, girls), basketball (b,g), cross-country running (b,g), floor hockey (b), golf (b,g), track and field (b,g), volleyball (b,g), wrestling (b,g); coed interscholastic: aerobics, soccer, track and field; coed intramural: aquatics, backpacking, badminton, ball hockey, baseball, basketball, bicycling, bowling, canoeing/kayaking, climbing, cooperative games, curling, fishing, fitness, flag football, floor hockey, football, Frisbee, handball, hiking/backpacking, indoor soccer, indoor track & field, jogging, juggling, jump rope, mountain biking, outdoor activities, physical fitness, project adventure, snowshoeing, soccer, softball, strength & conditioning, swimming and diving, team handball, touch football, track and field, ultimate Frisbee, volleyball, wall climbing, weight training, wilderness survival. 1 PE instructor.
Computers Computers are regularly used in animation, Bible studies, career education, data processing, English, graphics, information technology, keyboarding, mathematics, multimedia, photography, science, social studies classes. Computer network features include Internet access, Internet filtering or blocking technology. Student e-mail accounts are available to students. The school has a published electronic and media policy.
Contact Office. 403-219-3201. Fax: 403-219-3210. E-mail: heritage_info@pallisersd.ab.ca. Web site: www.hcacalgary.com.

HERITAGE CHRISTIAN SCHOOL

2850 Fourth Avenue
PO Box 400
Jordan, Ontario L0R 1S0, Canada
Head of School: Mr. A. Ben Harsevoort

General Information Coeducational day college-preparatory, general academic, arts, and religious studies school, affiliated with Reformed Church; primarily serves students with learning disabilities, individuals with Attention Deficit Disorder, individuals with emotional and behavioral problems, and dyslexic students. Grades K–12. Founded: 1992. Setting: rural. Nearest major city is St. Catharines, Canada. 26-acre campus. 1 building on campus. Approved or accredited by Ontario Department of Education. Language of instruction: English. Total enrollment: 568. Upper school average class size: 50. Upper school faculty-student ratio: 1:15.
Upper School Student Profile Grade 9: 31 students (21 boys, 10 girls); Grade 10: 49 students (23 boys, 26 girls); Grade 11: 41 students (20 boys, 21 girls); Grade 12: 43 students (22 boys, 21 girls). 95% of students are Reformed.
Faculty School total: 30. In upper school: 11 men, 4 women; 4 have advanced degrees.
Subjects Offered 20th century American writers, 20th century physics, 20th century world history, advanced chemistry, advanced math, algebra, analysis and differential calculus, art, Bible, biology, bookkeeping, British literature, business mathematics, business studies, calculus, Canadian geography, Canadian history, Canadian law, Canadian literature, career education, chemistry, choral music, Christian and Hebrew scripture, Christian doctrine, Christian education, Christian ethics, Christian studies, Christian testament, Christianity, church history, civics, classical civilization, computer education, computer keyboarding, computer programming, computer skills, consumer mathematics, creative writing, culinary arts, drafting, English, English composition, English literature, entrepreneurship, environmental education, ethics, European civilization, European history, family studies, finite math, foods, foundations of civilization, French as a second language, general math, geography, geometry, grammar, health, history, honors algebra, honors English, honors geometry, honors world history, humanities, independent living, language and composition, language arts, law and the legal system, life science, literature, marketing, mathematics, media literacy, modern civilization, modern European history, modern Western civilization, music, music appreciation, novels, personal finance, physical education, physics, practicum, public speaking, religion and culture, religious education, religious studies, Shakespeare, society challenge and change, speech communications, technical drawing, vocal music, word processing, world civilizations, world literature, writing.
Graduation Requirements Ontario Secondary School Diploma requirements.
Special Academic Programs Independent study; remedial reading and/or remedial writing; remedial math.
College Admission Counseling 38 students graduated in 2008; 30 went to college, including Calvin College; Covenant College. Other: 8 went to work.
Student Life Upper grades have uniform requirement, student council. Discipline rests primarily with faculty. Attendance at religious services is required.
Tuition and Aid Day student tuition: CAN$12,500. Tuition installment plan (monthly payment plans).
Admissions Traditional secondary-level entrance grade is 9. Deadline for receipt of application materials: none. No application fee required. On-campus interview required.
Athletics Interscholastic: badminton (boys, girls), basketball (b,g), ice hockey (b), soccer (b,g), volleyball (b,g). 3 coaches.
Computers Computers are regularly used in accounting, business, economics, information technology, keyboarding, mathematics, newspaper, typing, yearbook classes. The school has a published electronic and media policy.
Contact Mrs. Mariam Sinke, Administrative Assistant. 905-562-7303 Ext. 221. Fax: 905-562-0020. E-mail: heritage@hcsjordan.ca. Web site: www.hcsjordan.ca.

HERITAGE HALL

1800 Northwest 122nd Street
Oklahoma City, Oklahoma 73120-9524

Head of School: Guy A. Bramble

General Information Coeducational day college-preparatory, arts, and ESL school. Grades PS–12. Founded: 1969. Setting: suburban. 97-acre campus. 3 buildings on campus. Approved or accredited by Independent Schools Association of the Southwest and Oklahoma Department of Education. Member of National Association of Independent Schools and Secondary School Admission Test Board. Endowment: $1.4 million. Total enrollment: 860. Upper school average class size: 15. Upper school faculty-student ratio: 1:16.

Upper School Student Profile Grade 9: 94 students (54 boys, 40 girls); Grade 10: 89 students (47 boys, 42 girls); Grade 11: 68 students (42 boys, 26 girls); Grade 12: 92 students (48 boys, 44 girls).

Faculty School total: 116. In upper school: 13 men, 30 women; 27 have advanced degrees.

Subjects Offered Advanced chemistry, algebra, American history, American literature, art, art history, biology, calculus, ceramics, chemistry, community service, computer science, debate, earth science, economics, English, English literature, environmental science, ethics, European history, film and literature, French, geography, geometry, government/civics, grammar, history, journalism, mathematics, music, photography, physical education, physics, play production, psychology, science, social studies, Spanish, speech, trigonometry, world history, world literature, writing.

Graduation Requirements Arts and fine arts (art, music, dance, drama), computer education, English, foreign language, mathematics, physical education (includes health), science, social studies (includes history), 32 hours of documented community service each year in grades 9 through 12.

Special Academic Programs Advanced Placement exam preparation; honors section; independent study; academic accommodation for the gifted, the musically talented, and the artistically talented; programs in English, mathematics, general development for dyslexic students; ESL (12 students enrolled).

College Admission Counseling 66 students graduated in 2008; all went to college, including Oklahoma State University; Southern Methodist University; University of Oklahoma. Mean SAT critical reading: 600, mean SAT math: 581, mean SAT writing: 596, mean composite ACT: 27. 20% scored over 600 on SAT critical reading, 26% scored over 600 on SAT math, 20% scored over 600 on SAT writing, 42% scored over 26 on composite ACT.

Student Life Upper grades have specified standards of dress, student council, honor system. Discipline rests equally with students and faculty.

Summer Programs Remediation, enrichment, sports, art/fine arts, computer instruction programs offered; session focuses on arts, athletics, and academics; held on campus; accepts boys and girls; open to students from other schools. 416 students usually enrolled. 2009 schedule: June 4 to July 27.

Tuition and Aid Day student tuition: $14,665. Tuition installment plan (Insured Tuition Payment Plan, monthly payment plans). Merit scholarship grants, need-based scholarship grants, need-based loans available. In 2008–09, 22% of upper-school students received aid; total upper-school merit-scholarship money awarded: $92,000. Total amount of financial aid awarded in 2008–09: $5,110,000.

Admissions Traditional secondary-level entrance grade is 9. For fall 2008, 56 students applied for upper-level admission, 49 were accepted, 33 enrolled. ERB CTP (level F), ERB CTP IV, essay, Math Placement Exam, WISC-III and Woodcock-Johnson and writing sample required. Deadline for receipt of application materials: none. Application fee required: $35. On-campus interview required.

Athletics Interscholastic: baseball (boys), basketball (b,g), cheering (g), cross-country running (b,g), field hockey (g), fitness (b,g), football (b), golf (b,g), physical fitness (b,g), soccer (b,g), softball (g), strength & conditioning (b,g), swimming and diving (b,g), tennis (b,g), track and field (b,g), volleyball (g), weight training (b,g), wrestling (b); intramural: Frisbee (b). 5 PE instructors, 15 coaches, 1 athletic trainer.

Computers Computers are regularly used in art, college planning, computer applications, desktop publishing, English, ESL, foreign language, library, mathematics, multimedia, newspaper, programming, publishing, SAT preparation, science, speech, Web site design, word processing, writing, yearbook classes. Computer network features include on-campus library services, online commercial services, Internet access, wireless campus network, Internet filtering or blocking technology, homework assignments and test schedules available online. Campus intranet and computer access in designated common areas are available to students. Students grades are available online. The school has a published electronic and media policy.

Contact Mrs. Betsy Horn, Director of Admission. 405-749-3002. Fax: 405-751-7372. E-mail: bhorn@heritagehall.com. Web site: www.heritagehall.com.

THE HERITAGE SCHOOL

2093 Highway 29 North
Newnan, Georgia 30263

Head of School: Judith Griffith

General Information Coeducational day college-preparatory, arts, and technology school. Grades PK–12. Founded: 1970. Setting: suburban. Nearest major city is Atlanta. 62-acre campus. 10 buildings on campus. Approved or accredited by Georgia Independent School Association, Southern Association of Colleges and Schools, Southern Association of Independent Schools, and Georgia Department of Education. Member of National Association of Independent Schools. Endowment: $1.1 million. Total enrollment: 401. Upper school average class size: 18. Upper school faculty-student ratio: 1:7.

Upper School Student Profile Grade 9: 35 students (16 boys, 19 girls); Grade 10: 20 students (12 boys, 8 girls); Grade 11: 42 students (24 boys, 18 girls); Grade 12: 43 students (22 boys, 21 girls).

Faculty School total: 49. In upper school: 5 men, 15 women; 3 have advanced degrees.

Subjects Offered Advanced Placement courses, algebra, American history, American literature, art, art history, biology, calculus, chemistry, computer applications, drama, earth science, economics, English, English literature, environmental science, European history, French, geography, geometry, government/civics, grammar, health, history, mathematics, music, physical education, public speaking, science, social science, social studies, Spanish, speech, theater, world history, world literature.

Graduation Requirements Arts and fine arts (art, music, dance, drama), computer science, electives, English, foreign language, mathematics, physical education (includes health), public speaking, science, social studies (includes history).

Special Academic Programs 16 Advanced Placement exams for which test preparation is offered; independent study.

College Admission Counseling 33 students graduated in 2008; 31 went to college, including Auburn University; Furman University; Georgia Institute of Technology; Mercer University; University of Georgia; Wesleyan College. Other: 1 went to work, 1 entered a postgraduate year. Median SAT critical reading: 530, median SAT math: 530, median SAT writing: 520, median combined SAT: 1590.

Student Life Upper grades have specified standards of dress, student council, honor system. Discipline rests primarily with faculty.

Tuition and Aid Day student tuition: $6710–$12,705. Tuition installment plan (monthly payment plans). Tuition reduction for siblings, need-based scholarship grants available. In 2008–09, 19% of upper-school students received aid. Total amount of financial aid awarded in 2008–09: $154,588.

Admissions Traditional secondary-level entrance grade is 9. For fall 2008, 25 students applied for upper-level admission, 17 were accepted, 16 enrolled. Otis-Lennon School Ability Test required. Deadline for receipt of application materials: none. Application fee required: $50. On-campus interview required.

Athletics Interscholastic: aerobics/dance (girls), baseball (b), basketball (b,g), cheering (g), cross-country running (b,g), dance team (g), football (b), golf (b,g), soccer (b,g), softball (g), swimming and diving (b,g), tennis (b,g), weight training (b); coed interscholastic: equestrian sports, physical fitness, skeet shooting; coed intramural: backpacking, basketball, canoeing/kayaking, climbing, flag football, hiking/backpacking, juggling, kayaking, mountaineering, outdoor adventure, outdoor education, ropes courses, wilderness survival. 3 PE instructors.

Computers Computers are regularly used in college planning, creative writing, English, foreign language, publications, science, yearbook classes. Computer network features include on-campus library services, online commercial services, Internet access, wireless campus network, Internet filtering or blocking technology. Campus intranet, student e-mail accounts, and computer access in designated common areas are available to students. Students grades are available online.

Contact Amy Riley, Director of Advancement. 678-423-5393. Fax: 770-253-4850. E-mail: ariley@heritagehawks.org. Web site: www.heritagehawks.org.

HIDDEN LAKE ACADEMY

Dahlonega, Georgia

See Special Needs Schools section.

HIGHLAND HALL, A WALDORF SCHOOL

17100 Superior Street
Northridge, California 91325

Head of School: Jim Pedroja

General Information Coeducational day college-preparatory and arts school. Grades N–12. Founded: 1955. Setting: suburban. Nearest major city is Los Angeles. 11-acre campus. 4 buildings on campus. Approved or accredited by Association of Waldorf Schools of North America and Western Association of Schools and Colleges. Total enrollment: 390. Upper school average class size: 25. Upper school faculty-student ratio: 1:6.

Upper School Student Profile Grade 9: 22 students (12 boys, 10 girls); Grade 10: 22 students (12 boys, 10 girls); Grade 11: 25 students (14 boys, 11 girls); Grade 12: 29 students (16 boys, 13 girls).

Faculty School total: 59. In upper school: 16 men, 14 women; 3 have advanced degrees.

Subjects Offered Algebra, American history, American literature, anatomy, ancient history, architecture, art, art history, astronomy, biology, bookbinding, botany, calculus, career/college preparation, cell biology, chemistry, choral music, chorus, clayworking, conflict resolution, CPR, creative writing, drama, drawing, earth science, economics, English, English literature, ethnic studies, European history, eurythmy, expository writing, geography, geology, geometry, German, government/civics, grammar, guidance, guitar, handbells, health, history, honors U.S. history, jazz ensemble, marine biology, mathematics, metalworking, music, music history, Native American history, orchestra, painting, physical education, physics, physiology, pre-algebra, pre-calculus, SAT preparation, sculpture, sewing, social studies, Spanish, speech, stained glass, stone carving, theater, trigonometry, woodworking, world history, world literature, writing, yearbook, zoology.

Graduation Requirements Ancient history, art, art history, crafts, earth science, economics, English, foreign language, government, history of music, human sexuality, mathematics, music, physical education (includes health), science, sculpture, society and culture, U.S. history, world history. Community service is required.

Special Academic Programs Honors section; independent study; study abroad.

College Admission Counseling 25 students graduated in 2008; 24 went to college, including Eugene Lang College The New School for Liberal Arts; New York University; Occidental College; St. John's College; The Juilliard School; University of California, Berkeley. Other: 1 went to work. Mean SAT critical reading: 645, mean SAT math: 550, mean composite ACT: 27. 50% scored over 600 on SAT critical reading, 60% scored over 600 on SAT math, 50% scored over 26 on composite ACT.

Student Life Discipline rests primarily with faculty.

Tuition and Aid Day student tuition: $16,850. Tuition installment plan (Insured Tuition Payment Plan, FACTS Tuition Payment Plan, monthly payment plans). Need-based scholarship grants available. In 2008–09, 19% of upper-school students received aid. Total amount of financial aid awarded in 2008–09: $104,600.

Admissions Traditional secondary-level entrance grade is 9. For fall 2008, 31 students applied for upper-level admission, 21 were accepted, 14 enrolled. Essay, math and English placement tests and writing sample required. Deadline for receipt of application materials: January 31. Application fee required: $100. On-campus interview required.

Athletics Interscholastic: baseball (boys), basketball (b,g), softball (g), volleyball (b,g); coed interscholastic: soccer; coed intramural: golf. 2 PE instructors, 3 coaches.

Computers Computers are regularly used in newspaper, yearbook classes. Computer network features include on-campus library services, Internet access, wireless campus network.

Contact Lynn van Schilfgaarde, Enrollment Director. 818-349-1394 Ext. 211. Fax: 818-349-2390. E-mail: lvs@highlandhall.org. Web site: www.highlandhall.org.

HIGHLAND SCHOOL

597 Broadview Avenue
Warrenton, Virginia 20186

Head of School: Mr. Henry D. Berg

General Information Coeducational day college-preparatory school. Grades PK–12. Founded: 1928. Setting: small town. Nearest major city is Washington, DC. 42-acre campus. 4 buildings on campus. Approved or accredited by Virginia Association of Independent Schools and Virginia Department of Education. Member of National Association of Independent Schools. Endowment: $4 million. Total enrollment: 540. Upper school average class size: 11. Upper school faculty-student ratio: 1:6.

Upper School Student Profile Grade 9: 49 students (22 boys, 27 girls); Grade 10: 59 students (32 boys, 27 girls); Grade 11: 57 students (23 boys, 34 girls); Grade 12: 60 students (26 boys, 34 girls).

Faculty School total: 107. In upper school: 13 men, 23 women; 23 have advanced degrees.

Subjects Offered Algebra, American literature, art, art appreciation, biology, biotechnology, calculus-AP, chemistry, chemistry-AP, choir, choral music, chorus, college writing, composition, computer graphics, computer keyboarding, computer literacy, computer programming, computer programming-AP, computer science, computer science-AP, computer skills, computer studies, computer technologies, computer tools, computer-aided design, concert band, concert bell choir, drama, English, English-AP, environmental science, European history-AP, French, French-AP, geometry, Greek, honors English, international relations, intro to computers, journalism, Latin, Latin-AP, law, macroeconomics-AP, marine biology, microeconomics, modern European history, music appreciation, orchestra, physical education, physics, physics-AP, pre-calculus, probability and statistics, SAT preparation, Spanish, Spanish-AP, statistics-AP, study skills, trigonometry, U.S. history-AP, world cultures, world religions.

Graduation Requirements Arts and fine arts (art, music, dance, drama), computer science, English, foreign language, lab science, mathematics, physical education (includes health), social science, 20 hours of community service for each year of attendance.

Special Academic Programs Advanced Placement exam preparation; honors section; independent study; term-away projects; study at local college for college credit.

College Admission Counseling 53 students graduated in 2008; all went to college, including Davidson College; Hampden-Sydney College; James Madison University; Lynchburg College; The College of William and Mary; University of Virginia. Median SAT critical reading: 570, median SAT math: 530, median SAT writing: 570, median combined SAT: 1700, median composite ACT: 24. 37% scored over 600 on SAT critical reading, 17% scored over 600 on SAT math, 32% scored over 600 on SAT writing, 29% scored over 1800 on combined SAT, 36% scored over 26 on composite ACT.

Student Life Upper grades have specified standards of dress, student council, honor system. Discipline rests equally with students and faculty.

Summer Programs Enrichment, sports, art/fine arts, rigorous outdoor training, computer instruction programs offered; session focuses on recreation and academics; held both on and off campus; held at Warrenton (swimming) and various locations (camping and hiking); accepts boys and girls; open to students from other schools. 200 students usually enrolled. 2009 schedule: June 22 to August 7.

Tuition and Aid Day student tuition: $19,100. Tuition installment plan (Insured Tuition Payment Plan, FACTS Tuition Payment Plan, monthly payment plans, individually arranged payment plans). Merit scholarship grants, need-based scholarship grants, faculty/staff discounts available. In 2008–09, 20% of upper-school students received aid; total upper-school merit-scholarship money awarded: $80,000. Total amount of financial aid awarded in 2008–09: $465,000.

Admissions Traditional secondary-level entrance grade is 9. For fall 2008, 77 students applied for upper-level admission, 74 were accepted, 43 enrolled. SSAT, ERB, PSAT, SAT, PLAN or ACT or TOEFL or SLEP required. Deadline for receipt of application materials: January 30. Application fee required: $50. Interview required.

Athletics Interscholastic: aerobics/dance (girls), baseball (b), basketball (b,g), cheering (g), cross-country running (b,g), dance (g), dance squad (g), dance team (g), field hockey (g), lacrosse (b,g), modern dance (g), running (b,g), soccer (b,g), softball (g), tennis (b,g), volleyball (g); intramural: ball hockey (g), basketball (b,g), field hockey (g), lacrosse (b,g), soccer (b,g), volleyball (g); coed interscholastic: aquatics, cross-country running, golf, swimming and diving; coed intramural: aerobics/dance, backpacking, climbing, dance, fitness, freestyle skiing, outdoor activities, outdoor adventure, physical fitness, power lifting, ropes courses, running, skiing (downhill), snowboarding, strength & conditioning, volleyball, weight lifting, weight training. 2 PE instructors, 7 coaches, 1 athletic trainer.

Computers Computers are regularly used in all academic classes. Computer network features include on-campus library services, Internet access, Internet filtering or blocking technology. Students grades are available online. The school has a published electronic and media policy.

Contact Mr. Chris S. Pryor, Director of Admission and Financial Aid. 540-878-2700. Fax: 540-878-2731. E-mail: cpryor@highlandschool.org. Web site: www.highlandschool.org.

ANNOUNCEMENT FROM THE SCHOOL As an accredited PK–Grade 12, independent, co-ed, day school of 540 students in Warrenton, Virginia, Highland School provides its college-bound students the opportunity to develop their talents in a safe, well-rounded, academic environment. The School's athletic, artistic, and experiential education programs complement classroom learning by encouraging students to work as a team, be creative, and take risks. Highland School draws talented students from nine surrounding counties and offers bus service to Haymarket, Gainesville, Middleburg, Purcellville, Manassas, Leesburg, and Culpeper. Financial aid and merit-based grants are available. Please contact Chris Pryor or Laura McCauley in the Admission and Financial Aid Office at 540-878-2741 or admission@highlandschool.org to schedule a campus visit, request an application, or to ask any questions. Highland School hosts three open house programs each year for prospective students and their families in November, December or January, and May. Open house dates in 2009 are Sunday, January 11 and Sunday, May 3; please contact the School for the November 2009 date. All programs begin at 2 p.m. in the Center for the Arts. We look forward to welcoming you to Highland School.

HIGH MOWING SCHOOL

222 Isaac Frye Highway
Wilton, New Hampshire 03086

Head of School: Patrice Pinette

General Information Coeducational boarding and day college-preparatory and arts school. Grades 9–12. Founded: 1942. Setting: rural. Nearest major city is Boston, MA. Students are housed in single-sex dormitories. 125-acre campus. 17 buildings on campus. Approved or accredited by Association of Independent Schools in New England, Association of Waldorf Schools of North America, Independent Schools of Northern New England, New England Association of Schools and Colleges, The Association of Boarding Schools, and New Hampshire Department of Education. Member of National Association of Independent Schools and Secondary School Admission Test Board. Endowment: $1 million. Total enrollment: 112. Upper school average class size: 12. Upper school faculty-student ratio: 1:5.

Upper School Student Profile Grade 9: 19 students (7 boys, 12 girls); Grade 10: 24 students (10 boys, 14 girls); Grade 11: 34 students (15 boys, 19 girls); Grade 12: 35 students (17 boys, 18 girls). 50% of students are boarding students. 50% are state residents. 18 states are represented in upper school student body. 7% are international students. International students from France, Germany, Japan, Mexico, Republic of Korea, and Switzerland; 1 other country represented in student body.

Faculty School total: 26. In upper school: 10 men, 12 women; 16 have advanced degrees; 15 reside on campus.

Subjects Offered Advanced chemistry, algebra, American history, American literature, anatomy, ancient history, art, astronomy, batik, biology, botany, calculus, ceramics, chemistry, community service, computer math, computer programming, computer science, creative writing, dance, digital art, drama, driver education, earth

science, ecology, economics, English, English literature, environmental science, ESL, ethics, European history, expository writing, fiber arts, fine arts, French, geography, geology, geometry, German, government/civics, grammar, health, history, history of science, mathematics, meteorology, music, mythology, nature study, philosophy, photography, physical education, physics, physiology, Russian literature, science, social science, social studies, speech, theater, theory of knowledge, trigonometry, wilderness education, world history, world literature, writing, zoology.
Graduation Requirements Algebra, arts and fine arts (art, music, dance, drama), economics, English, foreign language, government, mathematics, performing arts, physical education (includes health), physics, science, social science, social studies (includes history), studio art. Community service is required.
Special Academic Programs Advanced Placement exam preparation; honors section; independent study; term-away projects; study abroad; academic accommodation for the musically talented and the artistically talented; programs in mathematics for dyslexic students; ESL (4 students enrolled).
College Admission Counseling 29 students graduated in 2008; 25 went to college, including Bennington College; Hampshire College; Mount Holyoke College; University of New Hampshire; Warren Wilson College. Other: 2 went to work, 2 had other specific plans.
Student Life Upper grades have specified standards of dress, student council. Discipline rests primarily with faculty.
Tuition and Aid Day student tuition: $24,400; 5-day tuition and room/board: $36,700; 7-day tuition and room/board: $38,900. Tuition installment plan (monthly payment plans, individually arranged payment plans). Need-based scholarship grants available. In 2008–09, 45% of upper-school students received aid. Total amount of financial aid awarded in 2008–09: $500,000.
Admissions Traditional secondary-level entrance grade is 9. Deadline for receipt of application materials: none. Application fee required: $50. Interview required.
Athletics Interscholastic: baseball (boys), basketball (b,g), cross-country running (b,g), lacrosse (g), soccer (b,g); coed interscholastic: Frisbee; coed intramural: aerobics, aerobics/dance, aerobics/Nautilus, alpine skiing, archery, backpacking, bicycling, billiards, Circus, climbing, cross-country running, dance, fitness, fitness walking, golf, handball, hiking/backpacking, jogging, juggling, Nautilus, outdoor activities, physical fitness, physical training, rock climbing, running, skiing (cross-country), skiing (downhill), snowboarding, ultimate Frisbee, walking, wall climbing, wilderness, wilderness survival, wildernessways, yoga. 1 PE instructor, 8 coaches.
Computers Computers are regularly used in graphic arts, graphic design, mathematics, science, technology classes. Computer resources include on-campus library services, Internet access, wireless campus network. The school has a published electronic and media policy.
Contact Patricia Meissner, Director of Admissions. 603-654-2391 Ext. 103. Fax: 603-654-6588. E-mail: admissions@highmowing.org. Web site: www.highmowing.org.

ANNOUNCEMENT FROM THE SCHOOL The expansion and renovation of High Mowing School's Main Building, built nearly 250 years ago and housing the assembly space and dining room, was completed in April 2008.

See Close-Up on page 786.

THE HILL CENTER, DURHAM ACADEMY

Durham, North Carolina
See Special Needs Schools section.

HILLCREST CHRISTIAN SCHOOL

384 Erbes Road
Thousand Oaks, California 91362
Head of School: Mr. Stephen Allen
General Information Coeducational day college-preparatory school, affiliated with Christian faith. Grades K–12. Founded: 1977. Setting: suburban. 4-acre campus. 7 buildings on campus. Approved or accredited by Association of Christian Schools International, Western Association of Schools and Colleges, and California Department of Education. Total enrollment: 335. Upper school average class size: 15. Upper school faculty-student ratio: 1:9.
Upper School Student Profile Grade 7: 27 students (16 boys, 11 girls); Grade 8: 27 students (17 boys, 10 girls); Grade 9: 13 students (4 boys, 9 girls); Grade 10: 9 students (6 boys, 3 girls); Grade 11: 13 students (6 boys, 7 girls); Grade 12: 17 students (8 boys, 9 girls). 90% of students are Christian faith.
Faculty School total: 17. In upper school: 4 men, 13 women; 9 have advanced degrees.
Subjects Offered Algebra, American literature, art, Bible, biology, British literature, British literature (honors), calculus, chemistry, computers, earth science, economics, geometry, health, home economics, honors English, honors U.S. history, honors world history, introduction to literature, keyboarding/computer, life science, marine biology, physical education, physics, physiology-anatomy, pre-algebra, pre-calculus, Spanish, trigonometry, U.S. government, U.S. history, world history, world literature, yearbook.
Graduation Requirements Algebra, American literature, Bible, Bible studies, biology, British literature, chemistry, economics, electives, English, foreign language, geology, geometry, introduction to literature, mathematics, physical education (includes health), U.S. government, U.S. history, world history, world literature, 20 hours of community service each year.
Special Academic Programs 3 Advanced Placement exams for which test preparation is offered; honors section; ESL (2 students enrolled).
College Admission Counseling 9 students graduated in 2008; all went to college, including Azusa Pacific University; California Institute of the Arts; Moorpark College; Santa Barbara City College. Mean SAT critical reading: 570, mean SAT math: 590. 10% scored over 600 on SAT critical reading, 10% scored over 600 on SAT math, 20% scored over 600 on SAT writing.
Student Life Upper grades have uniform requirement, student council, honor system. Discipline rests primarily with faculty. Attendance at religious services is required.
Tuition and Aid Day student tuition: $8260. Tuition installment plan (FACTS Tuition Payment Plan). Tuition reduction for siblings, need-based scholarship grants, tuition reduction for families of full-time pastors, tuition reduction for children of faculty and staff available. In 2008–09, 10% of upper-school students received aid. Total amount of financial aid awarded in 2008–09: $23,694.
Admissions Traditional secondary-level entrance grade is 10. For fall 2008, 14 students applied for upper-level admission, 6 were accepted, 5 enrolled. Admissions testing and Stanford Diagnostic Test required. Deadline for receipt of application materials: none. Application fee required: $100. On-campus interview required.
Athletics Interscholastic: basketball (boys, girls), cheering (g), football (b), golf (b), soccer (g), volleyball (b,g); coed intramural: flag football. 2 PE instructors, 4 coaches.
Computers Computers are regularly used in computer applications, economics, science, yearbook classes. Computer resources include on-campus library services, computer lab. Computer access in designated common areas is available to students. Students grades are available online. The school has a published electronic and media policy.
Contact Mrs. Gail Matheson, Office Manager. 805-497-7501 Ext. 200. Fax: 805-494-9355. E-mail: gmatheson@hillcrestcs.org. Web site: www.hillcrestcs.org.

HILLCREST SCHOOL

Midland, Texas
See Special Needs Schools section.

THE HILL SCHOOL

717 East High Street
Pottstown, Pennsylvania 19464-5791
Head of School: Mr. David R. Dougherty
General Information Coeducational boarding and day college-preparatory school, affiliated with Christian faith. Boarding grades 9–PG, day grades 9–12. Founded: 1851. Setting: small town. Nearest major city is Philadelphia. Students are housed in single-sex dormitories. 200-acre campus. 58 buildings on campus. Approved or accredited by Middle States Association of Colleges and Schools, The Association of Boarding Schools, and Pennsylvania Department of Education. Member of National Association of Independent Schools and Secondary School Admission Test Board. Endowment: $140.9 million. Total enrollment: 489. Upper school average class size: 13. Upper school faculty-student ratio: 1:7.
Upper School Student Profile Grade 9: 99 students (50 boys, 49 girls); Grade 10: 95 students (57 boys, 38 girls); Grade 11: 121 students (64 boys, 57 girls); Grade 12: 108 students (62 boys, 46 girls); Postgraduate: 15 students (14 boys, 1 girl). 80% of students are boarding students. 48% are state residents. 30 states are represented in upper school student body. 13% are international students. International students from Canada, Germany, Hong Kong, Malaysia, Republic of Korea, and Venezuela; 8 other countries represented in student body.
Faculty School total: 86. In upper school: 56 men, 30 women; 61 have advanced degrees; 80 reside on campus.
Subjects Offered Acting, advanced chemistry, advanced computer applications, advanced math, Advanced Placement courses, advanced studio art-AP, algebra, American Civil War, American history, American history-AP, American literature-AP, American studies, Ancient Greek, ancient world history, art, art history, art-AP, arts, astronomy, athletic training, basic language skills, Basic programming, Bible studies, biochemistry, biology, biology-AP, boat building, botany, British literature-AP, calculus, calculus-AP, chamber groups, chemistry, chemistry-AP, Chinese, choral music, Christian ethics, Christian scripture, Christian testament, college admission preparation, college counseling, college placement, college planning, college writing, composition-AP, computer math, computer programming, computer science, computer science-AP, concert choir, creative writing, digital art, earth science, ecology, economics, economics-AP, English, English language and composition-AP, English literature, English literature and composition-AP, environmental science, European history, European history-AP, expository writing, French, French language-AP, French literature-AP, geography, geometry, German, government/civics, grammar, Greek, history, honors algebra, honors English, honors geometry, humanities, independent study, instrumental music, jazz band, journalism, lab science, Latin, Latin-AP, life issues, linear algebra, mathematics, music, oral communications, orchestra, participation in sports, photography, physics, physics-AP, physiology-anatomy, pre-calculus, pre-college orientation, psychology, psychology-AP, radio broadcasting, religion, SAT/ACT preparation, science, sex education, sexuality, social

studies, sociology, Spanish, speech, sports medicine, theater, theology, trigonometry, typing, U.S. history-AP, woodworking, world history, world literature.

Graduation Requirements Art, English, foreign language, mathematics, religion (includes Bible studies and theology), science, social studies (includes history).

Special Academic Programs Advanced Placement exam preparation; honors section; independent study; study abroad.

College Admission Counseling 119 students graduated in 2008; all went to college, including Boston University; Cornell University; Trinity College; United States Naval Academy; University of Pennsylvania; University of Richmond. Mean SAT critical reading: 625, mean SAT math: 633, mean SAT writing: 625, mean composite ACT: 26. 62% scored over 600 on SAT critical reading, 66% scored over 600 on SAT math, 53% scored over 26 on composite ACT.

Student Life Upper grades have specified standards of dress, student council, honor system. Discipline rests equally with students and faculty. Attendance at religious services is required.

Tuition and Aid Day student tuition: $27,400; 7-day tuition and room/board: $39,400. Tuition installment plan (Insured Tuition Payment Plan, monthly payment plans, individually arranged payment plans). Need-based scholarship grants available. In 2008–09, 38% of upper-school students received aid. Total amount of financial aid awarded in 2008–09: $4,500,000.

Admissions Traditional secondary-level entrance grade is 9. For fall 2008, 700 students applied for upper-level admission, 305 were accepted, 168 enrolled. ACT, ISEE, PSAT or SAT for applicants to grade 11 and 12, SSAT or TOEFL required. Deadline for receipt of application materials: January 31. Application fee required: $50. Interview required.

Athletics Interscholastic: baseball (boys), basketball (b,g), cross-country running (b,g), field hockey (g), football (b), ice hockey (b,g), indoor track (b,g), lacrosse (b,g), soccer (b,g), softball (g), squash (b,g), swimming and diving (b,g), tennis (b,g), water polo (b,g), winter (indoor) track (b,g), wrestling (b); coed interscholastic: diving, golf, track and field; coed intramural: aerobics, basketball, golf, martial arts, riflery, soccer, squash, strength & conditioning, tennis, volleyball, weight lifting. 2 coaches, 2 athletic trainers.

Computers Computers are regularly used in all classes. Computer network features include on-campus library services, online commercial services, Internet access, wireless campus network. Student e-mail accounts are available to students. The school has a published electronic and media policy.

Contact Mr. Thomas Eccleston, IV, Director of Admission and Enrollment Management. 610-326-1000. Fax: 610-705-1753. E-mail: teccleston@thehill.org. Web site: www.thehill.org.

ANNOUNCEMENT FROM THE SCHOOL The Hill School's mission is to prepare young men and women from across the United States and around the world for excellence in school, college, career, and life. To achieve such scholastic excellence and character development, Hill students learn inside and outside the classroom: they learn in the dining hall, in the residence halls, through participation in extracurricular activities, via international exchange programs, and on the playing fields. Athletics are, in fact, part of The Hill School's curriculum, teaching sportsmanship and self-discipline. Traditions such as twice-weekly chapel services reinforce students' ethical development and nurture their individual spirituality. The top priority at Hill is to provide an outstanding, challenging academic environment. The Hill School's program is based on the liberal arts and sciences and is taught in small classes by faculty members who reside on campus and serve as dorm parents, coaches, and advisers.

See Close-Up on page 788.

HILLSIDE SCHOOL

Marlborough, Massachusetts

See Junior Boarding Schools section.

THE HILL TOP PREPARATORY SCHOOL

Rosemont, Pennsylvania

See Special Needs Schools section.

HILTON HEAD PREPARATORY SCHOOL

8 Fox Grape Road
Hilton Head Island, South Carolina 29928

Head of School: Mr. Peter Cooper

General Information Coeducational day college-preparatory, arts, and technology school. Grades K–12. Founded: 1965. Setting: small town. Nearest major city is Savannah, GA. 25-acre campus. 7 buildings on campus. Approved or accredited by South Carolina Independent School Association, Southern Association of Colleges and Schools, Southern Association of Independent Schools, The College Board, and South Carolina Department of Education. Member of National Association of Independent Schools and Secondary School Admission Test Board. Total enrollment: 439. Upper school average class size: 12. Upper school faculty-student ratio: 1:12.

Upper School Student Profile Grade 9: 47 students (22 boys, 25 girls); Grade 10: 45 students (22 boys, 23 girls); Grade 11: 43 students (23 boys, 20 girls); Grade 12: 45 students (27 boys, 18 girls).

Faculty School total: 63. In upper school: 14 men, 14 women; 12 have advanced degrees.

Subjects Offered Advanced studio art-AP, algebra, American literature-AP, art, biology-AP, British literature, calculus, calculus-AP, chemistry, chemistry-AP, Chinese, chorus, college counseling, community service, computer science-AP, computer studies, drama, English literature and composition-AP, French language-AP, French-AP, geography, geometry, guidance, guitar, health education, history-AP, journalism, Latin, leadership and service, library, literature and composition-AP, marine biology, newspaper, peer counseling, performing arts, physical education, physical fitness, physics-AP, piano, pre-calculus, SAT/ACT preparation, senior career experience, senior thesis, Spanish language-AP, Spanish-AP, statistics and probability, statistics-AP, strings, student government, studio art, trigonometry, U.S. history, U.S. history-AP, visual and performing arts, world history, world literature, yearbook.

Graduation Requirements Arts and fine arts (art, music, dance, drama), computer literacy, English, foreign language, internship, mathematics, physical education (includes health), science, social studies (includes history), senior speech, 10 hours of community service per school year.

Special Academic Programs Advanced Placement exam preparation; honors section.

College Admission Counseling 40 students graduated in 2008; all went to college, including Clemson University; Dartmouth College; Furman University; Northwestern University; Notre Dame de Namur University; Wake Forest University. Median SAT critical reading: 585, median SAT math: 561.

Student Life Upper grades have specified standards of dress, student council, honor system. Discipline rests equally with students and faculty.

Summer Programs Enrichment, sports, art/fine arts, computer instruction programs offered; held on campus; accepts boys and girls; open to students from other schools. 25 students usually enrolled. 2009 schedule: June 7 to July 31. Application deadline: none.

Tuition and Aid Day student tuition: $11,875–$15,295. Tuition installment plan (monthly payment plans, individually arranged payment plans, bank-arranged plan, self-insured tuition refund plan). Tuition reduction for siblings, need-based scholarship grants, tuition discounts for children of faculty available. In 2008–09, 23% of upper-school students received aid. Total amount of financial aid awarded in 2008–09: $250,000.

Admissions Traditional secondary-level entrance grade is 9. For fall 2008, 25 students applied for upper-level admission, 20 were accepted, 17 enrolled. School's own exam, SSAT or writing sample required. Deadline for receipt of application materials: none. Application fee required: $75. On-campus interview required.

Athletics Interscholastic: aerobics/dance (girls), baseball (b), basketball (b,g), cheering (g), dance team (g), football (b), soccer (b,g), tennis (b,g), volleyball (g); intramural: aerobics/dance (g), basketball (b,g), dance team (g), soccer (b,g); coed interscholastic: aquatics, cross-country running, golf; coed intramural: outdoor activities, physical fitness, strength & conditioning. 4 PE instructors, 4 coaches, 1 athletic trainer.

Computers Computers are regularly used in all academic, art, college planning, drawing and design, graphic arts, graphic design, library science, media arts, music, newspaper, photography, research skills, SAT preparation, senior seminar, speech, stock market, technical drawing, theater, theater arts, yearbook classes. Computer network features include on-campus library services, Internet access, wireless campus network, Internet filtering or blocking technology. Campus intranet is available to students. The school has a published electronic and media policy.

Contact Bobbie C. Somerville, Director of Admissions. 843-671-2286. Fax: 843-671-7624. E-mail: bsomerville@hhprep.org. Web site: www.hhprep.org.

THE HOCKADAY SCHOOL

11600 Welch Road
Dallas, Texas 75229-2999

Head of School: Jeanne P. Whitman

General Information Girls' boarding and day college-preparatory school. Boarding grades 8–12, day grades PK–12. Founded: 1913. Setting: suburban. Students are housed in single-sex dormitories. 100-acre campus. 12 buildings on campus. Approved or accredited by Independent Schools Association of the Southwest and The Association of Boarding Schools. Member of National Association of Independent Schools and Secondary School Admission Test Board. Endowment: $100 million. Total enrollment: 1,046. Upper school average class size: 16. Upper school faculty-student ratio: 1:14.

Upper School Student Profile Grade 9: 114 students (114 girls); Grade 10: 105 students (105 girls); Grade 11: 118 students (118 girls); Grade 12: 106 students (106 girls). 12% of students are boarding students. 9 states are represented in upper school student body. 3% are international students. International students from China, Japan, Mexico, Republic of Korea, Taiwan, and United Kingdom; 4 other countries represented in student body.

Faculty School total: 116. In upper school: 17 men, 44 women; 48 have advanced degrees.

Subjects Offered 3-dimensional art, 3-dimensional design, acting, advanced math, advanced studio art-AP, algebra, American biography, American history, American history-AP, American literature, analytic geometry, anatomy, applied arts, applied music, art history, Asian studies, astronomy, athletics, audio visual/media, backpacking, ballet, ballet technique, basketball, biology, biology-AP, body human, British literature, broadcast journalism, broadcasting, Broadway dance, calculus, calculus-AP, cell biology, ceramics, chemistry, chemistry-AP, comparative religion, computer applications, computer science, computer science-AP, concert choir, consumer economics, CPR, creative writing, current events, dance, dance performance, debate, digital art, digital imaging, digital music, digital photography, directing, discrete mathematics, drawing and design, ecology, environmental systems, economics-AP, English, English literature, English literature and composition-AP, environmental science, environmental science-AP, ESL, fencing, finite math, French, French language-AP, French literature-AP, genetics, geometry, guitar, health, health and wellness, honors English, humanities, information technology, interdisciplinary studies, journalism, Latin, Latin-AP, life management skills, madrigals, Mandarin, meteorology, microbiology, modern European history-AP, newspaper, non-Western literature, orchestra, philosophy, photography, physical education, physical fitness, physics, physics-AP, piano, pre-calculus, printmaking, probability and statistics, psychology, psychology-AP, self-defense, senior internship, set design, short story, Spanish, Spanish language-AP, Spanish literature-AP, stagecraft, studio art, studio art—AP, swimming, tennis, track and field, U.S. government, U.S. history, U.S. history-AP, Vietnam War, voice, volleyball, Web site design, wellness, world history, World War I, yearbook.

Graduation Requirements Algebra, American literature, applied arts, art history, audio visual/media, British literature, chemistry, computer literacy, computer skills, English, English literature, geometry, history of music, information technology, languages, physical education (includes health), physics, senior project, trigonometry, U.S. government, U.S. history, world history, one semester of a non-western course in any discipline, 60 hours of community service.

Special Academic Programs Advanced Placement exam preparation; honors section; independent study; term-away projects; study abroad; ESL (12 students enrolled).

College Admission Counseling 120 students graduated in 2008; all went to college, including Georgetown University; Harvard University; Stanford University; The University of Texas at Austin; University of Southern California; Vanderbilt University.

Student Life Upper grades have uniform requirement, student council, honor system. Discipline rests primarily with faculty.

Summer Programs Enrichment, advancement, ESL, sports, art/fine arts, computer instruction programs offered; session focuses on enrichment; held on campus; accepts boys and girls; open to students from other schools. 800 students usually enrolled. 2009 schedule: June 12 to July 21. Application deadline: none.

Tuition and Aid Day student tuition: $21,220–$21,850; 7-day tuition and room/board: $38,800–$42,755. Tuition installment plan (monthly payment plan at J.P. Morgan-Chase Bank). Need-based financial aid available. In 2008–09, 15% of upper-school students received aid. Total amount of financial aid awarded in 2008–09: $786,700.

Admissions Traditional secondary-level entrance grade is 9. For fall 2008, 194 students applied for upper-level admission, 57 were accepted, 40 enrolled. Admissions testing required. Deadline for receipt of application materials: none. Application fee required: $150. Interview required.

Athletics Interscholastic: basketball, cheering, crew, cross-country running, diving, fencing, field hockey, golf, lacrosse, rowing, soccer, softball, swimming and diving, tennis, track and field, volleyball, winter soccer; intramural: aerobics, aerobics/dance, aquatics, archery, badminton, bicycling, cooperative games, crew, dance, fitness, fitness walking, Frisbee, golf, hiking/backpacking, in-line hockey, in-line skating, independent competitive sports, jogging, life saving, martial arts, mountain biking, outdoor activities, outdoor adventure, paddle tennis, physical fitness, physical training, project adventure, racquetball, roller blading, ropes courses, running, self defense, strength & conditioning, swimming and diving, table tennis, tennis, ultimate Frisbee, walking, wallyball, weight lifting, weight training, yoga. 10 PE instructors, 10 coaches, 1 athletic trainer.

Computers Computers are regularly used in animation, art, computer applications, creative writing, dance, engineering, English, French, health, history, humanities, information technology, introduction to technology, journalism, Latin, mathematics, media, media production, media services, multimedia, music, newspaper, photography, photojournalism, psychology, publications, publishing, science, Spanish, technology, Web site design, yearbook classes. Computer network features include on-campus library services, online commercial services, Internet access, wireless campus network, Internet filtering or blocking technology. Student e-mail accounts and computer access in designated common areas are available to students. Students grades are available online. The school has a published electronic and media policy.

Contact Jen Liggitt, Director of Admission. 214-363-6311. Fax: 214-363-0942. E-mail: admissions@mail.hockaday.org. Web site: www.hockaday.org.

See Close-Up on page 790.

HOKKAIDO INTERNATIONAL SCHOOL

1-55 5-jo 19-chome
Hiragishi, Toyohira-ku
Sapporo 062-0935, Japan

Head of School: Mr. Richard Branson

General Information Coeducational boarding and day and distance learning college-preparatory school. Boarding grades 7–12, day grades PK–12. Distance learning grades 10–12. Founded: 1958. Setting: urban. Students are housed in coed dormitories. 4-acre campus. 2 buildings on campus. Approved or accredited by CITA (Commission on International and Trans-Regional Accreditation), East Asia Regional Council of Schools, and Western Association of Schools and Colleges. Member of Secondary School Admission Test Board. Language of instruction: English. Endowment: $10 million. Total enrollment: 198. Upper school average class size: 14. Upper school faculty-student ratio: 1:10.

Upper School Student Profile Grade 10: 14 students (5 boys, 9 girls); Grade 11: 13 students (1 boy, 12 girls); Grade 12: 18 students (8 boys, 10 girls). 24% of students are boarding students. 44% are international students. International students from Republic of Korea, Russian Federation, Taiwan, and United States; 10 other countries represented in student body.

Faculty School total: 25. In upper school: 8 men, 4 women; 5 have advanced degrees; 2 reside on campus.

Subjects Offered 1968, algebra, art, arts, biology, calculus, calculus-AP, chemistry, English, English literature-AP, fine arts, geography, history, Japanese, language arts, mathematics, music, physical education, physics, physics-AP, pre-calculus, science, social studies, Spanish, U.S. history.

Graduation Requirements Arts and fine arts (art, music, dance, drama), English, foreign language, mathematics, physical education (includes health), science, social science, social studies (includes history), extracurricular involvement requirement (EIR).

Special Academic Programs Advanced Placement exam preparation; independent study; ESL (20 students enrolled).

College Admission Counseling 17 students graduated in 2008; 15 went to college, including The University of British Columbia. Other: 1 went to work, 1 entered military service. Mean SAT critical reading: 500, mean SAT math: 610, mean SAT writing: 500.

Student Life Upper grades have student council. Discipline rests primarily with faculty.

Summer Programs Rigorous outdoor training programs offered; session focuses on Outdoor education and leadership; held on campus; accepts boys and girls; open to students from other schools. 12 students usually enrolled.

Tuition and Aid Day student tuition: ¥1,055,000; 7-day tuition and room/board: ¥1,700,000. Tuition reduction for siblings, need-based scholarship grants available. In 2008–09, 20% of upper-school students received aid. Total amount of financial aid awarded in 2008–09: ¥2,000,000.

Admissions Traditional secondary-level entrance grade is 10. For fall 2008, 10 students applied for upper-level admission, 9 were accepted, 9 enrolled. School's own exam required. Deadline for receipt of application materials: none. Application fee required: ¥17,300. Interview required.

Athletics Interscholastic: basketball (boys, girls), indoor soccer (b), soccer (b), volleyball (g); coed intramural: backpacking, freestyle skiing, hiking/backpacking, outdoor activities, outdoor recreation, skiing (downhill), snowboarding. 1 PE instructor.

Computers Computers are regularly used in English, foreign language, geography, history, mathematics, science classes. Computer network features include Internet access, wireless campus network. Students grades are available online.

Contact Mrs. Shimako Abe, Administrative Assistant. 81-11-816-5000. Fax: 81-11-816-2500. E-mail: shimakoa@his.ac.jp. Web site: www.his.ac.jp.

HOLDERNESS SCHOOL

Chapel Lane
PO Box 1879
Plymouth, New Hampshire 03264-1879

Head of School: Mr. R. Phillip Peck

General Information Coeducational boarding and day college-preparatory, arts, religious studies, bilingual studies, and technology school, affiliated with Episcopal Church. Grades 9–PG. Founded: 1879. Setting: small town. Nearest major city is Boston, MA. Students are housed in single-sex dormitories. 620-acre campus. 35 buildings on campus. Approved or accredited by Association of Independent Schools in New England, New England Association of Schools and Colleges, The Association of Boarding Schools, and New Hampshire Department of Education. Member of National Association of Independent Schools and Secondary School Admission Test Board. Endowment: $44 million. Total enrollment: 281. Upper school average class size: 12. Upper school faculty-student ratio: 1:6.

Upper School Student Profile Grade 9: 49 students (27 boys, 22 girls); Grade 10: 66 students (42 boys, 24 girls); Grade 11: 87 students (47 boys, 40 girls); Grade 12: 76 students (48 boys, 28 girls); Postgraduate: 3 students (3 boys). 79% of students are boarding students. 36% are state residents. 24 states are represented in upper school student body. 13% are international students. International students from Canada,

Cayman Islands, Lithuania, Republic of Korea, Saudi Arabia, and Spain; 5 other countries represented in student body. 20% of students are members of Episcopal Church.
Faculty School total: 49. In upper school: 29 men, 20 women; 29 have advanced degrees; 29 reside on campus.
Subjects Offered Advanced chemistry, Advanced Placement courses, algebra, anatomy and physiology, art, art history, Bible studies, biology, calculus, ceramics, chemistry, chorus, community service, drama, drawing, driver education, economics, economics and history, English, environmental science, ethics, ethics and responsibility, European history, fine arts, French, geometry, government/civics, history, human anatomy, human development, humanities, jazz band, Latin, mathematics, music, music composition, music theory, music theory-AP, painting, photography, physics, pre-calculus, religion, science, society and culture, Spanish, statistics, theater, theater arts, theater production, theology, trigonometry, U.S. history, women in world history, women's studies, world history, world religions, writing.
Graduation Requirements Arts and fine arts (art, music, dance, drama), English, foreign language, history, human development, humanities, mathematics, science, theology. Community service is required.
Special Academic Programs Advanced Placement exam preparation; honors section; independent study; term-away projects; study abroad; academic accommodation for the gifted, the musically talented, and the artistically talented.
College Admission Counseling 78 students graduated in 2008; 77 went to college, including Bates College; Dartmouth College; St. Lawrence University; University of New Hampshire; University of Vermont. Other: 1 entered a postgraduate year. Mean SAT critical reading: 555, mean SAT math: 577, mean SAT writing: 555. 37% scored over 600 on SAT critical reading, 39% scored over 600 on SAT math.
Student Life Upper grades have specified standards of dress, student council, honor system. Discipline rests equally with students and faculty. Attendance at religious services is required.
Tuition and Aid Day student tuition: $24,190; 7-day tuition and room/board: $40,700. Tuition installment plan (Insured Tuition Payment Plan, Key Tuition Payment Plan, monthly payment plans). Need-based scholarship grants available. In 2008–09, 39% of upper-school students received aid. Total amount of financial aid awarded in 2008–09: $2,200,000.
Admissions Traditional secondary-level entrance grade is 9. For fall 2008, 425 students applied for upper-level admission, 204 were accepted, 104 enrolled. SSAT or WISC III or TOEFL required. Deadline for receipt of application materials: February 1. Application fee required: $50. Interview required.
Athletics Interscholastic: alpine skiing (boys, girls), baseball (b), basketball (b,g), bicycling (b,g), cross-country running (b,g), field hockey (g), football (b), freestyle skiing (b,g), ice hockey (b,g), lacrosse (b,g), nordic skiing (b,g), skiing (cross-country) (b,g), skiing (downhill) (b,g), snowboarding (b,g), soccer (b,g), softball (g), tennis (b,g); coed interscholastic: golf, running, ski jumping; coed intramural: aerobics/dance, backpacking, canoeing/kayaking, climbing, dance, equestrian sports, fishing, fly fishing, Frisbee, hiking/backpacking, horseback riding, ice hockey, kayaking, mountain biking, mountaineering, outdoor activities, outdoor skills, physical fitness, rock climbing, skiing (cross-country), skiing (downhill), snowboarding, snowshoeing, softball, squash, strength & conditioning, table tennis, ultimate Frisbee, wall climbing, weight lifting, weight training, wilderness, wilderness survival. 21 coaches, 1 athletic trainer.
Computers Computers are regularly used in Bible studies, creative writing, English, foreign language, graphic arts, history, library, mathematics, music, photography, religious studies, science, technology, theater, video film production, Web site design, yearbook classes. Computer network features include on-campus library services, Internet access, wireless campus network, Internet filtering or blocking technology, four computer labs (3 PC, 1 Mac). Campus intranet, student e-mail accounts, and computer access in designated common areas are available to students. The school has a published electronic and media policy.
Contact Ms. Nancy Dalley, Director of Financial Aid and Admission Operations. 603-536-1747. Fax: 603-536-2125. E-mail: admissions@holderness.org. Web site: www.holderness.org.

See Close-Up on page 792.

HOLLAND HALL

5666 East 81st Street
Tulsa, Oklahoma 74137-2099

Head of School: Dr. Mark D. Desjardins

General Information Coeducational day college-preparatory, arts, religious studies, and technology school, affiliated with Episcopal Church. Grades PK–12. Founded: 1922. Setting: suburban. 162-acre campus. 5 buildings on campus. Approved or accredited by Independent Schools Association of the Southwest and Oklahoma Department of Education. Member of National Association of Independent Schools. Endowment: $87.9 million. Total enrollment: 993. Upper school average class size: 13. Upper school faculty-student ratio: 1:9.
Upper School Student Profile Grade 9: 81 students (42 boys, 39 girls); Grade 10: 77 students (36 boys, 41 girls); Grade 11: 93 students (53 boys, 40 girls); Grade 12: 89 students (48 boys, 41 girls). 10% of students are members of Episcopal Church.
Faculty School total: 119. In upper school: 25 men, 23 women; 30 have advanced degrees.
Subjects Offered Algebra, American history, American literature, art, art history, biology, calculus, calculus-AP, ceramics, chemistry, chemistry-AP, Chinese, computer programming, computer science, computer science-AP, creative writing, dance, debate, drama, driver education, earth science, ecology, economics, English, English literature, English literature-AP, environmental science, ethics, European history, expository writing, fine arts, French, French literature-AP, geology, geometry, government/civics, grammar, history, Latin, mathematics, music, photography, physical education, physics, physics-AP, physiology, religion, science, social studies, Spanish, Spanish-AP, speech, statistics-AP, theater, theology, trigonometry, world history, world literature, writing.
Graduation Requirements Arts and fine arts (art, music, dance, drama), English, foreign language, mathematics, physical education (includes health), religion (includes Bible studies and theology), science, social studies (includes history), senior intern program.
Special Academic Programs Advanced Placement exam preparation; honors section; independent study; study at local college for college credit.
College Admission Counseling 82 students graduated in 2007; 80 went to college, including Oklahoma State University; Princeton University; University of Oklahoma; University of Tulsa; Vanderbilt University. Other: 2 entered a postgraduate year. Mean SAT critical reading: 609, mean SAT math: 628, mean SAT writing: 597, mean composite ACT: 27.
Student Life Upper grades have uniform requirement, student council, honor system. Discipline rests equally with students and faculty. Attendance at religious services is required.
Tuition and Aid Day student tuition: $14,310. Tuition installment plan (monthly payment plans, school's own payment plan). Merit scholarship grants, need-based grants available. In 2007–08, 29% of upper-school students received aid; total upper-school merit-scholarship money awarded: $177,635. Total amount of financial aid awarded in 2007–08: $843,555.
Admissions Traditional secondary-level entrance grade is 9. For fall 2007, 91 students applied for upper-level admission, 56 were accepted, 28 enrolled. ERB required. Deadline for receipt of application materials: none. Application fee required: $25. On-campus interview required.
Athletics Interscholastic: baseball (boys), basketball (b,g), cheering (g), cross-country running (b,g), field hockey (g), football (b), golf (b,g), modern dance (b,g), soccer (b,g), softball (g), tennis (b,g), track and field (b,g), volleyball (g); intramural: aerobics (b,g), modern dance (b,g), soccer (b,g); coed interscholastic: cheering, modern dance, strength & conditioning; coed intramural: modern dance, soccer, tennis, weight lifting. 1 PE instructor, 7 coaches, 1 athletic trainer.
Computers Computers are regularly used in English, foreign language, history, mathematics, science classes. Computer network features include on-campus library services, online commercial services, Internet access, wireless campus network, Internet filtering or blocking technology. Student e-mail accounts and computer access in designated common areas are available to students.
Contact Lori Adams, Director of Admission and Financial Aid. 918-481-1111 Ext. 740. Fax: 918-481-1145. E-mail: ladams@hollandhall.org. Web site: www.hollandhall.org.

ANNOUNCEMENT FROM THE SCHOOL Holland Hall is an independent, coeducational, college-preparatory, Episcopal day school that educates, nurtures, and empowers the individual student for lifelong learning. Holland Hall is recognized for superior college preparation by the Oklahoma State Regents for Higher Education.

THE HOLTON-ARMS SCHOOL

7303 River Road
Bethesda, Maryland 20817

Head of School: Susanna A. Jones

General Information Girls' day college-preparatory school. Grades 3–12. Founded: 1901. Setting: suburban. Nearest major city is Washington, DC. 57-acre campus. 8 buildings on campus. Approved or accredited by Association of Independent Maryland Schools, Middle States Association of Colleges and Schools, and Maryland Department of Education. Member of National Association of Independent Schools and Secondary School Admission Test Board. Endowment: $51 million. Total enrollment: 644. Upper school average class size: 15. Upper school faculty-student ratio: 1:7.
Upper School Student Profile Grade 9: 77 students (77 girls); Grade 10: 83 students (83 girls); Grade 11: 77 students (77 girls); Grade 12: 89 students (89 girls).
Faculty School total: 64. In upper school: 20 men, 44 women; 47 have advanced degrees.
Subjects Offered Acting, algebra, American government-AP, American history, American history-AP, American literature, ancient world history, art, art history, art history-AP, Asian studies, biology, biology-AP, calculus, calculus-AP, ceramics, chemistry, Chinese, community service, contemporary history, creative writing, dance, drama, drawing, ecology, economics, economics and history, economics-AP, engineering, English, English literature, environmental science, environmental science-AP, European history, European history-AP, expository writing, forensic science, French, French-AP, geography, government/civics, grammar, health, history, history-AP, Latin, Latin American history, Latin-AP, macro/microeconomics-AP,

mathematics, medieval history, Middle Eastern history, music, music technology, painting, philosophy, photography, physical education, physics, physics-AP, psychology, science, science research, social studies, Spanish, Spanish-AP, speech, statistics, theater, trigonometry, U.S. government-AP, world history, world literature, writing.
Graduation Requirements Arts, English, foreign language, history, mathematics, physical education (includes health), science. Community service is required.
Special Academic Programs Advanced Placement exam preparation; honors section; independent study; academic accommodation for the gifted and the artistically talented.
College Admission Counseling 78 students graduated in 2008; all went to college, including Cornell University; Georgetown University; Harvard University; Middlebury College; Princeton University; Stanford University. Mean SAT critical reading: 687, mean SAT math: 673, mean SAT writing: 704, mean combined SAT: 2064.
Student Life Upper grades have uniform requirement, student council, honor system. Discipline rests equally with students and faculty.
Tuition and Aid Day student tuition: $27,200–$28,500. Tuition installment plan (Key Tuition Payment Plan, monthly payment plans). Need-based scholarship grants available. In 2008–09, 20% of upper-school students received aid. Total amount of financial aid awarded in 2008–09: $2,300,000.
Admissions Traditional secondary-level entrance grade is 9. ISEE or SSAT required. Deadline for receipt of application materials: February 1. Application fee required: $60. Interview required.
Athletics Interscholastic: basketball, crew, cross-country running, diving, field hockey, ice hockey, indoor track, lacrosse, soccer, softball, swimming and diving, tennis, track and field, volleyball, winter (indoor) track; intramural: dance, life saving, modern dance, physical fitness, strength & conditioning; coed intramural: water polo. 9 PE instructors, 10 coaches, 1 athletic trainer.
Computers Computers are regularly used in all classes. Computer network features include on-campus library services, online commercial services, Internet access, wireless campus network, laptop program (grades 7-12). Campus intranet and student e-mail accounts are available to students. Students grades are available online. The school has a published electronic and media policy.
Contact Sharron Rodgers, Director of Enrollment and Marketing. 301-365-5300. Fax: 301-365-6071. E-mail: admit@holton-arms.edu. Web site: www.holton-arms.edu.

HOLY INNOCENTS' EPISCOPAL SCHOOL

805 Mount Vernon Highway NW
Atlanta, Georgia 30327

Head of School: Mr. Kirk Duncan

General Information Coeducational day college-preparatory, arts, religious studies, and technology school, affiliated with Episcopal Church. Grades PS–12. Founded: 1959. Setting: suburban. 46-acre campus. 4 buildings on campus. Approved or accredited by Georgia Independent School Association, National Association of Episcopal Schools, Southern Association of Colleges and Schools, and Georgia Department of Education. Member of National Association of Independent Schools and Secondary School Admission Test Board. Endowment: $15.8 million. Total enrollment: 1,418. Upper school average class size: 16. Upper school faculty-student ratio: 1:10.
Upper School Student Profile Grade 9: 100 students (48 boys, 52 girls); Grade 10: 109 students (48 boys, 61 girls); Grade 11: 98 students (54 boys, 44 girls); Grade 12: 102 students (46 boys, 56 girls). 32% of students are members of Episcopal Church.
Faculty School total: 260. In upper school: 24 men, 23 women; 35 have advanced degrees.
Subjects Offered Algebra, American history, American history-AP, American literature, anatomy, art, art-AP, Bible studies, biology, biology-AP, calculus, calculus-AP, chemistry, chemistry-AP, chorus, computer science, creative writing, earth science, economics, electives, English, English literature, English literature-AP, European history-AP, French, French-AP, geometry, government, history, Latin, Latin-AP, mathematics, New Testament, orchestra, performing arts, photography, physical education, physics, physics-AP, pre-calculus, psychology, religion, science, social studies, Spanish, trigonometry, world history.
Graduation Requirements Arts and fine arts (art, music, dance, drama), English, foreign language, mathematics, physical education (includes health), religion (includes Bible studies and theology), science, social studies (includes history).
Special Academic Programs Advanced Placement exam preparation; honors section; study abroad.
College Admission Counseling 95 students graduated in 2008; all went to college, including Auburn University; College of Charleston; The University of Alabama; University of Georgia; University of Mississippi; Wake Forest University. 33% scored over 600 on SAT critical reading, 35% scored over 600 on SAT math, 32% scored over 600 on SAT writing, 30% scored over 1800 on combined SAT, 25% scored over 26 on composite ACT.
Student Life Upper grades have uniform requirement, student council, honor system. Discipline rests primarily with faculty. Attendance at religious services is required.
Summer Programs Enrichment, sports, art/fine arts programs offered; session focuses on athletics, fine arts, and academics; held on campus; accepts boys and girls; open to students from other schools. 50 students usually enrolled. 2009 schedule: June 2 to July 30. Application deadline: April 1.
Tuition and Aid Day student tuition: $18,110. Tuition installment plan (Insured Tuition Payment Plan). Need-based scholarship grants available. In 2008–09, 10% of upper-school students received aid. Total amount of financial aid awarded in 2008–09: $490,725.
Admissions Traditional secondary-level entrance grade is 9. For fall 2008, 107 students applied for upper-level admission, 60 were accepted, 30 enrolled. SSAT required. Deadline for receipt of application materials: February 15. Application fee required: $85. Interview required.
Athletics Interscholastic: baseball (boys), basketball (b,g), cheering (g), cross-country running (b,g), equestrian sports (g), football (b), golf (b,g), lacrosse (b,g), rafting (b,g), soccer (b,g), softball (g), swimming and diving (b,g), tennis (b,g), track and field (b,g), volleyball (g), wrestling (b); intramural: fitness (b,g); coed intramural: fitness. 2 PE instructors, 14 coaches, 1 athletic trainer.
Computers Computers are regularly used in art, English, foreign language, history, mathematics, science classes. Computer network features include on-campus library services, Internet access, wireless campus network, Internet filtering or blocking technology, 1-to-1 student laptops (grades 5 to 12). Campus intranet and student e-mail accounts are available to students. Students grades are available online. The school has a published electronic and media policy.
Contact Mr. Chris Pomar, Director of Admissions. 404-255-4026. Fax: 404-847-1156. E-mail: chris.pomar@hies.org. Web site: www.hies.org.

HOLY NAME HIGH SCHOOL

955 East Wyomissing Boulevard
Reading, Pennsylvania 19611

Head of School: Rev. John A. Frink

General Information Coeducational day college-preparatory school, affiliated with Roman Catholic Church. Grades 9–12. Founded: 1964. Setting: suburban. 18-acre campus. 1 building on campus. Approved or accredited by Middle States Association of Colleges and Schools and Pennsylvania Department of Education. Total enrollment: 456. Upper school average class size: 25. Upper school faculty-student ratio: 1:12.
Upper School Student Profile Grade 9: 113 students (58 boys, 55 girls); Grade 10: 112 students (55 boys, 57 girls); Grade 11: 113 students (52 boys, 61 girls); Grade 12: 118 students (48 boys, 70 girls). 94% of students are Roman Catholic.
Faculty School total: 35. In upper school: 18 men, 17 women; 11 have advanced degrees.
Graduation Requirements 4 years of theology.
Special Academic Programs Advanced Placement exam preparation; honors section; study at local college for college credit.
College Admission Counseling 111 students graduated in 2008; all went to college.
Student Life Upper grades have uniform requirement, student council. Discipline rests primarily with faculty. Attendance at religious services is required.
Summer Programs Sports programs offered; session focuses on basketball and volleyball; held on campus; accepts boys and girls; not open to students from other schools. 300 students usually enrolled. 2009 schedule: June 12 to August 11. Application deadline: none.
Tuition and Aid Day student tuition: $5500. Tuition installment plan (FACTS Tuition Payment Plan). Tuition reduction for siblings, need-based scholarship grants available. In 2008–09, 34% of upper-school students received aid. Total amount of financial aid awarded in 2008–09: $24,522.
Admissions Traditional secondary-level entrance grade is 9. For fall 2008, 117 students applied for upper-level admission, 115 were accepted, 115 enrolled. Math and English placement tests required. Deadline for receipt of application materials: none. Application fee required: $100. On-campus interview recommended.
Athletics Interscholastic: baseball (boys), basketball (b,g), cheering (g), field hockey (g), football (b), soccer (b,g), softball (g), swimming and diving (b,g), tennis (b,g), track and field (b,g), volleyball (g); coed interscholastic: cross-country running, golf; coed intramural: bowling, ice hockey, indoor track & field. 1 PE instructor, 52 coaches, 1 athletic trainer.
Computers Computers are regularly used in all academic classes. Computer resources include on-campus library services, Internet access, Internet filtering or blocking technology. Students grades are available online.
Contact Mr. Josh Ditsky, Director of College Counseling. 610-374-8361 Ext. 46. Fax: 610-374-4398. E-mail: jditsky@gohnhs.org. Web site: www.gohnhs.org.

HOLY NAMES HIGH SCHOOL

4660 Harbord Drive
Oakland, California 94618

Head of School: Sr. Sally Slyngstad

General Information Girls' day college-preparatory, arts, religious studies, and technology school, affiliated with Roman Catholic Church. Grades 9–12. Founded: 1868. Setting: urban. 5-acre campus. 1 building on campus. Approved or accredited by Western Association of Schools and Colleges and California Department of Education. Endowment: $5 million. Total enrollment: 300. Upper school average class size: 21. Upper school faculty-student ratio: 1:11.

Upper School Student Profile Grade 9: 75 students (75 girls); Grade 10: 75 students (75 girls); Grade 11: 79 students (79 girls); Grade 12: 71 students (71 girls). 51% of students are Roman Catholic.
Faculty School total: 28. In upper school: 5 men, 23 women; all have advanced degrees.
Subjects Offered Algebra, American history, American literature, art, biology, business skills, calculus, chemistry, computer programming, computer science, creative writing, drama, driver education, economics, English, English literature, fine arts, French, geometry, government/civics, health, history, mathematics, music, photography, physical education, physics, physiology, psychology, religion, science, social science, social studies, Spanish, speech, statistics, theater, theology, trigonometry, typing, world history, world literature.
Graduation Requirements Arts and fine arts (art, music, dance, drama), computer science, English, foreign language, mathematics, physical education (includes health), religion (includes Bible studies and theology), science, social science, social studies (includes history), technology.
Special Academic Programs 8 Advanced Placement exams for which test preparation is offered; honors section; independent study; term-away projects; study at local college for college credit; academic accommodation for the gifted, the musically talented, and the artistically talented.
College Admission Counseling 69 students graduated in 2008; all went to college, including California State University; Howard University; Saint Mary's College of California; University of California, Berkeley; University of Southern California. Mean SAT critical reading: 632, mean SAT math: 658. 99% scored over 600 on SAT critical reading, 99% scored over 600 on SAT math.
Student Life Upper grades have uniform requirement, student council, honor system. Discipline rests equally with students and faculty. Attendance at religious services is required.
Summer Programs Remediation, enrichment, art/fine arts, computer instruction programs offered; session focuses on enrichment; held on campus; accepts girls; not open to students from other schools. 10 students usually enrolled. 2009 schedule: June 25 to July 27. Application deadline: none.
Tuition and Aid Day student tuition: $10,800. Tuition installment plan (SMART Tuition Payment Plan, FACTS Tuition Payment Plan, monthly payment plans, individually arranged payment plans). Merit scholarship grants, need-based scholarship grants available. In 2008–09, 49% of upper-school students received aid; total upper-school merit-scholarship money awarded: $89,000. Total amount of financial aid awarded in 2008–09: $324,466.
Admissions Traditional secondary-level entrance grade is 9. For fall 2008, 210 students applied for upper-level admission, 180 were accepted, 75 enrolled. Catholic High School Entrance Examination and STS required. Deadline for receipt of application materials: January 9. Application fee required: $75. On-campus interview required.
Athletics Interscholastic: backpacking, basketball, cross-country running, dance squad, golf, indoor track & field, physical fitness, soccer, softball, swimming and diving, tennis, track and field, volleyball; intramural: backpacking, basketball, cross-country running, dance squad, golf, indoor track & field, physical fitness, soccer, softball, swimming and diving, tennis, track and field, volleyball. 2 PE instructors, 25 coaches, 8 athletic trainers.
Computers Computers are regularly used in English, foreign language, mathematics, religious studies, science classes. Computer network features include on-campus library services, Internet access, wireless campus network, Internet filtering or blocking technology. Campus intranet, student e-mail accounts, and computer access in designated common areas are available to students. Students grades are available online. The school has a published electronic and media policy.
Contact Sandra Carrillo, Director of Admissions. 510-450-1110 Ext. 119. Fax: 510-547-3111. E-mail: scarrillo@hnhsoakland.org. Web site: www.hnhsoakland.org/.

HOLY SAVIOR MENARD CATHOLIC HIGH SCHOOL

4603 Coliseum Boulevard
Alexandria, Louisiana 71303

Head of School: Mr. Joel Desselle

General Information Coeducational day college-preparatory and religious studies school, affiliated with Roman Catholic Church. Grades 7–12. Founded: 1930. Setting: suburban. 5-acre campus. 5 buildings on campus. Approved or accredited by National Catholic Education Association, Southern Association of Colleges and Schools, and Louisiana Department of Education. Total enrollment: 498. Upper school average class size: 19. Upper school faculty-student ratio: 1:14.
Upper School Student Profile Grade 9: 83 students (45 boys, 38 girls); Grade 10: 87 students (52 boys, 35 girls); Grade 11: 88 students (52 boys, 36 girls); Grade 12: 63 students (24 boys, 39 girls). 80% of students are Roman Catholic.
Faculty School total: 36. In upper school: 19 men, 15 women; 12 have advanced degrees.
Subjects Offered Advanced math, algebra, American history, art, athletics, biology, biology-AP, British literature, British literature (honors), calculus-AP, campus ministry, Catholic belief and practice, cheerleading, chemistry, civics/free enterprise, computer applications, computer science, digital photography, electives, English, English composition, English literature, English literature-AP, fine arts, French, general science, geometry, health, Holocaust studies, honors algebra, honors English, honors geometry, honors U.S. history, honors world history, human anatomy, journalism, language arts, moral reasoning, New Testament, newspaper, philosophy, physical education, physical science, physics, pre-algebra, pre-calculus, psychology, publications, reading/study skills, religion, Spanish, world geography, world history, yearbook.
Graduation Requirements Algebra, American history, arts and fine arts (art, music, dance, drama), biology, chemistry, civics/free enterprise, computer applications, English, foreign language, geometry, physical science, religion (includes Bible studies and theology), world history, 26 credits required.
Special Academic Programs 3 Advanced Placement exams for which test preparation is offered; honors section; independent study; study at local college for college credit.
College Admission Counseling 87 students graduated in 2008; 80 went to college, including Louisiana State University and Agricultural and Mechanical College; Louisiana Tech University; Northwestern State University of Louisiana; University of Louisiana at Lafayette. Other: 3 went to work, 3 entered military service, 1 had other specific plans. Mean composite ACT: 22. 21% scored over 26 on composite ACT.
Student Life Upper grades have uniform requirement, student council, honor system. Discipline rests primarily with faculty. Attendance at religious services is required.
Tuition and Aid Day student tuition: $4730. Tuition reduction for siblings, merit scholarship grants, need-based scholarship grants available. In 2008–09, 5% of upper-school students received aid; total upper-school merit-scholarship money awarded: $4000.
Admissions Traditional secondary-level entrance grade is 9. CTBS, Stanford Achievement Test, any other standardized test required. Deadline for receipt of application materials: March 15. Application fee required: $200. On-campus interview required.
Athletics Interscholastic: baseball (boys), basketball (b,g), cheering (g), cross-country running (b,g), danceline (g), football (b), golf (b), running (b,g), soccer (b,g), softball (g), tennis (b,g), track and field (b,g); coed interscholastic: swimming and diving. 2 coaches.
Computers Computers are regularly used in computer applications, journalism, publications, science classes. Computer network features include on-campus library services, Internet access, wireless campus network. Computer access in designated common areas is available to students. Students grades are available online.
Contact Mrs. Ashley Meadows, Guidance Secretary. 318-445-8233. Fax: 318-448-8170. E-mail: ameadows@holysaviormenard.com. Web site: www.holysaviormenard.com.

HOLY TRINITY DIOCESAN HIGH SCHOOL

98 Cherry Lane
Hicksville, New York 11801

Head of School: Mr. Gene Fennell

General Information Coeducational day college-preparatory school, affiliated with Roman Catholic Church. Grades 9–12. Founded: 1967. Setting: suburban. Nearest major city is New York. 1 building on campus. Approved or accredited by Middle States Association of Colleges and Schools, National Council for Private School Accreditation, National Private School Accreditation Alliance, New York State Board of Regents, and The College Board. Total enrollment: 1,496. Upper school average class size: 28.
Upper School Student Profile Grade 9: 382 students (190 boys, 192 girls); Grade 10: 389 students (185 boys, 204 girls); Grade 11: 340 students (137 boys, 203 girls); Grade 12: 385 students (157 boys, 228 girls). 90% of students are Roman Catholic.
Faculty School total: 110. In upper school: 43 men, 67 women; 91 have advanced degrees.
Subjects Offered Accounting, advanced math, Advanced Placement courses, American government, American government-AP, American history, American history-AP, American literature, American literature-AP, anatomy and physiology, architectural drawing, art, band, biology, biology-AP, British literature, British literature (honors), business law, calculus, calculus-AP, campus ministry, ceramics, chemistry, chemistry-AP, chorus, Christian scripture, Christian studies, Christian testament, comparative religion, composition, computer keyboarding, concert band, criminology, critical studies in film, dance, desktop publishing, earth science, economics, English, English composition, English language and composition-AP, English literature, English literature-AP, environmental science, film, food and nutrition, French, government and politics-AP, health, honors English, honors U.S. history, honors world history, intro to computers, jazz theory, keyboarding/computer, literature and composition-AP, mathematics, music, performing arts, physical education, physics, physics-AP, pre-calculus, public speaking, religion, Spanish, Spanish language-AP, stagecraft, statistics, theater arts, theology, U.S. government and politics, U.S. government and politics-AP, U.S. history, U.S. history-AP, world wide web design.
Graduation Requirements Arts and fine arts (art, music, dance, drama), economics, English, foreign language, mathematics, physical education (includes health), religion (includes Bible studies and theology), science, U.S. government and politics.
Special Academic Programs Advanced Placement exam preparation; honors section; study at local college for college credit.
College Admission Counseling 431 students graduated in 2008; all went to college, including Adelphi University; Hofstra University; Nassau Community College; Stony

Brook University, State University of New York. Mean SAT critical reading: 514, mean SAT math: 522, mean SAT writing: 520.

Student Life Upper grades have uniform requirement, student council. Discipline rests primarily with faculty.

Tuition and Aid Day student tuition: $7375. Tuition installment plan (monthly payment plans, individually arranged payment plans, 10-month tuition plan, 3-payment plan). Need-based scholarship grants available.

Admissions Traditional secondary-level entrance grade is 9. Catholic High School Entrance Examination required. Deadline for receipt of application materials: none. No application fee required.

Athletics Interscholastic: badminton (girls), baseball (b), basketball (b,g), cheering (g), cross-country running (b,g), dance team (g), football (b), golf (b), gymnastics (g), lacrosse (b,g), soccer (b,g), softball (g), swimming and diving (b,g), tennis (b,g), track and field (b,g), volleyball (b,g); intramural: physical training (b), weight training (b); coed interscholastic: bowling. 6 PE instructors, 1 athletic trainer.

Computers Computers are regularly used in English, graphic design, Web site design classes. Computer network features include on-campus library services, Internet access, Internet filtering or blocking technology. Student e-mail accounts are available to students. The school has a published electronic and media policy.

Contact Admissions. 516-433-2900. Fax: 516-433-2827. E-mail: hths98@holytrinityhs.echalk.com. Web site: www.holytrinityhs.org.

HOLY TRINITY HIGH SCHOOL

1443 West Division Street
Chicago, Illinois 60642

Head of School: Mr. Timothy M. Bopp

General Information Coeducational day college-preparatory, arts, business, religious studies, bilingual studies, and technology school. Grades 9–12. Founded: 1910. Setting: urban. 1 building on campus. Approved or accredited by North Central Association of Colleges and Schools and Illinois Department of Education. Total enrollment: 400. Upper school average class size: 23. Upper school faculty-student ratio: 1:13.

Faculty School total: 32. In upper school: 16 men, 16 women; 16 have advanced degrees.

Subjects Offered Algebra, American literature, animation, art, astronomy, biology, British literature, business, calculus, campus ministry, Catholic belief and practice, ceramics, chemistry, church history, composition, computer graphics, computers, conceptual physics, consumer economics, discrete mathematics, drawing, economics, environmental science, film studies, geography, geometry, government, health, Holocaust, Internet, media, painting, physical education, physical science, physics, pre-calculus, psychology, publications, sculpture, social justice, Spanish, speech, theater arts, trigonometry, U.S. history, wellness, wood processing, world history, world literature, world religions, writing workshop.

Graduation Requirements Business, English, mathematics, modern languages, physical education (includes health), religion (includes Bible studies and theology), science, social studies (includes history), visual and performing arts.

Special Academic Programs Advanced Placement exam preparation; honors section; study at local college for college credit.

College Admission Counseling 95 students graduated in 2008; all went to college, including DePaul University; Dominican University; Loyola University Chicago; Northern Illinois University; University of Illinois at Chicago; University of Illinois at Urbana–Champaign.

Student Life Upper grades have uniform requirement, student council, honor system. Discipline rests equally with students and faculty. Attendance at religious services is required.

Tuition and Aid Day student tuition: $6650. Tuition installment plan (monthly payment plans). Tuition reduction for siblings, merit scholarship grants, need-based scholarship grants available. In 2008–09, 95% of upper-school students received aid; total upper-school merit-scholarship money awarded: $126,500. Total amount of financial aid awarded in 2008–09: $1,547,085.

Admissions Traditional secondary-level entrance grade is 9. TerraNova required. Deadline for receipt of application materials: January 10. Application fee required: $25.

Athletics Interscholastic: baseball (boys), basketball (b,g), cross-country running (b,g), soccer (b,g), softball (g), track and field (b,g), volleyball (b,g); coed interscholastic: bowling, cheering, flag football. 2 PE instructors.

Computers Computer network features include on-campus library services, Internet access, wireless campus network, Internet filtering or blocking technology. Computer access in designated common areas is available to students. The school has a published electronic and media policy.

Contact Ms. Melinda J. Green, Director of Recruitment. 773-278-4212 Ext. 3023. Fax: 773-278-0729. E-mail: mgreen@holytrinity-hs.org. Web site: www.holytrinity-hs.org.

HOOSAC SCHOOL

PO Box 9
Hoosick, New York 12089

Head of School: Richard J. Lomuscio

General Information Coeducational boarding and day college-preparatory and arts school, affiliated with Episcopal Church. Grades 8–PG. Founded: 1889. Setting: rural. Nearest major city is Albany. Students are housed in single-sex dormitories. 350-acre campus. 16 buildings on campus. Approved or accredited by Middle States Association of Colleges and Schools, National Association of Episcopal Schools, New York State Association of Independent Schools, The Association of Boarding Schools, and New York Department of Education. Member of National Association of Independent Schools and Secondary School Admission Test Board. Endowment: $1 million. Total enrollment: 125. Upper school average class size: 8. Upper school faculty-student ratio: 1:5.

Upper School Student Profile Grade 8: 7 students (5 boys, 2 girls); Grade 9: 20 students (10 boys, 10 girls); Grade 10: 23 students (16 boys, 7 girls); Grade 11: 29 students (17 boys, 12 girls); Grade 12: 41 students (29 boys, 12 girls); Postgraduate: 5 students (5 boys). 88% of students are boarding students. 29% are state residents. 17 states are represented in upper school student body. 27% are international students. International students from Canada, China, Hungary, India, Jamaica, and Republic of Korea; 13 other countries represented in student body.

Faculty School total: 23. In upper school: 13 men, 10 women; 10 have advanced degrees; 15 reside on campus.

Subjects Offered Algebra, American history, American literature, art, art history, astronomy, biology, calculus, calculus-AP, ceramics, chemistry, computer science, creative writing, criminology, dance, drama, driver education, earth science, English, English literature, English-AP, ethics, European history, expository writing, fine arts, French, geometry, government/civics, grammar, history, history-AP, marketing, mathematics, music, photography, physical education, physics, science, social studies, theater, world history, world literature, writing.

Graduation Requirements Arts and fine arts (art, music, dance, drama), computer literacy, English, ethics, foreign language, mathematics, physical education (includes health), science, social studies (includes history), Ethics.

Special Academic Programs Advanced Placement exam preparation; accelerated programs; independent study; study at local college for college credit; academic accommodation for the musically talented and the artistically talented; remedial reading and/or remedial writing; remedial math; programs in English, mathematics, general development for dyslexic students; ESL (15 students enrolled).

College Admission Counseling 45 students graduated in 2008; all went to college, including Boston College; Boston University; Bowdoin College; Hamilton College; Penn State University Park; University of Michigan.

Student Life Upper grades have specified standards of dress, student council, honor system. Discipline rests primarily with faculty. Attendance at religious services is required.

Tuition and Aid Day student tuition: $15,300; 7-day tuition and room/board: $31,300. Tuition installment plan (Academic Management Services Plan, Key Tuition Payment Plan, monthly payment plans, individually arranged payment plans). Need-based scholarship grants available. In 2008–09, 30% of upper-school students received aid. Total amount of financial aid awarded in 2008–09: $500,000.

Admissions Traditional secondary-level entrance grade is 9. For fall 2008, 168 students applied for upper-level admission, 108 were accepted, 56 enrolled. Deadline for receipt of application materials: none. Application fee required: $30. Interview required.

Athletics Interscholastic: baseball (boys), basketball (b,g), cross-country running (b,g), ice hockey (b), lacrosse (b); intramural: bicycling (b,g), flag football (b,g), floor hockey (b,g); coed intramural: alpine skiing, aquatics, backpacking, ball hockey, billiards, bowling, cross-country running, dance, deck hockey, fishing, freestyle skiing, golf, indoor hockey, indoor soccer, life saving, outdoor activities, outdoor adventure, outdoor recreation, physical fitness. 1 PE instructor, 15 coaches.

Computers Computers are regularly used in all classes. Computer network features include on-campus library services, Internet access, wireless campus network. Campus intranet and student e-mail accounts are available to students. The school has a published electronic and media policy.

Contact Dean S. Foster, Assistant Headmaster. 800-822-0159. Fax: 518-686-3370. E-mail: admissions@hoosac.com. Web site: www.hoosac.com.

See Close-Up on page 794.

HOPE CHRISTIAN SCHOOL

PO Box 235
Champion, Alberta T0L 0R0, Canada

Head of School: Mr. Dale Anger

General Information Coeducational day college-preparatory, general academic, arts, vocational, and religious studies school, affiliated with Evangelical Free Church of America. Grades 1–12. Founded: 1980. Setting: small town. Nearest major city is Lethbridge, Canada. 2 buildings on campus. Approved or accredited by Alberta Department of Education. Language of instruction: English. Total enrollment: 19. Upper school average class size: 10. Upper school faculty-student ratio: 1:5.

Upper School Student Profile Grade 6: 4 students (4 girls); Grade 7: 2 students (2 boys); Grade 8: 3 students (1 boy, 2 girls). 20% of students are members of Evangelical Free Church of America.
Faculty School total: 2. In upper school: 1 man, 1 woman.
College Admission Counseling 4 students graduated in 2008; 1 went to college. Other: 3 went to work.
Student Life Upper grades have uniform requirement. Discipline rests primarily with faculty. Attendance at religious services is required.
Tuition and Aid Day student tuition: CAN$1000. Guaranteed tuition plan.
Admissions Deadline for receipt of application materials: none. No application fee required. Interview required.
Athletics 1 PE instructor.
Computers Computer resources include Internet filtering or blocking technology. Campus intranet and computer access in designated common areas are available to students. Students grades are available online.
Contact Mr. Dale Anger, Principal. 403-897-3019. Fax: 403-897-2392. E-mail: principal@hopechristianschool.ca. Web site: www.hopechristianschool.ca.

HOPKINS SCHOOL

986 Forest Road
New Haven, Connecticut 06515
Head of School: Ms. Barbara Masters Riley

General Information Coeducational day college-preparatory school. Grades 7–12. Founded: 1660. Setting: urban. Nearest major city is New York, NY. 108-acre campus. 9 buildings on campus. Approved or accredited by Connecticut Association of Independent Schools, New England Association of Schools and Colleges, and Connecticut Department of Education. Member of National Association of Independent Schools. Endowment: $60 million. Total enrollment: 670. Upper school average class size: 12. Upper school faculty-student ratio: 1:6.
Upper School Student Profile Grade 9: 129 students (65 boys, 64 girls); Grade 10: 131 students (64 boys, 67 girls); Grade 11: 130 students (65 boys, 65 girls); Grade 12: 130 students (66 boys, 64 girls).
Faculty School total: 113. In upper school: 54 men, 56 women; 75 have advanced degrees.
Subjects Offered African-American history, algebra, American history, American literature, ancient history, art, art history, art history-AP, art-AP, biology, biology-AP, British history, calculus, calculus-AP, ceramics, chemistry, chemistry-AP, chorus, classical music, computer math, computer programming, computer science, computer science-AP, creative writing, drama, earth science, English, English literature, environmental science-AP, European history, expository writing, film, fine arts, French, French-AP, geometry, government/civics, Greek, history, Holocaust studies, HTML design, human sexuality, Islamic history, Italian, jazz, Latin, Latin American history, Latin-AP, mathematics, military history, music, music theory, photography, physics, physics-AP, politics, psychology, public speaking, Russian history, Spanish, Spanish-AP, studio art, studio art-AP, theater, trigonometry, U.S. history-AP, video, Web site design, woodworking, world history, world literature, writing.
Graduation Requirements Arts and fine arts (art, music, dance, drama), English, foreign language, mathematics, physical education (includes health), science, social studies (includes history), swimming, grade 12 community service project.
Special Academic Programs Advanced Placement exam preparation; honors section; independent study; term-away projects; study abroad.
College Admission Counseling 124 students graduated in 2008; all went to college, including Boston College; Columbia College; Georgetown University; The Johns Hopkins University; University of Connecticut; Yale University. Mean SAT critical reading: 690, mean SAT math: 699.
Student Life Upper grades have specified standards of dress, student council, honor system. Discipline rests equally with students and faculty.
Summer Programs Remediation, enrichment, advancement, ESL, sports, art/fine arts, rigorous outdoor training, computer instruction programs offered; session focuses on academics and athletics; held on campus; accepts boys and girls; open to students from other schools. 290 students usually enrolled. 2009 schedule: June 29 to August 7. Application deadline: none.
Tuition and Aid Day student tuition: $28,400. Tuition installment plan (Academic Management Services Plan, Key Tuition Payment Plan). Need-based scholarship grants available. In 2008–09, 20% of upper-school students received aid. Total amount of financial aid awarded in 2008–09: $2,100,000.
Admissions Traditional secondary-level entrance grade is 9. For fall 2008, 270 students applied for upper-level admission, 89 were accepted, 70 enrolled. ISEE or SSAT required. Deadline for receipt of application materials: January 20. Application fee required: $50. On-campus interview required.
Athletics Interscholastic: baseball (boys), basketball (b,g), crew (b,g), cross-country running (b,g), diving (b,g), fencing (b,g), field hockey (g), football (b), independent competitive sports (b,g), indoor track (b), lacrosse (b,g), soccer (b,g), softball (g), swimming and diving (b,g), tennis (b,g), track and field (b,g), volleyball (g), wrestling (b); intramural: independent competitive sports (b,g); coed interscholastic: aquatics, golf, independent competitive sports, squash, water polo; coed intramural: aerobics, aerobics/dance, aerobics/Nautilus, ballet, basketball, climbing, cooperative games, dance, fencing, fitness, floor hockey, independent competitive sports, Nautilus, outdoor adventure, project adventure, ropes courses, running, soccer, swimming and diving, tennis, volleyball, weight lifting, weight training, wilderness, yoga. 5 coaches, 3 athletic trainers.
Computers Computers are regularly used in art, English, foreign language, history, mathematics, science classes. Computer network features include on-campus library services, Internet access, wireless campus network, Internet filtering or blocking technology. Campus intranet and student e-mail accounts are available to students. The school has a published electronic and media policy.
Contact Ms. Gena Eggert, Administrative Assistant to Director of Admissions. 203-397-1001 Ext. 211. Fax: 203-389-2249. E-mail: admissions@hopkins.edu. Web site: www.hopkins.edu.

THE HORACE MANN SCHOOL

231 West 246th Street
Bronx, New York 10471
Head of School: Dr. Thomas M. Kelly

General Information Coeducational day college-preparatory, arts, and technology school. Grades N–12. Founded: 1887. Setting: suburban. Nearest major city is New York. 18-acre campus. 6 buildings on campus. Approved or accredited by New York State Association of Independent Schools and New York Department of Education. Member of National Association of Independent Schools and Secondary School Admission Test Board. Endowment: $93 million. Total enrollment: 1,756. Upper school average class size: 17. Upper school faculty-student ratio: 1:9.
Upper School Student Profile Grade 9: 177 students (89 boys, 88 girls); Grade 10: 182 students (95 boys, 87 girls); Grade 11: 180 students (91 boys, 89 girls); Grade 12: 176 students (89 boys, 87 girls).
Faculty School total: 245.
Subjects Offered Advanced Placement courses, algebra, American history, anthropology, art, art history, astronomy, biology, business, calculus, ceramics, chemistry, community service, computer math, computer programming, computer science, creative writing, dance, drama, driver education, economics, English, English literature, environmental science, European history, expository writing, fine arts, French, French-AP, geology, geometry, German, government/civics, grammar, health, history, history of science, Italian, Japanese, journalism, Latin, logic, Mandarin, mathematics, music, philosophy, photography, physical education, physics, psychology, religion, Russian, science, social studies, Spanish, statistics, television, theater, trigonometry, typing, video, world history, writing.
Graduation Requirements Algebra, arts and fine arts (art, music, dance, drama), biology, computer science, CPR, English, foreign language, geometry, health and wellness, mathematics, physical education (includes health), science, social studies (includes history), trigonometry, U.S. history, world history. Community service is required.
Special Academic Programs Advanced Placement exam preparation; honors section; independent study.
College Admission Counseling 173 students graduated in 2008; 171 went to college, including Columbia College; Cornell University; Harvard University; University of Michigan; University of Pennsylvania; Yale University. Other: 1 entered a post-graduate year, 1 had other specific plans.
Student Life Upper grades have student council, honor system. Discipline rests primarily with faculty.
Summer Programs Remediation, enrichment, advancement, ESL, art/fine arts, computer instruction programs offered; session focuses on academics; held on campus; accepts boys and girls; open to students from other schools. 200 students usually enrolled. 2009 schedule: June 18 to July 31. Application deadline: none.
Tuition and Aid Day student tuition: $32,600. Tuition installment plan (Academic Management Services Plan, 3-payment plan). Need-based scholarship grants available. In 2008–09, 17% of upper-school students received aid. Total amount of financial aid awarded in 2008–09: $3,500,000.
Admissions Traditional secondary-level entrance grade is 9. ERB, ISEE or SSAT required. Deadline for receipt of application materials: December 1. Application fee required: $50. On-campus interview required.
Athletics Interscholastic: baseball (boys), basketball (b,g), crew (b,g), cross-country running (b,g), field hockey (g), football (b), gymnastics (g), lacrosse (b,g), soccer (b,g), softball (g), swimming and diving (b,g), tennis (b,g), track and field (b,g), volleyball (g), wrestling (b); intramural: baseball (b), basketball (b,g), field hockey (g), football (b), lacrosse (b,g), soccer (b,g), tennis (b,g); coed interscholastic: fencing, golf, indoor track & field, squash, water polo, winter (indoor) track; coed intramural: bowling, climbing, cross-country running, dance squad, dance team, fitness, Frisbee, golf, modern dance, outdoor education, paddle tennis, physical fitness, physical training, rock climbing, ropes courses, softball, strength & conditioning, swimming and diving, table tennis, track and field, ultimate Frisbee, volleyball, water polo, weight lifting, weight training. 14 PE instructors, 22 coaches, 2 athletic trainers.
Computers Computers are regularly used in English, foreign language, library skills, mathematics, media production, photography, science classes. Computer network features include on-campus library services, online commercial services, Internet access, wireless campus network. Campus intranet, student e-mail accounts, and computer access in designated common areas are available to students.
Contact Lisa J. Moreira, Director of Admissions and Financial Aid. 718-432-4100. Fax: 718-432-3610. E-mail: admissions@horacemann.org. Web site: www.horacemann.org/.

HORIZONS SCHOOL

1900 DeKalb Avenue
Atlanta, Georgia 30307

Head of School: Mr. Les Garber

General Information Coeducational boarding and day college-preparatory, arts, and ESL school. Boarding grades 8–PG, day grades K–PG. Founded: 1978. Setting: urban. Students are housed in single-sex dormitories and single-sex-by-hall dormitories. 4-acre campus. 4 buildings on campus. Approved or accredited by Georgia Accrediting Commission and Georgia Department of Education. Endowment: $100,000. Total enrollment: 100. Upper school average class size: 12. Upper school faculty-student ratio: 1:10.

Upper School Student Profile 15% of students are boarding students. 80% are state residents. 3 states are represented in upper school student body. 20% are international students. International students from Afghanistan, China, Japan, Myanmar, Republic of Korea, and Viet Nam; 5 other countries represented in student body.

Faculty School total: 12. In upper school: 4 men, 5 women; 4 have advanced degrees; 4 reside on campus.

Subjects Offered Algebra, American culture, American history, American literature, art, backpacking, biology, Black history, business mathematics, calculus, chemistry, computer graphics, computer literacy, contemporary history, crafts, creative writing, drama, economics, English, environmental science, ESL, film studies, filmmaking, French, geometry, government, interpersonal skills, Japanese, life management skills, literature and composition-AP, music, natural history, nature study, photography, physical science, physics, pre-algebra, pre-calculus, psychology, Spanish, theater, theater arts, theater design and production, theater production, U.S. history, video, video film production, wilderness camping, wilderness education, wilderness experience, wilderness studies, wilderness/outdoor program, woodworking, world history, world literature, zoology.

Graduation Requirements English, foreign language, independent study, mathematics, physical education (includes health), science, social studies (includes history). Community service is required.

Special Academic Programs Advanced Placement exam preparation; independent study; ESL (16 students enrolled).

College Admission Counseling 18 students graduated in 2007; 17 went to college, including Emory University; Georgia Perimeter College; Georgia State University; University of Georgia. Other: 1 went to work.

Student Life Upper grades have specified standards of dress, student council, honor system. Discipline rests equally with students and faculty.

Tuition and Aid Day student tuition: $10,500; 5-day tuition and room/board: $20,000; 7-day tuition and room/board: $20,000. Tuition installment plan (SMART Tuition Payment Plan, monthly payment plans). Tuition reduction for siblings, paying campus jobs available. In 2007–08, 70% of upper-school students received aid. Total amount of financial aid awarded in 2007–08: $56,000.

Admissions For fall 2007, 25 students applied for upper-level admission, 15 were accepted, 15 enrolled. Deadline for receipt of application materials: none. Application fee required: $200. Interview required.

Athletics Coed Intramural: soccer. 1 PE instructor.

Computers Computers are regularly used in animation, English, ESL, foreign language, history, mathematics, science, video film production classes. Computer network features include Internet access. Campus intranet and student e-mail accounts are available to students.

Contact Mr. Les Garber, Administrator. 404-378-2219. Fax: 404-378-8946. E-mail: horizonsschool@horizonsschool.com. Web site: www.horizonsschool.com.

ANNOUNCEMENT FROM THE SCHOOL Horizons School of Atlanta emphasizes education for families interested in the advantages of a small school community. High school classes (with an average size of 12 students) feature seminar-style approaches that maximize student participation and involvement. Elementary and middle school classes (with an average size of 14 students) provide a forum for optimal personalized and individualized education. Academically, Horizons offers a college-preparatory curriculum, with more than 90% of graduates enrolling in colleges and universities across the country. In addition, Horizons' philosophy and programs incorporate those experiences, skills, and values necessary for success. International students, an integral part of Horizons, graduate and then enroll in an American college or university. Some international students enroll for a transition year between high school and college in order to improve English proficiency and other skills required at a college level. There is no anonymity at Horizons School and no back of the classroom in which to hide. Education is active, not passive, and students learn responsibility by being given responsibility. Leadership skills are gained through experiences, and individual education is the empowerment of each student—the belief that he or she can accomplish anything. Students play an active role in all aspects of the School, from the traditional classroom expectations to the responsibilities each person has to the School community. The campus has four buildings, three of which (the high school, gymnasium, and theater) were built by students, on 3½ wooded acres. Students are involved in the decision-making process to constantly upgrade the campus. Horizons welcomes new students and families and extends an invitation to call 404-378-2219 for more information or to set up a visit.

HOSANNA CHRISTIAN SCHOOL

5000 Hosanna Way
Klamath Falls, Oregon 97603

Head of School: Mr. Jeff Mudrow

General Information Coeducational day college-preparatory, general academic, and religious studies school, affiliated with Evangelical faith. Grades PK–12. Founded: 1989. Setting: small town. 26-acre campus. 1 building on campus. Approved or accredited by Association of Christian Schools International, Northwest Association of Accredited Schools, and Oregon Department of Education. Endowment: $120,000. Total enrollment: 274. Upper school average class size: 20. Upper school faculty-student ratio: 1:15.

Upper School Student Profile Grade 9: 20 students (8 boys, 12 girls); Grade 10: 10 students (4 boys, 6 girls); Grade 11: 24 students (8 boys, 16 girls); Grade 12: 12 students (6 boys, 6 girls). 100% of students are members of Evangelical faith.

Faculty School total: 24. In upper school: 6 men, 4 women; 2 have advanced degrees.

Subjects Offered Algebra, American government, American history, American literature, anatomy, art, Bible, biology, British literature, chemistry, choir, Christian doctrine, Christian ethics, Christian testament, college writing, computer keyboarding, computer skills, computers, consumer economics, creative drama, critical thinking, dance, drama, economics, English, English literature, geometry, government/civics, intro to computers, keyboarding/computer, leadership skills, Life of Christ, Microsoft, personal finance, physical education, pre-algebra, reading/study skills, religious studies, service learning/internship, Spanish, speech, sports, track and field, trigonometry, U.S. government, U.S. history, volleyball, world history, yearbook.

Special Academic Programs Accelerated programs; study at local college for college credit; remedial reading and/or remedial writing; remedial math.

College Admission Counseling 18 students graduated in 2008; 16 went to college, including George Fox University; Oregon Institute of Technology; Portland State University; Southern Oregon University; University of Nevada, Reno; Western Oregon University. Other: 1 went to work, 1 had other specific plans.

Student Life Upper grades have specified standards of dress, student council, honor system. Discipline rests primarily with faculty. Attendance at religious services is required.

Tuition and Aid Day student tuition: $5000. Tuition installment plan (monthly payment plans). Tuition reduction for siblings, need-based scholarship grants available. In 2008–09, 10% of upper-school students received aid. Total amount of financial aid awarded in 2008–09: $12,000.

Admissions Traditional secondary-level entrance grade is 9. For fall 2008, 20 students applied for upper-level admission, 13 were accepted, 12 enrolled. Deadline for receipt of application materials: none. No application fee required. Interview required.

Athletics Interscholastic: basketball (boys, girls), cross-country running (b,g), dance team (g), track and field (b,g), volleyball (g); intramural: basketball (b,g); coed interscholastic: golf, track and field. 2 PE instructors, 8 coaches.

Computers Computers are regularly used in computer applications, economics, yearbook classes. Computer network features include on-campus library services, online commercial services, Internet access, Internet filtering or blocking technology. Computer access in designated common areas is available to students. Students grades are available online. The school has a published electronic and media policy.

Contact Mrs. Christi Garrison, Assistant. 541-882-7732. Fax: 541-882-6940. E-mail: admin@hosannachristian.org. Web site: www.hosannachristian.org.

THE HOTCHKISS SCHOOL

11 Interlaken Road
PO Box 800
Lakeville, Connecticut 06039

Head of School: Mr. Malcolm H. McKenzie

General Information Coeducational boarding and day college-preparatory school. Grades 9–PG. Founded: 1891. Setting: rural. Nearest major city is Hartford. Students are housed in single-sex dormitories. 540-acre campus. 80 buildings on campus. Approved or accredited by Connecticut Association of Independent Schools, New England Association of Schools and Colleges, The Association of Boarding Schools, and Connecticut Department of Education. Member of National Association of Independent Schools and Secondary School Admission Test Board. Endowment: $383 million. Total enrollment: 584. Upper school average class size: 12. Upper school faculty-student ratio: 1:6.

Upper School Student Profile Grade 9: 110 students (57 boys, 53 girls); Grade 10: 131 students (68 boys, 63 girls); Grade 11: 162 students (83 boys, 79 girls); Grade 12: 163 students (85 boys, 78 girls); Postgraduate: 18 students (13 boys, 5 girls). 91% of students are boarding students. 24% are state residents. 41 states are represented in upper school student body. 15% are international students. International students from Canada, China, Ghana, Hong Kong, Republic of Korea, and Thailand; 17 other countries represented in student body.

Faculty School total: 153. In upper school: 82 men, 71 women; 92 have advanced degrees; 119 reside on campus.

Subjects Offered 3-dimensional design, acting, advanced math, Advanced Placement courses, advanced studio art-AP, algebra, American history, American history-AP, American literature, American studies, anatomy and physiology, Ancient Greek, ancient history, architecture, art, art history-AP, astronomy, bioethics, biology, biology-AP, calculus, calculus-AP, ceramics, chemistry, chemistry-AP, China/Japan history, Chinese, chorus, classics, college counseling, comparative government and politics-AP, computer programming, computer science, computer science-AP, conceptual physics, constitutional history of U.S., creative writing, dance, digital photography, discrete math, drama, drawing, economics, economics-AP, English, English-AP, environmental science, environmental science-AP, ethics, European history, European history-AP, expository writing, fine arts, French, French language-AP, French literature-AP, geometry, German, history of music, Holocaust, humanities, independent study, jazz dance, jazz ensemble, Latin, Latin American history, Latin-AP, limnology, mathematics, music, music history, music technology, music theory, music theory-AP, musical productions, non-Western literature, orchestra, organic chemistry, philosophy, photography, physics, physics-AP, playwriting, pre-calculus, public speaking, religion, science, Spanish, Spanish language-AP, Spanish literature-AP, statistics-AP, studio art, the Sixties, theater, trigonometry, video, voice, world literature, writing.

Graduation Requirements American history, arts and fine arts (art, music, dance, drama), English, foreign language, mathematics, science.

Special Academic Programs Advanced Placement exam preparation; honors section; independent study; term-away projects; study abroad; academic accommodation for the gifted, the musically talented, and the artistically talented.

College Admission Counseling 177 students graduated in 2008; all went to college, including Dartmouth College; Middlebury College; Princeton University; University of Pennsylvania; Williams College; Yale University. Mean SAT critical reading: 667, mean SAT math: 675, mean SAT writing: 673, mean combined SAT: 2015. 83% scored over 600 on SAT critical reading, 85% scored over 600 on SAT math, 82% scored over 600 on SAT writing, 87% scored over 1800 on combined SAT.

Student Life Upper grades have specified standards of dress, student council. Discipline rests equally with students and faculty.

Summer Programs Art/fine arts programs offered; session focuses on chamber music, environmental studies; held on campus; accepts boys and girls; open to students from other schools. 92 students usually enrolled. 2009 schedule: June 28 to July 19. Application deadline: April 1.

Tuition and Aid Day student tuition: $34,250; 7-day tuition and room/board: $40,200. Tuition installment plan (Key Tuition Payment Plan). Need-based scholarship grants, need-based loans, middle-income loans available. In 2008–09, 35% of upper-school students received aid. Total amount of financial aid awarded in 2008–09: $6,849,356.

Admissions Traditional secondary-level entrance grade is 9. For fall 2008, 1,776 students applied for upper-level admission, 329 were accepted, 200 enrolled. ACT, ISEE, PSAT, SAT, or ACT for applicants to grade 11 and 12, SSAT or TOEFL required. Deadline for receipt of application materials: January 15. Application fee required: $50. Interview required.

Athletics Interscholastic: baseball (boys), basketball (b,g), cross-country running (b,g), diving (b,g), field hockey (g), football (b), golf (b,g), ice hockey (b,g), lacrosse (b,g), soccer (b,g), softball (g), squash (b,g), swimming and diving (b,g), tennis (b,g), touch football (b), track and field (b,g), volleyball (g), water polo (b), wrestling (b); coed interscholastic: Frisbee, sailing, ultimate Frisbee; coed intramural: aerobics, aerobics/Nautilus, ballet, basketball, canoeing/kayaking, climbing, combined training, dance, drill team, fitness, fitness walking, Frisbee, golf, hiking/backpacking, ice hockey, jogging, Nautilus, outdoor education, paddle tennis, physical fitness, physical training, rock climbing, running, squash, strength & conditioning, tennis, ultimate Frisbee, volleyball, walking, wall climbing, water polo, weight lifting, yoga. 2 coaches, 2 athletic trainers.

Computers Computers are regularly used in all academic classes. Computer network features include on-campus library services, online commercial services, Internet access, wireless campus network, Internet filtering or blocking technology. Campus intranet, student e-mail accounts, and computer access in designated common areas are available to students. The school has a published electronic and media policy.

Contact Ms. Rachael N. Beare, Dean of Admission and Financial Aid. 860-435-3102. Fax: 860-435-0042. E-mail: admission@hotchkiss.org. Web site: www.hotchkiss.org.

See Close-Up on page 796.

HOUGHTON ACADEMY

9790 Thayer Street
Houghton, New York 14744

Head of School: Philip G. Stockin

General Information Coeducational boarding and day college-preparatory, arts, religious studies, and ESL school, affiliated with Wesleyan Church. Boarding grades 9–PG, day grades 6–PG. Founded: 1883. Setting: rural. Nearest major city is Buffalo. Students are housed in single-sex dormitories and staff homes. 25-acre campus. 5 buildings on campus. Approved or accredited by Association of Christian Schools International, Middle States Association of Colleges and Schools, The Association of Boarding Schools, and New York Department of Education. Endowment: $90,000. Total enrollment: 177. Upper school average class size: 16. Upper school faculty-student ratio: 1:15.

Upper School Student Profile Grade 9: 19 students (9 boys, 10 girls); Grade 10: 39 students (17 boys, 22 girls); Grade 11: 41 students (17 boys, 24 girls); Grade 12: 49 students (26 boys, 23 girls). 51% of students are boarding students. 44% are state residents. 3 states are represented in upper school student body. 54% are international students. International students from China, Mexico, Republic of Korea, and Viet Nam; 7 other countries represented in student body. 25% of students are members of Wesleyan Church.

Faculty School total: 23. In upper school: 7 men, 16 women; 10 have advanced degrees; 3 reside on campus.

Subjects Offered Algebra, American history, American literature, art, band, Bible, Bible studies, biology, business, business skills, calculus, chemistry, chorus, community service, computer science, creative writing, desktop publishing, driver education, earth science, economics, English, English literature, environmental science, ESL, ethics, fine arts, geography, geometry, government/civics, grammar, history, home economics, industrial arts, mathematics, music, photography, physical education, physics, science, social science, social studies, Spanish, speech, trigonometry, word processing, world history, writing.

Graduation Requirements Arts and fine arts (art, music, dance, drama), Bible, electives, English, mathematics, physical education (includes health), science, social studies (includes history).

Special Academic Programs Honors section; independent study; study at local college for college credit; ESL (3 students enrolled).

College Admission Counseling 40 students graduated in 2008; all went to college, including Houghton College; LeTourneau University; Michigan State University; Penn State Erie, The Behrend College; Rice University; Rutgers, The State University of New Jersey, Newark. Median SAT critical reading: 455, median SAT math: 615. 35% scored over 600 on SAT critical reading, 42% scored over 600 on SAT math.

Student Life Upper grades have specified standards of dress, student council. Discipline rests primarily with faculty. Attendance at religious services is required.

Tuition and Aid Day student tuition: $6500; 7-day tuition and room/board: $22,445. Tuition installment plan (SMART Tuition Payment Plan, individually arranged payment plans). Need-based scholarship grants available. In 2008–09, 25% of upper-school students received aid. Total amount of financial aid awarded in 2008–09: $95,000.

Admissions Traditional secondary-level entrance grade is 9. For fall 2008, 138 students applied for upper-level admission, 90 were accepted, 62 enrolled. PSAT or SAT for applicants to grade 11 and 12, SLEP, SSAT or TOEFL required. Deadline for receipt of application materials: February 13. Application fee required: $50. Interview required.

Athletics Interscholastic: baseball (boys), basketball (b,g), cheering (g), soccer (b,g), volleyball (g); intramural: badminton (b,g), basketball (b,g), billiards (b,g), floor hockey (b,g), golf (b,g), indoor soccer (b,g), paddle tennis (b,g), racquetball (b,g), skiing (downhill) (b,g), soccer (b,g), table tennis (b,g), tennis (b,g), volleyball (b,g); coed interscholastic: golf; coed intramural: badminton, ball hockey, indoor soccer, paddle tennis, skiing (downhill), softball, table tennis. 2 PE instructors, 11 coaches, 1 athletic trainer.

Computers Computers are regularly used in accounting, Bible studies, college planning, English, graphic design, keyboarding, mathematics, multimedia, SAT preparation, science, word processing, yearbook classes. Computer network features include on-campus library services, Internet access, Internet filtering or blocking technology, electronic access to Houghton College Library holdings. Computer access in designated common areas is available to students. Students grades are available online. The school has a published electronic and media policy.

Contact Ronald J. Bradbury, Director of Admissions. 585-567-8115. Fax: 585-567-8048. E-mail: admissions@houghtonacademy.org. Web site: www.houghtonacademy.org.

HOWE MILITARY SCHOOL

PO Box 240
Howe, Indiana 46746

Head of School: Dr. Duane Van Orden

General Information Coeducational boarding and day college-preparatory, religious studies, bilingual studies, Junior ROTC, and military school, affiliated with Episcopal Church. Boarding grades 5–12, day grades 5–8. Founded: 1884. Setting: rural. Nearest major city is South Bend. Students are housed in single-sex dormitories. 100-acre campus. 15 buildings on campus. Approved or accredited by Independent Schools Association of the Central States, North Central Association of Colleges and Schools, The Association of Boarding Schools, and Indiana Department of Education. Member of National Association of Independent Schools. Endowment: $18 million. Total enrollment: 153. Upper school average class size: 10. Upper school faculty-student ratio: 1:9.

Upper School Student Profile Grade 9: 24 students (20 boys, 4 girls); Grade 10: 25 students (20 boys, 5 girls); Grade 11: 39 students (29 boys, 10 girls); Grade 12: 27 students (25 boys, 2 girls). 97% of students are boarding students. 28% are state residents. 13 states are represented in upper school student body. 9% are international students. International students from Canada, China, Republic of Korea, and Turkey. 5% of students are members of Episcopal Church.

Faculty School total: 30. In upper school: 12 men, 9 women; 5 have advanced degrees; 6 reside on campus.

Subjects Offered Accounting, algebra, American history, American literature, art, band, biology, biology-AP, broadcasting, cabinet making, calculus, calculus-AP, chemistry, chemistry-AP, chorus, comparative religion, computer graphics, computer programming, drafting, economics, English, English language and composition-AP, English literature, environmental science, French, geography, geometry, German, government/civics, grammar, history, industrial arts, journalism, JROTC, leadership training, mathematics, mechanical drawing, music, physical education, physics, pre-algebra, pre-calculus, religion, science, social studies, sociology, Spanish, speech, speech communications, trigonometry, world geography, world history, world literature, yearbook.

Graduation Requirements Computer education, English, foreign language, JROTC, leadership training, mathematics, physical education (includes health), religion (includes Bible studies and theology), science, social studies (includes history).

Special Academic Programs Advanced Placement exam preparation; honors section; accelerated programs; study at local college for college credit; ESL (8 students enrolled).

College Admission Counseling 20 students graduated in 2008; 18 went to college, including Adrian College; Lake Superior State University; Michigan State University; Rose-Hulman Institute of Technology; The College of Wooster. Other: 2 entered military service.

Student Life Upper grades have uniform requirement, student council, honor system. Discipline rests primarily with faculty. Attendance at religious services is required.

Summer Programs Remediation, advancement programs offered; session focuses on academics with a blend of recreation; held off campus; held at Cedar Lake, IN; accepts boys; open to students from other schools. 150 students usually enrolled. 2009 schedule: June 21 to July 31. Application deadline: July 8.

Tuition and Aid Day student tuition: $7515; 7-day tuition and room/board: $25,000. Tuition installment plan (monthly payment plans). Tuition reduction for siblings, need-based scholarship grants available. In 2008–09, 45% of upper-school students received aid. Total amount of financial aid awarded in 2008–09: $500,000.

Admissions Traditional secondary-level entrance grade is 10. For fall 2008, 74 students applied for upper-level admission, 64 were accepted, 46 enrolled. OLSAT, Stanford Achievement Test and TOEFL or SLEP required. Deadline for receipt of application materials: none. Application fee required: $100. Interview recommended.

Athletics Interscholastic: baseball (boys), basketball (b,g), tennis (b,g), track and field (b,g), volleyball (g), wrestling (b); intramural: baseball (b), football (b), physical training (b); coed interscholastic: basketball, golf, JROTC drill, riflery, soccer, wrestling; coed intramural: basketball, horseback riding, physical fitness, soccer, swimming and diving, volleyball. 1 PE instructor.

Computers Computers are regularly used in English, foreign language, JROTC, mathematics, newspaper, science, yearbook classes. Computer network features include on-campus library services, Internet access, Internet filtering or blocking technology, CAD, Microsoft Office. Campus intranet and student e-mail accounts are available to students. Students grades are available online.

Contact Dr. Brent E. Smith, Director of Admissions. 260-562-2131. Fax: 260-562-3678. E-mail: admissions@howemilitary.com. Web site: www.howemilitary.com.

See Close-Up on page 798.

THE HUDSON SCHOOL

601 Park Avenue
Hoboken, New Jersey 07030

Head of School: Mrs. Suellen F. Newman

General Information Coeducational day college-preparatory, arts, and music, theater, foreign languages school. Grades 5–12. Founded: 1978. Setting: urban. Nearest major city is New York, NY. 1 building on campus. Approved or accredited by Middle States Association of Colleges and Schools and New Jersey Department of Education. Member of National Association of Independent Schools. Endowment: $900,000. Total enrollment: 189. Upper school average class size: 18. Upper school faculty-student ratio: 1:10.

Upper School Student Profile Grade 9: 18 students (6 boys, 12 girls); Grade 10: 20 students (9 boys, 11 girls); Grade 11: 20 students (8 boys, 12 girls); Grade 12: 30 students (9 boys, 21 girls).

Faculty School total: 50. In upper school: 16 men, 18 women; 30 have advanced degrees.

Subjects Offered Algebra, American literature, anatomy and physiology, art, biology, British literature, calculus, chemistry, computer science, computer science-AP, computers, conceptual physics, contemporary issues, creative writing, English, English literature, English literature-AP, English-AP, environmental science, ethnic literature, film, French, gender issues, German, health, Japanese, Latin, learning strategies, mathematics, media studies, microbiology, music, music theory, mythology, physical education, physics-AP, psychology-AP, social science, Spanish, Spanish-AP, U.S. history, U.S. history-AP, world civilizations, world literature.

Graduation Requirements Arts and fine arts (art, music, dance, drama), computer science, English, foreign language, Latin, mathematics, physical education (includes health), science, social studies (includes history). Community service is required.

Special Academic Programs Advanced Placement exam preparation; honors section; accelerated programs; independent study; study at local college for college credit; study abroad; academic accommodation for the gifted, the musically talented, and the artistically talented; remedial reading and/or remedial writing; remedial math; ESL (6 students enrolled).

College Admission Counseling 27 students graduated in 2008; all went to college, including Boston University; Brown University; Columbia University; Swarthmore College; University of Pennsylvania; Vassar College. Median SAT critical reading: 612, median SAT math: 621, median SAT writing: 603, median combined SAT: 1816. 54% scored over 600 on SAT critical reading, 54% scored over 600 on SAT math, 54% scored over 600 on SAT writing, 58% scored over 1800 on combined SAT.

Student Life Upper grades have student council, honor system. Discipline rests primarily with faculty.

Tuition and Aid Day student tuition: $13,700. Tuition installment plan (monthly payment plans, individually arranged payment plans, semiannual and annual payment plans; quarterly by special arrangement). Need-based scholarship grants available. In 2008–09, 35% of upper-school students received aid. Total amount of financial aid awarded in 2008–09: $200,000.

Admissions Traditional secondary-level entrance grade is 9. For fall 2008, 96 students applied for upper-level admission, 60 were accepted, 28 enrolled. ERB, ISEE or SSAT required. Deadline for receipt of application materials: December 15. Application fee required: $50. On-campus interview required.

Athletics Interscholastic: basketball (boys, girls), dance (g), modern dance (g); coed interscholastic: bowling, cheering; coed intramural: aerobics/dance, fencing, Frisbee, outdoor education, physical fitness. 3 PE instructors, 4 coaches.

Computers Computers are regularly used in college planning, creative writing, desktop publishing, ESL, English, ethics, French, humanities, music, newspaper, philosophy, photography, photojournalism, programming, publications, Spanish, technology, theater, video film production, Web site design, word processing, writing, yearbook classes. Computer network features include Internet access.

Contact Mrs. Suellen F. Newman, Director. 201-659-8335 Ext. 107. Fax: 201-222-3669. E-mail: admissions@thehudsonschool.org. Web site: www.thehudsonschool.org.

ANNOUNCEMENT FROM THE SCHOOL The Hudson School provides intellectually inquisitive students in grades 5–12 with a rigorous college-preparatory education that inspires independent thinking, lifelong learning, and a sense of community. Hudson fosters an eclectic and supportive environment that challenges students and teachers to fully develop their talents through a creative and stimulating interdisciplinary curriculum.

HUMANEX ACADEMY

Englewood, Colorado

See Special Needs Schools section.

THE HUN SCHOOL OF PRINCETON

176 Edgerstoune Road
Princeton, New Jersey 08540

Head of School: Jonathan Brougham

General Information Coeducational boarding and day college-preparatory school. Boarding grades 9–PG, day grades 6–PG. Founded: 1914. Setting: small town. Nearest major city is New York, NY. Students are housed in single-sex dormitories. 45-acre campus. 7 buildings on campus. Approved or accredited by Middle States Association of Colleges and Schools, New Jersey Association of Independent Schools, and The Association of Boarding Schools. Member of National Association of Independent Schools and Secondary School Admission Test Board. Endowment: $15 million. Total enrollment: 595. Upper school average class size: 13. Upper school faculty-student ratio: 1:8.

Upper School Student Profile Grade 9: 113 students (59 boys, 54 girls); Grade 10: 110 students (61 boys, 49 girls); Grade 11: 126 students (73 boys, 53 girls); Grade 12: 126 students (67 boys, 59 girls); Postgraduate: 14 students (13 boys, 1 girl). 33% of students are boarding students. 15 states are represented in upper school student body. 10% are international students. International students from Bahrain, Republic of Korea, Russian Federation, Saudi Arabia, Taiwan, and Venezuela; 16 other countries represented in student body.

Faculty School total: 104. In upper school: 58 men, 46 women; 48 have advanced degrees; 32 reside on campus.

Subjects Offered 3-dimensional art, 3-dimensional design, advanced computer applications, Advanced Placement courses, advanced TOEFL/grammar, algebra, American government, American history, American history-AP, American literature, anatomy, architectural drawing, architecture, art, art history, art history-AP, astrophysics, biology, biology-AP, calculus, calculus-AP, ceramics, chemistry, chemistry-AP, chorus, community service, computer programming, computer science, drama, driver education, economics, engineering, English, English-AP, ESL, European history, fine arts, forensic science, French, French-AP, geometry, government/civics, health, history, interdisciplinary studies, jazz band, Latin, Latin-AP, marine biology, mathematics, mechanical drawing, music, photography, physical education, physics, physics-AP, physiology, public speaking, science, social studies, Spanish, Spanish-AP, statistics-AP, television, theater, trigonometry, U.S. history-AP, video, video film production, world history.

Graduation Requirements Arts and fine arts (art, music, dance, drama), computer science, English, foreign language, health, history, mathematics, science, 10-20 hours of community service per year, summer reading, extra-curricular activities.

Special Academic Programs Advanced Placement exam preparation; honors section; academic accommodation for the gifted; ESL (22 students enrolled).

College Admission Counseling 131 students graduated in 2008; all went to college, including Hobart and William Smith Colleges; Lehigh University; Penn State University Park; Princeton University; Syracuse University; Trinity College. Median SAT critical reading: 590, median SAT math: 620, median SAT writing: 610, median composite ACT: 27.

Student Life Upper grades have specified standards of dress, student council, honor system. Discipline rests equally with students and faculty.

Summer Programs Remediation, enrichment, advancement, ESL, art/fine arts, computer instruction programs offered; session focuses on make-up courses, enrichment, SAT and TOEFL preparation; held on campus; accepts boys and girls; open to students from other schools. 110 students usually enrolled. 2009 schedule: June 26 to July 28. Application deadline: none.

Tuition and Aid Day student tuition: $28,390; 7-day tuition and room/board: $41,670. Tuition installment plan (Academic Management Services Plan). Merit scholarship grants, need-based scholarship grants, prepGATE Loans available. In 2008–09, 25% of upper-school students received aid; total upper-school merit-scholarship money awarded: $50,000. Total amount of financial aid awarded in 2008–09: $2,150,000.

Admissions Traditional secondary-level entrance grade is 9. PSAT or SAT for applicants to grade 11 and 12, SSAT or TOEFL required. Deadline for receipt of application materials: January 31. Application fee required: $50. Interview required.

Athletics Interscholastic: baseball (boys), basketball (b,g), crew (b,g), cross-country running (b,g), fencing (b,g), field hockey (g), football (b), lacrosse (b,g), soccer (b,g), softball (g), tennis (b,g); intramural: dance squad (g), soccer (b,g), water polo (b,g), weight training (b,g); coed interscholastic: golf, ice hockey, swimming and diving, track and field; coed intramural: aerobics/dance, aerobics/Nautilus, ballet, basketball, cross-country running, dance, fitness, flag football, Frisbee, jogging, Nautilus, paint ball, physical fitness, running, skiing (downhill), strength & conditioning, touch football, ultimate Frisbee, volleyball, water polo, weight lifting. 3 coaches, 1 athletic trainer.

Computers Computers are regularly used in all academic classes. Computer network features include on-campus library services, online commercial services, Internet access, wireless campus network, Internet filtering or blocking technology. Campus intranet and student e-mail accounts are available to students. The school has a published electronic and media policy.

Contact Mr. P. Terence Beach, Director of Admissions. 609-921-7600. Fax: 609-279-9398. E-mail: admiss@hunschool.org. Web site: www.hunschool.org.

ANNOUNCEMENT FROM THE SCHOOL The Hun School of Princeton is located midway between New York City and Philadelphia in the university town of Princeton, New Jersey. Hun provides a traditional college-preparatory program that draws upon the cultural and scientific opportunities in the area. A full range of athletics and activities supplement a strong curriculum designed to stimulate critical thinking and analysis and inspire curiosity. Competent, caring faculty members work closely with students to promote excellence and self-esteem in an environment of high but fair expectations. Extensive weekend activities and a supportive adviser system are outstanding features of residential life. Academic learning skills and instruction in ESL are available.

See Close-Up on page 800.

HUNTINGTON-SURREY SCHOOL

4001 Speedway
Austin, Texas 78751

Head of School: Dr. Light Bailey German

General Information Coeducational day college-preparatory and Writing a special emphasis school. Grades 9–12. Founded: 1973. Setting: urban. 1 building on campus. Approved or accredited by Southern Association of Colleges and Schools and Texas Department of Education. Total enrollment: 61. Upper school average class size: 8. Upper school faculty-student ratio: 1:4.

Upper School Student Profile Grade 9: 9 students (2 boys, 7 girls); Grade 10: 11 students (6 boys, 5 girls); Grade 11: 21 students (10 boys, 11 girls); Grade 12: 20 students (12 boys, 8 girls).

Faculty School total: 20. In upper school: 9 men, 11 women; 16 have advanced degrees.

Subjects Offered Algebra, art, biology, calculus, chemistry, college planning, comparative religion, creative drama, discrete math, drama, ecology, environmental systems, English, film history, French, geometry, German, history, Latin, literature, math analysis, math review, mathematics, philosophy, physical science, physics, portfolio art, pre-algebra, pre-calculus, SAT preparation, senior science survey, social studies, Spanish, student publications, study skills, trigonometry, U.S. history, work-study, world history, writing.

Graduation Requirements American literature, biology, British literature, world history, world literature, writing, senior research project, school exit examinations: assertion with proof essay exam and mathematical competency exam, senior advisory course.

Special Academic Programs Accelerated programs; academic accommodation for the gifted.

College Admission Counseling 23 students graduated in 2008; 21 went to college, including Earlham College; St. Edward's University; Texas State University–San Marcos; The Evergreen State College; The University of Texas at Austin. Other: 1 entered military service, 1 entered a postgraduate year. Mean SAT critical reading: 570, mean SAT math: 530, mean SAT writing: 580, mean combined SAT: 1680. 10% scored over 600 on SAT critical reading, 10% scored over 600 on SAT math, 10% scored over 600 on SAT writing, 10% scored over 1800 on combined SAT.

Student Life Upper grades have student council, honor system. Discipline rests primarily with faculty.

Tuition and Aid Day student tuition: $7200. Tuition installment plan (monthly payment plans).

Admissions Traditional secondary-level entrance grade is 9. For fall 2008, 28 students applied for upper-level admission, 24 were accepted, 22 enrolled. Deadline for receipt of application materials: none. No application fee required. On-campus interview required.

Computers Computers are regularly used in study skills, writing classes. Computer resources include study hall computers and printers (available for student use). Computer access in designated common areas is available to students.

Contact Ms. Johni Walker-Little, Assistant Director. 512-478-4743. Fax: 512-457-0235. Web site: www.huntingtonsurrey.com.

HUTCHISON SCHOOL

1740 Ridgeway Road
Memphis, Tennessee 38119-5397

Head of School: Dr. Annette C. Smith

General Information Girls' day college-preparatory, arts, and technology school. Grades PK–12. Founded: 1902. Setting: suburban. 52-acre campus. 10 buildings on campus. Approved or accredited by Southern Association of Colleges and Schools, Southern Association of Independent Schools, and Tennessee Association of Independent Schools. Member of National Association of Independent Schools. Endowment: $14 million. Total enrollment: 931. Upper school average class size: 16. Upper school faculty-student ratio: 1:16.

Upper School Student Profile Grade 9: 63 students (63 girls); Grade 10: 64 students (64 girls); Grade 11: 60 students (60 girls); Grade 12: 46 students (46 girls).

Faculty School total: 122. In upper school: 3 men, 21 women; 19 have advanced degrees.

Subjects Offered Acting, advanced studio art-AP, algebra, American government, American history, American history-AP, American literature, American literature-AP, anatomy and physiology, art, biology, biology-AP, British literature, British literature (honors), British literature-AP, calculus, calculus-AP, chemistry, chemistry-AP, choral music, college writing, contemporary issues, creative writing, dance, digital photography, drama, earth science, economics, English, English language-AP, English literature, English literature-AP, environmental education, environmental science, European history, European history-AP, film and literature, film history, fine arts, foreign language, French, French language-AP, genetics, geography, geometry, global issues, government/civics, health, health and wellness, history, honors algebra, honors English, honors geometry, independent study, Latin, mathematics, music, music theory-AP, physical education, physics, physics-AP, pre-calculus, psychology, science, social studies, Spanish, speech, studio art, studio art—AP, theater, video film production, women's studies, world history, world history-AP, writing.

Graduation Requirements Alternative physical education, arts and fine arts (art, music, dance, drama), English, foreign language, humanities, mathematics, physical education (includes health), science, social studies (includes history), world history, annual community service, senior speaker program.

Special Academic Programs 20 Advanced Placement exams for which test preparation is offered; honors section; independent study; study abroad; academic accommodation for the gifted.

College Admission Counseling 48 students graduated in 2008; all went to college, including The University of Alabama; The University of Tennessee; University of Georgia; University of Mississippi; University of Virginia; Vanderbilt University. Mean SAT critical reading: 572, mean SAT math: 582, mean SAT writing: 597, mean combined SAT: 1759, mean composite ACT: 26. 33% scored over 600 on SAT critical reading, 41% scored over 600 on SAT math, 31% scored over 600 on SAT writing, 33% scored over 1800 on combined SAT, 47% scored over 26 on composite ACT.

Student Life Upper grades have uniform requirement, student council, honor system. Discipline rests equally with students and faculty.

Summer Programs Remediation, enrichment, advancement, sports, art/fine arts, computer instruction programs offered; session focuses on athletic skill development, academic enrichment, arts enrichment; held on campus; accepts boys and girls; open to students from other schools. 1,000 students usually enrolled. 2009 schedule: June 1 to August 10. Application deadline: none.

Tuition and Aid Day student tuition: $15,350. Tuition installment plan (Insured Tuition Payment Plan, monthly payment plans, individually arranged payment plans,

4-payment plan). Need-based scholarship grants available. In 2008–09, 12% of upper-school students received aid. Total amount of financial aid awarded in 2008–09: $138,774.

Admissions Traditional secondary-level entrance grade is 9. For fall 2008, 69 students applied for upper-level admission, 52 were accepted, 43 enrolled. Admissions testing, ERB CTP IV, ISEE, school's own test or writing sample required. Deadline for receipt of application materials: none. Application fee required: $50. Interview required.

Athletics Interscholastic: basketball (girls), bowling (g), cross-country running (g), dance (g), dance team (g), fitness (g), golf (g), lacrosse (g), soccer (g), swimming and diving (g), tennis (g), volleyball (g); intramural: basketball (g), bowling (g), cross-country running (g), lacrosse (g), soccer (g), softball (g), volleyball (g). 4 PE instructors, 12 coaches, 1 athletic trainer.

Computers Computers are regularly used in all academic, video film production classes. Computer network features include on-campus library services, online commercial services, Internet access, wireless campus network, Internet filtering or blocking technology. Campus intranet and student e-mail accounts are available to students. Students grades are available online. The school has a published electronic and media policy.

Contact Candy Covington, Advancement Director. 901-762-6672. Fax: 901-432-6655. E-mail: ccovington@hutchisonschool.org. Web site: www.hutchisonschool.org.

ANNOUNCEMENT FROM THE SCHOOL Hutchison School, founded in 1902, is located on 52 acres in East Memphis. The School serves more than 930 girls from prekindergarten to grade 12. This college-preparatory day school provides a challenging academic program framed by the balanced development of the mind, body, and spirit. The campus consists of nine buildings, including two gyms, a multimedia library and technology center, and a 630-seat theater. Hutchison offers a variety of athletic competition in twelve sports. The arts play an integral part in the curriculum, and instruction is further enhanced by the Arts Academy, a program that provides additional enrichment of the arts through its afterschool, weekend, and summer offerings. Hutchison is divided into four divisions. Early Childhood offers half-day and full-day programs, beginning with 3- and 4-year olds, and full-day programs for senior kindergarten. These programs focus on early literacy, fundamental math skills, Spanish, social studies, and science instruction. Classes of 15–17 girls are taught by a teacher and a teacher assistant. Lower School for grades 1–4 and Middle School for grades 5–8 offer interdisciplinary instruction in English, math, social studies, science, world languages, the arts, and PE. Latin is taught in grade 8. Upper School for grades 9–12 provides a rigorous college-preparatory program balanced by a variety of extracurricular activities. Hutchison students consistently rank above the national average on SAT/ACT tests, earn college credit through Advanced Placement classes, and are accepted at top colleges and universities across the country. A full-time college counseling staff works with students beginning in 9th grade, and 100% of the School's graduates attend four-year colleges and universities. With a low student-teacher ratio, the School maintains a focus on instruction that is student engaged and fosters an environment where students are encouraged to think critically, use original expression, and problem solve. The School seeks students who are intellectually inquisitive, strongly motivated, and highly committed to accepting the challenges and opportunities the School offers.

HYDE SCHOOL

PO Box 237
Woodstock, Connecticut 06281

Head of School: Laura Gauld

General Information Coeducational boarding and day college-preparatory and general academic school. Grades 9–12. Founded: 1996. Setting: rural. Nearest major city is Hartford. Students are housed in single-sex dormitories. 120-acre campus. 7 buildings on campus. Approved or accredited by Association of Independent Schools in New England, New England Association of Schools and Colleges, The Association of Boarding Schools, and Connecticut Department of Education. Endowment: $8 million. Total enrollment: 173. Upper school average class size: 12. Upper school faculty-student ratio: 1:12.

Upper School Student Profile Grade 9: 8 students (3 boys, 5 girls); Grade 10: 33 students (24 boys, 9 girls); Grade 11: 79 students (52 boys, 27 girls); Grade 12: 54 students (34 boys, 20 girls); Postgraduate: 3 students (3 boys). 98% of students are boarding students. 24% are state residents. 21 states are represented in upper school student body. 2% are international students. International students from Aland Islands, Canada, Japan, and Republic of Korea.

Faculty School total: 26. In upper school: 16 men, 10 women; 10 have advanced degrees; 24 reside on campus.

Subjects Offered 20th century history, advanced biology, advanced chemistry, advanced math, Advanced Placement courses, algebra, art history-AP, athletics, biology, calculus, calculus-AP, character education, chemistry, consumer education, English, English language and composition-AP, English language-AP, English literature, environmental science-AP, ethics, geometry, global issues, independent study, media arts, physics, pre-calculus, Spanish, Spanish-AP, sports, statistics, U.S. history, U.S. history-AP, wilderness experience, wilderness/outdoor program.

Graduation Requirements Electives, English, foreign language, mathematics, science, social studies (includes history), Hyde's graduation requirements embody academic achievement and character development. Character growth is determined through an intense 40-hour, evaluation process involving all members of the senior class and faculty. All students make a speech at graduation representing their principles.

Special Academic Programs 5 Advanced Placement exams for which test preparation is offered; honors section; independent study; remedial reading and/or remedial writing; remedial math.

College Admission Counseling 47 students graduated in 2008; 44 went to college, including Northeastern University. Other: 1 went to work, 1 entered military service, 1 entered a postgraduate year. Median SAT critical reading: 537, median SAT math: 535, median SAT writing: 515, median combined SAT: 1587, median composite ACT: 20.

Student Life Upper grades have specified standards of dress, honor system. Discipline rests equally with students and faculty.

Summer Programs Enrichment, sports, art/fine arts, rigorous outdoor training programs offered; session focuses on orientation for the Fall; held both on and off campus; held at Hyde's Wilderness Campus in Eustis, ME, and on Seguin Island off the coast of Maine; accepts boys and girls; open to students from other schools. 75 students usually enrolled. 2009 schedule: July 12 to August 10. Application deadline: none.

Tuition and Aid Day student tuition: $23,950; 5-day tuition and room/board: $44,750; 7-day tuition and room/board: $44,750. Tuition reduction for siblings, need-based scholarship grants available. In 2008–09, 25% of upper-school students received aid. Total amount of financial aid awarded in 2008–09: $258,000.

Admissions Traditional secondary-level entrance grade is 11. For fall 2008, 151 students applied for upper-level admission, 106 were accepted, 94 enrolled. Deadline for receipt of application materials: none. Application fee required: $100. Interview required.

Athletics Interscholastic: basketball (boys, girls), cross-country running (b,g), football (b), ice hockey (b,g), lacrosse (b,g), soccer (b,g), tennis (b,g), track and field (b,g), wrestling (b); coed interscholastic: equestrian sports, martial arts, ropes courses, wilderness, wrestling; coed intramural: backpacking, canoeing/kayaking, climbing, hiking/backpacking, outdoor adventure, outdoor skills, ropes courses, wilderness. 2 athletic trainers.

Computers Computer network features include on-campus library services, online commercial services, Internet access, Internet filtering or blocking technology. Student e-mail accounts are available to students. The school has a published electronic and media policy.

Contact MaryAnn Tingley, Admission Assistant. 860-963-4736. Fax: 860-928-0612. E-mail: mtingley@hyde.edu. Web site: www.hyde.edu.

See Close-Up on page 802.

HYDE SCHOOL

616 High Street
Bath, Maine 04530

Head of School: Don MacMillan

General Information Coeducational boarding and day college-preparatory and arts school. Grades 9–12. Founded: 1966. Setting: small town. Nearest major city is Portland. Students are housed in single-sex dormitories. 145-acre campus. 32 buildings on campus. Approved or accredited by Association of Independent Schools in New England, New England Association of Schools and Colleges, and The Association of Boarding Schools. Member of National Association of Independent Schools. Endowment: $8 million. Total enrollment: 129. Upper school average class size: 12. Upper school faculty-student ratio: 1:5.

Upper School Student Profile Grade 9: 8 students (5 boys, 3 girls); Grade 10: 19 students (11 boys, 8 girls); Grade 11: 55 students (29 boys, 26 girls); Grade 12: 42 students (28 boys, 14 girls); Postgraduate: 5 students (5 boys). 99% of students are boarding students. 21% are state residents. 27 states are represented in upper school student body. 8% are international students. International students from Canada, China, Democratic People's Republic of Korea, Rwanda, Spain, and United Kingdom.

Faculty School total: 25. In upper school: 17 men, 8 women; 9 have advanced degrees; 21 reside on campus.

Subjects Offered Algebra, American history, ancient history, art, biology, calculus, chemistry, composition-AP, creative writing, English, European history, geometry, government, history, music, physical education, physics-AP, pre-calculus, Spanish, statistics, technical theater, U.S. history, U.S. history-AP.

Graduation Requirements Electives, English, foreign language, history, mathematics, science, Hyde's graduation requirements embody academic achievement and character development. Character growth is determined through an intense 40-hour, evaluation process involving all members of the senior class and faculty. All students make a speech at graduation representing their principles.

Special Academic Programs Honors section; independent study; study at local college for college credit; remedial reading and/or remedial writing; remedial math.

College Admission Counseling 53 students graduated in 2008; 51 went to college, including Rhodes College; Southern Methodist University; The Colorado College;

University of Denver; University of Maryland, College Park; University of San Diego. Other: 1 went to work, 1 entered military service. Mean SAT critical reading: 530, mean SAT math: 520, mean SAT writing: 520, mean combined SAT: 1570, mean composite ACT: 21. 25% scored over 600 on SAT critical reading, 17% scored over 600 on SAT math, 14% scored over 600 on SAT writing, 18% scored over 1800 on combined SAT, 16% scored over 26 on composite ACT.

Student Life Upper grades have specified standards of dress, honor system. Discipline rests equally with students and faculty.

Summer Programs Enrichment, sports, art/fine arts programs offered; session focuses on orientation for the school year; held both on and off campus; held at wilderness preserve in Eustis, ME and on Seguin Island off the coast of Maine; accepts boys and girls; open to students from other schools. 80 students usually enrolled. 2009 schedule: July 9 to August 12. Application deadline: none.

Tuition and Aid Day student tuition: $22,500; 7-day tuition and room/board: $41,500. Tuition reduction for siblings, need-based scholarship grants, Sallie Mae Loan Program available. In 2008–09, 33% of upper-school students received aid. Total amount of financial aid awarded in 2008–09: $820,000.

Admissions For fall 2008, 137 students applied for upper-level admission, 83 were accepted, 68 enrolled. Deadline for receipt of application materials: none. Application fee required: $100. Interview required.

Athletics Interscholastic: basketball (boys, girls), football (b), lacrosse (b,g), soccer (b,g), track and field (b,g), wrestling (b); coed interscholastic: crew, cross-country running, nordic skiing, swimming and diving; coed intramural: hiking/backpacking, kayaking, life saving, outdoor adventure, outdoor skills, physical fitness, physical training, project adventure, ropes courses, snowshoeing, strength & conditioning, ultimate Frisbee, walking, weight lifting, weight training, wilderness, wilderness survival. 8 coaches, 1 athletic trainer.

Computers Computer network features include on-campus library services, online commercial services, Internet access, wireless campus network, Internet filtering or blocking technology. Student e-mail accounts are available to students. The school has a published electronic and media policy.

Contact Wanda Smith, Admission Assistant. 207-443-7101. Fax: 207-442-9346. E-mail: wsmith@hyde.edu. Web site: www.hyde.edu.

See Close-Up on page 802.

HYMAN BRAND HEBREW ACADEMY OF GREATER KANSAS CITY

5801 West 115th Street
Overland Park, Kansas 66211

Head of School: Mr. Howard Haas

General Information Coeducational day college-preparatory, general academic, and religious studies school, affiliated with Jewish faith. Grades K–12. Founded: 1966. Setting: suburban. Nearest major city is Kansas City, MO. 1 building on campus. Approved or accredited by Independent Schools Association of the Central States, International Baccalaureate Organization, and North Central Association of Colleges and Schools. Languages of instruction: English and Hebrew. Total enrollment: 227. Upper school average class size: 15. Upper school faculty-student ratio: 1:5.

Upper School Student Profile Grade 9: 8 students (4 boys, 4 girls); Grade 10: 13 students (5 boys, 8 girls); Grade 11: 14 students (8 boys, 6 girls); Grade 12: 23 students (11 boys, 12 girls). 100% of students are Jewish.

Faculty School total: 36. In upper school: 9 men, 9 women; 14 have advanced degrees.

Subjects Offered 3-dimensional design, algebra, American government, American history, American history-AP, American literature, anatomy and physiology, art, art history, Bible studies, biology, British literature, calculus-AP, chemistry, community service, computer applications, computer science, digital art, economics, English, English language and composition-AP, English literature, English literature and composition-AP, environmental science, ethics, European history, fine arts, geometry, health, Hebrew, Hebrew scripture, Holocaust seminar, Jewish studies, model United Nations, physical education, physics, statistics-AP, Talmud, trigonometry, U.S. government-AP, world history, world literature, yearbook.

Graduation Requirements Arts and fine arts (art, music, dance, drama), English, foreign language, mathematics, physical education (includes health), religion (includes Bible studies and theology), science, social studies (includes history). Community service is required.

Special Academic Programs Advanced Placement exam preparation; study at local college for college credit; academic accommodation for the gifted.

College Admission Counseling 21 students graduated in 2008; 13 went to college, including Boston University; Grinnell College; The University of Kansas; University of Denver; Yeshiva University. Other: 8 entered a postgraduate year.

Student Life Upper grades have specified standards of dress, student council. Discipline rests primarily with faculty. Attendance at religious services is required.

Tuition and Aid Day student tuition: $12,800. Tuition installment plan (FACTS Tuition Payment Plan). Tuition reduction for siblings, need-based scholarship grants available. In 2008–09, 50% of upper-school students received aid. Total amount of financial aid awarded in 2008–09: $800,000.

Admissions Traditional secondary-level entrance grade is 9. For fall 2008, 1 student applied for upper-level admission, 1 was accepted, 1 enrolled. Writing sample required. Deadline for receipt of application materials: none. Application fee required: $50. On-campus interview required.

Athletics Interscholastic: baseball (boys), basketball (b,g), cheering (g), soccer (b,g); coed intramural: golf, horseback riding, tennis, track and field. 2 PE instructors, 6 coaches.

Computers Computers are regularly used in computer applications, desktop publishing, digital applications, economics, English, humanities, mathematics, newspaper, psychology, religious studies, science, social studies, writing, yearbook classes. Computer network features include on-campus library services, online commercial services, Internet access, wireless campus network. Student e-mail accounts and computer access in designated common areas are available to students. Students grades are available online. The school has a published electronic and media policy.

Contact Mrs. Tamara Lawson Schuster, Director of Admissions. 913-327-8135. Fax: 913-327-8180. E-mail: tschuster@hbha.edu. Web site: www.hbha.edu.

IDYLLWILD ARTS ACADEMY

52500 Temecula Road
PO Box 38
Idyllwild, California 92549

Head of School: Dr. Karl L. Reiss

General Information Coeducational boarding and day college-preparatory and arts school. Grades 9–PG. Founded: 1986. Setting: rural. Nearest major city is Los Angeles. Students are housed in single-sex dormitories. 205-acre campus. 44 buildings on campus. Approved or accredited by California Association of Independent Schools and Western Association of Schools and Colleges. Member of National Association of Independent Schools and Secondary School Admission Test Board. Endowment: $3 million. Total enrollment: 261. Upper school average class size: 16. Upper school faculty-student ratio: 1:12.

Upper School Student Profile Grade 9: 40 students (13 boys, 27 girls); Grade 10: 58 students (16 boys, 42 girls); Grade 11: 96 students (34 boys, 62 girls); Grade 12: 65 students (32 boys, 33 girls); Postgraduate: 2 students (1 boy, 1 girl). 89% of students are boarding students. 38% are state residents. 30 states are represented in upper school student body. 32% are international students. International students from Bulgaria, China, Mexico, Republic of Korea, Singapore, and Taiwan; 16 other countries represented in student body.

Faculty School total: 65. In upper school: 24 men, 20 women; 30 have advanced degrees; 23 reside on campus.

Subjects Offered 3-dimensional art, 3-dimensional design, acting, advanced math, algebra, American government, American history, American literature, anatomy, art, art history, audio visual/media, audition methods, ballet, biology, Broadway dance, calculus, career/college preparation, ceramics, chemistry, choir, choral music, choreography, computer graphics, computer science, creative writing, critical studies in film, dance, digital art, directing, drama, drawing and design, driver education, economics, English, English literature, ensembles, environmental science, ESL, fiction, film and literature, film and new technologies, film appreciation, film history, film studies, filmmaking, fine arts, French, geography, geometry, government/civics, grammar, history, illustration, improvisation, jazz dance, jazz ensemble, jazz theory, mathematics, multimedia, music, music theater, music theory, musical productions, musical theater dance, orchestra, performing arts, photography, physical education, physics, play production, playwriting and directing, poetry, pottery, printmaking, science, social science, social studies, Spanish, tap dance, technical theater, technology/design, theater, video film production, vocal music, voice and diction, voice ensemble, world history, world literature, writing.

Graduation Requirements Art, arts and fine arts (art, music, dance, drama), English, foreign language, mathematics, performing arts, physical education (includes health), science, social science, social studies (includes history).

Special Academic Programs Advanced Placement exam preparation; honors section; ESL (31 students enrolled).

College Admission Counseling Colleges students went to include California Institute of the Arts; New York University; The Johns Hopkins University; The Juilliard School; University of California, Los Angeles; University of Rochester. Other: 1 had other specific plans.

Student Life Upper grades have student council. Discipline rests equally with students and faculty.

Summer Programs ESL, art/fine arts programs offered; session focuses on visual and performing arts; held on campus; accepts boys and girls; open to students from other schools. 600 students usually enrolled. 2009 schedule: July 10 to August 19. Application deadline: none.

Tuition and Aid Day student tuition: $28,950; 7-day tuition and room/board: $44,900. Tuition installment plan (Key Tuition Payment Plan, monthly payment plans, individually arranged payment plans, school's own payment plan). Need-based scholarship grants available. In 2008–09, 52% of upper-school students received aid. Total amount of financial aid awarded in 2008–09: $397,046.

Admissions Traditional secondary-level entrance grade is 10. For fall 2008, 233 students applied for upper-level admission, 201 were accepted, 119 enrolled. SLEP, SSAT or TOEFL required. Deadline for receipt of application materials: February 1. Application fee required: $50. Interview required.

Athletics Intramural: aerobics (boys, girls); coed intramural: aerobics, aerobics/dance, aerobics/Nautilus, ballet, basketball, bicycling, bowling, climbing, combined training, cooperative games, cross-country running, dance, fencing, fitness, Frisbee, hiking/backpacking, jogging, martial arts, modern dance, mountain biking, physical fitness, physical training, rock climbing, soccer, swimming and diving, tennis, ultimate Frisbee, volleyball, walking, weight training, yoga. 1 PE instructor.
Computers Computers are regularly used in art, design, drafting, drawing and design, English, ESL, graphic design, media production, science classes. Computer resources include on-campus library services, Internet access, Internet filtering or blocking technology. Computer access in designated common areas is available to students. Students grades are available online. The school has a published electronic and media policy.
Contact Ms. Karen R. Porter, Dean of Admission and Financial Aid. 951-659-2171 Ext. 2343. Fax: 951-659-2058. E-mail: admission@idyllwildarts.org. Web site: www.idyllwildarts.org.

ANNOUNCEMENT FROM THE SCHOOL Idyllwild Arts Academy now offers grades 9–12 and a postgraduate year. The priority deadline for admission and financial aid is February 1. Prospective students and their families should check the Web site at www.idyllwildarts.org for more details.

See Close-Up on page 804.

ILLIANA CHRISTIAN HIGH SCHOOL

2261 Indiana Avenue
Lansing, Illinois 60438

Head of School: Peter Boonstra

General Information Coeducational day college-preparatory, general academic, arts, business, vocational, religious studies, and technology school, affiliated with Christian Reformed Church, Reformed Church in America. Grades 9–12. Founded: 1945. Setting: suburban. Nearest major city is Chicago. 15-acre campus. 1 building on campus. Approved or accredited by Association of Christian Schools International, Christian Schools International, North Central Association of Colleges and Schools, and Illinois Department of Education. Endowment: $1.7 million. Total enrollment: 675. Upper school average class size: 23. Upper school faculty-student ratio: 1:18.
Upper School Student Profile Grade 9: 155 students (87 boys, 68 girls); Grade 10: 187 students (97 boys, 90 girls); Grade 11: 170 students (92 boys, 78 girls); Grade 12: 163 students (75 boys, 88 girls). 70% of students are members of Christian Reformed Church, Reformed Church in America.
Faculty School total: 41. In upper school: 20 men, 21 women; 32 have advanced degrees.
Subjects Offered Algebra, American history, American literature, art, arts, Bible studies, biology, botany, business, business skills, calculus, ceramics, chemistry, computer programming, computer science, drama, earth science, economics, English, environmental science, European history, expository writing, fine arts, geometry, German, government/civics, history, home economics, industrial arts, journalism, mathematics, music, physical education, physics, psychology, social studies, sociology, Spanish, theater, typing, world history, world literature, zoology.
Graduation Requirements Arts and fine arts (art, music, dance, drama), business skills (includes word processing), English, foreign language, mathematics, physical education (includes health), practical arts, religion (includes Bible studies and theology), science, social studies (includes history).
Special Academic Programs Advanced Placement exam preparation; honors section; remedial reading and/or remedial writing; remedial math; programs in English, mathematics for dyslexic students.
College Admission Counseling 155 students graduated in 2008; 121 went to college, including Calvin College; Dordt College; Hope College; Olivet Nazarene University; Purdue University; Trinity Christian College. Other: 3 entered military service, 31 had other specific plans.
Student Life Upper grades have specified standards of dress, student council. Discipline rests primarily with faculty. Attendance at religious services is required.
Summer Programs Sports, art/fine arts programs offered; session focuses on educational and recreational programs; held on campus; accepts boys and girls; open to students from other schools. 100 students usually enrolled. 2009 schedule: June 9 to July 18. Application deadline: none.
Tuition and Aid Day student tuition: $6900. Tuition installment plan (monthly payment plans). Need-based scholarship grants available. In 2008–09, 1% of upper-school students received aid.
Admissions Traditional secondary-level entrance grade is 9. For fall 2008, 163 students applied for upper-level admission, 162 were accepted, 155 enrolled. ACT-Explore required. No application fee required. On-campus interview required.
Athletics Interscholastic: baseball (boys), basketball (b,g), cheering (g), cross-country running (b,g), golf (b), indoor track & field (b,g), soccer (b,g), softball (g), tennis (b,g), track and field (b,g), volleyball (b,g), wrestling (b); coed intramural: bowling. 3 PE instructors, 37 coaches, 1 athletic trainer.
Computers Computers are regularly used in business applications, drawing and design, information technology classes. Computer network features include on-campus library services, online commercial services, Internet access.
Contact Peter Boonstra, Principal. 708-474-0515. Fax: 708-474-0581. E-mail: peter.boonstra@illianachristian.org. Web site: www.ichs.pvt.k12.il.us.

IMMACULATA HIGH SCHOOL

600 Shawnee
Leavenworth, Kansas 66048

Head of School: Mike Connelly

General Information Coeducational day college-preparatory, arts, business, and technology school, affiliated with Roman Catholic Church (Jesuit order). Grades 9–12. Founded: 1924. Setting: suburban. Nearest major city is Kansas City. 1 building on campus. Approved or accredited by North Central Association of Colleges and Schools and Kansas Department of Education. Total enrollment: 113. Upper school average class size: 15. Upper school faculty-student ratio: 1:9.
Upper School Student Profile Grade 9: 26 students (14 boys, 12 girls); Grade 10: 37 students (22 boys, 15 girls); Grade 11: 27 students (11 boys, 16 girls); Grade 12: 23 students (15 boys, 8 girls). 85% of students are Roman Catholic Church (Jesuit order).
Faculty School total: 13. In upper school: 5 men, 8 women; 6 have advanced degrees.
Student Life Upper grades have uniform requirement, student council. Discipline rests primarily with faculty. Attendance at religious services is required.
Admissions Traditional secondary-level entrance grade is 9. Achievement tests required. No application fee required.
Athletics Interscholastic: baseball (boys), basketball (b,g), cheering (g), football (b), golf (b), softball (g), tennis (b,g), track and field (b,g), volleyball (g), wrestling (b). 1 PE instructor, 3 coaches.
Computers Computer resources include Internet access.
Contact Nick Dannevik, Counselor. 913-682-3900. Fax: 913-682-9036. E-mail: ndannevik@archkckcs.org. Web site: www.archkckcs.org/immaculata.

IMMACULATE CONCEPTION HIGH SCHOOL

258 South Main Street
Lodi, New Jersey 07644-2199

Head of School: Sr. Mary Alicia Adametz, CSSF

General Information Girls' day college-preparatory, arts, and religious studies school, affiliated with Roman Catholic Church. Grades 9–12. Founded: 1915. Setting: suburban. Nearest major city is Paterson. 3-acre campus. 1 building on campus. Approved or accredited by Middle States Association of Colleges and Schools, National Catholic Education Association, and New Jersey Department of Education. Total enrollment: 172. Upper school average class size: 17. Upper school faculty-student ratio: 1:11.
Upper School Student Profile Grade 9: 39 students (39 girls); Grade 10: 50 students (50 girls); Grade 11: 40 students (40 girls); Grade 12: 43 students (43 girls). 85% of students are Roman Catholic.
Faculty School total: 17. In upper school: 5 men, 12 women.
Subjects Offered Advanced math, algebra, American government, American history, American history-AP, American literature, anatomy and physiology, art, Bible studies, biology, British literature, calculus, character education, chemistry, communications, computer graphics, computer skills, driver education, English, French, genetics, geometry, health and safety, honors algebra, honors English, honors geometry, honors U.S. history, lab science, musical productions, organic chemistry, performing arts, photography, physical education, physics, pre-calculus, psychology, religious education, social psychology, Spanish, women in society, world cultures, writing.
Graduation Requirements English, foreign language, lab science, mathematics, physical education (includes health), religious studies, social studies (includes history). Community service is required.
Special Academic Programs Advanced Placement exam preparation; honors section; study at local college for college credit.
College Admission Counseling 42 students graduated in 2008; all went to college, including Caldwell College; Felician College; Montclair State University; Seton Hall University; St. Thomas Aquinas College; William Paterson University of New Jersey. Mean SAT critical reading: 500, mean SAT math: 460, mean SAT writing: 510, mean combined SAT: 1470.
Student Life Upper grades have uniform requirement, student council. Discipline rests primarily with faculty. Attendance at religious services is required.
Summer Programs Enrichment, advancement programs offered; session focuses on Jump Start Program for incoming freshmen; held on campus; accepts girls; not open to students from other schools. 25 students usually enrolled. 2009 schedule: August 3 to August 20. Application deadline: February.
Tuition and Aid Day student tuition: $7800. Tuition installment plan (FACTS Tuition Payment Plan, annual payment plan). Tuition reduction for siblings, merit scholarship grants, need-based scholarship grants available. In 2008–09, 10% of upper-school students received aid; total upper-school merit-scholarship money awarded: $21,500. Total amount of financial aid awarded in 2008–09: $36,750.
Admissions Traditional secondary-level entrance grade is 9. For fall 2008, 225 students applied for upper-level admission, 179 were accepted, 47 enrolled. Cooperative Entrance Exam (McGraw-Hill) required. Deadline for receipt of application materials: none. Application fee required: $300. Interview recommended.

Athletics Interscholastic: basketball, bowling, cheering, cross-country running, soccer, softball, swimming and diving, tennis, track and field, volleyball; intramural: aerobics, basketball, dance, fitness, fitness walking, physical fitness, tennis, volleyball, walking. 2 PE instructors, 10 coaches.
Computers Computers are regularly used in graphics, newspaper, photography, yearbook classes. Computer resources include on-campus library services, Internet access, Internet filtering or blocking technology. Computer access in designated common areas is available to students. Students grades are available online. The school has a published electronic and media policy.
Contact Ms. Erica Kirsh, Director of Admissions. 973-773-2665. Fax: 973-614-0893. E-mail: Ekirsh@ichslodi.org. Web site: www.ichslodi.org.

IMMACULATE CONCEPTION SCHOOL

217 Cottage Hill Avenue
Elmhurst, Illinois 60126

Head of School: Pamela M. Levar

General Information Coeducational day college-preparatory, arts, religious studies, and technology school, affiliated with Roman Catholic Church. Grades 9–12. Founded: 1936. Setting: suburban. Nearest major city is Chicago. 2 buildings on campus. Approved or accredited by North Central Association of Colleges and Schools and Illinois Department of Education. Total enrollment: 254. Upper school average class size: 17. Upper school faculty-student ratio: 1:12.
Upper School Student Profile Grade 9: 79 students (42 boys, 37 girls); Grade 10: 71 students (35 boys, 36 girls); Grade 11: 59 students (32 boys, 27 girls); Grade 12: 45 students (27 boys, 18 girls). 95% of students are Roman Catholic.
Faculty School total: 20. In upper school: 5 men, 15 women; 6 have advanced degrees.
Subjects Offered 3-dimensional art, advanced chemistry, advanced math, algebra, American government, American history, anatomy and physiology, ancient world history, art, biology, biology-AP, British literature, business law, calculus, calculus-AP, campus ministry, career/college preparation, Catholic belief and practice, ceramics, chemistry, college counseling, computer applications, computer keyboarding, computer programming, constitutional history of U.S., consumer education, current events, drawing, ecology, environmental systems, economics, English, English-AP, environmental science, fitness, foreign language, French, geometry, government/civics, health education, honors algebra, honors English, honors geometry, honors U.S. history, humanities, library, musical theater, newspaper, painting, physical education, physics, pre-calculus, psychology, SAT/ACT preparation, sociology, Spanish, speech, student government, trigonometry, U.S. history-AP, yearbook.
Graduation Requirements Algebra, American government, American literature, art, biology, British literature, calculus, Catholic belief and practice, chemistry, computer applications, constitutional history of U.S., consumer education, English, environmental science, foreign language, geometry, grammar, health, history, human biology, language and composition, mathematics, physical science, political science, pre-calculus, trigonometry, U.S. history, world history, 40 hours of Christian Service, Attendance at retreat.
Special Academic Programs Advanced Placement exam preparation; honors section; study at local college for college credit.
College Admission Counseling 56 students graduated in 2008; 54 went to college, including DePauw University; Illinois State University; Indiana University Bloomington; Northwestern University; University of Illinois at Urbana–Champaign; University of Notre Dame. Other: 1 went to work, 1 entered military service. Median composite ACT: 21.
Student Life Upper grades have uniform requirement, student council. Discipline rests primarily with faculty. Attendance at religious services is required.
Summer Programs Remediation, sports programs offered; session focuses on sports; held on campus; accepts boys and girls; not open to students from other schools. 150 students usually enrolled.
Tuition and Aid Day student tuition: $7600. Tuition installment plan (SMART Tuition Payment Plan). Tuition reduction for siblings, merit scholarship grants, need-based scholarship grants, Merit scholarships (for placement test top scorers), Externally funded scholarships (alumni, memorials), Catholic School Teacher Grants (1/3 reduction) available. In 2008–09, 28% of upper-school students received aid; total upper-school merit-scholarship money awarded: $15,000. Total amount of financial aid awarded in 2008–09: $100,000.
Admissions Traditional secondary-level entrance grade is 9. For fall 2008, 90 students applied for upper-level admission, 85 were accepted, 79 enrolled. High School Placement Test (closed version) from Scholastic Testing Service required. Deadline for receipt of application materials: none. No application fee required.
Athletics Interscholastic: baseball (boys), basketball (b,g), bowling (b), cheering (g), cross-country running (b,g), dance team (g), football (b), pom squad (g), soccer (g), softball (g), track and field (b,g), volleyball (g), weight lifting (b), weight training (b,g); coed interscholastic: golf, tennis, winter (indoor) track. 2 PE instructors, 19 coaches, 2 athletic trainers.
Computers Computers are regularly used in business applications, career exploration, college planning, library, news writing, science, stock market, yearbook classes. Computer network features include on-campus library services, online commercial services, Internet access, Internet filtering or blocking technology. Student e-mail accounts are available to students. Students grades are available online. The school has a published electronic and media policy.
Contact Mrs. Jean Field, Director of Guidance. 630-530-3472. Fax: 630-530-2290. E-mail: jfield@ichsknights.org. Web site: www.ichsknights.org.

IMMACULATE HEART HIGH SCHOOL

5515 Franklin Avenue
Los Angeles, California 90028-5999

Head of School: Ms. Virginia Hurst

General Information Girls' day college-preparatory school, affiliated with Roman Catholic Church. Grades 6–12. Founded: 1906. Setting: urban. 7-acre campus. 7 buildings on campus. Approved or accredited by California Association of Independent Schools, Western Association of Schools and Colleges, and California Department of Education. Upper school average class size: 20.
Faculty School total: 48. In upper school: 9 men, 26 women; 22 have advanced degrees.
Student Life Upper grades have uniform requirement, student council, honor system. Discipline rests primarily with faculty. Attendance at religious services is required.
Admissions No application fee required.
Contact Ms. Kristy Nishina, Director of Admissions. 323-461-3651 Ext. 235. Fax: 323-462-0610. E-mail: knishina@immaculateheart.org. Web site: www.immaculateheart.org.

IMMACULATE HIGH SCHOOL

73 Southern Boulevard
Danbury, Connecticut 06810

Head of School: Mr. Richard T. Stoops

General Information Coeducational day college-preparatory, arts, and religious studies school, affiliated with Roman Catholic Church. Grades 9–12. Founded: 1962. Setting: urban. Nearest major city is Hartford. 17-acre campus. 1 building on campus. Approved or accredited by National Catholic Education Association, New England Association of Schools and Colleges, and Connecticut Department of Education. Total enrollment: 436. Upper school average class size: 19. Upper school faculty-student ratio: 1:10.
Upper School Student Profile Grade 9: 129 students (65 boys, 64 girls); Grade 10: 132 students (67 boys, 65 girls); Grade 11: 90 students (49 boys, 41 girls); Grade 12: 85 students (49 boys, 36 girls). 87% of students are Roman Catholic.
Faculty School total: 32. In upper school: 13 men, 19 women; 29 have advanced degrees.
Subjects Offered 20th century history, accounting, acting, advanced math, Advanced Placement courses, advanced studio art-AP, algebra, American government-AP, American history, American history-AP, American literature-AP, analytic geometry, anatomy and physiology, ancient history, art, athletic training, biochemistry, biology, biology-AP, business technology, calculus-AP, chemistry, chemistry-AP, choir, chorus, Christian and Hebrew scripture, Christian doctrine, Christian scripture, church history, civics, composition-AP, computer programming, computers, contemporary issues, creative dance, drama, drawing, electronic publishing, English language and composition-AP, English language-AP, English literature and composition-AP, English literature-AP, European civilization, geometry, government-AP, Hebrew scripture, history of the Catholic Church, history-AP, honors algebra, honors English, honors geometry, honors U.S. history, honors world history, jazz band, language, language-AP, physics, physics-AP, prayer/spirituality, psychology, religion, statistics-AP, world geography.
Graduation Requirements Arts and fine arts (art, music, dance, drama), business skills (includes word processing), computer science, English, foreign language, mathematics, physical education (includes health), religion (includes Bible studies and theology), science, social studies (includes history), 25 hours of community service.
Special Academic Programs Study at local college for college credit.
College Admission Counseling 99 students graduated in 2008; all went to college, including Boston College; Fairfield University; Fordham University; University of Connecticut; Western Connecticut State University; Yale University. Mean SAT critical reading: 537, mean SAT math: 536, mean SAT writing: 542, mean combined SAT: 1615. 36% scored over 600 on SAT critical reading, 34% scored over 600 on SAT math, 31% scored over 600 on SAT writing, 30% scored over 1800 on combined SAT.
Student Life Upper grades have uniform requirement, student council, honor system. Discipline rests primarily with faculty. Attendance at religious services is required.
Summer Programs Enrichment, advancement programs offered; session focuses on trigonometry enrichment; held on campus; accepts boys and girls; not open to students from other schools. 15 students usually enrolled. 2009 schedule: July 3 to August 9.
Tuition and Aid Day student tuition: $9200. Tuition installment plan (monthly payment plans, individually arranged payment plans). Tuition reduction for siblings, merit scholarship grants, need-based scholarship grants available. In 2008–09, 22% of upper-school students received aid; total upper-school merit-scholarship money awarded: $9000. Total amount of financial aid awarded in 2008–09: $80,000.
Admissions Traditional secondary-level entrance grade is 9. For fall 2008, 169 students applied for upper-level admission, 159 were accepted, 112 enrolled. ACT-Explore required. Deadline for receipt of application materials: none. Application fee required: $50. On-campus interview required.

Athletics Interscholastic: aerobics (girls), baseball (b), basketball (b,g), cheering (g), cross-country running (b,g), field hockey (g), football (b), hockey (b), ice hockey (b,g), indoor track & field (b,g), lacrosse (b), soccer (b,g), softball (g), tennis (b,g); intramural: basketball (b,g); coed interscholastic: aerobics/dance, aerobics/Nautilus, backpacking, bicycling, cross-country running, dance, dance team, fitness walking, golf, hiking/backpacking, indoor track, track and field; coed intramural: volleyball. 2 PE instructors, 19 coaches, 1 athletic trainer.
Computers Computers are regularly used in accounting, English, mathematics, science, social studies, writing fundamentals classes. Computer network features include on-campus library services, online commercial services, Internet access, Internet filtering or blocking technology. Campus intranet and computer access in designated common areas are available to students. Students grades are available online. The school has a published electronic and media policy.
Contact Mr. Michael Bonelli, Admissions/Director of Marketing. 203-744-1510 Ext. 157. Fax: 203-744-1275. E-mail: mbonelli@immaculatehs.org. Web site: www.immaculatehs.org.

IMMANUEL CHRISTIAN HIGH SCHOOL

802 6th Avenue N
Lethbridge, Alberta T1H 0S1, Canada
Head of School: Mr. Rob vanSpronsen

General Information Coeducational day college-preparatory and general academic school, affiliated with Christian Reformed Church, Reformed Church. Grades 7–12. Founded: 1962. Setting: urban. 4-acre campus. 1 building on campus. Approved or accredited by Christian Schools International and Alberta Department of Education. Language of instruction: English. Total enrollment: 261. Upper school average class size: 22. Upper school faculty-student ratio: 1:18.
Upper School Student Profile 70% of students are members of Christian Reformed Church, Reformed.
Faculty School total: 25. In upper school: 12 men, 13 women; 3 have advanced degrees.
Graduation Requirements Alberta Learning requirements.
College Admission Counseling 45 students graduated in 2008; 22 went to college, including Calvin College; Dordt College; Redeemer University College; Trinity Western University; University of Alberta; University of Lethbridge. Other: 23 went to work.
Student Life Upper grades have specified standards of dress, student council, honor system. Discipline rests primarily with faculty. Attendance at religious services is required.
Tuition and Aid Day student tuition: CAN$5750–CAN$6350. Tuition installment plan (monthly payment plans, individually arranged payment plans). Tuition reduction for siblings available.
Admissions Traditional secondary-level entrance grade is 10. For fall 2008, 6 students applied for upper-level admission, 4 were accepted, 4 enrolled. Deadline for receipt of application materials: none. No application fee required. On-campus interview required.
Athletics Interscholastic: badminton (boys, girls), basketball (b,g), golf (b,g), running (b,g), track and field (b,g), volleyball (b,g); intramural: badminton (b,g), basketball (b,g), outdoor education (b,g), track and field (b,g), volleyball (b,g); coed interscholastic: badminton, cross-country running; coed intramural: badminton, outdoor education, scuba diving.
Computers Computers are regularly used in all classes. Computer resources include on-campus library services, Internet access, Internet filtering or blocking technology.
Contact Mr. Rob vanSpronsen, Principal. 403-328-4783. Fax: 403-327-6333. E-mail: rvanspronsen@immanuelcs.ca. Web site: www.immanuelchristian.org.

IMPERIAL COLLEGE OF TORONTO

20 Queen Elizabeth Boulevard
Etobicoke, Ontario M8Z 1L8, Canada
Head of School: Mr. Daniel Crabb

General Information Coeducational boarding college-preparatory and general academic school. Grades 11–12. Founded: 1990. Setting: urban. Nearest major city is Toronto, Canada. Students are housed in coed dormitories. 2-acre campus. Approved or accredited by Ontario Department of Education. Language of instruction: English. Total enrollment: 202. Upper school average class size: 22. Upper school faculty-student ratio: 1:22.
Upper School Student Profile Grade 11: 30 students (16 boys, 14 girls); Grade 12: 172 students (88 boys, 84 girls). 25% of students are boarding students. 5% are province residents. 1 province is represented in upper school student body. 95% are international students. International students from China, Hong Kong, Malaysia, Republic of Korea, Taiwan, and Viet Nam; 2 other countries represented in student body.
Faculty School total: 17. In upper school: 10 men, 7 women; 6 have advanced degrees; 2 reside on campus.
Subjects Offered Accounting, advanced TOEFL/grammar, algebra, biology, chemistry, Chinese, college placement, computer applications, economics, finite math, geography, geometry, mathematics, physics.
Graduation Requirements Accounting, calculus, computer science, economics, English, mathematics, physics.
Special Academic Programs Accelerated programs; independent study; special instructional classes for students with emotional and behavioral problems; ESL (85 students enrolled).
College Admission Counseling 181 students graduated in 2008; 162 went to college, including McMaster University; Queen's University at Kingston; The University of Western Ontario; University of Manitoba; University of Toronto; University of Waterloo. Other: 10 had other specific plans.
Student Life Upper grades have honor system. Discipline rests primarily with faculty.
Summer Programs Enrichment, advancement, ESL, computer instruction programs offered; session focuses on ESL and pre-university program; held on campus; accepts boys and girls; open to students from other schools. 29 students usually enrolled. 2009 schedule: June 1 to August 26. Application deadline: May 1.
Tuition and Aid Day student tuition: CAN$8800; 7-day tuition and room/board: CAN$13,480. Guaranteed tuition plan.
Admissions Deadline for receipt of application materials: none. Application fee required: CAN$200.
Computers Computers are regularly used in accounting, business education, college planning, computer applications, creative writing, current events, data processing, design, desktop publishing, digital applications, economics, English, ESL, foreign language, geography, information technology, multimedia, science, study skills, Web site design, word processing, writing classes. Computer network features include Internet access. Campus intranet and computer access in designated common areas are available to students.
Contact Mr. Andrew Xu, Executive Assistant. 416-251-4970. Fax: 416-251-0259. E-mail: info@imperialcollege.org. Web site: www.imperialcollege.org.

INDEPENDENT SCHOOL

8317 East Douglas
Wichita, Kansas 67207
Head of School: Mr. Edward Walters

General Information Coeducational day college-preparatory school. Grades JK–12. Founded: 1980. Setting: suburban. 22-acre campus. 2 buildings on campus. Approved or accredited by North Central Association of Colleges and Schools and Kansas Department of Education. Candidate for accreditation by Independent Schools Association of the Central States. Endowment: $1.6 million. Total enrollment: 719. Upper school average class size: 18. Upper school faculty-student ratio: 1:10.
Faculty School total: 30. In upper school: 14 men, 16 women; 19 have advanced degrees.
Subjects Offered 3-dimensional art, advanced math, Advanced Placement courses, algebra, American government, American government-AP, American history, American history-AP, American literature, anatomy and physiology, art, biology, biology-AP, British literature, British literature (honors), British literature-AP, calculus, calculus-AP, ceramics, chemistry, chemistry-AP, choir, computer applications, computer art, computer keyboarding, debate, English literature-AP, foreign language, geometry, German, health, health and wellness, jazz band, Latin, music, newspaper, physics, physics-AP, Spanish, Spanish-AP, theater, theater arts, trigonometry, U.S. government-AP, Web site design, weight training, weightlifting, word processing, yearbook.
Graduation Requirements Algebra, American government, American history, American literature, arts and fine arts (art, music, dance, drama), biology, British literature, chemistry, computer applications, computer literacy, foreign language, geography, geometry, humanities, physical education (includes health), world history, world literature, 50 hours of community service.
Special Academic Programs Advanced Placement exam preparation; honors section; study at local college for college credit; academic accommodation for the gifted.
College Admission Counseling 53 students graduated in 2008; all went to college, including Creighton University; Kansas State University; Oklahoma State University; The University of Kansas; University of Tulsa. Mean SAT critical reading: 611, mean SAT math: 655, mean SAT writing: 620, mean combined SAT: 1887, mean composite ACT: 25. 29% scored over 600 on SAT critical reading, 71% scored over 600 on SAT math, 67% scored over 600 on SAT writing, 65% scored over 1800 on combined SAT, 41% scored over 26 on composite ACT.
Student Life Upper grades have specified standards of dress, student council. Discipline rests primarily with faculty.
Summer Programs Remediation, enrichment, advancement, art/fine arts, computer instruction programs offered; held on campus; accepts boys and girls; open to students from other schools. 125 students usually enrolled. 2009 schedule: June 16 to July 30. Application deadline: June 1.
Tuition and Aid Day student tuition: $8750. Tuition installment plan (monthly payment plans, individually arranged payment plans). Need-based scholarship grants available. In 2008–09, 22% of upper-school students received aid.
Admissions Traditional secondary-level entrance grade is 9. For fall 2008, 49 students applied for upper-level admission, 32 were accepted, 28 enrolled. Admissions testing, non-standardized placement tests and Otis-Lennon Ability or Stanford Achievement Test required. Deadline for receipt of application materials: none. Application fee required: $40. On-campus interview required.

Athletics Interscholastic: baseball (boys), basketball (b,g), cheering (g), cross-country running (b,g), dance team (g), football (b), golf (b,g), soccer (b,g), softball (g), strength & conditioning (b,g), swimming and diving (b,g), tennis (b,g), track and field (b,g), volleyball (g), weight training (b,g), wrestling (b); coed interscholastic: strength & conditioning, weight training. 2 PE instructors, 5 coaches, 1 athletic trainer.
Computers Computers are regularly used in art, college planning, economics, English, humanities, introduction to technology, keyboarding, library, literary magazine, mathematics, newspaper, photography, publications, Web site design, yearbook classes. Computer network features include on-campus library services, Internet access, Internet filtering or blocking technology, homework online. Students grades are available online. The school has a published electronic and media policy.
Contact Mrs. Jayme Davis, Director of Admissions. 316-686-0152 Ext. 405. Fax: 316-686-3918. E-mail: jayme.davis@theindependentschool.com. Web site: www.theindependentschool.com.

INDIAN MOUNTAIN SCHOOL

Lakeville, Connecticut
See Junior Boarding Schools section.

INDIAN SPRINGS SCHOOL

190 Woodward Drive
Indian Springs, Alabama 35124
Head of School: Mr. Gareth Vaughan

General Information Coeducational boarding and day college-preparatory, arts, and technology school. Boarding grades 9–12, day grades 8–12. Founded: 1952. Setting: suburban. Nearest major city is Birmingham. Students are housed in single-sex dormitories. 350-acre campus. 38 buildings on campus. Approved or accredited by Southern Association of Colleges and Schools, Southern Association of Independent Schools, The Association of Boarding Schools, and Alabama Department of Education. Member of National Association of Independent Schools and Secondary School Admission Test Board. Endowment: $25 million. Total enrollment: 297. Upper school average class size: 16. Upper school faculty-student ratio: 1:8.
Upper School Student Profile Grade 8: 26 students (14 boys, 12 girls); Grade 9: 53 students (23 boys, 30 girls); Grade 10: 72 students (37 boys, 35 girls); Grade 11: 73 students (34 boys, 39 girls); Grade 12: 73 students (36 boys, 37 girls). 28% of students are boarding students. 83% are state residents. 10 states are represented in upper school student body. 9% are international students. International students from China, Germany, Republic of Korea, Saudi Arabia, Switzerland, and Viet Nam; 1 other country represented in student body.
Faculty School total: 43. In upper school: 23 men, 20 women; 34 have advanced degrees; 23 reside on campus.
Subjects Offered Advanced Placement courses, algebra, American government-AP, American history, American literature, art, art history, astronomy, athletics, biology, biology-AP, calculus, calculus-AP, ceramics, chemistry, chemistry-AP, Chinese, computer applications, computer keyboarding, computer multimedia, computer science, concert choir, constitutional law, contemporary issues, creative writing, drama, economics, economics-AP, English, English literature, English-AP, environmental science-AP, European history, expository writing, film studies, fine arts, French, French-AP, geology, geometry, government-AP, government/civics, history, jazz, jazz ensemble, Latin, Latin-AP, mathematics, music, painting, philosophy, photo shop, physical education, physical fitness, physics, play production, pre-calculus, science, Shakespeare, social studies, Spanish, Spanish-AP, statistics-AP, theater, trigonometry, video film production, Western civilization-AP, world history, world literature, world religions, world wide web design, writing, yearbook.
Graduation Requirements Arts and fine arts (art, music, dance, drama), English, foreign language, mathematics, physical education (includes health), science, social studies (includes history), Art or Music History.
Special Academic Programs Advanced Placement exam preparation; independent study; academic accommodation for the gifted, the musically talented, and the artistically talented.
College Admission Counseling 65 students graduated in 2008; all went to college, including Bard College; Birmingham-Southern College; Georgia Institute of Technology; The University of Alabama; University of Kentucky. Median SAT critical reading: 660, median SAT math: 655. Mean SAT writing: 671, mean composite ACT: 27. 77% scored over 600 on SAT critical reading, 72% scored over 600 on SAT math, 65% scored over 26 on composite ACT.
Student Life Upper grades have student council, honor system. Discipline rests equally with students and faculty.
Tuition and Aid Day student tuition: $16,200; 5-day tuition and room/board: $28,000; 7-day tuition and room/board: $30,200. Tuition installment plan (Key Tuition Payment Plan, monthly payment plans). Need-based scholarship grants, middle-income loans, paying campus jobs, Key Education Resources available. In 2008–09, 27% of upper-school students received aid. Total amount of financial aid awarded in 2008–09: $987,748.
Admissions Traditional secondary-level entrance grade is 9. For fall 2008, 191 students applied for upper-level admission, 106 were accepted, 77 enrolled. SSAT required. Deadline for receipt of application materials: none. Application fee required: $65. Interview required.
Athletics Interscholastic: baseball (boys), basketball (b,g), soccer (b,g), softball (g), tennis (b,g), volleyball (g); intramural: basketball (b,g), flag football (b), soccer (b,g); coed interscholastic: cross-country running, golf, ultimate Frisbee; coed intramural: aerobics, aerobics/Nautilus, outdoor activities, paint ball, physical fitness, strength & conditioning, table tennis, ultimate Frisbee, yoga. 2 PE instructors, 5 coaches, 1 athletic trainer.
Computers Computers are regularly used in English, keyboarding, photography, technology, Web site design classes. Computer network features include on-campus library services, Internet access, wireless campus network, Internet filtering or blocking technology. Campus intranet, student e-mail accounts, and computer access in designated common areas are available to students.
Contact Mrs. Christine Copeland, Assistant Director of Admission and Financial Aid. 205-332-0582. Fax: 205-988-3797. E-mail: ccopeland@indiansprings.org. Web site: www.indiansprings.org.

INTERLOCHEN ARTS ACADEMY

PO Box 199
4000 Highway M-137
Interlochen, Michigan 49643-0199
Head of School: Mr. Jeffrey S. Kimpton

General Information Coeducational boarding and day college-preparatory and arts school. Grades 9–PG. Founded: 1962. Setting: rural. Nearest major city is Traverse City. Students are housed in single-sex dormitories. 1,200-acre campus. 225 buildings on campus. Approved or accredited by Independent Schools Association of the Central States, North Central Association of Colleges and Schools, The Association of Boarding Schools, and Michigan Department of Education. Member of National Association of Independent Schools and Secondary School Admission Test Board. Endowment: $32 million. Total enrollment: 455. Upper school average class size: 12. Upper school faculty-student ratio: 1:6.
Upper School Student Profile Grade 9: 27 students (14 boys, 13 girls); Grade 10: 62 students (18 boys, 44 girls); Grade 11: 160 students (71 boys, 89 girls); Grade 12: 188 students (95 boys, 93 girls); Postgraduate: 18 students (10 boys, 8 girls). 89% of students are boarding students. 20% are state residents. 48 states are represented in upper school student body. 21% are international students. International students from Canada, China, Germany, Japan, Republic of Korea, and Taiwan; 19 other countries represented in student body.
Faculty School total: 77. In upper school: 49 men, 28 women; 60 have advanced degrees; 36 reside on campus.
Subjects Offered Algebra, American history, American literature, art, ballet, ballet technique, biology, British literature, British literature (honors), calculus, ceramics, chamber groups, chemistry, chemistry-AP, choir, choral music, choreography, civil war history, computer math, computer science, contemporary art, creative writing, current events, dance, dance performance, drafting, drama, dramatic arts, earth science, ecology, English, English literature, environmental science, European history, expository writing, fine arts, French, geometry, German, government/civics, health, history, mathematics, music, philosophy, photography, physical education, physics, science, social studies, Spanish, speech, statistics, theater, trigonometry, world history, world literature, writing.
Graduation Requirements Arts and fine arts (art, music, dance, drama), English, mathematics, physical education (includes health), science, social studies (includes history).
Special Academic Programs Advanced Placement exam preparation; accelerated programs; independent study; term-away projects; academic accommodation for the gifted, the musically talented, and the artistically talented; ESL (54 students enrolled).
College Admission Counseling Colleges students went to include Cleveland Institute of Music; Eastman School of Music; Oberlin College; Peabody Conservatory of Music of The Johns Hopkins University; The Juilliard School; University of Michigan. Mean SAT critical reading: 609, mean SAT math: 577, mean composite ACT: 25.
Student Life Upper grades have uniform requirement, student council, honor system. Discipline rests primarily with faculty.
Summer Programs Art/fine arts programs offered; session focuses on fine and performing arts; held on campus; accepts boys and girls; open to students from other schools. 2,200 students usually enrolled. 2009 schedule: June 20 to August 3. Application deadline: February 1.
Tuition and Aid Day student tuition: $24,120; 7-day tuition and room/board: $38,890. Tuition installment plan (Key Tuition Payment Plan, payment plan). Merit scholarship grants, need-based scholarship grants available. In 2008–09, 70% of upper-school students received aid. Total amount of financial aid awarded in 2008–09: $5,000,000.
Admissions Traditional secondary-level entrance grade is 11. Achievement tests, any standardized test, audition, essay, placement test or SSAT required. Deadline for receipt of application materials: none. Application fee required: $50. Interview recommended.
Athletics Intramural: baseball (boys); coed intramural: aerobics, archery, badminton, basketball, canoeing/kayaking, climbing, cooperative games, cross-country running, fishing, fitness, fitness walking, flag football, floor hockey, fly fishing, Frisbee, hiking/backpacking, indoor soccer, jogging, modern dance, Newcombe ball, outdoor activities, physical fitness, pillo polo, project adventure, rappelling, ropes courses,

running, skiing (cross-country), skiing (downhill), snowshoeing, soccer, softball, table tennis, touch football, ultimate Frisbee, volleyball, wall climbing, whiffle ball, yoga. 1 PE instructor.

Computers Computers are regularly used in mathematics, music, science classes. Computer network features include on-campus library services, online commercial services, Internet access, wireless campus network. Student e-mail accounts are available to students. The school has a published electronic and media policy.

Contact Director of Admission. 231-276-7472. Fax: 231-276-7464. E-mail: admission@interlochen.org. Web site: www.interlochen.org.

INTERNATIONAL COLLEGE SPAIN

Calle Vereda Norte, #3
La Moraleja
Madrid 28109, Spain

Head of School: Mr. David Gatley

General Information Coeducational day college-preparatory and bilingual studies school. Grades PK–12. Founded: 1980. Setting: suburban. 3-hectare campus. 2 buildings on campus. Approved or accredited by European Council of International Schools, International Baccalaureate Organization, and New England Association of Schools and Colleges. Language of instruction: English. Total enrollment: 680. Upper school average class size: 18. Upper school faculty-student ratio: 1:10.

Faculty School total: 46. In upper school: 14 men, 23 women; 12 have advanced degrees.

Subjects Offered 20th century world history, advanced math, art, biology, chemistry, Danish, design, drama, Dutch, economics, English, English literature, European history, expressive arts, French, geography, global studies, history, humanities, information technology, interdisciplinary studies, International Baccalaureate courses, Italian, Japanese, mathematics, model United Nations, music, personal and social education, physical education, physics, science, social education, social studies, Spanish, Spanish literature, Swedish, technology, theory of knowledge, world cultures, world literature.

Graduation Requirements English, foreign language, mathematics, science, social science, social studies (includes history), 90% minimum attendance, minimum average effort grade of satisfactory. Community service is required.

Special Academic Programs International Baccalaureate program; ESL (56 students enrolled).

College Admission Counseling 46 students graduated in 2008; 42 went to college, including Hamilton College; New York University; Rhode Island School of Design; The George Washington University; Tufts University; Yale University. Other: 4 had other specific plans. 75% scored over 600 on SAT critical reading, 100% scored over 600 on SAT math.

Student Life Upper grades have specified standards of dress, student council. Discipline rests equally with students and faculty.

Summer Programs ESL, art/fine arts programs offered; session focuses on English and Spanish languages; held on campus; accepts boys and girls; open to students from other schools. 280 students usually enrolled. 2009 schedule: July 1 to July 26. Application deadline: none.

Tuition and Aid Day student tuition: €7950–€14,100. Tuition installment plan (Insured Tuition Payment Plan). Tuition reduction for siblings, bursaries, merit scholarship grants, need-based scholarship grants available. In 2008–09, 12% of upper-school students received aid; total upper-school merit-scholarship money awarded: €15,435. Total amount of financial aid awarded in 2008–09: €20,445.

Admissions Traditional secondary-level entrance grade is 11. For fall 2008, 23 students applied for upper-level admission, 15 were accepted, 9 enrolled. Admissions testing and math and English placement tests required. Deadline for receipt of application materials: none. Application fee required: €500. On-campus interview recommended.

Athletics Interscholastic: basketball (boys, girls), cross-country running (b,g), soccer (b,g), volleyball (b,g); intramural: aerobics/dance (b,g), badminton (b,g), ballet (b,g), field hockey (b,g), gymnastics (b,g), physical fitness (b,g), soccer (b,g), softball (b,g), swimming and diving (b,g), table tennis (b,g), tennis (b,g), volleyball (b,g); coed interscholastic: track and field; coed intramural: alpine skiing, dance, fencing, golf, horseback riding, judo, martial arts, modern dance, skiing (downhill), snowboarding. 2 PE instructors, 2 coaches.

Computers Computers are regularly used in art, career education, career exploration, college planning, economics, English, ESL, information technology, mathematics, science classes. Computer resources include on-campus library services, online commercial services, Internet access, wireless campus network, Internet filtering or blocking technology. Student e-mail accounts and computer access in designated common areas are available to students. Students grades are available online. The school has a published electronic and media policy.

Contact Mrs. Eunice Amondaray, Admissions Officer. 34-9-1-650-2398. Fax: 34-9-1-650-1035. E-mail: admissions@icsmadrid.org. Web site: www.icsmadrid.org.

INTERNATIONAL HIGH SCHOOL

150 Oak Street
San Francisco, California 94102

Head of School: Ms. Jane Camblin

General Information Coeducational day college-preparatory, arts, bilingual studies, and technology school. Grades PK–12. Founded: 1962. Setting: urban. 3-acre campus. 2 buildings on campus. Approved or accredited by California Association of Independent Schools, European Council of International Schools, French Ministry of Education, International Baccalaureate Organization, Western Association of Schools and Colleges, and California Department of Education. Member of National Association of Independent Schools and Secondary School Admission Test Board. Endowment: $4.7 million. Total enrollment: 944. Upper school average class size: 17. Upper school faculty-student ratio: 1:10.

Upper School Student Profile Grade 9: 84 students (40 boys, 44 girls); Grade 10: 76 students (33 boys, 43 girls); Grade 11: 71 students (27 boys, 44 girls); Grade 12: 96 students (38 boys, 58 girls).

Faculty School total: 139. In upper school: 30 men, 29 women; 35 have advanced degrees.

Subjects Offered Advanced chemistry, advanced math, algebra, American history, American literature, art, biology, calculus, chemistry, community service, computer science, creative writing, current events, drama, earth science, economics, English, English literature, environmental science, ESL, European history, expository writing, fine arts, French, geography, geometry, German, government/civics, history, International Baccalaureate courses, Mandarin, mathematics, music, philosophy, physical education, physics, science, social studies, Spanish, theater, theory of knowledge, trigonometry, world history, world literature, writing.

Graduation Requirements Arts and fine arts (art, music, dance, drama), English, foreign language, International Baccalaureate courses, mathematics, physical education (includes health), science, social studies (includes history), theory of knowledge, extended essay, 150 hours of CAS.

Special Academic Programs International Baccalaureate program; honors section; independent study; term-away projects; study abroad; academic accommodation for the gifted, the musically talented, and the artistically talented; ESL (10 students enrolled).

College Admission Counseling 96 students graduated in 2008; 94 went to college, including McGill University; New York University; Oberlin College; University of California, Berkeley; University of California, Santa Barbara; University of Southern California. Other: 2 had other specific plans. Mean SAT critical reading: 615, mean SAT math: 613, mean SAT writing: 611.

Student Life Upper grades have student council. Discipline rests equally with students and faculty.

Summer Programs Remediation, enrichment, advancement, art/fine arts programs offered; session focuses on Enrichment; held both on and off campus; held at France; accepts boys and girls; open to students from other schools.

Tuition and Aid Day student tuition: $27,670. Tuition installment plan (Insured Tuition Payment Plan, FACTS Tuition Payment Plan). Need-based scholarship grants, French bourse available. In 2008–09, 25% of upper-school students received aid. Total amount of financial aid awarded in 2008–09: $748,000.

Admissions Traditional secondary-level entrance grade is 9. For fall 2008, 236 students applied for upper-level admission, 201 were accepted, 70 enrolled. Any standardized test required. Deadline for receipt of application materials: none. Application fee required: $75. Interview required.

Athletics Interscholastic: baseball (boys, girls), basketball (b,g), football (b), soccer (b,g), volleyball (b,g); intramural: ballet (b,g), baseball (b), basketball (b,g), floor hockey (b,g), soccer (b,g), softball (g), tennis (b,g), volleyball (b,g); coed interscholastic: badminton, cross-country running, golf, swimming and diving, tennis, track and field; coed intramural: badminton, ballet, cross-country running, fencing, flagball, golf, handball, indoor hockey, outdoor activities, outdoor adventure, physical fitness, physical training, swimming and diving, water polo, weight training. 4 PE instructors, 8 coaches, 3 athletic trainers.

Computers Computers are regularly used in mathematics, science classes. Computer network features include on-campus library services, online commercial services, Internet access, wireless campus network, video editing, Web page creation. Computer access in designated common areas is available to students.

Contact Ms. Erin Cronin, Associate Director of Admission. 415-558-2093. Fax: 415-558-2085. E-mail: erinc@internationalsf.org. Web site: www.internationalsf.org.

INTERNATIONAL SCHOOL BANGKOK

39/7 Soi Nichada Thani, Samakee Road
Pakkret 11120, Thailand

Head of School: Dr. William Gerritz

General Information Coeducational day college-preparatory, arts, and technology school. Grades PK–12. Founded: 1951. Setting: suburban. Nearest major city is Bangkok, Thailand. 35-acre campus. 1 building on campus. Approved or accredited by Western Association of Schools and Colleges and state department of education. Affiliate member of National Association of Independent Schools; member of European Council of International Schools. Language of instruction: English. Total enrollment: 1,879. Upper school average class size: 18. Upper school faculty-student ratio: 1:10.

Upper School Student Profile Grade 9: 190 students (105 boys, 85 girls); Grade 10: 199 students (100 boys, 99 girls); Grade 11: 189 students (93 boys, 96 girls); Grade 12: 163 students (88 boys, 75 girls).
Faculty School total: 230. In upper school: 45 men, 41 women; 66 have advanced degrees.
Subjects Offered Algebra, American history, American literature, art, art history, biology, business, calculus, calculus-AP, ceramics, chemistry, computer math, computer programming, computer science, creative writing, dance, drafting, drama, earth science, ecology, economics, electives, English, English literature, environmental science, ESL, European history, expository writing, fine arts, French, geography, geology, geometry, German, government/civics, health, history, home economics, humanities, industrial arts, Japanese, journalism, language arts, languages, mathematics, mechanical drawing, music, performing arts, philosophy, photography, physical education, physics, psychology, reading, science, social studies, sociology, Spanish, speech, statistics, Thai, theater, theory of knowledge, trigonometry, typing, world history, world literature, writing.
Graduation Requirements Arts and fine arts (art, music, dance, drama), computers, English, mathematics, physical education (includes health), science, social studies (includes history). Community service is required.
Special Academic Programs International Baccalaureate program; Advanced Placement exam preparation; ESL (105 students enrolled).
College Admission Counseling 169 students graduated in 2008; 167 went to college, including Boston University; Brigham Young University; Louisiana State University and Agricultural and Mechanical College; The University of British Columbia; University of California, Los Angeles; University of Southern California.
Student Life Upper grades have uniform requirement, student council, honor system. Discipline rests primarily with faculty.
Summer Programs Remediation, enrichment, ESL, art/fine arts programs offered; held on campus; accepts boys and girls; open to students from other schools. 400 students usually enrolled. 2009 schedule: June 9 to July 31. Application deadline: June 6.
Tuition and Aid Day student tuition: 680,000 Thai bahts. Tuition installment plan (individually arranged payment plans).
Admissions Math and English placement tests required. Deadline for receipt of application materials: none. Application fee required: 4500 Thai bahts. On-campus interview required.
Athletics Interscholastic: aquatics (boys, girls), badminton (b,g), basketball (b,g), cross-country running (b,g), dance (b,g), football (b,g), rugby (b,g), running (b,g), soccer (b,g), softball (b,g), swimming and diving (b,g), tennis (b,g), track and field (b,g), volleyball (b,g); intramural: aquatics (b,g), badminton (b,g), basketball (b,g), cross-country running (b,g), dance (b,g), fencing (b), rugby (b,g), running (b,g), swimming and diving (b,g), track and field (b,g), volleyball (b,g). 5 PE instructors.
Computers Computers are regularly used in all academic classes. Computer network features include on-campus library services, Internet access, wireless campus network, Internet filtering or blocking technology. Campus intranet and computer access in designated common areas are available to students. Students grades are available online. The school has a published electronic and media policy.
Contact Ms. Wendy Van Bramer, Admissions Director. 662-963-5800 Ext. 125. Fax: 662-960-4103. E-mail: register@isb.ac.th. Web site: www.isb.ac.th.

INTERNATIONAL SCHOOL EERDE

Kasteellaan 1
Ommen 7731 PJ, Netherlands
Head of School: Mr. Herman Voogd

General Information Coeducational boarding and day college-preparatory and general academic school; primarily serves students with learning disabilities, individuals with Attention Deficit Disorder, individuals with emotional and behavioral problems, and dyslexic students. Boarding grades 9–12, day grades PS–12. Founded: 1934. Setting: rural. Nearest major city is Zwolle, Netherlands. Students are housed in coed dormitories. 7 buildings on campus. Approved or accredited by European Council of International Schools. Language of instruction: English. Upper school average class size: 10.
Faculty In upper school: 4 reside on campus.
Special Academic Programs International Baccalaureate program; ESL.
Student Life Upper grades have specified standards of dress, student council, honor system. Discipline rests primarily with faculty.
Tuition and Aid Day student tuition: €16,750; 5-day tuition and room/board: €39,350; 7-day tuition and room/board: €41,750. Guaranteed tuition plan. Tuition installment plan (monthly payment plans).
Admissions No application fee required. Interview required.
Athletics Coed Interscholastic: badminton, basketball, bicycling, dressage, equestrian sports, field hockey, fitness, golf, hockey, horseback riding, indoor hockey, indoor soccer. 2 PE instructors.
Computers Computers are regularly used in Web site design classes. Computer network features include Internet access, wireless campus network. Campus intranet and student e-mail accounts are available to students. Students grades are available online.
Contact Herman Voogd, Principal. 529-451452. Fax: 529-456377. E-mail: voogd@eerde.nl. Web site: www.eerde.nl.

INTERNATIONAL SCHOOL HAMBURG

Holmbrook 20
Hamburg 22605, Germany
Head of School: Mr. Peter Gittins

General Information Coeducational day college-preparatory, arts, and technology school. Grades PK–12. Founded: 1957. Setting: suburban. 3-acre campus. 1 building on campus. Approved or accredited by European Council of International Schools and New England Association of Schools and Colleges. Language of instruction: English. Total enrollment: 690. Upper school average class size: 20. Upper school faculty-student ratio: 1:7.
Upper School Student Profile Grade 9: 69 students (43 boys, 26 girls); Grade 10: 51 students (29 boys, 22 girls); Grade 11: 46 students (25 boys, 21 girls); Grade 12: 47 students (22 boys, 25 girls).
Faculty School total: 85. In upper school: 47 men, 25 women; 25 have advanced degrees.
Subjects Offered Art, biology, chemistry, computer math, drama, English, environmental science, ESL, European history, fine arts, French, geography, German, history, mathematics, music, photography, physical education, physics, science, social studies, Spanish, theater, theory of knowledge, world history.
Graduation Requirements Arts and fine arts (art, music, dance, drama), English, foreign language, mathematics, physical education (includes health), science, social studies (includes history).
Special Academic Programs International Baccalaureate program; ESL (80 students enrolled).
College Admission Counseling 42 students graduated in 2008; 35 went to college, including McGill University; University of Edinburgh; Yale University. Other: 1 entered military service, 3 had other specific plans.
Student Life Upper grades have student council. Discipline rests primarily with faculty.
Tuition and Aid Day student tuition: €13,300–€16,600. Tuition installment plan (2-payment plan).
Admissions Traditional secondary-level entrance grade is 9. For fall 2008, 50 students applied for upper-level admission, 45 were accepted, 44 enrolled. ACT, CTBS, Stanford Achievement Test, any other standardized test or PSAT and SAT for applicants to grade 11 and 12 required. Deadline for receipt of application materials: none. Application fee required: €100. On-campus interview required.
Athletics Interscholastic: basketball (boys, girls); intramural: basketball (b,g), cross-country running (b,g), field hockey (b,g). 5 PE instructors, 4 coaches.
Computers Computers are regularly used in English, foreign language, mathematics, music, science classes. Computer network features include on-campus library services, online commercial services, Internet access, Internet filtering or blocking technology. Campus intranet and student e-mail accounts are available to students. The school has a published electronic and media policy.
Contact Catherine Bissonnet, Director of Admissions. 49-40-883-00-133. Fax: 49-40-881-1405. E-mail: cbissonnet@ishamburg.org. Web site: www.ishamburg.org.

INTERNATIONAL SCHOOL MANILA

University Parkway
Fort Bonifacio
1634 Taguig City, Philippines
Head of School: Mr. David Toze

General Information Coeducational day college-preparatory, arts, business, bilingual studies, and technology school. Grades PS–12. Founded: 1920. Setting: urban. Nearest major city is Manila, Philippines. 7-hectare campus. 1 building on campus. Approved or accredited by European Council of International Schools and Western Association of Schools and Colleges. Affiliate member of National Association of Independent Schools; member of Secondary School Admission Test Board. Language of instruction: English. Total enrollment: 1,880. Upper school average class size: 16. Upper school faculty-student ratio: 1:9.
Upper School Student Profile Grade 9: 190 students (90 boys, 100 girls); Grade 10: 188 students (96 boys, 92 girls); Grade 11: 167 students (84 boys, 83 girls); Grade 12: 165 students (82 boys, 83 girls).
Faculty School total: 186. In upper school: 36 men, 40 women; 40 have advanced degrees.
Subjects Offered Acting, anthropology, art, athletic training, band, Basic programming, biology, business, calculus-AP, chemistry, Chinese, choir, college admission preparation, college awareness, college counseling, college placement, college planning, computer applications, computer graphics, computer literacy, computer multimedia, computer programming, computer science, creative writing, critical writing, dance, desktop publishing, digital photography, economics, economics and history, English, environmental science, ESL, film, filmmaking, foreign language, French, French as a second language, general science, geography, graphic design, health, health and wellness, health education, information technology, integrated mathematics, International Baccalaureate courses, international relations, Japanese, Japanese as Second Language, jazz band, leadership training, math applications, math methods, mathematics, media studies, music, orchestra, parenting, peer counseling, personal fitness, Philippine culture, physical science, physics, political science, pre-calculus, programming, psychology, reading/study skills, remedial study skills, research, service learning/internship, sex education, Spanish,

theater, theater arts, theory of knowledge, track and field, U.S. history, U.S. history-AP, video film production, visual and performing arts, visual arts, weight fitness, weight training, world history, world religions, writing.

Special Academic Programs International Baccalaureate program; Advanced Placement exam preparation; honors section; accelerated programs; independent study; ESL (166 students enrolled).

College Admission Counseling 171 students graduated in 2008; 165 went to college, including Boston University; Brown University; Santa Clara University; University of San Diego; University of Virginia. Other: 6 had other specific plans. Median SAT critical reading: 550, median SAT math: 600, median SAT writing: 560, median combined SAT: 1710, median composite ACT: 36. 40% scored over 600 on SAT critical reading, 63% scored over 600 on SAT math, 46% scored over 600 on SAT writing, 51% scored over 1800 on combined SAT, 100% scored over 26 on composite ACT.

Student Life Upper grades have uniform requirement, student council, honor system. Discipline rests equally with students and faculty.

Summer Programs ESL programs offered; session focuses on academics for ESL; held on campus; accepts boys and girls; open to students from other schools. 2009 schedule: June to July. Application deadline: none.

Tuition and Aid Day student tuition: $15,200–$17,000. Tuition installment plan (monthly payment plans, individually arranged payment plans, quarterly payment plan). Scholarships for low-income local students available. Total amount of financial aid awarded in 2008–09: $77,535.

Admissions Traditional secondary-level entrance grade is 9. For fall 2008, 240 students applied for upper-level admission, 210 were accepted, 190 enrolled. Deadline for receipt of application materials: none. Application fee required: $155. On-campus interview recommended.

Athletics Interscholastic: badminton (boys, girls), basketball (b,g), bowling (b,g), cheering (g), cross-country running (b,g), dance (b,g), golf (b,g), gymnastics (b,g), martial arts (b,g), rugby (b,g), soccer (b,g), softball (b,g), swimming and diving (b,g), table tennis (b,g), tennis (b,g), track and field (b,g), volleyball (b,g), wall climbing (b,g); intramural: rugby (b,g), wall climbing (b,g), water polo (b,g); coed interscholastic: wall climbing; coed intramural: volleyball, wall climbing. 4 PE instructors, 10 coaches.

Computers Computers are regularly used in art, English, foreign language, history, mathematics, music, science classes. Computer network features include on-campus library services, online commercial services, Internet access, wireless campus network, Internet filtering or blocking technology. Campus intranet and student e-mail accounts are available to students. Students grades are available online. The school has a published electronic and media policy.

Contact Gary Jerome, Director of Admission. 63-2-840-8488. Fax: 63-2-840-8489. E-mail: admission@ismanila.org. Web site: www.ismanila.org.

THE INTERNATIONAL SCHOOL OF ABERDEEN

296 North Deeside Road
Milltimber
Aberdeen AB13 OAB, United Kingdom

Head of School: Dr. Daniel A. Hovde

General Information Coeducational day college-preparatory, general academic, and arts school; primarily serves dyslexic students. Grades PK–12. Founded: 1972. Setting: suburban. 10-acre campus. 1 building on campus. Approved or accredited by European Council of International Schools, Independent Schools Council (UK), International Baccalaureate Organization, and Middle States Association of Colleges and Schools. Language of instruction: English. Total enrollment: 476. Upper school average class size: 17. Upper school faculty-student ratio: 1:3.

Upper School Student Profile Grade 9: 25 students (15 boys, 10 girls); Grade 10: 30 students (17 boys, 13 girls); Grade 11: 36 students (19 boys, 17 girls); Grade 12: 34 students (22 boys, 12 girls).

Faculty School total: 73. In upper school: 10 men, 28 women; 21 have advanced degrees.

Subjects Offered Art, biology, chemistry, computer science, drama, economics, English, fine arts, French, geography, government/civics, history, international relations, mathematics, music, physical education, physics, science, social studies, Spanish, speech, theater.

Graduation Requirements Arts and fine arts (art, music, dance, drama), computer science, economics, English, foreign language, mathematics, physical education (includes health), science, social studies (includes history).

Special Academic Programs International Baccalaureate program; independent study; ESL (45 students enrolled).

College Admission Counseling 27 students graduated in 2008; 26 went to college, including Boston University; Texas Tech University; The University of Texas at San Antonio; University of Delaware; Wheaton College. Other: 1 had other specific plans.

Student Life Upper grades have student council. Discipline rests equally with students and faculty.

Tuition and Aid Day student tuition: £16,775. Tuition installment plan (individually arranged payment plans). Bursaries, need-based scholarship grants available.

Admissions For fall 2008, 28 students applied for upper-level admission, 24 were accepted, 24 enrolled. Deadline for receipt of application materials: none. Application fee required: £500. On-campus interview required.

Athletics Interscholastic: badminton (boys, girls), basketball (b,g), football (b,g), golf (b,g), soccer (b), volleyball (b,g); intramural: aerobics (g), aerobics/dance (g), badminton (b,g), ball hockey (b,g), ballet (g), football (b,g), gymnastics (b,g), handball (b,g), hockey (b,g), lacrosse (b,g), table tennis (b,g), track and field (b,g), unicycling (b,g); coed interscholastic: badminton, basketball; coed intramural: badminton, basketball, soccer, softball, volleyball. 3 PE instructors, 6 coaches.

Computers Computers are regularly used in English, foreign language, mathematics, science classes. Computer network features include on-campus library services, Internet access, Internet filtering or blocking technology. Student e-mail accounts are available to students. The school has a published electronic and media policy.

Contact Mrs. Sheila Sibley, Admissions. 44-1224-732267. Fax: 44-1224-735648. E-mail: admin@isa.aberdeen.sch.uk. Web site: www.isa.aberdeen.sch.uk.

INTERNATIONAL SCHOOL OF AMSTERDAM

Sportlaan 45
Amstelveen 1185 TB, Netherlands

Head of School: Dr. Ed Greene

General Information Coeducational day college-preparatory, arts, bilingual studies, and technology school. Grades PS–12. Founded: 1964. Setting: suburban. Nearest major city is Amsterdam, Netherlands. 1-acre campus. 2 buildings on campus. Approved or accredited by European Council of International Schools and New England Association of Schools and Colleges. Language of instruction: English. Total enrollment: 933. Upper school average class size: 17. Upper school faculty-student ratio: 1:6.

Upper School Student Profile Grade 9: 62 students (34 boys, 28 girls); Grade 10: 63 students (33 boys, 30 girls); Grade 11: 55 students (25 boys, 30 girls); Grade 12: 45 students (22 boys, 23 girls).

Faculty School total: 162. In upper school: 27 men, 46 women; 21 have advanced degrees.

Subjects Offered Addiction, advanced math, algebra, American literature, art, biology, calculus, chemistry, community service, computer programming, computer science, drama, Dutch, economics, English, English literature, ESL, European history, food science, French, geography, geometry, German, history, Japanese, mathematics, music, photography, physical education, physics, science, social science, social studies, Spanish, technology, theater, theory of knowledge, trigonometry, world history, world literature.

Graduation Requirements Arts, computer science, English, foreign language, mathematics, physical education (includes health), science, social science, social studies (includes history). Community service is required.

Special Academic Programs International Baccalaureate program; independent study; academic accommodation for the gifted, the musically talented, and the artistically talented; remedial reading and/or remedial writing; remedial math; programs in English, mathematics, general development for dyslexic students; ESL (71 students enrolled).

College Admission Counseling 44 students graduated in 2008; 40 went to college, including Boston College; New York University; University of Oregon. Other: 1 entered military service, 2 had other specific plans. Median SAT critical reading: 580, median SAT math: 680, median SAT writing: 610, median combined SAT: 1870.

Student Life Upper grades have student council, honor system. Discipline rests primarily with faculty.

Summer Programs Sports programs offered; session focuses on one-week basketball camp; held on campus; accepts boys and girls; not open to students from other schools. 30 students usually enrolled.

Tuition and Aid Day student tuition: €19,575–€20,175. Tuition installment plan (monthly payment plans, individually arranged payment plans).

Admissions Traditional secondary-level entrance grade is 9. For fall 2008, 68 students applied for upper-level admission, 53 were accepted, 40 enrolled. Deadline for receipt of application materials: none. No application fee required. On-campus interview required.

Athletics Interscholastic: basketball (boys, girls), soccer (b,g), swimming and diving (b,g), tennis (b,g), track and field (b,g), volleyball (g); intramural: rugby (b); coed interscholastic: soccer, softball, volleyball; coed intramural: aerobics, aerobics/dance, aerobics/Nautilus, badminton, ballet, basketball, cricket, cross-country running, field hockey, fitness, floor hockey, gymnastics, hockey, indoor soccer, jogging, judo, life saving, martial arts, modern dance, netball, running, self defense, soccer, softball, swimming and diving, tennis, volleyball, weight lifting, weight training, yoga. 7 PE instructors, 14 coaches, 14 athletic trainers.

Computers Computers are regularly used in art, drawing and design, English, foreign language, information technology, keyboarding, library, mathematics, music, science, yearbook classes. Computer network features include on-campus library services, online commercial services, Internet access, Internet filtering or blocking technology. Campus intranet and student e-mail accounts are available to students.

Contact Julia True, Admissions Officer. 31-20-347-1111. Fax: 31-20-347-1105. E-mail: admissions@isa.nl. Web site: www.isa.nl.

INTERNATIONAL SCHOOL OF ARUBA

Wayaca 238A
Oranjenstad, Aruba

Head of School: Paul D. Sibley

General Information Coeducational day college-preparatory, business, and bilingual studies school. Grades PK–12. Founded: 1985. Setting: suburban. Nearest major city is Oranjestad, Aruba. 5-acre campus. 2 buildings on campus. Approved or accredited by Association of American Schools in South America, European Council of International Schools, Southern Association of Colleges and Schools, The College Board, and US Department of State. Language of instruction: English. Total enrollment: 158. Upper school average class size: 12. Upper school faculty-student ratio: 1:8.

Upper School Student Profile Grade 9: 13 students (7 boys, 6 girls); Grade 10: 10 students (5 boys, 5 girls); Grade 11: 15 students (7 boys, 8 girls); Grade 12: 7 students (4 boys, 3 girls).

Faculty School total: 25. In upper school: 6 men, 9 women; 3 have advanced degrees.

Subjects Offered Advanced Placement courses, algebra, American history, art, biology, calculus, chemistry, computer science, Dutch, English, English literature, environmental science, geometry, journalism, mathematics, oceanography, physical education, physics, physics-AP, science, social science, social studies, Spanish, world history.

Graduation Requirements Arts and fine arts (art, music, dance, drama), computer science, English, foreign language, mathematics, physical education (includes health), science, social science, social studies (includes history). Community service is required.

Special Academic Programs Advanced Placement exam preparation; independent study; remedial reading and/or remedial writing; ESL (23 students enrolled).

College Admission Counseling 10 students graduated in 2008; 8 went to college, including Boston University; Florida International University; Johnson & Wales University; Lynn University; University of Florida; York University. Other: 2 went to work. Median SAT critical reading: 500, median SAT math: 625. 25% scored over 600 on SAT critical reading, 50% scored over 600 on SAT math.

Student Life Upper grades have uniform requirement, student council, honor system. Discipline rests primarily with faculty.

Tuition and Aid Day student tuition: $10,000–$14,000. Tuition installment plan (3-payment plan). Tuition reduction for siblings available. In 2008–09, 2% of upper-school students received aid. Total amount of financial aid awarded in 2008–09: $26,000.

Admissions Traditional secondary-level entrance grade is 10. For fall 2008, 10 students applied for upper-level admission, 7 were accepted, 6 enrolled. Any standardized test and SLEP required. Deadline for receipt of application materials: none. No application fee required. On-campus interview required.

Athletics Interscholastic: basketball (boys, girls), scuba diving (b,g), soccer (b,g), softball (b,g), tennis (b,g), volleyball (b,g); intramural: aerobics/dance (b,g), basketball (b,g), soccer (b,g), track and field (b,g), volleyball (b,g); coed interscholastic: softball, tennis. 1 PE instructor.

Computers Computers are regularly used in college planning, computer applications, journalism, yearbook classes. Computer resources include Internet access, Internet filtering or blocking technology. Computer access in designated common areas is available to students. The school has a published electronic and media policy.

Contact Mary B. Sibley, Dean of Academics/Counselor. 297-583-5040. Fax: 297-583-6020. E-mail: info@isaruba.com.

INTERNATIONAL SCHOOL OF ATHENS

Xenias and Artemidos Streets
PO Box 51051
Kifissia—Athens GR-145 10, Greece

Head of School: Mr. C. N. Dardoufas

General Information Coeducational day and distance learning college-preparatory and arts school. Grades PK–12. Distance learning grades 9–12. Founded: 1972. Setting: suburban. Nearest major city is Athens, Greece. 2-acre campus. 1 building on campus. Approved or accredited by CITA (Commission on International and Trans-Regional Accreditation), Department of Defense Dependents Schools, International Baccalaureate Organization, and Middle States Association of Colleges and Schools. Language of instruction: English. Total enrollment: 378. Upper school average class size: 15. Upper school faculty-student ratio: 1:9.

Upper School Student Profile Grade 10: 46 students (30 boys, 16 girls); Grade 11: 50 students (33 boys, 17 girls); Grade 12: 29 students (16 boys, 13 girls).

Faculty School total: 67. In upper school: 13 men, 29 women; 27 have advanced degrees.

Subjects Offered American literature, Arabic, art, art history, biology, business studies, calculus, chemistry, cultural geography, design, drama, English, English literature, ESL, French, geography, Greek, history, information technology, mathematics, modern world history, music, physical education, physics, science, sociology, Spanish, studio art, theory of knowledge, world history, world literature, writing.

Graduation Requirements Art history, arts and fine arts (art, music, dance, drama), English, foreign language, history, information technology, mathematics, physical education (includes health), science, requirements for students in IB diploma program differ. Community service is required.

Special Academic Programs International Baccalaureate program; independent study; remedial reading and/or remedial writing; remedial math; programs in English, mathematics, general development for dyslexic students; ESL (49 students enrolled).

College Admission Counseling 20 students graduated in 2008; 16 went to college, including The American College of Greece; University of London. Other: 2 entered military service, 1 entered a postgraduate year, 1 had other specific plans.

Student Life Upper grades have uniform requirement, student council. Discipline rests primarily with faculty.

Summer Programs ESL, art/fine arts, computer instruction programs offered; session focuses on ESL, modern Greek, and French (subject to demand); held both on and off campus; held at archaeological sites, beaches, and pool; accepts boys and girls; open to students from other schools. 100 students usually enrolled. 2009 schedule: June 29 to July 24. Application deadline: none.

Tuition and Aid Day student tuition: €4700–€11,300. Tuition installment plan (monthly payment plans, individually arranged payment plans). Tuition reduction for siblings, need-based scholarship grants, Prepayment discount available.

Admissions Traditional secondary-level entrance grade is 10. For fall 2008, 41 students applied for upper-level admission, 39 were accepted, 36 enrolled. Math Placement Exam, Secondary Level English Proficiency or writing sample required. Deadline for receipt of application materials: none. Application fee required. On-campus interview required.

Athletics Interscholastic: basketball (boys, girls), cross-country running (b,g), soccer (b,g), track and field (b,g), volleyball (b,g); intramural: basketball (b,g), cross-country running (b,g), handball (b,g), soccer (b,g), swimming and diving (b,g), volleyball (b,g); coed intramural: tennis, water volleyball. 3 PE instructors.

Computers Computers are regularly used in English, foreign language, information technology, library, mathematics, science, social studies, yearbook classes. Computer resources include on-campus library services, online commercial services, Internet access, Internet filtering or blocking technology. Computer access in designated common areas is available to students.

Contact Ms. Betty Haniotakis, Director of Admissions. 30-210-623-3888. Fax: 30-210-623-3160. E-mail: bhani@isa.edu.gr. Web site: www.isa.edu.gr/home.htm.

INTERNATIONAL SCHOOL OF BERNE

Mattenstrasse 3
Guemligen 3073, Switzerland

Head of School: Kevin Thomas Page

General Information Coeducational day college-preparatory school. Grades PK–12. Founded: 1961. Setting: suburban. Nearest major city is Berne, Switzerland. 1-hectare campus. 4 buildings on campus. Approved or accredited by European Council of International Schools, International Baccalaureate Organization, New England Association of Schools and Colleges, and Swiss Federation of Private Schools. Language of instruction: English. Total enrollment: 277. Upper school average class size: 16. Upper school faculty-student ratio: 1:5.

Upper School Student Profile Grade 6: 22 students (11 boys, 11 girls); Grade 7: 25 students (14 boys, 11 girls); Grade 8: 20 students (12 boys, 8 girls); Grade 9: 31 students (15 boys, 16 girls); Grade 10: 25 students (17 boys, 8 girls); Grade 11: 20 students (10 boys, 10 girls); Grade 12: 20 students (12 boys, 8 girls).

Faculty School total: 50. In upper school: 15 men, 19 women; 18 have advanced degrees.

Subjects Offered Biology, chemistry, drama, economics, English, English literature, ESL, European history, fine arts, French, geography, German, history, mathematics, music, physical education, physics, science, social science, social studies, technology, theater, visual arts, world history, world literature.

Graduation Requirements Arts and fine arts (art, music, dance, drama), drama, English, foreign language, mathematics, physical education (includes health), science, social science, social studies (includes history), theory of knowledge, extended essay, Creative Action Service (CAS).

Special Academic Programs International Baccalaureate program; ESL (14 students enrolled).

College Admission Counseling 18 students graduated in 2008; 16 went to college, including Boston University; George Mason University; McGill University; Simon Fraser University. Other: 2 went to work. Mean SAT critical reading: 522, mean SAT math: 566, mean SAT writing: 506.

Student Life Upper grades have specified standards of dress, student council. Discipline rests primarily with faculty.

Tuition and Aid Day student tuition: 25,670 Swiss francs–28,850 Swiss francs. Tuition installment plan (monthly payment plans, individually arranged payment plans).

Admissions Traditional secondary-level entrance grade is 10. For fall 2008, 36 students applied for upper-level admission, 36 were accepted, 36 enrolled. Math and English placement tests required. Deadline for receipt of application materials: none. Application fee required: 250 Swiss francs. On-campus interview required.

Athletics Interscholastic: alpine skiing (boys, girls), basketball (b,g), cross-country running (b,g), indoor hockey (b,g), indoor soccer (b,g), running (b,g), skiing (downhill) (b,g), snowboarding (b,g), soccer (b,g), swimming and diving (b,g), track and field (b,g), volleyball (b,g); intramural: alpine skiing (b,g), basketball (b,g), cross-country running (b,g), ice skating (b,g), indoor hockey (b,g), indoor soccer (b,g), running (b,g), skiing (downhill) (b,g), snowboarding (b,g), soccer (b,g), swimming

and diving (b,g), track and field (b,g), volleyball (b,g); coed interscholastic: alpine skiing, swimming and diving; coed intramural: alpine skiing, ice skating, swimming and diving. 1 PE instructor, 4 coaches.
Computers Computers are regularly used in drawing and design, English, information technology, library skills, mathematics, science, yearbook classes. Computer network features include on-campus library services, online commercial services, Internet access, wireless campus network, Internet filtering or blocking technology. Computer access in designated common areas is available to students.
Contact Barry Mansfield, Secondary School Principal. +41-(0)31-951-2358. Fax: +41-(0)31-951-1710. E-mail: barry.mansfield@isberne.ch. Web site: www.isberne.ch.

ANNOUNCEMENT FROM THE SCHOOL The International School of Berne (ISBerne) is a nonprofit, parent-owned day school accredited by CIS and NEASC. It provides an education in English for 280 children, ages 3–19, of over forty nationalities. ISBerne is authorized to offer all three prestigious International Baccalaureate (IB) Programmes: the Primary Years Programme (ages 3–11); the Middle Years Programme (ages 11–16); and the Diploma Programme (ages 16–19). The strong educational curriculum follows a philosophy of education based on the principles of educating the whole person; of promoting international understanding; of education through a broad, balanced curriculum; and of respect for and tolerance of cultural diversity. The elementary and middle school programme includes French and German, music, visual arts, theatre arts, the sciences, humanities, mathematics, and English. The grade 5 students complete their elementary education with an Exhibition. The middle school students complete their educational programme through a Personal Project in grade 10. The IB Diploma programme in grades 11 and 12 is a comprehensive and rigorous two-year curriculum to prepare students for university entrance. Students choose six subjects to study, write an extended essay, follow a Theory of Knowledge Course, and complete a Community Service and Action Program. Specialist areas in the school include a gymnasium, two computer labs, three science labs, two art rooms, a theatre arts studio, and music rooms. Extensive use of local facilities for athletics, sports tournaments, theatre, and music productions enable the school to complement its programme. The physical education programme includes seven ice skating days for kindergarten and grade 1 and seven ski/snowboarding days for grades 2–12 during the winter term. The school is located in the suburb of Gümligen, 15 minutes from the centre of Berne, the capital of Switzerland. The three sections—Early Learning Centre, Elementary, and Secondary—are on three sites, all within 200 metres of one another

---

THE INTERNATIONAL SCHOOL OF GENEVA

62 Route de Chene
Geneva 1208, Switzerland
Head of School: Dr. Nicholas Tate

General Information Coeducational day college-preparatory, general academic, and bilingual studies school. Grades PK–13. Founded: 1924. Setting: urban. 15-acre campus. 16 buildings on campus. Approved or accredited by European Council of International Schools, International Baccalaureate Organization, Middle States Association of Colleges and Schools, Swiss Federation of Private Schools, and The College Board. Member of Secondary School Admission Test Board. Languages of instruction: English and French. Total enrollment: 4,010. Upper school average class size: 20. Upper school faculty-student ratio: 1:11.
Upper School Student Profile Grade 9: 340 students (175 boys, 165 girls); Grade 10: 330 students (170 boys, 160 girls); Grade 11: 350 students (180 boys, 170 girls); Grade 12: 375 students (190 boys, 185 girls); Grade 13: 320 students (165 boys, 155 girls).
Faculty School total: 420.
Subjects Offered Advanced chemistry, advanced math, art, biology, chemistry, computer skills, computer-aided design, drama, economics, English, English literature, ESL, fine arts, French, French as a second language, French literature-AP, general science, geography, German, history, International Baccalaureate courses, Italian, mathematics, music, performing arts, physical education, physics, psychology, science, social studies, Spanish, theater, theory of knowledge, world literature.
Graduation Requirements English, foreign language, lab science, mathematics, social studies (includes history).
Special Academic Programs International Baccalaureate program; academic accommodation for the musically talented and the artistically talented; remedial reading and/or remedial writing; remedial math; programs in general development for dyslexic students; ESL (150 students enrolled).
College Admission Counseling 335 students graduated in 2008; 325 went to college. Other: 4 went to work, 6 entered military service.
Student Life Upper grades have student council. Discipline rests primarily with faculty.
Tuition and Aid Day student tuition: 27,255 Swiss francs. Tuition installment plan (monthly payment plans, trimester payment plan). Tuition reduction for siblings, bursaries available.
Admissions Deadline for receipt of application materials: none. No application fee required. On-campus interview recommended.
Athletics Interscholastic: alpine skiing (boys, girls), basketball (b,g), cross-country running (b,g), indoor soccer (b,g), rugby (b,g), running (b,g), skiing (downhill) (b,g), soccer (b,g), swimming and diving (b,g), tennis (b,g), track and field (b,g); intramural: alpine skiing (b,g), badminton (b,g), basketball (b,g), climbing (b,g), crew (b,g), cross-country running (b,g), field hockey (b,g), indoor soccer (b,g), rugby (b,g), running (b,g), skiing (downhill) (b,g), soccer (b,g), swimming and diving (b,g), table tennis (b,g), tennis (b,g), track and field (b,g).
Computers Computers are regularly used in all academic classes. Computer network features include on-campus library services, Internet access, wireless campus network, Internet filtering or blocking technology. Students grades are available online. The school has a published electronic and media policy.
Contact Mr. John Douglas, Director of Admissions. 41-22-787 26 30. Fax: 41-22-787 26 32. E-mail: admissions@ecolint.ch. Web site: www.ecolint.ch.

ANNOUNCEMENT FROM THE SCHOOL In 1924, staff of the League of Nations founded The International School of Geneva and committed it to promoting international understanding and values now incorporated into the ideals of the United Nations. The School, with more than 130 nationalities and nearly as many mother tongues, is now one of the largest international schools in the world and Switzerland's largest private school. The School has three campuses, all with primary and secondary schools: La Grande Boissière (1,900 students) in Geneva; La Chataigneraie (1,150) in the canton of Vaud; and Campus des Nations (1,000), in the heart of Geneva's International Quarter. The School is a service school working for the benefit of the international community of Geneva. There are no entrance exams; the School is prepared to accept students throughout the year who can benefit from its programs based on previous academic records and recommendations. It is organized as a nonprofit foundation governed by a board of elected parent members and representatives of local authorities. School fees are the largest contributor to an annual operating budget of SF 75 million. Teachers come from more than thirty countries, reinforcing the School's commitment to an appreciation of cultural diversity. The learning languages are English and French; there is also a strong dual-language program. Children are encouraged to maintain contact with their mother languages. The School's educational programs are based on a multicultural view of the world and promote the development of the whole child. The School was the first in the world to offer the International Baccalaureate (IB Diploma) to its students. Students can also receive an American high school diploma or prepare for the International GCSE, the French brevet des collèges, and the Swiss maturité. The Council of International Schools and the Middle States Association of Colleges and Schools accredit the School.

INTERNATIONAL SCHOOL OF LAUSANNE

Chemin de la Grangette 2
Le Mont-sur-Lausanne 1052, Switzerland
Head of School: Ms. Lyn Cheetham

General Information Coeducational day college-preparatory school. Grades PK–12. Founded: 1962. Setting: suburban. Nearest major city is Lausanne, Switzerland. 8-acre campus. 1 building on campus. Approved or accredited by European Council of International Schools, International Baccalaureate Organization, and New England Association of Schools and Colleges. Language of instruction: English. Total enrollment: 617. Upper school average class size: 20. Upper school faculty-student ratio: 1:7.
Upper School Student Profile Grade 6: 44 students (24 boys, 20 girls); Grade 7: 44 students (21 boys, 23 girls); Grade 8: 44 students (26 boys, 18 girls); Grade 9: 49 students (25 boys, 24 girls); Grade 10: 47 students (21 boys, 26 girls); Grade 11: 52 students (28 boys, 24 girls); Grade 12: 52 students (27 boys, 25 girls).
Faculty School total: 86. In upper school: 21 men, 27 women; 16 have advanced degrees.
Subjects Offered Art, biology, chemistry, community service, design, drama, economics, English, ESL, French, geography, German, history, information technology, International Baccalaureate courses, library skills, mathematics, music, personal and social education, physics, science, Spanish, sports, Swedish, swimming, theory of knowledge.
Graduation Requirements English, foreign language, mathematics, physical education (includes health), science, social sciences. Community service is required.
Special Academic Programs International Baccalaureate program; special instructional classes for learning support classes for students with learning disabilities, dyslexia, etc; ESL (20 students enrolled).
College Admission Counseling 45 students graduated in 2008; 39 went to college, including Colgate University; Lewis & Clark College; Parsons The New School for Design; University of Pennsylvania; University of Southern California; Villanova University. Other: 1 went to work, 1 entered military service, 4 had other specific plans.
Student Life Upper grades have specified standards of dress, student council. Discipline rests equally with students and faculty.
Tuition and Aid Day student tuition: 29,000 Swiss francs. Bursaries available.

Admissions Traditional secondary-level entrance grade is 9. English for Non-native Speakers required. Deadline for receipt of application materials: none. Application fee required: 2500 Swiss francs. Interview recommended.
Athletics Interscholastic: basketball (boys), cross-country running (b,g), indoor soccer (b,g), soccer (b,g), swimming and diving (b,g), tennis (b,g), track and field (b,g), volleyball (g); coed interscholastic: alpine skiing, outdoor activities, running, skiing (downhill), tennis; coed intramural: aerobics/dance, badminton, basketball, climbing, dance, field hockey, fitness, floor hockey, indoor soccer, jogging, kayaking, mountain biking, nordic skiing, outdoor activities, rock climbing, rugby, skiing (downhill), soccer, softball, squash, swimming and diving, track and field, ultimate Frisbee, volleyball, water polo. 2 PE instructors, 3 coaches.
Computers Computers are regularly used in all classes. Computer resources include on-campus library services, Internet access, wireless campus network, Internet filtering or blocking technology. Student e-mail accounts are available to students. The school has a published electronic and media policy.
Contact Ms. Susy Weill, Admissions Office. 41-21-560 02 02. Fax: 41-21-560 02 03. E-mail: admissions@isl.ch. Web site: www.isl.ch.

THE INTERNATIONAL SCHOOL OF LONDON

139 Gunnersbury Avenue
London W3 8LG, United Kingdom
Head of School: Mr. Amin Makarem

General Information Coeducational day college-preparatory school. Grades K–13. Founded: 1972. Setting: urban. 2 buildings on campus. Approved or accredited by European Council of International Schools. Language of instruction: English. Total enrollment: 350. Upper school average class size: 18. Upper school faculty-student ratio: 1:8.
Faculty School total: 58. In upper school: 15 men, 15 women; 21 have advanced degrees.
Subjects Offered Art, economics, English, French, geography, history, languages, mathematics, music, physical education, science, social science, Spanish, world affairs.
Graduation Requirements Foreign language, mathematics, science, social science. Community service is required.
Special Academic Programs International Baccalaureate program; ESL (50 students enrolled).
College Admission Counseling 25 students graduated in 2008; all went to college, including University of London; University of Oxford.
Student Life Upper grades have student council. Discipline rests primarily with faculty.
Tuition and Aid Day student tuition: £18,250.
Admissions For fall 2008, 36 students applied for upper-level admission, 30 were accepted, 30 enrolled. Deadline for receipt of application materials: July 30. Application fee required: £150. Interview recommended.
Athletics Interscholastic: basketball (boys, girls), soccer (b); intramural: badminton (b,g), softball (b,g), swimming and diving (b,g), table tennis (b,g), tennis (b,g); coed interscholastic: soccer; coed intramural: softball, swimming and diving, table tennis, tennis. 2 PE instructors, 2 coaches.
Computers Computers are regularly used in English, foreign language, mathematics, science classes. Computer network features include on-campus library services, Internet access, wireless campus network, Internet filtering or blocking technology. Student e-mail accounts are available to students. The school has a published electronic and media policy.
Contact Yoel Gordon, Director of Admissions. 20-8992-5823. Fax: 44-8993-7012. E-mail: Mail@islondon.com. Web site: www.islondon.com.

INTERNATIONAL SCHOOL OF MILAN

Via G. Bellini 1
20146 Milan, Italy
Head of School: Mr. Terence F. Haywood

General Information Coeducational day college-preparatory school. Grades K–13. Founded: 1958. Setting: urban. Nearest major city is Milan, Italy. 3-acre campus. 1 building on campus. Approved or accredited by International Baccalaureate Organization. Member of European Council of International Schools. Language of instruction: English. Total enrollment: 1,300. Upper school average class size: 14. Upper school faculty-student ratio: 1:7.
Upper School Student Profile Grade 10: 60 students (29 boys, 31 girls); Grade 11: 57 students (29 boys, 28 girls); Grade 12: 67 students (32 boys, 35 girls); Grade 13: 56 students (29 boys, 27 girls).
Faculty School total: 145. In upper school: 17 men, 22 women; 36 have advanced degrees.
Subjects Offered Art, arts, biology, business, chemistry, ecology, environmental systems, economics, English, English literature, fine arts, French, geography, history, information technology, Italian, mathematics, music, music theory, philosophy, physical education, physics, science, social science, social studies, Spanish, theater arts, theory of knowledge.
Graduation Requirements Arts and fine arts (art, music, dance, drama), English, foreign language, mathematics, physical education (includes health), science, social studies (includes history), technology, theory of knowledge.
Special Academic Programs International Baccalaureate program; honors section; remedial reading and/or remedial writing; remedial math; programs in English for dyslexic students; ESL (40 students enrolled).
College Admission Counseling 64 students graduated in 2008; 60 went to college, including Emory University; London School of Economics and Political Science; The Johns Hopkins University; University of California, Los Angeles; University of Durham; University of Edinburgh. Other: 4 had other specific plans.
Student Life Upper grades have specified standards of dress, student council. Discipline rests primarily with faculty.
Tuition and Aid Day student tuition: €15,000. Tuition installment plan (individually arranged payment plans). Merit scholarship grants, need-based scholarship grants available. In 2008–09, 4% of upper-school students received aid; total upper-school merit-scholarship money awarded: €20,000. Total amount of financial aid awarded in 2008–09: €30,000.
Admissions Traditional secondary-level entrance grade is 10. For fall 2008, 60 students applied for upper-level admission, 25 were accepted, 21 enrolled. Academic Profile Tests, any standardized test, international math and English tests or math and English placement tests required. Deadline for receipt of application materials: none. No application fee required. On-campus interview recommended.
Athletics Interscholastic: basketball (boys, girls), cross-country running (b,g), field hockey (b,g), gymnastics (b,g), skiing (cross-country) (b,g), skiing (downhill) (b,g), soccer (b), squash (b,g), swimming and diving (b,g), track and field (b,g), volleyball (b,g); intramural: aerobics (g), basketball (b,g), cross-country running (b,g), field hockey (b,g), gymnastics (b,g), indoor soccer (b), skiing (cross-country) (b,g), skiing (downhill) (b,g), soccer (b), squash (b,g), swimming and diving (b,g), table tennis (b,g), tennis (b,g), track and field (b,g), volleyball (b,g); coed interscholastic: basketball, cross-country running, field hockey, gymnastics, skiing (cross-country), skiing (downhill), squash, swimming and diving, track and field, volleyball; coed intramural: aerobics/dance, alpine skiing, basketball, cross-country running, dance, field hockey, gymnastics, indoor hockey, modern dance, outdoor adventure, physical fitness, physical training, skiing (cross-country), skiing (downhill), squash, swimming and diving, table tennis, tennis, track and field, volleyball. 2 PE instructors.
Computers Computers are regularly used in all classes. Computer network features include on-campus library services, online commercial services, Internet access, wireless campus network, Internet filtering or blocking technology. Campus intranet and computer access in designated common areas are available to students. Students grades are available online. The school has a published electronic and media policy.
Contact Mr. Mark Dawson, High School Principal. 39-0242290577. Fax: 39-024235428. E-mail: ismhigh@ism-ac.it. Web site: www.ism-ac.it.

THE INTERNATIONAL SCHOOL OF PARIS

6, rue Beethoven
75016 Paris, France
Head of School: Mrs. Audrey Peverelli

General Information Coeducational day college-preparatory, general academic, and All programs of the IBO (PYP, MYP and IB Diploma) school. Grades N–12. Founded: 1964. Setting: urban. Nearest major city is Paris, France. 3 buildings on campus. Approved or accredited by European Council of International Schools, International Baccalaureate Organization, and New England Association of Schools and Colleges. Affiliate member of National Association of Independent Schools. Language of instruction: English. Endowment: €50,000. Upper school average class size: 14. Upper school faculty-student ratio: 1:8.
Faculty School total: 100. In upper school: 25 men, 32 women; 18 have advanced degrees.
Subjects Offered Algebra, art, biology, calculus, ceramics, chemistry, computer science, economics, English, English literature, ESL, fine arts, French, geography, geometry, Hindi, Japanese, Korean, mathematics, music, physical education, physics, Russian, science, social science, social studies, Swedish, theory of knowledge, trigonometry, world history.
Graduation Requirements Arts and fine arts (art, music, dance, drama), computer science, English, foreign language, mathematics, physical education (includes health), science, social science, social studies (includes history).
Special Academic Programs International Baccalaureate program; ESL (65 students enrolled).
College Admission Counseling 72 students graduated in 2008; 68 went to college, including Barnard College; Waseda University. Other: 4 had other specific plans. Median SAT critical reading: 550, median SAT math: 560, median SAT writing: 555.
Student Life Upper grades have student council. Discipline rests primarily with faculty.
Summer Programs Remediation, ESL, art/fine arts, computer instruction programs offered; session focuses on sports and intensive English and French; held on campus; accepts boys and girls; open to students from other schools. 160 students usually enrolled. 2009 schedule: July 7 to July 25. Application deadline: none.
Tuition and Aid Day student tuition: €21,600. Tuition installment plan (individually arranged payment plans). Need-based scholarship grants available. In 2008–09, 5% of upper-school students received aid. Total amount of financial aid awarded in 2008–09: $200,000.

Admissions For fall 2008, 50 students applied for upper-level admission, 44 were accepted, 44 enrolled. Deadline for receipt of application materials: none. No application fee required. Interview recommended.
Athletics Interscholastic: basketball (boys, girls), soccer (b,g), volleyball (b,g); intramural: basketball (b,g), gymnastics (b,g), lacrosse (b,g), skiing (downhill) (b,g), soccer (b,g), swimming and diving (b,g), table tennis (b,g), tennis (b,g), track and field (b,g), volleyball (b,g); coed intramural: aerobics/dance, ball hockey, dance, field hockey, juggling, physical fitness, running. 3 PE instructors.
Computers Computers are regularly used in English, foreign language, mathematics, science classes. Computer network features include on-campus library services, online commercial services, Internet access, wireless campus network. The school has a published electronic and media policy.
Contact Mrs. Catherine Hard, Director of Admissions. 33-1-42-24-09-54. Fax: 33-1-45-27-15-93. E-mail: chard@isparis.edu. Web site: www.isparis.edu.

INTERNATIONAL SCHOOL OF SOUTH AFRICA

Private Bag X 2114
Mafikeng 2745, South Africa
Head of School: Mr. James Haupt

General Information Coeducational boarding and day college-preparatory, general academic, arts, business, bilingual studies, and technology school. Grades 7–13. Founded: 1990. Setting: small town. Nearest major city is Johannesburg, South Africa. Students are housed in single-sex dormitories. 54-hectare campus. Approved or accredited by European Council of International Schools. Language of instruction: English. Total enrollment: 418. Upper school average class size: 15.
Upper School Student Profile Grade 7: 62 students (23 boys, 39 girls); Grade 8: 101 students (45 boys, 56 girls); Grade 9: 76 students (37 boys, 39 girls); Grade 10: 50 students (28 boys, 22 girls); Grade 11: 79 students (45 boys, 34 girls); Grade 12: 38 students (22 boys, 16 girls); Grade 13: 12 students (4 boys, 8 girls). 65% of students are boarding students. 60% are international students. International students from Botswana, Congo, Ghana, Malawi, Zambia, and Zimbabwe; 5 other countries represented in student body.
Student Life Upper grades have uniform requirement, student council, honor system. Discipline rests primarily with faculty.
Tuition and Aid Day student tuition: 31,698 South African rand–40,059 South African rand; 7-day tuition and room/board: 74,751 South African rand–83,109 South African rand. Tuition installment plan (monthly payment plans, individually arranged payment plans). Tuition reduction for siblings, bursaries, merit scholarship grants available. Total upper-school merit-scholarship money awarded for 2008–09: 100,000 South African rand.
Admissions Admissions testing required. Deadline for receipt of application materials: none. Application fee required: 500 South African rand. On-campus interview recommended.
Athletics Interscholastic: basketball (boys, girls), biathlon (b,g), cricket (b), football (b,g), hockey (b,g), netball (g), soccer (b,g), volleyball (b,g); intramural: basketball (b,g), cricket (b), football (b,g), hockey (b,g), netball (g), soccer (b,g), squash (b,g), volleyball (b,g); coed interscholastic: aquatics, swimming and diving, tennis; coed intramural: aquatics, swimming and diving, tennis. 2 PE instructors, 3 coaches, 3 athletic trainers.
Computers Computers are regularly used in aerospace science classes. Computer network features include Internet access, wireless campus network, Internet filtering or blocking technology. Campus intranet, student e-mail accounts, and computer access in designated common areas are available to students. The school has a published electronic and media policy.
Contact Mrs. Rani Chandramohan, Admissions Officer. 27 18 3811102. Fax: 27 18 3811187. E-mail: deputyhead@issa.co.za. Web site: www.issa.co.za.

IOLANI SCHOOL

563 Kamoku Street
Honolulu, Hawaii 96826
Head of School: Dr. Val T. Iwashita

General Information Coeducational day and distance learning college-preparatory and arts school, affiliated with Episcopal Church. Grades K–12. Distance learning grades 11–12. Founded: 1863. Setting: urban. 25-acre campus. 7 buildings on campus. Approved or accredited by National Association of Episcopal Schools, Western Association of Schools and Colleges, and Hawaii Department of Education. Member of National Association of Independent Schools and Secondary School Admission Test Board. Endowment: $100 million. Total enrollment: 1,842. Upper school average class size: 17. Upper school faculty-student ratio: 1:12.
Upper School Student Profile Grade 7: 183 students (91 boys, 92 girls); Grade 8: 192 students (92 boys, 100 girls); Grade 9: 234 students (111 boys, 123 girls); Grade 10: 231 students (118 boys, 113 girls); Grade 11: 225 students (107 boys, 118 girls); Grade 12: 237 students (115 boys, 122 girls).
Faculty School total: 182. In upper school: 63 men, 65 women; 90 have advanced degrees.
Subjects Offered 3-dimensional design, Advanced Placement courses, advanced studio art-AP, African American history, algebra, American government-AP, American history, American history-AP, American literature, American literature-AP, art, Asian studies, band, Basic programming, Bible, Bible studies, biology, biology-AP, British literature, calculus, calculus-AP, ceramics, chemistry, chemistry-AP, Chinese, chorus, computer programming, computer programming-AP, computer science, computer science-AP, conceptual physics, concert band, creative writing, dance, drama, earth science, economics, economics-AP, English, English as a foreign language, English language and composition-AP, English literature, English literature and composition-AP, English literature-AP, European history, European history-AP, expository writing, film and literature, fine arts, French, French language-AP, French literature-AP, geography, geometry, government-AP, government/civics, Hawaiian history, health, health education, history, Japanese, Japanese studies, jazz band, jazz ensemble, journalism, Latin, Latin-AP, leadership, macro/microeconomics-AP, macroeconomics-AP, Mandarin, marching band, mathematics, money management, music, newspaper, orchestra, photography, physical education, physics, physics-AP, pre-calculus, psychology, psychology-AP, religion, science, Shakespeare, social studies, Spanish, Spanish-AP, speech, statistics, statistics-AP, studio art-AP, theater, trigonometry, Web site design, world affairs, world history, world literature, writing fundamentals.
Graduation Requirements Algebra, arts and fine arts (art, music, dance, drama), Bible, biology, chemistry, computer science, English, European history, foreign language, geometry, literature, mathematics, physical education (includes health), physics, science, social studies (includes history), U.S. history.
Special Academic Programs Advanced Placement exam preparation; honors section; independent study; academic accommodation for the gifted, the musically talented, and the artistically talented; ESL (15 students enrolled).
College Admission Counseling 231 students graduated in 2008; all went to college, including Oregon State University; Santa Clara University; University of California, Los Angeles; University of Hawaii at Manoa; University of Southern California; University of Washington. 53% scored over 600 on SAT critical reading, 84% scored over 600 on SAT math, 62% scored over 600 on SAT writing, 65% scored over 26 on composite ACT.
Student Life Upper grades have specified standards of dress, student council. Discipline rests primarily with faculty. Attendance at religious services is required.
Summer Programs Enrichment, advancement, ESL, sports, art/fine arts, computer instruction programs offered; session focuses on reinforcement, enrichment, recreation, and sports; held on campus; accepts boys and girls; open to students from other schools. 3,000 students usually enrolled. 2009 schedule: June 12 to July 23. Application deadline: March 31.
Tuition and Aid Day student tuition: $14,900. Tuition installment plan (The Tuition Plan, monthly payment plans, semester and annual payment plans). Need-based scholarship grants available. In 2008–09, 12% of upper-school students received aid. Total amount of financial aid awarded in 2008–09: $1,580,000.
Admissions Traditional secondary-level entrance grade is 7. For fall 2008, 802 students applied for upper-level admission, 178 were accepted, 141 enrolled. SSAT required. Deadline for receipt of application materials: December 1. Application fee required: $100. On-campus interview recommended.
Athletics Interscholastic: aerobics/dance (girls), baseball (b), basketball (b,g), bowling (b,g), canoeing/kayaking (b,g), cheering (g), cross-country running (b,g), dance (b,g), dance team (g), diving (b,g), football (b), kayaking (b,g), modern dance (g), ocean paddling (b,g), soccer (b,g), softball (g), strength & conditioning (b,g), swimming and diving (b,g), tennis (b,g), track and field (b,g), volleyball (b,g), water polo (b,g), weight training (b,g), wrestling (b,g); coed interscholastic: ballet, golf, judo, tennis. 6 PE instructors, 170 coaches, 3 athletic trainers.
Computers Computers are regularly used in all academic classes. Computer network features include on-campus library services, online commercial services, Internet access, Internet filtering or blocking technology. Student e-mail accounts are available to students. The school has a published electronic and media policy.
Contact Patricia N. Liu, Director of Admission. 808-943-2222. Fax: 808-943-2375. E-mail: admission@iolani.org. Web site: www.iolani.org.

ISIDORE NEWMAN SCHOOL

1903 Jefferson Avenue
New Orleans, Louisiana 70115
Head of School: Dr. Thomas J. Locke

General Information Coeducational day college-preparatory school. Grades PK–12. Founded: 1903. Setting: urban. 11-acre campus. 11 buildings on campus. Approved or accredited by Independent Schools Association of the Southwest, Southern Association of Colleges and Schools, and Louisiana Department of Education. Member of National Association of Independent Schools. Endowment: $30 million. Total enrollment: 976. Upper school average class size: 18. Upper school faculty-student ratio: 1:18.
Upper School Student Profile Grade 6: 64 students (42 boys, 22 girls); Grade 7: 51 students (30 boys, 21 girls); Grade 8: 181 students (111 boys, 70 girls); Grade 9: 86 students (50 boys, 36 girls); Grade 10: 87 students (53 boys, 34 girls); Grade 11: 91 students (56 boys, 35 girls); Grade 12: 87 students (42 boys, 45 girls).
Faculty School total: 150. In upper school: 18 men, 40 women; 33 have advanced degrees.
Subjects Offered Advanced computer applications, Advanced Placement courses, algebra, American government-AP, American history, American history-AP, American literature, anatomy, art, art history, biology, biology-AP, calculus, calculus-AP, chemistry, Chinese, choral music, chorus, civics, communications,

computer science-AP, drama, English, English literature, environmental science, European history-AP, fine arts, French, French language-AP, French literature-AP, French-AP, genetics, geometry, government/civics, history, human development, humanities, Latin, Latin-AP, mathematics, modern European history, modern European history-AP, music, music theory, photojournalism, physical education, physics, physics-AP, physiology, science, sculpture, social studies, Spanish, Spanish language-AP, Spanish literature-AP, speech, statistics-AP, technical theater, theater, trigonometry, U.S. government-AP, U.S. history, U.S. history-AP, world history.

Graduation Requirements Arts and fine arts (art, music, dance, drama), computer science, English, foreign language, mathematics, physical education (includes health), science, social studies (includes history), speech, Senior Capstone Elective—one class each semester of senior year.

Special Academic Programs Advanced Placement exam preparation; honors section; independent study.

College Admission Counseling 97 students graduated in 2008; all went to college, including Boston College; Louisiana State University and Agricultural and Mechanical College; The University of Texas at Austin; Tulane University; University of Georgia; University of Pennsylvania. Mean SAT critical reading: 646, mean SAT math: 663, mean SAT writing: 661, mean combined SAT: 1970. 59% scored over 600 on SAT critical reading, 71% scored over 600 on SAT math, 62% scored over 600 on SAT writing, 61% scored over 1800 on combined SAT.

Student Life Upper grades have specified standards of dress, student council, honor system. Discipline rests equally with students and faculty.

Summer Programs Enrichment, art/fine arts, computer instruction programs offered; held both on and off campus; held at various locations; accepts boys and girls; open to students from other schools. 2009 schedule: June 1 to July 31. Application deadline: none.

Tuition and Aid Day student tuition: $16,431. Tuition installment plan (Sallie Mae tuition loans). Need-based scholarship grants, Sallie Mae Loans available. In 2008–09, 15% of upper-school students received aid. Total amount of financial aid awarded in 2008–09: $492,391.

Admissions Traditional secondary-level entrance grade is 9. For fall 2008, 72 students applied for upper-level admission, 42 were accepted, 27 enrolled. ERB (CTP-Verbal, Quantitative), ERB CTP III, independent norms, Individual IQ, Achievement and behavior rating scale, ISEE, school's own test and writing sample required. Deadline for receipt of application materials: none. Application fee required: $35. Interview required.

Athletics Interscholastic: aquatics (boys, girls), baseball (b), basketball (b,g), cross-country running (b,g), football (b), golf (b,g), gymnastics (b,g), indoor track & field (b), soccer (b,g), softball (g), swimming and diving (b,g), tennis (b,g), track and field (b,g), volleyball (g); coed interscholastic: cheering. 15 coaches, 2 athletic trainers.

Computers Computers are regularly used in all academic classes. Computer network features include on-campus library services, online commercial services, Internet access, wireless campus network, Internet filtering or blocking technology. Campus intranet and student e-mail accounts are available to students. Students grades are available online. The school has a published electronic and media policy.

Contact Mrs. Ladd Sheets, Admission Assistant. 504-896-6323. Fax: 504-896-8597. E-mail: lsheets@newmanschool.org. Web site: www.newmanschool.org.

ANNOUNCEMENT FROM THE SCHOOL For more than 100 years, Isidore Newman School has offered a challenging, sequential curriculum in a supportive learning environment. As they gain knowledge in the humanities, sciences, and fine arts, students demonstrate a mastery of material, meet high academic standards, and develop their capacity for critical thinking and creativity. A variety of extracurricular activities complements the program. For further information, families may access the Isidore Newman School Web site at www.newmanschool.org.

ISLAND SCHOOL

3-1875 Kaumualii Highway
Lihue, Hawaii 96766-9597

Head of School: Mr. Robert Springer

General Information Coeducational day college-preparatory, arts, bilingual studies, and technology school. Grades PK–12. Founded: 1977. Setting: small town. 38-acre campus. 11 buildings on campus. Approved or accredited by Academy of Orton-Gillingham Practitioners and Educators, The Hawaii Council of Private Schools, Western Association of Schools and Colleges, and Hawaii Department of Education. Language of instruction: Spanish. Endowment: $800,000. Total enrollment: 336. Upper school average class size: 15. Upper school faculty-student ratio: 1:11.

Upper School Student Profile Grade 9: 24 students (12 boys, 12 girls); Grade 10: 39 students (18 boys, 21 girls); Grade 11: 21 students (13 boys, 8 girls); Grade 12: 24 students (10 boys, 14 girls).

Faculty School total: 45. In upper school: 6 men, 17 women; 9 have advanced degrees.

Subjects Offered Intro to computers, introduction to literature, keyboarding/computer, language structure, literature, marine ecology, marine science, mathematics, medieval history, medieval literature, microeconomics, modern Western civilization, modern world history, money management, music, news writing, performing arts, photo shop, photography, physical education, physical fitness, poetry, pre-algebra, pre-calculus, religious studies, SAT/ACT preparation, sex education, Shakespeare, Shakespearean histories, short story, social studies, stagecraft, stock market, student government, theater, theater design and production, trigonometry, U.S. government, U.S. government and politics, U.S. government-AP, U.S. history, U.S. literature, world history, world religions, world studies, world wide web design, writing, writing workshop, yearbook.

Graduation Requirements Drama, electives, English, foreign language, life skills, mathematics, music, physical education (includes health), science, social studies (includes history), visual arts, technology tools.

Special Academic Programs Honors section; independent study; study at local college for college credit; academic accommodation for the gifted.

College Admission Counseling 24 students graduated in 2008; all went to college, including Pepperdine University; University of Denver. Mean SAT critical reading: 551, mean SAT math: 554.

Student Life Upper grades have specified standards of dress, student council, honor system. Discipline rests primarily with faculty.

Summer Programs Remediation, advancement programs offered; session focuses on broadening of students' academic abilities; held on campus; accepts boys and girls; open to students from other schools. 30 students usually enrolled. 2009 schedule: June 14 to July 31. Application deadline: June.

Tuition and Aid Day student tuition: $7860. Tuition installment plan (FACTS Tuition Payment Plan). Need-based scholarship grants available. In 2008–09, 41% of upper-school students received aid.

Admissions Traditional secondary-level entrance grade is 9. For fall 2008, 80 students applied for upper-level admission, 58 were accepted, 49 enrolled. Admissions testing, any standardized test, essay, Math Placement Exam and Stanford Achievement Test required. Deadline for receipt of application materials: none. Application fee required: $40. Interview required.

Athletics Interscholastic: basketball (boys), cross-country running (b,g), ocean paddling (b,g), riflery (b,g), swimming and diving (b,g), tennis (b,g), track and field (b,g); intramural: basketball (b,g), cross-country running (b,g), soccer (b,g), softball (b,g), volleyball (b,g); coed interscholastic: ocean paddling, riflery; coed intramural: baseball, basketball, dance, flag football, ocean paddling, roller hockey, running, scuba diving, self defense, soccer, softball, volleyball, yoga. 1 PE instructor, 11 coaches.

Computers Computers are regularly used in business, data processing, desktop publishing, English, history, information technology, introduction to technology, mathematics classes. Computer network features include on-campus library services, Internet access, Linux labs.

Contact Mr. Sean Magoun, Admission Director. 808-246-0233 Ext. 241. Fax: 808-245-6053. E-mail: sean@ischool.org. Web site: www.ischool.org.

JACK M. BARRACK HEBREW ACADEMY (FORMERLY AKIBA HEBREW ACADEMY)

272 South Bryn Mawr Avenue
Bryn Mawr, Pennsylvania 19010

Head of School: Dr. Steven M. Brown

General Information Coeducational day college-preparatory and religious studies school, affiliated with Jewish faith. Grades 6–12. Founded: 1946. Setting: suburban. Nearest major city is Philadelphia. 33-acre campus. 2 buildings on campus. Approved or accredited by Middle States Association of Colleges and Schools and Pennsylvania Department of Education. Member of National Association of Independent Schools. Languages of instruction: English and Hebrew. Endowment: $37 million. Total enrollment: 309. Upper school average class size: 14. Upper school faculty-student ratio: 1:8.

Upper School Student Profile Grade 9: 55 students (28 boys, 27 girls); Grade 10: 53 students (27 boys, 26 girls); Grade 11: 59 students (31 boys, 28 girls); Grade 12: 56 students (36 boys, 20 girls). 100% of students are Jewish.

Faculty School total: 62. In upper school: 19 men, 33 women; 48 have advanced degrees.

Subjects Offered Algebra, American history, American literature, art, astronomy, Bible studies, biology, calculus, chemistry, community service, computer math, computer programming, computer science, creative writing, earth science, English, English literature, environmental science, environmental science-AP, ethics, European history, French, geometry, government/civics, grammar, health, Hebrew, history, Jewish studies, Latin, mathematics, music, physical education, physics, public speaking, religion, science, social studies, Spanish, trigonometry, world history, writing.

Graduation Requirements English, foreign language, mathematics, physical education (includes health), religion (includes Bible studies and theology), science, social studies (includes history), senior community service project: 150 hours in the senior year in, order to graduate.

Special Academic Programs 8 Advanced Placement exams for which test preparation is offered; accelerated programs; independent study; term-away projects; study at local college for college credit; study abroad; academic accommodation for the gifted; remedial reading and/or remedial writing; remedial math; special instructional classes for deaf students.

College Admission Counseling 68 students graduated in 2008; all went to college, including Brandeis University; New York University; University of Maryland,

College Park; University of Pennsylvania; University of Pittsburgh. Median SAT critical reading: 610, median SAT math: 600.

Student Life Upper grades have specified standards of dress, student council. Discipline rests primarily with faculty.

Tuition and Aid Day student tuition: $21,350. Tuition installment plan (Key Tuition Payment Plan, monthly payment plans, individually arranged payment plans). Merit scholarship grants, need-based scholarship grants available. In 2008–09, 33% of upper-school students received aid; total upper-school merit-scholarship money awarded: $20,000. Total amount of financial aid awarded in 2008–09: $980,000.

Admissions Traditional secondary-level entrance grade is 9. For fall 2008, 97 students applied for upper-level admission, 84 were accepted, 75 enrolled. ISEE required. Deadline for receipt of application materials: none. Application fee required: $40. On-campus interview required.

Athletics Interscholastic: baseball (boys), basketball (b,g), soccer (b,g), softball (g), tennis (b,g), track and field (g); intramural: basketball (b,g), field hockey (b,g), golf (b,g), running (b,g), soccer (b,g), track and field (g), volleyball (b,g); coed interscholastic: cross-country running, soccer, swimming and diving. 2 PE instructors, 16 coaches.

Computers Computers are regularly used in foreign language, French, health, history, humanities, independent study, information technology, introduction to technology, journalism, keyboarding, Latin, library, literary magazine, mathematics, media production, multimedia, news writing, newspaper, photojournalism, programming, publications, remedial study skills, research skills, SAT preparation, science, social sciences, Spanish, study skills, technology, video film production, Web site design, word processing, writing, yearbook classes. Computer network features include on-campus library services, online commercial services, Internet access, wireless campus network, Internet filtering or blocking technology. Campus intranet, student e-mail accounts, and computer access in designated common areas are available to students. Students grades are available online. The school has a published electronic and media policy.

Contact Vivian Young, Director of Admissions. 610-922-2350. Fax: 610-922-2301. E-mail: vyoung@jbha.org. Web site: www.jbha.org.

JACKSON ACADEMY

4908 Ridgewood Road
PO Box 14978
Jackson, Mississippi 39236-4978

Head of School: Dr. Pat Taylor

General Information Coeducational day college-preparatory and technology school. Grades PK–12. Founded: 1959. Setting: urban. 48-acre campus. 6 buildings on campus. Approved or accredited by Mississippi Private School Association, Southern Association of Colleges and Schools, and Southern Association of Independent Schools. Member of National Association of Independent Schools. Endowment: $100,500. Total enrollment: 1,373. Upper school average class size: 21. Upper school faculty-student ratio: 1:15.

Upper School Student Profile Grade 10: 79 students (46 boys, 33 girls); Grade 11: 89 students (44 boys, 45 girls); Grade 12: 99 students (50 boys, 49 girls).

Faculty School total: 111. In upper school: 14 men, 32 women; 22 have advanced degrees.

Subjects Offered Accounting, algebra, American government, American history, American history-AP, American literature, anatomy and physiology, art, art history, band, Bible, biology, biology-AP, calculus, calculus-AP, chemistry, chemistry-AP, chorus, computer applications, computer programming, creative writing, driver education, economics, English, English language-AP, English literature, English literature-AP, film history, forensics, French, geography, geometry, Latin, physical education, physical science, physics, physics-AP, pre-calculus, sociology, Spanish, speech, state government, studio art, U.S. government and politics-AP, world history, world literature.

Graduation Requirements Electives, English, foreign language, mathematics, science, social studies (includes history).

Special Academic Programs Advanced Placement exam preparation; honors section; independent study; study at local college for college credit; programs in general development for dyslexic students.

College Admission Counseling 108 students graduated in 2008; all went to college, including Hinds Community College; Millsaps College; Mississippi College; Mississippi State University; University of Mississippi; University of Southern Mississippi. Median SAT critical reading: 580, median SAT math: 650, median SAT writing: 640, median combined SAT: 1870, median composite ACT: 27. 45% scored over 600 on SAT critical reading, 68% scored over 600 on SAT math, 60% scored over 600 on SAT writing, 60% scored over 1800 on combined SAT.

Student Life Upper grades have uniform requirement, student council. Discipline rests primarily with faculty.

Summer Programs Remediation, enrichment, advancement, sports, art/fine arts, computer instruction programs offered; session focuses on a well-rounded experience designed to meet children's needs; held on campus; accepts boys and girls; open to students from other schools. 125 students usually enrolled. 2009 schedule: June 1 to July 17. Application deadline: none.

Tuition and Aid Day student tuition: $9900. Tuition installment plan (monthly bank draft, biannual payment plan). Tuition reduction for siblings, need-based scholarship grants available. In 2008–09, 25% of upper-school students received aid. Total amount of financial aid awarded in 2008–09: $129,070.

Admissions Traditional secondary-level entrance grade is 10. For fall 2008, 13 students applied for upper-level admission, 11 were accepted, 11 enrolled. Otis-Lennon, Stanford Achievement Test required. Deadline for receipt of application materials: none. Application fee required: $50. On-campus interview required.

Athletics Interscholastic: baseball (boys), basketball (b,g), cheering (g), cross-country running (b,g), drill team (g), football (b), golf (b,g), soccer (b,g), softball (g), tennis (b,g), track and field (b,g); intramural: basketball (b,g); coed interscholastic: outdoor activities, swimming and diving. 2 PE instructors, 7 coaches.

Computers Computers are regularly used in English, history, mathematics, publishing, science classes. Computer network features include on-campus library services, Internet access, Internet filtering or blocking technology. Students grades are available online.

Contact Mrs. Linda C. Purviance, Director of Admissions. 601-362-9677. Fax: 601-364-5722. E-mail: lpurviance@jacksonacademy.org. Web site: www.jacksonacademy.org.

JACKSON CHRISTIAN SCHOOL

832 Country Club Lane
Jackson, Tennessee 38305

Head of School: Dr. Rick Brooks

General Information Coeducational day college-preparatory school, affiliated with Church of Christ. Grades JK–12. Founded: 1976. Setting: suburban. Nearest major city is Memphis. 30-acre campus. 6 buildings on campus. Approved or accredited by Southern Association of Colleges and Schools and Tennessee Department of Education. Endowment: $875,000. Total enrollment: 909. Upper school average class size: 19. Upper school faculty-student ratio: 1:19.

Upper School Student Profile Grade 6: 70 students (36 boys, 34 girls); Grade 7: 90 students (45 boys, 45 girls); Grade 8: 71 students (33 boys, 38 girls); Grade 9: 84 students (43 boys, 41 girls); Grade 10: 77 students (45 boys, 32 girls); Grade 11: 80 students (39 boys, 41 girls); Grade 12: 82 students (42 boys, 40 girls). 44% of students are members of Church of Christ.

Faculty School total: 65. In upper school: 13 men, 26 women; 13 have advanced degrees.

Subjects Offered Advanced chemistry, advanced computer applications, advanced studio art-AP, algebra, American government, American history, anatomy and physiology, art, baseball, basketball, Bible, Bible studies, biology, calculus, chemistry, choir, chorus, current events, ecology, economics, English, English composition, geometry, government, government/civics, honors English, journalism, keyboarding, life science, physical education, physical science, physics, pre-calculus, psychology, Spanish, state history, theater, theater arts, trigonometry, U.S. government, U.S. history, word processing, world geography, world history.

Graduation Requirements 20th century world history, 3-dimensional art, 3-dimensional design, arts and fine arts (art, music, dance, drama), English, foreign language, mathematics, physical education (includes health), religion (includes Bible studies and theology), science, social studies (includes history), must take the ACT test.

Special Academic Programs Honors section; study at local college for college credit.

College Admission Counseling 57 students graduated in 2008; all went to college, including Freed-Hardeman University; Harding University; Jackson State Community College; Middle Tennessee State University; The University of Tennessee at Martin; Union University.

Student Life Upper grades have uniform requirement, student council, honor system. Discipline rests primarily with faculty. Attendance at religious services is required.

Summer Programs Remediation programs offered; session focuses on make-up failed courses; held on campus; accepts boys and girls; not open to students from other schools. 8 students usually enrolled. 2009 schedule: June to July.

Tuition and Aid Day student tuition: $6545. Guaranteed tuition plan. Tuition installment plan (monthly payment plans, quarterly payment plan, semester payment plan, pay-in-full discount). Tuition reduction for siblings, need-based scholarship grants available. In 2008–09, 15% of upper-school students received aid. Total amount of financial aid awarded in 2008–09: $15,218.

Admissions Traditional secondary-level entrance grade is 9. For fall 2008, 63 students applied for upper-level admission, 57 were accepted, 55 enrolled. Deadline for receipt of application materials: none. Application fee required: $100. Interview required.

Athletics Interscholastic: baseball (boys), basketball (b,g), cheering (g), cross-country running (b,g), football (b), golf (b,g), soccer (b,g), softball (g), tennis (b,g), track and field (b,g); coed interscholastic: cheering. 3 PE instructors, 10 coaches.

Computers Computers are regularly used in science classes. Computer network features include Internet access, wireless campus network, Internet filtering or blocking technology. Student e-mail accounts and computer access in designated common areas are available to students. Students grades are available online.

Contact Jamie Gatlin, Director of Admissions. 731-668-8055. Fax: 731-664-5763. E-mail: jgatlin@jcseagles.org. Web site: www.jcseagles.org.

JACKSON PREPARATORY SCHOOL

3100 Lakeland Drive
Jackson, Mississippi 39232

Head of School: Susan Lindsay

General Information Coeducational day college-preparatory school. Grades 6–12. Founded: 1970. Setting: urban. 74-acre campus. 6 buildings on campus. Approved or accredited by Mississippi Private School Association, Southern Association of Colleges and Schools, Southern Association of Independent Schools, and The College Board. Member of National Association of Independent Schools. Endowment: $993,373. Total enrollment: 800. Upper school average class size: 16. Upper school faculty-student ratio: 1:11.

Upper School Student Profile Grade 10: 100 students (63 boys, 37 girls); Grade 11: 116 students (59 boys, 57 girls); Grade 12: 144 students (78 boys, 66 girls).

Faculty School total: 81. In upper school: 15 men, 37 women; 33 have advanced degrees.

Subjects Offered Accounting, advanced chemistry, Advanced Placement courses, algebra, American government, American history, American history-AP, American literature, art, Asian studies, Bible as literature, biology, biology-AP, British literature, calculus, calculus-AP, chemistry, chemistry-AP, choral music, civics, classical studies, computer science, creative writing, debate, discrete math, drama, driver education, earth science, economics, English, English literature, English literature-AP, European history, film, fine arts, finite math, French, geography, geometry, government-AP, government/civics, grammar, Greek, Greek culture, history, honors algebra, honors English, honors geometry, journalism, Latin, Latin-AP, mathematics, music, physical education, physics, physics-AP, pre-algebra, pre-calculus, science, social studies, Spanish, trigonometry, U.S. government, U.S. government-AP, U.S. history, U.S. history-AP, world history, world literature.

Graduation Requirements Arts and fine arts (art, music, dance, drama), computer applications, English, foreign language, mathematics, science, social studies (includes history).

Special Academic Programs Advanced Placement exam preparation; honors section; academic accommodation for the gifted, the musically talented, and the artistically talented; programs in English, mathematics, general development for dyslexic students.

College Admission Counseling 132 students graduated in 2007; all went to college, including Mississippi College; Mississippi State University; The University of Alabama; University of Mississippi; Vanderbilt University. Mean SAT critical reading: 567, mean SAT math: 604, mean SAT writing: 585, mean composite ACT: 26.

Student Life Upper grades have specified standards of dress, student council, honor system. Discipline rests primarily with faculty.

Tuition and Aid Day student tuition: $8100. Tuition installment plan (monthly payment plans). Need-based scholarship grants available. In 2007–08, 11% of upper-school students received aid. Total amount of financial aid awarded in 2007–08: $195,000.

Admissions Traditional secondary-level entrance grade is 10. For fall 2007, 18 students applied for upper-level admission, 11 were accepted, 10 enrolled. OLSAT, Stanford Achievement Test required. Deadline for receipt of application materials: none. Application fee required: $40. Interview required.

Athletics Interscholastic: baseball (boys), basketball (b,g), cheering (g), cross-country running (b,g), dance team (g), football (b), Frisbee (b), soccer (b,g), softball (g), swimming and diving (b,g), tennis (b,g), track and field (b,g), ultimate Frisbee (b); intramural: basketball (b,g), Frisbee (b), soccer (b,g), volleyball (b,g); coed interscholastic: cheering, golf. 4 coaches.

Computers Computers are regularly used in all classes. Computer network features include on-campus library services, online commercial services, Internet access, Electric Library, EBSCOhost®, GaleNet, Grolier Online, NewsBank, online subscription services. The school has a published electronic and media policy.

Contact Lesley W. Morton, Director of Admission. 601-932-8106 Ext. 1. Fax: 601-936-4068. E-mail: lmorton@jacksonprep.net. Web site: www.jacksonprep.net.

ANNOUNCEMENT FROM THE SCHOOL Specializing in secondary education since 1970, Jackson Preparatory School (Prep) has graduated more National Merit Semifinalists than any other school in the state, including 17 from the class of 2008. Prep offers the only Classical Heritage diploma in the state, and the School's curriculum includes thirteen Advanced Placement courses, as well as Greek and Mandarin Chinese. Complementing Prep's exemplary academic benchmarks are a rich palette of activities and a history of athletic achievements.

THE JANUS SCHOOL

Mount Joy, Pennsylvania
See Special Needs Schools section.

JESUIT COLLEGE PREPARATORY SCHOOL

12345 Inwood Road
Dallas, Texas 75244

Head of School: Mr. Mike Earsing

General Information Boys' day college-preparatory school, affiliated with Roman Catholic Church (Jesuit order). Grades 9–12. Founded: 1942. Setting: suburban. 27-acre campus. 2 buildings on campus. Approved or accredited by Jesuit Secondary Education Association, National Catholic Education Association, Southern Association of Colleges and Schools, Texas Catholic Conference, and Texas Department of Education. Endowment: $25.6 million. Total enrollment: 1,040. Upper school average class size: 17. Upper school faculty-student ratio: 1:11.

Upper School Student Profile Grade 9: 278 students (278 boys); Grade 10: 255 students (255 boys); Grade 11: 251 students (251 boys); Grade 12: 256 students (256 boys). 80.9% of students are Roman Catholic Church (Jesuit order).

Faculty School total: 109. In upper school: 76 men, 33 women; 61 have advanced degrees.

Subjects Offered Advanced chemistry, advanced computer applications, advanced math, American literature-AP, American studies, art, art appreciation, art-AP, arts, band, Bible, biology, biology-AP, British literature, British literature-AP, calculus, calculus-AP, Catholic belief and practice, ceramics, chemistry, chemistry-AP, choir, Christian ethics, church history, civics, college counseling, community service, composition, composition-AP, computer applications, computer graphics, computer science, computer science-AP, contemporary issues, discrete mathematics, drama, drama performance, drama workshop, drawing, drawing and design, driver education, earth science, economics, economics-AP, English, English composition, English language and composition-AP, English language-AP, English literature, English literature and composition-AP, English literature-AP, English-AP, English/composition-AP, ethical decision making, European history, fine arts, French, French-AP, general science, geometry, government, government-AP, grammar, guitar, health, history, history-AP, honors algebra, honors English, honors geometry, honors U.S. history, honors world history, instrumental music, jazz band, journalism, Latin, literature and composition-AP, marching band, mathematics, mathematics-AP, microcomputer technology applications, music, music appreciation, musical productions, orchestra, peace and justice, peer ministry, performing arts, physical education, physics, physics-AP, pottery, prayer/spirituality, pre-calculus, psychology, public speaking, publications, religion, scripture, social studies, Spanish, Spanish language-AP, Spanish literature-AP, Spanish-AP, speech, speech and debate, speech and oral interpretations, statistics, student government, student publications, studio art, studio art-AP, symphonic band, theater, theology, U.S. government, U.S. government-AP, U.S. history, U.S. history-AP, U.S. literature, world history, world history-AP.

Graduation Requirements Arts and fine arts (art, music, dance, drama), computer science, English, foreign language, mathematics, physical education (includes health), science, social studies (includes history), theology. Community service is required.

Special Academic Programs Advanced Placement exam preparation; honors section; study at local college for college credit.

College Admission Counseling 250 students graduated in 2008; all went to college, including Saint Louis University; Texas A&M University; Texas Christian University; The University of Kansas; The University of Texas at Austin. Mean SAT critical reading: 610, mean SAT math: 616, mean SAT writing: 605.

Student Life Upper grades have specified standards of dress, student council, honor system. Discipline rests primarily with faculty. Attendance at religious services is required.

Summer Programs Remediation, enrichment, advancement, sports, art/fine arts, computer instruction programs offered; session focuses on youth recreation; held on campus; accepts boys and girls; open to students from other schools. 800 students usually enrolled. 2009 schedule: June 15 to July 10. Application deadline: May 30.

Tuition and Aid Day student tuition: $11,800. Tuition installment plan (FACTS Tuition Payment Plan, individually arranged payment plans). Merit scholarship grants, need-based scholarship grants, paying campus jobs available. In 2008–09, 25% of upper-school students received aid; total upper-school merit-scholarship money awarded: $56,000. Total amount of financial aid awarded in 2008–09: $1,233,850.

Admissions Traditional secondary-level entrance grade is 9. For fall 2008, 486 students applied for upper-level admission, 318 were accepted, 278 enrolled. ISEE required. Deadline for receipt of application materials: January 9. Application fee required: $75. Interview required.

Athletics Interscholastic: baseball, basketball, crew, cross-country running, diving, fencing, football, golf, ice hockey, lacrosse, power lifting, rugby, soccer, swimming and diving, tennis, track and field, wrestling; intramural: basketball, flagball, indoor soccer, ultimate Frisbee; coed interscholastic: cheering, drill team. 6 PE instructors, 30 coaches, 2 athletic trainers.

Computers Computers are regularly used in college planning, desktop publishing, English, introduction to technology, literary magazine, newspaper, technology, Web site design, writing, yearbook classes. Computer network features include on-campus library services, online commercial services, Internet access, Internet filtering or blocking technology. Campus intranet, student e-mail accounts, and computer access in designated common areas are available to students. Students grades are available online. The school has a published electronic and media policy.

Contact Mrs. Susie Herrmann, Admissions Assistant. 972-387-8700 Ext. 453. Fax: 972-980-6707. E-mail: sherrmann@jesuitcp.org. Web site: www.jesuitcp.org.

JESUIT HIGH SCHOOL

1200 Jacob Lane
Carmichael, California 95608

Head of School: Rev. Edward S. Fassett, SJ

General Information Boys' day college-preparatory and religious studies school, affiliated with Roman Catholic Church. Grades 9–12. Founded: 1963. Setting: suburban. Nearest major city is Sacramento. 46-acre campus. 12 buildings on campus. Approved or accredited by National Catholic Education Association, Western Association of Schools and Colleges, and California Department of Education. Member of Secondary School Admission Test Board. Total enrollment: 1,088. Upper school average class size: 25. Upper school faculty-student ratio: 1:18.

Upper School Student Profile Grade 9: 283 students (283 boys); Grade 10: 283 students (283 boys); Grade 11: 263 students (263 boys); Grade 12: 259 students (259 boys). 80% of students are Roman Catholic.

Faculty School total: 81. In upper school: 58 men, 23 women; 48 have advanced degrees.

Subjects Offered Algebra, American history, American literature, art, art history, arts, biology, business, calculus, chemistry, computer programming, computer science, drama, driver education, earth science, economics, English, English literature, environmental science, ethics, European history, fine arts, French, geography, geometry, German, government/civics, grammar, health, history, journalism, Latin, mathematics, music, physical education, physics, religion, science, social science, social studies, Spanish, speech, theater, theology, trigonometry, typing, world history, world literature, writing.

Graduation Requirements Arts and fine arts (art, music, dance, drama), English, foreign language, mathematics, physical education (includes health), religion (includes Bible studies and theology), science, social studies (includes history), 60 hours of community service.

Special Academic Programs Advanced Placement exam preparation; honors section.

College Admission Counseling 252 students graduated in 2008; 247 went to college, including California Polytechnic State University, San Luis Obispo; California State University, Sacramento; Loyola Marymount University; Santa Clara University; University of California System; University of Southern California. Other: 2 went to work, 3 entered military service. Mean SAT critical reading: 574, mean SAT math: 592, mean SAT writing: 577, mean composite ACT: 24.

Student Life Upper grades have specified standards of dress, student council, honor system. Discipline rests primarily with faculty. Attendance at religious services is required.

Summer Programs Remediation, enrichment, advancement, computer instruction programs offered; held on campus; accepts boys and girls; open to students from other schools. 1,200 students usually enrolled. 2009 schedule: June 15 to July 24. Application deadline: June 1.

Tuition and Aid Day student tuition: $11,230. Tuition installment plan (monthly payment plans). Need-based scholarship grants, paying campus jobs available. In 2008–09, 15% of upper-school students received aid. Total amount of financial aid awarded in 2008–09: $740,000.

Admissions Traditional secondary-level entrance grade is 9. For fall 2008, 465 students applied for upper-level admission, 290 were accepted, 290 enrolled. High School Placement Test required. Deadline for receipt of application materials: February 6. Application fee required: $30. On-campus interview required.

Athletics Interscholastic: baseball, basketball, cross-country running, diving, football, golf, lacrosse, rugby, soccer, swimming and diving, tennis, track and field, volleyball, water polo, wrestling; intramural: baseball, basketball, bowling, football, soccer, volleyball. 6 PE instructors, 15 coaches, 1 athletic trainer.

Computers Computers are regularly used in English, mathematics, social studies classes. Computer resources include on-campus library services, online commercial services, Internet access.

Contact Mr. Gerry Lane, Director of Admissions. 916-482-6060 Ext. 227. Fax: 916-482-2310. E-mail: admissions@jhssac.org. Web site: www.jhssac.org.

JESUIT HIGH SCHOOL OF TAMPA

4701 North Himes Avenue
Tampa, Florida 33614-6694

Head of School: Mr. Joseph Sabin

General Information Boys' day college-preparatory and College Prep school, affiliated with Roman Catholic Church. Grades 9–12. Founded: 1899. Setting: urban. 40-acre campus. 9 buildings on campus. Approved or accredited by Jesuit Secondary Education Association, National Catholic Education Association, Southern Association of Colleges and Schools, and Florida Department of Education. Total enrollment: 675. Upper school average class size: 21. Upper school faculty-student ratio: 1:12.

Upper School Student Profile Grade 9: 194 students (194 boys); Grade 10: 168 students (168 boys); Grade 11: 153 students (153 boys); Grade 12: 160 students (160 boys). 75% of students are Roman Catholic.

Faculty School total: 50. In upper school: 35 men, 15 women; 41 have advanced degrees.

Subjects Offered Algebra, American foreign policy, American government, American history, analytic geometry, anatomy, art, biology, calculus, calculus-AP, chemistry, chemistry-AP, chorus, computer science, economics, English, English language and composition-AP, English literature and composition-AP, ethics, European history, French, geometry, global studies, health, Latin, marine biology, math analysis, music, physical education, physics, physiology, pre-calculus, psychology, sociology, Spanish, Spanish language-AP, speech, statistics, studio art—AP, theology, trigonometry, U.S. government and politics-AP, U.S. history-AP, world history, world history-AP, writing.

Graduation Requirements Arts and fine arts (art, music, dance, drama), English, foreign language, mathematics, physical education (includes health), science, social studies (includes history), theology, 150 hours of community service (additional 20 hours for National Honor Society members).

Special Academic Programs 9 Advanced Placement exams for which test preparation is offered; honors section.

College Admission Counseling 139 students graduated in 2008; all went to college, including Florida Gulf Coast University; Florida State University; Georgia Institute of Technology; University of Florida; University of South Florida. Median SAT critical reading: 585, median SAT math: 609, median SAT writing: 582, median combined SAT: 1776, median composite ACT: 25.

Student Life Upper grades have specified standards of dress, student council. Discipline rests primarily with faculty. Attendance at religious services is required.

Summer Programs Remediation programs offered; session focuses on remediation only; held on campus; accepts boys; not open to students from other schools. 2009 schedule: June 15 to July 17.

Tuition and Aid Day student tuition: $11,100. Tuition installment plan (FACTS Tuition Payment Plan). Need-based scholarship grants available. In 2008–09, 20% of upper-school students received aid. Total amount of financial aid awarded in 2008–09: $800,000.

Admissions Traditional secondary-level entrance grade is 9. For fall 2008, 302 students applied for upper-level admission, 281 were accepted, 199 enrolled. High School Placement Test (closed version) from Scholastic Testing Service required. Deadline for receipt of application materials: January 10. Application fee required: $50.

Athletics Interscholastic: baseball, basketball, bowling, cross-country running, diving, football, golf, soccer, swimming and diving, tennis, track and field, wrestling; intramural: basketball, football, Frisbee, sailing, softball, ultimate Frisbee. 2 PE instructors, 1 athletic trainer.

Computers Computer network features include on-campus library services, online commercial services, Internet access, Internet filtering or blocking technology. Campus intranet and computer access in designated common areas are available to students. Students grades are available online. The school has a published electronic and media policy.

Contact Mr. Steve Matesich, Director of Admissions. 813-877-5344 Ext. 264. Fax: 813-872-1853. E-mail: smatesich@jesuittampa.org. Web site: www.jesuittampa.org.

JOHN BAPST MEMORIAL HIGH SCHOOL

100 Broadway
Bangor, Maine 04401

Head of School: Mr. Melville MacKay

General Information Coeducational day college-preparatory school. Grades 9–12. Founded: 1928. Setting: urban. 1 building on campus. Approved or accredited by Association of Independent Schools in New England and New England Association of Schools and Colleges. Endowment: $860,000. Total enrollment: 467. Upper school average class size: 16. Upper school faculty-student ratio: 1:12.

Upper School Student Profile Grade 9: 121 students (53 boys, 68 girls); Grade 10: 121 students (57 boys, 64 girls); Grade 11: 102 students (35 boys, 67 girls); Grade 12: 123 students (60 boys, 63 girls).

Faculty School total: 40. In upper school: 19 men, 21 women; 22 have advanced degrees.

Subjects Offered 3-dimensional art, 3-dimensional design, advanced biology, advanced chemistry, advanced math, Advanced Placement courses, advanced studio art-AP, algebra, American history, American history-AP, American literature, anatomy, ancient world history, anthropology, art, art-AP, arts, astronomy, band, Basic programming, biology, biology-AP, British literature (honors), British literature-AP, calculus, calculus-AP, chemistry, chemistry-AP, chorus, college admission preparation, college awareness, college counseling, college placement, computer applications, computer graphics, computer multimedia, computer programming, concert band, concert choir, creative writing, drama, drawing, drawing and design, earth science, ecology, economics, English, English language and composition-AP, English literature, English literature and composition-AP, fine arts, foreign language, French, French studies, geology, geometry, graphic design, health and wellness, history-AP, Holocaust seminar, honors algebra, honors English, honors geometry, information technology, journalism, language-AP, Latin, mathematics-AP, modern Chinese history, music, music performance, music theory, oceanography, physical education, physical science, physics, physiology, political science, pre-calculus, programming, psychology, social sciences, social studies, sociology, Spanish, Spanish language-AP, speech and oral interpretations, statistics-AP, studio art, studio art-AP, trigonometry, world history.

Graduation Requirements Arts and fine arts (art, music, dance, drama), computer science, English, foreign language, health education, mathematics, physical education (includes health), science, social studies (includes history).

Special Academic Programs 11 Advanced Placement exams for which test preparation is offered; honors section; independent study; study at local college for college credit.

College Admission Counseling 109 students graduated in 2008; 105 went to college, including Colby College; Maine Maritime Academy; University of Maine; University of New Hampshire; University of Southern Maine. Other: 2 went to work, 1 entered military service, 1 had other specific plans. Mean SAT critical reading: 558, mean SAT math: 554, mean SAT writing: 538.

Student Life Upper grades have specified standards of dress, student council. Discipline rests primarily with faculty.

Tuition and Aid Day student tuition: $8700. Tuition installment plan (Insured Tuition Payment Plan, Academic Management Services Plan, monthly payment plans, individually arranged payment plans, biannual payment plan). Tuition reduction for siblings, need-based scholarship grants available. In 2008–09, 4% of upper-school students received aid. Total amount of financial aid awarded in 2008–09: $94,240.

Admissions Traditional secondary-level entrance grade is 9. For fall 2008, 173 students applied for upper-level admission, 157 were accepted, 135 enrolled. Academic Profile Tests and Achievement/Aptitude/Writing required. Deadline for receipt of application materials: March 1. No application fee required. Interview recommended.

Athletics Interscholastic: baseball (boys), basketball (b,g), cross-country running (b,g), diving (b,g), field hockey (g), football (b), gymnastics (g), ice hockey (b,g), skiing (downhill) (b,g), soccer (b,g), softball (g), swimming and diving (b,g), tennis (b,g), track and field (b,g), wrestling (b); coed interscholastic: alpine skiing, golf, nordic skiing; coed intramural: badminton, floor hockey. 2 PE instructors.

Computers Computers are regularly used in college planning, computer applications, creative writing, English, graphic design, library, literary magazine, mathematics, publications, technology classes. Computer network features include on-campus library services, online commercial services, Internet access, wireless campus network, Internet filtering or blocking technology. Campus intranet and computer access in designated common areas are available to students. Students grades are available online. The school has a published electronic and media policy.

Contact Mrs. Colleen C. Grover, Dean of Students. 207-947-0313. Fax: 207-941-2474. E-mail: cgrover@johnbapst.org. Web site: www.johnbapst.org.

JOHN BURROUGHS SCHOOL

755 South Price Road
St. Louis, Missouri 63124

Head of School: Keith E. Shahan

General Information Coeducational day college-preparatory school. Grades 7–12. Founded: 1923. Setting: suburban. 47-acre campus. 7 buildings on campus. Approved or accredited by Independent Schools Association of the Central States and North Central Association of Colleges and Schools. Member of National Association of Independent Schools and Secondary School Admission Test Board. Endowment: $41.4 million. Total enrollment: 600. Upper school average class size: 14. Upper school faculty-student ratio: 1:7.

Upper School Student Profile Grade 7: 95 students (48 boys, 47 girls); Grade 8: 101 students (50 boys, 51 girls); Grade 9: 103 students (48 boys, 55 girls); Grade 10: 102 students (52 boys, 50 girls); Grade 11: 103 students (52 boys, 51 girls); Grade 12: 96 students (45 boys, 51 girls).

Faculty School total: 101. In upper school: 47 men, 54 women; 84 have advanced degrees.

Subjects Offered Acting, Advanced Placement courses, African American history, algebra, American history, American literature, Ancient Greek, ancient world history, applied arts, architectural drawing, art, art history, art history-AP, astronomy, bioethics, biology, calculus, calculus-AP, ceramics, chemistry, chemistry-AP, choral music, chorus, classical language, community service, comparative religion, computer math, computer science, computer skills, computer-aided design, creative writing, dance, debate, drama, earth science, ecology, English, English literature, environmental science, environmental systems, expository writing, fine arts, finite math, foreign language, French, French language-AP, geology, geometry, German, global issues, global studies, Greek, Greek culture, health, history, home economics, honors English, industrial arts, jazz, jazz band, keyboarding/computer, lab science, Latin, Latin-AP, mathematics, mechanical drawing, meteorology, model United Nations, music, orchestra, organic chemistry, photography, physical education, physics, poetry, pre-algebra, pre-calculus, probability and statistics, psychology, public speaking, reading/study skills, religions, Russian, science, social science, social studies, Spanish, Spanish-AP, speech and debate, statistics, trigonometry, vocal music, word processing, world civilizations, world history, world literature, world religions, writing.

Graduation Requirements Arts and fine arts (art, music, dance, drama), English, foreign language, history, mathematics, performing arts, physical education (includes health), practical arts, science, Senior May Project.

Special Academic Programs Advanced Placement exam preparation; honors section; independent study.

College Admission Counseling 97 students graduated in 2008; all went to college, including Harvard University; University of Chicago; University of Denver; University of Pennsylvania; University of Virginia; Washington University in St. Louis. Median SAT critical reading: 710, median SAT math: 710, median SAT writing: 700, median combined SAT: 2120, median composite ACT: 31. 85% scored over 600 on SAT critical reading, 95% scored over 600 on SAT math, 90% scored over 600 on SAT writing, 91% scored over 1800 on combined SAT, 86% scored over 26 on composite ACT.

Student Life Upper grades have student council, honor system. Discipline rests equally with students and faculty.

Tuition and Aid Day student tuition: $19,450. Tuition installment plan (monthly payment plans). Need-based scholarship grants, need-based loans available. In 2008–09, 21% of upper-school students received aid. Total amount of financial aid awarded in 2008–09: $1,232,650.

Admissions Traditional secondary-level entrance grade is 7. For fall 2008, 261 students applied for upper-level admission, 134 were accepted, 114 enrolled. ISEE required. Deadline for receipt of application materials: January 15. Application fee required: $40. On-campus interview required.

Athletics Interscholastic: baseball (boys), basketball (b,g), cheering (g), cross-country running (b,g), dance (b,g), dance squad (g), diving (b,g), field hockey (g), fitness (b,g), football (b,g), golf (b,g), ice hockey (b), independent competitive sports (b,g), lacrosse (g), modern dance (b,g), outdoor education (b,g), physical fitness (b,g), physical training (b,g), racquetball (b,g), soccer (b,g), swimming and diving (b,g), tennis (b,g), track and field (b,g), volleyball (g), water polo (b,g), wrestling (b,g), yoga (b,g); intramural: hiking/backpacking (b,g), weight lifting (b,g). 46 coaches, 1 athletic trainer.

Computers Computers are regularly used in all academic, animation, architecture, art, basic skills, cabinet making, classics, college planning, current events, desktop publishing, drafting, drawing and design, industrial technology, keyboarding, lab/keyboard, library, library skills, media production, music, photography, photojournalism, remedial study skills, research skills, study skills, technical drawing, theater, video film production, Web site design, yearbook classes. Computer network features include on-campus library services, online commercial services, Internet access, wireless campus network, Internet filtering or blocking technology, monitoring software. The school has a published electronic and media policy.

Contact Caroline LaVigne, Director of Admissions and Tuition Aid. 314-993-4040. Fax: 314-567-2896. E-mail: clavigne@jburroughs.org. Web site: www.jburroughs.org.

THE JOHN COOPER SCHOOL

One John Cooper Drive
The Woodlands, Texas 77381

Head of School: Mr. Michael F. Maher

General Information Coeducational day college-preparatory, general academic, arts, technology, and competitive athletics school. Grades PK–12. Founded: 1988. Setting: suburban. Nearest major city is Houston. 43-acre campus. 6 buildings on campus. Approved or accredited by Independent Schools Association of the Southwest. Member of National Association of Independent Schools. Endowment: $800,000. Total enrollment: 949. Upper school average class size: 16. Upper school faculty-student ratio: 1:12.

Upper School Student Profile Grade 9: 79 students (41 boys, 38 girls); Grade 10: 82 students (37 boys, 45 girls); Grade 11: 81 students (38 boys, 43 girls); Grade 12: 82 students (35 boys, 47 girls).

Faculty School total: 89. In upper school: 13 men, 26 women; 26 have advanced degrees.

Subjects Offered 3-dimensional art, adolescent issues, advanced chemistry, advanced math, advanced studio art-AP, algebra, American history, American history-AP, American literature, anatomy and physiology, art, art history-AP, athletics, band, baseball, basketball, biology, biology-AP, British literature, calculus, calculus-AP, ceramics, cheerleading, chemistry, chemistry-AP, college planning, computer literacy, computer programming-AP, computer science, computer science-AP, concert choir, creative writing, drama, drawing, economics, economics and history, English, English literature-AP, European history, European history-AP, French, French-AP, geometry, glassblowing, golf, guitar, health, history, history-AP, jazz band, jewelry making, Latin, linear algebra, literary magazine, literature-AP, mathematical modeling, model United Nations, modern European history-AP, modern political theory, painting, photography, physical education, physics, physics-AP, political thought, pre-calculus, probability and statistics, psychology, social studies, softball, Spanish, Spanish-AP, statistics, statistics-AP, studio art-AP, symphonic band, tennis, theater, trigonometry, U.S. history-AP, volleyball, world history, world literature, world religions, yearbook.

Graduation Requirements Arts and fine arts (art, music, dance, drama), English, foreign language, mathematics, physical education (includes health), science, social studies (includes history).

Special Academic Programs Advanced Placement exam preparation; independent study.

College Admission Counseling 81 students graduated in 2008; all went to college, including Baylor University; Davidson College; Texas A&M University; Texas Christian University; The George Washington University; University of Southern California. Mean SAT critical reading: 653, mean SAT math: 656, mean SAT writing: 632, mean combined SAT: 1941, mean composite ACT: 29. 75% scored over 600 on SAT critical reading, 75% scored over 600 on SAT math, 70% scored over 600 on SAT writing, 72% scored over 1800 on combined SAT, 75% scored over 26 on composite ACT.

Student Life Upper grades have specified standards of dress, student council, honor system. Discipline rests primarily with faculty.
Summer Programs Enrichment, sports, art/fine arts, computer instruction programs offered; session focuses on academic enrichment; held both on and off campus; held at zoos, museums, and other field trip locations around town; accepts boys and girls; open to students from other schools. 980 students usually enrolled. 2009 schedule: June 1 to July 3. Application deadline: none.
Tuition and Aid Day student tuition: $16,550. Tuition installment plan (2-part, 4-part or 9-month payment plan). Need-based scholarship grants, need-based loans available. In 2008–09, 10% of upper-school students received aid. Total amount of financial aid awarded in 2008–09: $235,625.
Admissions Traditional secondary-level entrance grade is 9. For fall 2008, 77 students applied for upper-level admission, 38 were accepted, 31 enrolled. ISEE or Otis-Lennon School Ability Test required. Deadline for receipt of application materials: none. Application fee required: $125. Interview required.
Athletics Interscholastic: baseball (boys), basketball (b,g), cross-country running (b,g), golf (b,g), softball (g), swimming and diving (b,g), tennis (b,g), track and field (b,g), volleyball (g), winter soccer (b,g). 7 PE instructors, 8 coaches, 1 athletic trainer.
Computers Computers are regularly used in all academic, art, desktop publishing, foreign language, journalism, music, video film production, Web site design classes. Computer network features include on-campus library services, online commercial services, Internet access, Internet filtering or blocking technology.
Contact Mr. Craig Meredith, Director of Admission. 281-367-0900 Ext. 308. Fax: 281-298-5715. E-mail: cmeredith@johncooper.org. Web site: www.johncooper.org.

THE JOHN DEWEY ACADEMY

Great Barrington, Massachusetts
See Special Needs Schools section.

JOHN PAUL II CATHOLIC HIGH SCHOOL

5100 Terrebone Drive
Tallahassee, Florida 32311-7848
Head of School: Sr. Ellen Cronan

General Information Coeducational day college-preparatory and religious studies school, affiliated with Roman Catholic Church; primarily serves students with learning disabilities and individuals with Attention Deficit Disorder. Grades 9–12. Founded: 2001. Setting: suburban. 37-acre campus. 3 buildings on campus. Approved or accredited by Southern Association of Colleges and Schools and Florida Department of Education. Total enrollment: 129. Upper school average class size: 12. Upper school faculty-student ratio: 1:8.
Upper School Student Profile Grade 9: 21 students (10 boys, 11 girls); Grade 10: 41 students (19 boys, 22 girls); Grade 11: 44 students (22 boys, 22 girls); Grade 12: 23 students (9 boys, 14 girls). 83% of students are Roman Catholic.
Faculty School total: 19. In upper school: 8 men, 11 women; 14 have advanced degrees.
Special Academic Programs 6 Advanced Placement exams for which test preparation is offered; honors section; study at local college for college credit.
College Admission Counseling 5 students graduated in 2008; 3 went to college, including Georgia Institute of Technology. Other: 2 went to work. Mean SAT critical reading: 609, mean SAT math: 640. 43% scored over 600 on SAT critical reading, 57% scored over 600 on SAT math.
Student Life Upper grades have uniform requirement, student council. Discipline rests primarily with faculty. Attendance at religious services is required.
Tuition and Aid Day student tuition: $7400. Guaranteed tuition plan. Tuition installment plan (FACTS Tuition Payment Plan). Need-based scholarship grants available. In 2008–09, 17% of upper-school students received aid. Total amount of financial aid awarded in 2008–09: $40,000.
Admissions Traditional secondary-level entrance grade is 9. High School Placement Test required. Deadline for receipt of application materials: none. Application fee required: $150. On-campus interview recommended.
Athletics Interscholastic: baseball (boys), basketball (b,g), cheering (g), cross-country running (b,g), football (b), golf (b), soccer (b,g), tennis (b,g), volleyball (g). 1 PE instructor, 8 coaches, 1 athletic trainer.
Computers Computers are regularly used in drawing and design, technology classes. Computer resources include on-campus library services, Internet access, Internet filtering or blocking technology. Student e-mail accounts are available to students. Students grades are available online. The school has a published electronic and media policy.
Contact Mrs. Sharon Strohl, Office Administrator. 850-201-5744. Fax: 850-205-3299. E-mail: sstrohl@jpiichs.org. Web site: www.jpiichs.org.

JUNIPERO SERRA HIGH SCHOOL

451 West 20th Avenue
San Mateo, California 94403-1385
Head of School: Lars Lund

General Information Boys' day college-preparatory, arts, business, religious studies, and technology school, affiliated with Roman Catholic Church. Grades 9–12. Founded: 1944. Setting: suburban. Nearest major city is San Francisco. 13-acre campus. 8 buildings on campus. Approved or accredited by Western Association of Schools and Colleges. Endowment: $1.7 million. Total enrollment: 975. Upper school average class size: 27. Upper school faculty-student ratio: 1:27.
Upper School Student Profile Grade 9: 255 students (255 boys); Grade 10: 239 students (239 boys); Grade 11: 246 students (246 boys); Grade 12: 235 students (235 boys). 75% of students are Roman Catholic.
Faculty School total: 67. In upper school: 53 men, 14 women; 32 have advanced degrees.
Subjects Offered Algebra, American government-AP, American history, American history-AP, American literature, architecture, art, art history-AP, astronomy, band, biology, biology-AP, business, calculus, calculus-AP, chemistry, college admission preparation, college counseling, college planning, community service, comparative government and politics-AP, computer programming, computer science, creative writing, drafting, drama, driver education, earth science, economics, electronics, English, English literature, English literature and composition-AP, English literature-AP, ethics, European history, fine arts, French, French language-AP, geography, geology, geometry, German, government and politics-AP, government/civics, grammar, graphic design, health, history, instrumental music, journalism, keyboarding, library skills, library studies, literature and composition-AP, mathematics, mechanical drawing, music, photography, physical education, physics, religion, science, social science, social studies, Spanish, Spanish language-AP, speech, statistics, student government, theater, trigonometry, U.S. history-AP, world history, writing.
Graduation Requirements Arts and fine arts (art, music, dance, drama), computer science, English, foreign language, literature, mathematics, physical education (includes health), political systems, religion (includes Bible studies and theology), science, social science, social studies (includes history). Community service is required.
Special Academic Programs Advanced Placement exam preparation; honors section; study at local college for college credit.
College Admission Counseling 210 students graduated in 2008; 209 went to college, including College of San Mateo; Saint Mary's College; San Francisco State University; San Jose State University; Santa Clara University; University of California, Davis. Other: 1 entered military service.
Student Life Upper grades have specified standards of dress, student council, honor system. Discipline rests primarily with faculty. Attendance at religious services is required.
Summer Programs Remediation, enrichment, advancement, computer instruction programs offered; session focuses on enrichment and remediation; held on campus; accepts boys and girls; open to students from other schools. 460 students usually enrolled. 2009 schedule: June 15 to July 24. Application deadline: June 13.
Tuition and Aid Day student tuition: $13,450. Tuition installment plan (monthly payment plans, semester payment plan, annual payment plan, direct debit plan). Merit scholarship grants, need-based scholarship grants available. In 2008–09, 17% of upper-school students received aid; total upper-school merit-scholarship money awarded: $87,500. Total amount of financial aid awarded in 2008–09: $780,150.
Admissions Traditional secondary-level entrance grade is 9. For fall 2008, 500 students applied for upper-level admission, 350 were accepted, 255 enrolled. STS required. Deadline for receipt of application materials: January 4. Application fee required: $90. On-campus interview required.
Athletics Interscholastic: baseball, basketball, crew, cross-country running, diving, football, golf, soccer, swimming and diving, tennis, track and field, volleyball, water polo, wrestling; intramural: basketball, bicycling, bowling, fishing, flag football, Frisbee, soccer, softball, touch football, weight lifting. 3 PE instructors, 48 coaches, 1 athletic trainer.
Computers Computers are regularly used in English, foreign language, history, library, library skills, mathematics, music, science, social science classes. Computer network features include on-campus library services, Internet access.
Contact Randy Vogel, Director of Admissions. 650-345-8242. Fax: 650-573-6638. E-mail: padres@serrahs.com. Web site: www.serrahs.com.

KAPLAN COLLEGE PREPARATORY SCHOOL

4601 Sheridan Street
Suite 600
Hollywood, Florida 33021
Head of School: Miriam Rube

General Information Coeducational day and distance learning college-preparatory school. Grades 6–12. Distance learning grades 6–12. Founded: 2001. Setting: suburban. Nearest major city is Fort Lauderdale. Approved or accredited by CITA (Commission on International and Trans-Regional Accreditation), Southern Association of Colleges and Schools, and Florida Department of Education. Total enrollment: 260.
Upper School Student Profile Grade 9: 48 students (29 boys, 19 girls); Grade 10: 53 students (27 boys, 26 girls); Grade 11: 66 students (37 boys, 29 girls); Grade 12: 66 students (39 boys, 27 girls).
Faculty School total: 22. In upper school: 3 men, 19 women; 12 have advanced degrees.

Subjects Offered Advanced Placement courses, algebra, American government, American government-AP, American history, American history-AP, American literature, American literature-AP, art history, biology, biology-AP, business technology, chemistry, chemistry-AP, computer applications, earth and space science, economics, emerging technology, English, English language and composition-AP, English literature and composition-AP, English literature-AP, French, geometry, health, honors algebra, language, life management skills, marine science, mathematics, mathematics-AP, physical education, physical fitness, physics, pre-algebra, pre-calculus, psychology, SAT preparation, science, Spanish, U.S. history, world history, world literature.
Graduation Requirements American government, American history, American literature, biology, British literature, chemistry, economics, electives, English literature, foreign language, general science, life management skills, personal fitness, physical education (includes health), world history, world literature, The last six courses must be with KCPS for a Kaplan College Preparatory School diploma.
Special Academic Programs Advanced Placement exam preparation; honors section; accelerated programs.
College Admission Counseling 36 students graduated in 2008; 29 went to college, including University of Miami; University of Michigan; University of Oregon; University of South Carolina; University of Virginia; Wake Forest University. Other: 4 went to work, 3 had other specific plans.
Student Life Upper grades have student council, honor system. Discipline rests primarily with faculty.
Summer Programs Remediation, enrichment, advancement, art/fine arts, computer instruction programs offered; session focuses on Credit Recovery and Academic Enhancement; held on campus; accepts boys and girls; open to students from other schools. 650 students usually enrolled. 2009 schedule: May 1 to August 1.
Tuition and Aid Tuition installment plan (monthly payment plans, individually arranged payment plans).
Admissions Traditional secondary-level entrance grade is 9. Deadline for receipt of application materials: none. Application fee required: $100. Interview recommended.
Athletics 1 PE instructor.
Computers Computers are regularly used in all classes. Students grades are available online. The school has a published electronic and media policy.
Contact Alison Cohen, Registrar. 954-964-6502. Fax: 800-878-3152. E-mail: acohen2@kaplan.edu. Web site: www.kaplancollegepreparatory.com.

KARACHI AMERICAN SCHOOL

Amir Khusro Road, KDA Scheme No. 1
Karachi 75350, Pakistan

Head of School: Peter L. Pelosi, PhD

General Information Coeducational day college-preparatory, arts, bilingual studies, and technology school. Grades PS–12. Founded: 1953. Setting: urban. 12-acre campus. 6 buildings on campus. Approved or accredited by Middle States Association of Colleges and Schools. Member of European Council of International Schools. Language of instruction: English. Endowment: $7 million. Total enrollment: 331. Upper school average class size: 16. Upper school faculty-student ratio: 1:6.
Upper School Student Profile Grade 6: 25 students (11 boys, 14 girls); Grade 7: 24 students (18 boys, 6 girls); Grade 8: 35 students (23 boys, 12 girls); Grade 9: 23 students (12 boys, 11 girls); Grade 10: 34 students (21 boys, 13 girls); Grade 11: 29 students (16 boys, 13 girls); Grade 12: 28 students (10 boys, 18 girls).
Faculty School total: 39. In upper school: 11 men, 16 women; 24 have advanced degrees.
Subjects Offered Advanced Placement courses, band, biology, chemistry, chemistry-AP, computer science, concert band, desktop publishing, English, English-AP, French, general science, geometry, health, journalism, mathematics, physical education, physics-AP, psychology, science research, social studies, Spanish, Spanish-AP, studio art.
Graduation Requirements Arts and fine arts (art, music, dance, drama), computer studies, English, foreign language, mathematics, physical education (includes health), science, social studies (includes history), speech, writing, 26 credits are required. Community service is required.
Special Academic Programs Advanced Placement exam preparation; ESL (18 students enrolled).
College Admission Counseling 25 students graduated in 2008; all went to college, including Clark University; Hamilton College; McGill University; Mount Holyoke College; New York University; University of Massachusetts Amherst. Median composite ACT: 25. Mean SAT critical reading: 526, mean SAT math: 619, mean SAT writing: 548. 13% scored over 600 on SAT critical reading, 36% scored over 600 on SAT math, 31% scored over 600 on SAT writing, 25% scored over 1800 on combined SAT, 33% scored over 26 on composite ACT.
Student Life Upper grades have specified standards of dress, student council. Discipline rests primarily with faculty.
Tuition and Aid Day student tuition: $9830–$12,035. Tuition installment plan (pay in May and September (70%-30%)).
Admissions For fall 2008, 119 students applied for upper-level admission, 45 were accepted, 45 enrolled. Achievement tests, admissions testing, any standardized test, English proficiency, ESL, Iowa Test of Educational Development, Iowa Tests of Basic Skills, latest standardized score from previous school, PSAT or SAT, psychoeducational evaluation, SLEP for foreign students or writing sample required. Deadline for receipt of application materials: April 15. Application fee required: $250. On-campus interview required.
Athletics Interscholastic: badminton (boys, girls), baseball (b,g), basketball (b,g), cheering (b,g), cricket (b,g), cross-country running (b,g), flag football (b,g), floor hockey (b,g), football (b,g), physical fitness (b,g), physical training (b,g), running (b,g), soccer (b,g), softball (b,g), squash (b,g), swimming and diving (b,g), table tennis (b,g), tennis (b,g), track and field (b,g), volleyball (b,g); intramural: running (b,g); coed interscholastic: archery, badminton, baseball, cheering, cross-country running, floor hockey, football, physical fitness, physical training, running, soccer, softball, squash, swimming and diving, table tennis, tennis, track and field, volleyball; coed intramural: running. 5 PE instructors, 12 coaches, 3 athletic trainers.
Computers Computers are regularly used in all academic classes. Computer network features include on-campus library services, online commercial services, Internet access, wireless campus network, Internet filtering or blocking technology. Campus intranet, student e-mail accounts, and computer access in designated common areas are available to students. Students grades are available online. The school has a published electronic and media policy.
Contact Afshan Waris, Admission Officer. 92-21-453-9096. Fax: 92-21-454-7305. E-mail: admission@kas.edu.pk. Web site: www.kas.edu.pk.

THE KARAFIN SCHOOL

Mount Kisco, New York
See Special Needs Schools section.

KEITH COUNTRY DAY SCHOOL

1 Jacoby Place
Rockford, Illinois 61107

Head of School: Mrs. Elizabeth Giesen

General Information Coeducational day college-preparatory and arts school. Grades PK–12. Founded: 1916. Setting: suburban. Nearest major city is Chicago. 15-acre campus. 1 building on campus. Approved or accredited by Independent Schools Association of the Central States and Illinois Department of Education. Member of National Association of Independent Schools. Endowment: $920,000. Total enrollment: 329. Upper school average class size: 16. Upper school faculty-student ratio: 1:5.
Upper School Student Profile Grade 9: 23 students (9 boys, 14 girls); Grade 10: 36 students (21 boys, 15 girls); Grade 11: 30 students (18 boys, 12 girls); Grade 12: 22 students (13 boys, 9 girls).
Faculty School total: 51. In upper school: 11 men, 17 women; 20 have advanced degrees.
Subjects Offered Advanced math, Advanced Placement courses, algebra, American history, American literature, art, arts, Bible as literature, biology, biology-AP, calculus, ceramics, chemistry, chemistry-AP, college counseling, community service, computer science, design, drama, drawing, economics, English, English literature, English-AP, environmental science, European history, fine arts, French, geography, geometry, government/civics, health, history, Latin, mathematics, music, painting, photography, physical education, physics, pre-calculus, research skills, science, social studies, speech, study skills, theater, trigonometry, world history, world literature.
Graduation Requirements Arts and fine arts (art, music, dance, drama), college counseling, computer science, English, foreign language, mathematics, physical education (includes health), research skills, science, senior project, social studies (includes history), speech, 90 hours of community service.
Special Academic Programs Advanced Placement exam preparation; honors section; study at local college for college credit; study abroad; academic accommodation for the gifted, the musically talented, and the artistically talented; remedial reading and/or remedial writing; programs in general development for dyslexic students.
College Admission Counseling 24 students graduated in 2008; all went to college, including Knox College; Purdue University; University of Chicago; University of Illinois at Urbana–Champaign; University of Notre Dame. 50% scored over 600 on SAT math, 62% scored over 600 on SAT writing, 52% scored over 26 on composite ACT.
Student Life Upper grades have specified standards of dress, student council, honor system. Discipline rests equally with students and faculty.
Summer Programs Enrichment, sports, art/fine arts programs offered; session focuses on sports skills camps, math camp, music camp; held on campus; accepts boys and girls; open to students from other schools. 80 students usually enrolled. 2009 schedule: June 15 to August 15.
Tuition and Aid Day student tuition: $13,700. Tuition installment plan (monthly payment plans, school's own payment plan). Tuition reduction for siblings, merit scholarship grants, need-based scholarship grants available. In 2008–09, 44% of upper-school students received aid; total upper-school merit-scholarship money awarded: $28,000. Total amount of financial aid awarded in 2008–09: $358,970.
Admissions Traditional secondary-level entrance grade is 9. For fall 2008, 18 students applied for upper-level admission, 18 were accepted, 9 enrolled. ERB and school's own exam required. Deadline for receipt of application materials: none. Application fee required: $50. On-campus interview required.

Athletics Interscholastic: basketball (boys, girls), soccer (b,g), volleyball (g); coed interscholastic: cross-country running, golf, tennis; coed intramural: crew. 3 PE instructors, 6 coaches.
Computers Computers are regularly used in English, foreign language, history, mathematics, science, social studies, Spanish, writing, yearbook classes. Computer network features include on-campus library services, Internet access, wireless campus network, Internet filtering or blocking technology. Student e-mail accounts are available to students. The school has a published electronic and media policy.
Contact Marcia Aramovich, Director of Admissions. 815-399-8850 Ext. 144. Fax: 815-399-2470. E-mail: admissions@keithschool.com. Web site: www.keithschool.com.

KENT DENVER SCHOOL

4000 East Quincy Avenue
Englewood, Colorado 80113

Head of School: Todd Horn

General Information Coeducational day college-preparatory and arts school. Grades 6–12. Founded: 1922. Setting: suburban. Nearest major city is Denver. 220-acre campus. 6 buildings on campus. Approved or accredited by Association of Colorado Independent Schools and Colorado Department of Education. Member of National Association of Independent Schools and Secondary School Admission Test Board. Endowment: $35 million. Total enrollment: 659. Upper school average class size: 15. Upper school faculty-student ratio: 1:7.
Faculty School total: 81. In upper school: 30 men, 29 women; 41 have advanced degrees.
Subjects Offered African-American literature, algebra, American history, American history-AP, American literature, ancient history, anthropology, art, art history, art history-AP, Asian studies, biology, calculus, calculus-AP, career education internship, ceramics, chemistry, choir, clayworking, college counseling, community service, computer math, computer programming, computer programming-AP, computer science, creative writing, drama, earth science, economics, English, English language and composition-AP, English language-AP, English literature, English literature and composition-AP, environmental science, European history, European history-AP, fine arts, French, French language-AP, French literature-AP, French-AP, general science, genetics, geography, geology, geometry, government/civics, grammar, guitar, health and wellness, history, history-AP, human development, independent study, jazz band, Latin, mathematics, music, music performance, mythology, photography, physical education, physics, pre-calculus, science, social studies, Spanish, Spanish language-AP, Spanish literature-AP, statistics, studio art—AP, theater, Web site design, world history, world literature, writing.
Graduation Requirements Arts and fine arts (art, music, dance, drama), computer science, English, foreign language, history, internship, mathematics, participation in sports, physical education (includes health), science. Community service is required.
Special Academic Programs 16 Advanced Placement exams for which test preparation is offered; honors section; independent study; programs in general development for dyslexic students.
College Admission Counseling 107 students graduated in 2008; all went to college, including Claremont McKenna College; Dartmouth College; Middlebury College; Stanford University; The Colorado College; University of Southern California. Mean SAT critical reading: 642, mean SAT math: 641, mean SAT writing: 640.
Student Life Upper grades have specified standards of dress, student council. Discipline rests equally with students and faculty.
Summer Programs Enrichment, sports, art/fine arts, computer instruction programs offered; session focuses on skill building; held on campus; accepts boys and girls; open to students from other schools. 650 students usually enrolled. 2009 schedule: June 8 to July 13. Application deadline: none.
Tuition and Aid Day student tuition: $17,875. Tuition installment plan (Insured Tuition Payment Plan, Key Tuition Payment Plan, monthly payment plans). Need-based scholarship grants available. In 2008–09, 18% of upper-school students received aid. Total amount of financial aid awarded in 2008–09: $1,600,000.
Admissions Traditional secondary-level entrance grade is 9. For fall 2008, 152 students applied for upper-level admission, 61 were accepted, 50 enrolled. ISEE or SSAT required. Deadline for receipt of application materials: January 30. Application fee required: $60. Interview required.
Athletics Interscholastic: basketball (boys, girls), cross-country running (b,g), diving (g), field hockey (g), football (b), golf (b,g), hockey (b), ice hockey (b), lacrosse (b,g), soccer (b,g), swimming and diving (g), tennis (b,g), track and field (b,g), volleyball (g), wrestling (b); coed interscholastic: baseball, outdoor education; coed intramural: aerobics/Nautilus, bicycling, fitness, mountain biking, outdoor adventure, outdoor education, outdoor skills, physical fitness, physical training, strength & conditioning, weight lifting. 3 PE instructors, 17 coaches, 1 athletic trainer.
Computers Computers are regularly used in art, English, foreign language, history, mathematics, science classes. Computer network features include on-campus library services, online commercial services, Internet access, wireless campus network, Internet filtering or blocking technology. Student e-mail accounts and computer access in designated common areas are available to students. The school has a published electronic and media policy.
Contact Susan Green, Admission Office Manager. 303-770-7660 Ext. 237. Fax: 303-770-1398. E-mail: sgreen@kentdenver.org. Web site: www.kentdenver.org.

KENT PLACE SCHOOL

42 Norwood Avenue
Summit, New Jersey 07902-0308

Head of School: Mrs. Susan C. Bosland

General Information Coeducational day (boys' only in lower grades) college-preparatory school. Boys grades N–PK, girls grades N–12. Founded: 1894. Setting: suburban. Nearest major city is New York, NY. 25-acre campus. 6 buildings on campus. Approved or accredited by Middle States Association of Colleges and Schools and New Jersey Association of Independent Schools. Member of National Association of Independent Schools and Secondary School Admission Test Board. Endowment: $14.2 million. Total enrollment: 647. Upper school average class size: 16. Upper school faculty-student ratio: 1:7.
Upper School Student Profile Grade 9: 64 students (64 girls); Grade 10: 73 students (73 girls); Grade 11: 66 students (66 girls); Grade 12: 60 students (60 girls).
Faculty School total: 81. In upper school: 5 men, 28 women; 27 have advanced degrees.
Subjects Offered Advanced Placement courses, algebra, American history, American history-AP, American literature, anatomy and physiology, art, art history-AP, biology, biology-AP, calculus, calculus-AP, ceramics, chemistry, chemistry-AP, computer literacy, computer programming-AP, computer science, creative writing, dance, drama, driver education, economics, English, English language-AP, English literature, English literature-AP, environmental science, environmental science-AP, European history, expository writing, fine arts, French, French language-AP, French literature-AP, geometry, government/civics, grammar, health, history, independent study, Latin, Latin-AP, macroeconomics-AP, mathematics, modern European history-AP, music, music theory-AP, photography, physical education, physics, science, social studies, Spanish, Spanish language-AP, Spanish literature-AP, statistics, statistics-AP, theater, trigonometry, world history.
Graduation Requirements Arts and fine arts (art, music, dance, drama), computer science, English, foreign language, mathematics, physical education (includes health), science, social studies (includes history).
Special Academic Programs Advanced Placement exam preparation; independent study.
College Admission Counseling 61 students graduated in 2008; all went to college, including Boston College; Bucknell University; Cornell University; Princeton University; University of Pennsylvania; Yale University. Median SAT critical reading: 660, median SAT math: 670, median SAT writing: 630. 78% scored over 600 on SAT critical reading, 88% scored over 600 on SAT math.
Student Life Upper grades have specified standards of dress, student council, honor system. Discipline rests equally with students and faculty.
Tuition and Aid Day student tuition: $28,125. Tuition installment plan (Insured Tuition Payment Plan, Key Tuition Payment Plan, monthly payment plans). Need-based scholarship grants available. In 2008–09, 20% of upper-school students received aid. Total amount of financial aid awarded in 2008–09: $921,243.
Admissions Traditional secondary-level entrance grade is 9. ISEE or SSAT required. Deadline for receipt of application materials: January 9. Application fee required: $70. On-campus interview required.
Athletics Interscholastic: basketball, cross-country running, field hockey, indoor track, lacrosse, soccer, softball, swimming and diving, tennis, track and field, volleyball, winter (indoor) track; intramural: dance, fencing, modern dance, physical fitness, squash. 4 PE instructors, 19 coaches, 1 athletic trainer.
Computers Computers are regularly used in all classes. Computer network features include on-campus library services, online commercial services, Internet access, wireless campus network, Internet filtering or blocking technology. Student e-mail accounts are available to students. The school has a published electronic and media policy.
Contact Mrs. Nancy J. Humick, Director of Admission and Financial Aid. 908-273-0900 Ext. 254. Fax: 908-273-9390. E-mail: admission@kentplace.org. Web site: www.kentplace.org.

See Close-Up on page 806.

KENT SCHOOL

PO Box 2006
Kent, Connecticut 06757

Head of School: Rev. Richardson W. Schell

General Information Coeducational boarding and day college-preparatory, arts, religious studies, and technology school, affiliated with Episcopal Church. Grades 9–PG. Founded: 1906. Setting: small town. Nearest major city is Hartford. Students are housed in single-sex by floor dormitories and single-sex dormitories. 1,200-acre campus. 15 buildings on campus. Approved or accredited by Association of Independent Schools in New England, Connecticut Association of Independent Schools, National Association of Episcopal Schools, New England Association of Schools and Colleges, The Association of Boarding Schools, and Connecticut Department of Education. Member of National Association of Independent Schools and Secondary School Admission Test Board. Endowment: $73.5 million. Total enrollment: 574. Upper school average class size: 12. Upper school faculty-student ratio: 1:8.

Upper School Student Profile Grade 9: 83 students (38 boys, 45 girls); Grade 10: 138 students (63 boys, 75 girls); Grade 11: 167 students (95 boys, 72 girls); Grade 12: 166 students (105 boys, 61 girls); Postgraduate: 20 students (15 boys, 5 girls). 90% of students are boarding students. 31% are state residents. 35 states are represented in upper school student body. 18% are international students. International students from Canada, Germany, Hong Kong, Republic of Korea, Taiwan, and Thailand; 20 other countries represented in student body. 25% of students are members of Episcopal Church.

Faculty School total: 75. In upper school: 32 men, 42 women; 62 have advanced degrees; 30 reside on campus.

Subjects Offered Advanced studio art-AP, African-American history, algebra, American history, American history-AP, American literature, architecture, art, art history-AP, Asian history, astronomy, Bible studies, biology, biology-AP, biotechnology, calculus, calculus-AP, ceramics, chemistry, chemistry-AP, Chinese, classical Greek literature, classical studies, composition-AP, computer math, computer programming, computer science, computer science-AP, constitutional law, digital imaging, drama, ecology, economics, English, English literature, English literature-AP, environmental science-AP, European history, European history-AP, expository writing, fine arts, French, French language-AP, French literature-AP, genetics, geology, geometry, German, German-AP, government and politics-AP, Greek, history, Latin, Latin American history, Latin-AP, law and the legal system, mathematics, meteorology, Middle Eastern history, modern European history-AP, music, music theory-AP, photography, physical education, physics, physics-AP, psychology-AP, religion, science, sculpture, social studies, Spanish, Spanish language-AP, Spanish literature-AP, statistics and probability, statistics-AP, theater, theology, trigonometry, U.S. government-AP, world geography, world history, world literature.

Graduation Requirements Arts and fine arts (art, music, dance, drama), English, foreign language, history, mathematics, music, religion (includes Bible studies and theology), science, U.S. history.

Special Academic Programs Advanced Placement exam preparation; honors section; independent study; academic accommodation for the gifted, the musically talented, and the artistically talented; ESL (25 students enrolled).

College Admission Counseling 158 students graduated in 2007; all went to college, including Boston University; Carnegie Mellon University; Colgate University; Cornell University; Princeton University; St. Lawrence University.

Student Life Upper grades have specified standards of dress, student council. Discipline rests equally with students and faculty. Attendance at religious services is required.

Tuition and Aid Day student tuition: $33,000; 7-day tuition and room/board: $42,000. Guaranteed tuition plan. Tuition installment plan (Key Tuition Payment Plan, monthly payment plans, individually arranged payment plans). Need-based scholarship grants, need-based loans available. In 2008–09, 32% of upper-school students received aid. Total amount of financial aid awarded in 2008–09: $5,400,000.

Admissions Traditional secondary-level entrance grade is 9. For fall 2007, 922 students applied for upper-level admission, 427 were accepted, 200 enrolled. PSAT or SAT for applicants to grade 11 and 12, SSAT or TOEFL required. Deadline for receipt of application materials: January 15. Application fee required: $65. Interview required.

Athletics Interscholastic: baseball (boys), basketball (b,g), crew (b,g), cross-country running (b,g), diving (b,g), field hockey (g), football (b), hockey (b,g), ice hockey (b,g), lacrosse (b,g), rowing (b,g), soccer (b,g), softball (g), squash (b,g), swimming and diving (b,g), tennis (b,g); intramural: basketball (b), crew (b,g), rowing (b,g); coed interscholastic: crew, equestrian sports, golf, horseback riding; coed intramural: aerobics/dance, aerobics/Nautilus, ballet, bicycling, dance, equestrian sports, figure skating, fitness, hockey, horseback riding, life saving, modern dance, mountain biking, Nautilus, physical fitness, physical training, skiing (downhill), snowboarding, soccer, squash, strength & conditioning, swimming and diving, tennis, weight training, yoga. 1 athletic trainer.

Computers Computers are regularly used in all academic, journalism, newspaper, yearbook classes. Computer network features include on-campus library services, Internet access, wireless campus network, Internet filtering or blocking technology. Student e-mail accounts and computer access in designated common areas are available to students. The school has a published electronic and media policy.

Contact Ms. Kathryn F. Sullivan, Director of Admissions. 860-927-6111. Fax: 860-927-6109. E-mail: admissions@kent-school.edu. Web site: www.kent-school.edu.

ANNOUNCEMENT FROM THE SCHOOL There were many highlights for Kent students in the 2007–08 academic year. 100% of the Class of 2008 attend college—more than half (59%) matriculated at the most competitive and highly competitive schools. Kent computer science students took first place in the team competition of the General Electric Computer Science Contest. Three teams of Kent students participated in the High School Mathematical Contest in Modeling, and one of the teams earned a "Regional Outstanding" scoring in the top 10% of 270 teams from around the world. Kent community service clubs, in collaboration with the dining hall, hosted a Hunger Awareness Dinner in an effort to raise awareness of the issue of global hunger. For the second time in three years, the Kent Girls Varsity Soccer team was chosen by the Western Connecticut Soccer Officials Association for their annual Sportsmanship Award. The Boys Varsity Hockey Team defeated the first- and third–ranked hockey teams in New England on its way to an undefeated performance in the Christmas Hockey Classic. The Kent Girls Varsity Tennis Team placed third at the Annual DeVillafranca Tournament, the New England Championship. The three-time Founders League Champion Kent Girls Basketball team won their first Class A New England Prep School Championship. Twelve students represented Kent at the Scholastic Art Awards; 1 student won a gold key to advance to the national level. A Kent student's photographs were picked up by the Associated Press and published online. Finally, Kent students were represented at the Connecticut Northern Region Music Festival; the Connecticut All-State Music Festival; the New England Music Festival in Orchestra and Chorus; the Independent Schools Music Festival in Band, Orchestra, and Chorus; and in the Musical Club of Hartford Competition, where 1 student won first place in the flute competition.

See Close-Up on page 808.

KENTS HILL SCHOOL

PO Box 257
1614 Main Street, Route 17
Kents Hill, Maine 04349-0257

Head of School: Mr. Rist Bonnefond

General Information Coeducational boarding and day college-preparatory, arts, technology, Environmental Studies, and ESL school, affiliated with Methodist Church. Grades 9–PG. Founded: 1824. Setting: rural. Nearest major city is Portland. Students are housed in single-sex dormitories. 400-acre campus. 24 buildings on campus. Approved or accredited by Independent Schools of Northern New England, New England Association of Schools and Colleges, The Association of Boarding Schools, and Maine Department of Education. Member of National Association of Independent Schools and Secondary School Admission Test Board. Endowment: $4.7 million. Total enrollment: 226. Upper school average class size: 12. Upper school faculty-student ratio: 1:5.

Upper School Student Profile Grade 9: 33 students (23 boys, 10 girls); Grade 10: 56 students (32 boys, 24 girls); Grade 11: 75 students (48 boys, 27 girls); Grade 12: 49 students (29 boys, 20 girls); Postgraduate: 16 students (14 boys, 2 girls). 75% of students are boarding students. 33% are state residents. 22 states are represented in upper school student body. 20% are international students. International students from Canada, China, France, Germany, Japan, and Republic of Korea; 12 other countries represented in student body. 3% of students are Methodist.

Faculty School total: 45. In upper school: 26 men, 19 women; 17 have advanced degrees; 42 reside on campus.

Subjects Offered Acting, advanced math, Advanced Placement courses, advanced studio art-AP, African-American literature, algebra, American history, American literature, art, art history, astronomy, biology, biotechnology, calculus, calculus-AP, ceramics, chemistry, college counseling, computer graphics, computer science-AP, computer-aided design, concert choir, creative writing, dance, drama, Eastern religion and philosophy, ecology, economics, English, English literature, environmental science, environmental science-AP, environmental studies, ESL, ethics, ethics and responsibility, European history, filmmaking, fine arts, French, geology, geometry, government/civics, health, history, Holocaust, jazz ensemble, journalism, mathematics, music, photography, physics, psychology, religion, science, Shakespeare, Spanish, theater, U.S. history-AP, Western religions, woodworking, world history, writing.

Graduation Requirements English, environmental studies, foreign language, health, mathematics, science, social studies (includes history), visual and performing arts.

Special Academic Programs Advanced Placement exam preparation; honors section; independent study; term-away projects; study abroad; academic accommodation for the gifted and the artistically talented; programs in general development for dyslexic students; special instructional classes for students with learning differences (through the Learning Skills Center); ESL (20 students enrolled).

College Admission Counseling 76 students graduated in 2008; 69 went to college, including Syracuse University. Other: 1 entered military service, 5 entered a postgraduate year, 1 had other specific plans.

Student Life Upper grades have specified standards of dress, student council, honor system. Discipline rests equally with students and faculty.

Tuition and Aid Day student tuition: $22,900; 7-day tuition and room/board: $41,200. Tuition installment plan (Insured Tuition Payment Plan, FACTS Tuition Payment Plan, monthly payment plans, individually arranged payment plans, 2-payment plan). Need-based scholarship grants available. In 2008–09, 41% of upper-school students received aid. Total amount of financial aid awarded in 2008–09: $1,900,000.

Admissions Traditional secondary-level entrance grade is 9. Deadline for receipt of application materials: none. Application fee required: $50. Interview required.

Athletics Interscholastic: baseball (boys), basketball (b,g), field hockey (g), football (b), hockey (b,g), ice hockey (b,g), lacrosse (b,g), soccer (b,g), softball (g), tennis (b,g); coed interscholastic: alpine skiing, cross-country running, equestrian sports, fencing, golf, horseback riding, independent competitive sports, mountain biking, physical training, skiing (cross-country), skiing (downhill), snowboarding; coed intramural: alpine skiing, canoeing/kayaking, dance, equestrian sports, fencing, figure skating,

fitness, freestyle skiing, hiking/backpacking, horseback riding, ice skating, kayaking, mountain biking, nordic skiing, outdoor activities, outdoor recreation, outdoor skills, rock climbing, skiing (cross-country), skiing (downhill), snowboarding, snowshoeing, soccer, strength & conditioning, tennis. 4 coaches, 1 athletic trainer.
Computers Computers are regularly used in all academic, college planning, desktop publishing, graphic design, media production, newspaper, photojournalism, publications, SAT preparation, video film production, Web site design, yearbook classes. Computer network features include on-campus library services, online commercial services, Internet access, Internet filtering or blocking technology. Student e-mail accounts and computer access in designated common areas are available to students. The school has a published electronic and media policy.
Contact Ms. Amy Smucker, Director of Admissions. 207-685-4914 Ext. 152. Fax: 207-685-9529. E-mail: asmucker@kentshill.org. Web site: www.kentshill.org.

See Close-Up on page 810.

KENTUCKY COUNTRY DAY SCHOOL

4100 Springdale Road
Louisville, Kentucky 40241
Head of School: Mr. Bradley E. Lyman

General Information Coeducational day college-preparatory, arts, technology, Honors program, Independent Study, and Advanced programs for academically exceptional students school. Grades JK–12. Founded: 1972. Setting: suburban. 85-acre campus. 1 building on campus. Approved or accredited by Independent Schools Association of the Central States. Member of National Association of Independent Schools. Endowment: $10.3 million. Total enrollment: 902. Upper school average class size: 18. Upper school faculty-student ratio: 1:8.
Upper School Student Profile Grade 9: 68 students (30 boys, 38 girls); Grade 10: 75 students (37 boys, 38 girls); Grade 11: 59 students (32 boys, 27 girls); Grade 12: 69 students (36 boys, 33 girls).
Faculty School total: 107. In upper school: 19 men, 15 women; 26 have advanced degrees.
Subjects Offered Algebra, American history, American literature, art, biology, calculus, ceramics, chemistry, collage and assemblage, communications, computer math, computer programming, computer science, drama, economics, English, English literature, European history, fine arts, French, geology, geometry, government/civics, history, humanities, instrumental music, Latin, law, mathematics, multimedia, music, physical education, physics, play production, psychology, psychology-AP, science, sculpture, senior internship, senior project, social science, social studies, Spanish, Spanish language-AP, speech, stagecraft, statistics, studio art-AP, technical theater, theater, trigonometry, U.S. government-AP, U.S. history-AP.
Graduation Requirements Arts and fine arts (art, music, dance, drama), communications, English, foreign language, mathematics, physical education (includes health), science, social studies (includes history).
Special Academic Programs 20 Advanced Placement exams for which test preparation is offered; honors section; independent study; term-away projects; study abroad; academic accommodation for the gifted, the musically talented, and the artistically talented.
College Admission Counseling 51 students graduated in 2008; all went to college, including Davidson College; DePaul University; Emory University; Miami University; University of Kentucky; University of Louisville. Median SAT critical reading: 600, median SAT math: 600, median SAT writing: 600, median combined SAT: 1790, median composite ACT: 26. 50% scored over 600 on SAT critical reading, 52% scored over 600 on SAT math, 52% scored over 600 on SAT writing, 48% scored over 1800 on combined SAT, 57% scored over 26 on composite ACT.
Student Life Upper grades have specified standards of dress, student council, honor system. Discipline rests equally with students and faculty.
Summer Programs Remediation, enrichment, advancement, sports, art/fine arts, rigorous outdoor training, computer instruction programs offered; session focuses on enrichment; held on campus; accepts boys and girls; open to students from other schools. 200 students usually enrolled. 2009 schedule: June 7 to August 20. Application deadline: none.
Tuition and Aid Day student tuition: $15,490. Tuition installment plan (FACTS Tuition Payment Plan). Need-based scholarship grants available. In 2008–09, 13% of upper-school students received aid. Total amount of financial aid awarded in 2008–09: $398,816.
Admissions Traditional secondary-level entrance grade is 9. For fall 2008, 36 students applied for upper-level admission, 28 were accepted, 22 enrolled. ERB Reading and Math required. Deadline for receipt of application materials: none. Application fee required: $75. On-campus interview required.
Athletics Interscholastic: baseball (boys), basketball (b,g), cross-country running (b,g), diving (b,g), field hockey (g), football (b), golf (b,g), lacrosse (b,g), soccer (b,g), softball (g), swimming and diving (b,g), tennis (b,g), track and field (b,g), volleyball (g), wrestling (b); coed interscholastic: weight training; coed intramural: bowling, project adventure, ropes courses, weight lifting. 7 PE instructors, 39 coaches, 1 athletic trainer.
Computers Computers are regularly used in all classes. Computer network features include on-campus library services, online commercial services, Internet access, wireless campus network, Internet filtering or blocking technology. Campus intranet and student e-mail accounts are available to students. Students grades are available online. The school has a published electronic and media policy.
Contact Mr. Jeff Holbrook, Director of Admissions. 502-814-4375. Fax: 502-814-4381. E-mail: admissions@kcd.org. Web site: www.kcd.org.

KERR-VANCE ACADEMY

700 Vance Academy Road
Henderson, North Carolina 27537
Head of School: Mr. Paul Villatico

General Information Coeducational day college-preparatory school. Grades PK–12. Founded: 1968. Setting: rural. Nearest major city is Raleigh. 25-acre campus. 8 buildings on campus. Approved or accredited by North Carolina Association of Independent Schools, Southern Association of Colleges and Schools, and North Carolina Department of Education. Endowment: $40,000. Total enrollment: 472. Upper school average class size: 16. Upper school faculty-student ratio: 1:10.
Upper School Student Profile Grade 9: 33 students (15 boys, 18 girls); Grade 10: 44 students (18 boys, 26 girls); Grade 11: 32 students (13 boys, 19 girls); Grade 12: 23 students (14 boys, 9 girls).
Faculty School total: 41. In upper school: 5 men, 13 women; 12 have advanced degrees.
Subjects Offered Advanced Placement courses, algebra, American history, American literature, art, art history, biology, calculus, chemistry, computer programming, computer science, creative writing, driver education, earth science, economics, English, English literature, environmental science, French, geography, geometry, government/civics, grammar, Latin, mathematics, music, physical education, physics, psychology, SAT/ACT preparation, science, social science, social studies, sociology, Spanish, speech, trigonometry, world history, world literature, writing.
Graduation Requirements Computer science, English, English composition, English literature, foreign language, mathematics, physical education (includes health), science, social science, social studies (includes history), writing. Community service is required.
Special Academic Programs Advanced Placement exam preparation.
College Admission Counseling 27 students graduated in 2008; 25 went to college, including East Carolina University; Meredith College; North Carolina State University; The University of North Carolina at Chapel Hill; The University of North Carolina at Greensboro; The University of North Carolina Wilmington. Other: 2 went to work. Mean SAT critical reading: 508, mean SAT math: 517, mean composite ACT: 25. 16% scored over 600 on SAT critical reading, 21% scored over 600 on SAT math, 33% scored over 26 on composite ACT.
Student Life Upper grades have specified standards of dress, student council. Discipline rests primarily with faculty.
Summer Programs Enrichment, advancement programs offered; session focuses on academic advancement; held on campus; accepts boys and girls; open to students from other schools. 50 students usually enrolled. 2009 schedule: July 10 to August 11. Application deadline: May 15.
Tuition and Aid Day student tuition: $5684. Tuition installment plan (monthly payment plans). Tuition reduction for siblings, merit scholarship grants, need-based scholarship grants, paying campus jobs available. In 2008–09, 5% of upper-school students received aid; total upper-school merit-scholarship money awarded: $2000. Total amount of financial aid awarded in 2008–09: $15,000.
Admissions Admissions testing or writing sample required. Deadline for receipt of application materials: none. Application fee required: $50. On-campus interview required.
Athletics Interscholastic: baseball (boys), basketball (b,g), cheering (g), cross-country running (b,g), golf (b), soccer (b,g), softball (g), tennis (b,g), volleyball (g), weight training (b,g), wrestling (b); intramural: soccer (b,g), weight lifting (b); coed intramural: swimming and diving, volleyball. 3 PE instructors, 7 coaches, 1 athletic trainer.
Computers Computers are regularly used in art, English, history, library, literary magazine, newspaper, programming, reading, research skills, SAT preparation, science, technology, writing, yearbook classes. Computer network features include on-campus library services, online commercial services, Internet access.
Contact Rebecca W. Irvin, Admissions Coordinator. 252-492-0018. Fax: 252-438-4652. E-mail: rirvin@kerrvance.com. Web site: www.kerrvance.com.

THE KEY SCHOOL

534 Hillsmere Drive
Annapolis, Maryland 21403
Head of School: Marcella M. Yedid

General Information Coeducational day college-preparatory, arts, and outdoor education school. Grades PK–12. Founded: 1958. Setting: suburban. Nearest major city is Baltimore. 15-acre campus. 10 buildings on campus. Approved or accredited by Association of Independent Maryland Schools and Maryland Department of Education. Member of National Association of Independent Schools. Endowment: $4.4 million. Total enrollment: 700. Upper school average class size: 14. Upper school faculty-student ratio: 1:8.

Upper School Student Profile Grade 9: 48 students (21 boys, 27 girls); Grade 10: 42 students (14 boys, 28 girls); Grade 11: 53 students (29 boys, 24 girls); Grade 12: 49 students (22 boys, 27 girls).
Faculty School total: 111. In upper school: 15 men, 25 women; 28 have advanced degrees.
Subjects Offered Acting, algebra, American studies, ancient history, art, art history, biology, calculus, ceramics, chemistry, Chesapeake Bay studies, choir, computer science, conceptual physics, creative writing, dance, digital art, digital photography, drama, drama performance, drawing, economics, English, English literature, European history, fine arts, French, geometry, journalism, Latin, literature by women, music, photography, physical education, physics, physiology, playwriting, pre-calculus, printmaking, Russian literature, sculpture, Shakespeare, Spanish, Spanish literature, statistics, studio art, theater, theater production, trigonometry.
Graduation Requirements Arts and fine arts (art, music, dance, drama), English, foreign language, history, mathematics, performing arts, physical education (includes health), science.
Special Academic Programs Advanced Placement exam preparation; honors section; independent study; academic accommodation for the gifted.
College Admission Counseling 58 students graduated in 2008; all went to college, including Case Western Reserve University; Smith College; University of Chicago; University of Colorado at Boulder; University of Maryland, College Park; Washington University in St. Louis.
Student Life Upper grades have student council. Discipline rests equally with students and faculty.
Summer Programs Remediation, enrichment, sports, art/fine arts, rigorous outdoor training programs offered; held both on and off campus; held at area pools, area parks, and other off-site locations; accepts boys and girls; open to students from other schools. 475 students usually enrolled. 2009 schedule: June 15 to August 14.
Tuition and Aid Day student tuition: $21,500. Tuition installment plan (monthly payment plans, TuitionPay Plan from Sallie Mae, Management Services Plan)). Tuition reduction for siblings, need-based scholarship grants available. In 2008–09, 23% of upper-school students received aid. Total amount of financial aid awarded in 2008–09: $439,397.
Admissions Traditional secondary-level entrance grade is 9. For fall 2008, 53 students applied for upper-level admission, 37 were accepted, 23 enrolled. ERB or ISEE required. Deadline for receipt of application materials: none. Application fee required: $45. Interview required.
Athletics Interscholastic: baseball (boys), basketball (b,g), field hockey (g), indoor soccer (g), lacrosse (b,g), soccer (b,g); intramural: field hockey (g), lacrosse (b,g); coed interscholastic: cross-country running, golf, sailing, tennis; coed intramural: backpacking, basketball, canoeing/kayaking, climbing, cooperative games, dance, fitness, fitness walking, golf, hiking/backpacking, kayaking, kickball, modern dance, Newcombe ball, outdoor activities, project adventure, roller blading, running. 1 PE instructor, 44 coaches, 1 athletic trainer.
Computers Computers are regularly used in all academic classes. Computer network features include on-campus library services, online commercial services, Internet access, wireless campus network, online supplementary course materials. Campus intranet and student e-mail accounts are available to students. The school has a published electronic and media policy.
Contact Jessie D. Dunleavy, Director of Admission, Communication and Financial Aid. 410-263-9231. Fax: 410-280-5516. E-mail: jdunleavy@keyschool.org. Web site: www.keyschool.org.

ANNOUNCEMENT FROM THE SCHOOL The Key School has a strong academic curriculum that encourages intellectual rigor, independence of thought, curiosity, creativity, and openness to different ideas and perspectives. The tone of the campus is egalitarian, informal, and caring, with an academic focus that is both rigorous and innovative. Key School seeks to develop in its students an interest in learning and a sustaining degree of intellectual curiosity.

KILDONAN SCHOOL

Amenia, New York
See Special Needs Schools section.

KIMBALL UNION ACADEMY

PO Box 188
Main Street
Meriden, New Hampshire 03770
Head of School: Mr. Michael J. Schafer
General Information Coeducational boarding and day college-preparatory, arts, and environmental science school. Grades 9–PG. Founded: 1813. Setting: small town. Nearest major city is Boston, MA. Students are housed in single-sex dormitories. 1,300-acre campus. 35 buildings on campus. Approved or accredited by Independent Schools of Northern New England, New England Association of Schools and Colleges, The Association of Boarding Schools, The College Board, and New Hampshire Department of Education. Member of National Association of Independent Schools and Secondary School Admission Test Board. Endowment: $19.1 million. Total enrollment: 355. Upper school average class size: 12. Upper school faculty-student ratio: 1:6.
Upper School Student Profile Grade 9: 51 students (28 boys, 23 girls); Grade 10: 75 students (41 boys, 34 girls); Grade 11: 105 students (53 boys, 52 girls); Grade 12: 106 students (67 boys, 39 girls); Postgraduate: 18 students (18 boys). 67% of students are boarding students. 32% are state residents. 19 states are represented in upper school student body. 20% are international students. International students from Canada, China, Germany, Japan, Republic of Korea, and Spain; 13 other countries represented in student body.
Faculty School total: 49. In upper school: 28 men, 21 women; 34 have advanced degrees; 34 reside on campus.
Subjects Offered 3-dimensional design, Advanced Placement courses, algebra, American history, American literature, anatomy, anthropology, architectural drawing, architecture, art, art history, art history-AP, biology, biology-AP, calculus, calculus-AP, ceramics, chemistry, chemistry-AP, classical civilization, composition-AP, computer applications, computer programming, computer science, creative writing, criminal justice, dance, digital photography, drama, driver education, English, English language and composition-AP, English literature, English literature and composition-AP, English-AP, environmental science, environmental science-AP, environmental studies, European history, fine arts, French, French language-AP, French literature-AP, geology, geometry, government/civics, grammar, health, history, history-AP, honors English, honors geometry, human geography—AP, independent study, jazz ensemble, language-AP, Latin, Mandarin, marine biology, marine science, marine studies, mathematical modeling, mathematics, modern European history-AP, modern world history, music, music history, music theory, peer counseling, philosophy, photo shop, photography, physics, physics-AP, physiology, playwriting, pottery, probability and statistics, programming, psychology, public speaking, science, Shakespeare, social studies, Spanish, Spanish-AP, statistics-AP, student publications, studio art, theater, theater arts, theater design and production, trigonometry, U.S. history, U.S. history-AP, woodworking, world history, world literature, writing.
Graduation Requirements Art, English, foreign language, history, mathematics, science.
Special Academic Programs Advanced Placement exam preparation; honors section; independent study; study abroad.
College Admission Counseling 100 students graduated in 2008; 99 went to college, including Boston College; Boston University; Connecticut College; Lehigh University; University of New Hampshire; University of Vermont. Other: 1 had other specific plans. Mean SAT critical reading: 560, mean SAT math: 580, mean SAT writing: 550. 40% scored over 600 on SAT critical reading, 35% scored over 600 on SAT math.
Student Life Upper grades have specified standards of dress, student council, honor system. Discipline rests equally with students and faculty.
Summer Programs Enrichment, advancement, ESL, sports, art/fine arts, computer instruction programs offered; session focuses on environmental leadership (EE Just Institute) and enrichment, language, arts, athletic camps; held both on and off campus; held at Costa Rica; accepts boys and girls; open to students from other schools. 40 students usually enrolled. 2009 schedule: July 2 to August 3. Application deadline: April 15.
Tuition and Aid Day student tuition: $27,500; 7-day tuition and room/board: $42,500. Tuition installment plan (Insured Tuition Payment Plan, Academic Management Services Plan, Key Tuition Payment Plan, monthly payment plans). Need-based scholarship grants, paying campus jobs available. In 2008–09, 35% of upper-school students received aid. Total amount of financial aid awarded in 2008–09: $2,297,435.
Admissions Traditional secondary-level entrance grade is 9. For fall 2008, 475 students applied for upper-level admission, 268 were accepted, 124 enrolled. ACT, PSAT or SAT, SSAT or TOEFL required. Deadline for receipt of application materials: February 1. Application fee required: $50. Interview required.
Athletics Interscholastic: alpine skiing (boys, girls), baseball (b), basketball (b,g), bicycling (b,g), cross-country running (b,g), equestrian sports (b,g), field hockey (g), football (b), golf (b,g), hockey (b,g), horseback riding (b,g), ice hockey (b,g), lacrosse (b,g), mountain biking (b,g), nordic skiing (b,g), rugby (b), running (b,g), skiing (cross-country) (b,g), skiing (downhill) (b,g), snowboarding (b,g), soccer (b,g), softball (g), swimming and diving (b,g), tennis (b,g); coed intramural: alpine skiing, backpacking, canoeing/kayaking, dance, equestrian sports, fitness, freestyle skiing, hiking/backpacking, modern dance, outdoor activities, physical fitness, rock climbing, strength & conditioning, surfing, weight lifting. 1 coach, 2 athletic trainers.
Computers Computers are regularly used in architecture, art, drawing and design, English, foreign language, French, geography, graphic arts, graphic design, history, human geography—AP, literary magazine, mathematics, music, newspaper, photography, science, Spanish, technology, theater arts, video film production, woodworking, writing, yearbook classes. Computer network features include on-campus library services, Internet access, wireless campus network, Internet filtering or blocking technology, computer music studio/audio recording. Student e-mail accounts and computer access in designated common areas are available to students. Students grades are available online. The school has a published electronic and media policy.
Contact Mr. Rich Ryerson, Director of Admissions and Financial Aid. 603-469-2100. Fax: 603-469-2041. E-mail: admissions@kua.org. Web site: www.kua.org.

ANNOUNCEMENT FROM THE SCHOOL Founded in 1813, Kimball Union is a coeducational boarding and day school serving 345 students in grades 9–12 and a postgraduate year. Kimball Union's unique location in the Upper Connecticut River Valley and its proximity to Dartmouth College have long made it the preferred choice for students seeking an educational experience that develops the whole person as scholar, athlete, artist, and global citizen.

See Close-Up on page 812.

KIMBERTON WALDORF SCHOOL

PO Box 350
410 West Seven Stars Road
Kimberton, Pennsylvania 19442

Head of School: Lisa Faranda

General Information Coeducational day college-preparatory and arts school. Grades PK–12. Founded: 1941. Setting: rural. Nearest major city is Philadelphia. 350-acre campus. 3 buildings on campus. Approved or accredited by Association of Waldorf Schools of North America and Middle States Association of Colleges and Schools. Member of National Association of Independent Schools. Endowment: $2 million. Total enrollment: 306. Upper school average class size: 18. Upper school faculty-student ratio: 1:6.

Upper School Student Profile Grade 9: 20 students (13 boys, 7 girls); Grade 10: 28 students (14 boys, 14 girls); Grade 11: 20 students (8 boys, 12 girls); Grade 12: 20 students (9 boys, 11 girls).

Faculty School total: 40. In upper school: 18 men, 13 women; 15 have advanced degrees.

Subjects Offered Algebra, American history, American literature, anatomy, architecture, art, art history, astronomy, biology, botany, calculus, ceramics, chemistry, community service, creative writing, drama, earth science, English, English literature, environmental science, European history, expository writing, fine arts, gardening, geology, geometry, German, government/civics, grammar, health, history, history of ideas, history of science, mathematics, music, music history, physical education, physics, physiology, science, social studies, Spanish, speech, theater, trigonometry, world history, world literature, writing, zoology.

Graduation Requirements 20th century history, African history, agriculture, algebra, American Civil War, American government, American literature, ancient world history, art history, biology, botany, career education internship, Civil War, drama, East Asian history, English, European history, eurythmy, fiber arts, foreign language, geology, geometry, inorganic chemistry, mathematics, modern world history, organic chemistry, painting, physical education (includes health), physics, physiology, poetry, Russian literature, U.S. history, woodworking. Community service is required.

Special Academic Programs Honors section; independent study; term-away projects; study abroad.

College Admission Counseling 14 students graduated in 2008; 7 went to college, including Dickinson College; Indiana University of Pennsylvania; Marlboro College; Maryland Institute College of Art; Millersville University of Pennsylvania; West Chester University of Pennsylvania. Other: 7 had other specific plans. 29% scored over 600 on SAT critical reading, 29% scored over 600 on SAT writing.

Student Life Upper grades have specified standards of dress, student council. Discipline rests primarily with faculty.

Tuition and Aid Day student tuition: $17,530. Tuition installment plan (monthly payment plans, individually arranged payment plans, Biannual payment plan). Tuition reduction for siblings, need-based scholarship grants available. In 2008–09, 17% of upper-school students received aid. Total amount of financial aid awarded in 2008–09: $164,250.

Admissions Traditional secondary-level entrance grade is 9. For fall 2008, 5 students applied for upper-level admission, 5 were accepted, 3 enrolled. School placement exam required. Deadline for receipt of application materials: none. Application fee required: $50. On-campus interview required.

Athletics Interscholastic: basketball (boys, girls), field hockey (g), hiking/backpacking (b,g), lacrosse (b,g), soccer (b), tennis (b,g), volleyball (b,g); intramural: outdoor activities (b,g), rock climbing (b,g), ropes courses (b,g); coed interscholastic: hiking/backpacking, volleyball; coed intramural: outdoor activities, rock climbing, ropes courses. 3 PE instructors, 8 coaches.

Computers Computer resources include on-campus library services, Internet access, Internet filtering or blocking technology. The school has a published electronic and media policy.

Contact Danette Takahashi, Admissions Coordinator. 610-933-3635 Ext. 108. Fax: 610-935-6985. E-mail: dtakahashi@kimberton.org. Web site: www.kimberton.org.

KING GEORGE SCHOOL

Sutton, Vermont

See Special Needs Schools section.

KING LOW HEYWOOD THOMAS

1450 Newfield Avenue
Stamford, Connecticut 06905

Head of School: Thomas B. Main

General Information Coeducational day college-preparatory school. Grades PK–12. Founded: 1865. Setting: suburban. Nearest major city is New York, NY. 40-acre campus. 4 buildings on campus. Approved or accredited by Connecticut Association of Independent Schools and New England Association of Schools and Colleges. Member of National Association of Independent Schools. Endowment: $16.8 million. Total enrollment: 655. Upper school average class size: 12. Upper school faculty-student ratio: 1:7.

Upper School Student Profile Grade 9: 68 students (41 boys, 27 girls); Grade 10: 70 students (41 boys, 29 girls); Grade 11: 71 students (39 boys, 32 girls); Grade 12: 62 students (34 boys, 28 girls).

Faculty School total: 105. In upper school: 20 men, 23 women; 27 have advanced degrees.

Subjects Offered Acting, advanced chemistry, advanced computer applications, advanced math, algebra, American history, ancient history, ancient world history, art, biology, British literature, calculus, calculus-AP, chemistry, chemistry-AP, choral music, college counseling, college placement, computer applications, computer graphics, computer multimedia, computer programming, computer programming-AP, computer science, creative writing, discrete math, dramatic arts, economics, economics-AP, English, English literature, English literature-AP, ethics, ethics and responsibility, European history, European history-AP, expository writing, fine arts, French, French language-AP, general science, geometry, health, history, Holocaust, honors algebra, honors English, honors geometry, honors U.S. history, honors world history, independent study, introduction to theater, macroeconomics-AP, mathematics, mathematics-AP, microeconomics-AP, model United Nations, modern European history-AP, modern languages, musical productions, musical theater, performing arts, philosophy, physics, physics-AP, play production, pre-calculus, SAT preparation, science, social studies, Spanish, Spanish literature, Spanish literature-AP, statistics, statistics-AP, student government, student publications, studio art, theater arts, trigonometry, U.S. history-AP, U.S. literature, world history, writing workshop.

Graduation Requirements Arts and fine arts (art, music, dance, drama), English, ethics, foreign language, history, life skills, mathematics, science, sports, 2 participation in theater performance before graduation.

Special Academic Programs Advanced Placement exam preparation; honors section; independent study; academic accommodation for the gifted, the musically talented, and the artistically talented.

College Admission Counseling 59 students graduated in 2008; 55 went to college, including Boston University; Colgate University; Dartmouth College; Hamilton College; Lehigh University; University of Michigan. Other: 3 entered a postgraduate year, 1 had other specific plans. Mean SAT critical reading: 608, mean SAT math: 624, mean SAT writing: 609. 60% scored over 600 on SAT critical reading, 67% scored over 600 on SAT math, 60% scored over 600 on SAT writing, 60% scored over 1800 on combined SAT.

Student Life Upper grades have specified standards of dress, student council. Discipline rests equally with students and faculty.

Summer Programs Remediation, enrichment, advancement, sports, art/fine arts programs offered; session focuses on academics (grades 6-12), enrichment (elementary school), and sports (grades 4-8) enrichment; held on campus; accepts boys and girls; open to students from other schools. 260 students usually enrolled. 2009 schedule: June 15 to July 31. Application deadline: June 15.

Tuition and Aid Day student tuition: $30,200. Tuition installment plan (Key Tuition Payment Plan). Merit scholarship grants, need-based scholarship grants available. In 2008–09, 14% of upper-school students received aid; total upper-school merit-scholarship money awarded: $37,275. Total amount of financial aid awarded in 2008–09: $765,875.

Admissions Traditional secondary-level entrance grade is 9. For fall 2008, 176 students applied for upper-level admission, 60 were accepted, 40 enrolled. ISEE, school's own test or SSAT required. Deadline for receipt of application materials: January 15. Application fee required: $75. On-campus interview required.

Athletics Interscholastic: baseball (boys), basketball (b,g), cheering (g), cross-country running (b,g), field hockey (g), football (b), golf (b,g), ice hockey (b), independent competitive sports (b,g), lacrosse (b,g), soccer (b,g), softball (g), tennis (b,g), volleyball (g); intramural: dance (g), physical training (b,g); coed interscholastic: cheering, hockey, ice hockey, independent competitive sports, squash; coed intramural: aerobics, aerobics/dance, dance, fitness, physical training, strength & conditioning, weight lifting, weight training, yoga. 23 coaches, 2 athletic trainers.

Computers Computers are regularly used in college planning, creative writing, economics, English, ethics, foreign language, French, history, mathematics, science, technology, writing fundamentals, yearbook classes. Computer network features include on-campus library services, online commercial services, Internet access, wireless campus network, Internet filtering or blocking technology. Campus intranet, student e-mail accounts, and computer access in designated common areas are available to students. The school has a published electronic and media policy.

Contact Carrie Salvatore, Director of Admission and Financial Aid. 203-322-3496 Ext. 352. Fax: 203-505-6288. E-mail: csalvatore@klht.org. Web site: www.klht.org.

ANNOUNCEMENT FROM THE SCHOOL King Low Heywood Thomas (King) offers a comprehensive college-preparatory program that is responsive to the individual talents and needs of students and their changing environment. The School, which serves students from pre-kindergarten through twelfth grade, is noted for high academic standards and individual accountability in scholarship and leadership. King students are consistently recognized for their educational achievements. More than 60% of the Middle School qualifies annually for the Johns Hopkins Talent Search, and many graduating classes have had multiple National Merit Finalists. Honors and Advanced Placement courses are offered in all departments. Academics are balanced with full participation in athletics and a wide variety of clubs and organizations; opportunities for expression in the literary, performing, and visual arts abound. This balance is the framework for the development of the total child. King recognizes and rewards students' efforts to attain their full potential. The School's diverse community focuses on respect for the individual and high standards of conduct and behavior for everyone. College counseling includes full-time professionals, a resource library, workshops, and classes. More than 100 college representatives visit students on campus each year. Pre-kindergarten and kindergarten are taught by early childhood professionals in a comprehensive learning environment that emphasizes learning readiness within a developmental curriculum. The five-day program is a full-day program. King represents a merger of three schools, the oldest of which dates from 1865. Located on 36 acres in North Stamford, King draws from Fairfield and Westchester Counties. Financial aid is available. Thomas B. Main (B.A., Bates College; M.A., Wesleyan University) is Head of School. The School is accredited by the New England Association of Schools and Colleges (NEASC).

THE KING'S ACADEMY

202 Smothers Road
Seymour, Tennessee 37865

Head of School: Walter Grubb

General Information Coeducational boarding and day college-preparatory and religious studies school, affiliated with Southern Baptist Convention. Boarding grades 7–12, day grades K4–12. Founded: 1880. Setting: suburban. Nearest major city is Knoxville. Students are housed in single-sex dormitories. 67-acre campus. 8 buildings on campus. Approved or accredited by Association of Christian Schools International, Southern Association of Colleges and Schools, and Tennessee Department of Education. Endowment: $1.7 million. Total enrollment: 377. Upper school average class size: 14. Upper school faculty-student ratio: 1:14.

Upper School Student Profile Grade 9: 30 students (16 boys, 14 girls); Grade 10: 36 students (21 boys, 15 girls); Grade 11: 45 students (22 boys, 23 girls); Grade 12: 34 students (18 boys, 16 girls). 39% of students are boarding students. 65% are state residents. 1 state is represented in upper school student body. 33% are international students. International students from Brazil, China, Republic of Korea, Taiwan, Thailand, and United Kingdom; 13 other countries represented in student body. 80% of students are Southern Baptist Convention.

Faculty School total: 37. In upper school: 7 men, 10 women; 5 have advanced degrees; 7 reside on campus.

Subjects Offered Advanced Placement courses, algebra, American history, anatomy, art, Bible studies, biology, calculus, chemistry, choir, drama, economics, English, English-AP, ESL, fine arts, geometry, government/civics, grammar, health, health and wellness, history, journalism, keyboarding, mathematics, music, orchestra, physical education, physics, physiology, religion, science, social studies, Spanish, world history.

Graduation Requirements Arts and fine arts (art, music, dance, drama), computer science, English, foreign language, mathematics, religion (includes Bible studies and theology), science, social studies (includes history), wellness.

Special Academic Programs International Baccalaureate program; Advanced Placement exam preparation; honors section; independent study; ESL (12 students enrolled).

College Admission Counseling 45 students graduated in 2008; 42 went to college, including Liberty University; Michigan State University; Penn State University Park; The University of Arizona; The University of Tennessee; University of Washington. Other: 2 went to work, 1 entered military service.

Student Life Upper grades have uniform requirement, student council. Discipline rests primarily with faculty. Attendance at religious services is required.

Tuition and Aid Day student tuition: $4770–$5820; 5-day tuition and room/board: $14,100–$14,850; 7-day tuition and room/board: $18,980–$19,720. Tuition installment plan (monthly payment plans, individually arranged payment plans). Need-based scholarship grants, paying campus jobs available. In 2008–09, 14% of upper-school students received aid. Total amount of financial aid awarded in 2008–09: $189,364.

Admissions Traditional secondary-level entrance grade is 9. For fall 2008, 27 students applied for upper-level admission, 27 were accepted, 27 enrolled. Otis-Lennon School Ability Test required. Deadline for receipt of application materials: none. Application fee required: $50. Interview recommended.

Athletics Interscholastic: baseball (boys), basketball (b,g), cheering (g), football (b), golf (b,g), soccer (b,g), tennis (b,g), volleyball (g), weight lifting (b), weight training (b); intramural: basketball (b,g), billiards (b,g), table tennis (b,g), tennis (b,g), volleyball (g), weight lifting (b,g); coed interscholastic: backpacking, bowling, cross-country running, rappelling, rock climbing, strength & conditioning, track and field; coed intramural: canoeing/kayaking, cross-country running, outdoor education, physical fitness, volleyball. 4 coaches.

Computers Computers are regularly used in ESL, journalism, keyboarding classes. Computer network features include Internet access.

Contact Janice Mink, Director of Admissions. 865-573-8321. Fax: 865-573-8323. E-mail: jmink@thekingsacademy.net.

THE KING'S CHRISTIAN HIGH SCHOOL

5 Carnegie Plaza
Cherry Hill, New Jersey 08003-1020

Head of School: Rebecca B. Stiegel, EdD

General Information Coeducational day and distance learning college-preparatory and religious studies school, affiliated with Christian faith. Grades P3–12. Distance learning grades 6–12. Founded: 1946. Setting: suburban. Nearest major city is Philadelphia, PA. 11-acre campus. 1 building on campus. Approved or accredited by Association of Christian Schools International, Middle States Association of Colleges and Schools, and New Jersey Department of Education. Total enrollment: 363. Upper school average class size: 18. Upper school faculty-student ratio: 1:7.

Upper School Student Profile Grade 9: 35 students (19 boys, 16 girls); Grade 10: 33 students (16 boys, 17 girls); Grade 11: 26 students (11 boys, 15 girls); Grade 12: 44 students (23 boys, 21 girls). 100% of students are Christian faith.

Faculty School total: 36. In upper school: 7 men, 13 women; 5 have advanced degrees.

Subjects Offered Accounting, Advanced Placement courses, algebra, American history, American literature, anatomy, art, art appreciation, art history, art history-AP, band, bell choir, Bible, Bible studies, biology, biology-AP, British literature, business mathematics, calculus, calculus-AP, career and personal planning, career education, career/college preparation, chemistry, choir, Christian ethics, church history, college admission preparation, composition, computer education, computer graphics, computer keyboarding, computer skills, concert band, concert bell choir, concert choir, consumer mathematics, drama, economics, English literature, environmental science, ESL, fine arts, foreign language, general math, geometry, government-AP, handbells, health and safety, health and wellness, health education, honors algebra, honors English, honors geometry, honors U.S. history, instrumental music, jazz band, keyboarding/computer, language arts, library assistant, Life of Christ, marine science, music appreciation, music theory, music theory-AP, New Testament, physical education, physics, physiology-anatomy, SAT preparation, SAT/ACT preparation, senior project, Shakespeare, Spanish, speech, study skills, U.S. government, U.S. history, vocal ensemble, Web site design, world cultures, world history, yearbook.

Graduation Requirements Algebra, arts and fine arts (art, music, dance, drama), Bible, biology, British literature, career education, career technology, chemistry, Christian ethics, church history, computer technologies, English composition, English literature, ethics, human biology, Life of Christ, physical education (includes health), physical science, public speaking, SAT preparation, senior project, Spanish, study skills, U.S. government, U.S. history, world culture, world literature, writing, required volunteer service hours each year for grades 6-12.

Special Academic Programs Advanced Placement exam preparation; honors section; independent study; study at local college for college credit; programs in English, mathematics, general development for dyslexic students; special instructional classes for students with learning disabilities, Attention Deficit Disorder; ESL (5 students enrolled).

College Admission Counseling 34 students graduated in 2008; 33 went to college, including Cedarville University; Drexel University; Temple University. Other: 1 entered military service. Mean SAT critical reading: 561, mean SAT math: 546, mean SAT writing: 554, mean combined SAT: 1661, mean composite ACT: 22. 32% scored over 600 on SAT critical reading, 12% scored over 600 on SAT math, 20% scored over 600 on SAT writing.

Student Life Upper grades have specified standards of dress, student council, honor system. Discipline rests primarily with faculty. Attendance at religious services is required.

Summer Programs Remediation, enrichment, advancement, sports programs offered; session focuses on summer school programs; held on campus; accepts boys and girls; open to students from other schools. 2009 schedule: June 29 to August 14. Application deadline: May 1.

Tuition and Aid Day student tuition: $8500. Tuition installment plan (FACTS Tuition Payment Plan, annual and semi-annual payments). Need-based scholarship grants available. In 2008–09, 43% of upper-school students received aid. Total amount of financial aid awarded in 2008–09: $150,000.

Admissions Traditional secondary-level entrance grade is 9. For fall 2008, 18 students applied for upper-level admission, 18 were accepted, 10 enrolled. Deadline for receipt of application materials: none. Application fee required: $100. On-campus interview required.

Athletics Interscholastic: baseball (boys), basketball (b,g), physical fitness (b,g), soccer (b,g), softball (g), track and field (b,g); intramural: basketball (b), flag football (b), golf (b,g). 2 PE instructors.

Computers Computers are regularly used in career education, career exploration, college planning, computer applications, desktop publishing, keyboarding, Latin, library, life skills, SAT preparation, Web site design, yearbook classes. Computer network features include on-campus library services, Internet access, Internet filtering or blocking technology. Campus intranet and computer access in designated common areas are available to students. Students grades are available online. The school has a published electronic and media policy.

Contact Mrs. Jamie Sellers, Director of Student Recruitment. 856-489-6720 Ext. 117. Fax: 856-489-6727. E-mail: jsellers@tkcs.org. Web site: www.tkcs.org.

KINGS CHRISTIAN SCHOOL

900 East D Street
Lemoore, California 93245

Head of School: Mr. Duane E. Daniel

General Information Coeducational day and distance learning college-preparatory, general academic, arts, business, religious studies, and technology school. Grades PK–12. Distance learning grades 9–12. Founded: 1979. Setting: small town. Nearest major city is Fresno. 17-acre campus. 12 buildings on campus. Approved or accredited by Association of Christian Schools International and Western Association of Schools and Colleges. Total enrollment: 313. Upper school average class size: 20. Upper school faculty-student ratio: 1:15.

Upper School Student Profile Grade 6: 18 students (12 boys, 6 girls); Grade 7: 26 students (15 boys, 11 girls); Grade 8: 31 students (20 boys, 11 girls); Grade 9: 30 students (11 boys, 19 girls); Grade 10: 22 students (9 boys, 13 girls); Grade 11: 32 students (18 boys, 14 girls); Grade 12: 25 students (12 boys, 13 girls).

Faculty School total: 25. In upper school: 4 men, 6 women; 3 have advanced degrees.

Subjects Offered Accounting, advanced math, algebra, American government, art, Bible studies, biology, business, calculus-AP, career education, chemistry, choir, chorus, community service, computer literacy, computer programming, drama, drama performance, drawing, driver education, economics, English, English literature-AP, finance, fine arts, geography, geometry, health, keyboarding, life skills, literature, mathematics, music, music theory, novels, physical education, physical science, physics, pre-algebra, religion, SAT preparation, science, Shakespeare, sign language, social science, social studies, Spanish, speech, U.S. history, weight training, word processing, yearbook.

Graduation Requirements Arts and fine arts (art, music, dance, drama), English, foreign language, mathematics, physical education (includes health), science, social science, successfully pass Bible every year of attendance, proof of at least 9th grade proficiency (SAT Test). Community service is required.

Special Academic Programs 2 Advanced Placement exams for which test preparation is offered; honors section; accelerated programs; independent study; remedial reading and/or remedial writing; remedial math.

College Admission Counseling 27 students graduated in 2008; 23 went to college, including Biola University; California State University, Fresno; The Master's College and Seminary; University of California, Davis; Vanguard University of Southern California; West Hills Community College. Other: 1 went to work, 1 entered military service, 2 had other specific plans. Median SAT critical reading: 550, median SAT math: 500, median SAT writing: 550, median combined SAT: 1600. 35% scored over 600 on SAT critical reading, 1% scored over 600 on SAT math, 24% scored over 600 on SAT writing, 1% scored over 1800 on combined SAT.

Student Life Upper grades have specified standards of dress, student council. Discipline rests primarily with faculty.

Summer Programs Remediation, advancement programs offered; session focuses on on-line courses; held both on and off campus; held at students' homes; accepts boys and girls; not open to students from other schools. 8 students usually enrolled. 2009 schedule: June 9 to August 1. Application deadline: May 19.

Tuition and Aid Day student tuition: $5060. Tuition installment plan (monthly payment plans). Tuition reduction for siblings, need-based scholarship grants, paying campus jobs available. In 2008–09, 18% of upper-school students received aid. Total amount of financial aid awarded in 2008–09: $150,000.

Admissions Traditional secondary-level entrance grade is 9. PSAT or Stanford Achievement Test required. Deadline for receipt of application materials: none. Application fee required: $75.

Athletics Interscholastic: baseball (boys), basketball (b,g), football (b), softball (g), track and field (b,g), volleyball (g); intramural: physical fitness (b,g), physical training (b,g), power lifting (b), strength & conditioning (b,g), track and field (b,g), weight training (b,g); coed interscholastic: cheering, cross-country running, track and field; coed intramural: badminton, fitness, Frisbee, physical fitness, strength & conditioning, table tennis, track and field, volleyball. 5 PE instructors, 9 coaches, 2 athletic trainers.

Computers Computers are regularly used in Bible studies, college planning, English, introduction to technology, journalism, library skills, programming, SAT preparation, technical drawing, yearbook classes. Computer network features include on-campus library services, Internet access, wireless campus network, Internet filtering or blocking technology.

Contact Leslie Reynolds, Registrar. 559-924-8301 Ext. 107. Fax: 559-924-0607. E-mail: lreynolds@kcsnet.com. Web site: www.kcsnet.com.

KING'S-EDGEHILL SCHOOL

254 College Road
Windsor, Nova Scotia B0N 2T0, Canada

Head of School: Mr. Joseph Seagram

General Information Coeducational boarding and day college-preparatory school, affiliated with Church of England (Anglican). Grades 6–12. Founded: 1788. Setting: small town. Nearest major city is Halifax, Canada. Students are housed in single-sex dormitories. 65-acre campus. 17 buildings on campus. Approved or accredited by Canadian Association of Independent Schools, International Baccalaureate Organization, and Nova Scotia Department of Education. Language of instruction: English. Total enrollment: 365. Upper school average class size: 15. Upper school faculty-student ratio: 1:10.

Upper School Student Profile Grade 10: 70 students (38 boys, 32 girls); Grade 11: 95 students (55 boys, 40 girls); Grade 12: 90 students (50 boys, 40 girls). 68% of students are boarding students. 55% are province residents. 13 provinces are represented in upper school student body. 30% are international students. International students from Germany, Hong Kong, Mexico, Republic of Korea, and Taiwan; 13 other countries represented in student body. 40% of students are members of Church of England (Anglican).

Faculty School total: 46. In upper school: 19 men, 23 women; 15 have advanced degrees; 22 reside on campus.

Subjects Offered Art, biology, calculus, chemistry, current events, drama, economics, English, French, geography, geology, history, mathematics, music, physics, political science, religion, science, social science, social studies, theater, theory of knowledge, world history.

Graduation Requirements English, foreign language, mathematics, science, social science, social studies (includes history).

Special Academic Programs International Baccalaureate program; honors section; term-away projects; study abroad; academic accommodation for the gifted; ESL (22 students enrolled).

College Admission Counseling 78 students graduated in 2008; 77 went to college, including Acadia University; Bishop's University; Dalhousie University; McGill University; Queen's University at Kingston; The University of British Columbia. Other: 1 went to work.

Student Life Upper grades have uniform requirement, student council, honor system. Discipline rests primarily with faculty. Attendance at religious services is required.

Tuition and Aid Day student tuition: CAN$11,900; 7-day tuition and room/board: CAN$28,000–CAN$35,000. Bursaries, merit scholarship grants available. In 2008–09, 35% of upper-school students received aid. Total amount of financial aid awarded in 2008–09: CAN$700,000.

Admissions Traditional secondary-level entrance grade is 10. OLSAT and English Exam required. Deadline for receipt of application materials: none. Application fee required: CAN$100. Interview required.

Athletics Interscholastic: alpine skiing (boys, girls), aquatics (b,g), badminton (b,g), baseball (b,g), basketball (b,g), biathlon (b,g), bicycling (b,g), cross-country running (b,g), equestrian sports (b,g), fitness (b,g), Frisbee (b,g), golf (b,g), ice hockey (b,g), outdoor recreation (b,g), outdoor skills (b,g), physical fitness (b,g), rugby (b,g), skiing (cross-country) (b,g), skiing (downhill) (b,g), snowboarding (b,g), soccer (b,g), softball (b,g), table tennis (b,g), tennis (b,g), track and field (b,g), ultimate Frisbee (b,g), volleyball (b,g), weight lifting (b,g), wrestling (b,g); intramural: basketball (b,g), bicycling (b,g), cross-country running (b,g), golf (b,g), rugby (b,g), skiing (cross-country) (b,g), skiing (downhill) (b,g), snowboarding (b,g), soccer (b,g), softball (b,g), table tennis (b,g), tennis (b,g), track and field (b,g), weight lifting (b,g), yoga (b,g); coed interscholastic: alpine skiing, aquatics, bicycling, equestrian sports, fitness, Frisbee, outdoor recreation, outdoor skills, physical fitness, table tennis; coed intramural: bowling, curling, field hockey, table tennis, yoga. 2 PE instructors, 30 coaches.

Computers Computers are regularly used in computer applications, English, foreign language, mathematics, music, science classes. Computer network features include on-campus library services, online commercial services, Internet access, Internet filtering or blocking technology. Campus intranet, student e-mail accounts, and computer access in designated common areas are available to students.

Contact Mr. Chris B. Strickey, Director of Admission. 902-798-2278. Fax: 902-798-2105. E-mail: strickey@kes.ns.ca. Web site: www.kes.ns.ca.

KING'S HIGH SCHOOL

19303 Fremont Avenue North
Seattle, Washington 98133

Head of School: Bob Ruhlman

General Information Coeducational day college-preparatory, arts, business, religious studies, and technology school, affiliated with Christian faith. Grades PK–12. Founded: 1950. Setting: suburban. 55-acre campus. 6 buildings on campus. Approved or accredited by Association of Christian Schools International, Northwest Association of Schools and Colleges, and Washington Department of Education. Total enrollment: 1,160. Upper school average class size: 25. Upper school faculty-student ratio: 1:17.

Upper School Student Profile 80% of students are Christian faith.

Faculty School total: 93. In upper school: 13 men, 22 women; 19 have advanced degrees.

Subjects Offered Advanced Placement courses, algebra, American history, American literature, anatomy, anatomy and physiology, art, Bible, biology, business, calculus, calculus-AP, ceramics, chemistry, chemistry-AP, choir, choral music, computer science, culinary arts, drama, earth science, English, English literature, English-AP, environmental science, European history, European history-AP, expository writing, fine arts, geography, geometry, health, history, history-AP, honors algebra, honors English, honors geometry, honors U.S. history, jazz, journalism, leadership skills, mathematics, music, orchestra, photography, physical education, physics, pre-calculus, psychology, religion, SAT preparation, science, social studies, Spanish, speech, theater, trigonometry, U.S. history, U.S. history-AP, video film production, vocal ensemble, vocal jazz, world history, writing.
Graduation Requirements Arts and fine arts (art, music, dance, drama), computer science, English, foreign language, mathematics, physical education (includes health), religion (includes Bible studies and theology), science, social studies (includes history), speech, Senior Thesis, Senior Project, Senior Retreat.
Special Academic Programs Advanced Placement exam preparation; honors section.
College Admission Counseling 106 students graduated in 2008; 101 went to college, including Azusa Pacific University; Seattle Pacific University; University of Washington; Washington State University; Western Washington University; Westmont College. Other: 2 went to work, 1 entered military service, 2 had other specific plans. Mean SAT critical reading: 541, mean SAT math: 546, mean SAT writing: 525, mean combined SAT: 1612.
Student Life Upper grades have specified standards of dress, student council. Discipline rests primarily with faculty. Attendance at religious services is required.
Summer Programs Sports programs offered; session focuses on team and skill development; held both on and off campus; held at PLU, UW, WWU, and NW Basketball Camps; accepts boys and girls; open to students from other schools. 30 students usually enrolled. 2009 schedule: June 18 to July 30. Application deadline: none.
Tuition and Aid Day student tuition: $10,400. Tuition installment plan (monthly payment plans). Tuition reduction for siblings, need-based scholarship grants, paying campus jobs available. In 2008–09, 5% of upper-school students received aid.
Admissions Traditional secondary-level entrance grade is 9. For fall 2008, 60 students applied for upper-level admission, 58 were accepted, 55 enrolled. Gates MacGinite Placement Test or TOEFL required. Deadline for receipt of application materials: none. Application fee required: $50. On-campus interview required.
Athletics Interscholastic: basketball (boys, girls), cross-country running (b,g), football (b), golf (b,g), soccer (b,g), track and field (b,g), volleyball (g); coed interscholastic: cheering, physical fitness, physical training, power lifting, strength & conditioning, weight training. 3 PE instructors, 26 coaches, 1 athletic trainer.
Computers Computers are regularly used in English, introduction to technology, journalism, keyboarding, media production, photography, science, study skills, technology, video film production, Web site design, yearbook classes. Computer network features include on-campus library services, online commercial services, Internet access, Internet filtering or blocking technology. Students grades are available online. The school has a published electronic and media policy.
Contact Lynn Newcombe, Secondary Admissions Coordinator. 206-289-7783. Fax: 206-546-7214. E-mail: lnewcombe@crista.net. Web site: www.kingsschools.org.

KINGSHILL SCHOOL

St. Croix, Virgin Islands
See Special Needs Schools section.

KING'S RIDGE CHRISTIAN SCHOOL

2765 Bethany Bend
Alpharetta, Georgia 30004
Head of School: Mr. C. David Rhodes III

General Information Coeducational day and distance learning college-preparatory and technology school, affiliated with Christian faith. Grades K–12. Distance learning grades 9–12. Founded: 2001. Setting: suburban. Nearest major city is Atlanta. 70-acre campus. 3 buildings on campus. Approved or accredited by Georgia Accrediting Commission, Georgia Independent School Association, Southern Association of Colleges and Schools, and Southern Association of Independent Schools. Total enrollment: 625. Upper school average class size: 12. Upper school faculty-student ratio: 1:8.
Faculty School total: 110. In upper school: 12 men, 12 women; 14 have advanced degrees.
Graduation Requirements 50 hours of community service between grades 9-12.
Special Academic Programs Advanced Placement exam preparation; honors section.
College Admission Counseling 3 students graduated in 2008.
Student Life Upper grades have uniform requirement, student council, honor system. Discipline rests primarily with faculty. Attendance at religious services is required.
Tuition and Aid Day student tuition: $12,357. Tuition installment plan (Insured Tuition Payment Plan, FACTS Tuition Payment Plan). Tuition reduction for siblings, need-based scholarship grants available.
Admissions SSAT, ERB, PSAT, SAT, PLAN or ACT required. Deadline for receipt of application materials: none. Application fee required: $75. Interview required.
Athletics Interscholastic: baseball (boys), basketball (b,g), cheering (g), football (b), lacrosse (b), soccer (b,g), softball (g), strength & conditioning (b), swimming and diving (b,g), tennis (b,g), volleyball (g); coed interscholastic: cross-country running, equestrian sports, golf, horseback riding, track and field. 3 PE instructors, 3 coaches.
Computers Computers are regularly used in all academic classes. Computer network features include online commercial services, Internet access, wireless campus network, Internet filtering or blocking technology, online collaboration of classroom activities. Campus intranet, student e-mail accounts, and computer access in designated common areas are available to students. Students grades are available online. The school has a published electronic and media policy.
Contact Lisa K. McGuire, Director of Admission/Marketing. 770-754-5738 Ext. 118. Fax: 770-754-5544. E-mail: lmcguire@kingsridgecs.org. Web site: www.kingsridgecs.org/.

KINGSWAY COLLEGE

1200 Leland Road
Oshawa, Ontario L1K 2H4, Canada
Head of School: Mr. Gregory Bussey

General Information Coeducational boarding and day college-preparatory, general academic, and religious studies school, affiliated with Seventh-day Adventists. Grades 9–12. Founded: 1903. Setting: small town. Nearest major city is Toronto, Canada. Students are housed in single-sex dormitories. 100-acre campus. 9 buildings on campus. Approved or accredited by Ontario Ministry of Education and Ontario Department of Education. Language of instruction: English. Endowment: CAN$1.6 million. Total enrollment: 191. Upper school average class size: 25. Upper school faculty-student ratio: 1:11.
Upper School Student Profile Grade 9: 47 students (22 boys, 25 girls); Grade 10: 50 students (28 boys, 22 girls); Grade 11: 49 students (24 boys, 25 girls); Grade 12: 42 students (17 boys, 25 girls). 49% of students are boarding students. 83% are province residents. 9 provinces are represented in upper school student body. 9% are international students. International students from Bahamas, Bermuda, Democratic People's Republic of Korea, United States, and Venezuela. 90% of students are Seventh-day Adventists.
Faculty School total: 17. In upper school: 10 men, 7 women; 2 have advanced degrees; 10 reside on campus.
Subjects Offered Accounting, advanced chemistry, advanced computer applications, advanced math, algebra, American history, anthropology, band, biology, business studies, calculus, Canadian geography, Canadian history, Canadian law, career education, ceramics, chemistry, choir, civics, computer applications, computer information systems, computer programming, computer studies, concert band, English, English literature, ESL, French, healthful living, information processing, intro to computers, music, music performance, physical education, physics, psychology, religious education, science, sociology, U.S. history, visual arts, work-study, world civilizations, world religions.
Graduation Requirements Art, Canadian geography, Canadian history, careers, civics, English, French, mathematics, physical education (includes health), science, All students must take 1 religion course per year.
Special Academic Programs ESL (5 students enrolled).
College Admission Counseling 52 students graduated in 2008; 51 went to college, including Andrews University; Queen's University at Kingston; Southern Adventist University; The University of Western Ontario; University of Toronto; Walla Walla University. Other: 1 went to work.
Student Life Upper grades have specified standards of dress, student council. Discipline rests primarily with faculty. Attendance at religious services is required.
Tuition and Aid Day student tuition: CAN$9680; 7-day tuition and room/board: CAN$16,350. Tuition installment plan (monthly payment plans, individually arranged payment plans). Tuition reduction for siblings, merit scholarship grants, need-based scholarship grants, paying campus jobs available. In 2008–09, 45% of upper-school students received aid; total upper-school merit-scholarship money awarded: CAN$25,350. Total amount of financial aid awarded in 2008–09: CAN$205,365.
Admissions Traditional secondary-level entrance grade is 9. Deadline for receipt of application materials: none. No application fee required. Interview required.
Athletics Interscholastic: basketball (boys, girls); intramural: basketball (b,g), flag football (b,g), floor hockey (b,g), ice hockey (b), indoor hockey (b,g), soccer (b,g), softball (b,g), volleyball (b,g); coed intramural: backpacking, badminton, bicycling, canoeing/kayaking, gymnastics, hiking/backpacking, outdoor education, roller skating, skiing (downhill), snowboarding, volleyball. 1 PE instructor.
Computers Computers are regularly used in accounting, business, career education, computer applications, data processing, English, ESL, programming, science, social sciences classes. Computer network features include Internet access, Internet filtering or blocking technology. Student e-mail accounts are available to students. Students grades are available online. The school has a published electronic and media policy.
Contact Ms. Raelene Brower, Director of Enrolment Services. 905-433-1144 Ext. 212. Fax: 905-433-1156. E-mail: browerr@kingswaycollege.on.ca. Web site: www.kingswaycollege.on.ca.

KING'S WEST SCHOOL

4012 Chico Way NW
Bremerton, Washington 98312-1397

Head of School: Mr. Bryan Peterson

General Information Coeducational day college-preparatory, arts, religious studies, and technology school, affiliated with Christian faith. Grades K–12. Founded: 1991. Setting: small town. Nearest major city is Tacoma. 8-acre campus. 7 buildings on campus. Approved or accredited by Association of Christian Schools International, Northwest Association of Accredited Schools, and Washington Department of Education. Total enrollment: 380. Upper school average class size: 17. Upper school faculty-student ratio: 1:10.

Upper School Student Profile Grade 7: 32 students (16 boys, 16 girls); Grade 8: 29 students (15 boys, 14 girls); Grade 9: 27 students (12 boys, 15 girls); Grade 10: 45 students (25 boys, 20 girls); Grade 11: 35 students (16 boys, 19 girls); Grade 12: 30 students (14 boys, 16 girls). 70% of students are Christian faith.

Faculty School total: 21. In upper school: 8 men, 13 women; 12 have advanced degrees.

Subjects Offered 20th century world history, algebra, American literature, art, band, Bible, biology, calculus-AP, chemistry, chorus, comparative government and politics-AP, computers, desktop publishing, drama, earth science, English, English literature, ensembles, European literature, fine arts, geography, geometry, health, history, keyboarding, life science, mathematics, music, physical education, physical science, physics, practical living, religion, science, Spanish, speech, statistics-AP, theater, U.S. history, U.S. history-AP, weight training, world history, world literature, world wide web design, yearbook.

Graduation Requirements Arts and fine arts (art, music, dance, drama), Bible, computer science, English, foreign language, mathematics, physical education (includes health), practical living, science, social studies (includes history), speech.

Special Academic Programs Study at local college for college credit.

College Admission Counseling 30 students graduated in 2008; 29 went to college, including Biola University; Liberty University; Olympic College; Pacific Lutheran University; Seattle Pacific University; Trinity Western University. Other: 1 entered military service. Mean SAT critical reading: 548, mean SAT math: 522, mean SAT writing: 511, mean combined SAT: 1581, mean composite ACT: 24. 33% scored over 600 on SAT critical reading, 19% scored over 600 on SAT math, 15% scored over 600 on SAT writing, 19% scored over 1800 on combined SAT, 50% scored over 26 on composite ACT.

Student Life Upper grades have specified standards of dress, student council, honor system. Discipline rests primarily with faculty. Attendance at religious services is required.

Tuition and Aid Day student tuition: $8810. Tuition installment plan (monthly payment plans, prepayment discount plan). Tuition reduction for siblings, need-based scholarship grants available. In 2008–09, 39% of upper-school students received aid. Total amount of financial aid awarded in 2008–09: $190,000.

Admissions Traditional secondary-level entrance grade is 7. Comprehensive educational evaluation required. Deadline for receipt of application materials: none. Application fee required: $50. Interview required.

Athletics Interscholastic: basketball (boys, girls), cross-country running (b,g), golf (b), soccer (b,g), softball (g), track and field (b,g), volleyball (g), weight training (b,g).

Computers Computers are regularly used in publications, technology, video film production, Web site design, yearbook classes. Computer network features include Internet access, Internet filtering or blocking technology. The school has a published electronic and media policy.

Contact Mrs. Linda McClellan, Office Manager. 360-377-7700 Ext. 5011. Fax: 360-377-7795. E-mail: lmcclellan@crista.net. Web site: www.kingswest.org.

KINGSWOOD-OXFORD SCHOOL

170 Kingswood Road
West Hartford, Connecticut 06119-1430

Head of School: Mr. Dennis Bisgaard

General Information Coeducational day college-preparatory school. Grades 6–12. Founded: 1909. Setting: suburban. Nearest major city is Hartford. 30-acre campus. 10 buildings on campus. Approved or accredited by Connecticut Association of Independent Schools, New England Association of Schools and Colleges, and Connecticut Department of Education. Member of National Association of Independent Schools and Secondary School Admission Test Board. Endowment: $34.4 million. Total enrollment: 570. Upper school average class size: 13. Upper school faculty-student ratio: 1:8.

Upper School Student Profile Grade 9: 105 students (53 boys, 52 girls); Grade 10: 95 students (53 boys, 42 girls); Grade 11: 93 students (52 boys, 41 girls); Grade 12: 106 students (45 boys, 61 girls).

Faculty School total: 93. In upper school: 35 men, 33 women; 51 have advanced degrees.

Subjects Offered Algebra, American history, American literature, art, art history-AP, band, biology, biology-AP, calculus, calculus-AP, chemistry, chemistry-AP, Chinese, chorus, composition-AP, computer science, computer science-AP, concert band, concert choir, creative writing, digital music, digital photography, dramatic arts, drawing, economics, economics-AP, English, English language-AP, English literature, English literature-AP, environmental science, fine arts, forensic science, French, French language-AP, geography, geometry, government/civics, jazz band, jazz ensemble, journalism, Latin, Latin-AP, macroeconomics-AP, marine biology, mathematics, media, microeconomics-AP, music, mythology, orchestra, photography, physics, physics-AP, political science, public speaking, social studies, Spanish, Spanish language-AP, Spanish-AP, statistics, statistics-AP, theater, trigonometry, U.S. history-AP, visual arts, woodworking, world history, world literature, writing.

Graduation Requirements Computer science, English, foreign language, mathematics, performing arts, science, social studies (includes history), visual arts, participation on athletic teams, senior thesis in English. Community service is required.

Special Academic Programs 18 Advanced Placement exams for which test preparation is offered; honors section; independent study; term-away projects; study at local college for college credit; study abroad.

College Admission Counseling 95 students graduated in 2008; all went to college, including Boston University; Colby College; Cornell University; Trinity College; Union College; University of Connecticut. Median SAT critical reading: 640, median SAT math: 640, median SAT writing: 640.

Student Life Upper grades have specified standards of dress, student council. Discipline rests equally with students and faculty.

Tuition and Aid Day student tuition: $29,750. Tuition installment plan (Academic Management Services Plan). Merit scholarship grants, need-based scholarship grants available. In 2008–09, 30% of upper-school students received aid. Total amount of financial aid awarded in 2008–09: $2,658,775.

Admissions Traditional secondary-level entrance grade is 9. For fall 2008, 168 students applied for upper-level admission, 124 were accepted, 51 enrolled. SSAT required. Deadline for receipt of application materials: February 1. Application fee required: $50. On-campus interview required.

Athletics Interscholastic: baseball (boys), basketball (b,g), cross-country running (b,g), diving (b,g), field hockey (g), football (b), ice hockey (b,g), lacrosse (b,g), soccer (b,g), softball (g), squash (b,g), swimming and diving (b,g), tennis (b,g), track and field (b,g); intramural: basketball (b), soccer (b), yoga (g); coed interscholastic: golf, skiing (downhill); coed intramural: dance, strength & conditioning. 5 coaches, 2 athletic trainers.

Computers Computers are regularly used in English, foreign language, history, mathematics, music technology, photography, science classes. Computer resources include on-campus library services, Internet access, wireless campus network. Student e-mail accounts and computer access in designated common areas are available to students. Students grades are available online. The school has a published electronic and media policy.

Contact Mr. James E. O¿Donnell, Director of Enrollment Management. 860-727-5000. Fax: 860-236-3651. E-mail: odonnell.j@k-o.org. Web site: www.kingswood-oxford.org.

ANNOUNCEMENT FROM THE SCHOOL Located in West Hartford, Connecticut, Kingswood-Oxford School is a coeducational, college-preparatory day school serving students in grades 6 through 12, formed by the merger in 1969 of two long-standing independent day schools: Oxford School for girls (1909) and Kingswood School for boys (1916). Founders Mary Martin and George R.H. Nicholson sought to provide their students with the advantages of a rigorous independent school education while allowing them the benefits of family life. The mission of Kingswood-Oxford today is to help build and strengthen the intellectual, ethical, aesthetic, and physical capabilities of young people from diverse backgrounds, inspiring them to lead lives of integrity and involvement. The curriculum is designed to prepare students in the liberal arts as well as offer exposure to a variety of elective courses. The Middle School emphasizes the development of study skills and a sense of oneself as a learner. At the Upper School, seniors write a thesis, and the curriculum culminates in Advanced Placement courses in all disciplines. A rich array of athletic, extracurricular, travel, and service opportunities allow students to explore their interests, develop their self-confidence, hone their leadership skills, and contribute to the greater community. In addition to teaching and coaching, faculty members also serve as advisers—working closely with students and communicating regularly with parents. One hundred percent of graduates attend four-year colleges and universities. Recent building campaigns include the Estes Family Building, which houses the Middle School (2004), a renovated library and dining hall (2007), and synthetic turf fields (2008). The Chase Tallwood Science Math Technology Center is scheduled to open in September 2009. Other facilities include a 600-seat theater, a black box theater, music suites, a dance studio, three specialized labs (music technology, modern languages, and graphic arts), three gymnasiums, tennis and squash courts, and an ice rink.

THE KNOX SCHOOL

541 Long Beach Road
St. James, New York 11780

Head of School: Mr. George K Allison

General Information Coeducational boarding and day college-preparatory, arts, bilingual studies, and technology school. Boarding grades 7–12, day grades 6–12. Founded: 1904. Setting: suburban. Nearest major city is New York. Students are housed in single-sex dormitories. 48-acre campus. 12 buildings on campus. Approved or accredited by Middle States Association of Colleges and Schools, New York State Association of Independent Schools, The Association of Boarding Schools, and New York Department of Education. Member of National Association of Independent Schools. Total enrollment: 109. Upper school average class size: 12. Upper school faculty-student ratio: 1:5.

Upper School Student Profile Grade 9: 21 students (8 boys, 13 girls); Grade 10: 20 students (9 boys, 11 girls); Grade 11: 28 students (19 boys, 9 girls); Grade 12: 28 students (15 boys, 13 girls). 82% of students are boarding students. 47% are state residents. 5 states are represented in upper school student body. 52% are international students. International students from China, Japan, Republic of Korea, Spain, Sudan, and Taiwan; 2 other countries represented in student body.

Faculty School total: 29. In upper school: 9 men, 20 women; 14 have advanced degrees; 20 reside on campus.

Subjects Offered 20th century history, algebra, American literature, art history, biology, British literature, calculus, calculus-AP, chemistry, chemistry-AP, computer art, computer science, creative writing, earth science, economics, English, English composition, environmental science, ESL, European history, French, geometry, government, health and wellness, Italian, Latin, music, music history, photo shop, photography, physics, physics-AP, pre-algebra, pre-calculus, psychology, Spanish, studio art, theater, U.S. history, vocal music, world history, world literature.

Graduation Requirements Art, computer education, electives, English, foreign language, health, history, lab science, mathematics, senior project.

Special Academic Programs Advanced Placement exam preparation; honors section; independent study; term-away projects; study at local college for college credit; study abroad; ESL (32 students enrolled).

College Admission Counseling 22 students graduated in 2008; 21 went to college, including Boston University; Hofstra University; Lynn University; New York University; The George Washington University; University of Michigan. Other: 1 entered a postgraduate year.

Student Life Upper grades have uniform requirement, student council. Discipline rests primarily with faculty.

Tuition and Aid Day student tuition: $22,500; 5-day tuition and room/board: $38,700; 7-day tuition and room/board: $40,800. Tuition installment plan (individually arranged payment plans, Knight Tuition Plan). Need-based scholarship grants available. In 2008–09, 42% of upper-school students received aid. Total amount of financial aid awarded in 2008–09: $503,670.

Admissions Traditional secondary-level entrance grade is 9. For fall 2008, 96 students applied for upper-level admission, 68 were accepted, 29 enrolled. CCAT, ERB, SLEP, SSAT or TOEFL required. Deadline for receipt of application materials: none. Application fee required: $75. On-campus interview recommended.

Athletics Interscholastic: baseball (boys), basketball (b,g), soccer (b), softball (g), tennis (b,g), volleyball (g); coed interscholastic: crew, cross-country running, equestrian sports, fitness, golf, horseback riding, soccer; coed intramural: combined training, dance, dressage, equestrian sports, golf, horseback riding, outdoor activities, physical training, yoga. 19 coaches.

Computers Computers are regularly used in computer applications, graphic arts, graphic design classes. Computer network features include on-campus library services, Internet access, wireless campus network. Computer access in designated common areas is available to students. Students grades are available online. The school has a published electronic and media policy.

Contact Ms. Susan Day-Holsinger, Administrative Assistant. 631-686-1600 Ext. 414. Fax: 631-686-1650. E-mail: sdayholsinger@knoxschool.org. Web site: www.knoxschool.org.

ANNOUNCEMENT FROM THE SCHOOL Knox—the school by the city and the sea—is located 50 miles from New York City on Long Island's beautiful North Shore in St. James, New York. The Knox School is an independent college-preparatory day and boarding school for boys and girls in grades 6–12. Founded in 1904, Knox boasts over 100 years of a mission dedicated to providing capable students with the opportunity to excel within a liberal arts program infused with artistic and athletic pursuits in preparation for higher education at selective colleges and universities. Knox does so by inspiring in each student a love of learning and the desire to continually develop the skills necessary to lead happy, confident, and successful lives in a complex and changing world. Learning takes place in formal ways from the young scholar's programs at local colleges to AP classes to Honor's portfolio programs and senior projects, to extra help sessions in Knox's ACCESS program. The ACCESS program helps students with language-based learning disabilities develop learning strategies to master material. This program addresses such areas as time management, prioritizing, encoding, and decoding—among other skills developed. Knox has strength in the arts, with a fall play and a spring musical where everyone has an opportunity to get involved at the appropriate level. Athletics enjoys winning teams, and everyone gets a chance to play—even on some of the School's championship teams. Athletic options include an equestrian program equipped to handle the beginner to the highly competitive. Other sports teams include baseball, boys and girls basketball, boys and girls tennis, crew, cross-country, soccer, softball, and volleyball. Clubs include yearbook, chess, gourmet, art and fashion design, library, SADD, photography, outdoor club, tae kwon do, community service, GSA, Squibblers, and a very successful Model UN club that traveled to South Africa to compete.

KNOXVILLE CATHOLIC HIGH SCHOOL

9245 Fox Lonas Road
Knoxville, Tennessee 37923

Head of School: Mr. Dickie Sompayrac

General Information Coeducational day college-preparatory, arts, and religious studies school, affiliated with Roman Catholic Church. Grades 9–12. Founded: 1932. Setting: suburban. 20-acre campus. 3 buildings on campus. Approved or accredited by Southern Association of Colleges and Schools and Tennessee Department of Education. Total enrollment: 624. Upper school average class size: 19. Upper school faculty-student ratio: 1:13.

Upper School Student Profile Grade 9: 156 students (77 boys, 79 girls); Grade 10: 170 students (75 boys, 95 girls); Grade 11: 164 students (87 boys, 77 girls); Grade 12: 135 students (73 boys, 62 girls). 83% of students are Roman Catholic.

Faculty School total: 50. In upper school: 23 men, 26 women; 27 have advanced degrees.

Subjects Offered Accounting, ACT preparation, Advanced Placement courses, algebra, American government, American government-AP, American history, American history-AP, anatomy and physiology, art, art-AP, band, biology, biology-AP, business, calculus, calculus-AP, ceramics, chemistry, chemistry-AP, computers, current events, drama, drama performance, drawing, driver education, ecology, economics, English, English language and composition-AP, English language-AP, English literature, English literature and composition-AP, English literature-AP, English-AP, ESL, European history, forensic science, French, French language-AP, French-AP, geography, geometry, government, government-AP, government/civics, health and wellness, honors algebra, honors English, honors geometry, honors U.S. history, independent study, journalism, Latin, library assistant, music appreciation, newspaper, painting, personal finance, physical education, physical fitness, physical science, physics, physiology, pottery, pre-algebra, pre-calculus, psychology, religion, sociology, Spanish, Spanish-AP, speech, speech communications, statistics, statistics-AP, theater, theater arts, theater production, theology, U.S. government, U.S. government-AP, U.S. history, U.S. history-AP, United States government-AP, Web site design, weight training, weightlifting, wellness, world geography, world history, writing workshop, yearbook.

Graduation Requirements Arts and fine arts (art, music, dance, drama), electives, English, foreign language, mathematics, science, social studies (includes history), speech, theology, wellness.

Special Academic Programs Advanced Placement exam preparation; honors section; study at local college for college credit; ESL (9 students enrolled).

College Admission Counseling 160 students graduated in 2008; 145 went to college, including Middle Tennessee State University; The University of Tennessee; The University of Tennessee at Chattanooga. Other: 15 went to work.

Student Life Upper grades have uniform requirement, student council, honor system. Discipline rests primarily with faculty. Attendance at religious services is required.

Tuition and Aid Day student tuition: $7100–$8500. Tuition installment plan (FACTS Tuition Payment Plan).

Admissions Traditional secondary-level entrance grade is 9. High School Placement Test or High School Placement Test (closed version) from Scholastic Testing Service required. Deadline for receipt of application materials: February 15. Application fee required: $100. Interview required.

Athletics Interscholastic: aquatics (boys, girls), baseball (b), basketball (b,g), bowling (b,g), cheering (g), cross-country running (b,g), dance team (g), diving (b,g), football (b), golf (b,g), ice hockey (b), in-line hockey (b), rugby (b), soccer (b,g), softball (g), swimming and diving (b,g), tennis (b,g), track and field (b,g), volleyball (g), wrestling (b); intramural: dance (g). 2 PE instructors, 7 coaches, 1 athletic trainer.

Computers Computer network features include on-campus library services, Internet access. Students grades are available online. The school has a published electronic and media policy.

Contact Ms. Barrie Smith, Dean of Admissions. 865-560-0502. Fax: 865-560-0314. E-mail: bsmith@knoxvillecatholic.com. Web site: www.knoxvillecatholic.com.

KOINONIA CHRISTIAN SCHOOL

6014-57 Avenue
Red Deer, Alberta T4N 4S9, Canada

Head of School: Mr. Vern Rand

General Information Coeducational day and distance learning college-preparatory, general academic, and religious studies school, affiliated with Christian faith. Grades K–12. Distance learning grades 10–12. Founded: 1983. Setting: urban. Nearest major city is Calgary, Canada. 3-acre campus. 1 building on campus. Approved or accredited by Association of Christian Schools International and Alberta Department of Education. Language of instruction: English. Total enrollment: 189. Upper school average class size: 15. Upper school faculty-student ratio: 1:12.

Upper School Student Profile Grade 9: 13 students (6 boys, 7 girls); Grade 10: 18 students (8 boys, 10 girls); Grade 11: 18 students (12 boys, 6 girls); Grade 12: 12 students (8 boys, 4 girls). 100% of students are Christian faith.

Faculty School total: 12. In upper school: 2 men, 2 women; 1 has an advanced degree.

Special Academic Programs Independent study; ESL (10 students enrolled).
Student Life Upper grades have specified standards of dress. Discipline rests equally with students and faculty. Attendance at religious services is required.
Tuition and Aid Day student tuition: CAN$3180–CAN$4800. Guaranteed tuition plan. Tuition installment plan (monthly payment plans, individually arranged payment plans). Tuition reduction for siblings, bursaries, need-based scholarship grants available. In 2008–09, 20% of upper-school students received aid.
Admissions Traditional secondary-level entrance grade is 9. For fall 2008, 10 students applied for upper-level admission, 7 were accepted, 7 enrolled. Deadline for receipt of application materials: none. Application fee required: CAN$50. On-campus interview required.
Athletics Interscholastic: badminton (boys, girls), basketball (b,g), fitness (b,g), floor hockey (b), soccer (b,g), volleyball (b,g); intramural: basketball (b,g), fitness (b,g), soccer (b,g), volleyball (b); coed interscholastic: volleyball. 1 PE instructor, 6 coaches.
Computers Computer resources include Internet access, Internet filtering or blocking technology.
Contact Mr. Vern Rand, Principal. 403-346-1818. Fax: 403-347-3013. E-mail: vrrdkcs@shaw.ca. Web site: www.koinonia.ca/.

LA CHEIM SCHOOL

Antioch, California
See Special Needs Schools section.

LADYWOOD HIGH SCHOOL

14680 Newburgh Road
Livonia, Michigan 48154
Head of School: Sr. Mary Ann Smith, CSSF

General Information Girls' day college-preparatory, arts, and religious studies school, affiliated with Roman Catholic Church. Grades 9–12. Founded: 1950. Setting: suburban. Nearest major city is Detroit. 1 building on campus. Approved or accredited by National Catholic Education Association, North Central Association of Colleges and Schools, and Michigan Department of Education. Total enrollment: 410. Upper school average class size: 24. Upper school faculty-student ratio: 1:13.
Upper School Student Profile Grade 9: 121 students (121 girls); Grade 10: 94 students (94 girls); Grade 11: 101 students (101 girls); Grade 12: 94 students (94 girls). 93% of students are Roman Catholic.
Faculty School total: 34. In upper school: 8 men, 26 women; 11 have advanced degrees.
Subjects Offered Advanced chemistry, advanced math, algebra, American government, American history, American history-AP, American literature, anatomy and physiology, art, Asian history, Bible studies, biochemistry, biology, biology-AP, calculus-AP, career and personal planning, career exploration, Catholic belief and practice, ceramics, chemistry-AP, child development, choir, Christian and Hebrew scripture, college writing, composition, computer education, culinary arts, discrete math, drama, drama performance, drawing and design, economics, English, English composition, English literature and composition-AP, environmental science, environmental science-AP, environmental studies, European civilization, family and consumer sciences, film appreciation, food science, French, French language-AP, French-AP, geometry, global issues, government, graphic arts, health, history of the Catholic Church, independent living, Italian, keyboarding/computer, language and composition, language arts, leadership and service, leadership skills, library assistant, life management skills, novels, oil painting, orchestra, parent/child development, physical education, physics, poetry, prayer/spirituality, pre-calculus, psychology, religion, science, scripture, sewing, short story, sociology, Spanish, Spanish language-AP, Spanish-AP, speech, statistics and probability, studio art—AP, theater, theater arts, U.S. government, U.S. history, U.S. history-AP, Vietnam War, visual and performing arts, water color painting, world cultures, world studies, writing, yearbook.
Graduation Requirements Algebra, American government, American history, American literature, arts and fine arts (art, music, dance, drama), biology, British literature, Catholic belief and practice, chemistry, computer applications, computer keyboarding, computer science, economics, English composition, foreign language, geometry, global studies, health education, literature, mathematics, physical education (includes health), physical fitness, religion (includes Bible studies and theology), science, social science, speech communications.
Special Academic Programs Advanced Placement exam preparation; study at local college for college credit.
College Admission Counseling 135 students graduated in 2008; all went to college, including Central Michigan University; Michigan State University; University of Michigan; University of Notre Dame; Western Michigan University. Median composite ACT: 23. Mean SAT critical reading: 550, mean SAT math: 552, mean SAT writing: 546, mean combined SAT: 1648. 28% scored over 26 on composite ACT.
Student Life Upper grades have uniform requirement, student council, honor system. Discipline rests primarily with faculty. Attendance at religious services is required.
Tuition and Aid Day student tuition: $7000. Tuition installment plan (The Tuition Plan, monthly payment plans, individually arranged payment plans). Tuition reduction for siblings, need-based scholarship grants available. In 2008–09, 25% of upper-school students received aid. Total amount of financial aid awarded in 2008–09: $75,000.
Admissions Traditional secondary-level entrance grade is 9. High School Placement Test required. Deadline for receipt of application materials: none. Application fee required: $500. Interview recommended.
Athletics Interscholastic: basketball, bowling, cheering, cross-country running, diving, equestrian sports, field hockey, figure skating, flag football, golf, ice hockey, lacrosse, skiing (cross-country), skiing (downhill), soccer, softball, strength & conditioning, swimming and diving, tennis, track and field, volleyball, weight training; intramural: flagball. 2 PE instructors, 30 coaches, 1 athletic trainer.
Computers Computers are regularly used in accounting, computer applications, data processing, keyboarding, Web site design, word processing, yearbook classes. Computer network features include on-campus library services, Internet access, Internet filtering or blocking technology. Campus intranet is available to students. Students grades are available online. The school has a published electronic and media policy.
Contact Guidance Counselors. 734-591-5492 Ext. 226. Fax: 734-591-4214. Web site: www.ladywood.org.

LAKEFIELD COLLEGE SCHOOL

4391 County Road, #29
Lakefield, Ontario K0L 2H0, Canada
Head of School: Mr. David Thompson

General Information Coeducational boarding and day college-preparatory, arts, technology, and distance learning, outdoor education program school, affiliated with Church of England (Anglican). Boarding grades 9–12, day grades 7–12. Founded: 1879. Setting: small town. Nearest major city is Toronto, Canada. Students are housed in single-sex dormitories. 315-acre campus. 23 buildings on campus. Approved or accredited by Canadian Association of Independent Schools, Canadian Educational Standards Institute, The Association of Boarding Schools, and Ontario Department of Education. Affiliate member of National Association of Independent Schools; member of Secondary School Admission Test Board. Language of instruction: English. Endowment: CAN$17 million. Total enrollment: 366. Upper school average class size: 17. Upper school faculty-student ratio: 1:7.
Upper School Student Profile Grade 7: 15 students (10 boys, 5 girls); Grade 8: 15 students (9 boys, 6 girls); Grade 9: 72 students (39 boys, 33 girls); Grade 10: 60 students (29 boys, 31 girls); Grade 11: 96 students (45 boys, 51 girls); Grade 12: 108 students (56 boys, 52 girls). 70% of students are boarding students. 75% are province residents. 6 provinces are represented in upper school student body. 28% are international students. International students from Barbados, Bermuda, China, Germany, Saudi Arabia, and United States; 20 other countries represented in student body. 40% of students are members of Church of England (Anglican).
Faculty School total: 54. In upper school: 27 men, 26 women; 10 have advanced degrees; 22 reside on campus.
Subjects Offered Algebra, art, art history, biology, calculus, chemistry, computer science, creative writing, drama, driver education, earth science, economics, English, English literature, environmental science, fine arts, French, geography, geometry, government/civics, health, history, kinesiology, mathematics, music, outdoor education, physical education, physics, science, social studies, sociology, Spanish, theater, trigonometry, vocal music, world history, world literature.
Graduation Requirements English, foreign language, mathematics, physical education (includes health), science, social studies (includes history).
Special Academic Programs Advanced Placement exam preparation; honors section; accelerated programs; independent study; term-away projects; study at local college for college credit; study abroad; academic accommodation for the gifted, the musically talented, and the artistically talented.
College Admission Counseling 102 students graduated in 2008; 95 went to college, including McGill University; Queen's University at Kingston; The University of British Columbia; The University of Western Ontario; Trent University; University of Toronto. Other: 7 had other specific plans.
Student Life Upper grades have uniform requirement, student council, honor system. Discipline rests equally with students and faculty.
Summer Programs Session focuses on on-line courses for current students; held off campus; held at online; accepts boys and girls; not open to students from other schools. 100 students usually enrolled. 2009 schedule: June 22 to August 30.
Tuition and Aid Day student tuition: CAN$24,825; 7-day tuition and room/board: CAN$43,450. Tuition installment plan (Insured Tuition Payment Plan, monthly payment plans, individually arranged payment plans, 3-payment plan). Bursaries, need-based scholarship grants available. In 2008–09, 25% of upper-school students received aid. Total amount of financial aid awarded in 2008–09: CAN$140,000.
Admissions Traditional secondary-level entrance grade is 9. For fall 2008, 246 students applied for upper-level admission, 183 were accepted, 122 enrolled. Otis-Lennon School Ability Test or SSAT required. Deadline for receipt of application materials: none. Application fee required: CAN$100. Interview required.
Athletics Interscholastic: alpine skiing (boys, girls), baseball (b), basketball (g), crew (g), cross-country running (b,g), field hockey (g), golf (b,g), hockey (b,g), ice hockey (b,g), nordic skiing (b,g), outdoor education (b,g), ropes courses (b,g), rowing (b,g), rugby (b,g), skiing (cross-country) (b,g), skiing (downhill) (b,g), snowboarding (b,g), soccer (b,g), softball (b); intramural: aerobics/dance (g), basketball (b,g), cross-country running (b,g), skiing (cross-country) (b,g); coed interscholastic: alpine skiing, cross-country running, equestrian sports, Frisbee, golf, hockey, horseback riding, ice hockey, nordic skiing, outdoor education, sailing, skiing (cross-country), skiing

(downhill), snowboarding; coed intramural: aerobics/Nautilus, baseball, basketball, bicycling, canoeing/kayaking, climbing, cross-country running, dance, equestrian sports, fitness, ice hockey, kayaking, sailing, skiing (cross-country), skiing (downhill), softball.
Computers Computers are regularly used in art, English, foreign language, history, mathematics, music, science classes. Computer network features include on-campus library services, online commercial services, Internet access, Internet filtering or blocking technology. Student e-mail accounts are available to students. Students grades are available online. The school has a published electronic and media policy.
Contact Mrs. Barbara M. Rutherford, Assistant Director of Admissions. 705-652-3324 Ext. 345. Fax: 705-652-6320. E-mail: admissions@lcs.on.ca. Web site: www.lcs.on.ca.

LAKE FOREST ACADEMY

1500 West Kennedy Road
Lake Forest, Illinois 60045
Head of School: Dr. John Strudwick

General Information Coeducational boarding and day college-preparatory and arts school. Grades 9–12. Founded: 1857. Setting: suburban. Nearest major city is Chicago. Students are housed in single-sex dormitories. 150-acre campus. 30 buildings on campus. Approved or accredited by Independent Schools Association of the Central States, Midwest Association of Boarding Schools, The Association of Boarding Schools, The College Board, and Illinois Department of Education. Member of National Association of Independent Schools and Secondary School Admission Test Board. Endowment: $25.8 million. Total enrollment: 391. Upper school average class size: 12. Upper school faculty-student ratio: 1:6.
Upper School Student Profile Grade 9: 80 students (48 boys, 32 girls); Grade 10: 104 students (56 boys, 48 girls); Grade 11: 108 students (60 boys, 48 girls); Grade 12: 94 students (52 boys, 42 girls); Postgraduate: 5 students (4 boys, 1 girl). 50% of students are boarding students. 71% are state residents. 20 states are represented in upper school student body. 30% are international students. International students from Canada, China, Germany, Republic of Korea, Taiwan, and Thailand; 21 other countries represented in student body.
Faculty School total: 69. In upper school: 36 men, 33 women; 46 have advanced degrees; 53 reside on campus.
Subjects Offered 20th century history, 20th century world history, 3-dimensional art, 3-dimensional design, acting, advanced chemistry, advanced computer applications, advanced math, Advanced Placement courses, advanced studio art-AP, algebra, American government, American government-AP, American history, American history-AP, American literature, American literature-AP, American studies, anatomy and physiology, anthropology, applied arts, applied music, art, art appreciation, art education, art history, art history-AP, art-AP, astronomy, bioethics, bioethics, DNA and culture, biology, biology-AP, calculus, calculus-AP, ceramics, chemistry, chemistry-AP, Chinese, choir, choral music, chorus, cinematography, comparative government and politics-AP, computer applications, computer graphics, computer information systems, computer programming, computer science, computer science-AP, creative writing, drama, ecology, English, English literature, environmental science, ESL, fine arts, French, geometry, health and wellness, history, journalism, Latin, Latin American literature, Latin-AP, literature and composition-AP, mathematics, music, mythology, photography, physics, poetry, pre-calculus, science, Shakespeare, social studies, Spanish, speech, statistics-AP, theater, world history.
Graduation Requirements Arts and fine arts (art, music, dance, drama), athletics, English, foreign language, mathematics, science, social studies (includes history). Community service is required.
Special Academic Programs Advanced Placement exam preparation; honors section; independent study; study abroad; academic accommodation for the gifted, the musically talented, and the artistically talented; ESL (16 students enrolled).
College Admission Counseling 100 students graduated in 2008; 99 went to college, including Carnegie Mellon University; Emory University; Miami University; Northwestern University; University of Illinois at Urbana–Champaign; University of Michigan. Other: 1 entered a postgraduate year. Mean SAT critical reading: 580, mean SAT math: 640, mean SAT writing: 590, mean combined SAT: 1800, mean composite ACT: 26.
Student Life Upper grades have specified standards of dress, student council. Discipline rests equally with students and faculty.
Summer Programs ESL programs offered; session focuses on ESL; held on campus; accepts boys and girls; open to students from other schools. 85 students usually enrolled. 2009 schedule: July 13 to August 15. Application deadline: June 1.
Tuition and Aid Day student tuition: $28,500; 7-day tuition and room/board: $38,500. Tuition installment plan (FACTS Tuition Payment Plan). Merit scholarship grants, need-based scholarship grants available. In 2008–09, 30% of upper-school students received aid. Total amount of financial aid awarded in 2008–09: $2,875,100.
Admissions Traditional secondary-level entrance grade is 9. For fall 2008, 463 students applied for upper-level admission, 197 were accepted, 124 enrolled. SSAT or TOEFL required. Deadline for receipt of application materials: January 31. Application fee required: $50. Interview required.
Athletics Interscholastic: baseball (boys), basketball (b,g), cross-country running (b,g), field hockey (g), football (b), ice hockey (b,g), soccer (b,g), softball (g), swimming and diving (b,g), tennis (b,g), track and field (b,g), volleyball (b,g), wrestling (b); coed interscholastic: cheering, golf; coed intramural: bowling, dance, dance squad, fitness, martial arts, racquetball, sailing, squash, water polo, weight training, yoga. 3 coaches, 1 athletic trainer.
Computers Computers are regularly used in English, foreign language, history, mathematics, science classes. Computer network features include on-campus library services, online commercial services, Internet access, wireless campus network, Internet filtering or blocking technology, iPods, Smart Boards in classrooms. Campus intranet, student e-mail accounts, and computer access in designated common areas are available to students. The school has a published electronic and media policy.
Contact Admissions Office. 847-615-3267. Fax: 847-295-8149. E-mail: info@lfanet.org. Web site: www.lfanet.org.

See Close-Up on page 814.

LAKEHILL PREPARATORY SCHOOL

2720 Hillside Drive
Dallas, Texas 75214
Head of School: Roger L. Perry

General Information Coeducational day college-preparatory, arts, bilingual studies, and technology school. Grades K–12. Founded: 1971. Setting: urban. 23-acre campus. 2 buildings on campus. Approved or accredited by Independent Schools Association of the Southwest, Southern Association of Colleges and Schools, Texas Private School Accreditation Commission, The College Board, and Texas Department of Education. Endowment: $200,000. Total enrollment: 400. Upper school average class size: 15. Upper school faculty-student ratio: 1:12.
Faculty School total: 44. In upper school: 12 men, 10 women; 13 have advanced degrees.
Subjects Offered Advanced Placement courses, advanced studio art-AP, algebra, American history, American history-AP, American literature, art, art history, biology, calculus, calculus-AP, chemistry, college counseling, computer math, computer programming, computer programming-AP, computer science, digital photography, drama, earth science, economics, English, English language and composition-AP, English literature, European history, French, French language-AP, French literature-AP, geography, geometry, government/civics, grammar, health, history, journalism, Latin, mathematics, music, music theater, physical education, physics, psychology, public speaking, publications, science, senior career experience, Shakespeare, social science, social studies, Spanish, Spanish language-AP, Spanish literature-AP, speech, statistics, theater, trigonometry, Western civilization, world history, world literature, writing.
Graduation Requirements 1½ elective credits, computer science, English, foreign language, mathematics, physical education (includes health), science, social science, social studies (includes history), Senior Internship Program.
Special Academic Programs Advanced Placement exam preparation; honors section; independent study.
College Admission Counseling 27 students graduated in 2008; all went to college, including Southern Methodist University; The University of Texas at Austin. Median SAT critical reading: 620, median SAT math: 660.
Student Life Upper grades have specified standards of dress, student council, honor system. Discipline rests primarily with faculty.
Summer Programs Enrichment, sports, art/fine arts, computer instruction programs offered; session focuses on Enrichment; held on campus; accepts boys and girls; open to students from other schools. 2009 schedule: June to July.
Tuition and Aid Day student tuition: $14,453. Tuition installment plan (monthly payment plans). Tuition reduction for siblings, need-based scholarship grants available. In 2008–09, 19% of upper-school students received aid.
Admissions Traditional secondary-level entrance grade is 9. ERB CTP IV, ISEE or Stanford Achievement Test required. Deadline for receipt of application materials: January 9. Application fee required: $150. On-campus interview recommended.
Athletics Interscholastic: baseball (boys), basketball (b,g), cheering (g), cross-country running (b,g), football (b), golf (b,g), jogging (b,g), rock climbing (b,g), softball (g), tennis (b,g), track and field (b,g), volleyball (g), weight training (b,g); coed interscholastic: tennis; coed intramural: bowling. 3 PE instructors, 12 coaches.
Computers Computers are regularly used in college planning, creative writing, English, graphic design, journalism, mathematics, science, speech, Web site design, word processing, writing, yearbook classes. Computer network features include on-campus library services, online commercial services, Internet access, wireless campus network, Internet filtering or blocking technology. Students grades are available online. The school has a published electronic and media policy.
Contact Susanne Seitz, Director of Admissions. 214-826-2931. Fax: 214-826-4623. E-mail: sseitz@lakehillprep.org. Web site: www.lakehillprep.org.

LAKELAND CHRISTIAN ACADEMY

1093 South 250 East
Winona Lake, Indiana 46590
Head of School: Mrs. Joy Lavender

General Information Coeducational day college-preparatory, arts, religious studies, bilingual studies, and technology school, affiliated with Christian faith; primarily serves students with learning disabilities and individuals with Attention Deficit Disorder. Grades 7–12. Founded: 1974. Setting: small town. Nearest major city is Fort Wayne. 40-acre campus. 1 building on campus. Approved or accredited by Association of Christian Schools International, North Central Association of Colleges and Schools, and Indiana Department of Education. Endowment: $750,000. Total enrollment: 153. Upper school average class size: 24. Upper school faculty-student ratio: 1:15.

Upper School Student Profile Grade 9: 17 students (6 boys, 11 girls); Grade 10: 27 students (12 boys, 15 girls); Grade 11: 28 students (10 boys, 18 girls); Grade 12: 33 students (15 boys, 18 girls). 100% of students are Christian faith.

Faculty School total: 17. In upper school: 4 men, 13 women; 7 have advanced degrees.

Subjects Offered Acting, advanced biology, advanced chemistry, advanced math, algebra, American government, American history, analysis and differential calculus, analytic geometry, anatomy, art, band, baseball, Basic programming, basketball, Bible, biology, calculus, career and personal planning, chemistry, choir, computer applications, computer education, computer keyboarding, consumer economics, consumer education, consumer mathematics, CPR, desktop publishing, economics, electives, English, English literature, food science, government, grammar, health education, history, human anatomy, human biology, keyboarding, mathematics, physical fitness, physics, poetry, pre-algebra, pre-calculus, psychology, Shakespeare, Spanish, speech, U.S. government, U.S. history, world geography.

College Admission Counseling 33 students graduated in 2008; 20 went to college, including Indiana University–Purdue University Fort Wayne; Wheaton College. Other: 8 went to work.

Student Life Upper grades have specified standards of dress, student council, honor system. Discipline rests primarily with faculty. Attendance at religious services is required.

Tuition and Aid Day student tuition: $5300. Tuition installment plan (monthly payment plans, individually arranged payment plans). Need-based scholarship grants available. In 2008–09, 22% of upper-school students received aid. Total amount of financial aid awarded in 2008–09: $75,000.

Admissions Traditional secondary-level entrance grade is 9. For fall 2008, 25 students applied for upper-level admission, 24 were accepted, 24 enrolled. ACT or SAT required. Deadline for receipt of application materials: none. Application fee required: $75. Interview required.

Athletics Interscholastic: baseball (boys), basketball (b,g), cheering (g), soccer (b,g), softball (g), track and field (b,g), volleyball (g); intramural: basketball (b,g), physical training (b); coed interscholastic: soccer, track and field. 2 PE instructors, 8 coaches.

Computers Computer network features include on-campus library services, online commercial services, Internet access, Internet filtering or blocking technology. Campus intranet and computer access in designated common areas are available to students. The school has a published electronic and media policy.

Contact Joy Lavender, Administrator. 574-267-7265. Fax: 574-267-5687. E-mail: jlavender@lcacougars.com. Web site: www.lcacougars.com.

LAKE RIDGE ACADEMY

37501 Center Ridge Road
North Ridgeville, Ohio 44039

Head of School: Mrs. Carol L. Klimas

General Information Coeducational day college-preparatory, arts, business, technology, and Entrepreneurial Studies Program school. Grades K–12. Founded: 1963. Setting: suburban. Nearest major city is Cleveland. 88-acre campus. 5 buildings on campus. Approved or accredited by Independent Schools Association of the Central States and Ohio Department of Education. Member of National Association of Independent Schools. Endowment: $1.1 million. Total enrollment: 357. Upper school average class size: 12. Upper school faculty-student ratio: 1:8.

Upper School Student Profile Grade 9: 39 students (21 boys, 18 girls); Grade 10: 32 students (15 boys, 17 girls); Grade 11: 43 students (22 boys, 21 girls); Grade 12: 40 students (26 boys, 14 girls).

Faculty School total: 46. In upper school: 10 men, 13 women; 15 have advanced degrees.

Subjects Offered Algebra, American history, American literature, art, biology, biology-AP, calculus, calculus-AP, ceramics, chemistry, chemistry-AP, choir, computer applications, creative writing, design, digital imaging, discrete math, ecology, environmental systems, economics, electronic publishing, English, English-AP, entrepreneurship, ethics, expository writing, fine arts, French, French-AP, functions, geometry, graphic arts, health, humanities, instrumental music, interactive media, journalism, literature, mathematics, music composition, music theory, physical education, physics, physics-AP, play/screen writing, portfolio writing, pre-calculus, senior seminar, Shakespeare, social studies, Spanish, Spanish-AP, statistics, theater, U.S. history-AP, video film production, world civilizations, world history, world literature, writing.

Graduation Requirements Arts and fine arts (art, music, dance, drama), English, ethics, foreign language, mathematics, physical education (includes health), science, social studies (includes history), U.S. history.

Special Academic Programs Advanced Placement exam preparation; honors section; independent study; term-away projects; study at local college for college credit; academic accommodation for the gifted, the musically talented, and the artistically talented; programs in general development for dyslexic students; special instructional classes for deaf students; ESL (7 students enrolled).

College Admission Counseling 40 students graduated in 2008; all went to college, including Case Western Reserve University; Wittenberg University. Median SAT critical reading: 630, median SAT math: 670, median SAT writing: 620, median composite ACT: 26. 63% scored over 600 on SAT critical reading, 68% scored over 600 on SAT math, 40% scored over 600 on SAT writing, 70% scored over 26 on composite ACT.

Student Life Upper grades have specified standards of dress, student council, honor system. Discipline rests primarily with faculty.

Summer Programs Remediation, enrichment, advancement, sports, art/fine arts, computer instruction programs offered; session focuses on enrichment, learning, summer fun; held both on and off campus; held at various locations (for field trips); accepts boys and girls; open to students from other schools. 300 students usually enrolled. 2009 schedule: June 9 to July 18. Application deadline: June.

Tuition and Aid Day student tuition: $21,450–$23,225. Tuition installment plan (The Tuition Plan, Insured Tuition Payment Plan, monthly payment plans, individually arranged payment plans). Merit scholarship grants, need-based scholarship grants available. In 2008–09, 44% of upper-school students received aid. Total amount of financial aid awarded in 2008–09: $942,676.

Admissions Traditional secondary-level entrance grade is 9. For fall 2008, 34 students applied for upper-level admission, 29 were accepted, 20 enrolled. CTBS, OLSAT, essay, ISEE, mathematics proficiency exam, school's own exam, SLEP for foreign students and writing sample required. Deadline for receipt of application materials: none. Application fee required: $35. Interview required.

Athletics Interscholastic: baseball (boys), basketball (b,g), cross-country running (b), golf (b,g), indoor track & field (b), soccer (b,g), softball (g), tennis (b,g), track and field (b,g), volleyball (g), winter (indoor) track (b), wrestling (b); intramural: indoor soccer (b,g), strength & conditioning (b,g), winter soccer (b,g); coed intramural: backpacking, indoor soccer, outdoor adventure, outdoor recreation, physical fitness, physical training, strength & conditioning, ultimate Frisbee, weight lifting, weight training. 3 PE instructors, 12 coaches, 1 athletic trainer.

Computers Computers are regularly used in college planning, creative writing, drawing and design, English, history, journalism, mathematics, media production, research skills, science classes. Computer network features include on-campus library services, online commercial services, Internet access, wireless campus network, Internet filtering or blocking technology, intranet. Student e-mail accounts are available to students. The school has a published electronic and media policy.

Contact Mrs. Alexa C. Hansen, Director of Admission. 440-327-1175 Ext. 103. Fax: 440-327-3641. E-mail: admission@lakeridgeacademy.org. Web site: www.lakeridgeacademy.org.

LAKESIDE SCHOOL

14050 First Avenue NE
Seattle, Washington 98125-3099

Head of School: Mr. Bernard Noe

General Information Coeducational day college-preparatory, arts, and technology school. Grades 5–12. Founded: 1919. Setting: urban. 34-acre campus. 19 buildings on campus. Approved or accredited by Northwest Association of Schools and Colleges, Pacific Northwest Association of Independent Schools, and Washington Department of Education. Member of National Association of Independent Schools. Endowment: $163 million. Total enrollment: 776. Upper school average class size: 16. Upper school faculty-student ratio: 1:10.

Upper School Student Profile Grade 9: 127 students (70 boys, 57 girls); Grade 10: 131 students (70 boys, 61 girls); Grade 11: 129 students (68 boys, 61 girls); Grade 12: 131 students (65 boys, 66 girls).

Faculty School total: 98. In upper school: 37 men, 27 women; 50 have advanced degrees.

Subjects Offered Algebra, American history, American literature, art, biology, calculus, ceramics, chemistry, community service, computer programming, computer science, creative writing, drama, driver education, economics, English, English literature, environmental science, European history, expository writing, fine arts, French, geometry, government/civics, health, history, journalism, Latin, mathematics, music, outdoor education, philosophy, photography, physical education, physics, pre-calculus, science, social studies, Spanish, theater, trigonometry, world history, world literature, writing.

Graduation Requirements Arts, English, foreign language, history, mathematics, outdoor education, physical education (includes health), science. Community service is required.

Special Academic Programs Honors section; independent study; term-away projects; study abroad.

College Admission Counseling 126 students graduated in 2008; all went to college, including Harvard University; Princeton University; Stanford University; University of Washington; Williams College. Median SAT critical reading: 715, median SAT math: 700, median SAT writing: 705. 91% scored over 600 on SAT critical reading, 91% scored over 600 on SAT math, 90% scored over 600 on SAT writing.

Student Life Upper grades have student council. Discipline rests equally with students and faculty.

Summer Programs Enrichment, computer instruction programs offered; session focuses on enrichment for students from public middle schools; held on campus; accepts boys and girls; open to students from other schools. 92 students usually enrolled. 2009 schedule: June 22 to July 31. Application deadline: April 15.

Tuition and Aid Day student tuition: $23,500. Tuition installment plan (Key Tuition Payment Plan, monthly payment plans). Need-based scholarship grants, need-based loans, middle-income loans, CitiAssist K-12 Loans, prepGATE Loans available. In 2008–09, 26% of upper-school students received aid. Total amount of financial aid awarded in 2008–09: $2,562,130.

Admissions Traditional secondary-level entrance grade is 9. For fall 2008, 266 students applied for upper-level admission, 91 were accepted, 57 enrolled. ISEE or PSAT or SAT for applicants to grade 11 and 12 required. Deadline for receipt of application materials: January 29. Application fee required: $48. Interview required.

Athletics Interscholastic: baseball (boys), basketball (b,g), crew (b,g), football (b), lacrosse (b,g), soccer (b,g), softball (g), volleyball (g); coed interscholastic: cross-country running, golf, skiing (cross-country), swimming and diving, tennis, track and field, wrestling. 5 PE instructors, 47 coaches.

Computers Computers are regularly used in all academic classes. Computer network features include on-campus library services, online commercial services, Internet access, wireless campus network, Internet filtering or blocking technology. Student e-mail accounts are available to students. The school has a published electronic and media policy.

Contact Ms. Karen Weslander, Admissions/Financial Aid Assistant. 206-368-3605. Fax: 206-440-2777. E-mail: admissions@lakesideschool.org. Web site: www.lakesideschool.org.

LAKEVIEW ACADEMY

796 Lakeview Drive
Gainesville, Georgia 30501

Head of School: Dr. James Curry Robison

General Information Coeducational day college-preparatory and technology school. Grades PK–12. Founded: 1970. Setting: suburban. Nearest major city is Atlanta. 88-acre campus. 5 buildings on campus. Approved or accredited by Georgia Independent School Association, Southern Association of Colleges and Schools, and Southern Association of Independent Schools. Member of National Association of Independent Schools. Endowment: $1 million. Total enrollment: 598. Upper school average class size: 12. Upper school faculty-student ratio: 1:5.

Upper School Student Profile Grade 9: 28 students (13 boys, 15 girls); Grade 10: 32 students (20 boys, 12 girls); Grade 11: 43 students (20 boys, 23 girls); Grade 12: 35 students (19 boys, 16 girls).

Faculty School total: 119. In upper school: 12 men, 14 women; 16 have advanced degrees.

Subjects Offered Addiction, advanced biology, algebra, American history, American literature, American sign language, art, athletic training, biology, biology-AP, calculus, calculus-AP, chemistry, chemistry-AP, choral music, chorus, computer applications, computer art, computer graphics, computer information systems, computer keyboarding, computer processing, computer programming, computer science, computer science-AP, computer technologies, creative writing, drama, drawing, earth science, economics, economics and history, English, English language and composition-AP, English literature, English literature and composition-AP, environmental science, ethics, foreign language, forensics, geometry, government, government/civics, grammar, graphic arts, honors algebra, honors English, honors geometry, immunology, introduction to theater, journalism, literary magazine, literature, mathematics, multimedia, painting, physical education, physics, poetry, political science, pre-calculus, psychology, science, social studies, Spanish, Spanish language-AP, statistics, studio art—AP, technology, technology/design, television, theater, trigonometry, U.S. history-AP, video, world history, world history-AP, world literature, yearbook.

Graduation Requirements Algebra, American literature, arts, biology, chemistry, composition, computer science, electives, English, ethics, foreign language, mathematics, physical education (includes health), science, technology, U.S. government, U.S. history, world history, world studies, 60 hours of community service.

Special Academic Programs 9 Advanced Placement exams for which test preparation is offered; honors section; independent study; academic accommodation for the gifted, the musically talented, and the artistically talented; remedial reading and/or remedial writing; remedial math; programs in English, mathematics, general development for dyslexic students.

College Admission Counseling 43 students graduated in 2008; all went to college, including Clemson University; Furman University; Georgia College & State University; Georgia Institute of Technology; Samford University; University of Georgia. Median SAT critical reading: 595, median SAT math: 570, median SAT writing: 610, median combined SAT: 1780, median composite ACT: 24. 39.5% scored over 600 on SAT critical reading, 31.6% scored over 600 on SAT math, 50% scored over 600 on SAT writing, 42.1% scored over 1800 on combined SAT, 44.7% scored over 26 on composite ACT.

Student Life Upper grades have uniform requirement, student council, honor system. Discipline rests equally with students and faculty.

Summer Programs Enrichment, advancement, sports, art/fine arts, computer instruction programs offered; session focuses on instructional, fun summer activity camps; held on campus; accepts boys and girls; open to students from other schools. 350 students usually enrolled. 2009 schedule: June 4 to July 27. Application deadline: April 13.

Tuition and Aid Day student tuition: $13,400. Tuition installment plan (monthly payment plans, biannual payment plan). Tuition reduction for siblings, merit scholarship grants, need-based scholarship grants available. In 2008–09, 11% of upper-school students received aid; total upper-school merit-scholarship money awarded: $32,000. Total amount of financial aid awarded in 2008–09: $157,000.

Admissions Traditional secondary-level entrance grade is 9. For fall 2008, 20 students applied for upper-level admission, 15 were accepted, 15 enrolled. ERB or Otis-Lennon IQ required. Deadline for receipt of application materials: none. Application fee required: $75. On-campus interview required.

Athletics Interscholastic: baseball (boys), basketball (b,g), cheering (g), football (b), soccer (b,g), tennis (b,g), volleyball (g); coed interscholastic: cross-country running, golf, kayaking, physical fitness, physical training, strength & conditioning; coed intramural: aerobics/Nautilus, hiking/backpacking. 4 PE instructors, 4 coaches.

Computers Computers are regularly used in all classes. Computer network features include on-campus library services, Internet access, wireless campus network, Internet filtering or blocking technology, all upper school students have a laptop computer equipped with wireless internet access. Campus intranet and student e-mail accounts are available to students. Students grades are available online. The school has a published electronic and media policy.

Contact Mrs. Pat England, Director of Admission. 770-531-2603. Fax: 770-718-0768. E-mail: pat.england@lakeviewacademy.com. Web site: www.lakeviewacademy.com.

LA LUMIERE SCHOOL

6801 North Wilhelm Road
La Porte, Indiana 46350

Head of School: Michael H. Kennedy

General Information Coeducational boarding and day college-preparatory, arts, and religious studies school. Boarding grades 9–PG, day grades 9–12. Founded: 1963. Setting: rural. Nearest major city is Chicago, IL. Students are housed in single-sex dormitories. 155-acre campus. 18 buildings on campus. Approved or accredited by Independent Schools Association of the Central States, Midwest Association of Boarding Schools, North Central Association of Colleges and Schools, and The Association of Boarding Schools. Member of National Association of Independent Schools. Total enrollment: 179. Upper school average class size: 15. Upper school faculty-student ratio: 1:7.

Upper School Student Profile Grade 9: 38 students (23 boys, 15 girls); Grade 10: 55 students (25 boys, 30 girls); Grade 11: 41 students (25 boys, 16 girls); Grade 12: 42 students (25 boys, 17 girls); Postgraduate: 3 students (3 boys). 40% of students are boarding students. 57% are state residents. 9 states are represented in upper school student body. 11% are international students. International students from China, Croatia, Germany, Republic of Korea, Russian Federation, and Serbia and Montenegro.

Faculty School total: 27. In upper school: 14 men, 13 women; 15 have advanced degrees; 19 reside on campus.

Subjects Offered Advanced Placement courses, algebra, American history-AP, American literature, art, art history, biology, biology-AP, British literature, calculus, calculus-AP, chemistry, Christian and Hebrew scripture, college counseling, computer programming, conceptual physics, creative writing, drama, economics, English, English literature, English-AP, ESL, ethics, French, French-AP, geography, geometry, government/civics, graphic design, health, physics, physics-AP, pre-calculus, SAT/ACT preparation, Spanish, Spanish-AP, speech, study skills, trigonometry, U.S. history, U.S. history-AP, Web site design, world history, world literature, world religions.

Graduation Requirements American government, American history, American literature, arts and fine arts (art, music, dance, drama), Bible as literature, British literature, college writing, computer science, electives, English, English composition, English literature, ethics, foreign language, government, health education, leadership, mathematics, public service, science, social studies (includes history), theology, U.S. history, world history. Community service is required.

Special Academic Programs Advanced Placement exam preparation; honors section; independent study; study at local college for college credit; academic accommodation for the gifted and the artistically talented; ESL (2 students enrolled).

College Admission Counseling 32 students graduated in 2008; all went to college, including DePaul University; Michigan State University; Saint Louis University; University of Illinois at Urbana–Champaign; University of Notre Dame. Median SAT critical reading: 550, median SAT math: 530, median SAT writing: 510, median combined SAT: 1600, median composite ACT: 24. 24% scored over 600 on SAT critical reading, 28% scored over 600 on SAT math, 14% scored over 600 on SAT writing, 10% scored over 1800 on combined SAT, 27% scored over 26 on composite ACT.

Student Life Upper grades have uniform requirement, student council, honor system. Discipline rests primarily with faculty.

Summer Programs Enrichment, advancement, ESL programs offered; session focuses on academics; held on campus; accepts boys and girls; open to students from other schools. 25 students usually enrolled. Application deadline: June 1.

Tuition and Aid Day student tuition: $8780; 7-day tuition and room/board: $29,100. Tuition installment plan (Academic Management Services Plan, Key Tuition Payment Plan, FACTS Tuition Payment Plan, individually arranged payment plans). Tuition reduction for siblings, merit scholarship grants, need-based scholarship grants available. In 2008–09, 28% of upper-school students received aid; total upper-school merit-scholarship money awarded: $15,000. Total amount of financial aid awarded in 2008–09: $500,000.

Admissions Traditional secondary-level entrance grade is 9. For fall 2008, 127 students applied for upper-level admission, 71 were accepted, 59 enrolled.

Achievement tests, admissions testing, any standardized test, English proficiency, ERB or ISEE required. Deadline for receipt of application materials: none. Application fee required: $50. Interview required.
Athletics Interscholastic: basketball (boys, girls), football (b), golf (b,g), independent competitive sports (b,g), lacrosse (b), softball (g), tennis (b,g), track and field (b,g), volleyball (g); intramural: aerobics (g), aerobics/dance (g), dance team (g), volleyball (b,g); coed interscholastic: baseball, cross-country running, outdoor adventure, running, soccer; coed intramural: aerobics/Nautilus, basketball, billiards, canoeing/kayaking, combined training, cooperative games, cross-country running, dance, fishing, fitness, flag football, floor hockey, Frisbee, jogging, kayaking, martial arts, Nautilus, outdoor adventure, physical fitness, physical training, power lifting, ropes courses, skateboarding, strength & conditioning, table tennis, touch football, ultimate Frisbee, weight lifting, weight training, yoga. 10 coaches, 1 athletic trainer.
Computers Computers are regularly used in all academic, college planning, creative writing, programming, yearbook classes. Computer network features include on-campus library services, Internet access, wireless campus network, Internet filtering or blocking technology. Student e-mail accounts and computer access in designated common areas are available to students. Students grades are available online. The school has a published electronic and media policy.
Contact Ms. Mary C. O'Malley, Director of Admissions. 219-326-7450. Fax: 219-325-3185. E-mail: admissions@lalumiere.org. Web site: www.lalumiere.org.

LANCASTER COUNTRY DAY SCHOOL

725 Hamilton Road
Lancaster, Pennsylvania 17603
Head of School: Mr. Steven D. Lisk

General Information Coeducational day college-preparatory and arts school. Grades PS–12. Founded: 1943. Setting: suburban. Nearest major city is Philadelphia. 26-acre campus. 1 building on campus. Approved or accredited by Middle States Association of Colleges and Schools, Pennsylvania Association of Independent Schools, and Pennsylvania Department of Education. Member of National Association of Independent Schools. Endowment: $12.5 million. Total enrollment: 535. Upper school average class size: 12. Upper school faculty-student ratio: 1:6.
Upper School Student Profile Grade 9: 45 students (22 boys, 23 girls); Grade 10: 33 students (17 boys, 16 girls); Grade 11: 42 students (14 boys, 28 girls); Grade 12: 37 students (15 boys, 22 girls).
Faculty School total: 76. In upper school: 13 men, 16 women; 16 have advanced degrees.
Subjects Offered Algebra, Asian studies, athletic training, Basic programming, bioethics, DNA and culture, biology, biology-AP, calculus, calculus-AP, ceramics, chamber groups, chemistry, chemistry-AP, China/Japan history, chorus, computer art, computer graphics, computer programming, computer programming-AP, computer science, computer science-AP, conceptual physics, contemporary history, contemporary issues, contemporary issues in science, creative writing, critical thinking, critical writing, dance, desktop publishing, digital imaging, drama, drawing, driver education, economics, economics and history, English literature, English-AP, ensembles, environmental science, environmental science-AP, European civilization, European history, European literature, fine arts, French, French-AP, geometry, guitar, honors geometry, instrumental music, journalism, Latin, math applications, mathematics, model United Nations, music, music history, painting, photography, physical education, physics, pre-calculus, printmaking, programming, psychology, research seminar, senior project, service learning/internship, Spanish, Spanish-AP, sports medicine, statistics, statistics-AP, theater, trigonometry, U.S. history, U.S. history-AP, U.S. literature, United Nations and international issues, weight training, women in world history, world affairs, world civilizations, world history, world literature, writing skills, yearbook.
Graduation Requirements Algebra, arts, biology, chemistry, computer science, English, foreign language, geometry, history, Latin, mathematics, physical education (includes health), science, trigonometry, one-week off-campus senior project.
Special Academic Programs Advanced Placement exam preparation; accelerated programs; independent study; study at local college for college credit; academic accommodation for the gifted, the musically talented, and the artistically talented.
College Admission Counseling 53 students graduated in 2008; all went to college, including Bucknell University; Carnegie Mellon University; Dickinson College; Millersville University of Pennsylvania; University of Pennsylvania; University of Vermont. Median SAT critical reading: 620, median SAT math: 615, median SAT writing: 600, median combined SAT: 1835.
Student Life Upper grades have specified standards of dress, student council, honor system. Discipline rests primarily with faculty.
Tuition and Aid Day student tuition: $18,100. Tuition installment plan (monthly payment plans, 2-installment plan). Need-based scholarship grants available. In 2008–09, 28% of upper-school students received aid. Total amount of financial aid awarded in 2008–09: $435,250.
Admissions Traditional secondary-level entrance grade is 9. For fall 2008, 22 students applied for upper-level admission, 18 were accepted, 18 enrolled. ERB CTP III required. Deadline for receipt of application materials: none. Application fee required: $75. Interview required.
Athletics Interscholastic: baseball (boys), basketball (b,g), cross-country running (b,g), dance (b,g), field hockey (g), football (b), golf (b,g), lacrosse (b,g), modern dance (b,g), soccer (b,g), softball (g), squash (b,g), swimming and diving (b,g), tennis (b,g), track and field (b,g), weight training (b,g). 3 PE instructors, 5 coaches, 1 athletic trainer.
Computers Computers are regularly used in desktop publishing, ESL, English, graphic arts, history, information technology, journalism, literary magazine, newspaper, programming, psychology, research skills, science, technology, Web site design, word processing, writing, yearbook classes. Computer network features include on-campus library services, online commercial services, Internet access, Internet filtering or blocking technology, technology-rich environment with SmartBoards in every classroom. Student e-mail accounts and computer access in designated common areas are available to students. Students grades are available online. The school has a published electronic and media policy.
Contact Beth Townsend, Assistant Director of Admission. 717-392-2916 Ext. 228. Fax: 717-509-8912. E-mail: townsendb@e-lcds.org. Web site: www.lancastercountryday.org.

LANCASTER MENNONITE HIGH SCHOOL

2176 Lincoln Highway East
Lancaster, Pennsylvania 17602
Head of School: Mr. Miles Yoder

General Information Coeducational boarding and day college-preparatory, general academic, vocational, religious studies, and Agriculture school, affiliated with Mennonite Church; primarily serves students with learning disabilities. Boarding grades 9–12, day grades 6–12. Founded: 1942. Setting: suburban. Nearest major city is Philadelphia. Students are housed in coed dormitories and single-sex by wings. 100-acre campus. 8 buildings on campus. Approved or accredited by Mennonite Education Agency, Mennonite Schools Council, Middle States Association of Colleges and Schools, and Pennsylvania Department of Education. Endowment: $12 million. Total enrollment: 1,501. Upper school average class size: 18. Upper school faculty-student ratio: 1:15.
Upper School Student Profile Grade 9: 122 students (56 boys, 66 girls); Grade 10: 166 students (79 boys, 87 girls); Grade 11: 163 students (89 boys, 74 girls); Grade 12: 197 students (89 boys, 108 girls). 8% of students are boarding students. 89% are state residents. 7 states are represented in upper school student body. 11% are international students. International students from Ethiopia, Germany, Japan, Kenya, Republic of Korea, and Zimbabwe; 2 other countries represented in student body. 49% of students are Mennonite.
Faculty School total: 77. In upper school: 38 men, 37 women; 50 have advanced degrees; 4 reside on campus.
Subjects Offered 1½ elective credits, 1968, 20th century American writers, 20th century history, 20th century physics, 20th century world history, ACT preparation, addiction, ADL skills, adolescent issues, advertising design, aerobics, aerospace education, aerospace science, aesthetics, African American history, African American studies, African dance, African drumming, African history, African literature, African studies, African-American history, African-American literature, African-American studies, agroecology, Alabama history and geography, alternative physical education, American biography, American Civil War, American culture, American democracy, American foreign policy, American government-AP, American legal systems, American literature-AP, American minority experience, American politics in film, American sign language, American studies, Amharic, analysis, analysis of data, analytic geometry, anatomy, anatomy and physiology, Ancient Greek, ancient/medieval philosophy, animal behavior, animation.
Special Academic Programs Advanced Placement exam preparation; honors section; independent study; study at local college for college credit; remedial reading and/or remedial writing; remedial math; special instructional classes for deaf students, blind students; ESL (20 students enrolled).
College Admission Counseling 174 students graduated in 2008; 112 went to college, including Eastern Mennonite University; Goshen College; Hesston College; Messiah College; Penn State University Park; York College of Pennsylvania. Other: 27 went to work, 35 had other specific plans. Mean SAT critical reading: 570, mean SAT math: 562, mean SAT writing: 560, mean combined SAT: 1692.
Student Life Upper grades have specified standards of dress, student council. Discipline rests primarily with faculty. Attendance at religious services is required.
Summer Programs Sports programs offered; held on campus; accepts boys and girls; open to students from other schools. 200 students usually enrolled. 2009 schedule: June to August. Application deadline: none.
Tuition and Aid Day student tuition: $6360; 5-day tuition and room/board: $8995; 7-day tuition and room/board: $12,002. Tuition installment plan (monthly payment plans). Tuition reduction for siblings, merit scholarship grants, need-based scholarship grants, paying campus jobs available. In 2008–09, 30% of upper-school students received aid; total upper-school merit-scholarship money awarded: $20,000. Total amount of financial aid awarded in 2008–09: $600,000.
Admissions Traditional secondary-level entrance grade is 9. Deadline for receipt of application materials: none. Application fee required: $100. Interview recommended.
Athletics Interscholastic: ball hockey (girls), baseball (b), basketball (b,g), cross-country running (b,g), field hockey (g), golf (b), soccer (b,g), softball (g), tennis (b,g), track and field (b,g); coed interscholastic: baseball. 4 PE instructors, 20 coaches, 1 athletic trainer.

Computers Computer network features include on-campus library services, Internet access, Internet filtering or blocking technology. The school has a published electronic and media policy.
Contact Christy L. Horst, Administrative Assistant for Admissions. 717-299-0436 Ext. 312. Fax: 717-299-0823. E-mail: horstcl@lancastermennonite.org. Web site: www.lancastermennonite.org.

LANDMARK EAST SCHOOL

Wolfville, Nova Scotia, Canada
See Special Needs Schools section.

LANDMARK SCHOOL

Prides Crossing, Massachusetts
See Special Needs Schools section.

LANDON SCHOOL

6101 Wilson Lane
Bethesda, Maryland 20817
Head of School: Mr. David M. Armstrong

General Information Boys' day college-preparatory, arts, and music school. Grades 3–12. Founded: 1929. Setting: suburban. Nearest major city is Washington, DC. 75-acre campus. 13 buildings on campus. Approved or accredited by Association of Independent Maryland Schools, Middle States Association of Colleges and Schools, and Maryland Department of Education. Member of National Association of Independent Schools. Endowment: $10.4 million. Total enrollment: 679. Upper school average class size: 15. Upper school faculty-student ratio: 1:8.
Upper School Student Profile Grade 9: 86 students (86 boys); Grade 10: 87 students (87 boys); Grade 11: 88 students (88 boys); Grade 12: 82 students (82 boys).
Faculty School total: 110. In upper school: 66 men, 14 women; 34 have advanced degrees.
Subjects Offered Acting, algebra, American Civil War, American foreign policy, American history, American literature, American studies, art, art history-AP, biology, biology-AP, calculus, calculus-AP, ceramics, chemistry, chemistry-AP, Chinese, Chinese history, computer science, computer science-AP, conceptual physics, constitutional law, creative writing, digital art, drama, drawing, earth science, economics-AP, engineering, English, English literature, environmental science-AP, environmental studies, ethics, European history, expository writing, fine arts, foreign policy, forensic science, French, French language-AP, French literature-AP, French studies, geography, geology, geometry, government/civics, grammar, handbells, health, history, humanities, international relations, jazz band, Latin, mathematics, meteorology, Middle Eastern history, music, music history, music theory, music theory-AP, oceanography, painting, performing arts, photography, physical education, physics, physics-AP, pre-calculus, science, sculpture, senior project, Shakespeare, social studies, Spanish, Spanish language-AP, Spanish literature, statistics-AP, strings, technological applications, theater, trigonometry, typing, U.S. history, U.S. history-AP, world history, world literature, writing.
Graduation Requirements American Civil War, American government, arts and fine arts (art, music, dance, drama), biology, chemistry, English, ethics, foreign language, government, humanities, mathematics, music, physical education (includes health), pre-calculus, science, social studies (includes history), Senior Project, 2-year arts requirement.
Special Academic Programs Advanced Placement exam preparation; honors section; independent study; term-away projects; study abroad.
College Admission Counseling 76 students graduated in 2008; all went to college, including Davidson College; Dickinson College; Georgetown University; Miami University; Tufts University; Yale University. Mean SAT critical reading: 671, mean SAT math: 663, mean SAT writing: 663, mean combined SAT: 1997, mean composite ACT: 27.
Student Life Upper grades have specified standards of dress, student council, honor system. Discipline rests equally with students and faculty.
Summer Programs Remediation, enrichment, advancement, art/fine arts programs offered; session focuses on Enrichment, advancement, remediation, expanded time in art studios and travel abroad; held both on and off campus; held at locations in France, China, Europe, Italy, and Spain; accepts boys and girls; open to students from other schools. 200 students usually enrolled. 2009 schedule: June 15 to July 31. Application deadline: none.
Tuition and Aid Day student tuition: $28,400. Tuition installment plan (FACTS Tuition Payment Plan, 2 payment plan—June and December). Need-based scholarship grants available. In 2008–09, 18% of upper-school students received aid. Total amount of financial aid awarded in 2008–09: $1,900,000.
Admissions Traditional secondary-level entrance grade is 9. For fall 2008, 119 students applied for upper-level admission, 49 were accepted, 24 enrolled. ISEE or SSAT required. Deadline for receipt of application materials: January 31. Application fee required: $75. On-campus interview required.
Athletics Interscholastic: baseball (boys), basketball (b), cross-country running (b), diving (b), fencing (b), football (b), golf (b), ice hockey (b), indoor track (b), indoor track & field (b), lacrosse (b), riflery (b), rugby (b), soccer (b), squash (b), swimming and diving (b), tennis (b), track and field (b), water polo (b), winter (indoor) track (b), wrestling (b); intramural: basketball (b), climbing (b), Frisbee (b), physical fitness (b), softball (b), strength & conditioning (b), tennis (b), ultimate Frisbee (b), weight lifting (b). 9 coaches, 1 athletic trainer.
Computers Computers are regularly used in all classes. Computer network features include on-campus library services, online commercial services, Internet access, wireless campus network, Internet filtering or blocking technology, Password-Accessed Web Portals. Campus intranet, student e-mail accounts, and computer access in designated common areas are available to students. The school has a published electronic and media policy.
Contact Mr. George C. Mulligan, Director of Admissions. 301-320-1067. Fax: 301-320-1133. E-mail: george_mulligan@landon.net. Web site: www.landon.net.

LANSDALE CATHOLIC HIGH SCHOOL

700 Lansdale Avenue
Lansdale, Pennsylvania 19446-2995
Head of School: Mr. Timothy Quinn

General Information Coeducational day college-preparatory, general academic, and religious studies school, affiliated with Roman Catholic Church. Grades 9–12. Founded: 1949. Setting: suburban. Nearest major city is Philadelphia. 1 building on campus. Approved or accredited by Middle States Association of Colleges and Schools, National Catholic Education Association, and Pennsylvania Department of Education. Total enrollment: 820. Upper school average class size: 30.
Upper School Student Profile Grade 9: 174 students (79 boys, 95 girls); Grade 10: 220 students (113 boys, 107 girls); Grade 11: 228 students (118 boys, 110 girls); Grade 12: 184 students (102 boys, 82 girls). 99% of students are Roman Catholic.
Faculty School total: 43. In upper school: 21 men, 22 women; 26 have advanced degrees.
Subjects Offered Algebra, American government, American government-AP, American history, American history-AP, American literature, analytic geometry, art history-AP, Basic programming, biology-AP, business law, calculus, calculus-AP, career education, career planning, career/college preparation, Catholic belief and practice, chemistry, chorus, church history, classical language, college counseling, college placement, college planning, computer education, computer programming, drama, English language and composition-AP, English literature and composition-AP, English literature-AP, environmental science, European history, French, government and politics-AP, government-AP, Greek, health education, Italian, Latin, mathematics-AP, physical fitness, physical science, physics, pre-calculus, SAT/ACT preparation, Spanish, student government, trigonometry, U.S. government and politics-AP, United States government-AP, Western civilization.
Graduation Requirements Service requirement: 30 hours by the end of junior year.
Special Academic Programs 13 Advanced Placement exams for which test preparation is offered; honors section; study at local college for college credit; remedial reading and/or remedial writing; remedial math; ESL (20 students enrolled).
College Admission Counseling 185 students graduated in 2008; 181 went to college, including Gwynedd-Mercy College; Montgomery County Community College; Penn State University Park; Temple University. Other: 3 went to work, 1 entered military service.
Student Life Upper grades have uniform requirement, student council, honor system. Discipline rests primarily with faculty. Attendance at religious services is required.
Summer Programs Remediation, enrichment, advancement, sports, art/fine arts programs offered; held on campus; accepts boys and girls; open to students from other schools.
Tuition and Aid Day student tuition: $4860. Tuition installment plan (monthly payment plans, individually arranged payment plans). Tuition reduction for siblings, merit scholarship grants, need-based scholarship grants, TAP Program available. In 2008–09, 20% of upper-school students received aid.
Admissions Traditional secondary-level entrance grade is 9. Deadline for receipt of application materials: none. Application fee required. Interview recommended.
Athletics Interscholastic: baseball (boys), basketball (b,g), cheering (g), cross-country running (b,g), dance squad (b,g), field hockey (g), football (b), golf (b,g), ice hockey (b,g), lacrosse (b,g), rugby (b,g), soccer (b,g), softball (g), swimming and diving (b,g), tennis (b,g), track and field (b,g), volleyball (g), weight lifting (b), winter (indoor) track (b,g), wrestling (b); intramural: flag football (b), ice hockey (b,g); coed interscholastic: bowling, diving, indoor track. 2 PE instructors, 1 athletic trainer.
Computers Computers are regularly used in all classes. Computer network features include on-campus library services, online commercial services, Internet access, wireless campus network, Internet filtering or blocking technology. Computer access in designated common areas is available to students. Students grades are available online. The school has a published electronic and media policy.
Contact Mr. James Casey, President. 215-362-6160 Ext. 133. Fax: 215-362-5746. E-mail: jcasey@lansdalecatholic.com. Web site: www.lansdalecatholic.com.

LANSING CHRISTIAN SCHOOL

3405 Belle Chase
Lansing, Michigan 48911

Head of School: Mrs. Pamela Campbell

General Information Coeducational day college-preparatory, general academic, arts, business, religious studies, bilingual studies, and technology school, affiliated with Christian faith. Grades PK–12. Founded: 1950. Setting: suburban. 65-acre campus. 1 building on campus. Approved or accredited by Christian Schools International, Michigan Association of Non-Public Schools, and North Central Association of Colleges and Schools. Endowment: $14,500. Total enrollment: 618. Upper school average class size: 20. Upper school faculty-student ratio: 1:12.

Upper School Student Profile Grade 9: 53 students (26 boys, 27 girls); Grade 10: 36 students (14 boys, 22 girls); Grade 11: 61 students (37 boys, 24 girls); Grade 12: 41 students (26 boys, 15 girls). 100% of students are Christian faith.

Faculty School total: 50. In upper school: 10 men, 15 women; 10 have advanced degrees.

Subjects Offered Acting, advanced chemistry, advanced computer applications, advanced math, Advanced Placement courses, algebra, American Civil War, American government, American history, American literature, analytic geometry, art, art appreciation, Bible, Bible studies, biology, business, business education, calculus, calculus-AP, chemistry, choir, Christian doctrine, Christian testament, church history, civics, clinical chemistry, computer keyboarding, computer skills, concert band, concert choir, current history, drama, economics, English literature, French, general science, geometry, government, health, history, instruments, journalism, music, Spanish, Web site design, yearbook.

Special Academic Programs Advanced Placement exam preparation; academic accommodation for the gifted; programs in English, mathematics, general development for dyslexic students; ESL (3 students enrolled).

College Admission Counseling Colleges students went to include Calvin College; Cedarville University; Michigan State University; Taylor University; University of Michigan.

Student Life Upper grades have specified standards of dress, student council, honor system. Discipline rests equally with students and faculty. Attendance at religious services is required.

Admissions Traditional secondary-level entrance grade is 9. Any standardized test required. Deadline for receipt of application materials: none. Application fee required: $100. Interview required.

Athletics Interscholastic: baseball (boys), basketball (b,g), cheering (g). 2 PE instructors, 15 coaches.

Computers Computers are regularly used in all academic classes. Computer network features include on-campus library services, Internet access.

Contact Mrs. Kristen Salsbury, Director of Admissions. 517-882-5779 Ext. 107. Fax: 517-882-5849. E-mail: admissions@lansingchristianschool.org. Web site: www.lansingchristianschool.org.

LA PIETRA–HAWAII SCHOOL FOR GIRLS

2933 Poni Moi Road
Honolulu, Hawaii 96815

Head of School: Mrs. Mahina Eleneki Hugo

General Information Girls' day college-preparatory, arts, and technology school. Grades 6–12. Founded: 1962. Setting: suburban. 6-acre campus. 15 buildings on campus. Approved or accredited by Western Association of Schools and Colleges. Member of National Association of Independent Schools and Secondary School Admission Test Board. Endowment: $3 million. Total enrollment: 247. Upper school average class size: 6. Upper school faculty-student ratio: 1:10.

Upper School Student Profile Grade 9: 33 students (33 girls); Grade 10: 37 students (37 girls); Grade 11: 34 students (34 girls); Grade 12: 39 students (39 girls).

Faculty School total: 36. In upper school: 8 men, 28 women; 23 have advanced degrees.

Subjects Offered Advanced Placement courses, algebra, American history, American literature, art, art history, biology, calculus, ceramics, chemistry, creative writing, drama, earth science, ecology, English, English literature, European history, expository writing, fine arts, French, geography, geometry, grammar, health, history, Japanese, marine biology, mathematics, music, oceanography, photography, physical education, physics, physiology, psychology, science, social studies, Spanish, theater, trigonometry, world history, writing.

Graduation Requirements Arts and fine arts (art, music, dance, drama), English, foreign language, mathematics, physical education (includes health), science, social studies (includes history), independent project.

Special Academic Programs Advanced Placement exam preparation; honors section; independent study; remedial reading and/or remedial writing; remedial math.

College Admission Counseling 37 students graduated in 2008; all went to college, including University of Hawaii at Manoa. Mean SAT math: 562, mean SAT writing: 553.

Student Life Upper grades have uniform requirement, student council. Discipline rests primarily with faculty.

Tuition and Aid Day student tuition: $13,625. Guaranteed tuition plan. Tuition installment plan (monthly payment plans, individually arranged payment plans, tuition insurance). Need-based scholarship grants available. In 2008–09, 40% of upper-school students received aid. Total amount of financial aid awarded in 2008–09: $400,700.

Admissions Traditional secondary-level entrance grade is 9. For fall 2008, 104 students applied for upper-level admission, 67 were accepted, 38 enrolled. SSAT required. Deadline for receipt of application materials: none. Application fee required: $50. Interview required.

Athletics Interscholastic: basketball, bowling, canoeing/kayaking, cheering, cross-country running, diving, equestrian sports, golf, gymnastics, judo, kayaking, ocean paddling, paddling, riflery, sailing, soccer, softball, swimming and diving, synchronized swimming, tennis, track and field, volleyball, water polo, wrestling. 2 PE instructors, 10 coaches.

Computers Computers are regularly used in all academic, art classes. Computer network features include on-campus library services, online commercial services, Internet access, wireless campus network, Internet filtering or blocking technology, LavaNet. Students grades are available online. The school has a published electronic and media policy.

Contact Mrs. Sandra Robinson, Director of Admissions. 808-922-2744. Fax: 808-923-4514. E-mail: admissions@lapietra.edu. Web site: www.lapietra.edu.

LA SALLE ACADEMY

612 Academy Avenue
Providence, Rhode Island 02908

Head of School: Br. Michael McKenery, FSC

General Information Coeducational day college-preparatory, arts, religious studies, and technology school, affiliated with Roman Catholic Church. Grades 7–12. Founded: 1874. Setting: urban. 60-acre campus. 5 buildings on campus. Approved or accredited by New England Association of Schools and Colleges. Member of National Association of Independent Schools. Total enrollment: 1,460. Upper school average class size: 20. Upper school faculty-student ratio: 1:12.

Upper School Student Profile 85% of students are Roman Catholic.

Faculty School total: 108. In upper school: 59 men, 49 women; 76 have advanced degrees.

Subjects Offered Algebra, American history, American literature, anatomy, art, astronomy, biology, business, calculus, ceramics, chemistry, community service, computer programming, computer science, creative writing, dance, drama, drawing, economics, electronics, engineering, English, English literature, environmental science, ESL, film, fine arts, French, geology, geometry, history, Italian, journalism, law, mathematics, microbiology, music, painting, photography, physical education, physical science, physics, physiology, psychology, religion, science, social studies, sociology, Spanish, statistics, theater, trigonometry, world history, world literature, writing.

Graduation Requirements Arts and fine arts (art, music, dance, drama), computer science, English, foreign language, mathematics, physical education (includes health), religion (includes Bible studies and theology), science, social studies (includes history). Community service is required.

Special Academic Programs Advanced Placement exam preparation; honors section; study at local college for college credit; academic accommodation for the gifted, the musically talented, and the artistically talented.

College Admission Counseling 292 students graduated in 2008; 285 went to college, including Boston College; Brown University; Harvard University; United States Military Academy; University of Rhode Island; Yale University. Other: 6 went to work, 1 entered military service.

Student Life Upper grades have uniform requirement, student council, honor system. Discipline rests equally with students and faculty.

Tuition and Aid Day student tuition: $10,650. Tuition installment plan (FACTS Tuition Payment Plan). Merit scholarship grants, need-based scholarship grants available. In 2008–09, 35% of upper-school students received aid; total upper-school merit-scholarship money awarded: $600,000. Total amount of financial aid awarded in 2008–09: $1,400,000.

Admissions Traditional secondary-level entrance grade is 9. For fall 2008, 850 students applied for upper-level admission, 400 were accepted, 350 enrolled. STS, Diocese Test required. Deadline for receipt of application materials: December 31. Application fee required: $25.

Athletics Interscholastic: baseball (boys), basketball (b,g), cross-country running (b,g), football (b), golf (b,g), gymnastics (b,g), ice hockey (b,g), lacrosse (b,g), sailing (b,g), soccer (b,g), softball (g), swimming and diving (b,g), tennis (b,g), track and field (b,g), volleyball (b,g), wrestling (b,g); coed intramural: fencing, modern dance, physical fitness, physical training, table tennis, touch football, volleyball, walking, whiffle ball. 5 PE instructors, 61 coaches, 4 athletic trainers.

Computers Computers are regularly used in English, foreign language, history, mathematics, music, science classes. Computer network features include online commercial services, Internet access.

Contact Mr. George Aldrich, Director of Admissions and Public Relations. 401-351-7750 Ext. 122. Fax: 401-444-1782. E-mail: galdrich@lasalle-academy.org. Web site: www.lasalle-academy.org.

LA SALLE HIGH SCHOOL

3601 South Miami Avenue
Miami, Florida 33133

Head of School: Sr. Patricia Roche, FMA

General Information Coeducational day college-preparatory, arts, business, religious studies, and technology school, affiliated with Roman Catholic Church. Grades 9–12. Founded: 1959. Setting: urban. 13-acre campus. 7 buildings on campus. Approved or accredited by Southern Association of Colleges and Schools, The College Board, and Florida Department of Education. Endowment: $68,000. Total enrollment: 733. Upper school average class size: 27. Upper school faculty-student ratio: 1:15.
Upper School Student Profile Grade 9: 191 students (62 boys, 129 girls); Grade 10: 177 students (60 boys, 117 girls); Grade 11: 181 students (64 boys, 117 girls); Grade 12: 184 students (51 boys, 133 girls). 95% of students are Roman Catholic.
Faculty School total: 49. In upper school: 20 men, 29 women; 22 have advanced degrees.
Subjects Offered Advanced Placement courses, African American studies, algebra, American government-AP, American history, American history-AP, analytic geometry, anatomy, art, automated accounting, band, Bible studies, biology, calculus, chemistry, choral music, computer programming, computer programming-AP, computer science, desktop publishing, drama, economics, English, European history, fine arts, French, geometry, government/civics, health, history, humanities, Italian, marine biology, mathematics, music appreciation, physical education, physics, psychology, religion, science, social studies, sociology, Spanish, speech, trigonometry, world history.
Graduation Requirements Arts and fine arts (art, music, dance, drama), business skills (includes word processing), computer science, English, foreign language, mathematics, physical education (includes health), religion (includes Bible studies and theology), science, social studies (includes history), 20 hours of community service for each of the 4 years.
Special Academic Programs Advanced Placement exam preparation; honors section; independent study; study at local college for college credit; academic accommodation for the gifted.
College Admission Counseling 182 students graduated in 2008; 179 went to college, including Florida International University; Florida State University; Miami Dade College; University of Central Florida; University of Florida; University of Miami. Mean SAT critical reading: 499, mean SAT math: 477, mean SAT writing: 498, mean combined SAT: 1474, mean composite ACT: 20. 17% scored over 600 on SAT critical reading, 9% scored over 600 on SAT math, 10% scored over 600 on SAT writing, 36% scored over 1800 on combined SAT.
Student Life Upper grades have uniform requirement, student council. Discipline rests equally with students and faculty. Attendance at religious services is required.
Summer Programs Remediation, enrichment programs offered; session focuses on remediation and enrichment; held on campus; accepts boys and girls; open to students from other schools. 200 students usually enrolled. 2009 schedule: June 15 to July 10. Application deadline: June 12.
Tuition and Aid Day student tuition: $9635. Tuition installment plan (FACTS Tuition Payment Plan, monthly payment plans, individually arranged payment plans). Paying campus jobs available. In 2008–09, 5% of upper-school students received aid. Total amount of financial aid awarded in 2008–09: $165,000.
Admissions Traditional secondary-level entrance grade is 9. For fall 2008, 350 students applied for upper-level admission, 260 were accepted, 220 enrolled. Catholic High School Entrance Examination or PSAT and SAT for applicants to grade 11 and 12 required. Deadline for receipt of application materials: none. Application fee required: $350. On-campus interview required.
Athletics Interscholastic: baseball (boys), basketball (b,g), bicycling (b,g), cheering (b,g), cross-country running (b,g), dance team (g), football (b), lacrosse (b), soccer (b,g), softball (g), swimming and diving (b,g), tennis (b,g), track and field (b,g), trap and skeet (b,g), volleyball (g), weight training (b,g), winter soccer (b,g); intramural: football (b), volleyball (g); coed interscholastic: sailing, tennis, track and field; coed intramural: aerobics/dance, bicycling, dance, dance team, mountain biking, physical fitness, sailing, table tennis, weight training. 2 PE instructors, 15 coaches, 1 athletic trainer.
Computers Computers are regularly used in business, business applications, economics, French, journalism, mathematics, programming, science, technology, word processing, yearbook classes. Computer network features include on-campus library services, Internet access. Students grades are available online.
Contact Ms. Nancy Toruno, Admissions Director. 305-854-2334 Ext. 130. Fax: 305-858-5971. E-mail: admissions@lasallehighschool.com. Web site: www.lasallehighschool.com.

LA SALLE INSTITUTE

174 Williams Road
Troy, New York 12180

Head of School: Br. Carl J. Malacalza, FSC

General Information Boys' day college-preparatory, religious studies, technology, and military school, affiliated with Roman Catholic Church. Grades 6–12. Founded: 1850. Setting: suburban. Nearest major city is Albany. 25-acre campus. 2 buildings on campus. Approved or accredited by Christian Brothers Association, Middle States Association of Colleges and Schools, and New York Department of Education. Endowment: $1.5 million. Total enrollment: 440. Upper school average class size: 24. Upper school faculty-student ratio: 1:10.
Upper School Student Profile Grade 9: 82 students (82 boys); Grade 10: 68 students (68 boys); Grade 11: 92 students (92 boys); Grade 12: 98 students (98 boys). 70% of students are Roman Catholic.
Faculty School total: 44. In upper school: 29 men, 15 women; 25 have advanced degrees.
Subjects Offered Advanced chemistry, advanced math, algebra, American government-AP, American history, American literature, anatomy, art, band, biology, biology-AP, business, calculus, campus ministry, career education, Catholic belief and practice, chemistry, chorus, college counseling, computer programming, computer resources, computer science, computer skills, computer studies, concert band, drama, driver education, earth science, economics, economics and history, English, English literature, English literature and composition-AP, environmental studies, European history, fine arts, French, French language-AP, geometry, government and politics-AP, government/civics, grammar, health education, history, jazz band, JROTC or LEAD (Leadership Education and Development), logic, mathematics, mathematics-AP, military science, music, philosophy, physical education, physics, physiology, precalculus, public speaking, religion, science, social studies, Spanish, Spanish-AP, theater, trigonometry, typing, U.S. history-AP, world history, world literature, writing.
Graduation Requirements Successfully pass all senior subjects and take SAT/ACT, annual service requirement.
Special Academic Programs Advanced Placement exam preparation; honors section; study at local college for college credit; remedial reading and/or remedial writing.
College Admission Counseling 99 students graduated in 2008; 97 went to college, including Boston College; Le Moyne College; Manhattan College; Rensselaer Polytechnic Institute; Siena College; The Catholic University of America. Other: 2 entered military service.
Student Life Upper grades have uniform requirement, student council, honor system. Discipline rests primarily with faculty. Attendance at religious services is required.
Tuition and Aid Day student tuition: $6875–$9840. Tuition installment plan (FACTS Tuition Payment Plan, monthly payment plans, 3-payment plan). Merit scholarship grants, need-based scholarship grants available. In 2008–09, 47% of upper-school students received aid; total upper-school merit-scholarship money awarded: $145,483. Total amount of financial aid awarded in 2008–09: $372,768.
Admissions BASIS, essay, placement test, standardized test scores and Stanford Test of Academic Skills required. Deadline for receipt of application materials: none. No application fee required. On-campus interview required.
Athletics Interscholastic: alpine skiing, baseball, basketball, bowling, cross-country running, drill team, fencing, football, golf, ice hockey, indoor track, indoor track & field, JROTC drill, lacrosse, soccer, tennis, track and field, winter (indoor) track, wrestling; intramural: basketball, bicycling, bowling, paint ball, skiing (downhill), snowboarding, strength & conditioning, table tennis, weight lifting. 3 PE instructors, 1 athletic trainer.
Computers Computers are regularly used in accounting, career technology, college planning, economics, English, graphic design, introduction to technology, journalism, keyboarding, library, literary magazine, mathematics, media production, newspaper, publications, SAT preparation, science, typing, yearbook classes. Computer network features include on-campus library services, online commercial services, Internet access. The school has a published electronic and media policy.
Contact Mr. Gerald Washington, Admissions Coordinator. 518-283-2500 Ext. 237. Fax: 518-283-6265. E-mail: gwashington@lasalleinstitute.org. Web site: www.lasalleinstitute.org.

THE LAUREATE ACADEMY

Winnipeg, Manitoba, Canada
See Special Needs Schools section.

LAUREL SPRINGS SCHOOL

302 West El Paseo Road
Ojai, California 93023

Head of School: Marilyn Mosley

General Information Distance learning only college-preparatory, general academic, arts, vocational, technology, and distance learning school. Distance learning grades K–12. Founded: 1991. Setting: small town. Nearest major city is Los Angeles. 1 building on campus. Approved or accredited by Western Association of Schools and Colleges and California Department of Education. Total enrollment: 1,633.
Faculty School total: 72. In upper school: 15 men, 57 women; 30 have advanced degrees.
Subjects Offered Adolescent issues, Advanced Placement courses, algebra, American literature, art appreciation, art history, biology, biology-AP, British literature, British literature (honors), calculus, calculus-AP, calligraphy, career/college preparation, cartooning/animation, chemistry, chemistry-AP, college admission preparation, college counseling, composition, drama, driver education, earth science, economics, electives, English as a foreign language, English composition, English language-AP, English literature-AP, environmental education, environmental studies,

French, geometry, health, honors algebra, honors English, honors geometry, honors U.S. history, honors world history, independent study, Internet, media literacy, microeconomics-AP, music history, mythology, painting, photo shop, physical education, physics, pre-calculus, psychology, SAT/ACT preparation, Shakespeare, sociology, Spanish, Spanish-AP, trigonometry, U.S. government, U.S. government and politics-AP, U.S. history, world cultures, world history, world literature, writing fundamentals.

Graduation Requirements Arts and fine arts (art, music, dance, drama), electives, English, foreign language, mathematics, physical education (includes health), science, social studies (includes history).

Special Academic Programs Honors section; accelerated programs; independent study; term-away projects; academic accommodation for the gifted, the musically talented, and the artistically talented; remedial reading and/or remedial writing; remedial math; programs in English, mathematics, general development for dyslexic students; special instructional classes for students needing customized learning options; ESL.

College Admission Counseling 236 students graduated in 2008; 129 went to college, including Pace University; San Jose State University; Stanford University; The University of Texas at Austin; University of California, Santa Barbara; University of California, Santa Cruz. Other: 12 went to work, 1 entered military service, 25 had other specific plans. Median SAT critical reading: 540, median SAT math: 495, median SAT writing: 550, median combined SAT: 1545, median composite ACT: 21. 34% scored over 600 on SAT critical reading, 21% scored over 600 on SAT math, 24% scored over 600 on SAT writing, 25% scored over 1800 on combined SAT, 17% scored over 26 on composite ACT.

Student Life Upper grades have honor system. Discipline rests equally with students and faculty.

Summer Programs Remediation, enrichment, advancement, ESL, art/fine arts, computer instruction programs offered; session focuses on remediation and dual enrollment options; held both on and off campus; held at individual homes of enrolled students; accepts boys and girls; open to students from other schools. 1,231 students usually enrolled. 2009 schedule: July 1 to August 15. Application deadline: June 15.

Tuition and Aid Guaranteed tuition plan. Tuition installment plan (monthly payment plans, individually arranged payment plans). Tuition reduction for siblings, need-based scholarship grants available. In 2008–09, 1% of upper-school students received aid. Total amount of financial aid awarded in 2008–09: $22,538.

Admissions Traditional secondary-level entrance grade is 9. Deadline for receipt of application materials: none. Application fee required: $100. Interview required.

Computers Computers are regularly used in art, economics, English, ESL, foreign language, geography, health, history, independent study, information technology, language development, life skills, mathematics, psychology, SAT preparation, science, social studies, typing, writing classes. Computer network features include on-campus library services, Internet access, 100 online courses. Student e-mail accounts are available to students. Students grades are available online.

Contact Ms. Wendy Pilon, Heads of Enrollments. 805-646-2473 Ext. 121. Fax: 805-646-0186. E-mail: wpilon@laurelsprings.com. Web site: www.laurelsprings.com.

LAUREL VIEW ACADEMY

140 Mapleton Avenue
Barrie, Ontario L4N 9N7, Canada

Head of School: Mrs. Susi Rumney

General Information Coeducational day college-preparatory, general academic, arts, business, and technology school. Grades JK–12. Founded: 2001. Setting: suburban. 3-acre campus. 1 building on campus. Approved or accredited by Ontario Ministry of Education. Language of instruction: English. Upper school average class size: 10. Upper school faculty-student ratio: 1:10.

Faculty School total: 4. In upper school: 2 women; 1 has an advanced degree.

Subjects Offered 20th century history, 20th century physics, 20th century world history, advanced chemistry, advanced math, algebra, analysis of data, analytic geometry, anthropology, art, biology, business, calculus, Canadian geography, Canadian history, Canadian law, Canadian literature, career education, character education, chemistry, discrete math, English, English as a foreign language, ESL, French as a second language, general science, geography, government and politics-AP, grammar, health education, history, language arts, law, leadership, linear algebra, literature, math analysis, math applications, math methods, math review, mathematical modeling, mathematics, media, novels, oral communications, oral expression, parent/child development, performing arts, philosophy, physical education, physics, political science, politics, pre-algebra, pre-calculus, pre-college orientation, probability and statistics, projective geometry, psychology, reading, reading/study skills, research, research and reference, research skills, research techniques, science, science and technology, sex education, Shakespeare, short story, social education, social issues, social justice, social psychology, social sciences, social skills, social studies, society, society and culture, society challenge and change, society, politics and law, socioeconomic problems, sociology, statistics, statistics and probability, student government, study skills, technical education, The 20th Century, visual arts, world geography, world history, world issues, world literature, World War I, World War II, writing.

Graduation Requirements 20th century history, arts, careers, civics, English, French as a second language, general science, geography, mathematics, physical education (includes health).

Special Academic Programs Independent study; ESL.

College Admission Counseling 3 students graduated in 2008; all went to college, including Brock University; York University.

Student Life Upper grades have uniform requirement. Discipline rests primarily with faculty.

Tuition and Aid Day student tuition: CAN$9000. Tuition installment plan (monthly payment plans). Tuition reduction for siblings, need-based scholarship grants available.

Admissions For fall 2008, 2 students applied for upper-level admission, 2 were accepted. Deadline for receipt of application materials: none. Application fee required: CAN$150. Interview recommended.

Athletics Coed Interscholastic: alpine skiing, basketball, bowling, combined training, cooperative games, cross-country running, equestrian sports, horseback riding, outdoor activities, physical fitness, skiing (downhill), soccer.

Computers Computer resources include Internet access, wireless campus network.

Contact Mrs. Susi Rumney. 705-796-8295. Fax: 705-458-8296. E-mail: laurelview.academy@sympatico.ca. Web site: www.laurelviewacademy.ca.

LAUSANNE COLLEGIATE SCHOOL

1381 West Massey Road
Memphis, Tennessee 38120

Head of School: Mr. Stuart McCathie

General Information Coeducational day college-preparatory, arts, bilingual studies, technology, AP Courses Honors Curriculum, and Sports Education Electives school. Grades PK–12. Founded: 1926. Setting: suburban. 28-acre campus. 5 buildings on campus. Approved or accredited by National Independent Private Schools Association, Southern Association of Colleges and Schools, Southern Association of Independent Schools, Tennessee Association of Independent Schools, and Tennessee Department of Education. Member of National Association of Independent Schools. Endowment: $700,000. Total enrollment: 745. Upper school average class size: 18. Upper school faculty-student ratio: 1:9.

Upper School Student Profile Grade 9: 56 students (25 boys, 31 girls); Grade 10: 75 students (32 boys, 43 girls); Grade 11: 66 students (26 boys, 40 girls); Grade 12: 55 students (26 boys, 29 girls).

Faculty School total: 83. In upper school: 12 men, 15 women; 17 have advanced degrees.

Subjects Offered Acting, algebra, American government, ancient world history, art, art-AP, biology, biology-AP, calculus, chemistry, choir, college admission preparation, comparative government and politics-AP, computer programming, creative writing, discrete mathematics, economics, English, English-AP, French, French-AP, geometry, health and wellness, honors algebra, honors English, honors geometry, humanities, instrumental music, international studies, journalism, Latin, Latin-AP, modern world history, photography, physical education, physical science, physics, physics-AP, play production, pre-calculus, public policy, short story, Spanish, Spanish-AP, statistics, U.S. history, U.S. history-AP, World War II, writing workshop.

Graduation Requirements Arts and fine arts (art, music, dance, drama), English, foreign language, mathematics, physical education (includes health), science, social studies (includes history).

Special Academic Programs 12 Advanced Placement exams for which test preparation is offered; honors section; academic accommodation for the gifted, the musically talented, and the artistically talented; ESL (20 students enrolled).

College Admission Counseling 48 students graduated in 2008; all went to college, including Boston University; Mississippi State University; Rhodes College; The George Washington University; The University of Tennessee; University of Memphis. 53% scored over 600 on SAT critical reading, 57% scored over 600 on SAT math, 50% scored over 600 on SAT writing, 57% scored over 1800 on combined SAT, 36% scored over 26 on composite ACT.

Student Life Upper grades have specified standards of dress, student council, honor system. Discipline rests primarily with faculty.

Summer Programs Remediation, enrichment, advancement, sports, art/fine arts, computer instruction programs offered; session focuses on academics, athletics, and fun; held on campus; accepts boys and girls; open to students from other schools. 800 students usually enrolled. 2009 schedule: June 1 to July 31. Application deadline: none.

Tuition and Aid Day student tuition: $13,750. Tuition installment plan (monthly payment plans, Tuition Refund Plan). Need-based scholarship grants, tuition remission for children of faculty available. In 2008–09, 8% of upper-school students received aid. Total amount of financial aid awarded in 2008–09: $248,208.

Admissions Traditional secondary-level entrance grade is 9. For fall 2008, 59 students applied for upper-level admission, 39 were accepted, 32 enrolled. ISEE required. Deadline for receipt of application materials: none. Application fee required: $75. On-campus interview required.

Athletics Interscholastic: basketball (boys, girls), cheering (g), cross-country running (b,g), dance squad (g), dance team (g), golf (b,g), gymnastics (g), lacrosse (b,g), pom squad (g), soccer (b,g), swimming and diving (b,g), tennis (b,g), track and field (b,g), volleyball (g); intramural: backpacking (b,g), ballet (g), basketball (b,g), bowling (b,g), canoeing/kayaking (b,g), climbing (b,g), dance team (g), flag football (b,g), floor hockey (b,g), Frisbee (b,g), hiking/backpacking (b,g), indoor soccer (b,g), kayaking (b,g), lacrosse (b,g), mountain biking (b,g), mountaineering (b,g), outdoor activities (b,g), physical fitness (b,g), rafting (b,g), rappelling (b,g), rock climbing (b,g), ropes courses (b,g), rugby (b), soccer (b,g), strength & conditioning (b,g), tennis (b,g), track and field (b,g), ultimate Frisbee (b,g), volleyball (b,g), wall climbing (b,g), weight lifting (b,g), wilderness (b,g); coed interscholastic: swimming and diving; coed intramural: backpacking, basketball, bowling, canoeing/kayaking, climbing, fishing, flag football, floor hockey, Frisbee, hiking/backpacking, indoor soccer, kayaking, lacrosse, martial arts, mountain biking, mountaineering, outdoor activities, physical fitness, rafting, rappelling, rock climbing, ropes courses, soccer, strength & conditioning, tennis, track and field, ultimate Frisbee, volleyball, wall climbing, weight lifting, wilderness, yoga. 4 PE instructors, 2 coaches, 1 athletic trainer.

Computers Computers are regularly used in all academic, technology classes. Computer network features include on-campus library services, online commercial services, Internet access, wireless campus network, Internet filtering or blocking technology, homework assignments available online. Student e-mail accounts are available to students. Students grades are available online. The school has a published electronic and media policy.

Contact Mrs. Jennifer Saxton, Admission Coordinator. 901-474-1030. Fax: 901-474-1010. E-mail: jsaxton@lausanneschool.com. Web site: www.lausanneschool.com.

LAWRENCE ACADEMY

Powderhouse Road
Groton, Massachusetts 01450
Head of School: D. Scott Wiggins, Esq.

General Information Coeducational boarding and day college-preparatory, Interdisciplinary Ninth Grade Curriculum, and Student Centered Learning school; primarily serves students with learning disabilities and Limited academic support. Grades 9–12. Founded: 1793. Setting: small town. Nearest major city is Boston. Students are housed in single-sex dormitories. 100-acre campus. 31 buildings on campus. Approved or accredited by Association of Independent Schools in New England, New England Association of Schools and Colleges, The Association of Boarding Schools, and Massachusetts Department of Education. Member of National Association of Independent Schools and Secondary School Admission Test Board. Endowment: $16 million. Total enrollment: 396. Upper school average class size: 15. Upper school faculty-student ratio: 1:8.

Upper School Student Profile Grade 9: 79 students (40 boys, 39 girls); Grade 10: 108 students (61 boys, 47 girls); Grade 11: 108 students (59 boys, 49 girls); Grade 12: 101 students (51 boys, 50 girls). 50% of students are boarding students. 58% are state residents. 14 states are represented in upper school student body. 14% are international students. International students from Germany, Hong Kong, Japan, Republic of Korea, Taiwan, and Thailand; 15 other countries represented in student body.

Faculty School total: 75. In upper school: 41 men, 34 women; 50 have advanced degrees; 35 reside on campus.

Subjects Offered Advanced Placement courses, African-American literature, algebra, American government-AP, American history, anatomy, art, astronomy, biology, biology-AP, botany, calculus, calculus-AP, ceramics, chemistry, composition, creative writing, criminal justice, dance, drawing, ecology, electives, electronics, English, English literature, entomology, environmental science-AP, ESL, European history, fine arts, finite math, fractals, French, French-AP, government/civics, history, independent study, John F. Kennedy, Latin, Latin American literature, limnology, marine science, mathematics, microbiology, music, music composition, music technology, music theory, music-AP, ornithology, painting, photography, physics, physics-AP, playwriting, pre-calculus, psychology, scene study, science, sculpture, Shakespeare, social psychology, Spanish, Spanish-AP, studio art, theater, tropical biology, writing.

Graduation Requirements Arts and fine arts (art, music, dance, drama), English, foreign language, history, mathematics, science, Winterim participation.

Special Academic Programs Advanced Placement exam preparation; honors section; independent study; study abroad; academic accommodation for the musically talented and the artistically talented; special instructional classes for deaf students, blind students; ESL (20 students enrolled).

College Admission Counseling 101 students graduated in 2008; all went to college, including Boston College; Boston University; Colby College; Northeastern University; University of New Hampshire; University of Vermont. Mean SAT critical reading: 550, mean SAT math: 588, mean SAT writing: 566.

Student Life Upper grades have specified standards of dress, student council, honor system. Discipline rests primarily with faculty.

Tuition and Aid Day student tuition: $33,900; 7-day tuition and room/board: $44,200. Tuition installment plan (Key Tuition Payment Plan, monthly payment plans). Need-based scholarship grants, need-based loans, prepGATE Loans available. In 2008–09, 30% of upper-school students received aid. Total amount of financial aid awarded in 2008–09: $2,000,000.

Admissions Traditional secondary-level entrance grade is 9. For fall 2008, 602 students applied for upper-level admission, 269 were accepted, 132 enrolled. PSAT or SAT, SSAT or TOEFL required. Deadline for receipt of application materials: February 1. Application fee required: $50. Interview required.

Athletics Interscholastic: baseball (boys), basketball (b,g), cross-country running (b,g), field hockey (g), football (b), golf (b,g), ice hockey (b,g), lacrosse (b,g), soccer (b,g), softball (g), tennis (b,g), volleyball (g), wrestling (b); intramural: snowboarding (b,g), tennis (b,g); coed interscholastic: alpine skiing, independent competitive sports, skiing (downhill); coed intramural: dance, fitness, independent competitive sports, modern dance, outdoors, physical fitness, physical training, rappelling, skiing (downhill), strength & conditioning, volleyball, weight training. 5 coaches, 2 athletic trainers.

Computers Computers are regularly used in college planning, computer applications, ESL, library, media production, music, photography, SAT preparation, video film production, yearbook classes. Computer network features include on-campus library services, online commercial services, Internet access, wireless campus network, Internet filtering or blocking technology. Student e-mail accounts and computer access in designated common areas are available to students. The school has a published electronic and media policy.

Contact Tony Hawgood, Director of Admissions. 978-448-6535. Fax: 978-448-1519. E-mail: admiss@lacademy.edu. Web site: www.lacademy.edu.

ANNOUNCEMENT FROM THE SCHOOL Tradition and innovation meet at Lawrence Academy. More than 200 years of rigorous academic programs are preserved while the student-centered approach and hands-on learning prepare students for advanced academic study. Through the Ninth Grade Program, Winterim, and the Independent Immersion Program, students learn thinking skills that will allow them to arrive at their own interpretations, develop their own points of view, and learn the facts within the context of a meaningful question or problem. Extensive arts offerings in dance, drama, music, and visual arts, as well as competitive athletics, further the cocurricular experience. A warm community environment, international diversity, daily advisor meetings, extensive college counseling, and state-of-the-art facilities enhance the program.

See Close-Up on page 816.

LAWRENCE SCHOOL

Sagamore Hills, Ohio
See Special Needs Schools section.

THE LAWRENCEVILLE SCHOOL

PO Box 6008
2500 Main Street
Lawrenceville, New Jersey 08648
Head of School: Elizabeth A. Duffy

General Information Coeducational boarding and day college-preparatory, arts, religious studies, and technology school. Grades 9–PG. Founded: 1810. Setting: small town. Nearest major city is Philadelphia, PA. Students are housed in single-sex dormitories. 700-acre campus. 31 buildings on campus. Approved or accredited by Middle States Association of Colleges and Schools, New Jersey Association of Independent Schools, The Association of Boarding Schools, and New Jersey Department of Education. Member of National Association of Independent Schools and Secondary School Admission Test Board. Endowment: $300 million. Total enrollment: 795. Upper school average class size: 12. Upper school faculty-student ratio: 1:8.

Upper School Student Profile Grade 9: 152 students (76 boys, 76 girls); Grade 10: 207 students (112 boys, 95 girls); Grade 11: 205 students (116 boys, 89 girls); Grade 12: 209 students (116 boys, 93 girls); Postgraduate: 22 students (19 boys, 3 girls). 72% of students are boarding students. 39% are state residents. 40 states are represented in upper school student body. 10% are international students. International students from China, Hong Kong, Japan, Mexico, Republic of Korea, and United Kingdom; 30 other countries represented in student body.

Faculty School total: 163. In upper school: 87 men, 76 women; 96 have advanced degrees; 151 reside on campus.

Subjects Offered Acting, advanced chemistry, advanced computer applications, advanced studio art-AP, African-American literature, algebra, American Civil War, American foreign policy, American government, American history, American history-AP, American literature, American studies, architecture, art, art history, art history-AP, art-AP, arts, Asian history, astronomy, Basic programming, Bible, Bible studies, bioethics, bioethics, DNA and culture, biology, biology-AP, British literature, Buddhism, calculus, calculus-AP, Central and Eastern European history, ceramics, chamber groups, chemistry, chemistry-AP, China/Japan history, Chinese, Chinese studies, choir, chorus, Christian studies, Civil War, civil war history, classical Greek literature, classical language, comparative government and politics, conceptual physics, constitutional history of U.S., contemporary women writers, critical writing, dance, data analysis, design, digital applications, digital art, drama, dramatic arts, drawing, drawing and design, driver education, Eastern religion and philosophy, economics, electronic music, English, English literature, English literature-AP, English/composition-AP, environmental science, environmental studies, ethics, European history, European history-AP, European literature, evolution, field ecology, film and new technologies, film appreciation, filmmaking, foreign language, foreign policy, French, French language-AP, French literature-AP, French studies, French-AP, geometry, global science, Greek, health and wellness, Hebrew scripture, Hindi, historical foundations for arts, history of China and Japan, Holocaust, human biology, humanities, independent study, instruments, interdisciplinary studies, introduction to literature, introduction to theater, Irish literature, Irish studies, Islamic studies, Japanese, Japanese history, jazz, Jewish studies, John F. Kennedy, journalism, Latin, linear algebra, literature, medieval history, medieval literature, Middle East, Middle Eastern history, nature study, orchestra, organic chemistry, painting, participation in sports, personal development, philosophy, photography, physics, physics-AP, physiology, poetry, pre-algebra, pre-calculus, printmaking, probability and statistics, research seminar, robotics, science, set design, Shakespeare, short story, Southern literature, Spanish, Spanish language-AP, Spanish literature, studio art, the Presidency, the Sixties, theater, theater arts, U.S. constitutional history, U.S. government, U.S. government and politics, U.S. history, visual arts, water color painting, women in world history, world religions, world religions, writing.

Graduation Requirements Arts and fine arts (art, music, dance, drama), English, foreign language, interdisciplinary studies, mathematics, religion (includes Bible studies and theology), science, social science, social studies (includes history). Community service is required.

Special Academic Programs Honors section; independent study; term-away projects; study abroad.

College Admission Counseling 223 students graduated in 2008; 217 went to college, including Columbia College; Cornell University; New York University; Princeton University; University of Pennsylvania; University of Virginia. Other: 3 entered a postgraduate year, 3 had other specific plans. Median SAT critical reading: 680, median SAT math: 660, median SAT writing: 670.

Student Life Upper grades have specified standards of dress, student council, honor system. Discipline rests equally with students and faculty.

Tuition and Aid Day student tuition: $35,290; 7-day tuition and room/board: $43,320. Tuition installment plan (one, two, and ten month installment plans are available.). Need-based scholarship grants available. In 2008–09, 28% of upper-school students received aid. Total amount of financial aid awarded in 2008–09: $8,000,000.

Admissions Traditional secondary-level entrance grade is 9. For fall 2008, 1,871 students applied for upper-level admission, 389 were accepted, 246 enrolled. ISEE, PSAT and SAT for applicants to grade 11 and 12, SSAT or TOEFL or SLEP required. Deadline for receipt of application materials: January 31. Application fee required: $50. Interview required.

Athletics Interscholastic: baseball (boys), basketball (b,g), crew (b,g), cross-country running (b,g), fencing (b,g), field hockey (g), football (b), golf (b,g), hockey (b,g), ice hockey (b,g), indoor track (b,g), indoor track & field (b,g), lacrosse (b,g), rowing (b,g), soccer (b,g), softball (g), squash (b,g), swimming and diving (b,g), tennis (b,g), track and field (b,g), volleyball (b,g), water polo (b,g), winter (indoor) track (b,g); intramural: basketball (b,g), Frisbee (g), handball (b,g), team handball (b,g), ultimate Frisbee (g), weight lifting (b,g), weight training (b,g); coed interscholastic: wrestling; coed intramural: backpacking, bicycling, broomball, canoeing/kayaking, climbing, cricket, dance, fitness, hiking/backpacking, ice skating, kayaking, modern dance, Nautilus, outdoor activities, physical fitness, physical training, rock climbing, ropes courses, strength & conditioning, wall climbing, yoga. 26 coaches.

Computers Computers are regularly used in art, English, mathematics, music, science, technology classes. Computer network features include on-campus library services, online commercial services, Internet access, wireless campus network, Internet filtering or blocking technology. Campus intranet, student e-mail accounts, and computer access in designated common areas are available to students. Students grades are available online. The school has a published electronic and media policy.

Contact Gregg W. M. Maloberti, Dean of Admission. 800-735-2030. Fax: 609-895-2217. E-mail: admissions@lawrenceville.org. Web site: www.lawrenceville.org.

See Close-Up on page 818.

LEE ACADEMY

26 Winn Road
Lee, Maine 04455

Head of School: Mr. Bruce Lindberg

General Information Coeducational boarding and day college-preparatory, arts, vocational, and Vocational option is not available for international student school. Boarding grades 9–PG, day grades 9–12. Founded: 1845. Setting: rural. Nearest major city is Bangor. Students are housed in single-sex dormitories. 150-acre campus. 13 buildings on campus. Approved or accredited by Independent Schools of Northern New England, New England Association of Schools and Colleges, and Maine Department of Education. Total enrollment: 272. Upper school average class size: 12. Upper school faculty-student ratio: 1:10.

Upper School Student Profile Grade 9: 49 students (27 boys, 22 girls); Grade 10: 61 students (41 boys, 20 girls); Grade 11: 80 students (52 boys, 28 girls); Grade 12: 74 students (40 boys, 34 girls); Postgraduate: 8 students (8 boys). 30% of students are boarding students. 70% are state residents. 7 states are represented in upper school student body. 30% are international students. International students from China, Democratic People's Republic of Korea, Hong Kong, Israel, Taiwan, and Thailand; 3 other countries represented in student body.

Faculty School total: 29. In upper school: 15 men, 14 women; 9 have advanced degrees; 13 reside on campus.

Subjects Offered ACT preparation, Advanced Placement courses, advanced studio art-AP, architectural drawing, calculus, chemistry, chemistry-AP, chorus, civics, civil rights, electives, English, English language and composition-AP, English literature and composition-AP, ESL, foreign language, forensics, French, government/civics, health and wellness, honors algebra, honors geometry, honors U.S. history, integrated mathematics, peer counseling, physical education, physics, SAT/ACT preparation, Spanish, theater, TOEFL preparation, U.S. government, U.S. history-AP, world history, yearbook.

Graduation Requirements Algebra, American history, arts, biology, civics, computer skills, English, foreign language, health and wellness, mathematics, physical education (includes health), science.

Special Academic Programs Advanced Placement exam preparation; honors section; independent study; ESL (52 students enrolled).

College Admission Counseling 48 students graduated in 2008; 44 went to college, including University of Maine. Other: 2 went to work, 2 entered military service. Median SAT critical reading: 560, median SAT math: 622, median SAT writing: 570, median composite ACT: 26.

Student Life Upper grades have specified standards of dress, student council. Discipline rests primarily with faculty.

Summer Programs ESL, sports programs offered; session focuses on ESL, American culture, outdoor activities; held both on and off campus; held at off -campus includes whale watching in Bar Harbor, hiking Mt. Katahdin, swimming activities at the and local lake, canoeing & kayaking local rivers; accepts boys and girls; open to students from other schools. 30 students usually enrolled. 2009 schedule: August 1 to August 15. Application deadline: May 15.

Tuition and Aid Day student tuition: $8000; 5-day tuition and room/board: $21,000; 7-day tuition and room/board: $27,200. Guaranteed tuition plan. Tuition installment plan (monthly payment plans, individually arranged payment plans). Merit scholarship grants, need-based scholarship grants available. In 2008–09, 40% of upper-school students received aid.

Admissions Traditional secondary-level entrance grade is 9. For fall 2008, 92 students applied for upper-level admission, 65 were accepted, 57 enrolled. SAT, TOEFL or SLEP or writing sample required. Deadline for receipt of application materials: none. No application fee required. Interview recommended.

Athletics Interscholastic: baseball (boys), basketball (b,g), cross-country running (b,g), nordic skiing (b,g), skiing (cross-country) (b,g), skiing (downhill) (b,g), soccer (b,g), softball (g); intramural: backpacking (b,g); coed interscholastic: alpine skiing, cheering, golf, tennis; coed intramural: aerobics, aerobics/dance, aerobics/Nautilus, archery, badminton, ball hockey, bicycling, billiards, bowling, canoeing/kayaking, cooperative games, cross-country running, fishing, fitness, fitness walking, floor hockey, freestyle skiing, Frisbee, golf, hiking/backpacking, horseback riding, horseshoes, in-line skating, indoor soccer, jogging, kayaking, kickball, life saving, mountain biking, Nautilus, outdoor activities, paddle tennis, physical fitness, physical training, rafting, rock climbing, roller blading, ropes courses, running, self defense, skiing (cross-country), skiing (downhill), snowboarding, tennis, volleyball, walking, wall climbing, water skiing, weight training, wilderness, winter soccer, yoga. 2 PE instructors, 11 coaches, 2 athletic trainers.

Computers Computers are regularly used in architecture, drafting, English, ESL, independent study, library, literary magazine, SAT preparation, yearbook classes. Computer resources include on-campus library services, Internet access, wireless campus network, Internet filtering or blocking technology. Student e-mail accounts and computer access in designated common areas are available to students. Students grades are available online. The school has a published electronic and media policy.

Contact Mrs. Deborah Jacobs, Director of Admission. 207-738-2252. Fax: 207-738-3257. E-mail: admissions@leeacademy.org. Web site: www.leeacademy.org.

LEHIGH VALLEY CHRISTIAN HIGH SCHOOL

1414 East Cedar Street
Allentown, Pennsylvania 18109

Head of School: Mr. Robert J. Brennan, Jr.

General Information Coeducational day college-preparatory, general academic, and business school, affiliated with Protestant-Evangelical faith; primarily serves students with learning disabilities. Grades 9–12. Founded: 1988. Setting: urban. 4-acre campus. 2 buildings on campus. Approved or accredited by Association of Christian Schools International, Middle States Association of Colleges and Schools, and Pennsylvania Department of Education. Total enrollment: 167. Upper school average class size: 20. Upper school faculty-student ratio: 1:12.

Upper School Student Profile Grade 9: 37 students (19 boys, 18 girls); Grade 10: 55 students (18 boys, 37 girls); Grade 11: 32 students (14 boys, 18 girls); Grade 12: 44 students (18 boys, 26 girls). 90% of students are Protestant-Evangelical faith.

Faculty School total: 18. In upper school: 11 men, 7 women; 4 have advanced degrees.

Subjects Offered Accounting, advanced chemistry, advanced math, Advanced Placement courses, algebra, American history, American literature, ancient world history, art, Bible, biology, calculus-AP, chemistry, chorus, computer applications, computer keyboarding, consumer mathematics, economics, English, English literature, environmental science, geometry, German, government, health, history,

physical education, physical science, physics, physics-AP, pre-algebra, Spanish, state history, U.S. history, Western civilization.
Graduation Requirements Algebra, American history, American literature, art, Bible, Bible studies, biology, British literature, chemistry, choir, civics, computer applications, English, foreign language, geometry, mathematics, physical education (includes health), physical science, science, social sciences, Western civilization, general lifestyle not harmful to the testimony of the school as a Christian institution, minimum one year of full-time enrollment in LVCH or another Christian high school.
Special Academic Programs Advanced Placement exam preparation; honors section; accelerated programs; independent study; study at local college for college credit; academic accommodation for the gifted; programs in English, mathematics, general development for dyslexic students; special instructional classes for students needing learning support; ESL (10 students enrolled).
College Admission Counseling 35 students graduated in 2008; 33 went to college, including Eastern University; Lehigh University; Liberty University; Moravian College; Penn State University Park; Philadelphia Biblical University. Other: 1 went to work, 1 entered military service. Mean SAT critical reading: 519, mean SAT math: 518, mean SAT writing: 517, mean combined SAT: 1554.
Student Life Upper grades have uniform requirement, student council. Discipline rests primarily with faculty.
Summer Programs Remediation, advancement programs offered; session focuses on make-up courses; held both on and off campus; held at students' homes (for independent credit); accepts boys and girls; not open to students from other schools. 12 students usually enrolled. 2009 schedule: June 18 to August 11.
Tuition and Aid Day student tuition: $6215. Tuition installment plan (FACTS Tuition Payment Plan, individually arranged payment plans). Tuition reduction for siblings, merit scholarship grants, need-based scholarship grants available. In 2008–09, 14% of upper-school students received aid; total upper-school merit-scholarship money awarded: $54,975. Total amount of financial aid awarded in 2008–09: $54,975.
Admissions Traditional secondary-level entrance grade is 9. For fall 2008, 58 students applied for upper-level admission, 58 were accepted, 58 enrolled. Achievement tests, Gates MacGinite Reading Tests or Wide Range Achievement Test required. Deadline for receipt of application materials: none. Application fee required: $250. On-campus interview required.
Athletics Interscholastic: baseball (boys), basketball (b,g), cheering (g), field hockey (g), soccer (b,g), volleyball (g); coed interscholastic: track and field; coed intramural: skiing (downhill). 1 PE instructor, 13 coaches.
Computers Computers are regularly used in graphic arts, library, science, technology, writing fundamentals, yearbook classes. Computer network features include on-campus library services, Internet access, Internet filtering or blocking technology. Students grades are available online. The school has a published electronic and media policy.
Contact Mr. Robert J. Brennan, Jr., Head of School. 610-821-9443 Ext. 10. Fax: 610-821-5527. E-mail: bob.brennan@lvchs.org. Web site: www.lvchs.org.

LEHMAN HIGH SCHOOL

2400 Saint Mary Avenue
Sidney, Ohio 45365

Head of School: Mr. David Michael Barhorst

General Information Coeducational day and distance learning college-preparatory, arts, business, and religious studies school, affiliated with Roman Catholic Church. Grades 9–12. Distance learning grades 10–12. Founded: 1970. Setting: small town. Nearest major city is Dayton. 50-acre campus. 1 building on campus. Approved or accredited by North Central Association of Colleges and Schools, Ohio Catholic Schools Accreditation Association (OCSAA), and Ohio Department of Education. Endowment: $2.5 million. Total enrollment: 234. Upper school average class size: 15. Upper school faculty-student ratio: 1:15.
Upper School Student Profile Grade 9: 52 students (20 boys, 32 girls); Grade 10: 65 students (37 boys, 28 girls); Grade 11: 60 students (27 boys, 33 girls); Grade 12: 57 students (35 boys, 22 girls). 89% of students are Roman Catholic.
Faculty School total: 26. In upper school: 10 men, 15 women; 17 have advanced degrees.
Subjects Offered Accounting, algebra, American government, American literature, anatomy and physiology, architectural drawing, art, art history, biology, biology-AP, British literature, British literature (honors), business, calculus, calculus-AP, career and personal planning, ceramics, chemistry, chemistry-AP, child development, choir, computer applications, computer programming, concert band, earth science, English, English literature and composition-AP, environmental science, family and consumer science, geography, geometry, government, health education, history of the Catholic Church, integrated science, international foods, intro to computers, keyboarding, Latin, moral theology, music theory, newspaper, painting, peace and justice, physical education, physics, pre-algebra, pre-calculus, psychology, religious education, sociology, Spanish, studio art, U.S. history, vocal music, world history, yearbook.
Graduation Requirements Biology, chemistry, computer applications, electives, English composition, English literature, health education, life skills, mathematics, physical education (includes health), physical science, religion (includes Bible studies and theology), U.S. government, U.S. history.
Special Academic Programs Advanced Placement exam preparation; honors section; independent study; study at local college for college credit.
College Admission Counseling 70 students graduated in 2008; all went to college, including Ball State University; Bowling Green State University; Miami University; The Ohio State University; University of Dayton; Wright State University. Mean composite ACT: 24. 15% scored over 26 on composite ACT.
Student Life Upper grades have uniform requirement, student council, honor system. Discipline rests primarily with faculty. Attendance at religious services is required.
Tuition and Aid Day student tuition: $6195. Tuition installment plan (FACTS Tuition Payment Plan). Tuition reduction for siblings, need-based scholarship grants available. In 2008–09, 33% of upper-school students received aid. Total amount of financial aid awarded in 2008–09: $271,849.
Admissions Traditional secondary-level entrance grade is 9. For fall 2008, 4 students applied for upper-level admission, 4 were accepted, 4 enrolled. Any standardized test required. Deadline for receipt of application materials: none. Application fee required: $100. Interview recommended.
Athletics Interscholastic: aquatics (boys, girls), baseball (b), basketball (b,g), cheering (g), cross-country running (b,g), diving (b,g), football (b), soccer (b,g), softball (g), swimming and diving (b,g), tennis (b,g), track and field (b,g), volleyball (g), wrestling (b); intramural: strength & conditioning (b,g); coed interscholastic: golf. 42 coaches.
Computers Computers are regularly used in accounting, architecture, computer applications, drafting, keyboarding, newspaper, yearbook classes. Computer resources include on-campus library services, Internet access, Internet filtering or blocking technology. Computer access in designated common areas is available to students. Students grades are available online. The school has a published electronic and media policy.
Contact Mrs. Denise Stauffer, Principal. 937-498-1161 Ext. 115. Fax: 937-492-9877. E-mail: d.stauffer@lehmancatholic.com.

LE LYCEE FRANCAIS DE LOS ANGELES

3261 Overland Avenue
Los Angeles, California 90034-3589

Head of School: Mrs. Clara-Lisa Kabbaz

General Information Coeducational day college-preparatory, general academic, arts, and bilingual studies school. Grades PS–12. Founded: 1964. Setting: suburban. Nearest major city is West Los Angeles. 12-acre campus. 7 buildings on campus. Approved or accredited by French Ministry of Education and Western Association of Schools and Colleges. Member of European Council of International Schools. Languages of instruction: English and French. Endowment: $4.8 million. Total enrollment: 732. Upper school average class size: 16. Upper school faculty-student ratio: 1:15.
Upper School Student Profile Grade 6: 48 students (12 boys, 36 girls); Grade 7: 37 students (15 boys, 22 girls); Grade 8: 52 students (23 boys, 29 girls); Grade 9: 22 students (8 boys, 14 girls); Grade 10: 27 students (7 boys, 20 girls); Grade 11: 39 students (18 boys, 21 girls); Grade 12: 41 students (21 boys, 20 girls).
Faculty School total: 85. In upper school: 16 men, 26 women; 31 have advanced degrees.
Subjects Offered 20th century history, algebra, American history, American literature, anatomy, art, biology, calculus, ceramics, chemistry, computer programming, computer science, creative writing, dance, drama, earth science, economics, English, English literature, environmental science, ESL, European history, expository writing, fine arts, French, geography, geology, geometry, German, government/civics, grammar, history, Latin, mathematics, music, philosophy, photography, physical education, physics, science, social science, social studies, Spanish, statistics, theater, trigonometry, typing, world history, world literature, writing.
Graduation Requirements Arts and fine arts (art, music, dance, drama), English, foreign language, mathematics, physical education (includes health), science, social science, social studies (includes history).
Special Academic Programs International Baccalaureate program; Advanced Placement exam preparation; honors section; remedial reading and/or remedial writing; remedial math; ESL (25 students enrolled).
College Admission Counseling 25 students graduated in 2008; all went to college, including Loyola Marymount University; New York University; University of California, Berkeley; University of California, Los Angeles; University of California, San Diego; University of Southern California. 36% scored over 600 on SAT critical reading, 32% scored over 600 on SAT math, 32% scored over 600 on SAT writing, 32% scored over 1800 on combined SAT, 43% scored over 26 on composite ACT.
Student Life Upper grades have uniform requirement, student council, honor system. Discipline rests primarily with faculty.
Summer Programs Session focuses on social activities, sports, foreign languages; held both on and off campus; held at Field Trips; accepts boys and girls; open to students from other schools. 2009 schedule: June 29 to July 30. Application deadline: April 1.
Tuition and Aid Day student tuition: $11,200–$16,800. Bursaries, need-based scholarship grants available. In 2008–09, 12% of upper-school students received aid. Total amount of financial aid awarded in 2008–09: $63,000.
Admissions Traditional secondary-level entrance grade is 9. For fall 2008, 45 students applied for upper-level admission, 32 were accepted, 28 enrolled. School's own exam required. Deadline for receipt of application materials: February 28. Application fee required: $400. Interview required.

Athletics Interscholastic: basketball (boys); intramural: ballet (g), baseball (g), fencing (b,g), outdoor activities (b,g), outdoor recreation (b,g), physical fitness (b,g); coed intramural: martial arts. 6 PE instructors, 5 coaches, 4 athletic trainers.
Computers Computers are regularly used in English, foreign language, mathematics, science classes. Computer resources include on-campus library services, Internet access, wireless campus network, Internet filtering or blocking technology, Internet Café. Computer access in designated common areas is available to students. The school has a published electronic and media policy.
Contact Mme. Virginie Casarubbia, Admissions. 310-836-3464 Ext. 315. Fax: 310-558-8069. E-mail: admissions@lyceeonline.org. Web site: www.lyceeonline.org.

LESTER B. PEARSON UNITED WORLD COLLEGE OF THE PACIFIC

650 Pearson College Drive
Victoria, British Columbia V9C 4H7, Canada

Head of School: Dr. David Hawley

General Information Coeducational boarding and day college-preparatory and International Baccalaureate school. Grades 13–PG. Founded: 1974. Setting: rural. Approved or accredited by British Columbia Department of Education. Languages of instruction: English and French. Upper school average class size: 15.
Upper School Student Profile 100% of students are boarding students. 75% are international students.
Special Academic Programs International Baccalaureate program.
Tuition and Aid Financial aid available to upper-school students. In 2008–09, 100% of upper-school students received aid.
Admissions Deadline for receipt of application materials: February 15. Application fee required: CAN$50. Interview required.
Contact Canadian Selection Coordinator. 250-391-2411. E-mail: admin@pearsoncollege.ca. Web site: www.pearsoncollege.ca.

LEXINGTON CATHOLIC HIGH SCHOOL

2250 Clays Mill Road
Lexington, Kentucky 40503-1797

Head of School: Mr. David Hardin

General Information Coeducational day college-preparatory and religious studies school, affiliated with Roman Catholic Church. Grades 9–12. Founded: 1823. Setting: urban. 6-acre campus. 3 buildings on campus. Approved or accredited by National Catholic Education Association, Southern Association of Colleges and Schools, and Kentucky Department of Education. Endowment: $600,000. Total enrollment: 860. Upper school average class size: 22. Upper school faculty-student ratio: 1:14.
Upper School Student Profile Grade 9: 214 students (106 boys, 108 girls); Grade 10: 215 students (104 boys, 111 girls); Grade 11: 216 students (116 boys, 100 girls); Grade 12: 215 students (100 boys, 115 girls). 75% of students are Roman Catholic.
Faculty School total: 63. In upper school: 33 men, 30 women; 44 have advanced degrees.
Subjects Offered Accounting, advanced chemistry, Advanced Placement courses, advanced studio art-AP, algebra, American government, American government-AP, American history, American history-AP, American literature, anatomy and physiology, art, astronomy, band, Bible as literature, biology, biology-AP, British literature, British literature (honors), calculus, calculus-AP, Catholic belief and practice, ceramics, chemistry, chemistry-AP, choral music, Christian and Hebrew scripture, church history, comparative religion, computer applications, computer programming, creative writing, drama, economics, English-AP, ethics, film, French, French-AP, geography, geology, geometry, government and politics-AP, health, history of the Catholic Church, honors English, honors geometry, honors U.S. history, honors world history, humanities, introduction to literature, Latin, Latin-AP, physical education, physics, psychology, religious studies, sociology, Spanish, Spanish language-AP, U.S. government, U.S. government-AP, U.S. history, U.S. history-AP, world history, world literature.
Graduation Requirements American history, American literature, arts and fine arts (art, music, dance, drama), biology, British literature, Catholic belief and practice, chemistry, Christian and Hebrew scripture, church history, comparative religion, computer applications, English, foreign language, mathematics, physical education (includes health), religion (includes Bible studies and theology), science, U.S. government, U.S. government and politics, U.S. history, world history.
Special Academic Programs Advanced Placement exam preparation; honors section.
College Admission Counseling 196 students graduated in 2008; 194 went to college, including University of Kentucky. Other: 1 entered a postgraduate year, 1 had other specific plans. Median SAT critical reading: 540, median SAT math: 540, median SAT writing: 540, median composite ACT: 23. 24% scored over 600 on SAT critical reading, 28% scored over 600 on SAT math, 22% scored over 600 on SAT writing, 26% scored over 26 on composite ACT.
Student Life Upper grades have uniform requirement, student council, honor system. Discipline rests primarily with faculty. Attendance at religious services is required.
Tuition and Aid Day student tuition: $6040. Tuition installment plan (monthly payment plans, individually arranged payment plans). Merit scholarship grants, need-based scholarship grants available. In 2008–09, 10% of upper-school students received aid; total upper-school merit-scholarship money awarded: $5000. Total amount of financial aid awarded in 2008–09: $450,000.
Admissions Traditional secondary-level entrance grade is 9. For fall 2008, 254 students applied for upper-level admission, 254 were accepted, 223 enrolled. Scholastic Testing Service High School Placement Test required. Deadline for receipt of application materials: none. Application fee required: $150.
Athletics Interscholastic: baseball (boys), basketball (b,g), cheering (g), cross-country running (b,g), dance team (g), diving (b,g), football (b), golf (b,g), ice hockey (b), power lifting (b), soccer (b,g), softball (g), swimming and diving (b,g), tennis (b,g), track and field (b,g), volleyball (g); intramural: basketball (b,g), flag football (g), lacrosse (b), physical training (b,g); coed interscholastic: ultimate Frisbee; coed intramural: bowling, hiking/backpacking, outdoor activities. 2 athletic trainers.
Computers Computers are regularly used in all academic classes. Computer network features include on-campus library services, Internet access, wireless campus network. Students grades are available online. The school has a published electronic and media policy.
Contact Ms. Susie Fryer, Admissions Director. 859-277-7183 Ext. 231. Fax: 859-276-5086. E-mail: sfryer@lexingtoncatholic.com. Web site: www.lexingtoncatholic.com.

LEXINGTON CHRISTIAN ACADEMY

48 Bartlett Avenue
Lexington, Massachusetts 02420

Head of School: Mr. Mark R. Davis

General Information Coeducational day college-preparatory, arts, religious studies, and technology school, affiliated with Christian faith. Grades 6–12. Founded: 1946. Setting: suburban. Nearest major city is Boston. 30-acre campus. 1 building on campus. Approved or accredited by Association of Christian Schools International, Association of Independent Schools in New England, Christian Schools International, New England Association of Schools and Colleges, and Massachusetts Department of Education. Member of National Association of Independent Schools. Endowment: $3.6 million. Total enrollment: 333. Upper school average class size: 16. Upper school faculty-student ratio: 1:11.
Upper School Student Profile Grade 9: 59 students (30 boys, 29 girls); Grade 10: 64 students (34 boys, 30 girls); Grade 11: 57 students (28 boys, 29 girls); Grade 12: 53 students (29 boys, 24 girls).
Faculty School total: 42. In upper school: 22 men, 20 women; 29 have advanced degrees.
Subjects Offered Advanced Placement courses, algebra, American history-AP, anatomy, ancient history, art, Bible studies, biology, British literature, British literature-AP, calculus-AP, chemistry, choral music, Christian ethics, college counseling, community service, computer graphics, computer information systems, computers, concert band, creative writing, drama, economics, English, English literature, English literature-AP, ESL, European history-AP, French, general science, geography, geometry, health, history, independent study, journalism, Latin, mathematics, music, physical education, physical science, physics, physiology, psychology, religion, science, science research, senior internship, senior project, social studies, Spanish, theater, trigonometry, world history, world literature, writing.
Graduation Requirements Algebra, American history, American literature, Bible, British literature, college planning, computer literacy, English, English literature, ethics, European history, European literature, foreign language, health education, lab science, mathematics, physical education (includes health), religion (includes Bible studies and theology), science, senior internship, social studies (includes history), U.S. history, senior internship (3-week work experience in career of student's choice, including a journal of the experience), Interim (participation each year in one week of special Interim courses). Community service is required.
Special Academic Programs Advanced Placement exam preparation; honors section; independent study; term-away projects; study at local college for college credit; ESL (24 students enrolled).
College Admission Counseling 56 students graduated in 2008; 53 went to college, including Boston College; Boston University; Gordon College; Massachusetts Institute of Technology; Pepperdine University; Wheaton College. Other: 3 had other specific plans. Mean SAT critical reading: 607, mean SAT math: 613, mean SAT writing: 629.
Student Life Upper grades have specified standards of dress, student council. Discipline rests primarily with faculty. Attendance at religious services is required.
Tuition and Aid Day student tuition: $20,250. Tuition installment plan (Tuition Management Systems). Merit scholarship grants, need-based scholarship grants available. In 2008–09, 45% of upper-school students received aid; total upper-school merit-scholarship money awarded: $223,973. Total amount of financial aid awarded in 2008–09: $739,135.
Admissions Traditional secondary-level entrance grade is 9. ISEE or SSAT required. Deadline for receipt of application materials: February 15. Application fee required: $50. Interview required.
Athletics Interscholastic: baseball (boys), basketball (b,g), cheering (g), cross-country running (b,g), field hockey (g), lacrosse (b,g), soccer (b,g), softball (g), wrestling (b); intramural: basketball (b,g), cheering (g), gymnastics (b,g), lacrosse (b), physical training (b,g), soccer (b,g), tennis (b,g), volleyball (b,g), wrestling (b); coed interscholastic: golf; coed intramural: climbing, fitness, outdoor activities, rock climbing, ropes courses, skiing (downhill), snowboarding, strength & conditioning,

swimming and diving, ultimate Frisbee, volleyball, wall climbing, weight training. 2 PE instructors, 10 coaches, 1 athletic trainer.
Computers Computers are regularly used in library science, literary magazine, mathematics, media arts, music, photography, publications, science, yearbook classes. Computer network features include on-campus library services, online commercial services, Internet access, wireless campus network, Internet filtering or blocking technology. Campus intranet and computer access in designated common areas are available to students. The school has a published electronic and media policy.
Contact Mrs. Cynthia Torjesen, Director of Admission. 781-862-7850 Ext. 152. Fax: 781-863-8503. E-mail: cindy.torjesen@lca.edu. Web site: www.lca.edu.

ANNOUNCEMENT FROM THE SCHOOL Lexington Christian Academy is a coed, college-prep day school that educates students in grades 6–12 within the context of the historic Christian faith. LCA is a community in which students think critically, communicate effectively, and excel in academics, athletics, and the arts. Graduates of LCA perform with distinction in college and engage actively in communities both locally and abroad.

LEYSIN AMERICAN SCHOOL IN SWITZERLAND

Admissions Office
Beau Site
Leysin, Switzerland

See Close-Up on page 820.

LIFEGATE SCHOOL

1052 Fairfield Avenue
Eugene, Oregon 97402-2053

Head of School: Mr. Tom Gregersen

General Information Coeducational boarding and day and distance learning college-preparatory, general academic, arts, and religious studies school, affiliated with Christian faith. Grades 6–12. Distance learning grade X. Founded: 1994. Setting: suburban. 1-acre campus. 1 building on campus. Approved or accredited by Northwest Association of Schools and Colleges and Oregon Department of Education. Total enrollment: 44. Upper school average class size: 8. Upper school faculty-student ratio: 1:10.
Upper School Student Profile Grade 6: 5 students (4 boys, 1 girl); Grade 7: 4 students (2 boys, 2 girls); Grade 8: 5 students (2 boys, 3 girls); Grade 9: 7 students (4 boys, 3 girls); Grade 10: 10 students (5 boys, 5 girls); Grade 11: 9 students (4 boys, 5 girls); Grade 12: 6 students (3 boys, 3 girls). 100% are state residents. 50 states are represented in upper school student body. 95% of students are Christian faith.
Faculty School total: 16. In upper school: 3 men, 5 women; 5 have advanced degrees.
Subjects Offered Advanced math, algebra, American government, American history, ancient world history, art, audio visual/media, band, Bible, biology, career and personal planning, chemistry, computer applications, computer graphics, computer keyboarding, computer processing, cultural geography, drama, economics, English, English composition, English language and composition-AP, English literature-AP, geometry, health education, independent study, instrumental music, journalism, leadership training, life skills, physical education, physical science, physics, pre-algebra, pre-calculus, reading/study skills, Spanish, speech, world history, writing, yearbook.
Graduation Requirements Bible, computer keyboarding, English, government, history, life skills, mathematics, physical education (includes health), 25 hours of volunteer work per year.
Special Academic Programs Advanced Placement exam preparation; honors section; accelerated programs; independent study; academic accommodation for the gifted and the artistically talented; remedial math.
College Admission Counseling 12 students graduated in 2008; 9 went to college, including Georgia State University; Lane Community College. Other: 1 went to work, 2 entered military service.
Student Life Upper grades have specified standards of dress, student council. Discipline rests primarily with faculty. Attendance at religious services is required.
Tuition and Aid Day student tuition: $5550. Tuition installment plan (SMART Tuition Payment Plan, monthly payment plans). Tuition reduction for siblings, need-based scholarship grants available. In 2008–09, 14% of upper-school students received aid.
Admissions Traditional secondary-level entrance grade is 9. For fall 2008, 9 students applied for upper-level admission, 9 were accepted, 9 enrolled. Deadline for receipt of application materials: none. No application fee required. On-campus interview required.
Athletics Interscholastic: basketball (boys, girls), volleyball (g); intramural: golf (b,g); coed interscholastic: track and field. 2 PE instructors, 4 coaches.
Computers Computers are regularly used in desktop publishing, English, freshman foundations, lab/keyboard, media arts, video film production, writing, yearbook classes. Computer network features include on-campus library services, Internet access, Internet filtering or blocking technology. Student e-mail accounts are available to students. Students grades are available online.
Contact Ms. Donna Wickwire, Assistant Administrator. 541-689-5847. Fax: 541-689-6028. E-mail: donnaw@lifegatechristian.org. Web site: www.lifegatechristian.org.

LINCOLN SCHOOL

301 Butler Avenue
Providence, Rhode Island 02906-5556

Head of School: Julia Russell Eells

General Information Coeducational day (boys' only in lower grades) college-preparatory, arts, and technology school, affiliated with Society of Friends. Boys grades N–PK, girls grades N–12. Founded: 1884. Setting: urban. 46-acre campus. 5 buildings on campus. Approved or accredited by Association of Independent Schools in New England, Friends Council on Education, New England Association of Schools and Colleges, and Rhode Island Department of Education. Member of National Association of Independent Schools and Secondary School Admission Test Board. Endowment: $7 million. Total enrollment: 388. Upper school average class size: 12. Upper school faculty-student ratio: 1:4.
Upper School Student Profile Grade 9: 48 students (48 girls); Grade 10: 29 students (29 girls); Grade 11: 40 students (40 girls); Grade 12: 50 students (50 girls). 3% of students are members of Society of Friends.
Faculty School total: 75. In upper school: 11 men, 35 women.
Subjects Offered Algebra, American history, American literature, anatomy, Arabic, art, biology, biology-AP, calculus, calculus-AP, ceramics, chemistry, chemistry-AP, college awareness, community service, computer science, creative writing, dance, English, English literature, environmental science, ethics, European history, European history-AP, French, French-AP, geometry, health, history, Latin, music, photography, physical education, physics, pre-calculus, Spanish, Spanish language-AP, statistics-AP, theater, trigonometry, U.S. history-AP, visual literacy, women's studies, world history, world literature.
Graduation Requirements Arts and fine arts (art, music, dance, drama), college planning, computer science, English, ethics, foreign language, mathematics, physical education (includes health), science, social studies (includes history), senior internship. Community service is required.
Special Academic Programs Advanced Placement exam preparation; honors section; independent study; term-away projects; study at local college for college credit; study abroad; programs in general development for dyslexic students.
College Admission Counseling 40 students graduated in 2008; all went to college, including Boston University; Brown University; Hobart and William Smith Colleges; Lehigh University; Trinity College; Vanderbilt University. Median SAT critical reading: 590, median SAT math: 570, median SAT writing: 609.
Student Life Upper grades have uniform requirement, student council. Discipline rests equally with students and faculty.
Tuition and Aid Day student tuition: $9000–$24,650. Tuition installment plan (Academic Management Services Plan, monthly payment plans, Tuition Management Systems Plan). Merit scholarship grants, need-based scholarship grants, Achiever-Loans (Key Education Resources) available. In 2008–09, 25% of upper-school students received aid; total upper-school merit-scholarship money awarded: $7500. Total amount of financial aid awarded in 2008–09: $1,000,000.
Admissions Traditional secondary-level entrance grade is 9. For fall 2008, 88 students applied for upper-level admission, 55 were accepted, 28 enrolled. ISEE or SSAT required. Deadline for receipt of application materials: none. Application fee required: $50. Interview required.
Athletics Interscholastic: basketball, crew, cross-country running, field hockey, ice hockey, lacrosse, soccer, squash, swimming and diving, tennis. 4 PE instructors, 11 coaches, 1 athletic trainer.
Computers Computers are regularly used in English, history, science classes. Computer network features include on-campus library services, Internet access.
Contact Mrs. Diane Mota, Admission Office Administrative Assistant. 401-331-9696 Ext. 3157. Fax: 401-751-6670. E-mail: dmota@lincolnschool.org. Web site: www.lincolnschool.org.

LINDEN HALL

212 East Main Street
Lititz, Pennsylvania 17543

Head of School: Dr. Vincent M. Stumpo

General Information Girls' boarding and day college-preparatory, arts, bilingual studies, technology, and AP/Honors school. Grades 6–PG. Founded: 1746. Setting: small town. Nearest major city is Philadelphia. Students are housed in single-sex dormitories. 47-acre campus. 12 buildings on campus. Approved or accredited by Middle States Association of Colleges and Schools, Pennsylvania Association of Independent Schools, The Association of Boarding Schools, and Pennsylvania Department of Education. Member of National Association of Independent Schools and Secondary School Admission Test Board. Total enrollment: 173. Upper school average class size: 11. Upper school faculty-student ratio: 1:8.
Upper School Student Profile Grade 9: 19 students (19 girls); Grade 10: 41 students (41 girls); Grade 11: 44 students (44 girls); Grade 12: 14 students (14 girls). 80% of students are boarding students. 11 states are represented in upper school student body.

International students from Bahamas, Bermuda, China, Mexico, Republic of Korea, and Saudi Arabia; 3 other countries represented in student body.
Faculty School total: 26. In upper school: 5 men, 21 women; 14 have advanced degrees; 9 reside on campus.
Subjects Offered 20th century world history, acting, advanced chemistry, advanced math, Advanced Placement courses, advanced studio art-AP, algebra, American government, American literature, art, art history, art history-AP, athletics, bell choir, biology, biology-AP, botany, calculus, calculus-AP, career/college preparation, ceramics, chemistry, chemistry-AP, choir, chorus, college admission preparation, college counseling, college placement, college planning, communication arts, composition, computer applications, computer literacy, computer processing, computer skills, computers, CPR, creative writing, critical writing, dance, dance performance, digital photography, drama, drama performance, drawing and design, driver education, earth science, electives, English, English composition, English literature, English literature and composition-AP, English literature-AP, environmental science, environmental science-AP, equestrian sports, equine studies, equitation, ESL, ethics, ethics and responsibility, European history, European history-AP, European literature, film, fine arts, fitness, foreign language, French, French literature-AP, general science, genetics, geometry, global studies, government, grammar, handbells, health, health and wellness, history, history of drama, history-AP, honors English, honors world history, integrated arts, jewelry making, journalism, Latin, library skills, mathematics, media arts, music, music history, music performance, newspaper, painting, photography, photojournalism, physical education, physics, physics-AP, piano, pre-algebra, pre-calculus, printmaking, psychology, reading, SAT preparation, SAT/ACT preparation, social studies, Spanish, Spanish language-AP, Spanish-AP, speech, statistics, statistics-AP, student government, studio art-AP, study skills, theater, theater arts, TOEFL preparation, U.S. history, U.S. history-AP, visual and performing arts, vocal music, voice, Web site design, women in world history, world culture, world cultures, world history, world religions, writing, yearbook.
Graduation Requirements Arts and fine arts (art, music, dance, drama), college counseling, college placement, composition, critical writing, English, foreign language, mathematics, physical education (includes health), SAT preparation, science, social studies (includes history), speech, study skills, TOEFL review (for ESL students), Community Service Hours.
Special Academic Programs Advanced Placement exam preparation; honors section; independent study; study abroad; academic accommodation for the gifted, the musically talented, and the artistically talented; ESL.
College Admission Counseling 21 students graduated in 2008; all went to college, including Boston University; Carnegie Mellon University; Massachusetts Institute of Technology; Mount Holyoke College; Smith College; The George Washington University. Mean combined SAT: 1806.
Student Life Upper grades have uniform requirement, student council, honor system. Discipline rests equally with students and faculty. Attendance at religious services is required.
Summer Programs Enrichment, ESL, sports programs offered; session focuses on Science/ Riding/ Chinese Language/ ESL; held on campus; accepts boys and girls; open to students from other schools. 2009 schedule: June to August.
Tuition and Aid Day student tuition: $16,990; 5-day tuition and room/board: $37,590; 7-day tuition and room/board: $39,990. Tuition installment plan (monthly payment plans, individually arranged payment plans). Merit scholarship grants, need-based scholarship grants available. In 2008–09, 30% of upper-school students received aid. Total amount of financial aid awarded in 2008–09: $700,000.
Admissions Traditional secondary-level entrance grade is 9. Any standardized test, SSAT, TOEFL or writing sample required. Deadline for receipt of application materials: February 1. Application fee required: $45. On-campus interview required.
Athletics Interscholastic: basketball, cross-country running, equestrian sports, field hockey, lacrosse, soccer, softball, swimming and diving, tennis, track and field, volleyball; intramural: aerobics, aerobics/dance, dance, fitness, fitness walking, horseback riding, self defense, weight training, yoga. 1 PE instructor, 4 coaches, 1 athletic trainer.
Computers Computers are regularly used in all academic, career exploration, college planning, commercial art, desktop publishing, drawing and design, ESL, graphic arts, journalism, keyboarding, library skills, literary magazine, media production, newspaper, photojournalism, publications, SAT preparation, speech, theater arts, typing, video film production, Web site design, yearbook classes. Computer network features include on-campus library services, online commercial services, Internet access, wireless campus network, Internet filtering or blocking technology. Student e-mail accounts and computer access in designated common areas are available to students. Students grades are available online. The school has a published electronic and media policy.
Contact Amy A. Weaver, Assistant Director of Admissions. 717-626-8512. Fax: 717-627-1384. E-mail: admissions@lindenhall.org. Web site: www.lindenhall.org.

ANNOUNCEMENT FROM THE SCHOOL The 2008–09 school year at Linden Hall has been a year marked by growth. The strength of the school's academic program has led to a 54% increase in new applications this past admission season, with newly admitted students averaging in the 78th percentile on the SSAT test. This score ranks Linden Hall first among U.S. girls' boarding schools in average SSAT scores. Linden Hall is also pleased to announce at the start of the 2008 academic year that the average SAT score from last year's graduating class was 1806 (greatly exceeding the U.S. average of 1511) and that the average Advanced Placement (AP) Exam score of Linden Hall students was 4.0 (well above the U.S. average of 2.9). Both scores place Linden Hall notably ahead of national, state, and local norms and reflect the strength of the school's academic program as one of the finest among girls' schools in the nation.

See Close-Up on page 822.

LINDEN HILL SCHOOL

Northfield, Massachusetts
See Junior Boarding Schools section.

THE LINDEN SCHOOL

10 Rosehill Avenue
Toronto, Ontario M4T 1G5, Canada

Head of School: Ms. Dawn Chan

General Information Girls' day college-preparatory, arts, technology, humanities, and science school. Grades 1–12. Founded: 1993. Setting: urban. 2 buildings on campus. Approved or accredited by Ontario Department of Education. Language of instruction: English. Total enrollment: 141. Upper school average class size: 12. Upper school faculty-student ratio: 1:3.
Upper School Student Profile Grade 9: 19 students (19 girls); Grade 10: 18 students (18 girls); Grade 11: 11 students (11 girls); Grade 12: 5 students (5 girls).
Faculty School total: 30. In upper school: 4 men, 24 women; 10 have advanced degrees.
Subjects Offered Algebra, biology, calculus, chemistry, computer science, dramatic arts, English, English literature, French, geography, geometry, history, information technology, Latin, physics, Spanish, visual arts, writing workshop.
Graduation Requirements Ontario Secondary School Diploma requirements.
Special Academic Programs Advanced Placement exam preparation; honors section; independent study; academic accommodation for the gifted; ESL (6 students enrolled).
College Admission Counseling 13 students graduated in 2008; 10 went to college, including McGill University; The University of Western Ontario; University of Guelph; University of Toronto; University of Waterloo; York University. Other: 1 had other specific plans.
Student Life Upper grades have specified standards of dress, honor system. Discipline rests equally with students and faculty.
Tuition and Aid Day student tuition: CAN$13,885. Tuition installment plan (monthly payment plans, individually arranged payment plans). Bursaries, merit scholarship grants, need-based scholarship grants, paying campus jobs available. In 2008–09, 25% of upper-school students received aid; total upper-school merit-scholarship money awarded: CAN$100,000. Total amount of financial aid awarded in 2008–09: CAN$150,000.
Admissions Traditional secondary-level entrance grade is 9. School's own test required. Deadline for receipt of application materials: none. Application fee required: CAN$100. Interview required.
Athletics Interscholastic: cross-country running, dance, fitness, fitness walking, flag football, floor hockey, indoor hockey, indoor soccer, running, track and field, ultimate Frisbee, volleyball; intramural: alpine skiing, backpacking, badminton, ball hockey, baseball, basketball, boxing, canoeing/kayaking, climbing, combined training, cooperative games, cross-country running, dance, fitness, floor hockey, Frisbee, hiking/backpacking, ice skating, indoor hockey, indoor soccer, kickball, modern dance, outdoor activities, physical fitness, rock climbing, ropes courses, running, skiing (cross-country), skiing (downhill), snowboarding, soccer, track and field, ultimate Frisbee, volleyball, yoga. 2 PE instructors.
Computers Computers are regularly used in all classes. Computer network features include on-campus library services, Internet access, wireless campus network, Internet filtering or blocking technology. Computer access in designated common areas is available to students. The school has a published electronic and media policy.
Contact Ms. Ina Szekely, Co-Principal. 416-966-4406 Ext. 21. Fax: 416-966-9736. E-mail: admissions@lindenschool.ca. Web site: www.lindenschool.ca.

LINFIELD CHRISTIAN SCHOOL

31950 Pauba Road
Temecula, California 92592

Head of School: Karen Raftery

General Information Coeducational day college-preparatory, arts, religious studies, and technology school, affiliated with Christian faith. Grades K–12. Founded: 1936. Setting: suburban. Nearest major city is San Diego. 105-acre campus. 6 buildings on campus. Approved or accredited by Association of Christian Schools International, Western Association of Schools and Colleges, and California Department of Education. Total enrollment: 855. Upper school average class size: 20. Upper school faculty-student ratio: 1:19.
Upper School Student Profile Grade 9: 83 students (40 boys, 43 girls); Grade 10: 102 students (53 boys, 49 girls); Grade 11: 95 students (50 boys, 45 girls); Grade 12: 88 students (45 boys, 43 girls). 70% of students are Christian faith.

Faculty School total: 56. In upper school: 11 men, 16 women; 8 have advanced degrees.
Subjects Offered Advanced math, algebra, American sign language, anatomy and physiology, art, ASB Leadership, athletics, band, Bible, biology, calculus-AP, career/college preparation, chemistry, chemistry-AP, choir, computers, economics, English, English-AP, European history-AP, film, filmmaking, French, freshman foundations, general science, geometry, government, government-AP, health, physical education, physics, pre-calculus, public policy, senior seminar, service learning/internship, Spanish, Spanish-AP, speech and debate, sports medicine, theater, U.S. history, U.S. history-AP, world history, world religions, yearbook.
Graduation Requirements Arts and fine arts (art, music, dance, drama), computer science, economics, English, foreign language, freshman foundations, government, mathematics, physical education (includes health), religion (includes Bible studies and theology), science, senior seminar, social science, social studies (includes history), speech and debate. Community service is required.
Special Academic Programs Advanced Placement exam preparation; honors section; study at local college for college credit.
College Admission Counseling 95 students graduated in 2008; 92 went to college, including Azusa Pacific University; California State University, San Marcos; University of California, Riverside; University of California, San Diego. Other: 1 entered military service. Median SAT critical reading: 560, median SAT math: 540, median SAT writing: 520.
Student Life Upper grades have uniform requirement, student council, honor system. Discipline rests primarily with faculty. Attendance at religious services is required.
Summer Programs Sports, art/fine arts programs offered; held on campus; accepts boys and girls; open to students from other schools.
Tuition and Aid Day student tuition: $8580. Tuition installment plan (monthly payment plans). Need-based scholarship grants available. In 2008–09, 10% of upper-school students received aid.
Admissions Traditional secondary-level entrance grade is 9. For fall 2008, 63 students applied for upper-level admission, 55 were accepted, 40 enrolled. 3-R Achievement Test, SLEP and USC/UC Math Diagnostic Test required. Deadline for receipt of application materials: none. Application fee required: $50. On-campus interview required.
Athletics Interscholastic: baseball (boys), basketball (b,g), cheering (g), cross-country running (b,g), football (b), soccer (b,g), softball (g), tennis (b,g), track and field (b,g), volleyball (g); intramural: volleyball (g); coed interscholastic: golf; coed intramural: cross-country running. 2 PE instructors, 16 coaches, 1 athletic trainer.
Computers Computers are regularly used in computer applications, keyboarding, science, senior seminar, yearbook classes. Computer network features include on-campus library services, Internet access, wireless campus network, Internet filtering or blocking technology. Students grades are available online. The school has a published electronic and media policy.
Contact Mrs. Becky Swanson, Admissions Assistant. 951-676-8111 Ext. 1402. Fax: 951-695-1291. E-mail: bswanson@linfield.com. Web site: www.linfield.com.

THE LINSLY SCHOOL

60 Knox Lane
Wheeling, West Virginia 26003-6489

Head of School: Reno F. DiOrio

General Information Coeducational boarding and day college-preparatory, arts, technology, and science, mathematics, humanities, foreign language school. Boarding grades 7–12, day grades 5–12. Founded: 1814. Setting: suburban. Nearest major city is Pittsburgh, PA. Students are housed in single-sex dormitories. 60-acre campus. 19 buildings on campus. Approved or accredited by Independent Schools Association of the Central States, North Central Association of Colleges and Schools, The Association of Boarding Schools, and West Virginia Department of Education. Member of National Association of Independent Schools. Endowment: $15.8 million. Total enrollment: 443. Upper school average class size: 15. Upper school faculty-student ratio: 1:10.
Upper School Student Profile Grade 9: 55 students (32 boys, 23 girls); Grade 10: 46 students (17 boys, 29 girls); Grade 11: 44 students (25 boys, 19 girls); Grade 12: 51 students (31 boys, 20 girls). 32% of students are boarding students. 58% are state residents. 15 states are represented in upper school student body. 6% are international students. International students from China, Germany, Mexico, Republic of Korea, Russian Federation, and Rwanda.
Faculty School total: 48. In upper school: 24 men, 11 women; 17 have advanced degrees; 23 reside on campus.
Subjects Offered Algebra, American history, American literature, art, art history, biology, biology-AP, calculus-AP, character education, chemistry, chemistry-AP, Chinese, chorus, college counseling, communications, computer programming, computer science, concert band, contemporary issues, creative writing, drama, earth science, economics, English, English language-AP, English literature, English literature-AP, environmental science, expository writing, film, fine arts, French, geometry, German, government/civics, health, history, human geography—AP, humanities, Latin, mathematics, model United Nations, music, newspaper, physical education, physics, physics-AP, psychology, psychology-AP, science, social studies, Spanish, speech, statistics, theater, U.S. history-AP, world history, writing, yearbook.
Graduation Requirements Arts and fine arts (art, music, dance, drama), computer science, English, foreign language, mathematics, physical education (includes health), science, social studies (includes history).
Special Academic Programs 12 Advanced Placement exams for which test preparation is offered; honors section; academic accommodation for the gifted.
College Admission Counseling 66 students graduated in 2008; all went to college, including Duquesne University; Earlham College; The Ohio State University; University of California, San Diego; University of Virginia; West Virginia University. Mean SAT critical reading: 560, mean SAT math: 580, mean SAT writing: 564, mean combined SAT: 1706, mean composite ACT: 25.
Student Life Upper grades have uniform requirement, student council. Discipline rests primarily with faculty.
Summer Programs Enrichment, advancement, computer instruction programs offered; held on campus; accepts boys and girls; open to students from other schools. 100 students usually enrolled. 2009 schedule: June 12 to July 12. Application deadline: June 12.
Tuition and Aid Day student tuition: $12,330; 5-day tuition and room/board: $25,100; 7-day tuition and room/board: $25,100. Tuition installment plan (Academic Management Services Plan). Need-based scholarship grants available. In 2008–09, 40% of upper-school students received aid. Total amount of financial aid awarded in 2008–09: $900,000.
Admissions Traditional secondary-level entrance grade is 9. Otis-Lennon, Stanford Achievement Test required. Deadline for receipt of application materials: none. No application fee required. On-campus interview required.
Athletics Interscholastic: baseball (boys), basketball (b,g), cheering (g), cross-country running (b,g), diving (b,g), football (b), golf (b,g), ice hockey (b,g), lacrosse (b), soccer (b,g), softball (g), wrestling (b); intramural: flag football (b,g), floor hockey (b), football (b), hiking/backpacking (b,g), indoor soccer (b,g), indoor track (b,g), indoor track & field (b,g), life saving (b,g), mountain biking (b,g), outdoor activities (b,g), physical fitness (b,g), power lifting (b), rappelling (b,g), rock climbing (b,g), roller blading (b,g), ropes courses (b,g), running (b,g), street hockey (b); coed intramural: backpacking, badminton, bowling, canoeing/kayaking, climbing, combined training, cooperative games, cross-country running, fitness, Frisbee, ice skating, in-line skating, jogging, kayaking, kickball, life saving, mountain biking, Nautilus, physical fitness, physical training, rafting, rock climbing, ropes courses, running, scuba diving, soccer, softball. 4 PE instructors, 4 coaches, 1 athletic trainer.
Computers Computers are regularly used in economics, English, foreign language, humanities, mathematics, music, psychology, science classes. Computer network features include on-campus library services, Internet access, wireless campus network, Internet filtering or blocking technology. Student e-mail accounts are available to students.
Contact Chad Barnett, Director of Admissions. 304-233-1436. Fax: 304-234-4614. E-mail: admit@linsly.org. Web site: www.linsly.org.

ANNOUNCEMENT FROM THE SCHOOL Located on a beautiful campus in Wheeling, West Virginia, The Linsly School is a coeducational, college-preparatory school, founded in 1814 by former Wheeling mayor, Noah Linsly. Linsly's traditional, values-based curriculum is supported by a warm, community-spirited environment. Linsly combines the values of hard work, respect, honor, honesty, and self-discipline within a rigorous academic program that challenges students to reach their highest potential physically, socially, and morally. With a student-teacher ratio of 9:1 in the Upper School, Linsly offers small classes and individual attention for each student. Faculty members work closely with students and serve as role models and mentors in all areas of school activities. The Lower School, grades 5–8, develops sound work habits as well as academic preparation for the transition to the Upper School, grades 9–12. Students in the Upper School carry at least five core courses per semester, following a challenging college-preparatory curriculum. Advanced Placement instruction is offered in numerous disciplines. College counseling begins during the sophomore year, allowing each student the opportunity to arrive at an understanding of his or her academic and personal priorities when selecting a college. Students can choose from a variety of campus clubs, community service activities, and interscholastic athletics. Weekend activities for boarding students may include school dances, informal parties, recreational sports, and supervised off-campus trips to the mall or nearby Oglebay Park. An outdoor educational program unique to Linsly, The Linsly Outdoor Center, located in Pennsylvania's Raccoon Creek State Park, challenges students physically and mentally, builds self-esteem, and strengthens camaraderie among classmates. Linsly's 65-acre campus includes a central academic complex, a new visual arts center, music facilities, science/computer laboratories, a bookstore, the Coudon-Ogden Library, an athletic field house, and The Hess Center, a woodworking facility. Linsly is located 1 hour west of Pittsburgh and 2 hours east of Columbus.

LITTLE KESWICK SCHOOL

Keswick, Virginia
See Special Needs Schools section.

LITTLE RED SCHOOL HOUSE AND ELISABETH IRWIN HIGH SCHOOL

272 Sixth Avenue
New York, New York 10014

Head of School: Philip Kassen

General Information Coeducational day college-preparatory, arts, and technology school. Grades N–12. Founded: 1921. Setting: urban. 2 buildings on campus. Approved or accredited by New York State Association of Independent Schools and New York Department of Education. Member of National Association of Independent Schools. Total enrollment: 565. Upper school average class size: 15. Upper school faculty-student ratio: 1:7.

Faculty In upper school: 14 men, 22 women; 36 have advanced degrees.

Subjects Offered 20th century American writers, 20th century physics, advanced biology, advanced chemistry, African-American literature, American culture, American history, American literature, art, art history, Asian history, astronomy, biology, calculus, chemistry, chorus, college counseling, college placement, community service, computer graphics, creative dance, dance, data analysis, drama, economics, environmental science, European history, film and literature, filmmaking, French, global studies, human rights, independent study, introduction to literature, introduction to technology, jazz band, journalism, Latin American literature, law, library research, life issues, literary magazine, Mandarin, Middle Eastern history, modern dance, modern European history, multimedia design, music, music technology, newspaper, painting, peer counseling, photography, physical science, physics, play production, playwriting, pre-calculus, printmaking, research skills, sculpture, senior internship, Shakespeare, Spanish, Spanish literature, studio art, theater, trigonometry, U.S. history, urban studies, weight fitness, world literature.

Graduation Requirements Arts and fine arts (art, music, dance, drama), English, foreign language, history, life issues, mathematics, physical education (includes health), science, senior project, technology, urban studies, 25 hours of community service per year.

Special Academic Programs Honors section; independent study; study at local college for college credit; study abroad.

College Admission Counseling 44 students graduated in 2008; all went to college, including Cornell University; Hampshire College; Oberlin College; Occidental College; Skidmore College; Vassar College.

Student Life Upper grades have student council, honor system. Discipline rests equally with students and faculty.

Tuition and Aid Day student tuition: $30,810. Tuition installment plan (Insured Tuition Payment Plan, SMART Tuition Payment Plan, monthly payment plans). Need-based scholarship grants available. In 2008–09, 22% of upper-school students received aid.

Admissions Traditional secondary-level entrance grade is 9. For fall 2008, 182 students applied for upper-level admission, 68 were accepted, 20 enrolled. ISEE required. Deadline for receipt of application materials: December 1. Application fee required: $50. On-campus interview required.

Athletics Interscholastic: baseball (boys), basketball (b,g), soccer (b,g), softball (g), track and field (b,g), volleyball (g); coed interscholastic: cross-country running, golf, judo, tennis; coed intramural: aerobics, aerobics/dance, dance squad, fitness, martial arts, yoga. 5 PE instructors, 10 coaches, 1 athletic trainer.

Computers Computers are regularly used in all classes. Computer network features include on-campus library services, Internet access, wireless campus network, Internet filtering or blocking technology. Campus intranet, student e-mail accounts, and computer access in designated common areas are available to students. Students grades are available online. The school has a published electronic and media policy.

Contact Samantha Caruth, Director of Admissions. 212-477-5316 Ext. 210. E-mail: admissions@lrei.org. Web site: www.lrei.org.

LOGOS SCHOOL

St. Louis, Missouri
See Special Needs Schools section.

THE LOOMIS CHAFFEE SCHOOL

4 Batchelder Road
Windsor, Connecticut 06095

Head of School: Dr. Sheila A. Culbert

General Information Coeducational boarding and day college-preparatory school. Grades 9–PG. Founded: 1914. Setting: suburban. Nearest major city is Hartford. Students are housed in single-sex dormitories. 300-acre campus. 65 buildings on campus. Approved or accredited by New England Association of Schools and Colleges, The Association of Boarding Schools, and Connecticut Department of Education. Member of National Association of Independent Schools and Secondary School Admission Test Board. Endowment: $20 million. Total enrollment: 714. Upper school average class size: 12. Upper school faculty-student ratio: 1:5.

Upper School Student Profile Grade 9: 149 students (74 boys, 75 girls); Grade 10: 166 students (88 boys, 78 girls); Grade 11: 188 students (93 boys, 95 girls); Grade 12: 198 students (104 boys, 94 girls); Postgraduate: 13 students (13 boys). 56% of students are boarding students. 59% are state residents. 25 states are represented in upper school student body. 10% are international students. International students from Canada, China, Republic of Korea, Thailand, United Kingdom, and Viet Nam; 12 other countries represented in student body.

Faculty School total: 150. In upper school: 75 men, 75 women; 112 have advanced degrees; 70 reside on campus.

Subjects Offered Algebra, American history, American literature, anatomy, art, art history, astronomy, biology, calculus, ceramics, chemistry, computer math, computer science, creative writing, dance, drama, ecology, economics, English, English literature, environmental science, ethics, European history, expository writing, fine arts, French, geology, geometry, history, history of ideas, history of science, journalism, Latin, library studies, logic, Mandarin, mathematics, music, philosophy, photography, physical education, physics, physiology, religion, science, social studies, Spanish, statistics, theater, trigonometry, video film production, world history, world literature, writing.

Graduation Requirements Arts and fine arts (art, music, dance, drama), English, foreign language, history, mathematics, philosophy, physical education (includes health), religion (includes Bible studies and theology), science.

Special Academic Programs Advanced Placement exam preparation; honors section; independent study; term-away projects; study at local college for college credit; study abroad; academic accommodation for the gifted, the musically talented, and the artistically talented.

College Admission Counseling 200 students graduated in 2008; 197 went to college, including Boston College; Bucknell University; Connecticut College; The College of William and Mary; The George Washington University; The Johns Hopkins University. 74% scored over 600 on SAT critical reading, 77% scored over 600 on SAT math.

Student Life Upper grades have specified standards of dress, student council. Discipline rests primarily with faculty.

Tuition and Aid Day student tuition: $31,100; 7-day tuition and room/board: $41,200. Guaranteed tuition plan. Tuition installment plan (Insured Tuition Payment Plan, Key Tuition Payment Plan, monthly payment plans). Need-based scholarship grants, need-based loans available. In 2008–09, 30% of upper-school students received aid. Total amount of financial aid awarded in 2008–09: $6,000,000.

Admissions Traditional secondary-level entrance grade is 9. For fall 2008, 1,164 students applied for upper-level admission, 522 were accepted, 237 enrolled. ISEE, PSAT, SAT, SSAT or TOEFL required. Deadline for receipt of application materials: January 15. Application fee required: $75. Interview required.

Athletics Interscholastic: baseball (boys), basketball (b,g), cross-country running (b,g), field hockey (g), football (b), golf (b,g), ice hockey (b,g), lacrosse (b,g), soccer (b,g), softball (g), squash (b,g), swimming and diving (b,g), tennis (b,g), track and field (b,g), volleyball (b,g), water polo (b,g), wrestling (b); intramural: ice hockey (b,g), soccer (b,g), volleyball (b,g), yoga (b,g); coed interscholastic: alpine skiing, diving, skiing (downhill); coed intramural: aerobics, aerobics/dance, aerobics/Nautilus, backpacking, basketball, bicycling, canoeing/kayaking, climbing, dance, fencing, figure skating, fitness, Frisbee, hiking/backpacking, ice skating, jogging, kayaking, life saving, mountain biking, Nautilus, outdoor activities, outdoor adventure, physical fitness, physical training, ropes courses, running, soccer, softball, squash, strength & conditioning, ultimate Frisbee, weight training. 5 PE instructors, 2 athletic trainers.

Computers Computers are regularly used in English, foreign language, history, library skills, mathematics, science classes. Computer network features include on-campus library services, online commercial services, Internet access, wireless campus network, Internet filtering or blocking technology. Student e-mail accounts and computer access in designated common areas are available to students. The school has a published electronic and media policy.

Contact Thomas D. Southworth, Director of Admission. 860-687-6400. Fax: 860-298-8756. E-mail: tom_southworth@loomis.org. Web site: www.loomis.org.

ANNOUNCEMENT FROM THE SCHOOL Both traditional and innovative, the Loomis Chaffee School is an independent, coeducational, college-preparatory boarding and day school with 700 students from more than fifteen countries and thirty states. Academically and athletically rigorous, the School promotes active learning, moral values, and close faculty-student bonds within a community of respect and civility. Students enjoy up-to-date facilities, numerous extracurricular activities, community service opportunities, and individual guidance from a dedicated faculty of 150. Thirty percent of the students receive financial aid.

See Close-Up on page 824.

LORETTO ACADEMY

1300 Hardaway Street
El Paso, Texas 79903

Head of School: Sr. Mary E. (Buffy) Boesen, SL

General Information Coeducational day (boys' only in lower grades) college-preparatory, arts, religious studies, and technology school, affiliated with Roman Catholic Church. Boys grades PK–5, girls grades PK–12. Founded: 1923. Setting: urban. 17-acre campus. 3 buildings on campus. Approved or accredited by Southern

Association of Colleges and Schools and Texas Catholic Conference. Endowment: $3.3 million. Total enrollment: 707. Upper school average class size: 20. Upper school faculty-student ratio: 1:20.

Upper School Student Profile Grade 9: 89 students (89 girls); Grade 10: 116 students (116 girls); Grade 11: 87 students (87 girls); Grade 12: 104 students (104 girls). 85% of students are Roman Catholic.

Faculty School total: 51. In upper school: 5 men, 21 women; 12 have advanced degrees.

Subjects Offered Acting, advanced math, Advanced Placement courses, algebra, American government, American history, art, art appreciation, art-AP, arts, arts and crafts, Bible, biology, body human, business mathematics, calculus, calculus-AP, chemistry, choir, choral music, Christian and Hebrew scripture, college writing, computer applications, computer keyboarding, computer programming, computer science, English, environmental science, fine arts, French, geology, geometry, government, government-AP, health, honors algebra, honors English, honors geometry, integrated science, Internet, jewelry making, journalism, keyboarding, life issues, literature, literature-AP, mathematics, modern dance, moral theology, music appreciation, photo shop, physical education, physics, physics-AP, religion, science, social studies, Spanish, Spanish language-AP, Spanish-AP, speech, speech and debate, student government, study skills, technical writing, theater production, world geography, world history, world religions, yearbook, zoology.

Graduation Requirements Algebra, American government, arts and fine arts (art, music, dance, drama), biology, Christian and Hebrew scripture, Christian ethics, Christian studies, computer science, economics, English, English composition, English literature, environmental science, foreign language, geography, lab/keyboard, life issues, mathematics, moral reasoning, physical education (includes health), physical science, psychology, religion (includes Bible studies and theology), science, social studies (includes history), speech communications, world geography, world religions.

Special Academic Programs Advanced Placement exam preparation.

College Admission Counseling 116 students graduated in 2008; all went to college, including New Mexico State University; St. Edward's University; St. Mary's University; The University of Texas at El Paso; The University of Texas at San Antonio. Mean SAT critical reading: 481, mean SAT math: 470, mean SAT writing: 503. 14% scored over 600 on SAT critical reading, 3.1% scored over 600 on SAT math, 23.4% scored over 600 on SAT writing, 7% scored over 26 on composite ACT.

Student Life Upper grades have uniform requirement, student council, honor system. Discipline rests primarily with faculty.

Summer Programs Remediation programs offered; session focuses on remediation; held on campus; accepts girls; not open to students from other schools. 25 students usually enrolled. 2009 schedule: June 2 to July 3.

Tuition and Aid Day student tuition: $6200. Tuition installment plan (FACTS Tuition Payment Plan). Tuition reduction for siblings, need-based scholarship grants available. In 2008–09, 24% of upper-school students received aid. Total amount of financial aid awarded in 2008–09: $95,000.

Admissions Traditional secondary-level entrance grade is 9. For fall 2008, 149 students applied for upper-level admission, 131 were accepted, 109 enrolled. High School Placement Test (closed version) from Scholastic Testing Service required. Deadline for receipt of application materials: none. Application fee required: $30. On-campus interview required.

Athletics Interscholastic: aquatics, basketball, cheering, cross-country running, dance squad, dance team, golf, soccer, softball, swimming and diving, tennis, track and field, volleyball. 10 coaches, 2 athletic trainers.

Computers Computers are regularly used in all academic classes. Computer network features include Internet access, Internet filtering or blocking technology. The school has a published electronic and media policy.

Contact Mrs. Lily Miranda, Director of Admissions. 915-566-8400. Fax: 915-566-0636. E-mail: lmiranda@loretto.org. Web site: www.loretto.org.

LOS ANGELES BAPTIST JUNIOR/SENIOR HIGH SCHOOL

9825 Woodley Avenue
North Hills, California 91343

Head of School: Mr. Scott Marshall

General Information Coeducational day college-preparatory, arts, religious studies, and technology school, affiliated with Baptist Church. Grades 6–12. Founded: 1962. Setting: suburban. Nearest major city is Los Angeles. 11-acre campus. 5 buildings on campus. Approved or accredited by Association of Christian Schools International and Western Association of Schools and Colleges. Total enrollment: 858. Upper school average class size: 30. Upper school faculty-student ratio: 1:22.

Upper School Student Profile Grade 9: 126 students (69 boys, 57 girls); Grade 10: 163 students (83 boys, 80 girls); Grade 11: 153 students (82 boys, 71 girls); Grade 12: 155 students (74 boys, 81 girls).

Faculty School total: 48. In upper school: 20 men, 12 women; 27 have advanced degrees.

Subjects Offered 3-dimensional design, advanced computer applications, algebra, American history, American literature, American literature-AP, analysis and differential calculus, anatomy and physiology, art, art appreciation, ASB Leadership, band, Bible studies, biology, biology-AP, calculus-AP, ceramics, chemistry, chemistry-AP, choir, choral music, Christian doctrine, Christian education, Christian ethics, Civil War, computer applications, computer education, computer graphics, computer keyboarding, computer programming, computer science, computer skills, computer technologies, digital photography, drama, drama performance, earth science, economics, English, English literature, English-AP, European history-AP, expository writing, fine arts, French, French-AP, geography, geometry, government/civics, home economics, HTML design, intro to computers, jazz band, journalism, mathematics, music, photography, physical education, physics, physics-AP, practical arts, pre-calculus, psychology, psychology-AP, religion, science, social studies, Spanish, Spanish-AP, speech, statistics, statistics-AP, studio art, theater arts, trigonometry, typing, U.S. history-AP, world history, world history-AP.

Graduation Requirements Arts and fine arts (art, music, dance, drama), English, foreign language, mathematics, physical education (includes health), practical arts, religion (includes Bible studies and theology), science, social studies (includes history).

Special Academic Programs Advanced Placement exam preparation; honors section.

College Admission Counseling 144 students graduated in 2008; 141 went to college, including Biola University; California State University, Northridge; Concordia University; University of California, Los Angeles; University of California, Santa Barbara. Other: 3 entered military service. Median SAT critical reading: 545, median SAT math: 530, median SAT writing: 530, median combined SAT: 1595, median composite ACT: 22. 26.7% scored over 600 on SAT critical reading, 23.2% scored over 600 on SAT math, 17.4% scored over 600 on SAT writing, 20.9% scored over 1800 on combined SAT, 40% scored over 26 on composite ACT.

Student Life Upper grades have specified standards of dress, student council, honor system. Discipline rests primarily with faculty. Attendance at religious services is required.

Summer Programs Remediation, advancement, sports, computer instruction programs offered; session focuses on remediation and enrichment; held on campus; accepts boys and girls; open to students from other schools. 300 students usually enrolled. 2009 schedule: June 19 to August 5.

Tuition and Aid Day student tuition: $7000. Tuition installment plan (FACTS Tuition Payment Plan, monthly payment plans, 2-semester payment plan, annual payment plan). Merit scholarship grants, need-based scholarship grants available. In 2008–09, 26% of upper-school students received aid; total upper-school merit-scholarship money awarded: $2000. Total amount of financial aid awarded in 2008–09: $687,468.

Admissions Traditional secondary-level entrance grade is 9. For fall 2008, 147 students applied for upper-level admission, 123 were accepted, 105 enrolled. QUIC required. Deadline for receipt of application materials: August 18. Application fee required: $50. On-campus interview required.

Athletics Interscholastic: baseball (boys), basketball (b,g), cheering (g), cross-country running (b,g), football (b), soccer (b,g), softball (g), tennis (g), track and field (b,g), volleyball (b,g); coed interscholastic: golf. 26 coaches.

Computers Computers are regularly used in animation, business applications, career technology, French, graphic design, graphics, introduction to technology, keyboarding, lab/keyboard, library, programming, Spanish, technology, typing, Web site design, word processing classes. Computer network features include on-campus library services, Internet access, Internet filtering or blocking technology. The school has a published electronic and media policy.

Contact Mrs. Karnel Watkins, Admissions/Recruitment Coordinator. 818-894-5742 Ext. 322. Fax: 818-892-5018. E-mail: kwatkins@labaptist.org. Web site: www.labaptist.org/.

LOS ANGELES LUTHERAN HIGH SCHOOL

13570 Eldridge Avenue
Sylmar, California 91342

Head of School: Mrs. Ruth Peterson

General Information Coeducational day and distance learning college-preparatory, arts, and religious studies school, affiliated with Lutheran Church. Grades 6–12. Distance learning grades 11–12. Founded: 1953. Setting: urban. Nearest major city is Los Angeles. 4-acre campus. 1 building on campus. Approved or accredited by Western Association of Schools and Colleges and California Department of Education. Endowment: $450,000. Total enrollment: 212. Upper school average class size: 25. Upper school faculty-student ratio: 1:16.

Upper School Student Profile Grade 9: 31 students (17 boys, 14 girls); Grade 10: 31 students (20 boys, 11 girls); Grade 11: 43 students (18 boys, 25 girls); Grade 12: 23 students (11 boys, 12 girls). 30% of students are Lutheran.

Faculty School total: 17. In upper school: 7 men, 6 women; 5 have advanced degrees.

Subjects Offered 3-dimensional art, algebra, American literature, anatomy and physiology, band, Bible, biology, biology-AP, business applications, business law, business mathematics, calculus, choir, composition, drawing, economics, English literature, English-AP, ethics, family studies, German, government, jazz band, Life of Christ, math analysis, music theory, painting, physics, psychology, sociology, Spanish, U.S. history, world history, yearbook.

Graduation Requirements Advanced math, algebra, American government, American history, American literature, analytic geometry, ancient world history, biology, British literature, career education, chemistry, Christian doctrine, Christian testament, comparative religion, composition, computer keyboarding, economics,

English composition, English literature, geometry, government, physical education (includes health), religious education, Spanish, U.S. government, U.S. history, world history.

Special Academic Programs Advanced Placement exam preparation; honors section; study at local college for college credit; academic accommodation for the gifted, the musically talented, and the artistically talented; ESL (15 students enrolled).

College Admission Counseling 43 students graduated in 2008; 39 went to college, including California State University, Northridge; Concordia University; Loyola Marymount University; University of California, Irvine; University of Southern California. Other: 2 went to work, 2 entered military service.

Student Life Upper grades have specified standards of dress, student council. Discipline rests primarily with faculty. Attendance at religious services is required.

Summer Programs Remediation programs offered; session focuses on mathematics and English; held on campus; accepts boys and girls; not open to students from other schools. 15 students usually enrolled. 2009 schedule: July 7 to July 31. Application deadline: June 15.

Tuition and Aid Day student tuition: $6825. Tuition installment plan (SMART Tuition Payment Plan, monthly payment plans). Merit scholarship grants, need-based scholarship grants available. In 2008–09, 15% of upper-school students received aid; total upper-school merit-scholarship money awarded: $10,000. Total amount of financial aid awarded in 2008–09: $25,000.

Admissions Traditional secondary-level entrance grade is 9. For fall 2008, 34 students applied for upper-level admission, 27 were accepted, 24 enrolled. Achievement/Aptitude/Writing or placement test required. Deadline for receipt of application materials: none. Application fee required: $300. Interview required.

Athletics Interscholastic: baseball (boys), basketball (b,g), cheering (g), drill team (g), flag football (b), football (b), ropes courses (b,g), track and field (b,g), volleyball (g), weight training (b,g); coed interscholastic: soccer. 2 PE instructors, 8 coaches.

Computers Computers are regularly used in business, business applications, college planning, computer applications, desktop publishing, digital applications, journalism, keyboarding, lab/keyboard, media production, science, yearbook classes. Computer network features include on-campus library services, online commercial services, Internet access, Internet filtering or blocking technology. Students grades are available online. The school has a published electronic and media policy.

Contact Ms. Barbara Winslow, Admissions Counselor. 818-362-5861. Fax: 818-367-0043. E-mail: barbara.winslow@lalhs.org. Web site: www.lalhs.org.

LOUISVILLE COLLEGIATE SCHOOL

2427 Glenmary Avenue
Louisville, Kentucky 40204

Head of School: Junius Scott Prince

General Information Coeducational day college-preparatory and arts school. Grades JK–12. Founded: 1915. Setting: urban. 24-acre campus. 2 buildings on campus. Approved or accredited by Independent Schools Association of the Central States. Member of National Association of Independent Schools and Secondary School Admission Test Board. Endowment: $5.6 million. Total enrollment: 638. Upper school average class size: 13. Upper school faculty-student ratio: 1:8.

Upper School Student Profile Grade 9: 53 students (21 boys, 32 girls); Grade 10: 50 students (23 boys, 27 girls); Grade 11: 55 students (23 boys, 32 girls); Grade 12: 46 students (15 boys, 31 girls).

Faculty School total: 77. In upper school: 10 men, 11 women; 16 have advanced degrees.

Subjects Offered Algebra, American history, American literature, ancient history, art, art history, biology, calculus, chemistry, Chinese, chorus, community service, composition, computer science, creative writing, discrete math, drama, economics, English, English literature, ensembles, environmental science, European history, fine arts, French, geometry, German, government/civics, history, mathematics, media, music, music history, physical education, physics, physiology, pre-calculus, psychology, science, social studies, Spanish, statistics, studio art, theater, trigonometry, world history, world literature, writing.

Graduation Requirements Arts and fine arts (art, music, dance, drama), English, foreign language, mathematics, physical education (includes health), science, social studies (includes history), senior symposium in leadership and service, individual and class service projects, senior speech.

Special Academic Programs Advanced Placement exam preparation; honors section; independent study; term-away projects; study abroad.

College Admission Counseling 42 students graduated in 2008; all went to college, including Centre College; Emory University; Miami University; Rhodes College; University of Kentucky; Vanderbilt University. Median SAT critical reading: 611, median SAT math: 611, median SAT writing: 633, median combined SAT: 1855, median composite ACT: 25. 70% scored over 600 on SAT critical reading, 52% scored over 600 on SAT math, 76% scored over 600 on SAT writing.

Student Life Upper grades have uniform requirement, student council, honor system. Discipline rests equally with students and faculty.

Summer Programs Enrichment, advancement, sports, art/fine arts, computer instruction programs offered; session focuses on educational enrichment and sports; held both on and off campus; held at off-Campus athletic fields owned by Collegiate; accepts boys and girls; open to students from other schools. 400 students usually enrolled. 2009 schedule: June 8 to July 31. Application deadline: none.

Tuition and Aid Day student tuition: $17,400. Tuition installment plan (The Tuition Plan, FACTS Tuition Payment Plan, monthly payment plans, individually arranged payment plans). Merit scholarship grants, need-based scholarship grants available. In 2008–09, 22% of upper-school students received aid; total upper-school merit-scholarship money awarded: $34,800. Total amount of financial aid awarded in 2008–09: $528,150.

Admissions Traditional secondary-level entrance grade is 9. For fall 2008, 22 students applied for upper-level admission, 18 were accepted, 13 enrolled. School's own exam and SSAT required. Deadline for receipt of application materials: none. Application fee required: $50. Interview required.

Athletics Interscholastic: baseball (boys), basketball (b,g), crew (g), cross-country running (b,g), field hockey (g), golf (b,g), indoor track (b,g), lacrosse (b,g), rowing (b,g), soccer (b,g), softball (g), strength & conditioning (b,g), swimming and diving (b,g), tennis (b,g), track and field (b,g), winter (indoor) track (b,g); intramural: basketball (b,g), soccer (b,g), tennis (b,g); coed interscholastic: soccer, strength & conditioning; coed intramural: soccer. 4 PE instructors, 60 coaches, 1 athletic trainer.

Computers Computers are regularly used in art, English, foreign language, history, mathematics, science classes. Computer network features include on-campus library services, online commercial services, Internet access, wireless campus network, Internet filtering or blocking technology. Student e-mail accounts and computer access in designated common areas are available to students. Students grades are available online. The school has a published electronic and media policy.

Contact Lynne Age, Admission Office Administrative Assistant. 502-479-0378. Fax: 502-454-0549. E-mail: lynne_age@loucol.com. Web site: www.loucol.com.

LOUISVILLE HIGH SCHOOL

22300 Mulholland Drive
Woodland Hills, California 91364

Head of School: Mrs. Kathleen Vercillo

General Information Girls' day college-preparatory, arts, religious studies, and technology school, affiliated with Roman Catholic Church. Grades 9–12. Founded: 1960. Setting: suburban. Nearest major city is Encino. 17-acre campus. 7 buildings on campus. Approved or accredited by National Catholic Education Association, Western Association of Schools and Colleges, Western Catholic Education Association, and California Department of Education. Total enrollment: 454. Upper school average class size: 25. Upper school faculty-student ratio: 1:25.

Upper School Student Profile Grade 9: 86 students (86 girls); Grade 10: 109 students (109 girls); Grade 11: 135 students (135 girls); Grade 12: 124 students (124 girls). 86% of students are Roman Catholic.

Faculty School total: 42. In upper school: 9 men, 32 women; 26 have advanced degrees.

Subjects Offered Advanced Placement courses, advanced studio art-AP, algebra, American history, American literature, anatomy, art, Bible studies, biology, calculus, calculus-AP, campus ministry, ceramics, chemistry, computer science, creative writing, dance, drama, driver education, earth science, economics, English, English literature, European history, fine arts, French, geography, geometry, government/civics, grammar, history, journalism, law, mathematics, music, photography, physical education, physics, physiology, psychology, religion, science, social science, social studies, Spanish, speech, statistics, theater, trigonometry, video film production, Web site design, world history, world literature.

Graduation Requirements Arts and fine arts (art, music, dance, drama), computer science, English, foreign language, mathematics, performing arts, physical education (includes health), religion (includes Bible studies and theology), science, social science, social studies (includes history), visual arts. Community service is required.

Special Academic Programs Advanced Placement exam preparation.

College Admission Counseling 108 students graduated in 2008; 107 went to college, including California State University, Northridge; Loyola Marymount University; University of California, Berkeley; University of California, Los Angeles; University of California, San Diego; University of Southern California.

Student Life Upper grades have uniform requirement, student council, honor system. Discipline rests equally with students and faculty. Attendance at religious services is required.

Summer Programs Sports programs offered; session focuses on skill development; held both on and off campus; held at Los Angeles Pierce Community College and Balboa Park; accepts girls; open to students from other schools. 200 students usually enrolled. 2009 schedule: June 15 to August 14. Application deadline: May 26.

Tuition and Aid Day student tuition: $10,600. Tuition installment plan (FACTS Tuition Payment Plan). Merit scholarship grants, need-based scholarship grants available. In 2008–09, 15% of upper-school students received aid; total upper-school merit-scholarship money awarded: $41,000. Total amount of financial aid awarded in 2008–09: $250,000.

Admissions Traditional secondary-level entrance grade is 9. For fall 2008, 127 students applied for upper-level admission, 116 were accepted, 86 enrolled. High School Placement Test required. Deadline for receipt of application materials: January 23. Application fee required: $75. On-campus interview required.

Athletics Interscholastic: basketball, cross-country running, equestrian sports, field hockey, golf, soccer, softball, swimming and diving, tennis, track and field, volleyball, water polo. 2 PE instructors, 30 coaches, 1 athletic trainer.

Computers Computers are regularly used in English, foreign language, French, graphic design, graphics, journalism, library, literary magazine, media, media

production, photography, religion, religious studies, science, social studies, Spanish, speech, technology, Web site design, yearbook classes. Computer network features include on-campus library services, online commercial services, Internet access, Internet filtering or blocking technology.
Contact Mrs. Linda Klarin, Admissions Coordinator. 818-346-8812. Fax: 818-346-9483. E-mail: lklarin@louisvillehs.org. Web site: www.louisvillehs.org.

LOURDES CATHOLIC HIGH SCHOOL

PO Box 1865
Nogales, Arizona 85628

Head of School: Barbara Lorene Monsegur

General Information Coeducational day college-preparatory school, affiliated with Roman Catholic Church. Grades K–12. Founded: 1934. Setting: rural. Nearest major city is Tucson. 10-acre campus. 1 building on campus. Approved or accredited by National Catholic Education Association, North Central Association of Colleges and Schools, Western Catholic Education Association, and Arizona Department of Education. Languages of instruction: English and Spanish. Total enrollment: 331. Upper school average class size: 25. Upper school faculty-student ratio: 1:10.
Upper School Student Profile Grade 9: 22 students (13 boys, 9 girls); Grade 10: 22 students (14 boys, 8 girls); Grade 11: 15 students (8 boys, 7 girls); Grade 12: 18 students (8 boys, 10 girls). 99% of students are Roman Catholic.
Faculty In upper school: 3 men, 4 women; 4 have advanced degrees.
Subjects Offered Algebra, American government, American history, American literature, art, athletics, basketball, Bible, biology, British literature, calculus, campus ministry, character education, chemistry, choir, Christian and Hebrew scripture, Christian doctrine, Christian scripture, church history, college counseling, computer literacy, computer skills, computers, dance, economics, electives, English, English literature, ESL, folk dance, foreign language, geometry, government, Hebrew scripture, history, honors algebra, honors English, independent study, journalism, Life of Christ, Mexican history, Mexican literature, moral theology, photojournalism, religious studies, Shakespeare, social justice, Spanish, Spanish literature, student government, tennis, theology, U.S. government, U.S. history, world religions, yearbook.
Graduation Requirements Art, career/college preparation, computer education, economics, English, English literature, mathematics, physical education (includes health), religion (includes Bible studies and theology), science, social studies (includes history), student government, U.S. government, yearbook.
Special Academic Programs Independent study; remedial reading and/or remedial writing; remedial math; ESL (11 students enrolled).
College Admission Counseling 18 students graduated in 2008; all went to college, including Arizona State University; Northern Arizona University; Pima Community College; The University of Arizona.
Student Life Upper grades have uniform requirement, student council, honor system. Discipline rests primarily with faculty. Attendance at religious services is required.
Tuition and Aid Day student tuition: $7000. Guaranteed tuition plan. Tuition installment plan (monthly payment plans, individually arranged payment plans). Tuition reduction for siblings, merit scholarship grants, paying campus jobs available. In 2008–09, 8% of upper-school students received aid; total upper-school merit-scholarship money awarded: $500. Total amount of financial aid awarded in 2008–09: $18,840.
Admissions Traditional secondary-level entrance grade is 9. For fall 2008, 2 students applied for upper-level admission, 2 were accepted, 2 enrolled. SSTS Placement Test required. Deadline for receipt of application materials: July 31. No application fee required. Interview recommended.
Athletics Interscholastic: baseball (boys, girls), basketball (b,g), volleyball (b,g). 1 PE instructor.
Computers Computers are regularly used in yearbook classes. Computer resources include Internet access. Computer access in designated common areas is available to students. The school has a published electronic and media policy.
Contact Mrs. Bertha P. Ramirez, Registrar. 520-287-5659. Fax: 520-287-2910. E-mail: registrar@lourdescatholicschool.org. Web site: www.lcsnogales.org.

THE LOVETT SCHOOL

4075 Paces Ferry Road NW
Atlanta, Georgia 30327

Head of School: William S. Peebles

General Information Coeducational day college-preparatory school. Grades K–12. Founded: 1926. Setting: suburban. 100-acre campus. 8 buildings on campus. Approved or accredited by Southern Association of Colleges and Schools, Southern Association of Independent Schools, and Georgia Department of Education. Member of National Association of Independent Schools and Secondary School Admission Test Board. Endowment: $54.3 million. Total enrollment: 1,550. Upper school average class size: 15. Upper school faculty-student ratio: 1:7.
Upper School Student Profile Grade 9: 160 students (74 boys, 86 girls); Grade 10: 152 students (72 boys, 80 girls); Grade 11: 144 students (70 boys, 74 girls); Grade 12: 139 students (65 boys, 74 girls).
Faculty School total: 234. In upper school: 26 men, 32 women; 48 have advanced degrees.
Subjects Offered Advanced chemistry, advanced computer applications, advanced math, Advanced Placement courses, African American history, African history, African literature, African-American literature, algebra, American government, American history, American history-AP, American legal systems, American literature, ancient history, ancient world history, architecture, art, art history, Asian history, Asian studies, band, biology, botany, calculus, calculus-AP, career and personal planning, career/college preparation, ceramics, character education, chemistry, chorus, computer art, computer education, computer graphics, computer programming, computer science, creative writing, dance, debate, drama, driver education, earth science, ecology, economics, electronic music, English, English literature, English-AP, environmental science, ethics, European history, fiction, film history, fine arts, French, French language-AP, French literature-AP, French studies, French-AP, gender issues, genetics, geometry, German, history, human development, jazz dance, journalism, Latin, Latin-AP, leadership, marine biology, mathematics, medieval history, music theory, music theory-AP, newspaper, orchestra, painting, philosophy, photography, physical education, physics, portfolio art, pre-calculus, public speaking, religion, robotics, science, sculpture, social studies, Spanish, Spanish language-AP, Spanish literature-AP, speech, statistics, technical theater, theater, theater arts, trigonometry, U.S. government and politics-AP, video, Western civilization, Western philosophy, world cultures, world history, world literature, world religions, writing workshop, yearbook, zoology.
Graduation Requirements Algebra, American studies, arts and fine arts (art, music, dance, drama), biology, English, foreign language, geometry, history, mathematics, physical education (includes health), religion (includes Bible studies and theology), science, Western civilization.
Special Academic Programs Advanced Placement exam preparation; honors section; independent study; term-away projects; study abroad; academic accommodation for the gifted, the musically talented, and the artistically talented.
College Admission Counseling 162 students graduated in 2008; all went to college, including Furman University; Georgia Institute of Technology; The University of Alabama; University of Georgia; University of South Carolina; Vanderbilt University.
Student Life Upper grades have uniform requirement, student council, honor system. Discipline rests primarily with faculty. Attendance at religious services is required.
Summer Programs Remediation, enrichment, advancement programs offered; session focuses on academic course work; held on campus; accepts boys and girls; open to students from other schools. 35 students usually enrolled. 2009 schedule: June 8 to July 24. Application deadline: May 15.
Tuition and Aid Day student tuition: $16,365–$19,515. Tuition installment plan (The Tuition Plan, Key Tuition Payment Plan, monthly payment plans, individually arranged payment plans, 1/2 paid in July and 1/2 paid in November). Need-based scholarship grants, local bank loans available. In 2008–09, 11% of upper-school students received aid. Total amount of financial aid awarded in 2008–09: $1,870,000.
Admissions Traditional secondary-level entrance grade is 9. For fall 2008, 94 students applied for upper-level admission, 44 were accepted, 26 enrolled. SSAT required. Deadline for receipt of application materials: January 30. Application fee required: $75. On-campus interview required.
Athletics Interscholastic: artistic gym (girls), baseball (b), basketball (b,g), cheering (g), cross-country running (b,g), dance (g), diving (b,g), football (b), golf (b,g), gymnastics (g), lacrosse (b,g), modern dance (g), soccer (b,g), softball (g), swimming and diving (b,g), tennis (b,g), track and field (b,g), volleyball (g), wrestling (b); intramural: aerobics/dance (g), dance (g), in-line hockey (b), modern dance (g), roller hockey (b); coed intramural: backpacking, bicycling, bowling, canoeing/kayaking, climbing, fitness, flag football, Frisbee, hiking/backpacking, kayaking, mountain biking, outdoor activities, physical fitness, physical training, rappelling, rock climbing, ropes courses, strength & conditioning, ultimate Frisbee, wall climbing, weight lifting, weight training, yoga. 3 PE instructors, 40 coaches, 2 athletic trainers.
Computers Computers are regularly used in all academic classes. Computer network features include on-campus library services, online commercial services, Internet access, wireless campus network, Internet filtering or blocking technology, central file storage. Student e-mail accounts and computer access in designated common areas are available to students. Students grades are available online.
Contact Ms. Debbie Lange, Director of Admission. 404-262-3032. Fax: 404-479-8463. E-mail: dlange@lovett.org. Web site: www.lovett.org.

THE LOWELL WHITEMAN SCHOOL

42605 RCR 36
Steamboat Springs, Colorado 80487

Head of School: Walter Daub

General Information Coeducational boarding and day college-preparatory school. Grades 9–12. Founded: 1957. Setting: rural. Nearest major city is Denver. Students are housed in single-sex dormitories. 185-acre campus. 10 buildings on campus. Approved or accredited by Association of Colorado Independent Schools, Missouri Independent School Association, The Association of Boarding Schools, and Colorado Department of Education. Member of National Association of Independent Schools and Secondary School Admission Test Board. Endowment: $1 million. Total enrollment: 96. Upper school average class size: 8. Upper school faculty-student ratio: 1:7.
Upper School Student Profile Grade 9: 12 students (9 boys, 3 girls); Grade 10: 21 students (13 boys, 8 girls); Grade 11: 26 students (12 boys, 14 girls); Grade 12: 38 students (22 boys, 16 girls). 47% of students are boarding students. 65% are state

residents. 24 states are represented in upper school student body. 5% are international students. International students from Canada, China, Finland, Germany, United Arab Emirates, and United Kingdom.

Faculty School total: 21. In upper school: 13 men, 8 women; 7 have advanced degrees; 16 reside on campus.

Subjects Offered 20th century history, algebra, American history, American literature, American studies, anatomy, art, art history, biology, calculus, chemistry, computer math, computer programming, computer science, creative writing, drama, economics, English, English literature, expository writing, film, fine arts, French, geography, geology, geometry, government/civics, grammar, mathematics, physical education, physics, science, social science, social studies, Spanish, theater, trigonometry, typing, world history, writing.

Graduation Requirements Algebra, arts and fine arts (art, music, dance, drama), business skills (includes word processing), chemistry, computer science, English, foreign language, geography, geometry, mathematics, physical education (includes health), science, social science, social studies (includes history), Western civilization, foreign travel program, competitive ski/snowboarding program.

Special Academic Programs Advanced Placement exam preparation; honors section; independent study; study abroad.

College Admission Counseling 18 students graduated in 2008; all went to college, including Bates College; The Colorado College; University of Colorado at Boulder; University of Denver; Whitman College.

Student Life Upper grades have student council, honor system. Discipline rests equally with students and faculty.

Tuition and Aid Day student tuition: $17,350; 7-day tuition and room/board: $32,250. Tuition installment plan (individually arranged payment plans, school's own payment plan). Merit scholarship grants, need-based scholarship grants available. In 2008–09, 30% of upper-school students received aid; total upper-school merit-scholarship money awarded: $11,000. Total amount of financial aid awarded in 2008–09: $351,000.

Admissions Traditional secondary-level entrance grade is 9. For fall 2008, 62 students applied for upper-level admission, 51 were accepted, 42 enrolled. Deadline for receipt of application materials: none. Application fee required: $40. Interview required.

Athletics Interscholastic: alpine skiing (boys, girls), baseball (b), basketball (b,g), biathlon (b,g), cross-country running (b,g), dance team (g), freestyle skiing (b,g), golf (b,g), hockey (b,g), ice hockey (b,g), indoor hockey (b,g), mountain biking (b,g), mountaineering (b,g), nordic skiing (b,g), outdoor adventure (b,g), ski jumping (b,g), skiing (cross-country) (b,g), skiing (downhill) (b,g), snowboarding (b,g), soccer (b,g), tennis (b,g), wrestling (b); intramural: backpacking (b,g), basketball (b,g), bicycling (b,g), ice hockey (b,g), ice skating (b,g), independent competitive sports (b,g), indoor hockey (b,g), indoor soccer (b,g), lacrosse (g), mountain biking (b,g), mountaineering (b,g), outdoor adventure (b,g), rock climbing (b,g), skiing (cross-country) (b,g), skiing (downhill) (b,g), snowboarding (b,g), soccer (b,g); coed interscholastic: alpine skiing, biathlon, climbing, cross-country running, freestyle skiing, golf, ice hockey, indoor hockey, kayaking, mountain biking, mountaineering, nordic skiing, outdoor adventure, rock climbing, ski jumping, skiing (cross-country), skiing (downhill), snowboarding, soccer, telemark skiing, wall climbing; coed intramural: aerobics, backpacking, badminton, bicycling, billiards, canoeing/kayaking, climbing, figure skating, flag football, Frisbee, golf, hiking/backpacking, horseback riding, ice hockey, ice skating, independent competitive sports, indoor hockey, indoor soccer, kayaking, lacrosse, mountain biking, mountaineering, outdoor adventure, physical fitness, physical training, rafting, rappelling, rock climbing, running, skateboarding, skiing (cross-country), skiing (downhill), snowboarding, snowshoeing, soccer, strength & conditioning, swimming and diving, table tennis, telemark skiing, tennis, volleyball, wall climbing, weight lifting, weight training, wilderness, wilderness survival, wildernessways, winter soccer, winter walking, yoga.

Computers Computers are regularly used in all academic classes. Computer network features include on-campus library services, online commercial services, Internet access, wireless campus network, Internet filtering or blocking technology. Campus intranet and student e-mail accounts are available to students. The school has a published electronic and media policy.

Contact Jared Olson, Director of Admission. 970-879-1350 Ext. 15. Fax: 970-879-0506. E-mail: admissions@lws.edu. Web site: www.lws.edu.

See Close-Up on page 826.

LOYOLA-BLAKEFIELD

PO Box 6819
Baltimore, Maryland 21285-6819

Head of School: Mr. Anthony I. Day

General Information Boys' day college-preparatory, arts, and religious studies school, affiliated with Roman Catholic Church. Grades 6–12. Founded: 1852. Setting: suburban. 60-acre campus. 7 buildings on campus. Approved or accredited by Association of Independent Maryland Schools and Jesuit Secondary Education Association. Endowment: $9.9 million. Total enrollment: 1,009. Upper school average class size: 19. Upper school faculty-student ratio: 1:11.

Upper School Student Profile Grade 9: 191 students (191 boys); Grade 10: 174 students (174 boys); Grade 11: 197 students (197 boys); Grade 12: 204 students (204 boys). 80% of students are Roman Catholic.

Faculty School total: 88. In upper school: 53 men, 16 women; 53 have advanced degrees.

Subjects Offered Accounting, algebra, American government, American government-AP, American literature, American literature-AP, art, art history, band, biology, biology-AP, biotechnology, British literature, British literature (honors), calculus, calculus-AP, ceramics, chemistry, chemistry-AP, Chesapeake Bay studies, chorus, civil war history, composition, composition-AP, computer graphics, computer science, concert band, drawing, driver education, English, English language-AP, English literature-AP, European history-AP, film studies, fine arts, forensic science, French, French language-AP, German, German-AP, government and politics-AP, Greek, history, history of music, honors algebra, honors English, honors geometry, honors U.S. history, honors world history, instrumental music, jazz ensemble, journalism, Latin, Latin-AP, mathematics, music history, oil painting, painting, photography, physical education, physics, physics-AP, poetry, pre-calculus, psychology, public speaking, religion, science, Spanish, Spanish language-AP, stagecraft, statistics-AP, U.S. government and politics-AP, U.S. history, U.S. history-AP, yearbook.

Graduation Requirements Arts and fine arts (art, music, dance, drama), computer science, English, foreign language, mathematics, physical education (includes health), religion (includes Bible studies and theology), science, social studies (includes history), 40 hours of Christian service.

Special Academic Programs Advanced Placement exam preparation; honors section; independent study; academic accommodation for the gifted, the musically talented, and the artistically talented.

College Admission Counseling 176 students graduated in 2008; 172 went to college, including Randolph-Macon College; Saint Joseph's University; Towson University; University of Maryland, Baltimore County; University of Maryland, College Park; Virginia Polytechnic Institute and State University. Other: 3 entered a postgraduate year, 1 had other specific plans. Mean SAT critical reading: 603, mean SAT math: 610, mean SAT writing: 593, mean combined SAT: 1806.

Student Life Upper grades have specified standards of dress, student council, honor system. Discipline rests primarily with faculty. Attendance at religious services is required.

Summer Programs Remediation, enrichment, advancement, sports programs offered; held on campus; accepts boys and girls; open to students from other schools. 350 students usually enrolled. 2009 schedule: June 22 to July 24. Application deadline: none.

Tuition and Aid Day student tuition: $13,900. Tuition installment plan (Key Tuition Payment Plan). Merit scholarship grants, need-based scholarship grants available. In 2008–09, 37% of upper-school students received aid; total upper-school merit-scholarship money awarded: $267,420. Total amount of financial aid awarded in 2008–09: $1,717,524.

Admissions Traditional secondary-level entrance grade is 9. For fall 2008, 350 students applied for upper-level admission, 227 were accepted, 120 enrolled. ISEE or Scholastic Testing Service required. Deadline for receipt of application materials: December 15. Application fee required: $30. On-campus interview required.

Athletics Interscholastic: baseball, basketball, cross-country running, diving, football, golf, ice hockey, indoor track & field, lacrosse, rugby, soccer, squash, swimming and diving, tennis, track and field, volleyball, water polo, winter (indoor) track, wrestling; intramural: badminton, basketball, fishing, flag football, football, indoor soccer, lacrosse, martial arts, sailing, tennis, ultimate Frisbee. 4 PE instructors, 30 coaches, 1 athletic trainer.

Computers Computers are regularly used in all classes. Computer network features include on-campus library services, online commercial services, Internet access, wireless campus network, Internet filtering or blocking technology. Campus intranet, student e-mail accounts, and computer access in designated common areas are available to students. Students grades are available online. The school has a published electronic and media policy.

Contact Ms. Paddy M. Sachse, Admissions Assistant. 443-841-3680. Fax: 443-841-3105. E-mail: pmsachse@loyolablakefield.org. Web site: www.loyolablakefield.org.

LOYOLA HIGH SCHOOL, JESUIT COLLEGE PREPARATORY

1901 Venice Boulevard
Los Angeles, California 90006-4496

Head of School: Fr. Charles J. Tilley, SJ

General Information Boys' day college-preparatory, arts, religious studies, bilingual studies, and technology school, affiliated with Roman Catholic Church. Grades 9–12. Founded: 1865. Setting: urban. 23-acre campus. 12 buildings on campus. Approved or accredited by California Association of Independent Schools and Western Association of Schools and Colleges. Endowment: $20 million. Total enrollment: 1,212. Upper school average class size: 26. Upper school faculty-student ratio: 1:15.

Upper School Student Profile Grade 9: 314 students (314 boys); Grade 10: 306 students (306 boys); Grade 11: 300 students (300 boys); Grade 12: 292 students (292 boys). 85% of students are Roman Catholic.

Faculty School total: 89. In upper school: 60 men, 29 women; 72 have advanced degrees.

Subjects Offered African-American studies, algebra, American history, American history-AP, American literature, anatomy and physiology, art, art history, Bible studies, biology, biology-AP, calculus, calculus-AP, ceramics, chemistry, chemistry-AP, community service, composition, computer math, computer programming, computer science, computer science-AP, creative writing, drama, earth science, economics-AP, English, English literature, English-AP, environmental science-AP, ethics, European history, European history-AP, expository writing, fine arts, French, French-AP, geometry, German, German-AP, government/civics, grammar, health, history, Latin, Latin-AP, mathematics, Mexican history, music, music theory-AP, oceanography, philosophy, photography, physical education, physics, physics-AP, pre-calculus, psychology-AP, religion, rhetoric, science, Shakespeare, social studies, Spanish, Spanish language-AP, Spanish literature-AP, theater, theology, trigonometry, typing, Western civilization, world history, world literature, writing.
Graduation Requirements Arts and fine arts (art, music, dance, drama), English, foreign language, mathematics, physical education (includes health), religion (includes Bible studies and theology), science, social science, social studies (includes history), three-week internship in senior year. Community service is required.
Special Academic Programs Advanced Placement exam preparation; honors section; independent study; special instructional classes for deaf students.
College Admission Counseling 292 students graduated in 2008; all went to college, including Loyola Marymount University; University of California, Berkeley; University of California, Irvine; University of California, Los Angeles; University of California, Santa Barbara; University of Southern California. Mean SAT critical reading: 618, mean SAT math: 620, mean SAT writing: 620, mean combined SAT: 1858. 54% scored over 600 on SAT critical reading, 52% scored over 600 on SAT math, 53% scored over 600 on SAT writing.
Student Life Upper grades have specified standards of dress, student council, honor system. Discipline rests primarily with faculty. Attendance at religious services is required.
Summer Programs Remediation, enrichment, advancement, sports, art/fine arts, computer instruction programs offered; held on campus; accepts boys and girls; open to students from other schools. 1,400 students usually enrolled. 2009 schedule: June 22 to July 24. Application deadline: May 14.
Tuition and Aid Day student tuition: $12,500. Tuition installment plan (FACTS Tuition Payment Plan, semester payment plan). Merit scholarship grants, need-based scholarship grants available. In 2008–09, 20% of upper-school students received aid; total upper-school merit-scholarship money awarded: $215,000. Total amount of financial aid awarded in 2008–09: $1,380,000.
Admissions Traditional secondary-level entrance grade is 9. For fall 2008, 813 students applied for upper-level admission, 355 were accepted, 314 enrolled. High School Placement Test required. Deadline for receipt of application materials: January 9. Application fee required: $70.
Athletics Interscholastic: baseball, basketball, cross-country running, diving, football, golf, lacrosse, soccer, swimming and diving, tennis, track and field, volleyball, water polo; intramural: baseball, basketball, diving, football, paddle tennis, soccer, swimming and diving, tennis, volleyball, water polo. 2 PE instructors, 3 coaches, 2 athletic trainers.
Computers Computers are regularly used in English, history, journalism, keyboarding, mathematics, science, yearbook classes. Computer network features include on-campus library services, Internet access, wireless campus network, Internet filtering or blocking technology.
Contact Heath B. Utley, Director of Admissions. 213-381-5121 Ext. 219. Fax: 213-368-3819. E-mail: hutley@loyolahs.edu. Web site: www.loyolahs.edu.

LOYOLA SCHOOL

980 Park Avenue
New York, New York 10028-0020
Head of School: Mr. James F. X. Lyness Jr.

General Information Coeducational day college-preparatory school, affiliated with Roman Catholic Church (Jesuit order). Grades 9–12. Founded: 1900. Setting: urban. 2 buildings on campus. Approved or accredited by Jesuit Secondary Education Association, Middle States Association of Colleges and Schools, National Catholic Education Association, New York State Association of Independent Schools, and New York State Board of Regents. Member of National Association of Independent Schools. Endowment: $7 million. Total enrollment: 208. Upper school average class size: 17. Upper school faculty-student ratio: 1:8.
Upper School Student Profile Grade 9: 46 students (24 boys, 22 girls); Grade 10: 54 students (24 boys, 30 girls); Grade 11: 56 students (23 boys, 33 girls); Grade 12: 52 students (20 boys, 32 girls). 85% of students are Roman Catholic Church (Jesuit order).
Faculty School total: 32. In upper school: 17 men, 15 women; 28 have advanced degrees.
Subjects Offered Advanced Placement courses, algebra, American government, American history, American literature, art, art history, biology, calculus, chemistry, chorus, college counseling, community service, comparative religion, computer programming, computer science, creative writing, death and loss, discrete mathematics, drama, economics, English, English literature, ethics, European history, expository writing, film, film history, fine arts, French, geometry, grammar, health, history, instrumental music, Italian, journalism, language-AP, Latin, mathematics, music history, philosophy, photography, physical education, physics, political science, pre-calculus, religion, science, social studies, Spanish, speech, statistics-AP, student government, student publications, theater, theology, trigonometry, world history, writing.
Graduation Requirements Art history, computer literacy, English, foreign language, guidance, mathematics, music history, physical education (includes health), science, social studies (includes history), speech, theology, Christian Service Program in each year.
Special Academic Programs Advanced Placement exam preparation; honors section; independent study; study at local college for college credit; study abroad.
College Admission Counseling 49 students graduated in 2008; all went to college, including Boston College; College of the Holy Cross; Fordham University; The George Washington University; Vassar College; Villanova University. Median SAT critical reading: 610, median SAT math: 600, median SAT writing: 610.
Student Life Upper grades have specified standards of dress, student council, honor system. Discipline rests primarily with faculty. Attendance at religious services is required.
Tuition and Aid Day student tuition: $25,600. Tuition installment plan (Academic Management Services Plan). Merit scholarship grants, need-based scholarship grants available. In 2008–09, 33% of upper-school students received aid; total upper-school merit-scholarship money awarded: $175,000. Total amount of financial aid awarded in 2008–09: $725,000.
Admissions Traditional secondary-level entrance grade is 9. ISEE, school's own exam or SSAT required. Deadline for receipt of application materials: November 15. Application fee required: $75. On-campus interview recommended.
Athletics Interscholastic: baseball (boys), basketball (b,g), cross-country running (b,g), soccer (b), softball (g), track and field (b,g), volleyball (g); intramural: basketball (b,g), dance (g); coed interscholastic: golf, soccer; coed intramural: Frisbee, hiking/backpacking, outdoor activities, outdoor adventure, paddle tennis, physical fitness, physical training, track and field. 1 PE instructor, 9 coaches.
Computers Computers are regularly used in all academic classes. Computer network features include on-campus library services, online commercial services, Internet access, Internet filtering or blocking technology. Campus intranet and student e-mail accounts are available to students.
Contact Ms. Lillian Diaz-Imbelli, Director of Admissions. 646-346-8132. Fax: 646-346-8175. E-mail: limbelli@loyola-nyc.org. Web site: www.loyola-nyc.org.

ANNOUNCEMENT FROM THE SCHOOL Founded in 1900, Loyola School is an independent, coeducational, Jesuit high school—unique in the New York City area. A small school of approximately 200 students, Loyola provides an education that is marked by individual attention and by a close-knit, talented, and diverse community of students and parents, teachers, and administrators—all collaborating in the education of "women and men for others."

LUSTRE CHRISTIAN HIGH SCHOOL

HC 66, Box 57
Lustre, Montana 59225
Head of School: Al Leland

General Information Coeducational boarding and day college-preparatory, general academic, and religious studies school, affiliated with Mennonite Brethren Church. Grades 9–12. Founded: 1948. Setting: rural. Nearest major city is Glasgow. Students are housed in single-sex by floor dormitories. 20-acre campus. 1 building on campus. Approved or accredited by Association of Christian Schools International and Montana Department of Education. Endowment: $220,000. Total enrollment: 22. Upper school average class size: 6. Upper school faculty-student ratio: 1:3.
Upper School Student Profile Grade 9: 10 students (4 boys, 6 girls); Grade 10: 3 students (3 boys); Grade 11: 6 students (6 boys); Grade 12: 3 students (1 boy, 2 girls). 59% of students are boarding students. 64% are state residents. 5 states are represented in upper school student body. 14% are international students. International students from China and Republic of Korea. 14% of students are members of Mennonite Brethren Church.
Faculty School total: 6. In upper school: 1 man, 5 women; 1 has an advanced degree; 4 reside on campus.
Subjects Offered Algebra, American literature, band, Bible studies, biology, British literature, chemistry, choir, computer science, computers, English, fine arts, foreign language, geometry, health, journalism, mathematics, physical education, physical science, physics, pre-calculus, religion, science, social science, social studies, U.S. government, U.S. history, world history.
Graduation Requirements Arts and fine arts (art, music, dance, drama), computer science, English, mathematics, physical education (includes health), religion (includes Bible studies and theology), science, social studies (includes history), senior chapel message (as part of senior Bible program).
Special Academic Programs Independent study.
College Admission Counseling 11 students graduated in 2008; 9 went to college, including Montana State University; Montana State University–Billings. Other: 2 went to work. Median SAT critical reading: 445, median SAT math: 500, median SAT writing: 415, median combined SAT: 1360, median composite ACT: 21.
Student Life Upper grades have specified standards of dress, student council. Discipline rests primarily with faculty. Attendance at religious services is required.

Tuition and Aid Day student tuition: $1600; 7-day tuition and room/board: $3000. Tuition installment plan (monthly payment plans, individually arranged payment plans). Need-based scholarship grants available. In 2008–09, 14% of upper-school students received aid. Total amount of financial aid awarded in 2008–09: $2750.
Admissions Traditional secondary-level entrance grade is 9. ITBS achievement test, PSAT, SLEP for foreign students, Stanford Achievement Test, Otis-Lennon School Ability Test or TOEFL or SLEP required. Deadline for receipt of application materials: none. No application fee required. Interview recommended.
Athletics Interscholastic: basketball (boys, girls), football (b), track and field (b,g), volleyball (g). 2 coaches.
Computers Computers are regularly used in English, history, journalism, religious studies, science, yearbook classes. Computer network features include Internet access, wireless campus network.
Contact Al Leland, Supervising Teacher. 406-392-5735. Fax: 406-392-5765. E-mail: aleland@nemont.net. Web site: www.lustrechristian.org.

LUTHERAN HIGH NORTH

1130 West 34th Street
Houston, Texas 77018

Head of School: Mr. David Waterman

General Information Coeducational day college-preparatory, arts, religious studies, bilingual studies, and technology school, affiliated with Lutheran Church–Missouri Synod. Grades 9–12. Founded: 1982. Setting: urban. 10-acre campus. 3 buildings on campus. Approved or accredited by National Lutheran School Accreditation, Southern Association of Colleges and Schools, Texas Education Agency, and Texas Private School Accreditation Commission. Endowment: $1.5 million. Total enrollment: 295. Upper school average class size: 22. Upper school faculty-student ratio: 1:22.
Upper School Student Profile Grade 9: 68 students (33 boys, 35 girls); Grade 10: 82 students (33 boys, 49 girls); Grade 11: 71 students (30 boys, 41 girls); Grade 12: 70 students (33 boys, 37 girls). 50% of students are Lutheran Church–Missouri Synod.
Faculty School total: 26. In upper school: 13 men, 12 women; 11 have advanced degrees.
Subjects Offered 20th century American writers, 20th century history, 20th century physics, 20th century world history, 3-dimensional art, 3-dimensional design, ACT preparation, acting, advanced chemistry, advanced computer applications, advanced math, Advanced Placement courses, algebra, American Civil War, American government, American history, American literature, anatomy and physiology, ancient world history, applied arts, applied music, art, athletic training, athletics, band, baseball, Basic programming, basketball, Bible, Bible studies, biology, British literature, British literature (honors), business technology, cabinet making, calculus, calculus-AP, ceramics, cheerleading, chemistry, choir, choral music, chorus, Christian doctrine, Christian education, Christian scripture, Christian testament, civil war history, college counseling, college placement, college planning, college writing, computer applications, computer information systems, computer keyboarding, computer multimedia, computer programming, concert band, concert choir, digital imaging, digital photography, drafting, drama, drama performance, economics, English, English composition, English literature, English-AP, environmental science, foreign language, geometry, golf, government, health, history, honors algebra, honors English, honors geometry, human anatomy, human biology, instrumental music, jazz band, journalism, keyboarding, keyboarding/computer, language, Latin, marching band, music theory, musical productions, novels, oil painting, photojournalism, physical education, physics, pre-calculus, psychology, public speaking, SAT preparation, SAT/ACT preparation, senior career experience, social issues, softball, Spanish, swimming, travel, U.S. government, visual arts, volleyball, Web site design, weight training, weightlifting, woodworking, world history, yearbook.
Graduation Requirements Algebra, anatomy and physiology, art education, arts and fine arts (art, music, dance, drama), computer science, economics, electives, English, foreign language, geography, geometry, government, human biology, mathematics, physical education (includes health), public speaking, religion (includes Bible studies and theology), science, social studies (includes history), U.S. history, world history, Distinguished Diploma students must have an additional credit in foreign language, 2½ credits electives, 5 credits honors work, and 4 advanced measures with approved college courses with A or B.
Special Academic Programs Advanced Placement exam preparation; honors section; study at local college for college credit; programs in English, mathematics for dyslexic students.
College Admission Counseling 70 students graduated in 2008; 67 went to college, including Sam Houston State University; Texas A&M University; The University of Texas at Austin; The University of Texas at San Antonio; University of Houston. Other: 1 went to work, 2 entered military service. Mean SAT writing: 522, mean combined SAT: 1013, mean composite ACT: 21.
Student Life Upper grades have uniform requirement, student council, honor system. Discipline rests primarily with faculty. Attendance at religious services is required.
Summer Programs Enrichment, sports, art/fine arts, computer instruction programs offered; session focuses on sports and band/music; held on campus; accepts boys and girls; open to students from other schools. 125 students usually enrolled. 2009 schedule: June 1 to July 31. Application deadline: May 31.
Tuition and Aid Day student tuition: $9950. Tuition installment plan (FACTS Tuition Payment Plan, individually arranged payment plans, special tuition arrangements—full, half semester or monthly). Tuition reduction for siblings, merit scholarship grants, need-based scholarship grants available. In 2008–09, 30% of upper-school students received aid; total upper-school merit-scholarship money awarded: $8000. Total amount of financial aid awarded in 2008–09: $175,000.
Admissions Traditional secondary-level entrance grade is 9. For fall 2008, 110 students applied for upper-level admission, 83 were accepted, 75 enrolled. Admissions testing and High School Placement Test (closed version) from Scholastic Testing Service required. Deadline for receipt of application materials: none. Application fee required: $50. Interview required.
Athletics Interscholastic: aquatics (boys, girls), baseball (b), basketball (b,g), football (b), soccer (b,g), softball (g), volleyball (g), winter soccer (b,g); coed interscholastic: cheering, cross-country running, golf, outdoor activities, physical fitness, physical training, power lifting, swimming and diving, track and field, weight lifting, weight training. 3 PE instructors, 8 coaches, 2 athletic trainers.
Computers Computers are regularly used in current events, desktop publishing, drafting, English, graphic arts, graphic design, information technology, journalism, keyboarding, media arts, multimedia, news writing, publications, publishing, research skills, Spanish, theology, Web site design, word processing, writing, yearbook classes. Computer network features include on-campus library services, Internet access, Internet filtering or blocking technology. Student e-mail accounts are available to students. Students grades are available online. The school has a published electronic and media policy.
Contact Andy Manriquez, Admissions Director. 713-880-3131 Ext. 322. Fax: 713-880-5447. E-mail: andymanriquez@lea-hou.org. Web site: www.lutheranhighnorth.org/default.htm.

LUTHERAN HIGH SCHOOL

5555 South Arlington Avenue
Indianapolis, Indiana 46237-2366

Head of School: Mr. Gary St. Clair

General Information Coeducational day college-preparatory, general academic, and religious studies school, affiliated with Lutheran Church–Missouri Synod. Grades 9–12. Founded: 1975. Setting: suburban. 18-acre campus. 1 building on campus. Approved or accredited by National Lutheran School Accreditation, North Central Association of Colleges and Schools, and Indiana Department of Education. Endowment: $113,000. Total enrollment: 279. Upper school average class size: 18. Upper school faculty-student ratio: 1:14.
Upper School Student Profile Grade 9: 78 students (35 boys, 43 girls); Grade 10: 75 students (38 boys, 37 girls); Grade 11: 67 students (35 boys, 32 girls); Grade 12: 59 students (31 boys, 28 girls). 64% of students are Lutheran Church–Missouri Synod.
Faculty School total: 21. In upper school: 13 men, 7 women; 16 have advanced degrees.
Subjects Offered Accounting, advanced biology, advanced chemistry, advanced computer applications, advanced math, Advanced Placement courses, algebra, American government, American history, American literature-AP, American sign language, anatomy, anatomy and physiology, Basic programming, Bible, Bible studies, biology, biology-AP, bookkeeping, business, calculus-AP, ceramics, chemistry, chemistry-AP, choir, Christian doctrine, Christian ethics, church history, comparative religion, computer applications, computer graphics, computer programming, computer science-AP, concert band, concert choir, desktop publishing, developmental language skills, drawing, driver education, economics, English, English language and composition-AP, English literature and composition-AP, environmental studies, family living, general business, general math, geometry, German, graphic design, health and wellness, humanities, independent study, jazz band, music theory, oil painting, personal fitness, physical fitness, physics, pre-calculus, printmaking, probability and statistics, psychology, publishing, sculpture, sociology, Spanish, speech, sports conditioning, statistics and probability, student teaching, theater arts, U.S. government, vocational-technical courses, Web site design, world history, writing workshop.
Graduation Requirements Algebra, anatomy and physiology, arts and fine arts (art, music, dance, drama), biology-AP, chemistry-AP, computer applications, economics, English, foreign language, geometry, health and safety, physical education (includes health), physics, religious studies, U.S. government, U.S. history, world geography, world history.
Special Academic Programs 5 Advanced Placement exams for which test preparation is offered; honors section; independent study; study at local college for college credit; remedial reading and/or remedial writing; remedial math.
College Admission Counseling 87 students graduated in 2008; 84 went to college, including Ball State University; Indiana University Bloomington; Purdue University; University of Indianapolis; Valparaiso University. Other: 3 entered military service. Mean SAT critical reading: 531, mean SAT math: 522, mean SAT writing: 498, mean combined SAT: 1551, mean composite ACT: 24.
Student Life Upper grades have uniform requirement, student council, honor system. Discipline rests primarily with faculty. Attendance at religious services is required.
Tuition and Aid Day student tuition: $7600. Tuition installment plan (FACTS Tuition Payment Plan, individually arranged payment plans). Tuition reduction for siblings, need-based scholarship grants, paying campus jobs, Simply Giving (Thrivent), Church Worker Grants available. In 2008–09, 34% of upper-school students received aid. Total amount of financial aid awarded in 2008–09: $220,000.

Admissions Traditional secondary-level entrance grade is 9. Deadline for receipt of application materials: none. Application fee required: $150. On-campus interview required.
Athletics Interscholastic: baseball (boys), basketball (b,g), cheering (g), cross-country running (b,g), football (b), golf (b,g), soccer (b,g), softball (g), tennis (b,g), track and field (b,g), volleyball (g); coed interscholastic: physical fitness, weight training; coed intramural: basketball, bowling, football. 22 coaches.
Computers Computers are regularly used in accounting, art, Bible studies, business applications, career exploration, current events, design, desktop publishing, drawing and design, economics, English, foreign language, graphic design, historical foundations for arts, history, independent study, keyboarding, library skills, media production, publications, science, social sciences, yearbook classes. Computer network features include on-campus library services, online commercial services, Internet access, wireless campus network, Internet filtering or blocking technology, shared library catalog and Internet databases with Indianapolis-Marion County Public Library. Computer access in designated common areas is available to students. Students grades are available online. The school has a published electronic and media policy.
Contact Mrs. Margo Korb, Administrative Assistant. 317-787-5474 Ext. 211. Fax: 317-787-2794. E-mail: mkorb@lhsi.org. Web site: www.lhsi.org.

LUTHERAN HIGH SCHOOL
12411 Wornall Rd.
Kansas City, Missouri 64145-1736
Head of School: Mr. Chris Domsch
General Information Coeducational day college-preparatory and religious studies school, affiliated with Lutheran Church–Missouri Synod. Grades 9–12. Founded: 1980. Setting: suburban. 29-acre campus. 1 building on campus. Approved or accredited by Missouri Independent School Association, National Lutheran School Accreditation, North Central Association of Colleges and Schools, and Missouri Department of Education. Endowment: $97,000. Total enrollment: 113. Upper school average class size: 15. Upper school faculty-student ratio: 1:12.
Upper School Student Profile Grade 9: 36 students (10 boys, 26 girls); Grade 10: 35 students (19 boys, 16 girls); Grade 11: 29 students (19 boys, 10 girls); Grade 12: 13 students (8 boys, 5 girls). 80% of students are Lutheran Church–Missouri Synod.
Faculty School total: 13. In upper school: 7 men, 6 women; 5 have advanced degrees.
Subjects Offered Advanced math, African literature, algebra, American government, American literature, analysis, analytic geometry, anatomy and physiology, ancient world history, applied music, art, athletics, baseball, Basic programming, basketball, Bible studies, biology, biology-AP, calculus, cheerleading, chemistry, choir, Christian doctrine, Christian education, Christian ethics, Christian scripture, Christianity, church history, college counseling, communication skills, comparative religion, composition, computer keyboarding, consumer economics, consumer mathematics, contemporary art, earth science, economics, English composition, English literature, genetics, geometry, government, graphic arts, health education, history, history of religion, HTML design, instrumental music, Internet, Internet research, introduction to literature, keyboarding/computer, Life of Christ, math analysis, photography, physical education, physical science, physics, pre-algebra, psychology, sociology, Spanish, state history, student government, theater production, track and field, trigonometry, U.S. government, volleyball, Web site design, weightlifting.
Graduation Requirements Algebra, American government, American history, American literature, analytic geometry, art, arts and fine arts (art, music, dance, drama), Bible studies, biology, British literature, calculus, chemistry, church history, electives, geometry, health education, math analysis, modern world history, trigonometry, U.S. history.
Special Academic Programs Honors section; independent study; study at local college for college credit; study abroad.
College Admission Counseling 24 students graduated in 2008; 23 went to college, including Concordia University; Truman State University; University of Central Missouri; University of Missouri–Columbia. Other: 1 went to work. Mean SAT critical reading: 550, mean SAT math: 480, mean composite ACT: 24. 50% scored over 600 on SAT critical reading, 50% scored over 600 on SAT math, 25% scored over 26 on composite ACT.
Student Life Upper grades have specified standards of dress, student council, honor system. Discipline rests primarily with faculty.
Tuition and Aid Day student tuition: $5795–$9000. Tuition installment plan (monthly payment plans, individually arranged payment plans). Tuition reduction for siblings, merit scholarship grants, need-based scholarship grants available. In 2008–09, 20% of upper-school students received aid; total upper-school merit-scholarship money awarded: $2500. Total amount of financial aid awarded in 2008–09: $15,000.
Admissions Traditional secondary-level entrance grade is 9. For fall 2008, 125 students applied for upper-level admission, 112 were accepted, 112 enrolled. SLEP for foreign students required. Deadline for receipt of application materials: none. Application fee required: $275. On-campus interview required.
Athletics Interscholastic: baseball (boys), basketball (b,g), cheering (g), dance team (g), soccer (b,g), track and field (b,g), volleyball (g), weight lifting (b,g); coed intramural: basketball, bowling, golf, gymnastics, physical fitness, softball, volleyball, weight training.
Computers Computers are regularly used in accounting, business education, data processing, word processing classes. Computer network features include on-campus library services, Internet access, wireless campus network, Internet filtering or blocking technology. Student e-mail accounts and computer access in designated common areas are available to students. Students grades are available online.
Contact Mrs. Paula Meier, Registrar. 816-241-5478. Fax: 816-876-2069. E-mail: pmeier@lhskc.com. Web site: www.lhskc.com.

LUTHERAN HIGH SCHOOL NORTH
5401 Lucas Hunt Road
St. Louis, Missouri 63121
Head of School: Mr. Timothy Hipenbecker
General Information Coeducational day college-preparatory, arts, business, religious studies, and bilingual studies school, affiliated with Lutheran Church. Grades 9–12. Founded: 1946. Setting: urban. 47-acre campus. 1 building on campus. Approved or accredited by Lutheran School Accreditation Commission, National Lutheran School Accreditation, North Central Association of Colleges and Schools, and Missouri Department of Education. Endowment: $6.8 million. Total enrollment: 384. Upper school average class size: 22. Upper school faculty-student ratio: 1:13.
Upper School Student Profile Grade 9: 100 students (58 boys, 42 girls); Grade 10: 105 students (54 boys, 51 girls); Grade 11: 97 students (52 boys, 45 girls); Grade 12: 82 students (33 boys, 49 girls). 44% of students are Lutheran.
Faculty School total: 31. In upper school: 20 men, 11 women; 26 have advanced degrees.
Subjects Offered Accounting, advanced chemistry, Advanced Placement courses, algebra, American history, American history-AP, American literature, anatomy, art, Bible studies, biology, business, business law, business skills, calculus, calculus-AP, ceramics, chemistry, child development, choir, Christian doctrine, Christian education, Christian ethics, Christian scripture, Christian studies, Christianity, church history, computer applications, computer keyboarding, computer multimedia, computer science, concert band, concert choir, data analysis, design, drawing, drawing and design, economics, English, English composition, English literature, English literature-AP, entrepreneurship, European history, family and consumer sciences, fashion, fine arts, finite math, food and nutrition, foods, French, geography, geometry, government, government/civics, health education, history, human anatomy, keyboarding, literature-AP, marketing, mathematics, media studies, multimedia design, music, organic chemistry, painting, physical education, physics, physiology, play production, practical arts, pre-calculus, printmaking, probability and statistics, psychology, religion, research, science, social studies, society and culture, Spanish, speech, statistics, student publications, theology, U.S. government, U.S. history-AP, world geography, world history, world literature, world religions, writing.
Graduation Requirements Arts and fine arts (art, music, dance, drama), English, mathematics, physical education (includes health), practical arts, religion (includes Bible studies and theology), science, social studies (includes history), Saved to Serve (community service hours).
Special Academic Programs Advanced Placement exam preparation; honors section; independent study; study at local college for college credit.
College Admission Counseling 86 students graduated in 2008; 80 went to college, including Augustana College; Concordia University, Nebraska; Lindenwood University; Missouri University of Science and Technology; University of Missouri–Columbia; University of Missouri–St. Louis. Other: 6 had other specific plans. 25% scored over 26 on composite ACT.
Student Life Upper grades have uniform requirement, student council, honor system. Discipline rests primarily with faculty. Attendance at religious services is required.
Summer Programs Enrichment, sports programs offered; session focuses on Fundamentals & Enrichment; held on campus; accepts boys and girls; not open to students from other schools. 120 students usually enrolled. 2009 schedule: June 1 to July 31.
Tuition and Aid Day student tuition: $8225–$9425. Tuition installment plan (FACTS Tuition Payment Plan, monthly payment plans, individually arranged payment plans, semester payment plan, full-year payment plan with discount). Tuition reduction for siblings, merit scholarship grants, need-based scholarship grants available. In 2008–09, 60% of upper-school students received aid; total upper-school merit-scholarship money awarded: $22,000. Total amount of financial aid awarded in 2008–09: $600,000.
Admissions Traditional secondary-level entrance grade is 9. For fall 2008, 119 students applied for upper-level admission, 117 were accepted, 100 enrolled. ACT-Explore required. Deadline for receipt of application materials: none. Application fee required: $250. Interview recommended.
Athletics Interscholastic: baseball (boys), basketball (b,g), cheering (g), cross-country running (b,g), football (b), golf (b), pom squad (g), soccer (b,g), softball (g), tennis (b,g), track and field (b,g), volleyball (g). 2 PE instructors.
Computers Computers are regularly used in art, business education, English, history, mathematics, science, social studies, yearbook classes. Computer network features include on-campus library services, Internet access, wireless campus network, Internet filtering or blocking technology. Computer access in designated common areas is available to students. The school has a published electronic and media policy.
Contact Judy Knight, Records Clerk. 314-389-3100 Ext. 420. Fax: 314-389-3103. E-mail: jknight@lhsn.org. Web site: www.lhsn.org.

LUTHERAN HIGH SCHOOL NORTHWEST

1000 Bagley Avenue
Rochester Hills, Michigan 48309

Head of School: Mr. Paul Looker

General Information Coeducational day college-preparatory and religious studies school, affiliated with Lutheran Church–Missouri Synod. Grades 9–12. Founded: 1978. Setting: suburban. Nearest major city is Detroit. 30-acre campus. 1 building on campus. Approved or accredited by Michigan Association of Non-Public Schools, National Lutheran School Accreditation, North Central Association of Colleges and Schools, and Michigan Department of Education. Endowment: $1 million. Total enrollment: 308. Upper school average class size: 25. Upper school faculty-student ratio: 1:16.

Upper School Student Profile Grade 9: 76 students (36 boys, 40 girls); Grade 10: 67 students (44 boys, 23 girls); Grade 11: 76 students (38 boys, 38 girls); Grade 12: 89 students (40 boys, 49 girls). 75% of students are Lutheran Church–Missouri Synod.

Faculty School total: 19. In upper school: 11 men, 8 women; 15 have advanced degrees.

Subjects Offered Accounting, advanced chemistry, algebra, American government-AP, American history, American history-AP, art, audio visual/media, band, Basic programming, biology, biology-AP, bookkeeping, business, business mathematics, calculus, chemistry, chorus, computer science, Eastern world civilizations, economics, English, English-AP, geography, geometry, German, government/civics, law, mathematics, music, physical education, physical science, physics-AP, psychology, Spanish, statistics-AP, theology, trigonometry, world history.

Graduation Requirements Arts and fine arts (art, music, dance, drama), English, mathematics, physical education (includes health), religion (includes Bible studies and theology), science, social science, social studies (includes history). Community service is required.

Special Academic Programs Advanced Placement exam preparation; honors section; independent study; study at local college for college credit.

College Admission Counseling 61 students graduated in 2008; 59 went to college, including Central Michigan University; Concordia College; Michigan State University; Oakland University; University of Michigan; Western Michigan University. Other: 2 went to work. Median composite ACT: 22. Mean SAT critical reading: 662, mean SAT math: 702. 75% scored over 600 on SAT critical reading, 75% scored over 600 on SAT math, 26% scored over 26 on composite ACT.

Student Life Upper grades have specified standards of dress, student council. Discipline rests primarily with faculty. Attendance at religious services is required.

Tuition and Aid Day student tuition: $6550. Tuition installment plan (monthly payment plans). Merit scholarship grants, need-based scholarship grants available. In 2008–09, 2% of upper-school students received aid; total upper-school merit-scholarship money awarded: $2000. Total amount of financial aid awarded in 2008–09: $2000.

Admissions Traditional secondary-level entrance grade is 9. For fall 2008, 80 students applied for upper-level admission, 80 were accepted, 80 enrolled. High School Placement Test required. Deadline for receipt of application materials: none. Application fee required: $350. On-campus interview required.

Athletics Interscholastic: baseball (boys), basketball (b,g), cheering (g), cross-country running (b,g), football (b), golf (b), soccer (b,g), softball (g), track and field (b,g), volleyball (g), wrestling (b); intramural: dance squad (g), indoor soccer (b,g); coed intramural: badminton, fitness, physical fitness, physical training, weight training.

Computers Computers are regularly used in journalism, keyboarding, mathematics, media, research skills, word processing, yearbook classes. Computer network features include Internet access, Internet filtering or blocking technology. Students grades are available online. The school has a published electronic and media policy.

Contact Mr. Paul Looker, Principal. 248-852-6677. Fax: 248-852-2667. E-mail: plooker@lhsa.com. Web site: www.lhnw.lhsa.com.

LUTHERAN HIGH SCHOOL OF HAWAII

1404 University Avenue
Honolulu, Hawaii 96822-2494

Head of School: Arthur Gundell

General Information Coeducational day college-preparatory school, affiliated with Lutheran Church–Missouri Synod. Grades 9–12. Founded: 1988. Setting: urban. 1-acre campus. 3 buildings on campus. Approved or accredited by Lutheran School Accreditation Commission, The Hawaii Council of Private Schools, Western Association of Schools and Colleges, and Hawaii Department of Education. Member of Secondary School Admission Test Board. Endowment: $35,000. Total enrollment: 123. Upper school average class size: 12. Upper school faculty-student ratio: 1:10.

Upper School Student Profile Grade 9: 34 students (21 boys, 13 girls); Grade 10: 24 students (16 boys, 8 girls); Grade 11: 33 students (17 boys, 16 girls); Grade 12: 32 students (21 boys, 11 girls). 13% of students are Lutheran Church–Missouri Synod.

Faculty School total: 15. In upper school: 8 men, 7 women; 7 have advanced degrees.

Subjects Offered 20th century history, 3-dimensional art, advanced math, Advanced Placement courses, algebra, American government, American history, American literature, analytic geometry, art, art-AP, Bible studies, biology, British literature, calculus, calculus-AP, chemistry, choir, computer applications, computer programming, computer science, concert band, consumer economics, drama, earth science, economics, English, English literature, European history, expository writing, fine arts, food and nutrition, geometry, government/civics, grammar, health, history, home economics, Japanese, journalism, keyboarding, life skills, marine biology, mathematics, music, oceanography, photography, physical education, physics, psychology, religion, science, social science, social studies, Spanish, speech, theater, world history, world literature.

Graduation Requirements Arts and fine arts (art, music, dance, drama), computer science, English, mathematics, physical education (includes health), religion (includes Bible studies and theology), science, social science, social studies (includes history).

Special Academic Programs Advanced Placement exam preparation; honors section.

College Admission Counseling 31 students graduated in 2008; 30 went to college, including Kapiolani Community College; University of Hawaii at Mānoa. Other: 1 entered military service. Median composite ACT: 23. Mean SAT critical reading: 525, mean SAT math: 530, mean SAT writing: 525. 10% scored over 600 on SAT critical reading, 15% scored over 600 on SAT math.

Student Life Upper grades have specified standards of dress, student council, honor system. Discipline rests primarily with faculty. Attendance at religious services is required.

Tuition and Aid Day student tuition: $7290–$8290. Tuition installment plan (Insured Tuition Payment Plan). Tuition reduction for siblings, merit scholarship grants, need-based scholarship grants available. In 2008–09, 10% of upper-school students received aid; total upper-school merit-scholarship money awarded: $40,075. Total amount of financial aid awarded in 2008–09: $50,000.

Admissions Traditional secondary-level entrance grade is 9. For fall 2008, 75 students applied for upper-level admission, 48 were accepted, 38 enrolled. SSAT required. Deadline for receipt of application materials: none. Application fee required: $30. Interview recommended.

Athletics Interscholastic: baseball (boys), basketball (b,g), bowling (b,g), canoeing/kayaking (b,g), cross-country running (b,g), diving (b,g); coed interscholastic: cheering, football; coed intramural: dance. 1 PE instructor, 6 coaches, 1 athletic trainer.

Computers Computers are regularly used in mathematics, science classes. Computer network features include on-campus library services, Internet access, Internet filtering or blocking technology. Students grades are available online. The school has a published electronic and media policy.

Contact Arthur Gundell, Principal. 808-949-5302. Fax: 808-947-3701.

LUTHERAN HIGH SCHOOL OF SAN DIEGO

2755 55th Street
San Diego, California 92105

Head of School: Hanne Krause

General Information Coeducational day and distance learning college-preparatory and religious studies school, affiliated with Lutheran Church. Grades 9–12. Distance learning grades 9–12. Founded: 1975. Setting: urban. 9-acre campus. 2 buildings on campus. Approved or accredited by National Lutheran School Accreditation, Western Association of Schools and Colleges, and California Department of Education. Total enrollment: 92. Upper school average class size: 12. Upper school faculty-student ratio: 1:12.

Upper School Student Profile Grade 9: 17 students (11 boys, 6 girls); Grade 10: 27 students (11 boys, 16 girls); Grade 11: 22 students (8 boys, 14 girls); Grade 12: 26 students (13 boys, 13 girls). 45% of students are Lutheran.

Faculty School total: 11. In upper school: 4 men, 7 women; 8 have advanced degrees.

Subjects Offered Accounting, acting, Advanced Placement courses, algebra, American government, American history, American literature, American literature-AP, analytic geometry, anatomy and physiology, applied arts, applied music, art, art appreciation, art history-AP, ASB Leadership, athletics, band, baseball, basketball, bell choir, Bible, biology, biology-AP, British literature, British literature-AP, calculus-AP, campus ministry, chemistry, choir, choral music, Christian education, Christian ethics, comparative religion, computer literacy, creative writing, drama, driver education, economics, English, English language and composition-AP, English language-AP, English literature and composition-AP, English literature-AP, English-AP, English/composition-AP, European history-AP, French, geometry, government, health education, history, music appreciation, physical education, physics, pre-calculus, softball, Spanish, Spanish language-AP, speech, student government, U.S. government and politics, yearbook.

Special Academic Programs Advanced Placement exam preparation.

College Admission Counseling 17 students graduated in 2008; 16 went to college, including Concordia University; Humboldt State University; San Diego State University; University of California, Santa Barbara; Vanguard University of Southern California; Whitworth University. Other: 1 entered military service.

Student Life Upper grades have student council, honor system. Discipline rests primarily with faculty.

Tuition and Aid Day student tuition: $7500. Tuition installment plan (monthly payment plans, individually arranged payment plans, Simply Giving—Thrivent Financial for Lutherans). Tuition reduction for siblings, merit scholarship grants, need-based scholarship grants available. In 2008–09, 31% of upper-school students received aid; total upper-school merit-scholarship money awarded: $8000. Total amount of financial aid awarded in 2008–09: $28,000.

Admissions Traditional secondary-level entrance grade is 9. No application fee required. On-campus interview required.

Athletics Interscholastic: baseball (boys), basketball (b,g), cheering (g), cross-country running (b,g), football (b), softball (g), volleyball (g). 1 PE instructor, 7 coaches.

Computers Computer network features include on-campus library services, Internet access. Students grades are available online.

Contact Casey Kunde, Guidance Counselor. 619-262-4444 Ext. 15. E-mail: llhssd@cox.net.

LUTHERAN HIGH SCHOOL WEST

3850 Linden Road
Rocky River, Ohio 44116-4099

Head of School: Dale Wolfgram

General Information Coeducational day college-preparatory, general academic, and religious studies school, affiliated with Lutheran Church. Grades 9–12. Founded: 1948. Setting: suburban. Nearest major city is Cleveland. 17-acre campus. 1 building on campus. Approved or accredited by North Central Association of Colleges and Schools. Endowment: $2.4 million. Total enrollment: 460. Upper school faculty-student ratio: 1:14.

Upper School Student Profile Grade 9: 119 students (56 boys, 63 girls); Grade 10: 125 students (61 boys, 64 girls); Grade 11: 99 students (48 boys, 51 girls); Grade 12: 117 students (61 boys, 56 girls). 72% of students are Lutheran.

Faculty School total: 34. In upper school: 17 men, 17 women; 18 have advanced degrees.

Subjects Offered Accounting, algebra, American history, American history-AP, American literature, art, art history, arts, Bible studies, biology, biology-AP, business, business applications, business skills, calculus, chemistry, computer programming, computer science, creative writing, drafting, economics, engineering, English, English literature, ethics, European history, expository writing, fine arts, geography, geometry, German, government/civics, grammar, health, history, home economics, industrial arts, mathematics, mechanical drawing, music, physical education, physics, religion, science, social studies, Spanish, technology, theology, trigonometry, typing, world history, world literature, writing.

Graduation Requirements Arts and fine arts (art, music, dance, drama), business skills (includes word processing), English, foreign language, mathematics, physical education (includes health), religion (includes Bible studies and theology), science, social studies (includes history).

Special Academic Programs Advanced Placement exam preparation; honors section; accelerated programs; independent study; study at local college for college credit; remedial reading and/or remedial writing; remedial math.

College Admission Counseling 113 students graduated in 2008; 110 went to college, including Bowling Green State University; Cleveland State University; Kent State University; The College of Wooster. Other: 1 went to work, 2 entered military service.

Student Life Upper grades have specified standards of dress, student council, honor system. Discipline rests primarily with faculty. Attendance at religious services is required.

Tuition and Aid Day student tuition: $8150. Tuition installment plan (FACTS Tuition Payment Plan). Tuition reduction for siblings, merit scholarship grants, need-based scholarship grants available. In 2008–09, 80% of upper-school students received aid; total upper-school merit-scholarship money awarded: $40,000. Total amount of financial aid awarded in 2008–09: $1,100,000.

Admissions Traditional secondary-level entrance grade is 9. Math and English placement tests required. Deadline for receipt of application materials: none. Application fee required: $100. On-campus interview required.

Athletics Interscholastic: baseball (boys), basketball (b,g), bowling (b), cross-country running (b,g), drill team (g), football (b), golf (b), soccer (b), softball (g), track and field (b,g), volleyball (g), wrestling (b); intramural: basketball (b,g), power lifting (b,g), softball (b,g); coed intramural: badminton, skiing (downhill), volleyball. 3 PE instructors, 26 coaches, 1 athletic trainer.

Computers Computers are regularly used in art, business studies, computer applications, desktop publishing, English, history, journalism, mathematics, multimedia, science, word processing, yearbook classes. Computer resources include on-campus library services, Internet access, wireless campus network, Internet filtering or blocking technology. The school has a published electronic and media policy.

Contact Charlotte Fecht, Recruitment Coordinator. 440-333-1660 Ext. 150. Fax: 440-333-1729. E-mail: cfecht@lutheranwest.com.

LUTHER COLLEGE HIGH SCHOOL

1500 Royal Street
Regina, Saskatchewan S4T 5A5, Canada

Head of School: Mark Anderson

General Information Coeducational boarding and day college-preparatory, general academic, arts, religious studies, International Baccalaureate, and ESL school, affiliated with Lutheran Church. Grades 9–12. Founded: 1913. Setting: urban. Nearest major city is Winnipeg, MB, Canada. Students are housed in single-sex dormitories. 27-acre campus. 5 buildings on campus. Approved or accredited by Canadian Association of Independent Schools and Saskatchewan Department of Education. Language of instruction: English. Endowment: CAN$600,000. Total enrollment: 463. Upper school average class size: 22. Upper school faculty-student ratio: 1:16.

Upper School Student Profile Grade 9: 126 students (69 boys, 57 girls); Grade 10: 113 students (47 boys, 66 girls); Grade 11: 111 students (62 boys, 49 girls); Grade 12: 113 students (53 boys, 60 girls). 24% of students are boarding students. 81% are province residents. 5 provinces are represented in upper school student body. 19% are international students. International students from China, Germany, Hong Kong, Republic of Korea, Taiwan, and Thailand; 5 other countries represented in student body. 22% of students are Lutheran.

Faculty School total: 36. In upper school: 21 men, 15 women; 5 have advanced degrees; 2 reside on campus.

Subjects Offered Art-AP, band, biology, calculus, chemistry, choir, Christian ethics, computer science, drama, English, ESL, French, German, handbells, history, information processing, International Baccalaureate courses, Latin, mathematics, music, orchestra, physical fitness, physics, psychology, science, video film production.

Graduation Requirements Christian ethics, English, mathematics, science, social studies (includes history).

Special Academic Programs International Baccalaureate program; independent study; study at local college for college credit; study abroad; academic accommodation for the gifted; ESL (19 students enrolled).

College Admission Counseling 122 students graduated in 2008; 73 went to college, including Queen's University at Kingston; University of Alberta; University of Regina; University of Saskatchewan; University of Toronto. Other: 23 went to work, 26 had other specific plans.

Student Life Upper grades have specified standards of dress, student council. Discipline rests primarily with faculty. Attendance at religious services is required.

Tuition and Aid Day student tuition: CAN$3980; 7-day tuition and room/board: CAN$11,480. Tuition installment plan (monthly payment plans, individually arranged payment plans). Tuition reduction for siblings, bursaries, merit scholarship grants, need-based scholarship grants available. In 2008–09, 20% of upper-school students received aid; total upper-school merit-scholarship money awarded: CAN$30,000. Total amount of financial aid awarded in 2008–09: CAN$165,000.

Admissions Traditional secondary-level entrance grade is 9. For fall 2008, 170 students applied for upper-level admission, 161 were accepted, 158 enrolled. Deadline for receipt of application materials: none. Application fee required: CAN$150.

Athletics Interscholastic: badminton (boys, girls), baseball (b), basketball (b,g), bicycling (b,g), cheering (g), cross-country running (b,g), curling (b,g), football (b), golf (b,g), hockey (b,g), pom squad (g), rugby (b,g), soccer (b,g), volleyball (g); intramural: basketball (b,g), floor hockey (b,g), soccer (b,g), volleyball (g); coed interscholastic: badminton, curling, track and field; coed intramural: aerobics/dance, basketball, curling, floor hockey, football, outdoor education. 4 PE instructors, 28 coaches, 2 athletic trainers.

Computers Computers are regularly used in all academic classes. Computer network features include Internet access, wireless campus network, Internet filtering or blocking technology. Student e-mail accounts and computer access in designated common areas are available to students.

Contact Mrs. Jan Schmidt, Registrar. 306-791-9154. Fax: 306-359-6962. E-mail: lutherhs@luthercollege.edu. Web site: www.luthercollege.edu.

LUTHER HIGH SCHOOL NORTH

5700 West Berteau Avenue
Chicago, Illinois 60634

Head of School: Mr. Thomas E. Wiemann

General Information Coeducational day and distance learning college-preparatory, general academic, arts, business, religious studies, and technology school, affiliated with Lutheran Church–Missouri Synod, Evangelical Lutheran Church in America; primarily serves students with learning disabilities. Grades 9–12. Distance learning grades 10–12. Founded: 1909. Setting: urban. 10-acre campus. 1 building on campus. Approved or accredited by National Lutheran School Accreditation, North Central Association of Colleges and Schools, and Illinois Department of Education. Endowment: $965,000. Total enrollment: 224. Upper school average class size: 16. Upper school faculty-student ratio: 1:16.

Upper School Student Profile Grade 9: 45 students (25 boys, 20 girls); Grade 10: 54 students (25 boys, 29 girls); Grade 11: 75 students (40 boys, 35 girls); Grade 12: 50 students (30 boys, 20 girls). 47% of students are Lutheran Church–Missouri Synod, Evangelical Lutheran Church in America.

Faculty School total: 22. In upper school: 11 men, 10 women; 14 have advanced degrees.

Subjects Offered 20th century history, 3-dimensional art, accounting, ACT preparation, advanced computer applications, algebra, American legal systems, anatomy, art, astronomy, band, biology, business, calculus, ceramics, chemistry, chorus, composition, computer science, crafts, drawing, economics, English, English-AP, fine arts, geography, geometry, German, government-AP, government/civics, health, keyboarding/computer, law, mathematics, music, painting, photography, physical education, physics, physiology, psychology, public speaking, reading, science, sewing, social science, social studies, Spanish, study skills, theology, trigonometry, U.S. history, word processing.

Graduation Requirements Arts and fine arts (art, music, dance, drama), English, foreign language, mathematics, physical education (includes health), religion (includes Bible studies and theology), science, social science, social studies (includes history), word processing, summative portfolio demonstration of faculty selected, extra and co-curricular participation annually.

Special Academic Programs Advanced Placement exam preparation; honors section; accelerated programs; independent study; study at local college for college credit; academic accommodation for the gifted, the musically talented, and the artistically talented; remedial reading and/or remedial writing; remedial math; programs in general development for dyslexic students; special instructional classes for students with learning differences.
College Admission Counseling 54 students graduated in 2008; 48 went to college, including Concordia University; DePaul University; Northeastern Illinois University; University of Illinois at Chicago; University of Illinois at Urbana–Champaign; Valparaiso University. Other: 2 went to work, 2 entered military service, 2 had other specific plans. Median composite ACT: 23. 20% scored over 26 on composite ACT.
Student Life Upper grades have specified standards of dress, student council. Discipline rests primarily with faculty. Attendance at religious services is required.
Summer Programs Remediation, enrichment, advancement, sports, computer instruction programs offered; session focuses on academics and enrichment for credit; held on campus; accepts boys and girls; open to students from other schools. 300 students usually enrolled. 2009 schedule: June 23 to July 31. Application deadline: June 23.
Tuition and Aid Day student tuition: $7100. Tuition installment plan (Insured Tuition Payment Plan, Academic Management Services Plan, monthly payment plans, individually arranged payment plans). Tuition reduction for siblings, merit scholarship grants, need-based scholarship grants, paying campus jobs available. In 2008–09, 70% of upper-school students received aid; total upper-school merit-scholarship money awarded: $30,000.
Admissions Traditional secondary-level entrance grade is 9. For fall 2008, 75 students applied for upper-level admission, 64 were accepted, 62 enrolled. Stanford Achievement Test, Otis-Lennon School Ability Test required. Deadline for receipt of application materials: none. Application fee required: $150. On-campus interview recommended.
Athletics Interscholastic: baseball (boys), basketball (b,g), cross-country running (b,g), football (b), golf (b), indoor track & field (b,g), soccer (b,g), softball (g), tennis (g), track and field (b,g), volleyball (g); intramural: cheering (g); coed interscholastic: indoor track; coed intramural: bowling. 1 PE instructor, 8 coaches, 2 athletic trainers.
Computers Computers are regularly used in all academic classes. Computer network features include on-campus library services, online commercial services, Internet access, wireless campus network, Internet filtering or blocking technology, workshops for students and parents in technology. Computer access in designated common areas is available to students. The school has a published electronic and media policy.
Contact Mr. Sam Radom, Admissions Assistant. 773-286-3600 Ext. 0. Fax: 773-286-0304. E-mail: sradom@luthernorth.org. Web site: www.luthernorth.org.

LUTHER HIGH SCHOOL SOUTH

3130 West 87th Street
Chicago, Illinois 60652

Head of School: Anthony Rainey

General Information Coeducational day college-preparatory school, affiliated with Lutheran Church–Missouri Synod. Grades 6–12. Founded: 1951. Setting: urban. 22-acre campus. 1 building on campus. Approved or accredited by National Lutheran School Accreditation, North Central Association of Colleges and Schools, and Illinois Department of Education. Upper school average class size: 17. Upper school faculty-student ratio: 1:11.
Upper School Student Profile Grade 9: 26 students (15 boys, 11 girls); Grade 10: 31 students (19 boys, 12 girls); Grade 11: 27 students (20 boys, 7 girls); Grade 12: 47 students (30 boys, 17 girls). 10% of students are Lutheran Church–Missouri Synod.
Faculty School total: 17. In upper school: 8 men, 9 women; 8 have advanced degrees.
Subjects Offered African-American history, algebra, American history, ancient history, art, arts, biology, biology-AP, business skills, careers, chemistry, chemistry-AP, composition, computer programming, earth science, ecology, economics, English, English language and composition-AP, English literature, entrepreneurship, family living, fine arts, geography, geometry, government/civics, Internet, keyboarding/computer, literature, mathematics, music, physical education, physical science, physics, pre-calculus, psychology, religion, science, social studies, Spanish, speech, trigonometry, U.S. history-AP, world history.
Graduation Requirements ACT preparation, arts and fine arts (art, music, dance, drama), computer applications, computer keyboarding, English, mathematics, physical education (includes health), religion (includes Bible studies and theology), science, social studies (includes history), theology.
Special Academic Programs Advanced Placement exam preparation; honors section; study at local college for college credit; remedial reading and/or remedial writing; remedial math.
College Admission Counseling 54 students graduated in 2008; 51 went to college, including Chicago State University; Northern Illinois University; University of Illinois; University of Illinois at Chicago. Median composite ACT: 18. 1% scored over 26 on composite ACT.
Student Life Upper grades have specified standards of dress, student council. Discipline rests primarily with faculty.
Summer Programs Remediation, enrichment, advancement, sports, computer instruction programs offered; session focuses on make-up credits for failed classes; held on campus; accepts boys and girls; open to students from other schools. 200 students usually enrolled. 2009 schedule: June 30 to August 8. Application deadline: none.
Tuition and Aid Day student tuition: $7115. Tuition installment plan (monthly payment plans, individually arranged payment plans). Tuition reduction for siblings, merit scholarship grants, need-based scholarship grants available. In 2008–09, 15% of upper-school students received aid; total upper-school merit-scholarship money awarded: $4500. Total amount of financial aid awarded in 2008–09: $13,000.
Admissions Traditional secondary-level entrance grade is 9. For fall 2008, 118 students applied for upper-level admission, 112 were accepted, 53 enrolled. ACT-Explore required. Deadline for receipt of application materials: none. Application fee required: $40.
Athletics Interscholastic: baseball (boys), basketball (b,g), cheering (g), cross-country running (b,g), football (b), indoor track & field (b,g), softball (g), track and field (b,g), volleyball (g), wrestling (b); intramural: dance (g); coed intramural: bowling. 1 PE instructor, 11 coaches.
Computers Computers are regularly used in accounting, all academic, business applications, career exploration, music, yearbook classes. Computer network features include Internet access. The school has a published electronic and media policy.
Contact Ms. Sharon Mason, Assistant Principal. 773-737-1416 Ext. 2102. Fax: 773-737-2882. E-mail: smason@luthersouth.org. Web site: www.luthersouth.org.

LYCEE CLAUDEL

1635 Promenade Riverside
Ottawa, Ontario K1G 0E5, Canada

Head of School: Mme. Joëlle Emorine

General Information Coeducational day and distance learning college-preparatory school. Grades 5–12. Distance learning grades 5–12. Founded: 1962. Setting: suburban. 2-hectare campus. 2 buildings on campus. Approved or accredited by French Ministry of Education and Ontario Department of Education. Language of instruction: French. Endowment: CAN$6 million. Total enrollment: 154. Upper school average class size: 24. Upper school faculty-student ratio: 1:15.
Upper School Student Profile Grade 10: 60 students (30 boys, 30 girls); Grade 11: 40 students (18 boys, 22 girls); Grade 12: 54 students (26 boys, 28 girls).
Faculty School total: 45. In upper school: 15 men, 30 women; 30 have advanced degrees.
Special Academic Programs International Baccalaureate program; Advanced Placement exam preparation; academic accommodation for the musically talented; ESL (50 students enrolled).
College Admission Counseling 45 students graduated in 2008; all went to college, including Carleton University; McGill University; Queen's University at Kingston; University of Ottawa; University of Toronto; Wellesley College.
Student Life Upper grades have student council, honor system. Discipline rests equally with students and faculty.
Tuition and Aid Day student tuition: CAN$6500–CAN$7000. Tuition installment plan (monthly payment plans). Bursaries available. In 2008–09, 4% of upper-school students received aid.
Admissions Traditional secondary-level entrance grade is 10. For fall 2008, 15 students applied for upper-level admission, 15 were accepted, 15 enrolled. Deadline for receipt of application materials: June 15. Application fee required: CAN$100. Interview required.
Athletics Interscholastic: badminton (boys), judo (b,g), scooter football (b,g), soccer (b,g), tennis (b), volleyball (b,g); coed intramural: badminton, basketball, handball, jogging, judo, running, scooter football, soccer, swimming and diving, table tennis, team handball, tennis, volleyball. 4 PE instructors.
Computers Computer resources include on-campus library services, online commercial services, Internet access.
Contact Mme. Jacqueline Hessel, Registrar. 613-733-8522 Ext. 606. Fax: 613-733-3782. E-mail: secretariat.lycee@claudel.org.

LYCEE FRANÇAIS DE NEW YORK

505 East 75th Street
New York, New York 10021

Head of School: Yves Thézé

General Information Coeducational day college-preparatory and bilingual studies school. Grades N–12. Founded: 1935. Setting: urban. 7-acre campus. 1 building on campus. Approved or accredited by French Ministry of Education, New York State Association of Independent Schools, and New York Department of Education. Languages of instruction: English and French. Endowment: $11 million. Total enrollment: 1,376. Upper school average class size: 15. Upper school faculty-student ratio: 1:9.
Faculty School total: 141. In upper school: 27 men, 43 women; 63 have advanced degrees.
Subjects Offered Algebra, American history, American literature, art, art history, biology, calculus, chemistry, computer science, creative writing, earth science, economics, English, English literature, English literature-AP, European history, fine arts, French, French language-AP, French literature-AP, geography, geometry, German, German-AP, government/civics, Greek, health, history, Italian, Latin,

Mandarin, mathematics, music, philosophy, physical education, physics, science, social science, social studies, Spanish, Spanish language-AP, Spanish literature-AP, trigonometry, world history, world literature, writing.
Graduation Requirements Arts and fine arts (art, music, dance, drama), computer science, English, foreign language, French, Latin, mathematics, physical education (includes health), physical fitness, science, social science, requirements for the French baccalaureate differ.
Special Academic Programs International Baccalaureate program; Advanced Placement exam preparation; honors section; accelerated programs; independent study; term-away projects; study abroad; ESL (57 students enrolled).
College Admission Counseling 93 students graduated in 2008; 92 went to college, including Babson College; Brown University; McGill University; University of Pennsylvania. Other: 1 had other specific plans. Median SAT critical reading: 580, median SAT math: 590, median SAT writing: 570, median combined SAT: 1735. 41% scored over 600 on SAT critical reading, 49% scored over 600 on SAT math, 44% scored over 600 on SAT writing, 46% scored over 1800 on combined SAT.
Student Life Upper grades have specified standards of dress, student council, honor system. Discipline rests primarily with faculty.
Tuition and Aid Day student tuition: $22,650. Tuition installment plan (Academic Management Services Plan, individually arranged payment plans). Need-based scholarship grants, French government financial assistance available. In 2008–09, 25% of upper-school students received aid.
Admissions Traditional secondary-level entrance grade is 10. Deadline for receipt of application materials: none. Application fee required: $200. On-campus interview recommended.
Athletics Interscholastic: basketball (boys, girls), gymnastics (g), soccer (b,g), tennis (b,g), volleyball (g); coed interscholastic: cross-country running, golf, running, softball, swimming and diving, track and field; coed intramural: alpine skiing, badminton, ballet, basketball, dance, fencing, fitness, gymnastics, ice skating, in-line skating, indoor soccer, judo, martial arts, modern dance, physical fitness, physical training, roller blading, rugby, skiing (downhill), snowboarding, soccer, strength & conditioning, table tennis, tennis, volleyball, weight lifting, weight training, yoga. 8 PE instructors, 5 coaches.
Computers Computers are regularly used in all academic, yearbook classes. Computer network features include on-campus library services, online commercial services, Internet access, wireless campus network, Internet filtering or blocking technology.
Contact Martine Lala, Director of Admissions. 212-439-3827. Fax: 212-439-4215. E-mail: mlala@lfny.org. Web site: www.lfny.org.

THE LYCEE INTERNATIONAL, AMERICAN SECTION

rue du Fer-a-Cheval
BP 70107
Saint-Germain-en-Laye Cedex 78101, France
Head of School: Mr. Sean Lynch

General Information Coeducational day college-preparatory and bilingual studies school. Grades PK–12. Founded: 1952. Setting: suburban. Nearest major city is Paris, France. 10-acre campus. 6 buildings on campus. Approved or accredited by European Council of International Schools, French Ministry of Education, and The College Board. Languages of instruction: English and French. Total enrollment: 689. Upper school average class size: 20. Upper school faculty-student ratio: 1:18.
Upper School Student Profile Grade 10: 65 students (42 boys, 23 girls); Grade 11: 65 students (40 boys, 25 girls); Grade 12: 59 students (33 boys, 26 girls).
Faculty School total: 20. In upper school: 5 men, 4 women; 4 have advanced degrees.
Subjects Offered Algebra, American history, American literature, art, biology, botany, calculus, chemistry, computer math, computer programming, computer science, drama, Dutch, economics, English, English literature, English-AP, European history, French, geography, geometry, German, grammar, Greek, health, history, Italian, Latin, mathematics, music, philosophy, physical education, physics, Russian, science, social science, social studies, Spanish, statistics, theater, trigonometry, world history, world literature, writing, zoology.
Graduation Requirements English, foreign language, French, mathematics, physical education (includes health), science, social science, social studies (includes history), Examination (French Baccalaureate with International Option).
Special Academic Programs Advanced Placement exam preparation; honors section.
College Admission Counseling 58 students graduated in 2008; all went to college, including Duke University; Harvard University; McGill University; Stanford University; University of Virginia; Williams College. 73.4% scored over 600 on SAT critical reading, 73.4% scored over 600 on SAT math.
Student Life Upper grades have student council. Discipline rests primarily with faculty.
Tuition and Aid Day student tuition: €1550–€6900. Tuition installment plan (monthly payment plans). Tuition reduction for siblings, need-based scholarship grants available. In 2008–09, 5% of upper-school students received aid. Total amount of financial aid awarded in 2008–09: €30,000.
Admissions Traditional secondary-level entrance grade is 10. For fall 2008, 40 students applied for upper-level admission, 18 were accepted, 18 enrolled. Admissions testing required. Deadline for receipt of application materials: none. Application fee required: $250. On-campus interview recommended.
Athletics Intramural: badminton (boys, girls), basketball (b,g), climbing (b,g), judo (b), martial arts (b), rugby (b), soccer (b,g), tennis (b,g), track and field (b,g), volleyball (b,g), wall climbing (b,g); coed intramural: swimming and diving, table tennis. 9 PE instructors.
Computers Computers are regularly used in mathematics, technology classes. Computer network features include on-campus library services, Internet access.
Contact Mrs. Mary Friel, Director of Admissions. 33-1 34 51 90 92. Fax: 33-1 30 87 00 49. E-mail: admissions@americansection.org. Web site: www.americansection.org.

LYDIA PATTERSON INSTITUTE

517 South Florence Street
El Paso, Texas 79901-2998
Head of School: Mr. Hector Lachica

General Information Coeducational day and distance learning college-preparatory, arts, religious studies, bilingual studies, and technology school, affiliated with United Methodist Church. Grades 8–12. Distance learning grade 12. Founded: 1913. Setting: urban. 1-acre campus. 5 buildings on campus. Approved or accredited by Southern Association of Colleges and Schools, University Senate of United Methodist Church, and Texas Department of Education. Language of instruction: Spanish. Endowment: $5 million. Total enrollment: 440. Upper school average class size: 21. Upper school faculty-student ratio: 1:20.
Upper School Student Profile Grade 9: 28 students (12 boys, 16 girls); Grade 10: 80 students (42 boys, 38 girls); Grade 11: 77 students (45 boys, 32 girls); Grade 12: 73 students (44 boys, 29 girls). 0.2% of students are United Methodist Church.
Faculty School total: 27. In upper school: 5 men, 5 women; 3 have advanced degrees.
Subjects Offered Computer science, economics, English, fine arts, foreign language, health, mathematics, physical education, religion, U.S. government, U.S. history, world geography, world history.
Graduation Requirements Arts and fine arts (art, music, dance, drama), computer science, economics, English, foreign language, mathematics, physical education (includes health), religion (includes Bible studies and theology), science, U.S. government, U.S. history.
Special Academic Programs International Baccalaureate program; Advanced Placement exam preparation; honors section; accelerated programs; independent study; study at local college for college credit; academic accommodation for the gifted; special instructional classes for deaf students; ESL (182 students enrolled).
College Admission Counseling 94 students graduated in 2008; 91 went to college, including El Paso Community College; MacMurray College; Simpson University; Texas Wesleyan University; The University of Texas at El Paso. Other: 1 went to work, 2 entered military service. Median SAT critical reading: 390, median SAT math: 390, median SAT writing: 380, median combined SAT: 1160.
Student Life Upper grades have uniform requirement, student council, honor system. Discipline rests equally with students and faculty. Attendance at religious services is required.
Summer Programs Remediation, advancement, ESL programs offered; session focuses on advancement; held on campus; accepts boys and girls; not open to students from other schools. 180 students usually enrolled. 2009 schedule: June 21 to August 7. Application deadline: May 29.
Tuition and Aid Day student tuition: $2430. Tuition installment plan (monthly payment plans). Need-based scholarship grants available. In 2008–09, 25% of upper-school students received aid. Total amount of financial aid awarded in 2008–09: $157,950.
Admissions English entrance exam required. Deadline for receipt of application materials: none. Application fee required: $250. On-campus interview required.
Athletics Interscholastic: basketball (boys, girls), cross-country running (b,g), dance (b), soccer (b,g), track and field (b,g), volleyball (b,g), weight lifting (b,g); intramural: baseball (b), basketball (b,g), dance (b), soccer (b,g), track and field (b,g), volleyball (b,g); coed interscholastic: dance team. 2 PE instructors, 2 coaches.
Computers Computers are regularly used in word processing, yearbook classes. Computer network features include on-campus library services, online commercial services, Internet access, wireless campus network. Campus intranet and student e-mail accounts are available to students.
Contact Mr. Hector Lachica, Vice President for Academic Affairs. 915-533-8286 Ext. 20. Fax: 915-533-5236. E-mail: lasshika@yahoo.com. Web site: www.lydiapattersoninstitute.org.

LYMAN WARD MILITARY ACADEMY

PO Box 550 P
174 Ward Circle
Camp Hill, Alabama 36850-0550
Head of School: Col. Albert W. Jenrette

General Information Boys' boarding college-preparatory and military school, affiliated with Christian faith; primarily serves underachievers. Grades 6–12. Founded: 1898. Setting: small town. Nearest major city is Birmingham. Students are housed in single-sex dormitories. 300-acre campus. 23 buildings on campus.

Approved or accredited by Southern Association of Colleges and Schools and Alabama Department of Education. Total enrollment: 95. Upper school average class size: 12. Upper school faculty-student ratio: 1:12.

Upper School Student Profile Grade 9: 15 students (15 boys); Grade 10: 17 students (17 boys); Grade 11: 18 students (18 boys); Grade 12: 10 students (10 boys). 100% of students are boarding students. 25% are state residents. 15 states are represented in upper school student body. 1% are international students. International students from Germany, Guatemala, and Mexico. 85% of students are Christian faith.

Faculty School total: 12. In upper school: 8 men, 4 women; 6 have advanced degrees; 1 resides on campus.

Subjects Offered Advanced Placement courses, algebra, band, biology, chemistry, computers, economics, English, geometry, government, health, JROTC, physical science, physiology, pre-algebra, pre-calculus, reading, Spanish, trigonometry, U.S. history, world history.

Special Academic Programs Advanced Placement exam preparation; honors section; remedial reading and/or remedial writing; remedial math.

College Admission Counseling 10 students graduated in 2008; 7 went to college, including Auburn University; Clemson University; Florida State University; North Georgia College & State University; The Citadel, The Military College of South Carolina; The University of Alabama. Other: 1 went to work, 2 entered military service. 5% scored over 600 on SAT critical reading, 5% scored over 600 on SAT math, 5% scored over 26 on composite ACT.

Student Life Upper grades have uniform requirement, student council, honor system. Discipline rests primarily with faculty. Attendance at religious services is required.

Summer Programs Remediation, enrichment, advancement, rigorous outdoor training programs offered; session focuses on leadership training through challenging exercises; held both on and off campus; held at Lake Martin, Natahalla River, and Mt.Cheaha; accepts boys; open to students from other schools. 25 students usually enrolled. 2009 schedule: June 16 to July 11. Application deadline: none.

Tuition and Aid 7-day tuition and room/board: $16,000. Tuition installment plan (monthly payment plans). Tuition reduction for siblings, merit scholarship grants, need-based scholarship grants available. In 2008–09, 10% of upper-school students received aid. Total amount of financial aid awarded in 2008–09: $50,000.

Admissions Traditional secondary-level entrance grade is 10. Star-9 required. Deadline for receipt of application materials: none. Application fee required: $250. Interview recommended.

Athletics Interscholastic: baseball, basketball, drill team, football, JROTC drill, marksmanship, riflery, soccer; intramural: aquatics, archery, basketball, billiards, canoeing/kayaking, cross-country running, drill team, fishing, fitness, football, Frisbee, hiking/backpacking, JROTC drill, life saving, marksmanship, outdoor activities, physical fitness, physical training, project adventure, rafting, rappelling, riflery, ropes courses, soccer, softball, strength & conditioning, swimming and diving, table tennis, tennis, ultimate Frisbee, volleyball. 1 PE instructor, 1 coach.

Computers Computer resources include on-campus library services, Internet access, Internet filtering or blocking technology. Student e-mail accounts are available to students. The school has a published electronic and media policy.

Contact Maj. Joe C. Watson, Assistant to the President/Admissions. 256-896-4127. Fax: 256-896-4661. E-mail: info@lwma.org. Web site: www.lwma.org.

LYNDON INSTITUTE

PO Box 127
College Road
Lyndon Center, Vermont 05850-0127

Head of School: Richard D. Hilton

General Information Coeducational boarding and day college-preparatory, general academic, arts, business, technology, and ESL school. Boarding grades 8–12, day grades 9–12. Founded: 1867. Setting: small town. Nearest major city is Burlington. Students are housed in single-sex dormitories. 150-acre campus. 27 buildings on campus. Approved or accredited by Independent Schools of Northern New England, New England Association of Schools and Colleges, The Association of Boarding Schools, and Vermont Department of Education. Endowment: $8 million. Total enrollment: 626. Upper school average class size: 16. Upper school faculty-student ratio: 1:10.

Upper School Student Profile Grade 9: 145 students (62 boys, 83 girls); Grade 10: 158 students (84 boys, 74 girls); Grade 11: 143 students (78 boys, 65 girls); Grade 12: 180 students (91 boys, 89 girls). 12% of students are boarding students. 91% are state residents. 2 states are represented in upper school student body. 9% are international students. International students from China, Japan, Kazakhstan, Mexico, Republic of Korea, and Taiwan; 2 other countries represented in student body.

Faculty School total: 68. In upper school: 36 men, 32 women; 20 have advanced degrees; 3 reside on campus.

Subjects Offered 3-dimensional art, accounting, advanced chemistry, advanced math, algebra, American literature, ancient world history, animal science, art, auto mechanics, auto shop, band, Basic programming, biology, bookmaking, business, business education, business mathematics, business technology, calculus, chemistry, chemistry-AP, chorus, college counseling, computer applications, computer graphics, computer information systems, computer keyboarding, computer science, computer skills, computer technologies, computer-aided design, concert band, consumer economics, creative writing, desktop publishing, drafting, drawing, driver education, economics, English, English language and composition-AP, English literature, entrepreneurship, environmental science, European history, family and consumer science, fashion, fine arts, French, general math, geography, geometry, graphic design, health, history, honors algebra, honors English, honors U.S. history, honors world history, industrial arts, information processing, information technology, instrumental music, jazz ensemble, keyboarding/computer, Latin, literary magazine, mathematics, metalworking, music, music theory, philosophy, photography, physical education, physics, printmaking, science, social studies, Spanish, street law, studio art, studio art-AP, theater, theater arts, trigonometry, U.S. history, woodworking, word processing, world culture, world history, writing.

Graduation Requirements Arts and fine arts (art, music, dance, drama), electives, English, health education, mathematics, physical education (includes health), science, social studies (includes history), U.S. history.

Special Academic Programs Advanced Placement exam preparation; honors section; independent study; study at local college for college credit; remedial reading and/or remedial writing; remedial math; ESL (50 students enrolled).

College Admission Counseling 130 students graduated in 2007; 91 went to college, including Boston University; Norwich University; University of Vermont. Other: 33 went to work, 6 entered military service.

Student Life Upper grades have specified standards of dress, student council. Discipline rests primarily with faculty.

Tuition and Aid Day student tuition: $11,880; 5-day tuition and room/board: $21,150; 7-day tuition and room/board: $29,600. Tuition installment plan (monthly payment plans, individually arranged payment plans). Need-based scholarship grants, prepGATE Loans available. In 2007–08, 2% of upper-school students received aid. Total amount of financial aid awarded in 2007–08: $14,150.

Admissions Traditional secondary-level entrance grade is 9. SSAT, ERB, PSAT, SAT, PLAN or ACT or TOEFL or SLEP required. Deadline for receipt of application materials: March 31. Application fee required: $50. Interview recommended.

Athletics Interscholastic: alpine skiing (boys, girls), baseball (b), basketball (b,g), cross-country running (b,g), field hockey (g), golf (b,g), ice hockey (b), nordic skiing (b,g), running (b,g), skiing (cross-country) (b,g), skiing (downhill) (b,g), soccer (b,g), softball (g), track and field (b,g); intramural: ballet (g), dance (b,g), volleyball (b,g); coed interscholastic: cheering, football, ice hockey, outdoor activities; coed intramural: aerobics/dance, dance, dance team, fitness walking, marksmanship, modern dance, riflery, weight lifting. 2 PE instructors, 26 coaches, 2 athletic trainers.

Computers Computers are regularly used in architecture, business, business applications, business education, business skills, desktop publishing, drafting, engineering, graphic design, information technology, keyboarding, literary magazine, publishing, SAT preparation, science, technical drawing, technology, word processing, yearbook classes. Computer resources include on-campus library services, Internet access, Internet filtering or blocking technology, Big Chalk eLibrary, Vermont Online Library, NewsBank. Student e-mail accounts and computer access in designated common areas are available to students. The school has a published electronic and media policy.

Contact Mary B. Thomas, Assistant Head for Admissions. 802-626-5232. Fax: 802-626-6138. E-mail: mary.thomas@lyndoninstitute.org. Web site: www.LyndonInstitute.org.

See Close-Up on page 828.

MA'AYANOT YESHIVA HIGH SCHOOL FOR GIRLS OF BERGAN COUNTY

1650 Palisade Avenue
Teaneck, New Jersey 07666

Head of School: Mrs. Rookie Billet

General Information Girls' day college-preparatory and religious studies school, affiliated with Jewish faith. Grades 9–12. Founded: 1995. Setting: suburban. 1 building on campus. Approved or accredited by Middle States Association of Colleges and Schools and New Jersey Department of Education. Total enrollment: 246. Upper school average class size: 18. Upper school faculty-student ratio: 1:5.

Upper School Student Profile Grade 9: 55 students (55 girls); Grade 10: 69 students (69 girls); Grade 11: 54 students (54 girls); Grade 12: 68 students (68 girls). 100% of students are Jewish.

Faculty School total: 53. In upper school: 8 men, 45 women.

Subjects Offered 20th century world history, advanced biology, advanced chemistry, advanced math, Advanced Placement courses, algebra, American culture, American government, American literature, American sign language, Bible, Bible studies, biology, biology-AP, calculus, calculus-AP, chemistry, chemistry-AP, college writing, computer programming, computer skills, creative writing, desktop publishing, geometry, health education, Hebrew, Hebrew scripture, history, honors English, Jewish history, Jewish studies, Judaic studies, lab science, language and composition, literature, model United Nations, physical education, physics, pre-calculus, psychology-AP, senior internship, Spanish, speech, statistics-AP, Talmud, the Sixties, U.S. government, world history.

Graduation Requirements Algebra, art, biology, chemistry, English, geometry, Hebrew, history, physical education (includes health), physics, technology.

Special Academic Programs Advanced Placement exam preparation.

College Admission Counseling 32 students graduated in 2008; all went to college, including Queens College of the City University of New York; Rutgers, The State University of New Jersey, New Brunswick; Yeshiva University.

Student Life Upper grades have specified standards of dress, student council. Discipline rests primarily with faculty. Attendance at religious services is required.
Admissions Traditional secondary-level entrance grade is 9. For fall 2008, 100 students applied for upper-level admission, 80 were accepted, 55 enrolled. Board of Jewish Education Entrance Exam required. Deadline for receipt of application materials: none. No application fee required. Interview required.
Athletics Interscholastic: basketball, indoor soccer, softball, swimming and diving, track and field, volleyball. 2 PE instructors, 1 coach.
Computers Computers are regularly used in all academic classes. Computer resources include on-campus library services, Internet access, wireless campus network, Internet filtering or blocking technology. Student e-mail accounts and computer access in designated common areas are available to students.
Contact Mrs. Evelyn Gross, Assistant Principal Director of Admissions. 201-833-4307 Ext. 217. Fax: 201-833-0816. E-mail: egross@maayanot.org.

THE MACDUFFIE SCHOOL

1 Ames Hill Drive
Springfield, Massachusetts 01105
Head of School: Kathryn P. Gibson

General Information Coeducational boarding and day college-preparatory, arts, and technology school. Boarding grades 9–12, day grades 6–12. Founded: 1890. Setting: urban. Students are housed in single-sex dormitories. 14-acre campus. 15 buildings on campus. Approved or accredited by Association of Independent Schools in New England, New England Association of Schools and Colleges, The Association of Boarding Schools, and Massachusetts Department of Education. Member of National Association of Independent Schools and Secondary School Admission Test Board. Total enrollment: 232. Upper school average class size: 11. Upper school faculty-student ratio: 1:7.
Upper School Student Profile Grade 9: 40 students (30 boys, 10 girls); Grade 10: 43 students (23 boys, 20 girls); Grade 11: 52 students (28 boys, 24 girls); Grade 12: 51 students (27 boys, 24 girls). 24% of students are boarding students. 80% are state residents. 3 states are represented in upper school student body. 20% are international students. International students from China, Hong Kong, Jamaica, Republic of Korea, Switzerland, and Taiwan; 7 other countries represented in student body.
Faculty School total: 36. In upper school: 15 men, 21 women; 28 have advanced degrees; 4 reside on campus.
Subjects Offered Acting, Advanced Placement courses, African-American history, algebra, American literature, architecture, art, astronomy, biology, British literature, calculus, calculus-AP, chemistry, choreography, computer programming, conceptual physics, creative writing, dance, earth science, East European studies, English, English-AP, environmental science, ESL, European history, film studies, French, geometry, global studies, graphic design, health, journalism, Latin, modern dance, modern European history, modern European history-AP, music, painting, peace studies, physical education, physics, physiology, portfolio art, pre-calculus, psychology, SAT/ACT preparation, sculpture, Spanish, theater, U.S. history, U.S. history-AP, visual arts, Web site design, Western philosophy, women in literature, world literature, yearbook.
Graduation Requirements Algebra, arts and fine arts (art, music, dance, drama), English, foreign language, geometry, history, mathematics, physical education (includes health), science.
Special Academic Programs Advanced Placement exam preparation; honors section; independent study; study at local college for college credit; academic accommodation for the gifted; ESL (24 students enrolled).
College Admission Counseling 50 students graduated in 2007; 49 went to college, including Boston University; Fordham University; Georgetown University; Holy Cross College; Simmons College; Syracuse University. Other: 1 had other specific plans.
Student Life Upper grades have specified standards of dress, student council, honor system. Discipline rests primarily with faculty.
Tuition and Aid Day student tuition: $19,950; 7-day tuition and room/board: $34,600. Tuition installment plan (Academic Management Services Plan, monthly payment plans, individually arranged payment plans). Merit scholarship grants, need-based scholarship grants, tuition remission for children of faculty available. In 2007–08, 42% of upper-school students received aid; total upper-school merit-scholarship money awarded: $6000. Total amount of financial aid awarded in 2007–08: $500,000.
Admissions Traditional secondary-level entrance grade is 9. For fall 2007, 95 students applied for upper-level admission, 60 were accepted, 45 enrolled. SSAT or TOEFL or SLEP required. Deadline for receipt of application materials: none. Application fee required: $50. Interview required.
Athletics Interscholastic: baseball (boys), basketball (b,g), cross-country running (b,g), field hockey (g), lacrosse (g), soccer (b), softball (g), tennis (b,g), volleyball (g); coed interscholastic: ballet, soccer; coed intramural: aerobics/dance, badminton, ballet, blading, cooperative games, cricket, dance, fitness, fitness walking, flag football, football, Frisbee, handball, in-line skating, jogging, modern dance, physical fitness, pillo polo. 2 PE instructors, 10 coaches, 2 athletic trainers.
Computers Computers are regularly used in all academic, yearbook classes. Computer network features include on-campus library services, Internet access, campus computer labs. The school has a published electronic and media policy.
Contact Ms. Linda Keating, Director of Admissions. 413-734-4971 Ext. 140. Fax: 413-734-6693. E-mail: lkeating@macduffie.com. Web site: www.macduffie.com.

See Close-Up on page 830.

MACLACHLAN COLLEGE

337 Trafalgar Road
Oakville, Ontario L6J 3H3, Canada
Head of School: Ms. Diane Finlay

General Information Coeducational day college-preparatory, arts, business, and technology school. Grades PK–12. Founded: 1978. Setting: suburban. Nearest major city is Toronto, Canada. 2-acre campus. 1 building on campus. Approved or accredited by Canadian Association of Independent Schools, Canadian Educational Standards Institute, Ontario Ministry of Education, and Ontario Department of Education. Language of instruction: English. Total enrollment: 344. Upper school average class size: 18. Upper school faculty-student ratio: 1:10.
Upper School Student Profile Grade 9: 28 students (17 boys, 11 girls); Grade 10: 36 students (21 boys, 15 girls); Grade 11: 37 students (21 boys, 16 girls); Grade 12: 32 students (23 boys, 9 girls).
Faculty School total: 40. In upper school: 5 men, 17 women; 7 have advanced degrees.
Subjects Offered 20th century history, accounting, algebra, band, business, business law, business mathematics, calculus, Canadian geography, Canadian history, Canadian law, Canadian literature, career education, chemistry, civics, computer multimedia, computer programming, computer science, drama, economics, English, environmental science, ESL, finite math, French, geography, geometry, health, history, law, marketing, mathematics, multimedia, physical education, physics, science, society challenge and change, TOEFL preparation, visual arts.
Graduation Requirements Arts, careers, civics, English, French, geography, history, mathematics, physical education (includes health), science, pass the grade 10 Ontario Literacy test, 40 hours of community service.
Special Academic Programs Advanced Placement exam preparation; accelerated programs; independent study; ESL (30 students enrolled).
College Admission Counseling 36 students graduated in 2008; they went to Carleton University; Ryerson University; The University of Western Ontario; University of Toronto; University of Waterloo; York University. Other: 36 entered a postgraduate year.
Student Life Upper grades have uniform requirement, student council, honor system. Discipline rests primarily with faculty.
Summer Programs Remediation, ESL programs offered; session focuses on ESL and upgrading; held on campus; accepts boys and girls; open to students from other schools. 25 students usually enrolled. 2009 schedule: July 2 to August 2. Application deadline: June 30.
Tuition and Aid Day student tuition: CAN$17,200. Tuition installment plan (monthly payment plans). Tuition reduction for siblings, bursaries available. In 2008–09, 1% of upper-school students received aid. Total amount of financial aid awarded in 2008–09: CAN$9000.
Admissions Traditional secondary-level entrance grade is 11. Academic Profile Tests and SSAT required. Deadline for receipt of application materials: none. Application fee required: CAN$250. Interview required.
Athletics Interscholastic: aerobics (boys), wrestling (b); intramural: ball hockey (b), baseball (b,g), basketball (b,g), flag football (b,g), floor hockey (b,g), soccer (b,g), softball (b,g), touch football (b,g), ultimate Frisbee (b,g), volleyball (b,g), wilderness survival (b,g); coed interscholastic: aerobics, archery, backpacking, badminton, ball hockey, baseball, basketball, bowling, canoeing/kayaking, cooperative games, cricket, cross-country running, curling, field hockey, fitness, fitness walking, flag football, flagball, floor hockey, football, golf, gymnastics, hiking/backpacking, ice skating, lacrosse, outdoor activities, outdoor adventure, outdoor education, physical fitness, racquetball, running, soccer, softball, touch football, ultimate Frisbee, volleyball, wilderness survival; coed intramural: football, hiking/backpacking, independent competitive sports. 2 PE instructors.
Computers Computers are regularly used in accounting, art, basic skills, business, business applications, business education, business studies, career education, career exploration, career technology, commercial art, computer applications, creative writing, data processing, design, desktop publishing, digital applications, economics, English, ESL, French, geography, graphic arts, health, history, humanities, information technology, library, mathematics, media arts, multimedia, music, programming, reading, research skills, science, theology, Web site design, wilderness education, writing, writing, yearbook classes. Computer network features include on-campus library services, Internet access, wireless campus network, Internet filtering or blocking technology. Campus intranet, student e-mail accounts, and computer access in designated common areas are available to students. The school has a published electronic and media policy.
Contact Ms. Nancy Norcross, Director of Admissions. 905-844-0372 Ext. 235. Fax: 905-844-9369. E-mail: nnorcross@maclachlan.ca. Web site: www.maclachlan.ca.

MADISON ACADEMY

325 Slaughter Road
Madison, Alabama 35758
Head of School: Dr. Robert F. Burton

General Information Coeducational day college-preparatory and religious studies school, affiliated with Church of Christ. Grades PS–12. Founded: 1955. Setting: suburban. Nearest major city is Huntsville. 160-acre campus. 5 buildings on campus. Approved or accredited by Southern Association of Colleges and Schools. Endowment: $800,000. Total enrollment: 800. Upper school average class size: 20. Upper school faculty-student ratio: 1:15.

Upper School Student Profile 35% of students are members of Church of Christ.

Faculty School total: 70. In upper school: 14 men, 20 women; 14 have advanced degrees.

Subjects Offered Accounting, advanced math, Alabama history and geography, algebra, American literature, anatomy, art, art history, arts, band, Bible studies, biology, calculus, calculus-AP, chemistry, choral music, chorus, Christian education, Christian ethics, Christian scripture, Christian studies, church history, community service, computer science, concert choir, consumer mathematics, creative writing, drama, earth science, economics, English, English literature, English/composition-AP, environmental science, European history, expository writing, French, general math, geography, geology, geometry, government/civics, health, human anatomy, journalism, keyboarding/computer, music, photography, physical education, physical science, physics, physics-AP, physiology, pre-algebra, religion, Spanish, speech, studio art, trigonometry, U.S. government, U.S. government and politics, U.S. history, world geography, world history, world literature.

Graduation Requirements English, foreign language, mathematics, religion (includes Bible studies and theology), science, social science.

Special Academic Programs Honors section; accelerated programs; study at local college for college credit.

College Admission Counseling 70 students graduated in 2008; 69 went to college, including Abilene Christian University; Auburn University; Freed-Hardeman University; Lipscomb University; The University of Alabama. Other: 1 entered military service. Mean composite ACT: 23.

Student Life Upper grades have uniform requirement, student council, honor system. Discipline rests primarily with faculty. Attendance at religious services is required.

Tuition and Aid Day student tuition: $4450. Tuition installment plan (monthly payment plans). Tuition reduction for siblings, need-based scholarship grants available. In 2008–09, 10% of upper-school students received aid. Total amount of financial aid awarded in 2008–09: $100,000.

Admissions Traditional secondary-level entrance grade is 9. For fall 2008, 100 students applied for upper-level admission, 50 were accepted, 41 enrolled. Stanford Achievement Test required. Deadline for receipt of application materials: none. Application fee required: $200. On-campus interview required.

Athletics Interscholastic: baseball (boys), basketball (b,g), cheering (g), football (b), golf (b), softball (g), volleyball (g). 3 PE instructors, 36 coaches, 1 athletic trainer.

Computers Computers are regularly used in art, foreign language, science classes. Computer network features include on-campus library services, Internet access.

Contact Dr. Michael Weimer, High School Principal. 256-971-1624. Fax: 256-971-1436. E-mail: mweimer@macademy.org. Web site: www.macademy.org.

MADISON-RIDGELAND ACADEMY

7601 Old Canton Road
Madison, Mississippi 39110
Head of School: Mr. Tommy Thompson

General Information Coeducational day college-preparatory school. Grades 1–12. Founded: 1969. Setting: suburban. Nearest major city is Jackson. 25-acre campus. 6 buildings on campus. Approved or accredited by Mississippi Private School Association, Southern Association of Colleges and Schools, and Mississippi Department of Education. Endowment: $1 million. Total enrollment: 953. Upper school average class size: 20. Upper school faculty-student ratio: 1:13.

Upper School Student Profile Grade 9: 61 students (30 boys, 31 girls); Grade 10: 64 students (30 boys, 34 girls); Grade 11: 66 students (34 boys, 32 girls); Grade 12: 53 students (26 boys, 27 girls).

Faculty School total: 64. In upper school: 14 men, 23 women; 14 have advanced degrees.

Subjects Offered Accounting, algebra, American government, American government-AP, American history, American history-AP, anatomy and physiology, art, Bible, biology, biology-AP, chemistry, chemistry-AP, chorus, civics, communications, computer applications, computer programming, creative writing, debate, drama, driver education, economics, English, European history-AP, forensics, French, French-AP, geography, geometry, global studies, government, graphic arts, health, journalism, keyboarding, music, newspaper, physical fitness, physics, physics-AP, pre-calculus, probability and statistics, psychology, sociology, Spanish, Spanish-AP, speech, trigonometry, Web site design, world history, yearbook.

Graduation Requirements ACT preparation, advanced math, algebra, American government, biology, chemistry, civics, computer applications, computer keyboarding, economics, electives, English, foreign language, geometry, health, science, social studies (includes history).

Special Academic Programs Advanced Placement exam preparation; honors section; study at local college for college credit; academic accommodation for the gifted.

College Admission Counseling 49 students graduated in 2008; all went to college, including Belhaven College; Millsaps College; Mississippi College; Mississippi State University; University of Mississippi; University of Southern Mississippi. Median SAT critical reading: 705, median SAT math: 620, median composite ACT: 24. 100% scored over 600 on SAT critical reading, 100% scored over 600 on SAT math, 25% scored over 26 on composite ACT.

Student Life Upper grades have specified standards of dress, student council. Discipline rests primarily with faculty. Attendance at religious services is required.

Summer Programs Enrichment, sports programs offered; held on campus; accepts boys and girls; open to students from other schools. 300 students usually enrolled. 2009 schedule: June 1 to July 30. Application deadline: May 15.

Tuition and Aid Day student tuition: $6780. Tuition installment plan (monthly payment plans, semiannual payment plan). Tuition reduction for siblings, merit scholarship grants, need-based scholarship grants available. In 2008–09, 2% of upper-school students received aid; total upper-school merit-scholarship money awarded: $12,000. Total amount of financial aid awarded in 2008–09: $123,000.

Admissions Traditional secondary-level entrance grade is 9. For fall 2008, 60 students applied for upper-level admission, 54 were accepted, 38 enrolled. Admissions testing, BASIS or Otis-Lennon Ability or Stanford Achievement Test required. Deadline for receipt of application materials: none. Application fee required: $35. On-campus interview required.

Athletics Interscholastic: aquatics (boys, girls), baseball (b), basketball (b,g), cheering (g), cross-country running (b,g), dance team (b,g), football (b), golf (b), soccer (b,g), softball (g), strength & conditioning (b,g), tennis (b,g), track and field (b,g); coed interscholastic: aquatics, golf, tennis. 4 PE instructors, 12 coaches, 1 athletic trainer.

Computers Computers are regularly used in accounting, art, journalism, media, media services, Web site design classes. Computer network features include on-campus library services, Internet access, Internet filtering or blocking technology. Students grades are available online. The school has a published electronic and media policy.

Contact Mrs. Tammy Synder, Registrar. 601-856-4455. Fax: 601-853-3835. Web site: www.mrapats.com.

MAGNIFICAT HIGH SCHOOL

20770 Hilliard Road
Rocky River, Ohio 44116
Head of School: Sr. Mary Pat Cook, HM

General Information Girls' day college-preparatory school, affiliated with Roman Catholic Church. Grades 9–12. Founded: 1955. Setting: suburban. Nearest major city is Cleveland. 20-acre campus. 1 building on campus. Approved or accredited by North Central Association of Colleges and Schools, Ohio Catholic Schools Accreditation Association (OCSAA), and Ohio Department of Education. Total enrollment: 830. Upper school average class size: 22. Upper school faculty-student ratio: 1:12.

Upper School Student Profile Grade 9: 207 students (207 girls); Grade 10: 217 students (217 girls); Grade 11: 204 students (204 girls); Grade 12: 202 students (202 girls). 92% of students are Roman Catholic.

Faculty School total: 67. In upper school: 4 men, 63 women; 48 have advanced degrees.

Subjects Offered Accounting, algebra, American literature, art, art history, art history-AP, arts, band, biology, biology-AP, British literature, business, business technology, calculus-AP, chemistry, chemistry-AP, choir, chorus, clayworking, comparative religion, computer applications, computer science-AP, CPR, dance, design, drama, drawing, earth science, economics, economics-AP, electives, English, film and literature, first aid, French, French-AP, geometry, government, health, keyboarding/computer, life issues, mathematics, metalworking, modern languages, music, oral communications, orchestra, painting, photography, physical education, physics, pre-calculus, programming, psychology, science, social studies, sociology, Spanish, Spanish-AP, statistics, statistics and probability, statistics-AP, theology, trigonometry, U.S. history, U.S. history-AP, Web site design, world history, world literature, writing.

Graduation Requirements Art appreciation, electives, English, health education, keyboarding, mathematics, modern languages, physical education (includes health), social studies (includes history), theology, word processing, Service requirements and Senior Genesis Project.

Special Academic Programs 12 Advanced Placement exams for which test preparation is offered.

College Admission Counseling 236 students graduated in 2008; 234 went to college, including John Carroll University; Loyola University Chicago; The Ohio State University; University of Dayton; University of Notre Dame; Xavier University. Mean SAT critical reading: 541, mean SAT math: 540, mean SAT writing: 549, mean composite ACT: 25.

Student Life Upper grades have uniform requirement, student council. Attendance at religious services is required.

Tuition and Aid Day student tuition: $9200. Tuition installment plan (SMART Tuition Payment Plan). Need-based scholarship grants available. In 2008–09, 40% of upper-school students received aid. Total amount of financial aid awarded in 2008–09: $800,000.

Admissions Traditional secondary-level entrance grade is 9. High School Placement Test (closed version) from Scholastic Testing Service required. Deadline for receipt of application materials: January 30. No application fee required.

Athletics Interscholastic: basketball, cross-country running, dance team, diving, field hockey, golf, gymnastics, lacrosse, soccer, softball, swimming and diving, tennis, track and field, volleyball. 3 PE instructors, 50 coaches, 1 athletic trainer.

Computers Computers are regularly used in all academic classes. Computer network features include on-campus library services, Internet access. Students grades are available online. The school has a published electronic and media policy.

Contact Mrs. Maggie Gibbons Gedeon, Admissions Officer. 440-331-1572 Ext. 248. Fax: 440-331-7257. E-mail: mgedeon@magnificaths.org. Web site: www.magnificaths.org.

MAHARISHI ACADEMY OF TOTAL KNOWLEDGE

100 Old North Branch Road
Antrim, New Hampshire 03440

Head of School: Mr. Alan Colby

General Information Boys' boarding and day college-preparatory, the Transcendental Meditation® program, and sustainable living curriculum, outdoor adventure education school. Grades 9–12. Setting: rural. Nearest major city is Boston, MA. Students are housed in single-sex dormitories. 450-acre campus. 6 buildings on campus. Approved or accredited by New Hampshire Department of Education. Upper school average class size: 10.

Subjects Offered Algebra, American government, American history, American literature, art, athletics, biology, British literature, calculus, computer science, drama, ecology, English, film, filmmaking, geometry, health, integrated mathematics, music, outdoor education, physical education, physics, physiology, pre-calculus, research in consciousness, Sanskrit, senior thesis, social studies, state history, survival training, trigonometry, U.S. history, wilderness/outdoor program, world history, writing.

Special Academic Programs Honors section.

Student Life Upper grades have uniform requirement, student council, honor system. Discipline rests equally with students and faculty.

Tuition and Aid Day student tuition: $25,000; 7-day tuition and room/board: $38,250. Tuition installment plan (individually arranged payment plans).

Admissions SSAT required. Deadline for receipt of application materials: none. Application fee required: $30. Interview required.

Athletics Intramural: alpine skiing, basketball, bicycling, canoeing/kayaking, climbing, cooperative games, Frisbee, hiking/backpacking, nordic skiing, outdoor activities, outdoor adventure, paddling, rock climbing, skiing (cross-country), skiing (downhill), snowboarding, snowshoeing, soccer, swimming and diving, tennis, volleyball, walking, weight lifting, weight training, wilderness, wilderness survival, wildernessways.

Computers Computers are regularly used in all classes. Computer network features include online commercial services, Internet access, Internet filtering or blocking technology. Campus intranet and computer access in designated common areas are available to students. The school has a published electronic and media policy.

Contact Mr. Greg Monokian, Admissions Director. 603-588-0400. Fax: 603-588-4249. E-mail: Admissions@MaharishiAcademy.org. Web site: www.maharishiacademy.org.

MAHARISHI SCHOOL OF THE AGE OF ENLIGHTENMENT

804 Dr. Robert Keith Wallace Drive
Fairfield, Iowa 52556-2200

Head of School: Dr. Richard Beall

General Information Coeducational day college-preparatory, Science of Creative Intelligence: Study of Natural Law, and Transcendental Meditation: Research in Consciousness school. Grades PS–12. Founded: 1972. Setting: small town. Nearest major city is Iowa City. 10-acre campus. 5 buildings on campus. Approved or accredited by Independent Schools Association of the Central States and Iowa Department of Education. Member of National Association of Independent Schools. Total enrollment: 204. Upper school average class size: 11. Upper school faculty-student ratio: 1:10.

Upper School Student Profile Grade 10: 22 students (10 boys, 12 girls); Grade 11: 20 students (8 boys, 12 girls); Grade 12: 20 students (10 boys, 10 girls).

Faculty School total: 50. In upper school: 16 men, 11 women; 12 have advanced degrees.

Subjects Offered Algebra, American government, American history, American literature, art, art history, basketball, British literature, chemistry, desktop publishing, discrete math, drama performance, economics, English, geology, geometry, integrated mathematics, music performance, personal growth, photography, physical education, physics, physiology, pre-calculus, Sanskrit, science project, senior thesis, track and field, Vedic science, volleyball, world history, world literature, writing, yoga.

Graduation Requirements Economics, electives, English, foreign language, mathematics, physical education (includes health), science, senior thesis, social studies (includes history), Science of Creative Intelligence course, Student Etiquette.

Special Academic Programs Honors section; academic accommodation for the gifted, the musically talented, and the artistically talented; remedial reading and/or remedial writing; remedial math.

College Admission Counseling 29 students graduated in 2008; all went to college, including Emerson College; Maharishi University of Management; New York University; The University of Iowa; University of San Francisco; University of Vermont. Median SAT critical reading: 640, median SAT math: 535, median SAT writing: 540, median combined SAT: 1745, median composite ACT: 23. 56% scored over 600 on SAT critical reading, 44% scored over 600 on SAT math, 39% scored over 600 on SAT writing, 33% scored over 1800 on combined SAT, 25% scored over 26 on composite ACT.

Student Life Upper grades have uniform requirement, student council. Discipline rests primarily with faculty.

Summer Programs Enrichment, sports programs offered; session focuses on interscholastic sports; held on campus; accepts boys and girls. 40 students usually enrolled. 2009 schedule: June 15 to August 15. Application deadline: June 12.

Tuition and Aid Day student tuition: $13,900. Tuition installment plan (two semester payments). Tuition reduction for siblings, need-based scholarship grants available. In 2008–09, 69% of upper-school students received aid. Total amount of financial aid awarded in 2008–09: $535,923.

Admissions Traditional secondary-level entrance grade is 10. For fall 2008, 5 students applied for upper-level admission, 5 were accepted, 5 enrolled. Deadline for receipt of application materials: none. No application fee required. On-campus interview required.

Athletics Interscholastic: basketball (boys, girls), cross-country running (b,g), golf (b), soccer (b), tennis (b,g), track and field (b,g), volleyball (g); intramural: aerobics (b,g), aerobics/dance (g), basketball (b,g), bicycling (b,g), canoeing/kayaking (b,g), cheering (g), field hockey (b,g), fitness (b,g), flag football (b,g), Frisbee (b,g), gymnastics (g), hiking/backpacking (b,g), indoor soccer (b), indoor track (b,g), indoor track & field (b,g), kickball (b,g), outdoor activities (b,g), physical fitness (b,g), physical training (b,g), rock climbing (b), strength & conditioning (b,g), table tennis (b,g), team handball (b,g), tennis (b,g), track and field (b,g), volleyball (b,g), weight training (b,g), yoga (b,g). 4 PE instructors, 9 coaches.

Computers Computers are regularly used in creative writing, desktop publishing, economics, English, geography, independent study, library skills, mathematics, science, senior seminar, social sciences, social studies, writing classes. Computer network features include Internet access, Internet filtering or blocking technology. Campus intranet and computer access in designated common areas are available to students. Students grades are available online. The school has a published electronic and media policy.

Contact Ms. Tere Cutler, Director of Admissions. 641-472-9400 Ext. 5064. Fax: 641-472-1211. E-mail: tcutler@msae.edu. Web site: www.maharishischooliowa.org.

MAINE CENTRAL INSTITUTE

295 Main Street
Pittsfield, Maine 04967

Head of School: Christopher Hopkins

General Information Coeducational boarding and day college-preparatory, general academic, arts, vocational, bilingual studies, technology, humanities, and mathematics, the sciences school. Grades 9–PG. Founded: 1866. Setting: small town. Nearest major city is Portland. Students are housed in single-sex dormitories. 23-acre campus. 16 buildings on campus. Approved or accredited by Independent Schools of Northern New England, New England Association of Schools and Colleges, The Association of Boarding Schools, The Hawaii Council of Private Schools, and Maine Department of Education. Member of National Association of Independent Schools and Secondary School Admission Test Board. Endowment: $4 million. Total enrollment: 485. Upper school average class size: 15. Upper school faculty-student ratio: 1:15.

Upper School Student Profile 71% are state residents. 6 states are represented in upper school student body. 85% are international students.

Faculty School total: 41. In upper school: 20 men, 21 women; 14 have advanced degrees; 26 reside on campus.

Subjects Offered Algebra, American history, American literature, anatomy, art, art-AP, Asian studies, astronomy, audio visual/media, ballet, biology, botany, calculus, calculus-AP, career exploration, chemistry, chemistry-AP, child development, civil rights, computer science, concert band, concert choir, contemporary issues, creative writing, drafting, drama, earth science, ecology, economics, electronic publishing, English, English literature, environmental science, ESL, ethics, fine arts, French, geology, geometry, government/civics, health, history, humanities, integrated science, jazz band, jazz dance, jazz ensemble, Latin, life management skills, literature-AP, mathematics, meteorology, music, music appreciation, music composition, music theory, personal finance, philosophy, photography, physical education, physics, physics-AP, piano, psychology, reading/study skills, SAT preparation, science, social science, social studies, sociology, Spanish, statistics, theater, trigonometry, video film production, Web site design, world history.

Graduation Requirements Arts and fine arts (art, music, dance, drama), computer skills, English, mathematics, physical education (includes health), science, senior project, social studies (includes history), Manson Essay.

Special Academic Programs Advanced Placement exam preparation; honors section; accelerated programs; independent study; study at local college for college credit; study abroad; academic accommodation for the musically talented; remedial reading and/or remedial writing; remedial math; programs in English, mathematics, general development for dyslexic students; ESL.

College Admission Counseling 120 students graduated in 2008; 90 went to college, including Husson College; Maine Maritime Academy; University of Maine; University of Maine at Farmington; University of Southern Maine. Other: 20 went to work, 3 entered military service, 1 entered a postgraduate year, 6 had other specific plans. Median SAT critical reading: 428, median SAT math: 444, median SAT writing: 442, median combined SAT: 1314.

Student Life Upper grades have specified standards of dress, student council, honor system. Discipline rests primarily with faculty.

Tuition and Aid Day student tuition: $10,000; 7-day tuition and room/board: $35,500. Tuition installment plan (Key Tuition Payment Plan, SMART Tuition Payment Plan, school's own payment plan). Merit scholarship grants, need-based scholarship grants available. In 2008–09, 25% of upper-school students received aid; total upper-school merit-scholarship money awarded: $24,430. Total amount of financial aid awarded in 2008–09: $1,036,339.

Admissions Traditional secondary-level entrance grade is 9. For fall 2008, 275 students applied for upper-level admission, 177 were accepted, 139 enrolled. Deadline for receipt of application materials: none. Application fee required: $50. Interview recommended.

Athletics Interscholastic: baseball (boys), basketball (b,g), field hockey (g), football (b), riflery (b,g); intramural: football (b); coed interscholastic: aerobics/dance, ballet, cheering, cross-country running, dance, fencing, golf, modern dance, physical training; coed intramural: alpine skiing, billiards, canoeing/kayaking, climbing, cooperative games, fencing, fishing, flagball, floor hockey, handball, outdoor activities, rafting. 1 PE instructor, 30 coaches, 1 athletic trainer.

Computers Computer network features include on-campus library services, Internet access, Internet filtering or blocking technology.

Contact Mr. Clint M. Williams, Director of Admission. 207-487-2282 Ext. 128. Fax: 207-487-3512. E-mail: cwilliams@mci-school.org. Web site: www.mci-school.org.

See Close-Up on page 832.

MAINE SCHOOL OF SCIENCE AND MATHEMATICS

95 High Street
Limestone, Maine 04750

Head of School: Mr. Walter J. Warner

General Information Coeducational boarding college-preparatory, Mathematics and Science, and Computer Science school. Grades 10–12. Founded: 1995. Setting: rural. Nearest major city is Presque Isle. Students are housed in single-sex by floor dormitories. 5-acre campus. 9 buildings on campus. Approved or accredited by Maine Department of Education. Candidate for accreditation by New England Association of Schools and Colleges. Endowment: $190,000. Total enrollment: 120. Upper school average class size: 14. Upper school faculty-student ratio: 1:13.

Upper School Student Profile Grade 10: 38 students (22 boys, 16 girls); Grade 11: 33 students (17 boys, 16 girls); Grade 12: 49 students (30 boys, 19 girls). 100% of students are boarding students. 97% are state residents. 4 states are represented in upper school student body. 3% are international students. International students from Republic of Korea and Viet Nam; 1 other country represented in student body.

Faculty School total: 22. In upper school: 6 men, 3 women; 7 have advanced degrees; 5 reside on campus.

Subjects Offered Advanced biology, advanced chemistry, advanced math, Advanced Placement courses, American history, American literature, analysis and differential calculus, anatomy, art, astronomy, band, biology, biology-AP, British literature, calculus, calculus-AP, chemistry, chemistry-AP, Chinese, chorus, college awareness, composition, composition-AP, computer applications, computer programming, computer science, creative writing, data processing, economics, English composition, English language and composition-AP, English literature, English literature-AP, environmental science-AP, fine arts, French, French-AP, honors English, information technology, internship, linear algebra, mathematics-AP, medieval literature, physics, physics-AP, probability and statistics, psychology-AP, senior seminar, Spanish, Spanish-AP, theater, U.S. history, U.S. history-AP.

Graduation Requirements January-Term, Work Assignment, Recreation.

Special Academic Programs Advanced Placement exam preparation; honors section; accelerated programs; independent study; term-away projects; study at local college for college credit; study abroad; academic accommodation for the gifted.

College Admission Counseling 41 students graduated in 2008; all went to college, including Carnegie Mellon University; Maine Maritime Academy; Massachusetts Institute of Technology; Rensselaer Polytechnic Institute; University of Maine; Worcester Polytechnic Institute. Median SAT critical reading: 560, median SAT math: 640, median SAT writing: 570, median combined SAT: 1770, median composite ACT: 24. 39% scored over 600 on SAT critical reading, 68% scored over 600 on SAT math, 41% scored over 600 on SAT writing, 84% scored over 1800 on combined SAT, 44% scored over 26 on composite ACT.

Student Life Upper grades have specified standards of dress, student council, honor system. Discipline rests primarily with faculty.

Summer Programs Enrichment programs offered; session focuses on Mathematics, Science, and Technology; held on campus; accepts boys and girls; open to students from other schools. 250 students usually enrolled. 2009 schedule: June 28 to July 26. Application deadline: June 1.

Tuition and Aid 7-day tuition and room/board: $23,500. Tuition installment plan (monthly payment plans, individually arranged payment plans, Out-of-State Residents—Tuition and Room & Board). Discount to Room & Board based on NAIS/SSS Financial Aid Application available. In 2008–09, 30% of upper-school students received aid. Total amount of financial aid awarded in 2008–09: $237,000.

Admissions Traditional secondary-level entrance grade is 10. PSAT, SAT or SSAT required. Deadline for receipt of application materials: February 15. No application fee required. Interview required.

Athletics Interscholastic: baseball (boys), basketball (b,g), cross-country running (b,g), soccer (b,g), track and field (b,g); intramural: volleyball (b,g); coed interscholastic: biathlon, cheering, golf.

Computers Computers are regularly used in all academic classes. Computer network features include online commercial services, Internet access, wireless campus network, Internet filtering or blocking technology. Campus intranet, student e-mail accounts, and computer access in designated common areas are available to students. The school has a published electronic and media policy.

Contact Mrs. Danielle Deschaine, Administrative Assistant. 207-325-3303. Fax: 207-325-3340. E-mail: deschained@mssm.org. Web site: www.mssm.org.

See Close-Up on page 834.

MANLIUS PEBBLE HILL SCHOOL

5300 Jamesville Road
DeWitt, New York 13214

Head of School: Baxter F. Ball

General Information Coeducational day college-preparatory school. Grades PK–PG. Founded: 1869. Setting: suburban. Nearest major city is Syracuse. 25-acre campus. 10 buildings on campus. Approved or accredited by Middle States Association of Colleges and Schools. Member of National Association of Independent Schools. Endowment: $2.8 million. Total enrollment: 582. Upper school average class size: 16. Upper school faculty-student ratio: 1:6.

Upper School Student Profile Grade 9: 56 students (27 boys, 29 girls); Grade 10: 68 students (28 boys, 40 girls); Grade 11: 73 students (36 boys, 37 girls); Grade 12: 64 students (30 boys, 34 girls).

Faculty School total: 78. In upper school: 17 men, 24 women; 27 have advanced degrees.

Subjects Offered 3-dimensional design, advanced chemistry, advanced math, Advanced Placement courses, advanced studio art-AP, algebra, American history, American history-AP, American literature, American literature-AP, ancient world history, art history, ballet, Basic programming, biology, biology-AP, calculus, calculus-AP, ceramics, chemistry, chemistry-AP, Chinese, college counseling, comedy, computer math, computer science, creative writing, drama, driver education, earth science, English, English literature, environmental science, European history, expository writing, fine arts, French, geometry, government/civics, health, information technology, Latin, literature, marketing, mathematics, music, philosophy, photography, physical education, physics, science, social studies, sociology, Spanish, statistics, theater, trigonometry, world history.

Graduation Requirements Arts and fine arts (art, music, dance, drama), computer science, electives, English, foreign language, health and wellness, history, mathematics, performing arts, physical education (includes health), science.

Special Academic Programs Advanced Placement exam preparation; honors section; independent study; term-away projects; study at local college for college credit; study abroad; academic accommodation for the gifted; ESL (5 students enrolled).

College Admission Counseling 80 students graduated in 2008; 76 went to college, including Cornell University; Hamilton College; New York University; Princeton University; Syracuse University; Tufts University. Other: 4 had other specific plans. Mean SAT critical reading: 622, mean SAT math: 612, mean SAT writing: 618.

Student Life Upper grades have specified standards of dress, student council, honor system. Discipline rests primarily with faculty.

Summer Programs Enrichment, advancement, sports, art/fine arts, computer instruction programs offered; session focuses on summer camp; held on campus; accepts boys and girls; open to students from other schools. 900 students usually enrolled. 2009 schedule: June 29 to August 21. Application deadline: none.

Tuition and Aid Day student tuition: $15,550–$16,850. Tuition installment plan (Insured Tuition Payment Plan, FACTS Tuition Payment Plan). Merit scholarship grants, need-based scholarship grants available. In 2008–09, 40% of upper-school students received aid; total upper-school merit-scholarship money awarded: $690,000. Total amount of financial aid awarded in 2008–09: $880,000.

Admissions Traditional secondary-level entrance grade is 9. For fall 2008, 54 students applied for upper-level admission, 47 were accepted, 35 enrolled. ERB or PSAT or SAT for applicants to grade 11 and 12 required. Deadline for receipt of application materials: none. Application fee required: $50. On-campus interview required.

Athletics Interscholastic: basketball (boys), diving (g), lacrosse (b,g), soccer (b,g), softball (g), swimming and diving (g), tennis (b,g), volleyball (g); intramural: lacrosse

(g); coed interscholastic: alpine skiing, ballet, cheering, cross-country running, dance, equestrian sports, fitness, golf, indoor track, modern dance, outdoor education, skiing (downhill), snowboarding, strength & conditioning, track and field, winter (indoor) track; coed intramural: outdoor education, trap and skeet. 4 PE instructors, 9 coaches, 1 athletic trainer.
Computers Computers are regularly used in English, foreign language, graphic design, history, information technology, library skills, literary magazine, mathematics, newspaper, science, Web site design, yearbook classes. Computer network features include on-campus library services, online commercial services, Internet access, wireless campus network, Internet filtering or blocking technology. Campus intranet, student e-mail accounts, and computer access in designated common areas are available to students. The school has a published electronic and media policy.
Contact Lynne E. Allard, Director of Admission. 315-446-2452 Ext. 131. Fax: 315-446-2620. E-mail: lallard@mph.net. Web site: www.mph.net.

MAPLEBROOK SCHOOL

Amenia, New York
See Special Needs Schools section.

MARET SCHOOL

3000 Cathedral Avenue NW
Washington, District of Columbia 20008
Head of School: Marjo Talbott
General Information Coeducational day college-preparatory, arts, and technology school. Grades K–12. Founded: 1911. Setting: urban. 7-acre campus. 6 buildings on campus. Approved or accredited by Association of Independent Maryland Schools, Association of Independent Schools of Greater Washington, Middle States Association of Colleges and Schools, and District of Columbia Department of Education. Member of National Association of Independent Schools and Secondary School Admission Test Board. Endowment: $12 million. Total enrollment: 600. Upper school average class size: 14. Upper school faculty-student ratio: 1:6.
Upper School Student Profile Grade 9: 73 students (38 boys, 35 girls); Grade 10: 73 students (36 boys, 37 girls); Grade 11: 71 students (34 boys, 37 girls); Grade 12: 75 students (35 boys, 40 girls).
Faculty School total: 106. In upper school: 34 men, 72 women; 62 have advanced degrees.
Subjects Offered Acting, advanced computer applications, advanced studio art-AP, African-American literature, algebra, American history, American literature, anatomy, art, astronomy, biology, calculus-AP, ceramics, chemistry, civil rights, classical civilization, classical Greek literature, classical language, classics, computer graphics, computer math, computer programming, computer science, creative writing, drama, earth science, ecology, English, English literature, European history, film history, fine arts, French, gender issues, geometry, government/civics, history, humanities, Latin, marine biology, mathematics, music, philosophy, photography, physical education, physics, physiology, psychology, science, Spanish, statistics, technology, trigonometry, women in world history, world history, world literature, writing.
Graduation Requirements Arts and fine arts (art, music, dance, drama), English, foreign language, history, mathematics, music, performing arts, physical education (includes health), science, 15 hours of community service in grades 9 and 10, additional 15 hours in grades 11 and 12.
Special Academic Programs 15 Advanced Placement exams for which test preparation is offered; honors section; independent study; study at local college for college credit; study abroad; academic accommodation for the gifted, the musically talented, and the artistically talented.
College Admission Counseling 74 students graduated in 2008; all went to college, including Bates College; Emory University; Harvard University; Northwestern University; University of Pennsylvania; Washington University in St. Louis.
Student Life Upper grades have student council. Discipline rests primarily with faculty.
Summer Programs Advancement, sports, art/fine arts programs offered; session focuses on academics, athletics, and performing arts; held both on and off campus; held at locations in Costa Rica and Florida; accepts boys and girls; open to students from other schools. 100 students usually enrolled. 2009 schedule: June 15 to August 15. Application deadline: June 1.
Tuition and Aid Day student tuition: $28,430. Tuition installment plan (Key Tuition Payment Plan). Need-based scholarship grants available. In 2008–09, 19% of upper-school students received aid. Total amount of financial aid awarded in 2008–09: $995,000.
Admissions Traditional secondary-level entrance grade is 9. For fall 2008, 182 students applied for upper-level admission, 43 were accepted, 25 enrolled. ISEE, PSAT or SSAT required. Deadline for receipt of application materials: January 9. Application fee required: $65. On-campus interview required.
Athletics Interscholastic: baseball (boys), basketball (b,g), football (b), golf (b,g), lacrosse (b,g), soccer (b,g), softball (g), tennis (b,g), volleyball (g), wrestling (b); coed interscholastic: aerobics, cross-country running, diving, independent competitive sports, indoor soccer, martial arts, swimming and diving, track and field, ultimate Frisbee, weight training; coed intramural: weight lifting. 7 PE instructors, 2 coaches, 1 athletic trainer.
Computers Computers are regularly used in graphic design, graphics, programming, publications, Web site design classes. Computer network features include on-campus library services, online commercial services, Internet access, wireless campus network, Internet filtering or blocking technology. Campus intranet and student e-mail accounts are available to students. The school has a published electronic and media policy.
Contact Annie M. Farquhar, Director of Admission and Financial Aid. 202-939-8814. Fax: 202-939-8845. E-mail: admissions@maret.org. Web site: www.maret.org.

MARIANAPOLIS PREPARATORY SCHOOL

PO Box 304
26 Chase Road
Thompson, Connecticut 06277-0304
Head of School: Mrs. Marilyn S. Ebbitt
General Information Coeducational boarding and day college-preparatory, religious studies, and ESL school, affiliated with Roman Catholic Church. Grades 9–PG. Founded: 1926. Setting: suburban. Nearest major city is Boston, MA. Students are housed in single-sex dormitories. 300-acre campus. 11 buildings on campus. Approved or accredited by Connecticut Association of Independent Schools, New England Association of Schools and Colleges, The Association of Boarding Schools, and Connecticut Department of Education. Member of Secondary School Admission Test Board. Total enrollment: 315. Upper school average class size: 15. Upper school faculty-student ratio: 1:10.
Upper School Student Profile Grade 9: 70 students (35 boys, 35 girls); Grade 10: 75 students (35 boys, 40 girls); Grade 11: 85 students (45 boys, 40 girls); Grade 12: 80 students (35 boys, 45 girls); Postgraduate: 5 students (3 boys, 2 girls). 38% of students are boarding students. 30% are state residents. 4 states are represented in upper school student body. 33% are international students. International students from China, Mexico, Republic of Korea, Spain, Taiwan, and Viet Nam; 19 other countries represented in student body. 60% of students are Roman Catholic.
Faculty School total: 34. In upper school: 19 men, 15 women; 10 have advanced degrees; 14 reside on campus.
Subjects Offered Algebra, American government, American literature, art, Bible studies, biology, calculus, calculus-AP, chemistry, chemistry-AP, chorus, Christian and Hebrew scripture, Christian doctrine, Christian ethics, church history, comparative religion, computer programming, computer science, contemporary studies, drawing, English, English literature, English literature-AP, English-AP, ensembles, environmental science, ESL, fine arts, French, geometry, government/civics, guitar, history, honors algebra, honors English, honors geometry, mathematics, modern European history, moral theology, music, physics, physics-AP, piano, pre-calculus, probability and statistics, psychology, religion, science, social studies, Spanish, theology, trigonometry, U.S. history, world literature.
Graduation Requirements Arts and fine arts (art, music, dance, drama), computer science, electives, English, foreign language, mathematics, religion (includes Bible studies and theology), science, social studies (includes history). Community service is required.
Special Academic Programs Advanced Placement exam preparation; honors section; independent study; academic accommodation for the musically talented and the artistically talented; ESL (90 students enrolled).
College Admission Counseling 67 students graduated in 2007; all went to college, including College of the Holy Cross; Middlebury College; Providence College; Purdue University; Syracuse University; University of Connecticut.
Student Life Upper grades have specified standards of dress, student council. Discipline rests equally with students and faculty. Attendance at religious services is required.
Tuition and Aid Day student tuition: $10,250; 7-day tuition and room/board: $29,790. Tuition installment plan (Key Tuition Payment Plan, monthly payment plans, individually arranged payment plans). Tuition reduction for siblings, merit scholarship grants, need-based scholarship grants, tuition reduction for Diocese of Norwich affiliation available. In 2007–08, 62% of upper-school students received aid; total upper-school merit-scholarship money awarded: $100,000. Total amount of financial aid awarded in 2007–08: $800,000.
Admissions For fall 2007, 250 students applied for upper-level admission, 175 were accepted, 115 enrolled. Common entrance examinations, PSAT, SAT, SLEP, SSAT or TOEFL required. Deadline for receipt of application materials: none. Application fee required: $80. Interview required.
Athletics Interscholastic: baseball (boys), basketball (b,g), cross-country running (b,g), lacrosse (b,g), soccer (b,g), softball (g), tennis (b,g); intramural: basketball (b,g), dance (g), modern dance (g); coed interscholastic: golf, running, track and field, wrestling; coed intramural: aerobics/dance, alpine skiing, bicycling, billiards, cross-country running, dance, flag football, Frisbee, independent competitive sports, jogging, judo, martial arts, mountain biking, skiing (cross-country), skiing (downhill), snowboarding, snowshoeing, swimming and diving, table tennis, tai chi, tennis, ultimate Frisbee, volleyball, weight lifting, yoga. 24 coaches, 1 athletic trainer.
Computers Computers are regularly used in all academic, ESL classes. Computer network features include Internet access, wireless campus network, Internet filtering or blocking technology. Student e-mail accounts are available to students. The school has a published electronic and media policy.

Contact Mr. Daniel M. Harrop, Director of Admissions and Financial Aid. 860-923-9565 Ext. 233. Fax: 860-923-3730. E-mail: dharrop@marianapolis.org. Web site: www.marianapolis.org.

See Close-Up on page 836.

MARIAN BAKER SCHOOL

PO Box 4269-1000
San Jose 1000, Costa Rica

Head of School: Linda A. Niehaus

General Information Coeducational day college-preparatory, arts, bilingual studies, and technology school; primarily serves individuals with Attention Deficit Disorder, individuals with emotional and behavioral problems, and dyslexic students. Grades PK–12. Founded: 1984. Setting: suburban. Nearest major city is San Jose, Costa Rica, Costa Rica. 2-hectare campus. 5 buildings on campus. Approved or accredited by Southern Association of Colleges and Schools. Language of instruction: English. Total enrollment: 201. Upper school average class size: 14. Upper school faculty-student ratio: 1:12.

Upper School Student Profile Grade 9: 8 students (4 boys, 4 girls); Grade 10: 13 students (4 boys, 9 girls); Grade 11: 11 students (7 boys, 4 girls); Grade 12: 12 students (5 boys, 7 girls).

Faculty School total: 37. In upper school: 8 men, 10 women; 18 have advanced degrees.

Subjects Offered Acting, advanced biology, advanced chemistry, advanced math, Advanced Placement courses, algebra, American government, applied arts, applied music, art, art appreciation, basketball, biology, biology-AP, business mathematics, calculus, calculus-AP, career and personal planning, chemistry, chemistry-AP, choir, civics, composition, computer applications, computer education, computer graphics, computer keyboarding, computer skills, culinary arts, digital photography, drama, drama performance, drawing, earth science, ecology, English, English literature, English-AP, ESL, film appreciation, general science, geometry, government, graphic arts, health, honors English, honors U.S. history, honors world history, Latin American literature, library research, linear algebra, painting, physics, physics-AP, pre-algebra, pre-calculus, psychology-AP, science, social studies, Spanish, Spanish literature, Spanish-AP, speech, sports, standard curriculum, statistics, statistics and probability, theater design and production, theater production, trigonometry, U.S. government and politics, U.S. history, U.S. history-AP, values and decisions, Web site design, world civilizations, world culture, world history, world history-AP.

Graduation Requirements Latin American history or Costa Rican social studies, computer competency.

Special Academic Programs Advanced Placement exam preparation; honors section; independent study; study abroad; academic accommodation for the gifted; remedial reading and/or remedial writing; remedial math; programs in general development for dyslexic students; ESL (18 students enrolled).

College Admission Counseling 19 students graduated in 2008; all went to college, including Brown University; Princeton University; The College of William and Mary; The University of British Columbia. Median SAT critical reading: 520, median SAT math: 570, median SAT writing: 490, median combined SAT: 1640. 25% scored over 600 on SAT critical reading, 37% scored over 600 on SAT math, 38% scored over 600 on SAT writing, 25% scored over 1800 on combined SAT.

Student Life Upper grades have uniform requirement, student council, honor system. Discipline rests primarily with faculty.

Tuition and Aid Day student tuition: $7500. Tuition reduction for siblings available.

Admissions Traditional secondary-level entrance grade is 9. For fall 2008, 30 students applied for upper-level admission, 9 were accepted, 7 enrolled. Deadline for receipt of application materials: none. Application fee required: $50. Interview required.

Athletics Interscholastic: basketball (boys, girls), soccer (b,g), volleyball (b,g). 2 PE instructors, 2 coaches.

Computers Computers are regularly used in all academic, art, ESL, graphic arts, mathematics, photography classes. Computer network features include Internet access, wireless campus network, Internet filtering or blocking technology. Computer access in designated common areas is available to students. The school has a published electronic and media policy.

Contact Linda A. Niehaus, General Director. 506-2273-0024 Ext. 110. Fax: 506-2273-0280. E-mail: lniehaus@mbs.ed.cr. Web site: www.mbs.ed.cr.

MARIAN CENTRAL CATHOLIC HIGH SCHOOL

1001 McHenry Avenue
Woodstock, Illinois 60098

Head of School: Mr. Charles D. Rakers

General Information Coeducational day college-preparatory, arts, business, religious studies, bilingual studies, and technology school, affiliated with Roman Catholic Church. Grades 9–12. Founded: 1959. Setting: suburban. 42-acre campus. 1 building on campus. Approved or accredited by National Catholic Education Association, North Central Association of Colleges and Schools, and Illinois Department of Education. Endowment: $1.1 million. Total enrollment: 758. Upper school average class size: 24. Upper school faculty-student ratio: 1:14.

Upper School Student Profile Grade 9: 193 students (97 boys, 96 girls); Grade 10: 211 students (111 boys, 100 girls); Grade 11: 183 students (83 boys, 100 girls); Grade 12: 171 students (87 boys, 84 girls). 86.8% of students are Roman Catholic.

Faculty School total: 57. In upper school: 26 men, 25 women; 31 have advanced degrees.

Subjects Offered Accounting, advanced biology, advanced chemistry, advanced math, Advanced Placement courses, algebra, American government, art, band, biology, business law, calculus, calculus-AP, chemistry, chemistry-AP, chorus, composition, computer programming, consumer economics, English, English composition, English literature-AP, first aid, French, general science, geography, geometry, global issues, government, health, honors algebra, honors English, honors geometry, honors U.S. history, information processing, integrated science, marketing, physical education, physical fitness, physical science, physics, pre-calculus, psychology, psychology-AP, publications, religious studies, sociology, Spanish, speech, U.S. history, U.S. history-AP, world history-AP.

Graduation Requirements Art, biology, consumer economics, electives, English, foreign language, government, mathematics, music, physical education (includes health), religious studies, science, social studies (includes history), U.S. history.

Special Academic Programs Advanced Placement exam preparation; honors section; remedial reading and/or remedial writing; remedial math.

College Admission Counseling 168 students graduated in 2008; 161 went to college, including Augustana College; DePaul University; Loyola University Chicago; Marquette University; Northern Illinois University; University of Illinois at Urbana–Champaign. Other: 1 went to work, 6 had other specific plans. Mean composite ACT: 25. 32% scored over 26 on composite ACT.

Student Life Upper grades have uniform requirement, student council. Discipline rests primarily with faculty. Attendance at religious services is required.

Summer Programs Sports programs offered; session focuses on sports camps; held on campus; accepts boys and girls; open to students from other schools. 2009 schedule: June to August.

Tuition and Aid Day student tuition: $5370–$7175. Tuition installment plan (monthly payment plans, quarterly payment plan, yearly payment plans). Tuition reduction for siblings, need-based scholarship grants, paying campus jobs available. In 2008–09, 13% of upper-school students received aid. Total amount of financial aid awarded in 2008–09: $220,870.

Admissions Traditional secondary-level entrance grade is 9. High School Placement Test (closed version) from Scholastic Testing Service required. Deadline for receipt of application materials: none. No application fee required.

Athletics Interscholastic: baseball (boys), basketball (b,g), cheering (g), cross-country running (b,g), dance team (g), football (b), golf (b,g), pom squad (g), soccer (b,g), softball (g), tennis (b,g), track and field (b,g), volleyball (g), wrestling (b); intramural: fencing (b,g), floor hockey (b,g). 4 PE instructors, 36 coaches, 1 athletic trainer.

Computers Computers are regularly used in information technology, programming, publications classes. Computer resources include on-campus library services, online commercial services, Internet access, Internet filtering or blocking technology. The school has a published electronic and media policy.

Contact Ms. Jacqueline Hyzy, Curriculum Director. 815-338-4220 Ext. 105. Fax: 815-338-4253. E-mail: jhyzy@marian.com. Web site: www.marian.com.

MARIAN HIGH SCHOOL

1311 South Logan Street
Mishawaka, Indiana 46544

Head of School: Carl Loesch

General Information Coeducational day college-preparatory, arts, business, vocational, religious studies, bilingual studies, and technology school, affiliated with Roman Catholic Church. Grades 9–12. Founded: 1965. Setting: suburban. 135-acre campus. 1 building on campus. Approved or accredited by North Central Association of Colleges and Schools, The College Board, and Indiana Department of Education. Total enrollment: 730. Upper school average class size: 25. Upper school faculty-student ratio: 1:20.

Upper School Student Profile Grade 9: 201 students (107 boys, 94 girls); Grade 10: 165 students (83 boys, 82 girls); Grade 11: 174 students (87 boys, 87 girls); Grade 12: 190 students (89 boys, 101 girls). 82% of students are Roman Catholic.

Faculty School total: 52. In upper school: 19 men, 29 women; 20 have advanced degrees.

Subjects Offered 20th century history, 20th century physics, 20th century world history, 3-dimensional art, 3-dimensional design, accounting, advanced chemistry, advanced computer applications, advanced math, algebra, alternative physical education, American government, American literature, analysis and differential calculus, analytic geometry, anatomy, ancient world history, art, art history, arts and crafts, arts appreciation, business law, calculus, Catholic belief and practice, chemistry, drama, drawing, drawing and design, economics, English composition, English literature-AP, environmental science, environmental studies, environmental systems, family and consumer science, family living, fashion, fine arts, food and nutrition, foods, French, French language-AP, general business, general math, geography, geometry, German, government and politics-AP, government-AP, government/civics, Greek, guidance, health, histology, honors world history, independent living, integrated science, keyboarding/computer, Latin, Life of Christ, media, media arts, moral theology, music, music appreciation, music theory-AP, nutrition, physics, physics-AP, pre-algebra, pre-calculus, psychology, religion, scripture, senior project, sewing, sociology, Spanish, Spanish language-AP, Spanish-AP, study skills, theology, U.S. government-AP, U.S. history, U.S. history-AP, visual arts, vocal music, Western civilization.

Graduation Requirements Algebra, American government, American history, analytic geometry, arts and fine arts (art, music, dance, drama), biology, chemistry, computer information systems, computer keyboarding, computer skills, economics, English, English composition, English literature, family and consumer sciences, French, languages, mathematics, science, scripture, writing skills, four years of theology.

Special Academic Programs Advanced Placement exam preparation; study at local college for college credit; remedial reading and/or remedial writing; remedial math.

College Admission Counseling 212 students graduated in 2008; 201 went to college, including Ball State University; DePaul University; Indiana University Bloomington; Purdue University; University of Notre Dame. Other: 6 went to work, 3 entered military service, 2 had other specific plans. Mean SAT critical reading: 540, mean SAT math: 544, mean SAT writing: 528.

Student Life Upper grades have specified standards of dress, student council, honor system. Discipline rests equally with students and faculty. Attendance at religious services is required.

Summer Programs Sports, art/fine arts, computer instruction programs offered; session focuses on enrichment; held on campus; accepts boys and girls; open to students from other schools. 2009 schedule: June 9 to July 28.

Tuition and Aid Day student tuition: $5475–$6475. Tuition installment plan (The Tuition Plan, FACTS Tuition Payment Plan, individually arranged payment plans). Tuition reduction for siblings, need-based loans available. In 2008–09, 40% of upper-school students received aid. Total amount of financial aid awarded in 2008–09: $350,000.

Admissions Traditional secondary-level entrance grade is 9. For fall 2008, 222 students applied for upper-level admission, 220 were accepted, 200 enrolled. High School Placement Test, Math Placement Exam or placement test required. Deadline for receipt of application materials: August 13. Application fee required: $100. Interview required.

Athletics Interscholastic: aerobics/dance (girls), aquatics (b,g), baseball (b), basketball (b,g), cheering (b,g), Cosom hockey (b), cross-country running (b,g), dance team (g), diving (b,g), flag football (g), football (b), golf (b,g), gymnastics (g), hockey (b), ice hockey (b), indoor hockey (b), lacrosse (b,g), power lifting (b,g), rugby (b), soccer (b,g), softball (g), swimming and diving (b,g), tennis (b,g), track and field (b,g), volleyball (g), weight training (b,g), wrestling (b,g); intramural: basketball (b), flag football (g), pom squad (g); coed interscholastic: cheering, wrestling; coed intramural: alpine skiing, bowling. 2 PE instructors, 40 coaches, 1 athletic trainer.

Computers Computers are regularly used in business education, business skills, career education, career exploration, commercial art, economics, foreign language, graphic arts, history, library, media arts, occupational education, publications, religion, yearbook classes. Computer network features include on-campus library services, online commercial services, Internet access, Internet filtering or blocking technology. Students grades are available online. The school has a published electronic and media policy.

Contact Janet M. Hatfield, Dean. 574-259-5257. Fax: 574-258-7668. E-mail: jhatfield@marianhs.org. Web site: www.marianhs.org/.

MARIAN HIGH SCHOOL

7225 Lahser
Bloomfield Hills, Michigan 48301

Head of School: Sr. Lenore Pochelski, IHM

General Information Girls' day college-preparatory and religious studies school, affiliated with Roman Catholic Church. Grades 9–12. Founded: 1959. Setting: suburban. Nearest major city is Detroit. 1 building on campus. Approved or accredited by North Central Association of Colleges and Schools and Michigan Department of Education. Total enrollment: 580. Upper school average class size: 18. Upper school faculty-student ratio: 1:11.

Upper School Student Profile Grade 9: 160 students (160 girls); Grade 10: 151 students (151 girls); Grade 11: 146 students (146 girls); Grade 12: 123 students (123 girls). 88% of students are Roman Catholic.

Faculty School total: 44. In upper school: 4 men, 40 women; 27 have advanced degrees.

Special Academic Programs Advanced Placement exam preparation; honors section.

College Admission Counseling 129 students graduated in 2008; all went to college, including Michigan State University; University of Michigan.

Student Life Upper grades have uniform requirement, student council, honor system. Discipline rests primarily with faculty. Attendance at religious services is required.

Summer Programs Computer instruction programs offered; held on campus; accepts girls; not open to students from other schools.

Tuition and Aid Tuition installment plan (monthly payment plans). Tuition reduction for siblings, merit scholarship grants, need-based scholarship grants, paying campus jobs available.

Admissions Traditional secondary-level entrance grade is 9. Catholic High School Entrance Examination required. Deadline for receipt of application materials: none. No application fee required.

Athletics Interscholastic: basketball, cross-country running, dance team, diving, equestrian sports, field hockey, lacrosse, physical fitness, skiing (downhill), soccer, softball, swimming and diving, tennis, track and field, volleyball; intramural: badminton, basketball, bowling, volleyball. 1 PE instructor, 32 coaches, 1 athletic trainer.

Computers Computer network features include on-campus library services, Internet access, wireless campus network, Internet filtering or blocking technology. Campus intranet, student e-mail accounts, and computer access in designated common areas are available to students. Students grades are available online.

Contact Ms. Sherri McIntyre, Office of Admission. 248-644-1750. Fax: 248-644-6107. E-mail: smcintyre@marian-hs.org. Web site: www.marian-hs.org.

MARIN ACADEMY

1600 Mission Avenue
San Rafael, California 94901-1859

Head of School: Travis Brownley

General Information Coeducational day college-preparatory, arts, technology, and outdoor education program school. Grades 9–12. Founded: 1971. Setting: suburban. Nearest major city is San Francisco. 10-acre campus. 11 buildings on campus. Approved or accredited by California Association of Independent Schools, The College Board, and Western Association of Schools and Colleges. Member of National Association of Independent Schools and Secondary School Admission Test Board. Endowment: $9.1 million. Total enrollment: 406. Upper school average class size: 15. Upper school faculty-student ratio: 1:9.

Upper School Student Profile Grade 9: 108 students (53 boys, 55 girls); Grade 10: 103 students (52 boys, 51 girls); Grade 11: 95 students (43 boys, 52 girls); Grade 12: 100 students (48 boys, 52 girls).

Faculty School total: 55. In upper school: 23 men, 32 women; 36 have advanced degrees.

Subjects Offered 20th century history, 20th century world history, 3-dimensional art, acting, adolescent issues, Advanced Placement courses, African history, algebra, American culture, American government, American history, American literature, American minority experience, American studies, ancient world history, art, Asian history, Asian literature, biology, British literature (honors), calculus, ceramics, chemistry, chorus, college counseling, community service, creative writing, dance, digital imaging, digital photography, English, English literature, environmental science, European history, fine arts, French, French language-AP, French literature-AP, geology, geometry, government-AP, government/civics, health, history, honors U.S. history, human development, Islamic studies, Japanese, journalism, Mandarin, mathematics, music, oceanography, photography, physical education, physics, pre-calculus, science, social studies, Spanish, theater, trigonometry, world culture.

Graduation Requirements Arts and fine arts (art, music, dance, drama), English, foreign language, health and wellness, health education, mathematics, physical education (includes health), science, social studies (includes history), annual one-week experiential education course. Community service is required.

Special Academic Programs Advanced Placement exam preparation; honors section; independent study; term-away projects; study at local college for college credit; study abroad; academic accommodation for the gifted, the musically talented, and the artistically talented.

College Admission Counseling 99 students graduated in 2008; 98 went to college, including Bard College; New York University; Oberlin College; Stanford University; University of California, Berkeley; University of Southern California. Other: 1 had other specific plans. Median SAT critical reading: 670, median SAT math: 645, median SAT writing: 675, median combined SAT: 2000, median composite ACT: 28.

Student Life Upper grades have student council, honor system. Discipline rests primarily with faculty.

Tuition and Aid Day student tuition: $30,970. Tuition installment plan (Key Tuition Payment Plan). Need-based scholarship grants, need-based loans available. In 2008–09, 21% of upper-school students received aid. Total amount of financial aid awarded in 2008–09: $1,781,027.

Admissions Traditional secondary-level entrance grade is 9. For fall 2008, 472 students applied for upper-level admission, 158 were accepted, 110 enrolled. CTBS or ERB, ISEE, SSAT or Star-9 required. Deadline for receipt of application materials: January 10. Application fee required: $75. On-campus interview required.

Athletics Interscholastic: aquatics (boys, girls), baseball (b), basketball (b,g), combined training (b,g), cross-country running (b,g), fencing (b,g), golf (b,g), independent competitive sports (b,g), lacrosse (b), mountain biking (b,g), outdoor activities (b,g), physical fitness (b,g), rock climbing (b,g), sailing (b,g), soccer (b,g), softball (g), swimming and diving (b,g), tennis (b,g), track and field (b,g), volleyball (g), water polo (b,g); coed interscholastic: dance, golf; coed intramural: bicycling, climbing, fitness, flag football, Frisbee, hiking/backpacking, kayaking, martial arts, Nautilus, rock climbing, scuba diving, ultimate Frisbee. 28 coaches, 1 athletic trainer.

Computers Computers are regularly used in art, English, foreign language, history, mathematics, music, photography, science, yearbook classes. Computer network features include on-campus library services, online commercial services, Internet access, wireless campus network, multimedia hardware and production applications. Student e-mail accounts and computer access in designated common areas are available to students.

Contact Dan Babior, Director of Admissions and Financial Aid. 415-453-4550 Ext. 216. Fax: 415-453-8905. E-mail: dbabior@ma.org. Web site: www.ma.org.

ANNOUNCEMENT FROM THE SCHOOL Marin Academy, an independent, coeducational, college-preparatory high school, enrolls a diversely talented student body of 400. The campus is located in San Rafael, a community of 57,000 residents, 12 miles north of San Francisco. Facilities on the 10-acre campus include eleven buildings, new FieldTurf, two playing fields, two athletic centers, a swimming pool, three computer labs, a multimedia lab, a science center, a new library, the Performing Arts Center, and the Visual Arts Center. The curriculum features thirty-five honors and AP courses, sixty-three electives, and outstanding opportunities in performing and visual arts as part of an extensive academic program. Marin field teams in eleven different sports. Many trips are offered through a highly developed Outdoor Education Program. Independent study and study-abroad programs are available. Graduates of the school attend leading colleges and universities throughout the country. 2008–09 tuition: $30,970; Web site: www.ma.org.

MARION ACADEMY

2002 Prier Drive
Marion, Alabama 36756

Head of School: Mr. Anthony L. Yelverton

General Information Coeducational day college-preparatory, arts, bilingual studies, and technology school, affiliated with Christian faith. Grades K4–12. Founded: 1987. Setting: small town. Nearest major city is Tuscaloosa. 5-acre campus. 1 building on campus. Approved or accredited by Alabama Department of Education. Total enrollment: 82. Upper school average class size: 6. Upper school faculty-student ratio: 1:8.

Upper School Student Profile Grade 6: 8 students (3 boys, 5 girls); Grade 7: 7 students (3 boys, 4 girls); Grade 8: 6 students (2 boys, 4 girls); Grade 9: 5 students (3 boys, 2 girls); Grade 10: 7 students (3 boys, 4 girls); Grade 11: 6 students (2 boys, 4 girls); Grade 12: 2 students (2 girls). 98% of students are Christian.

Faculty School total: 14. In upper school: 2 men, 2 women; 3 have advanced degrees.

Subjects Offered 20th century history, 20th century world history, ACT preparation, advanced math, Alabama history and geography, algebra, American government, anatomy and physiology, art, athletics, basic language skills, biology, cheerleading, college planning, creative writing, drama, earth science, economics, English language and composition-AP, English language-AP, English literature, English literature and composition-AP, English/composition-AP, foreign language, general math, geography, German, German-AP, government, grammar, health education, history, honors algebra, honors English, honors geometry, honors U.S. history, honors world history, human anatomy, Internet, language, language and composition, language arts, library, math applications, math methods, math review, mathematics, mathematics-AP, physical education, SAT/ACT preparation, speech, U.S. government, U.S. history.

College Admission Counseling 3 students graduated in 2008; 2 went to college, including Samford University. Other: 1 went to work.

Student Life Upper grades have specified standards of dress, student council, honor system. Discipline rests primarily with faculty.

Tuition and Aid Guaranteed tuition plan.

Admissions Traditional secondary-level entrance grade is 9. Deadline for receipt of application materials: none. No application fee required. Interview required.

Athletics Interscholastic: baseball (boys), basketball (b,g), cheering (g), football (b), softball (g), track and field (b,g), volleyball (g); coed interscholastic: track and field. 1 PE instructor, 1 coach.

Computers Computers are regularly used in career education classes. Computer network features include Internet access. Student e-mail accounts are available to students.

Contact Mrs. Margaret S. Hallmon, Secretary. 334-683-8204. Fax: 334-683-4938. E-mail: marionacademy@hotmail.com. Web site: www.marionacademy.org.

MARIST HIGH SCHOOL

4200 West 115th Street
Chicago, Illinois 60655-4306

Head of School: Br. Patrick McNamara, FMS

General Information Coeducational day college-preparatory school, affiliated with Roman Catholic Church; primarily serves students with learning disabilities. Grades 9–12. Founded: 1963. Setting: suburban. 55-acre campus. 1 building on campus. Approved or accredited by National Catholic Education Association and Illinois Department of Education. Total enrollment: 1,810. Upper school average class size: 29. Upper school faculty-student ratio: 1:16.

Upper School Student Profile 93% of students are Roman Catholic.

Faculty School total: 102. In upper school: 63 men, 39 women; 74 have advanced degrees.

Subjects Offered Accounting, algebra, American legal systems, anatomy, architecture, art, band, biology, biology-AP, business mathematics, calculus, calculus-AP, chemistry, chemistry-AP, chorus, computer graphics, computer science, computer science-AP, creative writing, drafting, drawing, economics, English, English-AP, environmental science, film and literature, film studies, forensic science, French, French language-AP, geometry, information technology, journalism, painting, peer counseling, philosophy, physics, physics-AP, pottery, psychology, reading, religious studies, rhetoric, senior humanities, Spanish, Spanish-AP, studio art, U.S. history, U.S. history-AP, Web site design, wellness, Western civilization, world geography.

Graduation Requirements Electives, English, foreign language, mathematics, performing arts, physical education (includes health), religion (includes Bible studies and theology), science, social studies (includes history), technology, visual arts.

Special Academic Programs Advanced Placement exam preparation; honors section; study at local college for college credit; remedial reading and/or remedial writing; programs in English, mathematics, general development for dyslexic students.

College Admission Counseling 434 students graduated in 2008; 420 went to college, including DePaul University; Eastern Illinois University; Illinois State University; Loyola University Chicago; Marquette University; University of Illinois at Urbana–Champaign. Other: 11 went to work, 3 entered military service. Mean composite ACT: 23.

Student Life Upper grades have uniform requirement, student council, honor system. Discipline rests primarily with faculty. Attendance at religious services is required.

Tuition and Aid Day student tuition: $8200. Tuition installment plan (monthly payment plans). Tuition reduction for siblings, merit scholarship grants, need-based scholarship grants, paying campus jobs available. In 2008–09, 25% of upper-school students received aid.

Admissions For fall 2008, 696 students applied for upper-level admission, 490 enrolled. High School Placement Test required. Deadline for receipt of application materials: March 1. Application fee required: $25.

Athletics Interscholastic: baseball (boys), basketball (b,g), bordenball (b,g), boxing (b), cheering (b), cross-country running (b,g), dance team (g), flag football (g), football (b), golf (b,g), hockey (b), ice hockey (b), pom squad (b), soccer (b,g), softball (g), swimming and diving (g), tennis (b,g), track and field (b,g), volleyball (b,g), wrestling (b); intramural: basketball (b,g), boxing (b); coed interscholastic: billiards; coed intramural: bicycling, bowling, flag football, Frisbee, skiing (downhill). 8 PE instructors, 3 coaches, 1 athletic trainer.

Computers Computers are regularly used in architecture, drafting, graphic design, newspaper, Web site design classes. Computer network features include online commercial services, Internet access, wireless campus network, Internet filtering or blocking technology. Student e-mail accounts and computer access in designated common areas are available to students. Students grades are available online. The school has a published electronic and media policy.

Contact Mrs. Alex Brown, Director of Admissions. 773-881-5300 Ext. 5330. Fax: 773-881-0595. E-mail: alex@marist.net. Web site: www.marist.net.

MARIST HIGH SCHOOL

1241 Kennedy Boulevard
Bayonne, New Jersey 07002

Head of School: Br. Steve Schlitte, FMS

General Information Coeducational day college-preparatory, religious studies, and technology school, affiliated with Roman Catholic Church; primarily serves students with learning disabilities. Grades 9–12. Founded: 1954. Setting: urban. 1 building on campus. Approved or accredited by Middle States Association of Colleges and Schools, National Catholic Education Association, and New Jersey Department of Education. Total enrollment: 510. Upper school average class size: 25. Upper school faculty-student ratio: 1:25.

Upper School Student Profile Grade 9: 143 students (94 boys, 49 girls); Grade 10: 113 students (70 boys, 43 girls); Grade 11: 114 students (72 boys, 42 girls); Grade 12: 142 students (82 boys, 60 girls). 30% of students are Roman Catholic.

Faculty School total: 55. In upper school: 30 men, 25 women; 20 have advanced degrees.

Subjects Offered Advanced Placement courses, algebra, American history, American history-AP, art education, art history-AP, athletics, baseball, basketball, biology, biology-AP, bowling, British literature (honors), business education, calculus-AP, campus ministry, career/college preparation, character education, college awareness, college counseling, college placement, college planning, college writing, composition-AP, computer education, computer graphics, computer programming, computer skills, economics, English, geometry, health, history, history-AP, independent study, Internet, mathematics, mathematics-AP, programming, social sciences, Spanish, Spanish language-AP.

Graduation Requirements Advanced Placement courses, art, computer skills, driver education, English, foreign language, mathematics, physical education (includes health), religion (includes Bible studies and theology), SAT preparation, science, social studies (includes history), writing workshop.

Special Academic Programs Advanced Placement exam preparation; honors section; independent study; study at local college for college credit; academic accommodation for the gifted; remedial reading and/or remedial writing; remedial math; special instructional classes for students with learning disabilities.

College Admission Counseling 119 students graduated in 2008; 115 went to college, including New Jersey Institute of Technology; Pace University; Saint Peter's College; Seton Hall University; The College of New Jersey. Other: 3 went to work, 1 entered military service.

Student Life Upper grades have uniform requirement, student council, honor system. Discipline rests primarily with faculty. Attendance at religious services is required.
Summer Programs Remediation programs offered; held on campus; accepts boys and girls; open to students from other schools.
Tuition and Aid Day student tuition: $5800. Tuition installment plan (FACTS Tuition Payment Plan). Merit scholarship grants, need-based scholarship grants available.
Admissions Traditional secondary-level entrance grade is 9. For fall 2008, 600 students applied for upper-level admission, 154 enrolled. Cooperative Entrance Exam (McGraw-Hill) or Terra Nova-CTB required. Deadline for receipt of application materials: none. Application fee required: $425. On-campus interview recommended.
Athletics Interscholastic: baseball (boys), basketball (b,g), football (b), soccer (b,g), softball (g), tennis (b,g); coed interscholastic: bowling, cheering, cross-country running, track and field, weight lifting; coed intramural: weight lifting, whiffle ball. 1 PE instructor.
Computers Computers are regularly used in all academic classes. Computer network features include on-campus library services, Internet access, wireless campus network, Internet filtering or blocking technology. The school has a published electronic and media policy.
Contact Mr. John A. Taormina, Director of Marketing and Admissions. 201-437-4544 Ext. 202. Fax: 201-437-6013. E-mail: admissions@marist.org. Web site: www.marist.org.

MARIST SCHOOL

3790 Ashford-Dunwoody Road NE
Atlanta, Georgia 30319-1899

Head of School: Rev. Joel M. Konzen, SM

General Information Coeducational day college-preparatory, arts, religious studies, and technology school, affiliated with Roman Catholic Church. Grades 7–12. Founded: 1901. Setting: suburban. 68-acre campus. 18 buildings on campus. Approved or accredited by Georgia Independent School Association, National Catholic Education Association, Southern Association of Colleges and Schools, Southern Association of Independent Schools, and Georgia Department of Education. Member of National Association of Independent Schools and Secondary School Admission Test Board. Endowment: $14.5 million. Total enrollment: 1,070. Upper school average class size: 18. Upper school faculty-student ratio: 1:11.
Upper School Student Profile Grade 7: 144 students (77 boys, 67 girls); Grade 8: 144 students (75 boys, 69 girls); Grade 9: 203 students (101 boys, 102 girls); Grade 10: 191 students (97 boys, 94 girls); Grade 11: 200 students (101 boys, 99 girls); Grade 12: 188 students (89 boys, 99 girls). 77% of students are Roman Catholic.
Faculty School total: 98. In upper school: 50 men, 48 women; 71 have advanced degrees.
Subjects Offered ACT preparation, algebra, American history, American literature, ancient history, art, art history, biology, business skills, calculus, ceramics, chemistry, community service, computer programming, computer science, creative writing, dance, drama, driver education, economics, English, English literature, European history, fine arts, French, general science, geography, geology, geometry, German, government/civics, health, history, humanities, journalism, keyboarding, Latin, mathematics, music, peace and justice, philosophy, photography, physical education, physics, religion, science, social studies, Spanish, speech, statistics, studio art, theater, theology, world history, world literature, world religions, writing.
Graduation Requirements Arts and fine arts (art, music, dance, drama), business skills (includes word processing), computer science, English, foreign language, mathematics, physical education (includes health), religion (includes Bible studies and theology), science, social studies (includes history). Community service is required.
Special Academic Programs Advanced Placement exam preparation; honors section; independent study.
College Admission Counseling 193 students graduated in 2008; all went to college, including Auburn University; Clemson University; Georgia Institute of Technology; University of Georgia; University of Notre Dame. 61% scored over 600 on SAT critical reading, 60% scored over 600 on SAT math, 56% scored over 600 on SAT writing, 59% scored over 1800 on combined SAT, 62% scored over 26 on composite ACT.
Student Life Upper grades have uniform requirement, student council, honor system. Discipline rests primarily with faculty. Attendance at religious services is required.
Summer Programs Enrichment, sports, art/fine arts programs offered; held on campus; accepts boys and girls; open to students from other schools.
Tuition and Aid Day student tuition: $14,875. Tuition installment plan (Key Tuition Payment Plan). Need-based scholarship grants available. In 2008–09, 13% of upper-school students received aid. Total amount of financial aid awarded in 2008–09: $1,082,150.
Admissions Traditional secondary-level entrance grade is 7. SSAT required. Deadline for receipt of application materials: January 31. Application fee required: $75. On-campus interview required.
Athletics Interscholastic: baseball (boys), basketball (b,g), cheering (g), cross-country running (b,g), diving (b,g), football (b), golf (b,g), lacrosse (b,g), soccer (b,g), softball (g), swimming and diving (b,g), tennis (b,g), track and field (b,g), volleyball (g), weight lifting (b,g), wrestling (b); coed interscholastic: drill team; coed intramural: outdoor education, ultimate Frisbee.
Computers Computers are regularly used in accounting, English, foreign language, mathematics, music, science classes. Computer network features include on-campus library services, online commercial services, Internet access, wireless campus network, Internet filtering or blocking technology. Student e-mail accounts and computer access in designated common areas are available to students. Students grades are available online. The school has a published electronic and media policy.
Contact Mr. Jim Byrne, Director of Admissions. 770-936-2214. Fax: 770-457-8402. E-mail: admissions@marist.com. Web site: www.marist.com.

ANNOUNCEMENT FROM THE SCHOOL Marist School is an independent Catholic school of the Marist Fathers and Brothers and delivers a values-based education to seventh through twelfth graders. A close-knit and academically challenging community, Marist School gives students the tools for achievement and lifelong excellence in academics, the arts, and athletics in an environment that nurtures each student in the image of Christ.

MARLBOROUGH SCHOOL

250 South Rossmore Avenue
Los Angeles, California 90004

Head of School: Ms. Barbara E. Wagner

General Information Girls' day college-preparatory school. Grades 7–12. Founded: 1889. Setting: urban. 4-acre campus. 4 buildings on campus. Approved or accredited by California Association of Independent Schools, Western Association of Schools and Colleges, and California Department of Education. Member of National Association of Independent Schools. Endowment: $34.2 million. Total enrollment: 537. Upper school average class size: 12. Upper school faculty-student ratio: 1:5.
Upper School Student Profile Grade 10: 92 students (92 girls); Grade 11: 97 students (97 girls); Grade 12: 88 students (88 girls).
Faculty School total: 62. In upper school: 20 men, 33 women; 40 have advanced degrees.
Subjects Offered Algebra, American history, American literature, anatomy, art, art history, astronomy, biology, calculus, ceramics, chemistry, computer science, creative writing, dance, drama, economics, English, English literature, environmental science, European history, expository writing, fine arts, French, genetics, geometry, government/civics, health, history, journalism, Latin, mathematics, music, photography, physical education, physics, physiology, psychology, science, sculpture, social science, social studies, Spanish, Spanish language-AP, Spanish literature-AP, statistics, theater, trigonometry, world history, world literature, writing.
Graduation Requirements Arts and fine arts (art, music, dance, drama), computer science, English, foreign language, mathematics, physical education (includes health), science, social science, social studies (includes history).
Special Academic Programs Advanced Placement exam preparation; honors section; independent study.
College Admission Counseling 84 students graduated in 2007; all went to college, including New York University; Northwestern University; University of California, Berkeley; University of Pennsylvania; University of Southern California. Mean SAT critical reading: 675, mean SAT math: 664, mean SAT writing: 690, mean combined SAT: 2029.
Student Life Upper grades have uniform requirement, student council, honor system. Discipline rests primarily with faculty.
Tuition and Aid Day student tuition: $26,750. Tuition installment plan (Insured Tuition Payment Plan, FACTS Tuition Payment Plan, monthly payment plans). Need-based scholarship grants available. In 2007–08, 14% of upper-school students received aid. Total amount of financial aid awarded in 2007–08: $747,665.
Admissions For fall 2007, 9 students applied for upper-level admission, 1 was accepted, 1 enrolled. ISEE required. Deadline for receipt of application materials: January 17. Application fee required: $100. On-campus interview required.
Athletics Interscholastic: aquatics, basketball, cross-country running, dressage, equestrian sports, golf, independent competitive sports, soccer, softball, swimming and diving, tennis, track and field, volleyball. 8 PE instructors, 30 coaches.
Computers Computers are regularly used in all academic classes. Computer network features include on-campus library services, online commercial services, Internet access, videoconferencing. The school has a published electronic and media policy.
Contact Ms. Jeanette Woo Chitjian, Director of Admissions. 323-964-8451. Fax: 323-933-0542. E-mail: jeanette.woochitjian@marlboroughschool.org. Web site: www.marlboroughschool.org.

ANNOUNCEMENT FROM THE SCHOOL With an environment that values girls' individual interests, intellectual risk-taking, and passionate energy, Marlborough School is dedicated to creating a learning environment that is best suited for the development of successful young women. The School community is defined by its high ethical standards, commitment to diversity, and a deep desire to educate as well as expand horizons and exceed expectations. Rigorous academics, state-of-the-art facilities, competitive athletic programs, outstanding visual and performing arts offerings, and unique opportunities for research in the sciences place Marlborough among the top independent schools in the country.

MARMION ACADEMY

1000 Butterfield Road
Aurora, Illinois 60502

Head of School: John K. Milroy

General Information Boys' day college-preparatory, business, religious studies, Junior ROTC, and LEAD (Leadership Education And Development) school, affiliated with Roman Catholic Church. Grades 9–12. Founded: 1933. Setting: suburban. Nearest major city is Chicago. 325-acre campus. 5 buildings on campus. Approved or accredited by National Catholic Education Association, North Central Association of Colleges and Schools, and Illinois Department of Education. Member of Secondary School Admission Test Board. Endowment: $9 million. Total enrollment: 520. Upper school average class size: 27. Upper school faculty-student ratio: 1:11.

Upper School Student Profile Grade 9: 131 students (131 boys); Grade 10: 132 students (132 boys); Grade 11: 136 students (136 boys); Grade 12: 121 students (121 boys). 85% of students are Roman Catholic.

Faculty School total: 49. In upper school: 40 men, 9 women; 30 have advanced degrees.

Subjects Offered 1½ elective credits, accounting, algebra, American history, American literature, anatomy, art, astronomy, band, biology, biology-AP, botany, calculus, calculus-AP, chemistry, community service, computer science, computer science-AP, computer-aided design, creative writing, driver education, ecology, economics, English, English literature, English-AP, fine arts, French, general science, geometry, government/civics, history, history-AP, JROTC, Latin, leadership education training, leadership training, mathematics, mathematics-AP, meteorology, music, philosophy, physical education, physics, physics-AP, physiology, psychology, religion, science, social science, social studies, sociology, Spanish, Spanish language-AP, theology, trigonometry, Western civilization, zoology.

Graduation Requirements Arts and fine arts (art, music, dance, drama), English, foreign language, JROTC, leadership education training, mathematics, music appreciation, physical education (includes health), religion (includes Bible studies and theology), science, social science, social studies (includes history). Community service is required.

Special Academic Programs Advanced Placement exam preparation; honors section; independent study; academic accommodation for the gifted.

College Admission Counseling 101 students graduated in 2008; 100 went to college, including Marquette University; Purdue University; The University of Iowa; University of Illinois; Western Illinois University. Other: 1 entered military service. Mean composite ACT: 25.

Student Life Upper grades have uniform requirement, student council. Discipline rests primarily with faculty. Attendance at religious services is required.

Tuition and Aid Day student tuition: $8800. Tuition installment plan (SMART Tuition Payment Plan). Merit scholarship grants, need-based scholarship grants, paying campus jobs available. In 2008–09, 22% of upper-school students received aid; total upper-school merit-scholarship money awarded: $130,000. Total amount of financial aid awarded in 2008–09: $269,812.

Admissions Traditional secondary-level entrance grade is 9. For fall 2008, 220 students applied for upper-level admission, 180 were accepted, 131 enrolled. High School Placement Test (closed version) from Scholastic Testing Service required. Deadline for receipt of application materials: none. Application fee required: $50. On-campus interview required.

Athletics Interscholastic: baseball, basketball, cross-country running, diving, football, golf, riflery, soccer, swimming and diving, tennis, track and field, wrestling; intramural: baseball, basketball, fencing, floor hockey, football, JROTC drill, outdoor activities, outdoors, soccer, swimming and diving, table tennis, tennis, volleyball, water polo, weight lifting. 3 PE instructors, 3 coaches, 1 athletic trainer.

Computers Computers are regularly used in drafting, science classes. Computer network features include on-campus library services, Internet access. The school has a published electronic and media policy.

Contact William J. Dickson Jr., Director of Admissions. 630-897-6936. Fax: 630-897-7086. Web site: www.marmion.org.

ANNOUNCEMENT FROM THE SCHOOL Marmion Academy is a Catholic and Benedictine college-preparatory day high school for boys. The school is for average and above-average students whose goal is to attend college. Marmion was founded in 1933 and has been owned and operated ever since by the Benedictine Priests and Brothers of Marmion Abbey. Located on a scenic 325-acre campus just off Interstate 88 in the western Chicago suburb of Aurora, Illinois, the Academy is 35 miles west of downtown Chicago. The school's educational objective is to educate the whole man by establishing a climate conducive to spiritual growth, intellectual endeavors, and leadership training. This goal is based on a firm belief in the goodness of each individual as an image of God, graced with a unique spiritual, intellectual, and physical potential. Marmion has a history of challenging academics and strong leadership programs. These academic-based leadership programs include a Junior Officer Training (JROTC) Program and Marmion's own Leadership Education And Development (LEAD) Program. Approximately 70 percent of Marmion graduates receive merit-based scholarships, with an average of $7.3 million awarded during the past three years. Marmion is a nonprofit organization with a self-perpetuating advisory Board of Lay Trustees, 34 in number, which meets in full session quarterly. The Alumni Association, representing more than 7,600 graduates, organizes alumni events and aids in recruiting students, many of whom are the sons, grandsons, and brothers of alumni. Marmion Academy is fully accredited by the North Central Association of Colleges and Schools and the Illinois State Board of Education. Marmion is a member of the National Catholic Educational Association and the Secondary School Admission Test Board.

MARQUETTE UNIVERSITY HIGH SCHOOL

3401 West Wisconsin Avenue
Milwaukee, Wisconsin 53208

Head of School: Rev. John Belmonte, SJ

General Information Boys' day college-preparatory school, affiliated with Roman Catholic Church. Grades 9–12. Founded: 1857. Setting: urban. 1 building on campus. Approved or accredited by National Catholic Education Association, North Central Association of Colleges and Schools, and Wisconsin Department of Education. Total enrollment: 1,046. Upper school average class size: 24. Upper school faculty-student ratio: 1:14.

Upper School Student Profile Grade 9: 288 students (288 boys); Grade 10: 269 students (269 boys); Grade 11: 248 students (248 boys); Grade 12: 241 students (241 boys). 84% of students are Roman Catholic.

Faculty School total: 76. In upper school: 52 men, 23 women; 45 have advanced degrees.

Subjects Offered Algebra, American history, American literature, architectural drawing, architecture, art, art-AP, Bible studies, biology, biology-AP, calculus, calculus-AP, ceramics, chemistry, chemistry-AP, choral music, computer math, computer programming, computer science, computer science-AP, creative writing, drama, driver education, economics, English, English language-AP, English literature, English literature-AP, ethics, European history, European history-AP, expository writing, geography, geometry, German, government/civics, grammar, graphic design, health, history, jazz band, Latin, Latin-AP, macroeconomics-AP, mathematics, microeconomics-AP, music, philosophy, photography, physical education, physics, psychology, psychology-AP, religion, social studies, sociology, Spanish, Spanish language-AP, statistics-AP, studio art-AP, theology, trigonometry, U.S. government and politics-AP, U.S. history-AP, world history, world literature, World War I, World War II, writing.

Graduation Requirements Arts and fine arts (art, music, dance, drama), English, foreign language, mathematics, science, social studies (includes history), theology, retreats. Community service is required.

Special Academic Programs Advanced Placement exam preparation; honors section.

College Admission Counseling 263 students graduated in 2008; 261 went to college, including Creighton University; Marquette University; Saint Louis University; University of Minnesota, Twin Cities Campus; University of Wisconsin–Madison; University of Wisconsin–Milwaukee. Other: 2 went to work. Median SAT critical reading: 540, median SAT math: 670, median composite ACT: 26. 44% scored over 600 on SAT critical reading, 59% scored over 600 on SAT math, 48% scored over 26 on composite ACT.

Student Life Upper grades have specified standards of dress, student council, honor system. Discipline rests primarily with faculty. Attendance at religious services is required.

Tuition and Aid Day student tuition: $8440. Tuition installment plan (monthly payment plans, prepaid tuition loan program). Need-based scholarship grants, paying campus jobs, state-sponsored voucher program available. In 2008–09, 27% of upper-school students received aid. Total amount of financial aid awarded in 2008–09: $1,250,000.

Admissions Traditional secondary-level entrance grade is 9. Essay and STS—Educational Development Series required. Deadline for receipt of application materials: none. Application fee required: $25.

Athletics Interscholastic: baseball, basketball, cross-country running, diving, fitness, football, golf, hockey, ice hockey, indoor track, indoor track & field, lacrosse, physical fitness, physical training, power lifting, rugby, sailing, skiing (downhill), soccer, strength & conditioning, swimming and diving, tennis, track and field, volleyball, weight lifting, weight training, wrestling; intramural: basketball, bowling, soccer, softball, volleyball.

Computers Computers are regularly used in architecture, college planning, creative writing, data processing, desktop publishing, economics, English, graphic design, literary magazine, mathematics, music, newspaper, research skills, stock market, Web site design, word processing, writing, yearbook classes. Computer network features include on-campus library services, online commercial services, Internet access, Internet filtering or blocking technology, university and county library systems link. Student e-mail accounts are available to students.

Contact Mr. Casey Kowalewski, Director of Admissions. 414-933-7220 Ext. 3046. Fax: 414-937-6002. E-mail: admissions@muhs.edu. Web site: www.muhs.edu.

MARSHALL SCHOOL

1215 Rice Lake Road
Duluth, Minnesota 55811

Head of School: Ms. Barb Brueggemann

General Information Coeducational day college-preparatory, arts, religious studies, and technology school. Grades 5–12. Founded: 1904. Setting: suburban. Nearest major city is Minneapolis. 40-acre campus. 1 building on campus. Approved or accredited by Independent Schools Association of the Central States. Member of National Association of Independent Schools. Endowment: $3.2 million. Total enrollment: 432. Upper school average class size: 18. Upper school faculty-student ratio: 1:11.

Upper School Student Profile Grade 9: 63 students (43 boys, 20 girls); Grade 10: 61 students (34 boys, 27 girls); Grade 11: 75 students (42 boys, 33 girls); Grade 12: 68 students (40 boys, 28 girls).

Faculty School total: 51. In upper school: 18 men, 13 women; 12 have advanced degrees.

Subjects Offered Algebra, American history, American literature, anatomy, art, biology, botany, calculus, calculus-AP, chemistry, community service, computer science, computer science-AP, creative writing, drama, earth science, English, English literature, English literature-AP, environmental science, European history, expository writing, fine arts, French, French-AP, geography, geometry, German, government/civics, health, history, law, mathematics, music, outdoor education, physical education, physics, poetry, religion, science, social studies, Spanish, Spanish-AP, speech, theater, theology, trigonometry, world history, world literature, writing.

Graduation Requirements Arts and fine arts (art, music, dance, drama), computer science, English, foreign language, mathematics, outdoor education, physical education (includes health), religion (includes Bible studies and theology), science, social studies (includes history). Community service is required.

Special Academic Programs 10 Advanced Placement exams for which test preparation is offered; honors section; independent study; academic accommodation for the gifted; remedial reading and/or remedial writing; remedial math; programs in English, mathematics, general development for dyslexic students; special instructional classes for deaf students.

College Admission Counseling 87 students graduated in 2008; 85 went to college, including Saint John's University; University of Minnesota, Duluth; University of Minnesota, Twin Cities Campus; University of Wisconsin–Madison. Other: 2 had other specific plans. Median SAT critical reading: 630, median SAT math: 621, median composite ACT: 26.

Student Life Upper grades have student council. Discipline rests equally with students and faculty.

Summer Programs Remediation, enrichment, sports, art/fine arts, computer instruction programs offered; session focuses on enrichment and study skills; held both on and off campus; held at local parks; accepts boys and girls; open to students from other schools. 300 students usually enrolled. 2009 schedule: June 15 to August 18. Application deadline: none.

Tuition and Aid Day student tuition: $11,450. Tuition installment plan (Insured Tuition Payment Plan, Key Tuition Payment Plan, monthly payment plans). Need-based scholarship grants, paying campus jobs, AchieverLoans (Key Education Resources) available. In 2008–09, 27% of upper-school students received aid. Total amount of financial aid awarded in 2008–09: $680,000.

Admissions Traditional secondary-level entrance grade is 9. CTP or ERB required. Deadline for receipt of application materials: none. Application fee required: $50. On-campus interview required.

Athletics Interscholastic: baseball (boys), basketball (b,g), cheering (b,g), cross-country running (b,g), danceline (b,g), football (b), golf (b,g), ice hockey (b,g), nordic skiing (b,g), skiing (cross-country) (b,g), skiing (downhill) (b,g), soccer (b,g), softball (g), tennis (b,g), track and field (b,g), volleyball (g); coed interscholastic: alpine skiing, football; coed intramural: outdoor education. 4 PE instructors, 43 coaches, 1 athletic trainer.

Computers Computers are regularly used in English, foreign language, history, mathematics, science classes. Computer network features include on-campus library services, online commercial services, Internet access, wireless campus network, Internet filtering or blocking technology. Campus intranet and computer access in designated common areas are available to students. The school has a published electronic and media policy.

Contact Ms. Christa M. Knudsen, Director of Admissions, Public Relations and Financial Aid. 218-727-7266 Ext. 111. Fax: 218-727-1569. E-mail: cknudsen@marshallschool.org. Web site: www.marshallschool.org.

MARS HILL BIBLE SCHOOL

698 Cox Creek Parkway
Florence, Alabama 35630

Head of School: Dr. Kenny D Barfield

General Information Coeducational day college-preparatory, arts, and religious studies school, affiliated with Church of Christ; primarily serves students with learning disabilities, individuals with Attention Deficit Disorder, and dyslexic students. Grades K–12. Founded: 1947. Setting: suburban. Nearest major city is Huntsville. 80-acre campus. 6 buildings on campus. Approved or accredited by National Christian School Association and Southern Association of Colleges and Schools. Endowment: $3.2 million. Total enrollment: 611. Upper school average class size: 22. Upper school faculty-student ratio: 1:14.

Upper School Student Profile Grade 9: 64 students (34 boys, 30 girls); Grade 10: 52 students (31 boys, 21 girls); Grade 11: 47 students (22 boys, 25 girls); Grade 12: 48 students (17 boys, 31 girls). 81% of students are members of Church of Christ.

Faculty School total: 43. In upper school: 11 men, 12 women; 15 have advanced degrees.

Subjects Offered ACT preparation, algebra, American government, American literature, American literature-AP, anatomy and physiology, ancient world history, band, Bible studies, biology, biology-AP, calculus, calculus-AP, chemistry, chemistry-AP, chorus, computer literacy, computer programming, computer science, concert band, concert choir, current events, debate, drama, drama performance, driver education, ecology, economics, English, English composition, English literature, English literature and composition-AP, English literature-AP, ensembles, forensics, geometry, government-AP, Greek, health, honors English, human anatomy, Internet research, jazz band, Life of Christ, marine biology, musical productions, physical education, physical science, physics, pre-algebra, pre-calculus, psychology, psychology-AP, Spanish, speech, speech and debate, statistics-AP, student government, student publications, U.S. government-AP, U.S. history, U.S. history-AP, word processing, world geography, world history, yearbook.

Graduation Requirements Algebra, American government, American history, American literature, ancient world history, Bible, biology, British literature, chemistry, college writing, computer applications, computer literacy, English composition, foreign language, geometry, health and wellness, introduction to literature, mathematics, physical education (includes health), physical science, science, social studies (includes history), speech communications. Community service is required.

Special Academic Programs 3 Advanced Placement exams for which test preparation is offered; honors section; independent study; study at local college for college credit; special instructional classes for students with learning disabilities, Attention Deficit Disorder, and dyslexia.

College Admission Counseling 48 students graduated in 2008; all went to college, including Auburn University; Freed-Hardeman University; Harding University; The University of Alabama; University of North Alabama. Median composite ACT: 24. 43% scored over 26 on composite ACT.

Student Life Upper grades have specified standards of dress, student council. Discipline rests primarily with faculty. Attendance at religious services is required.

Tuition and Aid Day student tuition: $4880. Tuition installment plan (FACTS Tuition Payment Plan, monthly payment plans). Tuition reduction for siblings, need-based scholarship grants available. In 2008–09, 20% of upper-school students received aid. Total amount of financial aid awarded in 2008–09: $150,000.

Admissions Traditional secondary-level entrance grade is 9. For fall 2008, 31 students applied for upper-level admission, 24 were accepted, 24 enrolled. Achievement tests, ACT-Explore, PSAT or Stanford Achievement Test required. Deadline for receipt of application materials: none. Application fee required: $100. Interview required.

Athletics Interscholastic: baseball (boys), basketball (b,g), cheering (g), cross-country running (b,g), golf (b,g), soccer (b,g), softball (g), tennis (b,g), track and field (b,g), volleyball (g); intramural: basketball (b,g), bowling (b,g), fitness (b,g); coed intramural: badminton, bowling, cooperative games, fitness. 5 PE instructors, 7 coaches.

Computers Computers are regularly used in Bible studies, English, history, remedial study skills, yearbook classes. Computer resources include on-campus library services, online commercial services, Internet access, wireless campus network, Internet filtering or blocking technology. Computer access in designated common areas is available to students. Students grades are available online. The school has a published electronic and media policy.

Contact Mrs. Jeannie Garrett, Director of Admissions. 256-767-1203 Ext. 205. Fax: 256-767-6304. E-mail: jgarrett@mhbs.org. Web site: www.mhbs.org.

MARTIN LUTHER HIGH SCHOOL

60-02 Maspeth Avenue
Maspeth, New York 11378

Head of School: Ben Herbrich

General Information Coeducational day college-preparatory, arts, and business school, affiliated with Lutheran Church. Grades 9–12. Founded: 1960. Setting: urban. Nearest major city is New York. 1-acre campus. 1 building on campus. Approved or accredited by Middle States Association of Colleges and Schools and New York Department of Education. Endowment: $2.2 million. Total enrollment: 316. Upper school average class size: 25. Upper school faculty-student ratio: 1:15.

Upper School Student Profile Grade 9: 69 students (41 boys, 28 girls); Grade 10: 80 students (37 boys, 43 girls); Grade 11: 81 students (40 boys, 41 girls); Grade 12: 86 students (46 boys, 40 girls). 16% of students are Lutheran.

Faculty School total: 24. In upper school: 13 men, 11 women; 13 have advanced degrees.

Subjects Offered Algebra, American history, art, Bible studies, biology, business, business skills, calculus, chemistry, computer programming, computer science, drama, driver education, earth science, economics, English, English literature, ethics, European history, fine arts, French, geography, geometry, German, government/civics, grammar, health, history, journalism, marine biology, mathematics, music, philosophy,

photography, physical education, physics, psychology, religion, science, social studies, Spanish, speech, theater, theology, trigonometry, world history.
Graduation Requirements Arts and fine arts (art, music, dance, drama), business skills (includes word processing), English, foreign language, mathematics, physical education (includes health), religion (includes Bible studies and theology), science, social studies (includes history), service hours.
Special Academic Programs Advanced Placement exam preparation; honors section; accelerated programs; independent study; study at local college for college credit; remedial reading and/or remedial writing; remedial math; programs in general development for dyslexic students.
College Admission Counseling 89 students graduated in 2008; 83 went to college, including City College of the City University of New York; Hunter College of the City University of New York; Queens College of the City University of New York; St. Francis College; St. John's University; Stony Brook University, State University of New York. Other: 5 went to work, 1 entered military service.
Student Life Upper grades have uniform requirement, student council. Discipline rests primarily with faculty. Attendance at religious services is required.
Summer Programs Remediation, computer instruction programs offered; held on campus; accepts boys and girls; open to students from other schools. 250 students usually enrolled. 2009 schedule: July 2 to August 16. Application deadline: none.
Tuition and Aid Day student tuition: $8000–$9200. Tuition installment plan (monthly payment plans). Tuition reduction for siblings, merit scholarship grants, need-based scholarship grants available. In 2008–09, 30% of upper-school students received aid; total upper-school merit-scholarship money awarded: $87,940. Total amount of financial aid awarded in 2008–09: $103,400.
Admissions Traditional secondary-level entrance grade is 9. School's own exam required. Deadline for receipt of application materials: none. Application fee required: $50. On-campus interview recommended.
Athletics Interscholastic: baseball (boys), basketball (b,g), cheering (g), cross-country running (b,g), fitness (b,g), soccer (b), softball (g), tennis (b,g), track and field (b,g), volleyball (g), wrestling (b,g); intramural: basketball (b,g), cross-country running (b,g), floor hockey (b,g), indoor hockey (b,g), soccer (b,g), weight lifting (b,g), wrestling (b); coed interscholastic: cheering, cross-country running, fitness, soccer; coed intramural: archery, badminton, cross-country running, fitness, handball, paddle tennis, racquetball, track and field, volleyball, wrestling. 3 PE instructors, 18 coaches.
Computers Computers are regularly used in business education, career education, Christian doctrine, history, keyboarding, newspaper, yearbook classes. Computer resources include on-campus library services, Internet access.
Contact Mrs. Patricia Dee, Admissions Administrator. 718-894-4000. Fax: 718-894-1469. Web site: www.martinluthernyc.org.

THE MARVELWOOD SCHOOL

476 Skiff Mountain Road
PO Box 3001
Kent, Connecticut 06757-3001

Head of School: Mr. Scott E. Pottbecker

General Information Coeducational boarding and day college-preparatory, arts, technology, field science, and community service, and ESL school; primarily serves underachievers, students with learning disabilities, individuals with Attention Deficit Disorder, and dyslexic students. Grades 9–12. Founded: 1957. Setting: rural. Nearest major city is Hartford. Students are housed in single-sex dormitories. 83-acre campus. 10 buildings on campus. Approved or accredited by Association of Independent Schools in New England, Connecticut Association of Independent Schools, National Independent Private Schools Association, New England Association of Schools and Colleges, The Association of Boarding Schools, and Connecticut Department of Education. Member of National Association of Independent Schools. Endowment: $1.4 million. Total enrollment: 165. Upper school average class size: 8. Upper school faculty-student ratio: 1:4.
Upper School Student Profile Grade 9: 29 students (19 boys, 10 girls); Grade 10: 42 students (33 boys, 9 girls); Grade 11: 47 students (34 boys, 13 girls); Grade 12: 47 students (28 boys, 19 girls). 94% of students are boarding students. 21% are state residents. 14 states are represented in upper school student body. 33% are international students. International students from Afghanistan, China, Jamaica, Republic of Korea, Spain, and United Kingdom; 6 other countries represented in student body.
Faculty School total: 48. In upper school: 19 men, 27 women; 24 have advanced degrees; 34 reside on campus.
Subjects Offered Algebra, American history, American literature, anatomy and physiology, art, art history, biology, calculus, ceramics, chemistry, chorus, community service, creative writing, drama, driver education, English, English literature, ESL, ethology, European history, film, fine arts, French, geography, geometry, history of China and Japan, limnology, mathematics, music, ornithology, photography, physics, pre-algebra, psychology, religion, science, Shakespeare, social studies, Spanish, studio art, trigonometry, world culture, world history, world literature.
Graduation Requirements Arts and fine arts (art, music, dance, drama), English, foreign language, mathematics, science, social studies (includes history), senior service project, daily participation in sports, weekly community service program.
Special Academic Programs Advanced Placement exam preparation; honors section; remedial reading and/or remedial writing; remedial math; programs in general development for dyslexic students; ESL (42 students enrolled).
College Admission Counseling 44 students graduated in 2008; 41 went to college, including Hofstra University; New York University; Pace University; Purdue University; Syracuse University; University of Connecticut. Other: 3 had other specific plans. Median SAT critical reading: 458, median SAT math: 424, median SAT writing: 458.
Student Life Upper grades have specified standards of dress, student council. Discipline rests primarily with faculty.
Summer Programs Remediation, enrichment, ESL, art/fine arts, computer instruction programs offered; session focuses on study skills; held on campus; accepts boys and girls; open to students from other schools. 30 students usually enrolled. 2009 schedule: July 5 to August 2. Application deadline: none.
Tuition and Aid Day student tuition: $25,250; 7-day tuition and room/board: $41,500. Tuition installment plan (Insured Tuition Payment Plan, Academic Management Services Plan, Key Tuition Payment Plan, individually arranged payment plans). Need-based scholarship grants available. In 2008–09, 30% of upper-school students received aid. Total amount of financial aid awarded in 2008–09: $583,500.
Admissions Traditional secondary-level entrance grade is 9. For fall 2008, 226 students applied for upper-level admission, 174 were accepted, 83 enrolled. Deadline for receipt of application materials: none. Application fee required: $50. Interview required.
Athletics Interscholastic: baseball (boys), basketball (b,g), cross-country running (b,g), horseback riding (g), lacrosse (b), soccer (b,g), softball (g), tennis (b,g), volleyball (g), wrestling (b); intramural: lacrosse (g); coed interscholastic: alpine skiing, golf, skiing (downhill); coed intramural: bicycling, canoeing/kayaking, climbing, fishing, fly fishing, hiking/backpacking, horseback riding, mountain biking, mountaineering, outdoor activities, physical training, rock climbing, ropes courses, skiing (downhill), snowboarding, strength & conditioning, weight training, wilderness, wildernessways, yoga. 1 athletic trainer.
Computers Computers are regularly used in mathematics, newspaper, photography, science, writing classes. Computer network features include on-campus library services, Internet access, wireless campus network, Internet filtering or blocking technology. Campus intranet, student e-mail accounts, and computer access in designated common areas are available to students. The school has a published electronic and media policy.
Contact Mrs. Katherine Almquist, Director of Admissions. 860-927-0047 Ext. 1004. Fax: 860-927-0021. E-mail: katherine.almquist@marvelwood.org. Web site: www.marvelwood.org.

ANNOUNCEMENT FROM THE SCHOOL The Marvelwood Summer Program runs from July 5 through August 1, 2009, and features classes for credit or enrichment, SAT and TOEFL preparation, English language learning (ELL), and a Leadership Seminar. The four-week Marvelwood Summer Program recognizes that each student walks a unique path towards success—one that is not always easily recognized in traditional teaching environments. Small classes, an experienced faculty, and a dedication to each student's individual success distinguish Marvelwood's Summer Program and provide a solid foundation for academic success. The Leadership Seminar features rock climbing, white water canoeing and kayaking, hiking, and peer mediation. It is open to students entering grades 8–11. Marvelwood's two-week English Language Learners Program runs August 2–15, 2009. This program immerses students in the English language and culture and prepares them for their studies in the United States. It is open to any student entering grades 8–12 in an American school for the 2009–10 academic year.

See Close-Up on page 838.

MARY HELP OF CHRISTIANS ACADEMY

659 Belmont Avenue
North Haledon, New Jersey 07508

Head of School: Sr. Kim Keraitis, FMA

General Information Girls' day college-preparatory, business, religious studies, and health care studies school, affiliated with Roman Catholic Church. Grades 9–12. Founded: 1940. Setting: suburban. Nearest major city is Paterson. 16-acre campus. 6 buildings on campus. Approved or accredited by Middle States Association of Colleges and Schools and New Jersey Department of Education. Total enrollment: 230. Upper school average class size: 17. Upper school faculty-student ratio: 1:8.
Upper School Student Profile Grade 9: 62 students (62 girls); Grade 10: 57 students (57 girls); Grade 11: 59 students (59 girls); Grade 12: 52 students (52 girls). 80% of students are Roman Catholic.
Faculty School total: 28. In upper school: 8 men, 20 women; 15 have advanced degrees.
Subjects Offered Accounting, advanced chemistry, advanced math, Advanced Placement courses, advertising design, algebra, American literature, anatomy and physiology, art, art appreciation, art history, Bible studies, biology, biology-AP, British literature, British literature (honors), business, business studies, calculus-AP, career/college preparation, Catholic belief and practice, chemistry, choral music, Christian and Hebrew scripture, Christian ethics, communication skills, computer applications, computer graphics, computer literacy, consumer mathematics, driver education, English, English literature-AP, environmental science, fashion, first aid, forensics,

French, geometry, gymnastics, health science, history of the Catholic Church, home economics, honors English, human anatomy, instrumental music, journalism, marketing, music appreciation, music theory, photo shop, physical education, physical science, physics, political science, political systems, pre-algebra, pre-calculus, psychology, publications, SAT preparation, science and technology, social justice, Spanish, Spanish language-AP, student government, studio art, study skills, television, theology, trigonometry, video film production, vocal music, Web site design, world history, writing, yearbook.

Graduation Requirements Algebra, American history, American literature, art, biology, British literature, career/college preparation, Catholic belief and practice, Christian and Hebrew scripture, Christian doctrine, computer applications, computers, driver education, electives, English, first aid, foreign language, general science, geometry, health and safety, history of the Catholic Church, literature, moral theology, physical education (includes health), science, study skills, world history, world literature, 80 hours of service performed with a nonprofit community organization.

Special Academic Programs Advanced Placement exam preparation; honors section; independent study; study at local college for college credit; remedial reading and/or remedial writing; remedial math; special instructional classes for students with moderate learning disabilities.

College Admission Counseling 42 students graduated in 2008; all went to college, including Caldwell College; Felician College; Pace University; Rutgers, The State University of New Jersey, New Brunswick; William Paterson University of New Jersey.

Student Life Upper grades have uniform requirement, student council, honor system. Discipline rests primarily with faculty. Attendance at religious services is required.

Summer Programs Remediation, advancement programs offered; session focuses on mathematics advancement, remediation in mathematics, language arts for incoming freshmen, honors biology; held on campus; accepts girls; not open to students from other schools. 30 students usually enrolled. 2009 schedule: June 23 to July 25. Application deadline: May 15.

Tuition and Aid Day student tuition: $6000. Tuition installment plan (monthly payment plans, individually arranged payment plans). Tuition reduction for siblings, merit scholarship grants, need-based scholarship grants, paying campus jobs available. In 2008–09, 51% of upper-school students received aid; total upper-school merit-scholarship money awarded: $80,000. Total amount of financial aid awarded in 2008–09: $378,091.

Admissions Traditional secondary-level entrance grade is 9. Cooperative Entrance Exam (McGraw-Hill) and school placement exam required. Deadline for receipt of application materials: none. No application fee required. Interview required.

Athletics Interscholastic: basketball, bowling, cheering, soccer, softball, tennis, track and field, volleyball; intramural: basketball, cheering, volleyball. 1 PE instructor, 4 coaches.

Computers Computers are regularly used in accounting, English, graphic arts, graphics, journalism, publications, religion, SAT preparation, science, Spanish, video film production, Web site design, word processing, yearbook classes. Computer network features include on-campus library services, online commercial services, Internet access, wireless campus network, Internet filtering or blocking technology, EBSCOhost®, Kurzweil 3000 (assistive reading software). Campus intranet is available to students. Students grades are available online. The school has a published electronic and media policy.

Contact Sr. Maryann Schaefer, FMA, Admissions Director. 973-790-6200 Ext. 140. Fax: 973-790-6125. E-mail: admissions@maryhelp.org. Web site: www.maryhelp.org.

MARYKNOLL SCHOOL

1526 Alexander Street
Honolulu, Hawaii 96822

Head of School: Perry K. Martin

General Information Coeducational day college-preparatory school, affiliated with Roman Catholic Church. Grades PK–12. Founded: 1927. Setting: urban. 3-acre campus. 3 buildings on campus. Approved or accredited by National Catholic Education Association, Western Association of Schools and Colleges, Western Catholic Education Association, and Hawaii Department of Education. Member of National Association of Independent Schools and Secondary School Admission Test Board. Endowment: $3.5 million. Total enrollment: 1,372. Upper school average class size: 18. Upper school faculty-student ratio: 1:11.

Upper School Student Profile Grade 9: 152 students (69 boys, 83 girls); Grade 10: 147 students (71 boys, 76 girls); Grade 11: 128 students (68 boys, 60 girls); Grade 12: 136 students (64 boys, 72 girls). 50% of students are Roman Catholic.

Faculty School total: 104. In upper school: 26 men, 28 women; 30 have advanced degrees.

Subjects Offered Adolescent issues, algebra, American literature, art, art history-AP, biology, biology-AP, biotechnology, British literature, calculus-AP, chemistry, chemistry-AP, college counseling, college placement, computer programming, creative writing, drawing, economics, English language and composition-AP, English literature and composition-AP, ethics, European history-AP, French, geography, geometry, global science, golf, government, government-AP, guitar, Hawaiian history, Hawaiian language, human development, Japanese, journalism, library assistant, marine science, media, mythology, novels, Pacific art, painting, philosophy, physical education, physics, physics-AP, poetry, pre-calculus, psychology, psychology-AP, religion, religious studies, research, Russian history, science fiction, senior project, Shakespeare, sociology, Spanish, speech, statistics, studio art-AP, theater, U.S. history, U.S. history-AP, Web site design, weight training, world history, world literature, yearbook.

Graduation Requirements Arts and fine arts (art, music, dance, drama), English, foreign language, mathematics, physical education (includes health), religion (includes Bible studies and theology), science, senior project, social science, social studies (includes history), portfolio of student works. Community service is required.

Special Academic Programs Advanced Placement exam preparation; honors section; independent study.

College Admission Counseling 137 students graduated in 2008; all went to college, including Loyola Marymount University; Santa Clara University; University of Hawaii at Manoa; University of San Francisco; University of Southern California; University of Washington.

Student Life Upper grades have uniform requirement, student council. Discipline rests equally with students and faculty. Attendance at religious services is required.

Summer Programs Remediation, enrichment, advancement, sports, art/fine arts, computer instruction programs offered; session focuses on advancement and enrichment; held on campus; accepts boys and girls; open to students from other schools. 800 students usually enrolled. 2009 schedule: June 16 to July 28. Application deadline: May 15.

Tuition and Aid Day student tuition: $12,200. Tuition installment plan (Insured Tuition Payment Plan, monthly payment plans). Merit scholarship grants, need-based scholarship grants, paying campus jobs available. In 2008–09, 17% of upper-school students received aid; total upper-school merit-scholarship money awarded: $64,000. Total amount of financial aid awarded in 2008–09: $395,000.

Admissions Traditional secondary-level entrance grade is 9. For fall 2008, 182 students applied for upper-level admission, 121 were accepted, 61 enrolled. PSAT or SSAT required. Deadline for receipt of application materials: December 15. Application fee required: $75. On-campus interview required.

Athletics Interscholastic: aerobics/dance (girls), baseball (b), basketball (b,g), bowling (b,g), canoeing/kayaking (b,g), cross-country running (b,g), dance (g), diving (b,g), football (b), golf (b,g), gymnastics (b,g), judo (b,g), kayaking (b,g), martial arts (b,g), ocean paddling (b,g), paddling (b,g), power lifting (b,g), riflery (b,g), sailing (b,g), soccer (b,g), softball (g), strength & conditioning (b,g), swimming and diving (b,g), tennis (b,g), track and field (b,g), volleyball (b,g), water polo (b,g), weight lifting (b,g), weight training (b,g), wrestling (b,g); intramural: basketball (b,g), volleyball (b,g); coed interscholastic: canoeing/kayaking, cheering, football, ocean paddling, paddling, strength & conditioning, weight training, wrestling; coed intramural: basketball, bowling, floor hockey. 3 PE instructors, 50 coaches, 1 athletic trainer.

Computers Computers are regularly used in English, foreign language, history, mathematics, science classes. Computer network features include on-campus library services, online commercial services, Internet access, wireless campus network, Internet filtering or blocking technology. Student e-mail accounts are available to students.

Contact Mrs. Lori Carlos, Director of Admission. 808-952-7330. Fax: 808-952-7331. E-mail: admission@maryknollschool.org. Web site: www.maryknollschool.org.

MARYLAWN OF THE ORANGES

445 Scotland Road
South Orange, New Jersey 07079

Head of School: Mrs. Christine H. Lopez

General Information Girls' day college-preparatory, arts, business, religious studies, bilingual studies, and technology school, affiliated with Roman Catholic Church. Grades 9–12. Founded: 1935. Setting: suburban. Nearest major city is Newark. 2 buildings on campus. Approved or accredited by Middle States Association of Colleges and Schools and New Jersey Department of Education. Total enrollment: 156. Upper school average class size: 15. Upper school faculty-student ratio: 1:15.

Upper School Student Profile Grade 9: 37 students (37 girls); Grade 10: 36 students (36 girls); Grade 11: 42 students (42 girls); Grade 12: 41 students (41 girls). 25% of students are Roman Catholic.

Faculty School total: 19. In upper school: 8 men, 11 women; 9 have advanced degrees.

Subjects Offered Advanced chemistry, advanced computer applications, advanced math, African-American literature, algebra, American literature, anatomy and physiology, art, art history, athletics, biology, British literature (honors), calculus, campus ministry, career/college preparation, Catholic belief and practice, cheerleading, chemistry, choir, choral music, Christian ethics, Christian scripture, civics, classical studies, community service, constitutional law, dramatic arts, English, English-AP, environmental science, film, fine arts, French, geometry, global studies, grammar, guidance, handbells, health education, honors algebra, honors English, honors geometry, honors U.S. history, Internet research, journalism, language arts, Latin, mathematics, moral theology, music theory, physical education, physics, pre-calculus, psychology, SAT/ACT preparation, social studies, Spanish, trigonometry, U.S. history, world history, world religions, writing workshop, yearbook.

Graduation Requirements Arts and fine arts (art, music, dance, drama), English, foreign language, mathematics, physical education (includes health), religious studies, science, social studies (includes history), 25 hours of community service (junior year), 40 hours of community service (senior year).

Special Academic Programs 1 Advanced Placement exam for which test preparation is offered; honors section; independent study; academic accommodation for the gifted, the musically talented, and the artistically talented; remedial reading and/or remedial writing; remedial math; ESL (1 student enrolled).
College Admission Counseling 42 students graduated in 2008; all went to college, including Hampton University; Kean University; Rutgers, The State University of New Jersey, New Brunswick; Seton Hall University; University of Hartford. Median SAT critical reading: 464, median SAT math: 450, median SAT writing: 470. 10% scored over 600 on SAT critical reading, 3% scored over 600 on SAT math, 13% scored over 600 on SAT writing.
Student Life Upper grades have uniform requirement, student council. Discipline rests primarily with faculty. Attendance at religious services is required.
Summer Programs Remediation, enrichment, advancement, computer instruction programs offered; session focuses on prep and advancement for secondary school courses; make-up for failed classes; held on campus; accepts girls; not open to students from other schools. 60 students usually enrolled. 2009 schedule: June 25 to July 23. Application deadline: June 20.
Tuition and Aid Day student tuition: $6750. Tuition installment plan (monthly payment plans, Tuition Management Systems). Tuition reduction for siblings, merit scholarship grants, need-based scholarship grants available. In 2008–09, 37% of upper-school students received aid; total upper-school merit-scholarship money awarded: $24,000. Total amount of financial aid awarded in 2008–09: $81,200.
Admissions For fall 2008, 193 students applied for upper-level admission, 160 were accepted, 51 enrolled. Cooperative Entrance Exam (McGraw-Hill) required. Deadline for receipt of application materials: none. Application fee required: $125. On-campus interview required.
Athletics Interscholastic: basketball, cheering, dance team, drill team, softball, track and field, volleyball; intramural: basketball, physical fitness, tennis, weight training. 1 PE instructor, 2 coaches.
Computers Computers are regularly used in all classes. Computer resources include on-campus library services, Internet access, Internet filtering or blocking technology. The school has a published electronic and media policy.
Contact Mrs. Tanya Craig, Admissions Officer. 973-762-9222 Ext. 15. Fax: 973-378-7975. E-mail: admissions@marylawn.us. Web site: www.marylawn.us.

THE MARY LOUIS ACADEMY

176-21 Wexford Terrace
Jamaica Estates, New York 11432-2926
Head of School: Kathleen M. McKinney, CSJ

General Information Girls' day college-preparatory, arts, religious studies, and technology school, affiliated with Roman Catholic Church. Grades 9–12. Founded: 1936. Setting: urban. Nearest major city is New York. 2 buildings on campus. Approved or accredited by Middle States Association of Colleges and Schools and New York State Board of Regents. Endowment: $1.5 million. Total enrollment: 962. Upper school average class size: 28. Upper school faculty-student ratio: 1:13.
Upper School Student Profile Grade 9: 246 students (246 girls); Grade 10: 249 students (249 girls); Grade 11: 223 students (223 girls); Grade 12: 244 students (244 girls). 77.2% of students are Roman Catholic.
Faculty School total: 78. In upper school: 16 men, 62 women; 60 have advanced degrees.
Subjects Offered Advanced Placement courses, American history, art, astronomy, biology, calculus, career exploration, chemistry, college planning, composition, computer science, current events, drawing, driver education, earth science, economics, English, English literature, European history, family studies, fine arts, first aid, French, government/civics, history, human development, Italian, Latin, law, leadership training, literature, mathematics, microbiology, music, music theory, nutrition, painting, physical education, physics, political science, religion, science, sculpture, social studies, Spanish, vocal music, world history, world literature.
Graduation Requirements Arts and fine arts (art, music, dance, drama), English, foreign language, mathematics, music, physical education (includes health), religion (includes Bible studies and theology), science, social studies (includes history), technology, service project.
Special Academic Programs Advanced Placement exam preparation; honors section; study at local college for college credit; academic accommodation for the musically talented and the artistically talented; programs in general development for dyslexic students.
College Admission Counseling 221 students graduated in 2008; all went to college, including Fordham University. Mean SAT critical reading: 537, mean SAT math: 537. 21% scored over 600 on SAT critical reading, 21% scored over 600 on SAT math.
Student Life Upper grades have uniform requirement, student council. Discipline rests primarily with faculty. Attendance at religious services is required.
Summer Programs Remediation, enrichment programs offered; session focuses on Regents Competency Test preparation only; held on campus; accepts girls; open to students from other schools. 55 students usually enrolled. 2009 schedule: August 1 to August 15. Application deadline: June 30.
Tuition and Aid Day student tuition: $6600. Tuition installment plan (SMART Tuition Payment Plan, monthly payment plans, quarterly payment plan, Tuition in full (yearly), Tuition Guarantee Program). Tuition reduction for siblings, merit scholarship grants, need-based scholarship grants available. In 2008–09, 23% of upper-school students received aid; total upper-school merit-scholarship money awarded: $409,150. Total amount of financial aid awarded in 2008–09: $445,150.
Admissions Traditional secondary-level entrance grade is 9. Catholic High School Entrance Examination required. Deadline for receipt of application materials: February 15. Application fee required: $300. Interview recommended.
Athletics Interscholastic: basketball, cheering, cross-country running, dance, dance team, golf, gymnastics, indoor track, indoor track & field, lacrosse, running, soccer, softball, swimming and diving, tennis, track and field, volleyball, winter (indoor) track; intramural: basketball, billiards, fitness, self defense, soccer, yoga. 4 PE instructors, 17 coaches.
Computers Computers are regularly used in career exploration, college planning, English, foreign language, history, mathematics, music, science classes. Computer network features include on-campus library services, online commercial services, Internet access, Internet filtering or blocking technology. The school has a published electronic and media policy.
Contact Sr. Lorraine O'Neill, CSJ, Administrative Secretary. 718-297-2120. Fax: 718-739-0037. Web site: www.tmla.org.

MARYMOUNT HIGH SCHOOL

10643 Sunset Boulevard
Los Angeles, California 90077
Head of School: Dr. Mary Ellen Gozdecki

General Information Girls' day college-preparatory and religious studies school, affiliated with Roman Catholic Church. Grades 9–12. Founded: 1923. Setting: suburban. 6.5-acre campus. 6 buildings on campus. Approved or accredited by California Association of Independent Schools, National Catholic Education Association, The College Board, Western Association of Schools and Colleges, and California Department of Education. Member of National Association of Independent Schools and Secondary School Admission Test Board. Endowment: $5.3 million. Total enrollment: 402. Upper school average class size: 17. Upper school faculty-student ratio: 1:8.
Upper School Student Profile Grade 9: 97 students (97 girls); Grade 10: 101 students (101 girls); Grade 11: 109 students (109 girls); Grade 12: 95 students (95 girls). 68% of students are Roman Catholic.
Faculty School total: 56. In upper school: 15 men, 41 women; 42 have advanced degrees.
Subjects Offered Acting, advanced studio art-AP, aerobics, African literature, algebra, American history, American legal systems, American literature, anatomy, art, art history, art-AP, biology, biology-AP, British literature, calculus, calculus-AP, ceramics, chemistry, choir, Christian testament, community service, computer literacy, computer science, contemporary issues, dance, death and loss, design, drama, drawing, ecology, economics, English, English literature, environmental science, environmental science-AP, ethics, fencing, fine arts, French, French-AP, gender and religion, geography, geometry, government/civics, Hebrew scripture, human development, Japanese literature, jazz ensemble, journalism, language and composition, literary magazine, literature, literature-AP, music, musical productions, painting, peace studies, performing arts, photography, physical education, physics, physiology, pre-calculus, printmaking, psychology, religion, religious studies, robotics, science, self-defense, social justice, social studies, softball, Spanish, Spanish language-AP, Spanish literature-AP, speech, swimming, theology, trigonometry, U.S. government-AP, U.S. history, U.S. history-AP, vocal music, volleyball, women's studies, world religions, writing.
Graduation Requirements Arts and fine arts (art, music, dance, drama), computer science, English, foreign language, mathematics, physical education (includes health), religion (includes Bible studies and theology), science, social studies (includes history), 100 hours of community service.
Special Academic Programs 17 Advanced Placement exams for which test preparation is offered; honors section; independent study.
College Admission Counseling 103 students graduated in 2008; 102 went to college, including Loyola Marymount University; Santa Clara University; The University of Arizona; University of California, Berkeley; University of Colorado at Boulder; University of Southern California. Other: 1 had other specific plans. Mean SAT critical reading: 629, mean SAT math: 601, mean SAT writing: 647, mean combined SAT: 1997. 57% scored over 600 on SAT critical reading, 51% scored over 600 on SAT math, 72% scored over 600 on SAT writing, 60% scored over 1800 on combined SAT.
Student Life Upper grades have uniform requirement, student council, honor system. Discipline rests equally with students and faculty. Attendance at religious services is required.
Summer Programs Remediation, enrichment, advancement, sports, art/fine arts, computer instruction programs offered; session focuses on enrichment, advancement; held on campus; accepts boys and girls; open to students from other schools. 180 students usually enrolled. 2009 schedule: June 22 to July 24. Application deadline: May 15.
Tuition and Aid Day student tuition: $23,900. Tuition installment plan (FACTS Tuition Payment Plan). Merit scholarship grants, need-based scholarship grants available. In 2008–09, 21% of upper-school students received aid; total upper-school merit-scholarship money awarded: $11,000. Total amount of financial aid awarded in 2008–09: $1,028,517.

Admissions Traditional secondary-level entrance grade is 9. For fall 2008, 208 students applied for upper-level admission, 132 were accepted, 105 enrolled. ISEE required. Deadline for receipt of application materials: January 12. Application fee required: $100. Interview required.
Athletics Interscholastic: basketball, cross-country running, equestrian sports, fencing, golf, soccer, softball, swimming and diving, tennis, track and field, volleyball, water polo; intramural: aerobics, aerobics/dance, archery, crew, dance, physical fitness, self defense, strength & conditioning. 1 PE instructor, 24 coaches, 1 athletic trainer.
Computers Computers are regularly used in all academic classes. Computer network features include on-campus library services, online commercial services, Internet access, wireless campus network, Internet filtering or blocking technology, access to UCLA Library, Loyola Marymount University Library, 14 independent high school libraries. Campus intranet, student e-mail accounts, and computer access in designated common areas are available to students. Students grades are available online. The school has a published electronic and media policy.
Contact Mrs. Erica Huebner, Director of Admission. 310-472-1205 Ext. 220. Fax: 310-440-4316. E-mail: ehuebner@mhs-la.org. Web site: www.mhs-la.org.

ANNOUNCEMENT FROM THE SCHOOL Marymount High School, a Catholic, independent, college-preparatory day school established in 1923 by the Religious of the Sacred Heart of Mary (RSHM), shares the tradition of an international network of schools dedicated to the education of young women. Marymount maintains a philosophy deeply rooted in the RSHM mission of educating the heart and mind to prepare young women to make a better world. A hallmark of a Marymount education is a highly personalized, student-centered program. Each year, 100% of Marymount graduates are admitted to selective colleges and universities.

MARYMOUNT INTERNATIONAL SCHOOL

Via di Villa Lauchli 180
Rome 00191, Italy

Head of School: Dr. Yvonne Hennigan

General Information Coeducational day college-preparatory school, affiliated with Roman Catholic Church. Grades PK–12. Founded: 1946. Setting: suburban. 16-acre campus. 3 buildings on campus. Approved or accredited by European Council of International Schools and New England Association of Schools and Colleges. Language of instruction: English. Total enrollment: 715. Upper school average class size: 18. Upper school faculty-student ratio: 1:15.
Upper School Student Profile Grade 9: 62 students (21 boys, 41 girls); Grade 10: 53 students (32 boys, 21 girls); Grade 11: 49 students (26 boys, 23 girls); Grade 12: 60 students (30 boys, 30 girls). 75% of students are Roman Catholic.
Faculty School total: 98. In upper school: 15 men, 35 women; 40 have advanced degrees.
Subjects Offered Algebra, American history, American literature, art, art history, art history-AP, biology, calculus, ceramics, chemistry, computer programming, computer science, current events, drama, English, English literature, environmental science, ESL, European history, fine arts, French, geography, geometry, health, history, International Baccalaureate courses, international relations, Italian, Latin, mathematics, music, photography, physical education, physics, pre-calculus, religious education, science, social studies, Spanish, study skills, theater arts, theory of knowledge, trigonometry, world history.
Graduation Requirements Arts and fine arts (art, music, dance, drama), English, foreign language, mathematics, religion (includes Bible studies and theology), science, social studies (includes history).
Special Academic Programs International Baccalaureate program; 1 Advanced Placement exam for which test preparation is offered; ESL (24 students enrolled).
College Admission Counseling 45 students graduated in 2008; 40 went to college, including DePaul University; McGill University; Michigan State University; San Francisco State University; St. John's University; University of San Diego. Other: 5 had other specific plans. Median SAT critical reading: 520, median SAT math: 500, median SAT writing: 520. 15% scored over 600 on SAT critical reading, 15% scored over 600 on SAT math, 15% scored over 600 on SAT writing.
Student Life Upper grades have specified standards of dress, student council, honor system. Discipline rests primarily with faculty. Attendance at religious services is required.
Tuition and Aid Day student tuition: €16,100.
Admissions Traditional secondary-level entrance grade is 9. For fall 2008, 52 students applied for upper-level admission, 42 were accepted, 28 enrolled. Deadline for receipt of application materials: none. Application fee required: €350. On-campus interview recommended.
Athletics Interscholastic: basketball (boys, girls), cheering (g), cross-country running (b,g), soccer (b,g), tennis (b,g), track and field (b,g), volleyball (b,g). 2 PE instructors, 9 coaches.
Computers Computers are regularly used in graphic arts classes. Computer network features include on-campus library services, Internet access, wireless campus network, Internet filtering or blocking technology. Student e-mail accounts are available to students.
Contact Ms. Deborah Woods, Admissions Director. 39-063629101 Ext. 212. Fax: 39-36301738. E-mail: admissions@marymountrome.org. Web site: www.marymountrome.org.

MARYMOUNT INTERNATIONAL SCHOOL

George Road
Kingston upon Thames
Surrey KT2 7PE, United Kingdom

Head of School: Sr. Kathleen Fagan, RSHM

General Information Girls' boarding and day college-preparatory, general academic, arts, religious studies, and International Baccalaureate school, affiliated with Roman Catholic Church. Grades 6–12. Founded: 1955. Setting: suburban. Nearest major city is London, United Kingdom. Students are housed in single-sex dormitories. 7-acre campus. 9 buildings on campus. Approved or accredited by Boarding Schools Association (UK), Department for Education and Skills (UK), European Council of International Schools, Independent Schools Council (UK), International Baccalaureate Organization, and Middle States Association of Colleges and Schools. Member of Secondary School Admission Test Board. Language of instruction: English. Total enrollment: 247. Upper school average class size: 14. Upper school faculty-student ratio: 1:7.
Upper School Student Profile Grade 9: 23 students (23 girls); Grade 10: 54 students (54 girls); Grade 11: 67 students (67 girls); Grade 12: 46 students (46 girls). 44% of students are boarding students. 65% are international students. International students from China, Germany, Japan, Republic of Korea, Spain, and United States; 48 other countries represented in student body. 34% of students are Roman Catholic.
Faculty School total: 40. In upper school: 10 men, 30 women; 14 have advanced degrees.
Subjects Offered Advanced biology, advanced chemistry, advanced math, algebra, art, biology, chemistry, Chinese, Chinese literature, drama, economics, English, English literature, ESL, European history, French, general science, geography, German, German literature, history, information technology, Japanese, Japanese literature, mathematics, music, personal and social education, physical education, physics, religion, Spanish, theater, theory of knowledge, world history, world literature.
Graduation Requirements English, foreign language, mathematics, physical education (includes health), religion (includes Bible studies and theology), science, social studies (includes history), IB Diploma requirements—3 Higher Level, 3 Standard Level courses, Additional IB Diploma requirements—CAS program hours (Creativity, Action, Service), Theory of Knowledge Course, and Extended Essay.
Special Academic Programs International Baccalaureate program; honors section; independent study; ESL (43 students enrolled).
College Admission Counseling 43 students graduated in 2008; 41 went to college. Other: 2 had other specific plans.
Student Life Upper grades have uniform requirement, student council, honor system. Discipline rests primarily with faculty. Attendance at religious services is required.
Tuition and Aid Day student tuition: £14,895–£16,945; 5-day tuition and room/board: £25,135–£27,185; 7-day tuition and room/board: £26,340–£28,390. Tuition installment plan (individually arranged payment plans, two semester payments). Tuition reduction for siblings, bursaries, need-based scholarship grants available.
Admissions Traditional secondary-level entrance grade is 11. For fall 2008, 118 students applied for upper-level admission, 74 were accepted, 61 enrolled. English proficiency, mathematics proficiency exam, school's own test or writing sample required. Deadline for receipt of application materials: none. Application fee required: £100. Interview recommended.
Athletics Interscholastic: badminton (girls), basketball (g), cross-country running (g), soccer (g), softball (g), tennis (g), volleyball (g); intramural: aerobics/dance (g), badminton (g), basketball (g), cross-country running (g), dance (g), horseback riding (g), indoor soccer (g), modern dance (g), physical fitness (g), physical training (g), soccer (g), softball (g), strength & conditioning (g), tennis (g), volleyball (g), weight training (g). 3 PE instructors, 3 coaches.
Computers Computers are regularly used in all academic, information technology classes. Computer network features include on-campus library services, Internet access, wireless campus network, Internet filtering or blocking technology. Campus intranet, student e-mail accounts, and computer access in designated common areas are available to students. The school has a published electronic and media policy.
Contact Mr. Chris Hiscock, Marketing and Admissions Officer. 44-(0) 20 8949 0571. Fax: 44-(0) 20 8336 2485. E-mail: admissions@marymountlondon.com. Web site: www.marymountlondon.com.

MARYMOUNT SCHOOL

1026 Fifth Avenue
New York, New York 10028

Head of School: Mrs. Concepcion Alvar, EdD

General Information Coeducational day (boys' only in lower grades) college-preparatory, arts, religious studies, and technology school, affiliated with Roman Catholic Church. Boys grades N–PK, girls grades N–12. Founded: 1926. Setting: urban. 3 buildings on campus. Approved or accredited by New York State Association of Independent Schools. Member of National Association of Independent Schools. Endowment: $800,000. Total enrollment: 572. Upper school average class size: 15. Upper school faculty-student ratio: 1:6.

Upper School Student Profile Grade 8: 34 students (34 girls); Grade 9: 53 students (53 girls); Grade 10: 50 students (50 girls); Grade 11: 49 students (49 girls); Grade 12: 44 students (44 girls). 66% of students are Roman Catholic.

Faculty School total: 107. In upper school: 16 men, 37 women; 44 have advanced degrees.

Subjects Offered Advanced studio art-AP, algebra, American history, American literature, art, art history, astronomy, bell choir, Bible studies, biology, calculus, chemistry, chorus, community service, computer science, dance, economics, English, English literature, ethics, European history, fine arts, French, geometry, Greek, health, Latin, mathematics, music, music history, physical education, physics, political science, religion, science, Spanish, speech, statistics, studio art, studio art-AP, technological applications, technology, theater history, trigonometry, world history, world literature, writing.

Graduation Requirements Arts and fine arts (art, music, dance, drama), computer science, English, foreign language, history, mathematics, physical education (includes health), religion (includes Bible studies and theology), science, speech, senior internships, senior seminars, Class XII Retreat. Community service is required.

Special Academic Programs Advanced Placement exam preparation; honors section; study abroad; academic accommodation for the gifted.

College Admission Counseling 49 students graduated in 2008; all went to college, including Barnard College; Connecticut College; Duke University; Georgetown University; New York University; Wheaton College. Mean SAT critical reading: 630, mean SAT math: 610, mean SAT writing: 680.

Student Life Upper grades have uniform requirement, student council, honor system. Discipline rests primarily with faculty. Attendance at religious services is required.

Summer Programs Advancement, art/fine arts programs offered; session focuses on middle school performing arts and middle school science and technology; held on campus; accepts boys and girls; open to students from other schools. 150 students usually enrolled. 2009 schedule: June 22 to July 24. Application deadline: November 1.

Tuition and Aid Day student tuition: $19,595–$34,000. Tuition installment plan (Key Tuition Payment Plan). Need-based scholarship grants available. In 2008–09, 20% of upper-school students received aid. Total amount of financial aid awarded in 2008–09: $2,115,000.

Admissions Traditional secondary-level entrance grade is 9. ISEE or SSAT required. Deadline for receipt of application materials: November 30. Application fee required: $70. On-campus interview required.

Athletics Interscholastic: aerobics, badminton, basketball, bicycling, cross-country running, dance, fencing, field hockey, fitness, gymnastics, lacrosse, modern dance, physical fitness, soccer, softball, swimming and diving, tennis, track and field, volleyball, yoga; intramural: aerobics, badminton, basketball, bicycling, cross-country running, dance, fitness, gymnastics, lacrosse, martial arts, modern dance, outdoor adventure, physical fitness, soccer, softball, volleyball, yoga. 3 PE instructors, 32 coaches, 1 athletic trainer.

Computers Computers are regularly used in all classes. Computer network features include on-campus library services, Internet access, wireless campus network, Internet filtering or blocking technology. Student e-mail accounts and computer access in designated common areas are available to students. The school has a published electronic and media policy.

Contact Mrs. Lillian Issa, Director of Admissions. 212-744-4486 Ext. 152. Fax: 212-744-0716. E-mail: lillian_issa@marymount.k12.ny.us. Web site: www.marymount.k12.ny.us.

See Close-Up on page 840.

MARYVALE PREPARATORY SCHOOL

11300 Falls Road
Brooklandville, Maryland 21022

Head of School: Sr. Shawn Marie Maguire, SND

General Information Girls' day college-preparatory school, affiliated with Roman Catholic Church. Grades 6–12. Founded: 1945. Setting: suburban. Nearest major city is Baltimore. 113-acre campus. 4 buildings on campus. Approved or accredited by Association of Independent Maryland Schools, Middle States Association of Colleges and Schools, National Catholic Education Association, and Maryland Department of Education. Member of National Association of Independent Schools. Endowment: $1.4 million. Total enrollment: 392. Upper school average class size: 15. Upper school faculty-student ratio: 1:9.

Upper School Student Profile Grade 9: 73 students (73 girls); Grade 10: 85 students (85 girls); Grade 11: 74 students (74 girls); Grade 12: 72 students (72 girls). 82% of students are Roman Catholic.

Faculty School total: 40. In upper school: 6 men, 29 women; 27 have advanced degrees.

Subjects Offered Algebra, American history, American literature, anatomy and physiology, anthropology, art, art history, band, biology, biology-AP, British literature (honors), calculus, calculus-AP, chemistry, chorus, community service, computer science, digital photography, drama, economics, English, English literature, English literature-AP, English-AP, forensic science, French, French-AP, geography, geometry, grammar, health, history, Holocaust, honors algebra, honors English, honors U.S. history, honors world history, journalism, keyboarding, Latin, literary magazine, marine biology, mathematics, model United Nations, music, newspaper, physical education, physics, piano, pre-algebra, pre-calculus, psychology, public speaking, religion, research, science, Shakespeare, social studies, Spanish, Spanish-AP, speech, statistics, theater, theology, trigonometry, U.S. history-AP, voice, Web site design, world history, world literature, writing, yearbook.

Graduation Requirements Arts and fine arts (art, music, dance, drama), computer science, English, foreign language, mathematics, physical education (includes health), religion (includes Bible studies and theology), science, social studies (includes history), 100 hours of community service.

Special Academic Programs Advanced Placement exam preparation; honors section; accelerated programs; study at local college for college credit.

College Admission Counseling 58 students graduated in 2008; 57 went to college, including Loyola College in Maryland; Salisbury University; Stevenson University; Towson University; Virginia Polytechnic Institute and State University. Other: 1 had other specific plans. Mean SAT critical reading: 584, mean SAT math: 558, mean SAT writing: 623, mean combined SAT: 1766. 35% scored over 600 on SAT critical reading, 21% scored over 600 on SAT math, 62% scored over 600 on SAT writing, 38% scored over 1800 on combined SAT.

Student Life Upper grades have uniform requirement, student council, honor system. Discipline rests equally with students and faculty. Attendance at religious services is required.

Summer Programs Enrichment, sports, art/fine arts, computer instruction programs offered; session focuses on Enrichment in a unique setting for girls in grades 4-7; held on campus; accepts girls; open to students from other schools. 150 students usually enrolled. 2009 schedule: June 15 to July 3. Application deadline: June 1.

Tuition and Aid Day student tuition: $14,400. Tuition installment plan (Academic Management Services Plan). Bursaries, need-based scholarship grants available. In 2008–09, 25% of upper-school students received aid. Total amount of financial aid awarded in 2008–09: $480,000.

Admissions Traditional secondary-level entrance grade is 9. For fall 2008, 193 students applied for upper-level admission, 125 were accepted, 46 enrolled. High School Placement Test required. Deadline for receipt of application materials: January 9. Application fee required: $50. On-campus interview required.

Athletics Interscholastic: basketball, cross-country running, field hockey, indoor soccer, indoor track, indoor track & field, lacrosse, physical fitness, soccer, softball, track and field, volleyball, winter soccer, yoga. 3 PE instructors, 26 coaches, 1 athletic trainer.

Computers Computers are regularly used in all academic classes. Computer network features include on-campus library services, online commercial services, Internet access, wireless campus network, Internet filtering or blocking technology. Student e-mail accounts and computer access in designated common areas are available to students. Students grades are available online. The school has a published electronic and media policy.

Contact Monica C. Graham, Director of Admissions. 410-560-3243. Fax: 410-561-1826. E-mail: grahamm@maryvale.com. Web site: www.maryvale.com.

MASSANUTTEN MILITARY ACADEMY

614 South Main Street
Woodstock, Virginia 22664

Head of School: Col. Roy F. Zinser

General Information Coeducational boarding and day college-preparatory, arts, and military school, affiliated with Christian faith. Grades 7–PG. Founded: 1899. Setting: small town. Nearest major city is Washington, DC. Students are housed in single-sex dormitories. 40-acre campus. 11 buildings on campus. Approved or accredited by Southern Association of Colleges and Schools, The Association of Boarding Schools, Virginia Association of Independent Schools, and Virginia Department of Education. Endowment: $13 million. Total enrollment: 194. Upper school average class size: 10. Upper school faculty-student ratio: 1:8.

Upper School Student Profile Grade 9: 29 students (19 boys, 10 girls); Grade 10: 33 students (25 boys, 8 girls); Grade 11: 51 students (38 boys, 13 girls); Grade 12: 47 students (33 boys, 14 girls); Postgraduate: 9 students (9 boys). 99% of students are boarding students. 41% are state residents. 23 states are represented in upper school student body. 11% are international students. International students from Canada, China, France, Republic of Korea, and Senegal; 3 other countries represented in student body.

Faculty School total: 27. In upper school: 19 men, 8 women; 8 have advanced degrees; 6 reside on campus.

Subjects Offered Algebra, American history, American literature, art, art appreciation, band, biology, calculus, character education, chemistry, computer applications, criminal justice, earth science, English, English literature, equestrian sports, ESL, French, geometry, government/civics, grammar, health, history, Internet research, intro to computers, introduction to literature, JROTC, leadership training, mathematics, music, news writing, physical education, physical science, physics, pre-calculus, Russian, science, social science, social studies, Spanish, U.S. history, world history, world literature, writing.

Graduation Requirements Arts and fine arts (art, music, dance, drama), computer applications, English, foreign language, JROTC, mathematics, physical education (includes health), science, social studies (includes history), one year of JROTC for each year enrolled.
Special Academic Programs Advanced Placement exam preparation; independent study; study at local college for college credit; remedial reading and/or remedial writing; remedial math; ESL (8 students enrolled).
College Admission Counseling 43 students graduated in 2007; all went to college, including George Mason University; Mary Baldwin College; Radford University; The Citadel, The Military College of South Carolina; University of Georgia; Virginia Polytechnic Institute and State University. Median SAT critical reading: 470, median SAT math: 520, median composite ACT: 20. 10% scored over 600 on SAT critical reading, 7% scored over 600 on SAT math, 10% scored over 26 on composite ACT.
Student Life Upper grades have uniform requirement, student council, honor system. Discipline rests equally with students and faculty.
Tuition and Aid Day student tuition: $14,461; 7-day tuition and room/board: $23,489. Tuition installment plan (SMART Tuition Payment Plan, FACTS Tuition Payment Plan, monthly payment plans, individually arranged payment plans). Tuition reduction for siblings, merit scholarship grants, need-based scholarship grants, need-based loans, middle-income loans, paying campus jobs, USS Education Loan Program, PLATO Loans, legacy discounts available. In 2007–08, 50% of upper-school students received aid; total upper-school merit-scholarship money awarded: $75,000. Total amount of financial aid awarded in 2007–08: $150,000.
Admissions Traditional secondary-level entrance grade is 10. For fall 2007, 109 students applied for upper-level admission, 90 were accepted, 81 enrolled. Deadline for receipt of application materials: none. Application fee required: $50. Interview required.
Athletics Interscholastic: baseball (boys), basketball (b,g), cross-country running (b,g), fitness (b,g), football (b), independent competitive sports (b,g), lacrosse (b), rugby (b), softball (g), strength & conditioning (b), swimming and diving (b,g), tennis (b,g), track and field (b,g), volleyball (g), wrestling (b); intramural: aerobics (g), aerobics/Nautilus (g), field hockey (g), strength & conditioning (g); coed interscholastic: aquatics, drill team, golf, JROTC drill, marksmanship, pistol, riflery, soccer; coed intramural: aquatics, backpacking, billiards, canoeing/kayaking, cheering, climbing, cross-country running, diving, dressage, drill team, equestrian sports, hiking/backpacking, horseback riding, jogging, kickball, marksmanship, mountaineering, outdoor activities, outdoor adventure, outdoor education, outdoor recreation, outdoor skills, outdoors, paddle tennis, paint ball, physical fitness, physical training, pistol, power lifting, project adventure, rafting, rappelling, riflery, running, skiing (downhill), snowboarding, snowshoeing, soccer, swimming and diving, table tennis, tennis, walking, water polo, weight lifting, weight training, whiffle ball, wilderness, wilderness survival, winter walking. 2 PE instructors, 5 coaches, 1 athletic trainer.
Computers Computers are regularly used in all academic, business applications, business skills, business studies, computer applications, journalism, JROTC, SAT preparation, yearbook classes. Computer network features include on-campus library services, Internet access, wireless campus network, Internet filtering or blocking technology. Student e-mail accounts and computer access in designated common areas are available to students. Students grades are available online. The school has a published electronic and media policy.
Contact Mr. Murali Sinnathamby, Director of Admissions. 540-459-2167 Ext. 262. Fax: 540-459-5421. E-mail: admissions@militaryschool.com. Web site: www.militaryschool.com.

ANNOUNCEMENT FROM THE SCHOOL MMA was founded in 1899 in Woodstock, Virginia. Massanutten attracts students from all over the world who desire advanced preparation for college in a structured environment. Situated in a small town on 40 acres in the heart of the Shenandoah Valley, the Academy is only 90 minutes from downtown Washington, DC.

See Close-Up on page 842.

THE MASTER'S SCHOOL

36 Westledge Road
West Simsbury, Connecticut 06092-9400

Head of School: Jon F. Holley

General Information Coeducational day college-preparatory, arts, religious studies, and technology school, affiliated with Christian faith. Grades PK–12. Founded: 1970. Setting: suburban. Nearest major city is Hartford. 76-acre campus. 10 buildings on campus. Approved or accredited by Association of Christian Schools International, Connecticut Association of Independent Schools, New England Association of Schools and Colleges, and Connecticut Department of Education. Endowment: $34,000. Total enrollment: 275. Upper school average class size: 15. Upper school faculty-student ratio: 1:7.
Upper School Student Profile Grade 9: 34 students (14 boys, 20 girls); Grade 10: 30 students (16 boys, 14 girls); Grade 11: 31 students (19 boys, 12 girls); Grade 12: 31 students (15 boys, 16 girls).
Faculty School total: 40. In upper school: 9 men, 12 women; 7 have advanced degrees.
Subjects Offered Advanced computer applications, advanced studio art-AP, algebra, American history, American literature, applied music, art, art history, Bible studies, biology, biology-AP, British literature, British literature (honors), calculus, calculus-AP, chemistry, chemistry-AP, chorus, civics, community service, computer applications, computer education, computer keyboarding, computer literacy, computer math, computer programming, computer skills, creative writing, earth science, English, English literature, English literature-AP, English-AP, ethics, expository writing, fine arts, French, geometry, grammar, health education, history, honors algebra, honors English, honors geometry, honors U.S. history, independent study, instrumental music, mathematics, music, music composition, philosophy, photography, physical education, physics, science, senior seminar, social studies, Spanish, theology, trigonometry, Western civilization, world history, world literature, writing workshop, yearbook.
Graduation Requirements Arts and fine arts (art, music, dance, drama), computer education, English, foreign language, mathematics, physical education (includes health), religion (includes Bible studies and theology), science, senior seminar, social studies (includes history).
Special Academic Programs Advanced Placement exam preparation; honors section; independent study; study at local college for college credit; academic accommodation for the gifted, the musically talented, and the artistically talented.
College Admission Counseling 20 students graduated in 2008; 19 went to college, including Gordon College; Grove City College; Hofstra University; Houghton College; Messiah College; University of Connecticut. Other: 1 went to work. Mean SAT critical reading: 521, mean SAT math: 549, mean SAT writing: 530. 16% scored over 600 on SAT critical reading, 35% scored over 600 on SAT math, 19% scored over 600 on SAT writing.
Student Life Upper grades have specified standards of dress, student council, honor system. Discipline rests primarily with faculty. Attendance at religious services is required.
Summer Programs Enrichment, advancement, sports, art/fine arts, computer instruction programs offered; session focuses on academic enrichment and advancement for middle and secondary level students, sports clinics, art classes; held on campus; accepts boys and girls; open to students from other schools. 600 students usually enrolled. 2009 schedule: June 20 to August 12.
Tuition and Aid Day student tuition: $14,500. Tuition installment plan (FACTS Tuition Payment Plan, single payment plan). Tuition reduction for siblings, merit scholarship grants, need-based scholarship grants available. In 2008–09, 25% of upper-school students received aid; total upper-school merit-scholarship money awarded: $7000. Total amount of financial aid awarded in 2008–09: $194,507.
Admissions Traditional secondary-level entrance grade is 9. For fall 2008, 165 students applied for upper-level admission, 85 were accepted, 72 enrolled. SSAT required. Deadline for receipt of application materials: none. Application fee required: $50. On-campus interview required.
Athletics Interscholastic: baseball (boys), basketball (b,g), lacrosse (b,g), soccer (b,g), softball (g), ultimate Frisbee (b,g), volleyball (g); intramural: ballet (g); coed interscholastic: alpine skiing, Frisbee, golf, skiing (downhill); coed intramural: alpine skiing, cooperative games, fitness, nordic skiing, physical fitness, physical training, skiing (downhill), snowboarding, strength & conditioning, weight lifting, weight training. 3 PE instructors, 12 coaches, 1 athletic trainer.
Computers Computers are regularly used in career education, college planning, computer applications, data processing, desktop publishing, graphic design, keyboarding, mathematics, science, typing, Web site design, word processing, yearbook classes. Computer network features include on-campus library services, Internet access, Internet filtering or blocking technology, MS Office Suite, educational software, digital photography and darkroom facility. Students grades are available online. The school has a published electronic and media policy.
Contact Marion Dietrich, Director of Admissions. 860-651-9361. Fax: 860-651-9363. E-mail: mdietrich@masterschool.org. Web site: www.masterschool.org.

THE MASTERS SCHOOL

49 Clinton Avenue
Dobbs Ferry, New York 10522

Head of School: Dr. Maureen Fonseca

General Information Coeducational boarding and day college-preparatory, arts, and technology school. Boarding grades 9–12, day grades 5–12. Founded: 1877. Setting: suburban. Nearest major city is New York. Students are housed in single-sex dormitories. 96-acre campus. 12 buildings on campus. Approved or accredited by Middle States Association of Colleges and Schools, New York State Association of Independent Schools, The Association of Boarding Schools, and New York Department of Education. Member of National Association of Independent Schools and Secondary School Admission Test Board. Endowment: $27.5 million. Total enrollment: 580. Upper school average class size: 14. Upper school faculty-student ratio: 1:6.
Upper School Student Profile Grade 9: 97 students (50 boys, 47 girls); Grade 10: 103 students (50 boys, 53 girls); Grade 11: 109 students (45 boys, 64 girls); Grade 12: 105 students (43 boys, 62 girls). 40% of students are boarding students. 70% are state residents. 16 states are represented in upper school student body. 13% are international students. International students from China, Croatia, Germany, Jamaica, Republic of Korea, and Taiwan; 10 other countries represented in student body.

Faculty School total: 97. In upper school: 37 men, 50 women; 67 have advanced degrees; 55 reside on campus.

Subjects Offered Acting, algebra, American history, American literature, art, art history, biology, biology-AP, calculus, calculus-AP, ceramics, chemistry, chemistry-AP, computer math, computer programming, computer science, creative writing, dance, drama, driver education, earth science, electronics, English, English language-AP, English literature, English literature-AP, environmental science, ESL, ethics, European history, European history-AP, expository writing, fine arts, French, French language-AP, French literature-AP, geography, geometry, grammar, health, health and wellness, health education, jazz, jazz band, journalism, Latin, Latin-AP, mathematics, meteorology, music, music theory-AP, performing arts, photography, physical education, physics, physics-AP, pre-calculus, religion, science, senior thesis, social studies, Spanish, Spanish language-AP, Spanish literature-AP, speech, statistics, statistics-AP, studio art, studio art—AP, theater, trigonometry, U.S. history, U.S. history-AP, world history, world literature, world religions, writing, yearbook, yoga.

Graduation Requirements Art, arts, arts and fine arts (art, music, dance, drama), computer science, English, foreign language, mathematics, physical education (includes health), science, speech, U.S. history, world history, world religions.

Special Academic Programs 19 Advanced Placement exams for which test preparation is offered; honors section; independent study; term-away projects; study at local college for college credit; study abroad; academic accommodation for the gifted, the musically talented, and the artistically talented; ESL (20 students enrolled).

College Admission Counseling 95 students graduated in 2008; all went to college, including Carnegie Mellon University; Cornell University; Middlebury College; New York University; The Johns Hopkins University; Williams College. Mean SAT critical reading: 633, mean SAT math: 630, mean SAT writing: 627, mean combined SAT: 1890. 61% scored over 600 on SAT critical reading, 55% scored over 600 on SAT math, 54% scored over 600 on SAT writing, 58% scored over 1800 on combined SAT.

Student Life Upper grades have specified standards of dress, student council. Discipline rests equally with students and faculty.

Tuition and Aid Day student tuition: $30,250; 7-day tuition and room/board: $42,000. Tuition installment plan (Insured Tuition Payment Plan, Key Tuition Payment Plan, monthly payment plans, individually arranged payment plans). Need-based scholarship grants available. In 2008–09, 33% of upper-school students received aid. Total amount of financial aid awarded in 2008–09: $3,700,000.

Admissions Traditional secondary-level entrance grade is 9. For fall 2008, 510 students applied for upper-level admission, 250 were accepted, 156 enrolled. ISEE or SSAT required. Deadline for receipt of application materials: January 5. Application fee required: $50. Interview required.

Athletics Interscholastic: baseball (boys), basketball (b,g), cross-country running (b,g), fencing (b,g), field hockey (g), lacrosse (b,g), soccer (b,g), softball (g), tennis (b,g), volleyball (g); coed interscholastic: dance, dance team, golf; coed intramural: aerobics, aerobics/dance, aerobics/Nautilus, combined training, dance squad, dance team, fitness, Frisbee, martial arts, modern dance, outdoor activities, physical fitness, physical training, strength & conditioning, ultimate Frisbee, weight lifting, weight training, yoga. 2 PE instructors, 13 coaches, 1 athletic trainer.

Computers Computers are regularly used in computer applications, English, foreign language, graphic arts, graphic design, history, mathematics, newspaper, photography, programming, publications, science, senior seminar, study skills, video film production, Web site design, writing, yearbook classes. Computer network features include on-campus library services, online commercial services, Internet access, wireless campus network, Internet filtering or blocking technology. Student e-mail accounts and computer access in designated common areas are available to students. The school has a published electronic and media policy.

Contact Mary Schellhorn, Associate Head of School for Enrollment and Strategic Planning. 914-479-6432. Fax: 914-693-7295. E-mail: mary.schellhorn@mastersny.org. Web site: www.mastersny.org.

ANNOUNCEMENT FROM THE SCHOOL With nearly half boarding and half day in the Upper School, The Masters School opened in fall 2007 with a record enrollment of 560 students. The School continues its commitment to character, athletics, service, academic rigor, and the arts. These values permeate the academic day, the cocurricular activities, and the residential program.

See Close-Up on page 844.

MATER DEI HIGH SCHOOL

1300 Harmony Way
Evansville, Indiana 47720-6199

Head of School: Mr. Timothy Anderson Dickel

General Information Coeducational day college-preparatory, arts, business, religious studies, and technology school, affiliated with Roman Catholic Church. Grades 9–12. Founded: 1948. Setting: urban. 25-acre campus. 2 buildings on campus. Approved or accredited by National Christian School Association, North Central Association of Colleges and Schools, and Indiana Department of Education. Total enrollment: 560. Upper school average class size: 25. Upper school faculty-student ratio: 1:15.

Upper School Student Profile Grade 9: 155 students (82 boys, 73 girls); Grade 10: 138 students (69 boys, 69 girls); Grade 11: 132 students (65 boys, 67 girls); Grade 12: 135 students (74 boys, 61 girls). 98% of students are Roman Catholic.

Faculty School total: 40. In upper school: 18 men, 21 women; 28 have advanced degrees.

Graduation Requirements Service hours to church and community.

Special Academic Programs Advanced Placement exam preparation; honors section; study at local college for college credit; programs in English, mathematics for dyslexic students; special instructional classes for students with LD, ADD, emotional and behavioral problems.

College Admission Counseling 145 students graduated in 2008; 140 went to college, including University of Evansville. Median SAT math: 513, median SAT writing: 511, median combined SAT: 1024, median composite ACT: 23.

Student Life Upper grades have uniform requirement, student council, honor system. Discipline rests primarily with faculty. Attendance at religious services is required.

Tuition and Aid Need-based scholarship grants available. In 2008–09, 25% of upper-school students received aid.

Admissions Traditional secondary-level entrance grade is 9. Deadline for receipt of application materials: none. Application fee required: $170. Interview recommended.

Athletics Interscholastic: baseball (boys), basketball (b,g), cheering (g), cross-country running (b,g), dance squad (g), football (b), golf (b,g), soccer (b,g), softball (g), swimming and diving (b,g), tennis (b,g), track and field (b,g), volleyball (g), weight training (b,g), wrestling (b); coed interscholastic: bowling.

Computers Computer network features include on-campus library services, Internet access, wireless campus network, Internet filtering or blocking technology. The school has a published electronic and media policy.

Contact Admissions. 812-426-2258. Fax: 812-421-5717. E-mail: materdeiwildcats@evansville.net.

MATIGNON HIGH SCHOOL

1 Matignon Road
Cambridge, Massachusetts 02140

Head of School: Mr. Thomas Galligani

General Information Coeducational day college-preparatory, arts, business, religious studies, and technology school, affiliated with Roman Catholic Church. Grades 9–12. Founded: 1945. Setting: suburban. Nearest major city is Boston. 10-acre campus. 3 buildings on campus. Approved or accredited by Association of Independent Schools in New England, National Catholic Education Association, New England Association of Schools and Colleges, and Massachusetts Department of Education. Endowment: $253,000. Total enrollment: 350. Upper school average class size: 20. Upper school faculty-student ratio: 1:15.

Upper School Student Profile Grade 9: 105 students (53 boys, 52 girls); Grade 10: 105 students (42 boys, 63 girls); Grade 11: 55 students (30 boys, 25 girls); Grade 12: 88 students (37 boys, 51 girls). 75% of students are Roman Catholic.

Faculty School total: 30. In upper school: 12 men, 18 women; 15 have advanced degrees.

Subjects Offered 3-dimensional art, 3-dimensional design, accounting, adolescent issues, Advanced Placement courses, algebra, American history, American literature, anatomy and physiology, art, art history, Bible studies, biology, calculus, chemistry, community service, computer science, drawing and design, economics, English, English literature, environmental science, fine arts, French, geometry, government/civics, grammar, health, history, Latin, law, mathematics, physical education, physics, psychology, religion, science, social science, social studies, Spanish, theology, trigonometry, world history, writing.

Graduation Requirements 20th century history, accounting, Advanced Placement courses, algebra, American history, anatomy and physiology, arts and fine arts (art, music, dance, drama), chemistry, computer science, English-AP, French, French-AP, geometry, health education, honors algebra, honors English, honors geometry, honors world history, Latin, law, physical education (includes health), psychology, religious studies, SAT preparation, senior internship, Spanish, Spanish-AP, U.S. history, U.S. history-AP, world cultures, world history, Christian service, thirty hours of community service (before junior year).

Special Academic Programs Advanced Placement exam preparation; honors section; independent study; study abroad.

College Admission Counseling 65 students graduated in 2008; 60 went to college, including Boston University; Merrimack College; Saint Anselm College; University of Massachusetts Boston. Other: 2 went to work, 1 entered military service, 2 entered a postgraduate year. Median SAT critical reading: 500, median SAT math: 510, median SAT writing: 510, median combined SAT: 1520. 10% scored over 600 on SAT critical reading, 10% scored over 600 on SAT math, 10% scored over 600 on SAT writing.

Student Life Upper grades have uniform requirement, student council, honor system. Discipline rests primarily with faculty. Attendance at religious services is required.

Summer Programs Remediation, enrichment programs offered; held on campus; accepts boys and girls; open to students from other schools. 80 students usually enrolled. 2009 schedule: June 26 to July 26. Application deadline: June 23.

Tuition and Aid Day student tuition: $7700. Tuition installment plan (FACTS Tuition Payment Plan, monthly payment plans). Merit scholarship grants, need-based scholarship grants available. In 2008–09, 50% of upper-school students received aid; total upper-school merit-scholarship money awarded: $50,000. Total amount of financial aid awarded in 2008–09: $125,000.

Admissions Traditional secondary-level entrance grade is 9. For fall 2008, 450 students applied for upper-level admission, 150 were accepted, 105 enrolled. Catholic High School Entrance Examination, SSAT or TOEFL or SLEP required. Deadline for receipt of application materials: none. No application fee required. On-campus interview recommended.
Athletics Interscholastic: baseball (boys), basketball (b,g), cheering (g), cross-country running (b,g), football (b), golf (b,g), ice hockey (b,g), lacrosse (b,g), soccer (b,g), softball (g), swimming and diving (b,g), track and field (b,g), volleyball (g); intramural: aerobics/dance (b,g), dance (g), dance squad (g), dance team (g), physical training (b,g), strength & conditioning (b,g), weight lifting (b,g), weight training (b,g). 1 PE instructor, 20 coaches, 1 athletic trainer.
Computers Computers are regularly used in all academic classes. Computer network features include on-campus library services, Internet access, Internet filtering or blocking technology, all academic homework is provided on-line. Student e-mail accounts and computer access in designated common areas are available to students.
Contact Mr. Joseph DiSarcina, Principal. 617-876-1212 Ext. 14. Fax: 617-661-3905. E-mail: jdisarcina@matignon-hs.org. Web site: www.matignon-hs.org.

MAUMEE VALLEY COUNTRY DAY SCHOOL

1715 South Reynolds Road
Toledo, Ohio 43614-1499

Head of School: Gary Boehm

General Information Coeducational day college-preparatory and arts school. Grades P3–12. Founded: 1884. Setting: suburban. 72-acre campus. 4 buildings on campus. Approved or accredited by Independent Schools Association of the Central States, Ohio Association of Independent Schools, and Ohio Department of Education. Member of National Association of Independent Schools. Endowment: $10.5 million. Total enrollment: 479. Upper school average class size: 10. Upper school faculty-student ratio: 1:10.
Upper School Student Profile Grade 9: 44 students (28 boys, 16 girls); Grade 10: 36 students (21 boys, 15 girls); Grade 11: 58 students (35 boys, 23 girls); Grade 12: 49 students (27 boys, 22 girls).
Faculty School total: 55. In upper school: 13 men, 9 women; 17 have advanced degrees.
Subjects Offered Algebra, American government, American history, anthropology, art, biology, biology-AP, calculus-AP, chemistry, choir, computer graphics, computer science, creative writing, design, drama, earth science, ecology, English, environmental science, European history, expository writing, fine arts, French, geology, geometry, government/civics, grammar, health, history, human development, humanities, mathematics, microbiology, music, physical education, physics, science, social studies, Spanish, Spanish-AP, speech, statistics, statistics-AP, theater, trigonometry, women's studies, world history.
Graduation Requirements American government, arts and fine arts (art, music, dance, drama), English, foreign language, mathematics, physical education (includes health), science, social studies (includes history). Community service is required.
Special Academic Programs Advanced Placement exam preparation; honors section; independent study; term-away projects; study at local college for college credit; domestic exchange program (with The Athenian School, The Network Program Schools); study abroad; academic accommodation for the gifted, the musically talented, and the artistically talented; ESL (1 student enrolled).
College Admission Counseling 37 students graduated in 2008; all went to college, including Indiana University Bloomington; Miami University; Purdue University; The George Washington University; The University of Toledo. Mean SAT critical reading: 650, mean SAT math: 633, mean SAT writing: 612, mean combined SAT: 1895, mean composite ACT: 29. 50% scored over 600 on SAT critical reading, 50% scored over 600 on SAT math.
Student Life Upper grades have specified standards of dress, student council, honor system. Discipline rests equally with students and faculty.
Summer Programs Enrichment, sports, art/fine arts, computer instruction programs offered; session focuses on day camp and sports camps; held on campus; accepts boys and girls; open to students from other schools. 350 students usually enrolled. 2009 schedule: June 15 to August 14. Application deadline: May 15.
Tuition and Aid Day student tuition: $14,125–$15,125. Tuition installment plan (FACTS Tuition Payment Plan, monthly payment plans, individually arranged payment plans). Merit scholarship grants, need-based scholarship grants available. In 2008–09, 35% of upper-school students received aid; total upper-school merit-scholarship money awarded: $136,000. Total amount of financial aid awarded in 2008–09: $454,900.
Admissions Traditional secondary-level entrance grade is 9. For fall 2008, 23 students applied for upper-level admission, 22 were accepted, 22 enrolled. Brigance Test of Basic Skills, CTP, ERB—verbal abilities, reading comprehension, quantitative abilities (level F, form 1), OLSAT, ERB, Otis-Lennon Ability or Stanford Achievement Test, Otis-Lennon and 2 sections of ERB, Slosson Intelligence or writing sample required. Deadline for receipt of application materials: none. Application fee required: $50. On-campus interview required.
Athletics Interscholastic: baseball (boys), basketball (b,g), cheering (b,g), cross-country running (b,g), field hockey (g), golf (b,g), lacrosse (g), soccer (b,g), tennis (b,g), track and field (b,g); intramural: indoor soccer (g), lacrosse (g); coed intramural: strength & conditioning, weight training. 3 PE instructors, 10 coaches, 1 athletic trainer.
Computers Computers are regularly used in English, foreign language, graphic design, history, information technology, library skills, literary magazine, mathematics, music, newspaper, science, yearbook classes. Computer network features include on-campus library services, online commercial services, Internet access, wireless campus network, Internet filtering or blocking technology. Student e-mail accounts are available to students. Students grades are available online. The school has a published electronic and media policy.
Contact Sarah Bigenho, Admission Assistant. 419-381-1313 Ext. 3082. Fax: 419-381-9941. E-mail: sbigenho@mvcds.net. Web site: www.mvcds.org.

MAUR HILL-MOUNT ACADEMY

1000 Green Street
Atchison, Kansas 66002

Head of School: Mrs. Sharon Pruett

General Information Coeducational boarding and day college-preparatory, arts, religious studies, bilingual studies, and English as a Second language school, affiliated with Roman Catholic Church. Grades 9–12. Founded: 1863. Setting: small town. Nearest major city is Kansas City, MO. Students are housed in single-sex dormitories. 150-acre campus. 7 buildings on campus. Approved or accredited by North Central Association of Colleges and Schools, The Association of Boarding Schools, and Kansas Department of Education. Member of Secondary School Admission Test Board. Total enrollment: 198. Upper school average class size: 16. Upper school faculty-student ratio: 1:9.
Upper School Student Profile Grade 9: 53 students (29 boys, 24 girls); Grade 10: 45 students (24 boys, 21 girls); Grade 11: 56 students (32 boys, 24 girls); Grade 12: 54 students (27 boys, 27 girls). 40% of students are boarding students. 50% are state residents. 7 states are represented in upper school student body. 25% are international students. International students from China, Mexico, Pakistan, Republic of Korea, and Taiwan; 7 other countries represented in student body. 82% of students are Roman Catholic.
Faculty School total: 21. In upper school: 13 men, 8 women; 6 have advanced degrees; 3 reside on campus.
Subjects Offered Algebra, American history, American literature, anatomy, art, basketball, Bible studies, biology, business, business skills, calculus, chemistry, computer math, computer programming, computer science, current events, drama, economics, English, English literature, ESL, ethics, fine arts, French, geography, geometry, government/civics, grammar, health, history, humanities, journalism, mathematics, music, photography, physical education, physics, physiology, psychology, religion, science, social science, social studies, sociology, Spanish, speech, theater, theology, trigonometry, typing, world history, world literature, writing.
Graduation Requirements Arts and fine arts (art, music, dance, drama), business skills (includes word processing), computer science, English, foreign language, mathematics, physical education (includes health), religion (includes Bible studies and theology), science, social science, social studies (includes history).
Special Academic Programs Honors section; study at local college for college credit; special instructional classes for students with Attention Deficit Disorder; ESL (23 students enrolled).
College Admission Counseling 48 students graduated in 2008; all went to college, including Benedictine College; Creighton University; Saint Louis University; University of Minnesota, Twin Cities Campus; Washburn University.
Student Life Upper grades have uniform requirement, student council, honor system. Discipline rests primarily with faculty.
Summer Programs ESL programs offered; session focuses on activities camp, ESL program; held on campus; accepts boys and girls; open to students from other schools. 20 students usually enrolled. 2009 schedule: July 7 to August 8. Application deadline: June 10.
Tuition and Aid Day student tuition: $4200; 7-day tuition and room/board: $18,650. Tuition installment plan (individually arranged payment plans). Tuition reduction for siblings, merit scholarship grants available. In 2008–09, 20% of upper-school students received aid; total upper-school merit-scholarship money awarded: $22,000. Total amount of financial aid awarded in 2008–09: $100,000.
Admissions Traditional secondary-level entrance grade is 10. For fall 2008, 134 students applied for upper-level admission, 65 were accepted, 54 enrolled. Deadline for receipt of application materials: none. Application fee required: $100. On-campus interview recommended.
Athletics Interscholastic: aquatics (girls), baseball (b), basketball (b,g), cheering (g), cross-country running (b,g), dance (g), dance squad (g), dance team (g), drill team (g), football (b), swimming and diving (g), tennis (b,g), track and field (b,g), volleyball (g); intramural: boxing (b), field hockey (b), fitness (b), flag football (b), floor hockey (b), football (b), running (b,g), skateboarding (b), skiing (downhill) (b,g), soccer (b,g), swimming and diving (b,g), touch football (b), track and field (b,g), weight lifting (b,g), weight training (b,g); coed interscholastic: golf, physical fitness, physical training, running, soccer, wrestling; coed intramural: baseball, basketball, bowling, Nautilus, physical fitness, physical training, roller blading, table tennis, tennis, volleyball, walking. 2 PE instructors, 10 coaches, 2 athletic trainers.
Computers Computer network features include on-campus library services, Internet access. Students grades are available online.
Contact Mr. Deke Nolan, Admissions Director. 913-367-5482 Ext. 210. Fax: 913-367-5096. E-mail: admissions@mh-ma.com. Web site: www.mh-ma.com.

THE MCCALLIE SCHOOL

500 Dodds Avenue
Chattanooga, Tennessee 37404

Head of School: Dr. R. Kirk Walker

General Information Boys' boarding and day college-preparatory school, affiliated with Christian faith. Boarding grades 9–12, day grades 6–12. Founded: 1905. Setting: suburban. Nearest major city is Atlanta, GA. Students are housed in single-sex dormitories. 110-acre campus. 19 buildings on campus. Approved or accredited by Southern Association of Colleges and Schools, Southern Association of Independent Schools, Tennessee Association of Independent Schools, The Association of Boarding Schools, and Tennessee Department of Education. Member of National Association of Independent Schools and Secondary School Admission Test Board. Endowment: $53 million. Total enrollment: 919. Upper school average class size: 14. Upper school faculty-student ratio: 1:8.

Upper School Student Profile Grade 9: 163 students (163 boys); Grade 10: 162 students (162 boys); Grade 11: 170 students (170 boys); Grade 12: 158 students (158 boys). 42% of students are boarding students. 23 states are represented in upper school student body. 3% are international students. International students from Austria, Germany, Republic of Korea, Saudi Arabia, Switzerland, and United Kingdom.

Faculty School total: 133. In upper school: 93 men, 15 women; 77 have advanced degrees; 50 reside on campus.

Subjects Offered Algebra, American Civil War, American history, American literature, American studies, art, Bible studies, bioethics, biology, calculus, ceramics, chemistry, Chinese, computer science, creative writing, design, drama, economics, English, English literature, environmental science, European history, fine arts, French, geometry, German, government/civics, Greek, health, history, human development, Japanese, journalism, keyboarding, Latin, mathematics, music, music theory, photography, physical education, physical science, physics, poetry, political science, pottery, printmaking, public speaking, religion, rhetoric, science, social science, social studies, Spanish, speech, theater, trigonometry, world history, world literature, writing.

Graduation Requirements Arts and fine arts (art, music, dance, drama), English, foreign language, mathematics, physical education (includes health), public speaking, religion (includes Bible studies and theology), science, social science, social studies (includes history).

Special Academic Programs Advanced Placement exam preparation; honors section; independent study; study abroad; academic accommodation for the gifted, the musically talented, and the artistically talented.

College Admission Counseling 146 students graduated in 2008; all went to college, including Georgia Institute of Technology; North Carolina State University; The University of North Carolina at Chapel Hill; The University of Tennessee; The University of Tennessee at Chattanooga; University of Georgia. Mean SAT critical reading: 602, mean SAT math: 641, mean SAT writing: 607, mean combined SAT: 1849, mean composite ACT: 27.

Student Life Upper grades have specified standards of dress, student council, honor system. Discipline rests equally with students and faculty. Attendance at religious services is required.

Summer Programs Enrichment, sports, rigorous outdoor training programs offered; session focuses on introduction to McCallie School with special emphasis on fun and participation; held on campus; accepts boys; open to students from other schools. 2,000 students usually enrolled. 2009 schedule: June 1 to August 1.

Tuition and Aid Day student tuition: $17,895; 7-day tuition and room/board: $34,185. Tuition installment plan (Insured Tuition Payment Plan, monthly payment plans). Merit scholarship grants, need-based scholarship grants, need-based loans available. In 2008–09, 28% of upper-school students received aid; total upper-school merit-scholarship money awarded: $750,000. Total amount of financial aid awarded in 2008–09: $3,100,000.

Admissions Traditional secondary-level entrance grade is 9. ISEE or SSAT required. Deadline for receipt of application materials: February 1. Application fee required: $50. On-campus interview required.

Athletics Interscholastic: baseball, basketball, bowling, climbing, crew, cross-country running, diving, football, golf, indoor track, indoor track & field, lacrosse, physical training, rock climbing, rowing, skeet shooting, soccer, swimming and diving, tennis, track and field, trap and skeet, ultimate Frisbee, wall climbing, wrestling; intramural: backpacking, baseball, basketball, bicycling, billiards, bowling, canoeing/kayaking, climbing, fencing, fishing, fitness, flag football, fly fishing, football, Frisbee, golf, hiking/backpacking, indoor soccer, juggling, kayaking, lacrosse, martial arts, mountain biking, mountaineering, outdoor activities, paint ball, physical fitness, physical training, power lifting, racquetball, rappelling, rock climbing, ropes courses, scuba diving, soccer, softball, strength & conditioning, swimming and diving, table tennis, tennis, touch football, ultimate Frisbee, volleyball, wall climbing, water polo, weight lifting, weight training, whiffle ball, wilderness, wilderness survival, wrestling, yoga; coed interscholastic: cheering. 2 athletic trainers.

Computers Computers are regularly used in Bible studies, economics, English, foreign language, mathematics, science, writing classes. Computer network features include on-campus library services, online commercial services, Internet access, wireless campus network, Internet filtering or blocking technology. Campus intranet, student e-mail accounts, and computer access in designated common areas are available to students. Students grades are available online. The school has a published electronic and media policy.

Contact Mr. David L. Hughes, Director of Boarding Admissions. 423-624-8300. Fax: 423-493-5426. E-mail: admissions@mccallie.org. Web site: www.mccallie.org.

See Close-Up on page 846.

MCCURDY SCHOOL

261 McCurdy Road
Espanola, New Mexico 87532

Head of School: Rev. Daniel Garcia

General Information Coeducational day college-preparatory, general academic, arts, business, religious studies, and technology school, affiliated with United Methodist Church. Grades PK–12. Founded: 1912. Setting: small town. Nearest major city is Albuquerque. 44-acre campus. 8 buildings on campus. Approved or accredited by North Central Association of Colleges and Schools, University Senate of United Methodist Church, and New Mexico Department of Education. Endowment: $1 million. Total enrollment: 342. Upper school average class size: 14. Upper school faculty-student ratio: 1:14.

Upper School Student Profile Grade 9: 47 students (25 boys, 22 girls); Grade 10: 29 students (16 boys, 13 girls); Grade 11: 38 students (18 boys, 20 girls); Grade 12: 30 students (14 boys, 16 girls). 8% of students are United Methodist Church.

Faculty School total: 32. In upper school: 5 men, 9 women; 9 have advanced degrees.

Subjects Offered Advanced Placement courses, algebra, American history-AP, anatomy, art, athletic training, athletics, biology, business, calculus-AP, chemistry, choral music, Christian studies, computer applications, computer science, drama, English, English-AP, general science, geometry, government/civics, grammar, health, health education, journalism, Life of Christ, mathematics, physical education, religion, social studies, Spanish, speech.

Graduation Requirements Arts and fine arts (art, music, dance, drama), English, mathematics, physical education (includes health), religion (includes Bible studies and theology), science, social studies (includes history).

Special Academic Programs Advanced Placement exam preparation; honors section; independent study; study at local college for college credit.

College Admission Counseling 27 students graduated in 2008; all went to college, including New Mexico State University; Northern New Mexico College; Tufts University; University of New Mexico. Mean composite ACT: 20. 10% scored over 26 on composite ACT.

Student Life Upper grades have specified standards of dress, student council. Discipline rests primarily with faculty. Attendance at religious services is required.

Tuition and Aid Day student tuition: $4612. Tuition installment plan (FACTS Tuition Payment Plan, monthly payment plans). Tuition reduction for siblings, merit scholarship grants, need-based scholarship grants, paying campus jobs available. In 2008–09, 30% of upper-school students received aid; total upper-school merit-scholarship money awarded: $28,664. Total amount of financial aid awarded in 2008–09: $37,664.

Admissions Traditional secondary-level entrance grade is 9. For fall 2008, 12 students applied for upper-level admission, 10 were accepted, 10 enrolled. Deadline for receipt of application materials: none. Application fee required: $25. Interview required.

Athletics Interscholastic: baseball (boys), basketball (b,g), cheering (g), cross-country running (b,g), football (b), softball (b), track and field (b,g), volleyball (b); intramural: physical fitness (b,g), physical training (b,g), weight training (b,g); coed intramural: bowling, skiing (downhill). 2 PE instructors, 15 coaches.

Computers Computers are regularly used in accounting, business applications, computer applications, English, science classes. Computer resources include on-campus library services, Internet access.

Contact Ms. Pamela Miller, Business Manager. 505-753-7221. Fax: 505-753-7830. E-mail: busmgr@mccurdy.org. Web site: www.McCurdy.org.

MCDONOGH SCHOOL

8600 McDonogh Road
Owings Mills, Maryland 21117-0380

Head of School: Charles W. Britton

General Information Coeducational boarding and day college-preparatory school. Boarding grades 9–12, day grades K–12. Founded: 1873. Setting: suburban. Nearest major city is Baltimore. Students are housed in single-sex dormitories. 800-acre campus. 44 buildings on campus. Approved or accredited by Association of Independent Maryland Schools. Member of National Association of Independent Schools. Endowment: $83.1 million. Total enrollment: 1,293. Upper school average class size: 15. Upper school faculty-student ratio: 1:9.

Upper School Student Profile Grade 9: 143 students (79 boys, 64 girls); Grade 10: 145 students (80 boys, 65 girls); Grade 11: 144 students (75 boys, 69 girls); Grade 12: 137 students (72 boys, 65 girls). 15% of students are boarding students. 99% are state residents. 2 states are represented in upper school student body.

Faculty School total: 197. In upper school: 39 men, 48 women; 65 have advanced degrees; 31 reside on campus.

Subjects Offered 20th century American writers, acting, advanced chemistry, Advanced Placement courses, African history, African literature, African-American studies, algebra, American government-AP, American history, American history-AP, American literature, American literature-AP, anatomy, area studies, art, art history, art-AP, Asian studies, band, bioethics, biology, biology-AP, botany, calculus, calculus-AP, ceramics, chemistry, chemistry-AP, Chesapeake Bay studies, classical Greek literature, composition-AP, computer animation, computer graphics, computer music, computer programming, computer science, computer science-AP, concert band, concert choir, creative writing, dance, drama, drawing, ecology, economics, economics-AP, electives, engineering, English, English composition, English literature, English literature and composition-AP, English literature-AP, English-AP, English/composition-AP, environmental science, environmental science-AP, ethics, European history, film, film and literature, fine arts, fitness, foreign language, French, French language-AP, French literature-AP, French-AP, genetics, geology, geometry, German, German-AP, government and politics-AP, government-AP, government/civics, health and wellness, history, history-AP, honors algebra, honors English, honors geometry, honors U.S. history, honors world history, Irish literature, jazz band, jazz dance, journalism, language-AP, languages, Latin, Latin American literature, linguistics, literature and composition-AP, literature by women, marine biology, mathematics, Middle Eastern history, music, music theory, music theory-AP, oceanography, photography, physical education, physical fitness, physics, poetry, precalculus, psychology, religion, Russian history, science, senior project, set design, Shakespeare, short story, Spanish, Spanish language-AP, Spanish literature, Spanish literature-AP, Spanish-AP, speech, speech communications, statistics-AP, tap dance, theater, trigonometry, tropical ecology, U.S. government and politics-AP, U.S. government-AP, U.S. history, U.S. history-AP, video, visual arts, Web site design, woodworking, world history, world history-AP, world religions, world wide web design, writing workshop, yearbook.

Graduation Requirements Arts and fine arts (art, music, dance, drama), English, foreign language, mathematics, physical education (includes health), science, senior project, social studies (includes history). Community service is required.

Special Academic Programs Advanced Placement exam preparation; honors section; independent study; term-away projects.

College Admission Counseling 136 students graduated in 2008; 134 went to college, including Bucknell University; University of Maryland, College Park; University of Pennsylvania; University of Virginia; Virginia Polytechnic Institute and State University. Other: 2 entered a postgraduate year. Mean SAT critical reading: 616, mean SAT math: 631, mean SAT writing: 619, mean combined SAT: 1866, mean composite ACT: 27.

Student Life Upper grades have uniform requirement, student council, honor system. Discipline rests primarily with faculty.

Summer Programs Enrichment, sports, art/fine arts, computer instruction programs offered; session focuses on recreation and sports camps; held both on and off campus; held at Gunpowder Falls State Park and Chesapeake Bay; accepts boys and girls; open to students from other schools. 1,800 students usually enrolled. 2009 schedule: June 22 to July 31. Application deadline: May 1.

Tuition and Aid Day student tuition: $20,640; 5-day tuition and room/board: $27,770. Tuition installment plan (Key Tuition Payment Plan, monthly payment plans, individually arranged payment plans). Need-based scholarship grants, need-based loans, middle-income loans available. In 2008–09, 21% of upper-school students received aid. Total amount of financial aid awarded in 2008–09: $2,013,980.

Admissions Traditional secondary-level entrance grade is 9. For fall 2008, 313 students applied for upper-level admission, 83 were accepted, 51 enrolled. ISEE required. Deadline for receipt of application materials: December 15. Application fee required: $45. On-campus interview required.

Athletics Interscholastic: aquatics (boys, girls), baseball (b), basketball (b,g), cross-country running (b,g), equestrian sports (b,g), field hockey (g), football (b), golf (b,g), lacrosse (b,g), soccer (b,g), softball (g), swimming and diving (b,g), tennis (b,g), volleyball (g), water polo (b,g), winter (indoor) track (b,g), wrestling (b); coed interscholastic: cheering, equestrian sports, horseback riding; coed intramural: badminton, ballet, dance, fencing, fitness, squash. 10 PE instructors, 92 coaches, 2 athletic trainers.

Computers Computers are regularly used in all classes. Computer network features include on-campus library services, online commercial services, Internet access, wireless campus network, Internet filtering or blocking technology. Campus intranet, student e-mail accounts, and computer access in designated common areas are available to students. Students grades are available online. The school has a published electronic and media policy.

Contact Anita Hilson, Director of Admissions. 410-581-4719. Fax: 410-998-3537. E-mail: ahilson@mcdonogh.org. Web site: www.mcdonogh.org.

ANNOUNCEMENT FROM THE SCHOOL McDonogh School was established in 1873 with a bequest from philanthropist and merchant John McDonogh. Originally a free school for academically capable but economically disadvantaged boys, McDonogh has emerged as a nondenominational, college-preparatory, coeducational day and boarding school. John McDonogh's philosophy—to develop moral character, a sense of responsibility, and a capacity for leadership—still guides the School. There are 1,293 boys and girls in kindergarten through grade 12, including 72 students in grades 9–12 enrolled in the School's five-day boarding program. McDonogh is set on nearly 800 picturesque acres in Owings Mills, a suburb of Baltimore. Bus transportation and hot lunches are included in tuition. Exemplary facilities include a 580-seat theater, computer labs and libraries for all levels, dance and art studios, nineteen athletic fields, an outdoor stadium, a life fitness center, indoor multipurpose courts, a 50-meter indoor swimming pool, and riding rings. In the Upper School, the college-preparatory program includes Advanced Placement courses and honors classes in all major subjects. With an average class size of 15, students are guaranteed individual attention. McDonogh also offers interscholastic competition in twenty-seven different sports, and students are required to join teams or take physical education classes. Extracurriculars, which take place between the end of the academic day and athletic practices, include fifty clubs and activities. In addition, students must perform 40 hours of community service for graduation. One of McDonogh's strengths is its college counseling program. Experienced counselors serve as students' advocates through the process, and all graduates typically enroll in four-year colleges.

MCQUAID JESUIT

1800 South Clinton Avenue
Rochester, New York 14618

Head of School: Fr. James K. Coughlin, SJ

General Information Boys' day college-preparatory, arts, religious studies, and technology school, affiliated with Roman Catholic Church (Jesuit order). Grades 7–12. Founded: 1954. Setting: suburban. 33-acre campus. 1 building on campus. Approved or accredited by Jesuit Secondary Education Association, Middle States Association of Colleges and Schools, National Catholic Education Association, New York State Association of Independent Schools, and New York State Board of Regents. Endowment: $11 million. Total enrollment: 870. Upper school average class size: 21. Upper school faculty-student ratio: 1:15.

Upper School Student Profile Grade 9: 163 students (163 boys); Grade 10: 175 students (175 boys); Grade 11: 158 students (158 boys); Grade 12: 150 students (150 boys). 78% of students are Roman Catholic Church (Jesuit order).

Faculty School total: 69. In upper school: 43 men, 19 women; 55 have advanced degrees.

Subjects Offered 3-dimensional art, advanced computer applications, advanced math, algebra, American government, American history, American literature, art, band, Bible studies, biology, biology-AP, biotechnology, calculus, calculus-AP, Catholic belief and practice, chemistry, chemistry-AP, choir, classical language, community service, computer keyboarding, computer literacy, computer math, computer programming, computer programming-AP, computer science, creative writing, drama, dramatic arts, driver education, earth science, economics, economics-AP, English, English literature, English literature and composition-AP, English literature-AP, environmental science, environmental science-AP, European history, European history-AP, expository writing, fine arts, foreign language, French, geography, geometry, global studies, government/civics, grammar, health, history, honors English, instrumental music, Italian, jazz band, Latin, mathematics, modern European history-AP, music, musical theater, novels, physical education, physics, physics-AP, poetry, portfolio writing, pre-calculus, psychology, psychology-AP, religion, religious studies, robotics, science, senior seminar, Shakespeare, social studies, Spanish, Spanish language-AP, speech and debate, statistics-AP, studio art-AP, theology, U.S. history-AP, vocal ensemble, vocal music, word processing, world history-AP, writing.

Graduation Requirements Arts and fine arts (art, music, dance, drama), English, foreign language, health education, mathematics, physical education (includes health), religion (includes Bible studies and theology), science, social studies (includes history). Community service is required.

Special Academic Programs Advanced Placement exam preparation; honors section.

College Admission Counseling 172 students graduated in 2008; 171 went to college, including Boston College; John Carroll University; Le Moyne College; Rochester Institute of Technology; Syracuse University; University of Rochester. Other: 1 went to work. Mean SAT critical reading: 584, mean SAT math: 605.

Student Life Upper grades have specified standards of dress, student council, honor system. Discipline rests primarily with faculty. Attendance at religious services is required.

Tuition and Aid Day student tuition: $9400. Tuition installment plan (monthly payment plans, individually arranged payment plans). Merit scholarship grants, need-based scholarship grants available. In 2008–09, 38% of upper-school students received aid; total upper-school merit-scholarship money awarded: $11,000. Total amount of financial aid awarded in 2008–09: $1,225,000.

Admissions Traditional secondary-level entrance grade is 9. For fall 2008, 131 students applied for upper-level admission, 109 were accepted, 80 enrolled. STS required. Deadline for receipt of application materials: none. Application fee required: $10.

Athletics Interscholastic: alpine skiing, baseball, basketball, bowling, crew, cross-country running, football, golf, ice hockey, indoor track, indoor track & field, lacrosse, rowing, rugby, sailing, skiing (downhill), soccer, swimming and diving, tennis, track and field, volleyball, winter (indoor) track, wrestling; intramural: baseball, basketball, bicycling, billiards, bocce, fencing, flag football, floor hockey, football, Frisbee, handball, hiking/backpacking, martial arts, mountain biking, paint ball, physical fitness, physical training, power lifting, ropes courses, self defense, skiing (cross-country), soccer, softball, strength & conditioning, table tennis, tennis, touch football, ultimate Frisbee, volleyball, water polo, weight lifting, weight training, wrestling, yoga. 4 PE instructors, 20 coaches, 1 athletic trainer.

Computers Computers are regularly used in art, English, foreign language, graphic design, history, journalism, lab/keyboard, library, literary magazine, mathematics, music, newspaper, religious studies, research skills, science, word processing, yearbook classes. Computer network features include on-campus library services, online commercial services, Internet access, wireless campus network, Internet filtering or blocking technology. Computer access in designated common areas is available to students. The school has a published electronic and media policy.

Contact Mr. Christopher Parks, Dean of Admissions. 585-256-6117. Fax: 585-256-6171. E-mail: cparks@mcquaid.org. Web site: www.mcquaid.org.

MEADOWRIDGE SCHOOL

12224 240th Street
Maple Ridge, British Columbia V4R 1N1, Canada

Head of School: Mr. Hugh Burke

General Information Coeducational day college-preparatory, arts, and technology school. Grades JK–12. Founded: 1985. Setting: rural. Nearest major city is Vancouver, Canada. 16.4-acre campus. 1 building on campus. Approved or accredited by Canadian Association of Independent Schools, Canadian Educational Standards Institute, European Council of International Schools, International Baccalaureate Organization, and British Columbia Department of Education. Language of instruction: English. Total enrollment: 500. Upper school average class size: 18. Upper school faculty-student ratio: 1:9.

Upper School Student Profile Grade 8: 44 students (19 boys, 25 girls); Grade 9: 31 students (12 boys, 19 girls); Grade 10: 38 students (13 boys, 25 girls); Grade 11: 42 students (18 boys, 24 girls); Grade 12: 28 students (16 boys, 12 girls).

Faculty School total: 46. In upper school: 11 men, 9 women; 6 have advanced degrees.

Subjects Offered Accounting, Advanced Placement courses, art, biology, biology-AP, calculus, calculus-AP, career and personal planning, chemistry, comparative civilizations, computer science-AP, computer technologies, drama, English, English literature, English-AP, filmmaking, forensics, French, geography, history, humanities, marketing, mathematics, photography, physical education, physics, science, Spanish, weight training.

Graduation Requirements 3 provincially examinable courses.

Special Academic Programs International Baccalaureate program; Advanced Placement exam preparation; study abroad; academic accommodation for the gifted.

College Admission Counseling 36 students graduated in 2008; all went to college, including McGill University; Queen's University at Kingston; Simon Fraser University; The University of British Columbia; University of Toronto; University of Victoria.

Student Life Upper grades have uniform requirement, student council, honor system. Discipline rests equally with students and faculty.

Tuition and Aid Day student tuition: CAN$12,400. Tuition installment plan (Insured Tuition Payment Plan, monthly payment plans). Tuition reduction for siblings, bursaries, merit scholarship grants available. In 2008–09, 1% of upper-school students received aid; total upper-school merit-scholarship money awarded: CAN$22,000.

Admissions Traditional secondary-level entrance grade is 8. For fall 2008, 39 students applied for upper-level admission, 28 were accepted, 26 enrolled. Admissions testing and writing sample required. Deadline for receipt of application materials: none. Application fee required: CAN$150. On-campus interview required.

Athletics Interscholastic: aerobics/dance (boys, girls), badminton (b,g), basketball (b,g), physical fitness (b,g), rugby (b,g), soccer (b,g), volleyball (b,g); intramural: aerobics/dance (b,g), basketball (b,g); coed interscholastic: aerobics/dance, cross-country running, flag football, outdoor activities, swimming and diving, track and field; coed intramural: aerobics/dance. 2 PE instructors.

Computers Computers are regularly used in information technology, journalism, video film production, yearbook classes. Computer network features include on-campus library services, Internet access, wireless campus network, Internet filtering or blocking technology. Student e-mail accounts and computer access in designated common areas are available to students.

Contact Ms. Christine Bickle, Director of Admissions. 604-467-4444 Ext. 217. Fax: 604-467-4989. E-mail: christine.bickle@meadowridge.bc.ca. Web site: www.meadowridge.bc.ca.

ANNOUNCEMENT FROM THE SCHOOL Meadowridge is an exemplary destination school, welcoming students and their families from throughout British Columbia and the world. Located in Maple Ridge, British Columbia, Meadowridge is an independent, nondenominational, International Baccalaureate World School offering a university-preparatory education to students from Junior Kindergarten to Grade 12. With an emphasis on the development of well-rounded individuals, Meadowridge students learn to live well—with others and for others—in a just community. The foundation of that learning is the safe and supportive environment of the school. Class sizes are small in order to provide more individual instruction and to permit the full participation of every student as a member of the class and of the intellectual community. The School believes that these learning conditions help promote the strong motivation, diligence, and respect for others shown by Meadowridge students. The teaching staff members are selected for their high level of professionalism, dedication, and concern for the intellectual, emotional, and personal needs of the students. The Meadowridge Early Childhood Center offers innovative full-time programs for Junior Kindergarten and Kindergarten students, leading them to an easy transition into the primary years of school. Meadowridge School offers Advanced Placement courses for students in grades 10–12 and is extremely proud of its continued 100% rate of postsecondary placement for its graduates. Meadowridge is one of just three schools in British Columbia to be granted membership in the Canadian Educational Standards Institute (CESI), and it is one of only six schools in Canada accredited to offer both the IB Primary Years (PYP) and Middle Years (MYP) Programs. The School's modern facility is situated just 45 kilometers east of Vancouver. The proximity of Meadowridge to provincial parks and river systems provides students with the ideal opportunities for integrated learning in the Outdoor Education Program. We invite you to pay us a visit!

THE MEADOWS SCHOOL

8601 Scholar Lane
Las Vegas, Nevada 89128-7302

Head of School: Mrs. Carolyn G. Goodman

General Information Coeducational day college-preparatory, arts, technology, and Debate, Foreign Languages school. Grades PK–12. Founded: 1981. Setting: suburban. Nearest major city is Los Angeles, CA. 42-acre campus. 10 buildings on campus. Approved or accredited by CITA (Commission on International and Trans-Regional Accreditation), Northwest Association of Schools and Colleges, Pacific Northwest Association of Independent Schools, and Nevada Department of Education. Member of National Association of Independent Schools and Secondary School Admission Test Board. Endowment: $1.8 million. Total enrollment: 910. Upper school average class size: 18. Upper school faculty-student ratio: 1:11.

Upper School Student Profile Grade 9: 75 students (38 boys, 37 girls); Grade 10: 62 students (27 boys, 35 girls); Grade 11: 61 students (29 boys, 32 girls); Grade 12: 65 students (26 boys, 39 girls).

Faculty School total: 92. In upper school: 22 men, 16 women; 25 have advanced degrees.

Subjects Offered 20th century American writers, 3-dimensional art, acting, advanced chemistry, advanced math, Advanced Placement courses, advanced studio art-AP, American literature, anatomy and physiology, ancient history, anthropology, Arabic, architectural drawing, architecture, art, art history, art history-AP, athletics, band, banking, Basic programming, biology, biology-AP, British literature, British literature (honors), calculus, calculus-AP, ceramics, chemistry, chemistry-AP, choir, choral music, chorus, comparative religion, composition, composition-AP, computer applications, computer graphics, computer keyboarding, computer literacy, computer programming, computer programming-AP, computer science, computer science-AP, concert choir, constitutional law, creative writing, dance, digital art, digital photography, drama, drama performance, drawing, drawing and design, economics, economics-AP, English, English composition, English language and composition-AP, English literature, English literature and composition-AP, environmental science-AP, European history, European history-AP, finance, finite math, foreign language, forensics, French, French language-AP, French literature-AP, genetics, geometry, health, honors English, honors geometry, honors U.S. history, honors world history, human anatomy, human geography—AP, instrumental music, integrated mathematics, journalism, Latin, Latin-AP, law, literature and composition-AP, macroeconomics-AP, microeconomics-AP, money management, music theater, painting, philosophy, photography, physics, physics-AP, pre-calculus, psychology-AP, sculpture, Shakespeare, social justice, social sciences, Spanish, Spanish language-AP, Spanish literature, Spanish literature-AP, Spanish-AP, speech, speech and debate, speech and oral interpretations, statistics, statistics-AP, studio art, studio art-AP, technical theater, technology, trigonometry, U.S. government-AP, U.S. history, U.S. history-AP, yearbook.

Graduation Requirements American literature, ancient world history, arts and fine arts (art, music, dance, drama), biology, English, English composition, English literature, European history, foreign language, geometry, mathematics, physical education (includes health), physics, pre-calculus, science, social studies (includes history), technical skills, U.S. government, U.S. history, Seniors have a 24-hour per semester community service requirement.

Special Academic Programs 26 Advanced Placement exams for which test preparation is offered; honors section; academic accommodation for the gifted, the musically talented, and the artistically talented; special instructional classes for None.

College Admission Counseling 72 students graduated in 2008; all went to college, including University of California, Berkeley; University of California, Los Angeles; University of Nevada, Las Vegas; University of San Diego; University of San Francisco; University of Southern California. Median SAT critical reading: 660, median SAT math: 650, median SAT writing: 650, median combined SAT: 1990, median composite ACT: 28. 78% scored over 600 on SAT critical reading, 76% scored over 600 on SAT math, 84% scored over 600 on SAT writing, 80% scored over 1800 on combined SAT, 69% scored over 26 on composite ACT.

Student Life Upper grades have uniform requirement, student council, honor system. Discipline rests equally with students and faculty.

Summer Programs Enrichment programs offered; session focuses on enrichment; held on campus; accepts boys and girls; open to students from other schools. 50 students usually enrolled. 2009 schedule: June to July. Application deadline: May.

Tuition and Aid Day student tuition: $18,500. Tuition installment plan (Insured Tuition Payment Plan, monthly payment plans, individually arranged payment plans, 2-payment plan, 70% by July 15 and 30% by February 15, 10 monthly payment plan using electronic withdrawal only). Need-based scholarship grants, need-based loans available. In 2008–09, 16% of upper-school students received aid. Total amount of financial aid awarded in 2008–09: $555,245.
Admissions Traditional secondary-level entrance grade is 9. For fall 2008, 71 students applied for upper-level admission, 31 were accepted, 31 enrolled. ERB, ISEE, PSAT, SAT or SSAT required. Deadline for receipt of application materials: none. Application fee required: $100. On-campus interview required.
Athletics Interscholastic: baseball (boys), basketball (b,g), cheering (g), cross-country running (b,g), dance (g), diving (b,g), football (b), golf (b), softball (g), swimming and diving (b,g), tennis (b,g), track and field (b,g), volleyball (g), wrestling (b); coed interscholastic: soccer. 1 PE instructor, 1 athletic trainer.
Computers Computers are regularly used in college planning, desktop publishing, English, foreign language, graphic design, history, independent study, information technology, introduction to technology, library, mathematics, music, news writing, photography, photojournalism, programming, publications, publishing, science, speech, technology, yearbook classes. Computer network features include on-campus library services, online commercial services, Internet access, wireless campus network, Internet filtering or blocking technology, Neon, SMART boards, two wireless mobile computer labs with notebook computers, course syllabus and homework for upper and middle school. Computer access in designated common areas is available to students. The school has a published electronic and media policy.
Contact Upper School Admissions. 702-254-1610. Web site: www.themeadowsschool.org.

MEMORIAL HALL SCHOOL

3721 Dacoma
Houston, Texas 77092
Head of School: Rev. George C. Aurich

General Information Coeducational day college-preparatory, general academic, and bilingual studies school. Grades 4–12. Founded: 1966. Setting: urban. 2-acre campus. 2 buildings on campus. Approved or accredited by Southern Association of Colleges and Schools, Southern Association of Independent Schools, Texas Education Agency, and Texas Department of Education. Total enrollment: 110. Upper school average class size: 14. Upper school faculty-student ratio: 1:14.
Faculty School total: 14. In upper school: 4 men, 10 women; 3 have advanced degrees.
Subjects Offered Algebra, American history, art, biology, business mathematics, business skills, chemistry, computer science, economics, English, ESL, fine arts, geography, geometry, government/civics, health, history, journalism, mathematics, physical education, physics, psychology, science, social science, social studies, sociology, Spanish, trigonometry, world history.
Graduation Requirements Arts and fine arts (art, music, dance, drama), business skills (includes word processing), computer science, English, foreign language, mathematics, physical education (includes health), science, social science, social studies (includes history), community service, foreign credit accepted upon completion.
Special Academic Programs Honors section; accelerated programs; independent study; study at local college for college credit; academic accommodation for the gifted; remedial reading and/or remedial writing; remedial math; programs in English, mathematics, general development for dyslexic students; special instructional classes for students with learning disabilities, Attention Deficit Disorder, and dyslexia; ESL (60 students enrolled).
College Admission Counseling Colleges students went to include Baylor University; Sam Houston State University; St. Thomas University; Texas A&M University; The University of Texas at Austin; University of Houston.
Student Life Upper grades have uniform requirement, student council, honor system. Discipline rests equally with students and faculty.
Summer Programs Remediation, enrichment, advancement, ESL, computer instruction programs offered; session focuses on additional credit enrichment, study skills; held on campus; accepts boys and girls; open to students from other schools. 55 students usually enrolled. 2009 schedule: June 15 to July 30. Application deadline: none.
Tuition and Aid Day student tuition: $8115. Tuition installment plan (Insured Tuition Payment Plan, monthly payment plans, individually arranged payment plans). Tuition reduction for siblings available. In 2008–09, 5% of upper-school students received aid.
Admissions Traditional secondary-level entrance grade is 9. Stanford Achievement Test required. Deadline for receipt of application materials: none. Application fee required: $250. Interview required.
Athletics Interscholastic: basketball (boys, girls), flag football (b); intramural: baseball (b,g), basketball (b,g), cheering (g), flag football (b); coed intramural: dance, outdoor activities, physical fitness. 2 coaches.
Computers Computers are regularly used in all academic, basic skills, foreign language classes. Computer network features include Internet access.
Contact Kimberly Smith, Coordinator. 713-688-5566. Fax: 713-956-9751. E-mail: memhallsch@aol.com. Web site: www.memorialhall.org.

MEMPHIS UNIVERSITY SCHOOL

6191 Park Avenue
Memphis, Tennessee 38119-5399
Head of School: Mr. Ellis L. Haguewood

General Information Boys' day college-preparatory school. Grades 7–12. Founded: 1893. Setting: suburban. 94-acre campus. 8 buildings on campus. Approved or accredited by Southern Association of Colleges and Schools, Southern Association of Independent Schools, and Tennessee Association of Independent Schools. Member of National Association of Independent Schools. Endowment: $19 million. Total enrollment: 650. Upper school average class size: 17. Upper school faculty-student ratio: 1:10.
Upper School Student Profile Grade 9: 102 students (102 boys); Grade 10: 103 students (103 boys); Grade 11: 116 students (116 boys); Grade 12: 95 students (95 boys).
Faculty School total: 68. In upper school: 41 men, 12 women; 52 have advanced degrees.
Subjects Offered Algebra, American government, American literature, art, art history, art history-AP, arts and crafts, Bible, biology, biology-AP, British literature, calculus, calculus-AP, chemistry, chemistry-AP, choral music, college counseling, college placement, comparative government and politics-AP, comparative religion, composition-AP, computer education, computer programming, computer science, computer science-AP, driver education, earth science, economics, economics and history, English, English composition, English literature, English literature and composition-AP, environmental science, ethics, ethics and responsibility, European history, European history-AP, expository writing, fine arts, foreign language, French, geometry, German, global studies, government and politics-AP, government/civics, grammar, health, history, humanities, introduction to theater, keyboarding/computer, language and composition, Latin, library skills, literature, mathematics, music, music appreciation, music composition, music theory, physical education, physical science, physics, physics-AP, pre-algebra, pre-calculus, probability and statistics, psychology, religion, research skills, science, social science, social studies, Spanish, studio art, study skills, trigonometry, U.S. history, U.S. history-AP, United States government-AP, Western civilization, woodworking, world history, writing.
Graduation Requirements Arts and fine arts (art, music, dance, drama), computer science, English, foreign language, mathematics, physical education (includes health), religion (includes Bible studies and theology), science, social science, social studies (includes history).
Special Academic Programs Advanced Placement exam preparation; honors section; study abroad; remedial reading and/or remedial writing; remedial math.
College Admission Counseling 93 students graduated in 2008; all went to college, including Furman University; Rhodes College; The University of Alabama at Birmingham; The University of Tennessee; University of Mississippi; Vanderbilt University. Median composite ACT: 29. Mean SAT critical reading: 643, mean SAT math: 655, mean SAT writing: 641. 70% scored over 600 on SAT critical reading, 77% scored over 600 on SAT math, 65% scored over 600 on SAT writing, 76% scored over 1800 on combined SAT, 75% scored over 26 on composite ACT.
Student Life Upper grades have specified standards of dress, student council, honor system. Discipline rests primarily with faculty.
Summer Programs Remediation, enrichment, advancement, sports programs offered; session focuses on academics and athletics; held on campus; accepts boys and girls; open to students from other schools. 460 students usually enrolled. 2009 schedule: June 1 to July 25. Application deadline: none.
Tuition and Aid Day student tuition: $15,250. Tuition installment plan (monthly payment plans, individually arranged payment plans). Need-based scholarship grants available. In 2008–09, 28% of upper-school students received aid. Total amount of financial aid awarded in 2008–09: $843,680.
Admissions Traditional secondary-level entrance grade is 9. For fall 2008, 50 students applied for upper-level admission, 27 were accepted, 19 enrolled. ISEE required. Deadline for receipt of application materials: January 10. Application fee required: $50. On-campus interview recommended.
Athletics Interscholastic: baseball, basketball, cross-country running, football, golf, lacrosse, soccer, swimming and diving, tennis, track and field, trap and skeet, weight training, wrestling. 5 PE instructors, 9 coaches, 1 athletic trainer.
Computers Computers are regularly used in all academic, career exploration, college planning, graphic design, library science, newspaper, publications, yearbook classes. Computer network features include on-campus library services, online commercial services, Internet access, wireless campus network, Internet filtering or blocking technology. Campus intranet, student e-mail accounts, and computer access in designated common areas are available to students. Students grades are available online.
Contact Mr. Daniel H. Kahalley, Director of Admissions. 901-260-1349. Fax: 901-260-1301. E-mail: danny.kahalley@musowls.org. Web site: www.musowls.org.

MENAUL SCHOOL

301 Menaul Boulevard NE
Albuquerque, New Mexico 87107
Head of School: Mr. Lindsey R. Gilbert

General Information Coeducational day college-preparatory and arts school, affiliated with Presbyterian Church. Grades 6–12. Founded: 1896. Setting: urban.

35-acre campus. 10 buildings on campus. Approved or accredited by North Central Association of Colleges and Schools, The College Board, and New Mexico Department of Education. Candidate for accreditation by Independent Schools Association of the Southwest. Endowment: $3.3 million. Total enrollment: 154. Upper school average class size: 12. Upper school faculty-student ratio: 1:9.

Upper School Student Profile Grade 9: 30 students (12 boys, 18 girls); Grade 10: 18 students (11 boys, 7 girls); Grade 11: 21 students (9 boys, 12 girls); Grade 12: 25 students (14 boys, 11 girls). 20% of students are Presbyterian.

Faculty School total: 25. In upper school: 13 men, 11 women; 16 have advanced degrees.

Subjects Offered ACT preparation, Advanced Placement courses, algebra, American government, American government-AP, American history, American literature, art, arts and crafts, band, Bible studies, biology, calculus-AP, chemistry, clayworking, communications, computer graphics, computer programming, computer science, earth science, economics, English, English literature, English-AP, ethics, fine arts, geography, geometry, government/civics, history, Life of Christ, mathematics, music, Native American arts and crafts, physical education, physics, psychology, religion, science, social science, social studies, sociology, Spanish, theology, trigonometry, world history, world literature, writing, yearbook.

Graduation Requirements Arts and fine arts (art, music, dance, drama), communications, computer science, English, foreign language, mathematics, physical education (includes health), religion (includes Bible studies and theology), science, social science, social studies (includes history), 100 hours of community service.

Special Academic Programs Advanced Placement exam preparation; honors section; independent study; study at local college for college credit; academic accommodation for the gifted and the artistically talented; ESL (5 students enrolled).

College Admission Counseling 18 students graduated in 2008; 17 went to college, including New Mexico State University; University of New Mexico. Other: 1 went to work. Median SAT critical reading: 500, median SAT math: 450, median composite ACT: 21. 20% scored over 600 on SAT critical reading, 15% scored over 600 on SAT math, 5% scored over 26 on composite ACT.

Student Life Upper grades have uniform requirement, student council. Discipline rests primarily with faculty. Attendance at religious services is required.

Summer Programs Enrichment, advancement, art/fine arts, computer instruction programs offered; session focuses on Academic enrichment and arts; held on campus; accepts boys and girls; open to students from other schools. 100 students usually enrolled. 2009 schedule: June 8 to July 25. Application deadline: none.

Tuition and Aid Day student tuition: $12,350. Tuition installment plan (FACTS Tuition Payment Plan). Need-based scholarship grants available. In 2008–09, 55% of upper-school students received aid. Total amount of financial aid awarded in 2008–09: $267,000.

Admissions Traditional secondary-level entrance grade is 9. For fall 2008, 30 students applied for upper-level admission, 24 were accepted, 12 enrolled. Achievement tests, ERB, Gates MacGinite Reading Tests, ISEE or SSAT required. Deadline for receipt of application materials: none. Application fee required: $30. Interview required.

Athletics Interscholastic: baseball (boys), basketball (b,g), flag football (b), football (b), soccer (g), softball (g), volleyball (g); coed interscholastic: golf, outdoor education, running, track and field. 2 PE instructors, 6 coaches, 1 athletic trainer.

Computers Computers are regularly used in art, college planning, English, graphics, history, mathematics, psychology, science, yearbook classes. Computer network features include on-campus library services, online commercial services, Internet access, wireless campus network, Internet filtering or blocking technology. Campus intranet and student e-mail accounts are available to students. Students grades are available online.

Contact John B. Thayer, Director of Admission and Financial Aid. 505-341-7223. Fax: 505-344-2517. E-mail: jthayer@menaulschool.com. Web site: www.menaulschool.com.

MENLO SCHOOL

50 Valparaiso Avenue
Atherton, California 94027

Head of School: Norman M. Colb

General Information Coeducational day college-preparatory, arts, and technology school. Grades 6–12. Founded: 1915. Setting: suburban. Nearest major city is San Jose. 35-acre campus. 23 buildings on campus. Approved or accredited by California Association of Independent Schools, Western Association of Schools and Colleges, and California Department of Education. Member of National Association of Independent Schools. Endowment: $23 million. Total enrollment: 750. Upper school average class size: 16. Upper school faculty-student ratio: 1:10.

Upper School Student Profile Grade 9: 141 students (72 boys, 69 girls); Grade 10: 128 students (68 boys, 60 girls); Grade 11: 130 students (69 boys, 61 girls); Grade 12: 131 students (71 boys, 60 girls).

Faculty School total: 93. In upper school: 34 men, 37 women; 56 have advanced degrees.

Subjects Offered Advanced computer applications, algebra, American history, American history-AP, American literature, American literature-AP, analytic geometry, anatomy and physiology, ancient world history, art, art history, biology, biology-AP, calculus, calculus-AP, California writers, chemistry, chemistry-AP, chorus, computer graphics, computer literacy, computer multimedia, computer programming, computer science, computer science-AP, creative writing, dance, debate, drama, earth science, economics, English, English language and composition-AP, English literature, English literature-AP, English-AP, ethics, European history, European history-AP, fine arts, French, French language-AP, French literature-AP, French-AP, geometry, government, history, honors geometry, intro to computers, Japanese, Japanese as Second Language, jazz band, jazz dance, journalism, Latin, Latin-AP, macro/microeconomics-AP, Mandarin, martial arts, mathematics, mathematics-AP, methods of research, microeconomics-AP, multimedia, music, music theory-AP, music-AP, musical productions, newspaper, orchestra, performing arts, philosophy, photography, physical education, physics, physics-AP, play production, science, science research, senior internship, Shakespeare, society and culture, Spanish, Spanish language-AP, Spanish literature-AP, Spanish-AP, statistics-AP, student government, student publications, studio art, studio-art-AP, swimming, U.S. government and politics-AP, United States government-AP, wellness, world history, world religions, writing.

Graduation Requirements Arts and fine arts (art, music, dance, drama), English, foreign language, mathematics, physical education (includes health), science, social studies (includes history), senior project (3-week project at the end of senior year), Knight School. Community service is required.

Special Academic Programs Advanced Placement exam preparation; honors section; independent study; academic accommodation for the gifted, the musically talented, and the artistically talented.

College Admission Counseling 139 students graduated in 2008; all went to college, including Claremont McKenna College; Princeton University; Stanford University; University of California, Los Angeles; University of California, Santa Barbara; University of Southern California. Mean SAT critical reading: 662, mean SAT math: 672, mean SAT writing: 661. 82% scored over 600 on SAT critical reading, 85% scored over 600 on SAT math, 81% scored over 600 on SAT writing.

Student Life Upper grades have student council. Discipline rests equally with students and faculty.

Tuition and Aid Day student tuition: $30,800. Tuition installment plan (Key Tuition Payment Plan). Need-based scholarship grants, paying campus jobs available. In 2008–09, 20% of upper-school students received aid. Total amount of financial aid awarded in 2008–09: $3,500,000.

Admissions Traditional secondary-level entrance grade is 9. For fall 2008, 350 students applied for upper-level admission, 116 were accepted, 70 enrolled. ISEE, SSAT or TOEFL required. Deadline for receipt of application materials: January 15. Application fee required: $85. On-campus interview required.

Athletics Interscholastic: aerobics/dance (girls), baseball (b), basketball (b,g), cross-country running (b,g), dance (g), football (b), golf (b,g), lacrosse (b,g), soccer (b,g), softball (g), swimming and diving (b,g), tennis (b,g), track and field (b,g), volleyball (b,g), water polo (b,g); coed interscholastic: aerobics/dance, dance, martial arts. 67 coaches, 2 athletic trainers.

Computers Computers are regularly used in English, foreign language, history, journalism, mathematics, media arts, multimedia, newspaper, science, yearbook classes. Computer network features include on-campus library services, online commercial services, Internet access, wireless campus network. Student e-mail accounts are available to students.

Contact Mary Emery, Admissions and Financial Aid Assistant. 650-330-2000 Ext. 2601. Fax: 650-330-2012. Web site: www.menloschool.org.

ANNOUNCEMENT FROM THE SCHOOL Menlo promotes the development of mind, body, and character. In a framework of strong faculty and parent support, students are encouraged to fulfill their potential by engaging in a wide array of academic and extracurricular programs. Vital, energetic students of varied backgrounds and talents take ever-greater responsibility for their own learning and behavior. Graduates attend leading colleges and universities.

MENNONITE COLLEGIATE INSTITUTE

Box 250
Gretna, Manitoba R0G 0V0, Canada

Head of School: Mr. Darryl K. Loewen

General Information Coeducational boarding and day college-preparatory, general academic, arts, business, and religious studies school, affiliated with Mennonite Church, Mennonite Brethren Church; primarily serves individuals with emotional and behavioral problems and physical disabilities. Grades 9–12. Founded: 1889. Setting: small town. Nearest major city is Winnipeg, Canada. Students are housed in single-sex dormitories. 12-acre campus. 5 buildings on campus. Approved or accredited by Manitoba Department of Education. Language of instruction: English. Endowment: CAN$250,000. Total enrollment: 153. Upper school average class size: 20. Upper school faculty-student ratio: 1:11.

Upper School Student Profile Grade 9: 28 students (10 boys, 18 girls); Grade 10: 37 students (20 boys, 17 girls); Grade 11: 43 students (21 boys, 22 girls); Grade 12: 45 students (22 boys, 23 girls). 42% of students are boarding students. 95% are province residents. 2 provinces are represented in upper school student body. 3% are international students. International students from Hong Kong, Japan, and Mexico. 60% of students are Mennonite, members of Mennonite Brethren Church.

Faculty School total: 14. In upper school: 9 men, 5 women; 3 have advanced degrees; 1 resides on campus.

Graduation Requirements Bible, English, mathematics, physical education (includes health), compulsory religion courses at each grade level, compulsory religious history courses at one level.
Special Academic Programs Advanced Placement exam preparation; academic accommodation for the musically talented; remedial reading and/or remedial writing; remedial math; special instructional classes for blind students; ESL (4 students enrolled).
College Admission Counseling 40 students graduated in 2008; 17 went to college, including The University of Winnipeg; University of Manitoba. Other: 21 went to work, 2 had other specific plans.
Student Life Upper grades have uniform requirement, student council, honor system. Discipline rests primarily with faculty. Attendance at religious services is required.
Tuition and Aid Day student tuition: CAN$3900; 7-day tuition and room/board: CAN$8050. Tuition installment plan (monthly payment plans, individually arranged payment plans). Tuition reduction for siblings, bursaries, merit scholarship grants, need-based scholarship grants, need-based loans, middle-income loans available. In 2008–09, 40% of upper-school students received aid; total upper-school merit-scholarship money awarded: CAN$9000. Total amount of financial aid awarded in 2008–09: CAN$46,000.
Admissions Traditional secondary-level entrance grade is 9. Deadline for receipt of application materials: none. Application fee required: CAN$200. Interview required.
Athletics Interscholastic: badminton (boys, girls), baseball (g), basketball (b,g), cross-country running (b,g), curling (b,g), golf (b), hockey (b), ice hockey (b), soccer (b,g), volleyball (b,g); intramural: floor hockey (b,g); coed interscholastic: badminton, cross-country running, curling, golf; coed intramural: floor hockey. 1 PE instructor.
Computers Computers are regularly used in all academic classes. Computer network features include on-campus library services, Internet access, Internet filtering or blocking technology. The school has a published electronic and media policy.
Contact Mr. Jeremy Siemens, Admissions Counselor. 204-327-5891. Fax: 204-327-5872. E-mail: admissions@mciblues.net. Web site: www.mciblues.net.

MENTOR COLLEGE

40 Forest Avenue
Mississauga, Ontario L5G 1L1, Canada
Head of School: Mr. Ken Philbrook

General Information Coeducational day college-preparatory school. Grades JK–12. Founded: 1981. Setting: suburban. 20-hectare campus. 1 building on campus. Approved or accredited by Ontario Department of Education. Language of instruction: English. Total enrollment: 1,580. Upper school average class size: 16. Upper school faculty-student ratio: 1:14.
Faculty School total: 59. In upper school: 26 men, 33 women.
Subjects Offered Accounting, algebra, biology, business, calculus, Canadian geography, Canadian history, careers, chemistry, civics, computer multimedia, computer programming, data analysis, discrete mathematics, earth and space science, economics, English/composition-AP, environmental science, ESL, European history, exercise science, fine arts, French as a second language, history, law, literature, marine biology, mathematics, music, philosophy, physical education, physical science, physics, science, Spanish, visual arts, world issues.
Special Academic Programs Advanced Placement exam preparation; ESL (50 students enrolled).
College Admission Counseling 142 students graduated in 2008; 137 went to college, including McGill University; McMaster University; The University of Western Ontario; University of Toronto; University of Waterloo; Wilfrid Laurier University. Other: 4 went to work, 1 had other specific plans.
Student Life Upper grades have uniform requirement, student council. Discipline rests primarily with faculty.
Summer Programs Remediation, enrichment, advancement, ESL, computer instruction programs offered; session focuses on advancement; held on campus; accepts boys and girls; open to students from other schools. 100 students usually enrolled. 2009 schedule: June 26 to July 31. Application deadline: June 15.
Tuition and Aid Day student tuition: CAN$13,600. Merit scholarship grants available. Total upper-school merit-scholarship money awarded for 2008–09: CAN$3002. Total amount of financial aid awarded in 2008–09: CAN$3002.
Admissions Traditional secondary-level entrance grade is 9. School's own exam required. Deadline for receipt of application materials: none. Application fee required: CAN$100. Interview required.
Athletics Interscholastic: alpine skiing (boys, girls), aquatics (b,g), badminton (b,g), basketball (b,g), cheering (b,g), cricket (b), cross-country running (b,g), golf (b,g), hockey (b), indoor soccer (b,g), rowing (b,g), rugby (b,g), skiing (downhill) (b,g), soccer (b,g), swimming and diving (b,g), table tennis (b,g), tennis (b,g), track and field (b,g), volleyball (b,g), wrestling (b,g); intramural: badminton (b,g), basketball (b,g), floor hockey (b,g), indoor hockey (b,g), indoor soccer (b,g), lacrosse (b,g), soccer (b,g), volleyball (b,g); coed interscholastic: archery, mountain biking, softball, ultimate Frisbee; coed intramural: cricket, dance, outdoor education, physical fitness, physical training, scuba diving, table tennis. 4 PE instructors.
Computers Computers are regularly used in business, computer applications, geography, technology classes. Computer network features include online commercial services, Internet access, Internet filtering or blocking technology, Edline. The school has a published electronic and media policy.
Contact Anna Penney, Registrar. 905-271-3393. Fax: 905-271-8367. E-mail: admin@mentorcollege.edu. Web site: www.mentorcollege.edu.

MERCEDES COLLEGE

540 Fullarton Road
Springfield 5062, Australia
Head of School: Mr. Peter Howard Daw

General Information Coeducational day college-preparatory, general academic, arts, business, vocational, religious studies, and bilingual studies school, affiliated with Roman Catholic Church. Grades 1–12. Founded: 1954. Setting: suburban. Nearest major city is Adelaide, Australia. 7-hectare campus. 10 buildings on campus. Approved or accredited by International Baccalaureate Organization. Member of European Council of International Schools. Language of instruction: English. Total enrollment: 1,201. Upper school average class size: 16. Upper school faculty-student ratio: 1:12.
Upper School Student Profile Grade 10: 149 students (78 boys, 71 girls); Grade 11: 154 students (76 boys, 78 girls); Grade 12: 154 students (82 boys, 72 girls). 90% of students are Roman Catholic.
Faculty School total: 132. In upper school: 24 men, 38 women; 14 have advanced degrees.
Special Academic Programs International Baccalaureate program; academic accommodation for the gifted; remedial reading and/or remedial writing; programs in general development for dyslexic students; ESL.
College Admission Counseling 154 students graduated in 2008.
Student Life Upper grades have uniform requirement, student council, honor system. Discipline rests primarily with faculty. Attendance at religious services is required.
Admissions For fall 2008, 66 students applied for upper-level admission, 52 were accepted, 52 enrolled. Deadline for receipt of application materials: none. Application fee required. Interview required.
Athletics Interscholastic: cricket (boys), football (b), netball (g), water polo (b); coed interscholastic: alpine skiing, badminton, basketball, canoeing/kayaking, climbing, cross-country running, fitness, hiking/backpacking, hockey, outdoor education, physical fitness, physical training, rock climbing, running, soccer, swimming and diving, table tennis, tennis, track and field, triathlon, volleyball, winter soccer. 6 PE instructors.
Computers Computers are regularly used in all classes. Computer network features include on-campus library services, Internet access, wireless campus network, Internet filtering or blocking technology. Student e-mail accounts are available to students. The school has a published electronic and media policy.
Contact Mrs. Shirley Smith, Registrar. 618-83723200. Fax: 618-83799540 Ext. 252. E-mail: ssmith@mercedes.adl.catholic.edu.au. Web site: www.mercedes.adl.catholic.edu.au.

MERCERSBURG ACADEMY

300 East Seminary Street
Mercersburg, Pennsylvania 17236
Head of School: Mr. Doug Hale

General Information Coeducational boarding and day college-preparatory school. Boarding grades 9–PG, day grades 9–11. Founded: 1893. Setting: small town. Nearest major city is Washington, DC. Students are housed in single-sex dormitories. 300-acre campus. 28 buildings on campus. Approved or accredited by Association of Independent Schools of Greater Washington, Middle States Association of Colleges and Schools, Pennsylvania Association of Independent Schools, The Association of Boarding Schools, and Pennsylvania Department of Education. Member of National Association of Independent Schools and Secondary School Admission Test Board. Endowment: $195 million. Total enrollment: 437. Upper school average class size: 12. Upper school faculty-student ratio: 1:5.
Upper School Student Profile Grade 9: 74 students (31 boys, 43 girls); Grade 10: 113 students (66 boys, 47 girls); Grade 11: 123 students (70 boys, 53 girls); Grade 12: 108 students (54 boys, 54 girls); Postgraduate: 19 students (14 boys, 5 girls). 85% of students are boarding students. 30% are state residents. 31 states are represented in upper school student body. 15% are international students. International students from Ecuador, Germany, Jamaica, Republic of Korea, Saudi Arabia, and Taiwan; 33 other countries represented in student body.
Faculty School total: 97. In upper school: 64 men, 33 women; 63 have advanced degrees; 29 reside on campus.
Subjects Offered 20th century American writers, 20th century world history, 3-dimensional art, acting, advanced chemistry, advanced computer applications, Advanced Placement courses, African American history, African dance, African drumming, algebra, American Civil War, American government-AP, American history, American history-AP, American literature, American literature-AP, art, art history, art history-AP, Asian history, astronomy, ballet, band, biology, biology-AP, botany, British literature-AP, Buddhism, calculus, calculus-AP, ceramics, chemistry, chemistry-AP, Chinese, choral music, chorus, comparative government and politics-AP, computer graphics, computer math, computer programming-AP, computer science, computer science-AP, concert band, creative writing, dance, digital art, drama, economics-AP, English, English literature, English literature and composition-AP, environmental science-AP, ethics, European history, European

history-AP, fine arts, French, French language-AP, French literature-AP, genetics, geometry, German, German-AP, government and politics-AP, health, history, honors algebra, honors English, honors geometry, honors U.S. history, honors world history, humanities, Islamic studies, jazz band, Latin, Latin-AP, mathematics, modern European history-AP, music, music composition, music history, musical theater dance, orchestra, personal fitness, physical education, physical science, physics, physics-AP, public speaking, religion, robotics, SAT preparation, science, social studies, Spanish, Spanish language-AP, statistics-AP, studio art, theater, theater design and production, trigonometry, U.S. history-AP, United States government-AP, yoga, zoology.

Graduation Requirements Arts and fine arts (art, music, dance, drama), English, foreign language, history, mathematics, physical education (includes health), religion (includes Bible studies and theology), science, participation in sports, performing arts, or other activities.

Special Academic Programs Advanced Placement exam preparation; honors section; independent study; term-away projects; study abroad; academic accommodation for the gifted.

College Admission Counseling 123 students graduated in 2008; all went to college, including Bryn Mawr College; Bucknell University; Georgetown University; Sewanee: The University of the South; United States Naval Academy; University of Pennsylvania.

Student Life Upper grades have specified standards of dress, student council, honor system. Discipline rests primarily with faculty.

Summer Programs Enrichment, ESL, sports, art/fine arts, rigorous outdoor training programs offered; session focuses on enrichment; held both on and off campus; held at various locations; accepts boys and girls; open to students from other schools. 2,300 students usually enrolled. 2009 schedule: June 10 to August 17. Application deadline: none.

Tuition and Aid Day student tuition: $31,700; 7-day tuition and room/board: $41,350. Tuition installment plan (Insured Tuition Payment Plan, Key Tuition Payment Plan, monthly payment plans). Merit scholarship grants, need-based scholarship grants, need-based loans available. In 2008–09, 42% of upper-school students received aid; total upper-school merit-scholarship money awarded: $400,000. Total amount of financial aid awarded in 2008–09: $4,500,000.

Admissions Traditional secondary-level entrance grade is 9. For fall 2008, 614 students applied for upper-level admission, 271 were accepted, 163 enrolled. ISEE, PSAT and SAT for applicants to grade 11 and 12, SSAT or TOEFL required. Deadline for receipt of application materials: January 31. Application fee required: $50. Interview required.

Athletics Interscholastic: baseball (boys), basketball (b,g), cross-country running (b,g), diving (b,g), field hockey (g), football (b), lacrosse (b,g), soccer (b,g), softball (g), squash (b,g), swimming and diving (b,g), tennis (b,g), track and field (b,g), volleyball (g), winter (indoor) track (b,g), wrestling (b); coed interscholastic: golf; coed intramural: aerobics/dance, alpine skiing, backpacking, ballet, bicycling, canoeing/kayaking, climbing, dance, equestrian sports, freestyle skiing, Frisbee, golf, hiking/backpacking, horseback riding, kayaking, martial arts, modern dance, outdoor education, physical fitness, physical training, rafting, rappelling, rock climbing, skiing (downhill), snowboarding, strength & conditioning, ultimate Frisbee, wall climbing, weight lifting, weight training, wilderness survival, yoga. 4 PE instructors, 22 coaches, 2 athletic trainers.

Computers Computers are regularly used in art, English, foreign language, history, mathematics, music, science classes. Computer network features include on-campus library services, online commercial services, Internet access, wireless campus network. Student e-mail accounts and computer access in designated common areas are available to students. The school has a published electronic and media policy.

Contact Mr. Thomas W. Adams, Assistant Head of School for Enrollment. 717-328-6173. Fax: 717-328-6319. E-mail: admission@mercersburg.edu. Web site: www.mercersburg.edu.

MERCHISTON CASTLE SCHOOL

Colinton
Edinburgh EH13 0PU, United Kingdom
Head of School: Mr. A. R. Hunter

General Information Boys' boarding and day college-preparatory school, affiliated with Christian faith. Ungraded, ages 8–18. Founded: 1833. Setting: suburban. Students are housed in single-sex dormitories. 100-acre campus. 11 buildings on campus. Approved or accredited by Headmasters' Conference. Language of instruction: English. Upper school average class size: 10. Upper school faculty-student ratio: 1:9.

Upper School Student Profile 76% of students are boarding students. 20% are international students. International students from Belgium, Brazil, China, Germany, and United States; 10 other countries represented in student body. 50% of students are Christian faith.

Faculty School total: 60. In upper school: 32 men, 15 women; 37 have advanced degrees; 30 reside on campus.

Subjects Offered Algebra, art, biology, calculus, chemistry, Chinese, computer science, creative writing, design, drama, electronics, English, English literature, European history, French, geography, geometry, German, government/civics, grammar, history, Italian, Japanese, Latin, mathematics, music, physical education, physics, religion, Russian, science, social studies, Spanish, trigonometry, world history.

Graduation Requirements Any three A-level courses.

Special Academic Programs Study abroad; academic accommodation for the gifted, the musically talented, and the artistically talented; remedial reading and/or remedial writing; remedial math; special instructional classes for deaf students, blind students; ESL (10 students enrolled).

College Admission Counseling 65 students graduated in 2008; 62 went to college. Other: 3 had other specific plans.

Student Life Upper grades have specified standards of dress, student council, honor system. Discipline rests equally with students and faculty.

Tuition and Aid Day student tuition: £16,395; 5-day tuition and room/board: £22,845; 7-day tuition and room/board: £22,845. Tuition reduction for siblings, bursaries, merit scholarship grants available.

Admissions Achievement/Aptitude/Writing and school's own exam required. Deadline for receipt of application materials: none. Application fee required: £150. Interview recommended.

Athletics Interscholastic: basketball (boys), cricket (b), cross-country running (b), fencing (b), football (b), golf (b), riflery (b), rugby (b), sailing (b), scuba diving (b), skiing (downhill) (b), soccer (b), squash (b), swimming and diving (b), tennis (b), track and field (b); intramural: badminton (b), basketball (b), bicycling (b), cricket (b), cross-country running (b), diving (b), fencing (b), Fives (b), football (b), golf (b), gymnastics (b), martial arts (b), mountain biking (b), outdoor activities (b), riflery (b), rugby (b), sailing (b), scuba diving (b), skiing (downhill) (b), soccer (b), squash (b), swimming and diving (b), table tennis (b), tennis (b), track and field (b), volleyball (b). 2 PE instructors, 1 coach.

Computers Computer network features include Internet access. Campus intranet and student e-mail accounts are available to students. The school has a published electronic and media policy.

Contact Mrs. Anne Rickard, Director of Admissions. 44-131-312 Ext. 2201. Fax: 44-131-441 Ext. 6060. E-mail: admissions@merchiston.co.uk. Web site: www.merchiston.co.uk.

MERCY HIGH SCHOOL

233 Riverside Way
Red Bluff, California 96080
Head of School: Mrs. Cheryl A. Ramirez

General Information Coeducational day college-preparatory, arts, and religious studies school, affiliated with Roman Catholic Church. Grades 9–12. Founded: 1882. Setting: small town. Nearest major city is Chico. 1 building on campus. Approved or accredited by Western Association of Schools and Colleges and California Department of Education. Total enrollment: 104. Upper school average class size: 15. Upper school faculty-student ratio: 1:10.

Upper School Student Profile Grade 9: 14 students (8 boys, 6 girls); Grade 10: 33 students (18 boys, 15 girls); Grade 11: 22 students (13 boys, 9 girls); Grade 12: 35 students (17 boys, 18 girls). 70% of students are Roman Catholic.

Faculty School total: 10. In upper school: 4 men, 6 women; 2 have advanced degrees.

Graduation Requirements 20 community service hours per year.

Special Academic Programs Advanced Placement exam preparation; honors section; study at local college for college credit.

College Admission Counseling 28 students graduated in 2008; 27 went to college, including California State University, Chico; University of California, Berkeley; University of California, San Diego; University of San Diego. Other: 1 went to work.

Student Life Upper grades have specified standards of dress, student council. Discipline rests primarily with faculty. Attendance at religious services is required.

Tuition and Aid Tuition installment plan (FACTS Tuition Payment Plan, 2-payment plan, prepayment discount plan). Need-based scholarship grants available.

Admissions Traditional secondary-level entrance grade is 9. For fall 2008, 36 students applied for upper-level admission, 36 were accepted, 36 enrolled. Deadline for receipt of application materials: none. Application fee required: $50.

Athletics Interscholastic: baseball (boys), basketball (b,g), cheering (g), football (b), softball (g), tennis (b,g), volleyball (g); intramural: basketball (b,g), volleyball (b,g); coed interscholastic: cross-country running, golf, skiing (downhill), snowboarding, soccer, swimming and diving, track and field; coed intramural: badminton. 1 PE instructor, 2 coaches.

Computers Computer resources include Internet access. Students grades are available online.

Contact Mrs. Cheryl Ramirez, Principal/Counselor. 916-527-8313. Fax: 916-527-3058. E-mail: mercy@mercy-high.org.

MERCY HIGH SCHOOL

1740 Randolph Road
Middletown, Connecticut 06457-5155
Head of School: Sr. Mary McCarthy, RSM

General Information Girls' day college-preparatory, arts, and religious studies school, affiliated with Roman Catholic Church. Grades 9–12. Founded: 1963. Setting: rural. Nearest major city is Hartford. 26-acre campus. 1 building on campus. Approved or accredited by Mercy Secondary Education Association, National Catholic Education Association, New England Association of Schools and Colleges, and Connecticut Department of Education. Total enrollment: 697. Upper school average class size: 21. Upper school faculty-student ratio: 1:14.

Upper School Student Profile Grade 9: 186 students (186 girls); Grade 10: 181 students (181 girls); Grade 11: 173 students (173 girls); Grade 12: 157 students (157 girls). 82% of students are Roman Catholic.
Faculty School total: 55. In upper school: 8 men, 47 women; 39 have advanced degrees.
Subjects Offered Accounting, advanced math, algebra, American government, American literature, American literature-AP, anatomy and physiology, art, art appreciation, arts and crafts, biology, biology-AP, business, calculus, calculus-AP, Catholic belief and practice, ceramics, chamber groups, chemistry, chemistry-AP, choir, chorus, civics, comparative government and politics, computer applications, concert band, concert choir, creative writing, drama workshop, drawing and design, English, English literature, English-AP, European history, expository writing, French, French language-AP, French literature-AP, French-AP, geometry, government/civics, grammar, health, history, honors algebra, honors English, honors geometry, honors U.S. history, honors world history, humanities, independent study, journalism, keyboarding/computer, Latin, Latin-AP, law, literature-AP, mathematics, modern history, music, neuroscience, photography, physical education, physics, physics-AP, pottery, pre-algebra, pre-calculus, psychology, public speaking, reading/study skills, religious studies, science, social studies, sociology, Spanish, Spanish language-AP, Spanish-AP, statistics, statistics-AP, theater arts, trigonometry, U.S. history, U.S. history-AP, wind ensemble, word processing, world history, world literature, writing.
Graduation Requirements Civics, computer applications, English, foreign language, mathematics, physical education (includes health), religion (includes Bible studies and theology), science, social studies (includes history), 70 hours of community service.
Special Academic Programs 10 Advanced Placement exams for which test preparation is offered; honors section; independent study; study at local college for college credit; programs in English for dyslexic students.
College Admission Counseling 162 students graduated in 2008; 158 went to college, including Bryant University; Central Connecticut State University; College of the Holy Cross; Southern Connecticut State University; Stonehill College; University of Connecticut. Other: 1 went to work, 3 had other specific plans. Median SAT critical reading: 530, median SAT math: 510, median SAT writing: 540, median combined SAT: 1570, median composite ACT: 21. 22% scored over 600 on SAT critical reading, 14% scored over 600 on SAT math, 24% scored over 600 on SAT writing, 16% scored over 1800 on combined SAT, 14% scored over 26 on composite ACT.
Student Life Upper grades have uniform requirement, student council. Discipline rests primarily with faculty. Attendance at religious services is required.
Tuition and Aid Day student tuition: $8850–$9350. Tuition installment plan (FACTS Tuition Payment Plan, individually arranged payment plans). Tuition reduction for siblings, merit scholarship grants, need-based scholarship grants available.
Admissions Traditional secondary-level entrance grade is 9. For fall 2008, 349 students applied for upper-level admission, 295 were accepted, 198 enrolled. High School Placement Test (closed version) from Scholastic Testing Service required. Deadline for receipt of application materials: none. Application fee required: $50.
Athletics Interscholastic: basketball, cheering, cross-country running, diving, field hockey, golf, gymnastics, indoor track, lacrosse, soccer, softball, swimming and diving, tennis, track and field, volleyball; intramural: basketball, golf, soccer, tennis, volleyball. 2 PE instructors, 29 coaches, 1 athletic trainer.
Computers Computers are regularly used in accounting, all academic, computer applications, desktop publishing, journalism, newspaper, word processing classes. Computer network features include on-campus library services, Internet access, Internet filtering or blocking technology. Campus intranet, student e-mail accounts, and computer access in designated common areas are available to students.
Contact Sr. Patty Moriarty, RSM, Director of Admissions. 860-346-6659. Fax: 860-344-9887. E-mail: pmoriarty@mercyhigh.com. Web site: www.mercyhigh.com.

MERCY HIGH SCHOOL

1501 South 48th Street
Omaha, Nebraska 68106-2598

Head of School: Ms. Carolyn Jaworski

General Information Girls' day college-preparatory, general academic, arts, business, religious studies, and technology school, affiliated with Roman Catholic Church. Grades 9–12. Founded: 1955. Setting: urban. 2-acre campus. 1 building on campus. Approved or accredited by Mercy Secondary Education Association, National Catholic Education Association, North Central Association of Colleges and Schools, and Nebraska Department of Education. Total enrollment: 365. Upper school average class size: 22. Upper school faculty-student ratio: 1:12.
Upper School Student Profile Grade 9: 101 students (101 girls); Grade 10: 79 students (79 girls); Grade 11: 105 students (105 girls); Grade 12: 80 students (80 girls). 89% of students are Roman Catholic.
Faculty School total: 33. In upper school: 5 men, 28 women; 20 have advanced degrees.
Subjects Offered Accounting, algebra, American government, American history, American history-AP, American literature, anatomy and physiology, art, ballet, biology, British literature, British literature-AP, business applications, calculus, calculus-AP, chemistry, chemistry-AP, child development, choir, computer education, computer keyboarding, consumer mathematics, culinary arts, debate, drama, drawing, ecology, English, French, general math, geometry, health, honors English, honors geometry, journalism, keyboarding/computer, math review, moral theology, painting, participation in sports, peace and justice, physics, physics-AP, play production, pottery, pre-algebra, pre-calculus, psychology, social justice, Spanish, Spanish-AP, speech, speech and debate, sports medicine, stagecraft, statistics, theology, theology and the arts, trigonometry, U.S. government, U.S. history, U.S. history-AP, vocal music, world history, yearbook.
Graduation Requirements Advanced math, algebra, American government, anatomy and physiology, arts and fine arts (art, music, dance, drama), biology, chemistry, computer applications, debate, English, foreign language, geometry, mathematics, physical education (includes health), physics, social studies (includes history), speech, theology, U.S. history, world history, service hours.
Special Academic Programs Advanced Placement exam preparation; honors section; study at local college for college credit; remedial reading and/or remedial writing; remedial math; programs in general development for dyslexic students; special instructional classes for deaf students, blind students, students with LD, ADD, emotional and behavioral problems.
College Admission Counseling 75 students graduated in 2008; 66 went to college, including Creighton University; University of Nebraska–Lincoln; University of Nebraska at Omaha. Other: 4 went to work, 5 had other specific plans.
Student Life Upper grades have uniform requirement, student council, honor system. Discipline rests primarily with faculty. Attendance at religious services is required.
Tuition and Aid Day student tuition: $7300. Tuition installment plan (individually arranged payment plans, each family has an individualized tuition based upon their income). Tuition reduction for siblings, merit scholarship grants, need-based scholarship grants, paying campus jobs available. In 2008–09, 85% of upper-school students received aid; total upper-school merit-scholarship money awarded: $100,000. Total amount of financial aid awarded in 2008–09: $500,000.
Admissions Traditional secondary-level entrance grade is 9. For fall 2008, 101 students applied for upper-level admission, 101 were accepted, 101 enrolled. STS Examination required. Deadline for receipt of application materials: March 31. Application fee required: $100. Interview required.
Athletics Interscholastic: aerobics, archery, badminton, ballet, basketball, bowling, cheering, cross-country running, dance squad, dance team, diving, fitness walking, golf, independent competitive sports, physical fitness, self defense, soccer, softball, strength & conditioning, swimming and diving, tennis, track and field, volleyball, weight training; intramural: indoor soccer. 1 PE instructor, 15 coaches, 1 athletic trainer.
Computers Computers are regularly used in accounting, business, business applications, business education, business studies, history, journalism, keyboarding, lab/keyboard, library, library skills, mathematics, music, photojournalism, publications, religion, science, yearbook classes. Computer network features include on-campus library services, online commercial services, Internet access, wireless campus network, Internet filtering or blocking technology. Student e-mail accounts and computer access in designated common areas are available to students. Students grades are available online. The school has a published electronic and media policy.
Contact Ms. Anne Zadina, Recruitment Director. 402-553-9424. Fax: 402-553-0394. E-mail: zadinaa@mercyhigh.org. Web site: www.mercyhigh.org.

MERCY HIGH SCHOOL COLLEGE PREPARATORY

3250 19th Avenue
San Francisco, California 94132-2000

Head of School: Dr. Dorothy McCrea

General Information Girls' day college-preparatory, arts, business, vocational, religious studies, bilingual studies, and technology school, affiliated with Roman Catholic Church. Grades 9–12. Founded: 1952. Setting: urban. Nearest major city is Daly City. 6-acre campus. 2 buildings on campus. Approved or accredited by European Council of International Schools, Western Association of Schools and Colleges, and California Department of Education. Total enrollment: 509. Upper school average class size: 26. Upper school faculty-student ratio: 1:15.
Upper School Student Profile Grade 9: 149 students (149 girls); Grade 10: 135 students (135 girls); Grade 11: 116 students (116 girls); Grade 12: 109 students (109 girls). 67.8% of students are Roman Catholic.
Faculty School total: 34. In upper school: 7 men, 27 women; 28 have advanced degrees.
Subjects Offered Algebra, American history, American literature, art, biology, business, calculus, ceramics, chemistry, chorus, computer applications, computer programming, creative writing, dance, drama, English, English literature, environmental science, ethics, ethnic studies, expository writing, French, geometry, government/civics, keyboarding, mathematics, physical education, physics, religion, social studies, Spanish, speech, theater, trigonometry, world history.
Graduation Requirements 100 community service hours, Intersession.
Special Academic Programs Advanced Placement exam preparation; honors section.
College Admission Counseling 126 students graduated in 2008; all went to college, including City College of San Francisco; San Francisco State University; San Jose State University; University of California, Irvine; University of California, Santa Cruz; University of San Francisco. Mean SAT critical reading: 514, mean SAT math: 505, mean SAT writing: 521, mean combined SAT: 1540, mean composite ACT: 21. 14% scored over 600 on SAT critical reading, 15% scored over 600 on SAT math, 13% scored over 600 on SAT writing, 8.7% scored over 1800 on combined SAT, 4.7% scored over 26 on composite ACT.

Student Life Upper grades have uniform requirement, student council, honor system. Discipline rests primarily with faculty. Attendance at religious services is required.
Summer Programs Enrichment programs offered; session focuses on Pre-high program—enrichment only, secondary program—enrichment & remediation; held on campus; accepts boys and girls; open to students from other schools. 400 students usually enrolled. 2009 schedule: June 22 to July 17. Application deadline: June 18.
Tuition and Aid Day student tuition: $12,500. Guaranteed tuition plan. Tuition installment plan (full payment, 10 months payment (July-April), Semi-annual payment (July-December)). Need-based scholarship grants available. In 2008–09, 50% of upper-school students received aid. Total amount of financial aid awarded in 2008–09: $1,424,260.
Admissions Traditional secondary-level entrance grade is 9. For fall 2008, 337 students applied for upper-level admission, 227 were accepted, 149 enrolled. Comprehensive Test of Basic Skills and High School Placement Test required. Deadline for receipt of application materials: December 8. Application fee required: $80. Interview recommended.
Athletics Interscholastic: basketball, cross-country running, dance, self defense, soccer, softball, swimming and diving, tennis, track and field, volleyball. 10 coaches.
Computers Computers are regularly used in accounting, Bible studies, business education, business skills, English, religion, science classes. Computer network features include on-campus library services, Internet access, Internet filtering or blocking technology, Hunter Systems, Blackbaud. Computer access in designated common areas is available to students. Students grades are available online.
Contact Liz Belonogoff, Admissions Director. 415-584-5929. Fax: 415-334-9726. E-mail: lbelonogoff@mercyhs.org. Web site: www.mercyhs.org.

MERCYHURST PREPARATORY SCHOOL

538 East Grandview Boulevard
Erie, Pennsylvania 16504-2697

Head of School: Ms. Margaret M. Aste

General Information Coeducational day college-preparatory, arts, religious studies, and technology school, affiliated with Roman Catholic Church. Grades 9–12. Founded: 1926. Setting: urban. 5-acre campus. 1 building on campus. Approved or accredited by International Baccalaureate Organization, Middle States Association of Colleges and Schools, and Pennsylvania Department of Education. Total enrollment: 600. Upper school average class size: 25. Upper school faculty-student ratio: 1:13.
Upper School Student Profile Grade 9: 152 students (52 boys, 100 girls); Grade 10: 150 students (52 boys, 98 girls); Grade 11: 159 students (65 boys, 94 girls); Grade 12: 137 students (41 boys, 96 girls). 81% of students are Roman Catholic.
Faculty School total: 47. In upper school: 13 men, 33 women; 19 have advanced degrees.
Subjects Offered Accounting, algebra, American Civil War, American government, American history, American literature, anatomy, art, art appreciation, art education, art history, astronomy, athletic training, ballet, biology, business skills, calculus, campus ministry, career exploration, ceramics, chemistry, chorus, Christian ethics, civil war history, communications, community service, computer applications, computer keyboarding, computer programming, computer science, creative arts, dance, digital photography, drama, drama performance, drawing, drawing and design, earth science, English, English literature, environmental science, ethics, European history, expository writing, fine arts, first aid, French, geology, geometry, government/civics, guitar, health, Hebrew scripture, history, Holocaust, humanities, Internet, journalism, leadership training, mathematics, multimedia, music, music appreciation, music theory-AP, musical productions, orchestra, painting, photography, physical education, physics, physiology, piano, psychology, public speaking, publications, reading/study skills, religion, SAT preparation, SAT/ACT preparation, science, senior internship, set design, social studies, Spanish, speech, speech and debate, study skills, tap dance, technical theater, technology/design, theater, theater arts, theology, theory of knowledge, trigonometry, typing, U.S. government, U.S. history, visual and performing arts, weight fitness, weightlifting, word processing, world cultures, world history, writing, writing skills, yearbook.
Graduation Requirements Arts and fine arts (art, music, dance, drama), arts appreciation, business skills (includes word processing), computer science, creative arts, English, foreign language, mathematics, physical education (includes health), public speaking, religion (includes Bible studies and theology), science, social studies (includes history), technological applications, 25 service hours per year.
Special Academic Programs International Baccalaureate program; honors section; independent study; study at local college for college credit; academic accommodation for the gifted, the musically talented, and the artistically talented; remedial reading and/or remedial writing; remedial math; special instructional classes for deaf students.
College Admission Counseling 165 students graduated in 2008; 161 went to college, including Edinboro University of Pennsylvania; Gannon University; Mercyhurst College; Penn State University Park; University of Pittsburgh. Other: 4 went to work. Mean SAT critical reading: 519, mean SAT math: 507, mean SAT writing: 525, mean composite ACT: 22.
Student Life Upper grades have uniform requirement, student council, honor system. Discipline rests primarily with faculty. Attendance at religious services is required.
Summer Programs Remediation, enrichment, advancement, art/fine arts, computer instruction programs offered; session focuses on enrichment; held on campus; accepts boys and girls; open to students from other schools. 142 students usually enrolled. 2009 schedule: June 15 to August 7. Application deadline: none.
Tuition and Aid Day student tuition: $6400. Tuition installment plan (FACTS Tuition Payment Plan). Merit scholarship grants, need-based scholarship grants, creative arts scholarships, alumni scholarships, endowment scholarships available. In 2008–09, 50% of upper-school students received aid; total upper-school merit-scholarship money awarded: $94,400. Total amount of financial aid awarded in 2008–09: $492,600.
Admissions Traditional secondary-level entrance grade is 9. For fall 2008, 292 students applied for upper-level admission, 269 were accepted, 152 enrolled. Achievement tests, Iowa Tests of Basic Skills or Math Placement Exam required. Deadline for receipt of application materials: none. Application fee required: $10.
Athletics Interscholastic: baseball (boys), basketball (b,g), bowling (g), cheering (g), crew (b,g), cross-country running (b,g), dance team (g), football (b), golf (b,g), modern dance (g), rowing (b,g), skiing (downhill) (g), soccer (b,g), softball (g), swimming and diving (b,g), tennis (b,g), track and field (b,g), volleyball (g); coed interscholastic: tennis, weight training; coed intramural: weight lifting, weight training. 2 PE instructors, 40 coaches, 1 athletic trainer.
Computers Computers are regularly used in college planning, English, foreign language, history, journalism, mathematics, media, newspaper, photography, photojournalism, publications, publishing, SAT preparation, science, typing, word processing, writing, yearbook classes. Computer network features include on-campus library services, online commercial services, Internet access, wireless campus network, Internet filtering or blocking technology. Campus intranet is available to students. Students grades are available online. The school has a published electronic and media policy.
Contact Mrs. Marcia E. DiTullio, Administrative Assistant. 814-824-2323. Fax: 814-824-2116. E-mail: mditullio@mpslakers.com. Web site: www.mpslakers.com.

MERCY VOCATIONAL HIGH SCHOOL

2900 West Hunting Park Avenue
Philadelphia, Pennsylvania 19129

Head of School: Sr. Rosemary Herron, RSM

General Information Coeducational day college-preparatory and vocational school, affiliated with Roman Catholic Church. Grades 9–12. Founded: 1950. Setting: urban. 2 buildings on campus. Approved or accredited by Middle States Association of Colleges and Schools and Pennsylvania Department of Education. Upper school average class size: 22. Upper school faculty-student ratio: 1:16.
Faculty School total: 38. In upper school: 14 men, 24 women.
Student Life Upper grades have uniform requirement, student council. Discipline rests primarily with faculty. Attendance at religious services is required.
Admissions Traditional secondary-level entrance grade is 9. For fall 2008, 179 students applied for upper-level admission, 125 were accepted, 125 enrolled. Deadline for receipt of application materials: none. No application fee required.
Athletics 1 PE instructor, 3 coaches.
Contact Director of Admissions. 215-226-1225 Ext. 115. Fax: 215-228-6337. E-mail: wdonahue@mercyvhs.org. Web site: www.mercyvocational.org.

MESA GRANDE SEVENTH-DAY ACADEMY

975 South Fremont Street
Calimesa, California 92320

Head of School: Alfred J. Riddle

General Information Coeducational day college-preparatory, arts, religious studies, and technology school, affiliated with Seventh-day Adventists, Christian faith. Grades K–12. Founded: 1928. Setting: rural. Nearest major city is San Bernardino. 14-acre campus. 3 buildings on campus. Approved or accredited by Western Association of Schools and Colleges and California Department of Education. Endowment: $650,000. Total enrollment: 281. Upper school average class size: 30. Upper school faculty-student ratio: 1:10.
Upper School Student Profile Grade 9: 27 students (15 boys, 12 girls); Grade 10: 48 students (20 boys, 28 girls); Grade 11: 28 students (16 boys, 12 girls); Grade 12: 29 students (17 boys, 12 girls). 90% of students are Seventh-day Adventists, Christian.
Faculty School total: 25. In upper school: 9 men, 7 women; 9 have advanced degrees.
Subjects Offered Algebra, American literature, animal behavior, arts, ASB Leadership, auto mechanics, bell choir, biology, British literature, career education, chemistry, choral music, community service, composition, computer applications, computer-aided design, computers, concert choir, desktop publishing, drama, economics, economics and history, English, English composition, family living, fine arts, French, general math, geography, geometry, government/civics, graphic arts, handbells, health, instrumental music, keyboarding, lab science, marine biology, mathematics, music composition, music theory, physical education, physical science, physics, pre-calculus, printmaking, religion, religious education, science, social science, social studies, Spanish, U.S. government, U.S. history, video film production, world history, world literature, yearbook.
Graduation Requirements Algebra, American government, applied skills, arts and fine arts (art, music, dance, drama), biology, British literature, career education, chemistry, computer education, computer technologies, economics, English, English composition, family living, industrial technology, keyboarding, mathematics, modern languages, physical education (includes health), physical fitness, physical science,

physics, religious studies, science, social studies (includes history), Spanish, technical skills, writing fundamentals, work experience, community service.
College Admission Counseling 38 students graduated in 2008; 37 went to college, including Andrews University; California State University, San Bernardino; La Sierra University; Pacific Union College; University of California, Riverside; Walla Walla University. Other: 1 went to work. Median SAT critical reading: 540, median SAT math: 567, median composite ACT: 24. 10% scored over 600 on SAT critical reading, 10% scored over 600 on SAT math, 5% scored over 26 on composite ACT.
Student Life Upper grades have uniform requirement, student council, honor system. Discipline rests primarily with faculty. Attendance at religious services is required.
Summer Programs Sports programs offered; held both on and off campus; held at Drayson Center, Loma Linda, CA; accepts boys and girls; open to students from other schools. 50 students usually enrolled. 2009 schedule: June 8 to August 20. Application deadline: May 5.
Tuition and Aid Day student tuition: $7980. Tuition installment plan (monthly payment plans). Need-based loans, paying campus jobs available. In 2008–09, 25% of upper-school students received aid. Total amount of financial aid awarded in 2008–09: $35,000.
Admissions Traditional secondary-level entrance grade is 9. For fall 2008, 55 students applied for upper-level admission, 45 were accepted, 45 enrolled. Any standardized test, ITBS-TAP or Math Placement Exam required. Deadline for receipt of application materials: none. Application fee required: $50. On-campus interview required.
Athletics Interscholastic: baseball (boys), basketball (b,g), flag football (b,g), softball (g), volleyball (b,g); coed interscholastic: cross-country running, golf, weight lifting. 3 PE instructors, 12 coaches, 2 athletic trainers.
Computers Computers are regularly used in design, graphic design, journalism, library skills, science, technical drawing, technology, typing, video film production, writing, yearbook classes. Computer network features include on-campus library services, online commercial services, Internet access, Internet filtering or blocking technology. Student e-mail accounts and computer access in designated common areas are available to students. Students grades are available online. The school has a published electronic and media policy.
Contact Lois M. Myhre, Admissions Office. 909-795-1112 Ext. 257. Fax: 909-795-1653. E-mail: lois.myhre@mgak-12.org. Web site: www.mesagrandeacademy.org.

METAIRIE PARK COUNTRY DAY SCHOOL

300 Park Road
Metairie, Louisiana 70005-4199

Head of School: Ms. Carolyn Chandler

General Information Coeducational day college-preparatory and arts school. Grades K–12. Founded: 1929. Setting: suburban. Nearest major city is New Orleans. 14-acre campus. 24 buildings on campus. Approved or accredited by Independent Schools Association of the Southwest and Louisiana Department of Education. Member of National Association of Independent Schools and Secondary School Admission Test Board. Endowment: $6.3 million. Total enrollment: 685. Upper school average class size: 12. Upper school faculty-student ratio: 1:7.
Upper School Student Profile Grade 9: 69 students (33 boys, 36 girls); Grade 10: 51 students (25 boys, 26 girls); Grade 11: 45 students (15 boys, 30 girls); Grade 12: 61 students (30 boys, 31 girls).
Faculty School total: 96. In upper school: 18 men, 32 women; 28 have advanced degrees.
Subjects Offered Advanced Placement courses, aerospace science, algebra, American government-AP, American history, American history-AP, American literature, art, biology, biology-AP, calculus, calculus-AP, chemistry, chemistry-AP, chorus, classics, clayworking, computer graphics, concert band, creative writing, dance, drama, drawing, English, English composition, English literature, English literature-AP, English-AP, environmental science-AP, European history-AP, film studies, fine arts, French, French-AP, government-AP, government/civics, health, honors algebra, honors English, honors geometry, honors world history, independent study, instrumental music, jazz band, jewelry making, journalism, literary magazine, mathematics, metalworking, modern European history-AP, music, music theory, newspaper, oceanography, orchestra, painting, photography, physical education, physics, physics-AP, poetry, pre-calculus, psychology, robotics, sculpture, senior humanities, social studies, Spanish, Spanish-AP, video, vocal ensemble, Web site design, woodworking, world history, world literature, World-Wide-Web publishing, yearbook.
Graduation Requirements Arts and fine arts (art, music, dance, drama), electives, English, foreign language, mathematics; physical education (includes health), science, social studies (includes history).
Special Academic Programs Advanced Placement exam preparation; honors section; independent study; academic accommodation for the gifted, the musically talented, and the artistically talented; programs in general development for dyslexic students.
College Admission Counseling 42 students graduated in 2008; all went to college, including Tulane University. 35% scored over 600 on SAT critical reading, 62% scored over 600 on SAT math, 53% scored over 600 on SAT writing, 51% scored over 1800 on combined SAT, 39% scored over 26 on composite ACT.
Student Life Upper grades have specified standards of dress, student council, honor system. Discipline rests equally with students and faculty.
Tuition and Aid Day student tuition: $14,900. Tuition installment plan (Insured Tuition Payment Plan, monthly payment plans, individually arranged payment plans). Need-based scholarship grants available. In 2008–09, 26% of upper-school students received aid. Total amount of financial aid awarded in 2008–09: $325,000.
Admissions Traditional secondary-level entrance grade is 9. For fall 2008, 88 students applied for upper-level admission, 53 were accepted, 28 enrolled. Academic Profile Tests, SSAT or SSAT, ERB, PSAT, SAT, PLAN or ACT required. Deadline for receipt of application materials: none. Application fee required: $50. Interview required.
Athletics Interscholastic: baseball (boys), basketball (b,g), cheering (g), cross-country running (b,g), football (b), golf (b), power lifting (b,g), soccer (b,g), softball (g), strength & conditioning (b,g), swimming and diving (b,g), tennis (b,g), track and field (b,g), volleyball (g). 9 PE instructors, 35 coaches, 1 athletic trainer.
Computers Computers are regularly used in all classes. Computer network features include on-campus library services, online commercial services, Internet access.
Contact Amy White, Director of Admission. 504-849-3105. Fax: 504-837-0015. E-mail: amy_white@mpcds.com. Web site: www.mpcds.com.

METRO-EAST LUTHERAN HIGH SCHOOL

6305 Center Grove Road
Edwardsville, Illinois 62025

Head of School: Daniel S Kostencki

General Information Coeducational day college-preparatory and general academic school, affiliated with Lutheran Church. Grades 9–12. Founded: 1977. Setting: urban. Nearest major city is St. Louis. 15-acre campus. 1 building on campus. Approved or accredited by National Lutheran School Accreditation, North Central Association of Colleges and Schools, and Illinois Department of Education. Upper school average class size: 15. Upper school faculty-student ratio: 1:15.
Upper School Student Profile 75% of students are Lutheran.
Faculty School total: 22. In upper school: 12 men, 10 women; 11 have advanced degrees.
Subjects Offered Accounting, advanced biology, advanced chemistry, advanced math, algebra, American history, analytic geometry, anatomy and physiology, ancient history, ancient world history, art, arts and crafts, band, bioethics, DNA and culture, biology, calculus, chemistry, choir, Christian doctrine, Christian ethics, Christian studies, civics, communications, computer applications, concert band, drawing, earth and space science, economics, English, English literature, fine arts, general science, geography, geometry, health, honors English, honors geometry, honors U.S. history, independent study, journalism, mathematics, microbiology, modern history, New Testament, newspaper, oral communications, organic chemistry, physical education, physics, pottery, pre-calculus, psychology, religion, social studies, Spanish, Spanish language-AP, studio art, theology, world history.
Graduation Requirements Algebra, biology, civics, economics, foreign language, geography, geometry, health, religion (includes Bible studies and theology).
Student Life Upper grades have specified standards of dress, student council, honor system. Discipline rests primarily with faculty. Attendance at religious services is required.
Tuition and Aid Day student tuition: $6700. Tuition reduction for siblings, need-based scholarship grants available. Total amount of financial aid awarded in 2008–09: $30,000.
Admissions School's own exam required. Deadline for receipt of application materials: none. Application fee required: $250. On-campus interview required.
Athletics Interscholastic: baseball (boys), basketball (b), bowling (b,g), cheering (g), dance team (g), fishing (b), football (b), golf (b), indoor track & field (b,g), soccer (b,g), softball (g), swimming and diving (b,g), tennis (b,g), track and field (b,g), volleyball (g). 2 PE instructors.
Computers Computers are regularly used in accounting, business, computer applications, journalism, science classes. Computer network features include on-campus library services, Internet access, Internet filtering or blocking technology. Student e-mail accounts and computer access in designated common areas are available to students. Students grades are available online. The school has a published electronic and media policy.
Contact School Office. 618-656-0043. Fax: 618-565-3315. E-mail: sue.koenig@melhs.org.

MIAMI COUNTRY DAY SCHOOL

601 Northeast 107th Street
Miami, Florida 33161

Head of School: Dr. John P. Davies

General Information Coeducational day college-preparatory school. Grades PK–12. Founded: 1938. Setting: suburban. 16-acre campus. 6 buildings on campus. Approved or accredited by Florida Council of Independent Schools, Southern Association of Colleges and Schools, Southern Association of Independent Schools, The College Board, and Florida Department of Education. Member of National

Association of Independent Schools and Secondary School Admission Test Board. Endowment: $4.5 million. Total enrollment: 990. Upper school average class size: 18. Upper school faculty-student ratio: 1:9.

Upper School Student Profile Grade 9: 94 students (54 boys, 40 girls); Grade 10: 104 students (57 boys, 47 girls); Grade 11: 84 students (47 boys, 37 girls); Grade 12: 98 students (57 boys, 41 girls).

Faculty School total: 119. In upper school: 29 men, 26 women; 38 have advanced degrees.

Subjects Offered Advanced Placement courses, African-American studies, algebra, American government-AP, American history, American history-AP, American literature, ancient history, art, art history, backpacking, band, biology, calculus, ceramics, chemistry, community service, composition, computer programming, computer science, conflict resolution, creative writing, design, desktop publishing, drama, drawing, economics, English, English literature, ESL, European history, film, film and literature, fine arts, French, geography, geometry, government/civics, health, instrumental music, jewelry making, journalism, law, life management skills, literature, marine biology, mathematics, music theory, orchestra, painting, philosophy, photography, physical education, physical science, physics, psychology, public speaking, religion, science, sculpture, social science, social studies, Spanish, theater, trigonometry, video film production, world history, world literature, writing, yearbook.

Graduation Requirements Arts and fine arts (art, music, dance, drama), computer science, electives, English, foreign language, mathematics, philosophy, physical education (includes health), religion (includes Bible studies and theology), science, social studies (includes history), speech and debate, 100 hours of community service.

Special Academic Programs Advanced Placement exam preparation; honors section; independent study; study at local college for college credit.

College Admission Counseling 98 students graduated in 2008; all went to college, including Florida International University; Florida State University; Northwestern University; The George Washington University; University of Florida; University of Miami. Median SAT critical reading: 630, median SAT math: 660, median SAT writing: 630.

Student Life Upper grades have uniform requirement, student council, honor system. Discipline rests equally with students and faculty.

Summer Programs Remediation, enrichment, advancement, ESL, art/fine arts, computer instruction programs offered; session focuses on academics, enrichment, review, and recreation; held on campus; accepts boys and girls; open to students from other schools. 210 students usually enrolled. 2009 schedule: June 15 to July 24. Application deadline: none.

Tuition and Aid Day student tuition: $20,435–$20,914. Tuition installment plan (Academic Management Services Plan). Need-based scholarship grants available. In 2008–09, 14% of upper-school students received aid. Total amount of financial aid awarded in 2008–09: $550,000.

Admissions Traditional secondary-level entrance grade is 9. For fall 2008, 82 students applied for upper-level admission, 48 were accepted, 31 enrolled. ISEE, OLSAT, ERB, PSAT and SAT for applicants to grade 11 and 12 or writing sample required. Deadline for receipt of application materials: February 15. Application fee required: $85. On-campus interview required.

Athletics Interscholastic: baseball (boys), basketball (b,g), cheering (g), cross-country running (b,g), football (b), golf (b), lacrosse (b), soccer (b,g), softball (g), swimming and diving (b,g), tennis (b,g), track and field (b,g), volleyball (g), water polo (b,g); intramural: baseball (b), basketball (b,g), cheering (g), cross-country running (b,g), dance (g), lacrosse (b), volleyball (b), yoga (g); coed intramural: crew, flag football, outdoor education, outdoor skills, physical fitness, physical training, soccer, strength & conditioning, weight training. 5 PE instructors, 24 coaches, 1 athletic trainer.

Computers Computers are regularly used in all academic, graphic design, journalism, media, research skills, Web site design, yearbook classes. Computer network features include on-campus library services, online commercial services, Internet access, wireless campus network, Internet filtering or blocking technology, The Homework Site, faculty access via the Web (faweb). Student e-mail accounts and computer access in designated common areas are available to students. Students grades are available online. The school has a published electronic and media policy.

Contact Jasmine A. Lake, Director of Admission and Financial Aid. 305-779-7230. Fax: 305-758-5107. E-mail: lakej@miamicountryday.org. Web site: www.miamicountryday.org.

MIDDLESEX SCHOOL

1400 Lowell Road
Concord, Massachusetts 01742

Head of School: Kathleen C. Giles

General Information Coeducational boarding and day college-preparatory school. Grades 9–12. Founded: 1901. Setting: rural. Nearest major city is Boston. Students are housed in single-sex dormitories. 350-acre campus. 31 buildings on campus. Approved or accredited by Association of Independent Schools in New England, New England Association of Schools and Colleges, The Association of Boarding Schools, and The College Board. Member of National Association of Independent Schools and Secondary School Admission Test Board. Endowment: $110 million. Total enrollment: 342. Upper school average class size: 11. Upper school faculty-student ratio: 1:5.

Upper School Student Profile Grade 9: 77 students (41 boys, 36 girls); Grade 10: 85 students (44 boys, 41 girls); Grade 11: 93 students (48 boys, 45 girls); Grade 12: 87 students (45 boys, 42 girls). 72% of students are boarding students. 57% are state residents. 24 states are represented in upper school student body. 10% are international students. International students from Bermuda, Canada, China, Japan, Republic of Korea, and Switzerland; 6 other countries represented in student body.

Faculty School total: 62. In upper school: 35 men, 27 women; 51 have advanced degrees; 50 reside on campus.

Subjects Offered Acting, advanced biology, advanced chemistry, advanced computer applications, Advanced Placement courses, advanced studio art-AP, African American history, African history, African-American history, algebra, American government-AP, American literature, analytic geometry, art, art history, art history-AP, art-AP, Asian literature, astronomy, biology, biology-AP, British literature, calculus, calculus-AP, ceramics, chemistry, chemistry-AP, Chinese, classical Greek literature, computer programming, computer programming-AP, computer science, computer science-AP, creative writing, discrete math, DNA, drama, economics, economics-AP, English, English literature, English literature and composition-AP, environmental science, environmental science-AP, ethics, European history, European history-AP, finite math, forensic science, French, French language-AP, French literature-AP, geometry, Greek, history, history of jazz, Holocaust studies, independent study, jazz band, Latin, Latin American history, Latin-AP, marine studies, mathematics, media, Middle East, Middle Eastern history, model United Nations, music, music theory, music theory-AP, philosophy, photography, physics, physics-AP, political science, religion, Shakespeare, Spanish, Spanish language-AP, Spanish literature-AP, statistics, statistics-AP, studio art—AP, theater, trigonometry, U.S. government and politics-AP, U.S. history, U.S. history-AP, video film production, Vietnam history, Vietnam War, vocal ensemble, women in world history, woodworking, world history, writing, writing workshop.

Graduation Requirements Algebra, analytic geometry, arts, English, English literature and composition-AP, European history, foreign language, geometry, science, trigonometry, U.S. history, completion of a wooden plaque.

Special Academic Programs Advanced Placement exam preparation; honors section; independent study; academic accommodation for the gifted.

College Admission Counseling 98 students graduated in 2008; 97 went to college, including Boston College; Brown University; Colby College; Georgetown University; Tufts University; Williams College. Other: 1 had other specific plans. Median SAT critical reading: 670, median SAT math: 670, median SAT writing: 690, median combined SAT: 2030.

Student Life Upper grades have specified standards of dress, student council, honor system. Discipline rests primarily with faculty.

Summer Programs Art/fine arts programs offered; session focuses on arts; held on campus; accepts boys and girls; open to students from other schools. 180 students usually enrolled. 2009 schedule: June 29 to August 1.

Tuition and Aid Day student tuition: $34,250; 7-day tuition and room/board: $42,820. Guaranteed tuition plan. Tuition installment plan (Insured Tuition Payment Plan, Key Tuition Payment Plan, monthly payment plans, semiannual payment plan). Need-based scholarship grants, need-based loans, AchieverLoans (Key Education Resources) available. In 2008–09, 30% of upper-school students received aid. Total amount of financial aid awarded in 2008–09: $3,400,000.

Admissions Traditional secondary-level entrance grade is 9. For fall 2008, 935 students applied for upper-level admission, 256 were accepted, 108 enrolled. ISEE or SSAT required. Deadline for receipt of application materials: January 31. Application fee required: $50. On-campus interview recommended.

Athletics Interscholastic: alpine skiing (boys, girls), baseball (b), basketball (b,g), crew (b,g), cross-country running (b,g), field hockey (g), football (b), ice hockey (b,g), lacrosse (b,g), skiing (downhill) (b,g), soccer (b,g), softball (g), squash (b,g), tennis (b,g), wrestling (b); coed interscholastic: golf, physical training, track and field; coed intramural: dance, fitness, strength & conditioning, yoga. 16 coaches, 1 athletic trainer.

Computers Computers are regularly used in economics, English, foreign language, history, mathematics, science classes. Computer network features include on-campus library services, online commercial services, Internet access, Internet filtering or blocking technology. Student e-mail accounts and computer access in designated common areas are available to students. The school has a published electronic and media policy.

Contact Douglas C. Price, Director of Admissions. 978-371-6524. Fax: 978-402-1400. E-mail: dprice@mxschool.edu. Web site: www.mxschool.edu.

ANNOUNCEMENT FROM THE SCHOOL For more than a century, Middlesex School, located in historic Concord, Massachusetts, has committed to finding the promise in every student. A rich and demanding curriculum; small, interactive classes; outstanding opportunities in athletics and the arts; and talented and engaging faculty members enable students to discover their strengths and develop their talents.

See Close-Up on page 848.

MIDLAND SCHOOL

PO Box 8
5100 Figueroa Mountain Road
Los Olivos, California 93441

Head of School: Will Graham

General Information Coeducational boarding and day college-preparatory and environmental studies school. Boarding grades 9–12, day grades 9–11. Founded: 1932. Setting: rural. Nearest major city is Santa Barbara. Students are housed in single-sex cabins. 2,860-acre campus. Approved or accredited by California Association of Independent Schools, The Association of Boarding Schools, The College Board, US Department of State, and Western Association of Schools and Colleges. Member of National Association of Independent Schools and Secondary School Admission Test Board. Endowment: $8.5 million. Total enrollment: 91. Upper school average class size: 12. Upper school faculty-student ratio: 1:5.

Upper School Student Profile Grade 9: 25 students (14 boys, 11 girls); Grade 10: 28 students (17 boys, 11 girls); Grade 11: 16 students (9 boys, 7 girls); Grade 12: 22 students (14 boys, 8 girls). 98% of students are boarding students. 70% are state residents. 7 states are represented in upper school student body. 11% are international students. International students from China, Hong Kong, Republic of Korea, and United Kingdom; 1 other country represented in student body.

Faculty School total: 22. In upper school: 12 men, 10 women; 9 have advanced degrees; 20 reside on campus.

Subjects Offered 3-dimensional art, adolescent issues, advanced chemistry, advanced math, agroecology, algebra, American history, American literature, American studies, anthropology, backpacking, basketball, biology, calculus-AP, ceramics, character education, chemistry, Chinese history, clayworking, community service, composition, creative writing, drama, economics, environmental education, environmental studies, equestrian sports, film and literature, foreign language, gardening, geology, geometry, health education, human sexuality, hydrology, integrated science, land and ranch management, leadership skills, literature by women, metalworking, music, painting, physics, physics-AP, pre-calculus, senior project, senior seminar, senior thesis, sex education, Spanish, Spanish literature, Spanish-AP, statistics, U.S. history, utopia, volleyball, wilderness camping, wilderness education, world studies.

Graduation Requirements Arts and fine arts (art, music, dance, drama), English, foreign language, history, mathematics, science, senior thesis, Independent Senior Thesis.

Special Academic Programs 6 Advanced Placement exams for which test preparation is offered; honors section; independent study.

College Admission Counseling 22 students graduated in 2008; 20 went to college. Other: 2 went to work.

Student Life Upper grades have specified standards of dress, student council. Discipline rests equally with students and faculty.

Tuition and Aid Day student tuition: $20,200; 7-day tuition and room/board: $35,000. Need-based scholarship grants, need-based loans available. In 2008–09, 42% of upper-school students received aid. Total amount of financial aid awarded in 2008–09: $848,000.

Admissions Traditional secondary-level entrance grade is 9. For fall 2008, 74 students applied for upper-level admission, 59 were accepted, 37 enrolled. SSAT required. Deadline for receipt of application materials: February 15. Application fee required: $30. On-campus interview required.

Athletics Interscholastic: cross-country running (boys, girls), lacrosse (b,g), soccer (b,g), volleyball (g); intramural: table tennis (b,g); coed interscholastic: basketball; coed intramural: backpacking, bicycling, dance, equestrian sports, hiking/backpacking, horseback riding, mountain biking, outdoor adventure, outdoor education, outdoor skills, surfing, touch football, ultimate Frisbee. 10 coaches.

Computers Computer network features include on-campus library services, Internet access, Internet filtering or blocking technology. Student e-mail accounts are available to students.

Contact Derek Svennungsen, Director of Admissions. 805-688-5114 Ext. 14. Fax: 805-686-2470. E-mail: dsvennungsen@midland-school.org. Web site: www.midland-school.org.

MID-PACIFIC INSTITUTE

2445 Kaala Street
Honolulu, Hawaii 96822-2299

Head of School: Mr. Joe C. Rice

General Information Coeducational day college-preparatory, arts, bilingual studies, technology, and International Baccalaureate school, affiliated with Christian faith. Grades K–12. Founded: 1864. Setting: urban. 34-acre campus. 30 buildings on campus. Approved or accredited by International Baccalaureate Organization and Western Association of Schools and Colleges. Member of National Association of Independent Schools and Secondary School Admission Test Board. Endowment: $10 million. Total enrollment: 1,515. Upper school average class size: 20. Upper school faculty-student ratio: 1:19.

Upper School Student Profile 50% of students are Christian faith.

Faculty School total: 102. In upper school: 42 men, 54 women; 20 have advanced degrees.

Subjects Offered Algebra, American history, American literature, art, art history, astronomy, ballet, band, biology, business skills, calculus, career education, ceramics, chemistry, computer programming, computer science, creative writing, dance, debate, drama, drawing, economics, English, English literature, ESL, film, fine arts, first aid, French, general science, geography, geometry, Hawaiian history, health, history, instrumental music, Japanese, Latin, law, mathematics, oceanography, oral communications, painting, philosophy, photography, physical education, physics, printmaking, psychology, religion, science, sculpture, social science, social studies, Spanish, speech, swimming, swimming competency, technological applications, technology, theater, video, weight training, world history, world literature, writing.

Graduation Requirements Arts and fine arts (art, music, dance, drama), business skills (includes word processing), career education, computer science, English, foreign language, mathematics, oral communications, physical education (includes health), religion (includes Bible studies and theology), science, social science, social studies (includes history), speech, swimming competency.

Special Academic Programs International Baccalaureate program; Advanced Placement exam preparation; honors section; study at local college for college credit; academic accommodation for the gifted and the artistically talented; ESL (41 students enrolled).

College Admission Counseling 201 students graduated in 2008; all went to college, including Hawai'i Pacific University; Pacific University; University of Hawaii at Manoa; University of Southern California; University of Washington.

Student Life Upper grades have specified standards of dress, student council, honor system. Discipline rests primarily with faculty. Attendance at religious services is required.

Summer Programs Enrichment, advancement, ESL, art/fine arts, computer instruction programs offered; session focuses on physical fitness and skills; held on campus; accepts boys and girls; open to students from other schools. 950 students usually enrolled. 2009 schedule: June 5 to July 27. Application deadline: April 5.

Tuition and Aid Day student tuition: $15,000. Tuition installment plan (Insured Tuition Payment Plan, FACTS Tuition Payment Plan, monthly payment plans, semiannual payment plan). Merit scholarship grants, need-based scholarship grants, paying campus jobs, tuition reduction for children of employees available. In 2008–09, 15% of upper-school students received aid; total upper-school merit-scholarship money awarded: $305,000. Total amount of financial aid awarded in 2008–09: $644,000.

Admissions Traditional secondary-level entrance grade is 9. For fall 2008, 700 students applied for upper-level admission, 220 were accepted, 150 enrolled. SAT, SSAT and TOEFL required. Deadline for receipt of application materials: December 1. Application fee required: $75. Interview required.

Athletics Interscholastic: aquatics (boys, girls), baseball (b), basketball (b,g), bowling (b,g), canoeing/kayaking (b,g), cheering (g), cross-country running (b,g), football (b), golf (b,g), gymnastics (g), independent competitive sports (b,g), kayaking (b,g), ocean paddling (b,g), physical fitness (b,g), physical training (b,g), riflery (b,g), soccer (b,g), softball (g), strength & conditioning (b,g), surfing (b,g), swimming and diving (b,g), tennis (b,g), track and field (b,g), volleyball (b,g), water polo (b,g), wrestling (b,g); intramural: badminton (b,g), weight lifting (b,g), weight training (b,g); coed interscholastic: fitness, modern dance; coed intramural: badminton. 6 PE instructors, 15 coaches, 2 athletic trainers.

Computers Computers are regularly used in English, foreign language, mathematics, media arts, science classes. Computer network features include on-campus library services, online commercial services, Internet access, wireless campus network, Internet filtering or blocking technology. Campus intranet, student e-mail accounts, and computer access in designated common areas are available to students. Students grades are available online. The school has a published electronic and media policy.

Contact Mrs. Linda Oshio, Admissions Secretary. 808-973-5005. Fax: 808-973-5099. E-mail: admissions@midpac.edu. Web site: www.midpac.edu.

MID-PENINSULA HIGH SCHOOL

1340 Willow Road
Menlo Park, California 94025-1516

Head of School: Douglas C. Thompson, PhD

General Information Coeducational day college-preparatory, general academic, and arts school; primarily serves underachievers, individuals with Attention Deficit Disorder, individuals with emotional and behavioral problems, dyslexic students, and Asberger's. Grades 9–12. Founded: 1979. Setting: suburban. Nearest major city is San Jose. 2-acre campus. 1 building on campus. Approved or accredited by California Association of Independent Schools, Western Association of Schools and Colleges, and California Department of Education. Endowment: $1.4 million. Total enrollment: 109. Upper school average class size: 12. Upper school faculty-student ratio: 1:5.

Upper School Student Profile Grade 9: 23 students (9 boys, 14 girls); Grade 10: 29 students (16 boys, 13 girls); Grade 11: 27 students (20 boys, 7 girls); Grade 12: 28 students (18 boys, 10 girls).

Faculty School total: 22. In upper school: 11 men, 11 women; 6 have advanced degrees.

Subjects Offered Algebra, art, biology, calculus, calculus-AP, chemistry, composition, contemporary issues, drama, driver education, English, geometry, government, human relations, mathematics, music performance, physical education, physics, SAT/ACT preparation, science, Spanish, sports, study skills, trigonometry, U.S. history, world studies.

Graduation Requirements Government, human relations, mathematics, physical education (includes health), science, social science, U.S. history. Community service is required.
Special Academic Programs Accelerated programs; independent study; remedial reading and/or remedial writing; remedial math; special instructional classes for students with learning disabilities, ADD, dyslexia, emotional and behavioral problems.
College Admission Counseling 40 students graduated in 2008; 38 went to college, including California State University, Chico; San Francisco State University; The University of Arizona; University of California, Santa Cruz; University of the Pacific; Willamette University. Other: 2 entered military service. Median SAT critical reading: 630, median SAT math: 530, median SAT writing: 520, median combined SAT: 1680, median composite ACT: 24. 58% scored over 600 on SAT critical reading, 26% scored over 600 on SAT math, 26% scored over 600 on SAT writing, 47% scored over 1800 on combined SAT, 38% scored over 26 on composite ACT.
Student Life Discipline rests primarily with faculty.
Summer Programs Remediation, enrichment, art/fine arts programs offered; session focuses on academic support for current students; held on campus; accepts boys and girls; open to students from other schools. 60 students usually enrolled. 2009 schedule: June 22 to July 24. Application deadline: June 21.
Tuition and Aid Day student tuition: $24,960. Tuition installment plan (monthly payment plans, individually arranged payment plans, 2-payment plan). Tuition reduction for siblings, need-based scholarship grants available. In 2008–09, 24% of upper-school students received aid. Total amount of financial aid awarded in 2008–09: $630,000.
Admissions Traditional secondary-level entrance grade is 9. For fall 2008, 74 students applied for upper-level admission, 69 were accepted, 40 enrolled. Admissions testing required. Deadline for receipt of application materials: none. No application fee required. On-campus interview required.
Athletics Interscholastic: baseball (boys), basketball (b,g), softball (g), volleyball (b,g); coed interscholastic: cross-country running, soccer, track and field. 1 PE instructor, 4 coaches.
Computers Computers are regularly used in desktop publishing, English, mathematics, music, publications, social sciences classes. Computer network features include Internet access, wireless campus network, Internet filtering or blocking technology. Computer access in designated common areas is available to students. The school has a published electronic and media policy.
Contact Ms. Barbara Brown, Director of Admissions. 650-321-1991 Ext. 147. Fax: 650-321-9921. E-mail: barbara@mid-pen.com. Web site: www.mid-pen.com.

MILKEN COMMUNITY HIGH SCHOOL OF STEPHEN S. WISE TEMPLE

15800 Zeldins' Way at Mulholland Drive
Los Angeles, California 90049
Head of School: Jason Ablin

General Information Coeducational day college-preparatory and Jewish Studies school, affiliated with Jewish faith. Grades 7–12. Founded: 1990. Setting: suburban. 11-acre campus. 4 buildings on campus. Approved or accredited by California Association of Independent Schools, Western Association of Schools and Colleges, and California Department of Education. Total enrollment: 790. Upper school average class size: 18. Upper school faculty-student ratio: 1:7.
Upper School Student Profile Grade 7: 112 students (58 boys, 54 girls); Grade 8: 93 students (38 boys, 55 girls); Grade 9: 162 students (84 boys, 78 girls); Grade 10: 145 students (72 boys, 73 girls); Grade 11: 139 students (75 boys, 64 girls); Grade 12: 139 students (66 boys, 73 girls). 100% of students are Jewish.
Faculty In upper school: 42 men, 60 women; 78 have advanced degrees.
Subjects Offered Acting, algebra, American government, American government-AP, American literature, architectural drawing, art, art history, art history-AP, astronomy, audio visual/media, Basic programming, Bible studies, biology, biology-AP, broadcasting, calculus, calculus-AP, career education internship, ceramics, chamber groups, chemistry, chemistry-AP, choir, classical music, college placement, community service, composition, computer applications, computer graphics, computer programming, computer technologies, creative writing, current events, dance performance, debate, drama performance, drawing, ecology, environmental systems, economics, electronics, English, English language and composition-AP, English literature and composition-AP, equestrian sports, European history-AP, French, French-AP, general math, general science, geometry, government and politics-AP, graphic design, guitar, health, Hebrew, Hebrew scripture, history, history-AP, Holocaust studies, honors algebra, honors English, honors geometry, honors U.S. history, honors world history, instrumental music, Israeli studies, jazz dance, jazz ensemble, Jewish studies, journalism, Latin, leadership training, life science, literary magazine, literature and composition-AP, macro/microeconomics-AP, marine biology, media arts, media production, model United Nations, modern dance, modern world history, music appreciation, music composition, music performance, music theory, music theory-AP, musical theater, newspaper, oceanography, orchestra, painting, philosophy, physical science, physics, physics-AP, prayer/spirituality, pre-algebra, pre-calculus, pre-college orientation, psychology, psychology-AP, Rabbinic literature, religion, religion and culture, religious studies, science, science research, sculpture, senior career experience, senior seminar, set design, sex education, Spanish, Spanish-AP, speech and debate, stage design, statistics, statistics-AP, studio art, studio art-AP, study skills, Talmud, trigonometry, U.S. government and politics-AP, U.S. history, U.S. history-AP, video communication, video film production, water color painting, Web site design, world history, world history-AP.
Graduation Requirements Arts, electives, English, Hebrew, Jewish studies, mathematics, physical education (includes health), religion (includes Bible studies and theology), science, senior seminar, social science, senior sermon. Community service is required.
Special Academic Programs Advanced Placement exam preparation; honors section; independent study; study at local college for college credit; study abroad; academic accommodation for the gifted, the musically talented, and the artistically talented.
College Admission Counseling 138 students graduated in 2008; 137 went to college, including Boston University; Massachusetts Institute of Technology; University of California, Berkeley; University of California, Los Angeles; University of Pennsylvania; University of Southern California. Other: 1 entered military service. Mean SAT critical reading: 588, mean SAT math: 608, mean SAT writing: 627, mean combined SAT: 1823, mean composite ACT: 26.
Student Life Upper grades have specified standards of dress, student council, honor system. Discipline rests primarily with faculty. Attendance at religious services is required.
Summer Programs Remediation, enrichment, advancement, sports, art/fine arts, computer instruction programs offered; session focuses on enrichment, advancement, remediation; held on campus; accepts boys and girls; open to students from other schools. 180 students usually enrolled. 2009 schedule: June 22 to July 24. Application deadline: none.
Tuition and Aid Day student tuition: $27,380. Tuition installment plan (Insured Tuition Payment Plan, Key Tuition Payment Plan, monthly payment plans, individually arranged payment plans). Need-based scholarship grants available. Total amount of financial aid awarded in 2008–09: $1,414,100.
Admissions Traditional secondary-level entrance grade is 9. ISEE required. Deadline for receipt of application materials: December 15. Application fee required: $150. On-campus interview required.
Athletics Interscholastic: aquatics (boys, girls), baseball (b), basketball (b,g), cross-country running (b,g), soccer (b,g), swimming and diving (b,g), tennis (b,g), track and field (b,g), volleyball (b,g), water polo (b,g); coed interscholastic: dance team, dressage, equestrian sports, flag football, golf; coed intramural: dance. 7 PE instructors, 22 coaches, 1 athletic trainer.
Computers Computers are regularly used in architecture, art, design, drafting, drawing and design, economics, English, foreign language, graphic design, history, independent study, journalism, library, literary magazine, mathematics, multimedia, music, psychology, religious studies, research skills, science, video film production, Web site design, yearbook classes. Computer network features include on-campus library services, online commercial services, Internet access, wireless campus network, Internet filtering or blocking technology. Student e-mail accounts are available to students. The school has a published electronic and media policy.
Contact Rachelle Lobato, Admission Assistant. 310-440-3553. Fax: 310-471-5139. E-mail: admission@MilkenSchool.org. Web site: www.MilkenSchool.org.

MILLBROOK SCHOOL

131 Millbrook School Road
Millbrook, New York 12545
Head of School: Mr. Drew Casertano

General Information Coeducational boarding and day college-preparatory, arts, environmental stewardship, and community service school. Grades 9–12. Founded: 1931. Setting: rural. Nearest major city is New York. Students are housed in single-sex dormitories. 800-acre campus. 70 buildings on campus. Approved or accredited by National Independent Private Schools Association, New York State Association of Independent Schools, The Association of Boarding Schools, and New York Department of Education. Member of National Association of Independent Schools and Secondary School Admission Test Board. Endowment: $22 million. Total enrollment: 258. Upper school average class size: 14. Upper school faculty-student ratio: 1:5.
Upper School Student Profile Grade 9: 47 students (23 boys, 24 girls); Grade 10: 71 students (43 boys, 28 girls); Grade 11: 79 students (36 boys, 43 girls); Grade 12: 61 students (38 boys, 23 girls). 80% of students are boarding students. 49% are state residents. 21 states are represented in upper school student body. 10% are international students. International students from Canada, Costa Rica, Germany, Hong Kong, Japan, and Republic of Korea; 3 other countries represented in student body.
Faculty School total: 57. In upper school: 32 men, 25 women; 25 have advanced degrees; 44 reside on campus.
Subjects Offered Advanced chemistry, advanced math, Advanced Placement courses, advanced studio art-AP, aesthetics, algebra, American history, American literature, ancient world history, animal behavior, animal science, anthropology, art, art history, astronomy, biology, calculus, calculus-AP, ceramics, chemistry, choral music, choreography, constitutional law, creative writing, dance, dance performance, digital photography, drama, drama performance, drawing, ecology, English, English language-AP, English literature, English-AP, environmental science, European history, fine arts, French, French language-AP, French-AP, geometry, history, honors

English, human biology, independent study, jazz ensemble, journalism, mathematics, Middle Eastern history, music, music appreciation, painting, philosophy, photography, physics, pre-calculus, psychology, science, social science, social studies, Spanish, Spanish-AP, studio art, theater, trigonometry, world history.

Graduation Requirements Biology, English, foreign language, mathematics, physical education (includes health), science, social studies (includes history), visual and performing arts, Culminating Experience for Seniors.

Special Academic Programs 4 Advanced Placement exams for which test preparation is offered; honors section; independent study; term-away projects; study abroad.

College Admission Counseling 71 students graduated in 2008; 68 went to college, including College of Charleston; Elon University; Gettysburg College; St. Lawrence University; The George Washington University; University of Chicago. Other: 3 had other specific plans. Mean SAT critical reading: 583, mean SAT math: 589, mean SAT writing: 577, mean combined SAT: 1749, mean composite ACT: 23.

Student Life Upper grades have specified standards of dress, student council, honor system. Discipline rests primarily with faculty.

Tuition and Aid Day student tuition: $30,100; 7-day tuition and room/board: $41,400. Tuition installment plan (individually arranged payment plans, Tuition Management Services). Need-based scholarship grants, need-based loans available. In 2008–09, 25% of upper-school students received aid. Total amount of financial aid awarded in 2008–09: $1,963,750.

Admissions Traditional secondary-level entrance grade is 9. For fall 2008, 485 students applied for upper-level admission, 256 were accepted, 97 enrolled. ISEE, PSAT or SAT for applicants to grade 11 and 12, SSAT, TOEFL or writing sample required. Deadline for receipt of application materials: January 31. Application fee required: $50. On-campus interview required.

Athletics Interscholastic: baseball (boys), basketball (b,g), cross-country running (b,g), field hockey (g), ice hockey (b,g), lacrosse (b,g), soccer (b,g), softball (g), squash (b,g), tennis (b,g); coed interscholastic: golf; coed intramural: aerobics/dance, aerobics/Nautilus, alpine skiing, badminton, bicycling, dance, equestrian sports, fitness, horseback riding, modern dance, physical training, running, skiing (downhill), snowboarding, strength & conditioning, weight training, yoga. 2 coaches, 1 athletic trainer.

Computers Computers are regularly used in history, journalism, mathematics, photography, science, study skills, video film production, yearbook classes. Computer network features include on-campus library services, online commercial services, Internet access, wireless campus network, Internet filtering or blocking technology. Campus intranet, student e-mail accounts, and computer access in designated common areas are available to students. The school has a published electronic and media policy.

Contact Mrs. Cynthia S. McWilliams, Director of Admission. 845-677-8261 Ext. 111. Fax: 845-677-1265. E-mail: admissions@millbrook.org. Web site: www.millbrook.org.

See Close-Up on page 850.

MILLER SCHOOL

1000 Samuel Miller Loop
Charlottesville, Virginia 22903-9328

Head of School: Mr. Walter "Winn" Price

General Information Coeducational boarding and day college-preparatory and arts school. Grades 8–12. Founded: 1878. Setting: rural. Students are housed in single-sex dormitories. 1,600-acre campus. 6 buildings on campus. Approved or accredited by The Association of Boarding Schools and Virginia Association of Independent Schools. Member of National Association of Independent Schools. Endowment: $14 million. Total enrollment: 145. Upper school average class size: 10. Upper school faculty-student ratio: 1:6.

Upper School Student Profile Grade 8: 8 students (3 boys, 5 girls); Grade 9: 27 students (17 boys, 10 girls); Grade 10: 28 students (15 boys, 13 girls); Grade 11: 40 students (26 boys, 14 girls); Grade 12: 40 students (16 boys, 24 girls); Postgraduate: 1 student (1 boy). 68% of students are boarding students. 55% are state residents. 9 states are represented in upper school student body. 26% are international students. International students from Cameroon, China, Kazakhstan, Lithuania, Republic of Korea, and Ukraine; 6 other countries represented in student body.

Faculty School total: 26. In upper school: 15 men, 11 women; 19 have advanced degrees; 23 reside on campus.

Subjects Offered Algebra, American government, American government-AP, American literature, ancient history, art, arts, baseball, basketball, biology, calculus, calculus-AP, carpentry, chemistry, civics, CPR, creative writing, drama performance, driver education, earth science, economics, economics and history, electives, English, English composition, English language and composition-AP, English language-AP, English literature, English literature and composition-AP, English literature-AP, English-AP, English/composition-AP, environmental science, environmental science-AP, environmental studies, environmental systems, ESL, European history, European history-AP, fine arts, fitness, foreign language, French, French language-AP, French literature-AP, French studies, French-AP, geography, geometry, government, government and politics-AP, government-AP, government/civics, history-AP, independent study, instrumental music, Latin, macroeconomics-AP, mathematics-AP, modern European history, modern European history-AP, music, music performance, musical productions, musical theater, participation in sports, photography, physical education, physical fitness, physical science, physics, poetry, pre-algebra, pre-calculus, reading/study skills, Spanish, Spanish language-AP, Spanish literature-AP, Spanish-AP, sports conditioning, statistics, student government, studio art, studio art-AP, study skills, tennis, trigonometry, U.S. government, U.S. government and politics-AP, U.S. history, U.S. history-AP, visual arts, volleyball, woodworking, wrestling, yearbook.

Graduation Requirements Arts and fine arts (art, music, dance, drama), English, foreign language, mathematics, physical education (includes health), science, social studies (includes history). Community service is required.

Special Academic Programs Advanced Placement exam preparation; honors section; accelerated programs; independent study; academic accommodation for the gifted, the musically talented, and the artistically talented; ESL (8 students enrolled).

College Admission Counseling 42 students graduated in 2008; 39 went to college, including Duke University; James Madison University; Longwood University; Penn State University Park; University of Virginia; Virginia Polytechnic Institute and State University. Mean SAT critical reading: 561, mean SAT math: 568, mean SAT writing: 542. 35% scored over 600 on SAT critical reading, 35% scored over 600 on SAT math.

Student Life Upper grades have specified standards of dress, student council, honor system. Discipline rests equally with students and faculty.

Tuition and Aid Day student tuition: $14,350; 5-day tuition and room/board: $29,750; 7-day tuition and room/board: $33,000. Tuition installment plan (Insured Tuition Payment Plan, SMART Tuition Payment Plan, individually arranged payment plans). Tuition reduction for siblings, need-based scholarship grants available. In 2008–09, 33% of upper-school students received aid. Total amount of financial aid awarded in 2008–09: $525,000.

Admissions Traditional secondary-level entrance grade is 9. For fall 2008, 130 students applied for upper-level admission, 94 were accepted, 58 enrolled. ACT, any standardized test, California Achievement Test, Iowa Tests of Basic Skills, PSAT or SAT, SSAT, Stanford Achievement Test or TOEFL or SLEP required. Deadline for receipt of application materials: none. Application fee required: $50. Interview required.

Athletics Interscholastic: baseball (boys), basketball (b,g), cross-country running (b,g), lacrosse (b), soccer (b,g), tennis (b,g), volleyball (g), wrestling (b); coed interscholastic: golf, horseback riding; coed intramural: basketball, bicycling, canoeing/kayaking, cross-country running, fishing, fitness, Frisbee, hiking/backpacking, indoor soccer, jogging, mountain biking, outdoor activities, paint ball, physical fitness, physical training, power lifting, running, skateboarding, soccer, softball, street hockey, strength & conditioning, swimming and diving, table tennis, tennis, touch football, ultimate Frisbee, volleyball, walking, weight lifting, weight training. 5 coaches, 1 athletic trainer.

Computers Computers are regularly used in English, foreign language, history, mathematics, science classes. Computer network features include on-campus library services, online commercial services, Internet access, wireless campus network, Internet filtering or blocking technology. Campus intranet and student e-mail accounts are available to students. The school has a published electronic and media policy.

Contact Ms. Dee Gregory, Assistant Director of Admissions. 434-823-4805 Ext. 248. Fax: 434-205-5007. E-mail: dgregory@millerschool.org. Web site: www.millerschool.org.

See Close-Up on page 852.

MILTON ACADEMY

170 Centre Street
Milton, Massachusetts 02186

Head of School: Rick Hardy

General Information Coeducational boarding and day college-preparatory school. Boarding grades 9–12, day grades K–12. Founded: 1798. Setting: suburban. Nearest major city is Boston. Students are housed in single-sex dormitories. 125-acre campus. 24 buildings on campus. Approved or accredited by Association of Independent Schools in New England, New England Association of Schools and Colleges, The Association of Boarding Schools, and Massachusetts Department of Education. Member of National Association of Independent Schools and Secondary School Admission Test Board. Endowment: $190 million. Total enrollment: 964. Upper school average class size: 14. Upper school faculty-student ratio: 1:5.

Upper School Student Profile 50% of students are boarding students. 64% are state residents. 29 states are represented in upper school student body. 18% are international students. International students from Hong Kong, India, Jamaica, Japan, Republic of Korea, and Taiwan; 21 other countries represented in student body.

Faculty School total: 180. In upper school: 71 men, 68 women; 104 have advanced degrees; 111 reside on campus.

Subjects Offered Algebra, American history, American literature, anatomy, anthropology, archaeology, architecture, art, art history, arts, astronomy, biology, calculus, ceramics, chemistry, Chinese, computer math, computer programming, computer science, creative writing, current events, dance, drama, driver education, earth science, economics, English, English literature, ethics, European history, expository writing, fine arts, French, geography, geometry, German, government/civics, grammar, Greek, health, history, Italian, Latin, mathematics, music, philosophy, photography, physical education, physics, physiology, psychology, religion, science, social studies, sociology, Spanish, speech, statistics, theater, trigonometry, world history, world literature, writing.

Graduation Requirements Arts and fine arts (art, music, dance, drama), current events, English, foreign language, leadership skills, mathematics, physical education (includes health), public speaking, science, social studies (includes history).

Special Academic Programs Advanced Placement exam preparation; honors section; independent study; term-away projects; study abroad; academic accommodation for the gifted, the musically talented, and the artistically talented.

College Admission Counseling 185 students graduated in 2008; 182 went to college, including Brown University; Harvard University; The George Washington University; University of Pennsylvania; Wesleyan University; Yale University. Mean SAT critical reading: 679, mean SAT math: 688, mean SAT writing: 695.

Student Life Upper grades have student council. Discipline rests equally with students and faculty.

Tuition and Aid Day student tuition: $33,150; 7-day tuition and room/board: $40,395. Tuition installment plan (Key Tuition Payment Plan). Need-based scholarship grants available. In 2008–09, 32% of upper-school students received aid. Total amount of financial aid awarded in 2008–09: $6,100,000.

Admissions Traditional secondary-level entrance grade is 9. For fall 2008, 900 students applied for upper-level admission, 270 were accepted, 150 enrolled. ISEE, SSAT or TOEFL required. Deadline for receipt of application materials: January 15. Application fee required: $50. Interview required.

Athletics Interscholastic: baseball (boys), basketball (b,g), cross-country running (b,g), field hockey (g), football (b), ice hockey (b,g), lacrosse (b,g), soccer (b,g), softball (g), squash (b,g), tennis (b,g), track and field (b,g), volleyball (g); intramural: basketball (b,g), soccer (b,g), strength & conditioning (b,g); coed interscholastic: alpine skiing, diving, golf, rock climbing, sailing, skiing (downhill), swimming and diving, wrestling; coed intramural: climbing, martial arts, outdoor activities, outdoor education, project adventure, rock climbing, skiing (downhill), squash, tennis, ultimate Frisbee, yoga. 6 PE instructors, 3 athletic trainers.

Computers Computers are regularly used in mathematics, science classes. Computer network features include on-campus library services, online commercial services, Internet access. Student e-mail accounts are available to students.

Contact Mrs. Patricia Finn, Admission Assistant. 617-898-2227. Fax: 617-898-1701. E-mail: admissions@milton.edu. Web site: www.milton.edu.

ANNOUNCEMENT FROM THE SCHOOL Milton Academy engages students and faculty in intense and challenging preparation for college and for life, in an environment that stimulates and supports extraordinary intellectual and personal growth. Day in and day out, in and out of class, faculty members connect vitally with students—setting sights high, bringing opportunities to light, tackling big questions, affirming students' individuality, and building their confidence and skill. Not only do Milton graduates succeed at the most competitive universities in the country, their awareness, creativity, and competence empower them to fully commit themselves to meaningful endeavors of all kinds throughout the world. Milton Academy is an independent, college-preparatory, K–12 school, boarding and day in grades 9–12, located 8 miles south of Boston.

See Close-Up on page 854.

MINOT BISHOP RYAN

316 11th Avenue NW
Minot, North Dakota 58703

Head of School: Mr. Richard Limke

General Information Coeducational day college-preparatory and religious studies school, affiliated with Roman Catholic Church. Grades 7–12. Founded: 1958. 3-acre campus. 1 building on campus. Approved or accredited by North Central Association of Colleges and Schools and North Dakota Department of Education. Total enrollment: 420. Upper school average class size: 17. Upper school faculty-student ratio: 1:17.

Upper School Student Profile 90% of students are Roman Catholic.

Faculty School total: 25. In upper school: 9 men, 16 women.

Subjects Offered Accounting, algebra, American literature, art, arts and crafts, band, Basic programming, biology, calculus, career exploration, chemistry, choir, computer programming, computer science, creative writing, earth science, economics, English, English literature, food science, geography, geometry, German, government, health, home economics, human biology, keyboarding, law, life science, mathematics, parent/child development, physical science, physics, play production, pre-algebra, psychology, religion, social studies, sociology, Spanish, speech, trigonometry, U.S. history, world history, writing, writing fundamentals.

Student Life Upper grades have specified standards of dress, student council. Discipline rests primarily with faculty. Attendance at religious services is required.

Tuition and Aid Financial aid available to upper-school students. In 2008–09, 60% of upper-school students received aid. Total amount of financial aid awarded in 2008–09: $5000.

Admissions Deadline for receipt of application materials: none. No application fee required. On-campus interview required.

Athletics Interscholastic: baseball (boys), basketball (b,g), cross-country running (b,g), football (b), golf (b,g), gymnastics (g), hockey (b), ice hockey (b), soccer (b,g), swimming and diving (b,g), tennis (b,g), track and field (b,g), volleyball (g), wrestling (b). 2 PE instructors, 8 coaches.

Contact Mr. Terry Voiles, Principal. 701-852-4004. Fax: 701-839-4651. E-mail: tvoiles@brhs.com.

MISS EDGAR'S AND MISS CRAMP'S SCHOOL

525 Mount Pleasant Avenue
Montreal, Quebec H3Y 3H6, Canada

Head of School: Ms. Katherine Nikidis

General Information Girls' day college-preparatory, arts, bilingual studies, and technology school. Grades K–11. Founded: 1909. Setting: urban. 4-acre campus. 1 building on campus. Approved or accredited by Canadian Association of Independent Schools, Quebec Association of Independent Schools, and Quebec Department of Education. Affiliate member of National Association of Independent Schools; member of Secondary School Admission Test Board. Languages of instruction: English and French. Total enrollment: 345. Upper school average class size: 19. Upper school faculty-student ratio: 1:9.

Upper School Student Profile Grade 9: 40 students (40 girls); Grade 10: 44 students (44 girls); Grade 11: 44 students (44 girls).

Faculty School total: 40. In upper school: 3 men, 15 women; 8 have advanced degrees.

Subjects Offered Art, art history, biology, calculus, career exploration, chemistry, computer science, creative writing, drama, ecology, economics, English, environmental science, European history, French, geography, history, mathematics, media, music, physical education, physics, science, social studies, Spanish, theater, women's studies, world history.

Graduation Requirements English, foreign language, mathematics, science, social studies (includes history).

Special Academic Programs 2 Advanced Placement exams for which test preparation is offered; honors section.

College Admission Counseling 38 students graduated in 2008; all went to college, including John Abbott College; Lower Canada College; Marianopolis College.

Student Life Upper grades have uniform requirement, student council, honor system. Discipline rests primarily with faculty.

Tuition and Aid Day student tuition: CAN$13,800. Tuition installment plan (individually arranged payment plans). Bursaries, merit scholarship grants available. In 2008–09, 18% of upper-school students received aid; total upper-school merit-scholarship money awarded: CAN$76,700. Total amount of financial aid awarded in 2008–09: CAN$103,000.

Admissions Traditional secondary-level entrance grade is 9. For fall 2008, 11 students applied for upper-level admission, 10 were accepted, 4 enrolled. CCAT, SSAT or writing sample required. Deadline for receipt of application materials: none. Application fee required: CAN$50. On-campus interview required.

Athletics Interscholastic: badminton, basketball, cross-country running, golf, hockey, ice hockey, soccer, swimming and diving, tennis, touch football, track and field, volleyball; intramural: archery, badminton, baseball, basketball, cross-country running, field hockey, gymnastics, ice hockey, outdoor adventure, outdoor education, outdoor skills, rugby, skiing (cross-country), soccer, touch football, track and field, volleyball. 3 PE instructors, 11 coaches.

Computers Computers are regularly used in art, English, French, history, newspaper, writing, yearbook classes. Computer network features include on-campus library services, Internet access, wireless campus network, Internet filtering or blocking technology. Campus intranet, student e-mail accounts, and computer access in designated common areas are available to students. The school has a published electronic and media policy.

Contact Ms. Carla Bolsius, Admissions Co-coordinator. 514-935-6357 Ext. 254. Fax: 514-935-1099. E-mail: bolsiusc@ecs.qc.ca. Web site: www.ecs.qc.ca.

MISS HALL'S SCHOOL

492 Holmes Road
Pittsfield, Massachusetts 01201

Head of School: Ms. Jeannie Norris

General Information Girls' boarding and day college-preparatory, arts, technology, community service, and leadership development school. Grades 9–12. Founded: 1898. Setting: suburban. Nearest major city is Albany, NY. Students are housed in single-sex dormitories. 80-acre campus. 9 buildings on campus. Approved or accredited by Association of Independent Schools in New England, New England Association of Schools and Colleges, The Association of Boarding Schools, and Massachusetts Department of Education. Member of National Association of Independent Schools and Secondary School Admission Test Board. Endowment: $12 million. Total enrollment: 195. Upper school average class size: 11. Upper school faculty-student ratio: 1:6.

Upper School Student Profile Grade 9: 40 students (40 girls); Grade 10: 53 students (53 girls); Grade 11: 51 students (51 girls); Grade 12: 51 students (51 girls). 75% of students are boarding students. 41% are state residents. 20 states are represented in upper school student body. 30% are international students. International students from

British Virgin Islands, China, Hungary, Mexico, Republic of Korea, and Taiwan; 14 other countries represented in student body.
Faculty School total: 35. In upper school: 8 men, 27 women; 26 have advanced degrees; 18 reside on campus.
Subjects Offered Advanced Placement courses, algebra, American government, American history, American literature, anatomy, art, art history, biology, business skills, calculus, ceramics, chamber groups, chemistry, college counseling, community service, computer science, CPR, dance, drama, drawing, driver education, ecology, economics, English, English literature, English-AP, environmental science, ESL, ethics, ethics and responsibility, European history, European history-AP, expressive arts, fine arts, forensic science, forensics, French, geometry, government/civics, health, history, Latin, mathematics, music, music history, painting, photography, physics, physiology, political science, psychology, science, social studies, Spanish, theater, trigonometry, world culture, world history.
Graduation Requirements Arts and fine arts (art, music, dance, drama), English, foreign language, history, mathematics, physical education (includes health), science. Community service is required.
Special Academic Programs Advanced Placement exam preparation; honors section; independent study; academic accommodation for the gifted, the musically talented, and the artistically talented; special instructional classes for students with mild learning disabilities and Attention Deficit Disorder; ESL (20 students enrolled).
College Admission Counseling 42 students graduated in 2008; all went to college, including Babson College; Denison University; Northeastern University; The College of William and Mary; University of Pennsylvania; Williams College.
Student Life Upper grades have specified standards of dress, student council, honor system. Discipline rests equally with students and faculty.
Tuition and Aid Day student tuition: $25,850; 7-day tuition and room/board: $41,800. Tuition installment plan (Insured Tuition Payment Plan, Academic Management Services Plan, Key Tuition Payment Plan, monthly payment plans, individually arranged payment plans). Merit scholarship grants, need-based scholarship grants available. In 2008–09, 47% of upper-school students received aid; total upper-school merit-scholarship money awarded: $275,000. Total amount of financial aid awarded in 2008–09: $2,000,000.
Admissions Traditional secondary-level entrance grade is 9. For fall 2008, 237 students applied for upper-level admission, 107 were accepted, 74 enrolled. SSAT or TOEFL required. Deadline for receipt of application materials: February 15. Application fee required: $40. Interview required.
Athletics Interscholastic: alpine skiing, basketball, crew, cross-country running, field hockey, lacrosse, skiing (downhill), soccer, softball, tennis, volleyball; intramural: aerobics, aerobics/dance, alpine skiing, dance, equestrian sports, fitness, jogging, modern dance, outdoor activities, outdoor education, outdoor skills, physical fitness, rock climbing, ropes courses, running, skiing (cross-country), skiing (downhill), snowboarding, tennis, walking, wall climbing, wilderness, yoga. 3 coaches, 1 athletic trainer.
Computers Computers are regularly used in computer applications, English, foreign language, history, music, newspaper, photography, science, yearbook classes. Computer network features include on-campus library services, online commercial services, Internet access, wireless campus network. Student e-mail accounts and computer access in designated common areas are available to students. The school has a published electronic and media policy.
Contact Ms. Kimberly B. Boland, Director of Admission. 413-499-1300. Fax: 413-448-2994. E-mail: info@misshalls.org. Web site: www.misshalls.org.

See Close-Up on page 856.

MISSISSAUGA PRIVATE SCHOOL

30 Barrhead Crescent
Toronto, Ontario M9W 3Z7, Canada
Head of School: Mrs. Gabrielle Bush

General Information Coeducational day college-preparatory, arts, business, and technology school. Grades JK–12. Founded: 1977. Setting: urban. 1 building on campus. Approved or accredited by Ontario Ministry of Education and Ontario Department of Education. Language of instruction: English. Total enrollment: 320. Upper school average class size: 18. Upper school faculty-student ratio: 1:13.
Upper School Student Profile Grade 9: 39 students (25 boys, 14 girls); Grade 10: 40 students (18 boys, 22 girls); Grade 11: 23 students (11 boys, 12 girls); Grade 12: 18 students (9 boys, 9 girls).
Faculty School total: 35. In upper school: 5 men, 7 women; 5 have advanced degrees.
Subjects Offered Accounting, anthropology, biology, Canadian geography, Canadian history, Canadian law, chemistry, civics, communications, data processing, discrete math, dramatic arts, English, French, functions, geometry, healthful living, information technology, learning strategies, mathematics, organizational studies, personal finance, physics, psychology, reading, science, society challenge and change, sociology, visual arts, world history, writing.
Graduation Requirements Ontario Ministry of Education requirements.
Special Academic Programs ESL (30 students enrolled).
College Admission Counseling 33 students graduated in 2008; 30 went to college, including McMaster University; Ryerson University; University of Guelph; University of Toronto; University of Waterloo; York University.
Student Life Upper grades have uniform requirement, student council, honor system. Discipline rests primarily with faculty.
Summer Programs Remediation, enrichment, advancement, ESL, sports, art/fine arts, computer instruction programs offered; session focuses on academics; held on campus; accepts boys and girls; open to students from other schools. 100 students usually enrolled. 2009 schedule: July 6 to July 31. Application deadline: June 25.
Tuition and Aid Day student tuition: CAN$12,000. Tuition installment plan (individually arranged payment plans, MPS Payment Plan). Tuition reduction for siblings available.
Admissions Traditional secondary-level entrance grade is 9. For fall 2008, 15 students applied for upper-level admission, 11 were accepted, 11 enrolled. Admissions testing required. Deadline for receipt of application materials: October 31. No application fee required. Interview required.
Athletics Interscholastic: baseball (girls), basketball (b,g), flag football (b,g), football (b), indoor track & field (b,g), running (b,g), soccer (b,g), swimming and diving (b,g), track and field (b,g), volleyball (b,g); intramural: basketball (b,g), flag football (b,g), floor hockey (b,g), Frisbee (b,g), indoor hockey (b,g), physical fitness (b,g), rhythmic gymnastics (b,g), running (b,g), soccer (b,g), swimming and diving (b,g), touch football (b,g), track and field (b,g), ultimate Frisbee (b,g), volleyball (b,g), winter (indoor) track (b,g), winter soccer (b,g); coed interscholastic: aquatics, bowling, cross-country running, field hockey, flag football; coed intramural: badminton, baseball, basketball, bowling, cooperative games, cross-country running, flag football, table tennis, tennis. 3 PE instructors, 12 coaches.
Computers Computers are regularly used in art, business education, computer applications, graphic arts, media arts classes. Computer resources include Internet access, Internet filtering or blocking technology. The school has a published electronic and media policy.
Contact Mrs. Gabrielle Bush, Director. 416-745-1328. Fax: 416-745-4168. E-mail: gbushmps@rogers.com. Web site: www.mpsontario.com.

MISSOURI MILITARY ACADEMY

204 Grand Avenue
Mexico, Missouri 65265
Head of School: Gen. Robert M. Flanagan

General Information Boys' boarding college-preparatory, ESL, military science, and military school, affiliated with Christian faith; primarily serves individuals with Attention Deficit Disorder. Grades 6–PG. Founded: 1889. Setting: small town. Nearest major city is St. Louis. Students are housed in single-sex dormitories. 288-acre campus. 19 buildings on campus. Approved or accredited by Independent Schools Association of the Central States, North Central Association of Colleges and Schools, and The Association of Boarding Schools. Member of National Association of Independent Schools and Secondary School Admission Test Board. Endowment: $45 million. Total enrollment: 270. Upper school average class size: 10. Upper school faculty-student ratio: 1:11.
Upper School Student Profile Grade 9: 55 students (55 boys); Grade 10: 52 students (52 boys); Grade 11: 53 students (53 boys); Grade 12: 50 students (50 boys). 100% of students are boarding students. 20% are state residents. 30 states are represented in upper school student body. International students from Canada, China, Mexico, Republic of Korea, Russian Federation, and Taiwan; 10 other countries represented in student body.
Faculty School total: 47. In upper school: 27 men, 7 women; 27 have advanced degrees; 6 reside on campus.
Subjects Offered Algebra, American literature, art, biology, broadcasting, business, business skills, calculus, chemistry, computer science, drama, economics, English, ESL, fine arts, French, geography, geometry, government/civics, history, honors algebra, honors English, honors U.S. history, humanities, instrumental music, Internet, jazz band, journalism, JROTC or LEAD (Leadership Education and Development), keyboarding/computer, languages, Latin American studies, leadership, leadership skills, literary magazine, marching band, mathematics, military science, music, newspaper, physical education, physical science, physics, physics-AP, psychology, science, social studies, sociology, Spanish, speech, statistics, student government, student publications, swimming, theater, track and field, typing, U.S. government, U.S. history, vocal ensemble, vocal music, world history, wrestling, writing, yearbook.
Graduation Requirements Arts and fine arts (art, music, dance, drama), business skills (includes word processing), computer science, English, foreign language, JROTC, mathematics, physical education (includes health), science, social studies (includes history), 20 Hours of Community Service Per School Year.
Special Academic Programs 9 Advanced Placement exams for which test preparation is offered; honors section; independent study; study at local college for college credit; academic accommodation for the gifted, the musically talented, and the artistically talented; remedial math; special instructional classes for students with Attention Deficit Disorder; ESL (50 students enrolled).
College Admission Counseling 52 students graduated in 2008; all went to college, including Saint Louis University; Texas A&M University; The University of Arizona; The University of Texas at Austin; University of Miami; University of Missouri–Columbia. Median SAT critical reading: 525, median SAT math: 543, median combined SAT: 1068, median composite ACT: 23.
Student Life Upper grades have uniform requirement, student council, honor system. Discipline rests equally with students and faculty. Attendance at religious services is required.

Summer Programs Sports, rigorous outdoor training programs offered; session focuses on leadership; held both on and off campus; held at Water Park in Jefferson City, MO and Courtois River for float/canoe trips; accepts boys; open to students from other schools. 125 students usually enrolled. 2009 schedule: July 13 to July 26. Application deadline: July 3.
Tuition and Aid 7-day tuition and room/board: $22,715. Tuition installment plan (SMART Tuition Payment Plan, individually arranged payment plans, school's own payment plan). Merit scholarship grants, need-based scholarship grants, need-based loans available. In 2008–09, 24% of upper-school students received aid; total upper-school merit-scholarship money awarded: $120,000. Total amount of financial aid awarded in 2008–09: $476,000.
Admissions Traditional secondary-level entrance grade is 9. For fall 2008, 250 students applied for upper-level admission, 147 were accepted, 135 enrolled. Deadline for receipt of application materials: none. Application fee required: $100. Interview required.
Athletics Interscholastic: aquatics (boys), baseball (b), basketball (b), cross-country running (b), diving (b), drill team (b), football (b), golf (b), JROTC drill (b), marksmanship (b), outdoor activities (b), riflery (b), soccer (b), swimming and diving (b), tennis (b), track and field (b), wrestling (b); intramural: aquatics (b), basketball (b), canoeing/kayaking (b), equestrian sports (b), fencing (b), fishing (b), fitness (b), fitness walking (b), flag football (b), horseback riding (b), indoor track (b), marksmanship (b), martial arts (b), outdoor activities (b), outdoor recreation (b), outdoor skills (b), paint ball (b), physical fitness (b), physical training (b), rappelling (b), riflery (b), roller blading (b), ropes courses (b), running (b), skateboarding (b), soccer (b), softball (b), strength & conditioning (b), swimming and diving (b), table tennis (b), tennis (b), touch football (b), track and field (b), volleyball (b), weight lifting (b), weight training (b), winter (indoor) track (b), wrestling (b). 12 coaches, 1 athletic trainer.
Computers Computers are regularly used in business, English, history, journalism, library, mathematics, newspaper, science, yearbook classes. Computer network features include on-campus library services, online commercial services, Internet access, wireless campus network, Internet filtering or blocking technology. Campus intranet, student e-mail accounts, and computer access in designated common areas are available to students. Students grades are available online. The school has a published electronic and media policy.
Contact Lt. Col. Gregory W. Seibert, Director of Admissions. 573-581-1776 Ext. 323. Fax. 573-581-0081. E-mail: gsei@mma.mexico.mo.us. Web site: www.missourimilitaryacademy.com.

MISS PORTER'S SCHOOL

60 Main Street
Farmington, Connecticut 06032
Head of School: Ms. Katherine G. Windsor

General Information Girls' boarding and day college-preparatory and arts school. Grades 9–12. Founded: 1843. Setting: suburban. Nearest major city is Hartford. Students are housed in single-sex dormitories. 50-acre campus. 48 buildings on campus. Approved or accredited by New England Association of Schools and Colleges and Connecticut Department of Education. Member of National Association of Independent Schools and Secondary School Admission Test Board. Endowment: $103 million. Total enrollment: 330. Upper school average class size: 11. Upper school faculty-student ratio: 1:8.
Upper School Student Profile Grade 9: 75 students (75 girls); Grade 10: 88 students (88 girls); Grade 11: 86 students (86 girls); Grade 12: 81 students (81 girls). 66% of students are boarding students. 55% are state residents. 22 states are represented in upper school student body. 10% are international students. International students from China and Republic of Korea; 13 other countries represented in student body.
Faculty School total: 55. In upper school: 21 men, 34 women; 41 have advanced degrees; 28 reside on campus.
Subjects Offered Acting, advanced chemistry, advanced computer applications, advanced math, Advanced Placement courses, advanced studio art-AP, African history, algebra, American history, American literature, anatomy and physiology, aquatics, area studies, art history, art history-AP, arts, astronomy, athletics, ballet, biology, biology-AP, British literature, calculus, calculus-AP, career/college preparation, ceramics, chemistry, chemistry-AP, Chinese, Chinese history, classical language, college counseling, college planning, community service, computer applications, computer graphics, computer programming, computer science, creative writing, dance, dance performance, desktop publishing, drama, drama performance, economics, economics and history, engineering, English, English literature, environmental science, environmental science-AP, ethical decision making, ethics, European history, European history-AP, experiential education, expository writing, fitness, foreign language, forensic science, French, French language-AP, French literature-AP, geometry, global issues, golf, graphic design, health and wellness, history, honors geometry, human rights, international relations, intro to computers, Japanese history, jazz, jewelry making, languages, Latin, Latin American literature, Latin-AP, leadership, mathematics, Middle Eastern history, model United Nations, modern dance, modern European history-AP, multicultural literature, music, music history, music performance, music theory, participation in sports, performing arts, personal finance, photography, physics, physics-AP, pre-calculus, printmaking, psychology, public speaking, science, Shakespeare, social studies, Spanish, Spanish language-AP, Spanish literature-AP, sports, squash, statistics, statistics-AP, student government, studio art, studio art-AP, swimming, swimming test, tennis, textiles, theater, trigonometry, U.S. history, U.S. history-AP, video film production, visual arts, vocal music, Web site design, Western civilization, writing, yoga.
Graduation Requirements Arts and fine arts (art, music, dance, drama), athletics, computer science, English, experiential education, foreign language, leadership, mathematics, science, social studies (includes history). Community service is required.
Special Academic Programs 22 Advanced Placement exams for which test preparation is offered; honors section; independent study; term-away projects; study abroad; ESL (4 students enrolled).
College Admission Counseling 83 students graduated in 2008; 79 went to college, including Boston University; Brown University; New York University; Smith College; The Johns Hopkins University. Other: 4 had other specific plans. Mean SAT critical reading: 615, mean SAT math: 619, mean SAT writing: 627.
Student Life Upper grades have specified standards of dress, student council, honor system. Discipline rests equally with students and faculty.
Summer Programs Enrichment, advancement, sports, art/fine arts programs offered; session focuses on athletics, Daoyun Chinese, leadership, science and mathematics; held on campus; accepts girls; open to students from other schools. 60 students usually enrolled. 2009 schedule: June to July. Application deadline: none.
Tuition and Aid Day student tuition: $31,850; 7-day tuition and room/board: $41,100. Tuition installment plan (monthly payment plans, individually arranged payment plans). Merit scholarship grants, need-based scholarship grants, need-based loans available. In 2008–09, 40% of upper-school students received aid. Total amount of financial aid awarded in 2008–09: $3,500,000.
Admissions Traditional secondary-level entrance grade is 9. For fall 2008, 431 students applied for upper-level admission, 203 were accepted, 99 enrolled. ISEE, PSAT and SAT for applicants to grade 11 and 12, SSAT or TOEFL required. Deadline for receipt of application materials: January 15. Application fee required: $50. Interview required.
Athletics Interscholastic: alpine skiing (girls), badminton (g), basketball (g), crew (g), cross-country running (g), dance (g), diving (g), equestrian sports (g), field hockey (g), golf (g), horseback riding (g), independent competitive sports (g), lacrosse (g), skiing (downhill) (g), soccer (g), softball (g), squash (g), swimming and diving (g), tennis (g), track and field (g), ultimate Frisbee (g), volleyball (g); intramural: aerobics (g), aerobics/Nautilus (g), ballet (g), climbing (g), dance (g), equestrian sports (g), fencing (g), fitness (g), fitness walking (g), golf (g), horseback riding (g), jogging (g), life saving (g), martial arts (g), modern dance (g), physical fitness (g), self defense (g), skiing (downhill) (g), snowboarding (g), squash (g), strength & conditioning (g), swimming and diving (g), tennis (g), walking (g), wall climbing (g), yoga (g). 3 coaches, 1 athletic trainer.
Computers Computers are regularly used in computer applications, desktop publishing, graphic design, graphics, introduction to technology, publications, Web site design classes. Computer network features include on-campus library services, online commercial services, Internet access, wireless campus network, Internet filtering or blocking technology. Campus intranet, student e-mail accounts, and computer access in designated common areas are available to students. Students grades are available online. The school has a published electronic and media policy.
Contact Deborah Haskins, Director of Admission. 860-409-3530. Fax: 860-409-3531. E-mail: deborah_haskins@missporters.org. Web site: www.porters.org.

ANNOUNCEMENT FROM THE SCHOOL Located in the center of Farmington, Connecticut, Porter's is a college-preparatory boarding and day school for girls in grades 9 through 12. Founded in 1843 by lifelong scholar and educator, Sarah Porter, the School's innovative, rigorous, well-rounded approach to education prepares girls to expand their minds and grow into socially engaged, confident young women. With 330 students hailing from twenty-two states and twenty countries, Porter's provides a diverse high school experience that helps young women become local and global leaders of the future.

See Close-Up on page 858.

MMI PREPARATORY SCHOOL

154 Centre Street
Freeland, Pennsylvania 18224
Head of School: Mr. Thomas G. Hood

General Information Coeducational day college-preparatory, arts, and technology school. Grades 6–12. Founded: 1879. Setting: small town. Nearest major city is Hazleton. 20-acre campus. 1 building on campus. Approved or accredited by Middle States Association of Colleges and Schools and Pennsylvania Department of Education. Member of National Association of Independent Schools. Endowment: $10 million. Total enrollment: 251. Upper school average class size: 15. Upper school faculty-student ratio: 1:9.
Upper School Student Profile Grade 6: 25 students (7 boys, 18 girls); Grade 7: 30 students (18 boys, 12 girls); Grade 8: 45 students (21 boys, 24 girls); Grade 9: 47 students (26 boys, 21 girls); Grade 10: 39 students (21 boys, 18 girls); Grade 11: 38 students (24 boys, 14 girls); Grade 12: 29 students (15 boys, 14 girls).
Faculty School total: 25. In upper school: 13 men, 12 women; 18 have advanced degrees.

Subjects Offered Algebra, American history, American literature, anatomy, art, biology, calculus, chemistry, computer programming, computer science, consumer education, creative writing, earth science, economics, English, English literature, environmental science, European history, expository writing, fine arts, geography, geometry, German, government/civics, grammar, health, history, keyboarding, Latin, mathematics, music, physical education, physics, physiology, psychology, science, social studies, Spanish, speech, statistics, trigonometry, world history, world literature.
Graduation Requirements Analysis and differential calculus, arts and fine arts (art, music, dance, drama), college counseling, computer science, consumer education, economics, English, foreign language, mathematics, physical education (includes health), science, social studies (includes history), speech, independent research project presentation every spring, public speaking assembly project every year.
Special Academic Programs 8 Advanced Placement exams for which test preparation is offered; honors section; study at local college for college credit; academic accommodation for the gifted and the artistically talented.
College Admission Counseling 28 students graduated in 2008; all went to college, including Carnegie Mellon University; New York University; Penn State University Park; Saint Joseph's University; Temple University; The University of Scranton. Mean SAT critical reading: 610, mean SAT math: 620, mean SAT writing: 613, mean combined SAT: 1843.
Student Life Upper grades have specified standards of dress, student council, honor system. Discipline rests primarily with faculty.
Summer Programs Remediation, enrichment, advancement, computer instruction programs offered; session focuses on academics; held on campus; accepts boys and girls; open to students from other schools. 40 students usually enrolled. 2009 schedule: June 18 to July 27. Application deadline: June 15.
Tuition and Aid Day student tuition: $11,375. Tuition installment plan (monthly payment plans). Merit scholarship grants, need-based scholarship grants, paying campus jobs available. In 2008–09, 65% of upper-school students received aid; total upper-school merit-scholarship money awarded: $30,000. Total amount of financial aid awarded in 2008–09: $767,000.
Admissions Traditional secondary-level entrance grade is 9. For fall 2008, 71 students applied for upper-level admission, 69 were accepted, 59 enrolled. Iowa Silent Reading, Iowa Tests of Basic Skills and Otis-Lennon School Ability Test required. Deadline for receipt of application materials: none. Application fee required: $25. On-campus interview required.
Athletics Interscholastic: baseball (boys), basketball (b,g), cheering (g), cross-country running (b,g), soccer (b,g), softball (g), tennis (b,g), volleyball (g); intramural: bowling (b,g); coed interscholastic: golf; coed intramural: skiing (downhill), snowboarding. 2 PE instructors.
Computers Computers are regularly used in all classes. Computer network features include on-campus library services, Internet access, wireless campus network, Internet filtering or blocking technology. Students grades are available online. The school has a published electronic and media policy.
Contact Kim McNulty, Director of Admissions and Financial Aid. 570-636-1108. Fax: 570-636-0742. E-mail: kmcnulty@mmiprep.org. Web site: www.mmiprep.org.

MODESTO CHRISTIAN SCHOOL

5901 Sisk Road
Modesto, California 95356

Head of School: Rev. Ralph Sudfeld

General Information Coeducational day college-preparatory, arts, and religious studies school, affiliated with Assembly of God Church. Grades K–12. Founded: 1973. Setting: suburban. Nearest major city is Sacramento. 40-acre campus. 6 buildings on campus. Approved or accredited by Association of Christian Schools International, Western Association of Schools and Colleges, and California Department of Education. Total enrollment: 650. Upper school average class size: 20. Upper school faculty-student ratio: 1:9.
Upper School Student Profile Grade 9: 72 students (41 boys, 31 girls); Grade 10: 82 students (45 boys, 37 girls); Grade 11: 88 students (50 boys, 38 girls); Grade 12: 66 students (32 boys, 34 girls). 75% of students are members of Assembly of God Church.
Faculty School total: 26. In upper school: 10 men, 16 women; 3 have advanced degrees.
Subjects Offered Advanced biology, algebra, American literature, American sign language, arts, band, biology, biology-AP, calculus-AP, career education, chemistry, choir, church history, computer keyboarding, consumer education, digital photography, drama, economics, English, English literature, environmental science, fine arts, French language-AP, general math, geometry, grammar, health, history, honors English, keyboarding, keyboarding/computer, mathematics, physical education, physics, physiology-anatomy, political science, pre-algebra, pre-calculus, religion, science, social science, social studies, Spanish, Spanish language-AP, speech, studio art-AP, study skills, U.S. government, U.S. history, U.S. history-AP, word processing, world history.
Graduation Requirements Arts and fine arts (art, music, dance, drama), English, foreign language, mathematics, physical education (includes health), religion (includes Bible studies and theology), science, social studies (includes history), speech.
Special Academic Programs 7 Advanced Placement exams for which test preparation is offered; honors section; remedial reading and/or remedial writing; remedial math; programs in English, mathematics, general development for dyslexic students.
College Admission Counseling 71 students graduated in 2008; 68 went to college, including Azusa Pacific University; California Polytechnic State University, San Luis Obispo; California State University, Stanislaus; Modesto Junior College; San Francisco State University. Other: 1 entered military service, 1 entered a postgraduate year, 1 had other specific plans. Median SAT critical reading: 524, median SAT math: 513, median SAT writing: 505.
Student Life Upper grades have specified standards of dress, student council. Discipline rests primarily with faculty.
Tuition and Aid Day student tuition: $7295. Tuition installment plan (monthly payment plans, individually arranged payment plans). Tuition reduction for siblings available. In 2008–09, 5% of upper-school students received aid.
Admissions Traditional secondary-level entrance grade is 9. Admissions testing or Stanford Achievement Test required. Deadline for receipt of application materials: none. Application fee required: $200. On-campus interview required.
Athletics Interscholastic: baseball (boys), basketball (b,g), football (b), golf (b,g), soccer (b,g), softball (g), strength & conditioning (b,g), volleyball (g), wrestling (b); coed interscholastic: fitness, tennis, track and field, weight lifting. 2 PE instructors, 20 coaches.
Computers Computers are regularly used in career education, college planning, typing, yearbook classes. Computer resources include on-campus library services, Internet filtering or blocking technology. Students grades are available online. The school has a published electronic and media policy.
Contact Mrs. Lynn Olson, Admissions Office. 209-343-2225. Fax: 209-543-9930. E-mail: lolson@modestochristian.org. Web site: www.modestochristian.org.

MONMOUTH ACADEMY

152 Lanes Mill Road
Howell, New Jersey 07731

Head of School: Mr. Timothy Costello

General Information Coeducational day college-preparatory and arts school. Grades K–12. Founded: 1972. Setting: small town. Nearest major city is New York, NY. 31-acre campus. 2 buildings on campus. Approved or accredited by Commission on Secondary Schools, Middle States Association of Colleges and Schools, and New Jersey Association of Independent Schools. Total enrollment: 98. Upper school average class size: 13. Upper school faculty-student ratio: 1:8.
Upper School Student Profile Grade 6: 10 students (3 boys, 7 girls); Grade 7: 12 students (6 boys, 6 girls); Grade 8: 5 students (5 boys); Grade 9: 2 students (2 boys); Grade 10: 12 students (8 boys, 4 girls); Grade 11: 4 students (3 boys, 1 girl); Grade 12: 19 students (14 boys, 5 girls).
Faculty School total: 22. In upper school: 4 men, 7 women; 4 have advanced degrees.
Subjects Offered Algebra, American history, American literature, anatomy, art, art history, biology, calculus, career experience, chemistry, computer math, computer programming, computer science, creative writing, drama, economics, English, English literature, environmental science, European history, expository writing, fine arts, French, geography, geology, geometry, grammar, health, Hebrew, history, mathematics, music, mythology, philosophy, physical education, physics, physiology, poetry, science, social studies, Spanish, speech, theater, trigonometry, world history, world literature, writing.
Graduation Requirements Arts and fine arts (art, music, dance, drama), career experience, English, foreign language, mathematics, physical education (includes health), science, social studies (includes history).
Special Academic Programs Advanced Placement exam preparation; honors section; accelerated programs; independent study; study at local college for college credit; academic accommodation for the gifted and the artistically talented; remedial reading and/or remedial writing; remedial math.
College Admission Counseling 19 students graduated in 2008; all went to college, including Columbia College; Hofstra University; New York University; Penn State University Park; State University of New York at Binghamton. Median SAT critical reading: 570, median SAT math: 570. 20% scored over 600 on SAT critical reading, 25% scored over 600 on SAT math.
Student Life Upper grades have specified standards of dress, student council, honor system. Discipline rests primarily with faculty.
Tuition and Aid Day student tuition: $14,000–$15,500. Tuition installment plan (SMART Tuition Payment Plan, monthly payment plans, individually arranged payment plans, 3-payment plan). Tuition reduction for siblings, merit scholarship grants, need-based scholarship grants available. In 2008–09, 10% of upper-school students received aid; total upper-school merit-scholarship money awarded: $7250. Total amount of financial aid awarded in 2008–09: $21,750.
Admissions Traditional secondary-level entrance grade is 9. For fall 2008, 5 students applied for upper-level admission, 5 were accepted, 5 enrolled. Wechsler Intelligence Scale for Children required. Deadline for receipt of application materials: none. Application fee required: $125. On-campus interview required.
Athletics Interscholastic: baseball (boys), basketball (b,g), cross-country running (b,g); intramural: bowling (b,g); coed interscholastic: soccer, tennis, track and field; coed intramural: aerobics/dance, golf. 2 PE instructors, 4 coaches.
Computers Computers are regularly used in English, mathematics, science classes. Computer network features include on-campus library services, online commercial

services, Internet access, wireless campus network, Internet filtering or blocking technology. Student e-mail accounts are available to students.
Contact Mr. Timothy L. Costello, Dean of Admission. 732-364-2812 Ext. 106. Fax: 732-364-4004. E-mail: tcostello@monmouthacademy.org. Web site: www.monmouthacademy.org.

MONSIGNOR DONOVAN HIGH SCHOOL

711 Hooper Avenue
Toms River, New Jersey 08753
Head of School: Edward Gere

General Information Coeducational day college-preparatory school, affiliated with Roman Catholic Church; primarily serves students with learning disabilities, individuals with Attention Deficit Disorder, dyslexic students, and OHI (Other health impaired). Grades 9–12. Founded: 1962. Setting: suburban. 1 building on campus. Approved or accredited by Middle States Association of Colleges and Schools, National Catholic Education Association, and New Jersey Department of Education. Total enrollment: 957. Upper school average class size: 29. Upper school faculty-student ratio: 1:14.
Upper School Student Profile Grade 9: 233 students (121 boys, 112 girls); Grade 10: 243 students (124 boys, 119 girls); Grade 11: 234 students (111 boys, 123 girls); Grade 12: 247 students (118 boys, 129 girls). 85% of students are Roman Catholic.
Faculty School total: 72. In upper school: 28 men, 40 women; 36 have advanced degrees.
Special Academic Programs Advanced Placement exam preparation; honors section; independent study; study at local college for college credit; academic accommodation for the gifted, the musically talented, and the artistically talented; remedial reading and/or remedial writing; remedial math; ESL.
College Admission Counseling 243 students graduated in 2008; 239 went to college. Other: 2 went to work, 2 had other specific plans.
Student Life Upper grades have uniform requirement, student council, honor system. Discipline rests equally with students and faculty. Attendance at religious services is required.
Tuition and Aid Day student tuition: $8775. Tuition installment plan (FACTS Tuition Payment Plan, monthly payment plans, individually arranged payment plans). Merit scholarship grants, need-based scholarship grants, paying campus jobs available. In 2008–09, 20% of upper-school students received aid.
Admissions Traditional secondary-level entrance grade is 9. High School Placement Test (closed version) from Scholastic Testing Service or Scholastic Testing Service High School Placement Test required. Deadline for receipt of application materials: November 10. Application fee required: $50. On-campus interview recommended.
Athletics Interscholastic: baseball (boys), cheering (g), dance (g), football (b), golf (b), ice hockey (b), lacrosse (g), softball (g), wrestling (b); coed interscholastic: basketball, bowling, cross-country running, hiking/backpacking, sailing, skiing (cross-country), snowboarding, soccer, strength & conditioning, surfing, swimming and diving, tennis. 5 PE instructors, 22 coaches, 1 athletic trainer.
Computers Computers are regularly used in all academic classes. Computer network features include on-campus library services, Internet access, wireless campus network, Internet filtering or blocking technology. Student e-mail accounts are available to students. Students grades are available online.
Contact Mrs. Carol A. Gaspartich, Registrar. 732-349-8801 Ext. 2426. Fax: 732-505-8014. E-mail: cgaspartich@mondonhs.com. Web site: www.mondonhs.com.

MONTANA ACADEMY

Marion, Montana
See Special Needs Schools section.

MONTCLAIR COLLEGE PREPARATORY SCHOOL

8071 Sepulveda Boulevard
Van Nuys, California 91402-4420

See Close-Up on page 860.

MONTGOMERY BELL ACADEMY

4001 Harding Road
Nashville, Tennessee 37205
Head of School: Bradford Gioia

General Information Boys' day college-preparatory and arts school. Grades 7–12. Founded: 1867. Setting: urban. 43-acre campus. 9 buildings on campus. Approved or accredited by Southern Association of Colleges and Schools, Southern Association of Independent Schools, and Tennessee Association of Independent Schools. Member of National Association of Independent Schools and Secondary School Admission Test Board. Endowment: $60.1 million. Total enrollment: 700. Upper school average class size: 13. Upper school faculty-student ratio: 1:7.
Upper School Student Profile Grade 9: 128 students (128 boys); Grade 10: 123 students (123 boys); Grade 11: 119 students (119 boys); Grade 12: 100 students (100 boys).
Faculty School total: 90. In upper school: 67 men, 21 women; 71 have advanced degrees.
Subjects Offered Advanced Placement courses, algebra, American government-AP, American history, American history-AP, American literature, American literature-AP, art, art history, art history-AP, biology, biology-AP, calculus, calculus-AP, chemistry, chemistry-AP, computer programming, computer science, computer science-AP, drama, earth science, economics, English, English literature, environmental science-AP, European history, European history-AP, fine arts, French, French language-AP, French literature-AP, French-AP, geography, geology, geometry, German, German-AP, government/civics, grammar, Greek, history, Latin, Latin-AP, mathematics, music, music history, music theory, music theory-AP, physical education, physics, physics-AP, science, social studies, Spanish, Spanish-AP, speech, statistics, statistics-AP, theater, trigonometry, U.S. history-AP, world history, world history-AP, writing.
Graduation Requirements Arts and fine arts (art, music, dance, drama), English, foreign language, mathematics, physical education (includes health), science, social studies (includes history).
Special Academic Programs Advanced Placement exam preparation; honors section; term-away projects; study abroad.
College Admission Counseling 105 students graduated in 2008; 104 went to college, including Sewanee: The University of the South; Southern Methodist University; The University of Alabama; The University of Tennessee; University of Georgia; Vanderbilt University. Other: 1 entered a postgraduate year. Mean SAT critical reading: 636, mean SAT math: 651, mean SAT writing: 648, mean combined SAT: 1935, mean composite ACT: 28.
Student Life Upper grades have specified standards of dress, student council, honor system. Discipline rests primarily with faculty.
Summer Programs Remediation, enrichment, sports, computer instruction programs offered; held both on and off campus; held at Long Mountain, TN; accepts boys and girls; open to students from other schools. 2009 schedule: June 1 to July 31.
Tuition and Aid Day student tuition: $18,175. Tuition installment plan (monthly payment plans, Dewar Tuition Refund Plan). Need-based scholarship grants available. In 2008–09, 19% of upper-school students received aid. Total amount of financial aid awarded in 2008–09: $742,225.
Admissions Traditional secondary-level entrance grade is 9. For fall 2008, 69 students applied for upper-level admission, 35 were accepted, 30 enrolled. ISEE required. Deadline for receipt of application materials: February 1. Application fee required: $50. On-campus interview required.
Athletics Interscholastic: baseball, basketball, bowling, cross-country running, diving, football, golf, hockey, ice hockey, lacrosse; intramural: backpacking, baseball, basketball, cheering, flag football, football, Frisbee, hiking/backpacking, outdoor activities, paddle tennis. 2 PE instructors, 6 coaches, 2 athletic trainers.
Computers Computers are regularly used in all academic classes. Computer network features include on-campus library services, online commercial services, Internet access, wireless campus network, Internet filtering or blocking technology. Student e-mail accounts are available to students. Students grades are available online.
Contact Mr. Greg Ferrell, Director, Admission and Financial Aid. 615-298-5514 Ext. 251. Fax: 615-297-0271. E-mail: ferrelg@montgomerybell.com. Web site: www.montgomerybell.com.

MONTROSE SCHOOL

29 North Street
Medfield, Massachusetts 02052
Head of School: Dr. Karen E. Bohlin, EdD

General Information Girls' day college-preparatory school, affiliated with Roman Catholic Church. Grades 6–12. Founded: 1979. Setting: suburban. Nearest major city is Boston. 14-acre campus. 3 buildings on campus. Approved or accredited by Massachusetts Department of Education. Total enrollment: 140. Upper school average class size: 13. Upper school faculty-student ratio: 1:10.
Upper School Student Profile Grade 9: 23 students (23 girls); Grade 10: 20 students (20 girls); Grade 11: 20 students (20 girls); Grade 12: 15 students (15 girls). 70% of students are Roman Catholic.
Faculty School total: 28. In upper school: 28 women; 15 have advanced degrees.
Subjects Offered 20th century American writers, 20th century history, advanced biology, advanced math, Advanced Placement courses, algebra, American literature, biology, British literature, calculus-AP, chemistry, church history, computers, drama, English-AP, French, geometry, Life of Christ, medieval/Renaissance history, modern European history, moral theology, music, physical education, physics, pre-calculus, religion, social doctrine, Spanish, speech, studio art, trigonometry, U.S. history, world history, world literature.
Graduation Requirements Arts and fine arts (art, music, dance, drama), English, foreign language, mathematics, physical education (includes health), religion (includes Bible studies and theology), science, social studies (includes history).
Special Academic Programs Advanced Placement exam preparation; honors section; independent study.
College Admission Counseling 25 students graduated in 2008; all went to college, including Boston College; Georgia Institute of Technology; Hamilton College; Massachusetts Institute of Technology; Smith College; University of Notre Dame. Mean SAT critical reading: 640, mean SAT math: 640, mean SAT writing: 680. 53% scored over 600 on SAT critical reading, 53% scored over 600 on SAT math.

Student Life Upper grades have uniform requirement, student council, honor system. Discipline rests primarily with faculty.
Tuition and Aid Day student tuition: $15,600. Tuition installment plan (FACTS Tuition Payment Plan). Tuition reduction for siblings, merit scholarship grants, need-based scholarship grants available. In 2008–09, 38% of upper-school students received aid; total upper-school merit-scholarship money awarded: $5000. Total amount of financial aid awarded in 2008–09: $90,000.
Admissions Traditional secondary-level entrance grade is 9. For fall 2008, 25 students applied for upper-level admission, 20 were accepted, 16 enrolled. Admissions testing, ERB Reading and Math, ERB verbal, ERB math, essay or SSAT required. Deadline for receipt of application materials: February 1. Application fee required: $50. Interview required.
Athletics Interscholastic: basketball, cross-country running, lacrosse; intramural: dance, fitness. 1 PE instructor, 4 coaches.
Computers Computers are regularly used in English, foreign language, history, newspaper, philosophy, religion, Spanish, theology classes. Computer network features include Internet access, Internet filtering or blocking technology.
Contact Heather Roy, Office of Admissions. 508-359-2423 Ext. 387. Fax: 508-359-2597. E-mail: hroy@montroseschool.org. Web site: www.montroseschool.org.

MONTVERDE ACADEMY

17235 Seventh Street
Montverde, Florida 34756

Head of School: Mr. Kasey C. Kesselring

General Information Coeducational boarding and day college-preparatory and arts school. Boarding grades 7–PG, day grades PK–PG. Founded: 1912. Setting: small town. Nearest major city is Orlando. Students are housed in single-sex dormitories. 125-acre campus. 25 buildings on campus. Approved or accredited by Florida Council of Independent Schools, Southern Association of Colleges and Schools, Southern Association of Independent Schools, and The Association of Boarding Schools. Member of National Association of Independent Schools. Endowment: $8 million. Total enrollment: 665. Upper school average class size: 20. Upper school faculty-student ratio: 1:12.
Upper School Student Profile Grade 9: 63 students (26 boys, 37 girls); Grade 10: 65 students (38 boys, 27 girls); Grade 11: 79 students (47 boys, 32 girls); Grade 12: 76 students (46 boys, 30 girls); Postgraduate: 2 students (1 boy, 1 girl). 65% of students are boarding students. 30% are state residents. 9 states are represented in upper school student body. 65% are international students. International students from China, Germany, Puerto Rico, Republic of Korea, Thailand, and Viet Nam; 24 other countries represented in student body.
Faculty School total: 51. In upper school: 8 men, 12 women; 15 have advanced degrees; 25 reside on campus.
Subjects Offered 20th century history, 3-dimensional art, acting, advanced computer applications, algebra, American history, American literature, anatomy, anatomy and physiology, ancient world history, art, art history, biology, biology-AP, calculus, calculus-AP, ceramics, chemistry, chemistry-AP, choral music, clayworking, computer applications, computer keyboarding, computer science, concert choir, desktop publishing, drama, economics, English, English language and composition-AP, English literature, English literature and composition-AP, ESL, ethics, European history-AP, fitness, forensic science, French, French language-AP, geography, geometry, government, health, history, history of music, honors algebra, honors English, honors geometry, honors U.S. history, international affairs, introduction to theater, jazz band, marine biology, mathematics, modern world history, music appreciation, music theory-AP, photo shop, photography, physical education, physics, physics-AP, physiology, piano, politics, pre-calculus, programming, SAT/ACT preparation, science, Spanish, Spanish language-AP, statistics-AP, studio art, studio art-AP, study skills, theater history, trigonometry, U.S. government and politics-AP, U.S. history, U.S. history-AP, Web site design, woodworking, world history.
Graduation Requirements Arts and fine arts (art, music, dance, drama), computer science, electives, English, ethics, foreign language, mathematics, physical education (includes health), science, social studies (includes history), international students are not required to take a foreign language if their native language is not English.
Special Academic Programs Advanced Placement exam preparation; honors section; ESL (62 students enrolled).
College Admission Counseling 71 students graduated in 2008; all went to college. Median SAT critical reading: 423, median SAT math: 542, median SAT writing: 442, median combined SAT: 1364, median composite ACT: 18.
Student Life Upper grades have uniform requirement, student council, honor system. Discipline rests equally with students and faculty.
Summer Programs Remediation, advancement, ESL programs offered; session focuses on academics; held on campus; accepts boys and girls; open to students from other schools. 50 students usually enrolled. 2009 schedule: June 22 to August 4. Application deadline: none.
Tuition and Aid Day student tuition: $10,170; 7-day tuition and room/board: $29,500. Tuition installment plan (monthly payment plans). Tuition reduction for siblings, need-based scholarship grants available. Total amount of financial aid awarded in 2008–09: $1,000,000.
Admissions Traditional secondary-level entrance grade is 9. For fall 2008, 211 students applied for upper-level admission, 173 were accepted, 120 enrolled. ISEE and SSAT required. Deadline for receipt of application materials: none. Application fee required: $50. Interview recommended.
Athletics Interscholastic: baseball (boys), basketball (b,g), cheering (g), cross-country running (b,g), dance team (b,g), golf (b,g), soccer (b,g), tennis (b,g), track and field (b,g), volleyball (g); intramural: basketball (b,g), flag football (b), soccer (b,g), softball (b,g), table tennis (b,g), tennis (b,g); coed interscholastic: equestrian sports, horseback riding, track and field; coed intramural: aerobics/dance, aquatics, bicycling, billiards, canoeing/kayaking, equestrian sports, fishing, fitness, fitness walking, Frisbee, horseback riding, jogging, kayaking, physical fitness, physical training, running, soccer, strength & conditioning, ultimate Frisbee, walking. 2 PE instructors, 15 coaches.
Computers Computers are regularly used in all academic, computer applications, desktop publishing, information technology, introduction to technology, keyboarding, language development, library skills, newspaper, programming, publications classes. Computer network features include on-campus library services, online commercial services, Internet access, wireless campus network, Internet filtering or blocking technology. Computer access in designated common areas is available to students. Students grades are available online. The school has a published electronic and media policy.
Contact Mrs. Robin Revis-Pyke, Dean of Admission and Financial Aid. 407-469-2561 Ext. 204. Fax: 407-469-3711. E-mail: robin.pyke@montverde.org. Web site: www.montverde.org.

ANNOUNCEMENT FROM THE SCHOOL Founded in 1912, Montverde Academy is a college preparatory, coeducational independent school serving grades PK3-12. The boarding program serves boys and girls in grades 7–12 and the postgraduate program. Montverde Academy offers a challenging academic environment to students who have a strong desire to learn. Five generations of Montverde Academy graduates have been guided by three fundamental principles: Knowledge, Character, and Community. These principles are illustrated in the classroom through Advanced Placement and Honors courses. Performance on Advanced Placement exams achieved better than 82% passing rate, with 51% scoring 4 or higher. Achievement of college placement is evidenced by a 100% college acceptance rate. The athletic program is sanctioned through the Florida High School Athletic Association. A variety of individual and team sports at both the Varsity and Junior Varsity levels facilitate student development. The basketball program excelled as it captured the HoopsUSA.com 2007 National Championship. A World Championship equestrian program is also a part of Montverde Academy's extracurricular program. Through required involvement in fine arts, athletics, clubs, and service organizations, students become positive contributors to the school and community. The educational experience provided by Montverde Academy creates opportunities for lifelong learning and global leadership.

MOORESTOWN FRIENDS SCHOOL

110 East Main Street
Moorestown, New Jersey 08057

Head of School: Mr. Laurence Van Meter

General Information Coeducational day college-preparatory, arts, religious studies, and technology school, affiliated with Society of Friends. Grades PS–12. Founded: 1785. Setting: suburban. Nearest major city is Philadelphia, PA. 48-acre campus. 9 buildings on campus. Approved or accredited by Middle States Association of Colleges and Schools and New Jersey Department of Education. Member of National Association of Independent Schools. Total enrollment: 725. Upper school average class size: 18. Upper school faculty-student ratio: 1:9.
Upper School Student Profile Grade 9: 74 students (42 boys, 32 girls); Grade 10: 74 students (34 boys, 40 girls); Grade 11: 73 students (39 boys, 34 girls); Grade 12: 68 students (28 boys, 40 girls). 2% of students are members of Society of Friends.
Faculty School total: 90. In upper school: 20 men, 37 women; 38 have advanced degrees.
Subjects Offered Algebra, American history, American literature, art, art history, biology, calculus, ceramics, chemistry, Chinese, community service, computer programming, computer science, creative writing, drama, driver education, earth science, economics, English, English literature, environmental science, ethics, European history, expository writing, fine arts, French, geometry, government/civics, grammar, health, history, mathematics, music, philosophy, photography, physical education, physics, psychology, religion, science, social studies, Spanish, theater, trigonometry, world history, writing.
Graduation Requirements Arts and fine arts (art, music, dance, drama), English, foreign language, mathematics, physical education (includes health), science, senior project, social studies (includes history). Community service is required.
Special Academic Programs Advanced Placement exam preparation; honors section; independent study; term-away projects; study abroad.
College Admission Counseling 69 students graduated in 2008; all went to college, including Cornell University; Dickinson College; Lehigh University; Swarthmore

College; University of Delaware; University of Pennsylvania. Mean SAT critical reading: 629, mean SAT math: 633, mean SAT writing: 637, mean combined SAT: 1899.

Student Life Upper grades have specified standards of dress, student council, honor system. Discipline rests primarily with faculty. Attendance at religious services is required.

Tuition and Aid Day student tuition: $18,900. Tuition installment plan (Academic Management Services Plan, Tuition Refund Plan). Need-based scholarship grants, need-based loans, tuition reduction for children of faculty and staff available. In 2008–09, 29% of upper-school students received aid. Total amount of financial aid awarded in 2008–09: $905,350.

Admissions Traditional secondary-level entrance grade is 9. For fall 2008, 102 students applied for upper-level admission, 56 were accepted, 35 enrolled. ERB CTP required. Deadline for receipt of application materials: none. Application fee required: $45. On-campus interview required.

Athletics Interscholastic: baseball (boys), basketball (b,g), crew (b,g), cross-country running (b,g), fencing (b,g), field hockey (g), independent competitive sports (b,g), lacrosse (g), physical training (b,g), soccer (b,g), swimming and diving (b,g), tennis (b,g); intramural: floor hockey (b), roller hockey (b), street hockey (b), weight training (b,g); coed interscholastic: golf. 5 PE instructors, 24 coaches, 1 athletic trainer.

Computers Computers are regularly used in English, foreign language, mathematics, music, science classes. Computer network features include on-campus library services, Internet access, wireless campus network, Internet filtering or blocking technology. Campus intranet, student e-mail accounts, and computer access in designated common areas are available to students. Students grades are available online.

Contact Karin B. Miller, Director of Admission and Financial Aid. 856-235-2900 Ext. 227. Fax: 856-235-6684. E-mail: kmiller@mfriends.org. Web site: www.mfriends.org.

MOOSE KERR SCHOOL

PO Box 120
Aklavik, Northwest Territories X0E 0A0, Canada

Head of School: Ms. Velma Illasiak

General Information Coeducational day and distance learning general academic and vocational school; primarily serves underachievers and individuals with Attention Deficit Disorder. Grades K–12. Distance learning grades 10–12. Founded: 1967. Setting: rural. Nearest major city is Yellowknife, Canada. 1 building on campus. Approved or accredited by Northwest Territories Department of Education. Language of instruction: English. Total enrollment: 144. Upper school average class size: 25. Upper school faculty-student ratio: 1:15.

Upper School Student Profile Grade 6: 14 students (8 boys, 6 girls); Grade 7: 7 students (4 boys, 3 girls); Grade 8: 6 students (3 boys, 3 girls); Grade 9: 16 students (12 boys, 4 girls); Grade 10: 19 students (11 boys, 8 girls); Grade 11: 19 students (12 boys, 7 girls); Grade 12: 8 students (4 boys, 4 girls).

Faculty School total: 13. In upper school: 2 men, 1 woman; 1 has an advanced degree.

Special Academic Programs Remedial reading and/or remedial writing.

College Admission Counseling 11 students graduated in 2008; 4 went to college. Other: 3 went to work, 4 entered a postgraduate year.

Student Life Upper grades have honor system. Discipline rests primarily with faculty.

Admissions Traditional secondary-level entrance grade is 10. Deadline for receipt of application materials: none. No application fee required.

Athletics Interscholastic: soccer (boys, girls), softball (b,g), volleyball (b,g). 2 coaches.

Computers Computers are regularly used in career education, computer applications, construction, creative writing, current events, desktop publishing, English, geography, graphic design, independent study, information technology, literacy, mathematics, music, psychology, reading, social sciences, social studies, typing, woodworking classes. Computer network features include on-campus library services, Internet access, Internet filtering or blocking technology. Computer access in designated common areas is available to students.

Contact Ms. Velma Illasiak, Principal. 867-978-2536. Fax: 867-978-2829. E-mail: velma_illasiak@bdec.learnnet.nt.ca.

MORAVIAN ACADEMY

4313 Green Pond Road
Bethlehem, Pennsylvania 18020

Head of School: George N. King Jr.

General Information Coeducational day college-preparatory school, affiliated with Moravian Church. Grades PK–12. Founded: 1742. Setting: rural. Nearest major city is Philadelphia. 120-acre campus. 8 buildings on campus. Approved or accredited by Middle States Association of Colleges and Schools, Pennsylvania Association of Independent Schools, and Pennsylvania Department of Education. Member of National Association of Independent Schools and Secondary School Admission Test Board. Endowment: $11.5 million. Total enrollment: 814. Upper school average class size: 15. Upper school faculty-student ratio: 1:7.

Upper School Student Profile Grade 9: 67 students (25 boys, 42 girls); Grade 10: 72 students (31 boys, 41 girls); Grade 11: 78 students (36 boys, 42 girls); Grade 12: 70 students (39 boys, 31 girls).

Faculty School total: 100. In upper school: 22 men, 21 women; 36 have advanced degrees.

Subjects Offered Algebra, American history, American literature, anatomy, ancient history, art, biology, calculus, chemistry, Chinese, community service, drama, driver education, ecology, economics, English, English literature, European history, fine arts, French, geometry, government, health, history, Japanese, Japanese studies, mathematics, music, photography, physical education, physics, poetry, religion, science, Spanish, statistics, theater, trigonometry, woodworking, world history, world literature.

Graduation Requirements Arts and fine arts (art, music, dance, drama), English, foreign language, mathematics, physical education (includes health), religion (includes Bible studies and theology), science, social studies (includes history), service project.

Special Academic Programs 10 Advanced Placement exams for which test preparation is offered; honors section; independent study; study at local college for college credit; remedial reading and/or remedial writing.

College Admission Counseling 69 students graduated in 2008; all went to college, including Boston University; Cornell University; Drexel University; Hofstra University; New York University; University of Pennsylvania. Median SAT critical reading: 630, median SAT math: 610, median SAT writing: 630. 67% scored over 600 on SAT critical reading, 55% scored over 600 on SAT math, 63% scored over 600 on SAT writing, 43% scored over 1800 on combined SAT.

Student Life Upper grades have specified standards of dress, student council. Discipline rests equally with students and faculty. Attendance at religious services is required.

Summer Programs Remediation, enrichment, art/fine arts programs offered; session focuses on enrichment; held on campus; accepts boys and girls; open to students from other schools. 2009 schedule: June 15 to July 24.

Tuition and Aid Day student tuition: $19,380. Tuition installment plan (monthly payment plans). Need-based scholarship grants, need-based loans available. In 2008–09, 17% of upper-school students received aid. Total amount of financial aid awarded in 2008–09: $576,950.

Admissions Traditional secondary-level entrance grade is 9. For fall 2008, 50 students applied for upper level admission, 32 were accepted, 28 enrolled. ERB and Otis-Lennon School Ability Test required. Deadline for receipt of application materials: none. Application fee required: $65. On-campus interview required.

Athletics Interscholastic: baseball (boys), basketball (b,g), field hockey (g), lacrosse (b), soccer (b,g), softball (g), tennis (b,g); coed interscholastic: cross-country running, golf, swimming and diving. 3 PE instructors, 12 coaches, 1 athletic trainer.

Computers Computers are regularly used in art, English, foreign language, history, mathematics, music, science classes. Computer resources include on-campus library services, Internet access, wireless campus network.

Contact Daniel Axford, Director of Admissions. 610-691-1600. Fax: 610-691-3354. E-mail: daxford@moravianacademy.org. Web site: www.moravianacademy.org.

See Close-Up on page 862.

MOREAU CATHOLIC HIGH SCHOOL

27170 Mission Boulevard
Hayward, California 94544

Head of School: Mr. Terry Lee

General Information Coeducational day college-preparatory, arts, business, religious studies, and technology school, affiliated with Roman Catholic Church; primarily serves students with learning disabilities and Saints and Scholars program for students with documented learning disabilities who require accommodations. Grades 9–12. Founded: 1965. Setting: suburban. Nearest major city is Oakland. 14-acre campus. 6 buildings on campus. Approved or accredited by National Catholic Education Association, Western Association of Schools and Colleges, Western Catholic Education Association, and California Department of Education. Endowment: $2.5 million. Total enrollment: 930. Upper school average class size: 27. Upper school faculty-student ratio: 1:18.

Upper School Student Profile Grade 9: 227 students (104 boys, 123 girls); Grade 10: 227 students (107 boys, 120 girls); Grade 11: 242 students (124 boys, 118 girls); Grade 12: 234 students (124 boys, 110 girls). 72% of students are Roman Catholic.

Faculty School total: 60. In upper school: 25 men, 32 women; 34 have advanced degrees.

Subjects Offered Advanced Placement courses, aerobics, algebra, American Civil War, American government-AP, American history, American literature, anatomy, art, art history, ASB Leadership, astronomy, athletics, biology, biology-AP, business, business law, business skills, calculus, calculus-AP, campus ministry, ceramics, cheerleading, chemistry, choral music, Christian ethics, Christian scripture, Christianity, church history, community service, computer education, computer math, computer programming, computer science, concert band, creative writing, drafting, drama, drama performance, driver education, earth science, economics, electronics, engineering, English, English literature, English/composition-AP, ethics, ethics and responsibility, European history, expository writing, fine arts, French, French-AP, geometry, government-AP, government/civics, grammar, health, health education,

history, history of the Catholic Church, home economics, honors algebra, honors English, honors geometry, honors U.S. history, honors world history, human biology, instrumental music, jazz band, jazz ensemble, journalism, marching band, mathematics, mechanical drawing, media studies, moral and social development, moral theology, music, music appreciation, newspaper, physical education, physics, physics-AP, physiology, psychology, religion, science, sculpture, social science, social studies, Spanish, Spanish language-AP, speech, sports medicine, sports science, student government, student publications, symphonic band, the Sixties, theater, theology, trigonometry, typing, U.S. government, U.S. government-AP, U.S. history, U.S. history-AP, weight training, world history, world literature, writing, yearbook.
Graduation Requirements Arts and fine arts (art, music, dance, drama), computer science, English, foreign language, mathematics, physical education (includes health), religion (includes Bible studies and theology), science, social science, social studies (includes history). Community service is required.
Special Academic Programs Advanced Placement exam preparation; honors section.
College Admission Counseling 232 students graduated in 2008; 230 went to college, including California State University; Saint Mary's College of California; Santa Clara University; Stanford University; University of California, Berkeley; University of San Francisco. Other: 2 entered military service. Mean SAT critical reading: 555, mean SAT math: 559, mean composite ACT: 23.
Student Life Upper grades have specified standards of dress, student council. Discipline rests primarily with faculty. Attendance at religious services is required.
Summer Programs Remediation, enrichment, sports programs offered; session focuses on enrichment and remediation; held on campus; accepts boys and girls; open to students from other schools. 245 students usually enrolled. 2009 schedule: June 21 to July 30. Application deadline: May 31.
Tuition and Aid Day student tuition: $10,944. Tuition installment plan (FACTS Tuition Payment Plan). Tuition reduction for siblings, merit scholarship grants, need-based scholarship grants, paying campus jobs available. In 2008–09, 35% of upper-school students received aid. Total amount of financial aid awarded in 2008–09: $775,000.
Admissions Traditional secondary-level entrance grade is 9. For fall 2008, 312 students applied for upper-level admission, 295 were accepted, 232 enrolled. Scholastic Testing Service High School Placement Test required. Deadline for receipt of application materials: January 10. Application fee required: $75. On-campus interview required.
Athletics Interscholastic: aquatics (boys, girls), badminton (b,g), baseball (b), basketball (b,g), cheering (g), cross-country running (b,g), dance squad (g), football (b), golf (b,g), soccer (b,g), softball (g), swimming and diving (b,g), tennis (b,g), track and field (b,g), volleyball (b,g); intramural: lacrosse (g); coed interscholastic: aerobics/dance, modern dance; coed intramural: equestrian sports, skiing (downhill), strength & conditioning. 5 PE instructors, 50 coaches, 1 athletic trainer.
Computers Computers are regularly used in career exploration, college planning, English, foreign language, history, journalism, keyboarding, mathematics, newspaper, religious studies, science, technology, theology, yearbook classes. Computer network features include on-campus library services, online commercial services, Internet access, wireless campus network, PowerSchool grade program, 1:1 student laptop program (Every student at Moreau has a laptop). Campus intranet, student e-mail accounts, and computer access in designated common areas are available to students. Students grades are available online. The school has a published electronic and media policy.
Contact Patricia Bevilacqua, Admissions Assistant. 510-881-4320. Fax: 510-581-5669. E-mail: apply@moreaucatholic.org. Web site: www.moreaucatholic.org.

MORGAN PARK ACADEMY

2153 West 111th Street
Chicago, Illinois 60643

Head of School: Barbara Tubutis

General Information Coeducational day college-preparatory, arts, and technology school. Grades PK–12. Founded: 1873. Setting: urban. 20-acre campus. 5 buildings on campus. Approved or accredited by Independent Schools Association of the Central States and Illinois Department of Education. Member of National Association of Independent Schools. Endowment: $905,450. Total enrollment: 474. Upper school average class size: 14. Upper school faculty-student ratio: 1:5.
Upper School Student Profile Grade 9: 39 students (13 boys, 26 girls); Grade 10: 38 students (18 boys, 20 girls); Grade 11: 40 students (14 boys, 26 girls); Grade 12: 40 students (26 boys, 14 girls).
Faculty School total: 62. In upper school: 12 men, 14 women; 20 have advanced degrees.
Subjects Offered Accounting, algebra, American history, American literature, art, art history, biology, calculus, chemistry, Coming of Age in the 20th Century, computer programming, computer science, creative writing, current events, drama, driver education, English, English literature, expository writing, fine arts, French, general science, geography, geometry, health, history, humanities, journalism, mathematics, music, physical education, physics, political science, science, social studies, Spanish, speech, studio art, trigonometry, word processing, world history, world literature, writing.
Graduation Requirements Arts and fine arts (art, music, dance, drama), English, foreign language, history, lab science, mathematics, physical education (includes health).
Special Academic Programs Advanced Placement exam preparation; honors section; independent study; study abroad; academic accommodation for the gifted, the musically talented, and the artistically talented.
College Admission Counseling 48 students graduated in 2008; all went to college, including Brown University; Northwestern University; University of Illinois; University of Michigan; Washington University in St. Louis. Median composite ACT: 27. 50% scored over 600 on SAT critical reading, 80% scored over 600 on SAT math, 57% scored over 26 on composite ACT.
Student Life Upper grades have specified standards of dress, student council, honor system. Discipline rests equally with students and faculty.
Summer Programs Remediation, enrichment, advancement, art/fine arts, computer instruction programs offered; session focuses on academics, sports and recreation; held on campus; accepts boys and girls; open to students from other schools. 300 students usually enrolled. 2009 schedule: June 22 to July 31. Application deadline: none.
Tuition and Aid Day student tuition: $17,300. Tuition installment plan (FACTS Tuition Payment Plan). Tuition reduction for siblings, merit scholarship grants, need-based scholarship grants available. In 2008–09, 22% of upper-school students received aid. Total amount of financial aid awarded in 2008–09: $137,450.
Admissions Traditional secondary-level entrance grade is 9. For fall 2008, 65 students applied for upper-level admission, 40 were accepted, 30 enrolled. Admissions testing, OLSAT, Stanford Achievement Test and writing sample required. Deadline for receipt of application materials: none. Application fee required: $50. On-campus interview required.
Athletics Interscholastic: baseball (boys), basketball (b,g), cheering (b,g), cross-country running (b,g), golf (b,g), soccer (b,g), softball (b,g), tennis (b,g), volleyball (g); coed interscholastic: golf, soccer, track and field; coed intramural: archery, badminton, bowling, football, golf, paddle tennis, skiing (cross-country), table tennis, weight lifting. 4 PE instructors, 4 coaches.
Computers Computers are regularly used in art, economics, English, foreign language, graphic arts, history, humanities, journalism, mathematics, news writing, newspaper, science, Spanish, yearbook classes. Computer network features include on-campus library services, online commercial services, Internet access.
Contact Andrea Durbin-Odom, Director of Admissions. 773-881-6700 Ext. 232. Fax: 773-881-8409. E-mail: adurbin@morganparkacademy.org. Web site: www.MorganParkAcademy.org.

MORRISTOWN-BEARD SCHOOL

70 Whippany Road
Morristown, New Jersey 07960

Head of School: Dr. Alex D. Curtis, PhD

General Information Coeducational day college-preparatory and arts school. Grades 6–12. Founded: 1891. Setting: suburban. Nearest major city is New York, NY. 22-acre campus. 11 buildings on campus. Approved or accredited by Middle States Association of Colleges and Schools, New Jersey Association of Independent Schools, and New Jersey Department of Education. Member of National Association of Independent Schools and Secondary School Admission Test Board. Endowment: $100 million. Total enrollment: 529. Upper school average class size: 12. Upper school faculty-student ratio: 1:7.
Upper School Student Profile Grade 6: 42 students (26 boys, 16 girls); Grade 7: 52 students (23 boys, 29 girls); Grade 8: 52 students (29 boys, 23 girls); Grade 9: 99 students (56 boys, 43 girls); Grade 10: 96 students (47 boys, 49 girls); Grade 11: 103 students (59 boys, 44 girls); Grade 12: 94 students (50 boys, 44 girls).
Faculty School total: 93. In upper school: 54 have advanced degrees.
Subjects Offered 20th century history, acting, advanced chemistry, advanced math, Advanced Placement courses, advanced studio art-AP, African history, African literature, African studies, algebra, American history, American legal systems, American studies, anatomy and physiology, ancient world history, architecture, art, art history, Asian studies, astronomy, astrophysics, Bible as literature, biology, biology-AP, calculus, calculus-AP, career exploration, ceramics, chemistry, chemistry-AP, choir, chorus, community service, computer programming, computer science, computer science-AP, computer skills, computer studies, constitutional law, creative writing, dance, drama, drawing, earth science, ecology, engineering, English, English-AP, fine arts, French, geometry, health, instrumental music, journalism, Latin, Middle Eastern history, mythology, nature writers, painting, photography, physical education, physical science, physics, physics-AP, public speaking, regional literature, rite of passage, Spanish, Spanish-AP, speech, statistics, statistics-AP, studio art—AP, the comic tradition, theater, trigonometry, U.S. history-AP, women in literature, world history.
Graduation Requirements Arts and fine arts (art, music, dance, drama), English, foreign language, mathematics, physical education (includes health), science, service learning/internship, social studies (includes history). Community service is required.
Special Academic Programs Advanced Placement exam preparation; honors section; independent study; term-away projects; study abroad.
College Admission Counseling 76 students graduated in 2008; 74 went to college. Other: 2 entered a postgraduate year. Mean SAT critical reading: 572, mean SAT math: 598, mean SAT writing: 595, mean composite ACT: 24.

Student Life Upper grades have specified standards of dress, student council, honor system. Discipline rests equally with students and faculty.
Summer Programs Enrichment, advancement, sports, art/fine arts, computer instruction programs offered; session focuses on traditional day camp; held on campus; accepts boys and girls; open to students from other schools. 700 students usually enrolled. 2009 schedule: June 22 to August 4.
Tuition and Aid Day student tuition: $28,530. Tuition installment plan (Tuition Management Services). Merit scholarship grants, need-based scholarship grants, need-based loans available. In 2008–09, 13% of upper-school students received aid; total upper-school merit-scholarship money awarded: $85,500. Total amount of financial aid awarded in 2008–09: $1,000,000.
Admissions Traditional secondary-level entrance grade is 9. ISEE or SSAT required. Deadline for receipt of application materials: February 9. Application fee required: $55. On-campus interview required.
Athletics Interscholastic: baseball (boys), basketball (b,g), field hockey (g), football (b), ice hockey (b,g), lacrosse (b,g), skiing (downhill) (b,g), soccer (b,g), softball (g), swimming and diving (b,g), tennis (b,g), track and field (b,g), volleyball (g); coed interscholastic: alpine skiing, cross-country running, dance, golf, swimming and diving, track and field, yoga; coed intramural: dance, figure skating, fitness, mountain biking, Nautilus, physical fitness. 4 PE instructors, 3 coaches, 1 athletic trainer.
Computers Computers are regularly used in architecture, art, English, foreign language, history, mathematics, music, science classes. Computer network features include on-campus library services, online commercial services, Internet access, wireless campus network, Internet filtering or blocking technology, Jstor, Jerseycat. Student e-mail accounts are available to students.
Contact Mrs. Barbara Luperi, Admission Assistant. 973-539-3032. Fax: 973-539-1590. E-mail: bluperi@mobeard.org. Web site: www.mobeard.org.

See Close-Up on page 864.

MOSES BROWN SCHOOL

250 Lloyd Avenue
Providence, Rhode Island 02906

Head of School: Joanne P. Hoffman

General Information Coeducational day college-preparatory, arts, religious studies, and technology school, affiliated with Society of Friends. Grades N–12. Founded: 1784. Setting: urban. Nearest major city is Boston, MA. 32-acre campus. 16 buildings on campus. Approved or accredited by Association of Independent Schools in New England, New England Association of Schools and Colleges, and Rhode Island Department of Education. Member of National Association of Independent Schools and Secondary School Admission Test Board. Endowment: $13 million. Total enrollment: 787. Upper school average class size: 12. Upper school faculty-student ratio: 1:8.
Upper School Student Profile Grade 9: 101 students (49 boys, 52 girls); Grade 10: 100 students (52 boys, 48 girls); Grade 11: 97 students (51 boys, 46 girls); Grade 12: 95 students (46 boys, 49 girls). 3% of students are members of Society of Friends.
Faculty School total: 103. In upper school: 17 men, 34 women; 38 have advanced degrees.
Subjects Offered Acting, algebra, American history, American literature, art, art history, astronomy, Bible studies, biology, calculus, ceramics, chemistry, community service, computer graphics, computer programming, computer science, creative writing, dance, drama, English, English literature, environmental science, ethics, European history, evolution, expository writing, film, fine arts, French, geometry, government/civics, history, history of science, Italian, Japanese, jazz ensemble, Latin, marine biology, mathematics, music, music appreciation, music theory, philosophy, photography, physical education, physics, pre-calculus, religion, science, social studies, Spanish, statistics, studio art, theater, theology, trigonometry, world history, world literature, world wide web design, writing.
Graduation Requirements Arts and fine arts (art, music, dance, drama), English, foreign language, mathematics, religion (includes Bible studies and theology), science, social studies (includes history), technology, Quaker seminar, co-curricular subjects.
Special Academic Programs Advanced Placement exam preparation; honors section; independent study; remedial reading and/or remedial writing.
College Admission Counseling 96 students graduated in 2008; 95 went to college, including Boston University; Brown University; New York University; Northeastern University; The Johns Hopkins University; Tufts University. Other: 1 had other specific plans. Median SAT critical reading: 640, median SAT math: 650, median combined SAT: 1300, median composite ACT: 27. 56% scored over 600 on SAT critical reading, 70% scored over 600 on SAT math, 74% scored over 1800 on combined SAT, 59% scored over 26 on composite ACT.
Student Life Upper grades have specified standards of dress, student council, honor system. Discipline rests equally with students and faculty. Attendance at religious services is required.
Summer Programs Remediation, enrichment, advancement, ESL, art/fine arts, computer instruction programs offered; held on campus; accepts boys and girls; open to students from other schools. 175 students usually enrolled. 2009 schedule: June 27 to August 5. Application deadline: none.
Tuition and Aid Day student tuition: $23,620. Tuition installment plan (Academic Management Services Plan, monthly payment plans). Need-based scholarship grants available. In 2008–09, 24% of upper-school students received aid. Total amount of financial aid awarded in 2008–09: $798,040.
Admissions Traditional secondary-level entrance grade is 9. For fall 2008, 252 students applied for upper-level admission, 83 were accepted, 52 enrolled. ISEE or SSAT required. Deadline for receipt of application materials: February 11. Application fee required: $55. On-campus interview required.
Athletics Interscholastic: baseball (boys), basketball (b,g), cross-country running (b,g), field hockey (g), fitness (b,g), football (b), ice hockey (b,g), independent competitive sports (b,g), indoor track & field (b,g), lacrosse (b,g), physical fitness (b,g), soccer (b,g), softball (g), squash (b,g), tennis (b,g), track and field (b,g), wrestling (b); coed interscholastic: golf, sailing, swimming and diving, yoga; coed intramural: dance. 5 PE instructors, 20 coaches, 1 athletic trainer.
Computers Computers are regularly used in English, foreign language, history, mathematics, music, science classes. Computer network features include on-campus library services, Internet access, Internet filtering or blocking technology, scanners. Campus intranet, student e-mail accounts, and computer access in designated common areas are available to students. The school has a published electronic and media policy.
Contact Hugh A. Madden, Interim Director of Admissions. 401-831-7350. Fax: 401-455-0084. E-mail: hmadden@mosesbrown.org. Web site: www.mosesbrown.org.

MOTHER CABRINI HIGH SCHOOL

701 Fort Washington Avenue
New York, New York 10040

Head of School: Mrs. Rose K. McTague

General Information Girls' day college-preparatory school, affiliated with Roman Catholic Church. Grades 9–12. Founded: 1899. Setting: urban. 2-acre campus. 1 building on campus. Approved or accredited by Middle States Association of Colleges and Schools, National Catholic Education Association, New York State Board of Regents, and The College Board. Total enrollment: 350. Upper school average class size: 22. Upper school faculty-student ratio: 1:13.
Upper School Student Profile 75% of students are Roman Catholic.
Faculty School total: 35. In upper school: 8 men, 26 women; 25 have advanced degrees.
Subjects Offered Accounting, algebra, American literature, anatomy and physiology, art, art history, basketball, chemistry, computer applications, computer science, English literature, environmental science, forensic science, geometry, guidance, health, honors algebra, honors geometry, literature, peer counseling, photo shop, physics, pre-algebra, pre-calculus, religion, softball, Spanish, Spanish literature, Spanish-AP, speech, U.S. government, U.S. history-AP, volleyball, world literature.
Graduation Requirements Art, electives, English, language, mathematics, music, physical education (includes health), science, social studies (includes history).
Special Academic Programs 5 Advanced Placement exams for which test preparation is offered; honors section; study at local college for college credit.
College Admission Counseling 114 students graduated in 2008; all went to college, including City College of the City University of New York; Fairfield University; Fordham University; John Jay College of Criminal Justice of the City University of New York; Manhattan College.
Student Life Upper grades have uniform requirement, student council. Discipline rests equally with students and faculty. Attendance at religious services is required.
Summer Programs Remediation, enrichment programs offered; held on campus; accepts girls; not open to students from other schools.
Tuition and Aid Tuition installment plan (SMART Tuition Payment Plan). Tuition reduction for siblings, merit scholarship grants, need-based scholarship grants, paying campus jobs available. In 2008–09, 50% of upper-school students received aid.
Admissions Traditional secondary-level entrance grade is 9. For fall 2008, 364 students applied for upper-level admission, 306 were accepted, 86 enrolled. Catholic High School Entrance Examination, Gates MacGinite Reading Tests and Otis-Lennon School Ability Test required. Deadline for receipt of application materials: none. No application fee required.
Athletics Interscholastic: basketball, cheering, softball, volleyball; intramural: aerobics/dance, running.
Computers Computer resources include on-campus library services, Internet access, Internet filtering or blocking technology. Campus intranet and student e-mail accounts are available to students.
Contact Ms. Cheryl P. Hallenback, Director of Recruitment and Public Relations. 212-923-3540 Ext. 17. Fax: 212-923-3960. E-mail: Cheryl.Hallenback@cabrinihs.org. Web site: www.cabrinihs.com.

MOTHER MCAULEY HIGH SCHOOL

3737 West 99th Street
Chicago, Illinois 60655-3133

Head of School: Dr. Christine M. Melone

General Information Girls' day college-preparatory, arts, religious studies, and technology school, affiliated with Roman Catholic Church. Grades 9–12. Founded: 1846. Setting: urban. 21-acre campus. 2 buildings on campus. Approved or accredited by Mercy Secondary Education Association, National Catholic Education Association, North Central Association of Colleges and Schools, The College Board, and

Illinois Department of Education. Endowment: $2 million. Total enrollment: 1,393. Upper school average class size: 25. Upper school faculty-student ratio: 1:15.
Upper School Student Profile Grade 9: 339 students (339 girls); Grade 10: 382 students (382 girls); Grade 11: 341 students (341 girls); Grade 12: 331 students (331 girls). 87% of students are Roman Catholic.
Faculty School total: 92. In upper school: 12 men, 80 women; 56 have advanced degrees.
Subjects Offered Anatomy and physiology, art history, art history-AP, calculus-AP, ceramics, chemistry-AP, English, English literature, English literature and composition-AP, European history-AP, first aid, French, French-AP, general science, geography, geometry, geometry with art applications, global issues, graphic design, history of the Catholic Church, honors algebra, honors English, honors geometry, honors U.S. history, honors world history, introduction to theater, journalism, Latin, Latin-AP, Life of Christ, marching band, media literacy, music appreciation, newspaper, orchestra, painting, photography, physical education, physics, play production, scripture, Spanish, Spanish-AP, speech, studio art, studio art-AP, theater, theology, U.S. history, U.S. history-AP, U.S. literature, Web site design, wind ensemble, world history, world history-AP, yearbook.
Graduation Requirements Art history, English, lab science, language, mathematics, music, physical education (includes health), social sciences, speech, theology.
Special Academic Programs Advanced Placement exam preparation; honors section; study at local college for college credit.
College Admission Counseling 367 students graduated in 2008; 366 went to college, including Eastern Illinois University; Illinois State University; Loyola University Chicago; University of Illinois at Chicago; University of Illinois at Urbana–Champaign. Other: 1 went to work.
Student Life Upper grades have uniform requirement, student council. Discipline rests primarily with faculty. Attendance at religious services is required.
Summer Programs Remediation, enrichment, advancement, sports, art/fine arts, computer instruction programs offered; session focuses on academics; held on campus; accepts girls; open to students from other schools. 200 students usually enrolled. 2009 schedule: June 15 to July 24. Application deadline: June 12.
Tuition and Aid Day student tuition: $7950. Tuition installment plan (monthly payment plans, individually arranged payment plans). Tuition reduction for siblings, merit scholarship grants, need-based scholarship grants, paying campus jobs available. In 2008–09, 25% of upper-school students received aid; total upper-school merit-scholarship money awarded: $3500. Total amount of financial aid awarded in 2008–09: $495,100.
Admissions Traditional secondary-level entrance grade is 9. For fall 2008, 454 students applied for upper-level admission, 370 were accepted, 365 enrolled. ACT-Explore required. Deadline for receipt of application materials: August 15. Application fee required: $150. On-campus interview required.
Athletics Interscholastic: basketball, cross-country running, diving, golf, independent competitive sports, soccer, softball, swimming and diving, tennis, track and field, volleyball, water polo; intramural: aerobics, basketball, bowling, Frisbee, softball, ultimate Frisbee, volleyball. 3 PE instructors, 20 coaches, 1 athletic trainer.
Computers Computers are regularly used in accounting, art, basic skills, business education, drafting, drawing and design, English, foreign language, French, graphics, journalism, Latin, mathematics, music, newspaper, photography, science, social sciences, Spanish, theater, Web site design, writing, yearbook classes. Computer network features include on-campus library services, Internet access, Internet filtering or blocking technology. Computer access in designated common areas is available to students. Students grades are available online. The school has a published electronic and media policy.
Contact Mrs. Kathryn Klyczek, Director of Admissions. 773-881-6534. Fax: 773-429-4235. E-mail: kklyczek@mothermcauley.org. Web site: www.mothermcauley.org.

MOUNDS PARK ACADEMY

2051 Larpenteur Avenue East
St. Paul, Minnesota 55109

Head of School: Michael Downs

General Information Coeducational day college-preparatory, arts, bilingual studies, and technology school. Grades PK–12. Founded: 1982. Setting: suburban. 32-acre campus. 1 building on campus. Approved or accredited by Independent Schools Association of the Central States and Minnesota Department of Education. Member of National Association of Independent Schools. Endowment: $2.7 million. Total enrollment: 625. Upper school average class size: 16. Upper school faculty-student ratio: 1:9.
Upper School Student Profile Grade 9: 64 students (33 boys, 31 girls); Grade 10: 65 students (38 boys, 27 girls); Grade 11: 52 students (21 boys, 31 girls); Grade 12: 69 students (35 boys, 34 girls).
Faculty School total: 76. In upper school: 9 men, 18 women; 14 have advanced degrees.
Subjects Offered Algebra, American history, American literature, anatomy, area studies, art, biology, calculus, ceramics, chemistry, chorus, contemporary women writers, creative writing, debate, design, drama, drawing, economics, English literature, fine arts, French, geometry, health, history, independent study, law, literature, mathematics, media, men's studies, multicultural literature, music, painting, photography, physical education, physical science, physics, physiology, psychology, public policy issues and action, science, senior seminar, social science, social studies, Spanish, speech, statistics, theater, trigonometry, Western civilization, world literature, writing.
Graduation Requirements Arts and fine arts (art, music, dance, drama), English, foreign language, health education, mathematics, physical education (includes health), science, senior seminar, social studies (includes history), senior performance. Community service is required.
Special Academic Programs 4 Advanced Placement exams for which test preparation is offered; honors section; independent study; study at local college for college credit.
College Admission Counseling 56 students graduated in 2008; all went to college, including Dartmouth College; Hamline University; Macalester College; St. Olaf College; University of Wisconsin–Madison. Mean SAT critical reading: 629, mean SAT math: 597, mean SAT writing: 611, mean combined SAT: 1226, mean composite ACT: 27.
Student Life Upper grades have specified standards of dress, student council. Discipline rests equally with students and faculty.
Summer Programs Enrichment, sports, art/fine arts programs offered; held on campus; accepts boys and girls; open to students from other schools. 350 students usually enrolled. 2009 schedule: June 15 to August 15.
Tuition and Aid Day student tuition: $19,380. Tuition installment plan (monthly payment plans, 2-payment plan, 3-payment plan, 8-payment plan, 12-payment plan). Need-based scholarship grants available. In 2008–09, 10% of upper-school students received aid. Total amount of financial aid awarded in 2008–09: $312,705.
Admissions Traditional secondary-level entrance grade is 9. For fall 2008, 31 students applied for upper-level admission, 20 were accepted, 13 enrolled. Writing sample required. Deadline for receipt of application materials: March 2. Application fee required: $50. Interview required.
Athletics Interscholastic: alpine skiing (boys, girls), baseball (b), basketball (b,g), cross-country running (b,g), dance team (g), equestrian sports (g), football (b), golf (b,g), hockey (b), ice hockey (b), nordic skiing (b,g), skiing (cross-country) (b,g), skiing (downhill) (b,g), soccer (b,g), softball (g), swimming and diving (g), tennis (b,g), track and field (b,g), volleyball (g). 6 PE instructors.
Computers Computers are regularly used in English, foreign language, mathematics, science, social studies classes. Computer network features include on-campus library services, online commercial services, Internet access, wireless campus network, Internet filtering or blocking technology. Student e-mail accounts are available to students. Students grades are available online. The school has a published electronic and media policy.
Contact Linda Hoopes, Director of Admission. 651-748-5577. Fax: 651-748-5534. E-mail: lhoopes@moundsparkacademy.org. Web site: www.moundsparkacademy.org.

MOUNT BACHELOR ACADEMY

Prineville, Oregon
See Special Needs Schools section.

MOUNT MICHAEL BENEDICTINE SCHOOL

22520 Mount Michael Road
Elkhorn, Nebraska 68022-3400

Head of School: Mr. Tom Ridder

General Information Boys' boarding and day college-preparatory, arts, religious studies, and technology school, affiliated with Roman Catholic Church. Grades 9–12. Founded: 1970. Setting: suburban. Nearest major city is Omaha. Students are housed in single-sex dormitories and private homes. 440-acre campus. 1 building on campus. Approved or accredited by European Council of International Schools, National Catholic Education Association, North Central Association of Colleges and Schools, The College Board, and Nebraska Department of Education. Endowment: $2.5 million. Total enrollment: 172. Upper school average class size: 14. Upper school faculty-student ratio: 1:9.
Upper School Student Profile Grade 9: 75 students (75 boys); Grade 10: 55 students (55 boys); Grade 11: 44 students (44 boys); Grade 12: 37 students (37 boys). 18% of students are boarding students. 78% are state residents. 4 states are represented in upper school student body. 17% are international students. International students from Canada, China, Indonesia, Republic of Korea, Rwanda, and Thailand. 83% of students are Roman Catholic.
Faculty School total: 26. In upper school: 18 men, 5 women; 11 have advanced degrees; 11 reside on campus.
Subjects Offered Accounting, Advanced Placement courses, algebra, American history, American history-AP, American literature, architectural drawing, art, band, Basic programming, basketball, bioethics, DNA and culture, biology, business, business skills, calculus-AP, ceramics, chemistry, chemistry-AP, chorus, Christian doctrine, Christian ethics, Christian scripture, Christianity, community service, computer programming, computer science, critical writing, drafting, drama, economics, English, English literature, English literature and composition-AP, European history, European history-AP, film studies, forensics, French, French language-AP, geography, geometry, government/civics, health education, Hebrew scripture, history of the Catholic Church, journalism, keyboarding/computer, math applications,

mathematics, music, physical education, physics, physics-AP, reading, science, social science, social studies, Spanish, speech, theater, theology, trigonometry, weight training, Western civilization, world religions, wrestling, writing, yearbook.

Graduation Requirements Advanced math, algebra, American government, American history, biology, biology-AP, career/college preparation, chemistry, Christian studies, computer science, economics, economics and history, English, foreign language, geometry, government, mathematics, physical education (includes health), physics, physiology-anatomy, pre-calculus, social studies (includes history), speech, Western civilization, world culture, world religions, Service Hour Requirement. Community service is required.

Special Academic Programs Advanced Placement exam preparation; honors section; independent study; study at local college for college credit.

College Admission Counseling 33 students graduated in 2008; all went to college, including Benedictine College; Kansas State University; Marquette University; University of Nebraska–Lincoln; University of Nebraska at Omaha; University of Tulsa. Median SAT critical reading: 610, median SAT math: 780, median SAT writing: 670, median combined SAT: 2000, median composite ACT: 28. 66% scored over 600 on SAT critical reading, 77% scored over 600 on SAT math, 89% scored over 600 on SAT writing, 89% scored over 1800 on combined SAT, 70% scored over 26 on composite ACT.

Student Life Upper grades have specified standards of dress, student council, honor system. Discipline rests primarily with faculty. Attendance at religious services is required.

Tuition and Aid Day student tuition: $7720–$7995; 5-day tuition and room/board: $12,790–$13,065; 7-day tuition and room/board: $14,890–$15,165. Tuition installment plan (FACTS Tuition Payment Plan). Tuition reduction for siblings, bursaries, merit scholarship grants, need-based loans, paying campus jobs available. In 2008–09, 48% of upper-school students received aid; total upper-school merit-scholarship money awarded: $101,900. Total amount of financial aid awarded in 2008–09: $240,000.

Admissions Traditional secondary-level entrance grade is 9. For fall 2008, 87 students applied for upper-level admission, 55 were accepted, 51 enrolled. California Achievement Test, Explore, High School Placement Test, Iowa Tests of Basic Skills or Stanford Achievement Test required. Deadline for receipt of application materials: none. Application fee required: $30. Interview required.

Athletics Interscholastic: baseball (boys), basketball (b), bowling (b), cheering (b), cross-country running (b), diving (b), football (b), golf (b), soccer (b), swimming and diving (b), tennis (b), wrestling (b); intramural: ball hockey (b), basketball (b), flag football (b), floor hockey (b), physical fitness (b), physical training (b), soccer (b), strength & conditioning (b), ultimate Frisbee (b), weight lifting (b), weight training (b). 3 PE instructors, 11 coaches, 2 athletic trainers.

Computers Computers are regularly used in architecture, career education, career exploration, career technology, college planning, drafting, economics, French, geography, history, journalism, keyboarding, library, mathematics, newspaper, science, Spanish, stock market, Web site design, yearbook classes. Computer network features include on-campus library services, online commercial services, Internet access, Internet filtering or blocking technology. Campus intranet, student e-mail accounts, and computer access in designated common areas are available to students. Students grades are available online. The school has a published electronic and media policy.

Contact Mr. Eric Crawford, Director of Admissions. 402-253-0946. Fax: 402-289-4539. E-mail: ecrawford@mountmichael.org. Web site: www.mountmichaelhs.com.

MOUNT SAINT CHARLES ACADEMY

800 Logee Street
Woonsocket, Rhode Island 02895-5599

Head of School: Br. Robert R. Croteau, SC

General Information Coeducational day college-preparatory, arts, and religious studies school, affiliated with Roman Catholic Church. Grades 7–12. Founded: 1924. Setting: suburban. Nearest major city is Providence. 22-acre campus. 2 buildings on campus. Approved or accredited by New England Association of Schools and Colleges and Rhode Island Department of Education. Total enrollment: 993. Upper school average class size: 25. Upper school faculty-student ratio: 1:14.

Upper School Student Profile Grade 7: 117 students (48 boys, 69 girls); Grade 8: 151 students (68 boys, 83 girls); Grade 9: 198 students (95 boys, 103 girls); Grade 10: 181 students (79 boys, 102 girls); Grade 11: 173 students (81 boys, 92 girls); Grade 12: 173 students (84 boys, 89 girls). 85% of students are Roman Catholic.

Faculty School total: 55. In upper school: 26 men, 26 women; 30 have advanced degrees.

Subjects Offered Advanced computer applications, algebra, American literature, architecture, art, art history, art-AP, band, biology, biology-AP, British literature, calculus, calculus-AP, chemistry, chorus, computer science, creative writing, dance, drama, economics, English, English language and composition-AP, English literature, English literature and composition-AP, English literature-AP, environmental science, environmental science-AP, ethics, European history, European history-AP, expository writing, fine arts, forensic science, French, geography, geometry, government, government and politics-AP, government/civics, handbells, health education, history, history of the Catholic Church, honors U.S. history, honors world history, jazz band, mathematics, mathematics-AP, modern European history, music, music theory-AP, physical education, physics, physiology, psychology, psychology-AP, religion, science, social studies, Spanish, theater, trigonometry, U.S. history, U.S. history-AP, world history, world literature, writing, yearbook.

Graduation Requirements Arts and fine arts (art, music, dance, drama), computer science, English, foreign language, mathematics, physical education (includes health), religion (includes Bible studies and theology), science, social studies (includes history).

Special Academic Programs Advanced Placement exam preparation; honors section; study at local college for college credit; special instructional classes for Individualized programs through the Academic Support Program.

College Admission Counseling 161 students graduated in 2008; 160 went to college. Other: 1 entered a postgraduate year.

Student Life Upper grades have uniform requirement, student council. Discipline rests primarily with faculty. Attendance at religious services is required.

Summer Programs Sports, art/fine arts programs offered; session focuses on fine arts, soccer, hockey, basketball; held on campus; accepts boys and girls; open to students from other schools. 220 students usually enrolled. 2009 schedule: July. Application deadline: none.

Tuition and Aid Day student tuition: $9800. Tuition installment plan (FACTS Tuition Payment Plan, full-payment discount plan). Need-based scholarship grants available. In 2008–09, 25% of upper-school students received aid. Total amount of financial aid awarded in 2008–09: $600,000.

Admissions Traditional secondary-level entrance grade is 7. For fall 2008, 375 students applied for upper-level admission, 225 were accepted, 205 enrolled. Diocesan Entrance Exam, ISEE, SAS, STS-HSPT, SSAT or STS required. Deadline for receipt of application materials: none. Application fee required: $25.

Athletics Interscholastic: baseball (boys), basketball (b,g), cheering (g), cross-country running (b,g), gymnastics (g), ice hockey (b,g), indoor track (b,g), lacrosse (b,g), sailing (b,g), soccer (b,g), softball (g), swimming and diving (b,g), tennis (b,g), track and field (b,g), volleyball (b,g); intramural: aerobics/dance (g), basketball (b,g), dance (g); coed interscholastic: golf; coed intramural: billiards, bowling, dance team, flag football, indoor soccer, lacrosse, soccer, strength & conditioning. 4 PE instructors, 15 coaches, 1 athletic trainer.

Computers Computers are regularly used in accounting, architecture, art, computer applications, desktop publishing, graphic design, science, yearbook classes. Computer network features include on-campus library services, online commercial services, Internet access, Internet filtering or blocking technology, college/financial aid searches. Campus intranet and computer access in designated common areas are available to students. Students grades are available online. The school has a published electronic and media policy.

Contact Joseph J. O'Neill Jr., Registrar/Director of Admissions. 401-769-0310 Ext. 137. Fax: 401-762-2327. E-mail: admissions@mountsaintcharles.org. Web site: www.mountsaintcharles.org.

MT. SAINT DOMINIC ACADEMY

3 Ryerson Avenue
Caldwell, New Jersey 07006

Head of School: Sr. Frances Sullivan, OP

General Information Girls' day college-preparatory, arts, religious studies, and technology school, affiliated with Roman Catholic Church. Grades 9–12. Founded: 1892. Setting: suburban. Nearest major city is Newark. 70-acre campus. 3 buildings on campus. Approved or accredited by Middle States Association of Colleges and Schools, New Jersey Association of Independent Schools, and New Jersey Department of Education. Endowment: $1.6 million. Total enrollment: 330. Upper school average class size: 10. Upper school faculty-student ratio: 1:10.

Upper School Student Profile Grade 9: 94 students (94 girls); Grade 10: 69 students (69 girls); Grade 11: 100 students (100 girls); Grade 12: 67 students (67 girls). 88% of students are Roman Catholic.

Faculty School total: 40. In upper school: 5 men, 35 women; 30 have advanced degrees.

Subjects Offered Advanced math, algebra, American history-AP, American legal systems, American literature, American literature-AP, art, art appreciation, art history-AP, Bible studies, biology, biology-AP, British literature, British literature (honors), British literature-AP, calculus, calculus-AP, Catholic belief and practice, chemistry, choir, college placement, communication skills, computer applications, computer keyboarding, computer programming, computer science, CPR, creative writing, dance, debate, desktop publishing, drama, driver education, ecology, environmental systems, economics and history, English, English literature, English literature and composition-AP, environmental science, forensics, French, geometry, health, history, Holocaust studies, literature, mathematics, music, photography, physical education, physics, pre-calculus, psychology, public speaking, religion, SAT preparation, science, Spanish, studio art-AP, U.S. history, U.S. history-AP, U.S. literature, word processing, world history, world literature, world wide web design, World-Wide-Web publishing.

Graduation Requirements 4 years of community service.

Special Academic Programs Advanced Placement exam preparation; honors section; independent study; academic accommodation for the gifted, the musically talented, and the artistically talented.

College Admission Counseling 88 students graduated in 2008; all went to college, including Boston College; Boston University; Colgate University; College of the Holy Cross; Dartmouth College; Tufts University. Median SAT critical reading: 548,

median SAT math: 536, median SAT writing: 564. 23% scored over 600 on SAT critical reading, 26% scored over 600 on SAT math, 43% scored over 600 on SAT writing.
Student Life Upper grades have uniform requirement, student council, honor system. Discipline rests primarily with faculty. Attendance at religious services is required.
Summer Programs Enrichment, advancement, sports programs offered; session focuses on mathematics advancement, English and math enrichment; held on campus; accepts girls; open to students from other schools. 15 students usually enrolled. 2009 schedule: June to July. Application deadline: May.
Tuition and Aid Day student tuition: $12,850. Tuition installment plan (individually arranged payment plans, one payment in full, or otherwise monthly, quarterly, or semi-annually). Tuition reduction for siblings, merit scholarship grants, need-based scholarship grants available. In 2008–09, 15% of upper-school students received aid; total upper-school merit-scholarship money awarded: $12,850.
Admissions Traditional secondary-level entrance grade is 9. For fall 2008, 205 students applied for upper-level admission, 185 were accepted, 94 enrolled. Cooperative Entrance Exam (McGraw-Hill) required. Deadline for receipt of application materials: December 15. Application fee required: $40.
Athletics Interscholastic: aerobics/dance, aquatics, basketball, cheering, cross-country running, golf, indoor track, indoor track & field, lacrosse, soccer, softball, swimming and diving, tennis, track and field, volleyball; intramural: aerobics/dance, ballet, dance, dance squad, dance team, modern dance. 2 PE instructors, 20 coaches, 1 athletic trainer.
Computers Computers are regularly used in English, foreign language, history, mathematics, music, science classes. Computer network features include on-campus library services, online commercial services, Internet access, wireless campus network, Internet filtering or blocking technology. Student e-mail accounts are available to students. Students grades are available online. The school has a published electronic and media policy.
Contact Maryann Feuerstein, Director of Admission. 973-226-0660 Ext. 1114. Fax: 973-226-2135. E-mail: mfeuerstein@msdacademy.org. Web site: www.msdacademy.org.

MOUNT SAINT JOSEPH ACADEMY

120 West Wissahickon Avenue
Flourtown, Pennsylvania 19031
Head of School: Sr. Kathleen Brabson, SSJ

General Information Girls' day college-preparatory school, affiliated with Roman Catholic Church. Grades 9–12. Founded: 1858. Setting: suburban. Nearest major city is Philadelphia. 78-acre campus. 1 building on campus. Approved or accredited by Middle States Association of Colleges and Schools, Pennsylvania Association of Independent Schools, and Pennsylvania Department of Education. Member of National Association of Independent Schools. Endowment: $3 million. Total enrollment: 570. Upper school average class size: 19. Upper school faculty-student ratio: 1:10.
Upper School Student Profile Grade 9: 145 students (145 girls); Grade 10: 145 students (145 girls); Grade 11: 140 students (140 girls); Grade 12: 140 students (140 girls). 95% of students are Roman Catholic.
Faculty School total: 61. In upper school: 16 men, 45 women; 47 have advanced degrees.
Subjects Offered Accounting, algebra, American history, American history-AP, American literature, American studies, art, art history, astronomy, biochemistry, biology, calculus, calculus-AP, chemistry, chorus, communications, computer science, design, desktop publishing, drama, drawing, economics, English, English literature, English literature-AP, ethics, European history, film, fine arts, French, French-AP, geography, geometry, government/civics, health, history, human sexuality, instrumental music, journalism, keyboarding, Latin, literature, mathematics, music, music-AP, painting, physical education, physics, physics-AP, physiology, pre-calculus, psychology, religion, science, social studies, Spanish, Spanish-AP, speech, technology, theater, theology, trigonometry, word processing, world history, world literature, writing.
Graduation Requirements Arts and fine arts (art, music, dance, drama), computer science, English, foreign language, mathematics, physical education (includes health), religion (includes Bible studies and theology), science, social studies (includes history).
Special Academic Programs 13 Advanced Placement exams for which test preparation is offered; honors section; independent study; study at local college for college credit; academic accommodation for the gifted, the musically talented, and the artistically talented.
College Admission Counseling 134 students graduated in 2008; all went to college, including Drexel University; Fordham University; Penn State University Park; Saint Joseph's University; Temple University; University of Pennsylvania. Mean SAT critical reading: 616, mean SAT math: 593, mean SAT writing: 629, mean combined SAT: 1833. 64% scored over 600 on SAT critical reading, 51% scored over 600 on SAT math.
Student Life Upper grades have uniform requirement, student council, honor system. Discipline rests primarily with faculty. Attendance at religious services is required.
Tuition and Aid Day student tuition: $12,400. Tuition installment plan (Higher Education Service, Inc, semester payment plan). Tuition reduction for siblings, merit scholarship grants, need-based scholarship grants available. In 2008–09, 35% of upper-school students received aid; total upper-school merit-scholarship money awarded: $282,490. Total amount of financial aid awarded in 2008–09: $383,975.
Admissions Traditional secondary-level entrance grade is 9. For fall 2008, 327 students applied for upper-level admission, 148 were accepted, 145 enrolled. High School Placement Test, SAS, STS-HSPT or school's own test required. Deadline for receipt of application materials: October 28. Application fee required: $75.
Athletics Interscholastic: basketball, cheering, crew, cross-country running, diving, field hockey, golf, indoor track, lacrosse, soccer, softball, swimming and diving, tennis, track and field, volleyball. 2 PE instructors, 24 coaches, 1 athletic trainer.
Computers Computers are regularly used in art, English, foreign language, history, mathematics, music, science classes. Computer network features include on-campus library services, online commercial services, Internet access, video conferencing, SmartBoards. The school has a published electronic and media policy.
Contact Ms. Carol Finney, Director of Admissions. 215-233-9133. Fax: 215-233-5887. E-mail: cfinney@msjacad.org. Web site: www.msjacad.org.

MOUNT SAINT MARY ACADEMY

1645 Highway 22
Watchung, New Jersey 07069
See Close-Up on page 866.

MUNICH INTERNATIONAL SCHOOL

Schloss Buchhof
Starnberg D-82319, Germany
Head of School: Mary Seppala, EdD

General Information Coeducational day college-preparatory, arts, business, bilingual studies, and technology school. Grades PK–12. Founded: 1966. Setting: rural. Nearest major city is Munich, Germany. 26-acre campus. 5 buildings on campus. Approved or accredited by European Council of International Schools, International Baccalaureate Organization, and New England Association of Schools and Colleges. Affiliate member of National Association of Independent Schools; member of Secondary School Admission Test Board. Language of instruction: English. Total enrollment: 1,264. Upper school average class size: 21. Upper school faculty-student ratio: 1:8.
Upper School Student Profile Grade 9: 127 students (63 boys, 64 girls); Grade 10: 98 students (51 boys, 47 girls); Grade 11: 100 students (47 boys, 53 girls); Grade 12: 95 students (42 boys, 53 girls).
Faculty School total: 164. In upper school: 23 men, 29 women; 37 have advanced degrees.
Subjects Offered Adolescent issues, algebra, art, biology, business, calculus, chemistry, community service, computer science, computer-aided design, design, drama, earth science, economics, English, English literature, ESL, European history, film studies, fine arts, French, geography, geometry, German, grammar, health, health education, history, home economics, information technology, instrumental music, integrated mathematics, International Baccalaureate courses, Japanese, journalism, lab/keyboard, library skills, math methods, mathematics, model United Nations, music, personal and social education, physical education, physics, SAT preparation, science, senior thesis, social science, social studies, Spanish, speech and debate, student government, technology/design, theater, theory of knowledge, trigonometry, world history, world literature, writing, yearbook.
Graduation Requirements Arts and fine arts (art, music, dance, drama), English, foreign language, mathematics, philosophy, physical education (includes health), science, social science, social studies (includes history), theory of knowledge, extended essay. Community service is required.
Special Academic Programs International Baccalaureate program; academic accommodation for the gifted; remedial math; ESL (20 students enrolled).
College Admission Counseling 95 students graduated in 2008; 48 went to college, including California State University, Fullerton; Colgate University; Columbia College; Rhode Island School of Design; The George Washington University; Yale University. Other: 2 went to work, 1 entered military service, 43 had other specific plans. Mean SAT critical reading: 582, mean SAT math: 587, mean SAT writing: 588, mean composite ACT: 25. 52% scored over 600 on SAT critical reading, 52% scored over 600 on SAT math, 48% scored over 600 on SAT writing, 46% scored over 26 on composite ACT.
Student Life Upper grades have specified standards of dress, student council, honor system. Discipline rests equally with students and faculty.
Summer Programs Enrichment, sports, rigorous outdoor training programs offered; held both on and off campus; held at Lake Garda (Italy); accepts boys and girls; open to students from other schools. 120 students usually enrolled. 2009 schedule: June 30 to July 14. Application deadline: May 31.
Tuition and Aid Tuition installment plan (monthly payment plans, individually arranged payment plans). Tuition reduction for siblings, need-based tuition remission for current students available. In 2008–09, 5% of upper-school students received aid.
Admissions Traditional secondary-level entrance grade is 9. For fall 2008, 97 students applied for upper-level admission, 53 were accepted, 52 enrolled. English for Non-native Speakers or Secondary Level English Proficiency required. Deadline for receipt of application materials: none. Application fee required: €80. On-campus interview recommended.

Athletics Interscholastic: alpine skiing (boys, girls), basketball (b,g), cross-country running (b,g), freestyle skiing (b,g), golf (b,g), skiing (downhill) (b,g), soccer (b,g), softball (g), swimming and diving (b,g), tennis (b,g), track and field (b,g), volleyball (b,g); intramural: alpine skiing (b,g), badminton (b,g), ballet (b,g), basketball (b,g), canoeing/kayaking (b,g), climbing (b,g), cross-country running (b,g), dance (b,g), freestyle skiing (b,g), gymnastics (b,g), indoor hockey (b,g), indoor soccer (b,g), kayaking (b,g), outdoor skills (b,g), skiing (downhill) (b,g), soccer (b,g), softball (g), strength & conditioning (b,g), swimming and diving (b,g), table tennis (b,g), tennis (b,g), track and field (b,g), volleyball (b,g), wall climbing (b,g); coed interscholastic: alpine skiing, golf, track and field; coed intramural: alpine skiing, ballet, canoeing/kayaking, climbing, dance, gymnastics, kayaking, outdoor skills, swimming and diving, wall climbing. 5 PE instructors, 8 coaches.

Computers Computers are regularly used in all academic, current events, library skills, newspaper, research skills, yearbook classes. Computer network features include on-campus library services, Internet access, wireless campus network, Internet filtering or blocking technology. Campus intranet and student e-mail accounts are available to students. Students grades are available online. The school has a published electronic and media policy.

Contact Ms. Manuela Black, Director of Admissions. 49-8151-366 Ext. 120. Fax: 49-8151-366 Ext. 129. E-mail: admissions@mis-munich.de. Web site: www.mis-munich.de.

See Close-Up on page 868.

NANCY CAMPBELL COLLEGIATE INSTITUTE

451 Ridout Street North
London, Ontario N6A 2P6, Canada

Head of School: Ms. Cora McNamara

General Information Coeducational boarding and day college-preparatory, arts, technology, world citizenship, and leadership school, affiliated with Baha'i faith. Boarding grades 7–12, day grades JK–12. Founded: 1993. Setting: urban. Students are housed in single-sex dormitories and homes. 3 buildings on campus. Approved or accredited by Ontario Ministry of Education and Ontario Department of Education. Languages of instruction: English and French. Total enrollment: 219. Upper school average class size: 15. Upper school faculty-student ratio: 1:9.

Upper School Student Profile Grade 9: 18 students (12 boys, 6 girls); Grade 10: 29 students (16 boys, 13 girls); Grade 11: 44 students (22 boys, 22 girls); Grade 12: 94 students (50 boys, 44 girls). 75% of students are boarding students. 20% are province residents. 9 provinces are represented in upper school student body. 79% are international students. International students from China, Colombia, Japan, Mexico, Republic of Korea, and United States; 19 other countries represented in student body. 5% of students are Baha'i.

Faculty School total: 26. In upper school: 10 men, 10 women; 9 have advanced degrees.

Subjects Offered 20th century American writers, 20th century history, 20th century physics, 20th century world history, 3-dimensional art, 3-dimensional design, acting, advanced chemistry, advanced math, Advanced Placement courses, algebra, applied music, art, art appreciation, art education, arts, audio visual/media, basic language skills, biology, body human, business education, business skills, calculus, calculus-AP, Canadian geography, Canadian history, Canadian law, Canadian literature, character education, chemistry, chemistry-AP, civics, classical music, computer education, computer literacy, computer skills, contemporary art, contemporary history, contemporary issues, contemporary math, creative arts, creative dance, creative drama, creative writing, dance, dance performance, discrete math, discrete mathematics, drama, drama performance, dramatic arts, English, English as a foreign language, English composition, English literature, ESL, ethical decision making, fine arts, general science, geography, geometry, global issues, graphic arts, healthful living, history, human biology, information technology, language arts, law, law and the legal system, mathematics, moral and social development, moral reasoning, music appreciation, music performance, musical productions, musical theater, musical theater dance, North American literature, novels, outdoor education, performing arts, philosophy, physical education, physics, physics-AP, playwriting and directing, science, science and technology, science research, social issues, social justice, social sciences, social studies, society and culture, society challenge and change, Southern literature, space and physical sciences, Spanish, Spanish language-AP, speech and debate, speech and oral interpretations, theater, theater arts, values and decisions, visual arts, world history, writing fundamentals, writing skills.

Graduation Requirements Completion of 50 service hours per year of Upper School.

Special Academic Programs Advanced Placement exam preparation; ESL (75 students enrolled).

College Admission Counseling 55 students graduated in 2008; 50 went to college, including McMaster University; The University of Western Ontario; University of Guelph; University of Toronto; University of Waterloo; York University. Other: 5 had other specific plans.

Student Life Upper grades have uniform requirement, student council, honor system. Discipline rests primarily with faculty.

Summer Programs Enrichment, ESL programs offered; session focuses on ESL; held on campus; accepts boys and girls; open to students from other schools. 120 students usually enrolled. 2009 schedule: July 6 to August 14. Application deadline: April 30.

Tuition and Aid Day student tuition: CAN$10,800–CAN$13,300; 7-day tuition and room/board: CAN$21,000–CAN$24,400. Tuition installment plan (full-payment plan, 2-payment plan with 50% of tuition due by June 30 and balance by November 10, 10-month payment plan (for North American students only)). Tuition reduction for siblings, bursaries, merit scholarship grants available. In 2008–09, 20% of upper-school students received aid; total upper-school merit-scholarship money awarded: CAN$52,000. Total amount of financial aid awarded in 2008–09: CAN$298,600.

Admissions Traditional secondary-level entrance grade is 9. For fall 2008, 194 students applied for upper-level admission, 176 were accepted, 174 enrolled. Deadline for receipt of application materials: none. Application fee required: CAN$100. Interview required.

Athletics Coed Intramural: aquatics, basketball, cooperative games, cross-country running, dance team, fitness walking, floor hockey, indoor soccer, jogging, outdoor adventure, outdoor education, outdoor recreation, physical fitness, physical training, running, soccer. 1 PE instructor.

Computers Computer network features include Internet access, wireless campus network, Internet filtering or blocking technology, Internet access outside regular school hours in residence, Internet monitoring hardware. Computer access in designated common areas is available to students.

Contact Mr. John Pammer, Director of Communications. 519-641-6224 Ext. 501. Fax: 519-641-6233. E-mail: jpammer@nancycampbell.net. Web site: www.nancycampbell.net.

NATIONAL CATHEDRAL SCHOOL

Mount Saint Alban
Washington, District of Columbia 20016-5000

Head of School: Mrs. Kathleen O'Neill Jamieson

General Information Girls' day college-preparatory school, affiliated with Episcopal Church. Grades 4–12. Founded: 1900. Setting: urban. 59-acre campus. 7 buildings on campus. Approved or accredited by Association of Independent Maryland Schools, Association of Independent Schools of Greater Washington, Middle States Association of Colleges and Schools, National Association of Episcopal Schools, The College Board, and District of Columbia Department of Education. Member of National Association of Independent Schools and Secondary School Admission Test Board. Endowment: $19 million. Total enrollment: 582. Upper school average class size: 14. Upper school faculty-student ratio: 1:7.

Upper School Student Profile Grade 9: 71 students (71 girls); Grade 10: 77 students (77 girls); Grade 11: 78 students (78 girls); Grade 12: 78 students (78 girls).

Faculty School total: 101. In upper school: 11 men, 34 women; 36 have advanced degrees.

Subjects Offered Advanced Placement courses, African American history, African-American literature, algebra, American history, American literature, art, art history, art history-AP, biology, calculus, ceramics, chemistry, Chinese, community service, computer programming, computer science, creative writing, dance, drama, earth science, economics, English, English literature, ethics, European history, expository writing, fine arts, French, geography, geometry, government/civics, Greek, history, Japanese, Latin, mathematics, music, photography, physical education, physics, political science, psychology, public speaking, religion, science, social studies, Spanish, statistics, theater, trigonometry, world history, writing.

Graduation Requirements Arts and fine arts (art, music, dance, drama), English, foreign language, mathematics, physical education (includes health), religion (includes Bible studies and theology), science, social studies (includes history). Community service is required.

Special Academic Programs 17 Advanced Placement exams for which test preparation is offered; honors section; independent study; term-away projects; study abroad; academic accommodation for the gifted.

College Admission Counseling 75 students graduated in 2008; all went to college, including Brown University; Dartmouth College; Princeton University; Stanford University; University of Pennsylvania; Yale University. Mean SAT critical reading: 718, mean SAT math: 698, mean SAT writing: 724.

Student Life Upper grades have specified standards of dress, student council, honor system. Discipline rests equally with students and faculty. Attendance at religious services is required.

Summer Programs Enrichment, sports, art/fine arts programs offered; held on campus; accepts boys and girls; open to students from other schools. 2009 schedule: June 11 to July 30. Application deadline: June 1.

Tuition and Aid Day student tuition: $30,700. Tuition installment plan (FACTS Tuition Payment Plan). Need-based scholarship grants available. In 2008–09, 17% of upper-school students received aid. Total amount of financial aid awarded in 2008–09: $917,760.

Admissions Traditional secondary-level entrance grade is 9. For fall 2008, 105 students applied for upper-level admission, 32 were accepted, 19 enrolled. ERB CTP IV, ISEE, SSAT or Wechsler Intelligence Scale for Children required. Deadline for receipt of application materials: January 15. Application fee required: $75. On-campus interview required.

Athletics Interscholastic: basketball, crew, dance team, field hockey, ice hockey, indoor soccer, indoor track, indoor track & field, lacrosse, Nautilus, rowing, soccer, softball, tennis, track and field, volleyball, winter (indoor) track; intramural: aerobics, aerobics/dance, aerobics/Nautilus, backpacking, ballet, canoeing/kayaking, climbing, dance, fitness, hiking/backpacking, independent competitive sports, kayaking, modern dance, mountain biking, outdoor adventure, physical fitness, rafting, rappelling, rock climbing, strength & conditioning, weight lifting, weight training, yoga; coed interscholastic: cross-country running, diving, swimming and diving. 11 PE instructors, 11 coaches, 1 athletic trainer.
Computers Computers are regularly used in art, English, foreign language, mathematics, multimedia, science classes. Computer network features include on-campus library services, online commercial services, Internet access, wireless campus network, Internet filtering or blocking technology. Student e-mail accounts and computer access in designated common areas are available to students. The school has a published electronic and media policy.
Contact Ms. Elizabeth Wilson, Admission Assistant. 202-537-6374. Fax: 202-537-2382. E-mail: ncs_admissions@cathedral.org. Web site: www.ncs.cathedral.org.

NATIONAL HIGH SCHOOL

6685 Peachtree Industrial Boulevard
Atlanta, Georgia 30360
Head of School: Alex Mithani

General Information Distance learning only college-preparatory, general academic, arts, and business school; primarily serves students with learning disabilities, individuals with Attention Deficit Disorder, individuals with emotional and behavioral problems, and ADHD. Distance learning grades 9–12. Founded: 2000. Setting: urban. 1 building on campus. Approved or accredited by CITA (Commission on International and Trans-Regional Accreditation), Southern Association of Colleges and Schools, and Georgia Department of Education. Total enrollment: 91. Upper school faculty-student ratio: 1:12.
Upper School Student Profile Grade 9: 28 students (11 boys, 17 girls); Grade 10: 24 students (9 boys, 15 girls); Grade 11: 17 students (4 boys, 13 girls); Grade 12: 22 students (8 boys, 14 girls).
Faculty School total: 8. In upper school: 2 men, 6 women; all have advanced degrees.
Subjects Offered 1½ elective credits, advanced biology, advanced chemistry, advanced computer applications, advanced math, Advanced Placement courses, American history, American history-AP, American literature, American literature-AP, biology, biology-AP, British literature, chemistry, chemistry-AP, electives, English, French, general math, geography, geometry, German, health, keyboarding, keyboarding/computer, language arts, mathematical modeling, physical education, physical science, physics, physics-AP, pre-algebra, pre-calculus, U.S. history, world geography.
Graduation Requirements Algebra, American government, American history, American literature, biology, chemistry, earth science, economics and history, electives, English, English literature, foreign language, geography, geometry, grammar, history, physical fitness, physical science, physics, pre-calculus, U.S. government, U.S. history, world history, world literature, two elective credits.
Special Academic Programs Advanced Placement exam preparation; honors section; accelerated programs; academic accommodation for the gifted, the musically talented, and the artistically talented; remedial reading and/or remedial writing; remedial math; ESL.
College Admission Counseling 58 students graduated in 2008; 43 went to college, including University at Albany, State University of New York. Other: 12 went to work, 2 entered military service.
Student Life Upper grades have student council, honor system. Discipline rests primarily with faculty.
Summer Programs Remediation, enrichment, advancement, ESL, art/fine arts, computer instruction programs offered; held off campus; held at Web-based program; accepts boys and girls; open to students from other schools. 72 students usually enrolled. 2009 schedule: May to September. Application deadline: May.
Tuition and Aid Guaranteed tuition plan. Tuition installment plan (The Tuition Plan).
Admissions Traditional secondary-level entrance grade is 11. Admissions testing required. Deadline for receipt of application materials: none. No application fee required. Interview required.
Computers Computers are regularly used in all classes. Computer resources include Internet access, wireless campus network, Internet filtering or blocking technology. Campus intranet and student e-mail accounts are available to students. Students grades are available online. The school has a published electronic and media policy.
Contact Ms. Dona Mary Mathews, Senior Admissions Executive. 866-550-0210. Fax: 678-669-2439. E-mail: dmathews@nationalhighschool.com. Web site: www.nationalhighschool.com.

NATIONAL SPORTS ACADEMY AT LAKE PLACID

821 Mirror Lake Drive
Lake Placid, New York 12946
Head of School: David Wenn

General Information Coeducational boarding and day college-preparatory and student learning services school. Grades 8–PG. Founded: 1977. Setting: small town. Nearest major city is Albany. Students are housed in single-sex by floor dormitories. 2 buildings on campus. Approved or accredited by National Independent Private Schools Association, New York State Association of Independent Schools, and New York State Board of Regents. Member of National Association of Independent Schools. Total enrollment: 79. Upper school average class size: 8. Upper school faculty-student ratio: 1:7.
Upper School Student Profile Grade 8: 6 students (5 boys, 1 girl); Grade 9: 5 students (3 boys, 2 girls); Grade 10: 15 students (10 boys, 5 girls); Grade 11: 18 students (8 boys, 10 girls); Grade 12: 24 students (13 boys, 11 girls); Postgraduate: 11 students (9 boys, 2 girls). 79% of students are boarding students. 45% are state residents. 17 states are represented in upper school student body. 12% are international students. International students from Canada and United Kingdom.
Faculty School total: 15. In upper school: 9 men, 6 women; 10 have advanced degrees; 6 reside on campus.
Subjects Offered Algebra, American history, American literature, biology, biology-AP, calculus, calculus-AP, chemistry, computers, earth science, English, English literature, English-AP, environmental science, European history, French, geometry, government, health, history, history-AP, mathematics, physical education, physics, pre-calculus, science, social studies, Spanish, sports science, world history.
Graduation Requirements Algebra, biology, chemistry, earth science, English, English literature, environmental science, European history, French, geometry, history, physical education (includes health), physics, pre-calculus, Spanish, sports science, U.S. government, U.S. history, world history. Community service is required.
Special Academic Programs 4 Advanced Placement exams for which test preparation is offered; independent study.
College Admission Counseling 21 students graduated in 2008; 14 went to college, including Clarkson University; Queen's University at Kingston; St. Lawrence University; Union College; United States Naval Academy; University of Vermont. Other: 5 entered a postgraduate year, 2 had other specific plans. Mean SAT critical reading: 525, mean SAT math: 521, mean SAT writing: 500.
Student Life Upper grades have specified standards of dress, student council, honor system. Discipline rests primarily with faculty.
Summer Programs Sports programs offered; session focuses on sports-specific athletic training; held off campus; held at various sports venues; accepts boys and girls; open to students from other schools. 25 students usually enrolled. 2009 schedule: June to August.
Tuition and Aid Day student tuition: $13,000; 7-day tuition and room/board: $28,000. Tuition installment plan (Key Tuition Payment Plan, monthly payment plans). Tuition reduction for siblings, need-based scholarship grants, prepGATE Loans available. In 2008–09, 60% of upper-school students received aid.
Admissions Traditional secondary-level entrance grade is 10. For fall 2008, 115 students applied for upper-level admission, 49 were accepted, 38 enrolled. PSAT and SAT for applicants to grade 11 and 12 required. Deadline for receipt of application materials: none. Application fee required: $40. Interview required.
Athletics Interscholastic: alpine skiing (boys, girls), biathlon (b,g), bicycling (b,g), figure skating (b,g), freestyle skiing (b,g), ice hockey (b,g), ice skating (b,g), luge (b,g), nordic skiing (b,g), ski jumping (b,g), skiing (cross-country) (b,g), skiing (downhill) (b,g), snowboarding (b,g), speedskating (b,g), strength & conditioning (b,g), weight training (b,g); coed interscholastic: physical training, soccer; coed intramural: golf, lacrosse, rappelling, rock climbing, tennis, weight training, yoga. 17 coaches, 1 athletic trainer.
Computers Computers are regularly used in English, foreign language, history, mathematics, science classes. Computer network features include Internet access, wireless campus network, Internet filtering or blocking technology, E-Library.
Contact Gun Rand, Director of Admissions. 518-523-3460 Ext. 22. Fax: 518-523-3488. E-mail: grand@nationalsportsacademy.com. Web site: www.nationalsportsacademy.com.

NAVAJO PREPARATORY SCHOOL, INC.

1220 West Apache Street
Farmington, New Mexico 87401
Head of School: Mr. John C Tohtsoni Jr.

General Information Coeducational boarding and day college-preparatory, arts, and bilingual studies school. Grades 9–12. Founded: 1991. Setting: suburban. Nearest major city is Albuquerque. Students are housed in single-sex dormitories. 84-acre campus. 12 buildings on campus. Approved or accredited by National Council for Nonpublic Schools, North Central Association of Colleges and Schools, and New Mexico Department of Education. Upper school average class size: 15. Upper school faculty-student ratio: 1:15.
Upper School Student Profile Grade 9: 52 students (19 boys, 33 girls); Grade 10: 49 students (19 boys, 30 girls); Grade 11: 40 students (19 boys, 21 girls); Grade 12: 42 students (14 boys, 28 girls). 85% of students are boarding students. 100% are state residents.
Faculty School total: 19. In upper school: 10 men, 9 women; 16 have advanced degrees.
Graduation Requirements Navajo language, Navajo history, Navajo culture.
College Admission Counseling 39 students graduated in 2008; 36 went to college, including Fort Lewis College; San Juan College; The University of Arizona; University of New Mexico; Whittier College. Other: 2 went to work, 1 entered military service.

Student Life Upper grades have specified standards of dress, student council, honor system. Discipline rests primarily with faculty.
Admissions Traditional secondary-level entrance grade is 9. ACT-Explore required. Deadline for receipt of application materials: none. Application fee required: $20. Interview required.
Athletics Interscholastic: baseball (boys, girls), basketball (b,g), cheering (b,g), cross-country running (b,g), football (b,g), golf (b,g), softball (b,g), volleyball (b,g). 1 PE instructor, 19 coaches.
Computers Computer network features include on-campus library services, Internet access, wireless campus network. Student e-mail accounts are available to students. The school has a published electronic and media policy.
Contact Ms. Marilyn Holiday, Director of Federal Programs/Admissions. 505-326-6571 Ext. 126. Fax: 505-564-8099. E-mail: mharris@nps.bia.edu. Web site: www.nps.bia.edu.

NAZARETH ACADEMY

1209 West Ogden Avenue
LaGrange Park, Illinois 60526
Head of School: Ms. Deborah A. Vondrasek

General Information Coeducational day college-preparatory school, affiliated with Roman Catholic Church. Grades 9–12. Founded: 1900. Setting: suburban. Nearest major city is Chicago. 15-acre campus. 2 buildings on campus. Approved or accredited by North Central Association of Colleges and Schools and Illinois Department of Education. Total enrollment: 787. Upper school average class size: 24. Upper school faculty-student ratio: 1:17.
Upper School Student Profile Grade 9: 221 students (109 boys, 112 girls); Grade 10: 205 students (108 boys, 97 girls); Grade 11: 173 students (77 boys, 96 girls); Grade 12: 188 students (79 boys, 109 girls). 90% of students are Roman Catholic.
Faculty School total: 45. In upper school: 17 men, 27 women; 36 have advanced degrees.
Subjects Offered Algebra, American government, American literature, art, band, biology, biology-AP, calculus-AP, chemistry, chorus, computer programming, computer science-AP, conceptual physics, creative writing, drama, economics, English, English language and composition-AP, English literature and composition-AP, fine arts, French, geometry, German, health, humanities, Italian, journalism, photography, physical education, physics, pre-calculus, psychology, religion, Spanish, speech, studio art, theater, trigonometry, U.S. history, U.S. history-AP, Western civilization, world history, world literature, world religions.
Graduation Requirements Advanced math, algebra, American literature, arts and fine arts (art, music, dance, drama), biology, chemistry, church history, English, foreign language, geometry, physical education (includes health), physics, religion (includes Bible studies and theology), scripture, U.S. history, Western civilization, world literature, world religions, world studies, service hours, off-campus retreat for juniors.
Special Academic Programs 12 Advanced Placement exams for which test preparation is offered; honors section.
College Admission Counseling 188 students graduated in 2008; 186 went to college, including DePaul University; Marquette University; Northwestern University; University of Illinois at Chicago; University of Illinois at Urbana–Champaign; University of Notre Dame. Other: 2 entered military service. Median composite ACT: 24. 30% scored over 26 on composite ACT.
Student Life Upper grades have uniform requirement, student council, honor system. Discipline rests primarily with faculty. Attendance at religious services is required.
Tuition and Aid Day student tuition: $9100. Tuition installment plan (monthly payment plans). Tuition reduction for siblings, merit scholarship grants, need-based scholarship grants available. In 2008–09, 22% of upper-school students received aid; total upper-school merit-scholarship money awarded: $40,000. Total amount of financial aid awarded in 2008–09: $300,000.
Admissions Traditional secondary-level entrance grade is 9. For fall 2008, 350 students applied for upper-level admission, 221 enrolled. High School Placement Test (closed version) from Scholastic Testing Service required. Deadline for receipt of application materials: June 30. No application fee required. On-campus interview recommended.
Athletics Interscholastic: baseball (boys), basketball (b,g), cheering (g), cross-country running (b,g), football (b), golf (b,g), hockey (b), lacrosse (g), pom squad (g), soccer (b,g), softball (g), swimming and diving (b,g), tennis (b,g), track and field (b,g), volleyball (b,g); intramural: hockey (b). 2 PE instructors, 1 coach, 1 athletic trainer.
Computers Computers are regularly used in English, foreign language, history, mathematics, science classes. Computer network features include on-campus library services, Internet access, wireless campus network, Internet filtering or blocking technology. Students grades are available online. The school has a published electronic and media policy.
Contact Mr. John Bonk, Recruitment Director. 708-387-8538. Fax: 708-354-0109. E-mail: jbonk@nazarethacademy.com. Web site: www.nazarethacademy.com.

NEBRASKA CHRISTIAN SCHOOLS

1847 Inskip Avenue
Central City, Nebraska 68826
Head of School: Mr. Daniel R. Woods

General Information Coeducational boarding and day college-preparatory school, affiliated with Protestant-Evangelical faith. Boarding grades 7–12, day grades K–12. Founded: 1959. Setting: rural. Nearest major city is Lincoln. Students are housed in single-sex dormitories. 27-acre campus. 7 buildings on campus. Approved or accredited by Association of Christian Schools International and Nebraska Department of Education. Endowment: $35,000. Total enrollment: 181. Upper school average class size: 20. Upper school faculty-student ratio: 1:10.
Upper School Student Profile Grade 9: 16 students (9 boys, 7 girls); Grade 10: 27 students (16 boys, 11 girls); Grade 11: 18 students (9 boys, 9 girls); Grade 12: 29 students (15 boys, 14 girls). 23% of students are boarding students. 86% are state residents. 1 state is represented in upper school student body. 14% are international students. International students from China, Hong Kong, Japan, Republic of Korea, Taiwan, and Viet Nam. 90% of students are Protestant-Evangelical faith.
Faculty School total: 26. In upper school: 13 men, 13 women; 5 have advanced degrees; 5 reside on campus.
Subjects Offered Accounting, advanced math, algebra, American government, American history, American literature, anatomy and physiology, ancient world history, art, band, Bible, biology, business, business law, chemistry, choir, Christian doctrine, Christian ethics, composition, computer applications, computer keyboarding, computer programming, concert band, consumer mathematics, creation science, desktop publishing, economics, English, English composition, ESL, family living, fitness, general math, geography, geometry, health and safety, history, lab science, language arts, Life of Christ, life science, literature, mathematics, music, music theory, physical education, physical fitness, physical science, physics, pre-calculus, science, science project, social studies, Spanish, speech, trigonometry, vocal ensemble, vocal music, Web site design, word processing, world geography, world history, writing, yearbook.
Graduation Requirements Algebra, American government, American history, American literature, art, Bible, biology, Christian doctrine, computer keyboarding, economics, English, family living, geometry, history, Life of Christ, physical education (includes health), physical science, world history.
Special Academic Programs Independent study; study at local college for college credit; ESL (20 students enrolled).
College Admission Counseling 27 students graduated in 2008; all went to college, including California State University, Dominguez Hills; Cedarville University; Fashion Institute of Technology; John Brown University; University of Nebraska–Lincoln; University of Nebraska at Kearney. Median composite ACT: 21. 18% scored over 26 on composite ACT.
Student Life Upper grades have specified standards of dress, student council, honor system. Discipline rests primarily with faculty. Attendance at religious services is required.
Tuition and Aid Day student tuition: $5000; 5-day tuition and room/board: $8000; 7-day tuition and room/board: $23,000. Tuition installment plan (FACTS Tuition Payment Plan, individually arranged payment plans). Tuition reduction for siblings, merit scholarship grants, need-based scholarship grants available. In 2008–09, 44% of upper-school students received aid. Total amount of financial aid awarded in 2008–09: $90,000.
Admissions Traditional secondary-level entrance grade is 9. For fall 2008, 30 students applied for upper-level admission, 30 were accepted, 22 enrolled. SLEP for foreign students or TOEFL or SLEP required. Deadline for receipt of application materials: none. Application fee required: $300. Interview recommended.
Athletics Interscholastic: basketball (boys, girls), cross-country running (b,g), football (b), track and field (b,g), volleyball (g), wrestling (b). 2 PE instructors, 7 coaches.
Computers Computers are regularly used in business applications, desktop publishing, programming, Web site design, yearbook classes. Computer network features include Internet access, wireless campus network, Internet filtering or blocking technology. Students grades are available online.
Contact Mr. Larry Hoff, Director, International Programs. 308-946-3836. Fax: 308-946-3837. E-mail: lhoff@nebraskachristian.org. Web site: www.nebraskachristian.org.

NERINX HALL

530 East Lockwood Avenue
Webster Groves, Missouri 63119
Head of School: Sr. Barbara Roche, SL

General Information Girls' day college-preparatory and arts school, affiliated with Roman Catholic Church. Grades 9–12. Founded: 1924. Setting: suburban. Nearest major city is St. Louis. 4 buildings on campus. Approved or accredited by North Central Association of Colleges and Schools and Missouri Department of Education. Endowment: $2.3 million. Total enrollment: 620. Upper school average class size: 20. Upper school faculty-student ratio: 1:10.
Upper School Student Profile Grade 9: 166 students (166 girls); Grade 10: 157 students (157 girls); Grade 11: 150 students (150 girls); Grade 12: 147 students (147 girls). 94% of students are Roman Catholic.

Faculty School total: 54. In upper school: 14 men, 40 women; 49 have advanced degrees.
Subjects Offered Acting, advanced math, American government, American history, American literature, anatomy, anthropology, art, astronomy, athletics, biology, business, calculus, ceramics, chemistry, computer applications, computer graphics, conceptual physics, creative writing, death and loss, desktop publishing, drawing and design, Eastern world civilizations, economics, English composition, English literature, film appreciation, French, geology, German, graphics, health, history, Holocaust, honors algebra, honors English, honors geometry, honors U.S. history, instrumental music, jazz band, keyboarding, lab science, Latin, media, Middle East, model United Nations, multimedia, orchestra, painting, performing arts, personal finance, physics, pre-calculus, psychology, public speaking, religious education, Spanish, stagecraft, theology, Web site design, Western civilization.
Graduation Requirements Algebra, arts and fine arts (art, music, dance, drama), biology, chemistry, foreign language, geometry, physical education (includes health), physical fitness, physics, theology, U.S. government and politics, U.S. history, U.S. literature, world history, writing. Community service is required.
Special Academic Programs Honors section; study at local college for college credit.
College Admission Counseling 155 students graduated in 2008; all went to college, including DePaul University; Missouri State University; Saint Louis University; Truman State University; University of Dayton; University of Missouri–Columbia. Median SAT critical reading: 640, median SAT math: 623, median SAT writing: 646, median composite ACT: 26.
Student Life Upper grades have uniform requirement, student council, honor system. Discipline rests primarily with faculty. Attendance at religious services is required.
Summer Programs Advancement programs offered; session focuses on advancement; held on campus; accepts girls; not open to students from other schools. 175 students usually enrolled.
Tuition and Aid Day student tuition: $9600. Tuition installment plan (individually arranged payment plans). Tuition reduction for siblings, merit scholarship grants, need-based scholarship grants, paying campus jobs available. In 2008–09, 20% of upper-school students received aid. Total amount of financial aid awarded in 2008–09: $357,550.
Admissions For fall 2008, 211 students applied for upper-level admission, 171 were accepted, 166 enrolled. Any standardized test or CTBS (or similar from their school) required. Deadline for receipt of application materials: November 24. Application fee required: $10. Interview required.
Athletics Interscholastic: basketball, cross-country running, diving, field hockey, golf, lacrosse, racquetball, soccer, softball, swimming and diving, tennis, track and field, volleyball. 3 PE instructors, 25 coaches.
Computers Computers are regularly used in graphics, humanities, mathematics, science, speech, writing, writing classes. Computer network features include on-campus library services, Internet access, wireless campus network, Internet filtering or blocking technology. Student e-mail accounts are available to students. Students grades are available online. The school has a published electronic and media policy.
Contact Mrs. Joyce Bytnar. 314-968-1505 Ext. 151. Fax: 314-968-0604. E-mail: jbytnar@nerinxhs.org. Web site: www.nerinxhs.org.

NEUCHATEL JUNIOR COLLEGE

Cret-Taconnet 4
2002 Neuchâtel, Switzerland

Head of School: Mr. Norman Southward

General Information Coeducational boarding college-preparatory, arts, business, bilingual studies, and international development school. Grade 12. Founded: 1956. Setting: urban. Nearest major city is Berne, Switzerland. Students are housed in homes of host families. 1-acre campus. 3 buildings on campus. Approved or accredited by Canadian Association of Independent Schools, Canadian Educational Standards Institute, and state department of education. Languages of instruction: English and French. Endowment: CAN$350,000. Total enrollment: 97. Upper school average class size: 15. Upper school faculty-student ratio: 1:10.
Upper School Student Profile Grade 12: 74 students (27 boys, 47 girls); Postgraduate: 23 students (12 boys, 11 girls). 100% of students are boarding students. 4% are international students. International students from Bermuda, Canada, Mexico, United Arab Emirates, United Kingdom, and United States.
Faculty School total: 10. In upper school: 4 men, 6 women; 7 have advanced degrees; 1 resides on campus.
Subjects Offered 20th century world history, advanced chemistry, advanced math, Advanced Placement courses, advanced studio art-AP, algebra, analysis and differential calculus, ancient world history, applied arts, art, art history, art history-AP, athletics, biology, biology-AP, British history, calculus, calculus-AP, Canadian history, Canadian law, Canadian literature, chemistry, chemistry-AP, classical civilization, comparative government and politics-AP, comparative politics, debate, dramatic arts, earth science, economics, economics-AP, English, English language and composition-AP, English literature-AP, environmental science, European history, European history-AP, finite math, French as a second language, French language-AP, French literature-AP, German-AP, government and politics-AP, human geography—AP, law, personal and social education, physics, physics-AP, public speaking, studio art—AP, United Nations and international issues, world history-AP, world issues.
Graduation Requirements Minimum of 6 senior year university prep level courses.
Special Academic Programs Advanced Placement exam preparation; study abroad.
College Admission Counseling 105 students graduated in 2008; 103 went to college, including Dalhousie University; McGill University; McMaster University; Queen's University at Kingston; The University of Western Ontario; University of Toronto. Other: 2 had other specific plans.
Student Life Upper grades have specified standards of dress, student council, honor system. Discipline rests primarily with faculty.
Tuition and Aid 7-day tuition and room/board: 39,500 Swiss francs. Bursaries, merit scholarship grants available. In 2008–09, 8% of upper-school students received aid; total upper-school merit-scholarship money awarded: 9000 Swiss francs. Total amount of financial aid awarded in 2008–09: 75,000 Swiss francs.
Admissions Traditional secondary-level entrance grade is 12. For fall 2008, 145 students applied for upper-level admission, 103 were accepted, 97 enrolled. Deadline for receipt of application materials: December 9. Application fee required: CAN$175. Interview recommended.
Athletics Interscholastic: field hockey (boys, girls), rugby (b,g), soccer (b,g); intramural: hockey (b,g), ice hockey (b,g), indoor hockey (b,g), rugby (b,g), soccer (b,g); coed interscholastic: alpine skiing, aquatics, snowboarding, swimming and diving; coed intramural: alpine skiing, aquatics, basketball, bicycling, cross-country running, curling, floor hockey, jogging, sailing, snowboarding, volleyball.
Computers Computer network features include on-campus library services, Internet access, wireless campus network. Student e-mail accounts are available to students. The school has a published electronic and media policy.
Contact Ms. Anne Hamilton, Admission Officer. 416-368-8169 Ext. 222. Fax: 416-368-0956. E-mail: admissions@neuchatel.org. Web site: www.njc.ch/school/.

NEWARK ACADEMY

91 South Orange Avenue
Livingston, New Jersey 07039-4989

Head of School: M. Donald M. Austin

General Information Coeducational day college-preparatory, arts, technology, and International Baccalaureate school. Grades 6–12. Founded: 1774. Setting: suburban. Nearest major city is Morristown. 68-acre campus. 1 building on campus. Approved or accredited by Middle States Association of Colleges and Schools, New Jersey Association of Independent Schools, and New Jersey Department of Education. Member of National Association of Independent Schools and Secondary School Admission Test Board. Endowment: $20.3 million. Total enrollment: 559. Upper school average class size: 13. Upper school faculty-student ratio: 1:12.
Upper School Student Profile Grade 9: 99 students (51 boys, 48 girls); Grade 10: 100 students (52 boys, 48 girls); Grade 11: 96 students (49 boys, 47 girls); Grade 12: 101 students (48 boys, 53 girls).
Faculty School total: 74. In upper school: 33 men, 34 women; 59 have advanced degrees.
Subjects Offered Algebra, American history, American literature, anatomy, art, art history, arts, biology, botany, calculus, ceramics, chemistry, chorus, communications, community service, computer programming, computer science, creative writing, drama, driver education, ecology, economics, English, English literature, European history, finance, fine arts, French, geometry, government/civics, grammar, health, history, humanities, Latin, leadership training, Mandarin, mathematics, music, philosophy, physical education, physics, religion, SAT/ACT preparation, science, social studies, Spanish, theater, theory of knowledge, trigonometry, typing, world history, world literature, writing.
Graduation Requirements Arts and fine arts (art, music, dance, drama), computer science, English, foreign language, mathematics, physical education (includes health), science, social studies (includes history), 40-hour senior service project, community service.
Special Academic Programs International Baccalaureate program; Advanced Placement exam preparation; honors section; accelerated programs; independent study; term-away projects; study at local college for college credit; study abroad; academic accommodation for the gifted, the musically talented, and the artistically talented.
College Admission Counseling 102 students graduated in 2008; all went to college, including New York University; Stanford University; The George Washington University; Tufts University; University of Pennsylvania; Yale University. Median SAT math: 660, median SAT writing: 650, median composite ACT: 26. 83% scored over 600 on SAT math, 82% scored over 600 on SAT writing, 36% scored over 26 on composite ACT.
Student Life Upper grades have specified standards of dress, student council, honor system. Discipline rests equally with students and faculty.
Summer Programs Remediation, enrichment, advancement, ESL, sports, art/fine arts, computer instruction programs offered; session focuses on enrichment and advancement; held on campus; accepts boys and girls; open to students from other schools. 850 students usually enrolled. 2009 schedule: June 19 to August 11. Application deadline: June 1.
Tuition and Aid Day student tuition: $26,300. Tuition installment plan (Insured Tuition Payment Plan, Key Tuition Payment Plan, monthly payment plans, indi-

vidually arranged payment plans). Need-based scholarship grants available. In 2008–09, 15% of upper-school students received aid. Total amount of financial aid awarded in 2008–09: $1,400,000.
Admissions Traditional secondary-level entrance grade is 9. For fall 2008, 330 students applied for upper-level admission, 103 were accepted, 49 enrolled. ISEE or SSAT required. Deadline for receipt of application materials: January 9. Application fee required: $65. Interview required.
Athletics Interscholastic: baseball (boys), basketball (b,g), cross-country running (b,g), fencing (b,g), field hockey (g), football (b), golf (b,g), lacrosse (b,g), running (b,g), skiing (downhill) (b,g), soccer (b,g), softball (g), swimming and diving (b,g), tennis (b,g), track and field (b,g), volleyball (g), wrestling (b); intramural: aerobics/dance (b,g), aerobics/Nautilus (b,g), baseball (b), basketball (b,g), bicycling (b,g), cross-country running (b,g), dance (b,g), dance team (b,g), field hockey (g), fitness (b,g), football (b), golf (b,g), hockey (b), ice hockey (b), lacrosse (b,g), modern dance (b,g), soccer (b,g), softball (g), swimming and diving (b,g), tennis (b,g), track and field (b,g), volleyball (g), weight lifting (b,g), wrestling (b), yoga (b,g); coed intramural: aerobics/dance, aerobics/Nautilus, bicycling, cricket, dance, dance team, fitness, modern dance, mountain biking, skiing (downhill), table tennis, ultimate Frisbee, weight lifting, yoga. 5 PE instructors, 10 coaches, 1 athletic trainer.
Computers Computers are regularly used in all academic classes. Computer network features include on-campus library services, online commercial services, Internet access, wireless campus network. Student e-mail accounts are available to students.
Contact Mrs. Jennifer Blythe, Admissions Office manager. 973-992-7000 Ext. 323. Fax: 973-993-8962. E-mail: jblythe@newarka.edu. Web site: www.newarka.edu.

ANNOUNCEMENT FROM THE SCHOOL Founded in 1774, Newark Academy has a rich history as an independent, coeducational school that is located on a beautiful 68-acre campus in northern New Jersey. The Academy is a place where smart, motivated students are challenged by a broad and rigorous academic program taught by an energized faculty committed to excellence. The extracurricular programs and emphasis on life balance combine to make a wonderful environment for students to learn and grow into confident and secure young adults. Newark Academy produces young people who are prepared for the intellectual, political, and social challenges posed by the complexity of today's world. The Academy is characterized by a culture that prepares students for college and a lifetime of learning, while emphasizing the development of compassionate people.

NEWBURY PARK ADVENTIST ACADEMY

180 Academy Drive
Newbury Park, California 91320
Head of School: Harold Crook, Ed.D.

General Information Coeducational day college-preparatory, arts, religious studies, technology, and community service school, affiliated with Seventh-day Adventist Church. Grades 9–12. Founded: 1948. Setting: suburban. Nearest major city is Thousand Oaks. 436-acre campus. 6 buildings on campus. Approved or accredited by Association of Seventh-day Adventist Secondary Schools and Colleges, Western Association of Schools and Colleges, and California Department of Education. Upper school average class size: 25. Upper school faculty-student ratio: 1:25.
Upper School Student Profile 70% of students are Seventh-day Adventists.
Faculty School total: 15. In upper school: 9 men, 5 women; 1 has an advanced degree.
Subjects Offered Accounting, algebra, American government, art, biology, calculus, career education, chemistry, choir, computer applications, concert band, earth science, English, geography, geometry, health, industrial arts, instrumental music, keyboarding, life skills, organ, physical education, physical science, physics, piano, religion, Spanish, U.S. history, voice, world history, yearbook.
Graduation Requirements Arts and fine arts (art, music, dance, drama), business skills (includes word processing), career education, computer science, English, life skills, mathematics, physical education (includes health), religion (includes Bible studies and theology), science, social science, social studies (includes history), work experience. Community service is required.
Special Academic Programs Independent study; study at local college for college credit; remedial reading and/or remedial writing; remedial math; ESL (10 students enrolled).
Student Life Upper grades have specified standards of dress, student council, honor system. Discipline rests primarily with faculty. Attendance at religious services is required.
Tuition and Aid Tuition installment plan (monthly payment plans, individually arranged payment plans). Need-based scholarship grants, paying campus jobs available.
Admissions Deadline for receipt of application materials: none. Application fee required: $25. Interview required.
Athletics Interscholastic: basketball (boys, girls), volleyball (b,g); intramural: baseball (b,g), basketball (b,g), equestrian sports (b,g), golf (b,g), skiing (downhill) (b,g), soccer (b,g), softball (b,g), squash (b,g), swimming and diving (b,g), tennis (b,g), track and field (b,g), volleyball (b,g), weight lifting (b); coed interscholastic: baseball; coed intramural: skiing (downhill), softball, tennis, track and field, volleyball. 2 PE instructors, 4 coaches.
Computers Computers are regularly used in art, English, history, mathematics classes. Computer resources include on-campus library services, Internet access.
Contact Mary Hardin, Registrar. 805-498-2191. Fax: 805-499-1165. Web site: www.npaa.netadventist.org.

NEW COVENANT ACADEMY

3304 South Cox Road
Springfield, Missouri 65807
Head of School: Dr. Cindy Evans

General Information Coeducational day college-preparatory, arts, business, religious studies, and technology school, affiliated with Christian faith. Grades JK–12. Founded: 1979. Setting: suburban. 22-acre campus. 1 building on campus. Approved or accredited by Association of Christian Schools International and North Central Association of Colleges and Schools. Total enrollment: 405. Upper school average class size: 15. Upper school faculty-student ratio: 1:10.
Upper School Student Profile Grade 9: 31 students (21 boys, 10 girls); Grade 10: 39 students (17 boys, 22 girls); Grade 11: 35 students (20 boys, 15 girls); Grade 12: 27 students (13 boys, 14 girls). 100% of students are Christian.
Faculty In upper school: 6 men, 7 women; 8 have advanced degrees.
Special Academic Programs Study at local college for college credit.
College Admission Counseling 27 students graduated in 2008; 26 went to college, including Missouri State University.
Student Life Upper grades have specified standards of dress, student council, honor system. Discipline rests primarily with faculty. Attendance at religious services is required.
Tuition and Aid Guaranteed tuition plan. Tuition installment plan (monthly payment plans). Need-based scholarship grants available.
Admissions Otis-Lennon School Ability Test or SAT required. Deadline for receipt of application materials: none. Application fee required: $50. Interview required.
Athletics Interscholastic: basketball (boys, girls), cheering (g), golf (b); coed interscholastic: golf. 1 PE instructor, 12 coaches.
Computers Computers are regularly used in accounting classes. Computer network features include Internet access, Internet filtering or blocking technology. Computer access in designated common areas is available to students.
Contact Mrs. Delana Reynolds, Admissions Officer. 417-887-9848 Ext. 3. Fax: 417-887-2419. E-mail: dreynolds@newcovenant.net. Web site: www.newcovenant.net.

NEW HAMPTON SCHOOL

70 Main Street
New Hampton, New Hampshire 03256
Head of School: Andrew Menke

General Information Coeducational boarding and day college-preparatory, general academic, arts, and bilingual studies school. Grades 9–PG. Founded: 1821. Setting: small town. Nearest major city is Boston, MA. Students are housed in single-sex dormitories. 300-acre campus. 35 buildings on campus. Approved or accredited by Association of Independent Schools in New England, Independent Schools of Northern New England, New England Association of Schools and Colleges, The Association of Boarding Schools, and New Hampshire Department of Education. Member of National Association of Independent Schools and Secondary School Admission Test Board. Endowment: $10 million. Total enrollment: 321. Upper school average class size: 11. Upper school faculty-student ratio: 1:5.
Upper School Student Profile Grade 9: 55 students (32 boys, 23 girls); Grade 10: 58 students (34 boys, 24 girls); Grade 11: 83 students (54 boys, 29 girls); Grade 12: 99 students (67 boys, 32 girls); Postgraduate: 26 students (24 boys, 2 girls). 72% of students are boarding students. 50% are state residents. 26 states are represented in upper school student body. 14% are international students. International students from Bermuda, Canada, China, Germany, Republic of Korea, and United Kingdom; 6 other countries represented in student body.
Faculty School total: 82. In upper school: 38 men, 40 women; 42 have advanced degrees; 51 reside on campus.
Subjects Offered Algebra, American history, American literature, anatomy, art, art history, biology, broadcasting, calculus, ceramics, chemistry, community service, computer programming, computer science, creative writing, dance, drama, driver education, earth science, ecology, economics, electronics, English, English literature, environmental science, European history, expository writing, filmmaking, fine arts, French, geography, geometry, government/civics, grammar, health, history, human sexuality, journalism, Latin, logic, mathematics, music, music history, philosophy, photography, physical education, physics, physics-AP, physiology, psychology, science, senior seminar, social studies, sociology, Spanish, speech, statistics, theater, trigonometry, world history, world literature, writing.
Graduation Requirements Arts and fine arts (art, music, dance, drama), computer science, English, foreign language, mathematics, performing arts, science, social studies (includes history), speech. Community service is required.
Special Academic Programs Advanced Placement exam preparation; honors section; independent study; academic accommodation for the gifted, the musically talented, and the artistically talented; remedial reading and/or remedial writing; remedial math; programs in English for dyslexic students; ESL (15 students enrolled).

College Admission Counseling 112 students graduated in 2007; 109 went to college, including Colby College; Ithaca College; Northeastern University; St. Lawrence University; University of New Hampshire; University of Vermont. Other: 3 had other specific plans. Median SAT critical reading: 500, median SAT math: 530. 15% scored over 600 on SAT critical reading, 25% scored over 600 on SAT math.
Student Life Upper grades have student council, honor system. Discipline rests equally with students and faculty.
Tuition and Aid Day student tuition: $22,500; 7-day tuition and room/board: $38,500. Tuition installment plan (Insured Tuition Payment Plan, Academic Management Services Plan, Key Tuition Payment Plan, monthly payment plans, individually arranged payment plans). Need-based scholarship grants available. In 2007–08, 30% of upper-school students received aid. Total amount of financial aid awarded in 2007–08: $2,075,000.
Admissions Traditional secondary-level entrance grade is 9. For fall 2007, 408 students applied for upper-level admission, 284 were accepted, 142 enrolled. SSAT or TOEFL or SLEP required. Deadline for receipt of application materials: none. Application fee required: $50. Interview required.
Athletics Interscholastic: alpine skiing (boys, girls), baseball (b), basketball (b,g), bicycling (b,g), cross-country running (b,g), field hockey (g), football (b), golf (b,g), hockey (b,g), ice hockey (b,g), lacrosse (b,g), skiing (downhill) (b,g), soccer (b,g), softball (g), tennis (b,g), volleyball (g); coed interscholastic: alpine skiing, bicycling, canoeing/kayaking, equestrian sports, horseback riding, kayaking, mountain biking, snowboarding; coed intramural: aerobics/dance, ballet, bicycling, canoeing/kayaking, climbing, cross-country running, dance, equestrian sports, fitness, golf, hiking/backpacking, horseback riding, ice hockey, kayaking, modern dance, nordic skiing, outdoor activities, outdoor adventure, outdoor education, outdoor recreation, outdoor skills, physical training, rock climbing, ropes courses, skiing (downhill), snowboarding, tennis, wall climbing, weight lifting, weight training, yoga. 3 athletic trainers.
Computers Computers are regularly used in English, graphic design, introduction to technology, journalism, mathematics, media production, music, science, video film production, yearbook classes. Computer resources include on-campus library services, Internet access, Internet filtering or blocking technology. Student e-mail accounts are available to students. Students grades are available online.
Contact Ms. Suzanne Walker Buck, Director of Admission. 603-677-3402. Fax: 603-677-3481. E-mail: sbuck@newhampton.org. Web site: www.newhampton.org.

ANNOUNCEMENT FROM THE SCHOOL New Hampton School prepares students for lifelong learning through self-discovery, authentic relationships, civic responsibility, and global citizenship. Students are readied not only for the rigors of college and university study, but they are also thoughtfully prepared to become citizens of tomorrow's world.

See Close-Up on page 870.

NEW HAVEN

2172 East 7200 South
Spanish Fork, Utah 84660
Head of School: Laurie Laird
General Information Girls' boarding college-preparatory and general academic school; primarily serves students with learning disabilities, individuals with Attention Deficit Disorder, and individuals with emotional and behavioral problems. Grades 8–12. Founded: 1995. Setting: rural. Students are housed in single-sex dormitories. 20-acre campus. 4 buildings on campus. Approved or accredited by CITA (Commission on International and Trans-Regional Accreditation), Joint Commission on Accreditation of Healthcare Organizations, Northwest Association of Schools and Colleges, The College Board, and Utah Department of Education. Total enrollment: 64. Upper school average class size: 10. Upper school faculty-student ratio: 1:5.
Upper School Student Profile Grade 10: 20 students (20 girls); Grade 11: 20 students (20 girls); Grade 12: 14 students (14 girls). 100% of students are boarding students. 10% are state residents. 21 states are represented in upper school student body. 15% are international students. International students from Canada and Spain.
Faculty School total: 8. In upper school: 6 women; 2 have advanced degrees.
Special Academic Programs Honors section; accelerated programs; independent study.
College Admission Counseling 12 students graduated in 2008; 10 went to college, including Whittier College. Other: 2 went to work. Median SAT critical reading: 590, median SAT math: 545, median SAT writing: 590, median composite ACT: 25.
Student Life Upper grades have specified standards of dress, student council, honor system. Discipline rests primarily with faculty.
Admissions Deadline for receipt of application materials: none. No application fee required. Interview recommended.
Athletics Interscholastic: aerobics (girls), baseball (g), basketball (g), combined training (g), cooperative games (g), dance (g), equestrian sports (g), fitness (g), fitness walking (g), flag football (g), Frisbee (g), gymnastics (g), hiking/backpacking (g), horseback riding (g), jogging (g), outdoor activities (g), outdoor adventure (g), outdoor recreation (g), physical fitness (g), physical training (g), soccer (g), softball (g), strength & conditioning (g), volleyball (g), walking (g), weight training (g), winter soccer (g), yoga (g). 2 PE instructors.
Computers Computers are regularly used in history classes. Computer network features include on-campus library services, Internet access, wireless campus network, Internet filtering or blocking technology. Students grades are available online. The school has a published electronic and media policy.
Contact Kristie Jensen, Admissions Director. 801-794-1220 Ext. 5271. Fax: 801-794-9558. E-mail: Kristiej@newhavenrtc.com. Web site: www.newhavenrtc.com.

NEW HORIZON YOUTH MINISTRIES

Marion, Indiana
See Special Needs Schools section.

THE NEWMAN SCHOOL

247 Marlborough Street
Boston, Massachusetts 02116
Head of School: Mr. J. Harry Lynch
General Information Coeducational day college-preparatory and ESL school. Grades 9–PG. Founded: 1945. Setting: urban. 2 buildings on campus. Approved or accredited by Association of Independent Schools in New England, New England Association of Schools and Colleges, and Massachusetts Department of Education. Member of Secondary School Admission Test Board. Total enrollment: 230. Upper school average class size: 14. Upper school faculty-student ratio: 1:14.
Upper School Student Profile Grade 9: 45 students (20 boys, 25 girls); Grade 10: 51 students (25 boys, 26 girls); Grade 11: 69 students (32 boys, 37 girls); Grade 12: 65 students (27 boys, 38 girls).
Faculty School total: 25. In upper school: 11 men, 12 women; 9 have advanced degrees.
Subjects Offered Advanced chemistry, Advanced Placement courses, African-American history, algebra, American government-AP, American history, American history-AP, American literature, American literature-AP, anatomy and physiology, anthropology, art, art history, biology, biology-AP, British literature, calculus, calculus-AP, chemistry, computer programming, computer science, computer science-AP, creative writing, drama, earth science, English, English literature, environmental science, ESL, expository writing, fine arts, French, geography, geometry, government-AP, government/civics, grammar, international relations, journalism, Latin, marine biology, mathematics, moral reasoning, physics, psychology, religion, science, social studies, society, politics and law, sociology, Spanish, theater, trigonometry, word processing, world history, world literature, writing.
Graduation Requirements Arts and fine arts (art, music, dance, drama), computer science, English, foreign language, mathematics, science, senior project, social studies (includes history).
Special Academic Programs 7 Advanced Placement exams for which test preparation is offered; honors section; accelerated programs; study at local college for college credit; ESL (25 students enrolled).
College Admission Counseling 60 students graduated in 2008; 58 went to college, including Boston College; Boston University; Northeastern University; Suffolk University; University of Massachusetts Amherst; Worcester Polytechnic Institute. Other: 2 went to work.
Student Life Upper grades have specified standards of dress, student council. Discipline rests primarily with faculty.
Summer Programs Remediation, enrichment, advancement, ESL, computer instruction programs offered; session focuses on high school credits for courses never before taken; held on campus; accepts boys and girls; open to students from other schools. 100 students usually enrolled. 2009 schedule: June 20 to July 10. Application deadline: none.
Tuition and Aid Day student tuition: $14,200–$24,000. Tuition installment plan (monthly payment plans). Merit scholarship grants, need-based scholarship grants available. In 2008–09, 20% of upper-school students received aid; total upper-school merit-scholarship money awarded: $100,000. Total amount of financial aid awarded in 2008–09: $250,000.
Admissions Traditional secondary-level entrance grade is 9. For fall 2008, 165 students applied for upper-level admission, 95 were accepted, 60 enrolled. School's own exam or SSAT required. Deadline for receipt of application materials: none. Application fee required: $40. On-campus interview recommended.
Athletics Interscholastic: baseball (boys), basketball (b,g), cross-country running (b,g), dance (g), lacrosse (g), soccer (b,g), softball (g), tennis (b,g); coed interscholastic: crew, sailing; coed intramural: aerobics/dance, bicycling, fencing, fitness walking, flag football, hiking/backpacking, modern dance, outdoor activities, yoga.
Computers Computers are regularly used in English, ESL, history, library, mathematics, science classes. Computer network features include on-campus library services, Internet access, wireless campus network, Internet filtering or blocking technology. The school has a published electronic and media policy.
Contact Mr. Francis L. Donelan, Vice President. 617-267-4530. Fax: 617-267-7070. Web site: www.newmanboston.org.

See Close-Up on page 872.

NEW MEXICO MILITARY INSTITUTE

101 West College Boulevard
Roswell, New Mexico 88201
Head of School: Rear Adm. David Ellison

General Information Coeducational boarding college-preparatory, arts, and military school. Grades 9–12. Founded: 1891. Setting: small town. Nearest major city is Albuquerque. Students are housed in coed dormitories. 300-acre campus. 17 buildings on campus. Approved or accredited by Council of Accreditation and School Improvement, North Central Association of Colleges and Schools, and New Mexico Department of Education. Member of Secondary School Admission Test Board. Endowment: $130 million. Total enrollment: 380. Upper school average class size: 15. Upper school faculty-student ratio: 1:15.

Upper School Student Profile Grade 9: 96 students (82 boys, 14 girls); Grade 10: 88 students (73 boys, 15 girls); Grade 11: 111 students (94 boys, 17 girls); Grade 12: 86 students (68 boys, 18 girls). 100% of students are boarding students. 45% are state residents. 44 states are represented in upper school student body. 14% are international students. International students from China, Mexico, Poland, Republic of Korea, United Arab Emirates, and United States Minor Outlying Islands; 14 other countries represented in student body.

Faculty School total: 77. In upper school: 37 men, 31 women; 66 have advanced degrees.

Subjects Offered Algebra, American history, American literature, Arabic, art, art history, biology, business, business skills, calculus, chemistry, computer programming, computer science, creative writing, drafting, drama, driver education, earth science, ecology, economics, English, English literature, European history, fine arts, French, geology, geometry, government/civics, grammar, health, history, journalism, JROTC, mathematics, mechanical drawing, music, physical education, physics, science, social science, social studies, sociology, Spanish, speech, theater, trigonometry, typing, world history, writing.

Graduation Requirements Arts and fine arts (art, music, dance, drama), business skills (includes word processing), computer science, English, foreign language, JROTC, mathematics, physical education (includes health), science, social science, social studies (includes history).

Special Academic Programs Honors section; study at local college for college credit.

College Admission Counseling 62 students graduated in 2008; 61 went to college, including New Mexico Military Institute; New Mexico State University; United States Air Force Academy; University of Denver; University of New Mexico. Other: 1 went to work. Median composite ACT: 22. 24% scored over 26 on composite ACT.

Student Life Upper grades have uniform requirement, student council, honor system. Discipline rests equally with students and faculty.

Summer Programs Remediation, enrichment, advancement, sports, art/fine arts, rigorous outdoor training, computer instruction programs offered; session focuses on academics; held both on and off campus; held at online courses; accepts boys and girls; not open to students from other schools. 100 students usually enrolled. 2009 schedule: June 10 to July 15. Application deadline: June 9.

Tuition and Aid 7-day tuition and room/board: $11,261. Tuition installment plan (monthly payment plans, individually arranged payment plans). Merit scholarship grants, need-based scholarship grants available. In 2008–09, 70% of upper-school students received aid; total upper-school merit-scholarship money awarded: $450,000. Total amount of financial aid awarded in 2008–09: $750,000.

Admissions Traditional secondary-level entrance grade is 9. For fall 2008, 678 students applied for upper-level admission, 305 were accepted, 249 enrolled. Common entrance examinations required. Deadline for receipt of application materials: none. Application fee required: $85. Interview required.

Athletics Interscholastic: aquatics (boys, girls), baseball (b), basketball (b,g), cheering (b,g), cross-country running (b,g), diving (b,g), football (b), strength & conditioning (b,g), tennis (b,g), track and field (b,g), volleyball (g); coed interscholastic: drill team, golf, JROTC drill, life saving, marksmanship, riflery, soccer, swimming and diving, tennis; coed intramural: aerobics/Nautilus, alpine skiing, aquatics, archery, bowling, climbing, combined training, fencing, fitness, flag football, Frisbee, martial arts, Nautilus, paint ball, physical fitness, physical training, racquetball, ropes courses, self defense, skiing (downhill), softball, strength & conditioning, swimming and diving, touch football, ultimate Frisbee, weight lifting, weight training. 3 PE instructors, 11 coaches, 2 athletic trainers.

Computers Computers are regularly used in all classes. Computer network features include on-campus library services, online commercial services, Internet access, wireless campus network, Internet filtering or blocking technology. Campus intranet, student e-mail accounts, and computer access in designated common areas are available to students. Students grades are available online. The school has a published electronic and media policy.

Contact Maj. Sonya Rodriguez, Director of Admissions and Financial Aid. 575-624-8065. Fax: 575-624-8058. E-mail: admissions@nmmi.edu. Web site: www.nmmi.edu.

NEW SUMMIT SCHOOL

Jackson, Mississippi
See Special Needs Schools section.

NEW TRIBES MISSION ACADEMY

PO Box 707
Durham, Ontario N0G 1R0, Canada
Head of School: Helmut Penner

General Information Coeducational day college-preparatory school, affiliated with Baptist Bible Fellowship, Brethren Church. Grades K–12. Founded: 1992. Setting: small town. 1-acre campus. 1 building on campus. Approved or accredited by Association of Christian Schools International and Ontario Department of Education. Language of instruction: English. Total enrollment: 28. Upper school average class size: 4. Upper school faculty-student ratio: 1:3.

Upper School Student Profile Grade 6: 5 students (2 boys, 3 girls); Grade 8: 2 students (2 boys); Grade 9: 2 students (2 boys); Grade 10: 2 students (2 boys); Grade 12: 1 student (1 girl). 80% of students are Baptist Bible Fellowship, Brethren.

Faculty School total: 8. In upper school: 3 men, 2 women.

Subjects Offered Art, Bible studies, Canadian history, chemistry, consumer mathematics, English language and composition-AP, French, geometry, literature, music, physical education, world history.

Graduation Requirements Advanced math, algebra, Bible studies, biology, Canadian geography, Canadian history, chemistry, computer skills, consumer mathematics, English, English language and composition-AP, English literature and composition-AP, French, history, mathematics, physical education (includes health), physics, science.

College Admission Counseling 1 student graduated in 2008 and went to college.

Student Life Upper grades have specified standards of dress, honor system. Discipline rests equally with students and faculty.

Tuition and Aid Day student tuition: CAN$1200. Tuition installment plan (monthly payment plans).

Admissions CAT or SAT required. Deadline for receipt of application materials: August 15. No application fee required. Interview recommended.

Athletics Coed Intramural: archery, badminton, basketball, curling, floor hockey, golf, indoor soccer, soccer, tennis, track and field, volleyball. 1 PE instructor.

Computers Computer access in designated common areas is available to students.

Contact Helmut Penner, Principal. 519-369-2622. Fax: 519-369-5828. E-mail: academy@ntmc.ca.

NEW WAY LEARNING ACADEMY

Scottsdale, Arizona
See Special Needs Schools section.

NEW YORK MILITARY ACADEMY

78 Academy Avenue
Cornwall-on-Hudson, New York 12520
Head of School: Capt. Robert D. Watts

General Information Coeducational boarding and day college-preparatory, Junior ROTC, ESL, and military school. Grades 7–12. Founded: 1889. Setting: small town. Nearest major city is New York. Students are housed in single-sex dormitories. 165-acre campus. 11 buildings on campus. Approved or accredited by Middle States Association of Colleges and Schools, New York State Association of Independent Schools, The Association of Boarding Schools, and New York Department of Education. Member of National Association of Independent Schools and Secondary School Admission Test Board. Languages of instruction: English, Spanish, and French. Endowment: $2.6 million. Total enrollment: 146. Upper school average class size: 10. Upper school faculty-student ratio: 1:10.

Upper School Student Profile Grade 9: 23 students (18 boys, 5 girls); Grade 10: 33 students (24 boys, 9 girls); Grade 11: 39 students (36 boys, 3 girls); Grade 12: 28 students (23 boys, 5 girls); Grade 13: 123 students (101 boys, 22 girls). 71% of students are boarding students. 66% are state residents. 12 states are represented in upper school student body. 11% are international students. International students from Ethiopia, Hong Kong, Republic of Korea, Rwanda, and Zimbabwe.

Faculty School total: 26. In upper school: 13 men, 9 women; 8 have advanced degrees; 20 reside on campus.

Subjects Offered Algebra, American history, American history-AP, art, biology, business mathematics, chemistry, computer literacy, criminology, earth science, economics, English, English-AP, environmental science, French, geography, geometry, government, health, JROTC, Latin, physical science, physics, pre-calculus, social studies, Spanish, trigonometry, world history.

Graduation Requirements American history, art, biology, calculus, chemistry, computer science, economics, English, English composition, English literature, foreign language, global studies, government, JROTC or LEAD (Leadership Education and Development), mathematics, physical education (includes health), science, trigonometry. Community service is required.

Special Academic Programs Advanced Placement exam preparation; honors section; study at local college for college credit; ESL (15 students enrolled).

College Admission Counseling Colleges students went to include Embry-Riddle Aeronautical University; Norwich University; Penn State University Park; Rochester Institute of Technology; Stony Brook University, State University of New York; United States Military Academy.

Student Life Upper grades have uniform requirement, student council, honor system. Discipline rests equally with students and faculty. Attendance at religious services is required.
Tuition and Aid Day student tuition: $7800; 7-day tuition and room/board: $25,300. Tuition installment plan (individually arranged payment plans). Tuition reduction for siblings, merit scholarship grants, need-based scholarship grants, TERI Loans, PLATO Junior Loans, Sallie Mae Loans, prepGATE Loans, CitiAssist Loans available. In 2007–08, 46% of upper-school students received aid; total upper-school merit-scholarship money awarded: $36,000. Total amount of financial aid awarded in 2007–08: $280,000.
Admissions Traditional secondary-level entrance grade is 10. For fall 2007, 120 students applied for upper-level admission, 92 were accepted, 73 enrolled. California Achievement Test, Cooperative Entrance Exam (McGraw-Hill), Iowa Tests of Basic Skills, Otis-Lennon School Ability Test, PSAT and SAT for applicants to grade 11 and 12, SLEP, SSAT, Stanford Achievement Test or TOEFL required. Deadline for receipt of application materials: none. Application fee required: $100. On-campus interview required.
Athletics Interscholastic: baseball (boys), basketball (b,g), football (b), ice hockey (b), lacrosse (b); intramural: hockey (b); coed interscholastic: cross-country running, drill team, golf, JROTC drill, marksmanship; coed intramural: dance, dance team, equestrian sports, handball, ice skating, martial arts. 1 PE instructor, 1 coach, 1 athletic trainer.
Computers Computers are regularly used in all academic, keyboarding, lab/keyboard, word processing classes. Computer network features include on-campus library services, Internet access, Internet filtering or blocking technology. Student e-mail accounts are available to students. Students grades are available online. The school has a published electronic and media policy.
Contact Ms. Maureen T. Kelly, Director of Admissions. 845-534-3710 Ext. 4233. Fax: 845-534-7699. E-mail: mkelly@nyma.org. Web site: www.nyma.org.

See Close-Up on page 874.

NIAGARA CHRISTIAN COMMUNITY OF SCHOOLS

2619 Niagara Boulevard
Fort Erie, Ontario L2A 5M4, Canada
Head of School: Mr. Kevin Bayne

General Information Coeducational boarding and day college-preparatory, general academic, arts, business, and religious studies school, affiliated with Brethren in Christ Church. Boarding grades 9–12, day grades JK–12. Founded: 1932. Setting: rural. Nearest major city is Niagara Falls, Canada. Students are housed in single-sex dormitories. 121-acre campus. 15 buildings on campus. Approved or accredited by Association of Christian Schools International and Ontario Department of Education. Language of instruction: English. Total enrollment: 379. Upper school average class size: 17. Upper school faculty-student ratio: 1:17.
Upper School Student Profile Grade 9: 45 students (31 boys, 14 girls); Grade 10: 53 students (32 boys, 21 girls); Grade 11: 79 students (46 boys, 33 girls); Grade 12: 78 students (46 boys, 32 girls). 67% of students are boarding students. 65% are province residents. 3 provinces are represented in upper school student body. 35% are international students. International students from Cayman Islands, Hong Kong, Japan, Mexico, Republic of Korea, and Taiwan; 12 other countries represented in student body. 17% of students are Brethren in Christ Church.
Faculty School total: 23. In upper school: 10 men, 13 women; 5 have advanced degrees; 2 reside on campus.
Subjects Offered Accounting, advanced chemistry, advanced computer applications, advanced math, Advanced Placement courses, advanced TOEFL/grammar, algebra, American history, analysis and differential calculus, analysis of data, analytic geometry, anatomy, ancient history, anthropology, art, art history, athletics, Bible, biology, biology-AP, business, business applications, business education, business mathematics, business technology, calculus, calculus-AP, Canadian geography, Canadian history, Canadian literature, career education, chemistry, choir, civics, computer applications, computer keyboarding, computer programming, concert choir, CPR, data processing, discrete math, dramatic arts, early childhood, economics, English, English literature, ESL, European history, exercise science, family studies, French as a second language, general math, geography, geometry, guidance, health education, history, information technology, instrumental music, integrated science, international affairs, keyboarding/computer, leadership education training, Life of Christ, mathematics, media studies, medieval history, modern world history, music, parenting, physical education, physics, politics, pre-calculus, science, Spanish, TOEFL preparation, world history, world history-AP, world issues, world religions, writing, writing skills.
Special Academic Programs Advanced Placement exam preparation; special instructional classes for students with learning disabilities; ESL (125 students enrolled).
College Admission Counseling 83 students graduated in 2008; 76 went to college, including Brock University; McMaster University; The University of Western Ontario; University of Toronto; University of Waterloo; Wilfrid Laurier University. Other: 2 went to work, 5 had other specific plans.
Student Life Upper grades have uniform requirement, student council, honor system. Discipline rests primarily with faculty. Attendance at religious services is required.
Summer Programs ESL programs offered; session focuses on ESL; held both on and off campus; held at Toronto (3 days); accepts boys and girls; open to students from other schools. 50 students usually enrolled. 2009 schedule: July 6 to August 1. Application deadline: June 1.
Tuition and Aid Day student tuition: CAN$7260; 5-day tuition and room/board: CAN$16,055; 7-day tuition and room/board: CAN$29,890. Tuition installment plan (monthly payment plans, individually arranged payment plans, quarterly payment plan). Tuition reduction for siblings, bursaries, merit scholarship grants, need-based scholarship grants, paying campus jobs available. In 2008–09, 40% of upper-school students received aid; total upper-school merit-scholarship money awarded: CAN$5000. Total amount of financial aid awarded in 2008–09: CAN$250,000.
Admissions Traditional secondary-level entrance grade is 9. For fall 2008, 85 students applied for upper-level admission, 73 were accepted, 68 enrolled. Admissions testing and English proficiency required. Deadline for receipt of application materials: none. Application fee required: CAN$100. Interview required.
Athletics Interscholastic: badminton (boys, girls), basketball (b,g), cross-country running (b,g), golf (b), hockey (b,g), ice hockey (b,g), soccer (b,g), softball (g), swimming and diving (b,g), track and field (b,g), volleyball (b,g); intramural: basketball (b,g), indoor soccer (b,g), soccer (b,g), swimming and diving (b,g), volleyball (b,g); coed interscholastic: badminton; coed intramural: aerobics, alpine skiing, badminton, ball hockey, baseball, bowling, canoeing/kayaking, cross-country running, fitness, fitness walking, floor hockey, golf, ice skating, jogging, racquetball, running, skiing (downhill), snowboarding, softball, swimming and diving, table tennis, track and field, volleyball. 1 PE instructor.
Computers Computers are regularly used in accounting, business, data processing, economics, ESL, keyboarding, mathematics, science, yearbook classes. Computer network features include on-campus library services, Internet access, wireless campus network, Internet filtering or blocking technology. Computer access in designated common areas is available to students. Students grades are available online. The school has a published electronic and media policy.
Contact Mr. Tom Auld, Director of Student Life. 905-871-6980 Ext. 2280. Fax: 905-871-9260. E-mail: tomauld@niagaracc.com. Web site: www.niagaracc.com.

THE NICHOLS SCHOOL

1250 Amherst Street
Buffalo, New York 14216
Head of School: Richard C. Bryan Jr.

General Information Coeducational day college-preparatory, arts, and technology school. Grades 5–12. Founded: 1892. Setting: urban. 25-acre campus. 9 buildings on campus. Approved or accredited by New York State Association of Independent Schools and New York Department of Education. Member of National Association of Independent Schools. Endowment: $16 million. Total enrollment: 585. Upper school average class size: 14. Upper school faculty-student ratio: 1:8.
Upper School Student Profile Grade 9: 92 students (42 boys, 50 girls); Grade 10: 104 students (53 boys, 51 girls); Grade 11: 107 students (60 boys, 47 girls); Grade 12: 97 students (43 boys, 54 girls).
Faculty School total: 79. In upper school: 30 men, 24 women; 18 have advanced degrees.
Subjects Offered Algebra, American history, American literature, anatomy, art, art history, biology, calculus, chemistry, Chinese, community service, computer graphics, computer math, computer programming, computer science, creative writing, dance, drama, driver education, earth science, economics, English, English literature, environmental science, European history, expository writing, fine arts, French, geology, geometry, government/civics, history, Latin, mathematics, music, photography, physical education, physics, science, social studies, Spanish, speech, theater, trigonometry, world history, world literature.
Graduation Requirements Arts and fine arts (art, music, dance, drama), English, foreign language, mathematics, physical education (includes health), science, social studies (includes history).
Special Academic Programs Advanced Placement exam preparation; honors section; independent study; study abroad.
College Admission Counseling 82 students graduated in 2008; 80 went to college, including St. Lawrence University; Trinity College; Tufts University; Union College; University at Buffalo, the State University of New York; University of Pittsburgh. Other: 1 entered a postgraduate year, 1 had other specific plans. Median SAT critical reading: 600, median SAT math: 630, median SAT writing: 610. 50% scored over 600 on SAT critical reading, 60% scored over 600 on SAT math, 56% scored over 600 on SAT writing.
Student Life Upper grades have specified standards of dress, student council, honor system. Discipline rests equally with students and faculty.
Summer Programs Remediation, enrichment, advancement, art/fine arts programs offered; session focuses on academic enrichment; held on campus; accepts boys and girls; open to students from other schools. 68 students usually enrolled. 2009 schedule: June 15 to August 15. Application deadline: none.
Tuition and Aid Day student tuition: $16,200–$17,600. Tuition installment plan (Insured Tuition Payment Plan, monthly payment plans). Need-based scholarship grants available. In 2008–09, 30% of upper-school students received aid. Total amount of financial aid awarded in 2008–09: $1,400,000.
Admissions Traditional secondary-level entrance grade is 9. For fall 2008, 158 students applied for upper-level admission, 117 were accepted, 70 enrolled. Otis-

Lennon and 2 sections of ERB required. Deadline for receipt of application materials: none. Application fee required: $35. On-campus interview required.
Athletics Interscholastic: baseball (boys), basketball (b,g), crew (b,g), cross-country running (b,g), field hockey (g), football (b), golf (b,g), hockey (b,g), ice hockey (b,g), lacrosse (b,g), soccer (b,g), softball (g), squash (b,g), tennis (b,g), track and field (b,g), volleyball (g), wrestling (b); coed interscholastic: aerobics, aerobics/dance, bowling; coed intramural: aerobics/dance. 5 PE instructors, 12 coaches, 3 athletic trainers.
Computers Computers are regularly used in art, library skills, newspaper, photography, science, technology, yearbook classes. Computer network features include on-campus library services, online commercial services, Internet access. Student e-mail accounts are available to students. The school has a published electronic and media policy.
Contact Ms. Laura Yusick, Director of Admissions. 716-332-6325. Fax: 716-875-6474. E-mail: lyusick@nicholsschool.org. Web site: www.nicholsschool.org.

NOAH WEBSTER CHRISTIAN SCHOOL

3411 Cleveland Avenue
PO Box 21239
Cheyenne, Wyoming 82003
Head of School: Miss Shirley Falk

General Information Coeducational day college-preparatory and general academic school, affiliated with Evangelical/Fundamental faith. Grades K–12. Founded: 1987. Setting: small town. Nearest major city is Denver, CO. 1 building on campus. Approved or accredited by Wyoming Department of Education. Total enrollment: 89. Upper school average class size: 12. Upper school faculty-student ratio: 1:15.
Upper School Student Profile Grade 9: 4 students (2 boys, 2 girls); Grade 10: 3 students (1 boy, 2 girls); Grade 11: 1 student (1 girl); Grade 12: 2 students (2 boys).
Faculty School total: 16. In upper school: 9 women; 1 has an advanced degree.
Special Academic Programs Study at local college for college credit.
College Admission Counseling 2 students graduated in 2008; all went to college.
Student Life Upper grades have specified standards of dress, student council. Discipline rests primarily with faculty.
Admissions Deadline for receipt of application materials: none. Application fee required. On-campus interview required.
Athletics 1 PE instructor.
Computers Computer network features include Internet access, Internet filtering or blocking technology. Computer access in designated common areas is available to students.
Contact 307-635-2175. Fax: 307-773-8523. Web site: www.noahweb.org.

NOBLE AND GREENOUGH SCHOOL

10 Campus Drive
Dedham, Massachusetts 02026-4099
Head of School: Mr. Robert P. Henderson Jr.

General Information Coeducational boarding and day college-preparatory school. Boarding grades 9–12, day grades 7–12. Founded: 1866. Setting: suburban. Nearest major city is Boston. Students are housed in single-sex dormitories. 187-acre campus. 12 buildings on campus. Approved or accredited by Association of Independent Schools in New England, New England Association of Schools and Colleges, The College Board, and Massachusetts Department of Education. Member of National Association of Independent Schools and Secondary School Admission Test Board. Endowment: $80 million. Total enrollment: 569. Upper school average class size: 14. Upper school faculty-student ratio: 1:7.
Upper School Student Profile Grade 9: 108 students (54 boys, 54 girls); Grade 10: 118 students (58 boys, 60 girls); Grade 11: 118 students (58 boys, 60 girls); Grade 12: 111 students (57 boys, 54 girls). 9% of students are boarding students. 99% are state residents. 4 states are represented in upper school student body.
Faculty School total: 133. In upper school: 66 men, 67 women; 35 reside on campus.
Subjects Offered 20th century history, Advanced Placement courses, African-American literature, algebra, American history, American literature, anatomy, ancient history, art, art history, astronomy, biology, calculus, ceramics, chemistry, community service, computer programming, computer science, concert band, creative writing, drama, drawing, earth science, ecology, economics, English, English literature, environmental science, ethics, European history, expository writing, fine arts, French, genetics, geography, geometry, government/civics, grammar, health, history, independent study, Japanese, journalism, Latin, Latin American history, marine biology, mathematics, music, painting, philosophy, photography, physics, physiology, printmaking, psychology, Roman civilization, science, senior internship, senior project, social studies, Spanish, speech, statistics, theater, trigonometry, Vietnam, world history, world literature, writing.
Graduation Requirements Arts and fine arts (art, music, dance, drama), computer science, English, foreign language, mathematics, performing arts, physical education (includes health), science, social studies (includes history), 80 hours of community service must be completed.
Special Academic Programs Advanced Placement exam preparation; honors section; independent study; term-away projects; study abroad; academic accommodation for the gifted, the musically talented, and the artistically talented.
College Admission Counseling 113 students graduated in 2008; all went to college, including Boston College; Bowdoin College; Brown University; Cornell University; Duke University; Williams College. 72% scored over 600 on SAT critical reading, 75% scored over 600 on SAT math, 80% scored over 600 on SAT writing.
Student Life Upper grades have specified standards of dress, student council, honor system. Discipline rests equally with students and faculty.
Tuition and Aid Day student tuition: $32,400; 5-day tuition and room/board: $37,000. Tuition installment plan (Tuition Management Systems). Need-based scholarship grants, need-based loans available. In 2008–09, 15% of upper-school students received aid. Total amount of financial aid awarded in 2008–09: $2,148,500.
Admissions Traditional secondary-level entrance grade is 9. For fall 2008, 514 students applied for upper-level admission, 121 were accepted, 62 enrolled. ISEE or SSAT required. Deadline for receipt of application materials: January 15. Application fee required: $50. On-campus interview required.
Athletics Interscholastic: baseball (boys), basketball (b,g), crew (b,g), cross-country running (b,g), field hockey (g), football (b); coed intramural: aerobics/dance, dance. 12 coaches, 2 athletic trainers.
Computers Computers are regularly used in English, foreign language, history, journalism, Latin, mathematics, music, science classes. Computer network features include on-campus library services, online commercial services, Internet access, Internet filtering or blocking technology, NoblesNet (first class e-mail and bulletin board with electronic conferencing capability), Wireless iBooks. Campus intranet, student e-mail accounts, and computer access in designated common areas are available to students. The school has a published electronic and media policy.
Contact Ms. Jennifer Hines, Dean of Enrollment Management. 781-320-7100. Fax: 781-320-1329. E-mail: admission@nobles.edu. Web site: www.nobles.edu.

ANNOUNCEMENT FROM THE SCHOOL Located in Dedham, Massachusetts, Noble and Greenough School is a coeducational day and five-day boarding school of 560 students in grades 7–12. The School believes that education at its best is relational, and the bonds that develop between students and faculty members are strong and lifelong. Every day is started with an all-school assembly, generating a sense of community that permeates the School and carries through the day. The School's core principles are "honesty" and "respect for self and others." The academic curriculum, coupled with a required afternoon program, not only keeps students engaged throughout the entire day, but also challenges them to stretch beyond their comfort zones and tackle new experiences. Many students participate in programs away from the campus, including School Year Abroad and City Term. In addition, the programs in arts, athletics, and community service have all received national recognition. The campus facilities are peerless. The School's mission statement reads: "Noble and Greenough School is a rigorous academic community that strives for excellence in its classroom teaching, intellectual growth in its students, and commitment to the arts, athletics, and service to others. Our diverse community draws together the range of experience from people of different backgrounds and promotes the principles of respect for self and for others in all its activities. Further, the School encourages students to develop within themselves qualities of curiosity, integrity, civility, and humor. Nobles believes in the educational benefit of a supportive environment. The caring relationships between faculty and students develop confidence within young people and encourage them to work toward their highest potential."

THE NORA SCHOOL

955 Sligo Avenue
Silver Spring, Maryland 20910
Head of School: David E. Mullen

General Information Coeducational day college-preparatory, arts, and technology school. Grades 9–12. Founded: 1964. Setting: urban. Nearest major city is Washington, DC. 1-acre campus. 1 building on campus. Approved or accredited by Association of Independent Schools of Greater Washington, Middle States Association of Colleges and Schools, and Maryland Department of Education. Endowment: $208,000. Total enrollment: 60. Upper school average class size: 8. Upper school faculty-student ratio: 1:5.
Upper School Student Profile Grade 9: 14 students (11 boys, 3 girls); Grade 10: 14 students (8 boys, 6 girls); Grade 11: 17 students (4 boys, 13 girls); Grade 12: 15 students (8 boys, 7 girls).
Faculty School total: 12. In upper school: 8 men, 4 women; 10 have advanced degrees.
Subjects Offered African-American literature, algebra, American literature, American studies, art, art history, astronomy, biology, British literature, calculus, ceramics, chemistry, college writing, community service, computer graphics, conceptual physics, conflict resolution, crafts, creative writing, English composition, environmental science, expository writing, film and literature, forensic science, geography, geometry, German, graphic design, illustration, integrated science, peace studies, peer counseling, photo shop, photography, physical education, physics, political science, pre-algebra, pre-calculus, psychology, sculpture, Shakespeare, social justice, Spanish, street law, studio art, trigonometry, U.S. history, wilderness education, women's literature, world history, world religions, writing.

Graduation Requirements Arts and fine arts (art, music, dance, drama), English, foreign language, lab science, mathematics, personal fitness, science, social studies (includes history), sports, U.S. history, wilderness education, writing, graduation portfolio. Community service is required.
Special Academic Programs Independent study; term-away projects; study at local college for college credit; academic accommodation for the gifted and the artistically talented; remedial reading and/or remedial writing; remedial math; programs in English, mathematics, general development for dyslexic students; special instructional classes for students with Attention Deficit Disorder and learning disabilities, students who have been unsuccessful in a traditional learning environment.
College Admission Counseling 15 students graduated in 2008; all went to college, including Goucher College; Guilford College; Husson College; Mitchell College; New England College; Trinity College.
Student Life Upper grades have student council. Discipline rests primarily with faculty.
Summer Programs Remediation, enrichment, advancement, art/fine arts programs offered; held on campus; accepts boys and girls; not open to students from other schools. 8 students usually enrolled.
Tuition and Aid Day student tuition: $20,950. Tuition installment plan (Key Tuition Payment Plan, monthly payment plans, individually arranged payment plans). Need-based scholarship grants, Black student fund, Latino student fund, Washington Scholarship fund available. In 2008–09, 18% of upper-school students received aid. Total amount of financial aid awarded in 2008–09: $115,000.
Admissions Traditional secondary-level entrance grade is 9. For fall 2008, 41 students applied for upper-level admission, 32 were accepted, 20 enrolled. Deadline for receipt of application materials: none. Application fee required: $50. On-campus interview required.
Athletics Interscholastic: basketball (boys, girls); intramural: cheering (g); coed interscholastic: soccer, softball; coed intramural: alpine skiing, backpacking, bicycling, bowling, canoeing/kayaking, climbing, cooperative games, hiking/backpacking, ice skating, kayaking, outdoor activities, outdoor adventure, rafting, rock climbing, ropes courses, skiing (downhill), table tennis, tennis, volleyball, wilderness. 2 coaches.
Computers Computers are regularly used in art, college planning, creative writing, design, drawing and design, English, graphic arts, graphic design, independent study, literary magazine, mathematics, photography, SAT preparation, writing, writing, yearbook classes. Computer network features include on-campus library services, online commercial services, Internet access, wireless campus network, Internet filtering or blocking technology. Students grades are available online. The school has a published electronic and media policy.
Contact Janette Patterson, Director of Admissions. 301-495-6672. Fax: 301-495-7829. E-mail: janette@nora-school.org. Web site: www.nora-school.org.

NORFOLK ACADEMY

1585 Wesleyan Drive
Norfolk, Virginia 23502

Head of School: Mr. Dennis G. Manning

General Information Coeducational day college-preparatory school. Grades 1–12. Founded: 1728. Setting: suburban. 70-acre campus. 14 buildings on campus. Approved or accredited by Southern Association of Colleges and Schools, Virginia Association of Independent Schools, and Virginia Department of Education. Member of National Association of Independent Schools. Endowment: $39 million. Total enrollment: 1,233. Upper school average class size: 20. Upper school faculty-student ratio: 1:10.
Upper School Student Profile Grade 10: 117 students (57 boys, 60 girls); Grade 11: 116 students (62 boys, 54 girls); Grade 12: 116 students (61 boys, 55 girls).
Faculty School total: 124. In upper school: 39 men, 13 women; 32 have advanced degrees.
Subjects Offered Advanced Placement courses, algebra, American history, American literature, art, art history, band, biology, calculus, chemistry, chorus, computer math, computer programming, computer science, dance, driver education, economics, English, English literature, environmental science, European history, film studies, fine arts, French, geography, geometry, German, government/civics, health, history, instrumental music, Italian, Latin, mathematics, music, music history, music theory, physical education, physics, science, social studies, Spanish, speech, statistics, studio art, theater arts, world history.
Graduation Requirements Arts and fine arts (art, music, dance, drama), English, foreign language, mathematics, physical education (includes health), science, social studies (includes history), 8-minute senior speech, Seminar Program. Community service is required.
Special Academic Programs Advanced Placement exam preparation; study abroad; academic accommodation for the gifted, the musically talented, and the artistically talented.
College Admission Counseling 106 students graduated in 2008; all went to college, including The College of William and Mary; The Johns Hopkins University; University of Virginia; Virginia Polytechnic Institute and State University. Mean SAT critical reading: 634, mean SAT math: 660, mean SAT writing: 645.
Student Life Upper grades have specified standards of dress, student council, honor system. Discipline rests primarily with students.
Summer Programs Enrichment, advancement, sports, art/fine arts programs offered; session focuses on academics and athletics; held on campus; accepts boys and girls; open to students from other schools. 500 students usually enrolled. 2009 schedule: June 22 to July 31.
Tuition and Aid Day student tuition: $17,300. Tuition installment plan (Key Tuition Payment Plan, monthly payment plans). Need-based scholarship grants, need-based loans available. In 2008–09, 16% of upper-school students received aid.
Admissions Traditional secondary-level entrance grade is 10. For fall 2008, 17 students applied for upper-level admission, 5 were accepted, 5 enrolled. ERB Achievement Test, ERB CTP IV and Otis-Lennon School Ability Test required. Deadline for receipt of application materials: February 1. Application fee required: $35. Interview required.
Athletics Interscholastic: baseball (boys), basketball (b,g), cheering (g), crew (b,g), cross-country running (b,g), diving (b,g), field hockey (g), football (b), golf (b,g), indoor track (b,g), lacrosse (b,g), sailing (b,g), soccer (b,g), softball (g), swimming and diving (b,g), tennis (b,g), volleyball (g), winter (indoor) track (b,g), wrestling (b); intramural: ballet (g), dance (g), dance team (g), modern dance (g), physical fitness (b,g), physical training (b,g), weight training (b,g). 2 PE instructors, 2 coaches, 3 athletic trainers.
Computers Computers are regularly used in all academic classes. Computer network features include on-campus library services, Internet access, Internet filtering or blocking technology, online library resources, video production, curriculum-based software, desktop publishing, campus-wide media distribution system. Student e-mail accounts and computer access in designated common areas are available to students. The school has a published electronic and media policy.
Contact Mrs. Linda Gorsline, Director of Upper School. 757-461-6236 Ext. 5362. Fax: 757-455-3186. E-mail: lgorsline@norfolkacademy.org. Web site: www.norfolkacademy.org.

ANNOUNCEMENT FROM THE SCHOOL Founded in 1728, Norfolk Academy is a coeducational, college-preparatory day school enrolling 1,230 students in grades 1–12. Committed to excellence in the classroom, on the athletic fields, in the arts, and in service to others, all members of the Norfolk Academy community are bound together by an honor code. Located on 70 acres in the heart of Hampton Roads, the campus now includes the new 50,000-square-foot Tucker Arts Center and the new Athletic Pavilion, in addition to eight other school buildings, a 375-seat auditorium, two libraries, two gymnasiums, an aquatic center, fourteen playing fields, eight tennis courts, a football stadium, and a 400-meter track. The Lower School curriculum consists of language arts, mathematics, science, social studies, music, art, physical education, computers, library, Spanish, guidance and health, and research skills. The Middle and Upper Schools offer American and British literature; history; mathematics through Calculus BC; four years of French, German, and Spanish; six years of Latin; three years of Italian; science through advanced biology, chemistry, and physics; public speaking; and a seminar program. A campuswide computer network includes 500 workstations and eight computer labs. Internet access is available from each network computer. A campuswide media distribution system is available in all classrooms. Exchange programs with China, France, Germany, and Spain are offered. There are seventy-two athletic teams and nearly forty clubs. The faculty numbers 122: 78 women and 49 men; 97 hold advanced degrees. The highest average SAT or ACT equivalent of the Class of 2008 was 1281. Graduates (107 in 2008) entered such colleges and universities as Columbia, Davidson, Duke, Hampden-Sydney, Johns Hopkins, Virginia Tech, Wake Forest, Washington & Lee, William & Mary, and the Universities of North Carolina and Virginia.

NORFOLK CHRISTIAN SCHOOL

255 Thole Street
Norfolk, Virginia 23505

Head of School: Dr. Jane Duffey

General Information Coeducational day college-preparatory, religious studies, and Bible is part and parcel of our entire curriculum. school, affiliated with Christian faith. Grades PK–12. Founded: 1952. Setting: suburban. 9-acre campus. 1 building on campus. Approved or accredited by Association of Christian Schools International, Southern Association of Colleges and Schools, Virginia Association of Independent Schools, and Virginia Department of Education. Total enrollment: 759. Upper school average class size: 22. Upper school faculty-student ratio: 1:15.
Upper School Student Profile Grade 6: 64 students (34 boys, 30 girls); Grade 7: 54 students (29 boys, 25 girls); Grade 8: 74 students (41 boys, 33 girls); Grade 9: 51 students (30 boys, 21 girls); Grade 10: 54 students (23 boys, 31 girls); Grade 11: 52 students (25 boys, 27 girls); Grade 12: 69 students (33 boys, 36 girls). 100% of students are Christian faith.
Faculty School total: 76. In upper school: 16 men, 60 women; 43 have advanced degrees.
Subjects Offered Advanced chemistry, Advanced Placement courses, algebra, American government, American government-AP, American history, American history-AP, American literature, art, athletic training, Bible, biology, biology-AP, British literature, British literature-AP, calculus-AP, chemistry-AP, chorus, Christian

doctrine, Christian ethics, church history, communication skills, computer applications, computer graphics, computer keyboarding, computer multimedia, concert band, digital photography, drama performance, earth science, French, geometry, Latin, Life of Christ, physical education, physics, physics-AP, psychology, psychology-AP, sociology, Spanish, Spanish language-AP, speech, trigonometry, world history.

Graduation Requirements Bible classes are mandatory in grades PK-12. They are graded and become part of the students GPA.

Special Academic Programs Advanced Placement exam preparation; honors section; independent study; academic accommodation for the gifted; remedial reading and/or remedial writing; remedial math.

College Admission Counseling 56 students graduated in 2008; 54 went to college, including Christopher Newport University; Old Dominion University; The University of North Carolina Wilmington; United States Air Force Academy; University of Virginia; Virginia Polytechnic Institute and State University. Other: 2 went to work.

Student Life Upper grades have specified standards of dress, student council, honor system. Discipline rests primarily with faculty. Attendance at religious services is required.

Summer Programs Remediation, enrichment, advancement, sports, art/fine arts programs offered; session focuses on academic; held on campus; accepts boys and girls; open to students from other schools. 50 students usually enrolled. 2009 schedule: June 10 to August 14.

Tuition and Aid Day student tuition: $1050–$8775. Tuition installment plan (FACTS Tuition Payment Plan). Tuition reduction for siblings, need-based scholarship grants, paying campus jobs available. In 2008–09, 24% of upper-school students received aid. Total amount of financial aid awarded in 2008–09: $379,148.

Admissions Traditional secondary-level entrance grade is 9. For fall 2008, 211 students applied for upper-level admission, 156 were accepted, 156 enrolled. Admissions testing required. Deadline for receipt of application materials: none. Application fee required: $100. On-campus interview required.

Athletics Interscholastic: baseball (boys, girls), basketball (b,g), cheering (g), cross-country running (b,g), football (b), golf (b,g), tennis (b,g), track and field (b,g), volleyball (b,g); intramural: badminton (b,g), lacrosse (b), swimming and diving (b,g), wrestling (b); coed intramural: badminton, swimming and diving.

Computers Computers are regularly used in all academic, art, desktop publishing classes. Computer network features include on-campus library services, online commercial services, Internet access, wireless campus network, Internet filtering or blocking technology. Students grades are available online. The school has a published electronic and media policy.

Contact Mr. Ross W. McCloud, Director of Admissions. 757-423-5770 Ext. 116. Fax: 757-440-5388. E-mail: admissions@norfolkchristian.org. Web site: www.norfolkchristian.org.

NORFOLK COLLEGIATE SCHOOL

7336 Granby Street
Norfolk, Virginia 23505

Head of School: Mr. Scott G. Kennedy

General Information Coeducational day college-preparatory school. Grades K–12. Founded: 1948. Setting: urban. 10-acre campus. 1 building on campus. Approved or accredited by Southern Association of Colleges and Schools, Southern Association of Independent Schools, Virginia Association of Independent Schools, and Virginia Department of Education. Member of National Association of Independent Schools. Total enrollment: 896. Upper school average class size: 18. Upper school faculty-student ratio: 1:10.

Upper School Student Profile Grade 9: 70 students (38 boys, 32 girls); Grade 10: 89 students (50 boys, 39 girls); Grade 11: 85 students (44 boys, 41 girls); Grade 12: 89 students (48 boys, 41 girls).

Faculty School total: 95. In upper school: 15 men, 33 women; 31 have advanced degrees.

Subjects Offered Algebra, American history, American literature, analysis, ancient world history, art, art history, astronomy, band, biology, biology-AP, calculus-AP, chemistry, chemistry-AP, chorus, computer-aided design, concert band, cultural geography, drawing, driver education, English, English language-AP, English literature, English literature-AP, environmental science-AP, European history-AP, expository writing, family life, film studies, first aid, French, geology, geometry, German, global issues, government-AP, government/civics, graphic arts, history, human geography—AP, independent study, jazz band, journalism, Latin, Latin-AP, marine biology, mathematics, music, oceanography, painting, photography, physical education, physics, pottery, pre-calculus, psychology-AP, public speaking, publications, SAT preparation, science, social studies, Spanish, statistics-AP, trigonometry, U.S. and Virginia government-AP, U.S. government-AP, U.S. history-AP, video communication, video film production, world geography, world history-AP, yearbook.

Graduation Requirements Algebra, arts and fine arts (art, music, dance, drama), biology, chemistry, computer literacy, English composition, English literature, family life, first aid, foreign language, geometry, health education, mathematics, physical education (includes health), science, senior project, social studies (includes history), U.S. and Virginia government, U.S. and Virginia history, Western civilization.

Special Academic Programs 14 Advanced Placement exams for which test preparation is offered; honors section; independent study; academic accommodation for the gifted; remedial reading and/or remedial writing; remedial math; programs in English, mathematics, general development for dyslexic students.

College Admission Counseling 80 students graduated in 2008; 78 went to college, including George Mason University; James Madison University; Old Dominion University; The University of Alabama at Birmingham; University of Virginia; Virginia Polytechnic Institute and State University. Other: 2 entered a postgraduate year. Median SAT critical reading: 550, median SAT math: 570, median SAT writing: 570, median combined SAT: 1670.

Student Life Upper grades have specified standards of dress, student council, honor system. Discipline rests primarily with faculty.

Summer Programs Remediation, enrichment, sports, art/fine arts, rigorous outdoor training, computer instruction programs offered; session focuses on academic review, enrichment, sports; held on campus; accepts boys and girls; open to students from other schools. 30 students usually enrolled. 2009 schedule: June 15 to July 31. Application deadline: none.

Tuition and Aid Day student tuition: $12,400. Tuition installment plan (monthly payment plans, individually arranged payment plans, semiannual payment plan, The Tuition Refund Plan). Merit scholarship grants, need-based scholarship grants available. In 2008–09, 22% of upper-school students received aid; total upper-school merit-scholarship money awarded: $14,510. Total amount of financial aid awarded in 2008–09: $418,137.

Admissions Traditional secondary-level entrance grade is 9. For fall 2008, 59 students applied for upper-level admission, 45 were accepted, 25 enrolled. ERB CTP IV, ERB Reading and Math, essay and Otis-Lennon School Ability Test required. Deadline for receipt of application materials: February 14. Application fee required: $50. On-campus interview required.

Athletics Interscholastic: baseball (boys), basketball (b,g), cross-country running (b,g), field hockey (g), lacrosse (b,g), soccer (b,g), softball (g), swimming and diving (b,g), tennis (b,g), track and field (b,g), volleyball (b,g), wrestling (b); coed interscholastic: cheering, crew, golf, sailing. 3 PE instructors, 42 coaches, 1 athletic trainer.

Computers Computers are regularly used in art, career exploration, college planning, computer applications, current events, desktop publishing, drawing and design, English, foreign language, graphic arts, health, history, human geography—AP, humanities, independent study, journalism, library skills, literary magazine, mathematics, music, newspaper, photojournalism, publishing, research skills, SAT preparation, science, senior seminar, social science, stock market, video film production, Web site design, yearbook classes. Computer network features include on-campus library services, online commercial services, Internet access, Internet filtering or blocking technology, ProQuest, Biography Resource Center, Contemporary Literary Criticism, Expanded Academic ASAP, ELibrary, Health and Wellness Resource Center, InfoTrac. Students grades are available online. The school has a published electronic and media policy.

Contact Brenda H. Waters, Director of Admissions. 757-480-1495. Fax: 757-588-8655. E-mail: bwaters@norfolkcollegiate.org. Web site: www.norfolkcollegiate.org.

THE NORTH BROWARD PREPARATORY UPPER SCHOOL

7600 Lyons Road
Coconut Creek, Florida 33073

Head of School: David V. Hicks

General Information Coeducational boarding and day college-preparatory, arts, and technology school. Boarding grades 8–12, day grades PK–12. Founded: 1957. Setting: suburban. Students are housed in single-sex dormitories. 75-acre campus. 10 buildings on campus. Approved or accredited by Florida Council of Independent Schools and Southern Association of Colleges and Schools. Total enrollment: 1,583. Upper school average class size: 16. Upper school faculty-student ratio: 1:12.

Upper School Student Profile Grade 9: 132 students (62 boys, 70 girls); Grade 10: 197 students (132 boys, 65 girls); Grade 11: 166 students (90 boys, 76 girls); Grade 12: 203 students (119 boys, 84 girls). 10% of students are boarding students. 93% are state residents. 2 states are represented in upper school student body. 7% are international students. International students from Brazil, China, Germany, Italy, Republic of Korea, and Russian Federation; 6 other countries represented in student body.

Faculty School total: 90. In upper school: 35 men, 55 women; 49 have advanced degrees; 5 reside on campus.

Subjects Offered Algebra, American history-AP, analysis and differential calculus, analytic geometry, ancient world history, art, art history, audio visual/media, Basic programming, biology, biology-AP, British literature, broadcast journalism, business, calculus, calculus-AP, chemistry, chemistry-AP, choir, choral music, college counseling, computer applications, computer graphics, computer keyboarding, computer programming, computer programming-AP, computers, concert band, concert choir, contemporary women writers, drama workshop, dramatic arts, ecology, environmental systems, economics, English, English composition, English literature, English literature and composition-AP, environmental science, environmental science-AP, ESL, European history, European history-AP, forensic science, French, French language-AP, French literature-AP, geometry, guitar, honors algebra, honors English, honors geometry, honors U.S. history, honors world history, jazz band, jazz dance, jazz ensemble, Latin, model United Nations, modern European history, modern European history-AP, music, music appreciation, performing arts, physical education, physical fitness, physics-AP, psychology-AP, robotics, SAT preparation, Shakespeare, skills for success, sociology, Spanish, Spanish language-AP, Spanish literature, Spanish literature-AP, U.S. government, U.S. government-AP, U.S. history, U.S. literature, wind ensemble, wind instruments, women in literature, women's literature, world history-AP.

Graduation Requirements Algebra, American history, American literature, biology, calculus, chemistry, computer applications, electives, English, European history, foreign language, geometry, performing arts, physical education (includes health), physics, U.S. government, U.S. literature, world cultures. Community service is required.

Special Academic Programs International Baccalaureate program; Advanced Placement exam preparation; honors section; independent study; study at local college for college credit; academic accommodation for the gifted, the musically talented, and the artistically talented; remedial reading and/or remedial writing; remedial math; programs in English, mathematics, general development for dyslexic students; ESL (80 students enrolled).

College Admission Counseling 172 students graduated in 2008; 171 went to college, including Florida Atlantic University; Indiana University Bloomington; University of Central Florida; University of Florida; University of Miami. Mean SAT critical reading: 536, mean SAT math: 544, mean SAT writing: 535. 25% scored over 600 on SAT critical reading, 25% scored over 600 on SAT math.

Student Life Upper grades have uniform requirement, student council, honor system. Discipline rests equally with students and faculty.

Summer Programs Remediation, enrichment, advancement, sports, art/fine arts, computer instruction programs offered; session focuses on enrichment; held on campus; accepts boys and girls; open to students from other schools. 750 students usually enrolled. 2009 schedule: June 9 to August 1.

Tuition and Aid Day student tuition: $18,000–$20,000; 7-day tuition and room/board: $32,850–$34,850. Tuition installment plan (monthly payment plans). Tuition reduction for siblings, merit scholarship grants, need-based scholarship grants available. In 2008–09, 18% of upper-school students received aid; total upper-school merit-scholarship money awarded: $300,000. Total amount of financial aid awarded in 2008–09: $1,000,000.

Admissions Traditional secondary-level entrance grade is 9. For fall 2008, 300 students applied for upper-level admission, 258 were accepted, 185 enrolled. SSAT required. Deadline for receipt of application materials: none. Application fee required: $150. Interview required.

Athletics Interscholastic: aquatics (boys, girls), baseball (b), basketball (b,g), bowling (g), cross-country running (b,g), dance (g), dance squad (g), dance team (g), flag football (g), football (b), golf (b,g), ice hockey (b), lacrosse (b,g), physical fitness (b,g), rugby (b), soccer (b,g), softball (g), tennis (b,g), track and field (b,g), volleyball (g), water polo (b,g), winter soccer (b,g), wrestling (b); coed interscholastic: aquatics, bowling, cheering, cross-country running, dressage, fencing, golf, running, scuba diving, strength & conditioning, swimming and diving; coed intramural: basketball, flag football. 5 PE instructors, 17 coaches, 1 athletic trainer.

Computers Computers are regularly used in all academic classes. Computer network features include on-campus library services, online commercial services, Internet access, wireless campus network, Internet filtering or blocking technology. Campus intranet, student e-mail accounts, and computer access in designated common areas are available to students. Students grades are available online. The school has a published electronic and media policy.

Contact Jackie Fagan, Director of Admissions. 954-247-0011 Ext. 303. Fax: 954-247-0012. E-mail: faganj@nbps.org. Web site: www.nbps.org.

NORTH COBB CHRISTIAN SCHOOL

4500 Lakeview Drive
Kennesaw, Georgia 30144

Head of School: Mr. Todd Clingman

General Information Coeducational day college-preparatory, arts, business, and religious studies school, affiliated with Christian faith. Grades PK–12. Founded: 1983. Setting: suburban. Nearest major city is Atlanta. 16-acre campus. 3 buildings on campus. Approved or accredited by Association of Christian Schools International, Georgia Accrediting Commission, and Southern Association of Colleges and Schools. Endowment: $102,225. Total enrollment: 878. Upper school average class size: 20. Upper school faculty-student ratio: 1:6.

Upper School Student Profile Grade 9: 55 students (28 boys, 27 girls); Grade 10: 80 students (37 boys, 43 girls); Grade 11: 43 students (25 boys, 18 girls); Grade 12: 63 students (32 boys, 31 girls). 95% of students are Christian.

Faculty School total: 85. In upper school: 25 men, 30 women; 16 have advanced degrees.

Subjects Offered Acting, Advanced Placement courses, algebra, American government-AP, American literature, analysis, analysis and differential calculus, anatomy and physiology, band, Bible, Bible studies, biology, British literature, British literature (honors), British literature-AP, calculus, calculus-AP, chemistry, choral music, composition, computer graphics, computer keyboarding, computer programming, computer skills, computer technology certification, computers, concert band, concert choir, dance, desktop publishing, drama, ecology, economics, economics-AP, electives, English, English literature-AP, English-AP, English/composition-AP, fine arts, French, French-AP, geometry, government, graphic arts, health, honors algebra, honors geometry, honors U.S. history, HTML design, instrumental music, journalism, leadership skills, life management skills, literature, marching band, math analysis, physical education, physical science, physics, psychology, Spanish, Spanish-AP, statistics, student government, theater, trigonometry, U.S. government, U.S. government-AP, U.S. history, U.S. history-AP, U.S. literature, weight training, word processing, world governments, world history, world history-AP, world literature, world wide web design.

Graduation Requirements Arts and fine arts (art, music, dance, drama), Bible, computers, electives, English, foreign language, mathematics, physical education (includes health), science, social studies (includes history), Leadership Practicum, Apologetics. Community service is required.

Special Academic Programs Advanced Placement exam preparation; honors section; study at local college for college credit; academic accommodation for the musically talented and the artistically talented; programs in general development for dyslexic students; special instructional classes for deaf students.

College Admission Counseling 62 students graduated in 2008; all went to college, including Covenant College; Georgia College & State University; Georgia State University; Kennesaw State University; University of Georgia; Young Harris College.

Student Life Upper grades have specified standards of dress, student council, honor system. Discipline rests equally with students and faculty. Attendance at religious services is required.

Summer Programs Remediation, enrichment, sports, art/fine arts, computer instruction programs offered; session focuses on advancing skills and pleasure; held both on and off campus; held at other college campus for sports purposes; accepts boys and girls; open to students from other schools. 450 students usually enrolled. 2009 schedule: June 1 to July 24. Application deadline: May 1.

Tuition and Aid Day student tuition: $10,620–$11,151. Tuition installment plan (Insured Tuition Payment Plan, FACTS Tuition Payment Plan). Tuition reduction for siblings, need-based scholarship grants available. In 2008–09, 10% of upper-school students received aid. Total amount of financial aid awarded in 2008–09: $100,000.

Admissions Traditional secondary-level entrance grade is 9. For fall 2008, 54 students applied for upper-level admission, 40 were accepted, 39 enrolled. Otis-Lennon, Stanford Achievement Test required. Deadline for receipt of application materials: none. Application fee required: $100. Interview required.

Athletics Interscholastic: aerobics (boys, girls), aerobics/dance (g), ballet (g), baseball (b), basketball (b,g), cheering (g), cross-country running (b,g), dance (g), physical fitness (b,g), soccer (b,g), softball (g), swimming and diving (b,g), tennis (b,g), track and field (b,g), volleyball (g); coed interscholastic: aquatics, archery, golf, strength & conditioning, weight training. 6 PE instructors, 6 coaches, 2 athletic trainers.

Computers Computers are regularly used in art, basic skills, desktop publishing, drawing and design, graphic arts, graphic design, keyboarding, library skills, media production, video film production, word processing, yearbook classes. Computer network features include on-campus library services, Internet access, wireless campus network. Students grades are available online. The school has a published electronic and media policy.

Contact Mrs. Joan Carver, Admissions Assistant. 770-975-0252 Ext. 501. Fax: 770-975-9051. E-mail: jcarver@ncchristian.org. Web site: www.ncchristian.org.

NORTH COUNTRY SCHOOL

Lake Placid, New York

See Junior Boarding Schools section.

NORTH CROSS SCHOOL

4254 Colonial Avenue
Roanoke, Virginia 24018

Head of School: Mr. Timothy J. Seeley

General Information Coeducational day college-preparatory school. Grades JK–12. Founded: 1944. Setting: suburban. 77-acre campus. 6 buildings on campus. Approved or accredited by National Independent Private Schools Association, Virginia Association of Independent Schools, and Virginia Department of Education. Member of National Association of Independent Schools. Endowment: $8 million. Total enrollment: 521. Upper school average class size: 15. Upper school faculty-student ratio: 1:6.

Faculty School total: 54. In upper school: 9 men, 14 women; 14 have advanced degrees.

Subjects Offered Algebra, American history, art, biology, calculus, calculus-AP, chemistry, chemistry-AP, comparative religion, creative writing, drama, English, English literature, English-AP, environmental science-AP, European history, fine arts, French, French-AP, geology, government/civics, health, instrumental music, Latin, Latin-AP, mathematics, physical education, physics, pre-calculus, science, Spanish, Spanish language-AP, Spanish-AP, studio art, theater, writing.

Graduation Requirements Arts and fine arts (art, music, dance, drama), English, foreign language, mathematics, physical education (includes health), science, social studies (includes history), senior project or thesis paper and speech.

Special Academic Programs 36 Advanced Placement exams for which test preparation is offered; honors section; independent study.

College Admission Counseling 54% scored over 600 on SAT math.

Student Life Upper grades have specified standards of dress, student council, honor system. Discipline rests equally with students and faculty.

Summer Programs Enrichment, sports, art/fine arts programs offered; session focuses on Enrichment; held on campus; accepts boys and girls; open to students from other schools. 500 students usually enrolled. 2009 schedule: June 1 to August 20.
Tuition and Aid Tuition installment plan (FACTS Tuition Payment Plan, monthly payment plans). Need-based scholarship grants available.
Admissions Traditional secondary-level entrance grade is 9. Deadline for receipt of application materials: none. Application fee required: $40. Interview recommended.
Athletics Interscholastic: baseball (boys), basketball (b,g), cross-country running (b,g), field hockey (g), football (b), lacrosse (b), soccer (b,g), softball (g), swimming and diving (b,g), tennis (b,g), volleyball (g), wrestling (b); coed interscholastic: golf. 3 PE instructors, 3 coaches.
Computers Computers are regularly used in English, foreign language, history, mathematics, science classes. Computer network features include on-campus library services, online commercial services, Internet access, Internet filtering or blocking technology, VERN. Campus intranet and student e-mail accounts are available to students. The school has a published electronic and media policy.
Contact Mrs. Deborah C. Jessee, Director of Admission and Financial Assistance. 540-989-6641 Ext. 330. Fax: 540-989-7299. E-mail: djessee@northcross.org. Web site: www.northcross.org.

NORTHFIELD MOUNT HERMON SCHOOL

One Lamplighter Way
Mount Hermon, Massachusetts 01354
Head of School: Thomas K. Sturtevant

General Information Coeducational boarding and day college-preparatory, arts, religious studies, and technology school. Grades 9–PG. Founded: 1879. Setting: rural. Nearest major city is Hartford, CT. Students are housed in coed dormitories and single-sex dormitories. 1,100-acre campus. 73 buildings on campus. Approved or accredited by Association of Independent Schools in New England, New England Association of Schools and Colleges, The Association of Boarding Schools, and Massachusetts Department of Education. Member of National Association of Independent Schools and Secondary School Admission Test Board. Endowment: $148 million. Total enrollment: 620. Upper school average class size: 14. Upper school faculty-student ratio: 1:7.
Upper School Student Profile Grade 9: 75 students (38 boys, 37 girls); Grade 10: 138 students (70 boys, 68 girls); Grade 11: 176 students (87 boys, 89 girls); Grade 12: 207 students (101 boys, 106 girls); Postgraduate: 39 students (35 boys, 4 girls). 78% of students are boarding students. 31% are state residents. 28 states are represented in upper school student body. 21% are international students. International students from Germany, Hong Kong, Japan, Republic of Korea, Taiwan, and Thailand; 18 other countries represented in student body.
Faculty School total: 91. In upper school: 44 men, 47 women; 60 have advanced degrees; all reside on campus.
Subjects Offered Algebra, American history, American literature, anthropology, archaeology, art, art history, astronomy, athletics, Bible studies, biology, botany, calculus, ceramics, chemistry, Chinese, computer programming, computer science, creative writing, dance, drama, driver education, earth science, economics, English, English literature, environmental science, ethics, European history, expository writing, fine arts, French, geography, geology, geometry, German, government/civics, Greek, health, history, journalism, Latin, logic, mathematics, music, philosophy, photography, physical education, physics, physiology, psychology, religion, Russian, SAT/ACT preparation, science, social science, social studies, Spanish, speech, statistics, theater, trigonometry, typing, world history, world literature, writing.
Graduation Requirements Arts and fine arts (art, music, dance, drama), English, foreign language, mathematics, physical education (includes health), religion (includes Bible studies and theology), science, social studies (includes history), participation in work program.
Special Academic Programs Advanced Placement exam preparation; honors section; accelerated programs; independent study; term-away projects; study at local college for college credit; study abroad; academic accommodation for the gifted, the musically talented, and the artistically talented; ESL (32 students enrolled).
College Admission Counseling 247 students graduated in 2008; 238 went to college, including Connecticut College; Cornell University; Hamilton College; Ithaca College; New York University; The Johns Hopkins University. Other: 1 went to work, 3 entered military service, 5 had other specific plans. Mean SAT critical reading: 598, mean SAT math: 604, mean composite ACT: 24.
Student Life Upper grades have student council, honor system. Discipline rests primarily with faculty.
Summer Programs Remediation, enrichment, ESL programs offered; session focuses on Intense academic preparation; held both on and off campus; held at New Zealand; accepts boys and girls; open to students from other schools.
Tuition and Aid Day student tuition: $29,300; 7-day tuition and room/board: $41,700. Tuition installment plan (Academic Management Services Plan, monthly payment plans). Need-based scholarship grants, need-based loans, middle-income loans, AchieverLoans (Key Education Resources), prepGATE Loans, Sallie Mae Loans available. In 2008–09, 44% of upper-school students received aid. Total amount of financial aid awarded in 2008–09: $5,500,000.
Admissions Traditional secondary-level entrance grade is 9. For fall 2008, 1,009 students applied for upper-level admission, 519 were accepted, 231 enrolled. ACT, CTP, ISEE, PSAT, SAT, SSAT or TOEFL required. Deadline for receipt of application materials: February 1. Application fee required: $50. Interview recommended.
Athletics Interscholastic: alpine skiing (boys, girls), baseball (b), basketball (b,g), crew (b,g), cross-country running (b,g), field hockey (g), football (b), hockey (b,g), ice hockey (b,g), lacrosse (b,g); coed interscholastic: dance, dance team, Frisbee, golf, modern dance; coed intramural: aerobics, aerobics/dance, alpine skiing, aquatics, badminton, ballet, basketball, bicycling, canoeing/kayaking, climbing, dance, dance team, fencing, fitness, jogging, lacrosse, martial arts, modern dance. 8 PE instructors, 8 coaches, 2 athletic trainers.
Computers Computers are regularly used in desktop publishing, English, foreign language, mathematics, music, science classes. Computer network features include on-campus library services, online commercial services, Internet access, wireless campus network, Internet filtering or blocking technology. Campus intranet and student e-mail accounts are available to students. Students grades are available online. The school has a published electronic and media policy.
Contact Office of Admission. 413-498-3227. Fax: 413-498-3152. E-mail: admission@nmhschool.org. Web site: www.nmhschool.org.

ANNOUNCEMENT FROM THE SCHOOL The NMH academic program blends traditional values with the latest innovations in education. NMH provides focus (students take three major courses per semester), individual attention (Moody system of advising, college counseling), opportunity (200 courses, 60 sports teams, a new arts center with state-of-the-art facilities, more than 35 student groups, 11 study-abroad options), and values (work, service, and spirituality programs).

See Close-Up on page 876.

NORTH SHORE COUNTRY DAY SCHOOL

310 Green Bay Road
Winnetka, Illinois 60093-4094
Head of School: Mr. Tom Doar III

General Information Coeducational day college-preparatory, arts, technology, Global, and Service-learning school. Grades PK–12. Founded: 1919. Setting: suburban. Nearest major city is Chicago. 16-acre campus. 6 buildings on campus. Approved or accredited by Independent Schools Association of the Central States and Illinois Department of Education. Member of National Association of Independent Schools and Secondary School Admission Test Board. Endowment: $21 million. Total enrollment: 493. Upper school average class size: 14. Upper school faculty-student ratio: 1:8.
Upper School Student Profile Grade 9: 46 students (19 boys, 27 girls); Grade 10: 53 students (30 boys, 23 girls); Grade 11: 45 students (20 boys, 25 girls); Grade 12: 43 students (17 boys, 26 girls).
Faculty School total: 76. In upper school: 27 men, 35 women; 42 have advanced degrees.
Subjects Offered Algebra, American history, American literature, anatomy, art, art history, Asian studies, biology, biology-AP, calculus, calculus-AP, ceramics, chemistry, chemistry-AP, computer math, computer programming, computer science, creative writing, drama, earth science, ecology, economics, English, English literature, English-AP, environmental science, European history, expository writing, fine arts, French, French-AP, geography, geometry, government/civics, grammar, industrial arts, journalism, Mandarin, marine biology, mathematics, music, photography, physical education, physics, physics-AP, science, social studies, Spanish, Spanish-AP, speech, statistics, statistics-AP, technology, theater, trigonometry, U.S. history-AP, world history, world literature, writing.
Graduation Requirements Arts and fine arts (art, music, dance, drama), computer science, English, foreign language, mathematics, physical education (includes health), physical fitness, science, social studies (includes history), technology, one stage performance in four years, completion of senior service project in May, completion of one-week community service project in four years.
Special Academic Programs Advanced Placement exam preparation; independent study; term-away projects; study at local college for college credit; study abroad.
College Admission Counseling 48 students graduated in 2008; 46 went to college, including University of Illinois at Urbana–Champaign. Other: 2 had other specific plans.
Student Life Upper grades have specified standards of dress, student council, honor system. Discipline rests primarily with faculty.
Summer Programs Enrichment, sports, art/fine arts, rigorous outdoor training, computer instruction programs offered; session focuses on academic and artistic enrichment, outdoor expedition, soccer, basketball, field hockey; held both on and off campus; held at lakefront and local preserves and camp sites; accepts boys and girls; open to students from other schools. 750 students usually enrolled. 2009 schedule: June 16 to August 8. Application deadline: none.
Tuition and Aid Day student tuition: $20,791–$21,777. Tuition installment plan (Insured Tuition Payment Plan, Key Tuition Payment Plan, monthly payment plans, individually arranged payment plans, trimester payment plan). Merit scholarship grants, need-based scholarship grants, need-based loans, middle-income loans available. In 2008–09, 15% of upper-school students received aid. Total amount of financial aid awarded in 2008–09: $900,000.

North Shore Country Day School

Admissions Traditional secondary-level entrance grade is 9. ERB and writing sample required. Deadline for receipt of application materials: none. Application fee required: $50. On-campus interview required.
Athletics Interscholastic: baseball (boys), basketball (b,g), cross-country running (b,g), field hockey (g), football (b), golf (b,g), indoor track & field (b,g), soccer (b,g), tennis (b,g), track and field (b,g), volleyball (g); intramural: physical training (b,g), weight lifting (b,g); coed intramural: dance, sailing. 4 PE instructors, 24 coaches, 1 athletic trainer.
Computers Computers are regularly used in accounting, all academic classes. Computer network features include on-campus library services, online commercial services, Internet access, wireless campus network, Internet filtering or blocking technology. Campus intranet and student e-mail accounts are available to students. The school has a published electronic and media policy.
Contact Ms. Diane Olson, Admissions Associate. 847-441-3313. Fax: 847-446-0675. E-mail: dolson@nscds.org. Web site: www.nscds.org.

ANNOUNCEMENT FROM THE SCHOOL Committed to the academic, personal, and social development of its students, North Shore Country Day School offers a rigorous college-preparatory curriculum that includes AP courses along with community service, performing arts, and athletic requirements. The School has developed unique programs in languages, global consciousness, humanities, math, and science and technology. Call Admissions at 847-441-3313 or visit www.nscds.org.

NORTHSIDE CHRISTIAN SCHOOL

7777 62nd Avenue North
St. Petersburg, Florida 33709
Head of School: Mrs. Mary Brandes
General Information Coeducational day college-preparatory, arts, religious studies, and technology school, affiliated with Baptist Church. Grades PS–12. Founded: 1971. Setting: urban. 32-acre campus. 3 buildings on campus. Approved or accredited by Association of Christian Schools International, Scottish Education Department, Southern Association of Colleges and Schools, and Florida Department of Education. Endowment: $50,000. Total enrollment: 877. Upper school average class size: 20. Upper school faculty-student ratio: 1:11.
Upper School Student Profile 27% of students are Baptist.
Faculty School total: 65. In upper school: 10 men, 15 women; 10 have advanced degrees.
Subjects Offered 3-dimensional art, Advanced Placement courses, algebra, American government, American history, American history-AP, anatomy and physiology, band, Bible studies, biology, business mathematics, calculus-AP, chamber groups, chemistry, chemistry-AP, chorus, Christian education, communication skills, computer applications, computer information systems, computer keyboarding, computer multimedia, computers, drama, economics, economics and history, English, English literature and composition-AP, English-AP, eurythmics (guard), fine arts, fitness, foreign language, French, general science, geometry, health, health education, jazz band, journalism, keyboarding, language arts, marine biology, marine science, mathematics, mathematics-AP, music, music appreciation, music theory, physical education, physical science, physics, pre-algebra, pre-calculus, psychology, Spanish, Spanish literature, speech, sports, study skills, track and field, U.S. history, volleyball, weight fitness, weight training, world history, world religions, yearbook.
Graduation Requirements Arts and fine arts (art, music, dance, drama), business skills (includes word processing), computer science, English, foreign language, mathematics, physical education (includes health), religion (includes Bible studies and theology), science, social science, social studies (includes history), SAT and ACT testing. Community service is required.
Special Academic Programs Advanced Placement exam preparation; honors section; independent study; academic accommodation for the gifted; programs in English, mathematics, general development for dyslexic students.
College Admission Counseling 45 students graduated in 2008; all went to college, including Florida State University; St. Petersburg College; University of Central Florida; University of Florida; University of North Florida; University of South Florida. Mean SAT critical reading: 538, mean SAT math: 529, mean composite ACT: 23. 25% scored over 600 on SAT critical reading, 25% scored over 600 on SAT math.
Student Life Upper grades have specified standards of dress, student council, honor system. Discipline rests primarily with faculty. Attendance at religious services is required.
Summer Programs Enrichment, sports, art/fine arts, computer instruction programs offered; session focuses on enrichment; held on campus; accepts boys and girls; open to students from other schools. 70 students usually enrolled. 2009 schedule: June 1 to August 1. Application deadline: May 31.
Tuition and Aid Day student tuition: $6433. Tuition installment plan (monthly payment plans). Need-based scholarship grants available. In 2008–09, 10% of upper-school students received aid. Total amount of financial aid awarded in 2008–09: $20,000.
Admissions Traditional secondary-level entrance grade is 9. For fall 2008, 25 students applied for upper-level admission, 22 were accepted, 20 enrolled. PSAT or Stanford Achievement Test required. Deadline for receipt of application materials: none. Application fee required: $75. Interview required.
Athletics Interscholastic: baseball (boys), basketball (b,g), cheering (g), cross-country running (b,g), football (b), golf (b), soccer (g), softball (g), swimming and diving (b,g), track and field (b,g), volleyball (g), weight lifting (b), wrestling (b); intramural: basketball (b,g), fitness (b,g), flag football (b); coed interscholastic: cross-country running, track and field. 4 PE instructors, 4 coaches, 1 athletic trainer.
Computers Computers are regularly used in business, desktop publishing, ESL, library, mathematics, newspaper, science, typing, word processing, yearbook classes. Computer network features include on-campus library services, Internet access.
Contact Mrs. Joni McAlpin, Admissions/Registrar. 727-541-7593 Ext. 251. Fax: 727-546-5836. E-mail: joni.mcalpin@nck12.com. Web site: www.nck12.com.

NORTHWEST ACADEMY

Naples, Idaho
See Special Needs Schools section.

THE NORTHWEST ACADEMY

1130 Southwest Main Street
Portland, Oregon 97205
Head of School: Mary Vinton Folberg
General Information Coeducational day college-preparatory, arts, and technology school. Grades 6–12. Founded: 1995. Setting: urban. 4 buildings on campus. Approved or accredited by Northwest Association of Schools and Colleges, Pacific Northwest Association of Independent Schools, and Oregon Department of Education. Total enrollment: 120. Upper school average class size: 15. Upper school faculty-student ratio: 1:15.
Upper School Student Profile Grade 9: 15 students (7 boys, 8 girls); Grade 10: 18 students (10 boys, 8 girls); Grade 11: 18 students (9 boys, 9 girls); Grade 12: 17 students (8 boys, 9 girls).
Faculty School total: 38. In upper school: 16 men, 13 women; 8 have advanced degrees.
Subjects Offered 20th century history, acting, algebra, anatomy and physiology, animation, art history, ballet, biology, calculus, career/college preparation, cartooning, chamber groups, chemistry, comparative government and politics, comparative politics, comparative religion, computer animation, computer keyboarding, computer literacy, computer music, creative writing, critical thinking, dance performance, desktop publishing, digital art, drama workshop, drawing, earth and space science, ecology, environmental systems, English literature, European civilization, film studies, French, geometry, history of music, Holocaust studies, human anatomy, humanities, illustration, independent study, internship, introduction to digital multi-track recording techniques, jazz band, jazz dance, jazz ensemble, journalism, martial arts, media arts, medieval/Renaissance history, multimedia design, music composition, music history, music performance, musical theater, painting, photo shop, physics, play/screen writing, political systems, pre-calculus, printmaking, senior thesis, Shakespeare, social science, Spanish, student publications, tap dance, theater, trigonometry, U.S. government and politics, U.S. history, video film production, visual arts, vocal ensemble, vocal jazz, world cultures, world history, world wide web design, writing fundamentals.
Graduation Requirements 4 Years of English/Humanities, Senior Thesis Seminar, 3 Years of both Math & Science, 2 years of foreign language, 6 units of credit of arts electives, community service, computer literacy, PE.
Special Academic Programs Accelerated programs; independent study; study at local college for college credit; academic accommodation for the gifted, the musically talented, and the artistically talented.
College Admission Counseling 11 students graduated in 2008; all went to college, including California Institute of the Arts; Kenyon College; Marlboro College; New York University; Pratt Institute; Sarah Lawrence College.
Student Life Upper grades have student council, honor system. Discipline rests primarily with faculty.
Tuition and Aid Day student tuition: $17,500. Tuition installment plan (FACTS Tuition Payment Plan). Need-based scholarship grants available. In 2008–09, 20% of upper-school students received aid. Total amount of financial aid awarded in 2008–09: $150,000.
Admissions Traditional secondary-level entrance grade is 9. For fall 2008, 15 students applied for upper-level admission, 13 were accepted, 9 enrolled. Admissions testing, placement test and writing sample required. Deadline for receipt of application materials: February 13. Application fee required: $100. Interview required.
Athletics Coed Intramural: aerobics, aerobics/dance, artistic gym, ballet, cooperative games, dance, modern dance, tai chi, yoga.
Computers Computer network features include on-campus library services, Internet access, film and audio editing, sound design, animation, Flash. The school has a published electronic and media policy.
Contact Lainie Keslin Ettinger, Director of Admissions. 503-223-3367 Ext. 104. Fax: 503-402-1043. E-mail: lettinger@nwacademy.org. Web site: www.nwacademy.org.

NORTHWEST CATHOLIC HIGH SCHOOL

29 Wampanoag Drive
West Hartford, Connecticut 06117

Head of School: Mr. Matthew O'N. Fitzsimons

General Information Coeducational day college-preparatory school, affiliated with Roman Catholic Church. Grades 9–12. Founded: 1961. Setting: suburban. Nearest major city is Hartford. 1 building on campus. Approved or accredited by New England Association of Schools and Colleges and Connecticut Department of Education. Total enrollment: 620. Upper school average class size: 18. Upper school faculty-student ratio: 1:12.

Upper School Student Profile 80% of students are Roman Catholic.

Graduation Requirements Arts and fine arts (art, music, dance, drama), English, foreign language, health education, mathematics, physical education (includes health), religion (includes Bible studies and theology), science, social studies (includes history), 25 hours of community service.

Special Academic Programs 14 Advanced Placement exams for which test preparation is offered; honors section; study at local college for college credit.

College Admission Counseling 174 students graduated in 2008.

Student Life Upper grades have uniform requirement, student council. Discipline rests primarily with faculty. Attendance at religious services is required.

Tuition and Aid Day student tuition: $11,700. Tuition installment plan (monthly payment plans). Tuition reduction for siblings, merit scholarship grants, need-based scholarship grants available.

Admissions Traditional secondary-level entrance grade is 9. High School Placement Test required. Application fee required: $30.

Athletics Interscholastic: baseball (boys), basketball (b,g), cheering (g), cross-country running (b,g), field hockey (g), football (b), ice hockey (b), indoor track & field (b,g), lacrosse (b,g), soccer (b,g), softball (g), tennis (b,g), track and field (b,g), volleyball (g), winter (indoor) track (b,g); intramural: basketball (b,g); coed interscholastic: diving, golf, swimming and diving; coed intramural: dance team, flag football, indoor soccer, outdoor adventure, rafting, rappelling, rock climbing, ropes courses, scuba diving, skiing (downhill), snowboarding, strength & conditioning, ultimate Frisbee, weight training, whiffle ball. 1 PE instructor, 1 athletic trainer.

Computers Computers are regularly used in all academic classes. Computer network features include on-campus library services, Internet access, Internet filtering or blocking technology. Students grades are available online. The school has a published electronic and media policy.

Contact Mrs. Nancy Scully Bannon, Director of Admissions. 860-236-4221 Ext. 124. Fax: 860-570-0080. E-mail: nbannon@nwcath.org. Web site: www.northwestcatholic.org.

THE NORTHWEST SCHOOL

1415 Summit Avenue
Seattle, Washington 98122

Head of School: Ellen Taussig

General Information Coeducational boarding and day college-preparatory, arts, and ESL school. Boarding grades 9–12, day grades 6–12. Founded: 1978. Setting: urban. Students are housed in coed dormitories. 1-acre campus. 4 buildings on campus. Approved or accredited by Northwest Association of Accredited Schools, Pacific Northwest Association of Independent Schools, and Washington Department of Education. Member of National Association of Independent Schools. Endowment: $387,198. Total enrollment: 477. Upper school average class size: 17. Upper school faculty-student ratio: 1:9.

Upper School Student Profile Grade 9: 86 students (40 boys, 46 girls); Grade 10: 86 students (44 boys, 42 girls); Grade 11: 88 students (44 boys, 44 girls); Grade 12: 87 students (44 boys, 43 girls). 11% of students are boarding students. 80% are state residents. 2 states are represented in upper school student body. 20% are international students. International students from China, Hong Kong, Japan, Republic of Korea, Taiwan, and Thailand; 5 other countries represented in student body.

Faculty School total: 67. In upper school: 23 men, 34 women; 40 have advanced degrees.

Subjects Offered Advanced chemistry, algebra, astronomy, biology, calculus, cartooning, ceramics, chemistry, Chinese, chorus, computer skills, contemporary problems, dance, drama, drawing, driver education, earth science, English, ESL, evolution, fiber arts, film, fine arts, folk dance, French, geometry, health, history, humanities, illustration, improvisation, jazz dance, jazz ensemble, journalism, life science, literature, math analysis, mathematics, mentorship program, musical theater, orchestra, outdoor education, painting, performing arts, philosophy, photography, physical education, physical science, physics, play production, pre-algebra, pre-calculus, printmaking, Spanish, statistics, strings, textiles, theater, trigonometry, U.S. government and politics, U.S. history, visual arts, Washington State and Northwest History, water color painting, wilderness/outdoor program, world history, writing.

Graduation Requirements English, foreign language, humanities, mathematics, physical education (includes health), science, senior thesis, visual and performing arts, participation in environmental maintenance program.

Special Academic Programs Academic accommodation for the gifted, the musically talented, and the artistically talented; ESL (48 students enrolled).

College Admission Counseling 70 students graduated in 2008; 69 went to college, including Lewis & Clark College; New York University; Occidental College; University of Washington; University of Wisconsin–Madison; Wesleyan University. Other: 1 had other specific plans.

Student Life Upper grades have honor system. Discipline rests primarily with faculty.

Summer Programs Enrichment, ESL, sports, art/fine arts, computer instruction programs offered; session focuses on Global connections with International students; held on campus; accepts boys and girls; open to students from other schools. 325 students usually enrolled. 2009 schedule: July 6 to August 14. Application deadline: June 20.

Tuition and Aid Day student tuition: $25,095; 7-day tuition and room/board: $36,775. Tuition installment plan (school's own payment plan). Need-based scholarship grants available. In 2008–09, 16% of upper-school students received aid. Total amount of financial aid awarded in 2008–09: $932,170.

Admissions Traditional secondary-level entrance grade is 9. For fall 2008, 269 students applied for upper-level admission, 162 were accepted, 67 enrolled. ISEE required. Deadline for receipt of application materials: January 15. Application fee required: $55. On-campus interview required.

Athletics Interscholastic: basketball (boys, girls), cross-country running (b,g), soccer (b,g), track and field (b,g), ultimate Frisbee (b,g), volleyball (g); coed interscholastic: ultimate Frisbee; coed intramural: fitness, hiking/backpacking, outdoor education, rock climbing, ropes courses, skiing (cross-country), skiing (downhill), ultimate Frisbee. 6 PE instructors, 6 coaches.

Computers Computers are regularly used in art, English, ESL, foreign language, health, humanities, journalism, mathematics, science, video film production, writing, yearbook classes. Computer network features include on-campus library services, Internet access, wireless campus network, ProQuest, Big Chalk, and World Book Online databases. Computer access in designated common areas is available to students. The school has a published electronic and media policy.

Contact Anne Smith, Director of Admissions. 206-682-7309. Fax: 206-467-7353. E-mail: anne.smith@northwestschool.org. Web site: www.northwestschool.org.

NORTHWEST YESHIVA HIGH SCHOOL

5017 90th Avenue Southeast
Mercer Island, Washington 98040

Head of School: Rabbi Bernie Fox

General Information Coeducational day college-preparatory and religious studies school, affiliated with Jewish faith. Grades 9–12. Founded: 1974. Setting: suburban. Nearest major city is Seattle. 2-acre campus. 3 buildings on campus. Approved or accredited by Northwest Association of Schools and Colleges and Washington Department of Education. Languages of instruction: English and Hebrew. Endowment: $841,000. Total enrollment: 92. Upper school average class size: 12. Upper school faculty-student ratio: 1:4.

Upper School Student Profile Grade 9: 25 students (14 boys, 11 girls); Grade 10: 20 students (12 boys, 8 girls); Grade 11: 28 students (12 boys, 16 girls); Grade 12: 19 students (13 boys, 6 girls). 100% of students are Jewish.

Faculty School total: 30. In upper school: 15 men, 15 women; 15 have advanced degrees.

Subjects Offered 20th century history, algebra, American legal systems, art, art history, biology, calculus, chemistry, college admission preparation, college counseling, drama, economics, English, film appreciation, fine arts, geometry, Hebrew, Hebrew scripture, integrated mathematics, Jewish history, Judaic studies, lab science, language arts, modern Western civilization, newspaper, philosophy, physical education, physics, prayer/spirituality, pre-algebra, pre-calculus, psychology, Rabbinic literature, religious studies, Spanish, Talmud, U.S. government, U.S. history, U.S. literature, Western civilization, world history, writing, yearbook.

Graduation Requirements Advanced math, arts and fine arts (art, music, dance, drama), biology, conceptual physics, Hebrew, integrated mathematics, Judaic studies, language arts, physics, Spanish, Talmud, U.S. government, U.S. history, world history. Community service is required.

Special Academic Programs Independent study; academic accommodation for the gifted; remedial reading and/or remedial writing; remedial math; special instructional classes for deaf students; ESL (1 student enrolled).

College Admission Counseling Colleges students went to include Brandeis University; University of Washington; Yeshiva University. Other: 1 entered military service, 10 had other specific plans. Median SAT critical reading: 620, median SAT math: 550, median SAT writing: 590, median combined SAT: 1780. 40% scored over 600 on SAT critical reading, 53% scored over 600 on SAT math, 47% scored over 600 on SAT writing, 40% scored over 1800 on combined SAT.

Student Life Upper grades have specified standards of dress, student council, honor system. Discipline rests primarily with faculty. Attendance at religious services is required.

Tuition and Aid Day student tuition: $12,000. Tuition installment plan (monthly payment plans, individually arranged payment plans). Need-based scholarship grants available. In 2008–09, 34% of upper-school students received aid. Total amount of financial aid awarded in 2008–09: $154,000.

Admissions Traditional secondary-level entrance grade is 9. Deadline for receipt of application materials: February 14. Application fee required: $250. Interview required.

Athletics Interscholastic: basketball (boys, girls), crew (b,g), cross-country running (b,g), golf (b,g), volleyball (g); coed interscholastic: cross-country running, softball. 5 PE instructors, 5 coaches.
Computers Computer network features include Internet access.
Contact Mr. Ian Weiner, Director of Student Services. 206-232-5272. Fax: 206-232-2711. E-mail: admin@nyhs.com. Web site: www.nyhs.net.

NORTHWOOD SCHOOL

PO Box 1070
Lake Placid, New York 12946
Head of School: Edward M. Good

General Information Coeducational boarding and day college-preparatory school. Grades 9–PG. Founded: 1905. Setting: small town. Nearest major city is Albany. Students are housed in single-sex dormitories. 80-acre campus. 8 buildings on campus. Approved or accredited by New York State Association of Independent Schools and The Association of Boarding Schools. Member of National Association of Independent Schools and Secondary School Admission Test Board. Endowment: $8 million. Total enrollment: 174. Upper school average class size: 9. Upper school faculty-student ratio: 1:6.
Upper School Student Profile Grade 9: 22 students (11 boys, 11 girls); Grade 10: 40 students (27 boys, 13 girls); Grade 11: 50 students (35 boys, 15 girls); Grade 12: 56 students (37 boys, 19 girls); Postgraduate: 6 students (6 boys). 85% of students are boarding students. 35% are state residents. 24 states are represented in upper school student body. 30% are international students. International students from Canada, China, France, Republic of Korea, Spain, and United Kingdom; 6 other countries represented in student body.
Faculty School total: 34. In upper school: 24 men, 10 women; 18 have advanced degrees; 18 reside on campus.
Subjects Offered Algebra, American history, American literature, art, biology, calculus, ceramics, chemistry, computer science, drama, earth science, English, English literature, ensembles, environmental science, expository writing, fiber arts, French, geography, geology, geometry, government/civics, great issues, health, history, journalism, mathematics, music, photography, physical education, physics, psychology, SAT preparation, science, social studies, sociology, Spanish, theater, trigonometry, world history.
Graduation Requirements Arts and fine arts (art, music, dance, drama), English, foreign language, mathematics, physical education (includes health), science, social studies (includes history).
Special Academic Programs Advanced Placement exam preparation; honors section; independent study; remedial reading and/or remedial writing; ESL (18 students enrolled).
College Admission Counseling 62 students graduated in 2008; 54 went to college, including Boston College; Clarkson University; Colgate University; Queen's University at Kingston; St. Lawrence University; Wesleyan University. Other: 3 entered a postgraduate year, 4 had other specific plans. Median SAT critical reading: 520, median SAT math: 500, median SAT writing: 510.
Student Life Upper grades have specified standards of dress, student council, honor system. Discipline rests primarily with faculty.
Tuition and Aid Day student tuition: $20,975; 7-day tuition and room/board: $38,350. Tuition installment plan (The Tuition Plan, Key Tuition Payment Plan, monthly payment plans, individually arranged payment plans, 3-payment plan). Need-based scholarship grants available. In 2008–09, 50% of upper-school students received aid. Total amount of financial aid awarded in 2008–09: $1,150,000.
Admissions Traditional secondary-level entrance grade is 10. For fall 2008, 224 students applied for upper-level admission, 120 were accepted, 77 enrolled. SSAT or TOEFL or SLEP required. Deadline for receipt of application materials: none. Application fee required: $40. On-campus interview required.
Athletics Interscholastic: crew (boys, girls), hockey (b,g), ice hockey (b,g), ice skating (b,g), lacrosse (b,g), nordic skiing (b,g), ski jumping (b,g), skiing (downhill) (b,g), soccer (b,g), telemark skiing (b,g), tennis (b,g); intramural: hockey (b,g), ice hockey (b,g), ice skating (b,g), skiing (downhill) (b,g), snowboarding (b,g); coed interscholastic: alpine skiing, figure skating, fitness, freestyle skiing, golf, nordic skiing, skiing (cross-country), snowboarding, telemark skiing; coed intramural: alpine skiing, backpacking, bicycling, canoeing/kayaking, climbing, combined training, cross-country running, figure skating, fishing, fitness, fly fishing, freestyle skiing, golf, hiking/backpacking, jogging, kayaking, luge, mountain biking, mountaineering, nordic skiing, outdoor adventure, physical training, rafting, rappelling, rock climbing, ropes courses, rowing, running, skiing (cross-country), skiing (downhill), snowboarding, street hockey, strength & conditioning, tennis, walking, wall climbing, weight training, wilderness, wilderness survival, wildernessways, winter walking. 1 coach, 1 athletic trainer.
Computers Computers are regularly used in English, foreign language, history, mathematics, science classes. Computer network features include on-campus library services, online commercial services, Internet access, Internet filtering or blocking technology. The school has a published electronic and media policy.
Contact Timothy Weaver, Director of Admissions. 518-523-3382 Ext. 205. Fax: 518-523-3405. E-mail: weavert@northwoodschool.com. Web site: www.northwoodschool.com.

See Close-Up on page 878.

NORTH YARMOUTH ACADEMY

148 Main Street
Yarmouth, Maine 04096
Head of School: Peter W. Mertz

General Information Coeducational day college-preparatory, arts, and technology school. Grades 6–12. Founded: 1814. Setting: suburban. Nearest major city is Portland. 25-acre campus. 10 buildings on campus. Approved or accredited by Association of Independent Schools in New England, Independent Schools of Northern New England, New England Association of Schools and Colleges, and Maine Department of Education. Member of National Association of Independent Schools and Secondary School Admission Test Board. Endowment: $3 million. Total enrollment: 330. Upper school average class size: 14. Upper school faculty-student ratio: 1:8.
Upper School Student Profile Grade 9: 50 students (25 boys, 25 girls); Grade 10: 55 students (31 boys, 24 girls); Grade 11: 47 students (22 boys, 25 girls); Grade 12: 45 students (26 boys, 19 girls).
Faculty School total: 42. In upper school: 10 men, 16 women; 14 have advanced degrees.
Subjects Offered Algebra, American government, American history, American history-AP, ancient world history, art, art history-AP, biology-AP, calculus-AP, chemistry, chorus, composition-AP, computer graphics, contemporary issues, drama, drawing and design, earth science, English, English composition, English literature, English literature and composition-AP, environmental science-AP, European history, European history-AP, experiential education, fine arts, French, genetics, geometry, history, instrumental music, jazz, language-AP, Latin, Latin-AP, mathematics, music, music theory-AP, painting, photography, physical education, physical science, physics, pottery, pre-calculus, science, social issues, social studies, society challenge and change, Spanish, statistics, studio art—AP, technology, theater, trigonometry, U.S. history, U.S. history-AP, world history.
Graduation Requirements Arts and fine arts (art, music, dance, drama), English, foreign language, history, mathematics, science, senior project, speech, two-week volunteer senior service project, senior speech, participation in athletics or performing arts program each trimester.
Special Academic Programs Advanced Placement exam preparation; honors section; study abroad.
College Admission Counseling 45 students graduated in 2008; 44 went to college, including Boston University; Bowdoin College; Hamilton College; Haverford College; St. Lawrence University; University of Maine. Other: 1 had other specific plans. Median SAT critical reading: 600, median SAT math: 600. 50% scored over 600 on SAT critical reading, 50% scored over 600 on SAT math.
Student Life Upper grades have specified standards of dress, student council, honor system. Discipline rests primarily with faculty.
Tuition and Aid Day student tuition: $20,400. Tuition installment plan (Insured Tuition Payment Plan, monthly payment plans). Need-based scholarship grants available. In 2008–09, 30% of upper-school students received aid. Total amount of financial aid awarded in 2008–09: $689,404.
Admissions Traditional secondary-level entrance grade is 9. For fall 2008, 57 students applied for upper-level admission, 45 were accepted, 29 enrolled. SSAT required. Deadline for receipt of application materials: February 10. Application fee required: $35. On-campus interview required.
Athletics Interscholastic: baseball (boys), basketball (b,g), cross-country running (b,g), field hockey (g), golf (b,g), ice hockey (b,g), indoor track (b,g), indoor track & field (b,g), lacrosse (b,g), nordic skiing (b,g), sailing (b,g), soccer (b,g), softball (g), swimming and diving (b,g). 17 coaches.
Computers Computers are regularly used in English, foreign language, graphic design, history, mathematics, science, technology classes. Computer network features include on-campus library services, Internet access. Student e-mail accounts are available to students.
Contact Joseph P. Silvestri, Director of Admission. 207-846-2376. Fax: 207-846-2382. E-mail: admission@nya.org. Web site: www.nya.org.

THE NORWICH FREE ACADEMY

305 Broadway
Norwich, Connecticut 06360
Head of School: Dr. Mark Cohan, PhD

General Information Coeducational day college-preparatory, general academic, arts, business, vocational, bilingual studies, and technology school. Grades 9–12. Founded: 1856. Setting: suburban. 15-acre campus. 11 buildings on campus. Approved or accredited by New England Association of Schools and Colleges and Connecticut Department of Education. Upper school average class size: 22. Upper school faculty-student ratio: 1:22.
Faculty School total: 85. In upper school: 30 men, 55 women; 75 have advanced degrees.
Special Academic Programs Advanced Placement exam preparation; honors section; remedial reading and/or remedial writing; remedial math; special instructional classes for students with learning disabilities, Attention Deficit Disorder, emotional and behavioral problems, and dyslexia; ESL (90 students enrolled).
College Admission Counseling 507 students graduated in 2008; 396 went to college. Other: 56 went to work, 45 entered military service, 3 had other specific plans.

Student Life Upper grades have specified standards of dress, honor system. Discipline rests equally with students and faculty.
Summer Programs Remediation, enrichment, ESL, sports programs offered; held on campus; accepts boys and girls; open to students from other schools. 250 students usually enrolled. 2009 schedule: July 1 to July 29. Application deadline: June 1.
Tuition and Aid Day student tuition: $10,300.
Admissions ACT-Explore required. Deadline for receipt of application materials: none. No application fee required. Interview required.
Athletics Interscholastic: baseball (boys), basketball (b,g), cheering (b,g), cross-country running (b,g), drill team (g), field hockey (g), football (b), golf (b), indoor track (b,g), lacrosse (b), physical fitness (b,g), running (b,g), soccer (b,g), softball (g), Special Olympics (b,g), swimming and diving (b,g), volleyball (b,g), weight lifting (b), winter (indoor) track (b,g), wrestling (b); intramural: fencing (b,g), hockey (b), ice hockey (b), ice skating (b,g), skiing (cross-country) (b,g), skiing (downhill) (b,g), table tennis (b,g). 8 PE instructors, 25 coaches, 5 athletic trainers.
Computers Computer network features include on-campus library services, Internet access, Internet filtering or blocking technology. The school has a published electronic and media policy.
Contact Dr. Mark Cohan, PhD, Head of School. 860-425-5501. E-mail: cohanm@norwichfreeacademy.com. Web site: www.norwichfreeacademy.com.

NOTRE DAME ACADEMY

2851 Overland Avenue
Los Angeles, California 90064

Head of School: Mrs. Joan Gumaer Tyhurst

General Information Girls' day college-preparatory, arts, religious studies, technology, and fine arts school, affiliated with Roman Catholic Church. Grades 9–12. Founded: 1949. Setting: urban. 1 building on campus. Approved or accredited by Western Association of Schools and Colleges, Western Catholic Education Association, and California Department of Education. Total enrollment: 470. Upper school average class size: 28. Upper school faculty-student ratio: 1:12.
Upper School Student Profile 92% of students are Roman Catholic.
Faculty School total: 37. In upper school: 10 men, 27 women.
Subjects Offered Algebra, American history, American history-AP, American literature, art, art-AP, Bible studies, biology, biology-AP, calculus, calculus-AP, chemistry, community service, computer programming, computer science, dance, design, drama, economics, English, English literature, English-AP, fine arts, fitness, French, French-AP, functions, geometry, government/civics, health, history, Latin, law, leadership training, literature, physical education, physics, pre-calculus, psychology, religion, Spanish, speech, statistics, trigonometry, world affairs, world literature.
Graduation Requirements Arts and fine arts (art, music, dance, drama), computer science, English, foreign language, mathematics, physical education (includes health), religion (includes Bible studies and theology), science, social studies (includes history), speech. Community service is required.
Special Academic Programs Advanced Placement exam preparation; honors section.
College Admission Counseling 117 students graduated in 2008; all went to college, including Loyola Marymount University; University of California, Berkeley; University of California, Los Angeles; University of California, San Diego; University of California, Santa Barbara; University of Southern California.
Student Life Upper grades have uniform requirement, student council, honor system. Discipline rests primarily with faculty. Attendance at religious services is required.
Summer Programs Remediation, enrichment, advancement, art/fine arts, rigorous outdoor training programs offered; session focuses on assisting incoming students in attaining grade level; held on campus; accepts girls; not open to students from other schools. 200 students usually enrolled. 2009 schedule: June 16 to July 25. Application deadline: May 27.
Tuition and Aid Day student tuition: $8600–$9100. Tuition installment plan (monthly payment plans, quarterly and semester payment plans). Merit scholarship grants, need-based scholarship grants, paying campus jobs available. In 2008–09, 30% of upper-school students received aid.
Admissions For fall 2008, 280 students applied for upper-level admission, 128 were accepted, 128 enrolled. High School Placement Test (closed version) from Scholastic Testing Service required. Deadline for receipt of application materials: January 5. Application fee required: $65. On-campus interview required.
Athletics Interscholastic: aerobics/dance, basketball, cross-country running, dance, soccer, softball, swimming and diving, track and field, volleyball. 1 PE instructor, 8 coaches.
Computers Computers are regularly used in art, English, history classes. Computer network features include on-campus library services, Internet access. The school has a published electronic and media policy.
Contact Ms. Daryl Crowley, Director of Admissions. 310-839-5289. Fax: 310-839-7957. E-mail: dcrowley@ndala.com. Web site: www.ndala.com.

NOTRE DAME ACADEMY

1073 Main Street
Hingham, Massachusetts 02043

Head of School: Sr. Barbara A. Barry, SND

General Information Girls' day college-preparatory, arts, business, religious studies, and technology school, affiliated with Roman Catholic Church. Grades 9–12. Founded: 1853. Setting: suburban. Nearest major city is Boston. 68-acre campus. 1 building on campus. Approved or accredited by Association of Independent Schools in New England, National Catholic Education Association, New England Association of Schools and Colleges, and Massachusetts Department of Education. Endowment: $4.9 million. Total enrollment: 595. Upper school average class size: 20. Upper school faculty-student ratio: 1:10.
Upper School Student Profile Grade 9: 159 students (159 girls); Grade 10: 147 students (147 girls); Grade 11: 145 students (145 girls); Grade 12: 144 students (144 girls). 94% of students are Roman Catholic.
Faculty School total: 53. In upper school: 9 men, 44 women; 40 have advanced degrees.
Subjects Offered Acting, advanced chemistry, Advanced Placement courses, advanced studio art-AP, algebra, American government-AP, American history, American history-AP, American literature, anatomy, anatomy and physiology, art, art history, Bible studies, bioethics, biology, biology-AP, business, business skills, calculus, calculus-AP, campus ministry, Catholic belief and practice, ceramics, chemistry, community service, computer science, driver education, economics, English, English literature, ethics, European history, fine arts, French, geometry, government/civics, history, Latin, mathematics, music, photography, physical education, physics, physiology, psychology, religion, science, social science, social studies, Spanish, trigonometry, world history, world literature.
Graduation Requirements Art, computer applications, English, foreign language, guidance, mathematics, music, physical education (includes health), religion (includes Bible studies and theology), science, social studies (includes history).
Special Academic Programs Advanced Placement exam preparation; honors section; independent study; academic accommodation for the musically talented and the artistically talented.
College Admission Counseling 132 students graduated in 2008; all went to college, including Holy Cross College; Loyola College in Maryland; Northeastern University; Providence College; Saint Anselm College; University of Massachusetts Amherst.
Student Life Upper grades have uniform requirement, student council. Discipline rests primarily with faculty. Attendance at religious services is required.
Tuition and Aid Day student tuition: $13,800. Tuition installment plan (FACTS Tuition Payment Plan). Tuition reduction for siblings, merit scholarship grants, need-based scholarship grants available. In 2008–09, 33% of upper-school students received aid; total upper-school merit-scholarship money awarded: $200,000. Total amount of financial aid awarded in 2008–09: $600,000.
Admissions Traditional secondary-level entrance grade is 9. For fall 2008, 350 students applied for upper-level admission, 260 were accepted, 159 enrolled. Diocesan Entrance Exam required. Deadline for receipt of application materials: December 1. Application fee required: $30.
Athletics Interscholastic: alpine skiing, basketball, cheering, cross-country running, dance team, diving, field hockey, golf, gymnastics, ice hockey, indoor track & field, lacrosse, sailing, skiing (downhill), soccer, softball, strength & conditioning, swimming and diving, tennis, track and field, volleyball, weight training, winter (indoor) track; intramural: crew, dance team. 1 PE instructor, 26 coaches, 1 athletic trainer.
Computers Computers are regularly used in art, college planning, English, foreign language, history, mathematics, music, religion, science classes. Computer network features include on-campus library services, Internet access, wireless campus network, Internet filtering or blocking technology. Computer access in designated common areas is available to students. Students grades are available online. The school has a published electronic and media policy.
Contact Mrs. Patricia Spatola, Director of Admissions. 781-749-5930 Ext. 235. Fax: 781-749-8366. E-mail: pspatola@ndahingham.com. Web site: www.ndahingham.com.

NOTRE DAME ACADEMY

425 Salisbury Street
Worcester, Massachusetts 01609

Head of School: Sr. Ann E. Morrison, SND

General Information Girls' day and distance learning college-preparatory, arts, and religious studies school, affiliated with Roman Catholic Church. Grades 9–12. Distance learning grades 9–12. Founded: 1951. Setting: suburban. Nearest major city is Boston. 13-acre campus. 3 buildings on campus. Approved or accredited by Association of Independent Schools in New England. Member of National Association of Independent Schools. Total enrollment: 285. Upper school average class size: 17. Upper school faculty-student ratio: 1:11.
Upper School Student Profile 80% of students are Roman Catholic.
Faculty School total: 39. In upper school: 4 men, 32 women; 27 have advanced degrees.
Subjects Offered 20th century history, advanced chemistry, advanced math, advanced studio art-AP, algebra, American history, American literature, analysis and

differential calculus, anatomy and physiology, ancient world history, art, art history, art history-AP, Bible studies, biology, British literature, British literature (honors), British literature-AP, calculus, calculus-AP, career exploration, Catholic belief and practice, chamber groups, chemistry, chemistry-AP, choral music, Christian and Hebrew scripture, Christian doctrine, college planning, communication skills, community service, computer skills, creative writing, dance, drama, drawing and design, economics and history, English, English composition, English literature, English literature and composition-AP, English-AP, ethics, European history, European history-AP, expository writing, fine arts, French, French language-AP, geometry, grammar, graphic design, health, history, honors geometry, keyboarding/computer, Latin, literature seminar, mathematics, mathematics-AP, music, music theory-AP, photography, physical education, physics, pre-calculus, psychology, public service, religion, science, senior project, Shakespeare, social studies, sociology, Spanish, Spanish language-AP, studio art-AP, theater, theology, trigonometry, world history, world literature, world religions, writing.

Graduation Requirements Arts and fine arts (art, music, dance, drama), computer science, English, foreign language, Latin, mathematics, physical education (includes health), public service, religion (includes Bible studies and theology), science, social studies (includes history), guidance seminar. Community service is required.

Special Academic Programs Advanced Placement exam preparation; honors section.

College Admission Counseling 69 students graduated in 2008; all went to college, including Assumption College; Boston University; Northeastern University; Providence College. Mean SAT critical reading: 570, mean SAT math: 530, mean SAT writing: 570.

Student Life Upper grades have specified standards of dress, student council. Discipline rests equally with students and faculty. Attendance at religious services is required.

Tuition and Aid Day student tuition: $10,800. Tuition installment plan (Insured Tuition Payment Plan, monthly payment plans). Need-based scholarship grants available. In 2008–09, 7% of upper-school students received aid.

Admissions Traditional secondary-level entrance grade is 9. For fall 2008, 123 students applied for upper-level admission, 110 were accepted, 68 enrolled. Admissions testing, California Achievement Test and CAT 5 required. Deadline for receipt of application materials: December 1. Application fee required: $50. On-campus interview recommended.

Athletics Interscholastic: alpine skiing (girls), aquatics (g), basketball (g), cross-country running (g), curling (g), diving (g), field hockey (g), fitness walking (g), freestyle skiing (g), golf (g), indoor track (g), indoor track & field (g), Nautilus (g), physical fitness (g), physical training (g), running (g), skiing (downhill) (g), softball (g), swimming and diving (g), tennis (g), track and field (g), winter (indoor) track (g); intramural: dance (g), fitness walking (g). 1 PE instructor, 20 coaches.

Computers Computers are regularly used in English, foreign language, graphic design, history, library skills, literary magazine, mathematics, newspaper, psychology, religious studies, research skills, science, yearbook classes. Computer network features include on-campus library services, Internet access. Computer access in designated common areas is available to students. The school has a published electronic and media policy.

Contact Mrs. Mary F. Riordan, Admissions Director. 508-757-6200. Fax: 508-757-1800. E-mail: mriordan@nda-worc.org. Web site: www.nda-worc.org.

NOTRE DAME ACADEMY

35321 Notre Dame Lane
Middleburg, Virginia 20117-3621

Head of School: Ms. Elizabeth Manley Murray

General Information Coeducational day college-preparatory, arts, religious studies, and technology school, affiliated with Roman Catholic Church. Grades 9–12. Founded: 1965. Setting: rural. Nearest major city is Washington, DC. 90-acre campus. 8 buildings on campus. Approved or accredited by Association of Independent Schools of Greater Washington, Southern Association of Colleges and Schools, Southern Association of Independent Schools, and Virginia Association of Independent Schools. Endowment: $425,000. Total enrollment: 250. Upper school average class size: 14. Upper school faculty-student ratio: 1:9.

Upper School Student Profile Grade 9: 66 students (33 boys, 33 girls); Grade 10: 58 students (29 boys, 29 girls); Grade 11: 70 students (35 boys, 35 girls); Grade 12: 56 students (28 boys, 28 girls). 45% of students are Roman Catholic.

Faculty School total: 28. In upper school: 17 men, 11 women; 18 have advanced degrees.

Subjects Offered Accounting, Advanced Placement courses, advanced studio art-AP, algebra, American government-AP, American history-AP, American literature, anatomy, anthropology, archaeology, architectural drawing, architecture, art, biology, biology-AP, calculus, Catholic belief and practice, ceramics, chemistry, chemistry-AP, chorus, comparative government and politics-AP, composition-AP, computer applications, computer keyboarding, computer math, computer programming, computer-aided design, creative writing, design, drama, drama performance, drawing, English, English composition, English literature, English literature and composition-AP, English-AP, environmental science, fine arts, French, French-AP, geometry, government and politics-AP, government/civics, graphic arts, health, history, honors algebra, honors English, honors geometry, honors world history, human anatomy, independent study, instrumental music, Latin, literature, mathematics, music, music appreciation, painting, photography, physical education, physics, religion, SAT preparation, science, social science, social studies, Spanish, Spanish-AP, statistics, theater, writing.

Graduation Requirements Art, drama, English, foreign language, mathematics, music, science, social studies (includes history), theology, acceptance at a college or university, at least 25 hours of community service per year.

Special Academic Programs Advanced Placement exam preparation; honors section; study at local college for college credit; academic accommodation for the gifted, the musically talented, and the artistically talented.

College Admission Counseling 67 students graduated in 2008; all went to college, including James Madison University; Lynchburg College; The College of William and Mary; University of Virginia; Virginia Polytechnic Institute and State University. Mean SAT critical reading: 560, mean SAT math: 550, mean SAT writing: 560, mean combined SAT: 1670. 25% scored over 600 on SAT critical reading, 25% scored over 600 on SAT math, 28% scored over 600 on SAT writing, 27% scored over 1800 on combined SAT.

Student Life Upper grades have specified standards of dress, student council, honor system. Discipline rests primarily with faculty.

Summer Programs Remediation, enrichment, sports, art/fine arts programs offered; session focuses on sports camps, academics; held on campus; accepts boys and girls; open to students from other schools. 100 students usually enrolled. 2009 schedule: June 15 to August 15. Application deadline: none.

Tuition and Aid Day student tuition: $17,570. Tuition installment plan (SMART Tuition Payment Plan, semiannual payment plan). Need-based scholarship grants available. In 2008–09, 40% of upper-school students received aid. Total amount of financial aid awarded in 2008–09: $728,502.

Admissions Traditional secondary-level entrance grade is 9. For fall 2008, 160 students applied for upper-level admission, 140 were accepted, 90 enrolled. High School Placement Test, SLEP for foreign students, SSAT, WISC III or other aptitude measures; standardized achievement test or writing sample required. Deadline for receipt of application materials: none. Application fee required: $50. On-campus interview required.

Athletics Interscholastic: baseball (boys), basketball (b,g), field hockey (g), indoor soccer (b,g), lacrosse (b,g), soccer (b,g), softball (g), tennis (b,g), volleyball (g); intramural: strength & conditioning (b,g), weight training (b,g); coed interscholastic: cross-country running, golf, mountain biking, swimming and diving; coed intramural: flag football, outdoor activities, table tennis. 8 coaches, 1 athletic trainer.

Computers Computers are regularly used in all academic, art, literary magazine, music, newspaper, programming, yearbook classes. Computer network features include on-campus library services, Internet access, Internet filtering or blocking technology. Campus intranet and computer access in designated common areas are available to students. Students grades are available online. The school has a published electronic and media policy.

Contact Mrs. Catherine M. Struder, Director of Admission. 540-687-5581. Fax: 540-687-3552. E-mail: cstruder@notredameva.org. Web site: www.notredameva.org.

NOTRE DAME- BISHOP GIBBONS SCHOOL

2600 Albany Street
Schenectady, New York 12304

Head of School: Mr. Michael Piatek

General Information Coeducational day college-preparatory, arts, religious studies, bilingual studies, technology, and Music school, affiliated with Roman Catholic Church. Grades 6–12. Founded: 1958. Setting: urban. Nearest major city is Albany. 12-acre campus. 2 buildings on campus. Approved or accredited by Middle States Association of Colleges and Schools and New York State Board of Regents. Endowment: $250,000. Total enrollment: 316. Upper school average class size: 22. Upper school faculty-student ratio: 1:11.

Upper School Student Profile Grade 6: 33 students (18 boys, 15 girls); Grade 7: 40 students (19 boys, 21 girls); Grade 8: 46 students (21 boys, 25 girls); Grade 9: 56 students (38 boys, 18 girls); Grade 10: 41 students (24 boys, 17 girls); Grade 11: 45 students (27 boys, 18 girls); Grade 12: 55 students (24 boys, 31 girls). 73% of students are Roman Catholic.

Faculty School total: 28. In upper school: 8 men, 16 women; 22 have advanced degrees.

Subjects Offered Advanced math, Advanced Placement courses, American history, American history-AP, anatomy, art, Bible studies, biology, calculus, campus ministry, Catholic belief and practice, chemistry, church history, community service, computer applications, computer education, computer keyboarding, computer literacy, computer skills, earth science, economics, electives, English, English composition, English language and composition-AP, English literature-AP, European history-AP, foreign language, general math, global studies, government, health, history, history of the Catholic Church, Holocaust, honors English, honors U.S. history, honors world history, instrumental music, integrated mathematics, Internet, keyboarding/computer, lab science, language arts, library skills, mathematics, moral theology, musical theater, New Testament, peace and justice, peer ministry, physical education, physics, pre-calculus, psychology, religious studies, science, science project, social sciences, Spanish, Spanish literature, Spanish-AP, student government, student publications, theology, U.S. government, U.S. history, U.S. history-AP, weight training, word processing, world history, writing skills, yearbook.

Graduation Requirements Arts and fine arts (art, music, dance, drama), biology, chemistry, computer studies, earth science, economics, electives, English, government, health, mathematics, moral theology, peace and justice, religious studies, social studies (includes history), Spanish, U.S. government, U.S. history, world history, Each senior is expected to perform twenty-five hours of service before graduating.
Special Academic Programs 6 Advanced Placement exams for which test preparation is offered; honors section; study at local college for college credit; remedial reading and/or remedial writing; remedial math.
College Admission Counseling 66 students graduated in 2008; 65 went to college, including Albany College of Pharmacy and Health Sciences; Iona College; Nazareth College of Rochester; Russell Sage College; Siena College; The College of Saint Rose. Other: 1 went to work. Median SAT critical reading: 515, median SAT math: 505, median SAT writing: 505, median combined SAT: 1545. 27% scored over 600 on SAT critical reading, 13% scored over 600 on SAT math, 23% scored over 600 on SAT writing, 21% scored over 1800 on combined SAT.
Student Life Upper grades have uniform requirement, student council, honor system. Discipline rests primarily with faculty. Attendance at religious services is required.
Tuition and Aid Day student tuition: $5000–$6100. Tuition installment plan (FACTS Tuition Payment Plan, monthly payment plans). Tuition reduction for siblings, merit scholarship grants, need-based scholarship grants, paying campus jobs available. In 2008–09, 23% of upper-school students received aid. Total amount of financial aid awarded in 2008–09: $90,000.
Admissions Traditional secondary-level entrance grade is 9. For fall 2008, 31 students applied for upper-level admission, 28 were accepted, 27 enrolled. STS—Educational Development Series required. Deadline for receipt of application materials: none. Application fee required: $100. Interview required.
Athletics Interscholastic: baseball (boys), basketball (b,g), cheering (g), cross-country running (b,g), football (b), indoor track (b,g), soccer (b,g), softball (g), track and field (b,g), volleyball (g), weight training (b,g), winter (indoor) track (b,g); coed interscholastic: bowling, golf; coed intramural: paint ball. 2 PE instructors, 27 coaches.
Computers Computers are regularly used in computer applications, English, keyboarding, mathematics, Spanish, word processing, yearbook classes. Computer network features include Internet access, wireless campus network, Internet filtering or blocking technology. Students grades are available online. The school has a published electronic and media policy.
Contact Mrs. Pennie Agostara, Director of Recruitment and Marketing. 518-393-3131 Ext. 106. Fax: 518-370-3817. E-mail: agostara@nd-bg.org. Web site: www.nd-bg.org.

NOTRE DAME-CATHEDRAL LATIN SCHOOL

13000 Auburn Road
Chardon, Ohio 44024
Head of School: Mr. Joseph Waler
General Information Coeducational day college-preparatory and religious studies school, affiliated with Roman Catholic Church. Grades 9–12. Founded: 1988. Setting: suburban. Nearest major city is Cleveland. 100-acre campus. 2 buildings on campus. Approved or accredited by North Central Association of Colleges and Schools and Ohio Department of Education. Endowment: $900,000. Total enrollment: 749. Upper school average class size: 20. Upper school faculty-student ratio: 1:15.
Upper School Student Profile Grade 9: 206 students (105 boys, 101 girls); Grade 10: 171 students (80 boys, 91 girls); Grade 11: 172 students (78 boys, 94 girls); Grade 12: 200 students (105 boys, 95 girls). 95% of students are Roman Catholic.
Faculty School total: 57. In upper school: 19 men, 35 women; 32 have advanced degrees.
Subjects Offered Algebra, American history, American literature, anatomy, art, biology, business, calculus, ceramics, chemistry, community service, computer programming, computer science-AP, creative writing, desktop publishing, drawing, economics, electronic research, English, English literature, environmental science, film studies, fine arts, French, geography, geometry, German, government/civics, health, history, home economics, integrated science, journalism, keyboarding, mathematics, music, music theory, photography, physical education, physics, physiology, religion, science, senior career experience, social studies, sociology, Spanish, speech, statistics, studio art-AP, theology, trigonometry, world affairs, world history, world literature.
Graduation Requirements Arts and fine arts (art, music, dance, drama), English, foreign language, mathematics, physical education (includes health), religion (includes Bible studies and theology), science, senior career experience, social studies (includes history). Community service is required.
Special Academic Programs Advanced Placement exam preparation; honors section; study at local college for college credit; remedial reading and/or remedial writing; remedial math; programs in general development for dyslexic students.
College Admission Counseling 178 students graduated in 2008; 176 went to college, including John Carroll University; Kent State University; Miami University; Ohio University; The Ohio State University; University of Dayton. Other: 2 had other specific plans. Median SAT critical reading: 541, median SAT math: 536, median SAT writing: 530.
Student Life Upper grades have uniform requirement, student council. Discipline rests primarily with faculty. Attendance at religious services is required.
Tuition and Aid Day student tuition: $7550. Tuition installment plan (bank-arranged 10-month plan). Tuition reduction for siblings, merit scholarship grants, need-based scholarship grants, scholarships in specific academic disciplines available. In 2008–09, 30% of upper-school students received aid.
Admissions High School Placement Test required. Deadline for receipt of application materials: January 26. No application fee required. On-campus interview recommended.
Athletics Interscholastic: baseball (boys), basketball (b,g), cross-country running (b,g), dance team (g), football (b), gymnastics (g), ice hockey (b), soccer (b,g), softball (g), swimming and diving (b,g), tennis (b,g), track and field (b,g), volleyball (g), weight lifting (b,g); intramural: basketball (b,g), skiing (downhill) (b,g); coed interscholastic: cross-country running, diving, golf; coed intramural: skiing (downhill). 3 PE instructors.
Computers Computer network features include Internet access.
Contact Mr. Keith Corlew, Director of Admissions. 888-214-8108. Fax: 440-286-7199.

NOTRE DAME HIGH SCHOOL

1540 Ralston Avenue
Belmont, California 94002-1995
Head of School: Ms. Rita Gleason
General Information Girls' day college-preparatory, arts, religious studies, technology, and visual and performing arts school, affiliated with Roman Catholic Church. Grades 9–12. Founded: 1851. Setting: suburban. Nearest major city is San Francisco. 11-acre campus. 3 buildings on campus. Approved or accredited by Western Association of Schools and Colleges and California Department of Education. Endowment: $1.4 million. Total enrollment: 580. Upper school average class size: 23. Upper school faculty-student ratio: 1:16.
Upper School Student Profile Grade 9: 137 students (137 girls); Grade 10: 138 students (138 girls); Grade 11: 139 students (139 girls); Grade 12: 166 students (166 girls). 75% of students are Roman Catholic.
Faculty School total: 57. In upper school: 16 men, 41 women; 42 have advanced degrees.
Subjects Offered Advanced chemistry, advanced computer applications, advanced math, Advanced Placement courses, advanced studio art-AP, algebra, American government, American government-AP, American history, American literature, art, art history, art history-AP, band, bioethics, biology, biology-AP, British literature, British literature-AP, calculus, calculus-AP, chemistry, chemistry-AP, choir, choral music, chorus, Christian and Hebrew scripture, church history, computer applications, computer literacy, computer science, creative writing, dance, decision making, digital photography, driver education, economics, economics and history, economics-AP, English, English literature, English literature-AP, environmental science, ethics, European history, French, French language-AP, geometry, government and politics-AP, government-AP, health, Hebrew scripture, history, honors English, honors geometry, honors U.S. history, honors world history, integrated science, jazz band, journalism, leadership, leadership and service, modern world history, moral reasoning, newspaper, orchestra, photography, physical education, physical science, physics, pre-calculus, psychology, relationships, religion, science, sculpture, self-defense, social justice, social science, social sciences, Spanish, Spanish language-AP, Spanish-AP, sports conditioning, sports medicine, studio art-AP, television, trigonometry, U.S. government, U.S. government and politics-AP, U.S. history-AP, video film production, weight training, world history, world literature, world religions, yearbook.
Graduation Requirements Arts and fine arts (art, music, dance, drama), English, foreign language, mathematics, physical education (includes health), religion (includes Bible studies and theology), science, social science, social studies (includes history), 100 hours Community Service.
Special Academic Programs Advanced Placement exam preparation; honors section; independent study; study at local college for college credit; special instructional classes for deaf students, blind students, special needs program for students with learning differences.
College Admission Counseling 179 students graduated in 2008; all went to college, including San Francisco State University; Sonoma State University; The University of Arizona; University of California, Davis; University of San Francisco. Mean SAT critical reading: 558, mean SAT math: 547, mean SAT writing: 563.
Student Life Upper grades have uniform requirement, student council, honor system. Discipline rests primarily with faculty. Attendance at religious services is required.
Summer Programs Enrichment, advancement, sports, art/fine arts, computer instruction programs offered; session focuses on enrichment for grades 6-9; held on campus; accepts girls; open to students from other schools. 150 students usually enrolled. 2009 schedule: June 15 to July 10. Application deadline: May 1.
Tuition and Aid Day student tuition: $14,950. Guaranteed tuition plan. Tuition installment plan (Key Tuition Payment Plan, FACTS Tuition Payment Plan, individually arranged payment plans). Merit scholarship grants, need-based scholarship grants available. In 2008–09, 18% of upper-school students received aid; total upper-school merit-scholarship money awarded: $100,000. Total amount of financial aid awarded in 2008–09: $700,000.
Admissions Traditional secondary-level entrance grade is 9. For fall 2008, 351 students applied for upper-level admission, 295 were accepted, 137 enrolled. High School Placement Test (closed version) from Scholastic Testing Service and writing

sample required. Deadline for receipt of application materials: December 5. Application fee required: $50. On-campus interview required.
Athletics Interscholastic: aquatics, basketball, cheering, cross-country running, dance team, golf, physical training, soccer, softball, strength & conditioning, swimming and diving, tennis, track and field, volleyball, water polo; intramural: cheering, touch football. 1 PE instructor, 33 coaches, 2 athletic trainers.
Computers Computers are regularly used in college planning, creative writing, English, foreign language, health, history, independent study, journalism, mathematics, media production, newspaper, photography, publishing, religious studies, SAT preparation, science, social studies, video film production, yearbook classes. Computer network features include on-campus library services, Internet access, wireless campus network, Internet filtering or blocking technology. Student e-mail accounts and computer access in designated common areas are available to students. Students grades are available online. The school has a published electronic and media policy.
Contact Mrs. Shyrl McCormick, Director of Admissions. 650-595-1913 Ext. 320. Fax: 650-595-2643. E-mail: smccormick@ndhsb.org. Web site: www.ndhsb.org.

ANNOUNCEMENT FROM THE SCHOOL Notre Dame High School is a private Catholic college-preparatory school for young women located on 10 acres in Belmont, California. The essence of Notre Dame lies in a strong academic program and a caring, supportive environment rooted in Christian values. Notre Dame prepares young women for lives of leadership and service. Graduation requirements fulfill the course requirements for admission to the University of California. Historically, 100% of the graduates enroll in colleges and universities throughout the country. Notre Dame, Belmont; Mercy, Burlingame; and Junipero Serra High School participate in a Tri-School Program, which provides co-educational experiences in the areas of academics, campus ministry, athletics, performing and visual arts, and student activities. Notre Dame students develop the ability to think critically, logically, and creatively utilizing effective verbal and communication skills; develop resources of strength and self-confidence by challenging themselves physically on a variety of levels in the athletic program; develop creativity and imagination through activities such as drama, art, music, dance, photography, and creative writing; and develop the inner strength and moral conviction that is the foundation of a whole and fulfilling spiritual life. An excellent co-curricular program offers students the opportunity to become involved, make new friends, and take an active role in building a strong Christian community. Students are required to complete 100 hours of community service over four years. NDB Tigers participate in the Western Catholic Athletic League (WCAL) in ten sports. Through the award-winning Visual and Performing Arts Program, students participate in chorus, Tri-M Music Society, string orchestra, band, plays, and musicals; publish a newspaper, literary magazine, and yearbook; and produce a television broadcast. Tuition for 2008–09 is $13,950. Tuition assistance is available to students with demonstrated financial need and has no bearing on admission to Notre Dame High School.

NOTRE DAME HIGH SCHOOL

910 North Eastern Avenue
Crowley, Louisiana 70526

Head of School: Mrs. Cindy Istre

General Information Coeducational day college-preparatory, arts, vocational, religious studies, and technology school, affiliated with Roman Catholic Church. Grades 9–12. Founded: 1974. Setting: small town. Nearest major city is Lafayette. 10-acre campus. 7 buildings on campus. Approved or accredited by Southern Association of Colleges and Schools and Louisiana Department of Education. Total enrollment: 500. Upper school average class size: 25. Upper school faculty-student ratio: 1:25.
Upper School Student Profile 99% of students are Roman Catholic.
Faculty School total: 38. In upper school: 13 men, 25 women; 9 have advanced degrees.
Subjects Offered Accounting, adolescent issues, advanced math, agriculture, algebra, American history, anatomy and physiology, ancient world history, art, athletics, baseball, basketball, biology, calculus, chemistry, civics/free enterprise, computer applications, computer keyboarding, computer multimedia, computer technologies, dance, drama, driver education, early childhood, economics, English, environmental science, family and consumer sciences, fine arts, food and nutrition, French, geometry, health education, honors algebra, honors English, honors geometry, honors U.S. history, honors world history, physical education, physical science, physics, pre-calculus, psychology, publications, religion, softball, Spanish, speech, study skills, swimming, tennis, theater, track and field, U.S. history, volleyball, world history, yearbook.
Special Academic Programs Honors section; independent study; study at local college for college credit; academic accommodation for the gifted.
College Admission Counseling 127 students graduated in 2008; 120 went to college, including Louisiana State University and Agricultural and Mechanical College; Louisiana State University at Eunice; University of Louisiana at Lafayette. Other: 3 entered military service.
Student Life Upper grades have uniform requirement, student council. Discipline rests primarily with faculty. Attendance at religious services is required.
Summer Programs Sports programs offered; session focuses on training and fitness; held on campus; accepts boys and girls; not open to students from other schools.
Tuition and Aid Tuition installment plan (The Tuition Plan, monthly payment plans). Tuition reduction for siblings available.
Admissions Explore or Iowa Test of Educational Development required. Deadline for receipt of application materials: none. No application fee required. Interview required.
Athletics Interscholastic: baseball (boys), basketball (b,g), cheering (g), cross-country running (b,g), dance squad (g), football (b), softball (g), tennis (b,g), track and field (b,g), volleyball (g); coed interscholastic: drill team, golf, soccer, swimming and diving. 12 coaches, 2 athletic trainers.
Computers Computers are regularly used in computer applications, multimedia classes. Computer network features include on-campus library services, Internet access, Internet filtering or blocking technology. Students grades are available online.
Contact Mr. Nolan Theriot, Dean of Students. 337-783-3519. Fax: 337-788-2115. Web site: www.ndpios.com.

NOTRE DAME HIGH SCHOOL

601 Lawrence Road
Lawrenceville, New Jersey 08648

Head of School: Ms. Mary Liz Ivins

General Information Coeducational day college-preparatory school, affiliated with Roman Catholic Church. Grades 9–12. Founded: 1957. Setting: suburban. Nearest major city is Trenton. 100-acre campus. 1 building on campus. Approved or accredited by Middle States Association of Colleges and Schools, National Catholic Education Association, and New Jersey Department of Education. Total enrollment: 1,277. Upper school average class size: 24. Upper school faculty-student ratio: 1:24.
Upper School Student Profile Grade 9: 315 students (175 boys, 140 girls); Grade 10: 333 students (186 boys, 147 girls); Grade 11: 321 students (149 boys, 172 girls); Grade 12: 308 students (131 boys, 177 girls). 88% of students are Roman Catholic.
Faculty School total: 91. In upper school: 34 men, 54 women; 42 have advanced degrees.
Subjects Offered 20th century history, 3-dimensional art, 3-dimensional design, accounting, acting, advanced chemistry, advanced computer applications, advanced math, Advanced Placement courses, algebra, American history, American history-AP, American literature, ancient world history, applied music, art, art and culture, athletics, Basic programming, Bible studies, biology, biology-AP, British literature, business, business applications, business studies, calculus, calculus-AP, Catholic belief and practice, ceramics, chemistry, chemistry-AP, choir, Christian doctrine, comparative religion, computer applications, computer science, concert band, concert choir, constitutional law, contemporary issues, creative writing, dance, dance performance, discrete math, drama, driver education, ecology, environmental systems, economics, English, English composition, English literature-AP, environmental science-AP, etymology, European history-AP, first aid, French, geometry, German, German literature, health education, honors algebra, honors English, honors world history, Italian, Japanese, journalism, Latin, law, leadership and service, leadership education training, literature-AP, madrigals, math review, peer ministry, philosophy, photography, physical education, physics, physics-AP, piano, portfolio art, pre-algebra, pre-calculus, probability and statistics, psychology, psychology-AP, public speaking, reading/study skills, SAT preparation, scripture, senior internship, senior project, sociology, Spanish, Spanish literature, speech and debate, sports medicine, theater design and production, U.S. government, U.S. government-AP, U.S. literature, world history, world literature, writing.
Graduation Requirements Biology, English, foreign language, integrated technology fundamentals, lab science, mathematics, physical education (includes health), religion (includes Bible studies and theology), U.S. history, world history. Community service is required.
Special Academic Programs 13 Advanced Placement exams for which test preparation is offered; honors section; independent study; study at local college for college credit; remedial reading and/or remedial writing; remedial math.
College Admission Counseling 282 students graduated in 2008; 276 went to college, including Cabrini College; Drexel University; Rutgers, The State University of New Jersey, New Brunswick; Saint Joseph's University; Seton Hall University; The College of New Jersey. Other: 3 went to work, 3 entered military service. Mean SAT critical reading: 540, mean SAT math: 537, mean SAT writing: 544, mean combined SAT: 1621. 34% scored over 600 on SAT critical reading, 34% scored over 600 on SAT math, 24% scored over 600 on SAT writing, 27% scored over 1800 on combined SAT.
Student Life Upper grades have uniform requirement, student council, honor system. Discipline rests primarily with faculty. Attendance at religious services is required.
Summer Programs Enrichment, sports, art/fine arts programs offered; session focuses on sports, arts, and writing camps; held on campus; accepts boys and girls; open to students from other schools. 775 students usually enrolled. 2009 schedule: June 22 to August 7. Application deadline: June 22.
Tuition and Aid Day student tuition: $9500. Tuition installment plan (Tuition Management Systems Plan). Tuition reduction for siblings, need-based scholarship grants available. In 2008–09, 10% of upper-school students received aid. Total amount of financial aid awarded in 2008–09: $180,000.
Admissions Traditional secondary-level entrance grade is 9. For fall 2008, 525 students applied for upper-level admission, 420 were accepted, 316 enrolled.

Scholastic Testing Service High School Placement Test required. Deadline for receipt of application materials: November 27. Application fee required: $50. On-campus interview required.
Athletics Interscholastic: baseball (boys), basketball (b,g), cheering (g), cross-country running (b,g), dance (b,g), field hockey (g), football (b), golf (b), ice hockey (b), indoor track (b,g), lacrosse (b,g), soccer (b,g), softball (g), swimming and diving (b,g), tennis (b,g), track and field (b,g), winter (indoor) track (b,g), wrestling (b); intramural: touch football (g), volleyball (b,g); coed interscholastic: cheering, diving, fitness, strength & conditioning; coed intramural: Frisbee, outdoor activities, outdoor recreation, physical fitness, ultimate Frisbee, volleyball, weight lifting, weight training. 8 PE instructors, 71 coaches, 1 athletic trainer.
Computers Computers are regularly used in all academic classes. Computer network features include on-campus library services, online commercial services, Internet access, wireless campus network, Internet filtering or blocking technology. Campus intranet and computer access in designated common areas are available to students. Students grades are available online. The school has a published electronic and media policy.
Contact Ms. Peggy Miller, Admissions Coordinator. 609-882-7900 Ext. 139. Fax: 609-882-6599. E-mail: miller@ndnj.org. Web site: www.ndnj.org.

NOTRE DAME HIGH SCHOOL

2701 Vermont Avenue
Chattanooga, Tennessee 37404
Head of School: Mr. Perry L. Storey

General Information Coeducational day college-preparatory, arts, religious studies, and technology school, affiliated with Roman Catholic Church. Grades 9–12. Founded: 1876. Setting: urban. 22-acre campus. 5 buildings on campus. Approved or accredited by National Catholic Education Association, Southern Association of Colleges and Schools, Tennessee Association of Independent Schools, The College Board, and Tennessee Department of Education. Endowment: $1.5 million. Total enrollment: 509. Upper school average class size: 15. Upper school faculty-student ratio: 1:10.
Upper School Student Profile Grade 9: 110 students (53 boys, 57 girls); Grade 10: 130 students (62 boys, 68 girls); Grade 11: 128 students (58 boys, 70 girls); Grade 12: 141 students (55 boys, 86 girls). 71% of students are Roman Catholic.
Faculty School total: 54. In upper school: 24 men, 30 women; 27 have advanced degrees.
Subjects Offered 3-dimensional art, ACT preparation, Advanced Placement courses, algebra, American government-AP, American history-AP, American literature, anatomy, band, biology, biology-AP, British literature, British literature-AP, calculus, Catholic belief and practice, chemistry, choir, civics, conceptual physics, creative dance, criminal justice, drama, economics, electives, English composition, English literature, foreign language, French, geometry, government, health and wellness, honors algebra, honors English, honors geometry, honors U.S. history, honors world history, Latin, physics, religion, Spanish, weight training, wellness, world history, world history-AP, yoga.
Special Academic Programs Advanced Placement exam preparation; honors section; independent study; study at local college for college credit.
College Admission Counseling 127 students graduated in 2008; 125 went to college, including Auburn University; Middle Tennessee State University; The University of Tennessee; The University of Tennessee at Chattanooga; University of Georgia. Other: 2 entered military service.
Student Life Upper grades have uniform requirement, student council, honor system. Discipline rests primarily with faculty. Attendance at religious services is required.
Summer Programs Enrichment, sports programs offered; session focuses on enrichment; held both on and off campus; held at various sites in Chattanooga; accepts boys and girls; open to students from other schools. 250 students usually enrolled. 2009 schedule: June 1 to July 31. Application deadline: April 1.
Tuition and Aid Day student tuition: $8502–$11,444. Tuition installment plan (Insured Tuition Payment Plan, monthly payment plans). Tuition reduction for siblings, need-based scholarship grants, paying campus jobs available. In 2008–09, 12% of upper-school students received aid. Total amount of financial aid awarded in 2008–09: $195,000.
Admissions Traditional secondary-level entrance grade is 9. ACT-Explore required. Deadline for receipt of application materials: March 1. Application fee required: $100. On-campus interview required.
Athletics Interscholastic: aerobics/dance (girls), baseball (b), basketball (b,g), bowling (b,g), cross-country running (b,g), dance (g), dance squad (g), dance team (g), diving (b,g), football (b), golf (b,g), modern dance (g), physical training (b,g), running (b,g), soccer (b,g), softball (g), swimming and diving (b,g), tennis (b,g), track and field (b,g), volleyball (g), weight training (b,g), wrestling (b); intramural: aerobics/dance (g), cheering (g), indoor soccer (b), indoor track (b,g); coed interscholastic: cheering, yoga; coed intramural: backpacking, canoeing/kayaking, climbing, crew, hiking/backpacking, kayaking, mountaineering, outdoors, rafting, rappelling, rock climbing, rowing, skiing (downhill), snowboarding, wall climbing. 5 PE instructors, 30 coaches, 2 athletic trainers.
Computers Computer network features include on-campus library services, Internet access, wireless campus network, Internet filtering or blocking technology, calendar and sports updates by email or text. Students grades are available online. The school has a published electronic and media policy.
Contact Mr. Brantley Crowder, Admissions Director. 423-624-4618 Ext. 1004. Fax: 423-624-4621. E-mail: admissions@myndhs.com. Web site: www.myndhs.com.

NOTRE DAME JUNIOR/SENIOR HIGH SCHOOL

60 Spangenburg Avenue
East Stroudsburg, Pennsylvania 18301-2799
Head of School: Mr. Jeffrey Neill Lyons

General Information Coeducational day college-preparatory, arts, and religious studies school, affiliated with Roman Catholic Church. Grades 9–12. Founded: 1967. Setting: suburban. 40-acre campus. 4 buildings on campus. Approved or accredited by Middle States Association of Colleges and Schools, National Catholic Education Association, and Pennsylvania Department of Education. Total enrollment: 259. Upper school average class size: 25. Upper school faculty-student ratio: 1:15.
Upper School Student Profile Grade 9: 62 students (23 boys, 39 girls); Grade 10: 70 students (32 boys, 38 girls); Grade 11: 61 students (28 boys, 33 girls); Grade 12: 66 students (31 boys, 35 girls). 88% of students are Roman Catholic.
Faculty School total: 25. In upper school: 12 men, 13 women; 14 have advanced degrees.
Graduation Requirements Lab/keyboard, mathematics, moral theology, physical education (includes health), physical science, religion (includes Bible studies and theology), senior project, U.S. history, U.S. literature, word processing, world cultures, world religions.
Special Academic Programs Advanced Placement exam preparation; honors section; study at local college for college credit.
College Admission Counseling 60 students graduated in 2008; 57 went to college, including Marywood University; Mount St. Mary's University; Penn State University Park; Saint Joseph's University; Temple University; The University of Scranton. Other: 2 went to work, 1 entered military service.
Student Life Upper grades have uniform requirement, student council. Discipline rests primarily with faculty. Attendance at religious services is required.
Tuition and Aid Tuition installment plan (FACTS Tuition Payment Plan). Tuition reduction for siblings, need-based scholarship grants available. In 2008–09, 30% of upper-school students received aid.
Admissions Traditional secondary-level entrance grade is 9. Achievement tests or TerraNova required. Deadline for receipt of application materials: May 1. No application fee required. Interview required.
Athletics Interscholastic: baseball (boys), basketball (b,g), cheering (g), field hockey (g), soccer (b,g), softball (g), swimming and diving (b,g), tennis (b,g), winter soccer (b,g); coed interscholastic: golf, soccer; coed intramural: cross-country running, indoor soccer, jogging, strength & conditioning. 2 PE instructors, 19 coaches, 1 athletic trainer.
Computers Computer network features include on-campus library services, Internet access, Internet filtering or blocking technology. The school has a published electronic and media policy.
Contact Mr. Jeffrey Neill Lyons, Principal. 570-421-0466. Fax: 570-476-0629. E-mail: principal@ndhigh.org. Web site: www.ndhigh.org.

NOTRE DAME PREPARATORY SCHOOL

815 Hampton Lane
Towson, Maryland 21286

Head of School: Sr. Patricia McCarron, SSND

General Information Girls' day college-preparatory school, affiliated with Roman Catholic Church. Grades 6–12. Founded: 1873. Setting: suburban. Nearest major city is Baltimore. 60-acre campus. 3 buildings on campus. Approved or accredited by Association of Independent Maryland Schools, Middle States Association of Colleges and Schools, National Catholic Education Association, and Maryland Department of Education. Member of National Association of Independent Schools. Endowment: $7 million. Total enrollment: 756. Upper school average class size: 16. Upper school faculty-student ratio: 1:9.

Upper School Student Profile Grade 9: 156 students (156 girls); Grade 10: 134 students (134 girls); Grade 11: 147 students (147 girls); Grade 12: 135 students (135 girls). 85% of students are Roman Catholic.

Faculty School total: 91. In upper school: 13 men, 78 women; 70 have advanced degrees.

Subjects Offered Algebra, American history, American literature, anatomy, architectural drawing, art, Bible studies, biology, calculus, calculus-AP, ceramics, chemistry, community service, computer science, creative writing, drama, economics, English, English literature, environmental science, European history, fine arts, French, geometry, government/civics, grammar, history, Japanese, journalism, Latin, marine biology, mathematics, music, philosophy, photography, physical education, physics, religion, science, social issues, social justice, social studies, Spanish, statistics, swimming, theater, trigonometry, world history, world literature, writing.

Graduation Requirements Arts and fine arts (art, music, dance, drama), English, foreign language, mathematics, physical education (includes health), religion (includes Bible studies and theology), science, social studies (includes history), swimming. Community service is required.

Special Academic Programs 20 Advanced Placement exams for which test preparation is offered; honors section; independent study.

College Admission Counseling 161 students graduated in 2008; all went to college, including Loyola College in Maryland; Penn State University Park; Roanoke College; Towson University; University of Maryland, College Park; Virginia Polytechnic Institute and State University. Median SAT critical reading: 610, median SAT math: 620, median SAT writing: 630, median combined SAT: 1860. 57% scored over 600 on SAT critical reading, 53% scored over 600 on SAT math, 65% scored over 600 on SAT writing, 64% scored over 1800 on combined SAT.

Student Life Upper grades have uniform requirement, student council, honor system. Discipline rests equally with students and faculty. Attendance at religious services is required.

Tuition and Aid Day student tuition: $14,890. Tuition installment plan (FACTS Tuition Payment Plan). Need-based scholarship grants available. In 2008–09, 21% of upper-school students received aid. Total amount of financial aid awarded in 2008–09: $1,131,647.

Admissions Traditional secondary-level entrance grade is 9. For fall 2008, 243 students applied for upper-level admission, 141 were accepted, 100 enrolled. High School Placement Test and ISEE required. Deadline for receipt of application materials: December 1. Application fee required: $75. On-campus interview required.

Athletics Interscholastic: badminton, basketball, crew, cross-country running, field hockey, golf, indoor soccer, indoor track, lacrosse, soccer, softball, swimming and diving, tennis, track and field, volleyball, winter (indoor) track, winter soccer; intramural: aerobics, badminton, basketball, cheering, cooperative games, dance team, field hockey, skiing (downhill), soccer, tennis, volleyball, yoga. 6 PE instructors, 28 coaches, 1 athletic trainer.

Computers Computers are regularly used in all classes. Computer network features include on-campus library services, online commercial services, Internet access, wireless campus network, Internet filtering or blocking technology, computer-based science, music, language, publications and art labs, Microsoft Office, laptop program for grades 9-12; laptop carts for grades 6-8, automated library research databases; internet-based learning management systems. Student e-mail accounts and computer access in designated common areas are available to students. The school has a published electronic and media policy.

Contact Mrs. Katherine Goetz, Director of Admission. 410-825-0590. Fax: 410-825-0982. E-mail: goetzk@notredameprep.com. Web site: www.notredameprep.com.

OAK CREEK RANCH SCHOOL

West Sedona, Arizona
See Special Needs Schools section.

OAK GROVE LUTHERAN SCHOOL

124 North Terrace
Fargo, North Dakota 58102

Head of School: Bruce A. Messelt

General Information Coeducational day college-preparatory, general academic, religious studies, and music school, affiliated with Lutheran Church. Grades K–12. Founded: 1906. Setting: suburban. Nearest major city is Minneapolis, MN. 5-acre campus. 5 buildings on campus. Approved or accredited by North Central Association of Colleges and Schools and North Dakota Department of Education. Endowment: $6 million. Total enrollment: 505. Upper school average class size: 17. Upper school faculty-student ratio: 1:12.

Upper School Student Profile 75% of students are Lutheran.

Faculty School total: 40. In upper school: 10 men, 12 women; 6 have advanced degrees.

Subjects Offered Accounting, algebra, American history, American literature, art, band, Bible studies, biology, British literature, business law, business skills, calculus, chemistry, chorus, civics, computer programming, computer science, consumer mathematics, driver education, Eastern world civilizations, economics, English, ensembles, family studies, food science, geography, geometry, German, government, health, history, keyboarding, mathematics, music appreciation, nutrition, physical education, physical science, physics, pre-calculus, psychology, religion, science, social science, social studies, sociology, Spanish, speech, textiles, trigonometry, weight training, world affairs, world culture, world history.

Graduation Requirements Business skills (includes word processing), English, mathematics, physical education (includes health), religion (includes Bible studies and theology), science, social science, social studies (includes history).

Special Academic Programs Advanced Placement exam preparation; honors section; independent study; study at local college for college credit; study abroad; academic accommodation for the gifted and the musically talented; remedial reading and/or remedial writing; remedial math; programs in English, mathematics, general development for dyslexic students; special instructional classes for students with learning disabilities, Attention Deficit Disorder; ESL (15 students enrolled).

College Admission Counseling 50 students graduated in 2008; all went to college, including Concordia College; Gustavus Adolphus College; North Dakota State University; Northwestern University; St. Olaf College; University of North Dakota.

Student Life Upper grades have specified standards of dress, student council, honor system. Discipline rests equally with students and faculty. Attendance at religious services is required.

Summer Programs Enrichment, sports, art/fine arts programs offered; held on campus; accepts boys and girls; open to students from other schools. 50 students usually enrolled.

Tuition and Aid Day student tuition: $6400. Tuition installment plan (FACTS Tuition Payment Plan). Tuition reduction for siblings, merit scholarship grants, need-based scholarship grants, paying campus jobs, work-study tuition reduction plan available. In 2008–09, 46% of upper-school students received aid; total upper-school merit-scholarship money awarded: $12,000. Total amount of financial aid awarded in 2008–09: $250,000.

Admissions Traditional secondary-level entrance grade is 9. Achievement tests, ACT, Iowa Test, CTBS, or TAP, PSAT or SAT, Stanford Achievement Test, TOEFL or Woodcock-Johnson required. Deadline for receipt of application materials: none. Application fee required: $45. Interview recommended.

Athletics Interscholastic: aquatics (boys, girls), baseball (b,g), basketball (b,g), cheering (g), cross-country running (b,g), diving (b,g), football (b), golf (b,g), ice hockey (b), physical training (b,g), soccer (b,g), swimming and diving (g), tennis (b,g); coed intramural: billiards, table tennis. 1 PE instructor, 2 coaches, 1 athletic trainer.

Computers Computers are regularly used in business, college planning, English, history, independent study, library skills, mathematics, religious studies, science classes. Computer network features include on-campus library services, online commercial services, Internet access, wireless campus network, Internet filtering or blocking technology. Campus intranet and computer access in designated common areas are available to students. Students grades are available online. The school has a published electronic and media policy.

Contact Terry J. Haus, Director of Admissions. 701-373-7114. Fax: 701-237-4217. E-mail: terry.haus@oakgrovelutheran.com. Web site: www.oakgrovelutheran.com.

OAK GROVE SCHOOL

220 West Lomita Avenue
Ojai, California 93023

Head of School: Meredy Benson Rice

General Information Coeducational boarding and day college-preparatory and arts school. Boarding grades 9–12, day grades PK–12. Founded: 1975. Setting: small town. Nearest major city is Los Angeles. Students are housed in coed dormitories. 150-acre campus. 6 buildings on campus. Approved or accredited by California Association of Independent Schools, The Association of Boarding Schools, Western Association of Schools and Colleges, and California Department of Education. Member of Secondary School Admission Test Board. Endowment: $700,000. Total enrollment: 200. Upper school average class size: 12. Upper school faculty-student ratio: 1:7.

Upper School Student Profile Grade 9: 9 students (5 boys, 4 girls); Grade 10: 9 students (5 boys, 4 girls); Grade 11: 13 students (8 boys, 5 girls); Grade 12: 11 students (4 boys, 7 girls). 35% of students are boarding students. 83% are state residents. 2 states are represented in upper school student body. 23% are international students. International students from China, Mexico, and Republic of Korea.

Faculty School total: 30. In upper school: 4 men, 6 women; 5 have advanced degrees; 3 reside on campus.

Subjects Offered Algebra, American history, American literature, anatomy, art, art history, biology, calculus, ceramics, chemistry, community service, computer science, drama, earth science, economics, English, English literature, ethics, film and new technologies, fine arts, gardening, geography, geometry, global studies, history, horticulture, human development, inquiry into relationship, mathematics, music, permaculture, photography, physical education, physics, relationships, religion and culture, science, social studies, Spanish, studio art, theater, world culture, world history, world literature.

Graduation Requirements Algebra, American history, arts and fine arts (art, music, dance, drama), backpacking, biology, chemistry, college admission preparation, comparative religion, economics and history, English, ethics and responsibility, foreign language, geometry, mathematics, science, social studies (includes history), Spanish, world religions, participation in camping and travel programs, one year of Visual and Performing Arts. Community service is required.

Special Academic Programs Advanced Placement exam preparation; honors section; ESL (2 students enrolled).

College Admission Counseling 2 students graduated in 2008. Mean SAT critical reading: 627, mean SAT math: 580, mean SAT writing: 617. 57% scored over 600 on SAT critical reading, 28% scored over 600 on SAT math, 42% scored over 600 on SAT writing.

Student Life Upper grades have student council, honor system. Discipline rests equally with students and faculty.

Tuition and Aid Day student tuition: $15,400; 5-day tuition and room/board: $30,150; 7-day tuition and room/board: $34,100. Tuition installment plan (FACTS Tuition Payment Plan, annual and semiannual payment plans). Need-based scholarship grants, African-American scholarships available. In 2008–09, 40% of upper-school students received aid. Total amount of financial aid awarded in 2008–09: $60,000.

Admissions Traditional secondary-level entrance grade is 9. For fall 2008, 32 students applied for upper-level admission, 27 were accepted, 20 enrolled. SSAT or TOEFL or SLEP required. Deadline for receipt of application materials: none. Application fee required: $50. Interview required.

Athletics Interscholastic: soccer (boys, girls), volleyball (b,g); intramural: soccer (b,g), volleyball (g); coed interscholastic: backpacking, bicycling, cross-country running, fitness, hiking/backpacking, outdoor activities, physical training, ropes courses, running, skiing (downhill), table tennis, tennis, track and field, wilderness, yoga. 1 PE instructor, 2 coaches.

Computers Computers are regularly used in art, ESL, graphic arts, history, independent study, library, mathematics, multimedia, photography, SAT preparation, science, technology, typing, writing, yearbook classes. Computer resources include on-campus library services, online commercial services, Internet access, wireless campus network, Internet filtering or blocking technology. Computer access in designated common areas is available to students.

Contact Joy Maguire-Parsons, Director of Admissions and Financial Aid. 805-646-8236 Ext. 109. Fax: 805-646-6509. E-mail: enroll@oakgroveschool.com. Web site: www.oakgroveschool.com.

OAK HILL ACADEMY

2635 Oak Hill Road
Mouth of Wilson, Virginia 24363

Head of School: Dr. Michael D. Groves

General Information Coeducational boarding and day college-preparatory, general academic, Microsoft IT Academy, and Dual-Credit Courses school, affiliated with Baptist Church; primarily serves individuals with Attention Deficit Disorder. Grades 8–12. Founded: 1878. Setting: rural. Nearest major city is Charlotte, NC. Students are housed in single-sex dormitories. 400-acre campus. 21 buildings on campus. Approved or accredited by Southern Association of Independent Schools, The Association of Boarding Schools, Virginia Association of Independent Schools, and Virginia Department of Education. Member of Secondary School Admission Test Board. Endowment: $1.5 million. Total enrollment: 137. Upper school average class size: 10. Upper school faculty-student ratio: 1:10.

Upper School Student Profile Grade 8: 5 students (4 boys, 1 girl); Grade 9: 14 students (8 boys, 6 girls); Grade 10: 27 students (21 boys, 6 girls); Grade 11: 55 students (33 boys, 22 girls); Grade 12: 41 students (30 boys, 11 girls). 95% of students are boarding students. 20% are state residents. 24 states are represented in upper school student body. 18% are international students. International students from Bahamas, Hungary, Japan, Republic of Korea, Spain, and Switzerland; 4 other countries represented in student body. 23% of students are Baptist.

Faculty School total: 19. In upper school: 12 men, 7 women; 11 have advanced degrees; 14 reside on campus.

Subjects Offered Advanced math, algebra, art, biology, business, business mathematics, calculus, chemistry, choir, creative writing, desktop publishing, drama, earth science, English, equine studies, film history, fine arts, geometry, health, honors algebra, honors English, honors geometry, honors U.S. history, honors world history, instrumental music, intro to computers, keyboarding, mathematics, Microsoft, modern world history, photography, physical education, physics, psychology, reading/study skills, religion, science, social science, social studies, Spanish, study skills, theater, trigonometry, U.S. government, U.S. history, world geography, world history, world religions, world studies, yearbook.

Graduation Requirements Arts and fine arts (art, music, dance, drama), computer science, English, foreign language, mathematics, physical education (includes health), religion (includes Bible studies and theology), science, social science, social studies (includes history).

Special Academic Programs Honors section; study at local college for college credit; remedial reading and/or remedial writing; special instructional classes for students with Attention Deficit Disorder; ESL (20 students enrolled).

College Admission Counseling 33 students graduated in 2008; 29 went to college, including College of Charleston; Florida State University; North Carolina State University; The Ohio State University; University of Kentucky; Virginia Polytechnic Institute and State University. Other: 1 went to work, 2 entered a postgraduate year, 1 had other specific plans. Median SAT critical reading: 480, median SAT math: 470. 10% scored over 600 on SAT critical reading, 5% scored over 600 on SAT math, 5% scored over 26 on composite ACT.

Student Life Upper grades have uniform requirement, student council, honor system. Discipline rests primarily with faculty. Attendance at religious services is required.

Summer Programs Remediation, advancement programs offered; session focuses on advancement and remediation; held on campus; accepts boys and girls; open to students from other schools. 50 students usually enrolled. 2009 schedule: June 23 to July 26. Application deadline: none.

Tuition and Aid Day student tuition: $6000; 7-day tuition and room/board: $20,800. Tuition installment plan (monthly payment plans, individually arranged payment plans, 12-month interest-free payment plan for those students accepted by June 1). Tuition reduction for siblings, need-based scholarship grants available. In 2008–09, 29% of upper-school students received aid. Total amount of financial aid awarded in 2008–09: $350,000.

Admissions Traditional secondary-level entrance grade is 11. For fall 2008, 97 students applied for upper-level admission, 72 were accepted, 68 enrolled. Any standardized test or TOEFL or SLEP required. Deadline for receipt of application materials: none. Application fee required: $50. On-campus interview recommended.

Athletics Interscholastic: baseball (boys), basketball (b,g), cheering (g), tennis (b,g), volleyball (g); intramural: baseball (b), basketball (b,g), billiards (b,g), bowling (b,g), canoeing/kayaking (b,g), equestrian sports (b,g), fishing (b), golf (b,g), hiking/backpacking (b,g), horseback riding (b,g), jogging (b,g), Nautilus (b,g), outdoor recreation (b,g), running (b,g), softball (g), strength & conditioning (b,g), table tennis (b,g), tennis (b,g), walking (g), weight lifting (b,g); coed interscholastic: soccer, track and field; coed intramural: aquatics, fitness walking, Fives, flag football, paint ball, skiing (downhill), snowboarding, soccer, swimming and diving, ultimate Frisbee, volleyball, yoga. 1 PE instructor, 1 coach, 1 athletic trainer.

Computers Computers are regularly used in business education, creative writing, desktop publishing, English, ESL, mathematics, science, yearbook classes. Computer resources include on-campus library services, Internet access, wireless campus network, Internet filtering or blocking technology. Student e-mail accounts are available to students. The school has a published electronic and media policy.

Contact Dr. Michael D. Groves, President. 276-579-2619. Fax: 276-579-4722. E-mail: info@oak-hill.net. Web site: www.oak-hill.net.

OAK KNOLL SCHOOL OF THE HOLY CHILD

44 Blackburn Road
Summit, New Jersey 07901

Head of School: Timothy J. Saburn

General Information Coeducational day (boys' only in lower grades) college-preparatory, arts, and religious studies school, affiliated with Roman Catholic Church. Boys grades K–6, girls grades K–12. Founded: 1924. Setting: suburban. Nearest major city is New York, NY. 11-acre campus. 4 buildings on campus. Approved or accredited by Middle States Association of Colleges and Schools and New Jersey Department of Education. Member of National Association of Independent Schools and Secondary School Admission Test Board. Endowment: $9.5 million. Total enrollment: 556. Upper school average class size: 15. Upper school faculty-student ratio: 1:8.

Upper School Student Profile Grade 7: 37 students (37 girls); Grade 8: 37 students (37 girls); Grade 9: 58 students (58 girls); Grade 10: 64 students (64 girls); Grade 11: 60 students (60 girls); Grade 12: 57 students (57 girls). 87% of students are Roman Catholic.

Faculty School total: 72. In upper school: 7 men, 45 women; 38 have advanced degrees.

Subjects Offered 20th century American writers, addiction, adolescent issues, advanced studio art-AP, African American studies, African-American literature, algebra, alternative physical education, American history, American literature, American studies, anatomy, ancient world history, art, art appreciation, Asian studies, ballet, Basic programming, Bible studies, biology, biology-AP, British literature, calculus, calculus-AP, calligraphy, campus ministry, career/college preparation, Catholic belief and practice, chemistry, chemistry-AP, Christian and Hebrew scripture, church history, college counseling, computer literacy, computer programming-AP, computer science, computer science-AP, concert choir, creative writing, dance, dance performance, decision making skills, desktop publishing, digital photography, driver education, English, English literature, English literature-AP, English-AP, ensembles, ethics, ethnic studies, European history, European history-AP, expository writing, fine arts, French, French-AP, genetics, geometry, health and wellness, history, Latin, leadership and service, marine science, mathematics, modern world history, music, Native American history, oceanography, peer ministry, physical education, physics, physics-AP, physiology, pre-calculus, psychology, SAT preparation, science, social psychology, Spanish, Spanish-AP, studio art-AP, theology, trigonometry, U.S. history-AP, word processing, world history, world literature, writing.

Graduation Requirements Arts and fine arts (art, music, dance, drama), computer science, English, foreign language, mathematics, physical education (includes health), religion (includes Bible studies and theology), science, U.S. history, world history.
Special Academic Programs Advanced Placement exam preparation; honors section; independent study.
College Admission Counseling 63 students graduated in 2008; all went to college, including Fairfield University; Georgetown University; Lafayette College; Princeton University; University of Pennsylvania; Villanova University. Mean SAT critical reading: 620, mean SAT math: 642, mean SAT writing: 651.
Student Life Upper grades have uniform requirement, student council. Discipline rests primarily with faculty. Attendance at religious services is required.
Summer Programs Enrichment, sports programs offered; held on campus; accepts boys and girls; open to students from other schools. 2009 schedule: June 22 to August. Application deadline: April.
Tuition and Aid Day student tuition: $27,600. Tuition installment plan (Key Tuition Payment Plan). Merit scholarship grants, need-based scholarship grants available. In 2008–09, 15% of upper-school students received aid; total upper-school merit-scholarship money awarded: $79,700. Total amount of financial aid awarded in 2008–09: $1,100,000.
Admissions Traditional secondary-level entrance grade is 9. For fall 2008, 128 students applied for upper-level admission, 66 were accepted, 47 enrolled. ISEE required. Deadline for receipt of application materials: January 28. Application fee required: $50. Interview required.
Athletics Interscholastic: basketball, cross-country running, fencing, field hockey, lacrosse, soccer, softball, swimming and diving, tennis, track and field, volleyball, winter (indoor) track; intramural: dance squad, deck hockey, fitness, yoga. 3 PE instructors, 12 coaches, 1 athletic trainer.
Computers Computers are regularly used in all academic classes. Computer network features include on-campus library services, Internet access, wireless campus network, campus-wide laptop program grades 7-12. Campus intranet and student e-mail accounts are available to students. The school has a published electronic and media policy.
Contact Suzanne Kimm Lewis, Admissions Director. 908-522-8109. Fax: 908-277-1838. E-mail: okadmissions@oakknoll.org. Web site: www.oakknoll.org.

See Close-Up on page 880.

THE OAKLAND SCHOOL

362 McKee Place
Pittsburgh, Pennsylvania 15213

Head of School: Jack C. King

General Information Coeducational day college-preparatory and arts school. Grades 8–12. Founded: 1982. Setting: urban. 1 building on campus. Approved or accredited by United Private Schools Association of Pennsylvania and Pennsylvania Department of Education. Total enrollment: 60. Upper school average class size: 6. Upper school faculty-student ratio: 1:6.
Upper School Student Profile Grade 8: 1 student (1 boy); Grade 9: 13 students (6 boys, 7 girls); Grade 10: 10 students (6 boys, 4 girls); Grade 11: 22 students (15 boys, 7 girls); Grade 12: 14 students (8 boys, 6 girls).
Faculty School total: 12. In upper school: 6 men, 4 women; 7 have advanced degrees.
Subjects Offered Advanced math, algebra, American history, American literature, art, art history, biology, business skills, calculus, chemistry, computer math, computer science, creative writing, drama, earth science, ecology, economics, English, English literature, environmental science, ESL, expository writing, fine arts, French, geography, geometry, government/civics, history, Latin, mathematics, physical education, physics, pre-calculus, psychology, SAT/ACT preparation, science, social studies, Spanish, speech, trigonometry, world history, world literature, writing.
Graduation Requirements Arts and fine arts (art, music, dance, drama), computer literacy, English, mathematics, physical education (includes health), science, social studies (includes history), Community Service.
Special Academic Programs Honors section; accelerated programs; independent study; study at local college for college credit; academic accommodation for the gifted and the artistically talented; remedial reading and/or remedial writing; remedial math; ESL (2 students enrolled).
College Admission Counseling 14 students graduated in 2008; 11 went to college, including Chatham University; Edinboro University of Pennsylvania; Indiana University of Pennsylvania; University of Pittsburgh. Other: 2 went to work, 1 had other specific plans. Mean SAT critical reading: 560, mean SAT math: 512, mean SAT writing: 580.
Student Life Upper grades have student council. Discipline rests primarily with faculty.
Tuition and Aid Day student tuition: $9000. Tuition installment plan (monthly payment plans, individually arranged payment plans, quarterly payment plan, semiannual payment plan). Tuition reduction for siblings, merit scholarship grants, need-based scholarship grants available. In 2008–09, 25% of upper-school students received aid; total upper-school merit-scholarship money awarded: $6000. Total amount of financial aid awarded in 2008–09: $45,000.
Admissions Traditional secondary-level entrance grade is 10. WRAT required. Deadline for receipt of application materials: none. Application fee required: $100. On-campus interview required.
Athletics Intramural: aerobics/dance (girls), dance (g); coed intramural: baseball, basketball, bicycling, billiards, bowling, cooperative games, cross-country running, fitness, fitness walking, flag football, Frisbee, golf, hiking/backpacking, ice skating, jogging, jump rope, kickball, martial arts, racquetball, running, skateboarding, skiing (cross-country), skiing (downhill), snowboarding, softball, swimming and diving, tai chi, tennis, volleyball, walking.
Computers Computers are regularly used in all academic classes. Computer network features include Internet access, wireless campus network. Student e-mail accounts and computer access in designated common areas are available to students.
Contact Admissions Desk. 412-621-7878. Fax: 412-621-7881. E-mail: oschool@stargate.net. Web site: www.theoaklandschool.org.

OAKLAND SCHOOL

Keswick, Virginia
See Special Needs Schools section.

OAK MOUNTAIN ACADEMY

222 Cross Plains Road
Carrollton, Georgia 30116

Head of School: Mr. Ricky Parmer

General Information Coeducational day college-preparatory school, affiliated with Christian faith. Grades K4–12. Founded: 1962. Setting: small town. Nearest major city is Atlanta. 88-acre campus. 2 buildings on campus. Approved or accredited by Georgia Accrediting Commission, Georgia Independent School Association, Southern Association of Colleges and Schools, and Southern Association of Independent Schools. Endowment: $496,583. Total enrollment: 258. Upper school average class size: 12. Upper school faculty-student ratio: 1:5.
Upper School Student Profile Grade 9: 17 students (9 boys, 8 girls); Grade 10: 19 students (10 boys, 9 girls); Grade 11: 17 students (8 boys, 9 girls); Grade 12: 17 students (6 boys, 11 girls).
Faculty School total: 39. In upper school: 8 men, 11 women; 8 have advanced degrees.
Subjects Offered Advanced math, Advanced Placement courses, algebra, American government, American history, American literature, anatomy, ancient world history, art, athletic training, athletics, Bible, biology, biology-AP, calculus, calculus-AP, chemistry, chemistry-AP, chorus, college counseling, community service, computer graphics, computer science, discrete mathematics, drama, economics, electives, English composition, English language-AP, English literature, English literature-AP, English-AP, expository writing, French, geometry, government, graphic arts, guidance, independent study, Latin, modern civilization, music, physical fitness, physical science, physics, pre-calculus, public speaking, research skills, senior internship, senior project, Spanish, statistics, student government, U.S. history, U.S. history-AP, world literature, yearbook.
Graduation Requirements Algebra, ancient world history, Bible, biology, calculus, chemistry, economics, electives, English, foreign language, geometry, modern civilization, physical education (includes health), physical science, public speaking, senior internship, senior project, U.S. government, U.S. history, Senior Project, including research paper, oral presentation, creating a product and 50-hour internship. Community service is required.
Special Academic Programs Advanced Placement exam preparation; honors section; independent study; study at local college for college credit.
College Admission Counseling 13 students graduated in 2008; all went to college, including Kennesaw State University; LaGrange College; Samford University; The Citadel, The Military College of South Carolina; University of Georgia. Mean SAT critical reading: 627, mean SAT math: 617. 50% scored over 600 on SAT critical reading, 60% scored over 600 on SAT math.
Student Life Upper grades have specified standards of dress, student council. Discipline rests primarily with faculty.
Tuition and Aid Day student tuition: $9515. Tuition installment plan (monthly payment plans, three-payment plan). Tuition reduction for siblings, need-based scholarship grants available. In 2008–09, 16% of upper-school students received aid. Total amount of financial aid awarded in 2008–09: $94,000.
Admissions Traditional secondary-level entrance grade is 9. For fall 2008, 7 students applied for upper-level admission, 6 were accepted, 6 enrolled. School's own exam required. Deadline for receipt of application materials: none. Application fee required: $50. Interview required.
Athletics Interscholastic: baseball (boys), basketball (b,g), cheering (g), cross-country running (b,g), soccer (b,g), softball (g), swimming and diving (b,g), tennis (b,g), track and field (b,g), volleyball (g); coed interscholastic: golf. 2 PE instructors, 6 coaches.
Computers Computers are regularly used in English, foreign language, French, graphic arts, independent study, lab/keyboard, Latin, programming, science, Spanish, yearbook classes. Computer network features include on-campus library services, online commercial services, Internet access, Internet filtering or blocking technology. Student e-mail accounts and computer access in designated common areas are available to students. Students grades are available online. The school has a published electronic and media policy.

Contact Mrs. Susan Emmons, Director of Admissions. 770-834-6651. Fax: 770-834-6785. E-mail: admissions@oakmountain.us. Web site: www.oakmountain.us.

OAK RIDGE MILITARY ACADEMY

2317 Oak Ridge Road
PO Box 498
Oak Ridge, North Carolina 27310

Head of School: Col. Roy W. Berwick

General Information Coeducational boarding and day college-preparatory, leadership, and military school. Boarding grades 7–12, day grades 6–12. Founded: 1852. Setting: rural. Nearest major city is Greensboro. Students are housed in single-sex dormitories. 101-acre campus. 22 buildings on campus. Approved or accredited by North Carolina Association of Independent Schools, Southern Association of Colleges and Schools, Southern Association of Independent Schools, and North Carolina Department of Education. Member of National Association of Independent Schools. Total enrollment: 160. Upper school average class size: 9. Upper school faculty-student ratio: 1:11.

Upper School Student Profile Grade 9: 23 students (19 boys, 4 girls); Grade 10: 38 students (25 boys, 13 girls); Grade 11: 39 students (31 boys, 8 girls); Grade 12: 30 students (22 boys, 8 girls). 84% of students are boarding students. 49% are state residents. 16 states are represented in upper school student body. 14% are international students. International students from Bermuda, China, Honduras, Mexico, Philippines, and Republic of Korea; 4 other countries represented in student body.

Faculty School total: 25. In upper school: 12 men, 13 women; 8 have advanced degrees; 9 reside on campus.

Subjects Offered Algebra, American history, American literature, biology, calculus, chemistry, college writing, computer math, computer science, creative writing, driver education, earth science, English, English literature, environmental science, ESL, French, geometry, German, government/civics, grammar, health, JROTC, JROTC or LEAD (Leadership Education and Development), mathematics, military science, music, physical education, physics, SAT preparation, science, social studies, Spanish, trigonometry, world history, writing.

Graduation Requirements Computer science, English, foreign language, mathematics, physical education (includes health), ROTC, SAT preparation, science, social studies (includes history), writing, complete three college applications, 20 hours of community service.

Special Academic Programs Honors section; accelerated programs; study at local college for college credit; academic accommodation for the gifted; special instructional classes for students with Attention Deficit Disorder and Attention Deficit Hyperactivity Disorder; ESL (6 students enrolled).

College Admission Counseling 28 students graduated in 2008; 27 went to college, including Appalachian State University; East Carolina University; North Carolina State University; The Citadel, The Military College of South Carolina; The University of North Carolina at Chapel Hill; The University of North Carolina at Charlotte.

Student Life Upper grades have uniform requirement, student council, honor system. Discipline rests primarily with faculty. Attendance at religious services is required.

Summer Programs Remediation, enrichment, advancement, ESL programs offered; session focuses on leadership, adventure, academics, confidence building; held both on and off campus; held at Carowinds, Wet and Wild and white water rafting in WV; accepts boys and girls; open to students from other schools. 250 students usually enrolled. 2009 schedule: June 24 to August 5. Application deadline: June 1.

Tuition and Aid Day student tuition: $8990; 5-day tuition and room/board: $17,290; 7-day tuition and room/board: $19,990. Tuition installment plan (Key Tuition Payment Plan, SMART Tuition Payment Plan, monthly payment plans). Tuition reduction for siblings, merit scholarship grants, USS Education Loan Program available. In 2008–09, 24% of upper-school students received aid.

Admissions Deadline for receipt of application materials: none. Application fee required: $100. Interview recommended.

Athletics Interscholastic: baseball (boys), basketball (b,g), golf (b), soccer (b,g), swimming and diving (b,g), tennis (b), track and field (b,g), volleyball (g), wrestling (b); intramural: basketball (b,g), flag football (b), outdoor adventure (b,g), paint ball (b,g), rappelling (b,g), scuba diving (b,g), skydiving (b,g), strength & conditioning (b,g), weight lifting (b,g); coed interscholastic: cross-country running, drill team, JROTC drill, marksmanship, riflery, swimming and diving, track and field; coed intramural: outdoor adventure, paint ball, pistol, rappelling, scuba diving, skydiving, softball, strength & conditioning, weight lifting. 1 PE instructor, 22 coaches, 1 athletic trainer.

Computers Computers are regularly used in English, mathematics, science classes. Computer resources include on-campus library services, Internet access, Internet filtering or blocking technology. Students grades are available online. The school has a published electronic and media policy.

Contact Mrs. Amber W. Coble, Deputy Director of Admissions. 336-643-4131 Ext. 196. Fax: 336-643-1797. E-mail: acoble@ormila.com. Web site: www.oakridgemilitary.com.

See Close-Up on page 882.

THE OAKRIDGE SCHOOL

5900 West Pioneer Parkway
Arlington, Texas 76013-2899

Head of School: Mr. Jonathan Kellam

General Information Coeducational day college-preparatory, arts, and technology school. Grades PS–12. Founded: 1979. Setting: suburban. 82-acre campus. 6 buildings on campus. Approved or accredited by Independent Schools Association of the Southwest and Texas Department of Education. Member of National Association of Independent Schools. Endowment: $353,820. Total enrollment: 891. Upper school average class size: 16. Upper school faculty-student ratio: 1:10.

Upper School Student Profile Grade 9: 77 students (45 boys, 32 girls); Grade 10: 73 students (41 boys, 32 girls); Grade 11: 77 students (42 boys, 35 girls); Grade 12: 64 students (30 boys, 34 girls).

Faculty School total: 77. In upper school: 10 men, 16 women; 23 have advanced degrees.

Subjects Offered 3-dimensional art, acting, Advanced Placement courses, advanced studio art-AP, algebra, American government-AP, American history, American history-AP, American literature, anatomy, ancient world history, anthropology, archaeology, art, art history-AP, athletics, biology, British literature, calculus, calculus-AP, chemistry, chemistry-AP, Chinese, choir, choral music, classical civilization, college admission preparation, college counseling, college writing, community service, comparative religion, composition-AP, computer animation, computer applications, computer art, computer graphics, computer information systems, computer keyboarding, computer literacy, computer multimedia, computer processing, computer programming-AP, computer science-AP, computer skills, concert choir, creative writing, current events, desktop publishing, digital applications, digital art, digital imaging, digital music, digital photography, discrete mathematics, drafting, drama, drama performance, drama workshop, dramatic arts, drawing, drawing and design, economics, economics and history, English, English language and composition-AP, English literature and composition-AP, environmental science-AP, European civilization, European history-AP, expository writing, film and literature, fine arts, fractal geometry, fractals, French, French language-AP, French-AP, geometry, golf, government, government and politics-AP, government-AP, government/civics, graphic arts, graphic design, graphics, health, honors algebra, honors English, honors geometry, honors world history, human biology, independent study, keyboarding/computer, language and composition, language arts, Latin, literature and composition-AP, media literacy, modern European history-AP, modern world history, musical productions, organic chemistry, physics, physics-AP, play production, poetry, portfolio art, portfolio writing, pre-algebra, pre-calculus, printmaking, probability and statistics, programming, public service, public speaking, reading/study skills, SAT preparation, SAT/ACT preparation, Spanish, Spanish-AP, strings, theater, track and field, U.S. government, U.S. government and politics, U.S. government and politics-AP, U.S. government-AP, U.S. history, U.S. history-AP, United States government-AP, video, video and animation, video communication, video film production, visual and performing arts, voice, voice ensemble, Web site design, weightlifting, world history.

Graduation Requirements Arts and fine arts (art, music, dance, drama), English, foreign language, mathematics, physical education (includes health), science, social studies (includes history), participation in six seasons of athletics. Community service is required.

Special Academic Programs Advanced Placement exam preparation; honors section; independent study; study at local college for college credit; study abroad; academic accommodation for the gifted, the musically talented, and the artistically talented.

College Admission Counseling 73 students graduated in 2008; all went to college, including Baylor University; Southern Methodist University; Texas A&M University; Texas Christian University; The University of Texas at Austin; University of Southern California. Median SAT critical reading: 530, median SAT math: 570, median SAT writing: 540, median combined SAT: 1100, median composite ACT: 23. 27% scored over 600 on SAT critical reading, 44% scored over 600 on SAT math, 24% scored over 600 on SAT writing, 29% scored over 1800 on combined SAT, 38% scored over 26 on composite ACT.

Student Life Upper grades have uniform requirement, student council, honor system. Discipline rests primarily with faculty.

Summer Programs Remediation, enrichment, advancement, sports, art/fine arts, computer instruction programs offered; session focuses on enrichment and remediation; held both on and off campus; held at museums and recreational facilities; accepts boys and girls; open to students from other schools. 200 students usually enrolled. 2009 schedule: June 11 to July 13. Application deadline: none.

Tuition and Aid Day student tuition: $5200–$14,630. Tuition installment plan (FACTS Tuition Payment Plan, early discount option). Need-based scholarship grants, tuition remission for children of faculty and staff available. In 2008–09, 40% of upper-school students received aid. Total amount of financial aid awarded in 2008–09: $456,932.

Admissions Traditional secondary-level entrance grade is 9. For fall 2008, 64 students applied for upper-level admission, 40 were accepted, 33 enrolled. ERB Reading and Math, ISEE, Otis-Lennon School Ability Test or Stanford Achievement Test required. Deadline for receipt of application materials: none. Application fee required: $50. On-campus interview required.

Athletics Interscholastic: baseball (boys), basketball (b,g), cross-country running (b,g), field hockey (g), football (b), golf (b,g), soccer (b,g), softball (g), tennis (b,g), track and field (b,g), volleyball (g), weight lifting (b), winter soccer (b,g); intramural: weight training (b); coed interscholastic: cheering. 5 PE instructors, 10 coaches, 1 athletic trainer.
Computers Computers are regularly used in art, English, foreign language, history, mathematics, programming, science, stock market, technology, video film production, Web site design, writing, yearbook classes. Computer network features include on-campus library services, online commercial services, Internet access, wireless campus network, Internet filtering or blocking technology. Campus intranet and computer access in designated common areas are available to students. Students grades are available online. The school has a published electronic and media policy.
Contact Dr. Jerry Davis Jr., Director of Admissions. 817-451-4994 Ext. 708. Fax: 817-457-6681. E-mail: jadavis@theoakridgeschool.org. Web site: www.theoakridgeschool.org.

ANNOUNCEMENT FROM THE SCHOOL The Oakridge School is an independent college-preparatory school founded in 1979. Serving students in preschool through 12th grade, the School encourages students to develop a lifelong interest in learning and the arts, in staying physically fit, and in making contributions to their communities. At Oakridge, students experience a broad range of opportunities in a challenging academic environment. Athletics, the fine arts, and numerous extracurricular activities provide additional outlets for students' talents and interests. The School offers programs for preschool and prekindergarten and a full-day program for kindergarten. In Lower School, grades 1 and 2 are self-contained classrooms; grades 3 and 4 rotate among the 3 teachers at each grade level. In addition, children also work with specialists in mathematics, reading, science, Spanish, computer, art, music, and P.E. The Middle and Upper Schools offer honors courses, and all disciplines in Upper School offer Advanced Placement courses. The college adviser supports Upper School students and their parents in their search for the right colleges or universities and then becomes the students' advocate in the college admissions process. The arts at Oakridge flourish in the 32,000-square-foot fine arts center. The center includes a 400-seat performance hall. Oakridge students receive outstanding recognition throughout the state for their accomplishments in choral music, strings, drama, and art. In athletics, Oakridge students participate in interscholastic sports beginning in 7th grade. The School offers fifteen different sports during the fall, winter, and spring seasons. The full range of opportunities for students means that "everybody can be somebody at Oakridge."

OAKWOOD FRIENDS SCHOOL

22 Spackenkill Road
Poughkeepsie, New York 12603

Head of School: Peter F. Baily

General Information Coeducational boarding and day college-preparatory and arts school, affiliated with Society of Friends. Boarding grades 9–12, day grades 6–12. Founded: 1796. Setting: suburban. Nearest major city is New York. Students are housed in single-sex by floor dormitories and coed dormitories. 63-acre campus. 22 buildings on campus. Approved or accredited by Friends Council on Education, New York State Association of Independent Schools, The Association of Boarding Schools, and New York Department of Education. Member of National Association of Independent Schools and Secondary School Admission Test Board. Endowment: $3 million. Total enrollment: 179. Upper school average class size: 15. Upper school faculty-student ratio: 1:5.
Upper School Student Profile Grade 9: 25 students (13 boys, 12 girls); Grade 10: 48 students (26 boys, 22 girls); Grade 11: 46 students (24 boys, 22 girls); Grade 12: 39 students (26 boys, 13 girls). 49% of students are boarding students. 74% are state residents. 5 states are represented in upper school student body. 21% are international students. International students from China, Republic of Korea, Russian Federation, Taiwan, and Viet Nam. 4% of students are members of Society of Friends.
Faculty School total: 35. In upper school: 14 men, 16 women; 22 have advanced degrees; 26 reside on campus.
Subjects Offered Acting, algebra, American history, American literature, American sign language, anthropology, art, art history, biology, calculus, ceramics, chemistry, collage and assemblage, community service, computer applications, conceptual physics, creative writing, critical thinking, directing, drama, drawing, ecology, English, English literature, ensembles, environmental science, ESL, European history, existentialism, expository writing, fashion, fine arts, French, geometry, health, history, history of jazz, interdisciplinary studies, mathematics, media arts, music, music theater, painting, photography, physical education, physics, playwriting and directing, pre-calculus, printmaking, psychology, public speaking, Quakerism and ethics, robotics, science, sculpture, social studies, Spanish, theater, world history, writing.
Graduation Requirements Advanced math, algebra, American history, arts and fine arts (art, music, dance, drama), biology, chemistry, computer literacy, conceptual physics, English, foreign language, geometry, interdisciplinary studies, physical education (includes health), Quakerism and ethics, world history. Community service is required.
Special Academic Programs 9 Advanced Placement exams for which test preparation is offered; independent study; special instructional classes for Academic Support Center for students with mild learning differences; ESL (25 students enrolled).
College Admission Counseling 26 students graduated in 2008; all went to college, including Hampshire College; Hobart and William Smith Colleges; Manhattanville College; Syracuse University. Median SAT critical reading: 550, median SAT math: 580, median SAT writing: 520, median combined SAT: 1680. 32% scored over 600 on SAT critical reading, 21% scored over 600 on SAT math, 26% scored over 600 on SAT writing, 26% scored over 1800 on combined SAT.
Student Life Upper grades have specified standards of dress, student council. Discipline rests equally with students and faculty. Attendance at religious services is required.
Tuition and Aid Day student tuition: $21,195; 5-day tuition and room/board: $31,917; 7-day tuition and room/board: $36,741. Tuition installment plan (monthly payment plans, individually arranged payment plans). Tuition reduction for siblings, need-based scholarship grants available. In 2008–09, 38% of upper-school students received aid. Total amount of financial aid awarded in 2008–09: $747,000.
Admissions Traditional secondary-level entrance grade is 9. For fall 2008, 123 students applied for upper-level admission, 82 were accepted, 59 enrolled. SLEP for foreign students, TOEFL or writing sample required. Deadline for receipt of application materials: none. Application fee required: $40. Interview required.
Athletics Interscholastic: baseball (boys), basketball (b,g), cross-country running (b,g), soccer (b,g), softball (g), tennis (b,g), volleyball (g); coed interscholastic: aquatics, independent competitive sports, swimming and diving, ultimate Frisbee; coed intramural: bowling, cooperative games, cross-country running, fitness, fitness walking, jogging, martial arts, outdoor activities, physical training, ropes courses, running, strength & conditioning, table tennis, ultimate Frisbee, walking, weight lifting, yoga. 1 coach.
Computers Computers are regularly used in computer applications, English, foreign language, history, science, writing classes. Computer network features include on-campus library services, online commercial services, Internet access, wireless campus network, Internet filtering or blocking technology. Student e-mail accounts are available to students. The school has a published electronic and media policy.
Contact Susan Masciale-Lynch, Director of Admissions. 845-462-4200. Fax: 845-462-4251. E-mail: smascialelynch@oakwoodfriends.org. Web site: www.oakwoodfriends.org.

See Close-Up on page 884.

OAKWOOD SCHOOL

11600 Magnolia Boulevard
North Hollywood, California 91601-3098

Head of School: Dr. James Alan Astman

General Information Coeducational day college-preparatory and arts school. Grades K–12. Founded: 1951. Setting: urban. Nearest major city is Los Angeles. 5-acre campus. 6 buildings on campus. Approved or accredited by California Association of Independent Schools and Western Association of Schools and Colleges. Member of National Association of Independent Schools and Secondary School Admission Test Board. Total enrollment: 764. Upper school average class size: 15. Upper school faculty-student ratio: 1:7.
Upper School Student Profile Grade 7: 80 students (40 boys, 40 girls); Grade 8: 80 students (41 boys, 39 girls); Grade 9: 82 students (37 boys, 45 girls); Grade 10: 74 students (42 boys, 32 girls); Grade 11: 76 students (43 boys, 33 girls); Grade 12: 78 students (37 boys, 41 girls).
Faculty School total: 69. In upper school: 40 men, 29 women; 36 have advanced degrees.
Subjects Offered Algebra, American history, American literature, art, art history-AP, astronomy, ballet, Basic programming, biology, biology-AP, botany, calculus, calculus-AP, ceramics, chemistry, chemistry-AP, choir, community service, comparative religion, composition, computer keyboarding, computer literacy, computer math, computer programming, computer programming-AP, computer science, computer science-AP, computer skills, conceptual physics, constitutional law, creative writing, critical studies in film, dance, discrete math, drama, earth and space science, earth science, ecology, economics, English, English language and composition-AP, English literature, English literature and composition-AP, environmental science, ethics, European civilization, expository writing, film studies, fine arts, French, French language-AP, geography, geology, geometry, government and politics-AP, government/civics, grammar, health, health and wellness, history, history of jazz, honors algebra, honors English, honors geometry, honors U.S. history, HTML design, human development, human geography—AP, human sexuality, independent study, introduction to theater, Japanese, jazz band, jazz ensemble, lab science, Latin, life science, Mandarin, marine biology, mathematics, medieval/Renaissance history, modern dance, music, music composition, music theory, music theory-AP, musical theater, philosophy, photography, physical education, physics, physics-AP, pre-algebra, pre-calculus, psychology, psychology-AP, science, science fiction, senior project, Shakespeare, social studies, Spanish, Spanish language-AP, statistics, statistics-AP, theater, trigonometry, U.S. government and politics-AP, world history, world literature, writing.
Graduation Requirements Class trips.

Special Academic Programs Advanced Placement exam preparation; academic accommodation for the gifted.
College Admission Counseling 78 students graduated in 2008; 76 went to college, including Barnard College; Oberlin College; Pitzer College; University of Southern California; University of Wisconsin–Madison; Wesleyan University. Other: 2 had other specific plans. Mean SAT critical reading: 643, mean SAT math: 634, mean SAT writing: 639, mean combined SAT: 1917, mean composite ACT: 26. 80% scored over 600 on SAT critical reading, 75% scored over 600 on SAT math, 76% scored over 600 on SAT writing.
Student Life Upper grades have specified standards of dress, student council. Discipline rests primarily with faculty.
Summer Programs Enrichment, sports, art/fine arts programs offered; session focuses on sports (basketball); held on campus; accepts boys and girls; open to students from other schools. 15 students usually enrolled. 2009 schedule: June 16 to August 3. Application deadline: May 1.
Tuition and Aid Day student tuition: $26,800. Tuition installment plan (Key Tuition Payment Plan, monthly payment plans, individually arranged payment plans, 2- and 10-payment plans). Need-based scholarship grants, AchieverLoans (Key Education Resources) available. In 2008–09, 14% of upper-school students received aid.
Admissions Traditional secondary-level entrance grade is 7. For fall 2008, 317 students applied for upper-level admission, 138 were accepted, 51 enrolled. Deadline for receipt of application materials: January 19. Application fee required: $100. On-campus interview required.
Athletics Interscholastic: baseball (boys, girls), cross-country running (b,g), flag football (b), soccer (b,g), softball (g), tennis (b,g), track and field (b,g), volleyball (b,g); intramural: baseball (b,g), dance (b,g), golf (b,g); coed interscholastic: equestrian sports, horseback riding, track and field; coed intramural: aerobics, aerobics/dance, aerobics/Nautilus, ball hockey, combined training, Cosom hockey, fitness, floor hockey, Frisbee, jogging, lacrosse, martial arts, modern dance, Nautilus, outdoor activities, paddle tennis, physical fitness, physical training, power lifting, ropes courses, running, self defense, softball, speedball, street hockey, strength & conditioning, team handball, tennis, touch football, ultimate Frisbee, volleyball, walking, weight lifting, weight training, yoga. 4 PE instructors, 20 coaches, 1 athletic trainer.
Computers Computers are regularly used in history, humanities, mathematics, programming, science, video film production classes. Computer resources include on-campus library services, online commercial services, Internet access, Internet filtering or blocking technology. Campus intranet and student e-mail accounts are available to students. Students grades are available online. The school has a published electronic and media policy.
Contact Margie Llinas, Assistant to Director of Admission 7-12. 818-752-5277. Fax: 818-766-1285. E-mail: mllinas@oakwoodschool.org. Web site: www.oakwoodschool.org.

THE OAKWOOD SCHOOL

4000 MacGregor Downs Road
Greenville, North Carolina 27834
Head of School: Mr. Robert R. Peterson

General Information Coeducational day college-preparatory, arts, and technology school. Grades PK–12. Founded: 1996. Setting: small town. Nearest major city is Raleigh. 41-acre campus. 1 building on campus. Approved or accredited by Southern Association of Colleges and Schools and North Carolina Department of Education. Languages of instruction: English and Spanish. Total enrollment: 334. Upper school average class size: 15. Upper school faculty-student ratio: 1:8.
Upper School Student Profile Grade 8: 25 students (11 boys, 14 girls); Grade 9: 16 students (11 boys, 5 girls); Grade 10: 7 students (4 boys, 3 girls); Grade 11: 5 students (3 boys, 2 girls); Grade 12: 9 students (7 boys, 2 girls).
Faculty School total: 39. In upper school: 2 men, 16 women; 10 have advanced degrees.
Subjects Offered Algebra, American literature, American literature-AP, band, biology, biology-AP, calculus, calculus-AP, chemistry, chemistry-AP, chorus, conceptual physics, discrete math, environmental studies, European history, European history-AP, European literature, geometry, health and wellness, journalism, physics-AP, pre-calculus, Spanish, Spanish-AP, statistics, statistics-AP, studio art, Western civilization, Western literature, world history, world history-AP, world literature, yearbook.
Graduation Requirements Arts and fine arts (art, music, dance, drama), English, foreign language, history, mathematics, physical education (includes health), science, electives such as art, music, orchestra, journalism, creative writing, computer graphics.
Special Academic Programs Advanced Placement exam preparation; honors section; independent study; academic accommodation for the gifted and the musically talented.
Student Life Upper grades have specified standards of dress, student council, honor system. Discipline rests primarily with faculty.
Summer Programs Enrichment, advancement, sports programs offered; session focuses on summer camps; held on campus; accepts boys and girls; open to students from other schools. 130 students usually enrolled. 2009 schedule: June 20 to July 30. Application deadline: April 1.
Tuition and Aid Day student tuition: $9850. Tuition installment plan (Insured Tuition Payment Plan, monthly payment plans, individually arranged payment plans). Merit scholarship grants, need-based scholarship grants available. In 2008–09, 9% of upper-school students received aid; total upper-school merit-scholarship money awarded: $20,000. Total amount of financial aid awarded in 2008–09: $91,500.
Admissions Traditional secondary-level entrance grade is 8. For fall 2008, 8 students applied for upper-level admission, 6 were accepted, 6 enrolled. OLSAT, ERB, Woodcock-Johnson Revised Achievement Test and writing sample required. Deadline for receipt of application materials: none. Application fee required: $75. On-campus interview required.
Athletics Interscholastic: baseball (boys), basketball (b,g), cheering (g), independent competitive sports (b,g), soccer (b,g), softball (g), volleyball (g); intramural: softball (g); coed interscholastic: cross-country running, golf, physical fitness; coed intramural: basketball, cross-country running. 2 PE instructors, 5 coaches.
Computers Computers are regularly used in all classes. Computer network features include on-campus library services, online commercial services, Internet access, wireless campus network, Internet filtering or blocking technology. Student e-mail accounts and computer access in designated common areas are available to students. Students grades are available online. The school has a published electronic and media policy.
Contact Ms. Gini Peterson, Director of Admissions. 252-931-0760 Ext. 222. Fax: 252-931-0964. E-mail: gpeterson@theoakwoodschool.org. Web site: www.theoakwoodschool.org.

O'DEA HIGH SCHOOL

802 Terry Avenue
Seattle, Washington 98104-2018
Head of School: Br. Dominic Murray, CFC

General Information Boys' day college-preparatory, general academic, and religious studies school, affiliated with Roman Catholic Church. Grades 9–12. Founded: 1923. Setting: urban. 1-acre campus. 1 building on campus. Approved or accredited by National Catholic Education Association, Northwest Association of Schools and Colleges, and Washington Department of Education. Endowment: $3.5 million. Total enrollment: 466. Upper school average class size: 25. Upper school faculty-student ratio: 1:13.
Upper School Student Profile Grade 9: 135 students (135 boys); Grade 10: 118 students (118 boys); Grade 11: 103 students (103 boys); Grade 12: 110 students (110 boys). 81% of students are Roman Catholic.
Faculty School total: 41. In upper school: 33 men, 8 women; 25 have advanced degrees.
Subjects Offered Advanced chemistry, Advanced Placement courses, African-American history, algebra, American history, American literature, art, art appreciation, art education, art history, arts, band, biology, calculus, chemistry, Christian doctrine, Christian ethics, Christian scripture, church history, civics, college counseling, community service, computer music, computer programming, computer-aided design, contemporary problems, digital photography, drama performance, driver education, economics, English, fine arts, geometry, health, history, humanities, independent study, Japanese, jazz band, Latin, leadership training, math analysis, mathematics, mathematics-AP, photography, physical education, physics, publications, science, social science, Spanish, trigonometry, world literature, writing.
Graduation Requirements Arts and fine arts (art, music, dance, drama), English, foreign language, mathematics, physical education (includes health), religion (includes Bible studies and theology), science, social studies (includes history). Community service is required.
Special Academic Programs Advanced Placement exam preparation; honors section; study at local college for college credit; academic accommodation for the gifted; remedial reading and/or remedial writing.
College Admission Counseling 108 students graduated in 2008; 104 went to college, including Gonzaga University; Seattle University; University of Portland; University of Washington; Washington State University; Western Washington University. Other: 3 went to work, 1 entered military service.
Student Life Upper grades have specified standards of dress, student council, honor system. Discipline rests primarily with faculty. Attendance at religious services is required.
Tuition and Aid Day student tuition: $6900–$7900. Tuition installment plan (monthly payment plans). Tuition reduction for siblings, need-based scholarship grants available. In 2008–09, 29% of upper-school students received aid. Total amount of financial aid awarded in 2008–09: $340,000.
Admissions Traditional secondary-level entrance grade is 9. For fall 2008, 300 students applied for upper-level admission, 160 were accepted, 130 enrolled. Metropolitan Achievement Test required. Deadline for receipt of application materials: January 16. Application fee required: $50. Interview recommended.
Athletics Interscholastic: baseball, basketball, cross-country running, football, golf, soccer, swimming and diving, tennis, track and field, weight training, wrestling; intramural: basketball, bicycling, flag football, indoor soccer, physical training, soccer, touch football, volleyball, weight training. 1 PE instructor.
Computers Computers are regularly used in accounting, desktop publishing, ESL, English, graphic design, mathematics, photography, publications, SAT preparation, science, study skills, technical drawing, yearbook classes. Computer network features include on-campus library services, Internet access, Internet filtering or blocking technology. Students grades are available online. The school has a published electronic and media policy.

Contact Mrs. Jeanne Flohr, Director of Admissions. 206-622-1308. E-mail: jflohr@odea.org. Web site: www.odea.org.

OJAI VALLEY SCHOOL

723 El Paseo Road
Ojai, California 93023
Head of School: M. D. Hermes

General Information Coeducational boarding and day college-preparatory school. Boarding grades 3–12, day grades PK–12. Founded: 1911. Setting: rural. Nearest major city is Los Angeles. Students are housed in single-sex dormitories. 200-acre campus. 13 buildings on campus. Approved or accredited by California Association of Independent Schools, The Association of Boarding Schools, Western Association of Schools and Colleges, and California Department of Education. Member of National Association of Independent Schools and Secondary School Admission Test Board. Endowment: $1 million. Total enrollment: 328. Upper school average class size: 12. Upper school faculty-student ratio: 1:6.

Upper School Student Profile Grade 9: 31 students (14 boys, 17 girls); Grade 10: 43 students (27 boys, 16 girls); Grade 11: 26 students (17 boys, 9 girls); Grade 12: 25 students (12 boys, 13 girls). 77% of students are boarding students. 62% are state residents. 8 states are represented in upper school student body. 33% are international students. International students from China, Japan, Mexico, Republic of Korea, Taiwan, and Thailand; 7 other countries represented in student body.

Faculty School total: 54. In upper school: 11 men, 12 women; 10 have advanced degrees; 10 reside on campus.

Subjects Offered 20th century history, algebra, American history, American literature, art, art history, biology, biology-AP, calculus, calculus-AP, chemistry, chemistry-AP, community service, computer science, conceptual physics, creative writing, drama, ecology, economics, English, English literature, English-AP, environmental science, equestrian sports, ESL, European history, fine arts, French, French-AP, geography, geometry, government/civics, grammar, health, history, honors English, humanities, independent study, mathematics, music, music theory-AP, philosophy, photography, physical education, physics, psychology, science, social studies, Spanish, Spanish-AP, speech, statistics, studio art, studio art-AP, theater, trigonometry, typing, wilderness/outdoor program, world history, writing.

Graduation Requirements Arts and fine arts (art, music, dance, drama), economics, English, foreign language, government, mathematics, science, social studies (includes history).

Special Academic Programs Advanced Placement exam preparation; honors section; accelerated programs; independent study; study abroad; academic accommodation for the gifted and the artistically talented; remedial reading and/or remedial writing; remedial math; ESL (12 students enrolled).

College Admission Counseling 35 students graduated in 2007; all went to college, including Boston University; New York University; The Johns Hopkins University; University of California, Riverside; University of California, Santa Barbara. Median SAT critical reading: 537, median SAT math: 599, median combined SAT: 1136. 25% scored over 600 on SAT math.

Student Life Upper grades have specified standards of dress, student council, honor system. Discipline rests equally with students and faculty.

Tuition and Aid Day student tuition: $17,750; 7-day tuition and room/board: $39,000. Tuition installment plan (individually arranged payment plans). Need-based scholarship grants, need-based loans available. In 2007–08, 9% of upper-school students received aid. Total amount of financial aid awarded in 2007–08: $163,105.

Admissions Traditional secondary-level entrance grade is 9. For fall 2007, 160 students applied for upper-level admission, 82 were accepted, 37 enrolled. Any standardized test, SLEP for foreign students, SSAT or TOEFL required. Deadline for receipt of application materials: none. Application fee required: $50. Interview required.

Athletics Interscholastic: baseball (boys), basketball (b,g), cross-country running (b,g), dressage (b,g), flag football (b), lacrosse (b,g), soccer (b,g), volleyball (b,g); coed interscholastic: equestrian sports, golf, track and field; coed intramural: aerobics, aerobics/dance, backpacking, basketball, bicycling, canoeing/kayaking, climbing, cross-country running, equestrian sports, fencing, fitness, fitness walking, golf, hiking/backpacking, horseback riding, kayaking, martial arts, mountain biking, outdoor education, paddle tennis, rafting, rappelling, rock climbing, ropes courses, scuba diving, surfing, swimming and diving, wall climbing, weight training, yoga. 2 PE instructors, 2 coaches, 2 athletic trainers.

Computers Computers are regularly used in English, introduction to technology, mathematics, music, SAT preparation, science, yearbook classes. Computer resources include on-campus library services, online commercial services, Internet access. The school has a published electronic and media policy.

Contact Ms. Tracy Wilson, Director of Admission. 805-646-1423. Fax: 805-646-0362. E-mail: admission@ovs.org. Web site: www.ovs.org.

See Close-Up on page 886.

OKANAGAN ADVENTIST ACADEMY

1035 Hollywood Road
Kelowna, British Columbia V1X 4N3, Canada
Head of School: Mrs. Janice Harford

General Information Coeducational day college-preparatory, arts, religious studies, and technology school, affiliated with Seventh-day Adventist Church. Grades K–12. Founded: 1920. Setting: small town. Nearest major city is Vancouver, Canada. 10-acre campus. 2 buildings on campus. Approved or accredited by Association of Christian Schools International and British Columbia Department of Education. Language of instruction: English. Endowment: CAN$20,000. Total enrollment: 104. Upper school average class size: 15. Upper school faculty-student ratio: 1:11.

Upper School Student Profile Grade 8: 9 students (4 boys, 5 girls); Grade 9: 10 students (4 boys, 6 girls); Grade 10: 9 students (6 boys, 3 girls); Grade 11: 11 students (5 boys, 6 girls); Grade 12: 10 students (4 boys, 6 girls). 85% of students are Seventh-day Adventists.

Faculty School total: 10. In upper school: 5 men, 1 woman; 4 have advanced degrees.

Subjects Offered Art, biology, chemistry, choir, drama, English, French, health education, home economics, mathematics, physical education, physics, religion, science, social studies.

Graduation Requirements Applied skills, arts and fine arts (art, music, dance, drama), career planning, careers, English, mathematics, religion (includes Bible studies and theology), science, social studies (includes history).

College Admission Counseling 12 students graduated in 2008; 4 went to college. Other: 8 went to work.

Student Life Upper grades have specified standards of dress, student council, honor system. Discipline rests primarily with faculty.

Tuition and Aid Day student tuition: CAN$3100–CAN$3400. Guaranteed tuition plan. Tuition installment plan (monthly payment plans, individually arranged payment plans). Tuition reduction for siblings, need-based scholarship grants, church-based financial aid available. In 2008–09, 40% of upper-school students received aid. Total amount of financial aid awarded in 2008–09: CAN$55,000.

Admissions Traditional secondary-level entrance grade is 8. Deadline for receipt of application materials: none. Application fee required: CAN$160. Interview recommended.

Athletics Coed Interscholastic: badminton, ball hockey, baseball, basketball, bicycling, cooperative games, cross-country running, fitness, flag football, floor hockey, physical fitness, running, soccer, track and field, volleyball; coed intramural: badminton, ball hockey, baseball, basketball, flag football, floor hockey, independent competitive sports, soccer, volleyball. 2 PE instructors.

Computers Computers are regularly used in information technology classes. Computer network features include on-campus library services, Internet access, Internet filtering or blocking technology.

Contact Ms. Brittany Johnson, Treasurer. 250-860-5305. Fax: 250-868-9703. E-mail: okaa@shaw.ca.

OLDENBURG ACADEMY

1 Twister Circle
Oldenburg, Indiana 47036
Head of School: Sr. Therese Gillman, OSF

General Information Coeducational day college-preparatory, arts, and religious studies school, affiliated with Roman Catholic Church. Grades 9–12. Founded: 1852. Setting: small town. Nearest major city is Cincinnati, OH. 23-acre campus. 3 buildings on campus. Approved or accredited by North Central Association of Colleges and Schools and Indiana Department of Education. Total enrollment: 205. Upper school average class size: 15. Upper school faculty-student ratio: 1:12.

Upper School Student Profile Grade 9: 60 students (23 boys, 37 girls); Grade 10: 56 students (22 boys, 34 girls); Grade 11: 38 students (19 boys, 19 girls); Grade 12: 51 students (23 boys, 28 girls). 80% of students are Roman Catholic.

Faculty School total: 17. In upper school: 3 men, 14 women; 10 have advanced degrees.

Graduation Requirements 40 hours of community service.

Special Academic Programs Advanced Placement exam preparation; honors section.

College Admission Counseling Colleges students went to include Indiana University Bloomington; Purdue University.

Student Life Upper grades have uniform requirement, student council, honor system. Discipline rests primarily with faculty. Attendance at religious services is required.

Tuition and Aid Day student tuition: $6400. Tuition installment plan (FACTS Tuition Payment Plan). Tuition reduction for siblings, merit scholarship grants, need-based scholarship grants available. In 2008–09, 35% of upper-school students received aid. Total amount of financial aid awarded in 2008–09: $50,000.

Admissions Traditional secondary-level entrance grade is 9. High School Placement Test (closed version) from Scholastic Testing Service required. Deadline for receipt of application materials: none. Application fee required: $350. Interview recommended.

Athletics Interscholastic: baseball (boys), basketball (b,g), cheering (g), cross-country running (b,g), dance team (g). 1 PE instructor, 9 coaches.

Computers Computers are regularly used in all academic classes. Computer network features include on-campus library services, Internet access, wireless campus network,

Internet filtering or blocking technology. Student e-mail accounts and computer access in designated common areas are available to students. Students grades are available online. The school has a published electronic and media policy.
Contact Mrs. Bettina Rose, Principal. 812-934-4440 Ext. 223. Fax: 812-934-4838. E-mail: brose@oldenburgacademy.org.

OLDFIELDS SCHOOL

1500 Glencoe Road
Glencoe, Maryland 21152

Head of School: Mr. Taylor Smith

General Information Girls' boarding and day college-preparatory, arts, and technology school; primarily serves Learning support superior and deals with a few students who may be ADD, etc. Grades 8–PG. Founded: 1867. Setting: rural. Nearest major city is Baltimore. Students are housed in single-sex dormitories. 230-acre campus. 14 buildings on campus. Approved or accredited by Association of Independent Maryland Schools, Middle States Association of Colleges and Schools, The Association of Boarding Schools, and Maryland Department of Education. Member of National Association of Independent Schools and Secondary School Admission Test Board. Endowment: $15 million. Total enrollment: 164. Upper school average class size: 12. Upper school faculty-student ratio: 1:6.
Upper School Student Profile Grade 8: 12 students (12 girls); Grade 9: 28 students (28 girls); Grade 10: 47 students (47 girls); Grade 11: 30 students (30 girls); Grade 12: 47 students (47 girls). 70% of students are boarding students. 20% are state residents. 17 states are represented in upper school student body. 10% are international students. International students from Brazil, China, El Salvador, Germany, Mexico, and United Kingdom; 5 other countries represented in student body.
Faculty School total: 32. In upper school: 4 men, 28 women; 21 have advanced degrees; 24 reside on campus.
Subjects Offered 20th century history, 3-dimensional design, acting, advanced chemistry, algebra, American history, anatomy and physiology, art history, astronomy, biology, calculus, ceramics, chemistry, choreography, college counseling, computer science, dance, directing, drawing, English, equine science, ethics, French, geometry, government, graphic design, health, honors algebra, honors English, honors geometry, honors U.S. history, honors world history, HTML design, international relations, painting, photography, physics, pre-algebra, pre-calculus, psychology, publications, science, sociology, Spanish, technical theater, theater, trigonometry, voice, world history.
Graduation Requirements Arts and fine arts (art, music, dance, drama), computer literacy, English, foreign language, mathematics, physical education (includes health), science, social studies (includes history), participation in May Program, senior presentation.
Special Academic Programs Advanced Placement exam preparation; honors section; independent study; study abroad; academic accommodation for the gifted.
College Admission Counseling 39 students graduated in 2008; 38 went to college, including Rutgers, The State University of New Jersey, Newark; Syracuse University; The Johns Hopkins University; University of Maryland, College Park; University of Michigan. Other: 1 had other specific plans.
Student Life Upper grades have specified standards of dress, student council, honor system. Discipline rests equally with students and faculty.
Summer Programs Enrichment, sports, art/fine arts programs offered; session focuses on arts, SAT prep, sports; held on campus; accepts boys and girls; open to students from other schools. 2009 schedule: June 15 to July 30.
Tuition and Aid Day student tuition: $25,075; 5-day tuition and room/board: $37,948; 7-day tuition and room/board: $42,475. Tuition installment plan (Key Tuition Payment Plan, additional bank loans). Merit scholarship grants, need-based scholarship grants, middle-income loans available. In 2008–09, 27% of upper-school students received aid. Total amount of financial aid awarded in 2008–09: $1,200,000.
Admissions Traditional secondary-level entrance grade is 9. For fall 2008, 270 students applied for upper-level admission, 127 were accepted, 46 enrolled. ISEE, PSAT and SAT for applicants to grade 11 and 12, SSAT, TOEFL, Wechsler Intelligence Scale for Children or WISC/Woodcock-Johnson required. Deadline for receipt of application materials: February 1. Application fee required: $50. Interview recommended.
Athletics Interscholastic: badminton, basketball, cross-country running, equestrian sports, field hockey, horseback riding, indoor soccer, lacrosse, soccer, softball, tennis, volleyball, winter soccer; intramural: aerobics, aerobics/dance, aerobics/Nautilus, backpacking, ballet, dance, dance squad, dance team, dressage, equestrian sports, fitness, hiking/backpacking, horseback riding, jogging, modern dance, mountaineering, outdoor activities, physical fitness, running, sailing, strength & conditioning, surfing, table tennis, ultimate Frisbee, walking, weight lifting, weight training, wilderness, wilderness survival, yoga. 3 PE instructors, 8 coaches, 1 athletic trainer.
Computers Computers are regularly used in all academic classes. Computer network features include on-campus library services, online commercial services, Internet access, wireless campus network, Internet filtering or blocking technology. Campus intranet, student e-mail accounts, and computer access in designated common areas are available to students. Students grades are available online. The school has a published electronic and media policy.
Contact Dr. Parnell Hagerman, Associate Head of School. 410-472-4800. Fax: 410-472-6839. E-mail: hagermanp@oldfieldsschool.org. Web site: www.oldfieldsschool.org.

See Close-Up on page 888.

OLNEY FRIENDS SCHOOL

61830 Sandy Ridge Road
Barnesville, Ohio 43713

Head of School: Richard F. Sidwell

General Information Coeducational boarding and day college-preparatory and religious studies school, affiliated with Society of Friends. Grades 9–12. Founded: 1837. Setting: rural. Nearest major city is Pittsburgh, PA. Students are housed in single-sex dormitories. 350-acre campus. 10 buildings on campus. Approved or accredited by Friends Council on Education, Independent Schools Association of the Central States, Midwest Association of Boarding Schools, Ohio Association of Independent Schools, The Association of Boarding Schools, and Ohio Department of Education. Member of National Association of Independent Schools. Endowment: $600,000. Total enrollment: 62. Upper school average class size: 8. Upper school faculty-student ratio: 1:5.
Upper School Student Profile Grade 9: 7 students (5 boys, 2 girls); Grade 10: 13 students (7 boys, 6 girls); Grade 11: 18 students (8 boys, 10 girls); Grade 12: 24 students (11 boys, 13 girls). 97% of students are boarding students. 15% are state residents. 17 states are represented in upper school student body. 44% are international students. International students from China, Ethiopia, Japan, Republic of Korea, Rwanda, and Viet Nam; 5 other countries represented in student body. 21% of students are members of Society of Friends.
Faculty School total: 19. In upper school: 10 men, 9 women; 11 have advanced degrees; 11 reside on campus.
Subjects Offered Advanced math, agriculture, agroecology, algebra, alternative physical education, American studies, ancient history, art, astronomy, biology, calculus, calculus-AP, ceramics, chemistry, chorus, clayworking, college counseling, community service, drawing, English, English literature, English literature-AP, environmental science, ESL, fine arts, folk art, gardening, general science, geometry, global issues, government/civics, health, history, library research, library skills, mathematics, photography, physical education, physics, religion, social studies, Spanish, Western civilization, women in society, woodworking, world literature.
Graduation Requirements Algebra, arts and fine arts (art, music, dance, drama), calculus, English, foreign language, general science, geometry, humanities, lab science, mathematics, physical education (includes health), pre-calculus, religion (includes Bible studies and theology), science, social studies (includes history), research graduation essay. Community service is required.
Special Academic Programs Advanced Placement exam preparation; independent study; term-away projects; ESL (20 students enrolled).
College Admission Counseling 14 students graduated in 2007; 12 went to college, including Earlham College; Georgia Institute of Technology; Haverford College; Ohio Wesleyan University. Other: 2 went to work. Median SAT critical reading: 500, median SAT math: 560. 33% scored over 600 on SAT critical reading, 33% scored over 600 on SAT math.
Student Life Upper grades have student council, honor system. Discipline rests equally with students and faculty. Attendance at religious services is required.
Tuition and Aid Day student tuition: $13,050; 7-day tuition and room/board: $26,100. Tuition installment plan (monthly payment plans, individually arranged payment plans). Need-based scholarship grants, tuition discounts for children of faculty, tuition discounts for children of alumni and Quakers available. In 2007–08, 65% of upper-school students received aid. Total amount of financial aid awarded in 2007–08: $535,500.
Admissions Traditional secondary-level entrance grade is 9. For fall 2007, 41 students applied for upper-level admission, 35 were accepted, 28 enrolled. Skills for ESL students, SLEP for foreign students, TOEFL or TOEFL or SLEP required. Deadline for receipt of application materials: none. Application fee required: $50. On-campus interview required.
Athletics Interscholastic: basketball (boys); intramural: basketball (b,g), volleyball (b,g); coed interscholastic: soccer; coed intramural: aerobics, aerobics/dance, artistic gym, backpacking, bicycling, cooperative games, cross-country running, field hockey, fitness, fitness walking, Frisbee, gymnastics, hiking/backpacking, jump rope, outdoor activities, outdoor education, outdoor skills, running, soccer, softball, tennis, ultimate Frisbee, walking, wall climbing. 2 PE instructors, 3 coaches.
Computers Computers are regularly used in art, college planning, English, ESL, history, humanities, music, photography, social studies classes. Computer network features include on-campus library services, online commercial services, Internet access, wireless campus network, Internet filtering or blocking technology, PC computer classroom with a multimedia presentation system, Mac computers in designated areas. Student e-mail accounts and computer access in designated common areas are available to students. The school has a published electronic and media policy.
Contact Ela J. Robertson, Director of Admissions. 740-425-3655 Ext. 207. Fax: 740-425-3202. E-mail: admissions@olneyfriends.org. Web site: www.olneyfriends.org.

ANNOUNCEMENT FROM THE SCHOOL Founded in 1837 by the Religious Society of Friends, Olney Friends School is an independent Quaker high school, which strives to create a diverse and globally representative student body. Students and staff members celebrate intellectual vigor, provoke questions of conscience, and nurture the skills of living in a community. Olney offers a values-centered, college-directed, interactive curriculum that promotes the concepts and practice of sustainability.

See Close-Up on page 890.

THE O'NEAL SCHOOL

3300 Airport Road
PO Box 290
Southern Pines, North Carolina 28388-0290

Head of School: Mr. John Neiswender

General Information Coeducational day college-preparatory school. Grades PK–12. Founded: 1971. Setting: small town. Nearest major city is Raleigh. 40-acre campus. 3 buildings on campus. Approved or accredited by North Carolina Association of Independent Schools, Southern Association of Colleges and Schools, Southern Association of Independent Schools, and North Carolina Department of Education. Member of National Association of Independent Schools. Endowment: $1.3 million. Total enrollment: 440. Upper school average class size: 15. Upper school faculty-student ratio: 1:10.

Upper School Student Profile Grade 9: 31 students (13 boys, 18 girls); Grade 10: 44 students (22 boys, 22 girls); Grade 11: 47 students (22 boys, 25 girls); Grade 12: 41 students (18 boys, 23 girls).

Faculty School total: 53. In upper school: 10 men, 12 women; 9 have advanced degrees.

Subjects Offered Algebra, American history, American literature, art, art history, biology, biology-AP, calculus-AP, chemistry, community service, computer science, creative writing, economics, English, English literature, English literature and composition-AP, environmental science, environmental science-AP, ethics, European history, European history-AP, expository writing, film appreciation, fine arts, French, French-AP, geometry, journalism, Latin, Latin-AP, logic, mathematics, music, philosophy, photography, physical education, physics-AP, political science, pottery, public speaking, science, social studies, Spanish, Spanish-AP, speech, statistics-AP, U.S. history-AP, world history, world literature.

Graduation Requirements Arts and fine arts (art, music, dance, drama), computer science, English, foreign language, mathematics, physical education (includes health), science, social studies (includes history), speech, 36 hours of community service.

Special Academic Programs 14 Advanced Placement exams for which test preparation is offered; independent study; study at local college for college credit; remedial reading and/or remedial writing; remedial math; programs in English, mathematics, general development for dyslexic students.

College Admission Counseling 38 students graduated in 2008; all went to college, including Duke University; Emory University; The University of North Carolina at Chapel Hill; The University of North Carolina Wilmington; Wake Forest University. Median SAT critical reading: 570, median SAT math: 590, median SAT writing: 560. 40% scored over 600 on SAT critical reading, 50% scored over 600 on SAT math, 35% scored over 600 on SAT writing, 44% scored over 1800 on combined SAT.

Student Life Upper grades have specified standards of dress, student council, honor system. Discipline rests primarily with faculty.

Tuition and Aid Day student tuition: $13,950. Tuition installment plan (Insured Tuition Payment Plan, monthly payment plans, individually arranged payment plans). Merit scholarship grants, need-based scholarship grants available. In 2008–09, 24% of upper-school students received aid; total upper-school merit-scholarship money awarded: $33,387. Total amount of financial aid awarded in 2008–09: $274,063.

Admissions Traditional secondary-level entrance grade is 9. For fall 2008, 29 students applied for upper-level admission, 26 were accepted, 16 enrolled. Admissions testing, essay, OLSAT, Stanford Achievement Test, PSAT and SAT for applicants to grade 11 and 12, WRAT or writing sample required. Deadline for receipt of application materials: none. Application fee required: $75. On-campus interview required.

Athletics Interscholastic: baseball (boys), basketball (b,g), cheering (g), cross-country running (b,g), soccer (b,g), swimming and diving (b,g), tennis (b,g), track and field (b,g), volleyball (g); intramural: cheering (g); coed interscholastic: golf; coed intramural: martial arts. 2 PE instructors, 4 coaches.

Computers Computers are regularly used in all academic classes. Computer network features include on-campus library services, Internet access, wireless campus network, Internet filtering or blocking technology, EBSCO, World Book Online. Student e-mail accounts and computer access in designated common areas are available to students. The school has a published electronic and media policy.

Contact Mrs. Alice Droppers, Director of Admissions and Financial Aid. 910-692-6920 Ext. 103. Fax: 910-692-6930. E-mail: adroppers@onealschool.org.

ANNOUNCEMENT FROM THE SCHOOL O'Neal is a college-preparatory school dedicated to the development of academic excellence, strength of character, and physical well-being of its students in an environment where integrity, self-discipline, and consideration for others are fundamental. O'Neal enrolls approximately 460 students from prekindergarten through grade 12. Community service, athletics, and extracurricular activities are integral to O'Neal's mission. O'Neal also has an Academic Enrichment Program for students with learning differences. Financial aid is available. John Neiswender is Headmaster.

ONEIDA BAPTIST INSTITUTE

11 Mulberry Street
Oneida, Kentucky 40972

Head of School: Dr. W. F. Underwood

General Information Coeducational boarding and day college-preparatory, general academic, arts, vocational, religious studies, bilingual studies, and agriculture school, affiliated with Southern Baptist Convention. Grades 6–12. Founded: 1899. Setting: rural. Nearest major city is Lexington. Students are housed in single-sex dormitories. 200-acre campus. 15 buildings on campus. Approved or accredited by The Kentucky Non-Public School Commission, The National Non-Public School Commission, and Kentucky Department of Education. Endowment: $15 million. Total enrollment: 300. Upper school average class size: 11. Upper school faculty-student ratio: 1:11.

Upper School Student Profile Grade 9: 40 students (25 boys, 15 girls); Grade 10: 60 students (30 boys, 30 girls); Grade 11: 65 students (35 boys, 30 girls); Grade 12: 60 students (30 boys, 30 girls). 80% of students are boarding students. 60% are state residents. 28 states are represented in upper school student body. 15% are international students. International students from China, Ethiopia, Japan, Nigeria, Republic of Korea, and Thailand. 25% of students are Southern Baptist Convention.

Faculty School total: 45. In upper school: 20 men, 15 women; 9 have advanced degrees; all reside on campus.

Subjects Offered Agriculture, algebra, art, auto mechanics, band, Bible, biology, biology-AP, calculus, calculus-AP, chemistry, child development, choir, commercial art, computers, drama, earth and space science, English, English-AP, ESL, foods, geography, geometry, German, guitar, health, language arts, life skills, literature, mathematics, physical education, piano, political science, pre-algebra, pre-calculus, science, social science, social studies, Spanish, Spanish-AP, stagecraft, U.S. history, U.S. history-AP, weight training, welding, world history.

Graduation Requirements Arts and fine arts (art, music, dance, drama), Bible, computer literacy, English, foreign language, mathematics, physical education (includes health), science, social studies (includes history), field placement.

Special Academic Programs Advanced Placement exam preparation; independent study; remedial reading and/or remedial writing; remedial math; ESL (31 students enrolled).

College Admission Counseling 54 students graduated in 2008; 30 went to college, including Berea College; Lindsey Wilson College; Union College; University of Kentucky; University of the Cumberlands; Western Kentucky University. Other: 9 went to work, 1 entered military service.

Student Life Upper grades have specified standards of dress. Discipline rests primarily with faculty. Attendance at religious services is required.

Summer Programs Remediation, enrichment, advancement, ESL programs offered; session focuses on remediation and make-up courses; held on campus; accepts boys and girls; open to students from other schools. 125 students usually enrolled. 2009 schedule: June 7 to July 24. Application deadline: none.

Tuition and Aid 7-day tuition and room/board: $5350–$9400. Tuition installment plan (monthly payment plans). Need-based scholarship grants available. In 2008–09, 100% of upper-school students received aid.

Admissions Traditional secondary-level entrance grade is 9. Deadline for receipt of application materials: none. Application fee required: $35. On-campus interview required.

Athletics Interscholastic: baseball (boys), basketball (b,g), cheering (g), cross-country running (b,g), softball (g), swimming and diving (b,g), tennis (b,g), track and field (b,g), volleyball (g); coed interscholastic: soccer.

Computers Computers are regularly used in commercial art classes. Computer resources include Internet access, Internet filtering or blocking technology.

Contact Admissions. 606-847-4111 Ext. 233. Fax: 606-847-4496. E-mail: admissions4obi@yahoo.com. Web site: www.oneidaschool.org.

ORANGEWOOD ADVENTIST ACADEMY

13732 Clinton Street
Garden Grove, California 92843

Head of School: Mr. Ruben A. Escalante

General Information Coeducational day college-preparatory and religious studies school, affiliated with Seventh-day Adventist Church. Grades PK–12. Founded: 1956. Setting: urban. Nearest major city is Anaheim. 11-acre campus. 6 buildings on campus. Approved or accredited by Board of Regents, General Conference of Seventh-day Adventists, Western Association of Schools and Colleges, and California Department of Education. Total enrollment: 251. Upper school average class size: 24. Upper school faculty-student ratio: 1:10.

Upper School Student Profile Grade 9: 20 students (11 boys, 9 girls); Grade 10: 17 students (7 boys, 10 girls); Grade 11: 21 students (7 boys, 14 girls); Grade 12: 26 students (12 boys, 14 girls). 80% of students are Seventh-day Adventists.

Faculty School total: 20. In upper school: 5 men, 5 women; 4 have advanced degrees.

Subjects Offered Algebra, arts, biology, calculus, career education, chemistry, choir, computer science, computers, drama, English, family studies, fine arts, geometry, government, health, journalism, life skills, mathematics, photography, physical education, physical science, physics, pre-calculus, religion, science, silk screening, social studies, Spanish, technical arts, typing, U.S. history, world history, yearbook.
Graduation Requirements Arts and fine arts (art, music, dance, drama), business skills (includes word processing), computer science, English, foreign language, mathematics, physical education (includes health), religion (includes Bible studies and theology), science, social studies (includes history), work experience.
Special Academic Programs Advanced Placement exam preparation; honors section; ESL (21 students enrolled).
College Admission Counseling 24 students graduated in 2008; 22 went to college, including California State University; Loma Linda University; Pacific Union College. Other: 1 went to work, 1 had other specific plans. 4% scored over 600 on SAT critical reading, 3% scored over 600 on SAT math, 2% scored over 26 on composite ACT.
Student Life Upper grades have uniform requirement, student council, honor system. Discipline rests primarily with faculty. Attendance at religious services is required.
Summer Programs Enrichment programs offered; session focuses on math and reading; held on campus; accepts boys and girls; open to students from other schools. 50 students usually enrolled.
Tuition and Aid Day student tuition: $4680. Tuition installment plan (monthly payment plans). Tuition reduction for siblings, need-based scholarship grants, paying campus jobs available. In 2008–09, 45% of upper-school students received aid. Total amount of financial aid awarded in 2008–09: $75,000.
Admissions Traditional secondary-level entrance grade is 9. For fall 2008, 15 students applied for upper-level admission, 14 were accepted, 14 enrolled. Deadline for receipt of application materials: none. No application fee required. Interview required.
Athletics Interscholastic: basketball (boys, girls), cheering (g), flag football (b), soccer (b), softball (g), volleyball (b,g); intramural: basketball (b,g), flag football (b), volleyball (b,g); coed interscholastic: soccer; coed intramural: gymnastics. 1 PE instructor, 5 coaches.
Computers Computers are regularly used in all classes. Computer network features include on-campus library services, online commercial services, Internet access, wireless campus network, Internet filtering or blocking technology, One-to-One Apple Program. Student e-mail accounts are available to students. The school has a published electronic and media policy.
Contact Mrs. Martha Machado, Director of Admissions and Records. 714-534-4694 Ext. 214. Fax: 714-534-5931. E-mail: mrsmach57@aol.com. Web site: www.orangewoodacademy.com.

OREGON EPISCOPAL SCHOOL

6300 Southwest Nicol Road
Portland, Oregon 97223-7566
Head of School: Mr. Matthew H. Hanly

General Information Coeducational boarding and day college-preparatory, arts, religious studies, technology, and science school, affiliated with Episcopal Church. Boarding grades 9–12, day grades PK–12. Founded: 1869. Setting: suburban. Students are housed in single-sex dormitories. 59-acre campus. 9 buildings on campus. Approved or accredited by National Association of Episcopal Schools, Northwest Association of Schools and Colleges, Pacific Northwest Association of Independent Schools, and Oregon Department of Education. Member of National Association of Independent Schools and Secondary School Admission Test Board. Endowment: $20.9 million. Total enrollment: 845. Upper school average class size: 14. Upper school faculty-student ratio: 1:7.
Upper School Student Profile Grade 9: 78 students (38 boys, 40 girls); Grade 10: 77 students (43 boys, 34 girls); Grade 11: 80 students (38 boys, 42 girls); Grade 12: 70 students (38 boys, 32 girls). 17% of students are boarding students. 79% are state residents. 4 states are represented in upper school student body. 14% are international students. International students from China, Indonesia, Japan, Republic of Korea, Taiwan, and Thailand; 7 other countries represented in student body. 14% of students are members of Episcopal Church.
Faculty School total: 123. In upper school: 26 men, 32 women; 47 have advanced degrees; 13 reside on campus.
Subjects Offered Advanced chemistry, advanced math, Advanced Placement courses, algebra, American history, American literature, American studies, anatomy, anatomy and physiology, Arabic studies, art, Asian history, astronomy, athletic training, band, Basic programming, biology, Buddhism, calculus, calculus-AP, ceramics, chemistry, Chinese, chorus, Christian studies, Christianity, college counseling, college planning, college writing, community service, computer graphics, computer science, computer science-AP, constitutional law, creative writing, dance, debate, discrete math, discrete mathematics, drama, drawing, driver education, East Asian history, ecology, electronics, engineering, English, English literature, environmental science, ESL, ESL, European history, fencing, film, film and literature, filmmaking, fine arts, finite math, foreign language, foreign policy, French, French language-AP, French literature-AP, French-AP, freshman seminar, functions, gardening, geology, geometry, graphic arts, graphic design, graphics, health, health and wellness, history, history of China and Japan, history of ideas, history of rock and roll, history-AP, human anatomy, human relations, human sexuality, humanities, independent study, international affairs, international relations, Japanese, jazz band, jazz dance, jazz ensemble, journalism, literature, marine biology, marine ecology, mathematics, mathematics-AP, microbiology, model United Nations, modern Chinese history, music, music history, music technology, musical productions, musical theater, newspaper, painting, personal finance, personal fitness, philosophy, photography, photojournalism, physical education, physical fitness, physics, playwriting and directing, poetry, pre-algebra, pre-calculus, psychology, psychology-AP, religion, religion and culture, research, science, science project, science research, service learning/internship, sex education, sexuality, Shakespeare, social studies, Spanish, Spanish language-AP, Spanish literature, Spanish literature-AP, Spanish-AP, speech, stagecraft, statistics, statistics-AP, tennis, theater, theater design and production, theology, track and field, trigonometry, U.S. history, U.S. history-AP, urban studies, video and animation, video film production, visual arts, vocal ensemble, vocal music, weight training, weightlifting, wellness, wilderness education, wilderness experience, wilderness/outdoor program, world history, world literature, world religions, world religions, world wide web design, yearbook, yoga, zoology.
Graduation Requirements Arts and fine arts (art, music, dance, drama), electives, English, foreign language, health education, humanities, mathematics, philosophy, physical education (includes health), religion (includes Bible studies and theology), science, U.S. history, Winterim, College Decisions (for juniors), Senior Discovery Program, 120 hours of service learning.
Special Academic Programs Advanced Placement exam preparation; honors section; independent study; term-away projects; study abroad; academic accommodation for the gifted; ESL (13 students enrolled).
College Admission Counseling 69 students graduated in 2008; 67 went to college, including Boston University; Carleton College; Harvey Mudd College; Seattle University; University of Oregon; University of Washington. Other: 2 had other specific plans. Median SAT critical reading: 650, median SAT math: 670, median SAT writing: 660, median combined SAT: 1990. Mean composite ACT: 28. 67% scored over 600 on SAT critical reading, 71% scored over 600 on SAT math, 67% scored over 600 on SAT writing, 72% scored over 1800 on combined SAT.
Student Life Upper grades have specified standards of dress, student council. Discipline rests equally with students and faculty. Attendance at religious services is required.
Summer Programs Remediation, enrichment, advancement, sports, art/fine arts, computer instruction programs offered; session focuses on variety of academic, sports, and artistic enrichment programs; held both on and off campus; held at day trips around Oregon and overnight camping; accepts boys and girls; open to students from other schools. 800 students usually enrolled. 2009 schedule: June 15 to August 21. Application deadline: August 10.
Tuition and Aid Day student tuition: $21,370; 7-day tuition and room/board: $38,850. Tuition installment plan (Insured Tuition Payment Plan, monthly payment plans). Need-based scholarship grants available. In 2008–09, 11% of upper-school students received aid. Total amount of financial aid awarded in 2008–09: $1,131,531.
Admissions Traditional secondary-level entrance grade is 9. For fall 2008, 159 students applied for upper-level admission, 76 were accepted, 43 enrolled. SSAT or TOEFL required. Deadline for receipt of application materials: February 2. Application fee required: $75. Interview required.
Athletics Interscholastic: alpine skiing (boys, girls), basketball (b,g), cross-country running (b,g), fencing (b,g), lacrosse (b,g), skiing (downhill) (b,g), soccer (b,g), tennis (b,g), track and field (b,g), volleyball (g); intramural: snowboarding (b,g), yoga (b,g); coed intramural: outdoor education, ropes courses. 2 PE instructors, 22 coaches, 1 athletic trainer.
Computers Computers are regularly used in art, English, foreign language, history, humanities, independent study, mathematics, music, philosophy, religion, science, social sciences, technology classes. Computer network features include on-campus library services, online commercial services, Internet access, wireless campus network, Internet filtering or blocking technology. Campus intranet, student e-mail accounts, and computer access in designated common areas are available to students. The school has a published electronic and media policy.
Contact Ms. Emily Pritchard, Admissions Assistant. 503-768-3115. Fax: 503-768-3140. E-mail: admit@oes.edu. Web site: www.oes.edu.

See Close-Up on page 892.

ORINDA ACADEMY

19 Altarinda Road
Orinda, California 94563-2602
Head of School: Ron Graydon

General Information Coeducational day college-preparatory, general academic, arts, and technology school. Grades 7–12. Founded: 1982. Setting: suburban. Nearest major city is Walnut Creek. 1-acre campus. 3 buildings on campus. Approved or accredited by East Bay Independent Schools Association, The College Board, and Western Association of Schools and Colleges. Total enrollment: 104. Upper school average class size: 10. Upper school faculty-student ratio: 1:9.
Upper School Student Profile Grade 9: 17 students (10 boys, 7 girls); Grade 10: 20 students (10 boys, 10 girls); Grade 11: 29 students (22 boys, 7 girls); Grade 12: 31 students (22 boys, 9 girls).
Faculty School total: 16. In upper school: 9 men, 7 women; 10 have advanced degrees.

Subjects Offered Algebra, American history, American literature, art, basketball, biology, British literature, calculus, chemistry, chorus, community service, computer graphics, computer keyboarding, computer literacy, computer multimedia, computer music, computer processing, computer programming, contemporary issues, creative writing, dance, drama, earth science, economics, English, English literature, English literature and composition-AP, ensembles, environmental science, ESL, European history, film history, fine arts, French, geography, geometry, government/civics, health, history, history of music, introduction to theater, journalism, mathematics, music, music performance, musical productions, performing arts, physical education, physics, science, social studies, Spanish, Spanish language-AP, theater, trigonometry, visual arts, women's literature, yearbook.

Graduation Requirements Algebra, biology, civics, composition, economics, English, foreign language, geometry, physical education (includes health), science, trigonometry, U.S. history, visual and performing arts. Community service is required.

Special Academic Programs Advanced Placement exam preparation; honors section; accelerated programs; academic accommodation for the gifted; ESL (4 students enrolled).

College Admission Counseling 28 students graduated in 2008; 26 went to college, including Brown University; Dickinson College; Saint Mary's College of California; San Francisco State University; Sonoma State University; University of California, San Diego. Other: 2 had other specific plans. Mean SAT critical reading: 601, mean SAT math: 605, mean SAT writing: 591, mean combined SAT: 1797, mean composite ACT: 21. 37% scored over 600 on SAT critical reading, 37% scored over 600 on SAT math, 26% scored over 600 on SAT writing, 16% scored over 1800 on combined SAT, 40% scored over 26 on composite ACT.

Student Life Upper grades have specified standards of dress, student council, honor system. Discipline rests primarily with faculty.

Summer Programs Remediation, enrichment, advancement programs offered; session focuses on academics; held on campus; accepts boys and girls; open to students from other schools. 70 students usually enrolled. 2009 schedule: June 22 to August 7. Application deadline: none.

Tuition and Aid Day student tuition: $23,995. Tuition installment plan (FACTS Tuition Payment Plan). Tuition reduction for siblings, need-based scholarship grants available. In 2008–09, 20% of upper-school students received aid. Total amount of financial aid awarded in 2008–09: $400,000.

Admissions Traditional secondary-level entrance grade is 9. For fall 2008, 100 students applied for upper-level admission, 40 were accepted, 29 enrolled. ISEE required. Deadline for receipt of application materials: January 15. Application fee required: $75. On-campus interview required.

Athletics Interscholastic: baseball (boys), basketball (b,g), softball (g); coed interscholastic: soccer; coed intramural: soccer, softball.

Computers Computers are regularly used in English, journalism, social sciences, typing, writing, yearbook classes. Computer network features include Internet access. Student e-mail accounts are available to students. The school has a published electronic and media policy.

Contact Nettie Anthony-Harris, Director of Admissions. 925-250-7659 Ext. 305. Fax: 925-254-4768. E-mail: nettie@orindaacademy.org. Web site: www.orindaacademy.org.

THE ORME SCHOOL

HC 63, Box 3040
Mayer, Arizona 86333

Head of School: Mrs. Alyce Brownridge

General Information Coeducational boarding and day college-preparatory, arts, ESL Program, and Horsemanship school. Boarding grades 8–PG, day grades 1–PG. Founded: 1929. Setting: rural. Nearest major city is Phoenix. Students are housed in single-sex dormitories. 300-acre campus. 30 buildings on campus. Approved or accredited by Arizona Association of Independent Schools, North Central Association of Colleges and Schools, The Association of Boarding Schools, and Arizona Department of Education. Member of National Association of Independent Schools and Secondary School Admission Test Board. Endowment: $1 million. Total enrollment: 152. Upper school average class size: 14. Upper school faculty-student ratio: 1:7.

Upper School Student Profile Grade 9: 25 students (14 boys, 11 girls); Grade 10: 31 students (10 boys, 21 girls); Grade 11: 40 students (25 boys, 15 girls); Grade 12: 32 students (15 boys, 17 girls); Postgraduate: 2 students (2 girls). 76% of students are boarding students. 54% are state residents. 20 states are represented in upper school student body. 20% are international students. International students from China, Germany, Hong Kong, Republic of Korea, Taiwan, and Turkey; 2 other countries represented in student body.

Faculty School total: 25. In upper school: 12 men, 9 women; 10 have advanced degrees; 24 reside on campus.

Subjects Offered Advanced Placement courses, advanced TOEFL/grammar, algebra, American history, American history-AP, American literature, American literature-AP, ancient world history, art, art history, astronomy, band, biology, British literature (honors), calculus, calculus-AP, ceramics, chemistry, choir, college admission preparation, college counseling, community service, computer programming, computer science, creative writing, drama, drama performance, ecology, English, English language and composition-AP, English literature, English literature and composition-AP, European history, European history-AP, fine arts, French, geography, geology, geometry, government, grammar, history, history of music, honors English, honors U.S. history, humanities, Latin, mathematics, music, performing arts, photography, physics, physics-AP, psychology, science, social science, social studies, Spanish, statistics-AP, student government, theater, trigonometry, U.S. history, U.S. history-AP, weightlifting, world culture, world history, world literature, writing.

Graduation Requirements Arts and fine arts (art, music, dance, drama), computer science, English, foreign language, humanities, mathematics, science, social science, social studies (includes history), Students must participate in annual outdoor programs such as Fall outing and Caravan. Community service is required.

Special Academic Programs Advanced Placement exam preparation; honors section; independent study; remedial reading and/or remedial writing; remedial math; programs in English, mathematics, general development for dyslexic students; ESL (27 students enrolled).

College Admission Counseling 33 students graduated in 2008; 32 went to college, including Arizona State University; Boston University; Dartmouth College; Michigan State University; Northern Arizona University; Skidmore College. Other: 1 went to work. Mean SAT critical reading: 500, mean SAT math: 533, mean SAT writing: 495, mean combined SAT: 1528, mean composite ACT: 21. 19% scored over 600 on SAT critical reading, 12% scored over 1800 on combined SAT, 9% scored over 26 on composite ACT.

Student Life Upper grades have specified standards of dress, student council, honor system. Discipline rests equally with students and faculty.

Summer Programs Remediation, advancement, ESL programs offered; session focuses on advancement; held on campus; accepts boys and girls; open to students from other schools. 12 students usually enrolled. 2009 schedule: June 11 to August 5. Application deadline: none.

Tuition and Aid Day student tuition: $20,500; 5-day tuition and room/board: $25,500; 7-day tuition and room/board: $36,050. Tuition installment plan (monthly payment plans, individually arranged payment plans). Merit scholarship grants, need-based scholarship grants, need-based loans, middle-income loans available. In 2008–09, 31% of upper-school students received aid. Total amount of financial aid awarded in 2008–09: $914,450.

Admissions Traditional secondary-level entrance grade is 9. For fall 2008, 150 students applied for upper-level admission, 93 were accepted, 77 enrolled. PSAT and SAT for applicants to grade 11 and 12, SSAT or TOEFL or SLEP required. Deadline for receipt of application materials: February 15. Application fee required: $50. Interview required.

Athletics Interscholastic: baseball (boys), basketball (b,g), cheering (g), cross-country running (b,g), equestrian sports (b,g), football (b), pom squad (g), rodeo (b,g), softball (g), tennis (b,g), track and field (b,g), volleyball (g); intramural: aerobics/dance (g), backpacking (b,g), climbing (b,g), dressage (b,g), fitness (b,g), physical training (b,g), rappelling (b,g), rock climbing (b,g), rodeo (b,g), strength & conditioning (b,g), tennis (b,g), wall climbing (b,g), weight lifting (b,g), weight training (b,g), wilderness (b,g), wilderness survival (b,g), wrestling (b); coed interscholastic: equestrian sports, horseback riding, rodeo; coed intramural: backpacking, climbing, dressage, fitness, fitness walking, hiking/backpacking, horseback riding, mountain biking, mountaineering, outdoor activities, physical training, power lifting, rappelling, rock climbing, rodeo, skiing (downhill), snowboarding, soccer, strength & conditioning, tai chi, walking, wall climbing, weight lifting, weight training, wilderness, wilderness survival, yoga.

Computers Computers are regularly used in all academic classes. Computer network features include on-campus library services, Internet access, wireless campus network, Internet filtering or blocking technology. Student e-mail accounts and computer access in designated common areas are available to students. Students grades are available online.

Contact Mr. Kelly Johnston, Assistant Director of Admissions. 928-632-7601 Ext. 2350. Fax: 928-632-7605. E-mail: kjohnston@ormeschool.org. Web site: www.ormeschool.org.

OUR LADY ACADEMY

222 South Beach Boulevard
Bay St. Louis, Mississippi 38520-4320

Head of School: Mrs. Susan Goggins

General Information Girls' day college-preparatory and religious studies school, affiliated with Roman Catholic Church. Grades 7–12. Founded: 1971. Setting: small town. Nearest major city is New Orleans, LA. 3-acre campus. 4 buildings on campus. Approved or accredited by Mercy Secondary Education Association, National Catholic Education Association, Southern Association of Colleges and Schools, and Mississippi Department of Education. Endowment: $2 million. Total enrollment: 269. Upper school average class size: 22. Upper school faculty-student ratio: 1:13.

Upper School Student Profile Grade 9: 43 students (43 girls); Grade 10: 28 students (28 girls); Grade 11: 43 students (43 girls); Grade 12: 45 students (45 girls). 85% of students are Roman Catholic.

Faculty School total: 25. In upper school: 2 men, 23 women; 5 have advanced degrees.

Subjects Offered Accounting, ACT preparation, advanced biology, advanced math, Advanced Placement courses, algebra, aquatics, art, band, biology, biology-AP, calculus, Catholic belief and practice, ceramics, chemistry, choral music, Christian ethics, Christian studies, computers, desktop publishing, economics, English, English composition, English language-AP, English literature, entrepreneurship, environmental science, ESL, European history, European history-AP, fine arts, French, genetics, geology, geometry, graphic design, health, human anatomy, integrated science, journalism, Latin, law and the legal system, learning strategies, marine science, mathematics, minority studies, moral reasoning, music, mythology, oral communications, personal finance, physical education, physical science, physics, physics-AP, physiology, pre-algebra, pre-calculus, probability and statistics, psychology, reading, religious studies, scripture, service learning/internship, short story, Spanish, theater, theater arts, trigonometry, U.S. government, U.S. history, visual arts, word processing, world geography, world history, world religions.

Graduation Requirements Art, computers, English, foreign language, health, mathematics, religious studies, science, social science.

Special Academic Programs 9 Advanced Placement exams for which test preparation is offered; honors section; independent study; ESL (9 students enrolled).

College Admission Counseling Colleges students went to include Mississippi State University; University of Mississippi; University of South Alabama; University of Southern Mississippi. Median composite ACT: 20. 30% scored over 26 on composite ACT.

Student Life Upper grades have uniform requirement, student council, honor system. Discipline rests primarily with faculty. Attendance at religious services is required.

Tuition and Aid Day student tuition: $5200. Tuition installment plan (The Tuition Plan, monthly payment plans, individually arranged payment plans). Need-based scholarship grants available. In 2008–09, 5% of upper-school students received aid. Total amount of financial aid awarded in 2008–09: $10,000.

Admissions Traditional secondary-level entrance grade is 9. Metropolitan Achievement Short Form required. Deadline for receipt of application materials: none. No application fee required. On-campus interview required.

Athletics Interscholastic: basketball, cheering, cross-country running, dance squad, drill team, sailing, soccer, softball, swimming and diving, tennis, track and field, volleyball. 1 PE instructor, 8 coaches, 1 athletic trainer.

Computers Computers are regularly used in accounting, business, college planning, creative writing, desktop publishing, English, foreign language, keyboarding, library science, newspaper, typing, Web site design, word processing, writing, yearbook classes. Computer network features include Internet access, wireless campus network, Internet filtering or blocking technology. Campus intranet is available to students. Students grades are available online. The school has a published electronic and media policy.

Contact Mrs. Susan Goggins, Principal. 228-467-7048 Ext. 12. Fax: 228-467-1666. Web site: www.ourladyacademy.com.

OUR LADY OF MERCY ACADEMY

1001 Main Road
Newfield, New Jersey 08344

Head of School: Sr. Grace Marie Scandale

General Information Girls' day college-preparatory, arts, religious studies, and technology school, affiliated with Roman Catholic Church. Grades 9–12. Founded: 1962. Setting: rural. Nearest major city is Vineland. 58-acre campus. 2 buildings on campus. Approved or accredited by Middle States Association of Colleges and Schools and National Catholic Education Association. Endowment: $250,000. Total enrollment: 203. Upper school average class size: 20. Upper school faculty-student ratio: 1:11.

Upper School Student Profile Grade 9: 44 students (44 girls); Grade 10: 50 students (50 girls); Grade 11: 52 students (52 girls); Grade 12: 57 students (57 girls). 90% of students are Roman Catholic.

Faculty School total: 22. In upper school: 1 man, 21 women; 10 have advanced degrees.

Subjects Offered Algebra, American history, American literature, art, biology, botany, British literature (honors), career and personal planning, Catholic belief and practice, chemistry, choral music, chorus, Christian ethics, Christian scripture, Christian testament, Christianity, college counseling, computer technologies, CPR, current events, death and loss, driver education, economics, electronic publishing, English literature, first aid, food and nutrition, French, graphic design, honors algebra, honors geometry, horticulture, Middle Eastern history, physics, pre-calculus, probability and statistics, psychology, publications, religion, remedial/makeup course work, social justice, sociology, technology, Western civilization.

Graduation Requirements Algebra, biology, chemistry, English, geometry, physical education (includes health), religion (includes Bible studies and theology), technology, U.S. history, Western civilization.

Special Academic Programs Honors section; study at local college for college credit.

College Admission Counseling 71 students graduated in 2008; all went to college, including La Salle University; Rockhurst University; Rutgers, The State University of New Jersey, New Brunswick; Saint Joseph's University; Seton Hall University; University of Pennsylvania.

Student Life Upper grades have uniform requirement, student council, honor system. Discipline rests primarily with faculty. Attendance at religious services is required.

Tuition and Aid Day student tuition: $8100. Tuition installment plan (SMART Tuition Payment Plan, monthly payment plans, individually arranged payment plans). Tuition reduction for siblings, merit scholarship grants, need-based scholarship grants, paying campus jobs available. In 2008–09, 15% of upper-school students received aid; total upper-school merit-scholarship money awarded: $35,000. Total amount of financial aid awarded in 2008–09: $40,000.

Admissions Traditional secondary-level entrance grade is 9. For fall 2008, 70 students applied for upper-level admission, 68 were accepted, 44 enrolled. High School Placement Test (closed version) from Scholastic Testing Service required. Deadline for receipt of application materials: none. Application fee required: $200.

Athletics Interscholastic: basketball, cheering, crew, cross-country running, diving, indoor track & field, lacrosse, running, soccer, softball, strength & conditioning, swimming and diving, tennis, track and field, volleyball, winter (indoor) track; intramural: badminton, basketball, flag football, golf, gymnastics, physical fitness, soccer, softball, synchronized swimming, volleyball. 2 PE instructors, 12 coaches.

Computers Computers are regularly used in all academic, career exploration, college planning, creative writing, graphic design, graphics, library, library skills, photography, publications, research skills, technology, typing, Web site design, word processing, yearbook classes. Computer network features include on-campus library services, online commercial services, Internet access, wireless campus network, Internet filtering or blocking technology. Students grades are available online. The school has a published electronic and media policy.

Contact Sr. Grace Marie Scandale, Principal. 856-697-2008. Fax: 856-697-2887. E-mail: srgrace@olmanj.org. Web site: www.olmanj.org.

OUR LADY OF MERCY HIGH SCHOOL

1437 Blossom Road
Rochester, New York 14610

Head of School: Mr. Terence Quinn

General Information Girls' day college-preparatory, arts, business, and technology school, affiliated with Roman Catholic Church. Grades 7–12. Founded: 1928. Setting: suburban. 1 building on campus. Approved or accredited by Mercy Secondary Education Association, Middle States Association of Colleges and Schools, National Catholic Education Association, and New York State Board of Regents. Total enrollment: 645. Upper school average class size: 22. Upper school faculty-student ratio: 1:14.

Upper School Student Profile Grade 9: 142 students (142 girls); Grade 10: 118 students (118 girls); Grade 11: 118 students (118 girls); Grade 12: 117 students (117 girls). 80% of students are Roman Catholic.

Faculty School total: 60. In upper school: 8 men, 41 women; 45 have advanced degrees.

Subjects Offered Accounting, algebra, American history, American history-AP, American literature, art, biology, biology-AP, business, calculus-AP, ceramics, chemistry, chemistry-AP, creative writing, drama, earth science, economics, English, English literature, English literature-AP, entrepreneurship, European history-AP, finance, French, French-AP, geometry, government/civics, health, Latin, Latin-AP, mathematics, music, orchestra, photography, physical education, physics, physics-AP, prayer/spirituality, pre-calculus, psychology, psychology-AP, science, scripture, social justice, Spanish, Spanish-AP, speech, studio art, theater, theater arts, theology, world history, world history-AP, world literature, writing.

Graduation Requirements Arts and fine arts (art, music, dance, drama), English, foreign language, mathematics, physical education (includes health), science, social studies (includes history), theology.

Special Academic Programs 12 Advanced Placement exams for which test preparation is offered; honors section; study at local college for college credit; ESL (4 students enrolled).

College Admission Counseling 124 students graduated in 2008; 121 went to college, including Buffalo State College, State University of New York; State University of New York College at Geneseo; University of Notre Dame; University of Rochester. Other: 1 went to work, 2 had other specific plans. Mean SAT critical reading: 564, mean SAT math: 555, mean SAT writing: 600. 39% scored over 26 on composite ACT.

Student Life Upper grades have uniform requirement, student council, honor system. Discipline rests primarily with faculty. Attendance at religious services is required.

Summer Programs Remediation, sports, art/fine arts, computer instruction programs offered; held on campus; accepts girls; open to students from other schools.

Tuition and Aid Day student tuition: $7550. Tuition installment plan (monthly payment plans, individually arranged payment plans, 2-payment plan). Merit scholarship grants, need-based scholarship grants available. Total amount of financial aid awarded in 2008–09: $800,000.

Admissions Traditional secondary-level entrance grade is 9. For fall 2008, 70 students applied for upper-level admission, 60 were accepted, 55 enrolled. Educational Development Series, High School Placement Test (closed version) from Scholastic Testing Service or Scholastic Testing Service High School Placement Test required. Deadline for receipt of application materials: none. Application fee required: $200. On-campus interview recommended.

Athletics Interscholastic: basketball, bowling, cheering, crew, cross-country running, diving, golf, indoor track, lacrosse, sailing, skiing (downhill), soccer, softball, swimming and diving, tennis, track and field, volleyball. 3 PE instructors, 12 coaches, 1 athletic trainer.

Computers Computers are regularly used in accounting, all academic, business, business education, career exploration, college planning, English, keyboarding, library skills, literary magazine, mathematics, newspaper, photography, publications, research skills, science, technology, yearbook classes. Computer resources include on-campus library services, Internet access. The school has a published electronic and media policy.

Contact Mary Elizabeth McCahill, Director of Admissions. 716-288-7120 Ext. 310. Fax: 716-288-7966. E-mail: mmccahill@mercyhs.com. Web site: www.mercyhs.com.

OUR SAVIOUR LUTHERAN SCHOOL

1734 Williamsbridge Road
Bronx, New York 10461

Head of School: John Schmidt

General Information Coeducational day college-preparatory, arts, religious studies, and technology school, affiliated with Lutheran Church–Missouri Synod. Grades PK–12. Founded: 1942. Setting: urban. Nearest major city is New York. 2-acre campus. 1 building on campus. Approved or accredited by Middle States Association of Colleges and Schools, New York Department of Education, and New York Department of Education. Endowment: $100,000. Total enrollment: 348. Upper school average class size: 20. Upper school faculty-student ratio: 1:13.

Upper School Student Profile Grade 7: 22 students (8 boys, 14 girls); Grade 8: 24 students (13 boys, 11 girls); Grade 9: 22 students (9 boys, 13 girls); Grade 10: 24 students (11 boys, 13 girls); Grade 11: 27 students (13 boys, 14 girls); Grade 12: 32 students (20 boys, 12 girls). 5% of students are Lutheran Church–Missouri Synod.

Faculty School total: 30. In upper school: 11 men, 2 women; 13 have advanced degrees.

Subjects Offered Algebra, American history, American literature, art, art history, Bible studies, biology, chemistry, computer programming, computer science, drama, earth science, economics, English, English literature, English-AP, environmental science, ethics, European history, French, geography, geometry, government/civics, grammar, health, history, history-AP, Latin, mathematics, mathematics-AP, music, physical education, physics, psychology, religion, social studies, Spanish, theology, trigonometry, world history, world literature, writing.

Graduation Requirements Arts and fine arts (art, music, dance, drama), Bible studies, biology, British literature, chemistry, Christian doctrine, Christian ethics, Christian scripture, church history, computer education, computer science, English, English composition, European civilization, foreign language, geometry, government, Latin, mathematics, music, physical education (includes health), physical fitness, physics, Shakespeare, social studies (includes history), trigonometry, Western civilization.

Special Academic Programs 1 Advanced Placement exam for which test preparation is offered.

College Admission Counseling 22 students graduated in 2008; 18 went to college, including City College of the City University of New York; Concordia College; Hofstra University; Syracuse University; University at Albany, State University of New York. Other: 3 went to work, 1 entered military service. Median SAT critical reading: 420, median SAT math: 420, median SAT writing: 510, median combined SAT: 1300, median composite ACT: 20. 4% scored over 600 on SAT critical reading, 3% scored over 600 on SAT math, 2% scored over 600 on SAT writing, 3% scored over 1800 on combined SAT, 3% scored over 26 on composite ACT.

Student Life Upper grades have uniform requirement, student council. Discipline rests primarily with faculty. Attendance at religious services is required.

Summer Programs Remediation, enrichment programs offered; session focuses on remediation; held on campus; accepts boys and girls; open to students from other schools. 200 students usually enrolled. 2009 schedule: July 1 to August 15. Application deadline: none.

Tuition and Aid Day student tuition: $5700. Tuition installment plan (FACTS Tuition Payment Plan). Tuition reduction for siblings, merit scholarship grants, need-based scholarship grants available. In 2008–09, 10% of upper-school students received aid; total upper-school merit-scholarship money awarded: $10,000. Total amount of financial aid awarded in 2008–09: $30,000.

Admissions Traditional secondary-level entrance grade is 7. For fall 2008, 158 students applied for upper-level admission, 139 were accepted, 98 enrolled. Any standardized test or Stanford Achievement Test required. Deadline for receipt of application materials: none. Application fee required: $30.

Athletics Interscholastic: baseball (boys), basketball (b,g), softball (g), track and field (b,g), volleyball (b,g); intramural: basketball (b,g), track and field (b,g), volleyball (b,g); coed interscholastic: basketball, soccer, track and field, volleyball; coed intramural: basketball, track and field, volleyball. 2 PE instructors, 4 coaches.

Computers Computers are regularly used in English, foreign language, history, Latin, mathematics, programming, SAT preparation, science, word processing classes. Computer resources include Internet access.

Contact Ada Sierra, Secretary. 718-792-5665. Fax: 718-409-3877. E-mail: ousalubn@aol.com. Web site: www.oursaviourbronx.org.

OUT-OF-DOOR-ACADEMY

5950 Deer Drive
Sarasota, Florida 34240

Head of School: Mr. David Mahler

General Information Coeducational day college-preparatory school. Grades PK–12. Founded: 1924. Setting: suburban. Nearest major city is Tampa. 85-acre campus. 9 buildings on campus. Approved or accredited by Florida Council of Independent Schools. Member of National Association of Independent Schools. Endowment: $1.8 million. Total enrollment: 621. Upper school average class size: 16. Upper school faculty-student ratio: 1:8.

Upper School Student Profile Grade 9: 62 students (33 boys, 29 girls); Grade 10: 61 students (33 boys, 28 girls); Grade 11: 47 students (27 boys, 20 girls); Grade 12: 38 students (14 boys, 24 girls).

Faculty School total: 78. In upper school: 17 men, 17 women; 19 have advanced degrees.

Subjects Offered Advanced Placement courses, advanced studio art-AP, algebra, American history-AP, art history, biology, biology-AP, British literature, calculus, calculus-AP, chemistry, chemistry-AP, college counseling, computers, drama, drama performance, dramatic arts, English, English composition, English language and composition-AP, English literature, English literature and composition-AP, English-AP, European history-AP, expository writing, French, French language-AP, geometry, graphic design, health and wellness, history-AP, honors algebra, honors geometry, Latin, Latin-AP, literature, literature and composition-AP, music, newspaper, photography, portfolio art, Spanish, Spanish language-AP, studio art, studio art-AP, U.S. government, U.S. history, U.S. history-AP, women's studies, world culture, world literature, world studies, yearbook, zoology.

Graduation Requirements Arts and fine arts (art, music, dance, drama), electives, English, foreign language, health, history, mathematics, performing arts, personal fitness, science. Community service is required.

Special Academic Programs 17 Advanced Placement exams for which test preparation is offered; honors section; independent study.

College Admission Counseling 45 students graduated in 2008; all went to college, including Boston College; Dartmouth College; Duke University; University of Miami; University of Virginia; Vanderbilt University. Mean SAT critical reading: 622, mean SAT math: 618, mean SAT writing: 613, mean combined SAT: 1854. 59% scored over 600 on SAT critical reading, 59% scored over 600 on SAT math, 61% scored over 600 on SAT writing, 61% scored over 1800 on combined SAT.

Student Life Upper grades have specified standards of dress, student council, honor system. Discipline rests equally with students and faculty.

Summer Programs Enrichment, sports, art/fine arts programs offered; held on campus; accepts boys and girls; open to students from other schools. 100 students usually enrolled. 2009 schedule: June to August. Application deadline: May.

Tuition and Aid Day student tuition: $16,400. Tuition installment plan (FACTS Tuition Payment Plan). Need-based scholarship grants, faculty/staff tuition remission available. In 2008–09, 17% of upper-school students received aid. Total amount of financial aid awarded in 2008–09: $410,000.

Admissions Traditional secondary-level entrance grade is 9. For fall 2008, 36 students applied for upper-level admission, 22 were accepted, 17 enrolled. PSAT, SAT or SSAT required. Deadline for receipt of application materials: March 6. Application fee required: $100. Interview required.

Athletics Interscholastic: baseball (boys), basketball (b,g), cheering (g), cross-country running (b,g), football (b), golf (b,g), independent competitive sports (b,g), soccer (b,g), softball (g), swimming and diving (b,g), tennis (b,g), track and field (b,g), volleyball (g); intramural: fitness (b,g); coed interscholastic: sailing, ultimate Frisbee; coed intramural: physical fitness, physical training, strength & conditioning, weight training. 3 PE instructors, 20 coaches, 1 athletic trainer.

Computers Computers are regularly used in computer applications, English, foreign language, French, graphic design, history, Latin, mathematics, newspaper, science, senior seminar, social studies, Spanish, yearbook classes. Computer network features include on-campus library services, online commercial services, Internet access, wireless campus network, Internet filtering or blocking technology, digital video production. Student e-mail accounts are available to students. The school has a published electronic and media policy.

Contact Mr. Jamie Carver, Director of Middle and Upper School Admissions. 941-554-5954. Fax: 941-907-1251. E-mail: jcarver@oda.edu. Web site: www.oda.edu.

THE OVERLAKE SCHOOL

20301 Northeast 108th Street
Redmond, Washington 98053

Head of School: Francisco J. Grijalva, EdD

General Information Coeducational day college-preparatory, arts, and technology school. Grades 5–12. Founded: 1967. Setting: rural. Nearest major city is Seattle. 75-acre campus. 22 buildings on campus. Approved or accredited by Northwest Association of Accredited Schools, Pacific Northwest Association of Independent Schools, and Washington Department of Education. Member of National Association of Independent Schools. Endowment: $15 million. Total enrollment: 499. Upper school average class size: 13. Upper school faculty-student ratio: 1:9.

Upper School Student Profile Grade 9: 76 students (40 boys, 36 girls); Grade 10: 73 students (41 boys, 32 girls); Grade 11: 75 students (38 boys, 37 girls); Grade 12: 66 students (34 boys, 32 girls).

Faculty School total: 59. In upper school: 23 men, 31 women; 38 have advanced degrees.

Subjects Offered Algebra, American history, American history-AP, American literature, art-AP, biology-AP, botany, calculus, calculus-AP, ceramics, chemistry-AP, Chinese, chorus, community service, computer programming, computer science, concert band, creative writing, dance, drama, economics, English, English literature, English-AP, environmental science, ethics, European history-AP, European literature, film, fine arts, French, French-AP, geology, geometry, integrated science, Islamic history, Japanese, jazz band, journalism, Latin, Latin American literature, Latin-AP, life skills, literature, math review, mathematics, music, outdoor education, philosophy, photography, physical education, physics, physics-AP, pre-calculus, science, social studies, Spanish, Spanish-AP, statistics, studio art, study skills, theater, Vietnam War, woodworking, world history, world literature, World-Wide-Web publishing, yearbook, zoology.

Graduation Requirements Arts and fine arts (art, music, dance, drama), English, foreign language, history, lab science, mathematics, physical education (includes health), senior project, annual project week, 3 co-curricular activities, 15 hours of community service per year (60 total).

Special Academic Programs Advanced Placement exam preparation; honors section; independent study; term-away projects; study abroad; academic accommodation for the gifted, the musically talented, and the artistically talented.

College Admission Counseling 66 students graduated in 2008; all went to college, including Gonzaga University; Lewis & Clark College; Santa Clara University; University of Southern California; University of Washington; Western Washington University. Median SAT critical reading: 615, median SAT math: 630, median SAT writing: 630. 61% scored over 600 on SAT critical reading, 69% scored over 600 on SAT math, 66% scored over 600 on SAT writing.

Student Life Upper grades have student council. Discipline rests equally with students and faculty.

Summer Programs Sports programs offered; session focuses on skill-building sports camps; held on campus; accepts boys and girls; not open to students from other schools. 75 students usually enrolled. 2009 schedule: August 1 to August 15. Application deadline: June 30.

Tuition and Aid Day student tuition: $22,859. Tuition installment plan (Insured Tuition Payment Plan, monthly payment plans). Need-based scholarship grants, 50% tuition remission for faculty and staff, Malone Scholarship available. In 2008–09, 15% of upper-school students received aid. Total amount of financial aid awarded in 2008–09: $494,449.

Admissions Traditional secondary-level entrance grade is 9. For fall 2008, 70 students applied for upper-level admission, 29 were accepted, 20 enrolled. ISEE required. Deadline for receipt of application materials: January 15. Application fee required: $60. Interview required.

Athletics Interscholastic: baseball (boys), basketball (b,g), cross-country running (b,g), golf (b,g), lacrosse (b,g), outdoor education (b,g), physical fitness (b,g), rock climbing (b,g), ropes courses (b,g), soccer (b,g), tennis (b,g), track and field (b,g), volleyball (g); intramural: baseball (b), basketball (b,g), cross-country running (b,g), lacrosse (b,g), outdoor education (b,g), physical fitness (b,g), rock climbing (b,g), ropes courses (b,g), skiing (cross-country) (b,g), skiing (downhill) (b,g), soccer (b,g), strength & conditioning (b,g), tennis (b,g), track and field (b,g), ultimate Frisbee (b,g), volleyball (b,g), weight lifting (b,g), weight training (b,g); coed interscholastic: outdoor education, rock climbing, ropes courses, squash, tennis; coed intramural: basketball, bicycling, cross-country running, fencing, golf, outdoor education, rock climbing, ropes courses, skiing (cross-country), skiing (downhill), table tennis, tennis. 4 PE instructors, 22 coaches, 1 athletic trainer.

Computers Computers are regularly used in all classes. Computer network features include on-campus library services, online commercial services, Internet access, wireless campus network. Campus intranet and computer access in designated common areas are available to students. The school has a published electronic and media policy.

Contact Lori Maughan, Director of Admission. 425-868-1000. Fax: 425-868-5771. E-mail: lmaughan@overlake.org. Web site: www.overlake.org.

OVERSEAS FAMILY SCHOOL

25F Paterson Road
Singapore 238515, Singapore

See Close-Up on page 894.

THE OXFORD ACADEMY

1393 Boston Post Road
Westbrook, Connecticut 06498-0685

Head of School: Philip H. Davis

General Information Boys' boarding college-preparatory, general academic, arts, bilingual studies, and ESL school; primarily serves underachievers. Grades 9–PG. Founded: 1906. Setting: small town. Nearest major city is New Haven. Students are housed in single-sex dormitories. 13-acre campus. 8 buildings on campus. Approved or accredited by Connecticut Association of Independent Schools, New England Association of Schools and Colleges, The Association of Boarding Schools, and Connecticut Department of Education. Member of National Association of Independent Schools and Secondary School Admission Test Board. Endowment: $250,000. Total enrollment: 38. Upper school average class size: 1. Upper school faculty-student ratio: 1:1.

Upper School Student Profile Grade 9: 4 students (4 boys); Grade 10: 5 students (5 boys); Grade 11: 10 students (10 boys); Grade 12: 17 students (17 boys). 100% of students are boarding students. 35% are state residents. 8 states are represented in upper school student body. 33% are international students. International students from Bahamas, Bermuda, France, Mexico, Republic of Korea, and Saudi Arabia.

Faculty School total: 22. In upper school: 15 men, 7 women; 10 have advanced degrees; 12 reside on campus.

Subjects Offered Algebra, American history, American literature, anatomy, astronomy, biology, botany, calculus, chemistry, creative writing, earth science, ecology, economics, English, English literature, environmental science, ESL, European history, expository writing, French, geography, geology, geometry, German, government/civics, grammar, history, Latin, marine biology, mathematics, oceanography, paleontology, philosophy, physical education, physics, physiology, psychology, science, social studies, sociology, Spanish, study skills, trigonometry, world history, world literature, writing, zoology.

Graduation Requirements English, foreign language, mathematics, science, social studies (includes history). Community service is required.

Special Academic Programs Advanced Placement exam preparation; honors section; accelerated programs; independent study; academic accommodation for the gifted; remedial reading and/or remedial writing; remedial math; ESL (6 students enrolled).

College Admission Counseling 12 students graduated in 2008; 10 went to college, including Bucknell University; Georgia Southern University; Lynn University; Rhode Island School of Design; Suffolk University; Wheaton College. Other: 1 entered military service, 1 entered a postgraduate year.

Student Life Upper grades have specified standards of dress, student council, honor system. Discipline rests equally with students and faculty.

Summer Programs Remediation, enrichment, advancement, ESL programs offered; session focuses on acceleration of academics, study skills; held on campus; accepts boys; open to students from other schools. 25 students usually enrolled. 2009 schedule: June 17 to July 20. Application deadline: none.

Tuition and Aid 7-day tuition and room/board: $50,456. Tuition installment plan (monthly payment plans, individually arranged payment plans).

Admissions For fall 2008, 22 students applied for upper-level admission, 19 were accepted, 13 enrolled. SLEP for foreign students, Stanford Achievement Test, Otis-Lennon School Ability Test, TOEFL, WISC or WAIS or Woodcock-Johnson required. Deadline for receipt of application materials: none. Application fee required: $65. On-campus interview required.

Athletics Interscholastic: basketball, soccer, tennis; intramural: basketball, flag football, Frisbee, hiking/backpacking, paint ball, power lifting, roller blading, strength & conditioning, table tennis, weight lifting, weight training. 6 coaches.

Computers Computers are regularly used in mathematics classes. Computer network features include Internet access. Student e-mail accounts are available to students. The school has a published electronic and media policy.

Contact Mr. Philip H. Davis, Headmaster. 860-399-6247 Ext. 180. Fax: 860-399-6805. E-mail: admissions@oxfordacademy.net. Web site: www.oxfordacademy.net.

See Close-Up on page 896.

OXFORD SCHOOL

18760 East Colima Road
Rowland Heights, California 91748

Head of School: Mary Sue Lindsay

General Information Coeducational day college-preparatory and ESL school. Grades 7–12. Founded: 1980. Setting: suburban. Nearest major city is Los Angeles. 2-acre campus. 3 buildings on campus. Approved or accredited by Western Association of Schools and Colleges and California Department of Education. Endowment: $350,000. Total enrollment: 76. Upper school average class size: 15. Upper school faculty-student ratio: 1:11.

Upper School Student Profile Grade 8: 1 student (1 boy); Grade 9: 14 students (9 boys, 5 girls); Grade 10: 18 students (12 boys, 6 girls); Grade 11: 27 students (14 boys, 13 girls); Grade 12: 14 students (9 boys, 5 girls).

Faculty School total: 7. In upper school: 5 men, 2 women; 3 have advanced degrees.

Subjects Offered Advanced Placement courses, American history, American literature, art, arts, biology, British literature, calculus, chemistry, choir, college counseling, composition, computers, earth science, English, English as a foreign language, English composition, English literature, geography, history, lab science, language and composition, language arts, language development, mathematics, newspaper, physical education, physics, pre-calculus, pre-college orientation, reading/study skills, remedial/makeup course work, science, senior project, speech, student

publications, TOEFL preparation, U.S. government and politics, U.S. history, U.S. literature, Western literature, world civilizations, world history, writing, yearbook.
Graduation Requirements Arts and fine arts (art, music, dance, drama), English, foreign language, mathematics, physical education (includes health), physical fitness, portfolio writing, science, social studies (includes history), senior portfolio and oral presentation.
Special Academic Programs Advanced Placement exam preparation; study at local college for college credit; special instructional classes for students with limited English proficiency; ESL (50 students enrolled).
College Admission Counseling 27 students graduated in 2008; all went to college, including California State Polytechnic University, Pomona; California State University, Fullerton; California State University, Long Beach; Mt. San Antonio College; University of California, Irvine; University of California, Riverside.
Student Life Upper grades have uniform requirement, student council, honor system. Discipline rests equally with students and faculty.
Summer Programs Remediation, enrichment, ESL programs offered; session focuses on English Language Development; held on campus; accepts boys and girls; open to students from other schools. 40 students usually enrolled. 2009 schedule: June 29 to August 24. Application deadline: May 1.
Tuition and Aid Day student tuition: $8248. Tuition reduction for siblings available.
Admissions Traditional secondary-level entrance grade is 10. ESOL English Proficiency Test and mathematics proficiency exam required. Deadline for receipt of application materials: none. Application fee required: $190. Interview required.
Athletics Interscholastic: basketball (boys, girls), dance (b,g), physical fitness (b,g), soccer (b), table tennis (b,g), volleyball (g); intramural: basketball (b,g); coed interscholastic: basketball, dance, physical fitness, table tennis; coed intramural: basketball.
Computers Computers are regularly used in art, desktop publishing, ESL, English, ESL, foreign language, French, geography, history, independent study, language development, literacy, mathematics, newspaper, reading, religious studies, research skills, science, Spanish, stock market, writing, writing, yearbook classes. Computer network features include on-campus library services, Internet access, wireless campus network.
Contact Shenny Swain, Director of Admissions. 626-964-9588. Fax: 626-913-3919. E-mail: sswain@oxfordschool.org. Web site: www.oxfordschool.org.

PACE ACADEMY

966 West Paces Ferry Road NW
Atlanta, Georgia 30327

Head of School: Mr. Frederick G. Assaf

General Information Coeducational day college-preparatory, arts, and technology school. Grades K–12. Founded: 1958. Setting: suburban. 63-acre campus. 7 buildings on campus. Approved or accredited by Southern Association of Colleges and Schools and Southern Association of Independent Schools. Member of National Association of Independent Schools and Secondary School Admission Test Board. Endowment: $32.1 million. Total enrollment: 996. Upper school average class size: 11. Upper school faculty-student ratio: 1:7.
Upper School Student Profile Grade 9: 101 students (52 boys, 49 girls); Grade 10: 90 students (44 boys, 46 girls); Grade 11: 96 students (49 boys, 47 girls); Grade 12: 98 students (53 boys, 45 girls).
Faculty School total: 119. In upper school: 29 men, 23 women; 41 have advanced degrees.
Subjects Offered Acting, adolescent issues, advanced math, advanced studio art-AP, algebra, American history, American history-AP, American literature, ancient world history, architectural drawing, art, art history, art history-AP, arts, band, biology, biology-AP, British literature, British literature (honors), calculus, calculus-AP, ceramics, chemistry, chemistry-AP, Chinese history, chorus, community service, comparative government and politics-AP, comparative politics, computer keyboarding, computer science-AP, computer skills, creative writing, debate, digital imaging, digital photography, directing, drawing, earth science, economics, English, English literature, English-AP, environmental science-AP, European history, fine arts, French, French language-AP, geometry, history, honors algebra, honors English, honors geometry, honors U.S. history, honors world history, Japanese history, Latin, Latin-AP, leadership education training, mathematics, modern European history-AP, music history, music theory-AP, painting, photography, physical education, physics, physics-AP, political science, pre-algebra, psychology, public speaking, religion, science, social science, Spanish, Spanish language-AP, stagecraft, statistics-AP, student publications, trigonometry, world history, world literature, yearbook.
Graduation Requirements Arts and fine arts (art, music, dance, drama), English, foreign language, mathematics, physical education (includes health), science, social science, social studies (includes history), 40 hours of community service, one semester of public speaking.
Special Academic Programs 17 Advanced Placement exams for which test preparation is offered; honors section; independent study; term-away projects; study abroad; academic accommodation for the gifted, the musically talented, and the artistically talented.
College Admission Counseling 96 students graduated in 2008; 86 went to college, including College of Charleston; Southern Methodist University; The University of North Carolina at Chapel Hill; University of Chicago; University of Georgia; Vanderbilt University. Mean SAT critical reading: 660, mean SAT math: 651, mean SAT writing: 667, mean combined SAT: 1978.
Student Life Upper grades have specified standards of dress, student council, honor system. Discipline rests equally with students and faculty.
Summer Programs Remediation, enrichment, advancement, sports, art/fine arts, computer instruction programs offered; session focuses on traditional day camp with specialty academic, activity and athletic camps; held on campus; accepts boys and girls; open to students from other schools. 1,200 students usually enrolled. 2009 schedule: June 8 to July 24.
Tuition and Aid Day student tuition: $19,565. Tuition installment plan (FACTS Tuition Payment Plan). Need-based scholarship grants available. In 2008–09, 10% of upper-school students received aid. Total amount of financial aid awarded in 2008–09: $1,000,000.
Admissions Traditional secondary-level entrance grade is 9. For fall 2008, 104 students applied for upper-level admission, 41 were accepted, 20 enrolled. SSAT required. Deadline for receipt of application materials: February 17. Application fee required: $75. On-campus interview required.
Athletics Interscholastic: baseball (boys), basketball (b,g), cheering (g), cross-country running (b,g), diving (b,g), fitness (b,g), football (b), golf (b,g), gymnastics (g), lacrosse (b,g), soccer (b,g), softball (g), swimming and diving (b,g), tennis (b,g), track and field (b,g), volleyball (g), wrestling (b); intramural: squash (b,g), water polo (b); coed intramural: squash, ultimate Frisbee. 8 PE instructors, 6 coaches, 3 athletic trainers.
Computers Computers are regularly used in all classes. Computer network features include on-campus library services, online commercial services, Internet access, wireless campus network, classroom SmartBoards and ActivBoards; student laptop loaner program. Campus intranet, student e-mail accounts, and computer access in designated common areas are available to students. Students grades are available online. The school has a published electronic and media policy.
Contact Mrs. Jennifer McGurn, Associate Director of Admissions. 404-926-3710. Fax: 404-240-9124. E-mail: jmcgurn@paceacademy.org. Web site: www.paceacademy.org.

PACIFIC ACADEMY

679 Encinitas Boulevard
Suite 205
Encinitas, California 92024

Head of School: Mrs. Alexa Ann Greenland

General Information Coeducational day college-preparatory school. Grades 7–12. Founded: 1997. Setting: small town. Nearest major city is San Diego. 1 building on campus. Approved or accredited by Western Association of Schools and Colleges and California Department of Education. Total enrollment: 30. Upper school average class size: 6. Upper school faculty-student ratio: 1:5.
Faculty School total: 5. In upper school: 2 men, 3 women; all have advanced degrees.
Subjects Offered Algebra, American government, American literature, American studies, art history, biology, business mathematics, chemistry, computer applications, earth science, economics, English, ethnic studies, general math, geography, geometry, history, language arts, life science, literature, physical science, physics, pre-algebra, pre-calculus, Spanish, U.S. history, world history, world literature.
Graduation Requirements Arts and fine arts (art, music, dance, drama), computer studies, English, foreign language, mathematics, physical education (includes health), practical arts, science, social studies (includes history), community service hours in 11th and 12th grade.
Special Academic Programs Advanced Placement exam preparation; honors section; accelerated programs; academic accommodation for the gifted.
College Admission Counseling 5 students graduated in 2008.
Student Life Upper grades have honor system. Discipline rests primarily with faculty.
Summer Programs Remediation, enrichment, advancement programs offered; session focuses on academics; held on campus; accepts boys and girls; open to students from other schools. 38 students usually enrolled. 2009 schedule: June 23 to August 1. Application deadline: June 15.
Tuition and Aid Day student tuition: $13,600–$13,950. Tuition installment plan (monthly payment plans). Tuition reduction for siblings available. In 2008–09, 2% of upper-school students received aid.
Admissions Traditional secondary-level entrance grade is 10. California Achievement Test required. Deadline for receipt of application materials: none. Application fee required: $50. On-campus interview required.
Athletics 1 PE instructor.
Computers Computers are regularly used in all academic, yearbook classes. Computer network features include online commercial services, Internet access, wireless campus network.
Contact Mrs. Alexa Ann Greenland, Director of Admissions. 760-436-5718. Fax: 760-436-5718. E-mail: admissions@pacificacademy.org. Web site: www.pacificacademy.org.

PACIFIC CREST COMMUNITY SCHOOL

116 Northeast 29th Street
Portland, Oregon 97232

Head of School: Becky Lukens

General Information Coeducational day college-preparatory and arts school. Grades 7–12. Founded: 1993. Setting: urban. 1 building on campus. Approved or accredited by Northwest Association of Accredited Schools, Northwest Association of Schools and Colleges, and Oregon Department of Education. Total enrollment: 85. Upper school average class size: 10. Upper school faculty-student ratio: 1:9.

Faculty School total: 10. In upper school: 4 men, 6 women; 9 have advanced degrees.

Graduation Requirements Senior Seminar/Dissertation.

College Admission Counseling 13 students graduated in 2008; 10 went to college. Other: 3 had other specific plans.

Student Life Discipline rests equally with students and faculty.

Tuition and Aid Day student tuition: $9000. Tuition installment plan (monthly payment plans). Tuition reduction for siblings, need-based scholarship grants available. In 2008–09, 15% of upper-school students received aid. Total amount of financial aid awarded in 2008–09: $60,000.

Admissions Traditional secondary-level entrance grade is 9. Deadline for receipt of application materials: none. Application fee required: $100. Interview required.

Athletics Coed Intramural: artistic gym, basketball, bicycling, bowling, canoeing/kayaking, hiking/backpacking, outdoor adventure, outdoor education, outdoor skills, rock climbing, skiing (cross-country). 2 PE instructors.

Computers Computer resources include Internet access, wireless campus network. Student e-mail accounts are available to students.

Contact Jenny Osborne, Co-Director. 503-234-2826. Fax: 503-234-3186. E-mail: Jenny@pcrest.org. Web site: www.pcrest.org.

PACIFIC HILLS SCHOOL

8628 Holloway Drive
West Hollywood, California 90069

Head of School: Mr. Richard S. Makoff

General Information Coeducational day college-preparatory school. Grades 6–12. Founded: 1983. Setting: urban. Nearest major city is Beverly Hills. 2-acre campus. 2 buildings on campus. Approved or accredited by California Association of Independent Schools, Western Association of Schools and Colleges, and California Department of Education. Member of National Association of Independent Schools. Total enrollment: 245. Upper school average class size: 18. Upper school faculty-student ratio: 1:15.

Upper School Student Profile Grade 9: 51 students (29 boys, 22 girls); Grade 10: 50 students (33 boys, 17 girls); Grade 11: 60 students (36 boys, 24 girls); Grade 12: 33 students (17 boys, 16 girls).

Faculty School total: 31. In upper school: 20 men, 11 women; 11 have advanced degrees.

Subjects Offered Advanced Placement courses, aerobics, algebra, American history, American literature, anatomy, art, biology, calculus-AP, cheerleading, chemistry, computers, economics, English, English literature, film, French, geometry, government, human development, independent study, music, newspaper, photography, physical education, physics, pre-calculus, Spanish, speech, theater arts, yearbook.

Graduation Requirements Arts and fine arts (art, music, dance, drama), English, foreign language, mathematics, outdoor education, physical education (includes health), science, social science, social studies (includes history). Community service is required.

Special Academic Programs Advanced Placement exam preparation; honors section.

College Admission Counseling 47 students graduated in 2008; 40 went to college, including California State University, Long Beach; California State University, Northridge; The University of Arizona; University of California, San Diego; University of California, Santa Barbara; University of Southern California. Other: 3 went to work, 4 had other specific plans. Mean SAT critical reading: 525, mean SAT math: 510, mean SAT writing: 532. 17% scored over 600 on SAT critical reading, 15% scored over 600 on SAT math, 15% scored over 600 on SAT writing.

Student Life Upper grades have specified standards of dress, student council, honor system. Discipline rests primarily with faculty.

Summer Programs Remediation, enrichment programs offered; held on campus; accepts boys and girls; open to students from other schools. 170 students usually enrolled. 2009 schedule: June 22 to July 30. Application deadline: none.

Tuition and Aid Day student tuition: $19,500. Tuition installment plan (Insured Tuition Payment Plan, monthly payment plans, individually arranged payment plans). Tuition reduction for siblings, need-based scholarship grants, need-based loans available. In 2008–09, 51% of upper-school students received aid. Total amount of financial aid awarded in 2008–09: $1,895,845.

Admissions Traditional secondary-level entrance grade is 9. For fall 2008, 196 students applied for upper-level admission, 57 were accepted, 46 enrolled. CTBS (or similar from their school) or ISEE required. Deadline for receipt of application materials: none. Application fee required: $100. On-campus interview required.

Athletics Interscholastic: baseball (boys), basketball (b,g), cheering (g), softball (g), volleyball (b,g); coed interscholastic: aerobics, cross-country running, fencing, outdoor education, soccer, track and field, yoga. 5 PE instructors, 7 coaches.

Computers Computers are regularly used in graphic design, journalism, yearbook classes. Computer network features include Internet access, wireless campus network, Internet filtering or blocking technology. Students grades are available online. The school has a published electronic and media policy.

Contact Ms. Lynne Bradshaw, Admissions Assistant. 310-276-3068 Ext. 112. Fax: 310-657-3831. E-mail: lbradshaw@phschool.org. Web site: www.phschool.org.

PACIFIC LUTHERAN HIGH SCHOOL

2150 Sepulveda Boulevard
Torrance, California 90501

Head of School: Mr. Lucas Michael Fitzgerald

General Information college-preparatory, general academic, and religious studies school, affiliated with Lutheran Church–Missouri Synod; primarily serves underachievers. Founded: 1997. Setting: suburban. 2-acre campus. 2 buildings on campus. Approved or accredited by Western Association of Schools and Colleges and California Department of Education. Total enrollment: 83. Upper school average class size: 15. Upper school faculty-student ratio: 1:10.

Upper School Student Profile 15% of students are Lutheran Church–Missouri Synod.

Faculty In upper school: 5 men, 5 women; 6 have advanced degrees.

Subjects Offered 1½ elective credits, 1968, 3-dimensional art, 3-dimensional design, accounting, ACT preparation, acting, addiction, ADL skills, advanced biology, advanced chemistry, advanced computer applications, advanced studio art-AP, advanced TOEFL/grammar, advertising design, aerobics, aerospace education, aerospace science, aesthetics, African American history, African American studies, African dance, African drumming, African history, African literature, African studies.

Graduation Requirements Students are required to take four years of Theology courses.

Special Academic Programs International Baccalaureate program; Advanced Placement exam preparation; academic accommodation for the gifted; remedial reading and/or remedial writing.

College Admission Counseling 26 students graduated in 2008; 23 went to college. Other: 3 went to work.

Student Life Upper grades have specified standards of dress, student council, honor system. Discipline rests equally with students and faculty.

Summer Programs Remediation, enrichment, sports programs offered; session focuses on Remedial and Enrichment work has been offered in English and the sciences; held on campus; accepts boys and girls; open to students from other schools. 7 students usually enrolled.

Tuition and Aid Day student tuition: $6500. Tuition installment plan (SMART Tuition Payment Plan, monthly payment plans, individually arranged payment plans). Tuition reduction for siblings, merit scholarship grants, need-based scholarship grants, middle-income loans, We work with families to arrange payment plans where/if necessary available. In 2008–09, 5% of upper-school students received aid; total upper-school merit-scholarship money awarded: $10,000. Total amount of financial aid awarded in 2008–09: $20,000.

Admissions Iowa Test of Educational Development required. Deadline for receipt of application materials: none. Application fee required: $50. Interview required.

Athletics Interscholastic: baseball (boys), football (b); coed interscholastic: basketball, cheering, cross-country running, golf, winter soccer; coed intramural: flag football, outdoor activities, outdoor education, outdoor recreation, ropes courses, strength & conditioning, touch football. 1 PE instructor, 4 coaches.

Computers Computer network features include Internet access, wireless campus network, Internet filtering or blocking technology. Students grades are available online.

Contact Mrs. Denise Spartalis, Office Manager. 310-530-1231. Fax: 310-530-1215. E-mail: pacificlutheranhigh@yahoo.com. Web site: www.pacificlutheranhigh.com/.

THE PACKER COLLEGIATE INSTITUTE

170 Joralemon Street
Brooklyn, New York 11201

Head of School: Dr. Bruce L. Dennis

General Information Coeducational day college-preparatory school. Grades PK–12. Founded: 1845. Setting: urban. Nearest major city is New York. 5 buildings on campus. Approved or accredited by New York State Association of Independent Schools and New York Department of Education. Member of National Association of Independent Schools and Secondary School Admission Test Board. Endowment: $13 million. Total enrollment: 941. Upper school average class size: 15. Upper school faculty-student ratio: 1:7.

Upper School Student Profile Grade 9: 66 students (34 boys, 32 girls); Grade 10: 87 students (45 boys, 42 girls); Grade 11: 70 students (36 boys, 34 girls); Grade 12: 83 students (38 boys, 45 girls).

Faculty School total: 149. In upper school: 27 men, 42 women; 48 have advanced degrees.

Subjects Offered African literature, algebra, American history, American literature, art, art history, biology, calculus, chemistry, community service, computer math, computer programming, computer science, creative writing, dance, drama, English, English literature, ethics, European history, expository writing, fine arts, French,

geometry, government/civics, health, history, Latin, music, philosophy, photography, physical education, physics, science, sociology, Spanish, theater, trigonometry, women's studies, world history, world literature.
Graduation Requirements Arts and fine arts (art, music, dance, drama), English, foreign language, mathematics, physical education (includes health), science, social studies (includes history). Community service is required.
Special Academic Programs Advanced Placement exam preparation; honors section; independent study; term-away projects; study at local college for college credit; study abroad.
College Admission Counseling Colleges students went to include Brown University; Skidmore College; Wesleyan College; Williams College; Yale University.
Student Life Upper grades have student council. Discipline rests equally with students and faculty.
Admissions Traditional secondary-level entrance grade is 9. For fall 2008, 220 students applied for upper-level admission, 80 were accepted, 35 enrolled. ISEE or SSAT required. Deadline for receipt of application materials: December 1. Application fee required: $50. On-campus interview required.
Athletics Interscholastic: baseball (boys), basketball (b,g), cross-country running (b,g), dance (b,g). 10 PE instructors, 4 coaches, 2 athletic trainers.
Computers Computers are regularly used in mathematics, science, writing classes. Computer network features include on-campus library services, online commercial services, Internet access, laptop program (grades 6-12).
Contact Kati Crowley, Admissions Coordinator. 718-250-0385. Fax: 718-875-1363. E-mail: kcrowley@packer.edu. Web site: www.packer.edu.

PADUA FRANCISCAN HIGH SCHOOL

6740 State Road
Parma, Ohio 44134-4598
Head of School: Mr. David Stec

General Information Coeducational day college-preparatory, arts, business, religious studies, and technology school, affiliated with Roman Catholic Church; primarily serves students with learning disabilities. Grades 9–12. Founded: 1961. Setting: suburban. Nearest major city is Cleveland. 40-acre campus. 1 building on campus. Approved or accredited by North Central Association of Colleges and Schools, Ohio Catholic Schools Accreditation Association (OCSAA), and Ohio Department of Education. Endowment: $1.5 million. Total enrollment: 958. Upper school average class size: 24. Upper school faculty-student ratio: 1:18.
Upper School Student Profile Grade 9: 231 students (109 boys, 122 girls); Grade 10: 252 students (136 boys, 116 girls); Grade 11: 247 students (127 boys, 120 girls); Grade 12: 228 students (115 boys, 113 girls). 90% of students are Roman Catholic.
Faculty School total: 79. In upper school: 39 men, 40 women; 40 have advanced degrees.
Subjects Offered Accounting, algebra, American government, art appreciation, biology-AP, business, calculus-AP, chemistry, child development, Christian ethics, church history, computers, concert band, concert choir, consumer economics, current events, design, drawing, earth science, economics, English, English language-AP, ensembles, fitness, food and nutrition, French, French-AP, geography, geometry, German, German-AP, honors algebra, honors English, honors geometry, honors U.S. history, integrated science, interior design, Italian, Latin, Latin-AP, marching band, marketing, math analysis, music appreciation, music theory, orchestra, painting, photography, physics, pre-calculus, programming, psychology, social issues, social justice, sociology, Spanish, Spanish-AP, stagecraft, symphonic band, theater, trigonometry, U.S. history, U.S. history-AP, world cultures, world history.
Graduation Requirements Arts and fine arts (art, music, dance, drama), computer science, English, foreign language, lab science, mathematics, physical education (includes health), social studies (includes history), theology, four years of service projects.
Special Academic Programs Advanced Placement exam preparation; honors section; accelerated programs; study at local college for college credit; study abroad; remedial reading and/or remedial writing; special instructional classes for students with learning disabilities.
College Admission Counseling 218 students graduated in 2008; 212 went to college, including Bowling Green State University; Kent State University; Miami University; The University of Akron; The University of Toledo; University of Dayton. Other: 4 went to work, 2 entered military service. Median SAT critical reading: 537, median SAT math: 530, median composite ACT: 23.
Student Life Upper grades have uniform requirement, student council, honor system. Discipline rests primarily with faculty. Attendance at religious services is required.
Summer Programs Enrichment, sports, art/fine arts, computer instruction programs offered; session focuses on introducing students to school, programs, coaches, and other students; held on campus; accepts boys and girls; open to students from other schools. 150 students usually enrolled. 2009 schedule: June 15 to June 19. Application deadline: May 22.
Tuition and Aid Day student tuition: $8250. Tuition installment plan (monthly payment plans, individually arranged payment plans). Tuition reduction for siblings, merit scholarship grants, need-based scholarship grants, paying campus jobs available. In 2008–09, 48% of upper-school students received aid; total upper-school merit-scholarship money awarded: $181,000. Total amount of financial aid awarded in 2008–09: $777,980.
Admissions Traditional secondary-level entrance grade is 9. For fall 2008, 275 students applied for upper-level admission, 250 were accepted, 231 enrolled. STS required. Deadline for receipt of application materials: January 23. Application fee required: $100.
Athletics Interscholastic: aquatics (boys, girls), baseball (b), basketball (b,g), cheering (g), combined training (b,g), cross-country running (b,g), dance team (g), diving (b,g), football (b), golf (b,g), hockey (b), ice hockey (b), physical fitness (b,g), soccer (b,g), softball (g), strength & conditioning (b,g), swimming and diving (b,g), tennis (g), track and field (b,g), volleyball (g), wrestling (b); intramural: basketball (b), flag football (b), football (b), freestyle skiing (b,g), golf (g), gymnastics (g), power lifting (b), touch football (b), weight lifting (b), weight training (b,g), winter soccer (b); coed intramural: alpine skiing, backpacking, canoeing/kayaking, fishing, hiking/backpacking, skiing (downhill), snowboarding, wilderness, wilderness survival, wildernessways. 3 PE instructors, 30 coaches, 5 athletic trainers.
Computers Computers are regularly used in all academic classes. Computer network features include on-campus library services, online commercial services, Internet access. Computer access in designated common areas is available to students. Students grades are available online. The school has a published electronic and media policy.
Contact Mrs. Nancy Hodas, Admissions Coordinator. 440-845-2444 Ext. 112. Fax: 440-845-5710. E-mail: nhodas@paduafranciscan.com. Web site: www.paduafranciscan.com.

THE PAIDEIA SCHOOL

1509 Ponce de Leon Avenue
Atlanta, Georgia 30307
Head of School: Paul F. Bianchi

General Information Coeducational day college-preparatory, arts, and technology school. Grades PK–12. Founded: 1971. Setting: urban. 28-acre campus. 13 buildings on campus. Approved or accredited by Georgia Independent School Association, Southern Association of Colleges and Schools, Southern Association of Independent Schools, and Georgia Department of Education. Endowment: $16.5 million. Total enrollment: 923. Upper school average class size: 12. Upper school faculty-student ratio: 1:9.
Upper School Student Profile Grade 9: 99 students (49 boys, 50 girls); Grade 10: 97 students (52 boys, 45 girls); Grade 11: 96 students (49 boys, 47 girls); Grade 12: 97 students (54 boys, 43 girls).
Faculty School total: 119. In upper school: 30 men, 33 women; 55 have advanced degrees.
Subjects Offered African-American history, algebra, American culture, American government, American history, American literature, anatomy, archaeology, art, art history, Asian history, Asian studies, auto mechanics, bioethics, biology, biology-AP, calculus, ceramics, chemistry, chemistry-AP, chorus, community service, comparative religion, computer programming, creative writing, drama, drawing, ecology, environmental systems, economics, English, English literature, environmental science, ethics, European history-AP, expository writing, fine arts, forensics, French, French studies, geography, geology, geometry, government/civics, health, history, humanities, jazz, journalism, literature, mathematics, medieval history, organic chemistry, photography, physical education, physics, physics-AP, physiology, poetry, pre-calculus, psychology, psychology-AP, Shakespeare, social studies, sociology, Spanish, Spanish literature, speech, statistics, statistics-AP, theater, trigonometry, U.S. history, Web site design, weight training, women's health, women's studies, world history, world literature, writing.
Graduation Requirements Arts and fine arts (art, music, dance, drama), English, foreign language, mathematics, physical education (includes health), science, social studies (includes history). Community service is required.
Special Academic Programs 7 Advanced Placement exams for which test preparation is offered; honors section; independent study.
College Admission Counseling 101 students graduated in 2008; 95 went to college, including Emory University; Georgia Institute of Technology; New York University; The George Washington University; University of Georgia; Yale University. Other: 6 had other specific plans.
Student Life Upper grades have student council, honor system. Discipline rests equally with students and faculty.
Tuition and Aid Day student tuition: $17,790. Tuition installment plan (bank-arranged tuition loan program). Need-based tuition assistance available. In 2008–09, 17% of upper-school students received aid. Total amount of financial aid awarded in 2008–09: $1,099,107.
Admissions Traditional secondary-level entrance grade is 9. Deadline for receipt of application materials: February 2. Application fee required: $75. On-campus interview required.
Athletics Interscholastic: baseball (boys), basketball (b,g), cross-country running (b,g), diving (b,g), soccer (b,g), softball (g), swimming and diving (b,g), tennis (b,g), track and field (b,g), ultimate Frisbee (b,g), volleyball (g); coed interscholastic: ultimate Frisbee; coed intramural: aerobics, basketball, bicycling, bowling, fitness, flag football, hiking/backpacking, lacrosse, outdoor education, soccer, softball, tai chi, ultimate Frisbee, yoga. 2 PE instructors, 1 athletic trainer.
Computers Computers are regularly used in art, English, foreign language, graphic arts, history, journalism, mathematics, music, science classes. Computer network features include on-campus library services, Internet access, wireless campus network, Internet filtering or blocking technology, technology assistant program, computer

borrowing program for students, technology courses. Campus intranet, student e-mail accounts, and computer access in designated common areas are available to students. The school has a published electronic and media policy.
Contact Florence Henry, Admissions Office Administrator. 404-270-2312. Fax: 404-270-2312. E-mail: henry.flo@paideiaschool.org. Web site: www.paideiaschool.org.

ANNOUNCEMENT FROM THE SCHOOL The Paideia School is committed to a racial, socioeconomic, and cultural cross-section of students and faculty members. Students balance a rigorous academic program with independent projects, community service, the arts, and athletics. The philosophy is based on the belief that schools can be informal and individualized, yet still educate well.

PALMA HIGH SCHOOL

919 Iverson Street
Salinas, California 93901

Head of School: Br. Patrick D. Dunne, CFC

General Information Boys' day college-preparatory and religious studies school, affiliated with Roman Catholic Church. Grades 7–12. Founded: 1951. Setting: suburban. Nearest major city is San Jose. 25-acre campus. 16 buildings on campus. Approved or accredited by Western Association of Schools and Colleges, Western Catholic Education Association, and California Department of Education. Endowment: $200,000. Total enrollment: 625. Upper school average class size: 25. Upper school faculty-student ratio: 1:15.
Upper School Student Profile Grade 9: 88 students (88 boys); Grade 10: 121 students (121 boys); Grade 11: 116 students (116 boys); Grade 12: 119 students (119 boys). 69% of students are Roman Catholic.
Faculty School total: 41. In upper school: 31 men, 10 women; 22 have advanced degrees.
Subjects Offered Algebra, American history, American literature, anatomy, art, art history, band, biology, business, calculus, calculus-AP, chemistry, Chinese, Christian and Hebrew scripture, church history, civics, community service, computer applications, computer art, computer math, computer multimedia, computer programming, computer programming-AP, computer science, computer-aided design, creative writing, debate, digital art, driver education, earth science, economics, English, English language and composition-AP, English literature, English literature-AP, ethics, European history, European history-AP, expository writing, film, film studies, fine arts, French, geography, geometry, government/civics, grammar, health, health education, history, honors algebra, honors geometry, Japanese, jazz ensemble, journalism, Latin, mathematics, music, participation in sports, physical education, physical science, physics, pre-calculus, psychology, religion, Russian, Russian literature, science, social studies, Spanish, Spanish language-AP, speech, statistics-AP, student government, theology, trigonometry, typing, U.S. government and politics-AP, U.S. history-AP, video film production, world history, world literature, world religions, writing.
Graduation Requirements Arts and fine arts (art, music, dance, drama), English, foreign language, mathematics, physical education (includes health), religion (includes Bible studies and theology), science, social studies (includes history), religious retreat (8th, 9th, 10th grades), 60 hours of community service.
Special Academic Programs Advanced Placement exam preparation; honors section.
College Admission Counseling 109 students graduated in 2008; 100 went to college, including California Polytechnic State University, San Luis Obispo; California State University, Fresno; California State University, Monterey Bay; Saint Mary's College of California; Santa Clara University; University of California, Davis. Other: 2 went to work, 2 entered military service. Mean SAT critical reading: 539, mean SAT math: 550, mean SAT writing: 513, mean composite ACT: 22.
Student Life Upper grades have specified standards of dress, student council, honor system. Discipline rests primarily with faculty. Attendance at religious services is required.
Summer Programs Remediation, enrichment, advancement programs offered; session focuses on remediation and advancement; held on campus; accepts boys and girls; open to students from other schools. 150 students usually enrolled. 2009 schedule: June 15 to July 25. Application deadline: March 1.
Tuition and Aid Day student tuition: $9900. Tuition installment plan (monthly payment plans, 2-payment plan). Merit scholarship grants, need-based scholarship grants available. In 2008–09, 15% of upper-school students received aid. Total amount of financial aid awarded in 2008–09: $229,000.
Admissions Traditional secondary-level entrance grade is 9. For fall 2008, 50 students applied for upper-level admission, 25 were accepted, 13 enrolled. ETS high school placement exam required. Deadline for receipt of application materials: January 14. Application fee required: $75. On-campus interview required.
Athletics Interscholastic: baseball, basketball, cross-country running, diving, football, golf, soccer, swimming and diving, track and field, volleyball, water polo, wrestling; intramural: basketball, indoor soccer. 4 PE instructors, 15 coaches, 1 athletic trainer.
Computers Computers are regularly used in art, desktop publishing, economics, English, foreign language, history, mathematics, multimedia, music, newspaper, photography, science, social sciences, technical drawing, video film production, Web site design, word processing, writing, yearbook classes. Computer network features include on-campus library services, online commercial services, Internet access, wireless campus network, Internet filtering or blocking technology. Computer access in designated common areas is available to students. Students grades are available online. The school has a published electronic and media policy.
Contact Mr. Adam Fox, Director of Admissions. 831-422-6391. Fax: 831-422-5065. E-mail: fox@palmahs.org. Web site: www.palmahs.org.

PALMER TRINITY SCHOOL

7900 Southwest 176th Street
Miami, Florida 33157

ANNOUNCEMENT FROM THE SCHOOL Palmer Trinity School, a co-educational Episcopal day school, is committed to the academic, spiritual, physical, and creative growth of all members of its community. Through their dedication to excellence, students are inspired to lead lives of honor, integrity, and social responsibility. The best environment for young people is a school where students feel valued, affirmed, and supported while they explore their interests and develop their skills. Palmer Trinity provides a rigorous college-preparatory curriculum, a competitive athletics program, and one of the strongest music programs in Miami. The School serves a community of students in grades 6–12 from a broad range of socio-economic, ethnic, and religious backgrounds. Palmer Trinity is the only Episcopal Middle/Upper School in the Miami area and is an institution where values are celebrated as fervently as academic accomplishments. Palmer Trinity honors the unity of mind, body, and spirit. All graduating seniors attend four-year universities, with 80% matriculating outside Florida. The early admission deadline is November 15, and the regular admission and financial aid deadline is February 1. For more information about Palmer Trinity School or to apply online, please visit www.palmertrinity.org.

PARADISE ADVENTIST ACADEMY

5699 Academy Drive
PO Box 2169
Paradise, California 95969

Head of School: Mr. Ken Preston

General Information Coeducational day college-preparatory school, affiliated with Seventh-day Adventists. Grades K–12. Founded: 1908. Setting: small town. Nearest major city is Sacramento. 12-acre campus. 4 buildings on campus. Approved or accredited by Western Association of Schools and Colleges and California Department of Education. Endowment: $200,000. Total enrollment: 211. Upper school average class size: 25. Upper school faculty-student ratio: 1:10.
Upper School Student Profile Grade 9: 26 students (14 boys, 12 girls); Grade 10: 21 students (10 boys, 11 girls); Grade 11: 18 students (11 boys, 7 girls); Grade 12: 12 students (7 boys, 5 girls). 80% of students are Seventh-day Adventists.
Faculty School total: 20. In upper school: 7 men, 3 women; 4 have advanced degrees.
Subjects Offered Advanced math, algebra, American government, American history, auto shop, band, basketball, Bible, biology, career education, carpentry, chemistry, choir, computer applications, computer keyboarding, computers, drama, earth science, English, geometry, health, keyboarding, keyboarding/computer, physical education, physical science, physics, pre-algebra, pre-calculus, Spanish, speech, U.S. government, U.S. history, volleyball, weightlifting, woodworking, world history, yearbook.
Graduation Requirements Algebra, American government, American history, Bible, biology, career education, chemistry, computer keyboarding, computer literacy, English, physical education (includes health), physics, pre-calculus, Spanish, world history, 100 hours of community service, 20 credits of fine arts, 5 credits work experience (100 hours work).
Special Academic Programs Accelerated programs; independent study.
College Admission Counseling 20 students graduated in 2008; 17 went to college, including Andrews University; La Sierra University; Pacific Union College; University of California, Santa Barbara; Walla Walla University. Other: 1 went to work, 2 had other specific plans. Median SAT critical reading: 485, median SAT math: 490, median SAT writing: 490, median combined SAT: 1380, median composite ACT: 20. 9% scored over 600 on SAT critical reading, 27.5% scored over 600 on SAT math, 9% scored over 600 on SAT writing, 9% scored over 1800 on combined SAT.
Student Life Upper grades have specified standards of dress, student council. Discipline rests primarily with faculty. Attendance at religious services is required.
Tuition and Aid Day student tuition: $7540. Tuition installment plan (monthly payment plans). Tuition reduction for siblings, need-based scholarship grants, paying campus jobs available. In 2008–09, 25% of upper-school students received aid.
Admissions Traditional secondary-level entrance grade is 9. For fall 2008, 7 students applied for upper-level admission, 7 were accepted, 7 enrolled. Any standardized test required. Deadline for receipt of application materials: August 14. Application fee required: $35. Interview required.
Athletics Interscholastic: basketball (boys, girls), football (b,g), volleyball (g). 1 PE instructor.

Computers Computers are regularly used in all academic classes. Computer network features include on-campus library services, Internet access, Internet filtering or blocking technology. Campus intranet, student e-mail accounts, and computer access in designated common areas are available to students. Students grades are available online. The school has a published electronic and media policy.
Contact Mrs. Brenda Muth, Registrar. 530-877-6540 Ext. 3010. Fax: 530-877-0870. E-mail: bmuth@mypaa.net. Web site: www.mypaa.net.

PARISH EPISCOPAL SCHOOL

4101 Sigma Road
Dallas, Texas 75244
Head of School: Mrs. Gloria Hoffman Snyder

General Information Coeducational day college-preparatory school, affiliated with Episcopal Church. Grades PK–12. Founded: 1972. Setting: suburban. 50-acre campus. 1 building on campus. Approved or accredited by Independent Schools Association of the Southwest, Southwest Association of Episcopal Schools, and Texas Department of Education. Total enrollment: 1,101.
Upper School Student Profile Grade 9: 89 students (32 boys, 57 girls); Grade 10: 65 students (29 boys, 36 girls); Grade 11: 75 students (34 boys, 41 girls); Grade 12: 49 students (24 boys, 25 girls). 25% of students are members of Episcopal Church.
Special Academic Programs Honors section.
Student Life Upper grades have uniform requirement, student council, honor system. Discipline rests primarily with faculty. Attendance at religious services is required.
Summer Programs Enrichment, advancement, sports, art/fine arts, computer instruction programs offered; held on campus; accepts boys and girls; open to students from other schools. 2009 schedule: June to July. Application deadline: May.
Tuition and Aid Day student tuition: $14,400. Guaranteed tuition plan. Tuition installment plan (Insured Tuition Payment Plan, monthly payment plans). Need-based scholarship grants available.
Admissions Traditional secondary-level entrance grade is 9. ISEE required. Deadline for receipt of application materials: January 19. Application fee required: $150. Interview required.
Athletics Interscholastic: baseball (boys), basketball (b,g), cheering (g), field hockey (g), lacrosse (b,g), soccer (b,g), softball (g), winter soccer (b,g); intramural: aerobics/dance (g), dance (g); coed interscholastic: cross-country running, golf, tennis; coed intramural: physical fitness, strength & conditioning, weight training. 6 PE instructors, 12 coaches, 2 athletic trainers.
Computers Computer resources include Internet filtering or blocking technology. Campus intranet and computer access in designated common areas are available to students. Students grades are available online. The school has a published electronic and media policy.
Contact Mrs. Marci McLean, Director of Admission. 972-852-8750. Fax: 972-991-1237. E-mail: mmclean@parishepiscopal.org. Web site: www.parishepiscopal.org.

THE PARKER SCHOOL

65-1224 Lindsey Road
Kamuela, Hawaii 96743
Head of School: Dr. Carl Sturges

General Information Coeducational day college-preparatory, arts, and technology school. Grades K–12. Founded: 1976. Setting: rural. Nearest major city is Kona. 9-acre campus. 9 buildings on campus. Approved or accredited by Western Association of Schools and Colleges and Hawaii Department of Education. Member of National Association of Independent Schools. Endowment: $3 million. Total enrollment: 296. Upper school average class size: 12. Upper school faculty-student ratio: 1:8.
Upper School Student Profile Grade 9: 32 students (13 boys, 19 girls); Grade 10: 32 students (14 boys, 18 girls); Grade 11: 34 students (11 boys, 23 girls); Grade 12: 22 students (9 boys, 13 girls).
Faculty School total: 24. In upper school: 7 men, 9 women; 8 have advanced degrees.
Subjects Offered Advanced math, Advanced Placement courses, algebra, American literature, art, art and culture, biology, chemistry, college planning, computer programming, computer science, computer technologies, creative writing, drama, earth science, English, English literature, European history, film studies, fine arts, geography, geometry, government/civics, grammar, Hawaiian history, health, history, mathematics, music, Pacific Island studies, physical education, physics, pre-algebra, pre-calculus, science, senior seminar, social science, social studies, sociology, Spanish, theater, trigonometry, U.S. history, weight training, world history, world literature, writing.
Graduation Requirements Arts and fine arts (art, music, dance, drama), English, foreign language, mathematics, physical education (includes health), science, social studies (includes history).
Special Academic Programs Advanced Placement exam preparation; honors section; independent study.
College Admission Counseling 27 students graduated in 2008; 25 went to college, including University of Colorado at Boulder; University of Hawaii at Manoa. Other: 2 went to work. Mean SAT critical reading: 543, mean SAT math: 520, mean SAT writing: 536, mean combined SAT: 1599.
Student Life Upper grades have specified standards of dress, student council, honor system. Discipline rests primarily with faculty.
Summer Programs Remediation, enrichment programs offered; session focuses on remediation and enrichment; held on campus; accepts boys and girls; open to students from other schools. 20 students usually enrolled. 2009 schedule: June 9 to July 11. Application deadline: none.
Tuition and Aid Day student tuition: $9900. Tuition installment plan (Key Tuition Payment Plan, monthly payment plans, individually arranged payment plans). Merit scholarship grants, need-based scholarship grants, paying campus jobs available. In 2008–09, 46% of upper-school students received aid; total upper-school merit-scholarship money awarded: $59,500. Total amount of financial aid awarded in 2008–09: $117,000.
Admissions Traditional secondary-level entrance grade is 9. For fall 2008, 26 students applied for upper level admission, 21 were accepted, 21 enrolled. Admissions testing required. Deadline for receipt of application materials: none. Application fee required: $75. Interview required.
Athletics Interscholastic: basketball (boys, girls), canoeing/kayaking (b,g), cross-country running (b,g), golf (b,g), ocean paddling (b,g), soccer (b,g), swimming and diving (b,g), tennis (b,g), track and field (b,g), volleyball (b,g); coed intramural: cooperative games. 13 coaches.
Computers Computers are regularly used in drafting, English, graphics, independent study, science classes. Computer network features include Internet access.
Contact Ms. Ann Renick, Admission Director. 808-885-7933. Fax: 808-885-6233. E-mail: arenick@parkerschool.net. Web site: www.parkerschool.net/.

PARKLANE ACADEMY

1115 Parklane Road
McComb, Mississippi 39648
Head of School: Mr. Charles S. Siebert

General Information Coeducational day college-preparatory school, affiliated with Christian faith. Grades PK–12. Founded: 1970. Setting: small town. Nearest major city is Jackson. 44-acre campus. 4 buildings on campus. Approved or accredited by Southern Association of Colleges and Schools and Mississippi Department of Education. Total enrollment: 976. Upper school average class size: 25. Upper school faculty-student ratio: 1:16.
Upper School Student Profile Grade 7: 72 students (42 boys, 30 girls); Grade 8: 69 students (40 boys, 29 girls); Grade 9: 95 students (41 boys, 54 girls); Grade 10: 53 students (36 boys, 17 girls); Grade 11: 85 students (43 boys, 42 girls); Grade 12: 51 students (22 boys, 29 girls). 80% of students are Christian faith.
Faculty School total: 54. In upper school: 9 men, 18 women; 9 have advanced degrees.
Subjects Offered 20th century world history, advanced chemistry, algebra, ancient world history, art, band, basic language skills, Bible, biology, calculus, choral music, choreography, civics, composition, computer applications, computer keyboarding, computer science, concert band, consumer economics, creative writing, driver education, economics, economics and history, English composition, English language-AP, English literature and composition-AP, English-AP, French, geography, government, government and politics-AP, government-AP, grammar, health, history-AP, honors geometry, honors U.S. history, human anatomy, lab science, library, literature, literature and composition-AP, literature-AP, media services, musical productions, physical science, physics, public speaking, reading, SAT/ACT preparation, science, Spanish, speech, state government, U.S. history, U.S. literature, world history, world literature.
Graduation Requirements Algebra, American history, American literature, analytic geometry, applied music, biology, British literature, chemistry, civics/free enterprise, computer applications, economics, electives, English, English composition, foreign language, geometry, government, honors algebra, honors English, honors geometry, honors U.S. history, honors world history, human biology, lab science, language and composition, music appreciation, U.S. government, world history.
Special Academic Programs Advanced Placement exam preparation; honors section; study at local college for college credit.
College Admission Counseling 59 students graduated in 2008; 50 went to college, including Belhaven College; Mississippi College; Mississippi State University; University of Mississippi; University of Southern Mississippi. Other: 2 entered military service. Median composite ACT: 23. 19% scored over 26 on composite ACT.
Student Life Upper grades have specified standards of dress, student council, honor system. Discipline rests primarily with faculty.
Summer Programs Remediation, computer instruction programs offered; session focuses on earning make-up credits, keyboarding, and driver education; held on campus; accepts boys and girls; not open to students from other schools. 25 students usually enrolled. 2009 schedule: June 1 to July 30. Application deadline: May 10.
Tuition and Aid Day student tuition: $2700. Tuition installment plan (monthly payment plans). Tuition reduction for siblings available. In 2008–09, 1% of upper-school students received aid. Total amount of financial aid awarded in 2008–09: $3000.
Admissions Traditional secondary-level entrance grade is 9. Admissions testing required. Deadline for receipt of application materials: none. Application fee required: $150. On-campus interview required.
Athletics Interscholastic: baseball (boys), basketball (b,g), cheering (b,g), danceline (g), football (b), golf (b), soccer (b), softball (g), tennis (b), track and field (b,g), weight training (b,g). 1 PE instructor, 10 coaches.

Computers Computers are regularly used in computer applications, data processing, desktop publishing, keyboarding, science, typing, word processing, yearbook classes. Computer network features include on-campus library services, Internet access, wireless campus network. Campus intranet is available to students. Students grades are available online. The school has a published electronic and media policy.

Contact Mrs. Emma Lampton, Registrar/Technology Coordinator. 601-684-8113 Ext. 223. Fax: 601-684-4166 Ext. 256. E-mail: parklane@cableone.net. Web site: www.parklaneacademy.net.

THE PARK SCHOOL OF BUFFALO

4625 Harlem Road
Snyder, New York 14226

Head of School: Christopher J. Lauricella

General Information Coeducational day college-preparatory and arts school. Grades N–12. Founded: 1912. Setting: suburban. Nearest major city is Buffalo. 33-acre campus. 15 buildings on campus. Approved or accredited by New York Department of Education, New York State Association of Independent Schools, and New York State Board of Regents. Member of National Association of Independent Schools. Endowment: $1.3 million. Total enrollment: 239. Upper school average class size: 15. Upper school faculty-student ratio: 1:9.

Upper School Student Profile Grade 9: 19 students (8 boys, 11 girls); Grade 10: 30 students (14 boys, 16 girls); Grade 11: 30 students (12 boys, 18 girls); Grade 12: 26 students (13 boys, 13 girls).

Faculty School total: 39. In upper school: 14 men, 25 women; 20 have advanced degrees.

Subjects Offered Advanced studio art-AP, algebra, American government-AP, American history, American history-AP, American literature, American literature-AP, art, band, biology, biology-AP, calculus, calculus-AP, ceramics, chemistry, chorus, college admission preparation, college counseling, community service, computer applications, computer programming, critical thinking, drama, drawing, economics, English, environmental science, fine arts, forensic science, French, French language-AP, freshman seminar, geometry, government and politics-AP, government/civics, health, junior and senior seminars, marine biology, media, media production, metalworking, music, orchestra, organic chemistry, photography, physical education, physics, senior project, senior seminar, senior thesis, Spanish, Spanish-AP, studio art-AP, trigonometry, woodworking, world history, yearbook.

Graduation Requirements Arts and fine arts (art, music, dance, drama), computer science, English, foreign language, mathematics, physical education (includes health), science, senior project, senior thesis, social science, social studies (includes history). Community service is required.

Special Academic Programs Advanced Placement exam preparation; honors section; accelerated programs; independent study; study at local college for college credit; academic accommodation for the gifted; ESL (11 students enrolled).

College Admission Counseling 18 students graduated in 2008; 17 went to college, including Oberlin College; Sarah Lawrence College; University at Buffalo, the State University of New York. Other: 1 had other specific plans. 33% scored over 600 on SAT critical reading, 28% scored over 600 on SAT math, 39% scored over 600 on SAT writing.

Student Life Upper grades have specified standards of dress, student council. Discipline rests primarily with faculty.

Tuition and Aid Day student tuition: $16,200–$17,250. Tuition installment plan (Insured Tuition Payment Plan, FACTS Tuition Payment Plan). Tuition reduction for siblings, merit scholarship grants, need-based scholarship grants available. In 2008–09, 38% of upper-school students received aid; total upper-school merit-scholarship money awarded: $25,350. Total amount of financial aid awarded in 2008–09: $387,150.

Admissions Traditional secondary-level entrance grade is 9. For fall 2008, 88 students applied for upper-level admission, 60 were accepted, 48 enrolled. ERB Reading and Math and Otis-Lennon School Ability Test required. Deadline for receipt of application materials: none. Application fee required: $25. On-campus interview required.

Athletics Interscholastic: basketball (boys, girls), bowling (b), golf (b), soccer (b,g), softball (g), tennis (b,g); coed interscholastic: soccer; coed intramural: floor hockey, running, yoga. 2 PE instructors, 5 coaches.

Computers Computers are regularly used in creative writing, current events, data processing, English, graphic arts, independent study, mathematics, media, media arts, media services, newspaper, photography, science, word processing, yearbook classes. Computer network features include on-campus library services, online commercial services, Internet access, wireless campus network, Internet filtering or blocking technology. Campus intranet, student e-mail accounts, and computer access in designated common areas are available to students. Students grades are available online. The school has a published electronic and media policy.

Contact Jennifer A. Brady, Director of Admissions. 716-839-1242 Ext. 107. Fax: 716-839-2014. E-mail: jbrady@theparkschool.org. Web site: www.theparkschool.org.

PARK TUDOR SCHOOL

7200 North College Avenue
Indianapolis, Indiana 46240-3016

Head of School: Mr. Douglas S. Jennings

General Information Coeducational day college-preparatory, arts, and bilingual studies school. Grades PK–12. Founded: 1902. Setting: suburban. 55-acre campus. 6 buildings on campus. Approved or accredited by Independent Schools Association of the Central States and Indiana Department of Education. Member of National Association of Independent Schools and Secondary School Admission Test Board. Endowment: $89.6 million. Total enrollment: 982. Upper school average class size: 14. Upper school faculty-student ratio: 1:9.

Upper School Student Profile Grade 6: 60 students (28 boys, 32 girls); Grade 7: 69 students (39 boys, 30 girls); Grade 8: 72 students (33 boys, 39 girls); Grade 9: 104 students (54 boys, 50 girls); Grade 10: 108 students (55 boys, 53 girls); Grade 11: 109 students (54 boys, 55 girls); Grade 12: 105 students (58 boys, 47 girls).

Faculty School total: 158. In upper school: 31 men, 36 women; 49 have advanced degrees.

Subjects Offered 3-dimensional design, acting, advanced chemistry, advanced math, Advanced Placement courses, algebra, American history, American history-AP, American literature-AP, art, art history, art history-AP, ballet, biology, biology-AP, calculus, calculus-AP, Canadian history, ceramics, chemistry, chemistry-AP, choir, computer programming-AP, computer science, computer science-AP, creative writing, dance, drama, economics, economics-AP, electives, English, English language-AP, English literature-AP, English-AP, English/composition-AP, environmental science, environmental science-AP, ethics, etymology, film history, fine arts, French, French language-AP, French literature-AP, geography, geometry, German, government/civics, health, history, history-AP, jazz band, jazz ensemble, journalism, Latin, Latin-AP, madrigals, Mandarin, mathematics, multicultural literature, music, music history, music theory, music theory-AP, philosophy, photography, physical education, physics, physics-AP, physiology, printmaking, science, social science, social studies, sociology, Spanish, Spanish language-AP, speech, speech and debate, statistics, statistics-AP, studio art, studio art—AP, theater, theater design and production, theater history, trigonometry, U.S. government, U.S. history, U.S. history-AP, world history, world history-AP, world wide web design.

Graduation Requirements Arts and fine arts (art, music, dance, drama), English, foreign language, mathematics, physical education (includes health), science, social science, social studies (includes history).

Special Academic Programs 20 Advanced Placement exams for which test preparation is offered; honors section; accelerated programs; independent study; study abroad; academic accommodation for the gifted, the musically talented, and the artistically talented.

College Admission Counseling 100 students graduated in 2008; all went to college, including Bowdoin College; DePauw University; Emory University, Oxford College; Indiana University Bloomington; Purdue University; Vanderbilt University. Mean SAT critical reading: 627, mean SAT math: 617, mean SAT writing: 620, mean combined SAT: 1864, mean composite ACT: 28.

Student Life Upper grades have specified standards of dress, student council, honor system. Discipline rests equally with students and faculty.

Summer Programs Remediation, enrichment, advancement, sports, art/fine arts, rigorous outdoor training, computer instruction programs offered; session focuses on academics, fine arts, and athletics; held both on and off campus; held at Bradford Woods, Martinsville, IN; accepts boys and girls; open to students from other schools. 300 students usually enrolled. 2009 schedule: June 7 to August 7. Application deadline: none.

Tuition and Aid Day student tuition: $16,570. Tuition installment plan (annual, biannual or quarterly payment plans). Merit scholarship grants, need-based scholarship grants available. In 2008–09, 38% of upper-school students received aid. Total amount of financial aid awarded in 2008–09: $1,446,312.

Admissions Traditional secondary-level entrance grade is 9. For fall 2008, 112 students applied for upper-level admission, 81 were accepted, 52 enrolled. ERB CTP IV required. Deadline for receipt of application materials: December 12. Application fee required: $50. On-campus interview required.

Athletics Interscholastic: baseball (boys), basketball (b,g), crew (b,g), cross-country running (b,g), football (b), golf (b,g), ice hockey (b), lacrosse (b,g), soccer (b,g), softball (g), swimming and diving (b,g), tennis (b,g), track and field (b,g), volleyball (g), wrestling (b); intramural: basketball (b,g); coed interscholastic: cheering; coed intramural: running, soccer. 5 PE instructors, 21 coaches, 1 athletic trainer.

Computers Computers are regularly used in newspaper, yearbook classes. Computer network features include on-campus library services, online commercial services, Internet access, wireless campus network, Internet filtering or blocking technology. Campus intranet, student e-mail accounts, and computer access in designated common areas are available to students. Students grades are available online. The school has a published electronic and media policy.

Contact Mr. David Amstutz, Assistant Head and Director of Admissions. 317-415-2777. Fax: 317-254-2714. E-mail: damstutz@parktudor.org. Web site: www.parktudor.org.

ANNOUNCEMENT FROM THE SCHOOL Park Tudor School's exceptional educators and extraordinary opportunities prepare students to become confident and resourceful lifelong learners. The School community creates an inspiring college-preparatory learning environment for highly motivated young people in junior kindergarten through grade 12. The comprehensive curriculum includes foreign language study, twenty Advanced Placement classes, complete arts and athletics offerings, and before- and after-school programs.

See Close-Up on page 898.

PEDDIE SCHOOL

South Main Street
Hightstown, New Jersey 08520
Head of School: John F. Green

General Information Coeducational boarding and day college-preparatory, arts, and technology school. Grades 9–PG. Founded: 1864. Setting: small town. Nearest major city is Princeton. Students are housed in single-sex dormitories. 230-acre campus. 53 buildings on campus. Approved or accredited by Middle States Association of Colleges and Schools, New Jersey Association of Independent Schools, The Association of Boarding Schools, and New Jersey Department of Education. Member of National Association of Independent Schools and Secondary School Admission Test Board. Endowment: $280 million. Total enrollment: 527. Upper school average class size: 12. Upper school faculty-student ratio: 1:6.

Upper School Student Profile Grade 9: 129 students (67 boys, 62 girls); Grade 10: 103 students (51 boys, 52 girls); Grade 11: 122 students (62 boys, 60 girls); Grade 12: 123 students (57 boys, 66 girls); Postgraduate: 10 students (6 boys, 4 girls). 65% of students are boarding students. 23 states are represented in upper school student body. 11% are international students. International students from Canada, China, Hong Kong, Republic of Korea, Thailand, and United Kingdom; 21 other countries represented in student body.

Faculty School total: 94. In upper school: 50 men, 35 women; 66 have advanced degrees; 76 reside on campus.

Subjects Offered Acting, African studies, algebra, American history, American literature, American studies, anatomy, art, art history, art history-AP, Asian studies, astronomy, Bible studies, biology, biology-AP, calculus, calculus-AP, chemistry, Chinese, comedy, comparative religion, computer programming, computer science, creative writing, debate, digital imaging, DNA, DNA science lab, drama, earth science, ecology, economics, English, English literature, environmental science, environmental science-AP, European history, European history-AP, expository writing, film history, fine arts, forensics, French, French language-AP, French literature-AP, geometry, global issues, global science, government/civics, health, history, information technology, Latin, Latin-AP, mathematics, Middle East, music, music theory-AP, neuroscience, philosophy, photography, physical education, physics, physics-AP, psychology, psychology-AP, robotics, science, Shakespeare, social studies, Spanish, Spanish language-AP, Spanish literature-AP, speech, statistics, statistics-AP, studio art—AP, theater, trigonometry, U.S. history, U.S. history-AP, video film production, world history, world literature, World War I, World War II, writing.

Graduation Requirements Arts and fine arts (art, music, dance, drama), computer science, English, foreign language, history, mathematics, physical education (includes health), science. Community service is required.

Special Academic Programs Advanced Placement exam preparation; honors section; independent study; term-away projects; study abroad.

College Admission Counseling 140 students graduated in 2008; all went to college, including Boston College; Carnegie Mellon University; Cornell University; New York University; The George Washington University; University of Pennsylvania.

Student Life Upper grades have specified standards of dress, student council. Discipline rests primarily with faculty.

Summer Programs Enrichment, advancement programs offered; session focuses on enrichment; held on campus; accepts boys and girls; open to students from other schools. 175 students usually enrolled. 2009 schedule: June 22 to August 3. Application deadline: none.

Tuition and Aid Day student tuition: $30,200; 7-day tuition and room/board: $39,900. Tuition installment plan (Academic Management Services Plan, monthly payment plans, individually arranged payment plans). Merit scholarship grants, need-based scholarship grants, need-based loans available. In 2008–09, 40% of upper-school students received aid; total upper-school merit-scholarship money awarded: $86,350. Total amount of financial aid awarded in 2008–09: $5,000,000.

Admissions Traditional secondary-level entrance grade is 9. For fall 2008, 1,257 students applied for upper-level admission, 330 were accepted, 179 enrolled. ISEE or SSAT required. Deadline for receipt of application materials: January 15. Application fee required: $50. Interview required.

Athletics Interscholastic: baseball (boys), basketball (b,g), crew (b,g), cross-country running (b,g), diving (b,g), field hockey (g), fitness (b,g), football (b), golf (b,g), indoor track & field (b,g), lacrosse (b,g), soccer (b,g), softball (g), strength & conditioning (b,g), swimming and diving (b,g), tennis (b,g), track and field (b,g), winter (indoor) track (b,g), wrestling (b), yoga (b,g); intramural: weight lifting (b,g), weight training (b,g); coed intramural: bicycling, bowling, softball. 9 coaches, 3 athletic trainers.

Computers Computers are regularly used in English, foreign language, history, mathematics, science classes. Computer network features include on-campus library services, online commercial services, Internet access, wireless campus network, NewsBank, Britannica, GaleNet, Electric Library. Student e-mail accounts are available to students.

Contact Raymond H. Cabot, Director of Admissions. 609-490-7501. Fax: 609-944-7901. E-mail: admission@peddie.org. Web site: www.peddie.org.

ANNOUNCEMENT FROM THE SCHOOL Technology partners with curriculum at Peddie's extraordinary Walter and Leonore Annenberg Science Center. Multimedia stations support courses that include Forensics, Genetics, Robotics, and Global Warming: Science and Economics. Caspersen History House, with "tech pods" in every classroom, now offers Modern Africa, Modern East Asia: The Rise of China, and Modern India.

See Close-Up on page 900.

THE PENIKESE ISLAND SCHOOL

Woods Hole, Massachusetts
See Special Needs Schools section.

THE PENNINGTON SCHOOL

112 West Delaware Avenue
Pennington, New Jersey 08534-1601
Head of School: Mrs. Stephanie (Penny) G. Townsend

General Information Coeducational boarding and day college-preparatory school, affiliated with Methodist Church. Boarding grades 7–12, day grades 6–12. Founded: 1838. Setting: small town. Nearest major city is Philadelphia, PA. Students are housed in single-sex by floor dormitories and single-sex dormitories. 54-acre campus. 17 buildings on campus. Approved or accredited by Middle States Association of Colleges and Schools, National Independent Private Schools Association, New Jersey Association of Independent Schools, The Association of Boarding Schools, The College Board, University Senate of United Methodist Church, and New Jersey Department of Education. Member of National Association of Independent Schools and Secondary School Admission Test Board. Endowment: $24.5 million. Total enrollment: 478. Upper school average class size: 13. Upper school faculty-student ratio: 1:8.

Upper School Student Profile Grade 9: 97 students (54 boys, 43 girls); Grade 10: 97 students (55 boys, 42 girls); Grade 11: 100 students (56 boys, 44 girls); Grade 12: 93 students (50 boys, 43 girls). 26% of students are boarding students. 66% are state residents. 8 states are represented in upper school student body. 12% are international students. International students from China, Germany, Republic of Korea, South Africa, Taiwan, and Thailand; 14 other countries represented in student body. 5% of students are Methodist.

Faculty School total: 87. In upper school: 31 men, 38 women; 55 have advanced degrees; 49 reside on campus.

Subjects Offered Advanced studio art-AP, advanced TOEFL/grammar, African-American history, algebra, American history, American literature, anatomy, anatomy and physiology, art, bioethics, DNA and culture, biology, British literature-AP, calculus-AP, cheerleading, chemistry, chemistry-AP, Chinese, chorus, computer applications, computer skills, drama, economics, English, English literature, English literature-AP, English-AP, environmental science, ESL, fine arts, forensics, French, French language-AP, genetics, geometry, German, government and politics-AP, Greek, Greek culture, health, history-AP, honors algebra, honors English, honors geometry, honors U.S. history, jazz ensemble, Latin, macroeconomics-AP, music, music history, music theory, organic chemistry, photography, physics, physics-AP, pottery, pre-calculus, psychology, public speaking, religion, robotics, senior internship, Spanish, Spanish literature, Spanish-AP, stage design, stagecraft, technical theater, U.S. government and politics-AP, Web site design, weight training, world history, world history-AP.

Graduation Requirements Algebra, American history, arts and fine arts (art, music, dance, drama), athletics, biology, chemistry, computer education, English, foreign language, geometry, health education, public speaking, religion (includes Bible studies and theology), religion and culture, world history.

Special Academic Programs Advanced Placement exam preparation; honors section; independent study; term-away projects; study at local college for college credit; academic accommodation for the gifted; programs in English for dyslexic students; ESL (41 students enrolled).

College Admission Counseling 99 students graduated in 2008; all went to college, including Carnegie Mellon University; Georgetown University; Muhlenberg College; New York University; Penn State University Park; Quinnipiac University.

Student Life Upper grades have specified standards of dress, student council. Discipline rests equally with students and faculty. Attendance at religious services is required.

Tuition and Aid Day student tuition: $26,500; 7-day tuition and room/board: $39,400. Tuition installment plan (Key Tuition Payment Plan). Merit scholarship grants, need-based scholarship grants available. In 2008–09, 22% of upper-school students received aid; total upper-school merit-scholarship money awarded: $201,600. Total amount of financial aid awarded in 2008–09: $1,265,000.

Admissions Traditional secondary-level entrance grade is 9. For fall 2008, 467 students applied for upper-level admission, 154 were accepted, 117 enrolled.

Secondary Level English Proficiency, SLEP for foreign students, SSAT or TOEFL required. Deadline for receipt of application materials: February 1. Application fee required: $50. Interview required.
Athletics Interscholastic: baseball (boys), basketball (b,g), field hockey (g), football (b), ice hockey (b), lacrosse (b,g), soccer (b,g), softball (g), tennis (b,g), weight training (b); coed interscholastic: cheering, cross-country running, golf, indoor track, judo, swimming and diving, track and field, water polo, winter (indoor) track; coed intramural: fitness, strength & conditioning, weight training. 3 coaches, 2 athletic trainers.
Computers Computers are regularly used in art, college planning, computer applications, creative writing, desktop publishing, graphic design, library, literary magazine, mathematics, music, newspaper, research skills, science, video film production, yearbook classes. Computer network features include on-campus library services, online commercial services, Internet access, wireless campus network, Internet filtering or blocking technology, The Homework Site. Campus intranet, student e-mail accounts, and computer access in designated common areas are available to students. Students grades are available online. The school has a published electronic and media policy.
Contact Mr. Mark Saunders, Director of Admission. 609-737-6128. Fax: 609-730-1405. E-mail: msaunders@pennington.org. Web site: www.pennington.org.

See Close-Up on page 902.

PENSACOLA CATHOLIC HIGH SCHOOL

3043 West Scott Street
Pensacola, Florida 32505
Head of School: Sr. Kierstin Martin

General Information Coeducational day college-preparatory school, affiliated with Roman Catholic Church; primarily serves students with learning disabilities and individuals with Attention Deficit Disorder. Grades 9–12. Founded: 1941. Setting: urban. 25-acre campus. 5 buildings on campus. Approved or accredited by Southern Association of Colleges and Schools. Total enrollment: 599. Upper school average class size: 22. Upper school faculty-student ratio: 1:18.
Upper School Student Profile Grade 9: 141 students (79 boys, 62 girls); Grade 10: 151 students (80 boys, 71 girls); Grade 11: 144 students (72 boys, 72 girls); Grade 12: 163 students (87 boys, 76 girls). 70% of students are Roman Catholic.
Faculty School total: 50. In upper school: 15 men, 35 women; 15 have advanced degrees.
Subjects Offered Advanced math, Advanced Placement courses, algebra, American government, American government-AP, American history, American history-AP, American literature, analysis and differential calculus, analytic geometry, anatomy and physiology, art, art appreciation, arts and crafts, athletics, band, baseball, basketball, Bible, Bible studies, biology, botany, British literature, broadcast journalism, business law, calculus, calculus-AP, campus ministry, Catholic belief and practice, chemistry, Christian ethics, Christian scripture, Christian studies, Christian testament, church history, civics, college counseling, comparative religion, composition, composition-AP, computer applications, computer graphics, consumer mathematics, CPR, creative arts, criminal justice, desktop publishing, digital photography, drawing, earth science, economics, electives, English, English composition, English language and composition-AP, English literature, English literature and composition-AP, environmental science, fabric arts, film appreciation, film history, filmmaking, foreign language, French, general science, genetics, geography, geometry, government, government-AP, grammar, graphic arts, guidance, health education, history, history of the Catholic Church, honors algebra, honors English, honors geometry, honors U.S. history, honors world history, human sexuality, journalism, keyboarding/computer, lab science, library, library assistant, Life of Christ, literature and composition-AP, marine biology, music appreciation, music history, physical education, physical science, physics, pottery, pre-algebra, pre-calculus, probability and statistics, reading, religion, sex education, social studies, Spanish, student government, student publications, telecommunications and the Internet, television, the Web, trigonometry, U.S. government, U.S. government-AP, U.S. history, U.S. literature, vocal music, weight training, Western civilization, world geography, world history, world religions.
Special Academic Programs Advanced Placement exam preparation; honors section; study at local college for college credit; academic accommodation for the gifted; remedial reading and/or remedial writing; remedial math; programs in English, mathematics, general development for dyslexic students; special instructional classes for deaf students, blind students.
College Admission Counseling 146 students graduated in 2008; all went to college, including Florida State University; Pensacola Junior College; University of Central Florida; University of Florida. Mean SAT critical reading: 544, mean SAT math: 532, mean composite ACT: 23.
Student Life Upper grades have specified standards of dress, student council. Discipline rests primarily with faculty. Attendance at religious services is required.
Admissions Traditional secondary-level entrance grade is 9. ETS high school placement exam required. Deadline for receipt of application materials: none. No application fee required. On-campus interview required.
Computers Computers are regularly used in Bible studies, computer applications, creative writing, desktop publishing, foreign language, French, geography, graphic design, history, independent study, keyboarding, mathematics, publications, reading, religion, science, social studies, Spanish, stock market, study skills, video film production, Web site design, word processing, yearbook classes. Computer network features include on-campus library services, online commercial services, Internet access, wireless campus network, Internet filtering or blocking technology. Student e-mail accounts and computer access in designated common areas are available to students. Students grades are available online. The school has a published electronic and media policy.
Contact Mrs. Karen Adams, Senior Guidance Counselor. 850-436-6400 Ext. 119. Fax: 850-436-6405. E-mail: kadams@pensacolachs.org. Web site: www.pensacolachs.org.

PEOPLES CHRISTIAN ACADEMY

374 Sheppard Avenue East
Toronto, Ontario M2N 3B6, Canada
Head of School: Mrs. Sharon M Cracknell

General Information Coeducational day college-preparatory and religious studies school, affiliated with Christian faith. Grades JK–12. Founded: 1971. Setting: urban. 5-acre campus. 2 buildings on campus. Approved or accredited by Association of Christian Schools International, Ontario Ministry of Education, and Ontario Department of Education. Language of instruction: English. Total enrollment: 695. Upper school average class size: 20. Upper school faculty-student ratio: 1:10.
Upper School Student Profile Grade 7: 60 students (33 boys, 27 girls); Grade 8: 57 students (31 boys, 26 girls); Grade 9: 63 students (29 boys, 34 girls); Grade 10: 59 students (29 boys, 30 girls); Grade 11: 57 students (28 boys, 29 girls); Grade 12: 59 students (34 boys, 25 girls). 85% of students are Christian.
Faculty School total: 45. In upper school: 8 men, 13 women; 4 have advanced degrees.
Subjects Offered Accounting, Bible, biology, calculus, Canadian geography, Canadian history, Canadian law, careers, chemistry, civics, discrete mathematics, dramatic arts, economics, English, exercise science, family studies, French, functions, geography, geometry, health education, healthful living, ideas, information technology, instrumental music, journalism, keyboarding, literature, mathematics, media arts, organizational studies, philosophy, physical education, physics, psychology, science, sociology, visual arts, vocal music, world history, world religions, writing.
Graduation Requirements Arts, Canadian geography, Canadian history, careers, civics, English, French as a second language, mathematics, physical education (includes health), science, Must complete Bible course curriculum for all grades.
Special Academic Programs ESL (6 students enrolled).
College Admission Counseling 64 students graduated in 2008; 63 went to college, including McMaster University; The University of Western Ontario; University of Guelph; University of Toronto; Wilfrid Laurier University; York University. Other: 1 had other specific plans.
Student Life Upper grades have uniform requirement, student council, honor system. Discipline rests primarily with faculty. Attendance at religious services is required.
Tuition and Aid Day student tuition: CAN$8104. Tuition installment plan (monthly payment plans). Tuition reduction for siblings, bursaries, need-based scholarship grants, alumni scholarships, prepayment tuition reduction available. In 2008–09, 2% of upper-school students received aid. Total amount of financial aid awarded in 2008–09: CAN$30,000.
Admissions Traditional secondary-level entrance grade is 9. For fall 2008, 15 students applied for upper-level admission, 10 were accepted, 10 enrolled. CTBS (or similar from their school) required. Deadline for receipt of application materials: none. Application fee required: CAN$225. On-campus interview required.
Athletics Interscholastic: badminton (boys, girls), baseball (b,g), basketball (b,g), cross-country running (b,g), running (b,g), track and field (b,g), volleyball (b,g); intramural: badminton (b,g), basketball (b,g), cross-country running (b,g), floor hockey (b,g), running (b,g); coed interscholastic: badminton, baseball, basketball, cross-country running, running, swimming and diving, track and field; coed intramural: badminton, basketball, cross-country running, floor hockey, running, volleyball. 2 PE instructors, 5 coaches.
Computers Computers are regularly used in business studies, drawing and design, graphics, information technology, introduction to technology, journalism, mathematics, yearbook classes. Computer network features include Internet access, Internet filtering or blocking technology. The school has a published electronic and media policy.
Contact School Office. 416-222-3341. Fax: 416-222-3344. E-mail: academy-info@peoplesministries.org. Web site: www.peopleschristianacademy.ca.

PERKIOMEN SCHOOL

200 Seminary Street
Pennsburg, Pennsylvania 18073
Head of School: Mr. Christopher R. Tompkins

General Information Coeducational boarding and day college-preparatory school, affiliated with Schwenkfelder Church. Boarding grades 7–PG, day grades 5–PG. Founded: 1875. Setting: small town. Nearest major city is Philadelphia. Students are housed in single-sex dormitories. 165-acre campus. 23 buildings on campus. Approved or accredited by Middle States Association of Colleges and Schools, Pennsylvania Association of Independent Schools, The Association of Boarding Schools, The College Board, and Pennsylvania Department of Education. Member of

National Association of Independent Schools and Secondary School Admission Test Board. Endowment: $4.2 million. Total enrollment: 281. Upper school average class size: 12. Upper school faculty-student ratio: 1:7.

Upper School Student Profile Grade 9: 24 students (11 boys, 13 girls); Grade 10: 57 students (40 boys, 17 girls); Grade 11: 58 students (43 boys, 15 girls); Grade 12: 73 students (48 boys, 25 girls); Postgraduate: 3 students (1 boy, 2 girls). 64% of students are boarding students. 65% are state residents. 15 states are represented in upper school student body. 18% are international students. International students from Bermuda, China, Japan, Republic of Korea, Spain, and Taiwan; 10 other countries represented in student body. 1% of students are members of Schwenkfelder Church.

Faculty School total: 49. In upper school: 26 men, 23 women; 31 have advanced degrees; 36 reside on campus.

Subjects Offered African history, algebra, American history, American literature, art, art history, astronomy, Bible studies, biology, calculus, ceramics, chemistry, computer graphics, computer programming, computer science, creative writing, current events, dance, developmental language skills, drama, driver education, earth science, economics, English, English literature, environmental science, ESL, ethics, European history, fine arts, French, gender issues, geography, geology, geometry, government/civics, grammar, health, history, humanities, journalism, Latin, library studies, mathematics, music, painting, philosophy, photography, physical education, physics, physics-AP, psychology, religion, science, social studies, sociology, Spanish, speech, statistics, textiles, theater, trigonometry, world history, world literature.

Graduation Requirements Arts and fine arts (art, music, dance, drama), computer studies, English, foreign language, mathematics, physical education (includes health), religion (includes Bible studies and theology), science, social studies (includes history). Community service is required.

Special Academic Programs Advanced Placement exam preparation; honors section; independent study; academic accommodation for the gifted, the musically talented, and the artistically talented; programs in English, general development for dyslexic students; ESL (36 students enrolled).

College Admission Counseling 60 students graduated in 2008; all went to college, including Bryn Mawr College; Cornell University; Haverford College; Lehigh University; Northwestern University; University of Chicago. Mean SAT critical reading: 550, mean SAT math: 600, mean SAT writing: 560.

Student Life Upper grades have uniform requirement, student council. Discipline rests primarily with faculty. Attendance at religious services is required.

Summer Programs ESL, sports programs offered; held on campus; accepts boys and girls; open to students from other schools.

Tuition and Aid Day student tuition: $22,400; 7-day tuition and room/board: $38,200. Tuition installment plan (monthly payment plans). Need-based scholarship grants available. In 2008–09, 33% of upper-school students received aid. Total amount of financial aid awarded in 2008–09: $1,399,000.

Admissions Traditional secondary-level entrance grade is 10. For fall 2008, 419 students applied for upper-level admission, 238 were accepted, 107 enrolled. SSAT or TOEFL or SLEP required. Deadline for receipt of application materials: none. Application fee required: $50. Interview required.

Athletics Interscholastic: baseball (boys), basketball (b,g), field hockey (g), football (b), golf (b), lacrosse (b,g), power lifting (b), soccer (b), softball (g), tennis (b,g), weight lifting (b), wrestling (b); coed interscholastic: cheering, cross-country running, dance, martial arts, swimming and diving; coed intramural: dance, skateboarding. 1 PE instructor, 7 coaches, 1 athletic trainer.

Computers Computers are regularly used in all academic, art classes. Computer network features include on-campus library services, online commercial services, Internet access, Internet filtering or blocking technology. Campus intranet, student e-mail accounts, and computer access in designated common areas are available to students. The school has a published electronic and media policy.

Contact Carol Dougherty, Assistant Head of School. 215-679-9511. Fax: 215-679-1146. E-mail: cdougherty@perkiomen.org. Web site: www.perkiomen.org.

THE PHELPS SCHOOL

583 Sugartown Road
Malvern, Pennsylvania 19355

Head of School: Mr. F. Christopher Chirieleison

General Information Boys' boarding and day college-preparatory, general academic, Academic Support Program, and ESL Program school; primarily serves underachievers, students with learning disabilities, individuals with Attention Deficit Disorder, and dyslexic students. Grades 7–PG. Founded: 1946. Setting: suburban. Nearest major city is Philadelphia. Students are housed in single-sex dormitories. 75-acre campus. 18 buildings on campus. Approved or accredited by Academy of Orton-Gillingham Practitioners and Educators, Middle States Association of Colleges and Schools, Pennsylvania Association of Independent Schools, The Association of Boarding Schools, and Pennsylvania Department of Education. Total enrollment: 142. Upper school average class size: 7. Upper school faculty-student ratio: 1:5.

Upper School Student Profile Grade 7: 4 students (4 boys); Grade 8: 11 students (11 boys); Grade 9: 23 students (23 boys); Grade 10: 29 students (29 boys); Grade 11: 38 students (38 boys); Grade 12: 33 students (33 boys); Postgraduate: 4 students (4 boys). 81% of students are boarding students. 35% are state residents. 16 states are represented in upper school student body. 39% are international students. International students from Bermuda, China, Nigeria, Republic of Korea, Spain, and Taiwan; 7 other countries represented in student body.

Faculty School total: 25. In upper school: 18 men, 7 women; 8 have advanced degrees; 17 reside on campus.

Subjects Offered Algebra, American history, art, biology, calculus, calculus-AP, chemistry, college admission preparation, earth science, English, environmental science, ESL, fitness, general math, geometry, government, health, learning strategies, mathematics, participation in sports, photography, physical education, physical science, physics, pre-algebra, pre-calculus, psychology, reading, reading/study skills, remedial study skills, SAT preparation, scuba diving, shop, Spanish, study skills, weight training, world history, yearbook.

Graduation Requirements English, mathematics, physical education (includes health), science, social studies (includes history). Community service is required.

Special Academic Programs Advanced Placement exam preparation; independent study; academic accommodation for the gifted, the musically talented, and the artistically talented; remedial reading and/or remedial writing; remedial math; programs in English, mathematics, general development for dyslexic students; ESL (22 students enrolled).

College Admission Counseling 37 students graduated in 2008; 34 went to college, including College of Charleston; Drexel University; Lynn University; Rochester Institute of Technology; University of Oregon; University of Rochester. Other: 1 went to work, 1 entered military service, 1 entered a postgraduate year.

Student Life Upper grades have specified standards of dress, student council. Discipline rests primarily with faculty.

Tuition and Aid Day student tuition: $19,000; 7-day tuition and room/board: $32,000. Tuition installment plan (individually arranged payment plans). Tuition reduction for siblings, need-based scholarship grants available. In 2008–09, 15% of upper-school students received aid. Total amount of financial aid awarded in 2008–09: $250,000.

Admissions Traditional secondary-level entrance grade is 7. For fall 2008, 154 students applied for upper-level admission, 115 were accepted, 71 enrolled. Deadline for receipt of application materials: none. Application fee required: $50. Interview required.

Athletics Interscholastic: baseball, basketball, cross-country running, golf, lacrosse, soccer, tennis; intramural: bowling, climbing, fitness, flag football, Frisbee, golf, horseback riding, in-line skating, independent competitive sports, indoor soccer, martial arts, physical fitness, rock climbing, roller blading, ropes courses, scuba diving, softball, strength & conditioning, tennis, volleyball, wall climbing, weight lifting, weight training, winter soccer. 2 PE instructors.

Computers Computers are regularly used in college planning, English, ESL, remedial study skills, study skills, yearbook classes. Computer network features include Internet access, wireless campus network, Internet filtering or blocking technology. Campus intranet and computer access in designated common areas are available to students. Students grades are available online. The school has a published electronic and media policy.

Contact Mr. Michael J. Reardon, Assistant Headmaster for Enrollment. 610-644-1754 Ext. 210. Fax: 610-644-6679. E-mail: admis@thephelpsschool.org. Web site: www.thephelpsschool.org.

ANNOUNCEMENT FROM THE SCHOOL The Phelps School was founded in 1946 by Dr. Norman T. Phelps, fulfilling his dream of starting a boarding school for boys—in particular, those who need extra personal attention to help them reach their potential. The Phelps philosophy of dedication to the academic, personal, and social development of each boy is accentuated by a structured family atmosphere, small classes, and daily tutorial support. Fully accredited, Phelps offers a college-preparatory program for ineffective learners who may have attention issues or learning differences. The School is thoroughly aware that no two students are exactly alike and no two students have exactly the same needs. From the very first visit, The Phelps School focuses on getting to know each student well in order to help shape a course of study that will enable him to enhance his strengths and improve his skills. The School's mission is to create a nurturing and responsive climate that will bring out the best in each student and help him gain self-confidence and acquire respect for those around him. This effort is strengthened by the "family" atmosphere, small classes, and a strong tutorial component. The School also works to achieve a proper balance between every boy's academic performance and his physical, social, and moral development. The School is located 20 miles west of Philadelphia in the suburban community of Malvern (population 2,500). The campus comprises 75 acres. The cultural and recreational resources of a major metropolitan center are within 45 minutes of the campus. The Phelps School is a nonprofit corporation controlled by a Board of Trustees, which is composed of 11 individuals of varying backgrounds and professions. The board has a strong alumni component. There are approximately 1,300 alumni. Please visit the Web site at www.thephelpsschool.org or e-mail admis@thephelpsschool.org.

PHILLIPS ACADEMY (ANDOVER)

180 Main Street
Andover, Massachusetts 01810-4161
Head of School: Barbara L. Chase

General Information Coeducational boarding and day college-preparatory school. Grades 9–PG. Founded: 1778. Setting: suburban. Nearest major city is Boston. Students are housed in single-sex dormitories and 9th graders housed separately from other students. 500-acre campus. 160 buildings on campus. Approved or accredited by New England Association of Schools and Colleges and The Association of Boarding Schools. Member of National Association of Independent Schools and Secondary School Admission Test Board. Endowment: $670 million. Total enrollment: 1,090. Upper school average class size: 13. Upper school faculty-student ratio: 1:5.

Upper School Student Profile Grade 9: 232 students (115 boys, 117 girls); Grade 10: 264 students (136 boys, 128 girls); Grade 11: 288 students (136 boys, 152 girls); Grade 12: 291 students (136 boys, 155 girls); Postgraduate: 15 students (14 boys, 1 girl). 73% of students are boarding students. 46% are state residents. 46 states are represented in upper school student body. 9% are international students. International students from Canada, China, Hong Kong, Japan, Republic of Korea, and Saudi Arabia; 25 other countries represented in student body.

Faculty School total: 222. In upper school: 116 men, 106 women; 160 have advanced degrees; 196 reside on campus.

Subjects Offered Algebra, American history, American literature, ancient history, animal behavior, animation, Arabic, Arabic studies, architecture, art, art history, astronomy, band, Bible studies, biology, calculus, ceramics, chamber groups, chemistry, Chinese, chorus, computer graphics, computer programming, computer science, creative writing, dance, drama, drawing, driver education, ecology, economics, English, English literature, environmental science, ethics, European history, expository writing, film, fine arts, French, geology, geometry, German, government/civics, grammar, Greek, health, history, international relations, Japanese, jazz, Latin, Latin American studies, life issues, literature, mathematics, Middle Eastern history, music, mythology, oceanography, painting, philosophy, photography, physical education, physics, physiology, printmaking, psychology, religion, Russian, Russian studies, science, sculpture, social science, social studies, sociology, Spanish, speech, swimming, theater, trigonometry, video, world history, writing.

Graduation Requirements Arts and fine arts (art, music, dance, drama), English, foreign language, history, life issues, mathematics, philosophy, physical education (includes health), religion (includes Bible studies and theology), science, social science, swimming test.

Special Academic Programs Advanced Placement exam preparation; honors section; independent study; term-away projects; study abroad; academic accommodation for the gifted, the musically talented, and the artistically talented; programs in English, mathematics, general development for dyslexic students; special instructional classes for deaf students, blind students.

College Admission Counseling 303 students graduated in 2008; 290 went to college, including Georgetown University; Harvard University; Princeton University; Stanford University; University of Pennsylvania; Yale University. Other: 13 had other specific plans. Mean SAT critical reading: 685, mean SAT math: 698, mean SAT writing: 680.

Student Life Upper grades have student council, honor system. Discipline rests primarily with faculty.

Summer Programs Remediation, enrichment, advancement, ESL, art/fine arts, computer instruction programs offered; session focuses on academics; held both on and off campus; held at Colorado; accepts boys and girls; open to students from other schools. 550 students usually enrolled. 2009 schedule: June 30 to August 5. Application deadline: none.

Tuition and Aid Day student tuition: $29,000; 7-day tuition and room/board: $37,200. Tuition installment plan (individually arranged payment plans, The Andover Plan). Need-based scholarship grants, middle-income loans available. In 2008–09, 42% of upper-school students received aid. Total amount of financial aid awarded in 2008–09: $14,600,000.

Admissions For fall 2008, 2,410 students applied for upper-level admission, 474 were accepted, 350 enrolled. Iowa Test of Educational Development, ISEE, PSAT, SAT, SSAT or TOEFL required. Deadline for receipt of application materials: February 1. Application fee required: $40. Interview required.

Athletics Interscholastic: baseball (boys), basketball (b,g), bicycling (b,g), crew (b,g), cross-country running (b,g), diving (b,g), field hockey (g), football (b), golf (b,g), ice hockey (b,g), indoor track & field (b,g), lacrosse (b,g), nordic skiing (b,g), skiing (cross-country) (b,g), soccer (b,g), softball (g), squash (b,g), swimming and diving (b,g), tennis (b,g), track and field (b,g), volleyball (b,g), water polo (b,g), winter (indoor) track (b,g), wrestling (b); intramural: aerobics/dance (b,g), backpacking (b,g), basketball (b,g), crew (b,g), martial arts (b,g), physical fitness (b,g), physical training (b,g); coed interscholastic: bicycling, Frisbee, golf, ultimate Frisbee, wrestling; coed intramural: badminton, ballet, canoeing/kayaking, cheering, cross-country running, dance, fencing, fitness, fitness walking, hiking/backpacking, martial arts, modern dance, outdoor adventure, outdoor education, physical fitness, physical training, rappelling, rock climbing, ropes courses, soccer, softball, strength & conditioning, tennis, wall climbing. 7 PE instructors, 25 coaches, 3 athletic trainers.

Computers Computers are regularly used in animation, architecture, art, classics, computer applications, digital applications, English, foreign language, history, mathematics, music, photography, psychology, religious studies, science, theater, video film production classes. Computer network features include on-campus library services, online commercial services, Internet access. Campus intranet and student e-mail accounts are available to students. The school has a published electronic and media policy.

Contact Jane F. Fried, Dean of Admission. 978-749-4050. Fax: 978-749-4068. E-mail: admissions@andover.edu. Web site: www.andover.edu.

See Close-Up on page 904.

PHILLIPS EXETER ACADEMY

20 Main Street
Exeter, New Hampshire 03833-2460
Head of School: Mr. Tyler C. Tingley

General Information Coeducational boarding and day college-preparatory school. Grades 9–PG. Founded: 1781. Setting: small town. Nearest major city is Boston, MA. Students are housed in single-sex dormitories. 619-acre campus. 127 buildings on campus. Approved or accredited by Association of Independent Schools in New England, New England Association of Schools and Colleges, and The Association of Boarding Schools. Member of National Association of Independent Schools and Secondary School Admission Test Board. Endowment: $1 billion. Total enrollment: 1,045. Upper school average class size: 12. Upper school faculty-student ratio: 1:5.

Upper School Student Profile Grade 9: 176 students (87 boys, 89 girls); Grade 10: 247 students (109 boys, 138 girls); Grade 11: 293 students (150 boys, 143 girls); Grade 12: 329 students (174 boys, 155 girls). 80% of students are boarding students. 23% are state residents. 45 states are represented in upper school student body. 11% are international students. International students from Canada, China, Republic of Korea, Saudi Arabia, Singapore, and United Kingdom; 20 other countries represented in student body.

Faculty School total: 203. In upper school: 110 men, 93 women; 168 have advanced degrees; 110 reside on campus.

Subjects Offered Algebra, American history, American literature, anatomy, anthropology, Arabic, archaeology, architecture, art, art history, astronomy, biology, botany, calculus, ceramics, chemistry, Chinese, classics, computer programming, computer science, creative writing, dance, discrete math, drama, driver education, ecology, economics, electronics, English, English literature, environmental science, ethics, European history, evolution, existentialism, expository writing, film, fine arts, French, genetics, geology, geometry, German, Greek, health, history, Italian, Japanese, Latin, linear algebra, logic, marine biology, mathematics, music, music composition, ornithology, philosophy, photography, physical education, physics, physiology, psychology, religion, Russian, science, sculpture, Spanish, statistics, theater, trigonometry, world literature, writing, Zen Buddhism.

Graduation Requirements American history, art, biology, computer science, English, foreign language, mathematics, physical education (includes health), physical science, religion (includes Bible studies and theology), science.

Special Academic Programs Advanced Placement exam preparation; honors section; independent study; term-away projects; study abroad; academic accommodation for the gifted, the musically talented, and the artistically talented.

College Admission Counseling 330 students graduated in 2007; all went to college, including Harvard University; New York University; Stanford University; The George Washington University; The Johns Hopkins University; University of Pennsylvania. Mean SAT critical reading: 691, mean SAT math: 706, mean SAT writing: 688.

Student Life Upper grades have specified standards of dress, student council, honor system. Discipline rests primarily with faculty.

Tuition and Aid Day student tuition: $28,200; 7-day tuition and room/board: $36,500. Tuition installment plan (Academic Management Services Plan, Tuition Management Systems Plan). Need-based scholarship grants available. In 2007–08, 46% of upper-school students received aid. Total amount of financial aid awarded in 2007–08: $13,000,000.

Admissions Traditional secondary-level entrance grade is 9. For fall 2007, 2,286 students applied for upper-level admission, 502 were accepted, 345 enrolled. PSAT or SAT, SSAT or TOEFL required. Deadline for receipt of application materials: January 15. Application fee required: $50. Interview required.

Athletics Interscholastic: baseball (boys), basketball (b,g), crew (b,g), cross-country running (b,g), diving (b,g), field hockey (g), football (b), ice hockey (b,g), indoor track & field (b,g), lacrosse (b,g), soccer (b,g), softball (g), squash (b,g), swimming and diving (b,g), tennis (b,g), track and field (b,g), volleyball (g), water polo (b,g), winter (indoor) track (b,g), wrestling (b); intramural: crew (b,g), ice hockey (b,g), rugby (b,g); coed interscholastic: bicycling, golf; coed intramural: aerobics/dance, ballet, basketball, bicycling, dance, fencing, fitness, golf, lacrosse, life saving, martial arts, modern dance, outdoor activities, physical fitness, physical training, running, scuba diving, skiing (cross-country), skiing (downhill), soccer, softball, squash, strength & conditioning, tennis, ultimate Frisbee, volleyball, weight lifting, weight training, yoga. 12 PE instructors, 12 coaches, 3 athletic trainers.

Computers Computers are regularly used in computer applications, foreign language, mathematics, science classes. Computer network features include on-campus library services, Internet access, Internet filtering or blocking technology. Campus intranet and student e-mail accounts are available to students.

Contact Mr. Michael Gary, Director of Admissions. 603-777-3437. Fax: 603-777-4399. E-mail: admit@exeter.edu. Web site: www.exeter.edu.

See Close-Up on page 906.

PHOENIX CHRISTIAN UNIFIED SCHOOLS

1751 West Indian School Road
Phoenix, Arizona 85015

Head of School: Mr. James H. Koan II

General Information Coeducational day college-preparatory, general academic, and religious studies school, affiliated with Christian faith. Grades PS–12. Founded: 1949. Setting: suburban. 12-acre campus. 10 buildings on campus. Approved or accredited by Association of Christian Schools International, North Central Association of Colleges and Schools, and Arizona Department of Education. Total enrollment: 732. Upper school average class size: 20. Upper school faculty-student ratio: 1:20.

Upper School Student Profile Grade 9: 90 students (40 boys, 50 girls); Grade 10: 72 students (39 boys, 33 girls); Grade 11: 93 students (48 boys, 45 girls); Grade 12: 60 students (30 boys, 30 girls). 100% of students are Christian faith.

Faculty School total: 36. In upper school: 19 men, 17 women; 17 have advanced degrees.

Subjects Offered Advanced computer applications, algebra, American literature, American literature-AP, anatomy, art, band, Bible, biology, calculus, calculus-AP, career and personal planning, chemistry, choir, choral music, computer applications, computers, drama, drama performance, drawing, earth science, economics, English, English literature, English literature-AP, English-AP, fine arts, French, geometry, government, instrumental music, integrated science, intro to computers, language-AP, library, literature, literature-AP, marching band, physical education, physics, pre-algebra, pre-calculus, psychology, social studies, Spanish, Spanish language-AP, speech, student government, study skills, U.S. government, U.S. history, U.S. history-AP, Web site design, world history, yearbook.

Graduation Requirements Advanced math, algebra, arts and fine arts (art, music, dance, drama), biology, chemistry, computer education, earth and space science, economics, English, English composition, English literature, foreign language, geography, geometry, government, pre-calculus, religious studies, speech, U.S. history, world history, world literature.

Special Academic Programs Advanced Placement exam preparation; honors section; independent study; term-away projects; study at local college for college credit; ESL (25 students enrolled).

College Admission Counseling 108 students graduated in 2008; 91 went to college, including Arizona State University; Azusa Pacific University; Glendale Community College; Northern Arizona University; The University of Arizona. Other: 12 went to work, 3 entered military service. Median SAT critical reading: 538, median SAT math: 526, median SAT writing: 515.

Student Life Upper grades have uniform requirement, student council. Discipline rests primarily with faculty. Attendance at religious services is required.

Summer Programs Remediation, enrichment programs offered; session focuses on academics; held both on and off campus; held at online; accepts boys and girls; open to students from other schools. 25 students usually enrolled. 2009 schedule: June 1 to July 31. Application deadline: May 15.

Tuition and Aid Day student tuition: $7575. Tuition installment plan (monthly payment plans, individually arranged payment plans). Tuition reduction for siblings, need-based scholarship grants, ministerial discount available. In 2008–09, 11% of upper-school students received aid. Total amount of financial aid awarded in 2008–09: $83,725.

Admissions Traditional secondary-level entrance grade is 9. For fall 2008, 112 students applied for upper-level admission, 108 were accepted, 90 enrolled. Achievement tests or any standardized test required. Deadline for receipt of application materials: none. Application fee required: $300. Interview required.

Athletics Interscholastic: baseball (boys), basketball (b,g), cheering (g), drill team (g), football (b), softball (g), volleyball (g), wrestling (b); coed interscholastic: cross-country running, diving, golf, soccer, swimming and diving, tennis, track and field, weight lifting, weight training. 17 coaches, 1 athletic trainer.

Computers Computers are regularly used in career exploration, college planning, computer applications, creative writing, desktop publishing, journalism, keyboarding, library, media services, newspaper, publications, Web site design, yearbook classes. Computer resources include on-campus library services, Internet access, Internet filtering or blocking technology. Campus intranet and computer access in designated common areas are available to students. Students grades are available online. The school has a published electronic and media policy.

Contact Mrs. Nancy L. Smith, Student Recruitment Coordinator. 602-265-4707 Ext. 270. Fax: 602-277-7170. E-mail: nsmith@phoenixchristian.org.

PHOENIX COUNTRY DAY SCHOOL

3901 East Stanford Drive
Paradise Valley, Arizona 85253

Head of School: Geoff Campbell

General Information Coeducational day college-preparatory, arts, and music school. Grades PK–12. Founded: 1961. Setting: suburban. Nearest major city is Phoenix. 40-acre campus. 8 buildings on campus. Approved or accredited by Independent Schools Association of the Southwest and North Central Association of Colleges and Schools. Member of National Association of Independent Schools. Endowment: $16 million. Total enrollment: 728. Upper school average class size: 16. Upper school faculty-student ratio: 1:9.

Upper School Student Profile Grade 9: 59 students (28 boys, 31 girls); Grade 10: 61 students (29 boys, 32 girls); Grade 11: 65 students (28 boys, 37 girls); Grade 12: 67 students (38 boys, 29 girls).

Faculty School total: 90. In upper school: 18 men, 12 women; 25 have advanced degrees.

Subjects Offered Algebra, American history, American literature, anatomy, anthropology, art, art history, biology, calculus, ceramics, chemistry, computer programming, computer science, creative writing, ecology, English, English literature, environmental science, ethics, European history, fine arts, French, geography, geology, geometry, government/civics, history, journalism, Latin, marine biology, mathematics, music, oceanography, photography, physical education, physics, physiology, psychology, science, social science, social studies, Spanish, speech, statistics, theater, trigonometry, world history.

Graduation Requirements American history, American literature, ancient world history, arts and fine arts (art, music, dance, drama), biology, English, foreign language, mathematics, physical education (includes health), physics, science.

Special Academic Programs 15 Advanced Placement exams for which test preparation is offered; honors section; independent study; study abroad.

College Admission Counseling 66 students graduated in 2008; all went to college, including Northwestern University; Scripps College; Stanford University; The University of Arizona; University of Southern California. Median SAT critical reading: 640, median SAT math: 660, median SAT writing: 670, median composite ACT: 28.

Student Life Upper grades have specified standards of dress, student council, honor system. Discipline rests primarily with faculty.

Summer Programs Enrichment, advancement, sports, art/fine arts, computer instruction programs offered; session focuses on academics/sports camp/arts program; held on campus; accepts boys and girls; open to students from other schools. 450 students usually enrolled. 2009 schedule: June 8 to July 17. Application deadline: none.

Tuition and Aid Day student tuition: $21,000. Tuition installment plan (Insured Tuition Payment Plan, monthly payment plans, individually arranged payment plans, 10 months, quarterly, semiannual, and yearly payment plans). Need-based scholarship grants available. In 2008–09, 18% of upper-school students received aid.

Admissions Traditional secondary-level entrance grade is 9. For fall 2008, 54 students applied for upper-level admission, 43 were accepted, 33 enrolled. Achievement/Aptitude/Writing, ERB CTP IV and Otis-Lennon IQ required. Deadline for receipt of application materials: March 1. Application fee required: $100. On-campus interview required.

Athletics Interscholastic: baseball (boys), basketball (b,g), canoeing/kayaking (g), cross-country running (b,g), diving (b,g), flag football (b), golf (b,g), lacrosse (b,g), running (b,g), soccer (b,g), softball (g), swimming and diving (b,g), tennis (b,g), volleyball (g), winter soccer (g); intramural: archery (b,g), badminton (b,g), baseball (b), basketball (b,g), field hockey (b,g), flag football (b), lacrosse (b,g), outdoor education (b,g), outdoor recreation (b,g), physical fitness (b,g), soccer (b,g), softball (g), strength & conditioning (b,g), swimming and diving (b,g), volleyball (g), yoga (b,g). 5 PE instructors, 20 coaches.

Computers Computers are regularly used in art, college planning, creative writing, data processing, desktop publishing, economics, engineering, English, foreign language, French, history, humanities, independent study, information technology, keyboarding, library, library skills, literary magazine, mathematics, news writing, newspaper, photography, programming, publications, research skills, science, social sciences, social studies, Spanish, stock market, Web site design, writing, yearbook classes. Computer resources include on-campus library services, online commercial services, Internet access, wireless campus network, Internet filtering or blocking technology. Campus intranet, student e-mail accounts, and computer access in designated common areas are available to students. Students grades are available online. The school has a published electronic and media policy.

Contact Kelsey Neal, Director of Admissions. 602-955-8200 Ext. 2256. Fax: 602-381-4554. E-mail: kelsey.neal@pcds.org.

ANNOUNCEMENT FROM THE SCHOOL Founded in 1961, Phoenix Country Day School, PK–12, is a coeducational, nonsectarian college preparatory school. Its mission is to offer a distinguished liberal arts curriculum that fosters the growth of the whole person and the acquisition of thinking skills and cooperative behaviors to establish a foundation for success in college and in life. Intellectual, artistic, and communication skills, as well as physical development, share equal emphasis with self-discipline and sound moral and ethical values.

PIC RIVER PRIVATE HIGH SCHOOL

36 Pic River Road
PO Box 217
Heron Bay, Ontario P0T 1R0, Canada

Head of School: Mrs. Alison Hemingway Rayasi

General Information Coeducational day college-preparatory school. Grades K–12. Founded: 1993. Setting: rural. 1 building on campus. Approved or accredited by Ontario Department of Education. Language of instruction: English. Upper school faculty-student ratio: 1:10.

Faculty School total: 2. In upper school: 1 man, 1 woman; 1 has an advanced degree.

Student Life Discipline rests equally with students and faculty.

Admissions No application fee required.

Computers Computer network features include on-campus library services, Internet access, Internet filtering or blocking technology. Campus intranet and student e-mail accounts are available to students.

Contact Mrs. Jennifer Cress, Independent Study Coordinator. 807-229-2120. Fax: 807-229-3404. E-mail: jmcress@picriver.com.

PIEDMONT ACADEMY

PO Box 231
126 Highway 212 West
Monticello, Georgia 31064

Head of School: Dr. Michael Rossi

General Information Coeducational day college-preparatory, arts, business, vocational, religious studies, bilingual studies, technology, and Joint Enrollment with Georgia Military College school, affiliated with Protestant faith. Grades PK–12. Founded: 1970. Setting: small town. Nearest major city is Atlanta. 25-acre campus. 8 buildings on campus. Approved or accredited by Georgia Accrediting Commission and Georgia Independent School Association. Total enrollment: 399. Upper school average class size: 17. Upper school faculty-student ratio: 1:13.

Upper School Student Profile Grade 9: 34 students (23 boys, 11 girls); Grade 10: 33 students (15 boys, 18 girls); Grade 11: 25 students (11 boys, 14 girls); Grade 12: 24 students (12 boys, 12 girls). 98% of students are Protestant.

Faculty School total: 52. In upper school: 5 men, 14 women; 19 have advanced degrees.

Subjects Offered Advanced chemistry, advanced computer applications, advanced math, algebra, American government, American history, American history-AP, anatomy and physiology, band, biology, business law, calculus, calculus-AP, chemistry, chemistry-AP, civics, computer science, computer science-AP, computers, concert band, concert choir, consumer economics, consumer law, economics, English, English-AP, geometry, government and politics-AP, government-AP, government/civics, grammar, health education, honors algebra, honors English, honors geometry, Internet, intro to computers, keyboarding/computer, language arts, leadership and service, literature, mathematics, performing arts, personal finance, physical fitness, physical science, physics, pre-calculus, science, sociology, Spanish, student government, wind instruments, world history, yearbook.

Graduation Requirements Algebra, American government, American literature, biology, calculus, chemistry, civics, computer keyboarding, English composition, English literature, geometry, government, grammar, history, mathematics, physical education (includes health), physical science, science, Spanish.

Special Academic Programs Study at local college for college credit.

College Admission Counseling 27 students graduated in 2008; all went to college, including Georgia Perimeter College; North Georgia College & State University; University of Georgia.

Student Life Upper grades have uniform requirement, student council, honor system. Discipline rests primarily with faculty.

Summer Programs Sports, art/fine arts, rigorous outdoor training programs offered; session focuses on preparation for school year competition; held on campus; accepts boys and girls; open to students from other schools. 130 students usually enrolled. 2009 schedule: June 1 to August 2.

Tuition and Aid Day student tuition: $5568. Guaranteed tuition plan. Tuition installment plan (monthly payment plans, individually arranged payment plans). Tuition reduction for siblings, need-based scholarship grants available. In 2008–09, 7% of upper-school students received aid. Total amount of financial aid awarded in 2008–09: $15,000.

Admissions For fall 2008, 11 students applied for upper-level admission, 7 were accepted, 7 enrolled. OLSAT, Stanford Achievement Test required. Deadline for receipt of application materials: February 1. Application fee required: $75. Interview required.

Athletics Interscholastic: baseball (boys), basketball (b,g), cheering (b,g), fitness (b,g), flag football (b,g), football (b), golf (b,g), power lifting (b,g), soccer (b,g), softball (g), strength & conditioning (b,g), tennis (b,g), weight lifting (b,g), weight training (b,g), wrestling (b,g); coed interscholastic: track and field; coed intramural: flag football. 6 PE instructors, 10 coaches.

Computers Computers are regularly used in all academic classes. Computer network features include on-campus library services, online commercial services, Internet access, wireless campus network, Internet filtering or blocking technology. Campus intranet is available to students. Students grades are available online. The school has a published electronic and media policy.

Contact Judy M. Nelson, Director of Admissions/Public and Alumni Relations. 706-468-8818 Ext. 19. Fax: 706-468-2409. E-mail: judy_nelson@piedmontacademy.com. Web site: www.piedmontacademy.com.

PINE CREST SCHOOL

1501 Northeast 62nd Street
Fort Lauderdale, Florida 33334-5116

Head of School: Dr. Lourdes Cowgill

General Information Coeducational day college-preparatory school. Grades PK–12. Founded: 1934. Setting: urban. 49-acre campus. 22 buildings on campus. Approved or accredited by Florida Council of Independent Schools, Southern Association of Colleges and Schools, and Southern Association of Independent Schools. Member of National Association of Independent Schools and Secondary School Admission Test Board. Endowment: $47 million. Total enrollment: 1,715. Upper school average class size: 17. Upper school faculty-student ratio: 1:9.

Upper School Student Profile Grade 9: 212 students (103 boys, 109 girls); Grade 10: 217 students (107 boys, 110 girls); Grade 11: 195 students (102 boys, 93 girls); Grade 12: 189 students (92 boys, 97 girls).

Faculty School total: 131. In upper school: 29 men, 45 women; 42 have advanced degrees.

Subjects Offered Algebra, American history, art, art history, ballet, band, biology, calculus, ceramics, chemistry, Chinese, chorus, comparative government and politics-AP, computer graphics, computer programming, computer science, dance, drama, economics, English, environmental science, ethics, European history, fine arts, forensics, French, geometry, German, government/civics, history, mathematics, music, orchestra, photography, physical education, physics, psychology, Spanish, speech, statistics.

Graduation Requirements Arts and fine arts (art, music, dance, drama), computer science, English, ethics, foreign language, mathematics, physical education (includes health), science, social studies (includes history), speech.

Special Academic Programs Advanced Placement exam preparation; honors section.

College Admission Counseling 173 students graduated in 2008; all went to college, including Florida State University; Northwestern University; University of Central Florida; University of Florida; University of Pennsylvania; Washington University in St. Louis. Mean SAT critical reading: 651, mean SAT math: 649, mean SAT writing: 661, mean composite ACT: 29.

Student Life Upper grades have uniform requirement, student council, honor system. Discipline rests primarily with faculty.

Summer Programs Enrichment, advancement, sports programs offered; session focuses on competitive swimming, summer camp (ages 5-11), summer school (grades 9-12); held on campus; accepts boys and girls; open to students from other schools. 300 students usually enrolled. 2009 schedule: June 1 to August 7. Application deadline: none.

Tuition and Aid Day student tuition: $20,600. Tuition installment plan (Key Tuition Payment Plan). Need-based scholarship grants available. In 2008–09, 16% of upper-school students received aid. Total amount of financial aid awarded in 2008–09: $1,628,697.

Admissions Traditional secondary-level entrance grade is 9. For fall 2008, 164 students applied for upper-level admission, 94 were accepted, 62 enrolled. SSAT required. Deadline for receipt of application materials: none. Application fee required: $100. Interview required.

Athletics Interscholastic: aquatics (boys, girls), baseball (b), basketball (b,g), crew (b,g), cross-country running (b,g), diving (b,g), fitness (b,g), flag football (b), football (b), golf (b,g), lacrosse (b,g), physical fitness (b,g), soccer (b,g), softball (g), strength & conditioning (b,g), swimming and diving (b,g), tennis (b,g), track and field (b,g), volleyball (b,g), weight lifting (b,g); intramural: aquatics (b,g), swimming and diving (b,g); coed interscholastic: ballet, cheering; coed intramural: ballet, physical training, strength & conditioning. 8 PE instructors, 1 athletic trainer.

Computers Computer network features include on-campus library services, Internet access, wireless campus network, laptop program (grades 6-12), SmartBoards in classrooms.

Contact Mrs. Elena Del Alamo, Vice President for Admission. 954-492-4103. Fax: 954-492-4188. E-mail: pcadmit@pinecrest.edu. Web site: www.pinecrest.edu.

PINEHURST SCHOOL

St. Catharines, Ontario, Canada
See Special Needs Schools section.

PINE RIDGE SCHOOL

Williston, Vermont
See Special Needs Schools section.

PINEWOOD PREPARATORY SCHOOL

1114 Orangeburg Road
Summerville, South Carolina 29483
Head of School: Dr. Glyn Cowlishaw

General Information Coeducational day college-preparatory school. Grades PS–12. Founded: 1952. Setting: suburban. 6 buildings on campus. Approved or accredited by South Carolina Independent School Association, Southern Association of Colleges and Schools, and South Carolina Department of Education. Upper school average class size: 14. Upper school faculty-student ratio: 1:11.
Faculty In upper school: 18 men, 22 women; 27 have advanced degrees.
Special Academic Programs Advanced Placement exam preparation; honors section; independent study; study at local college for college credit.
College Admission Counseling Colleges students went to include Clemson University; College of Charleston; Converse College; Limestone College; University of South Carolina.
Student Life Upper grades have specified standards of dress, student council, honor system.
Admissions No application fee required.
Athletics Interscholastic: aquatics (boys, girls), baseball (b), basketball (b,g), cheering (b,g), cross-country running (b,g), football (b,g), golf (b,g), tennis (b,g), volleyball (g); intramural: flag football (b).
Computers Computers are regularly used in all academic classes. Computer network features include on-campus library services, Internet access, wireless campus network, Internet filtering or blocking technology. Campus intranet and computer access in designated common areas are available to students. Students grades are available online.
Contact 843-873-1643. Fax: 843-821-4257. Web site: www.pinewoodprep.com/.

PINEWOOD—THE INTERNATIONAL SCHOOL OF THESSALONIKI, GREECE

PO Box 60606
Thermi
Thessaloniki 57001, Greece
Head of School: Dr. Peter Nanos

General Information Coeducational boarding and day college-preparatory, general academic, arts, bilingual studies, and technology school. Boarding grades 7–12, day grades PK–12. Founded: 1950. Setting: suburban. Students are housed in coed dormitories. 4-acre campus. 1 building on campus. Approved or accredited by International Baccalaureate Organization, Middle States Association of Colleges and Schools, The College Board, US Department of State, and state department of education. Member of European Council of International Schools. Language of instruction: English. Total enrollment: 188. Upper school average class size: 10. Upper school faculty-student ratio: 1:5.
Upper School Student Profile Grade 10: 22 students (10 boys, 12 girls); Grade 11: 17 students (10 boys, 7 girls); Grade 12: 5 students (5 boys). 10% of students are boarding students. International students from Bulgaria, Greece, Italy, Spain, United Kingdom, and United States; 28 other countries represented in student body.
Faculty School total: 35. In upper school: 7 men, 14 women; 11 have advanced degrees.
Subjects Offered Algebra, American history, art, biology, chemistry, computer applications, computer science, computers, economics, electives, English, English literature, ESL, European history, French, general science, geography, geometry, Greek, Greek culture, history, honors English, honors U.S. history, library, literature, math methods, mathematics, music, physical education, physical science, physics, pre-algebra, psychology, science, social science, social studies, U.S. history, world culture, world geography, world history, world literature, yearbook.
Graduation Requirements Electives, English, European history, foreign language, mathematics, physical education (includes health), science, social studies (includes history), world history.
Special Academic Programs International Baccalaureate program; accelerated programs; study at local college for college credit; ESL (30 students enrolled).
College Admission Counseling 14 students graduated in 2008; 8 went to college, including University of Maryland, College Park. Other: 2 went to work, 4 entered a postgraduate year.
Student Life Upper grades have student council, honor system. Discipline rests equally with students and faculty.
Tuition and Aid Day student tuition: €9990; 7-day tuition and room/board: €20,000. Tuition installment plan (monthly payment plans, individually arranged payment plans, 3-payment plan). Need-based scholarship grants available. In 2008–09, 5% of upper-school students received aid. Total amount of financial aid awarded in 2008–09: €3000.
Admissions For fall 2008, 12 students applied for upper-level admission, 12 were accepted, 12 enrolled. English entrance exam or English language required. Deadline for receipt of application materials: none. No application fee required. On-campus interview required.
Athletics Interscholastic: aerobics/dance (girls), baseball (b), basketball (b,g), dance (g), fitness (b,g), football (b), volleyball (b,g); intramural: basketball (b,g), cheering (g), football (b,g); coed interscholastic: baseball, football, gymnastics, indoor soccer, juggling; coed intramural: aerobics, baseball, gymnastics, juggling, softball. 2 PE instructors, 3 coaches, 2 athletic trainers.
Computers Computers are regularly used in English, science, word processing, yearbook classes. Computer resources include Internet access. The school has a published electronic and media policy.
Contact Mrs. Youli Andrianopoulou, Administrative Assistant to the Director/Office of Admissions. 30-2310-301221 Ext. 13. Fax: 30-2310-323196. E-mail: administration@pinewood.gr. Web site: www.pinewood.gr.

THE PINGRY SCHOOL

Martinsville Road
PO Box 366
Martinsville, New Jersey 08836
Head of School: Mr. Nathaniel Conard

General Information Coeducational day college-preparatory and arts school. Grades K–12. Founded: 1861. Setting: suburban. Nearest major city is New York, NY. 240-acre campus. 1 building on campus. Approved or accredited by Middle States Association of Colleges and Schools, New Jersey Association of Independent Schools, and New Jersey Department of Education. Member of National Association of Independent Schools. Endowment: $66 million. Total enrollment: 1,055. Upper school average class size: 14. Upper school faculty-student ratio: 1:8.
Upper School Student Profile Grade 9: 133 students (74 boys, 59 girls); Grade 10: 128 students (67 boys, 61 girls); Grade 11: 136 students (68 boys, 68 girls); Grade 12: 131 students (66 boys, 65 girls).
Faculty School total: 160. In upper school: 58 men, 37 women; 86 have advanced degrees.
Subjects Offered Algebra, American literature, analysis, analysis and differential calculus, anatomy, architecture, art, art history-AP, biology, biology-AP, brass choir, calculus, chemistry, chemistry-AP, clayworking, comparative cultures, computer science-AP, creative writing, drafting, drama, driver education, English, ethics, European literature, filmmaking, French, French-AP, geometry, German, German-AP, Greek drama, health, jazz band, jewelry making, Latin, literature by women, macro/microeconomics-AP, macroeconomics-AP, modern European history, music theory, mythology, orchestra, painting, peer counseling, photography, physics, physics-AP, physiology, psychology, psychology-AP, sculpture, Shakespeare, Spanish, Spanish-AP, studio art-AP, trigonometry, U.S. government-AP, U.S. history-AP, wind ensemble, world literature, yearbook.
Graduation Requirements Arts and fine arts (art, music, dance, drama), English, foreign language, mathematics, physical education (includes health), science, social studies (includes history). Community service is required.
Special Academic Programs Advanced Placement exam preparation; honors section; independent study; academic accommodation for the gifted.
College Admission Counseling 122 students graduated in 2008; 121 went to college, including Cornell University; Harvard University; Princeton University; University of Pennsylvania; Yale University. Other: 1 entered a postgraduate year.
Student Life Upper grades have specified standards of dress, student council, honor system. Discipline rests equally with students and faculty.
Summer Programs Enrichment programs offered; session focuses on enrichment, writing and study skills; held on campus; accepts boys and girls; open to students from other schools. 2009 schedule: June 22 to July 31.
Tuition and Aid Day student tuition: $22,950–$27,500. Tuition installment plan (Key Tuition Payment Plan, individually arranged payment plans). Need-based scholarship grants available. In 2008–09, 9% of upper-school students received aid. Total amount of financial aid awarded in 2008–09: $1,521,010.
Admissions Traditional secondary-level entrance grade is 9. For fall 2008, 263 students applied for upper-level admission, 85 were accepted, 56 enrolled. ERB, ISEE, SSAT or Wechsler Intelligence Scale for Children required. Deadline for receipt of application materials: January 9. Application fee required: $75. On-campus interview required.
Athletics Interscholastic: baseball (boys), basketball (b,g), cheering (g), cross-country running (b,g), fencing (b,g), field hockey (g), football (b), golf (b,g), ice hockey (b,g), lacrosse (b,g), skiing (downhill) (b,g), soccer (b,g), softball (g), swimming and diving (b,g), tennis (b,g), track and field (b,g), wrestling (b); coed interscholastic: dance, physical fitness, physical training, squash, water polo. 2 PE instructors, 15 coaches, 1 athletic trainer.
Computers Computers are regularly used in all academic classes. Computer network features include on-campus library services, online commercial services, Internet access, wireless campus network, Internet filtering or blocking technology. Campus intranet, student e-mail accounts, and computer access in designated common areas are available to students. The school has a published electronic and media policy.
Contact Ms. Reena Kamins, Director of Admission. 908-647-5555 Ext. 1228. Fax: 908-647-4395. E-mail: rkamins@pingry.org. Web site: www.pingry.org.

ANNOUNCEMENT FROM THE SCHOOL Since its founding in 1861 by Dr. John F. Pingry, the Pingry School has stood for excellence in teaching, high moral standards, and the development of integrity and character among its students. Pingry is a coeducational, college-preparatory, country day school that enrolls approximately 1,050 students from 101 communities in New Jersey. The

School serves its students through two campuses. Situated on 28 acres, the Short Hills campus (257 students in grades K–5) houses twenty-eight classrooms, three science labs, a computer lab, a newly renovated media center, a gym, and two music rooms. The 230-acre Martinsville campus (800 students in grades 6–12) houses classrooms; science laboratories; a 732-seat auditorium; a 60-seat attic theater; music practice rooms; three computer labs; a multimedia library; world-class athletic facilities that support thirty-three different sports at the varsity, junior varsity, and middle school levels; and a 41,000-square-foot Academic Arts Center. Pingry's Smith Middle School is approximately 29,000 square feet and includes eighteen classrooms, four science labs, and a central gathering area. The School, accredited by the Middle States Association, the New Jersey Association of Independent Schools, and the state of New Jersey, is nationally recognized for its outstanding academic program—a solid liberal arts curriculum enriched by extracurricular activities and athletics. Pingry offers eighteen Advanced Placement courses, and any student may sit for AP exams. Class size in all grades averages 16 students. Fifty-four percent of Pingry's 156 full- and part-time faculty members hold advanced degrees, with an average tenure of thirteen years at Pingry. The School strongly upholds the student-initiated Honor System from 1926, and encourages the students to give back to the community by requiring 10 hours of community service. In 11th grade, each student is assigned a college counselor to help with the college admission process. The counselors work closely with students to select the most appropriate institution for them. The top 7 schools that Pingry graduates currently attend are Georgetown, University of Pennsylvania, Cornell, Harvard, Yale, Boston College, and Princeton. Tuition ranges from $22,950 for kindergarten to $27,500 for grades 9–12.

PIONEER VALLEY CHRISTIAN SCHOOL

965 Plumtree Road
Springfield, Massachusetts 01119

Head of School: Mr. Timothy L. Duff

General Information Coeducational day college-preparatory, religious studies, bilingual studies, and technology school, affiliated with Protestant faith, Evangelical faith. Grades PS–12. Founded: 1972. Setting: suburban. 25-acre campus. 1 building on campus. Approved or accredited by Association of Christian Schools International, New England Association of Schools and Colleges, and Massachusetts Department of Education. Total enrollment: 320. Upper school average class size: 16. Upper school faculty-student ratio: 1:7.

Upper School Student Profile Grade 9: 36 students (16 boys, 20 girls); Grade 10: 23 students (11 boys, 12 girls); Grade 11: 35 students (16 boys, 19 girls); Grade 12: 36 students (20 boys, 16 girls). 95% of students are Protestant, members of Evangelical faith.

Faculty School total: 38. In upper school: 7 men, 12 women; 6 have advanced degrees.

Subjects Offered Advanced math, Advanced Placement courses, algebra, American literature, American literature-AP, art, athletics, band, baseball, basketball, Bible, Bible studies, biology, biology-AP, British literature, British literature-AP, calculus-AP, chemistry, choir, drama, economics, English, English-AP, French, geometry, government, history, instrumental music, jazz band, Middle Eastern history, music, music technology, physical education, physical science, physics, pre-algebra, sociology, softball, Spanish, speech, sports, technology, tennis, U.S. history, volleyball, Western civilization, wind instruments, yearbook.

Graduation Requirements Algebra, American literature, Bible, biology, British literature, computer applications, economics, English, foreign language, geometry, government, physical education (includes health), physical science, sociology, speech, U.S. history, Western civilization, Christian/community service hours.

Special Academic Programs Advanced Placement exam preparation; honors section; remedial reading and/or remedial writing; remedial math; programs in English, mathematics, general development for dyslexic students; special instructional classes for deaf students, students with learning disabilities, Attention Deficit Disorder, and dyslexia.

College Admission Counseling 30 students graduated in 2008; 29 went to college, including Boston University; Cedarville University; Holyoke Community College; Messiah College. Other: 1 went to work. Median SAT critical reading: 508, median SAT math: 473. 23% scored over 600 on SAT critical reading, 30% scored over 600 on SAT math.

Student Life Upper grades have uniform requirement, honor system. Discipline rests primarily with faculty. Attendance at religious services is required.

Tuition and Aid Day student tuition: $8500. Tuition installment plan (Electronic Funds Transfer, Weekly, biweekly, monthly). Need-based scholarship grants, need-based financial aid and scholarship available. In 2008–09, 54% of upper-school students received aid. Total amount of financial aid awarded in 2008–09: $94,018.

Admissions Traditional secondary-level entrance grade is 9. For fall 2008, 34 students applied for upper-level admission, 29 were accepted, 27 enrolled. Admissions testing required. Deadline for receipt of application materials: none. Application fee required: $100. Interview required.

Athletics Interscholastic: baseball (boys), basketball (b,g), softball (g), tennis (b,g), volleyball (g); intramural: soccer (b,g); coed interscholastic: soccer; coed intramural: combined training, golf, indoor soccer, physical training, soccer, strength & conditioning, winter soccer. 2 PE instructors, 10 coaches.

Computers Computers are regularly used in all academic classes. Computer network features include on-campus library services, Internet access, Internet filtering or blocking technology, homework assignments available online. Students grades are available online.

Contact Mr. Pat Sterlacci, Admissions Director. 413-782-8031. Fax: 413-782-8033. E-mail: psterlacci@pvcs.org. Web site: www.pvcs.org.

PIUS X HIGH SCHOOL

6000 A Street
Lincoln, Nebraska 68510

Head of School: Fr. James J. Meysenburg

General Information Coeducational day college-preparatory, general academic, and religious studies school, affiliated with Roman Catholic Church; primarily serves students with learning disabilities, individuals with Attention Deficit Disorder, and individuals with emotional and behavioral problems. Grades 9–12. Founded: 1956. Setting: urban. 30-acre campus. 1 building on campus. Approved or accredited by Academy of Orton-Gillingham Practitioners and Educators, North Central Association of Colleges and Schools, and Nebraska Department of Education. Endowment: $6.2 million. Total enrollment: 1,024. Upper school average class size: 26. Upper school faculty-student ratio: 1:14.

Upper School Student Profile Grade 9: 297 students (134 boys, 163 girls); Grade 10: 232 students (101 boys, 131 girls); Grade 11: 248 students (130 boys, 118 girls); Grade 12: 228 students (117 boys, 111 girls). 98% of students are Roman Catholic.

Faculty School total: 72. In upper school: 35 men, 37 women; 25 have advanced degrees.

Subjects Offered Accounting, acting, advanced chemistry, advanced computer applications, advanced math, algebra, American government, American government-AP, American literature, anatomy, applied arts, applied music, architectural drawing, art, art appreciation, art history, Bible studies, biology, biology-AP, British literature, business, business law, calculus, calculus-AP, carpentry, Catholic belief and practice, chemistry, chemistry-AP, choir, choral music, civics, comparative government and politics-AP, comparative religion, composition, computer applications, computer graphics, computer keyboarding, computer literacy, concert band, concert choir, drafting, drama, drawing, drawing and design, English, English composition, English literature, English literature-AP, family living, fitness, food and nutrition, French, general math, geography, government and politics-AP, government-AP, graphic design, health, history of music, history of the Catholic Church, human anatomy, industrial arts, instrumental music, integrated science, interior design, jazz band, journalism, literature-AP, marching band, marketing, mechanical drawing, moral theology, music appreciation, personal money management, photography, physical education, physical science, physics, physics-AP, play production, pre-algebra, pre-calculus, psychology, religion, small engine repair, social justice, Spanish, speech and debate, stage design, student publications, studio art, symphonic band, textiles, U.S. history, U.S. history-AP, vocal music, world geography, world history, yearbook.

Graduation Requirements Arts and fine arts (art, music, dance, drama), civics, computer literacy, electives, English, geography, mathematics, physical education (includes health), religion (includes Bible studies and theology), science, speech communications, U.S. history, world history, senior service requirement, all-school retreat attendance.

Special Academic Programs 8 Advanced Placement exams for which test preparation is offered; independent study; study at local college for college credit; remedial reading and/or remedial writing; remedial math.

College Admission Counseling 234 students graduated in 2008; 220 went to college, including Benedictine College; Creighton University; University of Nebraska–Lincoln; University of Nebraska at Kearney; University of Nebraska at Omaha; Wesleyan University. Other: 2 went to work, 5 entered military service, 7 entered a postgraduate year. Mean SAT critical reading: 600, mean SAT math: 613, mean SAT writing: 605, mean composite ACT: 24. 64% scored over 600 on SAT critical reading, 61% scored over 600 on SAT math, 54% scored over 600 on SAT writing, 31% scored over 26 on composite ACT.

Student Life Upper grades have uniform requirement, student council. Discipline rests primarily with faculty. Attendance at religious services is required.

Tuition and Aid Day student tuition: $1500. Guaranteed tuition plan. Tuition installment plan (monthly payment plans, individually arranged payment plans). Need-based scholarship grants available. In 2008–09, 5% of upper-school students received aid. Total amount of financial aid awarded in 2008–09: $10,000.

Admissions Traditional secondary-level entrance grade is 9. Deadline for receipt of application materials: none. Application fee required: $70.

Athletics Interscholastic: baseball (boys), basketball (b,g), cheering (g), cross-country running (b,g), dance team (g), drill team (g), football (b), golf (b,g), soccer (b,g), softball (g), swimming and diving (b,g), tennis (b,g), track and field (b,g), volleyball (g), wrestling (b); intramural: running (g); coed intramural: basketball, bowling, running. 4 PE instructors, 2 coaches.

Computers Computers are regularly used in accounting, business, business applications, business education, business skills, business studies, computer applications, creative writing, drafting, journalism, multimedia, Web site design, yearbook classes. Computer network features include on-campus library services, Internet access, wireless campus network, Internet filtering or blocking technology. Computer access in designated common areas is available to students. Students grades are available online. The school has a published electronic and media policy.

Contact Mrs. Jan Frayser, Director of Guidance. 402-488-0931. Fax: 402-488-1061. E-mail: jan.frayser@piusx.net. Web site: www.piusx.net.

POLY PREP COUNTRY DAY SCHOOL

9216 Seventh Avenue
Brooklyn, New York 11228

Head of School: Mr. David B. Harman

General Information Coeducational day college-preparatory school. Grades N–12. Founded: 1854. Setting: urban. 24-acre campus. 3 buildings on campus. Approved or accredited by Middle States Association of Colleges and Schools and New York State Association of Independent Schools. Member of National Association of Independent Schools and Secondary School Admission Test Board. Endowment: $19.5 million. Total enrollment: 1,010. Upper school average class size: 17. Upper school faculty-student ratio: 1:7.

Upper School Student Profile Grade 9: 120 students (62 boys, 58 girls); Grade 10: 120 students (69 boys, 51 girls); Grade 11: 123 students (67 boys, 56 girls); Grade 12: 118 students (58 boys, 60 girls).

Faculty School total: 143. In upper school: 34 men, 38 women; 68 have advanced degrees.

Subjects Offered 20th century world history, Advanced Placement courses, African American history, algebra, American history, American literature, art, art history, art history-AP, astronomy, bioethics, biology, biology-AP, biotechnology, calculus, calculus-AP, Caribbean history, ceramics, chemistry, chemistry-AP, choral music, classics, computer programming, computer programming-AP, computer science, computer-aided design, creative writing, DNA research, drama, drawing, earth science, ecology, economics, English, English language-AP, English literature-AP, environmental science, environmental studies, European history, European history-AP, film and literature, filmmaking, fine arts, forensic science, forensics, French, French language-AP, French literature-AP, geology, geometry, history, international relations, jazz band, Latin, Latin-AP, mathematics, music, music theory-AP, paleontology, philosophy, physical education, physics, physics-AP, politics, psychology, science, senior project, social studies, Spanish, Spanish language-AP, Spanish literature-AP, speech, theater, theater arts, trigonometry, U.S. history-AP, world history, world history-AP, writing.

Graduation Requirements Arts and fine arts (art, music, dance, drama), English, foreign language, history, mathematics, music, physical education (includes health), science, speech, senior thesis with oral presentation. Community service is required.

Special Academic Programs 16 Advanced Placement exams for which test preparation is offered; honors section; independent study; term-away projects; academic accommodation for the gifted and the artistically talented.

College Admission Counseling 109 students graduated in 2008; 108 went to college, including Amherst College; Boston University; Franklin & Marshall College; New York University; Rutgers, The State University of New Jersey, Newark; The Catholic University of America. Other: 1 entered a postgraduate year.

Student Life Upper grades have specified standards of dress, student council, honor system. Discipline rests equally with students and faculty.

Summer Programs Remediation, enrichment, advancement, sports, art/fine arts, computer instruction programs offered; session focuses on recreational and sports camps and some academic programs; held on campus; accepts boys and girls; open to students from other schools. 700 students usually enrolled. 2009 schedule: June 15 to August 28. Application deadline: June 1.

Tuition and Aid Day student tuition: $8525–$29,075. Tuition installment plan (Academic Management Services Plan). Merit scholarship grants, need-based scholarship grants available. In 2008–09, 26% of upper-school students received aid. Total amount of financial aid awarded in 2008–09: $4,600,000.

Admissions Traditional secondary-level entrance grade is 9. ERB, ISEE or SSAT required. Deadline for receipt of application materials: December 1. Application fee required: $50. On-campus interview required.

Athletics Interscholastic: baseball (boys), basketball (b,g), cross-country running (b,g), football (b), lacrosse (b,g), soccer (b,g), softball (g), squash (b,g), swimming and diving (b,g), tennis (b,g), track and field (b,g), volleyball (g), winter (indoor) track (b,g), wrestling (b); coed interscholastic: golf; coed intramural: ballet, cheering, dance, dance team, fitness, Frisbee, outdoor adventure, physical fitness, physical training, strength & conditioning, ultimate Frisbee, weight training, yoga. 12 PE instructors, 24 coaches, 1 athletic trainer.

Computers Computers are regularly used in all academic, publications, yearbook classes. Computer network features include on-campus library services, Internet access, wireless campus network, Internet filtering or blocking technology. Campus intranet, student e-mail accounts, and computer access in designated common areas are available to students. The school has a published electronic and media policy.

Contact Ms. Lori W. Redell, Assistant Head for Admissions and Financial Aid. 718-663-6060. Fax: 718-238-3393. E-mail: polyadmissions@polyprep.org. Web site: www.polyprep.org.

POLYTECHNIC SCHOOL

1030 East California Boulevard
Pasadena, California 91106-4099

Head of School: Mrs. Deborah E. Reed

General Information Coeducational day college-preparatory school. Grades K–12. Founded: 1907. Setting: suburban. 15-acre campus. 7 buildings on campus. Approved or accredited by California Association of Independent Schools, The College Board, Western Association of Schools and Colleges, and California Department of Education. Member of National Association of Independent Schools. Endowment: $48.3 million. Total enrollment: 857. Upper school average class size: 17. Upper school faculty-student ratio: 1:17.

Upper School Student Profile Grade 9: 94 students (49 boys, 45 girls); Grade 10: 92 students (46 boys, 46 girls); Grade 11: 93 students (47 boys, 46 girls); Grade 12: 97 students (54 boys, 43 girls).

Faculty School total: 99. In upper school: 12 men, 25 women; 28 have advanced degrees.

Subjects Offered Acting, algebra, American history, American history-AP, analytic geometry, art history, athletics, audio visual/media, Basic programming, batik, biology, biology-AP, calculus, calculus-AP, ceramics, chamber groups, chemistry, chemistry-AP, choral music, communications, computer art, computer science, constitutional law, data analysis, drama, drama performance, drawing, East Asian history, economics, English, English language and composition-AP, English literature and composition-AP, ensembles, ethics, filmmaking, French, French literature-AP, functions, geometry, guitar, improvisation, jazz dance, jazz ensemble, Latin, Latin-AP, madrigals, math analysis, mathematical modeling, music history, music theory, musical productions, musical theater, orchestra, painting, photography, physical science, physics, physics-AP, Roman civilization, sculpture, silk screening, society, Spanish, Spanish literature-AP, statistics, tap dance, technical theater, theater, theater design and production, theater history, trigonometry, U.S. government and politics, U.S. history-AP, Vietnam War, visual arts, Western civilization, woodworking, world cultures, world religions.

Special Academic Programs Honors section; independent study; study abroad.

College Admission Counseling 87 students graduated in 2008; all went to college, including Duke University; New York University; Northwestern University; Princeton University; Stanford University; University of Southern California.

Student Life Upper grades have specified standards of dress, student council, honor system. Discipline rests equally with students and faculty.

Tuition and Aid Day student tuition: $25,225. Tuition installment plan (monthly payment plans). Need-based scholarship grants available. In 2008–09, 20% of upper-school students received aid. Total amount of financial aid awarded in 2008–09: $2,800,000.

Admissions Traditional secondary-level entrance grade is 9. For fall 2008, 177 students applied for upper-level admission, 26 enrolled. ISEE required. Deadline for receipt of application materials: January 9. Application fee required: $100. On-campus interview required.

Athletics Interscholastic: baseball (boys), basketball (b,g), cheering (g), cross-country running (b,g), diving (b,g), equestrian sports (g), football (b), golf (b,g), soccer (b,g), softball (g), swimming and diving (b,g), tennis (b,g), track and field (b,g), volleyball (b,g), water polo (b,g); coed interscholastic: badminton. 6 PE instructors, 19 coaches, 1 athletic trainer.

Computers Computers are regularly used in all classes. Computer network features include on-campus library services, Internet access.

Contact Ms. Sally Jeanne McKenna, Director of Admissions. 626-792-2147. Fax: 626-449-5727. E-mail: sjmckenna@polytechnic.org. Web site: www.polytechnic.org.

POMFRET SCHOOL

PO Box 128
398 Pomfret Street
Pomfret, Connecticut 06258-0128

Head of School: Mr. Bradford Hastings

General Information Coeducational boarding and day college-preparatory, arts, religious studies, and technology school, affiliated with Episcopal Church. Grades 9–PG. Founded: 1894. Setting: rural. Nearest major city is Hartford. Students are housed in single-sex dormitories. 500-acre campus. 62 buildings on campus. Approved or accredited by Connecticut Association of Independent Schools, New England Association of Schools and Colleges, The Association of Boarding Schools, and Connecticut Department of Education. Member of National Association of Independent Schools and Secondary School Admission Test Board. Endowment: $40 million. Total enrollment: 355. Upper school average class size: 11. Upper school faculty-student ratio: 1:6.

Upper School Student Profile Grade 9: 52 students (21 boys, 31 girls); Grade 10: 102 students (56 boys, 46 girls); Grade 11: 98 students (45 boys, 53 girls); Grade 12: 82 students (44 boys, 38 girls); Postgraduate: 12 students (9 boys, 3 girls). 80% of students are boarding students. 35% are state residents. 25 states are represented in upper school student body. 12% are international students. International students from Bermuda, Canada, Germany, and Republic of Korea; 5 other countries represented in student body. 22% of students are members of Episcopal Church.

Faculty School total: 74. In upper school: 43 men, 31 women; 40 have advanced degrees; 58 reside on campus.

Subjects Offered Advanced Placement courses, algebra, American history, American literature, anatomy, art, art history, astronomy, biology, botany, calculus, ceramics, chemistry, computer programming, computer science, creative writing, drama, driver education, earth science, ecology, economics, English, English literature, environmental science, ethics, European history, expository writing, fine arts, French, geometry, government/civics, history, Latin, marine biology, mathematics, music, photography, physics, psychology, religion, science, social studies, Spanish, statistics, theater, trigonometry, world history, writing.
Graduation Requirements Arts and fine arts (art, music, dance, drama), computer science, English, foreign language, mathematics, religion (includes Bible studies and theology), science, social studies (includes history).
Special Academic Programs Advanced Placement exam preparation; honors section; independent study; academic accommodation for the gifted, the musically talented, and the artistically talented.
College Admission Counseling 94 students graduated in 2008; all went to college, including Boston College; Colby College; Franklin & Marshall College; Hamilton College; Trinity College; Wesleyan University. Median SAT critical reading: 600, median SAT math: 600, median SAT writing: 610, median combined SAT: 1820, median composite ACT: 25. 55% scored over 600 on SAT critical reading, 59% scored over 600 on SAT math, 63% scored over 600 on SAT writing, 57% scored over 1800 on combined SAT, 35% scored over 26 on composite ACT.
Student Life Upper grades have specified standards of dress, student council. Discipline rests equally with students and faculty. Attendance at religious services is required.
Summer Programs Art/fine arts programs offered; session focuses on creative writing; held on campus; accepts boys and girls; open to students from other schools. 2009 schedule: June 24 to July 2. Application deadline: June 1.
Tuition and Aid Day student tuition: $26,750; 7-day tuition and room/board: $42,900. Guaranteed tuition plan. Tuition installment plan (The Tuition Plan, Insured Tuition Payment Plan, Academic Management Services Plan, monthly payment plans). Need-based scholarship grants available. In 2008–09, 33% of upper-school students received aid. Total amount of financial aid awarded in 2008–09: $2,751,000.
Admissions Traditional secondary-level entrance grade is 9. For fall 2008, 772 students applied for upper-level admission, 389 were accepted, 125 enrolled. SSAT and TOEFL required. Deadline for receipt of application materials: January 15. Application fee required: $50. On-campus interview required.
Athletics Interscholastic: baseball (boys), basketball (b,g), crew (b,g), cross-country running (b,g), field hockey (g), football (b), golf (b,g), hockey (b,g), horseback riding (b,g), ice hockey (b,g), lacrosse (b,g), soccer (b,g), softball (g), squash (b,g), tennis (b,g); coed interscholastic: outdoor adventure, wrestling; coed intramural: aerobics, aerobics/dance, alpine skiing, backpacking, dance, dance team, hiking/backpacking, mountaineering, skiing (cross-country), skiing (downhill), snowboarding, weight training, wilderness, yoga. 1 coach, 1 athletic trainer.
Computers Computers are regularly used in aerospace science, foreign language, history, mathematics, science classes. Computer network features include on-campus library services, Internet access, wireless campus network, Internet filtering or blocking technology. Campus intranet, student e-mail accounts, and computer access in designated common areas are available to students. Students grades are available online.
Contact Mr. Erik Bertelsen, Assistant Head for Enrollment. 860-963-6121. Fax: 860-963-2042. E-mail: bertelse@pomfretschool.org. Web site: www.pomfretschool.org.

ANNOUNCEMENT FROM THE SCHOOL In 2007–08, students worked with visiting Schwartz Fellow Carole Simpson, an Emmy Award-winning senior correspondent for ABC News and former anchor for "World News Tonight Sunday." Over the March break, there were over five school-led trips, including a tour of Japan by the Pomfret chorus, a community service trip to Tanzania, and a language trip to Spain, and several athletic teams traveled to warmer climates to prepare for their upcoming seasons. Pomfret's new athletic and student center, ice rink, tennis center, and boathouse are open for students and families to enjoy, and many dorms have been newly renovated.

See Close-Up on page 908.

POPE JOHN XXIII REGIONAL HIGH SCHOOL

28 Andover Road
Sparta, New Jersey 07871

Head of School: Rev. Msgr. Kieran McHugh

General Information Coeducational day college-preparatory, arts, business, religious studies, and technology school, affiliated with Roman Catholic Church. Grades 9–12. Founded: 1956. Setting: suburban. Nearest major city is New York, NY. 15-acre campus. 3 buildings on campus. Approved or accredited by Department of Defense Dependents Schools, Middle States Association of Colleges and Schools, and New Jersey Department of Education. Total enrollment: 965. Upper school average class size: 20. Upper school faculty-student ratio: 1:13.
Upper School Student Profile Grade 9: 278 students (148 boys, 130 girls); Grade 10: 246 students (132 boys, 114 girls); Grade 11: 204 students (109 boys, 95 girls); Grade 12: 239 students (124 boys, 115 girls). 82% of students are Roman Catholic.
Faculty School total: 75. In upper school: 31 men, 44 women.
Subjects Offered Advanced chemistry, advanced computer applications, advanced math, Advanced Placement courses, algebra, American literature, American studies, anatomy and physiology, art, biology, biology-AP, British literature, business, business law, calculus, calculus-AP, chemistry, chemistry-AP, choral music, computer literacy, computer science, computer science-AP, conceptual physics, concert choir, earth science, economics, English, English language-AP, English literature, English literature and composition-AP, environmental science, environmental science-AP, European history-AP, fine arts, French, French-AP, geometry, German, global issues, government and politics-AP, graphic arts, health and safety, history-AP, honors algebra, honors English, honors geometry, honors U.S. history, honors world history, Italian, Japanese, jazz band, journalism, lab science, Latin, macroeconomics-AP, microeconomics-AP, modern politics, music theory, physical education, physics, physics-AP, pre-calculus, psychology, public speaking, reading/study skills, Spanish, Spanish language-AP, statistics, theater arts, theology, U.S. government, U.S. government and politics-AP, U.S. history, U.S. history-AP, world cultures, world history-AP, writing skills, zoology.
Graduation Requirements Arts and fine arts (art, music, dance, drama), English, foreign language, health and safety, mathematics, science, social studies (includes history), theology, 60 hours of community service (15 hours per year).
Special Academic Programs Honors section; ESL.
College Admission Counseling 205 students graduated in 2008; 199 went to college, including Fordham University; Penn State University Park; Rutgers, The State University of New Jersey, New Brunswick; The Catholic University of America; The University of Scranton; Villanova University. Other: 1 entered military service, 5 entered a postgraduate year. Mean SAT critical reading: 544, mean SAT math: 555, mean SAT writing: 541, mean combined SAT: 1640.
Student Life Upper grades have uniform requirement, student council. Discipline rests primarily with faculty. Attendance at religious services is required.
Summer Programs Remediation, enrichment, sports programs offered; session focuses on sports; held on campus; accepts boys and girls; open to students from other schools. 200 students usually enrolled.
Tuition and Aid Day student tuition: $11,000. Guaranteed tuition plan. Tuition installment plan (FACTS Tuition Payment Plan). Need-based scholarship grants available.
Admissions Traditional secondary-level entrance grade is 9. CTB/McGraw-Hill/Macmillan Co-op Test, Math Placement Exam, placement test and writing sample required. Deadline for receipt of application materials: none. No application fee required.
Athletics Interscholastic: baseball (boys), basketball (b,g), cheering (g), field hockey (g), football (b), ice hockey (b), indoor track & field (b,g), lacrosse (b,g), skiing (downhill) (b,g), softball (g), swimming and diving (b,g), tennis (b,g), track and field (b,g), volleyball (g), winter (indoor) track (b,g), wrestling (b); coed interscholastic: golf.
Computers Computers are regularly used in graphic arts, programming classes. Computer network features include Internet access, Internet filtering or blocking technology. The school has a published electronic and media policy.
Contact Mrs. Anne Kaiser, Administrative Assistant for Admissions. 973-729-6125 Ext. 255. Fax: 973-729-4536. E-mail: annekaiser@popejohn.org. Web site: www.popejohn.org.

PORTER-GAUD SCHOOL

300 Albemarle Road
Charleston, South Carolina 29407

Head of School: Dr. Christian Jennings Proctor

General Information Coeducational day college-preparatory, arts, bilingual studies, and technology school, affiliated with Christian faith, Episcopal Church. Grades 1–12. Founded: 1867. Setting: suburban. 80-acre campus. 13 buildings on campus. Approved or accredited by National Association of Episcopal Schools, South Carolina Independent School Association, Southern Association of Colleges and Schools, Southern Association of Independent Schools, and South Carolina Department of Education. Member of National Association of Independent Schools. Endowment: $7 million. Total enrollment: 921. Upper school average class size: 12. Upper school faculty-student ratio: 1:12.
Upper School Student Profile Grade 9: 80 students (55 boys, 25 girls); Grade 10: 95 students (55 boys, 40 girls); Grade 11: 85 students (48 boys, 37 girls); Grade 12: 66 students (47 boys, 19 girls). 90% of students are Christian, members of Episcopal Church.
Faculty School total: 100. In upper school: 15 men, 25 women; 30 have advanced degrees.
Subjects Offered Advanced Placement courses, algebra, American history, American literature, art, art history, biology, calculus, chemistry, computer programming, computer science, drama, economics, English, English literature, ethics, European history, expository writing, fine arts, French, geometry, government/civics, health, Latin, modern European history-AP, music, music appreciation, physical education, physics, Spanish, world history, world literature.
Graduation Requirements Algebra, American history, American literature, art education, arts and fine arts (art, music, dance, drama), biology, calculus, chemistry, computer science, English, English composition, English literature, European history,

foreign language, geometry, physical education (includes health), physics, pre-calculus, religion (includes Bible studies and theology), trigonometry, world history.
Special Academic Programs 13 Advanced Placement exams for which test preparation is offered; honors section; independent study; ESL (2 students enrolled).
College Admission Counseling 81 students graduated in 2008; 79 went to college, including Clemson University; Duke University; University of Georgia; University of South Carolina; Washington and Lee University. Other: 2 entered a postgraduate year. Median SAT critical reading: 630, median SAT math: 620, median SAT writing: 640, median combined SAT: 1890. Mean composite ACT: 26. 72% scored over 600 on SAT critical reading, 69% scored over 600 on SAT math, 73% scored over 600 on SAT writing, 71% scored over 1800 on combined SAT, 57% scored over 26 on composite ACT.
Student Life Upper grades have uniform requirement, student council, honor system. Discipline rests equally with students and faculty. Attendance at religious services is required.
Tuition and Aid Day student tuition: $17,050. Tuition installment plan (monthly payment plans, individually arranged payment plans, 2-payment plan). Need-based scholarship grants available. In 2008–09, 10% of upper-school students received aid. Total amount of financial aid awarded in 2008–09: $900,000.
Admissions Traditional secondary-level entrance grade is 9. For fall 2008, 45 students applied for upper-level admission, 34 were accepted, 32 enrolled. ISEE required. Deadline for receipt of application materials: none. Application fee required: $75. On-campus interview recommended.
Athletics Interscholastic: aerobics (girls), baseball (b,g), basketball (b,g), field hockey (g), football (b), ice hockey (b), physical training (b,g), soccer (b,g), swimming and diving (b,g), tennis (b,g), track and field (b,g), volleyball (g), weight lifting (b), weight training (b), yoga (g); intramural: basketball (b,g), Frisbee (b,g), lacrosse (b), paddling (b), strength & conditioning (b,g), volleyball (b,g); coed interscholastic: aerobics/Nautilus, cheering, cross-country running, golf, Nautilus, sailing, strength & conditioning; coed intramural: Frisbee. 4 PE instructors, 8 coaches, 1 athletic trainer.
Computers Computers are regularly used in English, foreign language, history, mathematics, music, science, video film production, yearbook classes. Computer network features include on-campus library services, Internet access, wireless campus network, Internet filtering or blocking technology. Student e-mail accounts and computer access in designated common areas are available to students. Students grades are available online. The school has a published electronic and media policy.
Contact Mrs. Eleanor W. Hurtes, Director of Admissions. 843-402-4775. Fax: 843-556-7404. E-mail: eleanor.hurtes@portergaud.edu. Web site: www.portergaud.edu.

PORTLAND LUTHERAN SCHOOL

740 Southeast 182nd Avenue
Portland, Oregon 97233-4960

Head of School: Mr. Donn Maier

General Information Coeducational boarding and day college-preparatory and religious studies school, affiliated with Lutheran Church. Boarding grades 9–12, day grades PK–12. Founded: 1905. Setting: urban. Students are housed in homes of school families (international students). 15-acre campus. 5 buildings on campus. Approved or accredited by National Lutheran School Accreditation, Northwest Association of Schools and Colleges, and Oregon Department of Education. Endowment: $402,943. Total enrollment: 240. Upper school average class size: 16. Upper school faculty-student ratio: 1:15.
Upper School Student Profile Grade 9: 20 students (12 boys, 8 girls); Grade 10: 24 students (12 boys, 12 girls); Grade 11: 13 students (6 boys, 7 girls); Grade 12: 23 students (17 boys, 6 girls). 35% of students are boarding students. 65% are state residents. 2 states are represented in upper school student body. 35% are international students. International students from Germany, Hong Kong, Japan, Republic of Korea, Taiwan, and Viet Nam; 2 other countries represented in student body. 25% of students are Lutheran.
Faculty School total: 22. In upper school: 5 men, 6 women; 7 have advanced degrees.
Subjects Offered Advanced computer applications, Advanced Placement courses, algebra, American culture, American government, American history, art, astronomy, band, Bible studies, biology, British literature-AP, calculus, chemistry, choir, Christian ethics, college planning, computer applications, computer programming, drama performance, earth science, economics, English, English literature, ESL, expository writing, finite math, geology, geometry, government/civics, health, integrated science, keyboarding/computer, New Testament, physical education, physics, pre-algebra, pre-calculus, psychology, religion, Spanish, statistics and probability, student publications, studio art, trigonometry, weight training, world geography, world history, world literature.
Graduation Requirements American government, arts and fine arts (art, music, dance, drama), Bible studies, career education, Christian studies, college counseling, composition, computer applications, computer keyboarding, economics, English, foreign language, lab science, language, mathematics, physical education (includes health), political science, religion (includes Bible studies and theology), science, speech, U.S. history, world civilizations, world history. Community service is required.
Special Academic Programs 2 Advanced Placement exams for which test preparation is offered; honors section; independent study; study at local college for college credit; ESL (20 students enrolled).
College Admission Counseling 26 students graduated in 2008; 25 went to college, including Concordia University; Mt. Hood Community College; Oregon State University; Portland State University; University of Oregon; University of Portland. Other: 1 entered military service. Median SAT critical reading: 480, median SAT math: 600, median SAT writing: 485, median combined SAT: 1497. 29% scored over 600 on SAT critical reading, 50% scored over 600 on SAT math, 7% scored over 600 on SAT writing, 7% scored over 1800 on combined SAT.
Student Life Upper grades have specified standards of dress, student council, honor system. Discipline rests primarily with faculty. Attendance at religious services is required.
Tuition and Aid Day student tuition: $8115; 7-day tuition and room/board: $13,550. Tuition installment plan (monthly payment plans, individually arranged payment plans, quarterly, semiannual, and annual payment plans, Simply Giving). Tuition reduction for siblings, merit scholarship grants, need-based scholarship grants, tuition reduction for members of association congregations available. In 2008–09, 35% of upper-school students received aid; total upper-school merit-scholarship money awarded: $15,000. Total amount of financial aid awarded in 2008–09: $35,260.
Admissions Traditional secondary-level entrance grade is 9. For fall 2008, 30 students applied for upper-level admission, 30 were accepted, 30 enrolled. Any standardized test or High School Placement Test required. Deadline for receipt of application materials: none. No application fee required. On-campus interview required.
Athletics Interscholastic: aerobics/dance (girls), baseball (b), basketball (b,g), cheering (b,g), cross-country running (b,g), football (b), soccer (b), track and field (b,g), volleyball (g); intramural: badminton (b,g), basketball (b,g), flag football (b,g), volleyball (b,g); coed interscholastic: aerobics/dance, dance team, golf, soccer; coed intramural: badminton, basketball, skiing (downhill), speedball, team handball, ultimate Frisbee, volleyball. 2 PE instructors, 6 coaches.
Computers Computers are regularly used in data processing, foreign language, information technology, introduction to technology, keyboarding, programming, publications, publishing, science, technology, typing, Web site design, word processing, yearbook classes. Computer network features include on-campus library services, online commercial services, Internet access, wireless campus network, Internet filtering or blocking technology. Students grades are available online. The school has a published electronic and media policy.
Contact Ms. Pam Merritt, Admissions Officer. 503-667-3199 Ext. 354. Fax: 503-667-4520. E-mail: pmerritt@portland-lutheran.org. Web site: www.portland-lutheran.org.

PORTLEDGE SCHOOL

355 Duck Pond Road
Locust Valley, New York 11560

Head of School: Steven L. Hahn

General Information Coeducational day college-preparatory school. Grades N–12. Founded: 1965. Setting: suburban. Nearest major city is New York. 62-acre campus. 4 buildings on campus. Approved or accredited by New York State Association of Independent Schools and New York State Board of Regents. Member of National Association of Independent Schools and Secondary School Admission Test Board. Endowment: $1.5 million. Total enrollment: 407. Upper school average class size: 12. Upper school faculty-student ratio: 1:6.
Upper School Student Profile Grade 9: 44 students (27 boys, 17 girls); Grade 10: 51 students (29 boys, 22 girls); Grade 11: 42 students (19 boys, 23 girls); Grade 12: 35 students (21 boys, 14 girls).
Faculty School total: 78. In upper school: 16 men, 22 women; 23 have advanced degrees.
Subjects Offered 3-dimensional art, advanced biology, advanced chemistry, advanced computer applications, advanced math, Advanced Placement courses, advanced studio art-AP, algebra, American history, American history-AP, American literature, American literature-AP, ancient history, architectural drawing, architecture, art, art appreciation, art history, art-AP, Basic programming, biology, calculus, calculus-AP, ceramics, chemistry, chemistry-AP, chorus, community service, computer programming, computer science, computers, creative writing, digital music, drama, drama workshop, driver education, earth science, economics, English, English language-AP, English literature, English literature-AP, environmental science, European history, expository writing, fine arts, foreign language, French, French-AP, geography, geometry, government/civics, grammar, graphic design, health, health education, history, honors algebra, honors English, honors geometry, honors U.S. history, independent study, instrumental music, jazz ensemble, journalism, keyboarding, mathematics, music, Native American history, photography, physical education, physics, psychology, public policy, public service, public speaking, science, senior project, social science, social studies, Spanish, Spanish-AP, theater, trigonometry, U.S. history-AP, world history.
Graduation Requirements Arts and fine arts (art, music, dance, drama), computer science, English, foreign language, mathematics, performing arts, physical education (includes health), public speaking, science, senior project, social science, social studies (includes history). Community service is required.
Special Academic Programs Advanced Placement exam preparation; honors section; independent study; academic accommodation for the gifted, the musically talented, and the artistically talented.

College Admission Counseling 37 students graduated in 2008; 36 went to college. Other: 1 had other specific plans. Median SAT critical reading: 590, median SAT math: 600, median SAT writing: 610. 55% scored over 600 on SAT critical reading, 60% scored over 600 on SAT math, 60% scored over 600 on SAT writing.
Student Life Upper grades have specified standards of dress, student council, honor system. Discipline rests primarily with faculty.
Summer Programs Enrichment, sports, art/fine arts, computer instruction programs offered; session focuses on chess, computers, tennis, field hockey, lacrosse, soccer; held on campus; accepts boys and girls; open to students from other schools. 300 students usually enrolled. 2009 schedule: June 30 to August 22.
Tuition and Aid Day student tuition: $28,600. Tuition installment plan (Tuition Management Systems). Tuition reduction for siblings, need-based scholarship grants available. In 2008–09, 29% of upper-school students received aid. Total amount of financial aid awarded in 2008–09: $903,500.
Admissions Traditional secondary-level entrance grade is 9. For fall 2008, 168 students applied for upper-level admission, 120 were accepted, 72 enrolled. SSAT required. Deadline for receipt of application materials: February 10. Application fee required: $75. On-campus interview required.
Athletics Interscholastic: baseball (boys), basketball (b,g), fencing (b,g), ice hockey (b,g), lacrosse (b,g), soccer (b,g), softball (g), tennis (b,g); intramural: tennis (g); coed interscholastic: cross-country running, golf, squash. 3 PE instructors, 2 coaches.
Computers Computers are regularly used in art, English, foreign language, history, mathematics, music, science classes. Computer network features include on-campus library services, online commercial services, Internet access, wireless campus network, Internet filtering or blocking technology. Computer access in designated common areas is available to students. The school has a published electronic and media policy.
Contact Susan Simon, Director of Admissions. 516-750-3203. Fax: 516-674-7063. E-mail: ssimon@portledge.org. Web site: www.portledge.org.

PORTSMOUTH ABBEY SCHOOL

285 Cory's Lane
Portsmouth, Rhode Island 02871

Head of School: Dr. James De Vecchi

General Information Coeducational boarding and day college-preparatory, arts, religious studies, and Music, Classics, Humanities school, affiliated with Roman Catholic Church. Grades 9–12. Founded: 1926. Setting: small town. Nearest major city is Providence. Students are housed in single-sex dormitories. 500-acre campus. 36 buildings on campus. Approved or accredited by Association of Independent Schools in New England, New England Association of Schools and Colleges, and The Association of Boarding Schools. Member of National Association of Independent Schools and Secondary School Admission Test Board. Endowment: $32 million. Total enrollment: 340. Upper school average class size: 13. Upper school faculty-student ratio: 1:7.
Upper School Student Profile Grade 9: 66 students (34 boys, 32 girls); Grade 10: 85 students (38 boys, 47 girls); Grade 11: 106 students (61 boys, 45 girls); Grade 12: 83 students (43 boys, 40 girls). 70% of students are boarding students. 55% are state residents. 24 states are represented in upper school student body. 11% are international students. International students from Canada, Dominican Republic, Germany, Guatemala, Republic of Korea, and Spain; 11 other countries represented in student body. 62% of students are Roman Catholic.
Faculty School total: 52. In upper school: 30 men, 22 women; 50 have advanced degrees; 34 reside on campus.
Subjects Offered Algebra, American literature, art, art history, art history-AP, art-AP, biology, biology-AP, calculus, calculus-AP, chemistry, chemistry-AP, Christian doctrine, Christian ethics, church history, computer programming, computer programming-AP, computer science, computer science-AP, drama, economics, English, English language and composition-AP, English literature, English literature and composition-AP, ethics, European history, European history-AP, fine arts, French, French language-AP, French literature-AP, geometry, government/civics, Greek, health, history, history-AP, humanities, international relations, Latin, Latin-AP, Mandarin, marine biology, mathematics, mathematics-AP, modern European history, modern European history-AP, music, music appreciation, music composition, music history, music theory, music theory-AP, philosophy, photography, physical education, physics, physics-AP, physiology, political science, religion, science, social science, Spanish, Spanish language-AP, Spanish literature-AP, statistics and probability, statistics-AP, studio art-AP, theater, theology, trigonometry, U.S. history, U.S. history-AP, world history, writing workshop.
Graduation Requirements Arts and fine arts (art, music, dance, drama), English, foreign language, history, Latin, mathematics, religion (includes Bible studies and theology), science, Humanities.
Special Academic Programs Advanced Placement exam preparation; honors section; independent study; academic accommodation for the gifted.
College Admission Counseling 95 students graduated in 2008; 90 went to college, including Boston College; Fordham University; Northeastern University; The Catholic University of America; The George Washington University; United States Military Academy. Other: 5 entered military service. Median SAT critical reading: 600, median SAT math: 590, median SAT writing: 600, median combined SAT: 1830.
Student Life Upper grades have specified standards of dress, student council, honor system. Discipline rests primarily with faculty. Attendance at religious services is required.
Summer Programs Enrichment, advancement programs offered; held on campus; accepts boys and girls; open to students from other schools. 80 students usually enrolled. 2009 schedule: June 29 to July 24. Application deadline: none.
Tuition and Aid Day student tuition: $28,150; 7-day tuition and room/board: $41,150. Tuition installment plan (monthly payment plans, individually arranged payment plans, Tuition Management Systems Plan). Merit scholarship grants, need-based scholarship grants available. In 2008–09, 37% of upper-school students received aid; total upper-school merit-scholarship money awarded: $2,500,000. Total amount of financial aid awarded in 2008–09: $2,500,000.
Admissions Traditional secondary-level entrance grade is 9. For fall 2008, 331 students applied for upper-level admission, 208 were accepted, 122 enrolled. PSAT or SAT for applicants to grade 11 and 12, SSAT and SSAT or WISC III required. Deadline for receipt of application materials: January 31. Application fee required: $50. Interview required.
Athletics Interscholastic: baseball (boys), basketball (b,g), cross-country running (b,g), field hockey (g), football (b), golf (b,g), ice hockey (b,g), lacrosse (b,g), soccer (b,g), softball (g), squash (b,g), swimming and diving (b,g), track and field (b,g); coed interscholastic: cross-country running, sailing, tennis, track and field, weight training; coed intramural: ballet, dance, equestrian sports, fitness, horseback riding, modern dance. 2 athletic trainers.
Computers Computers are regularly used in science classes. Computer network features include on-campus library services, Internet access, wireless campus network. Student e-mail accounts are available to students.
Contact Mrs. Ann Motta, Admissions Coordinator. 401-643-1248. Fax: 401-643-1355. E-mail: admissions@portsmouthabbey.org. Web site: www.portsmouthabbey.org.

See Close-Up on page 910.

PORTSMOUTH CHRISTIAN ACADEMY

20 Seaborne Drive
Dover, New Hampshire 03820

Head of School: Mr. Brian Bell

General Information Coeducational day college-preparatory, arts, religious studies, science/mathematics, and communication school, affiliated with Christian faith. Grades K–12. Founded: 1979. Setting: rural. Nearest major city is Portsmouth. 50-acre campus. 3 buildings on campus. Approved or accredited by Association of Christian Schools International, New England Association of Schools and Colleges, and New Hampshire Department of Education. Total enrollment: 797. Upper school average class size: 17. Upper school faculty-student ratio: 1:11.
Upper School Student Profile Grade 9: 57 students (32 boys, 25 girls); Grade 10: 59 students (22 boys, 37 girls); Grade 11: 72 students (30 boys, 42 girls); Grade 12: 56 students (33 boys, 23 girls). 80% of students are Christian faith.
Faculty School total: 58. In upper school: 10 men, 9 women; 13 have advanced degrees.
Subjects Offered 20th century American writers, 20th century history, 3-dimensional art, 3-dimensional design, advanced chemistry, advanced math, Advanced Placement courses, algebra, alternative physical education, American history, analysis and differential calculus, art, art history, art history-AP, arts appreciation, band, baseball, basketball, Bible, Bible studies, biochemistry, biology, British literature, British literature (honors), calculus, calculus-AP, chemistry, chemistry-AP, choir, choral music, chorus, Christian doctrine, Christian education, Christian scripture, Christian studies, Christian testament, Christianity, church history, college admission preparation, college placement, college writing, comparative religion, composition, composition-AP, computer graphics, computer processing, computer resources, computer-aided design, contemporary issues, current history, digital photography, drama, drama performance, drawing, economics, economics and history, English, English composition, English language and composition-AP, English literature and composition-AP, environmental science, European history, foreign language, French, French language-AP, French studies, geometry, government, government/civics, guitar, health and wellness, honors algebra, honors English, honors geometry, jazz band, law studies, literature, literature and composition-AP, literature-AP, math review, mathematics, microbiology, modern history, music appreciation, musical productions, musical theater, New Testament, novels, photography, physics, physics-AP, political economics, pre-calculus, rhetoric, SAT preparation, SAT/ACT preparation, Shakespeare, Spanish, Spanish language-AP, student government, theology, U.S. history, world history, World War II, writing fundamentals, writing skills, writing workshop, yearbook.
Graduation Requirements 20th century history, algebra, arts and fine arts (art, music, dance, drama), biology, chemistry, comparative cultures, composition, computer skills, foreign language, geometry, physical education (includes health), physical science, U.S. history, writing, one Bible course for each year of Upper School attendance, service hours.
Special Academic Programs Advanced Placement exam preparation; honors section; accelerated programs; independent study; academic accommodation for the gifted and the musically talented; special instructional classes for students with Attention Deficit Disorder and dyslexia.

College Admission Counseling 59 students graduated in 2008; 47 went to college, including United States Military Academy; University of Maine at Farmington; University of New Hampshire; University of South Florida. Other: 8 went to work, 3 entered military service, 1 had other specific plans. Mean SAT critical reading: 670, mean SAT math: 637, mean SAT writing: 648.
Student Life Upper grades have specified standards of dress, student council, honor system. Discipline rests primarily with faculty.
Summer Programs Remediation, enrichment, sports programs offered; session focuses on soccer, basketball and volleyball; held on campus; accepts boys and girls; open to students from other schools. 40 students usually enrolled. 2009 schedule: July 10 to August 10. Application deadline: June 1.
Tuition and Aid Day student tuition: $8947. Tuition installment plan (FACTS Tuition Payment Plan). Tuition reduction for siblings, merit scholarship grants, need-based scholarship grants available. In 2008–09, 20% of upper-school students received aid. Total amount of financial aid awarded in 2008–09: $76,000.
Admissions Traditional secondary-level entrance grade is 9. Stanford Achievement Test required. Deadline for receipt of application materials: none. Application fee required: $100. Interview required.
Athletics Interscholastic: baseball (boys), basketball (b,g), cross-country running (b,g), indoor track & field (b,g), soccer (b,g), softball (g), tennis (b,g), track and field (b,g), volleyball (g); intramural: golf (b,g), skiing (cross-country) (b,g); coed interscholastic: alpine skiing. 1 PE instructor, 8 coaches.
Computers Computers are regularly used in art, Bible studies, career education, Christian doctrine, classics, college planning, desktop publishing, economics, English, foreign language, graphic design, history, humanities, independent study, library, library skills, mathematics, media arts, religion, religious studies, SAT preparation, science, social studies, writing classes. Computer network features include on-campus library services, online commercial services, Internet access, Internet filtering or blocking technology. Computer access in designated common areas is available to students. Students grades are available online. The school has a published electronic and media policy.
Contact Mrs. Diane Sipp, Director of Admissions. 603-742-3617 Ext. 116. Fax: 603-750-0490. E-mail: dsipp@pcaschool.org. Web site: www.pcaschool.org.

THE POTOMAC SCHOOL

Box 430
1301 Potomac School Road
McLean, Virginia 22101

Head of School: Geoffrey Jones

General Information Coeducational day college-preparatory, liberal arts, and strong emphasis: Academics, Arts, Athletics, Character Ed school. Grades K–12. Founded: 1904. Setting: suburban. Nearest major city is Washington, DC. 90-acre campus. 6 buildings on campus. Approved or accredited by Association of Independent Schools of Greater Washington and Virginia Association of Independent Schools. Member of National Association of Independent Schools and Secondary School Admission Test Board. Endowment: $26.5 million. Total enrollment: 956. Upper school average class size: 14. Upper school faculty-student ratio: 1:6.
Upper School Student Profile Grade 9: 109 students (51 boys, 58 girls); Grade 10: 103 students (55 boys, 48 girls); Grade 11: 93 students (41 boys, 52 girls); Grade 12: 69 students (38 boys, 31 girls).
Faculty School total: 150. In upper school: 20 men, 32 women; 42 have advanced degrees.
Subjects Offered 20th century American writers, 20th century history, 20th century world history, 3-dimensional art, 3-dimensional design, acting, advanced computer applications, advanced math, Advanced Placement courses, advanced studio art-AP, African history, African-American literature, African-American studies, algebra, American foreign policy, American government-AP, American literature, anatomy and physiology, ancient history, art, art history, Asian studies, athletics, band, bell choir, Bible as literature, bioethics, biology, British literature, calculus, calculus-AP, cell biology, ceramics, chamber groups, character education, chemistry, chemistry-AP, China/Japan history, Chinese history, Chinese studies, choral music, civil war history, college counseling, community service, comparative religion, computer programming, computer programming-AP, computer science, conceptual physics, concert band, creative writing, debate, directing, drama, drama performance, drawing and design, economics and history, electives, engineering, English, English literature, environmental science, ethics, European history, expository writing, film and literature, fine arts, French, French language-AP, French literature-AP, functions, geometry, global studies, government/civics, handbells, Harlem Renaissance, historical research, history of jazz, history of music, independent study, Japanese literature, jazz band, Latin, Latin American literature, Latin-AP, literary magazine, madrigals, mathematics, medieval history, Middle Eastern history, model United Nations, modern European history, music, music composition, music theory-AP, newspaper, painting, participation in sports, performing arts, photography, physical education, physics, physics-AP, portfolio art, pre-calculus, robotics, science, science and technology, sculpture, senior project, Shakespeare, short story, Spanish, Spanish language-AP, Spanish literature-AP, squash, stagecraft, statistics-AP, strings, student government, studio art-AP, theater arts, trigonometry, U.S. history-AP, vocal music, World War II, yearbook.
Graduation Requirements Arts and fine arts (art, music, dance, drama), English, ethics, foreign language, history, mathematics, physical education (includes health), science, senior project, month-long senior project.
Special Academic Programs Advanced Placement exam preparation; honors section; independent study.
College Admission Counseling 83 students graduated in 2008; 80 went to college, including Duke University; Georgetown University; Gettysburg College; Middlebury College; Southern Methodist University; The College of William and Mary. Other: 3 entered a postgraduate year. Median SAT critical reading: 664, median SAT math: 677.
Student Life Upper grades have specified standards of dress, student council. Discipline rests equally with students and faculty.
Summer Programs Enrichment, advancement, sports, art/fine arts programs offered; session focuses on academics and enrichment; held on campus; accepts boys and girls; open to students from other schools. 2009 schedule: June 22 to August 15. Application deadline: none.
Tuition and Aid Day student tuition: $27,445. Tuition installment plan (Insured Tuition Payment Plan, Key Tuition Payment Plan, monthly payment plans). Need-based scholarship grants available. In 2008–09, 13% of upper-school students received aid. Total amount of financial aid awarded in 2008–09: $944,995.
Admissions Traditional secondary-level entrance grade is 9. ISEE or SSAT required. Deadline for receipt of application materials: January 15. Application fee required: $65. On-campus interview required.
Athletics Interscholastic: baseball (boys), basketball (b,g), cross-country running (b,g), field hockey (g), football (b), lacrosse (b,g), soccer (b,g), softball (g), squash (b,g), tennis (b,g), track and field (b,g), wrestling (b); intramural: weight lifting (b,g); coed interscholastic: fitness, golf, swimming and diving, weight training, winter (indoor) track; coed intramural: canoeing/kayaking, hiking/backpacking, martial arts, outdoor education, physical fitness, physical training, strength & conditioning. 1 PE instructor, 65 coaches, 1 athletic trainer.
Computers Computers are regularly used in all academic, computer applications, drawing and design, independent study, literary magazine, newspaper, photography, programming, theater arts, yearbook classes. Computer network features include on-campus library services, online commercial services, Internet access, wireless campus network, Internet filtering or blocking technology. Campus intranet and student e-mail accounts are available to students. The school has a published electronic and media policy.
Contact Liza Hodskins, Admission Services Coordinator. 703-749-6313. Fax: 703-356-1764. Web site: www.potomacschool.org.

POUGHKEEPSIE DAY SCHOOL

260 Boardman Road
Poughkeepsie, New York 12603

Head of School: Josie Holford

General Information Coeducational day college-preparatory and arts school. Grades PK–12. Founded: 1934. Setting: suburban. Nearest major city is New York. 35-acre campus. 2 buildings on campus. Approved or accredited by New York State Association of Independent Schools and New York Department of Education. Member of National Association of Independent Schools. Endowment: $4.1 million. Total enrollment: 320. Upper school average class size: 12. Upper school faculty-student ratio: 1:6.
Upper School Student Profile Grade 9: 24 students (10 boys, 14 girls); Grade 10: 28 students (11 boys, 17 girls); Grade 11: 19 students (6 boys, 13 girls); Grade 12: 22 students (8 boys, 14 girls).
Faculty School total: 54. In upper school: 7 men, 13 women; 13 have advanced degrees.
Subjects Offered 3-dimensional art, acting, advanced math, Advanced Placement courses, African drumming, algebra, American literature, American literature-AP, analysis and differential calculus, analytic geometry, anatomy and physiology, ancient history, ancient world history, animal behavior, art history, arts, Basic programming, bioethics, biology, calculus, calculus-AP, chamber groups, chemistry, collage and assemblage, college admission preparation, college planning, community service, computer programming, computer science, conflict resolution, contemporary art, creative arts, creative drama, creative writing, decision making skills, digital photography, drama, drama performance, drawing, ecology, economics, English, English literature, English literature-AP, English-AP, ensembles, European civilization, European history, European literature, fiction, filmmaking, fine arts, French, French language-AP, French-AP, geology, geometry, guitar, history, Holocaust studies, independent study, instrumental music, integrated arts, interdisciplinary studies, jazz band, jazz ensemble, keyboarding/computer, lab science, leadership skills, life saving, life skills, literary magazine, literature, literature-AP, mathematics, modern European history, multicultural literature, multicultural studies, music, music appreciation, music composition, music performance, music theory, music theory-AP, musical productions, oil painting, painting, peer counseling, performing arts, photography, physical education, physical science, physics, physiology, play production, playwriting and directing, pre-calculus, printmaking, probability and statistics, religion and culture, SAT preparation, science, senior internship, service learning/internship, social issues, social studies, Spanish, Spanish language-AP, Spanish-AP, stained glass, strings, studio art, theater arts, theater production, trigonometry, U.S. history, video film production, visual arts, voice ensemble, Web site design, Western civilization, wind ensemble, writing workshop, yearbook, zoology.

Graduation Requirements Algebra, arts, biology, calculus, chemistry, classical Greek literature, college planning, electives, English, English literature, foreign language, geometry, interdisciplinary studies, life skills, mathematics, music, performing arts, physical education (includes health), physics, physiology, pre-calculus, SAT preparation, senior internship, senior thesis, trigonometry, visual arts, four-week off-campus senior internship. Community service is required.
Special Academic Programs Advanced Placement exam preparation; independent study; term-away projects; study at local college for college credit; academic accommodation for the gifted, the musically talented, and the artistically talented.
College Admission Counseling 33 students graduated in 2008; all went to college, including Clark University; Goucher College; Macalester College; Oberlin College; Skidmore College; St. Lawrence University. Mean SAT critical reading: 610, mean SAT math: 580, mean SAT writing: 600, mean combined SAT: 1790. 63% scored over 600 on SAT critical reading, 47% scored over 600 on SAT math, 50% scored over 600 on SAT writing, 56% scored over 1800 on combined SAT.
Student Life Upper grades have student council, honor system. Discipline rests primarily with faculty.
Summer Programs Art/fine arts programs offered; session focuses on visual and performing arts; held on campus; accepts boys and girls; open to students from other schools. 30 students usually enrolled. 2009 schedule: June 23 to August 7. Application deadline: May 15.
Tuition and Aid Day student tuition: $20,425. Tuition installment plan (monthly payment plans, individually arranged payment plans, The Tuition Refund Plan). Need-based scholarship grants, tuition reduction for children of full-time faculty and staff available. In 2008–09, 18% of upper-school students received aid. Total amount of financial aid awarded in 2008–09: $204,295.
Admissions Traditional secondary-level entrance grade is 9. For fall 2008, 26 students applied for upper-level admission, 12 were accepted, 8 enrolled. School's own exam required. Deadline for receipt of application materials: January 15. Application fee required: $50. On-campus interview required.
Athletics Interscholastic: basketball (boys, girls), cross-country running (b,g), soccer (b,g), softball (g); intramural: basketball (b,g), softball (g); coed interscholastic: cross-country running, Frisbee, soccer, ultimate Frisbee; coed intramural: alpine skiing, basketball, bicycling, cooperative games, cross-country running, dance, figure skating, fitness walking, Frisbee, hiking/backpacking, ice skating, jogging, life saving, outdoor education, outdoor skills, skiing (downhill), snowboarding, soccer, swimming and diving, tennis, ultimate Frisbee, volleyball, walking, yoga. 2 PE instructors, 5 coaches.
Computers Computers are regularly used in all academic, college planning, desktop publishing, journalism, library skills, literary magazine, media, music, newspaper, photography, photojournalism, programming, SAT preparation, video film production, Web site design, yearbook classes. Computer network features include on-campus library services, Internet access, wireless campus network, EBSCOhost®, Maps101, Web Feet Guides, Gale databases, ProQuest, unitedstreaming, Britannica Online, World Book Online, Grolier Online. Campus intranet and student e-mail accounts are available to students. The school has a published electronic and media policy.
Contact Tammy Reilly, Admissions Assistant. 845-462-7600 Ext. 201. Fax: 845-462-7602. E-mail: treilly@poughkeepsieday.org. Web site: www.poughkeepsieday.org/.

POWERS CATHOLIC HIGH SCHOOL

G-2040 West Carpenter Road
Flint, Michigan 48505-1028

Head of School: Mr. Thomas H. Furnas

General Information Coeducational day college-preparatory, arts, and religious studies school, affiliated with Roman Catholic Church. Grades 9–12. Founded: 1970. Setting: urban. 67-acre campus. 1 building on campus. Approved or accredited by North Central Association of Colleges and Schools and Michigan Department of Education. Endowment: $3 million. Total enrollment: 641. Upper school average class size: 25. Upper school faculty-student ratio: 1:16.
Upper School Student Profile Grade 9: 156 students (69 boys, 87 girls); Grade 10: 139 students (72 boys, 67 girls); Grade 11: 178 students (86 boys, 92 girls); Grade 12: 165 students (68 boys, 97 girls). 75% of students are Roman Catholic.
Faculty School total: 39. In upper school: 17 men, 22 women; 26 have advanced degrees.
Subjects Offered Art, art-AP, biology, biology-AP, calculus-AP, ceramics, chemistry, choir, computer skills, concert band, drafting, English, English literature and composition-AP, European history-AP, French, geometry, government, government-AP, health, honors algebra, honors English, honors geometry, integrated science, interdisciplinary studies, macroeconomics-AP, marching band, math analysis, math applications, mechanical drawing, mythology, orchestra, physics, pre-algebra, pre-calculus, psychology-AP, public speaking, religion, social justice, sociology, Spanish, state history, studio art—AP, theology, trigonometry, U.S. history, wind ensemble, world geography, world history, world issues, world religions, yearbook.
Graduation Requirements American history, English, government, health, mathematics, science, theology, world history, 40 hrs. of community service.
Special Academic Programs 8 Advanced Placement exams for which test preparation is offered; honors section; remedial reading and/or remedial writing; remedial math.
College Admission Counseling 186 students graduated in 2008; 183 went to college, including Central Michigan University; Grand Valley State University; Michigan State University; Saginaw Valley State University; University of Michigan. Other: 1 went to work, 2 had other specific plans. Mean SAT critical reading: 592, mean SAT math: 590, mean SAT writing: 599, mean composite ACT: 22.
Student Life Upper grades have specified standards of dress, student council. Discipline rests primarily with faculty. Attendance at religious services is required.
Tuition and Aid Day student tuition: $6900. Tuition installment plan (monthly payment plans, individually arranged payment plans). Tuition reduction for siblings, merit scholarship grants, need-based scholarship grants available. In 2008–09, 44% of upper-school students received aid; total upper-school merit-scholarship money awarded: $7000. Total amount of financial aid awarded in 2008–09: $505,838.
Admissions Traditional secondary-level entrance grade is 9. ACT-Explore required. Deadline for receipt of application materials: none. Application fee required: $50. Interview required.
Athletics Interscholastic: alpine skiing (boys, girls), baseball (b), basketball (b,g), bowling (b,g), cross-country running (b,g), dance squad (g), dance team (g), diving (b,g), football (b), golf (b,g), ice hockey (b), lacrosse (b,g), Nautilus (b,g), skiing (downhill) (b,g), soccer (b,g), softball (g), swimming and diving (b,g), tennis (b,g), track and field (b,g), volleyball (g), wrestling (b); coed interscholastic: cheering, equestrian sports, indoor track, power lifting, skeet shooting, strength & conditioning, weight lifting; coed intramural: ultimate Frisbee, weight training. 1 PE instructor.
Computers Computers are regularly used in accounting, business applications, drafting, graphic design, keyboarding, yearbook classes. Computer resources include on-campus library services, Internet access, Internet filtering or blocking technology. Computer access in designated common areas is available to students. Students grades are available online. The school has a published electronic and media policy.
Contact Ms. Sally Bartos, Assistant Principal for Instruction. 810-591-4741. Fax: 810-591-0383. E-mail: sbartos@powerscatholic.org. Web site: www.powerscatholic.org.

THE PRAIRIE SCHOOL

4050 Lighthouse Drive
Racine, Wisconsin 53402

Head of School: Mr. Wm. Mark H. Murphy

General Information Coeducational day college-preparatory, arts, and technology school. Grades PK–12. Founded: 1965. Setting: small town. Nearest major city is Milwaukee. 33-acre campus. 2 buildings on campus. Approved or accredited by Independent Schools Association of the Central States and Wisconsin Department of Education. Member of National Association of Independent Schools. Endowment: $38 million. Total enrollment: 723. Upper school average class size: 17. Upper school faculty-student ratio: 1:17.
Upper School Student Profile Grade 9: 79 students (43 boys, 36 girls); Grade 10: 73 students (35 boys, 38 girls); Grade 11: 60 students (29 boys, 31 girls); Grade 12: 64 students (34 boys, 30 girls).
Faculty School total: 75. In upper school: 18 men, 14 women; 18 have advanced degrees.
Subjects Offered Algebra, American history, American history-AP, American literature, art, astronomy, athletic training, biology, biology-AP, calculus, calculus-AP, ceramics, chemistry, chemistry-AP, choir, community service, comparative religion, computer science, CPR, creative writing, dance, digital imaging, drama, drawing and design, earth and space science, ecology, economics, English, English literature, English-AP, environmental science, environmental science-AP, European history, European history-AP, fine arts, French, French language-AP, geometry, glassblowing, government/civics, health, history, international relations, jazz ensemble, mathematics, multicultural literature, music, music theory-AP, orchestra, photography, physical education, physics, physics-AP, pre-calculus, probability and statistics, public speaking, science, social studies, Spanish, Spanish language-AP, speech, study skills, theater, trigonometry, Western literature, world history, world literature.
Graduation Requirements Arts and fine arts (art, music, dance, drama), English, foreign language, mathematics, physical education (includes health), science, social studies (includes history), study skills, Spring Interim Program (including on-campus seminars, community service, off-campus internships), 100-hour service requirement.
Special Academic Programs 13 Advanced Placement exams for which test preparation is offered; honors section; independent study; term-away projects; academic accommodation for the gifted, the musically talented, and the artistically talented; remedial reading and/or remedial writing; ESL (2 students enrolled).
College Admission Counseling 51 students graduated in 2008; all went to college, including Arizona State University; Carnegie Mellon University; Marquette University; St. Olaf College; University of Wisconsin–Madison. Median SAT math: 570, median SAT writing: 580, median combined SAT: 1150, median composite ACT: 28.
Student Life Upper grades have specified standards of dress, student council, honor system. Discipline rests primarily with faculty.
Summer Programs Enrichment, advancement, ESL, art/fine arts, computer instruction programs offered; session focuses on enrichment and athletics; held on campus; accepts boys and girls; open to students from other schools. 200 students usually enrolled. 2009 schedule: June 22 to August 21. Application deadline: June.
Tuition and Aid Day student tuition: $12,700. Tuition installment plan (FACTS Tuition Payment Plan). Tuition reduction for siblings, merit scholarship grants, need-based scholarship grants available. In 2008–09, 43% of upper-school students

received aid; total upper-school merit-scholarship money awarded: $146,000. Total amount of financial aid awarded in 2008–09: $620,000.
Admissions Traditional secondary-level entrance grade is 9. For fall 2008, 46 students applied for upper-level admission, 33 were accepted, 26 enrolled. Admissions testing, school's own exam or TerraNova required. Deadline for receipt of application materials: none. Application fee required: $50. On-campus interview required.
Athletics Interscholastic: baseball (boys), basketball (b,g), soccer (b,g), tennis (b,g), volleyball (g); coed interscholastic: cross-country running, golf, modern dance, outdoor activities, track and field. 7 PE instructors, 13 coaches, 1 athletic trainer.
Computers Computers are regularly used in all academic classes. Computer network features include on-campus library services, Internet access, wireless campus network, Internet filtering or blocking technology. Campus intranet and computer access in designated common areas are available to students. Students grades are available online. The school has a published electronic and media policy.
Contact Ms. Molly Lofquist, Director of Admissions. 262-260-4393. Fax: 262-260-3790. E-mail: mlofquist@prairieschool.com. Web site: www.prairieschool.com.

ANNOUNCEMENT FROM THE SCHOOL Serving over 725 students in early school through grade 12, Prairie provides a college-preparatory curriculum that combines challenging academics, comprehensive fine and creative arts, and a strong athletic program. The 22-acre campus is surrounded by meadowlands, overlooks Lake Michigan, and houses the Student Research Center, the Samuel C. Johnson Upper School, and the state-of-the-art Johnson Athletic Center.

PRESTON HIGH SCHOOL

2780 Schurz Avenue
Bronx, New York 10465

Head of School: Mrs. Jane Grendell

General Information Girls' day college-preparatory, arts, religious studies, and technology school, affiliated with Roman Catholic Church. Grades 9–12. Founded: 1947. Setting: urban. Nearest major city is New York. 5-acre campus. 2 buildings on campus. Approved or accredited by Middle States Association of Colleges and Schools and New York Department of Education. Total enrollment: 611. Upper school average class size: 25. Upper school faculty-student ratio: 1:15.
Upper School Student Profile Grade 9: 154 students (154 girls); Grade 10: 151 students (151 girls); Grade 11: 138 students (138 girls); Grade 12: 168 students (168 girls). 83% of students are Roman Catholic.
Faculty School total: 44. In upper school: 14 men, 30 women; 37 have advanced degrees.
Subjects Offered Advanced computer applications, advanced math, Advanced Placement courses, algebra, American government-AP, American history, American history-AP, anatomy and physiology, art, biology, biology-AP, British literature, British literature (honors), calculus-AP, Catholic belief and practice, chemistry, chorus, communication skills, computer education, computer graphics, computer programming, creative writing, earth science, economics and history, English, English literature and composition-AP, film history, foreign language, geometry, global studies, government-AP, graphic design, health, honors algebra, honors English, honors geometry, honors U.S. history, honors world history, Italian, Latin, law, media studies, moral theology, music, peer counseling, philosophy, physical education, physics, play/screen writing, religious studies, service learning/internship, Spanish, Spanish language-AP, Spanish literature-AP, women in world history, world literature.
Graduation Requirements Service.
Special Academic Programs Advanced Placement exam preparation; honors section; independent study; study at local college for college credit.
College Admission Counseling 139 students graduated in 2008; all went to college, including Fordham University; Iona College; Manhattan College; New York University; State University of New York at Binghamton; University at Albany, State University of New York. Mean SAT critical reading: 530, mean SAT math: 530, mean SAT writing: 541.
Student Life Upper grades have uniform requirement, student council, honor system. Discipline rests equally with students and faculty. Attendance at religious services is required.
Summer Programs Remediation, enrichment programs offered; session focuses on enrichment for incoming freshmen; held on campus; accepts girls; not open to students from other schools. 30 students usually enrolled. 2009 schedule: July 1 to July 31.
Tuition and Aid Day student tuition: $6915. Tuition installment plan (monthly payment plans, individually arranged payment plans). Tuition reduction for siblings, merit scholarship grants, need-based scholarship grants available. In 2008–09, 25% of upper-school students received aid.
Admissions Traditional secondary-level entrance grade is 9. Deadline for receipt of application materials: March 1. Application fee required: $75. Interview required.
Athletics Interscholastic: basketball, cheering, fitness, indoor track, soccer, softball, swimming and diving, track and field, volleyball. 2 PE instructors, 9 coaches.
Computers Computers are regularly used in graphic design, language development, mathematics, Web site design classes. Computer network features include on-campus library services, Internet access, Internet filtering or blocking technology. Students grades are available online. The school has a published electronic and media policy.
Contact Ms. Julia Wall, Director of Admissions. 718-863-9134 Ext. 132. Fax: 718-863-6125. E-mail: jwall@prestonhs.org. Web site: www.prestonhs.org.

PRESTONWOOD CHRISTIAN ACADEMY

6801 West Park Boulevard
Plano, Texas 75093

Head of School: Mr. Larry Taylor

General Information Coeducational day college-preparatory and Bible courses school, affiliated with Southern Baptist Convention. Grades PK–12. Founded: 1997. Setting: suburban. Nearest major city is Dallas. 44-acre campus. 2 buildings on campus. Approved or accredited by Southern Association of Colleges and Schools and Texas Department of Education. Total enrollment: 1,443. Upper school average class size: 18. Upper school faculty-student ratio: 1:9.
Upper School Student Profile Grade 9: 126 students (60 boys, 66 girls); Grade 10: 116 students (55 boys, 61 girls); Grade 11: 122 students (53 boys, 69 girls); Grade 12: 96 students (48 boys, 48 girls). 67% of students are Southern Baptist Convention.
Faculty School total: 118. In upper school: 14 men, 22 women; 18 have advanced degrees.
Subjects Offered 20th century history, 20th century physics, advanced chemistry, advanced math, Advanced Placement courses, algebra, American government-AP, American history-AP, American literature, anatomy and physiology, art, art-AP, band, Bible, biology, biology-AP, British literature, calculus-AP, ceramics, chemistry, choir, Christian doctrine, computer applications, conceptual physics, debate, drama, drawing, economics, ethics, fine arts, fitness, geometry, government, government-AP, health, honors algebra, honors English, honors geometry, honors U.S. history, honors world history, internship, language-AP, leadership education training, learning lab, literature-AP, logic, multimedia, multimedia design, newspaper, painting, performing arts, personal fitness, philosophy, photo shop, physical fitness, physics, physics-AP, pre-calculus, printmaking, sculpture, service learning/internship, Spanish, Spanish-AP, speech, statistics, student government, studio art, U.S. history, Web site design, Western literature, world history, world religions, yearbook.
Graduation Requirements 1½ elective credits, algebra, arts and fine arts (art, music, dance, drama), Bible, biology, British literature, chemistry, Christian doctrine, computer applications, economics, English, English literature, ethics, foreign language, geometry, government, philosophy, physical education (includes health), physics, speech, U.S. history, Western literature, world history.
Special Academic Programs Advanced Placement exam preparation; honors section; academic accommodation for the gifted.
College Admission Counseling 104 students graduated in 2008; 103 went to college, including Baylor University; Southern Methodist University; Texas A&M University; Texas Christian University; University of Arkansas; University of Oklahoma. Other: 1 entered military service. Mean SAT critical reading: 550, mean SAT math: 530, mean SAT writing: 560, mean combined SAT: 1640, mean composite ACT: 24. 39% scored over 600 on SAT critical reading, 30% scored over 600 on SAT math, 30% scored over 600 on SAT writing, 39% scored over 1800 on combined SAT, 31% scored over 26 on composite ACT.
Student Life Upper grades have uniform requirement, student council, honor system. Discipline rests primarily with faculty.
Summer Programs Remediation, enrichment, advancement, sports, art/fine arts, rigorous outdoor training, computer instruction programs offered; held on campus; accepts boys and girls; open to students from other schools. 800 students usually enrolled. 2009 schedule: June 1 to August 5. Application deadline: May 1.
Tuition and Aid Day student tuition: $14,217–$15,095. Tuition installment plan (FACTS Tuition Payment Plan, monthly payment plans, individually arranged payment plans). Tuition reduction for siblings, need-based scholarship grants available. In 2008–09, 18% of upper-school students received aid. Total amount of financial aid awarded in 2008–09: $365,693.
Admissions Traditional secondary-level entrance grade is 9. For fall 2008, 91 students applied for upper-level admission, 73 were accepted, 66 enrolled. ISEE or Stanford Achievement Test required. Deadline for receipt of application materials: none. Application fee required: $100. Interview required.
Athletics Interscholastic: baseball (boys), basketball (b,g), cheering (g), cross-country running (b,g), drill team (g), football (b), golf (b,g), soccer (b,g), softball (g), swimming and diving (b,g), tennis (b,g), track and field (b,g), volleyball (g). 1 PE instructor, 29 coaches, 1 athletic trainer.
Computers Computers are regularly used in all academic, technology classes. Computer network features include on-campus library services, Internet access, wireless campus network, Internet filtering or blocking technology. Students grades are available online. The school has a published electronic and media policy.
Contact Mrs. Marsha Backof, Admissions Assistant. 972-930-4010. Fax: 972-930-4008. E-mail: mbackof@prestonwoodchristian.org. Web site: www.prestonwoodchristian.org.

PRINCETON DAY SCHOOL

PO Box 75
The Great Road
Princeton, New Jersey 08542

ANNOUNCEMENT FROM THE SCHOOL The School complex is bright, modern, and comfortable. It offers exceptional educational resources, including three libraries, computers in every grade level linked through PDS Net, a newly renovated campus center, and a 400-seat theater. Beyond the buildings lie 105 acres that offer excellent sports facilities, including four new playing fields, a synthetic-turf field, and a skating rink. Over the past five years, more than 90% of Princeton Day School graduates have been accepted by colleges and universities that rate themselves "most difficult" according to Peterson's, a Nelnet company.

PROFESSIONAL CHILDREN'S SCHOOL

132 West 60th Street
New York, New York 10023
Head of School: Dr. James Dawson

General Information Coeducational day college-preparatory school. Grades 6–12. Founded: 1914. Setting: urban. 1 building on campus. Approved or accredited by New York State Association of Independent Schools. Member of National Association of Independent Schools. Endowment: $2.7 million. Total enrollment: 181. Upper school average class size: 10. Upper school faculty-student ratio: 1:8.

Upper School Student Profile Grade 9: 21 students (17 boys, 4 girls); Grade 10: 36 students (27 boys, 9 girls); Grade 11: 48 students (35 boys, 13 girls); Grade 12: 42 students (27 boys, 15 girls).

Faculty School total: 27. In upper school: 11 men, 16 women; 22 have advanced degrees.

Subjects Offered Advanced math, algebra, American government, American history, biology, calculus, chemistry, chorus, computer education, constitutional history of U.S., constitutional law, creative writing, drama, English, English literature, environmental science, ESL, foreign language, French, general math, geometry, health education, introduction to literature, keyboarding/computer, library research, library skills, physical education, physics, pre-algebra, pre-calculus, Spanish, studio art, U.S. government, U.S. history.

Graduation Requirements Art, English, foreign language, health, history, mathematics, science.

Special Academic Programs ESL (15 students enrolled).

College Admission Counseling 61 students graduated in 2008; 58 went to college, including Boston University; Duke University; Fordham University; Manhattan School of Music; New York University; The Juilliard School. Other: 3 had other specific plans.

Student Life Upper grades have student council, honor system. Discipline rests primarily with faculty.

Tuition and Aid Day student tuition: $28,250–$31,000. Tuition installment plan (Academic Management Services Plan, Sallie Mae). Need-based scholarship grants available. In 2008–09, 33% of upper-school students received aid. Total amount of financial aid awarded in 2008–09: $681,500.

Admissions Traditional secondary-level entrance grade is 9. For fall 2008, 109 students applied for upper-level admission, 76 were accepted, 51 enrolled. ERB, ISEE or Stanford Achievement Test required. Deadline for receipt of application materials: none. Application fee required: $50. On-campus interview recommended.

Athletics 1 PE instructor.

Computers Computers are regularly used in all academic classes. Computer network features include on-campus library services, Internet access, wireless campus network, Internet filtering or blocking technology. Student e-mail accounts are available to students.

Contact Sherrie A. Hinkle, Director of Admissions. 212-582-3116 Ext. 112. Fax: 212-307-6542. E-mail: admit@pcs-nyc.org. Web site: www.pcs-nyc.org.

ANNOUNCEMENT FROM THE SCHOOL Professional Children's School (PCS) provides a college-preparatory curriculum for young people engaged in professional training and/or performance in the arts or sports. Current PCS students include dancers with the New York City Ballet; actors from movies, TV, and Broadway shows; models at such agencies as Ford and Red Model Management; and athletes and musicians who study at institutions such as the Juilliard School.

See Close-Up on page 912.

THE PROUT SCHOOL

4640 Tower Hill Road
Wakefield, Rhode Island 02879
Head of School: Mr. Gary Delneo

General Information Coeducational day college-preparatory, arts, religious studies, and technology school, affiliated with Roman Catholic Church. Grades 9–12. Founded: 1966. Setting: small town. Nearest major city is Providence. 25-acre campus. 1 building on campus. Approved or accredited by International Baccalaureate Organization, New England Association of Schools and Colleges, Rhode Island State Certified Resource Progam, and Rhode Island Department of Education. Total enrollment: 657. Upper school average class size: 21. Upper school faculty-student ratio: 1:18.

Upper School Student Profile 75% of students are Roman Catholic.

Faculty School total: 53. In upper school: 25 men, 28 women; 40 have advanced degrees.

Subjects Offered Acting, American literature, anatomy and physiology, art education, art history, athletic training, ballet, ballet technique, band, biology, calculus, chemistry, Chinese, choir, chorus, Christian doctrine, Christian education, Christian ethics, Christian scripture, Christian studies, Christianity, church history, clayworking, college planning, college writing, community service, comparative religion, computer applications, computer art, computer education, computer graphics, computer keyboarding, computer multimedia, computer programming, computer science, computer skills, computer studies, contemporary history, contemporary issues, costumes and make-up, CPR, creative dance, creative drama, creative thinking, critical studies in film, critical writing, dance performance, drama performance, drama workshop, dramatic arts, drawing, drawing and design, earth science, economics, economics and history, English, English composition, English literature, environmental science, environmental studies, first aid, fitness, food and nutrition, foreign language, French, general science, government, graphic arts, graphic design, health, health and wellness, history, history of the Catholic Church, honors English, honors U.S. history, honors world history, human anatomy, instruments, introduction to theater, Italian, jazz band, keyboarding/computer, lab science, language, language and composition, law and the legal system, life science, marine science, mathematics, modern history, music performance, music theater, musical theater, musical theater dance, oceanography, personal fitness, physical fitness, physics, play production, portfolio art, pre-calculus, public service, religion, religion and culture, religions, religious education, religious studies, scene study, science, science research, scripture, set design, Spanish, sports nutrition, stage and body movement, stage design, theater, theater arts, theater design and production, theater history, visual and performing arts, yearbook.

Graduation Requirements Computers, English, foreign language, health education, history, lab science, mathematics, oceanography, physical education (includes health), religion (includes Bible studies and theology), science.

Special Academic Programs International Baccalaureate program; honors section.

College Admission Counseling 120 students graduated in 2008; 116 went to college, including Northeastern University; Providence College; Rhode Island College; Roger Williams University; University of Rhode Island. Other: 2 went to work, 1 entered military service, 1 had other specific plans.

Student Life Upper grades have uniform requirement, student council, honor system. Discipline rests primarily with faculty. Attendance at religious services is required.

Tuition and Aid Day student tuition: $9800. Tuition installment plan (FACTS Tuition Payment Plan). Tuition reduction for siblings, need-based scholarship grants available. In 2008–09, 23% of upper-school students received aid. Total amount of financial aid awarded in 2008–09: $210,000.

Admissions Traditional secondary-level entrance grade is 9. For fall 2008, 312 students applied for upper-level admission, 195 were accepted, 173 enrolled. Admissions testing and essay required. Deadline for receipt of application materials: January 10. Application fee required: $25.

Athletics Interscholastic: baseball (boys), basketball (b,g), cheering (g), cross-country running (b,g), gymnastics (g), lacrosse (b), soccer (b,g), softball (g), swimming and diving (b,g), tennis (b,g), track and field (b,g), volleyball (g); intramural: dance (g), outdoor recreation (b,g); coed interscholastic: aquatics, golf, ice hockey; coed intramural: aerobics, aerobics/dance, ballet, bicycling, fitness, outdoor recreation, sailing, strength & conditioning, table tennis, weight lifting, weight training. 3 PE instructors, 14 coaches.

Computers Computers are regularly used in all academic classes.

Contact Ms. Kristen Need, Director of Admissions. 401-789-9262 Ext. 515. Fax: 401-782-2262. E-mail: kneed@theproutschool.org. Web site: www.theproutschool.org.

PROVIDENCE COUNTRY DAY SCHOOL

660 Waterman Avenue
East Providence, Rhode Island 02914-1724
Head of School: Mrs. Susan M. Haberlandt

General Information Coeducational day college-preparatory, arts, and technology school. Grades 5–12. Founded: 1923. Setting: suburban. Nearest major city is Providence. 42-acre campus. 5 buildings on campus. Approved or accredited by Association of Independent Schools in New England, New England Association of Schools and Colleges, The College Board, and Rhode Island Department of Education. Member of National Association of Independent Schools and Secondary School

Admission Test Board. Endowment: $2.5 million. Total enrollment: 275. Upper school average class size: 12. Upper school faculty-student ratio: 1:6.
Faculty School total: 48. In upper school: 15 men, 16 women; 24 have advanced degrees.
Subjects Offered Advanced Placement courses, algebra, American government, American government-AP, American history, American history-AP, American literature, ancient history, art, art history, art history-AP, Asian studies, Bible as literature, bioethics, biology, biology-AP, British literature, calculus, calculus-AP, ceramics, chemistry, choir, college counseling, community service, computer graphics, computer science, conceptual physics, creative writing, drama, earth science, electives, English, English literature, English literature-AP, English-AP, European civilization, European history, expository writing, fine arts, foreign language, forensic science, French, geography, geometry, government/civics, graphic design, health, history, independent study, jazz ensemble, journalism, Latin, Latin-AP, mathematics, media production, model United Nations, modern European history, music, performing arts, photography, physical education, physics, pottery, pre-algebra, pre-calculus, public speaking, SAT preparation, science, senior internship, social studies, Spanish, student government, student publications, studio art, theater, trigonometry, visual arts, world history, writing.
Graduation Requirements Arts and fine arts (art, music, dance, drama), English, foreign language, history, mathematics, physical education (includes health), science, senior independent project.
Special Academic Programs 8 Advanced Placement exams for which test preparation is offered; honors section; independent study; term-away projects; study at local college for college credit; study abroad; academic accommodation for the gifted, the musically talented, and the artistically talented.
College Admission Counseling 52 students graduated in 2008; 49 went to college, including Brown University; Connecticut College; Fairfield University; Hobart and William Smith Colleges; Providence College; Roanoke College. Other: 2 entered a postgraduate year, 1 had other specific plans. Mean SAT critical reading: 586, mean SAT math: 578, mean SAT writing: 585. 45% scored over 600 on SAT critical reading, 41% scored over 600 on SAT math, 46% scored over 600 on SAT writing.
Student Life Upper grades have specified standards of dress, student council. Discipline rests equally with students and faculty.
Summer Programs Art/fine arts programs offered; session focuses on theater, writing; held on campus; accepts boys and girls; not open to students from other schools. 15 students usually enrolled. 2009 schedule: June 22 to July 10.
Tuition and Aid Day student tuition: $24,750–$25,200. Tuition installment plan (monthly payment plans). Need-based scholarship grants available. In 2008–09, 30% of upper-school students received aid. Total amount of financial aid awarded in 2008–09: $1,175,000.
Admissions Traditional secondary-level entrance grade is 9. For fall 2008, 113 students applied for upper-level admission, 82 were accepted, 36 enrolled. ISEE or SSAT required. Deadline for receipt of application materials: February 1. Application fee required: $55. On-campus interview required.
Athletics Interscholastic: baseball (boys), basketball (b,g), cross-country running (b,g), football (b), golf (b), ice hockey (b,g), lacrosse (b,g), sailing (b,g), soccer (b,g), tennis (b,g), track and field (b), wrestling (b); coed interscholastic: crew, physical fitness; coed intramural: fencing, strength & conditioning, volleyball, weight training. 2 PE instructors, 6 coaches, 1 athletic trainer.
Computers Computers are regularly used in art, English, foreign language, history, mathematics, music, science classes. Computer network features include on-campus library services, online commercial services, Internet access, Internet filtering or blocking technology. Computer access in designated common areas is available to students. The school has a published electronic and media policy.
Contact Ms. Whitney H. Russell, Senior Associate Director of Admissions. 401-438-5170 Ext. 102. Fax: 401-435-4514. E-mail: russell@providencecountryday.org. Web site: www.providencecountryday.org.

PROVIDENCE DAY SCHOOL

5800 Sardis Road
Charlotte, North Carolina 28270
Head of School: Dr. John E. Creeden

General Information Coeducational day college-preparatory school. Grades PK–12. Founded: 1970. Setting: suburban. 48-acre campus. 18 buildings on campus. Approved or accredited by North Carolina Association of Independent Schools, Southern Association of Colleges and Schools, Southern Association of Independent Schools, and North Carolina Department of Education. Member of National Association of Independent Schools. Endowment: $4 million. Total enrollment: 1,528. Upper school average class size: 15. Upper school faculty-student ratio: 1:7.
Upper School Student Profile Grade 9: 130 students (61 boys, 69 girls); Grade 10: 132 students (82 boys, 50 girls); Grade 11: 122 students (54 boys, 68 girls); Grade 12: 125 students (71 boys, 54 girls).
Faculty School total: 148. In upper school: 41 men, 31 women; 51 have advanced degrees.
Subjects Offered Accounting, African-American history, algebra, American history, American literature, art, art history-AP, Asian history, band, biology, biology-AP, calculus-AP, chemistry, chemistry-AP, chorus, Civil War, composition, computer graphics, computer programming, computer science, computer science-AP, drama, economics, English, English literature, English-AP, environmental science, environmental science-AP, fine arts, French, French-AP, geometry, German, German-AP, government-AP, government/civics, health, history, history-AP, instrumental music, international relations, journalism, Judaic studies, keyboarding, Latin, Latin-AP, literature, Mandarin, mathematics, music-AP, photography, physical education, physical science, physics, physics-AP, political science, pre-calculus, psychology, science, set design, social studies, Spanish, Spanish-AP, sports medicine, statistics-AP, theater, word processing, world history, writing, yearbook.
Graduation Requirements Arts and fine arts (art, music, dance, drama), computer science, English, foreign language, mathematics, physical education (includes health), science, social studies (includes history).
Special Academic Programs Advanced Placement exam preparation; honors section; accelerated programs; independent study; study abroad; academic accommodation for the gifted, the musically talented, and the artistically talented.
College Admission Counseling 129 students graduated in 2008; all went to college, including Appalachian State University; Duke University; North Carolina State University; The University of North Carolina at Chapel Hill; University of Virginia; Wake Forest University. Mean SAT critical reading: 717, mean SAT math: 710. 60% scored over 600 on SAT critical reading, 70% scored over 600 on SAT math.
Student Life Upper grades have specified standards of dress, student council, honor system. Discipline rests equally with students and faculty.
Summer Programs Remediation, enrichment, advancement, sports, art/fine arts, computer instruction programs offered; session focuses on academics, enrichment; held both on and off campus; held at various parks, recreation centers, museums; accepts boys and girls; open to students from other schools. 2,500 students usually enrolled. 2009 schedule: June 9 to August 8. Application deadline: none.
Tuition and Aid Day student tuition: $19,110. Tuition installment plan (Academic Management Services Plan, monthly payment plans). Need-based scholarship grants available. In 2008–09, 8% of upper-school students received aid. Total amount of financial aid awarded in 2008–09: $600,000.
Admissions Traditional secondary-level entrance grade is 9. For fall 2008, 110 students applied for upper-level admission, 56 were accepted, 33 enrolled. Cognitive Abilities Test, ERB CTP IV or ISEE required. Deadline for receipt of application materials: January 15. Application fee required: $90. On-campus interview required.
Athletics Interscholastic: aerobics/dance (girls), baseball (b), basketball (b,g), cheering (g), cross-country running (b,g), dance squad (g), field hockey (g), football (b), golf (b,g), lacrosse (b,g), soccer (b,g), softball (g), swimming and diving (b,g), tennis (b,g), track and field (b,g), volleyball (g), wrestling (b); intramural: indoor hockey (b,g), indoor soccer (b,g), Newcombe ball (b,g), physical fitness (b,g), pillo polo (b,g), soccer (b,g), softball (b,g), strength & conditioning (b,g), volleyball (b,g); coed intramural: indoor hockey, indoor soccer, Newcombe ball, physical fitness, pillo polo, soccer, softball, strength & conditioning, tennis, volleyball. 4 PE instructors, 36 coaches, 2 athletic trainers.
Computers Computers are regularly used in English, mathematics, science, technology, word processing classes. Computer network features include on-campus library services, online commercial services, Internet access, wireless campus network, Internet filtering or blocking technology, wireless iBook lab available for individual student check-out. Student e-mail accounts are available to students. The school has a published electronic and media policy.
Contact Mr. Scott C Siegfried, Director of Admissions. 704-887-7040. Fax: 704-887-7520. E-mail: scott.siegfried@providenceday.org. Web site: www.providenceday.org.

ANNOUNCEMENT FROM THE SCHOOL Providence Day School, located in Charlotte, North Carolina, is an independent, college-preparatory, coed school for Transitional Kindergarten through grade 12. Providence Day School exists to inspire in its students a passion for learning, a commitment to personal integrity, and a sense of social responsibility. Teachers at Providence Day School encourage their students to "think" and to not merely memorize facts. They want children to understand the concept, analyze, discuss, build models, debate, and defend viewpoints. The School embraces a global focus from the Lower School through the Upper School, culminating in the Global Studies Diploma in the Upper School. From the time students first enter Lower School, they are asked, "What do you think? How would you solve this task? Why do you think this happened?" The Lower School helps teach that childhood is a journey, not a race. The Middle School develops a student's sense of self-worth. By accepting students as they are, Providence Day School continually opens opportunities for them to take responsibility for their education and lives. Providence Day School helps students learn about themselves as individuals with unique learning styles, while carefully developing the skills needed for academic success. Excellence is the norm at Providence Day Upper School. In an environment where dedicated teachers listen, encourage, and inspire, students learn because they challenge themselves and are challenged to think at a high level. Providence Day School believes in developing the whole child: academically, socially, physically, and morally. To find this balance, the School offers a wide range of clubs, organizations, athletics, and after-school opportunities. Facility highlights include a state-of-the-art Technology Center, with lecture hall and computer, math, and science labs; a Lower School Library that is next to the Middle and Upper School Library Center; and the Fine Arts Center, with a 500-seat theater, a Black Box Theater, and art, music, and photography classrooms. Athletics are supported by a football/soccer/track stadium, athletic fields, tennis courts, and the Athletic Center, with a double gymnasium and state-of-the-art training center.

PROVIDENCE HIGH SCHOOL

511 South Buena Vista Street
Burbank, California 91505-4865

Head of School: Mrs. Michele Schulte

General Information Coeducational day college-preparatory, arts, religious studies, and technology school, affiliated with Roman Catholic Church. Grades 9–12. Founded: 1955. Setting: urban. Nearest major city is Los Angeles. 4-acre campus. 6 buildings on campus. Approved or accredited by National Catholic Education Association, The College Board, Western Association of Schools and Colleges, and California Department of Education. Endowment: $100,000. Total enrollment: 518. Upper school average class size: 22. Upper school faculty-student ratio: 1:15.

Upper School Student Profile Grade 9: 133 students (68 boys, 65 girls); Grade 10: 116 students (49 boys, 67 girls); Grade 11: 119 students (57 boys, 62 girls); Grade 12: 150 students (59 boys, 91 girls). 64% of students are Roman Catholic.

Faculty School total: 43. In upper school: 17 men, 26 women; 28 have advanced degrees.

Subjects Offered Accounting, algebra, American government-AP, American history, American literature, Bible studies, biology, biology-AP, calculus, ceramics, chemistry, chorus, communications, community service, computer science, drama, economics, economics-AP, English, English literature, English literature and composition-AP, environmental science, ethics, film, fine arts, French, French-AP, geography, geometry, graphic arts, health, history, journalism, law, mathematics, media studies, music, photography, physical education, physics, pre-calculus, psychology, religion, science, social studies, Spanish, Spanish-AP, theater, trigonometry, U.S. government, U.S. government-AP, U.S. history-AP, United States government-AP, video, video and animation, video film production, visual and performing arts, volleyball, weight fitness, weight training, world cultures, world geography, world history, world religions, world religions, writing, writing fundamentals, yearbook.

Graduation Requirements Art, computer science, economics, English, ethics, foreign language, humanities, mathematics, philosophy, physical education (includes health), religion (includes Bible studies and theology), science, social studies (includes history), sociology, speech, completion of Christian Service hours.

Special Academic Programs Advanced Placement exam preparation; honors section; academic accommodation for the musically talented and the artistically talented.

College Admission Counseling 155 students graduated in 2008; 149 went to college, including California State University, Northridge; Loyola Marymount University; Pasadena City College; University of California, Irvine; University of California, Riverside; University of Southern California. Other: 3 went to work, 2 entered military service, 1 had other specific plans. Mean SAT critical reading: 632, mean SAT math: 529, mean SAT writing: 538. 31% scored over 600 on SAT critical reading, 29% scored over 600 on SAT math, 29% scored over 600 on SAT writing.

Student Life Upper grades have uniform requirement, student council. Discipline rests equally with students and faculty. Attendance at religious services is required.

Summer Programs Remediation, enrichment, advancement, sports, art/fine arts, computer instruction programs offered; session focuses on remediation and extracurricular activities; held on campus; accepts boys and girls; open to students from other schools. 252 students usually enrolled. 2009 schedule: June 29 to July 30. Application deadline: June 19.

Tuition and Aid Day student tuition: $8900. Tuition installment plan (The Tuition Plan, 1-payment plan: payment in full due July 1st, 2-payment plan: 60% due July 1st—40% January 1st, 5-payment plan: 20% due July 1, September 1, November 1, January 1 and April 1). Tuition reduction for siblings, bursaries, merit scholarship grants, need-based scholarship grants, need-based loans, middle-income loans, paying campus jobs available. In 2008–09, 36% of upper-school students received aid; total upper-school merit-scholarship money awarded: $17,655. Total amount of financial aid awarded in 2008–09: $196,750.

Admissions Admissions testing or ETS high school placement exam required. Deadline for receipt of application materials: March 11. Application fee required: $65. On-campus interview required.

Athletics Interscholastic: aerobics (boys, girls), baseball (b), basketball (b,g), cross-country running (b,g), fitness (b,g), physical fitness (b,g), soccer (b,g), softball (g), strength & conditioning (b,g), volleyball (b,g), weight training (b,g); coed interscholastic: cheering, cross-country running, dance team, track and field. 4 PE instructors, 10 coaches.

Computers Computers are regularly used in yearbook classes. Computer network features include on-campus library services, online commercial services, Internet access, wireless campus network, Microsoft Office Suite XP Professional, extranet portal. Student e-mail accounts are available to students. Students grades are available online. The school has a published electronic and media policy.

Contact Mrs. Judy Umeck, Director of Admissions. 818-846-8141 Ext. 501. Fax: 818-843-8421. E-mail: judy.umeck@providencehigh.org. Web site: www.providencehigh.org.

PROVIDENCE HIGH SCHOOL

1215 North St. Mary's
San Antonio, Texas 78215-1787

Head of School: Mrs. Bristol

General Information Girls' day college-preparatory, arts, and religious studies school, affiliated with Roman Catholic Church. Grades 6–12. Founded: 1951. Setting: urban. 3-acre campus. 4 buildings on campus. Approved or accredited by Southern Association of Colleges and Schools, Southern Association of Independent Schools, Texas Catholic Conference, and Texas Education Agency. Total enrollment: 340. Upper school average class size: 22. Upper school faculty-student ratio: 1:10.

Upper School Student Profile Grade 6: 32 students (32 girls); Grade 7: 41 students (41 girls); Grade 8: 36 students (36 girls); Grade 9: 71 students (71 girls); Grade 10: 63 students (63 girls); Grade 11: 45 students (45 girls); Grade 12: 52 students (52 girls). 90% of students are Roman Catholic.

Faculty School total: 34. In upper school: 5 men, 26 women; 28 have advanced degrees.

Subjects Offered Acting, advanced chemistry, advanced math, Advanced Placement courses, aerobics, algebra, American government-AP, American history, American history-AP, American literature, American literature-AP, anatomy, ancient world history, art, athletics, audio visual/media, band, biology, biology-AP, British literature, British literature-AP, broadcast journalism, broadcasting, calculus-AP, career education internship, Catholic belief and practice, cheerleading, chemistry, choir, choral music, church history, composition-AP, computer information systems, concert band, concert choir, conflict resolution, creative writing, dance, dance performance, desktop publishing, drama, drama performance, drama workshop, economics, English, English language and composition-AP, English language-AP, English literature, English literature and composition-AP, English literature-AP, English-AP, film, fitness, foreign language, French, geography, government, government and politics-AP, history, history-AP, human anatomy, jazz band, journalism, JROTC, JROTC or LEAD (Leadership Education and Development), Latin, law, leadership, literature and composition-AP, music theory, newspaper, peer ministry, personal fitness, photography, photojournalism, physical education, physical fitness, physical science, physics, play production, psychology, social justice, sociology, softball, Spanish, Spanish language-AP, Spanish-AP, speech, sports, statistics-AP, student government, student publications, swimming, swimming competency, tennis, Texas history, the Web, theater, theater arts, theater design and production, theater production, theology, track and field, U.S. government and politics, U.S. government and politics-AP, U.S. history, U.S. history-AP, volleyball, Web site design, world geography, world history, yearbook.

Special Academic Programs Advanced Placement exam preparation; honors section; independent study; study at local college for college credit.

College Admission Counseling 57 students graduated in 2008; all went to college, including St. Mary's University; Texas A&M University; The University of Texas at Austin; The University of Texas at San Antonio.

Student Life Upper grades have uniform requirement, student council, honor system. Discipline rests primarily with faculty. Attendance at religious services is required.

Summer Programs Remediation, enrichment, advancement, sports, art/fine arts programs offered; session focuses on get ahead (improvement); held on campus; accepts girls; open to students from other schools. 50 students usually enrolled. 2009 schedule: June 6 to July 14. Application deadline: May 25.

Tuition and Aid Day student tuition: $7700. Tuition installment plan (monthly payment plans). Tuition reduction for siblings, merit scholarship grants, need-based scholarship grants available. In 2008–09, 50% of upper-school students received aid; total upper-school merit-scholarship money awarded: $45,000. Total amount of financial aid awarded in 2008–09: $200,000.

Admissions Traditional secondary-level entrance grade is 9. High School Placement Test required. Deadline for receipt of application materials: none. No application fee required.

Athletics Interscholastic: basketball, bowling, cheering, cross-country running, dance, golf, JROTC drill, soccer, softball, tennis, volleyball, winter soccer. 2 PE instructors, 7 coaches, 1 athletic trainer.

Computers Computers are regularly used in desktop publishing, journalism, newspaper, Web site design, yearbook classes. Computer network features include on-campus library services, online commercial services, Internet access, Internet filtering or blocking technology, online classrooms. Students grades are available online. The school has a published electronic and media policy.

Contact Mrs. Cerdedo, Admissions Director. 210-224-6651 Ext. 203. Fax: 210-224-6214. E-mail: ccerdedo@providencehs.net. Web site: www.providencehs.net.

PULASKI ACADEMY

12701 Hinson Road
Little Rock, Arkansas 72212

Head of School: Mr. Joe B Hatcher

General Information Coeducational day college-preparatory and arts school. Grades PK–12. Founded: 1971. Setting: urban. 32-acre campus. 4 buildings on campus. Approved or accredited by Independent Schools Association of the Central States. Member of National Association of Independent Schools and Secondary School Admission Test Board. Endowment: $1 million. Total enrollment: 1,313. Upper school average class size: 13. Upper school faculty-student ratio: 1:13.

Upper School Student Profile Grade 9: 94 students (48 boys, 46 girls); Grade 10: 86 students (43 boys, 43 girls); Grade 11: 91 students (43 boys, 48 girls); Grade 12: 104 students (54 boys, 50 girls).
Faculty School total: 112. In upper school: 19 men, 42 women; 14 have advanced degrees.
Subjects Offered Algebra, American government-AP, American history-AP, American literature, anatomy, art, art history, band, biology, biology-AP, calculus, calculus-AP, chemistry, chemistry-AP, chorus, community service, composition-AP, creative writing, debate, design, desktop publishing, drama, drawing, English, English literature, English literature-AP, European history-AP, fine arts, French, French-AP, geometry, German, government and politics-AP, grammar, health, humanities, journalism, Latin, Latin-AP, mathematics, music, music history, music theory, physical education, physical science, physics, physics-AP, physiology, pre-calculus, reading, science, social studies, Spanish, Spanish-AP, speech, statistics, theater, trigonometry, world civilizations, world history, yearbook.
Graduation Requirements Arts and fine arts (art, music, dance, drama), English, foreign language, history, mathematics, physical education (includes health), science. Community service is required.
Special Academic Programs Advanced Placement exam preparation; honors section; independent study; study abroad.
College Admission Counseling 86 students graduated in 2008; all went to college, including Baylor University; Harvard University; Southern Methodist University; University of Arkansas; Vanderbilt University. Mean SAT critical reading: 582, mean SAT math: 587, mean SAT writing: 620, mean combined SAT: 1789, mean composite ACT: 26.
Student Life Upper grades have specified standards of dress, student council, honor system. Discipline rests primarily with faculty.
Summer Programs Enrichment, art/fine arts, computer instruction programs offered; session focuses on enrichment opportunities; held on campus; accepts boys and girls; open to students from other schools. 700 students usually enrolled. 2009 schedule: June 15 to August 4. Application deadline: none.
Tuition and Aid Day student tuition: $3200–$9700. Tuition installment plan (monthly payment plans, individually arranged payment plans, school's own payment plan). Tuition reduction for siblings, need-based scholarship grants available. In 2008–09, 13% of upper-school students received aid. Total amount of financial aid awarded in 2008–09: $300,000.
Admissions Traditional secondary-level entrance grade is 9. For fall 2008, 32 students applied for upper-level admission, 27 were accepted, 24 enrolled. Stanford Achievement Test required. Deadline for receipt of application materials: none. Application fee required: $50. On-campus interview recommended.
Athletics Interscholastic: aerobics/dance (girls), aerobics/Nautilus (b), aquatics (b,g), baseball (b), basketball (b,g), cheering (g), cross-country running (b,g), dance (g), dance squad (g), dance team (g), diving (b,g), drill team (g), football (b), golf (b,g), pom squad (g), soccer (b,g), softball (g), swimming and diving (b,g), tennis (b,g); intramural: fitness (b,g); coed interscholastic: aerobics. 4 PE instructors, 10 coaches, 1 athletic trainer.
Computers Computers are regularly used in business, career exploration, college planning, creative writing, current events, data processing, economics, English, foreign language, geography, human geography—AP, information technology, introduction to technology, mathematics, newspaper, publications, SAT preparation, science, yearbook classes. Computer network features include on-campus library services, Internet access. The school has a published electronic and media policy.
Contact Gregg R. Ledbetter, JD, Head of Enrollment and Financial Aid. 501-604-1923. Fax: 501-225-1974. E-mail: gregg.ledbetter@pulaskiacademy.org. Web site: www.pulaskiacademy.org.

PUNAHOU SCHOOL

1601 Punahou Street
Honolulu, Hawaii 96822

Head of School: Dr. James K. Scott

General Information Coeducational day college-preparatory, arts, and technology school. Grades K–12. Founded: 1841. Setting: urban. 76-acre campus. 21 buildings on campus. Approved or accredited by Western Association of Schools and Colleges. Member of National Association of Independent Schools and Secondary School Admission Test Board. Endowment: $183.8 million. Total enrollment: 3,754. Upper school average class size: 21. Upper school faculty-student ratio: 1:12.
Upper School Student Profile Grade 9: 440 students (226 boys, 214 girls); Grade 10: 432 students (208 boys, 224 girls); Grade 11: 431 students (215 boys, 216 girls); Grade 12: 426 students (215 boys, 211 girls).
Faculty School total: 340. In upper school: 78 men, 79 women; 107 have advanced degrees.
Subjects Offered 20th century history, acting, algebra, American culture, American literature, American studies, anatomy and physiology, anthropology, Asian history, Asian literature, astronomy, Bible as literature, bioethics, biology, biology-AP, British literature, Buddhism, calculus-AP, calligraphy, ceramics, character education, chemistry, chemistry-AP, child development, Chinese history, chorus, composition, computer science, computer science-AP, conceptual physics, concert band, contemporary issues, creative writing, digital art, drawing, driver education, economics, English, environmental science-AP, European history, European history-AP, film and literature, French, French language-AP, genetics, geometry, glassblowing, global issues, government and politics-AP, guidance, Hawaiian history, Hawaiian language, history of jazz, humanities, independent study, integrated science, Japanese, Japanese history, jewelry making, journalism, JROTC or LEAD (Leadership Education and Development), keyboarding/computer, law, Mandarin, marching band, marine biology, mechanical drawing, media arts, medieval history, money management, music technology, music theory, oceanography, painting, peer counseling, photography, physical education, physics, physics-AP, pre-calculus, psychology, psychology-AP, religions, science research, sculpture, Shakespeare, social studies, Spanish, Spanish-AP, sports psychology, statistics-AP, studio art, studio art-AP, symphonic band, technical theater, the Sixties, theater design and production, trigonometry, U.S. government and politics-AP, U.S. history, U.S. history-AP, video, video film production, Western literature, wind ensemble, world civilizations, world literature, writing.
Graduation Requirements English, foreign language, mathematics, physical education (includes health), science, social studies (includes history), visual and performing arts, credits in critical thinking, ethical, spiritual, and community responsibility.
Special Academic Programs 32 Advanced Placement exams for which test preparation is offered; honors section; independent study; study abroad.
College Admission Counseling 425 students graduated in 2008; 423 went to college, including Boston University; Creighton University; Santa Clara University; University of Hawaii at Manoa; University of Southern California; University of Washington. Other: 2 had other specific plans. Mean SAT critical reading: 614, mean SAT math: 662, mean SAT writing: 613. 60% scored over 600 on SAT critical reading, 78% scored over 600 on SAT math, 59% scored over 600 on SAT writing.
Student Life Upper grades have specified standards of dress, student council, honor system. Discipline rests primarily with faculty. Attendance at religious services is required.
Summer Programs Enrichment, advancement, sports, art/fine arts programs offered; session focuses on enrichment and graduation credit; held both on and off campus; held at France, Italy, Spain, Rapa Nui, Japan, Costa Rica, China; accepts boys and girls; open to students from other schools. 4,000 students usually enrolled. 2009 schedule: June 16 to July 24. Application deadline: May 8.
Tuition and Aid Day student tuition: $16,675. Tuition installment plan (monthly payment plans, semester payment plan). Merit scholarship grants, need-based scholarship grants available. In 2008–09, 14% of upper-school students received aid; total upper-school merit-scholarship money awarded: $203,100. Total amount of financial aid awarded in 2008–09: $2,180,582.
Admissions Traditional secondary-level entrance grade is 9. For fall 2008, 431 students applied for upper-level admission, 134 were accepted, 98 enrolled. ERB CTP IV, Individual IQ, SSAT or TOEFL required. Deadline for receipt of application materials: December 1. Application fee required: $100. Interview required.
Athletics Interscholastic: baseball (boys), basketball (b,g), bowling (b,g), canoeing/kayaking (b,g), cheering (g), cross-country running (b,g), diving (b,g), football (b), golf (b,g), gymnastics (b,g), judo (b,g), kayaking (b,g), paddling (b,g), riflery (b,g), sailing (b,g), soccer (b,g), softball (g), swimming and diving (b,g), tennis (b,g), track and field (b,g), volleyball (b,g), water polo (b,g), wrestling (b,g); coed interscholastic: paddling. 4 PE instructors, 183 coaches, 3 athletic trainers.
Computers Computers are regularly used in all classes. Computer network features include on-campus library services, online commercial services, Internet access, wireless campus network, Internet filtering or blocking technology. Campus intranet, student e-mail accounts, and computer access in designated common areas are available to students. The school has a published electronic and media policy.
Contact Mrs. Betsy S. Hata, Director of Admission and Financial Aid. 808-944-5714. Fax: 808-943-3602. E-mail: admission@punahou.edu. Web site: www.punahou.edu.

PURNELL SCHOOL

Pottersville, New Jersey
See Special Needs Schools section.

THE PUTNEY SCHOOL

Elm Lea Farm
418 Houghton Brook Road
Putney, Vermont 05346-8675

Head of School: Emily Jones

General Information Coeducational boarding and day college-preparatory, arts, environmental science, and ESL school. Grades 9–12. Founded: 1935. Setting: rural. Nearest major city is Boston, MA. Students are housed in single-sex dormitories. 500-acre campus. 37 buildings on campus. Approved or accredited by Association of Independent Schools in New England, Independent Schools of Northern New England, New England Association of Schools and Colleges, The Association of Boarding Schools, and Vermont Department of Education. Member of National Association of Independent Schools and Secondary School Admission Test Board. Endowment: $18 million. Total enrollment: 226. Upper school average class size: 15. Upper school faculty-student ratio: 1:7.
Upper School Student Profile Grade 9: 39 students (18 boys, 21 girls); Grade 10: 58 students (21 boys, 37 girls); Grade 11: 65 students (32 boys, 33 girls); Grade 12:

64 students (31 boys, 33 girls). 75% of students are boarding students. 30% are state residents. 22 states are represented in upper school student body. 19% are international students. International students from China, France, Germany, Japan, Republic of Korea, and Russian Federation; 9 other countries represented in student body.
Faculty School total: 42. In upper school: 20 men, 22 women; 29 have advanced degrees; 26 reside on campus.
Subjects Offered Advanced chemistry, African dance, African drumming, African studies, agroecology, algebra, American history, American literature, anatomy, ancient history, art, art history, astronomy, biology, calculus, cartooning, ceramics, chamber groups, chemistry, chorus, college placement, comparative religion, computer science, conservation, creative writing, dance, design, digital photography, drama, drawing, ecology, economics, English, English literature, ensembles, environmental science, environmental systems, ESL, European history, expository writing, fabric arts, fiber arts, fine arts, foods, French, genetics, geometry, history, human development, instruments, jazz, jazz ensemble, Latin American history, literature, mathematics, Middle Eastern history, music, music appreciation, music composition, music history, music theory, musical theater, orchestra, painting, philosophy, photography, physical education, physics, physiology, post-calculus, printmaking, science, sculpture, sewing, Shakespeare, social studies, Spanish, stained glass, statistics, theater, U.S. history, video film production, vocal jazz, voice, weaving, women's studies, woodworking, work experience, world history, world literature, writing, yearbook, yoga.
Graduation Requirements Arts and fine arts (art, music, dance, drama), electives, English, foreign language, history, human development, lab science, mathematics, physical education (includes health), science, one trimester each of 6 required jobs, including lunch, dinner, barn, dishwashing, general substitute, and a land-use activity, Project Week: two projects each semester of dedicated work, one academic and one non-academic, participation in annual Long Spring camping/backpacking trips.
Special Academic Programs Advanced Placement exam preparation; independent study; term-away projects; academic accommodation for the gifted, the musically talented, and the artistically talented; ESL (17 students enrolled).
College Admission Counseling 62 students graduated in 2007; 60 went to college, including Columbia College; Dartmouth College; Earlham College; Hampshire College; Mount Holyoke College; New York University. Other: 2 had other specific plans. Mean SAT critical reading: 632, mean SAT math: 570, mean composite ACT: 25. 59% scored over 600 on SAT critical reading, 33% scored over 600 on SAT math, 50% scored over 26 on composite ACT.
Student Life Upper grades have student council, honor system. Discipline rests equally with students and faculty.
Tuition and Aid Day student tuition: $25,100; 7-day tuition and room/board: $38,600. Tuition installment plan (Academic Management Services Plan, Key Tuition Payment Plan, monthly payment plans, Tuition Management Systems Plan, prepayment discount plan). Need-based scholarship grants available. In 2007–08, 42% of upper-school students received aid. Total amount of financial aid awarded in 2007–08: $1,205,820.
Admissions Traditional secondary-level entrance grade is 9. For fall 2007, 157 students applied for upper-level admission, 137 were accepted, 81 enrolled. SSAT required. Deadline for receipt of application materials: January 15. Application fee required: $40. Interview required.
Athletics Interscholastic: bicycling (boys, girls), crew (b,g), cross-country running (b,g), lacrosse (b,g), nordic skiing (b,g), rowing (b,g), running (b,g), skiing (cross-country) (b,g), soccer (b,g); coed interscholastic: alpine skiing, basketball, Frisbee, skiing (downhill), ultimate Frisbee; coed intramural: aerobics/dance, aerobics/Nautilus, alpine skiing, backpacking, badminton, ballet, basketball, bicycling, boxing, broomball, canoeing/kayaking, Circus, climbing, crew, cross-country running, dance, equestrian sports, fencing, fitness, fitness walking, freestyle skiing, Frisbee, hiking/backpacking, horseback riding, jogging, modern dance, mountain biking, nordic skiing, outdoor activities, outdoor adventure, outdoor education, outdoor recreation, outdoor skills, outdoors, paddling, physical fitness, rappelling, rock climbing, running, sailboarding, skiing (cross-country), skiing (downhill), snowboarding, snowshoeing, soccer, strength & conditioning, table tennis, tennis, ultimate Frisbee, volleyball, walking, wall climbing, weight training, wilderness, wilderness survival, windsurfing, winter walking, yoga. 3 coaches.
Computers Computers are regularly used in English, foreign language, history, mathematics, music, science classes. Computer network features include on-campus library services, online commercial services, Internet access, wireless campus network, Internet filtering or blocking technology. Student e-mail accounts are available to students. The school has a published electronic and media policy.
Contact Ann McBroom, Admission Assistant. 802-387-6219. Fax: 802-387-6278. E-mail: admission@putneyschool.org. Web site: www.putneyschool.org.

See Close-Up on page 914.

QUEEN ANNE SCHOOL

14111 Oak Grove Road
Upper Marlboro, Maryland 20774
Head of School: Mr. J. Temple Blackwood

General Information Coeducational day college-preparatory, arts, religious studies, and technology school, affiliated with Episcopal Church. Grades 6–12. Founded: 1964. Setting: rural. Nearest major city is Washington, DC. 60-acre campus. 8 buildings on campus. Approved or accredited by Association of Independent Maryland Schools, National Association of Episcopal Schools, and Maryland Department of Education. Member of National Association of Independent Schools and Secondary School Admission Test Board. Total enrollment: 155. Upper school average class size: 13. Upper school faculty-student ratio: 1:7.
Upper School Student Profile Grade 6: 8 students (7 boys, 1 girl); Grade 7: 17 students (8 boys, 9 girls); Grade 8: 24 students (13 boys, 11 girls); Grade 9: 24 students (13 boys, 11 girls); Grade 10: 36 students (19 boys, 17 girls); Grade 11: 21 students (6 boys, 15 girls); Grade 12: 25 students (11 boys, 14 girls). 15% of students are members of Episcopal Church.
Faculty School total: 17. In upper school: 5 men, 9 women; 13 have advanced degrees.
Subjects Offered Algebra, American history, American history-AP, art, art history, arts, biology, biology-AP, calculus, calculus-AP, ceramics, chemistry, chemistry-AP, computer programming, computer science, creative writing, drama, earth science, economics, English, English literature, English literature and composition-AP, environmental science, ethics, fine arts, French, geography, geometry, government/civics, grammar, history, journalism, mathematics, music, philosophy, physical education, physics, physiology, psychology, religion, science, social studies, Spanish, theater, trigonometry, world history, world literature.
Graduation Requirements Arts and fine arts (art, music, dance, drama), English, foreign language, mathematics, physical education (includes health), religion (includes Bible studies and theology), science, social studies (includes history).
Special Academic Programs 10 Advanced Placement exams for which test preparation is offered.
College Admission Counseling 35 students graduated in 2008; all went to college, including Bowie State University; Drexel University; St. Mary's College of Maryland; Temple University. Mean SAT critical reading: 585, mean SAT math: 558.
Student Life Upper grades have specified standards of dress, student council, honor system. Discipline rests equally with students and faculty.
Summer Programs Enrichment, sports, computer instruction programs offered; session focuses on enrichment and sports; held on campus; accepts boys and girls; open to students from other schools. 300 students usually enrolled. 2009 schedule: June 16 to August 20. Application deadline: June 16.
Tuition and Aid Day student tuition: $18,850. Tuition installment plan (FACTS Tuition Payment Plan, monthly payment plans, full-payment discount plan, 2- and 10-payment plans). Need-based scholarship grants available. In 2008–09, 58% of upper-school students received aid. Total amount of financial aid awarded in 2008–09: $603,819.
Admissions Traditional secondary-level entrance grade is 9. For fall 2008, 94 students applied for upper-level admission, 33 were accepted, 33 enrolled. ISEE required. Deadline for receipt of application materials: none. Application fee required: $50. On-campus interview required.
Athletics Interscholastic: aerobics/dance (girls), ballet (g), baseball (b), basketball (b,g), cheering (g), dance (g), dance squad (g), dance team (g), lacrosse (b,g), soccer (b,g), softball (g), swimming and diving (b,g), tennis (b,g), volleyball (b,g), wrestling (b); intramural: aerobics/dance (g), ballet (b,g), dance (g), dance team (g), volleyball (b,g); coed interscholastic: cross-country running, outdoor education, tennis, track and field. 1 PE instructor, 4 coaches.
Computers Computers are regularly used in English, foreign language, mathematics, music, science classes. Computer network features include on-campus library services, online commercial services, Internet access, wireless campus network, Internet filtering or blocking technology. Student e-mail accounts are available to students. Students grades are available online. The school has a published electronic and media policy.
Contact Ms. Courtney Pouchet, Director of Admissions. 301-249-5000 Ext. 305. Fax: 301-249-3838. E-mail: cpouchet@queenanne.org. Web site: www.queenanne.org.

QUEEN MARGARET'S SCHOOL

660 Brownsey Avenue
Duncan, British Columbia V9L 1C2, Canada
Head of School: Pat Rowantree

General Information Girls' boarding and coeducational day college-preparatory, general academic, arts, and athletics and equestrian studies school. Boarding girls grades 7–12, day boys grades JK–7, day girls grades JK–12. Founded: 1921. Setting: small town. Nearest major city is Victoria, Canada. Students are housed in single-sex dormitories. 27-acre campus. 8 buildings on campus. Approved or accredited by Canadian Association of Independent Schools, Canadian Educational Standards Institute, Pacific Northwest Association of Independent Schools, The Association of Boarding Schools, and British Columbia Department of Education. Member of Canadian Association of Independent Schools. Language of instruction: English. Endowment: CAN$500,000. Total enrollment: 321. Upper school average class size: 18. Upper school faculty-student ratio: 1:7.
Upper School Student Profile 65% of students are boarding students. 53% are province residents. 11 provinces are represented in upper school student body. 47% are international students. International students from Hong Kong, Japan, Mexico, Republic of Korea, Taiwan, and United States; 17 other countries represented in student body.

Faculty School total: 36. In upper school: 8 men, 12 women; 8 have advanced degrees; 4 reside on campus.
Subjects Offered Advanced math, algebra, animal husbandry, animal science, applied skills, art, biology, business education, business skills, calculus, calculus-AP, Canadian history, career and personal planning, career exploration, chemistry, chemistry-AP, chorus, college planning, computer science, creative writing, drama, English, English literature, equine science, ESL, fine arts, French, geography, geometry, grammar, health, history, home economics, instrumental music, Japanese, journalism, mathematics, photography, physical education, physics, SAT preparation, science, social studies, speech, sports, sports psychology, theater, TOEFL preparation, trigonometry, visual arts, world history, writing.
Graduation Requirements Arts and fine arts (art, music, dance, drama), career and personal planning, computer science, English, finance, foreign language, mathematics, media production, physical education (includes health), science, social studies (includes history), women's studies. Community service is required.
Special Academic Programs Independent study; academic accommodation for the gifted, the musically talented, and the artistically talented; ESL (30 students enrolled).
College Admission Counseling 28 students graduated in 2008; 26 went to college, including McGill University; Queen's University at Kingston; The University of British Columbia; University of Toronto; University of Victoria; Washington State University. Other: 1 went to work, 1 had other specific plans.
Student Life Upper grades have uniform requirement, student council. Discipline rests primarily with faculty. Attendance at religious services is required.
Summer Programs Enrichment, ESL, sports programs offered; session focuses on equestrian sports; held on campus; accepts boys and girls; open to students from other schools. 100 students usually enrolled. 2009 schedule: July 6 to August 29. Application deadline: June 15.
Tuition and Aid Day student tuition: CAN$9400–CAN$11,680; 5-day tuition and room/board: CAN$25,700; 7-day tuition and room/board: CAN$28,500–CAN$38,270. Tuition installment plan (Insured Tuition Payment Plan, monthly payment plans, individually arranged payment plans). Tuition reduction for siblings, bursaries, merit scholarship grants, tuition reduction for children of staff available. In 2008–09, 30% of upper-school students received aid; total upper-school merit-scholarship money awarded: CAN$50,000. Total amount of financial aid awarded in 2008–09: CAN$100,000.
Admissions Traditional secondary-level entrance grade is 8. Otis-Lennon School Ability Test, SLEP or Stanford Achievement Test required. Deadline for receipt of application materials: none. Application fee required: CAN$200. Interview required.
Athletics Interscholastic: badminton (girls), basketball (g), canoeing/kayaking (g), cooperative games (g), cross-country running (g), dressage (g), equestrian sports (g), field hockey (g), golf (g), horseback riding (g), ocean paddling (g), outdoor activities (g), outdoor recreation (g), paddling (g), rugby (g), soccer (g), tennis (g), track and field (g), volleyball (g); intramural: aerobics (g), aerobics/dance (g), alpine skiing (g), aquatics (g), backpacking (g), badminton (g), ball hockey (g), basketball (g), canoeing/kayaking (g), cooperative games (g), Cosom hockey (g), cross-country running (g), dressage (g), equestrian sports (g), field hockey (g), floor hockey (g), Frisbee (g), golf (g), horseback riding (g), indoor hockey (g), indoor soccer (g), jogging (g), nordic skiing (g), ocean paddling (g), outdoor activities (g), outdoor recreation (g), paddling (g), physical fitness (g), physical training (g), rugby (g), skiing (downhill) (g), snowboarding (g), soccer (g), tennis (g), track and field (g), ultimate Frisbee (g), volleyball (g). 2 PE instructors, 2 coaches, 2 athletic trainers.
Computers Computers are regularly used in career education, career exploration, college planning, creative writing, English, ESL, French, information technology, introduction to technology, journalism, mathematics, media arts, media production, science, social science, technology classes. Computer network features include on-campus library services, Internet access, wireless campus network, Internet filtering or blocking technology. Student e-mail accounts are available to students. The school has a published electronic and media policy.
Contact Chad Holtum, Deputy Head, Office of Admissions and Advancement. 250-746-4185. Fax: 250-746-4187. E-mail: admissions@qms.bc.ca. Web site: www.qms.bc.ca.

QUEEN OF PEACE HIGH SCHOOL

7659 South Linder Avenue
Burbank, Illinois 60459

Head of School: Dr. Kathleen Hanlon

General Information Girls' day college-preparatory school, affiliated with Roman Catholic Church. Grades 9–12. Founded: 1962. Setting: suburban. Nearest major city is Chicago. Approved or accredited by Illinois Department of Education. Upper school average class size: 19. Upper school faculty-student ratio: 1:16.
Faculty School total: 42.
Student Life Upper grades have uniform requirement, student council. Attendance at religious services is required.
Admissions No application fee required.
Contact Ms. Sharon Geinosky, Director of Guidance. 708-458-7600 Ext. 290. Fax: 708-458-5734. Web site: www.queenofpeacehs.org.

QUEENSWAY CHRISTIAN COLLEGE

1536 The Queensway
Etobicoke, Ontario M8Z 1T5, Canada

Head of School: Mr. John Allardyce

General Information Coeducational day college-preparatory, arts, religious studies, and technology school, affiliated with Protestant faith. Grades JK–12. Founded: 1978. Setting: urban. Nearest major city is Toronto, Canada. 1 building on campus. Approved or accredited by Association of Christian Schools International and Ontario Department of Education. Language of instruction: English. Total enrollment: 106. Upper school average class size: 10. Upper school faculty-student ratio: 1:7.
Upper School Student Profile Grade 9: 5 students (3 boys, 2 girls); Grade 10: 7 students (4 boys, 3 girls); Grade 11: 11 students (5 boys, 6 girls); Grade 12: 17 students (12 boys, 5 girls). 80% of students are Protestant.
Faculty School total: 14. In upper school: 3 men, 4 women; 3 have advanced degrees.
Subjects Offered Algebra, biology, calculus, Canadian geography, Canadian history, career exploration, chemistry, Christian education, civics, computers, dramatic arts, English, family studies, French, geometry, health education, physical education, physics, visual arts, world history, world issues.
Graduation Requirements Arts, Canadian geography, Canadian history, career exploration, civics, English, French, mathematics, physical education (includes health), science, Bible, literacy test, 40 hours of community service.
Special Academic Programs Independent study; ESL (2 students enrolled).
College Admission Counseling 10 students graduated in 2008.
Student Life Upper grades have uniform requirement, student council, honor system. Discipline rests primarily with faculty. Attendance at religious services is required.
Tuition and Aid Day student tuition: CAN$8100. Tuition installment plan (monthly payment plans, individually arranged payment plans). Tuition reduction for siblings, need-based scholarship grants available. In 2008–09, 3% of upper-school students received aid. Total amount of financial aid awarded in 2008–09: CAN$5000.
Admissions Traditional secondary-level entrance grade is 9. For fall 2008, 7 students applied for upper-level admission, 7 were accepted, 7 enrolled. CTBS (or similar from their school) required. Deadline for receipt of application materials: none. Application fee required: CAN$400. On-campus interview required.
Athletics Interscholastic: basketball (boys, girls), cross-country running (b,g), flag football (b), floor hockey (b,g), running (b,g), soccer (b,g), softball (b,g), track and field (b,g), volleyball (b,g); intramural: badminton (b,g), ball hockey (b,g), baseball (b,g); coed interscholastic: badminton, ball hockey, baseball, cross-country running, fitness, life saving, outdoor activities, outdoor recreation, outdoor skills, physical fitness, physical training, running, strength & conditioning, track and field, volleyball; coed intramural: badminton, ball hockey, baseball, floor hockey, football. 1 PE instructor, 3 coaches.
Computers Computers are regularly used in information technology classes. Computer network features include on-campus library services, online commercial services, Internet access, Internet filtering or blocking technology. Students grades are available online. The school has a published electronic and media policy.
Contact Mrs. Sue Broomer, Secretary. 416-255-6033. Fax: 416-255-7389. E-mail: sbroomer@qccollege.com. Web site: www.qccollege.com.

QUIGLEY CATHOLIC HIGH SCHOOL

200 Quigley Drive
Baden, Pennsylvania 15005-1295

Head of School: Dr. Madonna J. Helbling

General Information Coeducational day college-preparatory, religious studies, and technology school, affiliated with Roman Catholic Church. Grades 9–12. Founded: 1967. Setting: suburban. Nearest major city is Pittsburgh. 19-acre campus. 1 building on campus. Approved or accredited by Middle States Association of Colleges and Schools, National Catholic Education Association, and Pennsylvania Department of Education. Endowment: $2.5 million. Total enrollment: 215. Upper school average class size: 20. Upper school faculty-student ratio: 1:12.
Upper School Student Profile Grade 9: 47 students (20 boys, 27 girls); Grade 10: 71 students (34 boys, 37 girls); Grade 11: 59 students (27 boys, 32 girls); Grade 12: 38 students (15 boys, 23 girls). 95% of students are Roman Catholic.
Faculty School total: 18. In upper school: 10 men, 6 women; 14 have advanced degrees.
Subjects Offered Advanced Placement courses, algebra, American government, American history-AP, American literature, anatomy and physiology, art, athletics, band, baseball, Basic programming, basketball, biology, bookbinding, bowling, British literature, British literature (honors), calculus, calculus-AP, campus ministry, ceramics, cheerleading, chemistry, choir, chorus, church history, composition-AP, computer programming, computer science, concert choir, debate, drawing, ecology, English-AP, European history-AP, French language-AP, geometry, government, guitar, health education, honors algebra, honors world history, library, physical education, physical science, physics, piano, play production, pottery, pre-algebra, pre-calculus, printmaking, religious education, SAT preparation, Spanish, speech and debate, sports, student government, studio art, trigonometry, yearbook.
Graduation Requirements Algebra, American government, American history, American history-AP, British literature, British literature (honors), chemistry, church history, computer science, English, English literature, European history, European history-AP, French, geometry, government, health, math review, music, physical

science, physics, religion (includes Bible studies and theology), Spanish, U.S. history, 125 hours of service completed by end of senior year.

Special Academic Programs Advanced Placement exam preparation; honors section; study at local college for college credit.

College Admission Counseling 38 students graduated in 2008; all went to college, including John Carroll University; University of Pittsburgh.

Student Life Upper grades have uniform requirement, student council, honor system. Discipline rests primarily with faculty. Attendance at religious services is required.

Tuition and Aid Day student tuition: $7450. Tuition installment plan (SMART Tuition Payment Plan, individually arranged payment plans, one time payment in full). Tuition reduction for siblings, merit scholarship grants, need-based scholarship grants, paying campus jobs available. In 2008–09, 48% of upper-school students received aid; total upper-school merit-scholarship money awarded: $33,660. Total amount of financial aid awarded in 2008–09: $299,953.

Admissions Traditional secondary-level entrance grade is 9. For fall 2008, 17 students applied for upper-level admission, 12 were accepted, 12 enrolled. Iowa Test, CTBS, or TAP, Math Placement Exam or PSAT required. Deadline for receipt of application materials: none. Application fee required: $30. Interview required.

Athletics Interscholastic: baseball (boys), basketball (b,g), bowling (b,g), cheering (g), cross-country running (b,g), dance team (g), golf (b), gymnastics (g), ice hockey (b), soccer (b,g), softball (g), swimming and diving (g), tennis (g), volleyball (g), wrestling (b). 2 PE instructors, 11 coaches, 1 athletic trainer.

Computers Computers are regularly used in newspaper, programming, yearbook classes. Computer resources include on-campus library services, Internet access.

Contact Sr. Bridget Reilly, Guidance Counselor. 724-869-2188. Fax: 724-869-2188. E-mail: reilly@qchs.org. Web site: www.qchs.org.

QUINTE CHRISTIAN HIGH SCHOOL

138 Wallbridge-Loyalist Road
RR 2
Belleville, Ontario K8N 4Z2, Canada

Head of School: Mr. Johan Cooke

General Information Coeducational day college-preparatory, general academic, arts, business, vocational, religious studies, bilingual studies, and technology school, affiliated with Christian faith, Protestant faith. Grades 9–12. Founded: 1977. Setting: suburban. Nearest major city is Toronto, Canada. 25-acre campus. 1 building on campus. Approved or accredited by Christian Schools International, Ontario Ministry of Education, and Ontario Department of Education. Language of instruction: English. Total enrollment: 157. Upper school average class size: 15. Upper school faculty-student ratio: 1:15.

Upper School Student Profile Grade 9: 38 students (14 boys, 24 girls); Grade 10: 46 students (22 boys, 24 girls); Grade 11: 39 students (16 boys, 23 girls); Grade 12: 33 students (11 boys, 22 girls). 90% of students are Christian, Protestant.

Faculty School total: 15. In upper school: 9 men, 6 women; 2 have advanced degrees.

Subjects Offered Accounting, art, Bible, biology, calculus, careers, chemistry, Christian education, civics, computers, drama, English, English literature, ESL, French, geography, history, law, leadership education training, mathematics, mathematics-AP, media, music, peer counseling, physical education, physics, religious education, science, shop, society challenge and change, technical education, transportation technology, world issues, world religions.

Graduation Requirements Accounting, applied arts, careers, Christian education, civics, computers, English, French, geography, mathematics, physical education (includes health), religious education, science, social studies (includes history), world religions, Ontario Christian School Diploma Requirements.

Special Academic Programs Special instructional classes for students with learning disabilities.

College Admission Counseling 27 students graduated in 2008; 20 went to college, including Calvin College; Dordt College; Queen's University at Kingston; Redeemer University College; University of Guelph; University of Waterloo. Other: 4 went to work, 3 had other specific plans. 100% scored over 26 on composite ACT.

Student Life Upper grades have specified standards of dress, student council, honor system. Discipline rests primarily with faculty. Attendance at religious services is required.

Tuition and Aid Day student tuition: CAN$11,200. Tuition installment plan (monthly payment plans, individually arranged payment plans). Tuition reduction for siblings, need-based scholarship grants available. In 2008–09, 18% of upper-school students received aid.

Admissions Traditional secondary-level entrance grade is 9. Deadline for receipt of application materials: March 31. Application fee required: CAN$250. Interview required.

Athletics Interscholastic: badminton (boys, girls), basketball (b,g), cross-country running (b,g), track and field (b,g), volleyball (b,g); coed interscholastic: badminton; coed intramural: badminton, basketball, fitness walking, indoor soccer, physical training, volleyball. 4 PE instructors.

Computers Computers are regularly used in all classes. Computer network features include on-campus library services, Internet access, wireless campus network, Internet filtering or blocking technology. Campus intranet, student e-mail accounts, and computer access in designated common areas are available to students. The school has a published electronic and media policy.

Contact Mrs. Hermien Hogewoning, Administrative Assistant. 613-968-7870. Fax: 613-968-7970. E-mail: admin@qchs.ca. Web site: www.qchs.ca.

RABBI ALEXANDER S. GROSS HEBREW ACADEMY

2425 Pine Tree Drive
Miami Beach, Florida 33140

Head of School: Dr. Roni Raab

General Information Coeducational day college-preparatory, general academic, religious studies, and technology school, affiliated with Jewish faith. Grades N–12. Founded: 1948. Setting: urban. 4-acre campus. 1 building on campus. Approved or accredited by Massachusetts Office of Child Care Services, Southern Association of Colleges and Schools, and Florida Department of Education. Member of Secondary School Admission Test Board. Languages of instruction: English and Hebrew. Endowment: $650,000. Total enrollment: 499. Upper school average class size: 18. Upper school faculty-student ratio: 1:4.

Upper School Student Profile Grade 9: 44 students (30 boys, 14 girls); Grade 10: 63 students (27 boys, 36 girls); Grade 11: 47 students (24 boys, 23 girls); Grade 12: 43 students (23 boys, 20 girls). 100% of students are Jewish.

Faculty School total: 70. In upper school: 21 men, 18 women; 23 have advanced degrees.

Subjects Offered Algebra, audio visual/media, Bible studies, biology, biology-AP, calculus, calculus-AP, chemistry, chemistry-AP, computers, economics, English, English-AP, environmental science, geometry, Jewish studies, life science, physical education, physics, political science, pre-calculus, SAT preparation, social studies, Spanish, Talmud, technology.

Graduation Requirements Arts and fine arts (art, music, dance, drama), business skills (includes word processing), computer science, English, foreign language, mathematics, physical education (includes health), religion (includes Bible studies and theology), science, social science, social studies (includes history). Community service is required.

Special Academic Programs Advanced Placement exam preparation; honors section; independent study; study at local college for college credit; academic accommodation for the gifted; ESL (3 students enrolled).

College Admission Counseling 51 students graduated in 2008; 50 went to college, including Florida International University; New York University; University of Florida; University of Maryland, College Park; Yeshiva University. Other: 1 went to work. Mean SAT critical reading: 562, mean SAT math: 558, mean SAT writing: 547, mean combined SAT: 1667, mean composite ACT: 26.

Student Life Upper grades have specified standards of dress, student council, honor system. Discipline rests primarily with faculty. Attendance at religious services is required.

Tuition and Aid Day student tuition: $14,000. Tuition installment plan (monthly payment plans, individually arranged payment plans). Tuition reduction for siblings, need-based scholarship grants available. In 2008–09, 46% of upper-school students received aid. Total amount of financial aid awarded in 2008–09: $300,000.

Admissions Traditional secondary-level entrance grade is 9. For fall 2008, 40 students applied for upper-level admission, 33 were accepted, 30 enrolled. SSAT required. Deadline for receipt of application materials: none. No application fee required. On-campus interview required.

Athletics Interscholastic: basketball (boys, girls), soccer (b), tennis (b,g), volleyball (g); intramural: basketball (b,g), soccer (b), tennis (b,g), volleyball (g). 2 PE instructors, 3 coaches.

Computers Computers are regularly used in English, mathematics, religion, science classes. Computer network features include Internet access. Student e-mail accounts are available to students.

Contact Rabbi Mordechai Shifman, Principal of Judaic Studies. 305-532-6421. Fax: 305-535-5670. E-mail: mshifman@rasg.org. Web site: www.rasg.org.

RABUN GAP-NACOOCHEE SCHOOL

339 Nacoochee Drive
Rabun Gap, Georgia 30568

Head of School: Mr. John D. Marshall

General Information Coeducational boarding and day college-preparatory, arts, ESL, and performing arts school, affiliated with Presbyterian Church. Boarding grades 7–12, day grades 6–12. Founded: 1903. Setting: rural. Nearest major city is Atlanta. Students are housed in single-sex dormitories. 1,400-acre campus. 14 buildings on campus. Approved or accredited by Evangelical Lutheran Church in America, Georgia Independent School Association, Southern Association of Colleges and Schools, Southern Association of Independent Schools, The Association of Boarding Schools, and Georgia Department of Education. Member of National Association of Independent Schools and Secondary School Admission Test Board. Endowment: $50 million. Total enrollment: 357. Upper school average class size: 16. Upper school faculty-student ratio: 1:8.

Upper School Student Profile Grade 9: 56 students (29 boys, 27 girls); Grade 10: 76 students (39 boys, 37 girls); Grade 11: 72 students (35 boys, 37 girls); Grade 12: 61 students (30 boys, 31 girls). 58% of students are boarding students. 41% are state residents. 18 states are represented in upper school student body. 19% are international

students. International students from China, Germany, Mexico, Republic of Korea, Taiwan, and Turks and Caicos Islands; 9 other countries represented in student body. 10% of students are Presbyterian.
Faculty School total: 52. In upper school: 19 men, 21 women; 26 have advanced degrees; 39 reside on campus.
Subjects Offered Advanced Placement courses, algebra, American government-AP, American literature, anatomy, ancient world history, art, art history, art history-AP, band, Bible studies, biology, biology-AP, botany, calculus-AP, chemistry, chemistry-AP, chorus, computer-aided design, creative writing, economics, English language-AP, English literature-AP, environmental science, environmental science-AP, ESL, European history-AP, French, French-AP, geography, geometry, government, government-AP, health, health education, history-AP, honors algebra, honors English, honors U.S. history, honors world history, industrial arts, journalism, life science, mathematics, modern European history-AP, modern world history, music, orchestra, physical education, physical science, physics, physics-AP, pre-algebra, pre-calculus, psychology, science, Spanish, Spanish language-AP, Spanish-AP, statistics and probability, studio art-AP, theater, U.S. history, U.S. history-AP, wind ensemble, world geography, world history, world literature, yearbook.
Graduation Requirements Algebra, ancient world history, arts and fine arts (art, music, dance, drama), biology, chemistry, English, foreign language, geometry, mathematics, modern world history, physical education (includes health), physics, religion (includes Bible studies and theology), science, social studies (includes history), U.S. history, participation in Intersession.
Special Academic Programs Advanced Placement exam preparation; honors section; independent study; ESL (16 students enrolled).
College Admission Counseling 69 students graduated in 2008; all went to college, including College of Charleston; Emory University; Georgia Institute of Technology; The University of North Carolina at Asheville; United States Naval Academy; University of Georgia.
Student Life Upper grades have uniform requirement, student council, honor system. Discipline rests primarily with faculty. Attendance at religious services is required.
Summer Programs Remediation, advancement, sports programs offered; session focuses on fall sports team preparation, ESL and math remedial and enrichment programs; held on campus; accepts boys and girls; not open to students from other schools. 130 students usually enrolled. 2009 schedule: July 30 to August 22. Application deadline: February 1.
Tuition and Aid Day student tuition: $15,220; 7-day tuition and room/board: $33,700. Tuition installment plan (Insured Tuition Payment Plan, monthly payment plans, semester payment plan). Merit scholarship grants, need-based scholarship grants, tuition remission for children of faculty and staff available. In 2008–09, 65% of upper-school students received aid; total upper-school merit-scholarship money awarded: $266,930. Total amount of financial aid awarded in 2008–09: $2,572,695.
Admissions Traditional secondary-level entrance grade is 9. For fall 2008, 308 students applied for upper-level admission, 196 were accepted, 117 enrolled. ISEE, SLEP for foreign students, SSAT or TOEFL required. Deadline for receipt of application materials: February 1. Application fee required: $85. Interview required.
Athletics Interscholastic: baseball (boys), basketball (b,g), cross-country running (b,g), football (b), soccer (b,g), softball (g), swimming and diving (b,g), tennis (b,g), volleyball (g); intramural: soccer (b,g), swimming and diving (b,g), tennis (b,g); coed interscholastic: Circus, dance team, golf, tennis; coed intramural: aerobics/dance, ballet, basketball, bicycling, canoeing/kayaking, Circus, climbing, combined training, dance, dance team, fitness, fitness walking, hiking/backpacking, kayaking, modern dance, mountain biking, Nautilus, outdoor activities, physical training, rafting, rock climbing, strength & conditioning, swimming and diving, tennis, triathlon, ultimate Frisbee, wall climbing, weight lifting, yoga. 1 PE instructor, 22 coaches, 1 athletic trainer.
Computers Computers are regularly used in English, library skills, literary magazine, technical drawing, theater arts, writing, yearbook classes. Computer network features include on-campus library services, online commercial services, Internet access, wireless campus network, Internet filtering or blocking technology, application and re-enrollment online services. Campus intranet and student e-mail accounts are available to students. The school has a published electronic and media policy.
Contact Mrs. Kathy Watts, Admission Assistant. 706-746-7720. Fax: 706-746-7797. E-mail: kwatts@rabungap.org. Web site: www.rabungap.org.

See Close-Up on page 916.

RAMBAM MESIVTA

15 Frost Lane
Lawrence, New York 11559
Head of School: Rabbi Zev Meir Friedman

General Information Boys' day college-preparatory, religious studies, and technology school, affiliated with Jewish faith; primarily serves students with learning disabilities and individuals with Attention Deficit Disorder. Grades 9–12. Founded: 1991. Setting: suburban. Nearest major city is New York. 1-acre campus. 1 building on campus. Approved or accredited by Middle States Association of Colleges and Schools and New York State Board of Regents. Languages of instruction: English and Hebrew. Total enrollment: 156. Upper school average class size: 23. Upper school faculty-student ratio: 1:3.
Upper School Student Profile Grade 9: 41 students (41 boys); Grade 10: 36 students (36 boys); Grade 11: 37 students (37 boys); Grade 12: 42 students (42 boys). 100% of students are Jewish.
Faculty School total: 46. In upper school: 41 men, 4 women; 40 have advanced degrees.
Subjects Offered Accounting, Advanced Placement courses, algebra, Bible studies, biology-AP, business, business applications, business mathematics, calculus-AP, chemistry-AP, computer literacy, economics, emergency medicine, English, English-AP, ethics, European history, European history-AP, freshman seminar, geometry, Hebrew, Hebrew scripture, Holocaust studies, independent study, Israeli studies, Jewish history, Jewish studies, Judaic studies, Middle Eastern history, moral reasoning, moral theology, philosophy, physical education, physics-AP, prayer/spirituality, pre-calculus, psychology-AP, Rabbinic literature, robotics, SAT preparation, Spanish, Talmud, trigonometry, U.S. history, U.S. history-AP, Web site design.
Special Academic Programs Advanced Placement exam preparation; honors section; independent study; study at local college for college credit; academic accommodation for the gifted.
College Admission Counseling 36 students graduated in 2008; they went to Columbia College; Harvard University; New York University; Queens College of the City University of New York; University of Pennsylvania; Yeshiva University. Other: 36 entered a postgraduate year. Median SAT critical reading: 570, median SAT math: 620, median SAT writing: 570.
Student Life Upper grades have specified standards of dress, student council, honor system. Discipline rests primarily with faculty. Attendance at religious services is required.
Tuition and Aid Day student tuition: $14,100. Tuition installment plan (monthly payment plans, individually arranged payment plans). Merit scholarship grants, need-based scholarship grants, need-based loans available. In 2008–09, 30% of upper-school students received aid; total upper-school merit-scholarship money awarded: $12,500. Total amount of financial aid awarded in 2008–09: $300,000.
Admissions Traditional secondary-level entrance grade is 9. For fall 2008, 110 students applied for upper-level admission, 42 were accepted, 42 enrolled. Board of Jewish Education Entrance Exam required. Deadline for receipt of application materials: none. Application fee required: $100. On-campus interview required.
Athletics Interscholastic: ball hockey, basketball, bowling, floor hockey, soccer, softball, tennis; intramural: basketball, table tennis, touch football. 4 coaches.
Computers Computers are regularly used in basic skills, video film production, Web site design classes. Computer resources include Internet access, wireless campus network, Internet filtering or blocking technology. Students grades are available online.
Contact Shirley Levy. 516-371-5824 Ext. 100. Fax: 516-371-4706. E-mail: info@rambam.org. Web site: www.rambam.org.

RANDOLPH-MACON ACADEMY

200 Academy Drive
Front Royal, Virginia 22630
Head of School: Maj. Gen. Henry M. Hobgood

General Information Coeducational boarding and day college-preparatory, religious studies, technology, Air Force Junior ROTC, ESL, and military school, affiliated with Methodist Church. Grades 6–PG. Founded: 1892. Setting: small town. Nearest major city is Washington, DC. Students are housed in single-sex dormitories. 135-acre campus. 8 buildings on campus. Approved or accredited by Southern Association of Colleges and Schools, The Association of Boarding Schools, University Senate of United Methodist Church, Virginia Association of Independent Schools, and Virginia Department of Education. Member of National Association of Independent Schools. Endowment: $3.8 million. Total enrollment: 373. Upper school average class size: 14. Upper school faculty-student ratio: 1:9.
Upper School Student Profile Grade 9: 51 students (42 boys, 9 girls); Grade 10: 64 students (42 boys, 22 girls); Grade 11: 91 students (68 boys, 23 girls); Grade 12: 94 students (68 boys, 26 girls). 77% of students are boarding students. 46% are state residents. 29 states are represented in upper school student body. 22% are international students. International students from China, Hong Kong, Republic of Korea, Saudi Arabia, Spain, and Viet Nam; 6 other countries represented in student body. 10% of students are Methodist.
Faculty School total: 49. In upper school: 24 men, 13 women; 18 have advanced degrees; 22 reside on campus.
Subjects Offered Advanced math, aerospace science, algebra, American government, American government-AP, American history, American history-AP, American literature, American literature-AP, anatomy and physiology, art, art history-AP, band, Bible studies, biology, biology-AP, British literature, calculus, calculus-AP, chemistry, chorus, Civil War, comparative religion, composition-AP, computer applications, computer keyboarding, computer literacy, conceptual physics, concert band, concert choir, critical thinking, desktop publishing, discrete math, drama, English, English composition, English literature, English literature and composition-AP, English-AP, ESL, European history-AP, flight instruction, French, French language-AP, geometry, geopolitics, German, German-AP, government/civics, handbells, history, honors algebra, honors English, honors geometry, honors U.S. history, independent study, JROTC, Latin, mathematics, music, music appreciation, New Testament, personal finance, personal fitness, photography, physical education, physics, physics-AP, pre-algebra, pre-calculus, religion, SAT preparation, science,

senior seminar, Shakespeare, social studies, Spanish, Spanish literature-AP, speech and debate, statistics-AP, studio art, theater arts, trigonometry, U.S. government, U.S. history, world history, yearbook.

Graduation Requirements Aerospace science, computer science, English, foreign language, mathematics, physical education (includes health), religion (includes Bible studies and theology), science, social studies (includes history), Air Force Junior ROTC for each year student is enrolled.

Special Academic Programs Advanced Placement exam preparation; honors section; independent study; study at local college for college credit; study abroad; academic accommodation for the gifted; ESL (18 students enrolled).

College Admission Counseling 89 students graduated in 2008; all went to college, including Embry-Riddle Aeronautical University; Lynchburg College; Old Dominion University; Penn State University Park; Purdue University; West Virginia University. Median SAT critical reading: 490, median SAT math: 580, median SAT writing: 510, median combined SAT: 1590. 22% scored over 600 on SAT critical reading, 48% scored over 600 on SAT math, 10% scored over 600 on SAT writing, 18% scored over 1800 on combined SAT.

Student Life Upper grades have uniform requirement, student council, honor system. Discipline rests equally with students and faculty. Attendance at religious services is required.

Summer Programs Remediation, enrichment, advancement, ESL, art/fine arts, computer instruction programs offered; session focuses on remediation, new courses, ESL, flight, college counseling; held on campus; accepts boys and girls; open to students from other schools. 180 students usually enrolled. 2009 schedule: June 28 to July 24. Application deadline: June 26.

Tuition and Aid Day student tuition: $13,656; 7-day tuition and room/board: $27,905. Tuition installment plan (monthly payment plans, 2-payment plan). Tuition reduction for siblings, merit scholarship grants, need-based scholarship grants, paying campus jobs, Methodist Church scholarships available. In 2008–09, 14% of upper-school students received aid; total upper-school merit-scholarship money awarded: $51,000. Total amount of financial aid awarded in 2008–09: $259,341.

Admissions Traditional secondary-level entrance grade is 9. For fall 2008, 226 students applied for upper-level admission, 137 were accepted, 81 enrolled. Any standardized test or SSAT required. Deadline for receipt of application materials: none. Application fee required: $75. Interview required.

Athletics Interscholastic: baseball (boys), basketball (b,g), cross-country running (b,g), football (b), lacrosse (b), soccer (b,g), softball (g), swimming and diving (b,g), tennis (b,g), track and field (b,g), volleyball (b,g), wrestling (b); intramural: basketball (b,g), horseback riding (g), independent competitive sports (b,g), soccer (b,g), softball (g), strength & conditioning (b,g), swimming and diving (b,g), tennis (b,g), track and field (b,g), volleyball (b,g); coed interscholastic: cheering, drill team, equestrian sports, golf, JROTC drill; coed intramural: golf, horseback riding, indoor soccer, jogging, JROTC drill, outdoor activities, outdoor recreation, physical fitness, soccer, strength & conditioning, swimming and diving, table tennis, volleyball, weight lifting, weight training. 2 PE instructors, 1 athletic trainer.

Computers Computers are regularly used in aerospace science, aviation, English, ESL, foreign language, independent study, Latin, mathematics, science, yearbook classes. Computer network features include on-campus library services, online commercial services, Internet access, Internet filtering or blocking technology. Student e-mail accounts are available to students. Students grades are available online. The school has a published electronic and media policy.

Contact Mrs. Paula Brady, Admissions Coordinator. 540-636-5200 Ext. 5484. Fax: 540-636-5419. E-mail: paulab@rma.edu. Web site: www.rma.edu.

RANDOLPH SCHOOL

1005 Drake Avenue
Huntsville, Alabama 35802

Head of School: Dr. Byron C. Hulsey

General Information Coeducational day college-preparatory school. Grades K–12. Founded: 1959. Setting: suburban. 67-acre campus. 10 buildings on campus. Approved or accredited by Southern Association of Colleges and Schools, Southern Association of Independent Schools, and The College Board. Member of National Association of Independent Schools. Endowment: $7 million. Total enrollment: 904. Upper school average class size: 13. Upper school faculty-student ratio: 1:12.

Upper School Student Profile Grade 9: 75 students (32 boys, 43 girls); Grade 10: 70 students (47 boys, 23 girls); Grade 11: 67 students (35 boys, 32 girls); Grade 12: 66 students (36 boys, 30 girls).

Faculty School total: 97. In upper school: 13 men, 22 women; 30 have advanced degrees.

Subjects Offered 3-dimensional art, acting, algebra, American history-AP, American literature, anatomy, art, art-AP, band, biology, biology-AP, calculus, calculus-AP, ceramics, chemistry, chemistry-AP, Chinese, comparative government and politics-AP, computer math, concert choir, consumer economics, creative writing, drama, drama workshop, economics, English, English literature, English-AP, environmental science, European history, European history-AP, film appreciation, filmmaking, fine arts, forensics, French, French-AP, geometry, history, Homeric Greek, journalism, Latin, marine biology, mathematics, music, music theory-AP, physical education, physics, physics-AP, physiology, psychology, science, social studies, Southern literature, Spanish, Spanish-AP, speech, stage design, stagecraft, student publications, studio art—AP, theater, trigonometry, U.S. government-AP, U.S. history-AP, world history, world history-AP, world literature, writing, yearbook.

Graduation Requirements Algebra, American literature, arts and fine arts (art, music, dance, drama), biology, British literature, chemistry, computer science, English, European history, foreign language, geometry, literature, mathematics, science, social studies (includes history), world literature.

Special Academic Programs 12 Advanced Placement exams for which test preparation is offered; honors section; independent study; study at local college for college credit.

College Admission Counseling 60 students graduated in 2008; all went to college, including Auburn University; Birmingham-Southern College; Sewanee: The University of the South; The University of Alabama; The University of Alabama at Birmingham; Vanderbilt University. Median SAT critical reading: 640, median SAT math: 670, median SAT writing: 640, median combined SAT: 1940, median composite ACT: 29. 65% scored over 600 on SAT critical reading, 72% scored over 600 on SAT math, 63% scored over 600 on SAT writing, 77% scored over 1800 on combined SAT, 67% scored over 26 on composite ACT.

Student Life Upper grades have specified standards of dress, student council, honor system. Discipline rests primarily with faculty.

Summer Programs Enrichment, sports programs offered; session focuses on sports, science, art, foreign language; held on campus; accepts boys and girls; open to students from other schools. 140 students usually enrolled. 2009 schedule: June 1 to July 31. Application deadline: April 30.

Tuition and Aid Day student tuition: $11,100–$13,760. Tuition installment plan (Insured Tuition Payment Plan, 2- and 10-payment plans). Merit scholarship grants, need-based scholarship grants available. In 2008–09, 4% of upper-school students received aid; total upper-school merit-scholarship money awarded: $21,932. Total amount of financial aid awarded in 2008–09: $88,875.

Admissions Traditional secondary-level entrance grade is 9. For fall 2008, 31 students applied for upper-level admission, 19 were accepted, 15 enrolled. ERB, ISEE or writing sample required. Deadline for receipt of application materials: none. Application fee required: $75. On-campus interview required.

Athletics Interscholastic: baseball (boys), basketball (b,g), cheering (g), cross-country running (b,g), diving (b,g), football (b), golf (b,g), indoor track & field (b,g), soccer (b,g), softball (g), swimming and diving (b,g), tennis (b,g), track and field (b,g), volleyball (g), winter (indoor) track (b,g); coed interscholastic: diving; coed intramural: flag football. 6 PE instructors, 5 coaches.

Computers Computers are regularly used in all academic classes. Computer network features include on-campus library services, online commercial services, Internet access, wireless campus network, Internet filtering or blocking technology, laptops. Campus intranet and student e-mail accounts are available to students. The school has a published electronic and media policy.

Contact Nancy Hodges, Director of Admissions. 256-881-1701 Ext. 104. Fax: 256-881-1784. E-mail: nhodges@randolphschool.net. Web site: www.randolphschool.net.

RANNEY SCHOOL

235 Hope Road
Tinton Falls, New Jersey 07724

Head of School: Dr. Lawrence S. Sykoff

General Information Coeducational day college-preparatory school. Grades N–12. Founded: 1960. Setting: suburban. Nearest major city is New York, NY. 60-acre campus. 3 buildings on campus. Approved or accredited by Middle States Association of Colleges and Schools and New Jersey Department of Education. Member of National Association of Independent Schools. Total enrollment: 815. Upper school average class size: 15.

Upper School Student Profile Grade 9: 63 students (27 boys, 36 girls); Grade 10: 58 students (30 boys, 28 girls); Grade 11: 63 students (27 boys, 36 girls); Grade 12: 57 students (24 boys, 33 girls).

Faculty School total: 96. In upper school: 14 men, 18 women; 19 have advanced degrees.

Subjects Offered Advanced Placement courses, algebra, American history, American literature, art, art history, art history-AP, biology, biology-AP, calculus, calculus-AP, ceramics, chemistry, chemistry-AP, computer programming, computer science, computer science-AP, economics, economics-AP, English, English language-AP, English literature, English literature-AP, European history, European history-AP, fine arts, French, French-AP, geometry, grammar, health, history, journalism, mathematics, music, physical education, physics, psychology, science, Spanish, Spanish language-AP, world history, world literature, writing.

Graduation Requirements Arts and fine arts (art, music, dance, drama), English, foreign language, history, mathematics, physical education (includes health), science.

Special Academic Programs Advanced Placement exam preparation; honors section.

College Admission Counseling 53 students graduated in 2007; all went to college, including Emory University; New York University; Princeton University; The Johns Hopkins University; University of Notre Dame; University of Pennsylvania. Median SAT critical reading: 603, median SAT math: 615, median SAT writing: 608, median combined SAT: 1826.

Student Life Upper grades have specified standards of dress, student council, honor system. Discipline rests equally with students and faculty.

Tuition and Aid Day student tuition: $20,600–$21,900. Tuition installment plan (Key Tuition Payment Plan). Tuition reduction for siblings, need-based scholarship grants, reduced tuition for children of employees available. In 2007–08, 5% of upper-school students received aid. Total amount of financial aid awarded in 2007–08: $43,000.
Admissions Traditional secondary-level entrance grade is 9. For fall 2007, 43 students applied for upper-level admission, 32 were accepted, 19 enrolled. ERB required. Deadline for receipt of application materials: none. Application fee required: $75. On-campus interview required.
Athletics Interscholastic: baseball (boys), basketball (b,g), cheering (g), field hockey (g), lacrosse (b), soccer (b,g), softball (g), tennis (b,g); coed interscholastic: aquatics, cross-country running, golf, swimming and diving, track and field; coed intramural: fencing, fitness, weight training. 6 PE instructors, 16 coaches, 1 athletic trainer.
Computers Computer resources include on-campus library services, Internet access, Internet filtering or blocking technology.
Contact Heather Rudisi, Associate Head for Admission and Marketing. 732-542-4777 Ext. 107. Fax: 732-460-1078. E-mail: hrudisi@ranneyschool.com. Web site: www.ranneyschool.com.

See Close-Up on page 918.

RANSOM EVERGLADES SCHOOL

3575 Main Highway
Miami, Florida 33133

Head of School: Mrs. Ellen Y. Moceri

General Information Coeducational day college-preparatory school. Grades 6–12. Founded: 1903. Setting: urban. 11-acre campus. 21 buildings on campus. Approved or accredited by Southern Association of Colleges and Schools, Southern Association of Independent Schools, and Florida Department of Education. Member of National Association of Independent Schools and Secondary School Admission Test Board. Endowment: $21.4 million. Total enrollment: 1,054. Upper school average class size: 14. Upper school faculty-student ratio: 1:14.
Upper School Student Profile Grade 9: 148 students (65 boys, 83 girls); Grade 10: 145 students (65 boys, 80 girls); Grade 11: 153 students (76 boys, 77 girls); Grade 12: 147 students (71 boys, 76 girls).
Faculty School total: 97. In upper school: 29 men, 27 women; 40 have advanced degrees.
Subjects Offered Advanced Placement courses, algebra, American government-AP, American history, American history-AP, American literature, anatomy and physiology, art, art history, art history-AP, astronomy, band, biology, calculus, calculus-AP, ceramics, chemistry, chemistry-AP, choir, chorus, college counseling, comparative government and politics-AP, computer math, computer programming, computer science, computer science-AP, computer-aided design, concert band, creative writing, dance, dance performance, debate, digital photography, drama, earth science, ecology, economics, economics-AP, engineering, English, English literature, English literature and composition-AP, English-AP, environmental science, environmental science-AP, environmental studies, ethical decision making, ethics, ethics and responsibility, European history, European history-AP, experiential education, fine arts, French, French language-AP, French-AP, geography, geology, geometry, government and politics-AP, government/civics, grammar, graphic design, guitar, health, health and wellness, history, history-AP, human anatomy, interdisciplinary studies, jazz ensemble, journalism, macro/microeconomics-AP, macroeconomics-AP, Mandarin, marine biology, mathematics, mathematics-AP, music, music theory, music theory-AP, music-AP, mythology, philosophy, photography, physical education, physics, physics-AP, probability and statistics, psychology, psychology-AP, robotics, science, sculpture, social studies, sociology, Spanish, Spanish language-AP, Spanish literature-AP, speech, speech and debate, statistics, statistics and probability, statistics-AP, theater, theory of knowledge, trigonometry, U.S. government and politics-AP, U.S. government-AP, U.S. history, U.S. history-AP, world history, world history-AP, world literature, writing, yearbook.
Graduation Requirements Arts and fine arts (art, music, dance, drama), computer science, English, foreign language, mathematics, physical education (includes health), science, social studies (includes history).
Special Academic Programs 23 Advanced Placement exams for which test preparation is offered; honors section.
College Admission Counseling 136 students graduated in 2008; all went to college, including Emory University; The George Washington University; University of Florida; University of Miami; Wake Forest University; Washington University in St. Louis. Median SAT critical reading: 660, median SAT math: 670, median SAT writing: 670.
Student Life Upper grades have specified standards of dress, student council, honor system. Discipline rests primarily with faculty.
Summer Programs Enrichment, advancement, computer instruction programs offered; session focuses on enrichment to reinforce basic skills and advancement for credit; held on campus; accepts boys and girls; open to students from other schools. 130 students usually enrolled. 2009 schedule: June 15 to July 19. Application deadline: June 8.
Tuition and Aid Day student tuition: $23,000. Tuition installment plan (monthly payment plans, 60%/40% payment plan). Need-based scholarship grants available. In 2008–09, 13% of upper-school students received aid. Total amount of financial aid awarded in 2008–09: $2,917,606.
Admissions Traditional secondary-level entrance grade is 9. For fall 2008, 151 students applied for upper-level admission, 34 were accepted, 24 enrolled. SSAT required. Deadline for receipt of application materials: February 15. Application fee required: $100. On-campus interview required.
Athletics Interscholastic: baseball (boys), basketball (b,g), canoeing/kayaking (b,g), cheering (g), crew (b,g), cross-country running (b,g), dance (g), dance team (g), football (b), golf (b,g), kayaking (b,g), lacrosse (b), physical training (b,g), sailing (b,g), soccer (b,g), softball (g), swimming and diving (b,g), tennis (b,g), track and field (b,g), volleyball (b,g), water polo (b,g), wrestling (b); coed interscholastic: crew, kayaking, sailing. 5 PE instructors, 75 coaches, 2 athletic trainers.
Computers Computers are regularly used in all classes. Computer network features include on-campus library services, online commercial services, Internet access, wireless campus network, Internet filtering or blocking technology. Student e-mail accounts and computer access in designated common areas are available to students. Students grades are available online. The school has a published electronic and media policy.
Contact Amy Sayfie, Director of Admission. 305-250-6875. Fax: 305-854-1846. E-mail: admission@ransomeverglades.org. Web site: www.ransomeverglades.org.

RAVENSCROFT SCHOOL

7409 Falls of the Neuse Road
Raleigh, North Carolina 27615

Head of School: Mrs. Doreen C. Kelly

General Information Coeducational day college-preparatory, arts, and technology school. Grades PK–12. Founded: 1862. Setting: suburban. 127-acre campus. 13 buildings on campus. Approved or accredited by Southern Association of Colleges and Schools, Southern Association of Independent Schools, and North Carolina Department of Education. Member of National Association of Independent Schools. Endowment: $12 million. Total enrollment: 1,229. Upper school average class size: 16. Upper school faculty-student ratio: 1:8.
Upper School Student Profile Grade 9: 115 students (61 boys, 54 girls); Grade 10: 117 students (62 boys, 55 girls); Grade 11: 118 students (64 boys, 54 girls); Grade 12: 96 students (44 boys, 52 girls).
Faculty School total: 146. In upper school: 30 men, 39 women; 47 have advanced degrees.
Subjects Offered Advanced Placement courses, algebra, American history, American literature, anatomy, art, art history, biology, biotechnology, calculus, chemistry, computer programming, computer science, discrete math, drama, economics, English, English literature, environmental science, environmental science-AP, European history, expository writing, fine arts, French, geometry, government/civics, Greek, health, history, journalism, Latin, mathematics, music, photography, physical education, physics, psychology, science, social science, social studies, Spanish, speech, sports medicine, stagecraft, statistics-AP, theater, typing, world history, writing.
Graduation Requirements Arts and fine arts (art, music, dance, drama), composition, English, foreign language, mathematics, physical education (includes health), science, social science, social studies (includes history). Community service is required.
Special Academic Programs Advanced Placement exam preparation; honors section; independent study; term-away projects; study at local college for college credit; study abroad; academic accommodation for the gifted, the musically talented, and the artistically talented; ESL (4 students enrolled).
College Admission Counseling 94 students graduated in 2008; all went to college, including Appalachian State University; East Carolina University; North Carolina State University; The University of North Carolina at Chapel Hill; University of Georgia; Wake Forest University. Median SAT critical reading: 630, median SAT math: 650, median SAT writing: 670, median combined SAT: 1930, median composite ACT: 26.
Student Life Upper grades have specified standards of dress, student council, honor system. Discipline rests equally with students and faculty.
Summer Programs Enrichment, advancement, sports, art/fine arts, computer instruction programs offered; session focuses on enrichment; held on campus; accepts boys and girls; open to students from other schools. 2,000 students usually enrolled. 2009 schedule: June 15 to August 7. Application deadline: none.
Tuition and Aid Day student tuition: $16,655. Tuition installment plan (individually arranged payment plans). Merit scholarship grants, need-based scholarship grants, need-based loans available. In 2008–09, 16% of upper-school students received aid; total upper-school merit-scholarship money awarded: $60,655. Total amount of financial aid awarded in 2008–09: $761,005.
Admissions Traditional secondary-level entrance grade is 9. For fall 2008, 118 students applied for upper-level admission, 76 were accepted, 57 enrolled. ERB required. Deadline for receipt of application materials: none. Application fee required: $125. On-campus interview required.
Athletics Interscholastic: baseball (boys), basketball (b,g), cheering (g), cross-country running (b,g), dance squad (g), field hockey (g), fitness (b,g), football (b), golf (b,g), lacrosse (b), physical training (b,g), soccer (b,g), softball (g), strength &

conditioning (b,g), swimming and diving (b,g), tennis (b,g), track and field (b,g), volleyball (g), weight training (b,g), wrestling (b); intramural: baseball (b), basketball (b,g), cheering (g), dance team (g), football (b,g), lacrosse (b), soccer (b,g), softball (g), strength & conditioning (b,g), swimming and diving (b,g), tennis (b,g), track and field (b,g), volleyball (g), wrestling (b); coed interscholastic: life saving. 10 PE instructors, 68 coaches, 2 athletic trainers.
Computers Computers are regularly used in economics, English, foreign language, history, mathematics, science, social studies, writing classes. Computer network features include on-campus library services, online commercial services, Internet access, Internet filtering or blocking technology. Student e-mail accounts and computer access in designated common areas are available to students. Students grades are available online. The school has a published electronic and media policy.
Contact Mrs. Pamela J. Jamison, Director of Admissions. 919-847-0900 Ext. 2226. Fax: 919-846-2371. E-mail: pjamison@ravenscroft.org. Web site: www.ravenscroft.org.

ANNOUNCEMENT FROM THE SCHOOL Located on a beautiful 125-acre campus in North Raleigh, Ravenscroft School is a coeducational, college-preparatory day school enrolling 1,250 students in pre-kindergarten through grade 12. The School mission states, "The Ravenscroft community, guided by our legacy of excellence, nurtures individual potential and prepares students to thrive in a complex and interdependent world." The School's campus features three academic classroom buildings, a dedicated library for the Lower School, a Middle and Upper School Library and Technology Center, a Fine Arts Center with a 460-seat theater and gallery space, a black box theater, and a state-of-the-art athletic complex that includes football and soccer stadiums, a baseball diamond, a regulation track, an aquatics center, six tennis courts, gymnasiums, and a fitness facility with trainer. A wide range of summer programs and off-campus learning experiences are offered. Need-based financial aid and academic scholarships are available.

THE RECTORY SCHOOL

Pomfret, Connecticut
See Junior Boarding Schools section.

REDEMPTION CHRISTIAN ACADEMY

192 Ninth Street
PO Box 753
Troy, New York 12181

Head of School: Elder John Massey Jr.

General Information Coeducational boarding and day college-preparatory and religious studies school, affiliated with Pentecostal Church. Boarding grades 7–PG, day grades K–PG. Founded: 1979. Setting: urban. Nearest major city is New York. Students are housed in single-sex dormitories. 2-acre campus. 1 building on campus. Approved or accredited by Association of Christian Schools International and New York Department of Education. Upper school average class size: 10. Upper school faculty-student ratio: 1:10.
Upper School Student Profile 40% of students are boarding students. 90% are state residents. 2 states are represented in upper school student body. 7% are international students. International students from Liberia. 80% of students are Pentecostal.
Faculty School total: 15. In upper school: 3 men, 8 women; 4 have advanced degrees; 6 reside on campus.
Subjects Offered African-American literature, algebra, American history, American literature, art, athletic training, basketball, Bible studies, biology, chemistry, choir, communication skills, computer science, creative writing, current events, earth science, economics, English, English literature, European history, expository writing, French, geometry, government/civics, grammar, health, history, keyboarding/computer, life skills, mathematics, music, physical education, physics, reading, religion, SAT preparation, science, social science, social studies, Spanish, study skills, trigonometry, world history, writing.
Graduation Requirements Art, English, foreign language, health science, mathematics, physical education (includes health), religion (includes Bible studies and theology), science, social science, social studies (includes history).
Special Academic Programs Accelerated programs; independent study; academic accommodation for the gifted; remedial reading and/or remedial writing; remedial math; programs in English, mathematics, general development for dyslexic students; special instructional classes for students with learning disabilities, Attention Deficit Disorder, emotional and behavioral problems, and dyslexia; ESL.
College Admission Counseling 2 students graduated in 2008; 1 went to college. Other: 1 had other specific plans.
Student Life Upper grades have uniform requirement, student council, honor system. Discipline rests primarily with faculty. Attendance at religious services is required.
Summer Programs Remediation, enrichment, ESL, sports, computer instruction programs offered; session focuses on program for new students; held on campus; accepts boys and girls; open to students from other schools. 2009 schedule: July to August. Application deadline: none.
Tuition and Aid Day student tuition: $5000; 5-day tuition and room/board: $12,000; 7-day tuition and room/board: $15,000. Tuition installment plan (individually arranged payment plans, 2-installment payment plan). Tuition reduction for siblings, merit scholarship grants, need-based scholarship grants, tuition work credit, parent fundraiser program available. In 2008–09, 80% of upper-school students received aid.
Admissions Traditional secondary-level entrance grade is 12. Deadline for receipt of application materials: none. Application fee required: $30. Interview required.
Athletics Interscholastic: basketball (boys, girls); intramural: aerobics (g), basketball (b,g), volleyball (g). 4 coaches, 1 athletic trainer.
Computers Computers are regularly used in English, social sciences classes. Computer network features include Internet access, wireless campus network, Internet filtering or blocking technology. The school has a published electronic and media policy.
Contact Laura Holmes, Vice Principal. 518-272-6679. Fax: 518-270-8039. E-mail: info@rcastudents.com. Web site: www.rcastudents.com.

REDWOOD CHRISTIAN SCHOOLS

4200 James Avenue
Castro Valley, California 94546

Head of School: Mr. Bruce D. Johnson

General Information Coeducational day college-preparatory and religious studies school. Grades K–12. Founded: 1970. Setting: urban. Nearest major city is Oakland. 10-acre campus. 11 buildings on campus. Approved or accredited by Association of Christian Schools International, Western Association of Schools and Colleges, and California Department of Education. Total enrollment: 702. Upper school average class size: 24. Upper school faculty-student ratio: 1:24.
Upper School Student Profile Grade 9: 67 students (35 boys, 32 girls); Grade 10: 60 students (28 boys, 32 girls); Grade 11: 63 students (35 boys, 28 girls); Grade 12: 63 students (31 boys, 32 girls).
Faculty School total: 26. In upper school: 18 men, 7 women; 9 have advanced degrees.
Subjects Offered Advanced math, algebra, art, Bible studies, biology, calculus, chemistry, choir, computer literacy, concert band, data processing, drama, economics, English, English-AP, European history-AP, French, geometry, honors English, physical education, physical science, physics, Spanish, speech, trigonometry, U.S. government, U.S. history, woodworking, world history, yearbook.
Graduation Requirements Arts and fine arts (art, music, dance, drama), Bible, computer literacy, electives, English, foreign language, mathematics, physical education (includes health), science, speech, world history.
Special Academic Programs Advanced Placement exam preparation; honors section; study at local college for college credit; remedial reading and/or remedial writing; remedial math; programs in English, mathematics, general development for dyslexic students.
College Admission Counseling 64 students graduated in 2008; 63 went to college, including Azusa Pacific University; Biola University; California Polytechnic State University, San Luis Obispo; California State University, East Bay; University of California, Davis; University of California, Irvine. Other: 1 went to work. Mean SAT critical reading: 586, mean SAT math: 597, mean SAT writing: 581. 53% scored over 600 on SAT critical reading, 50% scored over 600 on SAT math, 53% scored over 600 on SAT writing, 47% scored over 1800 on combined SAT.
Student Life Upper grades have specified standards of dress, student council, honor system. Discipline rests primarily with faculty. Attendance at religious services is required.
Tuition and Aid Day student tuition: $9063–$13,595. Tuition installment plan (monthly payment plans, individually arranged payment plans). Tuition reduction for siblings, need-based scholarship grants, paying campus jobs available. In 2008–09, 50% of upper-school students received aid. Total amount of financial aid awarded in 2008–09: $300,000.
Admissions Traditional secondary-level entrance grade is 9. For fall 2008, 52 students applied for upper-level admission, 45 were accepted, 36 enrolled. Stanford Achievement Test required. Deadline for receipt of application materials: none. Application fee required: $50. On-campus interview required.
Athletics Interscholastic: baseball (boys), basketball (b,g), cross-country running (b,g), soccer (b,g), softball (g), tennis (b,g), track and field (b,g), volleyball (b,g). 2 PE instructors, 1 coach.
Computers Computers are regularly used in yearbook classes. Students grades are available online.
Contact Mrs. Deborah Wright, Registrar. 510-889-7526. Fax: 510-881-0127. E-mail: deborahwright@rcs.edu. Web site: www.rcs.edu.

REGINA DOMINICAN HIGH SCHOOL

701 Locust Road
Wilmette, Illinois 60091

Head of School: Sr. Mary Margaret Pachucki, OP

General Information Girls' day college-preparatory, arts, business, religious studies, technology, Science, and Mathematics school, affiliated with Roman Catholic Church. Grades 9–12. Founded: 1957. Setting: suburban. Nearest major city is Chicago. 6-acre campus. 2 buildings on campus. Approved or accredited by North

Central Association of Colleges and Schools. Total enrollment: 400. Upper school average class size: 17. Upper school faculty-student ratio: 1:12.

Upper School Student Profile Grade 9: 100 students (100 girls); Grade 10: 100 students (100 girls); Grade 11: 100 students (100 girls); Grade 12: 100 students (100 girls). 87% of students are Roman Catholic.

Faculty School total: 38. In upper school: 10 men, 28 women; 36 have advanced degrees.

Subjects Offered 3-dimensional design, accounting, advanced biology, advanced chemistry, advanced math, Advanced Placement courses, algebra, American government, American government-AP, American history, American history-AP, American literature, American literature-AP, anatomy and physiology, Ancient Greek, art, Bible studies, biology, British literature, British literature (honors), British literature-AP, business, business education, calculus, calculus-AP, ceramics, chemistry, chemistry-AP, choir, choral music, Christian and Hebrew scripture, Christian scripture, college writing, consumer education, creative writing, current events, dance, drama, drawing, drawing and design, English, English language-AP, English literature, English literature-AP, English-AP, etymology, European history, European history-AP, fine arts, foreign language, French, French-AP, general science, geometry, government and politics-AP, government/civics, graphic design, health, history, journalism, Latin, Latin-AP, mathematics, music, philosophy, photography, physical education, physics, physics-AP, psychology, public speaking, religion, science, social studies, sociology, Spanish, Spanish literature-AP, Spanish-AP, speech, statistics, theater, theater arts, theater design and production, theology, trigonometry, U.S. government and politics-AP, word processing, world history, world literature, world religions, writing.

Graduation Requirements Arts and fine arts (art, music, dance, drama), English, foreign language, government, mathematics, physical education (includes health), religion (includes Bible studies and theology), science, social studies (includes history).

Special Academic Programs 16 Advanced Placement exams for which test preparation is offered; honors section; academic accommodation for the gifted, the musically talented, and the artistically talented; remedial reading and/or remedial writing; remedial math.

College Admission Counseling 98 students graduated in 2008; all went to college, including DePaul University; Loyola University Chicago; Marquette University; Northwestern University; Saint Louis University; University of Illinois at Urbana–Champaign. Mean SAT critical reading: 605, mean SAT math: 590, mean composite ACT: 23.

Student Life Upper grades have uniform requirement, student council, honor system. Discipline rests equally with students and faculty.

Summer Programs Remediation programs offered; held on campus; accepts girls; not open to students from other schools.

Tuition and Aid Day student tuition: $9950. Tuition installment plan (monthly payment plans, individually arranged payment plans). Merit scholarship grants, need-based scholarship grants available. In 2008–09, 33% of upper-school students received aid.

Admissions Traditional secondary-level entrance grade is 9. For fall 2008, 104 students applied for upper-level admission, 100 were accepted, 100 enrolled. TerraNova required. Deadline for receipt of application materials: January. No application fee required. On-campus interview required.

Athletics Interscholastic: basketball, bowling, cross-country running, dance team, fishing, golf, pom squad, soccer, softball, swimming and diving, tennis, track and field, volleyball; intramural: cheering, field hockey, lacrosse. 1 PE instructor, 15 coaches, 1 athletic trainer.

Computers Computer network features include on-campus library services, online commercial services, Internet access, wireless campus network, Internet filtering or blocking technology. Student e-mail accounts and computer access in designated common areas are available to students. Students grades are available online.

Contact Mrs. Patricia Fuentes, Director of Admissions. 847-256-7660. Fax: 847-256-3726. E-mail: pfuentes@rdhs.org. Web site: www.rdhs.org.

REGINA HIGH SCHOOL

1857 South Green Road
South Euclid, Ohio 44121

Head of School: Sr. Maureen Burke, SND

General Information Girls' day college-preparatory, arts, religious studies, and technology school, affiliated with Roman Catholic Church; primarily serves students with learning disabilities, individuals with Attention Deficit Disorder, individuals with emotional and behavioral problems, and dyslexic students. Grades 9–12. Founded: 1953. Setting: suburban. Nearest major city is Cleveland. 40-acre campus. 3 buildings on campus. Approved or accredited by National Catholic Education Association, North Central Association of Colleges and Schools, Ohio Catholic Schools Accreditation Association (OCSAA), and Ohio Department of Education. Endowment: $1 million. Total enrollment: 232. Upper school average class size: 20. Upper school faculty-student ratio: 1:12.

Upper School Student Profile Grade 9: 72 students (72 girls); Grade 10: 54 students (54 girls); Grade 11: 52 students (52 girls); Grade 12: 54 students (54 girls). 80% of students are Roman Catholic.

Faculty School total: 31. In upper school: 6 men, 25 women; 18 have advanced degrees.

Subjects Offered ACT preparation, advanced biology, advanced chemistry, Advanced Placement courses, African dance, algebra, American history-AP, American literature-AP, anatomy, art, arts, British literature, business, career/college preparation, chemistry, Christian and Hebrew scripture, college counseling, college planning, communications, computer math, computer science, CPR, creative arts, dance, discrete mathematics, drama, earth science, emerging technology, engineering, English, English literature-AP, environmental science, fine arts, French studies, German literature, government/civics, health, home economics, Internet, Japanese, library skills, music, peace education, performing arts, physical science, prayer/spirituality, pre-calculus, SAT/ACT preparation, science, social issues, social studies, Spanish literature, statistics and probability, telecommunications and the Internet, theater arts, trigonometry, world cultures, world literature, yearbook.

Graduation Requirements Portfolio.

Special Academic Programs Advanced Placement exam preparation; honors section; independent study; study at local college for college credit; study abroad; academic accommodation for the gifted, the musically talented, and the artistically talented; remedial reading and/or remedial writing; remedial math; programs in English, mathematics, general development for dyslexic students; special instructional classes for students with learning disabilities, Attention Deficit Disorder, and dyslexia.

College Admission Counseling 54 students graduated in 2008; 52 went to college, including John Carroll University; Kent State University; Mercyhurst College; Miami University; The Ohio State University; Xavier University. Other: 2 had other specific plans.

Student Life Upper grades have uniform requirement, student council, honor system. Discipline rests primarily with faculty. Attendance at religious services is required.

Summer Programs Remediation, enrichment, advancement, sports, art/fine arts programs offered; session focuses on drama; held on campus; accepts boys and girls; open to students from other schools. 20 students usually enrolled. 2009 schedule: June to July.

Tuition and Aid Day student tuition: $8450. Tuition installment plan (monthly payment plans). Tuition reduction for siblings, merit scholarship grants, need-based scholarship grants, need-based loans available. In 2008–09, 30% of upper-school students received aid; total upper-school merit-scholarship money awarded: $25,000. Total amount of financial aid awarded in 2008–09: $250,000.

Admissions Traditional secondary-level entrance grade is 9. For fall 2008, 100 students applied for upper-level admission, 84 were accepted, 72 enrolled. Scholastic Testing Service High School Placement Test required. Deadline for receipt of application materials: none. Application fee required: $250. Interview required.

Athletics Interscholastic: basketball, bowling, cheering, cross-country running, diving, lacrosse, softball, swimming and diving, tennis, track and field, volleyball, winter (indoor) track. 1 PE instructor, 17 coaches, 1 athletic trainer.

Computers Computer network features include on-campus library services, online commercial services, Internet access, wireless campus network, Internet filtering or blocking technology. Campus intranet, student e-mail accounts, and computer access in designated common areas are available to students. Students grades are available online. The school has a published electronic and media policy.

Contact Megan Schoene, Director of Admissions. 216-382-2110 Ext. 225. Fax: 216-382-3555. E-mail: schoenem@reginahigh.com. Web site: www.reginahigh.com.

REGIS HIGH SCHOOL

55 East 84th Street
New York, New York 10028-0884

Head of School: Dr. Gary J. Tocchet, PhD

General Information Boys' day college-preparatory school, affiliated with Roman Catholic Church. Grades 9–12. Founded: 1914. Setting: urban. 3-acre campus. 1 building on campus. Approved or accredited by Jesuit Secondary Education Association, Middle States Association of Colleges and Schools, New York State Association of Independent Schools, and New York Department of Education. Total enrollment: 536. Upper school average class size: 15. Upper school faculty-student ratio: 1:15.

Upper School Student Profile Grade 9: 136 students (136 boys); Grade 10: 139 students (139 boys); Grade 11: 129 students (129 boys); Grade 12: 132 students (132 boys). 100% of students are Roman Catholic.

Faculty School total: 62. In upper school: 41 men, 21 women; all have advanced degrees.

Subjects Offered Algebra, American history, American literature, architecture, art, art history, band, biology, calculus, chemistry, Chinese, computer programming, computer science, creative writing, drama, driver education, economics, English, English literature, ethics, European history, expository writing, film, French, geometry, German, health, history, Latin, mathematics, music, physical education, physics, psychology, social studies, Spanish, speech, statistics, theater, theology, trigonometry, writing.

Graduation Requirements Art, computer literacy, English, foreign language, history, mathematics, music, physical education (includes health), science, theology, Christian Service Program.

Special Academic Programs Advanced Placement exam preparation; independent study; study abroad.

College Admission Counseling 141 students graduated in 2008; all went to college, including Boston College; Brown University; College of the Holy Cross; Fordham

University; Georgetown University; Yale University. Mean SAT critical reading: 715, mean SAT math: 704, mean SAT writing: 713, mean combined SAT: 2133.
Student Life Upper grades have specified standards of dress, student council. Discipline rests primarily with faculty. Attendance at religious services is required.
Summer Programs Remediation programs offered; session focuses on remediation; held on campus; accepts boys; not open to students from other schools. 20 students usually enrolled. 2009 schedule: July 6 to August 1.
Tuition and Aid Tuition-free school available.
Admissions Traditional secondary-level entrance grade is 9. For fall 2008, 790 students applied for upper-level admission, 142 were accepted, 136 enrolled. Admissions testing required. Deadline for receipt of application materials: October 17. Application fee required: $40. On-campus interview required.
Athletics Interscholastic: baseball, basketball, bowling, cross-country running, indoor track & field, soccer, track and field, volleyball; intramural: basketball, floor hockey, indoor hockey, soccer. 2 PE instructors, 16 coaches.
Computers Computers are regularly used in all academic classes. Computer network features include on-campus library services, Internet access.
Contact Mr. Eric P. DiMichele, Director of Admissions. 212-288-1100 Ext. 2057. Fax: 212-794-1221. E-mail: edimiche@regis-nyc.org. Web site: www.regis-nyc.org.

REITZ MEMORIAL HIGH SCHOOL

1500 Lincoln Avenue
Evansville, Indiana 47714

Head of School: Mrs. Gwen Godsey

General Information Coeducational day college-preparatory and religious studies school, affiliated with Roman Catholic Church. Grades 9–12. Founded: 1924. Setting: urban. Nearest major city is Indianapolis. 2 buildings on campus. Approved or accredited by North Central Association of Colleges and Schools, The College Board, and Indiana Department of Education. Total enrollment: 791. Upper school average class size: 25. Upper school faculty-student ratio: 1:16.
Upper School Student Profile Grade 9: 203 students (97 boys, 106 girls); Grade 10: 202 students (104 boys, 98 girls); Grade 11: 208 students (106 boys, 102 girls); Grade 12: 179 students (84 boys, 95 girls). 90% of students are Roman Catholic.
Faculty School total: 54. In upper school: 18 men, 36 women; 28 have advanced degrees.
Subjects Offered 20th century American writers, 20th century history, 3-dimensional art, accounting, advanced biology, advanced chemistry, advanced computer applications, Advanced Placement courses, algebra, American government, American history, American literature, anthropology, applied music, art, art appreciation, art history, band, Basic programming, biology, biology-AP, British literature, business, business communications, business law, business skills, calculus-AP, Catholic belief and practice, ceramics, chemistry, chemistry-AP, choir, chorus, church history, composition, computer applications, computer keyboarding, computer programming, consumer economics, current events, digital photography, dramatic arts, drawing, driver education, earth and space science, ecology, environmental systems, English, English composition, English literature and composition-AP, entomology, environmental science, etymology, foreign language, forensics, French, French language-AP, geometry, German, government, grammar, guitar, health and wellness, history of the Catholic Church, honors algebra, honors English, honors geometry, honors U.S. history, honors world history, jewelry making, journalism, law, law and the legal system, library assistant, Life of Christ, literary genres, marching band, media arts, music appreciation, music composition, music history, New Testament, newspaper, oil painting, painting, peace and justice, personal finance, physical education, physics, physics-AP, piano, portfolio art, prayer/spirituality, pre-calculus, printmaking, psychology, Spanish, Spanish language-AP, studio art, theater arts, trigonometry, U.S. history, weight training, world history, world history-AP, yearbook.
Graduation Requirements Service Hours.
Special Academic Programs 8 Advanced Placement exams for which test preparation is offered; honors section; study at local college for college credit.
College Admission Counseling 216 students graduated in 2008; 213 went to college, including Indiana University Bloomington; Purdue University; University of Evansville; University of Kentucky. Other: 1 went to work, 2 entered military service.
Student Life Upper grades have uniform requirement, student council. Discipline rests primarily with faculty. Attendance at religious services is required.
Summer Programs Remediation, sports programs offered; held both on and off campus; held at city-owned local schools and fields; accepts boys and girls; open to students from other schools. 400 students usually enrolled. 2009 schedule: May 26 to July 31.
Tuition and Aid Day student tuition: $3128–$4795. Tuition installment plan (ETFCU Loans). Tuition reduction for siblings, need-based scholarship grants, need-based loans available. In 2008–09, 10% of upper-school students received aid.
Admissions Traditional secondary-level entrance grade is 9. ACT-Explore required. Deadline for receipt of application materials: none. Application fee required: $170.
Athletics Interscholastic: baseball (boys), basketball (b,g), cheering (g), dance squad (g), dance team (g), diving (b,g), drill team (g), football (b), golf (b,g), soccer (b,g), softball (g), swimming and diving (b,g), tennis (b,g), track and field (b,g), volleyball (g), wrestling (b); intramural: bowling (b,g); coed intramural: ice hockey, table tennis. 4 PE instructors, 1 athletic trainer.
Computers Computers are regularly used in all classes. Computer network features include on-campus library services, Internet access, wireless campus network, Internet filtering or blocking technology. Campus intranet and computer access in designated common areas are available to students. Students grades are available online. The school has a published electronic and media policy.
Contact Mrs. Lisa Popham, Assistant Principal. 812-476-4973 Ext. 205. Fax: 812-474-2942. E-mail: lpopham@mhs.evansville.net. Web site: www.mhs.evansville.net.

RICE HIGH SCHOOL

74 West 124th Street
New York, New York 10027

Head of School: Br. Michael Segvich, CFC

General Information Boys' day college-preparatory and religious studies school, affiliated with Roman Catholic Church. Grades 9–12. Founded: 1938. Setting: urban. 1 building on campus. Approved or accredited by Middle States Association of Colleges and Schools, National Catholic Education Association, and New York Department of Education. Languages of instruction: English and Spanish. Endowment: $2 million. Total enrollment: 276. Upper school average class size: 25. Upper school faculty-student ratio: 1:15.
Upper School Student Profile Grade 9: 85 students (85 boys); Grade 10: 89 students (89 boys); Grade 11: 62 students (62 boys); Grade 12: 40 students (40 boys). 40% of students are Roman Catholic.
Faculty School total: 24. In upper school: 17 men, 7 women; 16 have advanced degrees.
Graduation Requirements Algebra, American history, art, biology, chemistry, earth science, English, global studies, health education, mathematics, physical education (includes health), religion (includes Bible studies and theology), Spanish, U.S. history, 125 hours of community service.
Special Academic Programs Study at local college for college credit.
College Admission Counseling 46 students graduated in 2008; all went to college, including Cornell University; Fairfield University; Fordham University; New York University.
Student Life Upper grades have specified standards of dress, student council, honor system. Discipline rests primarily with faculty. Attendance at religious services is required.
Summer Programs Enrichment programs offered; session focuses on incoming freshmen preparation; held on campus; accepts boys; not open to students from other schools. 85 students usually enrolled. 2009 schedule: July 7 to August 1.
Tuition and Aid Day student tuition: $5550. Tuition installment plan (The Tuition Plan, monthly payment plans). Merit scholarship grants, need-based scholarship grants available. In 2008–09, 75% of upper-school students received aid. Total amount of financial aid awarded in 2008–09: $600,000.
Admissions Traditional secondary-level entrance grade is 9. For fall 2008, 300 students applied for upper-level admission, 150 were accepted, 85 enrolled. Admissions testing required. Deadline for receipt of application materials: none. No application fee required. Interview recommended.
Athletics Interscholastic: baseball, basketball, bowling, cross-country running, flag football, indoor track & field, jogging, soccer, track and field; intramural: baseball, flag football, tennis. 1 PE instructor, 7 coaches.
Computers Computer network features include on-campus library services, Internet access, wireless campus network, Internet filtering or blocking technology. Campus intranet and student e-mail accounts are available to students. Students grades are available online.
Contact Mr. W. Eric Crawford, Director of Admissions. 212-369-4100 Ext. 208. Fax: 212-369-5408. E-mail: wcrawford@ricehighschool.com. Web site: www.ricehighschool.com.

RICHMOND CHRISTIAN SCHOOL

10200 #5 Road
Richmond, British Columbia V7A 4E5, Canada

Head of School: Mr. Bob White

General Information Coeducational day college-preparatory, general academic, arts, vocational, religious studies, and technology school, affiliated with Christian faith; primarily serves students with learning disabilities, individuals with Attention Deficit Disorder, individuals with emotional and behavioral problems, and dyslexic students. Grades K–12. Founded: 1957. Setting: suburban. Nearest major city is Vancouver, Canada. 5-acre campus. 1 building on campus. Approved or accredited by Christian Schools International and British Columbia Department of Education. Languages of instruction: English and French. Upper school average class size: 25. Upper school faculty-student ratio: 1:16.
Upper School Student Profile Grade 8: 74 students (40 boys, 34 girls); Grade 9: 50 students (33 boys, 17 girls); Grade 10: 65 students (26 boys, 39 girls); Grade 11: 44 students (17 boys, 27 girls); Grade 12: 53 students (31 boys, 22 girls). 100% of students are Christian faith.
Faculty School total: 18. In upper school: 7 men, 9 women; 3 have advanced degrees.
Subjects Offered Biology, calculus, calculus-AP, career education, chemistry, choral music, Christian studies, communications, computers, concert band, drama, English, English language and composition-AP, English literature, English literature and composition-AP, ESL, foods, French, general math, general science, history, infor-

mation technology, instrumental music, journalism, Mandarin, mathematics, musicianship, outdoor education, physical education, physics, science and technology, social studies, theater production, visual arts, woodworking, work experience, yearbook.

Graduation Requirements Career planning, Christian education, general math, general science, language arts, physical education (includes health), social studies (includes history), Ministry of British Columbia requirements, Christian Studies classes each year of attendance.

Special Academic Programs Advanced Placement exam preparation; honors section; independent study; academic accommodation for the gifted; remedial reading and/or remedial writing; remedial math; programs in general development for dyslexic students; special instructional classes for students with learning disabilities; ESL (10 students enrolled).

College Admission Counseling 32 students graduated in 2008; 25 went to college, including Queen's University at Kingston; Simon Fraser University; The University of British Columbia; Trinity Western University. Other: 3 went to work, 1 entered military service, 3 had other specific plans.

Student Life Upper grades have specified standards of dress, student council, honor system. Discipline rests primarily with faculty. Attendance at religious services is required.

Summer Programs Advancement programs offered; session focuses on mathematics; held on campus; accepts boys and girls; open to students from other schools.

Tuition and Aid Day student tuition: CAN$4500–CAN$6000. Tuition installment plan (monthly payment plans). Tuition reduction for siblings, need-based scholarship grants available.

Admissions Traditional secondary-level entrance grade is 8. Deadline for receipt of application materials: June 15. Application fee required: CAN$100. On-campus interview required.

Athletics Interscholastic: badminton (boys, girls), ball hockey (b,g), basketball (b,g), floor hockey (b,g), indoor track & field (b,g), volleyball (b,g); coed intramural: badminton, ball hockey, basketball, floor hockey, indoor track & field, volleyball. 4 PE instructors, 6 coaches.

Computers Computers are regularly used in career education, English, information technology, journalism, mathematics, religious studies, science classes.

Contact Mrs. Judy Sawatsky, Secretary. 604-274-1122. Fax: 604-274-1128. E-mail: jsawatsky@richmondchristian.ca. Web site: www.richmondchristian.ca.

RIDGECROFT SCHOOL

420 NC 11 North
PO Box 1008
Ahoskie, North Carolina 27910

Head of School: Mr. Elton L. Winslow Sr.

General Information Coeducational day college-preparatory and arts school. Grades PK–12. Founded: 1968. Setting: rural. Nearest major city is Norfolk, VA. 52-acre campus. 3 buildings on campus. Approved or accredited by North Carolina Association of Independent Schools and Southern Association of Colleges and Schools. Endowment: $519,067. Total enrollment: 331. Upper school average class size: 15. Upper school faculty-student ratio: 1:11.

Upper School Student Profile Grade 9: 22 students (8 boys, 14 girls); Grade 10: 23 students (17 boys, 6 girls); Grade 11: 23 students (12 boys, 11 girls); Grade 12: 17 students (6 boys, 11 girls).

Faculty School total: 35. In upper school: 5 men, 13 women; 6 have advanced degrees.

Subjects Offered Accounting, algebra, art, band, biology, business, calculus-AP, chemistry, computer skills, computers, earth science, English, English-AP, environmental science, forensic science, functions, geometry, health, Latin, modeling, physical education, physical science, physics, pre-algebra, pre-calculus, Spanish, U.S. history, U.S. history-AP, weightlifting, world history, yearbook.

Graduation Requirements Algebra, American history, American legal systems, American literature, biology, British literature, chemistry, computer applications, earth science, English, English composition, English literature, European literature, geometry, mathematics, physical education (includes health), Spanish, world history, Community Service—70 hours.

Special Academic Programs Advanced Placement exam preparation; honors section; independent study; study at local college for college credit; special instructional classes for students with learning disabilities and Attention Deficit Disorder.

College Admission Counseling 25 students graduated in 2008; 23 went to college, including East Carolina University; Meredith College; North Carolina State University. Other: 1 went to work, 1 entered military service. Median SAT critical reading: 510, median SAT math: 540, median SAT writing: 560, median combined SAT: 1530. 27.7% scored over 600 on SAT critical reading, 27.7% scored over 600 on SAT math, 22.2% scored over 600 on SAT writing, 27.7% scored over 1800 on combined SAT.

Student Life Upper grades have specified standards of dress, student council, honor system. Discipline rests primarily with faculty.

Summer Programs Remediation programs offered; session focuses on make-up courses; held on campus; accepts boys and girls; not open to students from other schools. 5 students usually enrolled. 2009 schedule: June 16 to July 31. Application deadline: June 6.

Tuition and Aid Day student tuition: $4495. Tuition installment plan (monthly payment plans, individually arranged payment plans). Tuition reduction for siblings available.

Admissions Traditional secondary-level entrance grade is 9. For fall 2008, 3 students applied for upper-level admission, 3 were accepted, 3 enrolled. Deadline for receipt of application materials: none. No application fee required. Interview recommended.

Athletics Interscholastic: baseball (boys), basketball (b,g), cheering (g), soccer (b,g), softball (g), tennis (g), volleyball (g); coed interscholastic: archery, golf, marksmanship, riflery, weight training. 1 coach.

Computers Computers are regularly used in accounting, art, computer applications, English, history, science classes. Computer network features include on-campus library services, Internet access, wireless campus network, Internet filtering or blocking technology. Campus intranet and computer access in designated common areas are available to students. The school has a published electronic and media policy.

Contact Mrs. Cindy Burgess, Business Manager. 252-332-2964 Ext. 224. Fax: 252-332-7586. E-mail: cburgess@ridgecroft.org. Web site: www.ridgecroft.org.

RIDGEWOOD PREPARATORY SCHOOL

201 Pasadena Avenue
Metairie, Louisiana 70001

Head of School: Mr. M.J. Montgomery Jr.

General Information Coeducational day college-preparatory school. Grades PK–12. Founded: 1948. Setting: suburban. 4-acre campus. 3 buildings on campus. Approved or accredited by Southern Association of Colleges and Schools and Louisiana Department of Education. Endowment: $45,000. Total enrollment: 280. Upper school average class size: 25. Upper school faculty-student ratio: 1:25.

Upper School Student Profile Grade 9: 33 students (17 boys, 16 girls); Grade 10: 38 students (16 boys, 22 girls); Grade 11: 35 students (16 boys, 19 girls); Grade 12: 43 students (27 boys, 16 girls).

Faculty School total: 28. In upper school: 8 men, 13 women; 10 have advanced degrees.

Subjects Offered Advanced math, algebra, American government, American history, American literature, anatomy and physiology, ancient world history, art, art and culture, art appreciation, art history, band, biology, British literature, calculus, chemistry, civics, civics/free enterprise, civil war history, composition, computer applications, computer literacy, computer resources, computer science, critical writing, driver education, English, English composition, English literature, fine arts, foreign language, French, geography, health, history, human anatomy, human biology, journalism, literature, news writing, newspaper, physical science, physics, pre-calculus, public speaking, Spanish, speech.

Graduation Requirements Arts and fine arts (art, music, dance, drama), computer science, English, foreign language, mathematics, physical education (includes health), science, social studies (includes history).

Special Academic Programs Study at local college for college credit; academic accommodation for the gifted.

College Admission Counseling 63 students graduated in 2008; 62 went to college, including Louisiana State University and Agricultural and Mechanical College; Loyola Marymount University; Loyola University New Orleans; Tulane University; University of Louisiana at Lafayette; University of New Orleans. Other: 1 entered military service.

Student Life Upper grades have specified standards of dress, student council, honor system. Discipline rests primarily with faculty.

Tuition and Aid Day student tuition: $5450. Tuition installment plan (monthly payment plans).

Admissions Traditional secondary-level entrance grade is 9. School's own exam required. Deadline for receipt of application materials: none. Application fee required: $300. Interview required.

Athletics Interscholastic: baseball (boys), basketball (b,g), football (b), soccer (b,g), softball (g), track and field (b,g), volleyball (g); coed interscholastic: soccer.

Computers Computers are regularly used in computer applications, economics classes. Computer resources include on-campus library services, Internet access, wireless campus network, Internet filtering or blocking technology. Campus intranet and computer access in designated common areas are available to students. The school has a published electronic and media policy.

Contact Mr. M. J. Montgomery Jr., Headmaster. 504-835-2545. Fax: 504-837-1864. E-mail: mjmontgomery@ridgewoodprep.com. Web site: www.ridgewoodprep.com.

RIDLEY COLLEGE

2 Ridley Road
PO Box 3013
St. Catharines, Ontario L2R7C3, Canada

Head of School: Jonathan Leigh

General Information Coeducational boarding and day college-preparatory, arts, and technology school, affiliated with Church of England (Anglican). Boarding grades

5–PG, day grades 1–PG. Founded: 1889. Setting: suburban. Nearest major city is Buffalo, NY. Students are housed in single-sex dormitories. 100-acre campus. 11 buildings on campus. Approved or accredited by Canadian Association of Independent Schools, Canadian Educational Standards Institute, Conference of Independent Schools of Ontario, The Association of Boarding Schools, and Ontario Department of Education. Affiliate member of National Association of Independent Schools; member of Secondary School Admission Test Board. Language of instruction: English. Endowment: CAN$25 million. Total enrollment: 607. Upper school average class size: 17. Upper school faculty-student ratio: 1:9.

Upper School Student Profile Grade 9: 68 students (46 boys, 22 girls); Grade 10: 112 students (46 boys, 66 girls); Grade 11: 151 students (77 boys, 74 girls); Grade 12: 149 students (103 boys, 46 girls); Postgraduate: 7 students (7 boys). 67% of students are boarding students. 70% are province residents. 11 provinces are represented in upper school student body. 30% are international students. International students from China, Germany, Hong Kong, Mexico, Republic of Korea, and United States; 31 other countries represented in student body. 20% of students are members of Church of England (Anglican).

Faculty School total: 102. In upper school: 55 men, 46 women; 34 have advanced degrees; 39 reside on campus.

Subjects Offered Accounting, Advanced Placement courses, algebra, American history, art, art history, biology, business mathematics, business skills, calculus, Canadian history, Canadian law, chemistry, computer programming, computer science, creative writing, drafting, drama, dramatic arts, driver education, economics, English, English literature, ESL, fine arts, French, geography, German, kinesiology, Latin, Mandarin, mathematics, music, physical education, physics, science, social science, social studies, Spanish, theater, world history.

Graduation Requirements Arts and fine arts (art, music, dance, drama), business skills (includes word processing), English, foreign language, mathematics, physical education (includes health), science, social science, social studies (includes history).

Special Academic Programs Advanced Placement exam preparation; honors section; independent study; domestic exchange program; study abroad; academic accommodation for the musically talented and the artistically talented; ESL (15 students enrolled).

College Admission Counseling 175 students graduated in 2008; 169 went to college, including Brock University; Queen's University at Kingston; The University of Western Ontario; University of Toronto; University of Waterloo; Wilfrid Laurier University. Other: 2 entered a postgraduate year, 4 had other specific plans. Mean SAT critical reading: 570, mean SAT math: 590.

Student Life Upper grades have uniform requirement, student council, honor system. Discipline rests primarily with faculty. Attendance at religious services is required.

Summer Programs Advancement programs offered; session focuses on academics; held on campus; accepts boys and girls; open to students from other schools. 50 students usually enrolled. 2009 schedule: July 1 to July 28. Application deadline: May 31.

Tuition and Aid Day student tuition: CAN$23,025; 5-day tuition and room/board: CAN$27,750; 7-day tuition and room/board: CAN$42,100. Tuition installment plan (monthly payment plans, individually arranged payment plans). Tuition reduction for siblings, bursaries, merit scholarship grants, need-based loans available. In 2008–09, 38% of upper-school students received aid; total upper-school merit-scholarship money awarded: CAN$550,000. Total amount of financial aid awarded in 2008–09: CAN$1,800,000.

Admissions Traditional secondary-level entrance grade is 9. For fall 2008, 357 students applied for upper-level admission, 307 were accepted, 225 enrolled. Differential Aptitude Test or SSAT required. Deadline for receipt of application materials: none. Application fee required: CAN$150. Interview recommended.

Athletics Interscholastic: aerobics/dance (girls), artistic gym (g), baseball (b,g), basketball (b,g), crew (b,g), cross-country running (b,g), dance (g), dance team (g), field hockey (g), football (b), golf (b), gymnastics (g), hockey (b,g), ice hockey (b,g), lacrosse (b), modern dance (g), rowing (b,g), rugby (b,g), running (b,g), soccer (b,g), softball (b,g), squash (b,g), swimming and diving (b,g), tennis (b,g), track and field (b,g), volleyball (g); intramural: aerobics (g), aerobics/dance (g), ballet (g), Cosom hockey (g), ice hockey (b), modern dance (b), running (b,g); coed interscholastic: golf, tennis; coed intramural: aerobics/Nautilus, alpine skiing, aquatics, backpacking, badminton, baseball, basketball, bicycling, canoeing/kayaking, climbing, cooperative games, drill team, equestrian sports, fitness, Frisbee, handball, hiking/backpacking, horseback riding, ice skating, life saving, martial arts, outdoor activities, physical fitness, racquetball, rock climbing, ropes courses, scuba diving, self defense, skeet shooting, skiing (downhill), snowboarding, soccer, softball, squash, strength & conditioning, swimming and diving, table tennis, tennis, track and field, trap and skeet, ultimate Frisbee, volleyball, weight training, yoga. 6 PE instructors, 6 coaches, 3 athletic trainers.

Computers Computers are regularly used in all academic classes. Computer network features include on-campus library services, online commercial services, Internet access, wireless campus network, Internet filtering or blocking technology. Student e-mail accounts are available to students. Students grades are available online. The school has a published electronic and media policy.

Contact Marilyn Martin, Director of Admission. 905-684-1889 Ext. 2247. Fax: 905-684-8875. E-mail: admission@ridleycollege.com. Web site: www.ridleycollege.com.

ANNOUNCEMENT FROM THE SCHOOL Located only 20 minutes from Niagara Falls, Ridley attracts boys and girls from more than thirty countries, including many from the USA. Students have campuswide wireless Internet access, and dual-platform MacBook laptop computers are curriculum integrated. A new ice hockey arena and field house complex will be operational in 2009.

RIPON CHRISTIAN SCHOOLS

435 North Maple Avenue
Ripon, California 95366

Head of School: Mrs. Mary Ann Sybesma

General Information Coeducational day college-preparatory, arts, business, vocational, religious studies, and technology school, affiliated with Calvinist faith; primarily serves students with learning disabilities. Grades K–12. Founded: 1946. Setting: small town. Nearest major city is San Francisco. 34-acre campus. 5 buildings on campus. Approved or accredited by Association of Christian Schools International, Christian Schools International, Western Association of Schools and Colleges, and California Department of Education. Endowment: $2.5 million. Total enrollment: 703. Upper school average class size: 22. Upper school faculty-student ratio: 1:18.

Upper School Student Profile 60% of students are Calvinist.

Faculty School total: 47. In upper school: 12 men, 10 women; 11 have advanced degrees.

Subjects Offered 20th century American writers, accounting, advanced computer applications, algebra, American history, anatomy and physiology, animal science, art, band, Bible studies, biology, business, business mathematics, calculus, calculus-AP, ceramics, chemistry, choir, computer applications, computer education, computer keyboarding, computer science, computer-aided design, creative writing, drafting, English, English language and composition-AP, English literature and composition-AP, environmental education, environmental science, ethics, family living, fine arts, geography, geometry, government/civics, grammar, health, history, leadership, leadership skills, life skills, mathematics, music, physical education, physics, psychology, science, social science, social studies, Spanish, Spanish-AP, U.S. history-AP, weightlifting, welding, woodworking, world history, yearbook.

Graduation Requirements Computer science, English, mathematics, physical education (includes health), religion (includes Bible studies and theology), science, social science, social studies (includes history), 10 Service hours per semester are required of all students.

Special Academic Programs 4 Advanced Placement exams for which test preparation is offered; independent study; academic accommodation for the musically talented and the artistically talented; remedial math.

College Admission Counseling 56 students graduated in 2008; 54 went to college, including Azusa Pacific University; California Polytechnic State University, San Luis Obispo; California State University, Stanislaus; Calvin College; Dordt College; Modesto Junior College. Other: 2 entered military service.

Student Life Upper grades have specified standards of dress, student council. Discipline rests primarily with faculty. Attendance at religious services is required.

Tuition and Aid Day student tuition: $6885. Tuition installment plan (FACTS Tuition Payment Plan, individually arranged payment plans, 1-payment plan, biannual payment plan, quarterly payment plan). Tuition reduction for siblings, need-based scholarship grants, need-based financial assistance, TRIP program available. In 2008–09, 10% of upper-school students received aid. Total amount of financial aid awarded in 2008–09: $20,000.

Admissions Traditional secondary-level entrance grade is 9. For fall 2008, 21 students applied for upper-level admission, 20 were accepted, 17 enrolled. Kaufman Test of Educational Achievement or Woodcock-Johnson required. Deadline for receipt of application materials: none. No application fee required. On-campus interview required.

Athletics Interscholastic: baseball (boys), basketball (b,g), football (b), golf (b,g), physical fitness (b,g), physical training (b,g), soccer (b,g), softball (g), tennis (b,g), volleyball (g), weight training (b,g); intramural: indoor soccer (b); coed interscholastic: tennis; coed intramural: tennis. 2 PE instructors, 15 coaches.

Computers Computers are regularly used in business skills classes. Computer network features include on-campus library services, Internet access, wireless campus network, Internet filtering or blocking technology. Students grades are available online. The school has a published electronic and media policy.

Contact Mrs. Mary Ann Sybesma, Principal. 209-599-2155. Fax: 209-599-2170. E-mail: msybesma@rcschools.com. Web site: www.rcschools.com.

RIVERDALE COUNTRY SCHOOL

5250 Fieldston Road
Riverdale, New York 10471-2999

Head of School: Dominic A. A. Randolph

General Information Coeducational day college-preparatory school. Grades PK–12. Founded: 1907. Setting: suburban. Nearest major city is New York. 27-acre campus. 9 buildings on campus. Approved or accredited by New York State Association of Independent Schools and New York Department of Education. Member of National Association of Independent Schools and Secondary School Admission Test

Board. Endowment: $42.8 million. Total enrollment: 1,084. Upper school average class size: 16. Upper school faculty-student ratio: 1:8.

Faculty School total: 185. In upper school: 42 men, 51 women; 72 have advanced degrees.

Subjects Offered Algebra, American literature, anatomy, art, art history, biology, calculus, ceramics, chemistry, community service, computer math, computer programming, computer science, creative writing, drama, driver education, earth science, ecology, economics, English, English literature, environmental science, European history, expository writing, fine arts, French, geology, geometry, government/civics, grammar, health, history, history of science, introduction to liberal studies, Japanese, journalism, Latin, Mandarin, marine biology, mathematics, music, oceanography, philosophy, photography, physical education, physics, psychology, science, social studies, Spanish, speech, statistics, theater, theory of knowledge, trigonometry, world history, writing.

Graduation Requirements American studies, arts and fine arts (art, music, dance, drama), computer science, English, foreign language, mathematics, physical education (includes health), science, social studies (includes history), integrated liberal studies. Community service is required.

Special Academic Programs Advanced Placement exam preparation; honors section; independent study; term-away projects; study abroad; academic accommodation for the gifted, the musically talented, and the artistically talented.

College Admission Counseling 111 students graduated in 2008; all went to college, including Duke University; Hamilton College; Indiana University Bloomington; Princeton University; Skidmore College; University of Pennsylvania.

Student Life Upper grades have student council, honor system. Discipline rests primarily with faculty.

Tuition and Aid Day student tuition: $35,250. Tuition installment plan (Key Tuition Payment Plan, monthly payment plans). Need-based scholarship grants available. In 2008–09, 20% of upper-school students received aid. Total amount of financial aid awarded in 2008–09: $4,600,000.

Admissions Traditional secondary-level entrance grade is 9. ISEE or SSAT required. Deadline for receipt of application materials: December 3. Application fee required: $60. On-campus interview required.

Athletics Interscholastic: baseball (boys), basketball (b,g), field hockey (g), football (b), gymnastics (g), lacrosse (b,g), soccer (b,g), softball (g), tennis (b,g), volleyball (g), wrestling (b); intramural: baseball (b), basketball (b,g), field hockey (g), football (b), gymnastics (g), lacrosse (b,g), soccer (b,g), softball (g), tennis (b,g), volleyball (g), wrestling (b); coed interscholastic: cross-country running, fencing, golf, squash, swimming and diving, track and field; coed intramural: cross-country running, dance, fencing, fitness, physical fitness, squash, swimming and diving, tennis, track and field, ultimate Frisbee, yoga. 7 PE instructors, 31 coaches, 1 athletic trainer.

Computers Computers are regularly used in art, English, foreign language, history, mathematics, music, science classes. Computer network features include on-campus library services, online commercial services, Internet access, Internet filtering or blocking technology, off-campus e-mail, off-campus library services. Student e-mail accounts are available to students. The school has a published electronic and media policy.

Contact Jenna Rogers King, Director of Middle and Upper School Admission. 718-519-2715. Fax: 718-519-2793. E-mail: jrking@riverdale.edu. Web site: www.riverdale.edu.

ANNOUNCEMENT FROM THE SCHOOL Riverdale enrolls students from the New York metro area in Pre-Kindergarten through Grade 12. The country setting within a short distance of New York City provides a wide range of learning and enrichment experiences. Riverdale aims to cultivate the unique talents of its students and to nurture their intellectual, creative, physical, moral, emotional, and social development.

RIVERMONT COLLEGIATE

1821 Sunset Drive
Bettendorf, Iowa 52722

Head of School: Mr. Richard E. St. Laurent

General Information Coeducational day college-preparatory, arts, and technology school. Grades PS–12. Founded: 1884. Setting: suburban. Nearest major city is Davenport. 16-acre campus. 6 buildings on campus. Approved or accredited by Independent Schools Association of the Central States and Iowa Department of Education. Member of National Association of Independent Schools and Secondary School Admission Test Board. Endowment: $1.9 million. Total enrollment: 195. Upper school average class size: 10. Upper school faculty-student ratio: 1:4.

Upper School Student Profile Grade 9: 7 students (2 boys, 5 girls); Grade 10: 11 students (7 boys, 4 girls); Grade 11: 4 students (3 boys, 1 girl); Grade 12: 10 students (6 boys, 4 girls).

Faculty School total: 26. In upper school: 4 men, 11 women; 6 have advanced degrees.

Subjects Offered Acting, advanced chemistry, advanced math, algebra, anatomy and physiology, ancient world history, art, arts, band, biology, business law, calculus, calculus-AP, chemistry, chemistry-AP, Chinese, computer multimedia, computer programming, computer science, creative writing, drama, earth science, economics, English, English literature, English-AP, European history, fine arts, French, French language-AP, French literature-AP, French-AP, geography, geometry, German, global science, government/civics, grammar, health, health education, history, history-AP, Holocaust studies, honors algebra, honors English, HTML design, humanities, independent study, jazz band, Latin, Latin American history, life science, mathematics, music, photography, physical education, physical fitness, physics, piano, psychology, public speaking, science, senior project, social studies, Spanish, Spanish literature-AP, Spanish-AP, speech, speech and debate, theater, theater arts, theater design and production, U.S. government, U.S. history, U.S. history-AP, vocal ensemble, Web site design, writing.

Graduation Requirements Arts and fine arts (art, music, dance, drama), computer science, English, foreign language, mathematics, physical education (includes health), science, senior project, social studies (includes history).

Special Academic Programs Advanced Placement exam preparation; honors section; independent study; study at local college for college credit; academic accommodation for the gifted and the musically talented.

College Admission Counseling 4 students graduated in 2008. Median SAT critical reading: 670, median SAT math: 640, median composite ACT: 28.

Student Life Upper grades have specified standards of dress, student council. Discipline rests primarily with faculty.

Summer Programs Enrichment, sports programs offered; session focuses on enrichment; held on campus; accepts boys and girls; open to students from other schools. 75 students usually enrolled. 2009 schedule: June 21 to August 6. Application deadline: May 28.

Tuition and Aid Day student tuition: $10,220. Tuition installment plan (Insured Tuition Payment Plan, Key Tuition Payment Plan, monthly payment plans). Tuition reduction for siblings, merit scholarship grants, need-based scholarship grants available. In 2008–09, 45% of upper-school students received aid; total upper-school merit-scholarship money awarded: $13,240. Total amount of financial aid awarded in 2008–09: $309,755.

Admissions Traditional secondary-level entrance grade is 11. For fall 2008, 2 students applied for upper-level admission, 2 were accepted, 2 enrolled. Any standardized test, Iowa Tests of Basic Skills or Wide Range Achievement Test required. Deadline for receipt of application materials: none. Application fee required: $50. Interview recommended.

Athletics Interscholastic: basketball (boys, girls), cheering (g), cross-country running (b,g), golf (b,g), soccer (b), swimming and diving (g), track and field (b,g), volleyball (g); intramural: basketball (b,g), cheering (g), table tennis (b,g); coed interscholastic: soccer; coed intramural: bowling, floor hockey, indoor soccer, table tennis, volleyball. 1 PE instructor, 3 coaches.

Computers Computers are regularly used in English, foreign language, history, independent study, mathematics classes. Computer network features include on-campus library services, Internet access, wireless campus network, Internet filtering or blocking technology. Student e-mail accounts are available to students. The school has a published electronic and media policy.

Contact Miss Cindy M. Murray, Director of Admission/Marketing Coordinator. 563-359-1366 Ext. 302. Fax: 563-359-7576. E-mail: murray@rvmt.org. Web site: www.rivermontcollegiate.org.

RIVERSIDE MILITARY ACADEMY

2001 Riverside Drive
Gainesville, Georgia 30501

Head of School: Col. Guy S. Gardner

General Information Boys' boarding and day college-preparatory, arts, technology, JROTC (grades 9-12), and military school, affiliated with Christian faith. Grades 7–PG. Founded: 1907. Setting: suburban. Nearest major city is Atlanta. Students are housed in single-sex dormitories. 206-acre campus. 9 buildings on campus. Approved or accredited by Georgia Independent School Association, Southern Association of Colleges and Schools, Southern Association of Independent Schools, The Association of Boarding Schools, and Georgia Department of Education. Member of National Association of Independent Schools. Endowment: $84 million. Total enrollment: 358. Upper school average class size: 10. Upper school faculty-student ratio: 1:10.

Upper School Student Profile Grade 9: 61 students (61 boys); Grade 10: 78 students (78 boys); Grade 11: 86 students (86 boys); Grade 12: 75 students (75 boys). 90% of students are boarding students. 60% are state residents. 30 states are represented in upper school student body. 25% are international students. International students from Dominican Republic, Germany, Mexico, Republic of Korea, Taiwan, and United Kingdom; 8 other countries represented in student body. 95% of students are Christian.

Faculty School total: 55. In upper school: 44 men, 11 women; 38 have advanced degrees; 20 reside on campus.

Subjects Offered Advanced chemistry, algebra, American literature, American literature-AP, art, art appreciation, astronomy, band, biology, biology-AP, British literature-AP, calculus, calculus-AP, ceramics, chemistry, chemistry-AP, computer applications, computer education, computer keyboarding, computer math, computer programming, computer science, computer skills, computer studies, computer technologies, creative writing, desktop publishing, drama, drawing, earth science, economics, English, English literature, ESL, ethics, European history, fine arts, French, French language-AP, geography, geometry, German, government/civics, grammar, health, history-AP, honors English, honors geometry, honors U.S. history, honors world history, jazz ensemble, journalism, JROTC, leadership, mathematics, military science, modern world history, music, music technology, music theory, painting, photography, physical education, physics, physics-AP, political science, pre-algebra, pre-calculus, printmaking, science, sculpture, social science, social studies, Spanish, Spanish-AP, statistics, theater, typing, U.S. government, U.S. government-AP, U.S. history, U.S. history-AP, visual arts, weight training, world history, world history-AP, world literature, yearbook.

Graduation Requirements Arts and fine arts (art, music, dance, drama), computer science, English, foreign language, JROTC, mathematics, physical education (includes health), science, social studies (includes history).

Special Academic Programs Advanced Placement exam preparation; honors section; ESL (24 students enrolled).

College Admission Counseling 78 students graduated in 2008; 77 went to college, including Clemson University; Furman University; The Citadel, The Military College of South Carolina; The University of Alabama; The University of North Carolina at Charlotte; University of Georgia. Other: 1 entered military service.

Student Life Upper grades have uniform requirement, student council, honor system. Discipline rests equally with students and faculty. Attendance at religious services is required.

Summer Programs Remediation, enrichment, advancement, ESL, sports, art/fine arts, rigorous outdoor training, computer instruction programs offered; session focuses on academics; held on campus; accepts boys; open to students from other schools. 170 students usually enrolled. 2009 schedule: June 15 to July 27. Application deadline: none.

Tuition and Aid Day student tuition: $16,500; 7-day tuition and room/board: $28,500. Tuition installment plan (Key Tuition Payment Plan, FACTS Tuition Payment Plan, monthly payment plans). Tuition reduction for siblings, merit scholarship grants, need-based scholarship grants available. In 2008–09, 7% of upper-school students received aid; total upper-school merit-scholarship money awarded: $5000. Total amount of financial aid awarded in 2008–09: $18,000.

Admissions Traditional secondary-level entrance grade is 9. Any standardized test and writing sample required. Deadline for receipt of application materials: none. Application fee required: $100. Interview required.

Athletics Interscholastic: baseball, basketball, cross-country running, drill team, football, golf, JROTC drill, lacrosse, marksmanship, riflery, soccer, swimming and diving, tennis, track and field, wrestling; intramural: aquatics, backpacking, baseball, basketball, billiards, canoeing/kayaking, cheering, climbing, combined training, cross-country running, flag football, football, hiking/backpacking, indoor soccer, indoor track, indoor track & field, jogging, kayaking, marksmanship, mountaineering, outdoor activities, paddle tennis, paint ball, physical training, rappelling, rock climbing, ropes courses, running, skateboarding, soccer, softball, strength & conditioning, swimming and diving, table tennis, tennis, volleyball, wall climbing, water polo, water volleyball, weight lifting, weight training. 5 PE instructors, 12 coaches, 1 athletic trainer.

Computers Computers are regularly used in college planning, desktop publishing, English, ESL, foreign language, French, journalism, library, mathematics, music, newspaper, photography, SAT preparation, science, Spanish, technology, theater, yearbook classes. Computer network features include on-campus library services, Internet access, Internet filtering or blocking technology. Campus intranet, student e-mail accounts, and computer access in designated common areas are available to students. Students grades are available online. The school has a published electronic and media policy.

Contact Admissions Office. 770-532-6251 Ext. 2128. Fax: 678-291-3364. E-mail: admissions@cadet.com. Web site: www.cadet.com.

See Close-Up on page 920.

THE RIVERS SCHOOL

333 Winter Street
Weston, Massachusetts 02493-1040

Head of School: Thomas P. Olverson

General Information Coeducational day college-preparatory and arts school. Grades 6–12. Founded: 1915. Setting: suburban. Nearest major city is Boston. 53-acre campus. 8 buildings on campus. Approved or accredited by Association of Independent Schools in New England and New England Association of Schools and Colleges. Member of National Association of Independent Schools and Secondary School Admission Test Board. Endowment: $19.6 million. Total enrollment: 440. Upper school average class size: 12. Upper school faculty-student ratio: 1:8.

Upper School Student Profile Grade 9: 84 students (39 boys, 45 girls); Grade 10: 81 students (39 boys, 42 girls); Grade 11: 86 students (46 boys, 40 girls); Grade 12: 81 students (39 boys, 42 girls).

Faculty School total: 78. In upper school: 31 men, 27 women; 40 have advanced degrees.

Subjects Offered Advanced Placement courses, algebra, American history, American literature, art, art history, art history-AP, astronomy, biology, biology-AP, calculus, calculus-AP, ceramics, chamber groups, chemistry, chemistry-AP, chorus, civil rights, Civil War, computer graphics, computer science, computer science-AP, creative writing, drama, earth science, English, English language and composition-AP, English literature, English literature and composition-AP, environmental science-AP, European history, expository writing, film studies, filmmaking, fine arts, French, French-AP, geography, geometry, history, Holocaust, jazz band, journalism, kinesiology, Latin, Latin-AP, Mandarin, mathematics, modern European history-AP, music, photography, physics, physics-AP, science, Spanish, Spanish-AP, statistics-AP, theater, theater arts, trigonometry, U.S. history-AP, world history, world literature.

Graduation Requirements Algebra, athletics, English, foreign language, geometry, history, mathematics, modern European history, science, U.S. history, visual and performing arts, participation in athletics. Community service is required.

Special Academic Programs Advanced Placement exam preparation; honors section; independent study; study at local college for college credit.

College Admission Counseling 81 students graduated in 2008; 80 went to college, including Boston College; Brown University; Duke University; Tufts University; Union College; University of Vermont. Other: 1 entered a postgraduate year. Median SAT critical reading: 640, median SAT math: 660, median SAT writing: 660, median combined SAT: 1965. 72% scored over 600 on SAT critical reading, 85% scored over 600 on SAT math, 85% scored over 600 on SAT writing, 82% scored over 1800 on combined SAT.

Student Life Upper grades have specified standards of dress, student council, honor system. Discipline rests primarily with faculty.

Tuition and Aid Day student tuition: $32,300. Tuition installment plan (Academic Management Services Plan, Key Tuition Payment Plan, monthly payment plans). Need-based scholarship grants available. In 2008–09, 24% of upper-school students received aid. Total amount of financial aid awarded in 2008–09: $2,483,400.

Admissions Traditional secondary-level entrance grade is 9. For fall 2008, 351 students applied for upper-level admission, 104 were accepted, 54 enrolled. ISEE or SSAT required. Deadline for receipt of application materials: February 1. Application fee required: $40. On-campus interview required.

Athletics Interscholastic: alpine skiing (boys, girls), baseball (b), basketball (b,g), cross-country running (b,g), field hockey (g), football (b), ice hockey (b,g), lacrosse (b,g), skiing (downhill) (b,g), soccer (b,g), softball (g), strength & conditioning (b,g), tennis (b,g); intramural: basketball (b,g), tennis (g); coed interscholastic: fitness, physical training, track and field, weight lifting, weight training; coed intramural: strength & conditioning. 4 coaches, 2 athletic trainers.

Computers Computers are regularly used in art, aviation, English, foreign language, history, humanities, language development, mathematics, newspaper, publications, science, writing, yearbook classes. Computer network features include on-campus library services, online commercial services, Internet access, wireless campus network, Internet filtering or blocking technology, language lab. Campus intranet, student e-mail accounts, and computer access in designated common areas are available to students. Students grades are available online. The school has a published electronic and media policy.

Contact Gillian Lloyd, Director of Admissions. 781-235-9300. Fax: 781-239-3614. E-mail: g.lloyd@rivers.org. Web site: www.rivers.org.

RIVERSTONE INTERNATIONAL SCHOOL

5493 Warm Springs Avenue
Boise, Idaho 83716

Head of School: Mr. Andrew Derry

General Information Coeducational day college-preparatory school. Grades K–12. Founded: 1997. Setting: suburban. 14-acre campus. 1 building on campus. Approved or accredited by International Baccalaureate Organization, Northwest Association of Accredited Schools, Northwest Association of Schools and Colleges, Pacific Northwest Association of Independent Schools, and Idaho Department of Education. Total enrollment: 316. Upper school average class size: 11. Upper school faculty-student ratio: 1:5.

Upper School Student Profile Grade 9: 25 students (17 boys, 8 girls); Grade 10: 28 students (20 boys, 8 girls); Grade 11: 23 students (5 boys, 18 girls); Grade 12: 28 students (11 boys, 17 girls).

Faculty School total: 42. In upper school: 7 men, 9 women; 8 have advanced degrees.

Graduation Requirements Art, English, foreign language, history, mathematics, science.

Special Academic Programs International Baccalaureate program; independent study; study abroad; ESL (20 students enrolled).

College Admission Counseling 18 students graduated in 2008; all went to college, including Brown University; Middlebury College; New York University; Sarah Lawrence College; The College of Idaho; University of Southern California. Median SAT critical reading: 585, median SAT math: 605, median SAT writing: 620, median combined SAT: 1810. 42% scored over 600 on SAT critical reading, 67% scored over 600 on SAT math, 67% scored over 600 on SAT writing, 58% scored over 1800 on combined SAT.

Student Life Upper grades have specified standards of dress, student council, honor system. Discipline rests primarily with faculty.

Summer Programs Enrichment, ESL, art/fine arts, rigorous outdoor training programs offered; session focuses on camps, ESL, and outdoor education; held both on and off campus; held at Boise River and Boise foothills; accepts boys and girls; open to students from other schools. 100 students usually enrolled. 2009 schedule: July 7 to August 8. Application deadline: June 26.

Tuition and Aid Day student tuition: $10,936. Tuition installment plan (monthly payment plans). Tuition reduction for siblings, need-based scholarship grants available. In 2008–09, 38% of upper-school students received aid.

Admissions Traditional secondary-level entrance grade is 9. For fall 2008, 43 students applied for upper-level admission, 32 were accepted, 26 enrolled. Deadline for receipt of application materials: none. Application fee required: $50. Interview required.
Athletics Intramural: fitness (girls); coed interscholastic: indoor soccer, nordic skiing, skiing (cross-country), skiing (downhill), snowboarding; coed intramural: backpacking, fitness walking, golf, ice skating, kayaking, lacrosse, nordic skiing, outdoor activities, physical fitness, rafting, ropes courses, running, skiing (cross-country), skiing (downhill), snowboarding. 1 PE instructor.
Computers Computers are regularly used in art, college planning, data processing, English, ESL, foreign language, French, history, lab/keyboard, music, research skills, Spanish, writing, yearbook classes. Computer network features include Internet access, wireless campus network. The school has a published electronic and media policy.
Contact Ms. Rachel Pusch, Admissions Director. 208-424-5000 Ext. 2104. Fax: 208-424-0033. E-mail: rpusch@riverstoneschool.org. Web site: www.riverstoneschool.org.

RIVERVIEW SCHOOL

East Sandwich, Massachusetts
See Special Needs Schools section.

ROANOKE CATHOLIC SCHOOL

621 North Jefferson Street
Roanoke, Virginia 24016
Head of School: Mr. Ray-Eric Correia

General Information Coeducational day college-preparatory, arts, business, religious studies, and technology school, affiliated with Roman Catholic Church. Grades PK–12. Founded: 1889. Setting: suburban. Approved or accredited by European Council of International Schools, National Catholic Education Association, Southern Association of Colleges and Schools, and Virginia Department of Education. Total enrollment: 595. Upper school average class size: 18.
Upper School Student Profile 75% of students are Roman Catholic.
Faculty School total: 55.
Special Academic Programs Advanced Placement exam preparation; honors section; study at local college for college credit; special instructional classes for students with Attention Deficit Disorder.
College Admission Counseling Colleges students went to include Georgetown University; Johnson & Wales University; Pepperdine University; The University of North Carolina at Chapel Hill; University of Virginia; Virginia Polytechnic Institute and State University.
Student Life Upper grades have uniform requirement, student council, honor system. Discipline rests primarily with faculty. Attendance at religious services is required.
Tuition and Aid Day student tuition: $4650–$7705. Tuition installment plan (FACTS Tuition Payment Plan). Tuition reduction for siblings, need-based scholarship grants available.
Admissions Deadline for receipt of application materials: none. Application fee required: $75. Interview required.
Athletics Interscholastic: baseball (boys), basketball (b,g), cheering (g), cross-country running (b,g), football (b), indoor track (b,g), soccer (b,g), swimming and diving (b,g), track and field (b,g).
Computers Computer resources include on-campus library services, Internet access.
Contact Mrs. Dawn Galbraith, Admission/Enrollment. 540-982-3532 Ext. 103. Fax: 540-345-0785. E-mail: dgalbraith@roanokecatholic.com. Web site: www.roanokecatholic.com.

ROBERT LOUIS STEVENSON SCHOOL

New York, New York
See Special Needs Schools section.

ROCKLAND COUNTRY DAY SCHOOL

34 Kings Highway
Congers, New York 10920-2199
Head of School: Dr. E. Lee Hancock

General Information Coeducational day college-preparatory, arts, and technology school. Grades PK–12. Founded: 1959. Setting: suburban. Nearest major city is New York. 20-acre campus. 5 buildings on campus. Approved or accredited by New York State Association of Independent Schools and New York Department of Education. Member of National Association of Independent Schools. Total enrollment: 145. Upper school average class size: 16. Upper school faculty-student ratio: 1:6.
Upper School Student Profile Grade 9: 14 students (8 boys, 6 girls); Grade 10: 15 students (7 boys, 8 girls); Grade 11: 19 students (10 boys, 9 girls); Grade 12: 17 students (10 boys, 7 girls).
Faculty School total: 40. In upper school: 13 men, 17 women; 17 have advanced degrees.
Subjects Offered Algebra, American history, American literature, art, art history, band, biology, calculus, ceramics, chemistry, chorus, community service, computer math, creative writing, drama, drawing, English, English literature, environmental science, European history, expository writing, fine arts, forensics, French, geometry, government/civics, health, history, humanities, jazz ensemble, Latin, madrigals, mathematics, music, orchestra, painting, philosophy, photography, photojournalism, physical education, physics, psychology, science, social studies, sociology, Spanish, theater, world history, world literature, writing.
Graduation Requirements Arts and fine arts (art, music, dance, drama), computer science, English, experiential education, foreign language, mathematics, music, physical education (includes health), science, social studies (includes history), off-campus senior internship and/or independent senior project. Community service is required.
Special Academic Programs 15 Advanced Placement exams for which test preparation is offered; honors section; accelerated programs; independent study; term-away projects; study at local college for college credit; academic accommodation for the gifted, the musically talented, and the artistically talented; ESL (16 students enrolled).
College Admission Counseling Colleges students went to include Clarkson University; New York University; Oberlin College; Rutgers, The State University of New Jersey, New Brunswick; Syracuse University; Vassar College. Median SAT critical reading: 560, median SAT math: 600, median SAT writing: 590, median combined SAT: 1750. 41% scored over 600 on SAT critical reading, 50% scored over 600 on SAT math, 41% scored over 600 on SAT writing, 41% scored over 1800 on combined SAT.
Student Life Upper grades have specified standards of dress, student council, honor system. Discipline rests equally with students and faculty.
Tuition and Aid Day student tuition: $13,775–$29,475. Tuition installment plan (Insured Tuition Payment Plan, Key Tuition Payment Plan, monthly payment plans, individually arranged payment plans). Need-based scholarship grants available. In 2008–09, 28% of upper-school students received aid. Total amount of financial aid awarded in 2008–09: $409,744.
Admissions Traditional secondary-level entrance grade is 9. For fall 2008, 20 students applied for upper-level admission, 12 were accepted, 12 enrolled. Admissions testing, any standardized test, English entrance exam, English proficiency, ERB and writing sample required. Deadline for receipt of application materials: none. Application fee required: $50. On-campus interview required.
Athletics Interscholastic: basketball (boys, girls), cheering (g), softball (g); intramural: cheering (g); coed interscholastic: aerobics/dance, dance, soccer, tennis; coed intramural: dance, flag football, Frisbee, golf, lacrosse, martial arts, paddle tennis, skateboarding, skiing (downhill), snowboarding, soccer, softball, table tennis, tennis, yoga. 2 PE instructors, 8 coaches.
Computers Computers are regularly used in art, desktop publishing, English, history, humanities, keyboarding, lab/keyboard, newspaper, photography, research skills, science, video film production, word processing, yearbook classes. Computer network features include online commercial services, Internet access, wireless campus network, Internet filtering or blocking technology, E-Library. The school has a published electronic and media policy.
Contact Ms. Lorraine Greenwell, Admissions Director. 845-268-6802 Ext. 201. Fax: 845-268-4644. E-mail: lgreenwell@rocklandcds.org. Web site: www.rocklandcds.org.

ROCK POINT SCHOOL

1 Rock Point Road
Burlington, Vermont 05408
Head of School: John Rouleau

General Information Coeducational boarding and day college-preparatory and arts school, affiliated with Episcopal Church. Grades 9–12. Founded: 1928. Setting: small town. Students are housed in single-sex by floor dormitories. 150-acre campus. 1 building on campus. Approved or accredited by Independent Schools of Northern New England, National Association of Episcopal Schools, New England Association of Schools and Colleges, The Association of Boarding Schools, and Vermont Department of Education. Endowment: $2.7 million. Total enrollment: 37. Upper school average class size: 11. Upper school faculty-student ratio: 1:5.
Upper School Student Profile Grade 9: 4 students (3 boys, 1 girl); Grade 10: 10 students (7 boys, 3 girls); Grade 11: 12 students (7 boys, 5 girls); Grade 12: 11 students (5 boys, 6 girls). 89% of students are boarding students. 35% are state residents. 16 states are represented in upper school student body. International students from Bermuda. 12% of students are members of Episcopal Church.
Faculty School total: 9. In upper school: 2 men, 6 women; 1 has an advanced degree.
Subjects Offered Algebra, American history, American literature, ancient history, art, art history, biology, calculus, chemistry, drawing, earth science, English, geometry, health, historical foundations for arts, history, mathematics, painting, photography, physical education, poetry, pottery, pre-calculus, science, sculpture, stained glass, Western civilization, world history, world literature.
Graduation Requirements Art, art history, English, history, mathematics, physical education (includes health), science. Community service is required.
Special Academic Programs Independent study; term-away projects; study at local college for college credit; special instructional classes for students who need structure and personal attention; ESL.

College Admission Counseling 12 students graduated in 2007; 11 went to college, including Lawrence University; St. John's College; The College of Wooster; University of New Hampshire. Other: 1 went to work. Median SAT critical reading: 540, median SAT math: 490, median SAT writing: 490, median combined SAT: 1500. 29% scored over 600 on SAT critical reading, 14% scored over 600 on SAT math, 14% scored over 600 on SAT writing, 29% scored over 1800 on combined SAT.
Student Life Upper grades have specified standards of dress. Discipline rests primarily with faculty.
Tuition and Aid Day student tuition: $23,300; 7-day tuition and room/board: $42,200. Tuition installment plan (deposit and two installment plan (September 1 and December 1)). Need-based scholarship grants available. In 2007–08, 13% of upper-school students received aid. Total amount of financial aid awarded in 2007–08: $95,800.
Admissions Traditional secondary-level entrance grade is 10. For fall 2007, 35 students applied for upper-level admission, 27 were accepted, 23 enrolled. Writing sample required. Deadline for receipt of application materials: none. Application fee required: $45. On-campus interview required.
Athletics Coed Interscholastic: basketball; coed intramural: alpine skiing, backpacking, ball hockey, basketball, bicycling, broomball, canoeing/kayaking, climbing, cooperative games, fitness, fitness walking, Frisbee, hiking/backpacking, jogging, kickball, martial arts, outdoor activities, outdoor adventure, outdoor recreation, physical fitness, physical training, rock climbing, running, skateboarding, skiing (downhill), snowboarding, soccer, softball, touch football, walking, weight training, yoga. 4 PE instructors.
Computers Computers are regularly used in all academic, art, college planning, creative writing, music, photography, video film production, word processing classes. Computer network features include Internet access, Internet filtering or blocking technology. Student e-mail accounts are available to students.
Contact Hillary Kramer, Director of Admissions. 802-863-1104 Ext. 12. Fax: 802-863-6628. E-mail: hkramer@rockpoint.org. Web site: www.rockpoint.org.

ANNOUNCEMENT FROM THE SCHOOL Rock Point School is a small, coeducational, boarding/day, college-preparatory school, located in Burlington, Vermont. The program, accredited by the New England Association of Schools and Colleges and approved by the Vermont State Board of Education, is designed to meet the needs of average to above-average students who have found themselves off-track academically or socially/emotionally and who want the structure and support of a close-knit community of 42 students and 25 staff members. Rock Point students are typically creative, bright, free-thinking individuals who have struggled in other school settings. Rock Point School was founded in 1928 by Bishop Booth of the Episcopal Diocese, replacing an earlier school located on the same grounds since 1889. The School is located on 150 acres bordering Lake Champlain, within minutes of downtown Burlington. Students come from across the country, with the largest percentage coming from New England. All students enroll in a core curriculum of English, history, science, math, art, and physical education. The academic program emphasizes writing across the curriculum. The art program includes art history, theater, painting, stained glass, photography, and video arts. Classes range from 6 to 12 students in size. Students attend two supervised study halls each day, and they have access to tutoring and organizational support. A senior seminar helps with college applications. Rock Point recognizes the equally important roles that the dormitory and academic programs play in a student's ability to get back on track and experience success and satisfaction. Students are offered a rich after-school and weekend program that includes community service (with local and international opportunities), skiing and snowboarding, hiking, camping, and many art and cultural activities. As needed, students can access community-based services, such as counseling and AA meetings. They have the opportunity to explore downtown Burlington, as well as many locations throughout Vermont. Some students earn the privilege of taking an outside class, getting a job, or participating in an internship.

ROCKY HILL SCHOOL

530 Ives Road
East Greenwich, Rhode Island 02818
Head of School: James J. Young III

General Information Coeducational day college-preparatory, arts, technology, and Marine Studies school. Grades PS–12. Founded: 1934. Setting: rural. Nearest major city is Providence. 88-acre campus. 16 buildings on campus. Approved or accredited by Association of Independent Schools in New England, New England Association of Schools and Colleges, and Rhode Island Department of Education. Member of National Association of Independent Schools and Secondary School Admission Test Board. Endowment: $1.5 million. Total enrollment: 352. Upper school average class size: 12. Upper school faculty-student ratio: 1:7.
Upper School Student Profile Grade 9: 41 students (26 boys, 15 girls); Grade 10: 43 students (20 boys, 23 girls); Grade 11: 42 students (23 boys, 19 girls); Grade 12: 38 students (17 boys, 21 girls).
Faculty School total: 67. In upper school: 12 men, 19 women; 17 have advanced degrees.
Subjects Offered African-American history, algebra, American foreign policy, American history, American literature, ancient history, art, art history, biology, biology-AP, calculus, chemistry, Chinese, computer math, computer programming, computer science, constitutional history of U.S., creative writing, drama, earth science, ecology, English, English literature, English-AP, environmental education, environmental science, ESL, European history, expository writing, fine arts, finite math, French, French-AP, geography, geometry, government, government/civics, health, history, history-AP, Latin, Latin-AP, marine biology, marine science, marine studies, mathematics, medieval history, modern European history, music, oceanography, physical education, physics, psychology, publications, robotics, SAT preparation, science, Shakespeare, social studies, sociology, Spanish, Spanish-AP, speech, statistics, statistics-AP, student government, student publications, studio art—AP, the Sixties, theater, TOEFL preparation, trigonometry, U.S. history-AP, voice, Western civilization, wilderness experience, woodworking, world history, world literature, writing.
Graduation Requirements Arts and fine arts (art, music, dance, drama), English, foreign language, history, mathematics, physical education (includes health), science, senior internship. Community service is required.
Special Academic Programs Advanced Placement exam preparation; honors section; independent study; term-away projects; study at local college for college credit; study abroad; academic accommodation for the gifted, the musically talented, and the artistically talented; ESL (3 students enrolled).
College Admission Counseling 33 students graduated in 2008; all went to college, including Bates College; Cornell University; Georgetown University; Gettysburg College; Smith College; Williams College. Median SAT critical reading: 587, median SAT math: 589, median SAT writing: 616.
Student Life Upper grades have specified standards of dress, student council. Discipline rests primarily with faculty.
Summer Programs Enrichment, sports, art/fine arts, computer instruction programs offered; session focuses on sports, arts, and enrichment activities; held on campus; accepts boys and girls; open to students from other schools. 450 students usually enrolled. 2009 schedule: June 18 to July 27. Application deadline: none.
Tuition and Aid Day student tuition: $25,500. Tuition installment plan (Insured Tuition Payment Plan, individually arranged payment plans, Tuition Management Services). Need-based scholarship grants available. In 2008–09, 19% of upper-school students received aid. Total amount of financial aid awarded in 2008–09: $1,020,500.
Admissions Traditional secondary-level entrance grade is 9. For fall 2008, 65 students applied for upper-level admission, 54 were accepted, 39 enrolled. ISEE, SSAT or TOEFL or SLEP required. Deadline for receipt of application materials: February 16. Application fee required: $50. Interview required.
Athletics Interscholastic: basketball (boys, girls), field hockey (g), ice hockey (b,g), lacrosse (b,g), soccer (b,g); coed interscholastic: cross-country running, fitness, golf, sailing, tennis; coed intramural: canoeing/kayaking, climbing, fitness, kayaking, mountain biking, outdoor adventure, rock climbing, sailing, tennis, wall climbing, yoga. 2 PE instructors, 15 coaches, 1 athletic trainer.
Computers Computers are regularly used in all classes. Computer network features include on-campus library services, Internet access, wireless campus network, Internet filtering or blocking technology, laptop/tablet program required and integrated into the curriculum. Campus intranet, student e-mail accounts, and computer access in designated common areas are available to students. Students grades are available online. The school has a published electronic and media policy.
Contact Maria T. Emmons, Admission Associate. 401-884-9070 Ext. 107. Fax: 401-885-4985. E-mail: memmons@rockyhill.org. Web site: www.rockyhill.org.

ROCKY MOUNT ACADEMY

1313 Avondale Avenue
Rocky Mount, North Carolina 27803
Head of School: Mr. Thomas R. Stevens

General Information Coeducational day college-preparatory school. Grades PK–12. Founded: 1968. Setting: small town. Nearest major city is Raleigh. 44-acre campus. 9 buildings on campus. Approved or accredited by Southern Association of Colleges and Schools. Member of National Association of Independent Schools. Endowment: $640,116. Total enrollment: 447. Upper school average class size: 12. Upper school faculty-student ratio: 1:8.
Upper School Student Profile Grade 9: 49 students (19 boys, 30 girls); Grade 10: 31 students (17 boys, 14 girls); Grade 11: 44 students (20 boys, 24 girls); Grade 12: 35 students (20 boys, 15 girls).
Faculty School total: 52. In upper school: 9 men, 11 women; 13 have advanced degrees.
Subjects Offered Adolescent issues, advanced computer applications, Advanced Placement courses, algebra, American history, American history-AP, American literature, anatomy, art, art appreciation, art history, astronomy, athletics, biology, biology-AP, calculus, calculus-AP, ceramics, cheerleading, chemistry, civics, community service, composition, computer education, creative writing, criminal justice, drama, earth science, economics-AP, English, English literature, English literature-AP, European history, fine arts, French, French-AP, geography, geology, geometry, government and politics-AP, government/civics, grammar, history, honors English, honors U.S. history, HTML design, human sexuality, keyboarding/computer, Latin, mathematics, music appreciation, newspaper, North Carolina history, novels, participation in sports, photography, photojournalism, physical education, physics, pottery,

pre-algebra, pre-calculus, psychology, psychology-AP, public speaking, publications, research skills, science, social studies, Spanish, student government, studio art-AP, technology, theater, trigonometry, visual arts, Web site design, word processing, world history, world literature, yearbook.
Graduation Requirements Arts and fine arts (art, music, dance, drama), computer science, English, foreign language, mathematics, physical education (includes health), public speaking, science, social studies (includes history). Community service is required.
Special Academic Programs 13 Advanced Placement exams for which test preparation is offered; honors section; independent study; study at local college for college credit; academic accommodation for the gifted; remedial reading and/or remedial writing; remedial math.
College Admission Counseling 27 students graduated in 2008; all went to college, including Duke University; Elon University; Furman University; North Carolina State University; The University of North Carolina at Chapel Hill; The University of North Carolina Wilmington. Mean SAT critical reading: 520, mean SAT math: 490, mean SAT writing: 560. 44% scored over 600 on SAT critical reading, 44% scored over 600 on SAT math, 48% scored over 600 on SAT writing.
Student Life Upper grades have specified standards of dress, student council, honor system. Discipline rests primarily with faculty.
Summer Programs Enrichment, sports, art/fine arts, computer instruction programs offered; session focuses on enrichment; held on campus; accepts boys and girls; open to students from other schools. 75 students usually enrolled. 2009 schedule: June 10 to August 15.
Tuition and Aid Day student tuition: $9385–$9790. Tuition installment plan (monthly payment plans, 3-payment plan, full-year payment plan). Merit scholarship grants, need-based scholarship grants available. In 2008–09, 22% of upper-school students received aid; total upper-school merit-scholarship money awarded: $52,300. Total amount of financial aid awarded in 2008–09: $180,000.
Admissions Traditional secondary-level entrance grade is 9. For fall 2008, 15 students applied for upper-level admission, 11 were accepted, 11 enrolled. QUIC required. Deadline for receipt of application materials: none. Application fee required: $75. On-campus interview required.
Athletics Interscholastic: baseball (boys), basketball (b,g), cheering (g), cross-country running (b,g), football (b), physical fitness (b,g), soccer (b,g), softball (g), tennis (b,g), volleyball (g); coed interscholastic: golf, physical fitness, swimming and diving; coed intramural: table tennis, ultimate Frisbee. 4 PE instructors, 4 coaches.
Computers Computers are regularly used in English, foreign language, graphics, health, history, independent study, library, mathematics, news writing, photojournalism, reading, research skills, science, speech, technology, writing fundamentals, yearbook classes. Computer resources include on-campus library services, Internet access, Internet filtering or blocking technology, INET Library. Computer access in designated common areas is available to students. The school has a published electronic and media policy.
Contact Mrs. Millie Harris Walker, Director of Enrollment Management. 252-443-4126 Ext. 224. Fax: 252-937-7922. E-mail: mwalker@rmacademy.com. Web site: www.rmacademy.com.

THE ROEPER SCHOOL

41190 Woodward Avenue
Bloomfield Hills, Michigan 48304
Head of School: Randall C. Dunn

General Information Coeducational day college-preparatory school. Grades PK–12. Founded: 1941. Setting: urban. Nearest major city is Birmingham. 1-acre campus. 1 building on campus. Approved or accredited by Independent Schools Association of the Central States. Member of National Association of Independent Schools. Endowment: $4.1 million. Total enrollment: 625. Upper school average class size: 14. Upper school faculty-student ratio: 1:6.
Upper School Student Profile Grade 9: 49 students (28 boys, 21 girls); Grade 10: 45 students (24 boys, 21 girls); Grade 11: 54 students (35 boys, 19 girls); Grade 12: 50 students (24 boys, 26 girls).
Faculty School total: 90. In upper school: 14 men, 24 women; 21 have advanced degrees.
Subjects Offered Algebra, American history, American literature, art, art history, biology, calculus, chemistry, computer programming, computer science, creative writing, dance, drama, English, English literature, European history, fine arts, French, geometry, government/civics, health, history, journalism, Latin, mathematics, music, philosophy, photography, physical education, physics, science, social studies, Spanish, speech, statistics, theater, trigonometry, world history, world literature, writing.
Graduation Requirements Arts and fine arts (art, music, dance, drama), computer science, English, foreign language, government, health, mathematics, science, social studies (includes history).
Special Academic Programs Advanced Placement exam preparation; independent study; academic accommodation for the gifted, the musically talented, and the artistically talented; programs in English, mathematics, general development for dyslexic students.
College Admission Counseling 46 students graduated in 2008; 44 went to college, including Kalamazoo College; Michigan State University; University of Michigan; University of Michigan–Dearborn. Other: 1 went to work, 1 had other specific plans.
Student Life Upper grades have student council, honor system. Discipline rests primarily with faculty.
Summer Programs Art/fine arts programs offered; session focuses on theater; held on campus; accepts boys and girls; open to students from other schools. 40 students usually enrolled. 2009 schedule: June 22 to August 14.
Tuition and Aid Day student tuition: $20,550. Tuition installment plan (FACTS Tuition Payment Plan, individually arranged payment plans). Need-based scholarship grants available. In 2008–09, 32% of upper-school students received aid. Total amount of financial aid awarded in 2008–09: $680,572.
Admissions Traditional secondary-level entrance grade is 9. For fall 2008, 53 students applied for upper-level admission, 38 were accepted, 28 enrolled. Individual IQ required. Deadline for receipt of application materials: none. Application fee required: $75. On-campus interview required.
Athletics Interscholastic: baseball (boys), basketball (b,g), cross-country running (b,g), physical training (b,g), soccer (b,g), strength & conditioning (b,g), track and field (b,g), volleyball (g), weight lifting (b,g); intramural: indoor soccer (b,g); coed intramural: physical training, strength & conditioning, weight lifting.
Computers Computers are regularly used in English, journalism, library, mathematics, publishing, science, yearbook classes. Computer network features include on-campus library services, online commercial services, Internet access.
Contact Lori Zinser, Director of Admissions. 248-203-7302. Fax: 248-203-7310. E-mail: lori.zinser@roeper.org.

ANNOUNCEMENT FROM THE SCHOOL The Roeper School is a private, coeducational day school for gifted and talented students, pre-kindergarten through grade 12, with campuses in Bloomfield Hills (pre-K through 5th grade) and Birmingham (grades 6–12). Roeper provides a personal, stimulating, and solid education in all academic disciplines. Students become increasingly self-directed and confident and develop an appreciation for individual differences.

ROLAND PARK COUNTRY SCHOOL

5204 Roland Avenue
Baltimore, Maryland 21210
Head of School: Mrs. Jean Waller Brune

General Information Girls' day college-preparatory and arts school. Grades K–12. Founded: 1901. Setting: suburban. 21-acre campus. 1 building on campus. Approved or accredited by Association of Independent Maryland Schools. Member of National Association of Independent Schools and Secondary School Admission Test Board. Endowment: $48 million. Total enrollment: 710. Upper school average class size: 14. Upper school faculty-student ratio: 1:7.
Upper School Student Profile Grade 9: 65 students (65 girls); Grade 10: 75 students (75 girls); Grade 11: 69 students (69 girls); Grade 12: 76 students (76 girls).
Faculty School total: 117. In upper school: 7 men, 42 women; 39 have advanced degrees.
Subjects Offered Advanced Placement courses, algebra, American literature, anatomy, Arabic, art, art history, astronomy, biology, calculus, ceramics, chemistry, chemistry-AP, Chinese, community service, computer programming, computer science, creative writing, dance, drama, ecology, economics, engineering, English, English literature, environmental science, European history, French, geometry, German, government/civics, Greek, health, Latin, music, philosophy, photography, physical education, physics, physiology, religion, Russian, science, social studies, Spanish, speech, statistics, theater, trigonometry, world history.
Graduation Requirements Adolescent issues, arts and fine arts (art, music, dance, drama), biology, chemistry, English, foreign language, history, mathematics, physical education (includes health), physics, public speaking, science. Community service is required.
Special Academic Programs Advanced Placement exam preparation; honors section; independent study; term-away projects; study abroad.
College Admission Counseling 59 students graduated in 2008; all went to college, including Boston University; Brown University; Tulane University; University of Delaware; University of Maryland, College Park; Vanderbilt University. Median SAT critical reading: 610, median SAT math: 620, median SAT writing: 630, median combined SAT: 1770, median composite ACT: 25. 47% scored over 600 on SAT critical reading, 57% scored over 600 on SAT math, 52% scored over 600 on SAT writing, 46% scored over 1800 on combined SAT, 42% scored over 26 on composite ACT.
Student Life Upper grades have uniform requirement, student council, honor system. Discipline rests equally with students and faculty.
Summer Programs Remediation, enrichment, advancement, sports, art/fine arts programs offered; session focuses on summer camp, arts, some academics; held both on and off campus; held at off-site pool and venues for outdoor education programs and various sites around Baltimore for art projects; accepts boys and girls; open to students from other schools. 90 students usually enrolled. 2009 schedule: June 22 to August 28. Application deadline: none.
Tuition and Aid Day student tuition: $21,250. Tuition installment plan (Academic Management Services Plan, monthly payment plans). Need-based scholarship grants, paying campus jobs available. In 2008–09, 23% of upper-school students received aid. Total amount of financial aid awarded in 2008–09: $804,325.

Admissions Traditional secondary-level entrance grade is 9. For fall 2008, 99 students applied for upper-level admission, 68 were accepted, 22 enrolled. CTP, ERB CTP IV or ISEE required. Deadline for receipt of application materials: Jahuary 15. Application fee required: $40. On-campus interview required.
Athletics Interscholastic: badminton, basketball, crew, cross-country running, field hockey, golf, indoor soccer, indoor track, lacrosse, soccer, softball, squash, swimming and diving, tennis, volleyball, winter (indoor) track, winter soccer; intramural: dance, fitness, modern dance, outdoor education, physical fitness, strength & conditioning. 5 PE instructors, 1 athletic trainer.
Computers Computers are regularly used in all classes. Computer network features include on-campus library services, online commercial services, Internet access, wireless campus network, Internet filtering or blocking technology, online database. Campus intranet, student e-mail accounts, and computer access in designated common areas are available to students. Students grades are available online. The school has a published electronic and media policy.
Contact Peggy Wolf, Director of Admissions. 410-323-5500. Fax: 410-323-2164. E-mail: admissions@rpcs.org. Web site: www.rpcs.org.

ROLLING HILLS PREPARATORY SCHOOL

One Rolling Hills Prep Way
San Pedro, California 90732
Head of School: Peter McCormack

General Information Coeducational day college-preparatory, arts, and technology school. Grades 6–12. Founded: 1981. Setting: suburban. Nearest major city is Los Angeles. 20-acre campus. 20 buildings on campus. Approved or accredited by California Association of Independent Schools, Western Association of Schools and Colleges, and California Department of Education. Member of National Association of Independent Schools. Endowment: $10,000. Total enrollment: 240. Upper school average class size: 16. Upper school faculty-student ratio: 1:9.
Upper School Student Profile Grade 9: 38 students (19 boys, 19 girls); Grade 10: 32 students (16 boys, 16 girls); Grade 11: 32 students (15 boys, 17 girls); Grade 12: 38 students (20 boys, 18 girls).
Faculty School total: 36. In upper school: 6 men, 21 women; 15 have advanced degrees.
Subjects Offered Algebra, American history, American literature, American sign language, anatomy, art, biology, calculus, ceramics, chemistry, computer science, creative writing, drama, economics, English, English literature, European history, fine arts, French, geography, geometry, government/civics, history, mathematics, music, photography, physical education, physics, pre-calculus, robotics, science, social studies, Spanish, speech, statistics, theater, trigonometry, world history.
Graduation Requirements Arts and fine arts (art, music, dance, drama), English, foreign language, mathematics, outdoor education, physical education (includes health), science, social studies (includes history), two-week senior internship, senior speech.
Special Academic Programs Advanced Placement exam preparation; honors section; independent study; academic accommodation for the gifted; programs in general development for dyslexic students; ESL (18 students enrolled).
College Admission Counseling 31 students graduated in 2008; all went to college, including New York University; University of California, Berkeley; University of California, Los Angeles; University of California, Santa Barbara; University of Southern California. Mean SAT critical reading: 590, mean SAT math: 590, mean SAT writing: 620. 45% scored over 600 on SAT critical reading, 40% scored over 600 on SAT math, 45% scored over 600 on SAT writing.
Student Life Upper grades have specified standards of dress, student council. Discipline rests primarily with faculty.
Tuition and Aid Day student tuition: $20,100. Tuition installment plan (Insured Tuition Payment Plan, Key Tuition Payment Plan, monthly payment plans). Merit scholarship grants, need-based scholarship grants available. In 2008–09, 30% of upper-school students received aid. Total amount of financial aid awarded in 2008–09: $410,000.
Admissions Traditional secondary-level entrance grade is 9. For fall 2008, 36 students applied for upper-level admission, 15 were accepted, 12 enrolled. ISEE required. Deadline for receipt of application materials: none. Application fee required: $150. On-campus interview required.
Athletics Interscholastic: baseball (boys), basketball (b,g), cheering (g), football (b), soccer (g), softball (g), volleyball (b,g); intramural: cheering (g), dance (g); coed interscholastic: cross-country running, golf, roller hockey, running, soccer; coed intramural: backpacking, climbing, hiking/backpacking, outdoor education, rock climbing, ropes courses. 4 PE instructors, 9 coaches, 1 athletic trainer.
Computers Computers are regularly used in English, foreign language, mathematics, science classes. Computer network features include on-campus library services, Internet access. The school has a published electronic and media policy.
Contact Bryonna Fisco, Director of Admission. 310-791-1101 Ext. 148. Fax: 310-373-4931. E-mail: bfisco@rhps-k12.com. Web site: www.rollinghillsprep.org.

RONCALLI HIGH SCHOOL

3300 Prague Road
Indianapolis, Indiana 46227
Head of School: Mr. Joseph D. Hollowell

General Information Coeducational day college-preparatory and religious studies school, affiliated with Roman Catholic Church. Grades 9–12. Founded: 1969. Setting: suburban. 38-acre campus. 3 buildings on campus. Approved or accredited by National Catholic Education Association, North Central Association of Colleges and Schools, and Indiana Department of Education. Total enrollment: 1,142. Upper school average class size: 22. Upper school faculty-student ratio: 1:14.
Upper School Student Profile Grade 9: 317 students (172 boys, 145 girls); Grade 10: 266 students (141 boys, 125 girls); Grade 11: 292 students (144 boys, 148 girls); Grade 12: 268 students (134 boys, 134 girls). 96% of students are Roman Catholic.
Faculty School total: 78. In upper school: 31 men, 47 women; 42 have advanced degrees.
Subjects Offered ACT preparation, addiction, ADL skills, adolescent issues, advanced TOEFL/grammar, advertising design, aerobics, African American history, African American studies, African dance, African drumming, African history, African literature, African studies, African-American history, African-American literature, African-American studies, agriculture, agroecology, Alabama history and geography, American biography, American culture, American democracy, American foreign policy.
Graduation Requirements Biology, computer applications, English, mathematics, physical education (includes health), physical science, religious studies, U.S. government, U.S. history, service requirements each year of school.
Special Academic Programs 13 Advanced Placement exams for which test preparation is offered; honors section; independent study; study at local college for college credit; study abroad; academic accommodation for the gifted, the musically talented, and the artistically talented; remedial reading and/or remedial writing; remedial math; programs in English, mathematics, general development for dyslexic students; special instructional classes for blind students, students with autism, learning disabilities, Attention Deficit Disorder.
College Admission Counseling 278 students graduated in 2008; 264 went to college, including Ball State University; Indiana University Bloomington; Purdue University. Other: 10 went to work, 4 entered military service. Mean SAT critical reading: 510, mean SAT math: 540, mean SAT writing: 510, mean combined SAT: 1560, mean composite ACT: 23. 25.3% scored over 600 on SAT critical reading, 26% scored over 600 on SAT math, 18% scored over 600 on SAT writing, 19.5% scored over 1800 on combined SAT, 23% scored over 26 on composite ACT.
Student Life Upper grades have uniform requirement, student council. Discipline rests primarily with faculty. Attendance at religious services is required.
Tuition and Aid Day student tuition: $7500. Tuition installment plan (monthly payment plans). Tuition reduction for siblings, merit scholarship grants, need-based scholarship grants, paying campus jobs available. In 2008–09, 24% of upper-school students received aid; total upper-school merit-scholarship money awarded: $10,000. Total amount of financial aid awarded in 2008–09: $725,000.
Admissions Traditional secondary-level entrance grade is 9. High School Placement Test or High School Placement Test (closed version) from Scholastic Testing Service required. Deadline for receipt of application materials: none. Application fee required: $100. On-campus interview required.
Athletics Interscholastic: baseball (boys), basketball (b,g), bowling (b,g), cheering (g), cross-country running (b,g), diving (b,g), football (b), golf (b,g), gymnastics (g), soccer (b,g), softball (g), strength & conditioning (b), swimming and diving (b,g), tennis (b,g), track and field (b,g), volleyball (b,g), wrestling (b); intramural: backpacking (b,g), boxing (b,g), dance team (g), ice hockey (b), lacrosse (b), power lifting (b), rugby (b), weight lifting (b,g); coed intramural: climbing, Frisbee, hiking/backpacking, mountaineering, rock climbing, ultimate Frisbee, wilderness. 5 PE instructors, 2 athletic trainers.
Computers Computer network features include on-campus library services, Internet access, wireless campus network, Internet filtering or blocking technology. Campus intranet, student e-mail accounts, and computer access in designated common areas are available to students. Students grades are available online. The school has a published electronic and media policy.
Contact Mr. James Kedra, Assistant Principal for Academic Affairs. 317-787-8277 Ext. 222. Fax: 317-788-4095. E-mail: jkedra@roncallihs.org. Web site: www.roncalli.org.

RON PETTIGREW CHRISTIAN SCHOOL

1761 110th Avenue
Dawson Creek, British Columbia V1G 4X4, Canada
Head of School: Phyllis L. Roch

General Information Coeducational day college-preparatory and general academic school, affiliated with Christian faith. Grades K–12. Founded: 1989. Setting: small town. Nearest major city is Prince George, Canada. 1-acre campus. 1 building on campus. Approved or accredited by Association of Christian Schools International and British Columbia Department of Education. Language of instruction: English. Total enrollment: 88. Upper school faculty-student ratio: 1:5.
Upper School Student Profile 76% of students are Christian faith.
Faculty School total: 6. In upper school: 2 men, 4 women.

College Admission Counseling 2 students graduated in 2008. Other: 2 went to work.
Student Life Upper grades have uniform requirement, student council, honor system. Discipline rests primarily with faculty. Attendance at religious services is required.
Admissions No application fee required. Interview required.
Computers Computer network features include Internet access, wireless campus network, Internet filtering or blocking technology.
Contact Phyllis L. Roch, Head of School. 250-782-4580. Fax: 250-782-9805. E-mail: rpcs@pris.ca.

ROSSEAU LAKE COLLEGE

1967 Bright Street
Rosseau, Ontario P0C 1J0, Canada
Head of School: Mr. Graham Hookey

General Information Coeducational boarding and day college-preparatory, arts, and business school. Grades 7–12. Founded: 1967. Setting: rural. Nearest major city is Toronto, Canada. Students are housed in single-sex dormitories. 53-acre campus. 13 buildings on campus. Approved or accredited by Canadian Association of Independent Schools, Canadian Educational Standards Institute, and Ontario Department of Education. Languages of instruction: English and French. Endowment: CAN$100,000. Total enrollment: 141. Upper school average class size: 12. Upper school faculty-student ratio: 1:7.
Upper School Student Profile Grade 9: 26 students (17 boys, 9 girls); Grade 10: 25 students (17 boys, 8 girls); Grade 11: 21 students (17 boys, 4 girls); Grade 12: 41 students (29 boys, 12 girls). 60% of students are boarding students. 82% are province residents. 2 provinces are represented in upper school student body. 18% are international students. International students from Bermuda, Democratic People's Republic of Korea, Mexico, Spain, Taiwan, and United States; 15 other countries represented in student body.
Faculty School total: 20. In upper school: 7 men, 12 women; 5 have advanced degrees; 11 reside on campus.
Subjects Offered Accounting, algebra, art, art history, biology, business, calculus, Canadian law, career and personal planning, chemistry, civics, computer programming, computer science, data analysis, economics, English, entrepreneurship, ESL, European history, experiential education, fine arts, French, geography, geometry, health, history, information technology, marketing, mathematics, music, outdoor education, physical education, physics, political science, science, social science, trigonometry, visual arts, world governments, writing skills.
Graduation Requirements Arts and fine arts (art, music, dance, drama), business skills (includes word processing), career planning, civics, computer science, English, foreign language, mathematics, physical education (includes health), science, social studies (includes history).
Special Academic Programs Accelerated programs; independent study; term-away projects; study abroad; academic accommodation for the gifted; remedial reading and/or remedial writing; remedial math; ESL (25 students enrolled).
College Admission Counseling 27 students graduated in 2008; 26 went to college, including McMaster University; Queen's University at Kingston; The University of Western Ontario; University of Guelph; University of Toronto; York University. Other: 1 went to work.
Student Life Upper grades have uniform requirement, student council, honor system. Discipline rests equally with students and faculty.
Summer Programs Remediation, enrichment, sports, rigorous outdoor training, computer instruction programs offered; session focuses on academics; held on campus; accepts boys and girls; open to students from other schools. 30 students usually enrolled. 2009 schedule: July 1 to July 30. Application deadline: June 15.
Tuition and Aid Day student tuition: CAN$17,350; 7-day tuition and room/board: CAN$39,650. Tuition installment plan (monthly payment plans, individually arranged payment plans). Tuition reduction for siblings, bursaries, merit scholarship grants, need-based scholarship grants available. In 2008–09, 10% of upper-school students received aid; total upper-school merit-scholarship money awarded: CAN$40,000. Total amount of financial aid awarded in 2008–09: CAN$160,000.
Admissions Traditional secondary-level entrance grade is 9. For fall 2008, 87 students applied for upper-level admission, 42 were accepted, 40 enrolled. Admissions testing and English Composition Test for ESL students required. Deadline for receipt of application materials: none. Application fee required: CAN$100. Interview required.
Athletics Interscholastic: baseball (boys), basketball (b,g), cross-country running (b,g), field hockey (g), hockey (b), ice hockey (b), mountain biking (b,g), nordic skiing (b,g), rugby (b), running (b,g), skiing (cross-country) (b,g), snowboarding (b,g), soccer (b,g), softball (b), swimming and diving (b,g), tennis (b,g), track and field (b,g), volleyball (b,g); intramural: alpine skiing (b,g), baseball (b), basketball (b,g), cross-country running (b,g), field hockey (g), hockey (b,g), ice hockey (b,g), rugby (b), running (b,g), skiing (cross-country) (b,g), snowboarding (b,g); coed interscholastic: bicycling, canoeing/kayaking, climbing, golf, kayaking, mountain biking, nordic skiing, running, skiing (cross-country), skiing (downhill), snowboarding, softball, track and field; coed intramural: aerobics, aquatics, backpacking, baseball, basketball, bicycling, billiards, bowling, broomball, canoeing/kayaking, climbing, combined training, cooperative games, Cosom hockey, cross-country running, curling, equestrian sports, fishing, fitness, fitness walking, flag football, floor hockey, fly fishing, freestyle skiing, Frisbee, golf, hiking/backpacking, horseback riding, ice skating, indoor hockey, indoor soccer, jogging, kayaking, life saving, mountain biking, mountaineering, nordic skiing, outdoor activities, paddle tennis, paddling, physical fitness, physical training, rappelling, rock climbing, ropes courses, sailboarding, sailing, scuba diving, skateboarding, skiing (cross-country), skiing (downhill), snowboarding, snowshoeing, soccer, softball, squash, street hockey, strength & conditioning, swimming and diving, table tennis, tennis, track and field, triathlon, ultimate Frisbee, volleyball, walking, wall climbing, water skiing, weight lifting, weight training, wilderness, wilderness survival, wildernessways, windsurfing, winter walking, yoga. 2 coaches, 1 athletic trainer.
Computers Computers are regularly used in accounting, geography, graphic arts, information technology classes. Computer network features include on-campus library services, Internet access, wireless campus network, Internet filtering or blocking technology. Campus intranet, student e-mail accounts, and computer access in designated common areas are available to students. The school has a published electronic and media policy.
Contact Ms. Jeanette Turvey, Admissions Assistant. 705-732-4351 Ext. 21. Fax: 705-732-6319. E-mail: admissions@rlc.on.ca. Web site: www.rosseaulakecollege.com.

ROSS SCHOOL

18 Goodfriend Drive
East Hampton, New York 11937
Head of School: Michele Claeys

General Information Coeducational boarding and day college-preparatory, Globally focused, integrated curriculum, and ESL support school. Boarding grades 9–12, day grades N–12. Founded: 1991. Setting: small town. Nearest major city is New York. Students are housed in single-sex dormitories and host family homes. 100-acre campus. 6 buildings on campus. Approved or accredited by Middle States Association of Colleges and Schools, New York State Association of Independent Schools, and New York Department of Education. Total enrollment: 580. Upper school average class size: 16.
Upper School Student Profile Grade 9: 59 students (29 boys, 30 girls); Grade 10: 63 students (29 boys, 34 girls); Grade 11: 48 students (22 boys, 26 girls); Grade 12: 50 students (27 boys, 23 girls). 10% of students are boarding students. 90% are state residents. 10% are international students. International students from China, Germany, Norway, Republic of Korea, Sweden, and Taiwan; 3 other countries represented in student body.
Faculty School total: 106. In upper school: 14 men, 22 women; 28 have advanced degrees.
Subjects Offered Advanced biology, advanced chemistry, advanced math, art history, athletics, Chinese, college counseling, computer multimedia, English literature, ESL, French, health and wellness, independent study, media studies, model United Nations, physics, SAT preparation, senior project, Spanish, theater arts, world history.
Graduation Requirements 30 hours of community service.
Special Academic Programs Independent study; term-away projects; ESL (9 students enrolled).
College Admission Counseling 43 students graduated in 2008; 42 went to college, including Bowdoin College; Columbia College; New York University; The College of William and Mary; Trinity College; Wake Forest University.
Student Life Upper grades have uniform requirement, student council, honor system. Discipline rests primarily with faculty.
Summer Programs Sports, art/fine arts programs offered; session focuses on Sports and Fine Arts; held on campus; accepts boys and girls; open to students from other schools. 180 students usually enrolled. 2009 schedule: July to August. Application deadline: June.
Tuition and Aid Day student tuition: $24,800; 5-day tuition and room/board: $32,500; 7-day tuition and room/board: $41,700. Tuition installment plan (monthly payment plans). Tuition reduction for siblings, need-based scholarship grants available. In 2008–09, 40% of upper-school students received aid. Total amount of financial aid awarded in 2008–09: $2,000,000.
Admissions Traditional secondary-level entrance grade is 9. Any standardized test required. Deadline for receipt of application materials: January 31. Application fee required: $50. Interview required.
Athletics Interscholastic: baseball (boys), basketball (b,g), lacrosse (b,g), soccer (b,g), softball (g), tennis (b,g), track and field (b,g), volleyball (b,g); coed interscholastic: cheering, golf; coed intramural: sailing. 4 PE instructors, 5 coaches.
Computers Computers are regularly used in all classes. Computer network features include on-campus library services, online commercial services, Internet access, wireless campus network, Internet filtering or blocking technology. Campus intranet and student e-mail accounts are available to students. Students grades are available online. The school has a published electronic and media policy.
Contact Ms. Kristen Kaschub, Director of Upper School Admission, Director of Boarding Program. 631-907-5400. Fax: 631-907-5563. E-mail: kkaschub@ross.org. Web site: www.ross.org/.

ROTHESAY NETHERWOOD SCHOOL

40 College Hill Road
Rothesay, New Brunswick E2E 5H1, Canada

Head of School: Mr. Paul G. Kitchen

General Information Coeducational boarding and day college-preparatory, arts, and technology school, affiliated with Anglican Church of Canada. Grades 6–12. Founded: 1877. Setting: small town. Nearest major city is Saint John, Canada. Students are housed in single-sex dormitories. 180-acre campus. 25 buildings on campus. Approved or accredited by Canadian Association of Independent Schools, Canadian Educational Standards Institute, Conference of Independent Schools of Ontario, International Baccalaureate Organization, The Association of Boarding Schools, and New Brunswick Department of Education. Languages of instruction: English and French. Endowment: CAN$3 million. Total enrollment: 250. Upper school average class size: 15. Upper school faculty-student ratio: 1:8.

Upper School Student Profile Grade 9: 42 students (22 boys, 20 girls); Grade 10: 56 students (32 boys, 24 girls); Grade 11: 55 students (32 boys, 23 girls); Grade 12: 49 students (27 boys, 22 girls). 58% of students are boarding students. 64% are province residents. 12 provinces are represented in upper school student body. 14% are international students. International students from Bermuda, Germany, Japan, Mexico, Republic of Korea, and United States; 5 other countries represented in student body. 30% of students are members of Anglican Church of Canada.

Faculty School total: 44. In upper school: 13 men, 17 women; 9 have advanced degrees; 24 reside on campus.

Subjects Offered Advanced chemistry, art, art history, biology, Canadian history, chemistry, computer programming, computer science, CPR, digital art, drama, driver education, English, English literature, ESL, European history, fine arts, French, geography, geometry, health, history, information technology, International Baccalaureate courses, leadership, math applications, mathematical modeling, mathematics, music, outdoor education, physical education, physics, science, social studies, theater arts, world history, writing.

Graduation Requirements Arts and fine arts (art, music, dance, drama), computer science, English, foreign language, mathematics, physical education (includes health), science, social science, social studies (includes history), IB Theory of Knowledge, IB designation CAS hours (creativity, action, service), Extended Essay, Outward Bound adventure.

Special Academic Programs International Baccalaureate program; honors section; independent study; term-away projects; study at local college for college credit; academic accommodation for the gifted, the musically talented, and the artistically talented; ESL (14 students enrolled).

College Admission Counseling 49 students graduated in 2008; all went to college, including Acadia University; Dalhousie University; McGill University; Mount Allison University; Saint Mary's University; University of Toronto.

Student Life Upper grades have uniform requirement, student council, honor system. Discipline rests primarily with faculty. Attendance at religious services is required.

Tuition and Aid Day student tuition: CAN$17,750; 7-day tuition and room/board: CAN$34,900. Tuition installment plan (monthly payment plans, individually arranged payment plans). Tuition reduction for siblings, bursaries, merit scholarship grants, need-based scholarship grants available. In 2008–09, 30% of upper-school students received aid; total upper-school merit-scholarship money awarded: CAN$146,000. Total amount of financial aid awarded in 2008–09: CAN$460,000.

Admissions Traditional secondary-level entrance grade is 9. For fall 2008, 117 students applied for upper-level admission, 84 were accepted, 71 enrolled. School's own exam or SSAT required. Deadline for receipt of application materials: none. Application fee required: CAN$200. Interview required.

Athletics Interscholastic: badminton (boys, girls), basketball (b,g), crew (b,g), cross-country running (b,g), golf (b,g), ice hockey (b,g), rowing (b,g), rugby (b,g), running (b,g), soccer (b,g), squash (b,g), tennis (b,g), track and field (b,g), volleyball (b,g); intramural: aerobics/dance (g), badminton (b,g), bicycling (b), cross-country running (b,g), golf (b,g), ice hockey (b,g), indoor soccer (b), squash (b,g), tennis (b,g), track and field (b,g), yoga (g); coed interscholastic: badminton, crew, cross-country running, golf, rowing, tennis, track and field; coed intramural: aerobics, backpacking, badminton, bicycling, billiards, bowling, broomball, canoeing/kayaking, climbing, cooperative games, cross-country running, fitness, fitness walking, floor hockey, Frisbee, golf, hiking/backpacking, ice hockey, ice skating, indoor soccer, jogging, kayaking, mountain biking, outdoor activities, physical fitness, physical training, running, skiing (downhill), snowboarding, squash, street hockey, strength & conditioning, tennis, track and field, ultimate Frisbee, volleyball, walking, wall climbing, weight training. 3 PE instructors.

Computers Computers are regularly used in all classes. Computer network features include on-campus library services, Internet access, wireless campus network, Internet filtering or blocking technology, informative, interactive online community for parents, teachers and students, Website for each academic course. Campus intranet and student e-mail accounts are available to students. Students grades are available online. The school has a published electronic and media policy.

Contact Ms. Jayne Fillman, Director of Admission. 506-847-8224. Fax: 506-848-0851. E-mail: fillmanj@rns.cc. Web site: www.rns.cc.

ROTTERDAM INTERNATIONAL SECONDARY SCHOOL, WOLFERT VAN BORSELEN

Bentincklaan 294
Rotterdam 3039 KK, Netherlands

Head of School: Aidan Campbell

General Information Coeducational day college-preparatory, bilingual studies, and languages school. Grades 6–12. Founded: 1988. Setting: urban. 2-hectare campus. 2 buildings on campus. Approved or accredited by state department of education. Member of European Council of International Schools. Language of instruction: English. Total enrollment: 175. Upper school average class size: 15. Upper school faculty-student ratio: 1:10.

Upper School Student Profile Grade 6: 16 students (8 boys, 8 girls); Grade 7: 15 students (10 boys, 5 girls); Grade 8: 19 students (12 boys, 7 girls); Grade 9: 25 students (17 boys, 8 girls); Grade 10: 33 students (16 boys, 17 girls); Grade 11: 40 students (23 boys, 17 girls); Grade 12: 26 students (17 boys, 9 girls).

Faculty School total: 32. In upper school: 13 men, 18 women; 13 have advanced degrees.

Special Academic Programs International Baccalaureate program; ESL.

College Admission Counseling 24 students graduated in 2008; 15 went to college. Other: 9 had other specific plans.

Student Life Upper grades have student council. Discipline rests primarily with faculty.

Tuition and Aid Day student tuition: €4930–€5800. Tuition installment plan (monthly payment plans, eight yearly payments).

Admissions Traditional secondary-level entrance grade is 11. For fall 2008, 58 students applied for upper-level admission, 58 were accepted, 58 enrolled. Admissions testing required. Deadline for receipt of application materials: none. Application fee required: €250. On-campus interview required.

Athletics Coed Interscholastic: basketball, soccer; coed intramural: baseball, basketball, bicycling, rowing, soccer, tai chi, track and field, volleyball. 4 PE instructors.

Computers Computers are regularly used in all academic classes. Computer network features include Internet access. Student e-mail accounts are available to students. Students grades are available online. The school has a published electronic and media policy.

Contact Alexa Nijpels, Admissions Officer. 31-10 890 7745. Fax: 31-10 8907755. E-mail: info.riss@wolfert.nl. Web site: www.wolfert.nl/riss/.

ROWLAND HALL-ST. MARK'S SCHOOL

843 South Lincoln Street
Salt Lake City, Utah 84102

Head of School: Mr. Alan C. Sparrow

General Information Coeducational day college-preparatory school. Grades PK–12. Founded: 1880. Setting: urban. 4-acre campus. 1 building on campus. Approved or accredited by National Association of Episcopal Schools, Northwest Association of Accredited Schools, Northwest Association of Schools and Colleges, Pacific Northwest Association of Independent Schools, The College Board, and Utah Department of Education. Member of National Association of Independent Schools. Endowment: $4 million. Total enrollment: 996. Upper school average class size: 16. Upper school faculty-student ratio: 1:8.

Upper School Student Profile Grade 9: 66 students (29 boys, 37 girls); Grade 10: 64 students (35 boys, 29 girls); Grade 11: 69 students (41 boys, 28 girls); Grade 12: 72 students (36 boys, 36 girls).

Faculty School total: 36. In upper school: 15 men, 19 women; 19 have advanced degrees.

Subjects Offered Adolescent issues, advanced studio art-AP, algebra, art history-AP, band, biology, biology-AP, calculus, calculus-AP, ceramics, chemistry, chemistry-AP, chorus, computer graphics, computer programming, creative writing, dance, debate, drama, English, English language and composition-AP, English literature and composition-AP, environmental science, ethics, European history-AP, filmmaking, French, French language-AP, French literature-AP, geometry, graphic arts, graphic design, history, human development, intro to computers, jazz band, Latin, Latin-AP, math applications, modern European history-AP, music theory-AP, newspaper, photography, physical education, physics, physics-AP, political science, pre-calculus, psychology-AP, Spanish, Spanish-AP, speech and debate, statistics-AP, studio art, studio art-AP, theater, trigonometry, U.S. history, U.S. history-AP, Web site design, weight training, Western civilization, world cultures, world religions, yearbook.

Graduation Requirements American history, arts and fine arts (art, music, dance, drama), biology, chemistry, computer skills, English, ethics, foreign language, health education, mathematics, physical education (includes health), science, social studies (includes history), world religions.

Special Academic Programs Advanced Placement exam preparation; honors section; independent study.

College Admission Counseling 78 students graduated in 2008; 73 went to college, including Seattle University; St. Olaf College; University of Denver; University of Puget Sound; University of Utah; Westminster College. Other: 5 had other specific plans. Mean SAT critical reading: 604, mean SAT math: 603, mean SAT writing: 599, mean combined SAT: 1208, mean composite ACT: 26. 54% scored over 600 on SAT critical reading, 45% scored over 600 on SAT math, 43% scored over 600 on SAT writing, 54% scored over 26 on composite ACT.

Student Life Upper grades have specified standards of dress, student council, honor system. Discipline rests equally with students and faculty.
Summer Programs Enrichment, advancement, computer instruction programs offered; session focuses on advancement; held on campus; accepts boys and girls; not open to students from other schools. 60 students usually enrolled. 2009 schedule: June 15 to July 31. Application deadline: none.
Tuition and Aid Day student tuition: $15,430. Tuition installment plan (monthly payment plans, individually arranged payment plans, 2-installment plan). Merit scholarship grants, need-based scholarship grants, diversity scholarship grants available. In 2008–09, 21% of upper-school students received aid; total upper-school merit-scholarship money awarded: $48,000. Total amount of financial aid awarded in 2008–09: $481,088.
Admissions Traditional secondary-level entrance grade is 9. For fall 2008, 48 students applied for upper-level admission, 34 were accepted, 31 enrolled. ACT-Explore, ERB CTP IV, ISEE, TOEFL or writing sample required. Deadline for receipt of application materials: none. Application fee required: $50. Interview recommended.
Athletics Interscholastic: alpine skiing (boys, girls), baseball (b), basketball (b,g), diving (b,g), skiing (downhill) (b,g), soccer (b,g), softball (g), swimming and diving (b,g), tennis (b,g), track and field (b,g), volleyball (g); intramural: skiing (downhill) (b,g), soccer (b,g); coed interscholastic: crew, cross-country running, dance, golf, modern dance, ropes courses, skiing (downhill), swimming and diving, track and field; coed intramural: alpine skiing, archery, bowling, climbing, deck hockey, hiking/backpacking, ice hockey, ice skating, mountain biking, outdoor activities, outdoor education, physical fitness, physical training, rock climbing, skiing (cross-country), snowboarding, strength & conditioning, swimming and diving, telemark skiing, weight training, yoga. 4 PE instructors, 12 coaches, 2 athletic trainers.
Computers Computers are regularly used in desktop publishing, graphic design, yearbook classes. Computer network features include on-campus library services, Internet access, wireless campus network, Internet filtering or blocking technology, all students have their own laptop computer. Campus intranet, student e-mail accounts, and computer access in designated common areas are available to students. Students grades are available online. The school has a published electronic and media policy.
Contact Karen Hyde, Director of Admission. 801-924-5940. Fax: 801-355-0474. E-mail: karenhyde@rhsm.org. Web site: www.rhsm.org.

See Close-Up on page 922.

THE ROXBURY LATIN SCHOOL

101 St. Theresa Avenue
West Roxbury, Massachusetts 02132
Head of School: Mr. Kerry Paul Brennan

General Information Boys' day college-preparatory school. Grades 7–12. Founded: 1645. Setting: urban. Nearest major city is Boston. 70-acre campus. 1 building on campus. Approved or accredited by Association of Independent Schools in New England, and New England Association of Schools and Colleges. Member of National Association of Independent Schools and Secondary School Admission Test Board. Endowment: $147 million. Total enrollment: 291. Upper school average class size: 14. Upper school faculty-student ratio: 1:7.
Upper School Student Profile Grade 7: 43 students (43 boys); Grade 8: 45 students (45 boys); Grade 9: 52 students (52 boys); Grade 10: 50 students (50 boys); Grade 11: 51 students (51 boys); Grade 12: 50 students (50 boys).
Faculty School total: 39. In upper school: 33 men, 6 women; 30 have advanced degrees.
Subjects Offered Advanced chemistry, advanced math, advanced studio art-AP, algebra, American Civil War, American government, American government-AP, American history, American literature, analytic geometry, Ancient Greek, ancient history, ancient world history, art, art history, art history-AP, arts, biology, calculus, calculus-AP, chemistry, classical Greek literature, classical language, college counseling, college placement, computer science, computer science-AP, creative writing, drama, earth science, economics, economics-AP, English, English literature, European history, expository writing, fine arts, French, French literature-AP, geometry, government/civics, grammar, Greek, history, history-AP, Latin, Latin-AP, life science, macro/microeconomics-AP, mathematics, mathematics-AP, Middle East, music, music theory-AP, personal development, photography, physical education, physical science, physics, science, senior project, Spanish, statistics-AP, studio art, studio art-AP, theater, trigonometry, U.S. history-AP, Western civilization, world history, writing.
Graduation Requirements Arts and fine arts (art, music, dance, drama), computer science, English, foreign language, Latin, mathematics, physical education (includes health), science, social studies (includes history), U.S. history-AP, independent senior project.
Special Academic Programs Advanced Placement exam preparation; honors section; independent study; academic accommodation for the gifted, the musically talented, and the artistically talented.
College Admission Counseling 50 students graduated in 2008; 49 went to college, including Amherst College; Brown University; Dartmouth College; Duke University; Harvard University; Massachusetts Institute of Technology. Other: 1 entered a postgraduate year. Median SAT critical reading: 750, median SAT math: 750, median SAT writing: 750, median combined SAT: 2250. 92% scored over 600 on SAT critical reading, 96% scored over 600 on SAT math, 96% scored over 600 on SAT writing, 98% scored over 1800 on combined SAT.
Student Life Upper grades have specified standards of dress, student council, honor system. Discipline rests equally with students and faculty.
Summer Programs Enrichment, sports programs offered; held on campus; accepts boys; open to students from other schools.
Tuition and Aid Day student tuition: $17,900. Tuition installment plan (Insured Tuition Payment Plan, Key Tuition Payment Plan, 2-payment plan). Need-based scholarship grants available. In 2008–09, 36% of upper-school students received aid. Total amount of financial aid awarded in 2008–09: $1,324,550.
Admissions Traditional secondary-level entrance grade is 7. For fall 2008, 362 students applied for upper-level admission, 64 were accepted, 57 enrolled. ISEE or SSAT required. Deadline for receipt of application materials: January 9. No application fee required. On-campus interview required.
Athletics Interscholastic: baseball, basketball, cross-country running, football, ice hockey, lacrosse, soccer, tennis, track and field, wrestling. 1 PE instructor, 6 coaches, 1 athletic trainer.
Computers Computers are regularly used in all academic, desktop publishing, literary magazine, newspaper, yearbook classes. Computer network features include on-campus library services, online commercial services, Internet access, Internet filtering or blocking technology. Campus intranet, student e-mail accounts, and computer access in designated common areas are available to students. The school has a published electronic and media policy.
Contact Mrs. Velura Perry, Assistant Director of Admission. 617-325-4920. Fax: 617-325-3585. E-mail: admission@roxburylatin.org. Web site: www.roxburylatin.org.

ANNOUNCEMENT FROM THE SCHOOL Roxbury Latin is a small, diverse community, unified by a common purpose and shared values. It instills in its students a capacity for rigorous analysis, disciplined reflection, and lucid expression. Students come to experience the excitement and joy that result from hard and deep thinking. The School stresses standards of honesty, simplicity, and respect and concern for others, and it tries to practice these values in its life as a community.

ROYAL CANADIAN COLLEGE

8610 Ash Street
Vancouver, British Columbia V6P 3M2, Canada
Head of School: Mr. Howard H. Jiang

General Information Coeducational day college-preparatory and general academic school. Grades 8–12. Founded: 1989. Setting: suburban. 1-acre campus. 1 building on campus. Approved or accredited by British Columbia Department of Education. Language of instruction: English. Total enrollment: 56. Upper school average class size: 20. Upper school faculty-student ratio: 1:15.
Upper School Student Profile Grade 8: 2 students (2 boys); Grade 9: 5 students (4 boys, 1 girl); Grade 10: 11 students (6 boys, 5 girls); Grade 11: 14 students (6 boys, 8 girls); Grade 12: 24 students (12 boys, 12 girls).
Faculty School total: 5. In upper school: 5 men.
Subjects Offered 20th century world history, accounting, applied skills, biology, calculus, Canadian geography, Canadian history, career planning, chemistry, communications, comparative civilizations, computer science, computer science-AP, drama, economics, English, ESL, fine arts, general science, history, information technology, Mandarin, mathematics, physical education, physics, social sciences, world history, writing.
Graduation Requirements Applied skills, arts and fine arts (art, music, dance, drama), career and personal planning, language arts, mathematics, science, social studies (includes history).
Special Academic Programs ESL (20 students enrolled).
College Admission Counseling 34 students graduated in 2008; 33 went to college, including Boston University; McGill University; Simon Fraser University; The University of British Columbia; University of Southern California; University of Toronto. Other: 1 had other specific plans. Median SAT critical reading: 700, median SAT math: 770, median SAT writing: 710. 100% scored over 600 on SAT critical reading, 100% scored over 600 on SAT math, 100% scored over 600 on SAT writing.
Student Life Upper grades have honor system. Discipline rests primarily with faculty.
Summer Programs ESL programs offered; session focuses on learning survival English conversational skills, and Canadian cultural experience; held on campus; accepts boys and girls; open to students from other schools. 30 students usually enrolled. 2009 schedule: July 1 to August 29. Application deadline: May 31.
Tuition and Aid Day student tuition: CAN$11,600. Merit scholarship grants available. Total upper-school merit-scholarship money awarded for 2008–09: CAN$10,000.
Admissions Traditional secondary-level entrance grade is 11. For fall 2008, 25 students applied for upper-level admission, 24 were accepted, 24 enrolled. English language required. Deadline for receipt of application materials: none. Application fee required: CAN$150.

Athletics Intramural: badminton (boys, girls), baseball (b,g), basketball (b,g), soccer (b,g), ultimate Frisbee (b,g); coed intramural: badminton, baseball, soccer, ultimate Frisbee. 2 PE instructors.
Computers Computers are regularly used in accounting, career exploration, information technology, programming classes. Computer network features include Internet access, Internet filtering or blocking technology.
Contact Mr. Jeffry Yip, Senior Administrator. 604-738-2221. Fax: 604-738-2282. E-mail: info@royalcanadiancollege.com. Web site: www.royalcanadiancollege.com.

ROYCEMORE SCHOOL

640 Lincoln Street
Evanston, Illinois 60201

Head of School: Mr. Joseph A. Becker

General Information Coeducational day college-preparatory and arts school. Grades PK–12. Founded: 1915. Setting: suburban. Nearest major city is Chicago. 1-acre campus. 1 building on campus. Approved or accredited by Independent Schools Association of the Central States and Illinois Department of Education. Member of National Association of Independent Schools. Endowment: $1 million. Total enrollment: 249. Upper school average class size: 9. Upper school faculty-student ratio: 1:9.
Upper School Student Profile Grade 9: 26 students (13 boys, 13 girls); Grade 10: 19 students (13 boys, 6 girls); Grade 11: 16 students (10 boys, 6 girls); Grade 12: 23 students (13 boys, 10 girls).
Faculty School total: 35. In upper school: 4 men, 12 women; 10 have advanced degrees.
Subjects Offered African-American literature, algebra, American literature, art, biology, biology-AP, calculus-AP, chemistry, choir, comedy, composition, cultural geography, drawing, English language and composition-AP, English literature, environmental science, European history-AP, French, French-AP, geometry, government/civics, human development, independent study, international relations, introduction to theater, literature-AP, microeconomics, modern European history, music composition, music history, music theory, music theory-AP, mythology, painting, physical education, physics, physics-AP, pottery, public speaking, sculpture, society, politics and law, sociology, Spanish, Spanish-AP, studio art-AP, trigonometry, U.S. history, U.S. history-AP, world history, world literature, world religions, yearbook.
Graduation Requirements Arts and fine arts (art, music, dance, drama), English, foreign language, mathematics, physical education (includes health), science, social studies (includes history), participation in a January short-term project each year.
Special Academic Programs Advanced Placement exam preparation; accelerated programs; independent study; study at local college for college credit.
College Admission Counseling 23 students graduated in 2008; all went to college, including DePaul University; Grinnell College; Knox College; Northwestern University; Oberlin College. Median SAT critical reading: 600, median SAT math: 585, median SAT writing: 575, median combined SAT: 1740, median composite ACT: 24. 45% scored over 600 on SAT critical reading, 45% scored over 600 on SAT math, 32% scored over 600 on SAT writing, 41% scored over 1800 on combined SAT, 38% scored over 26 on composite ACT.
Student Life Upper grades have specified standards of dress, student council, honor system. Discipline rests primarily with faculty.
Tuition and Aid Day student tuition: $21,310. Tuition installment plan (individually arranged payment plans, semiannual payment plan, 9-month payment plan). Merit scholarship grants, need-based scholarship grants, discounts for children of Northwestern University & Evanston Northwestern, Healthcare employees available. In 2008–09, 53% of upper-school students received aid; total upper-school merit-scholarship money awarded: $134,190. Total amount of financial aid awarded in 2008–09: $731,056.
Admissions Traditional secondary-level entrance grade is 9. Any standardized test or writing sample required. Deadline for receipt of application materials: none. Application fee required: $75. Interview required.
Athletics Interscholastic: basketball (boys, girls), volleyball (g); coed interscholastic: soccer; coed intramural: gymnastics. 3 PE instructors, 1 coach.
Computers Computers are regularly used in all academic classes. Computer network features include on-campus library services, Internet access, wireless campus network. The school has a published electronic and media policy.
Contact Ms. Jessica Acee, Director of Admissions. 847-866-6055. Fax: 847-866-6545. E-mail: jacee@roycemoreschool.org. Web site: www.roycemoreschool.org.

RUMSEY HALL SCHOOL

Washington Depot, Connecticut
See Junior Boarding Schools section.

RUNDLE COLLEGE

4411 Manitoba Road SE
Calgary, Alberta T2G 4B9, Canada

Head of School: Mtro. David Hauk

General Information Coeducational day college-preparatory, arts, business, bilingual studies, and technology school. Grades PK–12. Founded: 1985. Setting: suburban. 5-acre campus. 1 building on campus. Approved or accredited by Association of Independent Schools and Colleges of Alberta, Canadian Association of Independent Schools, and Alberta Department of Education. Language of instruction: English. Total enrollment: 771. Upper school average class size: 14. Upper school faculty-student ratio: 1:14.
Upper School Student Profile Grade 6: 56 students (21 boys, 35 girls); Grade 7: 84 students (49 boys, 35 girls); Grade 8: 84 students (43 boys, 41 girls); Grade 9: 84 students (43 boys, 41 girls); Grade 10: 84 students (43 boys, 41 girls); Grade 11: 83 students (46 boys, 37 girls); Grade 12: 81 students (42 boys, 39 girls).
Faculty School total: 78. In upper school: 11 men, 11 women.
Subjects Offered Accounting, art, band, biology, calculus, chemistry, computer science, drama, English, French, general science, mathematics, physical education, physics, science, social studies, Spanish, theater.
Graduation Requirements Career and personal planning, English, mathematics, physical education (includes health), science, social science.
College Admission Counseling 77 students graduated in 2008; 75 went to college, including The University of British Columbia; The University of Western Ontario; University of Alberta; University of Calgary; University of Victoria; University of Waterloo. Other: 2 had other specific plans.
Student Life Upper grades have uniform requirement, student council, honor system. Discipline rests primarily with faculty.
Tuition and Aid Day student tuition: CAN$10,990. Tuition installment plan (monthly payment plans). Bursaries available. In 2008–09, 1% of upper-school students received aid. Total amount of financial aid awarded in 2008–09: CAN$22,250.
Admissions For fall 2008, 50 students applied for upper-level admission, 35 were accepted, 30 enrolled. Achievement tests or SSAT or WISC III required. Deadline for receipt of application materials: none. Application fee required: CAN$100. On-campus interview required.
Athletics Interscholastic: badminton (boys, girls), basketball (b,g), cross-country running (b,g), curling (b,g), dance squad (b,g), flag football (b,g), floor hockey (b,g), football (b), golf (b,g), rugby (b,g), soccer (b,g), track and field (b,g), volleyball (b,g), wrestling (b,g); intramural: badminton (b,g), dance (g), football (b); coed interscholastic: badminton, softball; coed intramural: badminton, baseball, basketball, cross-country running, flag football, football, lacrosse, outdoor recreation, skiing (downhill), soccer, table tennis, track and field, volleyball, weight lifting, wrestling. 4 PE instructors.
Computers Computers are regularly used in all classes. Computer network features include Internet access, wireless campus network, web page hosting, multimedia productions, streaming video student news. Student e-mail accounts are available to students. The school has a published electronic and media policy.
Contact Lynn Moriarity, Director of Admissions. 403-291-3866 Ext. 106. Fax: 403-291-5458. E-mail: moriarity@rundle.ab.ca. Web site: www.rundle.ab.ca.

RUTGERS PREPARATORY SCHOOL

1345 Easton Avenue
Somerset, New Jersey 08873

Head of School: Dr. Steven A. Loy

General Information Coeducational day college-preparatory and arts school. Grades PK–12. Founded: 1766. Setting: suburban. Nearest major city is New York, NY. 35-acre campus. 8 buildings on campus. Approved or accredited by Middle States Association of Colleges and Schools and New Jersey Association of Independent Schools. Member of National Association of Independent Schools and Secondary School Admission Test Board. Endowment: $6 million. Total enrollment: 702. Upper school average class size: 14. Upper school faculty-student ratio: 1:6.
Upper School Student Profile Grade 9: 85 students (44 boys, 41 girls); Grade 10: 87 students (53 boys, 34 girls); Grade 11: 74 students (38 boys, 36 girls); Grade 12: 89 students (43 boys, 46 girls).
Faculty School total: 105. In upper school: 29 men, 31 women; 42 have advanced degrees.
Subjects Offered Algebra, American history, American literature, architecture, art, art history, astronomy, biology, calculus, ceramics, chemistry, classics, community service, comparative religion, computer programming, computer science, creative writing, discrete math, drama, driver education, economics, English, English literature, environmental science, European history, fine arts, foundations of civilization, French, geometry, government/civics, health, history, Japanese, Latin, literature, mathematics, media, multimedia, music, photography, physical education, physical science, physics, poetry, psychology, psychology-AP, science, Shakespeare, social studies, Spanish, statistics, theater, word processing, world history, writing.
Graduation Requirements Arts and fine arts (art, music, dance, drama), computer science, English, foreign language, mathematics, physical education (includes health), science, social studies (includes history). Community service is required.

Special Academic Programs Advanced Placement exam preparation; honors section; independent study; term-away projects; academic accommodation for the gifted, the musically talented, and the artistically talented.
College Admission Counseling 89 students graduated in 2008; all went to college, including American University; Brown University; Rutgers, The State University of New Jersey, Rutgers College; Syracuse University; The George Washington University; University of Pennsylvania. Mean SAT critical reading: 624, mean SAT math: 632, mean SAT writing: 640. 60.7% scored over 600 on SAT critical reading, 64% scored over 600 on SAT math, 65% scored over 600 on SAT writing.
Student Life Upper grades have specified standards of dress, student council, honor system. Discipline rests primarily with faculty.
Summer Programs Remediation, enrichment, advancement, computer instruction programs offered; session focuses on academics and sports; held on campus; accepts boys and girls; open to students from other schools. 500 students usually enrolled. 2009 schedule: June 8 to August 21. Application deadline: June 8.
Tuition and Aid Day student tuition: $24,270. Tuition installment plan (individually arranged payment plans, Tuition Management Systems). Need-based scholarship grants, need-based financial aid, Key Education Resources available. In 2008–09, 20% of upper-school students received aid. Total amount of financial aid awarded in 2008–09: $1,011,793.
Admissions Traditional secondary-level entrance grade is 9. For fall 2008, 129 students applied for upper-level admission, 76 were accepted, 46 enrolled. Iowa Tests of Basic Skills and SSAT required. Deadline for receipt of application materials: none. Application fee required: $75. On-campus interview required.
Athletics Interscholastic: baseball (boys), basketball (b,g), lacrosse (b,g), soccer (b,g), softball (g), tennis (b,g), volleyball (g), wrestling (b); intramural: dance team (g); coed interscholastic: cross-country running, golf, swimming and diving. 6 PE instructors, 8 coaches, 1 athletic trainer.
Computers Computers are regularly used in English, foreign language, history, mathematics, music, science classes. Computer network features include on-campus library services, online commercial services, Internet access, wireless campus network, Internet filtering or blocking technology, laptops.
Contact Audrey Forte, Admission Assistant. 732-545-5600 Ext. 261. Fax: 732-214-1819. E-mail: forte@rutgersprep.org. Web site: www.rutgersprep.org.

RYE COUNTRY DAY SCHOOL

Cedar Street
Rye, New York 10580-2034

Head of School: Mr. Scott A. Nelson

General Information Coeducational day college-preparatory, arts, and technology school. Grades PK–12. Founded: 1869. Setting: suburban. Nearest major city is New York. 28-acre campus. 7 buildings on campus. Approved or accredited by Middle States Association of Colleges and Schools, New York State Association of Independent Schools, and New York Department of Education. Member of National Association of Independent Schools and Secondary School Admission Test Board. Endowment: $23 million. Total enrollment: 871. Upper school average class size: 13. Upper school faculty-student ratio: 1:7.
Upper School Student Profile Grade 9: 97 students (47 boys, 50 girls); Grade 10: 96 students (50 boys, 46 girls); Grade 11: 97 students (53 boys, 44 girls); Grade 12: 93 students (45 boys, 48 girls).
Faculty School total: 117. In upper school: 27 men, 31 women; 47 have advanced degrees.
Subjects Offered 20th century history, algebra, American history, American history-AP, American literature, American literature-AP, art, art history, art history-AP, art-AP, astronomy, biology, biology-AP, calculus, calculus-AP, ceramics, chemistry, chemistry-AP, chorus, classics, computer music, computer programming, computer science-AP, computer-aided design, CPR, creative writing, dance, drama, driver education, economics, English, English literature, English literature-AP, English-AP, environmental science, environmental science-AP, European history, European history-AP, expository writing, fencing, fine arts, forensic science, forensics, French, French-AP, geometry, government, government and politics-AP, government-AP, Greek, health, history, honors English, honors geometry, independent study, instrumental music, interdisciplinary studies, jazz band, Latin, Latin-AP, Mandarin, mathematics, mechanical drawing, modern European history-AP, music, music theory-AP, oceanography, philosophy, photography, physical education, physics, physics-AP, psychology, psychology-AP, science, social studies, Spanish, Spanish-AP, speech, squash, statistics-AP, studio art-AP, The 20th Century, the Sixties, theater, theater arts, trigonometry, U.S. government-AP, U.S. history, U.S. history-AP, U.S. literature, weight training, wind ensemble, world civilizations, writing.
Graduation Requirements Arts and fine arts (art, music, dance, drama), English, foreign language, life management skills, mathematics, physical education (includes health), science, social studies (includes history).
Special Academic Programs 25 Advanced Placement exams for which test preparation is offered; honors section; independent study; academic accommodation for the gifted; special instructional classes for deaf students.
College Admission Counseling 94 students graduated in 2008; all went to college, including Boston College; Harvard University; Middlebury College; Syracuse University; Trinity College; University of Pennsylvania. Mean SAT critical reading: 675, mean SAT math: 676, mean SAT writing: 690, mean combined SAT: 2040.
Student Life Upper grades have student council. Discipline rests primarily with faculty.
Summer Programs Remediation, enrichment, advancement, ESL, art/fine arts, computer instruction programs offered; session focuses on remediation; held on campus; accepts boys and girls; open to students from other schools. 200 students usually enrolled. 2009 schedule: June 29 to August 7. Application deadline: June 22.
Tuition and Aid Day student tuition: $28,900–$29,200. Tuition installment plan (FACTS Tuition Payment Plan). Need-based scholarship grants available. In 2008–09, 20% of upper-school students received aid. Total amount of financial aid awarded in 2008–09: $2,013,540.
Admissions Traditional secondary-level entrance grade is 9. For fall 2008, 265 students applied for upper-level admission, 55 were accepted, 38 enrolled. ISEE or SSAT required. Deadline for receipt of application materials: December 15. Application fee required: $60. On-campus interview required.
Athletics Interscholastic: baseball (boys), basketball (b,g), cross-country running (b,g), fencing (b,g), field hockey (g), football (b), golf (b,g), ice hockey (b,g), lacrosse (b,g), sailing (b,g), soccer (b,g), softball (g), squash (b,g), tennis (b,g), wrestling (b); intramural: basketball (b), fitness (b,g), physical fitness (b,g), physical training (b,g), squash (b,g), strength & conditioning (b,g), tennis (b,g), ultimate Frisbee (b), weight training (b,g), wrestling (b); coed intramural: aerobics/dance, cross-country running, dance, fitness, ice skating, modern dance, running, squash, yoga. 4 PE instructors, 14 coaches, 2 athletic trainers.
Computers Computers are regularly used in art, classics, English, foreign language, history, mathematics, music, photography, publishing, science, technology, yearbook classes. Computer network features include on-campus library services, online commercial services, Internet access, wireless campus network, Internet filtering or blocking technology, student and faculty schedules online. Student e-mail accounts are available to students. The school has a published electronic and media policy.
Contact Mr. Matthew J.M. Suzuki, Director of Admissions. 914-925-4513. Fax: 914-921-2147. E-mail: matt_suzuki@ryecountryday.org. Web site: www.ryecountryday.org.

See Close-Up on page 924.

SACRAMENTO ADVENTIST ACADEMY

5601 Winding Way
Carmichael, California 95608-1298

Head of School: Bettesue Constanzo

General Information Coeducational day college-preparatory, general academic, arts, business, vocational, religious studies, bilingual studies, and technology school, affiliated with Seventh-day Adventist Church. Grades K–12. Founded: 1957. Setting: suburban. Nearest major city is Sacramento. 36-acre campus. 5 buildings on campus. Approved or accredited by Board of Regents, General Conference of Seventh-day Adventists, National Council for Private School Accreditation, Western Association of Schools and Colleges, and California Department of Education. Total enrollment: 291. Upper school average class size: 29. Upper school faculty-student ratio: 1:12.
Upper School Student Profile 96% of students are Seventh-day Adventists.
Faculty School total: 25. In upper school: 8 men, 4 women; 4 have advanced degrees.
Subjects Offered Accounting, advanced math, algebra, art, biology, chemistry, choir, computer applications, conceptual physics, concert band, consumer mathematics, driver education, economics, English, geometry, health, keyboarding, life skills, microcomputer technology applications, photography, physical education, physics, religion, Spanish, U.S. government, U.S. history, word processing, world history.
Graduation Requirements Arts and fine arts (art, music, dance, drama), biology, computer applications, economics, English, keyboarding, life skills, mathematics, physical education (includes health), religion (includes Bible studies and theology), science, U.S. government, U.S. history, 100 hours of documented work experience, 25 hours of documented community service per year of attendance.
Special Academic Programs Honors section; accelerated programs; study at local college for college credit; remedial math.
College Admission Counseling 27 students graduated in 2008; 25 went to college, including American River College; La Sierra University; Pacific Union College; Sierra College; Walla Walla University. Other: 2 went to work. Mean SAT critical reading: 559, mean SAT math: 566, mean composite ACT: 23. 22% scored over 600 on SAT critical reading, 44% scored over 600 on SAT math, 45% scored over 26 on composite ACT.
Student Life Upper grades have specified standards of dress, student council. Discipline rests primarily with faculty.
Tuition and Aid Day student tuition: $4310–$8790. Tuition installment plan (monthly payment plans, individually arranged payment plans). Tuition reduction for siblings, paying campus jobs, academy day scholarships available. In 2008–09, 5% of upper-school students received aid. Total amount of financial aid awarded in 2008–09: $10,000.
Admissions Traditional secondary-level entrance grade is 9. Deadline for receipt of application materials: none. Application fee required: $25. Interview required.
Athletics Interscholastic: baseball (girls), basketball (b,g), flag football (b,g), golf (b), softball (b,g), volleyball (g). 1 PE instructor, 1 coach.

Computers Computers are regularly used in accounting, business applications, English, history, keyboarding, religion, word processing classes. Computer network features include on-campus library services, online commercial services, Internet access.

Contact Mrs. Sheri Miller, Registrar/Guidance Counselor. 916-481-2300 Ext. 102. Fax: 916-481-7426. E-mail: smiller@sacaa.org. Web site: www.sacaa.org.

SACRAMENTO COUNTRY DAY SCHOOL

2636 Latham Drive
Sacramento, California 95864-7198

Head of School: Stephen T. Repsher

General Information Coeducational day college-preparatory, arts, and technology school. Grades PK–12. Founded: 1964. Setting: urban. 12-acre campus. 8 buildings on campus. Approved or accredited by California Association of Independent Schools and Western Association of Schools and Colleges. Member of National Association of Independent Schools. Total enrollment: 512. Upper school average class size: 12. Upper school faculty-student ratio: 1:9.

Upper School Student Profile Grade 9: 32 students (18 boys, 14 girls); Grade 10: 39 students (18 boys, 21 girls); Grade 11: 36 students (15 boys, 21 girls); Grade 12: 42 students (25 boys, 17 girls).

Faculty School total: 110. In upper school: 18 men, 10 women; 19 have advanced degrees.

Subjects Offered Acting, algebra, American history, American literature, ancient history, ancient/medieval philosophy, art, art history, art history-AP, art-AP, band, biology, biology-AP, British literature, calculus, calculus-AP, ceramics, chamber groups, chemistry, chemistry-AP, community service, computer programming, computer programming-AP, computer science, computer skills, computer technologies, concert band, creative writing, digital imaging, digital music, drama, drama performance, drawing, earth science, ecology, economics, English, English literature, European history, fine arts, French, French-AP, geography, geometry, government/civics, grammar, history, international relations, Japanese studies, jazz band, journalism, language and composition, Latin, Latin-AP, mathematics, model United Nations, newspaper, nutrition, orchestra, physical education, physics, physics-AP, physiology, pre-calculus, public speaking, science, social studies, Spanish, Spanish-AP, speech, studio art, studio art-AP, technology/design, theater, trigonometry, U.S. history, U.S. history-AP, world history, world literature, writing.

Graduation Requirements Arts and fine arts (art, music, dance, drama), computer science, electives, English, foreign language, history, mathematics, physical education (includes health), science, 40-hour senior project. Community service is required.

Special Academic Programs Advanced Placement exam preparation; independent study; study at local college for college credit.

College Admission Counseling 27 students graduated in 2008; all went to college, including American University; Boston University; Middlebury College; Occidental College; University of California, Santa Cruz; University of Puget Sound. Median SAT critical reading: 605, median SAT math: 614, median SAT writing: 626.

Student Life Upper grades have specified standards of dress, student council, honor system. Discipline rests primarily with faculty.

Tuition and Aid Day student tuition: $17,300. Tuition installment plan (Insured Tuition Payment Plan, monthly payment plans, individually arranged payment plans). Need-based scholarship grants available. In 2008–09, 18% of upper-school students received aid.

Admissions Traditional secondary-level entrance grade is 9. For fall 2008, 36 students applied for upper-level admission, 21 were accepted, 17 enrolled. ERB, Otis-Lennon Mental Ability Test and writing sample required. Deadline for receipt of application materials: none. Application fee required: $25. Interview required.

Athletics Interscholastic: baseball (boys), basketball (b,g), cross-country running (b,g), flag football (b), soccer (b,g), swimming and diving (b,g), track and field (b,g), volleyball (b,g); coed interscholastic: golf, paint ball, skiing (downhill), tennis. 5 PE instructors, 14 coaches.

Computers Computer network features include on-campus library services, online commercial services, Internet access, Internet filtering or blocking technology. Campus intranet and student e-mail accounts are available to students. The school has a published electronic and media policy.

Contact Lonna Bloedau, Director of Admission. 916-481-8811. Fax: 916-481-6016. E-mail: lbloedau@saccds.org. Web site: www.saccds.org.

SACRAMENTO WALDORF SCHOOL

3750 Bannister Road
Fair Oaks, California 95628

Head of School: Elizabeth Beaven

General Information Coeducational day college-preparatory, general academic, and arts school. Grades PK–12. Founded: 1959. Setting: suburban. Nearest major city is Sacramento. 22-acre campus. 8 buildings on campus. Approved or accredited by Association of Waldorf Schools of North America and Western Association of Schools and Colleges. Endowment: $40,000. Total enrollment: 433. Upper school average class size: 20. Upper school faculty-student ratio: 1:7.

Upper School Student Profile Grade 9: 33 students (18 boys, 15 girls); Grade 10: 36 students (15 boys, 21 girls); Grade 11: 46 students (20 boys, 26 girls); Grade 12: 40 students (21 boys, 19 girls).

Faculty School total: 53. In upper school: 14 men, 11 women; 9 have advanced degrees.

Subjects Offered 20th century American writers, 20th century history, 20th century world history, 3-dimensional art, 3-dimensional design, acting, advanced math, aesthetics, algebra, American government, American history, American literature, anatomy, animal husbandry, applied arts, applied music, architectural drawing, architecture, art, art history, arts, astronomy, band, biology, bookbinding, bookmaking, botany, British literature, calculus, calligraphy, chemistry, choir, choral music, chorus, classical Greek literature, community service, computer education, computer literacy, concert choir, crafts, creative arts, creative thinking, drama, drama performance, drama workshop, dramatic arts, drawing, electives, English, English composition, English literature, ensembles, European civilization, European history, European literature, eurythmy, expressive arts, fabric arts, fiber arts, fine arts, gardening, general math, general science, geology, geometry, German, government/civics, Greek drama, health, honors English, human sexuality, literature, mathematics, medieval history, medieval literature, medieval/Renaissance history, music, music appreciation, music performance, musical productions, orchestra, parent/child development, parenting, participation in sports, performing arts, physical education, physical science, physics, physiology, play production, pottery, pre-calculus, printmaking, Russian literature, science, sculpture, senior career experience, senior project, sex education, sexuality, Shakespeare, Shakespearean histories, social science, social studies, Spanish, strings, student publications, studio art, theater, theater arts, theater design and production, theater production, theory of knowledge, trigonometry, U.S. literature, visual and performing arts, visual arts, vocal ensemble, vocal jazz, vocal music, wood lab, woodworking, world arts, world civilizations, world culture, world cultures, world geography, world history, world literature, writing fundamentals, writing skills, writing workshop, yearbook, zoology.

Graduation Requirements Aesthetics, arts and fine arts (art, music, dance, drama), computer literacy, English, foreign language, mathematics, physical education (includes health), science, senior project, social science, social studies (includes history). Community service is required.

Special Academic Programs Honors section; independent study; term-away projects; study abroad.

College Admission Counseling 24 students graduated in 2008; 20 went to college, including Macalester College; Occidental College; Sonoma State University; University of California, Santa Cruz; Whittier College. Other: 2 went to work, 2 had other specific plans. Median SAT critical reading: 590, median SAT math: 580, median SAT writing: 590, median combined SAT: 1680. 40% scored over 600 on SAT critical reading, 40% scored over 600 on SAT math, 40% scored over 600 on SAT writing, 20% scored over 1800 on combined SAT.

Student Life Upper grades have specified standards of dress, student council, honor system. Discipline rests equally with students and faculty.

Tuition and Aid Day student tuition: $12,130–$12,435. Tuition installment plan (Insured Tuition Payment Plan, monthly payment plans, semi-annual and annual payment plans). Tuition reduction for siblings, need-based scholarship grants available. In 2008–09, 25% of upper-school students received aid. Total amount of financial aid awarded in 2008–09: $126,438.

Admissions Traditional secondary-level entrance grade is 9. For fall 2008, 61 students applied for upper-level admission, 55 were accepted, 43 enrolled. Math Placement Exam or TOEFL required. Deadline for receipt of application materials: none. Application fee required: $50. Interview required.

Athletics Interscholastic: baseball (boys), basketball (b,g), golf (b), running (b,g), soccer (b,g), volleyball (g); coed interscholastic: aerobics/Nautilus, ball hockey, climbing, combined training, cooperative games, cross-country running, dance, fitness, flag football, floor hockey, Frisbee, kickball, martial arts, outdoor activities, paddle tennis, physical fitness, physical training, pillo polo, rock climbing, touch football, track and field, ultimate Frisbee, winter soccer, yoga; coed intramural: fencing. 1 PE instructor, 8 coaches.

Computers Computers are regularly used in college planning, independent study, introduction to technology, mathematics, photography, Web site design, word processing, yearbook classes. Computer network features include Internet access, wireless campus network, Internet filtering or blocking technology, online college and career searches. Campus intranet and computer access in designated common areas are available to students. The school has a published electronic and media policy.

Contact Sharon Caraccio, High School Coordinator. 916-860-2525. Fax: 916-961-3970. E-mail: scaraccio@sacwaldorf.org. Web site: www.sacwaldorf.org.

SACRED HEART SCHOOL OF HALIFAX

5820 Spring Garden Road
Halifax, Nova Scotia B3H 1X8, Canada

Head of School: Ms. Patricia Donnelly

General Information Coeducational day college-preparatory and religious studies school, affiliated with Roman Catholic Church. Boys grades K–11, girls grades K–12. Founded: 1849. Setting: urban. 1 building on campus. Approved or accredited by Canadian Association of Independent Schools, Canadian Educational Standards

Institute, and Nova Scotia Department of Education. Language of instruction: English. Total enrollment: 480. Upper school average class size: 18. Upper school faculty-student ratio: 1:15.
Upper School Student Profile Grade 7: 50 students (18 boys, 32 girls); Grade 8: 48 students (16 boys, 32 girls); Grade 9: 49 students (8 boys, 41 girls); Grade 10: 41 students (11 boys, 30 girls); Grade 11: 33 students (9 boys, 24 girls); Grade 12: 33 students (33 girls). 60% of students are Roman Catholic.
Faculty School total: 50. In upper school: 1 man, 24 women; 10 have advanced degrees.
Subjects Offered 20th century history, 20th century world history, algebra, art, Bible studies, biology, calculus, Canadian history, chemistry, creative writing, earth science, economics, English, English literature, environmental science, European history, expository writing, French, geography, geometry, government/civics, grammar, health, history, mathematics, music, physical education, physics, religion, science, social studies, sociology, Spanish, theater, trigonometry, world history, writing.
Graduation Requirements Arts and fine arts (art, music, dance, drama), English, foreign language, history, mathematics, physical education (includes health), religion (includes Bible studies and theology), science. Community service is required.
Special Academic Programs Advanced Placement exam preparation; honors section; domestic exchange program (with Network of Sacred Heart Schools); study abroad; ESL (19 students enrolled).
College Admission Counseling 27 students graduated in 2008; all went to college, including Acadia University; Carleton University; Dalhousie University; Mount Allison University; Saint Mary's University; St. Francis Xavier University.
Student Life Upper grades have uniform requirement, student council, honor system. Discipline rests primarily with faculty. Attendance at religious services is required.
Summer Programs Remediation programs offered; session focuses on French remediation; held on campus; accepts boys and girls; open to students from other schools. 10 students usually enrolled. Application deadline: none.
Tuition and Aid Day student tuition: CAN$10,551. Tuition installment plan (monthly payment plans, individually arranged payment plans). Tuition reduction for siblings, bursaries, merit scholarship grants, need-based scholarship grants available. In 2008–09, 12% of upper-school students received aid; total upper-school merit-scholarship money awarded: CAN$25,000. Total amount of financial aid awarded in 2008–09: CAN$65,000.
Admissions Traditional secondary-level entrance grade is 7. For fall 2008, 53 students applied for upper-level admission, 52 were accepted, 50 enrolled. SCAT and school's own test required. Deadline for receipt of application materials: none. Application fee required: CAN$100. On-campus interview required.
Athletics Interscholastic: aquatics (girls), badminton (b,g), basketball (b,g), cross-country running (b,g), field hockey (g), ice hockey (b), soccer (b,g), swimming and diving (b,g), tennis (g), volleyball (g); intramural: alpine skiing (b,g), badminton (b,g), basketball (b,g), cross-country running (b,g), curling (g), fitness walking (g), jogging (b,g), running (b,g), skiing (downhill) (b,g), soccer (b,g), swimming and diving (b), tennis (g), track and field (g), volleyball (g). 3 PE instructors.
Computers Computer network features include on-campus library services, Internet access, wireless campus network, Internet filtering or blocking technology. Campus intranet and student e-mail accounts are available to students. The school has a published electronic and media policy.
Contact Pauline Mary Scott, Principal, Girls' High School. 902-422-4459 Ext. 209. Fax: 902-423-7691. E-mail: pscott@shsh.ca. Web site: www.sacredheartschool.ns.ca.

SADDLE RIVER DAY SCHOOL

147 Chestnut Ridge Road
Saddle River, New Jersey 07458

Head of School: Michael N. Eanes

General Information Coeducational day college-preparatory, arts, bilingual studies, and technology school. Grades K–12. Founded: 1957. Setting: suburban. Nearest major city is New York, NY. 26-acre campus. 3 buildings on campus. Approved or accredited by Middle States Association of Colleges and Schools, New Jersey Association of Independent Schools, and New Jersey Department of Education. Member of National Association of Independent Schools and Secondary School Admission Test Board. Endowment: $5 million. Total enrollment: 276. Upper school average class size: 14. Upper school faculty-student ratio: 1:7.
Upper School Student Profile Grade 9: 31 students (15 boys, 16 girls); Grade 10: 29 students (16 boys, 13 girls); Grade 11: 48 students (24 boys, 24 girls); Grade 12: 29 students (15 boys, 14 girls).
Faculty School total: 56. In upper school: 20 men, 36 women; 20 have advanced degrees.
Subjects Offered Advanced Placement courses, algebra, American history, American literature, anatomy, art, astronomy, bell choir, biology, calculus, chemistry, computer programming, computer science, concert choir, creative writing, drama, driver education, earth science, economics, English, English literature, European history, finance, fine arts, French, geography, geometry, government/civics, grammar, history, Latin, mathematics, music, physical education, physics, psychology, science, social science, social studies, Spanish, theater, trigonometry, world history, writing.
Graduation Requirements Arts and fine arts (art, music, dance, drama), computer science, English, foreign language, mathematics, physical education (includes health), science, social science, social studies (includes history).
Special Academic Programs 12 Advanced Placement exams for which test preparation is offered; honors section; term-away projects; study abroad; academic accommodation for the gifted, the musically talented, and the artistically talented.
College Admission Counseling 54 students graduated in 2008; all went to college, including Boston University; Brandeis University; Brown University; Franklin & Marshall College; Lafayette College; Rutgers, The State University of New Jersey, New Brunswick. Median SAT critical reading: 560, median SAT math: 590, median SAT writing: 580.
Student Life Upper grades have specified standards of dress, student council, honor system. Discipline rests primarily with faculty.
Tuition and Aid Day student tuition: $25,812. Tuition installment plan (The Tuition Plan, Insured Tuition Payment Plan, monthly payment plans). Tuition reduction for siblings, merit scholarship grants, need-based scholarship grants available. In 2008–09, 15% of upper-school students received aid; total upper-school merit-scholarship money awarded: $71,000. Total amount of financial aid awarded in 2008–09: $662,800.
Admissions Traditional secondary-level entrance grade is 9. For fall 2008, 98 students applied for upper-level admission, 54 were accepted, 20 enrolled. ISEE, placement test, SSAT or writing sample required. Deadline for receipt of application materials: none. Application fee required: $50. On-campus interview required.
Athletics Interscholastic: baseball (boys), basketball (b,g), cross-country running (b,g), golf (b), soccer (b,g), softball (g), tennis (b,g), track and field (b,g), volleyball (g), winter (indoor) track (b,g); intramural: tennis (b,g); coed intramural: fitness, fly fishing, Frisbee, lacrosse, skiing (downhill), snowboarding, weight training. 3 PE instructors, 15 coaches.
Computers Computers are regularly used in English, foreign language, mathematics, science, social studies classes. Computer network features include on-campus library services, online commercial services, Internet access, wireless campus network.
Contact Kris Sweeny, Assistant to the Director of Admissions. 201-327-4050 Ext. 1105. Fax: 201-327-6161. E-mail: ksweeny@saddleriverday.org. Web site: www.saddleriverday.org.

ANNOUNCEMENT FROM THE SCHOOL Saddle River Day School (SRDS) in Saddle River, New Jersey, is a coeducational, college-preparatory day school enrolling students in kindergarten through grade 12. Located in the northeastern corner of the state, SRDS is 18 miles from New York City and benefits from the cultural opportunities available in the metropolitan area. Founded in 1957 by John and Diane Alford and Headmaster Douglas Olgilvie, Saddle River Day was created to provide families with school choice and to create lasting educational value for the community. SRDS seeks to provide a safe, intellectually challenging environment where children are encouraged to learn, to question, and to grow as individuals while being part of a community. With its goal of helping students become caring, competent adults able to succeed in and contribute to society, the School best serves those who have the ability to thrive in a traditional college-preparatory curriculum. The 26-acre campus provides a view of the Ramapo Mountains and includes two soccer fields, a softball field, a baseball diamond, six tennis courts, two playgrounds, three academic buildings, and the Headmaster's house as well as formal gardens, lawns, and woods. Grades K–5 combine classroom learning with hands-on experiences in an integrated curriculum. Students are engaged in reading/ language arts, mathematics, science, and social studies. Art, music, world languages, physical education, and computer lab supplement the core curriculum. Middle School students follow a fully departmentalized curriculum. Core courses include literature, composition, research skills, mathematics, laboratory science, calculator skills, history and world cultures, and world languages, including Latin, French, and Spanish. Upper School students follow a rigorous, traditional, college-preparatory curriculum that may include honors and AP-level courses in all subject areas. College counseling is a four-year process. Typically, 100% of the senior class matriculates at colleges and universities such as Amherst, Boston College, Brown, Brandeis, Carnegie Mellon, Cornell, Hamilton, Ithaca, Johns Hopkins, Princeton, Union, University of Chicago, Wesleyan, Williams, and Yale.

SAGE HILL SCHOOL

20402 Newport Coast Drive
Newport Coast, California 92657-0300

Head of School: Mr. Gordon McNeill

General Information Coeducational day college-preparatory and arts school. Grades 9–12. Founded: 2000. Setting: suburban. Nearest major city is Newport Beach. 30-acre campus. 4 buildings on campus. Approved or accredited by California Association of Independent Schools and Western Association of Schools and Colleges. Endowment: $1 million. Total enrollment: 454. Upper school average class size: 15. Upper school faculty-student ratio: 1:14.
Upper School Student Profile Grade 9: 103 students (55 boys, 48 girls); Grade 10: 124 students (59 boys, 65 girls); Grade 11: 119 students (57 boys, 62 girls); Grade 12: 108 students (58 boys, 50 girls).

Faculty School total: 44. In upper school: 20 men, 23 women; 30 have advanced degrees.
Subjects Offered Algebra, art, art history, art-AP, biology, biology-AP, calculus, calculus-AP, chemistry, chemistry-AP, Chinese, dance, dance performance, digital art, economics, English, English-AP, environmental science-AP, European history, European history-AP, forensic science, French, French language-AP, French literature-AP, geometry, Latin, Latin-AP, marine science, music, physical science, physics-AP, pre-calculus, Spanish, Spanish literature-AP, Spanish-AP, statistics, statistics-AP, theater.
Graduation Requirements Arts, English, history, languages, mathematics, physical education (includes health), science.
Special Academic Programs 18 Advanced Placement exams for which test preparation is offered; honors section; independent study; academic accommodation for the gifted, the musically talented, and the artistically talented.
College Admission Counseling 108 students graduated in 2008; all went to college, including Chapman University; Columbia College; Loyola Marymount University; Stanford University; University of Southern California.
Student Life Upper grades have specified standards of dress, student council, honor system. Discipline rests equally with students and faculty.
Summer Programs Remediation, enrichment, advancement, sports, art/fine arts programs offered; session focuses on academics; held on campus; accepts boys and girls; not open to students from other schools. 50 students usually enrolled. 2009 schedule: June 19 to July 29.
Tuition and Aid Day student tuition: $27,000. Tuition installment plan (Insured Tuition Payment Plan, Key Tuition Payment Plan, monthly payment plans). Need-based scholarship grants available. In 2008–09, 15% of upper-school students received aid. Total amount of financial aid awarded in 2008–09: $1,068,750.
Admissions Traditional secondary-level entrance grade is 9. For fall 2008, 248 students applied for upper-level admission, 185 were accepted, 124 enrolled. ISEE required. Deadline for receipt of application materials: none. Application fee required: $100. On-campus interview required.
Athletics Interscholastic: baseball (boys), basketball (b,g), football (b), golf (b,g), lacrosse (b,g), outdoor activities (b,g), soccer (b,g), softball (g), swimming and diving (b,g), tennis (b,g), volleyball (b,g), water polo (b,g); coed interscholastic: aerobics/dance, aquatics, flag football, track and field; coed intramural: cross-country running, dance, fitness, modern dance, outdoor recreation, physical fitness, sailing, strength & conditioning, surfing, weight training, yoga. 3 PE instructors, 15 coaches, 1 athletic trainer.
Computers Computers are regularly used in digital applications classes. Computer network features include on-campus library services, online commercial services, Internet access, wireless campus network, Internet filtering or blocking technology. Student e-mail accounts and computer access in designated common areas are available to students. Students grades are available online.
Contact Ms. Elaine Mijalis-Kahn, Director of Enrollment Services. 949-219-1337. Fax: 949-219-1399. E-mail: mijaliskahne@sagehillschool.org. Web site: www.sagehillschool.org.

SAGE RIDGE SCHOOL

2515 Crossbow Court
Reno, Nevada 89511

Head of School: Mr. William H. Heim III

General Information Coeducational day college-preparatory, arts, and technology school. Grades 5–12. Founded: 1997. Setting: suburban. 44-acre campus. 2 buildings on campus. Approved or accredited by Pacific Northwest Association of Independent Schools and Nevada Department of Education. Total enrollment: 234. Upper school average class size: 14. Upper school faculty-student ratio: 1:8.
Upper School Student Profile Grade 9: 32 students (15 boys, 17 girls); Grade 10: 21 students (10 boys, 11 girls); Grade 11: 18 students (9 boys, 9 girls); Grade 12: 11 students (2 boys, 9 girls).
Faculty School total: 27. In upper school: 9 men, 7 women; 8 have advanced degrees.
Subjects Offered Advanced chemistry, algebra, American history-AP, American literature, American literature-AP, analytic geometry, anatomy and physiology, ancient world history, art history, biology, biology-AP, British literature, British literature-AP, calculus, calculus-AP, ceramics, chemistry, choir, classical language, college counseling, conceptual physics, creative writing, debate, drama performance, electives, English language and composition-AP, English language-AP, English literature and composition-AP, English literature-AP, European history, European literature, foreign language, geometry, honors algebra, honors English, lab science, language-AP, Latin, Latin-AP, medieval history, modern European history, music history, music performance, music theory, outdoor education, philosophy, physical education, physical fitness, physics, playwriting and directing, poetry, pre-algebra, pre-calculus, probability and statistics, public speaking, senior internship, senior seminar, senior thesis, Spanish, Spanish language-AP, Spanish literature, Spanish literature-AP, Spanish-AP, statistics, studio art, studio art—AP, theater, theater arts, theater history, theory of knowledge, trigonometry, U.S. government and politics-AP, U.S. government-AP, U.S. history, U.S. history-AP, Western literature, world history.
Graduation Requirements 20th century world history, algebra, American history, American literature, analytic geometry, ancient world history, art history, biology, British literature, chemistry, conceptual physics, English composition, European history, foreign language, history of music, modern European history, music, outdoor education, participation in sports, pre-calculus, public speaking, science, senior internship, senior thesis, speech, theater history, trigonometry, U.S. history, 15 hours of community service per year, senior thesis and senior internship, two mini-semester seminars per year.
Special Academic Programs Honors section; independent study; academic accommodation for the gifted.
College Admission Counseling 13 students graduated in 2008; all went to college, including Brown University; Kenyon College; New York University; University of Southern California; Vanderbilt University; Yale University. Mean SAT critical reading: 600, mean SAT math: 616, mean SAT writing: 604, mean combined SAT: 1819, mean composite ACT: 29.
Student Life Upper grades have uniform requirement, student council, honor system. Discipline rests equally with students and faculty.
Tuition and Aid Day student tuition: $16,250–$17,500. Tuition installment plan (Insured Tuition Payment Plan, FACTS Tuition Payment Plan). Need-based scholarship grants available. In 2008–09, 24% of upper-school students received aid. Total amount of financial aid awarded in 2008–09: $159,290.
Admissions Traditional secondary-level entrance grade is 9. For fall 2008, 23 students applied for upper-level admission, 16 were accepted, 11 enrolled. ERB required. Deadline for receipt of application materials: none. Application fee required: $50. Interview required.
Athletics Interscholastic: alpine skiing (boys, girls), basketball (b), cross-country running (b,g), golf (b), skiing (downhill) (b,g), tennis (b,g), track and field (b,g), volleyball (g), wrestling (b,g); intramural: alpine skiing (b,g), basketball (b,g), cross-country running (b,g), golf (b,g), skiing (downhill) (b,g), track and field (b,g), volleyball (g); coed intramural: bicycling, Frisbee, lacrosse, outdoor education, ropes courses, soccer. 2 PE instructors, 12 coaches.
Computers Computers are regularly used in art, classics, college planning, current events, English, foreign language, history, humanities, independent study, Latin, literary magazine, mathematics, newspaper, publications, SAT preparation, science, senior seminar, social sciences, social studies, Spanish, speech, word processing, writing, yearbook classes. Computer network features include on-campus library services, online commercial services, Internet access, wireless campus network. Student e-mail accounts are available to students. Students grades are available online.
Contact Ms. Carol Murphy, Director of Admission. 775-852-6222 Ext. 503. Fax: 775-852-6228. E-mail: cmurphy@sageridge.org. Web site: www.sageridge.org.

ST. AGNES ACADEMY

9000 Bellaire Boulevard
Houston, Texas 77036

Head of School: Sr. Jane Meyer

General Information Girls' day college-preparatory, arts, business, religious studies, and technology school, affiliated with Roman Catholic Church. Grades 9–12. Founded: 1906. Setting: urban. 15-acre campus. 3 buildings on campus. Approved or accredited by Southern Association of Colleges and Schools, Texas Education Agency, and Texas Department of Education. Endowment: $4 million. Total enrollment: 861. Upper school average class size: 22. Upper school faculty-student ratio: 1:15.
Upper School Student Profile Grade 9: 236 students (236 girls); Grade 10: 216 students (216 girls); Grade 11: 209 students (209 girls); Grade 12: 200 students (200 girls). 78% of students are Roman Catholic.
Faculty School total: 83. In upper school: 21 men, 62 women; 52 have advanced degrees.
Subjects Offered Accounting, acting, algebra, American history, American literature, art, art history, biology, business law, business skills, calculus, chemistry, community service, computer programming, computer science, creative writing, dance, drama, economics, English, English literature, European history, fine arts, French, geology, geometry, government/civics, health, history, integrated physics, journalism, keyboarding, Latin, marine biology, mathematics, music, philosophy, photography, physical education, physics, physiology, psychology, religion, science, social science, social studies, Spanish, speech, theater, theology, trigonometry, video film production, world history, world literature.
Graduation Requirements Arts and fine arts (art, music, dance, drama), computer science, electives, English, foreign language, mathematics, physical education (includes health), religion (includes Bible studies and theology), science, social science, social studies (includes history), speech, 100 hours of community service.
Special Academic Programs Advanced Placement exam preparation; honors section; independent study.
College Admission Counseling 196 students graduated in 2008; all went to college, including St. Edward's University; Texas A&M University; The University of Texas at Austin; The University of Texas at San Antonio; University of Houston. Mean SAT critical reading: 620, mean SAT math: 620, mean composite ACT: 26. 56% scored over 600 on SAT critical reading, 58% scored over 600 on SAT math, 50% scored over 26 on composite ACT.
Student Life Upper grades have uniform requirement, student council, honor system. Discipline rests primarily with faculty. Attendance at religious services is required.
Summer Programs Remediation, art/fine arts, computer instruction programs offered; session focuses on remediation and elective credit; held on campus; accepts girls; not open to students from other schools. 100 students usually enrolled.
Tuition and Aid Day student tuition: $10,750. Tuition installment plan (plans arranged through local bank). Merit scholarship grants, need-based scholarship grants

available. In 2008–09, 25% of upper-school students received aid; total upper-school merit-scholarship money awarded: $24,000. Total amount of financial aid awarded in 2008–09: $300,000.

Admissions Traditional secondary-level entrance grade is 9. For fall 2008, 527 students applied for upper-level admission, 313 were accepted, 236 enrolled. ISEE required. Deadline for receipt of application materials: February 1. Application fee required: $50. On-campus interview required.

Athletics Interscholastic: aquatics, basketball, cheering, cross-country running, dance team, diving, golf, soccer, softball, swimming and diving, tennis, track and field, volleyball, water polo, winter soccer; intramural: badminton, floor hockey, volleyball. 4 PE instructors, 6 coaches, 1 athletic trainer.

Computers Computers are regularly used in all classes. Computer network features include on-campus library services, online commercial services, Internet access, wireless campus network, Internet filtering or blocking technology. Campus intranet and student e-mail accounts are available to students. Students grades are available online. The school has a published electronic and media policy.

Contact Deborah Whalen, Director of Admission. 713-219-5400. Fax: 713-219-5499. E-mail: dwhalen@st-agnes.org. Web site: www.st-agnes.org.

ANNOUNCEMENT FROM THE SCHOOL St. Agnes Academy is very proud of the 25 members of the class of 2009 named by the National Merit Corporation for awards in the NMSQT competition. In addition, the College Board has recognized 8 National Hispanic Scholars and 1 Honorable Mention winner.

ST. ALBANS SCHOOL

Mount Saint Alban
Washington, District of Columbia 20016

Head of School: Mr. Vance Wilson

General Information Boys' boarding and day college-preparatory school, affiliated with Episcopal Church. Boarding grades 9–12, day grades 4–12. Founded: 1909. Setting: urban. Students are housed in single-sex dormitories. 57-acre campus. 7 buildings on campus. Approved or accredited by Association of Independent Maryland Schools and District of Columbia Department of Education. Member of National Association of Independent Schools and Secondary School Admission Test Board. Endowment: $51 million. Total enrollment: 578. Upper school average class size: 13. Upper school faculty-student ratio: 1:7.

Upper School Student Profile Grade 9: 82 students (82 boys); Grade 10: 84 students (84 boys); Grade 11: 80 students (80 boys); Grade 12: 71 students (71 boys). 9% of students are boarding students. 43% are state residents. 8 states are represented in upper school student body. 2% are international students. International students from China, Czech Republic, Ireland, and Republic of Korea. 20% of students are members of Episcopal Church.

Faculty School total: 80. In upper school: 43 men, 14 women; 42 have advanced degrees; 6 reside on campus.

Subjects Offered Algebra, American history, American literature, art, art history, Bible studies, biology, calculus, ceramics, chemistry, Chinese, community service, computer math, computer programming, computer science, creative writing, dance, drama, earth science, economics, English, English literature, ethics, European history, expository writing, fine arts, French, geography, geometry, government/civics, Greek, history, Japanese, Latin, marine biology, mathematics, music, photography, physical education, physics, religion, science, social studies, Spanish, speech, theater.

Graduation Requirements American history, ancient history, arts and fine arts (art, music, dance, drama), English, ethics, foreign language, mathematics, physical education (includes health), science, participation in athletic program. Community service is required.

Special Academic Programs Advanced Placement exam preparation; honors section; independent study; term-away projects.

College Admission Counseling 76 students graduated in 2008; 73 went to college, including Georgetown University; Harvard University; The Johns Hopkins University; University of Pennsylvania; University of Virginia; Yale University. Other: 3 had other specific plans.

Student Life Upper grades have specified standards of dress, student council, honor system. Discipline rests equally with students and faculty. Attendance at religious services is required.

Summer Programs Remediation, enrichment, advancement, ESL, sports, art/fine arts, rigorous outdoor training, computer instruction programs offered; session focuses on academics and day camp; held on campus; accepts boys and girls; open to students from other schools. 1,500 students usually enrolled. 2009 schedule: June 9 to August 22. Application deadline: none.

Tuition and Aid Day student tuition: $31,428; 7-day tuition and room/board: $44,457. Tuition installment plan (Insured Tuition Payment Plan, monthly payment plans, individually arranged payment plans). Need-based scholarship grants, need-based loans available. In 2008–09, 26% of upper-school students received aid. Total amount of financial aid awarded in 2008–09: $2,849,889.

Admissions Traditional secondary-level entrance grade is 9. For fall 2008, 136 students applied for upper-level admission, 47 were accepted, 32 enrolled. ISEE or SSAT required. Deadline for receipt of application materials: January 15. Application fee required: $80. Interview required.

Athletics Interscholastic: aquatics, baseball, basketball, canoeing/kayaking, climbing, crew, cross-country running, diving, football, golf, ice hockey, independent competitive sports, indoor soccer, indoor track, indoor track & field, kayaking, lacrosse, rappelling, rock climbing, soccer, swimming and diving, tennis, track and field, weight training, winter (indoor) track, winter soccer, wrestling; intramural: aquatics, basketball, combined training, dance, fitness, indoor soccer, outdoor activities, physical training, tennis, track and field, yoga. 5 coaches, 2 athletic trainers.

Computers Computers are regularly used in mathematics, programming, science classes. Computer network features include on-campus library services, online commercial services, Internet access, wireless campus network. Campus intranet and student e-mail accounts are available to students. The school has a published electronic and media policy.

Contact Mrs. Laura Capito, Admissions and Financial Aid Coordinator. 202-537-6440. Fax: 202-537-2225. E-mail: lcapito@cathedral.org. Web site: www.stalbansschool.org/.

ST. ANDREW'S COLLEGE

15800 Yonge Street
Aurora, Ontario L4G 3H7, Canada

Head of School: Mr. E.G. Ted Staunton

General Information Boys' boarding and day college-preparatory, arts, business, and technology school. Grades 6–12. Founded: 1899. Setting: small town. Nearest major city is Toronto, Canada. Students are housed in single-sex dormitories. 110-acre campus. 24 buildings on campus. Approved or accredited by Canadian Association of Independent Schools, Canadian Educational Standards Institute, Conference of Independent Schools of Ontario, The Association of Boarding Schools, and Ontario Department of Education. Affiliate member of National Association of Independent Schools; member of Secondary School Admission Test Board. Language of instruction: English. Endowment: CAN$20 million. Total enrollment: 560. Upper school average class size: 17. Upper school faculty-student ratio: 1:9.

Upper School Student Profile Grade 9: 91 students (91 boys); Grade 10: 119 students (119 boys); Grade 11: 107 students (107 boys); Grade 12: 116 students (116 boys). 52% of students are boarding students. 47% are province residents. 12 provinces are represented in upper school student body. 53% are international students. International students from China, Hong Kong, Jamaica, Mexico, Republic of Korea, and United States; 25 other countries represented in student body.

Faculty School total: 62. In upper school: 43 men, 6 women; 13 have advanced degrees; 25 reside on campus.

Subjects Offered Accounting, Advanced Placement courses, algebra, American history, art, biology, business, calculus, chemistry, communications, community service, computer science, creative writing, drama, economics, English, English literature, environmental science, fine arts, French, geography, geometry, health, history, mathematics, music, physical education, physics, physiology, science, social science, social studies, sociology, Spanish, statistics, world history, world religions.

Graduation Requirements Arts, arts and fine arts (art, music, dance, drama), business, careers, civics, computer science, dance, drama, English, foreign language, French, geography, health education, history, mathematics, physical education (includes health), science, science and technology, social science. Community service is required.

Special Academic Programs 9 Advanced Placement exams for which test preparation is offered; honors section; accelerated programs; independent study; term-away projects; study abroad; ESL (21 students enrolled).

College Admission Counseling 93 students graduated in 2008; all went to college, including McGill University; New York University; Queen's University at Kingston; The University of British Columbia; The University of Western Ontario; University of Toronto. Median SAT critical reading: 539, median SAT math: 673, median SAT writing: 555, median combined SAT: 1767.

Student Life Upper grades have uniform requirement, student council, honor system. Discipline rests equally with students and faculty. Attendance at religious services is required.

Summer Programs Sports, art/fine arts programs offered; session focuses on Scottish music (piping and drumming), sports/arts camps, leadership camps, academics; held on campus; accepts boys and girls; open to students from other schools. 260 students usually enrolled. 2009 schedule: June 28 to August 13. Application deadline: none.

Tuition and Aid Day student tuition: CAN$24,450; 5-day tuition and room/board: CAN$39,300; 7-day tuition and room/board: CAN$39,300. Tuition installment plan (monthly payment plans, one time payment, Three Installments Plan). Bursaries, merit scholarship grants, need-based scholarship grants available. In 2008–09, 17% of upper-school students received aid; total upper-school merit-scholarship money awarded: CAN$145,000. Total amount of financial aid awarded in 2008–09: CAN$1,200,000.

Admissions Traditional secondary-level entrance grade is 9. For fall 2008, 173 students applied for upper-level admission, 131 were accepted, 107 enrolled. SLEP, SSAT or TOEFL required. Deadline for receipt of application materials: none. Application fee required: CAN$150. Interview required.

Athletics Interscholastic: alpine skiing, aquatics, badminton, baseball, basketball, biathlon, cricket, cross-country running, curling, fencing, football, golf, ice hockey, indoor track, indoor track & field, lacrosse, marksmanship, nordic skiing, rugby, running, skiing (cross-country), skiing (downhill), soccer, squash, swimming and diving, table tennis, tennis, track and field, triathlon, volleyball, winter (indoor) track; intramural: aquatics, archery, backpacking, badminton, ball hockey, baseball, basketball, canoeing/kayaking, climbing, cooperative games, cross-country running, curling, fencing, fitness, flag football, floor hockey, football, Frisbee, golf, hiking/backpacking, ice hockey, ice skating, jogging, lacrosse, marksmanship, mountain biking, nordic skiing, outdoor activities, outdoor education, outdoor skills, physical fitness, rock climbing, ropes courses, running, scuba diving, self defense, skiing (cross-country), skiing (downhill), snowboarding, soccer, softball, squash, strength & conditioning, swimming and diving, table tennis, tennis, touch football, track and field, triathlon, ultimate Frisbee, volleyball, wall climbing, water polo, weight training, wilderness survival. 7 athletic trainers.

Computers Computers are regularly used in all academic classes. Computer network features include on-campus library services, online commercial services, Internet access, wireless campus network, Internet filtering or blocking technology. The school has a published electronic and media policy.

Contact Mrs. Natascia Stewart, Admission Associate. 905-727-3178 Ext. 303. Fax: 905-727-9032. E-mail: admission@sac.on.ca. Web site: www.sac.on.ca.

ST. ANDREW'S EPISCOPAL SCHOOL

8804 Postoak Road
Potomac, Maryland 20854

Head of School: Mr. Robert Kosasky

General Information Coeducational day college-preparatory, arts, and religious studies school, affiliated with Episcopal Church. Grades PS–12. Founded: 1978. Setting: suburban. Nearest major city is Washington, DC. 19-acre campus. 5 buildings on campus. Approved or accredited by Association of Independent Maryland Schools, Association of Independent Schools of Greater Washington, Middle States Association of Colleges and Schools, and National Association of Episcopal Schools. Member of National Association of Independent Schools and Secondary School Admission Test Board. Endowment: $3.7 million. Total enrollment: 455. Upper school average class size: 15. Upper school faculty-student ratio: 1:7.

Upper School Student Profile Grade 6: 21 students (12 boys, 9 girls); Grade 7: 41 students (22 boys, 19 girls); Grade 8: 58 students (30 boys, 28 girls); Grade 9: 75 students (42 boys, 33 girls); Grade 10: 69 students (36 boys, 33 girls); Grade 11: 87 students (52 boys, 35 girls); Grade 12: 82 students (42 boys, 40 girls). 22% of students are members of Episcopal Church.

Faculty School total: 80. In upper school: 27 men, 25 women; 39 have advanced degrees.

Subjects Offered 20th century history, 3-dimensional art, 3-dimensional design, acting, Advanced Placement courses, advanced studio art-AP, algebra, American history, American literature, art, art history, art history-AP, art-AP, athletics, band, Bible, biology, biology-AP, British literature, calculus, calculus-AP, ceramics, chemistry, chorus, civics, college counseling, composition-AP, computer animation, computer art, computer graphics, computer science, creative writing, dance, digital photography, drama, dramatic arts, earth science, English, English literature, English literature and composition-AP, English-AP, ethics, European history, fine arts, French, French language-AP, French literature-AP, geography, geometry, global studies, government/civics, guitar, health, history, instrumental music, jazz band, journalism, Latin, Latin American studies, Latin-AP, mathematics, modern European history, music, musical theater, newspaper, orchestra, organic biochemistry, painting, photography, physical education, physical science, physics, physics-AP, pre-algebra, pre-calculus, public speaking, religion, robotics, science, service learning/internship, Spanish, Spanish language-AP, Spanish literature-AP, Spanish-AP, sports, stage design, statistics, student publications, studio art, studio art—AP, theater, theater design and production, theology, trigonometry, U.S. history, U.S. history-AP, video, visual and performing arts, vocal music, world cultures, world history, world religions, writing, yearbook.

Graduation Requirements English, foreign language, history, mathematics, performing arts, physical education (includes health), religion (includes Bible studies and theology), science, senior thesis, visual arts. Community service is required.

Special Academic Programs Advanced Placement exam preparation; independent study.

College Admission Counseling 65 students graduated in 2008; all went to college, including Bucknell University; Cornell University; Harvard University; Tulane University; University of Virginia; Wake Forest University.

Student Life Upper grades have specified standards of dress, student council, honor system. Discipline rests primarily with faculty. Attendance at religious services is required.

Summer Programs Enrichment, advancement, sports, art/fine arts programs offered; session focuses on advancement and enrichment; held on campus; accepts boys and girls; open to students from other schools. 400 students usually enrolled. 2009 schedule: June 8 to July 31. Application deadline: none.

Tuition and Aid Day student tuition: $29,960. Tuition installment plan (Key Tuition Payment Plan, FACTS Tuition Payment Plan, monthly payment plans). Need-based scholarship grants, AchieverLoans (Key Education Resources) available. In 2008–09, 16% of upper-school students received aid. Total amount of financial aid awarded in 2008–09: $1,030,500.

Admissions Traditional secondary-level entrance grade is 9. ISEE or SSAT required. Deadline for receipt of application materials: February 1. Application fee required: $50. On-campus interview required.

Athletics Interscholastic: baseball (boys), basketball (b,g), cross-country running (b,g), lacrosse (b,g), soccer (b,g), softball (g), tennis (b,g), volleyball (g); coed interscholastic: equestrian sports, golf, track and field, wrestling; coed intramural: dance, fitness, physical fitness, weight training. 2 PE instructors, 32 coaches, 1 athletic trainer.

Computers Computers are regularly used in English, foreign language, graphic arts, history, journalism, mathematics, music, science classes. Computer network features include on-campus library services, online commercial services, Internet access, wireless campus network, Internet filtering or blocking technology. Campus intranet and student e-mail accounts are available to students. Students grades are available online. The school has a published electronic and media policy.

Contact Mrs. Aileen Moodie, Admission Coordinator. 301-983-5200 Ext. 236. Fax: 301-983-4620. E-mail: admission@saes.org. Web site: www.saes.org.

ST. ANDREW'S EPISCOPAL SCHOOL

370 Old Agency Road
Ridgeland, Mississippi 39157

Head of School: Dr. George D. Penick Jr.

General Information Coeducational day college-preparatory, arts, religious studies, technology, and Global Studies school, affiliated with Episcopal Church. Grades PK–12. Founded: 1947. Setting: suburban. Nearest major city is Jackson. 108-acre campus. 12 buildings on campus. Approved or accredited by National Association of Episcopal Schools, Southern Association of Colleges and Schools, and Southern Association of Independent Schools. Member of National Association of Independent Schools. Endowment: $5.8 million. Total enrollment: 1,217. Upper school average class size: 18. Upper school faculty-student ratio: 1:9.

Upper School Student Profile Grade 9: 77 students (31 boys, 46 girls); Grade 10: 93 students (43 boys, 50 girls); Grade 11: 90 students (40 boys, 50 girls); Grade 12: 86 students (42 boys, 44 girls). 29% of students are members of Episcopal Church.

Faculty School total: 131. In upper school: 17 men, 18 women; 28 have advanced degrees.

Subjects Offered 3-dimensional design, algebra, American government-AP, American history, American literature, art, art history-AP, astronomy, biology, biology-AP, calculus, calculus-AP, chemistry, chemistry-AP, community service, computer programming, computers, creative writing, drama, driver education, engineering, English, English literature, English literature-AP, English-AP, European history, European literature, film, French, French language-AP, freshman seminar, geometry, government-AP, government/civics, grammar, history-AP, honors algebra, honors English, honors geometry, honors U.S. history, international studies, Latin, Latin-AP, literature-AP, Mandarin, mathematics, modern European history, music, physics, physics-AP, probability and statistics, psychology, Spanish, Spanish language-AP, speech, speech and debate, studio art-AP, theater arts, U.S. history-AP, visual arts, world history, world literature.

Graduation Requirements Arts and fine arts (art, music, dance, drama), English, foreign language, mathematics, science, social studies (includes history), speech. Community service is required.

Special Academic Programs Advanced Placement exam preparation; honors section; study abroad; academic accommodation for the gifted, the musically talented, and the artistically talented.

College Admission Counseling 73 students graduated in 2008; all went to college, including Harvard University; Millsaps College; Mississippi State University; Southern Methodist University; University of Mississippi; Vanderbilt University. Mean SAT critical reading: 657, mean SAT math: 626, mean SAT writing: 665, mean combined SAT: 1948, mean composite ACT: 28.

Student Life Upper grades have specified standards of dress, student council, honor system. Discipline rests primarily with faculty. Attendance at religious services is required.

Tuition and Aid Day student tuition: $10,985. Tuition installment plan (monthly payment plans, semester payment plan). Merit scholarship grants, need-based scholarship grants available. In 2008–09, 7% of upper-school students received aid; total upper-school merit-scholarship money awarded: $104,509. Total amount of financial aid awarded in 2008–09: $167,124.

Admissions Traditional secondary-level entrance grade is 9. For fall 2008, 38 students applied for upper-level admission, 30 were accepted, 23 enrolled. ERB Reading and Math, PSAT, SAT, or ACT for applicants to grade 11 and 12 or writing sample required. Deadline for receipt of application materials: none. Application fee required: $35. On-campus interview required.

Athletics Interscholastic: baseball (boys), basketball (b,g), cross-country running (b,g), dance (g), fitness (b,g), football (b), golf (b), power lifting (b), soccer (b,g), softball (g), tennis (b,g), track and field (b,g), volleyball (g); coed interscholastic: bowling, cheering, lacrosse, physical fitness, sailing, swimming and diving, tennis; coed intramural: equestrian sports. 10 coaches.

Computers Computers are regularly used in all academic, college planning, geography, journalism, newspaper, theater, yearbook classes. Computer network features include on-campus library services, online commercial services, Internet access, wireless campus network, Internet filtering or blocking technology, laptop requirement for all students in grades 9 through 12. Student e-mail accounts and computer access in designated common areas are available to students. Students grades are available online. The school has a published electronic and media policy.

Contact Mrs. Dawn McCarley, Director of Admissions and Financial Aid. 601-853-6042. Fax: 601-853-6001. E-mail: mccarleyd@gosaints.org. Web site: www.gosaints.org.

ST. ANDREW'S ON THE MARSH SCHOOL

601 Penn Waller Road
Savannah, Georgia 31410

Head of School: Mr. Gil Webb

General Information Coeducational day college-preparatory, arts, and bilingual studies school. Grades PK–12. Founded: 1947. Setting: suburban. 28-acre campus. 6 buildings on campus. Approved or accredited by Georgia Independent School Association, South Carolina Independent School Association, Southern Association of Colleges and Schools, Southern Association of Independent Schools, and Georgia Department of Education. Member of National Association of Independent Schools. Endowment: $150,000. Total enrollment: 482. Upper school average class size: 16. Upper school faculty-student ratio: 1:9.

Upper School Student Profile Grade 9: 32 students (18 boys, 14 girls); Grade 10: 45 students (28 boys, 17 girls); Grade 11: 36 students (21 boys, 15 girls); Grade 12: 51 students (31 boys, 20 girls).

Faculty School total: 64. In upper school: 11 men, 14 women; 13 have advanced degrees.

Subjects Offered Algebra, American history, American literature, anatomy, art, art history, biology, calculus, chemistry, classical studies, community service, computer programming, computer science, creative writing, drama, earth science, economics, English, English literature, environmental science, European history, fine arts, French, geography, geometry, government/civics, health, history, mathematics, music, physical education, physics, psychology, science, social studies, Spanish, theater, trigonometry, Web site design, world history.

Graduation Requirements Arts and fine arts (art, music, dance, drama), computer science, English, foreign language, mathematics, physical education (includes health), science, social studies (includes history), senior work project. Community service is required.

Special Academic Programs Advanced Placement exam preparation; honors section; accelerated programs; independent study; study at local college for college credit; study abroad.

College Admission Counseling 31 students graduated in 2008; all went to college, including Appalachian State University; Auburn University; Georgia Institute of Technology; Georgia Southern University; University of Georgia; Valdosta State University. Median SAT critical reading: 535, median SAT math: 545, median SAT writing: 550.

Student Life Upper grades have specified standards of dress, student council, honor system. Discipline rests equally with students and faculty.

Summer Programs Remediation, enrichment, sports, art/fine arts programs offered; session focuses on enrichment; held on campus; accepts boys and girls; open to students from other schools. 100 students usually enrolled. 2009 schedule: June 7 to August 6.

Tuition and Aid Day student tuition: $9500. Tuition installment plan (monthly payment plans, individually arranged payment plans). Need-based scholarship grants, need-based grants available. In 2008–09, 30% of upper-school students received aid. Total amount of financial aid awarded in 2008–09: $150,000.

Admissions Traditional secondary-level entrance grade is 9. For fall 2008, 35 students applied for upper-level admission, 31 were accepted, 24 enrolled. ERB, Iowa Tests of Basic Skills or Stanford Achievement Test required. Deadline for receipt of application materials: none. Application fee required: $100. Interview required.

Athletics Interscholastic: baseball (boys), basketball (b,g), cheering (g), cross-country running (b,g), football (b), golf (b,g), physical fitness (b,g), soccer (b,g), softball (g), strength & conditioning (b,g), swimming and diving (g), tennis (b,g), track and field (b,g), volleyball (g), weight lifting (b,g), weight training (b,g); intramural: basketball (b,g), soccer (b,g), softball (g), volleyball (b,g), weight lifting (b,g), weight training (b,g); coed interscholastic: cheering, cross-country running, physical fitness, weight lifting, weight training. 4 PE instructors, 3 coaches, 1 athletic trainer.

Computers Computers are regularly used in history, science, Spanish, yearbook classes. Computer network features include on-campus library services, Internet access, Internet filtering or blocking technology. The school has a published electronic and media policy.

Contact Mrs. Beth G. Aldrich, Director of Admissions. 912-897-4941 Ext. 303. Fax: 912-897-4943. E-mail: Aldrichb@saintschool.com. Web site: www.saintschool.com.

ST. ANDREW'S PRIORY SCHOOL

224 Queen Emma Square
Honolulu, Hawaii 96813

Head of School: Ms. Sandra J. Theunick

General Information Girls' day college-preparatory, arts, and technology school, affiliated with Episcopal Church. Grades K–12. Founded: 1867. Setting: urban. 3-acre campus. 7 buildings on campus. Approved or accredited by National Association of Episcopal Schools, The College Board, The Hawaii Council of Private Schools, Western Association of Schools and Colleges, and Hawaii Department of Education. Member of National Association of Independent Schools and Secondary School Admission Test Board. Endowment: $3.2 million. Total enrollment: 491. Upper school average class size: 12. Upper school faculty-student ratio: 1:8.

Upper School Student Profile Grade 6: 29 students (29 girls); Grade 7: 41 students (41 girls); Grade 8: 45 students (45 girls); Grade 9: 33 students (33 girls); Grade 10: 47 students (47 girls); Grade 11: 64 students (64 girls); Grade 12: 44 students (44 girls). 15% of students are members of Episcopal Church.

Faculty School total: 65. In upper school: 12 men, 32 women; 30 have advanced degrees.

Subjects Offered Algebra, American government, American history, American literature, ancient history, applied arts, applied music, art, art history, Asian studies, Bible studies, biology, biology-AP, British literature, British literature-AP, calculus, calculus-AP, ceramics, chemistry, chemistry-AP, choir, college counseling, college placement, community service, competitive science projects, computer art, computer education, computer graphics, computer literacy, computer multimedia, computer programming, computer science, computer technology certification, creative writing, drama, economics, economics and history, English, English literature, English literature-AP, ESL, European history, expository writing, fine arts, French, geography, geometry, government/civics, grammar, guidance, handbells, Hawaiian history, Hawaiian language, health, history, honors U.S. history, humanities, Japanese, journalism, Latin, leadership training, life skills, mathematics, mechanical drawing, medieval history, microbiology, modern world history, music, Pacific Island studies, photography, physical education, physics, physics-AP, physiology, Polynesian dance, pre-algebra, pre-calculus, psychology, religion, science, science research, social science, social studies, sociology, Spanish, Spanish-AP, speech, speech communications, theater, theology, trigonometry, U.S. history-AP, United States government-AP, video and animation, visual and performing arts, wind ensemble, women's studies, world civilizations, world history, world literature, world wide web design, writing workshop, yearbook.

Graduation Requirements Advanced Placement courses, arts and fine arts (art, music, dance, drama), computer science, English, foreign language, Hawaiian history, humanities, mathematics, physical education (includes health), religion (includes Bible studies and theology), science, science research, social science, social studies (includes history), speech, technological applications. Community service is required.

Special Academic Programs Advanced Placement exam preparation; honors section; independent study; study at local college for college credit; academic accommodation for the musically talented and the artistically talented; ESL (5 students enrolled).

College Admission Counseling 40 students graduated in 2008; all went to college, including Brown University; Santa Clara University; Tufts University; University of Hawaii at Manoa; University of San Francisco.

Student Life Upper grades have uniform requirement, student council, honor system. Discipline rests primarily with faculty. Attendance at religious services is required.

Summer Programs Remediation, enrichment, advancement, ESL, sports, art/fine arts, rigorous outdoor training, computer instruction programs offered; session focuses on academics, arts, sports; held on campus; accepts boys and girls; open to students from other schools. 600 students usually enrolled. 2009 schedule: June 12 to July 24. Application deadline: March.

Tuition and Aid Day student tuition: $12,960. Tuition installment plan (FACTS Tuition Payment Plan, monthly payment plans, individually arranged payment plans). Tuition reduction for siblings, merit scholarship grants, need-based scholarship grants available. In 2008–09, 30% of upper-school students received aid; total upper-school merit-scholarship money awarded: $162,000. Total amount of financial aid awarded in 2008–09: $497,989.

Admissions Traditional secondary-level entrance grade is 9. PSAT or SAT for applicants to grade 11 and 12 or SSAT required. Deadline for receipt of application materials: none. Application fee required: $50. On-campus interview required.

Athletics Interscholastic: basketball, bowling, canoeing/kayaking, cheering, cross-country running, dance team, diving, golf, gymnastics, martial arts, ocean paddling, soccer, softball, swimming and diving, tennis, track and field, volleyball, water polo, wrestling; intramural: aerobics/dance, dance squad, drill team, fitness, flag football, jogging, outdoor activities, outdoor adventure, physical fitness, ropes courses, self defense, strength & conditioning, tai chi, weight training, windsurfing. 4 PE instructors, 18 coaches.

Computers Computers are regularly used in animation, art, college planning, English, ESL, foreign language, graphic design, history, humanities, independent study, library, literary magazine, mathematics, media arts, music, newspaper, photojournalism, psychology, religion, science, speech, technology, writing, yearbook classes. Computer network features include on-campus library services, online commercial services, Internet access, wireless campus network, Internet filtering or blocking technology. Campus intranet and student e-mail accounts are available to students. Students grades are available online. The school has a published electronic and media policy.

Contact Sue Ann Wargo, Director of Admissions. 808-532-2418. Fax: 808-531-8426. E-mail: sawargo@priory.net. Web site: www.priory.net.

SAINT ANDREW'S SCHOOL

3900 Jog Road
Boca Raton, Florida 33434

Head of School: Dr. Ann Marie Krejcarek

General Information Coeducational boarding and day college-preparatory school, affiliated with Episcopal Church. Boarding grades 9–12, day grades JK–12. Founded: 1961. Setting: suburban. Nearest major city is West Palm Beach. Students are housed in single-sex dormitories. 80-acre campus. 18 buildings on campus. Approved or accredited by Florida Council of Independent Schools, The Association of Boarding Schools, and Florida Department of Education. Member of National Association of Independent Schools and Secondary School Admission Test Board. Endowment: $10 million. Total enrollment: 1,288. Upper school average class size: 15. Upper school faculty-student ratio: 1:9.

Upper School Student Profile Grade 9: 148 students (74 boys, 74 girls); Grade 10: 154 students (85 boys, 69 girls); Grade 11: 158 students (89 boys, 69 girls); Grade 12: 144 students (71 boys, 73 girls). 17% of students are boarding students. 82% are state residents. 11 states are represented in upper school student body. 12% are international students. International students from Bahamas, China, Germany, Jamaica, Japan, and Republic of Korea; 17 other countries represented in student body. 15% of students are members of Episcopal Church.

Faculty School total: 210. In upper school: 55 men, 75 women; 80 have advanced degrees; 35 reside on campus.

Subjects Offered Advanced studio art-AP, algebra, American history, American literature, American studies, anatomy, archaeology, art, art history, Bible studies, biology, biology-AP, calculus, calculus-AP, chemistry, chemistry-AP, Chinese, community service, computer math, computer programming, computer science, computer science-AP, creative writing, drafting, drama, earth science, ecology, economics, English, English literature, English-AP, environmental science, ethics, European history, expository writing, fine arts, French, French-AP, geography, geometry, German, German-AP, government/civics, grammar, history, journalism, Latin, marine biology, mathematics, music, photography, physical education, physics, physics-AP, pre-calculus, psychology, science, social studies, Spanish, Spanish-AP, speech, statistics, theater, theology, trigonometry, U.S. history-AP, world history, world history-AP, world literature, writing.

Graduation Requirements Arts and fine arts (art, music, dance, drama), computer science, English, foreign language, mathematics, physical education (includes health), religion (includes Bible studies and theology), science, social studies (includes history), speech, visual and performing arts, Participation in sports, Community service hours. Community service is required.

Special Academic Programs 21 Advanced Placement exams for which test preparation is offered; honors section; academic accommodation for the gifted; ESL (20 students enrolled).

College Admission Counseling 151 students graduated in 2008; 148 went to college, including Boston University; Indiana University–Purdue University Fort Wayne; Northwestern University; The George Washington University; University of Florida; University of Miami. Mean SAT critical reading: 596, mean SAT math: 634, mean SAT writing: 610, mean combined SAT: 1839, mean composite ACT: 27. 48% scored over 600 on SAT critical reading, 64% scored over 600 on SAT math, 57% scored over 600 on SAT writing, 58% scored over 1800 on combined SAT, 47% scored over 26 on composite ACT.

Student Life Upper grades have specified standards of dress, student council, honor system. Discipline rests primarily with faculty. Attendance at religious services is required.

Summer Programs Remediation, enrichment, advancement, ESL, sports, art/fine arts, computer instruction programs offered; session focuses on Academics; held on campus; accepts boys and girls; not open to students from other schools. 225 students usually enrolled. 2009 schedule: June 10 to July 20. Application deadline: none.

Tuition and Aid Day student tuition: $21,950; 7-day tuition and room/board: $39,000. Tuition installment plan (Insured Tuition Payment Plan, FACTS Tuition Payment Plan, monthly payment plans, individually arranged payment plans). Need-based scholarship grants available. In 2008–09, 17% of upper-school students received aid. Total amount of financial aid awarded in 2008–09: $1,960,000.

Admissions Traditional secondary-level entrance grade is 9. SSAT and TOEFL or SLEP required. Deadline for receipt of application materials: February 1. Application fee required: $75. Interview required.

Athletics Interscholastic: baseball (boys), basketball (b,g), cheering (g), cross-country running (b,g), danceline (g), diving (b,g), football (b), golf (b,g), lacrosse (b,g), soccer (b,g), softball (g), swimming and diving (b,g), tennis (b,g), track and field (b,g), volleyball (g), water polo (b,g), wrestling (b); intramural: weight lifting (b,g); coed interscholastic: bowling, water polo. 48 coaches.

Computers Computers are regularly used in college planning, English, foreign language, history, mathematics, science classes. Computer network features include on-campus library services, online commercial services, Internet access, wireless campus network, Internet filtering or blocking technology. Computer access in designated common areas is available to students. Students grades are available online. The school has a published electronic and media policy.

Contact Kilian J. Forgus, Associate Headmaster for Enrollment and Strategic Planning. 561-210-2000. Fax: 561-210-2027. E-mail: admission@saintandrews.net. Web site: www.saintandrewsschool.net.

ANNOUNCEMENT FROM THE SCHOOL Saint Andrew's School, situated on an 80-acre campus 5 miles from the Atlantic Ocean in south Florida, is an independent, college-preparatory school for grades JK–12. The upper school curriculum is distinguished by a number of honors courses, along with twenty-three Advanced Placement classes. Elective courses include anatomy and physiology, marine science, comparative government, expository writing, comparative religion, music appreciation, and art appreciation. Athletic programs are offered in eighteen different interscholastic sports, with the swimming, tennis, golf, basketball, and lacrosse teams having recently received statewide recognition. Students have benefited from $18 million in new facilities, including a state-of-the-art science center; an athletic and aquatics complex with two gymnasiums, a modern fitness center, and a 50-meter pool; and a center for the performing arts, which includes a 650-seat auditorium. Saint Andrew's offers a family-like community and distinguished, nurturing faculty members who help students develop in mind, body, and spirit.

ST. ANDREW'S SCHOOL

63 Federal Road
Barrington, Rhode Island 02806

Head of School: Mr. John D. Martin

General Information Coeducational boarding and day college-preparatory and arts school, affiliated with Episcopal Church. Boarding grades 9–12, day grades 3–12. Founded: 1893. Setting: suburban. Nearest major city is Providence. Students are housed in single-sex dormitories. 100-acre campus. 33 buildings on campus. Approved or accredited by Massachusetts Department of Education, National Association of Episcopal Schools, New England Association of Schools and Colleges, Rhode Island State Certified Resource Progam, The Association of Boarding Schools, and Rhode Island Department of Education. Member of National Association of Independent Schools and Secondary School Admission Test Board. Endowment: $19 million. Total enrollment: 223. Upper school average class size: 11. Upper school faculty-student ratio: 1:5.

Upper School Student Profile Grade 9: 25 students (13 boys, 12 girls); Grade 10: 44 students (32 boys, 12 girls); Grade 11: 48 students (29 boys, 19 girls); Grade 12: 48 students (36 boys, 12 girls). 30% of students are boarding students. 65% are state residents. 9 states are represented in upper school student body. 12% are international students. International students from China, India, Republic of Korea, and Taiwan; 1 other country represented in student body.

Faculty School total: 49. In upper school: 20 men, 21 women; 29 have advanced degrees; 23 reside on campus.

Subjects Offered Advanced Placement courses, algebra, American history, American literature, American studies, ancient history, art, astronomy, biology, calculus, calculus-AP, ceramics, chemistry, chorus, college counseling, computer applications, computer graphics, computer science, consumer mathematics, digital photography, drama, drama workshop, drawing, English, environmental science, ESL, ethics, European history, fine arts, French, geometry, global issues, graphic arts, graphic design, history of music, human anatomy, literature, mathematics, oceanography, oral communications, photography, physical education, physics, portfolio art, pre-calculus, probability and statistics, remedial study skills, SAT preparation, science, social studies, Spanish, statistics-AP, study skills, theater, theater arts, TOEFL preparation, trigonometry, word processing, yearbook.

Graduation Requirements Arts and fine arts (art, music, dance, drama), English, mathematics, physical education (includes health), science, social studies (includes history), Community Service.

Special Academic Programs Advanced Placement exam preparation; honors section; independent study; academic accommodation for the musically talented and the artistically talented; remedial reading and/or remedial writing; programs in English for dyslexic students; special instructional classes for students with mild language-based learning disabilities, students with attention/organizational issues (ADHD); ESL (19 students enrolled).

College Admission Counseling 46 students graduated in 2008; 45 went to college, including Boston College; Plymouth State University; Pratt Institute; Suffolk University; The George Washington University; Wheaton College. Other: 1 entered a postgraduate year. Median SAT critical reading: 490, median SAT math: 490, median SAT writing: 480, median combined SAT: 1460. 2% scored over 600 on SAT critical reading, 15% scored over 600 on SAT math, 2% scored over 600 on SAT writing, 4% scored over 1800 on combined SAT.

Student Life Upper grades have specified standards of dress, student council. Discipline rests primarily with faculty.

Summer Programs Enrichment, advancement, sports, art/fine arts, rigorous outdoor training, computer instruction programs offered; session focuses on skills development; held on campus; accepts boys and girls; open to students from other schools. 1,200 students usually enrolled. 2009 schedule: June 22 to August 14. Application deadline: June 21.

Tuition and Aid Day student tuition: $25,800; 7-day tuition and room/board: $39,500. Tuition installment plan (Academic Management Services Plan). Need-based scholarship grants, need-based loans, paying campus jobs available. In 2008–09, 38% of upper-school students received aid. Total amount of financial aid awarded in 2008–09: $1,223,225.

Admissions Traditional secondary-level entrance grade is 9. For fall 2008, 281 students applied for upper-level admission, 135 were accepted, 71 enrolled. Any standardized test required. Deadline for receipt of application materials: January 15. Application fee required: $50. Interview required.
Athletics Interscholastic: basketball (boys, girls), cross-country running (b,g), lacrosse (b,g), soccer (b,g), tennis (b,g); coed interscholastic: golf, soccer; coed intramural: badminton, ball hockey, basketball, bicycling, bocce, cooperative games, crew, croquet, fitness, fitness walking, flag football, floor hockey, Frisbee, horseshoes, jogging, physical fitness, project adventure, ropes courses, running, soccer, strength & conditioning, tennis, touch football, ultimate Frisbee, volleyball, walking, weight lifting, weight training, yoga. 1 PE instructor, 20 coaches, 1 athletic trainer.
Computers Computers are regularly used in all academic, computer applications, library skills, multimedia, photography, SAT preparation, yearbook classes. Computer network features include on-campus library services, Internet access, wireless campus network, Internet filtering or blocking technology, NetClassroom is available for parents and students. Campus intranet, student e-mail accounts, and computer access in designated common areas are available to students. Students grades are available online. The school has a published electronic and media policy.
Contact Mary Bishop, Admissions Assistant. 401-246-1230 Ext. 3025. Fax: 401-246-0510. E-mail: admissions@standrews-ri.org. Web site: www.standrews-ri.org.

See Close-Up on page 926.

ST. ANDREW'S–SEWANEE SCHOOL

290 Quintard Road
Sewanee, Tennessee 37375-3000

Head of School: Rev. John T. Thomas

General Information Coeducational boarding and day college-preparatory, arts, and theater school, affiliated with Episcopal Church. Boarding grades 9–12, day grades 6–12. Founded: 1868. Setting: small town. Nearest major city is Chattanooga. Students are housed in single-sex dormitories. 550-acre campus. 19 buildings on campus. Approved or accredited by National Association of Episcopal Schools, Southern Association of Colleges and Schools, Tennessee Association of Independent Schools, The Association of Boarding Schools, and Tennessee Department of Education. Member of National Association of Independent Schools and Secondary School Admission Test Board. Endowment: $11.5 million. Total enrollment: 262. Upper school average class size: 13. Upper school faculty-student ratio: 1:7.
Upper School Student Profile Grade 9: 34 students (18 boys, 16 girls); Grade 10: 53 students (31 boys, 22 girls); Grade 11: 48 students (23 boys, 25 girls); Grade 12: 51 students (32 boys, 19 girls). 46% of students are boarding students. 25% are state residents. 16 states are represented in upper school student body. 32% are international students. International students from Germany, Honduras, Jamaica, Republic of Korea, and Taiwan; 6 other countries represented in student body. 36% of students are members of Episcopal Church.
Faculty School total: 47. In upper school: 21 men, 26 women; 36 have advanced degrees; 22 reside on campus.
Subjects Offered 20th century history, acting, adolescent issues, advanced chemistry, algebra, American history, American literature, art, band, biology, calculus, chamber groups, chemistry, Chinese, choir, civil rights, college counseling, community service, comparative religion, drama, dramatic arts, ecology, emergency medicine, English, English literature, environmental systems, ESL, fine arts, French, general science, geometry, history, Holocaust, humanities, Latin, mathematics, music, physical education, physics, pottery, pre-algebra, religion, science, social studies, Spanish, statistics, theater, trigonometry, world history, yearbook.
Graduation Requirements Arts and fine arts (art, music, dance, drama), English, foreign language, mathematics, physical education (includes health), religion (includes Bible studies and theology), science, social studies (includes history), junior essay, Senior Lecture Series, outreach, credal statement. Community service is required.
Special Academic Programs Independent study; term-away projects; study at local college for college credit; academic accommodation for the gifted, the musically talented, and the artistically talented; remedial reading and/or remedial writing; remedial math; ESL (22 students enrolled).
College Admission Counseling 55 students graduated in 2008; 51 went to college, including Middle Tennessee State University; Sewanee: The University of the South; The University of Tennessee; The University of Tennessee at Chattanooga; University of Georgia; Vanderbilt University. Other: 3 entered military service, 1 had other specific plans.
Student Life Upper grades have specified standards of dress, student council, honor system. Discipline rests equally with students and faculty. Attendance at religious services is required.
Tuition and Aid Day student tuition: $14,500–$14,655; 7-day tuition and room/board: $32,500. Tuition installment plan (monthly payment plans, Tuition Management Systems Plan). Merit scholarship grants, need-based scholarship grants available. In 2008–09, 51% of upper-school students received aid; total upper-school merit-scholarship money awarded: $45,000. Total amount of financial aid awarded in 2008–09: $1,550,000.
Admissions Traditional secondary-level entrance grade is 9. For fall 2008, 105 students applied for upper-level admission, 73 were accepted, 49 enrolled. SLEP, TOEFL or writing sample required. Deadline for receipt of application materials: none. Application fee required: $50. On-campus interview required.
Athletics Interscholastic: baseball (boys), basketball (b,g), cross-country running (b,g), dance squad (g), football (b), modern dance (b), soccer (b,g), softball (g), swimming and diving (b,g), tennis (b,g), track and field (b,g), volleyball (g), wrestling (b); intramural: cheering (g), dance team (g); coed interscholastic: equestrian sports, golf, mountain biking, outdoor skills, rock climbing, strength & conditioning; coed intramural: aerobics/dance, bicycling, canoeing/kayaking, climbing, fitness, outdoor adventure, outdoor education, physical training, rappelling, ropes courses, weight training. 1 PE instructor, 12 coaches, 1 athletic trainer.
Computers Computers are regularly used in art, English, foreign language, history, introduction to technology, mathematics, SAT preparation, science, yearbook classes. Computer network features include on-campus library services, online commercial services, Internet access, wireless campus network, Internet filtering or blocking technology, access to University of the South technology facilities. Student e-mail accounts and computer access in designated common areas are available to students.
Contact Mr. Jim Tucker, Director of Admission and Financial Aid. 931-598-5651 Ext. 3217. Fax: 931-968-0208. E-mail: admissions@sasweb.org. Web site: www.sasweb.org.

ST. ANNE'S–BELFIELD SCHOOL

2132 Ivy Road
Charlottesville, Virginia 22903

Head of School: Mr. David S. Lourie

General Information Coeducational boarding and day college-preparatory, arts, religious studies, and ESL school, affiliated with Christian faith, Jewish faith. Boarding grades 9–12, day grades PK–12. Founded: 1910. Setting: suburban. Nearest major city is Richmond. Students are housed in coed dormitories. 49-acre campus. 6 buildings on campus. Approved or accredited by The Association of Boarding Schools and Virginia Association of Independent Schools. Member of National Association of Independent Schools and Secondary School Admission Test Board. Endowment: $4.3 million. Total enrollment: 841. Upper school average class size: 12. Upper school faculty-student ratio: 1:7.
Upper School Student Profile Grade 9: 80 students (40 boys, 40 girls); Grade 10: 75 students (44 boys, 31 girls); Grade 11: 89 students (58 boys, 31 girls); Grade 12: 89 students (41 boys, 48 girls). 18% of students are boarding students. 87% are state residents. 7 states are represented in upper school student body. 9% are international students. International students from China, Italy, Morocco, Republic of Korea, South Africa, and Taiwan; 17 other countries represented in student body.
Faculty School total: 95. In upper school: 19 men, 21 women; 32 have advanced degrees; 6 reside on campus.
Subjects Offered Algebra, art, art history, biology, biology-AP, calculus-AP, ceramics, chemistry, chemistry-AP, choir, Civil War, conceptual physics, drama, economics, English, environmental science-AP, ESL, French, French language-AP, French literature-AP, geometry, honors algebra, honors geometry, human development, humanities, Latin, Latin-AP, model United Nations, modern European history-AP, modern world history, music theory, music theory-AP, orchestra, photography, physics, physics-AP, pre-calculus, religion, sculpture, Shakespeare, short story, Spanish, Spanish language-AP, Spanish literature-AP, statistics, statistics-AP, theology, trigonometry, U.S. history, U.S. history-AP, video, world history, World War II, writing workshop.
Graduation Requirements Art, English, foreign language, history, mathematics, physical education (includes health), religion (includes Bible studies and theology), science. Community service is required.
Special Academic Programs Advanced Placement exam preparation; honors section; independent study; study at local college for college credit; ESL (12 students enrolled).
College Admission Counseling 76 students graduated in 2008; 75 went to college, including James Madison University; Lynchburg College; The College of William and Mary; University of Mary Washington; University of Virginia; Virginia Commonwealth University. Other: 1 had other specific plans. Median SAT critical reading: 630, median SAT math: 620. Mean SAT writing: 622. 59% scored over 600 on SAT critical reading, 57% scored over 600 on SAT math, 68% scored over 600 on SAT writing, 72% scored over 1800 on combined SAT.
Student Life Upper grades have specified standards of dress, student council, honor system. Discipline rests primarily with faculty. Attendance at religious services is required.
Summer Programs Remediation, enrichment, sports programs offered; session focuses on academic enrichment and remediation through 8th grade; held on campus; accepts boys and girls; open to students from other schools. 350 students usually enrolled. 2009 schedule: June 15 to July 31. Application deadline: none.
Tuition and Aid Day student tuition: $18,700–$18,950; 5-day tuition and room/board: $31,450–$31,700; 7-day tuition and room/board: $40,450–$40,700. Tuition installment plan (The Tuition Plan, Insured Tuition Payment Plan, FACTS Tuition Payment Plan, Your Tuition Solution). Need-based scholarship grants, need-based financial aid available. In 2008–09, 36% of upper-school students received aid. Total amount of financial aid awarded in 2008–09: $1,633,575.
Admissions Traditional secondary-level entrance grade is 9. For fall 2008, 104 students applied for upper-level admission, 60 were accepted, 45 enrolled. ERB

verbal, ERB math, SSAT, TOEFL or writing sample required. Deadline for receipt of application materials: February 20. Application fee required: $30. Interview recommended.

Athletics Interscholastic: baseball (boys), basketball (b,g), cross-country running (b,g), field hockey (g), football (b), golf (b,g), lacrosse (b,g), soccer (b,g), softball (g), squash (b,g), swimming and diving (b,g), tennis (b,g), track and field (b,g), volleyball (g), wrestling (b); coed interscholastic: cross-country running, golf, squash, swimming and diving, track and field; coed intramural: aerobics, aerobics/dance, dance, fitness, physical fitness, yoga. 6 PE instructors, 8 coaches, 2 athletic trainers.

Computers Computer network features include on-campus library services, online commercial services, Internet access, wireless campus network. The school has a published electronic and media policy.

Contact Mrs. Stacey Gearhart, Assistant Director of Admission for Grades 5—12. 434-296-5106. Fax: 434-979-1486. E-mail: sgearhart@stab.org. Web site: www.stab.org.

See Close-Up on page 928.

ST. ANSELM'S ABBEY SCHOOL

4501 South Dakota Avenue NE
Washington, District of Columbia 20017

Head of School: Mr. Louis Silvano

General Information Boys' day college-preparatory school, affiliated with Roman Catholic Church. Grades 6–12. Founded: 1942. Setting: urban. 40-acre campus. 4 buildings on campus. Approved or accredited by Association of Independent Maryland Schools, Association of Independent Schools of Greater Washington, Middle States Association of Colleges and Schools, and National Catholic Education Association. Member of National Association of Independent Schools. Endowment: $2.8 million. Total enrollment: 238. Upper school average class size: 14. Upper school faculty-student ratio: 1:5.

Upper School Student Profile Grade 9: 36 students (36 boys); Grade 10: 34 students (34 boys); Grade 11: 34 students (34 boys); Grade 12: 39 students (39 boys). 65% of students are Roman Catholic.

Faculty School total: 46. In upper school: 30 men, 10 women; 31 have advanced degrees.

Subjects Offered Advanced Placement courses, advanced studio art-AP, algebra, American government-AP, American history, American history-AP, American literature, American literature-AP, anatomy, Ancient Greek, ancient world history, anthropology, applied music, Arabic, art, art history, art history-AP, athletics, bell choir, Bible studies, biology, botany, British literature-AP, calculus, calculus-AP, career planning, career/college preparation, Catholic belief and practice, ceramics, chemistry, chemistry-AP, choir, choral music, church history, classical Greek literature, classical language, classical music, college counseling, college placement, comparative government and politics-AP, computer education, computer graphics, computer math, computer programming, computer science, creative drama, drama, earth science, economics, economics-AP, English, English language and composition-AP, English literature, English literature and composition-AP, English-AP, environmental science, environmental science-AP, ethics, European history, European history-AP, expository writing, fencing, fine arts, foreign language, forensics, French, French as a second language, French language-AP, French literature-AP, French-AP, geography, geology, geometry, government and politics-AP, government/civics, grammar, Greek, history, history of music, history of science, history-AP, instrumental music, international relations-AP, journalism, Latin, Latin-AP, mathematics, mathematics-AP, medieval history, medieval literature, medieval/Renaissance history, model United Nations, modern European history, modern languages, modern politics, modern Western civilization, modern world history, music, music appreciation, music history, music performance, music theory-AP, Native American studies, Navajo, non-Western societies, opera, oral communications, oral expression, organizational studies, performing arts, philosophy, physical education, physical fitness, physics, physics-AP, pre-calculus, religion, religious education, religious studies, robotics, Roman civilization, Roman culture, science, Shakespeare, social studies, Spanish, Spanish language-AP, Spanish literature-AP, Spanish-AP, speech, speech and debate, speech and oral interpretations, speech communications, statistics, statistics-AP, studio art-AP, theater, theology, trigonometry, U.S. government and politics-AP, vocal music, weightlifting, Western civilization-AP, world history, world history-AP, world literature, writing.

Graduation Requirements Arts and fine arts (art, music, dance, drama), English, foreign language, mathematics, physical education (includes health), religion (includes Bible studies and theology), science, social studies (includes history), community service for 11th and 12th grade.

Special Academic Programs Advanced Placement exam preparation; academic accommodation for the gifted.

College Admission Counseling 33 students graduated in 2008; all went to college, including Boston College; Georgetown University; New York University; The College of William and Mary; University of Maryland, College Park; University of Notre Dame. Median SAT critical reading: 675, median SAT math: 675, median SAT writing: 672, median combined SAT: 2022. 100% scored over 600 on SAT critical reading, 100% scored over 600 on SAT math, 100% scored over 600 on SAT writing, 100% scored over 1800 on combined SAT.

Student Life Upper grades have specified standards of dress, student council. Discipline rests primarily with faculty.

Summer Programs Remediation, enrichment, advancement, sports, art/fine arts programs offered; session focuses on academic enrichment; held on campus; accepts boys and girls; open to students from other schools. 50 students usually enrolled. 2009 schedule: June 16 to July 18. Application deadline: June 16.

Tuition and Aid Day student tuition: $19,990. Tuition installment plan (monthly payment plans, individually arranged payment plans, two payments (one prior to each semester), 10-month (June-March)). Need-based scholarship grants, Archdiocese of Washington financial aid program, Washington Scholarship Fund, Latino Student Fund available. In 2008–09, 28% of upper-school students received aid. Total amount of financial aid awarded in 2008–09: $500,000.

Admissions Traditional secondary-level entrance grade is 9. For fall 2008, 29 students applied for upper-level admission, 12 were accepted, 5 enrolled. Admissions testing and OLSAT and SCAT required. Deadline for receipt of application materials: none. Application fee required: $35. On-campus interview required.

Athletics Interscholastic: baseball, basketball, cross-country running, fencing, golf, soccer, tennis, track and field; intramural: baseball, basketball, bicycling, fitness, flag football, football, outdoor activities, physical fitness, strength & conditioning, weight lifting, weight training. 3 PE instructors, 8 coaches.

Computers Computers are regularly used in art, Christian doctrine, classics, college planning, computer applications, creative writing, design, desktop publishing, drawing and design, economics, engineering, English, ethics, French, geography, graphic design, graphics, health, history, humanities, Latin, library, literary magazine, mathematics, music, news writing, newspaper, philosophy, photography, reading, religion, science, social sciences, Spanish, speech, study skills, theater, theology, Web site design, writing, yearbook classes. Computer network features include on-campus library services, online commercial services, Internet access, Internet filtering or blocking technology. The school has a published electronic and media policy.

Contact Mrs. E.V. Downey, Director of Admissions. 202-269-2379. Fax: 202-269-2373. E-mail: admissions@saintanselms.org. Web site: www.saintanselms.org.

ANNOUNCEMENT FROM THE SCHOOL Located on the wooded grounds of a Benedictine monastery, St. Anselm's Abbey School provides a rigorous classical education to gifted and motivated young men in grades 6 through 12. The low student-faculty ratio, nurturing community, and high academic standards create an environment where high-achieving students can thrive, preparing them for placement in America's top colleges and universities. Students take advantage of a well-rounded program of academics and extra-curricular activities, including a comprehensive interscholastic sports program and opportunities in music, drama, and the visual arts; student-run publications; and a wide range of other activities.

ST. ANTHONY CATHOLIC HIGH SCHOOL

3200 McCullough Avenue
San Antonio, Texas 78212-3099

Head of School: Mr. Henry Galindo

General Information Coeducational boarding and day college-preparatory, arts, business, religious studies, bilingual studies, and technology school, affiliated with Roman Catholic Church. Grades 9–12. Founded: 1905. Setting: urban. Students are housed in single-sex by floor dormitories. 14-acre campus. 3 buildings on campus. Approved or accredited by National Catholic Education Association, Southern Association of Colleges and Schools, Texas Education Agency, and The College Board. Total enrollment: 453. Upper school average class size: 23. Upper school faculty-student ratio: 1:22.

Upper School Student Profile Grade 9: 110 students (65 boys, 45 girls); Grade 10: 121 students (76 boys, 45 girls); Grade 11: 115 students (65 boys, 50 girls); Grade 12: 105 students (67 boys, 38 girls). 7% of students are boarding students. 95% are state residents. 5 states are represented in upper school student body. 6% are international students. International students from China, Hong Kong, Japan, Mexico, Republic of Korea, and Spain; 3 other countries represented in student body. 85% of students are Roman Catholic.

Faculty School total: 34. In upper school: 17 men, 17 women; 21 have advanced degrees.

Subjects Offered Acting, advanced biology, advanced chemistry, advanced math, Advanced Placement courses, algebra, aquatics, art, Bible studies, biology, calculus, Catholic belief and practice, chemistry, choir, computer graphics, computer keyboarding, computer literacy, economics, English, English literature, environmental science, ESL, French, geometry, government, graphic arts, graphic design, health, history, Japanese, jazz band, language, Latin, mathematical modeling, photography, photojournalism, physical education, physics, physics-AP, physiology-anatomy, pre-calculus, psychology, robotics, sexuality, sociology, Spanish, Spanish-AP, speech, technical writing, theater, theology, trigonometry, typing, U.S. government, U.S. history, U.S. literature, world history, world religions, writing, yearbook.

Graduation Requirements Arts and fine arts (art, music, dance, drama), computer applications, economics, English, foreign language, government, mathematics, physical education (includes health), religion (includes Bible studies and theology), science, speech, U.S. history, word processing, world history.

Special Academic Programs Advanced Placement exam preparation; study at local college for college credit; study abroad; academic accommodation for the gifted; ESL (15 students enrolled).
College Admission Counseling 113 students graduated in 2008; 111 went to college, including Texas A&M University; Texas State University–San Marcos; The University of Texas at Austin; Trinity University; United States Air Force Academy; University of the Incarnate Word. Other: 2 entered military service.
Student Life Upper grades have uniform requirement, student council, honor system. Discipline rests primarily with faculty. Attendance at religious services is required.
Summer Programs Remediation, enrichment, advancement, ESL, sports programs offered; session focuses on enrichment/advancement; held on campus; accepts boys and girls; open to students from other schools. 200 students usually enrolled. 2009 schedule: June to July.
Tuition and Aid Day student tuition: $5400; 5-day tuition and room/board: $14,000; 7-day tuition and room/board: $14,000. Tuition installment plan (monthly payment plans). Tuition reduction for siblings, need-based scholarship grants available. In 2008–09, 35% of upper-school students received aid. Total amount of financial aid awarded in 2008–09: $95,000.
Admissions Traditional secondary-level entrance grade is 9. For fall 2008, 207 students applied for upper-level admission, 150 were accepted, 110 enrolled. High School Placement Test required. Deadline for receipt of application materials: none. No application fee required. Interview required.
Athletics Interscholastic: baseball (boys), basketball (b,g), cheering (g), dance (g), dance team (g), football (b), lacrosse (b), soccer (b,g), softball (g), swimming and diving (b,g), tennis (b,g), volleyball (g), wrestling (b); coed interscholastic: cross-country running, golf, track and field. 3 PE instructors, 15 coaches, 2 athletic trainers.
Computers Computers are regularly used in all classes. Computer network features include on-campus library services, Internet access, Internet filtering or blocking technology. Students grades are available online. The school has a published electronic and media policy.
Contact Mr. Bart Zavaletta, Director of Enrollment. 210-832-5632. Fax: 210-832-5633. E-mail: zavalett@uiwtx.edu. Web site: www.sachs.org.

SAINT ANTHONY HIGH SCHOOL

304 East Roadway Avenue
Effingham, Illinois 62401

Head of School: Miss Marianne Larimer

General Information Coeducational day college-preparatory, arts, business, religious studies, bilingual studies, and technology school, affiliated with Roman Catholic Church; primarily serves students with learning disabilities. Grades 9–12. Setting: small town. Nearest major city is St. Louis, MO. 1 building on campus. Approved or accredited by Illinois Department of Education. Total enrollment: 214. Upper school average class size: 20. Upper school faculty-student ratio: 1:10.
Upper School Student Profile Grade 9: 51 students (33 boys, 18 girls); Grade 10: 53 students (33 boys, 20 girls); Grade 11: 61 students (36 boys, 25 girls); Grade 12: 49 students (20 boys, 29 girls). 95% of students are Roman Catholic.
Faculty School total: 24. In upper school: 8 men, 14 women; 8 have advanced degrees.
Subjects Offered Accounting, advanced math, algebra, American government, anatomy, art appreciation, band, biology, British literature, calculus-AP, career exploration, Catholic belief and practice, ceramics, chemistry, chorus, communications, composition, computer applications, conceptual physics, concert band, consumer education, criminal justice, current events, drawing, earth science, English literature, English-AP, environmental science, finite math, forensic science, general math, geography, geometry, health, microbiology, music appreciation, physical education, physical science, physics, pre-algebra, psychology, publications, Spanish, statistics-AP, U.S. history, world history, world wide web design.
Graduation Requirements American government, arts and fine arts (art, music, dance, drama), computer science, consumer education, English, mathematics, physical education (includes health), religion (includes Bible studies and theology), science, social science, speech, U.S. history, world history.
Special Academic Programs International Baccalaureate program; 3 Advanced Placement exams for which test preparation is offered; independent study; study at local college for college credit; remedial math; special instructional classes for deaf students.
College Admission Counseling 55 students graduated in 2008; 53 went to college, including Eastern Illinois University; Southern Illinois University Edwardsville; University of Illinois at Urbana–Champaign. Other: 1 went to work, 1 entered military service. Median composite ACT: 23.
Student Life Upper grades have specified standards of dress, student council. Discipline rests primarily with faculty. Attendance at religious services is required.
Tuition and Aid Tuition installment plan (monthly payment plans). Need-based scholarship grants available.
Admissions Traditional secondary-level entrance grade is 9. No application fee required.
Athletics Interscholastic: baseball (boys), basketball (b,g), cheering (g), dance team (g), golf (b,g), soccer (b,g), softball (g), tennis (b,g), track and field (b,g), volleyball (g), wrestling (b); coed interscholastic: cross-country running. 3 PE instructors, 19 coaches.
Computers Computers are regularly used in drafting, publications, yearbook classes. Computer network features include on-campus library services, Internet access, Internet filtering or blocking technology. Student e-mail accounts are available to students. The school has a published electronic and media policy.
Contact Miss Marianne Larimer, Principal. 217-342-6969. Fax: 217-342-6997. E-mail: mlarimer@stanthony.com. Web site: www.stanthony.com.

ST. ANTHONY'S JUNIOR-SENIOR HIGH SCHOOL

1618 Lower Main Street
Wailuku, Hawaii 96793

Head of School: Fr. Orsini James

General Information Coeducational day college-preparatory, general academic, arts, religious studies, and technology school, affiliated with Roman Catholic Church. Grades 7–12. Founded: 1848. Setting: small town. 15-acre campus. 13 buildings on campus. Approved or accredited by National Catholic Education Association, Western Association of Schools and Colleges, and Hawaii Department of Education. Endowment: $216,177. Total enrollment: 242. Upper school average class size: 22. Upper school faculty-student ratio: 1:10.
Upper School Student Profile Grade 9: 30 students (11 boys, 19 girls); Grade 10: 42 students (24 boys, 18 girls); Grade 11: 46 students (29 boys, 17 girls); Grade 12: 44 students (30 boys, 14 girls). 50% of students are Roman Catholic.
Faculty School total: 26. In upper school: 9 men, 17 women; 8 have advanced degrees.
Subjects Offered Advanced math, American government, American government-AP, American history, American history-AP, American literature, American literature-AP, anatomy and physiology, applied arts, art, athletic training, athletics, baseball, basic skills, basketball, Bible, Bible as literature, Bible studies, biology, biology-AP, bowling, British literature, British literature (honors), British literature-AP, business, calculus, calculus-AP, campus ministry, chemistry, chemistry-AP, college counseling, college planning, computer education, computer graphics, computer keyboarding, computer literacy, computer skills, computer technologies, computer technology certification, computer tools, computer-aided design, computers, consumer mathematics, creative arts, dance, drama, drama performance, drama workshop, dramatic arts, drawing, drawing and design, driver education, electives, English, English language and composition-AP, English language-AP, English literature, English literature and composition-AP, English literature-AP, English-AP, English/composition-AP, environmental science, environmental science-AP, foreign language, health, mathematics, music, physical education, play production, Polynesian dance, pre-algebra, pre-calculus, religions, religious studies, SAT preparation, SAT/ACT preparation, science, social studies, Spanish language-AP, sports medicine, standard curriculum, technology, U.S. history-AP, world geography, writing, writing skills, yearbook, zoology.
Graduation Requirements English, languages, mathematics, physical education (includes health), religion (includes Bible studies and theology), science, social studies (includes history), technology.
Special Academic Programs Advanced Placement exam preparation; study at local college for college credit.
College Admission Counseling 42 went to college, including Fordham University; Pacific Lutheran University; University of San Diego; University of San Francisco; University of Washington; Vanguard University of Southern California. Other: 1 had other specific plans. 50% scored over 600 on SAT critical reading, 50% scored over 600 on SAT math, 50% scored over 600 on SAT writing, 50% scored over 1800 on combined SAT, 50% scored over 26 on composite ACT.
Student Life Upper grades have uniform requirement, student council. Discipline rests primarily with faculty. Attendance at religious services is required.
Summer Programs Remediation, enrichment programs offered; session focuses on remediation; held on campus; accepts boys and girls; open to students from other schools. 100 students usually enrolled. 2009 schedule: June 13 to July 15. Application deadline: June 1.
Tuition and Aid Day student tuition: $8730–$9200. Tuition installment plan (FACTS Tuition Payment Plan). Merit scholarship grants available. In 2008–09, 33% of upper-school students received aid.
Admissions Traditional secondary-level entrance grade is 9. For fall 2008, 40 students applied for upper-level admission, 40 were accepted, 40 enrolled. Achievement tests or Educational Development Series required. Deadline for receipt of application materials: none. Application fee required: $300. Interview required.
Athletics Interscholastic: aquatics (boys, girls), baseball (b), basketball (b,g), bowling (b,g), canoeing/kayaking (b,g), cross-country running (b,g), curling (g), football (b), golf (b,g), judo (b,g), ocean paddling (b,g), riflery (b,g), running (b,g), soccer (b,g), softball (g), strength & conditioning (b,g), surfing (b,g), swimming and diving (g), tennis (b,g), track and field (b,g), volleyball (g), weight lifting (b,g), weight training (b,g), wrestling (b,g); intramural: basketball (b,g); coed interscholastic: cheering, flag football. 2 PE instructors, 36 coaches, 1 athletic trainer.
Computers Computers are regularly used in aerospace science classes. Computer network features include on-campus library services, Internet access, Internet filtering or blocking technology. Student e-mail accounts are available to students. Students grades are available online. The school has a published electronic and media policy.
Contact Mr. Michael Weddington, Registrar. 808-244-4190 Ext. 224. Fax: 808-242-8081. E-mail: mweddington@sasmaui.org. Web site: www.sasmaui.org.

ST. AUGUSTINE HIGH SCHOOL

3266 Nutmeg Street
San Diego, California 92104-5199

Head of School: James Walter Horne

General Information Boys' day college-preparatory and religious studies school, affiliated with Roman Catholic Church. Grades 9–12. Founded: 1922. Setting: urban. 6-acre campus. 10 buildings on campus. Approved or accredited by National Catholic Education Association, Western Association of Schools and Colleges, and Western Catholic Education Association. Endowment: $1 million. Total enrollment: 700. Upper school average class size: 28. Upper school faculty-student ratio: 1:28.

Upper School Student Profile Grade 9: 190 students (190 boys); Grade 10: 180 students (180 boys); Grade 11: 170 students (170 boys); Grade 12: 160 students (160 boys). 95% of students are Roman Catholic.

Faculty School total: 45. In upper school: 34 men, 11 women; 28 have advanced degrees.

Subjects Offered Algebra, American history, American literature, anatomy, art, art history, arts, Bible studies, biology, calculus, chemistry, computer science, driver education, economics, economics-AP, English, English literature, English-AP, ethics, fine arts, French, geometry, government/civics, grammar, health, history, Latin, mathematics, music, philosophy, physical education, physics, physiology, psychology, religion, science, social studies, Spanish, speech, theology, trigonometry, Western civilization-AP, world history, world literature, writing.

Graduation Requirements Arts and fine arts (art, music, dance, drama), English, foreign language, mathematics, physical education (includes health), religion (includes Bible studies and theology), science, social studies (includes history), speech, 100 hours of Christian Service over four years.

Special Academic Programs Advanced Placement exam preparation; honors section; academic accommodation for the gifted; remedial reading and/or remedial writing; remedial math; programs in English, mathematics, general development for dyslexic students.

College Admission Counseling 162 students graduated in 2008; all went to college, including Gonzaga University; San Diego State University; University of California, Los Angeles; University of California, San Diego; University of Notre Dame; University of San Diego. 45% scored over 600 on SAT critical reading, 45% scored over 600 on SAT math, 45% scored over 600 on SAT writing, 55% scored over 26 on composite ACT.

Student Life Upper grades have specified standards of dress, student council, honor system. Discipline rests primarily with faculty. Attendance at religious services is required.

Summer Programs Remediation, enrichment, advancement, sports, rigorous outdoor training programs offered; session focuses on preparing students for fall semester; held on campus; accepts boys and girls; open to students from other schools. 150 students usually enrolled. 2009 schedule: June 15 to July 31. Application deadline: none.

Tuition and Aid Day student tuition: $10,970. Tuition installment plan (monthly payment plans, quarterly and annual payment plans). Merit scholarship grants, need-based scholarship grants, paying campus jobs available. In 2008–09, 30% of upper-school students received aid.

Admissions For fall 2008, 345 students applied for upper-level admission, 200 were accepted, 190 enrolled. High School Placement Test required. Deadline for receipt of application materials: January 24. Application fee required: $50. Interview required.

Athletics Interscholastic: baseball, basketball, bicycling, cross-country running, football, golf, mountain biking, soccer, street hockey, surfing, swimming and diving, tennis, track and field, volleyball, wrestling; intramural: basketball, flag football, volleyball. 5 PE instructors, 26 coaches, 1 athletic trainer.

Computers Computers are regularly used in foreign language, mathematics, science, writing classes. Computer resources include on-campus library services, online commercial services, Internet access, wireless campus network, Internet filtering or blocking technology, online databases; remote access. Campus intranet and computer access in designated common areas are available to students. The school has a published electronic and media policy.

Contact Jeannie Oliwa, Registrar. 619-282-2184 Ext. 5512. Fax: 619-282-1203. E-mail: joliwa@sahs.org. Web site: www.sahs.org.

ST. AUGUSTINE HIGH SCHOOL

1300 Galveston
Laredo, Texas 78040

Head of School: Mrs. Olga P. Gentry

General Information Coeducational day college-preparatory and religious studies school, affiliated with Roman Catholic Church. Grades 9–12. Founded: 1927. Setting: urban. Nearest major city is San Antonio. 3-acre campus. 5 buildings on campus. Approved or accredited by National Catholic Education Association, Texas Catholic Conference, Texas Education Agency, and Texas Department of Education. Endowment: $1.4 million. Total enrollment: 650. Upper school average class size: 30. Upper school faculty-student ratio: 1:20.

Upper School Student Profile Grade 9: 124 students (68 boys, 56 girls); Grade 10: 95 students (38 boys, 57 girls); Grade 11: 122 students (50 boys, 72 girls); Grade 12: 126 students (59 boys, 67 girls). 98% of students are Roman Catholic.

Faculty School total: 34. In upper school: 14 men, 20 women; 11 have advanced degrees.

Subjects Offered Accounting, algebra, American history, art, art appreciation, biology, calculus, chemistry, Christian scripture, church history, computer applications, computer literacy, computer programming, creative writing, critical writing, drawing, economics, English, geography, geometry, government, health, language arts, mathematics, novels, painting, physical education, physics, pre-calculus, psychology, reading, religion, science, social justice, social studies, Spanish, speech, Texas history, theater arts, world history, world religions, yearbook.

Graduation Requirements Arts and fine arts (art, music, dance, drama), computer science, English, foreign language, mathematics, physical education (includes health), religion (includes Bible studies and theology), science, social studies (includes history), 100 hours of community service.

Special Academic Programs Advanced Placement exam preparation; study at local college for college credit.

College Admission Counseling 126 students graduated in 2008; 123 went to college, including St. Mary's University; Texas A&M International University; Texas A&M University; The University of Texas at San Antonio; University of the Incarnate Word. Other: 3 entered a postgraduate year. Mean SAT critical reading: 486, mean SAT math: 465, mean composite ACT: 20.

Student Life Upper grades have uniform requirement, student council, honor system. Discipline rests primarily with faculty. Attendance at religious services is required.

Summer Programs Remediation, enrichment, advancement programs offered; session focuses on remediation as well as course recovery; held on campus; accepts boys and girls; not open to students from other schools. 50 students usually enrolled. 2009 schedule: June 1 to July 31. Application deadline: May 31.

Tuition and Aid Day student tuition: $4350. Tuition installment plan (monthly payment plans). Tuition reduction for siblings, need-based scholarship grants available. In 2008–09, 18% of upper-school students received aid. Total amount of financial aid awarded in 2008–09: $46,000.

Admissions Traditional secondary-level entrance grade is 9. For fall 2008, 25 students applied for upper-level admission, 21 were accepted, 21 enrolled. Admissions testing, High School Placement Test or mathematics proficiency exam required. Deadline for receipt of application materials: February 28. Application fee required: $150. On-campus interview required.

Athletics Interscholastic: baseball (boys), basketball (b,g), cheering (g), cross-country running (b,g), dance team (g), golf (b,g), softball (g), tennis (b,g), track and field (b,g); coed interscholastic: tennis, track and field. 4 PE instructors, 6 coaches.

Computers Computers are regularly used in accounting, art, English, history, mathematics, science, Web site design classes. Computer network features include on-campus library services, Internet access. The school has a published electronic and media policy.

Contact Mrs. Frances Wawroski, Director of Academic Affairs/Registrars. 956-724-8131 Ext. 1005. Fax: 956-725-9241. E-mail: fwawroski@st-augustine.org. Web site: www.st-augustine.org.

SAINT AUGUSTINE PREPARATORY SCHOOL

611 Cedar Avenue
PO Box 279
Richland, New Jersey 08350

Head of School: Rev. Francis J. Horn, OSA

General Information Boys' day college-preparatory and religious studies school, affiliated with Roman Catholic Church. Grades 9–12. Founded: 1959. Setting: rural. Nearest major city is Vineland. 125-acre campus. 4 buildings on campus. Approved or accredited by Middle States Association of Colleges and Schools, National Catholic Education Association, and New Jersey Department of Education. Endowment: $250,000. Total enrollment: 647. Upper school average class size: 17. Upper school faculty-student ratio: 1:13.

Upper School Student Profile Grade 9: 199 students (199 boys); Grade 10: 157 students (157 boys); Grade 11: 148 students (148 boys); Grade 12: 143 students (143 boys). 76% of students are Roman Catholic.

Faculty School total: 51. In upper school: 36 men, 15 women; 20 have advanced degrees.

Subjects Offered 20th century history, accounting, Advanced Placement courses, algebra, American Civil War, American legal systems, American literature, anatomy and physiology, ancient world history, art, art appreciation, band, Bible, Bible studies, biology, biology-AP, British literature, British literature (honors), British literature-AP, business, business applications, calculus, calculus-AP, Catholic belief and practice, chemistry, chemistry-AP, choir, Christian and Hebrew scripture, Christian doctrine, Christian ethics, church history, Civil War, classical language, community service, comparative religion, computer applications, computer programming, computer science, computer-aided design, constitutional law, creative writing, culinary arts, drama, driver education, engineering, English, English composition, English language-AP, English literature, English literature-AP, environmental education, ethics and responsibility, European history, European history-AP, finance, forensic science, forensics, French, French language-AP, French-AP, geometry, grammar, guitar, history, history of the Catholic Church, honors algebra, honors English, honors geometry, honors U.S. history, independent study, Italian, jazz band, jazz ensemble, lab science, language-AP, Latin, Latin-AP, law and the legal system, marine biology, mathematics-AP, model United Nations, moral reasoning, moral theology, music appreciation, music theory, music theory-AP, music-AP, peer ministry, philosophy, physical education, physics, physics-AP, political science, pre-calculus, psychology, psychology-AP, religion, religious studies, SAT preparation, scripture, service learning/internship, sociology, Spanish, Spanish language-AP, Spanish literature-AP, Spanish-AP, sports medicine, statistics-AP, studio art, U.S. history-AP, vocal music, world cultures, world religions, writing skills.

Graduation Requirements Electives, English, foreign language, lab science, mathematics, religion (includes Bible studies and theology), U.S. history, world cultures, social service hours, retreat experiences, third semester experiences.

Special Academic Programs 13 Advanced Placement exams for which test preparation is offered; honors section; independent study; study at local college for college credit; study abroad; programs in general development for dyslexic students; special instructional classes for blind students; ESL (4 students enrolled).

College Admission Counseling 141 students graduated in 2008; 140 went to college, including Drexel University; La Salle University; Rutgers, The State University of New Jersey, Newark; Saint Joseph's University; Seton Hall University; Villanova University. Other: 1 entered a postgraduate year. Mean SAT critical reading: 579, mean SAT math: 593, mean SAT writing: 582, mean combined SAT: 1754. 33% scored over 600 on SAT critical reading, 46% scored over 600 on SAT math, 26% scored over 600 on SAT writing, 34% scored over 1800 on combined SAT.

Student Life Upper grades have uniform requirement, student council, honor system. Discipline rests primarily with faculty. Attendance at religious services is required.

Summer Programs Enrichment, advancement, sports, art/fine arts, rigorous outdoor training, computer instruction programs offered; session focuses on academic enrichment, community relations; held on campus; accepts boys and girls; open to students from other schools. 500 students usually enrolled. 2009 schedule: June 18 to August 10. Application deadline: May 15.

Tuition and Aid Day student tuition: $11,950. Tuition installment plan (FACTS Tuition Payment Plan, monthly payment plans, individually arranged payment plans, credit card payment). Merit scholarship grants, need-based scholarship grants available. In 2008–09, 31% of upper-school students received aid; total upper-school merit-scholarship money awarded: $75,000. Total amount of financial aid awarded in 2008–09: $675,000.

Admissions Traditional secondary-level entrance grade is 9. For fall 2008, 300 students applied for upper-level admission, 233 were accepted, 200 enrolled. School's own exam required. Deadline for receipt of application materials: January 30. Application fee required: $75. On-campus interview recommended.

Athletics Interscholastic: baseball, basketball, bowling, crew, cross-country running, fencing, football, golf, ice hockey, indoor track, lacrosse, rowing, sailing, soccer, surfing, swimming and diving, tennis, track and field, volleyball, winter (indoor) track, wrestling; intramural: basketball, rugby, ultimate Frisbee, weight training. 2 PE instructors, 11 coaches, 1 athletic trainer.

Computers Computers are regularly used in all academic, art classes. Computer network features include on-campus library services, online commercial services, Internet access, wireless campus network, Internet filtering or blocking technology, syllabus, current grades, and assignments available online for all courses. Computer access in designated common areas is available to students. Students grades are available online. The school has a published electronic and media policy.

Contact Mrs. Linda Pine, Director of Admissions. 856-697-2600 Ext. 112. Fax: 856-697-8389. E-mail: mrs.pine@hermits.com. Web site: www.hermits.com.

SAINT BASIL ACADEMY

711 Fox Chase Road
Jenkintown, Pennsylvania 19046

Head of School: Sr. Carla Hernandez

General Information Girls' day college-preparatory, arts, business, religious studies, bilingual studies, and technology school, affiliated with Roman Catholic Church. Grades 9–12. Founded: 1931. Setting: suburban. Nearest major city is Philadelphia. 28-acre campus. 1 building on campus. Approved or accredited by Middle States Association of Colleges and Schools and Pennsylvania Department of Education. Endowment: $600,000. Total enrollment: 410. Upper school average class size: 24. Upper school faculty-student ratio: 1:13.

Upper School Student Profile Grade 9: 101 students (101 girls); Grade 10: 107 students (107 girls); Grade 11: 103 students (103 girls); Grade 12: 99 students (99 girls). 93% of students are Roman Catholic.

Faculty School total: 38. In upper school: 8 men, 27 women; 22 have advanced degrees.

Subjects Offered Accounting, advanced biology, algebra, American government-AP, American history, American history-AP, American literature, anatomy, art, biology, business, calculus-AP, chemistry, Christian and Hebrew scripture, Christian ethics, computer applications, concert choir, desktop publishing, earth science, economics, English, English language-AP, English literature, English literature-AP, ensembles, environmental science, European history, fine arts, French, French literature-AP, geometry, German, government/civics, history, honors algebra, honors English, honors geometry, journalism, keyboarding/computer, Latin, mathematics, music, physical education, physics, pre-calculus, religion, science, social studies, Spanish, Spanish literature-AP, statistics, trigonometry, Ukrainian, world history.

Graduation Requirements Arts and fine arts (art, music, dance, drama), English, foreign language, keyboarding, mathematics, physical education (includes health), religion (includes Bible studies and theology), science, social studies (includes history). Community service is required.

Special Academic Programs Advanced Placement exam preparation; honors section; study at local college for college credit.

College Admission Counseling 107 students graduated in 2008; all went to college, including La Salle University; Saint Joseph's University; Temple University; University of Pittsburgh; West Chester University of Pennsylvania. Mean SAT critical reading: 546, mean SAT math: 501, mean SAT writing: 548, mean combined SAT: 1595, mean composite ACT: 21.

Student Life Upper grades have uniform requirement, student council. Discipline rests primarily with faculty. Attendance at religious services is required.

Summer Programs Sports programs offered; session focuses on sports camps; held on campus; accepts girls; open to students from other schools. 50 students usually enrolled. 2009 schedule: June 15 to June 30. Application deadline: May 31.

Tuition and Aid Tuition installment plan (monthly payment plans, 2-installments (pay 1/2 tuition July 15—1/2 tuition November 15), 1st installment (due July 15 (3 months)—7 installments—(pay Oct. 15—April 15)). Tuition reduction for siblings, merit scholarship grants, need-based scholarship grants, Ellis Grant for children of single parents living in Philadelphia, BLOCS Scholarships and Foundations available. In 2008–09, 13% of upper-school students received aid; total upper-school merit-scholarship money awarded: $128,500. Total amount of financial aid awarded in 2008–09: $171,400.

Admissions Traditional secondary-level entrance grade is 9. For fall 2008, 253 students applied for upper-level admission, 101 enrolled. High School Placement Test required. Deadline for receipt of application materials: November 8. Application fee required: $40.

Athletics Interscholastic: basketball, cheering, cross-country running, field hockey, indoor track, soccer, softball, tennis, track and field, volleyball, winter (indoor) track. 1 PE instructor, 25 coaches.

Computers Computers are regularly used in accounting, computer applications, creative writing, desktop publishing, digital applications, economics, journalism, keyboarding, science classes. Computer network features include Internet access, wireless campus network, Internet filtering or blocking technology, student accessible server storage space, on-campus and Web-based library services (catalog and book request). Student e-mail accounts are available to students. The school has a published electronic and media policy.

Contact Mrs. Maureen Walsh, Director of Admissions. 215-885-6952. Fax: 215-885-0395. E-mail: mwalsh@stbasilacademy.org. Web site: www.stbasilacademy.org.

ANNOUNCEMENT FROM THE SCHOOL Saint Basil Academy offers each student a liberal arts education with the goal of deepening her powers of critical and analytical thinking, effective communication, and appreciation of aesthetic values. It encourages a student's thirst for knowledge, a positive outlook on life, and a confidence to help develop her unique talents and abilities.

ST. BENEDICT AT AUBURNDALE

8250 Varnavas Drive
Cordova, Tennessee 38016

Head of School: Mr. George D. Valadie

General Information Coeducational day college-preparatory, arts, business, religious studies, bilingual studies, and technology school, affiliated with Roman Catholic Church; primarily serves students with learning disabilities, individuals with Attention Deficit Disorder, and dyslexic students. Grades 9–12. Founded: 1966. Setting: suburban. Nearest major city is Memphis. 40-acre campus. 1 building on campus. Approved or accredited by National Catholic Education Association, Southern Association of Colleges and Schools, Tennessee Association of Independent Schools, and Tennessee Department of Education. Endowment: $100,000. Total enrollment: 941. Upper school average class size: 26. Upper school faculty-student ratio: 1:13.

Upper School Student Profile Grade 9: 250 students (115 boys, 135 girls); Grade 10: 234 students (100 boys, 134 girls); Grade 11: 267 students (117 boys, 150 girls); Grade 12: 190 students (80 boys, 110 girls). 70% of students are Roman Catholic.

Faculty School total: 65. In upper school: 15 men, 50 women; 40 have advanced degrees.

Subjects Offered Accounting, algebra, American government-AP, American history-AP, American literature-AP, anatomy and physiology, applied music, art, art appreciation, art education, art history, art-AP, band, biology, calculus-AP, chemistry, chorus, cinematography, computer graphics, computer keyboarding, computer multimedia, computers, creative writing, dance, digital photography, drama, drama performance, ecology, economics, English, etymology, European history, forensics, French, general business, geometry, German, government, health and wellness, instrumental music, internship, jazz band, keyboarding/computer, Latin, marketing, modern history, music appreciation, music history, music theory, newspaper, performing arts, personal finance, photography, physical education, physical science, physics, play production, pre-algebra, pre-calculus, psychology, religion, sociology, Spanish, speech, sports conditioning, U.S. history-AP, world geography, world history, yearbook.

Graduation Requirements Arts and fine arts (art, music, dance, drama), English, foreign language, government, mathematics, physical education (includes health), religion (includes Bible studies and theology), science, social studies (includes history), technology.
Special Academic Programs 8 Advanced Placement exams for which test preparation is offered; honors section; independent study; study at local college for college credit; academic accommodation for the gifted, the musically talented, and the artistically talented; remedial reading and/or remedial writing; remedial math; programs in English, mathematics, general development for dyslexic students; special instructional classes for students with diagnosed learning disabilities and Attention Deficit Disorder.
College Admission Counseling 182 students graduated in 2008; all went to college, including Christian Brothers University; Middle Tennessee State University; The University of Tennessee; The University of Tennessee at Martin; University of Memphis; University of Mississippi. Mean SAT critical reading: 570, mean SAT math: 560, mean composite ACT: 24. 38% scored over 600 on SAT critical reading, 37% scored over 600 on SAT math, 30% scored over 26 on composite ACT.
Student Life Upper grades have uniform requirement, student council, honor system. Discipline rests primarily with faculty. Attendance at religious services is required.
Summer Programs Remediation, enrichment programs offered; session focuses on enrichment for math and language; held on campus; accepts boys and girls; open to students from other schools. 30 students usually enrolled. 2009 schedule: July 5 to July 31. Application deadline: none.
Tuition and Aid Day student tuition: $7150. Tuition installment plan (FACTS Tuition Payment Plan, monthly payment plans, individually arranged payment plans). Merit scholarship grants, need-based scholarship grants available. In 2008–09, 4% of upper-school students received aid; total upper-school merit-scholarship money awarded: $30,000. Total amount of financial aid awarded in 2008–09: $35,000.
Admissions Traditional secondary-level entrance grade is 9. High School Placement Test required. Deadline for receipt of application materials: none. Application fee required: $50. Interview required.
Athletics Interscholastic: baseball (boys), basketball (b,g), bowling (b,g), cheering (g), cross-country running (b,g), dance (g), dance squad (g), dance team (g), football (b), golf (b,g), lacrosse (b,g), pom squad (g), soccer (b,g), softball (g), strength & conditioning (b), swimming and diving (b,g), tennis (b,g), track and field (b,g), volleyball (g), weight lifting (b), weight training (b), wrestling (b); coed intramural: Frisbee. 4 PE instructors, 17 coaches, 1 athletic trainer.
Computers Computers are regularly used in art, desktop publishing, mathematics, newspaper, science, technology, yearbook classes. Computer network features include on-campus library services, Internet access, wireless campus network, Internet filtering or blocking technology. Students grades are available online. The school has a published electronic and media policy.
Contact Mrs. Ann O'Leary, Director of Admissions. 901-260-2875. Fax: 901-260-2850. E-mail: olearya@sbaeagles.org. Web site: www.sbaeagles.org.

ST. BENEDICT'S PREPARATORY SCHOOL

520 Dr. Martin Luther King, Jr. Boulevard
Newark, New Jersey 07102-1314

Head of School: Rev. Edwin D. Leahy, OSB

General Information Boys' day college-preparatory school, affiliated with Roman Catholic Church. Grades 7–12. Founded: 1868. Setting: urban. 12-acre campus. 15 buildings on campus. Approved or accredited by Middle States Association of Colleges and Schools, New Jersey Association of Independent Schools, and New Jersey Department of Education. Endowment: $28 million. Total enrollment: 550. Upper school average class size: 20. Upper school faculty-student ratio: 1:11.
Upper School Student Profile Grade 9: 137 students (137 boys); Grade 10: 116 students (116 boys); Grade 11: 133 students (133 boys); Grade 12: 97 students (97 boys). 40% of students are Roman Catholic.
Faculty School total: 55. In upper school: 44 men, 8 women; 40 have advanced degrees.
Subjects Offered Algebra, American history, American literature, architecture, art, astronomy, Bible studies, biology, Black history, calculus, chemistry, computer science, creative writing, drama, economics, English, English literature, ESL, European history, French, geometry, health, Hispanic literature, history, Latin, mathematics, mechanical drawing, music, physical education, physics, religion, social studies, sociology, Spanish, theater, trigonometry, world history.
Graduation Requirements English, foreign language, mathematics, physical education (includes health), religion (includes Bible studies and theology), science, social studies (includes history), spring projects, summer phase courses.
Special Academic Programs Term-away projects; domestic exchange program (with The Network Program Schools); remedial reading and/or remedial writing; remedial math; ESL (20 students enrolled).
College Admission Counseling 111 students graduated in 2008; 104 went to college, including Boston College; College of the Holy Cross; Rutgers, The State University of New Jersey, Newark; Saint John's University; Saint Peter's College; University of Notre Dame. Other: 7 went to work. Mean SAT critical reading: 468, mean SAT math: 492, mean SAT writing: 476, mean combined SAT: 1436.
Student Life Upper grades have uniform requirement, student council, honor system. Discipline rests equally with students and faculty. Attendance at religious services is required.
Summer Programs Remediation, enrichment, ESL, art/fine arts, computer instruction programs offered; session focuses on enrichment or remedial academic courses as appropriate; held on campus; accepts boys; not open to students from other schools. 550 students usually enrolled. 2009 schedule: July 28 to August 29.
Tuition and Aid Day student tuition: $7470. Tuition installment plan (FACTS Tuition Payment Plan). Need-based scholarship grants available. In 2008–09, 60% of upper-school students received aid. Total amount of financial aid awarded in 2008–09: $1,186,372.
Admissions Traditional secondary-level entrance grade is 9. For fall 2008, 280 students applied for upper-level admission, 144 were accepted, 120 enrolled. Deadline for receipt of application materials: December 31. No application fee required. On-campus interview required.
Athletics Interscholastic: baseball, basketball, cross-country running, fencing, golf, indoor track & field, soccer, swimming and diving, tennis, track and field, water polo, winter (indoor) track, wrestling; intramural: basketball, flag football, floor hockey, hiking/backpacking, life saving, outdoor adventure, outdoor skills, physical training, soccer, swimming and diving, weight lifting. 2 PE instructors, 20 coaches.
Computers Computers are regularly used in English, information technology, journalism, science classes. Computer network features include on-campus library services, online commercial services, Internet access, wireless campus network, Internet filtering or blocking technology. Student e-mail accounts are available to students. The school has a published electronic and media policy.
Contact Ms. Doris Lamourt, Admissions Administrative Assistant. 973-792-5744. Fax: 973-792-5706. E-mail: DLamourt@sbp.org. Web site: www.sbp.org.

ST. BRENDAN HIGH SCHOOL

2950 Southwest 87th Avenue
Miami, Florida 33165-3295

Head of School: Br. Felix Elardo

General Information Coeducational day college-preparatory, general academic, arts, business, religious studies, bilingual studies, and technology school, affiliated with Roman Catholic Church; primarily serves students with learning disabilities. Grades 9–12. Founded: 1975. Setting: urban. 34-acre campus. 3 buildings on campus. Approved or accredited by Southern Association of Colleges and Schools and Florida Department of Education. Total enrollment: 1,187. Upper school average class size: 28. Upper school faculty-student ratio: 1:15.
Upper School Student Profile Grade 9: 281 students (78 boys, 203 girls); Grade 10: 281 students (88 boys, 193 girls); Grade 11: 312 students (84 boys, 228 girls); Grade 12: 313 students (101 boys, 212 girls). 98% of students are Roman Catholic.
Faculty School total: 82. In upper school: 22 men, 60 women; 47 have advanced degrees.
Graduation Requirements Students must complete 100 community service hours in their four years of high school.
Special Academic Programs Advanced Placement exam preparation; honors section; study at local college for college credit; remedial reading and/or remedial writing.
College Admission Counseling 316 students graduated in 2008; 310 went to college, including Florida International University; Miami Dade College; St. Thomas University; University of Florida; University of Miami. Mean combined SAT: 960, mean composite ACT: 20.
Student Life Upper grades have uniform requirement, student council, honor system. Discipline rests primarily with faculty. Attendance at religious services is required.
Tuition and Aid Guaranteed tuition plan. Tuition installment plan (monthly payment plans). Need-based scholarship grants, paying campus jobs available. In 2008–09, 13% of upper-school students received aid.
Admissions Traditional secondary-level entrance grade is 9. Catholic High School Entrance Examination or placement test required. Deadline for receipt of application materials: January 23. Application fee required: $50.
Athletics Interscholastic: baseball (boys, girls), basketball (b,g), cheering (g), cross-country running (b,g), dance team (g), soccer (b,g), softball (g), swimming and diving (b,g), tennis (b,g), track and field (b,g), volleyball (g). 3 PE instructors, 17 coaches.
Computers Computers are regularly used in all classes. Computer network features include on-campus library services, wireless campus network, Internet filtering or blocking technology. Computer access in designated common areas is available to students. Students grades are available online. The school has a published electronic and media policy.
Contact Candice Barket, Director of Admissions. 305-223-5181 Ext. 578. Fax: 305-220-7434. E-mail: cbarket@stbhs.org. Web site: www.stbhs.org.

ST. CATHERINE'S MILITARY ACADEMY

Anaheim, California
See Junior Boarding Schools section.

ST. CATHERINE'S SCHOOL

6001 Grove Avenue
Richmond, Virginia 23226

Head of School: Laura J. Erickson

General Information Girls' day college-preparatory school, affiliated with Episcopal Church. Grades PK–12. Founded: 1890. Setting: suburban. Nearest major city is Washington, DC. 17-acre campus. 22 buildings on campus. Approved or accredited by New Jersey Association of Independent Schools, Virginia Association of Independent Schools, and Virginia Department of Education. Member of National Association of Independent Schools and Secondary School Admission Test Board. Endowment: $61.7 million. Total enrollment: 878. Upper school average class size: 16. Upper school faculty-student ratio: 1:5.

Upper School Student Profile Grade 9: 69 students (69 girls); Grade 10: 52 students (52 girls); Grade 11: 58 students (58 girls); Grade 12: 57 students (57 girls). 46% of students are members of Episcopal Church.

Faculty School total: 127. In upper school: 18 men, 29 women; 36 have advanced degrees.

Subjects Offered Acting, adolescent issues, advanced chemistry, advanced computer applications, advanced math, African-American literature, algebra, American government, American history, American history-AP, American literature, ancient history, architecture, art, art and culture, art history, art history-AP, band, Bible, biology, British literature-AP, calculus, calculus-AP, ceramics, chamber groups, chemistry, chemistry-AP, Chinese, choir, choral music, choreography, chorus, comparative government and politics-AP, comparative religion, computer applications, computer math, computer programming, computer science, computer science-AP, constitutional law, creative writing, dance, dance performance, desktop publishing, drama, driver education, economics, economics-AP, English, English language and composition-AP, English literature, English literature and composition-AP, environmental science, environmental science-AP, ethics, ethics and responsibility, European history, expository writing, film and literature, fine arts, French, French language-AP, French literature-AP, gender issues, geography, geometry, government and politics-AP, government/civics, grammar, Greek, guitar, health and wellness, health education, history, history of jazz, honors algebra, honors English, honors geometry, independent study, Latin, Latin-AP, macro/microeconomics-AP, mathematics, modern dance, moral and social development, moral theology, music, music history, music theory, music theory-AP, orchestra, painting, performing arts, philosophy, photography, physical education, physical fitness, physics, physics-AP, playwriting and directing, portfolio art, post-calculus, pre-calculus, printmaking, regional literature, religion, rhetoric, robotics, science, sculpture, short story, social studies, Southern literature, Spanish, Spanish language-AP, Spanish literature, Spanish literature-AP, speech, speech communications, statistics, statistics-AP, theater, theater arts, theology, trigonometry, U.S. government and politics-AP, Vietnam, world cultures, world geography, world history, world literature, writing.

Graduation Requirements Arts and fine arts (art, music, dance, drama), computer science, English, foreign language, mathematics, physical education (includes health), religion (includes Bible studies and theology), science, social science, social studies (includes history).

Special Academic Programs Advanced Placement exam preparation; honors section; independent study; term-away projects; study abroad.

College Admission Counseling 59 students graduated in 2008; all went to college, including James Madison University; The College of William and Mary; University of Virginia; Wake Forest University; Washington and Lee University. Median SAT critical reading: 630, median SAT math: 640, median SAT writing: 660, median combined SAT: 1930, median composite ACT: 26. 72% scored over 600 on SAT critical reading, 66.7% scored over 600 on SAT math, 82.5% scored over 600 on SAT writing, 77.2% scored over 1800 on combined SAT, 60% scored over 26 on composite ACT.

Student Life Upper grades have specified standards of dress, student council, honor system. Discipline rests equally with students and faculty. Attendance at religious services is required.

Summer Programs Sports, art/fine arts programs offered; session focuses on creative arts program and sports camps; held both on and off campus; held at James River (rafting) outdoor adventures; accepts boys and girls; open to students from other schools. 1,200 students usually enrolled. 2009 schedule: June 22 to July 30. Application deadline: March 1.

Tuition and Aid Day student tuition: $13,900–$18,850. Tuition installment plan (monthly payment plans, Tuition Management Systems Plan). Need-based scholarship grants available. In 2008–09, 13% of upper-school students received aid. Total amount of financial aid awarded in 2008–09: $448,800.

Admissions Traditional secondary-level entrance grade is 9. For fall 2008, 62 students applied for upper-level admission, 34 were accepted, 21 enrolled. SSAT, TOEFL and TOEFL or SLEP required. Deadline for receipt of application materials: none. Application fee required: $50. Interview required.

Athletics Interscholastic: basketball, cross-country running, diving, field hockey, golf, indoor track, indoor track & field, lacrosse, soccer, softball, squash, swimming and diving, tennis, track and field, volleyball, winter (indoor) track; intramural: aerobics, aerobics/dance, aerobics/Nautilus, aquatics, ballet, basketball, canoeing/kayaking, climbing, dance, equestrian sports, field hockey, golf, lacrosse, martial arts, modern dance, physical fitness, physical training, soccer, softball, strength & conditioning, swimming and diving, tennis, track and field, volleyball, weight lifting, weight training, wilderness, yoga; coed interscholastic: indoor track & field, track and field; coed intramural: aerobics/dance, backpacking, ballet, canoeing/kayaking, climbing, dance, modern dance, outdoor adventure, wilderness. 3 PE instructors, 50 coaches, 2 athletic trainers.

Computers Computers are regularly used in all classes. Computer network features include on-campus library services, online commercial services, Internet access, wireless campus network. Campus intranet and student e-mail accounts are available to students. Students grades are available online. The school has a published electronic and media policy.

Contact Kelly Jones Wilbanks, Director of Admission. 804-288-2804. Fax: 804-285-8169. E-mail: kwilbanks@st.catherines.org. Web site: www.st.catherines.org.

ST. CECILIA ACADEMY

4210 Harding Road
Nashville, Tennessee 37205

Head of School: Sr. Mary Thomas, OP

General Information Girls' day college-preparatory, arts, religious studies, and technology school, affiliated with Roman Catholic Church. Grades 9–12, Founded: 1860. Setting: suburban. 83-acre campus. 6 buildings on campus. Approved or accredited by National Catholic Education Association, Southern Association of Colleges and Schools, Southern Association of Independent Schools, Tennessee Association of Independent Schools, The College Board, and Tennessee Department of Education. Total enrollment: 239. Upper school average class size: 13. Upper school faculty-student ratio: 1:9.

Upper School Student Profile Grade 9: 75 students (75 girls); Grade 10: 66 students (66 girls); Grade 11: 55 students (55 girls); Grade 12: 43 students (43 girls). 70% of students are Roman Catholic.

Faculty School total: 32. In upper school: 4 men, 26 women; 23 have advanced degrees.

Subjects Offered Algebra, American history-AP, American literature, anatomy and physiology, biology, biology-AP, British literature, calculus, calculus-AP, Catholic belief and practice, chamber groups, chemistry, chemistry-AP, chorus, church history, computer programming, computer science, current events, dance, drawing, economics, economics and history, English literature, English-AP, ethics, European civilization, European history, European history-AP, fine arts, French, French language-AP, geometry, German, German-AP, government, government/civics, Internet research, journalism, Latin, microcomputer technology applications, moral theology, music, music appreciation, music theory, natural history, photography, physical education, physics, physics-AP, religion, scripture, Spanish language-AP, Spanish-AP, speech, studio art-AP, tap dance, theology, trigonometry, U.S. history, U.S. history-AP, visual and performing arts, visual arts, world history, yearbook.

Graduation Requirements Arts and fine arts (art, music, dance, drama), computer science, English, foreign language, history, mathematics, physical education (includes health), religion (includes Bible studies and theology), science.

Special Academic Programs Advanced Placement exam preparation; honors section; study at local college for college credit; academic accommodation for the gifted, the musically talented, and the artistically talented.

College Admission Counseling 59 students graduated in 2008; all went to college, including Samford University; Southern Methodist University; The University of Alabama; The University of Tennessee; The University of Tennessee at Chattanooga; University of Mississippi. Median SAT critical reading: 615, median SAT math: 555, median SAT writing: 645. Mean composite ACT: 25.

Student Life Upper grades have uniform requirement, student council, honor system. Discipline rests primarily with faculty. Attendance at religious services is required.

Tuition and Aid Day student tuition: $13,000. Tuition installment plan (Tuition Management Systems Plan). Need-based scholarship grants available. In 2008–09, 38% of upper-school students received aid. Total amount of financial aid awarded in 2008–09: $430,000.

Admissions Traditional secondary-level entrance grade is 9. For fall 2008, 140 students applied for upper-level admission, 91 were accepted, 75 enrolled. High School Placement Test and ISEE required. Deadline for receipt of application materials: January 12. Application fee required: $60. Interview required.

Athletics Interscholastic: aquatics, basketball, cross-country running, golf, running, soccer, softball, swimming and diving, tennis, track and field, volleyball; intramural: dance, dance team, independent competitive sports, modern dance, physical training, self defense, strength & conditioning, weight lifting, weight training. 1 PE instructor, 16 coaches, 1 athletic trainer.

Computers Computers are regularly used in art, English, foreign language, history, journalism, mathematics, newspaper, publications, science, Spanish, writing classes. Computer network features include on-campus library services, online commercial services, Internet access, Internet filtering or blocking technology. Students grades are available online. The school has a published electronic and media policy.

Contact Mrs. Betty Bader, Director of Enrollment Management. 615-298-4525 Ext. 377. Fax: 615-783-0561. E-mail: baderb@stcecilia.edu. Web site: www.stcecilia.edu.

SAINT CECILIA HIGH SCHOOL

521 North Kansas Avenue
Hastings, Nebraska 68901-7594

Head of School: Rev. Fr. Troy J. Schweiger

General Information Coeducational day and distance learning college-preparatory, arts, business, vocational, religious studies, and technology school, affiliated with Roman Catholic Church. Grades 6–12. Distance learning grades 11–12. Founded: 1912. Setting: small town. Nearest major city is Lincoln. 1-acre campus. 2 buildings on campus. Approved or accredited by National Catholic Education Association, North Central Association of Colleges and Schools, Northwest Association of Accredited Schools, and Nebraska Department of Education. Endowment: $4.5 million. Total enrollment: 296. Upper school average class size: 23. Upper school faculty-student ratio: 1:8.

Upper School Student Profile Grade 9: 41 students (18 boys, 23 girls); Grade 10: 44 students (27 boys, 17 girls); Grade 11: 48 students (26 boys, 22 girls); Grade 12: 50 students (28 boys, 22 girls). 98% of students are Roman Catholic.

Faculty School total: 35. In upper school: 15 men, 20 women; 9 have advanced degrees.

Subjects Offered Accounting, aerospace education, algebra, American history, American literature-AP, art history, automated accounting, band, Basic programming, biology, business law, business mathematics, calculus-AP, career education, Catholic belief and practice, chemistry, chorus, computer applications, computer programming, computer technology certification, computer-aided design, consumer economics, drafting, drawing, driver education, economics, English, environmental science, ESL, family and consumer science, fashion, fine arts, foods, French, French studies, geometry, health, history and culture of Portugal, history of the Catholic Church, instrumental music, interior design, Internet, introduction to technology, jazz band, language arts, library skills, Life of Christ, marketing, music, musical productions, newspaper, painting, peace and justice, physical education, physics, play production, portfolio art, pre-calculus, probability and statistics, psychology, religion, science, science project, sculpture, social science, social studies, sociology, Spanish, Spanish literature, speech, statistics, textiles, theater arts, TOEFL preparation, trigonometry, U.S. government, video film production, vocational arts, weight training, world history, yearbook.

Graduation Requirements Algebra, American government, American history, American literature, arts and fine arts (art, music, dance, drama), British literature, career education, computer skills, economics, English, foreign language, mathematics, physical education (includes health), practical arts, religion (includes Bible studies and theology), science, social studies (includes history), speech, vocational arts, vocational-technical courses, 45-50 volunteer service hours.

Special Academic Programs 1 Advanced Placement exam for which test preparation is offered; honors section; independent study; study at local college for college credit; remedial reading and/or remedial writing; remedial math; special instructional classes for students with learning disabilities and Attention Deficit Disorder; ESL (20 students enrolled).

College Admission Counseling 46 students graduated in 2008; 43 went to college, including Avila University; Benedictine College; Creighton University; University of Nebraska–Lincoln; University of Nebraska at Kearney; University of Nebraska at Omaha. Other: 3 went to work. Median composite ACT: 22. 8% scored over 26 on composite ACT.

Student Life Upper grades have uniform requirement, student council, honor system. Discipline rests primarily with faculty. Attendance at religious services is required.

Summer Programs Sports programs offered; session focuses on driver's education; held on campus; accepts boys and girls; open to students from other schools. 22 students usually enrolled. 2009 schedule: May 29 to July 25. Application deadline: April 1.

Tuition and Aid Day student tuition: $1375. Guaranteed tuition plan. Tuition installment plan (monthly payment plans, individually arranged payment plans). Tuition reduction for siblings, merit scholarship grants, scrip participation program, tuition assistance with parish pastors, Parish Pastor will pay or match family contribution to reach the total tuition available. In 2008–09, 3% of upper-school students received aid; total upper-school merit-scholarship money awarded: $5250. Total amount of financial aid awarded in 2008–09: $5250.

Admissions Traditional secondary-level entrance grade is 9. For fall 2008, 6 students applied for upper-level admission, 6 were accepted, 6 enrolled. English proficiency, PSAT, Terra Nova-CTB or writing sample required. Deadline for receipt of application materials: none. No application fee required. Interview required.

Athletics Interscholastic: aerobics/dance (girls), basketball (b,g), bowling (b,g), drill team (g), football (b), golf (b,g), running (b,g), tennis (g), volleyball (g), wrestling (b); intramural: dance team (g), drill team (g), power lifting (b); coed interscholastic: track and field; coed intramural: badminton, bowling, juggling, jump rope, life saving, physical fitness, physical training, weight lifting, weight training. 2 PE instructors, 2 athletic trainers.

Computers Computers are regularly used in accounting, business, career education, career exploration, career technology, Christian doctrine, college planning, computer applications, desktop publishing, ESL, drafting, drawing and design, English, ESL, foreign language, graphic design, graphics, health, journalism, keyboarding, mathematics, media production, music, newspaper, reading, science, Spanish, speech, video film production, vocational-technical courses, Web site design, word processing, writing, writing, yearbook classes. Computer network features include online commercial services, Internet access, wireless campus network, Internet filtering or blocking technology, SmartBoards. Computer access in designated common areas is available to students. The school has a published electronic and media policy.

Contact Mrs. Marie K. Butler, Principal. 402-462-2105. Fax: 402-462-2106. E-mail: mbutler@esu9.org. Web site: www.stchastings.org.

ST. CHRISTOPHER ACADEMY

Seattle, Washington

See Special Needs Schools section.

ST. CHRISTOPHER'S SCHOOL

711 St. Christopher's Road
Richmond, Virginia 23226

Head of School: Mr. Charles M. Stillwell

General Information Boys' day college-preparatory school, affiliated with Episcopal Church. Grades JK–12. Founded: 1911. Setting: suburban. 46-acre campus. 9 buildings on campus. Approved or accredited by National Association of Episcopal Schools and Virginia Association of Independent Schools. Member of National Association of Independent Schools and Secondary School Admission Test Board. Endowment: $61.7 million. Total enrollment: 955. Upper school average class size: 15. Upper school faculty-student ratio: 1:7.

Upper School Student Profile Grade 9: 76 students (76 boys); Grade 10: 74 students (74 boys); Grade 11: 80 students (80 boys); Grade 12: 79 students (79 boys). 40% of students are members of Episcopal Church.

Faculty School total: 152. In upper school: 27 men, 18 women; 29 have advanced degrees.

Subjects Offered Algebra, American history, American literature, ancient history, architecture, art, art history, astronomy, Bible studies, biology, calculus, ceramics, chemistry, Chinese, community service, computer math, computer programming, computer science, creative writing, dance, drama, driver education, ecology, economics, English, English literature, environmental science, ethics, European history, expository writing, fine arts, French, geography, geology, geometry, government/civics, grammar, Greek, health, history, industrial arts, journalism, Latin, mathematics, music, philosophy, photography, physics, public speaking, religion, science, social studies, Spanish, speech, statistics, theater, theology, trigonometry, typing, woodworking, writing.

Graduation Requirements 1½ elective credits, algebra, American history, American literature, ancient history, arts and fine arts (art, music, dance, drama), biology, British literature, chemistry, church history, computer science, English, English literature, European history, foreign language, geometry, physical education (includes health), physics, public speaking, religion (includes Bible studies and theology), speech, U.S. history. Community service is required.

Special Academic Programs Advanced Placement exam preparation; honors section; independent study; academic accommodation for the gifted, the musically talented, and the artistically talented.

College Admission Counseling 78 students graduated in 2008; all went to college, including Hampden-Sydney College; University of Virginia; Virginia Military Institute; Virginia Polytechnic Institute and State University. 75% scored over 600 on SAT critical reading, 75% scored over 600 on SAT math, 75% scored over 600 on SAT writing.

Student Life Upper grades have specified standards of dress, student council, honor system. Discipline rests equally with students and faculty. Attendance at religious services is required.

Summer Programs Advancement programs offered; session focuses on enrichment, sports, day camp, leadership; held on campus; accepts boys and girls; open to students from other schools. 750 students usually enrolled. 2009 schedule: June 15 to July 24. Application deadline: none.

Tuition and Aid Day student tuition: $16,950. Tuition installment plan (Academic Management Services Plan, Tuition Refund Plan). Merit scholarship grants, need-based scholarship grants available. In 2008–09, 19% of upper-school students received aid; total upper-school merit-scholarship money awarded: $6000. Total amount of financial aid awarded in 2008–09: $1,766,800.

Admissions Traditional secondary-level entrance grade is 9. For fall 2008, 56 students applied for upper-level admission, 28 were accepted, 16 enrolled. SSAT and writing sample required. Deadline for receipt of application materials: none. Application fee required: $50. On-campus interview recommended.

Athletics Interscholastic: baseball, basketball, football, golf, indoor soccer, lacrosse, sailing, soccer, strength & conditioning, tennis, weight lifting, weight training, wrestling; intramural: martial arts; coed interscholastic: canoeing/kayaking, climbing, cross-country running, dance, indoor track & field, martial arts, rappelling, swimming and diving, track and field, winter (indoor) track; coed intramural: swimming and diving. 5 coaches, 2 athletic trainers.

Computers Computers are regularly used in English, foreign language, history, mathematics, music, science classes. Computer network features include on-campus library services, online commercial services, Internet access, wireless campus network. Student e-mail accounts and computer access in designated common areas are available to students. Students grades are available online.

Contact Anne D. Booker, Director of Admissions. 804-282-3185 Ext. 387. Fax: 804-673-6632. E-mail: bookera@stcva.org. Web site: www.stchristophers.com.

ANNOUNCEMENT FROM THE SCHOOL St. Christopher's is committed to educating the whole boy for college and for life. Academics, athletics, art, and student life are major components of the whole-boy development. Small classes and individual attention from caring and talented teachers influence college choices and provide life-shaping experiences. A coordinate program with St. Catherine's at the Upper School level provides a broad curriculum with a wide selection of electives and AP courses in a coeducational context.

ST. CLEMENT SCHOOL

87 Mann Avenue
Ottawa, Ontario K1N 6Y8, Canada
Head of School: Mrs. Beryl Devine

General Information Coeducational day college-preparatory school, affiliated with Roman Catholic Church. Grades 7–12. Founded: 1996. Setting: urban. Approved or accredited by Ontario Department of Education. Language of instruction: English. Total enrollment: 33. Upper school average class size: 9. Upper school faculty-student ratio: 1:5.
Upper School Student Profile Grade 9: 8 students (2 boys, 6 girls); Grade 10: 4 students (3 boys, 1 girl); Grade 11: 4 students (2 boys, 2 girls); Grade 12: 4 students (2 boys, 2 girls). 100% of students are Roman Catholic.
Faculty School total: 14. In upper school: 7 men, 5 women; 9 have advanced degrees.
Subjects Offered Advanced math, algebra, arts and crafts, calculus, Canadian geography, Canadian history, Catholic belief and practice, chemistry, choir, church history, English literature and composition-AP, French, French as a second language, geometry, Greek, history, Latin, mathematics, music history, music theory, physical education, science, world history.
Graduation Requirements Biology, calculus, chemistry, church history, English, French, French as a second language, Greek, Latin, mathematics, music history, music theory, physics, religion (includes Bible studies and theology).
Special Academic Programs Honors section; ESL.
College Admission Counseling 4 students graduated in 2008; 3 went to college. Other: 1 went to work.
Student Life Upper grades have uniform requirement, honor system. Discipline rests primarily with faculty. Attendance at religious services is required.
Tuition and Aid Day student tuition: CAN$3500. Tuition installment plan (full payment in advance, 5-month payment plan). Tuition reduction for siblings available.
Admissions Traditional secondary-level entrance grade is 9. Canadian Standardized Test required. Deadline for receipt of application materials: April 1. No application fee required. On-campus interview required.
Athletics Coed Intramural: ice hockey, independent competitive sports, paddle tennis, physical training, running, soccer, tennis, touch football, track and field, volleyball. 2 PE instructors.
Computers Computer resources include Internet access, word processing, encyclopedia.
Contact Mrs. Beryl Devine, Headmistress. 613-236-7231. Fax: 613-236-9159. E-mail: stclementschool@bellnet.ca.

ST. CLEMENT'S SCHOOL

21 St. Clements Avenue
Toronto, Ontario M4R 1G8, Canada
Head of School: Ms. Patricia D. Parisi

General Information Girls' day college-preparatory, arts, business, and technology school, affiliated with Anglican Church of Canada. Grades 1–12. Founded: 1901. Setting: urban. 1 building on campus. Approved or accredited by Canadian Association of Independent Schools, Canadian Educational Standards Institute, Conference of Independent Schools of Ontario, and Ontario Department of Education. Affiliate member of National Association of Independent Schools; member of Secondary School Admission Test Board. Language of instruction: English. Total enrollment: 448. Upper school average class size: 16. Upper school faculty-student ratio: 1:9.
Upper School Student Profile Grade 10: 60 students (60 girls); Grade 11: 57 students (57 girls); Grade 12: 60 students (60 girls).
Faculty School total: 54. In upper school: 8 men, 39 women; 20 have advanced degrees.
Subjects Offered Algebra, American history, art, art history-AP, biology, biology-AP, business, business skills, calculus, calculus-AP, Canadian geography, Canadian history, Canadian law, career education, chemistry, chemistry-AP, civics, computer science, creative writing, data processing, drama, economics, economics-AP, English, English literature, English literature and composition-AP, environmental science, European history, fine arts, finite math, French, French-AP, geography, geometry, German, grammar, Greek, guidance, health, history, history-AP, instrumental music, jazz ensemble, keyboarding/computer, language and composition, language arts, Latin, Latin-AP, law, mathematics, modern Western civilization, music, philosophy, photography, physical education, physics, physics-AP, physiology, religion, science, social science, social studies, Spanish, Spanish-AP, theater, trigonometry, Western civilization, world history, writing workshop.
Graduation Requirements Arts and fine arts (art, music, dance, drama), business skills (includes word processing), computer science, English, foreign language, mathematics, physical education (includes health), science, social science, social studies (includes history).
Special Academic Programs Advanced Placement exam preparation; accelerated programs; independent study.
College Admission Counseling 52 students graduated in 2008; all went to college, including McGill University; McMaster University; Queen's University at Kingston; The University of Western Ontario; University of Toronto.
Student Life Upper grades have uniform requirement, student council, honor system. Discipline rests equally with students and faculty. Attendance at religious services is required.
Summer Programs Advancement, art/fine arts programs offered; session focuses on cooperative program and summer school credit courses; held both on and off campus; held at Europe; accepts boys and girls; open to students from other schools. 15 students usually enrolled. 2009 schedule: July 1 to July 30. Application deadline: March.
Tuition and Aid Day student tuition: CAN$20,700. Tuition installment plan (monthly payment plans, individually arranged payment plans). Bursaries, merit scholarship grants, need-based scholarship grants available.
Admissions Deadline for receipt of application materials: January 30. Application fee required: CAN$100. On-campus interview required.
Athletics Interscholastic: alpine skiing, badminton, basketball, cross-country running, curling, dance, dance team, equestrian sports, field hockey, golf, hockey, ice hockey, nordic skiing, running, skiing (downhill), soccer, softball, swimming and diving, tennis, track and field, volleyball; intramural: aerobics, aerobics/dance, backpacking, badminton, basketball, bocce, canoeing/kayaking, cooperative games, cross-country running, dance, dance team, field hockey, fitness, floor hockey, hiking/backpacking, indoor soccer, jogging, life saving, outdoor education, paddle tennis, running, soccer, softball, swimming and diving, table tennis, tennis, track and field, ultimate Frisbee, volleyball, walking, wilderness survival, yoga. 5 PE instructors, 12 coaches.
Computers Computers are regularly used in economics, English, geography, history, independent study, media arts, science, social science, yearbook classes. Computer network features include on-campus library services, online commercial services, Internet access, wireless campus network, Internet filtering or blocking technology. Campus intranet, student e-mail accounts, and computer access in designated common areas are available to students. The school has a published electronic and media policy.
Contact Ms. Elena Holeton, Director of Admissions. 416-483-4414 Ext. 2227. Fax: 416-483-8242. E-mail: elena.holeton@scs.on.ca. Web site: www.stclementsschool.ca.

ST. CROIX COUNTRY DAY SCHOOL

RR #1, Box 6199
Kingshill, Virgin Islands 00850-9807
Head of School: Mr. William D. Sinfield

General Information Coeducational day college-preparatory and technology school. Grades N–12. Founded: 1964. Setting: rural. Nearest major city is Christiansted, U.S. Virgin Islands. 25-acre campus. 6 buildings on campus. Approved or accredited by Middle States Association of Colleges and Schools and Virgin Islands Department of Education. Member of National Association of Independent Schools. Endowment: $574,000. Total enrollment: 478. Upper school average class size: 14. Upper school faculty-student ratio: 1:12.
Upper School Student Profile Grade 9: 40 students (21 boys, 19 girls); Grade 10: 47 students (17 boys, 30 girls); Grade 11: 44 students (20 boys, 24 girls); Grade 12: 38 students (15 boys, 23 girls).
Faculty School total: 51. In upper school: 6 men, 17 women; 11 have advanced degrees.
Subjects Offered Algebra, American history, American literature, art, art history, arts, band, biology, calculus, ceramics, chemistry, chorus, community service, computer programming, computer science, creative writing, current events, dance, drama, earth science, ecology, economics, electronics, English, English literature, film, fine arts, French, geometry, government/civics, health, history, journalism, keyboarding, marine biology, mathematics, music, Native American studies, photography, physical education, physical science, physics, pre-calculus, psychology, public speaking, science, social studies, sociology, Spanish, statistics, swimming, theater, trigonometry, world history.
Graduation Requirements Arts and fine arts (art, music, dance, drama), computer science, English, foreign language, mathematics, physical education (includes health), science, social studies (includes history), swimming, typing. Community service is required.
Special Academic Programs Advanced Placement exam preparation.
College Admission Counseling 38 students graduated in 2008; all went to college, including Michigan Technological University; University of Pennsylvania; University of Pittsburgh; Vassar College. Median SAT critical reading: 520, median SAT math: 540, median composite ACT: 22. 35% scored over 600 on SAT critical reading, 25% scored over 600 on SAT math, 19% scored over 26 on composite ACT.
Student Life Upper grades have specified standards of dress, student council, honor system. Discipline rests primarily with faculty.

Tuition and Aid Day student tuition: $11,800. Tuition installment plan (monthly payment plans, individually arranged payment plans, semiannual and annual payment plans). Merit scholarship grants, need-based scholarship grants available. In 2008–09, 35% of upper-school students received aid; total upper-school merit-scholarship money awarded: $17,700. Total amount of financial aid awarded in 2008–09: $251,360.

Admissions Traditional secondary-level entrance grade is 9. For fall 2008, 45 students applied for upper-level admission, 30 were accepted, 19 enrolled. Essay and Test of Achievement and Proficiency required. Deadline for receipt of application materials: none. Application fee required: $150. On-campus interview required.

Athletics Interscholastic: baseball (boys), cheering (g), football (b), softball (g), tennis (b,g), volleyball (b,g); intramural: volleyball (b,g); coed interscholastic: aquatics, basketball, cross-country running, golf, soccer; coed intramural: basketball, soccer, ultimate Frisbee. 4 PE instructors, 5 coaches.

Computers Computers are regularly used in mathematics, music, science, yearbook classes. Computer network features include on-campus library services, online commercial services, Internet access. The school has a published electronic and media policy.

Contact Mrs. Alma V. Castro-Nieves, Registrar. 340-778-1974 Ext. 2108. Fax: 340-779-3331. E-mail: anieves@stxcountryday.com. Web site: www.stxcountryday.com.

ST. CROIX LUTHERAN HIGH SCHOOL

1200 Oakdale Avenue
West St. Paul, Minnesota 55118

Head of School: Mr. Gene Pfeifer

General Information Coeducational boarding and day college-preparatory, general academic, arts, business, vocational, religious studies, bilingual studies, technology, and ESL school, affiliated with Wisconsin Evangelical Lutheran Synod, Christian faith. Grades 6–12. Founded: 1958. Setting: suburban. Nearest major city is St. Paul. Students are housed in single-sex dormitories. 30-acre campus. 3 buildings on campus. Approved or accredited by Minnesota Non-Public School Accrediting Association and Minnesota Department of Education. Endowment: $1.6 million. Total enrollment: 430. Upper school average class size: 22. Upper school faculty-student ratio: 1:15.

Upper School Student Profile Grade 6: 4 students (2 boys, 2 girls); Grade 7: 7 students (4 boys, 3 girls); Grade 8: 7 students (3 boys, 4 girls); Grade 9: 100 students (48 boys, 52 girls); Grade 10: 94 students (50 boys, 44 girls); Grade 11: 111 students (55 boys, 56 girls); Grade 12: 105 students (57 boys, 48 girls). 30% of students are boarding students. 78% are state residents. 7 states are represented in upper school student body. 16% are international students. International students from China, Japan, Kazakhstan, Republic of Korea, Taiwan, and Viet Nam; 2 other countries represented in student body. 70% of students are Wisconsin Evangelical Lutheran Synod, Christian.

Faculty School total: 32. In upper school: 19 men, 10 women; 16 have advanced degrees; 4 reside on campus.

Subjects Offered Accounting, advanced math, Advanced Placement courses, algebra, American history, American literature, art, band, Bible studies, biology, business skills, calculus, chemistry, chorus, computer programming, computer science, drama, economics, English, English literature, environmental science, general science, geography, geology, geometry, German, home economics, keyboarding, Latin, literature, Mandarin, mathematics, music, physical education, physics, pre-algebra, reading, religion, science, social science, social studies, Spanish, speech, trigonometry, world history, writing.

Graduation Requirements Algebra, arts and fine arts (art, music, dance, drama), biology, chemistry, English, English composition, English literature, foreign language, geometry, government, grammar, literature, physical education (includes health), physics, religion (includes Bible studies and theology), science, social studies (includes history), speech, world geography.

Special Academic Programs Advanced Placement exam preparation; honors section; independent study; academic accommodation for the artistically talented; remedial reading and/or remedial writing; remedial math; programs in English for dyslexic students; special instructional classes for students with learning disabilities; ESL (30 students enrolled).

College Admission Counseling 98 students graduated in 2008; 95 went to college, including Bethany Lutheran College; Hamline University; Martin Luther College; Minnesota State University Mankato; University of Minnesota, Twin Cities Campus; University of Wisconsin–Madison. Other: 1 went to work, 2 entered military service.

Student Life Upper grades have specified standards of dress, student council. Discipline rests primarily with faculty. Attendance at religious services is required.

Tuition and Aid 7-day tuition and room/board: $22,600. Tuition installment plan (SMART Tuition Payment Plan). Merit scholarship grants, need-based scholarship grants available. In 2008–09, 30% of upper-school students received aid; total upper-school merit-scholarship money awarded: $25,000. Total amount of financial aid awarded in 2008–09: $300,000.

Admissions Traditional secondary-level entrance grade is 9. For fall 2008, 68 students applied for upper-level admission, 40 were accepted, 38 enrolled. Secondary Level English Proficiency and writing sample required. Deadline for receipt of application materials: none. Application fee required: $100. Interview recommended.

Athletics Interscholastic: baseball (boys), basketball (b,g), cheering (g), dance team (g), football (b), golf (b); coed interscholastic: cross-country running; coed intramural: basketball.

Computers Computers are regularly used in accounting, computer applications, desktop publishing, economics, keyboarding, yearbook classes. Computer network features include on-campus library services, Internet access, Internet filtering or blocking technology. Computer access in designated common areas is available to students. Students grades are available online. The school has a published electronic and media policy.

Contact Mr. Jeff Lemke, Admissions Director. 651-455-1521. Fax: 651-451-3968. E-mail: international@stcroixschools.org. Web site: www.stcroixschools.org.

ST. DAVID'S SCHOOL

3400 White Oak Road
Raleigh, North Carolina 27609

Head of School: Mr. Kevin J. Lockerbie

General Information Coeducational day college-preparatory, arts, religious studies, and technology school, affiliated with Episcopal Church, Christian faith. Grades K–12. Founded: 1972. Setting: suburban. 16-acre campus. 7 buildings on campus. Approved or accredited by National Association of Episcopal Schools, North Carolina Association of Independent Schools, Southern Association of Colleges and Schools, Southern Association of Independent Schools, and North Carolina Department of Education. Member of Secondary School Admission Test Board. Endowment: $175,000. Total enrollment: 558. Upper school average class size: 16. Upper school faculty-student ratio: 1:10.

Upper School Student Profile Grade 9: 45 students (30 boys, 15 girls); Grade 10: 59 students (31 boys, 28 girls); Grade 11: 53 students (22 boys, 31 girls); Grade 12: 57 students (27 boys, 30 girls).

Faculty School total: 65. In upper school: 13 men, 13 women; 15 have advanced degrees.

Subjects Offered Algebra, American history, American literature, art, art history, biology, calculus, ceramics, chemistry, community service, composition, computer science, drama, drawing, earth science, English, English literature, European history, film studies, French, geography, geometry, government/civics, Greek, Latin, mathematics, music, physical education, physical science, physics, religion, science, social studies, Spanish, speech, studio art, theater, world history, world literature.

Graduation Requirements English, foreign language, mathematics, physical education (includes health), religion (includes Bible studies and theology), science, social studies (includes history), 40 hours of community service.

Special Academic Programs Advanced Placement exam preparation; honors section; independent study.

College Admission Counseling 46 students graduated in 2008; all went to college, including Appalachian State University; Davidson College; Elon University; North Carolina State University; The University of North Carolina at Chapel Hill; Wake Forest University.

Student Life Upper grades have specified standards of dress, student council, honor system. Discipline rests equally with students and faculty. Attendance at religious services is required.

Summer Programs Enrichment, advancement, sports, art/fine arts, computer instruction programs offered; held on campus; accepts boys and girls; open to students from other schools. 100 students usually enrolled.

Tuition and Aid Day student tuition: $15,500. Tuition installment plan (Insured Tuition Payment Plan, monthly payment plans, 10-month payment plan). Need-based scholarship grants available.

Admissions Traditional secondary-level entrance grade is 9. ISEE and writing sample required. Deadline for receipt of application materials: February 20. Application fee required: $75. On-campus interview required.

Athletics Interscholastic: baseball (boys, girls), basketball (b,g), cheering (g), cross-country running (b,g), football (b), indoor track & field (b,g); lacrosse (b), soccer (b,g), softball (g), tennis (b,g), track and field (b,g), volleyball (g), winter (indoor) track (b,g), wrestling (b); intramural: basketball (b,g), soccer (b,g); coed interscholastic: golf, swimming and diving. 3 PE instructors, 3 coaches, 1 athletic trainer.

Computers Computers are regularly used in all academic classes. Computer network features include on-campus library services, Internet access.

Contact Mrs. Teresa Wilson, Director of Admissions. 919-782-3331 Ext. 230. Fax: 919-571-3330. E-mail: twilson@sdsw.org. Web site: www.sdsw.org.

SAINT DOMINIC ACADEMY

2572 Kennedy Boulevard
Jersey City, New Jersey 07304

Head of School: Deborah Egan

General Information Girls' day college-preparatory, arts, business, religious studies, and technology school, affiliated with Roman Catholic Church. Grades 9–12. Founded: 1878. Setting: urban. Nearest major city is New York, NY. 2-acre campus. 1 building on campus. Approved or accredited by Middle States Association of Colleges and Schools, National Catholic Education Association, and New Jersey Association of Independent Schools. Endowment: $37,000. Total enrollment: 527. Upper school average class size: 24. Upper school faculty-student ratio: 1:12.

Upper School Student Profile Grade 9: 128 students (128 girls); Grade 10: 132 students (132 girls); Grade 11: 130 students (130 girls); Grade 12: 138 students (138 girls). 77% of students are Roman Catholic.
Faculty School total: 48. In upper school: 12 men, 29 women; 20 have advanced degrees.
Subjects Offered Accounting, advanced chemistry, algebra, American history, American literature, anatomy, art, art appreciation, art history, art history-AP, Bible studies, biology, business, business applications, business education, business skills, calculus, calculus-AP, chemistry, collage and assemblage, college counseling, college placement, college writing, computer applications, computer education, computer keyboarding, computer literacy, computer math, computer processing, computer programming, computer science, CPR, creative writing, critical thinking, critical writing, drama, driver education, economics, English, English language and composition-AP, English literature, European history, fine arts, French, French language-AP, geometry, government/civics, health, history, history-AP, International Baccalaureate courses, Italian, Latin, mathematics, music, music performance, music theory, peer counseling, peer ministry, physical education, physics, physiology, psychology, psychology-AP, religion, science, social studies, sociology, Spanish, Spanish language-AP, theater, theology, trigonometry, women in literature, women's studies, world history, world literature, writing.
Graduation Requirements Arts and fine arts (art, music, dance, drama), business skills (includes word processing), computer science, English, foreign language, mathematics, physical education (includes health), religion (includes Bible studies and theology), science, social studies (includes history), 40 hours of community service, term paper.
Special Academic Programs International Baccalaureate program; Advanced Placement exam preparation; honors section; study at local college for college credit; remedial reading and/or remedial writing; remedial math.
College Admission Counseling 118 students graduated in 2008; 116 went to college, including Caldwell College; Montclair State University; New Jersey City University; Rutgers, The State University of New Jersey, New Brunswick; Saint Peter's College; Seton Hall University. Other: 2 went to work. Median SAT critical reading: 470, median SAT math: 470, median SAT writing: 520. Mean composite ACT: 23. 10% scored over 600 on SAT critical reading, 7.5% scored over 600 on SAT math, 15% scored over 600 on SAT writing, 32.5% scored over 1800 on combined SAT, 29% scored over 26 on composite ACT.
Student Life Upper grades have uniform requirement, student council, honor system. Discipline rests primarily with faculty. Attendance at religious services is required.
Summer Programs Remediation, enrichment, advancement, computer instruction programs offered; session focuses on preparing students for a successful high school career; held on campus; accepts girls; open to students from other schools. 127 students usually enrolled. 2009 schedule: June 29 to August 6. Application deadline: June 8.
Tuition and Aid Day student tuition: $7100. Tuition installment plan (SMART Tuition Payment Plan, monthly payment plans, individually arranged payment plans, quarterly payment plan, semiannual payment plan, prepayment plan). Tuition reduction for siblings, merit scholarship grants, need-based scholarship grants, paying campus jobs available. In 2008–09, 35% of upper-school students received aid; total upper-school merit-scholarship money awarded: $113,400. Total amount of financial aid awarded in 2008–09: $163,900.
Admissions Traditional secondary-level entrance grade is 9. For fall 2008, 420 students applied for upper-level admission, 320 were accepted, 128 enrolled. Cooperative Entrance Exam (McGraw-Hill) required. Deadline for receipt of application materials: none. Application fee required: $40. On-campus interview required.
Athletics Interscholastic: basketball (girls), cross-country running (g), dance team (g), diving (g), indoor track & field (g), outdoor activities (g), soccer (g), softball (g), swimming and diving (g), tennis (g), track and field (g); intramural: volleyball (g). 4 PE instructors, 16 coaches.
Computers Computers are regularly used in accounting, art, basic skills, business applications, business education, business skills, business studies, career education, career exploration, career technology, creative writing, economics, introduction to technology, keyboarding, programming classes. Computer network features include on-campus library services, Internet access, Internet filtering or blocking technology. Campus intranet and student e-mail accounts are available to students. Students grades are available online. The school has a published electronic and media policy.
Contact Ms. Carolyn Smith, Director of Public Relations. 201-434-5938 Ext. 35. Fax: 201-434-2603. E-mail: csmith@stdominicacad.com. Web site: www.stdominicacad.com.

SAINT DOMINIC REGIONAL HIGH SCHOOL

Bishop Joseph OSB Boulevard
121 Gracelawn Road
Auburn, Maine 04210
Head of School: Mr. Donald Fournier

General Information Coeducational day college-preparatory, arts, business, and religious studies school, affiliated with Roman Catholic Church. Grades 9–12. Founded: 1941. Setting: rural. Nearest major city is Lewiston. 70-acre campus. 1 building on campus. Approved or accredited by National Catholic Education Association and Maine Department of Education. Total enrollment: 276. Upper school average class size: 17. Upper school faculty-student ratio: 1:12.
Upper School Student Profile Grade 9: 67 students (35 boys, 32 girls); Grade 10: 81 students (40 boys, 41 girls); Grade 11: 54 students (26 boys, 28 girls); Grade 12: 74 students (40 boys, 34 girls). 70% of students are Roman Catholic.
Faculty School total: 31. In upper school: 14 men, 12 women.
Special Academic Programs International Baccalaureate program; Advanced Placement exam preparation; honors section; independent study.
College Admission Counseling 98 students graduated in 2008; 96 went to college, including Boston College; Bowdoin College; Massachusetts Institute of Technology; Saint Anselm College; University of Maine; University of New Hampshire. Other: 2 went to work. Median SAT critical reading: 554, median SAT math: 543, median SAT writing: 549.
Student Life Upper grades have specified standards of dress. Discipline rests primarily with faculty. Attendance at religious services is required.
Summer Programs Enrichment, sports, art/fine arts, computer instruction programs offered; session focuses on recreational fun, sports, activities; held on campus; accepts boys and girls; not open to students from other schools. 150 students usually enrolled. 2009 schedule: June 15 to August 5.
Tuition and Aid Tuition installment plan (FACTS Tuition Payment Plan). Need-based scholarship grants available. In 2008–09, 33% of upper-school students received aid.
Admissions Traditional secondary-level entrance grade is 9. Scholastic Testing Service High School Placement Test required. Deadline for receipt of application materials: none. Application fee required: $50. On-campus interview required.
Athletics Interscholastic: baseball (boys), basketball (b,g), field hockey (g), hockey (b,g), indoor hockey (b,g), soccer (b,g), softball (g); coed interscholastic: aquatics, cheering, cross-country running, dance team, golf, swimming and diving. 1 PE instructor, 30 coaches.
Computers Computer network features include on-campus library services, online commercial services, Internet access, Internet filtering or blocking technology. Campus intranet, student e-mail accounts, and computer access in designated common areas are available to students. Students grades are available online. The school has a published electronic and media policy.
Contact Mr. James Boulet, Director of Admissions. 207-782-6911 Ext. 2110. Fax: 207-795-6439. E-mail: james.boulet@portlanddiocese.org.

ST. DOMINIC'S INTERNATIONAL SCHOOL, PORTUGAL

Rua Maria Brown
Outeiro de Polima
Sao Domingos de Rana 2785-816, Portugal
Head of School: Dra. Maria do Rosário Empis

General Information Coeducational day college-preparatory and general academic school. Grades 1–13. Founded: 1974. Setting: suburban. Nearest major city is Lisbon, Portugal. 5-acre campus. 5 buildings on campus. Approved or accredited by European Council of International Schools, International Baccalaureate Organization, and New England Association of Schools and Colleges. Language of instruction: English. Endowment: €7 million. Total enrollment: 654. Upper school average class size: 18. Upper school faculty-student ratio: 1:3.
Upper School Student Profile Grade 12: 56 students (26 boys, 30 girls); Grade 13: 45 students (22 boys, 23 girls).
Faculty School total: 75. In upper school: 11 men, 23 women; 20 have advanced degrees.
Graduation Requirements Arts, humanities, languages, mathematics, science.
Special Academic Programs International Baccalaureate program; academic accommodation for the gifted, the musically talented, and the artistically talented; remedial reading and/or remedial writing; remedial math; programs in English, mathematics, general development for dyslexic students; ESL (27 students enrolled).
College Admission Counseling 36 students graduated in 2008; 35 went to college.
Student Life Upper grades have uniform requirement, student council, honor system. Discipline rests equally with students and faculty.
Tuition and Aid Day student tuition: €12,079–€17,869. Merit scholarship grants available. In 2008–09, total upper-school merit-scholarship money awarded: €3,677,940.
Admissions Traditional secondary-level entrance grade is 12. For fall 2008, 8 students applied for upper-level admission, 8 were accepted, 8 enrolled. Math and English placement tests required. Deadline for receipt of application materials: none. No application fee required.
Athletics Interscholastic: badminton (boys, girls), basketball (b,g), fitness (b,g), floor hockey (b,g), gymnastics (b,g), independent competitive sports (b,g), judo (b,g), martial arts (b,g), outdoor adventure (b,g), physical training (b,g), soccer (b,g), table tennis (b,g), tennis (b,g), track and field (b,g), volleyball (b,g); intramural: badminton (b,g), basketball (b,g), fitness (b,g), floor hockey (b,g), gymnastics (b,g), independent competitive sports (b,g), judo (b,g), martial arts (b,g), outdoor adventure (b,g), physical training (b,g), soccer (b,g), table tennis (b,g), tennis (b,g), track and field (b,g), volleyball (b,g). 4 PE instructors.

Computers Computers are regularly used in all academic classes. Computer network features include on-campus library services, Internet access, wireless campus network. The school has a published electronic and media policy.

Contact Admissions. 351-214440434. E-mail: school@dominics-int.org. Web site: www.dominics-int.org.

SAINT EDMUND HIGH SCHOOL

2474 Ocean Avenue
Brooklyn, New York 11229

Head of School: Mr. John P. Lorenzetti

General Information Coeducational day college-preparatory and arts school, affiliated with Roman Catholic Church. Grades 9–12. Founded: 1932. Setting: urban. Nearest major city is New York. 1 building on campus. Approved or accredited by International Baccalaureate Organization, Middle States Association of Colleges and Schools, and New York State Board of Regents. Upper school average class size: 33. Upper school faculty-student ratio: 1:15.

Upper School Student Profile 95% of students are Roman Catholic.

Faculty School total: 50. In upper school: 20 men, 30 women; 34 have advanced degrees.

Subjects Offered 3-dimensional design, accounting, advanced biology, advanced chemistry, advanced computer applications, advanced math, Advanced Placement courses, advanced studio art-AP, African American studies, algebra, American government-AP, American history-AP, analysis and differential calculus, anthropology, applied music, architecture, art, art-AP, Asian studies, athletic training, Basic programming, Bible studies, biology, biology-AP, broadcast journalism, business law, calculus-AP, chemistry, chemistry-AP, chorus, Christian education, computer education, computer graphics, computer programming, computer science, consumer mathematics, CPR, dance, desktop publishing, discrete math, drawing, driver education, earth science, economics, English, English composition, English literature, English literature and composition-AP, environmental science, ethics, European history, European history-AP, film studies, forensic science, French, geometry, global studies, government, government and politics-AP, history, history of the Americas, history of the Catholic Church, honors algebra, honors geometry, instruments, International Baccalaureate courses, intro to computers, Irish literature, jazz, jazz band, Life of Christ, mathematics-AP, music, poetry, pre-calculus, science, Spanish-AP, sports, studio art-AP, U.S. government and politics-AP, U.S. history-AP, Web authoring, Web site design, weight fitness, women's literature, world religions, world wide web design, World-Wide-Web publishing.

Special Academic Programs International Baccalaureate program; Advanced Placement exam preparation; honors section; study at local college for college credit; academic accommodation for the artistically talented; remedial reading and/or remedial writing; remedial math; programs in English for dyslexic students.

College Admission Counseling 172 students graduated in 2008; they went to City College of the City University of New York; St. Francis College; St. John's University; State University of New York at Binghamton. Other: 1 entered military service.

Student Life Upper grades have uniform requirement, student council. Discipline rests primarily with faculty. Attendance at religious services is required.

Summer Programs Remediation programs offered; session focuses on make-up courses for failed classes and incoming students in need of development; held on campus; accepts boys and girls; open to students from other schools. 300 students usually enrolled. 2009 schedule: July 2 to August 18. Application deadline: June 26.

Tuition and Aid Day student tuition: $7200. Tuition installment plan (monthly payment plans, individually arranged payment plans). Tuition reduction for siblings, merit scholarship grants, need-based scholarship grants available. In 2008–09, 5% of upper-school students received aid; total upper-school merit-scholarship money awarded: $50,000. Total amount of financial aid awarded in 2008–09: $72,000.

Admissions Traditional secondary-level entrance grade is 9. Cooperative Entrance Exam (McGraw-Hill) required. No application fee required.

Athletics Interscholastic: baseball (boys, girls), basketball (b,g), bowling (b), cheering (g), cross-country running (b,g), handball (b), hockey (b), ice hockey (b), rugby (b), soccer (b,g), swimming and diving (b,g), volleyball (g), wrestling (b); coed intramural: volleyball. 3 PE instructors, 20 coaches.

Computers Computers are regularly used in accounting, business, business studies, computer applications, desktop publishing, English, foreign language, history, literary magazine, mathematics, media, newspaper, religion, science, technology, Web site design, yearbook classes. Computer resources include online commercial services, Internet access, wireless campus network, Internet filtering or blocking technology. Students grades are available online.

Contact Deacon Ron Rizzuto, Director of Admissions. 718-743-6100 Ext. 42. Fax: 718-743-5243. E-mail: rrizzuto@stedmundprep.org. Web site: www.stedmundprep.org.

SAINT EDWARD'S SCHOOL

1895 Saint Edward's Drive
Vero Beach, Florida 32963

Head of School: Dr. Charles F. Clark

General Information Coeducational day college-preparatory and technology school, affiliated with Episcopal Church; primarily serves students with learning disabilities, individuals with Attention Deficit Disorder, and dyslexic students. Grades PK–12. Founded: 1965. Setting: small town. Nearest major city is West Palm Beach. 33-acre campus. 8 buildings on campus. Approved or accredited by Florida Council of Independent Schools, National Association of Episcopal Schools, Southern Association of Colleges and Schools, and The College Board. Member of National Association of Independent Schools and Secondary School Admission Test Board. Endowment: $4.1 million. Total enrollment: 819. Upper school average class size: 17. Upper school faculty-student ratio: 1:9.

Upper School Student Profile Grade 9: 70 students (30 boys, 40 girls); Grade 10: 59 students (29 boys, 30 girls); Grade 11: 83 students (48 boys, 35 girls); Grade 12: 59 students (32 boys, 27 girls). 15% of students are members of Episcopal Church.

Faculty School total: 91. In upper school: 14 men, 18 women; 20 have advanced degrees.

Subjects Offered Algebra, American history, American literature, anatomy and physiology, art, art history, biology, biology-AP, calculus, calculus-AP, chemistry, chemistry-AP, drama, economics, English, English language and composition-AP, English literature and composition-AP, ethics, European history, fine arts, French, French language-AP, geography, geometry, government, government-AP, grammar, health, history, Latin American studies, Mandarin, marine biology, mathematics, Middle Eastern history, modern European history-AP, music, music appreciation, music theory, musical theater, physical education, physics, physics-AP, psychology, religion, science, social science, social studies, sociology, Spanish, Spanish language-AP, statistics, theater arts, U.S. government and politics-AP, U.S. history-AP, video film production, Western civilization-AP, world history, world history-AP.

Graduation Requirements Arts and fine arts (art, music, dance, drama), English, foreign language, mathematics, physical education (includes health), religion (includes Bible studies and theology), science, social science, social studies (includes history), 20 hours of community service each year of high school.

Special Academic Programs Advanced Placement exam preparation; honors section; independent study; study at local college for college credit; study abroad; academic accommodation for the gifted, the musically talented, and the artistically talented; ESL (6 students enrolled).

College Admission Counseling 90 students graduated in 2008; all went to college, including Auburn University Montgomery; Florida State University; University of Florida; University of Miami; University of South Carolina; Wake Forest University.

Student Life Upper grades have specified standards of dress, student council, honor system. Discipline rests primarily with faculty. Attendance at religious services is required.

Summer Programs Remediation, enrichment, sports, art/fine arts, computer instruction programs offered; session focuses on lifelong learning; held on campus; accepts boys and girls; open to students from other schools. 2009 schedule: June 15 to August 1.

Tuition and Aid Day student tuition: $7880–$21,060. Tuition installment plan (FACTS Tuition Payment Plan, 1-, 2-, and 10-payment plans). Need-based scholarship grants available. In 2008–09, 26% of upper-school students received aid. Total amount of financial aid awarded in 2008–09: $845,400.

Admissions Traditional secondary-level entrance grade is 9. For fall 2008, 39 students applied for upper-level admission, 36 were accepted, 22 enrolled. SSAT required. Deadline for receipt of application materials: February 15. Application fee required: $50. Interview required.

Athletics Interscholastic: baseball (boys), basketball (b,g), cheering (g), crew (b,g), cross-country running (b,g), football (b), golf (b,g), lacrosse (b,g), soccer (b,g), swimming and diving (b,g), tennis (b,g), track and field (b,g), volleyball (g), weight lifting (b,g); intramural: physical fitness (b,g), sailing (b,g); coed interscholastic: crew, swimming and diving, track and field; coed intramural: outdoor education, physical fitness. 1 PE instructor, 13 coaches, 1 athletic trainer.

Computers Computers are regularly used in all academic classes. Computer network features include on-campus library services, online commercial services, Internet access, wireless campus network, Internet filtering or blocking technology. Campus intranet and student e-mail accounts are available to students. Students grades are available online. The school has a published electronic and media policy.

Contact Mr. Bob Gregg, Director of Admission and Financial Aid. 772-492-2364. Fax: 772-231-2427. E-mail: bgregg@steds.org. Web site: www.steds.org.

ANNOUNCEMENT FROM THE SCHOOL Saint Edward's School is a pre-K–12, independent, coeducational, college-preparatory school with an enrollment of 845 students. Since its founding in 1965, Saint Edward's has been one of the leading independent schools in the state of Florida. Located 2 miles apart on 33 acres in Vero Beach, two campuses are situated between the Indian River lagoon and the Atlantic Ocean, providing a unique learning environment for students. The Lower School campus (pre-K–grade 5: 360 students) is located on Club Drive adjacent to the Riomar Country Club, while the Middle and Upper School campus (grades 6–12: 485 students) is located on Saint Edward's Drive off of A1A. Saint Edward's is committed to educational excellence through an environment of advocacy that promotes a lifelong passion for learning. Small class sizes, experienced faculty, and first-rate academic facilities offer Saint Edward's students an opportunity to excel in the classroom. The School offers numerous extracurricular opportunities in interscholastic athletics, fine and performing arts, music, student clubs, and community service. A strong Episcopal tradition cultivates moral courage and spiritual growth. Members of the class of 2008 were accepted at Auburn, Boston College, Bucknell, Clemson, Duke, Elon, Florida State, Georgetown, Northwestern, Rollins, Stanford, Stetson, Vanderbilt, and Wake Forest and the Universities of Florida, Maryland, Miami, Mississippi, North Carolina at Chapel Hill, Pennsylvania, South Carolina, and Virginia. The admission deadline is February 15, with applicant notification on March 15. Late applications for all grades are reviewed if space is available. Financial aid applications are due February 1. Financial aid is awarded on a need basis to 26% of the student body.

SAINT ELIZABETH HIGH SCHOOL

1530 34th Avenue
Oakland, California 94601

Head of School: Sr. Mary Liam Brock, OP

General Information Coeducational day college-preparatory, arts, and religious studies school, affiliated with Roman Catholic Church. Grades 9–12. Founded: 1921. Setting: urban. Nearest major city is Berkeley. 2-acre campus. 1 building on campus. Approved or accredited by National Catholic Education Association, Western Association of Schools and Colleges, and California Department of Education. Endowment: $580,000. Total enrollment: 225. Upper school average class size: 17. Upper school faculty-student ratio: 1:15.
Upper School Student Profile Grade 9: 51 students (27 boys, 24 girls); Grade 10: 47 students (23 boys, 24 girls); Grade 11: 77 students (42 boys, 35 girls); Grade 12: 50 students (30 boys, 20 girls). 65% of students are Roman Catholic.
Faculty School total: 22. In upper school: 10 men, 12 women; 14 have advanced degrees.
Subjects Offered Advanced math, algebra, American literature, American literature-AP, anatomy and physiology, art and culture, biology, British literature, business mathematics, calculus-AP, Catholic belief and practice, chemistry, Christian and Hebrew scripture, Christian testament, civics, composition, computer applications, computer graphics, computer literacy, creative writing, dance, desktop publishing, drama, drawing and design, economics, economics and history, English, English literature and composition-AP, geometry, journalism, learning strategies, moral and social development, physical education, physical science, physics, pre-algebra, pre-calculus, psychology, social justice, Spanish, Spanish language-AP, Spanish literature-AP, speech, speech communications, trigonometry, U.S. history, Web site design, world cultures, world geography, world history, world religions.
Graduation Requirements Arts and fine arts (art, music, dance, drama), electives, English, foreign language, mathematics, physical education (includes health), religious studies, science, social science, 100 hours of community service.
Special Academic Programs 2 Advanced Placement exams for which test preparation is offered; honors section; remedial reading and/or remedial writing; remedial math; programs in English, mathematics for dyslexic students; special instructional classes for students with learning disabilities, Attention Deficit Disorder, dyslexia, and emotional and behavioral problems.
College Admission Counseling 57 students graduated in 2008; 56 went to college, including California State University, East Bay; San Francisco State University; San Jose State University; University of California, Berkeley. Other: 1 went to work.
Student Life Upper grades have specified standards of dress, honor system. Discipline rests primarily with faculty. Attendance at religious services is required.
Summer Programs Remediation programs offered; session focuses on academics; held on campus; accepts boys and girls; not open to students from other schools. 50 students usually enrolled. 2009 schedule: June 20 to July 19. Application deadline: June 1.
Tuition and Aid Day student tuition: $9000. Tuition reduction for siblings, merit scholarship grants, need-based scholarship grants available. In 2008–09, 74% of upper-school students received aid; total upper-school merit-scholarship money awarded: $42,000. Total amount of financial aid awarded in 2008–09: $450,000.
Admissions Traditional secondary-level entrance grade is 9. For fall 2008, 88 students applied for upper-level admission, 73 were accepted, 58 enrolled. High School Placement Test required. Deadline for receipt of application materials: none. Application fee required: $75. Interview required.
Athletics Interscholastic: baseball (boys), basketball (b,g), football (b), soccer (b,g), softball (g), track and field (b,g), volleyball (b,g). 1 PE instructor, 5 coaches.
Computers Computer network features include on-campus library services, Internet access, wireless campus network, Internet filtering or blocking technology. Students grades are available online. The school has a published electronic and media policy.
Contact Lillie Fitzpatrick, Secretary. 510-532-8947 Ext. 0. Fax: 510-532-9754. E-mail: lfitzpatrick@stliz-hs.org. Web site: www.stliz-hs.org.

ST. FRANCIS DE SALES HIGH SCHOOL

2323 West Bancroft Street
Toledo, Ohio 43607

Head of School: Mr. Eric J. Smola

General Information Boys' day college-preparatory, religious studies, and AP Courses school, affiliated with Roman Catholic Church. Grades 9–12. Founded: 1955. Setting: urban. Nearest major city is Cleveland. 25-acre campus. 1 building on campus. Approved or accredited by Ohio Catholic Schools Accreditation Association (OCSAA) and Ohio Department of Education. Endowment: $6.9 million. Total enrollment: 617. Upper school average class size: 24. Upper school faculty-student ratio: 1:14.
Upper School Student Profile Grade 9: 186 students (186 boys); Grade 10: 151 students (151 boys); Grade 11: 143 students (143 boys); Grade 12: 137 students (137 boys). 72% of students are Roman Catholic.
Faculty School total: 61. In upper school: 45 men, 16 women; 33 have advanced degrees.
Subjects Offered Advanced Placement courses, algebra, American government-AP, American history, American history-AP, American literature, American literature-AP, anatomy, art, biology, biology-AP, calculus, calculus-AP, chemistry, chemistry-AP, Chinese, chorus, church history, community service, computer programming, computer science, creative writing, criminal justice, economics, English literature, English-AP, environmental science, expository writing, French, French-AP, geometry, German, German-AP, government/civics, grammar, graphic arts, health, Latin, Latin-AP, macroeconomics-AP, math analysis, mathematics, microeconomics-AP, military history, music, New Testament, physical education, physical science, physics, physics-AP, physiology, pre-algebra, pre-calculus, psychology, psychology-AP, science, social justice, social studies, Spanish, Spanish-AP, statistics, theology, trigonometry, U.S. government, U.S. history, U.S. history-AP, Web site design, world history, world literature, yearbook.
Graduation Requirements Art, computer science, English, foreign language, mathematics, physical education (includes health), religion (includes Bible studies and theology), science, social studies (includes history), participation in religious retreats 4 of 4 years. Community service is required.
Special Academic Programs Advanced Placement exam preparation; honors section; study at local college for college credit.
College Admission Counseling 140 students graduated in 2008; 138 went to college, including Bowling Green State University; Miami University; Ohio University; The Ohio State University; The University of Toledo; University of Dayton. Other: 2 entered military service. Mean SAT critical reading: 545, mean SAT math: 558, mean SAT writing: 527, mean composite ACT: 24.
Student Life Upper grades have specified standards of dress, student council. Discipline rests primarily with faculty. Attendance at religious services is required.
Summer Programs Remediation, enrichment programs offered; session focuses on mathematics, English, reading; held on campus; accepts boys; not open to students from other schools. 100 students usually enrolled. 2009 schedule: June 15 to July 10. Application deadline: June 1.
Tuition and Aid Day student tuition: $7950. Tuition installment plan (monthly payment plans, quarterly payment plan). Tuition reduction for siblings, merit scholarship grants, need-based scholarship grants, paying campus jobs available. In 2008–09, 69% of upper-school students received aid; total upper-school merit-scholarship money awarded: $441,127. Total amount of financial aid awarded in 2008–09: $1,051,630.
Admissions Traditional secondary-level entrance grade is 9. For fall 2008, 236 students applied for upper-level admission, 227 were accepted, 193 enrolled. STS required. Deadline for receipt of application materials: none. Application fee required: $200. Interview required.
Athletics Interscholastic: baseball, basketball, bowling, crew, cross-country running, diving, football, golf, ice hockey, lacrosse, soccer, swimming and diving, tennis, track and field, water polo, winter (indoor) track, wrestling; intramural: basketball, football. 24 coaches, 1 athletic trainer.
Computers Computers are regularly used in animation, art, desktop publishing, English, mathematics, science, Web site design classes. Computer network features include on-campus library services, Internet access. Student e-mail accounts are available to students. Students grades are available online. The school has a published electronic and media policy.
Contact Mrs. Jacqueline VanDemark, Administrative Assistant. 419-531-1618. Fax: 419-531-9740. E-mail: jvandemark@sfstoledo.org. Web site: www.sfstoledo.org.

SAINT FRANCIS HIGH SCHOOL

1885 Miramonte Avenue
Mountain View, California 94040

Head of School: Mr. Kevin Makley

General Information Coeducational day college-preparatory, arts, religious studies, and technology school, affiliated with Roman Catholic Church, Advent Christian Church. Grades 9–12. Founded: 1954. Setting: suburban. Nearest major city is San Jose. 25-acre campus. 8 buildings on campus. Approved or accredited by Western Association of Schools and Colleges and California Department of Education. Total enrollment: 1,666. Upper school average class size: 29. Upper school faculty-student ratio: 1:29.
Upper School Student Profile Grade 9: 449 students (224 boys, 225 girls); Grade 10: 415 students (207 boys, 208 girls); Grade 11: 407 students (196 boys, 211 girls); Grade 12: 395 students (188 boys, 207 girls). 70% of students are Roman Catholic, Advent Christian Church.
Faculty In upper school: 51 men, 45 women; 52 have advanced degrees.
Subjects Offered 20th century American writers, 3-dimensional design, accounting, algebra, American literature, analytic geometry, anatomy and physiology, Arabic studies, band, biology, biology-AP, British literature, British literature (honors), business, calculus-AP, chemistry, chemistry-AP, Christianity, computer graphics,

computer literacy, computer programming, computer science, computer science-AP, concert band, concert choir, contemporary issues, contemporary problems, creative writing, design, drama, drawing, economics, electronic music, English, English literature-AP, film and literature, French, French-AP, geography, geometry, German, German-AP, global science, graphics, health science, human biology, information technology, Irish literature, jazz band, jazz ensemble, journalism, music, oil painting, philosophy, physical education, physical science, pre-calculus, printmaking, psychology, religious studies, science fiction, short story, social justice, Spanish, Spanish-AP, speech, statistics, symphonic band, technical drawing, technology, trigonometry, typing, U.S. government, U.S. government-AP, U.S. history, U.S. history-AP, water color painting, word processing, world history, world religions.

Graduation Requirements Computer literacy, English, foreign language, human biology, mathematics, physical education (includes health), religious studies, science, social studies (includes history).

Special Academic Programs Advanced Placement exam preparation; honors section; study at local college for college credit.

College Admission Counseling 368 students graduated in 2008; all went to college, including Loyola Marymount University; Stanford University; University of California, Berkeley; University of California, Los Angeles. Mean SAT critical reading: 684, mean SAT math: 733, mean SAT writing: 694.

Student Life Upper grades have specified standards of dress, student council. Discipline rests primarily with faculty. Attendance at religious services is required.

Summer Programs Remediation, enrichment, advancement, sports, art/fine arts, computer instruction programs offered; session focuses on academics and fun; held on campus; accepts boys and girls; open to students from other schools. 1,000 students usually enrolled. 2009 schedule: June 15 to July 24. Application deadline: June 10.

Tuition and Aid Day student tuition: $12,200. Tuition installment plan (monthly payment plans, individually arranged payment plans). Need-based scholarship grants, paying campus jobs available. In 2008–09, 18% of upper-school students received aid. Total amount of financial aid awarded in 2008–09: $1,100,000.

Admissions Traditional secondary-level entrance grade is 9. For fall 2008, 1,235 students applied for upper-level admission, 650 were accepted, 462 enrolled. High School Placement Test required. Deadline for receipt of application materials: December 17. Application fee required: $65. On-campus interview required.

Athletics Interscholastic: aquatics (boys, girls), baseball (b,g), basketball (b,g), cheering (g), cross-country running (b,g), dance squad (g), diving (b,g), drill team (b,g), field hockey (g), football (b), golf (b,g), gymnastics (g), lacrosse (b,g), soccer (b,g), softball (g), strength & conditioning (b,g), swimming and diving (b,g), track and field (b,g), volleyball (b,g), water polo (b,g), wrestling (b); intramural: cooperative games (b,g), crew (g), dance (b,g), dance squad (b,g), flag football (b,g), floor hockey (b,g), indoor soccer (b,g), jogging (b,g), physical fitness (b,g), rugby (b,g), soccer (b,g), softball (b,g), strength & conditioning (b,g), swimming and diving (b,g), table tennis (b,g), touch football (b,g), track and field (b,g), ultimate Frisbee (b,g), volleyball (b,g), weight lifting (b,g); coed interscholastic: cheering; coed intramural: basketball, cooperative games, dance, dance squad, Frisbee. 6 PE instructors, 51 coaches, 1 athletic trainer.

Computers Computers are regularly used in creative writing, current events, graphic arts, graphic design, photography, publications classes. Computer network features include on-campus library services, Internet access, wireless campus network, Internet filtering or blocking technology. Campus intranet, student e-mail accounts, and computer access in designated common areas are available to students. Students grades are available online.

Contact Mr. Michael Speckman, Director of Admissions. 650-968-1213 Ext. 213. Fax: 650-968-1706. E-mail: mispeckm@sfhs.com. Web site: www.sfhs.com.

ST. FRANCIS HIGH SCHOOL

233 West Broadway
Louisville, Kentucky 40202

Head of School: Ms. Alexandra Schreiber Thurstone

General Information Coeducational day college-preparatory and arts school. Grades 9–12. Founded: 1976. Setting: urban. 2-acre campus. 1 building on campus. Approved or accredited by Independent Schools Association of the Central States and Kentucky Department of Education. Member of National Association of Independent Schools. Endowment: $1 million. Total enrollment: 126. Upper school average class size: 11. Upper school faculty-student ratio: 1:7.

Upper School Student Profile Grade 9: 21 students (10 boys, 11 girls); Grade 10: 32 students (13 boys, 19 girls); Grade 11: 41 students (24 boys, 17 girls); Grade 12: 32 students (18 boys, 14 girls).

Faculty School total: 21. In upper school: 12 men, 9 women; 16 have advanced degrees.

Subjects Offered African studies, algebra, American history, ancient history, ancient world history, art, biology, biology-AP, business, calculus, calculus-AP, chemistry, chemistry-AP, Chinese, Chinese history, civil rights, community service, creative writing, drama, drawing, English, English literature, English literature-AP, environmental science, environmental science-AP, European history, European history-AP, filmmaking, fine arts, finite math, French, French language-AP, French literature-AP, French-AP, gender and religion, gender issues, geometry, health, history-AP, journalism, law, medieval history, modern civilization, photography, physical education, physics, physics-AP, playwriting, pre-calculus, senior project, Spanish, Spanish language-AP, Spanish literature-AP, Spanish-AP, statistics, statistics-AP, The 20th Century, U.S. history-AP, world history, writing, zoology.

Graduation Requirements Arts and fine arts (art, music, dance, drama), English, foreign language, history, mathematics, physical education (includes health), science, senior project (year-long research project on a topic of student's choice). Community service is required.

Special Academic Programs Advanced Placement exam preparation; independent study; study abroad; academic accommodation for the gifted and the artistically talented.

College Admission Counseling 34 students graduated in 2008; 33 went to college. Other: 1 had other specific plans.

Student Life Upper grades have student council. Discipline rests equally with students and faculty.

Summer Programs Remediation, enrichment, advancement, sports programs offered; session focuses on enrichment; held on campus; accepts boys and girls; open to students from other schools. 40 students usually enrolled. 2009 schedule: June 1 to August 13. Application deadline: April 1.

Tuition and Aid Day student tuition: $15,800. Tuition installment plan (Insured Tuition Payment Plan, FACTS Tuition Payment Plan, monthly payment plans). Merit scholarship grants, need-based scholarship grants, tuition remission for children of faculty and staff available. In 2008–09, 48% of upper-school students received aid; total upper-school merit-scholarship money awarded: $44,710. Total amount of financial aid awarded in 2008–09: $615,000.

Admissions Traditional secondary-level entrance grade is 9. For fall 2008, 47 students applied for upper-level admission, 42 were accepted, 39 enrolled. Deadline for receipt of application materials: January 15. Application fee required: $50. On-campus interview required.

Athletics Interscholastic: basketball (boys, girls), field hockey (g), lacrosse (b), running (b,g), tennis (b,g), track and field (b,g), volleyball (g); intramural: indoor hockey (g), indoor soccer (b); coed interscholastic: indoor track & field, soccer; coed intramural: dance team, fitness, physical fitness, physical training, power lifting, racquetball, rowing, ultimate Frisbee, wall climbing, wallyball, weight lifting, weight training, yoga. 1 PE instructor, 12 coaches.

Computers Computers are regularly used in English, French, history, mathematics, science, Spanish classes. Computer network features include Internet access, wireless campus network, word processing, publishing, and Web page programs. Student e-mail accounts and computer access in designated common areas are available to students. The school has a published electronic and media policy.

Contact Ms. Stephanie Darst, Director of Admissions and Marketing. 502-736-1009. Fax: 502-736-1049. E-mail: darst@stfrancishighschool.com. Web site: www.stfrancishighschool.com.

ST. FRANCIS SCHOOL

13440 Cogburn Road
Alpharetta, Georgia 30004

Head of School: Mr. Drew Buccellato

General Information Coeducational day college-preparatory, arts, and technology school. Grades K–12. Founded: 1976. Setting: suburban. Nearest major city is Atlanta. 43-acre campus. 5 buildings on campus. Approved or accredited by Georgia Accrediting Commission, Georgia Independent School Association, Southern Association of Colleges and Schools, and Southern Association of Independent Schools. Endowment: $2 million. Total enrollment: 827. Upper school average class size: 14. Upper school faculty-student ratio: 1:14.

Upper School Student Profile Grade 9: 73 students (53 boys, 20 girls); Grade 10: 79 students (41 boys, 38 girls); Grade 11: 70 students (39 boys, 31 girls); Grade 12: 65 students (38 boys, 27 girls).

Faculty School total: 52. In upper school: 18 men, 34 women; 22 have advanced degrees.

Subjects Offered Algebra, American literature, art-AP, biology, British literature, calculus, character education, cheerleading, chemistry, chorus, college counseling, computer processing, computer programming, drama, drawing, economics, English, English literature-AP, English-AP, geography, geometry, government, graphic design, health, history-AP, honors algebra, honors English, honors geometry, honors U.S. history, honors world history, instrumental music, journalism, keyboarding, Latin, mathematics, newspaper, painting, physical education, physical science, physics, play production, psychology, public speaking, SAT preparation, science, social studies, Spanish, studio art, study skills, trigonometry, U.S. government, U.S. government-AP, U.S. history, U.S. history-AP, word processing, world history, writing, yearbook.

Graduation Requirements Arts and fine arts (art, music, dance, drama), electives, English, foreign language, mathematics, physical education (includes health), science, social studies (includes history), technology, writing, community service hours.

Special Academic Programs Honors section; study at local college for college credit; remedial reading and/or remedial writing; remedial math; special instructional classes for students with learning disabilities and Attention Deficit Disorder.

College Admission Counseling 82 students graduated in 2008; they went to Kennesaw State University; The University of Alabama; University of Georgia.

Student Life Upper grades have uniform requirement, student council, honor system. Discipline rests primarily with faculty.

Tuition and Aid Day student tuition: $16,900. Tuition installment plan (FACTS Tuition Payment Plan). Tuition reduction for siblings, need-based scholarship grants available. In 2008–09, 4% of upper-school students received aid. Total amount of financial aid awarded in 2008–09: $80,000.

Admissions Traditional secondary-level entrance grade is 9. For fall 2008, 75 students applied for upper-level admission, 47 were accepted, 39 enrolled. School placement exam required. Deadline for receipt of application materials: none. Application fee required: $100. On-campus interview required.

Athletics Interscholastic: baseball (boys), basketball (b,g), cheering (g), equestrian sports (g), golf (b), physical fitness (b,g), soccer (b,g), softball (g), swimming and diving (b,g), volleyball (g), wrestling (b); intramural: equestrian sports (g), horseback riding (g); coed interscholastic: cross-country running, swimming and diving, tennis, track and field, weight lifting. 3 PE instructors, 6 coaches, 1 athletic trainer.

Computers Computers are regularly used in English, graphic design, journalism, keyboarding, newspaper, research skills, science, typing, word processing, writing, yearbook classes. Computer network features include on-campus library services, Internet access, Internet filtering or blocking technology. Students grades are available online. The school has a published electronic and media policy.

Contact Mr. Brandon Bryan, Asst. Admissions Director. 678-339-9989 Ext. 33. Fax: 678-339-0473. E-mail: bbryan@stfranschool.com. Web site: www.saintfrancischools.com.

SAINT FRANCIS SCHOOL

2707 Pamoa Road
Honolulu, Hawaii 96822

Head of School: Sr. Joan of Arc Souza

General Information Coeducational day (boys' only in lower grades) college-preparatory, general academic, arts, business, religious studies, bilingual studies, technology, and ESL school, affiliated with Roman Cathoiic Church. Boys grades K–8, girls grades K–12. Founded: 1924. Setting: suburban. 11-acre campus. 8 buildings on campus. Approved or accredited by Western Association of Schools and Colleges, Western Catholic Education Association, and Hawaii Department of Education. Total enrollment: 353. Upper school average class size: 20. Upper school faculty-student ratio: 1:20.

Upper School Student Profile Grade 6: 8 students (3 boys, 5 girls); Grade 7: 32 students (11 boys, 21 girls); Grade 8: 33 students (5 boys, 28 girls); Grade 9: 65 students (65 girls); Grade 10: 51 students (51 girls); Grade 11: 58 students (58 girls); Grade 12: 65 students (65 girls). 65% of students are Roman Catholic.

Faculty School total: 27. In upper school: 9 men, 14 women; 18 have advanced degrees.

Subjects Offered Algebra, American history, American history-AP, American literature, ancient history, art, Asian history, band, Bible studies, biology, ceramics, chemistry, chemistry-AP, chorus, college admission preparation, college counseling, college planning, community service, computer literacy, computer programming, computer technologies, creative writing, drama, earth science, English, English literature, English literature-AP, environmental science, ESL, European history, family life, fine arts, geography, geometry, government and politics-AP, government/civics, grammar, health, history, humanities, Japanese, journalism, keyboarding, marine biology, mathematics, medieval/Renaissance history, music, newspaper, photography, physical education, physical science, physics, psychology, religion, science, social studies, sociology, Spanish, Spanish language-AP, speech, theater, trigonometry, world history, world literature, writing, yearbook.

Graduation Requirements Algebra, American history, American literature, arts and fine arts (art, music, dance, drama), biology, business skills (includes word processing), computer applications, computer keyboarding, computer literacy, English, foreign language, humanities, mathematics, physical education (includes health), religion (includes Bible studies and theology), science, social studies (includes history), U.S. history. Community service is required.

Special Academic Programs Advanced Placement exam preparation; honors section; independent study; study at local college for college credit; special instructional classes for deaf students; ESL (4 students enrolled).

College Admission Counseling 79 students graduated in 2008; 75 went to college, including Chaminade University of Honolulu; Hawai'i Pacific University; Seattle University; Southern Oregon University; University of Hawaii at Manoa; University of Oregon. Other: 4 had other specific plans.

Student Life Upper grades have uniform requirement, student council, honor system. Discipline rests primarily with faculty. Attendance at religious services is required.

Summer Programs Remediation, enrichment, ESL, computer instruction programs offered; held on campus; accepts boys and girls; open to students from other schools. 80 students usually enrolled. 2009 schedule: June 13 to July 11.

Tuition and Aid Day student tuition: $8600. Guaranteed tuition plan. Tuition installment plan (FACTS Tuition Payment Plan, individually arranged payment plans, quarterly, semiannual, and full payment plans, SFS/Damien discount plan). Tuition reduction for siblings, merit scholarship grants, need-based scholarship grants, alumni scholarships available. Total upper-school merit-scholarship money awarded for 2008–09: $15,450. Total amount of financial aid awarded in 2008–09: $80,620.

Admissions Traditional secondary-level entrance grade is 9. For fall 2008, 184 students applied for upper-level admission, 150 were accepted, 82 enrolled. School placement exam or SSAT required. Deadline for receipt of application materials: none. Application fee required: $40. Interview required.

Athletics Interscholastic: archery (girls), basketball (g), bowling (g), canoeing/kayaking (g), cheering (g), cross-country running (g), diving (g), golf (g), JROTC drill (g), kayaking (g), ocean paddling (g), paddling (g), riflery (g), running (g), soccer (g), softball (g), swimming and diving (g), tennis (g), track and field (g), volleyball (g), water polo (g), weight training (g), wrestling (g). 1 PE instructor, 30 coaches.

Computers Computers are regularly used in English, foreign language, mathematics, music, newspaper, religion, science, yearbook classes. Computer network features include on-campus library services, Internet access, wireless campus network, Internet filtering or blocking technology, database, word processing and spreadsheet applications, Web programming, web design. Computer access in designated common areas is available to students. Students grades are available online.

Contact Karen Curry, Director of Admissions. 808-988-4111 Ext. 712. Fax: 808-988-5497. E-mail: kcurry@stfrancis-oahu.org. Web site: www.stfrancis-oahu.org.

ST. GEORGE'S INDEPENDENT SCHOOL

1880 Wolf River Road
Collierville, Tennessee 38117

Head of School: Mr. William W. Taylor

General Information Coeducational day college-preparatory school, affiliated with Christian faith. Grades PK–12. Founded: 1959. Setting: suburban. Nearest major city is Memphis. 125-acre campus. 5 buildings on campus. Approved or accredited by Southern Association of Colleges and Schools and Southern Association of Independent Schools. Endowment: $2.2 million. Total enrollment: 1,235. Upper school average class size: 20. Upper school faculty-student ratio: 1:9.

Upper School Student Profile Grade 9: 106 students (47 boys, 59 girls); Grade 10: 102 students (54 boys, 48 girls); Grade 11: 84 students (49 boys, 35 girls); Grade 12: 77 students (38 boys, 39 girls).

Faculty School total: 39. In upper school: 18 men, 21 women; 21 have advanced degrees.

Graduation Requirements Art, electives, English, history, independent study, language, mathematics, religion (includes Bible studies and theology), science, wellness, Senior Independent Study, Senior Global Challenge.

Special Academic Programs Advanced Placement exam preparation; honors section; independent study.

College Admission Counseling 70 students graduated in 2008; all went to college. Mean SAT critical reading: 595, mean SAT math: 584, mean SAT writing: 595, mean composite ACT: 26.

Student Life Upper grades have specified standards of dress, student council, honor system. Discipline rests equally with students and faculty. Attendance at religious services is required.

Summer Programs Remediation, enrichment, advancement, sports, art/fine arts, computer instruction programs offered; session focuses on Enrichment; held on campus; accepts boys and girls; open to students from other schools. 2009 schedule: June to August. Application deadline: June.

Tuition and Aid Day student tuition: $13,982. Need-based scholarship grants available.

Admissions Traditional secondary-level entrance grade is 9. Admissions testing or ISEE required. Deadline for receipt of application materials: none. Application fee required: $100. Interview required.

Athletics Interscholastic: baseball (boys), basketball (b,g), cheering (g), cross-country running (b,g), football (b), golf (b,g), lacrosse (b,g), pom squad (g), soccer (b,g), softball (g), tennis (b,g), track and field (b,g), volleyball (g), wrestling (b); coed interscholastic: swimming and diving; coed intramural: riflery, unicycling. 5 PE instructors, 3 coaches, 2 athletic trainers.

Computers Computers are regularly used in all classes. Computer network features include on-campus library services, Internet access, wireless campus network, Internet filtering or blocking technology, leased laptops for all middle and upper school students. Campus intranet, student e-mail accounts, and computer access in designated common areas are available to students. Students grades are available online. The school has a published electronic and media policy.

Contact Mrs. Julie Loftin, Director of Admissions. 901-457-2150. Fax: 901-457-2111. E-mail: jloftin@sgis.org. Web site: www.sgsi.org.

ST. GEORGE'S SCHOOL

372 Purgatory Road
Middletown, Rhode Island 02842-5984

Head of School: Eric F. Peterson

General Information Coeducational boarding and day college-preparatory, arts, religious studies, technology, and marine sciences school, affiliated with Episcopal Church. Grades 9–12. Founded: 1896. Setting: suburban. Nearest major city is Providence. Students are housed in single-sex dormitories. 150-acre campus. 43 buildings on campus. Approved or accredited by Association of Independent Schools in New England, National Association of Episcopal Schools, New England Association of Schools and Colleges, The Association of Boarding Schools, and Rhode Island Department of Education. Member of National Association of Independent Schools and Secondary School Admission Test Board. Endowment: $115 million. Total enrollment: 357. Upper school average class size: 11. Upper school faculty-student ratio: 1:5.

Upper School Student Profile Grade 9: 72 students (33 boys, 39 girls); Grade 10: 98 students (44 boys, 54 girls); Grade 11: 97 students (48 boys, 49 girls); Grade 12: 90 students (42 boys, 48 girls). 87% of students are boarding students. 22% are state residents. 30 states are represented in upper school student body. 10% are international students. International students from Bermuda, China, Republic of Korea, and Thailand; 10 other countries represented in student body.
Faculty School total: 61. In upper school: 34 men, 27 women; 50 have advanced degrees; 55 reside on campus.
Subjects Offered Acting, algebra, American history, American literature, architecture, art, art history, Asian studies, astronomy, Bible studies, biology, calculus, ceramics, chemistry, computer graphics, computer math, computer programming, computer science, creative writing, dance, drama, driver education, ecology, economics, English, English literature, environmental science, ethics, European history, expository writing, fine arts, French, geometry, government/civics, grammar, health, history, journalism, Latin, law, logic, Mandarin, marine biology, mathematics, microbiology, music, navigation, oceanography, philosophy, photography, physics, psychology, public speaking, religion, science, sculpture, social studies, Spanish, statistics, theater, theology, trigonometry, veterinary science, world history, world literature, writing.
Graduation Requirements Arts and fine arts (art, music, dance, drama), computer science, English, foreign language, mathematics, physical education (includes health), religion (includes Bible studies and theology), science, social studies (includes history).
Special Academic Programs Advanced Placement exam preparation; honors section; independent study; term-away projects; study abroad; academic accommodation for the gifted, the musically talented, and the artistically talented.
College Admission Counseling 85 students graduated in 2008; all went to college, including Connecticut College; Georgetown University; Gettysburg College; Smith College; Wake Forest University. Mean SAT critical reading: 624, mean SAT math: 641, mean combined SAT: 1265.
Student Life Upper grades have specified standards of dress, student council, honor system. Discipline rests primarily with faculty. Attendance at religious services is required.
Tuition and Aid Day student tuition: $28,000; 7-day tuition and room/board: $41,000. Tuition installment plan (Insured Tuition Payment Plan, Academic Management Services Plan, Key Tuition Payment Plan, monthly payment plans, individually arranged payment plans). Need-based scholarship grants, need-based loans, middle-income loans available. In 2008–09, 32% of upper-school students received aid. Total amount of financial aid awarded in 2008–09: $2,700,000.
Admissions Traditional secondary-level entrance grade is 9. For fall 2008, 775 students applied for upper-level admission, 212 were accepted, 102 enrolled. ISEE, PSAT, SSAT or TOEFL required. Deadline for receipt of application materials: February 1. Application fee required: $50. Interview required.
Athletics Interscholastic: baseball (boys), basketball (b,g), cross-country running (b,g), field hockey (g), football (b), ice hockey (b,g), lacrosse (b,g), sailing (b,g), soccer (b,g), softball (g), squash (b,g), swimming and diving (b,g), tennis (b,g), track and field (b,g); coed interscholastic: dance, sailing; coed intramural: aerobics/dance, dance, modern dance, mountain biking, Nautilus, soccer, softball, squash, strength & conditioning. 2 coaches, 1 athletic trainer.
Computers Computers are regularly used in art, English, foreign language, history, mathematics, music, religion, science, theater classes. Computer network features include on-campus library services, online commercial services, Internet access, wireless campus network, Internet filtering or blocking technology, scanners, digital cameras, and access to printers. Campus intranet, student e-mail accounts, and computer access in designated common areas are available to students. Students grades are available online. The school has a published electronic and media policy.
Contact James A. Hamilton, Director of Admission. 401-842-6600. Fax: 401-842-6696. E-mail: admission@stgeorges.edu. Web site: www.stgeorges.edu.

See Close-Up on page 930.

SAINT GEORGE'S SCHOOL

2929 West Waikiki Road
Spokane, Washington 99208

Head of School: Mo Copeland

General Information Coeducational day college-preparatory, arts, and technology school. Grades K–12. Founded: 1955. Setting: suburban. 120-acre campus. 10 buildings on campus. Approved or accredited by Northwest Association of Schools and Colleges, Pacific Northwest Association of Independent Schools, and Washington Department of Education. Member of National Association of Independent Schools. Endowment: $3 million. Total enrollment: 398. Upper school average class size: 15. Upper school faculty-student ratio: 1:7.
Upper School Student Profile Grade 9: 30 students (18 boys, 12 girls); Grade 10: 40 students (26 boys, 14 girls); Grade 11: 44 students (22 boys, 22 girls); Grade 12: 30 students (20 boys, 10 girls).
Faculty School total: 47. In upper school: 14 men, 9 women; 12 have advanced degrees.
Subjects Offered Algebra, American history, American literature, art, biology, calculus, ceramics, chemistry, community service, computer science, creative writing, drama, earth science, ecology, economics, English, English literature, environmental science, European history, fine arts, French, geography, geometry, grammar, health, history, humanities, journalism, Mandarin, mathematics, music, photography, physical education, physical science, physics, science, social studies, Spanish, theater, trigonometry, world history, writing.
Graduation Requirements Arts and fine arts (art, music, dance, drama), computer science, English, foreign language, history, mathematics, physical education (includes health), science. Community service is required.
Special Academic Programs Advanced Placement exam preparation; honors section; study at local college for college credit.
College Admission Counseling 41 students graduated in 2008; 40 went to college, including Embry-Riddle Aeronautical University; Middlebury College; Stanford University; The University of Montana–Western; University of Washington; Western Washington University. Other: 1 entered military service. Mean SAT critical reading: 597, mean SAT math: 618, mean SAT writing: 603, mean combined SAT: 1893.
Student Life Upper grades have student council, honor system. Discipline rests equally with students and faculty.
Tuition and Aid Day student tuition: $16,220. Tuition installment plan (Insured Tuition Payment Plan, monthly payment plans, individually arranged payment plans). Merit scholarship grants, need-based scholarship grants available. In 2008–09, 26% of upper-school students received aid; total upper-school merit-scholarship money awarded: $19,220. Total amount of financial aid awarded in 2008–09: $301,781.
Admissions Traditional secondary-level entrance grade is 9. For fall 2008, 27 students applied for upper-level admission, 17 were accepted, 14 enrolled. School's own test or TOEFL required. Deadline for receipt of application materials: none. Application fee required: $50. On-campus interview required.
Athletics Interscholastic: baseball (boys), basketball (b,g), cross-country running (b,g), soccer (b), softball (g), tennis (b,g), track and field (b,g), volleyball (g); coed interscholastic: rock climbing. 3 PE instructors, 10 coaches.
Computers Computers are regularly used in all academic classes. Computer network features include on-campus library services, Internet access. Computer access in designated common areas is available to students. Students grades are available online. The school has a published electronic and media policy.
Contact Debra Duvoisin, Director of Admissions. 509-466-1636 Ext. 304. Fax: 509-467-3258. E-mail: debbie.duvoisin@sgs.org. Web site: www.sgs.org.

ST. GEORGE'S SCHOOL

4175 West 29th Avenue
Vancouver, British Columbia V6S 1V1, Canada

Head of School: Mr. Nigel R. L. Toy

General Information Boys' boarding and day college-preparatory, arts, bilingual studies, and technology school. Boarding grades 6–12, day grades 1–12. Founded: 1930. Setting: suburban. Students are housed in single-sex dormitories. 27-acre campus. 1 building on campus. Approved or accredited by Canadian Association of Independent Schools, The Association of Boarding Schools, and British Columbia Department of Education. Affiliate member of National Association of Independent Schools; member of Secondary School Admission Test Board. Language of instruction: English. Total enrollment: 1,157. Upper school average class size: 19. Upper school faculty-student ratio: 1:10.
Upper School Student Profile Grade 8: 144 students (144 boys); Grade 9: 149 students (149 boys); Grade 10: 157 students (157 boys); Grade 11: 156 students (156 boys); Grade 12: 155 students (155 boys). 18% of students are boarding students. 91% are province residents. 9 provinces are represented in upper school student body. 9% are international students. International students from Germany, Hong Kong, Mexico, Republic of Korea, Taiwan, and United States; 4 other countries represented in student body.
Faculty School total: 130. In upper school: 63 men, 23 women; 35 have advanced degrees; 9 reside on campus.
Subjects Offered Advanced chemistry, advanced computer applications, advanced math, algebra, analysis and differential calculus, applied arts, applied music, applied skills, architecture, art, art history, art history-AP, biology, biology-AP, business, business skills, calculus, calculus-AP, Canadian geography, Canadian history, Canadian literature, career and personal planning, ceramics, chemistry, chemistry-AP, comparative government and politics-AP, computer graphics, computer programming, computer programming-AP, computer science, computer science-AP, creative writing, critical thinking, debate, drama, drama performance, dramatic arts, earth science, economics, economics-AP, English, English literature, English literature-AP, environmental science, European history, expository writing, film, fine arts, French, French-AP, geography, geology, geometry, German, German-AP, government/civics, grammar, history, industrial arts, introduction to theater, Japanese, journalism, Latin, Latin-AP, law, library, Mandarin, mathematics, mathematics-AP, music, music-AP, performing arts, photography, physical education, physical fitness, physics, physics-AP, psychology, psychology-AP, science, social studies, society, politics and law, Spanish, Spanish-AP, speech and debate, studio art, studio art-AP, technical theater, theater, trigonometry, typing, U.S. history-AP, United States government-AP, Western civilization, world history, world literature, writing.
Graduation Requirements Arts and fine arts (art, music, dance, drama), business skills (includes word processing), English, foreign language, mathematics, physical education (includes health), science, social studies (includes history).
Special Academic Programs Advanced Placement exam preparation; honors section; remedial reading and/or remedial writing.

College Admission Counseling 155 students graduated in 2008; 152 went to college, including McGill University; Queen's University at Kingston; The University of British Columbia; The University of Western Ontario; University of Toronto; University of Victoria.
Student Life Upper grades have uniform requirement, student council, honor system. Discipline rests primarily with faculty.
Summer Programs Advancement, ESL, sports, art/fine arts, computer instruction programs offered; session focuses on recreation and enrichment; held both on and off campus; held at other schools in area (outdoor education); accepts boys and girls; open to students from other schools. 1,000 students usually enrolled. 2009 schedule: July 2 to August 15. Application deadline: none.
Tuition and Aid Day student tuition: CAN$14,200–CAN$24,675; 7-day tuition and room/board: CAN$34,975–CAN$43,175. Tuition installment plan (monthly payment plans, individually arranged payment plans, term payment plan, 1-time payment plan). Tuition reduction for siblings, bursaries, merit scholarship grants, need-based scholarship grants available. In 2008–09, 12% of upper-school students received aid; total upper-school merit-scholarship money awarded: CAN$75,000. Total amount of financial aid awarded in 2008–09: CAN$800,000.
Admissions Traditional secondary-level entrance grade is 8. For fall 2008, 250 students applied for upper-level admission, 90 were accepted, 50 enrolled. School's own exam and SSAT required. Deadline for receipt of application materials: February 10. Application fee required: CAN$200. Interview required.
Athletics Interscholastic: badminton, basketball, cricket, cross-country running, field hockey, golf, ice hockey, rowing, rugby, soccer, swimming and diving, tennis, track and field, triathlon, volleyball, water polo; intramural: badminton, ball hockey, basketball, bicycling, canoeing/kayaking, cross-country running, flag football, floor hockey, ice hockey, martial arts, outdoor education, outdoor recreation, physical fitness, rugby, running, sailing, skiing (downhill), soccer, softball, squash, swimming and diving, table tennis, tennis, track and field, ultimate Frisbee, volleyball, water polo, weight lifting. 4 PE instructors, 8 coaches.
Computers Computers are regularly used in desktop publishing, history, information technology, mathematics, media, publications, science, technology classes. Computer network features include on-campus library services, online commercial services, Internet access. The school has a published electronic and media policy.
Contact Mr. Lindsay Thierry, Director of Senior School Admissions. 604-222-5810. Fax: 604-224-5820. E-mail: lthierry@stgeorges.bc.ca. Web site: www.stgeorges.bc.ca.

ST. GEORGE'S SCHOOL OF MONTREAL

3100 The Boulevard
Montreal, Quebec H3Y 1R9, Canada
Head of School: Mr. James A. Officer

General Information Coeducational day college-preparatory, arts, bilingual studies, and technology school. Grades K–11. Founded: 1930. Setting: urban. 2-acre campus. 1 building on campus. Approved or accredited by Canadian Association of Independent Schools, Quebec Association of Independent Schools, and Quebec Department of Education. Affiliate member of National Association of Independent Schools. Languages of instruction: English and French. Total enrollment: 503. Upper school average class size: 17. Upper school faculty-student ratio: 1:17.
Upper School Student Profile Grade 6: 29 students (13 boys, 16 girls); Grade 7: 55 students (40 boys, 15 girls); Grade 8: 46 students (31 boys, 15 girls); Grade 9: 62 students (36 boys, 26 girls); Grade 10: 72 students (45 boys, 27 girls); Grade 11: 81 students (46 boys, 35 girls).
Faculty School total: 42. In upper school: 19 men, 23 women; 18 have advanced degrees.
Subjects Offered Advanced chemistry, advanced math, Advanced Placement courses, algebra, art, art history, art-AP, biology, biology-AP, calculus, Canadian history, chemistry, civics, computer art, computer math, computer programming, computer science, creative writing, dance, debate, drama, earth science, ecology, economics, English, English literature, English-AP, environmental science, expository writing, film, fine arts, French, French as a second language, French studies, French-AP, general math, general science, geography, government/civics, Internet research, leadership, library research, mathematics, media, moral and social development, moral reasoning, music, music appreciation, musical productions, newspaper, outdoor education, performing arts, physical education, physics, pre-calculus, psychology, science, science project, set design, social studies, theater, writing.
Graduation Requirements Economics, English, French as a second language, mathematics, physical education (includes health), science, social studies (includes history).
Special Academic Programs Advanced Placement exam preparation; honors section; independent study; academic accommodation for the gifted, the musically talented, and the artistically talented; remedial reading and/or remedial writing; remedial math; programs in English, mathematics, general development for dyslexic students; special instructional classes for deaf students; ESL (6 students enrolled).
College Admission Counseling 76 students graduated in 2008; all went to college.
Student Life Upper grades have specified standards of dress, student council. Discipline rests primarily with faculty.
Admissions Traditional secondary-level entrance grade is 7. For fall 2008, 24 students applied for upper-level admission, 24 were accepted, 24 enrolled. Admissions testing, school's own exam or SSAT required. Deadline for receipt of application materials: none. Application fee required: CAN$125. Interview required.
Athletics Interscholastic: badminton (boys, girls), basketball (b,g), flag football (g), hockey (g), ice hockey (g), indoor track & field (b,g); intramural: basketball (b,g); coed interscholastic: aquatics, cross-country running, dance, Frisbee; coed intramural: aerobics, alpine skiing, aquatics, badminton, ball hockey, baseball, basketball, canoeing/kayaking, climbing, cooperative games, Cosom hockey, cross-country running, fencing, fitness, flag football, floor hockey, Frisbee, golf, ice hockey, indoor track & field, life saving, outdoor education. 3 PE instructors, 5 coaches.
Computers Computers are regularly used in all academic classes. Campus intranet and student e-mail accounts are available to students.
Contact Ms. Kathay Carson, Director of High School Admissions. 514-904-0542. Fax: 514-933-3621. E-mail: kathay.carson@stgeorges.qc.ca. Web site: www.stgeorges.qc.ca.

SAINT GERTRUDE HIGH SCHOOL

3215 Stuart Avenue
Richmond, Virginia 23221
Head of School: Mrs. Susan Walker

General Information Girls' day college-preparatory and religious studies school, affiliated with Roman Catholic Church. Grades 9–12. Founded: 1922. Setting: urban. Nearest major city is Norfolk. 1 building on campus. Approved or accredited by Southern Association of Colleges and Schools and Virginia Association of Independent Schools. Member of National Association of Independent Schools. Total enrollment: 273. Upper school average class size: 15. Upper school faculty-student ratio: 1:9.
Upper School Student Profile Grade 9: 70 students (70 girls); Grade 10: 69 students (69 girls); Grade 11: 75 students (75 girls); Grade 12: 59 students (59 girls). 66% of students are Roman Catholic.
Faculty School total: 28. In upper school: 2 men, 26 women; 26 have advanced degrees.
Subjects Offered Advanced Placement courses, algebra, American government-AP, American history, American history-AP, American literature, American literature-AP, anatomy, art, bell choir, Bible studies, biology, calculus, calculus-AP, ceramics, chemistry, chemistry-AP, chorus, church history, community service, computer keyboarding, computer science, drama, drawing, driver education, English, English language and composition-AP, English language-AP, English literature, English literature and composition-AP, environmental science, European history, expository writing, fine arts, French, geometry, government and politics-AP, government/civics, grammar, history, honors algebra, honors English, honors world history, humanities, keyboarding, Latin, mathematics, media, music, painting, physical education, physics, physics-AP, pre-calculus, probability and statistics, psychology, religion, science, social science, social studies, sociology, Spanish, Spanish literature, studio art—AP, theater, theology, trigonometry, world history, world literature, writing, yearbook.
Graduation Requirements Arts and fine arts (art, music, dance, drama), computer science, English, keyboarding, mathematics, physical education (includes health), religion (includes Bible studies and theology), science, social science, social studies (includes history). Community service is required.
Special Academic Programs Advanced Placement exam preparation; honors section.
College Admission Counseling 66 students graduated in 2008; all went to college, including James Madison University; The College of William and Mary; University of Richmond; University of Virginia; Virginia Commonwealth University; Virginia Polytechnic Institute and State University.
Student Life Upper grades have uniform requirement, student council, honor system. Discipline rests primarily with faculty. Attendance at religious services is required.
Tuition and Aid Day student tuition: $11,050. Tuition installment plan (FACTS Tuition Payment Plan). Tuition reduction for siblings, merit scholarship grants, need-based scholarship grants available. In 2008–09, 21% of upper-school students received aid; total upper-school merit-scholarship money awarded: $20,200.
Admissions Traditional secondary-level entrance grade is 9. For fall 2008, 130 students applied for upper-level admission, 109 were accepted, 70 enrolled. Admissions testing, latest standardized score from previous school, Otis-Lennon School Ability Test and writing sample required. Deadline for receipt of application materials: January 31. Application fee required: $50. On-campus interview required.
Athletics Interscholastic: basketball, cross-country running, diving, field hockey, golf, indoor track, lacrosse, soccer, softball, swimming and diving, tennis, track and field, volleyball. 1 PE instructor, 14 coaches, 1 athletic trainer.
Computers Computers are regularly used in all academic classes. Computer network features include on-campus library services, Internet access, wireless campus network. Student e-mail accounts and computer access in designated common areas are available to students. The school has a published electronic and media policy.
Contact Maureen Williams, Director of Admission. 804-358-9885 Ext. 341. Fax: 804-353-8929. E-mail: mwilliams@saintgertrude.org. Web site: www.saintgertrude.org.

ST. GREGORY COLLEGE PREPARATORY SCHOOL

3231 North Craycroft Road
Tucson, Arizona 85712

Head of School: Mr. Bill Creeden

General Information Coeducational day college-preparatory and arts school. Grades 6–PG. Founded: 1980. Setting: suburban. 40-acre campus. 9 buildings on campus. Approved or accredited by Independent Schools Association of the Southwest, The College Board, and Arizona Department of Education. Member of National Association of Independent Schools and Secondary School Admission Test Board. Total enrollment: 310. Upper school average class size: 10. Upper school faculty-student ratio: 1:10.

Upper School Student Profile Grade 9: 30 students (15 boys, 15 girls); Grade 10: 42 students (24 boys, 18 girls); Grade 11: 38 students (15 boys, 23 girls); Grade 12: 54 students (30 boys, 24 girls).

Faculty School total: 38. In upper school: 7 men, 17 women; 20 have advanced degrees.

Subjects Offered Advanced studio art-AP, algebra, American history, American literature, anatomy and physiology, ancient world history, art, art history, band, biology, biology-AP, calculus, ceramics, chemistry, chemistry-AP, choir, chorus, college counseling, college placement, community service, comparative government and politics-AP, computer programming, creative writing, drama, earth science, ecology, economics, English, English literature, English-AP, ethics, European history, European history-AP, expository writing, fine arts, finite math, French, French language-AP, French-AP, geography, geology, geometry, government and politics-AP, government/civics, government/civics-AP, grammar, history, history of drama, history of music, humanities, independent study, jazz band, journalism, Latin, Latin-AP, literature, marine biology, mathematics, music, music theory, music theory-AP, newspaper, photography, physical education, physical science, physics, pre-calculus, religion, SAT preparation, science, social studies, Spanish, Spanish language-AP, Spanish-AP, speech, stage design, stagecraft, studio art-AP, theater, trigonometry, U.S. government-AP, U.S. history-AP, world history, writing.

Graduation Requirements Arts and fine arts (art, music, dance, drama), English, foreign language, history, humanities, mathematics, science, senior internships. Community service is required.

Special Academic Programs Advanced Placement exam preparation; honors section; accelerated programs; independent study; term-away projects; study at local college for college credit; academic accommodation for the gifted, the musically talented, and the artistically talented.

College Admission Counseling 55 students graduated in 2008; all went to college, including Brown University; Massachusetts Institute of Technology; The University of Arizona; University of California, San Diego; University of Pennsylvania; University of Southern California. Mean SAT critical reading: 591, mean SAT math: 590, mean composite ACT: 26.

Student Life Upper grades have specified standards of dress, student council, honor system. Discipline rests primarily with faculty.

Summer Programs Remediation, enrichment, advancement, sports, art/fine arts, computer instruction programs offered; session focuses on academics, arts, sports; held on campus; accepts boys and girls; open to students from other schools. 75 students usually enrolled. 2009 schedule: June 10 to July 28. Application deadline: April 30.

Tuition and Aid Day student tuition: $14,300–$15,300. Tuition installment plan (Insured Tuition Payment Plan, monthly payment plans, individually arranged payment plans, 2- and 10-payment plans). Need-based scholarship grants available. In 2008–09, 25% of upper-school students received aid. Total amount of financial aid awarded in 2008–09: $383,420.

Admissions Traditional secondary-level entrance grade is 9. For fall 2008, 20 students applied for upper-level admission, 18 were accepted, 8 enrolled. Any standardized test and writing sample required. Deadline for receipt of application materials: February 6. Application fee required: $45. Interview recommended.

Athletics Interscholastic: baseball (boys), basketball (b,g), golf (b,g), soccer (b,g), softball (g), swimming and diving (b,g), tennis (b,g), volleyball (b,g); intramural: touch football (b); coed interscholastic: cross-country running, hiking/backpacking, outdoor education, ropes courses, strength & conditioning; coed intramural: basketball, cooperative games, cross-country running, dance, flag football, football, hiking/backpacking, outdoor education, outdoor recreation, outdoor skills, physical training, ropes courses, strength & conditioning, volleyball, weight training, yoga. 2 PE instructors, 12 coaches.

Computers Computers are regularly used in foreign language, mathematics, science classes. Computer network features include on-campus library services, online commercial services, Internet access, wireless campus network, Internet filtering or blocking technology. Campus intranet, student e-mail accounts, and computer access in designated common areas are available to students. Students grades are available online. The school has a published electronic and media policy.

Contact Debby R. Kennedy, Director of Admissions. 520-327-6395 Ext. 213. Fax: 520-327-8276. E-mail: dkennedy@stgregoryschool.org. Web site: www.stgregoryschool.org.

See Close-Up on page 932.

ST. GREGORY'S HIGH SCHOOL

1677 West Bryn Mawr Avenue
Chicago, Illinois 60660-4195

Head of School: Mr. Tony DeSapio

General Information Coeducational day college-preparatory, general academic, business, vocational, religious studies, and technology school, affiliated with Roman Catholic Church; primarily serves students with learning disabilities and individuals with Attention Deficit Disorder. Grades 9–12. Founded: 1937. Setting: urban. 3 buildings on campus. Approved or accredited by North Central Association of Colleges and Schools and Illinois Department of Education. Total enrollment: 331. Upper school average class size: 18.

Upper School Student Profile 60% of students are Roman Catholic.

Faculty School total: 25.

Subjects Offered ACT preparation, algebra, art, biochemistry, biology, business, career planning, chemistry, chorus, computer graphics, computer programming, computer-aided design, consumer economics, drama, economics, electronics, English, ESL, first aid, French, general science, geometry, health, humanities, mathematics, music, physical education, physics, pre-calculus, psychology, Shakespeare, sociology, Spanish, studio art, technology, theater, typing, U.S. history, urban studies, word processing, world culture, yearbook.

Student Life Upper grades have uniform requirement, student council, honor system. Attendance at religious services is required.

Summer Programs Remediation, enrichment, advancement programs offered; held on campus; accepts boys and girls; open to students from other schools.

Tuition and Aid Tuition installment plan (monthly payment plans). Tuition reduction for siblings, need-based scholarship grants available.

Admissions ACT-Explore and CAT required. Deadline for receipt of application materials: none. No application fee required. On-campus interview recommended.

Athletics Interscholastic: baseball (boys), basketball (b,g), cross-country running (b,g), football (b), soccer (b,g), softball (g), track and field (b,g), volleyball (g).

Contact Mr. Kyle Martin, Director of Admissions. 773-907-2127. Fax: 773-907-2120. Web site: www.stgregory.org.

SAINT JAMES SCHOOL

17641 College Road
St. James, Maryland 21781-9999

Head of School: Rev. Dr. D. Stuart Dunnan

General Information Coeducational boarding and day college-preparatory school, affiliated with Episcopal Church. Grades 8–12. Founded: 1842. Setting: rural. Nearest major city is Washington, DC. Students are housed in single-sex dormitories. 900-acre campus. 36 buildings on campus. Approved or accredited by Association of Independent Maryland Schools, Association of Independent Schools of Greater Washington, Middle States Association of Colleges and Schools, National Association of Episcopal Schools, The Association of Boarding Schools, and Maryland Department of Education. Member of National Association of Independent Schools and Secondary School Admission Test Board. Endowment: $21 million. Total enrollment: 225. Upper school average class size: 12. Upper school faculty-student ratio: 1:7.

Upper School Student Profile Grade 9: 60 students (33 boys, 27 girls); Grade 10: 58 students (36 boys, 22 girls); Grade 11: 47 students (30 boys, 17 girls); Grade 12: 36 students (27 boys, 9 girls). 75% of students are boarding students. 55% are state residents. 17 states are represented in upper school student body. 9% are international students. International students from Bermuda, Cote d'Ivoire, Japan, Nigeria, Republic of Korea, and Taiwan; 4 other countries represented in student body. 20% of students are members of Episcopal Church.

Faculty School total: 31. In upper school: 18 men, 13 women; 17 have advanced degrees; 29 reside on campus.

Subjects Offered Algebra, American history-AP, American literature, ancient history, art, art history, art-AP, biology-AP, calculus-AP, chemistry, chemistry-AP, choir, community service, economics, English, English literature, environmental science, European history-AP, fine arts, French-AP, geography, geometry, government-AP, keyboarding, Latin-AP, mathematics, modern European history, music, music history, physical science, physics, physics-AP, political science, science, Spanish-AP, theology, voice, world literature, writing workshop.

Graduation Requirements Arts and fine arts (art, music, dance, drama), English, foreign language, history, mathematics, science. Community service is required.

Special Academic Programs Advanced Placement exam preparation; independent study; study abroad.

College Admission Counseling 51 students graduated in 2008; all went to college, including Amherst College; Hampden-Sydney College; Sewanee: The University of the South; The George Washington University; University of Maryland, College Park; University of Virginia. Mean SAT critical reading: 630, mean SAT math: 633. 51% scored over 600 on SAT critical reading, 58% scored over 600 on SAT math.

Student Life Upper grades have specified standards of dress, student council, honor system. Discipline rests equally with students and faculty. Attendance at religious services is required.

Tuition and Aid Day student tuition: $21,000; 7-day tuition and room/board: $33,200. Tuition installment plan (Insured Tuition Payment Plan, Academic Management Services Plan). Tuition reduction for siblings, merit scholarship grants,

need-based scholarship grants available. In 2008–09, 25% of upper-school students received aid; total upper-school merit-scholarship money awarded: $20,000. Total amount of financial aid awarded in 2008–09: $1,500,000.
Admissions Traditional secondary-level entrance grade is 9. For fall 2008, 204 students applied for upper-level admission, 107 were accepted, 70 enrolled. PSAT or SAT or SSAT required. Deadline for receipt of application materials: January 31. Application fee required: $50. Interview required.
Athletics Interscholastic: baseball (boys), basketball (b,g), cross-country running (b), field hockey (g), football (b), golf (b), lacrosse (b,g), soccer (b,g), softball (g), tennis (b,g), volleyball (g), wrestling (b); intramural: aerobics/dance (g), ballet (g), dance (g), fencing (b,g), modern dance (g), weight training (b,g); coed intramural: alpine skiing, indoor soccer, martial arts, skiing (downhill), strength & conditioning. 2 coaches, 1 athletic trainer.
Computers Computers are regularly used in all academic classes. Computer network features include on-campus library services, online commercial services, Internet access, wireless campus network, Internet filtering or blocking technology. Student e-mail accounts are available to students. The school has a published electronic and media policy.
Contact Lawrence J. Jensen, Director of Admissions. 301-733-9330. Fax: 301-739-1310. E-mail: admissions@stjames.edu. Web site: www.stjames.edu.

See Close-Up on page 934.

SAINT JOAN ANTIDA HIGH SCHOOL

1341 North Cass Street
Milwaukee, Wisconsin 53202
Head of School: Ms. Mary Kurhajetz

General Information Girls' day college-preparatory, arts, business, religious studies, technology, and Engineering school, affiliated with Roman Catholic Church. Grades 9–12. Founded: 1954. Setting: urban. 2 buildings on campus. Approved or accredited by North Central Association of Colleges and Schools and Wisconsin Department of Education. Total enrollment: 346. Upper school average class size: 25. Upper school faculty-student ratio: 1:14.
Upper School Student Profile Grade 9: 103 students (103 girls); Grade 10: 84 students (84 girls); Grade 11: 97 students (97 girls); Grade 12: 62 students (62 girls). 50% of students are Roman Catholic.
Faculty School total: 25. In upper school: 7 men, 18 women; 9 have advanced degrees.
Subjects Offered 3-dimensional art, advanced chemistry, advanced math, Advanced Placement courses, African drumming, algebra, American history-AP, American literature, American literature-AP, art, bell choir, biology, British literature, business, calculus, campus ministry, career/college preparation, Catholic belief and practice, chemistry, chemistry-AP, choir, choral music, Christian and Hebrew scripture, church history, college admission preparation, college counseling, composition, composition-AP, computer keyboarding, concert choir.
Graduation Requirements Advanced Placement courses, algebra, American history, chemistry, Christian studies, church history, composition, electives, English composition, English literature, history, history of the Americas, history of the Catholic Church, physics, religion (includes Bible studies and theology), science, speech.
Special Academic Programs Advanced Placement exam preparation; honors section; independent study; study at local college for college credit; remedial reading and/or remedial writing; remedial math.
College Admission Counseling 65 students graduated in 2008; 56 went to college, including University of Wisconsin–Milwaukee. Other: 2 went to work, 1 entered military service, 6 had other specific plans.
Student Life Upper grades have uniform requirement, student council. Discipline rests primarily with faculty. Attendance at religious services is required.
Tuition and Aid Day student tuition: $5150. Tuition installment plan (SMART Tuition Payment Plan). Merit scholarship grants, need-based scholarship grants available. In 2008–09, 95% of upper-school students received aid.
Admissions Traditional secondary-level entrance grade is 9. For fall 2008, 167 students applied for upper-level admission, 136 were accepted, 103 enrolled. Scholastic Testing Service High School Placement Test required. Deadline for receipt of application materials: none. Application fee required: $10. Interview recommended.
Athletics Interscholastic: basketball, cheering, cross-country running, drill team, soccer, tennis, volleyball. 1 PE instructor.
Computers Computers are regularly used in business, engineering, keyboarding classes. Computer network features include on-campus library services, Internet access, wireless campus network, Internet filtering or blocking technology. The school has a published electronic and media policy.
Contact Mrs. Elizabeth A. Lingen, Director of Admissions. 414-274-4709. Fax: 414-272-3135. E-mail: elingen@saintjoanantida.org. Web site: www.saintjoanantida.org.

SAINT JOHN BOSCO HIGH SCHOOL

13460 Bellflower Boulevard
Bellflower, California 90706
Head of School: Fr. Leo Baysinger

General Information Boys' day college-preparatory and religious studies school, affiliated with Roman Catholic Church. Grades 9–12. Founded: 1940. Setting: suburban. Nearest major city is Los Angeles. 35-acre campus. 5 buildings on campus. Approved or accredited by Western Association of Schools and Colleges and California Department of Education. Total enrollment: 956. Upper school average class size: 30. Upper school faculty-student ratio: 1:16.
Upper School Student Profile Grade 9: 227 students (227 boys); Grade 10: 262 students (262 boys); Grade 11: 217 students (217 boys); Grade 12: 250 students (250 boys). 92% of students are Roman Catholic.
Faculty School total: 63. In upper school: 47 men, 16 women; 25 have advanced degrees.
Subjects Offered Advanced computer applications, algebra, American government-AP, American history, American literature, American literature-AP, art history, art history-AP, Bible studies, biology, biology-AP, British literature, business, business law, calculus-AP, chemistry, civics, computer applications, computer programming, cultural geography, desktop publishing, drama, drawing, ecology, economics, electronics, English language and composition-AP, English literature and composition-AP, English literature-AP, French, French language-AP, geology, geometry, government and politics-AP, government-AP, health, history-AP, instrumental music, journalism, modern world history, moral theology, music appreciation, music theory, oceanography, painting, physical education, physical science, physics, pre-calculus, psychology, religious studies, social justice, Spanish, Spanish language-AP, Spanish literature-AP, trigonometry, U.S. government and politics-AP, U.S. history, U.S. history-AP, Web site design, world history, world history-AP, world literature, world religions.
Graduation Requirements Arts and fine arts (art, music, dance, drama), computer science, English, foreign language, mathematics, physical education (includes health), religion (includes Bible studies and theology), science, social studies (includes history).
Special Academic Programs 12 Advanced Placement exams for which test preparation is offered.
College Admission Counseling 242 students graduated in 2008; 237 went to college, including California State University, Fullerton; California State University, Long Beach; Long Beach City College; University of California, Irvine; University of California, Riverside. Other: 3 went to work, 2 entered military service. Mean SAT critical reading: 460, mean SAT math: 480, mean SAT writing: 460, mean combined SAT: 1400, mean composite ACT: 21.
Student Life Upper grades have specified standards of dress, student council. Discipline rests primarily with faculty. Attendance at religious services is required.
Summer Programs Remediation, enrichment, advancement, sports, art/fine arts, computer instruction programs offered; session focuses on enrichment and make-up courses; held on campus; accepts boys and girls; open to students from other schools. 800 students usually enrolled. 2009 schedule: June 16 to July 18. Application deadline: June 1.
Tuition and Aid Day student tuition: $8600. Need-based scholarship grants available. In 2008–09, 20% of upper-school students received aid. Total amount of financial aid awarded in 2008–09: $350,000.
Admissions Traditional secondary-level entrance grade is 9. For fall 2008, 400 students applied for upper-level admission, 320 were accepted, 292 enrolled. STS required. Deadline for receipt of application materials: February 1. Application fee required: $50.
Athletics Interscholastic: baseball, basketball, cross-country running, football, golf, lacrosse, soccer, swimming and diving, tennis, track and field, volleyball, water polo, wrestling; intramural: flag football, football, soccer, softball, touch football. 3 PE instructors, 1 athletic trainer.
Computers Computers are regularly used in computer applications, desktop publishing, graphic design classes. Computer network features include on-campus library services, online commercial services, Internet access, wireless campus network, Internet filtering or blocking technology. Computer access in designated common areas is available to students. Students grades are available online. The school has a published electronic and media policy.
Contact Mr. Ernie Antonelli, Admissions Director. 562-920-1734 Ext. 232. Fax: 562-867-2408. E-mail: eantonel@bosco.org. Web site: www.bosco.org.

ST. JOHNSBURY ACADEMY

PO Box 906
1000 Main Street
St. Johnsbury, Vermont 05819
Head of School: Mr. Thomas W. Lovett

General Information Coeducational boarding and day college-preparatory, general academic, arts, business, vocational, bilingual studies, and technology school; primarily serves students with learning disabilities, individuals with Attention Deficit Disorder, and dyslexic students. Grades 9–PG. Approved or accredited by Independent Schools of Northern New England, New England Association of Schools and Colleges, and The Association of Boarding Schools. Member of National Association of Independent Schools and Secondary School Admission Test Board. Total enrollment: 1,005. Upper school average class size: 12.

Upper School Student Profile Grade 9: 212 students (125 boys, 87 girls); Grade 10: 243 students (132 boys, 111 girls); Grade 11: 290 students (141 boys, 149 girls); Grade 12: 253 students (135 boys, 118 girls); Postgraduate: 7 students (6 boys, 1 girl). 24% of students are boarding students. 70% are state residents. 15 states are represented in upper school student body. 20% are international students. International students from Bermuda, Germany, Hong Kong, Republic of Korea, Spain, and Taiwan; 18 other countries represented in student body.

Subjects Offered Accounting, acting, Advanced Placement courses, advanced studio art-AP, advanced TOEFL/grammar, algebra, American government, American government-AP, American history, American history-AP, American literature, analysis, anatomy and physiology, ancient world history, architectural drawing, architecture, art, astronomy, audio visual/media, auto body, auto mechanics, auto shop, automated accounting, band, basic skills, biology, biology-AP, British literature, business, business communications, business skills, calculus-AP, career education, career experience, carpentry, chemistry, chemistry-AP, Chinese, chorus, civics, college writing, Coming of Age in the 20th Century, composition-AP, computer keyboarding, computer math, computer programming, computer science-AP, concert band, construction, CPR, culinary arts, dance, dance performance, desktop publishing, developmental math, digital art, directing, discrete math, drafting, drama, drama performance, drama workshop, dramatic arts, drawing and design, driver education, earth science, economics, electronics, engineering, English, English language and composition-AP, English literature, English literature and composition-AP, environmental education, environmental science, environmental science-AP, ESL, European history, European history-AP, expository writing, fashion, film studies, forest resources, forestry, French, French language-AP, French literature-AP, French-AP, geometry, government, government-AP, government/civics, guitar, health, health education, history, industrial arts, introduction to theater, Japanese, jazz band, journalism, land management, Latin, mathematics, mechanical drawing, media production, modern European history-AP, music, music appreciation, music theory, navigation, newspaper, nutrition, oil painting, photography, physical education, physics, physics-AP, playwriting and directing, portfolio art, pottery, pre-algebra, pre-calculus, pre-vocational education, psychology, psychology-AP, reading/study skills, science, sculpture, small engine repair, social science, social studies, sociology, Spanish, Spanish literature, sports medicine, sports science, stagecraft, statistics and probability, statistics-AP, studio art-AP, study skills, technical education, technical writing, technology, theater, theater design and production, TOEFL preparation, trigonometry, U.S. government-AP, U.S. history-AP, video communication, video film production, visual and performing arts, vocal ensemble, Web site design, welding, wilderness/outdoor program, wind ensemble, wind instruments, woodworking, word processing, world civilizations, world history, world literature, yearbook.

Graduation Requirements Economics, English, keyboarding/computer, mathematics, physical education (includes health), science, U.S. government, U.S. history, Senior Capstone Project.

Special Academic Programs Advanced Placement exam preparation; honors section; term-away projects; academic accommodation for the gifted and the artistically talented; remedial reading and/or remedial writing; remedial math; programs in English, mathematics, general development for dyslexic students; ESL (73 students enrolled).

College Admission Counseling 267 students graduated in 2008; 240 went to college, including Northeastern University; Rochester Institute of Technology; University of New Hampshire; University of Vermont; University of Wisconsin–Madison; Washington University in St. Louis. Other: 16 went to work, 8 entered military service, 2 entered a postgraduate year.

Summer Programs ESL programs offered; session focuses on English language; held on campus; accepts boys and girls; open to students from other schools. 30 students usually enrolled. 2009 schedule: July 11 to August 22. Application deadline: none.

Tuition and Aid Day student tuition: $12,980; 7-day tuition and room/board: $38,500. Tuition installment plan (individually arranged payment plans, two payments (August 1 and November 25)). Need-based scholarship grants available. In 2008–09, 4% of upper-school students received aid. Total amount of financial aid awarded in 2008–09: $782,900.

Admissions Traditional secondary-level entrance grade is 9. For fall 2008, 468 students applied for upper-level admission, 391 were accepted, 329 enrolled. Deadline for receipt of application materials: none. Application fee required: $20. Interview recommended.

Athletics Interscholastic: alpine skiing (boys, girls), baseball (b), basketball (b,g), cross-country running (b,g), field hockey (g), football (b), golf (b,g), gymnastics (g), ice hockey (b), lacrosse (b,g), nordic skiing (b,g), skiing (cross-country) (b,g), skiing (downhill) (b,g), soccer (b,g), softball (g), tennis (b,g), track and field (b,g), ultimate Frisbee (b,g), wrestling (b); intramural: ice hockey (g), volleyball (b,g); coed interscholastic: cheering, indoor track & field, ultimate Frisbee; coed intramural: aerobics/dance, badminton, basketball, bowling, canoeing/kayaking, cricket, dance, fencing, fishing, flag football, floor hockey, hiking/backpacking, hockey, indoor soccer, martial arts, mountain biking, outdoor adventure, paddle tennis, swimming and diving, ultimate Frisbee, volleyball, weight lifting, wilderness. 3 PE instructors, 10 coaches, 1 athletic trainer.

Computers Computers are regularly used in business education, career education, computer applications, desktop publishing, drafting, English, foreign language, journalism, keyboarding, mathematics, newspaper, publications, science, senior seminar, technical drawing, technology, video film production, Web site design, yearbook classes. Computer network features include on-campus library services, online commercial services, Internet access, wireless campus network, Internet filtering or blocking technology. Computer access in designated common areas is available to students. The school has a published electronic and media policy.

Contact Mrs. MaryAnn Gessner, Director of Admissions. 802-751-2130. Fax: 802-748-5463. E-mail: mgessner@stjacademy.org. Web site: www.stjohnsburyacademy.org.

ANNOUNCEMENT FROM THE SCHOOL Celebrating record enrollment for the 2008–09 school year, St. Johnsbury Academy is pleased to announce initial plans to build a new resident student dormitory and an athletic field. The Academy was the recipient of the 2007 Siemens Award for Achievement in Advanced Placement. For the third consecutive year, an Academy graduate has been awarded Vermont AP Scholar. St. Johnsbury Academy welcomes boarding students from two new countries: Oman and Kazakhstan.

See Close-Up on page 936.

ST. JOHN'S CATHOLIC PREP

889 Butterfly Lane
Frederick, Maryland 21703

Head of School: Dr. Robert A. Pastoor

General Information Coeducational day college-preparatory school, affiliated with Roman Catholic Church. Grades 9–12. Founded: 1829. Setting: suburban. Nearest major city is Baltimore. 31-acre campus. 9 buildings on campus. Approved or accredited by Association of Independent Maryland Schools and Maryland Department of Education. Total enrollment: 283. Upper school average class size: 18. Upper school faculty-student ratio: 1:11.

Upper School Student Profile Grade 9: 100 students (45 boys, 55 girls); Grade 10: 67 students (38 boys, 29 girls); Grade 11: 62 students (30 boys, 32 girls); Grade 12: 54 students (31 boys, 23 girls). 75% of students are Roman Catholic.

Faculty School total: 26. In upper school: 11 men, 15 women.

Special Academic Programs Advanced Placement exam preparation; honors section; study at local college for college credit; ESL (5 students enrolled).

College Admission Counseling 69 students graduated in 2008; all went to college, including University of Maryland, College Park. Median SAT critical reading: 602, median SAT math: 596, median SAT writing: 576.

Student Life Upper grades have uniform requirement, honor system. Discipline rests primarily with faculty. Attendance at religious services is required.

Summer Programs Sports, art/fine arts, computer instruction programs offered; held on campus; accepts boys and girls; open to students from other schools. 2009 schedule: June to August.

Tuition and Aid Day student tuition: $11,900. Tuition installment plan (FACTS Tuition Payment Plan). Tuition reduction for siblings, merit scholarship grants, need-based scholarship grants available. In 2008–09, 33% of upper-school students received aid; total upper-school merit-scholarship money awarded: $20,000. Total amount of financial aid awarded in 2008–09: $250,000.

Admissions Traditional secondary-level entrance grade is 9. For fall 2008, 146 students applied for upper-level admission, 142 were accepted, 100 enrolled. High School Placement Test (closed version) from Scholastic Testing Service required. Deadline for receipt of application materials: none. Application fee required: $95. On-campus interview required.

Athletics Interscholastic: baseball (boys), basketball (b,g), cheering (g), cross-country running (b,g), football (b), golf (b,g), lacrosse (b,g), soccer (b,g), softball (g), swimming and diving (b,g), tennis (b,g), volleyball (g), wrestling (b); coed interscholastic: indoor track & field, track and field; coed intramural: equestrian sports, horseback riding, indoor hockey, skiing (downhill), snowboarding, strength & conditioning, weight training. 2 PE instructors, 14 coaches, 1 athletic trainer.

Computers Computer network features include on-campus library services, Internet access. Student e-mail accounts are available to students.

Contact Mr. Michael W. Schultz, Director of Enrollment Management. 301-662-4210 Ext. 121. Fax: 301-662-5166. E-mail: mschultz@saintjohnsprep.org. Web site: www.saintjohnsprep.org.

ST. JOHN'S COLLEGE HIGH SCHOOL

2607 Military Road NW
Washington, District of Columbia 20015

Head of School: Mr. Jeffrey W. Mancabelli

General Information Coeducational day college-preparatory, arts, religious studies, and technology school, affiliated with Roman Catholic Church. Grades 9–12. Founded: 1851. Setting: urban. 30-acre campus. 5 buildings on campus. Approved or accredited by Middle States Association of Colleges and Schools and District of Columbia Department of Education. Endowment: $5 million. Total enrollment: 1,056. Upper school average class size: 22. Upper school faculty-student ratio: 1:13.

Upper School Student Profile Grade 9: 278 students (157 boys, 121 girls); Grade 10: 246 students (137 boys, 109 girls); Grade 11: 285 students (167 boys, 118 girls); Grade 12: 247 students (141 boys, 106 girls). 70% of students are Roman Catholic.
Faculty School total: 83. In upper school: 42 men, 41 women; 57 have advanced degrees.
Subjects Offered 3-dimensional design, accounting, Advanced Placement courses, algebra, American history, American literature, anatomy, art, band, biology, business, calculus, ceramics, chemistry, chorus, community service, computer math, computer programming, computer science, creative writing, earth science, economics, English, English literature, European history, fine arts, French, genetics, geometry, government/civics, history, journalism, JROTC, leadership training, mathematics, military science, music, physical education, physics, physiology, religion, science, Shakespeare, social science, social studies, Spanish, trigonometry, typing, weight training, world history, world literature.
Graduation Requirements Arts and fine arts (art, music, dance, drama), computer science, English, foreign language, mathematics, physical education (includes health), religion (includes Bible studies and theology), science, social science, social studies (includes history). Community service is required.
Special Academic Programs Advanced Placement exam preparation; honors section; independent study; academic accommodation for the gifted.
College Admission Counseling 228 students graduated in 2008; all went to college, including James Madison University; St. Mary's College of Maryland; The Catholic University of America; University of Maryland, College Park; University of Virginia. Mean SAT critical reading: 610, mean SAT math: 600.
Student Life Upper grades have uniform requirement, student council. Discipline rests primarily with faculty. Attendance at religious services is required.
Summer Programs Remediation, enrichment, advancement, sports, computer instruction programs offered; session focuses on remediation and advancement; held on campus; accepts boys and girls; not open to students from other schools. 75 students usually enrolled. 2009 schedule: June 22 to July 22.
Tuition and Aid Day student tuition: $13,500. Tuition installment plan (FACTS Tuition Payment Plan). Merit scholarship grants, need-based scholarship grants available. In 2008–09, 25% of upper-school students received aid; total upper-school merit-scholarship money awarded: $400,000. Total amount of financial aid awarded in 2008–09: $1,700,000.
Admissions Traditional secondary-level entrance grade is 9. For fall 2008, 870 students applied for upper-level admission, 380 were accepted, 280 enrolled. High School Placement Test (closed version) from Scholastic Testing Service required. Deadline for receipt of application materials: December 15. Application fee required: $50. Interview recommended.
Athletics Interscholastic: baseball (boys), basketball (b,g), cheering (g), crew (b,g), cross-country running (b,g), field hockey (g), football (b), ice hockey (b), lacrosse (b,g), soccer (b,g), softball (g), tennis (b,g), track and field (b,g), volleyball (g), wrestling (b); intramural: dance (g), dance squad (g), pom squad (g); coed interscholastic: archery, diving, drill team, golf, ice hockey, JROTC drill, marksmanship, physical fitness, riflery, rugby, swimming and diving; coed intramural: alpine skiing, bowling, equestrian sports, fishing, Frisbee, martial arts, outdoor activities, riflery, skiing (downhill), snowboarding, strength & conditioning, ultimate Frisbee, weight training. 1 PE instructor, 26 coaches, 1 athletic trainer.
Computers Computers are regularly used in all classes. Computer network features include on-campus library services, online commercial services, Internet access, wireless campus network. Students grades are available online.
Contact Mrs. Susan M. Hinton, Director of Admissions. 202-363-2316 Ext. 1070. Fax: 202-363-2916 Ext. 1070. E-mail: shinton@stjohns-chs.org. Web site: www.stjohns-chs.org.

ST. JOHN'S INTERNATIONAL

#300—1885 West Broadway
Vancouver, British Columbia V6J 1Y5, Canada

Head of School: Mr. Rick Shelly

General Information Coeducational day college-preparatory and sciences school. Grades 8–12. Founded: 1988. Setting: urban. 1 building on campus. Approved or accredited by British Columbia Department of Education. Language of instruction: English. Upper school average class size: 10. Upper school faculty-student ratio: 1:10.
Upper School Student Profile Grade 11: 17 students (11 boys, 6 girls); Grade 12: 5 students (5 boys).
Faculty School total: 9. In upper school: 5 men, 4 women; all have advanced degrees.
Graduation Requirements General science, language, math applications, physical education (includes health).
Special Academic Programs ESL (30 students enrolled).
College Admission Counseling 16 students graduated in 2008; 14 went to college, including Queen's University at Kingston; University of Hawaii at Manoa; York University. Other: 2 went to work.
Student Life Upper grades have uniform requirement, honor system. Discipline rests primarily with faculty.
Summer Programs ESL programs offered; session focuses on ESL; held on campus; accepts boys and girls; open to students from other schools. 20 students usually enrolled.
Tuition and Aid Day student tuition: CAN$13,500.
Admissions For fall 2008, 50 students applied for upper-level admission, 40 were accepted. English for Non-native Speakers required. Deadline for receipt of application materials: none. Application fee required: CAN$150.
Athletics 1 PE instructor.
Computers Computer network features include Internet access, open lab for assignments.
Contact Admissions Officer. 604-683-4572. Fax: 604-683-4579. E-mail: general@stjohnsis.com. Web site: www.stjohnsis.com.

ST. JOHN'S NORTHWESTERN MILITARY ACADEMY

1101 Genesee Street
Delafield, Wisconsin 53018-1498

Head of School: Mr. Jack H. Albert Jr.

General Information Boys' boarding and day college-preparatory, arts, business, and military school, affiliated with Episcopal Church; primarily serves underachievers. Grades 7–12. Founded: 1884. Setting: small town. Nearest major city is Milwaukee. Students are housed in single-sex dormitories. 150-acre campus. 15 buildings on campus. Approved or accredited by Independent Schools Association of the Central States, Midwest Association of Boarding Schools, National Association of Episcopal Schools, North Central Association of Colleges and Schools, The Association of Boarding Schools, and Wisconsin Department of Education. Member of National Association of Independent Schools and Secondary School Admission Test Board. Endowment: $6.5 million. Total enrollment: 300. Upper school average class size: 12. Upper school faculty-student ratio: 1:12.
Upper School Student Profile Grade 9: 56 students (56 boys); Grade 10: 63 students (63 boys); Grade 11: 51 students (51 boys); Grade 12: 55 students (55 boys). 98% of students are boarding students. 22% are state residents. 22 states are represented in upper school student body. 28% are international students. International students from Canada, China, Mexico, Republic of Korea, Russian Federation, and Thailand; 6 other countries represented in student body. 4% of students are members of Episcopal Church.
Faculty School total: 40. In upper school: 34 men, 6 women; 16 have advanced degrees; 12 reside on campus.
Subjects Offered Advanced math, algebra, American government, American literature, art, aviation, band, biology, British literature, calculus, ceramics, chemistry, choir, Christianity, computer programming, computer science, current events, drama, driver education, earth science, economics, English, entrepreneurship, environmental science, ESL, geography, geometry, German, government/civics, grammar, health, history, honors English, honors U.S. history, journalism, JROTC, mathematics, music, physical science, physics, psychology, reading, science, social studies, sociology, Spanish, statistics, strings, trigonometry, U.S. history, world geography, world history, world literature.
Graduation Requirements Advanced math, algebra, American government, American literature, arts and fine arts (art, music, dance, drama), biology, British literature, chemistry, computer science, electives, foreign language, geometry, introduction to literature, JROTC, physical science, U.S. history, world history, world literature. Community service is required.
Special Academic Programs Honors section; independent study; study at local college for college credit; ESL (10 students enrolled).
College Admission Counseling 56 students graduated in 2008; all went to college, including DePaul University; Embry-Riddle Aeronautical University; Marquette University; Purdue University; University of Illinois at Urbana–Champaign; University of Wisconsin–Madison.
Student Life Upper grades have uniform requirement, student council, honor system. Discipline rests primarily with faculty. Attendance at religious services is required.
Summer Programs Remediation, enrichment, advancement, ESL, computer instruction programs offered; session focuses on Academics; held on campus; accepts boys; open to students from other schools.
Tuition and Aid 7-day tuition and room/board: $31,000. Tuition installment plan (Key Tuition Payment Plan, FACTS Tuition Payment Plan, TeriPlease Tuition Payment Plans). Tuition reduction for siblings, merit scholarship grants, need-based scholarship grants, tuition remission for children of employees, endowed scholarships, alumni scholarships available. In 2008–09, 29% of upper-school students received aid; total upper-school merit-scholarship money awarded: $113,500. Total amount of financial aid awarded in 2008–09: $950,000.
Admissions Traditional secondary-level entrance grade is 9. For fall 2008, 430 students applied for upper-level admission, 236 were accepted, 125 enrolled. Kuhlmann-Anderson, SSAT or TOEFL required. Deadline for receipt of application materials: none. Application fee required: $100. On-campus interview required.
Athletics Interscholastic: archery, baseball, basketball, cross-country running, equestrian sports, football, golf, hockey, ice hockey, lacrosse, scuba diving; intramural: billiards, fishing, handball. 2 PE instructors.
Computers Computers are regularly used in all academic classes. Computer network features include on-campus library services, Internet access, Internet filtering or blocking technology. Campus intranet and student e-mail accounts are available to students. Students grades are available online. The school has a published electronic and media policy.

Contact Duane E. Rutherford, Director of Enrollment Services. 262-646-7122. Fax: 262-646-7128. E-mail: admissions@sjnma.org. Web site: www.sjnma.org.

ST. JOHN'S PREPARATORY SCHOOL

72 Spring Street
Danvers, Massachusetts 01923

Head of School: Mr. Albert J. Shannon, PhD

General Information Boys' day college-preparatory, arts, religious studies, and technology school, affiliated with Roman Catholic Church. Grades 9–12. Founded: 1907. Setting: suburban. Nearest major city is Boston. 175-acre campus. 9 buildings on campus. Approved or accredited by National Catholic Education Association and New England Association of Schools and Colleges. Endowment: $6.3 million. Total enrollment: 1,200. Upper school average class size: 19. Upper school faculty-student ratio: 1:12.

Upper School Student Profile Grade 9: 300 students (300 boys); Grade 10: 300 students (300 boys); Grade 11: 300 students (300 boys); Grade 12: 300 students (300 boys). 70% of students are Roman Catholic.

Faculty School total: 109. In upper school: 69 men, 40 women; 74 have advanced degrees.

Subjects Offered Accounting, acting, algebra, American government-AP, American history, American history-AP, American literature, anatomy and physiology, art, biology, biology-AP, business, calculus, calculus-AP, ceramics, chemistry, chemistry-AP, chorus, computer programming, computer science, computer science-AP, desktop publishing, drama, driver education, economics, economics-AP, English, English literature, English-AP, environmental science, environmental studies, ethics, European history, European history-AP, French, French-AP, geometry, German, German-AP, government/civics, Latin, Latin-AP, mathematics, music, neuroscience, physical education, physics, physics-AP, religion, science, sculpture, social studies, society, politics and law, Spanish, Spanish-AP, statistics, statistics-AP, studio art, technology, trigonometry, U.S. history-AP, world history, world religions.

Graduation Requirements Arts and fine arts (art, music, dance, drama), computer science, English, foreign language, mathematics, physical education (includes health), religion (includes Bible studies and theology), science, social studies (includes history).

Special Academic Programs Advanced Placement exam preparation; honors section; independent study; study abroad; academic accommodation for the gifted, the musically talented, and the artistically talented.

College Admission Counseling 247 students graduated in 2008; 245 went to college, including Boston College; Boston University; Northeastern University; Providence College; University of Massachusetts Amherst; Villanova University. Other: 2 entered a postgraduate year. Mean SAT critical reading: 603, mean SAT math: 626.

Student Life Upper grades have specified standards of dress, student council. Discipline rests primarily with faculty. Attendance at religious services is required.

Summer Programs Enrichment programs offered; session focuses on academic enrichment and study skills; held on campus; accepts boys and girls; open to students from other schools.

Tuition and Aid Day student tuition: $16,300. Tuition installment plan (monthly payment plans). Need-based scholarship grants available. In 2008–09, 30% of upper-school students received aid. Total amount of financial aid awarded in 2008–09: $2,800,000.

Admissions Traditional secondary-level entrance grade is 9. SSAT or STS, Diocese Test required. Deadline for receipt of application materials: December 15. No application fee required.

Athletics Interscholastic: alpine skiing, baseball, basketball, cross-country running, fencing, football, golf, hockey, ice hockey, indoor track, lacrosse, rugby, sailing, skiing (downhill), soccer, swimming and diving, tennis, track and field, volleyball, water polo, winter (indoor) track, wrestling; intramural: baseball, basketball, bicycling, bocce, bowling, climbing, combined training, cooperative games, crew, flag football, floor hockey, Frisbee, golf, in-line hockey, martial arts, mountain biking, Nautilus, physical fitness, rowing, sailing, skiing (downhill), snowboarding, strength & conditioning, surfing, table tennis, tennis, touch football, ultimate Frisbee, volleyball, weight lifting, weight training, whiffle ball. 3 PE instructors, 57 coaches, 2 athletic trainers.

Computers Computers are regularly used in all academic, career exploration, college planning, research skills classes. Computer network features include on-campus library services, Internet access, wireless campus network, Internet filtering or blocking technology, student access to 300 computer workstations. Student e-mail accounts are available to students. Students grades are available online. The school has a published electronic and media policy.

Contact Mr. Philip McManus, Associate Dean of Admissions. 978-774-1050 Ext. 372. Fax: 978-624-1315. E-mail: pmcmanus@stjohnsprep.org. Web site: www.stjohnsprep.org.

SAINT JOHN'S PREPARATORY SCHOOL

Box 4000
1857 Watertower Road
Collegeville, Minnesota 56321

Head of School: Fr. Timothy Backous, OSB

General Information Coeducational boarding and day college-preparatory, arts, religious studies, bilingual studies, and Theatre school, affiliated with Roman Catholic Church. Boarding grades 9–PG, day grades 7–PG. Founded: 1857. Setting: rural. Nearest major city is St. Cloud. Students are housed in single-sex dormitories. 2,700-acre campus. 23 buildings on campus. Approved or accredited by Independent Schools Association of the Central States, Midwest Association of Boarding Schools, The Association of Boarding Schools, and Minnesota Department of Education. Member of National Association of Independent Schools. Endowment: $6.9 million. Total enrollment: 338. Upper school average class size: 16. Upper school faculty-student ratio: 1:10.

Upper School Student Profile Grade 9: 45 students (26 boys, 19 girls); Grade 10: 69 students (28 boys, 41 girls); Grade 11: 81 students (49 boys, 32 girls); Grade 12: 62 students (37 boys, 25 girls); Postgraduate: 2 students (2 boys). 37% of students are boarding students. 55% are state residents. 12 states are represented in upper school student body. 25% are international students. International students from Austria, China, Japan, Mexico, Republic of Korea, and Taiwan; 10 other countries represented in student body. 50% of students are Roman Catholic.

Faculty School total: 35. In upper school: 21 men, 14 women; 26 have advanced degrees.

Subjects Offered 3-dimensional design, advanced chemistry, Advanced Placement courses, algebra, American history, American literature, art, art history, band, Bible studies, biology, biology-AP, British literature, calculus, ceramics, chemistry, Chinese, choir, civics, conceptual physics, creative writing, current events, drawing, driver education, earth science, economics, English, English literature, English-AP, environmental science-AP, ESL, European history, fine arts, geometry, German, government/civics, health, history, mathematics, music, orchestra, photography, physical education, physics, pre-calculus, religion, science, social studies, Spanish, speech, statistics, theology, trigonometry, world history, world literature, writing.

Special Academic Programs Advanced Placement exam preparation; honors section; independent study; term-away projects; study at local college for college credit; study abroad; academic accommodation for the gifted, the musically talented, and the artistically talented; ESL (27 students enrolled).

College Admission Counseling 58 students graduated in 2008; 57 went to college, including College of Saint Benedict; St. John's University; University of Illinois at Urbana–Champaign; University of Minnesota, Twin Cities Campus; University of Portland. Other: 1 had other specific plans. Mean SAT critical reading: 655, mean SAT math: 643, mean SAT writing: 610, mean combined SAT: 1908, mean composite ACT: 26.

Student Life Upper grades have specified standards of dress, student council, honor system. Discipline rests primarily with faculty. Attendance at religious services is required.

Summer Programs Enrichment, advancement, art/fine arts programs offered; session focuses on fun camp experiences; held on campus; accepts boys and girls; open to students from other schools. 1,000 students usually enrolled. 2009 schedule: June 14 to August 6. Application deadline: June 1.

Tuition and Aid Day student tuition: $12,739; 5-day tuition and room/board: $25,757; 7-day tuition and room/board: $28,918. Tuition installment plan (monthly payment plans, individually arranged payment plans, semester payment plan). Merit scholarship grants, need-based scholarship grants, paying campus jobs available. In 2008–09, 57% of upper-school students received aid; total upper-school merit-scholarship money awarded: $35,170. Total amount of financial aid awarded in 2008–09: $1,100,000.

Admissions Traditional secondary-level entrance grade is 9. For fall 2008, 140 students applied for upper-level admission, 97 were accepted, 77 enrolled. Differential Aptitude Test required. Deadline for receipt of application materials: none. Application fee required: $30. Interview required.

Athletics Interscholastic: alpine skiing (boys, girls), aquatics (g), baseball (b), basketball (b,g), cross-country running (b,g), diving (g), football (b), gymnastics (g), ice hockey (b,g), indoor track & field (b,g), nordic skiing (b,g), soccer (b,g), softball (g), swimming and diving (g), tennis (b,g), track and field (b,g); intramural: aerobics (g), aerobics/dance (g), dance (g), equestrian sports (g), figure skating (g), golf (b,g), ice skating (g); coed intramural: bicycling, canoeing/kayaking, cross-country running, fitness, fitness walking, flag football, floor hockey, Frisbee, indoor soccer, mountain biking, nordic skiing, physical fitness, physical training, racquetball, rock climbing, roller blading, skiing (cross-country), skiing (downhill), soccer, strength & conditioning, swimming and diving, ultimate Frisbee, volleyball, walking, wall climbing, wallyball, weight lifting, weight training, winter (indoor) track, winter walking, yoga. 1 PE instructor, 21 coaches.

Computers Computers are regularly used in English, mathematics, science classes. Computer network features include on-campus library services, Internet access, Internet filtering or blocking technology. Student e-mail accounts and computer access in designated common areas are available to students. Students grades are available online. The school has a published electronic and media policy.

Contact Bryan Backes, Director of Admissions. 320-363-3321. Fax: 320-363-3322. E-mail: bbackes@csbsju.edu. Web site: www.sjprep.net.

See Close-Up on page 938.

ST. JOHN'S-RAVENSCOURT SCHOOL

400 South Drive
Winnipeg, Manitoba R3T 3K5, Canada
Head of School: Dr. Stephen Johnson

General Information Coeducational boarding and day college-preparatory school. Boarding grades 8–12, day grades K–12. Founded: 1820. Setting: suburban. Students are housed in single-sex dormitories. 23-acre campus. 6 buildings on campus. Approved or accredited by Canadian Association of Independent Schools, Canadian Educational Standards Institute, The Association of Boarding Schools, and Manitoba Department of Education. Language of instruction: English. Endowment: CAN$8.3 million. Total enrollment: 806. Upper school average class size: 20. Upper school faculty-student ratio: 1:9.

Upper School Student Profile Grade 9: 88 students (53 boys, 35 girls); Grade 10: 86 students (58 boys, 28 girls); Grade 11: 85 students (48 boys, 37 girls); Grade 12: 91 students (57 boys, 34 girls). 13% of students are boarding students. 92% are province residents. 3 provinces are represented in upper school student body. 7% are international students. International students from China, Democratic People's Republic of Korea, Germany, Hong Kong, Japan, and Taiwan; 1 other country represented in student body.

Faculty School total: 75. In upper school: 23 men, 15 women; 12 have advanced degrees; 11 reside on campus.

Subjects Offered Algebra, American history, animation, art, biology, biology-AP, calculus, calculus-AP, Canadian geography, Canadian history, chemistry, chemistry-AP, computer science, debate, drama, driver education, economics, English, English literature, European history, European history-AP, French, French-AP, geography, geometry, history, information technology, law, linear algebra, mathematics, music, physical education, physics, physics-AP, pre-calculus, psychology, psychology-AP, science, social studies, Spanish, theater, visual arts, Web site design, world issues.

Graduation Requirements Canadian geography, Canadian history, computer science, English, French, geography, history, mathematics, physical education (includes health), pre-calculus, science, social science.

Special Academic Programs Advanced Placement exam preparation; honors section; independent study; study at local college for college credit; ESL (27 students enrolled).

College Admission Counseling 86 students graduated in 2008; 82 went to college, including McGill University; Queen's University at Kingston; The University of British Columbia; The University of Western Ontario; University of Manitoba; University of Toronto. Other: 4 had other specific plans.

Student Life Upper grades have uniform requirement, student council, honor system. Discipline rests equally with students and faculty.

Tuition and Aid Day student tuition: CAN$13,800; 7-day tuition and room/board: CAN$27,140–CAN$35,910. Tuition installment plan (monthly payment plans, individually arranged payment plans). Bursaries, merit scholarship grants available. In 2008–09, 21% of upper-school students received aid; total upper-school merit-scholarship money awarded: CAN$95,000. Total amount of financial aid awarded in 2008–09: CAN$262,250.

Admissions Traditional secondary-level entrance grade is 9. For fall 2008, 72 students applied for upper-level admission, 45 were accepted, 35 enrolled. Otis-Lennon School Ability Test, school's own exam or TOEFL or SLEP required. Deadline for receipt of application materials: none. Application fee required: CAN$100. Interview recommended.

Athletics Interscholastic: aerobics (boys, girls), badminton (b,g), basketball (b,g), cross-country running (b,g), Frisbee (b,g), golf (b), hockey (b,g), ice hockey (b,g), indoor track (b,g), indoor track & field (b,g), lacrosse (b,g), rugby (b,g), soccer (b,g), track and field (b,g), ultimate Frisbee (b,g), volleyball (b,g); intramural: badminton (b,g), basketball (b,g), cross-country running (b,g), dance (b,g), hockey (b,g), rock climbing (b,g), rugby (b,g), self defense (g), soccer (b,g), strength & conditioning (b,g), ultimate Frisbee (b,g), volleyball (g), wall climbing (b,g), weight training (b,g), yoga (b,g); coed interscholastic: badminton, Frisbee, physical fitness, running, skiing (cross-country), softball, speedball, ultimate Frisbee, water polo; coed intramural: badminton, flag football, floor hockey, rock climbing, running, skiing (cross-country), ultimate Frisbee. 6 PE instructors.

Computers Computers are regularly used in business skills, career exploration, college planning, creative writing, English, history, library skills, newspaper, science, social studies, yearbook classes. Computer network features include on-campus library services, Internet access, wireless campus network, Internet filtering or blocking technology, EBSCO. Campus intranet and student e-mail accounts are available to students. The school has a published electronic and media policy.

Contact Mrs. Lisa Kachulak-Babey, Director of Admissions. 204-477-2400. Fax: 204-477-2429. E-mail: admissions@sjr.mb.ca. Web site: www.sjr.mb.ca.

ST. JOSEPH ACADEMY

155 State Road 207
St. Augustine, Florida 32084
Head of School: Mr. Michael H. Heubeck

General Information Coeducational day college-preparatory, arts, religious studies, and technology school, affiliated with Roman Catholic Church; primarily serves individuals with Attention Deficit Disorder. Grades 9–12. Founded: 1866. Setting: suburban. 33-acre campus. 13 buildings on campus. Approved or accredited by National Council for Nonpublic Schools, Southern Association of Colleges and Schools, and Florida Department of Education. Total enrollment: 335. Upper school average class size: 20. Upper school faculty-student ratio: 1:13.

Upper School Student Profile Grade 9: 79 students (31 boys, 48 girls); Grade 10: 84 students (40 boys, 44 girls); Grade 11: 86 students (43 boys, 43 girls); Grade 12: 85 students (42 boys, 43 girls). 82% of students are Roman Catholic.

Faculty School total: 27. In upper school: 13 men, 14 women; 10 have advanced degrees.

Subjects Offered Advanced computer applications, advanced math, Advanced Placement courses, advanced studio art-AP, algebra, American government, American history, American sign language, anatomy and physiology, ancient world history, applied arts, art, art history, Bible studies, biology, calculus-AP, career education, career exploration, career planning, Catholic belief and practice, chemistry, Christianity, church history, clayworking, college counseling, college placement, college planning, community service, computer applications, computer education, computer keyboarding, computer skills, costumes and make-up, creative drama, drama, drama performance, drama workshop, drawing, English, English composition, English language-AP, environmental science, government, history of the Catholic Church, honors algebra, honors English, honors geometry, honors U.S. history, honors world history, integrated math, Internet research, life management skills, marine biology, Microsoft, moral theology, peer ministry, personal fitness, physical education, physics, play production, playwriting and directing, portfolio art, pottery, pre-algebra, pre-calculus, psychology, religious education, senior career experience, Shakespeare, Spanish, Spanish language-AP, Spanish literature-AP, theology, U.S. history, weight training.

Graduation Requirements Advanced Placement courses, career/college preparation, Catholic belief and practice, college writing, computer literacy, dramatic arts, economics, English, environmental science, foreign language, government, mathematics, physical education (includes health), religion (includes Bible studies and theology), social studies (includes history), theology.

Special Academic Programs Advanced Placement exam preparation; study at local college for college credit; academic accommodation for the gifted and the artistically talented.

College Admission Counseling 75 students graduated in 2008; all went to college, including University of Central Florida; University of Florida; University of North Florida.

Student Life Upper grades have uniform requirement, student council, honor system. Discipline rests primarily with faculty. Attendance at religious services is required.

Summer Programs Sports programs offered; session focuses on Football conditioning, weight training, basketball clinics and tournaments; held both on and off campus; accepts boys and girls; not open to students from other schools. 80 students usually enrolled. 2009 schedule: June 1 to July 1. Application deadline: August 1.

Tuition and Aid Day student tuition: $7015–$9095. Tuition installment plan (FACTS Tuition Payment Plan). Need-based scholarship grants available. In 2008–09, 18% of upper-school students received aid. Total amount of financial aid awarded in 2008–09: $126,535.

Admissions Traditional secondary-level entrance grade is 9. ACT-Explore, any standardized test, Gates MacGinite Reading Tests, Iowa Tests of Basic Skills, Iowa Tests of Basic Skills-Grades 7-8, Archdiocese HSEPT-Grade 9, PSAT or SAT required. Deadline for receipt of application materials: none. Application fee required: $630. Interview required.

Athletics Interscholastic: baseball (boys), basketball (b,g), cross-country running (b,g), flag football (g), football (b), golf (b), physical fitness (b,g), soccer (b,g), softball (g), swimming and diving (b,g), tennis (b,g), track and field (b,g), volleyball (g), weight training (b), winter soccer (b,g), wrestling (b). 2 coaches, 2 athletic trainers.

Computers Computer network features include on-campus library services, Internet access, Internet filtering or blocking technology. Students grades are available online. The school has a published electronic and media policy.

Contact Mrs. Diane M. Albano, Director, Admissions and Development. 904-824-0431 Ext. 307. Fax: 904-824-4412. E-mail: admissions@sjaweb.org. Web site: www.sjaweb.org.

SAINT JOSEPH CENTRAL CATHOLIC HIGH SCHOOL

702 Croghan Street
Fremont, Ohio 43420
Head of School: Mr. Michael Gabel

General Information Coeducational day college-preparatory, arts, business, religious studies, bilingual studies, and technology school, affiliated with Roman Catholic Church. Grades 9–12. Founded: 1893. Setting: small town. Nearest major city is Toledo. 5-acre campus. 1 building on campus. Approved or accredited by Ohio

Department of Education. Endowment: $540,000. Total enrollment: 243. Upper school average class size: 20. Upper school faculty-student ratio: 1:15.
Upper School Student Profile Grade 9: 58 students (24 boys, 34 girls); Grade 10: 72 students (38 boys, 34 girls); Grade 11: 51 students (23 boys, 28 girls); Grade 12: 62 students (23 boys, 39 girls). 94% of students are Roman Catholic.
Faculty School total: 22. In upper school: 8 men, 14 women; 5 have advanced degrees.
Subjects Offered Advanced computer applications, advanced math, advanced TOEFL/grammar, American history, American literature, art, band, biology, biology-AP, bookkeeping, calculus, Catholic belief and practice, chemistry, choir, desktop publishing, drama, earth science, English, environmental science, family and consumer science, French, general business, graphic design, health education, honors English, human biology, integrated math, philosophy, physical education, physics, probability and statistics, programming, psychology, public speaking, reading/study skills, religion, senior project, social justice, social studies, Spanish, yearbook.
Graduation Requirements Computer literacy, English, government, humanities, mathematics, physical education (includes health), religion (includes Bible studies and theology), science, social studies (includes history), citizenship.
Special Academic Programs Advanced Placement exam preparation; honors section; study at local college for college credit; remedial reading and/or remedial writing; remedial math.
College Admission Counseling 54 students graduated in 2008; 51 went to college, including Bowling Green State University; Miami University; Ohio University; The Ohio State University; The University of Toledo; University of Dayton. Other: 3 went to work.
Student Life Upper grades have uniform requirement, student council, honor system. Discipline rests primarily with faculty. Attendance at religious services is required.
Tuition and Aid Day student tuition: $4050. Tuition reduction for siblings, merit scholarship grants, need-based scholarship grants available. In 2008–09, 20% of upper-school students received aid; total upper-school merit-scholarship money awarded: $2000. Total amount of financial aid awarded in 2008–09: $20,000.
Admissions Traditional secondary-level entrance grade is 9. High School Placement Test required. Deadline for receipt of application materials: none. Application fee required: $100.
Athletics Interscholastic: baseball (boys), basketball (b), bowling (b,g), cheering (g), cross-country running (b,g), football (b), golf (b), soccer (b,g), softball (g), swimming and diving (b,g), tennis (b,g), track and field (b,g), volleyball (g), wrestling (b); intramural: indoor track & field (b,g); coed intramural: basketball. 1 PE instructor, 10 coaches.
Computers Computers are regularly used in Spanish, yearbook classes. Computer network features include Internet access, wireless campus network. Student e-mail accounts are available to students. Students grades are available online.
Contact Mrs. Angie Ritzman, Development Director. 419-332-9947. Fax: 419-332-4945. E-mail: aritzman@fremontstjoe.org. Web site: www.fremontstjoe.org.

ST. JOSEPH HIGH SCHOOL

4120 Bradley Road
Santa Maria, California 93455
Head of School: Mr. Joseph Thomas Myers

General Information Coeducational day college-preparatory, arts, religious studies, and technology school, affiliated with Roman Catholic Church. Grades 9–12. Founded: 1964. Setting: suburban. 15-acre campus. 8 buildings on campus. Approved or accredited by California Association of Independent Schools, National Catholic Education Association, Western Association of Schools and Colleges, and Western Catholic Education Association. Endowment: $3.6 million. Total enrollment: 599. Upper school average class size: 25. Upper school faculty-student ratio: 1:18.
Upper School Student Profile Grade 9: 128 students (64 boys, 64 girls); Grade 10: 181 students (94 boys, 87 girls); Grade 11: 142 students (73 boys, 69 girls); Grade 12: 148 students (72 boys, 76 girls). 65% of students are Roman Catholic.
Faculty School total: 42. In upper school: 15 men, 24 women; 17 have advanced degrees.
Subjects Offered Art, biology, biology-AP, computer keyboarding, computer literacy, economics, English literature, English literature-AP, ethics, European history-AP, French, general science, grammar, Hebrew scripture, language and composition, marine science, New Testament, painting, peace and justice, physical science, physics, pre-algebra, psychology, remedial study skills, scripture, sculpture, sociology, Spanish, Spanish language-AP, speech, U.S. government, U.S. history, U.S. history-AP, U.S. literature, weight training, Western civilization.
Graduation Requirements Arts and fine arts (art, music, dance, drama), Catholic belief and practice, Christian and Hebrew scripture, Christian doctrine, Christian ethics, church history, civics, communication arts, composition, computer keyboarding, computer skills, economics, English, English literature, ethics, foreign language, health, history, human biology, introduction to literature, language structure, life science, literature, mathematics, religion (includes Bible studies and theology), science, U.S. government, Western civilization, world geography.
Special Academic Programs Remedial reading and/or remedial writing; remedial math.
College Admission Counseling 149 students graduated in 2008; 138 went to college, including California Polytechnic State University, San Luis Obispo; Loyola Marymount University; Santa Clara University; University of California, Santa Barbara. Other: 1 went to work, 2 entered military service. Mean SAT critical reading: 538, mean SAT math: 531, mean SAT writing: 518. 42% scored over 600 on SAT critical reading, 39% scored over 600 on SAT math, 34% scored over 600 on SAT writing.
Student Life Upper grades have specified standards of dress, student council. Discipline rests primarily with faculty. Attendance at religious services is required.
Summer Programs Remediation, advancement, sports programs offered; held on campus; accepts boys and girls; not open to students from other schools. 400 students usually enrolled. 2009 schedule: June 22 to July 31. Application deadline: June 15.
Tuition and Aid Day student tuition: $6775. Tuition installment plan (monthly payment plans). Tuition reduction for siblings, merit scholarship grants, need-based scholarship grants, paying campus jobs available. In 2008–09, 16% of upper-school students received aid; total upper-school merit-scholarship money awarded: $2000. Total amount of financial aid awarded in 2008–09: $250,000.
Admissions Traditional secondary-level entrance grade is 9. For fall 2008, 145 students applied for upper-level admission, 140 were accepted, 128 enrolled. High School Placement Test required. Deadline for receipt of application materials: February 5. Application fee required: $50.
Athletics Interscholastic: baseball (boys), basketball (b,g), cross-country running (b,g), football (b), golf (b,g), soccer (b,g), softball (g), swimming and diving (b,g), tennis (b,g), track and field (b,g), volleyball (b,g), water polo (b,g); intramural: dance team (g), flag football (g); coed interscholastic: cheering; coed intramural: basketball. 3 PE instructors, 35 coaches, 1 athletic trainer.
Computers Computers are regularly used in computer applications, economics, English, history, keyboarding, mathematics, religion, Spanish, theology, yearbook classes. Computer network features include on-campus library services, online commercial services, Internet access, Internet filtering or blocking technology. Computer access in designated common areas is available to students. Students grades are available online. The school has a published electronic and media policy.
Contact Joanne Poloni, Director of Admissions. 805-937-2038 Ext. 114. Fax: 805-937-4248. E-mail: poloni@sjhsknights.com. Web site: www.sjhsknights.com.

ST. JOSEPH HIGH SCHOOL

2320 Huntington Turnpike
Trumbull, Connecticut 06611
Head of School: Pres. William J Fitzgerald, PhD

General Information Coeducational day college-preparatory, arts, business, religious studies, and technology school, affiliated with Roman Catholic Church; primarily serves students with learning disabilities, individuals with Attention Deficit Disorder, and Mild Learning Disabilities. Grades 9–12. Founded: 1962. Setting: suburban. Nearest major city is Bridgeport. 25-acre campus. 2 buildings on campus. Approved or accredited by New England Association of Schools and Colleges and Connecticut Department of Education. Total enrollment: 848. Upper school average class size: 24. Upper school faculty-student ratio: 1:14.
Upper School Student Profile Grade 9: 222 students (116 boys, 106 girls); Grade 10: 212 students (101 boys, 111 girls); Grade 11: 205 students (95 boys, 110 girls); Grade 12: 209 students (98 boys, 111 girls). 85% of students are Roman Catholic.
Faculty School total: 64. In upper school: 25 men, 39 women; 41 have advanced degrees.
Subjects Offered Accounting, Advanced Placement courses, algebra, American history, American literature, art, art history, band, biology, business skills, calculus, chemistry, chorus, community service, computer applications, current events, design, drawing, earth science, ecology, economics, English, English literature, European history, finance, fine arts, French, geography, geometry, government/civics, health, history, international relations, Italian, journalism, law, mathematics, music, painting, philosophy, physical education, physics, poetry, pre-calculus, psychology, religion, science, sculpture, Shakespeare, social studies, sociology, Spanish, statistics, study skills, theology, trigonometry, word processing.
Graduation Requirements Arts and fine arts (art, music, dance, drama), English, foreign language, mathematics, physical education (includes health), religion (includes Bible studies and theology), science, social studies (includes history). Community service is required.
Special Academic Programs 7 Advanced Placement exams for which test preparation is offered; honors section; study at local college for college credit; academic accommodation for the gifted; special instructional classes for students with learning disabilities and Attention Deficit Disorder.
College Admission Counseling 182 students graduated in 2008; 175 went to college, including Boston College; Boston University; Fairfield University; Providence College; Southern Connecticut State University; University of Connecticut. Other: 1 entered military service, 1 entered a postgraduate year. Mean SAT critical reading: 535, mean SAT math: 515, mean SAT writing: 546, mean combined SAT: 1597, mean composite ACT: 22.
Student Life Upper grades have uniform requirement, student council. Discipline rests primarily with faculty. Attendance at religious services is required.
Tuition and Aid Day student tuition: $9775. Tuition installment plan (monthly payment plans, one lump sum payment with discount by June 1 or two payments by semester, payment plan through People's Bank). Tuition reduction for siblings, merit scholarship grants, need-based scholarship grants available. In 2008–09, 34% of upper-school students received aid; total upper-school merit-scholarship money awarded: $148,000. Total amount of financial aid awarded in 2008–09: $235,000.

Admissions Admissions testing, High School Placement Test and STS—Educational Development Series required. Deadline for receipt of application materials: December 1. Application fee required: $50.

Athletics Interscholastic: baseball (boys), basketball (b,g), cheering (g), cross-country running (b,g), diving (g), football (b), hockey (b,g), ice hockey (b), indoor track & field (b,g), lacrosse (b,g), softball (g), swimming and diving (g), tennis (b,g), track and field (b,g), volleyball (b,g); coed interscholastic: bowling, golf. 2 PE instructors, 61 coaches, 2 athletic trainers.

Computers Computer network features include on-campus library services, online commercial services, Internet access. The school has a published electronic and media policy.

Contact Peggy Kuhar Marino '71, Director of Admission. 203-378-9378 Ext. 308. Fax: 203-378-7306. E-mail: pmarino@sjcadets.org. Web site: www.sjcadets.org.

SAINT JOSEPH HIGH SCHOOL

10900 West Cermak Road
Westchester, Illinois 60154-4299

Head of School: Ms. Donna Kiel

General Information Coeducational day college-preparatory, arts, business, vocational, religious studies, bilingual studies, and technology school, affiliated with Christian faith. Grades 9–12. Founded: 1960. Setting: suburban. Nearest major city is Chicago. 21-acre campus. 2 buildings on campus. Approved or accredited by Christian Brothers Association, North Central Association of Colleges and Schools, and Illinois Department of Education. Total enrollment: 827. Upper school average class size: 25. Upper school faculty-student ratio: 1:17.

Upper School Student Profile Grade 9: 238 students (142 boys, 96 girls); Grade 10: 220 students (132 boys, 88 girls); Grade 11: 208 students (125 boys, 83 girls); Grade 12: 161 students (97 boys, 64 girls). 95% of students are Christian.

Faculty School total: 68. In upper school: 36 men, 32 women; 23 have advanced degrees.

Subjects Offered Accounting, acting, advanced studio art-AP, algebra, American history, anatomy and physiology, art, band, biology, business law, calculus, calculus-AP, ceramics, chemistry, Christian ethics, computer applications, computer graphics, computer programming, computer science-AP, computer-aided design, concert band, concert choir, consumer economics, creative writing, current events, digital photography, economics, English, English-AP, environmental science, European history-AP, film studies, fine arts, French, geography, geometry, graphic arts, health, human biology, internship, Italian, jazz band, journalism, marching band, marketing, men's studies, moral and social development, music appreciation, peace and justice, peer ministry, photography, physical education, physics, physics-AP, pre-algebra, pre-calculus, reading, reading/study skills, sociology, Spanish, Spanish-AP, speech, sports conditioning, sports medicine, studio art, studio art-AP, theater production, U.S. history, Web site design, women spirituality and faith, world cultures, world religions.

Graduation Requirements Arts and fine arts (art, music, dance, drama), computer applications, economics, English, foreign language, mathematics, physical education (includes health), religion (includes Bible studies and theology), science, social studies (includes history), Each student must complete 40 community service hours.

Special Academic Programs Advanced Placement exam preparation; honors section; study at local college for college credit; academic accommodation for the gifted, the musically talented, and the artistically talented; remedial reading and/or remedial writing; remedial math.

College Admission Counseling 139 students graduated in 2008; 135 went to college, including Brown University; DePaul University; Loyola University Chicago; The Ohio State University; University of Illinois at Urbana–Champaign; University of Notre Dame. Other: 3 went to work, 1 entered military service. Median composite ACT: 22. 10% scored over 26 on composite ACT.

Student Life Upper grades have specified standards of dress, student council, honor system. Discipline rests primarily with faculty. Attendance at religious services is required.

Summer Programs Remediation programs offered; session focuses on make-up credit for failed courses; held on campus; accepts boys and girls; open to students from other schools. 200 students usually enrolled. 2009 schedule: June 15 to July 30. Application deadline: June 5.

Tuition and Aid Day student tuition: $7450. Merit scholarship grants, need-based scholarship grants, paying campus jobs available. In 2008–09, 40% of upper-school students received aid; total upper-school merit-scholarship money awarded: $75,000. Total amount of financial aid awarded in 2008–09: $500,000.

Admissions Traditional secondary-level entrance grade is 9. For fall 2008, 315 students applied for upper-level admission, 275 were accepted, 238 enrolled. TerraNova required. Deadline for receipt of application materials: none. Application fee required: $250. Interview required.

Athletics Interscholastic: aerobics/dance (girls), baseball (b), basketball (b,g), bowling (b,g), boxing (b), cheering (g), cross-country running (b,g), dance team (g), football (b), golf (b,g), hockey (g), ice hockey (g), soccer (b,g), softball (g), strength & conditioning (b,g), tennis (b,g), track and field (b,g), volleyball (b,g), wrestling (b). 22 coaches.

Computers Computers are regularly used in business applications, computer applications, current events, desktop publishing, drafting, economics, English, French, geography, graphic arts, graphic design, health, history, journalism, mathematics, music, newspaper, photography, reading, religion, science, social studies, Spanish, speech, technology, theater arts, writing, yearbook classes. Computer network features include on-campus library services, online commercial services, Internet access, wireless campus network, Internet filtering or blocking technology, all students have a laptop computer with wireless access to the Internet, anywhere on campus. Campus intranet and student e-mail accounts are available to students. Students grades are available online. The school has a published electronic and media policy.

Contact Mr. Joseph Tortorich, Director of Finance and Admissions. 708-562-4433 Ext. 114. Fax: 708-562-4459. E-mail: jtortorich@stjoeshs.org.

SAINT JOSEPH HIGH SCHOOL

800 Montana Avenue
Natrona Heights, Pennsylvania 15065

Head of School: Ms. Beverly K. Kaniecki

General Information Coeducational day college-preparatory school, affiliated with Roman Catholic Church. Grades 9–12. Founded: 1916. Setting: suburban. Nearest major city is Pittsburgh. 2 buildings on campus. Approved or accredited by Middle States Association of Colleges and Schools and Pennsylvania Department of Education. Total enrollment: 180. Upper school average class size: 20. Upper school faculty-student ratio: 1:14.

Upper School Student Profile Grade 9: 48 students (22 boys, 26 girls); Grade 10: 52 students (29 boys, 23 girls); Grade 11: 45 students (21 boys, 24 girls); Grade 12: 34 students (18 boys, 16 girls). 90% of students are Roman Catholic.

Faculty School total: 18. In upper school: 6 men, 12 women; 10 have advanced degrees.

Subjects Offered American history, American literature, art, art history, biology, British literature, calculus, Catholic belief and practice, chemistry, choir, composition, French, freshman seminar, geometry, Latin, macroeconomics-AP, physical education, physics, pre-calculus, psychology, religion, robotics, Spanish, statistics, trigonometry, U.S. history, Web site design, world history, world literature.

Special Academic Programs Honors section; study at local college for college credit.

College Admission Counseling 47 students graduated in 2008; 46 went to college, including Duquesne University; John Carroll University; Penn State University Park; University of Notre Dame; University of Pittsburgh. Other: 1 entered a postgraduate year. Mean SAT critical reading: 506, mean SAT math: 508.

Student Life Upper grades have uniform requirement. Discipline rests primarily with faculty. Attendance at religious services is required.

Summer Programs Enrichment programs offered; session focuses on developing skills; held on campus; accepts boys and girls; open to students from other schools.

Tuition and Aid Day student tuition: $6450. Tuition installment plan (FACTS Tuition Payment Plan). Tuition reduction for siblings, merit scholarship grants, need-based scholarship grants available. In 2008–09, 60% of upper-school students received aid; total upper-school merit-scholarship money awarded: $16,000.

Admissions Traditional secondary-level entrance grade is 9. High School Placement Test (closed version) from Scholastic Testing Service required. Deadline for receipt of application materials: none. Application fee required: $25. Interview recommended.

Athletics Interscholastic: baseball (boys), basketball (b,g), cheering (g), golf (b,g), softball (g), swimming and diving (b,g), tennis (b,g); intramural: flag football (b), touch football (b), volleyball (g); coed interscholastic: golf, soccer, volleyball. 2 PE instructors, 15 coaches.

Computers Computers are regularly used in graphic design classes. Computer network features include Internet access, wireless campus network, Internet filtering or blocking technology. Students grades are available online. The school has a published electronic and media policy.

Contact Mrs. Christine Anne Harmon, Guidance Counselor. 724-224-5552. Fax: 724-224-3205. E-mail: charmon@salsgiver.com. Web site: www.saintjosehhs.com.

SAINT JOSEPH HIGH SCHOOL

2401 69th Street
Kenosha, Wisconsin 53143

Head of School: Mr. Robert Freund

General Information Coeducational day college-preparatory, general academic, arts, religious studies, and technology school, affiliated with Roman Catholic Church; primarily serves students with learning disabilities. Grades 7–12. Founded: 1957. Setting: suburban. Nearest major city is Milwaukee. 1 building on campus. Approved or accredited by National Catholic Education Association, North Central Association of Colleges and Schools, and Wisconsin Department of Education. Endowment: $100,000. Total enrollment: 461. Upper school average class size: 20. Upper school faculty-student ratio: 1:20.

Upper School Student Profile Grade 9: 88 students (44 boys, 44 girls); Grade 10: 78 students (44 boys, 34 girls); Grade 11: 60 students (33 boys, 27 girls); Grade 12: 80 students (36 boys, 44 girls). 80% of students are Roman Catholic.

Faculty School total: 34. In upper school: 9 men, 19 women; 12 have advanced degrees.

Subjects Offered Algebra, American government, anatomy and physiology, architecture, art, band, biology, biology-AP, calculus-AP, ceramics, chemistry, chemistry-AP, choir, Christian scripture, computer applications, computers, consumer mathematics, creative writing, critical writing, drafting, drama, drawing, economics, English, English-AP, film, French, geometry, health, Hebrew scripture, Italian, journalism, keyboarding, mathematics, newspaper, photography, physical education, physical science, physics-AP, pre-algebra, pre-calculus, psychology, reading/study skills, science, social studies, Spanish, speech, statistics, studio art, theater, theology, trigonometry, U.S. history, world history, world religions, yearbook.

Graduation Requirements Arts and fine arts (art, music, dance, drama), computers, electives, English, mathematics, physical education (includes health), religion (includes Bible studies and theology), science, social studies (includes history).

Special Academic Programs Advanced Placement exam preparation; honors section.

College Admission Counseling 66 students graduated in 2008; 55 went to college, including Marquette University; University of Wisconsin–Madison; University of Wisconsin–Milwaukee. Other: 5 went to work, 6 had other specific plans. Mean composite ACT: 23. 25% scored over 26 on composite ACT.

Student Life Upper grades have specified standards of dress, student council, honor system. Discipline rests primarily with faculty. Attendance at religious services is required.

Tuition and Aid Day student tuition: $6750. Tuition installment plan (monthly payment plans, individually arranged payment plans). Tuition reduction for siblings, merit scholarship grants, need-based scholarship grants available. In 2008–09, 29% of upper-school students received aid; total upper-school merit-scholarship money awarded: $45,000. Total amount of financial aid awarded in 2008–09: $100,000.

Admissions Traditional secondary-level entrance grade is 9. For fall 2008, 100 students applied for upper-level admission, 100 were accepted, 88 enrolled. ACT-Explore or admissions testing required. Deadline for receipt of application materials: none. Application fee required: $100.

Athletics Interscholastic: baseball (boys), basketball (b,g), cheering (b,g), cross-country running (b,g), football (b), golf (b,g), soccer (b,g), softball (g). 2 PE instructors, 15 coaches, 1 athletic trainer.

Computers Computers are regularly used in all classes. Computer resources include Internet access, Internet filtering or blocking technology. Campus intranet is available to students. Students grades are available online.

Contact Mrs. Linda Browne, Admissions Director. 262-654-8651 Ext. 108. Fax: 262-654-1615. E-mail: lbrowne@kenoshastjoseph.com. Web site: www.kenoshastjoseph.com.

SAINT JOSEPH REGIONAL HIGH SCHOOL

40 Chestnut Ridge Road
Montvale, New Jersey 07645

Head of School: Mr. Barry Donnelly

General Information Boys' day college-preparatory school, affiliated with Roman Catholic Church. Grades 9–12. Founded: 1962. Setting: suburban. Nearest major city is New York, NY. 33-acre campus. 1 building on campus. Approved or accredited by Middle States Association of Colleges and Schools and New Jersey Department of Education. Total enrollment: 501. Upper school average class size: 23. Upper school faculty-student ratio: 1:12.

Upper School Student Profile Grade 9: 142 students (142 boys); Grade 10: 131 students (131 boys); Grade 11: 112 students (112 boys); Grade 12: 116 students (116 boys).

Faculty School total: 35. In upper school: 27 men, 8 women; 21 have advanced degrees.

Subjects Offered Accounting, advanced chemistry, advanced math, Advanced Placement courses, algebra, American government, American history, American history-AP, American literature, anatomy, art, art appreciation, Bible studies, biology, biology-AP, British literature, calculus, calculus-AP, Catholic belief and practice, chemistry, chemistry-AP, Christian doctrine, church history, computer applications, computer keyboarding, computer science, driver education, economics, English, English-AP, European history-AP, French, geography, geometry, health education, honors algebra, honors English, honors geometry, honors U.S. history, honors world history, keyboarding/computer, Latin, law, New Testament, physical education, physics, physics-AP, pre-calculus, psychology, religion, science, social studies, Spanish, Spanish-AP, studio art, The 20th Century, theology, U.S. government, U.S. history, U.S. history-AP, Western civilization, word processing, world cultures, world geography, world history.

Special Academic Programs Advanced Placement exam preparation; honors section; study at local college for college credit.

College Admission Counseling 116 students graduated in 2008; all went to college, including Fairfield University; Iona College; Penn State University Park; Rutgers, The State University of New Jersey, New Brunswick; The University of Scranton.

Student Life Upper grades have specified standards of dress, student council, honor system. Discipline rests primarily with faculty. Attendance at religious services is required.

Tuition and Aid Day student tuition: $10,200. Tuition installment plan (FACTS Tuition Payment Plan). Tuition reduction for siblings, merit scholarship grants, need-based scholarship grants, need-based loans available.

Admissions Traditional secondary-level entrance grade is 9. Cooperative Entrance Exam (McGraw-Hill) required. Deadline for receipt of application materials: none. No application fee required. Interview required.

Athletics Interscholastic: baseball, basketball, bowling, cross-country running, football, golf, ice hockey, indoor track & field, lacrosse, physical fitness, running, soccer, tennis, track and field, weight lifting, weight training, winter (indoor) track, wrestling.

Computers Computers are regularly used in all classes. Computer network features include Internet access, wireless campus network, Internet filtering or blocking technology. Campus intranet is available to students. The school has a published electronic and media policy.

Contact Mr. Michael J. Doherty, Director of Admissions. 201-391-3300 Ext. 19. Fax: 201-391-8073. E-mail: mdoherty@saintjosephregional.org. Web site: www.saintjosephregional.org.

ST. JOSEPH'S ACADEMY

3015 Broussard Street
Baton Rouge, Louisiana 70808

Head of School: Linda Fryoux Harvison

General Information Girls' day college-preparatory, arts, religious studies, and technology school, affiliated with Roman Catholic Church. Grades 9–12. Founded: 1868. Setting: urban. 14-acre campus. 6 buildings on campus. Approved or accredited by National Catholic Education Association, Southern Association of Colleges and Schools, Southern Association of Independent Schools, and Louisiana Department of Education. Endowment: $3.6 million. Total enrollment: 877. Upper school average class size: 23. Upper school faculty-student ratio: 1:14.

Upper School Student Profile Grade 9: 230 students (230 girls); Grade 10: 230 students (230 girls); Grade 11: 218 students (218 girls); Grade 12: 199 students (199 girls). 94% of students are Roman Catholic.

Faculty School total: 67. In upper school: 6 men, 61 women; 35 have advanced degrees.

Subjects Offered Accounting, acting, advanced chemistry, advanced computer applications, advanced math, Advanced Placement courses, algebra, American history, American history-AP, American literature, American literature-AP, analysis, analysis and differential calculus, art, art appreciation, band, Basic programming, biology, biology-AP, business law, calculus-AP, campus ministry, Catholic belief and practice, chemistry, child development, choir, choral music, chorus, Christian and Hebrew scripture, church history, civics, civics/free enterprise, computer applications, computer information systems, computer multimedia, computer programming, computer technologies, computer technology certification, CPR, critical studies in film, dance, desktop publishing, drama, drama performance, economics, English, English literature-AP, English-AP, entrepreneurship, environmental science, European history-AP, family and consumer science, family and consumer sciences, film and literature, fine arts, foreign language, French, French as a second language, geometry, grammar, health, health and safety, health education, Hebrew scripture, honors algebra, honors English, honors geometry, human sexuality, independent study, information technology, Latin, marching band, media arts, media production, music, novels, physical education, physical fitness, physics, poetry, pre-calculus, public speaking, religion, research, Shakespeare, social justice, Spanish, speech, speech communications, technology, the Web, transition mathematics, U.S. history, U.S. history-AP, U.S. literature, visual arts, vocal ensemble, vocal music, Web authoring, Web site design, world history-AP.

Graduation Requirements Advanced math, algebra, American history, arts and fine arts (art, music, dance, drama), biology, chemistry, civics, computer applications, English, foreign language, geometry, physical education (includes health), physical science, physics, religion (includes Bible studies and theology), world history, service hours.

Special Academic Programs Advanced Placement exam preparation; honors section; independent study; study at local college for college credit.

College Admission Counseling 192 students graduated in 2008; all went to college, including Auburn University; Louisiana State University and Agricultural and Mechanical College; Louisiana Tech University; Loyola University New Orleans; University of Louisiana at Lafayette; University of Mississippi. 69% scored over 26 on composite ACT.

Student Life Upper grades have uniform requirement, student council, honor system. Discipline rests primarily with faculty. Attendance at religious services is required.

Summer Programs Computer instruction programs offered; session focuses on computer orientation for incoming 9th grade students; held on campus; accepts girls; not open to students from other schools. 230 students usually enrolled. 2009 schedule: June 5 to June 25. Application deadline: March 16.

Tuition and Aid Day student tuition: $8349. Tuition installment plan (monthly debit plan). Need-based scholarship grants available. In 2008–09, 6% of upper-school students received aid. Total amount of financial aid awarded in 2008–09: $218,295.

Admissions Traditional secondary-level entrance grade is 9. For fall 2008, 245 students applied for upper-level admission, 240 were accepted, 230 enrolled. STS required. Deadline for receipt of application materials: November 21. Application fee required: $35. On-campus interview required.

Athletics Interscholastic: basketball, bowling, cheering, cross-country running, dance squad, golf, gymnastics, running, soccer, softball, strength & conditioning, swimming and diving, tennis, track and field, volleyball; coed intramural: volleyball. 6 PE instructors, 9 coaches, 1 athletic trainer.

Computers Computers are regularly used in all classes. Computer network features include on-campus library services, online commercial services, Internet access,

wireless campus network, Internet filtering or blocking technology, administrative software/grading/scheduling. Student e-mail accounts are available to students. Students grades are available online. The school has a published electronic and media policy.

Contact Kathy Meares, Assistant Principal of Records. 225-388-2213. Fax: 225-344-5714. E-mail: mearesk@sjabr.org. Web site: www.sjabr.org.

ST. JOSEPH'S CATHOLIC SCHOOL

100 St. Joseph's Drive
Greenville, South Carolina 29607

Head of School: Mr. Keith F. Kiser

General Information Coeducational day college-preparatory school, affiliated with Roman Catholic Church. Grades 6–12. Founded: 1993. Setting: suburban. 36-acre campus. 3 buildings on campus. Approved or accredited by South Carolina Independent School Association and South Carolina Department of Education. Total enrollment: 540. Upper school average class size: 17. Upper school faculty-student ratio: 1:13.

Upper School Student Profile Grade 9: 81 students (35 boys, 46 girls); Grade 10: 81 students (35 boys, 46 girls); Grade 11: 65 students (22 boys, 43 girls); Grade 12: 57 students (30 boys, 27 girls). 78% of students are Roman Catholic.

Faculty School total: 45. In upper school: 13 men, 20 women; 16 have advanced degrees.

Subjects Offered Algebra, American history, American literature, art, arts appreciation, bell choir, biology, biology-AP, calculus-AP, chemistry, chemistry-AP, chorus, Christian doctrine, Christian ethics, church history, composition, computer applications, computer graphics, dance, drama workshop, drawing, economics, economics-AP, English literature and composition-AP, English-AP, ensembles, European history, European history-AP, European literature, exercise science, film studies, fine arts, forensic science, French, geometry, government, government-AP, honors algebra, honors English, honors geometry, human movement and its application to health, Latin, literature, medieval/Renaissance history, moral theology, newspaper, personal money management, physical education, physics, physics-AP, pre-calculus, science fiction, Shakespeare, Spanish, Spanish-AP, speech, statistics-AP, strings, theater arts, theater production, U.S. history, U.S. history-AP, yearbook.

Graduation Requirements 65 hours of community service.

Special Academic Programs Advanced Placement exam preparation; honors section.

College Admission Counseling 50 students graduated in 2008; all went to college, including Clemson University; College of Charleston; Furman University; University of South Carolina. Median SAT critical reading: 593, median SAT math: 603, median SAT writing: 604, median combined SAT: 1800, median composite ACT: 25.

Student Life Upper grades have uniform requirement, student council, honor system. Discipline rests primarily with faculty. Attendance at religious services is required.

Summer Programs Sports, art/fine arts programs offered; held on campus; accepts boys and girls; open to students from other schools.

Tuition and Aid Day student tuition: $8340. Tuition installment plan (monthly payment plans, yearly payment plan, semiannual payment plan). Tuition reduction for siblings, merit scholarship grants, need-based scholarship grants, tuition reduction for staff available. In 2008–09, 40% of upper-school students received aid; total upper-school merit-scholarship money awarded: $27,790. Total amount of financial aid awarded in 2008–09: $140,500.

Admissions Traditional secondary-level entrance grade is 9. For fall 2008, 53 students applied for upper-level admission, 41 were accepted, 28 enrolled. High School Placement Test (closed version) from Scholastic Testing Service required. Deadline for receipt of application materials: May 31. Application fee required: $125. On-campus interview required.

Athletics Interscholastic: baseball (boys), basketball (b,g), cheering (g), cross-country running (b,g), golf (b), soccer (b,g), softball (g), swimming and diving (b,g), tennis (b,g), volleyball (g), wrestling (b); intramural: flag football (b); coed intramural: dance, weight training.

Computers Computers are regularly used in computer applications, graphic design, keyboarding, programming, yearbook classes. Computer network features include Internet access.

Contact Mrs. Barbara L. McGrath, Director of Admissions. 864-234-9009 Ext. 104. Fax: 864-234-5516. E-mail: bmcgrath@sjcatholicschool.org. Web site: www.sjcatholicschool.org.

ST. JOSEPH'S PREPARATORY SCHOOL

1733 Girard Avenue
Philadelphia, Pennsylvania 19130

Head of School: Rev. George W. Bur, SJ

General Information Boys' day college-preparatory, arts, and religious studies school, affiliated with Roman Catholic Church. Grades 9–12. Founded: 1851. Setting: urban. 7-acre campus. 3 buildings on campus. Approved or accredited by Jesuit Secondary Education Association, Middle States Association of Colleges and Schools, National Catholic Education Association, and Pennsylvania Department of Education. Member of National Association of Independent Schools. Endowment: $3.5 million. Total enrollment: 976. Upper school average class size: 26. Upper school faculty-student ratio: 1:16.

Upper School Student Profile Grade 9: 230 students (230 boys); Grade 10: 259 students (259 boys); Grade 11: 236 students (236 boys); Grade 12: 251 students (251 boys). 95% of students are Roman Catholic.

Faculty School total: 65. In upper school: 49 men, 13 women; 40 have advanced degrees.

Subjects Offered Algebra, American history, American literature, anatomy, archaeology, art, biology, business, calculus, chemistry, classics, computer math, computer programming, computer science, driver education, earth science, economics, English, English literature, environmental science, ethics, European history, fine arts, French, geometry, German, government/civics, Greek, history, Latin, Mandarin, marine biology, mathematics, photography, physical education, physics, physiology, religion, science, social science, social studies, Spanish, speech, trigonometry, world history, world literature.

Graduation Requirements Arts and fine arts (art, music, dance, drama), classics, computer science, English, foreign language, mathematics, physical education (includes health), religion (includes Bible studies and theology), science, social science, social studies (includes history), Christian service hours in junior and senior year.

Special Academic Programs Advanced Placement exam preparation; honors section; accelerated programs; independent study; study at local college for college credit; study abroad; academic accommodation for the gifted, the musically talented, and the artistically talented.

College Admission Counseling 234 students graduated in 2008; 231 went to college, including Fordham University; Georgetown University; Penn State University Park; Saint Joseph's University; Temple University; University of Pennsylvania. Other: 3 entered a postgraduate year. Mean SAT critical reading: 615, mean SAT math: 613, mean SAT writing: 614, mean combined SAT: 1852. 55% scored over 600 on SAT critical reading, 55% scored over 600 on SAT math, 55% scored over 600 on SAT writing, 55% scored over 1800 on combined SAT.

Student Life Upper grades have specified standards of dress, student council. Discipline rests primarily with faculty. Attendance at religious services is required.

Summer Programs Remediation, enrichment, art/fine arts programs offered; session focuses on pre-8th grade enrichment; held on campus; accepts boys and girls; open to students from other schools. 500 students usually enrolled. 2009 schedule: June 25 to July 25. Application deadline: none.

Tuition and Aid Day student tuition: $16,600. Tuition installment plan (monthly payment plans). Tuition reduction for siblings, merit scholarship grants, need-based scholarship grants, need-based loans, middle-income loans, paying campus jobs available. In 2008–09, 66% of upper-school students received aid; total upper-school merit-scholarship money awarded: $500,000. Total amount of financial aid awarded in 2008–09: $2,000,000.

Admissions Traditional secondary-level entrance grade is 9. For fall 2008, 663 students applied for upper-level admission, 270 were accepted, 230 enrolled. 3-R Achievement Test required. Deadline for receipt of application materials: November 11. Application fee required: $60. On-campus interview recommended.

Athletics Interscholastic: baseball, basketball, bowling, crew, cross-country running, football, Frisbee, golf, ice hockey, indoor track & field, lacrosse, rowing, rugby, soccer, squash, swimming and diving, tennis, track and field, ultimate Frisbee, wrestling; intramural: basketball, flag football, juggling, martial arts, table tennis, volleyball. 35 coaches, 1 athletic trainer.

Computers Computers are regularly used in English, mathematics, science classes. Computer network features include on-campus library services, Internet access, wireless campus network, Internet filtering or blocking technology. Student e-mail accounts are available to students. Students grades are available online. The school has a published electronic and media policy.

Contact Jason M. Zazyczny, Director of Admission. 215-978-1958. Fax: 215-978-1920. E-mail: jzazyczny@sjprep.org. Web site: www.sjprep.org.

ST. JUDE'S SCHOOL

420 Weber Street North
Waterloo, Ontario N2L 3X2, Canada

Head of School: Mr. Frederick T. Gore

General Information Coeducational day college-preparatory, arts, temporary alternative to the Publicly Funded System or, and Bright Learning Disabled school; primarily serves underachievers, students with learning disabilities, individuals with Attention Deficit Disorder, dyslexic students, and auditory processing. Grades 1–12. Founded: 1982. Setting: small town. Nearest major city is Toronto. 1-acre campus. 1 building on campus. Approved or accredited by Conference of Independent Schools of Ontario, Ontario Ministry of Education, and Ontario Department of Education. Language of instruction: English. Total enrollment: 30. Upper school average class size: 10. Upper school faculty-student ratio: 1:5.

Upper School Student Profile Grade 6: 3 students (2 boys, 1 girl); Grade 7: 5 students (3 boys, 2 girls); Grade 8: 5 students (3 boys, 2 girls); Grade 9: 7 students (4 boys, 3 girls); Grade 10: 2 students (2 boys); Grade 11: 1 student (1 boy).

Faculty School total: 6. In upper school: 3 men, 3 women; 3 have advanced degrees.

Subjects Offered 20th century history, 20th century physics, 20th century world history, accounting, acting, adolescent issues, advanced chemistry, advanced math, algebra, analytic geometry, ancient history, ancient world history, ancient/medieval philosophy, anthropology, applied arts, art, art appreciation, art education, art history, basic skills, biology, bookkeeping, business education, business law, business mathematics, business studies, calculus, Canadian history, Canadian law, Canadian literature, career and personal planning, career education, chemistry, civics, college counseling, communication skills, computer keyboarding, computer literacy, computer science, computer skills, computer studies, discrete math, discrete mathematics, dramatic arts, drawing and design, earth and space science, ecology, ecology, environmental systems, economics, economics and history, English, English literature, environmental studies, ESL, family studies, fencing, finite math, French as a second language, general science, geography, health, health education, history, honors algebra, honors English, honors geometry, independent study, intro to computers, keyboarding, law, law studies, marketing, media studies, modern Western civilization, modern world history, philosophy, physical education, physical fitness, physics-AP, remedial study skills, remedial/makeup course work, science, science and technology, society, politics and law, sociology, Spanish, study skills, visual arts, Western philosophy, world issues.

Graduation Requirements Ontario requirements.

Special Academic Programs Remedial reading and/or remedial writing; remedial math; programs in English, mathematics, general development for dyslexic students; special instructional classes for students with learning disabilities, Attention Deficit Disorder, and dyslexia; ESL (5 students enrolled).

College Admission Counseling 3 students graduated in 2008; all went to college, including University of Waterloo; Wilfrid Laurier University.

Student Life Upper grades have uniform requirement, student council, honor system. Discipline rests primarily with faculty.

Summer Programs Session focuses on English and Math; held on campus; accepts boys and girls; open to students from other schools. 15 students usually enrolled. 2009 schedule: July 1 to July 30. Application deadline: June 1.

Tuition and Aid Day student tuition: CAN$16,900. Tuition installment plan (monthly payment plans, individually arranged payment plans).

Admissions For fall 2008, 5 students applied for upper-level admission, 5 were accepted, 5 enrolled. Academic Profile Tests, achievement tests and Woodcock-Johnson Educational Evaluation, WISC III required. No application fee required. Interview required.

Athletics Interscholastic: synchronized swimming (girls); coed interscholastic: basketball, bowling, cross-country running, fencing, golf; coed intramural: badminton, ball hockey, baseball, basketball, bowling, cross-country running, curling, fencing, fitness, floor hockey, golf, martial arts. 2 PE instructors.

Computers Computers are regularly used in all classes. Computer network features include Internet access, Internet filtering or blocking technology.

Contact Frederick T. Gore, Director of Education. 519-888-6620. Fax: 519-888-0316. E-mail: director2@stjudes.com. Web site: www.stjudes.com.

ST. LAWRENCE SEMINARY

301 Church Street
Mount Calvary, Wisconsin 53057

Head of School: Fr. Dennis Druggan, OFMCAP

General Information Boys' boarding college-preparatory and religious studies school, affiliated with Roman Catholic Church. Grades 9–12. Founded: 1860. Setting: rural. Nearest major city is Milwaukee. Students are housed in single-sex dormitories. 150-acre campus. 11 buildings on campus. Approved or accredited by National Catholic Education Association, North Central Association of Colleges and Schools, and Wisconsin Department of Education. Total enrollment: 200. Upper school average class size: 17. Upper school faculty-student ratio: 1:10.

Upper School Student Profile Grade 9: 47 students (47 boys); Grade 10: 55 students (55 boys); Grade 11: 52 students (52 boys); Grade 12: 47 students (47 boys). 100% of students are boarding students. 30% are state residents. 16 states are represented in upper school student body. 14% are international students. International students from India, Mali, Philippines, Republic of Korea, Saudi Arabia, and Viet Nam; 4 other countries represented in student body. 100% of students are Roman Catholic.

Faculty School total: 26. In upper school: 20 men, 6 women; 10 have advanced degrees; 7 reside on campus.

Subjects Offered Accounting, algebra, American history, American literature, art, biology, business, business law, calculus, chemistry, classical studies, computer science, English, English literature, fine arts, geometry, German, government/civics, health, health and wellness, humanities, industrial arts, lab/keyboard, Latin, literary genres, mathematics, mechanical drawing, music, physical education, physics, psychology, religion, science, socioeconomic problems, Spanish, theology, trigonometry, world history, world literature.

Graduation Requirements Arts and fine arts (art, music, dance, drama), business skills (includes word processing), computer science, English, foreign language, health education, humanities, mathematics, physical education (includes health), religion (includes Bible studies and theology), science, social studies (includes history), study skills, Ministry hours.

Special Academic Programs Study at local college for college credit.

College Admission Counseling 43 students graduated in 2008; 41 went to college, including Marquette University; Saint Xavier University; University of Chicago; University of Dallas; University of Minnesota, Duluth; University of Wisconsin–Madison. Other: 1 went to work, 1 had other specific plans. Median SAT critical reading: 550, median SAT math: 600, median SAT writing: 540, median combined SAT: 1630, median composite ACT: 23. 10% scored over 600 on SAT critical reading, 50% scored over 600 on SAT math, 20% scored over 600 on SAT writing, 30% scored over 1800 on combined SAT, 23% scored over 26 on composite ACT.

Student Life Upper grades have specified standards of dress, student council, honor system. Discipline rests primarily with faculty. Attendance at religious services is required.

Tuition and Aid 7-day tuition and room/board: $8400. Tuition installment plan (monthly payment plans, individually arranged payment plans). Need-based scholarship grants available. In 2008–09, 73% of upper-school students received aid. Total amount of financial aid awarded in 2008–09: $778,110.

Admissions Traditional secondary-level entrance grade is 9. For fall 2008, 77 students applied for upper-level admission, 65 were accepted, 57 enrolled. 3-R Achievement Test and any standardized test required. Deadline for receipt of application materials: May 31. Application fee required: $25. Interview recommended.

Athletics Interscholastic: baseball, basketball, cross-country running, soccer, track and field, wrestling; intramural: basketball, billiards, bowling, floor hockey, Frisbee, handball, kickball, outdoor activities, outdoor recreation, physical fitness, physical training, racquetball, skiing (downhill), softball, table tennis, tennis, volleyball, wallyball, weight lifting, winter soccer. 3 PE instructors, 8 coaches, 1 athletic trainer.

Computers Computers are regularly used in accounting, business education, classics, creative writing, drafting, economics, English, keyboarding, mathematics, psychology, science, typing, writing, yearbook classes. Computer network features include on-campus library services, Internet access, Internet filtering or blocking technology. Campus intranet, student e-mail accounts, and computer access in designated common areas are available to students. The school has a published electronic and media policy.

Contact Mr. Timothy Alan Guiden, Director of Admissions. 920-753-7522. Fax: 920-753-7507. E-mail: tguiden@stlawrence.edu. Web site: www.stlawrence.edu.

ST. MARGARET'S EPISCOPAL SCHOOL

31641 La Novia Avenue
San Juan Capistrano, California 92675

Head of School: Mr. Marcus D. Hurlbut

General Information Coeducational day college-preparatory, arts, religious studies, and technology school, affiliated with Episcopal Church. Grades PS–12. Founded: 1979. Setting: suburban. Nearest major city is Los Angeles. 21-acre campus. 6 buildings on campus. Approved or accredited by California Association of Independent Schools, National Association of Episcopal Schools, Western Association of Schools and Colleges, and California Department of Education. Member of National Association of Independent Schools. Endowment: $2.5 million. Total enrollment: 1,227. Upper school average class size: 13. Upper school faculty-student ratio: 1:6.

Upper School Student Profile Grade 9: 109 students (52 boys, 57 girls); Grade 10: 103 students (52 boys, 51 girls); Grade 11: 106 students (59 boys, 47 girls); Grade 12: 86 students (39 boys, 47 girls). 13% of students are members of Episcopal Church.

Faculty School total: 118. In upper school: 21 men, 33 women; 42 have advanced degrees.

Subjects Offered Algebra, American history, American literature, anatomy and physiology, anthropology, art, art history, art history-AP, art-AP, astronomy, Bible studies, biology, biology-AP, calculus, calculus-AP, chemistry, chemistry-AP, Chinese, community service, computer math, computer programming, computer science, computer science-AP, creative writing, drama, economics, English, English language and composition-AP, English language-AP, English literature, English literature and composition-AP, environmental science, environmental science-AP, ethics, European history, expository writing, fine arts, French, French language-AP, French literature-AP, French-AP, geography, geometry, government-AP, government/civics, history, history-AP, human development, Japanese, Japanese literature, journalism, Latin, Latin-AP, mathematics, music, music theory-AP, philosophy, physical education, physics, physics-AP, religion, science, social science, social studies, Spanish, Spanish language-AP, Spanish literature-AP, Spanish-AP, speech, statistics-AP, theater, trigonometry, world history, world history-AP, world literature, world religions, writing.

Graduation Requirements Arts and fine arts (art, music, dance, drama), computer science, English, foreign language, mathematics, physical education (includes health), religion (includes Bible studies and theology), science, social science, social studies (includes history). Community service is required.

Special Academic Programs 24 Advanced Placement exams for which test preparation is offered; honors section; independent study; study at local college for college credit; academic accommodation for the gifted, the musically talented, and the artistically talented.

College Admission Counseling 99 students graduated in 2008; all went to college, including Arizona State University; Southern Methodist University; University of California, San Diego; University of California, Santa Barbara; University of Southern California. Mean SAT critical reading: 618, mean SAT math: 630, mean SAT writing: 628, mean combined SAT: 1876.

Student Life Upper grades have specified standards of dress, student council, honor system. Discipline rests equally with students and faculty. Attendance at religious services is required.

Summer Programs Enrichment, advancement, sports, art/fine arts programs offered; session focuses on academic enrichment; held on campus; accepts boys and girls; open to students from other schools. 250 students usually enrolled. 2009 schedule: June 29 to July 31.
Tuition and Aid Day student tuition: $20,455. Tuition installment plan (monthly payment plans). Need-based scholarship grants available. In 2008–09, 20% of upper-school students received aid. Total amount of financial aid awarded in 2008–09: $1,431,790.
Admissions Traditional secondary-level entrance grade is 9. For fall 2008, 76 students applied for upper-level admission, 64 were accepted, 42 enrolled. ISEE required. Deadline for receipt of application materials: February 7. Application fee required: $75. Interview required.
Athletics Interscholastic: baseball (boys), basketball (b,g), cheering (g), cross-country running (b,g), football (b), golf (b,g), lacrosse (b,g), modern dance (g), soccer (b,g), softball (g), swimming and diving (b,g), tennis (b,g), track and field (b,g), volleyball (b,g), wrestling (b); intramural: aerobics/dance (b,g), badminton (g), paint ball (b), strength & conditioning (b,g); coed interscholastic: dance, diving, dressage, equestrian sports, independent competitive sports; coed intramural: badminton, fencing, physical fitness. 3 PE instructors, 10 coaches, 1 athletic trainer.
Computers Computers are regularly used in English, foreign language, history, mathematics, science, technology classes. Computer network features include on-campus library services, Internet access, wireless campus network, Internet filtering or blocking technology. Campus intranet, student e-mail accounts, and computer access in designated common areas are available to students. Students grades are available online. The school has a published electronic and media policy.
Contact Mr. Ryan S. Dahlem, Director of Admission and Financial Aid. 949-661-0108 Ext. 251. Fax: 949-240-1748. E-mail: ryan.dahlem@smes.org. Web site: www.smes.org.

ST. MARGARET'S SCHOOL

444 Water Lane
PO Box 158
Tappahannock, Virginia 22560
Head of School: Margaret R. Broad

General Information Girls' boarding and day college-preparatory and religious studies school, affiliated with Episcopal Church. Grades 8–12. Founded: 1921. Setting: small town. Nearest major city is Richmond. Students are housed in single-sex dormitories. 51-acre campus. 9 buildings on campus. Approved or accredited by Southern Association of Colleges and Schools, Virginia Association of Independent Schools, and Virginia Department of Education. Member of National Association of Independent Schools and Secondary School Admission Test Board. Endowment: $5.7 million. Total enrollment: 152. Upper school average class size: 10. Upper school faculty-student ratio: 1:6.
Upper School Student Profile Grade 8: 10 students (10 girls); Grade 9: 24 students (24 girls); Grade 10: 36 students (36 girls); Grade 11: 39 students (39 girls); Grade 12: 43 students (43 girls). 75% of students are boarding students. 47% are state residents. 17 states are represented in upper school student body. 23% are international students. International students from China, Japan, Mexico, Republic of Korea, and Taiwan; 4 other countries represented in student body. 25% of students are members of Episcopal Church.
Faculty School total: 34. In upper school: 6 men, 28 women; 15 have advanced degrees; 30 reside on campus.
Subjects Offered Algebra, American literature, anatomy and physiology, ancient history, art, art history, biology, biology-AP, British literature, calculus, calculus-AP, ceramics, chemistry, chorus, community service, computer science, conceptual physics, creative writing, drama, driver education, ecology, English, English-AP, ESL, European history, finance, fine arts, French, French-AP, geography, geometry, government/civics, health, history, history-AP, illustration, journalism, Latin, leadership, mathematics, music, music history, painting, photography, physical education, physics, piano, pre-algebra, religion, science, social studies, Spanish, U.S. government, world history, world literature, writing.
Graduation Requirements Arts and fine arts (art, music, dance, drama), computer science, English, foreign language, history, mathematics, physical education (includes health), religion (includes Bible studies and theology), science. Community service is required.
Special Academic Programs Advanced Placement exam preparation; honors section; independent study; study abroad; ESL (19 students enrolled).
College Admission Counseling 28 students graduated in 2008; all went to college, including Lynchburg College; Parsons The New School for Design; Saint Joseph's University; The College of William and Mary; Virginia Commonwealth University; Wofford College. Median SAT critical reading: 500, median SAT math: 510, median SAT writing: 535. 18% scored over 600 on SAT critical reading, 36% scored over 600 on SAT math, 25% scored over 600 on SAT writing.
Student Life Upper grades have uniform requirement, student council, honor system. Discipline rests equally with students and faculty. Attendance at religious services is required.
Tuition and Aid Day student tuition: $14,950; 7-day tuition and room/board: $37,500. Tuition installment plan (monthly payment plans). Need-based scholarship grants available. In 2008–09, 32% of upper-school students received aid. Total amount of financial aid awarded in 2008–09: $790,000.
Admissions Traditional secondary-level entrance grade is 9. For fall 2008, 111 students applied for upper-level admission, 86 were accepted, 58 enrolled. SSAT required. Deadline for receipt of application materials: none. Application fee required: $40. On-campus interview required.
Athletics Interscholastic: basketball, crew, cross-country running, field hockey, golf, indoor track & field, lacrosse, soccer, softball, swimming and diving, tennis, volleyball, winter (indoor) track; intramural: ballet, canoeing/kayaking, crew, dance, fitness, fitness walking, horseback riding, kayaking, modern dance, outdoor activities, strength & conditioning, tennis, ultimate Frisbee, walking, weight training. 1 PE instructor, 7 coaches, 1 athletic trainer.
Computers Computers are regularly used in English, foreign language, history, journalism, science, yearbook classes. Computer network features include on-campus library services, online commercial services, Internet access, wireless campus network, Internet filtering or blocking technology. Campus intranet, student e-mail accounts, and computer access in designated common areas are available to students. The school has a published electronic and media policy.
Contact Kimberly McDowell, Assistant Head, External Affairs, Director of Admission. 804-443-3357. Fax: 804-443-6781. E-mail: admit@sms.com. Web site: www.sms.org.

ANNOUNCEMENT FROM THE SCHOOL It is an exciting time to be at St. Margaret's School. Forty-two acres near the campus have been developed into a multi-field athletic complex, which also includes a cross-country course. The School opened its fall 2007 sports season on the new facilities. St. Margaret's programs are growing, too, from student leadership to the life-skills co-curriculum. Come join us!

See Close-Up on page 940.

ST. MARGARET'S SCHOOL

1080 Lucas Avenue
Victoria, British Columbia V8X 3P7, Canada
Head of School: Linda McGregor

General Information Girls' boarding and day college-preparatory, general academic, arts, technology, and ESL school. Boarding grades 7–12, day grades JK–12. Founded: 1908. Setting: suburban. Students are housed in single-sex dormitories. 22-acre campus. 10 buildings on campus. Approved or accredited by Canadian Association of Independent Schools, The Association of Boarding Schools, and British Columbia Department of Education. Language of instruction: English. Total enrollment: 346. Upper school average class size: 18. Upper school faculty-student ratio: 1:8.
Upper School Student Profile 30% of students are boarding students. 70% are province residents. 6 provinces are represented in upper school student body. 30% are international students. International students from China, Hong Kong, Japan, Mexico, Republic of Korea, and Taiwan; 6 other countries represented in student body.
Faculty School total: 38. In upper school: 7 men, 30 women; 12 have advanced degrees.
Subjects Offered Advanced Placement courses, algebra, applied skills, art, biology, calculus, Canadian geography, Canadian history, career and personal planning, chemistry, Chinese, choir, communications, comparative civilizations, computer science, creative writing, dance, drama, English, English literature, ESL, fine arts, French, geography, history, information technology, Japanese, journalism, law, leadership training, Mandarin, mathematics, music, music appreciation, outdoor education, performing arts, photography, physical education, physics, science, social studies, Spanish, theater, Western civilization, writing.
Graduation Requirements Applied skills, arts and fine arts (art, music, dance, drama), English, foreign language, mathematics, science, social studies (includes history).
Special Academic Programs Advanced Placement exam preparation; ESL (38 students enrolled).
College Admission Counseling 48 students graduated in 2008; 46 went to college, including McGill University; Simon Fraser University; The University of British Columbia; University of Toronto; University of Victoria; University of Waterloo. Other: 2 had other specific plans.
Student Life Upper grades have uniform requirement, student council. Discipline rests primarily with faculty.
Summer Programs ESL programs offered; session focuses on ESL combined with recreational activities and sightseeing; held both on and off campus; held at various locations for the local homestay program; accepts girls; open to students from other schools. 20 students usually enrolled. 2009 schedule: July 5 to July 31. Application deadline: May 1.
Tuition and Aid Day student tuition: CAN$6054–CAN$16,301; 7-day tuition and room/board: CAN$31,831–CAN$39,411. Tuition installment plan (Insured Tuition Payment Plan, monthly payment plans). Tuition reduction for siblings, bursaries, merit scholarship grants, need-based scholarship grants available. In 2008–09, 17% of

upper-school students received aid; total upper-school merit-scholarship money awarded: CAN$30,000. Total amount of financial aid awarded in 2008–09: CAN$70,000.

Admissions Traditional secondary-level entrance grade is 7. For fall 2008, 115 students applied for upper-level admission, 97 were accepted, 92 enrolled. School's own exam required. Deadline for receipt of application materials: none. Application fee required. Interview required.

Athletics Interscholastic: aerobics/dance, aquatics, badminton, basketball, cross-country running, dance, field hockey, fitness, rowing, running, soccer, swimming and diving, synchronized swimming, track and field, volleyball; intramural: aerobics, aerobics/dance, alpine skiing, aquatics, backpacking, badminton, baseball, basketball, bicycling, canoeing/kayaking, climbing, cooperative games, cross-country running, dance, equestrian sports, field hockey, figure skating, fitness, floor hockey, Frisbee, golf, gymnastics, hiking/backpacking, horseback riding, ice skating, indoor soccer, jogging, jump rope, kayaking, martial arts, modern dance, mountain biking, ocean paddling, outdoor activities, paddle tennis, physical fitness, rock climbing, ropes courses, rugby, running, sailing, skiing (cross-country), skiing (downhill), snowboarding, soccer, softball, squash, strength & conditioning, surfing, swimming and diving, table tennis, tennis, track and field, ultimate Frisbee, volleyball, wallyball, weight training, wilderness, wilderness survival, yoga. 4 PE instructors, 3 coaches, 1 athletic trainer.

Computers Computers are regularly used in career exploration, English, ESL, foreign language, French, history, journalism, mathematics, science classes. Computer network features include Internet access, wireless campus network, Internet filtering or blocking technology. Student e-mail accounts and computer access in designated common areas are available to students.

Contact Mrs. Kathy Parsons, Director of Admissions. 250-479-7171. Fax: 250-479-8976. E-mail: stmarg@stmarg.ca. Web site: www.stmarg.ca.

SAINT MARK'S SCHOOL

25 Marlborough Road
Southborough, Massachusetts 01772

Head of School: Mr. John Warren

General Information Coeducational boarding and day college-preparatory, arts, religious studies, and classics, math school, affiliated with Episcopal Church. Grades 9–12. Founded: 1865. Setting: suburban. Nearest major city is Boston. Students are housed in single-sex dormitories. 250-acre campus. 15 buildings on campus. Approved or accredited by New England Association of Schools and Colleges and Massachusetts Department of Education. Member of National Association of Independent Schools and Secondary School Admission Test Board. Endowment: $133 million. Total enrollment: 336. Upper school average class size: 10. Upper school faculty-student ratio: 1:5.

Upper School Student Profile Grade 9: 63 students (30 boys, 33 girls); Grade 10: 95 students (50 boys, 45 girls); Grade 11: 88 students (51 boys, 37 girls); Grade 12: 89 students (44 boys, 45 girls). 78% of students are boarding students. 54% are state residents. 18 states are represented in upper school student body. 10% are international students. International students from Australia, Canada, Hong Kong, Republic of Korea, Taiwan, and Thailand; 14 other countries represented in student body. 30% of students are members of Episcopal Church.

Faculty School total: 71. In upper school: 40 men, 31 women; 48 have advanced degrees; 68 reside on campus.

Subjects Offered 20th century history, Advanced Placement courses, algebra, American history, American literature, art, art history, biology, calculus, ceramics, chemistry, civil war history, computer math, computer science, computer science-AP, computer skills, computer studies, constitutional history of U.S., creative writing, DNA, drama, drama workshop, driver education, earth science, Eastern religion and philosophy, ecology, economics, English, English literature, environmental science, ethics, European history, expository writing, fine arts, French, geography, geometry, German, government/civics, Greek, history, Latin, Latin-AP, logic, mathematics, music, music history, music theory, music theory-AP, music-AP, photography, physics, physiology, psychology, religion, science, scripture, social studies, Spanish, Spanish language-AP, Spanish literature, Spanish literature-AP, statistics, studio art, studio art—AP, theater, trigonometry, world history, world literature.

Graduation Requirements Arts and fine arts (art, music, dance, drama), English, foreign language, mathematics, religion (includes Bible studies and theology), science, social studies (includes history).

Special Academic Programs Advanced Placement exam preparation; honors section; independent study; term-away projects; study abroad; academic accommodation for the gifted, the musically talented, and the artistically talented.

College Admission Counseling 89 students graduated in 2008; all went to college, including Boston University; Bucknell University; Georgetown University; Hobart and William Smith Colleges; The George Washington University; Tufts University. Mean SAT critical reading: 623, mean SAT math: 652.

Student Life Upper grades have specified standards of dress, student council, honor system. Discipline rests equally with students and faculty.

Tuition and Aid Day student tuition: $33,000; 7-day tuition and room/board: $41,300. Tuition installment plan (Key Tuition Payment Plan, monthly payment plans). Need-based scholarship grants, need-based loans available. In 2008–09, 26% of upper-school students received aid. Total amount of financial aid awarded in 2008–09: $2,700,000.

Admissions Traditional secondary-level entrance grade is 9. For fall 2008, 649 students applied for upper-level admission, 187 were accepted, 81 enrolled. SSAT and TOEFL required. Deadline for receipt of application materials: January 31. Application fee required: $50. Interview required.

Athletics Interscholastic: baseball (boys), basketball (b,g), crew (b,g), cross-country running (b,g), field hockey (g), Fives (b), football (b), golf (b,g), ice hockey (b,g), lacrosse (b,g), soccer (b,g), softball (g), squash (b,g), tennis (b,g), volleyball (g), wrestling (b); intramural: aerobics/dance (g), volleyball (b,g), weight lifting (b,g); coed interscholastic: dance; coed intramural: aerobics, aerobics/Nautilus, billiards, outdoor activities, yoga. 15 coaches, 2 athletic trainers.

Computers Computers are regularly used in English, foreign language, mathematics, science classes. Computer network features include on-campus library services, Internet access, wireless campus network, Internet filtering or blocking technology. Student e-mail accounts and computer access in designated common areas are available to students. The school has a published electronic and media policy.

Contact Anne E. Behnke, Director of Admission. 508-786-6000. Fax: 508-786-6120. E-mail: annebehnke@stmarksschool.org. Web site: www.stmarksschool.org.

ST. MARK'S SCHOOL OF TEXAS

10600 Preston Road
Dallas, Texas 75230-4000

Head of School: Mr. Arnold E. Holtberg

General Information Boys' day college-preparatory, arts, technology, and Advanced Placement school. Grades 1–12. Founded: 1906. Setting: urban. 40-acre campus. 13 buildings on campus. Approved or accredited by Independent Schools Association of the Southwest. Member of National Association of Independent Schools. Endowment: $107.3 million. Total enrollment: 841. Upper school average class size: 15. Upper school faculty-student ratio: 1:8.

Upper School Student Profile Grade 9: 96 students (96 boys); Grade 10: 85 students (85 boys); Grade 11: 95 students (95 boys); Grade 12: 88 students (88 boys).

Faculty School total: 105. In upper school: 41 men, 18 women; 51 have advanced degrees.

Subjects Offered 3-dimensional art, acting, algebra, American history-AP, ancient world history, art, art history, astronomy, Basic programming, biology, biology-AP, calculus, calculus-AP, ceramics, chemistry, chemistry-AP, Chinese, choir, community service, computer programming, computer science, computer science-AP, concert band, creative writing, digital art, digital photography, DNA, DNA science lab, drama, drama workshop, economics, economics-AP, English, English literature and composition-AP, English literature-AP, environmental science-AP, European history, European history-AP, fine arts, geology, geometry, German-AP, history, honors English, honors geometry, independent study, Japanese, journalism, Latin, Latin-AP, macroeconomics-AP, mathematics, microeconomics-AP, modern European history-AP, modern world history, music, photography, physical education, physics, physics-AP, pottery, psychology, science, senior project, Spanish, Spanish language-AP, Spanish literature-AP, statistics-AP, studio art-AP, theater, trigonometry, U.S. history, video film production, woodworking, world history, world religions.

Graduation Requirements Arts and fine arts (art, music, dance, drama), English, foreign language, mathematics, physical education (includes health), science, social studies (includes history), senior exhibition. Community service is required.

Special Academic Programs Advanced Placement exam preparation; honors section; independent study; term-away projects.

College Admission Counseling 75 students graduated in 2008; all went to college, including Duke University; Harvard University; Northwestern University; Stanford University; The University of Texas at Austin; University of Virginia. Median SAT critical reading: 700, median SAT math: 730, median SAT writing: 700. Mean composite ACT: 30. 81% scored over 600 on SAT critical reading, 92% scored over 600 on SAT math, 85% scored over 600 on SAT writing, 89% scored over 26 on composite ACT.

Student Life Upper grades have uniform requirement, student council, honor system. Discipline rests primarily with faculty. Attendance at religious services is required.

Tuition and Aid Day student tuition: $21,489–$22,874. Tuition installment plan (Insured Tuition Payment Plan, financial aid student monthly payment plan). Need-based scholarship grants, tuition remission for sons of faculty and staff, need-based middle-income financial aid available. In 2008–09, 17% of upper-school students received aid. Total amount of financial aid awarded in 2008–09: $1,916,667.

Admissions Traditional secondary-level entrance grade is 9. For fall 2008, 88 students applied for upper-level admission, 17 were accepted, 14 enrolled. ISEE required. Deadline for receipt of application materials: January 9. Application fee required: $125. Interview required.

Athletics Interscholastic: backpacking, baseball, basketball, cheering, climbing, crew, cross-country running, diving, fencing, football, golf, hiking/backpacking, hockey, ice hockey, lacrosse, outdoor education, outdoor skills, physical fitness, physical training, soccer, strength & conditioning, swimming and diving, tennis, track and field, volleyball, wall climbing, water polo, weight training, wilderness, winter soccer, wrestling; intramural: basketball, bicycling, cooperative games, cross-country running, fitness, flag football, floor hockey, jump rope, kickball, lacrosse, physical fitness, physical training, soccer, softball, swimming and diving, table tennis, team handball, tennis, track and field, volleyball, water polo, weight training, winter soccer, wrestling. 8 PE instructors, 9 coaches, 2 athletic trainers.

Computers Computers are regularly used in English, foreign language, humanities, mathematics, science classes. Computer network features include on-campus library services, online commercial services, Internet access, wireless campus network, Internet filtering or blocking technology. Student e-mail accounts are available to students. The school has a published electronic and media policy.
Contact Mr. David P. Baker, Director of Admission and Financial Aid. 214-346-8700. Fax: 214-346-8701. E-mail: admission@smtexas.org. Web site: www.smtexas.org.

See Close-Up on page 942.

ST. MARTIN'S EPISCOPAL SCHOOL

5309 Airline Drive
Metairie, Louisiana 70003-2499
Head of School: Dr. Jeffrey Pratt Beedy

General Information Coeducational day college-preparatory school, affiliated with Episcopal Church. Grades PK–12. Founded: 1947. Setting: suburban. Nearest major city is New Orleans. 18-acre campus. 13 buildings on campus. Approved or accredited by Independent Schools Association of the Southwest, National Association of Episcopal Schools, Southern Association of Colleges and Schools, Southwest Association of Episcopal Schools, The College Board, and Louisiana Department of Education. Member of National Association of Independent Schools. Endowment: $5.6 million. Total enrollment: 613. Upper school average class size: 17. Upper school faculty-student ratio: 1:9.
Upper School Student Profile Grade 9: 55 students (20 boys, 35 girls); Grade 10: 48 students (22 boys, 26 girls); Grade 11: 65 students (33 boys, 32 girls); Grade 12: 58 students (29 boys, 29 girls). 15% of students are members of Episcopal Church.
Faculty School total: 77. In upper school: 12 men, 19 women; 21 have advanced degrees.
Subjects Offered Advanced chemistry, advanced math, Advanced Placement courses, advanced studio art-AP, algebra, American history, American history-AP, American literature, American literature-AP, art, art history, baseball, basketball, bell choir, Bible studies, biology, biology-AP, business skills, calculus, calculus-AP, career education internship, career/college preparation, ceramics, chemistry, chemistry-AP, Chinese, choir, chorus, civics, college counseling, community service, computer literacy, computer programming, computer science, computer skills, creative writing, discrete math, drama, earth science, economics, economics and history, economics-AP, English, English language and composition-AP, English language-AP, English literature, English literature and composition-AP, English literature-AP, environmental science, environmental studies, film and literature, film studies, fine arts, French, French-AP, geography, geology, geometry, government/civics, grammar, history-AP, honors algebra, honors English, honors geometry, humanities, internship, journalism, lab science, Latin, Latin-AP, law, law studies, life management skills, life skills, literary magazine, mathematics, music, music appreciation, music theory-AP, musical productions, newspaper, philosophy, physical education, physics, pre-algebra, public speaking, publications, religion, SAT preparation, science, senior internship, social studies, softball, Southern literature, Spanish, Spanish-AP, student government, studio art, studio art-AP, swimming, theater, track and field, trigonometry, U.S. history-AP, world history, world literature, world religions, writing.
Graduation Requirements Arts and fine arts (art, music, dance, drama), computer science, electives, English, foreign language, mathematics, physical education (includes health), religion (includes Bible studies and theology), science, senior internship, social science, social studies (includes history), senior intern program, 50 hours of community service.
Special Academic Programs 10 Advanced Placement exams for which test preparation is offered; honors section; independent study.
College Admission Counseling 64 students graduated in 2008; all went to college, including College of Charleston; Louisiana State University and Agricultural and Mechanical College; Loyola University New Orleans; Rhodes College; Tulane University; University of Mississippi. Median SAT critical reading: 560, median SAT math: 580, median SAT writing: 555, median combined SAT: 1675, median composite ACT: 24. 30% scored over 600 on SAT critical reading, 40% scored over 600 on SAT math, 27% scored over 600 on SAT writing, 27% scored over 1800 on combined SAT, 30% scored over 26 on composite ACT.
Student Life Upper grades have specified standards of dress, student council, honor system. Discipline rests primarily with faculty. Attendance at religious services is required.
Summer Programs Remediation, enrichment, advancement, sports programs offered; session focuses on academics, athletics, creative arts, and enrichment; held on campus; accepts boys and girls; open to students from other schools. 400 students usually enrolled. 2009 schedule: June 1 to August 13. Application deadline: May 15.
Tuition and Aid Day student tuition: $16,400. Tuition installment plan (local bank-arranged plan). Merit scholarship grants, need-based scholarship grants available. In 2008–09, 30% of upper-school students received aid; total upper-school merit-scholarship money awarded: $268,850. Total amount of financial aid awarded in 2008–09: $568,210.
Admissions Traditional secondary-level entrance grade is 9. For fall 2008, 46 students applied for upper-level admission, 34 were accepted, 19 enrolled. ISEE or WISC III or other aptitude measures; standardized achievement test required. Deadline for receipt of application materials: none. Application fee required: $40. On-campus interview required.
Athletics Interscholastic: baseball (boys), basketball (b,g), cheering (b,g), cross-country running (b,g), flag football (b), football (b), golf (b,g), running (b,g), soccer (b,g), softball (g), swimming and diving (b,g), tennis (b,g), track and field (b,g), volleyball (g); intramural: basketball (b,g), cheering (b,g), cross-country running (b,g), golf (b,g), ropes courses (b,g), running (b,g), soccer (b,g), swimming and diving (b,g), tennis (b,g), track and field (b,g), volleyball (g); coed interscholastic: cheering; coed intramural: cheering. 2 PE instructors, 7 coaches, 1 athletic trainer.
Computers Computers are regularly used in all academic classes. Computer network features include on-campus library services, online commercial services, Internet access, wireless campus network, Internet filtering or blocking technology, VPN for teachers, staff and students. Campus intranet, student e-mail accounts, and computer access in designated common areas are available to students. Students grades are available online. The school has a published electronic and media policy.
Contact Mary White, Assistant Director of Admission. 504-736-9918. Fax: 504-736-8802. E-mail: mary.white@stmsaints.com. Web site: www.stmsaints.com.

SAINT MARY HIGH SCHOOL

64 Chestnut Street
Rutherford, New Jersey 07070
Head of School: Roy Corso

General Information Coeducational day college-preparatory school, affiliated with Roman Catholic Church; primarily serves students with learning disabilities, individuals with Attention Deficit Disorder, individuals with emotional and behavioral problems, and dyslexic students. Grades 9–12. Founded: 1929. Setting: suburban. Nearest major city is New York, NY. 2-acre campus. 2 buildings on campus. Approved or accredited by Middle States Association of Colleges and Schools and New Jersey Department of Education. Upper school average class size: 17. Upper school faculty-student ratio: 1:10.
Upper School Student Profile Grade 9: 70 students (35 boys, 35 girls); Grade 10: 90 students (45 boys, 45 girls); Grade 11: 90 students (45 boys, 45 girls); Grade 12: 92 students (46 boys, 46 girls). 90% of students are Roman Catholic.
Faculty School total: 30. In upper school: 14 men, 16 women; 15 have advanced degrees.
Special Academic Programs International Baccalaureate program; Advanced Placement exam preparation; independent study.
College Admission Counseling 92 students graduated in 2008; 91 went to college, including Montclair State University; Rutgers, The State University of New Jersey, New Brunswick; Saint Joseph's University. Other: 1 went to work.
Student Life Upper grades have uniform requirement, student council, honor system. Discipline rests equally with students and faculty. Attendance at religious services is required.
Summer Programs Remediation programs offered; held on campus; accepts boys and girls; open to students from other schools. 100 students usually enrolled. 2009 schedule: June 28 to July 31.
Tuition and Aid Day student tuition: $7000. Tuition reduction for siblings, merit scholarship grants, need-based scholarship grants, middle-income loans available.
Admissions Traditional secondary-level entrance grade is 9. For fall 2008, 300 students applied for upper-level admission, 100 were accepted, 70 enrolled. Cooperative Entrance Exam (McGraw-Hill) required. Deadline for receipt of application materials: none. Application fee required.
Athletics Interscholastic: baseball (boys), basketball (b,g), cheering (g), football (b), soccer (b,g), softball (g), volleyball (b), wrestling (g); coed interscholastic: bowling, cross-country running, track and field. 2 PE instructors, 8 coaches, 1 athletic trainer.
Computers Computers are regularly used in business applications, computer applications, desktop publishing, English, graphic design, history, information technology, keyboarding, library, multimedia, newspaper, programming, science, technology, typing, video film production, Web site design, yearbook classes. Computer network features include on-campus library services, online commercial services, Internet access, wireless campus network, Internet filtering or blocking technology. Campus intranet, student e-mail accounts, and computer access in designated common areas are available to students. The school has a published electronic and media policy.
Contact Mr. John Galka, Director of Admissions. 201-933-5220 Ext. 251. Fax: 201-933-0834. E-mail: jgalka@stmaryhs.org. Web site: www.stmaryhs.org.

ST. MARY'S ACADEMY

4545 South University Boulevard
Englewood, Colorado 80113-6059
Head of School: Deirdre Cryor

General Information Coeducational day (boys' only in lower grades) college-preparatory, arts, religious studies, and technology school, affiliated with Roman Catholic Church. Boys grades K–8, girls grades K–12. Founded: 1864. Setting: suburban. Nearest major city is Denver. 24-acre campus. 5 buildings on campus. Approved or accredited by Association of Colorado Independent Schools, National Independent Private Schools Association, North Central Association of Colleges and

Schools, and Colorado Department of Education. Member of National Association of Independent Schools. Endowment: $4.2 million. Total enrollment: 738. Upper school average class size: 16. Upper school faculty-student ratio: 1:10.

Upper School Student Profile Grade 9: 73 students (73 girls); Grade 10: 59 students (59 girls); Grade 11: 72 students (72 girls); Grade 12: 65 students (65 girls). 50% of students are Roman Catholic.

Faculty School total: 79. In upper school: 9 men, 28 women; 27 have advanced degrees.

Subjects Offered Algebra, American history, American literature, anatomy, art, art history, astronomy, biology, calculus, ceramics, chemistry, community service, creative writing, cultural criticism, dance, drama, ecology, economics, English, English literature, European history, expository writing, fine arts, French, genetics, geography, geometry, government/civics, grammar, history, mathematics, music, philosophy, philosophy of government, photography, physical education, physics, physiology, psychology, religion, science, social studies, Spanish, theater, theology, trigonometry, women's studies, world history, world literature, writing, zoology.

Graduation Requirements Arts and fine arts (art, music, dance, drama), English, foreign language, mathematics, physical education (includes health), religion (includes Bible studies and theology), science, social studies (includes history). Community service is required.

Special Academic Programs 12 Advanced Placement exams for which test preparation is offered; honors section; independent study.

College Admission Counseling 55 students graduated in 2008; all went to college, including Boston University; Creighton University; University of Colorado at Boulder; University of Denver; University of Notre Dame. Mean SAT critical reading: 589, mean SAT math: 584, mean SAT writing: 605.

Student Life Upper grades have specified standards of dress, student council. Discipline rests primarily with faculty.

Tuition and Aid Day student tuition: $12,000. Tuition installment plan (FACTS Tuition Payment Plan, monthly payment plans). Merit scholarship grants, need-based scholarship grants available. In 2008–09, 36% of upper-school students received aid; total upper-school merit-scholarship money awarded: $76,800. Total amount of financial aid awarded in 2008–09: $535,289.

Admissions Traditional secondary-level entrance grade is 9. High School Placement Test (closed version) from Scholastic Testing Service required. Deadline for receipt of application materials: January 11. Application fee required: $60. Interview required.

Athletics Interscholastic: aerobics/dance, badminton, basketball, cross-country running, dance team, diving, field hockey, golf, independent competitive sports, lacrosse, running, soccer, softball, swimming and diving, tennis, track and field, volleyball. 3 PE instructors, 18 coaches, 1 athletic trainer.

Computers Computers are regularly used in art, college planning, drawing and design, English, foreign language, history, journalism, mathematics, science, technology, writing classes. Computer network features include on-campus library services, online commercial services, Internet access, wireless campus network, Internet filtering or blocking technology. Campus intranet and student e-mail accounts are available to students. Students grades are available online. The school has a published electronic and media policy.

Contact Linda Ticer, Director of Admissions. 303-762-8300. Fax: 303-783-6201. E-mail: linda_ticer@smanet.org. Web site: www.smanet.org.

SAINT MARY'S COLLEGE HIGH SCHOOL

1294 Albina Avenue
Peralta Park
Berkeley, California 94706

Head of School: Peter Imperial

General Information Coeducational day college-preparatory school, affiliated with Roman Catholic Church. Grades 9–12. Founded: 1863. Setting: urban. Nearest major city is Oakland. 13-acre campus. 9 buildings on campus. Approved or accredited by National Catholic Education Association, Western Association of Schools and Colleges, and Western Catholic Education Association. Endowment: $638,000. Total enrollment: 620. Upper school average class size: 28. Upper school faculty-student ratio: 1:16.

Upper School Student Profile Grade 9: 169 students (83 boys, 86 girls); Grade 10: 156 students (78 boys, 78 girls); Grade 11: 142 students (74 boys, 68 girls); Grade 12: 153 students (70 boys, 83 girls). 55% of students are Roman Catholic.

Faculty School total: 41. In upper school: 28 men, 13 women; 20 have advanced degrees.

Subjects Offered Algebra, American history, American literature, art, band, biology, biology-AP, calculus-AP, chemistry, chorus, conceptual physics, concert band, dance, diversity studies, economics, English, English language and composition-AP, English literature, English literature-AP, French, French language-AP, geometry, government-AP, government/civics, graphic design, health education, jazz band, journalism, mathematics, philosophy, photography, physical education, physics, physics-AP, psychology, religion, Spanish, Spanish language-AP, sports medicine, studio art-AP, theater, trigonometry, U.S. history-AP, world history, world religions, yearbook.

Graduation Requirements Electives, English, foreign language, health and wellness, lab science, mathematics, physical education (includes health), religious studies, U.S. history, visual and performing arts, world history, service learning, enrichment week mini-course (once a year).

Special Academic Programs 10 Advanced Placement exams for which test preparation is offered; honors section.

College Admission Counseling 156 students graduated in 2008; 154 went to college, including San Francisco State University; San Jose State University; University of California, Berkeley; University of California, Davis; University of California, Santa Cruz; University of Oregon. Other: 1 went to work, 1 had other specific plans.

Student Life Upper grades have specified standards of dress, student council. Discipline rests primarily with faculty. Attendance at religious services is required.

Summer Programs Remediation programs offered; held on campus; accepts boys and girls; not open to students from other schools. 45 students usually enrolled.

Tuition and Aid Day student tuition: $13,200. Tuition installment plan (monthly payment plans). Need-based scholarship grants available. In 2008–09, 35% of upper-school students received aid. Total amount of financial aid awarded in 2008–09: $900,000.

Admissions Traditional secondary-level entrance grade is 9. For fall 2008, 420 students applied for upper-level admission, 260 were accepted, 167 enrolled. High School Placement Test and writing sample required. Deadline for receipt of application materials: January 2. Application fee required: $75. Interview required.

Athletics Interscholastic: baseball (boys), basketball (b,g), cross-country running (b,g), football (b), golf (b,g), lacrosse (b), soccer (b,g), softball (g); coed interscholastic: cheering, diving, swimming and diving; coed intramural: basketball. 1 PE instructor, 1 athletic trainer.

Computers Computers are regularly used in all academic, art, college planning, graphic arts, newspaper, yearbook classes. Computer network features include online commercial services, Internet access, wireless campus network, Internet filtering or blocking technology. Students grades are available online. The school has a published electronic and media policy.

Contact Lawrence Puck, Director of Admissions. 510-559-6235. Fax: 510-559-6277. E-mail: lpuck@stmchs.org. Web site: www.saintmaryschs.org.

ST. MARY'S DOMINICAN HIGH SCHOOL

7701 Walmsley Avenue
New Orleans, Louisiana 70125-0000

Head of School: Ms. Cynthia A. Thomas

General Information Girls' day college-preparatory school, affiliated with Roman Catholic Church. Grades 8–12. Founded: 1860. Setting: urban. 3 buildings on campus. Approved or accredited by Southern Association of Colleges and Schools and Louisiana Department of Education. Total enrollment: 927. Upper school average class size: 27. Upper school faculty-student ratio: 1:13.

Faculty School total: 76. In upper school: 11 men, 57 women; 29 have advanced degrees.

Special Academic Programs Advanced Placement exam preparation; honors section.

College Admission Counseling 247 students graduated in 2008.

Student Life Upper grades have uniform requirement, student council, honor system. Discipline rests primarily with faculty. Attendance at religious services is required.

Tuition and Aid Merit scholarship grants, need-based scholarship grants, paying campus jobs available.

Admissions Traditional secondary-level entrance grade is 8. High School Placement Test required. No application fee required. On-campus interview required.

Athletics Interscholastic: basketball (girls), bowling (g), cheering (g), dance squad (g), dance team (g), danceline (g), golf (g), gymnastics (g), indoor track (g), indoor track & field (g), soccer (g), softball (g), swimming and diving (g), tennis (g), track and field (g), volleyball (g); intramural: flag football (g), kickball (g). 4 PE instructors, 18 coaches, 1 athletic trainer.

Computers Computer network features include on-campus library services, Internet access, Internet filtering or blocking technology. The school has a published electronic and media policy.

Contact Mrs. Cathy Rice, Director of Admissions. 504-865-9401. Fax: 504-866-5958. E-mail: recruitment@stmarysdominican.org.

ST. MARY'S EPISCOPAL SCHOOL

60 Perkins Extended
Memphis, Tennessee 38117-3199

Head of School: Ms. Marlene R. Shaw

General Information Girls' day college-preparatory, arts, religious studies, technology, and Global Issues school, affiliated with Episcopal Church. Grades PK–12. Founded: 1847. Setting: urban. 25-acre campus. 8 buildings on campus. Approved or accredited by National Association of Episcopal Schools, Southern Association of Colleges and Schools, Southern Association of Independent Schools, Tennessee Association of Independent Schools, The College Board, and Tennessee Department of Education. Member of National Association of Independent Schools. Endowment: $15 million. Total enrollment: 866. Upper school average class size: 13. Upper school faculty-student ratio: 1:13.

Upper School Student Profile Grade 9: 62 students (62 girls); Grade 10: 61 students (61 girls); Grade 11: 55 students (55 girls); Grade 12: 51 students (51 girls). 15% of students are members of Episcopal Church.
Faculty School total: 104. In upper school: 5 men, 25 women; 22 have advanced degrees.
Subjects Offered 1½ elective credits, algebra, art, art history, art history-AP, biology, biology-AP, calculus, calculus-AP, chemistry, chemistry-AP, choir, chorus, composition, creative writing, economics, English, English language and composition-AP, English literature and composition-AP, European history-AP, French, French-AP, geometry, global issues, government, guitar, health, humanities, instrumental music, Latin, Latin-AP, microbiology, music, music history, music theory-AP, physical education, physics, physics-AP, physiology-anatomy, pre-calculus, psychology, religion, robotics, Spanish, Spanish-AP, speech, studio art-AP, technology, theater, U.S. history, U.S. history-AP, world history.
Graduation Requirements 1½ elective credits, algebra, arts and fine arts (art, music, dance, drama), biology, calculus, chemistry, comparative religion, English, English language-AP, English literature-AP, foreign language, geometry, physical education (includes health), physics, pre-calculus, religion (includes Bible studies and theology), social studies (includes history), U.S. history, world history.
Special Academic Programs Advanced Placement exam preparation; honors section; independent study; academic accommodation for the gifted, the musically talented, and the artistically talented.
College Admission Counseling 65 students graduated in 2008; all went to college, including American University; Boston University; Furman University; Kenyon College; Southern Methodist University; Vanderbilt University. Median SAT critical reading: 660, median SAT math: 650, median SAT writing: 690, median combined SAT: 2010, median composite ACT: 29. 88% scored over 600 on SAT critical reading, 79% scored over 600 on SAT math, 97% scored over 600 on SAT writing, 94% scored over 1800 on combined SAT, 86% scored over 26 on composite ACT.
Student Life Upper grades have specified standards of dress, student council, honor system. Discipline rests equally with students and faculty. Attendance at religious services is required.
Summer Programs Enrichment, sports, art/fine arts programs offered; session focuses on summer enrichment; held on campus; accepts boys and girls; open to students from other schools. 200 students usually enrolled. 2009 schedule: June 8 to July 24. Application deadline: none.
Tuition and Aid Day student tuition: $15,100. Tuition installment plan (Insured Tuition Payment Plan, monthly payment plans, credit card payment). Need-based scholarship grants, discounts for children of faculty, staff, and clergy available. In 2008–09, 12% of upper-school students received aid. Total amount of financial aid awarded in 2008–09: $192,584.
Admissions Traditional secondary-level entrance grade is 9. For fall 2008, 23 students applied for upper-level admission, 22 were accepted, 18 enrolled. ISEE and writing sample required. Deadline for receipt of application materials: none. Application fee required: $75. On-campus interview required.
Athletics Interscholastic: basketball, bowling, cross-country running, dance team, golf, lacrosse, soccer, softball, swimming and diving, tennis, track and field, volleyball. 1 PE instructor, 9 coaches, 1 athletic trainer.
Computers Computers are regularly used in all academic, career exploration, college planning, creative writing, library, literary magazine, music, newspaper, research skills, SAT preparation, speech, theater arts, yearbook classes. Computer network features include on-campus library services, Internet access, wireless campus network, Internet filtering or blocking technology, full-text databases. Campus intranet and computer access in designated common areas are available to students. The school has a published electronic and media policy.
Contact Ms. Nicole Hernandez, Director of Admission and Financial Aid. 901-537-1405. Fax: 901-685-1098. E-mail: nhernandez@stmarysschool.org. Web site: www.stmarysschool.org.

SAINT MARY'S HALL

9401 Starcrest Drive
San Antonio, Texas 78217

Head of School: Mr. Bob Windham

General Information Coeducational day college-preparatory and arts school. Grades PK–12. Founded: 1879. Setting: suburban. 60-acre campus. 13 buildings on campus. Approved or accredited by Independent Schools Association of the Southwest and Southern Association of Independent Schools. Member of National Association of Independent Schools and Secondary School Admission Test Board. Endowment: $35.6 million. Total enrollment: 964. Upper school average class size: 14. Upper school faculty-student ratio: 1:6.
Upper School Student Profile Grade 9: 95 students (46 boys, 49 girls); Grade 10: 73 students (37 boys, 36 girls); Grade 11: 84 students (39 boys, 45 girls); Grade 12: 79 students (43 boys, 36 girls).
Faculty School total: 94. In upper school: 18 men, 17 women; 34 have advanced degrees.
Subjects Offered 3-dimensional art, Advanced Placement courses, algebra, American history-AP, American literature, anatomy and physiology, art, art history, art history-AP, art-AP, athletic training, ballet, baseball, basketball, biology, biology-AP, British literature, calculus, calculus-AP, cell biology, ceramics, chemistry, chemistry-AP, choir, college counseling, composition, computer science, computer science-AP, concert choir, creative writing, dance, digital photography, directing, drama, drawing, drawing and design, economics, English language and composition-AP, English literature and composition-AP, environmental science-AP, European history, European history-AP, fitness, French, French language-AP, genetics, geology, geometry, golf, government/civics, great books, guitar, health, Japanese, jazz band, Latin, Latin-AP, literary magazine, marine biology, model United Nations, music theory, painting, photography, physical education, physics, physics-AP, piano, pre-calculus, religious studies, science research, sculpture, set design, softball, Spanish, Spanish language-AP, Spanish literature-AP, speech, statistics-AP, swimming, technical theater, tennis, track and field, U.S. history, voice, volleyball, Web site design, world geography, world history, world literature, world religions, yearbook, zoology.
Graduation Requirements Arts and fine arts (art, music, dance, drama), athletics, electives, English, foreign language, mathematics, physical education (includes health), science, social studies (includes history), theology, 40 hours of campus service.
Special Academic Programs Advanced Placement exam preparation; honors section; independent study; study abroad.
College Admission Counseling 81 students graduated in 2008; 80 went to college, including Massachusetts Institute of Technology; Rice University; The University of Texas at Austin; University of Southern California; Yale University. Other: 1 had other specific plans. Median SAT critical reading: 634, median SAT math: 636, median SAT writing: 654, median composite ACT: 27.
Student Life Upper grades have uniform requirement, student council, honor system. Discipline rests primarily with faculty. Attendance at religious services is required.
Summer Programs Enrichment, sports, art/fine arts, computer instruction programs offered; held on campus; accepts boys and girls; open to students from other schools. 785 students usually enrolled. 2009 schedule: June 1 to August 14. Application deadline: May 15.
Tuition and Aid Day student tuition: $18,175. Tuition installment plan (monthly payment plans, individually arranged payment plans, full-year payment plan, 2-payment plan). Merit scholarship grants, need-based scholarship grants available. In 2008–09, 30% of upper-school students received aid; total upper-school merit-scholarship money awarded: $422,075. Total amount of financial aid awarded in 2008–09: $509,630.
Admissions Traditional secondary-level entrance grade is 9. For fall 2008, 152 students applied for upper-level admission, 113 were accepted, 47 enrolled. ISEE required. Deadline for receipt of application materials: February 17. Application fee required: $50. Interview required.
Athletics Interscholastic: ballet (boys, girls), baseball (b), basketball (b,g), dance (b,g), field hockey (g), fitness (b,g), golf (b,g), independent competitive sports (b,g), lacrosse (b), soccer (b,g), softball (g), volleyball (b,g); coed interscholastic: cross-country running, physical fitness, physical training, strength & conditioning, tennis, track and field, weight training. 7 PE instructors, 52 coaches, 1 athletic trainer.
Computers Computers are regularly used in media arts classes. Computer network features include on-campus library services, Internet access, wireless campus network, Internet filtering or blocking technology, SmartBoards. Students grades are available online. The school has a published electronic and media policy.
Contact Mrs. Amy Rose Anderson, Director of Admission. 210-483-9234. Fax: 210-655-5211. E-mail: aanderson@smhall.org. Web site: www.smhall.org.

See Close-Up on page 944.

ST. MARY'S HALL–DOANE ACADEMY

350 Riverbank
Burlington, New Jersey 08016-2199

Head of School: Mr. John F. McGee

General Information Coeducational day college-preparatory and arts school, affiliated with Episcopal Church. Grades PK–12. Founded: 1837. Setting: suburban. Nearest major city is Philadelphia, PA. 10-acre campus. 5 buildings on campus. Approved or accredited by Middle States Association of Colleges and Schools and National Association of Episcopal Schools. Member of National Association of Independent Schools. Total enrollment: 197. Upper school average class size: 10. Upper school faculty-student ratio: 1:5.
Upper School Student Profile Grade 6: 10 students (6 boys, 4 girls); Grade 7: 11 students (7 boys, 4 girls); Grade 8: 12 students (7 boys, 5 girls); Grade 9: 20 students (11 boys, 9 girls); Grade 10: 22 students (10 boys, 12 girls); Grade 11: 18 students (11 boys, 7 girls); Grade 12: 24 students (13 boys, 11 girls). 10% of students are members of Episcopal Church.
Faculty School total: 34. In upper school: 7 men, 14 women; 10 have advanced degrees.
Subjects Offered African American history, algebra, American Civil War, American literature, ancient world history, arts and crafts, band, biology, biology-AP, British literature, calculus, calculus-AP, chemistry, chemistry-AP, choir, Civil War, computer graphics, computer literacy, computer science, creative writing, cultural geography, digital photography, drama, drawing, economics, English literature and composition-AP, environmental science, ethics, European history, European history-AP, French, geometry, government-AP, graphic design, health and wellness, honors algebra, instrumental music, Latin, Latin-AP, life science, music, novel, painting, physical education, physical science, physics, piano, poetry, pre-algebra,

psychology, psychology-AP, research skills, SAT preparation, sculpture, Shakespeare, short story, Spanish, Spanish-AP, speech and debate, studio art—AP, trigonometry, U.S. history, U.S. history-AP, Web site design, world history, world literature, world religions, writing skills.

Graduation Requirements Arts and fine arts (art, music, dance, drama), computer skills, English, ethics, foreign language, lab science, mathematics, physical education (includes health), science, social studies (includes history), world religions, Ethics—1 semester.

Special Academic Programs Advanced Placement exam preparation; honors section; independent study; academic accommodation for the gifted, the musically talented, and the artistically talented; remedial reading and/or remedial writing; remedial math.

College Admission Counseling 23 students graduated in 2008; all went to college, including Babson College; Carnegie Mellon University; Harvard University; Tulane University; United States Air Force Academy; Wellesley College. Mean SAT critical reading: 570, mean SAT math: 548, mean SAT writing: 553, mean combined SAT: 1671.

Student Life Upper grades have uniform requirement, student council, honor system. Discipline rests primarily with faculty. Attendance at religious services is required.

Tuition and Aid Day student tuition: $11,950–$12,890. Tuition installment plan (monthly payment plans). Tuition reduction for siblings, need-based scholarship grants, tuition remission for children of faculty and staff available. In 2008–09, 25% of upper-school students received aid. Total amount of financial aid awarded in 2008–09: $100,000.

Admissions Traditional secondary-level entrance grade is 9. For fall 2008, 28 students applied for upper-level admission, 23 were accepted, 17 enrolled. ISEE or SSAT required. Deadline for receipt of application materials: none. Application fee required: $35. On-campus interview required.

Athletics Interscholastic: baseball (boys), basketball (b,g), crew (b,g), cross-country running (b,g), golf (b,g), soccer (b,g), softball (g); coed interscholastic: outdoor adventure, soccer, strength & conditioning; coed intramural: alpine skiing, basketball, kickball, outdoor activities, soccer, softball, table tennis, volleyball. 2 PE instructors, 11 coaches.

Computers Computers are regularly used in graphic design, lab/keyboard, mathematics, photography, research skills, SAT preparation, science, Web site design, yearbook classes. Computer network features include on-campus library services, Internet access, Internet filtering or blocking technology, homework assignments available online. Campus intranet is available to students. The school has a published electronic and media policy.

Contact Miss Sue Gillespie, Dean of Admission. 609-386-3500 Ext. 15. Fax: 609-386-5878. E-mail: sgillespie@doaneacademy.org. Web site: www.doaneacademy.org.

SAINT MARY'S HIGH SCHOOL

2525 North Third Street
Phoenix, Arizona 85004

Head of School: Mr. Mark A. Mauro

General Information Coeducational day college-preparatory, general academic, arts, and religious studies school, affiliated with Roman Catholic Church. Grades 9–12. Founded: 1917. Setting: urban. 6-acre campus. 5 buildings on campus. Approved or accredited by North Central Association of Colleges and Schools, Western Catholic Education Association, and Arizona Department of Education. Endowment: $1 million. Total enrollment: 774. Upper school average class size: 27. Upper school faculty-student ratio: 1:17.

Upper School Student Profile Grade 9: 231 students (128 boys, 103 girls); Grade 10: 206 students (106 boys, 100 girls); Grade 11: 197 students (82 boys, 115 girls); Grade 12: 189 students (98 boys, 91 girls). 89% of students are Roman Catholic.

Faculty School total: 44. In upper school: 25 men, 19 women; 26 have advanced degrees.

Subjects Offered Advanced Placement courses, algebra, American government, American government-AP, American history, American history-AP, American literature, art, band, biology, British literature, British literature (honors), calculus-AP, Catholic belief and practice, chemistry, chorus, Christian and Hebrew scripture, composition, computer graphics, computer keyboarding, conceptual physics, dance, drama, economics, electives, English, English composition, English language and composition-AP, English literature, English literature and composition-AP, fine arts, foreign language, French, geometry, health, history, history of the Catholic Church, honors algebra, honors English, honors geometry, honors U.S. history, intro to computers, journalism, Life of Christ, personal finance, physical education, physical science, physics, prayer/spirituality, pre-algebra, pre-calculus, religious education, remedial study skills, social studies, Spanish, Spanish language-AP, standard curriculum, state government, state history, theology, trigonometry, world geography, world history, world religions, yearbook.

Graduation Requirements Advanced math, algebra, American government, American history, American literature, anatomy and physiology, arts and fine arts (art, music, dance, drama), biology, British literature, Catholic belief and practice, chemistry, Christian and Hebrew scripture, composition, economics, electives, English, foreign language, geometry, health education, history of the Catholic Church, language and composition, physical education (includes health), physics, pre-calculus, theology, trigonometry, world history, world literature, 90 hours of Christian community service.

Special Academic Programs 8 Advanced Placement exams for which test preparation is offered; honors section; study at local college for college credit; remedial reading and/or remedial writing; remedial math.

College Admission Counseling 183 students graduated in 2008; 176 went to college, including Arizona State University; Northern Arizona University; The University of Arizona. Other: 3 went to work, 1 entered military service, 3 had other specific plans. Median composite ACT: 21. Mean SAT critical reading: 485, mean SAT math: 462, mean SAT writing: 471. 14% scored over 600 on SAT critical reading, 12% scored over 600 on SAT math, 9% scored over 600 on SAT writing, 20% scored over 26 on composite ACT.

Student Life Upper grades have uniform requirement, student council. Discipline rests primarily with faculty. Attendance at religious services is required.

Summer Programs Remediation, enrichment, advancement, sports, art/fine arts programs offered; session focuses on high school preparation for incoming freshmen; held on campus; accepts boys and girls; not open to students from other schools. 250 students usually enrolled. 2009 schedule: June 2 to July 10. Application deadline: May 15.

Tuition and Aid Day student tuition: $7675–$9975. Tuition installment plan (FACTS Tuition Payment Plan, monthly payment plans, individually arranged payment plans, quarterly and semester payment plans). Need-based scholarship grants, paying campus jobs available. In 2008–09, 59% of upper-school students received aid. Total amount of financial aid awarded in 2008–09: $2,230,000.

Admissions Traditional secondary-level entrance grade is 9. For fall 2008, 350 students applied for upper-level admission, 300 were accepted, 210 enrolled. High School Placement Test required. Deadline for receipt of application materials: none. Application fee required: $300. On-campus interview required.

Athletics Interscholastic: baseball (boys), basketball (b,g), cheering (g), football (b), golf (b,g), physical fitness (b,g), soccer (b,g), softball (g), strength & conditioning (b,g), tennis (b,g), volleyball (b,g), weight training (b,g), winter soccer (b,g), wrestling (b); intramural: dance (g); coed interscholastic: cross-country running, physical fitness, strength & conditioning, swimming and diving, track and field, weight training; coed intramural: bowling. 4 PE instructors, 20 coaches, 1 athletic trainer.

Computers Computers are regularly used in computer applications, graphics, journalism, keyboarding, newspaper, Web site design, yearbook classes. Computer resources include on-campus library services, Internet access, Internet filtering or blocking technology. Students grades are available online. The school has a published electronic and media policy.

Contact Mrs. Linda Schmaltz, Office Manager. 602-251-2500. Fax: 602-251-2595. E-mail: lschmaltz@smknights.org. Web site: www.smknights.org.

ST. MARY'S HIGH SCHOOL

2501 East Yampa Street
Colorado Springs, Colorado 80909

Head of School: Ms. Patty Beckert

General Information Coeducational day college-preparatory and religious studies school, affiliated with Roman Catholic Church. Grades 9–12. Founded: 1885. Setting: urban. 5-acre campus. 4 buildings on campus. Approved or accredited by National Catholic Education Association, North Central Association of Colleges and Schools, and Colorado Department of Education. Total enrollment: 389. Upper school average class size: 18. Upper school faculty-student ratio: 1:11.

Upper School Student Profile Grade 9: 78 students (37 boys, 41 girls); Grade 10: 99 students (45 boys, 54 girls); Grade 11: 90 students (39 boys, 51 girls); Grade 12: 95 students (41 boys, 54 girls). 70% of students are Roman Catholic.

Faculty School total: 31. In upper school: 16 men, 15 women; 16 have advanced degrees.

Subjects Offered 3-dimensional art, advanced biology, advanced chemistry, advanced computer applications, advanced math, Advanced Placement courses, advanced studio art-AP, algebra, American government, American history, American history-AP, American literature, anatomy and physiology, art, Basic programming, biology, business, calculus, calculus-AP, ceramics, choir, Christian studies, computer applications, computer programming, computer studies, contemporary history, drama, earth science, ecology, economics, English, English-AP, finance, French, geometry, health.

Graduation Requirements Biology, computer applications, English, foreign language, geometry, mathematics, physical education (includes health), religious studies, science, social studies (includes history), speech, world geography, Community Service—25 hours each year, Theology.

Special Academic Programs Advanced Placement exam preparation; honors section; independent study.

College Admission Counseling 95 students graduated in 2008; 93 went to college, including Colorado School of Mines; Colorado State University; Gonzaga University; University of Colorado at Boulder; University of Northern Colorado. Other: 2 went to work.

Student Life Upper grades have specified standards of dress, student council. Discipline rests primarily with faculty. Attendance at religious services is required.

Summer Programs Enrichment, advancement, computer instruction programs offered; session focuses on academics; held on campus; accepts boys and girls; not open to students from other schools. 220 students usually enrolled. 2009 schedule: June 4 to June 26.
Tuition and Aid Day student tuition: $6800. Tuition installment plan (SMART Tuition Payment Plan). Merit scholarship grants, need-based scholarship grants available. In 2008–09, 30% of upper-school students received aid; total upper-school merit-scholarship money awarded: $10,000. Total amount of financial aid awarded in 2008–09: $190,000.
Admissions Traditional secondary-level entrance grade is 9. For fall 2008, 118 students applied for upper-level admission, 109 were accepted, 104 enrolled. High School Placement Test (closed version) from Scholastic Testing Service required. Deadline for receipt of application materials: February 27. Application fee required: $400. Interview required.
Athletics Interscholastic: baseball (boys), basketball (b,g), cheering (b,g), cross-country running (b,g), football (b), golf (b,g), lacrosse (b), soccer (b,g), softball (g), swimming and diving (g), tennis (g), track and field (b,g), volleyball (g), wrestling (b). 2 PE instructors, 25 coaches, 2 athletic trainers.
Computers Computers are regularly used in computer applications classes. Computer network features include Internet filtering or blocking technology. Campus intranet is available to students. Students grades are available online.
Contact Mrs. Leah Ramzy, Director of Admissions. 719-635-7540 Ext. 16. Fax: 719-471-7623. E-mail: lramzy@smhscs.org. Web site: www.smhscs.org.

SAINT MARY'S HIGH SCHOOL

113 Duke of Gloucester Street
Annapolis, Maryland 21401
Head of School: Mr. Richard Bayhan

General Information Coeducational day college-preparatory, arts, religious studies, bilingual studies, and technology school, affiliated with Roman Catholic Church. Grades 9–12. Founded: 1946. Setting: small town. 5-acre campus. 3 buildings on campus. Approved or accredited by Middle States Association of Colleges and Schools and Maryland Department of Education. Total enrollment: 520. Upper school average class size: 22. Upper school faculty-student ratio: 1:17.
Upper School Student Profile 80% of students are Roman Catholic.
Faculty School total: 47. In upper school: 32 men, 15 women; 37 have advanced degrees.
Subjects Offered Accounting, algebra, American government, American government-AP, American literature, art, art history, art history-AP, band, biology, biology-AP, British literature, calculus-AP, Catholic belief and practice, chemistry, chemistry-AP, chorus, Christian scripture, Christianity, cinematography, computer applications, creative writing, current events, drama, economics, environmental science, European history-AP, fiction, French, geography, geometry, guitar, health, integrated mathematics, interdisciplinary studies, Irish literature, Latin, literature and composition-AP, math analysis, mathematics, mechanical drawing, microbiology, musical theater, peace and justice, physical education, physical science, physics, physics-AP, pre-calculus, psychology, public speaking, senior project, Shakespeare, social justice, sociology, Spanish, sports conditioning, studio art, trigonometry, U.S. history, U.S. history-AP, weight training, world arts, world history, world literature, writing, zoology.
Graduation Requirements Arts and fine arts (art, music, dance, drama), computers, English, foreign language, mathematics, physical education (includes health), religion (includes Bible studies and theology), science, social studies (includes history).
Special Academic Programs Advanced Placement exam preparation; honors section; study at local college for college credit; study abroad; academic accommodation for the gifted.
College Admission Counseling 154 students graduated in 2008; all went to college, including American University; Gettysburg College; Princeton University; Stanford University; United States Naval Academy; University of Notre Dame. Median combined SAT: 1637. 35% scored over 1800 on combined SAT.
Student Life Upper grades have uniform requirement, honor system. Discipline rests primarily with faculty. Attendance at religious services is required.
Tuition and Aid Day student tuition: $11,640. Tuition installment plan (monthly payment plans). Merit scholarship grants, need-based scholarship grants available. In 2008–09, 40% of upper-school students received aid; total upper-school merit-scholarship money awarded: $25,000. Total amount of financial aid awarded in 2008–09: $250,000.
Admissions Traditional secondary-level entrance grade is 9. For fall 2008, 300 students applied for upper-level admission, 175 were accepted, 130 enrolled. High School Placement Test required. Deadline for receipt of application materials: January 11. Application fee required: $100.
Athletics Interscholastic: baseball (boys), basketball (b,g), cross-country running (b,g), diving (b,g), field hockey (g), football (b), golf (b,g), ice hockey (b), lacrosse (b,g), sailing (b,g), soccer (b,g), softball (g), swimming and diving (b,g), tennis (b,g), volleyball (g), wrestling (b); intramural: crew (g); coed interscholastic: cross-country running, golf, sailing, tennis, weight training; coed intramural: dance team, Frisbee, yoga. 2 PE instructors, 56 coaches, 1 athletic trainer.
Computers Computer network features include on-campus library services, online commercial services, Internet access.
Contact Mrs. Chrissie Chomo, Director of Admissions. 410-990-4236. Fax: 410-269-7843. E-mail: cchomo@stmarysannapolis.org. Web site: www.stmarysannapolis.org.

ST. MARY'S INTERNATIONAL SCHOOL

1-6-19 Seta, Setagaya-ku
Tokyo 158-8668, Japan
Head of School: Br. Michel Jutras

General Information Boys' day college-preparatory school, affiliated with Roman Catholic Church. Grades K–12. Founded: 1954. Setting: urban. 9-acre campus. 1 building on campus. Approved or accredited by East Asia Regional Council of Schools, European Council of International Schools, International Baccalaureate Organization, The College Board, and Western Association of Schools and Colleges. Language of instruction: English. Total enrollment: 923. Upper school average class size: 15. Upper school faculty-student ratio: 1:10.
Upper School Student Profile Grade 9: 78 students (78 boys); Grade 10: 74 students (74 boys); Grade 11: 68 students (68 boys); Grade 12: 78 students (78 boys). 20% of students are Roman Catholic.
Faculty School total: 102. In upper school: 40 men, 20 women; 45 have advanced degrees.
Subjects Offered Algebra, American history, architecture, art, Asian studies, band, biology, calculus, ceramics, chemistry, Chinese, computer programming, computer science, earth science, economics, English, English literature, ESL, ethics, fine arts, French, geometry, German, health, history, Italian, Japanese, journalism, mathematics, mechanical drawing, music, photography, physical education, physics, religion, science, social science, social studies, Spanish, statistics, Swedish, television, theory of knowledge, trigonometry, video, world history, world literature, writing.
Graduation Requirements Arts and fine arts (art, music, dance, drama), English, foreign language, mathematics, physical education (includes health), religion (includes Bible studies and theology), science, social science, social studies (includes history), community service (for IB students).
Special Academic Programs International Baccalaureate program; honors section; ESL (2 students enrolled).
College Admission Counseling 72 students graduated in 2008; 69 went to college, including Boston University; Brown University; Columbia College; McGill University; San Francisco State University; The University of British Columbia. Other: 1 entered military service, 2 had other specific plans. Mean SAT critical reading: 542, mean SAT math: 643, mean SAT writing: 542.
Student Life Upper grades have uniform requirement, student council. Discipline rests primarily with faculty.
Tuition and Aid Day student tuition: ¥1,930,000. Need-based scholarship grants available.
Admissions Deadline for receipt of application materials: none. No application fee required. Interview recommended.
Athletics Interscholastic: baseball, basketball, cross-country running, soccer, swimming and diving, tennis, track and field, wrestling; intramural: badminton, ball hockey, baseball, basketball, cricket, golf, ice hockey, indoor soccer, judo, martial arts, table tennis, volleyball, water polo, weight lifting, weight training. 6 PE instructors.
Computers Computers are regularly used in architecture, art, career exploration, college planning, literary magazine, mathematics, music, newspaper, science, yearbook classes. Computer network features include on-campus library services, online commercial services, Internet access, Internet filtering or blocking technology. The school has a published electronic and media policy.
Contact Mrs. Bedos Santos, Admissions Office. 81-3-3709-3411. Fax: 81-3-3707-1950. E-mail: admissions@smis.ac.jp. Web site: www.smis.ac.jp.

ST. MARY'S PREPARATORY SCHOOL

3535 Indian Trail
Orchard Lake, Michigan 48324
Head of School: James Glowacki

General Information Boys' boarding and day college-preparatory school, affiliated with Roman Catholic Church. Grades 9–12. Founded: 1885. Setting: suburban. Nearest major city is Detroit. Students are housed in single-sex dormitories. 80-acre campus. 12 buildings on campus. Approved or accredited by Michigan Association of Non-Public Schools and Michigan Department of Education. Total enrollment: 500. Upper school average class size: 18. Upper school faculty-student ratio: 1:10.
Upper School Student Profile Grade 9: 118 students (118 boys); Grade 10: 128 students (128 boys); Grade 11: 140 students (140 boys); Grade 12: 124 students (124 boys). 15% of students are boarding students. 80% are state residents. 5 states are represented in upper school student body. 15% are international students. International students from Brazil, Japan, Poland, Republic of Korea, Russian Federation, and Taiwan. 80% of students are Roman Catholic.
Faculty School total: 58. In upper school: 43 men, 15 women; 16 have advanced degrees; 6 reside on campus.
Subjects Offered Algebra, American history, American literature, art, band, Bible studies, biology, business, business skills, calculus, chemistry, computer programming, computer science, creative writing, drafting, driver education, earth science, ecology, economics, English, English literature, expository writing, fine arts,

French, geometry, government/civics, grammar, health, history, journalism, law, mathematics, music technology, mythology, physical education, physics, Polish, psychology, religion, robotics, science, social science, social studies, Spanish, speech, theology, trigonometry, world history, writing.
Graduation Requirements Arts and fine arts (art, music, dance, drama), business skills (includes word processing), computer science, English, foreign language, mathematics, physical education (includes health), religion (includes Bible studies and theology), science, social science, social studies (includes history).
Special Academic Programs Advanced Placement exam preparation; honors section; study at local college for college credit; academic accommodation for the musically talented and the artistically talented; programs in general development for dyslexic students; special instructional classes for students with learning disabilities, Attention Deficit Disorder, and dyslexia; ESL (20 students enrolled).
College Admission Counseling 126 students graduated in 2008; 125 went to college, including Michigan State University; Oakland University; University of Detroit Mercy; University of Michigan; Wayne State University; Western Michigan University. Other: 1 entered a postgraduate year. Median SAT critical reading: 503, median SAT math: 600, median SAT writing: 510, median combined SAT: 1613, median composite ACT: 25. 5% scored over 600 on SAT critical reading, 15% scored over 600 on SAT math, 40% scored over 26 on composite ACT.
Student Life Upper grades have specified standards of dress, student council, honor system. Discipline rests primarily with faculty. Attendance at religious services is required.
Summer Programs Remediation, sports programs offered; session focuses on football, basketball, and lacrosse; held on campus; accepts boys and girls; open to students from other schools. 400 students usually enrolled. 2009 schedule: June to August. Application deadline: June.
Tuition and Aid Day student tuition: $9150; 5-day tuition and room/board: $18,100; 7-day tuition and room/board: $21,700. Tuition installment plan (FACTS Tuition Payment Plan, individually arranged payment plans). Tuition reduction for siblings, merit scholarship grants, need-based scholarship grants available. In 2008–09, 50% of upper-school students received aid.
Admissions Traditional secondary-level entrance grade is 9. For fall 2008, 250 students applied for upper-level admission, 180 were accepted, 130 enrolled. STS and TOEFL required. Deadline for receipt of application materials: none. Application fee required: $35. Interview recommended.
Athletics Interscholastic: alpine skiing, baseball, basketball, crew, cross-country running, football, freestyle skiing, golf, hockey, ice hockey, indoor track, indoor track & field, jogging, lacrosse, rowing, skiing (downhill), soccer, track and field, wrestling; intramural: aerobics/Nautilus, aquatics, basketball, bicycling, billiards, bowling, broomball, fitness, Frisbee, golf, hockey, ice hockey, ice skating, indoor hockey, indoor soccer, indoor track, jogging, lacrosse, mountain biking, Nautilus, physical fitness, physical training, rowing, running, skiing (downhill), snowboarding, soccer, strength & conditioning, swimming and diving, table tennis, tennis, weight lifting, weight training, whiffle ball. 2 PE instructors, 25 coaches, 3 athletic trainers.
Computers Computers are regularly used in desktop publishing, drafting, engineering, yearbook classes. Computer network features include Internet access, Internet filtering or blocking technology. Student e-mail accounts are available to students.
Contact Leonard Karschnia, Dean of Admissions. 248-683-0514. Fax: 248-683-1740. E-mail: lkarschnia@stmarysprep.com. Web site: www.stmarysprep.com/.

See Close-Up on page 946.

SAINT MARY'S SCHOOL

900 Hillsborough Street
Raleigh, North Carolina 27603-1689
Head of School: Ms. Theo W. Coonrod

General Information Girls' boarding and day college-preparatory, arts, religious studies, and technology school, affiliated with Episcopal Church. Grades 9–12. Founded: 1842. Setting: urban. Students are housed in single-sex dormitories. 23-acre campus. 26 buildings on campus. Approved or accredited by National Association of Episcopal Schools, North Carolina Association of Independent Schools, Southern Association of Colleges and Schools, Southern Association of Independent Schools, and The Association of Boarding Schools. Member of National Association of Independent Schools and Secondary School Admission Test Board. Endowment: $22.6 million. Total enrollment: 297. Upper school average class size: 13. Upper school faculty-student ratio: 1:8.
Upper School Student Profile Grade 9: 64 students (64 girls); Grade 10: 85 students (85 girls); Grade 11: 72 students (72 girls); Grade 12: 76 students (76 girls). 41% of students are boarding students. 84% are state residents. 12 states are represented in upper school student body. 5% are international students. International students from China, India, Panama, Republic of Korea, Switzerland, and United Kingdom; 2 other countries represented in student body. 20% of students are members of Episcopal Church.
Faculty School total: 47. In upper school: 13 men, 34 women; 36 have advanced degrees; 39 reside on campus.
Subjects Offered Acting, advanced chemistry, advanced math, Advanced Placement courses, advanced studio art-AP, algebra, American government, American government-AP, American history, American history-AP, American literature, anatomy, art, art-AP, astronomy, athletic training, athletics, ballet, biology, biology-AP, calculus, calculus-AP, ceramics, chemistry, chemistry-AP, choir, choral music, computer science, creative writing, dance, drama, drama performance, drawing, drawing and design, earth science, ecology, English, English literature, English literature-AP, European history, French, French language-AP, geometry, government, government-AP, government/civics, honors English, honors geometry, honors U.S. history, honors world history, Latin, Latin-AP, mathematics, philosophy, physical education, physics, physics-AP, piano, psychology, psychology-AP, religion, senior project, social studies, Spanish, Spanish language-AP, speech, studio art-AP, U.S. history, U.S. history-AP, Western civilization, women's studies, world literature, yearbook.
Graduation Requirements Algebra, arts and fine arts (art, music, dance, drama), biology, electives, English, foreign language, geography, geometry, government, physical education (includes health), physical science, religion (includes Bible studies and theology), social sciences, U.S. history, Western civilization.
Special Academic Programs Advanced Placement exam preparation; honors section; independent study; study at local college for college credit.
College Admission Counseling 70 students graduated in 2008; all went to college, including Appalachian State University; College of Charleston; Meredith College; North Carolina State University; The University of North Carolina at Chapel Hill; University of South Carolina.
Student Life Upper grades have specified standards of dress, student council, honor system. Discipline rests equally with students and faculty. Attendance at religious services is required.
Summer Programs Enrichment, sports, art/fine arts, computer instruction programs offered; session focuses on sports, fine arts, and enrichment; held on campus; accepts girls; open to students from other schools. 450 students usually enrolled. 2009 schedule: June 1 to July 31.
Tuition and Aid Day student tuition: $16,417; 7-day tuition and room/board: $34,950. Tuition installment plan (monthly payment plans). Merit scholarship grants, need-based scholarship grants available. In 2008–09, 41% of upper-school students received aid; total upper-school merit-scholarship money awarded: $624,701. Total amount of financial aid awarded in 2008–09: $1,133,000.
Admissions Traditional secondary-level entrance grade is 9. For fall 2008, 209 students applied for upper-level admission, 161 were accepted, 104 enrolled. SSAT required. Deadline for receipt of application materials: none. Application fee required: $50. Interview required.
Athletics Interscholastic: basketball (girls), cross-country running (g), field hockey (g), golf (g), lacrosse (g), soccer (g), softball (g), swimming and diving (g), tennis (g), track and field (g), volleyball (g); intramural: ballet (g), dance (g), dance team (g), modern dance (g), weight training (g). 2 PE instructors, 32 coaches, 1 athletic trainer.
Computers Computers are regularly used in dance, English, foreign language, history, introduction to technology, mathematics, newspaper, publications, science, senior seminar, writing, yearbook classes. Computer network features include on-campus library services, online commercial services, Internet access, wireless campus network, Internet filtering or blocking technology. Student e-mail accounts are available to students. The school has a published electronic and media policy.
Contact Ms. Carol DeWitt, Admission Assistant. 800-948-2557. Fax: 919-424-4122. E-mail: cdewitt@sms.edu. Web site: www.sms.edu.

ANNOUNCEMENT FROM THE SCHOOL Dedicated to academic excellence and personal achievement for girls in grades 9–12, Saint Mary's School in Raleigh, North Carolina, offers a full complement of college-preparatory, AP, and honors courses; competition in eleven sports; a comprehensive fine arts program; and a signature co-curricular life skills program to prepare young women for independence.

ST. MARY'S SCHOOL

816 Black Oak Drive
Medford, Oregon 97504-8504
Head of School: Mr. Frank Phillips

General Information Coeducational day college-preparatory, arts, and religious studies school, affiliated with Roman Catholic Church. Grades 6–12. Founded: 1865. Setting: small town. Nearest major city is Eugene. 23-acre campus. 9 buildings on campus. Approved or accredited by National Catholic Education Association, Northwest Association of Schools and Colleges, Pacific Northwest Association of Independent Schools, and Oregon Department of Education. Member of National Association of Independent Schools. Total enrollment: 432. Upper school average class size: 18. Upper school faculty-student ratio: 1:11.
Upper School Student Profile Grade 9: 70 students (32 boys, 38 girls); Grade 10: 85 students (35 boys, 50 girls); Grade 11: 66 students (39 boys, 27 girls); Grade 12: 64 students (28 boys, 36 girls). 35% of students are Roman Catholic.
Faculty School total: 48. In upper school: 22 men, 26 women; 21 have advanced degrees.
Subjects Offered Advanced Placement courses, algebra, American history, American history-AP, American literature, ancient history, art, art history-AP, biology, biology-AP, calculus-AP, chamber groups, chemistry, chemistry-AP, chorus, community service, computer programming-AP, computer science, creative writing, drama, earth science, economics-AP, English, English-AP, environmental science-AP, ethics, European history, European history-AP, expository writing, fine arts, general

science, geometry, German, government/civics, government/civics-AP, grammar, health, history, human geography—AP, instrumental music, jazz band, Latin, Latin-AP, mathematics, music theory-AP, physical education, physics, physics-AP, religion, science, social science, social studies, Spanish, Spanish-AP, speech, studio art-AP, theater, trigonometry, world history, world literature, writing.

Graduation Requirements Arts and fine arts (art, music, dance, drama), electives, English, foreign language, mathematics, physical education (includes health), religion (includes Bible studies and theology), science, social science, social studies (includes history), 100 hours of community service (25 each year in upper school).

Special Academic Programs 18 Advanced Placement exams for which test preparation is offered; independent study; study at local college for college credit; academic accommodation for the gifted, the musically talented, and the artistically talented.

College Admission Counseling 63 students graduated in 2008; 61 went to college, including Oregon State University; Portland State University; Santa Clara University; University of Oregon; University of Portland; University of San Diego. Other: 2 had other specific plans. Mean SAT critical reading: 580, mean SAT math: 569, mean SAT writing: 573, mean combined SAT: 1722. 47% scored over 600 on SAT critical reading, 39% scored over 600 on SAT math, 47% scored over 600 on SAT writing, 42% scored over 1800 on combined SAT.

Student Life Upper grades have specified standards of dress, student council, honor system. Discipline rests equally with students and faculty. Attendance at religious services is required.

Summer Programs Remediation, enrichment, advancement, sports, art/fine arts, computer instruction programs offered; session focuses on enrichment and SAT prep; held on campus; accepts boys and girls; open to students from other schools. 196 students usually enrolled. 2009 schedule: June 15 to August 27. Application deadline: none.

Tuition and Aid Day student tuition: $10,250. Tuition installment plan (monthly payment plans, semiannual and annual payment plans). Tuition reduction for siblings, merit scholarship grants, need-based scholarship grants available. In 2008–09, 31% of upper-school students received aid; total upper-school merit-scholarship money awarded: $11,000. Total amount of financial aid awarded in 2008–09: $580,000.

Admissions Traditional secondary-level entrance grade is 9. For fall 2008, 127 students applied for upper-level admission, 116 were accepted, 95 enrolled. Deadline for receipt of application materials: February 15. Application fee required: $50. Interview required.

Athletics Interscholastic: baseball (boys), basketball (b,g), cross-country running (b,g), football (b), golf (b,g), independent competitive sports (b,g), soccer (b,g), softball (g), tennis (b,g), track and field (b,g), volleyball (g); intramural: alpine skiing (b,g), flag football (g); coed interscholastic: martial arts; coed intramural: back-packing, fitness, floor hockey, skiing (cross-country), strength & conditioning, tennis, weight lifting. 2 PE instructors.

Computers Computers are regularly used in English, history, mathematics, science, speech classes. Computer network features include on-campus library services, online commercial services, Internet access, wireless campus network, Internet filtering or blocking technology, access to homework, daily bulletins and teachers via e-mail. Campus intranet and computer access in designated common areas are available to students. Students grades are available online. The school has a published electronic and media policy.

Contact Michelle Tresemer, Director of Admissions. 541-773-7877 Ext. 3108. Fax: 541-772-8973. E-mail: admissions@smschool.us. Web site: www.smschool.us.

SAINT MATTHIAS HIGH SCHOOL

7851 Gardendale Street
Downey, California 90242-4199

Head of School: Mrs. Margaret Meland

General Information Girls' day college-preparatory, arts, business, religious studies, and technology school, affiliated with Roman Catholic Church. Grades 9–12. Founded: 1960. Setting: urban. 19-acre campus. 4 buildings on campus. Approved or accredited by Western Association of Schools and Colleges, Western Catholic Education Association, and California Department of Education. Total enrollment: 271. Upper school average class size: 21. Upper school faculty-student ratio: 1:21.

Upper School Student Profile Grade 9: 60 students (60 girls); Grade 10: 55 students (55 girls); Grade 11: 67 students (67 girls); Grade 12: 87 students (87 girls). 98% of students are Roman Catholic.

Faculty School total: 18. In upper school: 7 men, 11 women; 15 have advanced degrees.

Subjects Offered Acting, Advanced Placement courses, algebra, American history, American history-AP, art, art-AP, arts, ASB Leadership, athletics, Basic programming, basketball, bell choir, Bible studies, biology, calculus, calculus-AP, campus ministry, Catholic belief and practice, cheerleading, chemistry, choir, chorus, Christian and Hebrew scripture, Christian scripture, community service, composition-AP, computer programming, computer science, computer science-AP, computers, concert bell choir, CPR, crafts, current events, decision making, desktop publishing, digital photography, drama, drawing, driver education, economics, economics-AP, English, English language and composition-AP, English literature-AP, English-AP, ensembles, European history-AP, expository writing, first aid, French, French language-AP, French-AP, gender issues, general science, geography, geometry, government, government and politics-AP, government-AP, government/civics-AP, handbells, health education, Hebrew scripture, Hispanic literature, history of the Catholic Church, history-AP, honors algebra, honors English, honors geometry, human sexuality, humanities, integrated science, Internet, intro to computers, keyboarding, leadership training, life science, literature, mathematics, mathematics-AP, mentorship program, modern European history, music, painting, peace and justice, peace education, performing arts, personal development, physical education, physical science, physics, physics-AP, physiology, play production, post-calculus, pre-algebra, pre-calculus, pre-college orientation, psychology, public speaking, reading, religion, SAT/ACT preparation, senior project, service learning/internship, set design, social studies, Spanish, Spanish language-AP, Spanish-AP, speech, stagecraft, statistics, statistics-AP, student publications, studio art-AP, study skills, swimming, technology, trigonometry, U.S. government, U.S. history, vocal music, voice, volleyball, weight reduction, weight training, weightlifting, women's studies, word processing, work-study, world history, World-Wide-Web publishing, writing, yearbook.

Graduation Requirements Students must produce portfolio demonstrating achievement of Expected School wide Learning Results, presentation of portfolio to panel of school and community leaders.

Special Academic Programs Advanced Placement exam preparation; honors section; academic accommodation for the gifted, the musically talented, and the artistically talented; remedial reading and/or remedial writing; remedial math; programs in English, mathematics, general development for dyslexic students; special instructional classes for deaf students.

College Admission Counseling 100 students graduated in 2008; 98 went to college, including California State University, Long Beach; California State University, Los Angeles; Loyola Marymount University; Mount St. Mary's College; University of California, Irvine; University of California, Los Angeles. Other: 1 went to work.

Student Life Upper grades have uniform requirement, student council, honor system. Discipline rests primarily with faculty. Attendance at religious services is required.

Summer Programs Remediation, enrichment, advancement, ESL, art/fine arts, computer instruction programs offered; session focuses on academic advancement and remediation; held on campus; accepts boys and girls; open to students from other schools. 325 students usually enrolled. 2009 schedule: June 17 to July 24. Application deadline: May 15.

Tuition and Aid Day student tuition: $5700. Tuition installment plan (FACTS Tuition Payment Plan, monthly payment plans, individually arranged payment plans). Tuition reduction for siblings, merit scholarship grants, need-based scholarship grants available. In 2008–09, 60% of upper-school students received aid; total upper-school merit-scholarship money awarded: $25,000. Total amount of financial aid awarded in 2008–09: $250,000.

Admissions Traditional secondary-level entrance grade is 9. Admissions testing, High School Placement Test and writing sample required. Deadline for receipt of application materials: January 30. Application fee required: $75. Interview required.

Athletics Interscholastic: aerobics/dance, aquatics, basketball, cheering, cross-country running, dance squad, fitness, running, scooter football, soccer, softball, track and field, volleyball, winter soccer. 1 PE instructor.

Computers Computers are regularly used in all classes. Computer network features include on-campus library services, online commercial services, Internet access, Internet filtering or blocking technology. Students grades are available online. The school has a published electronic and media policy.

Contact Roxanne Santiago, Main Office Secretary Receptionist. 562-861-2271 Ext. 1400. Fax: 562-869-8652. E-mail: rsantiago@stmatthiashs.org. Web site: www.stmatthiashs.org.

SAINT MAUR INTERNATIONAL SCHOOL

83 Yamate-cho, Naka-ku
Yokohama 231-8654, Japan

Head of School: Jeanette K. Thomas

General Information Coeducational day college-preparatory, general academic, and arts school, affiliated with Roman Catholic Church. Grades PK–12. Founded: 1872. Setting: urban. 1-hectare campus. 6 buildings on campus. Approved or accredited by East Asia Regional Council of Schools, European Council of International Schools, International Baccalaureate Organization, Ministry of Education, Japan, and New England Association of Schools and Colleges. Language of instruction: English. Total enrollment: 468. Upper school average class size: 15. Upper school faculty-student ratio: 1:5.

Upper School Student Profile Grade 6: 34 students (13 boys, 21 girls); Grade 7: 30 students (13 boys, 17 girls); Grade 8: 27 students (11 boys, 16 girls); Grade 9: 33 students (12 boys, 21 girls); Grade 10: 42 students (22 boys, 20 girls); Grade 11: 33 students (12 boys, 21 girls); Grade 12: 30 students (12 boys, 18 girls). 16% of students are Roman Catholic.

Faculty School total: 63. In upper school: 18 men, 24 women; 21 have advanced degrees.

Subjects Offered Art, Asian studies, biology, chemistry, computer science, drama, drama performance, economics, English, fine arts, French, information technology, Japanese, Japanese history, mathematics, music, physical education, physics, psychology, religious education, science, social studies, Spanish, visual arts, world history.

Graduation Requirements Arts and fine arts (art, music, dance, drama), English, foreign language, mathematics, physical education (includes health), religion

(includes Bible studies and theology), science, social studies (includes history), graduation requirements for IB diploma differ.
Special Academic Programs International Baccalaureate program; 11 Advanced Placement exams for which test preparation is offered; independent study; academic accommodation for the gifted, the musically talented, and the artistically talented; ESL (16 students enrolled).
College Admission Counseling 23 students graduated in 2008; 22 went to college, including Harvard University; International Christian University; McGill University; Sophia Universtiy; The University of British Columbia. Median SAT critical reading: 560, median SAT math: 640, median SAT writing: 570, median combined SAT: 1770. 38% scored over 600 on SAT critical reading, 67% scored over 600 on SAT math, 33% scored over 600 on SAT writing, 39% scored over 1800 on combined SAT.
Student Life Upper grades have uniform requirement, student council. Discipline rests primarily with faculty. Attendance at religious services is required.
Summer Programs Enrichment, advancement, ESL, sports, art/fine arts, computer instruction programs offered; session focuses on TOEFL and SAT preparation; held both on and off campus; held at off-campus locations; accepts boys and girls; open to students from other schools. 65 students usually enrolled. 2009 schedule: June 15 to July 3. Application deadline: May 15.
Tuition and Aid Day student tuition: ¥1,990,000.
Admissions For fall 2008, 67 students applied for upper-level admission, 48 were accepted, 35 enrolled. School's own test required. Deadline for receipt of application materials: none. Application fee required: ¥20,000. On-campus interview required.
Athletics Interscholastic: baseball (boys), basketball (b,g), cross-country running (b,g), soccer (b,g), volleyball (g); intramural: soccer (b); coed intramural: hiking/backpacking, tennis. 3 PE instructors.
Computers Computers are regularly used in computer applications, economics, English, foreign language, French, geography, information technology, mathematics, SAT preparation, science, social studies classes. Computer network features include on-campus library services, Internet access, wireless campus network. The school has a published electronic and media policy.
Contact Jeanette K. Thomas, School Head. 81-45-641-5751. Fax: 81-45-641-6688. E-mail: jthomas@stmaur.ac.jp. Web site: www.stmaur.ac.jp.

ST. MICHAEL'S COLLEGE SCHOOL

1515 Bathurst Street
Toronto, Ontario M5P 3H4, Canada

Head of School: Fr. Joseph Redican, CSB

General Information Boys' day college-preparatory and religious studies school, affiliated with Roman Catholic Church. Grades 7–12. Founded: 1852. Setting: urban. 10-acre campus. 2 buildings on campus. Approved or accredited by Ontario Department of Education. Language of instruction: English. Total enrollment: 1,083. Upper school average class size: 24. Upper school faculty-student ratio: 1:16.
Upper School Student Profile Grade 9: 218 students (218 boys); Grade 10: 215 students (215 boys); Grade 11: 242 students (242 boys); Grade 12: 206 students (206 boys). 95% of students are Roman Catholic.
Faculty School total: 73. In upper school: 59 men, 13 women; 20 have advanced degrees.
Special Academic Programs Advanced Placement exam preparation.
College Admission Counseling 228 students graduated in 2008; 213 went to college, including Queen's University at Kingston; The University of Western Ontario; University of Guelph; University of Toronto; University of Waterloo; York University. Other: 1 went to work, 14 had other specific plans.
Student Life Upper grades have uniform requirement, student council, honor system. Discipline rests primarily with faculty. Attendance at religious services is required.
Tuition and Aid Day student tuition: CAN$12,800. Tuition installment plan (monthly payment plans, individually arranged payment plans). Bursaries, merit scholarship grants, need-based scholarship grants available. In 2008–09, 13% of upper-school students received aid; total upper-school merit-scholarship money awarded: CAN$105,000. Total amount of financial aid awarded in 2008–09: CAN$1,300,000.
Admissions Traditional secondary-level entrance grade is 9. For fall 2008, 233 students applied for upper-level admission, 170 were accepted, 129 enrolled. SSAT required. Deadline for receipt of application materials: none. Application fee required: CAN$100.
Athletics Interscholastic: alpine skiing, aquatics, archery, badminton, baseball, basketball, cross-country running, football, golf, ice hockey, lacrosse, mountain biking, skiing (downhill), snowboarding, soccer, softball, swimming and diving, tennis, track and field, volleyball; intramural: archery, badminton, basketball, flag football, outdoor education, power lifting.
Computers Computer resources include on-campus library services, Internet access, Internet filtering or blocking technology. The school has a published electronic and media policy.
Contact Mr. Greg Paolini, Director of Admissions. 416-653-3180 Ext. 195. Fax: 416-653-7704. E-mail: paolini@smcs.toronto.on.ca. Web site: www.stmichaelscollegeschool.com.

ST. MICHAEL'S PREPARATORY SCHOOL OF THE NORBERTINE FATHERS

19292 El Toro Road
Silverado, California 92676-9710

Head of School: Rev. Gabriel D. Stack, OPRAEM

General Information Boys' boarding college-preparatory and religious studies school, affiliated with Roman Catholic Church. Grades 9–12. Founded: 1961. Setting: suburban. Nearest major city is Los Angeles. Students are housed in single-sex dormitories. 35-acre campus. 2 buildings on campus. Approved or accredited by Western Association of Schools and Colleges and California Department of Education. Total enrollment: 64. Upper school average class size: 6. Upper school faculty-student ratio: 1:3.
Upper School Student Profile Grade 9: 17 students (17 boys); Grade 10: 14 students (14 boys); Grade 11: 19 students (19 boys); Grade 12: 14 students (14 boys). 100% of students are boarding students. 90% are state residents. 4 states are represented in upper school student body. 4% are international students. International students from Mexico and Republic of Korea; 2 other countries represented in student body. 98% of students are Roman Catholic.
Faculty School total: 20. In upper school: 18 men, 2 women; 18 have advanced degrees; 13 reside on campus.
Subjects Offered Algebra, American history, American history-AP, American literature, ancient history, art history, Bible studies, biology, calculus-AP, chemistry, chorus, economics, economics-AP, English, English literature, ethics, fine arts, geography, geometry, government-AP, government/civics, health, history, Latin, Latin-AP, mathematics, philosophy, physical education, physical science, physics, pre-calculus, religion, science, social studies, Spanish, Spanish-AP, theology, trigonometry, world literature.
Graduation Requirements Arts and fine arts (art, music, dance, drama), English, foreign language, mathematics, physical education (includes health), religion (includes Bible studies and theology), science, social studies (includes history), Senior Matura.
Special Academic Programs Advanced Placement exam preparation; honors section; independent study.
College Admission Counseling 11 students graduated in 2008; all went to college, including California State Polytechnic University, Pomona; California State University, Fullerton; California State University, Long Beach; Thomas Aquinas College; University of California, Davis; University of Notre Dame. Mean SAT critical reading: 514, mean SAT math: 530.
Student Life Upper grades have uniform requirement, student council, honor system. Discipline rests equally with students and faculty. Attendance at religious services is required.
Tuition and Aid 5-day tuition and room/board: $14,800; 7-day tuition and room/board: $16,800. Tuition installment plan (FACTS Tuition Payment Plan, monthly payment plans, individually arranged payment plans). Need-based scholarship grants available. Total amount of financial aid awarded in 2008–09: $350,000.
Admissions Traditional secondary-level entrance grade is 9. High School Placement Test required. Deadline for receipt of application materials: June 30. Application fee required: $100. Interview required.
Athletics Interscholastic: baseball, cross-country running, football, soccer; intramural: basketball, field hockey, outdoor activities, swimming and diving, table tennis, volleyball, weight lifting. 1 PE instructor, 2 coaches.
Computers Computers are regularly used in English, mathematics, science classes. Computer resources include on-campus library services, Internet access, Internet filtering or blocking technology. Computer access in designated common areas is available to students. Students grades are available online.
Contact Mrs. Pamela M. Christian, School Secretary. 949-858-0222 Ext. 237. Fax: 949-858-7365. E-mail: admissions@stmichaelsprep.org. Web site: www.stmichaelsprep.org.

SAINT MONICA'S HIGH SCHOOL

1030 Lincoln Boulevard
Santa Monica, California 90403-4096

Head of School: Mr. Thom Gasper

General Information Coeducational day college-preparatory, arts, and religious studies school, affiliated with Roman Catholic Church. Grades 9–12. Founded: 1937. Setting: urban. Nearest major city is Los Angeles. 5-acre campus. 4 buildings on campus. Approved or accredited by National Catholic Education Association, Western Association of Schools and Colleges, and California Department of Education. Total enrollment: 625. Upper school average class size: 25. Upper school faculty-student ratio: 1:14.
Upper School Student Profile 75% of students are Roman Catholic.
Faculty School total: 46. In upper school: 22 men, 24 women; 20 have advanced degrees.
Subjects Offered Accounting, acting, Advanced Placement courses, algebra, American government-AP, American history, American history-AP, applied music, art, arts, Bible studies, calculus, calculus-AP, campus ministry, ceramics, chemistry, chorus, college counseling, community service, drama, driver education, economics, English, English-AP, European history-AP, film, fine arts, French, geometry, government/civics, graphic arts, health, Japanese, keyboarding, marine biology,

mathematics, physical education, physics, psychology, reading, religion, science, social studies, Spanish, Spanish language-AP, theater, trigonometry, U.S. history-AP, world history, yearbook.
Graduation Requirements Arts and fine arts (art, music, dance, drama), English, foreign language, mathematics, physical education (includes health), religion (includes Bible studies and theology), science, social studies (includes history). Community service is required.
Special Academic Programs Advanced Placement exam preparation; honors section; study at local college for college credit; remedial reading and/or remedial writing; remedial math.
College Admission Counseling 119 students graduated in 2008; 118 went to college. Other: 1 had other specific plans.
Student Life Upper grades have uniform requirement, student council, honor system. Discipline rests primarily with faculty. Attendance at religious services is required.
Summer Programs Remediation, enrichment, advancement, sports, art/fine arts, computer instruction programs offered; held on campus; accepts boys and girls; open to students from other schools. 180 students usually enrolled. 2009 schedule: June 22 to July 24. Application deadline: May 30.
Tuition and Aid Day student tuition: $6700. Tuition installment plan (monthly payment plans, individually arranged payment plans). Merit scholarship grants, need-based scholarship grants available. In 2008–09, 20% of upper-school students received aid.
Admissions Traditional secondary-level entrance grade is 9. High School Placement Test (closed version) from Scholastic Testing Service required. Deadline for receipt of application materials: January 16. Application fee required: $60. On-campus interview required.
Athletics Interscholastic: baseball (boys), basketball (b,g), cheering (g), cross-country running (b,g), dance squad (b,g), football (b), golf (b,g), soccer (b,g), softball (g), tennis (b,g), track and field (b,g), volleyball (b,g); coed interscholastic: bowling, surfing. 2 PE instructors, 12 coaches, 1 athletic trainer.
Computers Computers are regularly used in all academic classes. Computer network features include on-campus library services, online commercial services, Internet access. Computer access in designated common areas is available to students. Students grades are available online. The school has a published electronic and media policy.
Contact Mrs. Michele Rice, Director of Admissions. 310-394-3701 Ext. 448. Fax: 310-458-1353. E-mail: mrice@stmonicahs.net. Web site: www.stmonicahs.org.

SAINT PATRICK HIGH SCHOOL

5900 West Belmont Avenue
Chicago, Illinois 60634
Head of School: Br. Konrad Diebold

General Information Boys' day college-preparatory, arts, and religious studies school, affiliated with Roman Catholic Church. Grades 9–12. Founded: 1861. Setting: urban. 1 building on campus. Approved or accredited by Christian Brothers Association, North Central Association of Colleges and Schools, and Illinois Department of Education. Endowment: $4.5 million. Total enrollment: 915. Upper school average class size: 25. Upper school faculty-student ratio: 1:25.
Upper School Student Profile Grade 9: 238 students (238 boys); Grade 10: 229 students (229 boys); Grade 11: 222 students (222 boys); Grade 12: 226 students (226 boys). 85% of students are Roman Catholic.
Faculty School total: 71. In upper school: 54 men, 17 women; 44 have advanced degrees.
Subjects Offered Accounting, algebra, American history, American literature, anatomy, art, art history, biology, broadcasting, business, business skills, calculus, chemistry, Chinese, chorus, computer graphics, computer science, creative writing, drama, driver education, ecology, economics, English, English literature, ESL, ethics, European history, fine arts, French, geography, geometry, German, government/civics, grammar, health, history, journalism, keyboarding, mathematics, music, physical education, physics, psychology, religion, science, social science, social studies, sociology, Spanish, speech, theater, trigonometry, word processing, world history, writing.
Graduation Requirements Arts and fine arts (art, music, dance, drama), business skills (includes word processing), computer science, English, mathematics, physical education (includes health), religion (includes Bible studies and theology), science, service learning/internship, social science, social studies (includes history), participation in a retreat program. Community service is required.
Special Academic Programs Advanced Placement exam preparation; honors section; study at local college for college credit; remedial reading and/or remedial writing; ESL (4 students enrolled).
College Admission Counseling 224 students graduated in 2008; 203 went to college, including DePaul University; Dominican University; Northeastern Illinois University; Northern Illinois University; University of Illinois at Chicago; University of Illinois at Urbana–Champaign. Other: 11 went to work, 1 entered military service, 9 had other specific plans. Mean composite ACT: 22. 16% scored over 26 on composite ACT.
Student Life Upper grades have specified standards of dress, student council, honor system. Discipline rests primarily with faculty. Attendance at religious services is required.
Summer Programs Remediation, enrichment, sports, art/fine arts, computer instruction programs offered; session focuses on remediation; held on campus; accepts boys and girls; open to students from other schools. 525 students usually enrolled. 2009 schedule: June 15 to August 7. Application deadline: June 8.
Tuition and Aid Day student tuition: $8100. Tuition installment plan (monthly payment plans, quarterly payment plan): Need-based scholarship grants, paying campus jobs available. In 2008–09, 31% of upper-school students received aid. Total amount of financial aid awarded in 2008–09: $690,000.
Admissions Traditional secondary-level entrance grade is 9. For fall 2008, 301 students applied for upper-level admission, 299 were accepted, 238 enrolled. ACT-Explore or any standardized test required. Deadline for receipt of application materials: none. Application fee required: $250. On-campus interview required.
Athletics Interscholastic: baseball, basketball, bowling, cross-country running, diving, fishing, football, golf, soccer, swimming and diving, tennis, track and field, volleyball, water polo, wrestling; intramural: basketball, football, volleyball. 5 PE instructors, 34 coaches, 1 athletic trainer.
Computers Computers are regularly used in business, English, foreign language, geography, graphic arts, graphic design, graphics, history, information technology, introduction to technology, library skills, mathematics, media arts, media production, media services, newspaper, photojournalism, religion, remedial study skills, research skills, science, typing, word processing, yearbook classes. Computer network features include on-campus library services, online commercial services, Internet access, Internet filtering or blocking technology. Students grades are available online. The school has a published electronic and media policy.
Contact Christopher Perez, Director of Curriculum. 773-282-8844 Ext. 228. Fax: 773-282-2361. E-mail: cperez@stpatrick.org. Web site: www.stpatrick.org.

ST. PATRICK HIGH SCHOOL

PO Box 2880
Yellowknife, Northwest Territories X1A 2P2, Canada
Head of School: Mr. John Bowden

General Information Coeducational day college-preparatory and general academic school, affiliated with Roman Catholic Church. Grades 9–12. Founded: 1949. Setting: small town. Nearest major city is Edmonton, AB, Canada. Approved or accredited by Northwest Territories Department of Education. Languages of instruction: English and French. Total enrollment: 525.
Upper School Student Profile Grade 9: 119 students (55 boys, 64 girls); Grade 10: 204 students (109 boys, 95 girls); Grade 11: 107 students (55 boys, 52 girls); Grade 12: 95 students (45 boys, 50 girls). 48% of students are Roman Catholic.
Student Life Upper grades have specified standards of dress. Attendance at religious services is required.
Admissions No application fee required.
Contact Ms. Eletha Curran, Secretary. 867-873-4888. Fax: 867-873-5732. E-mail: eletha_curran@mail.ycs.nt.ca.

SAINT PATRICK—SAINT VINCENT HIGH SCHOOL

1500 Benicia Road
Vallejo, California 94591
Head of School: Ms. Mary Ellen Ryan

General Information Coeducational day college-preparatory, arts, business, religious studies, and technology school, affiliated with Roman Catholic Church. Grades 9–12. Founded: 1870. Setting: suburban. 31-acre campus. 8 buildings on campus. Approved or accredited by Western Association of Schools and Colleges, Western Catholic Education Association, and California Department of Education. Total enrollment: 642. Upper school average class size: 30. Upper school faculty-student ratio: 1:30.
Upper School Student Profile Grade 9: 161 students (79 boys, 82 girls); Grade 10: 165 students (72 boys, 93 girls); Grade 11: 166 students (86 boys, 80 girls); Grade 12: 149 students (73 boys, 76 girls). 80% of students are Roman Catholic.
Faculty School total: 49. In upper school: 19 men, 30 women; 20 have advanced degrees.
Subjects Offered Algebra, art, biology, calculus, calculus-AP, campus ministry, Catholic belief and practice, chemistry, chemistry-AP, choir, civics, college counseling, college planning, computer keyboarding, computer multimedia, concert bell choir, concert choir, economics, English, English language-AP, English-AP, environmental science, environmental studies, ethnic studies, film appreciation, French, French language-AP, geometry, government-AP, health, history-AP, honors algebra, honors English, honors geometry, honors U.S. history, honors world history, human biology, leadership training, organic chemistry, physical education, physics, psychology, religion, science, Spanish, Spanish language-AP, statistics, statistics-AP, theater arts, U.S. history, vocal jazz, world history.
Graduation Requirements English, foreign language, mathematics, physical education (includes health), religion (includes Bible studies and theology), science, social studies (includes history), Christian service.
Special Academic Programs Advanced Placement exam preparation; honors section; academic accommodation for the gifted; remedial math.
College Admission Counseling 167 students graduated in 2008; 162 went to college, including California State University, Sacramento; San Francisco State University;

San Jose State University; Santa Clara University; Sonoma State University; University of San Francisco. Other: 2 entered military service, 3 had other specific plans.
Student Life Upper grades have uniform requirement, student council, honor system. Discipline rests primarily with faculty. Attendance at religious services is required.
Tuition and Aid Day student tuition: $9775. Tuition installment plan (FACTS Tuition Payment Plan). Need-based scholarship grants available. In 2008–09, 14% of upper-school students received aid. Total amount of financial aid awarded in 2008–09: $205,750.
Admissions Traditional secondary-level entrance grade is 9. For fall 2008, 208 students applied for upper-level admission, 198 were accepted, 163 enrolled. High School Placement Test required. Deadline for receipt of application materials: none. Application fee required: $40. Interview required.
Athletics Interscholastic: baseball (boys), basketball (b,g), football (b), golf (b,g), soccer (b,g), softball (g), water polo (b,g), wrestling (b); coed interscholastic: cross-country running, swimming and diving, tennis, track and field, volleyball. 4 PE instructors, 44 coaches, 1 athletic trainer.
Computers Computers are regularly used in Web site design, yearbook classes. Computer resources include on-campus library services, Internet access. Student e-mail accounts are available to students. Students grades are available online. The school has a published electronic and media policy.
Contact Mrs. Sheila Williams, Director of Admissions. 707-644-4425 Ext. 448. Fax: 707-644-3107. Web site: spsv.org.

ST. PATRICK'S REGIONAL SECONDARY

115 East 11th Avenue
Vancouver, British Columbia V5T 2C1, Canada

Head of School: Mr. John V. Bevacqua

General Information Coeducational day college-preparatory, general academic, arts, business, religious studies, and technology school, affiliated with Roman Catholic Church. Grades 8–12. Founded: 1923. Setting: urban. Approved or accredited by British Columbia Department of Education. Total enrollment: 500.
Upper School Student Profile 97% of students are Roman Catholic.
Faculty School total: 35.
Special Academic Programs Advanced Placement exam preparation; ESL (15 students enrolled).
College Admission Counseling 100 students graduated in 2008.
Student Life Upper grades have uniform requirement. Attendance at religious services is required.
Admissions Application fee required: CAN$50. Interview required.
Contact Mr. John V. Bevacqua, Principal. 604-874-6422. Fax: 604-874-5176. E-mail: administration@stpats.bc.ca. Web site: www.stpats.bc.ca.

SAINT PATRICK'S SCHOOL

318 Limestone Street
Maysville, Kentucky 41056

Head of School: Mrs. Jennifer Griffith

General Information Coeducational day college-preparatory school, affiliated with Roman Catholic Church. Grades 1–12. Founded: 1926. Setting: small town. Nearest major city is Cincinnati, OH. 1-acre campus. 1 building on campus. Approved or accredited by Southern Association of Colleges and Schools and Kentucky Department of Education. Total enrollment: 290. Upper school average class size: 22. Upper school faculty-student ratio: 1:13.
Upper School Student Profile 75% of students are Roman Catholic.
Faculty School total: 13. In upper school: 4 men, 9 women; 11 have advanced degrees.
Subjects Offered Accounting, ACT preparation, advanced biology, advanced math, algebra, analytic geometry, art, art appreciation, biology, bookkeeping, calculus, chemistry, college admission preparation, college awareness, college counseling, college placement, college planning, college writing, computer applications, computer keyboarding, computer literacy, drama, earth and space science, economics, English, English composition, English literature, general science, government/civics, guidance, health, health education, language arts, library, library assistant, mathematics, music, music appreciation, physical education, physical science, physics, pre-algebra, pre-calculus, psychology, religion, senior composition, senior humanities, social studies, sociology, Spanish, student government, U.S. government, U.S. history, vocal music, world geography, world history, yearbook.
Graduation Requirements Arts and fine arts (art, music, dance, drama), computer applications, electives, English, foreign language, mathematics, physical education (includes health), religion (includes Bible studies and theology), science, social studies (includes history). Community service is required.
Special Academic Programs Independent study.
College Admission Counseling 24 students graduated in 2008; 22 went to college, including Eastern Kentucky University; Loyola University New Orleans; Northern Kentucky University; University of Kentucky; University of Louisville. Other: 2 went to work.
Student Life Upper grades have uniform requirement, student council. Discipline rests primarily with faculty. Attendance at religious services is required.
Tuition and Aid Day student tuition: $3456. Tuition installment plan (The Tuition Plan). Tuition reduction for siblings available.
Admissions Traditional secondary-level entrance grade is 9. For fall 2008, 6 students applied for upper-level admission, 5 were accepted, 5 enrolled. Deadline for receipt of application materials: none. No application fee required. Interview required.
Athletics Interscholastic: baseball (boys, girls), basketball (b,g), cheering (g), cross-country running (b,g), golf (b), soccer (b,g), swimming and diving (b,g), tennis (b,g), track and field (b,g), volleyball (g); coed interscholastic: tennis, track and field. 1 PE instructor, 2 coaches.
Computers Computers are regularly used in accounting, business applications, data processing, economics, newspaper classes. Computer network features include Internet access. The school has a published electronic and media policy.
Contact Mr. Douglas K. Calland, Counselor. 606-564-5949 Ext. 238. Fax: 606-564-8795. E-mail: dcalland@stpatschool.com.

ST. PAUL ACADEMY AND SUMMIT SCHOOL

1712 Randolph Avenue
St. Paul, Minnesota 55105

Head of School: Bryn S. Roberts

General Information Coeducational day college-preparatory school. Grades K–12. Founded: 1900. Setting: urban. Nearest major city is Saint Paul. 32-acre campus. 4 buildings on campus. Approved or accredited by Independent Schools Association of the Central States and Minnesota Department of Education. Member of National Association of Independent Schools. Endowment: $39.2 million. Total enrollment: 862. Upper school average class size: 15. Upper school faculty-student ratio: 1:7.
Upper School Student Profile Grade 9: 81 students (37 boys, 44 girls); Grade 10: 92 students (50 boys, 42 girls); Grade 11: 93 students (46 boys, 47 girls); Grade 12: 79 students (39 boys, 40 girls).
Faculty School total: 104. In upper school: 30 men, 28 women; 48 have advanced degrees.
Subjects Offered Algebra, American literature, art, biology, calculus, ceramics, chemistry, Chinese, creative writing, current events, debate, drama, earth science, economics, English, English literature, European history, expository writing, fine arts, French, geometry, German, journalism, law and the legal system, marine biology, mathematics, multicultural studies, music, music theory, newspaper, photography, physical education, physics, psychology, science, senior project, Shakespeare, social psychology, social studies, sociology, space and physical sciences, Spanish, trigonometry, world history, world literature, world religions, yearbook.
Graduation Requirements Arts and fine arts (art, music, dance, drama), English, foreign language, mathematics, physical education (includes health), science, social studies (includes history), participation in athletics, month-long senior project, senior speech.
Special Academic Programs Honors section; independent study; term-away projects; study abroad.
College Admission Counseling 79 students graduated in 2008; all went to college, including Boston University; Carleton College; St. Olaf College; University of Minnesota, Twin Cities Campus; University of Puget Sound; Yale University. Mean SAT critical reading: 630, mean SAT math: 656, mean SAT writing: 633, mean combined SAT: 1919, mean composite ACT: 28. 61% scored over 600 on SAT critical reading, 70% scored over 600 on SAT math, 66% scored over 600 on SAT writing, 65% scored over 1800 on combined SAT, 73% scored over 26 on composite ACT.
Student Life Upper grades have specified standards of dress, student council. Discipline rests equally with students and faculty.
Tuition and Aid Day student tuition: $20,520–$22,410. Tuition installment plan (Insured Tuition Payment Plan, monthly payment plans). Need-based scholarship grants available. In 2008–09, 15% of upper-school students received aid. Total amount of financial aid awarded in 2008–09: $750,000.
Admissions Traditional secondary-level entrance grade is 9. For fall 2008, 70 students applied for upper-level admission, 25 were accepted, 17 enrolled. SSAT, ERB, PSAT, SAT, PLAN or ACT or writing sample required. Deadline for receipt of application materials: February 1. Application fee required: $80. Interview required.
Athletics Interscholastic: alpine skiing (boys, girls), baseball (b), basketball (b,g), cross-country running (b,g), dance (g), dance team (g), diving (b,g), fencing (b,g), football (b), golf (b,g), ice hockey (b,g), skiing (cross-country) (b,g), skiing (downhill) (b,g), soccer (b,g), softball (g), swimming and diving (b,g), tennis (b,g); intramural: outdoor adventure (b,g); coed interscholastic: lacrosse, strength & conditioning, track and field; coed intramural: hiking/backpacking, physical fitness, snowboarding, table tennis. 3 PE instructors, 101 coaches, 1 athletic trainer.
Computers Computers are regularly used in all academic classes. Computer network features include on-campus library services, online commercial services, Internet access, wireless campus network, Internet filtering or blocking technology, laptop program (beginning in grade 7). Student e-mail accounts and computer access in designated common areas are available to students. The school has a published electronic and media policy.
Contact Mrs. Heather Cameron Ploen, Director of Admission and Financial Aid. 651-698-2451. Fax: 651-698-6787. E-mail: hploen@spa.edu. Web site: www.spa.edu.

SAINT PAUL LUTHERAN HIGH SCHOOL

205 South Main Street
PO Box 719
Concordia, Missouri 64020

Head of School: Rev. Paul M. Mehl

General Information Coeducational boarding and day college-preparatory, general academic, arts, and religious studies school, affiliated with Lutheran Church–Missouri Synod. Grades 9–12. Founded: 1883. Setting: small town. Nearest major city is Kansas City. Students are housed in single-sex dormitories. 50-acre campus. 9 buildings on campus. Approved or accredited by Lutheran School Accreditation Commission, Midwest Association of Boarding Schools, North Central Association of Colleges and Schools, and Missouri Department of Education. Endowment: $1.5 million. Total enrollment: 186. Upper school average class size: 20. Upper school faculty-student ratio: 1:11.

Upper School Student Profile Grade 9: 30 students (14 boys, 16 girls); Grade 10: 47 students (21 boys, 26 girls); Grade 11: 74 students (39 boys, 35 girls); Grade 12: 35 students (15 boys, 20 girls). 73% of students are boarding students. 39% are state residents. 11 states are represented in upper school student body. 50% are international students. International students from Norway, Republic of Korea, Slovakia, Spain, Taiwan, and Viet Nam; 6 other countries represented in student body. 70% of students are Lutheran Church–Missouri Synod.

Faculty School total: 21. In upper school: 12 men, 9 women; 17 have advanced degrees; 10 reside on campus.

Subjects Offered Accounting, ADL skills, advanced biology, algebra, American history, American literature, analytic geometry, art, athletic training, band, Bible studies, biology, business law, calculus, ceramics, chemistry, child development, chorus, Christian doctrine, church history, community service, comparative religion, composition, computer science, concert choir, creative writing, current events, drama, drawing, economics, English, English literature, ESL, family studies, freshman seminar, general science, geography, geometry, German, government/civics, health, human anatomy, music appreciation, music theory, novels, painting, physical education, physical science, physics, poetry, pre-algebra, psychology, religion, Shakespeare, sociology, Spanish, speech, statistics, theology, trigonometry, world history, world literature, writing.

Graduation Requirements Arts and fine arts (art, music, dance, drama), computer science, English, foreign language, mathematics, physical education (includes health), practical arts, religion (includes Bible studies and theology), science, social studies (includes history), 3.0 grade point average on a 4.0 scale for college preparatory students, above (national) average score on ACT or SAT. Community service is required.

Special Academic Programs International Baccalaureate program; independent study; study at local college for college credit.

College Admission Counseling 39 students graduated in 2008; 36 went to college, including Concordia University; University of Central Missouri; University of Missouri–Columbia; Willamette University. Other: 2 entered military service, 1 entered a postgraduate year. Median SAT critical reading: 465, median SAT math: 630, median SAT writing: 490, median combined SAT: 1580, median composite ACT: 25. 19% scored over 600 on SAT critical reading, 63% scored over 600 on SAT math, 13% scored over 600 on SAT writing, 25% scored over 1800 on combined SAT, 40% scored over 26 on composite ACT.

Student Life Upper grades have specified standards of dress, student council, honor system. Discipline rests primarily with faculty. Attendance at religious services is required.

Tuition and Aid Day student tuition: $8000; 7-day tuition and room/board: $12,375. Guaranteed tuition plan. Tuition installment plan (monthly payment plans, individually arranged payment plans, lump-sum payment discount plan). Tuition reduction for siblings, need-based scholarship grants, paying campus jobs, LCMS Grants for church vocation students, early bird tuition grants available. In 2008–09, 16% of upper-school students received aid. Total amount of financial aid awarded in 2008–09: $185,285.

Admissions Traditional secondary-level entrance grade is 9. For fall 2008, 105 students applied for upper-level admission, 100 were accepted, 85 enrolled. School placement exam and SLEP for foreign students required. Deadline for receipt of application materials: none. Application fee required: $100. On-campus interview recommended.

Athletics Interscholastic: baseball (boys), basketball (b,g), cheering (g), cross-country running (b,g), football (b), golf (b,g), soccer (b,g), softball (g), track and field (b,g), volleyball (g); intramural: baseball (b), basketball (b,g), dance team (g), football (b), golf (b,g), jogging (b,g), roller blading (b,g), running (b,g), soccer (b,g), softball (g), strength & conditioning (b,g), tennis (b,g), volleyball (b,g), weight lifting (b,g); coed interscholastic: cross-country running, track and field; coed intramural: jogging, roller blading, running, soccer, table tennis, ultimate Frisbee. 2 PE instructors, 1 coach.

Computers Computers are regularly used in Christian doctrine, creative writing, data processing, English, freshman foundations, history, keyboarding, lab/keyboard, library skills, religious studies, speech, study skills, word processing, writing, writing classes. Computer resources include Internet access, wireless campus network. Students grades are available online. The school has a published electronic and media policy.

Contact Mrs. Gloria A. Burrow, Public Relations and Communications. 660-463-2238 Ext. 231. Fax: 660-463-7621. E-mail: gburrow@splhs.org. Web site: www.splhs.org.

ANNOUNCEMENT FROM THE SCHOOL Students from around the world study and learn together in an atmosphere of Christian commitment at Saint Paul Lutheran in Concordia, Missouri. The School provides general and college-preparatory curriculums, college-level courses, and excellence in education. A full range of athletic, academic, and fine art extracurricular activities are available for all students. Saint Paul's is fully accredited. Established in 1883, Saint Paul provides a rich heritage, a safe environment, and a location just 50 minutes from a major city. For more information, visit the School's Web site at www.splhs.org.

ST. PAUL'S EPISCOPAL SCHOOL

161 Dogwood Lane
Mobile, Alabama 36608

Head of School: Mr. F. Martin Lester Jr.

General Information Coeducational day college-preparatory, arts, and technology school, affiliated with Episcopal Church. Grades PK–12. Founded: 1947. Setting: suburban. 35-acre campus. 10 buildings on campus. Approved or accredited by National Association of Episcopal Schools, Southern Association of Colleges and Schools, Southern Association of Independent Schools, and Alabama Department of Education. Member of National Association of Independent Schools and Secondary School Admission Test Board. Endowment: $1.5 million. Total enrollment: 1,491. Upper school average class size: 21. Upper school faculty-student ratio: 1:12.

Upper School Student Profile Grade 9: 131 students (78 boys, 53 girls); Grade 10: 145 students (73 boys, 72 girls); Grade 11: 146 students (71 boys, 75 girls); Grade 12: 136 students (75 boys, 61 girls). 24% of students are members of Episcopal Church.

Faculty School total: 150. In upper school: 19 men, 34 women; 39 have advanced degrees.

Subjects Offered Algebra, American history, American literature, art, band, biology, British literature-AP, calculus, chemistry, composition, computer science, drama, driver education, economics, English, English literature, English-AP, European history, fine arts, French, geometry, government/civics, grammar, history, human anatomy, instrumental music, journalism, Latin, marching band, marine biology, mathematics, music, oil painting, painting, photography, physical education, physics, playwriting, pre-calculus, Spanish, speech, theater, theater arts, trigonometry, weight training, world history, yearbook.

Graduation Requirements Arts and fine arts (art, music, dance, drama), English, foreign language, history, mathematics, physical education (includes health), science. Community service is required.

Special Academic Programs Advanced Placement exam preparation; honors section; special instructional classes for students with diagnosed learning disabilities.

College Admission Counseling 156 students graduated in 2008; all went to college, including Auburn University; Birmingham-Southern College; The University of Alabama; University of Mississippi; University of South Alabama; University of Southern Mississippi.

Student Life Upper grades have uniform requirement, student council, honor system. Discipline rests primarily with faculty. Attendance at religious services is required.

Summer Programs Remediation, enrichment, advancement, sports, art/fine arts, computer instruction programs offered; session focuses on enrichment; held both on and off campus; held at European trips; accepts boys and girls; open to students from other schools. 560 students usually enrolled. 2009 schedule: May 27 to August 1. Application deadline: none.

Tuition and Aid Day student tuition: $8180. Tuition installment plan (monthly payment plans, semiannual payment plan). Need-based scholarship grants available. In 2008–09, 9% of upper-school students received aid. Total amount of financial aid awarded in 2008–09: $212,518.

Admissions Traditional secondary-level entrance grade is 9. For fall 2008, 60 students applied for upper-level admission, 44 were accepted, 35 enrolled. ERB CTP IV or Otis-Lennon and 2 sections of ERB required. Deadline for receipt of application materials: none. No application fee required. On-campus interview required.

Athletics Interscholastic: baseball (boys), basketball (b,g), cheering (g), cross-country running (b,g), dance team (g), football (b), golf (b,g), indoor track & field (b,g), soccer (b,g), softball (g), swimming and diving (b,g), tennis (b,g), track and field (b,g), volleyball (g), weight training (b), winter (indoor) track (b,g); intramural: basketball (b,g), cheering (g), soccer (b,g), volleyball (g), weight training (b). 6 PE instructors, 13 coaches, 4 athletic trainers.

Computers Computers are regularly used in economics, English, history, journalism, keyboarding, mathematics, newspaper, science, video film production, yearbook classes. Computer network features include on-campus library services, online commercial services, Internet access, wireless campus network, Internet filtering or blocking technology. Student e-mail accounts and computer access in designated common areas are available to students. Students grades are available online. The school has a published electronic and media policy.

Contact Ms. Julie L. Taylor, Admissions Office. 251-461-2129. Fax: 251-342-1844. E-mail: jtaylor@stpaulsmobile.net. Web site: www.stpaulsmobile.net.

ST. PAUL'S HIGH SCHOOL

2200 Grant Avenue
Winnipeg, Manitoba R3P 0P8, Canada

Head of School: Fr. Alan Fogarty, SJ

General Information Boys' day college-preparatory, arts, religious studies, and technology school, affiliated with Roman Catholic Church. Grades 9–12. Founded: 1926. Setting: suburban. 18-acre campus. 5 buildings on campus. Approved or accredited by Jesuit Secondary Education Association and Manitoba Department of Education. Language of instruction: English. Endowment: CAN$4.5 million. Total enrollment: 586. Upper school average class size: 26. Upper school faculty-student ratio: 1:14.

Upper School Student Profile Grade 9: 150 students (150 boys); Grade 10: 150 students (150 boys); Grade 11: 150 students (150 boys); Grade 12: 136 students (136 boys). 70% of students are Roman Catholic.

Faculty School total: 42. In upper school: 38 men, 4 women; 14 have advanced degrees.

Subjects Offered Algebra, American history, art, biology, calculus, chemistry, classics, computer science, current events, economics, English, ethics, French, geography, geometry, history, law, mathematics, media, multimedia, multimedia design, music, physical education, physics, political science, psychology, religion, science, social studies, speech, theology.

Graduation Requirements English, mathematics, physical education (includes health), religion (includes Bible studies and theology), science, social studies (includes history), completion of Christian service program.

Special Academic Programs Advanced Placement exam preparation; honors section; remedial math.

College Admission Counseling 137 students graduated in 2008; 130 went to college, including Carleton University; McGill University; Queen's University at Kingston; The University of Winnipeg; University of Manitoba; University of Toronto. Other: 7 had other specific plans.

Student Life Upper grades have specified standards of dress, student council, honor system. Discipline rests primarily with faculty. Attendance at religious services is required.

Summer Programs Sports programs offered; session focuses on sport skills and relationship building; held on campus; accepts boys; open to students from other schools. 2009 schedule: August 15 to August 29.

Tuition and Aid Day student tuition: CAN$5990. Tuition installment plan (Insured Tuition Payment Plan, monthly payment plans, individually arranged payment plans). Bursaries, need-based loans available. In 2008–09, 12% of upper-school students received aid. Total amount of financial aid awarded in 2008–09: CAN$240,000.

Admissions Traditional secondary-level entrance grade is 9. For fall 2008, 350 students applied for upper-level admission, 159 were accepted, 159 enrolled. Achievement tests and STS required. Deadline for receipt of application materials: February 7. Application fee required: CAN$75. On-campus interview required.

Athletics Interscholastic: badminton, basketball, cross-country running, curling, football, golf, ice hockey, indoor track, indoor track & field, rugby, soccer, track and field, volleyball, wrestling; intramural: basketball, curling, football, golf, physical fitness, physical training, skiing (downhill), strength & conditioning, table tennis, volleyball, weight training. 4 PE instructors, 1 athletic trainer.

Computers Computers are regularly used in French, French as a second language, geography, mathematics, multimedia, religious studies, science classes. Computer network features include on-campus library services, online commercial services, Internet access, Internet filtering or blocking technology. Campus intranet, student e-mail accounts, and computer access in designated common areas are available to students. Students' grades are available online. The school has a published electronic and media policy.

Contact Mr. Tom Lussier, Principal. 204-831-2300. Fax: 204-831-2340. E-mail: tlussier@stpauls.mb.ca. Web site: www.stpauls.mb.ca.

ST. PAUL'S SCHOOL

11152 Falls Road
PO Box 8100
Brooklandville, Maryland 21022-8100

Head of School: Mr. Thomas J. Reid

General Information Coeducational day (girls' only in lower grades) college-preparatory school, affiliated with Episcopal Church. Boys grades K–12, girls grades K–4. Founded: 1849. Setting: suburban. Nearest major city is Baltimore. 95-acre campus. 23 buildings on campus. Approved or accredited by Association of Independent Maryland Schools and Maryland Department of Education. Member of National Association of Independent Schools. Endowment: $26 million. Total enrollment: 851. Upper school average class size: 17. Upper school faculty-student ratio: 1:9.

Upper School Student Profile Grade 9: 91 students (91 boys); Grade 10: 84 students (84 boys); Grade 11: 85 students (85 boys); Grade 12: 80 students (80 boys).

Faculty School total: 119. In upper school: 34 men, 6 women; 29 have advanced degrees.

Subjects Offered Acting, algebra, American history, American literature, anatomy, art, art history, biology, biology-AP, calculus, calculus-AP, chemistry, community service, design, drama, drawing, economics, English, ethics, forensics, French, French-AP, geometry, German, German-AP, International Baccalaureate courses, Japanese, mathematics, model United Nations, music, painting, photography, physical education, physics, physics-AP, psychology, religion, Spanish, Spanish-AP, statistics, statistics-AP, theater, trigonometry, world history, world literature.

Graduation Requirements Arts and fine arts (art, music, dance, drama), English, foreign language, mathematics, physical education (includes health), religion (includes Bible studies and theology), science, social science, social studies (includes history). Community service is required.

Special Academic Programs International Baccalaureate program; Advanced Placement exam preparation; honors section; independent study; term-away projects; study abroad; academic accommodation for the gifted; programs in general development for dyslexic students.

College Admission Counseling 77 students graduated in 2008; all went to college, including Elon University; The University of North Carolina Wilmington; Tulane University; University of Colorado at Boulder.

Student Life Upper grades have specified standards of dress, student council, honor system. Discipline rests equally with students and faculty. Attendance at religious services is required.

Tuition and Aid Day student tuition: $19,750. Tuition installment plan (Key Tuition Payment Plan). Need-based scholarship grants available. In 2008–09, 20% of upper-school students received aid. Total amount of financial aid awarded in 2008–09: $741,975.

Admissions Traditional secondary-level entrance grade is 9. For fall 2008, 90 students applied for upper-level admission, 54 were accepted, 25 enrolled. CTP III, ERB, ISEE or SSAT required. Deadline for receipt of application materials: January 15. Application fee required: $50. On-campus interview required.

Athletics Interscholastic: baseball, basketball, crew, cross-country running, football, golf, ice hockey, independent competitive sports, lacrosse, soccer, squash, swimming and diving, tennis, volleyball, wrestling; intramural: bicycling, combined training, Frisbee, mountain biking, outdoor activities, physical fitness, physical training, ropes courses, running, soccer, strength & conditioning, ultimate Frisbee, weight training. 3 PE instructors, 3 coaches, 2 athletic trainers.

Computers Computers are regularly used in all classes. Computer network features include on-campus library services, online commercial services, Internet access, wireless campus network, Internet filtering or blocking technology. Student e-mail accounts are available to students. The school has a published electronic and media policy.

Contact Ms. Amy Hall Furlong, Director of Admissions. 410-821-3034. Fax: 410-427-0380. E-mail: admissions@stpaulsschool.org. Web site: www.stpaulsschool.org.

ST. PAUL'S SCHOOL

325 Pleasant Street
Concord, New Hampshire 03301-2591

Head of School: Mr. William R. Matthews Jr.

General Information Coeducational boarding college-preparatory and arts school, affiliated with Episcopal Church. Grades 9–12. Founded: 1856. Setting: rural. Nearest major city is Manchester. Students are housed in single-sex dormitories. 2,000-acre campus. 75 buildings on campus. Approved or accredited by Association of Independent Schools in New England, National Association of Episcopal Schools, New England Association of Schools and Colleges, The Association of Boarding Schools, and New Hampshire Department of Education. Member of National Association of Independent Schools and Secondary School Admission Test Board. Endowment: $438.2 million. Total enrollment: 533. Upper school average class size: 11. Upper school faculty-student ratio: 1:5.

Upper School Student Profile Grade 9: 102 students (54 boys, 48 girls); Grade 10: 149 students (77 boys, 72 girls); Grade 11: 141 students (66 boys, 75 girls); Grade 12: 141 students (70 boys, 71 girls). 100% of students are boarding students. 12% are state residents. 33 states are represented in upper school student body. 17% are international students. International students from Canada, China, Democratic People's Republic of Korea, Hong Kong, Japan, and United Kingdom; 11 other countries represented in student body. 33% of students are members of Episcopal Church.

Faculty School total: 81. In upper school: 46 men, 33 women; 76 have advanced degrees; all reside on campus.

Subjects Offered 3-dimensional design, algebra, American history, American literature, applied arts, applied music, architecture, art, art history, astronomy, ballet, biology, calculus, ceramics, chemistry, Chinese, classical civilization, classical Greek literature, classical language, computer math, computer programming, computer science, creative writing, drama, driver education, ecology, English, English literature, environmental science, ethics, European history, fine arts, French, geometry, German, government/civics, grammar, Greek, health, history, humanities, independent study, instrumental music, Japanese, Latin, mathematics, music, photography, physical education, physics, religion, robotics, science, social studies, Spanish, speech, statistics, theater, trigonometry, writing.

Graduation Requirements Art, athletics, humanities, language, mathematics, music, religion (includes Bible studies and theology), science, residential life. Community service is required.

Special Academic Programs Advanced Placement exam preparation; honors section; accelerated programs; independent study; term-away projects; study abroad; academic accommodation for the gifted, the musically talented, and the artistically talented.
College Admission Counseling 135 students graduated in 2008; 133 went to college, including Harvard University; Princeton University; Stanford University; Tufts University; University of Pennsylvania; Yale University. Other: 2 entered a postgraduate year. Median SAT math: 688, median SAT writing: 673.
Student Life Upper grades have specified standards of dress, student council, honor system. Discipline rests primarily with faculty. Attendance at religious services is required.
Summer Programs Enrichment programs offered; session focuses on enrichment for New Hampshire public high school juniors only; held on campus; accepts boys and girls; open to students from other schools. 245 students usually enrolled. 2009 schedule: June 20 to July 27. Application deadline: December 1.
Tuition and Aid 7-day tuition and room/board: $41,250. Tuition installment plan (Academic Management Services Plan, monthly payment plans). Merit scholarship grants, need-based scholarship grants, tuition remission for children of faculty and staff available. In 2008–09, 34% of upper-school students received aid; total upper-school merit-scholarship money awarded: $548,570. Total amount of financial aid awarded in 2008–09: $6,056,858.
Admissions Traditional secondary-level entrance grade is 9. For fall 2008, 1,190 students applied for upper-level admission, 260 were accepted, 153 enrolled. SSAT required. Deadline for receipt of application materials: January 15. Application fee required: $50. Interview required.
Athletics Interscholastic: alpine skiing (boys, girls), baseball (b), basketball (b,g), crew (b,g), cross-country running (b,g), field hockey (g), football (b), ice hockey (b,g), lacrosse (b,g), rowing (b,g), skiing (cross-country) (b,g), skiing (downhill) (b,g), soccer (b,g), softball (g), squash (b,g), tennis (b,g), track and field (b,g), volleyball (g), wrestling (b); intramural: crew (b,g), ice hockey (b,g), rowing (b,g), soccer (b,g); coed interscholastic: ballet; coed intramural: aerobics, aerobics/Nautilus, alpine skiing, backpacking, baseball, basketball, crew, equestrian sports, fitness, fly fishing, horseback riding, ice hockey, physical fitness, rowing, skeet shooting, skiing (cross-country), skiing (downhill), snowboarding, soccer, squash, tai chi, tennis, weight training. 2 coaches, 2 athletic trainers.
Computers Computers are regularly used in English, foreign language, humanities, mathematics, science classes. Computer network features include on-campus library services, online commercial services, Internet access, wireless campus network, Internet filtering or blocking technology. Student e-mail accounts and computer access in designated common areas are available to students. Students grades are available online. The school has a published electronic and media policy.
Contact Ms. Holly Foote, Office Manager. 603-229-4700. Fax: 603-229-4771. E-mail: admissions@sps.edu. Web site: www.sps.edu.

See Close-Up on page 948.

ST. PAUL'S SCHOOL FOR GIRLS

11232 Falls Road
Brooklandville, Maryland 21022

Head of School: Dr. Monica M. Gillespie

General Information Girls' day college-preparatory, arts, religious studies, technology, and AP and honors, leadership school, affiliated with Episcopal Church. Grades 5–12. Founded: 1959. Setting: suburban. Nearest major city is Baltimore. 38-acre campus. 4 buildings on campus. Approved or accredited by Association of Independent Maryland Schools, National Association of Episcopal Schools, and Maryland Department of Education. Member of National Association of Independent Schools. Endowment: $5.9 million. Total enrollment: 465. Upper school average class size: 15. Upper school faculty-student ratio: 1:7.
Upper School Student Profile Grade 9: 77 students (77 girls); Grade 10: 64 students (64 girls); Grade 11: 71 students (71 girls); Grade 12: 71 students (71 girls).
Faculty School total: 65. In upper school: 13 men, 36 women; 28 have advanced degrees.
Subjects Offered Algebra, American history, American literature, anatomy, ancient history, art, biology, biology-AP, biotechnology, calculus, calculus-AP, chemistry, chemistry-AP, Chinese, chorus, community service, computer science, dance, drama, economics, economics-AP, English, English language and composition-AP, English literature and composition-AP, English-AP, environmental science, environmental science-AP, ethics, fine arts, forensic science, forensics, French, French-AP, genetics, geography, geometry, German, German-AP, health, history, Japanese, journalism, leadership and service, literary magazine, literature, mathematics, mechanics, medieval history, modern history, music, newspaper, optics, photography, physical education, physics, physics-AP, physiology, pre-calculus, programming, psychology-AP, religion, research skills, science, senior project, social studies, Spanish, Spanish language-AP, speech, statistics, studio art-AP, theater, trigonometry, U.S. history-AP, world culture, world history.
Graduation Requirements Arts and fine arts (art, music, dance, drama), English, foreign language, mathematics, physical education (includes health), religion (includes Bible studies and theology), science, social studies (includes history), senior work project, senior speech. Community service is required.
Special Academic Programs Advanced Placement exam preparation; honors section; independent study; term-away projects; domestic exchange program; study abroad; academic accommodation for the gifted, the musically talented, and the artistically talented.
College Admission Counseling 65 students graduated in 2008; all went to college, including Bucknell University; Dartmouth College; Dickinson College; Georgetown University; University of Delaware; Wake Forest University.
Student Life Upper grades have uniform requirement, student council, honor system. Discipline rests equally with students and faculty. Attendance at religious services is required.
Summer Programs Enrichment, sports programs offered; session focuses on skills development, leadership; held both on and off campus; held at downtown Baltimore and local outdoor facilities; accepts boys and girls; open to students from other schools.
Tuition and Aid Day student tuition: $21,500. Tuition installment plan (Key Tuition Payment Plan, monthly payment plans). Merit scholarship grants, need-based scholarship grants, paying campus jobs available. In 2008–09, 18% of upper-school students received aid; total upper-school merit-scholarship money awarded: $21,500. Total amount of financial aid awarded in 2008–09: $1,200,000.
Admissions Traditional secondary-level entrance grade is 9. ISEE required. Deadline for receipt of application materials: January 15. Application fee required: $50. On-campus interview required.
Athletics Interscholastic: aerobics/dance, aquatics, badminton, ballet, basketball, crew, cross-country running, dance, field hockey, golf, ice hockey, indoor soccer, lacrosse, modern dance, physical fitness, rowing, soccer, softball, squash, swimming and diving, tennis, volleyball; coed intramural: sailing. 4 PE instructors, 12 coaches, 1 athletic trainer.
Computers Computers are regularly used in college planning, creative writing, current events, English, French, geography, history, introduction to technology, journalism, language development, library science, literary magazine, mathematics, newspaper, photography, psychology, religious studies, research skills, SAT preparation, science, Spanish, study skills, technology, yearbook classes. Computer network features include on-campus library services, online commercial services, Internet access, wireless campus network, Internet filtering or blocking technology, Moodle, Senior Systems, 200 free tablets. Campus intranet, student e-mail accounts, and computer access in designated common areas are available to students. The school has a published electronic and media policy.
Contact Debbie Awalt, Assistant Director of Admission. 443-632-1002. Fax: 410-828-7238. E-mail: dwalt@spsfg.org. Web site: www.spsfg.org.

ST. PETER'S PREPARATORY SCHOOL

144 Grand Street
Jersey City, New Jersey 07302

Head of School: Rev. Robert E. Reiser, SJ

General Information Boys' day college-preparatory, arts, technology, and music school, affiliated with Roman Catholic Church. Grades 9–12. Founded: 1872. Setting: urban. Nearest major city is New York, NY. 7-acre campus. 8 buildings on campus. Approved or accredited by Jesuit Secondary Education Association, Middle States Association of Colleges and Schools, and New Jersey Department of Education. Endowment: $18 million. Total enrollment: 919. Upper school average class size: 22. Upper school faculty-student ratio: 1:12.
Upper School Student Profile Grade 9: 272 students (272 boys); Grade 10: 205 students (205 boys); Grade 11: 223 students (223 boys); Grade 12: 219 students (219 boys). 80% of students are Roman Catholic.
Faculty School total: 76. In upper school: 53 men, 22 women; 48 have advanced degrees.
Subjects Offered Advanced Placement courses, algebra, American history, American history-AP, American legal systems, American literature, Ancient Greek, art, art history, Bible studies, biology, biology-AP, calculus, calculus-AP, ceramics, chemistry, chemistry-AP, choral music, Christian ethics, community service, computer programming, computer science, computer science-AP, concert band, contemporary issues, creative writing, drawing, driver education, English, English language-AP, English literature, English literature-AP, European history, French, geometry, German, health, history, human anatomy, Irish studies, Italian, jazz band, Latin, Latin-AP, mathematics, music, music theory, physical education, physics, religion, sculpture, social justice, Spanish, Spanish language-AP, Spanish literature-AP, statistics-AP, studio art, theology, trigonometry, Web site design, world civilizations, world history, world literature, writing.
Graduation Requirements Algebra, American history, American literature, ancient world history, art, Basic programming, biology, British literature, chemistry, computer education, English, geometry, Latin, modern languages, music, physical education (includes health), physics, religion (includes Bible studies and theology), U.S. history, world civilizations, 20 hours of community service in freshman and sophomore years and 60 hours in the third (junior) year.
Special Academic Programs International Baccalaureate program; 12 Advanced Placement exams for which test preparation is offered; honors section; study at local college for college credit; study abroad.
College Admission Counseling 209 students graduated in 2008; all went to college, including Rutgers, The State University of New Jersey, Rutgers College; Saint Joseph's University; Saint Peter's College; Seton Hall University; The College of New Jersey; The University of Scranton. Median SAT critical reading: 570, median SAT

math: 590. Mean SAT writing: 559, mean combined SAT: 1687. 40% scored over 600 on SAT critical reading, 49% scored over 600 on SAT math.
Student Life Upper grades have specified standards of dress, student council, honor system. Discipline rests primarily with faculty.
Summer Programs Remediation, art/fine arts programs offered; session focuses on make-up course work for failed classes; held on campus; accepts boys and girls; open to students from other schools. 100 students usually enrolled. 2009 schedule: June 29 to August 3. Application deadline: June 19.
Tuition and Aid Day student tuition: $8650. Tuition installment plan (SMART Tuition Payment Plan, monthly payment plans). Merit scholarship grants, need-based scholarship grants, paying campus jobs available. In 2008–09, 48% of upper-school students received aid; total upper-school merit-scholarship money awarded: $225,000. Total amount of financial aid awarded in 2008–09: $800,000.
Admissions Traditional secondary-level entrance grade is 9. For fall 2008, 910 students applied for upper-level admission, 350 were accepted, 245 enrolled. Cooperative Entrance Exam (McGraw-Hill) or SSAT required. Deadline for receipt of application materials: November 15. No application fee required.
Athletics Interscholastic: baseball, basketball, bowling, cross-country running, diving, fencing, football, golf, ice hockey, indoor track, indoor track & field, lacrosse, rugby, soccer, swimming and diving, tennis, track and field, volleyball, winter (indoor) track, wrestling; intramural: basketball, flag football, Frisbee, indoor soccer, outdoor recreation, team handball, touch football, ultimate Frisbee, weight lifting, whiffle ball. 3 PE instructors, 20 coaches, 1 athletic trainer.
Computers Computers are regularly used in all academic classes. Computer network features include on-campus library services, online commercial services, Internet access, wireless campus network, Internet filtering or blocking technology. Campus intranet and student e-mail accounts are available to students. Students grades are available online. The school has a published electronic and media policy.
Contact Mr. John T. Irvine, Director of Admissions. 201-547-6389. Fax: 201-547-6421. E-mail: Irvinej@spprep.org. Web site: www.spprep.org.

ST. PIUS X CATHOLIC HIGH SCHOOL

2674 Johnson Road NE
Atlanta, Georgia 30345

Head of School: Mr. Steve Spellman

General Information Coeducational day college-preparatory school, affiliated with Roman Catholic Church. Grades 9–12. Founded: 1958. Setting: suburban. 25-acre campus. 8 buildings on campus. Approved or accredited by National Catholic Education Association, Southern Association of Colleges and Schools, and Georgia Department of Education. Member of Secondary School Admission Test Board. Total enrollment: 1,000. Upper school average class size: 21. Upper school faculty-student ratio: 1:15.
Upper School Student Profile Grade 9: 260 students (130 boys, 130 girls); Grade 10: 250 students (125 boys, 125 girls); Grade 11: 250 students (125 boys, 125 girls); Grade 12: 240 students (120 boys, 120 girls). 82% of students are Roman Catholic.
Faculty School total: 85. In upper school: 40 men, 45 women; 55 have advanced degrees.
Subjects Offered Accounting, algebra, American history, American literature, anatomy, art, band, biology, business, business law, calculus, ceramics, chemistry, chorus, computer programming, computer science, creative writing, current events, dance, drama, driver education, economics, English, English literature, European history, expository writing, French, geography, geometry, German, government/civics, health, history, instrumental music, journalism, Latin, mathematics, music, physical education, physical science, physics, physiology, psychology, religion, science, social studies, sociology, Spanish, speech, statistics, theater, trigonometry, word processing, world history, world literature.
Graduation Requirements Computer science, English, foreign language, mathematics, physical education (includes health), religion (includes Bible studies and theology), religious studies, science, social studies (includes history).
Special Academic Programs 21 Advanced Placement exams for which test preparation is offered; honors section; special instructional classes for students with learning disabilities and Attention Deficit Disorder.
College Admission Counseling 255 students graduated in 2008; 254 went to college, including Emory University; Furman University; Georgia Institute of Technology; Georgia State University; University of Georgia; University of Notre Dame. Other: 1 had other specific plans. 60% scored over 600 on SAT critical reading, 60% scored over 600 on SAT math, 50% scored over 26 on composite ACT.
Student Life Upper grades have uniform requirement, student council, honor system. Discipline rests equally with students and faculty. Attendance at religious services is required.
Tuition and Aid Day student tuition: $10,200. Tuition installment plan (FACTS Tuition Payment Plan, monthly payment plans). Tuition reduction for siblings, need-based scholarship grants, paying campus jobs available. In 2008–09, 18% of upper-school students received aid. Total amount of financial aid awarded in 2008–09: $400,000.
Admissions Traditional secondary-level entrance grade is 9. For fall 2008, 480 students applied for upper-level admission, 310 were accepted, 270 enrolled. SSAT required. Deadline for receipt of application materials: February 2. Application fee required: $75.
Athletics Interscholastic: baseball (boys), basketball (b,g), cheering (b,g), cross-country running (b,g), dance squad (g), dance team (g), diving (b,g), dressage (g), football (b), golf (b,g), lacrosse (b,g), soccer (b,g), softball (g), strength & conditioning (b,g), swimming and diving (b,g), tennis (b,g), track and field (b,g), volleyball (g), water polo (b,g), weight training (b,g), wrestling (b). 4 PE instructors, 32 coaches, 1 athletic trainer.
Computers Computers are regularly used in science classes. Computer network features include on-campus library services, online commercial services, Internet access.
Contact Stephanie Dunn, Coordinator of Admissions. 404-636-0323 Ext. 291. Fax: 404-636-2118. E-mail: sdunn@spx.org. Web site: www.spx.org.

ST. SEBASTIAN'S SCHOOL

1191 Greendale Avenue
Needham, Massachusetts 02492

Head of School: William L. Burke III

General Information Boys' day college-preparatory school, affiliated with Roman Catholic Church. Grades 7–12. Founded: 1941. Setting: suburban. Nearest major city is Boston. 25-acre campus. 5 buildings on campus. Approved or accredited by New England Association of Schools and Colleges and Massachusetts Department of Education. Member of National Association of Independent Schools and Secondary School Admission Test Board. Endowment: $10.4 million. Total enrollment: 355. Upper school average class size: 11. Upper school faculty-student ratio: 1:7.
Upper School Student Profile Grade 9: 66 students (66 boys); Grade 10: 62 students (62 boys); Grade 11: 63 students (63 boys); Grade 12: 66 students (66 boys). 80% of students are Roman Catholic.
Faculty School total: 61. In upper school: 48 men, 13 women; 35 have advanced degrees.
Subjects Offered Algebra, American history, American literature, art, art history, biology, calculus, chemistry, computer science, drama, economics, English, English literature, ethics, European history, fine arts, geography, geometry, government/civics, Greek, history, Latin, mathematics, music, philosophy, photography, physical education, physics, religion, science, social studies, Spanish, speech, theater, trigonometry, world history, world literature, writing.
Graduation Requirements Arts and fine arts (art, music, dance, drama), English, foreign language, mathematics, physical education (includes health), religion (includes Bible studies and theology), science, social studies (includes history), senior service, chapel speaking program.
Special Academic Programs Advanced Placement exam preparation; honors section; independent study; academic accommodation for the gifted, the musically talented, and the artistically talented.
College Admission Counseling 61 students graduated in 2008; all went to college, including College of the Holy Cross; Hobart and William Smith Colleges; Loyola College in Maryland; Stonehill College; University of Richmond; Villanova University. Median SAT critical reading: 640, median SAT math: 640.
Student Life Upper grades have specified standards of dress, student council, honor system. Discipline rests primarily with faculty. Attendance at religious services is required.
Tuition and Aid Day student tuition: $30,200. Tuition installment plan (Academic Management Services Plan, Key Tuition Payment Plan). Need-based scholarship grants, need-based loans available. In 2008–09, 26% of upper-school students received aid. Total amount of financial aid awarded in 2008–09: $1,445,000.
Admissions Traditional secondary-level entrance grade is 9. For fall 2008, 100 students applied for upper-level admission, 34 were accepted, 17 enrolled. ISEE or SSAT required. Deadline for receipt of application materials: January 15. Application fee required: $40. On-campus interview required.
Athletics Interscholastic: baseball, basketball, cross-country running, football, golf, ice hockey, lacrosse, sailing, skiing (downhill), soccer, squash, swimming and diving, tennis; intramural: strength & conditioning, ultimate Frisbee, weight lifting, whiffle ball, wrestling. 1 athletic trainer.
Computers Computers are regularly used in English, foreign language, mathematics, science, social studies, writing classes. Computer network features include on-campus library services, Internet access, wireless campus network, Internet filtering or blocking technology. Campus intranet is available to students. The school has a published electronic and media policy.
Contact Mrs. Deborah Sewall, Assistant to Dean of Admissions. 781-449-5200 Ext. 125. Fax: 781-449-5630. E-mail: admissions@stsebs.org. Web site: www.saintsebastiansschool.org.

SAINTS PETER AND PAUL HIGH SCHOOL

900 High Street
Easton, Maryland 21601

Head of School: Mr. James Edward Nemeth

General Information Coeducational day college-preparatory school, affiliated with Roman Catholic Church. Grades 9–12. Founded: 1958. Setting: small town. Nearest major city is Baltimore. 4-acre campus. 4 buildings on campus. Approved or accredited by Middle States Association of Colleges and Schools, National Catholic

Education Association, and Maryland Department of Education. Total enrollment: 201. Upper school average class size: 15. Upper school faculty-student ratio: 1:8.

Upper School Student Profile Grade 9: 55 students (18 boys, 37 girls); Grade 10: 47 students (21 boys, 26 girls); Grade 11: 36 students (14 boys, 22 girls); Grade 12: 63 students (28 boys, 35 girls). 71% of students are Roman Catholic.

Faculty School total: 25. In upper school: 10 men, 13 women; 14 have advanced degrees.

Subjects Offered Advanced computer applications, algebra, American government, American literature, anatomy and physiology, art and culture, biology, biology-AP, British literature, British literature (honors), calculus, calculus-AP, campus ministry, Catholic belief and practice, chemistry, chemistry-AP, Christian and Hebrew scripture, Christian ethics, Christianity, church history, computer multimedia, computer programming, computer science, conceptual physics, creative writing, drama, earth science, economics, English literature and composition-AP, environmental science, French, geography, geometry, health and wellness, Hebrew scripture, honors algebra, honors English, honors geometry, honors U.S. history, honors world history, Microsoft, moral theology, music appreciation, music theory, philosophy, physical education, physics, pre-calculus, probability and statistics, Spanish, speech, studio art-AP, theology, U.S. government and politics-AP, U.S. history, U.S. history-AP, Web site design, world history, yearbook.

Graduation Requirements Algebra, American literature, arts and fine arts (art, music, dance, drama), biology, British literature, Catholic belief and practice, chemistry, Christian and Hebrew scripture, Christianity, computer applications, computer science, English, foreign language, geometry, history of the Catholic Church, mathematics, moral theology, physical education (includes health), physics, social justice, U.S. government, U.S. history, world history.

Special Academic Programs Advanced Placement exam preparation; honors section; independent study.

College Admission Counseling 44 students graduated in 2008; 42 went to college, including Loyola College in Maryland; Saint Joseph's University; Salisbury University; University of Maryland, College Park; Virginia Polytechnic Institute and State University. Other: 1 went to work, 1 had other specific plans. Median SAT critical reading: 560, median SAT math: 510, median SAT writing: 560. 35% scored over 600 on SAT critical reading, 25% scored over 600 on SAT math, 29% scored over 600 on SAT writing.

Student Life Upper grades have uniform requirement. Discipline rests primarily with faculty. Attendance at religious services is required.

Tuition and Aid Day student tuition: $7850. Tuition installment plan (FACTS Tuition Payment Plan). Tuition reduction for siblings, need-based scholarship grants, parish subsidies available. In 2008–09, 4% of upper-school students received aid. Total amount of financial aid awarded in 2008–09: $10,350.

Admissions Traditional secondary-level entrance grade is 9. For fall 2008, 68 students applied for upper-level admission, 65 were accepted, 56 enrolled. Diocesan Entrance Exam required. Deadline for receipt of application materials: March 15. Application fee required: $50. On-campus interview required.

Athletics Interscholastic: baseball (boys), basketball (b,g), cross-country running (b,g), field hockey (g), ice hockey (b), lacrosse (b,g), soccer (b,g), softball (g), swimming and diving (b,g); coed interscholastic: golf, tennis. 1 PE instructor, 23 coaches.

Computers Computers are regularly used in all academic classes. Computer network features include on-campus library services, Internet access, wireless campus network, Internet filtering or blocking technology. Students grades are available online. The school has a published electronic and media policy.

Contact Mrs. Carolyn Smith Hayman, Administrative Assistant. 410-822-2275 Ext. 150. Fax: 410-822-1767. E-mail: chayman@ssppeaston.org. Web site: www.ssppeaston.org.

ST. STANISLAUS COLLEGE

304 South Beach Boulevard
Bay St. Louis, Mississippi 39520

Head of School: Br. Ronald Hingle, SC

General Information Boys' boarding and day college-preparatory, general academic, and religious studies school, affiliated with Roman Catholic Church. Boarding grades 6–12, day grades 7–12. Founded: 1854. Setting: small town. Nearest major city is New Orleans, LA. Students are housed in single-sex dormitories. 30-acre campus. 7 buildings on campus. Approved or accredited by National Catholic Education Association, Southern Association of Colleges and Schools, and Mississippi Department of Education. Member of Secondary School Admission Test Board. Endowment: $7 million. Total enrollment: 427. Upper school average class size: 23. Upper school faculty-student ratio: 1:23.

Upper School Student Profile Grade 9: 67 students (67 boys); Grade 10: 93 students (93 boys); Grade 11: 79 students (79 boys); Grade 12: 70 students (70 boys). 24% of students are boarding students. 76% are state residents. 8 states are represented in upper school student body. 10% are international students. International students from Brazil, China, Guatemala, Mexico, and Republic of Korea. 70% of students are Roman Catholic.

Faculty School total: 42. In upper school: 28 men, 14 women; 21 have advanced degrees; 8 reside on campus.

Subjects Offered Accounting, algebra, American history, American literature, art, astronomy, biology, business, business law, calculus, chemistry, computer programming, computer science, creative writing, drama, economics, English, English literature, finance, French, geography, geometry, government/civics, grammar, health, history, journalism, marine biology, marine science, mathematics, music, physical education, physics, psychology, religion, science, short story, social science, social studies, Spanish, speech, theater, theology, trigonometry, typing, world history, world literature.

Graduation Requirements Arts and fine arts (art, music, dance, drama), computer science, English, foreign language, mathematics, physical education (includes health), religion (includes Bible studies and theology), science, social science, social studies (includes history).

Special Academic Programs 8 Advanced Placement exams for which test preparation is offered; honors section; remedial reading and/or remedial writing; remedial math; programs in English, mathematics, general development for dyslexic students; special instructional classes for students with Attention Deficit Disorder; ESL (10 students enrolled).

College Admission Counseling 62 students graduated in 2008; 57 went to college, including Louisiana State University and Agricultural and Mechanical College; Mississippi State University; University of Mississippi; University of New Orleans; University of South Alabama; University of Southern Mississippi.

Student Life Upper grades have uniform requirement, student council. Discipline rests primarily with faculty. Attendance at religious services is required.

Tuition and Aid Day student tuition: $5170; 7-day tuition and room/board: $19,325. Tuition installment plan (monthly payment plans). Need-based scholarship grants available.

Admissions Traditional secondary-level entrance grade is 10. Deadline for receipt of application materials: none. Application fee required: $100. On-campus interview required.

Athletics Interscholastic: baseball, basketball, cross-country running, football, golf, power lifting, sailing, soccer, swimming and diving, tennis, track and field; intramural: baseball, basketball, billiards, cheering, jogging, scuba diving. 5 PE instructors, 16 coaches, 1 athletic trainer.

Computers Computers are regularly used in accounting, desktop publishing, English, graphic design, mathematics, religion, SAT preparation, science, Spanish, typing classes. Computer network features include on-campus library services, online commercial services, Internet access, wireless campus network, Internet filtering or blocking technology. Students grades are available online.

Contact Mrs. Dolores Richmond, Director of Admissions. 228-467-9057 Ext. 226. Fax: 228-466-2972. E-mail: admissions@ststan.com. Web site: www.ststan.com.

See Close-Up on page 950.

ST. STEPHEN'S & ST. AGNES SCHOOL

1000 St. Stephen's Road
Alexandria, Virginia 22304

Head of School: Mrs. Joan G. Ogilvy Holden

General Information Coeducational day college-preparatory, arts, religious studies, and technology school, affiliated with Episcopal Church. Grades JK–12. Founded: 1924. Setting: suburban. Nearest major city is Washington, DC. 35-acre campus. 5 buildings on campus. Approved or accredited by Association of Independent Schools of Greater Washington, National Association of Episcopal Schools, and Virginia Association of Independent Schools. Member of National Association of Independent Schools and Secondary School Admission Test Board. Endowment: $18.2 million. Total enrollment: 1,124. Upper school average class size: 15. Upper school faculty-student ratio: 1:9.

Upper School Student Profile Grade 9: 113 students (53 boys, 60 girls); Grade 10: 109 students (60 boys, 49 girls); Grade 11: 118 students (63 boys, 55 girls); Grade 12: 109 students (46 boys, 63 girls). 28% of students are members of Episcopal Church.

Faculty School total: 131. In upper school: 23 men, 28 women; 37 have advanced degrees.

Subjects Offered 1½ elective credits, Advanced Placement courses, algebra, American history, American literature, art, art history, art history-AP, bioethics, biology, biology-AP, calculus, calculus-AP, ceramics, chemistry, chemistry-AP, Christian and Hebrew scripture, Christian education, Christian ethics, Christian scripture, Christian testament, comparative government and politics-AP, computer graphics, computer programming, concert choir, creative writing, directing, drama, drawing, economics, English, English literature, English literature-AP, English-AP, ensembles, environmental science-AP, ethics, European history, European history-AP, forensics, French, French language-AP, French literature-AP, geometry, government/civics, graphic design, Hebrew scripture, history, honors English, honors geometry, honors U.S. history, honors world history, instrumental music, jazz, jazz ensemble, journalism, Latin, Latin-AP, macroeconomics-AP, Mandarin, mathematics, medieval history, medieval/Renaissance history, microeconomics-AP, music, music theory-AP, newspaper, painting, physical education, physics, physics-AP, playwriting and directing, pre-calculus, psychology-AP, religion, robotics, sculpture, senior project, Spanish, Spanish language-AP, Spanish literature-AP, sports, sports medicine, statistics-AP, studio art, studio art-AP, technical theater, theater, theater arts, trigonometry, U.S. history-AP, video communication, world history, world literature, writing, yearbook.

Graduation Requirements Arts and fine arts (art, music, dance, drama), English, family studies, foreign language, history, mathematics, physical education (includes health), religion (includes Bible studies and theology), science, technological applications, senior year independent off-campus project, 40 hours of community service.
Special Academic Programs 25 Advanced Placement exams for which test preparation is offered; honors section; independent study; term-away projects; study abroad; academic accommodation for the gifted, the musically talented, and the artistically talented.
College Admission Counseling 106 students graduated in 2008; all went to college, including Boston College; Bucknell University; Stanford University; The College of William and Mary; University of Virginia; Virginia Polytechnic Institute and State University. Mean SAT critical reading: 626, mean SAT math: 641, mean SAT writing: 644. 57% scored over 600 on SAT critical reading, 74% scored over 600 on SAT math, 68% scored over 600 on SAT writing.
Student Life Upper grades have specified standards of dress, student council, honor system. Discipline rests equally with students and faculty. Attendance at religious services is required.
Summer Programs Enrichment, advancement, art/fine arts, computer instruction programs offered; session focuses on enrichment; held both on and off campus; held at Chesapeake Bay, DC, VA and MD area; accepts boys and girls; open to students from other schools. 1,500 students usually enrolled. 2009 schedule: June 15 to August 14. Application deadline: none.
Tuition and Aid Day student tuition: $26,425. Tuition installment plan (FACTS Tuition Payment Plan). Need-based scholarship grants available. In 2008–09, 24% of upper-school students received aid. Total amount of financial aid awarded in 2008–09: $1,728,163.
Admissions Traditional secondary-level entrance grade is 9. ISEE or SSAT required. Deadline for receipt of application materials: January 15. Application fee required: $70. Interview required.
Athletics Interscholastic: baseball (boys), basketball (b,g), field hockey (g), football (b), golf (b,g), ice hockey (b), independent competitive sports (b,g), lacrosse (b,g), soccer (b,g), softball (g), tennis (b,g), track and field (b,g), volleyball (g), winter soccer (g), wrestling (b); intramural: crew (g), rowing (g); coed interscholastic: cross-country running, diving, independent competitive sports, swimming and diving; coed intramural: basketball, fitness, golf, jogging, physical fitness, physical training, strength & conditioning, weight training, yoga. 6 PE instructors, 14 coaches, 2 athletic trainers.
Computers Computers are regularly used in all academic classes. Computer network features include on-campus library services, online commercial services, Internet access, wireless campus network, Internet filtering or blocking technology, computer labs for foreign language, math, technology, library, newspaper, physics and chemistry, homework assignments posted online, mobile wireless laptop cart (180 laptops), computers available in study hall and library. Campus intranet and computer access in designated common areas are available to students. Students grades are available online. The school has a published electronic and media policy.
Contact Mr. Jon Kunz, Director of Admission, Grades 6-12. 703-212-2706. Fax: 703-212-2788. E-mail: jkunz@sssas.org. Web site: www.sssas.org.

SAINT STEPHEN'S EPISCOPAL SCHOOL

315 41st Street West
Bradenton, Florida 34209

Head of School: Janet S. Pullen

General Information Coeducational day college-preparatory, arts, religious studies, and Marine Science school, affiliated with Episcopal Church. Grades PK–12. Founded: 1970. Setting: small town. Nearest major city is Tampa. 35-acre campus. 3 buildings on campus. Approved or accredited by Florida Council of Independent Schools, National Association of Episcopal Schools, and Southern Association of Colleges and Schools. Member of National Association of Independent Schools. Endowment: $958,000. Total enrollment: 725. Upper school average class size: 16. Upper school faculty-student ratio: 1:10.
Upper School Student Profile Grade 9: 62 students (28 boys, 34 girls); Grade 10: 68 students (33 boys, 35 girls); Grade 11: 55 students (25 boys, 30 girls); Grade 12: 72 students (43 boys, 29 girls). 14% of students are members of Episcopal Church.
Faculty School total: 87. In upper school: 7 men, 17 women; 20 have advanced degrees.
Subjects Offered 3-dimensional art, Advanced Placement courses, advanced studio art-AP, algebra, American government, American history, American history-AP, American literature, art, art history, art history-AP, art-AP, astronomy, band, biology, biology-AP, British literature, broadcast journalism, broadcasting, calculus, calculus-AP, ceramics, chemistry, chemistry-AP, choir, chorus, community service, comparative religion, composition, composition-AP, computer programming, computer programming-AP, computer science, computer science-AP, conceptual physics, debate, digital art, digital photography, discrete math, discrete mathematics, drama, economics, English, English language and composition-AP, English language-AP, English literature, English literature and composition-AP, English literature-AP, English-AP, environmental science-AP, European history, European history-AP, filmmaking, French, French language-AP, geometry, graphic design, humanities, international relations, journalism, Latin, Latin-AP, marine biology, marine science, music, newspaper, organic chemistry, painting, photography, physical education, physics, physics-AP, portfolio art, pre-calculus, probability and statistics, psychology, public speaking, science research, Spanish, Spanish language-AP, speech and debate, studio art, studio art-AP, trigonometry, U.S. history, U.S. history-AP, weight training, Western civilization, world history, world history-AP.
Graduation Requirements Arts and fine arts (art, music, dance, drama), electives, English, foreign language, mathematics, physical education (includes health), science, social studies (includes history), senior speech. Community service is required.
Special Academic Programs Advanced Placement exam preparation; honors section.
College Admission Counseling 79 students graduated in 2008; 78 went to college, including Florida State University; Southern Methodist University; University of Florida; University of Miami. Other: 1 had other specific plans. Mean SAT critical reading: 607, mean SAT math: 625, mean SAT writing: 589, mean composite ACT: 25. 52% scored over 600 on SAT critical reading, 58% scored over 600 on SAT math, 39% scored over 600 on SAT writing, 49% scored over 26 on composite ACT.
Student Life Upper grades have specified standards of dress, student council, honor system. Discipline rests primarily with faculty. Attendance at religious services is required.
Summer Programs Enrichment, advancement, sports programs offered; session focuses on academic enrichment; held on campus; accepts boys and girls; open to students from other schools. 100 students usually enrolled. 2009 schedule: June 8 to August 7. Application deadline: May 1.
Tuition and Aid Day student tuition: $10,800–$15,550. Tuition installment plan (monthly payment plans). Need-based scholarship grants available. In 2008–09, 13% of upper-school students received aid. Total amount of financial aid awarded in 2008–09: $250,000.
Admissions Traditional secondary-level entrance grade is 9. For fall 2008, 53 students applied for upper-level admission, 37 were accepted, 34 enrolled. School's own exam required. Deadline for receipt of application materials: none. Application fee required: $200. Interview recommended.
Athletics Interscholastic: aerobics/dance (girls), aquatics (b,g), baseball (b), basketball (b,g), cheering (g), cross-country running (b,g), dance (g), dance team (g), diving (b,g), golf (b,g), independent competitive sports (b,g), soccer (b,g), softball (g), swimming and diving (b,g), tennis (b,g), track and field (b,g), volleyball (g), winter soccer (b,g); intramural: aerobics/dance (g), ballet (g), basketball (b,g), cheering (g), cross-country running (b,g), dance (g), fitness (b,g), horseback riding (b,g), jogging (b,g), physical fitness (b,g), physical training (b,g), running (b,g), soccer (b,g), softball (b,g), strength & conditioning (b,g), track and field (b,g), weight training (b,g). 9 PE instructors, 14 coaches, 2 athletic trainers.
Computers Computers are regularly used in art, computer applications, foreign language, journalism, library, mathematics, media, science, social science, word processing, writing, yearbook classes. Computer network features include on-campus library services, online commercial services, Internet access, wireless campus network, Internet filtering or blocking technology, Microsoft Office. Computer access in designated common areas is available to students. The school has a published electronic and media policy.
Contact Linda G. Lutz, Director of Admissions. 941-746-2121 Ext. 568. Fax: 941-345-1237. E-mail: llutz@saintstephens.org. Web site: www.saintstephens.org.

ANNOUNCEMENT FROM THE SCHOOL Saint Stephen's is a coeducational independent day school located in Bradenton, Florida. The 35-acre campus serves students of all faiths in prekindergarten 3 through grade 12. The curriculum is based on traditional goals of university preparation enriched with programs in the fine arts, athletics, and global cultural awareness. With a student-faculty ratio of 11:1, Saint Stephen's provides an educational environment that holds high, yet attainable, standards for all students, allowing them to develop a deep sense of self-worth and independence.

ST. STEPHEN'S EPISCOPAL SCHOOL

2900 Bunny Run
Austin, Texas 78746

Head of School: Mr. Robert "Bob" Kirkpatrick

General Information Coeducational boarding and day college-preparatory and theater school, affiliated with Episcopal Church. Boarding grades 8–12, day grades 6–12. Founded: 1950. Setting: suburban. Students are housed in single-sex dormitories. 400-acre campus. 40 buildings on campus. Approved or accredited by Independent Schools Association of the Southwest, National Association of Episcopal Schools, Southwest Association of Episcopal Schools, Texas Education Agency, The Association of Boarding Schools, and Texas Department of Education. Member of National Association of Independent Schools. Endowment: $7.5 million. Total enrollment: 646. Upper school average class size: 16. Upper school faculty-student ratio: 1:7.
Upper School Student Profile Grade 9: 102 students (53 boys, 49 girls); Grade 10: 122 students (73 boys, 49 girls); Grade 11: 114 students (62 boys, 52 girls); Grade 12: 114 students (53 boys, 61 girls). 35% of students are boarding students. 82% are state residents. 12 states are represented in upper school student body. 17% are international students. International students from China, Germany, Mexico, Republic of Korea, Saudi Arabia, and Taiwan; 14 other countries represented in student body. 18% of students are members of Episcopal Church.

Faculty School total: 98. In upper school: 40 men, 34 women; 47 have advanced degrees; 36 reside on campus.
Subjects Offered 3-dimensional design, acting, algebra, American history, American history-AP, anthropology, art, art history, art history-AP, astrophysics, ballet, band, biology, biology-AP, calculus, calculus-AP, ceramics, chamber groups, chemistry, chemistry-AP, Chinese, choreography, classics, computer applications, computer math, computer science, computer studies, creative writing, directing, drama, English, English literature, environmental science, European history, European history-AP, fine arts, French, French-AP, geology, geometry, government/civics, history, jazz band, Latin, mathematics, music, music theory-AP, musical theater, photography, physical education, physics, physics-AP, play/screen writing, pre-calculus, psychology, public policy issues and action, public speaking, religion, religions, science, social studies, Spanish, Spanish-AP, statistics-AP, studio art-AP, theater arts, theology, video, world history, world literature.
Graduation Requirements Arts and fine arts (art, music, dance, drama), electives, English, foreign language, mathematics, physical education (includes health), religion (includes Bible studies and theology), science, social studies (includes history), community service requirement in middle and upper schools.
Special Academic Programs Advanced Placement exam preparation; honors section; independent study; study abroad; ESL (21 students enrolled).
College Admission Counseling 120 students graduated in 2007; all went to college, including The University of Texas at Austin; University of Washington. Median SAT critical reading: 650, median SAT math: 670, median SAT writing: 650.
Student Life Upper grades have specified standards of dress, student council. Discipline rests equally with students and faculty. Attendance at religious services is required.
Tuition and Aid Day student tuition: $19,350; 7-day tuition and room/board: $35,550. Tuition installment plan (Insured Tuition Payment Plan, Key Tuition Payment Plan, individually arranged payment plans, Compass Bank Educational Loans). Merit scholarship grants, need-based scholarship grants, partial tuition remission for children of faculty and staff available. In 2007–08, 13% of upper-school students received aid; total upper-school merit-scholarship money awarded: $20,000. Total amount of financial aid awarded in 2007–08: $1,200,000.
Admissions Traditional secondary-level entrance grade is 9. For fall 2007, 270 students applied for upper-level admission, 120 were accepted, 87 enrolled. ISEE or SSAT required. Deadline for receipt of application materials: February 1. Application fee required: $50. Interview required.
Athletics Interscholastic: baseball (boys), basketball (b,g), cheering (g), crew (b,g), cross-country running (b,g), dance (g), field hockey (g), football (b), golf (b,g), lacrosse (b,g), soccer (b,g), softball (g), swimming and diving (b,g), tennis (b,g), track and field (b,g), volleyball (g), winter soccer (b,g); intramural: bicycling (b,g), climbing (b,g), combined training (b,g), dance (b,g), fitness (b,g), hiking/backpacking (b,g), modern dance (b,g), mountain biking (b,g), mountaineering (b,g), outdoor adventure (b,g), outdoor education (b,g), physical fitness (b,g), rock climbing (b,g), ropes courses (b,g), strength & conditioning (b,g), surfing (b,g), triathlon (b,g), weight training (b,g). 2 PE instructors, 7 coaches, 1 athletic trainer.
Computers Computer network features include on-campus library services, online commercial services, Internet access, wireless campus network, Internet filtering or blocking technology, online schedules, syllabi, homework, examples, and links to information sources. Student e-mail accounts and computer access in designated common areas are available to students. Students grades are available online.
Contact Lawrence Sampleton, Director of Admission. 512-327-1213 Ext. 210. Fax: 512-327-6771. E-mail: admission@sstx.org. Web site: www.sstx.org.

ANNOUNCEMENT FROM THE SCHOOL St. Stephen's Episcopal School, a coeducational boarding and day school of the Diocese of Texas, is a caring, diverse community, inclusive of all faiths and grounded in the Christian tradition, which nurtures moral growth and values the potential and dignity of every human being. St. Stephen's Episcopal challenges motivated students to live intelligently, creatively, and humanely as contributing members of society. The School develops the whole person by providing rigorous academic preparation, stimulating physical activities, and rich opportunities in the fine arts. The scenic 370-acre campus, overlooking Lake Austin, is ideal for outdoor activities and study.

See Close-Up on page 952.

ST. STEPHEN'S SCHOOL, ROME

Via Aventina 3
Rome 00153, Italy

Head of School: Lesley Jane Murphy

General Information Coeducational boarding and day college-preparatory, arts, and bilingual studies school. Grades 9–PG. Founded: 1964. Setting: urban. Students are housed in single-sex by floor dormitories. 2-acre campus. 2 buildings on campus. Approved or accredited by European Council of International Schools, International Baccalaureate Organization, New England Association of Schools and Colleges, and US Department of State. Affiliate member of National Association of Independent Schools. Language of instruction: English. Endowment: €2 million. Total enrollment: 229. Upper school average class size: 13. Upper school faculty-student ratio: 1:7.
Upper School Student Profile Grade 9: 50 students (28 boys, 22 girls); Grade 10: 44 students (16 boys, 28 girls); Grade 11: 80 students (37 boys, 43 girls); Grade 12: 53 students (28 boys, 25 girls); Postgraduate: 2 students (2 girls). 14% of students are boarding students. 73% are international students. International students from China, Germany, India, Netherlands, United Kingdom, and United States; 27 other countries represented in student body.
Faculty School total: 40. In upper school: 10 men, 30 women; 29 have advanced degrees; 6 reside on campus.
Subjects Offered Algebra, American literature, art, art history, biology, calculus, chemistry, chorus, classical studies, dance, drama, economics, English, English literature, European history, French, geometry, health, Islamic studies, Italian, Latin, music appreciation, physical education, physics, pre-calculus, Roman civilization, sculpture, theory of knowledge, trigonometry, U.S. history, world literature.
Graduation Requirements Arts and fine arts (art, music, dance, drama), English, foreign language, mathematics, physical education (includes health), science, social studies (includes history), senior essay, computer proficiency examination.
Special Academic Programs International Baccalaureate program; 10 Advanced Placement exams for which test preparation is offered; domestic exchange program (with Buckingham Browne & Nichols School, Friends Seminary, Choate Rosemary Hall); ESL (7 students enrolled).
College Admission Counseling 56 students graduated in 2008; 48 went to college, including Boston College; Boston University; Brown University; Reed College; The George Washington University; Wesleyan College. Other: 8 had other specific plans. Mean SAT critical reading: 623, mean SAT math: 593, mean SAT writing: 608, mean combined SAT: 1823.
Student Life Upper grades have student council. Discipline rests equally with students and faculty.
Tuition and Aid Day student tuition: €19,850–€20,250; 7-day tuition and room/board: €30,000–€30,400. Tuition installment plan (individually arranged payment plans). Tuition reduction for siblings, need-based scholarship grants available. In 2008–09, 18% of upper-school students received aid. Total amount of financial aid awarded in 2008–09: €336,000.
Admissions Traditional secondary-level entrance grade is 9. For fall 2008, 157 students applied for upper-level admission, 126 were accepted, 97 enrolled. School's own exam required. Deadline for receipt of application materials: February 27. Application fee required: €100. Interview recommended.
Athletics Interscholastic: basketball (boys, girls), soccer (b,g), volleyball (b,g); intramural: basketball (b,g), dance (b,g), soccer (b,g), tennis (b,g), track and field (b,g), volleyball (b,g); coed interscholastic: tennis, track and field; coed intramural: dance, softball, tennis, track and field, ultimate Frisbee, volleyball, yoga. 1 coach.
Computers Computers are regularly used in English, foreign language, mathematics, science, social studies classes. Computer network features include on-campus library services, Internet access, wireless campus network, Internet filtering or blocking technology. Campus intranet, student e-mail accounts, and computer access in designated common areas are available to students. Students grades are available online. The school has a published electronic and media policy.
Contact Alex Perniciaro, Admissions Coordinator. 39-06-575-0605. Fax: 39-06-574-1941. E-mail: ststephens@ststephens-rome.com. Web site: www.ststephens-rome.com.

SAINT TERESA'S ACADEMY

5600 Main Street
Kansas City, Missouri 64113

Head of School: Mrs. Nan Tiehen Bone

General Information Girls' day college-preparatory school, affiliated with Roman Catholic Church. Grades 9–12. Founded: 1866. Setting: urban. 20-acre campus. 3 buildings on campus. Approved or accredited by North Central Association of Colleges and Schools and Missouri Department of Education. Endowment: $150,000. Total enrollment: 533. Upper school average class size: 21. Upper school faculty-student ratio: 1:12.
Upper School Student Profile Grade 9: 140 students (140 girls); Grade 10: 139 students (139 girls); Grade 11: 124 students (124 girls); Grade 12: 130 students (130 girls). 87% of students are Roman Catholic.
Faculty School total: 47. In upper school: 9 men, 38 women; 31 have advanced degrees.
Subjects Offered Advanced chemistry, advanced math, algebra, American government, American history, American literature, analysis, anatomy and physiology, art, athletics, basketball, biology, biology-AP, botany, British literature, calculus, career/college preparation, chamber groups, chemistry, chemistry-AP, choir, chorus, computer graphics, computer programming, computer science-AP, current events, dance, directing, drama, drawing, ecology, English, English language-AP, English literature, European history-AP, fiber arts, fitness, foreign language, forensics, French, French language-AP, French-AP, freshman seminar, geometry, golf, graphic design, health, independent study, journalism, keyboarding/computer, language arts, Latin, Latin History, music-AP, newspaper, painting, physical education, portfolio art, psychology, Shakespeare, social issues, social studies, sociology, softball, Spanish, Spanish language-AP, Spanish-AP, speech, sports conditioning, sports performance development, stagecraft, swimming, tennis, theater, theology and the arts, track and field,

trigonometry, U.S. government, U.S. government-AP, U.S. history, volleyball, Western civilization, women spirituality and faith, world geography, world religions, writing, yearbook.

Graduation Requirements Arts and fine arts (art, music, dance, drama), computer science, electives, English, foreign language, mathematics, physical education (includes health), science, social studies (includes history), theology. Community service is required.

Special Academic Programs Honors section; study at local college for college credit.

College Admission Counseling 131 students graduated in 2008; 129 went to college, including Kansas State University; Saint Louis University; The University of Kansas; University of Missouri–Columbia; University of Notre Dame. Other: 2 had other specific plans. Mean SAT critical reading: 600, mean SAT math: 580, mean SAT writing: 610, mean combined SAT: 1780, mean composite ACT: 26.

Student Life Upper grades have uniform requirement. Discipline rests primarily with faculty. Attendance at religious services is required.

Summer Programs Sports, art/fine arts, computer instruction programs offered; session focuses on fine arts, sports and remedial summer school programs; held on campus; accepts girls; open to students from other schools. 100 students usually enrolled. 2009 schedule: June 25 to July 8. Application deadline: May 1.

Tuition and Aid Day student tuition: $8950. Tuition installment plan (SMART Tuition Payment Plan). Tuition reduction for siblings, merit scholarship grants, need-based scholarship grants available. In 2008–09, 17% of upper-school students received aid; total upper-school merit-scholarship money awarded: $125,000. Total amount of financial aid awarded in 2008–09: $137,000.

Admissions Traditional secondary-level entrance grade is 9. For fall 2008, 174 students applied for upper-level admission, 165 were accepted, 140 enrolled. Placement test required. Deadline for receipt of application materials: February 28. No application fee required.

Athletics Interscholastic: aerobics/dance, basketball, cross-country running, diving, drill team, golf, soccer, softball, swimming and diving, tennis, track and field, volleyball; intramural: aerobics/dance, badminton, basketball, fitness, fitness walking, jogging, physical fitness, physical training, running, strength & conditioning, table tennis, volleyball, walking, weight lifting, weight training. 2 PE instructors, 25 coaches, 1 athletic trainer.

Computers Computers are regularly used in business education, creative writing, graphics, journalism, library, newspaper, research skills, science, writing, yearbook classes. Computer network features include on-campus library services, Internet access, wireless campus network, Internet filtering or blocking technology. Campus intranet is available to students. The school has a published electronic and media policy.

Contact Mrs. Roseann Hudnall, Admissions Director. 816-501-0011 Ext. 135. Fax: 816-523-0232. E-mail: rhudnall@stteresasacademy.org. Web site: www.stteresasacademy.org.

SAINT THOMAS ACADEMY

949 Mendota Heights Road
Mendota Heights, Minnesota 55120

Head of School: Thomas B. Mich, PhD

General Information Boys' day college-preparatory and military school, affiliated with Roman Catholic Church. Grades 7–12. Founded: 1885. Setting: suburban. Nearest major city is St. Paul. 72-acre campus. 3 buildings on campus. Approved or accredited by Independent Schools Association of the Central States. Endowment: $17.6 million. Total enrollment: 694. Upper school average class size: 18. Upper school faculty-student ratio: 1:10.

Upper School Student Profile Grade 7: 58 students (58 boys); Grade 8: 94 students (94 boys); Grade 9: 143 students (143 boys); Grade 10: 138 students (138 boys); Grade 11: 138 students (138 boys); Grade 12: 123 students (123 boys). 75% of students are Roman Catholic.

Faculty School total: 64. In upper school: 27 men, 23 women; 39 have advanced degrees.

Subjects Offered Advanced Placement courses, algebra, American history, American literature, art, art history, biology, calculus, campus ministry, chemistry, Chinese, computer science, creative writing, earth science, economics, English, English literature, environmental studies, European history, fine arts, French, geometry, government/civics, health, history, JROTC, Latin, mathematics, military science, music, physical education, physics, psychology, religion, science, social studies, Spanish, trigonometry, world history, world literature, writing.

Graduation Requirements Arts and fine arts (art, music, dance, drama), English, foreign language, health education, JROTC or LEAD (Leadership Education and Development), mathematics, physical education (includes health), religion (includes Bible studies and theology), science, social studies (includes history), U.S. history, world history, 100 hours of community service in 12th grade.

Special Academic Programs 10 Advanced Placement exams for which test preparation is offered; honors section; independent study.

College Admission Counseling 123 students graduated in 2008; 118 went to college, including Gustavus Adolphus College; Iowa State University of Science and Technology; Saint John's University; University of Minnesota, Twin Cities Campus; University of Notre Dame; University of St. Thomas. Other: 1 entered military service, 4 had other specific plans. Mean SAT critical reading: 584, mean SAT math: 620, mean composite ACT: 25. 38% scored over 600 on SAT critical reading, 64% scored over 600 on SAT math, 43% scored over 26 on composite ACT.

Student Life Upper grades have uniform requirement, student council, honor system. Discipline rests primarily with faculty. Attendance at religious services is required.

Summer Programs Remediation, enrichment programs offered; session focuses on study skills and remediation/make-up; held on campus; accepts boys; not open to students from other schools. 12 students usually enrolled. 2009 schedule: June 15 to July 17. Application deadline: March 16.

Tuition and Aid Day student tuition: $15,225. Tuition installment plan (monthly payment plans, individually arranged payment plans, quarterly payment plan). Merit scholarship grants, need-based scholarship grants available. In 2008–09, 33% of upper-school students received aid; total upper-school merit-scholarship money awarded: $49,500. Total amount of financial aid awarded in 2008–09: $1,300,000.

Admissions Traditional secondary-level entrance grade is 9. For fall 2008, 147 students applied for upper-level admission, 125 were accepted, 80 enrolled. Cognitive Abilities Test required. Deadline for receipt of application materials: January 15. No application fee required. On-campus interview recommended.

Athletics Interscholastic: alpine skiing, baseball, basketball, cross-country running, diving, drill team, fitness, football, golf, hockey, ice hockey, JROTC drill, lacrosse, marksmanship, nordic skiing, outdoor skills, physical fitness, riflery, skiing (cross-country), skiing (downhill), soccer, swimming and diving, tennis, track and field, wrestling; intramural: basketball, football, physical training, strength & conditioning, table tennis, weight lifting, weight training. 3 PE instructors, 1 athletic trainer.

Computers Computers are regularly used in all academic, art, foreign language, music classes. Computer network features include on-campus library services, online commercial services, Internet access, wireless campus network, Internet filtering or blocking technology. Students grades are available online. The school has a published electronic and media policy.

Contact Peggy Mansur, Admissions Assistant. 651-683-1515. Fax: 651-683-1576. E-mail: pmansur@cadets.com. Web site: www.cadets.com.

ST. THOMAS AQUINAS HIGH SCHOOL

2801 Southwest 12th Street
Fort Lauderdale, Florida 33312-2999

Head of School: Mrs. Tina Jones

General Information Coeducational day college-preparatory, arts, religious studies, and technology school, affiliated with Roman Catholic Church. Grades 9–12. Founded: 1936. Setting: suburban. 24-acre campus. 23 buildings on campus. Approved or accredited by National Catholic Education Association, Southern Association of Colleges and Schools, and Florida Department of Education. Total enrollment: 2,152. Upper school average class size: 25. Upper school faculty-student ratio: 1:18.

Upper School Student Profile Grade 9: 561 students (273 boys, 288 girls); Grade 10: 541 students (254 boys, 287 girls); Grade 11: 516 students (264 boys, 252 girls); Grade 12: 534 students (266 boys, 268 girls). 96% of students are Roman Catholic.

Faculty School total: 121. In upper school: 68 men, 47 women; 66 have advanced degrees.

Subjects Offered 20th century history, 20th century world history, 3-dimensional art, acting, advanced chemistry, advanced computer applications, advanced math, Advanced Placement courses, algebra, American government, American government-AP, American history, American history-AP, American literature, anatomy and physiology, art, art appreciation, art history-AP, athletics, biology, biology-AP, British literature, British literature (honors), British literature-AP, broadcast journalism, calculus, calculus-AP, chemistry, chemistry-AP, Chinese, choir, choral music, chorus, Christianity, church history, comparative government and politics-AP, comparative political systems-AP, composition-AP, computer art, computer graphics, computer keyboarding, computer programming-AP, computer science-AP, debate, desktop publishing, digital art, digital imaging, directing, drama, drama performance, drawing, economics-AP, electives, English, English language and composition-AP, English literature, English literature and composition-AP, English literature-AP, English-AP, English/composition-AP, environmental science, environmental science-AP, European history, European history-AP, film and literature, film and new technologies, fitness, food science, forensics, French, French language-AP, French literature-AP, French-AP, general science, geometry, government, government and politics-AP, government-AP, government/civics-AP, grammar, graphic arts, graphic design, health, health and safety, health and wellness, health education, health enhancement, health science, healthful living, Hispanic literature, history, history of drama, history-AP, Holocaust, honors algebra, honors English, honors geometry, honors U.S. history, honors world history, human anatomy, human geography—AP, jazz, jazz band, journalism, lab science, language, language and composition, language arts, language-AP, Latin, Latin-AP, leadership, leadership and service, leadership education training, leadership skills, leadership training, Life of Christ, literature, literature and composition-AP, literature-AP, macro/microeconomics-AP, macroeconomics-AP, marine biology, marine studies, mathematics-AP, media, microeconomics, microeconomics-AP, model United Nations, modern European history, modern European history-AP, news writing, newspaper, nutrition, oral expression, orchestra, peace and justice, peace education, peace studies, performing arts, photography, photojournalism, physical education, physical fitness, physics, physics-AP, play production, playwriting and directing, poetry, political systems, pottery, pre-algebra, pre-calculus, psychology, psychology-AP, public speaking,

reading, SAT preparation, SAT/ACT preparation, Spanish, Spanish language-AP, Spanish literature, Spanish literature-AP, Spanish-AP, speech, speech and debate, speech and oral interpretations, speech communications, sports team management, stage design, stagecraft, statistics, statistics and probability, statistics-AP, student government, student publications, studio art, technical theater, television, trigonometry, U.S. government and politics-AP, U.S. government-AP, U.S. history, U.S. history-AP, United States government-AP, world history, world history-AP.
Graduation Requirements Arts and fine arts (art, music, dance, drama), computer science, electives, English, foreign language, health, mathematics, personal fitness, science, social science, theology.
Special Academic Programs Advanced Placement exam preparation; honors section; remedial reading and/or remedial writing; remedial math.
College Admission Counseling 537 students graduated in 2008; 536 went to college, including Florida Atlantic University; Florida State University; University of Central Florida; University of Florida; University of Miami; University of North Florida. Other: 1 entered military service. Mean SAT critical reading: 578, mean SAT math: 576, mean SAT writing: 578, mean combined SAT: 1730, mean composite ACT: 24.
Student Life Upper grades have uniform requirement, student council, honor system. Discipline rests primarily with faculty. Attendance at religious services is required.
Summer Programs Remediation, enrichment, advancement, art/fine arts programs offered; session focuses on enrichment; held on campus; accepts boys and girls; not open to students from other schools. 1,000 students usually enrolled. 2009 schedule: June 8 to June 24. Application deadline: May 22.
Tuition and Aid Day student tuition: $7200. Need-based scholarship grants available.
Admissions Traditional secondary-level entrance grade is 9. For fall 2008, 903 students applied for upper-level admission, 570 were accepted, 560 enrolled. High School Placement Test required. Deadline for receipt of application materials: March 15. Application fee required: $50. Interview required.
Athletics Interscholastic: baseball (boys), basketball (b,g), cheering (g), cross-country running (b,g), diving (b,g), drill team (g), football (b), golf (b,g), soccer (b,g), softball (g), swimming and diving (b,g), tennis (b,g), track and field (b,g), volleyball (b,g), water polo (b); intramural: dance team (g), danceline (g), drill team (g); coed interscholastic: ice hockey, indoor hockey, physical training; coed intramural: physical training, running. 3 PE instructors, 25 coaches, 1 athletic trainer.
Computers Computers are regularly used in all academic, data processing, desktop publishing, graphic arts, graphic design, graphics, journalism, keyboarding, lab/keyboard, media, media arts, media production, media services, news writing, newspaper, programming, publications, publishing, technology, video film production, Web site design, word processing classes. Computer network features include on-campus library services, online commercial services, Internet access, Internet filtering or blocking technology. Computer access in designated common areas is available to students. The school has a published electronic and media policy.
Contact Admissions Office. 954-581-2127 Ext. 8623. Fax: 954-581-8263. E-mail: mfacella@aquinas-sta.org. Web site: www.aquinas-sta.org.

SAINT THOMAS AQUINAS HIGH SCHOOL

11411 Pflumm Road
Overland Park, Kansas 66215-4816
Head of School: Dr. William P. Ford

General Information Coeducational day college-preparatory, religious studies, and technology school, affiliated with Roman Catholic Church. Grades 9–12. Founded: 1988. Setting: suburban. Nearest major city is Kansas City, MO. 44-acre campus. 2 buildings on campus. Approved or accredited by National Catholic Education Association, North Central Association of Colleges and Schools, and Kansas Department of Education. Total enrollment: 1,092. Upper school average class size: 25. Upper school faculty-student ratio: 1:15.
Upper School Student Profile Grade 9: 270 students (121 boys, 149 girls); Grade 10: 270 students (129 boys, 141 girls); Grade 11: 282 students (121 boys, 161 girls); Grade 12: 270 students (124 boys, 146 girls). 97% of students are Roman Catholic.
Faculty School total: 77. In upper school: 33 men, 44 women; 57 have advanced degrees.
Graduation Requirements Arts and fine arts (art, music, dance, drama), computer technologies, electives, English, Latin, mathematics, modern languages, physical education (includes health), science, social studies (includes history), speech, theology, service (one fourth credit each of 4 years).
Special Academic Programs Advanced Placement exam preparation; honors section; study at local college for college credit; academic accommodation for the gifted; remedial reading and/or remedial writing; remedial math.
College Admission Counseling 336 students graduated in 2008; 331 went to college, including Benedictine College; Johnson County Community College; Kansas State University; The University of Kansas; University of Arkansas; University of Notre Dame. Other: 1 went to work, 4 entered military service. Mean SAT critical reading: 644, mean SAT math: 630, mean composite ACT: 25. 65% scored over 600 on SAT critical reading, 60% scored over 600 on SAT math, 33% scored over 26 on composite ACT.
Student Life Upper grades have uniform requirement, student council. Discipline rests primarily with faculty. Attendance at religious services is required.
Summer Programs Remediation, advancement, sports programs offered; session focuses on sports; held on campus; accepts boys and girls; open to students from other schools.
Tuition and Aid Day student tuition: $7050–$8050. Tuition installment plan (SMART Tuition Payment Plan). Need-based scholarship grants available.
Admissions Traditional secondary-level entrance grade is 9. ACT-Explore required. Deadline for receipt of application materials: none. Application fee required: $125. Interview required.
Athletics Interscholastic: baseball (boys), basketball (b,g), bowling (b,g), dance team (g), diving (b,g), football (b), golf (b,g), soccer (b,g), softball (g), swimming and diving (b,g), tennis (b,g), track and field (b,g), volleyball (g), wrestling (b); coed interscholastic: cheering, cross-country running; coed intramural: table tennis, ultimate Frisbee. 3 PE instructors, 1 athletic trainer.
Computers Computers are regularly used in all academic, computer applications, desktop publishing, programming, video film production, Web site design classes. Computer network features include on-campus library services, Internet access, wireless campus network, computer labs and laptop carts. Student e-mail accounts are available to students. Students grades are available online. The school has a published electronic and media policy.
Contact Mrs. Diane Pyle, Director of Admissions. 913-319-2423. Fax: 913-345-2319. E-mail: dpyle@stasaints.net. Web site: www.stasaints.net.

ST. THOMAS AQUINAS HIGH SCHOOL

197 Dover Point Road
Dover, New Hampshire 03820
Head of School: Mr. Ron Holtz

General Information Coeducational day college-preparatory and religious studies school, affiliated with Roman Catholic Church. Grades 9–12. Founded: 1960. Setting: small town. Nearest major city is Boston, MA. 11-acre campus. 2 buildings on campus. Approved or accredited by New England Association of Schools and Colleges and New Hampshire Department of Education. Total enrollment: 719. Upper school average class size: 21. Upper school faculty-student ratio: 1:15.
Upper School Student Profile Grade 9: 181 students (107 boys, 74 girls); Grade 10: 189 students (91 boys, 98 girls); Grade 11: 168 students (72 boys, 96 girls); Grade 12: 181 students (88 boys, 93 girls).
Faculty School total: 49. In upper school: 25 men, 23 women; 20 have advanced degrees.
Subjects Offered Algebra, anatomy and physiology, biology, biology-AP, calculus, calculus-AP, chemistry, chorus, Christian ethics, concert band, contemporary studies, drawing, economics, English, environmental science-AP, finite math, French, geography, geometry, honors algebra, honors English, honors geometry, humanities, introduction to technology, Latin, marine biology, math applications, media arts, music appreciation, music theory, painting, physics, prayer/spirituality, pre-calculus, psychology, science, scripture, sculpture, social justice, sociology, Spanish, statistics-AP, studio art, theology, trigonometry, U.S. government and politics-AP, U.S. history, U.S. history-AP, wellness, Western civilization, world religions.
Graduation Requirements Arts and fine arts (art, music, dance, drama), Christian ethics, electives, English, foreign language, freshman seminar, mathematics, prayer/spirituality, science, scripture, social justice, social studies (includes history), theology, world religions, 40 hour community service requirement.
Special Academic Programs Advanced Placement exam preparation; honors section.
College Admission Counseling 171 students graduated in 2008; 165 went to college, including Saint Anselm College; Stonehill College; University of New Hampshire. Mean SAT critical reading: 566, mean SAT math: 563, mean SAT writing: 569.
Student Life Upper grades have specified standards of dress, student council. Discipline rests primarily with faculty. Attendance at religious services is required.
Tuition and Aid Day student tuition: $9100. Tuition installment plan (annual, semiannual, and 10-month payment plans). Need-based scholarship grants available. In 2008–09, 12% of upper-school students received aid. Total amount of financial aid awarded in 2008–09: $270,000.
Admissions Traditional secondary-level entrance grade is 9. For fall 2008, 290 students applied for upper-level admission, 250 were accepted, 185 enrolled. Scholastic Testing Service High School Placement Test required. Deadline for receipt of application materials: December 31. Application fee required: $40.
Athletics Interscholastic: baseball (boys), basketball (b,g), cross-country running (b,g), field hockey (g), football (b), golf (b,g), gymnastics (g), ice hockey (b,g), lacrosse (b,g), skiing (downhill) (b,g), soccer (b,g), softball (g), swimming and diving (b,g), tennis (b,g), track and field (b,g), volleyball (g), winter (indoor) track (b,g), wrestling (b). 51 coaches, 1 athletic trainer.
Computers Computers are regularly used in introduction to technology, media arts classes. Computer network features include on-campus library services, Internet access, wireless campus network. Student e-mail accounts are available to students. Students grades are available online.
Contact Mrs. Patricia Krupsky, Director of Admissions. 603-742-3206. Fax: 603-749-7822. E-mail: pkrupsky@stalux.org. Web site: www.stalux.org.

ST. THOMAS CHOIR SCHOOL

New York, New York

See Junior Boarding Schools section.

ST. THOMAS HIGH SCHOOL

4500 Memorial Drive
Houston, Texas 77007-7332

Head of School: Rev. John Huber, CSB

General Information Boys' day college-preparatory and religious studies school, affiliated with Roman Catholic Church. Grades 9–12. Founded: 1900. Setting: urban. 37-acre campus. 6 buildings on campus. Approved or accredited by Southern Association of Colleges and Schools, Texas Catholic Conference, Texas Education Agency, and Texas Department of Education. Endowment: $12 million. Total enrollment: 711. Upper school average class size: 22. Upper school faculty-student ratio: 1:13.

Upper School Student Profile Grade 9: 197 students (197 boys); Grade 10: 189 students (189 boys); Grade 11: 176 students (176 boys); Grade 12: 149 students (149 boys). 83% of students are Roman Catholic.

Faculty School total: 49. In upper school: 35 men, 14 women; 30 have advanced degrees.

Subjects Offered Algebra, American government, American government-AP, American history, American history-AP, American literature, ancient history, art, arts, Basic programming, Bible studies, bioethics, biology, biology-AP, British literature, calculus, calculus-AP, ceramics, chemistry, chemistry-AP, civics/free enterprise, classical civilization, college counseling, comparative government and politics-AP, computer applications, computer information systems, computer programming, computer studies, creative writing, critical thinking, critical writing, decision making, drama, drawing, ecology, environmental systems, economics, economics-AP, English, English language-AP, English literature, English literature-AP, environmental science, ethics, European history, fine arts, forensics, French, geography, geology, geometry, government and politics-AP, government/civics, grammar, guidance, health, health education, history of the Catholic Church, Holocaust studies, instrumental music, jazz band, journalism, Latin, marine biology, mathematics, oceanography, oral communications, orchestra, painting, photography, physical education, physics, physics-AP, pre-calculus, programming, public speaking, publications, religion, social studies, Spanish, Spanish language-AP, speech, student government, student publications, theater, theology, trigonometry, world history, world literature.

Graduation Requirements Arts and fine arts (art, music, dance, drama), computer applications, English, foreign language, mathematics, physical education (includes health), religion (includes Bible studies and theology), science, social studies (includes history).

Special Academic Programs Advanced Placement exam preparation; honors section.

College Admission Counseling 174 students graduated in 2008; all went to college, including Texas A&M University; Texas Christian University; Texas Tech University; The University of Texas at Austin; University of Houston; University of St. Thomas. Mean composite ACT: 25.

Student Life Upper grades have specified standards of dress, student council. Discipline rests primarily with faculty. Attendance at religious services is required.

Admissions Traditional secondary-level entrance grade is 9. For fall 2008, 400 students applied for upper-level admission, 250 were accepted, 185 enrolled. High School Placement Test required. Deadline for receipt of application materials: February 3. Application fee required: $25.

Athletics Interscholastic: baseball, basketball, cross-country running, football, golf, roller hockey, soccer; intramural: basketball, bowling, flag football, rugby. 2 PE instructors, 2 coaches, 1 athletic trainer.

Computers Computers are regularly used in data processing, desktop publishing, multimedia, newspaper, programming, publications, word processing classes.

Contact Ms. Christine Westman, Assistant Principal. 713-864-6348. Fax: 713-864-5750. E-mail: chris.westman@sths.org. Web site: www.sths.org.

SAINT THOMAS MORE SCHOOL

45 Cottage Road
Oakdale, Connecticut 06370

Head of School: James F. Hanrahan Jr.

General Information Boys' boarding college-preparatory, arts, and religious studies school, affiliated with Roman Catholic Church; primarily serves underachievers, students with learning disabilities, individuals with Attention Deficit Disorder, and ADD, ADHD, Processing Disorders. Grades 8–PG. Founded: 1962. Setting: rural. Nearest major city is Hartford. Students are housed in single-sex dormitories. 100-acre campus. 14 buildings on campus. Approved or accredited by Connecticut Association of Independent Schools, New England Association of Schools and Colleges, The Association of Boarding Schools, and Connecticut Department of Education. Member of National Association of Independent Schools and Secondary School Admission Test Board. Endowment: $9.1 million. Total enrollment: 210. Upper school average class size: 12. Upper school faculty-student ratio: 1:7.

Upper School Student Profile Grade 9: 21 students (21 boys); Grade 10: 32 students (32 boys); Grade 11: 55 students (55 boys); Grade 12: 60 students (60 boys); Postgraduate: 26 students (26 boys). 100% of students are boarding students. 16% are state residents. 14 states are represented in upper school student body. 32% are international students. International students from China, Japan, Mexico, Republic of Korea, Spain, and Taiwan; 9 other countries represented in student body. 65% of students are Roman Catholic.

Faculty School total: 30. In upper school: 24 men, 5 women; 17 have advanced degrees; 27 reside on campus.

Subjects Offered Algebra, American literature, ancient history, arts appreciation, biology, British literature, calculus, chemistry, comparative religion, death and loss, earth science, economics, English, environmental science, ESL, geometry, global studies, grammar, intro to computers, language arts, life science, medieval history, moral theology, mythology, physics, political thought, pre-algebra, pre-calculus, programming, reading, Spanish, speech, studio art, U.S. history, world history, world literature, writing.

Graduation Requirements Arts and fine arts (art, music, dance, drama), English, foreign language, mathematics, religion (includes Bible studies and theology), science, social studies (includes history).

Special Academic Programs Remedial reading and/or remedial writing; remedial math; programs in general development for dyslexic students; special instructional classes for students with learning disabilities and Attention Deficit Disorder; ESL (40 students enrolled).

College Admission Counseling 50 students graduated in 2008; all went to college, including Bentley University; Michigan State University; Northeastern University; Rutgers, The State University of New Jersey, New Brunswick; University of Massachusetts Amherst; University of New Hampshire. Median SAT critical reading: 500, median SAT math: 520, median SAT writing: 500. 15% scored over 600 on SAT critical reading, 15% scored over 600 on SAT math, 15% scored over 600 on SAT writing.

Student Life Upper grades have uniform requirement, student council, honor system. Discipline rests primarily with faculty. Attendance at religious services is required.

Summer Programs Remediation, enrichment, ESL, sports, art/fine arts, computer instruction programs offered; session focuses on study skills, make-up credits, enrichment; held on campus; accepts boys; open to students from other schools. 50 students usually enrolled. 2009 schedule: June 28 to July 31. Application deadline: none.

Tuition and Aid 7-day tuition and room/board: $34,900–$38,400. Tuition installment plan (Key Tuition Payment Plan, monthly payment plans, individually arranged payment plans). Merit scholarship grants, need-based scholarship grants available. In 2008–09, 25% of upper-school students received aid; total upper-school merit-scholarship money awarded: $64,200. Total amount of financial aid awarded in 2008–09: $728,900.

Admissions Traditional secondary-level entrance grade is 10. For fall 2008, 274 students applied for upper-level admission, 212 were accepted, 92 enrolled. Otis-Lennon School Ability Test, SAT, SLEP, SSAT or TOEFL required. Deadline for receipt of application materials: none. Application fee required: $50. Interview required.

Athletics Interscholastic: baseball, basketball, cross-country running, football, golf, hockey, ice hockey, lacrosse, sailing, soccer, tennis, track and field; intramural: alpine skiing, baseball, basketball, billiards, canoeing/kayaking, fishing, fitness, flag football, Frisbee, jogging, kickball, martial arts, nordic skiing, outdoor activities, outdoor recreation, paddle tennis, physical fitness, physical training, roller blading, rowing, sailing, skateboarding, skiing (downhill), snowboarding, soccer, strength & conditioning, swimming and diving, table tennis, tennis, ultimate Frisbee, volleyball, weight lifting, weight training. 27 coaches, 1 athletic trainer.

Computers Computers are regularly used in college planning, newspaper, research skills, yearbook classes. Computer resources include on-campus library services, Internet access.

Contact Timothy P. Riordan, Director of Admissions. 860-823-3861. Fax: 860-823-3863. E-mail: triordan@stmct.org. Web site: www.stmct.org.

See Close-Up on page 954.

ST. TIMOTHY'S SCHOOL

8400 Greenspring Avenue
Stevenson, Maryland 21153

Head of School: Randy S. Stevens

General Information Girls' boarding and day college-preparatory, arts, and Cambridge (UK) General Certificate of Secondary Education school, affiliated with Episcopal Church. Grades 9–12. Founded: 1882. Setting: rural. Nearest major city is Baltimore. Students are housed in single-sex dormitories. 145-acre campus. 23 buildings on campus. Approved or accredited by Association of Independent Maryland Schools, International Baccalaureate Organization, Middle States Association of Colleges and Schools, National Association of Episcopal Schools, The Association of Boarding Schools, and Maryland Department of Education. Member of National Association of Independent Schools and Secondary School Admission Test Board. Endowment: $10 million. Total enrollment: 155. Upper school average class size: 10. Upper school faculty-student ratio: 1:5.

Upper School Student Profile Grade 9: 22 students (22 girls); Grade 10: 50 students (50 girls); Grade 11: 45 students (45 girls); Grade 12: 38 students (38 girls). 70% of students are boarding students. 40% are state residents. 16 states are represented in upper school student body. 30% are international students. International students from Bahamas, China, Germany, Mexico, Republic of Korea, and Spain; 11 other countries represented in student body.

Faculty School total: 38. In upper school: 12 men, 18 women; 21 have advanced degrees; 29 reside on campus.

Subjects Offered Algebra, American literature, art, art history, biology, British literature, calculus, chemistry, Chinese, comparative politics, creative writing, dance, drama, drama performance, drama workshop, economics, English, English composition, English literature, ESL, ethics, European history, fine arts, foreign language, French, geometry, history, International Baccalaureate courses, Latin, Mandarin, mathematics, modern dance, music, music theory, photography, physics, piano, religion, science, Spanish, U.S. history, world history, world literature, writing.

Graduation Requirements Arts and fine arts (art, music, dance, drama), English, foreign language, history, mathematics, physical education (includes health), religion (includes Bible studies and theology), science, independent senior project, extended essay, Community, Action and Service (CAS). Community service is required.

Special Academic Programs International Baccalaureate program; honors section; independent study; ESL (9 students enrolled).

College Admission Counseling 34 students graduated in 2008; all went to college, including Colby College; Princeton University; Skidmore College; University of Maryland, College Park; University of Pennsylvania; University of Virginia. Mean SAT critical reading: 570, mean SAT math: 560, mean combined SAT: 1130.

Student Life Upper grades have uniform requirement, student council, honor system. Discipline rests equally with students and faculty. Attendance at religious services is required.

Summer Programs Enrichment, ESL programs offered; session focuses on leadership and intensive language; held on campus; accepts boys and girls; open to students from other schools. 2009 schedule: July 1 to July 28. Application deadline: May 1.

Tuition and Aid Day student tuition: $24,200; 5-day tuition and room/board: $41,000; 7-day tuition and room/board: $41,000. Tuition installment plan (FACTS Tuition Payment Plan). Merit scholarship grants, need-based scholarship grants, need-based loans available. In 2008–09, 42% of upper-school students received aid; total upper-school merit-scholarship money awarded: $30,000. Total amount of financial aid awarded in 2008–09: $1,450,000.

Admissions Traditional secondary-level entrance grade is 9. For fall 2008, 184 students applied for upper-level admission, 106 were accepted, 57 enrolled. ISEE, SLEP for foreign students, SSAT or TOEFL required. Deadline for receipt of application materials: February 10. Application fee required: $45. Interview required.

Athletics Interscholastic: badminton, basketball, dressage, equestrian sports, field hockey, golf, horseback riding, ice hockey, indoor soccer, lacrosse, soccer, softball, squash, tennis, volleyball; intramural: ballet, cross-country running, dance, dance squad, equestrian sports, horseback riding, modern dance, outdoor adventure, weight training, yoga. 2 coaches, 1 athletic trainer.

Computers Computers are regularly used in art, college planning, English, mathematics, publications, SAT preparation, science, yearbook classes. Computer network features include on-campus library services, online commercial services, Internet access, wireless campus network, Internet filtering or blocking technology. Student e-mail accounts are available to students. The school has a published electronic and media policy.

Contact Patrick M. Finn, Director of Admissions and Assistant Head of School. 410-486-7401. Fax: 410-486-1167. E-mail: admis@stt.org. Web site: www.stt.org.

ANNOUNCEMENT FROM THE SCHOOL Established in 1882 as a college-preparatory boarding and day school for girls (grades 9–12), St. Tim's offers small class size, rigorous academics that are based on the International Baccalaureate (IB) Diploma Program, excellent fine arts, and athletics. The School is located on a large, rural campus near Baltimore, Maryland, and includes an athletic complex, equestrian center, an art barn, and a 350-seat theater. For more information, contact the Admission Office (phone: 410-486-7401; Web site: www.stt.org).

See Close-Up on page 956.

SAINT VIATOR HIGH SCHOOL

1213 East Oakton Street
Arlington Heights, Illinois 60004

Head of School: Rev. Robert M. Egan, CSV

General Information Coeducational day college-preparatory, arts, religious studies, bilingual studies, and technology school, affiliated with Roman Catholic Church. Grades 9–12. Founded: 1961. Setting: suburban. Nearest major city is Chicago. Approved or accredited by Illinois Department of Education. Upper school average class size: 25. Upper school faculty-student ratio: 1:12.

Faculty School total: 74. In upper school: 29 men, 45 women; 48 have advanced degrees.

Graduation Requirements 25 hours of Christian Service each year; 100 total hours.

College Admission Counseling 264 students graduated in 2008; 260 went to college, including DePaul University; Marquette University; The University of Iowa; University of Illinois at Urbana–Champaign; University of Notre Dame; University of Wisconsin–Madison. Other: 4 had other specific plans.

Student Life Upper grades have specified standards of dress, student council, honor system. Discipline rests primarily with faculty. Attendance at religious services is required.

Tuition and Aid Day student tuition: $9800. Need-based scholarship grants available. In 2008–09, 21% of upper-school students received aid. Total amount of financial aid awarded in 2008–09: $858,000.

Admissions ETS high school placement exam required. Application fee required: $400.

Athletics Interscholastic: baseball (boys), basketball (b,g), cheering (g), cross-country running (b,g), dance (g), football (b), golf (b,g), ice hockey (b), lacrosse (b), pom squad (g), soccer (b,g), softball (g), swimming and diving (b,g), tennis (b,g), track and field (b,g), volleyball (b,g), water polo (b,g), wrestling (b); coed intramural: outdoor adventure.

Computers Computer resources include Internet access, Faculty web pages. Students grades are available online.

Contact Mrs. Eileen Manno, Principal. 847-392-4050 Ext. 229. Fax: 847-392-8305. E-mail: emanno@saintviator.com. Web site: www.saintviator.com.

SAINT XAVIER HIGH SCHOOL

1609 Poplar Level Road
Louisville, Kentucky 40217

Head of School: Dr. Perry Sangalli

General Information Boys' day college-preparatory, arts, business, religious studies, bilingual studies, and technology school, affiliated with Roman Catholic Church. Grades 9–12. Founded: 1864. Setting: suburban. 72-acre campus. 6 buildings on campus. Approved or accredited by Southern Association of Colleges and Schools and Kentucky Department of Education. Endowment: $10 million. Total enrollment: 1,402. Upper school average class size: 23. Upper school faculty-student ratio: 1:12.

Upper School Student Profile Grade 9: 381 students (381 boys); Grade 10: 362 students (362 boys); Grade 11: 317 students (317 boys); Grade 12: 342 students (342 boys). 75% of students are Roman Catholic.

Faculty School total: 117. In upper school: 93 men, 24 women; 98 have advanced degrees.

Subjects Offered Accounting, acting, Advanced Placement courses, algebra, American government, anatomy and physiology, band, biology, business law, ceramics, chemistry, chorus, computer applications, computer programming, computer-aided design, creative writing, desktop publishing, drafting, economics, English, environmental science, fitness, French, geometry, German, global issues, health, humanities, journalism, keyboarding, mathematics, mechanical drawing, music, music history, music theory, philosophy, photography, physical education, physics, probability and statistics, psychology, reading, sculpture, sociology, Spanish, speech, theology, trigonometry, U.S. history, world civilizations, world geography, yearbook.

Graduation Requirements Arts and fine arts (art, music, dance, drama), electives, English, foreign language, mathematics, physical education (includes health), science, social studies (includes history), theology, U.S. history.

Special Academic Programs Advanced Placement exam preparation; honors section; study at local college for college credit; academic accommodation for the gifted, the musically talented, and the artistically talented; remedial reading and/or remedial writing; remedial math; programs in English, mathematics, general development for dyslexic students; special instructional classes for students with Attention Deficit Disorder, Attention Deficit Hyperactivity Disorder, dyslexia, and central auditory processing disorder.

College Admission Counseling 326 students graduated in 2008; 218 went to college, including Bellarmine University; Saint Louis University; University of Dayton; University of Kentucky; University of Louisville; Xavier University. Other: 8 went to work, 4 entered military service.

Student Life Upper grades have specified standards of dress, student council, honor system. Discipline rests primarily with faculty. Attendance at religious services is required.

Admissions Traditional secondary-level entrance grade is 9. For fall 2008, 475 students applied for upper-level admission, 475 were accepted, 381 enrolled. STS required. Deadline for receipt of application materials: none. Application fee required: $100. On-campus interview recommended.

Athletics Interscholastic: baseball, basketball, bowling, cheering, cross-country running, diving, fishing, fly fishing, football, golf, ice hockey, indoor track, indoor track & field, lacrosse, power lifting, running, soccer, strength & conditioning, swimming and diving, tennis, track and field, volleyball, weight lifting, weight training, wrestling; intramural: alpine skiing, basketball, billiards, bowling, cooperative games, fishing, flag football, football, Frisbee, golf, ice hockey, kickball, mountain biking, outdoor activities, skiing (downhill), snowboarding, soccer, table tennis, tennis, touch football, ultimate Frisbee, weight training. 3 PE instructors, 63 coaches, 1 athletic trainer.

Computers Computers are regularly used in all classes. Computer network features include on-campus library services, online commercial services, Internet access, Internet filtering or blocking technology. Students grades are available online.

Contact Br. Edwards Driscoll, CFX, Principal. 502-637-4712. Fax: 502-634-2171. E-mail: edriscoll@saintx.com. Web site: www.saintx.com.

SAINT XAVIER HIGH SCHOOL

600 North Bend Road
Cincinnati, Ohio 45224

Head of School: Rev. Walter C. Deye, SJ

General Information Boys' day college-preparatory, arts, religious studies, technology, and service learning school, affiliated with Roman Catholic Church. Grades 9–12. Founded: 1831. Setting: suburban. 100-acre campus. 1 building on campus. Approved or accredited by Jesuit Secondary Education Association, North Central Association of Colleges and Schools, Ohio Catholic Schools Accreditation Association (OCSAA), and Ohio Department of Education. Endowment: $37 million. Total enrollment: 1,560. Upper school average class size: 28. Upper school faculty-student ratio: 1:15.

Upper School Student Profile Grade 9: 408 students (408 boys); Grade 10: 412 students (412 boys); Grade 11: 367 students (367 boys); Grade 12: 373 students (373 boys). 81% of students are Roman Catholic.

Faculty School total: 100. In upper school: 72 men, 28 women; 88 have advanced degrees.

Subjects Offered Arts, biology, chemistry, computer science, English, fine arts, French, German, Greek, health, Latin, mathematics, physical education, physics, religion, science, social studies, Spanish.

Graduation Requirements Arts and fine arts (art, music, dance, drama), computer science, English, foreign language, forensics, mathematics, physical education (includes health), religion (includes Bible studies and theology), science, social studies (includes history).

Special Academic Programs Advanced Placement exam preparation; independent study; term-away projects; study at local college for college credit.

College Admission Counseling 390 students graduated in 2008; all went to college, including Miami University; Saint Louis University; The Ohio State University; University of Cincinnati; University of Notre Dame; Xavier University. Median SAT critical reading: 630, median SAT math: 640, median composite ACT: 27. 64% scored over 600 on SAT critical reading, 72% scored over 600 on SAT math, 60% scored over 26 on composite ACT.

Student Life Upper grades have specified standards of dress, student council. Discipline rests primarily with faculty. Attendance at religious services is required.

Tuition and Aid Day student tuition: $10,250. Merit scholarship grants, need-based scholarship grants, paying campus jobs available. In 2008–09, 28% of upper-school students received aid. Total amount of financial aid awarded in 2008–09: $2,300,000.

Admissions Traditional secondary-level entrance grade is 9. For fall 2008, 880 students applied for upper-level admission, 450 were accepted, 408 enrolled. High School Placement Test required. Deadline for receipt of application materials: December 1. Application fee required: $20.

Athletics Interscholastic: baseball, basketball, bowling, crew, cross-country running, diving, football, golf, ice hockey, lacrosse, soccer, swimming and diving, tennis, track and field, volleyball, wrestling; intramural: basketball, football, golf, soccer, table tennis, tennis, volleyball. 3 PE instructors, 2 athletic trainers.

Computers Computers are regularly used in art, design, drawing and design, foreign language, graphic arts, graphic design, graphics, keyboarding, lab/keyboard, language development, library, programming, research skills, science classes. Computer network features include on-campus library services, online commercial services, Internet access, wireless campus network, Internet filtering or blocking technology. Campus intranet, student e-mail accounts, and computer access in designated common areas are available to students. Students grades are available online. The school has a published electronic and media policy.

Contact Mr. Roderick D. Hinton, Director of Admissions. 513-761-7815 Ext. 106. Fax: 513-761-3811. E-mail: rhinton@stxavier.org. Web site: www.stxavier.org.

SALEM ACADEMY

500 Salem Avenue
Winston-Salem, North Carolina 27108-0578

Head of School: Mr. Karl Sjolund

General Information Girls' boarding and day college-preparatory and arts school, affiliated with Moravian Church. Grades 9–12. Founded: 1772. Setting: urban. Students are housed in single-sex dormitories. 60-acre campus. 4 buildings on campus. Approved or accredited by North Carolina Association of Independent Schools, Southern Association of Colleges and Schools, The Association of Boarding Schools, and North Carolina Department of Education. Member of National Association of Independent Schools and Secondary School Admission Test Board. Endowment: $7 million. Total enrollment: 175. Upper school average class size: 10. Upper school faculty-student ratio: 1:7.

Upper School Student Profile Grade 9: 39 students (39 girls); Grade 10: 38 students (38 girls); Grade 11: 50 students (50 girls); Grade 12: 45 students (45 girls). 50% of students are boarding students. 70% are state residents. 12 states are represented in upper school student body. 21% are international students. International students from China, Democratic People's Republic of Korea, Germany, Japan, Sweden, and Taiwan; 6 other countries represented in student body. 4% of students are Moravian.

Faculty School total: 24. In upper school: 3 men, 21 women; 13 have advanced degrees; 3 reside on campus.

Subjects Offered Algebra, American history, art, biology, calculus, chemistry, dance, drama, economics, English, European history, fine arts, French, geometry, government/civics, Latin, mathematics, music, physical education, physics, pre-calculus, psychology, religion, science, social science, social studies, Spanish, theater, trigonometry, world history.

Graduation Requirements Arts and fine arts (art, music, dance, drama), English, foreign language, mathematics, physical education (includes health), religion (includes Bible studies and theology), science, social science, social studies (includes history).

Special Academic Programs 10 Advanced Placement exams for which test preparation is offered; honors section; term-away projects; study at local college for college credit; study abroad; ESL (6 students enrolled).

College Admission Counseling 44 students graduated in 2008; all went to college, including Furman University; North Carolina State University; The University of North Carolina at Chapel Hill; University of Illinois at Urbana–Champaign; Wake Forest University. Mean SAT critical reading: 622, mean SAT math: 623, mean SAT writing: 623.

Student Life Upper grades have specified standards of dress, student council, honor system. Discipline rests equally with students and faculty.

Tuition and Aid Day student tuition: $17,000; 7-day tuition and room/board: $33,800. Tuition installment plan (Key Tuition Payment Plan, monthly payment plans). Merit scholarship grants, need-based scholarship grants available. In 2008–09, 45% of upper-school students received aid; total upper-school merit-scholarship money awarded: $123,100. Total amount of financial aid awarded in 2008–09: $1,033,794.

Admissions Traditional secondary-level entrance grade is 9. For fall 2008, 150 students applied for upper-level admission, 79 were accepted, 57 enrolled. ACT, PSAT, SAT, SSAT or TOEFL required. Deadline for receipt of application materials: none. Application fee required: $50. Interview required.

Athletics Interscholastic: basketball, cross-country running, field hockey, golf, soccer, softball, swimming and diving, tennis, track and field, volleyball; intramural: aerobics/dance, archery, badminton, dance, fitness, flag football, floor hockey, golf, horseback riding, indoor hockey, indoor soccer, self defense. 2 PE instructors, 15 coaches, 1 athletic trainer.

Computers Computers are regularly used in all academic classes. Computer network features include on-campus library services, online commercial services, Internet access, wireless campus network. Student e-mail accounts are available to students. Students grades are available online.

Contact C. Lucia Uldrick, Director of Admissions. 336-721-2643. Fax: 336-917-5340. E-mail: academy@salem.edu. Web site: www.salemacademy.com.

See Close-Up on page 958.

SALEM BAPTIST CHRISTIAN SCHOOL

429 South Broad Street
Winston Salem, North Carolina 27101

Head of School: Ms. Martha Drake

General Information Coeducational day college-preparatory school, affiliated with Baptist Church. Grades P3–12. Founded: 1950. Setting: urban. Nearest major city is Winston-Salem. 6-acre campus. 13 buildings on campus. Approved or accredited by Association of Christian Schools International, Southern Association of Colleges and Schools, and North Carolina Department of Education. Total enrollment: 391. Upper school average class size: 17. Upper school faculty-student ratio: 1:10.

Upper School Student Profile 50% of students are Baptist.

Faculty School total: 35. In upper school: 5 men, 5 women; 3 have advanced degrees.

Subjects Offered Advanced computer applications, advanced math, Advanced Placement courses, algebra, American government, American history, American history-AP, American literature, anatomy and physiology, ancient world history, art, art history, band, Bible, biology, biology-AP, business mathematics, calculus-AP, campus ministry, chemistry, choir, Christian doctrine, church history, civics, computer applications, consumer mathematics, drama, earth science, economics, English composition, English literature, English literature-AP, European history, fine arts, geography, geometry, government, honors algebra, honors English, honors geometry, honors U.S. history, honors world history, Life of Christ, music, personal money management, psychology, theater, U.S. history, U.S. history-AP, world history, world wide web design.

Special Academic Programs Advanced Placement exam preparation; honors section; study at local college for college credit; academic accommodation for the gifted.

College Admission Counseling 26 students graduated in 2008; 24 went to college, including Cedarville University; North Carolina State University; The University of North Carolina at Charlotte; The University of North Carolina at Greensboro. Other: 1 went to work, 1 entered military service.

Student Life Upper grades have specified standards of dress, student council, honor system. Discipline rests primarily with faculty.

Admissions Traditional secondary-level entrance grade is 9. Application fee required: $125. Interview required.

Athletics Interscholastic: baseball (boys), basketball (b,g), golf (b,g), soccer (b,g), track and field (b,g), volleyball (g). 1 PE instructor, 8 coaches.

Computers Computer network features include on-campus library services, Internet access, Internet filtering or blocking technology. Students grades are available online.

Contact 336-725-6113. Fax: 336-725-8455. Web site: www.mysbcs.com.

SALESIAN HIGH SCHOOL

2851 Salesian Avenue
Richmond, California 94804

Head of School: Mr. Timothy J. Chambers

General Information Coeducational day college-preparatory, arts, and religious studies school, affiliated with Roman Catholic Church. Grades 9–12. Founded: 1960. Setting: urban. Nearest major city is San Francisco. 25-acre campus. 3 buildings on campus. Approved or accredited by Association of Christian Schools International, Western Association of Schools and Colleges, Western Catholic Education Association, and California Department of Education. Endowment: $100,000. Total enrollment: 580. Upper school average class size: 27. Upper school faculty-student ratio: 1:25.

Upper School Student Profile Grade 9: 169 students (74 boys, 95 girls); Grade 10: 135 students (68 boys, 67 girls); Grade 11: 153 students (84 boys, 69 girls); Grade 12: 130 students (64 boys, 66 girls). 67% of students are Roman Catholic.

Faculty School total: 46. In upper school: 21 men, 25 women; 30 have advanced degrees.

Subjects Offered 20th century history, advanced math, advanced studio art-AP, algebra, American history-AP, American legal systems, American literature, American literature-AP, anatomy, ancient world history, art, art history, art history-AP, biology, calculus, calculus-AP, Catholic belief and practice, Christian scripture, Christianity, classical language, computer literacy, drama, dramatic arts, economics, English, English composition, English language and composition-AP, English literature, English literature-AP, English-AP, environmental science, French, French language-AP, French-AP, geometry, government, government/civics, health and wellness, history of the Catholic Church, history-AP, honors U.S. history, mathematics, mathematics-AP, performing arts, physical education, physics, pre-algebra, pre-calculus, psychology, religion, SAT preparation, science, Spanish, Spanish language-AP, Spanish-AP, U.S. government, U.S. history, visual and performing arts, world history, world religions.

Graduation Requirements Arts and fine arts (art, music, dance, drama), English, foreign language, mathematics, physical education (includes health), religion (includes Bible studies and theology), science, social science, 20 hours of Christian service per year.

Special Academic Programs Advanced Placement exam preparation; honors section.

College Admission Counseling 146 students graduated in 2008; 144 went to college, including California State University, East Bay; Saint Mary's College of California; San Francisco State University; University of California, Berkeley; University of California, Davis; University of California, Santa Cruz. Other: 2 entered military service.

Student Life Upper grades have specified standards of dress, student council. Discipline rests primarily with faculty. Attendance at religious services is required.

Summer Programs Remediation, enrichment, sports, art/fine arts, computer instruction programs offered; session focuses on Enrichment, Remediation and Recruitment of 6, 7, 8th grade students; held on campus; accepts boys and girls; not open to students from other schools. 250 students usually enrolled. 2009 schedule: June 22 to July 24. Application deadline: June 19.

Tuition and Aid Day student tuition: $10,540. Tuition installment plan (monthly payment plans, individually arranged payment plans). Merit scholarship grants, need-based scholarship grants available. In 2008–09, 30% of upper-school students received aid; total upper-school merit-scholarship money awarded: $30,000. Total amount of financial aid awarded in 2008–09: $900,000.

Admissions Traditional secondary-level entrance grade is 9. For fall 2008, 295 students applied for upper-level admission, 180 were accepted, 169 enrolled. High School Placement Test, High School Placement Test (closed version) from Scholastic Testing Service and Standardized Diocesan Test required. Deadline for receipt of application materials: December 19. Application fee required: $75. On-campus interview required.

Athletics Interscholastic: baseball (boys), basketball (b,g), cheering (g), cross-country running (b,g), football (b), soccer (b,g), softball (g), volleyball (b,g), winter soccer (b,g); intramural: basketball (b,g), football (b), roller hockey (b), weight training (b); coed interscholastic: golf. 3 PE instructors, 25 coaches.

Computers Computers are regularly used in computer applications, history, library, yearbook classes. Computer resources include on-campus library services, Internet access, Internet filtering or blocking technology. The school has a published electronic and media policy.

Contact Mrs. Dina Trombettas, Director of Admissions. 510-234-4433 Ext. 1128. Fax: 510-236-4636. E-mail: dtrombettas@salesian.com. Web site: www.salesian.com.

SALESIAN HIGH SCHOOL

148 Main Street
New Rochelle, New York 10801

Head of School: Mr. John P. Flaherty

General Information Boys' day college-preparatory, general academic, arts, religious studies, technology, and American studies school, affiliated with Roman Catholic Church. Grades 9–12. Founded: 1920. Setting: suburban. Nearest major city is New York. 19-acre campus. 4 buildings on campus. Approved or accredited by Middle States Association of Colleges and Schools and New York Department of Education. Endowment: $500,000. Total enrollment: 500. Upper school average class size: 25. Upper school faculty-student ratio: 1:11.

Upper School Student Profile 80% of students are Roman Catholic.

Faculty School total: 37. In upper school: 28 men, 9 women; 28 have advanced degrees.

Subjects Offered Algebra, American history, American history-AP, American literature, art, arts, Bible studies, biology, British literature, business, calculus, chemistry, community service, computer math, computer science, creative writing, driver education, earth science, economics, English, English literature, environmental science, ethics, European history, fine arts, geography, geometry, government/civics, grammar, health, history, Italian, law, mathematics, music, physical education, physics, physiology, psychology, religion, science, social studies, sociology, Spanish, theology, trigonometry, world affairs, world history, world literature, writing.

Graduation Requirements Arts and fine arts (art, music, dance, drama), computer science, English, foreign language, mathematics, physical education (includes health), religion (includes Bible studies and theology), science, social studies (includes history). Community service is required.

Special Academic Programs Advanced Placement exam preparation; honors section; study at local college for college credit.

College Admission Counseling 107 students graduated in 2008; 87 went to college.

Student Life Upper grades have uniform requirement, student council, honor system. Discipline rests equally with students and faculty. Attendance at religious services is required.

Summer Programs Remediation, enrichment, sports programs offered; session focuses on Remediation; held on campus; accepts boys and girls; open to students from other schools. 150 students usually enrolled. 2009 schedule: July 5 to July 30.

Tuition and Aid Day student tuition: $5675. Tuition installment plan (FACTS Tuition Payment Plan). Tuition reduction for siblings, merit scholarship grants available. Total amount of financial aid awarded in 2008–09: $100,000.

Admissions Traditional secondary-level entrance grade is 9. School's own test required. Deadline for receipt of application materials: none. No application fee required. On-campus interview required.

Athletics Interscholastic: baseball, basketball, bowling, cross-country running, golf, indoor track, soccer, tennis, track and field, volleyball, winter (indoor) track, wrestling; intramural: backpacking, baseball, basketball, bowling, flag football, floor hockey, football, hiking/backpacking, martial arts, physical fitness, softball, track and field, volleyball, weight training. 2 PE instructors, 6 coaches.

Computers Computers are regularly used in drafting, yearbook classes. Computer network features include on-campus library services, Internet access, Internet filtering or blocking technology.

Contact Sr. Barbara Wright, Assistant Principal. 914-632-0248. Fax: 914-632-1362. E-mail: bwright@salesianhigh.com. Web site: www.salesianhigh.org.

SALESIANUM SCHOOL

1801 North Broom Street
Wilmington, Delaware 19802-3891

Head of School: Rev. William T. McCandless OSFS

General Information Boys' day college-preparatory school, affiliated with Roman Catholic Church. Grades 9–12. Founded: 1903. Setting: suburban. 22-acre campus. 1 building on campus. Approved or accredited by Middle States Association of Colleges and Schools and Delaware Department of Education. Total enrollment: 1,019. Upper school average class size: 20. Upper school faculty-student ratio: 1:12.

Upper School Student Profile Grade 9: 268 students (268 boys); Grade 10: 261 students (261 boys); Grade 11: 245 students (245 boys); Grade 12: 245 students (245 boys). 87% of students are Roman Catholic.

Faculty School total: 86. In upper school: 64 men, 22 women; 53 have advanced degrees.

Subjects Offered Algebra, American history, American history-AP, American literature, anatomy, architecture, art, art-AP, band, biology, biology-AP, business, business law, calculus, calculus-AP, career/college preparation, chemistry, chemistry-AP, chorus, community service, computer applications, computer programming, computer science, computer science-AP, consumer economics, drafting, driver education, ecology, economics, English, English literature, English-AP, ensembles, environmental science-AP, European history-AP, fine arts, foreign policy, French, French-AP, geometry, German, German-AP, government/civics, health, journalism, Latin, law, literature, marketing, mathematics, physical education, physics, physics-AP, pre-calculus, psychology, psychology-AP, religion, science, social science, social studies, Spanish, Spanish-AP, statistics, statistics-AP, television, trigonometry, U.S. government-AP, video, Western literature, world affairs, world history, world literature.

Graduation Requirements Arts and fine arts (art, music, dance, drama), college planning, computer science, driver education, electives, English, foreign language, mathematics, physical education (includes health), religion (includes Bible studies and theology), science, social science, social studies (includes history). Community service is required.

Special Academic Programs Advanced Placement exam preparation; honors section; independent study; study at local college for college credit; domestic exchange program (with Ursuline Academy, Padua Academy); academic accommodation for the gifted; remedial reading and/or remedial writing; remedial math.

College Admission Counseling 261 students graduated in 2008; 257 went to college, including Penn State University Park; Saint Joseph's University; Temple University; University of Delaware; University of South Carolina; Villanova University. Other: 3 went to work, 1 entered military service. Mean SAT critical reading: 565, mean SAT math: 573, mean SAT writing: 545, mean combined SAT: 561. 34% scored over 600 on SAT critical reading, 44% scored over 600 on SAT math, 28% scored over 600 on SAT writing, 35% scored over 1800 on combined SAT.
Student Life Upper grades have specified standards of dress, student council. Discipline rests primarily with faculty. Attendance at religious services is required.
Tuition and Aid Day student tuition: $10,475. Tuition installment plan (Insured Tuition Payment Plan, monthly payment plans, semester payment plan, annual payment plan, monthly payment plan). Merit scholarship grants, need-based scholarship grants, paying campus jobs available. In 2008–09, 16% of upper-school students received aid; total upper-school merit-scholarship money awarded: $315,000. Total amount of financial aid awarded in 2008–09: $500,000.
Admissions Traditional secondary-level entrance grade is 9. Scholastic Testing Service High School Placement Test required. Deadline for receipt of application materials: November 25. Application fee required: $55.
Athletics Interscholastic: baseball (boys), basketball (b), cross-country running (b), diving (b), football (b), golf (b), ice hockey (b), lacrosse (b), soccer (b), swimming and diving (b), tennis (b), track and field (b), volleyball (b), wrestling (b); intramural: basketball (b), bowling (b), flag football (b), Frisbee (b), lacrosse (b), roller hockey (b), skateboarding (b), tennis (b), ultimate Frisbee (b), weight lifting (b). 4 PE instructors, 58 coaches, 1 athletic trainer.
Computers Computers are regularly used in architecture, college planning, drafting, English, foreign language, mathematics, science, social studies, yearbook classes. Computer network features include on-campus library services, online commercial services, Internet access, wireless campus network, Internet filtering or blocking technology. Campus intranet and computer access in designated common areas are available to students. Students grades are available online.
Contact Mrs. Connie Eastlack, Administrative Assistant to the Admissions Office. 302-654-2495 Ext. 121. Fax: 302-654-7767. E-mail: ceastlack@salesianum.org. Web site: www.salesianum.org.

SALISBURY SCHOOL

251 Canaan Road
Salisbury, Connecticut 06068

Head of School: Mr. Chisholm S. Chandler

General Information Boys' boarding and day college-preparatory school, affiliated with Episcopal Church. Grades 9–PG. Founded: 1901. Setting: rural. Nearest major city is Hartford. Students are housed in single-sex dormitories. 668-acre campus. 35 buildings on campus. Approved or accredited by Connecticut Association of Independent Schools, National Association of Episcopal Schools, National Independent Private Schools Association, New England Association of Schools and Colleges, and Connecticut Department of Education. Member of National Association of Independent Schools. Endowment: $43.3 million. Total enrollment: 295. Upper school average class size: 12. Upper school faculty-student ratio: 1:6.
Upper School Student Profile Grade 9: 50 students (50 boys); Grade 10: 75 students (75 boys); Grade 11: 85 students (85 boys); Grade 12: 70 students (70 boys); Postgraduate: 15 students (15 boys). 93% of students are boarding students. 28% are state residents. 24 states are represented in upper school student body. 16% are international students. International students from Canada, China, Democratic People's Republic of Korea, Panama, Spain, and Thailand; 5 other countries represented in student body.
Faculty School total: 67. In upper school: 52 men, 15 women; 31 have advanced degrees; 48 reside on campus.
Subjects Offered Algebra, American Civil War, American history-AP, ancient history, art, biology, biology-AP, boat building, calculus, calculus-AP, chemistry, chemistry-AP, Chinese history, civil rights, Civil War, computer science-AP, drawing, economics, economics and history, economics-AP, electronic music, English, English language and composition-AP, entrepreneurship, environmental science, field ecology, forestry, French, French language-AP, geology, history, history of jazz, history of rock and roll, history-AP, honors English, honors geometry, honors world history, instrumental music, international relations, Latin, Mandarin, philosophy, photography, physics, physics-AP, physiology-anatomy, pottery, pre-calculus, religion, sculpture, Spanish, Spanish language-AP, studio art, U.S. history, U.S. history-AP, woodworking, world history-AP.
Graduation Requirements Arts, English, foreign language, history, mathematics, philosophy, science, Students must pass all courses in their sixth form year to graduate.
Special Academic Programs 12 Advanced Placement exams for which test preparation is offered; honors section; independent study; term-away projects.
College Admission Counseling 89 students graduated in 2008; 85 went to college, including Cornell University; Lynchburg College; Roanoke College; Rollins College; Southern Methodist University; Trinity College. Other: 2 entered a postgraduate year, 2 had other specific plans. Mean SAT critical reading: 600, mean SAT math: 540, mean SAT writing: 540, mean combined SAT: 1680.
Student Life Upper grades have specified standards of dress, student council, honor system. Discipline rests primarily with faculty. Attendance at religious services is required.
Summer Programs Remediation, enrichment, ESL programs offered; session focuses on reading, writing, mathematics, and study skills; held on campus; accepts boys and girls; open to students from other schools. 105 students usually enrolled. 2009 schedule: June 27 to August 1. Application deadline: none.
Tuition and Aid Day student tuition: $31,700; 7-day tuition and room/board: $41,700. Tuition installment plan (individually arranged payment plans, Salisbury School Tuition Payment Plan). Merit scholarship grants, need-based scholarship grants, need-based loans, Patrick Stern '66 Memorial Scholarship, Freedom Fund Scholarship available. In 2008–09, 30% of upper-school students received aid; total upper-school merit-scholarship money awarded: $90,000. Total amount of financial aid awarded in 2008–09: $2,410,000.
Admissions Traditional secondary-level entrance grade is 9. For fall 2008, 550 students applied for upper-level admission, 200 were accepted, 110 enrolled. PSAT or SAT or SSAT required. Deadline for receipt of application materials: February 1. Application fee required: $50. Interview required.
Athletics Interscholastic: alpine skiing, baseball, basketball, crew, cross-country running, football, golf, ice hockey, lacrosse, sailing, soccer, squash, tennis, wrestling; intramural: alpine skiing, basketball, bicycling, climbing, ice hockey, paddle tennis, snowboarding, soccer, tennis, volleyball, wilderness. 2 coaches.
Computers Computers are regularly used in all academic classes. Computer network features include on-campus library services, Internet access, wireless campus network, Internet filtering or blocking technology. Campus intranet, student e-mail accounts, and computer access in designated common areas are available to students. Students grades are available online. The school has a published electronic and media policy.
Contact Mr. Peter Gilbert, Director of Admissions and Financial Aid. 860-435-5732. Fax: 860-435-5750. E-mail: pgilbert@salisburyschool.org. Web site: www.salisburyschool.org.

See Close-Up on page 960.

SALPOINTE CATHOLIC HIGH SCHOOL

1545 East Copper Street
Tucson, Arizona 85719-3199

Head of School: Rev. Frederick J. Tillotson, OCARM

General Information Coeducational day college-preparatory, arts, and religious studies school, affiliated with Roman Catholic Church. Grades 9–12. Founded: 1950. Setting: urban. 40-acre campus. 10 buildings on campus. Approved or accredited by National Catholic Education Association, North Carolina Department of Exceptional Children, North Central Association of Colleges and Schools, Western Catholic Education Association, and Arizona Department of Education. Endowment: $3.5 million. Total enrollment: 1,196. Upper school average class size: 24. Upper school faculty-student ratio: 1:14.
Upper School Student Profile 75% of students are Roman Catholic.
Faculty School total: 83. In upper school: 35 men, 48 women; 43 have advanced degrees.
Subjects Offered Algebra, American history, American literature, art, art history, Bible studies, biology, business, calculus, ceramics, chemistry, computer programming, computer science, creative writing, drama, driver education, economics, English, English literature, ethics, European history, expository writing, French, geography, geometry, government/civics, grammar, history, history of ideas, home economics, journalism, logic, mathematics, music, philosophy, photography, physical education, physics, psychology, religion, science, social studies, Spanish, speech, theater, theology, trigonometry, typing, world history, world literature, writing.
Graduation Requirements English, humanities, mathematics, modern languages, religion (includes Bible studies and theology), science, social studies (includes history).
Special Academic Programs Advanced Placement exam preparation; honors section; study at local college for college credit; remedial reading and/or remedial writing; remedial math; programs in English, mathematics, general development for dyslexic students.
College Admission Counseling 265 students graduated in 2008; 259 went to college, including Arizona State University; Gonzaga University; Northern Arizona University; Pima Community College; The University of Arizona. Other: 1 entered military service, 1 entered a postgraduate year, 3 had other specific plans. Median SAT critical reading: 534, median SAT math: 529, median SAT writing: 534, median composite ACT: 23.
Student Life Upper grades have specified standards of dress, student council, honor system. Discipline rests equally with students and faculty. Attendance at religious services is required.
Summer Programs Remediation, enrichment, advancement, sports, art/fine arts, rigorous outdoor training, computer instruction programs offered; session focuses on advancement and remediation; held on campus; accepts boys and girls; not open to students from other schools. 100 students usually enrolled. 2009 schedule: June 1 to June 25. Application deadline: June 1.
Tuition and Aid Day student tuition: $6180–$7135. Tuition installment plan (monthly payment plans, individually arranged payment plans). Tuition reduction for siblings, merit scholarship grants, need-based scholarship grants, USS Education Loan Program available. In 2008–09, 23% of upper-school students received aid; total upper-school merit-scholarship money awarded: $8000. Total amount of financial aid awarded in 2008–09: $1,000,000.

Admissions Traditional secondary-level entrance grade is 9. High School Placement Test required. Deadline for receipt of application materials: none. Application fee required: $45. On-campus interview required.
Athletics Interscholastic: aerobics/dance (girls), baseball (b), basketball (b,g), cross-country running (b,g), dance team (g), diving (b,g), football (b), golf (b,g), soccer (b,g), softball (g), swimming and diving (b,g), tennis (b,g), track and field (b,g), volleyball (b,g), weight lifting (b,g), wrestling (b); intramural: bicycling (b,g), ice hockey (b); coed interscholastic: cheering; coed intramural: basketball, bowling, outdoor adventure, ultimate Frisbee, volleyball. 2 PE instructors, 75 coaches, 2 athletic trainers.
Computers Computers are regularly used in English, mathematics, science classes. Computer network features include on-campus library services, Internet access, Internet filtering or blocking technology. Students grades are available online. The school has a published electronic and media policy.
Contact Ms. Meg Gossmann, Admissions Coordinator. 520-547-4460. Fax: 520-327-8477. E-mail: mgossmann@salpointe.org. Web site: www.salpointe.org.

SALT LAKE LUTHERAN HIGH SCHOOL

4020 South 900 East
Salt Lake City, Utah 84124-1169
Head of School: Mr. Charles Gebhardt

General Information Coeducational day and distance learning college-preparatory, general academic, and religious studies school, affiliated with Lutheran Church. Grades 9–12. Distance learning grades 11–12. Founded: 1984. Setting: urban. 3-acre campus. 1 building on campus. Approved or accredited by National Lutheran School Accreditation, Northwest Association of Accredited Schools, Northwest Association of Schools and Colleges, and Utah Department of Education. Total enrollment: 82. Upper school average class size: 15. Upper school faculty-student ratio: 1:7.
Upper School Student Profile Grade 9: 18 students (8 boys, 10 girls); Grade 10: 29 students (16 boys, 13 girls); Grade 11: 22 students (13 boys, 9 girls); Grade 12: 13 students (12 boys, 1 girl). 90% are state residents. 10% are international students. 42% of students are Lutheran.
Faculty School total: 13. In upper school: 5 men, 8 women; 7 have advanced degrees.
Subjects Offered Advanced biology, advanced chemistry, advanced computer applications, advanced math, Advanced Placement courses, algebra, American history, American literature, art, band, bell choir, Bible studies, biology, calculus, chemistry, chorus, computer science, drama, English, general science, geography, geometry, government/civics, health, journalism, keyboarding, literature, mathematics, novels, physical education, physics, psychology, religion, science, social science, sociology, Spanish, speech, vocal music, word processing, world history, world literature.
Graduation Requirements Arts and fine arts (art, music, dance, drama), business skills (includes word processing), computer science, English, mathematics, physical education (includes health), religion (includes Bible studies and theology), science, social science.
Special Academic Programs Honors section; accelerated programs; independent study; academic accommodation for the gifted; remedial reading and/or remedial writing.
College Admission Counseling 13 students graduated in 2008; 12 went to college, including Boise State University; Concordia College; Salt Lake Community College; University of Utah; Utah State University; Westminster College. Other: 1 went to work. Median composite ACT: 24. 23% scored over 26 on composite ACT.
Student Life Upper grades have specified standards of dress, student council, honor system. Discipline rests equally with students and faculty. Attendance at religious services is required.
Summer Programs Sports programs offered; session focuses on fundamentals and fun; held on campus; accepts boys and girls; open to students from other schools. 50 students usually enrolled. 2009 schedule: July 1 to August 15.
Tuition and Aid Day student tuition: $7200. Tuition installment plan (monthly payment plans). Tuition reduction for siblings, merit scholarship grants, need-based scholarship grants available. In 2008–09, 30% of upper-school students received aid; total upper-school merit-scholarship money awarded: $16,500. Total amount of financial aid awarded in 2008–09: $48,000.
Admissions Traditional secondary-level entrance grade is 9. For fall 2008, 100 students applied for upper-level admission, 90 were accepted, 82 enrolled. School placement exam, SLEP for foreign students, TOEFL or SLEP or writing sample required. Deadline for receipt of application materials: none. Application fee required: $25. Interview required.
Athletics Interscholastic: baseball (boys), basketball (b,g), cross-country running (b,g), golf (b,g), soccer (b,g), track and field (b,g), volleyball (g); coed interscholastic: cross-country running, golf, track and field; coed intramural: badminton, basketball, cross-country running, fencing, golf, outdoors, physical fitness, physical training, soccer, track and field, volleyball, weight training. 2 PE instructors, 8 coaches.
Computers Computers are regularly used in history, writing, yearbook classes. Computer network features include on-campus library services, Internet access.
Contact Mr. Charles Gebhardt, Principal/Executive Director. 801-266-6676. Fax: 801-266-1953. E-mail: sllhs@hotmail.com. Web site: www.sllhs.org.

SALTUS GRAMMAR SCHOOL

PO Box HM 2224
Hamilton HMJX, Bermuda
Head of School: Mr. Nigel J.G. Kermode

General Information Coeducational day college-preparatory, general academic, arts, business, and technology school, affiliated with Church of England (Anglican). Grades K–12. Founded: 1888. Setting: small town. Nearest major city is Hamilton, Bermuda. 6 buildings on campus. Approved or accredited by Canadian Educational Standards Institute. Affiliate member of National Association of Independent Schools. Language of instruction: English. Endowment: 5 million Bermuda dollars. Total enrollment: 1,083. Upper school average class size: 18. Upper school faculty-student ratio: 1:13.
Upper School Student Profile Grade 9: 77 students (44 boys, 33 girls); Grade 10: 70 students (42 boys, 28 girls); Grade 11: 52 students (26 boys, 26 girls); Grade 12: 59 students (30 boys, 29 girls). 60% of students are members of Church of England (Anglican).
Faculty School total: 90. In upper school: 18 men, 18 women; 20 have advanced degrees.
Subjects Offered Advanced Placement courses, American history, art, art history, biology, business, chemistry, computer programming, computer science, design, drama, earth science, economics, electronics, English, English literature, environmental science, European history, French, geography, health, history, mathematics, music, photography, physical education, physics, psychology, social studies, sociology, Spanish, speech, statistics, theater, trigonometry, world history.
Special Academic Programs 17 Advanced Placement exams for which test preparation is offered.
College Admission Counseling 60 students graduated in 2008; 57 went to college, including Brock University; Dalhousie University; McGill University; Queen's University at Kingston; University of Guelph; University of Toronto. Other: 3 went to work.
Student Life Upper grades have uniform requirement, student council. Discipline rests primarily with faculty.
Tuition and Aid Day student tuition: 16,642 Bermuda dollars. Tuition installment plan (monthly payment plans). Bursaries, merit scholarship grants, need-based scholarship grants available. In 2008–09, 15% of upper-school students received aid; total upper-school merit-scholarship money awarded: 120,000 Bermuda dollars. Total amount of financial aid awarded in 2008–09: 300,000 Bermuda dollars.
Admissions Traditional secondary-level entrance grade is 9. Grade equivalent tests required. Deadline for receipt of application materials: none. Application fee required: 50 Bermuda dollars. On-campus interview required.
Athletics Interscholastic: badminton (boys, girls), basketball (b,g), cricket (b), cross-country running (b,g), field hockey (g), football (b,g), golf (b), rugby (b), running (b,g), soccer (b,g), softball (b,g), swimming and diving (b,g), track and field (b,g), volleyball (b,g); intramural: badminton (b,g), basketball (b,g), cricket (b), cross-country running (b,g), field hockey (b,g), football (b,g), golf (b), rugby (b), running (b,g), soccer (b,g), softball (b,g), swimming and diving (b,g), table tennis (b,g), track and field (b,g), volleyball (b,g); coed interscholastic: badminton, basketball, field hockey, football, running, swimming and diving, water polo; coed intramural: badminton, field hockey, running, swimming and diving, table tennis, water polo. 4 PE instructors.
Computers Computers are regularly used in all classes. Computer network features include on-campus library services, Internet access, wireless campus network, Internet filtering or blocking technology. Campus intranet and student e-mail accounts are available to students. The school has a published electronic and media policy.
Contact Mr. Malcolm J. Durrant, Deputy Headmaster. 441-292-6177. Fax: 441-295-4977. E-mail: mdurrant@saltus.bm. Web site: www.saltus.bm.

THE SAMUEL SCHECK HILLEL COMMUNITY DAY SCHOOL

19000 25th Avenue
North Miami Beach, Florida 33180
Head of School: Dr. Adam Holden

General Information Coeducational day college-preparatory, religious studies, and bilingual studies school, affiliated with Jewish faith; primarily serves students with learning disabilities and dyslexic students. Grades PK–12. Founded: 1970. Setting: suburban. 3 buildings on campus. Approved or accredited by Southern Association of Colleges and Schools and Florida Department of Education. Total enrollment: 1,053. Upper school average class size: 20.
Upper School Student Profile 100% of students are Jewish.
Faculty School total: 250.
Special Academic Programs Advanced Placement exam preparation; honors section; study at local college for college credit; academic accommodation for the gifted and the artistically talented; remedial reading and/or remedial writing; remedial math; programs in English for dyslexic students.
College Admission Counseling 77 students graduated in 2008; all went to college.
Student Life Upper grades have uniform requirement, student council, honor system. Discipline rests primarily with faculty. Attendance at religious services is required.

Tuition and Aid Day student tuition: $19,400. Tuition installment plan (Tuition Management Systems). Need-based scholarship grants available. In 2008–09, 20% of upper-school students received aid.
Admissions Traditional secondary-level entrance grade is 9. SSAT required. Deadline for receipt of application materials: February 15. Application fee required: $200. Interview required.
Athletics Interscholastic: baseball (boys), basketball (b,g), crew (b,g), cross-country running (b,g), fencing (b,g), flag football (b), football (b), soccer (b,g), softball (g), tennis (b,g), volleyball (g); coed interscholastic: crew, cross-country running, fencing, tennis.
Computers Computer network features include Internet access, Internet filtering or blocking technology. Campus intranet, student e-mail accounts, and computer access in designated common areas are available to students. Students grades are available online.
Contact Mrs. Betty Salinas, Admissions Associate. 305-931-2831 Ext. 136. Fax: 305-932-7463. E-mail: salinas@hillel-nmb.net.

SANDIA PREPARATORY SCHOOL

532 Osuna Road NE
Albuquerque, New Mexico 87113
Head of School: Richard L. Heath

General Information Coeducational day college-preparatory and arts school. Grades 6–12. Founded: 1966. Setting: suburban. 27-acre campus. 12 buildings on campus. Approved or accredited by Independent Schools Association of the Southwest and New Mexico Department of Education. Member of National Association of Independent Schools. Endowment: $4 million. Total enrollment: 664. Upper school average class size: 17. Upper school faculty-student ratio: 1:10.
Upper School Student Profile Grade 9: 101 students (51 boys, 50 girls); Grade 10: 103 students (59 boys, 44 girls); Grade 11: 79 students (42 boys, 37 girls); Grade 12: 100 students (49 boys, 51 girls).
Faculty School total: 74. In upper school: 40 men, 33 women; 47 have advanced degrees.
Subjects Offered 20th century American writers, 3-dimensional art, adolescent issues, advanced biology, advanced chemistry, advanced computer applications, advanced math, algebra, American history, American literature, American politics in film, anatomy and physiology, ancient world history, art, astronomy, band, biology, calculus, ceramics, chemistry, chorus, computer programming, computer science, creative writing, drawing, earth science, ecology, environmental systems, economics, English, English literature, environmental science, film, film history, filmmaking, fine arts, foreign language, French, French as a second language, geology, geometry, global issues, grammar, guitar, healthful living, history, jazz band, journalism, language arts, library skills, life science, mathematics, media communications, modern world history, music, newspaper, orchestra, outdoor education, painting, performing arts, personal development, philosophy, photography, physical education, physics, pottery, pre-algebra, pre-calculus, science, Shakespearean histories, social studies, Spanish, state history, statistics, technical theater, technology, theater, trigonometry, women in world history, world history, world literature, World War I, World War II, yearbook.
Graduation Requirements Arts and fine arts (art, music, dance, drama), electives, English, foreign language, mathematics, physical education (includes health), science, social studies (includes history), completion of a one-month volunteer Senior Experience in a professional, academic or volunteer area of interest during May of the Senior year.
Special Academic Programs Independent study; study at local college for college credit; study abroad; academic accommodation for the gifted.
College Admission Counseling 91 students graduated in 2008; all went to college, including Carnegie Mellon University; Duke University; Knox College; Lake Forest Academy; Trinity University; University of New Mexico. Median SAT critical reading: 660, median SAT math: 610, median composite ACT: 27. 65% scored over 600 on SAT critical reading, 59% scored over 600 on SAT math, 60% scored over 26 on composite ACT.
Student Life Upper grades have specified standards of dress, student council. Discipline rests primarily with faculty.
Summer Programs Enrichment, sports, art/fine arts, computer instruction programs offered; session focuses on summer enrichment; held on campus; accepts boys and girls; open to students from other schools. 350 students usually enrolled. 2009 schedule: June 1 to July 18. Application deadline: May 1.
Tuition and Aid Day student tuition: $14,700. Tuition installment plan (FACTS Tuition Payment Plan). Need-based scholarship grants available. In 2008–09, 20% of upper-school students received aid. Total amount of financial aid awarded in 2008–09: $403,500.
Admissions Traditional secondary-level entrance grade is 9. For fall 2008, 66 students applied for upper-level admission, 43 were accepted, 30 enrolled. Deadline for receipt of application materials: February 6. Application fee required: $25. On-campus interview required.
Athletics Interscholastic: baseball (boys), basketball (b,g), cross-country running (b,g), golf (b,g), soccer (b,g), softball (g), swimming and diving (b,g), tennis (b,g), track and field (b,g), volleyball (g); intramural: basketball (b,g), self defense (g); coed intramural: backpacking, bocce, canoeing/kayaking, climbing, Frisbee, hiking/backpacking, kayaking, lacrosse, modern dance, nordic skiing, ocean paddling, outdoor adventure, outdoor education, outdoor skills, rock climbing, yoga. 5 PE instructors, 40 coaches, 1 athletic trainer.
Computers Computers are regularly used in art, college planning, graphic arts, history, information technology, journalism, library skills, literacy, mathematics, multimedia, newspaper, photography, publications, science, study skills, technology, typing, word processing, yearbook classes. Computer network features include on-campus library services, online commercial services, Internet access, Internet filtering or blocking technology, individual student accounts, productivity software. Students grades are available online. The school has a published electronic and media policy.
Contact Ester Tomelloso, Director of Admissions. 505-338-3000. Fax: 505-338-3099. E-mail: etomelloso@sandiaprep.org. Web site: www.sandiaprep.org.

SAN DIEGO ACADEMY

2800 East 4th Street
National City, California 91950-3097
Head of School: Mr. Mervin Kesler

General Information Coeducational day college-preparatory school, affiliated with Seventh-day Adventist Church. Grades K–12. Founded: 1899. Setting: suburban. Nearest major city is San Diego. 4 buildings on campus. Approved or accredited by Western Association of Schools and Colleges and California Department of Education. Upper school average class size: 25. Upper school faculty-student ratio: 1:12.
Upper School Student Profile 80% of students are Seventh-day Adventists.
Faculty School total: 20. In upper school: 5 men, 6 women; 6 have advanced degrees.
College Admission Counseling 18 students graduated in 2008; all went to college.
Student Life Upper grades have specified standards of dress. Discipline rests primarily with faculty. Attendance at religious services is required.
Admissions Traditional secondary-level entrance grade is 9. Deadline for receipt of application materials: none. No application fee required. Interview required.
Athletics Interscholastic: basketball (boys, girls), flag football (b), volleyball (g).
Contact Mrs. Mary Mendoza, Administrative Assistant. 619-267-9550 Ext. 153. E-mail: school@sdacademy.com.

SAN DIEGO JEWISH ACADEMY

11860 Carmel Creek Road
San Diego, California 92130
Head of School: Larry Acheatel

General Information Coeducational day college-preparatory, arts, and religious studies school, affiliated with Jewish faith. Grades K–12. Founded: 1979. Setting: suburban. 56-acre campus. 3 buildings on campus. Approved or accredited by California Association of Independent Schools, European Council of International Schools, National Independent Private Schools Association, Western Association of Schools and Colleges, and California Department of Education. Languages of instruction: English and Hebrew. Endowment: $2.5 million. Total enrollment: 622. Upper school average class size: 20. Upper school faculty-student ratio: 1:18.
Upper School Student Profile Grade 9: 37 students (16 boys, 21 girls); Grade 10: 56 students (35 boys, 21 girls); Grade 11: 36 students (19 boys, 17 girls); Grade 12: 52 students (27 boys, 25 girls). 99% of students are Jewish.
Faculty School total: 35. In upper school: 12 men, 19 women; 17 have advanced degrees.
Subjects Offered 20th century history, 20th century world history, advanced chemistry, Advanced Placement courses, algebra, American government, American history, American history-AP, American literature, American literature-AP, analytic geometry, art, art history-AP, athletics, baseball, basketball, Bible, Bible studies, biology, biology-AP, British history, British literature, British literature (honors), calculus-AP, chemistry, college admission preparation, college counseling, community service, competitive science projects, composition-AP, conceptual physics, creative drama, digital photography, dramatic arts, economics, economics and history, electives, English, English composition, English language and composition-AP, English language-AP, English literature, English literature and composition-AP, English literature-AP, English/composition-AP, European history, European literature, fitness, foreign language, golf, government, government/civics, guitar, Hebrew, Hebrew scripture, history, Holocaust, Holocaust studies, honors algebra, honors English, honors geometry, honors world history, humanities, independent study, instrumental music, instruments, Jewish history, Jewish studies, Judaic studies, languages, literature and composition-AP, literature-AP, music, musical theater dance, photography, physical education, physics, physics-AP, prayer/spirituality, pre-algebra, pre-calculus, pre-college orientation, psychology, Rabbinic literature, religious education, religious studies, social science, Spanish, standard curriculum, statistics-AP, student government, theater, trigonometry, U.S. government, U.S. history, U.S. history-AP, U.S. literature, video film production, visual arts, volleyball, weight fitness, weightlifting, world history, world literature, yearbook.
Special Academic Programs Advanced Placement exam preparation; honors section; independent study.
College Admission Counseling 43 students graduated in 2008; 42 went to college, including San Diego State University; University of California, San Diego; University of California, Santa Barbara; University of Southern California. Other: 1 had other

specific plans. Mean SAT critical reading: 534, mean SAT writing: 546. 50% scored over 600 on SAT critical reading, 58% scored over 600 on SAT math.
Student Life Upper grades have specified standards of dress, student council, honor system. Discipline rests primarily with faculty. Attendance at religious services is required.
Summer Programs Sports, rigorous outdoor training programs offered; session focuses on complete athletic development; held on campus; accepts boys and girls; open to students from other schools. 40 students usually enrolled. 2009 schedule: June 17 to August 22. Application deadline: June 1.
Tuition and Aid Day student tuition: $15,060–$15,430. Tuition installment plan (FACTS Tuition Payment Plan). Tuition reduction for siblings, merit scholarship grants, need-based scholarship grants available. In 2008–09, 20% of upper-school students received aid; total upper-school merit-scholarship money awarded: $50,000. Total amount of financial aid awarded in 2008–09: $553,000.
Admissions Traditional secondary-level entrance grade is 9. For fall 2008, 35 students applied for upper-level admission, 32 were accepted, 27 enrolled. Deadline for receipt of application materials: none. Application fee required. On-campus interview required.
Athletics Interscholastic: baseball (boys), basketball (b,g), cross-country running (b,g), football (b), golf (b), soccer (b,g), softball (g), tennis (b,g), volleyball (g), winter soccer (b,g); coed interscholastic: flag football, in-line hockey, roller hockey, track and field; coed intramural: aerobics/dance, baseball, basketball, dance, fencing, fitness, flag football, martial arts, physical fitness, physical training, self defense, soccer, strength & conditioning, tennis, track and field, volleyball, weight lifting, weight training, winter soccer. 3 PE instructors, 27 coaches, 1 athletic trainer.
Computers Computers are regularly used in college planning, English, foreign language, history, humanities, mathematics, psychology, religious studies, science, video film production, writing, yearbook classes. Computer network features include on-campus library services, online commercial services, Internet access, Internet filtering or blocking technology. Student e-mail accounts are available to students. Students grades are available online.
Contact Gabriela Stratton, Admissions Director. 858-704-3716. Fax: 858-704-3850. E-mail: gstratton@sdja.com. Web site: www.sdja.com.

SAN DOMENICO SCHOOL

1500 Butterfield Road
San Anselmo, California 94960
Head of School: Dr. Mathew Heersche

General Information Girls' boarding and coeducational day college-preparatory, arts, religious studies, music, and theater arts, dance school, affiliated with Roman Catholic Church. Boarding girls grades 9–12, day boys grades PK–8, day girls grades PK–12. Founded: 1850. Setting: suburban. Nearest major city is San Francisco. Students are housed in single-sex dormitories. 515-acre campus. 10 buildings on campus. Approved or accredited by California Association of Independent Schools, Western Association of Schools and Colleges, and Western Catholic Education Association. Member of National Association of Independent Schools. Endowment: $7.1 million. Total enrollment: 529. Upper school average class size: 12. Upper school faculty-student ratio: 1:8.
Upper School Student Profile Grade 9: 24 students (24 girls); Grade 10: 33 students (33 girls); Grade 11: 41 students (41 girls); Grade 12: 37 students (37 girls). 41% of students are boarding students. 75% are state residents. 2 states are represented in upper school student body. 25% are international students. International students from China, Hong Kong, Republic of Korea, Serbia and Montenegro, Taiwan, and Thailand; 5 other countries represented in student body. 30% of students are Roman Catholic.
Faculty School total: 33. In upper school: 9 men, 24 women; 31 have advanced degrees; 7 reside on campus.
Subjects Offered Acting, algebra, American history, American literature, art, art history, biology, biology-AP, calculus, ceramics, chemistry, community service, drama, English, English literature, environmental science, ESL, ethics, European history, expository writing, fine arts, French, freshman foundations, geometry, government/civics, grammar, history, mathematics, modern world history, music, music composition, music theater, music theory, musical productions, musicianship, photography, physical education, physics, religion, science, social studies, sociology, Spanish, studio art—AP, theater, theology, trigonometry, world history, world literature.
Graduation Requirements Arts and fine arts (art, music, dance, drama), English, foreign language, mathematics, physical education (includes health), religion (includes Bible studies and theology), science, social studies (includes history). Community service is required.
Special Academic Programs Advanced Placement exam preparation; honors section; independent study; academic accommodation for the musically talented; ESL (10 students enrolled).
College Admission Counseling 40 students graduated in 2008; all went to college, including Bryn Mawr College; Carnegie Mellon University; Massachusetts Institute of Technology; Northwestern University; Stanford University; University of California, Berkeley. Mean SAT critical reading: 592, mean SAT math: 563, mean SAT writing: 645, mean combined SAT: 1765.
Student Life Upper grades have specified standards of dress, student council, honor system. Discipline rests primarily with faculty. Attendance at religious services is required.
Tuition and Aid Day student tuition: $27,000; 5-day tuition and room/board: $39,500; 7-day tuition and room/board: $39,500. Tuition installment plan (Insured Tuition Payment Plan, monthly payment plans). Need-based scholarship grants available. In 2008–09, 30% of upper-school students received aid. Total amount of financial aid awarded in 2008–09: $1,000,000.
Admissions Traditional secondary-level entrance grade is 9. For fall 2008, 59 students applied for upper-level admission, 47 were accepted, 21 enrolled. High School Placement Test, ISEE or SSAT required. Deadline for receipt of application materials: January 15. Application fee required: $100. Interview required.
Athletics Interscholastic: badminton, basketball; intramural: dance, equestrian sports, horseback riding, modern dance. 1 PE instructor, 5 coaches.
Computers Computers are regularly used in freshman foundations, mathematics, science, social studies, yearbook classes. Computer network features include on-campus library services, online commercial services, Internet access, wireless campus network, Internet filtering or blocking technology. Student e-mail accounts are available to students. The school has a published electronic and media policy.
Contact Ms. Risa Oganesoff Heersche, Director of Upper School Admissions/International Student Relations. 415-258-1905 Ext. 1124. Fax: 415-258-1906. E-mail: rheersche@sandomenico.org. Web site: www.sandomenico.org/.

SANDY SPRING FRIENDS SCHOOL

16923 Norwood Road
Sandy Spring, Maryland 20860
Head of School: Kenneth W. Smith

General Information Coeducational boarding and day college-preparatory, arts, and ESL school, affiliated with Society of Friends. Boarding grades 9–12, day grades PK–12. Founded: 1961. Setting: suburban. Nearest major city is Washington, DC. Students are housed in single-sex by floor dormitories. 140-acre campus. 15 buildings on campus. Approved or accredited by Association of Independent Maryland Schools, Association of Independent Schools of Greater Washington, Friends Council on Education, The Association of Boarding Schools, and Maryland Department of Education. Member of National Association of Independent Schools and Secondary School Admission Test Board. Endowment: $1 million. Total enrollment: 571. Upper school average class size: 15. Upper school faculty-student ratio: 1:8.
Upper School Student Profile Grade 9: 51 students (28 boys, 23 girls); Grade 10: 76 students (37 boys, 39 girls); Grade 11: 57 students (24 boys, 33 girls); Grade 12: 67 students (37 boys, 30 girls). 9% of students are boarding students. 93% are state residents. 6 states are represented in upper school student body. 7% are international students. International students from China, Ethiopia, Republic of Korea, Sierra Leone, Taiwan, and Viet Nam; 1 other country represented in student body. 13% of students are members of Society of Friends.
Faculty School total: 75. In upper school: 14 men, 16 women; 18 have advanced degrees; 12 reside on campus.
Subjects Offered Algebra, American history, American literature, art, biology, British literature-AP, calculus, calculus-AP, ceramics, chemistry, chemistry-AP, choral music, creative writing, cultural geography, dance, dance performance, desktop publishing, drama, drawing, English, English as a foreign language, English literature and composition-AP, English literature-AP, environmental science-AP, ESL, ESL, French, French language-AP, geology, geometry, grammar, history, mathematics, music, music theory-AP, Native American history, painting, photography, physical education, physics, poetry, Quakerism and ethics, Russian literature, science, Spanish, Spanish language-AP, statistics-AP, trigonometry, U.S. history-AP, weaving, Western civilization, world literature.
Graduation Requirements Art, English, foreign language, history, mathematics, physical education (includes health), religion (includes Bible studies and theology), science. Community service is required.
Special Academic Programs 9 Advanced Placement exams for which test preparation is offered; independent study; ESL (25 students enrolled).
College Admission Counseling 67 students graduated in 2008; 66 went to college, including Dartmouth College; Haverford College; The College of Wooster; The Johns Hopkins University; University of Maryland, Baltimore; University of Virginia. Other: 1 had other specific plans. Median SAT critical reading: 600, median SAT math: 630, median SAT writing: 620, median combined SAT: 1850.
Student Life Upper grades have specified standards of dress, student council. Discipline rests equally with students and faculty. Attendance at religious services is required.
Summer Programs Enrichment, ESL, sports, art/fine arts programs offered; held on campus; accepts boys and girls; open to students from other schools. 600 students usually enrolled. 2009 schedule: June 9 to August 8. Application deadline: May 1.
Tuition and Aid Day student tuition: $24,400; 5-day tuition and room/board: $34,900; 7-day tuition and room/board: $42,900. Tuition installment plan (Insured Tuition Payment Plan, Key Tuition Payment Plan). Need-based scholarship grants available. In 2008–09, 27% of upper-school students received aid. Total amount of financial aid awarded in 2008–09: $1,089,967.
Admissions Traditional secondary-level entrance grade is 9. For fall 2008, 144 students applied for upper-level admission, 92 were accepted, 53 enrolled. SSAT or TOEFL or SLEP required. Deadline for receipt of application materials: January 15. Application fee required: $75. Interview required.
Athletics Interscholastic: baseball (boys), basketball (b,g), cross-country running (b,g), lacrosse (b,g), soccer (b,g), softball (g), tennis (b,g), volleyball (g); coed

interscholastic: cooperative games, golf, modern dance, track and field; coed intramural: dance, flag football, Frisbee, table tennis, track and field, ultimate Frisbee, walking, weight lifting, yoga. 5 PE instructors, 3 coaches, 1 athletic trainer.

Computers Computers are regularly used in all academic classes. Computer network features include on-campus library services, Internet access. Student e-mail accounts and computer access in designated common areas are available to students.

Contact Kent Beck, Director of Upper School Admissions. 301-774-7455 Ext. 203. Fax: 301-924-1115. E-mail: kent.beck@ssfs.org. Web site: www.ssfs.org.

See Close-Up on page 962.

SANFORD SCHOOL

6900 Lancaster Pike
PO Box 888
Hockessin, Delaware 19707-0888

Head of School: Douglas MacKelcan

General Information Coeducational day college-preparatory school. Grades PK–12. Founded: 1930. Setting: suburban. Nearest major city is Wilmington. 100-acre campus. 6 buildings on campus. Approved or accredited by Middle States Association of Colleges and Schools and Delaware Department of Education. Member of National Association of Independent Schools and Secondary School Admission Test Board. Total enrollment: 665. Upper school average class size: 14.

Upper School Student Profile Grade 9: 60 students (28 boys, 32 girls); Grade 10: 55 students (25 boys, 30 girls); Grade 11: 62 students (24 boys, 38 girls); Grade 12: 63 students (28 boys, 35 girls).

Faculty School total: 82. In upper school: 11 men, 21 women.

Subjects Offered Algebra, American history, American history-AP, American literature, American literature-AP, anatomy and physiology, art, biology, calculus, calculus-AP, ceramics, chemistry, chemistry-AP, collage and assemblage, computer art, computer programming, computer science, computer science-AP, drawing, driver education, ecology, economics, engineering, English, English language-AP, English literature, English literature-AP, environmental science, European history, European history-AP, fine arts, French, geometry, German, health, history, journalism, Latin, mathematics, music, painting, photography, physics, physics-AP, pre-calculus, printmaking, psychology, social studies, Spanish, Spanish-AP, statistics, statistics-AP, studio art-AP, technology, trigonometry, U.S. history, U.S. history-AP, video film production, visual arts, vocal ensemble, voice, world civilizations, world history, world history-AP, world literature, writing.

Graduation Requirements Arts and fine arts (art, music, dance, drama), athletics, computer science, electives, English, foreign language, health, lab science, mathematics, music, social science.

Special Academic Programs Advanced Placement exam preparation; honors section.

College Admission Counseling 56 students graduated in 2008; all went to college, including Elizabethtown College; Hofstra University; Muhlenberg College; Susquehanna University; University of Delaware; Ursinus College.

Student Life Upper grades have specified standards of dress, student council, honor system. Discipline rests equally with students and faculty.

Summer Programs Remediation, enrichment, advancement, art/fine arts, computer instruction programs offered; session focuses on enrichment; held on campus; accepts boys and girls; open to students from other schools. 2009 schedule: June 29 to August 7. Application deadline: none.

Tuition and Aid Day student tuition: $20,500. Tuition installment plan (Key Tuition Payment Plan). Need-based scholarship grants available. In 2008–09, 33% of upper-school students received aid. Total amount of financial aid awarded in 2008–09: $933,650.

Admissions Traditional secondary-level entrance grade is 9. For fall 2008, 73 students applied for upper-level admission, 60 were accepted, 34 enrolled. ERB CTP IV, ISEE or SSAT required. Deadline for receipt of application materials: January 9. Application fee required: $40. On-campus interview required.

Athletics Interscholastic: baseball (boys), basketball (b,g), cross-country running (b,g), field hockey (g), lacrosse (b,g), soccer (b,g), swimming and diving (b,g), tennis (b,g), volleyball (g), wrestling (b); coed interscholastic: golf, indoor track; coed intramural: physical fitness. 18 coaches, 2 athletic trainers.

Computers Computers are regularly used in art, computer applications, English, foreign language, history, mathematics, newspaper, science, yearbook classes. Computer network features include on-campus library services, Internet access, Blackboard. Campus intranet and student e-mail accounts are available to students. The school has a published electronic and media policy.

Contact Ceil Baum, Admission Administrative Assistant. 302-239-5263 Ext. 265. Fax: 302-239-1912. E-mail: admission@sanfordschool.org. Web site: www.sanfordschool.org.

SAN FRANCISCO UNIVERSITY HIGH SCHOOL

3065 Jackson Street
San Francisco, California 94115

Head of School: Dr. Michael Diamonti

General Information Coeducational day college-preparatory, arts, technology, and community service school. Grades 9–12. Founded: 1973. Setting: urban. 2.5-acre campus. 4 buildings on campus. Approved or accredited by Western Association of Schools and Colleges and California Department of Education. Member of National Association of Independent Schools and Secondary School Admission Test Board. Endowment: $20.5 million. Total enrollment: 395. Upper school average class size: 14. Upper school faculty-student ratio: 1:8.

Upper School Student Profile Grade 9: 100 students (43 boys, 57 girls); Grade 10: 100 students (45 boys, 55 girls); Grade 11: 105 students (44 boys, 61 girls); Grade 12: 90 students (42 boys, 48 girls).

Faculty School total: 53. In upper school: 25 men, 28 women; 43 have advanced degrees.

Subjects Offered 20th century physics, adolescent issues, advanced chemistry, advanced math, advanced studio art-AP, African American studies, African-American literature, algebra, American government-AP, American history, American literature, American literature-AP, analysis and differential calculus, anatomy, art, art history, Asian history, astronomy, band, Bible as literature, biochemistry, biology, calculus, calculus-AP, cell biology, ceramics, chamber groups, chemistry, chemistry-AP, chorus, clayworking, college counseling, community service, computer programming, computer science, creative writing, drawing, economics, economics and history, economics-AP, electronic music, English, English language and composition-AP, English literature, English literature-AP, environmental science, environmental science-AP, European history, European history-AP, film, fine arts, fractals, French, French language-AP, French literature-AP, French-AP, genetics, geography, geometry, global issues, grammar, health education, instrumental music, introduction to theater, jazz band, jazz ensemble, Latin, Latin-AP, marine biology, mathematics, mathematics-AP, Mexican history, microbiology, music, music theory, music theory-AP, music-AP, musical productions, musical theater, orchestra, peer counseling, philosophy, photography, physical education, physics, physics-AP, physiology, pre-calculus, probability and statistics, psychology, science, senior internship, senior project, senior seminar, social studies, Spanish, Spanish language-AP, Spanish literature, Spanish literature-AP, Spanish-AP, studio art-AP, theater, trigonometry, U.S. history-AP, Western civilization, world history, world literature, writing.

Graduation Requirements American history-AP, art, English, foreign language, mathematics, physical education (includes health), science, social studies (includes history). Community service is required.

Special Academic Programs Advanced Placement exam preparation; honors section; independent study; term-away projects; domestic exchange program (with The Masters School); study abroad; academic accommodation for the gifted, the musically talented, and the artistically talented.

College Admission Counseling 101 students graduated in 2008; all went to college, including Brown University; New York University; Stanford University; Tufts University; University of California, Berkeley; University of California, Los Angeles. Mean SAT critical reading: 691, mean SAT math: 700, mean SAT writing: 702.

Student Life Upper grades have student council, honor system. Discipline rests equally with students and faculty.

Tuition and Aid Day student tuition: $29,750. Tuition installment plan (monthly payment plans). Need-based scholarship grants available. In 2008–09, 21% of upper-school students received aid. Total amount of financial aid awarded in 2008–09: $1,680,000.

Admissions Traditional secondary-level entrance grade is 9. For fall 2008, 499 students applied for upper-level admission, 200 were accepted, 107 enrolled. PSAT or SAT for applicants to grade 11 and 12, SSAT or TOEFL required. Deadline for receipt of application materials: January 15. Application fee required: $75. On-campus interview required.

Athletics Interscholastic: baseball (boys), basketball (b,g), cross-country running (b,g), field hockey (g), lacrosse (b), soccer (b,g), swimming and diving (b,g), tennis (b,g), track and field (b,g), volleyball (g); intramural: basketball (b,g), cross-country running (b,g), field hockey (g), lacrosse (b), soccer (b,g), strength & conditioning (b,g), volleyball (g); coed intramural: badminton, bowling, canoeing/kayaking, climbing, crew, dance, fencing, golf, hiking/backpacking, outdoor education, yoga. 4 PE instructors, 43 coaches.

Computers Computers are regularly used in all academic classes. Computer network features include on-campus library services, online commercial services, Internet access.

Contact Sarah Anderson, Administrative Assistant to the Office of Admission. 415-447-3100 Ext. 106. Fax: 415-447-5801. E-mail: sarah.anderson@sfuhs.org. Web site: www.sfuhs.org.

SAN FRANCISCO WALDORF HIGH SCHOOL

470 West Portal Avenue
San Francisco, California 94127

Head of School: Dave Alsop

General Information Coeducational day college-preparatory, arts, and music school. Grades 9–12. Founded: 1997. Setting: urban. 1-acre campus. 1 building on campus. Approved or accredited by Association of Waldorf Schools of North America, Western Association of Schools and Colleges, and California Department of Education. Total enrollment: 148. Upper school average class size: 12. Upper school faculty-student ratio: 1:15.

Upper School Student Profile Grade 9: 39 students (20 boys, 19 girls); Grade 10: 46 students (24 boys, 22 girls); Grade 11: 25 students (12 boys, 13 girls); Grade 12: 38 students (14 boys, 24 girls).

Faculty School total: 36. In upper school: 15 men, 21 women; 17 have advanced degrees.

Subjects Offered 20th century American writers, 20th century history, 20th century world history, acting, adolescent issues, advanced chemistry, advanced computer applications, advanced math, African American history, African studies, algebra, American Civil War, American government, American history, American literature, anatomy and physiology, ancient world history, Arabic studies, architecture, art, art history, arts and crafts, Asian studies, astronomy, athletic training, backpacking, basketball, biochemistry, biology, bookbinding, botany, calculus, cell biology, chemistry, choir, choral music, civics, composition, computer skills, computer studies, contemporary art, CPR, drama, drawing, earth science, ecology, environmental systems, economics, economics and history, English, English composition, environmental science, eurythmy, fabric arts, fencing, fiber arts, film, fine arts, fitness, genetics, geometry, German, German literature, government, grammar, Greek culture, guitar, Harlem Renaissance, health education, HTML design, human anatomy, human biology, inorganic chemistry, internship, introduction to technology, jazz band, lab science, Latin American studies, mechanics, medieval history, medieval/Renaissance history, metalworking, Middle Eastern history, modern history, modern politics, modern world history, music, music history, nature writers, optics, orchestra, organic chemistry, outdoor education, painting, performing arts, personal fitness, photography, physical education, physical fitness, physics, play production, poetry, political economics, pottery, pre-algebra, pre-calculus, printmaking, robotics, Russian literature, sculpture, senior composition, senior internship, senior project, senior seminar, set design, sewing, Spanish, sports conditioning, stagecraft, stained glass, state government, stone carving, studio art, theater arts, theater design and production, trigonometry, U.S. history, video film production, vocal ensemble, volleyball, weaving, weight training, wilderness camping, wilderness/outdoor program, world civilizations, world geography, world history, world issues, zoology.

Graduation Requirements African studies, algebra, architecture, art, art history, Asian studies, classical Greek literature, comparative religion, drama, economics and history, English, eurythmy, foreign language, geography, geometry, Greek culture, health education, independent study, internship, Islamic studies, Latin American studies, modern politics, music, music history, physics, reading/study skills, Roman civilization, science, social skills, world governments, Independent Junior Project, Junior and Senior Internships in the Work World.

Special Academic Programs Honors section; independent study; study abroad; remedial math.

College Admission Counseling 21 students graduated in 2008; 16 went to college, including Eugene Lang College The New School for Liberal Arts; Lewis & Clark College; Occidental College; San Francisco State University; Seattle University; University of California, Santa Barbara. Other: 2 went to work, 3 had other specific plans. Mean SAT critical reading: 609, mean SAT math: 560, mean SAT writing: 590. 77% scored over 600 on SAT critical reading, 62% scored over 600 on SAT math, 77% scored over 600 on SAT writing.

Student Life Upper grades have specified standards of dress, student council, honor system. Discipline rests primarily with faculty.

Tuition and Aid Day student tuition: $24,700. Tuition installment plan (SMART Tuition Payment Plan). Tuition reduction for siblings, need-based scholarship grants available. In 2008–09, 32% of upper-school students received aid.

Admissions Traditional secondary-level entrance grade is 9. Deadline for receipt of application materials: January 15. Application fee required: $75. Interview required.

Athletics Interscholastic: baseball (boys), basketball (b,g), cross-country running (b,g), sailing (b,g), soccer (b,g), volleyball (g); coed interscholastic: backpacking, badminton, climbing, dance, fencing, floor hockey, hiking/backpacking, outdoor activities, outdoor education, strength & conditioning, ultimate Frisbee. 4 PE instructors, 14 coaches.

Computers Computers are regularly used in data processing, independent study, introduction to technology, library skills, mathematics, music, photography, science, video film production, Web site design, yearbook classes. Computer network features include on-campus library services, online commercial services, Internet access, wireless campus network. The school has a published electronic and media policy.

Contact Lisa Barry, Director of Admission. 415-431-2736 Ext. 139. Fax: 415-431-1712. E-mail: lbarry@sfwaldorf.org. Web site: www.sfwaldorfhighschool.org.

SAN MARCOS BAPTIST ACADEMY

2801 Ranch Road Twelve
San Marcos, Texas 78666-9406

Head of School: Dr. John H. Garrison

General Information Coeducational boarding and day college-preparatory, general academic, arts, religious studies, technology, and learning skills school, affiliated with Baptist Church. Grades 7–12. Founded: 1907. Setting: small town. Nearest major city is Austin. Students are housed in single-sex dormitories. 220-acre campus. 8 buildings on campus. Approved or accredited by Accreditation Commission of the Texas Association of Baptist Schools, Southern Association of Colleges and Schools, Texas Education Agency, The Association of Boarding Schools, and Texas Department of Education. Member of National Association of Independent Schools. Endowment: $5 million. Total enrollment: 262. Upper school average class size: 12. Upper school faculty-student ratio: 1:5.

Upper School Student Profile Grade 9: 50 students (31 boys, 19 girls); Grade 10: 36 students (21 boys, 15 girls); Grade 11: 58 students (38 boys, 20 girls); Grade 12: 69 students (44 boys, 25 girls). 76% of students are boarding students. 58% are state residents. 12 states are represented in upper school student body. 35% are international students. International students from China, Hong Kong, Mexico, Republic of Korea, Taiwan, and Viet Nam; 6 other countries represented in student body. 20% of students are Baptist.

Faculty School total: 38. In upper school: 17 men, 19 women; 18 have advanced degrees; 4 reside on campus.

Subjects Offered Advanced math, Advanced Placement courses, algebra, American government, American history, American literature, analysis and differential calculus, analytic geometry, anatomy and physiology, ancient world history, applied arts, applied music, art, athletic training, athletics, band, baseball, Basic programming, basketball, Bible, Bible studies, biology, biology-AP, British literature, British literature (honors), British literature-AP, business applications, calculus, calculus-AP, career/college preparation, character education, cheerleading, chemistry, choir, Christian scripture, Christian testament, Christianity, civics, civics/free enterprise, clayworking, college admission preparation, college counseling, college planning, communication skills, community service, comparative religion, computer applications, computer information systems, computer keyboarding, computer programming, computer science, computers, concert band, concert choir, contemporary art, critical thinking, desktop publishing, digital photography, drama, drama performance, drama workshop, dramatic arts, drawing, driver education, earth and space science, earth science, economics, economics and history, English, English as a foreign language, English composition, English literature, English literature and composition-AP, English literature-AP, English-AP, ESL, fine arts, foreign language, French, geography, geometry, golf, government/civics, grammar, guidance, health, health education, history, history of the Americas, honors algebra, honors geometry, honors U.S. history, honors world history, HTML design, human anatomy, human biology, instrumental music, instruments, intro to computers, introduction to theater, jazz band, journalism, JROTC, JROTC or LEAD (Leadership Education and Development), language and composition, language arts, leadership, leadership education training, leadership skills, leadership training, learning strategies, library, library skills, library studies, Life of Christ, life skills, literature, literature and composition-AP, literature-AP, logic, mathematical modeling, mathematics, mathematics-AP, military science, music, music appreciation, music performance, music theory, musical productions, musical theater, musicianship, New Testament, news writing, newspaper, novels, painting, participation in sports, personal and social education, personal fitness, personal growth, photography, photojournalism, physical education, physical fitness, physical science, physics, piano, play production, pottery, prayer/spirituality, pre-calculus, psychology, public speaking, reading, reading/study skills, religion, religious education, remedial study skills, research skills, SAT preparation, SAT/ACT preparation, science, social skills, social studies, society and culture, sociology, softball, Spanish, speech, speech and debate, speech communications, sports, sports conditioning, sports performance development, sports team management, state government, state history, stock market, student government, student publications, study skills, swimming, tennis, Texas history, theater, theater arts, theater production, theology, TOEFL preparation, track and field, U.S. government, U.S. government and politics, U.S. history, U.S. literature, visual arts, vocal ensemble, vocal jazz, vocal music, voice, voice and diction, voice ensemble, volleyball, Web authoring, Web site design, weight training, weightlifting, Western civilization, world civilizations, world culture, world cultures, world geography, world history, world issues, world literature, world religions, world religions, world studies, world wide web design, World-Wide-Web publishing, yearbook.

Graduation Requirements Arts and fine arts (art, music, dance, drama), computer science, economics, electives, English, foreign language, JROTC or LEAD (Leadership Education and Development), mathematics, physical education (includes health), religion (includes Bible studies and theology), science, social studies (includes history), speech.

Special Academic Programs Advanced Placement exam preparation; honors section; accelerated programs; independent study; study at local college for college credit; academic accommodation for the gifted, the musically talented, and the artistically talented; remedial reading and/or remedial writing; remedial math; programs in general development for dyslexic students; special instructional classes for students with Section 504 learning disabilities, Attention Deficit Disorder, and dyslexia; ESL (51 students enrolled).

College Admission Counseling 58 students graduated in 2008; 57 went to college, including Purdue University; Texas A&M University; Texas State University–San Marcos; Texas Tech University; The University of Texas at San Antonio; University of Houston. Other: 1 had other specific plans. Median SAT critical reading: 440, median SAT math: 545, median SAT writing: 445, median combined SAT: 1430, median composite ACT: 19. 28% scored over 600 on SAT critical reading, 30% scored over 600 on SAT math, 13% scored over 600 on SAT writing, 17% scored over 1800 on combined SAT, 11% scored over 26 on composite ACT.

Student Life Upper grades have uniform requirement, student council, honor system. Discipline rests primarily with faculty. Attendance at religious services is required.

Tuition and Aid Day student tuition: $7770; 7-day tuition and room/board: $24,768. Guaranteed tuition plan. Tuition installment plan (Key Tuition Payment Plan, monthly payment plans, Sallie Mae). Need-based scholarship grants available. In 2008–09, 24% of upper-school students received aid. Total amount of financial aid awarded in 2008–09: $325,000.
Admissions Traditional secondary-level entrance grade is 9. For fall 2008, 130 students applied for upper-level admission, 112 were accepted, 69 enrolled. Deadline for receipt of application materials: none. Application fee required: $100. Interview required.
Athletics Interscholastic: baseball (boys), basketball (b,g), cross-country running (b,g), flag football (b), football (b), golf (b,g), JROTC drill (b,g), power lifting (b,g), softball (g), swimming and diving (b,g), tennis (b,g), track and field (b,g), volleyball (g), weight lifting (b,g); coed interscholastic: cheering, drill team, equestrian sports, marksmanship, soccer, winter soccer; coed intramural: billiards, fitness walking, Frisbee, horseback riding, soccer, table tennis, weight lifting, weight training, winter soccer. 2 PE instructors, 7 coaches, 1 athletic trainer.
Computers Computers are regularly used in computer applications, desktop publishing, information technology, keyboarding, newspaper, photojournalism, technology, typing, Web site design, yearbook classes. Computer network features include on-campus library services, Internet access, wireless campus network, Internet filtering or blocking technology. Student e-mail accounts are available to students. Students grades are available online. The school has a published electronic and media policy.
Contact Mr. Jeffrey D. Baergen, Director of Admissions. 800-428-5120. Fax: 512-753-8031. E-mail: admissions@smba.org. Web site: www.smba.org.

ANNOUNCEMENT FROM THE SCHOOL Located 45 miles northeast of San Antonio and 30 miles south of Austin, San Marcos Baptist Academy is a coeducational college-preparatory school with a boarding and day program for boys and girls in grades 7–12. Founded in 1907, San Marcos Baptist Academy is beginning a second century of fulfilling its mission: educating young men and women in a nurturing community based upon Christian values. The school is accredited by the Southern Association of Colleges and Schools and the Accreditation Committee of the Texas Association of Baptist Schools and is recognized by the Texas Education Agency. The Academy seeks to provide for the intellectual, physical, and spiritual development of each student. The highly structured residential life program offers dormitory supervision in a 1:8 staff-to-student ratio. A school-wide Leadership, Education and Development (LEAD) program coaches students in key life skills and includes a Junior Reserve Officers' Training Corps unit. Male high school students who are U.S. citizens are required to participate in JROTC during their first semester at the Academy. Additional participation is voluntary. While the primary academic emphasis is college preparation, the curriculum at SMBA is designed to meet the individual needs of each student. The Learning Skills Program, staffed by 4 full-time learning specialists, provides one-on-one assistance for students with documented mild to moderate learning differences. Highly structured study halls are also available for students at risk of failing. Opportunities exist for advanced students to take more than 50 hours of dual-credit college courses as well as AP courses. The Academy's English as a Second Language program helps assimilate international students from a number of different countries. Rounding out the academic program are fine arts opportunities in visual arts, vocal and instrumental music, and theater. With a full complement of sports and student activities offered, the Academy is a wonderful place for young people to grow and mature as they prepare for college and life afterward.

SANTA FE PREPARATORY SCHOOL

1101 Camino Cruz Blanca
Santa Fe, New Mexico 87505

Head of School: Mr. James W. Leonard

General Information Coeducational day college-preparatory, arts, and community service school. Grades 7–12. Founded: 1961. Setting: suburban. 13-acre campus. 4 buildings on campus. Approved or accredited by Independent Schools Association of the Southwest and New Mexico Department of Education. Member of National Association of Independent Schools. Endowment: $5 million. Total enrollment: 350. Upper school average class size: 12. Upper school faculty-student ratio: 1:10.
Faculty School total: 82. In upper school: 43 men, 39 women; 61 have advanced degrees.
Subjects Offered Acting, advanced chemistry, advanced computer applications, advanced math, algebra, American Civil War, American culture, American democracy, American government, American history, American history-AP, American literature, analytic geometry, art, art appreciation, art history, art history-AP, arts, athletics, basketball, biology, calculus, calculus-AP, ceramics, chemistry, chemistry-AP, chorus, clayworking, college counseling, community service, computer applications, computer graphics, computer keyboarding, computer literacy, computer programming, computer science, conceptual physics, creative writing, drama, drama performance, dramatic arts, driver education, earth science, English, English literature, European history, fine arts, French, geography, geometry, health, history, humanities, journalism, Latin, mathematics, music, photography, physical education, physics, psychology, science, social studies, Spanish, theater, trigonometry, world history, world literature, writing.
Graduation Requirements Arts and fine arts (art, music, dance, drama), computer science, English, foreign language, humanities, mathematics, music appreciation, physical education (includes health), science, social studies (includes history), Senior Seminar Program. Community service is required.
Special Academic Programs Advanced Placement exam preparation; honors section; independent study; study at local college for college credit; study abroad.
College Admission Counseling 56 students graduated in 2008; all went to college, including Bard College; Brown University; Columbia College; Lewis & Clark College; The George Washington University; University of New Mexico. Mean SAT critical reading: 617, mean SAT math: 579, mean composite ACT: 26.
Student Life Upper grades have specified standards of dress, student council. Discipline rests equally with students and faculty.
Tuition and Aid Day student tuition: $16,965. Tuition installment plan (individually arranged payment plans, Tuition Management Systems Plan). Need-based scholarship grants available. In 2008–09, 19% of upper-school students received aid. Total amount of financial aid awarded in 2008–09: $631,194.
Admissions Traditional secondary-level entrance grade is 9. For fall 2008, 60 students applied for upper-level admission, 24 enrolled. Admissions testing required. Deadline for receipt of application materials: March 1. Application fee required: $35. On-campus interview required.
Athletics Interscholastic: baseball (boys), basketball (b,g), cross-country running (b,g), diving (b,g), lacrosse (b,g), soccer (b,g), softball (g), swimming and diving (b,g), tennis (b,g), track and field (b,g), volleyball (g); intramural: basketball (b,g), cross-country running (b,g), football (b,g), soccer (b,g), tennis (b,g), track and field (b,g), volleyball (g); coed interscholastic: aerobics/dance, dance team; coed intramural: basketball, bowling, skiing (downhill), swimming and diving. 1 PE instructor, 16 coaches, 1 athletic trainer.
Computers Computers are regularly used in current events, English, French, freshman foundations, geography, graphic arts, history, humanities, journalism, library, literary magazine, mathematics, newspaper, photography, photojournalism, science, social science, writing, yearbook classes. Computer network features include on-campus library services, Internet access.
Contact Marta M. Miskolczy, Director of Admissions. 505-982-1829 Ext. 1212. Fax: 505-982-2897. E-mail: admissions@sfprep.org. Web site: www.santafeprep.org.

SANTA MARGARITA CATHOLIC HIGH SCHOOL

22062 Antonio Parkway
Rancho Santa Margarita, California 92688

Head of School: Mr. Ray Dunne

General Information Coeducational day college-preparatory, arts, religious studies, technology, International Baccalaureate, and Auxiliary Studies Program school, affiliated with Roman Catholic Church. Grades 9–12. Founded: 1987. Setting: suburban. Nearest major city is Mission Viejo. 42-acre campus. 15 buildings on campus. Approved or accredited by Western Association of Schools and Colleges and California Department of Education. Total enrollment: 1,650. Upper school average class size: 25. Upper school faculty-student ratio: 1:16.
Upper School Student Profile Grade 9: 486 students (239 boys, 247 girls); Grade 10: 440 students (211 boys, 229 girls); Grade 11: 448 students (236 boys, 212 girls); Grade 12: 436 students (227 boys, 209 girls). 60% of students are Roman Catholic.
Faculty School total: 114. In upper school: 59 men, 55 women; 59 have advanced degrees.
Subjects Offered 20th century world history, advanced chemistry, advanced math, Advanced Placement courses, aerobics, algebra, American Civil War, American government, American government-AP, American history, American history-AP, American legal systems, anatomy, anatomy and physiology, Ancient Greek, ancient history, ancient world history, art, art and culture, art appreciation, art education, art history, art history-AP, art-AP, ASB Leadership, athletic training, athletics, ballet, ballet technique, band, baseball, Basic programming, basketball, bell choir, Bible studies, biology, biology-AP, British history, British literature, British literature (honors), British literature-AP, broadcast journalism, broadcasting, business, business applications, business communications, business education, business law, business mathematics, business skills, business studies, business technology, calculus, calculus-AP, campus ministry, career/college preparation, Catholic belief and practice, cell biology, ceramics, chamber groups, cheerleading, chemistry, chemistry-AP, Chinese, Chinese history, Chinese literature, Chinese studies, choir, choral music, choreography, chorus, Christian and Hebrew scripture, Christian doctrine, Christian education, Christian ethics, Christian scripture, Christian studies, Christian testament, Christianity, church history, cinematography, civics, civil war history, classical Greek literature, classical language, classical music, classical studies, community service, comparative government and politics, comparative government and politics-AP, comparative political systems-AP, comparative politics, comparative religion, computer education, computer graphics, computer information systems, computer literacy, computer math, computer programming, computer science, computer science-AP, computers, concert band, concert bell choir, concert choir, CPR, creative arts, creative dance, creative drama, creative thinking, creative writing, cultural geography, current events, current history, dance, dance performance, design, developmental language skills, developmental math, digital photography, drama, drama performance, drama

workshop, dramatic arts, drawing, drawing and design, earth science, East Asian history, East European studies, Eastern religion and philosophy, Eastern world civilizations, economics, economics and history, economics-AP, electives, English, English composition, English literature, English literature and composition-AP, English literature-AP, English-AP, English/composition-AP, environmental geography, environmental science, environmental science-AP, ethics, ethics and responsibility, European civilization, European history, European history-AP, European literature, film, film and literature, film appreciation, film history, film studies, finance, fine arts, forensic science, forensics, French, French language-AP, French literature-AP, French studies, French-AP, geography, geology, geometry, geometry with art applications, German-AP, government and politics-AP, government-AP, government/civics, government/civics-AP, Greek, Greek culture, guitar, handbells, health, health and safety, health and wellness, health education, health science, history, history of dance, history of religion, history of the Americas, history of the Catholic Church, history-AP, Holocaust, Holocaust and other genocides, Holocaust legacy, Holocaust seminar, Holocaust studies, honors algebra, honors English, honors geometry, honors U.S. history, honors world history, human biology, instrumental music, International Baccalaureate courses, international relations, jazz, jazz band, jazz dance, jazz ensemble, journalism, language and composition, language arts, language-AP, languages, Latin, Latin-AP, law, literacy, literature and composition-AP, literature-AP, macro/microeconomics-AP, macroeconomics-AP, marching band, marine biology, mathematics, mathematics-AP, microeconomics-AP, model United Nations, music, music appreciation, music history, music performance, music theater, musical productions, news writing, newspaper, nutrition, orchestra, painting, personal fitness, philosophy, photography, photojournalism, physical education, physical science, physics, physics-AP, physiology, play production, playwriting and directing, poetry, political science, politics, pre-algebra, pre-calculus, probability, probability and statistics, psychology, psychology-AP, public speaking, reading/study skills, religion, religion and culture, religions, religious education, religious studies, remedial/makeup course work, SAT preparation, SAT/ACT preparation, science, social science, social studies, sociology, softball, Spanish, Spanish language-AP, Spanish literature, Spanish literature-AP, Spanish-AP, speech, speech and debate, speech and oral interpretations, speech communications, sports, sports conditioning, statistics, statistics and probability, statistics-AP, student government, student publications, studio art, studio art—AP, swimming, tap dance, television, The 20th Century, the Presidency, theater production, theology and the arts, theory of knowledge, trigonometry, U.S. constitutional history, U.S. government, U.S. government and politics, U.S. government and politics-AP, U.S. government-AP, U.S. history, U.S. history-AP, United States government-AP, video, Vietnam, Vietnam history, Vietnam War, vocal ensemble, vocal jazz, vocal music, volleyball, water color painting, water polo, weight training, weightlifting, Western civilization-AP, wind ensemble, wind instruments, world governments, world history, world history-AP, world issues, world literature, world religions, World War I, World War II, wrestling, writing, writing skills, yearbook.

Graduation Requirements Arts and fine arts (art, music, dance, drama), business skills (includes word processing), computer science, English, foreign language, mathematics, physical education (includes health), religion (includes Bible studies and theology), science, social science, social studies (includes history). Community service is required.

Special Academic Programs International Baccalaureate program; Advanced Placement exam preparation; honors section; independent study; study at local college for college credit; academic accommodation for the gifted, the musically talented, and the artistically talented; remedial reading and/or remedial writing; remedial math; programs in English, mathematics, general development for dyslexic students; special instructional classes for deaf students, blind students, students with learning disabilities, attention deficit disorder, and dyslexia.

College Admission Counseling 416 students graduated in 2008; all went to college, including Loyola Marymount University; Santa Clara University; University of Notre Dame; University of San Diego; University of San Francisco; University of Southern California. Mean SAT critical reading: 564, mean SAT math: 573, mean SAT writing: 579, mean combined SAT: 1719, mean composite ACT: 25.

Student Life Upper grades have uniform requirement, student council, honor system. Discipline rests primarily with faculty. Attendance at religious services is required.

Summer Programs Remediation, enrichment, advancement, sports, art/fine arts, computer instruction programs offered; session focuses on enrichment; held on campus; accepts boys and girls; open to students from other schools. 300 students usually enrolled. 2009 schedule: June 22 to July 31. Application deadline: none.

Tuition and Aid Day student tuition: $10,000. Tuition installment plan (monthly payment plans). Tuition reduction for siblings, need-based scholarship grants available. In 2008–09, 12% of upper-school students received aid. Total amount of financial aid awarded in 2008–09: $560,000.

Admissions Traditional secondary-level entrance grade is 9. For fall 2008, 556 students applied for upper-level admission, 550 were accepted, 404 enrolled. High School Placement Test required. Deadline for receipt of application materials: none. Application fee required: $50.

Athletics Interscholastic: aerobics/dance (girls), aquatics (b,g), ballet (g), baseball (b), basketball (b,g), cheering (g), cross-country running (b,g), dance (g), dance squad (g), dance team (g), diving (b,g), dressage (b,g), drill team (g), equestrian sports (b,g), football (b), golf (b,g), hockey (b), ice hockey (b), in-line hockey (b), lacrosse (b,g), modern dance (g), roller hockey (b), running (b,g), soccer (b,g), softball (g), surfing (b,g), swimming and diving (b,g), tennis (b,g), track and field (b,g), volleyball (b,g), water polo (b,g), wrestling (b); intramural: aerobics (g), aerobics/Nautilus (g), ballet (g), fitness (b,g), flag football (b), jogging (b,g), physical fitness (b,g), physical training (b,g), power lifting (b), running (b,g), self defense (b,g), touch football (b), walking (g), weight lifting (b,g), weight training (b,g), yoga (g); coed intramural: bowling, Frisbee, Special Olympics, table tennis, ultimate Frisbee. 4 PE instructors, 40 coaches, 2 athletic trainers.

Computers Computers are regularly used in all academic classes. Computer network features include on-campus library services, online commercial services, Internet access, wireless campus network, Internet filtering or blocking technology, ISIS Program, Aeries. Campus intranet is available to students. Students grades are available online. The school has a published electronic and media policy.

Contact Mr. Ron Blanc, Admissions Director. 949-766-6076. Fax: 949-766-6005. E-mail: admissions@smhs.org. Web site: www.smhs.org.

SANTIAM CHRISTIAN SCHOOL

7220 Northeast Arnold Avenue
Corvallis, Oregon 97330-9498

Head of School: Mr. Stan Baker

General Information Coeducational day college-preparatory, arts, business, vocational, religious studies, bilingual studies, and technology school, affiliated with Christian faith. Grades PS–12. Founded: 1978. Setting: small town. Nearest major city is Salem. 18-acre campus. 14 buildings on campus. Approved or accredited by Association of Christian Schools International, Northwest Association of Schools and Colleges, and Oregon Department of Education. Total enrollment: 831. Upper school average class size: 22. Upper school faculty-student ratio: 1:17.

Upper School Student Profile Grade 9: 70 students (42 boys, 28 girls); Grade 10: 80 students (39 boys, 41 girls); Grade 11: 86 students (46 boys, 40 girls); Grade 12: 70 students (34 boys, 36 girls). 95% of students are Christian faith.

Faculty School total: 41. In upper school: 17 men, 17 women; 12 have advanced degrees.

Subjects Offered 20th century American writers, 20th century physics, 20th century world history, 3-dimensional art, 3-dimensional design, acting, advanced computer applications, advanced math, advanced studio art-AP, algebra, American biography, American Civil War, American culture, American democracy, American foreign policy, American literature, anatomy and physiology, ancient world history, animal science, art, art appreciation, band, Bible studies, biology, body human, British history, business applications, calculus, career and personal planning, career education, carpentry, character education, chemistry, child development, choir, choral music, Christian doctrine, Christian education, Christian ethics, Christian testament, Christianity, church history, civics, Civil War, college counseling, college writing, comparative government and politics, computer applications, computer education, computer graphics, computer keyboarding, computer programming, concert band, concert choir, drama, drama performance, drawing, early childhood, earth science, economics, English, English composition, English literature, ethics, family living, fine arts, first aid, fitness, food and nutrition, foods, French, general math, general science, geography, geometry, global studies, government, grammar, graphic arts, guidance, health and wellness, health education, human anatomy, instrumental music, Internet, intro to computers, introduction to literature, journalism, language arts, leadership, library, Life of Christ, literature, marine biology, marketing, mathematics, moral and social development, music, music appreciation, music composition, music performance, occupational education, oral expression, physics, play production, playwriting and directing, poetry, pre-algebra, pre-calculus, public speaking, science, sewing, Spanish, speech, stage design, studio art-AP, theater, theater arts, theater production, U.S. government, U.S. history, vocal music, Western civilization, woodworking, world history, world literature, writing.

Graduation Requirements Arts and fine arts (art, music, dance, drama), computer science, English, mathematics, physical education (includes health), religion (includes Bible studies and theology), science, social science, social studies (includes history).

Special Academic Programs 3 Advanced Placement exams for which test preparation is offered; honors section; independent study; study at local college for college credit.

College Admission Counseling 82 students graduated in 2008; 81 went to college, including Corban College; George Fox University; Linn-Benton Community College; Oregon State University; Western Oregon University. Other: 1 went to work. Mean SAT critical reading: 570, mean SAT math: 549, mean SAT writing: 552. 34.5% scored over 600 on SAT critical reading, 17.2% scored over 600 on SAT math, 20.7% scored over 600 on SAT writing, 24.1% scored over 1800 on combined SAT.

Student Life Upper grades have specified standards of dress, student council. Discipline rests primarily with faculty. Attendance at religious services is required.

Tuition and Aid Day student tuition: $5140. Tuition installment plan (monthly payment plans, individually arranged payment plans, prepayment discount plan). Tuition reduction for siblings, need-based scholarship grants, paying campus jobs available. Total amount of financial aid awarded in 2008–09: $130,000.

Admissions Traditional secondary-level entrance grade is 9. For fall 2008, 90 students applied for upper-level admission, 75 were accepted, 70 enrolled. Deadline for receipt of application materials: none. Application fee required: $35. Interview required.

Athletics Interscholastic: baseball (boys), basketball (b,g), cheering (g), cross-country running (b,g), equestrian sports (g), football (b), golf (b,g), soccer (b,g), softball (g), track and field (b,g), volleyball (g), wrestling (b). 4 PE instructors, 3 coaches.
Computers Computers are regularly used in career education, computer applications, keyboarding, yearbook classes. Computer network features include on-campus library services, Internet access, Internet filtering or blocking technology. Student e-mail accounts are available to students. Students grades are available online.
Contact Mrs. Sami Beam, Registrar. 541-745-5524 Ext. 203. Fax: 541-745-6338. E-mail: beams@santiam.org.

SAVANNAH CHRISTIAN PREPARATORY SCHOOL

PO Box 2848
Savannah, Georgia 31402-2848
Head of School: Mr. Roger L. Yancey

General Information Coeducational day college-preparatory school, affiliated with Christian faith. Grades PK–12. Founded: 1951. Setting: suburban. 236-acre campus. 6 buildings on campus. Approved or accredited by Georgia Independent School Association, Southern Association of Colleges and Schools, and Georgia Department of Education. Endowment: $1.4 million. Total enrollment: 1,492. Upper school average class size: 23. Upper school faculty-student ratio: 1:14.
Upper School Student Profile Grade 9: 118 students (61 boys, 57 girls); Grade 10: 126 students (73 boys, 53 girls); Grade 11: 109 students (44 boys, 65 girls); Grade 12: 110 students (58 boys, 52 girls). 95% of students are Christian faith.
Faculty School total: 125. In upper school: 11 men, 24 women; 26 have advanced degrees.
Subjects Offered 20th century history, accounting, algebra, American Civil War, American history, American history-AP, art, astronomy, band, Bible, biology, botany, business law, calculus-AP, chemistry, chemistry-AP, chorus, Christian ethics, computer applications, computer-aided design, creative writing, design, drama, driver education, earth science, ecology, economics, English, English-AP, European history-AP, French, geometry, government/civics, graphic arts, health, marine biology, mathematics, mechanical drawing, music appreciation, physical education, physics, probability and statistics, psychology, science, social studies, sociology, Spanish, speech, technical theater, theater, trigonometry, typing, world history, yearbook.
Graduation Requirements Accounting, algebra, biology, chemistry, economics, English, foreign language, geometry, mathematics, physical education (includes health), religion (includes Bible studies and theology), science, social studies (includes history).
Special Academic Programs Advanced Placement exam preparation; honors section; study at local college for college credit.
College Admission Counseling 102 students graduated in 2008; all went to college, including Armstrong Atlantic State University; Auburn University; Georgia Southern University; Savannah College of Art and Design; University of Georgia; Valdosta State University. Mean SAT critical reading: 545, mean SAT math: 550, mean SAT writing: 506, mean combined SAT: 1638, mean composite ACT: 24.
Student Life Upper grades have uniform requirement, student council, honor system. Discipline rests primarily with faculty.
Tuition and Aid Day student tuition: $6760. Tuition installment plan (monthly payment plans). Tuition reduction for siblings, merit scholarship grants, need-based scholarship grants available. In 2008–09, 15% of upper-school students received aid; total upper-school merit-scholarship money awarded: $104,000. Total amount of financial aid awarded in 2008–09: $134,000.
Admissions Traditional secondary-level entrance grade is 9. For fall 2008, 51 students applied for upper-level admission, 38 were accepted, 30 enrolled. Stanford Achievement Test and writing sample required. Deadline for receipt of application materials: January 31. Application fee required: $175. On-campus interview required.
Athletics Interscholastic: baseball (boys), basketball (b,g), cheering (g), cross-country running (b,g), dance team (g), football (b), golf (b,g), soccer (b,g), softball (g), tennis (b,g), track and field (b,g), volleyball (g); coed intramural: sailing. 3 PE instructors, 3 coaches, 1 athletic trainer.
Computers Computers are regularly used in accounting, business applications, computer applications, English, graphic arts, history, science, word processing, yearbook classes. Computer network features include on-campus library services, Internet access, wireless campus network, Internet filtering or blocking technology. Computer access in designated common areas is available to students. Students grades are available online. The school has a published electronic and media policy.
Contact Mrs. Debbie Fairbanks, Director of Admissions and Alumni Relations. 912-234-1653 Ext. 106. Fax: 912-234-0491. E-mail: dfairbanks@savcps.com. Web site: www.savcps.com.

THE SAVANNAH COUNTRY DAY SCHOOL

824 Stillwood Drive
Savannah, Georgia 31419-2643
Head of School: Mr. Thomas C. Bonnell

General Information Coeducational day college-preparatory, arts, and technology school. Grades PK–12. Founded: 1955. Setting: suburban. 65-acre campus. 11 buildings on campus. Approved or accredited by Georgia Independent School Association, Southern Association of Colleges and Schools, and Southern Association of Independent Schools. Member of National Association of Independent Schools. Endowment: $13.8 million. Total enrollment: 1,002. Upper school average class size: 16. Upper school faculty-student ratio: 1:10.
Upper School Student Profile Grade 9: 67 students (27 boys, 40 girls); Grade 10: 74 students (42 boys, 32 girls); Grade 11: 71 students (33 boys, 38 girls); Grade 12: 79 students (34 boys, 45 girls).
Faculty School total: 94. In upper school: 15 men, 19 women; 24 have advanced degrees.
Subjects Offered Advanced Placement courses, algebra, American history, American literature, analysis and differential calculus, anatomy and physiology, art, art history, biology, biology-AP, British literature-AP, calculus, calculus-AP, ceramics, chemistry, chemistry-AP, chorus, composition, computer education, computer science, dance, drama, drama performance, economics and history, English, English literature, English-AP, environmental science, environmental science-AP, European history, European history-AP, fine arts, French, geometry, government-AP, government/civics, guidance, health, honors algebra, honors English, honors geometry, honors U.S. history, honors world history, independent study, instrumental music, intro to computers, jazz band, language-AP, Latin, Latin-AP, music, photography, physical education, physics, physics-AP, pre-calculus, public speaking, Spanish, Spanish language-AP, statistics, studio art—AP, theater, U.S. history-AP, world history, world history-AP, yearbook.
Graduation Requirements Arts and fine arts (art, music, dance, drama), English, foreign language, health education, history, mathematics, physical education (includes health), science, speech.
Special Academic Programs Advanced Placement exam preparation; honors section; independent study; study at local college for college credit.
College Admission Counseling 68 students graduated in 2008; all went to college, including Auburn University; College of Charleston; Sewanee: The University of the South; University of Georgia; University of Virginia; Wofford College. Mean SAT critical reading: 680, mean SAT math: 690, mean SAT writing: 690, mean combined SAT: 2060.
Student Life Upper grades have specified standards of dress, student council, honor system. Discipline rests equally with students and faculty.
Summer Programs Remediation, enrichment, advancement, sports, art/fine arts, computer instruction programs offered; session focuses on recreation and enrichment; held both on and off campus; held at Coastal Ecology at the beach; accepts boys and girls; open to students from other schools. 1,400 students usually enrolled. 2009 schedule: June 5 to August 14. Application deadline: May 1.
Tuition and Aid Day student tuition: $15,690. Tuition installment plan (Insured Tuition Payment Plan, FACTS Tuition Payment Plan, monthly payment plans, individually arranged payment plans). Merit scholarship grants, need-based scholarship grants available. In 2008–09, 18% of upper-school students received aid; total upper-school merit-scholarship money awarded: $2000. Total amount of financial aid awarded in 2008–09: $389,900.
Admissions Traditional secondary-level entrance grade is 9. For fall 2008, 21 students applied for upper-level admission, 14 were accepted, 12 enrolled. ERB Reading and Math, Math Placement Exam, Otis-Lennon Mental Ability Test or writing sample required. Deadline for receipt of application materials: none. Application fee required: $175. Interview required.
Athletics Interscholastic: baseball (boys), basketball (b,g), cheering (g), crew (b,g), cross-country running (b,g), football (b), golf (b,g), soccer (b,g), softball (g), tennis (b,g), track and field (b,g), volleyball (g), wrestling (b); intramural: basketball (b,g), bocce (b,g), cheering (g), climbing (b,g), cross-country running (b,g), dance (b,g), in-line hockey (b), outdoor adventure (b,g), outdoor education (b,g), physical training (b,g), power lifting (b,g), project adventure (b,g), ropes courses (b,g), strength & conditioning (b,g), track and field (b,g), volleyball (g), water polo (g), weight lifting (b,g), weight training (b,g). 1 coach, 1 athletic trainer.
Computers Computers are regularly used in college planning, creative writing, English, foreign language, history, library skills, mathematics, publications, publishing, research skills, SAT preparation, science, yearbook classes. Computer network features include on-campus library services, online commercial services, Internet access, wireless campus network, Internet filtering or blocking technology. Campus intranet and student e-mail accounts are available to students. The school has a published electronic and media policy.
Contact Mrs. Josceline Reardon, Assistant Director of Admissions and Financial Aid Officer. 912-961-8807. Fax: 912-920-7800. E-mail: reardon@savcds.org. Web site: www.savcds.org.

ANNOUNCEMENT FROM THE SCHOOL Savannah Country Day School traces its origins back to the 1905 founding of the Pape School, long recognized for its academic excellence and college-preparatory curriculum. Led by a group of visionary parents who saw the continued need for a national caliber college-preparatory school in Savannah, the founders of Savannah Country Day acquired the assets of the Pape School, including its faculty, curriculum, the majority of its student body, and its facilities east of Forsyth Park. Drawing on the principles of the Judeo-Christian faiths, Savannah Country Day School seeks to prepare students of academic and personal promise to meet the challenges of college and of life with confidence, imagination, and integrity. In partnership with supportive families, the School strives to cultivate in each student the desire and the discipline to grow in wisdom, to lead lives of personal honor, to appreciate beauty, to pursue physical well-being, and to serve others with a generous and compassionate spirit. In fulfilling this mission, the School subscribes to the following core beliefs: that the ultimate goal of education is to cultivate in each student a lifelong passion for learning; each student's academic potential is most fully realized through a challenging and varied curriculum that has appropriate support; students learn best in a respectful, supportive community of trust where each student's learning needs and abilities are understood and accommodated as fully as possible; intellectual growth requires not only the acquisition of knowledge but also its application in analytical, creative, and expressive ways that make learning meaningful to the student; physical and emotional health is critical to the development of each student's personal potential; each student's life is enriched in a diverse community where differences among people are affirmed and celebrated; the School shares with families the responsibility for fostering in each student strength of character, a sense of personal responsibility, and an attitude of faith, reverence, and tolerance; and the development of leadership in each student should include instilling a commitment to use one's knowledge, skills, and resources in service to others.

SAYRE SCHOOL

194 North Limestone Street
Lexington, Kentucky 40507

Head of School: Mr. Clayton G. Chambliss

General Information Coeducational day college-preparatory, arts, and technology school. Grades PK–12. Founded: 1854. Setting: urban. 60-acre campus. 10 buildings on campus. Approved or accredited by Independent Schools Association of the Central States and Kentucky Department of Education. Member of National Association of Independent Schools and Secondary School Admission Test Board. Endowment: $14 million. Total enrollment: 628. Upper school average class size: 15. Upper school faculty-student ratio: 1:9.

Upper School Student Profile Grade 9: 44 students (17 boys, 27 girls); Grade 10: 71 students (29 boys, 42 girls); Grade 11: 59 students (34 boys, 25 girls); Grade 12: 56 students (30 boys, 26 girls).

Faculty School total: 32. In upper school: 12 men, 16 women; 22 have advanced degrees.

Subjects Offered Algebra, American history, American literature, art, art history, biology, calculus, chemistry, community service, computer science, creative writing, drama, earth science, English, English literature, fine arts, French, geometry, government/civics, health, history, journalism, mathematics, music, photography, physical education, physics, public speaking, science, social studies, Spanish, speech, statistics, theater, U.S. constitutional history, world history, writing.

Graduation Requirements Arts and fine arts (art, music, dance, drama), computer science, creative writing, English, foreign language, mathematics, physical education (includes health), public speaking, science, social studies (includes history), senior project internship. Community service is required.

Special Academic Programs 13 Advanced Placement exams for which test preparation is offered; honors section; independent study; term-away projects; study at local college for college credit; academic accommodation for the gifted and the artistically talented.

College Admission Counseling 53 students graduated in 2008; all went to college, including Centre College; Sewanee: The University of the South; The George Washington University; University of Georgia; University of Kentucky; Vanderbilt University. Median SAT critical reading: 570, median SAT math: 580, median SAT writing: 580, median combined SAT: 1760, median composite ACT: 25. 37% scored over 600 on SAT critical reading, 41% scored over 600 on SAT math, 43% scored over 600 on SAT writing, 40% scored over 1800 on combined SAT, 38% scored over 26 on composite ACT.

Student Life Upper grades have specified standards of dress, student council, honor system. Discipline rests equally with students and faculty.

Tuition and Aid Day student tuition: $16,000–$18,000. Tuition installment plan (Insured Tuition Payment Plan, monthly payment plans, individually arranged payment plans). Merit scholarship grants, need-based scholarship grants available. In 2008–09, 27% of upper-school students received aid; total upper-school merit-scholarship money awarded: $9000. Total amount of financial aid awarded in 2008–09: $360,550.

Admissions Traditional secondary-level entrance grade is 9. For fall 2008, 30 students applied for upper-level admission, 24 were accepted, 15 enrolled. Admissions testing, Math Placement Exam, PSAT and SAT for applicants to grade 11 and 12, school's own exam or writing sample required. Deadline for receipt of application materials: none. Application fee required: $75. On-campus interview required.

Athletics Interscholastic: baseball (boys), basketball (b,g), cheering (g), cross-country running (b,g), diving (b,g), golf (b,g), lacrosse (b), physical fitness (b), physical training (b,g), soccer (b,g), softball (g), swimming and diving (b,g), tennis (b,g). 5 PE instructors, 4 coaches, 1 athletic trainer.

Computers Computers are regularly used in English, foreign language, mathematics, music, science classes. Computer network features include on-campus library services, online commercial services, Internet access, wireless campus network, Internet filtering or blocking technology. Student e-mail accounts are available to students. The school has a published electronic and media policy.

Contact Mrs. Barbara N. Parsons, Assistant Head of School and Director of Admission. 859-254-1361 Ext. 202. Fax: 859-254-5627. E-mail: bparsons@sayreschool.org. Web site: www.sayreschool.org.

SCARBOROUGH CHRISTIAN SCHOOL

95 Jonesville Crescent
North York, Ontario M4A 1H2, Canada

Head of School: Mr. Glenn Mallory

General Information Coeducational day college-preparatory and business school, affiliated with Christian faith, Advent Christian Church. Grades JK–12. Founded: 1975. Setting: urban. Nearest major city is Toronto, Canada. 1-acre campus. 1 building on campus. Approved or accredited by Association of Christian Schools International and Ontario Department of Education. Language of instruction: English. Total enrollment: 120. Upper school average class size: 15. Upper school faculty-student ratio: 1:7.

Upper School Student Profile Grade 9: 7 students (4 boys, 3 girls); Grade 10: 14 students (8 boys, 6 girls); Grade 11: 7 students (4 boys, 3 girls); Grade 12: 17 students (13 boys, 4 girls). 50% of students are Christian, Advent Christian Church.

Faculty School total: 15. In upper school: 3 men, 4 women.

Subjects Offered Biology, business studies, calculus, Canadian geography, Canadian history, career education, chemistry, civics, English, ESL, French as a second language, math analysis, math applications, physics, science, visual arts.

Graduation Requirements Ontario Ministry of Education requirements.

Special Academic Programs Independent study; ESL (8 students enrolled).

Student Life Upper grades have uniform requirement, student council. Discipline rests primarily with faculty. Attendance at religious services is required.

Tuition and Aid Day student tuition: CAN$6000. Tuition installment plan (individually arranged payment plans). Tuition reduction for siblings available. In 2008–09, 20% of upper-school students received aid.

Admissions Traditional secondary-level entrance grade is 12. For fall 2008, 16 students applied for upper-level admission, 16 were accepted, 11 enrolled. SLEP required. Deadline for receipt of application materials: none. No application fee required.

Athletics Intramural: soccer (boys); coed intramural: badminton, baseball, basketball, physical fitness.

Computers Computers are regularly used in English, mathematics, technology classes. Computer network features include Internet access.

Contact Admissions. 416-750-7515. Fax: 416-750-7720. E-mail: scs@titan.tcn.net. Web site: www.scarboroughchristianschool.com.

SCATTERGOOD FRIENDS SCHOOL

1951 Delta Avenue
West Branch, Iowa 52358-8507

Head of School: Ms. Jan Luchini

General Information Coeducational boarding and day college-preparatory and arts school, affiliated with Society of Friends. Boarding grades 9–PG, day grades 9–12. Founded: 1890. Setting: rural. Nearest major city is Iowa City. Students are housed in single-sex dormitories. 120-acre campus. 15 buildings on campus. Approved or accredited by Friends Council on Education, Independent Schools Association of the Central States, Midwest Association of Boarding Schools, The Association of Boarding Schools, and Iowa Department of Education. Member of National Association of Independent Schools. Endowment: $3.5 million. Total enrollment: 45. Upper school average class size: 10. Upper school faculty-student ratio: 1:2.

Upper School Student Profile Grade 9: 8 students (6 boys, 2 girls); Grade 10: 14 students (6 boys, 8 girls); Grade 11: 11 students (4 boys, 7 girls); Grade 12: 12 students (8 boys, 4 girls). 100% of students are boarding students. 37% are state residents. 13 states are represented in upper school student body. 26% are international students. International students from China, Ethiopia, India, Mexico, Republic of Korea, and Rwanda. 14% of students are members of Society of Friends.

Faculty School total: 24. In upper school: 13 men, 11 women; 5 have advanced degrees; 21 reside on campus.

Subjects Offered 3-dimensional art, advanced TOEFL/grammar, agriculture, algebra, alternative physical education, American government, American history, art, biology, calculus, career/college preparation, ceramics, chemistry, choreography, college admission preparation, community service, conflict resolution, creative writing, critical thinking, dance, dance performance, digital art, drama, drama performance, drawing and design, ecology, environmental systems, electronic music, environmental science, ESL, ethics, expository writing, fencing, fine arts, gardening, geometry, glassblowing, government/civics, grammar, history, horticulture, independent study, industrial arts, Internet research, library research, martial arts, mathematics, organic gardening, physics, portfolio writing, pottery, Quakerism and ethics, religion, research seminar, SAT/ACT preparation, science, senior seminar, set design, social studies, Spanish, stained glass, studio art, swimming, U.S. history, wilderness/outdoor program, woodworking, writing workshop, yearbook, yoga.

Graduation Requirements Algebra, American literature, art, biology, chemistry, English, foreign language, geometry, government, history, humanities, junior and senior seminars, physical education (includes health), physics, portfolio writing, Quakerism and ethics, SAT/ACT preparation, U.S. history, world history, world literature, 30 hours of community service per year in attendance, 20-page senior research paper with a thesis defense presentation, acceptance at 4-year college or university.

Special Academic Programs Honors section; accelerated programs; independent study; term-away projects; study abroad; ESL (15 students enrolled).

College Admission Counseling 18 students graduated in 2008; 12 went to college, including Clark University; Cornell College; Earlham College; Grinnell College; The University of Iowa; Warren Wilson College. Other: 6 went to work. Mean SAT critical reading: 570, mean SAT math: 578, mean SAT writing: 540, mean combined SAT: 1688, mean composite ACT: 24.

Student Life Upper grades have specified standards of dress, student council. Discipline rests equally with students and faculty. Attendance at religious services is required.

Tuition and Aid Day student tuition: $13,950; 5-day tuition and room/board: $21,250; 7-day tuition and room/board: $22,750. Tuition installment plan (Academic Management Services Plan, monthly payment plans, individually arranged payment plans). Merit scholarship grants, need-based scholarship grants, paying campus jobs, scholarships for Quaker students available. In 2008–09, 76% of upper-school students received aid; total upper-school merit-scholarship money awarded: $1000. Total amount of financial aid awarded in 2008–09: $534,000.

Admissions Traditional secondary-level entrance grade is 10. For fall 2008, 31 students applied for upper-level admission, 29 were accepted, 21 enrolled. Deadline for receipt of application materials: none. Application fee required: $50. Interview required.

Athletics Coed Interscholastic: basketball, fencing, indoor soccer, soccer; coed intramural: aquatics, archery, backpacking, ball hockey, bicycling, canoeing/kayaking, combined training, cooperative games, dance, fitness, hiking/backpacking, in-line hockey, jogging, juggling, martial arts, modern dance, physical fitness, roller hockey, running, skateboarding, strength & conditioning, swimming and diving, ultimate Frisbee, volleyball, yoga.

Computers Computers are regularly used in all classes. Computer network features include online commercial services, Internet access, wireless campus network, Internet filtering or blocking technology, laptop computers for each student. Campus intranet, student e-mail accounts, and computer access in designated common areas are available to students. The school has a published electronic and media policy.

Contact Glenn Singer, Director of Admissions. 319-643-7628. Fax: 319-643-7638. E-mail: admissions@scattergood.org. Web site: www.scattergood.org.

SCECGS REDLANDS

272 Military Road
Cremorne 2090, Australia

Head of School: Dr. Peter Lennox

General Information Coeducational day college-preparatory school, affiliated with Church of England (Anglican). Grades PK–12. Founded: 1884. Setting: suburban. Nearest major city is Sydney, Australia. 14-acre campus. 11 buildings on campus. Approved or accredited by New South Wales Department of School Education. Language of instruction: English. Total enrollment: 1,550. Upper school average class size: 20.

Upper School Student Profile 60% of students are members of Church of England (Anglican).

Faculty School total: 111.

Subjects Offered Ancient history, art, ballet, biology, business studies, chemistry, computer math, computer science, computer studies, creative arts, dance, drama, economics, English, ESL, French, geography, geology, German, government/civics, Greek, health, history, industrial arts, information processing, information technology, Japanese, JROTC, language, Latin, Mandarin, mathematics, modern history, music, personal development, photography, physical education, physics, religion, science, social studies, software design, speech, textiles, theater, visual arts.

Graduation Requirements English, foreign language, mathematics, physical education (includes health), religion (includes Bible studies and theology), science, social studies (includes history).

Special Academic Programs International Baccalaureate program; honors section; accelerated programs; independent study; remedial reading and/or remedial writing; remedial math; programs in English, mathematics, general development for dyslexic students; special instructional classes for students with learning disabilities; ESL.

College Admission Counseling 173 students graduated in 2008; 136 went to college, including Macquarie University; University of New South Wales.

Student Life Upper grades have uniform requirement, student council, honor system. Discipline rests equally with students and faculty. Attendance at religious services is required.

Tuition and Aid Day student tuition: 16,780 Australian dollars–22,560 Australian dollars. Merit scholarship grants available.

Admissions For fall 2008, 364 students applied for upper-level admission, 119 were accepted. Deadline for receipt of application materials: none. Application fee required. On-campus interview recommended.

Athletics Interscholastic: basketball (boys, girls), crew (b), cricket (b), cross-country running (b,g), diving (b), golf (b), riflery (b), rugby (b), soccer (b,g), squash (b), swimming and diving (b,g), tennis (b,g), track and field (b); intramural: badminton (b,g), basketball (b,g), crew (b), cricket (b), cross-country running (b,g), diving (b), equestrian sports (b,g), riflery (b), rugby (b), sailing (b,g), soccer (b,g), softball (b,g), squash (b), swimming and diving (b,g), tennis (b,g), touch football (b), track and field (b), water polo (b,g).

Computers Computer resources include on-campus library services, wireless campus network. Student e-mail accounts are available to students.

Contact Ms. Terese Kielt, Registrar. 61-2-9909-3133. Fax: 61-2-9909-3228. E-mail: registrar@redlands.nsw.edu.au. Web site: www.redlands.nsw.edu.au.

SCHLARMAN HIGH SCHOOL

2112 North Vemilion
Danville, Illinois 61832

Head of School: Adm. Robert A. Rice

General Information Coeducational day college-preparatory, arts, business, religious studies, and technology school, affiliated with Roman Catholic Church. Grades 9–12. Founded: 1945. Setting: small town. 15-acre campus. 1 building on campus. Approved or accredited by North Central Association of Colleges and Schools and Illinois Department of Education. Endowment: $1 million. Total enrollment: 183. Upper school average class size: 18. Upper school faculty-student ratio: 1:17.

Upper School Student Profile Grade 9: 48 students (33 boys, 15 girls); Grade 10: 51 students (26 boys, 25 girls); Grade 11: 46 students (20 boys, 26 girls); Grade 12: 38 students (23 boys, 15 girls). 85% of students are Roman Catholic.

Faculty School total: 22. In upper school: 8 men, 14 women; 9 have advanced degrees.

Special Academic Programs Advanced Placement exam preparation; honors section; independent study; study at local college for college credit.

College Admission Counseling 44 students graduated in 2008; 43 went to college, including University of Illinois at Urbana–Champaign. Other: 1 entered military service. Mean composite ACT: 25.

Student Life Upper grades have specified standards of dress, student council. Discipline rests primarily with faculty. Attendance at religious services is required.

Tuition and Aid Day student tuition: $4980. Tuition installment plan (FACTS Tuition Payment Plan). Tuition reduction for siblings, need-based scholarship grants available. In 2008–09, 35% of upper-school students received aid. Total amount of financial aid awarded in 2008–09: $120,000.

Admissions Traditional secondary-level entrance grade is 9. Deadline for receipt of application materials: none. No application fee required. Interview recommended.

Athletics Interscholastic: aerobics/dance (girls), baseball (b), basketball (b), cheering (g), cross-country running (b,g), dance squad (g), dance team (g), diving (b,g), football (b), golf (b), indoor track (b,g), indoor track & field (b,g), soccer (b), softball (g), swimming and diving (b,g), tennis (b,g), track and field (b,g), volleyball (g), wrestling (b). 2 PE instructors, 20 coaches.

Computers Computer network features include wireless campus network, Internet filtering or blocking technology. Student e-mail accounts are available to students. Students grades are available online. The school has a published electronic and media policy.

Contact Adm. Robert A. Rice, Principal. 217-442-2725. Fax: 217-442-0293. E-mail: brice@schlarman.com.

SCHOOL FOR YOUNG PERFORMERS

175 West 92nd Street
Suite 1D
New York, New York 10025

Head of School: Ms. Alison Pitt

General Information Coeducational day college-preparatory, general academic, and arts school. Grades K–12. Founded: 1995. Setting: urban. Approved or accredited by New York Department of Education. Upper school average class size: 1. Upper school faculty-student ratio: 1:1.

Faculty School total: 45. In upper school: 15 have advanced degrees.

Graduation Requirements Electives, English, history, mathematics, science, foreign language requirement.

Special Academic Programs Advanced Placement exam preparation; honors section; accelerated programs; independent study; term-away projects; study abroad; academic accommodation for the gifted, the musically talented, and the artistically talented; remedial reading and/or remedial writing; remedial math; programs in English, mathematics, general development for dyslexic students; special instructional classes for deaf students, blind students; ESL.

College Admission Counseling Colleges students went to include Columbia College; Harvard University; New York University; University of California, Los Angeles.

Student Life Upper grades have honor system. Discipline rests equally with students and faculty.

Summer Programs Remediation, enrichment, advancement, art/fine arts programs offered; session focuses on academics; held off campus; held at in the home or at the job site of the student; accepts boys and girls; open to students from other schools. 3 students usually enrolled.

Tuition and Aid Day student tuition: $6000. Tuition installment plan (semester payment plan). Tuition reduction for siblings, need-based scholarship grants available.

Admissions Deadline for receipt of application materials: none. No application fee required. Interview recommended.
Computers Computers are regularly used in all classes.
Contact Ms. Alison Pitt, Head of School. 212-663-3921. Fax: 914-666-3810. E-mail: alison@schoolforyoungperformers.org. Web site: www.schoolforyoungperformers.org.

ANNOUNCEMENT FROM THE SCHOOL The School for Young Performers offers a K–12, college-preparatory curriculum in a nontraditional academic environment. The personalized educational program allows children with professional and creative pursuits, children from high-profile families, and children who travel frequently the convenience of learning at home, at work, or wherever schedules dictate. Highly qualified and dynamic professional teachers implement the School's New York State–registered nonpublic school curriculum, which is based on individualized course programming commensurate with national standards.

SCHOOL OF THE HOLY CHILD

2225 Westchester Avenue
Rye, New York 10580

Head of School: Ann F. Sullivan

General Information Girls' day college-preparatory school, affiliated with Roman Catholic Church. Grades 5–12. Founded: 1904. Setting: suburban. Nearest major city is White Plains. 17-acre campus. 2 buildings on campus. Approved or accredited by New York State Association of Independent Schools, North Carolina Association of Independent Schools, The College Board, and New York Department of Education. Member of National Association of Independent Schools and Secondary School Admission Test Board. Endowment: $3 million. Total enrollment: 344. Upper school average class size: 14. Upper school faculty-student ratio: 1:7.
Upper School Student Profile Grade 9: 61 students (61 girls); Grade 10: 60 students (60 girls); Grade 11: 60 students (60 girls); Grade 12: 56 students (56 girls). 85% of students are Roman Catholic.
Faculty School total: 51. In upper school: 5 men, 28 women; 26 have advanced degrees.
Subjects Offered Algebra, American history, American literature, anatomy, art, art history, art history-AP, arts, arts and crafts, astronomy, Bible studies, bioethics, biology, biology-AP, calculus, ceramics, chamber groups, chemistry, chorus, community service, computer programming, computer science, creative writing, dance, design, drama, drawing, driver education, economics, English, English literature, ethics, European history, expository writing, film, fine arts, French, French-AP, geometry, government/civics, grammar, health, history, illustration, Latin, Mandarin, mathematics, music, music theory-AP, physical education, physics, psychology, religion, science, Shakespeare, social studies, Spanish, Spanish-AP, speech, statistics, studio art-AP, theater, trigonometry, world history, writing.
Graduation Requirements Arts and fine arts (art, music, dance, drama), English, foreign language, independent study, mathematics, physical education (includes health), religion (includes Bible studies and theology), science, social studies (includes history), senior internship project, life skills for 9th and 10th grades, guidance for 11th and 12th grades, 100 hours of community service.
Special Academic Programs Advanced Placement exam preparation; honors section; independent study; term-away projects; domestic exchange program; study abroad.
College Admission Counseling 52 students graduated in 2008; all went to college, including Boston College; Bucknell University; College of the Holy Cross; Georgetown University; Trinity College; University of Notre Dame.
Student Life Upper grades have uniform requirement, student council. Discipline rests primarily with faculty. Attendance at religious services is required.
Summer Programs Enrichment, sports, art/fine arts programs offered; session focuses on performing and fine arts immersion and sports camps; held on campus; accepts boys and girls; open to students from other schools. 120 students usually enrolled. 2009 schedule: June 1 to August 31.
Tuition and Aid Day student tuition: $24,000. Tuition installment plan (Key Tuition Payment Plan, monthly payment plans). Merit scholarship grants, need-based scholarship grants, need-based loans, merit-based scholarships/grants (9th Grade Only) available. In 2008–09, 20% of upper-school students received aid.
Admissions Traditional secondary-level entrance grade is 9. Catholic High School Entrance Examination, ISEE or SSAT required. Deadline for receipt of application materials: January 4. Application fee required: $50. On-campus interview required.
Athletics Interscholastic: basketball, cross-country running, field hockey, golf, indoor track & field, lacrosse, soccer, softball, squash, swimming and diving, tennis, track and field, volleyball, winter (indoor) track; intramural: basketball, dance, dance squad, dance team, fitness, fitness walking, modern dance, volleyball, winter (indoor) track. 2 PE instructors, 37 coaches, 1 athletic trainer.
Computers Computers are regularly used in all academic classes. Computer network features include on-campus library services, online commercial services, Internet access, wireless campus network, Internet filtering or blocking technology. Campus intranet, student e-mail accounts, and computer access in designated common areas are available to students. The school has a published electronic and media policy.
Contact Admission Office. 914-967-5622 Ext. 227. Fax: 914-967-6476. E-mail: admissions@holychildrye.org. Web site: www.holychildrye.org.

SCOTUS CENTRAL CATHOLIC HIGH SCHOOL

1554 18th Avenue
Columbus, Nebraska 68601-5132

Head of School: Mr. Wayne Morfeld

General Information Coeducational day college-preparatory, arts, business, religious studies, and technology school, affiliated with Roman Catholic Church. Grades 7–12. Founded: 1884. Setting: rural. Nearest major city is Omaha. 1-acre campus. 1 building on campus. Approved or accredited by National Catholic Education Association, North Central Association of Colleges and Schools, and Nebraska Department of Education. Endowment: $65 million. Total enrollment: 359. Upper school average class size: 20. Upper school faculty-student ratio: 1:12.
Upper School Student Profile Grade 9: 68 students (38 boys, 30 girls); Grade 10: 46 students (20 boys, 26 girls); Grade 11: 50 students (24 boys, 26 girls); Grade 12: 54 students (27 boys, 27 girls). 97% of students are Roman Catholic.
Faculty School total: 27. In upper school: 10 men, 17 women; 9 have advanced degrees.
Subjects Offered Accounting, advanced math, Advanced Placement courses, algebra, American history, art, Bible studies, biology, bookkeeping, calculus, campus ministry, career/college preparation, character education, chemistry, choir, computer applications, computer keyboarding, CPR, digital applications, drama, earth science, economics, English, family and consumer science, guidance, jazz band, life skills, modern world history, personal fitness, physical science, physics, physiology, pottery, psychology, sociology, Spanish, speech, speech and debate, textiles, theater, vocal ensemble, volleyball, yearbook.
Special Academic Programs Advanced Placement exam preparation; study at local college for college credit.
College Admission Counseling 63 students graduated in 2008; 62 went to college, including Creighton University; University of Nebraska–Lincoln; University of Nebraska at Kearney; University of Nebraska at Omaha. Other: 1 went to work. Median composite ACT: 24. 27% scored over 26 on composite ACT.
Student Life Upper grades have uniform requirement, student council. Discipline rests equally with students and faculty. Attendance at religious services is required.
Tuition and Aid Day student tuition: $2115–$2215. Tuition installment plan (monthly payment plans). Need-based scholarship grants available. In 2008–09, 23% of upper-school students received aid. Total amount of financial aid awarded in 2008–09: $81,087.
Admissions Traditional secondary-level entrance grade is 9. Deadline for receipt of application materials: none. No application fee required.
Athletics Interscholastic: baseball (boys), basketball (b,g), cross-country running (b,g), football (b), golf (b,g), soccer (b,g), softball (g), swimming and diving (b,g), tennis (b,g), track and field (b,g), volleyball (g), wrestling (b); coed interscholastic: weight training. 3 PE instructors, 15 coaches, 2 athletic trainers.
Computers Computers are regularly used in business, newspaper, Web site design, word processing, yearbook classes. Computer network features include Internet access, Internet filtering or blocking technology. Student e-mail accounts are available to students. Students grades are available online. The school has a published electronic and media policy.
Contact Mrs. Pamela K. Weir, 7-12 Guidance Counselor. 402-564-7165. Fax: 402-564-6004. E-mail: pweir@esu7.org. Web site: www.scotuscc.org.

SEABURY HALL

480 Olinda Road
Makawao, Hawaii 96768-9399

Head of School: Mr. Joseph J. Schmidt

General Information Coeducational day college-preparatory, arts, and technology school, affiliated with Episcopal Church. Grades 6–12. Founded: 1964. Setting: rural. Nearest major city is Kahului. 52-acre campus. 8 buildings on campus. Approved or accredited by National Association of Episcopal Schools, Western Association of Schools and Colleges, and Hawaii Department of Education. Member of National Association of Independent Schools and Secondary School Admission Test Board. Endowment: $26.8 million. Total enrollment: 421. Upper school average class size: 18. Upper school faculty-student ratio: 1:10.
Upper School Student Profile Grade 9: 80 students (40 boys, 40 girls); Grade 10: 76 students (39 boys, 37 girls); Grade 11: 70 students (39 boys, 31 girls); Grade 12: 62 students (25 boys, 37 girls). 10% of students are members of Episcopal Church.
Faculty School total: 52. In upper school: 23 men, 13 women; 19 have advanced degrees.
Subjects Offered Acting, algebra, American history, American literature, art, band, biology, biology-AP, calculus-AP, ceramics, chemistry, chorus, community service, comparative religion, computer programming, dance, drawing, economics, English, English literature, ethics, European history-AP, expository writing, fine arts, geometry, global studies, government, history, Japanese, keyboarding, mathematics, mythology, painting, philosophy, physical education, physical science, physics, physics-AP,

political science, pre-algebra, pre-calculus, religion, science, set design, social studies, Spanish, Spanish-AP, speech, studio art-AP, yearbook.
Graduation Requirements Arts and fine arts (art, music, dance, drama), English, foreign language, mathematics, physical education (includes health), religion (includes Bible studies and theology), science, social studies (includes history), speech. Community service is required.
Special Academic Programs 13 Advanced Placement exams for which test preparation is offered; honors section; independent study.
College Admission Counseling 71 students graduated in 2008; all went to college, including Humboldt State University; New York University; Northern Arizona University; University of Hawaii at Hilo; Western Washington University; Whitworth University. Mean SAT critical reading: 563, mean SAT math: 559, mean SAT writing: 579, mean combined SAT: 1701, mean composite ACT: 25.
Student Life Upper grades have specified standards of dress, student council, honor system. Discipline rests primarily with faculty.
Summer Programs Enrichment, sports, art/fine arts programs offered; session focuses on enrichment; held on campus; accepts boys and girls; open to students from other schools. 200 students usually enrolled. 2009 schedule: June 15 to July 10. Application deadline: June 15.
Tuition and Aid Day student tuition: $15,630. Tuition installment plan (FACTS Tuition Payment Plan). Need-based scholarship grants available. In 2008–09, 33% of upper-school students received aid. Total amount of financial aid awarded in 2008–09: $664,660.
Admissions Traditional secondary-level entrance grade is 9. For fall 2008, 97 students applied for upper-level admission, 63 were accepted, 43 enrolled. ERB CTP III, ISEE or SSAT required. Deadline for receipt of application materials: February 28. Application fee required: $55. Interview required.
Athletics Interscholastic: basketball (boys, girls), cross-country running (b,g), dance (g), football (b), golf (b,g), soccer (b,g), swimming and diving (b,g), tennis (b,g), track and field (b,g), volleyball (b,g); intramural: basketball (b,g), dance (g), fitness (b,g), strength & conditioning (b,g); coed interscholastic: baseball, dance, physical fitness; coed intramural: ballet, baseball, cross-country running, dance, fitness, track and field, volleyball. 4 PE instructors, 12 coaches, 1 athletic trainer.
Computers Computers are regularly used in art, economics, English, foreign language, history, journalism, mathematics, newspaper, science, speech, yearbook classes. Computer network features include on-campus library services, online commercial services, Internet access, wireless campus network, Internet filtering or blocking technology. Campus intranet, student e-mail accounts, and computer access in designated common areas are available to students. The school has a published electronic and media policy.
Contact Elaine V. Nelson, Director of Admissions. 808-572-0807. Fax: 808-572-2042. E-mail: enelson@seaburyhall.org. Web site: www.seaburyhall.org.

SEATTLE ACADEMY OF ARTS AND SCIENCES

1201 East Union Street
Seattle, Washington 98122
Head of School: Jean Marie Orvis

General Information Coeducational day college-preparatory, arts, and technology school. Grades 6–12. Founded: 1983. Setting: urban. 3-acre campus. 5 buildings on campus. Approved or accredited by Northwest Association of Accredited Schools, Pacific Northwest Association of Independent Schools, and Washington Department of Education. Member of National Association of Independent Schools. Endowment: $3.6 million. Total enrollment: 592. Upper school average class size: 18. Upper school faculty-student ratio: 1:8.
Upper School Student Profile Grade 9: 86 students (34 boys, 52 girls); Grade 10: 84 students (42 boys, 42 girls); Grade 11: 88 students (38 boys, 50 girls); Grade 12: 93 students (48 boys, 45 girls).
Faculty School total: 83. In upper school: 40 men, 43 women; 58 have advanced degrees.
Subjects Offered Acting, advanced chemistry, algebra, American history, American literature, Asian studies, biology, biotechnology, calculus, chemistry, choir, civics, community service, dance, debate, drawing, economics, English, French, geometry, health, history, humanities, independent study, instrumental music, lab science, literature, Mandarin, marine science, math analysis, musical productions, painting, physical education, physics, printmaking, sculpture, Spanish, speech, stagecraft, statistics, visual arts, vocal music, world literature, yearbook.
Graduation Requirements Arts and fine arts (art, music, dance, drama), English, foreign language, mathematics, physical education (includes health), science, social studies (includes history). Community service is required.
Special Academic Programs Honors section; independent study; term-away projects; study abroad; academic accommodation for the gifted, the musically talented, and the artistically talented; remedial reading and/or remedial writing; remedial math; programs in English, mathematics, general development for dyslexic students.
College Admission Counseling 72 students graduated in 2008; 70 went to college. Other: 2 had other specific plans. Median combined SAT: 1823, median composite ACT: 27. 58% scored over 600 on SAT critical reading, 58% scored over 600 on SAT math, 62% scored over 600 on SAT writing, 58% scored over 1800 on combined SAT, 68% scored over 26 on composite ACT.
Student Life Upper grades have student council, honor system. Discipline rests equally with students and faculty.
Summer Programs Enrichment, sports, art/fine arts programs offered; held on campus; accepts boys and girls; not open to students from other schools. 60 students usually enrolled. 2009 schedule: June 15 to August 15.
Tuition and Aid Day student tuition: $23,226. Tuition installment plan (Academic Management Services Plan, monthly payment plans). Need-based scholarship grants available. In 2008–09, 20% of upper-school students received aid.
Admissions Traditional secondary-level entrance grade is 9. ISEE required. Deadline for receipt of application materials: January 15. Application fee required: $50. Interview required.
Athletics Interscholastic: basketball (boys, girls), cross-country running (b,g), golf (b,g), soccer (b,g), tennis (b,g), track and field (b,g), ultimate Frisbee (b,g), volleyball (g); intramural: fly fishing (b); coed interscholastic: dance, dance squad, dance team, Frisbee; coed intramural: bowling, in-line skating, outdoor activities, paint ball, roller blading, roller skating, skateboarding, skiing (downhill), snowboarding, squash. 5 PE instructors, 30 coaches, 1 athletic trainer.
Computers Computers are regularly used in English, foreign language, history, mathematics, science, speech, video film production, yearbook classes. Computer network features include on-campus library services, online commercial services, Internet access, wireless campus network, Internet filtering or blocking technology. Student e-mail accounts are available to students. The school has a published electronic and media policy.
Contact Jim Rupp, Admission Director. 206-324-7227. Fax: 206-323-6618. E-mail: jrupp@seattleacademy.org. Web site: www.seattleacademy.org.

SEATTLE CHRISTIAN SCHOOLS

18301 Military Road South
Seattle, Washington 98188
Head of School: Ms. Gloria Hunter

General Information Coeducational day college-preparatory, arts, religious studies, bilingual studies, and technology school, affiliated with Christian faith. Grades K–12. Founded: 1946. Setting: suburban. 13-acre campus. 1 building on campus. Approved or accredited by Association of Christian Schools International, CITA (Commission on International and Trans-Regional Accreditation), Northwest Association of Accredited Schools, and Washington Department of Education. Endowment: $899,468. Total enrollment: 662. Upper school average class size: 22. Upper school faculty-student ratio: 1:22.
Upper School Student Profile Grade 9: 73 students (31 boys, 42 girls); Grade 10: 59 students (27 boys, 32 girls); Grade 11: 60 students (32 boys, 28 girls); Grade 12: 73 students (28 boys, 45 girls). 100% of students are Christian faith.
Faculty School total: 50. In upper school: 13 men, 13 women; 13 have advanced degrees.
Subjects Offered Advanced Placement courses, algebra, American literature, art, band, Bible, biology, business mathematics, calculus, calculus-AP, chemistry, Christian education, Christian studies, civics, computer applications, computer education, computer skills, desktop publishing, drama, English, English-AP, ensembles, foreign language, French, geometry, health, keyboarding, math analysis, multimedia, music, Pacific Northwest seminar, photography, physical education, physical science, physics, physics-AP, physiology, pre-algebra, psychology, Spanish, U.S. history, U.S. history-AP, weight training, world history, yearbook.
Graduation Requirements Algebra, arts and fine arts (art, music, dance, drama), Bible, biology, chemistry, civics, English, English composition, foreign language, geometry, Life of Christ, mathematics, occupational education, physical education (includes health), physics, science, U.S. history, Washington State and Northwest History, world history, UTT-Understanding the Times, Acts and Paul.
Special Academic Programs Advanced Placement exam preparation; honors section; independent study; study at local college for college credit; remedial reading and/or remedial writing; programs in English for dyslexic students.
College Admission Counseling 56 students graduated in 2008; all went to college, including Bellevue Community College; Seattle Pacific University; University of Idaho; University of Washington; Washington State University; Western Washington University. Median SAT critical reading: 580, median SAT math: 560, median SAT writing: 570, median combined SAT: 1710, median composite ACT: 16. 38% scored over 600 on SAT critical reading, 23% scored over 600 on SAT math, 34% scored over 600 on SAT writing, 33% scored over 1800 on combined SAT, 33% scored over 26 on composite ACT.
Student Life Upper grades have specified standards of dress, student council, honor system. Discipline rests primarily with faculty. Attendance at religious services is required.
Tuition and Aid Day student tuition: $8130. Tuition installment plan (FACTS Tuition Payment Plan, monthly payment plans, individually arranged payment plans). Tuition reduction for siblings, need-based scholarship grants available. In 2008–09, 10% of upper-school students received aid. Total amount of financial aid awarded in 2008–09: $81,058.
Admissions Traditional secondary-level entrance grade is 9. For fall 2008, 21 students applied for upper-level admission, 16 were accepted, 15 enrolled. Admissions testing required. Deadline for receipt of application materials: none. Application fee required: $75. On-campus interview required.

Athletics Interscholastic: baseball (boys), basketball (b,g), cheering (g), cross-country running (b,g), golf (b,g), soccer (b,g), softball (g), track and field (b,g), volleyball (g); coed interscholastic: cross-country running, track and field; coed intramural: archery, badminton, ball hockey, baseball, basketball, combined training, field hockey, floor hockey, juggling, lacrosse, softball, strength & conditioning, touch football, weight training, whiffle ball. 1 PE instructor.
Computers Computers are regularly used in art, computer applications, desktop publishing, keyboarding, library, mathematics, multimedia, science, social studies, Web site design, yearbook classes. Computer network features include on-campus library services, Internet access, Internet filtering or blocking technology, Accelerated Reading and Math program and Nettrekker search engine for secondary students. Computer access in designated common areas is available to students. Students grades are available online. The school has a published electronic and media policy.
Contact Fran Hubeek, Admissions Coordinator. 206-246-8241 Ext. 1301. Fax: 206-246-9066. E-mail: admissions@seattlechristian.org. Web site: www.seattlechristian.org.

SEATTLE LUTHERAN HIGH SCHOOL

4141 41st Avenue SW
Seattle, Washington 98116

Head of School: Adair Hinds

General Information Coeducational day college-preparatory, general academic, arts, and religious studies school, affiliated with Lutheran Church; primarily serves dyslexic students. Grades 9–12. Founded: 1977. Setting: urban. 2-acre campus. 1 building on campus. Approved or accredited by Lutheran School Accreditation Commission, National Lutheran School Accreditation, Northwest Association of Schools and Colleges, and Washington Department of Education. Endowment: $385,000. Total enrollment: 186. Upper school average class size: 18. Upper school faculty-student ratio: 1:9.
Upper School Student Profile Grade 9: 43 students (22 boys, 21 girls); Grade 10: 49 students (22 boys, 27 girls); Grade 11: 49 students (21 boys, 28 girls); Grade 12: 45 students (23 boys, 22 girls). 40% of students are Lutheran.
Faculty School total: 23. In upper school: 10 men, 12 women; 4 have advanced degrees.
Subjects Offered 3-dimensional art, Advanced Placement courses, algebra, American government, American history, American history-AP, American literature, American sign language, art, art history, band, biology, boating, British literature (honors), British literature-AP, calculus, calculus-AP, ceramics, chemistry, choir, Christian doctrine, Christian education, Christian ethics, community service, design, drama, earth science, economics, English, English composition, English literature, ESL, French, geography, geometry, handbells, health, history, jazz band, journalism, keyboarding/computer, life skills, newspaper, painting, physical education, physics, portfolio art, pre-algebra, pre-calculus, psychology, publications, religion, robotics, science, senior project, social science, social studies, Spanish, Spanish-AP, state history, student government, study skills, world culture, world history, world literature.
Graduation Requirements American government, American history, arts and fine arts (art, music, dance, drama), biology, computer keyboarding, English, foreign language, life skills, mathematics, physical education (includes health), religion (includes Bible studies and theology), science, senior project, social science, world culture. Community service is required.
Special Academic Programs 3 Advanced Placement exams for which test preparation is offered; honors section; independent study; remedial reading and/or remedial writing; remedial math; programs in English, mathematics, general development for dyslexic students; ESL (1 student enrolled).
College Admission Counseling 32 students graduated in 2008; 31 went to college, including Concordia University; Pacific Lutheran University; South Seattle Community College; University of Idaho; University of Washington; Western Washington University. Other: 1 went to work.
Student Life Upper grades have specified standards of dress, student council, honor system. Discipline rests equally with students and faculty. Attendance at religious services is required.
Summer Programs Sports programs offered; session focuses on basketball, volleyball, soccer; held both on and off campus; held at Fairmount Park; accepts boys and girls; not open to students from other schools. 50 students usually enrolled. 2009 schedule: June 2 to July 31.
Tuition and Aid Day student tuition: $8900. Tuition installment plan (SMART Tuition Payment Plan, monthly payment plans). Tuition reduction for siblings, merit scholarship grants, need-based scholarship grants, honors scholarship at entrance to incoming valedictorians of 8th grade class available. In 2008–09, 21% of upper-school students received aid; total upper-school merit-scholarship money awarded: $1000. Total amount of financial aid awarded in 2008–09: $92,710.
Admissions Traditional secondary-level entrance grade is 9. For fall 2008, 67 students applied for upper-level admission, 47 were accepted, 47 enrolled. School's own exam and TAP required. Deadline for receipt of application materials: February 27. Application fee required: $50. Interview required.
Athletics Interscholastic: baseball (boys), basketball (b,g), cheering (b,g), cross-country running (b,g), football (b), physical training (b,g), soccer (g), softball (g), strength & conditioning (b,g), tennis (g), track and field (b,g), volleyball (g), weight training (b,g); intramural: yoga (g); coed interscholastic: golf; coed intramural: fencing, fitness, sailing. 3 PE instructors, 25 coaches.
Computers Computers are regularly used in English, keyboarding, life skills, newspaper, publications, social sciences, study skills, yearbook classes. Computer network features include on-campus library services, Internet access, wireless campus network, Internet filtering or blocking technology. Computer access in designated common areas is available to students. Students grades are available online. The school has a published electronic and media policy.
Contact Rachel Bigliardi, Director of Admissions. 206-937-7722 Ext. 18. Fax: 206-937-6781. E-mail: rbigliardi@seattlelutheran.org. Web site: www.seattlelutheran.org.

SECOND BAPTIST SCHOOL

6410 Woodway Drive
Houston, Texas 77057

Head of School: Dr. J. Brett Jacobsen

General Information Coeducational day college-preparatory and religious studies school, affiliated with Baptist Church. Grades PK–12. Founded: 1946. Setting: suburban. 42-acre campus. 4 buildings on campus. Approved or accredited by Southern Association of Colleges and Schools, Southern Association of Independent Schools, and Texas Department of Education. Upper school average class size: 13.
Upper School Student Profile 65% of students are Baptist.
Faculty In upper school: 49 have advanced degrees.
Subjects Offered 3-dimensional art, Advanced Placement courses, algebra, American literature, anatomy and physiology, art, art-AP, band, Bible, biology, biology-AP, British literature, British literature-AP, broadcasting, calculus, calculus-AP, chemistry, chemistry-AP, choir, computer programming, computer programming-AP, computer science, computer science-AP, concert band, concert choir, debate, desktop publishing, drama, economics, English, English-AP, European history-AP, French, French language-AP, French literature-AP, geometry, government, health, honors algebra, honors geometry, jazz ensemble, journalism, Latin, marching band, music theory-AP, photography, physical education, physics, physics-AP, pre-calculus, Spanish, Spanish language-AP, Spanish literature-AP, speech, statistics-AP, U.S. history, U.S. history-AP, world geography, world history.
Graduation Requirements Arts and fine arts (art, music, dance, drama), Bible, computer science, economics, electives, English, foreign language, government, mathematics, physical education (includes health), science, social studies (includes history), speech.
Special Academic Programs Advanced Placement exam preparation; honors section; accelerated programs; independent study; term-away projects; study at local college for college credit; study abroad.
College Admission Counseling 81 students graduated in 2008; all went to college.
Student Life Upper grades have specified standards of dress, student council. Discipline rests primarily with faculty. Attendance at religious services is required.
Tuition and Aid Day student tuition: $13,116. Tuition installment plan (monthly payment plans). Merit scholarship grants, need-based scholarship grants available. In 2008–09, 20% of upper-school students received aid.
Admissions ISEE and writing sample required. Deadline for receipt of application materials: none. Application fee required: $50. Interview required.
Athletics Interscholastic: baseball (boys), basketball (b,g), cross-country running (b,g), diving (b,g), drill team (g), fitness (b,g), football (b), golf (b,g); coed interscholastic: cheering. 9 PE instructors, 37 coaches, 2 athletic trainers.
Computers Computers are regularly used in all academic classes. Computer network features include on-campus library services, online commercial services, Internet access, wireless campus network, Internet filtering or blocking technology, science student interactive programs and computer-based labs. The school has a published electronic and media policy.
Contact Mrs. Andrea Prothro, Director of Admissions. 713-365-2314. Fax: 713-365-2445. E-mail: aprothro@secondbaptistschool.org. Web site: www.secondbaptistschool.org.

SEDBERGH SCHOOL

810 Côte Azélie
Montebello, Quebec J0V 1L0, Canada

Head of School: Andrew Blair

General Information Coeducational boarding and day college-preparatory, outdoor education, and military school. Grades 7–12. Founded: 1939. Setting: rural. Nearest major city is Ottawa, ON, Canada. Students are housed in single-sex dormitories. 1,200-acre campus. 3 buildings on campus. Approved or accredited by Canadian Association of Independent Schools, Canadian Educational Standards Institute, Quebec Association of Independent Schools, The Association of Boarding Schools, and Quebec Department of Education. Language of instruction: English. Total enrollment: 60. Upper school average class size: 15. Upper school faculty-student ratio: 1:5.
Upper School Student Profile Grade 7: 4 students (2 boys, 2 girls); Grade 8: 6 students (6 boys); Grade 9: 8 students (5 boys, 3 girls); Grade 10: 16 students (12 boys, 4 girls); Grade 11: 18 students (14 boys, 4 girls); Grade 12: 15 students (11 boys, 4

girls). 85% of students are boarding students. 20% are province residents. 7 provinces are represented in upper school student body. 20% are international students. International students from China, Hong Kong, Ireland, Mexico, Saudi Arabia, and United States; 3 other countries represented in student body.

Faculty School total: 16. In upper school: 9 men, 3 women; 5 have advanced degrees; 11 reside on campus.

Subjects Offered Algebra, art, biology, calculus, Canadian literature, character education, chemistry, communication skills, conflict resolution, contemporary issues, creative writing, decision making skills, earth science, economics, economics and history, English, English literature, environmental education, environmental geography, environmental science, environmental studies, ESL, ethics, expository writing, French, geography, geology, geometry, grammar, health and wellness, history, home economics, linear algebra, marine biology, mathematics, outdoor education, physical education, physics, physiology, science, senior thesis, social science, social studies, trigonometry, world history.

Graduation Requirements English, environmental studies, French, history, mathematics, physical education (includes health), science, province-wide exams.

Special Academic Programs Independent study; term-away projects; study abroad; remedial reading and/or remedial writing; remedial math; programs in English, mathematics, general development for dyslexic students; ESL (10 students enrolled).

College Admission Counseling 15 students graduated in 2008; 13 went to college, including Dalhousie University; Ottawa University; Queen's University at Kingston; St. Francis Xavier University; The University of Western Ontario; University of Toronto. Other: 1 had other specific plans.

Student Life Upper grades have uniform requirement, student council, honor system. Discipline rests equally with students and faculty.

Tuition and Aid Day student tuition: CAN$16,600; 5-day tuition and room/board: CAN$37,600; 7-day tuition and room/board: CAN$37,600. Tuition installment plan (monthly payment plans). Tuition reduction for siblings, bursaries, merit scholarship grants, need-based scholarship grants available. In 2008–09, 25% of upper-school students received aid; total upper-school merit-scholarship money awarded: CAN$50,000. Total amount of financial aid awarded in 2008–09: CAN$250,000.

Admissions Traditional secondary-level entrance grade is 9. For fall 2008, 35 students applied for upper-level admission, 25 were accepted, 20 enrolled. Secondary Level English Proficiency and SLEP for foreign students required. Deadline for receipt of application materials: none. No application fee required. Interview required.

Athletics Coed Interscholastic: canoeing/kayaking, kayaking, mountain biking, nordic skiing, rugby, running, skiing (cross-country), soccer, ultimate Frisbee; coed intramural: alpine skiing, backpacking, badminton, ball hockey, baseball, basketball, bicycling, billiards, broomball, canoeing/kayaking, climbing, combined training, cross-country running, fishing, fitness, flag football, floor hockey, Frisbee, hiking/backpacking, hockey, ice hockey, ice skating, jogging, kayaking, mountain biking, nordic skiing, outdoor activities, paddling, physical fitness, power lifting, rock climbing, rugby, running, skateboarding, skiing (cross-country), skiing (downhill), snowboarding, snowshoeing, soccer, softball, squash, strength & conditioning, swimming and diving, tennis, touch football, ultimate Frisbee, volleyball, wall climbing, weight lifting, weight training, wilderness survival, winter soccer, yoga.

Computers Computers are regularly used in all academic classes. Computer network features include online commercial services, Internet access, wireless campus network, Internet filtering or blocking technology. Student e-mail accounts are available to students. The school has a published electronic and media policy.

Contact Ms. Barbara Wilkinson, Admissions. 819-423-5523. Fax: 819-423-5769. E-mail: bwilkinson@sedbergh.com. Web site: www.sedbergh.com.

SEISEN INTERNATIONAL SCHOOL

12-15 Yoga 1-chome, Setagaya-ku

Tokyo 158-0097, Japan

Head of School: Sr. Concesa Martin

General Information Coeducational day (boys' only in lower grades) college-preparatory school, affiliated with Roman Catholic Church. Boys grade K, girls grades K–12. Founded: 1962. Setting: urban. 2-hectare campus. 3 buildings on campus. Approved or accredited by Department of Defense Dependents Schools, East Asia Regional Council of Schools, European Council of International Schools, International Baccalaureate Organization, Ministry of Education, Japan, National Catholic Education Association, and New England Association of Schools and Colleges. Member of Secondary School Admission Test Board. Language of instruction: English. Total enrollment: 711. Upper school average class size: 23. Upper school faculty-student ratio: 1:4.

Upper School Student Profile Grade 9: 50 students (50 girls); Grade 10: 43 students (43 girls); Grade 11: 46 students (46 girls); Grade 12: 33 students (33 girls). 21% of students are Roman Catholic.

Faculty School total: 85. In upper school: 13 men, 29 women; 24 have advanced degrees.

Subjects Offered 3-dimensional art, advanced math, art, bell choir, biology, business, career planning, chemistry, Chinese, choir, college planning, computer graphics, drama, English, ESL, French, geography, geometry, history, information technology, International Baccalaureate courses, Japanese, journalism, library assistant, math methods, mathematics, model United Nations, music, music composition, music performance, painting, performing arts, physical education, physics, pottery, psychology, religion, science, social science, social studies, Spanish, speech, theory of knowledge, visual arts, world history, yearbook.

Graduation Requirements Electives, English, foreign language, mathematics, physical education (includes health), religion (includes Bible studies and theology), science, social studies (includes history).

Special Academic Programs International Baccalaureate program; honors section; independent study; remedial reading and/or remedial writing; remedial math; ESL (20 students enrolled).

College Admission Counseling 41 students graduated in 2008; 40 went to college, including New York University; Northeastern University; Sophia Universtiy; Temple University, Japan Campus; University of California, San Diego; University of Toronto. Mean SAT critical reading: 537, mean SAT math: 616, mean SAT writing: 553, mean combined SAT: 1706. 16% scored over 600 on SAT critical reading, 63% scored over 600 on SAT math, 47% scored over 600 on SAT writing, 42% scored over 1800 on combined SAT.

Student Life Upper grades have uniform requirement, student council, honor system. Discipline rests primarily with faculty.

Summer Programs Remediation, ESL programs offered; session focuses on high school remedial work only; held on campus; accepts girls; not open to students from other schools. 17 students usually enrolled. 2009 schedule: June 15 to June 26. Application deadline: May 1.

Tuition and Aid Day student tuition: ¥1,940,000. Tuition installment plan (monthly payment plans, individually arranged payment plans). Tuition reduction for siblings, need-based scholarship grants available. In 2008–09, 2% of upper-school students received aid. Total amount of financial aid awarded in 2008–09: ¥2,910,000.

Admissions Traditional secondary-level entrance grade is 9. For fall 2008, 36 students applied for upper-level admission, 14 were accepted, 11 enrolled. Admissions testing, mathematics proficiency exam, Reading for Understanding or writing sample required. Deadline for receipt of application materials: none. Application fee required: ¥20,000. On-campus interview required.

Athletics Interscholastic: basketball, cross-country running, running, soccer, swimming and diving, tennis, track and field, volleyball; intramural: badminton, ballet, cooperative games, dance, indoor soccer, modern dance, outdoor activities, running, soccer, table tennis, tennis, winter soccer, yoga; coed interscholastic: aquatics. 2 PE instructors.

Computers Computers are regularly used in art, business studies, career education, career exploration, college planning, design, English, graphic design, history, information technology, journalism, mathematics, music, science, social studies, writing, yearbook classes. Computer network features include on-campus library services, online commercial services, Internet access, wireless campus network, Internet filtering or blocking technology. Campus intranet and computer access in designated common areas are available to students.

Contact Sr. Concesa Martin, School Head. 81-3-3704-2661. Fax: 81-3-3701-1033. E-mail: sisadmissions@seisen.com. Web site: www.seisen.com.

See Close-Up on page 964.

SELWYN HOUSE SCHOOL

95 chemin Côte St-Antoine

Westmount, Quebec H3Y 2H8, Canada

Head of School: Mr. William Mitchell

General Information Boys' day college-preparatory, bilingual studies, and technology school. Grades K–11. Founded: 1908. Setting: urban. Nearest major city is Montreal, Canada. 2-acre campus. 3 buildings on campus. Approved or accredited by Canadian Association of Independent Schools, Canadian Educational Standards Institute, International Coalition of Boys Schools, National Institute of Independent Schools, Quebec Association of Independent Schools, and Quebec Department of Education. Affiliate member of National Association of Independent Schools; member of Secondary School Admission Test Board. Languages of instruction: English and French. Endowment: CAN$5.4 million. Total enrollment: 555. Upper school average class size: 15. Upper school faculty-student ratio: 1:8.

Upper School Student Profile Grade 9: 64 students (64 boys); Grade 10: 65 students (65 boys); Grade 11: 60 students (60 boys).

Faculty School total: 72. In upper school: 27 men, 12 women; 16 have advanced degrees.

Subjects Offered Art, calculus, Canadian history, chemistry, computer multimedia, computer programming, computer science, debate, drama, economics, English, English literature, French, geography, golf, history, Japanese, jazz band, jazz ensemble, law, mathematics, music, outdoor education, photography, physical education, physics, public speaking, publishing, robotics, Spanish, world history, world issues, yearbook.

Graduation Requirements English, French, history, mathematics, physical science.

Special Academic Programs Honors section.

College Admission Counseling 65 students graduated in 2008; all went to college, including Choate Rosemary Hall; Kent School; Phillips Exeter Academy; St. Paul's School; The Hotchkiss School.

Student Life Upper grades have uniform requirement, student council, honor system. Discipline rests primarily with faculty.

Summer Programs Sports programs offered; session focuses on football, basketball, hockey and cycling camps; held both on and off campus; held at sixteen rented facilities along with two on-site gyms, Fitness centre, and Combatives room; accepts boys; open to students from other schools. 2009 schedule: June 22 to August 28. Application deadline: May 1.
Tuition and Aid Day student tuition: CAN$17,280. Guaranteed tuition plan. Tuition installment plan (monthly payment plans, individually arranged payment plans, 2- and 4-installment plans, credit card payments). Bursaries, merit scholarship grants, need-based scholarship grants, three-year merit-based scholarship to a new Grade 9 student, staff tuition discount available. In 2008–09, 16% of upper-school students received aid; total upper-school merit-scholarship money awarded: CAN$20,000. Total amount of financial aid awarded in 2008–09: CAN$115,400.
Admissions For fall 2008, 19 students applied for upper-level admission, 12 were accepted, 11 enrolled. English, French, and math proficiency required. Deadline for receipt of application materials: October 17. Application fee required: CAN$125. On-campus interview required.
Athletics Interscholastic: badminton, ball hockey, baseball, basketball, cross-country running, curling, fitness, football, golf, ice hockey, rock climbing, rowing, rugby, skiing (cross-country), soccer, tennis, track and field, wrestling; intramural: badminton, ball hockey, fitness, golf, ice hockey, rowing, rugby, skiing (cross-country), soccer, tennis, track and field, weight lifting. 7 PE instructors, 7 coaches, 1 athletic trainer.
Computers Computers are regularly used in all classes. Computer network features include on-campus library services, online commercial services, Internet access, wireless campus network, Internet filtering or blocking technology, one-to-one laptop program for grades 7 to 11, course conferences, Lon Capa—online tutorial for grades 9 to 11 math and science students. Student e-mail accounts are available to students. Students grades are available online. The school has a published electronic and media policy.
Contact Ms. Nathalie Gervais, Director of Admission. 514-931-2775. Fax: 514-932-8776. E-mail: admission@selwyn.ca. Web site: www.selwyn.ca.

SEOUL FOREIGN SCHOOL

55 Yonhi-Dong
Sodaemun-Gu
Seoul 120-113, Republic of Korea
Head of School: Dr. Nancy Price

General Information Coeducational day college-preparatory and International Baccalaureate school, affiliated with Christian faith. Grades PK–12. Founded: 1912. Setting: urban. 25-acre campus. 8 buildings on campus. Approved or accredited by International Baccalaureate Organization and Western Association of Schools and Colleges. Affiliate member of National Association of Independent Schools; member of European Council of International Schools. Language of instruction: English. Endowment: $2.7 million. Total enrollment: 1,462. Upper school average class size: 18. Upper school faculty-student ratio: 1:9.
Upper School Student Profile Grade 9: 111 students (63 boys, 48 girls); Grade 10: 122 students (64 boys, 58 girls); Grade 11: 108 students (52 boys, 56 girls); Grade 12: 84 students (44 boys, 40 girls). 80% of students are Christian faith.
Faculty School total: 157. In upper school: 20 men, 28 women; 34 have advanced degrees.
Subjects Offered Algebra, American history, art, art history, Bible studies, biology, calculus, chemistry, computer science, creative writing, drama, earth science, economics, English, ESL, ethics, European history, expository writing, French, health, integrated mathematics, international relations, Korean, Korean culture, mathematics, music, philosophy, photography, physical education, physics, psychology, religion, Spanish, speech, theory of knowledge, world history, world literature.
Graduation Requirements Arts and fine arts (art, music, dance, drama), biology, computers, English, foreign language, Korean culture, mathematics, physical education (includes health), physical science, religion (includes Bible studies and theology), social studies (includes history).
Special Academic Programs International Baccalaureate program; 1 Advanced Placement exam for which test preparation is offered; honors section; academic accommodation for the gifted, the musically talented, and the artistically talented; ESL (18 students enrolled).
College Admission Counseling 96 students graduated in 2008; 90 went to college, including Carnegie Mellon University; New York University; Northwestern University; University of Illinois at Urbana–Champaign; University of Pennsylvania; University of Southern California. Other: 6 had other specific plans. Mean SAT critical reading: 620, mean SAT math: 680, mean SAT writing: 640.
Student Life Upper grades have specified standards of dress, student council, honor system. Discipline rests primarily with faculty.
Tuition and Aid Day student tuition: $21,500. Tuition installment plan (2-payment plan with final payment due in January). Need-based scholarship grants available. In 2008–09, 8% of upper-school students received aid. Total amount of financial aid awarded in 2008–09: $365,000.
Admissions Traditional secondary-level entrance grade is 9. For fall 2008, 99 students applied for upper-level admission, 65 were accepted, 57 enrolled. Deadline for receipt of application materials: none. Application fee required: $250. On-campus interview required.
Athletics Interscholastic: basketball (boys, girls), cheering (b,g), cross-country running (b,g), dance squad (g), soccer (b,g), swimming and diving (b,g), tennis (b,g), volleyball (b,g); coed intramural: badminton, lacrosse, weight lifting. 2 PE instructors.
Computers Computers are regularly used in English, history, mathematics, music, science classes. Computer network features include on-campus library services, Internet access, wireless campus network, Internet filtering or blocking technology.
Contact Mrs. Esther Myong, Admissions Director. 822-330-3100 Ext. 121. Fax: 822-335-2045. E-mail: admissions@seoulforeign.org. Web site: www.seoulforeign.org.

ANNOUNCEMENT FROM THE SCHOOL Seoul Foreign School provides programs and an atmosphere that develop the body, mind, and spirit. The academically challenging curriculum includes a program that leads to the International Baccalaureate diploma and incorporates advanced educational technological resources. Faculty members are certified, caring, and experienced. The 25-acre campus is located adjacent to a greenbelt near the heart of Seoul.

SETON CATHOLIC CENTRAL HIGH SCHOOL

70 Seminary Avenue
Binghamton, New York 13905
Head of School: Miss Kathleen M. Dwyer

General Information Coeducational day college-preparatory, arts, business, vocational, and religious studies school, affiliated with Roman Catholic Church; primarily serves individuals with emotional and behavioral problems. Grades 9–12. Founded: 1963. Setting: suburban. Nearest major city is Syracuse. 4-acre campus. 1 building on campus. Approved or accredited by Middle States Association of Colleges and Schools, National Catholic Education Association, New York State Board of Regents, and The College Board. Total enrollment: 350. Upper school average class size: 23. Upper school faculty-student ratio: 1:23.
Upper School Student Profile 90% of students are Roman Catholic.
Faculty School total: 35. In upper school: 19 men, 13 women; 27 have advanced degrees.
Subjects Offered 3-dimensional design, accounting, advanced computer applications, Advanced Placement courses, advertising design, algebra, alternative physical education, American government, American history-AP, American legal systems, American literature, American literature-AP, ancient world history, applied music, architectural drawing, art-AP, band, Bible, biology, biology-AP, business, business law, business mathematics, calculus, calculus-AP, chemistry, chemistry-AP, chorus, Christian scripture, church history, comparative religion, computer applications, computer programming, computer programming-AP, creative drama, criminal justice, dramatic arts, economics, English, English language and composition-AP, English literature and composition-AP, entrepreneurship, environmental science, ethical decision making, ethics and responsibility, European history-AP, food and nutrition, foreign language, forensic science, French, government/civics, guitar, health, honors English, honors geometry, instrumental music, integrated mathematics, keyboarding/computer, Latin, Latin-AP, law and the legal system, literature and composition-AP, math applications, mathematics-AP, music theater, music theory, performing arts, photography, physical education, physics, physics-AP, pre-algebra, religions, social psychology, Spanish, Spanish-AP, studio art-AP, theater arts, theology, U.S. history, U.S. history-AP, wood processing, work-study, world history-AP, world religions.
Graduation Requirements Arts and fine arts (art, music, dance, drama), English, foreign language, mathematics, physical education (includes health), science, social studies (includes history), theology.
Special Academic Programs Advanced Placement exam preparation; honors section; study at local college for college credit; academic accommodation for the gifted; remedial reading and/or remedial writing; remedial math.
College Admission Counseling 108 students graduated in 2008; 107 went to college, including Le Moyne College; Marywood University; State University of New York at Binghamton; The University of Scranton; Villanova University. Other: 1 entered military service. Mean SAT critical reading: 560, mean SAT math: 569, mean SAT writing: 550.
Student Life Upper grades have specified standards of dress, student council, honor system. Discipline rests primarily with faculty.
Summer Programs Enrichment, sports programs offered; held on campus; accepts boys and girls; open to students from other schools. 200 students usually enrolled.
Tuition and Aid Tuition installment plan (monthly payment plans). Tuition reduction for siblings, merit scholarship grants, need-based scholarship grants available. In 2008–09, 40% of upper-school students received aid.
Admissions Traditional secondary-level entrance grade is 9. High School Placement Test required. Deadline for receipt of application materials: none. Application fee required: $50. Interview required.
Athletics Interscholastic: baseball (boys), basketball (b,g), cross-country running (b,g), football (b), ice hockey (b), indoor track & field (b,g), lacrosse (b,g), soccer (b,g), softball (g), swimming and diving (b,g), tennis (b,g), track and field (b,g), winter (indoor) track (b,g); intramural: snowboarding (b,g), strength & conditioning (b,g), weight training (b,g); coed interscholastic: cheering, golf; coed intramural: alpine skiing. 2 PE instructors, 25 coaches, 1 athletic trainer.

Computers Computers are regularly used in business applications, computer applications, desktop publishing, economics, English, foreign language, history, keyboarding, Latin, mathematics, science, social studies, Spanish, technology, yearbook classes. Computer network features include on-campus library services, online commercial services, Internet access, wireless campus network, Internet filtering or blocking technology. Computer access in designated common areas is available to students. The school has a published electronic and media policy.
Contact Guidance Office. 607-723-5307. Fax: 607-723-4811. E-mail: secathb@syrdiocese.org. Web site: www.setoncchs.com.

SETON CATHOLIC HIGH SCHOOL

1150 North Dobson Road
Chandler, Arizona 85224

Head of School: Patricia L. Collins

General Information Coeducational day college-preparatory and Dual enrollment w/ Seton Hill Univ in specific classes school, affiliated with Roman Catholic Church. Grades 9–12. Founded: 1954. Setting: suburban. Nearest major city is Phoenix. 30-acre campus. 10 buildings on campus. Approved or accredited by North Central Association of Colleges and Schools, Western Catholic Education Association, and Arizona Department of Education. Endowment: $342,000. Total enrollment: 544. Upper school average class size: 26. Upper school faculty-student ratio: 1:14.
Upper School Student Profile Grade 9: 141 students (71 boys, 70 girls); Grade 10: 142 students (78 boys, 64 girls); Grade 11: 151 students (77 boys, 74 girls); Grade 12: 110 students (57 boys, 53 girls). 95% of students are Roman Catholic.
Faculty School total: 42. In upper school: 19 men, 23 women; 29 have advanced degrees.
Subjects Offered Aerobics, algebra, American government, American history, anatomy, art, athletic training, Basic programming, biology, biology-AP, calculus, chemistry, chemistry-AP, choir, Christian and Hebrew scripture, Christian scripture, church history, computer applications, dance, drama, drawing, economics, English, English-AP, European history-AP, fitness, foreign language, French, geometry, government, guitar, health, honors English, honors geometry, honors U.S. history, keyboarding, Latin, Latin-AP, personal fitness, photography, physics, pre-calculus, psychology, reading/study skills, religion, scripture, social justice, Spanish, Spanish-AP, study skills, television, theology, U.S. government, U.S. history, video film production, weight training, world history, world religions, yearbook.
Graduation Requirements Arts and fine arts (art, music, dance, drama), computer applications, computer literacy, English, foreign language, mathematics, physical education (includes health), religion (includes Bible studies and theology), science, social studies (includes history), study skills.
Special Academic Programs Advanced Placement exam preparation; honors section.
College Admission Counseling 111 students graduated in 2008; 109 went to college, including Arizona State University; Northern Arizona University; The University of Arizona. Other: 1 went to work, 1 entered military service. Mean SAT critical reading: 552, mean SAT math: 566, mean SAT writing: 533, mean composite ACT: 24.
Student Life Upper grades have uniform requirement, student council, honor system. Discipline rests primarily with faculty. Attendance at religious services is required.
Summer Programs Remediation programs offered; session focuses on remediation for incoming students; held on campus; accepts boys and girls; not open to students from other schools. 60 students usually enrolled. 2009 schedule: June 1 to June 26.
Tuition and Aid Day student tuition: $10,220. Tuition installment plan (FACTS Tuition Payment Plan). Merit scholarship grants, need-based scholarship grants, Catholic Tuition Organization of Diocese of Phoenix available. In 2008–09, 33% of upper-school students received aid. Total amount of financial aid awarded in 2008–09: $605,000.
Admissions Traditional secondary-level entrance grade is 9. For fall 2008, 236 students applied for upper-level admission, 170 were accepted, 141 enrolled. Scholastic Testing Service High School Placement Test required. Deadline for receipt of application materials: none. Application fee required: $50. Interview required.
Athletics Interscholastic: baseball (boys), basketball (b,g), cross-country running (b,g), diving (b,g), football (b), golf (b,g), swimming and diving (b,g), tennis (b,g), track and field (b,g), volleyball (g), wrestling (b); coed interscholastic: aerobics/dance, cheering, dance, football, physical fitness. 2 PE instructors, 1 athletic trainer.
Computers Computers are regularly used in all academic, religious studies, yearbook classes. Computer network features include on-campus library services, Internet access, Internet filtering or blocking technology, Turnitin®. Student e-mail accounts are available to students. Students grades are available online. The school has a published electronic and media policy.
Contact Mr. James Felton, Admissions and Recruitment Director. 480-963-1900 Ext. 2008. Fax: 480-963-1974. E-mail: jfelton@setonchs.org. Web site: www.setoncatholic.org.

THE SEVEN HILLS SCHOOL

5400 Red Bank Road
Cincinnati, Ohio 45227

Head of School: Mr. Christopher P. Garten

General Information Coeducational day college-preparatory, arts, and technology school. Grades PK–12. Founded: 1974. Setting: suburban. 35-acre campus. 16 buildings on campus. Approved or accredited by Independent Schools Association of the Central States. Member of National Association of Independent Schools and Secondary School Admission Test Board. Endowment: $18 million. Total enrollment: 1,040. Upper school average class size: 15. Upper school faculty-student ratio: 1:9.
Upper School Student Profile Grade 9: 70 students (33 boys, 37 girls); Grade 10: 76 students (35 boys, 41 girls); Grade 11: 78 students (40 boys, 38 girls); Grade 12: 72 students (33 boys, 39 girls).
Faculty School total: 145. In upper school: 23 men, 29 women; 45 have advanced degrees.
Subjects Offered Acting, advanced computer applications, Advanced Placement courses, African-American studies, algebra, American history, American literature, ancient history, art, art history, biology, British literature, calculus, ceramics, chemistry, computer programming, computer science, economics, English, European history, fine arts, French, geometry, journalism, Latin, linear algebra, medieval/Renaissance history, modern political theory, music, physical education, physics, pre-calculus, psychology, Spanish, speech, theater, world history, world literature, writing.
Graduation Requirements Algebra, arts and fine arts (art, music, dance, drama), biology, chemistry, computer science, English, foreign language, geometry, performing arts, physical education (includes health), physics, U.S. history, U.S. literature, completion of a personal challenge project, successfully pass writing competency exam, 30 hours of community service.
Special Academic Programs 16 Advanced Placement exams for which test preparation is offered; honors section; independent study; term-away projects; academic accommodation for the gifted.
College Admission Counseling 77 students graduated in 2008; all went to college, including Duke University; Kenyon College; Miami University; Northwestern University; Tufts University; Washington University in St. Louis. Median SAT critical reading: 641, median SAT math: 670, median SAT writing: 655. 70% scored over 600 on SAT critical reading, 87% scored over 600 on SAT math, 80% scored over 600 on SAT writing.
Student Life Upper grades have specified standards of dress, student council. Discipline rests primarily with faculty.
Summer Programs Enrichment programs offered; session focuses on SAT review, sports clinics, and acting workshop; held on campus; accepts boys and girls; open to students from other schools. 400 students usually enrolled. 2009 schedule: June 15 to August 14. Application deadline: none.
Tuition and Aid Day student tuition: $17,950–$18,420. Tuition installment plan (monthly payment plans, individually arranged payment plans). Need-based scholarship grants available. In 2008–09, 15% of upper-school students received aid. Total amount of financial aid awarded in 2008–09: $500,000.
Admissions Traditional secondary-level entrance grade is 9. For fall 2008, 55 students applied for upper-level admission, 24 were accepted, 18 enrolled. ISEE required. Deadline for receipt of application materials: December 1. Application fee required: $50. On-campus interview required.
Athletics Interscholastic: baseball (boys), basketball (b,g), cheering (g), cross-country running (b,g), golf (b), gymnastics (g), lacrosse (b,g), soccer (b,g), softball (g), swimming and diving (b,g), tennis (b,g), volleyball (g); coed interscholastic: track and field. 3 PE instructors, 9 coaches.
Computers Computers are regularly used in foreign language, mathematics, science classes. Computer network features include on-campus library services, online commercial services, Internet access.
Contact Mr. Peter C. Egan, Director of Admission and Financial Aid. 513-271-9027. Fax: 513-271-2471. E-mail: peter.egan@7hills.org. Web site: www.7hills.org.

ANNOUNCEMENT FROM THE SCHOOL The Seven Hills School is a nonprofit school with 1,050 students in PK–12 from sixty greater Cincinnati zip codes. The Upper School combines academic rigor, freedom, and accountability. Honors and AP courses are offered in all disciplines along with a wide selection of electives. The School is also widely recognized for its excellence in the fine and performing arts. The 74,000-square-foot Upper School building features twenty-four classrooms that support wired and wireless technologies, six state-of-the-art science labs, and a library/media center for grades 6–12. Highly individualized counseling is provided by 3 college counselors, and each student has a faculty adviser. Graduation requirements include community service and the completion of a personal challenge, which is an independent project of each student's own design. Challenge projects foster creative thinking and decision making, encourage students to persevere and go beyond perceived limitations, and give them the satisfaction of personal accomplishment. The 77 members of the class of 2008 received 284 offers from 163 colleges and universities in thirty-three states and Canada. SAT scores for the class of 2008 at the mid-50% were 650 verbal and 675 math. Eighty-four percent of 135 students taking 265 AP exams earned a score of 3 or better, qualifying them for advanced standing in college. Twenty-two percent of the class of 2008 qualified for National Merit/National Achievement recognition. Approximately 80% of those in the Upper School play at least one interscholastic sport. Miami Valley Conference teams include boys' and girls' basketball, cross-country, soccer, swimming, tennis, and track; boys' baseball, golf, and lacrosse; and girls' cheerleading, gymnastics, lacrosse, softball, and volleyball. The School's athletes are consistently selected for All-State, All-City, and All-League honors. Facilities include two gyms, an all-weather track, and a weight training area.

SEVERN SCHOOL

201 Water Street
Severna Park, Maryland 21146

ANNOUNCEMENT FROM THE SCHOOL Severn School is a coed day school for grades 6–12 with a current enrollment of 595 students. Severn is the oldest independent school in Anne Arundel County, founded in 1914. Severn believes in educating the whole person in a student-centered, supportive educational community and challenges its students to pursue personal excellence in character, conduct, and scholarship.

SEWICKLEY ACADEMY

315 Academy Avenue
Sewickley, Pennsylvania 15143

Head of School: Kolia J. O'Connor

General Information Coeducational day college-preparatory, arts, and technology school. Grades PK–12. Founded: 1838. Setting: suburban. Nearest major city is Pittsburgh. 30-acre campus. 10 buildings on campus. Approved or accredited by Middle States Association of Colleges and Schools, National Independent Private Schools Association, Pennsylvania Association of Independent Schools, and Pennsylvania Department of Education. Member of National Association of Independent Schools. Endowment: $27.8 million. Total enrollment: 775. Upper school average class size: 15. Upper school faculty-student ratio: 1:8.

Upper School Student Profile Grade 9: 78 students (41 boys, 37 girls); Grade 10: 72 students (36 boys, 36 girls); Grade 11: 82 students (41 boys, 41 girls); Grade 12: 73 students (35 boys, 38 girls).

Faculty School total: 106. In upper school: 28 men, 28 women; 32 have advanced degrees.

Subjects Offered Advanced chemistry, advanced studio art-AP, African studies, algebra, American history, American history-AP, American literature, American literature-AP, art, art-AP, astronomy, band, biology, biology-AP, calculus, calculus-AP, ceramics, chemistry, chemistry-AP, choral music, chorus, clayworking, computer applications, computer art, computer keyboarding, computer programming, computer science, computer science-AP, concert band, concert choir, contemporary issues, creative writing, dance, dance performance, digital art, drama, drama performance, drama workshop, drawing, driver education, economics, English, English literature, environmental science, ethics, European history, European history-AP, expository writing, fine arts, French, French language-AP, French literature-AP, geometry, German, German-AP, government/civics, health, health education, history, Italian, keyboarding/computer, Mandarin, music, musical theater, performing arts, photography, physical education, physics, physics-AP, pre-calculus, psychology, psychology-AP, senior project, Spanish, Spanish literature, Spanish-AP, speech and debate, statistics, statistics-AP, studio art, theater, trigonometry, U.S. history-AP, U.S. literature, Vietnam War, world history, world literature, writing.

Graduation Requirements Arts and fine arts (art, music, dance, drama), English, foreign language, health education, mathematics, physical education (includes health), science, social studies (includes history), U.S. history, world cultures, world studies. Community service is required.

Special Academic Programs Advanced Placement exam preparation; honors section; independent study; term-away projects; study at local college for college credit; study abroad.

College Admission Counseling 68 students graduated in 2008; all went to college, including Carnegie Mellon University; Colgate University; The College of Wooster; The George Washington University; University of Colorado at Boulder; University of Pittsburgh.

Student Life Upper grades have specified standards of dress, student council, honor system. Discipline rests equally with students and faculty.

Summer Programs Enrichment, advancement, sports, art/fine arts programs offered; session focuses on academics, athletics, and musical theater; held on campus; accepts boys and girls; open to students from other schools. 150 students usually enrolled. 2009 schedule: June 11 to August 10. Application deadline: none.

Tuition and Aid Day student tuition: $19,800. Tuition installment plan (monthly payment plans). Need-based scholarship grants available. In 2008–09, 20% of upper-school students received aid. Total amount of financial aid awarded in 2008–09: $600,000.

Admissions Traditional secondary-level entrance grade is 9. For fall 2008, 64 students applied for upper-level admission, 40 were accepted, 28 enrolled. ISEE required. Deadline for receipt of application materials: February 6. Application fee required: $50. On-campus interview required.

Athletics Interscholastic: baseball (boys), basketball (b,g), golf (b), ice hockey (b,g), lacrosse (b,g), physical fitness (b,g), soccer (b,g), softball (g), tennis (b,g); coed interscholastic: cross-country running, diving, field hockey, physical fitness, swimming and diving, track and field. 5 PE instructors, 5 coaches, 1 athletic trainer.

Computers Computers are regularly used in all academic classes. Computer network features include on-campus library services, online commercial services, Internet access, wireless campus network, Internet filtering or blocking technology. Campus intranet, student e-mail accounts, and computer access in designated common areas are available to students. The school has a published electronic and media policy.

Contact Wendy Berns, Admission Assistant. 412-741-2230 Ext. 3056. Fax: 412-741-1411. E-mail: wberns@sewickley.org. Web site: www.sewickley.org.

SHADES MOUNTAIN CHRISTIAN SCHOOL

2290 Old Tyler Road
Hoover, Alabama 35226

Head of School: Mr. Laird Crump

General Information Coeducational day college-preparatory and Biblical studies school, affiliated with Christian faith; primarily serves students with learning disabilities and dyslexic students. Grades K4–12. Founded: 1974. Setting: suburban. Nearest major city is Birmingham. 30-acre campus. 3 buildings on campus. Approved or accredited by Association of Christian Schools International, Southern Association of Colleges and Schools, and Alabama Department of Education. Total enrollment: 463. Upper school average class size: 22. Upper school faculty-student ratio: 1:22.

Upper School Student Profile Grade 9: 39 students (22 boys, 17 girls); Grade 10: 33 students (15 boys, 18 girls); Grade 11: 36 students (20 boys, 16 girls); Grade 12: 33 students (17 boys, 16 girls). 50% of students are Christian faith.

Faculty School total: 51. In upper school: 11 men, 13 women; 12 have advanced degrees.

Subjects Offered Advanced chemistry, advanced math, algebra, American government, American literature, anatomy and physiology, ancient world history, art, band, Bible studies, business applications, calculus-AP, character education, chemistry, choir, choral music, Christian doctrine, Christian education, Christian ethics, Christian scripture, Christian studies, Christianity, civics, competitive science projects, composition, composition-AP, computer applications, computer keyboarding, computer literacy, consumer economics, CPR, creative thinking, creative writing, decision making, driver education, earth and space science, economics, English, English composition, English language and composition-AP, English literature, ensembles, ethics and responsibility, finance, first aid, general science, geography, geometry, government/civics, guitar, instruments, jazz band, junior and senior seminars, leadership training, Life of Christ, marching band, math applications, math methods, math review, mathematics, mathematics-AP, music appreciation, mythology, news writing, personal finance, philosophy, physical education, physical science, physics, pre-algebra, pre-calculus, psychology, reading/study skills, relationships, religion, research and reference, research skills, rhetoric, science, science project, science research, social science, social skills, social studies, Spanish, sports medicine, technology, trigonometry, typing, U.S. government and politics, U.S. history, values and decisions, world history, yearbook.

Graduation Requirements American history, Bible, computers, economics, English, foreign language, government, mathematics, philosophy, physical education (includes health), science, world history.

Special Academic Programs Advanced Placement exam preparation; honors section; independent study; study at local college for college credit; special instructional classes for students with learning disabilities.

College Admission Counseling 42 students graduated in 2008; 35 went to college, including Auburn University; Samford University; The University of Alabama; The University of Alabama at Birmingham; University of Montevallo. Other: 6 went to work, 1 entered military service. Mean SAT critical reading: 533, mean SAT math: 495, mean composite ACT: 24. 28% scored over 26 on composite ACT.

Student Life Upper grades have specified standards of dress, student council, honor system. Discipline rests primarily with faculty. Attendance at religious services is required.

Summer Programs Remediation programs offered; session focuses on make-up courses; held on campus; accepts boys and girls; not open to students from other schools. 2 students usually enrolled. 2009 schedule: June 1 to July 31. Application deadline: May 1.

Tuition and Aid Day student tuition: $5800. Tuition installment plan (monthly payment plans). Tuition reduction for siblings, need-based scholarship grants available. In 2008–09, 5% of upper-school students received aid. Total amount of financial aid awarded in 2008–09: $19,000.

Admissions Traditional secondary-level entrance grade is 9. For fall 2008, 18 students applied for upper-level admission, 14 were accepted, 14 enrolled. Admissions testing or any standardized test required. Deadline for receipt of application materials: none. Application fee required: $500. Interview required.

Athletics Interscholastic: baseball (boys), basketball (b,g), cheering (g), cross-country running (b,g), football (b), golf (b,g), independent competitive sports (b,g),

physical fitness (b,g), physical training (b,g), soccer (b,g), softball (g), strength & conditioning (b,g), swimming and diving (b,g), volleyball (g), wrestling (b). 3 PE instructors, 4 coaches, 1 athletic trainer.
Computers Computers are regularly used in keyboarding classes. Computer resources include on-campus library services, online commercial services, Internet access, Internet filtering or blocking technology. Students grades are available online. The school has a published electronic and media policy.
Contact Mrs. Beth Buyck, School Secretary. 205-978-6001. Fax: 205-978-9120. E-mail: bethbuyck@smcs.org.

SHADY SIDE ACADEMY

423 Fox Chapel Road
Pittsburgh, Pennsylvania 15238

Head of School: Mr. Thomas N. Southard

General Information Coeducational boarding and day college-preparatory school. Boarding grades 9–12, day grades PK–12. Founded: 1883. Setting: suburban. Students are housed in single-sex dormitories. 130-acre campus. 26 buildings on campus. Approved or accredited by Middle States Association of Colleges and Schools, Pennsylvania Association of Independent Schools, The Association of Boarding Schools, and Pennsylvania Department of Education. Member of National Association of Independent Schools. Endowment: $51.7 million. Total enrollment: 960. Upper school average class size: 13. Upper school faculty-student ratio: 1:8.
Upper School Student Profile Grade 9: 131 students (80 boys, 51 girls); Grade 10: 125 students (64 boys, 61 girls); Grade 11: 131 students (74 boys, 57 girls); Grade 12: 118 students (61 boys, 57 girls). 10% of students are boarding students. 99% are state residents. 2 states are represented in upper school student body.
Faculty School total: 112. In upper school: 27 men, 31 women; 33 have advanced degrees; 17 reside on campus.
Subjects Offered Advanced Placement courses, algebra, American history, American literature, architectural drawing, architecture, art, art history, biology, calculus, calculus-AP, ceramics, chemistry, Chinese, Chinese history, computer graphics, computer math, computer programming, computer science, computer science-AP, creative writing, drama, driver education, economics, English, English literature, ethics, European history, expository writing, fine arts, fractal geometry, French, French-AP, gender issues, geography, geometry, German, German-AP, health, history, Latin, linear algebra, logic, mathematics, music, music technology, musical theater, philosophy, photography, physical education, physics, religion and culture, science, social studies, Spanish, Spanish-AP, speech, statistics, studio art, technical theater, trigonometry, world history, world literature, writing.
Graduation Requirements Arts and fine arts (art, music, dance, drama), athletics, computer science, English, foreign language, mathematics, physical education (includes health), science, social studies (includes history), CPR certification, participation in five seasons of athletics.
Special Academic Programs Advanced Placement exam preparation; honors section; accelerated programs; independent study; term-away projects; study abroad; academic accommodation for the gifted, the musically talented, and the artistically talented.
College Admission Counseling 125 students graduated in 2008; 124 went to college, including Carnegie Mellon University; Georgetown University; New York University; Stanford University; University of Pittsburgh; Wake Forest University. Other: 1 entered a postgraduate year. Mean SAT critical reading: 627, mean SAT math: 646, mean SAT writing: 639, mean combined SAT: 1912, mean composite ACT: 26. 61% scored over 600 on SAT critical reading, 67% scored over 600 on SAT math, 70% scored over 600 on SAT writing, 67% scored over 1800 on combined SAT, 51% scored over 26 on composite ACT.
Student Life Upper grades have specified standards of dress, student council. Discipline rests primarily with faculty.
Summer Programs Remediation, enrichment, advancement, sports, art/fine arts, computer instruction programs offered; session focuses on academic and non-academic enrichment; held on campus; accepts boys and girls; open to students from other schools. 1,400 students usually enrolled. 2009 schedule: June 15 to July 24. Application deadline: none.
Tuition and Aid Day student tuition: $23,100; 5-day tuition and room/board: $32,400. Tuition installment plan (Academic Management Services Plan, monthly payment plans). Tuition reduction for siblings, merit scholarship grants, need-based scholarship grants, Merit-based aid for Day students (some need required), FAME awards, partial tuition remission for children of full-time employees available. In 2008–09, 16% of upper-school students received aid; total upper-school merit-scholarship money awarded: $45,000. Total amount of financial aid awarded in 2008–09: $1,364,550.
Admissions Traditional secondary-level entrance grade is 9. For fall 2008, 178 students applied for upper-level admission, 109 were accepted, 75 enrolled. ISEE, SSAT or TOEFL required. Deadline for receipt of application materials: January 30. Application fee required: $50. On-campus interview required.
Athletics Interscholastic: baseball (boys), basketball (b,g), crew (g), cross-country running (b,g), field hockey (g), football (b), golf (b,g), ice hockey (b,g), lacrosse (b,g), soccer (b,g), softball (g), squash (b,g), swimming and diving (b,g), tennis (b,g), track and field (b,g), wrestling (b); intramural: cheering (g); coed intramural: aerobics/dance, backpacking, badminton, bowling, cricket, ultimate Frisbee, weight lifting. 1 PE instructor, 47 coaches, 1 athletic trainer.
Computers Computers are regularly used in all classes. Computer network features include on-campus library services, online commercial services, Internet access, Internet filtering or blocking technology. Student e-mail accounts are available to students. The school has a published electronic and media policy.
Contact Ms. Katherine H. Mihm, Director of Enrollment Management and Marketing. 412-447-2228. Fax: 412-968-3213. E-mail: kmihm@shadysideacademy.org. Web site: www.shadysideacademy.org.

ANNOUNCEMENT FROM THE SCHOOL Celebrating 125 years, Shady Side Academy is a coeducational independent school serving 950 students in grades pre-k through 12 across three unique campuses in the Pittsburgh area. At all levels of the Shady Side Academy experience, students are offered academic and personal growth opportunities and are supported by a committed, talented, and caring faculty. At the Junior School (grades pre-k–5), located in the Point Breeze section of Pittsburgh, the curriculum is guided by the philosophy of the Responsive Classroom, focusing on interdisciplinary teaching and learning through play and investigation. Students have a range of special courses in addition to their regular subjects in small classroom settings. An After-School Discovery program offers further support and enrichment opportunities. At the Middle School (grades 6–8), located in suburban Fox Chapel, Pennsylvania, students are encouraged to take on greater personal responsibility in their learning and to delve deeper into their individual strengths and abilities. Daily meetings with advisers and conference periods allow students the opportunity to discuss class work individually with teachers. More than thirty different athletic and activity options are available to students each year. At the Senior School (grades 9–12), also in Fox Chapel, students further develop and refine critical thinking, writing, and analytical skills that distinguish them in the college search. Dedicated college counselors guide students through a process with final results meant to fulfill their ambitions and further prepare them for their future. A five-day boarding program is also available for students in grades 9–12. The average SAT score for Shady Side Academy students is more than 400 points above the national average, with 76 percent of students scoring above 1800 (on the 2400 scale). Shady Side Academy enjoys a 100 percent college placement for graduating seniors. Ignite your child's potential today. Call 412-968-3206 or visit www.shadysideacademy.org.

SHANNON FOREST CHRISTIAN SCHOOL

829 Garlington Road
Greenville, South Carolina 29615

Head of School: Ms. Brenda K. Hillman

General Information Coeducational day college-preparatory, arts, religious studies, and technology school, affiliated with Presbyterian Church. Grades PK–12. Founded: 1968. Setting: small town. 50-acre campus. 7 buildings on campus. Approved or accredited by Association of Christian Schools International and Southern Association of Colleges and Schools. Endowment: $200,000. Total enrollment: 568. Upper school average class size: 20. Upper school faculty-student ratio: 1:17.
Upper School Student Profile Grade 6: 50 students (20 boys, 30 girls); Grade 7: 42 students (22 boys, 20 girls); Grade 8: 40 students (18 boys, 22 girls); Grade 9: 44 students (18 boys, 26 girls); Grade 10: 30 students (13 boys, 17 girls); Grade 11: 50 students (21 boys, 29 girls); Grade 12: 32 students (14 boys, 18 girls). 3% of students are Presbyterian.
Faculty School total: 49. In upper school: 7 men, 20 women; 16 have advanced degrees.
Subjects Offered Algebra, American literature, art, Bible, Bible studies, biology, biology-AP, calculus, calculus-AP, career/college preparation, chemistry, choir, college planning, computer keyboarding, computer science, drama, economics, English, English literature-AP, English-AP, European history-AP, French, geometry, government, health, journalism, literature, music, physical education, physical science, physics, pre-algebra, pre-calculus, psychology, SAT preparation, sociology, Spanish, theater arts, U.S. history, U.S. history-AP, world geography, world history, yearbook.
Graduation Requirements Computer science, English, foreign language, mathematics, physical education (includes health), religion (includes Bible studies and theology), SAT preparation, science, social science, social studies (includes history), annual attendance at two fine arts programs (grades 9—12), 30 hours of community service per year.
Special Academic Programs Advanced Placement exam preparation; honors section; programs in English, mathematics, general development for dyslexic students; special instructional classes for students with emotional/behavioral problems, learning disabilities, Attention Deficit Hyperactivity Disorder.
College Admission Counseling 29 students graduated in 2008; all went to college, including Anderson University; Clemson University; Converse College; Furman University; University of South Carolina; Wofford College.
Student Life Upper grades have uniform requirement, student council, honor system. Discipline rests primarily with faculty. Attendance at religious services is required.

Summer Programs Enrichment, sports, art/fine arts, computer instruction programs offered; held on campus; accepts boys and girls; not open to students from other schools. 150 students usually enrolled. 2009 schedule: June 1 to August 1. Application deadline: June 1.
Tuition and Aid Day student tuition: $7200. Tuition installment plan (FACTS Tuition Payment Plan). Need-based scholarship grants, Scholar Loans available. In 2008–09, 19% of upper-school students received aid. Total amount of financial aid awarded in 2008–09: $32,734.
Admissions Traditional secondary-level entrance grade is 7. For fall 2008, 80 students applied for upper-level admission, 51 were accepted, 40 enrolled. Stanford Achievement Test required. Deadline for receipt of application materials: none. Application fee required: $100. Interview required.
Athletics Interscholastic: baseball (boys), basketball (b,g), cheering (g), cross-country running (b,g), golf (b,g), soccer (b,g), swimming and diving (b,g), tennis (b,g), volleyball (g); intramural: baseball (b), flag football (b,g), soccer (b,g), tennis (b,g). 3 PE instructors, 18 coaches, 1 athletic trainer.
Computers Computers are regularly used in English, journalism, keyboarding, yearbook classes. Computer network features include on-campus library services, online commercial services, Internet access, wireless campus network, Internet filtering or blocking technology. Campus intranet is available to students. Students grades are available online. The school has a published electronic and media policy.
Contact Mrs. Andrea Culpepper, Admissions Coordinator. 864-678-5112. Fax: 864-281-9372. E-mail: aculpepper@shannonforest.com. Web site: www.shannonforest.com.

SHATTUCK-ST. MARY'S SCHOOL

1000 Shumway Avenue
PO Box 218
Faribault, Minnesota 55021

Head of School: Nicholas J.B. Stoneman

General Information Coeducational boarding and day college-preparatory and arts school, affiliated with Episcopal Church. Grades 6–12. Founded: 1858. Setting: small town. Nearest major city is Minneapolis/St. Paul. Students are housed in single-sex dormitories. 250-acre campus. 10 buildings on campus. Approved or accredited by Independent Schools Association of the Central States, Midwest Association of Boarding Schools, National Association of Episcopal Schools, The Association of Boarding Schools, and Minnesota Department of Education. Member of National Association of Independent Schools and Secondary School Admission Test Board. Endowment: $15.9 million. Total enrollment: 434. Upper school average class size: 15. Upper school faculty-student ratio: 1:9.
Upper School Student Profile Grade 9: 71 students (38 boys, 33 girls); Grade 10: 110 students (76 boys, 34 girls); Grade 11: 108 students (65 boys, 43 girls); Grade 12: 91 students (51 boys, 40 girls); Postgraduate: 1 student (1 boy). 72% of students are boarding students. 39 states are represented in upper school student body. 32% are international students. International students from Canada, China, Japan, Republic of Korea, Sweden, and Taiwan; 11 other countries represented in student body.
Faculty School total: 95. In upper school: 27 have advanced degrees; 50 reside on campus.
Subjects Offered 20th century world history, Advanced Placement courses, advanced studio art-AP, advanced TOEFL/grammar, algebra, American Civil War, American history, American history-AP, American literature, American sign language, art, art history, ballet, band, Bible studies, biology, British literature, calculus, calculus-AP, ceramics, chamber groups, chemistry, chemistry-AP, choir, choral music, community service, composition, dance, digital photography, drama, drawing, economics, English, English language and composition-AP, English literature, English literature and composition-AP, ESL, ethics, European history, expository writing, fine arts, French, French language-AP, geography, geometry, grammar, high adventure outdoor program, history, human anatomy, Latin, Latin American history, Mandarin, mathematics, Middle Eastern history, music, Native American history, oil painting, orchestra, physics, physics-AP, piano, pottery, pre-algebra, pre-calculus, psychology, public speaking, religion, robotics, science, social studies, Spanish, Spanish-AP, speech, statistics-AP, theater, trigonometry, U.S. history-AP, world history, writing.
Graduation Requirements Arts and fine arts (art, music, dance, drama), English, foreign language, mathematics, religion (includes Bible studies and theology), science, social studies (includes history), 20 hours of community service per year.
Special Academic Programs 14 Advanced Placement exams for which test preparation is offered; honors section; independent study; academic accommodation for the gifted and the musically talented; remedial reading and/or remedial writing; remedial math; ESL (40 students enrolled).
College Admission Counseling 76 students graduated in 2008; 59 went to college, including Cornell University; Harvard University; Lake Forest Academy; Princeton University; University of Minnesota, Twin Cities Campus. Other: 1 entered a postgraduate year, 16 had other specific plans.
Student Life Upper grades have specified standards of dress, student council. Discipline rests primarily with faculty. Attendance at religious services is required.
Summer Programs Sports, art/fine arts programs offered; session focuses on challenging, diversified instruction in the arts and athletics; held on campus; accepts boys and girls; open to students from other schools.
Tuition and Aid Day student tuition: $23,200; 7-day tuition and room/board: $35,950. Tuition installment plan (monthly payment plans). Merit scholarship grants, need-based scholarship grants, performing arts scholarship, Headmasters Scholarship available. In 2008–09, 47% of upper-school students received aid. Total amount of financial aid awarded in 2008–09: $3,300,000.
Admissions Traditional secondary-level entrance grade is 9. For fall 2008, 334 students applied for upper-level admission, 169 were accepted, 113 enrolled. Any standardized test, SLEP, SSAT, ERB, PSAT, SAT, PLAN or ACT or TOEFL required. Deadline for receipt of application materials: none. Application fee required: $50. Interview required.
Athletics Interscholastic: baseball (boys), basketball (b,g), fencing (b,g), golf (b,g), ice hockey (b,g), indoor soccer (b,g), lacrosse (b,g), soccer (b,g), tennis (b,g); intramural: drill team (b,g), volleyball (g), weight training (b,g); coed interscholastic: figure skating; coed intramural: aerobics/dance, dance, ice skating, jogging, outdoor activities, outdoor recreation, ropes courses, strength & conditioning, table tennis. 20 coaches, 2 athletic trainers.
Computers Computers are regularly used in animation, college planning, creative writing, English, ESL, foreign language, history, independent study, mathematics, photography, SAT preparation, science, senior seminar, speech, writing, writing, yearbook classes. Computer network features include on-campus library services, Internet access, wireless campus network, Internet filtering or blocking technology. Campus intranet, student e-mail accounts, and computer access in designated common areas are available to students. Students grades are available online. The school has a published electronic and media policy.
Contact Amy D. Wolf, Director of Admissions and Communications. 800-421-2724. Fax: 507-333-1661. E-mail: awolf@s-sm.org. Web site: www.s-sm.org.

SHEILA MORRISON SCHOOL

Utopia, Ontario, Canada
See Special Needs Schools section.

SHELTON SCHOOL AND EVALUATION CENTER

Dallas, Texas
See Special Needs Schools section.

SHENANDOAH VALLEY ACADEMY

234 West Lee Highway
New Market, Virginia 22844

Head of School: Mr. Spencer Hannah

General Information Coeducational boarding and day college-preparatory, general academic, business, vocational, religious studies, bilingual studies, and technology school, affiliated with Seventh-day Adventist Church. Grades 9–12. Founded: 1908. Setting: rural. Nearest major city is Harrisonburg. Students are housed in single-sex dormitories. 380-acre campus. 15 buildings on campus. Approved or accredited by Southern Association of Colleges and Schools, Virginia Association of Independent Schools, and Virginia Department of Education. Total enrollment: 221. Upper school average class size: 20. Upper school faculty-student ratio: 1:14.
Upper School Student Profile Grade 9: 58 students (32 boys, 26 girls); Grade 10: 57 students (23 boys, 34 girls); Grade 11: 60 students (28 boys, 32 girls); Grade 12: 46 students (21 boys, 25 girls). 81% of students are boarding students. 47% are state residents. 12 states are represented in upper school student body. 10% are international students. International students from Angola, Colombia, Republic of Korea, and Spain. 80% of students are Seventh-day Adventists.
Faculty School total: 16. In upper school: 9 men, 7 women; 10 have advanced degrees; 2 reside on campus.
Subjects Offered Accounting, algebra, anatomy and physiology, art, band, basketball, biology, business education, calculus-AP, chemistry, choir, Christianity, computer applications, concert choir, drama, driver education, English, English-AP, foreign language, general science, geometry, government/civics, health, honors English, mathematics, music, orchestra, organ, physical education, physics, piano, pre-calculus, religion, social studies, softball, Spanish, strings, swimming, symphonic band, tennis, U.S. government, U.S. history, U.S. history-AP, voice, volleyball, welding, world history.
Graduation Requirements One year of religion for each year in school.
Special Academic Programs Advanced Placement exam preparation; honors section; term-away projects; study at local college for college credit; academic accommodation for the gifted, the musically talented, and the artistically talented; remedial reading and/or remedial writing; remedial math; programs in English, mathematics, general development for dyslexic students; ESL (10 students enrolled).
College Admission Counseling 39 students graduated in 2008; 36 went to college, including Andrews University; Southern Adventist University; University of Georgia. Other: 2 went to work, 1 entered military service.
Student Life Upper grades have specified standards of dress, student council, honor system. Discipline rests primarily with faculty. Attendance at religious services is required.

Tuition and Aid Day student tuition: $9850; 7-day tuition and room/board: $6550. Tuition installment plan (FACTS Tuition Payment Plan). Merit scholarship grants, need-based scholarship grants, paying campus jobs available. In 2008–09, 70% of upper-school students received aid; total upper-school merit-scholarship money awarded: $50,000.
Admissions Traditional secondary-level entrance grade is 9. TOEFL required. Deadline for receipt of application materials: August 1. Application fee required: $50. Interview required.
Athletics Interscholastic: baseball (boys), basketball (b,g), soccer (b,g), softball (g), volleyball (g); intramural: softball (b,g); coed interscholastic: gymnastics; coed intramural: aerobics/Nautilus, backpacking, basketball, field hockey, flag football, floor hockey, indoor hockey, life saving, paddle tennis, physical fitness, skiing (downhill), snowboarding, soccer, volleyball. 1 PE instructor, 1 coach.
Computers Computers are regularly used in accounting, art, Bible studies, business education, career education, career exploration, history, library skills, newspaper, psychology, religion, research skills, SAT preparation, science, Spanish, word processing, writing, yearbook classes. Computer network features include on-campus library services, Internet access, wireless campus network, Internet filtering or blocking technology. Student e-mail accounts and computer access in designated common areas are available to students. Students grades are available online. The school has a published electronic and media policy.
Contact Mrs. Wendy Dean, Director of Admissions. 540-740-2206. Fax: 540-740-3336. E-mail: wendy.dean@sva-va.org. Web site: www.shenandoahvalleyacademy.org.

THE SHIPLEY SCHOOL

814 Yarrow Street
Bryn Mawr, Pennsylvania 19010-3598

Head of School: Dr. Steven S. Piltch

General Information Coeducational day college-preparatory school. Grades PK–12. Founded: 1894. Setting: suburban. Nearest major city is Philadelphia. 36-acre campus. 4 buildings on campus. Approved or accredited by Middle States Association of Colleges and Schools and Pennsylvania Association of Independent Schools. Member of National Association of Independent Schools and Secondary School Admission Test Board. Endowment: $16.2 million. Total enrollment: 882. Upper school average class size: 15. Upper school faculty-student ratio: 1:7.
Upper School Student Profile Grade 9: 86 students (42 boys, 44 girls); Grade 10: 88 students (49 boys, 39 girls); Grade 11: 85 students (39 boys, 46 girls); Grade 12: 84 students (43 boys, 41 girls).
Faculty School total: 108. In upper school: 23 men, 25 women; 30 have advanced degrees.
Subjects Offered Advanced chemistry, Advanced Placement courses, advanced studio art-AP, algebra, American history, American history-AP, American literature, American studies, ancient history, ancient world history, art, art history, art history-AP, band, biology, biology-AP, calculus, calculus-AP, chemistry, chemistry-AP, China/Japan history, choir, chorus, college counseling, computer keyboarding, computer literacy, computer programming, computer science, computer science-AP, concert bell choir, CPR, creative writing, desktop publishing, drama, drama performance, dramatic arts, driver education, economics, economics and history, English, English literature, English-AP, European history, European history-AP, expository writing, film studies, fine arts, finite math, French, French language-AP, geometry, global issues, global studies, government/civics, grammar, health education, history of religion, honors English, honors geometry, honors U.S. history, honors world history, humanities, jazz band, Latin, Latin American literature, Latin-AP, library skills, mathematics, mathematics-AP, medieval history, Middle East, Middle Eastern history, modern European history-AP, music, music theory, music theory-AP, musical productions, orchestra, philosophy, photography, physical education, physics, physics-AP, pre-calculus, Russia and contemporary Europe, science, sex education, Shakespeare, Shakespearean histories, social studies, Spanish, Spanish language-AP, statistics, studio art-AP, theater, theater arts, trigonometry, word processing, world affairs, world history, world literature.
Graduation Requirements Arts and fine arts (art, music, dance, drama), computer science, English, foreign language, mathematics, physical education (includes health), science, senior project, senior seminar, social studies (includes history), 40 hours of community service/service learning.
Special Academic Programs Advanced Placement exam preparation; honors section; accelerated programs; independent study; term-away projects; domestic exchange program (with The Masters School); study abroad; academic accommodation for the gifted.
College Admission Counseling 84 students graduated in 2008; 83 went to college, including Cornell University; Haverford College; Massachusetts Institute of Technology; Penn State University Park; Temple University; University of Pennsylvania. Other: 1 had other specific plans. 64% scored over 1800 on combined SAT.
Student Life Upper grades have specified standards of dress, student council, honor system. Discipline rests equally with students and faculty.
Tuition and Aid Day student tuition: $26,500. Tuition installment plan (monthly payment plans). Need-based scholarship grants, Centennial Scholarships (grade 9 need- and merit-based), prepGATE Loans available. In 2008–09, 24% of upper-school students received aid. Total amount of financial aid awarded in 2008–09: $1,652,300.
Admissions Traditional secondary-level entrance grade is 9. For fall 2008, 137 students applied for upper-level admission, 50 were accepted, 29 enrolled. ISEE, SSAT or WISC-R or WISC-III required. Deadline for receipt of application materials: January 15. Application fee required: $60. On-campus interview required.
Athletics Interscholastic: baseball (boys), basketball (b,g), crew (b,g), cross-country running (b,g), field hockey (g), independent competitive sports (b,g), lacrosse (b,g), rowing (b,g), soccer (b,g), softball (g), squash (b,g), tennis (b,g), volleyball (g), weight training (b,g); intramural: aerobics (b,g), aerobics/Nautilus (b,g), dance (g), modern dance (g), Nautilus (b,g); coed interscholastic: diving, golf, independent competitive sports, swimming and diving, weight training; coed intramural: aerobics, aerobics/Nautilus, fitness, Nautilus, physical fitness, yoga. 6 PE instructors, 51 coaches, 2 athletic trainers.
Computers Computers are regularly used in all academic classes. Computer network features include on-campus library services, online commercial services, Internet access, wireless campus network, Internet filtering or blocking technology. Campus intranet, student e-mail accounts, and computer access in designated common areas are available to students. The school has a published electronic and media policy.
Contact Mrs. Zoe Marshall, Assistant to the Director of Admissions. 610-525-4300 Ext. 4118. Fax: 610-525-5082. E-mail: zmarshall@shipleyschool.org. Web site: www.shipleyschool.org.

See Close-Up on page 966.

SHORECREST PREPARATORY SCHOOL

5101 First Street NE
Saint Petersburg, Florida 33703

Head of School: Mr. Michael A. Murphy

General Information Coeducational day college-preparatory and arts school. Grades PK–12. Founded: 1923. Setting: suburban. Nearest major city is Tampa. 28-acre campus. 3 buildings on campus. Approved or accredited by Florida Council of Independent Schools, Southern Association of Colleges and Schools, Southern Association of Independent Schools, The College Board, and Florida Department of Education. Member of National Association of Independent Schools and Secondary School Admission Test Board. Endowment: $1.5 million. Total enrollment: 968. Upper school average class size: 15. Upper school faculty-student ratio: 1:12.
Upper School Student Profile Grade 9: 66 students (38 boys, 28 girls); Grade 10: 76 students (32 boys, 44 girls); Grade 11: 77 students (31 boys, 46 girls); Grade 12: 56 students (27 boys, 29 girls).
Faculty School total: 104. In upper school: 20 men, 15 women; 23 have advanced degrees.
Subjects Offered 3-dimensional design, algebra, American literature, anatomy and physiology, ancient history, art, art history, art history-AP, band, biology, biology-AP, calculus, calculus-AP, chemistry, chemistry-AP, computer graphics, computer music, computer science, computer science-AP, conceptual physics, contemporary issues, creative writing, dance, digital imaging, drama, drawing and design, economics, economics-AP, English, English language-AP, English literature-AP, European history, European history-AP, film history, fine arts, fitness, French, French language-AP, French literature-AP, geometry, guitar, health, history of ideas, history of rock and roll, human geography—AP, humanities, journalism, Latin, Latin-AP, macroeconomics-AP, marine biology, music, music theory-AP, musical productions, musical theater, photography, physical education, physics, physics-AP, play/screen writing, political science, portfolio art, pre-calculus, psychology, psychology-AP, social studies, Spanish, Spanish language-AP, statistics and probability, studio art-AP, theater, trigonometry, U.S. history, U.S. history-AP, video film production, Web site design, weight training, Western civilization, world civilizations, world history, world history-AP, world literature, world religions, world wide web design, writing, yearbook.
Graduation Requirements Arts and fine arts (art, music, dance, drama), English, foreign language, health education, mathematics, science, social studies (includes history).
Special Academic Programs Advanced Placement exam preparation; honors section; independent study; academic accommodation for the gifted.
College Admission Counseling 63 students graduated in 2008; all went to college, including Boston College; Florida State University; University of Central Florida; University of Florida; University of Miami; University of Michigan. Mean SAT critical reading: 612, mean SAT math: 634, mean SAT writing: 605, mean combined SAT: 1851, mean composite ACT: 29.
Student Life Upper grades have specified standards of dress, student council, honor system. Discipline rests primarily with faculty.
Summer Programs Enrichment, sports, art/fine arts programs offered; session focuses on athletics and recreational activities; held on campus; accepts boys and girls; open to students from other schools. 2009 schedule: June 8 to July 31.
Tuition and Aid Day student tuition: $17,000. Tuition installment plan (monthly payment plans, semi-annual payment plan). Need-based scholarship grants available. In 2008–09, 14% of upper-school students received aid. Total amount of financial aid awarded in 2008–09: $923,650.
Admissions Traditional secondary-level entrance grade is 9. For fall 2008, 38 students applied for upper-level admission, 26 were accepted, 19 enrolled. ERB, ISEE,

PSAT or SAT, school's own test or SSAT required. Deadline for receipt of application materials: none. Application fee required: $75. On-campus interview required.
Athletics Interscholastic: baseball (boys), basketball (b,g), cheering (g), cross-country running (b,g), diving (b,g), football (b), golf (b,g), soccer (b,g), softball (g), swimming and diving (b,g), tennis (b,g), track and field (b,g), volleyball (g); coed interscholastic: sailing. 4 PE instructors, 28 coaches, 1 athletic trainer.
Computers Computers are regularly used in all academic classes. Computer network features include on-campus library services, online commercial services, Internet access, wireless campus network, Internet filtering or blocking technology. Student e-mail accounts and computer access in designated common areas are available to students. Students grades are available online. The school has a published electronic and media policy.
Contact Mrs. Diana Craig, Director of Admissions. 727-456-7511. Fax: 727-527-4191. E-mail: admissions@shorecrest.org. Web site: www.shorecrest.org.

See Close-Up on page 968.

SHORELINE CHRISTIAN

2400 Northeast 147th Street
Shoreline, Washington 98155

Head of School: Mr. Timothy E. Visser

General Information Coeducational day college-preparatory and general academic school, affiliated with Christian faith. Grades PS–12. Founded: 1952. Setting: suburban. Nearest major city is Seattle. 7-acre campus. 2 buildings on campus. Approved or accredited by Christian Schools International, Northwest Association of Accredited Schools, Northwest Association of Schools and Colleges, and Washington Department of Education. Endowment: $520,000. Total enrollment: 270. Upper school average class size: 25. Upper school faculty-student ratio: 1:7.
Upper School Student Profile Grade 9: 19 students (15 boys, 4 girls); Grade 10: 20 students (12 boys, 8 girls); Grade 11: 26 students (10 boys, 16 girls); Grade 12: 24 students (15 boys, 9 girls). 100% of students are Christian faith.
Faculty School total: 30. In upper school: 8 men, 9 women; 8 have advanced degrees.
Subjects Offered 20th century history, advanced computer applications, advanced math, Advanced Placement courses, algebra, American history, American literature, art, band, Bible, biology, British literature, calculus, chemistry, choir, Christian doctrine, college writing, composition, computer applications, consumer education, creative writing, current events, current history, drama, drawing, English, film, film appreciation, geometry, global studies, government, health, human anatomy, jazz band, keyboarding/computer, life science, life skills, literature, media, music appreciation, physical education, physical science, physics, psychology, sculpture, sociology, Spanish, speech, study skills, Washington State and Northwest History, weight training, Western civilization, world literature, world religions, yearbook.
Graduation Requirements American government, American literature, Bible, British literature, college writing, composition, electives, English, foreign language, global issues, keyboarding/computer, life skills, mathematics, occupational education, physical education (includes health), science, social science, speech, U.S. history, Washington State and Northwest History, Western civilization, world literature.
Special Academic Programs Independent study; study at local college for college credit; remedial reading and/or remedial writing.
College Admission Counseling 24 students graduated in 2008; 22 went to college, including Azusa Pacific University; Calvin College; Dordt College; Seattle Pacific University; University of Washington; Western Washington University. Other: 2 went to work. Median SAT critical reading: 520, median SAT math: 540, median SAT writing: 560, median composite ACT: 26. 38% scored over 600 on SAT critical reading, 40% scored over 600 on SAT math, 26% scored over 600 on SAT writing, 80% scored over 26 on composite ACT.
Student Life Upper grades have specified standards of dress, student council. Discipline rests primarily with faculty. Attendance at religious services is required.
Tuition and Aid Day student tuition: $8600–$8957. Tuition installment plan (monthly payment plans, individually arranged payment plans, prepaid cash tuition discount, quarterly or semi-annual payment plans). Tuition reduction for siblings, need-based scholarship grants, discount for qualifying Pastor families available. In 2008–09, 18% of upper-school students received aid. Total amount of financial aid awarded in 2008–09: $41,869.
Admissions Traditional secondary-level entrance grade is 9. For fall 2008, 15 students applied for upper-level admission, 10 were accepted, 8 enrolled. Deadline for receipt of application materials: none. Application fee required: $100. Interview required.
Athletics Interscholastic: baseball (boys), basketball (b,g), soccer (b), softball (g), volleyball (g); coed interscholastic: cheering, golf, soccer, track and field. 1 PE instructor.
Computers Computers are regularly used in all academic, art, library, media, music, occupational education, research skills, yearbook classes. Computer network features include on-campus library services, Internet access.
Contact Mrs. Laurie Dykstra, Director of Development. 206-364-7777 Ext. 308. Fax: 206-364-0349. E-mail: ldykstra@shorelinechristian.org. Web site: www.shorelinechristian.org.

SIOUX FALLS CHRISTIAN HIGH SCHOOL

6120 S Charger Avenue
Sioux Falls, South Dakota 57108

Head of School: Supt. Jay Woudstra

General Information Coeducational day college-preparatory, arts, business, religious studies, bilingual studies, and technology school, affiliated with Christian faith; primarily serves students with learning disabilities and individuals with Attention Deficit Disorder. Grades K–12. Founded: 1976. Setting: suburban. 40-acre campus. 1 building on campus. Approved or accredited by Christian Schools International and South Dakota Department of Education. Endowment: $200,000. Total enrollment: 764. Upper school average class size: 22. Upper school faculty-student ratio: 1:19.
Upper School Student Profile Grade 9: 55 students (25 boys, 30 girls); Grade 10: 55 students (36 boys, 19 girls); Grade 11: 44 students (20 boys, 24 girls); Grade 12: 60 students (31 boys, 29 girls). 100% of students are Christian faith.
Faculty School total: 21. In upper school: 8 men, 11 women; 11 have advanced degrees.
Subjects Offered Advanced Placement courses, algebra, American history, American literature, art, Bible studies, biology, business, calculus, chemistry, computer math, computer programming, computer science, earth science, economics, English, English literature, environmental science, ethics, geography, geology, government/civics, grammar, history, mathematics, media, music, physical education, physics, physiology, pre-calculus, psychology, religion, social studies, sociology, Spanish, speech, trigonometry, typing, world history, writing.
Graduation Requirements Algebra, American government, American history, American literature, Bible, biology, British literature, calculus-AP, chemistry, English, English composition, ethics, keyboarding/computer, literature, mathematics, physical education (includes health), physical science, physics-AP, physiology, physiology-anatomy, Spanish, speech, U.S. history, world geography, world history, service project for seniors.
Special Academic Programs Advanced Placement exam preparation; study at local college for college credit.
College Admission Counseling 50 students graduated in 2008; 40 went to college, including Bethel College; Calvin College; Dordt College; Northwestern College; South Dakota State University; University of Sioux Falls. Other: 4 went to work, 2 entered military service, 2 entered a postgraduate year, 2 had other specific plans. Median composite ACT: 24.
Student Life Upper grades have specified standards of dress, student council, honor system. Discipline rests primarily with faculty. Attendance at religious services is required.
Tuition and Aid Day student tuition: $5350. Need-based scholarship grants available. In 2008–09, 10% of upper-school students received aid. Total amount of financial aid awarded in 2008–09: $100,000.
Admissions Traditional secondary-level entrance grade is 9. For fall 2008, 25 students applied for upper-level admission, 22 were accepted, 20 enrolled. Deadline for receipt of application materials: none. Application fee required: $60. On-campus interview required.
Athletics Interscholastic: basketball (boys, girls), cross-country running (b,g), football (b), golf (b,g), soccer (b,g), track and field (b,g), volleyball (g); intramural: dance squad (g). 1 PE instructor, 16 coaches.
Computers Computers are regularly used in accounting, desktop publishing, economics, mathematics, multimedia, word processing classes. Computer network features include Internet access, Internet filtering or blocking technology. Students grades are available online. The school has a published electronic and media policy.
Contact Jay Woudstra, Superintendent. 605-334-1422. Fax: 605-334-6928. E-mail: sfchristian@sfchristian.org.

SKY RANCH FOR BOYS, INC.

Sky Ranch, South Dakota
See Special Needs Schools section.

SMITH SCHOOL

New York, New York
See Special Needs Schools section.

SMITHVILLE DISTRICT CHRISTIAN HIGH SCHOOL

6488 Smithville Road
Smithville, Ontario L0R 2A0, Canada

Head of School: Mr. Ted W. Harris

General Information Coeducational day college-preparatory, general academic, arts, business, vocational, religious studies, bilingual studies, and technology school, affiliated with Christian faith, Christian Reformed Church. Grades 9–12. Founded: 1980. Setting: small town. Nearest major city is Hamilton, Canada. 4-acre campus. 1 building on campus. Approved or accredited by Christian Schools International,

Ontario Ministry of Education, and Ontario Department of Education. Language of instruction: English. Total enrollment: 225. Upper school average class size: 18. Upper school faculty-student ratio: 1:11.
Upper School Student Profile 95% of students are Christian, members of Christian Reformed Church.
Faculty School total: 19. In upper school: 12 men, 7 women; 3 have advanced degrees.
Subjects Offered 20th century history, accounting, advanced math, ancient history, arts, athletics, Bible, biology, business, calculus, Canadian geography, Canadian history, careers, chemistry, civics, computer applications, computer information systems, computer science, construction, data analysis, discrete math, drama, dramatic arts, English, finance, fitness, food and nutrition, French, French as a second language, functions, general math, geography, geometry, health, health education, healthful living, history, instrumental music, integrated technology fundamentals, mathematics, media, parenting, personal finance, physical education, physics, science, society challenge and change, transportation technology, urban studies, visual arts, world geography, world history, writing fundamentals.
Graduation Requirements Arts, Bible, Canadian geography, Canadian history, careers, civics, electives, English, French, mathematics, physical education (includes health), science, society challenge and change.
Special Academic Programs Independent study; remedial reading and/or remedial writing; remedial math; programs in English for dyslexic students; special instructional classes for students with learning disabilities, Attention Deficit Disorder, emotional and behavioral problems.
College Admission Counseling 65 students graduated in 2008; 60 went to college, including Calvin College; Dordt College; Redeemer University College. Other: 5 went to work.
Student Life Upper grades have uniform requirement, student council, honor system. Discipline rests primarily with faculty.
Tuition and Aid Day student tuition: CAN$11,950. Tuition installment plan (monthly payment plans, individually arranged payment plans). Tuition reduction for siblings, bursaries available.
Admissions Traditional secondary-level entrance grade is 9. Deadline for receipt of application materials: none. No application fee required. Interview required.
Athletics Interscholastic: badminton (boys, girls), basketball (b,g), cross-country running (b,g), soccer (b,g), track and field (b,g), volleyball (b,g); coed interscholastic: badminton; coed intramural: ball hockey, basketball, field hockey, hockey, winter soccer. 2 PE instructors, 10 coaches.
Computers Computers are regularly used in Bible studies, business education, college planning, construction, current events, data processing, design, drafting, English, geography, history, independent study, introduction to technology, keyboarding, library, occupational education, photography, reading, social sciences, social studies, technical drawing, word processing, writing, writing, writing fundamentals, yearbook classes. Computer network features include Internet access. Student e-mail accounts are available to students.
Contact Mr. Al Korvemaker, Director of Program. 905-957-3255. Fax: 905-957-3431. E-mail: akorvemaker@sdch.on.ca. Web site: www.sdch.on.ca.

SOLEBURY SCHOOL

6832 Phillips Mill Road
New Hope, Pennsylvania 18938-9682

Head of School: Mr. Thomas G Wilschutz

General Information Coeducational boarding and day college-preparatory and arts school. Boarding grades 9–12, day grades 7–12. Founded: 1925. Setting: small town. Nearest major city is Philadelphia. Students are housed in single-sex dormitories. 90-acre campus. 22 buildings on campus. Approved or accredited by Middle States Association of Colleges and Schools, Pennsylvania Association of Independent Schools, The Association of Boarding Schools, and Pennsylvania Department of Education. Member of National Association of Independent Schools and Secondary School Admission Test Board. Endowment: $4 million. Total enrollment: 220. Upper school average class size: 11. Upper school faculty-student ratio: 1:5.
Upper School Student Profile Grade 9: 44 students (21 boys, 23 girls); Grade 10: 41 students (25 boys, 16 girls); Grade 11: 62 students (35 boys, 27 girls); Grade 12: 48 students (31 boys, 17 girls); Postgraduate: 1 student (1 boy). 30% of students are boarding students. 42% are state residents. 7 states are represented in upper school student body. 14% are international students. International students from China, Germany, Japan, Republic of Korea, Taiwan, and Viet Nam; 3 other countries represented in student body.
Faculty School total: 55. In upper school: 30 men, 25 women; 25 have advanced degrees; 24 reside on campus.
Subjects Offered Acting, advanced biology, advanced chemistry, advanced computer applications, Advanced Placement courses, advanced TOEFL/grammar, algebra, American government-AP, American history-AP, American studies, anatomy and physiology, ancient history, applied music, art, art history, art-AP, audio visual/media, biology, calculus, calculus-AP, ceramics, chemistry, chorus, computer graphics, computer music, computer programming, conceptual physics, creative writing, criminal justice, current events, digital photography, drama, drawing, English, English-AP, environmental science-AP, ESL, ethics, fine arts, food and nutrition, forensics, fractal geometry, French, French-AP, geometry, government and politics-AP, health, honors geometry, Middle East, music, painting, performing arts, photography, physical education, pre-algebra, pre-calculus, printmaking, psychology, public speaking, sculpture, senior project, Shakespeare, Spanish, Spanish-AP, statistics-AP, studio art, theater, theater design and production, trigonometry, U.S. history, world history, writing.
Graduation Requirements Art, computers, electives, English, foreign language, health, mathematics, science, social studies (includes history), 10 hours of community service per year.
Special Academic Programs Advanced Placement exam preparation; honors section; independent study; term-away projects; academic accommodation for the gifted, the musically talented, and the artistically talented; remedial reading and/or remedial writing; programs in English, general development for dyslexic students; ESL (23 students enrolled).
College Admission Counseling 49 students graduated in 2008; 47 went to college, including American University; Colgate University; Fashion Institute of Technology; Fordham University; New York University; Rhode Island School of Design. Other: 2 went to work. Mean SAT critical reading: 541, mean SAT math: 564, mean SAT writing: 555, mean combined SAT: 1660. 37% scored over 600 on SAT critical reading, 39% scored over 600 on SAT math, 35% scored over 600 on SAT writing, 30% scored over 1800 on combined SAT.
Student Life Upper grades have student council. Discipline rests equally with students and faculty.
Summer Programs ESL programs offered; session focuses on ESL; held both on and off campus; held at Washington, DC; Philadelphia, PA; New York, NY; Baltimore, MD; accepts boys and girls; open to students from other schools. 36 students usually enrolled. 2009 schedule: July 6 to August 14. Application deadline: April 30.
Tuition and Aid Day student tuition: $25,650; 7-day tuition and room/board: $38,500. Tuition installment plan (Key Tuition Payment Plan, monthly payment plans). Merit scholarship grants, need-based scholarship grants available. In 2008–09, 36% of upper-school students received aid; total upper-school merit-scholarship money awarded: $70,000. Total amount of financial aid awarded in 2008–09: $1,500,000.
Admissions Traditional secondary-level entrance grade is 9. For fall 2008, 157 students applied for upper-level admission, 109 were accepted, 67 enrolled. Any standardized test, SSAT or TOEFL or SLEP required. Deadline for receipt of application materials: January 15. Application fee required: $50. Interview required.
Athletics Interscholastic: baseball (boys), basketball (b,g), field hockey (g), lacrosse (g), soccer (b,g), softball (g), wrestling (b); coed interscholastic: cross-country running, tennis, track and field; coed intramural: bicycling, canoeing/kayaking, dance, fitness, fitness walking, golf, hiking/backpacking, horseback riding, independent competitive sports, outdoor activities, rock climbing, skiing (downhill), tennis, ultimate Frisbee, walking, weight training, yoga. 1 PE instructor, 1 coach.
Computers Computers are regularly used in art, college planning, English, ESL, foreign language, independent study, language development, literary magazine, mathematics, music, news writing, newspaper, research skills, science, social studies, theater, yearbook classes. Computer network features include on-campus library services, online commercial services, Internet access, wireless campus network, Internet filtering or blocking technology, AV room. Campus intranet, student e-mail accounts, and computer access in designated common areas are available to students. The school has a published electronic and media policy.
Contact Mr. Scott Eckstein, Director of Admission. 215-862-5261. Fax: 215-862-3366. E-mail: admissions@solebury.org. Web site: www.solebury.org.

See Close-Up on page 970.

SOLOMON LEARNING INSTITUTE, LTD.

#228, 10621 100th Avenue
Edmonton, Alberta T5J 0B3, Canada

Head of School: Ms. Ping Ping Lee

General Information Coeducational day and distance learning college-preparatory and general academic school. Grades 10–12. Distance learning grades 10–12. Founded: 1994. Setting: urban. 1 building on campus. Approved or accredited by Association of Independent Schools and Colleges of Alberta and Alberta Department of Education. Language of instruction: English. Upper school average class size: 10. Upper school faculty-student ratio: 1:10.
Upper School Student Profile Grade 10: 3 students (3 girls); Grade 11: 11 students (5 boys, 6 girls); Grade 12: 26 students (15 boys, 11 girls).
Faculty School total: 5. In upper school: 2 men, 2 women; 4 have advanced degrees.
Subjects Offered Biology, calculus, career and personal planning, chemistry, Chinese, computer information systems, computer keyboarding, computer skills, computer technologies, English literature, ESL, mathematics, physics, social studies.
Special Academic Programs ESL (55 students enrolled).
College Admission Counseling Colleges students went to include University of Alberta; University of Calgary; University of Lethbridge.
Student Life Discipline rests equally with students and faculty.
Tuition and Aid Day student tuition: CAN$5800. Financial aid available to upper-school students. In 2008–09, 10% of upper-school students received aid. Total amount of financial aid awarded in 2008–09: CAN$5500.

Admissions For fall 2008, 40 students applied for upper-level admission, 40 were accepted, 40 enrolled. Placement test required. Deadline for receipt of application materials: August 1. Application fee required: CAN$200.
Computers Computers are regularly used in information technology classes. Computer network features include Internet access, wireless campus network, Internet filtering or blocking technology. Campus intranet is available to students.
Contact Mr. Sunny Ip, Registrar. 780-431-1516. Fax: 780-431-1644. E-mail: admin@solomoncollege.ca.

SORENSON'S RANCH SCHOOL

Koosharem, Utah
See Special Needs Schools section.

SOUNDVIEW PREPARATORY SCHOOL

370 Underhill Avenue
Yorktown Heights, New York 10598
Head of School: W. Glyn Hearn

General Information Coeducational day college-preparatory, arts, and technology school. Grades 6–PG. Founded: 1989. Setting: suburban. Nearest major city is New York. 13-acre campus. 7 buildings on campus. Approved or accredited by New York State Association of Independent Schools and New York Department of Education. Total enrollment: 65. Upper school average class size: 7. Upper school faculty-student ratio: 1:5.
Upper School Student Profile Grade 9: 15 students (9 boys, 6 girls); Grade 10: 20 students (16 boys, 4 girls); Grade 11: 10 students (5 boys, 5 girls); Grade 12: 10 students (8 boys, 2 girls).
Faculty School total: 18. In upper school: 3 men, 15 women; 15 have advanced degrees.
Subjects Offered Advanced Placement courses, algebra, American history, American literature, art, art history, biology, calculus, chemistry, computer literacy, creative writing, drama, earth science, English, English literature, environmental studies, European history, expository writing, forensics, French, geometry, grammar, health, Italian, Latin, mathematics, philosophy, physical education, physics, psychology, science, social studies, Spanish, trigonometry, U.S. government, world history.
Graduation Requirements Arts and fine arts (art, music, dance, drama), English, foreign language, mathematics, physical education (includes health), science, social studies (includes history).
Special Academic Programs Advanced Placement exam preparation; honors section; accelerated programs; independent study; academic accommodation for the gifted, the musically talented, and the artistically talented; special instructional classes for students needing wheelchair accessibility.
College Admission Counseling 14 students graduated in 2008; 13 went to college, including Bard College; Brown University; Dickinson State University; Maryland Institute College of Art; Northeastern University; Syracuse University. Other: 1 entered a postgraduate year. Median SAT critical reading: 560, median SAT math: 560, median SAT writing: 554, median composite ACT: 24.
Student Life Discipline rests primarily with faculty.
Summer Programs Remediation, enrichment, advancement programs offered; session focuses on enrichment and remediation; held on campus; accepts boys and girls; open to students from other schools. 10 students usually enrolled. 2009 schedule: July 7 to August 15. Application deadline: none.
Tuition and Aid Day student tuition: $29,750–$30,650. Need-based scholarship grants available. In 2008–09, 15% of upper-school students received aid. Total amount of financial aid awarded in 2008–09: $240,000.
Admissions Traditional secondary-level entrance grade is 9. ERB (CTP-Verbal, Quantitative) or ERB Mathematics required. Deadline for receipt of application materials: none. Application fee required: $50. On-campus interview required.
Athletics Coed Interscholastic: basketball, soccer, ultimate Frisbee; coed intramural: bowling, cheering, ice skating, juggling, martial arts, tennis, volleyball. 1 coach.
Computers Computers are regularly used in all academic classes. Computer network features include Internet access, wireless campus network, Internet filtering or blocking technology. Campus intranet and student e-mail accounts are available to students. The school has a published electronic and media policy.
Contact Mary E. Ivanyi, Assistant Head. 914-962-2780. Fax: 914-302-2769. E-mail: mivanyi@soundviewprep.org. Web site: www.soundviewprep.org.

See Close-Up on page 972.

SOUTHFIELD CHRISTIAN HIGH SCHOOL

28650 Lahser Road
Southfield, Michigan 48034-2099
Head of School: Mrs. Margie Baldwin

General Information Coeducational day college-preparatory, arts, religious studies, and technology school, affiliated with Christian faith, Evangelical faith. Grades K–12. Founded: 1970. Setting: suburban. Nearest major city is Detroit. 28-acre campus. 1 building on campus. Approved or accredited by Association of Christian Schools International, Independent Schools Association of the Central States, North Central Association of Colleges and Schools, and Michigan Department of Education. Endowment: $1.5 million. Total enrollment: 578. Upper school average class size: 22. Upper school faculty-student ratio: 1:20.
Upper School Student Profile Grade 9: 39 students (17 boys, 22 girls); Grade 10: 53 students (24 boys, 29 girls); Grade 11: 59 students (33 boys, 26 girls); Grade 12: 65 students (25 boys, 40 girls). 100% of students are Christian faith, members of Evangelical faith.
Faculty School total: 24. In upper school: 12 men, 12 women; 18 have advanced degrees.
Subjects Offered Accounting, Advanced Placement courses, algebra, American government, American history, American history-AP, American literature, American literature-AP, ancient world history, art, band, Bible, biology, biology-AP, British literature, calculus-AP, chemistry, chemistry-AP, choir, chorus, communication arts, composition-AP, computer applications, computer programming, conceptual physics, creative writing, drawing and design, economics, English language-AP, English literature and composition-AP, film and literature, French, geography, geometry, government, graphic design, health, instrumental music, Life of Christ, literature and composition-AP, Middle Eastern history, New Testament, organic chemistry, photography, physical education, physics-AP, pre-calculus, probability and statistics, Russian history, senior project, Spanish, speech and debate, U.S. history, vocal music, Web site design, world studies, yearbook.
Special Academic Programs Advanced Placement exam preparation; honors section; independent study.
College Admission Counseling 63 students graduated in 2008; all went to college, including Cedarville University; Central Michigan University; Grand Valley State University; Michigan State University; University of Michigan; Wheaton College. Median SAT critical reading: 612, median SAT math: 589, median composite ACT: 25. 62% scored over 600 on SAT critical reading, 42% scored over 600 on SAT math, 46% scored over 26 on composite ACT.
Student Life Upper grades have uniform requirement, student council. Discipline rests primarily with faculty. Attendance at religious services is required.
Summer Programs Rigorous outdoor training programs offered; session focuses on physical education; held on campus; accepts boys and girls; not open to students from other schools. 10 students usually enrolled. 2009 schedule: June 8 to July 3. Application deadline: May 1.
Tuition and Aid Day student tuition: $8100. Tuition installment plan (FACTS Tuition Payment Plan). Tuition reduction for siblings, need-based scholarship grants available. In 2008–09, 5% of upper-school students received aid. Total amount of financial aid awarded in 2008–09: $50,000.
Admissions Traditional secondary-level entrance grade is 9. For fall 2008, 46 students applied for upper-level admission, 19 were accepted, 19 enrolled. Any standardized test required. Deadline for receipt of application materials: none. No application fee required. On-campus interview required.
Athletics Interscholastic: baseball (boys), cheering (g), football (b), softball (g), volleyball (g); coed interscholastic: basketball, cross-country running, golf, soccer, track and field; coed intramural: archery, backpacking, badminton, bicycling, flag football, floor hockey, Frisbee, skiing (cross-country), weight lifting. 2 PE instructors, 1 athletic trainer.
Computers Computers are regularly used in accounting, art, commercial art, computer applications, creative writing, drawing and design, graphic arts, graphic design, independent study, media production, programming, publishing, Web site design, writing, yearbook classes. Computer network features include on-campus library services, Internet access, wireless campus network, Internet filtering or blocking technology. Students grades are available online. The school has a published electronic and media policy.
Contact Dr. Phil Ackley, High School Principal. 248-357-3660 Ext. 247. Fax: 248-357-5271. E-mail: packley@southfieldchristian.org. Web site: www.southfieldchristian.org.

SOUTH KENT SCHOOL

40 Bull's Bridge Road
South Kent, Connecticut 06785
Head of School: Mr. Andrew J. Vadnais

General Information Boys' boarding and day college-preparatory, arts, and technology school, affiliated with Episcopal Church. Grades 9–PG. Founded: 1923. Setting: rural. Nearest major city is New York, NY. Students are housed in single-sex dormitories. 320-acre campus. 30 buildings on campus. Approved or accredited by National Association of Episcopal Schools, New England Association of Schools and Colleges, The Association of Boarding Schools, and Connecticut Department of Education. Member of National Association of Independent Schools and Secondary School Admission Test Board. Endowment: $4 million. Total enrollment: 145. Upper school average class size: 7. Upper school faculty-student ratio: 1:4.
Upper School Student Profile Grade 9: 18 students (18 boys); Grade 10: 28 students (28 boys); Grade 11: 42 students (42 boys); Grade 12: 42 students (42 boys); Postgraduate: 15 students (15 boys). 88% of students are boarding students. 28% are state residents. 17 states are represented in upper school student body. 17% are

international students. International students from Bermuda, China, Japan, Republic of Korea, Slovakia, and Thailand; 2 other countries represented in student body. 35% of students are members of Episcopal Church.

Faculty School total: 34. In upper school: 23 men, 11 women; 11 have advanced degrees; 25 reside on campus.

Subjects Offered Algebra, American history, American literature, art, art history, biology, calculus, ceramics, chemistry, creative writing, driver education, English, English literature, ESL, European history, expository writing, fine arts, French, geometry, grammar, health, history, mathematics, Native American history, photography, physics, physiology, psychology, science, Spanish, world history, writing.

Graduation Requirements Art, English, foreign language, lab science, mathematics, U.S. history.

Special Academic Programs Advanced Placement exam preparation; honors section; independent study; ESL (9 students enrolled).

College Admission Counseling 40 students graduated in 2007; 38 went to college, including Charleston Southern University; Clemson University; Hobart and William Smith Colleges; Lafayette College; Northeastern University; Purdue University. Other: 2 entered a postgraduate year. Median SAT critical reading: 520, median SAT math: 500. 18% scored over 600 on SAT critical reading, 24% scored over 600 on SAT math.

Student Life Upper grades have specified standards of dress, student council, honor system. Discipline rests primarily with faculty. Attendance at religious services is required.

Tuition and Aid Day student tuition: $24,000; 7-day tuition and room/board: $37,000. Tuition installment plan (Key Tuition Payment Plan, SMART Tuition Payment Plan, monthly payment plans, individually arranged payment plans). Merit scholarship grants, need-based scholarship grants, need-based loans, middle-income loans available. In 2007–08, 27% of upper-school students received aid. Total amount of financial aid awarded in 2007–08: $1,370,000.

Admissions Traditional secondary-level entrance grade is 9. For fall 2007, 185 students applied for upper-level admission, 120 were accepted, 67 enrolled. SSAT and writing sample required. Deadline for receipt of application materials: none. Application fee required: $40. Interview required.

Athletics Interscholastic: baseball, basketball, crew, cross-country running, football, golf, ice hockey, lacrosse, ropes courses, soccer, tennis; intramural: alpine skiing, baseball, basketball, bicycling, canoeing/kayaking, climbing, crew, golf, hiking/backpacking, ice hockey, outdoor activities, skiing (cross-country), skiing (downhill), snowboarding, soccer, strength & conditioning, ultimate Frisbee, wall climbing, weight lifting, weight training. 28 coaches, 2 athletic trainers.

Computers Computers are regularly used in art classes. Computer network features include on-campus library services, online commercial services, Internet access, wireless campus network, Internet filtering or blocking technology. Student e-mail accounts are available to students. The school has a published electronic and media policy.

Contact Mr. Richard A. Brande, Director of Admissions and Financial Aid. 860-927-3539 Ext. 202. Fax: 860-927-0024. E-mail: brander@southkentschool.net. Web site: www.southkentschool.net.

See Close-Up on page 974.

SOUTHRIDGE SCHOOL

2656 160th Street
Surrey, British Columbia V3S 0B7, Canada

Head of School: Mr. Drew Stephens

General Information Coeducational day college-preparatory, arts, and technology school. Grades K–12. Founded: 1994. Setting: suburban. Nearest major city is Vancouver, Canada. 17-acre campus. 2 buildings on campus. Approved or accredited by California Association of Independent Schools, Canadian Association of Independent Schools, and British Columbia Department of Education. Language of instruction: English. Endowment: CAN$500,000. Total enrollment: 662. Upper school average class size: 22. Upper school faculty-student ratio: 1:10.

Upper School Student Profile Grade 6: 44 students (23 boys, 21 girls); Grade 7: 44 students (22 boys, 22 girls); Grade 8: 66 students (32 boys, 34 girls); Grade 9: 66 students (33 boys, 33 girls); Grade 10: 67 students (34 boys, 33 girls); Grade 11: 68 students (32 boys, 36 girls); Grade 12: 66 students (31 boys, 35 girls).

Faculty School total: 58. In upper school: 12 men, 17 women; 17 have advanced degrees.

Subjects Offered Biology, biology-AP, calculus-AP, chemistry, chemistry-AP, computer science-AP, drama, economics, English, English language-AP, English literature-AP, French, geography, history-AP, information technology, jazz band, mathematics, media arts, physical education, physics, physics-AP, science, social studies, Spanish, studio art, studio art—AP, world civilizations.

Graduation Requirements Applied skills, arts and fine arts (art, music, dance, drama), athletics, career planning, language arts, mathematics, science, social studies or BC First Nations studies, 30 hours of service per year.

Special Academic Programs Advanced Placement exam preparation; honors section; term-away projects; study abroad.

College Admission Counseling 64 students graduated in 2008; 63 went to college, including Carleton University; Queen's University at Kingston; The University of British Columbia; The University of Western Ontario; University of Alberta; University of Victoria. Other: 1 went to work. Mean SAT critical reading: 628, mean SAT math: 650. 80% scored over 600 on SAT critical reading, 90% scored over 600 on SAT math.

Student Life Upper grades have uniform requirement, student council, honor system. Discipline rests primarily with faculty.

Summer Programs Enrichment, ESL, sports, art/fine arts, computer instruction programs offered; session focuses on K-12 academic and extracurricular activities; held both on and off campus; held at various nearby locations especially relating to outdoor education; accepts boys and girls; open to students from other schools. 900 students usually enrolled. 2009 schedule: July 1 to July 30. Application deadline: June 15.

Tuition and Aid Day student tuition: CAN$10,000–CAN$12,000. Tuition installment plan (individually arranged payment plans, quarterly payment plan). Tuition reduction for siblings, bursaries available. In 2008–09, 1% of upper-school students received aid. Total amount of financial aid awarded in 2008–09: CAN$50,000.

Admissions Traditional secondary-level entrance grade is 8. For fall 2008, 160 students applied for upper-level admission, 38 were accepted, 32 enrolled. Achievement/Aptitude/Writing, CCAT, PSAT and SAT for applicants to grade 11 and 12 or SSAT required. Deadline for receipt of application materials: January 15. Application fee required: CAN$250. On-campus interview required.

Athletics Interscholastic: field hockey (girls), rugby (b), soccer (b,g), swimming and diving (b,g), synchronized swimming (g), track and field (b,g), volleyball (g); intramural: ice hockey (g); coed interscholastic: aquatics, basketball, cross-country running, golf, tennis; coed intramural: aerobics/Nautilus, alpine skiing, backpacking, badminton, ball hockey, bicycling, canoeing/kayaking, cross-country running, floor hockey, hiking/backpacking, jogging, kayaking, ocean paddling, outdoor education, running, skiing (cross-country), skiing (downhill), snowboarding, snowshoeing, ultimate Frisbee, volleyball, wall climbing, weight lifting, weight training, yoga. 2 PE instructors.

Computers Computers are regularly used in all academic classes. Computer network features include on-campus library services, Internet access, wireless campus network, Internet filtering or blocking technology, grades 5-12 laptop program. Campus intranet and student e-mail accounts are available to students. The school has a published electronic and media policy.

Contact Ms. Kristine Mathiasen, Admissions Officer. 604-542-2345. Fax: 604-542-3767. E-mail: kmathias@southridge.bc.ca. Web site: www.southridge.bc.ca.

SOUTHWESTERN ACADEMY

Beaver Creek Ranch Campus
Rimrock, Arizona 86335

Head of School: Mr. Kenneth Veronda

General Information Coeducational boarding and day college-preparatory and general academic school. Grades 9–PG. Founded: 1963. Setting: rural. Nearest major city is Sedona. Students are housed in single-sex dormitories. 180-acre campus. 24 buildings on campus. Approved or accredited by Arizona Association of Independent Schools, The Association of Boarding Schools, Western Association of Schools and Colleges, and Arizona Department of Education. Endowment: $9.2 million. Total enrollment: 32. Upper school average class size: 6. Upper school faculty-student ratio: 1:3.

Upper School Student Profile Grade 9: 7 students (3 boys, 4 girls); Grade 10: 5 students (3 boys, 2 girls); Grade 11: 12 students (5 boys, 7 girls); Grade 12: 5 students (3 boys, 2 girls); Postgraduate: 3 students (2 boys, 1 girl). 100% of students are boarding students. 3% are state residents. 5 states are represented in upper school student body. 53% are international students. International students from China, Nepal, Republic of Korea, Serbia and Montenegro, Taiwan, and Thailand; 3 other countries represented in student body.

Faculty School total: 12. In upper school: 5 men, 7 women; 4 have advanced degrees; 7 reside on campus.

Subjects Offered Advanced math, Advanced Placement courses, algebra, American history, American literature, American literature-AP, art, art appreciation, art history, astronomy, biology, biology-AP, British literature, calculus, chemistry, earth science, ecology, economics, English, English composition, environmental education, environmental science, environmental studies, ESL, fashion, fine arts, general math, geometry, health, integrated science, Latin, math review, mathematics, music, music appreciation, outdoor education, physics, pre-algebra, Spanish, studio art, U.S. government, world cultures, yearbook.

Graduation Requirements Algebra, American government, American history, American literature, British literature, computer literacy, economics, electives, English, foreign language, geometry, lab science, mathematics, physical education (includes health), visual and performing arts, world cultures. Community service is required.

Special Academic Programs Advanced Placement exam preparation; honors section; accelerated programs; independent study; term-away projects; study at local college for college credit; ESL (6 students enrolled).

College Admission Counseling 4 students graduated in 2007; all went to college, including Arizona State University; California State University, Long Beach; Pacific Lutheran University; Trent University. Median SAT critical reading: 450, median SAT math: 600, median SAT writing: 550.
Student Life Upper grades have specified standards of dress, student council, honor system. Discipline rests primarily with faculty.
Tuition and Aid Day student tuition: $14,400; 7-day tuition and room/board: $31,400. Tuition installment plan (monthly payment plans, individually arranged payment plans). Need-based scholarship grants available. In 2007–08, 43% of upper-school students received aid. Total amount of financial aid awarded in 2007–08: $392,300.
Admissions Traditional secondary-level entrance grade is 9. For fall 2007, 33 students applied for upper-level admission, 24 were accepted, 11 enrolled. Any standardized test required. Deadline for receipt of application materials: none. Application fee required: $100. Interview recommended.
Athletics Interscholastic: basketball (boys, girls), volleyball (g); coed interscholastic: golf, soccer; coed intramural: alpine skiing, archery, backpacking, ballet, baseball, basketball, bicycling, billiards, climbing, cross-country running, equestrian sports, fishing, fitness, golf, hiking/backpacking, horseback riding, horseshoes, ice skating, mountain biking, outdoor activities, outdoor adventure, outdoor education, outdoor recreation, outdoor skills, paint ball, rock climbing, ropes courses, skiing (cross-country), skiing (downhill), snowboarding, soccer, softball, swimming and diving, table tennis, tennis, track and field, volleyball. 1 PE instructor, 1 coach.
Computers Computers are regularly used in all classes. Computer network features include on-campus library services, Internet access, wireless campus network, Internet filtering or blocking technology. Student e-mail accounts are available to students.
Contact Office of Admissions. 626-799-5010 Ext. 5. Fax: 626-799-0407. E-mail: bthomas@southwesternacademy.edu. Web site: www.southwesternacademy.edu.

See Close-Up on page 976.

SOUTHWESTERN ACADEMY

2800 Monterey Road
San Marino, California 91108
Head of School: Kenneth R. Veronda

General Information Coeducational boarding and day college-preparatory, general academic, arts, and ESL school. Grades 6–PG. Founded: 1924. Setting: suburban. Nearest major city is Pasadena. Students are housed in single-sex dormitories. 8-acre campus. 9 buildings on campus. Approved or accredited by The Association of Boarding Schools, Western Association of Schools and Colleges, and California Department of Education. Member of Secondary School Admission Test Board. Endowment: $15 million. Total enrollment: 123. Upper school average class size: 12. Upper school faculty-student ratio: 1:6.
Upper School Student Profile Grade 9: 21 students (9 boys, 12 girls); Grade 10: 20 students (13 boys, 7 girls); Grade 11: 39 students (25 boys, 14 girls); Grade 12: 27 students (19 boys, 8 girls); Postgraduate: 1 student (1 boy). 72% of students are boarding students. 40% are state residents. 4 states are represented in upper school student body. 55% are international students. International students from China, Japan, Republic of Korea, Rwanda, Serbia and Montenegro, and Viet Nam; 12 other countries represented in student body.
Faculty School total: 29. In upper school: 12 men, 11 women; 12 have advanced degrees; 10 reside on campus.
Subjects Offered Algebra, American history, American literature, animation, art, art history, audio visual/media, biology, calculus, calculus-AP, chemistry, college counseling, creative writing, drama, earth science, economics, English, English literature, ESL, European history, expository writing, fashion, fine arts, geography, geology, geometry, government/civics, grammar, health, history, journalism, mathematics, music, photography, physical education, physics, psychology, science, social science, social studies, Spanish, speech, world culture, world history, world literature, writing.
Graduation Requirements Algebra, American government, American history, American literature, British literature, computer literacy, economics, electives, English, foreign language, geometry, lab science, mathematics, physical education (includes health), visual and performing arts, world cultures. Community service is required.
Special Academic Programs Advanced Placement exam preparation; honors section; accelerated programs; independent study; study at local college for college credit; ESL (27 students enrolled).
College Admission Counseling 28 students graduated in 2007; all went to college, including California State University, Northridge; Occidental College; Pepperdine University; University of California, Irvine; University of California, San Diego; University of La Verne.
Student Life Upper grades have specified standards of dress, student council, honor system. Discipline rests primarily with faculty.
Tuition and Aid Day student tuition: $14,400; 7-day tuition and room/board: $29,500. Tuition installment plan (monthly payment plans, individually arranged payment plans). Need-based scholarship grants available. In 2007–08, 20% of upper-school students received aid. Total amount of financial aid awarded in 2007–08: $750,000.
Admissions Traditional secondary-level entrance grade is 9. For fall 2007, 122 students applied for upper-level admission, 103 were accepted, 68 enrolled. Any standardized test required. Deadline for receipt of application materials: none. Application fee required: $100. Interview recommended.
Athletics Interscholastic: baseball (boys), basketball (b,g), track and field (b,g), volleyball (b,g); intramural: baseball (b), basketball (b,g), track and field (b,g), volleyball (b,g); coed interscholastic: baseball, bowling, climbing, cross-country running, fishing, horseback riding, soccer, tennis; coed intramural: archery, backpacking, baseball, bicycling, bowling, climbing, cross-country running, fishing, golf, hiking/backpacking, horseback riding, outdoor activities, physical fitness, skiing (downhill), snowboarding, soccer, table tennis, tennis, weight training. 2 PE instructors, 4 coaches, 1 athletic trainer.
Computers Computers are regularly used in art, English, ESL, foreign language, history, mathematics, music, science, yearbook classes. Computer network features include on-campus library services, online commercial services, Internet access, wireless campus network, Internet filtering or blocking technology. Student e-mail accounts are available to students.
Contact Miss Ellesse Goodman, Assistant Admissions Director. 626-799-5010 Ext. 1204. Fax: 626-799-0407. E-mail: Admissions@southwesternacademy.edu. Web site: www.SouthwesternAcademy.edu.

See Close-Up on page 976.

THE SPENCE SCHOOL

22 East 91st Street
New York, New York 10128-0657
Head of School: Ellanor N. (Bodie) Brizendine

General Information Girls' day college-preparatory school. Grades K–12. Founded: 1892. Setting: urban. 1 building on campus. Approved or accredited by New York State Association of Independent Schools. Member of National Association of Independent Schools and Secondary School Admission Test Board. Endowment: $85 million. Total enrollment: 658. Upper school average class size: 14. Upper school faculty-student ratio: 1:7.
Upper School Student Profile Grade 9: 49 students (49 girls); Grade 10: 51 students (51 girls); Grade 11: 49 students (49 girls); Grade 12: 49 students (49 girls).
Faculty School total: 112. In upper school: 19 men, 58 women; 59 have advanced degrees.
Subjects Offered Acting, advanced math, African history, African literature, African-American literature, algebra, American literature, art, art history, art-AP, Asian literature, astronomy, bioethics, biology, calculus, ceramics, chemistry, Chinese history, computer science, critical writing, design, drama, dramatic arts, earth science, English, European history, exercise science, fiber arts, French, French literature-AP, geometry, health, history, Indian studies, Japanese history, Latin, Latin American literature, Latin American studies, Mandarin, mathematics, Middle East, music, music composition, Native American studies, novel, nutrition, painting, photo shop, photography, physical education, physics, poetry, pre-algebra, robotics, science, sculpture, Shakespeare, Spanish, Spanish literature, speech, statistics, technology, theater production, U.S. history, women's studies, world religions, world studies.
Graduation Requirements Advanced math, algebra, American literature, art, biology, chemistry, computer science, dance, drama, English, European history, foreign language, geometry, history, music, non-Western societies, physical education (includes health), physics, pre-algebra, science, Shakespeare, speech, technology, U.S. history, visual and performing arts, world religions, world studies.
Special Academic Programs 2 Advanced Placement exams for which test preparation is offered; independent study; term-away projects; study abroad.
College Admission Counseling 56 students graduated in 2008; 55 went to college, including Boston University; Brown University; Harvard University; Northwestern University; Princeton University; The Johns Hopkins University. Other: 1 had other specific plans. Median SAT critical reading: 700, median SAT math: 705, median SAT writing: 725.
Student Life Upper grades have uniform requirement, student council. Discipline rests primarily with faculty.
Tuition and Aid Day student tuition: $32,500. Tuition installment plan (Academic Management Services Plan). Need-based scholarship grants, prepGATE Loans, Academic Management Services Private Loans available. In 2008–09, 32% of upper-school students received aid. Total amount of financial aid awarded in 2008–09: $1,416,000.
Admissions Traditional secondary-level entrance grade is 9. ERB, ISEE and school's own test required. Deadline for receipt of application materials: December 1. Application fee required: $65. On-campus interview required.
Athletics Interscholastic: badminton, basketball, fencing, field hockey, soccer, softball, swimming and diving, tennis, track and field, volleyball. 9 PE instructors, 20 coaches, 2 athletic trainers.
Computers Computers are regularly used in art, basic skills, design, independent study, library, library skills, literary magazine, mathematics, news writing, newspaper, programming, publications, research skills, science, yearbook classes. Computer network features include on-campus library services, online commercial services, Internet access, wireless campus network, Internet filtering or blocking technology.

Campus intranet, student e-mail accounts, and computer access in designated common areas are available to students. The school has a published electronic and media policy.
Contact Susan Parker, Director of Admissions. 212-710-8140. Fax: 212-289-6025. E-mail: sparker@spenceschool.org.

SPRING RIDGE ACADEMY

Spring Valley, Arizona
See Special Needs Schools section.

SPRINGSIDE SCHOOL

8000 Cherokee Street
Philadelphia, Pennsylvania 19118

ANNOUNCEMENT FROM THE SCHOOL Springside School, founded in 1879 and the oldest school for girls in Philadelphia, enrolls 670 students in prekindergarten through grade 12, drawing students and faculty members from over 65 Zip codes throughout the city and its suburbs. Springside offers a comprehensive and rigorous college-preparatory curriculum that includes opportunities in visual and performing arts, athletics, service, and technology and extensive leadership and extracurricular activities. The 30-acre campus includes playing fields, tennis courts, and land in the Wissahickon watershed, which is used by the fully integrated environmental education program as an outdoor classroom to combine science, technology, and environmental stewardship for this urban forest. In 2004, Springside opened a new academic wing with twelve classrooms, five science laboratories, art studios and gallery space, commons space for students, and a library with dedicated reading and study areas and a technology suite. The Vare Field House, an athletic facility that houses three full basketball/volleyball courts, four squash courts, a crew tank, a dance studio, and a weight and fitness center, hosts Springside's teams and others in the local vicinity. From Springside's Mission Statement: "All college-preparatory schools expect their students to excel in a rigorous academic program. Springside asks more: that girls discover how they learn, that they take intellectual delight in their education, and that they gain the courage and integrity to negotiate the breadth of their complex futures. In every way, Springside School educates girls and young women to develop their capacities for leadership in the 21st century." For more information, please visit www.springside.org.

SQUAW VALLEY ACADEMY

235 Squaw Valley Road
Olympic Valley, California 96146
Head of School: Donald Rees

General Information Coeducational boarding and day college-preparatory and arts school. Grades 6–12. Founded: 1978. Setting: rural. Nearest major city is Reno, NV. Students are housed in single-sex dormitories. 3-acre campus. 5 buildings on campus. Approved or accredited by Western Association of Schools and Colleges. Total enrollment: 84. Upper school average class size: 9. Upper school faculty-student ratio: 1:7.
Upper School Student Profile Grade 9: 9 students (7 boys, 2 girls); Grade 10: 19 students (13 boys, 6 girls); Grade 11: 33 students (25 boys, 8 girls); Grade 12: 15 students (10 boys, 5 girls). 93% of students are boarding students. 46% are state residents. 12 states are represented in upper school student body. 25% are international students. International students from China, Czech Republic, Germany, Hong Kong, Republic of Korea, and Taiwan; 3 other countries represented in student body.
Faculty School total: 17. In upper school: 5 men, 12 women; 6 have advanced degrees; 6 reside on campus.
Subjects Offered Algebra, American history, American literature, anatomy, art, biology, calculus, ceramics, chemistry, computer programming, computer science, creative writing, drama, English, English literature, environmental science, expository writing, fine arts, French, geography, geometry, government/civics, grammar, health, history, mathematics, music appreciation, outdoor education, photography, physical education, physics, psychology, publications, science, social science, social studies, Spanish, trigonometry, typing, video, world history, writing.
Graduation Requirements Arts and fine arts (art, music, dance, drama), English, foreign language, mathematics, outdoor education, physical education (includes health), science, social science, social studies (includes history), participation in skiing and snowboarding.
Special Academic Programs Advanced Placement exam preparation; honors section; independent study; academic accommodation for the gifted and the artistically talented; ESL (18 students enrolled).
College Admission Counseling 13 students graduated in 2007; all went to college, including California State University, Sacramento; Humboldt State University; Montana State University; University of California, Davis; University of Colorado at Boulder; University of Nevada, Reno. Median SAT critical reading: 410, median SAT math: 550, median SAT writing: 445, median combined SAT: 1405. 20% scored over 600 on SAT critical reading, 40% scored over 600 on SAT math, 20% scored over 600 on SAT writing, 20% scored over 1800 on combined SAT.
Student Life Upper grades have specified standards of dress, student council, honor system. Discipline rests primarily with faculty.
Tuition and Aid Day student tuition: $15,390; 7-day tuition and room/board: $35,820. Tuition installment plan (individually arranged payment plans). Tuition reduction for siblings, need-based scholarship grants available. In 2007–08, 5% of upper-school students received aid.
Admissions Traditional secondary-level entrance grade is 9. For fall 2007, 86 students applied for upper-level admission, 80 were accepted, 76 enrolled. School's own exam required. Deadline for receipt of application materials: none. Application fee required: $100. Interview required.
Athletics Interscholastic: alpine skiing (boys, girls), freestyle skiing (b,g), golf (b,g), skiing (downhill) (b,g), snowboarding (b,g); intramural: aerobics (b,g), aerobics/Nautilus (b,g), alpine skiing (b,g), aquatics (b,g), backpacking (b,g), badminton (b,g), bicycling (b,g), billiards (b,g), blading (b,g), bocce (b,g), bowling (b,g), canoeing/kayaking (b,g), climbing (b,g), combined training (b,g), croquet (b,g), cross-country running (b,g), fishing (b,g), fitness (b,g), fitness walking (b,g), fly fishing (b,g), freestyle skiing (b,g), Frisbee (b,g), golf (b,g), hiking/backpacking (b,g), horseback riding (b,g), ice skating (b,g), jogging (b,g), kayaking (b,g), martial arts (b,g), mountain biking (b,g), mountaineering (b,g), nordic skiing (b,g), outdoor activities (b,g), outdoor adventure (b,g), outdoor education (b,g), outdoor recreation (b,g), outdoor skills (b,g), outdoors (b,g), paddling (b,g), paint ball (b,g), physical fitness (b,g), physical training (b,g), rafting (b,g), rock climbing (b,g), ropes courses (b,g), running (b,g), self defense (b,g), skateboarding (b,g), skiing (cross-country) (b,g), skiing (downhill) (b,g), snowboarding (b,g), snowshoeing (b,g), strength & conditioning (b,g), swimming and diving (b,g), table tennis (b,g), tai chi (b,g), telemark skiing (b,g), tennis (b,g), ultimate Frisbee (b,g), volleyball (b,g), walking (b,g), wall climbing (b,g), weight lifting (b,g), weight training (b,g), yoga (b,g); coed interscholastic: alpine skiing, bowling, freestyle skiing, golf, skiing (downhill), snowboarding, soccer; coed intramural: aerobics, aerobics/Nautilus, alpine skiing, aquatics, backpacking, badminton, baseball, bicycling, billiards, blading, bocce, bowling, canoeing/kayaking, climbing, combined training, croquet, cross-country running, fishing, fitness, fitness walking, fly fishing, freestyle skiing, Frisbee, golf, hiking/backpacking, horseback riding, ice skating, jogging, kayaking, martial arts, mountain biking, mountaineering, nordic skiing, outdoor activities, outdoor adventure, outdoor education, outdoor recreation, outdoor skills, outdoors, paddling, paint ball, physical fitness, physical training, rafting, rock climbing, ropes courses, running, self defense, skateboarding, skiing (cross-country), skiing (downhill), snowboarding, snowshoeing, soccer, softball, strength & conditioning, swimming and diving, table tennis, tai chi, telemark skiing, tennis, ultimate Frisbee, volleyball, walking, wall climbing, weight lifting, weight training, yoga.
Computers Computers are regularly used in English, graphic arts, health, history, journalism, publications, SAT preparation, science, typing, wilderness education, word processing, writing classes. Computer network features include on-campus library services, online commercial services, Internet access, wireless campus network, Internet filtering or blocking technology.
Contact Adrienne Forbes, M.Ed., Admissions Director. 530-583-9393 Ext. 14. Fax: 530-581-1111. E-mail: enroll@sva.org. Web site: www.sva.org.

See Close-Up on page 978.

STANBRIDGE ACADEMY

San Mateo, California
See Special Needs Schools section.

STARKVILLE ACADEMY

505 Academy Road
Starkville, Mississippi 39759
Head of School: Mr. Bobby Eiland

General Information Coeducational day college-preparatory, arts, and technology school. Grades K4–12. Founded: 1970. Setting: small town. Nearest major city is Jackson. 30-acre campus. 5 buildings on campus. Approved or accredited by Mississippi Private School Association, Southern Association of Colleges and Schools, and Southern Association of Independent Schools. Total enrollment: 795. Upper school average class size: 23. Upper school faculty-student ratio: 1:14.
Upper School Student Profile Grade 7: 64 students (32 boys, 32 girls); Grade 8: 67 students (31 boys, 36 girls); Grade 9: 55 students (28 boys, 27 girls); Grade 10: 63 students (31 boys, 32 girls); Grade 11: 40 students (24 boys, 16 girls); Grade 12: 62 students (30 boys, 32 girls).
Faculty School total: 26. In upper school: 9 men, 17 women.
Subjects Offered Advanced chemistry, advanced math, Advanced Placement courses, algebra, American government, American history, anatomy and physiology, art, athletics, baseball, basketball, biology, business mathematics, calculus-AP, cheerleading, chemistry, chemistry-AP, chorus, computer literacy, computer programming, desktop publishing, driver education, earth science, English, environ-

mental science, ethics, foreign language, geography, geometry, government, government/civics, health, honors English, jazz ensemble, library assistant, musical productions, physical science, physics-AP, pre-algebra, public speaking, publications, softball, Spanish, speech, state government, U.S. government, U.S. history, weight-lifting, world geography, world history, yearbook.

Graduation Requirements Computers, English, foreign language, history, mathematics, science, students must take the ACT.

Special Academic Programs Advanced Placement exam preparation; honors section.

College Admission Counseling 60 students graduated in 2008; 59 went to college, including Mississippi State University; University of Mississippi; University of Southern Mississippi. Other: 1 entered military service. Median composite ACT: 22. 20% scored over 26 on composite ACT.

Student Life Upper grades have specified standards of dress, student council. Discipline rests primarily with faculty.

Tuition and Aid Day student tuition: $2910. Tuition installment plan (monthly payment plans). Tuition reduction for siblings available.

Admissions Traditional secondary-level entrance grade is 9. For fall 2008, 30 students applied for upper-level admission, 30 were accepted, 30 enrolled. Admissions testing required. Deadline for receipt of application materials: none. Application fee required: $300. Interview required.

Athletics Interscholastic: baseball (boys, girls), basketball (b,g), cheering (g), cross-country running (b,g), dance team (g), football (b), golf (b,g), soccer (b,g), softball (g), tennis (b,g), track and field (b,g); intramural: strength & conditioning (b,g), weight lifting (b).

Computers Computers are regularly used in all academic classes. Computer network features include on-campus library services, Internet access. Students grades are available online.

Contact Mrs. Julie MacGown, Secretary. 662-323-7814 Ext. 101. Fax: 662-323-5480. E-mail: jmacgown@starkvilleacademy.org.

STATEN ISLAND ACADEMY

715 Todt Hill Road
Staten Island, New York 10304

Head of School: Mrs. Diane J. Hulse

General Information Coeducational day college-preparatory, arts, and technology school. Grades PK–12. Founded: 1886. Setting: urban. Nearest major city is New York. 12-acre campus. 7 buildings on campus. Approved or accredited by Middle States Association of Colleges and Schools and New York State Association of Independent Schools. Member of National Association of Independent Schools. Endowment: $5 million. Total enrollment: 400. Upper school average class size: 17. Upper school faculty-student ratio: 1:10.

Upper School Student Profile Grade 9: 42 students (22 boys, 20 girls); Grade 10: 32 students (16 boys, 16 girls); Grade 11: 33 students (16 boys, 17 girls); Grade 12: 37 students (20 boys, 17 girls).

Faculty School total: 58. In upper school: 21 men, 37 women; 41 have advanced degrees.

Subjects Offered Algebra, American history, American literature, anatomy, art, art history, astronomy, biology, calculus, ceramics, chemistry, community service, computer science, creative writing, dance, drama, economics, English, English literature, European history, expository writing, fine arts, French, geometry, grammar, health, human relations, journalism, Latin, law, mathematics, meteorology, music, oceanography, photography, physical education, physical science, physics, psychology, public speaking, robotics, science, social science, social studies, Spanish, speech, statistics, theater, trigonometry, visual and performing arts, Web site design, world history, writing.

Graduation Requirements Arts and fine arts (art, music, dance, drama), computer science, English, foreign language, human relations, mathematics, physical education (includes health), public speaking, science, science and technology, social science, social studies (includes history), Senior Year Internship Program. Community service is required.

Special Academic Programs Advanced Placement exam preparation; honors section; independent study; study at local college for college credit; study abroad; academic accommodation for the gifted, the musically talented, and the artistically talented.

College Admission Counseling 27 students graduated in 2008; all went to college, including Brown University; Cornell University; Dartmouth College; New York University; University of Pennsylvania. Mean SAT critical reading: 612, mean SAT math: 637, mean SAT writing: 627, mean combined SAT: 1876.

Student Life Upper grades have uniform requirement, student council. Discipline rests primarily with faculty.

Tuition and Aid Day student tuition: $20,130–$26,750. Tuition installment plan (monthly payment plans, SML Tuition Plan). Need-based scholarship grants available. In 2008–09, 26% of upper-school students received aid. Total amount of financial aid awarded in 2008–09: $1,000,000.

Admissions Traditional secondary-level entrance grade is 9. For fall 2008, 110 students applied for upper-level admission, 80 were accepted, 20 enrolled. ERB or ISEE required. Deadline for receipt of application materials: January 15. Application fee required: $50. On-campus interview required.

Athletics Interscholastic: baseball (boys), basketball (b,g), lacrosse (g), soccer (b,g), softball (g), tennis (b,g), volleyball (b,g); coed interscholastic: cheering, cross-country running, dance, golf; coed intramural: physical fitness. 7 PE instructors, 19 coaches.

Computers Computers are regularly used in art, data processing, English, graphic design, independent study, journalism, keyboarding, library, mathematics, newspaper, publications, research skills, SAT preparation, science, social sciences, word processing, writing, yearbook classes. Computer network features include on-campus library services, online commercial services, Internet access, wireless campus network. Campus intranet and student e-mail accounts are available to students. The school has a published electronic and media policy.

Contact Mrs. Linda Shuffman, Director of Admission. 718-303-7803. Fax: 718-979-7641. E-mail: lshuffman@statenislandacademy.org. Web site: www.statenislandacademy.org.

STELLA MARIS HIGH SCHOOL

Beach 112 Street
Rockaway Park, New York 11694

Head of School: Miss Geri Martinez

General Information Girls' day college-preparatory, arts, religious studies, program for students of average intelligence who have, and diagnosed learning disabilities school, affiliated with Roman Catholic Church. Grades 9–12. Founded: 1943. Setting: urban. Nearest major city is New York. 3-acre campus. 1 building on campus. Approved or accredited by Middle States Association of Colleges and Schools, National Catholic Education Association, and New York State Board of Regents. Total enrollment: 299. Upper school average class size: 22. Upper school faculty-student ratio: 1:8.

Upper School Student Profile Grade 9: 55 students (55 girls); Grade 10: 90 students (90 girls); Grade 11: 74 students (74 girls); Grade 12: 80 students (80 girls). 85% of students are Roman Catholic.

Faculty School total: 32. In upper school: 3 men, 29 women; 23 have advanced degrees.

Subjects Offered Accounting, algebra, American literature, anatomy, art, bioethics, biology-AP, British literature (honors), calculus, career exploration, career/college preparation, Catholic belief and practice, chemistry, child development, chorus, Christian ethics, Christian scripture, college planning, computer keyboarding, death and loss, desktop publishing, earth science, economics, English, English literature, family and consumer sciences, fashion, food and nutrition, French, geometry, health education, honors algebra, honors English, honors geometry, honors U.S. history, human anatomy, Italian, library, marketing, mathematics, music appreciation, painting, parent/child development, parenting, peer counseling, physical education, portfolio art, pre-calculus, psychology, SAT preparation, scripture, sewing, Spanish, studio art, technology, U.S. government, U.S. history, word processing, world geography, world history.

Graduation Requirements Arts and fine arts (art, music, dance, drama), computer skills, English, foreign language, health education, mathematics, physical education (includes health), religious studies, science, social studies (includes history), passing grade in required NY State Regents examinations.

Special Academic Programs 2 Advanced Placement exams for which test preparation is offered; honors section; study at local college for college credit; academic accommodation for the gifted and the artistically talented; programs in general development for dyslexic students.

College Admission Counseling 101 students graduated in 2008; 97 went to college, including John Jay College of Criminal Justice of the City University of New York; Nassau Community College; Queens College of the City University of New York; St. John's University; St. Joseph's College, New York; Stony Brook University, State University of New York. Other: 4 went to work. Mean SAT critical reading: 432, mean SAT math: 420, mean SAT writing: 434, mean combined SAT: 1286. 1% scored over 600 on SAT critical reading, 2% scored over 600 on SAT math, 1% scored over 600 on SAT writing, 4% scored over 1800 on combined SAT.

Student Life Upper grades have uniform requirement, student council. Discipline rests primarily with faculty. Attendance at religious services is required.

Summer Programs Remediation, sports programs offered; session focuses on remediation and make-up (courses and state exams), basketball camp for grades 3 to 9; held on campus; accepts boys and girls; open to students from other schools. 175 students usually enrolled. 2009 schedule: July 9 to August 14. Application deadline: June 30.

Tuition and Aid Day student tuition: $7100. Tuition installment plan (SMART Tuition Payment Plan, monthly payment plans). Merit scholarship grants, need-based scholarship grants available. In 2008–09, 16% of upper-school students received aid; total upper-school merit-scholarship money awarded: $65,000. Total amount of financial aid awarded in 2008–09: $85,700.

Admissions Traditional secondary-level entrance grade is 9. Catholic High School Entrance Examination or TerraNova required. Deadline for receipt of application materials: none. Application fee required: $50. Interview recommended.

Athletics Interscholastic: basketball, cheering, soccer, softball, volleyball; intramural: aerobics, aerobics/dance, dance, fitness, golf, gymnastics. 2 PE instructors, 6 coaches.

Computers Computers are regularly used in accounting, business applications, business education, career exploration, college planning, computer applications, data

processing, foreign language, keyboarding, mathematics, religious studies, remedial study skills, SAT preparation, science, social studies, technology, word processing classes. Computer network features include on-campus library services, Internet access, Internet filtering or blocking technology, homework assignments available online. Computer access in designated common areas is available to students.
Contact Sr. Barbara Buckbee, CSJ, Assistant Principal. 718-634-4994. Fax: 718-634-5267. E-mail: sbabuckbee@stellamarishigh.org. Web site: www.stellamarishs.org.

STEPHEN T. BADIN HIGH SCHOOL

571 New London Road
Hamilton, Ohio 45013
Head of School: Frank Margello

General Information Coeducational day college-preparatory, general academic, arts, business, vocational, and religious studies school, affiliated with Roman Catholic Church. Grades 9–12. Founded: 1966. Setting: urban. Nearest major city is Cincinnati. 22-acre campus. 2 buildings on campus. Approved or accredited by National Catholic Education Association, North Central Association of Colleges and Schools, Ohio Catholic Schools Accreditation Association (OCSAA), and Ohio Department of Education. Endowment: $125,000. Total enrollment: 575. Upper school average class size: 27. Upper school faculty-student ratio: 1:18.
Upper School Student Profile Grade 9: 125 students (60 boys, 65 girls); Grade 10: 140 students (70 boys, 70 girls); Grade 11: 155 students (81 boys, 74 girls); Grade 12: 155 students (80 boys, 75 girls). 90% of students are Roman Catholic.
Faculty School total: 40. In upper school: 22 men, 18 women; 21 have advanced degrees.
Subjects Offered Accounting, algebra, American history, American literature, art, band, biology, British literature, calculus, calculus-AP, chemistry, chorus, computer programming, computer resources, computer science, consumer economics, consumer mathematics, drawing and design, economics, English, English literature, English-AP, French, geometry, government-AP, government/civics, grammar, history, integrated science, intro to computers, journalism, Latin, marketing, mathematics, music, music theory, physical education, physical science, physics, physiology, pre-calculus, publications, religion, science, senior science survey, social studies, Spanish, trigonometry, Web site design, Western literature, word processing, world history.
Graduation Requirements Computer science, English, mathematics, physical education (includes health), religion (includes Bible studies and theology), science, social studies (includes history), 10 hours of community service per year.
Special Academic Programs Advanced Placement exam preparation; honors section; study at local college for college credit; study abroad; remedial reading and/or remedial writing; remedial math.
College Admission Counseling 163 students graduated in 2008; 150 went to college, including College of Mount St. Joseph; Miami University; The Ohio State University; University of Cincinnati; Wright State University; Xavier University. Other: 1 went to work, 4 entered military service, 8 had other specific plans. Median SAT critical reading: 523, median SAT math: 519, median composite ACT: 22. 22% scored over 600 on SAT critical reading, 18% scored over 600 on SAT math, 20% scored over 26 on composite ACT.
Student Life Upper grades have uniform requirement, student council. Discipline rests primarily with faculty. Attendance at religious services is required.
Tuition and Aid Day student tuition: $4900. Tuition installment plan (monthly payment plans, individually arranged payment plans, quarterly payment plan). Merit scholarship grants, need-based scholarship grants, paying campus jobs available. In 2008–09, 20% of upper-school students received aid; total upper-school merit-scholarship money awarded: $8000. Total amount of financial aid awarded in 2008–09: $270,000.
Admissions Traditional secondary-level entrance grade is 9. For fall 2008, 575 students applied for upper-level admission, 575 were accepted. Deadline for receipt of application materials: none. No application fee required. On-campus interview recommended.
Athletics Interscholastic: baseball (boys), basketball (b,g). 35 coaches.
Computers Computers are regularly used in drawing and design, mathematics, music, science, Web site design classes. Computer network features include on-campus library services, Internet access, scanners, travelling laptops, digital cameras.
Contact Mr. Dirk Allen, Director of recruitment. 513-863-3993 Ext. 145. Fax: 513-785-2844. E-mail: dallen@mail.badinhs.org. Web site: www.stephen-t-badin.cnd.pvt.k12.oh.us.

STEVENSON SCHOOL

3152 Forest Lake Road
Pebble Beach, California 93953
Head of School: Mr. Joseph E. Wandke

General Information Coeducational boarding and day college-preparatory and arts school. Boarding grades 9–12, day grades PK–12. Founded: 1952. Setting: suburban. Nearest major city is San Francisco. Students are housed in single-sex by floor dormitories. 60-acre campus. 22 buildings on campus. Approved or accredited by Western Association of Schools and Colleges and California Department of Education. Member of National Association of Independent Schools and Secondary School Admission Test Board. Endowment: $24 million. Total enrollment: 756. Upper school average class size: 14. Upper school faculty-student ratio: 1:10.
Upper School Student Profile Grade 9: 134 students (76 boys, 58 girls); Grade 10: 139 students (68 boys, 71 girls); Grade 11: 134 students (74 boys, 60 girls); Grade 12: 141 students (67 boys, 74 girls). 49% of students are boarding students. 77% are state residents. 23 states are represented in upper school student body. 15% are international students. International students from China, Germany, Hong Kong, Republic of Korea, Taiwan, and Thailand; 9 other countries represented in student body.
Faculty School total: 65. In upper school: 35 men, 22 women; 45 have advanced degrees; 28 reside on campus.
Subjects Offered 3-dimensional art, advanced chemistry, Advanced Placement courses, algebra, American history, American literature, American literature-AP, architecture, art, art history, art-AP, biology, biology-AP, broadcasting, calculus, calculus-AP, ceramics, chemistry, chemistry-AP, computer programming, computer science, concert band, creative writing, dance, dance performance, drama, drama performance, drama workshop, dramatic arts, drawing, drawing and design, driver education, economics, economics-AP, English, English literature, English-AP, environmental science, environmental science-AP, ethics, European civilization, European history, expository writing, fine arts, French, French-AP, geometry, German-AP, government/civics, grammar, history of ideas, history-AP, honors algebra, honors English, honors geometry, honors U.S. history, Japanese, jazz, jazz band, jazz ensemble, jazz theory, journalism, Latin, Latin-AP, macroeconomics-AP, marine biology, mathematics, mathematics-AP, microbiology, music, musical productions, musical theater, ornithology, photography, physical education, physics, physics-AP, portfolio art, pre-calculus, psychology, science, social studies, Spanish, Spanish-AP, speech, stage design, stagecraft, studio art—AP, tap dance, theater, trigonometry, U.S. history-AP, visual and performing arts, visual arts, vocal ensemble, wilderness experience, wilderness/outdoor program, wind ensemble, world cultures, world history, world literature, world studies, writing, yearbook.
Graduation Requirements Arts and fine arts (art, music, dance, drama), English, foreign language, mathematics, physical education (includes health), science, social studies (includes history).
Special Academic Programs Advanced Placement exam preparation; honors section; independent study; term-away projects; study abroad.
College Admission Counseling 140 students graduated in 2008; 136 went to college, including Santa Clara University; The University of Arizona; University of California, Berkeley; University of California, Davis; University of California, San Diego; University of California, Santa Barbara. Other: 2 entered military service, 2 had other specific plans. Mean SAT critical reading: 619, mean SAT math: 631, mean SAT writing: 615, mean combined SAT: 1864, mean composite ACT: 26. 63% scored over 600 on SAT critical reading, 67% scored over 600 on SAT math, 60% scored over 600 on SAT writing, 70% scored over 1800 on combined SAT, 57% scored over 26 on composite ACT.
Student Life Upper grades have student council, honor system. Discipline rests equally with students and faculty.
Summer Programs Enrichment programs offered; held on campus; accepts boys and girls; open to students from other schools. 140 students usually enrolled. 2009 schedule: June 26 to July 28. Application deadline: none.
Tuition and Aid Day student tuition: $26,100; 7-day tuition and room/board: $42,800. Tuition installment plan (Insured Tuition Payment Plan, monthly payment plans). Need-based scholarship grants available. In 2008–09, 15% of upper-school students received aid. Total amount of financial aid awarded in 2008–09: $2,100,000.
Admissions Traditional secondary-level entrance grade is 9. For fall 2008, 563 students applied for upper-level admission, 235 were accepted, 143 enrolled. SSAT required. Deadline for receipt of application materials: February 15. Application fee required: $75. Interview required.
Athletics Interscholastic: baseball (boys), basketball (b,g), cross-country running (b,g), diving (b,g), field hockey (g), football (b), golf (b,g), lacrosse (b,g), sailing (b,g), soccer (b,g), softball (g), swimming and diving (b,g), tennis (b,g), track and field (b,g), volleyball (g), water polo (b,g); intramural: dance (b,g), golf (b,g), horseback riding (b,g), kayaking (b,g), modern dance (b,g), mountaineering (b,g), outdoor education (b,g), outdoors (b,g), power lifting (b,g), rock climbing (b,g), strength & conditioning (b,g), table tennis (b,g), weight lifting (b,g), wilderness (b,g), yoga (b,g); coed interscholastic: sailing; coed intramural: basketball, bicycling, climbing, dance, equestrian sports, fencing, horseback riding, kayaking, modern dance, mountaineering, outdoor education, outdoors, rock climbing, sailing, softball, strength & conditioning, table tennis, weight lifting, wilderness, yoga. 22 coaches.
Computers Computers are regularly used in all classes. Computer network features include on-campus library services, online commercial services, Internet access, wireless campus network, Internet filtering or blocking technology. Campus intranet and student e-mail accounts are available to students. Students grades are available online. The school has a published electronic and media policy.
Contact Mr. Thomas W. Sheppard, Director of Admission. 831-625-8309. Fax: 831-625-5208. E-mail: info@stevensonschool.org. Web site: www.stevensonschool.org.

STILL CREEK CHRISTIAN SCHOOL

6055 Hearne Road
Bryan, Texas 77808-8262

Head of School: Brad Raphel

General Information Coeducational boarding and day and distance learning college-preparatory, general academic, and vocational school, affiliated with Christian faith; primarily serves underachievers and individuals with Attention Deficit Disorder. Grades K–12. Distance learning grades K–12. Founded: 1993. Setting: rural. Nearest major city is Houston. Students are housed in single-sex dormitories. 10-acre campus. 3 buildings on campus. Approved or accredited by European Council of International Schools, Southern Association of Colleges and Schools, and Texas Department of Education. Total enrollment: 47. Upper school average class size: 10. Upper school faculty-student ratio: 1:6.

Upper School Student Profile 9% of students are boarding students. 94% are state residents. 4 states are represented in upper school student body. 80% of students are Christian faith.

Faculty School total: 8. In upper school: 5 men, 3 women; 2 have advanced degrees; all reside on campus.

Subjects Offered Agriculture, algebra, biology, carpentry, Christianity, computer information systems, computer keyboarding, computer literacy, English, fitness, grammar, health, history, language arts, law and the legal system, physical science, reading/study skills, remedial/makeup course work, Spanish.

Graduation Requirements Algebra, American government, American history, Bible, biology, chemistry, computer information systems, computer literacy, economics, English, foreign language, geometry, physical education (includes health), yearbook, elective credits from vocational area.

Special Academic Programs Accelerated programs; independent study; study at local college for college credit; remedial reading and/or remedial writing; remedial math.

Student Life Upper grades have specified standards of dress, student council. Discipline rests primarily with faculty. Attendance at religious services is required.

Summer Programs Session focuses on horsemanship; held both on and off campus; held at various camps; accepts boys and girls; not open to students from other schools. 25 students usually enrolled. 2009 schedule: June 15 to July 31.

Tuition and Aid Tuition installment plan (monthly payment plans). Financial aid available to upper-school students. In 2008–09, 80% of upper-school students received aid.

Admissions Traditional secondary-level entrance grade is 10. School placement exam required. Deadline for receipt of application materials: none. No application fee required. Interview required.

Athletics 1 PE instructor.

Computers The school has a published electronic and media policy.

Contact Margaret O'Quinn, Ranch Administration. 979-589-3206. Fax: 979-589-2152. E-mail: stillcreek@wicksonwireless.com. Web site: www.iolbv.com/stillcreek.

ST LEONARDS SCHOOL AND SIXTH FORM COLLEGE

St. Andrews
Fife, Scotland KY16 9QJ, United Kingdom

Head of School: Dr. Michael Carslaw, PhD

General Information Coeducational boarding and day college-preparatory, general academic, arts, business, bilingual studies, and technology school. Boarding grades 8–13, day grades 1–13. Founded: 1877. Setting: small town. Nearest major city is Edinburgh, United Kingdom. Students are housed in single-sex dormitories. 26-acre campus. 8 buildings on campus. Approved or accredited by Boarding Schools Association (UK), Independent Schools Council (UK), International Baccalaureate Organization, and Scottish Education Department. Language of instruction: English. Total enrollment: 453. Upper school average class size: 16. Upper school faculty-student ratio: 1:7.

Upper School Student Profile Grade 8: 39 students (18 boys, 21 girls); Grade 9: 33 students (14 boys, 19 girls); Grade 10: 40 students (17 boys, 23 girls); Grade 11: 45 students (19 boys, 26 girls); Grade 12: 73 students (38 boys, 35 girls); Grade 13: 53 students (27 boys, 26 girls). 65% of students are boarding students. 60% are international students. International students from Austria, China, Germany, Hong Kong, and Russian Federation; 11 other countries represented in student body.

Faculty In upper school: 17 men, 29 women; 4 have advanced degrees; 5 reside on campus.

Subjects Offered 20th century physics, 20th century world history, 3-dimensional art, 3-dimensional design, acting, adolescent issues, advanced chemistry, advanced computer applications, advanced math, advanced TOEFL/grammar, Ancient Greek, art, art history, arts, biology, British history, business, career and personal planning, chemistry, classics, computer literacy, computer skills, creative arts, design, drama, economics, English, English as a foreign language, European history, geography, German, Greek, history, humanities, Latin, mathematics, modern history, modern languages, music, personal and social education, physics, politics, psychology, religious studies, science, theater design and production, vocal ensemble, voice, wind ensemble, wind instruments, word processing, work experience, world geography, world history.

Special Academic Programs International Baccalaureate program; study at local college for college credit; academic accommodation for the gifted, the musically talented, and the artistically talented; programs in English, mathematics, general development for dyslexic students; ESL (25 students enrolled).

College Admission Counseling 56 students graduated in 2008; 54 went to college. Other: 2 had other specific plans.

Student Life Upper grades have specified standards of dress, student council, honor system. Discipline rests equally with students and faculty.

Tuition and Aid Day student tuition: £9807; 7-day tuition and room/board: £23,346. Tuition installment plan (monthly payment plans, individually arranged payment plans). Need-based scholarship grants available.

Admissions Traditional secondary-level entrance grade is 12. For fall 2008, 74 students applied for upper-level admission, 70 were accepted, 70 enrolled. School's own exam required. Deadline for receipt of application materials: none. Application fee required: £100. Interview required.

Athletics Intramural: aerobics (girls), aerobics/dance (g), ballet (g), cricket (b), netball (g), yoga (g); coed interscholastic: alpine skiing, cross-country running, equestrian sports, freestyle skiing, golf, horseback riding, lacrosse, skiing (downhill), squash, swimming and diving, tennis, track and field, winter soccer; coed intramural: archery, backpacking, badminton, ball hockey, basketball, bicycling, canoeing/kayaking, cross-country running, dance, equestrian sports, fencing, field hockey, fitness, freestyle skiing, golf, gymnastics, hiking/backpacking, hockey, horseback riding, indoor hockey, indoor soccer, judo, kayaking, lacrosse, life saving, outdoor activities, physical fitness, rock climbing, rugby, running, sailing, self defense, skiing (downhill), soccer, squash, surfing, swimming and diving, table tennis, tennis, track and field, volleyball, wall climbing, weight training, wilderness survival, windsurfing, winter soccer. 4 PE instructors, 13 coaches.

Computers Computers are regularly used in art, career exploration, English, French, geography, history, information technology, language development, library skills, mathematics, music, research skills, Spanish, technical drawing classes. Computer network features include on-campus library services, Internet access, wireless campus network, Internet filtering or blocking technology. Campus intranet, student e-mail accounts, and computer access in designated common areas are available to students. The school has a published electronic and media policy.

Contact Dr. Caroline Routledge, Registrar. 44-1334-472126. Fax: 44-1334 476152. E-mail: info@stleonards-fife.org. Web site: www.stleonards-fife.org/.

STONELEIGH–BURNHAM SCHOOL

574 Bernardston Road
Greenfield, Massachusetts 01301

Head of School: Sally Mixsell

General Information Girls' boarding and day college-preparatory and arts school. Grades 7–PG. Founded: 1869. Setting: small town. Nearest major city is Boston. Students are housed in single-sex dormitories. 100-acre campus. 7 buildings on campus. Approved or accredited by Association of Independent Schools in New England, New England Association of Schools and Colleges, The Association of Boarding Schools, and Massachusetts Department of Education. Member of National Association of Independent Schools. Endowment: $2.8 million. Total enrollment: 127. Upper school average class size: 10. Upper school faculty-student ratio: 1:6.

Upper School Student Profile Grade 9: 21 students (21 girls); Grade 10: 24 students (24 girls); Grade 11: 35 students (35 girls); Grade 12: 18 students (18 girls). 71% of students are boarding students. 35% are state residents. 17 states are represented in upper school student body. 40% are international students. International students from China, Japan, Mexico, Republic of Korea, Rwanda, and Taiwan; 5 other countries represented in student body.

Faculty School total: 33. In upper school: 8 men, 25 women; 30 have advanced degrees; 16 reside on campus.

Subjects Offered Acting, Advanced Placement courses, algebra, American history, anatomy, art, astronomy, band, biology, biology-AP, botany, calculus, calculus-AP, ceramics, chemistry, Chinese, conceptual physics, dance, desktop publishing, drama, drawing, ecology, English, English-AP, environmental science-AP, equine science, ESL, ethical decision making, European history, European history-AP, fine arts, French, French-AP, gender issues, geometry, graphic arts, health, history, mathematics, music, music theory, nutrition, photography, physics, poetry, political science, psychology, public speaking, science, senior seminar, social studies, Spanish, Spanish-AP, sports medicine, theater, U.S. history-AP, values and decisions, water color painting, weaving, Web site design, yearbook.

Graduation Requirements Art, arts and fine arts (art, music, dance, drama), English, foreign language, history, mathematics, physical education (includes health), science, U.S. history.

Special Academic Programs Advanced Placement exam preparation; honors section; independent study; ESL (9 students enrolled).

College Admission Counseling 26 students graduated in 2008; all went to college, including Georgetown University; Hamilton College; Mount Holyoke College; Smith College; The George Washington University; Tufts University.

Student Life Upper grades have specified standards of dress, student council, honor system. Discipline rests equally with students and faculty.

Summer Programs Enrichment, ESL, sports, art/fine arts programs offered; session focuses on debate, softball, dance, riding, soccer, academic (math and English); held

on campus; accepts girls; open to students from other schools. 210 students usually enrolled. 2009 schedule: July 3 to August 13. Application deadline: none.
Tuition and Aid Day student tuition: $24,595; 7-day tuition and room/board: $41,500. Tuition installment plan (Academic Management Services Plan, monthly payment plans). Merit scholarship grants, need-based scholarship grants available. In 2008–09, 42% of upper-school students received aid; total upper-school merit-scholarship money awarded: $2500. Total amount of financial aid awarded in 2008–09: $904,000.
Admissions Traditional secondary-level entrance grade is 9. For fall 2008, 95 students applied for upper-level admission, 64 were accepted, 52 enrolled. ISEE, SAT, SSAT or TOEFL or SLEP required. Deadline for receipt of application materials: February 16. Application fee required: $40. Interview required.
Athletics Interscholastic: aerobics/dance, ballet, basketball, cross-country running, dance, dressage, equestrian sports, field hockey, horseback riding, lacrosse, modern dance, soccer, softball, tennis, volleyball; intramural: alpine skiing, fitness, golf, skiing (downhill), snowboarding, strength & conditioning. 1 PE instructor, 2 athletic trainers.
Computers Computers are regularly used in all classes. Computer network features include on-campus library services, online commercial services, Internet access, wireless campus network, Internet filtering or blocking technology. Campus intranet, student e-mail accounts, and computer access in designated common areas are available to students. The school has a published electronic and media policy.
Contact Laura Lavallee, Associate Director of Admissions. 413-774-2711 Ext. 257. Fax: 413-772-2602. E-mail: admissions@sbschool.org. Web site: www.sbschool.org.

STONE MOUNTAIN SCHOOL

Black Mountain, North Carolina
See Special Needs Schools section.

THE STONY BROOK SCHOOL

1 Chapman Parkway
Stony Brook, New York 11790
Head of School: Mr. Robert E. Gustafson Jr.

General Information Coeducational boarding and day college-preparatory, arts, and religious studies school, affiliated with Christian faith. Grades 7–12. Founded: 1922. Setting: suburban. Nearest major city is New York. Students are housed in single-sex dormitories. 55-acre campus. 14 buildings on campus. Approved or accredited by Council of Accreditation and School Improvement, Middle States Association of Colleges and Schools, New York State Association of Independent Schools, New York State Board of Regents, and The Association of Boarding Schools. Member of National Association of Independent Schools and Secondary School Admission Test Board. Endowment: $13.6 million. Total enrollment: 337. Upper school average class size: 13. Upper school faculty-student ratio: 1:8.
Upper School Student Profile Grade 9: 55 students (32 boys, 23 girls); Grade 10: 63 students (29 boys, 34 girls); Grade 11: 72 students (38 boys, 34 girls); Grade 12: 63 students (37 boys, 26 girls). 62% of students are boarding students. 80% are state residents. 11 states are represented in upper school student body. 37% are international students.
Faculty School total: 49. In upper school: 22 men, 17 women; 28 have advanced degrees; 46 reside on campus.
Subjects Offered Algebra, American history, American history-AP, ancient history, art, art-AP, Bible, Bible studies, biology, biology-AP, calculus, calculus-AP, ceramics, chamber groups, character education, chemistry, chemistry-AP, chorus, comparative government and politics, concert choir, creative writing, drawing, English, English literature, English-AP, environmental science-AP, ESL, European history, European history-AP, expository writing, fine arts, French, French-AP, general science, geometry, health, history, humanities, instrumental music, instruments, intro to computers, Islamic studies, jazz, jazz band, Jewish studies, Latin, Latin-AP, marine science, mathematics, modern European history, music, orchestra, painting, photography, physical education, physical science, physics, physics-AP, piano, political science, pre-algebra, pre-calculus, psychology, psychology-AP, science, social studies, Spanish, Spanish-AP, statistics-AP, studio art-AP, study skills, theater arts, U.S. government and politics-AP, U.S. history, U.S. history-AP, visual arts, world history, writing.
Graduation Requirements Algebra, arts and fine arts (art, music, dance, drama), Bible, biology, English, European history, foreign language, geometry, Islamic studies, Jewish studies, mathematics, physical education (includes health), science, social studies (includes history), U.S. history.
Special Academic Programs Advanced Placement exam preparation; honors section; independent study; study at local college for college credit; ESL (19 students enrolled).
College Admission Counseling 63 students graduated in 2008; all went to college, including Boston University; Eastern University; Emory University; New York University; Syracuse University; University of Illinois at Urbana–Champaign. Mean SAT critical reading: 612, mean SAT math: 628, mean SAT writing: 301, mean combined SAT: 1841.
Student Life Upper grades have specified standards of dress, student council, honor system. Discipline rests equally with students and faculty. Attendance at religious services is required.
Summer Programs Enrichment programs offered; session focuses on athletics, recreation and/or writing; held on campus; accepts boys and girls; open to students from other schools.
Tuition and Aid Day student tuition: $21,400; 5-day tuition and room/board: $30,200; 7-day tuition and room/board: $36,000. Tuition installment plan (Key Tuition Payment Plan, monthly payment plans). Need-based scholarship grants available. In 2008–09, 30% of upper-school students received aid.
Admissions Traditional secondary-level entrance grade is 9. SSAT required. Deadline for receipt of application materials: none. Application fee required. Interview required.
Athletics Interscholastic: baseball (boys), basketball (b,g), cross-country running (b,g), football (b), soccer (b,g), softball (g), tennis (b,g), track and field (b,g), volleyball (g), wrestling (b); intramural: football (b), weight lifting (b,g); coed interscholastic: golf, sailing; coed intramural: flag football, physical fitness. 13 coaches, 1 athletic trainer.
Computers Computers are regularly used in Bible studies, English, foreign language, history, mathematics, science classes. Computer network features include Internet access, Internet filtering or blocking technology. Campus intranet and student e-mail accounts are available to students. Students grades are available online. The school has a published electronic and media policy.
Contact Mr. Joseph R. Austin, Director of Admissions. 631-751-1800 Ext. 1. Fax: 631-751-4211. E-mail: admissions@stonybrookschool.org. Web site: www.stonybrookschool.org.

STORM KING SCHOOL

314 Mountain Road
Cornwall-on-Hudson, New York 12520-1899
Head of School: Helen S. Chinitz

General Information Coeducational boarding and day college-preparatory, arts, and bilingual studies school; primarily serves students with learning disabilities. Boarding grades 9–12, day grades 8–12. Founded: 1867. Setting: small town. Nearest major city is New York. Students are housed in single-sex dormitories. 40-acre campus. 24 buildings on campus. Approved or accredited by Middle States Association of Colleges and Schools, New York State Association of Independent Schools, The Association of Boarding Schools, and New York Department of Education. Member of National Association of Independent Schools and Secondary School Admission Test Board. Endowment: $1 million. Total enrollment: 143. Upper school average class size: 8. Upper school faculty-student ratio: 1:6.
Upper School Student Profile Grade 8: 9 students (8 boys, 1 girl); Grade 9: 21 students (14 boys, 7 girls); Grade 10: 30 students (17 boys, 13 girls); Grade 11: 48 students (28 boys, 20 girls); Grade 12: 35 students (19 boys, 16 girls). 74% of students are boarding students. 47% are state residents. 10 states are represented in upper school student body. 40% are international students. International students from China, Hong Kong, Republic of Korea, Spain, Taiwan, and Thailand; 4 other countries represented in student body.
Faculty School total: 33. In upper school: 19 men, 14 women; 22 have advanced degrees; 26 reside on campus.
Subjects Offered Acting, Advanced Placement courses, advanced studio art-AP, advanced TOEFL/grammar, algebra, American history, American sign language, art, art history-AP, biology, calculus, calculus-AP, ceramics, chemistry, choral music, college counseling, community service, creative writing, dance, drama, drawing, economics, English, English literature, English literature-AP, environmental science, ESL, expository writing, fine arts, foreign language, geometry, government/civics, guitar, health, history, Mandarin, mathematics, mechanical drawing, music, painting, performing arts, photography, physical education, physics, piano, playwriting, psychology, SAT preparation, science, social studies, Spanish, stagecraft, studio art—AP, theater, theater history, U.S. history-AP, wilderness/outdoor program, world history, writing.
Graduation Requirements English, foreign language, mathematics, outdoor education, performing arts, physical education (includes health), public speaking, science, social studies (includes history), visual arts. Community service is required.
Special Academic Programs Advanced Placement exam preparation; academic accommodation for the gifted, the musically talented, and the artistically talented; remedial reading and/or remedial writing; remedial math; ESL (30 students enrolled).
College Admission Counseling 37 students graduated in 2008; all went to college, including Cornell University; Florida State University; Pratt Institute; Skidmore College; Smith College. Median SAT critical reading: 510, median SAT math: 540, median SAT writing: 470, median combined SAT: 1470. 22% scored over 600 on SAT critical reading, 35% scored over 600 on SAT math, 19% scored over 600 on SAT writing, 22% scored over 1800 on combined SAT.
Student Life Upper grades have specified standards of dress, student council, honor system. Discipline rests equally with students and faculty.
Tuition and Aid Day student tuition: $19,950; 7-day tuition and room/board: $35,950. Tuition installment plan (individually arranged payment plans). Tuition reduction for siblings, merit scholarship grants, need-based scholarship grants

available. In 2008–09, 35% of upper-school students received aid; total upper-school merit-scholarship money awarded: $35,500. Total amount of financial aid awarded in 2008–09: $325,000.
Admissions Traditional secondary-level entrance grade is 9. For fall 2008, 138 students applied for upper-level admission, 107 were accepted, 53 enrolled. Admissions testing and SLEP for foreign students required. Deadline for receipt of application materials: none. Application fee required: $85. Interview required.
Athletics Interscholastic: basketball (boys, girls), lacrosse (b), soccer (b,g), softball (g), volleyball (b,g); coed interscholastic: cross-country running, freestyle skiing, Frisbee, golf, jogging, skiing (downhill), snowboarding, tennis, ultimate Frisbee; coed intramural: aerobics/dance, aerobics/Nautilus, alpine skiing, backpacking, ballet, bicycling, billiards, blading, bocce, bowling, canoeing/kayaking, cheering, climbing, dance, fitness, fitness walking, flag football, freestyle skiing, golf, hiking/backpacking, ice skating, jogging, martial arts, modern dance, mountain biking, Nautilus, outdoor adventure, paddle tennis, paint ball, physical fitness, power lifting, rafting, rock climbing, ropes courses, running, skiing (cross-country), skiing (downhill), snowboarding, strength & conditioning, table tennis, tai chi, tennis, touch football, track and field, ultimate Frisbee, volleyball, weight lifting, wilderness, yoga. 2 PE instructors, 12 coaches, 1 athletic trainer.
Computers Computers are regularly used in art, ESL, historical foundations for arts, history, journalism, library, library skills, mathematics, music, newspaper, research skills, SAT preparation, science, social sciences, social studies, theater, theater arts, writing, yearbook classes. Computer network features include on-campus library services, Internet access, wireless campus network, Internet filtering or blocking technology. Student e-mail accounts and computer access in designated common areas are available to students. The school has a published electronic and media policy.
Contact Mrs. Caroline A. Petro, Admissions and Communications Coordinator. 845-534-9860 Ext. 210. Fax: 845-534-4128. E-mail: cpetro@sks.org. Web site: www.sks.org.

See Close-Up on page 980.

STRAKE JESUIT COLLEGE PREPARATORY

8900 Bellaire Boulevard
Houston, Texas 77036

Head of School: Fr. Dan Lahart, SJ

General Information Boys' day college-preparatory school, affiliated with Roman Catholic Church (Jesuit order). Grades 9–12. Founded: 1960. Setting: suburban. 44-acre campus. 13 buildings on campus. Approved or accredited by Jesuit Secondary Education Association, Southern Association of Colleges and Schools, Texas Catholic Conference, Texas Education Agency, and Texas Department of Education. Endowment: $6 million. Total enrollment: 899. Upper school average class size: 20. Upper school faculty-student ratio: 1:11.
Upper School Student Profile Grade 9: 233 students (233 boys); Grade 10: 228 students (228 boys); Grade 11: 219 students (219 boys); Grade 12: 219 students (219 boys). 75% of students are Roman Catholic Church (Jesuit order).
Faculty School total: 81. In upper school: 64 men, 17 women; 26 have advanced degrees.
Subjects Offered Accounting, algebra, American history, American literature, art, art history, band, biology, broadcasting, calculus, chemistry, chorus, community service, computer science, debate, drama, drawing, economics, English, English literature, French, geometry, government/civics, health, journalism, Latin, mathematics, music, music theory, oceanography, orchestra, painting, physical education, physical science, physics, physiology, pre-calculus, reading, religion, science, social studies, Spanish, speech, television, theater, theology, trigonometry, video, word processing, world history, world literature.
Graduation Requirements Arts and fine arts (art, music, dance, drama), business skills (includes word processing), computer science, English, foreign language, mathematics, physical education (includes health), religion (includes Bible studies and theology), science, social studies (includes history), speech. Community service is required.
Special Academic Programs Advanced Placement exam preparation; honors section; study at local college for college credit.
College Admission Counseling 210 students graduated in 2008; all went to college, including Loyola University New Orleans; Texas A&M University; Texas Tech University; The University of Texas at Austin; University of Dallas; University of Notre Dame. Median SAT critical reading: 610, median SAT math: 645, median SAT writing: 610, median combined SAT: 1865, median composite ACT: 26. 62% scored over 600 on SAT critical reading, 81% scored over 600 on SAT math, 58% scored over 600 on SAT writing, 69% scored over 1800 on combined SAT, 52% scored over 26 on composite ACT.
Student Life Upper grades have specified standards of dress, student council, honor system. Discipline rests primarily with faculty. Attendance at religious services is required.
Tuition and Aid Need-based scholarship grants available. In 2008–09, 12% of upper-school students received aid. Total amount of financial aid awarded in 2008–09: $1,000,000.
Admissions Traditional secondary-level entrance grade is 9. For fall 2008, 578 students applied for upper-level admission, 318 were accepted, 244 enrolled. STS required. Deadline for receipt of application materials: February 2. Application fee required: $50.
Athletics Interscholastic: baseball, basketball, cross-country running, football, golf, lacrosse, soccer, swimming and diving, track and field, water polo. 4 PE instructors, 33 coaches, 1 athletic trainer.
Computers Computer resources include on-campus library services, online commercial services, Internet access. Student e-mail accounts are available to students. Students grades are available online.
Contact Mrs. Patti Ledesma, Assistant to the Director of Admissions. 713-490-8113. Fax: 713-774-6427. E-mail: pledesma@strakejesuit.org. Web site: www.strakejesuit.org.

STRATFORD ACADEMY

6010 Peake Road
Macon, Georgia 31220-3903

Head of School: Dr. Robert E. Veto

General Information Coeducational day college-preparatory, arts, and technology school. Grades PK–12. Founded: 1960. Setting: suburban. Nearest major city is Atlanta. 65-acre campus. 3 buildings on campus. Approved or accredited by Georgia Independent School Association, Southern Association of Colleges and Schools, Southern Association of Independent Schools, and Georgia Department of Education. Member of National Association of Independent Schools. Endowment: $1 million. Total enrollment: 888. Upper school average class size: 17. Upper school faculty-student ratio: 1:13.
Faculty School total: 88. In upper school: 24 men, 23 women; 25 have advanced degrees.
Subjects Offered Advanced Placement courses, algebra, American history, American literature, anatomy, art, art history, art-AP, athletics, baseball, basketball, biology, biology-AP, calculus, calculus-AP, chemistry, chemistry-AP, community service, comparative government and politics-AP, computer keyboarding, computer programming, computer science, creative writing, drama, drama performance, driver education, earth science, economics, English, English literature, English literature-AP, English-AP, European history, European history-AP, expository writing, French, French-AP, geography, geometry, government/civics, grammar, history, history-AP, humanities, journalism, Latin, Latin-AP, madrigals, mathematics, mathematics-AP, music, physical education, physical science, physics, pre-calculus, science, social science, social studies, sociology, Spanish, Spanish-AP, speech, theater, trigonometry, U.S. government and politics-AP, world history, world literature, writing.
Graduation Requirements English, foreign language, math applications, mathematics, science, senior seminar, social science, social studies (includes history). Community service is required.
Special Academic Programs Advanced Placement exam preparation; independent study; special instructional classes for students with learning disabilities, Attention Deficit Disorder, and dyslexia.
College Admission Counseling 73 students graduated in 2008; all went to college, including Auburn University; Georgia Institute of Technology; Georgia Southern University; Harvard University; University of Georgia; University of Mississippi.
Student Life Upper grades have uniform requirement, student council, honor system. Discipline rests primarily with faculty.
Tuition and Aid Day student tuition: $11,569. Tuition installment plan (Insured Tuition Payment Plan, monthly payment plans, individually arranged payment plans). Merit scholarship grants, need-based scholarship grants available. Total upper-school merit-scholarship money awarded for 2008–09: $11,569.
Admissions Traditional secondary-level entrance grade is 9. ERB required. Deadline for receipt of application materials: none. Application fee required: $50. On-campus interview required.
Athletics Interscholastic: aquatics (boys, girls), baseball (b), basketball (b,g), cheering (g), cross-country running (b,g), dance team (g), drill team (g), football (b), physical training (b,g), soccer (b,g), tennis (b,g), wrestling (b); coed interscholastic: badminton, golf. 8 PE instructors, 4 coaches, 1 athletic trainer.
Computers Computers are regularly used in art, creative writing, English, French, graphics, information technology, Spanish classes. Computer network features include on-campus library services, Internet access, wireless campus network. The school has a published electronic and media policy.
Contact Ms. Marilyn Holton-Walker, Registrar/Admissions Assistant. 478-477-8073 Ext. 205. Fax: 478-477-0299. E-mail: marilyn.walker@stratford.org. Web site: www.stratford.org.

STRATHCONA-TWEEDSMUIR SCHOOL

RR #2
Okotoks, Alberta T1S 1A2, Canada

Head of School: Mr. William Jones

General Information Coeducational day college-preparatory, arts, and technology school. Grades 1–12. Founded: 1905. Setting: rural. Nearest major city is Calgary, Canada. 160-acre campus. 1 building on campus. Approved or accredited by Canadian

Association of Independent Schools, Canadian Educational Standards Institute, International Baccalaureate Organization, and Alberta Department of Education. Affiliate member of National Association of Independent Schools. Language of instruction: English. Endowment: CAN$5 million. Total enrollment: 690. Upper school average class size: 20. Upper school faculty-student ratio: 1:20.
Upper School Student Profile Grade 10: 85 students (51 boys, 34 girls); Grade 11: 82 students (40 boys, 42 girls); Grade 12: 74 students (38 boys, 36 girls).
Faculty School total: 70. In upper school: 24 men, 27 women; 15 have advanced degrees.
Subjects Offered Art, band, biology, calculus, chemistry, computer science, drama, English, fine arts, French, Latin, mathematics, music, outdoor education, physical education, physics, science, social science, social studies, Spanish, theater.
Graduation Requirements Arts and fine arts (art, music, dance, drama), business skills (includes word processing), English, foreign language, mathematics, physical education (includes health), science, social science, social studies (includes history).
Special Academic Programs International Baccalaureate program; term-away projects.
College Admission Counseling 98 students graduated in 2008; 92 went to college, including Acadia University; Queen's University at Kingston; The University of British Columbia; The University of Western Ontario; University of Calgary; University of Victoria. Other: 6 had other specific plans.
Student Life Upper grades have uniform requirement, student council, honor system. Discipline rests primarily with faculty.
Tuition and Aid Day student tuition: CAN$13,200–CAN$15,750. Tuition installment plan (monthly payment plans). Bursaries, need-based scholarship grants available. In 2008–09, 2% of upper-school students received aid. Total amount of financial aid awarded in 2008–09: CAN$37,250.
Admissions Traditional secondary-level entrance grade is 10. For fall 2008, 56 students applied for upper-level admission, 28 were accepted, 25 enrolled. CTBS, OLSAT, Henmon-Nelson or SSAT required. Deadline for receipt of application materials: none. Application fee required: CAN$100. Interview required.
Athletics Interscholastic: badminton (boys, girls), basketball (b,g), cross-country running (b,g), field hockey (g), golf (b,g), outdoor education (b,g), rugby (b), soccer (g), telemark skiing (b,g), track and field (b,g), triathlon (b,g), volleyball (b,g), wall climbing (b,g); coed interscholastic: backpacking, badminton, climbing, outdoor education; coed intramural: basketball, volleyball. 10 PE instructors, 38 coaches, 2 athletic trainers.
Computers Computers are regularly used in all classes. Computer network features include on-campus library services, online commercial services, Internet access, wireless campus network, Internet filtering or blocking technology. Student e-mail accounts are available to students. Students grades are available online. The school has a published electronic and media policy.
Contact Ms. Tina Ierakidis, Director of Admissions. 403-938-8303. Fax: 403-938-4492. E-mail: ierakit@sts.ab.ca. Web site: www.sts.ab.ca.

STRATTON MOUNTAIN SCHOOL

World Cup Circle
Stratton Mountain, Vermont 05155

Head of School: Christopher G. Kaltsas

General Information Coeducational boarding and day college-preparatory, arts, bilingual studies, and technology school. Grades 7–PG. Founded: 1972. Setting: rural. Nearest major city is Albany, NY. Students are housed in single-sex by floor dormitories. 12-acre campus. 7 buildings on campus. Approved or accredited by Independent Schools of Northern New England, New England Association of Schools and Colleges, and Vermont Department of Education. Member of National Association of Independent Schools. Total enrollment: 130. Upper school average class size: 10. Upper school faculty-student ratio: 1:6.
Upper School Student Profile Grade 9: 23 students (13 boys, 10 girls); Grade 10: 31 students (16 boys, 15 girls); Grade 11: 29 students (17 boys, 12 girls); Grade 12: 22 students (10 boys, 12 girls); Postgraduate: 10 students (4 boys, 6 girls). 55% of students are boarding students. 48% are state residents. 22 states are represented in upper school student body. 10% are international students. International students from Australia, Canada, Italy, Republic of Korea, Spain, and Switzerland; 3 other countries represented in student body.
Faculty School total: 18. In upper school: 7 men, 11 women; 7 have advanced degrees; 17 reside on campus.
Subjects Offered Algebra, American history, American literature, art, biology, calculus, chemistry, computer science, English, English literature, environmental science, French, geography, geometry, grammar, health, history, journalism, mathematics, nutrition, physical education, physics, science, social studies, Spanish, speech, trigonometry, world history, writing.
Graduation Requirements Arts and fine arts (art, music, dance, drama), computer education, English, foreign language, mathematics, science, social studies (includes history), superior competence in winter sports (skiing/snowboarding). Community service is required.
Special Academic Programs ESL (8 students enrolled).
College Admission Counseling 23 students graduated in 2008; 18 went to college, including Dartmouth College; St. Lawrence University; University of New Hampshire; University of Utah; University of Vermont; Williams College. Other: 5 entered a postgraduate year. Mean SAT critical reading: 580, mean SAT math: 600, mean SAT writing: 610.
Student Life Upper grades have specified standards of dress, honor system. Discipline rests primarily with faculty.
Tuition and Aid Day student tuition: $27,500; 7-day tuition and room/board: $37,750. Tuition installment plan (individually arranged payment plans, two tuition installments and advance deposit). Need-based scholarship grants available. In 2008–09, 40% of upper-school students received aid. Total amount of financial aid awarded in 2008–09: $689,894.
Admissions Traditional secondary-level entrance grade is 9. For fall 2008, 96 students applied for upper-level admission, 68 were accepted, 54 enrolled. Deadline for receipt of application materials: March 15. Application fee required: $100. On-campus interview required.
Athletics Interscholastic: alpine skiing (boys, girls), bicycling (b,g), cross-country running (b,g), freestyle skiing (b,g), golf (b,g), lacrosse (b,g), nordic skiing (b,g), skiing (cross-country) (b,g), skiing (downhill) (b,g), snowboarding (b,g), soccer (b,g); intramural: tennis (b,g); coed intramural: skateboarding. 24 coaches, 1 athletic trainer.
Computers Computers are regularly used in computer applications, graphic design, mathematics, media production, research skills, science, Web site design, yearbook classes. Computer network features include on-campus library services, online commercial services, Internet access, Internet filtering or blocking technology. Student e-mail accounts are available to students. The school has a published electronic and media policy.
Contact Mrs. Kate Nolan Joyce, Director of Admissions. 802-856-1124. Fax: 802-297-0020. E-mail: knolan@gosms.org. Web site: www.gosms.org.

STUART COUNTRY DAY SCHOOL OF THE SACRED HEART

1200 Stuart Road
Princeton, New Jersey 08540-1219

Head of School: Frances de la Chapelle, RSCJ

General Information Coeducational day (boys' only in lower grades) college-preparatory, arts, religious studies, and technology school, affiliated with Roman Catholic Church. Boys grade PS, girls grades PS–12. Founded: 1963. Setting: suburban. 55-acre campus. 1 building on campus. Approved or accredited by Middle States Association of Colleges and Schools, Network of Sacred Heart Schools, New Jersey Association of Independent Schools, and New Jersey Department of Education. Member of National Association of Independent Schools and Secondary School Admission Test Board. Endowment: $7.5 million. Total enrollment: 507. Upper school average class size: 12. Upper school faculty-student ratio: 1:12.
Upper School Student Profile Grade 9: 37 students (37 girls); Grade 10: 33 students (33 girls); Grade 11: 34 students (34 girls); Grade 12: 40 students (40 girls). 50% of students are Roman Catholic.
Faculty School total: 123. In upper school: 3 men, 39 women; 14 have advanced degrees.
Subjects Offered African studies, algebra, American culture, American literature, anatomy, art, art history, Bible studies, biology, biology-AP, calculus, calculus-AP, ceramics, chemistry, college counseling, communications, community service, computer programming, computer science, conceptual physics, creative writing, dance, drama, drawing and design, economics, English, English literature, English-AP, environmental science, environmental science-AP, ethics, European history, European history-AP, expository writing, film, fine arts, French, French-AP, geometry, government/civics, handbells, health education, independent study, Latin, Latin-AP, mathematics, music, music history, music theory, philosophy, photography, physical education, physical fitness, physics, physics-AP, physiology, portfolio art, pre-calculus, probability and statistics, religion, religious studies, science, senior project, social studies, Spanish, Spanish-AP, speech, stagecraft, studio art, studio art—AP, theater, theology, trigonometry, U.S. history, U.S. history-AP, visual arts, vocal ensemble, world culture, world cultures, world literature, world religions, writing.
Graduation Requirements Arts and fine arts (art, music, dance, drama), computer science, English, foreign language, history, lab science, mathematics, physical education (includes health), religious studies, 50 hours of community service per year for each year of high school.
Special Academic Programs Advanced Placement exam preparation; honors section; accelerated programs; independent study; term-away projects; study at local college for college credit; study abroad.
College Admission Counseling 40 students graduated in 2008; 38 went to college, including Georgetown University; Princeton University; Rensselaer Polytechnic Institute; Villanova University; Yale University. Mean SAT critical reading: 602, mean SAT math: 627, mean composite ACT: 27. 60% scored over 600 on SAT critical reading, 60% scored over 600 on SAT math, 64% scored over 26 on composite ACT.
Student Life Upper grades have specified standards of dress, student council, honor system. Discipline rests equally with students and faculty. Attendance at religious services is required.
Summer Programs Enrichment, art/fine arts programs offered; session focuses on various course selections for enrichment, remediation, and athletic development; held on campus; accepts boys and girls; open to students from other schools. 65 students usually enrolled. 2009 schedule: June 15 to August 29. Application deadline: April 1.

Tuition and Aid Day student tuition: $26,980. Tuition installment plan (Academic Management Services Plan). Merit scholarship grants, need-based scholarship grants, prepGATE Loans available. In 2008–09, 26% of upper-school students received aid; total upper-school merit-scholarship money awarded: $47,215. Total amount of financial aid awarded in 2008–09: $692,800.
Admissions Traditional secondary-level entrance grade is 9. For fall 2008, 38 students applied for upper-level admission, 26 were accepted, 14 enrolled. SSAT required. Deadline for receipt of application materials: January 26. Application fee required: $75. On-campus interview required.
Athletics Interscholastic: aerobics/dance, basketball, cross-country running, dance, field hockey, fitness, lacrosse, squash, tennis, track and field; intramural: basketball, dance, fitness. 2 PE instructors, 16 coaches, 1 athletic trainer.
Computers Computers are regularly used in all academic classes. Computer network features include on-campus library services, Internet access, wireless campus network, Internet filtering or blocking technology. Student e-mail accounts are available to students. The school has a published electronic and media policy.
Contact Stephanie Lupero, Director of Admissions. 609-921-2330 Ext. 235. Fax: 609-497-0784. E-mail: slupero@stuartschool.org. Web site: www.stuartschool.org.

THE STUDY SCHOOL
3233 The Boulevard
Westmount, Quebec H3Y 1S4, Canada
Head of School: Elizabeth Falco
General Information Girls' day college-preparatory, arts, bilingual studies, technology, and Science school. Grades K–11. Founded: 1915. Setting: urban. Nearest major city is Montreal, Canada. 2 buildings on campus. Approved or accredited by Canadian Association of Independent Schools and Quebec Department of Education. Affiliate member of National Association of Independent Schools. Languages of instruction: English and French. Endowment: CAN$4.2 million. Total enrollment: 387. Upper school average class size: 18. Upper school faculty-student ratio: 1:8.
Upper School Student Profile Grade 7: 36 students (36 girls); Grade 8: 33 students (33 girls); Grade 9: 33 students (33 girls); Grade 10: 30 students (30 girls); Grade 11: 35 students (35 girls).
Faculty School total: 55. In upper school: 3 men, 28 women; 8 have advanced degrees.
Subjects Offered Algebra, art, art history, arts appreciation, biology, chemistry, computer science, ecology, economics, English, entrepreneurship, environmental science, ethics, European history, French, gender issues, geography, geometry, history, Mandarin, mathematics, music, philosophy, physical education, physics, religion and culture, science, social studies, Spanish, stagecraft, technology, theater, world history.
Graduation Requirements English, ethics, foreign language, French, mathematics, physical education (includes health), science, social studies (includes history), technology. Community service is required.
College Admission Counseling 36 students graduated in 2008; all went to college.
Student Life Upper grades have uniform requirement, student council, honor system. Discipline rests primarily with faculty.
Tuition and Aid Day student tuition: CAN$14,000. Tuition installment plan (monthly payment plans, individually arranged payment plans, 2-payment plan). Bursaries, merit scholarship grants, need-based scholarship grants available. In 2008–09, 16% of upper-school students received aid; total upper-school merit-scholarship money awarded: CAN$26,000. Total amount of financial aid awarded in 2008–09: CAN$169,750.
Admissions Traditional secondary-level entrance grade is 7. For fall 2008, 42 students applied for upper-level admission, 31 were accepted, 18 enrolled. SSAT required. Deadline for receipt of application materials: none. Application fee required: CAN$125. On-campus interview required.
Athletics Interscholastic: alpine skiing, aquatics, badminton, basketball, crew, cross-country running, flag football, golf, hockey, ice hockey, rowing, running, skiing (cross-country), soccer, swimming and diving, tennis, touch football, track and field, volleyball; intramural: aerobics, aerobics/dance, aerobics/Nautilus, badminton, ballet, basketball, bicycling, cooperative games, dance, fitness, ice hockey, jump rope, martial arts, outdoor activities, soccer, squash, touch football, track and field, ultimate Frisbee, volleyball. 3 PE instructors, 8 coaches.
Computers Computers are regularly used in art, English, history, mathematics, science classes. Computer network features include on-campus library services, Internet access, wireless campus network, Internet filtering or blocking technology. Campus intranet, student e-mail accounts, and computer access in designated common areas are available to students. The school has a published electronic and media policy.
Contact Pattie Edwards, Director of Admissions. 514-935-9352. Fax: 514-935-1721. E-mail: admissions@thestudy.qc.ca.

SUBIACO ACADEMY
405 North Subiaco Avenue
Subiaco, Arkansas 72865
Head of School: Mr. Michael Burke
General Information Boys' boarding and day college-preparatory, arts, religious studies, bilingual studies, technology, and Art and Performing Art school, affiliated with Roman Catholic Church. Grades 8–12. Founded: 1887. Setting: rural. Nearest major city is Little Rock. Students are housed in single-sex dormitories. 100-acre campus. 8 buildings on campus. Approved or accredited by Independent Schools Association of the Central States, Midwest Association of Boarding Schools, National Catholic Education Association, North Central Association of Colleges and Schools, The Association of Boarding Schools, and Arkansas Department of Education. Member of National Association of Independent Schools. Endowment: $3.5 million. Total enrollment: 175. Upper school average class size: 12. Upper school faculty-student ratio: 1:9.
Upper School Student Profile Grade 8: 14 students (14 boys); Grade 9: 32 students (32 boys); Grade 10: 40 students (40 boys); Grade 11: 45 students (45 boys); Grade 12: 44 students (44 boys). 89% of students are boarding students. 45% are state residents. 16 states are represented in upper school student body. 20% are international students. International students from Canada, China, Mexico, Netherlands Antilles, Republic of Korea, and Taiwan. 65% of students are Roman Catholic.
Faculty School total: 24. In upper school: 17 men, 7 women; 20 have advanced degrees; 9 reside on campus.
Subjects Offered Algebra, American history, American history-AP, American literature, anthropology, art, art-AP, band, biology, biology-AP, calculus, calculus-AP, chemistry, chemistry-AP, choral music, chorus, Christian and Hebrew scripture, Christian doctrine, Christian education, Christian scripture, Christian studies, Christian testament, church history, communications, computer art, computer science, drama, drama workshop, driver education, earth and space science, earth science, economics, English, English literature, English literature and composition-AP, English-AP, European history, finance, fine arts, geography, geometry, government/civics, international relations, jazz ensemble, journalism, Latin, Latin-AP, mathematics-AP, music, physical education, physics, piano, psychology, religion, sociology, Spanish, Spanish language-AP, speech, statistics-AP, Western civilization, world history.
Graduation Requirements Arts and fine arts (art, music, dance, drama), computer science, English, foreign language, mathematics, physical education (includes health), religion (includes Bible studies and theology), science, social studies (includes history), Western civilization, A student must complete at least two (2) years at Subiaco Academy to graduate. Community service is required.
Special Academic Programs 9 Advanced Placement exams for which test preparation is offered; honors section; academic accommodation for the gifted, the musically talented, and the artistically talented; ESL (15 students enrolled).
College Admission Counseling 37 students graduated in 2008; all went to college, including Texas A&M University–Commerce; The University of Texas at Austin; University of Arkansas.
Student Life Upper grades have uniform requirement, student council, honor system. Discipline rests equally with students and faculty. Attendance at religious services is required.
Tuition and Aid Day student tuition: $5400; 5-day tuition and room/board: $16,000; 7-day tuition and room/board: $17,300. Tuition installment plan (monthly payment plans, individually arranged payment plans). Need-based scholarship grants, paying campus jobs available. In 2008–09, 40% of upper-school students received aid.
Admissions Traditional secondary-level entrance grade is 10. SSAT or TOEFL or SLEP required. Deadline for receipt of application materials: July 1. Application fee required: $50. Interview required.
Athletics Interscholastic: baseball, basketball, cross-country running, football, golf, soccer; intramural: archery, backpacking, baseball, basketball, bicycling, billiards, blading, bowling, canoeing/kayaking, cheering, climbing, cross-country running, diving, fishing, fitness, fly fishing, football, Frisbee, golf, handball, hiking/backpacking, horseshoes, in-line skating, indoor soccer, jogging, kayaking, marksmanship, outdoor activities, physical fitness, physical training, power lifting, riflery, rock climbing, roller blading, running, skateboarding, skeet shooting, skiing (downhill), soccer, softball, strength & conditioning. 1 PE instructor, 9 coaches.
Computers Computers are regularly used in art, Christian doctrine, commercial art, creative writing, desktop publishing, digital applications, drawing and design, economics, English, geography, graphic arts, history, journalism, keyboarding, literary magazine, mathematics, news writing, newspaper, photography, photojournalism, publications, religion, religious studies, SAT preparation, science, Spanish, stock market, video film production, word processing, writing, yearbook classes. Computer resources include Internet access, wireless campus network, Internet filtering or blocking technology. Computer access in designated common areas is available to students. Students grades are available online. The school has a published electronic and media policy.
Contact Ms. Evelyn Bauer, Assistant Director of Admissions. 800-364-7824. Fax: 479-934-1033. E-mail: ebauer@subi.org. Web site: www.subi.org.

THE SUDBURY VALLEY SCHOOL
2 Winch Street
Framingham, Massachusetts 01701
Head of School: Michael Sadofsky
General Information Coeducational day college-preparatory, general academic, arts, business, and vocational school. Grades PS–12. Founded: 1968. Setting: suburban. Nearest major city is Boston. 10-acre campus. 2 buildings on campus.

Approved or accredited by Massachusetts Department of Education. Total enrollment: 180. Upper school faculty-student ratio: 1:16.
Faculty School total: 10. In upper school: 4 men, 6 women; 3 have advanced degrees.
Subjects Offered Algebra, American history, American literature, anatomy, anthropology, archaeology, art, art history, Bible studies, biology, botany, business, calculus, ceramics, chemistry, computer programming, computer science, creative writing, dance, drama, economics, English, English literature, ethics, European history, expository writing, French, geography, geometry, German, government/civics, grammar, Hebrew, history, history of ideas, history of science, home economics, Latin, mathematics, music, philosophy, photography, physical education, physics, physiology, psychology, religion, social studies, Spanish, speech, theater, trigonometry, typing, world history, world literature, writing.
Graduation Requirements Students must successfully defend the thesis that they have taken responsibility for preparing themselves to be an effective adult in the community.
Special Academic Programs Independent study.
College Admission Counseling 14 students graduated in 2008; 9 went to college. Other: 5 went to work.
Student Life Upper grades have student council, honor system. Discipline rests equally with students and faculty.
Tuition and Aid Day student tuition: $6130.
Admissions Deadline for receipt of application materials: none. Application fee required: $30. On-campus interview required.
Computers Computer resources include on-campus library services, Internet access.
Contact Hanna Greenberg, Admissions Clerk. 508-877-3030. Fax: 508-788-0674. E-mail: sudval@aol.com. Web site: www.sudval.org.

SUFFIELD ACADEMY

185 North Main Street
Suffield, Connecticut 06078
Head of School: Charles Cahn III

General Information Coeducational boarding and day college-preparatory, arts, technology, and leadership school. Grades 9–PG. Founded: 1833. Setting: small town. Nearest major city is Hartford. Students are housed in single-sex dormitories. 340-acre campus. 49 buildings on campus. Approved or accredited by Connecticut Association of Independent Schools, New England Association of Schools and Colleges, and The Association of Boarding Schools. Member of National Association of Independent Schools and Secondary School Admission Test Board. Endowment: $29 million. Total enrollment: 405. Upper school average class size: 10. Upper school faculty-student ratio: 1:5.
Upper School Student Profile Grade 9: 68 students (26 boys, 42 girls); Grade 10: 112 students (69 boys, 43 girls); Grade 11: 116 students (60 boys, 56 girls); Grade 12: 117 students (68 boys, 49 girls); Postgraduate: 9 students (7 boys, 2 girls). 68% of students are boarding students. 45% are state residents. 19 states are represented in upper school student body. 14% are international students. International students from Bermuda, Japan, Norway, Republic of Korea, Thailand, and United Kingdom; 22 other countries represented in student body.
Faculty School total: 82. In upper school: 40 men, 28 women; 51 have advanced degrees; 65 reside on campus.
Subjects Offered Acting, Advanced Placement courses, algebra, American history, American literature, anatomy and physiology, archaeology, art, art history, biology, biology-AP, calculus, calculus-AP, ceramics, chemistry, chemistry-AP, Chinese, computer math, computer programming, computer programming-AP, computer science, computer science-AP, constitutional law, dance, drama, economics, economics-AP, English, English literature, English-AP, environmental science, ESL, ethics, European history, expository writing, fine arts, French, French-AP, geometry, government-AP, government/civics, grammar, great books, health, history, jazz band, Latin, Latin-AP, leadership skills, leadership training, mathematics, mechanical drawing, music, music theory, news writing, philosophy, photography, physical education, physics, physics-AP, religion, science, senior seminar, short story, social studies, sociology, Spanish, Spanish-AP, statistics, statistics and probability, statistics-AP, technology, theater, theater arts, trigonometry, U.S. history, U.S. history-AP, visual and performing arts, visual arts, voice ensemble, wilderness/outdoor program, wind ensemble, wind instruments, woodworking, world history, writing.
Graduation Requirements Arts and fine arts (art, music, dance, drama), English, foreign language, leadership, mathematics, physical education (includes health), religion (includes Bible studies and theology), science, social studies (includes history), technology portfolio.
Special Academic Programs Advanced Placement exam preparation; honors section; independent study; academic accommodation for the gifted, the musically talented, and the artistically talented; ESL (12 students enrolled).
College Admission Counseling 109 students graduated in 2008; 108 went to college, including Bates College; Cornell University; New York University; The George Washington University; Trinity College. Other: 1 entered a postgraduate year. Mean SAT critical reading: 557, mean SAT math: 584, mean SAT writing: 561, mean combined SAT: 1702, mean composite ACT: 23. 29% scored over 600 on SAT critical reading, 36% scored over 600 on SAT math, 27% scored over 600 on SAT writing, 28% scored over 1800 on combined SAT, 21% scored over 26 on composite ACT.
Student Life Upper grades have specified standards of dress, student council, honor system. Discipline rests primarily with faculty.
Summer Programs Enrichment, ESL, art/fine arts, computer instruction programs offered; held on campus; accepts boys and girls; open to students from other schools. 2009 schedule: June 28 to July 31. Application deadline: June 1.
Tuition and Aid Day student tuition: $29,500; 7-day tuition and room/board: $41,500. Tuition installment plan (Key Tuition Payment Plan, monthly payment plans). Merit scholarship grants, need-based scholarship grants, need-based loans, middle-income loans, tuition remission for children of faculty and staff who meet years of service requirement available. In 2008–09, 32% of upper-school students received aid; total upper-school merit-scholarship money awarded: $202,000. Total amount of financial aid awarded in 2008–09: $2,605,410.
Admissions Traditional secondary-level entrance grade is 9. For fall 2008, 885 students applied for upper-level admission, 286 were accepted, 150 enrolled. PSAT or SAT, SSAT or TOEFL required. Deadline for receipt of application materials: February 1. Application fee required: $50. Interview required.
Athletics Interscholastic: alpine skiing (boys, girls), aquatics (b,g), baseball (b), basketball (b,g), cross-country running (b,g), field hockey (g), football (b), lacrosse (b,g), skiing (downhill) (b,g), soccer (b,g), softball (g), squash (b,g), swimming and diving (b,g), tennis (b,g), track and field (b,g), volleyball (g), water polo (b,g); coed interscholastic: alpine skiing, backpacking, dance, diving, fitness, golf, outdoors, riflery, snowboarding; coed intramural: rock climbing, ropes courses, weight lifting. 2 athletic trainers.
Computers Computers are regularly used in English, foreign language, history, mathematics, science classes. Computer network features include on-campus library services, Internet access, wireless campus network. Student e-mail accounts are available to students. The school has a published electronic and media policy.
Contact Terry Breault, Director of Admissions and Financial Aid. 860-386-4440. Fax: 860-668-2966. E-mail: saadmit@suffieldacademy.org. Web site: www.suffieldacademy.org.

See Close-Up on page 982.

SUMMERFIELD WALDORF SCHOOL

655 Willowside Road
Santa Rosa, California 95472
Head of School: Mr. Robert Flagg

General Information Coeducational day college-preparatory and arts school. Grades 1–12. Founded: 1974. Setting: rural. 38-acre campus. 5 buildings on campus. Approved or accredited by Association of Waldorf Schools of North America, Western Association of Schools and Colleges, and California Department of Education. Total enrollment: 380. Upper school average class size: 28. Upper school faculty-student ratio: 1:7.
Upper School Student Profile Grade 9: 31 students (13 boys, 18 girls); Grade 10: 21 students (8 boys, 13 girls); Grade 11: 20 students (7 boys, 13 girls); Grade 12: 25 students (6 boys, 19 girls).
Faculty School total: 23. In upper school: 11 men, 12 women; all have advanced degrees.
Subjects Offered Arts, history, humanities, literature, mathematics, music, science.
Special Academic Programs Advanced Placement exam preparation; study abroad.
College Admission Counseling 24 students graduated in 2008; 21 went to college, including Bard College; Rhode Island School of Design; University of California, Berkeley; University of California, San Diego; University of California, Santa Cruz; University of Colorado at Boulder. Other: 2 went to work, 1 entered a postgraduate year.
Student Life Upper grades have specified standards of dress, student council. Discipline rests primarily with faculty.
Tuition and Aid Day student tuition: $15,500. Tuition installment plan (FACTS Tuition Payment Plan). Tuition reduction for siblings, need-based scholarship grants available. In 2008–09, 30% of upper-school students received aid.
Admissions Traditional secondary-level entrance grade is 9. For fall 2008, 50 students applied for upper-level admission, 36 were accepted, 31 enrolled. Deadline for receipt of application materials: none. Application fee required: $75. On-campus interview required.
Athletics Interscholastic: baseball (boys, girls), soccer (b,g); intramural: basketball (b,g), volleyball (b,g); coed interscholastic: tennis. 1 PE instructor, 4 coaches.
Contact Ms. Sallie Miller, Admissions Director. 707-575-7194 Ext. 102. Fax: 707-575-3217. E-mail: sallie@summerfieldwaldof.org. Web site: www.summerfieldwaldorf.org.

THE SUMMIT COUNTRY DAY SCHOOL

2161 Grandin Road
Cincinnati, Ohio 45208-3300
Head of School: Mr. Jerry Jellig

General Information Coeducational day college-preparatory school, affiliated with Roman Catholic Church. Grades PK–12. Founded: 1890. Setting: suburban. 24-acre campus. 2 buildings on campus. Approved or accredited by Independent Schools

Association of the Central States, Ohio Association of Independent Schools, The College Board, and Ohio Department of Education. Member of Secondary School Admission Test Board. Endowment: $11 million. Total enrollment: 1,100. Upper school average class size: 16. Upper school faculty-student ratio: 1:9.

Upper School Student Profile Grade 9: 90 students (40 boys, 50 girls); Grade 10: 99 students (43 boys, 56 girls); Grade 11: 91 students (37 boys, 54 girls); Grade 12: 95 students (54 boys, 41 girls). 60% of students are Roman Catholic.

Faculty School total: 136. In upper school: 14 men, 23 women; 31 have advanced degrees.

Subjects Offered 1968, Advanced Placement courses, algebra, American government-AP, American history, American history-AP, American literature, anatomy and physiology, archaeology, area studies, art, Basic programming, Bible studies, biology, biology-AP, business, business law, calculus, calculus-AP, ceramics, chemistry, chemistry-AP, chorus, college admission preparation, college placement, community service, computer applications, computer programming, computer science, computer science-AP, concert choir, creative writing, critical studies in film, critical thinking, drama, earth science, economics, English, English literature, English-AP, environmental science, European history, European history-AP, expository writing, fine arts, French, French-AP, geometry, government-AP, government/civics, grammar, graphic design, health, history, history of science, history-AP, Holocaust studies, language-AP, Latin, Latin-AP, leadership and service, leadership education training, leadership training, literary magazine, mathematics, music, music theory-AP, music-AP, philosophy, physical education, physics, physics-AP, pre-calculus, psychology, psychology-AP, public speaking, religion, religious studies, science, senior career experience, service learning/internship, social studies, Spanish, Spanish language-AP, Spanish-AP, speech, speech communications, statistics-AP, student government, studio art, studio art—AP, study skills, theater, theology, trigonometry, world history, world history-AP, world literature, world religions, writing.

Graduation Requirements Arts and fine arts (art, music, dance, drama), computer applications, computer science, English, foreign language, mathematics, physical education (includes health), religion (includes Bible studies and theology), science, social science, social studies (includes history), speech communications, junior year leadership course (one semester), junior year speech course, 40 hours of Christian service, senior search (2-week field experience in career of interest area).

Special Academic Programs 19 Advanced Placement exams for which test preparation is offered; honors section; independent study; study abroad; academic accommodation for the gifted.

College Admission Counseling 67 students graduated in 2008; all went to college, including Boston University; Miami University; The Ohio State University; Washington University in St. Louis; Xavier University. Median SAT critical reading: 650, median SAT math: 610, median composite ACT: 28.

Student Life Upper grades have uniform requirement, student council, honor system. Discipline rests equally with students and faculty. Attendance at religious services is required.

Summer Programs Enrichment, advancement, sports, art/fine arts, computer instruction programs offered; session focuses on enrichment, academic advancement; held both on and off campus; held at sports may be held at 16-acre athletic complex; accepts boys and girls; open to students from other schools. 2009 schedule: June 8 to August 16. Application deadline: none.

Tuition and Aid Day student tuition: $16,400–$16,700. Tuition installment plan (monthly payment plans, individually arranged payment plans). Merit scholarship grants, need-based scholarship grants available. In 2008–09, 50% of upper-school students received aid.

Admissions Traditional secondary-level entrance grade is 9. For fall 2008, 80 students applied for upper-level admission, 72 were accepted, 47 enrolled. High School Placement Test or ISEE required. Deadline for receipt of application materials: December 19. Application fee required: $50. On-campus interview recommended.

Athletics Interscholastic: baseball (boys, girls), basketball (b,g), cheering (g), cross-country running (b,g), diving (b,g), field hockey (g), football (b), golf (b,g), lacrosse (b), soccer (b,g), softball (g), swimming and diving (b,g), tennis (b,g), track and field (b,g), volleyball (g), wrestling (b); intramural: dance team (g); coed interscholastic: weight lifting. 13 coaches, 1 athletic trainer.

Computers Computers are regularly used in all classes. Computer network features include on-campus library services, online commercial services, Internet access, wireless campus network, Internet filtering or blocking technology, mobile laptop computer lab, Basmati Grades, Blackboard, Sketchpad, 8 full-text databases including Big Chalk, World Book, Children's Lit, SIRS, Biography Resource Center, Wilson Web, INFOhio, JSTOR. Campus intranet, student e-mail accounts, and computer access in designated common areas are available to students. Students grades are available online. The school has a published electronic and media policy.

Contact Mrs. Kelley Schiess, Director of Admission. 513-871-4700 Ext. 207. Fax: 513-533-5350. E-mail: schiess_k@summitcds.org. Web site: www.summitcds.org.

ANNOUNCEMENT FROM THE SCHOOL Founded in 1890, the Summit Country Day School is Cincinnati's only Catholic, independent, college-preparatory school for students age 2 to grade 12. The School is situated in Hyde Park, on a beautiful 24-acre campus, with a separate 16-acre Athletic Complex, offering four sports fields, five tennis courts, and a 20,000-square-foot gymnasium. The Summit has three contiguous divisions: Lower School includes a Montessori toddler–kindergarten program and grades 1–4; Middle School, grades 5–8; and Upper School, grades 9–12. The Summit is a Christian learning environment in which values are fostered and students are challenged to bring forth their best efforts spiritually, academically, physically, socially, and artistically. Paramount to The Summit's education is its nationally recognized Educating for Character program, *CREDO,* which instills those qualities that define good character: respect, responsibility, and honesty. The educational environment is complemented by the religious and ethnic diversity of the 1,060 students, of whom 15% are members of minority groups. Students in all grades participate in field trips, leadership workshops, performing arts, academic and artistic competitions, and extensive athletic programs. As part of The Summit technology initiative, keyboarding begins in grade 1 and wireless laptops are used in grades 4–12 to enhance learning in all areas of study. This, along with access to more than 700 computers and leading-edge hardware, software, and Web resources, makes The Summit one of the most technologically advanced independent schools in the country. Through scholarship, service, creativity, and physical drive, Summit graduates have distinguished themselves nationally among other graduating seniors. Annually, more than 20% of Summit seniors are recognized by the National Merit Scholarship Corporation, 77% receive college scholarships, and 100% of graduating students successfully pursue college degrees. Tuition ranges from $5000 to $16,700, depending on the grade level. Financial aid is available to qualifying families in grades 1–12, and merit-based scholarships are available to Upper School students. For more information, visit www.summitcds.org.

SUMMIT PREPARATORY SCHOOL

Kalispell, Montana

See Special Needs Schools section.

SUNRISE ACADEMY

Hurricane, Utah

See Special Needs Schools section.

TABOR ACADEMY

66 Spring Street
Marion, Massachusetts 02738

Head of School: Mr. Jay S. Stroud

General Information Coeducational boarding and day college-preparatory and arts school. Grades 9–12. Founded: 1876. Setting: suburban. Nearest major city is Boston. Students are housed in single-sex dormitories. 85-acre campus. 42 buildings on campus. Approved or accredited by Association of Independent Schools in New England, New England Association of Schools and Colleges, and The Association of Boarding Schools. Member of National Association of Independent Schools and Secondary School Admission Test Board. Endowment: $39 million. Total enrollment: 500. Upper school average class size: 12. Upper school faculty-student ratio: 1:6.

Upper School Student Profile Grade 9: 88 students (42 boys, 46 girls); Grade 10: 125 students (70 boys, 55 girls); Grade 11: 147 students (79 boys, 68 girls); Grade 12: 140 students (72 boys, 68 girls). 71% of students are boarding students. 63% are state residents. 22 states are represented in upper school student body. 14% are international students. International students from Bermuda, Canada, China, Republic of Korea, Taiwan, and Thailand; 9 other countries represented in student body.

Faculty School total: 86. In upper school: 52 men, 34 women; 55 have advanced degrees; 59 reside on campus.

Subjects Offered Algebra, American history, American literature, ancient history, architecture, art, art history, astronomy, biology, calculus, celestial navigation, ceramics, chemistry, creative writing, drama, ecology, economics, English, English literature, European history, fine arts, French, freshman foundations, geology, geometry, German, Greek, health, history, Latin, maritime history, mathematics, meteorology, microbiology, music, navigation, oceanography, photography, physics, physiology, science, social science, social studies, Spanish, speech, statistics, theater, trigonometry, world history, world literature.

Graduation Requirements Algebra, arts and fine arts (art, music, dance, drama), biology, English, foreign language, geometry, mathematics, science, social science, social studies (includes history).

Special Academic Programs Advanced Placement exam preparation; honors section; independent study; term-away projects; academic accommodation for the gifted, the musically talented, and the artistically talented; ESL (5 students enrolled).

College Admission Counseling 140 students graduated in 2008; all went to college, including Boston University; New York University; Union College. Mean SAT critical reading: 600, mean SAT math: 620, mean SAT writing: 592, mean combined SAT: 1812.

Student Life Upper grades have specified standards of dress, student council. Discipline rests equally with students and faculty.

Tuition and Aid Day student tuition: $29,100; 7-day tuition and room/board: $41,400. Tuition installment plan (Academic Management Services Plan, Key Tuition Payment Plan, monthly payment plans, Tuition Management Systems Plan). Need-based scholarship grants available. In 2008–09, 30% of upper-school students received aid. Total amount of financial aid awarded in 2008–09: $2,100,000.
Admissions Traditional secondary-level entrance grade is 9. For fall 2008, 762 students applied for upper-level admission, 414 were accepted, 168 enrolled. ISEE, PSAT or SSAT required. Deadline for receipt of application materials: January 31. Application fee required: $50. Interview required.
Athletics Interscholastic: baseball (boys), basketball (b,g), crew (b,g), cross-country running (b,g), field hockey (g), football (b), ice hockey (b,g), lacrosse (b,g), soccer (b,g), softball (g), squash (b,g), tennis (b,g), track and field (b,g), wrestling (b); intramural: crew (b,g), ice hockey (g), squash (b,g), tennis (b,g); coed interscholastic: golf, sailing; coed intramural: aerobics, dance, fitness, sailing, strength & conditioning, weight training. 2 athletic trainers.
Computers Computers are regularly used in English, foreign language, history, literary magazine, mathematics, newspaper, photography, publications, science, yearbook classes. Computer network features include on-campus library services, online commercial services, Internet access, wireless campus network, digital media labs. Student e-mail accounts and computer access in designated common areas are available to students. The school has a published electronic and media policy.
Contact Mr. Andrew L. McCain, Director of Admissions. 508-291-8322. Fax: 508-748-0353. E-mail: admissions@taboracademy.org. Web site: www.taboracademy.org.

THE TAFT SCHOOL

110 Woodbury Road
Watertown, Connecticut 06795

Head of School: Mr. William R. MacMullen

General Information Coeducational boarding and day college-preparatory, arts, and humanities school. Grades 9–PG. Founded: 1890. Setting: small town. Nearest major city is Waterbury. Students are housed in single-sex dormitories. 220-acre campus. 20 buildings on campus. Approved or accredited by Connecticut Association of Independent Schools, New England Association of Schools and Colleges, The Association of Boarding Schools, The College Board, and Connecticut Department of Education. Member of National Association of Independent Schools and Secondary School Admission Test Board. Endowment: $203 million. Total enrollment: 577. Upper school average class size: 12. Upper school faculty-student ratio: 1:6.
Upper School Student Profile Grade 9: 94 students (45 boys, 49 girls); Grade 10: 162 students (81 boys, 81 girls); Grade 11: 148 students (80 boys, 68 girls); Grade 12: 158 students (88 boys, 70 girls); Postgraduate: 15 students (12 boys, 3 girls). 80% of students are boarding students. 38% are state residents. 33 states are represented in upper school student body. 13% are international students. International students from Canada, China, Hong Kong, Japan, Republic of Korea, and Taiwan; 20 other countries represented in student body.
Faculty School total: 93. In upper school: 58 men, 35 women; 91 have advanced degrees; all reside on campus.
Subjects Offered Acting, adolescent issues, advanced biology, advanced chemistry, advanced computer applications, advanced math, Advanced Placement courses, advanced studio art-AP, African-American literature, algebra, American government-AP, American history, American history-AP, American literature, anatomy, anatomy and physiology, animal behavior, architectural drawing, architecture, art, art history, art history-AP, astronomy, biology, biology-AP, calculus, calculus-AP, ceramics, chamber groups, character education, chemistry, chemistry-AP, Chinese, computer math, computer programming, computer science, computer science-AP, concert choir, creative writing, dance, design, digital imaging, drama, drawing, ecology, economics, economics-AP, English, English literature, English literature-AP, environmental science, environmental science-AP, ethics, European history, European history-AP, expository writing, film studies, fine arts, forensic science, French, French language-AP, geography, geology, geometry, government-AP, government/civics, grammar, Greek, history, history of rock and roll, history of science, honors algebra, honors English, honors geometry, human rights, humanities, Islamic studies, Japanese, jazz band, Latin, Mandarin, marine biology, mathematics, music, music theory-AP, philosophy, photography, physical education, physics, physics-AP, physiology, pre-calculus, psychology, religion, science, senior project, senior thesis, service learning/internship, sex education, South African history, Spanish, Spanish literature-AP, Spanish-AP, speech, statistics, statistics-AP, studio art-AP, theater, theology, trigonometry, U.S. government-AP, U.S. history-AP, video film production, world history, world literature, writing, zoology.
Graduation Requirements American history, arts and fine arts (art, music, dance, drama), English, foreign language, mathematics, science, social studies (includes history), three semesters of arts, senior thesis.
Special Academic Programs 27 Advanced Placement exams for which test preparation is offered; honors section; independent study; term-away projects; study abroad; academic accommodation for the gifted, the musically talented, and the artistically talented.
College Admission Counseling 165 students graduated in 2008; 164 went to college, including Amherst College; Cornell University; The George Washington University; Trinity College; University of Pennsylvania; Wake Forest University. Other: 1 entered a postgraduate year. Mean SAT critical reading: 639, mean SAT math: 644, mean SAT writing: 641, mean combined SAT: 1924. 65% scored over 600 on SAT critical reading, 67% scored over 600 on SAT math, 69% scored over 600 on SAT writing, 69% scored over 1800 on combined SAT.
Student Life Upper grades have specified standards of dress, student council, honor system. Discipline rests equally with students and faculty.
Summer Programs Enrichment, ESL, sports, art/fine arts programs offered; session focuses on Academic Enrichment; held on campus; accepts boys and girls; open to students from other schools. 150 students usually enrolled. 2009 schedule: June 28 to August 1. Application deadline: none.
Tuition and Aid Day student tuition: $30,700; 7-day tuition and room/board: $41,300. Tuition installment plan (Key Tuition Payment Plan). Need-based scholarship grants, need-based loans available. In 2008–09, 33% of upper-school students received aid. Total amount of financial aid awarded in 2008–09: $5,600,000.
Admissions Traditional secondary-level entrance grade is 9. For fall 2008, 1,367 students applied for upper-level admission, 377 were accepted, 185 enrolled. SSAT required. Deadline for receipt of application materials: January 15. Application fee required: $50. Interview required.
Athletics Interscholastic: alpine skiing (boys, girls), baseball (b), basketball (b,g), crew (b,g), cross-country running (b,g), field hockey (g), football (b), golf (b,g), hockey (b,g), ice hockey (b,g), lacrosse (b,g), rowing (b,g), soccer (b,g), softball (g), squash (b,g), tennis (b,g), track and field (b,g), ultimate Frisbee (b,g), volleyball (g), wrestling (b); coed interscholastic: dressage, equestrian sports, horseback riding; coed intramural: aerobics, aerobics/dance, ballet, basketball, climbing, cross-country running, dance, dressage, equestrian sports, figure skating, fitness, fitness walking, Frisbee, hockey, horseback riding, ice hockey, ice skating, jogging, martial arts, modern dance, outdoor activities, physical fitness, rock climbing, rowing, running, soccer, squash, strength & conditioning, tennis, track and field, ultimate Frisbee, walking, wall climbing, weight lifting, weight training, yoga. 1 coach, 3 athletic trainers.
Computers Computers are regularly used in art, English, foreign language, geography, history, mathematics, music, science classes. Computer network features include on-campus library services, online commercial services, Internet access, wireless campus network. Campus intranet, student e-mail accounts, and computer access in designated common areas are available to students. The school has a published electronic and media policy.
Contact Mr. Peter A. Frew, Director of Admissions. 860-945-7700. Fax: 860-945-7808. E-mail: admissions@taftschool.org. Web site: www.taftschool.org.

ANNOUNCEMENT FROM THE SCHOOL Known for intellectual rigor, extracurricular excellence, and its warm, spirited community, the Taft School seeks students who are intellectually curious, who will become involved, and who will commit themselves to the highest standard of academic and personal growth. Taft emphasizes individual development through rigorous academic, artistic, athletic, and extracurricular programs. In 2008, 212 Taft students took 510 Advanced Placement examinations and achieved an average score of 3.9. This achievement places Taft among the finest secondary schools in the country.

See Close-Up on page 984.

TALLULAH FALLS SCHOOL

PO Box 249
Tallulah Falls, Georgia 30573

Head of School: Mr. Larry Peevy

General Information Coeducational boarding and day college-preparatory school, affiliated with Christian faith. Boarding grades 7–12, day grades 6–12. Founded: 1909. Setting: rural. Nearest major city is Atlanta. Students are housed in single-sex dormitories. 500-acre campus. 16 buildings on campus. Approved or accredited by Georgia Independent School Association, Southern Association of Colleges and Schools, and The Association of Boarding Schools. Member of NAFSA: Association of International Educators. Endowment: $26 million. Total enrollment: 137. Upper school average class size: 12. Upper school faculty-student ratio: 1:10.
Upper School Student Profile 67% of students are boarding students. 80% are state residents. 9 states are represented in upper school student body. 15% are international students. International students from China, Hong Kong, Japan, Republic of Korea, Spain, and Viet Nam; 2 other countries represented in student body. 75% of students are Christian faith.
Faculty School total: 24. In upper school: 7 men, 11 women; 12 have advanced degrees; 3 reside on campus.
Subjects Offered Advanced chemistry, advanced math, Advanced Placement courses, algebra, American culture, American government, American history, American literature, American literature-AP, anatomy, animation, art, arts appreciation, athletics, biology, calculus, chemistry, chorus, computer animation, computer applications, computer education, computer graphics, computer information systems, computer literacy, computer multimedia, computer processing, computer programming, computer science, computer studies, computer technologies, computer-aided design, creative writing, earth science, English literature, English literature and composition-AP, French, geometry, government/civics, health, history, home eco-

nomics, industrial arts, journalism, keyboarding, mathematics, music, physical education, physical science, physics, physiology, Spanish, technology, trigonometry, world literature.
Graduation Requirements Algebra, American government, American literature, biology, British literature, chemistry, computer science, English, foreign language, geometry, government, mathematics, physical education (includes health), physical fitness, physical science, physics, political science, pre-calculus, science, social science, social studies (includes history).
Special Academic Programs Advanced Placement exam preparation; honors section; independent study; study at local college for college credit; ESL (20 students enrolled).
College Admission Counseling 25 students graduated in 2008; 24 went to college, including Georgia State University; North Georgia College & State University; University of Georgia. Other: 1 entered military service. Median SAT critical reading: 520, median SAT math: 530. 40% scored over 600 on SAT critical reading, 50% scored over 600 on SAT math.
Student Life Upper grades have uniform requirement, student council, honor system. Discipline rests primarily with faculty. Attendance at religious services is required.
Summer Programs ESL, sports programs offered; session focuses on ESL, volleyball, soccer; held on campus; accepts boys and girls; not open to students from other schools. 40 students usually enrolled. 2009 schedule: August to August.
Tuition and Aid Day student tuition: $8000–$8500; 5-day tuition and room/board: $14,500; 7-day tuition and room/board: $19,000–$25,000. Tuition installment plan (monthly payment plans, individually arranged payment plans). Tuition reduction for siblings, need-based scholarship grants available. In 2008–09, 70% of upper-school students received aid. Total amount of financial aid awarded in 2008–09: $1,000,000.
Admissions Traditional secondary-level entrance grade is 9. Admissions testing, SSAT or TOEFL required. Deadline for receipt of application materials: February 15. Application fee required: $30. Interview required.
Athletics Interscholastic: aerobics/dance (boys, girls), basketball (b,g), cheering (g), cross-country running (b,g), soccer (b), tennis (b,g), track and field (b,g), volleyball (g); intramural: dance (b,g); coed interscholastic: baseball, fishing, golf, running; coed intramural: backpacking, bicycling, canoeing/kayaking, climbing, fishing, fitness, flag football, hiking/backpacking, kayaking, martial arts, mountain biking, outdoor activities, paint ball, physical fitness, ropes courses, skiing (downhill), table tennis, track and field, volleyball, weight lifting, weight training. 2 PE instructors, 8 coaches, 1 athletic trainer.
Computers Computers are regularly used in career exploration, college planning, commercial art, graphic design, SAT preparation, yearbook classes. Computer network features include on-campus library services, online commercial services, Internet access, wireless campus network, Internet filtering or blocking technology. Student e-mail accounts and computer access in designated common areas are available to students. Students grades are available online. The school has a published electronic and media policy.
Contact Mrs. Tish M. Roller, Director of Enrollment Services. 706-754-0400 Ext. 5149. Fax: 706-754-5757. E-mail: troller@tfs.pvt.k12.ga.us. Web site: www.tallulahfalls.org.

See Close-Up on page 986.

TAMPA PREPARATORY SCHOOL

727 West Cass Street
Tampa, Florida 33606
Head of School: Mr. Kevin M. Plummer

General Information Coeducational day college-preparatory, arts, and technology school. Grades 6–12. Founded: 1974. Setting: urban. 12-acre campus. 3 buildings on campus. Approved or accredited by Association of Independent Schools of Florida, Southern Association of Colleges and Schools, and Florida Department of Education. Member of National Association of Independent Schools and Secondary School Admission Test Board. Endowment: $2.5 million. Total enrollment: 643. Upper school average class size: 18. Upper school faculty-student ratio: 1:10.
Upper School Student Profile Grade 9: 119 students (65 boys, 54 girls); Grade 10: 102 students (53 boys, 49 girls); Grade 11: 118 students (51 boys, 67 girls); Grade 12: 102 students (44 boys, 58 girls).
Faculty School total: 66. In upper school: 28 men, 38 women; 31 have advanced degrees.
Subjects Offered Advanced Placement courses, advanced studio art-AP, African-American literature, algebra, American government-AP, American history, American history-AP, American literature, anatomy, animal behavior, anthropology, art, art history, art history-AP, astronomy, biology, biology-AP, calculus, calculus-AP, ceramics, chemistry, chemistry-AP, chorus, classical language, computer math, computer science, computer science-AP, creative writing, dance, drama, ecology, economics, English, English literature, English literature-AP, environmental science, ethics, European history, fine arts, French, French-AP, geography, geometry, government/civics, journalism, Latin, Latin-AP, marine biology, mathematics, microeconomics, modern European history-AP, music, music theory-AP, photography, physical education, physics, physics-AP, physiology, psychology, religion, SAT preparation, science, social studies, Spanish, Spanish-AP, statistics-AP, studio art—AP, theater, theater arts, trigonometry, U.S. history-AP, visual arts, world affairs, world history, world literature.
Graduation Requirements Algebra, arts and fine arts (art, music, dance, drama), English, foreign language, geometry, history, physical education (includes health), pre-calculus, science.
Special Academic Programs 19 Advanced Placement exams for which test preparation is offered; honors section; accelerated programs; independent study; term-away projects; academic accommodation for the gifted, the musically talented, and the artistically talented.
College Admission Counseling 123 students graduated in 2008; 122 went to college, including Emory University; Florida State University; University of Central Florida; University of Florida; University of Pennsylvania; University of South Florida. Other: 1 entered military service. Mean composite ACT: 26.
Student Life Upper grades have specified standards of dress, student council, honor system. Discipline rests equally with students and faculty.
Summer Programs Remediation, enrichment, advancement, sports, computer instruction programs offered; session focuses on Summer Camp academics, enrichment, and sports; held on campus; accepts boys and girls; open to students from other schools. 400 students usually enrolled. 2009 schedule: June 8 to July 31. Application deadline: none.
Tuition and Aid Day student tuition: $13,240. Tuition installment plan (FACTS Tuition Payment Plan, individually arranged payment plans). Merit scholarship grants, need-based scholarship grants available. In 2008–09, 15% of upper-school students received aid; total upper-school merit-scholarship money awarded: $90,610. Total amount of financial aid awarded in 2008–09: $523,787.
Admissions Traditional secondary-level entrance grade is 9. For fall 2008, 264 students applied for upper-level admission, 210 were accepted, 163 enrolled. ISEE, PSAT or SAT or SSAT required. Deadline for receipt of application materials: none. Application fee required: $75. On-campus interview required.
Athletics Interscholastic: baseball (boys), basketball (b,g), crew (b,g), cross-country running (b,g), dance team (g), diving (b,g), golf (b,g), rowing (b,g), soccer (b,g), softball (g), swimming and diving (b,g), tennis (b,g), track and field (b,g), volleyball (g); intramural: dance team (g), physical fitness (b,g), racquetball (b,g); coed interscholastic: aquatics, bowling, wrestling; coed intramural: badminton, dance, fitness, modern dance, scuba diving, strength & conditioning, table tennis, weight training. 4 PE instructors, 57 coaches, 2 athletic trainers.
Computers Computers are regularly used in creative writing, economics, graphic design, introduction to technology, journalism, mathematics, science, word processing, yearbook classes. Computer network features include on-campus library services, online commercial services, Internet access.
Contact Mr. W. Dennis Facciolo, Director of Admissions. 813-251-8481 Ext. 4011. Fax: 813-254-2106. E-mail: dfacciolo@tampaprep.org. Web site: www.tampaprep.org.

TANDEM FRIENDS SCHOOL

279 Tandem Lane
Charlottesville, Virginia 22902
Head of School: Paul B. Perkinson

General Information Coeducational day college-preparatory and arts school, affiliated with Society of Friends. Grades 5–12. Founded: 1970. Setting: small town. Nearest major city is Richmond. 23-acre campus. 6 buildings on campus. Approved or accredited by Friends Council on Education and Virginia Association of Independent Schools. Member of National Association of Independent Schools. Endowment: $1.3 million. Total enrollment: 237. Upper school average class size: 12. Upper school faculty-student ratio: 1:8.
Upper School Student Profile Grade 9: 37 students (19 boys, 18 girls); Grade 10: 41 students (21 boys, 20 girls); Grade 11: 17 students (9 boys, 8 girls); Grade 12: 37 students (13 boys, 24 girls). 3% of students are members of Society of Friends.
Faculty School total: 42. In upper school: 10 men, 18 women; 16 have advanced degrees.
Subjects Offered Algebra, American literature, art, Asian studies, bioethics, biology, biology-AP, calculus, calculus-AP, ceramics, chemistry, chemistry-AP, college counseling, computer applications, creative writing, cultural geography, discrete math, drama, economics, English, English-AP, expository writing, fine arts, French, French-AP, geometry, health and wellness, jazz ensemble, Latin, media studies, music, musical productions, newspaper, performing arts, photography, physics, playwriting and directing, Quakerism and ethics, senior project, Spanish, Spanish-AP, statistics, statistics-AP, student government, student publications, studio art, theater, trigonometry, U.S. government, U.S. history, U.S. history-AP, weaving, world history, world literature, writing, yearbook.
Graduation Requirements Arts and fine arts (art, music, dance, drama), computer science, English, foreign language, government/civics, history, mathematics, science, senior year independent experiential learning project. Community service is required.
Special Academic Programs Advanced Placement exam preparation; independent study; academic accommodation for the gifted; remedial reading and/or remedial writing; remedial math.

College Admission Counseling 33 students graduated in 2008; 30 went to college, including Brown University; Guilford College; Haverford College; James Madison University; University of Virginia; Vassar College. Other: 2 went to work, 1 had other specific plans.
Student Life Upper grades have student council. Discipline rests equally with students and faculty. Attendance at religious services is required.
Tuition and Aid Day student tuition: $15,045. Tuition installment plan (Insured Tuition Payment Plan, monthly payment plans, individually arranged payment plans). Need-based scholarship grants, tuition remission for children of full-time faculty available. In 2008–09, 24% of upper-school students received aid. Total amount of financial aid awarded in 2008–09: $205,000.
Admissions Traditional secondary-level entrance grade is 9. For fall 2008, 33 students applied for upper-level admission, 18 were accepted, 14 enrolled. Deadline for receipt of application materials: March 15. Application fee required: $50. Interview required.
Athletics Interscholastic: basketball (boys, girls), field hockey (g), lacrosse (b,g), soccer (b,g); coed interscholastic: cross-country running, golf, tennis, volleyball, wrestling; coed intramural: fencing. 2 PE instructors.
Computers Computers are regularly used in all academic classes. Computer network features include on-campus library services, online commercial services, Internet access, virtual classroom. Student e-mail accounts and computer access in designated common areas are available to students. Students grades are available online. The school has a published electronic and media policy.
Contact Nica Waters, Director of Admissions. 434-296-1303 Ext. 225. Fax: 434-296-1886. E-mail: nwaters@tandemfs.org. Web site: www.tandemfs.org.

TASIS THE AMERICAN SCHOOL IN ENGLAND

Coldharbour Lane
Thorpe, Surrey TW20 8TE, United Kingdom
Head of School: Dr. James A. Doran

General Information Coeducational boarding and day college-preparatory and arts school. Boarding grades 9–13, day grades N–13. Founded: 1976. Setting: rural. Nearest major city is London, United Kingdom. Students are housed in single-sex dormitories. 43-acre campus. 23 buildings on campus. Approved or accredited by European Council of International Schools, International Baccalaureate Organization, New England Association of Schools and Colleges, Office for Standards in Education (OFSTED), The Association of Boarding Schools, and state department of education. Affiliate member of National Association of Independent Schools; member of Secondary School Admission Test Board. Language of instruction: English. Total enrollment: 750. Upper school average class size: 15. Upper school faculty-student ratio: 1:7.
Upper School Student Profile Grade 9: 80 students (38 boys, 42 girls); Grade 10: 100 students (46 boys, 54 girls); Grade 11: 110 students (46 boys, 64 girls); Grade 12: 80 students (28 boys, 52 girls). 43% of students are boarding students. 36% are international students. International students from Germany, Mexico, Republic of Korea, Russian Federation, Spain, and United States; 49 other countries represented in student body.
Faculty School total: 110. In upper school: 29 men, 28 women; 35 have advanced degrees; 19 reside on campus.
Subjects Offered 20th century history, acting, algebra, American history, American history-AP, American literature, ancient history, art, art history, art history-AP, biology, biology-AP, calculus-AP, ceramics, chemistry, chemistry-AP, choir, computer graphics, computer keyboarding, computer science, computer science-AP, drawing, earth science, economics, economics-AP, English, English language and composition-AP, English literature, English literature and composition-AP, ensembles, environmental science, environmental science-AP, ESL, European history, European history-AP, fine arts, French, French-AP, geometry, German, government and politics-AP, health and wellness, humanities, international affairs, international relations, journalism, Latin, mathematics, music theory, music theory-AP, painting, photography, physical education, physical science, physics, physics-AP, pre-calculus, printmaking, sculpture, senior humanities, Shakespeare, Spanish, Spanish-AP, statistics-AP, theater arts, theory of knowledge, visual arts, Web site design, Western civilization, world history, yearbook.
Graduation Requirements Arts and fine arts (art, music, dance, drama), computer science, English, foreign language, health, history, lab science, mathematics, physical education (includes health), senior humanities. Community service is required.
Special Academic Programs International Baccalaureate program; Advanced Placement exam preparation; independent study; academic accommodation for the gifted; remedial reading and/or remedial writing; ESL (75 students enrolled).
College Admission Counseling 95 students graduated in 2008; 92 went to college. Other: 1 entered a postgraduate year, 2 had other specific plans. Mean SAT critical reading: 598, mean SAT math: 593, mean SAT writing: 600.
Student Life Upper grades have uniform requirement, student council. Discipline rests primarily with faculty.
Summer Programs Remediation, enrichment, advancement, ESL, sports, art/fine arts, computer instruction programs offered; session focuses on ESL, academics, enrichment, theater; held on campus; accepts boys and girls; open to students from other schools. 250 students usually enrolled. 2009 schedule: June 21 to August 9. Application deadline: none.
Tuition and Aid Day student tuition: £17,500; 7-day tuition and room/board: £26,750. Tuition installment plan (monthly payment plans, individually arranged payment plans). Merit scholarship grants, need-based scholarship grants available.
Admissions TOEFL or SLEP required. Deadline for receipt of application materials: none. Application fee required: £95. Interview recommended.
Athletics Interscholastic: baseball (boys), basketball (b,g), cross-country running (b,g), rugby (b), soccer (b,g), softball (g), tennis (b,g), volleyball (b,g); intramural: aerobics (g), aerobics/dance (g), badminton (b,g), ballet (g), cricket (b,g), dance (g), dance team (g), equestrian sports (g), field hockey (b,g), fitness (b,g), floor hockey (b,g), gymnastics (b,g), handball (b,g), indoor soccer (b,g), jump rope (b,g), lacrosse (b,g), modern dance (b,g), outdoor activities (b,g), outdoor adventure (b,g), physical fitness (b,g), physical training (b,g), rhythmic gymnastics (b,g), rugby (b), running (b,g), scooter football (b,g), soccer (b,g), softball (b,g), strength & conditioning (b,g), team handball (b,g), weight training (b,g), winter soccer (b,g); coed interscholastic: cheering, golf; coed intramural: basketball, bicycling, equestrian sports, golf, gymnastics, handball, horseback riding, indoor soccer, lacrosse, martial arts, outdoor activities, outdoor adventure, squash, strength & conditioning, swimming and diving, table tennis, team handball, tennis, track and field, volleyball, weight training, winter soccer. 5 PE instructors, 12 coaches, 1 athletic trainer.
Computers Computers are regularly used in all academic classes. Computer network features include on-campus library services, online commercial services, Internet access, wireless campus network, Internet filtering or blocking technology. Campus intranet, student e-mail accounts, and computer access in designated common areas are available to students. The school has a published electronic and media policy.
Contact Mrs. Bronwyn Thorburn-Riseley, Director of Admissions. 44-1932-565252. Fax: 44-1932-564644. E-mail: ukadmissions@tasisengland.org. Web site: www.tasis.com/England/.

See Close-Up on page 988.

TASIS, THE AMERICAN SCHOOL IN SWITZERLAND

Via Collina d'Oro
Montagnola-Lugano CH-6926, Switzerland
Head of School: Mr. Michael Ulku-Steiner

General Information Coeducational boarding and day college-preparatory, arts, and sports school. Boarding grades 7–PG, day grades 1–PG. Founded: 1956. Setting: small town. Nearest major city is Lugano, Switzerland. Students are housed in single-sex dormitories. 9-acre campus. 19 buildings on campus. Approved or accredited by European Council of International Schools, New England Association of Schools and Colleges, and Swiss Federation of Private Schools. Affiliate member of National Association of Independent Schools; member of Secondary School Admission Test Board. Language of instruction: English. Total enrollment: 581. Upper school average class size: 13. Upper school faculty-student ratio: 1:5.
Upper School Student Profile Grade 7: 26 students (17 boys, 9 girls); Grade 8: 37 students (19 boys, 18 girls); Grade 9: 63 students (33 boys, 30 girls); Grade 10: 79 students (31 boys, 48 girls); Grade 11: 115 students (47 boys, 68 girls); Grade 12: 78 students (32 boys, 46 girls); Postgraduate: 6 students (3 boys, 3 girls). 80% of students are boarding students. 82% are international students. International students from Brazil, Germany, Italy, and United States; 44 other countries represented in student body.
Faculty School total: 58. In upper school: 30 men, 28 women; 34 have advanced degrees; 30 reside on campus.
Subjects Offered Advanced Placement courses, algebra, American history, American literature, ancient history, art, art history, art history-AP, biology, biology-AP, calculus, calculus-AP, ceramics, chemistry, chemistry-AP, digital photography, drama, economics, economics-AP, English, English language and composition-AP, English literature, English literature and composition-AP, environmental science, ESL, European history, European history-AP, fine arts, French, French language-AP, geography, geometry, German-AP, graphic design, health, history, international relations, Italian, mathematics, medieval/Renaissance history, music, photography, physical education, physics, science, social studies, Spanish, Spanish language-AP, theater, theory of knowledge, U.S. government, U.S. history-AP, world culture, world history, world literature.
Graduation Requirements Arts, English, European history, foreign language, mathematics, science, senior humanities, sports, U.S. history. Community service is required.
Special Academic Programs International Baccalaureate program; Advanced Placement exam preparation; honors section; ESL (205 students enrolled).
College Admission Counseling 93 students graduated in 2008; all went to college, including Pace University; The American University of Paris; The George Washington University. Median SAT critical reading: 551, median SAT math: 530. 30% scored over 600 on SAT critical reading, 33% scored over 600 on SAT math.
Student Life Upper grades have specified standards of dress, student council, honor system. Discipline rests equally with students and faculty.
Summer Programs ESL, sports, art/fine arts programs offered; session focuses on languages, sports, and arts; held both on and off campus; held at TASIS Lugano

TASIS, The American School in Switzerland

Campus and Chateau d'Oex; accepts boys and girls; open to students from other schools. 650 students usually enrolled. 2009 schedule: June 26 to July 26. Application deadline: none.

Tuition and Aid Day student tuition: 39,800 Swiss francs; 7-day tuition and room/board: 65,000 Swiss francs. Tuition installment plan (individually arranged payment plans). Need-based scholarship grants available. In 2008–09, 15% of upper-school students received aid. Total amount of financial aid awarded in 2008–09: 787,000 Swiss francs.

Admissions Traditional secondary-level entrance grade is 11. For fall 2008, 264 students applied for upper-level admission, 182 were accepted, 174 enrolled. TOEFL or SLEP required. Deadline for receipt of application materials: none. Application fee required: 300 Swiss francs. Interview recommended.

Athletics Interscholastic: basketball (boys, girls), golf (b), rugby (b), soccer (b,g), swimming and diving (b,g), tennis (b,g), track and field (b,g), volleyball (b,g); intramural: basketball (b,g), rugby (b); coed interscholastic: softball, swimming and diving, track and field; coed intramural: aerobics, aerobics/dance, aerobics/Nautilus, basketball, climbing, combined training, cross-country running, dance, fitness, flag football, floor hockey, golf, horseback riding, indoor soccer, jogging, lacrosse, martial arts, modern dance, physical fitness, physical training, rock climbing, running, sailing, soccer, softball, squash, strength & conditioning, swimming and diving, tennis, ultimate Frisbee, volleyball, weight lifting, weight training. 2 PE instructors.

Computers Computers are regularly used in art, English, ESL, foreign language, history, photography, science classes. Computer network features include on-campus library services, Internet access, wireless campus network, Internet filtering or blocking technology. Student e-mail accounts are available to students. The school has a published electronic and media policy.

Contact William E. Eichner, Director of Admissions. 41-91-960-5151. Fax: 41-91-993-2979. E-mail: admissions@tasis.ch. Web site: www.tasis.com.

See Close-Up on page 990.

THE TATNALL SCHOOL

1501 Barley Mill Road
Wilmington, Delaware 19807

Head of School: Eric G. Ruoss

General Information Coeducational day college-preparatory school. Grades N–12. Founded: 1930. Setting: suburban. 110-acre campus. 5 buildings on campus. Approved or accredited by Middle States Association of Colleges and Schools and Delaware Department of Education. Member of National Association of Independent Schools. Endowment: $23 million. Total enrollment: 688. Upper school average class size: 15. Upper school faculty-student ratio: 1:8.

Upper School Student Profile Grade 9: 66 students (33 boys, 33 girls); Grade 10: 62 students (33 boys, 29 girls); Grade 11: 71 students (37 boys, 34 girls); Grade 12: 71 students (34 boys, 37 girls).

Faculty School total: 108. In upper school: 18 men, 24 women; 26 have advanced degrees.

Subjects Offered 20th century American writers, 20th century world history, 3-dimensional art, 3-dimensional design, acting, advanced chemistry, advanced computer applications, advanced math, Advanced Placement courses, advanced studio art-AP, African-American literature, algebra, American Civil War, American government, American history, American history-AP, American literature, analysis and differential calculus, anatomy, art, athletic training, athletics, baseball, biology, biology-AP, botany, calculus, calculus-AP, ceramics, chemistry, chemistry-AP, college counseling, community service, computer programming, computer science, concert band, concert choir, drama, driver education, ecology, economics, English, English literature, English literature-AP, environmental science, environmental science-AP, European history, European history-AP, film, fine arts, French, French language-AP, geometry, health, history, Holocaust, Latin, Latin-AP, literature and composition-AP, marine biology, mathematics, modern European history-AP, music, newspaper, physical education, physics, physics-AP, psychology, psychology-AP, science, service learning/internship, social studies, Spanish, Spanish-AP, statistics, statistics-AP, theater, theater arts, theater production, trigonometry, U.S. history-AP, video, Vietnam War, world history, world literature, writing, yearbook.

Graduation Requirements Arts and fine arts (art, music, dance, drama), computer literacy, English, foreign language, mathematics, physical education (includes health), science, social studies (includes history). Community service is required.

Special Academic Programs Advanced Placement exam preparation; honors section; accelerated programs; independent study; term-away projects; study abroad; academic accommodation for the gifted, the musically talented, and the artistically talented.

College Admission Counseling 66 students graduated in 2008; 65 went to college, including Clemson University; Franklin & Marshall College; Georgetown University; Grinnell College; Penn State University Park; University of Delaware. Other: 1 had other specific plans. Mean SAT critical reading: 607, mean SAT math: 631, mean SAT writing: 635.

Student Life Upper grades have specified standards of dress, student council. Discipline rests primarily with faculty.

Summer Programs Enrichment, advancement, art/fine arts programs offered; session focuses on sports, the arts; held on campus; accepts boys and girls; open to students from other schools. 250 students usually enrolled. 2009 schedule: June to August.

Tuition and Aid Day student tuition: $20,780. Tuition installment plan (Key Tuition Payment Plan). Need-based scholarship grants, need-based loans available. In 2008–09, 30% of upper-school students received aid. Total amount of financial aid awarded in 2008–09: $971,786.

Admissions Traditional secondary-level entrance grade is 9. For fall 2008, 73 students applied for upper-level admission, 44 were accepted, 28 enrolled. ERB CTP IV required. Deadline for receipt of application materials: January 16. Application fee required: $40. On-campus interview required.

Athletics Interscholastic: baseball (boys), basketball (b,g), cheering (g), cross-country running (b,g), field hockey (g), football (b), ice hockey (b), indoor track & field (b,g), lacrosse (b,g), soccer (b,g), swimming and diving (b,g), tennis (b,g), track and field (b,g), volleyball (g), winter (indoor) track (b,g), wrestling (b); coed interscholastic: golf; coed intramural: ultimate Frisbee. 3 PE instructors, 1 athletic trainer.

Computers Computers are regularly used in all classes. Computer network features include on-campus library services, online commercial services, Internet access, wireless campus network, Internet filtering or blocking technology. The school has a published electronic and media policy.

Contact Judith M. Bagdon, Admissions Coordinator. 302-892-4285. Fax: 302-892-4387. E-mail: jbagdon@tatnall.org. Web site: www.tatnall.org.

TELLURIDE MOUNTAIN SCHOOL

200 San Miguel River Drive
Telluride, Colorado 81435

Head of School: Mr. Ernest S. Patterson

General Information Coeducational day college-preparatory, arts, technology, and music, visual and dramatic arts school. Grades PK–12. Founded: 1999. Setting: small town. Nearest major city is Denver. 2-acre campus. 1 building on campus. Approved or accredited by Association of Colorado Independent Schools. Total enrollment: 85. Upper school average class size: 8. Upper school faculty-student ratio: 1:5.

Upper School Student Profile Grade 9: 6 students (4 boys, 2 girls); Grade 10: 2 students (2 girls); Grade 11: 2 students (2 girls).

Faculty School total: 21. In upper school: 6 men, 2 women; 4 have advanced degrees.

Subjects Offered Algebra, alternative physical education, American Civil War, American history, American literature, ancient world history, applied music, art, backpacking, biology, calculus, character education, chemistry, civil rights, college admission preparation, college counseling, college planning, community service, computer education, computer literacy, computer multimedia, computer music, CPR, creative writing, critical thinking, critical writing, digital music, drama, dramatic arts, English composition, English literature, environmental education, European history, film studies, geography, geology, geometry, grammar, guitar, history, history of rock and roll, instrumental music, Internet research, keyboarding/computer, Latin American literature, leadership and service, leadership skills, music, music performance, music technology, outdoor education, painting, portfolio writing, pre-algebra, pre-calculus, public speaking, reading/study skills, Spanish, Spanish literature, studio art, trigonometry, video film production, visual arts, white-water trips, wilderness education, wilderness/outdoor program, world history.

Graduation Requirements Algebra, biology, chemistry, college admission preparation, college counseling, dramatic arts, English, English composition, English literature, geometry, grammar, history, music, physics, pre-calculus, Spanish, trigonometry, U.S. history, visual arts, wilderness/outdoor program, world history.

Special Academic Programs Study abroad.

College Admission Counseling 1 student graduated in 2008 and went to college.

Student Life Upper grades have specified standards of dress, honor system. Discipline rests primarily with faculty.

Tuition and Aid Day student tuition: $17,250. Tuition installment plan (monthly payment plans, individually arranged payment plans). Need-based scholarship grants available. In 2008–09, 25% of upper-school students received aid. Total amount of financial aid awarded in 2008–09: $56,000.

Admissions Traditional secondary-level entrance grade is 9. For fall 2008, 10 students applied for upper-level admission, 10 were accepted, 10 enrolled. Deadline for receipt of application materials: none. Application fee required: $50. Interview required.

Athletics Interscholastic: alpine skiing (boys, girls), freestyle skiing (b,g), hockey (b), ice hockey (b), lacrosse (b), skiing (cross-country) (b,g), skiing (downhill) (b,g), snowboarding (b,g), soccer (b); coed interscholastic: nordic skiing; coed intramural: alpine skiing, backpacking, canoeing/kayaking, climbing, cooperative games, fly fishing, hiking/backpacking, kayaking, mountaineering, outdoor activities, rappelling, rock climbing, snowshoeing, telemark skiing, wilderness. 1 PE instructor, 5 coaches.

Computers Computers are regularly used in all classes. Computer network features include Internet access, wireless campus network. Campus intranet, student e-mail accounts, and computer access in designated common areas are available to students. The school has a published electronic and media policy.

Contact Mrs. Robin Hope, Program Coordinator. 970-728-1969. Fax: 970-369-4412. E-mail: rhope@telluridemtnschool.org. Web site: www.telluridemtnschool.org/.

THE TENNEY SCHOOL

2055 South Gessner
Houston, Texas 77063

Head of School: Mr. George Edward Tenney

General Information Coeducational day college-preparatory and general academic school; primarily serves students with learning disabilities and individuals with Attention Deficit Disorder. Grades 6–12. Founded: 1973. Setting: urban. 1-acre campus. 1 building on campus. Approved or accredited by Southern Association of Colleges and Schools and Texas Department of Education. Total enrollment: 42. Upper school average class size: 1.

Upper School Student Profile Grade 6: 1 student (1 boy); Grade 7: 4 students (3 boys, 1 girl); Grade 8: 6 students (5 boys, 1 girl); Grade 9: 3 students (1 boy, 2 girls); Grade 10: 7 students (5 boys, 2 girls); Grade 11: 9 students (6 boys, 3 girls); Grade 12: 12 students (8 boys, 4 girls).

Faculty School total: 27. In upper school: 2 men, 25 women; 12 have advanced degrees.

Subjects Offered Accounting, algebra, American history, American literature, biology, British literature, business law, calculus, chemistry, computer programming, computer studies, creative writing, economics, English, fine arts, geometry, government, health, independent study, journalism, keyboarding, mathematics, microcomputer technology applications, physical education, physical science, physics, pre-calculus, psychology, science, social studies, sociology, Spanish, studio art, theater arts, world geography, world history, world literature, yearbook.

Special Academic Programs Advanced Placement exam preparation; honors section; academic accommodation for the gifted, the musically talented, and the artistically talented; remedial reading and/or remedial writing; remedial math; special instructional classes for deaf students.

College Admission Counseling 10 students graduated in 2008; all went to college, including Arizona State University; Eckerd College; Sam Houston State University; Texas State University–San Marcos; The University of Arizona; University of Colorado at Boulder.

Student Life Upper grades have specified standards of dress. Discipline rests primarily with faculty.

Summer Programs Remediation, enrichment, advancement, computer instruction programs offered; session focuses on academic course work; held on campus; accepts boys and girls; open to students from other schools. 20 students usually enrolled. 2009 schedule: June 2 to June 22. Application deadline: May 25.

Tuition and Aid Day student tuition: $21,000. Guaranteed tuition plan.

Admissions Traditional secondary-level entrance grade is 10. For fall 2008, 30 students applied for upper-level admission, 20 were accepted, 15 enrolled. Scholastic Achievement Test required. Deadline for receipt of application materials: none. No application fee required. On-campus interview required.

Athletics 1 PE instructor.

Computers Computers are regularly used in computer applications, creative writing, desktop publishing, English, foreign language, journalism, keyboarding, speech, word processing, yearbook classes. Computer network features include on-campus library services, Internet access, Internet filtering or blocking technology. Computer access in designated common areas is available to students.

Contact Michael E. Tenney, Director. 713-783-6990. Fax: 713-783-0786. E-mail: mtenney@tenneyschool.com. Web site: www.tenneyschool.com.

TEURLINGS CATHOLIC HIGH SCHOOL

139 Teurlings Drive
Lafayette, Louisiana 70501-0000

Head of School: Mr. Michael Harrison Boyer

General Information Coeducational day and distance learning college-preparatory and religious studies school, affiliated with Roman Catholic Church. Grades 9–12. Distance learning grades 10–12. Founded: 1955. Setting: urban. Nearest major city is Baton Rouge. 25-acre campus. 13 buildings on campus. Approved or accredited by National Catholic Education Association, Southern Association of Colleges and Schools, and Louisiana Department of Education. Endowment: $125,000. Total enrollment: 662. Upper school average class size: 21. Upper school faculty-student ratio: 1:21.

Upper School Student Profile Grade 9: 184 students (103 boys, 81 girls); Grade 10: 154 students (73 boys, 81 girls); Grade 11: 169 students (92 boys, 77 girls); Grade 12: 155 students (80 boys, 75 girls). 93% of students are Roman Catholic.

Faculty School total: 44. In upper school: 13 men, 31 women; 14 have advanced degrees.

Subjects Offered 20th century history, accounting, acting, advanced chemistry, advanced computer applications, advanced math, algebra, American history, American history-AP, American literature, anatomy and physiology, art, biology, business applications, business law, calculus, campus ministry, chemistry, choral music, civics/free enterprise, computer keyboarding, computer science, drama, earth science, English, English literature and composition-AP, entrepreneurship, environmental science, fine arts, French, geography, geometry, health, honors algebra, honors English, honors geometry, honors U.S. history, honors world history, interpersonal skills, Latin, newspaper, physical education, physical science, physics, psychology, public speaking, publications, Spanish, speech, theology, Web site design, world history, world history-AP.

Graduation Requirements Advanced math, algebra, American history, American literature, biology, chemistry, civics, civics/free enterprise, computer applications, computer literacy, electives, English, geometry, literature, physical education (includes health), physical science, public speaking, theology, world geography, world history.

Special Academic Programs Advanced Placement exam preparation; honors section; study at local college for college credit; remedial math.

College Admission Counseling 151 students graduated in 2008; 140 went to college, including Centenary College of Louisiana; Louisiana State University and Agricultural and Mechanical College; Louisiana State University at Eunice; Northwestern State University of Louisiana; Spring Hill College; University of Louisiana at Lafayette. Other: 11 had other specific plans. Median composite ACT: 21. 12% scored over 26 on composite ACT.

Student Life Upper grades have uniform requirement, student council, honor system. Discipline rests equally with students and faculty. Attendance at religious services is required.

Tuition and Aid Day student tuition: $4635. Tuition installment plan (monthly payment plans). Need-based scholarship grants, paying campus jobs available. In 2008–09, 4% of upper-school students received aid. Total amount of financial aid awarded in 2008–09: $29,664.

Admissions Traditional secondary-level entrance grade is 9. For fall 2008, 246 students applied for upper-level admission, 220 were accepted, 184 enrolled. Any standardized test required. Deadline for receipt of application materials: January 30. No application fee required.

Athletics Interscholastic: baseball (boys), basketball (b,g), bowling (b,g), cheering (b,g), cross-country running (b,g), dance team (g), football (b), golf (b,g), gymnastics (b), indoor track & field (b,g), soccer (b,g), softball (g), strength & conditioning (b,g), swimming and diving (b,g), tennis (b,g), track and field (b,g), volleyball (g), winter (indoor) track (b,g), wrestling (b); intramural: cheering (g); coed interscholastic: archery, riflery, skeet shooting, trap and skeet. 3 coaches.

Computers Computers are regularly used in all classes. Computer network features include on-campus library services, Internet access, wireless campus network, Internet filtering or blocking technology. Student e-mail accounts and computer access in designated common areas are available to students. Students grades are available online. The school has a published electronic and media policy.

Contact Mrs. Kathy Dodson, Administrative Secretary. 337-235-5711 Ext. 101. Fax: 337-234-8057. E-mail: kdodson@tchs.net. Web site: www.tchs.net.

THE THACHER SCHOOL

5025 Thacher Road
Ojai, California 93023

Head of School: Michael K. Mulligan

General Information Coeducational boarding and day college-preparatory, arts, and technology school. Grades 9–12. Founded: 1889. Setting: small town. Nearest major city is Santa Barbara. Students are housed in single-sex dormitories. 450-acre campus. 89 buildings on campus. Approved or accredited by California Association of Independent Schools, The Association of Boarding Schools, Western Association of Schools and Colleges, and California Department of Education. Member of National Association of Independent Schools and Secondary School Admission Test Board. Endowment: $106 million. Total enrollment: 249. Upper school average class size: 11. Upper school faculty-student ratio: 1:5.

Upper School Student Profile Grade 9: 54 students (28 boys, 26 girls); Grade 10: 69 students (34 boys, 35 girls); Grade 11: 62 students (29 boys, 33 girls); Grade 12: 64 students (31 boys, 33 girls). 90% of students are boarding students. 58% are state residents. 25 states are represented in upper school student body. 10% are international students. International students from Australia, Canada, Hong Kong, Japan, Saudi Arabia, and Taiwan; 5 other countries represented in student body.

Faculty School total: 46. In upper school: 22 men, 20 women; 37 have advanced degrees; 42 reside on campus.

Subjects Offered 3-dimensional art, ACT preparation, acting, advanced chemistry, advanced math, Advanced Placement courses, advanced studio art-AP, algebra, American history, American history-AP, American literature, art, art history, art history-AP, astronomy, biology, biology-AP, calculus, calculus-AP, ceramics, chemistry, chemistry-AP, Chinese, computer math, computer science, computer science-AP, conceptual physics, creative writing, dance, drama, ecology, economics, economics and history, electronic music, English, English literature, English literature-AP, English/composition-AP, environmental science, environmental science-AP, European history, European history-AP, film, fine arts, French, French language-AP, French literature-AP, geography, geometry, health, history, journalism, Latin, logic, marine biology, mathematics, music, music theory-AP, philosophy, photography, physical education, physics, physics-AP, psychology, religion, science, social studies, Spanish, Spanish language-AP, Spanish literature-AP, statistics, studio art-AP, theater, trigonometry, U.S. history-AP, world history, world literature, writing.

Graduation Requirements Arts and fine arts (art, music, dance, drama), English, foreign language, mathematics, physical education (includes health), science, social studies (includes history), Senior Exhibition Program (students choose an academic topic of interest and study it for one year, culminating in a school wide presentation).
Special Academic Programs Advanced Placement exam preparation; honors section; independent study; study abroad; academic accommodation for the gifted, the musically talented, and the artistically talented.
College Admission Counseling 63 students graduated in 2008; all went to college, including Brown University; Columbia College; Dartmouth College; Stanford University; The Colorado College; University of California, Berkeley. Mean SAT critical reading: 650, mean SAT math: 620, mean SAT writing: 650, mean combined SAT: 1950.
Student Life Upper grades have specified standards of dress, student council, honor system. Discipline rests equally with students and faculty.
Tuition and Aid Day student tuition: $27,300; 7-day tuition and room/board: $40,950. Tuition installment plan (Key Tuition Payment Plan, monthly payment plans). Need-based scholarship grants available. In 2008–09, 30% of upper-school students received aid. Total amount of financial aid awarded in 2008–09: $1,853,000.
Admissions Traditional secondary-level entrance grade is 9. For fall 2008, 410 students applied for upper-level admission, 82 were accepted, 65 enrolled. ISEE, PSAT or SSAT required. Deadline for receipt of application materials: February 1. Application fee required: $75. Interview required.
Athletics Interscholastic: baseball (boys), basketball (b,g), cross-country running (b,g), dance (b,g), football (b), lacrosse (b,g), soccer (b,g), tennis (b,g), track and field (b,g), volleyball (g); intramural: backpacking (b,g), ballet (g), bicycling (b,g), canoeing/kayaking (b,g), climbing (b,g), dance (b,g), horseback riding (b,g), outdoor activities (b,g), weight training (b,g), wilderness (b,g), wilderness survival (b,g), yoga (b,g); coed interscholastic: dance, equestrian sports; coed intramural: backpacking, bicycling, bowling, canoeing/kayaking, climbing, dance, equestrian sports, fencing, golf, handball, hiking/backpacking, horseback riding, modern dance, outdoor activities, pistol, polo, Polocrosse, riflery, rock climbing, rodeo, skiing (downhill), surfing, trap and skeet, ultimate Frisbee, wall climbing, weight lifting, yoga. 4 coaches.
Computers Computers are regularly used in English, foreign language, history, mathematics, science classes. Computer network features include on-campus library services, online commercial services, Internet access, wireless campus network, Internet filtering or blocking technology. Campus intranet and student e-mail accounts are available to students. Students grades are available online. The school has a published electronic and media policy.
Contact Mr. William P. McMahon, Director of Admission. 805-640-3210. Fax: 805-640-9377. E-mail: admission@thacher.org. Web site: www.thacher.org.

THOMAS JEFFERSON SCHOOL

4100 South Lindbergh Boulevard
St. Louis, Missouri 63127
Head of School: Mr. William C. Rowe

General Information Coeducational boarding and day college-preparatory school. Grades 7–PG. Founded: 1946. Setting: suburban. Students are housed in single-sex dormitories. 20-acre campus. 12 buildings on campus. Approved or accredited by Independent Schools Association of the Central States, Midwest Association of Boarding Schools, and The Association of Boarding Schools. Member of National Association of Independent Schools and Secondary School Admission Test Board. Endowment: $800,000. Total enrollment: 78. Upper school average class size: 10. Upper school faculty-student ratio: 1:7.
Upper School Student Profile Grade 9: 12 students (5 boys, 7 girls); Grade 10: 18 students (6 boys, 12 girls); Grade 11: 17 students (11 boys, 6 girls); Grade 12: 13 students (8 boys, 5 girls); Postgraduate: 1 student (1 boy). 57% of students are boarding students. 61% are state residents. 6 states are represented in upper school student body. 27% are international students. International students from China, Poland, Republic of Korea, and Venezuela.
Faculty School total: 18. In upper school: 6 men, 7 women; 10 have advanced degrees; 7 reside on campus.
Subjects Offered Advanced Placement courses, algebra, American history-AP, ancient history, ancient world history, art, art history, biology, biology-AP, calculus, calculus-AP, ceramics, chemistry, chemistry-AP, dance, earth science, English, English language-AP, English literature-AP, ESL, European history-AP, fine arts, French, geography, geometry, government/civics, Greek, history, Homeric Greek, Italian, Latin, life science, mathematics, music, physical science, physics, physics-AP, science, social studies, trigonometry, U.S. history-AP, world history, world history-AP.
Graduation Requirements Arts and fine arts (art, music, dance, drama), English, foreign language, mathematics, science, social studies (includes history). Community service is required.
Special Academic Programs 10 Advanced Placement exams for which test preparation is offered; honors section; academic accommodation for the gifted; ESL (6 students enrolled).
College Admission Counseling 17 students graduated in 2008; all went to college, including Cornell University; Northwestern University; Rensselaer Polytechnic Institute; Rhodes College; Saint Louis University; Washington University in St. Louis. Median SAT critical reading: 710, median SAT math: 680, median SAT writing: 700, median combined SAT: 2090.
Student Life Upper grades have specified standards of dress, student council, honor system. Discipline rests equally with students and faculty.
Tuition and Aid Day student tuition: $20,250; 5-day tuition and room/board: $32,000; 7-day tuition and room/board: $33,900. Tuition installment plan (Academic Management Services Plan, monthly payment plans, individually arranged payment plans). Merit scholarship grants, need-based scholarship grants, paying campus jobs available. In 2008–09, 35% of upper-school students received aid.
Admissions Traditional secondary-level entrance grade is 9. For fall 2008, 38 students applied for upper-level admission, 14 were accepted, 13 enrolled. ISEE, school's own exam, SSAT or TOEFL or SLEP required. Deadline for receipt of application materials: February 15. Application fee required: $40. Interview required.
Athletics Interscholastic: basketball (boys, girls), soccer (b,g), volleyball (b,g); intramural: basketball (b,g), soccer (b,g), volleyball (b,g); coed interscholastic: soccer; coed intramural: dance, fitness, martial arts, physical fitness, tai chi, tennis, volleyball, weight training, yoga. 5 coaches.
Computers Computers are regularly used in mathematics, science classes. Computer network features include online commercial services, Internet access, wireless campus network, Internet filtering or blocking technology. Campus intranet and student e-mail accounts are available to students. The school has a published electronic and media policy.
Contact Ms. Marie De Jesus, Director of Admissions. 314-843-4151 Ext. 128. Fax: 314-843-3527. E-mail: admissions@tjs.org. Web site: www.tjs.org.

See Close-Up on page 992.

THORNTON FRIENDS SCHOOL

13925 New Hampshire Avenue
Silver Spring, Maryland 20904
Head of School: Norman Maynard

General Information Coeducational day college-preparatory, general academic, and arts school, affiliated with Society of Friends; primarily serves underachievers. Grades 6–12. Founded: 1973. Setting: suburban. Nearest major city is Washington, DC. 2-acre campus. 2 buildings on campus. Approved or accredited by Association of Independent Schools of Greater Washington, Friends Council on Education, and Maryland Department of Education. Endowment: $33,528. Total enrollment: 58. Upper school average class size: 9. Upper school faculty-student ratio: 1:6.
Upper School Student Profile Grade 9: 8 students (6 boys, 2 girls); Grade 10: 12 students (9 boys, 3 girls); Grade 11: 16 students (10 boys, 6 girls); Grade 12: 21 students (9 boys, 12 girls). 3% of students are members of Society of Friends.
Faculty School total: 18. In upper school: 5 men, 5 women; 4 have advanced degrees.
Subjects Offered Algebra, American literature, art, biology, calculus, chemistry, community service, comparative religion, computer art, computer multimedia, creative writing, critical thinking, current events, digital art, digital photography, drama, English, English literature, environmental science, environmental studies, expository writing, field ecology, forensics, functions, geography, geometry, history, independent study, journalism, Latin, literary magazine, logic, mathematics, media literacy, peace studies, philosophy, physical education, physical fitness, physics, pre-calculus, probability and statistics, Quakerism and ethics, science, social studies, Spanish, stained glass, theater, trigonometry, wilderness education, world culture, world history, world literature, writing, yearbook.
Graduation Requirements English, mathematics, science, senior project, social studies (includes history), U.S. history. Community service is required.
Special Academic Programs Accelerated programs; independent study; term-away projects; academic accommodation for the gifted.
College Admission Counseling 12 students graduated in 2008; 8 went to college, including Guilford College; The College of Wooster; University of Maryland, College Park. Other: 2 went to work, 1 entered military service, 1 entered a postgraduate year.
Student Life Upper grades have specified standards of dress, student council. Discipline rests primarily with faculty. Attendance at religious services is required.
Tuition and Aid Day student tuition: $21,950. Tuition installment plan (FACTS Tuition Payment Plan, prepayment discount plan, 60%/40% option (due August 1 and December 1)). Need-based scholarship grants, tuition reduction for children of employees available. In 2008–09, 24% of upper-school students received aid. Total amount of financial aid awarded in 2008–09: $230,000.
Admissions Traditional secondary-level entrance grade is 9. For fall 2008, 20 students applied for upper-level admission, 16 were accepted, 12 enrolled. Deadline for receipt of application materials: none. Application fee required: $50. On-campus interview required.
Athletics Interscholastic: basketball (boys, girls); coed interscholastic: soccer, softball; coed intramural: basketball, bowling, cooperative games, fitness, flag football, flagball, Frisbee, hiking/backpacking, outdoor skills, rafting, rock climbing, ropes courses, soccer, softball, swimming and diving, touch football, ultimate Frisbee.
Computers Computers are regularly used in art, English, foreign language, geography, history, journalism, literary magazine, mathematics, science, social science, yearbook classes. Computer network features include Internet access, wireless campus network, Internet filtering or blocking technology. Computer access in designated common areas is available to students. Students grades are available online. The school has a published electronic and media policy.

Contact Norman Maynard, Principal. 301-384-0320. Fax: 301-236-9481. E-mail: nmaynard@thorntonfriends.org. Web site: www.thorntonfriends.org.

TILTON SCHOOL

30 School Street
Tilton, New Hampshire 03276

Head of School: James R. Clements

General Information Coeducational boarding and day college-preparatory school, affiliated with Methodist Church. Grades 9–PG. Founded: 1845. Setting: small town. Nearest major city is Concord. Students are housed in single-sex dormitories. 146-acre campus. 29 buildings on campus. Approved or accredited by Association of Independent Schools in New England, Independent Schools of Northern New England, New England Association of Schools and Colleges, The Association of Boarding Schools, and New Hampshire Department of Education. Member of National Association of Independent Schools and Secondary School Admission Test Board. Endowment: $16 million. Total enrollment: 256. Upper school average class size: 12. Upper school faculty-student ratio: 1:5.

Upper School Student Profile Grade 9: 22 students (13 boys, 9 girls); Grade 10: 60 students (32 boys, 28 girls); Grade 11: 67 students (46 boys, 21 girls); Grade 12: 83 students (56 boys, 27 girls); Postgraduate: 24 students (18 boys, 6 girls). 79% of students are boarding students. 32% are state residents. 24 states are represented in upper school student body. 21% are international students. International students from Canada, China, Japan, Nigeria, Republic of Korea, and Spain; 11 other countries represented in student body. 2% of students are Methodist.

Faculty School total: 44. In upper school: 28 men, 16 women; 18 have advanced degrees; 40 reside on campus.

Subjects Offered Advanced chemistry, advanced math, advanced studio art-AP, algebra, American history, American literature, anatomy and physiology, art, band, biology, biology-AP, calculus, calculus-AP, chemistry, chemistry-AP, chorus, clay-working, college counseling, community service, computer graphics, criminal justice, debate, drama, drawing, ecology, economics, English, English language and composition-AP, English literature-AP, ESL, European history-AP, forensic science, French, French-AP, functions, geology, geometry, honors algebra, honors English, honors geometry, independent study, integrated mathematics, integrated science, leadership training, marine ecology, music, music appreciation, music theory, musical productions, newspaper, painting, photography, physics, physics-AP, politics, pre-calculus, psychology-AP, SAT preparation, sociology, Spanish, Spanish-AP, statistics, studio art, studio art-AP, theater, trigonometry, wilderness/outdoor program, world cultures, world literature, world religions, yearbook.

Graduation Requirements American history, arts and fine arts (art, music, dance, drama), English, foreign language, history, lab science, mathematics, science, annual participation in Plus/5 (including activities in art and culture, athletics, community service, leadership, and outdoor experience).

Special Academic Programs Advanced Placement exam preparation; honors section; independent study; ESL (16 students enrolled).

College Admission Counseling 80 students graduated in 2008; 77 went to college, including Babson College; Boston University; Stonehill College; University of Illinois at Urbana–Champaign; University of Massachusetts Dartmouth. Other: 3 had other specific plans. Mean SAT critical reading: 500, mean SAT math: 510, mean SAT writing: 490, mean combined SAT: 1500.

Student Life Upper grades have specified standards of dress, student council, honor system. Discipline rests primarily with faculty.

Tuition and Aid Day student tuition: $23,750; 7-day tuition and room/board: $40,750. Tuition installment plan (FACTS Tuition Payment Plan, individually arranged payment plans). Merit scholarship grants, need-based scholarship grants, need-based loans available. In 2008–09, 43% of upper-school students received aid; total upper-school merit-scholarship money awarded: $221,200. Total amount of financial aid awarded in 2008–09: $2,063,364.

Admissions Traditional secondary-level entrance grade is 9. For fall 2008, 433 students applied for upper-level admission, 304 were accepted, 107 enrolled. PSAT or SAT for applicants to grade 11 and 12, SSAT or writing sample required. Deadline for receipt of application materials: February 1. Application fee required: $50. Interview required.

Athletics Interscholastic: baseball (boys), basketball (b,g), field hockey (g), football (b), ice hockey (b,g), lacrosse (b,g), soccer (b,g), softball (g), tennis (b,g), wrestling (b); coed interscholastic: alpine skiing, cross-country running, golf, mountain biking, skiing (downhill), snowboarding; coed intramural: canoeing/kayaking, hiking/backpacking, outdoor activities, outdoor education, outdoor skills, rock climbing, squash, strength & conditioning, wall climbing, weight training, wilderness survival. 1 athletic trainer.

Computers Computers are regularly used in English, foreign language, graphic arts, history, mathematics, newspaper, science, yearbook classes. Computer network features include on-campus library services, online commercial services, Internet access, wireless campus network, Internet filtering or blocking technology, USB Ports, Smart Media Readers. Campus intranet, student e-mail accounts, and computer access in designated common areas are available to students. The school has a published electronic and media policy.

Contact Beth A. Skoglund, Director of Admissions. 603-286-1733. Fax: 603-286-1705. E-mail: bskoglund@tiltonschool.org. Web site: www.tiltonschool.org.

See Close-Up on page 994.

TIMBER RIDGE SCHOOL

Cross Junction, Virginia
See Special Needs Schools section.

TIMOTHY CHRISTIAN HIGH SCHOOL

1061 South Prospect Avenue
Elmhurst, Illinois 60126

Head of School: Mr. Clyde Rinsema

General Information Coeducational day college-preparatory, general academic, arts, business, vocational, religious studies, and technology school, affiliated with Christian faith. Grades K–12. Founded: 1911. Setting: suburban. Nearest major city is Chicago. 26-acre campus. 1 building on campus. Approved or accredited by Christian Schools International, North Carolina Association of Independent Schools, North Central Association of Colleges and Schools, and Illinois Department of Education. Endowment: $4.8 million. Total enrollment: 1,036. Upper school average class size: 13. Upper school faculty-student ratio: 1:13.

Upper School Student Profile Grade 9: 105 students (51 boys, 54 girls); Grade 10: 88 students (38 boys, 50 girls); Grade 11: 91 students (40 boys, 51 girls); Grade 12: 114 students (55 boys, 59 girls). 100% of students are Christian.

Faculty School total: 30. In upper school: 21 men, 9 women; 22 have advanced degrees.

Subjects Offered Advanced math, algebra, American literature, anatomy and physiology, art, band, Bible, biology, British literature, British literature-AP, calculus, calculus-AP, ceramics, chemistry, choir, Christian ethics, communication skills, community service, computer applications, computer graphics, concert choir, creative writing, drafting, drama, economics, electives, English, European history, expository writing, family living, food and nutrition, French, geometry, German, health, home economics, independent living, industrial arts, instrumental music, music, oil painting, parent/child development, photography, physical education, physical science, physics, physics-AP, pre-algebra, psychology, sewing, sociology, Spanish, Spanish literature-AP, strings, study skills, theater, theater production, trigonometry, U.S. government, U.S. history, U.S. history-AP, United States government-AP, Western civilization, world history, world literature.

Graduation Requirements English, mathematics, music, physical education (includes health), religious studies, science, social studies (includes history), technological applications, theology, senior service retreat at end of 12th grade, service requirement in grades 9-11(10 hours per year).

Special Academic Programs Advanced Placement exam preparation; honors section; study at local college for college credit.

College Admission Counseling 97 students graduated in 2008; 91 went to college, including Calvin College; Hope College; Samford University; Texas Christian University; Trinity Christian College. Other: 1 entered military service, 5 had other specific plans. Mean composite ACT: 25.

Student Life Upper grades have specified standards of dress, student council, honor system. Discipline rests primarily with faculty. Attendance at religious services is required.

Summer Programs Enrichment, sports, art/fine arts programs offered; session focuses on athletics; held on campus; accepts boys and girls; not open to students from other schools. 2009 schedule: June to July. Application deadline: May.

Tuition and Aid Day student tuition: $7275. Tuition installment plan (monthly payment plans). Some financial assistance through the school foundation available. In 2008–09, 4% of upper-school students received aid.

Admissions Traditional secondary-level entrance grade is 9. Scholastic Testing Service High School Placement Test and school's own exam required. Deadline for receipt of application materials: none. Application fee required: $100. On-campus interview required.

Athletics Interscholastic: baseball (boys), basketball (b,g), cheering (g), cross-country running (b,g), golf (b,g), pom squad (g), soccer (b,g), softball (g), tennis (b,g), track and field (b,g), volleyball (g); intramural: basketball (b), flag football (b); coed interscholastic: golf; coed intramural: volleyball. 2 PE instructors, 1 athletic trainer.

Computers Computers are regularly used in art, business applications, English, science classes. Computer network features include on-campus library services, Internet access, wireless campus network, Internet filtering or blocking technology. Student e-mail accounts are available to students. Students grades are available online. The school has a published electronic and media policy.

Contact Mr. Rudi Gesch, Marketing Director. 630-782-4043. Fax: 630-833-9238. E-mail: gesch@timothychristian.com. Web site: www.timothychristian.com.

TMI—THE EPISCOPAL SCHOOL OF TEXAS

20955 West Tejas Trail
San Antonio, Texas 78257

Head of School: Dr. James A. Freeman

General Information Coeducational boarding and day college-preparatory, arts, and religious studies school, affiliated with Episcopal Church. Boarding grades 9–12, day grades 6–12. Founded: 1893. Setting: suburban. Students are housed in single-sex dormitories. 80-acre campus. 17 buildings on campus. Approved or accredited by Independent Schools Association of the Southwest, National Association of Episcopal Schools, Southwest Association of Episcopal Schools, The Association of Boarding Schools, and Texas Department of Education. Total enrollment: 400. Upper school average class size: 15. Upper school faculty-student ratio: 1:8.

Upper School Student Profile Grade 9: 73 students (46 boys, 27 girls); Grade 10: 64 students (39 boys, 25 girls); Grade 11: 68 students (40 boys, 28 girls); Grade 12: 62 students (35 boys, 27 girls). 18% of students are boarding students. 97% are state residents. 5 states are represented in upper school student body. 3% are international students. International students from Australia, Mexico, Panama, Republic of Korea, Saudi Arabia, and Viet Nam; 2 other countries represented in student body. 18% of students are members of Episcopal Church.

Faculty School total: 43. In upper school: 12 men, 16 women; 24 have advanced degrees; 17 reside on campus.

Subjects Offered 20th century history, acting, Advanced Placement courses, advanced studio art-AP, algebra, American Civil War, American history, American literature, anatomy and physiology, astronomy, athletics, biology, British literature, calculus, ceramics, chemistry, choir, computer programming, conceptual physics, earth science, economics, English, English literature, environmental science, fine arts, geometry, government, Greek, history, JROTC, Latin, meteorology, military history, philosophy, photography, physics, playwriting, religion, Spanish, statistics, studio art, theater arts, theater design and production, world history, writing.

Graduation Requirements Arts and fine arts (art, music, dance, drama), electives, English, foreign language, history, mathematics, philosophy, physical education (includes health), religion (includes Bible studies and theology), science, students must pass the Assessment of Basic English Skills.

Special Academic Programs Advanced Placement exam preparation; honors section; independent study.

College Admission Counseling 52 students graduated in 2008; all went to college, including Baylor University; Harvard University; Rice University; Southern Methodist University; Texas A&M University; Texas Christian University. Median SAT critical reading: 600, median SAT math: 590, median SAT writing: 610, median combined SAT: 1800.

Student Life Upper grades have uniform requirement, student council, honor system. Discipline rests equally with students and faculty. Attendance at religious services is required.

Summer Programs Enrichment, advancement, sports programs offered; session focuses on academics and enrichment; held on campus; accepts boys and girls; open to students from other schools. 30 students usually enrolled. 2009 schedule: June 8 to July 17. Application deadline: May 28.

Tuition and Aid Day student tuition: $17,355; 5-day tuition and room/board: $29,380; 7-day tuition and room/board: $34,205. Tuition installment plan (Academic Management Services Plan, FACTS Tuition Payment Plan, monthly payment plans). Merit scholarship grants, need-based scholarship grants, tuition remission for children of faculty available. In 2008–09, 20% of upper-school students received aid; total upper-school merit-scholarship money awarded: $230,000. Total amount of financial aid awarded in 2008–09: $500,000.

Admissions Traditional secondary-level entrance grade is 9. For fall 2008, 254 students applied for upper-level admission, 175 were accepted, 128 enrolled. ISEE required. Deadline for receipt of application materials: January 16. Application fee required: $75. Interview required.

Athletics Interscholastic: baseball (boys), basketball (b,g), cheering (g), cross-country running (b,g), diving (b,g), fitness (b,g), football (b), golf (b,g), lacrosse (b,g), soccer (b,g), softball (g), strength & conditioning (b,g), swimming and diving (b,g), tennis (b,g), volleyball (g), weight training (b,g); coed interscholastic: JROTC drill, marksmanship, physical training, riflery, strength & conditioning. 10 coaches, 1 athletic trainer.

Computers Computers are regularly used in journalism, language development, literary magazine, newspaper, programming, science, yearbook classes. Computer network features include on-campus library services, online commercial services, Internet access, Internet filtering or blocking technology. Campus intranet, student e-mail accounts, and computer access in designated common areas are available to students. Students grades are available online. The school has a published electronic and media policy.

Contact Mr. Aaron Hawkins, Associate Director. 210-564-6152. Fax: 210-698-0715. E-mail: a.hawkins@tmi-sa.org. Web site: www.tmi-sa.org.

TORONTO DISTRICT CHRISTIAN HIGH SCHOOL

377 Woodbridge Avenue
Woodbridge, Ontario L4L 2V7, Canada

Head of School: Ren Siebenga

General Information Coeducational day college-preparatory, general academic, arts, business, religious studies, bilingual studies, and technology school, affiliated with Christian Reformed Church, Christian faith. Grades 9–12. Founded: 1963. Setting: urban. Nearest major city is Toronto, Canada. 16-acre campus. 1 building on campus. Approved or accredited by Christian Schools International, Ontario Ministry of Education, and Ontario Department of Education. Language of instruction: English. Endowment: CAN$100,000. Total enrollment: 454. Upper school average class size: 25. Upper school faculty-student ratio: 1:14.

Upper School Student Profile Grade 9: 104 students (46 boys, 58 girls); Grade 10: 117 students (68 boys, 49 girls); Grade 11: 121 students (57 boys, 64 girls); Grade 12: 112 students (59 boys, 53 girls). 99% of students are members of Christian Reformed Church, Christian.

Faculty School total: 33. In upper school: 19 men, 12 women; 8 have advanced degrees.

Subjects Offered 20th century history, advanced math, ancient history, art, athletic training, Bible, biology, bookkeeping, business applications, business education, business mathematics, business technology, cabinet making, calculus, Canadian geography, Canadian history, career and personal planning, chemistry, choir, civics, computer applications, computer keyboarding, computer multimedia, computer programming, concert band, creative writing, discrete math, dramatic arts, economics, English, English literature, environmental studies, ESL, family living, family studies, French, geography, global issues, guitar, health, history, industrial arts, law, media studies, modern Western civilization, music, philosophy, physical education, physics, remedial study skills, science, social justice, theater arts, video film production, visual arts, Western civilization, world issues, world religions.

Graduation Requirements Ontario Ministry of Education requirements, family studies or philosophy.

Special Academic Programs Honors section; term-away projects; study abroad; remedial reading and/or remedial writing; remedial math; programs in English, mathematics, general development for dyslexic students; ESL (8 students enrolled).

College Admission Counseling 109 students graduated in 2008; 87 went to college, including McMaster University; Redeemer University College; University of Guelph; University of Toronto; University of Waterloo; York University. Other: 10 went to work, 12 had other specific plans.

Student Life Upper grades have specified standards of dress, student council, honor system. Discipline rests equally with students and faculty. Attendance at religious services is required.

Summer Programs Sports programs offered; session focuses on entry-level sports for incoming grade 9 students; held on campus; accepts boys and girls; not open to students from other schools. 24 students usually enrolled.

Tuition and Aid Day student tuition: CAN$9250–CAN$12,020. Tuition installment plan (monthly payment plans, individually arranged payment plans). Tuition reduction for siblings, need-based scholarship grants available.

Admissions Traditional secondary-level entrance grade is 9. For fall 2008, 104 students applied for upper-level admission, 104 were accepted, 104 enrolled. Deadline for receipt of application materials: February 1. Application fee required: CAN$400. On-campus interview required.

Athletics Interscholastic: basketball (boys, girls), hockey (b), soccer (b,g), volleyball (b,g); coed interscholastic: cross-country running, track and field, ultimate Frisbee; coed intramural: ice hockey. 5 PE instructors, 5 coaches.

Computers Computers are regularly used in accounting, all academic, business applications, programming, technology, video film production, yearbook classes. Computer network features include on-campus library services, Internet access, wireless campus network, Internet filtering or blocking technology. Campus intranet and student e-mail accounts are available to students. Students grades are available online. The school has a published electronic and media policy.

Contact Mr. Tim Bentum, Vice Principal, Students and Admissions. 905-851-1772 Ext. 202. Fax: 905-851-9992. E-mail: bentum@tdchristian.ca. Web site: tdchristian.ca.

TORONTO WALDORF SCHOOL

9100 Bathurst Street
Thornhill, Ontario L4J 8C7, Canada

Head of School: Mr. Todd Royer

General Information Coeducational day college-preparatory, general academic, arts, business, vocational, bilingual studies, and technology school; primarily serves underachievers. Grades JK–12. Founded: 1968. Setting: suburban. Nearest major city is Toronto, Canada. 25-acre campus. 2 buildings on campus. Approved or accredited by Association of Waldorf Schools of North America, Canadian Educational Standards Institute, and Ontario Department of Education. Language of instruction: English. Endowment: CAN$200,000. Total enrollment: 294. Upper school average class size: 23. Upper school faculty-student ratio: 1:5.

Upper School Student Profile Grade 9: 29 students (14 boys, 15 girls); Grade 10: 25 students (12 boys, 13 girls); Grade 11: 23 students (10 boys, 13 girls); Grade 12: 18 students (7 boys, 11 girls).
Faculty School total: 55. In upper school: 8 men, 12 women; 10 have advanced degrees.
Subjects Offered Acting, advanced computer applications, algebra, American history, ancient history, art, art history, astronomy, atomic theory, biochemistry, botany, business mathematics, business studies, Canadian geography, Canadian history, careers, chemistry, choir, civics, clayworking, composition, computer science, crafts, drama, drama performance, drawing, English composition, English literature, ESL, eurythmy, evolution, family studies, French, gardening, genetics, geography, geology, geometry, German, grammar, health, history, history of architecture, history of drama, history of music, human anatomy, inorganic chemistry, literature, mathematics, mechanics, medieval/Renaissance history, meteorology, microbiology, modeling, modern history, music, mythology, novel, nutrition, optics, orchestra, organic chemistry, painting, performing arts, philosophy, physical education, physics, physiology, practical arts, reading, Shakespeare, trigonometry, visual arts, water color painting, woodworking, writing, zoology.
Special Academic Programs Term-away projects; study abroad; ESL (10 students enrolled).
College Admission Counseling 30 students graduated in 2008; 25 went to college.
Student Life Upper grades have specified standards of dress, student council. Discipline rests primarily with faculty.
Tuition and Aid Day student tuition: CAN$16,200. Tuition installment plan (monthly payment plans). Bursaries, need-based scholarship grants available.
Admissions For fall 2008, 25 students applied for upper-level admission, 15 were accepted, 10 enrolled. Deadline for receipt of application materials: none. Application fee required: CAN$100. On-campus interview required.
Athletics Intramural: badminton (boys, girls), basketball (b,g), cross-country running (b,g), mountain biking (b,g); coed interscholastic: artistic gym, badminton, basketball, canoeing/kayaking, Circus, cooperative games, cross-country running, fitness, indoor track & field, juggling, outdoor adventure, outdoor education, physical fitness, physical training, rhythmic gymnastics, running, skiing (cross-country), skiing (downhill), strength & conditioning, track and field, unicycling, wallyball, wilderness survival, wildernessways, yoga. 2 PE instructors, 2 coaches.
Computers Computers are regularly used in yearbook classes. Computer resources include Internet access, Internet filtering or blocking technology.
Contact Ms. Aileen Stewart, Admissions Coordinator. 905-881-1611 Ext. 314. Fax: 905-881-6710. E-mail: astewart@torontowaldorfschool.com. Web site: www.torontowaldorfschool.com.

TOWER HILL SCHOOL

2813 West 17th Street
Wilmington, Delaware 19806

Head of School: Dr. Christopher D. Wheeler

General Information Coeducational day college-preparatory, arts, and technology school. Grades PK–12. Founded: 1919. Setting: suburban. Nearest major city is Philadelphia, PA. 40-acre campus. 4 buildings on campus. Approved or accredited by Middle States Association of Colleges and Schools and Delaware Department of Education. Member of National Association of Independent Schools and Secondary School Admission Test Board. Endowment: $33 million. Total enrollment: 725. Upper school average class size: 14. Upper school faculty-student ratio: 1:7.
Upper School Student Profile Grade 9: 55 students (23 boys, 32 girls); Grade 10: 56 students (26 boys, 30 girls); Grade 11: 49 students (29 boys, 20 girls); Grade 12: 50 students (26 boys, 24 girls).
Faculty School total: 86. In upper school: 31 men, 13 women; 26 have advanced degrees.
Subjects Offered Acting, algebra, American history, American literature, analysis, art, art history, band, biology, biology-AP, calculus, calculus-AP, ceramics, chemistry, chorus, community service, computer science, creative writing, drama, drawing, driver education, English, English literature, European history, European history-AP, film, fine arts, French, French language-AP, geometry, historical research, history, human anatomy, Internet, jazz band, Latin, Latin-AP, mathematics, music, music theory, organic chemistry, painting, photography, physical science, physics, physics-AP, poetry, pre-calculus, psychology, science, sculpture, Shakespeare, shop, sociology, Spanish, Spanish language-AP, stagecraft, statistics-AP, strings, theater, trigonometry, urban studies, woodworking, world history, writing.
Graduation Requirements Arts and fine arts (art, music, dance, drama), athletics, English, foreign language, mathematics, science, social studies (includes history). Community service is required.
Special Academic Programs Advanced Placement exam preparation; honors section; independent study; academic accommodation for the gifted, the musically talented, and the artistically talented.
College Admission Counseling 58 students graduated in 2008; all went to college, including Colgate University; Duke University; Massachusetts Institute of Technology; Syracuse University; University of Delaware. Mean SAT critical reading: 649, mean SAT math: 658, mean SAT writing: 664. 81% scored over 600 on SAT critical reading, 78% scored over 600 on SAT math, 78% scored over 600 on SAT writing.
Student Life Upper grades have specified standards of dress, student council, honor system. Discipline rests equally with students and faculty.
Tuition and Aid Day student tuition: $22,400–$22,900. Tuition installment plan (Key Tuition Payment Plan, monthly payment plans, individually arranged payment plans). Need-based scholarship grants available. In 2008–09, 15% of upper-school students received aid. Total amount of financial aid awarded in 2008–09: $565,325.
Admissions Traditional secondary-level entrance grade is 9. For fall 2008, 57 students applied for upper-level admission, 34 were accepted, 21 enrolled. ERB CTP IV, PSAT or SAT for applicants to grade 11 and 12, SSAT or writing sample required. Deadline for receipt of application materials: January 9. Application fee required: $40. On-campus interview required.
Athletics Interscholastic: baseball (boys), basketball (b,g), cross-country running (b,g), field hockey (g), football (b), indoor track (b,g), lacrosse (b,g), soccer (b,g), swimming and diving (b,g), tennis (b,g), track and field (b,g), volleyball (g), winter (indoor) track (b,g), wrestling (b); intramural: tennis (g); coed interscholastic: aerobics, aerobics/Nautilus, crew, golf, Nautilus, self defense; coed intramural: speedball, weight lifting. 21 coaches, 1 athletic trainer.
Computers Computers are regularly used in all academic classes. Computer network features include on-campus library services, Internet access, wireless campus network, Internet filtering or blocking technology. Student e-mail accounts and computer access in designated common areas are available to students. Students grades are available online. The school has a published electronic and media policy.
Contact Mr. William R. Ushler, Associate Director of Admission. 302-657-8350. Fax: 302-657-8377. E-mail: wushler@towerhill.org. Web site: www.towerhill.org.

TOWN CENTRE PRIVATE HIGH SCHOOL

155 Clayton Drive
Markham, Ontario L3R 7P3, Canada

Head of School: Mr. Jim Parsons

General Information Coeducational day college-preparatory school. Grades PS–12. Founded: 1986. Setting: suburban. Nearest major city is Toronto, Canada. 5-acre campus. 1 building on campus. Approved or accredited by Ontario Ministry of Education. Language of instruction: English. Total enrollment: 1,400. Upper school average class size: 15. Upper school faculty-student ratio: 1:15.
Faculty School total: 17. In upper school: 11 men, 6 women; 6 have advanced degrees.
Subjects Offered Accounting, advanced chemistry, advanced computer applications, advanced math, Advanced Placement courses, algebra, anthropology, applied music, art, band, biology, biology-AP, business, business applications, business studies, calculus, calculus-AP, Canadian geography, Canadian history, Canadian law, career education, chemistry, civics, computer information systems, computer keyboarding, computer programming, discrete mathematics, economics, English, English as a foreign language, English-AP, ESL, family living, French, geography, health education, health science, history, history-AP, law, music, music theory, physics, religions, science, sociology, visual arts, world religions.
Special Academic Programs Advanced Placement exam preparation; ESL (25 students enrolled).
College Admission Counseling Colleges students went to include McMaster University; Queen's University at Kingston; The University of Western Ontario; University of Toronto; University of Waterloo; York University. Other: 50 entered a postgraduate year.
Student Life Upper grades have uniform requirement, student council, honor system. Discipline rests primarily with faculty.
Tuition and Aid Day student tuition: CAN$12,600. Tuition installment plan (monthly payment plans, individually arranged payment plans, 2 installments and full payment). Tuition reduction for siblings available.
Admissions Traditional secondary-level entrance grade is 9. For fall 2008, 30 students applied for upper-level admission, 25 were accepted, 23 enrolled. High School Placement Test (closed version) from Scholastic Testing Service required. Deadline for receipt of application materials: none. Application fee required: CAN$200. Interview required.
Athletics Intramural: ball hockey (boys), ballet (g), basketball (b,g), soccer (b,g), volleyball (b,g); coed interscholastic: badminton, ball hockey, basketball, cooperative games, fitness, floor hockey, physical fitness, soccer, volleyball; coed intramural: archery, badminton, baseball, bowling, cricket, cross-country running, flag football, golf, softball, table tennis, tennis, ultimate Frisbee. 1 PE instructor, 4 coaches.
Computers Computers are regularly used in accounting, business, information technology classes. Computer network features include Internet access, Internet filtering or blocking technology. The school has a published electronic and media policy.
Contact Ms. Patricia Ego, Admissions. 905-470-1200. Fax: 905-470-1721. E-mail: pat.ego@tcphs.com. Web site: www.tcphs.com.

TRAFALGAR CASTLE SCHOOL

401 Reynolds Street
Whitby, Ontario L1N 3W9, Canada
Head of School: Mr. Brian McClure

General Information Girls' boarding and day college-preparatory, arts, business, and technology school. Boarding grades 7–12, day grades 6–12. Founded: 1874. Setting: small town. Nearest major city is Toronto, Canada. Students are housed in single-sex dormitories. 28-acre campus. 2 buildings on campus. Approved or accredited by Canadian Association of Independent Schools, Canadian Educational Standards Institute, Conference of Independent Schools of Ontario, Ontario Ministry of Education, The Association of Boarding Schools, and Ontario Department of Education. Language of instruction: English. Endowment: CAN$153,000. Total enrollment: 216. Upper school average class size: 15. Upper school faculty-student ratio: 1:9.

Upper School Student Profile Grade 6: 15 students (15 girls); Grade 7: 25 students (25 girls); Grade 8: 31 students (31 girls); Grade 9: 33 students (33 girls); Grade 10: 32 students (32 girls); Grade 11: 40 students (40 girls); Grade 12: 40 students (40 girls). 24% of students are boarding students. 79% are province residents. 2 provinces are represented in upper school student body. 21% are international students. International students from Bahamas, China, Hong Kong, Mexico, Republic of Korea, and Trinidad and Tobago; 4 other countries represented in student body.

Faculty School total: 25. In upper school: 4 men, 21 women; 6 have advanced degrees; 5 reside on campus.

Subjects Offered Algebra, art, art history, biology, business skills, calculus, chemistry, computer math, computer science, creative writing, drama, earth science, economics, English, English literature, environmental science, ESL, European history, fine arts, French, geography, geometry, grammar, law, mathematics, music, photography, physical education, physics, science, social studies, world history, world literature, writing.

Graduation Requirements Arts and fine arts (art, music, dance, drama), business skills (includes word processing), computer science, English, foreign language, mathematics, physical education (includes health), science, social studies (includes history).

Special Academic Programs Advanced Placement exam preparation; honors section; term-away projects; domestic exchange program (with Sedbergh School); special instructional classes for students with slight learning disabilities; ESL (19 students enrolled).

College Admission Counseling 40 students graduated in 2008; 39 went to college, including Ryerson University; The University of Western Ontario; University of Toronto; University of Waterloo; Wilfrid Laurier University. Other: 1 had other specific plans.

Student Life Upper grades have uniform requirement, student council. Discipline rests primarily with faculty.

Tuition and Aid Day student tuition: CAN$17,500–CAN$19,575; 7-day tuition and room/board: CAN$37,000–CAN$39,500. Tuition installment plan (monthly payment plans, individually arranged payment plans, early payment discounts). Tuition reduction for siblings, bursaries, merit scholarship grants, need-based scholarship grants available. In 2008–09, 3% of upper-school students received aid; total upper-school merit-scholarship money awarded: CAN$14,000. Total amount of financial aid awarded in 2008–09: CAN$43,000.

Admissions Traditional secondary-level entrance grade is 9. For fall 2008, 76 students applied for upper-level admission, 75 were accepted, 67 enrolled. Cognitive Abilities Test required. Deadline for receipt of application materials: none. Application fee required: CAN$2000. Interview required.

Athletics Interscholastic: badminton, baseball, basketball, cross-country running, field hockey, golf, gymnastics, horseback riding, ice hockey, rugby, soccer, softball, swimming and diving, synchronized swimming, tennis, track and field, volleyball; intramural: badminton, baseball, basketball, cross-country running, dance team, field hockey, fitness, fitness walking, golf, gymnastics, ice hockey, outdoor activities, outdoor adventure, physical fitness, ropes courses, skiing (cross-country), skiing (downhill), snowboarding, soccer, softball, swimming and diving, synchronized swimming, tennis, track and field, volleyball, yoga. 3 PE instructors.

Computers Computers are regularly used in all academic classes. Computer network features include on-campus library services, Internet access, wireless campus network, Internet filtering or blocking technology. Campus intranet and student e-mail accounts are available to students. Students grades are available online. The school has a published electronic and media policy.

Contact Irene Talent, Admissions Officer. 905-668-3358 Ext. 227. Fax: 905-668-4136. E-mail: talenti@castle-ed.com. Web site: www.castle-ed.com.

TRI-CITY CHRISTIAN SCHOOLS

1737 West Vista Way
Vista, California 92083
Head of School: Mr. Clark Gilbert

General Information Coeducational day college-preparatory, general academic, arts, vocational, religious studies, bilingual studies, and technology school, affiliated with Christian faith. Grades PK–12. Founded: 1971. Setting: suburban. Nearest major city is San Diego. 4-acre campus. 4 buildings on campus. Approved or accredited by Association of Christian Schools International and Western Association of Schools and Colleges. Endowment: $100,000. Total enrollment: 1,132. Upper school average class size: 22. Upper school faculty-student ratio: 1:12.

Upper School Student Profile Grade 6: 82 students (39 boys, 43 girls); Grade 7: 77 students (44 boys, 33 girls); Grade 8: 89 students (47 boys, 42 girls); Grade 9: 79 students (40 boys, 39 girls); Grade 10: 94 students (47 boys, 47 girls); Grade 11: 73 students (39 boys, 34 girls); Grade 12: 58 students (22 boys, 36 girls). 25% of students are Christian faith.

Faculty School total: 37. In upper school: 14 men, 23 women; 12 have advanced degrees.

Subjects Offered Algebra, American literature, American sign language, art, band, Bible studies, biology, biology-AP, British literature (honors), business communications, business mathematics, calculus, calculus-AP, chemistry, civics, computer science, dance, drama, economics, English, English language-AP, English literature, English literature-AP, ensembles, environmental science, European history, French, geometry, government/civics, guitar, health education, history, honors English, honors U.S. history, honors world history, jazz band, journalism, library studies, mathematics, music, philosophy, physical education, physical science, physiology, religion, science, social studies, Spanish, speech, trigonometry, typing, U.S. history, U.S. history-AP, world history, world literature.

Graduation Requirements Arts and fine arts (art, music, dance, drama), computer studies, English, foreign language, mathematics, physical education (includes health), religion (includes Bible studies and theology), science, social studies (includes history), speech, student portfolio. Community service is required.

Special Academic Programs International Baccalaureate program; Advanced Placement exam preparation; honors section.

College Admission Counseling 72 students graduated in 2008; 70 went to college, including Azusa Pacific University; Biola University; MiraCosta College; Palomar College; Point Loma Nazarene University; San Diego State University. Other: 1 entered military service. Mean SAT critical reading: 546, mean SAT math: 532, mean SAT writing: 544.

Student Life Upper grades have specified standards of dress, student council. Discipline rests primarily with faculty. Attendance at religious services is required.

Summer Programs Remediation, advancement, sports programs offered; session focuses on development; held both on and off campus; held at other area schools; accepts boys and girls; open to students from other schools. 60 students usually enrolled. 2009 schedule: June 15 to August 31.

Tuition and Aid Day student tuition: $7950. Tuition installment plan (monthly payment plans, individually arranged payment plans). Tuition reduction for siblings, need-based scholarship grants, paying campus jobs, church affiliation grants available. In 2008–09, 5% of upper-school students received aid. Total amount of financial aid awarded in 2008–09: $50,000.

Admissions Traditional secondary-level entrance grade is 9. For fall 2008, 56 students applied for upper-level admission, 53 were accepted, 49 enrolled. Any standardized test, English entrance exam and Math Placement Exam required. Deadline for receipt of application materials: none. Application fee required: $425. On-campus interview required.

Athletics Interscholastic: aerobics/dance (girls), baseball (b), basketball (b,g), cheering (g), cross-country running (b,g), dance (g), flag football (b), football (b), soccer (b,g), softball (g), tennis (b,g), touch football (b), track and field (b,g), volleyball (b,g), weight training (b,g); intramural: dance (g), physical fitness (b,g); coed interscholastic: equestrian sports, golf. 2 PE instructors, 20 coaches, 1 athletic trainer.

Computers Computers are regularly used in animation, business applications, career exploration, college planning, computer applications, English, journalism, library, media, media arts, media production, news writing, newspaper, SAT preparation, science, senior seminar, video film production, Web site design, yearbook classes. Computer network features include on-campus library services, Internet access, Internet filtering or blocking technology. Campus intranet and student e-mail accounts are available to students. Students grades are available online. The school has a published electronic and media policy.

Contact Mrs. Liz Myatt, Registrar. 760-806-8247 Ext. 200. Fax: 760-906-9002. E-mail: Liz.Myatt@tccs.org. Web site: www.tccs.org.

TRIDENT ACADEMY

Mt. Pleasant, South Carolina
See Special Needs Schools section.

TRINITY CATHOLIC HIGH SCHOOL

575 Washington Street
Newton, Massachusetts 02458-1493
Head of School: Mrs. Kelly Ann Surapaneni

General Information Coeducational day college-preparatory school, affiliated with Roman Catholic Church. Grades 9–12. Founded: 1894. Setting: suburban. Nearest major city is Boston. 4-acre campus. 2 buildings on campus. Approved or accredited by National Catholic Education Association, New England Association of Schools and

Colleges, and Massachusetts Department of Education. Endowment: $43,000. Upper school average class size: 23. Upper school faculty-student ratio: 1:13.

Upper School Student Profile Grade 9: 50 students (25 boys, 25 girls); Grade 10: 64 students (31 boys, 33 girls); Grade 11: 45 students (24 boys, 21 girls); Grade 12: 75 students (34 boys, 41 girls). 80% of students are Roman Catholic.

Faculty School total: 28. In upper school: 13 men, 15 women; 10 have advanced degrees.

Subjects Offered 20th century history, advanced computer applications, advanced math, algebra, American history, American history-AP, art, British literature, British literature-AP, calculus, calculus-AP, chemistry, choir, Christianity, civics, debate, earth science, English, English-AP, environmental science, French, freshman seminar, global studies, government, health, history, honors algebra, honors English, honors geometry, honors U.S. history, honors world history, introduction to literature, language, literature and composition-AP, mathematics, media, moral theology, philosophy, physical education, physics, pre-algebra, pre-calculus, religion, Spanish.

Graduation Requirements Art, computers, English, foreign language, mathematics, science, social studies (includes history), theology, senior service. Community service is required.

Special Academic Programs Advanced Placement exam preparation; honors section; independent study.

College Admission Counseling 64 students graduated in 2008; 54 went to college, including Providence College; Suffolk University; University of Hartford; University of Massachusetts Boston; University of Massachusetts Dartmouth. Other: 10 went to work. Mean SAT critical reading: 472, mean SAT math: 474, mean SAT writing: 465, mean combined SAT: 1410, mean composite ACT: 18. 1% scored over 600 on SAT critical reading, 5% scored over 600 on SAT math, 3% scored over 600 on SAT writing, 4% scored over 1800 on combined SAT.

Student Life Upper grades have uniform requirement, student council, honor system. Discipline rests primarily with faculty. Attendance at religious services is required.

Tuition and Aid Day student tuition: $8550. Tuition installment plan (FACTS Tuition Payment Plan). Tuition reduction for siblings, merit scholarship grants, need-based scholarship grants available. In 2008–09, 50% of upper-school students received aid; total upper-school merit-scholarship money awarded: $25,000. Total amount of financial aid awarded in 2008–09: $90,000.

Admissions Traditional secondary-level entrance grade is 9. For fall 2008, 175 students applied for upper-level admission, 120 were accepted, 65 enrolled. Catholic High School Entrance Examination required. Deadline for receipt of application materials: January 9. Application fee required: $20. On-campus interview required.

Athletics Interscholastic: baseball (boys), basketball (b,g), football (b), soccer (b,g), softball (g), volleyball (g); coed interscholastic: cheering, golf, ice hockey, track and field; coed intramural: dance, kickball, lacrosse, table tennis, tennis, ultimate Frisbee, weight lifting, whiffle ball, yoga. 5 coaches, 1 athletic trainer.

Computers Computers are regularly used in all academic, basic skills, publications classes. Computer network features include on-campus library services, Internet access, wireless campus network, Internet filtering or blocking technology, student server accounts. Students grades are available online. The school has a published electronic and media policy.

Contact Mrs. Lori Winer, Director of Admissions. 617-244-1841 Ext. 312. Fax: 617-796-9175. E-mail: lwiner@trinitycatholic.com. Web site: www.trinitycatholic.com/.

TRINITY CHRISTIAN ACADEMY

17001 Addison Road
Addison, Texas 75001-5096

Head of School: Mr. David Delph

General Information Coeducational day college-preparatory, arts, religious studies, bilingual studies, and technology school, affiliated with Christian faith. Grades K–12. Founded: 1970. Setting: suburban. Nearest major city is Dallas. 40-acre campus. 1 building on campus. Approved or accredited by Association of Christian Schools International, Christian Schools International, Southern Association of Colleges and Schools, The College Board, and Texas Department of Education. Endowment: $8.2 million. Total enrollment: 1,515. Upper school average class size: 18. Upper school faculty-student ratio: 1:10.

Upper School Student Profile 100% of students are Christian faith.

Faculty School total: 130. In upper school: 15 men, 35 women; 31 have advanced degrees.

Subjects Offered Advanced biology, advanced computer applications, advanced math, Advanced Placement courses, advanced studio art-AP, algebra, American government, American government-AP, American history, American history-AP, American literature, American literature-AP, anatomy and physiology, art, athletics, Bible, Bible studies, biology, biology-AP, calculus, calculus-AP, chemistry, community service, computer animation, computer applications, computer art, computer graphics, computer information systems, computer literacy, computer multimedia, computer programming, computer science, computer science-AP, desktop publishing, digital art, digital photography, drama, drama performance, drawing, economics, economics-AP, English, English language and composition-AP, English literature, European history, European history-AP, European literature, expository writing, fine arts, French, French-AP, geography, geometry, government, government-AP, government/civics, health, history, history of ideas, history-AP, honors algebra, honors English, honors geometry, honors world history, keyboarding, Latin, literature and composition-AP, mathematics, music, painting, performing arts, photography, physical education, physics, printmaking, psychology, religion, science, social science, social studies, Spanish, Spanish-AP, speech, speech communications, studio art—AP, theater, theater arts, trigonometry, U.S. government-AP, vocal music, Web site design, world history, world literature.

Graduation Requirements Arts and fine arts (art, music, dance, drama), Bible, economics, English, foreign language, government, mathematics, physical education (includes health), science, social science, social studies (includes history), speech communications, technology. Community service is required.

Special Academic Programs Advanced Placement exam preparation; honors section; independent study; study abroad.

College Admission Counseling 118 students graduated in 2008; all went to college, including Baylor University; Texas A&M University; The University of Texas at Austin; University of Oklahoma; Wake Forest University; Wheaton College. Mean SAT critical reading: 593, mean SAT math: 611, mean SAT writing: 607, mean combined SAT: 1811, mean composite ACT: 26.

Student Life Upper grades have uniform requirement, student council, honor system. Discipline rests equally with students and faculty. Attendance at religious services is required.

Summer Programs Enrichment, advancement, sports, art/fine arts, computer instruction programs offered; session focuses on enhancement; held on campus; accepts boys and girls; open to students from other schools. 700 students usually enrolled. 2009 schedule: June 15 to July 31. Application deadline: March 15.

Tuition and Aid Day student tuition: $12,550–$13,450. Tuition installment plan (monthly payment plans). Need-based scholarship grants available. In 2008–09, 5% of upper-school students received aid. Total amount of financial aid awarded in 2008–09: $190,000.

Admissions Traditional secondary-level entrance grade is 9. For fall 2008, 58 students applied for upper-level admission, 44 were accepted, 29 enrolled. ISEE and Stanford Achievement Test required. Deadline for receipt of application materials: February 1. Application fee required: $100. On-campus interview required.

Athletics Interscholastic: baseball (boys), basketball (b,g), cheering (g), drill team (g), football (b), golf (b,g), running (b,g), soccer (b,g), softball (g), strength & conditioning (b,g), volleyball (g), weight lifting (b), weight training (b), winter soccer (b,g), wrestling (b); coed interscholastic: cross-country running, swimming and diving, tennis, track and field. 2 PE instructors, 39 coaches, 1 athletic trainer.

Computers Computers are regularly used in animation, art, Bible studies, career exploration, college planning, desktop publishing, digital applications, English, foreign language, mathematics, multimedia, photojournalism, publications, science, technology, video film production, Web site design, word processing, yearbook classes. Computer network features include on-campus library services, Internet access, Internet filtering or blocking technology. Computer access in designated common areas is available to students. Students grades are available online.

Contact Mary Helen Noland, Admission Director. 972-931-8325. Fax: 972-931-8923. E-mail: mhnoland@trinitychristian.org. Web site: www.trinitychristian.org.

TRINITY COLLEGE SCHOOL

55 Deblaquire Street North
Port Hope, Ontario L1A 4K7, Canada

Head of School: Mr. Stuart K. C. Grainger

General Information Coeducational boarding and day college-preparatory school, affiliated with Church of England (Anglican). Boarding grades 9–12, day grades 5–12. Founded: 1865. Setting: small town. Nearest major city is Toronto, Canada. Students are housed in single-sex dormitories. 100-acre campus. 15 buildings on campus. Approved or accredited by Canadian Association of Independent Schools, Canadian Educational Standards Institute, Conference of Independent Schools of Ontario, The Association of Boarding Schools, and Ontario Department of Education. Affiliate member of National Association of Independent Schools; member of Secondary School Admission Test Board. Language of instruction: English. Endowment: CAN$25 million. Total enrollment: 608. Upper school average class size: 16. Upper school faculty-student ratio: 1:8.

Upper School Student Profile Grade 9: 96 students (52 boys, 44 girls); Grade 10: 106 students (53 boys, 53 girls); Grade 11: 158 students (80 boys, 78 girls); Grade 12: 150 students (87 boys, 63 girls). 60% of students are boarding students. 61% are province residents. 8 provinces are represented in upper school student body. 33% are international students. International students from Bahamas, Bermuda, China, Germany, Mexico, and Republic of Korea; 23 other countries represented in student body. 30% of students are members of Church of England (Anglican).

Faculty School total: 65. In upper school: 37 men, 27 women; 17 have advanced degrees; 11 reside on campus.

Subjects Offered Algebra, art, art history-AP, astronomy, biology, biology-AP, calculus, calculus-AP, Canadian geography, Canadian history, career education, career/college preparation, chemistry, chemistry-AP, civics, classical civilization, classics, community service, computer programming, computer science, creative writing, dramatic arts, earth science, economics, English, English literature, English-AP, environmental science, environmental studies, ESL, European history, fine arts, finite math, French, French-AP, general science, geography, geometry, German, guidance, health, history, independent study, Latin, law, mathematics,

modern Western civilization, music, philosophy, physical education, physics, physics-AP, political science, science, social science, social studies, Spanish.
Graduation Requirements Arts and fine arts (art, music, dance, drama), Canadian geography, Canadian history, civics, English, French, guidance, mathematics, physical education (includes health), science, social science, technology, minimum 40 hours of community service.
Special Academic Programs Advanced Placement exam preparation; independent study; term-away projects; study abroad; ESL (15 students enrolled).
College Admission Counseling 94 students graduated in 2008; all went to college, including Dalhousie University; McGill University; Queen's University at Kingston; The University of Western Ontario; University of Guelph; University of Toronto. 25.5% scored over 600 on SAT critical reading, 30% scored over 600 on SAT math, 23% scored over 600 on SAT writing, 30% scored over 1800 on combined SAT.
Student Life Upper grades have uniform requirement, student council, honor system. Discipline rests primarily with faculty. Attendance at religious services is required.
Summer Programs Advancement, art/fine arts, computer instruction programs offered; session focuses on advancement through cultural enrichment; held off campus; held at England and Spain; accepts boys and girls; open to students from other schools. 30 students usually enrolled. 2009 schedule: June 28 to July 26. Application deadline: April 28.
Tuition and Aid Day student tuition: CAN$22,980; 5-day tuition and room/board: CAN$39,990–CAN$41,250; 7-day tuition and room/board: CAN$39,990–CAN$41,250. Tuition installment plan (monthly payment plans, quarterly payment plan). Bursaries, need-based scholarship grants available. In 2008–09, 30% of upper-school students received aid. Total amount of financial aid awarded in 2008–09: CAN$1,000,000.
Admissions Traditional secondary-level entrance grade is 9. For fall 2008, 500 students applied for upper-level admission, 338 were accepted, 256 enrolled. CCAT, SSAT, ERB, PSAT, SAT, PLAN or ACT or TOEFL required. Deadline for receipt of application materials: none. Application fee required: CAN$200. Interview required.
Athletics Interscholastic: baseball (boys), basketball (b,g), cricket (b), field hockey (g), football (b), ice hockey (b,g), rugby (b,g), soccer (b,g), softball (g), squash (b,g), tennis (b,g), volleyball (b,g); coed interscholastic: badminton, cross-country running, dressage, equestrian sports, golf, nordic skiing, outdoor education, rowing, skiing (cross-country), swimming and diving, track and field; coed intramural: aerobics, aerobics/dance, alpine skiing, badminton, basketball, bicycling, cricket, cross-country running, dance, equestrian sports, fitness, golf, horseback riding, ice hockey, mountain biking, paddling, skiing (downhill), snowboarding, soccer, softball, squash, strength & conditioning, swimming and diving, table tennis, tennis, water polo, weight lifting, weight training. 4 PE instructors, 5 coaches, 2 athletic trainers.
Computers Computers are regularly used in career education, college planning, English, ESL, foreign language, French, geography, history, humanities, independent study, information technology, mathematics, music, science, technology classes. Computer network features include on-campus library services, Internet access, wireless campus network. Student e-mail accounts are available to students.
Contact Ms. Kathryn A. LaBranche, Director of Admissions. 905-885-3209. Fax: 905-885-7444. E-mail: admissions@tcs.on.ca. Web site: www.tcs.on.ca.

TRINITY EPISCOPAL SCHOOL

3850 Pittaway Drive
Richmond, Virginia 23235
Head of School: Dr. Thomas G. Aycock

General Information Coeducational day college-preparatory, arts, and International Baccalaureate school, affiliated with Episcopal Church. Grades 8–12. Founded: 1972. Setting: suburban. 40-acre campus. 6 buildings on campus. Approved or accredited by National Association of Episcopal Schools, Virginia Association of Independent Schools, and Virginia Department of Education. Member of National Association of Independent Schools. Endowment: $150,000. Total enrollment: 441. Upper school average class size: 13. Upper school faculty-student ratio: 1:10.
Upper School Student Profile Grade 8: 33 students (16 boys, 17 girls); Grade 9: 98 students (50 boys, 48 girls); Grade 10: 97 students (50 boys, 47 girls); Grade 11: 101 students (65 boys, 36 girls); Grade 12: 112 students (48 boys, 64 girls).
Faculty School total: 53. In upper school: 26 men, 27 women; 31 have advanced degrees.
Subjects Offered 20th century history, 20th century world history, 3-dimensional art, Advanced Placement courses, advanced studio art-AP, algebra, American government, American government-AP, American history, American history-AP, American literature, American politics in film, anatomy, art, astronomy, band, Bible studies, biology, biology-AP, calculus, calculus-AP, chemistry, chemistry-AP, chorus, computer graphics, computer keyboarding, computer programming, computer science, concert band, concert choir, creative writing, digital music, drama, driver education, earth science, economics, English, English literature, English-AP, environmental science, European history, European history-AP, foreign policy, French, French-AP, geography, geology, geometry, German, German-AP, government-AP, government/civics, International Baccalaureate courses, jazz band, keyboarding, Latin, math analysis, mathematics, music, physics, physics-AP, pre-calculus, religion, science, social science, social studies, Southern literature, Spanish, studio art-AP, theater, theology, theory of knowledge, trigonometry, U.S. history-AP, Web site design, word processing, world history, world literature, world religions, writing.
Graduation Requirements Arts and fine arts (art, music, dance, drama), computer science, English, foreign language, mathematics, religion (includes Bible studies and theology), science, social science, social studies (includes history). Community service is required.
Special Academic Programs International Baccalaureate program; 12 Advanced Placement exams for which test preparation is offered; honors section; independent study; study at local college for college credit; academic accommodation for the gifted, the musically talented, and the artistically talented.
College Admission Counseling 100 students graduated in 2008; 96 went to college, including Hampden-Sydney College; James Madison University; Longwood University; University of Virginia; Virginia Polytechnic Institute and State University. Other: 1 had other specific plans.
Student Life Upper grades have specified standards of dress, student council, honor system. Discipline rests equally with students and faculty. Attendance at religious services is required.
Tuition and Aid Day student tuition: $15,925. Tuition installment plan (Key Tuition Payment Plan, monthly payment plans). Merit scholarship grants, need-based scholarship grants available. In 2008–09, 24% of upper-school students received aid; total upper-school merit-scholarship money awarded: $149,400. Total amount of financial aid awarded in 2008–09: $781,887.
Admissions Traditional secondary-level entrance grade is 9. For fall 2008, 264 students applied for upper-level admission, 234 were accepted, 132 enrolled. English entrance exam and Otis-Lennon School Ability Test required. Deadline for receipt of application materials: February 20. Application fee required: $50. On-campus interview required.
Athletics Interscholastic: baseball (boys), basketball (b,g), cross-country running (b,g), field hockey (g), football (b), indoor soccer (b,g), lacrosse (b,g), soccer (b,g), softball (g), tennis (b,g), track and field (b,g), volleyball (b,g), winter soccer (b,g); coed interscholastic: aquatics, crew, diving, golf, indoor track, rowing, running, swimming and diving, winter (indoor) track; coed intramural: aerobics/dance, canoeing/kayaking, climbing, dance, fitness, physical fitness, physical training, rock climbing, scuba diving, strength & conditioning, wall climbing, weight training, yoga. 14 coaches, 1 athletic trainer.
Computers Computers are regularly used in all academic classes. Computer resources include on-campus library services, online commercial services, Internet access, wireless campus network. The school has a published electronic and media policy.
Contact Mrs. Emily H. McLeod, Director of Admission. 804-327-3156. Fax: 804-272-4652. E-mail: emilymcleod@trinityes.org. Web site: www.trinityes.org.

TRINITY HIGH SCHOOL

7574 West Division Street
River Forest, Illinois 60305
Head of School: Mrs. Antonia C Bouillette, PhD

General Information Girls' day college-preparatory, arts, and religious studies school, affiliated with Roman Catholic Church. Grades 9–12. Founded: 1918. Setting: suburban. Nearest major city is Chicago. 1-acre campus. 2 buildings on campus. Approved or accredited by International Baccalaureate Organization, National Catholic Education Association, North Central Association of Colleges and Schools, The College Board, and Illinois Department of Education. Endowment: $2 million. Total enrollment: 521. Upper school average class size: 20. Upper school faculty-student ratio: 1:14.
Upper School Student Profile Grade 9: 163 students (163 girls); Grade 10: 113 students (113 girls); Grade 11: 137 students (137 girls); Grade 12: 108 students (108 girls). 80% of students are Roman Catholic.
Faculty School total: 38. In upper school: 4 men, 34 women; 30 have advanced degrees.
Subjects Offered Algebra, British literature, choir, comparative religion, computer art, computer graphics, computer keyboarding, creative dance, creative drama, dance, desktop publishing, digital art, ecology, environmental systems, economics, English, environmental science, European history, film studies, French, geometry, government, graphic design, health, honors algebra, honors English, honors geometry, honors U.S. history, honors world history, integrated mathematics, Italian, math methods, moral theology, newspaper, painting, physical education, physics, pre-calculus, pre-college orientation, probability and statistics, psychology, religious studies, scripture, Spanish, speech, speech and debate, theater, theology, theory of knowledge, U.S. government, U.S. government and politics, U.S. history, vocal music, women in society, word processing, world civilizations, world geography, world governments, world history, world religions, world studies, yearbook.
Graduation Requirements Algebra, American literature, arts and fine arts (art, music, dance, drama), biology, British literature, Catholic belief and practice, chemistry, Christian ethics, Christian scripture, church history, computer applications, computer keyboarding, English composition, foreign language, geometry, health education, physical education (includes health), speech, theology, U.S. history, world history, world literature, world religions, world studies.
Special Academic Programs International Baccalaureate program; honors section; independent study; academic accommodation for the gifted.
College Admission Counseling 91 students graduated in 2008; all went to college, including DePaul University; Dominican University; Illinois State University; Loyola

University Chicago; Triton College; University of Illinois at Urbana–Champaign. Median composite ACT: 22. 19% scored over 26 on composite ACT.

Student Life Upper grades have uniform requirement, student council. Discipline rests primarily with faculty. Attendance at religious services is required.

Summer Programs Enrichment, advancement, sports, art/fine arts, computer instruction programs offered; session focuses on enrichment; held on campus; accepts girls; not open to students from other schools. 20 students usually enrolled. 2009 schedule: June 16 to July 24. Application deadline: May 1.

Tuition and Aid Day student tuition: $8200. Tuition installment plan (FACTS Tuition Payment Plan, monthly payment plans, individually arranged payment plans). Tuition reduction for siblings, merit scholarship grants, need-based scholarship grants, paying campus jobs available. In 2008–09, 31% of upper-school students received aid; total upper-school merit-scholarship money awarded: $26,050. Total amount of financial aid awarded in 2008–09: $427,700.

Admissions Traditional secondary-level entrance grade is 9. For fall 2008, 235 students applied for upper-level admission, 215 were accepted, 163 enrolled. ACT-Explore required. Deadline for receipt of application materials: none. No application fee required. On-campus interview recommended.

Athletics Interscholastic: basketball, bowling, cross-country running, golf, soccer, softball, swimming and diving, tennis, track and field, volleyball, water polo. 2 PE instructors, 28 coaches, 1 athletic trainer.

Computers Computers are regularly used in all classes. Computer network features include on-campus library services, online commercial services, Internet access, wireless campus network, Internet filtering or blocking technology, Edline. Campus intranet and computer access in designated common areas are available to students. Students grades are available online. The school has a published electronic and media policy.

Contact Miss Deborah Murphy, Assistant Principal. 708-771-8383. Fax: 708-488-2014. E-mail: dmurphy@trinityhs.org. Web site: www.trinityhs.org.

TRINITY HIGH SCHOOL

4011 Shelbyville Road
Louisville, Kentucky 40207-9427

Head of School: Robert J. Mullen, EdD

General Information Boys' day college-preparatory, arts, business, religious studies, and technology school, affiliated with Roman Catholic Church. Grades 9–12. Founded: 1953. Setting: suburban. 110-acre campus. 11 buildings on campus. Approved or accredited by National Catholic Education Association, Southern Association of Colleges and Schools, and Kentucky Department of Education. Endowment: $9 million. Total enrollment: 1,351. Upper school average class size: 21. Upper school faculty-student ratio: 1:13.

Upper School Student Profile Grade 9: 366 students (366 boys); Grade 10: 321 students (321 boys); Grade 11: 380 students (380 boys); Grade 12: 284 students (284 boys). 84% of students are Roman Catholic.

Faculty School total: 110. In upper school: 81 men, 29 women; 100 have advanced degrees.

Subjects Offered 20th century history, 3-dimensional art, accounting, acting, adolescent issues, advanced chemistry, advanced computer applications, advanced math, Advanced Placement courses, advanced studio art-AP, algebra, American Civil War, American democracy, American foreign policy, American government, American government-AP, American history, American history-AP, American literature, American literature-AP, analysis and differential calculus, analysis of data, anatomy and physiology, ancient history, ancient world history, applied arts, applied music, art, art and culture, art appreciation, art education, art history, art-AP, arts, arts appreciation, athletic training, athletics, band, banking, Basic programming, Bible as literature, biology, biology-AP, broadcasting, business, business education, business law, business mathematics, business studies, business technology, calculus, calculus-AP, campus ministry, career exploration, career planning, career/college preparation, cell biology, character education, cheerleading, chemistry, chemistry-AP, choir, choral music, chorus, Christian doctrine, Christian ethics, Christian scripture, church history, cinematography, civics, Civil War, classical civilization, classical Greek literature, classical music, college admission preparation, college awareness, college counseling, college placement, college planning, communication arts, communication skills, community service, comparative cultures, comparative government and politics, composition-AP, computer animation, computer applications, computer art, computer education, computer graphics, computer information systems, computer keyboarding, computer literacy, computer math, computer multimedia, computer music, computer processing, computer programming, computer science, computer skills, computer studies, computer technologies, computer technology certification, computer tools, computers, concert band, concert choir, conflict resolution, constitutional law, contemporary art, CPR, creative writing, critical studies in film, critical thinking, critical writing, data analysis, data processing, death and loss, decision making skills, developmental math, digital photography, DNA research, drama, drama performance, drawing, drawing and design, earth and space science, earth science, ecology, economics, economics and history, economics-AP, English, English language and composition-AP, English literature, English-AP, environmental studies, European civilization, European history, evolution, family life, fencing, film, film studies, finite math, first aid, forensics, French, general science, geography, geometry, German, health, health science, Hebrew scripture, Holocaust studies, HTML design, humanities, independent study, information technology, instrumental music, integrated math, interdisciplinary studies, Internet, jazz band, journalism, language arts, leadership and service, literature, literature-AP, martial arts, mathematics, modern civilization, moral and social development, multimedia design, music performance, musical theater, New Testament, news writing, newspaper, oil painting, painting, peace and justice, philosophy, photography, photojournalism, physical education, physical fitness, physical science, physics, physics-AP, post-calculus, pottery, pre-algebra, pre-calculus, probability and statistics, programming, psychology, public speaking, religion, religious studies, Roman civilization, Romantic period literature, Russian history, SAT/ACT preparation, science, sculpture, senior seminar, social justice, social psychology, social sciences, social studies, sociology, software design, space and physical sciences, Spanish, Spanish literature, Spanish-AP, speech and debate, sports medicine, sports nutrition, stage design, stained glass, statistics, student government, student publications, technology, trigonometry, U.S. history-AP, video film production, Web site design, weight training, Western civilization, Western civilization-AP, work-study, world civilizations, world history, world history-AP, yearbook.

Graduation Requirements Communication arts, English, ensembles, foreign language, humanities, mathematics, physical education (includes health), religion (includes Bible studies and theology), science, social studies (includes history), Several elective offerings. Community service is required.

Special Academic Programs Advanced Placement exam preparation; honors section; independent study; study at local college for college credit; study abroad; academic accommodation for the gifted, the musically talented, and the artistically talented; remedial reading and/or remedial writing; remedial math; programs in English, mathematics, general development for dyslexic students; special instructional classes for deaf students, blind students.

College Admission Counseling 319 students graduated in 2008; 310 went to college, including Bellarmine University; Eastern Kentucky University; Indiana University Bloomington; University of Dayton; University of Kentucky; University of Louisville. Other: 9 had other specific plans. Mean combined SAT: 1748, mean composite ACT: 24.

Student Life Upper grades have specified standards of dress, student council, honor system. Discipline rests primarily with faculty. Attendance at religious services is required.

Summer Programs Remediation, enrichment, advancement, sports, art/fine arts, computer instruction programs offered; session focuses on academic advancement & enrichment/sports camps; held on campus; accepts boys; not open to students from other schools. 1,000 students usually enrolled. 2009 schedule: June 1 to August 3. Application deadline: May 15.

Tuition and Aid Day student tuition: $9225. Guaranteed tuition plan. Tuition installment plan (monthly payment plans, individually arranged payment plans, Tuition Management Systems). Merit scholarship grants, need-based scholarship grants, paying campus jobs available. In 2008–09, 45% of upper-school students received aid. Total amount of financial aid awarded in 2008–09: $1,000,000.

Admissions Traditional secondary-level entrance grade is 9. High School Placement Test required. Deadline for receipt of application materials: none. Application fee required: $75. Interview required.

Athletics Interscholastic: baseball, basketball, bicycling, bowling, cheering, crew, cross-country running, diving, football, golf, hockey, ice hockey, lacrosse, power lifting, soccer, swimming and diving, tennis, track and field, volleyball, wrestling; intramural: alpine skiing, basketball, bocce, climbing, cricket, fencing, fishing, flag football, freestyle skiing, Frisbee, golf, hiking/backpacking, indoor soccer, kickball, life saving, martial arts, mountain biking, paddle tennis, rock climbing, skiing (downhill), snowboarding, soccer, softball, strength & conditioning, table tennis, ultimate Frisbee, volleyball, weight lifting, weight training; coed intramural: bowling. 5 PE instructors, 30 coaches, 3 athletic trainers.

Computers Computers are regularly used in all classes. Computer network features include on-campus library services, online commercial services, Internet access, wireless campus network, Internet filtering or blocking technology. Campus intranet, student e-mail accounts, and computer access in designated common areas are available to students. Students grades are available online. The school has a published electronic and media policy.

Contact Mr. Joseph M. Porter Jr., Vice President for Advancement. 502-736-2119. Fax: 502-899-2052. E-mail: porter@thsrock.net. Web site: www.trinityrocks.com.

TRINITY HIGH SCHOOL

581 Bridge Street
Manchester, New Hampshire 03104

Head of School: Mr. Denis Mailloux

General Information Coeducational day college-preparatory, arts, religious studies, and technology school, affiliated with Roman Catholic Church. Grades 9–12. Founded: 1886. Setting: urban. Nearest major city is Boston, MA. 5-acre campus. 2 buildings on campus. Approved or accredited by New England Association of Schools and Colleges and New Hampshire Department of Education. Total enrollment: 442. Upper school average class size: 15. Upper school faculty-student ratio: 1:16.

Upper School Student Profile Grade 9: 106 students (65 boys, 41 girls); Grade 10: 114 students (55 boys, 59 girls); Grade 11: 101 students (52 boys, 49 girls); Grade 12: 121 students (60 boys, 61 girls). 75% of students are Roman Catholic.

Faculty School total: 32. In upper school: 14 men, 18 women; 21 have advanced degrees.
Subjects Offered 3-dimensional art, advanced biology, advanced math, Advanced Placement courses, algebra, American history, American literature, art, Bible studies, biology, calculus, calculus-AP, chemistry, computer science, driver education, English, English literature, English-AP, ethics, French, geometry, grammar, health, history, human development, journalism, Latin, mathematics, physical education, physics, psychology, religion, science, social studies, sociology, Spanish, theology, trigonometry, U.S. history-AP, world history, world literature.
Special Academic Programs Advanced Placement exam preparation; honors section; study at local college for college credit.
College Admission Counseling 119 students graduated in 2008; all went to college, including Saint Anselm College; University of New Hampshire. Mean SAT critical reading: 546, mean SAT math: 540. 32% scored over 600 on SAT critical reading, 27% scored over 600 on SAT math.
Student Life Upper grades have specified standards of dress, student council, honor system. Discipline rests primarily with faculty. Attendance at religious services is required.
Tuition and Aid Day student tuition: $7740. Tuition installment plan (FACTS Tuition Payment Plan). Need-based scholarship grants available. In 2008–09, 10% of upper-school students received aid.
Admissions Traditional secondary-level entrance grade is 9. STS required. Deadline for receipt of application materials: none. Application fee required: $50. On-campus interview recommended.
Athletics Interscholastic: baseball (boys), basketball (b,g), cheering (g), cross-country running (b,g), football (b), gymnastics (g), hockey (b), ice hockey (b), indoor track & field (b,g), lacrosse (b), skiing (cross-country) (b,g), skiing (downhill) (b,g), soccer (b,g), softball (g), swimming and diving (b,g), tennis (b,g), volleyball (g), winter (indoor) track (b,g), wrestling (b); coed interscholastic: alpine skiing, golf, track and field; coed intramural: gymnastics. 1 PE instructor, 25 coaches, 1 athletic trainer.
Computers Computers are regularly used in desktop publishing, English, journalism, science, social science, yearbook classes. Computer resources include Internet access. Students grades are available online.
Contact Mr. Patrick Smith, Admissions Director. 603-668-2910 Ext. 18. Fax: 603-668-2913. E-mail: psmith@trinity-hs.org. Web site: www.trinity-hs.org.

TRINITY HIGH SCHOOL

12425 Granger Road
Garfield Heights, Ohio 44125

Head of School: Ms. Carla Fritsch

General Information Coeducational day college-preparatory, arts, business, religious studies, technology, Technical, and Medical school, affiliated with Roman Catholic Church. Grades 9–12. Founded: 1926. Setting: suburban. Nearest major city is Cleveland. 26-acre campus. 3 buildings on campus. Approved or accredited by National Catholic Education Association, North Central Association of Colleges and Schools, Ohio Catholic Schools Accreditation Association (OCSAA), and Ohio Department of Education. Total enrollment: 367. Upper school average class size: 17. Upper school faculty-student ratio: 1:10.
Upper School Student Profile Grade 9: 93 students (51 boys, 42 girls); Grade 10: 84 students (41 boys, 43 girls); Grade 11: 103 students (64 boys, 39 girls); Grade 12: 87 students (41 boys, 46 girls). 89% of students are Roman Catholic.
Faculty School total: 37. In upper school: 16 men, 21 women; 18 have advanced degrees.
Subjects Offered 3-dimensional art, accounting, advanced biology, advanced chemistry, advanced computer applications, advanced math, Advanced Placement courses, advanced studio art-AP, algebra, American government, American government-AP, American history, American history-AP, American literature, analysis and differential calculus, anatomy and physiology, animation, art, athletics, automated accounting, band, Bible, Bible studies, biology, bookkeeping, British literature, British literature (honors), business applications, business skills, business technology, calculus-AP, campus ministry, career and personal planning, career education, career education internship, career experience, career exploration, career planning, career/college preparation, Catholic belief and practice, ceramics, chemistry, choir, Christian and Hebrew scripture, Christian doctrine, Christian ethics, Christian scripture, Christian testament, church history, college admission preparation, college awareness, college counseling, college placement, college planning, college writing, communication skills, community service, comparative religion, competitive science projects, computer animation, computer applications, computer art, computer education, computer graphics, computer information systems, computer multimedia, computer technologies, computer technology certification, computer-aided design, concert band, concert choir, consumer economics, creative writing, critical thinking, critical writing, culinary arts, digital applications, drama performance, drawing and design, earth science, economics and history, electives, English, English literature and composition-AP, environmental science, ethics, European history, food and nutrition, foods, foreign language, four units of summer reading, geometry, global studies, government-AP, graphic arts, graphic design, graphics, guidance, health education, honors algebra, honors English, honors geometry, human anatomy, human biology, instrumental music, integrated math, Internet research, internship, lab science, library, life issues, Life of Christ, marching band, marine biology, Microsoft, moral theology, musical theater, neuroscience, oral communications, participation in sports, peace and justice, peer ministry, personal finance, photo shop, physical education, physics, play production, portfolio art, prayer/spirituality, pre-algebra, pre-calculus, psychology, public speaking, SAT/ACT preparation, speech, sports, studio art-AP, study skills, symphonic band, theology, U.S. government and politics-AP, video, video and animation, vocal ensemble, Web site design, wind ensemble, word processing, world history, yearbook.
Graduation Requirements Arts and fine arts (art, music, dance, drama), electives, English, government, human relations, mathematics, physical education (includes health), science, social studies (includes history), theology, Western civilization, service hours, internship.
Special Academic Programs Advanced Placement exam preparation; honors section; independent study; academic accommodation for the gifted and the artistically talented; remedial math; programs in English, mathematics, general development for dyslexic students.
College Admission Counseling 115 students graduated in 2008; 114 went to college, including Baldwin-Wallace College; Bowling Green State University; Cleveland State University; John Carroll University; Kent State University; The University of Akron. Other: 1 went to work. Median SAT critical reading: 500, median SAT math: 520, median SAT writing: 520, median combined SAT: 1540, median composite ACT: 20. 13% scored over 600 on SAT critical reading, 26% scored over 600 on SAT math, 16% scored over 600 on SAT writing, 15% scored over 1800 on combined SAT, 15% scored over 26 on composite ACT.
Student Life Upper grades have uniform requirement, student council. Discipline rests primarily with faculty. Attendance at religious services is required.
Summer Programs Enrichment, advancement, sports, art/fine arts programs offered; session focuses on recruitment; held both on and off campus; held at other schools; accepts boys and girls; open to students from other schools. 141 students usually enrolled. 2009 schedule: June to August. Application deadline: May.
Tuition and Aid Day student tuition: $8800. Tuition installment plan (individually arranged payment plans, private bank loans). Tuition reduction for siblings, need-based scholarship grants, middle-income loans, private bank loans available. In 2008–09, 25% of upper-school students received aid. Total amount of financial aid awarded in 2008–09: $356,000.
Admissions Traditional secondary-level entrance grade is 9. For fall 2008, 110 students applied for upper-level admission, 100 were accepted, 93 enrolled. Scholastic Testing Service High School Placement Test required. Deadline for receipt of application materials: none. Application fee required: $20. On-campus interview required.
Athletics Interscholastic: baseball (boys), basketball (b,g), cheering (g), cross-country running (b,g), danceline (g), football (b), ice hockey (b), soccer (g), softball (g), track and field (b,g), volleyball (g), wrestling (b); intramural: danceline (g); coed interscholastic: golf, indoor track & field; coed intramural: skiing (downhill), snowboarding. 1 PE instructor, 34 coaches, 1 athletic trainer.
Computers Computers are regularly used in all academic classes. Computer network features include on-campus library services, online commercial services, Internet access, wireless campus network, Internet filtering or blocking technology, Citrix, network printing, personal storage on network, weekly email grade reports, electronic newsletters, remote access, school website, online homework tracking system. Computer access in designated common areas is available to students. Students grades are available online. The school has a published electronic and media policy.
Contact Sr. Dian Majsterek, Administrative Assistant, Admissions and Marketing. 216-581-1644 Ext. 113. Fax: 216-581-9348. E-mail: SisterDian@ths.org. Web site: www.ths.org.

TRINITY-PAWLING SCHOOL

700 Route 22
Pawling, New York 12564

Head of School: Mr. Archibald A. Smith III

General Information Boys' boarding and day college-preparatory, arts, religious studies, technology, and ESL school, affiliated with Episcopal Church. Boarding grades 9–PG, day grades 7–PG. Founded: 1907. Setting: small town. Nearest major city is New York. Students are housed in single-sex dormitories. 140-acre campus. 23 buildings on campus. Approved or accredited by New York State Association of Independent Schools, New York State Board of Regents, and The Association of Boarding Schools. Member of National Association of Independent Schools and Secondary School Admission Test Board. Endowment: $32 million. Total enrollment: 320. Upper school average class size: 12. Upper school faculty-student ratio: 1:8.
Upper School Student Profile Grade 9: 43 students (43 boys); Grade 10: 64 students (64 boys); Grade 11: 80 students (80 boys); Grade 12: 71 students (71 boys); Postgraduate: 21 students (21 boys). 80% of students are boarding students. 20% are state residents. 34 states are represented in upper school student body. 20% are international students. International students from Canada, China, Ecuador, Republic of Korea, Saudi Arabia, and United Kingdom; 10 other countries represented in student body. 20% of students are members of Episcopal Church.
Faculty School total: 53. In upper school: 36 men, 15 women; 33 have advanced degrees; 49 reside on campus.
Subjects Offered Advanced Placement courses, advanced studio art-AP, algebra, American government, American history, American legal systems, American lit-

erature, American studies, anatomy, anatomy and physiology, architectural drawing, art, art history, art history-AP, Asian history, Asian studies, astronomy, Bible, biology, biology-AP, calculus, calculus-AP, ceramics, chemistry, chemistry-AP, choir, chorus, Christian ethics, civil rights, composition-AP, computer applications, computer information systems, computer math, computer music, computer programming, computer science, computer science-AP, computer technologies, constitutional history of U.S., data analysis, drafting, drama, drama performance, earth science, East Asian history, ecology, economics, economics-AP, English, English language-AP, English literature, English literature-AP, English-AP, English/composition-AP, environmental science, environmental science-AP, environmental studies, ESL, ethics, European history, European history-AP, fine arts, French, French language-AP, French studies, geology, geometry, government, government and politics-AP, government/civics, grammar, health science, history, honors algebra, honors English, honors geometry, honors U.S. history, honors world history, human anatomy, keyboarding, Latin, Latin American literature, Latin-AP, law and the legal system, literature, literature and composition-AP, Mandarin, mathematics, mechanical drawing, model United Nations, music, philosophy, photography, physical education, physics, physics-AP, physiology, political science, pre-calculus, psychology, public speaking, reading/study skills, religion, religious education, religious studies, SAT preparation, science, Shakespeare, social justice, social sciences, social studies, Spanish, Spanish language-AP, Spanish literature-AP, statistics and probability, statistics-AP, studio art, studio art-AP, study skills, theater, theology, trigonometry, U.S. government and politics, U.S. history, U.S. history-AP, Vietnam War, word processing, world history, writing, yearbook.

Graduation Requirements Arts and fine arts (art, music, dance, drama), English, foreign language, mathematics, physical education (includes health), religion (includes Bible studies and theology), science, social studies (includes history).

Special Academic Programs 17 Advanced Placement exams for which test preparation is offered; honors section; remedial reading and/or remedial writing; programs in English for dyslexic students; ESL (25 students enrolled).

College Admission Counseling 93 students graduated in 2008; all went to college, including Salve Regina University. Mean SAT critical reading: 580, mean SAT math: 570.

Student Life Upper grades have specified standards of dress, student council, honor system. Discipline rests equally with students and faculty. Attendance at religious services is required.

Tuition and Aid Day student tuition: $29,150; 7-day tuition and room/board: $41,250. Guaranteed tuition plan. Tuition installment plan (Insured Tuition Payment Plan, Key Tuition Payment Plan, monthly payment plans). Need-based scholarship grants, need-based loans available. In 2008–09, 35% of upper-school students received aid. Total amount of financial aid awarded in 2008–09: $2,000,000.

Admissions Traditional secondary-level entrance grade is 9. For fall 2008, 341 students applied for upper-level admission, 233 were accepted, 121 enrolled. PSAT or SAT, SLEP, SSAT, TOEFL, Wechsler Intelligence Scale for Children III or WISC-R required. Deadline for receipt of application materials: February 1. Application fee required: $40. On-campus interview required.

Athletics Interscholastic: alpine skiing, baseball, basketball, cross-country running, football, golf, hockey, ice hockey, lacrosse, ropes courses, skiing (downhill), soccer, squash, strength & conditioning, tennis, track and field, weight lifting, weight training, wrestling; intramural: alpine skiing, basketball, bicycling, climbing, fishing, fitness, floor hockey, fly fishing, Frisbee, golf, hiking/backpacking, ice skating, mountain biking, outdoor education, outdoor recreation, physical training, rock climbing, running, skiing (downhill), snowboarding, soccer, softball, squash, strength & conditioning, tennis, trap and skeet, ultimate Frisbee, wall climbing, weight lifting.

Computers Computers are regularly used in English, history, mathematics, remedial study skills, science classes. Computer network features include on-campus library services, online commercial services, Internet access, wireless campus network, Internet filtering or blocking technology. Campus intranet, student e-mail accounts, and computer access in designated common areas are available to students. Students grades are available online. The school has a published electronic and media policy.

Contact Mr. MacGregor Robinson, Director of Admission. 845-855-4825. Fax: 845-855-4827. E-mail: grobinson@trinitypawling.org. Web site: www.trinitypawling.org.

See Close-Up on page 996.

TRINITY PREPARATORY SCHOOL

5700 Trinity Prep Lane
Winter Park, Florida 32792

Head of School: Craig S. Maughan

General Information Coeducational day college-preparatory, arts, and technology school, affiliated with Episcopal Church. Grades 6–12. Founded: 1966. Setting: suburban. Nearest major city is Orlando. 100-acre campus. 12 buildings on campus. Approved or accredited by Florida Council of Independent Schools, National Association of Episcopal Schools, The College Board, and Florida Department of Education. Member of National Association of Independent Schools and Secondary School Admission Test Board. Endowment: $7.3 million. Total enrollment: 827. Upper school average class size: 17. Upper school faculty-student ratio: 1:12.

Upper School Student Profile Grade 9: 128 students (72 boys, 56 girls); Grade 10: 114 students (51 boys, 63 girls); Grade 11: 112 students (51 boys, 61 girls); Grade 12: 133 students (63 boys, 70 girls). 12% of students are members of Episcopal Church.

Faculty School total: 79. In upper school: 22 men, 38 women; 39 have advanced degrees.

Subjects Offered 20th century American writers, 20th century world history, 3-dimensional art, advanced math, Advanced Placement courses, advanced studio art-AP, algebra, American history, American literature, anatomy, animal science, art, athletic training, audio visual/media, band, Basic programming, Bible, biology, biology-AP, calculus, calculus-AP, character education, chemistry, chemistry-AP, civics, comparative religion, computer graphics, computer multimedia, computer processing, computer programming, computer programming-AP, concert band, concert choir, creative writing, critical studies in film, drama, economics, economics-AP, English, English language and composition-AP, English literature, English literature and composition-AP, environmental science, environmental science-AP, ethics, European history, European history-AP, fine arts, forensics, French, French language-AP, French literature-AP, geography, geometry, government and politics-AP, health, honors algebra, honors English, honors geometry, journalism, Latin, Latin-AP, life management skills, mathematics, music, music theory-AP, newspaper, painting, photography, physical education, physics, physics-AP, portfolio art, pottery, pre-algebra, pre-calculus, probability and statistics, psychology, psychology-AP, science, sculpture, social studies, Spanish, Spanish language-AP, Spanish literature-AP, speech, strings, studio art-AP, theater, trigonometry, U.S. government and politics-AP, U.S. history-AP, weight training, world history, world wide web design, writing, yearbook.

Graduation Requirements Arts and fine arts (art, music, dance, drama), computer science, electives, English, foreign language, life management skills, mathematics, physical education (includes health), science, social sciences.

Special Academic Programs Advanced Placement exam preparation; honors section; independent study; study at local college for college credit; academic accommodation for the gifted, the musically talented, and the artistically talented.

College Admission Counseling 128 students graduated in 2008; all went to college, including Duke University; Florida State University; Georgetown University; Northwestern University; University of Central Florida; University of Florida. Median SAT critical reading: 620, median SAT math: 650, median SAT writing: 620, median combined SAT: 1890, median composite ACT: 28. 62% scored over 600 on SAT critical reading, 76% scored over 600 on SAT math, 66% scored over 600 on SAT writing, 66% scored over 1800 on combined SAT, 71% scored over 26 on composite ACT.

Student Life Upper grades have specified standards of dress, student council, honor system. Discipline rests primarily with faculty. Attendance at religious services is required.

Summer Programs Remediation, enrichment, advancement, sports, art/fine arts, computer instruction programs offered; session focuses on enrichment; held on campus; accepts boys and girls; open to students from other schools. 300 students usually enrolled. 2009 schedule: June 9 to August 8. Application deadline: none.

Tuition and Aid Day student tuition: $15,200. Tuition installment plan (Insured Tuition Payment Plan, FACTS Tuition Payment Plan, monthly payment plans, semiannual and annual payment plans). Need-based scholarship grants, middle-income loans available. In 2008–09, 9% of upper-school students received aid. Total amount of financial aid awarded in 2008–09: $1,317,500.

Admissions Traditional secondary-level entrance grade is 9. For fall 2008, 82 students applied for upper-level admission, 35 were accepted, 27 enrolled. CTP, ISEE, PSAT, SAT or SSAT required. Deadline for receipt of application materials: February 12. Application fee required: $50. On-campus interview required.

Athletics Interscholastic: baseball (boys), basketball (b,g), bowling (b,g), cheering (g), cross-country running (b,g), diving (b,g), flag football (b), football (b), golf (b,g), lacrosse (b), physical fitness (b,g), soccer (b,g), softball (g), strength & conditioning (b,g), swimming and diving (b,g), tennis (b,g), track and field (b,g), volleyball (g), weight lifting (b,g), weight training (b,g); intramural: ropes courses (b,g), sailing (b,g), strength & conditioning (b,g). 5 PE instructors, 48 coaches, 1 athletic trainer.

Computers Computers are regularly used in animation, art, basic skills, career exploration, college planning, computer applications, creative writing, digital applications, economics, English, ethics, foreign language, keyboarding, library, mathematics, multimedia, music, newspaper, photography, photojournalism, programming, psychology, publications, religious studies, science, senior seminar, social sciences, social studies, stock market, study skills, theater, video film production, word processing, writing, yearbook classes. Computer network features include on-campus library services, online commercial services, Internet access, wireless campus network, Internet filtering or blocking technology. Computer access in designated common areas is available to students. Students grades are available online. The school has a published electronic and media policy.

Contact Sherryn M. Hay, Director of Admission. 321-282-2523. Fax: 407-671-6935. E-mail: hays@trinityprep.org. Web site: www.trinityprep.org.

ANNOUNCEMENT FROM THE SCHOOL Trinity Preparatory School has a rich tradition of excellence. Small class size and an exceptional faculty create the perfect environment for learning at the highest level. As an Episcopal school, students are encouraged to become stronger in their own faiths. Athletics, fine arts, and service are part of the student experience.

TRINITY PRESBYTERIAN SCHOOL

1700 East Trinity Boulevard
Montgomery, Alabama 36106

Head of School: Bob Neu

General Information Coeducational day college-preparatory, arts, religious studies, and technology school, affiliated with Christian faith. Grades K–12. Founded: 1970. Setting: urban. Nearest major city is Birmingham. 36-acre campus. 5 buildings on campus. Approved or accredited by Southern Association of Colleges and Schools and Alabama Department of Education. Total enrollment: 980. Upper school average class size: 25. Upper school faculty-student ratio: 1:15.

Upper School Student Profile Grade 9: 80 students (39 boys, 41 girls); Grade 10: 70 students (35 boys, 35 girls); Grade 11: 77 students (36 boys, 41 girls); Grade 12: 78 students (36 boys, 42 girls).

Faculty School total: 80. In upper school: 12 men, 32 women; 29 have advanced degrees.

Subjects Offered Accounting, Advanced Placement courses, algebra, American history, American history-AP, anatomy, art, band, biology, biology-AP, calculus, chemistry, chemistry-AP, Christian education, computer science, computers, debate, driver education, economics, English, English-AP, finite math, forensics, French, general science, geography, geometry, government/civics, graphic arts, health, history, humanities, keyboarding, Latin, mathematics, physical education, physical science, physics, physiology, religion, science, social science, social studies, Spanish, speech, world history.

Graduation Requirements Computer science, English, foreign language, humanities, mathematics, physical education (includes health), religion (includes Bible studies and theology), science, social science, social studies (includes history).

Special Academic Programs Advanced Placement exam preparation; honors section; independent study.

College Admission Counseling 78 students graduated in 2008; all went to college, including Auburn University; Auburn University Montgomery; Samford University; The University of Alabama; The University of Alabama at Birmingham; University of Mississippi. 35% scored over 26 on composite ACT.

Student Life Upper grades have uniform requirement, student council, honor system. Discipline rests primarily with faculty. Attendance at religious services is required.

Tuition and Aid Day student tuition: $6700. Tuition installment plan (2, 4, and 8-payment plans). Tuition reduction for siblings, merit scholarship grants, need-based scholarship grants available. In 2008–09, 2% of upper-school students received aid; total upper-school merit-scholarship money awarded: $1500. Total amount of financial aid awarded in 2008–09: $8000.

Admissions Traditional secondary-level entrance grade is 9. For fall 2008, 165 students applied for upper-level admission, 150 were accepted, 147 enrolled. Deadline for receipt of application materials: none. Application fee required: $150. On-campus interview required.

Athletics Interscholastic: aerobics/dance (girls), baseball (b), basketball (b,g), cheering (g), cross-country running (b,g), dance squad (g), dance team (g), football (b), golf (b,g), physical training (b,g), power lifting (b), soccer (b,g), softball (g), strength & conditioning (b,g), tennis (b,g), track and field (b,g), volleyball (g); coed interscholastic: golf. 1 PE instructor, 15 coaches, 1 athletic trainer.

Computers Computers are regularly used in all academic classes. Computer network features include on-campus library services, Internet access. Student e-mail accounts are available to students.

Contact Elizabeth Mosley, College Counselor. 334-213-2134. Fax: 334-277-6788. E-mail: emosley@trinitywildcats.com. Web site: www.trinitywildcats.com.

TRINITY SCHOOL

139 West 91st Street
New York, New York 10024

Head of School: Scull Preston Suellyn

General Information Coeducational day college-preparatory school, affiliated with Episcopal Church. Grades K–12. Founded: 1709. Setting: urban. 1 building on campus. Approved or accredited by National Association of Private Schools for Exceptional Children, New York State Association of Independent Schools, and New York Department of Education. Member of National Association of Independent Schools. Endowment: $50 million. Total enrollment: 976. Upper school average class size: 15. Upper school faculty-student ratio: 1:7.

Upper School Student Profile Grade 9: 110 students (55 boys, 55 girls); Grade 10: 110 students (55 boys, 55 girls); Grade 11: 110 students (55 boys, 55 girls); Grade 12: 110 students (55 boys, 55 girls). 15% of students are members of Episcopal Church.

Faculty School total: 163. In upper school: 50 men, 43 women; 72 have advanced degrees.

Subjects Offered Algebra, American history, American literature, art, art history, biology, calculus, ceramics, chemistry, computer math, computer programming, computer science, creative writing, dance, drama, driver education, economics, English, English literature, environmental science, ethics, European history, expository writing, fine arts, French, geometry, German, government/civics, Greek, history, Latin, marine biology, mathematics, music, photography, physical education, physics, psychology, religion, science, social studies, Spanish, speech, statistics, theater, trigonometry.

Graduation Requirements Arts and fine arts (art, music, dance, drama), English, foreign language, mathematics, physical education (includes health), religion (includes Bible studies and theology), science, social studies (includes history).

Special Academic Programs Advanced Placement exam preparation; honors section; independent study.

College Admission Counseling 110 students graduated in 2008; all went to college, including Brown University; Columbia College; Harvard University; University of Pennsylvania; Yale University.

Student Life Upper grades have specified standards of dress, student council. Discipline rests primarily with faculty. Attendance at religious services is required.

Tuition and Aid Day student tuition: $31,715. Middle-income loans, need-based grants available. In 2008–09, 20% of upper-school students received aid. Total amount of financial aid awarded in 2008–09: $2,500,000.

Admissions Traditional secondary-level entrance grade is 9. For fall 2008, 400 students applied for upper-level admission, 90 were accepted, 55 enrolled. Deadline for receipt of application materials: January 15. Application fee required: $60. On-campus interview required.

Athletics Interscholastic: baseball (boys), basketball (b,g), golf (b,g), indoor track & field (b,g), lacrosse (b,g), soccer (b,g), softball (g), tennis (b,g), track and field (b,g), volleyball (g), winter (indoor) track (b,g), wrestling (b); coed interscholastic: cross-country running, swimming and diving, water polo. 16 PE instructors, 45 coaches, 1 athletic trainer.

Computers Computers are regularly used in art, mathematics, science classes. Computer network features include on-campus library services, Internet access. The school has a published electronic and media policy.

Contact Lindsey Davis, Admissions Coordinator. 212-932-6819. Fax: 212-932-6812. E-mail: Lindsey.Davis@trinityschoolnyc.org. Web site: www.trinityschoolnyc.org.

TRINITY SCHOOL OF MIDLAND

3500 West Wadley Avenue
Midland, Texas 79707

Head of School: Mr. Geoffrey Butler

General Information Coeducational day college-preparatory, arts, bilingual studies, and technology school, affiliated with Episcopal Church. Grades PK–12. Founded: 1958. Setting: suburban. 20-acre campus. 7 buildings on campus. Approved or accredited by Independent Schools Association of the Southwest, Texas Education Agency, and Texas Department of Education. Member of National Association of Independent Schools. Endowment: $3.3 million. Total enrollment: 512. Upper school average class size: 16. Upper school faculty-student ratio: 1:8.

Upper School Student Profile Grade 9: 44 students (21 boys, 23 girls); Grade 10: 46 students (20 boys, 26 girls); Grade 11: 26 students (12 boys, 14 girls); Grade 12: 41 students (18 boys, 23 girls).

Faculty School total: 67. In upper school: 12 men, 13 women; 13 have advanced degrees.

Subjects Offered 3-dimensional art, advanced computer applications, algebra, American history, American literature, anatomy and physiology, art, art history, band, biology, British literature, British literature (honors), calculus, calculus-AP, chemistry, chemistry-AP, choir, college counseling, computer applications, computer graphics, computer science-AP, English language and composition-AP, English literature, English literature-AP, foreign language, French, French-AP, geometry, health, honors algebra, honors English, honors geometry, honors U.S. history, honors world history, instrumental music, jazz band, Latin, Latin-AP, modern European history, modern European history-AP, musical theater, photography, physical education, physics, pre-calculus, senior seminar, Spanish, Spanish-AP, strings, studio art, studio art-AP, U.S. government, U.S. government-AP, world history, world history-AP, world religions, yearbook.

Graduation Requirements Algebra, American government, American history, American literature, biology, chemistry, computer applications, English, English literature, foreign language, geometry, modern European history, physical education (includes health), physics, senior seminar, world history, Service Hours.

Special Academic Programs Advanced Placement exam preparation; honors section; independent study; study at local college for college credit; study abroad; academic accommodation for the musically talented.

College Admission Counseling 32 students graduated in 2008; all went to college, including Texas A&M University; Texas Christian University; Texas Tech University; The University of Texas at Austin. Mean SAT critical reading: 613, mean SAT math: 632. 49% scored over 600 on SAT critical reading, 64% scored over 600 on SAT math.

Student Life Upper grades have specified standards of dress, student council, honor system. Discipline rests equally with students and faculty. Attendance at religious services is required.

Tuition and Aid Day student tuition: $13,505. Tuition installment plan (monthly payment plans). Tuition reduction for siblings, merit scholarship grants, need-based scholarship grants available. In 2008–09, 20% of upper-school students received aid; total upper-school merit-scholarship money awarded: $26,950. Total amount of financial aid awarded in 2008–09: $219,785.

Admissions Traditional secondary-level entrance grade is 9. For fall 2008, 9 students applied for upper-level admission, 9 were accepted, 9 enrolled. Otis-Lennon School Ability Test and writing sample required. Deadline for receipt of application materials: none. Application fee required: $50.

Athletics Interscholastic: baseball (boys), basketball (b,g), cheering (g), cross-country running (b,g), football (b), golf (b,g), swimming and diving (b,g), tennis (b,g), track and field (b,g), volleyball (g); intramural: fitness (b,g), floor hockey (b,g), physical fitness (b,g), weight training (b,g); coed intramural: bowling, field hockey, kickball, soccer, table tennis, wall climbing. 8 coaches, 1 athletic trainer.

Computers Computers are regularly used in all academic, graphics, yearbook classes. Computer network features include on-campus library services, Internet access, wireless campus network, Internet filtering or blocking technology. The school has a published electronic and media policy.

Contact Mrs. Adrianne Clifton, Director of Admissions. 432-697-3281 Ext. 202. Fax: 432-697-7403. E-mail: a_clifton@trinitymidland.org. Web site: www.trinitymidland.org.

TRINITY VALLEY SCHOOL

7500 Dutch Branch Road
Fort Worth, Texas 76132

Head of School: Dr. Gary Krahn

General Information Coeducational day college-preparatory school. Grades K–12. Founded: 1959. Setting: urban. 75-acre campus. 7 buildings on campus. Approved or accredited by Independent Schools Association of the Southwest, Texas Education Agency, and Texas Department of Education. Member of National Association of Independent Schools. Endowment: $20 million. Total enrollment: 971. Upper school average class size: 16. Upper school faculty-student ratio: 1:8.

Upper School Student Profile Grade 9: 88 students (45 boys, 43 girls); Grade 10: 85 students (38 boys, 47 girls); Grade 11: 85 students (38 boys, 47 girls); Grade 12: 86 students (39 boys, 47 girls).

Faculty School total: 95. In upper school: 22 men, 19 women; 34 have advanced degrees.

Subjects Offered Algebra, American history, American history-AP, ancient history, art, Asian history, biology, biology-AP, British history, calculus, calculus-AP, ceramics, chemistry, chemistry-AP, Chinese, choir, computer science, computer science-AP, constitutional law, creative writing, debate, drama, economics, economics-AP, English, English language-AP, English literature-AP, French, French-AP, geometry, government-AP, government/civics, humanities, Latin, Latin-AP, leadership, medieval/Renaissance history, music theory, photography, physical education, physics, physics-AP, psychology-AP, Spanish, Spanish-AP, speech, statistics, statistics-AP, video film production, writing workshop, yearbook.

Graduation Requirements Algebra, American government, American history, arts and fine arts (art, music, dance, drama), biology, chemistry, economics, English, foreign language, geometry, physical education (includes health), physics, pre-calculus, Western civilization. Community service is required.

Special Academic Programs 22 Advanced Placement exams for which test preparation is offered; honors section; academic accommodation for the gifted, the musically talented, and the artistically talented.

College Admission Counseling 82 students graduated in 2008; all went to college, including Baylor University; Southern Methodist University; Texas A&M University; Texas Christian University; The University of Texas at Austin; University of Oklahoma. Mean SAT critical reading: 638, mean SAT math: 654, mean SAT writing: 641, mean combined SAT: 1933.

Student Life Upper grades have uniform requirement, student council, honor system. Discipline rests equally with students and faculty.

Summer Programs Enrichment, sports, art/fine arts, rigorous outdoor training programs offered; session focuses on enrichment; held both on and off campus; held at New Mexico and Colorado (backpacking); accepts boys and girls; open to students from other schools. 200 students usually enrolled. 2009 schedule: June 1 to June 12.

Tuition and Aid Day student tuition: $14,885. Tuition installment plan (monthly payment plans). Need-based scholarship grants, loans from bank associated with school available. In 2008–09, 13% of upper-school students received aid. Total amount of financial aid awarded in 2008–09: $423,128.

Admissions Traditional secondary-level entrance grade is 9. For fall 2008, 41 students applied for upper-level admission, 16 were accepted, 14 enrolled. CTP or ISEE required. Deadline for receipt of application materials: March 6. Application fee required: $75. Interview recommended.

Athletics Interscholastic: baseball (boys), basketball (b,g), cross-country running (b,g), field hockey (g), football (b), golf (b,g), soccer (b,g), softball (g), tennis (b,g), track and field (b,g), volleyball (b,g). 10 PE instructors, 2 athletic trainers.

Computers Computers are regularly used in all academic classes. Computer network features include on-campus library services, online commercial services, Internet access, Internet filtering or blocking technology. Campus intranet, student e-mail accounts, and computer access in designated common areas are available to students. Students grades are available online. The school has a published electronic and media policy.

Contact Judith Kinser, Director of Admissions and Financial Aid. 817-321-0116. Fax: 817-321-0105. E-mail: kinserj@trinityvalleyschool.org. Web site: www.trinityvalleyschool.org.

UNITED MENNONITE EDUCATIONAL INSTITUTE

614 Mersea Road 6, RR 5
Leamington, Ontario N8H 3V8, Canada

Head of School: Mr. Victor Winter

General Information Coeducational day college-preparatory, arts, and religious studies school, affiliated with Mennonite Church USA. Grades 9–12. Founded: 1945. Setting: rural. Nearest major city is Windsor, Canada. 12-acre campus. 3 buildings on campus. Approved or accredited by Ontario Department of Education. Language of instruction: English. Total enrollment: 80. Upper school average class size: 18. Upper school faculty-student ratio: 1:15.

Upper School Student Profile 65% of students are Mennonite Church USA.

Faculty School total: 10. In upper school: 5 men, 5 women; 1 has an advanced degree.

Subjects Offered 20th century physics, advanced chemistry, advanced math, algebra, American history, ancient world history, art, Bible, biology, business studies, career exploration, chemistry, choir, choral music, Christian ethics, church history, civics, communication arts, computer applications, computer studies, computer technologies, English, environmental geography, family studies, film and new technologies, foreign language, French as a second language, German, instrumental music, introduction to theater, mathematics, orchestra, parenting, religious studies, society challenge and change, theater arts.

Graduation Requirements Arts, Canadian geography, Canadian history, careers, civics, English, French, mathematics, physical education (includes health), science.

College Admission Counseling 19 students graduated in 2008; 16 went to college. Other: 2 went to work, 1 had other specific plans.

Student Life Upper grades have specified standards of dress, student council. Discipline rests equally with students and faculty. Attendance at religious services is required.

Tuition and Aid Day student tuition: CAN$5300. Tuition installment plan (monthly payment plans). Tuition reduction for siblings, need-based scholarship grants, need-based loans available. In 2008–09, 5% of upper-school students received aid. Total amount of financial aid awarded in 2008–09: CAN$4000.

Admissions Traditional secondary-level entrance grade is 9. For fall 2008, 19 students applied for upper-level admission, 19 were accepted, 19 enrolled. Deadline for receipt of application materials: none. No application fee required.

Athletics Interscholastic: badminton (boys, girls), baseball (b,g), basketball (b,g), cross-country running (b,g), floor hockey (b,g), golf (b), softball (g), volleyball (b,g); intramural: badminton (b,g), baseball (b,g), basketball (b,g), bicycling (b), football (b), indoor soccer (b,g), volleyball (b,g); coed intramural: skiing (downhill), ultimate Frisbee. 1 PE instructor.

Computers Computers are regularly used in all classes. Computer network features include on-campus library services, Internet access, Internet filtering or blocking technology.

Contact Mr. Victor J. Winter, Principal. 519-326 7448. Fax: 519-326-0278. E-mail: umeiadmi@mnsi.net. Web site: www.umei.on.ca.

UNITED NATIONS INTERNATIONAL SCHOOL

24-50 Franklin Roosevelt Drive
New York, New York 10010-4046

Head of School: Dr. Kenneth J. Wrye

General Information Coeducational day college-preparatory, arts, technology, English as Second Language & Eight Mother Tongue Programs, and International Baccalaureate school. Grades K–12. Founded: 1947. Setting: urban. 3-acre campus. 1 building on campus. Approved or accredited by International Baccalaureate Organization, New York State Association of Independent Schools, and New York State Board of Regents. Member of National Association of Independent Schools and European Council of International Schools. Endowment: $16.9 million. Total enrollment: 1,541. Upper school average class size: 20. Upper school faculty-student ratio: 1:10.

Upper School Student Profile Grade 9: 107 students (52 boys, 55 girls); Grade 10: 113 students (58 boys, 55 girls); Grade 11: 122 students (61 boys, 61 girls); Grade 12: 122 students (59 boys, 63 girls).

Faculty School total: 215. In upper school: 46 men, 56 women; 82 have advanced degrees.

Subjects Offered 3-dimensional art, algebra, American history, American literature, American studies, anthropology, Arabic, art, biology, calculus, chemistry, Chinese, community service, computer applications, computer science, creative writing, drama, economics, English, English literature, ESL, European history, expository writing, fine arts, French, geometry, German, history, humanities, Italian, Japanese, journalism, languages, library, mathematics, media production, modern languages, music, philosophy, photography, physical education, physics, psychology, Russian, science, social science, social studies, Spanish, theater arts, theory of knowledge, United Nations and international issues, world history, world literature, writing.

Graduation Requirements Art, electives, English, health and wellness, humanities, mathematics, modern languages, music, physical education (includes health), science, United Nations and international issues, International Baccalaureate, Theory of Knowledge, Extended Essay, Creative Aesthetic Service, individual project. Community service is required.
Special Academic Programs International Baccalaureate program; independent study; academic accommodation for the gifted, the musically talented, and the artistically talented; ESL (60 students enrolled).
College Admission Counseling 126 students graduated in 2008; 120 went to college, including American University; Cornell University; Duke University; McGill University; Smith College; The George Washington University. Other: 6 had other specific plans. Median SAT critical reading: 600, median SAT math: 600, median SAT writing: 600. 44% scored over 600 on SAT critical reading, 56% scored over 600 on SAT math, 48% scored over 600 on SAT writing.
Student Life Upper grades have specified standards of dress, student council. Discipline rests primarily with faculty.
Summer Programs Enrichment, ESL programs offered; session focuses on providing recreational enrichment in an international environment; held on campus; accepts boys and girls; open to students from other schools. 300 students usually enrolled. 2009 schedule: June 22 to July 31. Application deadline: May 30.
Tuition and Aid Day student tuition: $23,570–$24,110. Tuition installment plan (Key Education Resources—Monthly Payment Plan). Bursaries available. In 2008–09, 7% of upper-school students received aid. Total amount of financial aid awarded in 2008–09: $476,947.
Admissions Traditional secondary-level entrance grade is 9. For fall 2008, 82 students applied for upper-level admission, 40 were accepted, 33 enrolled. ISEE, PSAT and SAT for applicants to grade 11 and 12 or SSAT required. Deadline for receipt of application materials: November 15. Application fee required: $75. On-campus interview required.
Athletics Interscholastic: baseball (boys), basketball (b,g), soccer (b,g), softball (g), track and field (b,g), volleyball (b,g); intramural: volleyball (b,g); coed interscholastic: swimming and diving; coed intramural: aerobics, aerobics/dance, aerobics/Nautilus, aquatics, badminton, ball hockey, basketball, bicycling, canoeing/kayaking, climbing, cooperative games, dance, fitness, flag football, floor hockey, gymnastics, hiking/backpacking, independent competitive sports, indoor hockey, indoor soccer, indoor track, indoor track & field, jogging, jump rope, life saving, martial arts, modern dance, outdoor activities, physical fitness, physical training, rock climbing, ropes courses, rounders, running, soccer, softball, strength & conditioning, swimming and diving, table tennis, team handball, tennis, touch football, track and field, volleyball, wall climbing, weight training. 10 PE instructors, 28 coaches.
Computers Computers are regularly used in all classes. Computer network features include on-campus library services, online commercial services, Internet access, wireless campus network, media lab, TV studio, digital video streaming, digital video editing. Campus intranet, student e-mail accounts, and computer access in designated common areas are available to students. Students grades are available online.
Contact Admissions Office. 212-584-3071. Fax: 212-685-5023. E-mail: admissions@unis.org. Web site: www.unis.org.

THE UNITED WORLD COLLEGE—USA

PO Box 248
Montezuma, New Mexico 87731
Head of School: Lisa Darling

General Information Coeducational boarding college-preparatory, arts, bilingual studies, wilderness, search and rescue, conflict resolution, and service, science, humanities school. Grades 11–12. Founded: 1982. Setting: small town. Nearest major city is Santa Fe. Students are housed in single-sex dormitories. 168-acre campus. 20 buildings on campus. Approved or accredited by Independent Schools Association of the Southwest, International Baccalaureate Organization, and New Mexico Department of Education. Languages of instruction: English, Spanish, and French. Endowment: $12.2 million. Total enrollment: 200. Upper school average class size: 8. Upper school faculty-student ratio: 1:8.
Upper School Student Profile Grade 11: 100 students (50 boys, 50 girls); Grade 12: 100 students (50 boys, 50 girls). 100% of students are boarding students. 42 states are represented in upper school student body. 75% are international students. International students from Canada, Germany, Hong Kong, Mexico, Spain, and Venezuela; 75 other countries represented in student body.
Faculty School total: 30. In upper school: 17 men, 13 women; 25 have advanced degrees; 22 reside on campus.
Subjects Offered Anthropology, art, biology, calculus, chemistry, community service, conflict resolution, economics, English, English literature, environmental science, ESL, fine arts, French, German, history, information technology, International Baccalaureate courses, mathematics, music, physics, science, social science, social studies, Spanish, theater arts, theory of knowledge, world history, world literature, world religions.
Graduation Requirements Arts and fine arts (art, music, dance, drama), foreign language, International Baccalaureate courses, literature, mathematics, science, social science, theory of knowledge, extended essay, independent research, theory of knowledge. Community service is required.
Special Academic Programs International Baccalaureate program; honors section; independent study; academic accommodation for the musically talented and the artistically talented; ESL (40 students enrolled).
College Admission Counseling 100 students graduated in 2008; 94 went to college, including Brown University; Clark University; Dartmouth College; Earlham College; Harvard University; Princeton University. Other: 3 entered military service, 3 entered a postgraduate year. 25% scored over 600 on SAT critical reading, 75% scored over 600 on SAT math, 95% scored over 26 on composite ACT.
Student Life Upper grades have student council, honor system. Discipline rests equally with students and faculty.
Tuition and Aid 7-day tuition and room/board: $18,000. Guaranteed tuition plan. Tuition installment plan (all accepted U.S. students are awarded full merit scholarships, Need based financial assistance available to those who qualify). Merit scholarship grants, need-based scholarship grants, full-tuition merit scholarships awarded to all admitted U.S. citizens available. In 2008–09, 90% of upper-school students received aid; total upper-school merit-scholarship money awarded: $2,700,000. Total amount of financial aid awarded in 2008–09: $2,700,000.
Admissions Traditional secondary-level entrance grade is 11. For fall 2008, 385 students applied for upper-level admission, 50 were accepted, 50 enrolled. ACT, PSAT or SAT or PSAT, SAT, or ACT for applicants to grade 11 and 12 required. Deadline for receipt of application materials: January 15. No application fee required. Interview required.
Athletics Coed Intramural: aerobics, aerobics/dance, aerobics/Nautilus, alpine skiing, aquatics, backpacking, badminton, ballet, baseball, basketball, bicycling, billiards, canoeing/kayaking, climbing, combined training, cooperative games, cricket, cross-country running, dance, fitness, Frisbee, hiking/backpacking, jogging, modern dance, mountaineering, nordic skiing, outdoor activities, physical training, racquetball, ropes courses, running, sailing, skiing (cross-country), skiing (downhill), snowboarding, snowshoeing, soccer, softball, squash, strength & conditioning, swimming and diving, table tennis, tennis, volleyball, walking, weight lifting, weight training, wilderness, wilderness survival, yoga. 1 PE instructor, 12 athletic trainers.
Computers Computers are regularly used in art, foreign language, mathematics, music, science classes. Computer network features include on-campus library services, Internet access, wireless campus network, Internet filtering or blocking technology. Campus intranet, student e-mail accounts, and computer access in designated common areas are available to students. Students grades are available online.
Contact Tim Smith, Director of Admissions. 505-454-4201. Fax: 505-454-4294. E-mail: tim.smith@uwc-usa.org. Web site: www.uwc-usa.org.

See Close-Up on page 998.

UNIVERSITY CHRISTIAN PREPARATORY SCHOOL

4800 Mooringsport Road
Shreveport, Louisiana 71107
Head of School: Mrs. Susie Jefferson

General Information Coeducational day college-preparatory, general academic, arts, religious studies, and technology school, affiliated with Christian faith. Grades K–12. Founded: 1970. Setting: urban. Nearest major city is Bossier City. 25-acre campus. 14 buildings on campus. Approved or accredited by European Council of International Schools, Southern Association of Colleges and Schools, and Louisiana Department of Education. Total enrollment: 127. Upper school average class size: 14. Upper school faculty-student ratio: 1:14.
Upper School Student Profile Grade 9: 13 students (9 boys, 4 girls); Grade 10: 14 students (8 boys, 6 girls); Grade 11: 15 students (9 boys, 6 girls); Grade 12: 9 students (5 boys, 4 girls). 98% of students are Christian faith.
Faculty School total: 16. In upper school: 4 men, 4 women; 2 have advanced degrees.
Subjects Offered Advanced math, algebra, American government, American history, art, Bible, biology, business mathematics, chemistry, choral music, civics/free enterprise, computer applications, computer keyboarding, computer literacy, dance performance, earth science, English literature, general math, general science, geography, geometry, grammar, health, integrated math, Internet research, language arts, library, mathematics, physical education, physical science, pre-algebra, reading, reading/study skills, student government, student teaching, world geography, world history, yearbook.
Graduation Requirements Advanced math, algebra, American history, American literature, Bible, biology, British literature, chemistry, civics/free enterprise, computer applications, earth and space science, electives, foreign language, geometry, grammar, language arts, life science, literature, physical education (includes health), physical science, state history, world geography, world history.
College Admission Counseling 10 students graduated in 2008; 6 went to college, including University of Nebraska–Lincoln. Other: 3 went to work, 1 entered military service.
Student Life Upper grades have uniform requirement, student council, honor system. Discipline rests primarily with faculty. Attendance at religious services is required.
Tuition and Aid Day student tuition: $3800. Tuition installment plan (SMART Tuition Payment Plan, individually arranged payment plans). Tuition reduction for siblings available. In 2008–09, 14% of upper-school students received aid.

Admissions Traditional secondary-level entrance grade is 9. For fall 2008, 8 students applied for upper-level admission, 8 were accepted, 8 enrolled. Deadline for receipt of application materials: none. No application fee required. On-campus interview recommended.
Athletics Interscholastic: baseball (boys, girls), basketball (b,g), cheering (g), cross-country running (b,g), danceline (g), football (b), golf (b), softball (g), track and field (b,g); intramural: badminton (b,g), baseball (b,g), basketball (b,g), fitness (b,g), football (b), gymnastics (b,g), horseshoes (b,g), kickball (b,g), outdoor activities (b,g), physical fitness (b,g), physical training (b,g), pom squad (g), running (b,g), softball (b,g), strength & conditioning (b,g), tennis (b,g), track and field (b,g), walking (b,g), weight training (b,g); coed intramural: volleyball. 1 PE instructor, 2 coaches, 2 athletic trainers.
Computers Computers are regularly used in desktop publishing, graphic design, library, yearbook classes. Computer network features include Internet access.
Contact Office Manager. 318-221-2697. Fax: 318-221-2790. Web site: www.universitychristianprep.com.

UNIVERSITY LAKE SCHOOL

4024 Nagawicka Road
Hartland, Wisconsin 53029

Head of School: Mr. Bradley F. Ashley

General Information Coeducational day college-preparatory, arts, and technology school. Grades PK–12. Founded: 1956. Setting: small town. Nearest major city is Milwaukee. 180-acre campus. 5 buildings on campus. Approved or accredited by Independent Schools Association of the Central States. Member of National Association of Independent Schools. Endowment: $12.1 million. Total enrollment: 325. Upper school average class size: 12. Upper school faculty-student ratio: 1:9.
Upper School Student Profile Grade 9: 14 students (6 boys, 8 girls); Grade 10: 21 students (8 boys, 13 girls); Grade 11: 29 students (12 boys, 17 girls); Grade 12: 24 students (14 boys, 10 girls).
Faculty School total: 48. In upper school: 9 men, 5 women; 11 have advanced degrees.
Subjects Offered Algebra, American history, American literature, art, biology, calculus, chemistry, cinematography, computer science, creative writing, design, drama, English, English literature, environmental science, fine arts, French, geometry, government/civics, journalism, mathematics, music, photography, physical education, physics, science, social studies, Spanish, speech, statistics, theater, video film production, Web site design, world history, world literature, writing.
Graduation Requirements Art, arts and fine arts (art, music, dance, drama), computer science, English, foreign language, literature, mathematics, physical education (includes health), science, social studies (includes history), speech.
Special Academic Programs Advanced Placement exam preparation; honors section; independent study; study at local college for college credit; academic accommodation for the gifted, the musically talented, and the artistically talented; remedial reading and/or remedial writing; remedial math; programs in English for dyslexic students; special instructional classes for blind students.
College Admission Counseling 18 students graduated in 2008; 16 went to college, including Butler University; Dartmouth College; Drake University; Marquette University; Michigan Technological University; University of Wisconsin–Madison. Other: 2 had other specific plans. Mean SAT critical reading: 573, mean SAT math: 546, mean composite ACT: 25.
Student Life Upper grades have specified standards of dress, student council, honor system. Discipline rests equally with students and faculty.
Summer Programs Remediation, enrichment, advancement, sports, art/fine arts, computer instruction programs offered; session focuses on academics, arts, and athletics; held on campus; accepts boys and girls; open to students from other schools. 500 students usually enrolled. 2009 schedule: June 16 to August 6. Application deadline: May 31.
Tuition and Aid Day student tuition: $13,365. Tuition installment plan (Insured Tuition Payment Plan, FACTS Tuition Payment Plan, monthly payment plans). Merit scholarship grants, need-based scholarship grants available. In 2008–09, 25% of upper-school students received aid; total upper-school merit-scholarship money awarded: $37,000. Total amount of financial aid awarded in 2008–09: $128,541.
Admissions Traditional secondary-level entrance grade is 9. For fall 2008, 18 students applied for upper-level admission, 18 were accepted, 18 enrolled. Admissions testing, Kuhlmann-Anderson and Kulhmann-Anderson Level G (for grades 7-9) or Level H (for grades 10-12) required. Deadline for receipt of application materials: none. Application fee required: $25. On-campus interview recommended.
Athletics Interscholastic: basketball (boys, girls), field hockey (g), skiing (downhill) (b,g), soccer (b,g), softball (b,g), tennis (b,g), volleyball (g); coed interscholastic: alpine skiing, cross-country running, golf, ice hockey; coed intramural: alpine skiing, aquatics, volleyball, wall climbing. 2 PE instructors, 7 coaches.
Computers Computers are regularly used in all academic classes. Computer network features include on-campus library services, Internet access, wireless campus network, Internet filtering or blocking technology. Campus intranet and student e-mail accounts are available to students. Students grades are available online. The school has a published electronic and media policy.
Contact Mrs. Angela Wenger, Director of Admissions. 262-367-6011 Ext. 1455. Fax: 262-367-3146. E-mail: awenger@universitylake.org. Web site: www.universitylake.org.

UNIVERSITY LIGGETT SCHOOL

1045 Cook Road
Grosse Pointe Woods, Michigan 48236

Head of School: Dr. Joseph P. Healey

General Information Coeducational day college-preparatory, arts, and technology school. Grades PK–12. Founded: 1878. Setting: suburban. Nearest major city is Detroit. 50-acre campus. 4 buildings on campus. Approved or accredited by Independent Schools Association of the Central States. Member of National Association of Independent Schools. Endowment: $58 million. Total enrollment: 538. Upper school average class size: 14. Upper school faculty-student ratio: 1:8.
Upper School Student Profile Grade 9: 75 students (37 boys, 38 girls); Grade 10: 45 students (16 boys, 29 girls); Grade 11: 56 students (27 boys, 29 girls); Grade 12: 52 students (26 boys, 26 girls).
Faculty School total: 94. In upper school: 18 men, 15 women; 25 have advanced degrees.
Subjects Offered Advanced Placement courses, algebra, American history, American literature, art, art history, biology, calculus, ceramics, chemistry, creative writing, drama, engineering, English, English literature, environmental science-AP, European history, fine arts, French, geology, geometry, government/civics, Greek, health and wellness, history of jazz, instrumental music, Latin, mathematics, media arts, modern languages, photography, physical education, physical fitness, physics, physiology, psychology, SAT preparation, science, social studies, Spanish, technology, theater, Vietnam, world history.
Graduation Requirements Algebra, arts and fine arts (art, music, dance, drama), biology, chemistry, computer science, English, foreign language, geometry, government, mathematics, physical education (includes health), science, U.S. history, world history. Community service is required.
Special Academic Programs Advanced Placement exam preparation; honors section; independent study; term-away projects; study abroad; academic accommodation for the gifted, the musically talented, and the artistically talented; special instructional classes for deaf students.
College Admission Counseling 63 students graduated in 2008; all went to college, including DePaul University; Kalamazoo College; Loyola University Chicago; Michigan State University; University of Michigan. Mean SAT critical reading: 600, mean SAT math: 550, mean SAT writing: 600, mean composite ACT: 25. 54% scored over 600 on SAT critical reading, 43% scored over 600 on SAT math, 54% scored over 600 on SAT writing.
Student Life Upper grades have specified standards of dress, student council, honor system. Discipline rests primarily with faculty.
Summer Programs Remediation, enrichment, sports programs offered; session focuses on SAT preparation; held on campus; accepts boys and girls; open to students from other schools. 400 students usually enrolled. 2009 schedule: June 22 to August 12. Application deadline: none.
Tuition and Aid Day student tuition: $18,170–$18,830. Tuition installment plan (Insured Tuition Payment Plan, monthly payment plans, individually arranged payment plans, 2- and 4-payment plans). Merit scholarship grants, need-based scholarship grants, scholarships for children of alumni available. In 2008–09, 35% of upper-school students received aid; total upper-school merit-scholarship money awarded: $250,000. Total amount of financial aid awarded in 2008–09: $1,500,000.
Admissions Traditional secondary-level entrance grade is 9. For fall 2008, 400 students applied for upper-level admission, 109 were accepted, 63 enrolled. ERB CTP III or SSAT required. Deadline for receipt of application materials: none. Application fee required: $50. Interview required.
Athletics Interscholastic: baseball (boys), basketball (b,g), field hockey (g), football (b), golf (b), ice hockey (b,g), lacrosse (b,g), soccer (b,g), softball (g), tennis (b,g), volleyball (g); coed interscholastic: aerobics/dance, physical training, swimming and diving; coed intramural: ultimate Frisbee, weight lifting. 4 PE instructors, 15 coaches, 1 athletic trainer.
Computers Computers are regularly used in all academic classes. Computer network features include on-campus library services, online commercial services, Internet access, wireless campus network, Internet filtering or blocking technology. Campus intranet, student e-mail accounts, and computer access in designated common areas are available to students. Students grades are available online. The school has a published electronic and media policy.
Contact Mr. Kevin Breen, Director of Admissions. 313-884-4444 Ext. 218. Fax: 313-884-1775. E-mail: kbreen@uls.org. Web site: www.uls.org.

UNIVERSITY OF CHICAGO LABORATORY SCHOOLS

1362 East 59th Street
Chicago, Illinois 60637

Head of School: Dr. David W. Magill

General Information Coeducational day college-preparatory school. Grades N–12. Founded: 1896. Setting: urban. 11-acre campus. 3 buildings on campus. Approved or accredited by Independent Schools Association of the Central States, North Central Association of Colleges and Schools, and Illinois Department of Education. Member of National Association of Independent Schools. Endowment: $18.4 million. Total enrollment: 1,774. Upper school average class size: 16. Upper school faculty-student ratio: 1:10.

Upper School Student Profile Grade 9: 130 students (61 boys, 69 girls); Grade 10: 120 students (65 boys, 55 girls); Grade 11: 119 students (61 boys, 58 girls); Grade 12: 129 students (61 boys, 68 girls).

Faculty School total: 212. In upper school: 29 men, 33 women; 52 have advanced degrees.

Subjects Offered Acting, African-American history, algebra, American history, art, art history, art history-AP, biology, biology-AP, calculus, calculus-AP, chemistry, chemistry-AP, Chinese, community service, computer science, creative writing, drama, drawing, driver education, economics-AP, English, English literature, European history, European history-AP, expository writing, fine arts, French, French-AP, geometry, German, German-AP, government/civics, history, Holocaust, jazz band, journalism, Latin, mathematics, modern European history, modern European history-AP, music, music theory-AP, orchestra, painting, photography, physical education, physics, physics-AP, post-calculus, science, sculpture, social studies, Spanish, Spanish-AP, statistics, statistics-AP, studio art, theater, trigonometry, U.S. history-AP, Web site design, Western civilization, world history, writing skills, yearbook.

Graduation Requirements Arts and fine arts (art, music, dance, drama), English, foreign language, mathematics, music, physical education (includes health), science, social studies (includes history). Community service is required.

Special Academic Programs 17 Advanced Placement exams for which test preparation is offered; accelerated programs; independent study; study at local college for college credit; remedial reading and/or remedial writing; remedial math.

College Admission Counseling 128 students graduated in 2008; 127 went to college, including Northwestern University; The George Washington University; University of Chicago; University of Illinois at Urbana–Champaign; Wellesley College; Yale University. Other: 1 had other specific plans. Median SAT critical reading: 669, median SAT math: 677, median SAT writing: 676, median composite ACT: 29. 80% scored over 600 on SAT critical reading, 75% scored over 600 on SAT math, 75% scored over 600 on SAT writing, 75% scored over 26 on composite ACT.

Student Life Upper grades have student council. Discipline rests primarily with faculty.

Summer Programs Enrichment, advancement, sports programs offered; session focuses on advancement of placement in courses; held on campus; accepts boys and girls; open to students from other schools. 200 students usually enrolled. 2009 schedule: June 22 to July 31. Application deadline: May 15.

Tuition and Aid Day student tuition: $21,480. Tuition installment plan (monthly payment plans, quarterly payment plan). Need-based scholarship grants available. In 2008–09, 16% of upper-school students received aid. Total amount of financial aid awarded in 2008–09: $866,043.

Admissions Traditional secondary-level entrance grade is 9. For fall 2008, 174 students applied for upper-level admission, 79 were accepted, 54 enrolled. ISEE required. Deadline for receipt of application materials: December 1. Application fee required: $75. On-campus interview required.

Athletics Interscholastic: baseball (boys), basketball (b,g), cross-country running (b,g), soccer (b,g), swimming and diving (b,g), tennis (b,g), track and field (b,g), volleyball (g), winter (indoor) track (b,g); intramural: dance squad (g), weight training (b,g); coed interscholastic: cross-country running, golf; coed intramural: fencing, life saving. 12 PE instructors, 31 coaches, 1 athletic trainer.

Computers Computers are regularly used in mathematics, music, newspaper, science, yearbook classes. Computer network features include on-campus library services, Internet access, wireless campus network. Student e-mail accounts are available to students. The school has a published electronic and media policy.

Contact William Newman, Director of Admissions and Financial Aid. 773-702-9451. Fax: 773-702-7455. E-mail: wnewman@ucls.uchicago.edu. Web site: www.ucls.uchicago.edu/.

ANNOUNCEMENT FROM THE SCHOOL Students at the University of Chicago Laboratory Schools take advantage of many opportunities available at the University of Chicago, where they may study world history with museum materials, receive library privileges at the University libraries, work with professors on research, and enroll as high school students in University courses.

UNIVERSITY OF TORONTO SCHOOLS

371 Bloor Street West
Toronto, Ontario M5S 2R7, Canada

Head of School: Ms. Michaele Robertson

General Information Coeducational day college-preparatory, arts, bilingual studies, and liberal arts and sciences school. Grades 7–12. Founded: 1910. Setting: urban. 3-acre campus. 1 building on campus. Approved or accredited by Ontario Ministry of Education. Candidate for accreditation by North Central Association of Colleges and Schools. Language of instruction: English. Total enrollment: 640. Upper school average class size: 25. Upper school faculty-student ratio: 1:12.

Faculty School total: 65.

Subjects Offered 20th century history, Advanced Placement courses, American history, ancient world history, art, biology, calculus, Canadian geography, Canadian history, Canadian literature, career education, chemistry, chemistry-AP, civics, drama, economics, English, English literature, European history, French, French-AP, general science, geometry, German, German-AP, history, history-AP, language, language-AP, Latin, law, mathematics, mathematics-AP, music composition, philosophy, physical education, physics, physics-AP, science, Spanish, Spanish-AP, studio art, visual arts, world history, world issues.

Graduation Requirements Arts, business studies, Canadian geography, Canadian history, career education, civics, computer studies, English, French, mathematics, physical education (includes health), science, 40 hours of community service, literacy test, additional language.

Special Academic Programs Advanced Placement exam preparation; honors section; independent study; study abroad; academic accommodation for the gifted.

College Admission Counseling 100 students graduated in 2008; 99 went to college, including McGill University; McMaster University; Queen's University at Kingston; The University of Western Ontario; University of Toronto; University of Waterloo. Other: 1 had other specific plans.

Student Life Upper grades have student council, honor system. Discipline rests primarily with faculty.

Tuition and Aid Day student tuition: CAN$15,900. Tuition installment plan (monthly payment plans, 2-installment plan). Bursaries, merit scholarship grants available.

Admissions Traditional secondary-level entrance grade is 9. School's own test and SSAT required. Deadline for receipt of application materials: March 1. Application fee required: CAN$100. On-campus interview required.

Athletics Interscholastic: aquatics (boys, girls), badminton (b,g), basketball (b,g), cross-country running (b,g), curling (b,g), field hockey (g), Frisbee (b,g), golf (b,g), ice hockey (b), independent competitive sports (b,g), indoor hockey (b,g), indoor track (b,g), outdoor activities (b,g), rugby (b,g), running (b,g), skiing (cross-country) (b,g), skiing (downhill) (b,g), soccer (b,g), swimming and diving (b,g), tennis (b,g), track and field (b,g), ultimate Frisbee (b,g), volleyball (b,g), wrestling (b,g); intramural: aerobics (b,g), aerobics/dance (b,g), aquatics (b,g), badminton (b,g), ball hockey (b,g), basketball (b,g), combined training (b,g), cooperative games (b,g), cross-country running (b,g), fitness (b,g), fitness walking (b,g), floor hockey (b,g), Frisbee (b,g), outdoor activities (b,g), physical fitness (b,g), physical training (b,g), self defense (b,g), soccer (b,g), strength & conditioning (b,g), swimming and diving (b,g), table tennis (b,g), volleyball (b,g), walking (b,g), weight lifting (b,g), weight training (b,g), yoga (b,g); coed interscholastic: aquatics, badminton, basketball, cross-country running, curling, Frisbee, golf, independent competitive sports, indoor hockey, indoor track, outdoor activities, rugby, running, skiing (cross-country), skiing (downhill), soccer, swimming and diving, tennis, track and field, ultimate Frisbee, volleyball, wrestling; coed intramural: aerobics, aerobics/dance, aquatics, badminton, ball hockey, basketball, climbing, combined training, cooperative games, cross-country running, fitness, fitness walking, floor hockey, Frisbee, outdoor activities, physical fitness, physical training, rock climbing, ropes courses, self defense, soccer, strength & conditioning, swimming and diving, table tennis, volleyball, walking, weight lifting, weight training, yoga. 6 PE instructors, 40 coaches, 1 athletic trainer.

Computers Computers are regularly used in all academic classes. Computer resources include on-campus library services, Internet access, wireless campus network, Internet filtering or blocking technology. Campus intranet and student e-mail accounts are available to students. The school has a published electronic and media policy.

Contact Ms. Kristine Maitland, Admission Assistant. 416-946-7995. Fax: 416-978-6775. E-mail: info@utschools.ca. Web site: www.utschools.ca.

UNIVERSITY PREP

8000 25th Avenue NE
Seattle, Washington 98115

Head of School: Erica L. Hamlin

General Information Coeducational day college-preparatory, arts, bilingual studies, technology, and Global Education school; primarily serves dyslexic students. Grades 6–12. Founded: 1976. Setting: urban. 6-acre campus. 5 buildings on campus. Approved or accredited by Northwest Association of Schools and Colleges, Pacific Northwest Association of Independent Schools, and Washington Department of

Education. Member of National Association of Independent Schools. Endowment: $5 million. Total enrollment: 484. Upper school average class size: 16. Upper school faculty-student ratio: 1:9.

Upper School Student Profile Grade 6: 60 students (34 boys, 26 girls); Grade 7: 68 students (34 boys, 34 girls); Grade 8: 69 students (33 boys, 36 girls); Grade 9: 73 students (40 boys, 33 girls); Grade 10: 71 students (35 boys, 36 girls); Grade 11: 66 students (34 boys, 32 girls); Grade 12: 76 students (36 boys, 40 girls).

Faculty School total: 59. In upper school: 16 men, 20 women; 29 have advanced degrees.

Subjects Offered 3-dimensional art, advanced chemistry, advanced math, algebra, American history, American literature, art, art history, Asian literature, astronomy, band, biology, British literature, calculus, career and personal planning, career/college preparation, chemistry, Chinese, civil rights, classical civilization, community service, comparative religion, computer art, computer science, conceptual physics, creative writing, dance, decision making skills, digital art, drafting, drama, drama performance, dramatic arts, drawing, ecology, economics, English, English literature, ensembles, European history, expository writing, film studies, fine arts, French, geography, geometry, government/civics, history, history of religion, independent study, information technology, introduction to technology, Japanese, Japanese history, Japanese studies, jazz ensemble, journalism, Latin American studies, life skills, literary magazine, mathematics, medieval/Renaissance history, minority studies, music, music theory, Pacific Northwest seminar, painting, philosophy, photography, physical education, physics, poetry, programming, psychology, public policy, Russian studies, science, senior thesis, social justice, Spanish, stagecraft, student publications, theater, trigonometry, vocal ensemble, women in society, world literature, yearbook.

Graduation Requirements American history, arts and fine arts (art, music, dance, drama), biology, chemistry, English, foreign language, life skills, mathematics, Pacific Northwest seminar, physical education (includes health), physics, science, senior thesis, social studies (includes history). Community service is required.

Special Academic Programs Advanced Placement exam preparation; independent study; study abroad; programs in English, mathematics, general development for dyslexic students; special instructional classes for college-bound students with high intellectual potential who have diagnosed specific learning disability.

College Admission Counseling 59 students graduated in 2008; 57 went to college, including Santa Clara University; The George Washington University; University of Pennsylvania; University of Redlands; University of Washington; Washington State University. Other: 1 went to work, 1 had other specific plans. Median SAT critical reading: 615, median SAT math: 620, median SAT writing: 620, median combined SAT: 1820, median composite ACT: 27. 66% scored over 600 on SAT critical reading, 61% scored over 600 on SAT math, 63% scored over 600 on SAT writing, 57% scored over 1800 on combined SAT, 59% scored over 26 on composite ACT.

Student Life Upper grades have student council, honor system. Discipline rests equally with students and faculty.

Tuition and Aid Day student tuition: $22,310–$23,490. Tuition installment plan (Insured Tuition Payment Plan, Key Tuition Payment Plan, monthly payment plans, Dewar Tuition Refund Plan). Need-based scholarship grants available. In 2008–09, 16% of upper-school students received aid. Total amount of financial aid awarded in 2008–09: $918,780.

Admissions Traditional secondary-level entrance grade is 9. For fall 2008, 164 students applied for upper-level admission, 74 were accepted, 25 enrolled. ISEE required. Deadline for receipt of application materials: January 15. Application fee required: $65. On-campus interview required.

Athletics Interscholastic: baseball (boys), basketball (b,g), cross-country running (b,g), Frisbee (b,g), soccer (b,g), softball (g), tennis (b,g), track and field (b,g), volleyball (g); intramural: ultimate Frisbee (b,g); coed interscholastic: ultimate Frisbee; coed intramural: aerobics, aerobics/dance, hiking/backpacking, rock climbing, skiing (downhill), snowboarding, strength & conditioning, ultimate Frisbee, weight training, yoga. 4 PE instructors, 65 coaches.

Computers Computers are regularly used in English, foreign language, history, information technology, journalism, library, mathematics, music, publications, science, technology, yearbook classes. Computer network features include on-campus library services, online commercial services, Internet access, wireless campus network, Internet filtering or blocking technology. Campus intranet, student e-mail accounts, and computer access in designated common areas are available to students. The school has a published electronic and media policy.

Contact Melaine Taylor, Associate Director of Admission. 206-523-6407. Fax: 206-525-5320. E-mail: admissionoffice@universityprep.org. Web site: www.universityprep.org.

ANNOUNCEMENT FROM THE SCHOOL University Prep is committed to developing each student's potential to become an intellectually courageous, socially responsible citizen of the world. The curriculum is designed to inspire students' natural curiosity and to instill within them the desire for lifelong learning. Small classes, exceptional teachers, and innovative course work challenge students to develop creativity and critical-thinking skills. University Prep students learn to solve problems and make mature decisions, as well as learn the value of diversity and the importance of giving back to their community.

UNIVERSITY SCHOOL OF JACKSON

232/240 McClellan Road
Jackson, Tennessee 38305

Head of School: Clay Lilienstern

General Information Coeducational day college-preparatory, arts, and technology school. Grades PK–12. Founded: 1970. Setting: suburban. 148-acre campus. 2 buildings on campus. Approved or accredited by Southern Association of Colleges and Schools and Tennessee Department of Education. Member of National Association of Independent Schools. Endowment: $85,000. Total enrollment: 1,221. Upper school average class size: 20. Upper school faculty-student ratio: 1:11.

Upper School Student Profile Grade 9: 106 students (56 boys, 50 girls); Grade 10: 89 students (48 boys, 41 girls); Grade 11: 81 students (38 boys, 43 girls); Grade 12: 75 students (39 boys, 36 girls).

Faculty School total: 100. In upper school: 12 men, 19 women; 26 have advanced degrees.

Subjects Offered 3-dimensional art, 3-dimensional design, accounting, advanced chemistry, advanced math, Advanced Placement courses, algebra, American history, American history-AP, anatomy and physiology, art, biology, biology-AP, calculus, calculus-AP, chemistry, chemistry-AP, chorus, community service, computer applications, computer keyboarding, computer programming, computer science, computer science-AP, creative writing, current events, dramatic arts, ecology, ecology, environmental systems, economics, English, English language-AP, English literature-AP, environmental science-AP, European history-AP, fine arts, French, geography, geology, geometry, government/civics, honors algebra, honors English, honors geometry, humanities, mathematics, music theory, music theory-AP, performing arts, physical education, physical science, physics, pre-calculus, psychology, science, social studies, Spanish, Spanish language-AP, speech and debate, trigonometry, U.S. history, U.S. history-AP, vocal ensemble, world history, world religions, yearbook.

Graduation Requirements Arts and fine arts (art, music, dance, drama), computer science, English, foreign language, mathematics, science, social studies (includes history), 50 hours of community service.

Special Academic Programs Advanced Placement exam preparation; honors section; academic accommodation for the gifted, the musically talented, and the artistically talented; ESL (12 students enrolled).

College Admission Counseling 109 students graduated in 2008; all went to college, including Lambuth University; Rhodes College; The University of Tennessee; The University of Tennessee at Martin; Union University; University of Mississippi. Median SAT critical reading: 540, median SAT math: 560, median SAT writing: 560, median combined SAT: 1660, median composite ACT: 24. 27% scored over 600 on SAT critical reading, 32% scored over 600 on SAT math, 27% scored over 600 on SAT writing, 25% scored over 1800 on combined SAT, 30% scored over 26 on composite ACT.

Student Life Upper grades have uniform requirement, student council, honor system. Discipline rests primarily with faculty.

Summer Programs Remediation, enrichment, sports, art/fine arts, computer instruction programs offered; session focuses on enrichment and remediation; held on campus; accepts boys and girls; open to students from other schools. 500 students usually enrolled. 2009 schedule: June 1 to July 31. Application deadline: none.

Tuition and Aid Day student tuition: $5160–$6825. Tuition installment plan (monthly payment plans, quarterly payment plan). Tuition reduction for siblings, need-based financial aid available. In 2008–09, 3% of upper-school students received aid. Total amount of financial aid awarded in 2008–09: $150,000.

Admissions Traditional secondary-level entrance grade is 9. For fall 2008, 193 students applied for upper-level admission, 162 were accepted, 153 enrolled. Math Placement Exam, Otis-Lennon School Ability Test, SCAT and writing sample required. Deadline for receipt of application materials: none. Application fee required: $50. On-campus interview required.

Athletics Interscholastic: baseball (boys), basketball (b,g), cheering (g), cross-country running (b,g), football (b), golf (b,g), soccer (b,g), softball (g), tennis (b,g), track and field (b,g), volleyball (g), weight lifting (b,g), weight training (b,g); intramural: bowling (b,g); coed interscholastic: trap and skeet; coed intramural: bowling. 2 coaches.

Computers Computers are regularly used in art, English, foreign language, history, journalism, keyboarding, music, science, technology, theater arts, word processing, writing, yearbook classes. Computer network features include on-campus library services, online commercial services, Internet access. Students grades are available online. The school has a published electronic and media policy.

Contact Kay Shearin, Director of Admissions. 731-660-1692. Fax: 731-668-6910. E-mail: kshearin@usjbruins.org. Web site: www.usjbruins.org.

UNIVERSITY SCHOOL OF MILWAUKEE

2100 West Fairy Chasm Road
Milwaukee, Wisconsin 53217

Head of School: Ward J. Ghory, EdD

General Information Coeducational day college-preparatory, arts, and technology school. Grades PK–12. Founded: 1851. Setting: suburban. 127-acre campus. 2 buildings on campus. Approved or accredited by Independent Schools Association of the Central States and Wisconsin Department of Education. Member of National

Association of Independent Schools and Secondary School Admission Test Board. Endowment: $53 million. Total enrollment: 1,082. Upper school average class size: 15. Upper school faculty-student ratio: 1:9.

Upper School Student Profile Grade 9: 93 students (42 boys, 51 girls); Grade 10: 90 students (55 boys, 35 girls); Grade 11: 89 students (43 boys, 46 girls); Grade 12: 94 students (59 boys, 35 girls).

Faculty School total: 103. In upper school: 19 men, 17 women; 29 have advanced degrees.

Subjects Offered Algebra, American history, American literature, art, art history, band, biology, calculus, chemistry, computer programming, computer science, concert choir, discrete math, drama, drawing, economics, English, English literature, European history, expository writing, French, geometry, health, Latin, mathematics, music, orchestra, painting, photography, physical education, physics, printmaking, psychology, SAT/ACT preparation, sculpture, Spanish, statistics, theater, U.S. history, world history, world literature.

Graduation Requirements Arts and fine arts (art, music, dance, drama), English, foreign language, history, mathematics, physical education (includes health), science, 40 hours of community service.

Special Academic Programs Advanced Placement exam preparation; honors section; independent study; study at local college for college credit.

College Admission Counseling 86 students graduated in 2008; all went to college, including Dartmouth College; Georgetown University; Northwestern University; University of Wisconsin–Madison; Washington University in St. Louis. Median SAT critical reading: 647, median SAT math: 635, median SAT writing: 646, median combined SAT: 1928, median composite ACT: 28. 69% scored over 600 on SAT critical reading, 67% scored over 600 on SAT math, 69% scored over 600 on SAT writing, 67% scored over 1800 on combined SAT, 80% scored over 26 on composite ACT.

Student Life Upper grades have specified standards of dress, student council, honor system. Discipline rests equally with students and faculty.

Summer Programs Enrichment, sports, art/fine arts, computer instruction programs offered; session focuses on reading, writing, math, science, sports, visual arts, music, drama, and computer enrichment/ instruction; held on campus; accepts boys and girls; open to students from other schools. 1,500 students usually enrolled. 2009 schedule: June 15 to August 21. Application deadline: none.

Tuition and Aid Day student tuition: $18,495. Tuition installment plan (FACTS Tuition Payment Plan, monthly payment plans). Need-based scholarship grants available. In 2008–09, 21% of upper-school students received aid. Total amount of financial aid awarded in 2008–09: $742,991.

Admissions Traditional secondary-level entrance grade is 9. For fall 2008, 53 students applied for upper-level admission, 25 were accepted, 19 enrolled. ERB Achievement Test required. Deadline for receipt of application materials: none. Application fee required: $50. On-campus interview required.

Athletics Interscholastic: baseball (boys), basketball (b,g), cross-country running (b,g), diving (b,g), field hockey (g), football (b), golf (b), ice hockey (b,g), lacrosse (b), skiing (downhill) (b,g), soccer (b,g), swimming and diving (b,g), tennis (b,g), track and field (b,g), volleyball (g). 2 PE instructors, 42 coaches, 2 athletic trainers.

Computers Computers are regularly used in college planning, creative writing, English, foreign language, history, journalism, mathematics, science, yearbook classes. Computer network features include on-campus library services, online commercial services, Internet access, wireless campus network, Internet filtering or blocking technology. Student e-mail accounts are available to students. Students grades are available online. The school has a published electronic and media policy.

Contact Kathleen Friedman, Director of Admissions. 414-540-3321. Fax: 414-352-8076. E-mail: kfriedman@usmk12.org. Web site: www.usmk12.org.

ANNOUNCEMENT FROM THE SCHOOL USM is a prekindergarten (age 3) through grade 12, coeducational, college-preparatory school. A diverse student body of 1,081 benefits from an outstanding faculty, small classes, and a challenging curriculum in an atmosphere of mutual respect. Features of the School include foreign language instruction (prekindergarten-grade 12), a focus on writing, integration of technology in the classroom, a successful Advanced Placement program, competitive sports, and a variety of visual and performing arts opportunities.

UNIVERSITY SCHOOL OF NOVA SOUTHEASTERN UNIVERSITY

3301 College Avenue
Sonken Building
Fort Lauderdale, Florida 33314

Head of School: Dr. Jerome S. Chermak

General Information Coeducational day college-preparatory school. Grades PK–12. Founded: 1970. Setting: suburban. 300-acre campus. 2 buildings on campus. Approved or accredited by Association of Independent Schools of Florida, Florida Council of Independent Schools, Southern Association of Colleges and Schools, and Florida Department of Education. Member of National Association of Independent Schools. Endowment: $735,000. Total enrollment: 1,851. Upper school average class size: 20. Upper school faculty-student ratio: 1:11.

Upper School Student Profile Grade 9: 165 students (80 boys, 85 girls); Grade 10: 179 students (82 boys, 97 girls); Grade 11: 163 students (69 boys, 94 girls); Grade 12: 141 students (71 boys, 70 girls).

Faculty School total: 164. In upper school: 26 men, 35 women; 43 have advanced degrees.

Subjects Offered Advanced Placement courses, advanced studio art-AP, algebra, American government, American history, American literature, anatomy, art, band, biology, calculus, ceramics, chemistry, chorus, community service, computer programming, computer science, concert choir, creative writing, debate, directing, drawing and design, economics, English, English literature, environmental science, expository writing, fine arts, forensics, French, geometry, grammar, guitar, Internet, journalism, keyboarding, Latin, media production, music, music appreciation, music theory, orchestra, performing arts, personal fitness, physical education, physics, physiology, portfolio art, pre-calculus, psychology, public speaking, Spanish, speech, theater, trigonometry, video film production, Web site design, world geography, world history, world literature, writing.

Graduation Requirements Art, computer science, electives, English, expository writing, foreign language, health education, journalism, mathematics, music, personal fitness, physical education (includes health), public speaking, science, social studies (includes history), speech and debate, Senior Capstone Project-internship, Community Service. Community service is required.

Special Academic Programs Advanced Placement exam preparation; honors section; accelerated programs; term-away projects; study at local college for college credit; academic accommodation for the gifted, the musically talented, and the artistically talented; remedial reading and/or remedial writing.

College Admission Counseling 164 students graduated in 2008; all went to college, including Emory University; Florida State University; University of Central Florida; University of Florida; University of Miami; University of Michigan.

Student Life Upper grades have uniform requirement, student council, honor system. Discipline rests primarily with faculty.

Summer Programs Remediation, enrichment, advancement, sports, art/fine arts programs offered; session focuses on sports, arts, and academics; held on campus; accepts boys and girls; open to students from other schools. 400 students usually enrolled. 2009 schedule: June 4 to August 11. Application deadline: none.

Tuition and Aid Day student tuition: $16,100–$16,750. Tuition installment plan (Key Tuition Payment Plan). Tuition reduction for siblings, need-based scholarship grants available. In 2008–09, 11% of upper-school students received aid. Total amount of financial aid awarded in 2008–09: $915,000.

Admissions Traditional secondary-level entrance grade is 9. For fall 2008, 159 students applied for upper-level admission, 131 were accepted, 85 enrolled. SSAT required. Deadline for receipt of application materials: none. Application fee required: $100. On-campus interview required.

Athletics Interscholastic: baseball (boys), basketball (b,g), cheering (g), crew (b,g), cross-country running (b,g), dance team (g), diving (b,g), football (b), golf (b,g), ice hockey (b), lacrosse (g), roller hockey (b), soccer (b,g), softball (g), swimming and diving (b,g), tennis (b,g), track and field (b,g), volleyball (b,g). 3 PE instructors, 43 coaches, 1 athletic trainer.

Computers Computers are regularly used in English, foreign language, mathematics, science, social science classes. Computer network features include on-campus library services, Internet access, wireless campus network, Internet filtering or blocking technology. Student e-mail accounts and computer access in designated common areas are available to students. Students grades are available online. The school has a published electronic and media policy.

Contact Ms. Allison Musso, Coordinator of Admission. 954-262-4405. Fax: 954-262-3535. E-mail: amusso@nova.edu. Web site: www.uschool.nova.edu.

THE URBAN SCHOOL OF SAN FRANCISCO

1563 Page Street
San Francisco, California 94117

Head of School: Mark Salkind

General Information Coeducational day college-preparatory, arts, technology, and service learning (community service) school. Grades 9–12. Founded: 1966. Setting: urban. 2 buildings on campus. Approved or accredited by California Association of Independent Schools, Western Association of Schools and Colleges, and California Department of Education. Member of National Association of Independent Schools and Secondary School Admission Test Board. Endowment: $1 million. Total enrollment: 344. Upper school average class size: 13. Upper school faculty-student ratio: 1:9.

Upper School Student Profile Grade 9: 87 students (41 boys, 46 girls); Grade 10: 87 students (42 boys, 45 girls); Grade 11: 90 students (45 boys, 45 girls); Grade 12: 80 students (40 boys, 40 girls).

Faculty School total: 55. In upper school: 27 men, 24 women; 23 have advanced degrees.

Subjects Offered 20th century history, advanced chemistry, advanced math, African American history, African history, algebra, American Civil War, American culture, American history, American literature, animal behavior, art, art history, art-AP, Asian history, Asian literature, astronomy, audio visual/media, Bible studies, biochemistry, biology, bookmaking, British literature, calculus, calculus-AP, cell biology, ceramics, chemistry, chemistry-AP, Chinese history, chorus, circus acts, classical Greek literature, college counseling, community service, comparative religion, computer literacy, computer multimedia, computer programming, conflict resolution, constitutional law, creative writing, current events, dance, digital photography, diversity studies, drama, drama performance, drawing, drawing and design, English, English literature, environmental science, European history, expository writing, female experience in America, field ecology, fine arts, French, French-AP, genetics, geometry, health, history, Holocaust seminar, improvisation, independent study, instrumental music, jazz band, Latin American literature, literature, logic, Mandarin, marine biology, mathematics, medieval literature, music, music theory, neurobiology, ornithology, painting, peer counseling, photography, physics, play production, play/screen writing, printmaking, religion, science, sex education, Shakespeare, social studies, sophomore skills, Spanish, speech, statistics, stone carving, studio art-AP, theater, trigonometry, video, water color painting, Web site design, women in world history, women's literature, women's studies, woodworking, world history, writing.

Graduation Requirements Arts and fine arts (art, music, dance, drama), English, foreign language, history, mathematics, science. Community service is required.

Special Academic Programs Advanced Placement exam preparation; honors section; independent study; term-away projects; domestic exchange program; study abroad; academic accommodation for the gifted and the artistically talented.

College Admission Counseling 80 students graduated in 2007; all went to college, including Brown University; New York University; Oberlin College; University of California, Berkeley; University of California, Los Angeles; University of Southern California. Median SAT critical reading: 650, median SAT math: 650.

Student Life Upper grades have student council, honor system. Discipline rests equally with students and faculty.

Tuition and Aid Day student tuition: $29,300. Tuition installment plan (monthly payment plans, 2-payment plan). Need-based scholarship grants, AchieverLoans (Key Education Resources) available. In 2007–08, 22% of upper-school students received aid. Total amount of financial aid awarded in 2007–08: $1,600,000.

Admissions Traditional secondary-level entrance grade is 9. For fall 2007, 572 students applied for upper-level admission, 92 enrolled. SSAT required. Deadline for receipt of application materials: January 10. Application fee required: $75. On-campus interview recommended.

Athletics Interscholastic: baseball (boys), basketball (b,g), cross-country running (b,g), soccer (b,g), softball (g), tennis (b,g), volleyball (b,g); intramural: golf (g); coed interscholastic: fencing, golf; coed intramural: aerobics/dance, backpacking, bowling, canoeing/kayaking, Circus, climbing, fencing, fitness, gatorball, hiking/backpacking, jogging, juggling, kayaking, martial arts, outdoor activities, outdoor education, physical fitness, physical training, rafting, rock climbing, skiing (cross-country), skiing (downhill), strength & conditioning, ultimate Frisbee, weight training, yoga. 28 coaches.

Computers Computers are regularly used in all classes. Computer network features include on-campus library services, online commercial services, Internet access, wireless campus network, laptop program (for all incoming students). Student e-mail accounts are available to students. The school has a published electronic and media policy.

Contact Liz Calderwood, Assistant Director of Admissions. 415-593-9555. Fax: 415-626-1125. E-mail: lcalderwood@urbanschool.org. Web site: www.urbanschool.org.

ANNOUNCEMENT FROM THE SCHOOL The Urban School seeks to ignite a passion for learning, inspiring students to become self-motivated participants in their education. The School emphasizes learning as a process of discovery, the use of city resources to extend learning beyond the classroom, respect between students and teachers, and strong commitments to diversity and inclusion.

URSULINE ACADEMY

1106 Pennsylvania Avenue
Wilmington, Delaware 19806

Head of School: Ms. Cathie Field Lloyd

General Information Coeducational day (boys' only in lower grades) college-preparatory school, affiliated with Roman Catholic Church. Boys grades PK–3, girls grades PK–12. Founded: 1893. Setting: urban. 5-acre campus. 4 buildings on campus. Approved or accredited by Middle States Association of Colleges and Schools, National Catholic Education Association, and Delaware Department of Education. Member of National Association of Independent Schools. Endowment: $3 million. Total enrollment: 638. Upper school average class size: 17. Upper school faculty-student ratio: 1:14.

Upper School Student Profile Grade 9: 61 students (61 girls); Grade 10: 45 students (45 girls); Grade 11: 64 students (64 girls); Grade 12: 54 students (54 girls). 75% of students are Roman Catholic.

Faculty School total: 85. In upper school: 9 men, 35 women; 27 have advanced degrees.

Subjects Offered Advanced chemistry, advanced math, Advanced Placement courses, advanced studio art-AP, algebra, American government-AP, American history, American history-AP, American literature, American literature-AP, anthropology, art, art history, art history-AP, art-AP, biology, biology-AP, business law, calculus, calculus-AP, Catholic belief and practice, chemistry, chemistry-AP, chorus, college counseling, college planning, creative arts, driver education, earth science, economics, English language and composition-AP, English literature, English literature and composition-AP, English literature-AP, environmental science, European history, European history-AP, fine arts, French, French literature-AP, French-AP, geometry, government/civics, grammar, health, history, history-AP, journalism, Latin, mathematics, music appreciation, painting, photography, physical education, physical science, physics, physics-AP, psychology, psychology-AP, religion, religious education, science, social studies, Spanish, Spanish language-AP, Spanish literature-AP, statistics, statistics-AP, studio art-AP, theater, theology, trigonometry, word processing, world history, world literature.

Graduation Requirements Arts and fine arts (art, music, dance, drama), computer science, English, foreign language, mathematics, physical education (includes health), religion (includes Bible studies and theology), science, social studies (includes history), 80-hour community service project.

Special Academic Programs 16 Advanced Placement exams for which test preparation is offered; honors section.

College Admission Counseling 56 students graduated in 2008; all went to college, including Columbia College; Fairfield University; Penn State University Park; Saint Joseph's University; University of Delaware; University of Pittsburgh. Median SAT critical reading: 571, median SAT math: 541, median SAT writing: 586.

Student Life Upper grades have uniform requirement, student council, honor system. Discipline rests primarily with faculty. Attendance at religious services is required.

Tuition and Aid Day student tuition: $14,670. Tuition installment plan (monthly payment plans, 2-payment plan, 1-payment plan). Merit scholarship grants, need-based scholarship grants available. In 2008–09, 30% of upper-school students received aid; total upper-school merit-scholarship money awarded: $96,000. Total amount of financial aid awarded in 2008–09: $497,000.

Admissions Traditional secondary-level entrance grade is 9. For fall 2008, 224 students applied for upper-level admission, 224 were accepted, 224 enrolled. CTP III required. Deadline for receipt of application materials: none. Application fee required: $75. On-campus interview required.

Athletics Interscholastic: aquatics (girls), basketball (g), cross-country running (g), diving (g), field hockey (g), golf (g), indoor track & field (g), lacrosse (g), soccer (g), softball (g), swimming and diving (g), tennis (g), track and field (g), volleyball (g), winter (indoor) track (g); intramural: basketball (g), dance squad (g), field hockey (g), golf (g), indoor soccer (g), volleyball (g). 3 PE instructors, 25 coaches, 1 athletic trainer.

Computers Computers are regularly used in art, English, foreign language, history, mathematics, religion, science classes. Computer network features include on-campus library services, online commercial services, Internet access, wireless campus network, Internet filtering or blocking technology. Campus intranet and student e-mail accounts are available to students. Students grades are available online. The school has a published electronic and media policy.

Contact Jennifer Callahan, Director of Admission, Lower School. 302-658-7158 Ext. 210. Fax: 302-658-4297. E-mail: jcallahan@ursuline.org. Web site: www.ursuline.org.

URSULINE ACADEMY

85 Lowder Street
Dedham, Massachusetts 02026-4299

Head of School: Ms. Rosann Whiting

General Information Girls' day college-preparatory school, affiliated with Roman Catholic Church. Grades 7–12. Founded: 1946. Setting: suburban. Nearest major city is Boston. 28-acre campus. 3 buildings on campus. Approved or accredited by Association of Independent Schools in New England, National Catholic Education Association, New England Association of Schools and Colleges, The College Board, and Massachusetts Department of Education. Member of National Association of Independent Schools. Total enrollment: 388. Upper school average class size: 18. Upper school faculty-student ratio: 1:9.

Upper School Student Profile Grade 7: 43 students (43 girls); Grade 8: 57 students (57 girls); Grade 9: 85 students (85 girls); Grade 10: 67 students (67 girls); Grade 11: 63 students (63 girls); Grade 12: 73 students (73 girls). 90% of students are Roman Catholic.

Faculty School total: 43. In upper school: 4 men, 32 women; 34 have advanced degrees.

Subjects Offered Algebra, American history, American literature, anatomy and physiology, art, art history, biology, biology-AP, British literature (honors), calculus, calculus-AP, chemistry, chemistry-AP, communication arts, computer studies, English, English literature, English-AP, European history, French, geography, geometry, government/civics, grammar, history, Latin, life science, mathematics, music, physical education, physical science, physics, pre-algebra, pre-calculus, psychology, public speaking, social studies, Spanish, Spanish language-AP, studio art, study skills, theology, trigonometry, U.S. history, U.S. history-AP, world history, world literature.

Graduation Requirements Arts and fine arts (art, music, dance, drama), computer science, English, foreign language, mathematics, physical education (includes health), public speaking, religion (includes Bible studies and theology), science, social studies (includes history), study skills, Senior year community service field project.

Special Academic Programs 6 Advanced Placement exams for which test preparation is offered; honors section.
College Admission Counseling 68 students graduated in 2008; all went to college, including Boston College; Boston University; College of the Holy Cross; Northeastern University; Providence College; Trinity College. Mean SAT critical reading: 638, mean SAT math: 623, mean SAT writing: 659, mean combined SAT: 1920.
Student Life Upper grades have uniform requirement, student council, honor system. Discipline rests primarily with faculty. Attendance at religious services is required.
Tuition and Aid Day student tuition: $11,700. Tuition installment plan (Insured Tuition Payment Plan, monthly payment plans, individually arranged payment plans, semester and quarterly payment plans). Need-based scholarship grants available. In 2008–09, 10% of upper-school students received aid.
Admissions Traditional secondary-level entrance grade is 9. Archdiocese of Boston or STS or school's own exam required. Deadline for receipt of application materials: December 15. Application fee required: $30.
Athletics Interscholastic: basketball, cross-country running, diving, field hockey, golf, ice hockey, lacrosse, soccer, softball, swimming and diving, tennis, track and field, volleyball, winter (indoor) track; intramural: dance, golf, skiing (downhill), tennis. 3 PE instructors, 26 coaches.
Computers Computers are regularly used in foreign language, mathematics, science, social studies classes. Computer network features include on-campus library services, online commercial services, Internet access, wireless campus network, Internet filtering or blocking technology. Campus intranet, student e-mail accounts, and computer access in designated common areas are available to students. Students grades are available online. The school has a published electronic and media policy.
Contact Catherine Spencer, Director of Admissions. 781-326-6161 Ext. 107. Fax: 781-329-3926. E-mail: admissions@ursulineacademy.net. Web site: www.ursulineacademy.net.

THE URSULINE ACADEMY OF DALLAS

4900 Walnut Hill Lane
Dallas, Texas 75229

Head of School: Ms. Elizabeth Bourgeois

General Information Girls' day college-preparatory and technology school, affiliated with Roman Catholic Church. Grades 9–12. Founded: 1874. Setting: suburban. 29-acre campus. 4 buildings on campus. Approved or accredited by Independent Schools Association of the Southwest, Southern Association of Colleges and Schools, Texas Catholic Conference, Texas Education Agency, and Texas Department of Education. Endowment: $1.4 million. Total enrollment: 800. Upper school average class size: 18. Upper school faculty-student ratio: 1:10.
Upper School Student Profile Grade 9: 200 students (200 girls); Grade 10: 200 students (200 girls); Grade 11: 200 students (200 girls); Grade 12: 200 students (200 girls). 84% of students are Roman Catholic.
Faculty School total: 78. In upper school: 21 men, 57 women; 50 have advanced degrees.
Subjects Offered Algebra, American history, American literature, anatomy, band, biology, botany, calculus, ceramics, chemistry, Chinese, choir, community service, computer science, creative writing, dance, design, discrete math, drama, drawing, economics, English, English literature, environmental science, European history, fitness, French, genetics, geometry, government/civics, health, journalism, Latin, orchestra, photography, physical education, physics, physiology, pre-calculus, printmaking, psychology, sculpture, Spanish, speech, statistics, theater, theology, Western civilization, world history, world literature.
Graduation Requirements Arts and fine arts (art, music, dance, drama), computer science, English, foreign language, mathematics, physical education (includes health), religion (includes Bible studies and theology), science, social studies (includes history), speech. Community service is required.
Special Academic Programs Advanced Placement exam preparation; honors section; independent study; study at local college for college credit; academic accommodation for the gifted, the musically talented, and the artistically talented.
College Admission Counseling 202 students graduated in 2008; all went to college, including Baylor University; Southern Methodist University; Texas A&M University; Texas Tech University; The University of Texas at Austin; University of Dallas. Mean SAT critical reading: 612, mean SAT math: 613, mean composite ACT: 27.
Student Life Upper grades have uniform requirement, student council, honor system. Discipline rests equally with students and faculty. Attendance at religious services is required.
Summer Programs Remediation, advancement, computer instruction programs offered; session focuses on remediation and advancement; held on campus; accepts boys and girls; open to students from other schools. 200 students usually enrolled. 2009 schedule: June 6 to July 3. Application deadline: none.
Tuition and Aid Day student tuition: $13,650. Tuition installment plan (individually arranged payment plans, annual, biannual and monthly (by bank draft) payment plans). Merit scholarship grants, need-based scholarship grants available. In 2008–09, 20% of upper-school students received aid. Total amount of financial aid awarded in 2008–09: $732,000.
Admissions Traditional secondary-level entrance grade is 9. ISEE required. Deadline for receipt of application materials: January 9. Application fee required: $50. Interview required.
Athletics Interscholastic: basketball, cheering, crew, cross-country running, diving, drill team, golf, lacrosse, soccer, softball, swimming and diving, tennis, track and field, volleyball; intramural: crew, drill team. 3 PE instructors, 15 coaches, 1 athletic trainer.
Computers Computers are regularly used in English, foreign language, history, mathematics, science classes. Computer network features include on-campus library services, Internet access, wireless campus network, Internet filtering or blocking technology. Student e-mail accounts are available to students. Students grades are available online.
Contact Mrs. Mary Campise, Admission Associate. 469-232-1800 Ext. 1839. Fax: 469-232-1836. E-mail: mcampise@ursulinedallas.org. Web site: www.ursulinedallas.org.

URSULINE HIGH SCHOOL

90 Ursuline Road
Santa Rosa, California 95403

Head of School: Ms. Julie Carver

General Information Girls' day college-preparatory, arts, business, religious studies, and technology school, affiliated with Roman Catholic Church. Grades 9–12. Founded: 1880. Setting: suburban. 51-acre campus. 5 buildings on campus. Approved or accredited by Western Association of Schools and Colleges, Western Catholic Education Association, and California Department of Education. Endowment: $800,000. Total enrollment: 296. Upper school average class size: 20. Upper school faculty-student ratio: 1:14.
Upper School Student Profile Grade 9: 64 students (64 girls); Grade 10: 74 students (74 girls); Grade 11: 82 students (82 girls); Grade 12: 76 students (76 girls). 65% of students are Roman Catholic.
Faculty School total: 28. In upper school: 5 men, 23 women; 13 have advanced degrees.
Subjects Offered 20th century world history, algebra, art, ASB Leadership, biology, biology-AP, calculus, calculus-AP, chemistry, choir, Christian and Hebrew scripture, computers, conceptual physics, creative writing, cultural geography, dance, design, desktop publishing, drama, drawing, economics, English, English literature-AP, ensembles, ethics, film, fine arts, French, geometry, health, honors English, journalism, Latin, literature-AP, photography, physical education, physical science, physics-AP, pre-algebra, pre-calculus, psychology, public speaking, social justice, Spanish, Spanish language-AP, studio art—AP, trigonometry, U.S. government, U.S. history-AP, water color painting, world history, world religions, yearbook.
Graduation Requirements Bible studies, biology, Christian ethics, church history, cultural geography, economics, English, foreign language, government, mathematics, physical education (includes health), physical science, public speaking, social justice, visual and performing arts, world history, world religions, 25 hours of student service per year, cumulative 2.0 GPA (8 semesters).
Special Academic Programs Advanced Placement exam preparation; honors section; study at local college for college credit; special instructional classes for In Grade 9 Ursuline offers an Academic Strategies class that strengthens skills needed for high school success.
College Admission Counseling 72 students graduated in 2008; all went to college, including University of California, Davis; University of California, Santa Barbara.
Student Life Upper grades have uniform requirement, student council, honor system. Discipline rests primarily with faculty. Attendance at religious services is required.
Summer Programs Remediation, enrichment, advancement programs offered; session focuses on enrichment, advancement, math make-up courses; held on campus; accepts girls; not open to students from other schools. 80 students usually enrolled. 2009 schedule: June 8 to July 10. Application deadline: May 22.
Tuition and Aid Day student tuition: $11,600. Tuition installment plan (monthly payment plans, semiannual and annual payment plans). Merit scholarship grants, need-based scholarship grants available. In 2008–09, 32% of upper-school students received aid; total upper-school merit-scholarship money awarded: $12,000. Total amount of financial aid awarded in 2008–09: $290,000.
Admissions Traditional secondary-level entrance grade is 9. STS Examination required. Deadline for receipt of application materials: none. Application fee required: $100. On-campus interview required.
Athletics Interscholastic: basketball, cross-country running, diving, golf, lacrosse, soccer, softball, swimming and diving, tennis, track and field, volleyball, water polo. 2 PE instructors, 33 coaches.
Computers Computers are regularly used in business applications, computer applications, media, Web site design, yearbook classes. Computer network features include on-campus library services, online commercial services, Internet access, Internet filtering or blocking technology, Bridges, Atomic Learning, Family Connection by Naviance, Blackboard, MyAccess. Campus intranet and computer access in designated common areas are available to students. The school has a published electronic and media policy.
Contact Ms. Lisa Ormond, Admissions Director. 707-524-1133. Fax: 707-542-0131. E-mail: lormond@ursulinehs.org. Web site: www.ursulinehs.org.

THE URSULINE SCHOOL

1354 North Avenue
New Rochelle, New York 10804-2192

Head of School: Sr. Jean Baptiste Nicholson

General Information Girls' day college-preparatory, arts, religious studies, and technology school, affiliated with Roman Catholic Church. Grades 6–12. Founded: 1897. Setting: suburban. Nearest major city is New York. 11-acre campus. 5 buildings on campus. Approved or accredited by Middle States Association of Colleges and Schools, National Catholic Education Association, New York Department of Education, New York State Association of Independent Schools, The College Board, and New York Department of Education. Endowment: $500,000. Total enrollment: 823. Upper school average class size: 22. Upper school faculty-student ratio: 1:18.
Upper School Student Profile Grade 9: 183 students (183 girls); Grade 10: 171 students (171 girls); Grade 11: 145 students (145 girls); Grade 12: 164 students (164 girls). 89% of students are Roman Catholic.
Faculty School total: 97. In upper school: 12 men, 85 women; 82 have advanced degrees.
Subjects Offered Adolescent issues, Advanced Placement courses, algebra, American history, American literature, Ancient Greek, art, art history, art-AP, Bible studies, biology, biology-AP, British literature, British literature (honors), calculus, calculus-AP, chemistry, Chinese, chorus, Christian and Hebrew scripture, church history, classical Greek literature, college counseling, computer applications, computer graphics, computer literacy, computer science, computer skills, CPR, creative writing, dance, drawing, driver education, earth science, economics, economics and history, engineering, English, English literature and composition-AP, ethical decision making, European history, European history-AP, European literature, French, French language-AP, geometry, global studies, government, Homeric Greek, honors algebra, honors English, honors geometry, honors U.S. history, Italian, jazz dance, journalism, Latin, law, library skills, marine science, mathematics, music, music appreciation, music technology, New Testament, novel, orchestra, painting, peer counseling, peer ministry, physical education, physical fitness, physics, physics-AP, physiology, poetry, portfolio art, pottery, prayer/spirituality, pre-calculus, psychology, reading, religion, religious studies, science research, social justice, Spanish, Spanish language-AP, statistics, studio art—AP, studio art-AP, theology, trigonometry, U.S. government and politics-AP, U.S. history-AP, women spirituality and faith, world religions, writing workshop.
Graduation Requirements Arts and fine arts (art, music, dance, drama), English, foreign language, Latin, mathematics, physical education (includes health), religion (includes Bible studies and theology), science, social studies (includes history).
Special Academic Programs 13 Advanced Placement exams for which test preparation is offered; honors section; study at local college for college credit; academic accommodation for the gifted and the artistically talented; remedial reading and/or remedial writing; programs in English for dyslexic students.
College Admission Counseling 164 students graduated in 2008; all went to college, including Fordham University; Villanova University. Mean SAT critical reading: 590, mean SAT math: 580, mean SAT writing: 610. 25% scored over 600 on SAT critical reading, 25% scored over 600 on SAT math, 35% scored over 600 on SAT writing.
Student Life Upper grades have uniform requirement, student council. Discipline rests primarily with faculty. Attendance at religious services is required.
Tuition and Aid Day student tuition: $13,000. Tuition installment plan (monthly payment plans, individually arranged payment plans). Merit scholarship grants, paying campus jobs available. In 2008–09, 25% of upper-school students received aid; total upper-school merit-scholarship money awarded: $633,400. Total amount of financial aid awarded in 2008–09: $825,750.
Admissions Traditional secondary-level entrance grade is 9. For fall 2008, 426 students applied for upper-level admission, 286 were accepted, 140 enrolled. ISEE or New York Archdiocesan Cooperative Entrance Examination required. Deadline for receipt of application materials: none. No application fee required. On-campus interview recommended.
Athletics Interscholastic: basketball (girls), cheering (g), crew (g), cross-country running (g), diving (g), field hockey (g), golf (g), indoor track (g), indoor track & field (g), soccer (g), softball (g), swimming and diving (g), tennis (g), track and field (g), volleyball (g). 4 PE instructors, 34 coaches.
Computers Computers are regularly used in art, classics, English, foreign language, history, mathematics, music, religion, science classes. Computer network features include on-campus library services, online commercial services, Internet access, wireless campus network, Internet filtering or blocking technology. Campus intranet, student e-mail accounts, and computer access in designated common areas are available to students. The school has a published electronic and media policy.
Contact Mrs. Rose Trapani, Secretary. 914-636-3950 Ext. 212. Fax: 914-636-3949. E-mail: trapanir@ursuline.pvt.k12.ny.us. Web site: www.ursuline.pvt.k12.ny.us.

VALLE CATHOLIC HIGH SCHOOL

40 North Fourth Street
Ste. Genevieve, Missouri 63670

Head of School: Ms. Sara C. Menard

General Information Coeducational day college-preparatory, arts, business, vocational, religious studies, and technology school, affiliated with Roman Catholic Church; primarily serves students with learning disabilities and individuals with Attention Deficit Disorder. Grades 9–12. Founded: 1837. Setting: small town. Nearest major city is St. Louis. 3-acre campus. 3 buildings on campus. Approved or accredited by North Central Association of Colleges and Schools and Missouri Department of Education. Endowment: $2 million. Total enrollment: 152. Upper school average class size: 15. Upper school faculty-student ratio: 1:8.
Upper School Student Profile Grade 9: 36 students (18 boys, 18 girls); Grade 10: 40 students (24 boys, 16 girls); Grade 11: 42 students (24 boys, 18 girls); Grade 12: 32 students (15 boys, 17 girls). 97% of students are Roman Catholic.
Faculty School total: 15. In upper school: 6 men, 9 women; 7 have advanced degrees.
Subjects Offered 20th century American writers, accounting, advanced chemistry, advanced computer applications, advanced math, algebra, American democracy, American history, American literature, analysis and differential calculus, anatomy and physiology, architectural drawing, art, art history, arts, band, biology, British literature, business, business applications, business communications, business law, business mathematics, business skills, business studies, calculus, calculus-AP, Catholic belief and practice, chemistry-AP, Christian and Hebrew scripture, Christian scripture, church history, civics, civics/free enterprise, classics, communications, comparative religion, composition, computer applications, computer keyboarding, computer multimedia, computer science, computer skills, concert band, consumer economics, consumer education, consumer law, consumer mathematics, drafting, drama, drama performance, dramatic arts, drawing, earth science, ecology, environmental systems, economics, economics and history, English, entrepreneurship, environmental science, environmental systems, foreign language, freshman seminar, geography, geometry, history of the Catholic Church, honors algebra, honors English, honors U.S. history, human anatomy, journalism, marching band, math analysis, mathematics, media communications, moral theology, novels, orchestra, painting, peace and justice, physical education, physics, practical arts, psychology, religion, science, social studies, sociology, Spanish, technical drawing, U.S. government, values and decisions, visual arts, Western civilization, yearbook.
Graduation Requirements Advanced math, algebra, American history, American literature, biology, Catholic belief and practice, chemistry, Christian and Hebrew scripture, civics, English, English composition, ethical decision making, foreign language, geometry, government/civics, history of the Catholic Church, mathematics, physical education (includes health), practical arts, religion (includes Bible studies and theology), science, senior composition, social justice, social studies (includes history), Spanish, 80 hours of community service.
Special Academic Programs International Baccalaureate program; 1 Advanced Placement exam for which test preparation is offered; honors section; study at local college for college credit; academic accommodation for the gifted and the artistically talented; remedial reading and/or remedial writing; remedial math.
College Admission Counseling 24 students graduated in 2008; 22 went to college, including Missouri State University; Saint Louis University; Southeast Missouri State University; Truman State University; University of Missouri–Columbia. Other: 2 entered a postgraduate year. Mean SAT critical reading: 720, mean SAT math: 780, mean composite ACT: 24. 100% scored over 600 on SAT critical reading, 100% scored over 600 on SAT math, 26% scored over 26 on composite ACT.
Student Life Upper grades have uniform requirement, student council, honor system. Discipline rests primarily with faculty. Attendance at religious services is required.
Summer Programs Remediation, enrichment, advancement programs offered; session focuses on advancement and remediation/make-up; held on campus; accepts boys and girls; not open to students from other schools. 8 students usually enrolled. 2009 schedule: June 3 to July 31.
Tuition and Aid Day student tuition: $4500. Tuition installment plan (The Tuition Plan, monthly payment plans, individually arranged payment plans, tuition assistance through the St. Louis Archdiocese and Scholarships available through the School.). Tuition reduction for siblings, merit scholarship grants, need-based scholarship grants, tuition relief funds available from St. Louis Archdiocese available. In 2008–09, 30% of upper-school students received aid; total upper-school merit-scholarship money awarded: $10,000. Total amount of financial aid awarded in 2008–09: $165,000.
Admissions Traditional secondary-level entrance grade is 9. Any standardized test, school placement exam and writing sample required. Deadline for receipt of application materials: none. Application fee required: $20. Interview recommended.
Athletics Interscholastic: baseball (boys), basketball (b,g), dance team (g), drill team (g), football (b), track and field (b,g), volleyball (g), weight training (b); coed interscholastic: cheering, golf, physical training, strength & conditioning, weight lifting. 1 PE instructor.
Computers Computers are regularly used in accounting, business, career exploration, classics, college planning, economics, English, foreign language, geography, history, humanities, journalism, mathematics, psychology, religion, science, Spanish, writing, yearbook classes. Computer network features include Internet access, Internet filtering or blocking technology. Student e-mail accounts and computer access in designated common areas are available to students. The school has a published electronic and media policy.
Contact Ms. Sara C. Menard, Principal. 573-883-7496 Ext. 241. Fax: 573-883-9142. E-mail: menards@valleschools.org. Web site: www.valleschools.org.

VALLEY CHRISTIAN HIGH SCHOOL

7500 Inspiration Drive
Dublin, California 94568
Head of School: Mrs. RoseMary Tuu

General Information Coeducational day college-preparatory and religious studies school, affiliated with Assemblies of God. Grades 7–12. Founded: 1981. Setting: suburban. Nearest major city is Pleasanton. 49-acre campus. 3 buildings on campus. Approved or accredited by Association of Christian Schools International, Western Association of Schools and Colleges, and California Department of Education. Total enrollment: 450. Upper school average class size: 22. Upper school faculty-student ratio: 1:13.

Upper School Student Profile 10% of students are Assemblies of God.

Faculty School total: 39. In upper school: 11 men, 27 women; 7 have advanced degrees.

Subjects Offered Acting, advanced math, Advanced Placement courses, advanced studio art-AP, aerobics, algebra, American government, American history, American history-AP, American literature, American sign language, anatomy and physiology, art, arts, ASB Leadership, athletics, baseball, basketball, Bible, Bible studies, biology, British literature, calculus, calculus-AP, campus ministry, career and personal planning, career education, career exploration, career planning, career/college preparation, careers, character education, cheerleading, chemistry, choir, choral music, Christian doctrine, Christian ethics, Christian scripture, Christian studies, Christian testament, church history, college admission preparation, college awareness, college counseling, college planning, competitive science projects, composition, computer keyboarding, computer literacy, computer resources, conceptual physics, constitutional history of U.S., creation science, creative writing, critical thinking, critical writing, decision making, decision making skills, directing, drama, drama performance, drama workshop, earth science, economics, electives, English, English language and composition-AP, English literature, English literature and composition-AP, English literature-AP, English-AP, English/composition-AP, epic literature, ESL, ethical decision making, ethics, European literature, expository writing, expressive arts, fiction, fine arts, fitness, foreign language, French, French language-AP, French-AP, geography, geometry, German, German-AP, golf, government, grammar, great books, Harlem Renaissance, health and wellness, health education, history, history of religion, history-AP, Holocaust, honors algebra, honors English, honors geometry, human anatomy, humanities, ideas, illustration, improvisation, Japanese, journalism, keyboarding, keyboarding/computer, lab science, language arts, language structure, language-AP, languages, leadership, leadership and service, leadership skills, library, Life of Christ, life science, literary genres, literature, literature and composition-AP, literature-AP, marine biology, math analysis, math applications, mathematics, mathematics-AP, mechanics of writing, medieval literature, methods of research, modern history, modern languages, moral theology, music, music theory, newspaper, novels, oral communications, oral expression, painting, participation in sports, performing arts, physical education, physical fitness, physics, physics-AP, play production, poetry, pre-algebra, pre-calculus, pre-college orientation, psychology, public speaking, reading, reading/study skills, regional literature, religion, religious education, religious studies, remedial study skills, research and reference, research skills, research techniques, Russian literature, science fiction, science project, scripture, Shakespeare, Shakespearean histories, short story, softball, Spanish, Spanish language-AP, Spanish-AP, speech, sports, student government, studio art, studio art-AP, study skills, theater, theater arts, theater design and production, U.S. government, U.S. government and politics, U.S. history, U.S. history-AP, U.S. literature, values and decisions, visual and performing arts, volleyball, weight training, world geography, world history, world literature, world religions, yearbook.

Graduation Requirements Art, Christian doctrine, Christian ethics, Christian scripture, composition, economics, foreign language, geography, grammar, health, history, keyboarding/computer, literature, mathematics, moral reasoning, religious studies, science, U.S. government, World War II.

Special Academic Programs Academic accommodation for the gifted; remedial reading and/or remedial writing; programs in English, general development for dyslexic students; ESL (5 students enrolled).

College Admission Counseling 74 students graduated in 2008; 60 went to college, including Biola University; University of California, Los Angeles; University of California, Riverside. Median SAT critical reading: 574, median SAT math: 570, median SAT writing: 561, median composite ACT: 24.

Student Life Upper grades have specified standards of dress, student council, honor system. Discipline rests primarily with faculty. Attendance at religious services is required.

Tuition and Aid Tuition installment plan (monthly payment plans). Tuition reduction for siblings, need-based scholarship grants available. In 2008–09, 10% of upper-school students received aid. Total amount of financial aid awarded in 2008–09: $25,000.

Admissions Traditional secondary-level entrance grade is 9. SSAT and writing sample required. Deadline for receipt of application materials: none. Application fee required: $350. On-campus interview required.

Athletics Interscholastic: baseball (boys, girls), basketball (b,g), cheering (g), cross-country running (b,g), golf (b), soccer (b,g), softball (g), tennis (b,g), volleyball (b,g). 5 PE instructors, 10 coaches.

Computers Computers are regularly used in journalism, keyboarding, lab/keyboard, yearbook classes. Computer network features include on-campus library services, online commercial services, Internet access. Campus intranet is available to students.

Contact Mrs. Teresa Higuera, Office Manager. 925-560-6241. Fax: 925-828-5658. E-mail: thiguera@dublinvcc.org. Web site: www.dublinvcc.org.

VALLEY CHRISTIAN SCHOOL

100 Skyway Drive
San Jose, California 95111-3636
Head of School: Dr. Clifford Daugherty

General Information Coeducational day college-preparatory, arts, religious studies, technology, Music Conservatory, and Theatre Conservatory school, affiliated with Christian faith. Grades K–12. Founded: 1960. Setting: suburban. 53-acre campus. 4 buildings on campus. Approved or accredited by Association of Christian Schools International, Western Association of Schools and Colleges, and California Department of Education. Endowment: $1.5 million. Total enrollment: 2,285. Upper school average class size: 28. Upper school faculty-student ratio: 1:17.

Upper School Student Profile Grade 9: 322 students (162 boys, 160 girls); Grade 10: 333 students (171 boys, 162 girls); Grade 11: 304 students (151 boys, 153 girls); Grade 12: 274 students (140 boys, 134 girls). 85% of students are Christian.

Faculty School total: 139. In upper school: 28 men, 50 women; 23 have advanced degrees.

Subjects Offered 20th century American writers, acting, advanced chemistry, advanced computer applications, advanced math, Advanced Placement courses, advanced studio art-AP, algebra, American history, American literature, American sign language, anatomy and physiology, ancient world history, applied music, art, audio visual/media, Basic programming, Bible, Bible studies, biology, biology-AP, British literature-AP, broadcasting, calculus-AP, career and personal planning, cheerleading, chemistry, chemistry-AP, Chinese, choir, choral music, choreography, Christian doctrine, Christian ethics, Christian scripture, Christian studies, college admission preparation, college counseling, college planning, comparative political systems-AP, composition-AP, computer art, computer keyboarding, computer literacy, computer music, computer science-AP, concert choir, consumer mathematics, dance, dance performance, digital art, drama, drama performance, dramatic arts, English, English language and composition-AP, English literature-AP, European history-AP, filmmaking, finite math, foreign language, French, French studies, geometry, global studies, government, grammar, health education, health science, history, history of music, honors English, honors U.S. history, honors world history, HTML design, instrumental music, introduction to theater, Japanese, Japanese as Second Language, jazz band, jazz dance, jazz ensemble, journalism, Latin, leadership, leadership and service, literature and composition-AP, macro/microeconomics-AP, Mandarin, marching band, mathematics, mathematics-AP, Microsoft, music theory-AP, musical productions, musical theater, photo shop, photojournalism, physical science, physics, physics-AP, play/screen writing, pre-algebra, pre-calculus, radio broadcasting, SAT preparation, sign language, Spanish, Spanish-AP, stage design, statistics, statistics-AP, student government, studio art-AP, symphonic band, tap dance, technical theater, telecommunications, theater arts, theater production, trigonometry, typing, U.S. government, U.S. government-AP, U.S. history, U.S. history-AP, video film production, vocal ensemble, weight training, wind ensemble, world history, yearbook.

Graduation Requirements Arts and fine arts (art, music, dance, drama), biology, Christian and Hebrew scripture, Christian doctrine, Christian studies, computers, economics, English, English composition, English literature, global studies, mathematics, physical education (includes health), science, technology, U.S. government, U.S. history.

Special Academic Programs 22 Advanced Placement exams for which test preparation is offered; honors section.

College Admission Counseling 280 students graduated in 2008; 274 went to college, including California Polytechnic State University, San Luis Obispo; San Diego State University; San Jose State University; Sonoma State University; University of California, Davis; University of California, Irvine. Other: 4 went to work, 2 entered military service. Median SAT critical reading: 590, median SAT math: 580, median SAT writing: 580, median combined SAT: 1740. 47% scored over 600 on SAT critical reading, 46% scored over 600 on SAT math, 38% scored over 600 on SAT writing, 40% scored over 1800 on combined SAT.

Student Life Upper grades have specified standards of dress, student council, honor system. Discipline rests primarily with faculty.

Summer Programs Remediation, enrichment, advancement, sports, art/fine arts programs offered; session focuses on Advancement, Remediation and Enrichment; held on campus; accepts boys and girls; open to students from other schools. 300 students usually enrolled. 2009 schedule: June 23 to August 1. Application deadline: none.

Tuition and Aid Day student tuition: $13,400. Tuition installment plan (FACTS Tuition Payment Plan). Tuition reduction for siblings, need-based scholarship grants available. In 2008–09, 9% of upper-school students received aid. Total amount of financial aid awarded in 2008–09: $200,000.

Admissions Traditional secondary-level entrance grade is 9. For fall 2008, 272 students applied for upper-level admission, 180 were accepted, 140 enrolled. Admissions testing, essay, Iowa Subtests, mathematics proficiency exam, school's own test or SLEP for foreign students required. Deadline for receipt of application materials: none. Application fee required: $70. Interview required.

Athletics Interscholastic: aquatics (boys, girls), baseball (b), basketball (b,g), cheering (b,g), cross-country running (b,g), dance (b,g), dance squad (b,g), diving (b,g), football (b), golf (b,g), rugby (b), soccer (b,g), softball (g), swimming and diving (b,g), tennis (b,g), track and field (b,g), volleyball (b,g), water polo (b,g), wrestling (b); intramural: weight training (b,g). 3 PE instructors, 23 coaches, 2 athletic trainers.

Computers Computers are regularly used in computer applications, digital applications, foreign language, graphic arts, graphic design, journalism, keyboarding, lab/keyboard, library, mathematics, media arts, music, music technology, news writing, newspaper, photography, photojournalism, typing, video film production, Web site design, word processing, yearbook classes. Computer network features include on-campus library services, Internet access, wireless campus network, Internet filtering or blocking technology. Computer access in designated common areas is available to students. Students grades are available online. The school has a published electronic and media policy.

Contact Linda Kohlmoos, High School Admissions Coordinator. 408-513-2512. Fax: 408-513-2527. E-mail: lkohlmoos@vcs.net. Web site: www.vcs.net.

VALLEY FORGE MILITARY ACADEMY & COLLEGE

1001 Eagle Road
Wayne, Pennsylvania 19087-3695

Head of School: Mr. Charles A. McGeorge

General Information Boys' boarding and day college-preparatory, arts, business, religious studies, music, and military school. Boarding grades 7–PG, day grades 7–12. Founded: 1928. Setting: suburban. Nearest major city is Philadelphia. Students are housed in single-sex dormitories. 120-acre campus. 83 buildings on campus. Approved or accredited by Middle States Association of Colleges and Schools, The Association of Boarding Schools, and Pennsylvania Department of Education. Member of National Association of Independent Schools and Secondary School Admission Test Board. Endowment: $12 million. Total enrollment: 319. Upper school average class size: 12. Upper school faculty-student ratio: 1:13.

Upper School Student Profile Grade 9: 55 students (55 boys); Grade 10: 60 students (60 boys); Grade 11: 81 students (81 boys); Grade 12: 81 students (81 boys); Postgraduate: 18 students (18 boys). 100% of students are boarding students. 26% are state residents. 28 states are represented in upper school student body. 11% are international students. International students from Canada, China, Jordan, Mexico, Republic of Korea, and Venezuela; 10 other countries represented in student body.

Faculty School total: 50. In upper school: 22 men, 18 women; 20 have advanced degrees; 26 reside on campus.

Subjects Offered ACT preparation, advanced biology, advanced computer applications, algebra, American foreign policy, American government, American history, American history-AP, anatomy and physiology, ancient world history, applied music, art, art education, auto shop, band, biology, brass choir, business, business law, business studies, calculus, calculus-AP, character education, chemistry, Chinese, choir, comparative religion, computer keyboarding, computer math, computer programming, computer science, concert band, concert choir, drama, driver education, earth science, ecology, economics, English, English literature and composition-AP, equestrian sports, equitation, ESL, ESL, ethics, European history, fencing, fine arts, flight instruction, foreign language, French, French studies, geometry, German, government/civics, grammar, health, health education, honors algebra, honors English, honors geometry, honors U.S. history, honors world history, instrumental music, journalism, lab science, Latin, leadership, leadership and service, leadership education training, leadership skills, leadership training, marching band, mathematics, mathematics-AP, military science, modern world history, music, music performance, music theory, newspaper, official social customs, personal growth, physical education, physics, physics-AP, pre-algebra, reading, reading/study skills, ROTC (for boys), Russian, science, social science, social studies, sociology, Spanish, speech, sports, statistics and probability, swimming, theater, therapeutic horseback riding, TOEFL preparation, trigonometry, typing, U.S. government, U.S. history, U.S. history-AP, video communication, video film production, Web site design, world history, world religions, world religions, world wide web design, writing, writing skills.

Special Academic Programs Advanced Placement exam preparation; honors section; independent study; study at local college for college credit; study abroad; academic accommodation for the musically talented and the artistically talented; remedial reading and/or remedial writing; remedial math.

College Admission Counseling 91 students graduated in 2008; 89 went to college, including Drexel University; Tulane University; United States Air Force Academy; United States Military Academy; United States Naval Academy. Other: 1 went to work, 1 entered a postgraduate year. Median SAT critical reading: 495, median SAT math: 525. 12% scored over 600 on SAT critical reading, 26% scored over 600 on SAT math.

Student Life Upper grades have uniform requirement, student council, honor system. Discipline rests equally with students and faculty. Attendance at religious services is required.

Tuition and Aid Day student tuition: $19,900; 7-day tuition and room/board: $35,041. Tuition installment plan (monthly payment plans, individually arranged payment plans). Tuition reduction for siblings, merit scholarship grants, need-based scholarship grants, middle-income loans, paying campus jobs available. In 2008–09, 73% of upper-school students received aid; total upper-school merit-scholarship money awarded: $2,230,907. Total amount of financial aid awarded in 2008–09: $2,230,907.

Admissions Traditional secondary-level entrance grade is 9. For fall 2008, 366 students applied for upper-level admission, 244 were accepted, 165 enrolled. Iowa Test, CTBS, or TAP, ISEE, OLSAT and English Exam, SSAT, ERB, PSAT, SAT, PLAN or ACT or TOEFL or SLEP required. Deadline for receipt of application materials: none. Application fee required: $100. Interview required.

Athletics Interscholastic: baseball, basketball, climbing, cross-country running, dressage, drill team, equestrian sports, fitness, football, golf, horseback riding, indoor track, judo, lacrosse, marksmanship, outdoor activities, outdoor recreation, paint ball, physical fitness, physical training, soccer, swimming and diving, weight lifting, weight training, wrestling; intramural: blading, boxing, fencing, hockey, indoor soccer, life saving, martial arts, physical training, rugby, scuba diving, soccer. 3 PE instructors, 12 coaches, 2 athletic trainers.

Computers Computers are regularly used in accounting, aerospace science, basic skills, business applications, business education, business skills, business studies, college planning, data processing, English, journalism, keyboarding, lab/keyboard, library, library skills, mathematics, music, news writing, newspaper, photography, photojournalism, SAT preparation, science, video film production, Web site design classes. Computer network features include on-campus library services, Internet access, wireless campus network, Internet filtering or blocking technology, Blackboard. Campus intranet, student e-mail accounts, and computer access in designated common areas are available to students. The school has a published electronic and media policy.

Contact Capt. Gerald Hale, Dean of Enrollment Management. 610-989-1300. Fax: 610-688-1545. E-mail: admissions@vfmac.edu. Web site: www.vfmac.edu.

See Close-Up on page 1000.

VALLEY LUTHERAN HIGH SCHOOL

5199 North 7th Avenue
Phoenix, Arizona 85013-2043

Head of School: Dr. Jay A. Krause

General Information Coeducational day college-preparatory, arts, religious studies, and technology school, affiliated with Lutheran Church–Missouri Synod. Grades 9–12. Founded: 1981. Setting: urban. 10-acre campus. 4 buildings on campus. Approved or accredited by North Central Association of Colleges and Schools and Arizona Department of Education. Total enrollment: 170. Upper school average class size: 12. Upper school faculty-student ratio: 1:8.

Upper School Student Profile Grade 9: 54 students (23 boys, 31 girls); Grade 10: 49 students (28 boys, 21 girls); Grade 11: 45 students (24 boys, 21 girls); Grade 12: 22 students (10 boys, 12 girls). 73% of students are Lutheran Church–Missouri Synod.

Faculty School total: 16. In upper school: 7 men, 9 women; 7 have advanced degrees.

Special Academic Programs Honors section; academic accommodation for the gifted and the musically talented; remedial math; special instructional classes for deaf students.

College Admission Counseling 27 students graduated in 2008; 25 went to college, including Arizona State University; Concordia University Wisconsin; Glendale Community College; Northern Arizona University; The University of Arizona; University of California, Irvine. Other: 2 entered military service. Median SAT critical reading: 530, median SAT math: 500, median SAT writing: 530, median combined SAT: 1560, median composite ACT: 22.

Student Life Upper grades have specified standards of dress, student council, honor system. Discipline rests primarily with faculty. Attendance at religious services is required.

Tuition and Aid Day student tuition: $7500. Tuition installment plan (monthly payment plans, individually arranged payment plans, Vanco Services/Thrivent Financial for Lutherans). Merit scholarship grants, need-based scholarship grants, foundation grants, Christian worker discounts available. In 2008–09, 25% of upper-school students received aid. Total amount of financial aid awarded in 2008–09: $166,770.

Admissions Traditional secondary-level entrance grade is 9. School's own test required. Deadline for receipt of application materials: none. Application fee required: $50. Interview required.

Athletics Interscholastic: aerobics/dance (girls), baseball (b), basketball (b,g), cheering (g), dance (g), dance squad (g), fitness (b,g), football (b), physical fitness (b,g), pom squad (g), power lifting (b,g), softball (g), track and field (b,g), volleyball (g), wrestling (b); coed interscholastic: fitness, golf, physical fitness, power lifting, running, soccer, strength & conditioning, tennis, weight training. 1 PE instructor, 4 coaches.

Computers Computers are regularly used in desktop publishing, keyboarding, research skills, study skills, typing, Web site design, word processing, yearbook classes. Computer network features include Internet access, wireless campus network, Internet filtering or blocking technology. Student e-mail accounts are available to students. The school has a published electronic and media policy.

Contact Mrs. Teri K. Billaber, Office Manager. 602-230-1600 Ext. 100. Fax: 602-230-1602. E-mail: tbillaber@vlhs.org. Web site: www.vlhs.org/.

VALLEY LUTHERAN HIGH SCHOOL

3560 McCarty Road
Saginaw, Michigan 48603

Head of School: Dr. John M. Brandt

General Information Coeducational day college-preparatory, arts, and religious studies school, affiliated with Lutheran Church–Missouri Synod. Grades 9–12. Founded: 1977. Setting: suburban. Nearest major city is Detroit. 50-acre campus. 1 building on campus. Approved or accredited by Lutheran School Accreditation Commission, Michigan Association of Non-Public Schools, North Central Association of Colleges and Schools, and Michigan Department of Education. Endowment: $1 million. Total enrollment: 354. Upper school average class size: 23. Upper school faculty-student ratio: 1:17.

Upper School Student Profile Grade 9: 102 students (54 boys, 48 girls); Grade 10: 88 students (37 boys, 51 girls); Grade 11: 85 students (37 boys, 48 girls); Grade 12: 90 students (43 boys, 47 girls). 80% of students are Lutheran Church–Missouri Synod.

Faculty School total: 24. In upper school: 12 men, 11 women; 18 have advanced degrees.

Subjects Offered Accounting, algebra, American history, American literature, art, band, Bible studies, biology, business, calculus-AP, chemistry, chorus, composition, computer graphics, computer programming, drama, economics, English, ethics, fine arts, French, general science, geography, geometry, government/civics, health, keyboarding, Latin, mathematics, physical education, physics, pre-algebra, pre-calculus, psychology, reading, religion, science, social studies, Spanish, speech, word processing, world history, world literature, writing.

Graduation Requirements Arts and fine arts (art, music, dance, drama), English, mathematics, physical education (includes health), religion (includes Bible studies and theology), science, social studies (includes history).

Special Academic Programs Advanced Placement exam preparation; honors section.

College Admission Counseling 78 students graduated in 2008; 71 went to college, including Central Michigan University; Concordia University; Delta College; Grand Valley State University; Saginaw Valley State University. Other: 5 went to work, 2 entered military service. Median composite ACT: 23. 14% scored over 26 on composite ACT.

Student Life Upper grades have specified standards of dress, student council. Discipline rests primarily with faculty. Attendance at religious services is required.

Tuition and Aid Day student tuition: $4400–$5700. Tuition installment plan (monthly payment plans). Need-based scholarship grants available. In 2008–09, 30% of upper-school students received aid. Total amount of financial aid awarded in 2008–09: $150,000.

Admissions Traditional secondary-level entrance grade is 9. For fall 2008, 95 students applied for upper-level admission, 94 were accepted, 94 enrolled. Deadline for receipt of application materials: none. Application fee required: $200. Interview recommended.

Athletics Interscholastic: baseball (boys), basketball (b,g), cross-country running (b,g), football (b), golf (b), pom squad (g); coed interscholastic: pom squad. 2 PE instructors.

Computers Computers are regularly used in art, English, history classes. Computer network features include Internet access, Internet filtering or blocking technology. Students grades are available online.

Contact Mr. Randy Rogers, Guidance Director. 989-790-1676. Fax: 989-790-1680. E-mail: rrogers@vlhs.com. Web site: www.vlhs.com.

THE VALLEY SCHOOL

2474 South Ballenger Highway
Flint, Michigan 48507

Head of School: Kaye C. Panchula

General Information Coeducational day college-preparatory and arts school. Grades PK–12. Founded: 1970. Setting: urban. 1-acre campus. 1 building on campus. Approved or accredited by Independent Schools Association of the Central States. Total enrollment: 41. Upper school average class size: 16. Upper school faculty-student ratio: 1:8.

Upper School Student Profile Grade 9: 2 students (2 girls); Grade 10: 6 students (3 boys, 3 girls); Grade 11: 2 students (1 boy, 1 girl); Grade 12: 5 students (2 boys, 3 girls).

Faculty School total: 10. In upper school: 4 men, 3 women; 3 have advanced degrees.

Subjects Offered Algebra, American history, American literature, art, art history, biology, ceramics, chemistry, current events, earth science, English, English literature, European history, expository writing, fine arts, geometry, government/civics, grammar, history, mathematics, music, physical education, physics, SAT/ACT preparation, science, social science, Spanish, statistics and probability, trigonometry, world culture, world history, world literature, writing.

Graduation Requirements Arts and fine arts (art, music, dance, drama), English, foreign language, mathematics, physical education (includes health), science, social science, social studies (includes history), Senior project off campus.

Special Academic Programs Honors section; independent study; term-away projects; study at local college for college credit; academic accommodation for the gifted and the artistically talented.

College Admission Counseling 6 students graduated in 2008; all went to college, including Albion College; Eastern Michigan University; Kalamazoo College; Michigan State University; University of Michigan. Mean composite ACT: 25. 29% scored over 26 on composite ACT.

Student Life Discipline rests equally with students and faculty.

Tuition and Aid Day student tuition: $9399. Tuition installment plan (FACTS Tuition Payment Plan). Tuition reduction for siblings, merit scholarship grants, need-based scholarship grants available. In 2008–09, 30% of upper-school students received aid; total upper-school merit-scholarship money awarded: $50,000. Total amount of financial aid awarded in 2008–09: $74,992.

Admissions Traditional secondary-level entrance grade is 9. School's own exam required. Deadline for receipt of application materials: none. No application fee required. On-campus interview required.

Athletics Interscholastic: basketball (boys, girls), soccer (b,g), tennis (b), volleyball (g). 1 PE instructor, 2 coaches.

Computers Computers are regularly used in English, mathematics, science, social sciences classes. Computer resources include Internet access, wireless campus network.

Contact Minka Owens, Director of Admissions. 810-767-4004. Fax: 810-767-0841. E-mail: email@valleyschool.org. Web site: www.valleyschool.org.

VALLEY VIEW SCHOOL

North Brookfield, Massachusetts

See Special Needs Schools section.

VALWOOD SCHOOL

4380 US Hwy 41 North
Hahira, Georgia 31632

Head of School: Cobb Atkinson

General Information Coeducational day college-preparatory school. Grades PK–12. Founded: 1969. Setting: rural. Nearest major city is Jacksonville, FL. 45-acre campus. 7 buildings on campus. Approved or accredited by Georgia Accrediting Commission, Georgia Independent School Association, Southern Association of Colleges and Schools, and Southern Association of Independent Schools. Member of National Association of Independent Schools and Secondary School Admission Test Board. Upper school average class size: 15. Upper school faculty-student ratio: 1:6.

Upper School Student Profile Grade 9: 24 students (16 boys, 8 girls); Grade 10: 33 students (17 boys, 16 girls); Grade 11: 20 students (5 boys, 15 girls); Grade 12: 18 students (12 boys, 6 girls).

Faculty School total: 45. In upper school: 10 men, 13 women; 6 have advanced degrees.

Subjects Offered Algebra, American history, anatomy and physiology, art, biology, business skills, calculus, calculus-AP, chemistry, chemistry-AP, composition, drama, economics, English, English language-AP, English literature-AP, fitness, French, French-AP, geography, geometry, global issues, government/civics, health, honors algebra, honors English, honors geometry, instruments, Latin, literature, mathematics, model United Nations, music, music appreciation, physical education, physical science, physics, physics-AP, pre-calculus, psychology, science, senior project, Spanish, speech, strings, technology, trigonometry, U.S. history, U.S. history-AP, world history, world history-AP, yearbook.

Graduation Requirements Arts and fine arts (art, music, dance, drama), composition, computer science, English, foreign language, mathematics, physical education (includes health), science, social science, social studies (includes history), speech, technology, 20 hrs of community service annually.

Special Academic Programs 9 Advanced Placement exams for which test preparation is offered; honors section; independent study; academic accommodation for the gifted and the musically talented.

College Admission Counseling 31 students graduated in 2008; all went to college, including Auburn University; Georgia Institute of Technology; University of Georgia; University of Mississippi; Valdosta State University; Wake Forest University. Median SAT critical reading: 570, median SAT math: 540, median SAT writing: 550, median combined SAT: 1490, median composite ACT: 24. 48% scored over 600 on SAT critical reading, 19% scored over 600 on SAT math, 33% scored over 600 on SAT writing, 29% scored over 1800 on combined SAT, 33% scored over 26 on composite ACT.

Student Life Upper grades have specified standards of dress, student council, honor system. Discipline rests equally with students and faculty.

Tuition and Aid Day student tuition: $8460. Tuition installment plan (monthly payment plans). Tuition reduction for siblings, merit scholarship grants, need-based scholarship grants available. In 2008–09, 25% of upper-school students received aid; total upper-school merit-scholarship money awarded: $44,000. Total amount of financial aid awarded in 2008–09: $139,000.

Admissions Traditional secondary-level entrance grade is 9. For fall 2008, 14 students applied for upper-level admission, 12 were accepted, 11 enrolled. ACT, admissions testing, Explore, latest standardized score from previous school, PSAT or SAT, Stanford Achievement Test or writing sample required. Deadline for receipt of application materials: none. Application fee required: $50. Interview required.

Athletics Interscholastic: baseball (boys), basketball (b,g), cheering (g), cross-country running (b,g), football (b), golf (b,g), soccer (b,g), softball (g), tennis (b,g), track and field (b,g), wrestling (b). 1 PE instructor, 3 coaches, 1 athletic trainer.
Computers Computers are regularly used in creative writing, mathematics, science, technology, writing classes. Computer network features include on-campus library services, Internet access, wireless campus network, Internet filtering or blocking technology. Student e-mail accounts are available to students. Students grades are available online.
Contact Ginger D. Holley, Director of Admission. 229-242-8491. Fax: 229-245-7894. E-mail: gholley@valwood.org. Web site: www.valwood.org.

VANDEBILT CATHOLIC HIGH SCHOOL

209 South Hollywood Road
Houma, Louisiana 70360
Head of School: Mr. David Keife

General Information Coeducational day college-preparatory, arts, business, religious studies, and technology school, affiliated with Roman Catholic Church; primarily serves individuals with Attention Deficit Disorder and dyslexic students. Grades 8–12. Founded: 1965. Setting: suburban. Nearest major city is New Orleans. 29-acre campus. 8 buildings on campus. Approved or accredited by Southern Association of Colleges and Schools and Louisiana Department of Education. Endowment: $355,000. Total enrollment: 921. Upper school average class size: 25. Upper school faculty-student ratio: 1:25.
Upper School Student Profile Grade 8: 198 students (95 boys, 103 girls); Grade 9: 201 students (98 boys, 103 girls); Grade 10: 173 students (90 boys, 83 girls); Grade 11: 199 students (97 boys, 102 girls); Grade 12: 150 students (61 boys, 89 girls). 85% of students are Roman Catholic.
Faculty School total: 63. In upper school: 25 men, 38 women; 20 have advanced degrees.
Subjects Offered 20th century world history, 3-dimensional art, accounting, advanced chemistry, advanced math, algebra, American history, art, band, biology, bookkeeping, business education, business law, calculus, chemistry, choir, Christian education, civics, civics/free enterprise, computer applications, computer keyboarding, computer science, driver education, earth science, English, English literature, French, general business, geography, history of music, honors algebra, honors English, honors geometry, honors U.S. history, Latin, leadership, mathematics, media, music appreciation, physical education, physical science, physics, pre-algebra, reading, reading/study skills, religion, Spanish, speech, world history.
Graduation Requirements Algebra, American history, athletics, biology, chemistry, civics, computer applications, English, geometry, physical education (includes health), religion (includes Bible studies and theology), science, social studies (includes history).
Special Academic Programs Honors section; programs in English, mathematics for dyslexic students; special instructional classes for students with Attention Deficit Disorder and dyslexia.
College Admission Counseling 166 students graduated in 2008; 165 went to college, including Louisiana State University and Agricultural and Mechanical College; Louisiana Tech University; Loyola University New Orleans; Nicholls State University; Tulane University; University of Louisiana at Lafayette. Other: 1 went to work. Mean composite ACT: 23. 40% scored over 26 on composite ACT.
Student Life Upper grades have uniform requirement, student council. Discipline rests primarily with faculty. Attendance at religious services is required.
Tuition and Aid Day student tuition: $5355. Tuition installment plan (monthly payment plans). Tuition reduction for siblings, need-based scholarship grants, middle-income loans available. In 2008–09, 10% of upper-school students received aid. Total amount of financial aid awarded in 2008–09: $90,000.
Admissions Traditional secondary-level entrance grade is 8. For fall 2008, 895 students applied for upper-level admission, 894 were accepted, 894 enrolled. Admissions testing required. Deadline for receipt of application materials: none. No application fee required. On-campus interview required.
Athletics Interscholastic: baseball (boys), basketball (b,g), cheering (g), cross-country running (b,g), dance squad (g), football (b), golf (b), gymnastics (b,g), soccer (b,g), tennis (b,g), track and field (b,g), weight training (b,g). 5 PE instructors, 15 coaches.
Computers Computers are regularly used in all academic classes. Computer network features include on-campus library services, Internet access, Internet filtering or blocking technology. Computer access in designated common areas is available to students. Students grades are available online. The school has a published electronic and media policy.
Contact Mr. Quinn Moreaux, Assistant Principal. 985-876-2551. Fax: 985-868-9774. E-mail: qmoreaux@htdiocese.org. Web site: www.vandebiltcatholic.org.

VANGUARD PREPARATORY SCHOOL

4240 Sigma Road
Dallas, Texas 75244
Head of School: Ms. Rosalind Funderburgh

General Information Coeducational day college-preparatory school; primarily serves students with learning disabilities, individuals with Attention Deficit Disorder, individuals with emotional and behavioral problems, dyslexic students, and Mood disorder. Grades PK–12. Founded: 1993. Setting: suburban. 2-acre campus. 1 building on campus. Approved or accredited by Southern Association of Colleges and Schools and Texas Department of Education. Upper school average class size: 8. Upper school faculty-student ratio: 1:6.
Faculty School total: 30. In upper school: 5 men, 5 women.
Special Academic Programs Programs in English, mathematics, general development for dyslexic students.
Student Life Upper grades have specified standards of dress, student council, honor system. Discipline rests primarily with faculty.
Tuition and Aid Tuition installment plan (monthly payment plans). Tuition reduction for siblings, need-based scholarship grants available.
Admissions No application fee required. Interview required.
Computers Computers are regularly used in all classes. Computer resources include Internet access, Internet filtering or blocking technology.
Contact 972-404-1616. Fax: 972-404-1641. Web site: www.vanguardprepschool.com/.

THE VANGUARD SCHOOL

Lake Wales, Florida
See Special Needs Schools section.

VERDALA INTERNATIONAL SCHOOL

Fort Pembroke
Pembroke PBK1641, Malta
Head of School: Mr. Adam Pleasance

General Information Coeducational boarding and day college-preparatory and general academic school. Boarding grades 7–12, day grades PK–12. Founded: 1977. Setting: suburban. Nearest major city is Valletta, Malta. Students are housed in host family homes. 6-acre campus. 6 buildings on campus. Approved or accredited by International Baccalaureate Organization and Middle States Association of Colleges and Schools. Member of European Council of International Schools. Language of instruction: English. Endowment: €91,000. Total enrollment: 315. Upper school average class size: 15. Upper school faculty-student ratio: 1:7.
Upper School Student Profile Grade 9: 21 students (8 boys, 13 girls); Grade 10: 32 students (14 boys, 18 girls); Grade 11: 29 students (12 boys, 17 girls); Grade 12: 30 students (14 boys, 16 girls). 22% of students are boarding students. 90% are international students. International students from Austria, Germany, Netherlands, Russian Federation, United Kingdom, and United States; 32 other countries represented in student body.
Faculty School total: 44. In upper school: 7 men, 22 women; 7 have advanced degrees; 1 resides on campus.
Subjects Offered Algebra, art, art history, biology, calculus, chemistry, computer programming, computer science, drama, English, English literature, fine arts, French, geography, geometry, grammar, health, history, Italian, mathematics, music, physical education, physics, psychology, science, social studies, Spanish, theory of knowledge, trigonometry, world history, world literature, writing.
Graduation Requirements Arts and fine arts (art, music, dance, drama), computer science, English, foreign language, mathematics, physical education (includes health), science, social studies (includes history).
Special Academic Programs International Baccalaureate program; honors section; accelerated programs; ESL (50 students enrolled).
College Admission Counseling 24 students graduated in 2008; 19 went to college. Other: 1 went to work, 2 entered military service, 2 had other specific plans. Median SAT critical reading: 660, median SAT math: 610, median SAT writing: 550, median combined SAT: 1820. 80% scored over 600 on SAT critical reading, 60% scored over 600 on SAT math, 40% scored over 600 on SAT writing.
Student Life Upper grades have specified standards of dress, student council, honor system. Discipline rests primarily with faculty.
Tuition and Aid Day student tuition: €5950; 7-day tuition and room/board: €12,710. Tuition installment plan (monthly payment plans, individually arranged payment plans). Tuition reduction for siblings, need-based scholarship grants available. In 2008–09, 7% of upper-school students received aid. Total amount of financial aid awarded in 2008–09: $23,018.
Admissions Traditional secondary-level entrance grade is 9. For fall 2008, 18 students applied for upper-level admission, 15 were accepted, 15 enrolled. Academic Profile Tests required. Deadline for receipt of application materials: none. No application fee required. On-campus interview required.

Athletics Interscholastic: basketball (boys), volleyball (b,g); intramural: physical fitness (b,g), soccer (b,g), swimming and diving (b,g), track and field (b,g); coed intramural: physical fitness, swimming and diving. 2 coaches, 1 athletic trainer.

Computers Computer resources include on-campus library services, online commercial services, Internet access. Computer access in designated common areas is available to students.

Contact Mrs. Daphne Baldacchino, Secretary. 356-21375133. Fax: 356-21372387. E-mail: vis1@verdala.org. Web site: www.verdala.org.

VERDE VALLEY SCHOOL

3511 Verde Valley School Road
Sedona, Arizona 86351

Head of School: Paul Domingue

General Information Coeducational boarding and day college-preparatory and International Baccalaureate Programme school. Grades 9–12. Founded: 1948. Setting: rural. Nearest major city is Phoenix. Students are housed in single-sex dormitories. 160-acre campus. 20 buildings on campus. Approved or accredited by International Baccalaureate Organization, North Carolina Association of Independent Schools, and Arizona Department of Education. Candidate for accreditation by Independent Schools Association of the Southwest and North Central Association of Colleges and Schools. Member of National Association of Independent Schools and Secondary School Admission Test Board. Endowment: $2 million. Total enrollment: 116. Upper school average class size: 9. Upper school faculty-student ratio: 1:6.

Upper School Student Profile Grade 9: 24 students (11 boys, 13 girls); Grade 10: 32 students (17 boys, 15 girls); Grade 11: 36 students (16 boys, 20 girls); Grade 12: 22 students (15 boys, 7 girls). 83% of students are boarding students. 37% are state residents. 12 states are represented in upper school student body. 41% are international students. International students from China, Germany, Guatemala, Republic of Korea, Saudi Arabia, and Viet Nam; 9 other countries represented in student body.

Faculty School total: 24. In upper school: 13 men, 8 women; 11 have advanced degrees; 22 reside on campus.

Subjects Offered Algebra, American history, American literature, anthropology, art, art and culture, art history, biology, calculus, ceramics, chemistry, creative writing, dance, drama, drawing, earth science, ecology, English, English literature, environmental science, ESL, European history, expository writing, fine arts, geography, geometry, grammar, history, journalism, mathematics, music, Native American studies, painting, photography, physical education, physics, poetry, science, social studies, Spanish, theater, trigonometry, world history.

Graduation Requirements Arts and fine arts (art, music, dance, drama), English, foreign language, mathematics, science, social studies (includes history), participation in annual Project Period and Field Trip program, meet requirements of International Baccalaureate Programme.

Special Academic Programs International Baccalaureate program; independent study; academic accommodation for the gifted, the musically talented, and the artistically talented; ESL (12 students enrolled).

College Admission Counseling 26 students graduated in 2008; 24 went to college, including Columbia College; Northern Arizona University; Rochester Institute of Technology; Smith College; Stanford University; University of Colorado at Boulder. Other: 2 had other specific plans. Median SAT critical reading: 562, median SAT math: 556, median composite ACT: 23. 40% scored over 600 on SAT critical reading, 34% scored over 600 on SAT math, 31% scored over 26 on composite ACT.

Student Life Upper grades have student council. Discipline rests equally with students and faculty.

Tuition and Aid Day student tuition: $20,600; 5-day tuition and room/board: $38,300; 7-day tuition and room/board: $38,300. Tuition installment plan (FACTS Tuition Payment Plan, monthly payment plans). Need-based scholarship grants, need- and merit-based program available. In 2008–09, 53% of upper-school students received aid. Total amount of financial aid awarded in 2008–09: $1,403,600.

Admissions Traditional secondary-level entrance grade is 9. For fall 2008, 110 students applied for upper-level admission, 70 were accepted, 55 enrolled. SLEP for foreign students or SSAT required. Deadline for receipt of application materials: none. Application fee required: $50. Interview required.

Athletics Interscholastic: basketball (boys, girls), golf (b,g), soccer (b,g); coed interscholastic: bicycling, horseback riding; coed intramural: aerobics/dance, aerobics/Nautilus, aquatics, archery, backpacking, bicycling, canoeing/kayaking, climbing, cross-country running, dressage, equestrian sports, fitness, fitness walking, golf, hiking/backpacking, horseback riding, jogging, kayaking, martial arts, modern dance, mountain biking, mountaineering, Nautilus, outdoor activities, physical fitness, rappelling, rock climbing, ropes courses, running, skiing (cross-country), skiing (downhill), snowboarding, strength & conditioning, swimming and diving, table tennis, tai chi, tennis, walking, wall climbing, wilderness, yoga.

Computers Computers are regularly used in English, mathematics, science classes. Computer network features include on-campus library services, Internet access, wireless campus network, Internet filtering or blocking technology. Student e-mail accounts are available to students.

Contact Erin Fanelli, Admission Office Manager. 928-284-2272 Ext. 31. Fax: 928-284-0432. E-mail: admission@verdevalleyschool.org. Web site: www.vvsaz.org.

VERMONT ACADEMY

20 Pleasant Street
PO Box 500
Saxtons River, Vermont 05154

ANNOUNCEMENT FROM THE SCHOOL Vermont Academy offers an exciting college-preparatory curriculum designed for the development of confident and independent learners. Small classes and personal attention put each student in the front row. Everyone makes the team in Vermont Academy's eighteen sports offerings. Students discover their talents in visual and performing arts classes. Highlights include a new 350-seat state-of-the-art theater; an HP Tablet PC program with wireless Internet access; the Winter Sports Park for skiing, jumping, and snowboarding; a 22-student girls' dormitory and a renovated boys' dormitory; a renovated gym with new locker rooms, a fitness center, and a dance studio; and an observatory with a high-powered telescope.

See Close-Up on page 1002.

VIANNEY HIGH SCHOOL

1311 South Kirkwood Road
St. Louis, Missouri 63122

Head of School: Mr. Lawrence D. Keller

General Information Boys' day college-preparatory, arts, business, religious studies, and technology school, affiliated with Roman Catholic Church. Grades 9–12. Founded: 1960. Setting: suburban. 37-acre campus. 6 buildings on campus. Approved or accredited by National Catholic Education Association, North Central Association of Colleges and Schools, and The College Board. Total enrollment: 622. Upper school average class size: 26. Upper school faculty-student ratio: 1:12.

Upper School Student Profile Grade 9: 167 students (167 boys); Grade 10: 151 students (151 boys); Grade 11: 140 students (140 boys); Grade 12: 164 students (164 boys). 98% of students are Roman Catholic.

Faculty School total: 46. In upper school: 38 men, 8 women; 38 have advanced degrees.

Subjects Offered Accounting, advanced chemistry, Advanced Placement courses, algebra, American government, American history, American literature, analysis, analytic geometry, architectural drawing, art, art education, art history, arts appreciation, athletic training, band, British literature (honors), business law, business mathematics, calculus, calculus-AP, Catholic belief and practice, chemistry, Christian and Hebrew scripture, Christian ethics, Christian studies, college writing, communication skills, composition, computer applications, computer keyboarding, computer programming, computer skills, constitutional history of U.S., consumer education, current events, drama, economics, English composition, English literature, European history, expository writing, foreign language, fractal geometry, French, geometry, German, German literature, government, health and wellness, honors algebra, honors English, honors geometry, honors U.S. history, journalism, keyboarding, leadership skills, mythology, publications, research skills, scripture, sex education, Shakespeare, Spanish, Spanish literature, sports conditioning, stage design, stagecraft, statistics and probability, technical drawing, technology, technology/design, the Web, theater arts, theater design and production, theater history, trigonometry, U.S. government, U.S. history, U.S. literature, Web site design, weight training, world civilizations, world history, writing fundamentals, writing skills.

Graduation Requirements American history, American literature, arts and fine arts (art, music, dance, drama), biology, English, English composition, foreign language, government/civics, history, keyboarding/computer, mathematics, physical education (includes health), physical fitness, religious studies, science, social issues, 100 hours of community service.

Special Academic Programs 2 Advanced Placement exams for which test preparation is offered; honors section; study at local college for college credit; special instructional classes for students with learning disabilities, Attention Deficit Disorder, dyslexia, emotional and behavioral problems.

College Admission Counseling 130 students graduated in 2008; 107 went to college, including Missouri State University; St. Louis Community College at Meramec; Truman State University; University of Missouri–Columbia; Webster University. Other: 22 went to work, 1 entered military service. Median composite ACT: 20. 32% scored over 26 on composite ACT.

Student Life Upper grades have specified standards of dress, student council, honor system. Discipline rests equally with students and faculty. Attendance at religious services is required.

Summer Programs Enrichment, sports programs offered; session focuses on reinforcing athletic skills; held on campus; accepts boys and girls; open to students from other schools. 1,100 students usually enrolled. 2009 schedule: June 4 to July 27. Application deadline: June 1.

Tuition and Aid Day student tuition: $9350. Tuition installment plan (The Tuition Plan, SMART Tuition Payment Plan, FACTS Tuition Payment Plan, monthly payment plans, individually arranged payment plans). Tuition reduction for siblings, merit scholarship grants, need-based scholarship grants, paying campus jobs available. In

2008–09, 35% of upper-school students received aid; total upper-school merit-scholarship money awarded: $14,750. Total amount of financial aid awarded in 2008–09: $528,479.

Admissions Traditional secondary-level entrance grade is 9. For fall 2008, 179 students applied for upper-level admission, 173 were accepted, 167 enrolled. High School Placement Test (closed version) from Scholastic Testing Service required. Deadline for receipt of application materials: none. No application fee required. On-campus interview required.

Athletics Interscholastic: aquatics, baseball, basketball, cross-country running, diving, football, golf, ice hockey, in-line hockey, indoor hockey, lacrosse, racquetball, running, soccer, swimming and diving, tennis, track and field, volleyball, wrestling; intramural: bowling, fitness, flag football, paint ball, physical fitness, physical training, Special Olympics, strength & conditioning, touch football, weight training. 3 PE instructors, 36 coaches, 1 athletic trainer.

Computers Computers are regularly used in all academic, computer applications, creative writing, drafting, journalism, yearbook classes. Computer network features include on-campus library services, online commercial services, Internet access, wireless campus network, Internet filtering or blocking technology. Campus intranet, student e-mail accounts, and computer access in designated common areas are available to students. Students grades are available online. The school has a published electronic and media policy.

Contact Mr. Terry Cochran, Director of Admissions. 314-965-4853 Ext. 142. Fax: 314-965-1950. E-mail: tcochran@vianney.com. Web site: www.vianney.com.

VICTOR VALLEY CHRISTIAN SCHOOL

15260 Nisqually Road
Victorville, California 92395

Head of School: Mr. David B. Schnurstein

General Information Coeducational day college-preparatory, arts, and religious studies school, affiliated with Assemblies of God. Grades K–12. Founded: 1972. Setting: suburban. Nearest major city is Los Angeles. 8-acre campus. 5 buildings on campus. Approved or accredited by Association of Christian Schools International and Western Association of Schools and Colleges. Total enrollment: 419. Upper school average class size: 20. Upper school faculty-student ratio: 1:15.

Upper School Student Profile Grade 9: 43 students (26 boys, 17 girls); Grade 10: 51 students (19 boys, 32 girls); Grade 11: 41 students (27 boys, 14 girls); Grade 12: 30 students (18 boys, 12 girls). 15% of students are Assemblies of God.

Faculty School total: 17. In upper school: 6 men, 11 women; 2 have advanced degrees.

Subjects Offered Algebra, American history, art, arts, Bible studies, biology, biology-AP, calculus-AP, career education, chemistry, chorus, Christian education, computer literacy, computer science, drama, earth science, English, English language and composition-AP, English literature-AP, family studies, fine arts, geometry, government, health, mathematics, physical education, physics, pre-calculus, psychology-AP, religion, science, social science, social studies, Spanish, theater, U.S. history, U.S. history-AP, word processing, world history, world history-AP, yearbook.

Graduation Requirements Arts and fine arts (art, music, dance, drama), English, foreign language, health, mathematics, religion (includes Bible studies and theology), science, social science.

Special Academic Programs Advanced Placement exam preparation; study at local college for college credit; academic accommodation for the gifted; special instructional classes for students with learning disabilities; ESL (4 students enrolled).

College Admission Counseling 32 students graduated in 2008; 30 went to college, including California State University, Fullerton; California State University, San Bernardino; The University of Arizona; University of California, Irvine; University of Redlands; University of San Diego. Other: 2 went to work. Median SAT critical reading: 480, median SAT math: 470, median SAT writing: 475, median composite ACT: 19. 10% scored over 600 on SAT math.

Student Life Upper grades have uniform requirement, student council. Discipline rests primarily with faculty.

Summer Programs Remediation programs offered; session focuses on make-up credits; held on campus; accepts boys and girls; open to students from other schools. 8 students usually enrolled. 2009 schedule: June 22 to August 1. Application deadline: June 19.

Tuition and Aid Day student tuition: $4950. Tuition installment plan (monthly payment plans, individually arranged payment plans). Tuition reduction for siblings, need-based scholarship grants available. In 2008–09, 5% of upper-school students received aid. Total amount of financial aid awarded in 2008–09: $20,000.

Admissions Traditional secondary-level entrance grade is 9. For fall 2008, 19 students applied for upper-level admission, 18 were accepted, 18 enrolled. Deadline for receipt of application materials: none. No application fee required. On-campus interview required.

Athletics Interscholastic: baseball (boys), basketball (b,g), cheering (g), cross-country running (b,g), football (b), softball (g), track and field (b,g), volleyball (g); coed interscholastic: golf, soccer. 2 PE instructors, 7 coaches.

Computers Computers are regularly used in graphic arts, journalism, yearbook classes. Computer resources include on-campus library services, Internet access, wireless campus network, Internet filtering or blocking technology. Campus intranet is available to students. Students grades are available online.

Contact Mr. David B. Schnurstein, Principal. 760-241-8827. Fax: 760-243-0654. E-mail: davids@vfassembly.org. Web site: www.vvcs.org.

VIEWPOINT SCHOOL

23620 Mulholland Highway
Calabasas, California 91302

Head of School: Dr. Robert J. Dworkoski

General Information Coeducational day college-preparatory and arts school. Grades K–12. Founded: 1961. Setting: suburban. Nearest major city is Los Angeles. 25-acre campus. 5 buildings on campus. Approved or accredited by California Association of Independent Schools and Western Association of Schools and Colleges. Member of National Association of Independent Schools. Endowment: $5 million. Total enrollment: 1,210. Upper school average class size: 18. Upper school faculty-student ratio: 1:10.

Upper School Student Profile Grade 9: 132 students (70 boys, 62 girls); Grade 10: 128 students (64 boys, 64 girls); Grade 11: 114 students (57 boys, 57 girls); Grade 12: 106 students (58 boys, 48 girls).

Faculty School total: 154. In upper school: 22 men, 40 women; 46 have advanced degrees.

Subjects Offered Adolescent issues, advanced chemistry, advanced computer applications, advanced studio art-AP, African literature, algebra, American history, American history-AP, American literature, ancient history, ancient world history, animation, art, art appreciation, art history, art history-AP, Asian history, Asian studies, ballet, Basic programming, basic skills, Bible as literature, biology, biology-AP, British literature, business skills, calculus, calculus-AP, California writers, ceramics, character education, chemistry, chemistry-AP, Chinese, Chinese studies, choir, choreography, chorus, clayworking, college admission preparation, community service, comparative government and politics, comparative government and politics-AP, comparative politics, computer animation, computer keyboarding, computer programming, computer science, computer science-AP, concert band, contemporary women writers, creative writing, critical studies in film, dance, debate, decision making skills, diversity studies, drama, drama performance, dramatic arts, drawing and design, earth science, economics, English, English language-AP, English literature, English literature-AP, ensembles, environmental education, environmental science, environmental science-AP, European history, European history-AP, film, film appreciation, filmmaking, fine arts, French, French language-AP, French literature-AP, geometry, global science, government/civics, history, history-AP, Holocaust and other genocides, honors algebra, honors English, honors geometry, human development, humanities, instrumental music, international relations, jazz, jazz band, jazz dance, jazz ensemble, journalism, Latin, Latin American history, Latin History, Latin-AP, library skills, literary magazine, literature by women, mathematics, medieval history, multicultural literature, music, music composition, music history, music theory-AP, newspaper, oceanography, outdoor education, performing arts, photography, physical education, physics, physics-AP, physiology, poetry, psychology, psychology-AP, public speaking, robotics, science, sculpture, senior project, Shakespeare, short story, social studies, sociology, Spanish, Spanish language-AP, Spanish literature-AP, speech and debate, statistics and probability, student publications, studio art-AP, study skills, swimming, theater, trigonometry, U.S. government-AP, video, vocal jazz, women's literature, word processing, world history, yearbook.

Graduation Requirements Arts and fine arts (art, music, dance, drama), computer science, English, foreign language, mathematics, physical education (includes health), science, social studies (includes history). Community service is required.

Special Academic Programs 29 Advanced Placement exams for which test preparation is offered; honors section; independent study; study abroad.

College Admission Counseling 101 students graduated in 2008; all went to college, including University of California, Berkeley; University of California, Davis; University of California, Los Angeles; University of California, San Diego; University of Colorado at Boulder; University of Southern California. Mean SAT critical reading: 642, mean SAT math: 652, mean SAT writing: 660, mean composite ACT: 26.

Student Life Upper grades have specified standards of dress, student council, honor system. Discipline rests primarily with faculty.

Summer Programs Remediation, enrichment, advancement, sports, art/fine arts, computer instruction programs offered; session focuses on academics, arts, sports, and recreation; held on campus; accepts boys and girls; open to students from other schools. 315 students usually enrolled. 2009 schedule: June 16 to July 30. Application deadline: none.

Tuition and Aid Day student tuition: $22,150. Tuition installment plan (monthly payment plans). Tuition reduction for siblings, need-based scholarship grants available. In 2008–09, 14% of upper-school students received aid. Total amount of financial aid awarded in 2008–09: $886,690.

Admissions Traditional secondary-level entrance grade is 9. For fall 2008, 115 students applied for upper-level admission, 70 were accepted, 42 enrolled. ISEE required. Deadline for receipt of application materials: January 10. Application fee required: $125. Interview required.

Athletics Interscholastic: ballet (boys, girls), baseball (b), basketball (b,g), cooperative games (b,g), football (b), soccer (b,g), softball (g), volleyball (b,g); intramural: backpacking (b,g), ball hockey (b,g), ballet (b,g), baseball (b), basketball (b,g), soccer (b,g), softball (g), volleyball (b,g); coed interscholastic: cross-country running, dance, dressage, equestrian sports, flag football, golf, modern dance, swimming and diving, tennis; coed intramural: cheering, cross-country running, dance, dance team, fencing, football, golf, hiking/backpacking, modern dance, outdoor education, physical fitness, strength & conditioning, swimming and diving, weight training. 15 PE instructors, 15 coaches, 1 athletic trainer.

Computers Computers are regularly used in animation, basic skills, college planning, English, foreign language, history, keyboarding, library skills, mathematics, multimedia, music, newspaper, publications, science, video film production, Web site design, word processing, yearbook classes. Computer network features include on-campus library services, online commercial services, Internet access, wireless campus network, Internet filtering or blocking technology.

Contact Mrs. Julie Montgomery, Coordinator of Admission and Financial Aid Offices. 818-591-6560. Fax: 818-591-0834. E-mail: admission@viewpoint.org. Web site: www.viewpoint.org.

ANNOUNCEMENT FROM THE SCHOOL Viewpoint is an independent, nonprofit, coeducational college-preparatory day school for grades K–12. Viewpoint is located in the foothills of the Santa Monica Mountains on a 25-acre campus with scenic vistas, rolling hillsides, and large heritage oaks. For 49 years, families have been attracted to Viewpoint's excellent academic programs, its tranquil and nurturing environment, and its extensive facilities for academics, athletics, film, computer science, arts (both visual and dramatic), and music.

See Close-Up on page 1004.

VILLA DUCHESNE/OAK HILL SCHOOL

801 South Spoede Road
St. Louis, Missouri 63131

Head of School: Dr. Jack Rizzo, EdD

General Information Coeducational day (boys' only in lower grades) college-preparatory, arts, religious studies, and technology school, affiliated with Roman Catholic Church. Boys grades JK–6, girls grades JK–12. Founded: 1929. Setting: suburban. 60-acre campus. 2 buildings on campus. Approved or accredited by Independent Schools Association of the Central States, National Catholic Education Association, Network of Sacred Heart Schools, North Central Association of Colleges and Schools, and Missouri Department of Education. Total enrollment: 760. Upper school average class size: 16. Upper school faculty-student ratio: 1:9.

Upper School Student Profile Grade 7: 68 students (68 girls); Grade 8: 51 students (51 girls); Grade 9: 100 students (100 girls); Grade 10: 80 students (80 girls); Grade 11: 82 students (82 girls); Grade 12: 69 students (69 girls). 92% of students are Roman Catholic.

Faculty School total: 56. In upper school: 13 men, 43 women; 42 have advanced degrees.

Subjects Offered American government, American literature, American literature-AP, anatomy and physiology, art, biology, biology-AP, British literature, calculus, calculus-AP, campus ministry, ceramics, chemistry, chorus, civics, computers, creative writing, discrete math, drawing, economics, English, European history, European history-AP, Far Eastern history, French, geography, geometry, health, integrated physics, math analysis, Middle East, music, newspaper, painting, personal development, physical education, physics, pre-algebra, pre-calculus, printmaking, psychology, public speaking, religion, scripture, sculpture, social justice, Spanish, studio art, studio art-AP, theater arts, U.S. history, U.S. history-AP, Western civilization, women's studies, world literature, yearbook.

Graduation Requirements Students must perform community service to graduate.

Special Academic Programs International Baccalaureate program; Advanced Placement exam preparation; honors section; independent study; term-away projects; study at local college for college credit; domestic exchange program (with Network of Sacred Heart Schools); study abroad.

College Admission Counseling 69 students graduated in 2008; all went to college, including Saint Louis University; University of Missouri–Columbia; Washington University in St. Louis. Mean SAT critical reading: 580, mean SAT math: 572, mean SAT writing: 598, mean combined SAT: 1750, mean composite ACT: 27.

Student Life Upper grades have uniform requirement, student council, honor system. Discipline rests primarily with faculty. Attendance at religious services is required.

Summer Programs Enrichment, advancement, sports, art/fine arts, computer instruction programs offered; session focuses on enrichment and college preparation; held on campus; accepts boys and girls; open to students from other schools. 150 students usually enrolled. 2009 schedule: June to July. Application deadline: May.

Tuition and Aid Day student tuition: $13,450–$15,500. Tuition installment plan (monthly payment plans, 8-month plan, trimester plan, or full-payment plan). Tuition reduction for siblings, merit scholarship grants, need-based scholarship grants available. In 2008–09, 15% of upper-school students received aid. Total amount of financial aid awarded in 2008–09: $800,000.

Admissions Traditional secondary-level entrance grade is 7. Admissions testing required. Deadline for receipt of application materials: January 25. Application fee required: $40. On-campus interview required.

Athletics Interscholastic: basketball, cross-country running, diving, field hockey, golf, lacrosse, racquetball, soccer, softball, swimming and diving, tennis, track and field, volleyball. 7 PE instructors, 34 coaches, 1 athletic trainer.

Computers Computers are regularly used in all academic classes. Computer network features include on-campus library services, online commercial services, Internet access, wireless campus network, Internet filtering or blocking technology, students in grades 7 to12 have personal HP tablet PCs. Campus intranet, student e-mail accounts, and computer access in designated common areas are available to students. Students grades are available online. The school has a published electronic and media policy.

Contact Mrs. Suzy Grow, Admissions Assistant. 314-810-3451. Fax: 314-432-0199. E-mail: sgrow@vdoh.org. Web site: www.vdoh.org.

VILLA JOSEPH MARIE HIGH SCHOOL

1180 Holland Road
Holland, Pennsylvania 18966

Head of School: Mrs. Mary T. Michel

General Information Girls' day college-preparatory, arts, religious studies, and Drama school, affiliated with Roman Catholic Church. Grades 9–12. Founded: 1932. Setting: suburban. Nearest major city is Philadelphia. 55-acre campus. 3 buildings on campus. Approved or accredited by Middle States Association of Colleges and Schools and Pennsylvania Department of Education. Total enrollment: 381. Upper school average class size: 15. Upper school faculty-student ratio: 1:14.

Upper School Student Profile Grade 9: 95 students (95 girls); Grade 10: 93 students (93 girls); Grade 11: 106 students (106 girls); Grade 12: 88 students (88 girls). 98% of students are Roman Catholic.

Faculty School total: 37. In upper school: 9 men, 28 women; 30 have advanced degrees.

Subjects Offered Algebra, American government, American history, American history-AP, anatomy and physiology, ancient history, art, art appreciation, biology, biology-AP, business mathematics, calculus-AP, chemistry, chemistry-AP, chorus, conceptual physics, dance, drama, earth science, English, English literature-AP, environmental science, environmental science-AP, European history-AP, film and literature, forensic science, French, geometry, health, Latin, music, physical education, physics, physics-AP, pre-calculus, psychology, psychology-AP, sociology, Spanish, speech, studio art, theology, trigonometry, world history, writing.

Graduation Requirements Arts and fine arts (art, music, dance, drama), English, foreign language, mathematics, physical education (includes health), religion (includes Bible studies and theology), science, social science, social studies (includes history).

Special Academic Programs 9 Advanced Placement exams for which test preparation is offered; honors section; study at local college for college credit; academic accommodation for the gifted, the musically talented, and the artistically talented.

College Admission Counseling 88 students graduated in 2008; all went to college, including Loyola College in Maryland; Penn State University Park; Saint Joseph's University; The University of Scranton; Villanova University. Mean SAT critical reading: 580, mean SAT math: 555, mean SAT writing: 603.

Student Life Upper grades have uniform requirement, student council, honor system. Discipline rests primarily with faculty. Attendance at religious services is required.

Summer Programs Enrichment, sports programs offered; session focuses on enrichment; held on campus; accepts boys and girls; open to students from other schools. 45 students usually enrolled.

Tuition and Aid Day student tuition: $9950. Tuition installment plan (monthly payment plans). Tuition reduction for siblings, merit scholarship grants, need-based scholarship grants available. Total upper-school merit-scholarship money awarded for 2008–09: $160,000.

Admissions Traditional secondary-level entrance grade is 9. For fall 2008, 200 students applied for upper-level admission, 125 were accepted, 95 enrolled. High School Placement Test required. Deadline for receipt of application materials: November 14. Application fee required: $55. On-campus interview required.

Athletics Interscholastic: basketball, cheering, cross-country running, field hockey, golf, indoor track, lacrosse, soccer, softball, tennis, track and field, volleyball, winter (indoor) track. 1 PE instructor, 14 coaches, 1 athletic trainer.

Computers Computers are regularly used in art, English, foreign language, history, library, literary magazine, mathematics, religion, science, yearbook classes. Computer network features include on-campus library services, Internet access, wireless campus network, Internet filtering or blocking technology. The school has a published electronic and media policy.

Contact Mrs. Maureen Cleary, Director of Institutional Advancement. 215-357-8810 Ext. 124. Fax: 215-357-9410. E-mail: mclea@vjmhs.org. Web site: www.vjmhs.org.

VILLA MARIA ACADEMY

2403 West Eighth Street
Erie, Pennsylvania 16505-4492

Head of School: Ms. Geri Cicchetti

General Information Coeducational day college-preparatory and general academic school, affiliated with Roman Catholic Church. Grades 9–12. Founded: 1892. Setting:

suburban. 3 buildings on campus. Approved or accredited by Middle States Association of Colleges and Schools and National Catholic Education Association. Total enrollment: 295. Upper school average class size: 15. Upper school faculty-student ratio: 1:9.

Upper School Student Profile Grade 9: 67 students (13 boys, 54 girls); Grade 10: 81 students (15 boys, 66 girls); Grade 11: 69 students (17 boys, 52 girls); Grade 12: 78 students (14 boys, 64 girls). 87% of students are Roman Catholic.

Faculty School total: 33. In upper school: 6 men, 27 women; 13 have advanced degrees.

Subjects Offered Arts, community service, computer science, English, fine arts, health, keyboarding, Latin, mathematics, newspaper, physical education, practical arts, science, social studies, Spanish, theology, word processing, yearbook.

Graduation Requirements Arts and fine arts (art, music, dance, drama), English, foreign language, mathematics, physical education (includes health), religion (includes Bible studies and theology), science, social studies (includes history). Community service is required.

Special Academic Programs Advanced Placement exam preparation; honors section; study at local college for college credit.

College Admission Counseling 84 students graduated in 2008; 82 went to college, including Edinboro University of Pennsylvania; Gannon University; Mercyhurst College; Penn State Erie, The Behrend College; Penn State University Park; University of Pittsburgh. Other: 1 went to work, 1 entered military service.

Student Life Upper grades have uniform requirement, student council, honor system. Discipline rests primarily with faculty.

Tuition and Aid Day student tuition: $5660–$5960. Tuition installment plan (FACTS Tuition Payment Plan). Tuition reduction for siblings, merit scholarship grants, need-based scholarship grants available. Total upper-school merit-scholarship money awarded for 2008–09: $36,400. Total amount of financial aid awarded in 2008–09: $330,210.

Admissions Traditional secondary-level entrance grade is 9. Placement test required. Deadline for receipt of application materials: January 23. Application fee required: $10.

Athletics Interscholastic: baseball (boys), basketball (b,g), bowling (g), cheering (g), golf (b,g), lacrosse (g), soccer (b,g), softball (g), swimming and diving (g), tennis (b,g), volleyball (g), water polo (g); coed interscholastic: cross-country running, track and field. 1 PE instructor.

Computers Computers are regularly used in computer applications, graphic design, keyboarding, literary magazine, newspaper, Spanish, yearbook classes. Computer network features include on-campus library services, Internet access, wireless campus network, Internet filtering or blocking technology. Students grades are available online. The school has a published electronic and media policy.

Contact Mrs. Mary Mulard, Director of Admissions. 814-838-2061 Ext. 239. Fax: 814-836-0881. E-mail: mmulard@villamaria.com. Web site: www.villamaria.com.

VILLANOVA PREPARATORY SCHOOL

12096 North Ventura Avenue
Ojai, California 93023-3999

Head of School: Rev. Gregory Heidenblut

General Information Coeducational boarding and day college-preparatory, arts, religious studies, and ESL school, affiliated with Roman Catholic Church. Grades 9–12. Founded: 1924. Setting: rural. Nearest major city is Los Angeles. Students are housed in single-sex dormitories. 131-acre campus. 11 buildings on campus. Approved or accredited by National Catholic Education Association, The Association of Boarding Schools, Western Association of Schools and Colleges, and Western Catholic Education Association. Member of Secondary School Admission Test Board. Endowment: $7.6 million. Total enrollment: 315. Upper school average class size: 16. Upper school faculty-student ratio: 1:10.

Upper School Student Profile Grade 9: 88 students (47 boys, 41 girls); Grade 10: 83 students (45 boys, 38 girls); Grade 11: 70 students (40 boys, 30 girls); Grade 12: 74 students (44 boys, 30 girls). 32% of students are boarding students. 68% are state residents. International students from China, Guam, Republic of Korea, Rwanda, Taiwan, and Viet Nam; 5 other countries represented in student body. 54% of students are Roman Catholic.

Faculty School total: 41. In upper school: 20 men, 21 women; 26 have advanced degrees; 8 reside on campus.

Subjects Offered Algebra, American history, American literature, arts, biology, calculus, chemistry, computer programming, computer science, creative writing, drama, economics, English, English literature, English-AP, ESL, European history, expository writing, fine arts, geography, geometry, government/civics, health and wellness, history, history-AP, honors algebra, honors English, honors geometry, honors U.S. history, honors world history, Japanese, Latin, Latin-AP, marine science, mathematics, photography, physical education, physical science, physics, play production, psychology, religion, religious education, science, social studies, sociology, Spanish, Spanish-AP, speech, theater, theology, trigonometry, U.S. history-AP, world history, world literature, writing.

Graduation Requirements Arts and fine arts (art, music, dance, drama), electives, English, physical education (includes health), religion (includes Bible studies and theology), science, social studies (includes history). Community service is required.

Special Academic Programs 5 Advanced Placement exams for which test preparation is offered; honors section; ESL (54 students enrolled).

College Admission Counseling 89 students graduated in 2008; all went to college, including Boston University; Stanford University; University of California, Berkeley; University of California, Los Angeles; University of California, Santa Barbara; University of Southern California. Mean SAT critical reading: 562, mean SAT math: 595, mean SAT writing: 565, mean combined SAT: 1721, mean composite ACT: 26.

Student Life Upper grades have specified standards of dress, student council. Discipline rests primarily with faculty. Attendance at religious services is required.

Tuition and Aid Day student tuition: $14,000; 7-day tuition and room/board: $40,000. Tuition installment plan (monthly payment plans, school's own payment plan). Tuition reduction for siblings, merit scholarship grants, need-based scholarship grants available. In 2008–09, 40% of upper-school students received aid; total upper-school merit-scholarship money awarded: $35,000. Total amount of financial aid awarded in 2008–09: $800,000.

Admissions Traditional secondary-level entrance grade is 9. For fall 2008, 255 students applied for upper-level admission, 135 were accepted, 85 enrolled. High School Placement Test, SSAT or TOEFL required. Deadline for receipt of application materials: January 26. Application fee required: $125. On-campus interview required.

Athletics Interscholastic: aquatics (boys, girls), baseball (b), basketball (b,g), cross-country running (b,g), football (b), soccer (b,g), softball (g), surfing (b,g), swimming and diving (b,g), tennis (b,g), track and field (b,g), volleyball (g), water polo (b,g); intramural: cheering (b,g), weight training (b,g); coed interscholastic: golf, surfing, swimming and diving; coed intramural: cheering, ultimate Frisbee. 1 PE instructor.

Computers Computers are regularly used in English, ESL, foreign language, history, mathematics, publishing, science, yearbook classes. Computer network features include on-campus library services, online commercial services, Internet access, wireless campus network, Internet filtering or blocking technology, Microsoft Office Suite. Campus intranet, student e-mail accounts, and computer access in designated common areas are available to students. Students grades are available online. The school has a published electronic and media policy.

Contact Mrs. Michelle M. Kolbeck, Admission Assistant. 805-646-1464 Ext. 161. Fax: 805-646-4430. E-mail: admissions@villanovaprep.org. Web site: www.villanovaprep.org.

ANNOUNCEMENT FROM THE SCHOOL Villanova was founded in 1924 as a Catholic school in the Augustinian tradition. Through a balanced program of academic courses, athletics, community service, art, and extracurricular activities, Villanova channels students' curiosity, enthusiasm, and energy so they can reach the full potential of their abilities and interests.

See Close-Up on page 1006.

VILLA WALSH ACADEMY

455 Western Avenue
Morristown, New Jersey 07960

Head of School: Sr. Patricia Pompa

General Information Girls' day college-preparatory, arts, religious studies, and technology school, affiliated with Roman Catholic Church. Grades 7–12. Founded: 1967. Setting: suburban. Nearest major city is New York, NY. 130-acre campus. 3 buildings on campus. Approved or accredited by Middle States Association of Colleges and Schools, National Catholic Education Association, New Jersey Association of Independent Schools, and New Jersey Department of Education. Endowment: $5 million. Total enrollment: 245. Upper school average class size: 12. Upper school faculty-student ratio: 1:8.

Upper School Student Profile Grade 7: 15 students (15 girls); Grade 8: 12 students (12 girls); Grade 9: 56 students (56 girls); Grade 10: 58 students (58 girls); Grade 11: 57 students (57 girls); Grade 12: 47 students (47 girls). 90% of students are Roman Catholic.

Faculty School total: 35. In upper school: 3 men, 32 women; 20 have advanced degrees.

Subjects Offered Advanced Placement courses, algebra, American history, American literature, anatomy and physiology, art, Bible as literature, biology, biology-AP, British literature, British literature (honors), calculus, calculus-AP, career/college preparation, chemistry, chemistry-AP, choral music, chorus, church history, college admission preparation, computer applications, computer graphics, computer keyboarding, computer literacy, computer processing, computer programming, computer science, computer skills, CPR, creative writing, desktop publishing, driver education, economics, economics and history, English, English language and composition-AP, English literature, ethics, European civilization, family life, finite math, first aid, French, French-AP, geometry, health education, honors English, honors geometry, honors U.S. history, Italian; life science, mathematics, modern European history, modern European history-AP, moral theology, philosophy, physical education, physics, physics-AP, pre-algebra, pre-calculus, psychology, psychology-AP, religion, Spanish, Spanish-AP, statistics-AP, studio art, theology, U.S. government and politics, U.S. government and politics-AP, U.S. history, U.S. history-AP, voice ensemble, Web site design, world history, world literature.

Graduation Requirements Arts and fine arts (art, music, dance, drama), English, foreign language, mathematics, physical education (includes health), science, social studies (includes history), theology.

Special Academic Programs Advanced Placement exam preparation; honors section; independent study; academic accommodation for the gifted, the musically talented, and the artistically talented.

College Admission Counseling 52 students graduated in 2008; all went to college, including Bucknell University; Georgetown University; Princeton University; University of Notre Dame; Villanova University. Mean SAT critical reading: 650, mean SAT math: 660, mean SAT writing: 690, mean combined SAT: 2000. 60% scored over 600 on SAT critical reading, 65% scored over 600 on SAT math, 70% scored over 600 on SAT writing, 65% scored over 1800 on combined SAT.

Student Life Upper grades have uniform requirement, student council, honor system. Discipline rests primarily with faculty. Attendance at religious services is required.

Tuition and Aid Day student tuition: $14,700. Tuition installment plan (Insured Tuition Payment Plan, Key Tuition Payment Plan, individually arranged payment plans). Merit scholarship grants, need-based scholarship grants available. In 2008–09, 10% of upper-school students received aid; total upper-school merit-scholarship money awarded: $20,000. Total amount of financial aid awarded in 2008–09: $80,000.

Admissions Traditional secondary-level entrance grade is 9. For fall 2008, 165 students applied for upper-level admission, 70 were accepted, 65 enrolled. Math, reading, and mental ability tests required. Deadline for receipt of application materials: none. Application fee required: $50. On-campus interview required.

Athletics Interscholastic: basketball, cross-country running, indoor track, lacrosse, soccer, softball, swimming and diving, tennis, track and field, volleyball, winter (indoor) track. 1 PE instructor, 22 coaches, 2 athletic trainers.

Computers Computers are regularly used in college planning, desktop publishing, independent study, keyboarding, library science, mathematics, newspaper, programming, SAT preparation, science, technology, Web site design, word processing, yearbook classes. Computer network features include on-campus library services, Internet access, wireless campus network, Internet filtering or blocking technology. The school has a published electronic and media policy.

Contact Sr. Doris Lavinthal, Director. 973-538-3680 Ext. 175. Fax: 973-538-6733. E-mail: lavinthald@aol.com. Web site: www.villawalsh.org.

VIRGINIA BEACH FRIENDS SCHOOL

1537 Laskin Road
Virginia Beach, Virginia 23451

Head of School: Mr. Jonathan K. Alden

General Information Coeducational day college-preparatory, arts, religious studies, and technology school, affiliated with Society of Friends. Grades PK–12. Founded: 1955. Setting: suburban. 11-acre campus. 4 buildings on campus. Approved or accredited by Friends Council on Education, Virginia Association of Independent Schools, and Virginia Department of Education. Endowment: $109,000. Total enrollment: 210. Upper school average class size: 12. Upper school faculty-student ratio: 1:5.

Upper School Student Profile Grade 9: 17 students (10 boys, 7 girls); Grade 10: 13 students (7 boys, 6 girls); Grade 11: 11 students (6 boys, 5 girls); Grade 12: 14 students (9 boys, 5 girls). 5% of students are members of Society of Friends.

Faculty School total: 45. In upper school: 2 men, 9 women; 4 have advanced degrees.

Subjects Offered 3-dimensional design, Advanced Placement courses, American government, Arabic, art education, art history, arts appreciation, Asian literature, athletics, audio visual/media, Basic programming, basketball, Bible as literature, biology, British literature, Buddhism, calculus, calculus-AP, ceramics, chemistry, Chinese, college admission preparation, college counseling, college placement, college planning, community service, computer applications, computer art, computer graphics, computer keyboarding, computer literacy, computer multimedia, computer programming, computer programming-AP, computer skills, computer technologies, computer tools, computers, conflict resolution, contemporary art, desktop publishing, digital art, drawing, drawing and design, electives, English composition, English language and composition-AP, English literature, English literature and composition-AP, English-AP, English/composition-AP, environmental education, environmental science, environmental science-AP, environmental studies, film and literature, filmmaking, fitness, foreign language, general science, geometry, government, grammar, graphic arts, graphic design, graphics, guidance, history of the Americas, introduction to technology, Japanese, jewelry making, Jewish studies, journalism, junior and senior seminars, Korean literature, lab science, language and composition, language arts, language-AP, Latin, Latin-AP, leadership, leadership training, leatherworking, library, library skills, literature seminar, literature-AP, math applications, mathematics, mathematics-AP, media arts, media communications, media literacy, media services, media studies, modern world history, multicultural literature, multicultural studies, multimedia, multimedia design, music appreciation, music composition, neuroanatomy, neuroscience, non-Western literature, non-Western societies, North American literature, oceanography, oil painting, organic chemistry, participation in sports, peace and justice, peace studies, photography, photojournalism, physical education, physical fitness, physical science, physics, physics-AP, portfolio art, pre-algebra, pre-calculus, programming, psychology, psychology-AP, reading, reading/study skills, religion and culture, SAT preparation, science and technology, science project, sculpture, senior composition, senior internship, senior project, sex education, Shakespeare, Shakespearean histories, short story, Spanish, sports, sports conditioning, sports psychology, stained glass, statistics, statistics and probability, student government, student publications, student teaching, studio art, study skills, substance abuse, technical arts, technology, technology/design, telecommunications, telecommunications and the Internet, travel, U.S. and Virginia government, U.S. and Virginia history, U.S. constitutional history, U.S. government, U.S. government and politics, U.S. history, values and decisions, video, video and animation, video communication, Web authoring, Web site design, weight fitness, weight training, Western civilization, Western literature, Western religions, woodworking, world civilizations, world culture, world cultures, world geography, world governments, world history, world history-AP, world issues, world literature, world religions, world religions, world studies, world wide web design, World-Wide-Web publishing, writing fundamentals, writing skills, writing workshop, yearbook, youth culture.

Graduation Requirements Peace studies, physical education (includes health), practical arts, Quakerism and ethics, science, senior internship, senior project, U.S. history, Quaker Studies. Community service is required.

Special Academic Programs Advanced Placement exam preparation; honors section; accelerated programs; independent study; term-away projects; academic accommodation for the gifted, the musically talented, and the artistically talented.

College Admission Counseling 12 students graduated in 2008; 11 went to college, including Old Dominion University; Virginia Wesleyan College. Other: 1 went to work. Median SAT critical reading: 600, median SAT math: 550, median composite ACT: 22.

Student Life Upper grades have specified standards of dress, student council, honor system. Discipline rests equally with students and faculty. Attendance at religious services is required.

Tuition and Aid Day student tuition: $11,300. Tuition installment plan (Insured Tuition Payment Plan, monthly payment plans, individually arranged payment plans, Layaway Plans, Balloon Payment Plans, Extended Payment Plans). Merit scholarship grants, need-based scholarship grants available. In 2008–09, 25% of upper-school students received aid; total upper-school merit-scholarship money awarded: $10,000. Total amount of financial aid awarded in 2008–09: $45,000.

Admissions Traditional secondary-level entrance grade is 9. For fall 2008, 22 students applied for upper-level admission, 21 were accepted, 16 enrolled. Achievement tests or admissions testing required. Deadline for receipt of application materials: none. Application fee required: $25. Interview required.

Athletics Interscholastic: basketball (boys, girls), lacrosse (b), volleyball (g); coed interscholastic: independent competitive sports, soccer, softball; coed intramural: fitness, hiking/backpacking, indoor soccer, physical fitness. 2 PE instructors, 8 coaches.

Computers Computers are regularly used in all academic, animation, architecture, art, commercial art, design, drawing and design, media arts, multimedia, newspaper, photography, photojournalism, publishing, technology, video film production, Web site design, yearbook classes. Computer network features include on-campus library services, online commercial services, Internet access. The school has a published electronic and media policy.

Contact Ms. Jacquie Whitt, Director of Admissions. 757-428-7534 Ext. 104. Fax: 757-428-7511. E-mail: tjacquie@friends-school.org. Web site: www.friends-school.org.

VIRGINIA EPISCOPAL SCHOOL

400 VES Road
Lynchburg, Virginia 24503

Head of School: Dr. Phillip L. Hadley

General Information Coeducational boarding and day college-preparatory, arts, religious studies, and technology school, affiliated with Episcopal Church. Grades 9–12. Founded: 1916. Setting: suburban. Nearest major city is Richmond. Students are housed in single-sex dormitories. 160-acre campus. 15 buildings on campus. Approved or accredited by National Association of Episcopal Schools, The Association of Boarding Schools, Virginia Association of Independent Schools, and Virginia Department of Education. Member of National Association of Independent Schools and Secondary School Admission Test Board. Endowment: $19 million. Total enrollment: 262. Upper school average class size: 12. Upper school faculty-student ratio: 1:8.

Upper School Student Profile Grade 9: 43 students (28 boys, 15 girls); Grade 10: 56 students (32 boys, 24 girls); Grade 11: 76 students (44 boys, 32 girls); Grade 12: 87 students (55 boys, 32 girls). 65% of students are boarding students. 56% are state residents. 17 states are represented in upper school student body. 11% are international students. International students from China, Germany, Greece, India, Republic of Korea, and Serbia and Montenegro; 11 other countries represented in student body. 50% of students are members of Episcopal Church.

Faculty School total: 44. In upper school: 28 men, 14 women; 26 have advanced degrees; 26 reside on campus.

Subjects Offered Advanced math, algebra, American history, American history-AP, American literature, analysis, ancient history, art, art history, biology, biology-AP, calculus, calculus-AP, chemistry, choir, computer graphics, computer keyboarding, computer math, computer programming, computer programming-AP, computer science, computer science-AP, creative writing, drama, economics, English, English literature, English-AP, environmental science, ethics, ethics and responsibility, European history, European history-AP, fine arts, French, French language-AP, geometry, grammar, graphic design, health education, history, honors algebra, honors English, honors geometry, honors U.S. history, honors world history, instrumental music, Latin, life issues, mathematics, medieval history, modern European history-AP, music, music history, music theory-AP, musical theater, physical education, physics, pre-calculus, religion, SAT preparation, science, Spanish, Spanish language-AP, sports medicine, theater, theater history, trigonometry, Web site design, world history, world literature, writing.

Graduation Requirements Arts and fine arts (art, music, dance, drama), computer science, English, foreign language, life issues, mathematics, physical education (includes health), religion (includes Bible studies and theology), science, social studies (includes history).

Special Academic Programs Advanced Placement exam preparation; honors section; independent study; study abroad.

College Admission Counseling 65 students graduated in 2007; all went to college, including North Carolina State University; The University of North Carolina at Chapel Hill; The University of North Carolina Wilmington; University of Virginia.

Student Life Upper grades have specified standards of dress, student council, honor system. Discipline rests equally with students and faculty. Attendance at religious services is required.

Tuition and Aid Day student tuition: $16,950; 5-day tuition and room/board: $25,300; 7-day tuition and room/board: $33,500. Tuition installment plan (FACTS Tuition Payment Plan, individually arranged payment plans). Tuition reduction for siblings, merit scholarship grants, need-based scholarship grants available. In 2007–08, 20% of upper-school students received aid; total upper-school merit-scholarship money awarded: $96,000. Total amount of financial aid awarded in 2007–08: $860,000.

Admissions Traditional secondary-level entrance grade is 9. For fall 2007, 221 students applied for upper-level admission, 152 were accepted, 90 enrolled. SAT or SSAT required. Deadline for receipt of application materials: none. Application fee required: $50. Interview required.

Athletics Interscholastic: baseball (boys), basketball (b,g), field hockey (g), football (b), indoor soccer (b,g), lacrosse (b,g), soccer (b,g), softball (g), tennis (b,g), volleyball (g), winter soccer (g), wrestling (b); intramural: bicycling (b,g), weight lifting (b), yoga (g); coed interscholastic: cross-country running, equestrian sports, fitness, golf, horseback riding, indoor track, indoor track & field, swimming and diving, track and field, winter (indoor) track; coed intramural: fencing, outdoor activities, paint ball, physical fitness, physical training, strength & conditioning, ultimate Frisbee. 1 coach.

Computers Computers are regularly used in all academic classes. Computer network features include on-campus library services, online commercial services, Internet access, wireless campus network, Internet filtering or blocking technology, off-campus e-mail, Internet connections in each dorm room. Campus intranet and student e-mail accounts are available to students.

Contact Katharine Saunders, Director of Admission. 434-385-3605. Fax: 434-385-3603. E-mail: ksaunders@ves.org. Web site: www.ves.org.

See Close-Up on page 1008.

VISITATION ACADEMY OF ST. LOUIS COUNTY

3020 North Ballas Road
St. Louis, Missouri 63131

Head of School: Mrs. Rosalie Henry

General Information Coeducational day (boys' only in lower grades) college-preparatory, arts, and technology school, affiliated with Roman Catholic Church. Boys grades PK–K, girls grades PK–12. Founded: 1833. Setting: suburban. 30-acre campus. 1 building on campus. Approved or accredited by Independent Schools Association of the Central States, National Catholic Education Association, North Central Association of Colleges and Schools, and Missouri Department of Education. Member of National Association of Independent Schools. Endowment: $6 million. Total enrollment: 623. Upper school average class size: 18. Upper school faculty-student ratio: 1:9.

Upper School Student Profile Grade 7: 73 students (73 girls); Grade 8: 62 students (62 girls); Grade 9: 68 students (68 girls); Grade 10: 85 students (85 girls); Grade 11: 65 students (65 girls); Grade 12: 67 students (67 girls). 85% of students are Roman Catholic.

Faculty School total: 77. In upper school: 9 men, 39 women; 29 have advanced degrees.

Subjects Offered Algebra, American history, American literature, anatomy, art, art history, Bible studies, biology, calculus, ceramics, chemistry, computer art, computer math, computer programming, computer science, creative writing, drama, earth science, economics, English, English literature, European history, expository writing, fine arts, French, geography, geometry, government/civics, grammar, health, history, journalism, keyboarding, Latin, mathematics, music, photography, physical education, physical science, physics, psychology, science, social studies, Spanish, speech, theater, theology, trigonometry, world literature.

Graduation Requirements Arts and fine arts (art, music, dance, drama), computers, electives, English, foreign language, mathematics, physical education (includes health), science, social studies (includes history), theology, 120 hours of community service.

Special Academic Programs 12 Advanced Placement exams for which test preparation is offered; honors section; independent study; study at local college for college credit.

College Admission Counseling 76 students graduated in 2008; all went to college, including Saint Louis University; Santa Clara University; Southern Methodist University; The University of Kansas; University of Missouri–Columbia; Washington University in St. Louis. Median SAT critical reading: 634, median SAT math: 624, median composite ACT: 28. 67% scored over 600 on SAT critical reading, 60% scored over 600 on SAT math, 66% scored over 26 on composite ACT.

Student Life Upper grades have uniform requirement, student council. Discipline rests primarily with faculty. Attendance at religious services is required.

Summer Programs Sports programs offered; session focuses on sport camps; held on campus; accepts girls; open to students from other schools. 100 students usually enrolled.

Tuition and Aid Day student tuition: $14,310. Tuition installment plan (FACTS Tuition Payment Plan). Need-based scholarship grants available. In 2008–09, 10% of upper-school students received aid.

Admissions Traditional secondary-level entrance grade is 7. For fall 2008, 79 students applied for upper-level admission, 70 were accepted, 56 enrolled. ISEE required. Deadline for receipt of application materials: January 23. Application fee required: $75. Interview required.

Athletics Interscholastic: basketball, cheering, cross-country running, diving, field hockey, golf, lacrosse, racquetball, soccer, softball, swimming and diving, tennis, volleyball; intramural: basketball, dance, field hockey, soccer, softball, volleyball. 3 PE instructors, 17 coaches, 1 athletic trainer.

Computers Computers are regularly used in art, English, history, mathematics, science, theology classes. Computer network features include on-campus library services, Internet access, wireless campus network, Internet filtering or blocking technology. Student e-mail accounts are available to students. Students grades are available online. The school has a published electronic and media policy.

Contact Mrs. Ashley Giljum, Director of Admission. 314-625-9102. Fax: 314-432-7210. E-mail: agiljum@visitationacademy.org. Web site: www.visitationacademy.org.

WAKEFIELD SCHOOL

4439 Old Tavern Road
PO Box 107
The Plains, Virginia 20198

Head of School: Mr. Peter A. Quinn

General Information Coeducational day college-preparatory and arts school. Grades PS–12. Founded: 1972. Setting: rural. Nearest major city is Washington, DC. 65-acre campus. 6 buildings on campus. Approved or accredited by Association of Independent Schools of Greater Washington, Virginia Association of Independent Schools, and Virginia Department of Education. Total enrollment: 461. Upper school average class size: 12. Upper school faculty-student ratio: 1:12.

Upper School Student Profile Grade 6: 38 students (20 boys, 18 girls); Grade 7: 30 students (15 boys, 15 girls); Grade 8: 41 students (20 boys, 21 girls); Grade 9: 40 students (22 boys, 18 girls); Grade 10: 41 students (21 boys, 20 girls); Grade 11: 26 students (11 boys, 15 girls); Grade 12: 35 students (15 boys, 20 girls).

Faculty School total: 69. In upper school: 17 men, 13 women; 25 have advanced degrees.

Subjects Offered Acting, Advanced Placement courses, algebra, American government, American history-AP, American literature, art, art history, bell choir, biology, biology-AP, British history, British literature, calculus, calculus-AP, chemistry, chemistry-AP, chorus, classical language, composition, computer applications, computer programming, conservation, drama, dramatic arts, earth science, Eastern world civilizations, English language and composition-AP, English literature and composition-AP, environmental science, environmental science-AP, European history-AP, French, French language-AP, geometry, geopolitics, government and politics-AP, government/civics, Latin, Latin-AP, model United Nations, music, music composition, music history, music theory, music theory-AP, physical fitness, physics, physics-AP, political science, psychology, publications, Spanish, Spanish language-AP, statistics, statistics-AP, studio art, studio art-AP, U.S. history, world civilizations.

Graduation Requirements Advanced math, algebra, American history, American literature, arts, biology, British literature, chemistry, computer literacy, English, geometry, government/civics, grammar, language, physical education (includes health), pre-calculus, world civilizations, 2 interdisciplinary compositions, 2 thesis and portfolio projects, including Senior Thesis.

Special Academic Programs 11 Advanced Placement exams for which test preparation is offered; honors section; independent study.

College Admission Counseling 37 students graduated in 2008; all went to college, including James Madison University; The University of Alabama; University of Mary Washington; University of Virginia; Virginia Polytechnic Institute and State University. Mean SAT critical reading: 649, mean SAT math: 594, mean SAT writing:

609, mean combined SAT: 1852. 79% scored over 600 on SAT critical reading, 47% scored over 600 on SAT math, 63% scored over 600 on SAT writing, 47% scored over 1800 on combined SAT.

Student Life Upper grades have uniform requirement, student council, honor system. Discipline rests equally with students and faculty.

Summer Programs Enrichment, sports, art/fine arts, computer instruction programs offered; session focuses on academics, athletics, fine arts; held both on and off campus; held at various locations; accepts boys and girls; open to students from other schools. 200 students usually enrolled. 2009 schedule: June 22 to July 31.

Tuition and Aid Day student tuition: $9600–$19,500. Tuition installment plan (FACTS Tuition Payment Plan, monthly payment plans, The Tuition Refund Plan). Need-based scholarship grants available. In 2008–09, 15% of upper-school students received aid.

Admissions Traditional secondary-level entrance grade is 9. Admissions testing or SSAT required. Deadline for receipt of application materials: none. Application fee required: $60. Interview required.

Athletics Interscholastic: baseball (boys), basketball (b,g), field hockey (g), lacrosse (b,g), soccer (b,g), squash (b), tennis (b,g), volleyball (g); intramural: field hockey (g), fitness (b,g), marksmanship (b,g), outdoor activities (b,g), soccer (b,g), squash (b), strength & conditioning (b,g), tennis (b,g), volleyball (g), weight training (b,g); coed interscholastic: aquatics, cross-country running, fitness, golf, swimming and diving; coed intramural: aquatics, cross-country running, marksmanship, swimming and diving. 4 PE instructors, 3 coaches.

Computers Computers are regularly used in computer applications, English, independent study, publications, writing, yearbook classes. Computer network features include on-campus library services, online commercial services, Internet access, wireless campus network, Internet filtering or blocking technology, New Science and Technology Building opened in January, 2007, student center login/password protected portal for students on new website. Campus intranet and computer access in designated common areas are available to students. Students grades are available online. The school has a published electronic and media policy.

Contact Office of Admissions. 540-253-7600. Fax: 540-253-5492. E-mail: admissions@wakefieldschool.org. Web site: www.wakefieldschool.org.

ANNOUNCEMENT FROM THE SCHOOL Wakefield School, an independent, co-educational day school in The Plains, Virginia, serves students in preschool through 12th grade. The School provides a rigorous liberal arts education through a challenging, content-rich curriculum and extracurricular activities that are delivered by skilled, supportive, and creative teachers, coaches, and advisers. Wakefield believes in broad knowledge, the equal importance of character and intellect, the benefits of hard work, and the limitless potential of its students. The School fosters self-discipline, independence, creativity, and curiosity and welcomes families who will embrace Wakefield's ambitious vision: to develop capable, ethical, and articulate citizens who will seek the challenge, make a difference, and live extraordinary lives—each in his or her own way. Wakefield's traditional approach to education is evident in the celebration the students find in learning, their active role in the community, their outstanding college preparation (86% say they are better prepared than their peers, 98% say they are better at writing), and their successes as citizens. Students have an opportunity to participate in eleven sports consisting of thirty-seven different teams, an active Student Government, and a wide range of extracurricular activities, all designed to support the School's fundamental mission. Seniors design a year-long thesis project according to their passions and strengths. The Arts and Music Department provides more than thirty-five opportunities for students to actively participate in drama, music, drawing, painting, and photography. The newly opened Science and Technology Building provides new laboratories, a state-of-the-art library, and a technology lab. College matriculations include Boston College, Corcoran College of Art, Cornell, Emory, Georgetown, Hollins, James Madison, Middlebury, NYU, Princeton, Tulane, United States Air Force Academy, United States Military Academy, Ursinus, Virginia Tech, Washington (St. Louis), Wellesley, William and Mary, Yale, and the Universities of Alabama, Iowa, Mississippi, North Carolina at Chapel Hill, Pennsylvania, Tampa, Vermont, and Virginia. Wakefield School focuses on matching the student with the right college or university that best fits his or her individual academic, personal, and extracurricular interests and abilities. Wakefield School offers transportation from surrounding areas to and from the campus.

WALDORF HIGH SCHOOL OF MASSACHUSETTS BAY

160 Lexington Street
Belmont, Massachusetts 02478

Head of School: Mara D. White

General Information Coeducational day college-preparatory and arts school. Grades 9–12. Founded: 1996. Setting: suburban. Nearest major city is Boston. 1 building on campus. Approved or accredited by Association of Waldorf Schools of North America, New England Association of Schools and Colleges, and Massachusetts Department of Education. Total enrollment: 58. Upper school average class size: 15. Upper school faculty-student ratio: 1:6.

Upper School Student Profile Grade 9: 14 students (5 boys, 9 girls); Grade 10: 16 students (11 boys, 5 girls); Grade 11: 15 students (7 boys, 8 girls); Grade 12: 13 students (4 boys, 9 girls).

Faculty School total: 20. In upper school: 12 men, 8 women; 10 have advanced degrees.

Subjects Offered Algebra, American history, American literature, American studies, analysis and differential calculus, anatomy and physiology, ancient history, ancient world history, art, art history, astronomy, athletics, Bible as literature, biology, bookbinding, botany, calculus, calligraphy, chamber groups, chemistry, child development, chorus, classical Greek literature, college admission preparation, college counseling, college placement, community service, computer applications, computer resources, creative writing, current events, drama, drama performance, earth science, electives, English, English literature, epic literature, European history, expository writing, fine arts, fitness, geography, geometry, global studies, grammar, guitar, history of architecture, history of music, Internet research, jazz ensemble, mathematics, medieval/Renaissance history, model United Nations, modern history, music, Native American history, orchestra, painting, photography, physical education, physics, play production, poetry, projective geometry, Russian literature, SAT preparation, senior internship, senior seminar, Spanish, stone carving, swimming, theory of knowledge, trigonometry, U.S. government, woodworking, world history, world literature, writing, yearbook, zoology.

Graduation Requirements Algebra, arts and fine arts (art, music, dance, drama), chemistry, English, English literature, foreign language, geometry, global studies, mathematics, music, performing arts, physical education (includes health), physics, practical arts, science, social studies (includes history). Community service is required.

Special Academic Programs Honors section; independent study; study abroad.

College Admission Counseling 13 students graduated in 2008; 8 went to college, including Hampshire College; Occidental College; Simmons College; State University of New York at New Paltz; University of Massachusetts Lowell; Wellesley College. Other: 5 had other specific plans.

Student Life Upper grades have specified standards of dress, student council. Discipline rests primarily with faculty.

Tuition and Aid Day student tuition: $21,100. Tuition installment plan (Insured Tuition Payment Plan, monthly payment plans). Tuition reduction for siblings, merit scholarship grants, need-based scholarship grants available. In 2008–09, 44% of upper-school students received aid; total upper-school merit-scholarship money awarded: $29,648. Total amount of financial aid awarded in 2008–09: $263,200.

Admissions Traditional secondary-level entrance grade is 9. For fall 2008, 25 students applied for upper-level admission, 23 were accepted, 18 enrolled. Essay, grade equivalent tests or math and English placement tests required. Deadline for receipt of application materials: none. Application fee required: $50. On-campus interview required.

Athletics Interscholastic: basketball (boys, girls), soccer (b,g); coed intramural: running. 2 PE instructors, 3 coaches.

Computers Computers are regularly used in college planning, creative writing, current events, independent study, mathematics, research skills, SAT preparation, Spanish, yearbook classes. Computer network features include Internet access, Internet filtering or blocking technology. Computer access in designated common areas is available to students. The school has a published electronic and media policy.

Contact Susan Morris, Admissions. 617-489-6600 Ext. 11. Fax: 617-489-6619. E-mail: s.morris@waldorfhighschool.org. Web site: www.waldorfhighschool.org.

ANNOUNCEMENT FROM THE SCHOOL Waldorf High School of Massachusetts Bay, one of 800 Waldorf schools worldwide, offers a secondary school education to students in the greater Boston area. These students have a passion for learning and exploring. They are more interested in depth than acceleration, in collaboration than competition. The faculty has an equal passion for teaching and supporting teenagers as they develop into flexible, confident thinkers who address life's big questions with creativity and optimism. Waldorf High School of Massachusetts Bay offers an encompassing curriculum that integrates the arts into vigorous academic exploration and experiential learning. Topics in science, literature, history, and mathematics are taught intensively in a 90-minute class called the Main Lesson. With three to four weeks dedicated to each block, students explore primary source materials, do independent research and projects, and take field trips to deepen understanding with firsthand experience. Students create Main Lesson books that are filled with research, essays, observations, and artistic work. In addition, there are required courses in English, history, mathematics, Spanish, civics, current events, and music. Each student also takes classes in physical education, fine arts, and electives such as photography, computer programming, woodworking, chess, bookbinding, Model UN, and yearbook. All students must complete community service requirements. They participate in student council, team sports, and extracurricular activities like the drama and Spanish clubs. Seniors do a two-week internship with businesses or nonprofit organizations. Opportunities to study abroad are abundant through the foreign exchange program. High faculty-student ratios, mentors, and small classes create an environment where each student is valued and given the opportunity to reach his or her fullest potential. Graduates attend Boston

University, Brandeis, Earlham, Hampshire, Oberlin, St. John's College, Wellesley, and other fine colleges and universities.

THE WALDORF SCHOOL OF GARDEN CITY

225 Cambridge Avenue
Garden City, New York 11530

Head of School: Ms. Sabine Kully

General Information Coeducational day college-preparatory, arts, and Liberal Arts school. Grades N–12. Founded: 1947. Setting: suburban. Nearest major city is New York. 10-acre campus. 1 building on campus. Approved or accredited by Association of Waldorf Schools of North America, New York State Association of Independent Schools, and New York Department of Education. Member of National Association of Independent Schools and Secondary School Admission Test Board. Total enrollment: 349. Upper school average class size: 23. Upper school faculty-student ratio: 1:7.

Upper School Student Profile Grade 6: 24 students (14 boys, 10 girls); Grade 7: 21 students (6 boys, 15 girls); Grade 8: 24 students (15 boys, 9 girls); Grade 9: 24 students (11 boys, 13 girls); Grade 10: 27 students (17 boys, 10 girls); Grade 11: 17 students (8 boys, 9 girls); Grade 12: 21 students (9 boys, 12 girls).

Faculty School total: 50. In upper school: 9 men, 12 women; 14 have advanced degrees.

Subjects Offered Algebra, American history, American literature, anatomy, art, art history, biology, botany, calculus, cartography, chemistry, computer science, creative writing, dance, drama, earth science, economics, English, English literature, European history, expository writing, fine arts, French, geography, geology, geometry, German, government/civics, grammar, health, history, mathematics, model United Nations, music, physical education, physics, physiology, science, sculpture, social studies, speech, trigonometry, woodworking, world history, world literature, writing, zoology.

Graduation Requirements Applied arts, arts and fine arts (art, music, dance, drama), English, French, German, history of architecture, history of drama, history of music, history of science, literature, medieval history, medieval/Renaissance history, music, organic chemistry, physical education (includes health), science, social studies (includes history).

Special Academic Programs 3 Advanced Placement exams for which test preparation is offered; independent study; study abroad; academic accommodation for the musically talented and the artistically talented.

College Admission Counseling Colleges students went to include American University; Boston College; Dartmouth College; Fordham University; Rochester Institute of Technology; Wellesley College. Mean SAT critical reading: 551, mean SAT math: 579, mean SAT writing: 539, mean combined SAT: 556, mean composite ACT: 23. 35% scored over 600 on SAT critical reading, 40% scored over 600 on SAT math, 14% scored over 600 on SAT writing, 45% scored over 26 on composite ACT.

Student Life Upper grades have specified standards of dress, student council, honor system. Discipline rests equally with students and faculty.

Summer Programs Enrichment programs offered; session focuses on music, drama, field trips, tennis, painting, crafts, puppetry, swimming, athletics; held both on and off campus; held at Camp Glen Brook (programs in summer and winter); accepts boys and girls; open to students from other schools. 80 students usually enrolled. 2009 schedule: June 25 to August 3. Application deadline: none.

Tuition and Aid Day student tuition: $19,000. Tuition installment plan (FACTS Tuition Payment Plan). Merit scholarship grants, need-based scholarship grants available. In 2008–09, 35% of upper-school students received aid; total upper-school merit-scholarship money awarded: $30,000. Total amount of financial aid awarded in 2008–09: $180,000.

Admissions Traditional secondary-level entrance grade is 9. For fall 2008, 31 students applied for upper-level admission, 18 were accepted, 9 enrolled. SSAT required. Deadline for receipt of application materials: none. Application fee required: $50. On-campus interview required.

Athletics Interscholastic: baseball (boys, girls), basketball (b,g), cross-country running (b,g), independent competitive sports (b,g), physical fitness (b,g), soccer (b,g), softball (g), volleyball (g); intramural: artistic gym (b,g), cooperative games (b,g), dance (b,g), fitness (b,g), volleyball (b,g); coed interscholastic: baseball, outdoor education, ropes courses, soccer; coed intramural: artistic gym, dance, fitness, volleyball. 2 PE instructors, 6 coaches.

Computers Computers are regularly used in research skills, science, yearbook classes. Computer network features include Internet access, wireless campus network, Internet filtering or blocking technology. Computer access in designated common areas is available to students. The school has a published electronic and media policy.

Contact Mrs. Carol Proctor, Admissions Assistant. 516-742-3434 Ext. 129. Fax: 516-742-3457. E-mail: proctorc@waldorfgarden.org. Web site: www.waldorfgarden.org.

THE WALKER SCHOOL

700 Cobb Parkway North
Marietta, Georgia 30062

Head of School: Donald B. Robertson

General Information Coeducational day college-preparatory, arts, bilingual studies, and technology school. Grades PK–12. Founded: 1957. Setting: suburban. Nearest major city is Atlanta. 45-acre campus. 7 buildings on campus. Approved or accredited by Southern Association of Colleges and Schools and Georgia Department of Education. Member of National Association of Independent Schools and Secondary School Admission Test Board. Endowment: $5 million. Total enrollment: 1,066. Upper school average class size: 14. Upper school faculty-student ratio: 1:14.

Upper School Student Profile Grade 9: 86 students (40 boys, 46 girls); Grade 10: 85 students (41 boys, 44 girls); Grade 11: 100 students (54 boys, 46 girls); Grade 12: 88 students (48 boys, 40 girls).

Faculty School total: 135. In upper school: 27 men, 15 women; 42 have advanced degrees.

Subjects Offered Acting, advanced chemistry, advanced computer applications, algebra, American history, American literature, anatomy, art, art education, art history, art-AP, astronomy, athletics, band, Bible, biology, biology-AP, botany, calculus, calculus-AP, ceramics, chemistry, chemistry-AP, computer programming, computer science, computer science-AP, computer technologies, creative writing, dance, drama, driver education, economics, economics-AP, English, English-AP, environmental science-AP, ethics, European history, expository writing, film history, fine arts, fitness, French, French language-AP, French literature-AP, genetics, geometry, German, German-AP, government and politics-AP, government-AP, government/civics, grammar, history, history-AP, Latin, Latin-AP, literature and composition-AP, mathematics, music, musical theater, newspaper, orchestra, personal finance, physical education, physics, physics-AP, play production, psychology, public speaking, science, social studies, Spanish, Spanish-AP, statistics, statistics-AP, trigonometry, U.S. history-AP, Web site design, world history, world history-AP, world literature, writing, zoology.

Graduation Requirements American government, arts and fine arts (art, music, dance, drama), computer science, economics, English, English composition, English literature, foreign language, mathematics, physical education (includes health), science, social studies (includes history).

Special Academic Programs 25 Advanced Placement exams for which test preparation is offered; honors section; independent study; study abroad; academic accommodation for the gifted and the artistically talented.

College Admission Counseling 95 students graduated in 2008; 94 went to college, including Davidson College; Furman University; Georgia Institute of Technology; University of Georgia; Vanderbilt University; Virginia Polytechnic Institute and State University. Other: 1 had other specific plans. Median SAT critical reading: 600, median SAT math: 640, median SAT writing: 590, median combined SAT: 1810, median composite ACT: 27. 43% scored over 600 on SAT critical reading, 64% scored over 600 on SAT math, 47% scored over 600 on SAT writing, 59% scored over 1800 on combined SAT.

Student Life Upper grades have specified standards of dress, student council, honor system. Discipline rests equally with students and faculty.

Summer Programs Enrichment programs offered; session focuses on prep for school for new students; held on campus; accepts boys and girls; open to students from other schools. 60 students usually enrolled. 2009 schedule: June 15 to August 10.

Tuition and Aid Day student tuition: $16,055. Tuition installment plan (monthly payment plans, school's own payment plan). Need-based scholarship grants available. In 2008–09, 18% of upper-school students received aid. Total amount of financial aid awarded in 2008–09: $1,000,000.

Admissions Traditional secondary-level entrance grade is 9. For fall 2008, 80 students applied for upper-level admission, 45 were accepted, 35 enrolled. Otis-Lennon School Ability Test, SSAT or WISC III or Stanford Achievement Test required. Deadline for receipt of application materials: February 21. Application fee required: $75. On-campus interview required.

Athletics Interscholastic: aquatics (boys, girls), baseball (b), basketball (b,g), cheering (g), dance (g), dance squad (g), dance team (g), football (b), golf (b,g), physical training (b,g), soccer (b,g), softball (g), swimming and diving (b,g), tennis (b,g), track and field (b,g), volleyball (g), wrestling (b); intramural: aerobics (g), bowling (b,g), flag football (g), golf (b,g), strength & conditioning (b,g), weight training (b,g); coed interscholastic: cricket, cross-country running, dance, diving, fitness, golf, swimming and diving; coed intramural: bowling, cricket, fencing, fishing, fly fishing, golf, rugby. 8 PE instructors, 9 coaches, 2 athletic trainers.

Computers Computers are regularly used in art, drawing and design, English, foreign language, history, information technology, introduction to technology, literary magazine, mathematics, news writing, newspaper, science, writing classes. Computer network features include on-campus library services, online commercial services, Internet access, wireless campus network, Internet filtering or blocking technology. Student e-mail accounts are available to students. Students grades are available online. The school has a published electronic and media policy.

Contact Patricia H. Mozley, Director of Admission. 678-581-6921. Fax: 770-514-8122. E-mail: mozleyp@thewalkerschool.org. Web site: www.thewalkerschool.org.

ANNOUNCEMENT FROM THE SCHOOL Walker's traditional curriculum, master teachers, and incorporation of current technology work together to prepare students for success in the 21st century. Students are encouraged to explore opportunities for academic challenge and self-expression through art, literature, music, drama, and sports. Twenty-four Advanced Placement courses are available. For more information, students should visit the School's Web site at www.thewalkerschool.org.

WALNUT HILL SCHOOL

12 Highland Street
Natick, Massachusetts 01760-2199

Head of School: Eileen Soskin

General Information Coeducational boarding and day college-preparatory and arts school. Grades 9–12. Founded: 1893. Setting: suburban. Nearest major city is Boston. Students are housed in single-sex dormitories. 38-acre campus. 19 buildings on campus. Approved or accredited by New England Association of Schools and Colleges and Massachusetts Department of Education. Member of National Association of Independent Schools and Secondary School Admission Test Board. Endowment: $12 million. Total enrollment: 298. Upper school average class size: 14. Upper school faculty-student ratio: 1:6.

Upper School Student Profile Grade 9: 43 students (15 boys, 28 girls); Grade 10: 71 students (19 boys, 52 girls); Grade 11: 86 students (27 boys, 59 girls); Grade 12: 98 students (36 boys, 62 girls). 81% of students are boarding students. 31% are state residents. 32 states are represented in upper school student body. 30% are international students. International students from Brazil, Canada, China, Japan, Republic of Korea, and Taiwan; 11 other countries represented in student body.

Faculty School total: 51. In upper school: 24 men, 27 women; 47 have advanced degrees; 20 reside on campus.

Subjects Offered 20th century world history, 3-dimensional art, acting, advanced chemistry, advanced math, algebra, American history, American literature, art history, arts, ballet, ballet technique, biology, calculus, ceramics, chemistry, choral music, choreography, chorus, classical music, college counseling, community service, creative writing, dance, directing, drama, drawing, English, English literature, environmental science, ESL, fine arts, French, geometry, health, history, history of dance, jazz dance, mathematics, modern dance, music history, music theory, musical theater, musical theater dance, opera, orchestra, painting, photography, physics, piano, poetry, pre-calculus, research seminar, science, sculpture, set design, Shakespeare, social studies, Spanish, stage design, technical theater, theater, theater design and production, theater production, U.S. history, visual and performing arts, visual arts, vocal music, voice, voice ensemble, world history, writing.

Graduation Requirements Arts, English, foreign language, mathematics, science, social studies (includes history), U.S. history, completion of arts portfolio, body of writing, or participation in performing arts ensembles and/or solo recital.

Special Academic Programs Advanced Placement exam preparation; honors section; independent study; academic accommodation for the gifted, the musically talented, and the artistically talented; ESL (35 students enrolled).

College Admission Counseling 98 students graduated in 2008; 96 went to college, including McGill University; New England Conservatory of Music; Rice University; School of the Art Institute of Chicago; Smith College; The Boston Conservatory. Other: 2 had other specific plans. Median SAT critical reading: 580, median SAT math: 570, median SAT writing: 580, median composite ACT: 26.

Student Life Upper grades have student council. Discipline rests equally with students and faculty.

Summer Programs Art/fine arts programs offered; session focuses on theater, ballet, writing, and opera; held both on and off campus; held at Italy (opera) and England (writing); accepts boys and girls; open to students from other schools. 300 students usually enrolled. 2009 schedule: June to August. Application deadline: none.

Tuition and Aid Day student tuition: $32,800; 7-day tuition and room/board: $42,000. Tuition installment plan (Insured Tuition Payment Plan, Academic Management Services Plan, monthly payment plans). Need-based scholarship grants available. In 2008–09, 52% of upper-school students received aid. Total amount of financial aid awarded in 2008–09: $2,800,000.

Admissions Traditional secondary-level entrance grade is 10. For fall 2008, 407 students applied for upper-level admission, 178 were accepted, 119 enrolled. Any standardized test, audition, TOEFL or SLEP or writing sample required. Deadline for receipt of application materials: February 1. Application fee required: $65. Interview recommended.

Athletics Intramural: self defense (girls); coed intramural: aerobics, aerobics/dance, ballet, dance, fitness, modern dance, outdoor activities, physical fitness, physical training, self defense, yoga. 3 athletic trainers.

Computers Computer network features include on-campus library services, Internet access, wireless campus network, Internet filtering or blocking technology. Campus intranet, student e-mail accounts, and computer access in designated common areas are available to students. The school has a published electronic and media policy.

Contact Lorie K. Komlyn '88, J.D., Dean for Admission and Placement. 508-650-5020. Fax: 508-655-3726. E-mail: admissions@walnuthillarts.org. Web site: www.walnuthillarts.org.

See Close-Up on page 1010.

THE WARDLAW-HARTRIDGE SCHOOL

1295 Inman Avenue
Edison, New Jersey 08820

Head of School: Andrew Webster

General Information Coeducational day college-preparatory and arts school. Grades PK–12. Founded: 1882. Setting: suburban. Nearest major city is New York, NY. 36-acre campus. 1 building on campus. Approved or accredited by Middle States Association of Colleges and Schools, New Jersey Association of Independent Schools, and New Jersey Department of Education. Member of National Association of Independent Schools. Languages of instruction: English and Spanish. Endowment: $2 million. Total enrollment: 429. Upper school average class size: 16. Upper school faculty-student ratio: 1:4.

Upper School Student Profile Grade 9: 35 students (15 boys, 20 girls); Grade 10: 35 students (17 boys, 18 girls); Grade 11: 31 students (18 boys, 13 girls); Grade 12: 47 students (24 boys, 23 girls).

Faculty School total: 102. In upper school: 11 men, 11 women; 14 have advanced degrees.

Subjects Offered Algebra, American history, American history-AP, American literature, ancient history, art, art history, astronomy, band, biology, biology-AP, calculus, calculus-AP, chemistry, computer programming, computer science, computer science-AP, discrete math, drama, driver education, economics, English, English literature, English-AP, environmental science, ESL, European history, film, fine arts, French, French-AP, geometry, government/civics, health, history, independent study, journalism, Latin, Latin-AP, macroeconomics-AP, marine biology, math analysis, mathematics, modern European history-AP, music, music theory-AP, peer counseling, physical education, physical science, physics, physics-AP, pre-calculus, science, senior project, senior thesis, Shakespeare, short story, Spanish, Spanish-AP, studio art-AP, TOEFL preparation, U.S. government and politics-AP, world history.

Graduation Requirements Arts and fine arts (art, music, dance, drama), computer science, English, foreign language, history, mathematics, physical education (includes health), public speaking, science.

Special Academic Programs 20 Advanced Placement exams for which test preparation is offered; honors section; accelerated programs; independent study; study abroad; academic accommodation for the gifted, the musically talented, and the artistically talented.

College Admission Counseling 47 students graduated in 2008; all went to college, including Duke University; Mount Holyoke College; Muhlenberg College; Princeton University; Rutgers, The State University of New Jersey, New Brunswick. Median SAT critical reading: 590, median SAT math: 620.

Student Life Upper grades have uniform requirement, student council, honor system. Discipline rests equally with students and faculty.

Summer Programs Remediation, enrichment, advancement programs offered; session focuses on academics; held on campus; accepts boys and girls; open to students from other schools. 350 students usually enrolled. 2009 schedule: June 27 to August 5. Application deadline: June 21.

Tuition and Aid Day student tuition: $23,300. Tuition installment plan (Insured Tuition Payment Plan, monthly payment plans). Merit scholarship grants, need-based scholarship grants available. In 2008–09, 33% of upper-school students received aid; total upper-school merit-scholarship money awarded: $53,575. Total amount of financial aid awarded in 2008–09: $522,326.

Admissions Traditional secondary-level entrance grade is 9. For fall 2008, 86 students applied for upper-level admission, 40 were accepted, 24 enrolled. ISEE required. Deadline for receipt of application materials: December 17. Application fee required: $60. On-campus interview required.

Athletics Interscholastic: baseball (boys), basketball (b,g), cheering (g), dance team (g), soccer (b,g), softball (g), tennis (b,g), track and field (b,g), volleyball (g); coed interscholastic: cross-country running, fitness, golf, physical fitness, physical training, strength & conditioning, swimming and diving; coed intramural: outdoor activities, table tennis. 5 PE instructors, 10 coaches, 2 athletic trainers.

Computers Computers are regularly used in all academic classes. Computer network features include on-campus library services, Internet access, wireless campus network, Internet filtering or blocking technology. Campus intranet and student e-mail accounts are available to students. Students grades are available online. The school has a published electronic and media policy.

Contact Mrs. Charlotte Vigeant, Director of Admission. 908-754-1882 Ext. 110. Fax: 908-754-9678. E-mail: cvigeant@whschool.org. Web site: www.whschool.org.

ANNOUNCEMENT FROM THE SCHOOL The Wardlaw-Hartridge School prepares students to lead and succeed in a world of global interconnection. The School provides an educational atmosphere characterized by academic challenge, support for individual excellence, diversity, and a familial sense of community. In addition to its comprehensive and rigorous academic preparation, the School seeks to instill in its students the intellectual open-mindedness, love of learning, and courage needed to sustain personal integrity in their daily lives. The Wardlaw-Hartridge School graduates young men and women who are as intellectually curious about what is unknown to them as they are confident in their understanding of the traditional arts and sciences. Trained in critical thinking, they are capable of both independent and collaborative learning. They begin their collegiate studies able to articulate ideas and opinions persuasively and accurately, both orally and in writing. They have developed an appreciation for the fine and performing arts. They have become competent in both electronic and traditional research methods and enjoy a firm grasp of scientific and quantitative skills. Indeed, Wardlaw-Hartridge graduates, reflecting the motto of the School, are committed "to learn and to achieve" and to provide leadership and service in a rapidly changing world.

WARING SCHOOL

35 Standley Street
Beverly, Massachusetts 01915

Head of School: Mr. Peter L. Smick

General Information Coeducational day college-preparatory school. Grades 6–12. Founded: 1972. Setting: suburban. Nearest major city is Boston. 32-acre campus. 6 buildings on campus. Approved or accredited by New England Association of Schools and Colleges. Languages of instruction: English and French. Endowment: $4.6 million. Total enrollment: 149. Upper school average class size: 14. Upper school faculty-student ratio: 1:8.

Upper School Student Profile Grade 9: 24 students (8 boys, 16 girls); Grade 10: 22 students (9 boys, 13 girls); Grade 11: 25 students (10 boys, 15 girls); Grade 12: 18 students (7 boys, 11 girls).

Faculty School total: 52. In upper school: 16 men, 17 women; 17 have advanced degrees.

Subjects Offered 3-dimensional design, adolescent issues, advanced biology, advanced math, Advanced Placement courses, algebra, Asian studies, athletics, biology, calculus, chemistry, chorus, classical studies, college counseling, drama, earth science, fine arts, French, French language-AP, functions, medieval literature, medieval/Renaissance history, music appreciation, music performance, music theory, photography, physics, statistics, theater, theater arts, trigonometry, writing, yearbook.

Graduation Requirements Arts and fine arts (art, music, dance, drama), English, foreign language, mathematics, music, physical education (includes health), science, social science, writing.

Special Academic Programs 2 Advanced Placement exams for which test preparation is offered; honors section; independent study; term-away projects; study at local college for college credit; study abroad; academic accommodation for the gifted, the musically talented, and the artistically talented.

College Admission Counseling 22 students graduated in 2008; all went to college, including Boston University; Bryn Mawr College; Kenyon College; Swarthmore College; University of Virginia; Vassar College. Median SAT critical reading: 640, median SAT math: 620, median SAT writing: 650. Mean combined SAT: 1900. 76% scored over 600 on SAT critical reading, 71% scored over 600 on SAT math, 81% scored over 600 on SAT writing, 71% scored over 1800 on combined SAT.

Student Life Upper grades have specified standards of dress, honor system. Discipline rests equally with students and faculty.

Summer Programs Art/fine arts programs offered; session focuses on arts camp & music camp; held on campus; accepts boys and girls; open to students from other schools. 75 students usually enrolled. 2009 schedule: July 1 to August 1. Application deadline: April 1.

Tuition and Aid Day student tuition: $23,373. Tuition installment plan (Insured Tuition Payment Plan, individually arranged payment plans, TMS). Need-based scholarship grants available. In 2008–09, 30% of upper-school students received aid. Total amount of financial aid awarded in 2008–09: $425,000.

Admissions Traditional secondary-level entrance grade is 9. For fall 2008, 40 students applied for upper-level admission, 7 were accepted, 6 enrolled. Deadline for receipt of application materials: January 20. Application fee required: $40. On-campus interview required.

Athletics Interscholastic: basketball (boys, girls), lacrosse (b,g), soccer (b,g); coed interscholastic: cross-country running; coed intramural: basketball, dance, fitness, lacrosse, running, soccer, tennis, yoga. 1 PE instructor, 15 coaches, 1 athletic trainer.

Computers Computers are regularly used in literary magazine, mathematics, music, publications, science, writing, yearbook classes. Computer network features include Internet access, Internet filtering or blocking technology. Computer access in designated common areas is available to students. The school has a published electronic and media policy.

Contact Ms. Dorothy Wang, Assistant Head of School and Director of Admissions. 978-927-8793 Ext. 226. Fax: 978-921-2107. E-mail: dwang@waringschool.org. Web site: www.waringschool.org.

ANNOUNCEMENT FROM THE SCHOOL Waring's principal mission is to establish, sustain, and strengthen a community of motivated students and teachers who work and learn together for the common as well as the individual good. The Waring School offers a highly demanding college-preparatory education, which stresses the liberal arts and French (language and culture). The School supports an atmosphere in which both teachers and students will want to learn and believes that school is not an end in itself but is the beginning of a lifelong learning process. The student-teacher ratio is 7.5:1. Dorothy Wang is Assistant Head of School and Director of Admissions.

WASATCH ACADEMY

120 South 100 West
Mt. Pleasant, Utah 84647

Head of School: Mr. Joseph Loftin

General Information Coeducational boarding and day college-preparatory, arts, bilingual studies, technology, and debate, school; primarily serves students with learning disabilities. Grades 9–12. Founded: 1875. Setting: small town. Nearest major city is Provo. Students are housed in single-sex dormitories. 30-acre campus. 19 buildings on campus. Approved or accredited by European Council of International Schools, Northwest Association of Schools and Colleges, Pacific Northwest Association of Independent Schools, The Association of Boarding Schools, and Utah Department of Education. Member of National Association of Independent Schools. Endowment: $1.3 million. Upper school average class size: 10. Upper school faculty-student ratio: 1:10.

Upper School Student Profile Grade 9: 25 students (13 boys, 12 girls); Grade 10: 70 students (36 boys, 34 girls); Grade 11: 70 students (40 boys, 30 girls); Grade 12: 43 students (33 boys, 10 girls). 98% of students are boarding students. 19% are state residents. 24 states are represented in upper school student body. 41% are international students. International students from China, Germany, Mali, Mexico, Republic of Korea, and Taiwan; 30 other countries represented in student body.

Faculty School total: 53. In upper school: 25 men, 26 women; 19 have advanced degrees; 48 reside on campus.

Subjects Offered Acting, advanced studio art-AP, advanced TOEFL/grammar, algebra, anatomy, ballet, biology, biology-AP, calculus-AP, ceramics, chemistry, chemistry-AP, choir, college counseling, college placement, comedy, community garden, community service, dance, design, drama, drawing, drawing and design, driver education, earth science, electronic music, English, English-AP, equine studies, ESL, European history-AP, fencing, film, filmmaking, fine arts, forensic science, French, geography, geology, global issues, golf, guitar, honors algebra, honors English, honors U.S. history, Japanese, jewelry making, Latin, learning strategies, math applications, music, music theory, outdoor education, painting, performing arts, philosophy, photography, physical education, physical science, physics, piano, play production, pottery, pre-calculus, reading, SAT/ACT preparation, Spanish, Spanish-AP, speech and debate, stained glass, statistics-AP, study skills, theater, TOEFL preparation, U.S. history, U.S. history-AP, weightlifting, Western civilization, woodworking, world religions, yoga.

Graduation Requirements Arts and fine arts (art, music, dance, drama), computer literacy, English, foreign language, mathematics, physical education (includes health), science, social science, social studies (includes history), U.S. history, outdoor, cultural, community service, and recreational requirements.

Special Academic Programs Advanced Placement exam preparation; honors section; accelerated programs; independent study; study at local college for college credit; programs in English, mathematics, general development for dyslexic students; ESL (29 students enrolled).

College Admission Counseling 50 students graduated in 2008; 49 went to college, including Boston University; Lewis & Clark College; University of California, Berkeley; University of Pennsylvania; University of San Diego; University of Utah. Other: 1 went to work. Median SAT critical reading: 500, median SAT math: 480, median composite ACT: 22. 13% scored over 600 on SAT critical reading, 9% scored over 600 on SAT math, 27% scored over 26 on composite ACT.

Student Life Upper grades have specified standards of dress, student council, honor system. Discipline rests primarily with faculty. Attendance at religious services is required.

Summer Programs Remediation, enrichment, advancement, ESL programs offered; session focuses on boarding program transition; held on campus; accepts boys and girls; open to students from other schools. 25 students usually enrolled. 2009 schedule: June 23 to August 8. Application deadline: May 15.

Tuition and Aid Day student tuition: $20,000; 5-day tuition and room/board: $40,500; 7-day tuition and room/board: $44,500. Tuition installment plan (Key Tuition Payment Plan, monthly payment plans, individually arranged payment plans). Merit scholarship grants, need-based scholarship grants, need-based loans available. In 2008–09, 40% of upper-school students received aid; total upper-school merit-scholarship money awarded: $55,000. Total amount of financial aid awarded in 2008–09: $600,000.

Admissions For fall 2008, 146 students applied for upper-level admission, 110 were accepted, 101 enrolled. ACT, ISEE, SSAT, Stanford Achievement Test or TOEFL or SLEP required. Deadline for receipt of application materials: May 15. Application fee required: $50. Interview required.

Athletics Interscholastic: alpine skiing (boys, girls), baseball (b), basketball (b,g), climbing (b,g), cross-country running (b,g), dance (b,g), dressage (b,g), equestrian sports (b,g), fencing (b,g), golf (b,g), horseback riding (b,g), outdoor activities (b,g), outdoor education (b,g), paint ball (b,g), physical training (b,g), rodeo (b,g), running (b,g), skiing (cross-country) (b,g), skiing (downhill) (b,g), snowboarding (b,g), snowshoeing (b,g), soccer (b,g), tennis (b,g), track and field (b,g), volleyball (g), weight training (b,g); intramural: dance (g), skiing (downhill) (b,g), soccer (b,g), table tennis (b,g); coed interscholastic: aerobics/dance, archery, backpacking, ballet, bicycling, canoeing/kayaking, cheering, climbing, combined training, cross-country running, dance, dressage, equestrian sports, fencing, fishing, fly fishing, golf, hiking/backpacking, horseback riding, kayaking, life saving, martial arts, modern dance, mountain biking, nordic skiing, outdoor activities, paint ball, physical training, rock climbing, rodeo, running, ski jumping, skiing (cross-country), skiing (downhill), snowboarding, snowshoeing, swimming and diving, table tennis, telemark skiing, tennis, track and field, weight training, yoga; coed intramural: aerobics/dance, aquatics, archery, backpacking, badminton, ballet, bicycling, billiards, blading, bowling, canoeing/kayaking, climbing, combined training, cooperative games, dance team, equestrian sports, fishing, fitness, flag football, fly fishing, freestyle skiing, Frisbee, golf, hiking/backpacking, horseback riding, horseshoes, jogging, lacrosse, life saving, modern dance, mountain biking, nordic skiing, outdoor activities, paint ball, physical training, power lifting, rafting, rappelling, rock climbing, running, skateboarding, skiing (downhill), snowshoeing, swimming and diving, table tennis, telemark skiing, ultimate Frisbee, volleyball, weight lifting, weight training, yoga. 2 coaches, 1 athletic trainer.

Computers Computers are regularly used in all academic classes. Computer network features include on-campus library services, online commercial services, Internet access, wireless campus network, Internet filtering or blocking technology. Campus intranet and student e-mail accounts are available to students. Students grades are available online.

Contact Mrs. Kim Stephens, Director of Admission. 435-462-1443. Fax: 435-462-1450. E-mail: kimberly.stephens@wasatchacademy.org. Web site: www.wasatchacademy.org.

ANNOUNCEMENT FROM THE SCHOOL Wasatch Academy provides a nurturing community that empowers young men and women to develop academically, socially, and morally, while preparing them for college and the challenges of living in the 21st century.

See Close-Up on page 1012.

WASHINGTON ACADEMY

66 Cutler Road, PO Box 190
East Machias, Maine 04630

Head of School: Judson McBrine

General Information Coeducational boarding and day college-preparatory, general academic, arts, business, and vocational school; primarily serves students with learning disabilities and individuals with Attention Deficit Disorder. Grades 9–12. Founded: 1792. Setting: small town. Nearest major city is Bangor. Students are housed in single-sex dormitories and host family homes. 55-acre campus. 9 buildings on campus. Approved or accredited by Independent Schools of Northern New England, New England Association of Schools and Colleges, and Maine Department of Education. Endowment: $1.2 million. Total enrollment: 438. Upper school average class size: 16. Upper school faculty-student ratio: 1:11.

Upper School Student Profile Grade 9: 102 students (54 boys, 48 girls); Grade 10: 97 students (48 boys, 49 girls); Grade 11: 136 students (80 boys, 56 girls); Grade 12: 103 students (59 boys, 44 girls). 24% of students are boarding students. 78% are state residents. 4 states are represented in upper school student body. 22% are international students. International students from Bermuda, China, Jamaica, Republic of Korea, Spain, and Viet Nam; 10 other countries represented in student body.

Faculty School total: 41. In upper school: 17 men, 24 women; 19 have advanced degrees; 12 reside on campus.

Subjects Offered Accounting, Advanced Placement courses, algebra, American culture, American history-AP, architectural drawing, art, art history, art-AP, band, basic language skills, Basic programming, biology, biology-AP, boat building, business, calculus, calculus-AP, career education internship, carpentry, chemistry, Chinese, Chinese history, chorus, computer programming, computer science, computer-aided design, consumer mathematics, creative writing, desktop publishing, digital photography, drafting, drama, earth science, ecology, economics, English, English-AP, environmental science, environmental systems, ESL, ESL, field ecology, film, film studies, foreign language, French, geography, geometry, government/civics, guitar, honors algebra, HTML design, industrial technology, jazz band, journalism, keyboarding, Latin, Latin-AP, literature, marine studies, mathematics, metalworking, Microsoft, music, music appreciation, music history, music theory, photography, physical education, physical science, physics, pre-calculus, psychology, sociology, Spanish, Spanish-AP, speech, technical drawing, theater, TOEFL preparation, U.S. history, U.S. history-AP, video, video film production, vocational-technical courses, welding, woodworking, world history, writing.

Graduation Requirements Arts and fine arts (art, music, dance, drama), English, mathematics, physical education (includes health), science, social studies (includes history), 1 credit of advisor/advisee.

Special Academic Programs Advanced Placement exam preparation; study at local college for college credit; remedial reading and/or remedial writing; remedial math; programs in general development for dyslexic students; special instructional classes for students with learning disabilities; ESL (78 students enrolled).

College Admission Counseling 89 students graduated in 2008; 75 went to college, including Bowdoin College; Middlebury College; University of Maine. Other: 11 went to work, 2 entered military service, 1 entered a postgraduate year. Mean SAT critical reading: 451, mean SAT math: 452, mean SAT writing: 458. 8% scored over 600 on SAT critical reading, 9% scored over 600 on SAT math, 8% scored over 600 on SAT writing.

Student Life Upper grades have specified standards of dress, student council. Discipline rests primarily with faculty.

Summer Programs Remediation, enrichment, ESL programs offered; held on campus; accepts boys and girls; open to students from other schools. 95 students usually enrolled. 2009 schedule: June 25 to August 28. Application deadline: June 1.

Tuition and Aid Day student tuition: $12,000; 7-day tuition and room/board: $32,500. Tuition installment plan (Insured Tuition Payment Plan). Need-based scholarship grants available. In 2008–09, 12% of upper-school students received aid. Total amount of financial aid awarded in 2008–09: $515,561.

Admissions Traditional secondary-level entrance grade is 9. SLEP or TOEFL required. Deadline for receipt of application materials: none. Application fee required: $50. Interview recommended.

Athletics Interscholastic: baseball (boys), basketball (b,g), cross-country running (b,g), football (b), golf (b,g), soccer (b,g), softball (g), swimming and diving (b,g), tennis (b,g), volleyball (g), wrestling (b,g); intramural: indoor soccer (b,g); coed interscholastic: cheering; coed intramural: bowling, fencing, outdoor activities, sailing, skiing (cross-country), skiing (downhill), snowboarding, table tennis. 3 PE instructors, 30 coaches.

Computers Computers are regularly used in desktop publishing, mathematics, video film production, yearbook classes. Computer network features include on-campus library services, online commercial services, Internet access, wireless campus network, Internet filtering or blocking technology. Students grades are available online. The school has a published electronic and media policy.

Contact Kim Gardner, Admissions Coordinator. 207-255-8301 Ext. 207. Fax: 207-255-8303. E-mail: admissions@washingtonacademy.org. Web site: www.washingtonacademy.org.

See Close-Up on page 1014.

WASHINGTON COUNTY DAY SCHOOL

1605 East Reed Road
Greenville, Mississippi 38703-7297

Head of School: Mr. Rodney Brown

General Information Coeducational day college-preparatory, arts, bilingual studies, and technology school. Grades PK–12. Founded: 1969. Setting: suburban. Nearest major city is Jackson. 30-acre campus. 2 buildings on campus. Approved or accredited by Mississippi Private School Association and Southern Association of Colleges and Schools. Total enrollment: 753. Upper school average class size: 20. Upper school faculty-student ratio: 1:20.

Upper School Student Profile Grade 9: 72 students (38 boys, 34 girls); Grade 10: 61 students (30 boys, 31 girls); Grade 11: 61 students (31 boys, 30 girls); Grade 12: 62 students (30 boys, 32 girls).

Faculty School total: 65. In upper school: 9 men, 27 women; 17 have advanced degrees.

Subjects Offered Advanced chemistry, algebra, American history-AP, American literature, anatomy and physiology, art, band, biology, business skills, calculus, calculus-AP, chemistry, chemistry-AP, computer keyboarding, computer multimedia, computer science, computers, concert band, creative writing, drama, drama performance, driver education, economics, English, English literature, English-AP, French, French studies, geography, geometry, government, government/civics, history, honors U.S. history, journalism, marching band, mathematics, music, physical education, physics, political systems, pre-algebra, pre-calculus, psychology, publications, science, social science, social studies, Spanish, speech, speech and debate, world history, yearbook.

Graduation Requirements Algebra, American government, arts, biology, chemistry, computer science, economics, English, English composition, foreign language, mathematics, physics, science, social science, social studies (includes history), speech, student government.

Special Academic Programs Honors section.

College Admission Counseling 63 students graduated in 2008; all went to college, including Delta State University; Millsaps College; Mississippi College; Mississippi State University; The University of Alabama; University of Mississippi.

Student Life Upper grades have uniform requirement, student council. Discipline rests primarily with faculty.

Tuition and Aid Day student tuition: $4320. Tuition installment plan (monthly payment plans). Need-based scholarship grants available. In 2008–09, 2% of upper-school students received aid. Total amount of financial aid awarded in 2008–09: $18,000.

Admissions Traditional secondary-level entrance grade is 9. For fall 2008, 5 students applied for upper-level admission, 5 were accepted, 5 enrolled. Deadline for receipt of application materials: none. Application fee required: $80. On-campus interview required.

Athletics Interscholastic: baseball (boys), basketball (b,g), cheering (g), cross-country running (b,g), drill team (g), football (b), soccer (b,g), softball (g), tennis (b,g), track and field (b,g); coed interscholastic: golf. 2 PE instructors, 15 coaches, 1 athletic trainer.
Computers Computers are regularly used in computer applications, data processing, keyboarding, typing classes. Computer network features include on-campus library services, Internet access, wireless campus network. Computer access in designated common areas is available to students. Students grades are available online.
Contact Mrs. Ruth Vowell, Administrative Assistant. 662-332-0786. Fax: 662-332-0434. E-mail: generals@generals.ws. Web site: www.generals.ws.

WASHINGTON INTERNATIONAL SCHOOL

3100 Macomb Street NW
Washington, District of Columbia 20008

Head of School: Clayton W. Lewis

General Information Coeducational day college-preparatory, bilingual studies, International Baccalaureate, and Dual Language instruction through the end of Middle School school. Grades PK–12. Founded: 1966. Setting: urban. 6-acre campus. 8 buildings on campus. Approved or accredited by Association of Independent Schools of Greater Washington, European Council of International Schools, International Baccalaureate Organization, Middle States Association of Colleges and Schools, and District of Columbia Department of Education. Member of National Association of Independent Schools and Secondary School Admission Test Board. Languages of instruction: English, Spanish, and French. Endowment: $1 million. Total enrollment: 894. Upper school average class size: 15. Upper school faculty-student ratio: 1:7.
Upper School Student Profile Grade 9: 59 students (24 boys, 35 girls); Grade 10: 63 students (36 boys, 27 girls); Grade 11: 64 students (33 boys, 31 girls); Grade 12: 68 students (27 boys, 41 girls).
Faculty School total: 103. In upper school: 12 men, 25 women; 18 have advanced degrees.
Subjects Offered Advanced chemistry, advanced math, art, arts, biology, calculus, chemistry, chorus, community service, comparative government and politics, contemporary history, drama, Dutch, economics, English, English literature, environmental science, ESL, fine arts, French, geography, history, information technology, integrated mathematics, International Baccalaureate courses, Italian, Japanese, literature seminar, music, musical productions, physical education, physics, science, social science, Spanish, theater, theory of knowledge, world history.
Graduation Requirements Algebra, arts and fine arts (art, music, dance, drama), biology, chemistry, computer science, English, foreign language, geography, geometry, physical education (includes health), physics, trigonometry, world history, world literature, IB program. Community service is required.
Special Academic Programs International Baccalaureate program; ESL (7 students enrolled).
College Admission Counseling 51 students graduated in 2007; all went to college, including Columbia College; McGill University; New York University; University of Virginia. Mean SAT math: 646, mean SAT writing: 610.
Student Life Upper grades have specified standards of dress, student council, honor system. Discipline rests primarily with faculty.
Tuition and Aid Day student tuition: $25,030. Tuition installment plan (Key Tuition Payment Plan, monthly payment plans, 2-payment plan). Need-based scholarship grants available. In 2007–08, 12% of upper-school students received aid. Total amount of financial aid awarded in 2007–08: $446,960.
Admissions Traditional secondary-level entrance grade is 9. For fall 2007, 63 students applied for upper-level admission, 32 were accepted, 17 enrolled. School's own exam required. Deadline for receipt of application materials: January 10. Application fee required: $50. On-campus interview required.
Athletics Interscholastic: baseball (boys), basketball (b,g), soccer (b,g), softball (g), tennis (b,g), track and field (b,g), volleyball (g); coed interscholastic: cross-country running, golf; coed intramural: equestrian sports. 3 PE instructors, 2 coaches.
Computers Computers are regularly used in all classes. Computer network features include on-campus library services, online commercial services, Internet access, wireless campus network, Internet filtering or blocking technology. Campus intranet and student e-mail accounts are available to students.
Contact Ms. Priscilla Lund, Associate Director for Middle and Upper School Admissions. 202-243-1815. Fax: 202-243-1807. E-mail: lund@wis.edu. Web site: www.wis.edu.

ANNOUNCEMENT FROM THE SCHOOL Washington International School (WIS) offers 890 students a challenging International Baccalaureate curriculum and rich language program from pre-kindergarten to grade 12. The Primary Years Program (PYP), the Middle Years Program (MYP), and Diploma program culminate in the prestigious International Baccalaureate Diploma. The School's rigorous academic program and international focus prepare students to meet the challenges of a global world.

WASHINGTON WALDORF SCHOOL

4800 Sangamore Road
Bethesda, Maryland 20816

Head of School: Mrs. Natalie Adams

General Information Coeducational day college-preparatory and arts school. Grades PS–12. Founded: 1969. Setting: suburban. Nearest major city is Washington, DC. 6-acre campus. 1 building on campus. Approved or accredited by Association of Independent Schools of Greater Washington, Association of Waldorf Schools of North America, Middle States Association of Colleges and Schools, and Maryland Department of Education. Total enrollment: 290. Upper school average class size: 20. Upper school faculty-student ratio: 1:7.
Upper School Student Profile Grade 9: 21 students (9 boys, 12 girls); Grade 10: 17 students (5 boys, 12 girls); Grade 11: 13 students (4 boys, 9 girls); Grade 12: 23 students (14 boys, 9 girls).
Faculty School total: 38. In upper school: 6 men, 9 women; 8 have advanced degrees.
Subjects Offered 3-dimensional art, African-American history, algebra, American Civil War, American literature, anatomy and physiology, ancient world history, art, art and culture, art history, biochemistry, biology, bookbinding, botany, British literature, calculus, calculus-AP, chamber groups, chemistry, choir, chorus, civil rights, classical civilization, crafts, critical thinking, critical writing, drama performance, ecology, epic literature, eurythmy, fine arts, general math, general science, geology, geometry, German, grammar, history of architecture, history of music, human anatomy, human development, lab science, medieval literature, metalworking, modern history, modern world history, mythology, oil painting, optics, physical education, pre-calculus, printmaking, research skills, sculpture, Shakespeare, Spanish, stone carving, trigonometry, U.S. constitutional history, weaving, Western literature, writing, zoology.
Graduation Requirements Arts and fine arts (art, music, dance, drama), crafts, English, eurythmy, foreign language, mathematics, physical education (includes health), science, social studies (includes history).
Special Academic Programs Advanced Placement exam preparation; study abroad; academic accommodation for the musically talented and the artistically talented.
College Admission Counseling 17 students graduated in 2008; all went to college, including Bennington College; Haverford College; Kenyon College; Smith College; The University of North Carolina at Chapel Hill; University of Vermont. Mean SAT critical reading: 639, mean SAT math: 582, mean SAT writing: 675, mean combined SAT: 1896.
Student Life Upper grades have specified standards of dress, student council. Discipline rests primarily with faculty.
Summer Programs Sports programs offered; session focuses on basketball and baseball camps; held on campus; accepts boys and girls; open to students from other schools. 18 students usually enrolled.
Tuition and Aid Day student tuition: $20,400. Tuition installment plan (FACTS Tuition Payment Plan, monthly payment plans, individually arranged payment plans, self-insured tuition insurance). Tuition reduction for siblings, need-based scholarship grants, need-based assistance grants, tuition remission for children of faculty, one full scholarship for an inner-city student available. In 2008–09, 20% of upper-school students received aid. Total amount of financial aid awarded in 2008–09: $14,950.
Admissions Traditional secondary-level entrance grade is 9. For fall 2008, 17 students applied for upper-level admission, 9 were accepted, 7 enrolled. Math and English placement tests required. Deadline for receipt of application materials: none. Application fee required: $60. On-campus interview required.
Athletics Interscholastic: baseball (boys), basketball (b,g), cross-country running (b,g), soccer (b,g), softball (g). 1 PE instructor, 3 coaches.
Computers Computers are regularly used in graphic design, technology classes. Computer resources include Internet access.
Contact Ms. Lezlie Lawson, Admissions/Enrollment Director. 301-229-6107 Ext. 154. Fax: 301-229-9379. E-mail: llawson@washingtonwaldorf.org. Web site: www.washingtonwaldorf.org.

THE WATERFORD SCHOOL

1480 East 9400 South
Sandy, Utah 84093

Head of School: Mrs. Nancy M. Heuston

General Information Coeducational day college-preparatory, arts, technology, and visual arts, music, photography, dance, and theater school. Grades PK–12. Founded: 1981. Setting: suburban. Nearest major city is Salt Lake City. 50-acre campus. 10 buildings on campus. Approved or accredited by Northwest Association of Schools and Colleges, Pacific Northwest Association of Independent Schools, and Utah Department of Education. Member of National Association of Independent Schools. Total enrollment: 992. Upper school average class size: 16. Upper school faculty-student ratio: 1:5.
Upper School Student Profile Grade 9: 72 students (35 boys, 37 girls); Grade 10: 60 students (27 boys, 33 girls); Grade 11: 73 students (36 boys, 37 girls); Grade 12: 63 students (33 boys, 30 girls).
Faculty School total: 137. In upper school: 46 men, 37 women; 64 have advanced degrees.
Subjects Offered 20th century history, 3-dimensional design, acting, advanced math, Advanced Placement courses, aerobics, algebra, American history, American

history-AP, American literature, art, Asian history, baseball, basketball, biology, biology-AP, British literature, calculus, calculus-AP, ceramics, chemistry, chemistry-AP, chorus, computer applications, computer art, computer graphics, computer programming, computer science, computer science-AP, creative writing, debate, drama, drama performance, drama workshop, drawing, ecology, economics, English-AP, European history, European history-AP, French, French-AP, geology, geometry, German, German-AP, Japanese, jazz ensemble, Latin, Latin American literature, music history, music performance, music theater, newspaper, outdoor education, painting, philosophy, photography, physical education, physics, physics-AP, pre-calculus, psychology, sculpture, Spanish, Spanish-AP, statistics and probability, statistics-AP, strings, studio art—AP, trigonometry, voice ensemble, volleyball, weight training, wind ensemble, world literature, writing workshop, yearbook, zoology.

Graduation Requirements 20th century world history, algebra, American history, American literature, biology, British literature, calculus, chemistry, computer science, English, European history, foreign language, geometry, music performance, physics, pre-calculus, trigonometry, visual arts, world history, writing workshop, six terms of physical education or participation on athletic teams.

Special Academic Programs Advanced Placement exam preparation; honors section; independent study; term-away projects; academic accommodation for the gifted, the musically talented, and the artistically talented.

College Admission Counseling 71 students graduated in 2008; all went to college. Mean SAT critical reading: 604, mean SAT math: 623, mean SAT writing: 578, mean combined SAT: 1805, mean composite ACT: 27.

Student Life Upper grades have uniform requirement, student council, honor system. Discipline rests equally with students and faculty.

Summer Programs Enrichment, advancement, sports, art/fine arts, computer instruction programs offered; session focuses on enrichment and advancement; held both on and off campus; held at various locations in Utah and abroad; accepts boys and girls; not open to students from other schools. 100 students usually enrolled. 2009 schedule: June 10 to August 10. Application deadline: March 15.

Tuition and Aid Day student tuition: $16,925. Guaranteed tuition plan. Tuition installment plan (Insured Tuition Payment Plan, monthly payment plans). Tuition reduction for siblings, need-based scholarship grants available.

Admissions Traditional secondary-level entrance grade is 9. For fall 2008, 35 students applied for upper-level admission, 29 were accepted, 22 enrolled. ERB CTP IV required. Deadline for receipt of application materials: none. Application fee required: $35. On-campus interview required.

Athletics Interscholastic: basketball (boys, girls), crew (b,g), cross-country running (b,g), golf (b,g), lacrosse (b,g), soccer (b,g), swimming and diving (b,g), tennis (b,g), track and field (b,g), volleyball (g); intramural: indoor soccer (b,g); coed interscholastic: alpine skiing, ballet, dance, Frisbee, outdoor education, racquetball, skiing (downhill); coed intramural: aerobics, alpine skiing, backpacking, climbing, crew, mountain biking, nordic skiing, outdoor recreation, rock climbing, wall climbing, weight training. 7 PE instructors, 6 coaches.

Computers Computers are regularly used in animation, college planning, graphic design, library, literary magazine, newspaper, photography, publications, yearbook classes. Computer network features include on-campus library services, Internet access.

Contact Mr. Todd Winters, Director of Admissions. 801-816-2213. Fax: 801-572-1787. E-mail: toddwinters@waterfordschool.org. Web site: www.waterfordschool.org.

ANNOUNCEMENT FROM THE SCHOOL Nestled near the base of Utah's majestic Wasatch mountains, Waterford, which sits on 50 acres, reflects the grandeur of its dramatic setting. The School's tradition is liberal arts. The focus is on each student learning. Here, expectations are high, the curriculum rich, and the scholarship engaging and renewing. Founded in 1981, the School instills qualities of independent thought, responsibility, and service as it helps students lay a solid foundation for college and prepares them to lead purposeful and honorable lives. Parents trust Waterford to deliver the finest education based on the richness of its curriculum, the quality of its faculty, the commitment of its students, and the safety of its environment. Using classical ideals for learning and life, Waterford teachers measure their effectiveness by the growth and development of each student. Upper School students are taught to be self-reflective in their learning and to acquire a repertoire of learning styles, which may be used across subject matter that varies widely and is freshly challenging. In the process, students learn the merits of primary sources, class discussions, and personal discipline. A majority of students in grades 10–12 take honors classes; many enroll in AP courses, which culminate in the AP examinations. The fine arts also receive strong emphasis. Students may sample widely or focus on a particular specialty in the arts. In every case, the teachers are specialists in the fields they teach, from choral music to strings or band, watercolor to oil painting and ceramics, photography to drama and dance. This much is certain: When they graduate, Waterford students are primed for lifelong learning and are ready to contribute that learning to the common good.

WATKINSON SCHOOL

180 Bloomfield Avenue
Hartford, Connecticut 06105

Head of School: Mr. John W. Bracker

General Information Coeducational day college-preparatory, arts, technology, and athletics, global studies school. Grades 6–PG. Founded: 1881. Setting: suburban. 40-acre campus. 5 buildings on campus. Approved or accredited by Association of Independent Schools in New England, Connecticut Association of Independent Schools, National Association of Episcopal Schools, New England Association of Schools and Colleges, and Connecticut Department of Education. Member of National Association of Independent Schools and Secondary School Admission Test Board. Endowment: $2.9 million. Total enrollment: 284. Upper school average class size: 13. Upper school faculty-student ratio: 1:4.

Upper School Student Profile Grade 9: 49 students (26 boys, 23 girls); Grade 10: 45 students (22 boys, 23 girls); Grade 11: 58 students (26 boys, 32 girls); Grade 12: 42 students (22 boys, 20 girls).

Faculty School total: 58. In upper school: 16 men, 30 women; 34 have advanced degrees.

Subjects Offered African history, algebra, American history, American literature, American sign language, anatomy, ancient world history, art, Asian history, athletics, biology, calculus, ceramics, chemistry, creative writing, dance, drama, drawing, earth science, English, English literature, environmental science, environmental studies, European history, expository writing, fine arts, French, geography, geometry, health, history, internship, life skills, mathematics, modern European history, painting, photography, physical education, physics, pottery, science, social studies, Spanish, theater, U.S. history, world history, world literature, writing.

Graduation Requirements Arts and fine arts (art, music, dance, drama), English, foreign language, health and wellness, mathematics, science, social studies (includes history), technology.

Special Academic Programs Honors section; accelerated programs; independent study; term-away projects; study at local college for college credit; study abroad; academic accommodation for the gifted, the musically talented, and the artistically talented; ESL (2 students enrolled).

College Admission Counseling 43 students graduated in 2008; all went to college, including Johnson & Wales University; Sacred Heart University; University of Connecticut. Median SAT critical reading: 570, median SAT math: 560, median SAT writing: 560, median combined SAT: 1690, median composite ACT: 24. 28% scored over 600 on SAT critical reading, 26% scored over 600 on SAT math, 31% scored over 600 on SAT writing, 28% scored over 1800 on combined SAT, 39% scored over 26 on composite ACT.

Student Life Upper grades have specified standards of dress, student council, honor system. Discipline rests equally with students and faculty.

Summer Programs Remediation, enrichment, art/fine arts, computer instruction programs offered; session focuses on enrichment and tutorial support; held on campus; accepts boys and girls; open to students from other schools. 80 students usually enrolled. 2009 schedule: June 29 to August 7. Application deadline: none.

Tuition and Aid Day student tuition: $28,726. Tuition installment plan (Insured Tuition Payment Plan, Academic Management Services Plan). Need-based scholarship grants, Limited work study jobs. available. In 2008–09, 36% of upper-school students received aid. Total amount of financial aid awarded in 2008–09: $1,374,748.

Admissions Traditional secondary-level entrance grade is 9. For fall 2008, 95 students applied for upper-level admission, 64 were accepted, 29 enrolled. ISEE or SSAT required. Deadline for receipt of application materials: February 1. Application fee required: $50. On-campus interview required.

Athletics Interscholastic: baseball (boys), basketball (b,g), crew (b,g), cross-country running (b,g), lacrosse (b,g), soccer (b,g), softball (g), volleyball (g); coed interscholastic: crew, cross-country running, tennis, ultimate Frisbee; coed intramural: alpine skiing, ballet, climbing, combined training, dance, fencing, fitness, golf, outdoor adventure, physical fitness, skiing (cross-country), skiing (downhill), strength & conditioning, tennis, ultimate Frisbee, volleyball, weight lifting, yoga. 1 PE instructor, 9 coaches, 1 athletic trainer.

Computers Computers are regularly used in all classes. Computer network features include on-campus library services, online commercial services, Internet access, wireless campus network, Internet filtering or blocking technology. Campus intranet and student e-mail accounts are available to students. The school has a published electronic and media policy.

Contact Mrs. Cathy Batson, Admissions Office Assistant. 860-236-5618 Ext. 136. Fax: 860-233-8295. E-mail: cathy_batson@watkinson.org. Web site: www.watkinson.org.

ANNOUNCEMENT FROM THE SCHOOL Lead school for the Coalition of Essential Schools, Watkinson's award-winning college-preparatory curriculum serves grades 6–PG. Emphasis is on the mastery of essential skills and concepts. Ninety-minute classes allow for in-depth study. Special programs include creative arts, learning skills, and global studies. College credits are available at the adjacent University of Hartford.

THE WAVERLY SCHOOL

67 West Bellevue Drive
Pasadena, California 91105

Head of School: Ms. Heidi Johnson

General Information Coeducational day college-preparatory and arts school. Grades PK–12. Founded: 1993. Setting: urban. Nearest major city is Los Angeles. 1-acre campus. 7 buildings on campus. Approved or accredited by Western Association of Schools and Colleges. Total enrollment: 327. Upper school average class size: 12. Upper school faculty-student ratio: 1:8.

Upper School Student Profile Grade 9: 33 students (18 boys, 15 girls); Grade 10: 17 students (9 boys, 8 girls); Grade 11: 21 students (11 boys, 10 girls); Grade 12: 22 students (12 boys, 10 girls).

Faculty School total: 49. In upper school: 5 men, 9 women; 9 have advanced degrees.

Subjects Offered 20th century history, algebra, American history-AP, American literature, ancient history, art, biology, biology-AP, calculus-AP, chemistry, college counseling, composition, contemporary issues, creative writing, English composition, English language-AP, English-AP, environmental science-AP, environmental studies, ethics, European history-AP, European literature, filmmaking, French-AP, geometry, history, modern civilization, performing arts, physical science, physics-AP, physiology, pre-calculus, Spanish-AP, statistics, world religions, yearbook.

Graduation Requirements Algebra, American history, American literature, ancient history, art, biology, chemistry, foreign language, geometry, performing arts, physical science, world history. Community service is required.

Special Academic Programs Advanced Placement exam preparation; independent study.

College Admission Counseling 17 students graduated in 2008; all went to college, including Occidental College; Pitzer College; Trinity College; University of California, Berkeley; University of California, Santa Barbara; University of California, Santa Cruz. Median SAT critical reading: 640, median SAT math: 610. 57% scored over 600 on SAT critical reading, 71% scored over 600 on SAT math.

Student Life Upper grades have student council, honor system. Discipline rests primarily with faculty.

Summer Programs Remediation, enrichment, advancement, art/fine arts programs offered; session focuses on remediation; held on campus; accepts boys and girls; open to students from other schools. 25 students usually enrolled. 2009 schedule: July to August. Application deadline: none.

Tuition and Aid Day student tuition: $16,380. Tuition installment plan (monthly payment plans). Need-based scholarship grants available. In 2008–09, 8% of upper-school students received aid. Total amount of financial aid awarded in 2008–09: $17,000.

Admissions Traditional secondary-level entrance grade is 9. For fall 2008, 30 students applied for upper-level admission, 15 were accepted, 10 enrolled. Nonstandardized placement tests required. Deadline for receipt of application materials: February 1. Application fee required: $75. On-campus interview required.

Athletics Interscholastic: baseball (boys), basketball (b,g), cross-country running (b,g), softball (g), volleyball (g); intramural: cooperative games (b,g), yoga (b,g); coed interscholastic: equestrian sports, flag football, golf; coed intramural: basketball, cooperative games, fencing, fitness, yoga. 2 PE instructors, 10 coaches.

Computers Computers are regularly used in science classes.

Contact Jennifer Dakan, Admissions Director. 626-792-5940. Fax: 626-683-5460. E-mail: Jennifer@thewaverlyschool.org. Web site: www.thewaverlyschool.org.

WAYNE COUNTRY DAY SCHOOL

480 Country Day Road
Goldsboro, North Carolina 27530

Head of School: Mr. Todd Anderson

General Information Coeducational day college-preparatory school. Grades PK–12. Founded: 1968. Setting: rural. Nearest major city is Raleigh. 40-acre campus. 5 buildings on campus. Approved or accredited by Southern Association of Colleges and Schools and North Carolina Department of Education. Total enrollment: 253. Upper school average class size: 19. Upper school faculty-student ratio: 1:15.

Upper School Student Profile Grade 7: 15 students (8 boys, 7 girls); Grade 8: 26 students (15 boys, 11 girls); Grade 9: 24 students (16 boys, 8 girls); Grade 10: 21 students (8 boys, 13 girls); Grade 11: 21 students (12 boys, 9 girls); Grade 12: 17 students (6 boys, 11 girls).

Faculty School total: 36. In upper school: 5 men, 15 women; 6 have advanced degrees.

Subjects Offered Algebra, art, athletics, baseball, basketball, biology, biology-AP, calculus, calculus-AP, cheerleading, chemistry, choir, civics, college counseling, composition, composition-AP, computers, creative writing, critical writing, earth science, ecology, electives, English, English composition, English language and composition-AP, English language-AP, English literature, English literature and composition-AP, English literature-AP, English-AP, environmental science, film and literature, film history, geography, geometry, health, honors English, honors geometry, honors U.S. history, honors world history, keyboarding, life science, marine biology, multimedia design, music, music theory-AP, North Carolina history, photography, physical education, physical science, physics, pre-algebra, pre-calculus, Spanish, studio art, study skills, theater, theater production, U.S. history, U.S. history-AP, weightlifting, Western civilization, world history, world history-AP, yearbook.

Graduation Requirements Arts and fine arts (art, music, dance, drama), composition, computer science, English, foreign language, mathematics, physical education (includes health), science, social studies (includes history). Community service is required.

Special Academic Programs Advanced Placement exam preparation; honors section; independent study; academic accommodation for the gifted.

College Admission Counseling 29 students graduated in 2008; all went to college, including Amherst College; East Carolina University; New York University; North Carolina State University; The University of North Carolina at Chapel Hill; The University of North Carolina Wilmington.

Student Life Upper grades have specified standards of dress, student council, honor system. Discipline rests equally with students and faculty.

Summer Programs Advancement programs offered; session focuses on academic advancement; held on campus; accepts boys and girls; not open to students from other schools. 20 students usually enrolled. 2009 schedule: June 2 to June 30. Application deadline: May 23.

Tuition and Aid Day student tuition: $7600. Guaranteed tuition plan. Need-based scholarship grants available. In 2008–09, 30% of upper-school students received aid.

Admissions Traditional secondary-level entrance grade is 9. Admissions testing required. Deadline for receipt of application materials: none. Application fee required: $60. Interview required.

Athletics Interscholastic: baseball (boys), basketball (b,g), field hockey (g), soccer (b,g), tennis (b,g), volleyball (g), weight training (b,g); coed interscholastic: golf, strength & conditioning, swimming and diving, weight training; coed intramural: soccer. 3 PE instructors, 5 coaches.

Computers Computers are regularly used in English, foreign language, history, science classes. Computer network features include online commercial services, Internet access. The school has a published electronic and media policy.

Contact Ms. Elidia M. Eason, Director of Admissions. 919-736-1045 Ext. 233. Fax: 919-583-9493. E-mail: wcdsadmissions@waynecountryday.com. Web site: www.waynecountryday.com.

WAYNFLETE SCHOOL

360 Spring Street
Portland, Maine 04102

Head of School: Dr. Mark Segar

General Information Coeducational day college-preparatory school. Grades PK–12. Founded: 1898. Setting: urban. Nearest major city is Boston, MA. 30-acre campus. 11 buildings on campus. Approved or accredited by Association of Independent Schools in New England, Independent Schools of Northern New England, New England Association of Schools and Colleges, The College Board, and Maine Department of Education. Member of National Association of Independent Schools. Endowment: $11 million. Total enrollment: 568. Upper school average class size: 12. Upper school faculty-student ratio: 1:13.

Upper School Student Profile Grade 9: 52 students (26 boys, 26 girls); Grade 10: 61 students (29 boys, 32 girls); Grade 11: 57 students (30 boys, 27 girls); Grade 12: 63 students (24 boys, 39 girls).

Faculty School total: 102. In upper school: 25 men, 46 women.

Subjects Offered Algebra, American history, American literature, art history, biology, calculus, ceramics, chemistry, computer science, creative writing, dance, drama, earth science, ecology, English, English literature, environmental science, ethics, European history, expository writing, film, fine arts, French, geography, geometry, government/civics, grammar, health, Latin, marine biology, mathematics, music, physical education, physics, psychology, social studies, Spanish, studio art, theater, trigonometry, world history, world literature, writing.

Graduation Requirements Arts, biology, English, foreign language, geometry, history, mathematics, science, sports, U.S. history. Community service is required.

Special Academic Programs Independent study; term-away projects; study abroad.

College Admission Counseling 67 students graduated in 2008; 66 went to college, including Bates College; Brown University; Connecticut College; The George Washington University; University of Colorado Denver; Wheaton College. Other: 1 entered a postgraduate year. Median SAT critical reading: 620, median SAT math: 580, median SAT writing: 630, median combined SAT: 1860. 67% scored over 600 on SAT critical reading, 55% scored over 600 on SAT math, 64% scored over 600 on SAT writing, 62% scored over 1800 on combined SAT.

Student Life Upper grades have student council. Discipline rests primarily with faculty.

Summer Programs Enrichment, sports, art/fine arts programs offered; session focuses on fine arts, sports camps, gymnastics, performing arts, & science; held both on and off campus; held at Fore River Fields, Portland, ME; accepts boys and girls; open to students from other schools. 800 students usually enrolled. 2009 schedule: June 9 to August 1. Application deadline: June 1.

Tuition and Aid Day student tuition: $21,615. Tuition installment plan (Insured Tuition Payment Plan, monthly payment plans). Need-based scholarship grants available. In 2008–09, 18% of upper-school students received aid. Total amount of financial aid awarded in 2008–09: $787,383.

Admissions Traditional secondary-level entrance grade is 9. For fall 2008, 63 students applied for upper-level admission, 32 were accepted, 21 enrolled. Writing sample required. Deadline for receipt of application materials: February 10. Application fee required: $40. Interview required.
Athletics Interscholastic: baseball (boys), basketball (b,g), cross-country running (b,g), field hockey (g), golf (b,g), lacrosse (b,g), skiing (cross-country) (b,g), soccer (b,g), tennis (b,g); intramural: backpacking (b,g), handball (b); coed interscholastic: crew, nordic skiing, rowing, track and field; coed intramural: alpine skiing, bowling, combined training, dance, fitness walking, Frisbee, modern dance, physical fitness, sailing, swimming and diving, tennis, ultimate Frisbee, weight lifting, weight training, yoga. 4 PE instructors, 20 coaches, 1 athletic trainer.
Computers Computers are regularly used in all academic classes. Computer network features include on-campus library services, online commercial services, Internet access, Internet filtering or blocking technology. Student e-mail accounts and computer access in designated common areas are available to students.
Contact Admission Office. 207-774-5721 Ext. 224. Fax: 207-772-4782. E-mail: admission_office@waynflete.org. Web site: www.waynflete.org.

THE WEBB SCHOOL

319 Webb Road East
PO Box 488
Bell Buckle, Tennessee 37020
Head of School: Mr. Albert Cauz

General Information Coeducational boarding and day college-preparatory, arts, technology, and wilderness leadership school. Boarding grades 7–12, day grades 6–12. Founded: 1870. Setting: rural. Nearest major city is Nashville. Students are housed in single-sex dormitories. 150-acre campus. 17 buildings on campus. Approved or accredited by Southern Association of Colleges and Schools, Southern Association of Independent Schools, Tennessee Association of Independent Schools, The Association of Boarding Schools, and Tennessee Department of Education. Member of National Association of Independent Schools and Secondary School Admission Test Board. Endowment: $24 million. Total enrollment: 303. Upper school average class size: 12. Upper school faculty-student ratio: 1:7.
Upper School Student Profile Grade 9: 61 students (22 boys, 39 girls); Grade 10: 49 students (25 boys, 24 girls); Grade 11: 59 students (30 boys, 29 girls); Grade 12: 49 students (29 boys, 20 girls). 33% of students are boarding students. 73% are state residents. 15 states are represented in upper school student body. 15% are international students. International students from China, Germany, Republic of Korea, Taiwan, United Kingdom, and Viet Nam; 8 other countries represented in student body.
Faculty School total: 47. In upper school: 21 men, 23 women; 19 have advanced degrees; 21 reside on campus.
Subjects Offered Advanced Placement courses, algebra, American Civil War, American government, American history, American literature, American literature-AP, anatomy, art, art appreciation, art education, art history, arts appreciation, biology, business skills, calculus, ceramics, chemistry, chemistry-AP, computer programming, computer science, creative writing, drama, driver education, earth science, ecology, economics, English, English literature, ESL, ethical decision making, ethics, European history, fine arts, French, geography, geometry, German, government/civics, grammar, health, history, history-AP, journalism, Latin, mathematics, music, music appreciation, music history, music performance, music theory, physical education, physics, physics-AP, physiology, piano, poetry, psychology, religion, Russian history, science, Shakespeare, social science, social studies, Spanish, speech, statistics, theater, trigonometry, Western civilization, wilderness education, world history, world literature.
Graduation Requirements American government, American history, arts and fine arts (art, music, dance, drama), computer science, economics, English, ethical decision making, ethics, foreign language, mathematics, physical education (includes health), science, senior thesis, social science, social studies (includes history), speech, declamation.
Special Academic Programs 7 Advanced Placement exams for which test preparation is offered; honors section; independent study; study abroad; academic accommodation for the gifted; programs in general development for dyslexic students; special instructional classes for deaf students; ESL (7 students enrolled).
College Admission Counseling 49 students graduated in 2008; all went to college, including Birmingham-Southern College; Georgia Institute of Technology; Queens University of Charlotte; Reed College; Sewanee: The University of the South; Wake Forest University. Mean SAT critical reading: 640, mean SAT math: 632, mean SAT writing: 622, mean combined SAT: 1894, mean composite ACT: 26.
Student Life Upper grades have uniform requirement, student council, honor system. Discipline rests equally with students and faculty.
Tuition and Aid Day student tuition: $10,600–$14,100; 7-day tuition and room/board: $33,600–$41,000. Tuition installment plan (monthly payment plans, individually arranged payment plans). Merit scholarship grants, need-based scholarship grants available. In 2008–09, 34% of upper-school students received aid; total upper-school merit-scholarship money awarded: $201,600. Total amount of financial aid awarded in 2008–09: $920,000.
Admissions Traditional secondary-level entrance grade is 9. For fall 2008, 142 students applied for upper-level admission, 74 were accepted, 36 enrolled. ERB (grade level), ISEE, Otis-Lennon School Ability Test, PSAT, SLEP for foreign students, SSAT, Stanford Achievement Test or TOEFL or SLEP required. Deadline for receipt of application materials: none. Application fee required: $35. Interview required.
Athletics Interscholastic: baseball (boys), basketball (b,g), cross-country running (b,g), golf (b,g), lacrosse (b,g), soccer (b,g), volleyball (g); intramural: aerobics (g), aerobics/Nautilus (b,g); coed interscholastic: marksmanship, running, trap and skeet; coed intramural: aerobics/Nautilus, aquatics, backpacking, badminton, ballet, bowling, canoeing/kayaking, climbing, combined training, fishing, fitness, fitness walking, fly fishing, Frisbee, hiking/backpacking, horseback riding, kayaking, mountain biking, outdoor activities, physical fitness, physical training, rock climbing, ropes courses, skeet shooting, table tennis, ultimate Frisbee, weight lifting, weight training, wilderness survival. 1 PE instructor, 15 coaches, 1 athletic trainer.
Computers Computers are regularly used in computer applications, English, foreign language, history, journalism, mathematics, science, writing classes. Computer network features include on-campus library services, online commercial services, Internet access, wireless campus network, Internet filtering or blocking technology. Campus intranet, student e-mail accounts, and computer access in designated common areas are available to students. The school has a published electronic and media policy.
Contact Mrs. Julie Harris, Director of Admissions. 931-389-6003. Fax: 931-389-6657. E-mail: admissions@webbschool.com. Web site: www.thewebbschool.com.

See Close-Up on page 1016.

WEBB SCHOOL OF KNOXVILLE

9800 Webb School Drive
Knoxville, Tennessee 37923-3399
Head of School: Mr. Scott L. Hutchinson

General Information Coeducational day college-preparatory, arts, religious studies, and technology school. Grades K–12. Founded: 1955. Setting: urban. Nearest major city is Chattanooga. 108-acre campus. 9 buildings on campus. Approved or accredited by Southern Association of Colleges and Schools, Southern Association of Independent Schools, and Tennessee Department of Education. Member of National Association of Independent Schools and Secondary School Admission Test Board. Endowment: $6.7 million. Total enrollment: 1,049. Upper school average class size: 15. Upper school faculty-student ratio: 1:10.
Upper School Student Profile Grade 9: 127 students (64 boys, 63 girls); Grade 10: 107 students (59 boys, 48 girls); Grade 11: 123 students (63 boys, 60 girls); Grade 12: 118 students (61 boys, 57 girls).
Faculty School total: 100. In upper school: 19 men, 26 women; 38 have advanced degrees.
Subjects Offered 3-dimensional design, advanced math, algebra, art history-AP, biology, biology-AP, calculus, calculus-AP, ceramics, chamber groups, chemistry, chemistry-AP, computer science, computer science-AP, concert choir, drama, dramatic arts, drawing, economics, English composition, English language and composition-AP, English literature, English literature and composition-AP, English-AP, environmental science-AP, film, French, French-AP, freshman foundations, geometry, German, German-AP, handbells, history of music, history of rock and roll, honors algebra, honors English, honors geometry, honors world history, human biology, independent study, journalism, Latin, Latin-AP, macroeconomics-AP, Mandarin, modern European history-AP, modern world history, music theory-AP, painting, photography, physics, physics-AP, playwriting, pre-calculus, probability and statistics, psychology-AP, Spanish, Spanish-AP, speech communications, stage design, statistics-AP, strings, studio art-AP, U.S. government and politics, U.S. government and politics-AP, U.S. history, U.S. history-AP, wind ensemble, world history, world history-AP, world religions, yearbook.
Graduation Requirements Algebra, American history, arts and fine arts (art, music, dance, drama), biology, chemistry, electives, English, foreign language, freshman foundations, geometry, mathematics, philosophy, physical education (includes health), psychology, public service, religion (includes Bible studies and theology), science, world history, world religions, public speaking (two chapel talks), 25 hours of service learning per year.
Special Academic Programs 25 Advanced Placement exams for which test preparation is offered; honors section; independent study; study abroad.
College Admission Counseling 117 students graduated in 2008; all went to college, including Georgia Institute of Technology; The University of North Carolina at Chapel Hill; The University of Tennessee; The University of Tennessee at Chattanooga; Tufts University; Virginia Polytechnic Institute and State University. Mean SAT critical reading: 608, mean SAT math: 605, mean SAT writing: 598, mean composite ACT: 27. 66% scored over 600 on SAT critical reading, 65% scored over 600 on SAT math, 64% scored over 600 on SAT writing, 60% scored over 26 on composite ACT.
Student Life Upper grades have uniform requirement, student council, honor system. Discipline rests equally with students and faculty.
Summer Programs Remediation, enrichment, advancement, sports, art/fine arts programs offered; session focuses on camp and sports-oriented fun; held on campus; accepts boys and girls; open to students from other schools. 1,389 students usually enrolled. 2009 schedule: June 1 to July 31. Application deadline: June 1.
Tuition and Aid Day student tuition: $14,336. Tuition installment plan (Key Tuition Payment Plan, monthly payment plans, individually arranged payment plans). Need-based scholarship grants available. In 2008–09, 10% of upper-school students received aid. Total amount of financial aid awarded in 2008–09: $799,351.

Admissions Traditional secondary-level entrance grade is 9. For fall 2008, 52 students applied for upper-level admission, 43 were accepted, 33 enrolled. SSAT required. Deadline for receipt of application materials: January 9. Application fee required: $40. On-campus interview required.

Athletics Interscholastic: baseball (boys), basketball (b,g), bowling (b,g), cheering (g), climbing (b,g), cross-country running (b,g), diving (b,g), field hockey (g), football (b), golf (b,g), lacrosse (b), soccer (b,g), softball (g), swimming and diving (b,g), tennis (b,g), track and field (b,g), volleyball (g), wrestling (b); coed interscholastic: sailing; coed intramural: weight training. 27 coaches, 1 athletic trainer.

Computers Computers are regularly used in art, English, foreign language, graphic design, history, journalism, mathematics, science, technology, yearbook classes. Computer network features include on-campus library services, Internet access, wireless campus network, Internet filtering or blocking technology. Student e-mail accounts are available to students. Students grades are available online. The school has a published electronic and media policy.

Contact Mrs. Sarah Lowe, Admissions Administrative Assistant. 865-291-3830. Fax: 865-291-1532. E-mail: sarah_lowe@webbschool.org. Web site: www.webbschool.org.

THE WEBB SCHOOLS

1175 West Baseline Road
Claremont, California 91711

Head of School: Mrs. Susan A. Nelson

General Information Coeducational boarding and day college-preparatory school. Grades 9–12. Founded: 1922. Setting: suburban. Nearest major city is Pasadena. Students are housed in single-sex dormitories. 70-acre campus. 57 buildings on campus. Approved or accredited by California Association of Independent Schools, The Association of Boarding Schools, Western Association of Schools and Colleges, and California Department of Education. Member of National Association of Independent Schools and Secondary School Admission Test Board. Endowment: $20 million. Total enrollment: 391. Upper school average class size: 16. Upper school faculty-student ratio: 1:7.

Upper School Student Profile Grade 9: 89 students (40 boys, 49 girls); Grade 10: 104 students (55 boys, 49 girls); Grade 11: 98 students (52 boys, 46 girls); Grade 12: 100 students (53 boys, 47 girls). 62% of students are boarding students. 67% are state residents. 16 states are represented in upper school student body. 13% are international students. International students from China, Democratic People's Republic of Korea, Germany, Hong Kong, Kazakhstan, and Nigeria; 16 other countries represented in student body.

Faculty School total: 56. In upper school: 31 men, 25 women; 42 have advanced degrees; 44 reside on campus.

Subjects Offered Algebra, American history, American literature, art, biology, biology-AP, calculus-AP, chemistry, chemistry-AP, chorus, composition-AP, computer math, computer science, discrete math, drama, economics, English, English language and composition-AP, English literature, English literature and composition-AP, environmental science, European history, European history-AP, fine arts, French, French language-AP, French literature-AP, geometry, government/civics, history, leadership skills, literature, modern European history-AP, museum science, music, orchestra, paleontology, physical education, physical science, physics, physics-AP, poetry, pre-calculus, psychology, SAT preparation, science, social studies, Spanish, Spanish language-AP, Spanish literature-AP, speech, statistics-AP, technology, theater, trigonometry, U.S. history-AP, world history, world history-AP, writing, yearbook.

Graduation Requirements Arts and fine arts (art, music, dance, drama), computer science, English, foreign language, mathematics, physical education (includes health), science, social studies (includes history).

Special Academic Programs Advanced Placement exam preparation; honors section; independent study; study at local college for college credit; academic accommodation for the gifted.

College Admission Counseling 97 students graduated in 2008; 96 went to college, including Harvard University; Stanford University; University of California, Berkeley; University of Pennsylvania; University of Southern California; Wellesley College. Other: 1 had other specific plans. Mean combined SAT: 1940.

Student Life Upper grades have specified standards of dress, student council, honor system. Discipline rests equally with students and faculty.

Summer Programs Enrichment, advancement, art/fine arts, computer instruction programs offered; session focuses on academic enrichment; held on campus; accepts boys and girls; open to students from other schools. 300 students usually enrolled. 2009 schedule: June 21 to July 23. Application deadline: none.

Tuition and Aid Day student tuition: $31,300; 7-day tuition and room/board: $44,010. Tuition installment plan (Insured Tuition Payment Plan, monthly payment plans). Need-based scholarship grants, AchieverLoans (Key Education Resources) available. In 2008–09, 27% of upper-school students received aid. Total amount of financial aid awarded in 2008–09: $2,600,000.

Admissions Traditional secondary-level entrance grade is 9. For fall 2008, 267 students applied for upper-level admission, 168 were accepted, 114 enrolled. ISEE or SSAT required. Deadline for receipt of application materials: January 30. Application fee required: $50. On-campus interview required.

Athletics Interscholastic: baseball (boys), basketball (b,g), cross-country running (b,g), diving (b,g), football (b), golf (b,g), independent competitive sports (b,g), soccer (b,g), softball (g), swimming and diving (b,g), tennis (b,g), track and field (b,g), volleyball (g), water polo (b,g), winter soccer (g), wrestling (b); intramural: physical fitness (g), weight lifting (b); coed intramural: backpacking, climbing, dance, fitness, fitness walking, Frisbee, hiking/backpacking, outdoor activities, physical fitness, rock climbing, strength & conditioning, surfing, ultimate Frisbee. 12 coaches, 1 athletic trainer.

Computers Computers are regularly used in English, foreign language, graphic design, health, history, mathematics, science classes. Computer network features include on-campus library services, Internet access, Internet filtering or blocking technology. Student e-mail accounts are available to students. The school has a published electronic and media policy.

Contact Mr. Leo G. Marshall, Director of Admission and Financial Aid. 909-482-5214. Fax: 909-445-8269. E-mail: admissions@webb.org. Web site: www.webb.org/admission.

WEDIKO SCHOOL AND TREATMENT PROGRAM

Windsor, New Hampshire
See Special Needs Schools section.

THE WELLINGTON SCHOOL

3650 Reed Road
Columbus, Ohio 43220

Head of School: Mr. Robert D. Brisk

General Information Coeducational day college-preparatory, arts, and bilingual studies school. Grades PK–12. Founded: 1982. Setting: suburban. 21-acre campus. 1 building on campus. Approved or accredited by Independent Schools Association of the Central States, Ohio Association of Independent Schools, and Ohio Department of Education. Member of National Association of Independent Schools. Total enrollment: 616. Upper school average class size: 15. Upper school faculty-student ratio: 1:12.

Upper School Student Profile Grade 9: 53 students (29 boys, 24 girls); Grade 10: 52 students (30 boys, 22 girls); Grade 11: 60 students (30 boys, 30 girls); Grade 12: 45 students (22 boys, 23 girls).

Faculty School total: 56. In upper school: 14 men, 11 women; 16 have advanced degrees.

Subjects Offered Algebra, art and culture, band, biology, biology-AP, calculus-AP, ceramics, chemistry, chemistry-AP, choir, chorus, computer graphics, creative arts, drama, drawing, earth and space science, economics, English, English-AP, European history-AP, film, finite math, French, French-AP, geometry, government, issues of the 90's, journalism, Latin, Latin-AP, mathematics, modern history, music appreciation, music theory-AP, painting, photography, physical education, physics, physics-AP, printmaking, Spanish, Spanish-AP, speech, strings, studio art-AP, U.S. history, U.S. history-AP, visual arts, voice, Western civilization, word processing, writing, yearbook.

Graduation Requirements 3-dimensional art, arts and fine arts (art, music, dance, drama), English, foreign language, government, lab science, mathematics, physical education (includes health), science, social science, social studies (includes history), speech, senior independent project. Community service is required.

Special Academic Programs Advanced Placement exam preparation; honors section; accelerated programs; independent study; study at local college for college credit; study abroad; academic accommodation for the gifted, the musically talented, and the artistically talented.

College Admission Counseling 36 students graduated in 2008; all went to college, including Case Western Reserve University; Denison University; John Carroll University; Lehigh University; Miami University; The Ohio State University.

Student Life Upper grades have specified standards of dress, student council. Discipline rests equally with students and faculty.

Summer Programs Enrichment, advancement, sports programs offered; session focuses on advancement; held on campus; accepts boys and girls; open to students from other schools. 50 students usually enrolled. 2009 schedule: June 11 to August 17. Application deadline: none.

Tuition and Aid Day student tuition: $16,500–$17,150. Tuition installment plan (Key Tuition Payment Plan, monthly payment plans, individually arranged payment plans, 2-, 6-, and 10-month payment plans). Merit scholarship grants, need-based scholarship grants, need-based loans available.

Admissions Traditional secondary-level entrance grade is 9. Admissions testing or ERB required. Deadline for receipt of application materials: none. Application fee required: $50. On-campus interview required.

Athletics Interscholastic: baseball (boys), basketball (b,g), crew (b,g), fencing (b,g), golf (b,g), lacrosse (b,g), soccer (b,g), softball (g), tennis (b,g); intramural: basketball (b,g), lacrosse (g); coed interscholastic: crew, fencing, swimming and diving; coed intramural: climbing, flag football, martial arts. 2 PE instructors, 1 coach, 1 athletic trainer.

Computers Computers are regularly used in English, foreign language, library, mathematics, music, newspaper, research skills, science, senior seminar, theater arts, typing, yearbook classes. Computer network features include on-campus library services, online commercial services, Internet access, wireless campus network, Internet filtering or blocking technology, SmartBoards. Campus intranet, student e-mail accounts, and computer access in designated common areas are available to students. Students grades are available online. The school has a published electronic and media policy.

Contact Ms. Lynne Steger, Assistant Director of Admission. 614-324-1647. Fax: 614-442-3286. E-mail: steger@wellington.org. Web site: www.wellington.org.

WESLEYAN ACADEMY

PO Box 1489
Guaynabo, Puerto Rico 00970-1489
Head of School: Dra. Gloria Cordero

General Information Coeducational day college-preparatory school, affiliated with Wesleyan Church. Grades PK–12. Founded: 1955. Setting: urban. Nearest major city is San Juan. 6-acre campus. 1 building on campus. Approved or accredited by Association of Christian Schools International, Middle States Association of Colleges and Schools, and Puerto Rico Department of Education. Languages of instruction: English and Spanish. Total enrollment: 922. Upper school average class size: 25. Upper school faculty-student ratio: 1:23.

Upper School Student Profile Grade 7: 75 students (42 boys, 33 girls); Grade 8: 56 students (24 boys, 32 girls); Grade 9: 60 students (27 boys, 33 girls); Grade 10: 64 students (35 boys, 29 girls); Grade 11: 58 students (28 boys, 30 girls); Grade 12: 35 students (20 boys, 15 girls). 50% of students are members of Wesleyan Church.

Faculty School total: 72. In upper school: 10 men, 12 women; 12 have advanced degrees.

Subjects Offered Accounting, algebra, American history, anatomy and physiology, art, Bible, biology, calculus, career and personal planning, choir, college planning, computer keyboarding, computer skills, critical writing, English, general math, general science, geography, geometry, global studies, golf, guidance, handbells, health, history, Internet, intro to computers, lab science, library, mathematics, music, music appreciation, personal development, poetry, pre-algebra, pre-calculus, pre-college orientation, Puerto Rican history, science, social science, Spanish, swimming, trigonometry, U.S. government, volleyball, world affairs, world history, yearbook.

Graduation Requirements American government, American history, Bible, computer science, electives, English, foreign language, mathematics, physical education (includes health), religion (includes Bible studies and theology), science, social science, social studies (includes history), Spanish, 30 hours community service.

Special Academic Programs Advanced Placement exam preparation; honors section; independent study.

College Admission Counseling 35 students graduated in 2008; all went to college, including Abilene Christian University; University of Puerto Rico, Cayey University College; University of Puerto Rico, Río Piedras. Mean SAT critical reading: 487, mean SAT math: 458, mean SAT writing: 471, mean combined SAT: 1416. 11% scored over 600 on SAT critical reading, 6% scored over 600 on SAT writing.

Student Life Upper grades have uniform requirement, student council, honor system. Discipline rests primarily with faculty.

Summer Programs Remediation, enrichment, advancement programs offered; session focuses on remediation and enrichment classes; held on campus; accepts boys and girls; open to students from other schools. 100 students usually enrolled. 2009 schedule: June 2 to June 29. Application deadline: May 31.

Tuition and Aid Day student tuition: $6700. Guaranteed tuition plan. Tuition installment plan (monthly payment plans, full-payment discount plan, semester payment plan). Need-based scholarship grants, need-based financial aid available. In 2008–09, 2% of upper-school students received aid. Total amount of financial aid awarded in 2008–09: $5600.

Admissions Traditional secondary-level entrance grade is 7. For fall 2008, 80 students applied for upper-level admission, 45 were accepted, 45 enrolled. Academic Profile Tests, admissions testing, MAT 7 Metropolitan Achievement Test and mathematics proficiency exam required. Deadline for receipt of application materials: none. Application fee required: $30. On-campus interview required.

Athletics Interscholastic: basketball (boys, girls), cross-country running (b), golf (b), indoor soccer (b,g), soccer (b,g), softball (b,g), swimming and diving (b,g), track and field (b,g), volleyball (b,g); intramural: basketball (b,g), cross-country running (b), indoor soccer (b,g), soccer (b,g), softball (b,g), track and field (b,g), volleyball (b,g); coed interscholastic: cheering, tennis; coed intramural: cheering, tennis. 3 PE instructors, 3 coaches.

Computers Computers are regularly used in accounting, business, college planning, mathematics, Spanish classes. Computer network features include on-campus library services, Internet access, Internet filtering or blocking technology. Computer access in designated common areas is available to students. The school has a published electronic and media policy.

Contact Mrs. Carol Rampolla, Director of Admissions and Records. 787-720-8959 Ext. 237. Fax: 787-790-0730. E-mail: crampolla@wesleyanacademy.org. Web site: www.wesleyanacademy.org.

WESTBURY CHRISTIAN SCHOOL

10420 Hillcroft
Houston, Texas 77096
Head of School: Mr. Greg J. Glenn

General Information Coeducational day college-preparatory and religious studies school, affiliated with Church of Christ. Grades PK–12. Founded: 1975. Setting: urban. 13-acre campus. 1 building on campus. Approved or accredited by National Christian School Association, Southern Association of Colleges and Schools, Texas Education Agency, and Texas Department of Education. Endowment: $300,000. Total enrollment: 553. Upper school average class size: 22. Upper school faculty-student ratio: 1:11.

Upper School Student Profile Grade 9: 49 students (26 boys, 23 girls); Grade 10: 72 students (41 boys, 31 girls); Grade 11: 79 students (40 boys, 39 girls); Grade 12: 53 students (24 boys, 29 girls). 18% of students are members of Church of Christ.

Faculty School total: 56. In upper school: 21 men, 15 women; 9 have advanced degrees.

Subjects Offered Accounting, algebra, anatomy and physiology, art, athletics, band, basketball, Bible, biology, biology-AP, business, calculus-AP, cheerleading, chemistry, chemistry-AP, community service, computer applications, drama, economics, economics-AP, English, English language and composition-AP, English literature and composition-AP, entrepreneurship, environmental science, European history-AP, geography, geometry, government, government-AP, health, human geography—AP, marching band, marketing, photography, physical education, physical science, physics, pre-calculus, psychology-AP, Spanish, speech, statistics-AP, studio art-AP, U.S. history, weight training, world history, yearbook.

Graduation Requirements Arts and fine arts (art, music, dance, drama), Bible, computer science, electives, English, foreign language, mathematics, physical education (includes health), science, social studies (includes history), speech, continuous participation in student activities programs, community service each semester.

Special Academic Programs 13 Advanced Placement exams for which test preparation is offered.

College Admission Counseling 59 students graduated in 2008; 53 went to college, including Houston Baptist University; Houston Community College System; Rice University; Sam Houston State University; Stephen F. Austin State University; University of Houston. Other: 3 went to work, 3 had other specific plans. Mean SAT critical reading: 472, mean SAT math: 516, mean SAT writing: 475, mean combined SAT: 1504, mean composite ACT: 22. 21% scored over 600 on SAT critical reading, 23% scored over 600 on SAT math, 17% scored over 600 on SAT writing, 13% scored over 1800 on combined SAT, 28% scored over 26 on composite ACT.

Student Life Upper grades have uniform requirement, student council, honor system. Discipline rests primarily with faculty.

Summer Programs Sports programs offered; session focuses on basketball instruction camps; held on campus; accepts boys and girls; open to students from other schools. 320 students usually enrolled. 2009 schedule: June 1 to June 19. Application deadline: none.

Tuition and Aid Day student tuition: $7500. Tuition installment plan (FACTS Tuition Payment Plan, tuition discount if entire year paid by enrollment date). Tuition reduction for siblings, need-based scholarship grants available. In 2008–09, 15% of upper-school students received aid. Total amount of financial aid awarded in 2008–09: $95,000.

Admissions Traditional secondary-level entrance grade is 9. For fall 2008, 119 students applied for upper-level admission, 82 were accepted, 69 enrolled. ISEE, Otis-Lennon School Ability Test or SLEP for foreign students required. Deadline for receipt of application materials: none. Application fee required: $75. Interview required.

Athletics Interscholastic: baseball (boys), basketball (b,g), cheering (g), cross-country running (b,g), football (b), golf (b,g), soccer (b,g), softball (g), strength & conditioning (b,g), swimming and diving (b,g), tennis (b,g), track and field (b,g), volleyball (g); intramural: weight training (b); coed interscholastic: cheering. 1 PE instructor, 5 coaches.

Computers Computers are regularly used in English, library, publications, social sciences, yearbook classes. Computer network features include on-campus library services, online commercial services, Internet access, Internet filtering or blocking technology. Students grades are available online. The school has a published electronic and media policy.

Contact Mrs. Ann Arnold, Director of Admissions. 713-551-8100 Ext. 1015. Fax: 713-551-8117. E-mail: admissions@westburychristian.org. Web site: www.westburychristian.org.

WEST CATHOLIC HIGH SCHOOL

1801 Bristol Avenue NW
Grand Rapids, Michigan 49504
Head of School: Mr. Stan Spetoskey

General Information Coeducational day college-preparatory and religious studies school, affiliated with Roman Catholic Church. Grades 9–12. Founded: 1962. Setting: urban. 20-acre campus. 1 building on campus. Approved or accredited by National Catholic Education Association, North Central Association of Colleges and Schools,

and Michigan Department of Education. Endowment: $1 million. Total enrollment: 640. Upper school average class size: 23. Upper school faculty-student ratio: 1:23.
Upper School Student Profile Grade 9: 179 students (99 boys, 80 girls); Grade 10: 155 students (85 boys, 70 girls); Grade 11: 149 students (80 boys, 69 girls); Grade 12: 157 students (83 boys, 74 girls). 95% of students are Roman Catholic.
Faculty School total: 40. In upper school: 17 men, 21 women; 20 have advanced degrees.
Subjects Offered 20th century world history, 3-dimensional art, accounting, acting, adolescent issues, advanced chemistry, advanced computer applications, advanced math, American government, American government-AP, American history-AP, American literature, American literature-AP, analytic geometry, anatomy, art, band, basic language skills, Basic programming, Bible studies, biology, biology-AP, British literature, British literature (honors), British literature-AP, business studies, calculus, calculus-AP, career planning, chemistry, chemistry-AP, choir, Christian and Hebrew scripture, Christian doctrine, college writing, composition, composition-AP, computer applications, computer programming, concert band, culinary arts, debate, desktop publishing, drama, drawing, earth science, economics, economics-AP, English, English language and composition-AP, English language-AP, English literature, English literature and composition-AP, English literature-AP, English-AP, environmental science, family life, French, general business, general math, genetics, geometry, government, government and politics-AP, government-AP, government/civics, history, history of the Catholic Church, honors algebra, honors English, honors geometry, honors world history, human anatomy, Internet, intro to computers, jazz band, journalism, keyboarding/computer, marching band, physics, physics-AP, pre-algebra, pre-calculus, printmaking, psychology, public speaking, sex education, sexuality, social justice, sociology, Spanish, Spanish language-AP, speech, survival training, U.S. history, Web site design, world history, world history-AP, yearbook.
Graduation Requirements Economics, electives, English composition, foreign language, government, health, mathematics, religion (includes Bible studies and theology), science, social studies (includes history), U.S. history, visual arts.
Special Academic Programs Advanced Placement exam preparation; honors section; study at local college for college credit.
College Admission Counseling 172 students graduated in 2008; 164 went to college, including Central Michigan University; Grand Valley State University; Michigan State University; University of Michigan; Western Michigan University. Other: 5 went to work, 3 entered military service. Mean SAT critical reading: 650, mean SAT math: 660, mean SAT writing: 610, mean combined SAT: 1920, mean composite ACT: 23. 50% scored over 600 on SAT critical reading, 50% scored over 600 on SAT math, 50% scored over 600 on SAT writing, 50% scored over 1800 on combined SAT, 25% scored over 26 on composite ACT.
Student Life Upper grades have uniform requirement, student council, honor system. Discipline rests primarily with faculty. Attendance at religious services is required.
Summer Programs Sports programs offered; session focuses on sports enrichment; held both on and off campus; held at Union High School; accepts boys and girls; open to students from other schools. 100 students usually enrolled. 2009 schedule: June 8 to August 24. Application deadline: June 1.
Tuition and Aid Day student tuition: $7060. Tuition installment plan (monthly payment plans, individually arranged payment plans). Need-based scholarship grants available. In 2008–09, 25% of upper-school students received aid. Total amount of financial aid awarded in 2008–09: $330,000.
Admissions Traditional secondary-level entrance grade is 9. For fall 2008, 155 students applied for upper-level admission, 155 were accepted, 155 enrolled. High School Placement Test, Iowa Tests of Basic Skills and mathematics proficiency exam required. Deadline for receipt of application materials: none. No application fee required. Interview required.
Athletics Interscholastic: baseball (boys), basketball (b,g), bowling (b,g), cheering (g), cross-country running (b,g), diving (b,g), football (b), golf (b,g), gymnastics (g), hockey (b), ice hockey (b), pom squad (g), skiing (downhill) (b,g), soccer (b,g), softball (g), swimming and diving (b,g), tennis (b,g), track and field (b,g), volleyball (g), weight lifting (b), weight training (b), wrestling (b); intramural: bowling (b,g). 1 PE instructor, 66 coaches, 1 athletic trainer.
Computers Computers are regularly used in all academic classes. Computer network features include Internet access, Internet filtering or blocking technology. Student e-mail accounts and computer access in designated common areas are available to students. Students grades are available online. The school has a published electronic and media policy.
Contact Mrs. Marzi Johnson, Guidance Secretary. 616-233-5909. Fax: 616-453-8470. E-mail: marzijohnson@grcss.org. Web site: www.grwestcatholic.org.

WESTCHESTER COUNTRY DAY SCHOOL

2045 North Old Greensboro Road
High Point, North Carolina 27265

Head of School: Mr. Charles A. Hamblet

General Information Coeducational day college-preparatory, arts, bilingual studies, and technology school. Grades K–12. Founded: 1967. Setting: rural. Nearest major city is Greensboro. 53-acre campus. 6 buildings on campus. Approved or accredited by North Carolina Association of Independent Schools, Southern Association of Colleges and Schools, and Southern Association of Independent Schools. Member of National Association of Independent Schools. Endowment: $2.5 million. Total enrollment: 419. Upper school average class size: 15. Upper school faculty-student ratio: 1:6.
Upper School Student Profile Grade 9: 31 students (20 boys, 11 girls); Grade 10: 34 students (19 boys, 15 girls); Grade 11: 31 students (15 boys, 16 girls); Grade 12: 27 students (15 boys, 12 girls).
Faculty School total: 58. In upper school: 4 men, 17 women; 14 have advanced degrees.
Subjects Offered Advanced Placement courses, advanced studio art-AP, algebra, American history, American literature, art, art history-AP, art-AP, biology, biology-AP, British literature, calculus, chemistry, chemistry-AP, community service, computer science, creative writing, earth science, economics, English, English literature, environmental science, European history, fine arts, French, geography, geometry, government/civics, grammar, health, history, Mandarin, mathematics, music, physical education, physics, science, social studies, Spanish, speech, statistics and probability, statistics-AP, theater, Web site design, world history, world literature, writing.
Graduation Requirements Arts and fine arts (art, music, dance, drama), civics, English, foreign language, mathematics, physical education (includes health), science, social studies (includes history), Community Service project.
Special Academic Programs Advanced Placement exam preparation; honors section.
College Admission Counseling 31 students graduated in 2008; all went to college, including Appalachian State University; East Carolina University; Elon University; North Carolina State University; The University of North Carolina at Chapel Hill; The University of North Carolina at Greensboro. Mean SAT critical reading: 578, mean SAT math: 576, mean SAT writing: 551, mean combined SAT: 1186.
Student Life Upper grades have specified standards of dress, student council, honor system. Discipline rests primarily with faculty.
Summer Programs Enrichment, sports, art/fine arts, computer instruction programs offered; session focuses on academics, sports, hobby-related; held on campus; accepts boys and girls; open to students from other schools. 300 students usually enrolled. 2009 schedule: June 15 to August 14. Application deadline: none.
Tuition and Aid Day student tuition: $11,800–$12,070. Tuition installment plan (FACTS Tuition Payment Plan, monthly payment plans). Need-based scholarship grants available. In 2008–09, 4% of upper-school students received aid. Total amount of financial aid awarded in 2008–09: $109,140.
Admissions Traditional secondary-level entrance grade is 9. For fall 2008, 12 students applied for upper-level admission, 10 were accepted, 9 enrolled. Brigance Test of Basic Skills, ERB CTP IV, Kaufman Test of Educational Achievement, Wide Range Achievement Test or Woodcock-Johnson Revised Achievement Test required. Deadline for receipt of application materials: none. Application fee required: $75. On-campus interview recommended.
Athletics Interscholastic: baseball (boys), basketball (b,g), cheering (g), soccer (b,g), tennis (b,g), volleyball (g); coed interscholastic: cross-country running, golf, physical fitness, swimming and diving, track and field. 2 PE instructors, 14 coaches.
Computers Computers are regularly used in English, foreign language, history, library science, mathematics, science, Web site design, yearbook classes. Computer network features include on-campus library services, Internet access, wireless campus network, Internet filtering or blocking technology. Student e-mail accounts and computer access in designated common areas are available to students. Students grades are available online. The school has a published electronic and media policy.
Contact Mrs. Kerie Beth Scott, Director of Admissions. 336-822-4005. Fax: 336-869-6685. E-mail: keriebeth.scott@westchestercds.org. Web site: www.westchestercds.org.

WESTERN CHRISTIAN SCHOOLS

1115 East Puente Street
Covina, California 91724

Head of School: Robert Yovino

General Information Coeducational day college-preparatory, arts, and religious studies school, affiliated with Christian faith. Grades 7–12. Founded: 1920. Setting: suburban. Approved or accredited by Association of Christian Schools International, Western Association of Schools and Colleges, and California Department of Education. Member of European Council of International Schools. Total enrollment: 483. Upper school average class size: 17.
Upper School Student Profile 75% of students are Christian.
Faculty School total: 32. In upper school: 10 men, 20 women.
Subjects Offered Advanced Placement courses, aerobics, algebra, American history, anatomy, art, band, Bible studies, biology, calculus, calculus-AP, ceramics, chemistry, chorus, computer science, consumer mathematics, drama, ecology, economics, English, film, food science, geography, geometry, government/civics, health, journalism, math analysis, mathematics, physical education, physics, physiology, psychology, sociology, study skills, theater, world history.
Special Academic Programs 6 Advanced Placement exams for which test preparation is offered.
College Admission Counseling 132 students graduated in 2008; 82 went to college.
Student Life Upper grades have uniform requirement. Discipline rests primarily with faculty.

Summer Programs Remediation, enrichment, ESL programs offered; held on campus; accepts boys and girls; open to students from other schools. 75 students usually enrolled. 2009 schedule: June 20 to August 10. Application deadline: June 15.
Admissions School's own test required. Deadline for receipt of application materials: none. No application fee required. On-campus interview required.
Athletics Interscholastic: baseball (boys), basketball (b,g), cheering (g), cross-country running (b,g), football (b), golf (b), soccer (b,g), softball (g), track and field (b,g), volleyball (g). 1 PE instructor, 9 coaches.
Contact John Attwood, Vice-Principal. 626-967-0733. Fax: 626-915-8824.

WESTERN RESERVE ACADEMY

115 College Street
Hudson, Ohio 44236
Head of School: Christopher D. Burner

General Information Coeducational boarding and day college-preparatory and arts school. Grades 9–PG. Founded: 1826. Setting: small town. Nearest major city is Cleveland. Students are housed in single-sex dormitories. 190-acre campus. 49 buildings on campus. Approved or accredited by Independent Schools Association of the Central States, Midwest Association of Boarding Schools, North Central Association of Colleges and Schools, Ohio Association of Independent Schools, The Association of Boarding Schools, and Ohio Department of Education. Member of National Association of Independent Schools and Secondary School Admission Test Board. Endowment: $113.7 million. Total enrollment: 370. Upper school average class size: 12. Upper school faculty-student ratio: 1:6.
Upper School Student Profile Grade 9: 70 students (39 boys, 31 girls); Grade 10: 95 students (49 boys, 46 girls); Grade 11: 105 students (60 boys, 45 girls); Grade 12: 105 students (58 boys, 47 girls). 68% of students are boarding students. 70% are state residents. 27 states are represented in upper school student body. 18% are international students. International students from Canada, China, Germany, Jamaica, Republic of Korea, and Thailand; 12 other countries represented in student body.
Faculty School total: 69. In upper school: 41 men, 28 women; 41 have advanced degrees; 55 reside on campus.
Subjects Offered Algebra, American history, American literature, architecture, art, art history, astronomy, band, biology, calculus, ceramics, chemistry, chorus, computer programming, creative writing, dance, drafting, drama, economics, engineering, English, English literature, environmental science, European history, fine arts, French, geometry, German, health, history, humanities, independent study, industrial arts, Latin, Mandarin, mathematics, mechanical drawing, music, music history, music theory, orchestra, photography, physical education, physics, science, social studies, Spanish, speech, statistics, theater, trigonometry, world history, zoology.
Graduation Requirements Arts and fine arts (art, music, dance, drama), English, foreign language, history, mathematics, physical education (includes health), science, senior seminar, senior thesis.
Special Academic Programs 19 Advanced Placement exams for which test preparation is offered; honors section; independent study; study at local college for college credit; study abroad; academic accommodation for the gifted, the musically talented, and the artistically talented.
College Admission Counseling 112 students graduated in 2008; all went to college, including Case Western Reserve University; Cornell University; Duke University; Kenyon College; United States Naval Academy; University of Virginia.
Student Life Upper grades have specified standards of dress, student council. Discipline rests equally with students and faculty.
Tuition and Aid Day student tuition: $27,000; 7-day tuition and room/board: $37,900. Tuition installment plan (The Tuition Plan, Insured Tuition Payment Plan, Key Tuition Payment Plan, monthly payment plans, individually arranged payment plans). Merit scholarship grants, need-based scholarship grants, need-based loans available. In 2008–09, 34% of upper-school students received aid. Total amount of financial aid awarded in 2008–09: $3,600,000.
Admissions Traditional secondary-level entrance grade is 9. For fall 2008, 364 students applied for upper-level admission, 229 were accepted, 154 enrolled. ISEE, SSAT or TOEFL required. Deadline for receipt of application materials: January 15. Application fee required: $25. Interview required.
Athletics Interscholastic: baseball (boys), basketball (b,g), cross-country running (b,g), diving (b,g), field hockey (g), football (b), golf (b), ice hockey (b), lacrosse (b,g), soccer (b,g), softball (g), swimming and diving (b,g), tennis (b,g), track and field (b,g), volleyball (g), wrestling (b); intramural: basketball (b); coed interscholastic: marksmanship, riflery; coed intramural: aerobics, aerobics/dance, aerobics/Nautilus, backpacking, bicycling, dance, fitness, fly fishing, hiking/backpacking, jogging, martial arts, Nautilus, outdoor recreation, paddle tennis, physical fitness, physical training, running, sailing, skeet shooting, skiing (downhill), snowboarding, soccer, strength & conditioning, weight lifting, weight training, winter (indoor) track, yoga. 1 coach, 3 athletic trainers.
Computers Computers are regularly used in architecture, drawing and design, economics, engineering, English, foreign language, history, mathematics, science, technical drawing classes. Computer network features include on-campus library services, online commercial services, Internet access, wireless campus network, Internet filtering or blocking technology. Student e-mail accounts are available to students. The school has a published electronic and media policy.
Contact Mrs. Laura Hudak, Admission Office Coordinator. 330-650-9717. Fax: 330-650-5858. E-mail: admission@wra.net. Web site: www.wra.net.

ANNOUNCEMENT FROM THE SCHOOL As one of the oldest and most respected independent boarding schools, WRA offers an academically challenging, affordable secondary education. A large endowment supports a significant financial aid program. Honors, AP, independent study, and college-credit courses provide students with an academic profile demanding notice at the college level. Annual college placement speaks to the strength of this experience.

See Close-Up on page 1018.

WEST ISLAND COLLEGE

7410 Blackfoot Trail SE
Calgary, Alberta T2H IM5, Canada
Head of School: Mr. Jack A. Grant

General Information Coeducational day college-preparatory, arts, business, bilingual studies, technology, and Advanced Placement school. Grades 7–12. Founded: 1982. Setting: urban. 18-acre campus. 2 buildings on campus. Approved or accredited by Canadian Association of Independent Schools and Alberta Department of Education. Languages of instruction: English, Spanish, and French. Total enrollment: 473. Upper school average class size: 18. Upper school faculty-student ratio: 1:17.
Upper School Student Profile Grade 10: 74 students (39 boys, 35 girls); Grade 11: 64 students (39 boys, 25 girls); Grade 12: 80 students (44 boys, 36 girls).
Faculty School total: 45. In upper school: 20 men, 18 women; 14 have advanced degrees.
Subjects Offered Advanced Placement courses, anthropology, art, arts, biology, chemistry, choral music, communications, debate, drama, English, European history, experiential education, French, French studies, health, information processing, information technology, leadership, literature, mathematics, modern languages, music, outdoor education, philosophy, physical education, physics, political thought, politics, psychology, public speaking, science, social science, social studies, sociology, Spanish, standard curriculum, study skills, world geography, world history, world religions.
Graduation Requirements Alberta Education requirements.
Special Academic Programs 10 Advanced Placement exams for which test preparation is offered; honors section; independent study; study abroad; academic accommodation for the gifted.
College Admission Counseling 73 students graduated in 2008; 72 went to college, including McGill University; Queen's University at Kingston; The University of British Columbia; University of Alberta; University of Calgary; University of Victoria. Other: 1 had other specific plans.
Student Life Upper grades have uniform requirement, student council, honor system. Discipline rests equally with students and faculty.
Summer Programs Enrichment, advancement, sports, computer instruction programs offered; session focuses on study skills and academic preparedness; held both on and off campus; held at various public parks in the city; accepts boys and girls; open to students from other schools. 40 students usually enrolled. 2009 schedule: August 17 to August 21. Application deadline: March 31.
Tuition and Aid Day student tuition: CAN$11,200. Tuition installment plan (monthly payment plans).
Admissions Traditional secondary-level entrance grade is 10. For fall 2008, 37 students applied for upper-level admission, 8 were accepted, 8 enrolled. 3-R Achievement Test, CCAT, CTBS, OLSAT, Gates MacGinite Reading Tests and Otis-Lennon IQ Test required. Deadline for receipt of application materials: none. Application fee required: CAN$100. Interview required.
Athletics Interscholastic: basketball (boys, girls), field hockey (g), rugby (b), volleyball (b,g); intramural: aquatics (b,g), basketball (b,g), floor hockey (b,g), volleyball (b,g); coed interscholastic: badminton, climbing, cross-country running, soccer; coed intramural: alpine skiing, backpacking, badminton, bicycling, bowling, canoeing/kayaking, climbing, cross-country running, curling, dance, fitness, golf, hiking/backpacking, kayaking, mountaineering, nordic skiing, outdoor activities, physical fitness, physical training, rock climbing, sailing, skiing (cross-country), skiing (downhill), snowboarding, soccer, swimming and diving, touch football, wilderness survival, wildernessways. 4 PE instructors, 10 coaches, 2 athletic trainers.
Computers Computers are regularly used in career education, career exploration, career technology, economics, English, French, independent study, mathematics, media arts, media production, multimedia, science, social studies, technology, word processing classes. Computer network features include on-campus library services, online commercial services, Internet access, wireless campus network, Internet filtering or blocking technology. Campus intranet and student e-mail accounts are available to students. The school has a published electronic and media policy.
Contact Ms. Nicole Bernard, Assistant Director of Admissions. 403-444-0023. Fax: 403-444-2820. E-mail: admissions@westislandcollege.ab.ca. Web site: www.westislandcollege.ab.ca.

WESTMINSTER CATAWBA CHRISTIAN

2650 India Hook Road
Rock Hill, South Carolina 29732

Head of School: Mrs. Sandi Jolly

General Information Coeducational day college-preparatory and religious studies school, affiliated with Presbyterian Church in America; primarily serves students with learning disabilities and individuals with Attention Deficit Disorder. Grades PK–12. Founded: 1993. Setting: suburban. Nearest major city is Charlotte, NC. 22-acre campus. 8 buildings on campus. Approved or accredited by Association of Christian Schools International, Southern Association of Colleges and Schools, and South Carolina Department of Education. Endowment: $200,000. Total enrollment: 633. Upper school average class size: 22.

Upper School Student Profile Grade 7: 59 students (29 boys, 30 girls); Grade 8: 60 students (33 boys, 27 girls); Grade 9: 44 students (19 boys, 25 girls); Grade 10: 44 students (26 boys, 18 girls); Grade 11: 44 students (23 boys, 21 girls); Grade 12: 35 students (11 boys, 24 girls). 35% of students are Presbyterian Church in America.

Faculty School total: 102. In upper school: 5 men, 21 women; 16 have advanced degrees.

Subjects Offered ACT preparation, advanced computer applications, Advanced Placement courses, advanced studio art-AP, algebra, American literature-AP, art, art-AP, Bible studies, biology, biology-AP, British literature-AP, calculus, calculus-AP, career planning, career/college preparation, chemistry, choir, Christian ethics, Christian scripture, Christian studies, Christian testament, Christianity, college counseling, college placement, college planning, college writing, computer keyboarding, computer skills, concert band, drama, economics, English, English language-AP, English literature-AP, fine arts, foreign language, geography, geometry, government, human anatomy, Latin, library research, Life of Christ, physical education, physical science, physics, U.S. history, world history.

Graduation Requirements Arts and fine arts (art, music, dance, drama), Bible, English, foreign language, mathematics, physical education (includes health), science, social studies (includes history). Community service is required.

Special Academic Programs Advanced Placement exam preparation; honors section.

College Admission Counseling 25 students graduated in 2008; all went to college, including Clemson University; Furman University; University of South Carolina; Wofford College; York Technical College. Mean SAT critical reading: 569, mean SAT math: 530, mean SAT writing: 573, mean combined SAT: 1672, mean composite ACT: 23.

Student Life Upper grades have specified standards of dress, student council, honor system. Discipline rests primarily with faculty.

Tuition and Aid Day student tuition: $6015–$6355. Tuition installment plan (FACTS Tuition Payment Plan, monthly payment plans). Tuition reduction for siblings, need-based scholarship grants available.

Admissions For fall 2008, 15 students applied for upper-level admission, 10 were accepted, 8 enrolled. School's own test and WRAT required. Deadline for receipt of application materials: none. Application fee required: $50. Interview required.

Athletics Interscholastic: baseball (boys), basketball (b,g), cheering (g), cross-country running (b,g), football (b), golf (b,g), soccer (b,g), softball (g), tennis (b,g), volleyball (g). 2 PE instructors, 10 coaches.

Computers Computers are regularly used in all classes. Computer network features include on-campus library services, Internet access, Internet filtering or blocking technology. Campus intranet is available to students. The school has a published electronic and media policy.

Contact Mrs. Patty Limerick, Admissions Coordinator. 803-366-6703. Fax: 803-325-8191. E-mail: plimerick@wccs.org. Web site: www.wccs.org.

WESTMINSTER CHRISTIAN ACADEMY

3911 & 3913 Pulaski Pike
POBox 5680
Huntsville, Alabama 35810

Head of School: Mr. Craig L. Bouvier

General Information Coeducational day college-preparatory, general academic, arts, religious studies, and technology school, affiliated with Presbyterian Church. Grades K4–12. Founded: 1964. Setting: suburban. Nearest major city is Birmingham. 15-acre campus. 4 buildings on campus. Approved or accredited by Christian Schools International, Southern Association of Colleges and Schools, and Alabama Department of Education. Member of Secondary School Admission Test Board. Endowment: $3.9 million. Total enrollment: 629. Upper school average class size: 16. Upper school faculty-student ratio: 1:12.

Upper School Student Profile 14% of students are Presbyterian.

Faculty School total: 69. In upper school: 11 men, 18 women; 18 have advanced degrees.

Subjects Offered Advanced computer applications, algebra, American history, American history-AP, art, band, Bible studies, biology, botany, business mathematics, business skills, calculus, calculus-AP, chemistry, choir, civics, computer programming, computer programming-AP, concert choir, consumer mathematics, CPR, drama, drama performance, economics-AP, English, English-AP, ensembles, environmental science, first aid, fitness, French, geography, geometry, government, government-AP, health education, home economics, interior design, journalism, keyboarding, Latin, modern dance, painting, photography, physical education, physical science, physics, physiology, pre-calculus, psychology, Spanish, Web site design, world history, yearbook.

Graduation Requirements Arts and fine arts (art, music, dance, drama), computer applications, electives, English, foreign language, mathematics, physical education (includes health), religion (includes Bible studies and theology), science, social studies (includes history).

Special Academic Programs Advanced Placement exam preparation; honors section; independent study; study at local college for college credit; academic accommodation for the gifted, the musically talented, and the artistically talented; remedial reading and/or remedial writing; remedial math.

College Admission Counseling 51 students graduated in 2008; they went to Auburn University; Calhoun Community College; Covenant College; The University of Alabama; The University of Alabama in Huntsville. 35% scored over 600 on SAT critical reading, 50% scored over 600 on SAT math.

Student Life Upper grades have specified standards of dress, student council. Discipline rests primarily with faculty. Attendance at religious services is required.

Tuition and Aid Day student tuition: $6181. Guaranteed tuition plan. Tuition installment plan (monthly payment plans, individually arranged payment plans). Tuition reduction for siblings, need-based scholarship grants, free tuition for children of faculty available. In 2008–09, 15% of upper-school students received aid. Total amount of financial aid awarded in 2008–09: $200,000.

Admissions Traditional secondary-level entrance grade is 9. Any standardized test, school's own test or writing sample required. Deadline for receipt of application materials: none. Application fee required: $25. Interview required.

Athletics Interscholastic: baseball (boys), basketball (b,g), cheering (g), cross-country running (b,g), dance (g), football (b), golf (b,g), modern dance (g), physical training (b,g), soccer (b,g), softball (g), swimming and diving (b,g), track and field (b,g), volleyball (g), weight training (b,g), wrestling (b); intramural: physical fitness (b,g), physical training (b,g), strength & conditioning (b,g), weight training (b,g); coed interscholastic: cheering; coed intramural: weight training. 6 coaches, 1 athletic trainer.

Computers Computers are regularly used in all academic classes. Computer network features include on-campus library services, Internet access, wireless campus network, Internet filtering or blocking technology. Student e-mail accounts and computer access in designated common areas are available to students. Students grades are available online. The school has a published electronic and media policy.

Contact Mrs. Mary Cooper, Admissions Director. 256-705-8400. Fax: 256-705-8001. E-mail: mary.cooper@wca-hsv.org. Web site: www.wcahsv.org.

WESTMINSTER CHRISTIAN SCHOOL

6855 Southwest 152nd Street
Miami, Florida 33157

Head of School: Mr. George J.W. Lawrence Jr.

General Information Coeducational day and distance learning college-preparatory, arts, and religious studies school, affiliated with Christian faith. Grades PK–12. Distance learning grades 9–12. Founded: 1961. Setting: suburban. 26-acre campus. 9 buildings on campus. Approved or accredited by Christian Schools of Florida, Florida Council of Independent Schools, Southern Association of Colleges and Schools, and Florida Department of Education. Endowment: $2.2 million. Total enrollment: 1,162. Upper school average class size: 17. Upper school faculty-student ratio: 1:11.

Upper School Student Profile Grade 9: 108 students (49 boys, 59 girls); Grade 10: 113 students (51 boys, 62 girls); Grade 11: 109 students (56 boys, 53 girls); Grade 12: 117 students (52 boys, 65 girls). 100% of students are Christian.

Faculty School total: 103. In upper school: 29 men, 25 women; 31 have advanced degrees.

Subjects Offered Advanced Placement courses, algebra, American history, American literature, anatomy, art, Bible studies, biology, biology-AP, business law, business skills, calculus, ceramics, chemistry, chemistry-AP, community service, computer programming, computer science, creative writing, drama, economics, English, English literature, fine arts, French, French-AP, general science, geometry, government-AP, government/civics, grammar, health, history, macroeconomics-AP, marine biology, mathematics, music, organic chemistry, photography, physical education, physics, physiology, psychology, religion, SAT preparation, science, scripture, sculpture, sex education, social studies, sociology, softball, Spanish, Spanish language-AP, Spanish-AP, speech, sports, statistics-AP, strings, study skills, swimming, theater, track and field, trigonometry, typing, U.S. government, U.S. government-AP, U.S. history, U.S. history-AP, vocal ensemble, volleyball, weightlifting, wind ensemble, world history, world literature, wrestling, writing, yearbook.

Graduation Requirements Arts and fine arts (art, music, dance, drama), Bible, computer science, electives, English, foreign language, health science, lab science, mathematics, physical education (includes health), science, social studies (includes history), speech. Community service is required.

Special Academic Programs 13 Advanced Placement exams for which test preparation is offered; honors section; accelerated programs; independent study; academic accommodation for the gifted, the musically talented, and the artistically talented; programs in English, mathematics for dyslexic students.

College Admission Counseling 85 students graduated in 2008; 84 went to college, including Florida International University; Florida State University; Miami Dade College; University of Central Florida; University of Florida; University of Miami. Other: 1 went to work. Mean SAT critical reading: 532, mean SAT math: 544, mean SAT writing: 530, mean combined SAT: 1607, mean composite ACT: 22. 26% scored over 600 on SAT critical reading, 18% scored over 600 on SAT math, 19% scored over 600 on SAT writing, 11% scored over 1800 on combined SAT, 16.5% scored over 26 on composite ACT.
Student Life Upper grades have uniform requirement, student council, honor system. Discipline rests primarily with faculty. Attendance at religious services is required.
Summer Programs Remediation, advancement, computer instruction programs offered; session focuses on academics and athletics; held on campus; accepts boys and girls; open to students from other schools. 50 students usually enrolled. 2009 schedule: June 8 to July 10.
Tuition and Aid Day student tuition: $15,100. Tuition installment plan (monthly payment plans, individually arranged payment plans, semiannual and annual payment plans). Need-based scholarship grants available. In 2008–09, 10% of upper-school students received aid. Total amount of financial aid awarded in 2008–09: $500,000.
Admissions Traditional secondary-level entrance grade is 9. For fall 2008, 119 students applied for upper-level admission, 60 were accepted, 50 enrolled. Iowa Tests of Basic Skills and writing sample required. Deadline for receipt of application materials: February 1. Application fee required: $125. On-campus interview required.
Athletics Interscholastic: baseball (boys), basketball (b,g), cheering (g), cross-country running (b,g), football (b), golf (b,g), soccer (b,g), softball (g), swimming and diving (b,g), tennis (b,g), track and field (b,g), volleyball (b,g), wrestling (b). 8 PE instructors, 75 coaches, 2 athletic trainers.
Computers Computers are regularly used in accounting, art, Bible studies, business applications, career exploration, college planning, computer applications, creative writing, economics, English, foreign language, keyboarding, mathematics, music, photography, programming, science, word processing, writing, writing, yearbook classes. Computer network features include on-campus library services, Internet access, wireless campus network, Internet filtering or blocking technology. Students grades are available online. The school has a published electronic and media policy.
Contact Ms. Caroline H. Stone, Director of Admission. 305-233-2030 Ext. 1246. Fax: 305-253-9623. E-mail: cstone@wcsmiami.org. Web site: www.wcsmiami.org.

WESTMINSTER SCHOOL

995 Hopmeadow Street
Simsbury, Connecticut 06070

Head of School: Mr. W. Graham Cole Jr.

General Information Coeducational boarding and day college-preparatory, arts, and technology school. Grades 9–PG. Founded: 1888. Setting: suburban. Nearest major city is Hartford. Students are housed in single-sex dormitories. 230-acre campus. 38 buildings on campus. Approved or accredited by Connecticut Association of Independent Schools, New England Association of Schools and Colleges, The Association of Boarding Schools, and Connecticut Department of Education. Member of National Association of Independent Schools and Secondary School Admission Test Board. Endowment: $82 million. Total enrollment: 385. Upper school average class size: 12. Upper school faculty-student ratio: 1:5.
Upper School Student Profile Grade 9: 78 students (36 boys, 42 girls); Grade 10: 100 students (57 boys, 43 girls); Grade 11: 99 students (52 boys, 47 girls); Grade 12: 98 students (49 boys, 49 girls); Postgraduate: 10 students (9 boys, 1 girl). 67% of students are boarding students. 48% are state residents. 26 states are represented in upper school student body. 11% are international students. International students from Bermuda, Canada, China, Hong Kong, Mexico, and Republic of Korea; 14 other countries represented in student body.
Faculty School total: 59. In upper school: 33 men, 26 women; 48 have advanced degrees; 47 reside on campus.
Subjects Offered Acting, advanced chemistry, advanced computer applications, advanced math, Advanced Placement courses, advanced studio art-AP, African American history, algebra, American history, American history-AP, American literature, American literature-AP, anatomy and physiology, Ancient Greek, architecture, art, art history, art history-AP, art-AP, Asian history, astronomy, athletics, band, biology, biology-AP, calculus, calculus-AP, character education, chemistry, chemistry-AP, choir, choral music, comparative government and politics-AP, computer programming, computer science-AP, creative writing, dance, discrete mathematics, drama, drama workshop, drawing, drawing and design, driver education, ecology, economics, economics-AP, English, English literature, English-AP, English/composition-AP, environmental science-AP, ethics, ethics and responsibility, European history, European history-AP, female experience in America, fine arts, French, French language-AP, French literature-AP, geology, geometry, graphic design, health, history, honors algebra, honors English, honors geometry, illustration, Latin, Latin-AP, literature and composition-AP, macro/microeconomics-AP, mathematics, mathematics-AP, mechanical drawing, modern European history-AP, music, music appreciation, music composition, music theory-AP, musical theater, Native American history, painting, philosophy, photography, physics, physics-AP, pre-calculus, probability and statistics, SAT preparation, SAT/ACT preparation, science, set design, social studies, Spanish, Spanish language-AP, Spanish literature, Spanish literature-AP, stagecraft, statistics, statistics-AP, studio art—AP, theater, trigonometry, U.S. history-AP, world history, writing.
Graduation Requirements Arts, English, foreign language, history, mathematics, science.
Special Academic Programs 23 Advanced Placement exams for which test preparation is offered; honors section; independent study; term-away projects; study at local college for college credit; study abroad.
College Admission Counseling 104 students graduated in 2008; all went to college, including Boston College; Columbia College; Hamilton College; Trinity College; Yale University. Mean SAT critical reading: 602, mean SAT math: 621, mean SAT writing: 618, mean combined SAT: 1841.
Student Life Upper grades have specified standards of dress, student council. Discipline rests primarily with faculty.
Summer Programs Sports programs offered; session focuses on soccer; held on campus; accepts boys and girls; open to students from other schools. 350 students usually enrolled. 2009 schedule: July 6 to August 1.
Tuition and Aid Day student tuition: $31,100; 7-day tuition and room/board: $41,700. Tuition installment plan (Academic Management Services Plan, Key Tuition Payment Plan). Need-based scholarship grants available. In 2008–09, 29% of upper-school students received aid. Total amount of financial aid awarded in 2008–09: $3,440,000.
Admissions Traditional secondary-level entrance grade is 9. For fall 2008, 1,003 students applied for upper-level admission, 247 were accepted, 129 enrolled. PSAT and SAT for applicants to grade 11 and 12 or SSAT, ERB, PSAT, SAT, PLAN or ACT required. Deadline for receipt of application materials: January 15. Application fee required: $75. On-campus interview required.
Athletics Interscholastic: baseball (boys), basketball (b,g), cross-country running (b,g), diving (b,g), field hockey (g), football (b), golf (b,g), hockey (b,g), ice hockey (b,g), lacrosse (b,g), soccer (b,g), softball (g), squash (b,g), swimming and diving (b,g), tennis (b,g), track and field (b,g); intramural: strength & conditioning (b,g); coed interscholastic: dance, martial arts, modern dance, paddle tennis; coed intramural: aerobics/dance, ballet, bowling, dance, ice skating, modern dance, mountain biking, skiing (cross-country), skiing (downhill), table tennis, unicycling. 2 athletic trainers.
Computers Computers are regularly used in English, foreign language, history, mathematics, science classes. Computer network features include on-campus library services, online commercial services, Internet access, wireless campus network, Internet filtering or blocking technology. Campus intranet, student e-mail accounts, and computer access in designated common areas are available to students. The school has a published electronic and media policy.
Contact Mr. Jon C. Deveaux, Director of Admissions. 860-408-3060. Fax: 860-408-3042. E-mail: admit@westminster-school.org. Web site: www.westminster-school.org.

See Close-Up on page 1020.

THE WESTMINSTER SCHOOLS

1424 West Paces Ferry Road NW
Atlanta, Georgia 30327

Head of School: Dr. William Clarkson, IV

General Information Coeducational day college-preparatory, arts, business, religious studies, bilingual studies, and technology school, affiliated with Christian faith. Grades K–12. Founded: 1951. Setting: suburban. 200-acre campus. 7 buildings on campus. Approved or accredited by Georgia Independent School Association, Southern Association of Colleges and Schools, and Southern Association of Independent Schools. Member of National Association of Independent Schools and Secondary School Admission Test Board. Endowment: $229 million. Total enrollment: 1,819. Upper school average class size: 15. Upper school faculty-student ratio: 1:15.
Upper School Student Profile Grade 9: 208 students (106 boys, 102 girls); Grade 10: 202 students (104 boys, 98 girls); Grade 11: 188 students (96 boys, 92 girls); Grade 12: 205 students (96 boys, 109 girls). 80% of students are Christian.
Faculty School total: 259. In upper school: 54 men, 52 women; 89 have advanced degrees.
Subjects Offered Advanced Placement courses, advanced studio art-AP, algebra, American history, art, art history, Bible studies, biology, calculus, ceramics, chemistry, Chinese, choral music, Christian education, computer math, computer programming, computer science, drama, driver education, earth science, economics, English, English literature, ethics, European history, fine arts, French, geometry, grammar, health, history, Latin, leadership education training, mathematics, music, natural history, outdoor education, philosophy, photography, physical education, physics, political systems, psychology, religion, science, social studies, sociology, Spanish, speech, statistics, studio art—AP, theater, theater arts, trigonometry, visual and performing arts, world history, writing.
Graduation Requirements Arts and fine arts (art, music, dance, drama), English, experiential education, foreign language, history, mathematics, physical education (includes health), religion (includes Bible studies and theology), science.

Special Academic Programs Advanced Placement exam preparation; honors section; independent study; term-away projects; study abroad; academic accommodation for the gifted, the musically talented, and the artistically talented.

College Admission Counseling 197 students graduated in 2008; 195 went to college, including Auburn University; The University of North Carolina at Chapel Hill; University of Georgia; University of Virginia; Vanderbilt University; Williams College. Other: 1 entered a postgraduate year, 1 had other specific plans.

Student Life Upper grades have specified standards of dress, student council, honor system. Discipline rests equally with students and faculty.

Summer Programs Remediation, enrichment, advancement, sports, art/fine arts, rigorous outdoor training, computer instruction programs offered; session focuses on academics and sports/arts camps, philanthropy; held on campus; accepts boys and girls; open to students from other schools. 190 students usually enrolled. 2009 schedule: June 1 to July 10. Application deadline: February 2.

Tuition and Aid Day student tuition: $19,080. Tuition installment plan (Key Tuition Payment Plan). Need-based scholarship grants available. In 2008–09, 13% of upper-school students received aid. Total amount of financial aid awarded in 2008–09: $2,800,000.

Admissions Traditional secondary-level entrance grade is 9. For fall 2008, 157 students applied for upper-level admission, 37 were accepted, 27 enrolled. Admissions testing, Individual IQ, PSAT or SAT for applicants to grade 11 and 12 or SSAT required. Deadline for receipt of application materials: February 2. Application fee required: $75. On-campus interview required.

Athletics Interscholastic: baseball (boys), basketball (b,g), cheering (g), crew (g), cross-country running (b,g), diving (b,g), football (b), golf (b,g), gymnastics (g), lacrosse (b,g), soccer (b,g), softball (g), swimming and diving (b,g), tennis (b,g), track and field (b,g), volleyball (g), water polo (b), wrestling (b); intramural: climbing (b,g), crew (g), dance (g), fencing (b,g), physical fitness (b,g), polo (b,g), squash (b,g), strength & conditioning (b,g); coed intramural: backpacking, dance squad, dance team, flag football, hiking/backpacking, paddle tennis, rappelling, rock climbing, ropes courses, table tennis, tennis, ultimate Frisbee. 2 PE instructors, 4 coaches, 4 athletic trainers.

Computers Computers are regularly used in art, Bible studies, desktop publishing, economics, English, foreign language, keyboarding, mathematics, multimedia, music, science, technology, video film production, writing classes. Computer network features include on-campus library services, online commercial services, Internet access, wireless campus network, Internet filtering or blocking technology, language learning laboratory, writing laboratory staffed with English teachers. Campus intranet, student e-mail accounts, and computer access in designated common areas are available to students. The school has a published electronic and media policy.

Contact Mrs. Julie Williams, Assistant Director of Admissions. 404-609-6202. Fax: 404-367-7894. E-mail: admissions@westminster.net. Web site: www.westminster.net.

ANNOUNCEMENT FROM THE SCHOOL Westminster offers the opportunity to serve those students who are looking for an excellent education while balancing their involvement in the arts, athletics, and other extracurricular activities that enrich the body and spirit along with the mind. Westminster looks for students who are intellectually curious and interested in being active participants in school life while developing relationships with other students and faculty members.

WESTMINSTER SCHOOLS OF AUGUSTA

3067 Wheeler Road
Augusta, Georgia 30909

Head of School: Mr. Stephen D. O'Neil

General Information Coeducational day college-preparatory, arts, religious studies, and music, debate and drama school, affiliated with Presbyterian Church in America. Grades PK–12. Founded: 1972. Setting: suburban. 30-acre campus. 7 buildings on campus. Approved or accredited by Georgia Independent School Association, Southern Association of Colleges and Schools, and Southern Association of Independent Schools. Member of National Association of Independent Schools. Endowment: $290,000. Total enrollment: 535. Upper school average class size: 14. Upper school faculty-student ratio: 1:8.

Upper School Student Profile Grade 6: 28 students (19 boys, 9 girls); Grade 7: 39 students (22 boys, 17 girls); Grade 8: 40 students (29 boys, 11 girls); Grade 9: 52 students (23 boys, 29 girls); Grade 10: 36 students (16 boys, 20 girls); Grade 11: 33 students (17 boys, 16 girls); Grade 12: 32 students (16 boys, 16 girls). 40% of students are Presbyterian Church in America.

Faculty School total: 54. In upper school: 18 men, 14 women; 26 have advanced degrees.

Subjects Offered Algebra, analysis and differential calculus, analysis of data, analytic geometry, anatomy and physiology, Ancient Greek, art, arts, band, Bible studies, biology, biology-AP, British literature (honors), calculus, calculus-AP, chemistry, chemistry-AP, choir, chorus, Christian scripture, classical Greek literature, community service, computer keyboarding, computer programming, computer skills, computers, concert band, concert choir, drama, drama performance, dramatic arts, earth science, economics, English, English language and composition-AP, English language-AP, English literature, English literature and composition-AP, English literature-AP, European history, family life, French, French language-AP, French-AP, geography, geometry, government/civics, Greek, guidance, health, health education, history, history-AP, honors algebra, honors English, honors geometry, honors U.S. history, lab science, Latin, Latin-AP, mathematics, modern European history, modern European history-AP, modern history, modern world history, music, physical education, physical science, physics, physics-AP, pre-algebra, pre-calculus, psychology, religion, SAT preparation, science, social studies, Spanish, Spanish language-AP, Spanish-AP, speech, studio art, study skills, swimming, trigonometry, U.S. government and politics-AP, U.S. history, U.S. history-AP, U.S. literature, United States government-AP, weight training, word processing, world history, world literature, writing, yearbook.

Graduation Requirements Arts and fine arts (art, music, dance, drama), electives, English, foreign language, mathematics, physical education (includes health), religion (includes Bible studies and theology), science, social studies (includes history).

Special Academic Programs Advanced Placement exam preparation; honors section; academic accommodation for the gifted; programs in general development for dyslexic students.

College Admission Counseling 38 students graduated in 2008; all went to college, including Augusta State University; Clemson University; Covenant College; Samford University; University of Georgia; University of South Carolina. Median SAT critical reading: 625, median SAT math: 620, median SAT writing: 620. 59% scored over 600 on SAT critical reading, 68% scored over 600 on SAT math, 62% scored over 600 on SAT writing.

Student Life Upper grades have specified standards of dress, honor system. Discipline rests primarily with faculty.

Summer Programs Sports programs offered; session focuses on sports; held on campus; accepts boys and girls; open to students from other schools. 76 students usually enrolled. 2009 schedule: June 2 to August 1. Application deadline: May 1.

Tuition and Aid Day student tuition: $9949. Tuition installment plan (monthly payment plans). Tuition reduction for siblings, need-based scholarship grants available. In 2008–09, 20% of upper-school students received aid. Total amount of financial aid awarded in 2008–09: $152,000.

Admissions Traditional secondary-level entrance grade is 9. For fall 2008, 23 students applied for upper-level admission, 20 were accepted, 19 enrolled. ERB—verbal abilities, reading comprehension, quantitative abilities (level F, form 1), mathematics proficiency exam and writing sample required. Deadline for receipt of application materials: none. Application fee required: $75. On-campus interview required.

Athletics Interscholastic: baseball (boys), basketball (b,g), cheering (g), cross-country running (b,g), golf (b), soccer (b,g), swimming and diving (b,g), tennis (b,g), track and field (b,g), volleyball (g). 3 PE instructors, 4 coaches, 1 athletic trainer.

Computers Computers are regularly used in college planning, keyboarding, programming, SAT preparation, technology, yearbook classes. Computer network features include Internet access, Internet filtering or blocking technology. Students grades are available online. The school has a published electronic and media policy.

Contact Mrs. Aimee C. Lynch, Director of Admissions. 706-731-5260 Ext. 2220. Fax: 706-261-7786. E-mail: alynch@wsa.net. Web site: www.wsa.net.

WEST NOTTINGHAM ACADEMY

1079 Firetower Road
Colora, Maryland 21917-1599

Head of School: Dr. D. John Watson, PhD

General Information Coeducational boarding and day college-preparatory, arts, and ESL school. Grades 9–PG. Founded: 1744. Setting: rural. Nearest major city is Baltimore. Students are housed in single-sex dormitories. 120-acre campus. 12 buildings on campus. Approved or accredited by Association of Independent Maryland Schools, Middle States Association of Colleges and Schools, National Commission of Accreditation of Special Education Services, The Association of Boarding Schools, and Maryland Department of Education. Member of National Association of Independent Schools and Secondary School Admission Test Board. Total enrollment: 123. Upper school average class size: 10. Upper school faculty-student ratio: 1:6.

Upper School Student Profile Grade 9: 22 students (10 boys, 12 girls); Grade 10: 37 students (20 boys, 17 girls); Grade 11: 38 students (23 boys, 15 girls); Grade 12: 24 students (18 boys, 6 girls); Postgraduate: 1 student (1 boy). 61% of students are boarding students. 22% are state residents. 9 states are represented in upper school student body. 26% are international students. International students from China, Japan, Republic of Korea, Russian Federation, Taiwan, and Thailand; 2 other countries represented in student body.

Faculty School total: 28. In upper school: 13 men, 10 women; 16 have advanced degrees; 23 reside on campus.

Subjects Offered Advanced chemistry, advanced math, advanced TOEFL/grammar, African-American history, algebra, American literature, anatomy, ancient world history, applied arts, art, art history, Asian history, astronomy, basic language skills, biology, biology-AP, body human, British literature, British literature (honors), calculus, calculus-AP, ceramics, chemistry, chemistry-AP, clayworking, college counseling, comparative religion, computer education, drama, drama performance, drawing, earth science, English, English literature, English literature-AP, English-AP, environmental science, equestrian sports, ESL, ethics, ethics and responsibility, European history, European history-AP, fine arts, French, French-AP, geography, geometry, government/civics, guitar, health, history, history-AP, honors algebra, honors English, honors geometry, honors U.S. history, human anatomy, human biology, humanities, independent study, instrumental music, Latin, mathematics, modern European history, modern European history-AP, multicultural studies, music, music appreciation, photography, physical education, physics, physics-AP, physiology, piano, play production, pottery, pre-calculus, psychology, religion, SAT preparation, science, senior humanities, senior project, senior thesis, social studies, Spanish, Spanish-AP, sports, stage design, student government, student publications, studio art, studio art-AP, U.S. history, U.S. history-AP, visual and performing arts, voice, voice ensemble, weight training, wellness, world history, world literature, world religions, wrestling, writing fundamentals, yearbook.

Graduation Requirements Senior research paper.

Special Academic Programs Advanced Placement exam preparation; honors section; independent study; study at local college for college credit; academic accommodation for the gifted, the musically talented, and the artistically talented; remedial reading and/or remedial writing; remedial math; programs in English, mathematics, general development for dyslexic students; ESL (10 students enrolled).

College Admission Counseling 26 students graduated in 2008; all went to college, including Colby College; Gettysburg College; Syracuse University; University of Maryland, Baltimore; University of Southern California.

Student Life Upper grades have specified standards of dress, student council. Discipline rests primarily with faculty.

Tuition and Aid Day student tuition: $18,800; 7-day tuition and room/board: $36,300. Tuition installment plan (monthly payment plans, individually arranged payment plans). Need-based scholarship grants available. In 2008–09, 35% of upper-school students received aid. Total amount of financial aid awarded in 2008–09: $721,000.

Admissions Traditional secondary-level entrance grade is 9. For fall 2008, 184 students applied for upper-level admission, 91 were accepted, 45 enrolled. ISEE, SSAT, TOEFL or TOEFL or SLEP required. Deadline for receipt of application materials: none. Application fee required: $50. On-campus interview required.

Athletics Interscholastic: baseball (boys), basketball (b,g), cheering (g), cross-country running (b,g), field hockey (g), football (b), golf (b), lacrosse (b), soccer (b,g), tennis (b,g), track and field (b,g), volleyball (g), wrestling (b); intramural: bicycling (b); coed interscholastic: cross-country running, power lifting, tennis, track and field, weight training; coed intramural: equestrian sports, horseback riding, strength & conditioning, weight training. 2 coaches, 1 athletic trainer.

Computers Computers are regularly used in computer applications, introduction to technology, mathematics, SAT preparation, science classes. Computer network features include on-campus library services, Internet access, wireless campus network, Internet filtering or blocking technology. Campus intranet and student e-mail accounts are available to students. The school has a published electronic and media policy.

Contact Mr. Jesse Wilson Roberts, IV, Director of Admission. 410-658-5556 Ext. 9224. Fax: 410-658-9264. E-mail: admissions@wna.org. Web site: www.wna.org.

ANNOUNCEMENT FROM THE SCHOOL An important aspect of life at West Nottingham Academy is the emphasis on values and personal growth, both academic and social. Through service learning and culture credit programs, active participation in the classroom, and leadership opportunities in the school community, students discover the importance of sharing, critical thinking, working hard, and helping others. *Nihil Sine Labore*—Nothing Without Work.

See Close-Up on page 1022.

WESTOVER SCHOOL

1237 Whittemore Road
Middlebury, Connecticut 06762

Head of School: Mrs. Ann S. Pollina

General Information Girls' boarding and day college-preparatory, arts, technology, and mathematics and science school. Grades 9–12. Founded: 1909. Setting: small town. Nearest major city is New York, NY. Students are housed in single-sex dormitories. 133-acre campus. 11 buildings on campus. Approved or accredited by Association of Independent Schools in New England, Connecticut Association of Independent Schools, New England Association of Schools and Colleges, The Association of Boarding Schools, and Connecticut Department of Education. Member of National Association of Independent Schools and Secondary School Admission Test Board. Endowment: $42 million. Total enrollment: 200. Upper school average class size: 11. Upper school faculty-student ratio: 1:8.

Upper School Student Profile Grade 9: 52 students (52 girls); Grade 10: 51 students (51 girls); Grade 11: 51 students (51 girls); Grade 12: 46 students (46 girls). 60% of students are boarding students. 57% are state residents. 18 states are represented in upper school student body. 16% are international students. International students from Australia, Bermuda, Japan, Republic of Korea, Saudi Arabia, and Viet Nam; 12 other countries represented in student body.

Faculty School total: 48. In upper school: 20 men, 28 women; 21 have advanced degrees; 38 reside on campus.

Subjects Offered Advanced chemistry, Advanced Placement courses, African-American studies, algebra, American history, American history-AP, American literature, art, art history, art-AP, astronomy, ballet technique, bell choir, biology, biology-AP, calculus, calculus-AP, ceramics, chemistry, chemistry-AP, clayworking, community service, computer literacy, computer programming, computer science, computer science-AP, creative writing, dance, drama, drawing, English, English language and composition-AP, English literature, environmental science, environmental science-AP, ESL, etymology, European history, European history-AP, fabric arts, filmmaking, fine arts, French, French-AP, geography, geometry, grammar, health and wellness, history of mathematics, honors algebra, journalism, Latin, Latin-AP, marine biology, mathematics, model United Nations, modern European history-AP, music, music theory-AP, musical productions, painting, performing arts, photo shop, photography, physics, physics-AP, poetry, politics, portfolio art, pre-calculus, religion, robotics, science, sculpture, Shakespeare, short story, social studies, Spanish, Spanish-AP, speech, studio art-AP, theater, trigonometry, wilderness/outdoor program, women's studies, world history, writing.

Graduation Requirements American history, art, arts and fine arts (art, music, dance, drama), athletics, computer skills, English, foreign language, library studies, mathematics, science, social studies (includes history), summer reading. Community service is required.

Special Academic Programs Advanced Placement exam preparation; honors section; independent study; term-away projects; study abroad; academic accommodation for the gifted, the musically talented, and the artistically talented; ESL (5 students enrolled).

College Admission Counseling 47 students graduated in 2008; all went to college, including Columbia College; Franklin & Marshall College; Skidmore College; University of Connecticut; Vanderbilt University; Vassar College. Median composite ACT: 27. Mean SAT critical reading: 597, mean SAT math: 594, mean SAT writing: 621. 61% scored over 600 on SAT critical reading, 59% scored over 600 on SAT math, 64% scored over 600 on SAT writing, 54% scored over 1800 on combined SAT, 56% scored over 26 on composite ACT.

Student Life Upper grades have specified standards of dress, student council, honor system. Discipline rests equally with students and faculty.

Tuition and Aid Day student tuition: $28,000; 7-day tuition and room/board: $39,900. Tuition installment plan (The Tuition Plan, Insured Tuition Payment Plan, FACTS Tuition Payment Plan). Need-based scholarship grants, need-based loans, middle-income loans available. In 2008–09, 49% of upper-school students received aid. Total amount of financial aid awarded in 2008–09: $2,194,674.

Admissions Traditional secondary-level entrance grade is 9. For fall 2008, 236 students applied for upper-level admission, 137 were accepted, 69 enrolled. SSAT or TOEFL required. Deadline for receipt of application materials: February 1. Application fee required: $45. On-campus interview required.

Athletics Interscholastic: ballet, basketball, cross-country running, dance, field hockey, golf, independent competitive sports, lacrosse, modern dance, outdoor activities, paddle tennis, soccer, softball, squash, tennis, volleyball; intramural: aerobics, aerobics/dance, alpine skiing, backpacking, ballet, canoeing/kayaking, climbing, dance, fitness, fitness walking, Frisbee, hiking/backpacking, jogging, kayaking, modern dance, outdoor activities, physical fitness, physical training, rappelling, rock climbing, running, self defense, skiing (downhill), snowboarding, squash, strength & conditioning, tennis, walking, wall climbing, weight lifting, weight training, wilderness, yoga. 2 PE instructors, 5 coaches, 1 athletic trainer.

Computers Computers are regularly used in art, college planning, engineering, English, foreign language, graphic arts, history, keyboarding, language development, library science, literary magazine, mathematics, music, photography, photojournalism, science, video film production, Web site design classes. Computer network features include on-campus library services, online commercial services, Internet access, Internet filtering or blocking technology. Campus intranet, student e-mail accounts, and computer access in designated common areas are available to students. Students grades are available online. The school has a published electronic and media policy.

Contact Mrs. Laura Volovski, Director of Admission. 203-577-4521. Fax: 203-577-4588. E-mail: admission@westoverschool.org. Web site: www.westoverschool.org.

ANNOUNCEMENT FROM THE SCHOOL A leader in girls' education, Westover is an academically rigorous school dedicated to challenging and encouraging young women to participate in all aspects of academic, community, and athletic life. The Westover community is diverse, with students representing eighteen countries and eighteen states. Westover offers excellent college placement and its students continue outstanding success in twenty-one AP programs, particularly in mathematics and science. Three programs enhance the curriculum: Women in Science and Engineering (WISE), a joint, cocurricular program with Rensselaer Polytechnic Institute in Troy, New York; a joint program for preprofessional musicians with the Manhattan School of Music Pre-College Division; and a program with the Brass City Ballet of Middlebury for talented dancers.

See Close-Up on page 1024.

WESTRIDGE SCHOOL

324 Madeline Drive
Pasadena, California 91105-3399
Head of School: Ms. Rosemary C. Evans

General Information Girls' day college-preparatory, arts, and technology school. Grades 4–12. Founded: 1913. Setting: suburban. Nearest major city is Los Angeles. 10-acre campus. 11 buildings on campus. Approved or accredited by California Association of Independent Schools, National Independent Private Schools Association, The College Board, Western Association of Schools and Colleges, and California Department of Education. Member of National Association of Independent Schools. Endowment: $17.1 million. Total enrollment: 502. Upper school average class size: 18. Upper school faculty-student ratio: 1:9.

Upper School Student Profile Grade 9: 74 students (74 girls); Grade 10: 68 students (68 girls); Grade 11: 74 students (74 girls); Grade 12: 72 students (72 girls).

Faculty School total: 60. In upper school: 16 men, 21 women; 24 have advanced degrees.

Subjects Offered Acting, Advanced Placement courses, algebra, American history, American literature, art, art history, Asian history, biology, calculus, ceramics, chemistry, chorus, classical language, college counseling, computer applications, computer science, creative writing, dance, directing, drama, earth science, English, English literature, environmental science, European history, fine arts, French, geometry, government/civics, history, Latin, life science, mathematics, modern languages, music, orchestra, photography, physical education, physical science, physics, physiology, pre-calculus, psychology, science, social science, social studies, Spanish, Spanish literature, statistics, studio art, theater, trigonometry, video, visual and performing arts, world history, world literature, writing.

Graduation Requirements Art, college counseling, cultural arts, English, foreign language, history, mathematics, music, physical education (includes health), science, senior project. Community service is required.

Special Academic Programs Advanced Placement exam preparation; honors section; independent study.

College Admission Counseling 68 students graduated in 2008; all went to college, including Cornell University; Stanford University; University of Chicago; University of Pennsylvania; University of San Diego; University of Southern California. Median SAT critical reading: 600, median SAT math: 570, median SAT writing: 610.

Student Life Upper grades have uniform requirement, student council. Discipline rests primarily with faculty.

Summer Programs Enrichment, sports, art/fine arts programs offered; session focuses on non-academic activities; held on campus; accepts boys and girls; open to students from other schools. 150 students usually enrolled. 2009 schedule: June 22 to July 17. Application deadline: May 1.

Tuition and Aid Day student tuition: $25,300. Tuition installment plan (monthly payment plans, full payment, Two payment plan). Need-based scholarship grants available. In 2008–09, 33% of upper-school students received aid. Total amount of financial aid awarded in 2008–09: $1,318,800.

Admissions Traditional secondary-level entrance grade is 9. For fall 2008, 94 students applied for upper-level admission, 42 were accepted, 21 enrolled. ISEE, school's own exam or writing sample required. Deadline for receipt of application materials: February 2. Application fee required: $60. On-campus interview required.

Athletics Interscholastic: basketball, cross-country running, dance, diving, fencing, golf, lacrosse, modern dance, soccer, softball, tennis, track and field, volleyball, water polo, yoga. 4 PE instructors, 22 coaches, 1 athletic trainer.

Computers Computers are regularly used in art, English, foreign language, history, mathematics, science classes. Computer network features include on-campus library services, online commercial services, Internet access, wireless campus network, Internet filtering or blocking technology. Student e-mail accounts are available to students. Students grades are available online. The school has a published electronic and media policy.

Contact Ms. Helen V. Hopper, Director of Admissions. 626-799-1153 Ext. 213. Fax: 626-799-7068. E-mail: hhopper@westridge.org. Web site: www.westridge.org.

ANNOUNCEMENT FROM THE SCHOOL For 95 years, Westridge School has offered girls and young women an educational program rich in tradition, yet committed to innovation. In grades 4 through 12, 500 girls pursue a multifaceted academic, athletic, and extracurricular program that supports leadership training and community service learning. The academic curriculum is enhanced by study of art, dance, drama, foreign language, humanities, music, science, and technology.

WESTTOWN SCHOOL

Westtown Road
P.O. Box 1799
Westtown, Pennsylvania 19395-1799
Head of School: John W. Baird

General Information Coeducational boarding and day college-preparatory, arts, and religious studies school, affiliated with Society of Friends. Boarding grades 9–12, day grades PK–10. Founded: 1799. Setting: suburban. Nearest major city is Philadelphia. Students are housed in single-sex by floor dormitories and single-sex dormitories. 600-acre campus. 38 buildings on campus. Approved or accredited by Middle States Association of Colleges and Schools, Pennsylvania Association of Independent Schools, and Pennsylvania Department of Education. Member of National Association of Independent Schools and Secondary School Admission Test Board. Endowment: $75 million. Total enrollment: 789. Upper school average class size: 15. Upper school faculty-student ratio: 1:8.

Upper School Student Profile Grade 9: 91 students (49 boys, 42 girls); Grade 10: 107 students (61 boys, 46 girls); Grade 11: 123 students (50 boys, 73 girls); Grade 12: 89 students (46 boys, 43 girls). 75% of students are boarding students. 62% are state residents. 22 states are represented in upper school student body. 13% are international students. International students from China, Germany, Hong Kong, Nigeria, Republic of Korea, and Thailand; 7 other countries represented in student body. 16% of students are members of Society of Friends.

Faculty School total: 113. In upper school: 36 men, 33 women; 45 have advanced degrees; 55 reside on campus.

Subjects Offered 3-dimensional art, ACT preparation, advanced biology, advanced chemistry, advanced math, African dance, algebra, American culture, American foreign policy, American history, American literature, Ancient Greek, ancient history, Arabic, art, Asian history, astronomy, astrophysics, ballet, band, baseball, basketball, Bible, Bible studies, biology, botany, British literature, calculus, Chinese, choir, choral music, chorus, Christian and Hebrew scripture, classical language, classical studies, comparative religion, computer applications, concert band, concert choir, crafts, creative dance, creative writing, dance, dance performance, drama, drama performance, drama workshop, drawing, drawing and design, earth science, Eastern religion and philosophy, ecology, ecology, environmental systems, electives, English, English as a foreign language, English composition, English literature, environmental science, environmental studies, ESL, European history, film and literature, folk art, foreign language, foreign policy, fractal geometry, French, functions, geometry, German, graphic design, Greek, Holocaust and other genocides, honors algebra, honors geometry, honors U.S. history, honors world history, Italian, Japanese, jazz, jazz band, jazz dance, jazz ensemble, lab science, language, Latin, Latin American history, leadership training, library research, linear algebra, literature, literature seminar, Mandarin, mathematics, model United Nations, modern dance, music, music composition, music performance, music theater, musical theater, mythology, nature writers, non-Western literature, peace and justice, physics, piano, play production, playwriting and directing, pre-algebra, pre-calculus, Quakerism and ethics, religion, robotics, SAT preparation, science, senior project, senior seminar, Shakespeare, Spanish, Spanish literature, stage design, statistics, student government, student publications, studio art, swimming, tap dance, tennis, theater, theater design and production, theater history, theater production, trigonometry, U.S. history, U.S. literature, visual and performing arts, visual arts, vocal ensemble, vocal music, water color painting, weight fitness, Western civilization, Western literature, Western religions, woodworking, work-study, world history, world literature, world religions, wrestling, writing, writing workshop, yearbook.

Graduation Requirements Arts and fine arts (art, music, dance, drama), English, foreign language, mathematics, physical education (includes health), religion (includes Bible studies and theology), religious studies, science, senior project, social science, Required boarding in 11th and 12th grade.

Special Academic Programs Advanced Placement exam preparation; honors section; independent study; study abroad; academic accommodation for the gifted, the musically talented, and the artistically talented; remedial math; ESL (18 students enrolled).

College Admission Counseling 115 students graduated in 2008; all went to college, including Connecticut College; Earlham College; Haverford College; New York University; Northwestern University; Penn State University Park.

Student Life Upper grades have specified standards of dress, student council. Discipline rests equally with students and faculty. Attendance at religious services is required.

Summer Programs Remediation, enrichment, advancement, sports, art/fine arts programs offered; session focuses on fun and educational activities; held on campus; accepts boys and girls; open to students from other schools. 130 students usually enrolled. 2009 schedule: June 22 to August 14. Application deadline: none.

Tuition and Aid Day student tuition: $25,300; 7-day tuition and room/board: $40,250. Tuition installment plan (The IPP/HES Plan-Wachovia Bank). Need-based scholarship grants, need-based loans available. In 2008–09, 40% of upper-school students received aid. Total amount of financial aid awarded in 2008–09: $3,997,138.

Admissions Traditional secondary-level entrance grade is 9. For fall 2008, 275 students applied for upper-level admission, 147 were accepted, 89 enrolled. ISEE, SSAT or TOEFL required. Deadline for receipt of application materials: none. Application fee required: $50. On-campus interview required.

Athletics Interscholastic: baseball (boys), basketball (b,g), cross-country running (b,g), field hockey (g), independent competitive sports (b,g), lacrosse (b,g), soccer (b,g), softball (g), swimming and diving (b,g), tennis (b,g), track and field (b,g), volleyball (g), wrestling (b); coed interscholastic: dance team, golf, independent competitive sports, indoor track, indoor track & field; coed intramural: aquatics, ballet, basketball, canoeing/kayaking, combined training, dance, fitness, hiking/backpacking, indoor soccer, life saving, modern dance, outdoor activities, physical fitness, physical training, ropes courses, running, strength & conditioning, swimming and diving, tennis, ultimate Frisbee, weight lifting, weight training, winter (indoor) track, winter soccer, yoga. 18 coaches, 1 athletic trainer.

Computers Computers are regularly used in all academic, animation, art, career exploration, college planning, current events, desktop publishing, digital applications, graphic arts, introduction to technology, library, library skills, literary magazine, newspaper, publications, research skills, theater, yearbook classes. Computer network features include on-campus library services, online commercial services, Internet access, wireless campus network, Internet filtering or blocking technology. Campus intranet, student e-mail accounts, and computer access in designated common areas are available to students. Students grades are available online. The school has a published electronic and media policy.
Contact Kate Holz, Director of Admissions and Financial Aid. 610-399-7900. Fax: 610-399-7909. E-mail: admissions@westtown.edu. Web site: www.westtown.edu.

WHEATON ACADEMY

900 Prince Crossing Road
West Chicago, Illinois 60185
Head of School: Dr. Gene Frost

General Information Coeducational day college-preparatory and religious studies school, affiliated with Christian faith. Grades 9–12. Founded: 1853. Setting: suburban. Nearest major city is Chicago. 43-acre campus. 7 buildings on campus. Approved or accredited by Association of Christian Schools International, North Central Association of Colleges and Schools, and Illinois Department of Education. Total enrollment: 647. Upper school average class size: 20. Upper school faculty-student ratio: 1:14.
Upper School Student Profile Grade 9: 146 students (71 boys, 75 girls); Grade 10: 170 students (81 boys, 89 girls); Grade 11: 174 students (82 boys, 92 girls); Grade 12: 153 students (77 boys, 76 girls). 99% of students are Christian faith.
Faculty School total: 46. In upper school: 24 men, 22 women; 34 have advanced degrees.
Subjects Offered 20th century history, ACT preparation, algebra, art, arts and crafts, band, Bible, Bible studies, biology, biology-AP, British literature, business, business applications, calculus, calculus-AP, ceramics, chemistry, child development, choir, Christian doctrine, Christian education, classics, computer art, computer education, computer graphics, computer keyboarding, computer multimedia, computer processing, computer programming-AP, computer science, concert choir, consumer economics, creative writing, debate, desktop publishing, drama, drama workshop, drawing, driver education, earth science, economics, English, English language and composition-AP, English literature, English literature and composition-AP, environmental science, European history, European history-AP, family living, fiber arts, fine arts, foods, French, freshman seminar, geology, geometry, government/civics, graphic design, Greek, health, health and wellness, history, honors English, honors geometry, honors U.S. history, industrial arts, internship, journalism, leadership, literature, mathematics, multimedia design, music, music theory-AP, novels, orchestra, personal growth, physical education, physics, portfolio art, pre-algebra, psychology, publications, science, social science, social studies, sociology, Spanish, Spanish language-AP, speech, statistics, student publications, theater, theology, trigonometry, U.S. government, U.S. history, U.S. history-AP, U.S. literature, world history, world literature, writing.
Graduation Requirements Arts and fine arts (art, music, dance, drama), English, mathematics, physical education (includes health), religion (includes Bible studies and theology), science, social science, social studies (includes history), Winterim (3-week period during January allowing students to take two classes beyond the typical curriculum).
Special Academic Programs 11 Advanced Placement exams for which test preparation is offered; honors section; independent study; term-away projects; study at local college for college credit; academic accommodation for the gifted, the musically talented, and the artistically talented; remedial reading and/or remedial writing; remedial math; special instructional classes for students with learning disabilities.
College Admission Counseling 139 students graduated in 2008; 132 went to college, including Calvin College; Gordon College; Olivet Nazarene University; Taylor University; University of Illinois at Chicago; Wheaton College. Other: 2 went to work, 1 entered military service, 4 had other specific plans. Median composite ACT: 25. 40% scored over 26 on composite ACT.
Student Life Upper grades have specified standards of dress, honor system. Discipline rests primarily with faculty. Attendance at religious services is required.
Summer Programs Advancement, sports, art/fine arts, computer instruction programs offered; held on campus; accepts boys and girls; open to students from other schools. 65 students usually enrolled. 2009 schedule: June 9 to June 27.
Tuition and Aid Day student tuition: $11,500. Tuition installment plan (monthly payment plans, semester payment plan). Tuition reduction for siblings, merit scholarship grants, need-based scholarship grants, paying campus jobs available. In 2008–09, 30% of upper-school students received aid; total upper-school merit-scholarship money awarded: $14,000. Total amount of financial aid awarded in 2008–09: $540,000.
Admissions Traditional secondary-level entrance grade is 9. ACT-Explore or placement test required. Deadline for receipt of application materials: none. Application fee required: $50. On-campus interview required.
Athletics Interscholastic: baseball (boys), basketball (b,g), cheering (g), cross-country running (b,g), dance team (g), football (b), golf (b,g), ice hockey (b), pom squad (g), soccer (b,g), softball (g), tennis (b,g), track and field (b,g), volleyball (b,g); intramural: aerobics (g), flagball (g), ice hockey (b), wilderness survival (b); coed interscholastic: modern dance, physical training, running; coed intramural: climbing, floor hockey, hiking/backpacking, outdoor education, outdoor skills, power lifting, project adventure, rock climbing, skiing (cross-country), strength & conditioning, wall climbing, weight lifting, weight training. 2 PE instructors, 6 coaches.
Computers Computers are regularly used in Bible studies, graphic design, independent study, mathematics, multimedia, writing, yearbook classes. Computer network features include on-campus library services, online commercial services, Internet access, Internet filtering or blocking technology. Student e-mail accounts are available to students. Students grades are available online.
Contact Ms. Rachel Swanson, Admissions Assistant. 630-562-7500 Ext. 7501. Fax: 630-231-0842. E-mail: rswanson@wheatonacademy.org. Web site: www.wheatonacademy.org.

THE WHEELER SCHOOL

216 Hope Street
Providence, Rhode Island 02906
Head of School: Dan Miller, PhD

General Information Coeducational day college-preparatory and arts school. Grades N–12. Founded: 1889. Setting: urban. 5-acre campus. 7 buildings on campus. Approved or accredited by New England Association of Schools and Colleges and Rhode Island Department of Education. Member of National Association of Independent Schools. Endowment: $12.5 million. Total enrollment: 795. Upper school average class size: 15. Upper school faculty-student ratio: 1:13.
Upper School Student Profile Grade 9: 76 students (37 boys, 39 girls); Grade 10: 90 students (44 boys, 46 girls); Grade 11: 83 students (41 boys, 42 girls); Grade 12: 81 students (42 boys, 39 girls).
Faculty School total: 114. In upper school: 23 men, 35 women; 35 have advanced degrees.
Subjects Offered 20th century world history, acting, Advanced Placement courses, advanced studio art-AP, algebra, American history, anatomy, art, art history, biology, biology-AP, business skills, calculus, calculus-AP, ceramics, chemistry, Chinese, Chinese studies, computer programming, computer science, dance, drama, earth science, economics, English, English literature, English-AP, environmental science, environmental science-AP, European history, fine arts, forensic science, French, geometry, Japanese, Latin, mathematics, music, photography, physical education, physics, physiology, psychology, science, social studies, Spanish, theater, trigonometry.
Graduation Requirements Arts and fine arts (art, music, dance, drama), English, foreign language, mathematics, physical education (includes health), science, social studies (includes history), Community Service Component.
Special Academic Programs Advanced Placement exam preparation; honors section; accelerated programs; independent study; term-away projects; study at local college for college credit; study abroad.
College Admission Counseling 84 students graduated in 2008; all went to college, including Bates College; Boston University; Ithaca College; Rensselaer Polytechnic Institute; School of the Art Institute of Chicago; The George Washington University. Median SAT critical reading: 590, median SAT math: 580, median SAT writing: 570, median combined SAT: 1740.
Student Life Upper grades have specified standards of dress, student council. Discipline rests equally with students and faculty.
Tuition and Aid Day student tuition: $24,105. Tuition installment plan (Insured Tuition Payment Plan, Key Tuition Payment Plan, monthly payment plans). Need-based scholarship grants available. In 2008–09, 20% of upper-school students received aid. Total amount of financial aid awarded in 2008–09: $979,495.
Admissions Traditional secondary-level entrance grade is 9. For fall 2008, 133 students applied for upper-level admission, 59 were accepted, 29 enrolled. ISEE or SSAT required. Deadline for receipt of application materials: January 30. Application fee required: $60. On-campus interview required.
Athletics Interscholastic: baseball (boys), basketball (b,g), field hockey (g), football (b), ice hockey (b,g), independent competitive sports (b,g), lacrosse (b,g), soccer (b,g), softball (g), tennis (b,g), track and field (b,g), winter (indoor) track (b,g); intramural: field hockey (g), lacrosse (b,g), soccer (b,g), tennis (g), weight training (b,g); coed interscholastic: cross-country running, golf, sailing, squash; coed intramural: fencing, rock climbing, strength & conditioning. 7 PE instructors, 22 coaches, 1 athletic trainer.
Computers Computers are regularly used in mathematics, science classes. Computer network features include on-campus library services, Internet access.
Contact Jeanette Epstein, Director of Admission. 401-421-8100. Fax: 401-751-7674. E-mail: jeanetteepstein@wheelerschool.org. Web site: www.wheelerschool.org.

ANNOUNCEMENT FROM THE SCHOOL The Wheeler School, established in 1889, is an N–12, coed, independent day school in Providence, Rhode Island. The main campus houses all academic and administrative buildings, a field house, and a playground. The School today has approximately 3,700 alumni and 800 students, with 200 faculty and staff members. In addition to its main campus in Providence, the School has a 120-acre farm facility with an athletic complex, Sixth Grade Farm Program, Raku kiln, summer camp, and areas for academic programs, conferences, and environmental research.

WHITEFIELD ACADEMY

One Whitefield Drive
Mableton, Georgia 30126

Head of School: Dr. John H. Lindsell

General Information Coeducational day college-preparatory, arts, religious studies, technology, and life and career planning school, affiliated with Christian faith. Grades PK–12. Founded: 1996. Setting: suburban. Nearest major city is Atlanta. 74-acre campus. 2 buildings on campus. Approved or accredited by Association of Christian Schools International, Georgia Accrediting Commission, Southern Association of Colleges and Schools, and The College Board. Member of Secondary School Admission Test Board. Endowment: $1.7 million. Total enrollment: 691. Upper school average class size: 18. Upper school faculty-student ratio: 1:8.

Upper School Student Profile Grade 9: 72 students (46 boys, 26 girls); Grade 10: 64 students (38 boys, 26 girls); Grade 11: 54 students (31 boys, 23 girls); Grade 12: 61 students (38 boys, 23 girls). 100% of students are Christian faith.

Faculty School total: 81. In upper school: 14 men, 21 women; 20 have advanced degrees.

Graduation Requirements Algebra, American history, American literature, arts and fine arts (art, music, dance, drama), biology, British literature, chemistry, Christian studies, English, foreign language, geometry, health education, modern European history, physical fitness, physics, pre-calculus, public speaking, Western civilization, Life and Career Planning. Community service is required.

Special Academic Programs Advanced Placement exam preparation; honors section; independent study; special instructional classes for deaf students, blind students.

College Admission Counseling 55 students graduated in 2008; all went to college, including Auburn University; Furman University; The University of Alabama; University of Georgia.

Student Life Upper grades have uniform requirement, student council, honor system. Discipline rests equally with students and faculty. Attendance at religious services is required.

Summer Programs Remediation, enrichment, sports, art/fine arts programs offered; session focuses on skills improvement; held on campus; accepts boys and girls; open to students from other schools. 150 students usually enrolled.

Tuition and Aid Day student tuition: $16,975. Need-based financial assistance (through SSS application), PLEASE Loan Program, AchieverLoans, and PrepGATE Loans available. In 2008–09, 20% of upper-school students received aid. Total amount of financial aid awarded in 2008–09: $800,000.

Admissions Traditional secondary-level entrance grade is 9. SSAT required. Deadline for receipt of application materials: February 13. Application fee required: $65. On-campus interview required.

Athletics Interscholastic: baseball (boys), basketball (b,g), cheering (g), cross-country running (b,g), football (b), golf (b), physical fitness (b,g), soccer (b,g), softball (g), strength & conditioning (b), swimming and diving (b,g), tennis (b,g), track and field (b,g), volleyball (g), weight lifting (b), wrestling (b); coed interscholastic: cross-country running, physical fitness, tennis, track and field; coed intramural: golf. 2 PE instructors, 5 coaches, 2 athletic trainers.

Computers Computer network features include on-campus library services, online commercial services, Internet access, wireless campus network, Internet filtering or blocking technology. Students grades are available online. The school has a published electronic and media policy.

Contact Mrs. Linda J. Simpson, Admission Director. 678-305-3027. Fax: 678-305-3010. E-mail: lindas@whitefieldacademy.com. Web site: www.whitefieldacademy.com.

THE WHITE MOUNTAIN SCHOOL

West Farm Road
Bethlehem, New Hampshire 03574

Head of School: Brian Morgan

General Information Coeducational boarding and day college-preparatory, arts, and sustainability studies school, affiliated with Episcopal Church. Grades 9–PG. Founded: 1886. Setting: rural. Nearest major city is Concord. Students are housed in single-sex dormitories. 250-acre campus. 13 buildings on campus. Approved or accredited by National Association of Episcopal Schools, New England Association of Schools and Colleges, The Association of Boarding Schools, and New Hampshire Department of Education. Member of National Association of Independent Schools and Secondary School Admission Test Board. Endowment: $1.5 million. Total enrollment: 95. Upper school average class size: 9. Upper school faculty-student ratio: 1:5.

Upper School Student Profile 80% of students are boarding students. 25% are state residents. 22 states are represented in upper school student body. 14% are international students. International students from Bulgaria, Colombia, Ethiopia, Kenya, Republic of Korea, and Zambia; 1 other country represented in student body. 5% of students are members of Episcopal Church.

Faculty School total: 28. In upper school: 15 men, 13 women; 13 have advanced degrees; 23 reside on campus.

Subjects Offered Algebra, American literature, American studies, biology, calculus, Caribbean history, ceramics, chemistry, Chinese history, college counseling, community garden, community service, creative writing, drawing and design, earth science, economics, English, environmental education, environmental science, environmental studies, ESL, ethics, French, geometry, health, human development, independent study, Japanese history, jazz theory, learning strategies, literature, Middle Eastern history, music history, painting, philosophy, photography, physics, physiology-anatomy, pre-calculus, printmaking, senior project, social justice, Spanish, studio art, theater arts, theater production, U.S. history, Vietnam, world history, writing.

Graduation Requirements Algebra, American history, arts and fine arts (art, music, dance, drama), English, geometry, health, literature, non-Western societies, physical science, theology, Western civilization, writing, wilderness skills and outdoor learning expeditions, sustainability studies, Community Service. Community service is required.

Special Academic Programs Advanced Placement exam preparation; honors section; independent study; term-away projects; academic accommodation for the gifted, the musically talented, and the artistically talented; remedial reading and/or remedial writing; remedial math; programs in English, mathematics, general development for dyslexic students; special instructional classes for students with dysgraphia and other learning differences; ESL (2 students enrolled).

College Admission Counseling 24 students graduated in 2007; 22 went to college, including Fort Lewis College; Guilford College; St. Lawrence University; The College of Wooster; University of Vermont; Western State College of Colorado. Other: 2 went to work. 10% scored over 600 on SAT critical reading, 24% scored over 600 on SAT math.

Student Life Upper grades have specified standards of dress, student council, honor system. Discipline rests primarily with faculty.

Tuition and Aid Day student tuition: $18,000; 7-day tuition and room/board: $39,100. Tuition installment plan (Insured Tuition Payment Plan, Academic Management Services Plan, 2-payment plan). Merit scholarship grants, need-based scholarship grants available. In 2007–08, 37% of upper-school students received aid. Total amount of financial aid awarded in 2007–08: $798,570.

Admissions Traditional secondary-level entrance grade is 10. For fall 2007, 117 students applied for upper-level admission, 58 were accepted, 36 enrolled. TOEFL or SLEP, WISC III or other aptitude measures; standardized achievement test or writing sample required. Deadline for receipt of application materials: none. Application fee required: $50. Interview required.

Athletics Interscholastic: lacrosse (boys, girls), soccer (b,g); intramural: dance (g); coed interscholastic: mountain biking; coed intramural: aerobics/Nautilus, alpine skiing, backpacking, bicycling, canoeing/kayaking, climbing, combined training, fitness, freestyle skiing, hiking/backpacking, kayaking, martial arts, mountain biking, mountaineering, Nautilus, nordic skiing, outdoor activities, outdoor adventure, outdoor education, outdoor recreation, outdoor skills, outdoors, paddling, rappelling, rock climbing, running, skiing (cross-country), skiing (downhill), snowboarding, snowshoeing, squash, strength & conditioning, telemark skiing, tennis, ultimate Frisbee, wall climbing, wilderness, wilderness survival. 1 athletic trainer.

Computers Computers are regularly used in college planning, foreign language, library skills, mathematics, media arts, science, yearbook classes. Computer network features include on-campus library services, online commercial services, Internet access, wireless campus network, Internet filtering or blocking technology. Student e-mail accounts and computer access in designated common areas are available to students.

Contact Joanna Evans, Director of Admissions. 603-444-2928 Ext. 19. Fax: 603-444-5568. E-mail: joanna.evans@whitemountain.org. Web site: www.whitemountain.org.

ANNOUNCEMENT FROM THE SCHOOL The White Mountain School is an independent boarding and day school dedicated to preparing young people for college studies and life beyond formal academics. Through a robust curriculum and interactive classes, the White Mountain experience allows students in grades 9–12/PG to own their education and become responsible and innovative young adults.

See Close-Up on page 1026.

WICHITA COLLEGIATE SCHOOL

9115 East 13th Street
Wichita, Kansas 67206

Head of School: Mr. Chris Ashbrook

General Information Coeducational day college-preparatory, arts, and technology school. Grades PS–12. Founded: 1963. Setting: urban. 42-acre campus. 1 building on campus. Approved or accredited by Independent Schools Association of the

Southwest. Member of National Association of Independent Schools. Endowment: $3.3 million. Total enrollment: 1,018. Upper school average class size: 10. Upper school faculty-student ratio: 1:10.

Upper School Student Profile Grade 9: 53 students (30 boys, 23 girls); Grade 10: 60 students (27 boys, 33 girls); Grade 11: 65 students (33 boys, 32 girls); Grade 12: 48 students (24 boys, 24 girls).

Faculty School total: 99. In upper school: 13 men, 14 women; 15 have advanced degrees.

Subjects Offered Algebra, American history, American literature, art, biology, calculus, chemistry, computer programming, computer science, drama, economics, English, English literature, European history, fine arts, French, geometry, government/civics, history, humanities, journalism, Latin, mathematics, medieval/Renaissance history, music, photography, physical education, physics, science, social studies, Spanish, statistics, theater, trigonometry, video, video film production, world history, world literature, writing, yearbook.

Graduation Requirements Arts and fine arts (art, music, dance, drama), computer science, economics, English, foreign language, humanities, mathematics, physical education (includes health), science, social studies (includes history).

Special Academic Programs 18 Advanced Placement exams for which test preparation is offered; study at local college for college credit; academic accommodation for the gifted.

College Admission Counseling 59 students graduated in 2008; all went to college, including Baylor University; The Colorado College; The University of Kansas; University of Tulsa. Median SAT critical reading: 620, median SAT math: 630, median SAT writing: 600, median combined SAT: 1840, median composite ACT: 26. 51% scored over 600 on SAT critical reading, 58% scored over 600 on SAT math, 51% scored over 600 on SAT writing, 50% scored over 26 on composite ACT.

Student Life Upper grades have specified standards of dress, student council, honor system. Discipline rests primarily with faculty.

Summer Programs Remediation, enrichment, sports, art/fine arts, computer instruction programs offered; held on campus; accepts boys and girls; open to students from other schools. 700 students usually enrolled. 2009 schedule: June 8 to August 7. Application deadline: none.

Tuition and Aid Day student tuition: $12,575. Tuition installment plan (monthly payment plans, individually arranged payment plans, 3-payment plan). Need-based scholarship grants available. In 2008–09, 17% of upper-school students received aid. Total amount of financial aid awarded in 2008–09: $272,225.

Admissions Traditional secondary-level entrance grade is 9. For fall 2008, 25 students applied for upper-level admission, 22 were accepted, 15 enrolled. Otis-Lennon, Stanford Achievement Test and Stanford Achievement Test, Otis-Lennon School Ability Test required. Deadline for receipt of application materials: none. Application fee required: $35. Interview recommended.

Athletics Interscholastic: baseball (boys), basketball (b,g), cheering (b,g), cross-country running (b,g), dance team (g), football (b), golf (b), softball (g), strength & conditioning (b,g), tennis (b,g), track and field (b,g), volleyball (g); coed interscholastic: bowling, cross-country running, track and field. 2 PE instructors, 16 coaches, 1 athletic trainer.

Computers Computers are regularly used in video film production classes. Computer network features include on-campus library services, Internet access, Internet filtering or blocking technology. Students grades are available online. The school has a published electronic and media policy.

Contact Ms. Susie Steed, Director of Admission and Communication. 316-771-2203. Fax: 316-634-0598. E-mail: ssteed@wcsks.com. Web site: www.wcsks.com.

ANNOUNCEMENT FROM THE SCHOOL Wichita Collegiate School is a student-centered, coeducational, college-preparatory day school for age 2 through Grade 12. The School offers individual attention in small classes, a dynamic faculty, rigorous academics, and opportunities to participate in outstanding cocurricular programs in the arts, athletics, debate, and other areas for a balanced educational experience. Wichita Collegiate School is accredited by the ISAS and is a member of the NAIS. For more information, please visit www.wcsks.com.

WILLIAM PENN CHARTER SCHOOL

3000 West School House Lane
Philadelphia, Pennsylvania 19144

Head of School: Darryl J. Ford

General Information Coeducational day college-preparatory school, affiliated with Society of Friends. Grades PK–12. Founded: 1689. Setting: urban. 44-acre campus. 8 buildings on campus. Approved or accredited by Pennsylvania Association of Independent Schools. Member of National Association of Independent Schools. Endowment: $53 million. Total enrollment: 929. Upper school average class size: 16. Upper school faculty-student ratio: 1:9.

Upper School Student Profile Grade 9: 97 students (48 boys, 49 girls); Grade 10: 113 students (65 boys, 48 girls); Grade 11: 115 students (59 boys, 56 girls); Grade 12: 90 students (51 boys, 39 girls). 3% of students are members of Society of Friends.

Faculty School total: 134. In upper school: 39 men, 31 women; 55 have advanced degrees.

Subjects Offered Algebra, American history, American literature, architectural drawing, art, art history-AP, Asian studies, band, Bible studies, bioethics, biology, biology-AP, botany, British literature, calculus, calculus-AP, calligraphy, ceramics, chemistry, chemistry-AP, choral music, chorus, college counseling, computer math, computer programming, computer science, creative writing, design, drama, drawing, earth science, Eastern religion and philosophy, ecology, economics, electronic music, English, English literature, environmental science, environmental science-AP, ethics, European history, European history-AP, film, filmmaking, fine arts, French, French-AP, genetics, geology, geometry, government and politics-AP, health, Hebrew scripture, history, history of rock and roll, history of science, human anatomy, independent study, Irish literature, jazz band, junior and senior seminars, Latin, learning cognition classes, learning strategies, marine biology, mathematics, Middle East, model United Nations, modern European history-AP, music, music performance, oceanography, organic chemistry, painting, peace and justice, photography, physical education, physics, physics-AP, pottery, pre-calculus, public speaking, Quakerism and ethics, religion, science, sculpture, senior project, service learning/internship, Shakespeare, social studies, Spanish, Spanish-AP, speech, statistics-AP, symphonic band, theater, theater arts, theater design and production, theater production, trigonometry, U.S. history-AP, United States government-AP, video, visual and performing arts, world history, world literature, world religions, writing.

Graduation Requirements Computer science, English, foreign language, mathematics, music, physical education (includes health), religious studies, science, social studies (includes history), theater, visual arts.

Special Academic Programs Advanced Placement exam preparation; honors section; independent study; study at local college for college credit; academic accommodation for the gifted, the musically talented, and the artistically talented.

College Admission Counseling 110 students graduated in 2008; 109 went to college, including Harvard University; Northwestern University; Princeton University; The Johns Hopkins University; Tufts University; University of Pennsylvania. Other: 1 entered a postgraduate year. Mean SAT critical reading: 643, mean SAT math: 640, mean SAT writing: 650, mean combined SAT: 1933, mean composite ACT: 26. 61% scored over 600 on SAT critical reading, 65% scored over 600 on SAT math, 71% scored over 600 on SAT writing, 69% scored over 1800 on combined SAT, 46% scored over 26 on composite ACT.

Student Life Upper grades have specified standards of dress, student council, honor system. Discipline rests equally with students and faculty. Attendance at religious services is required.

Summer Programs Enrichment, advancement, sports, art/fine arts programs offered; held on campus; accepts boys and girls; open to students from other schools. 522 students usually enrolled. 2009 schedule: June 16 to August 1. Application deadline: June 16.

Tuition and Aid Day student tuition: $23,220. Tuition installment plan (Academic Management Services Plan, Key Tuition Payment Plan, Sallie Mae, Tuition Pay). Need-based scholarship grants available. In 2008–09, 36% of upper-school students received aid. Total amount of financial aid awarded in 2008–09: $2,259,910.

Admissions Traditional secondary-level entrance grade is 9. For fall 2008, 238 students applied for upper-level admission, 72 were accepted, 32 enrolled. ISEE or SSAT required. Deadline for receipt of application materials: none. Application fee required: $30. On-campus interview required.

Athletics Interscholastic: baseball (boys), basketball (b,g), cross-country running (b,g), diving (b,g), field hockey (g), football (b), golf (b,g), lacrosse (b,g), soccer (b,g), softball (g), squash (b,g), swimming and diving (b,g), tennis (b,g), track and field (b,g), water polo (b,g), wrestling (b); intramural: basketball (b,g); coed intramural: ultimate Frisbee. 9 PE instructors, 46 coaches, 2 athletic trainers.

Computers Computers are regularly used in all academic classes. Computer network features include on-campus library services, online commercial services, Internet access, wireless campus network, Internet filtering or blocking technology. Student e-mail accounts are available to students. The school has a published electronic and media policy.

Contact Stephen A. Bonnie, Director of Admissions. 215-844-3460. Fax: 215-843-3939. E-mail: sbonnie@penncharter.com. Web site: www.penncharter.com.

THE WILLIAMS SCHOOL

182 Mohegan Avenue
New London, Connecticut 06320-4110

Head of School: Mark Fader

General Information Coeducational day college-preparatory school. Grades 7–12. Founded: 1891. Setting: small town. 25-acre campus. 2 buildings on campus. Approved or accredited by Connecticut Association of Independent Schools, New England Association of Schools and Colleges, and Connecticut Department of Education. Member of National Association of Independent Schools and Secondary School Admission Test Board. Endowment: $4 million. Total enrollment: 315. Upper school average class size: 13. Upper school faculty-student ratio: 1:6.

Upper School Student Profile Grade 9: 61 students (27 boys, 34 girls); Grade 10: 59 students (28 boys, 31 girls); Grade 11: 60 students (25 boys, 35 girls); Grade 12: 67 students (32 boys, 35 girls).

Faculty School total: 43. In upper school: 17 men, 23 women; 30 have advanced degrees.

Subjects Offered Algebra, American history, art, band, biology, biology-AP, calculus, calculus-AP, chemistry, chemistry-AP, chorus, computer science, dance, digital art, drama, economics, English, English literature, English-AP, environmental science, European history, expository writing, fine arts, French, French-AP, geography, geometry, Greek, history, jazz, journalism, Latin-AP, mathematics, modern European history, music, music composition, music history, music theory, music theory-AP, physical education, physics, physics-AP, pre-calculus, science, social studies, Spanish, Spanish-AP, theater, trigonometry, world history, world literature.
Graduation Requirements Arts and fine arts (art, music, dance, drama), classical language, English, foreign language, mathematics, physical education (includes health), science, senior project, social studies (includes history).
Special Academic Programs 10 Advanced Placement exams for which test preparation is offered; honors section; independent study; study at local college for college credit; study abroad; academic accommodation for the gifted, the musically talented, and the artistically talented.
College Admission Counseling 67 students graduated in 2008; all went to college, including Boston University; New York University; St. Lawrence University; The George Washington University; University of Connecticut; University of Maryland, College Park. Mean SAT critical reading: 630, mean SAT math: 623, mean SAT writing: 608, mean combined SAT: 1861, mean composite ACT: 29. 62% scored over 600 on SAT critical reading, 64% scored over 600 on SAT math, 59% scored over 600 on SAT writing, 63% scored over 1800 on combined SAT, 60% scored over 26 on composite ACT.
Student Life Upper grades have specified standards of dress, student council. Discipline rests primarily with faculty.
Summer Programs Sports programs offered; session focuses on lacrosse and field hockey; held on campus; accepts boys and girls; open to students from other schools. 160 students usually enrolled. 2009 schedule: June 22 to August 21. Application deadline: June 15.
Tuition and Aid Day student tuition: $22,980. Tuition installment plan (Insured Tuition Payment Plan, FACTS Tuition Payment Plan, monthly payment plans, individually arranged payment plans). Need-based scholarship grants available. In 2008–09, 30% of upper-school students received aid. Total amount of financial aid awarded in 2008–09: $1,000,000.
Admissions Traditional secondary-level entrance grade is 9. For fall 2008, 88 students applied for upper-level admission, 70 were accepted, 35 enrolled. SSAT required. Deadline for receipt of application materials: February 15. Application fee required: $50. On-campus interview required.
Athletics Interscholastic: baseball (boys), basketball (b,g), cross-country running (b,g), field hockey (g), lacrosse (b,g), sailing (b,g), soccer (b,g), softball (g), swimming and diving (b,g), tennis (b,g); intramural: dance (b,g), dance team (b,g), squash (b,g); coed interscholastic: cross-country running, golf, sailing, swimming and diving; coed intramural: dance, dance team, fishing, golf, squash. 2 PE instructors, 7 coaches, 1 athletic trainer.
Computers Computers are regularly used in all classes. Computer network features include on-campus library services, online commercial services, Internet access, wireless campus network, Internet filtering or blocking technology. Campus intranet, student e-mail accounts, and computer access in designated common areas are available to students. The school has a published electronic and media policy.
Contact Julie Way, Admission Office Counselor. 860-439-2756. Fax: 860-439-2796. E-mail: jway@williamsschool.org. Web site: www.williamsschool.org.

THE WILLISTON NORTHAMPTON SCHOOL

19 Payson Avenue
Easthampton, Massachusetts 01027

Head of School: Dr. Brian R. Wright

General Information Coeducational boarding and day college-preparatory school. Boarding grades 9–PG, day grades 7–12. Founded: 1841. Setting: small town. Nearest major city is Northampton. Students are housed in single-sex dormitories. 125-acre campus. 57 buildings on campus. Approved or accredited by Association of Independent Schools in New England, New England Association of Schools and Colleges, and The Association of Boarding Schools. Member of National Association of Independent Schools and Secondary School Admission Test Board. Endowment: $40 million. Total enrollment: 536. Upper school average class size: 13. Upper school faculty-student ratio: 1:7.
Upper School Student Profile Grade 9: 74 students (41 boys, 33 girls); Grade 10: 102 students (53 boys, 49 girls); Grade 11: 130 students (70 boys, 60 girls); Grade 12: 119 students (60 boys, 59 girls); Postgraduate: 14 students (12 boys, 2 girls). 60% of students are boarding students. 39% are state residents. 20 states are represented in upper school student body. 16% are international students. International students from Bermuda, China, Hong Kong, Republic of Korea, Taiwan, and Viet Nam; 17 other countries represented in student body.
Faculty School total: 90. In upper school: 41 men, 40 women; 60 have advanced degrees; 59 reside on campus.
Subjects Offered African-American history, algebra, American history, American literature, anatomy and physiology, animal behavior, art, art history, astronomy, biology, biology-AP, calculus, calculus-AP, chemistry, chemistry-AP, China/Japan history, Chinese, choral music, choreography, Christian and Hebrew scripture, comparative government and politics-AP, comparative politics, computer math, computer programming, computer science, computer science-AP, constitutional law, creative writing, dance, discrete mathematics, drama, economics, economics and history, economics-AP, English, English language-AP, English literature, English literature-AP, environmental science, ESL, ethics, European history, expository writing, fine arts, French, French language-AP, French literature-AP, French-AP, genetics, geometry, global studies, government/civics, health, history, history of jazz, honors algebra, honors English, honors geometry, Islamic studies, Latin, Latin American history, Latin-AP, mathematics, music, music theory, organic biochemistry, organic chemistry, philosophy, photography, photojournalism, physics, physics-AP, play production, playwriting, poetry, psychology, psychology-AP, religion, religion and culture, Russian history, science, sculpture, social studies, Spanish, Spanish language-AP, Spanish literature-AP, statistics-AP, theater, theology, trigonometry, U.S. history-AP, world history, world literature, writing workshop.
Graduation Requirements Arts and fine arts (art, music, dance, drama), English, foreign language, history, mathematics, philosophy, religion (includes Bible studies and theology), science.
Special Academic Programs Advanced Placement exam preparation; honors section; independent study; term-away projects; study abroad; academic accommodation for the gifted, the musically talented, and the artistically talented; special instructional classes for deaf students; ESL (6 students enrolled).
College Admission Counseling 142 students graduated in 2008; all went to college, including Bates College; Boston College; Boston University; Colby College; Connecticut College; University of Vermont.
Student Life Upper grades have specified standards of dress, student council, honor system. Discipline rests equally with students and faculty.
Summer Programs Sports, art/fine arts programs offered; session focuses on sports camps and summer theater; held on campus; accepts boys and girls; open to students from other schools. 2009 schedule: June 19 to August 19.
Tuition and Aid Day student tuition: $29,500; 7-day tuition and room/board: $42,000. Tuition installment plan (Academic Management Services Plan, Key Tuition Payment Plan). Need-based scholarship grants, need-based loans available. In 2008–09, 42% of upper-school students received aid. Total amount of financial aid awarded in 2008–09: $5,197,000.
Admissions Traditional secondary-level entrance grade is 9. For fall 2008, 673 students applied for upper-level admission, 275 were accepted, 122 enrolled. ACT, ISEE, PSAT or SAT for applicants to grade 11 and 12, SSAT or TOEFL required. Deadline for receipt of application materials: February 1. Application fee required: $50. Interview required.
Athletics Interscholastic: alpine skiing (boys, girls), baseball (b), basketball (b,g), crew (b,g), cross-country running (b,g), field hockey (g), football (b), golf (b,g), ice hockey (b,g), lacrosse (b,g), soccer (b,g), softball (g), squash (b,g), swimming and diving (b,g), tennis (b,g), track and field (b,g), volleyball (g), water polo (b,g), wrestling (b); intramural: self defense (g); coed interscholastic: dance, diving; coed intramural: aerobics, aerobics/dance, dance, dance team, equestrian sports, fitness, fly fishing, Frisbee, horseback riding, judo, martial arts, modern dance, mountain biking, snowboarding, weight lifting, weight training, yoga. 1 PE instructor, 5 coaches, 2 athletic trainers.
Computers Computers are regularly used in college planning, geography, graphic design, history, library, mathematics, newspaper, photography, photojournalism, programming, science, yearbook classes. Computer network features include on-campus library services, online commercial services, Internet access, wireless campus network, Internet filtering or blocking technology. Campus intranet, student e-mail accounts, and computer access in designated common areas are available to students. The school has a published electronic and media policy.
Contact Jeffrey E. Pilgrim, Associate Director of Admission. 413-529-3258. Fax: 413-527-9494. E-mail: admission@williston.com. Web site: www.williston.com.

See Close-Up on page 1028.

WILLOW HILL SCHOOL

Sudbury, Massachusetts
See Special Needs Schools section.

THE WILLOWS ACADEMY

1012 Thacker Street
Des Plaines, Illinois 60016

Head of School: Mary J. Keenley

General Information Girls' day college-preparatory, arts, religious studies, and technology school, affiliated with Roman Catholic Church. Grades 6–12. Founded: 1974. Setting: suburban. Nearest major city is Chicago. 4-acre campus. 1 building on campus. Approved or accredited by Illinois Department of Education. Total enrollment: 229. Upper school average class size: 18. Upper school faculty-student ratio: 1:10.
Upper School Student Profile Grade 9: 30 students (30 girls); Grade 10: 31 students (31 girls); Grade 11: 48 students (48 girls); Grade 12: 48 students (48 girls). 85% of students are Roman Catholic.

Faculty School total: 35. In upper school: 1 man, 23 women; 15 have advanced degrees.
Subjects Offered Algebra, American history, American literature, art, biology, calculus, chemistry, choir, choral music, computer graphics, computer programming, computer science, economics, English, English literature, ethics, European history, fine arts, four units of summer reading, French, geography, geometry, government/civics, grammar, health, history, Latin, mathematics, music, music history, music theory, philosophy, physical education, physics, pre-calculus, science, social studies, Spanish, statistics, theology, visual arts, vocal music, world history, world literature, writing.
Graduation Requirements Arts and fine arts (art, music, dance, drama), English, foreign language, four units of summer reading, mathematics, physical education (includes health), religion (includes Bible studies and theology), science, social studies (includes history), 40 hours of service work per year.
Special Academic Programs Advanced Placement exam preparation; honors section.
College Admission Counseling 48 students graduated in 2008; all went to college, including Marquette University; Northwestern University; Purdue University; University of Dallas; University of Illinois at Urbana–Champaign; University of Notre Dame. Mean composite ACT: 25.
Student Life Upper grades have uniform requirement, student council, honor system. Discipline rests primarily with faculty.
Summer Programs Enrichment, sports programs offered; session focuses on athletic camps and enrichment; held on campus; accepts girls; open to students from other schools. 30 students usually enrolled. 2009 schedule: June 1 to July 31. Application deadline: none.
Tuition and Aid Day student tuition: $12,300. Tuition installment plan (Insured Tuition Payment Plan, monthly payment plans, quarterly, semiannual, and annual payment plans). Tuition reduction for siblings, need-based scholarship grants available. In 2008–09, 30% of upper-school students received aid.
Admissions Traditional secondary-level entrance grade is 9. ISEE required. Deadline for receipt of application materials: none. Application fee required: $50. On-campus interview required.
Athletics Interscholastic: basketball, cross-country running, dance team, golf, soccer, softball, swimming and diving, track and field, volleyball. 1 PE instructor, 8 coaches.
Computers Computers are regularly used in mathematics, science classes. Computer network features include Internet access. Students grades are available online.
Contact Stephanie Sheffield, Director of Admissions. 847-824-6927. Fax: 847-824-7089. E-mail: sheffield@willows.org. Web site: www.willows.org.

WILLOW WOOD SCHOOL

55 Scarsdale Road
Don Mills, Ontario M3B 2R3, Canada

Head of School: Ms. Joy Kurtz

General Information Coeducational day college-preparatory, general academic, arts, and technology school; primarily serves students with learning disabilities, individuals with Attention Deficit Disorder, dyslexic students, and gifted students. Grades 1–12. Founded: 1980. Setting: suburban. Nearest major city is Toronto, Canada. 3-acre campus. 1 building on campus. Approved or accredited by Ontario Ministry of Education. Languages of instruction: English and French. Total enrollment: 216. Upper school average class size: 16. Upper school faculty-student ratio: 1:7.
Upper School Student Profile Grade 9: 30 students (25 boys, 5 girls); Grade 10: 25 students (20 boys, 5 girls); Grade 11: 32 students (24 boys, 8 girls); Grade 12: 38 students (30 boys, 8 girls).
Faculty School total: 35. In upper school: 9 men, 8 women; 4 have advanced degrees.
Subjects Offered 20th century world history, accounting, advanced chemistry, advanced math, algebra, ancient world history, applied arts, art, art history, biology, business applications, business mathematics, calculus, Canadian geography, Canadian history, Canadian law, Canadian literature, career and personal planning, chemistry, civics, computer applications, computer graphics, computer information systems, computer literacy, computer multimedia, computer science, creative writing, data processing, dramatic arts, economics, English, English composition, English literature, environmental science, ESL, family studies, finite math, French, geography, geometry, global issues, guidance, health education, history, independent study, journalism, keyboarding/computer, learning cognition classes, learning strategies, mathematics, media studies, medieval history, modern Western civilization, philosophy, physical education, physics, politics, psychology, reading/study skills, research skills, science and technology, social skills, society challenge and change, society, politics and law, Spanish, study skills, The 20th Century, visual arts, world history, world religions, yearbook.
Graduation Requirements Arts, business, Canadian geography, Canadian history, career education, civics, electives, English, French, history, mathematics, physical education (includes health), science, social sciences, Provincial Literacy Test requirement, community service hours.
Special Academic Programs Accelerated programs; independent study; study abroad; academic accommodation for the gifted and the artistically talented; remedial reading and/or remedial writing; remedial math; programs in English, mathematics, general development for dyslexic students; special instructional classes for students with learning disabilities and Attention Deficit Disorder; ESL (25 students enrolled).
College Admission Counseling 23 students graduated in 2008; 21 went to college, including Carleton University; McMaster University; Ryerson University; University of Toronto; York University. Other: 1 went to work, 1 had other specific plans.
Student Life Upper grades have uniform requirement, student council, honor system. Discipline rests primarily with faculty.
Summer Programs Remediation, enrichment, advancement, ESL, computer instruction programs offered; session focuses on acquiring secondary school credits; held on campus; accepts boys and girls; open to students from other schools. 40 students usually enrolled. 2009 schedule: July 6 to August 7. Application deadline: June 1.
Tuition and Aid Day student tuition: CAN$14,900. Tuition installment plan (individually arranged payment plans, 10% due upon acceptance; balance divided into three equal payments due June 1, October 1, December 1). Tuition reduction for siblings available.
Admissions Traditional secondary-level entrance grade is 9. For fall 2008, 20 students applied for upper-level admission, 15 were accepted, 15 enrolled. Achievement/Aptitude/Writing, Canada Quick Individual Educational Test, CTBS, Stanford Achievement Test, any other standardized test, Henmon-Nelson or writing sample required. Deadline for receipt of application materials: none. No application fee required. On-campus interview required.
Athletics Interscholastic: badminton (boys, girls), ball hockey (b,g), basketball (b,g), cooperative games (b,g), croquet (b,g), flag football (b,g), floor hockey (b,g), hockey (b), track and field (b,g), volleyball (b,g); intramural: ball hockey (b,g), basketball (b,g), cooperative games (b,g), flag football (b,g), floor hockey (b,g), track and field (b,g); coed interscholastic: badminton, ball hockey, baseball, bowling, cross-country running, curling, fitness walking, Frisbee, golf, indoor soccer, jogging, soccer, softball, table tennis, ultimate Frisbee, walking; coed intramural: badminton, ball hockey, baseball, fitness, fitness walking, indoor soccer, jogging, outdoor education, outdoor recreation, soccer, softball, strength & conditioning, table tennis, ultimate Frisbee, volleyball, walking. 2 PE instructors, 1 athletic trainer.
Computers Computers are regularly used in accounting, business applications, career exploration, college planning, creative writing, data processing, English, ESL, geography, graphic arts, independent study, learning cognition, publishing, remedial study skills, typing, Web site design, writing, yearbook classes. Computer network features include on-campus library services, online commercial services, Internet access, Internet filtering or blocking technology. Computer access in designated common areas is available to students. Students grades are available online. The school has a published electronic and media policy.
Contact Ms. Joy Kurtz, Principal. 416-444-7644. Fax: 416-444-1801. E-mail: joykurtz@willowwoodschool.ca. Web site: www.willowwoodschool.ca.

WILMINGTON FRIENDS SCHOOL

101 School Road
Wilmington, Delaware 19803

Head of School: Bryan K. Garman

General Information Coeducational day college-preparatory school, affiliated with Society of Friends. Grades PS–12. Founded: 1748. Setting: suburban. Nearest major city is Philadelphia, PA. 57-acre campus. 4 buildings on campus. Approved or accredited by Friends Council on Education, International Baccalaureate Organization, Middle States Association of Colleges and Schools, and Delaware Department of Education. Member of National Association of Independent Schools. Endowment: $17.5 million. Total enrollment: 836. Upper school average class size: 16. Upper school faculty-student ratio: 1:9.
Upper School Student Profile Grade 9: 62 students (25 boys, 37 girls); Grade 10: 70 students (29 boys, 41 girls); Grade 11: 56 students (30 boys, 26 girls); Grade 12: 71 students (35 boys, 36 girls). 5% of students are members of Society of Friends.
Faculty School total: 101. In upper school: 12 men, 15 women; 23 have advanced degrees.
Subjects Offered 3-dimensional art, advanced chemistry, algebra, American history, art, art history, Bible as literature, biology, calculus, chemistry, community service, computer art, computer programming, drama, driver education, earth science, economics, English, environmental science, ethics, European history, French, geometry, global science, history, history of the Americas, improvisation, independent study, integrated mathematics, Internet, jazz ensemble, journalism, mathematics, media studies, music, music theory, physical education, physics, pre-calculus, Quakerism and ethics, religion, science, social science, Spanish, studio art, theater, theater arts, Web site design, wellness, wind ensemble, world history.
Graduation Requirements Computer science, English, foreign language, mathematics, participation in sports, performing arts, religion (includes Bible studies and theology), science, service learning/internship, social science, visual arts, wellness, 50 hours of community service (single organization) before senior year.
Special Academic Programs International Baccalaureate program; 2 Advanced Placement exams for which test preparation is offered; honors section; independent study; term-away projects; study abroad; academic accommodation for the gifted, the musically talented, and the artistically talented.
College Admission Counseling 57 students graduated in 2008; 54 went to college, including Eckerd College; Emory University; Franklin & Marshall College; North-

eastern University; Swarthmore College; University of Delaware. Other: 1 entered a postgraduate year, 2 had other specific plans. Mean SAT critical reading: 603, mean SAT math: 596, mean SAT writing: 613, mean combined SAT: 1812, mean composite ACT: 26.

Student Life Upper grades have specified standards of dress, student council. Discipline rests primarily with faculty. Attendance at religious services is required.

Tuition and Aid Day student tuition: $19,775. Tuition installment plan (Tuition Management Systems (purchased Key Tuition Plan)). Need-based scholarship grants available. In 2008–09, 23% of upper-school students received aid. Total amount of financial aid awarded in 2008–09: $640,685.

Admissions Traditional secondary-level entrance grade is 9. For fall 2008, 61 students applied for upper-level admission, 29 were accepted, 14 enrolled. CTP and ERB required. Deadline for receipt of application materials: none. Application fee required: $40. On-campus interview required.

Athletics Interscholastic: baseball (boys), basketball (b,g), cross-country running (b,g), field hockey (g), football (b), lacrosse (b,g), soccer (b,g), swimming and diving (b,g), tennis (b,g), volleyball (g), wrestling (b); coed intramural: aerobics/Nautilus. 25 coaches, 1 athletic trainer.

Computers Computers are regularly used in art, English, library skills, literary magazine, mathematics, music, newspaper, science, social studies, yearbook classes. Computer network features include on-campus library services, Internet access, document storage, backup, and security, off-campus library services (catalog and book request), Blackbaud's Netcommunity and Netclassroom. The school has a published electronic and media policy.

Contact Ms. Kathleen Hopkins, Director of Admissions and Financial Aid. 302-576-2930. Fax: 302-576-2939. E-mail: khopkins@wilmingtonfriends.org. Web site: www.wilmingtonfriends.org.

WILSON HALL

520 Wilson Hall Road
Sumter, South Carolina 29150

Head of School: Mr. Frederick B. Moulton

General Information Coeducational day college-preparatory, arts, and technology school. Grades PS–12. Founded: 1966. Setting: small town. Nearest major city is Columbia. 17-acre campus. 6 buildings on campus. Approved or accredited by South Carolina Independent School Association, Southern Association of Colleges and Schools, Southern Association of Independent Schools, and South Carolina Department of Education. Endowment: $280,000. Total enrollment: 854. Upper school average class size: 20. Upper school faculty-student ratio: 1:13.

Upper School Student Profile Grade 9: 63 students (40 boys, 23 girls); Grade 10: 53 students (26 boys, 27 girls); Grade 11: 66 students (31 boys, 35 girls); Grade 12: 61 students (26 boys, 35 girls).

Faculty School total: 80. In upper school: 15 men, 27 women; 21 have advanced degrees.

Subjects Offered 3-dimensional design, algebra, anatomy, biology-AP, calculus-AP, chemistry-AP, computer applications, computer programming, computer programming-AP, drawing, economics, English, English language-AP, English literature-AP, environmental science, European history-AP, French, French language-AP, government, government-AP, journalism, Latin, Latin-AP, multimedia, music theory-AP, philosophy, physical education, physical science, physics-AP, pottery, Spanish, Spanish language-AP, studio art-AP, trigonometry, U.S. history-AP, world history.

Graduation Requirements Arts and fine arts (art, music, dance, drama), business skills (includes word processing), computer science, English, foreign language, mathematics, physical education (includes health), science, social studies (includes history), acceptance into four-year college or university, 20 hours community service.

Special Academic Programs Advanced Placement exam preparation; honors section.

College Admission Counseling 50 students graduated in 2008; all went to college, including Clemson University; College of Charleston; The Citadel, The Military College of South Carolina; University of South Carolina; University of Virginia; Wofford College. Median SAT critical reading: 586, median SAT math: 602.

Student Life Upper grades have specified standards of dress, honor system. Discipline rests primarily with faculty.

Summer Programs Enrichment, sports, art/fine arts, computer instruction programs offered; session focuses on enrichment; held on campus; accepts boys and girls; not open to students from other schools. 100 students usually enrolled. 2009 schedule: June 1 to July 15. Application deadline: May 20.

Tuition and Aid Day student tuition: $4940–$5340. Tuition installment plan (monthly payment plans). Need-based scholarship grants available. In 2008–09, 8% of upper-school students received aid. Total amount of financial aid awarded in 2008–09: $115,000.

Admissions Traditional secondary-level entrance grade is 9. For fall 2008, 150 students applied for upper-level admission, 114 were accepted, 113 enrolled. ACT, CTBS, OLSAT, Iowa Tests of Basic Skills, PSAT and SAT for applicants to grade 11 and 12, school's own test or Stanford Achievement Test, Otis-Lennon School Ability Test required. Deadline for receipt of application materials: none. Application fee required: $150. On-campus interview required.

Athletics Interscholastic: baseball (boys), basketball (b,g), bowling (b,g), cheering (g), cross-country running (b,g), football (b), golf (b), Nautilus (b,g), softball (g), strength & conditioning (b,g), swimming and diving (b,g), tennis (b,g), track and field (b,g), trap and skeet (b), volleyball (g), wrestling (b); intramural: equestrian sports (g), weight lifting (b,g), weight training (b,g); coed interscholastic: climbing, hiking/backpacking, mountain biking, outdoor adventure, outdoor education, paint ball, soccer; coed intramural: outdoor adventure, rafting, rock climbing, ropes courses. 3 PE instructors.

Computers Computers are regularly used in English, journalism, literary magazine, technology, yearbook classes. Computer network features include on-campus library services, online commercial services, Internet access, Internet filtering or blocking technology. The school has a published electronic and media policy.

Contact Sean Hoskins, Director of Admissions and Public Relations. 803-469-3475 Ext. 107. Fax: 803-469-3477. E-mail: sean_hoskins@hotmail.com. Web site: www.wilsonhall.org.

THE WINCHENDON SCHOOL

172 Ash Street
Winchendon, Massachusetts 01475

Head of School: J. William LaBelle

General Information Coeducational boarding and day college-preparatory, arts, and technology school; primarily serves underachievers, students with learning disabilities, and individuals with Attention Deficit Disorder. Grades 8–PG. Founded: 1926. Setting: small town. Nearest major city is Boston. Students are housed in single-sex by floor dormitories. 375-acre campus. 27 buildings on campus. Approved or accredited by Association of Independent Schools in New England, New England Association of Schools and Colleges, and The Association of Boarding Schools. Member of National Association of Independent Schools and Secondary School Admission Test Board. Endowment: $20 million. Total enrollment: 240. Upper school average class size: 8. Upper school faculty-student ratio: 1:8.

Upper School Student Profile Grade 8: 8 students (5 boys, 3 girls); Grade 9: 18 students (11 boys, 7 girls); Grade 10: 39 students (31 boys, 8 girls); Grade 11: 66 students (43 boys, 23 girls); Grade 12: 65 students (56 boys, 9 girls); Postgraduate: 44 students (42 boys, 2 girls). 90% of students are boarding students. 21% are state residents. 21 states are represented in upper school student body. 65% are international students. International students from Brazil, Canada, China, Japan, Republic of Korea, and Taiwan; 19 other countries represented in student body.

Faculty School total: 30. In upper school: 21 men, 9 women; 12 have advanced degrees; 26 reside on campus.

Subjects Offered Algebra, American history, American literature, anatomy, art, biology, calculus, ceramics, chemistry, computer programming, computer science, creative writing, drama, driver education, earth science, ecology, English, English literature, environmental science, ESL, European history, expository writing, French, geography, geometry, government/civics, grammar, health, history, mathematics, physical education, physics, physiology, psychology, science, social science, social studies, Spanish, speech, trigonometry, typing, world history, writing.

Graduation Requirements Computer science, English, mathematics, physical education (includes health), science, social science, social studies (includes history).

Special Academic Programs Advanced Placement exam preparation; academic accommodation for the gifted; remedial reading and/or remedial writing; remedial math; programs in English, mathematics for dyslexic students; special instructional classes for students with learning disabilities and Attention Deficit Disorder; ESL (100 students enrolled).

College Admission Counseling 98 students graduated in 2007; 93 went to college, including Bentley University; Boston University; Curry College; Northeastern University; Penn State University Park; University of Massachusetts Amherst. Other: 3 entered a postgraduate year, 2 had other specific plans. Median SAT critical reading: 510, median SAT math: 550. 3% scored over 600 on SAT critical reading, 5% scored over 600 on SAT math.

Student Life Upper grades have specified standards of dress, student council. Discipline rests primarily with faculty.

Tuition and Aid Day student tuition: $22,100; 7-day tuition and room/board: $36,900. Tuition installment plan (SMART Tuition Payment Plan). Tuition reduction for siblings, need-based scholarship grants available. In 2007–08, 37% of upper-school students received aid. Total amount of financial aid awarded in 2007–08: $2,000,000.

Admissions Traditional secondary-level entrance grade is 10. For fall 2007, 376 students applied for upper-level admission, 372 were accepted, 240 enrolled. Deadline for receipt of application materials: none. Application fee required: $50. Interview recommended.

Athletics Interscholastic: baseball (boys), basketball (b,g), ice hockey (b), lacrosse (b), soccer (b), tennis (b,g), volleyball (b,g); intramural: aerobics/dance (g), basketball (b,g), dance (g), ice skating (b,g), winter soccer (b); coed interscholastic: alpine skiing, bicycling, cross-country running, golf, running; coed intramural: aerobics, aerobics/Nautilus, alpine skiing, bicycling, cross-country running, equestrian sports, fitness, fitness walking, floor hockey, freestyle skiing, golf, horseback riding, in-line skating, indoor soccer, jogging, mountain biking, Nautilus, nordic skiing, outdoor activities, outdoor adventure, outdoor recreation, physical fitness, power lifting, running, skiing

(cross-country), skiing (downhill), snowboarding, snowshoeing, strength & conditioning, swimming and diving, tennis, ultimate Frisbee, volleyball, walking, weight lifting, weight training, winter walking.
Computers Computer network features include on-campus library services, Internet access, wireless campus network, Internet filtering or blocking technology. Campus intranet and student e-mail accounts are available to students.
Contact Ellyn Baldini, Director of Admissions. 978-297-4476. Fax: 978-297-0911. E-mail: admissions@winchendon.org. Web site: www.winchendon.org.

See Close-Up on page 1030.

WINCHESTER THURSTON SCHOOL

555 Morewood Avenue
Pittsburgh, Pennsylvania 15213-2899
Head of School: Mr. Gary J. Niels

General Information Coeducational day college-preparatory and arts school. Grades PK–12. Founded: 1887. Setting: urban. 5-acre campus. 2 buildings on campus. Approved or accredited by Middle States Association of Colleges and Schools, Pennsylvania Association of Independent Schools, The College Board, and Pennsylvania Department of Education. Member of National Association of Independent Schools. Endowment: $9 million. Total enrollment: 627. Upper school average class size: 13. Upper school faculty-student ratio; 1:7.
Upper School Student Profile Grade 6: 38 students (22 boys, 16 girls); Grade 7: 45 students (26 boys, 19 girls); Grade 8: 42 students (22 boys, 20 girls); Grade 9: 61 students (39 boys, 22 girls); Grade 10: 60 students (37 boys, 23 girls); Grade 11: 42 students (18 boys, 24 girls); Grade 12: 40 students (16 boys, 24 girls).
Faculty School total: 97. In upper school: 14 men, 17 women; 21 have advanced degrees.
Subjects Offered Algebra, American history, American history-AP, American literature, art, art history, biology, biology-AP, calculus, calculus-AP, ceramics, chemistry, choir, chorus, classics, composition-AP, computer programming, computer science, computer science-AP, creative writing, dance, drama, drawing, economics, economics-AP, English, English literature, English literature-AP, English-AP, European history, European history-AP, expository writing, filmmaking, French, French-AP, geometry, government/civics, health, history, journalism, Latin, Latin-AP, mathematics, music, music theory, philosophy, photography, physical education, physics, physics-AP, psychology, SAT preparation, science, social studies, Spanish, Spanish-AP, speech, statistics-AP, visual arts, world history, world literature, writing, yearbook.
Graduation Requirements Arts and fine arts (art, music, dance, drama), computer science, English, foreign language, mathematics, physical education (includes health), science, social studies (includes history), speech.
Special Academic Programs Advanced Placement exam preparation; independent study; term-away projects; study at local college for college credit; study abroad; academic accommodation for the gifted, the musically talented, and the artistically talented.
College Admission Counseling 44 students graduated in 2008; 43 went to college, including Boston University; Carnegie Mellon University; Oberlin College; The College of Wooster; University of Pennsylvania; University of Pittsburgh. Other: 1 entered a postgraduate year. Median SAT critical reading: 605, median SAT math: 595, median SAT writing: 620, median combined SAT: 1820. 60% scored over 600 on SAT critical reading, 52.5% scored over 600 on SAT math, 65% scored over 600 on SAT writing, 59.2% scored over 1800 on combined SAT.
Student Life Upper grades have specified standards of dress, student council. Discipline rests equally with students and faculty.
Summer Programs Enrichment, sports, art/fine arts programs offered; session focuses on adventure and play, sports and physical fitness, creative arts, and academics; held on campus; accepts boys and girls; open to students from other schools. 500 students usually enrolled. 2009 schedule: June 22 to July 31. Application deadline: May 15.
Tuition and Aid Day student tuition: $20,500–$21,800. Tuition installment plan (10-month payment plan managed by an outside company). Need-based scholarship grants available. In 2008–09, 39% of upper-school students received aid. Total amount of financial aid awarded in 2008–09: $1,085,000.
Admissions Traditional secondary-level entrance grade is 9. For fall 2008, 80 students applied for upper-level admission, 63 were accepted, 33 enrolled. CTP III, ISEE or writing sample required. Deadline for receipt of application materials: December 15. Application fee required: $50. Interview required.
Athletics Interscholastic: basketball (boys, girls), cross-country running (b,g), drill team (g), field hockey (g), lacrosse (b,g), rowing (b,g), running (b,g), tennis (g); intramural: squash (b); coed interscholastic: crew, fencing, golf, soccer; coed intramural: basketball, dance, Frisbee, golf, independent competitive sports, outdoor activities, physical fitness, physical training, soccer, strength & conditioning, weight training, winter soccer, yoga. 4 PE instructors, 20 coaches, 1 athletic trainer.
Computers Computers are regularly used in art, college planning, creative writing, English, foreign language, history, library, mathematics, music, photography, science, senior seminar, social studies, writing, writing, yearbook classes. Computer network features include on-campus library services, online commercial services, Internet access, wireless campus network, Internet filtering or blocking technology. Campus intranet, student e-mail accounts, and computer access in designated common areas are available to students. Students grades are available online. The school has a published electronic and media policy.
Contact Mr. Scot Lorenzi, Director of Upper School Admission. 412-578-3738. Fax: 412-578-7504. E-mail: lorenzis@winchesterthurston.org. Web site: www.winchesterthurston.org.

WINDERMERE PREPARATORY SCHOOL

6189 Winter Garden-Vineland Road
Windermere, Florida 34786
Head of School: Mr. William Ford

General Information Coeducational day college-preparatory, arts, and technology school. Grades PK–12. Founded: 2000. Setting: small town. Nearest major city is Orlando. 48-acre campus. 3 buildings on campus. Approved or accredited by Southern Association of Colleges and Schools and Florida Department of Education. Total enrollment: 817. Upper school average class size: 17. Upper school faculty-student ratio: 1:17.
Upper School Student Profile Grade 9: 50 students (25 boys, 25 girls); Grade 10: 37 students (21 boys, 16 girls); Grade 11: 28 students (9 boys, 19 girls); Grade 12: 20 students (7 boys, 13 girls).
Faculty School total: 75. In upper school: 6 men, 10 women; 10 have advanced degrees.
Subjects Offered 20th century history, 3-dimensional art, acting, Advanced Placement courses, algebra, American government, American history, American literature, art, biology, biology-AP, business, calculus, calculus-AP, chemistry, chemistry-AP, composition-AP, drama, drama performance, economics, economics-AP, electives, engineering, English, English composition, English language and composition-AP, English literature, English literature and composition-AP, ethics, French, geometry, honors algebra, honors English, honors U.S. history, honors world history, Latin, music, music theory, personal fitness, physical education, physics, physics-AP, pre-calculus, psychology, psychology-AP, Spanish, speech and debate, world history, world history-AP, yearbook.
Graduation Requirements Arts and fine arts (art, music, dance, drama), electives, English, foreign language, history, mathematics, performing arts, physical fitness, science, 6 additional elective credits. Community service is required.
Special Academic Programs International Baccalaureate program; 11 Advanced Placement exams for which test preparation is offered; academic accommodation for the musically talented and the artistically talented.
College Admission Counseling 8 students graduated in 2008; all went to college. Median SAT critical reading: 580, median SAT math: 616, median SAT writing: 573.
Student Life Upper grades have uniform requirement, student council, honor system. Discipline rests primarily with faculty.
Summer Programs Enrichment, sports, art/fine arts programs offered; session focuses on enrichment academics and athletics; held on campus; accepts boys and girls; open to students from other schools. 200 students usually enrolled. 2009 schedule: June to August. Application deadline: May.
Tuition and Aid Day student tuition: $13,000. Tuition installment plan (monthly payment plans). Need-based scholarship grants available. In 2008–09, 15% of upper-school students received aid. Total amount of financial aid awarded in 2008–09: $188,900.
Admissions Traditional secondary-level entrance grade is 9. For fall 2008, 38 students applied for upper-level admission, 34 were accepted, 29 enrolled. Achievement tests, PSAT or Stanford 9 required. Deadline for receipt of application materials: none. Application fee required: $100. Interview required.
Athletics Interscholastic: baseball (boys), basketball (b,g), cheering (g), golf (b,g), lacrosse (b), soccer (b,g), swimming and diving (b,g), tennis (b,g), track and field (b,g), volleyball (g); coed interscholastic: crew, cross-country running, golf, soccer, track and field; coed intramural: ballet, basketball, cheering, dance, equestrian sports, fencing, flag football, golf, lacrosse, running, soccer, softball, swimming and diving, tennis, track and field, volleyball. 5 PE instructors, 10 coaches.
Computers Computers are regularly used in all academic classes. Computer network features include on-campus library services, Internet access, wireless campus network, Internet filtering or blocking technology. Student e-mail accounts are available to students. Students grades are available online. The school has a published electronic and media policy.
Contact Mrs. Carol Riggs, Director of Admissions. 407-905-7737. Fax: 407-905-7710. E-mail: carol.riggs@windermereprep.com. Web site: www.windermereprep.com.

THE WINDSOR SCHOOL

Administration Building
136-23 Sanford Avenue
Flushing, New York 11355
Head of School: Mr. James Seery

General Information Coeducational day college-preparatory and arts school. Grades 6–PG. Founded: 1968. Setting: urban. Nearest major city is New York. 2-acre campus. 3 buildings on campus. Approved or accredited by Middle States Association of Colleges and Schools, New York Department of Education, New York State Association of Independent Schools, New York State Board of Regents, The College Board, and US Department of State. Total enrollment: 147. Upper school average class size: 14. Upper school faculty-student ratio: 1:14.

Upper School Student Profile Grade 9: 11 students (6 boys, 5 girls); Grade 10: 24 students (15 boys, 9 girls); Grade 11: 42 students (25 boys, 17 girls); Grade 12: 61 students (34 boys, 27 girls).

Faculty School total: 11. In upper school: 7 men, 4 women; 10 have advanced degrees.

Subjects Offered Advanced Placement courses, algebra, American history, American literature, art, basic skills, biology, business, business applications, calculus, ceramics, chemistry, computer programming, computer science, computer skills, computer studies, creative writing, driver education, economics, English, English literature, environmental science, ESL, European history, fine arts, French, geometry, government/civics, grammar, health, marketing, mathematics, music, physical education, physics, pre-calculus, psychology, science, social science, social studies, Spanish, trigonometry, world affairs, world history.

Graduation Requirements Arts and fine arts (art, music, dance, drama), English, foreign language, mathematics, physical education (includes health), science, social science, social studies (includes history).

Special Academic Programs Advanced Placement exam preparation; honors section; accelerated programs; independent study; academic accommodation for the gifted, the musically talented, and the artistically talented; remedial reading and/or remedial writing; remedial math; ESL (36 students enrolled).

College Admission Counseling 53 students graduated in 2008; 50 went to college, including Queens College of the City University of New York; St. John's University; State University of New York at Binghamton. Other: 3 went to work. Median SAT critical reading: 440, median SAT math: 550. 10% scored over 600 on SAT critical reading, 23% scored over 600 on SAT math.

Student Life Upper grades have specified standards of dress. Discipline rests primarily with faculty.

Summer Programs Remediation, enrichment, advancement, ESL, art/fine arts, computer instruction programs offered; session focuses on advancement, enrichment, remediation; held on campus; accepts boys and girls; open to students from other schools. 600 students usually enrolled. 2009 schedule: July 1 to August 18. Application deadline: June 30.

Tuition and Aid Day student tuition: $17,400. Tuition installment plan (individually arranged payment plans).

Admissions Traditional secondary-level entrance grade is 9. For fall 2008, 65 students applied for upper-level admission, 59 were accepted, 54 enrolled. School's own exam required. Deadline for receipt of application materials: none. No application fee required. On-campus interview required.

Athletics Interscholastic: basketball (boys, girls), soccer (b,g), softball (b,g); intramural: aerobics (b,g), basketball (b,g), cooperative games (b,g), fitness (b,g), jump rope (g), physical fitness (b,g), soccer (b,g), softball (b,g), tennis (b,g), volleyball (b,g); coed interscholastic: basketball, soccer, softball; coed intramural: basketball, fitness, jump rope, physical fitness, soccer, softball, table tennis, tennis, volleyball. 2 PE instructors, 2 coaches.

Computers Computers are regularly used in art, business applications, mathematics, research skills, typing, yearbook classes. Computer resources include Internet access.

Contact Dr. Philip A. Stewart, Director of Admissions. 718-359-8300. Fax: 718-359-1876. E-mail: admin@thewindsorschool.com. Web site: www.windsorschool.com.

WINDWARD SCHOOL

11350 Palms Boulevard
Los Angeles, California 90066

Head of School: Tom Gilder

General Information Coeducational day college-preparatory school. Grades 7–12. Founded: 1971. Setting: urban. 9-acre campus. 9 buildings on campus. Approved or accredited by California Association of Independent Schools and Western Association of Schools and Colleges. Member of National Association of Independent Schools. Total enrollment: 477. Upper school average class size: 16. Upper school faculty-student ratio: 1:7.

Upper School Student Profile Grade 9: 79 students (41 boys, 38 girls); Grade 10: 87 students (46 boys, 41 girls); Grade 11: 79 students (38 boys, 41 girls); Grade 12: 83 students (40 boys, 43 girls).

Faculty School total: 65. In upper school: 32 men, 27 women; 37 have advanced degrees.

Subjects Offered Algebra, American history, American literature, art, art history, biology, calculus, ceramics, chemistry, chorus, computer science, creative writing, dance, drama, English, English literature, environmental science, European history, fine arts, French, geometry, government/civics, health, history, Japanese, journalism, Latin, marine biology, mathematics, music, photography, physical education, physiology, science, social studies, Spanish, theater, trigonometry, world history.

Graduation Requirements Arts and fine arts (art, music, dance, drama), English, foreign language, mathematics, physical education (includes health), science, social studies (includes history).

Special Academic Programs Advanced Placement exam preparation; honors section; independent study; study at local college for college credit.

College Admission Counseling 79 students graduated in 2008; all went to college, including Boston College; New York University; University of California, Berkeley; University of Southern California; Wesleyan University. Mean SAT critical reading: 639, mean SAT math: 622, mean SAT writing: 641, mean combined SAT: 1902.

Student Life Upper grades have specified standards of dress, student council, honor system. Discipline rests primarily with faculty.

Summer Programs Sports programs offered; session focuses on skill development and team play; held on campus; accepts boys and girls; open to students from other schools. 75 students usually enrolled. 2009 schedule: June 22 to August 21.

Tuition and Aid Day student tuition: $29,110. Tuition installment plan (Key Tuition Payment Plan, monthly payment plans). Need-based scholarship grants, need-based loans available. In 2008–09, 12% of upper-school students received aid. Total amount of financial aid awarded in 2008–09: $941,310.

Admissions Traditional secondary-level entrance grade is 9. For fall 2008, 138 students applied for upper-level admission, 26 were accepted, 19 enrolled. ISEE required. Deadline for receipt of application materials: December 19. Application fee required: $100. On-campus interview required.

Athletics Interscholastic: baseball (boys), basketball (b,g), football (b); coed interscholastic: cross-country running, flag football, lacrosse. 5 PE instructors, 15 coaches, 2 athletic trainers.

Computers Computers are regularly used in art, English, history, mathematics, science classes. Computer network features include on-campus library services, online commercial services, Internet access, wireless campus network, Internet filtering or blocking technology. Student e-mail accounts are available to students. The school has a published electronic and media policy.

Contact Sharon Pearline, Director of Admissions. 310-391-7127. Fax: 310-397-5655.

See Close-Up on page 1032.

THE WINSOR SCHOOL

103 Pilgrim Road
Boston, Massachusetts 02215

Head of School: Mrs. Rachel Friis Stettler

General Information Girls' day college-preparatory school. Grades 5–12. Founded: 1886. Setting: urban. 8-acre campus. 2 buildings on campus. Approved or accredited by Association of Independent Schools in New England, New England Association of Schools and Colleges, and Massachusetts Department of Education. Member of National Association of Independent Schools. Endowment: $55.4 million. Total enrollment: 425. Upper school average class size: 13. Upper school faculty-student ratio: 1:7.

Upper School Student Profile Grade 9: 60 students (60 girls); Grade 10: 59 students (59 girls); Grade 11: 52 students (52 girls); Grade 12: 62 students (62 girls).

Faculty School total: 69. In upper school: 11 men, 52 women; 45 have advanced degrees.

Subjects Offered Acting, advanced studio art-AP, African history, African literature, algebra, architecture, art, art history, astronomy, biology, calculus, ceramics, chemistry, Chinese, Chinese literature, contemporary history, creative writing, digital art, drama, engineering, English, environmental science, expository writing, fine arts, French, geometry, health, Islamic history, Latin, Latin American history, literature, marine biology, Middle Eastern history, music, photography, physical education, physics, pre-calculus, psychology, Russian history, sculpture, Spanish, theater, U.S. history, U.S. literature.

Graduation Requirements Algebra, art, biology, English, European history, French, geometry, Latin, physical education (includes health), Spanish, U.S. history.

Special Academic Programs Advanced Placement exam preparation; honors section.

College Admission Counseling 63 students graduated in 2008; all went to college, including Amherst College; Boston College; Brown University; Columbia College; Harvard University; The George Washington University. Median SAT critical reading: 700, median SAT math: 680, median SAT writing: 730, median combined SAT: 2100. 95% scored over 600 on SAT critical reading, 92% scored over 600 on SAT math, 100% scored over 600 on SAT writing.

Student Life Upper grades have specified standards of dress, student council, honor system. Discipline rests primarily with faculty.

Tuition and Aid Day student tuition: $30,500. Tuition installment plan (Academic Management Services Plan, FACTS Tuition Payment Plan, individually arranged payment plans). Need-based scholarship grants available. In 2008–09, 20% of upper-school students received aid. Total amount of financial aid awarded in 2008–09: $1,163,898.

Admissions Traditional secondary-level entrance grade is 9. For fall 2008, 133 students applied for upper-level admission, 21 were accepted, 10 enrolled. ISEE or SSAT required. Deadline for receipt of application materials: December 17. Application fee required: $45. On-campus interview required.

Athletics Interscholastic: basketball, crew, cross-country running, field hockey, ice hockey, lacrosse, sailing, soccer, softball, squash, swimming and diving, tennis, track and field. 4 PE instructors, 3 coaches, 1 athletic trainer.

Computers Computers are regularly used in photography, programming classes. Computer network features include on-campus library services, Internet access, wireless campus network, Internet filtering or blocking technology. Student e-mail accounts are available to students. The school has a published electronic and media policy.
Contact Mrs. Pamela Parks McLaurin, Director of Admission. 617-735-9503. Fax: 617-912-1381. Web site: www.winsor.edu/.

ANNOUNCEMENT FROM THE SCHOOL Founded in 1886 by Mary Pickard Winsor, the Winsor School is an independent day school for academically motivated and promising girls in grades 5–12. Winsor offers a rigorous academic program balanced by the arts and physical education in an environment of warmth and personal attention. Winsor is set on a 7-acre campus in Boston, and makes frequent use of the city's resources. Facilities include a renovated library with 27,000 volumes plus access to 850 periodicals, a multimedia language lab, three computer labs, three art studios, eight science laboratories, acres of playing fields, tennis courts, and a gymnasium. The Lower School comprises grades 5 through 8. In this supportive environment, teachers foster natural curiosity through active, hands-on lessons. The Upper School is an energetic learning community of students in grades 9 through 12. The faculty encourages girls to think logically, creatively, and compassionately and to take increasing responsibility for their own learning. At all levels, students enjoy dedicated, caring teachers who know their subjects intimately. "Global citizenship is a core part of the School's philosophy; international exchanges, service learning, and other programs augment the lessons within courses and open girls' eyes to the world." Beyond the classroom, clubs, the arts, and sports offer ways for girls to explore interests. Winsor offers teams in fourteen sports and has more than thirty clubs. Girls approach extracurriculars passionately and have won national honors in crew, debate, engineering, and choral competitions. Girls also work with boys from the Belmont Hill and Roxbury Latin schools on coordinated drama, music, and newspaper activities. The majority of students go on to attend the most selective colleges and universities. Experienced college counselors guide and support girls through the process. In the last five years, the students' most common college choices were Boston College, Brown, Columbia, Dartmouth, Harvard, MIT, Princeton, Yale, and the University of Pennsylvania. As a community, Winsor cherishes respect and generosity of spirit and its mission underscores a commitment to diversity. Its size means girls build lasting friendships, and it encourages each girl to realize her own uniqueness and promise.

WINSTON PREPARATORY SCHOOL
New York, New York
See Special Needs Schools section.

THE WINSTON SCHOOL
Dallas, Texas
See Special Needs Schools section.

THE WINSTON SCHOOL SAN ANTONIO
San Antonio, Texas
See Special Needs Schools section.

WISCONSIN ACADEMY
N2355 DuBorg Road
Columbus, Wisconsin 53925
Head of School: Mr. Marshall W. Bowers

General Information Coeducational boarding and day college-preparatory, general academic, and religious studies school, affiliated with Seventh-day Adventist Church. Grades 9–12. Founded: 1950. Setting: rural. Nearest major city is Madison. Students are housed in single-sex dormitories. 50-acre campus. 7 buildings on campus. Approved or accredited by Board of Regents, General Conference of Seventh-day Adventists, North Central Association of Colleges and Schools, and Wisconsin Department of Education. Endowment: $100,000. Total enrollment: 108. Upper school average class size: 30. Upper school faculty-student ratio: 1:6.
Upper School Student Profile 90% of students are boarding students. 88% are state residents. 5 states are represented in upper school student body. 3% are international students. 85% of students are Seventh-day Adventists.
Faculty School total: 15. In upper school: 9 men, 5 women; 5 have advanced degrees; all reside on campus.
Subjects Offered Advanced math, algebra, American government, American history, American literature, anatomy and physiology, art, bell choir, Bible, biology, chemistry, choir, chorus, composition, computer applications, computer graphics, computer keyboarding, computer literacy, driver education, economics, English, English-AP, general math, geography, geometry, guitar, gymnastics, handbells, health, home economics, newspaper, photo shop, physical education, physical science, physics, piano, pre-algebra, pre-calculus, religion, Spanish, work-study.
Graduation Requirements Algebra, American government, American history, American literature, Bible, biology, computer literacy, computer skills, English, foreign language, geometry, lab/keyboard, physical education (includes health), science, social studies (includes history), U.S. government.
College Admission Counseling 30 students graduated in 2008; 21 went to college. Other: 6 went to work, 3 had other specific plans.
Student Life Upper grades have specified standards of dress, student council, honor system. Discipline rests primarily with faculty. Attendance at religious services is required.
Tuition and Aid Day student tuition: $8450; 7-day tuition and room/board: $13,470. Tuition installment plan (monthly payment plans, individually arranged payment plans). Tuition reduction for siblings, need-based scholarship grants, paying campus jobs available. In 2008–09, 55% of upper-school students received aid. Total amount of financial aid awarded in 2008–09: $190,000.
Admissions Traditional secondary-level entrance grade is 9. For fall 2008, 102 students applied for upper-level admission, 102 were accepted, 91 enrolled. Iowa Test, CTBS, or TAP or TOEFL required. Deadline for receipt of application materials: none. No application fee required. Interview recommended.
Athletics Intramural: basketball (boys, girls), flag football (b,g), flagball (b,g), floor hockey (b,g), soccer (b,g), softball (b,g), volleyball (b,g); coed intramural: volleyball. 1 PE instructor.
Computers Computers are regularly used in all academic classes. Computer resources include on-campus library services, Internet access, Internet filtering or blocking technology. Student e-mail accounts are available to students. Students grades are available online. The school has a published electronic and media policy.
Contact Mrs. Stephanie Gottfried, Registrar. 920-623-3300 Ext. 13. Fax: 920-623-3318. E-mail: registrar@wisacad.org. Web site: www.wisacad.org.

WOODBERRY FOREST SCHOOL
10 Woodberry Station
Woodberry Forest, Virginia 22989

ANNOUNCEMENT FROM THE SCHOOL Woodberry Forest School is one of the nation's leading boarding schools for boys. Founded in 1889, this traditional, highly selective school educates nearly 400 boys in grades 9 through 12 from thirty-one states and eight other countries. Woodberry has recently opened Dowd-Finch, a state-of-the-art dormitory; Johnson Stadium, a new home for football and lacrosse; a climate-controlled squash pavilion; and the Class of 2006 Track and Field Complex, featuring an eight-lane, NCAA-quality track and Bermuda grass field. The School has also installed two new artificial turf playing fields.

See Close-Up on page 1034.

THE WOODHALL SCHOOL
58 Harrison Lane
Bethlehem, Connecticut 06751
Head of School: Matthew C. Woodhall

General Information Boys' boarding and day college-preparatory, arts, and ESL school. Grades 9–PG. Founded: 1982. Setting: rural. Nearest major city is Hartford. Students are housed in single-sex dormitories. 40-acre campus. 10 buildings on campus. Approved or accredited by Association of Independent Schools in New England, Connecticut Association of Independent Schools, New England Association of Schools and Colleges, and Connecticut Department of Education. Member of National Association of Independent Schools. Endowment: $120,000. Total enrollment: 42. Upper school average class size: 4. Upper school faculty-student ratio: 1:4.
Upper School Student Profile Grade 9: 8 students (8 boys); Grade 10: 16 students (16 boys); Grade 11: 10 students (10 boys); Grade 12: 8 students (8 boys). 100% of students are boarding students. 12% are state residents. 14 states are represented in upper school student body. 10% are international students. International students from El Salvador, Hong Kong, Philippines, and United Kingdom.
Faculty School total: 17. In upper school: 13 men, 4 women; 11 have advanced degrees; 14 reside on campus.
Subjects Offered Algebra, American history, anatomy, art, biology, calculus, chemistry, comparative government and politics, drama, English, environmental science, geometry, Greek, language and composition, Latin, physics, pre-calculus, Spanish, world civilizations.
Graduation Requirements Arts and fine arts (art, music, dance, drama), communication skills, English, foreign language, mathematics, physical education (includes health), science, social studies (includes history).

Special Academic Programs Advanced Placement exam preparation; independent study; special instructional classes for students with Attention Deficit Disorder and non-verbal learning disabilities; ESL.

College Admission Counseling 13 students graduated in 2007; all went to college, including Guilford College; Hartwick College; Mount Ida College; Northeastern University; Queen's University at Kingston; University of Vermont. Median SAT critical reading: 652, median SAT math: 500, median SAT writing: 569, median combined SAT: 574.

Student Life Upper grades have specified standards of dress, student council, honor system. Discipline rests primarily with faculty.

Tuition and Aid Day student tuition: $40,500; 7-day tuition and room/board: $52,000. Tuition installment plan (individually arranged payment plans).

Admissions Traditional secondary-level entrance grade is 10. For fall 2007, 34 students applied for upper-level admission, 25 were accepted, 18 enrolled. Deadline for receipt of application materials: none. Application fee required: $100. On-campus interview required.

Athletics Interscholastic: basketball, cross-country running, lacrosse, soccer; intramural: alpine skiing, basketball, bicycling, billiards, bowling, canoeing/kayaking, cross-country running, fishing, fitness, fitness walking, Frisbee, hiking/backpacking, ice skating, jogging, lacrosse, mountain biking, outdoor activities, outdoor education, outdoor recreation, physical fitness, physical training, rafting, running, skiing (cross-country), skiing (downhill), snowboarding, soccer, street hockey, strength & conditioning, table tennis, volleyball, walking, weight lifting, winter walking.

Computers Computers are regularly used in art, English, foreign language, history, mathematics, science, social science classes. Computer resources include Internet access. The school has a published electronic and media policy.

Contact Matthew C. Woodhall, Head of School. 203-266-7788. Fax: 203-266-5896. E-mail: mwoodhall@woodhallschool.org. Web site: www.woodhallschool.org.

ANNOUNCEMENT FROM THE SCHOOL Woodhall School's individualized approach includes an interpersonal component that recognizes the psychological aspects of education and that permeates all areas of the school—academics, communications, athletics, and student life. Unique to Woodhall, the Communications Program offers students and teachers the opportunity to be accountable to each other and to act with compassion, integrity, and respect.

WOODLANDS ACADEMY OF THE SACRED HEART

760 East Westleigh Road
Lake Forest, Illinois 60045-3298

Head of School: Mr. Gerald Grossman

General Information Girls' boarding and day college-preparatory, arts, technology, and music school, affiliated with Roman Catholic Church. Grades 9–12. Founded: 1858. Setting: suburban. Nearest major city is Chicago. Students are housed in single-sex dormitories. 20-acre campus. 1 building on campus. Approved or accredited by Independent Schools Association of the Central States, Network of Sacred Heart Schools, North Central Association of Colleges and Schools, The Association of Boarding Schools, and Illinois Department of Education. Endowment: $6 million. Total enrollment: 166. Upper school average class size: 15. Upper school faculty-student ratio: 1:9.

Upper School Student Profile Grade 9: 35 students (35 girls); Grade 10: 46 students (46 girls); Grade 11: 49 students (49 girls); Grade 12: 36 students (36 girls). 30% of students are boarding students. 58% are state residents. 6 states are represented in upper school student body. 30% are international students. International students from Canada, Japan, Mexico, Republic of Korea, Taiwan, and Thailand; 9 other countries represented in student body. 67% of students are Roman Catholic.

Faculty School total: 34. In upper school: 5 men, 29 women; 26 have advanced degrees; 3 reside on campus.

Subjects Offered Algebra, American history, American literature, anatomy, art, art history, Bible studies, biology, calculus, ceramics, chemistry, chorus, computer math, computer programming, computer science, creative writing, drama, drawing, driver education, earth science, English, English literature, ESL, ethics, European history, expository writing, fine arts, French, geometry, government/civics, grammar, health, history, Japanese, Latin, Mandarin, mathematics, music, painting, philosophy, photography, physical education, physical science, physics, physiology, psychology, religion, Russian, Russian history, science, social studies, sociology, Spanish, speech, theater, theology, trigonometry, world history, world literature, writing.

Graduation Requirements Arts and fine arts (art, music, dance, drama), English, foreign language, mathematics, physical education (includes health), religion (includes Bible studies and theology), science, social studies (includes history). Community service is required.

Special Academic Programs Advanced Placement exam preparation; honors section; study at local college for college credit; domestic exchange program; study abroad; academic accommodation for the gifted; ESL (15 students enrolled).

College Admission Counseling 50 students graduated in 2008; all went to college, including Boston College; Georgetown University; Princeton University; University of Notre Dame; University of Pennsylvania; Washington University in St. Louis.

Student Life Upper grades have uniform requirement, student council. Discipline rests equally with students and faculty. Attendance at religious services is required.

Tuition and Aid Day student tuition: $17,710; 7-day tuition and room/board: $35,310. Tuition installment plan (Academic Management Services Plan, monthly payment plans, individually arranged payment plans). Merit scholarship grants, need-based scholarship grants, need-based loans available. In 2008–09, 27% of upper-school students received aid.

Admissions Traditional secondary-level entrance grade is 9. For fall 2008, 95 students applied for upper-level admission, 72 were accepted, 60 enrolled. SSAT, ERB, PSAT, SAT, PLAN or ACT required. Deadline for receipt of application materials: none. Application fee required: $50. Interview required.

Athletics Interscholastic: basketball, crew, field hockey, golf; intramural: aerobics/dance, dance. 2 PE instructors, 5 coaches.

Computers Computers are regularly used in English, foreign language, mathematics, science classes. Computer network features include on-campus library services, online commercial services, Internet access.

Contact Kathleen Creed, Director of Admission and Financial Aid. 847-234-4300 Ext. 213. Fax: 847-234-0865. E-mail: admissions@woodlands.lfc.edu. Web site: www.woodlands.lfc.edu.

See Close-Up on page 1036.

WOODSIDE PRIORY SCHOOL

302 Portola Road
Founders Hall
Portola Valley, California 94028

Head of School: Mr. Tim J. Molak

General Information Coeducational boarding and day college-preparatory, arts, religious studies, and technology school, affiliated with Roman Catholic Church. Boarding grades 9–12, day grades 6–12. Founded: 1957. Setting: suburban. Nearest major city is San Francisco. Students are housed in single-sex dormitories. 50-acre campus. 25 buildings on campus. Approved or accredited by California Association of Independent Schools, National Catholic Education Association, The Association of Boarding Schools, The College Board, Western Association of Schools and Colleges, Western Catholic Education Association, and California Department of Education. Member of National Association of Independent Schools and Secondary School Admission Test Board. Endowment: $10 million. Total enrollment: 352. Upper school average class size: 18. Upper school faculty-student ratio: 1:10.

Upper School Student Profile Grade 9: 68 students (36 boys, 32 girls); Grade 10: 56 students (27 boys, 29 girls); Grade 11: 70 students (37 boys, 33 girls); Grade 12: 63 students (34 boys, 29 girls). 14% of students are boarding students. 85% are state residents. 4 states are represented in upper school student body. 10% are international students. International students from China, Hungary, India, Lithuania, Republic of Korea, and Taiwan; 10 other countries represented in student body. 40% of students are Roman Catholic.

Faculty School total: 70. In upper school: 28 men, 27 women; 48 have advanced degrees; 30 reside on campus.

Subjects Offered 20th century physics, 3-dimensional art, acting, advanced chemistry, advanced computer applications, advanced math, algebra, American democracy, American government, American history, American literature, analysis and differential calculus, animation, architecture, art, art history, art-AP, ASB Leadership, astronomy, Basic programming, biology, biology-AP, British literature, calculus, calculus-AP, ceramics, chemistry, chemistry-AP, choir, choral music, Christian and Hebrew scripture, church history, classics, college admission preparation, college counseling, community garden, community service, comparative cultures, computer applications, computer art, computer graphics, computer keyboarding, computer math, computer programming, computer science, computer science-AP, computer technologies, computers, constitutional history of U.S., contemporary issues, creative arts, creative writing, desktop publishing, drama, drama performance, earth and space science, earth science, ecology, economics, economics-AP, English, English composition, English literature, English literature-AP, English-AP, environmental science-AP, ethics, European history, European history-AP, expository writing, fine arts, French, French-AP, geography, geometry, government/civics, grammar, health and wellness, history of ideas, honors English, humanities, Japanese, journalism, Latin, life science, mathematics, music, music appreciation, music performance, peer counseling, personal fitness, philosophy, photography, physical education, physics, physics-AP, play production, portfolio art, pre-algebra, pre-calculus, probability and statistics, psychology, religion, science, social science, social studies, sociology, Spanish, Spanish language-AP, Spanish literature-AP, speech, studio art-AP, theater, theology, trigonometry, typing, U.S. history-AP, world history, world literature, writing.

Graduation Requirements Algebra, arts and fine arts (art, music, dance, drama), biology, British literature, calculus, chemistry, Christian and Hebrew scripture, comparative religion, computer science, earth science, English, environmental science, expository writing, foreign language, geometry, mathematics, physical education (includes health), physics, science, social science, social studies (includes history), theology. Community service is required.

Special Academic Programs Advanced Placement exam preparation; honors section; independent study; academic accommodation for the gifted, the musically talented, and the artistically talented.

College Admission Counseling 65 students graduated in 2008; all went to college, including Princeton University; Santa Clara University; Stanford University; University of California, Berkeley; University of California, Los Angeles; Yale University.

Student Life Upper grades have specified standards of dress, student council, honor system. Discipline rests equally with students and faculty.

Tuition and Aid Day student tuition: $29,950; 7-day tuition and room/board: $42,500. Tuition installment plan (monthly payment plans, individually arranged payment plans). Merit scholarship grants, need-based scholarship grants available. In 2008–09, 20% of upper-school students received aid. Total amount of financial aid awarded in 2008–09: $1,600,000.

Admissions Traditional secondary-level entrance grade is 9. For fall 2008, 227 students applied for upper-level admission, 115 were accepted, 55 enrolled. High School Placement Test (closed version) from Scholastic Testing Service, ISEE, PSAT or SAT for applicants to grade 11 and 12, SLEP for foreign students, SSAT, TOEFL or writing sample required. Deadline for receipt of application materials: January 15. Application fee required: $75. On-campus interview required.

Athletics Interscholastic: baseball (boys), basketball (b,g), cross-country running (b,g), flag football (b), football (b), golf (b,g), soccer (b,g), softball (g), swimming and diving (g), track and field (b,g), volleyball (g), water polo (b); intramural: alpine skiing (b,g); coed interscholastic: cross-country running, dance, golf, outdoor education, tennis; coed intramural: alpine skiing, bowling, canoeing/kayaking, cross-country running, fitness, ropes courses. 4 PE instructors, 10 coaches, 1 athletic trainer.

Computers Computers are regularly used in all academic, animation, art, college planning, drafting, library, literary magazine, media arts, research skills, senior seminar, study skills, technology, yearbook classes. Computer network features include on-campus library services, online commercial services, Internet access, wireless campus network, Internet filtering or blocking technology. Campus intranet and student e-mail accounts are available to students. Students grades are available online. The school has a published electronic and media policy.

Contact Mr. Al D. Zappelli, Dean of Admissions and Financial Aid. 650-851-8223 Ext. 101. Fax: 650-851-2839. E-mail: azappelli@PrioryCA.org. Web site: www.PrioryCA.org.

See Close-Up on page 1038.

WOODSTOCK SCHOOL

Mussoorie
Uttarakhand 248 179, India

Head of School: Dr. David Laurenson

General Information Coeducational boarding and day college-preparatory, music, and science school, affiliated with Christian faith. Boarding grades 3–12, day grades N–12. Founded: 1854. Setting: rural. Nearest major city is New Delhi, India. Students are housed in single-sex dormitories. 290-acre campus. 6 buildings on campus. Approved or accredited by Middle States Association of Colleges and Schools and New York State Association of Independent Schools. Member of European Council of International Schools. Language of instruction: English. Total enrollment: 475. Upper school average class size: 15. Upper school faculty-student ratio: 1:15.

Upper School Student Profile Grade 9: 61 students (33 boys, 28 girls); Grade 10: 67 students (30 boys, 37 girls); Grade 11: 69 students (37 boys, 32 girls); Grade 12: 76 students (34 boys, 42 girls). 95% of students are boarding students. 62% are international students. International students from Canada, Democratic People's Republic of Korea, Japan, Nepal, Thailand, and United States; 17 other countries represented in student body. 47% of students are Christian.

Faculty School total: 65. In upper school: 18 men, 15 women; 15 have advanced degrees; 55 reside on campus.

Subjects Offered Algebra, American history, American history-AP, American literature, American studies, art, art history, Asian studies, Bible, Bible studies, biology, biology-AP, calculus, calculus-AP, ceramics, chemistry, chemistry-AP, choir, choral music, Christianity, community service, comparative religion, computer science, concert band, drama, economics, English, English language-AP, English literature, English-AP, environmental science, environmental science-AP, ethics, European history, fine arts, French, French-AP, geometry, government, government and politics-AP, health education, Hindi, Indian studies, jazz band, journalism, macro/microeconomics-AP, macroeconomics-AP, mathematics, mathematics-AP, microeconomics-AP, music, philosophy, physical education, physics, physics-AP, religion, science, social studies, theater, trigonometry, U.S. government and politics-AP, vocal music, world history, world history-AP, world literature, world religions, writing, yearbook.

Graduation Requirements Arts and fine arts (art, music, dance, drama), Christian studies, computer literacy, English, foreign language, mathematics, physical education (includes health), science, social studies (includes history). Community service is required.

Special Academic Programs Advanced Placement exam preparation; independent study; study abroad; academic accommodation for the gifted, the musically talented, and the artistically talented; ESL (25 students enrolled).

College Admission Counseling 77 students graduated in 2008; they went to Barnard College; Carleton College; Embry-Riddle Aeronautical University; Georgia Institute of Technology; University of Illinois at Urbana–Champaign; University of Waterloo. Other: 4 had other specific plans. Median SAT critical reading: 510, median SAT math: 570, median SAT writing: 530, median combined SAT: 1610, median composite ACT: 24. 15% scored over 600 on SAT critical reading, 36% scored over 600 on SAT math, 20% scored over 600 on SAT writing, 19% scored over 1800 on combined SAT, 33% scored over 26 on composite ACT.

Student Life Upper grades have specified standards of dress, student council. Discipline rests primarily with faculty. Attendance at religious services is required.

Tuition and Aid Day student tuition: $16,795; 7-day tuition and room/board: $16,795. Tuition installment plan (individually arranged payment plans). Need-based scholarship grants available. In 2008–09, 20% of upper-school students received aid.

Admissions Traditional secondary-level entrance grade is 11. For fall 2008, 400 students applied for upper-level admission, 75 were accepted, 64 enrolled. TOEFL or SLEP required. Deadline for receipt of application materials: none. Application fee required: $75. Interview recommended.

Athletics Interscholastic: basketball (boys, girls), cricket (b), cross-country running (b,g), field hockey (b,g), track and field (b,g); intramural: backpacking (b,g), badminton (b,g), basketball (b,g), climbing (b,g), cricket (b), cross-country running (b,g), field hockey (b,g), gymnastics (b,g), hiking/backpacking (b,g), hockey (b,g), outdoor activities (b,g), outdoor education (b,g), running (b,g), soccer (b,g), table tennis (b,g), tennis (b,g), track and field (b,g); coed intramural: backpacking, hiking/backpacking, outdoor education. 3 PE instructors.

Computers Computers are regularly used in all academic classes. Computer network features include on-campus library services, Internet access, Internet filtering or blocking technology. Campus intranet, student e-mail accounts, and computer access in designated common areas are available to students. Students grades are available online. The school has a published electronic and media policy.

Contact Ms. Cathy E. Holmes, Director of Admissions. 91-135-2632547 Ext. 104. Fax: 91-135-2630897. E-mail: admissions@woodstock.ac.in. Web site: www.woodstock.ac.in.

WOODWARD ACADEMY

1662 Rugby Avenue
College Park, Georgia 30337

Head of School: Mr. Ron McCollum

General Information Coeducational day college-preparatory and arts school. Grades PK–12. Founded: 1900. Setting: suburban. Nearest major city is Atlanta. 90-acre campus. 50 buildings on campus. Approved or accredited by Georgia Independent School Association, Southern Association of Colleges and Schools, and Georgia Department of Education. Member of National Association of Independent Schools and Secondary School Admission Test Board. Endowment: $99 million. Total enrollment: 2,924. Upper school average class size: 17.

Faculty School total: 340. In upper school: 45 men, 68 women; 85 have advanced degrees.

Subjects Offered 20th century world history, 3-dimensional art, 3-dimensional design, acting, Advanced Placement courses, algebra, American government, American government-AP, American history, American history-AP, anatomy and physiology, art, astronomy, audio visual/media, band, biology, biology-AP, calculus, calculus-AP, ceramics, chemistry, chemistry-AP, choir, choral music, chorus, comparative religion, computer education, computer programming, computer programming-AP, computer science, computer science-AP, concert band, contemporary history, contemporary issues, creative writing, dance, debate, digital music, drama, drama performance, drawing, drawing and design, earth science, ecology, economics, economics and history, economics-AP, English, English language and composition-AP, English literature, English literature and composition-AP, English-AP, environmental science, environmental science-AP, European history, European history-AP, fine arts, French, French language-AP, French-AP, geography, geometry, government and politics-AP, government/civics, grammar, health, history, history-AP, honors English, honors geometry, honors U.S. history, honors world history, independent study, Japanese, jewelry making, journalism, Latin, literature and composition-AP, marching band, marine ecology, mathematics, meteorology, microeconomics-AP, Middle East, modern European history-AP, multicultural literature, music, oceanography, performing arts, personal fitness, photography, physical education, physics, physics-AP, pre-calculus, science, social studies, Spanish, Spanish language-AP, Spanish-AP, speech communications, statistics, statistics and probability, statistics-AP, television, the Sixties, theater, trigonometry, U.S. government and politics, U.S. government and politics-AP, U.S. government-AP, U.S. history, U.S. history-AP, video, voice ensemble, world history, world literature, world religions, yearbook.

Graduation Requirements Arts and fine arts (art, music, dance, drama), computer science, English, foreign language, mathematics, physical education (includes health), religion (includes Bible studies and theology), science, social studies (includes history).

Special Academic Programs Advanced Placement exam preparation; honors section; independent study.

College Admission Counseling 243 students graduated in 2008; all went to college, including Auburn University; Georgia Institute of Technology; University of Georgia; University of Michigan; Vanderbilt University.
Student Life Upper grades have uniform requirement, student council, honor system. Discipline rests primarily with faculty.
Tuition and Aid Day student tuition: $19,100. Tuition installment plan (Key Tuition Payment Plan). Need-based scholarship grants available. In 2008–09, 10% of upper-school students received aid. Total amount of financial aid awarded in 2008–09: $1,600,000.
Admissions Traditional secondary-level entrance grade is 9. SSAT required. Deadline for receipt of application materials: February 27. Application fee required: $75. On-campus interview required.
Athletics Interscholastic: baseball (boys), basketball (b,g), cheering (g), cross-country running (b,g), diving (b,g), football (b), golf (b,g), lacrosse (b,g), soccer (b,g), softball (g), swimming and diving (b,g), tennis (b,g), track and field (b,g), volleyball (g); intramural: basketball (b,g), cheering (g), football (b), soccer (b,g), softball (g), swimming and diving (b,g), tennis (b,g), track and field (b,g), volleyball (g); coed interscholastic: Frisbee, power lifting, ultimate Frisbee, weight lifting; coed intramural: fencing, horseback riding. 4 PE instructors, 34 coaches, 1 athletic trainer.
Computers Computers are regularly used in creative writing, English, foreign language, graphic design, journalism, literary magazine, mathematics, media production, newspaper, science, yearbook classes. Computer network features include on-campus library services, online commercial services, Internet access. Student e-mail accounts are available to students. Students grades are available online.
Contact Russell L. Slider, Vice President/Dean of Admissions. 404-765-4001. Fax: 404-765-4009. E-mail: rusty.slider@woodward.edu. Web site: www.woodward.edu.

WOOSTER SCHOOL

91 Miry Brook Road
Danbury, Connecticut 06810

Head of School: Mr. Timothy B. Golding

General Information Coeducational day college-preparatory, arts, and technology school, affiliated with Episcopal Church. Grades PK–12. Founded: 1926. Setting: suburban. 100-acre campus. 15 buildings on campus. Approved or accredited by Connecticut Association of Independent Schools, National Association of Episcopal Schools, New England Association of Schools and Colleges, and Connecticut Department of Education. Member of National Association of Independent Schools. Endowment: $8 million. Total enrollment: 350. Upper school average class size: 12. Upper school faculty-student ratio: 1:10.
Upper School Student Profile Grade 9: 35 students (20 boys, 15 girls); Grade 10: 48 students (29 boys, 19 girls); Grade 11: 32 students (13 boys, 19 girls); Grade 12: 32 students (16 boys, 16 girls). 8% of students are members of Episcopal Church.
Faculty School total: 97. In upper school: 13 men, 11 women; 14 have advanced degrees.
Subjects Offered Algebra, American government, American history, American history-AP, ancient history, Arabic, art, art history-AP, art-AP, biology, biology-AP, calculus, calculus-AP, chemistry, community service, computer animation, computer science, computer science-AP, earth science, economics, English, English literature-AP, English/composition-AP, ESL, ethics, European history-AP, fine arts, French, French-AP, general science, geography, geometry, mathematics, music, music-AP, Pacific art, photography, physical education, physics, political science, pottery, religion, science, social studies, Spanish, Spanish-AP, statistics, statistics-AP, U.S. history-AP.
Graduation Requirements 20th century history, arts and fine arts (art, music, dance, drama), computer science, English, foreign language, mathematics, physical education (includes health), religion (includes Bible studies and theology), science, social studies (includes history), 100 hours of community service, senior independent study and senior colloquium, Leadership in Self-help (jobs) Program.
Special Academic Programs Advanced Placement exam preparation; honors section; accelerated programs; independent study; term-away projects; study at local college for college credit; study abroad; ESL (5 students enrolled).
College Admission Counseling 39 students graduated in 2008; all went to college, including Carnegie Mellon University; Sarah Lawrence College; Skidmore College; Tufts University; Vassar College. Mean SAT critical reading: 626, mean SAT math: 616, mean SAT writing: 638, mean combined SAT: 1881.
Student Life Upper grades have specified standards of dress, student council, honor system. Discipline rests equally with students and faculty. Attendance at religious services is required.
Summer Programs Enrichment, sports, art/fine arts, computer instruction programs offered; session focuses on enrichment (ages PK-15) and physical education (PK-6); held on campus; accepts boys and girls; open to students from other schools. 800 students usually enrolled. 2009 schedule: June 23 to July 25. Application deadline: none.
Tuition and Aid Day student tuition: $14,950–$27,750. Tuition installment plan (The Tuition Plan, Insured Tuition Payment Plan, monthly payment plans, individually arranged payment plans, school's own payment plan). Need-based scholarship grants available. In 2008–09, 28% of upper-school students received aid. Total amount of financial aid awarded in 2008–09: $945,305.
Admissions Traditional secondary-level entrance grade is 9. For fall 2008, 66 students applied for upper-level admission, 47 were accepted, 19 enrolled. ISEE or SSAT required. Deadline for receipt of application materials: none. Application fee required: $50. On-campus interview required.
Athletics Interscholastic: baseball (boys), basketball (b,g), cross-country running (b,g), golf (b), lacrosse (b,g), soccer (b,g), softball (g), tennis (b,g), volleyball (g); intramural: dance (g), strength & conditioning (b,g), weight training (g); coed interscholastic: Frisbee, golf; coed intramural: basketball, outdoor education, ropes courses, soccer, weight lifting, weight training. 3 PE instructors, 15 coaches, 1 athletic trainer.
Computers Computers are regularly used in all classes. Computer network features include on-campus library services, Internet access, wireless campus network, Internet filtering or blocking technology. Campus intranet, student e-mail accounts, and computer access in designated common areas are available to students. The school has a published electronic and media policy.
Contact Grant Jacks, Director of Admissions. 203-830-3916. Fax: 203-790-7147. E-mail: admissions@woosterschool.org. Web site: www.woosterschool.org.

WORCESTER ACADEMY

81 Providence Street
Worcester, Massachusetts 01604

Head of School: Dexter P. Morse

General Information Coeducational boarding and day college-preparatory, arts, technology, and ESL school. Boarding grades 9–PG, day grades 6–12. Founded: 1834. Setting: urban. Nearest major city is Boston. Students are housed in single-sex dormitories. 60-acre campus. 14 buildings on campus. Approved or accredited by Association of Independent Schools in New England, New England Association of Schools and Colleges, and The Association of Boarding Schools. Member of National Association of Independent Schools and Secondary School Admission Test Board. Endowment: $38 million. Total enrollment: 657. Upper school average class size: 15. Upper school faculty-student ratio: 1:7.
Upper School Student Profile Grade 9: 101 students (51 boys, 50 girls); Grade 10: 120 students (65 boys, 55 girls); Grade 11: 128 students (67 boys, 61 girls); Grade 12: 122 students (61 boys, 61 girls); Postgraduate: 25 students (24 boys, 1 girl). 30% of students are boarding students. 70% are state residents. 12 states are represented in upper school student body. 15% are international students. International students from China, Hong Kong, Japan, Republic of Korea, Taiwan, and Viet Nam; 11 other countries represented in student body.
Faculty School total: 103. In upper school: 58 men, 45 women; 54 have advanced degrees; 29 reside on campus.
Subjects Offered Acting, advanced studio art-AP, algebra, American government-AP, American history, American history-AP, anatomy, art, art-AP, biology, biology-AP, British literature, calculus, calculus-AP, ceramics, chemistry, chemistry-AP, Chinese, chorus, computer programming, computer science-AP, contemporary issues, directing, economics, English, English language-AP, English literature, English literature-AP, environmental science, ESL, ethics, European history, European history-AP, French, French literature-AP, geography, geometry, government-AP, health, history, Holocaust studies, honors English, honors world history, human anatomy, Latin, mathematics, music, physical education, physics, post-calculus, pre-algebra, pre-calculus, Spanish, studio art-AP, U.S. history-AP, Vietnam history, world history.
Graduation Requirements Arts and fine arts (art, music, dance, drama), English, foreign language, mathematics, physical education (includes health), science, social studies (includes history), senior projects. Community service is required.
Special Academic Programs 15 Advanced Placement exams for which test preparation is offered; honors section; independent study; ESL (15 students enrolled).
College Admission Counseling 147 students graduated in 2008; all went to college, including Boston College; Boston University; New York University; Northeastern University; The George Washington University; Union College. Mean SAT critical reading: 560, mean SAT math: 620, mean composite ACT: 26. 35% scored over 600 on SAT critical reading, 40% scored over 600 on SAT math, 50% scored over 26 on composite ACT.
Student Life Upper grades have specified standards of dress, student council, honor system. Discipline rests equally with students and faculty.
Tuition and Aid Day student tuition: $23,910; 5-day tuition and room/board: $37,790; 7-day tuition and room/board: $42,290. Tuition installment plan (Academic Management Services Plan). Merit scholarship grants, need-based scholarship grants, paying campus jobs available. In 2008–09, 30% of upper-school students received aid; total upper-school merit-scholarship money awarded: $50,000. Total amount of financial aid awarded in 2008–09: $3,000,000.
Admissions Traditional secondary-level entrance grade is 9. For fall 2008, 363 students applied for upper-level admission, 202 were accepted, 114 enrolled. ACT, ISEE, PSAT or SAT for applicants to grade 11 and 12, SSAT or TOEFL required. Deadline for receipt of application materials: January 15. Application fee required: $50. Interview required.
Athletics Interscholastic: baseball (boys), basketball (b,g), cross-country running (b,g), field hockey (g), football (b), ice hockey (b), lacrosse (b,g), skiing (downhill) (b,g), soccer (b,g), softball (g), swimming and diving (b,g), tennis (b,g), track and field (b,g), volleyball (g), wrestling (b); intramural: aerobics/dance (g), basketball (b,g),

dance squad (g), dance team (g), snowboarding (b,g); coed interscholastic: crew, golf, water polo; coed intramural: paddle tennis, softball, tennis, volleyball. 3 PE instructors, 5 coaches, 3 athletic trainers.
Computers Computers are regularly used in art, college planning, economics, English, ESL, foreign language, French, history, journalism, lab/keyboard, library, mathematics, media arts, multimedia, music, science, Spanish, theater arts, video film production, Web site design, writing, yearbook classes. Computer network features include on-campus library services, online commercial services, Internet access, wireless campus network, Internet filtering or blocking technology. Campus intranet, student e-mail accounts, and computer access in designated common areas are available to students. Students grades are available online. The school has a published electronic and media policy.
Contact Susanne C. Carpenter, Director of Admission and Financial Aid. 508-754-5302 Ext. 199. Fax: 508-752-2382. E-mail: susanne.carpenter@worcesteracademy.org. Web site: www.worcesteracademy.org.

ANNOUNCEMENT FROM THE SCHOOL Worcester Academy is a co-ed day and boarding school for grades 6–12 and postgraduates. The school's urban setting, diverse community, and challenging curriculum provide students with a solid, real-world education.

See Close-Up on page 1040.

WORCESTER PREPARATORY SCHOOL

508 South Main Street
PO Box 1006
Berlin, Maryland 21811
Head of School: Dr. Barry W. Tull

General Information Coeducational day college-preparatory, arts, and technology school. Grades PK–12. Founded: 1970. Setting: small town. Nearest major city is Ocean City. 45-acre campus. 7 buildings on campus. Approved or accredited by Association of Independent Maryland Schools, Middle States Association of Colleges and Schools, and Maryland Department of Education. Member of National Association of Independent Schools. Total enrollment: 618. Upper school average class size: 14. Upper school faculty-student ratio: 1:9.
Upper School Student Profile Grade 9: 62 students (28 boys, 34 girls); Grade 10: 46 students (26 boys, 20 girls); Grade 11: 52 students (22 boys, 30 girls); Grade 12: 53 students (26 boys, 27 girls).
Faculty School total: 65. In upper school: 13 men, 23 women; 29 have advanced degrees.
Subjects Offered Advanced Placement courses, algebra, American history, American literature, art, art history, biology, biology-AP, calculus, calculus-AP, chemistry, chemistry-AP, computer programming, computer science, creative writing, dance, drama, earth science, economics, English, English literature, English literature and composition-AP, English-AP, European history, fine arts, French, geography, geometry, government/civics, Latin, literature and composition-AP, literature-AP, mathematics, military history, music, music theory, paleontology, physical education, physics, physics-AP, psychology, SAT preparation, science, social science, social studies, Spanish, speech, statistics, technological applications, technology/design, theater, typing, U.S. history-AP, vocal music, world history, world history-AP, world literature, writing.
Graduation Requirements Art appreciation, arts and fine arts (art, music, dance, drama), computer science, English, foreign language, mathematics, music appreciation, physical education (includes health), science, social science, social studies (includes history).
Special Academic Programs 8 Advanced Placement exams for which test preparation is offered; honors section; independent study; academic accommodation for the gifted.
College Admission Counseling 53 students graduated in 2008; all went to college, including Furman University; Harvard University; University of Delaware; University of Pennsylvania; University of Virginia; Washington College.
Student Life Upper grades have uniform requirement, student council, honor system. Discipline rests primarily with faculty.
Tuition and Aid Day student tuition: $10,825. Tuition installment plan (Key Tuition Payment Plan, monthly payment plans, individually arranged payment plans). Need-based scholarship grants available. In 2008–09, 1% of upper-school students received aid.
Admissions Traditional secondary-level entrance grade is 9. For fall 2008, 33 students applied for upper-level admission, 19 were accepted, 12 enrolled. Achievement/Aptitude/Writing and writing sample required. Deadline for receipt of application materials: none. Application fee required: $50. On-campus interview required.
Athletics Interscholastic: basketball (boys, girls), field hockey (g), lacrosse (b,g), soccer (b,g), tennis (b,g), weight training (b,g), winter soccer (b,g); intramural: basketball (b,g), dance (b,g), dance squad (b,g), flag football (b,g), soccer (b,g); coed interscholastic: cheering, golf, tennis; coed intramural: dance, dance squad. 3 PE instructors, 54 coaches, 1 athletic trainer.
Computers Computers are regularly used in all classes. Computer network features include on-campus library services, online commercial services, Internet access, wireless campus network, Internet filtering or blocking technology. Campus intranet, student e-mail accounts, and computer access in designated common areas are available to students. The school has a published electronic and media policy.
Contact Lisa B. Cook, Director of Admissions. 410-641-3575. Fax: 410-641-3586. E-mail: lcook@worcesterprep.org. Web site: www.worcesterprep.org.

WORLD HOPE ACADEMY

10691 North Kendall Drive
Suite 105
Miami, Florida 33176
Head of School: Dr. Alan Goldstein

General Information Distance learning only college-preparatory, general academic, religious studies, Advanced Placement, and medical curriculum school; primarily serves underachievers, students with learning disabilities, individuals with Attention Deficit Disorder, individuals with emotional and behavioral problems, and dyslexic students. Distance learning grades PK–12. Founded: 1978. 1 building on campus. Approved or accredited by Florida Department of Education. Language of instruction: Spanish. Total enrollment: 305. Upper school average class size: 20. Upper school faculty-student ratio: 1:20.
Faculty School total: 16. In upper school: 8 men, 7 women; 11 have advanced degrees.
Special Academic Programs International Baccalaureate program; Advanced Placement exam preparation; honors section; accelerated programs; independent study; study at local college for college credit; academic accommodation for the gifted; remedial reading and/or remedial writing; remedial math; programs in English, mathematics, general development for dyslexic students.
College Admission Counseling 320 students graduated in 2008; 150 went to college.
Student Life Upper grades have honor system. Discipline rests primarily with faculty.
Tuition and Aid Day student tuition: $500–$2600. Guaranteed tuition plan. Tuition installment plan (Insured Tuition Payment Plan, FACTS Tuition Payment Plan). Tuition reduction for siblings, need-based scholarship grants available. In 2008–09, 75% of upper-school students received aid.
Admissions Traditional secondary-level entrance grade is 9. Any standardized test required. Deadline for receipt of application materials: none. Application fee required: $150. Interview required.
Contact Grisel Macareno, Admissions. 305-270-9830. Web site: www.worldhopeacademy.org.

ANNOUNCEMENT FROM THE SCHOOL World Hope Academy is an accredited private high school that offers prekindergarten through 12th grade education through home schooling and regular attendance. Whether parents are concerned for their child's safety due to the environment of other schools, question the moral and religious character of their child's current teachers, are dissatisfied with the subjects covered, or have a child with special needs, World Hope Academy is there to help. The secret of World Hope's success is that it focuses on each student and develops an individual academic assessment plan according to the student's own strengths and weaknesses. All of World Hope's personal academic assessment plans and classes meet Florida's graduation requirements. Other schools might focus on tuition, fast graduation, easy exams, or some other distraction from success, but World Hope Academy focuses on the student's development for success in today's uncertain world. The teaching methods and books supplied are geared for regular students, learning disabled students, and Advanced Placement students. In a community committed to diversity in its student body, faculty, and staff, the school provides academic, extracurricular, and other resources that help students achieve at the highest scholarly levels and prepare students for lives of service in many fields of human endeavor. Today, World Hope Academy is led by Dr. Alan Goldstein, and the Trustees of World Hope Academy are responsible for the overall direction of the school. The trustees approve the operating and capital budgets, supervise the investment of the school, and oversee real estate and long-range physical planning. The trustees also exercise prior review and approval concerning changes in major policies, such as those in instructional programs and admission, as well as tuition and fees and the hiring of faculty members. So whether students are located in sunny Miami, Florida, or in stone-cold Alaska, World Hope Academy can help students graduate with success. Interested families should visit World Hope's Web site to read more about the school or call 305-270-9830 and speak with an admissions counselor.

WYOMING SEMINARY

201 North Sprague Avenue
Kingston, Pennsylvania 18704-3593

Head of School: Dr. Kip P. Nygren

General Information Coeducational boarding and day college-preparatory school, affiliated with United Methodist Church. Boarding grades 9–PG, day grades PK–PG. Founded: 1844. Setting: suburban. Nearest major city is Wilkes-Barre. Students are housed in single-sex dormitories. 22-acre campus. 12 buildings on campus. Approved or accredited by Middle States Association of Colleges and Schools, Pennsylvania Association of Independent Schools, The Association of Boarding Schools, The College Board, and Pennsylvania Department of Education. Member of National Association of Independent Schools and Secondary School Admission Test Board. Endowment: $51.7 million. Total enrollment: 782. Upper school average class size: 14. Upper school faculty-student ratio: 1:10.

Upper School Student Profile Grade 9: 92 students (42 boys, 50 girls); Grade 10: 125 students (62 boys, 63 girls); Grade 11: 110 students (54 boys, 56 girls); Grade 12: 120 students (56 boys, 64 girls); Postgraduate: 14 students (14 boys). 43% of students are boarding students. 64% are state residents. 18 states are represented in upper school student body. 20% are international students. International students from Canada, Germany, Japan, Republic of Korea, Taiwan, and Thailand; 20 other countries represented in student body. 10% of students are United Methodist Church.

Faculty School total: 124. In upper school: 42 men, 34 women; 46 have advanced degrees; 46 reside on campus.

Subjects Offered 20th century world history, 3-dimensional design, advanced computer applications, African American history, African history, algebra, alternative physical education, American Civil War, American government-AP, American history, American literature, analysis, analysis and differential calculus, analytic geometry, anatomy and physiology, ancient world history, animal behavior, art, art appreciation, art history, art history-AP, astronomy, Bible studies, biology, biology-AP, botany, British literature, calculus, calculus-AP, ceramics, chemistry, chemistry-AP, choral music, civil rights, college admission preparation, college counseling, community service, computer education, computer graphics, computer programming, computer science, conceptual physics, creative writing, critical writing, dance, discrete math, drama, drawing and design, ecology, economics, economics and history, English, English literature, environmental science, environmental science-AP, ESL, European history, European history-AP, expository writing, fine arts, forensic science, French, French-AP, geometry, health education, history, history of music, honors geometry, independent study, Judaic studies, Latin, Latin-AP, marine biology, mathematics, microeconomics, music, music theory, music theory-AP, philosophy, photography, physical education, physics, poetry, pre-calculus, printmaking, psychology, psychology-AP, public speaking, religion, Russian, Russian literature, science, science research, Shakespeare, social studies, sociology, Spanish, Spanish-AP, statistics, statistics-AP, studio art-AP, theater, trigonometry, U.S. history-AP, women in literature, world civilizations, world geography, world history, world literature, world religions, World War II, zoology.

Graduation Requirements Art history, Bible as literature, biology, computer science, English, foreign language, health education, mathematics, music history, physical education (includes health), public speaking, science, social studies (includes history), U.S. history, world civilizations, 40 hours of community service, extracurricular participation.

Special Academic Programs 26 Advanced Placement exams for which test preparation is offered; honors section; independent study; term-away projects; study at local college for college credit; study abroad; ESL (37 students enrolled).

College Admission Counseling 133 students graduated in 2008; 132 went to college, including Boston University; Pratt Institute; Princeton University; The George Washington University; The University of Scranton; United States Naval Academy. Other: 1 entered a postgraduate year. Mean SAT critical reading: 568, mean SAT math: 597, mean SAT writing: 571, mean combined SAT: 1736, mean composite ACT: 25.

Student Life Upper grades have specified standards of dress, student council, honor system. Discipline rests equally with students and faculty.

Summer Programs Enrichment, advancement, ESL, sports, art/fine arts, computer instruction programs offered; session focuses on performing arts and ESL; held on campus; accepts boys and girls; open to students from other schools. 700 students usually enrolled. 2009 schedule: June 30 to August 21. Application deadline: June 30.

Tuition and Aid Day student tuition: $19,200; 7-day tuition and room/board: $38,000. Tuition installment plan (Key Tuition Payment Plan, monthly payment plans). Merit scholarship grants, need-based scholarship grants, need-based loans, prepGATE Loans available. In 2008–09, 54% of upper-school students received aid; total upper-school merit-scholarship money awarded: $400,000. Total amount of financial aid awarded in 2008–09: $5,900,000.

Admissions Traditional secondary-level entrance grade is 9. For fall 2008, 355 students applied for upper-level admission, 187 were accepted, 127 enrolled. ACT, PSAT or SAT for applicants to grade 11 and 12, SSAT or TOEFL or SLEP required. Deadline for receipt of application materials: none. Application fee required: $75. Interview required.

Athletics Interscholastic: baseball (boys), basketball (b,g), cross-country running (b,g), diving (b,g), field hockey (g), football (b), ice hockey (b,g), lacrosse (b,g), soccer (b,g), softball (g), swimming and diving (b,g), tennis (b,g), wrestling (b,g); intramural: paint ball (b), power lifting (b); coed interscholastic: golf, strength & conditioning; coed intramural: alpine skiing, backpacking, badminton, ballet, bicycling, bowling, combined training, dance, fencing, fitness, flag football, Frisbee, martial arts, modern dance, Nautilus, outdoor activities, outdoor recreation, physical training, skiing (downhill), tai chi, wall climbing, yoga. 2 PE instructors, 4 coaches, 2 athletic trainers.

Computers Computers are regularly used in art, English, foreign language, history, mathematics, music, science classes. Computer network features include on-campus library services, online commercial services, Internet access, wireless campus network, Internet filtering or blocking technology. Campus intranet, student e-mail accounts, and computer access in designated common areas are available to students. The school has a published electronic and media policy.

Contact Mr. David R. Damico, Director of Admission. 570-270-2160. Fax: 570-270-2191. E-mail: admission@wyomingseminary.org. Web site: www.wyomingseminary.org.

See Close-Up on page 1042.

XAVERIAN BROTHERS HIGH SCHOOL

800 Clapboardtree Street
Westwood, Massachusetts 02090-1799

Head of School: Br. Daniel E. Skala, CFX

General Information Boys' day college-preparatory, arts, religious studies, and technology school, affiliated with Roman Catholic Church. Grades 9–12. Founded: 1963. Setting: suburban. Nearest major city is Boston. 35-acre campus. 1 building on campus. Approved or accredited by Association of Independent Schools in New England and New England Association of Schools and Colleges. Endowment: $27 million. Total enrollment: 973. Upper school average class size: 22. Upper school faculty-student ratio: 1:22.

Upper School Student Profile Grade 9: 274 students (274 boys); Grade 10: 241 students (241 boys); Grade 11: 218 students (218 boys); Grade 12: 240 students (240 boys). 85% of students are Roman Catholic.

Faculty School total: 86. In upper school: 72 men, 14 women; 63 have advanced degrees.

Subjects Offered Algebra, American history, American history-AP, American literature, art, biology, biology-AP, business, calculus, calculus-AP, chemistry, chemistry-AP, computer applications, computer math, computer programming, computer science, creative writing, driver education, economics, English, English literature, English-AP, European history, French, French-AP, government/civics, history, law, marine biology, mathematics, modern European history-AP, music, oceanography, physical education, physics, physics-AP, psychology, science, social science, social studies, Spanish, Spanish-AP, studio art-AP, theology, world history.

Graduation Requirements Arts and fine arts (art, music, dance, drama), computer science, English, foreign language, mathematics, physical education (includes health), religion (includes Bible studies and theology), science, social studies (includes history).

Special Academic Programs International Baccalaureate program; Advanced Placement exam preparation; honors section; term-away projects; academic accommodation for the gifted, the musically talented, and the artistically talented; remedial reading and/or remedial writing; remedial math; special instructional classes for deaf students, blind students.

College Admission Counseling 230 students graduated in 2008; 223 went to college, including Fairfield University; Northeastern University; Providence College; Quinnipiac University; Saint Michael's College; Villanova University. Other: 3 went to work, 1 entered military service, 1 entered a postgraduate year. Median SAT critical reading: 591, median SAT math: 608, median SAT writing: 587. 49% scored over 600 on SAT critical reading, 56% scored over 600 on SAT math, 43% scored over 600 on SAT writing.

Student Life Upper grades have specified standards of dress, student council, honor system. Discipline rests primarily with faculty. Attendance at religious services is required.

Summer Programs Remediation, enrichment, advancement, art/fine arts, computer instruction programs offered; session focuses on remediation and enrichment; held on campus; accepts boys and girls; open to students from other schools. 50 students usually enrolled. 2009 schedule: June 20 to August 20.

Tuition and Aid Day student tuition: $12,400. Tuition installment plan (monthly payment plans, individually arranged payment plans, The Tuition Solution). Merit scholarship grants, need-based scholarship grants available. In 2008–09, 35% of upper-school students received aid; total upper-school merit-scholarship money awarded: $536,000. Total amount of financial aid awarded in 2008–09: $1,200,000.

Admissions Traditional secondary-level entrance grade is 9. For fall 2008, 725 students applied for upper-level admission, 500 were accepted, 275 enrolled. Archdiocese of Boston High School entrance exam provided by STS required. Deadline for receipt of application materials: December 31. No application fee required. Interview recommended.

Athletics Interscholastic: alpine skiing, baseball, basketball, cross-country running, diving, football, golf, ice hockey, lacrosse, rugby, skiing (downhill), soccer, strength & conditioning, swimming and diving, tennis, track and field, volleyball, weight training, winter (indoor) track, wrestling; intramural: baseball, basketball, bicycling, billiards, bowling, floor hockey, football, Frisbee, golf, handball, racquetball, skiing (downhill), snowboarding, strength & conditioning, touch football, weight training. 2 PE instructors, 100 coaches, 2 athletic trainers.

Computers Computers are regularly used in business, mathematics, music, science classes. Computer network features include on-campus library services, online commercial services, Internet access, wireless campus network, Internet filtering or blocking technology, common desktop applications: MS office and Adobe Creative Suite, printing, access to digital and video cameras for music/video production. Campus intranet and computer access in designated common areas are available to students. Students grades are available online. The school has a published electronic and media policy.

Contact Mr. Tim McDonough, Director of Admissions. 781-326-6392. Fax: 781-320-0458. E-mail: tmcdonough@xbhs.com.

ANNOUNCEMENT FROM THE SCHOOL Xaverian Brothers High School is a high school for young men sponsored by the Xaverian Brothers. It offers intelligent, talented young men of faith the opportunity to become leaders, thinkers, entrepreneurs, educators, and active contributors in an increasingly competitive world. The School for the last five years has invested more than $23 million to make Xaverian Brothers High one of the most technologically advanced schools in New England. This past summer, the School added twenty-five additional SMARTBoards, which provide multimedia systems in every classroom. Xaverian also completed building digital laboratories for both visual fine arts and music centers that provide the highest state-of-the-art learning experience. For more information, prospective students and their families should visit the Web site at www.xbhs.com.

XAVIER COLLEGE PREPARATORY

4710 North Fifth Street
Phoenix, Arizona 85012

Head of School: Sr. Joan Fitzgerald, BVM

General Information Girls' day college-preparatory, arts, religious studies, technology, and Great Books, accelerated science, Advanced Placement school, affiliated with Roman Catholic Church. Grades 9–12. Founded: 1943. Setting: urban. 13-acre campus. 7 buildings on campus. Approved or accredited by National Catholic Education Association, North Central Association of Colleges and Schools, Western Catholic Education Association, and Arizona Department of Education. Endowment: $1.2 million. Total enrollment: 1,198. Upper school average class size: 26. Upper school faculty-student ratio: 1:22.

Upper School Student Profile Grade 9: 328 students (328 girls); Grade 10: 301 students (301 girls); Grade 11: 281 students (281 girls); Grade 12: 288 students (288 girls). 75% of students are Roman Catholic.

Faculty School total: 95. In upper school: 20 men, 75 women; 70 have advanced degrees.

Subjects Offered Accounting, advanced chemistry, advanced computer applications, Advanced Placement courses, advanced studio art-AP, algebra, American government, American government-AP, American history, American history-AP, American literature, analysis and differential calculus, anatomy and physiology, architecture, art, art history, art history-AP, astronomy, athletic training, audition methods, band, bell choir, biology, biology-AP, calculus, calculus-AP, ceramics, chemistry, chemistry-AP, child development, Chinese, choir, community service, computer programming-AP, computer science, computer studies, concert choir, contemporary issues, culinary arts, dance, dance performance, digital photography, drama, economics, English, English language-AP, English literature, English literature-AP, environmental science-AP, ethics, European history-AP, family and consumer science, film studies, fine arts, French, French language-AP, geography, geometry, graphic design, great books, guitar, jazz band, Latin, Latin-AP, music, music theory-AP, musical theater, New Testament, newspaper, philosophy, physical education, physics, physics-AP, pre-calculus, psychology, sociology, Spanish, Spanish language-AP, Spanish literature-AP, sports medicine, stagecraft, statistics-AP, student government, theology, trigonometry, visual arts, weight training, world history-AP, world literature, world wide web design.

Graduation Requirements American literature, arts and fine arts (art, music, dance, drama), computer science, English, foreign language, mathematics, physical education (includes health), religion (includes Bible studies and theology), science, social studies (includes history), AZ History and Free Enterprise Independent Study, Summer Reading Program, 50 hours of community service.

Special Academic Programs Advanced Placement exam preparation; honors section; independent study; study at local college for college credit; academic accommodation for the gifted and the artistically talented.

College Admission Counseling 244 students graduated in 2008; all went to college, including Arizona State University; Loyola Marymount University; Northern Arizona University; The University of Arizona; University of San Diego; University of Southern California. Median composite ACT: 25.

Student Life Upper grades have uniform requirement, student council, honor system. Discipline rests primarily with faculty. Attendance at religious services is required.

Summer Programs Enrichment, advancement, sports, art/fine arts, computer instruction programs offered; session focuses on academic advancement; held on campus; accepts girls; not open to students from other schools. 700 students usually enrolled. 2009 schedule: May 27 to June 27. Application deadline: April 1.

Tuition and Aid Day student tuition: $9963–$12,861. Tuition installment plan (monthly payment plans, semester payment plan). Need-based scholarship grants, reduced tuition rate for Catholic families registered in Catholic parishes of the Diocese of Phoenix available. In 2008–09, 20% of upper-school students received aid. Total amount of financial aid awarded in 2008–09: $850,000.

Admissions Traditional secondary-level entrance grade is 9. For fall 2008, 525 students applied for upper-level admission, 375 were accepted, 350 enrolled. High School Placement Test required. Deadline for receipt of application materials: January 30. Application fee required: $50.

Athletics Interscholastic: aerobics/dance, badminton, basketball, cheering, crew, cross-country running, dance team, danceline, diving, golf, ice hockey, lacrosse, pom squad, rowing, soccer, softball, swimming and diving, tennis, track and field, volleyball, winter soccer; intramural: basketball, crew, dance, fencing, fitness, floor hockey, modern dance, strength & conditioning, weight training; coed intramural: badminton, basketball, flag football, soccer, softball, tennis, volleyball. 4 PE instructors, 21 coaches, 2 athletic trainers.

Computers Computers are regularly used in all classes. Computer network features include on-campus library services, online commercial services, Internet access, Internet filtering or blocking technology, Blackboard Learning Systems, Blackbaud NetClassroom. Computer access in designated common areas is available to students. Students grades are available online. The school has a published electronic and media policy.

Contact Mrs. Paula Petrowski, Director of Admissions. 602-277-3772. Fax: 602-240-3175. E-mail: petrowski@xcp.org. Web site: www.xcp.org.

XAVIER UNIVERSITY PREPARATORY SCHOOL

5116 Magazine Street
New Orleans, Louisiana 70115-1699

Head of School: Mrs. Carolyn Oubre

General Information Girls' day college-preparatory, arts, religious studies, technology, honors, and Advanced Placement school, affiliated with Roman Catholic Church. Grades 7–12. Founded: 1915. Setting: urban. 2-acre campus. 4 buildings on campus. Approved or accredited by National Catholic Education Association, Southern Association of Colleges and Schools, Southern Association of Independent Schools, and Louisiana Department of Education. Total enrollment: 324. Upper school average class size: 25. Upper school faculty-student ratio: 1:11.

Upper School Student Profile Grade 7: 16 students (16 girls); Grade 8: 28 students (28 girls); Grade 9: 85 students (85 girls); Grade 10: 64 students (64 girls); Grade 11: 62 students (62 girls); Grade 12: 69 students (69 girls). 50% of students are Roman Catholic.

Faculty School total: 25. In upper school: 6 men, 17 women; 9 have advanced degrees.

Subjects Offered ACT preparation, African American studies, algebra, American history, art, art appreciation, art history, band, Bible, biology, British literature, British literature (honors), calculus, chemistry, chorus, civics, computer applications, computer literacy, conceptual physics, concert band, drama, drama performance, drawing, drawing and design, driver education, earth science, English, English literature, French, geometry, health and wellness, health education, history, honors algebra, honors English, honors geometry, honors U.S. history, honors world history, Latin, moral theology, music, music appreciation, New Testament, newspaper, psychology, religion, SAT/ACT preparation, science, sculpture, senior thesis, Shakespeare, Spanish, speech, studio art, technical theater, theater arts, U.S. history, U.S. literature, world geography, world history.

Graduation Requirements Advanced math, algebra, American history, American literature, biology, calculus, chemistry, civics, computer applications, computer literacy, English, foreign language, French, Latin, Spanish, U.S. history, U.S. literature, completion of a Senior Thesis.

Special Academic Programs Honors section; independent study; study at local college for college credit; academic accommodation for the musically talented and the artistically talented.

College Admission Counseling 63 students graduated in 2008; 58 went to college, including Dillard University; Northwestern State University of Louisiana; University of New Orleans; Xavier University of Louisiana. Other: 5 went to work. 16% scored over 600 on SAT critical reading, 10% scored over 600 on SAT math, 16% scored over 600 on SAT writing, 10% scored over 1800 on combined SAT, 10% scored over 26 on composite ACT.

Student Life Upper grades have uniform requirement, student council, honor system. Discipline rests primarily with faculty. Attendance at religious services is required.

Summer Programs Enrichment programs offered; session focuses on summer orientation for incoming students; held on campus; accepts girls; not open to students from other schools. 150 students usually enrolled. 2009 schedule: June 1 to June 25. Application deadline: January 10.

Tuition and Aid Day student tuition: $5400. Tuition installment plan (The Tuition Plan, monthly payment plans). Tuition reduction for siblings, merit scholarship grants, middle-income loans, paying campus jobs available. In 2008–09, 1% of upper-school students received aid; total upper-school merit-scholarship money awarded: $17,000. Total amount of financial aid awarded in 2008–09: $20,000.

Admissions Traditional secondary-level entrance grade is 9. For fall 2008, 165 students applied for upper-level admission, 113 were accepted, 98 enrolled. Iowa Tests of Basic Skills-Grades 7-8, Archdiocese HSEPT-Grade 9 required. Deadline for receipt of application materials: none. Application fee required: $20. On-campus interview required.
Athletics Interscholastic: baseball, basketball, cross-country running, softball, track and field, volleyball; intramural: cheering, dance team, golf. 1 PE instructor, 4 coaches.
Computers Computers are regularly used in computer applications, foreign language, publications, SAT preparation, study skills, yearbook classes. Computer network features include on-campus library services, Internet access, wireless campus network, Internet filtering or blocking technology. Computer access in designated common areas is available to students. Students grades are available online. The school has a published electronic and media policy.
Contact Mrs. Tiffany Neville Cambre, Director of Admissions and Student Activities. 504-899-6061 Ext. 324. Fax: 504-899-0547. E-mail: tcambre@xavierprep.com. Web site: www.xavierprep.com.

YOKOHAMA INTERNATIONAL SCHOOL

258 Yamate-cho, Naka-ku
Yokohama 231-0862, Japan

Head of School: Mr. Simon Taylor

General Information Coeducational day college-preparatory, arts, bilingual studies, and technology school. Grades N–12. Founded: 1924. Setting: urban. 3-acre campus. 8 buildings on campus. Approved or accredited by European Council of International Schools, International Baccalaureate Organization, and New England Association of Schools and Colleges. Language of instruction: English. Total enrollment: 724. Upper school average class size: 14. Upper school faculty-student ratio: 1:5.
Upper School Student Profile Grade 9: 59 students (24 boys, 35 girls); Grade 10: 61 students (32 boys, 29 girls); Grade 11: 59 students (25 boys, 34 girls); Grade 12: 54 students (26 boys, 28 girls).
Faculty School total: 85. In upper school: 32 men, 19 women; 20 have advanced degrees.
Subjects Offered Advanced chemistry, advanced math, art, band, biology, ceramics, chemistry, choir, computer programming, drama, Dutch, economics, English, English literature, environmental science, European history, French, geography, German, information technology, International Baccalaureate courses, Japanese, mathematics, modern languages, music composition, music theory, physical education, physics, Spanish, studio art, theater, theater arts, theory of knowledge, world history, world literature.
Graduation Requirements Arts, English, foreign language, information technology, mathematics, physical education (includes health), science, senior thesis, social studies (includes history), theory of knowledge, 50 hours of community service.
Special Academic Programs International Baccalaureate program.
College Admission Counseling 50 students graduated in 2008; 47 went to college, including The University of British Columbia. Other: 3 had other specific plans. Mean SAT critical reading: 516, mean SAT math: 554, mean SAT writing: 513.
Student Life Upper grades have specified standards of dress, student council. Discipline rests primarily with faculty.
Summer Programs Remediation, enrichment, sports programs offered; session focuses on English, mathematics, and basketball; held on campus; accepts boys and girls; open to students from other schools. 30 students usually enrolled. 2009 schedule: June to July. Application deadline: May.
Tuition and Aid Day student tuition: ¥2,200,000. Tuition installment plan (individually arranged payment plans).
Admissions Traditional secondary-level entrance grade is 9. For fall 2008, 60 students applied for upper-level admission, 25 were accepted, 20 enrolled. School's own test required. Deadline for receipt of application materials: none. Application fee required: ¥20,000. Interview recommended.
Athletics Interscholastic: baseball (boys), basketball (b,g), cross-country running (b,g), field hockey (g), soccer (b,g), track and field (b,g), volleyball (g); coed interscholastic: tennis; coed intramural: backpacking, ball hockey, bicycling, canoeing/kayaking, diving, floor hockey, gymnastics, hiking/backpacking, kayaking, netball, outdoor education, skateboarding, skiing (downhill), yoga. 4 PE instructors.
Computers Computers are regularly used in college planning, geography, graphic arts, graphic design, mathematics, media, music, science, social sciences, yearbook classes. Computer network features include on-campus library services, online commercial services, Internet access, wireless campus network, Internet filtering or blocking technology. Campus intranet and student e-mail accounts are available to students. Students grades are available online. The school has a published electronic and media policy.
Contact Ms. Susan Chen, Administrative Officer. 81-45-622-0084. Fax: 81-45-621-0379. E-mail: admissions@yis.ac.jp. Web site: www.yis.ac.jp.

YORK COUNTRY DAY SCHOOL

1071 Regents Glen Boulevard
York, Pennsylvania 17403

Head of School: Nathaniel W. Coffman

General Information Coeducational day college-preparatory, arts, and bilingual studies school. Grades PS–12. Founded: 1953. Setting: suburban. Nearest major city is Baltimore, MD. 15-acre campus. 1 building on campus. Approved or accredited by Middle States Association of Colleges and Schools, Pennsylvania Association of Independent Schools, and Pennsylvania Department of Education. Member of National Association of Independent Schools. Endowment: $1.3 million. Total enrollment: 212. Upper school average class size: 12. Upper school faculty-student ratio: 1:4.
Upper School Student Profile Grade 9: 15 students (7 boys, 8 girls); Grade 10: 10 students (7 boys, 3 girls); Grade 11: 15 students (7 boys, 8 girls); Grade 12: 16 students (7 boys, 9 girls).
Faculty School total: 42. In upper school: 10 men, 7 women; 10 have advanced degrees.
Subjects Offered Advanced Placement courses, algebra, American history, American history-AP, American literature, art, art history, biochemistry, biology, biology-AP, calculus, calculus-AP, chemistry, chemistry-AP, choral music, community service, computer programming, computer science, creative writing, drama, English, English literature, English literature-AP, European history, fine arts, French, French-AP, geography, geometry, government/civics, health, history, Latin, literature, mathematics, music, physical education, physics, psychology, public speaking, science, social studies, Spanish, Spanish language-AP, studio art-AP, theater, world history, world history-AP.
Graduation Requirements Arts and fine arts (art, music, dance, drama), English, foreign language, history, independent study, mathematics, physical education (includes health), public speaking, science, visual arts, Independent Study (3 semesters) through our Magnet Program. Community service is required.
Special Academic Programs Advanced Placement exam preparation; honors section; independent study; term-away projects; study at local college for college credit; study abroad; academic accommodation for the gifted, the musically talented, and the artistically talented; remedial reading and/or remedial writing; ESL (2 students enrolled).
College Admission Counseling 16 students graduated in 2008; all went to college, including Ithaca College; New York University; Towson University; University of Delaware; University of Richmond; Washington College. Median SAT critical reading: 650, median SAT math: 590.
Student Life Upper grades have specified standards of dress, student council, honor system. Discipline rests equally with students and faculty.
Tuition and Aid Day student tuition: $14,990. Tuition installment plan (Insured Tuition Payment Plan, monthly payment plans, semester payment plan). Need-based scholarship grants available. In 2008–09, 22% of upper-school students received aid. Total amount of financial aid awarded in 2008–09: $215,000.
Admissions Traditional secondary-level entrance grade is 9. 3-R Achievement Test, Academic Profile Tests, California Achievement Test, ISEE, Otis-Lennon Ability or Stanford Achievement Test or PSAT and SAT for applicants to grade 11 and 12 required. Deadline for receipt of application materials: none. Application fee required: $35. On-campus interview required.
Athletics Interscholastic: basketball (boys, girls), cross-country running (g), field hockey (g), football (b), independent competitive sports (b,g), soccer (b,g), swimming and diving (g), tennis (b,g), volleyball (g); intramural: basketball (b,g); coed interscholastic: golf. 2 PE instructors, 6 coaches.
Computers Computers are regularly used in all academic classes. Computer network features include on-campus library services, online commercial services, Internet access, Internet filtering or blocking technology. Student e-mail accounts are available to students.
Contact Ms. Alison C. Greer, Director of Admission and Communication. 717-843-9805. Fax: 717-815-6769. E-mail: agreer@ycds.org. Web site: www.ycds.org.

YORK PREPARATORY SCHOOL

40 West 68th Street
New York, New York 10023-6092

Head of School: Ronald P. Stewart

General Information Coeducational day college-preparatory, arts, technology, music (practical and theory), and drama school. Grades 6–12. Founded: 1969. Setting: urban. 1 building on campus. Approved or accredited by Middle States Association of Colleges and Schools. Total enrollment: 336. Upper school average class size: 15. Upper school faculty-student ratio: 1:5.
Upper School Student Profile Grade 9: 62 students (41 boys, 21 girls); Grade 10: 63 students (39 boys, 24 girls); Grade 11: 61 students (39 boys, 22 girls); Grade 12: 48 students (28 boys, 20 girls).
Faculty School total: 54. In upper school: 15 men, 39 women; 50 have advanced degrees.
Subjects Offered 20th century history, 20th century world history, 3-dimensional art, advanced chemistry, advanced computer applications, Advanced Placement courses,

advanced studio art-AP, algebra, American history, American history-AP, American literature, anatomy, animation, anthropology, art, art appreciation, astronomy, biology, calculus, calculus-AP, ceramics, chemistry, chemistry-AP, community service, comparative religion, computer math, computer programming, computer science, computer skills, concert band, creative writing, current events, drama, drama performance, driver education, earth science, economics, English, English literature, English-AP, environmental science, ethics, European history, expository writing, filmmaking, fine arts, French, genetics, geography, geology, geometry, government/civics, grammar, health education, Holocaust studies, law, literary magazine, mathematics, music, music history, philosophy, photography, physical education, physics, physiology, political science, politics, pre-calculus, psychology, reading/study skills, research skills, SAT preparation, science, science project, social studies, Spanish, statistics, theater, trigonometry, typing, world history, world literature, writing, zoology.
Graduation Requirements Arts and fine arts (art, music, dance, drama), English, foreign language, mathematics, physical education (includes health), science, social studies (includes history), 100 Hours of Community Service. Community service is required.
Special Academic Programs Advanced Placement exam preparation; honors section; accelerated programs; independent study; study at local college for college credit; academic accommodation for the gifted, the musically talented, and the artistically talented; programs in English, mathematics, general development for dyslexic students; special instructional classes for students with mild learning issues (extra tutoring program).
College Admission Counseling 61 students graduated in 2007; all went to college, including Boston University; Cornell University; New York University; Syracuse University; University of Vermont; Vassar College.
Student Life Upper grades have specified standards of dress, student council, honor system. Discipline rests primarily with faculty.
Tuition and Aid Day student tuition: $28,000–$30,200. Tuition installment plan (The Tuition Plan, Insured Tuition Payment Plan, Academic Management Services Plan, Key Tuition Payment Plan, monthly payment plans, individually arranged payment plans). Tuition reduction for siblings, bursaries, merit scholarship grants, need-based scholarship grants available. In 2007–08, 20% of upper-school students received aid. Total amount of financial aid awarded in 2007–08: $650,000.
Admissions Traditional secondary-level entrance grade is 9. ISEE required. Deadline for receipt of application materials: January 15. Application fee required: $50. On-campus interview required.
Athletics Interscholastic: basketball (boys, girls), softball (b,g), volleyball (g); intramural: dance squad (g), volleyball (g); coed interscholastic: baseball, basketball, cross-country running, fencing, golf, hockey, soccer, tennis, track and field; coed intramural: aerobics, aquatics, basketball, bicycling, billiards, bowling, climbing, cross-country running, dance, equestrian sports, fencing, Frisbee, golf, horseback riding, judo, roller hockey, soccer, softball, swimming and diving, ultimate Frisbee. 4 PE instructors, 6 coaches, 3 athletic trainers.
Computers Computers are regularly used in all academic classes. Computer network features include on-campus library services, online commercial services, Internet access, wireless campus network, Internet filtering or blocking technology, T1 Internet connection in every class. Students grades are available online. The school has a published electronic and media policy.
Contact Elizabeth Norton, Director of Enrollment. 212-362-0400 Ext. 106. Fax: 212-362-7424. E-mail: enorton@yorkprep.org. Web site: www.yorkprep.org.

ANNOUNCEMENT FROM THE SCHOOL York Prep, founded in 1969, is a college-preparatory school, enrolling students in grades 6–12, where contemporary methods enliven a strong, academically challenging, and traditional curriculum. The School's approach emphasizes independent thought, builds confidence, and sends graduates to the finest colleges and universities. York Prep offers state-of-the-art computer labs, varsity and junior varsity athletics, and many extracurricular activities.

See Close-Up on page 1044.

ZURICH INTERNATIONAL SCHOOL

Steinacherstrasse 140
Wädenswil 8820, Switzerland

Head of School: Peter C. Mott

General Information Coeducational day college-preparatory, arts, and technology school. Grades PS–13. Founded: 1963. Setting: suburban. Nearest major city is Zurich, Switzerland. 6-acre campus. 1 building on campus. Approved or accredited by European Council of International Schools, International Baccalaureate Organization, New England Association of Schools and Colleges, and Swiss Federation of Private Schools. Language of instruction: English. Total enrollment: 1,313. Upper school average class size: 14. Upper school faculty-student ratio: 1:7.
Upper School Student Profile Grade 9: 109 students (62 boys, 47 girls); Grade 10: 108 students (55 boys, 53 girls); Grade 11: 117 students (71 boys, 46 girls); Grade 12: 104 students (47 boys, 57 girls); Grade 13: 3 students (2 boys, 1 girl).
Faculty School total: 153. In upper school: 29 men, 33 women; 34 have advanced degrees.
Subjects Offered Acting, advanced math, Advanced Placement courses, American history, art history, art history-AP, biology, biology-AP, calculus, calculus-AP, chemistry-AP, community service, concert band, drama, drama performance, economics, English, English literature, English literature and composition-AP, ESL, European history-AP, fine arts, French, French language-AP, German, German-AP, global studies, health, health education, history, history-AP, International Baccalaureate courses, jazz band, journalism, math methods, mathematics, model United Nations, music, music theory-AP, philosophy, photography, physical education, physics-AP, pre-calculus, science, social studies, sports, statistics and probability, statistics-AP, studio art, studio art-AP, theater, trigonometry, U.S. history-AP, visual arts, world history, writing, yearbook.
Graduation Requirements 1½ elective credits, algebra, arts and fine arts (art, music, dance, drama), English, foreign language, geometry, history, mathematics, physical education (includes health), science, CAS (with IB Diploma), extended essay (IB), theory of knowledge. Community service is required.
Special Academic Programs International Baccalaureate program; 11 Advanced Placement exams for which test preparation is offered; honors section; independent study; academic accommodation for the gifted, the musically talented, and the artistically talented; remedial reading and/or remedial writing; remedial math; programs in English, mathematics, general development for dyslexic students; ESL (51 students enrolled).
College Admission Counseling 86 students graduated in 2008; 48 went to college, including Bentley University; Boston University; University of Colorado at Boulder. Other: 5 went to work, 3 entered military service, 15 had other specific plans. 35% scored over 600 on SAT critical reading, 50% scored over 600 on SAT math, 48% scored over 600 on SAT writing, 42% scored over 1800 on combined SAT.
Student Life Upper grades have specified standards of dress, student council, honor system. Discipline rests primarily with faculty.
Tuition and Aid Day student tuition: 31,000 Swiss francs. Tuition installment plan (monthly payment plans, individually arranged payment plans). Need-based scholarship grants available. In 2008–09, 5% of upper-school students received aid. Total amount of financial aid awarded in 2008–09: 97,500 Swiss francs.
Admissions Traditional secondary-level entrance grade is 9. For fall 2008, 124 students applied for upper-level admission, 87 were accepted, 87 enrolled. English for Non-native Speakers required. Deadline for receipt of application materials: none. Application fee required: 4500 Swiss francs. Interview recommended.
Athletics Interscholastic: basketball (boys, girls), rugby (b), soccer (b,g), softball (g), tennis (b,g), volleyball (b,g); intramural: indoor soccer (b,g); coed interscholastic: alpine skiing, cross-country running, golf, skiing (cross-country), skiing (downhill), swimming and diving, track and field; coed intramural: aerobics/dance, badminton, basketball, canoeing/kayaking, climbing, dance, fitness, Frisbee, kayaking, outdoor activities, rock climbing, swimming and diving, wall climbing, yoga. 5 PE instructors, 15 coaches.
Computers Computers are regularly used in art, English, foreign language, history, mathematics, science classes. Computer network features include on-campus library services, online commercial services, Internet access, wireless campus network, Internet filtering or blocking technology, Moodle, VHS. Campus intranet, student e-mail accounts, and computer access in designated common areas are available to students. The school has a published electronic and media policy.
Contact Dale Braunschweig, Head Admissions. 41-76 337 05 50. Fax: 41-43 244 20 51. E-mail: dbraunschweig@zis.ch. Web site: www.zis.ch.

ANNOUNCEMENT FROM THE SCHOOL Zurich International School is an internationally accredited independent school in Zurich spanning Pre-school through Grade 12. ZIS offers the IB Primary Years Programme, Advanced Placement courses, and the IB Diploma. Over 1,300 students from more than forty-five countries attend ZIS at one of the School's five campuses.

Traditional Day and Boarding School Close-Ups

ACCELERATED SCHOOLS

Denver, Colorado

Type: Coeducational boarding and day college-preparatory school
Grades: K–16; Elementary School, Kindergarten–6; Middle School, 7–8; High School, 9–12; postgraduate years
Enrollment: School total: 100; High School: 75
Head of School: John Klieforth

THE SCHOOL

Accelerated Schools was established in 1920. The School has many winning systems in its design that benefit the instructional process. Its individualized and tutorial program is designed to quickly improve a student's performance in every academic and social area. Student progress is so rapid that most students starting below grade level are effectively doing superior work after one or two semesters. Gifted and talented students find maximum challenge in the high performance, Honors, Advanced Placement, and Accelerated Thinking curriculums.

With 1 teacher for every 7 students, teachers have time to counsel, advise, tutor, and manage a very effective motivation system. Students learn to write and speak fluently. The average student completes 2,000 to 3,000 pages of notetaking, writing, and word processing during one school year. The School measures its accountability with standardized testing, mastery tests, and extensive writing portfolios.

Accelerated Schools provides a computer-intensive education and heavily emphasizes thinking, speaking, and writing skills. All students have access to a microcomputer for at least 3 hours per day. More than 150 microcomputers are available. The School's library of more than 2,000 educational and business computer programs meets a wide range of skill needs. In addition, computers can be borrowed for the school year.

Students' academic progress averages a three-year grade-level gain on standardized tests every nine months. Students raise their scores an average of three times more rapidly than the average school program, as measured by standardized tests.

Accelerated Schools is highly successful in its mission of educating students of any age, race, or creed. Each student has a completely individualized program dealing with his or her particular needs. There is extensive coordination with the student's home to develop and maintain a positive educational environment.

Accelerated Schools headquarters is located on the grounds of the historic Fitzroy Place in Denver, Colorado. In reality, the School has few boundaries. Its ten vans crisscross the metro area and a 150-mile radius with hundreds of daylong tours and afternoon field trips scheduled each year. Trips include tours of factories, gold mines, museums, historical and geological sites, dinosaur nests, and early Indian dwellings. The School is within 1½ hours of several popular ski areas. Optional ski school trips are scheduled every Wednesday during the long ski season from November to June.

Denver is located on the plains at 5,280 feet, but half the School's trips are in the mountains 10 miles to the west at elevations of 8,000 to 12,000 feet. The Denver metro area is an ideal resource for a well-rounded education. The high academic standards of the community have supported an abundance of exceptional educational and cultural happenings.

The Denver metro area, with a population of 2 million, is noted for its abundance of mild, sunny days, water sports, and a wide range of recreational activities. Denver is a beautiful city, renowned for its tree-lined streets, 205 parks, and many miles of biking and hiking trails.

Accelerated Schools is a private nonprofit corporation operated by an 8-member Board of Trustees composed of education and business leaders from the Denver area. The School plant is valued at $2.5 million.

Accelerated Schools also has a similar facility in Kansas City, Missouri, which may be reached at 913-341-6666.

Accelerated Schools are fully accredited by the North Central Association of Colleges and Schools and accepted by the Colorado State Board of Education.

ACADEMIC PROGRAMS

Accelerated Schools offers highly accelerated programs for students who are gifted and talented as well as those students who need remedial help. All student enrollments are individualized; students may start any day of the year. Their school year ends when attendance and course mastery requirements have been met. Attendance and work on a subject are equivalent to 1 Carnegie unit.

To graduate high school, students must complete a minimum of 22 approved credits as follows: 5 credits in English (including a senior research paper); 3 credits in social studies (1 of which must be in U.S. history); 7 credits in math, science, and computer science; 1 credit in physical education or health; ½ credit in reading; ½ credit in study skills; and 5 in academic electives.

Advanced Placement courses are available in many areas; study in most AP subjects can be arranged on an individual basis. In addition, Accelerated offers a post–high school, advanced studies program.

An average student-teacher ratio of 7:1 allows substantial faculty-student interaction. Each student receives a report card at the close of every school day. This daily evaluation ensures a close and constant screening of the student's progress toward fulfilling identified needs.

Students are graded by letter grades, A through C. No failing grades are given. If a student has not mastered a subject adequately, an "incomplete" is given until the student meets the mastery requirements of the subject. Daily grades are based upon the average of the day's report card scores.

Fifteen percent of the students are from other countries. In 1989, the School pioneered the computer-based Accelerated Language courses for its international students. English language classroom results improved markedly. In 1990, the School added an ESL version of its Accelerated Thinking procedures (listening, memory, speaking, and writing), which has rapidly improved the speaking and writing fluency of its ESL students. Results have been documented by improved TOEFL, mastery, and standardized test scores and by the number of writing portfolios completed.

Accelerated Schools specializes in preparing all students in the English as a second language program for more advanced college courses. It offers both regular and intensive tracks toward a certificate of completion from its International Student Department. Accelerated Thinking, Think Tank, and field trip procedures create many small conversation groups for practicing English.

Some students stay at the School after earning their diploma for more college prep, TOEFL prep, intensive English, or other college courses. The Accelerated Advanced Studies program is a great way to become more competitive in college while mastering more of the English language. Extra preparation for the demands of competitive college work gives students an additional edge over other students when applying to other colleges.

FACULTY AND ADVISERS

Accelerated Schools employs carefully screened professionals in every area of administration and instruction. All teachers are certified in the specific fields of their assignments, and all have a specialty that complements the backgrounds of their associates. Many teachers hold advanced degrees in education, special education, psychology, sociology, mathematics, and reading. Each teacher must also complete extensive independent study courses in behavior and computer classroom management.

In addition to the teaching staff, head teachers and educational counselors with special training in behavior management analyze the educational background and factors of psychological motivation affecting each student. They hold regular conferences with students and parents throughout the school year.

Because the faculty holds itself responsible for the student's education, weekly staff-training and review sessions are held. This allows the entire staff the opportunity to contribute to an individual's progress.

Of the 18 high school faculty members, 10 are women and 8 are men. Five hold master's degrees, and 3 have Ph.D.'s. Accelerated selects and retains only those teachers who are willing to accept the level of responsibility required by young students.

Principal John Klieforth is noted in Colorado as an outstanding teacher and school administrator. Carl Peterson, the Director of the School and founder of the Accelerated Schools concept, is the author of the book *Winning Systems,* a guide for student motivation. More than 100,000 students and teachers have attended classes directed by Mr. Peterson.

COLLEGE ADMISSION COUNSELING

College counseling is extensive for all students. The head teachers and educational counselors advise students on the college application process. All seniors are expected to take both the ACT and SAT. A complete library of college catalogs is available.

More than 75 percent of the graduates since 1980 enrolled in and were successful at the colleges or universities of their choice. Recent graduates are attending such schools as Arapahoe Community, Metropolitan State, and the Universities of Colorado, Denver, and Northern Colorado.

STUDENT BODY AND CONDUCT

The School's enrollment in 2007–08 was 100 students: 75 in high school, 20 in middle school, and 5 in elementary school. These students were from across the United States, Canada, Russia, Europe, the Middle East, and Asia.

The School has one primary rule—no student has the right to interfere with the rights of another student to learn, to be comfortable, and to be safe.

The School works to create and develop its students' self-control and self-esteem through accelerated academic development. Each student is treated as a complete individual in terms of social behavior, educational accomplishment, and personal discipline. Disciplinary action is seldom necessary, but if it becomes necessary, the student's family, or the host family in the case of boarding students, is the final arbiter.

The School's location in Denver, Colorado, provides an international crossroads and rich multicultural experiences for students from both the Atlantic and Pacific basins.

ACADEMIC FACILITIES

The main buildings on campus are the Mansion and the science and art building. The library is located in the Mansion and contains more than 2,000 volumes and more than 100 CD-ROM computers are located in the classrooms.

By providing one computer for each student, the School is set apart from most education facilities. Many brands of computers are available for students, as is a large accumulation of educational software. Computers do not replace books, paper, and pencils as tools for learning, but they are a very important part of the overall program for academic excellence.

BOARDING AND GENERAL FACILITIES

Room, board, and supervision for out-of-town students are provided by host families who can give students valuable attention and include them in social activities. The supportive family environment provided by host parents has proven most effective. The families whom the School recommends have been screened and trained to support the positive reinforcement program by awarding students extra privileges based on their work.

Students are treated as members of the host family and are responsible for the care of their own room. The host family's proximity to the School is not important—instructors pick up the students and take them home every day.

ATHLETICS

The School offers some sports on a noncompetitive basis. These include basketball, hiking, jogging, running, soccer, softball, snow skiing, swimming, tennis, and volleyball. Facilities for athletics are available locally.

EXTRACURRICULAR OPPORTUNITIES

There are frequent educational tours and trips for such activities as snow skiing, camping, and backpacking. All trips are well supervised by recreation professionals.

DAILY LIFE

The School is informal and nonstressful. It is a warm and friendly yet studious environment. Students quickly adapt to the high-level challenges being presented.

The student is picked up at the door of his or her residence and brought to school by 9 a.m. From 9 a.m. to 1:05 p.m. the student is under the supervision of one teacher for academics. This person does not teach all subjects but rather is responsible for the student's schedule, behavior, and progress.

The student has supervised breaks at 10:30 and 11:30 a.m. The balance of school time is spent working as directed on a teacher-monitored contract that results in a report card at the end of each day. Lunch is at 1:05 p.m. A student may bring a lunch or purchase a lunch from a catering truck that comes to the School. At 1:35, afternoon activities begin. Regularly scheduled activities are Accelerated Thinking, Accelerated Think Tank, computer lab, science lab, art, study hall, and library. Special activities such as swimming, jogging, and bowling may be scheduled by the staff. School ends at 3 p.m.

WEEKEND LIFE

Day students spend weekends with their families, and boarding students with their host families. Many of the host families organize activities and trips. There are optional escorted tours on some Saturdays, Sundays, and holidays.

SUMMER PROGRAMS

Accelerated Schools maintains a regular summer program that is just like that of the rest of the year. Features of the summer program include special trips and tours; supervised study in specific areas, particularly for gifted and talented students; special library and research programs; and many outdoor activities.

The summer program lasts from 40 hours to three months, depending on the student's progress, and is taught by regular faculty members. Students earn credit for their work.

COSTS AND FINANCIAL AID

Day student tuition in 2009–10 is $22,750 (meals not included). Boarding student tuition, room, and board cost $29,950. A monthly payment plan is available.

Some need-based scholarships are awarded. In 2008–09, 10 percent of the students received $90,000 in financial aid.

ADMISSIONS INFORMATION

Any student is eligible for admission. Placement within the program is determined by the student's needs and by free testing prior to admission. An application form should be submitted and an academic transcript forwarded to the School.

APPLICATION TIMETABLE

Accelerated is an individualized year-round school. A student may start any day of the year. Students take vacations when it is convenient for their parents or when they have met their course requirements. The year-round school allows fast track students to graduate from high school or the college within 36 months. Candidates are notified of the admission decision as soon as their applications have been reviewed.

ADMISSIONS CORRESPONDENCE

Jane Queen
Associate Director of Admissions
Accelerated Schools
2160 South Cook Street
Denver, Colorado 80210

Phone: 303-758-2003
Fax: 303-757-4336
E-mail: info@acceleratedschools.org
Web site: http://www.acceleratedschools.org

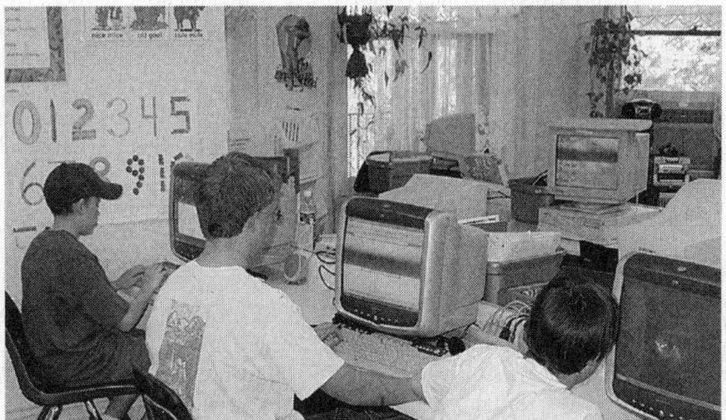

ACS INTERNATIONAL SCHOOLS

Cobham, Surrey; Egham, Surrey; and Hillingdon, Middlesex, England

Type: Coeducational boarding and day college-preparatory schools
Grades: Preschool (age 2 at Cobham and Egham, age 4 at Hillingdon) to grade 12
Enrollment: School total: 2,600; Upper Schools: 436 (Cobham), 242 (Hillingdon), 143 (Egham)
Heads of Schools: Tom Lehman, Cobham; Moyra Hadley, Egham; Ginger Apple, Hillingdon

THE SCHOOLS

The three ACS International Schools are nonsectarian and coeducational (with boarding at ACS Cobham), enrolling students from 2 to 18 years of age from more than seventy countries. ACS International Schools offer the International Baccalaureate (IB) Middle Years Programme, Primary Years Programme, Diploma, and an International curriculum, including Advanced Placement (AP) courses, leading to a high school diploma. ACS International Schools' excellent exam results have ensured that its graduates attend the world's finest universities.

ACS inspires its students to become successful lifelong learners and responsible global citizens. The Schools promote high standards of scholarship and challenge all members of the community to fulfill their potential.

ACS is accredited by the New England Association of Schools and Colleges and is authorized by the International Baccalaureate Organization to offer the IB Diploma. In addition, ACS Egham is one of only three schools in the U.K. to also offer the IB Primary Years Programme (3–11) and the IB Middle Years Programme (11–16). The Schools hold memberships in the U.S. College Board Advanced Placement (AP) Program, the European Council of International Schools, the Council of International Schools, and the Independent Schools Association. The Schools are inspected by the Independent Schools Inspectorate (ISI) on behalf of OFSTED, and the results are available on the ISI Web site (http://www.isinspect.org.uk)

The campuses are situated southwest of central London, offering families spacious suburban homes with direct public transportation links to central London. The Surrey campuses, ACS Cobham International School (23 miles south of London) and ACS Egham International School (25 miles southwest of London), are both served by direct rail links, while ACS Hillingdon International School (15 miles west of London) is served by London Underground and direct rail links.

The schools set the benchmark standard for high-quality facilities and grounds. Each campus is built around a spacious country estate, enhanced by modern, purpose-built classrooms, libraries, cafeterias, and sports facilities. Lower, Middle, and High Schools have designated computer rooms, libraries, science laboratories, and art studios. The organisation's robust program of development and renewal has invested more than £80 million into the campus facilities over the past ten years.

ACADEMIC PROGRAMS

All three campuses accept students from preschool through high school. ACS Cobham and ACS Egham accept students from age 2; ACS Hillingdon accepts students from age 4. All students graduate a with high school diploma and have the option of studying for the full IB Diploma. In addition, ACS Cobham and ACS Hillingdon campuses offer American AP courses. ACS Egham offers the IB Primary Years and Middle Years Programmes. ACS Hillingdon offers the IB Middle Years Programme.

Specialized learning support is available in the Lower, Middle, and High Schools for students with mild learning differences. English as an Additional Language (EAL) is available on all three campuses. Students should be intermediate English speakers before entering high school. The Schools also offer strong native language support as needed.

To graduate with the High School Diploma, High School students must complete at least 20 credits, including 6 in social studies and foreign language, 6 in mathematics and science, 4 in English, 1 in fine arts, and physical education in grades 9–12.

While courses may vary slightly, the full-year courses offered are English I–IV, French I–V, German I–IV, Spanish I–IV, world history I–II, contemporary history, U.S. history, economics, algebra I–II, plane geometry, advanced algebra II, trigonometry/analytic geometry, biology, chemistry, physics, drawing and painting, crafts, ceramics and sculpture, advanced art, advanced music, advanced drama, and word processing. Depending on student interest, AP or IB courses may be offered in English, French, German, Spanish, U.S. history, European history, calculus, biology, chemistry, physics, computer science, art, psychology, economics, and government.

The full International Baccalaureate Diploma Programme is offered on all three campuses. In 2008, the combined IB Diploma pass rate of 99 percent was well above the international average of 80 percent, and ACS International Schools' average IB Diploma score of 33 points clearly surpassed the international average of 30. These results continue to place ACS International among the highest achieving independent schools in the U.K.

Average class sizes range from 15 to 20 students. Teachers are available for extra help sessions during and after school. School reports are issued every quarter (approximately every nine weeks). Regular parent-teacher conferences are scheduled twice per year and on an occasional basis, as necessary. All schools have thriving parent communities, including parent-teacher organisations and associations, and families are made to feel welcome at the schools and are encouraged to be involved in school life.

FACULTY AND ADVISERS

There are 139 full-time teachers at ACS Cobham, 99 women and 40 men. At ACS Hillingdon, there are 78 full-time teachers, 51 women and 27 men. There are 78 full-time teachers, 58 women and 20 men, at ACS Egham. All teachers hold bachelor's degrees, and 120 have graduate degrees. There are 21 part-time instructors. Full-time nurses at all schools provide health care. Faculty benefits include a variety of options, such as health insurance, home leave, housing allowance, and a pension plan. Other benefits include a professional development allowance and bereavement fund.

COLLEGE ADMISSION COUNSELING

Assisted by university placement counselors on the Cobham, Egham, and Hillingdon campuses, nearly all ACS students attend institutions of higher education. ACS graduates attend leading universities around the world, including Cambridge, Imperial College London, London School of Economics, and Oxford in the U.K.; Harvard, Penn State, Princeton, and Stanford in the U.S.; and Delft University of Technology, Keio, McGill, Stockholm School of Economics, and the Universities of Oslo and Tokyo throughout the rest of the world.

STUDENT BODY AND CONDUCT

Fifty percent of the student body at ACS Cobham is American, with other major nationality groups being British, Canadian, Norwegian, Dutch, Swedish, Danish, and Australian. The total enrollment is approximately 1,369 students, consisting of 763 boys and 606 girls. The boarding school has 54 boys and 43 girls.

Approximately 45 percent of the student body at ACS Hillingdon is from the United States, with other main student populations from Japan, Britain, Canada, Norway, the Netherlands, and Sweden. The total enrollment at ACS Hillingdon is 577, 294 boys and 283 girls.

Approximately 43 percent of the student population at ACS Egham is American, with the other major nationality groups being Dutch, British, Canadian, Mexican, Belgian, and Danish. The Egham campus currently enrolls 586 students, 302 boys and 284 girls.

Approximately 47 percent of the total number of students at the ACS International Schools are American; 15 percent are British and Canadian. The remaining 35 percent represent more than sixty-five other nationalities. Most of the children are from families in business or government on assignment in London, and the Schools also attract a growing local British following.

ACADEMIC FACILITIES

Situated on a beautiful 128-acre country estate, ACS Cobham International School has purpose-built Lower, Middle, and High School buildings. In addition, the campus has premier sports facilities that include on-site soccer and rugby fields, softball and baseball diamonds, an all-weather Olympic-sized track, tennis courts, a six-hole golf course, and a new Sports Centre, which houses a basketball/volleyball show court, a 25-metre competition-class swimming pool, a dance studio, a fitness suite, and a cafeteria. The recently completed, purpose-built Early Childhood Village expansion project offers additional purpose-built classrooms and office space

Situated on a superbly kept 11-acre site, ACS Hillingdon International School has excellent facilities augmented by a new purpose-built music centre, complete with a digital recording studio, rehearsal rooms, practice studios, and a computer lab for music technology. There are on-site playing fields, tennis courts, and playgrounds, with additional off-site soccer, rugby, track, baseball, softball, swimming, and golf facilities available.

The 20-acre ACS Egham International School has superb teaching, sports, and extracurricular facilities and a newly refurbished cafeteria and kitchen. The campuswide wireless and cabled IT network makes working with laptop or desktop computers an effortless and integral part of the learning process.

BOARDING AND GENERAL FACILITIES

Staffed by teachers and full-time houseparents, the coeducational boarding house at ACS Cobham has separate-wing accommodation for 100 students ranging in age from 12 (grade 7) to 18 (grade 12). The ergonomically designed 2-person rooms have en-suite facilities and Internet connections. There are game and television rooms, kitchens, and common rooms for the students. A variety of weekend and afterschool trips and activities ensure a lively, active life for boarders.

Nurses at all schools provide health care in modern, purpose-built health centers. Each of the three schools has a Housing Department that offers a complimentary house-finding service for parents wishing to relocate to an ACS catchment area. The Schools provide an extensive door-to-door bus service within their catchment areas, which is popular with families.

ATHLETICS

School teams compete with local American and British schools as well as with international schools. Boys' and girls' varsity teams compete in basketball, cross-country, soccer, swimming, tennis, track and field, and volleyball. There are also boys' rugby and baseball teams and girls' softball and cheerleading teams. Intramural sports and non-competitive physical activities include badminton, basketball, dance, darts, "fun runs," gymnastics, soccer, tennis, and volleyball.

EXTRACURRICULAR OPPORTUNITIES

The three schools provide a variety of different after-school clubs, sports, and activities for Lower, Middle, and High School students. Optional Lower School activities may include various arts and crafts clubs, Scouts, music (additional choir or band), dance, chess, tennis, bowling, golf, dance, or other sports. Middle School activities and clubs may include a similar variety but also cooking clubs, safe-sitter programs, and a Middle School musical production. Both the High Schools and Middle Schools also have student councils, peer counsellors, cheerleaders, student newspapers, literary magazines, and yearbooks as well as recycling and environmental clubs. High School students may participate in up to three drama productions per year, math teams, Model United Nations, National Honor Society, International Schools Thespian Association, choir, speech and debate competitions, quiz bowls, and various community service organizations, such as Habitat for Humanity, the Duke of Edinburgh Award scheme, and World Challenge projects.

In addition to extensive field trips that enliven classroom learning, students also participate in more extended trips. Typical examples include trips to Stratford-upon-Avon and environmental or history centers in England; foreign language, skiing, and arts trips in Europe; and community-service activities in Africa or Asia. The Schools regularly host visiting artists, writers, and musicians and hold arts festivals, international celebrations, and a variety of community-service events.

DAILY LIFE

The school year, from the end of August to mid-June, is divided into two semesters. There are vacations in October, December, February, and April. The daily schedule for all grades extends from 8:30 a.m. to 3:10 p.m. each day. Middle and High School students have eight instructional periods each day, with extracurricular activities held after 3 p.m. Faculty members are available to provide individual help after school.

WEEKEND LIFE

Boarding students participate in planned trips to various cultural and sports events on weekends, virtually all of which are included in the basic fee. The prearranged programs for each weekend include attending concerts and plays in London, visiting such historic sites as the Naval Museum in Portsmouth, and attending ACS sports games.

SUMMER PROGRAMS

The ACS International Schools offer academic and recreational programs to fit the needs of participating students. Pioneered in 1996, the British Studies course is an interdisciplinary, three-week study and travel course for talented high school students 15–19 years old. The course offers enrichment in European history, English literature, art, and music.

COSTS AND FINANCIAL AID

For 2008–09, semester tuition for day students is £9140 for grades 9–12; semester fees are an additional £5025 for five-day boarding students and £6880 for seven-day boarding students. Bus service is extra, with a reduced rate for siblings. In addition, all families must pay a one-time £500 debenture subscription for each student enrolled.

ADMISSIONS INFORMATION

The ACS International Schools seek to enroll motivated students of all nationalities with the potential to succeed in a challenging college-preparatory curriculum. New students are accepted in all grades throughout the year (except grade 12—first-semester entry only) on the basis of the completed application form, previous school records, standardized test results, a student questionnaire, and recommendations from the previous school. The Schools administer placement exams as necessary. High school students whose native language is not English must take a language test for entrance. Those interested should note that if students have mild learning disabilities, additional information is requested.

APPLICATION TIMETABLE

Students may apply at any time. Preregistration for returning families begins in April. There is a registration fee.

ADMISSIONS CORRESPONDENCE

Admissions Office
ACS Cobham International School
Heywood, Portsmouth Road
Cobham, Surrey KT11 1BL
Phone: 44-1-932-869744
Fax: 44-1-932-869789
E-mail: cobhamadmissions@acs-england.co.uk
Web site: http://www.acs-england.co.uk

Admissions Office
ACS Hillingdon International School
Hillingdon Court, 108 Vine Lane
Hillingdon, Uxbridge
Middlesex UB10 0BE
Phone: 44-1-895-818402
Fax: 44-1-895-818404
E-mail: hillingdonadmissions@acs-england.co.uk
Web site: http://www.acs-england.co.uk

Admissions Office
ACS Egham International School
Woodlee, London Road (A30)
Egham, Surrey TW20 0HS
Phone: 44-1-784-430611
Fax: 44-1-784-430626
E-mail: eghamadmissions@acs-england.co.uk
Web site: http://www.acs-england.co.uk

THE AGNES IRWIN SCHOOL

Rosemont, Pennsylvania

The Agnes Irwin School

Type: Girls' day college-preparatory school
Grades: Pre-K–12
Enrollment: 681
Head of School: Helen Rowland Marter, Interim Head of School

THE SCHOOL

At the entrance to the Admissions Office at Harvard University, there is a plaque honoring Miss Agnes Irwin, who was chosen by Harvard to be the first dean of Radcliffe College. Her selection was not surprising; she was highly regarded as a pioneering educator of women and the founder in 1869 of one of the first schools in the United States devoted to girls—The Agnes Irwin School. The School was at the forefront in developing academic opportunities for girls and continues today to be a nationally recognized leader in this field. The atmosphere is both nurturing and challenging, with a faculty and program attuned specifically to the developmental strengths and needs of girls.

The School is located 10 miles west of Philadelphia on an 18-acre suburban campus. Twenty school districts provide bus transportation, enabling girls to attend the School from more than seventy-seven zip code areas in Philadelphia and suburban communities. Public transportation is available close to the School, and the School offers a free shuttle to and from public transportation.

A 31-member Board of Trustees, including alumnae, parents, and members of local education and business communities, governs Agnes Irwin. There is an active Alumnae Association with more than 4,000 members and a supportive Parent Association. Sponsored programs in recent years have included a Science Symposium for Girls, a day of workshops with ABC Congressional Correspondent and leading political pundit Cokie Roberts and literary giants Nikki Giovanni and Lisa See, and faculty and parents' workshops with Mel Levine, JoAnn Deak, Edward Hallowell, Michael Thompson, Lyn Michel Brown, and Leonard Sax exploring the current research on gender and learning. This year's annual giving and fund-raising activities totaled more than $1 million and the endowment currently stands at $23 million.

Accreditations include Middle States Association of Colleges and Schools and Pennsylvania Association of Private Academic Schools. Memberships include National Association of Independent Schools, Pennsylvania Association of Independent Schools, the National Coalition of Girls' Schools, and the Cum Laude Society.

ACADEMIC PROGRAMS

Graduation requirements include 4 years of English; 3 years of French or Spanish or completion of Latin III; 3 years of mathematics; 3 years of history; 3 years of lab science, including physics, chemistry, and biology; 1 year of fine arts; and 4 years of physical education. Students are expected to take five subjects per year. Grading is on a trimester system.

Electives are available in all areas and include bioethics, economics, international politics, Middle Eastern history, media arts and graphic design, robotics, the craft of writing, financial literacy, and advanced topics in math; the courses Banned Books: Censorship Today and Order and Chaos: What Lies Beneath; and independent science research.

Honors and Advanced Placement (AP) courses are available in English, U.S. history, European history, calculus, Latin, French, Spanish, physics, chemistry, biology, and environmental science. In the class of 2008, 60 percent were honored by the AP Scholars Program, and 43 percent took five or more AP courses. Ninety-two percent of the class took AP tests in sixteen subjects.

Visual and Performing Arts courses include AP photography, studio art, AP drawing/painting, AP mixed portfolio with 2-D design, computer graphics, 3-D design in pottery and/or sculpture, drama, communications and the media, dance, glee club, and the School's a cappella singing group, the Bel Cantos.

A unique feature of an Agnes Irwin education is the Special Studies Program. For two weeks in February, sophomores and juniors leave the School to explore careers or special interests in the greater classroom of the "real world." Students choose one of the School-sponsored courses offered, an independent program, or a combination of the two. The goals of the program are to enrich the student's educational experience by expanding her understanding of the world beyond Agnes Irwin through internships, community service, cultural immersion, and wilderness exploration as well as provide opportunities to pursue special talents and interests. In 2008, 70 percent of the girls were involved with the following programs: Habitat for Humanity, Santa Fe Photography Workshop, Presidential Classroom, Marine Ecology, a homestay in France or Mexico, Theater Arts, Teton Science School, Philadelphia Exploration, Shakespeare Theater and Stage Combat, and community service programs, including a week at an orphanage in the Dominican Republic. The remainder of the girls pursued independent projects, such as working in a law firm, interning in an architect's office, shadowing a Division I women's basketball coach, assisting a molecular biologist conducting research, and interning at a radio station.

The Senior Assembly is another treasured tradition at Agnes Irwin. Each senior is required to present a 10-minute speech in the theater before her peers and faculty members on a topic of her choosing. Recent topics include China's Century, Cole Porter, Is Turkey the New Iran, Medical Ethics, Positive Psychology, Stephen Colbert, and Time Travel. This special feature emphasizes the School's belief that each and every girl has something important to say and the confidence and the ability to address an audience of 300 people.

FACULTY AND ADVISERS

Of the 49 teaching faculty members in the Upper School, 67 percent hold advanced degrees and 31 percent are men. The average class size is 15, with a 7:1 student-teacher ratio.

In addition to teaching responsibilities, some faculty members also serve as advisers. Seven girls are grouped with 1 adviser and meet twice a week for a school period and then individually as needed. In addition, girls receive guidance and assistance through Support Services, which includes guidance counselors, learning specialists, psychologists, and academic tutors.

COLLEGE ADMISSION COUNSELING

In January of their junior year, the girls meet with the Director of College Counseling for twelve small-group seminars to learn how to conduct a successful college search. Topics include interview skills, effective college application essay writing, information regarding athletic recruitment, and financial aid. In the spring of junior year, girls and their parents have individual meetings with their college guidance counselor to help them plan for school visits over the summer and for the more than 75 college reps who visit Agnes Irwin in the fall. Each girl works closely with her college counselor throughout the fall of her senior year and into the spring until her choice has been made.

Typically, 20–25 percent of each graduating class is recognized by the National Merit Program. One hundred percent of the seniors attend college, and, in the last five years, they have matriculated at more than ninety different colleges and universities. Four or more members of the last three graduating classes have attended the University of Pennsylvania (20), Georgetown (11), NYU (8), Boston University (7), Tulane (7), Trinity (Hartford) (6), Dartmouth (5), University of Delaware (6), Princeton (5), University of Virginia (5), Wake Forest (5), Cornell (4), Duke (4), Franklin & Marshall (4), Lehigh (4), Penn State (4), Princeton (4), Skidmore (4), Stanford (4), and University of Richmond (4).

STUDENT BODY

The enrollment for 2008-09 was 681 and breaks down as follows: twelfth grade, 67; eleventh grade, 51; tenth grade, 61; ninth grade, 65; eighth grade, 57; seventh grade, 53; sixth grade, 60; fifth grade, 51; fourth grade, 43; third grade, 31; second grade, 44; first grade, 41; kindergarten, 42 and prekindergarten, 15.

Agnes Irwin fosters an environment where respect for the individual, appreciation of differences, and supportive, lasting friendships are developed and nurtured. The students represent an array of racial, ethnic, religious, socioeconomic, and geographic backgrounds. Students of color represent 20 percent of the student body, and more than 50 girls have a parent(s) who was born in another country and for whom English is a second language.

All students are expected to abide by the Code of Conduct: Respect yourself, respect others, respect property, and act responsibly. In addition, all Upper School girls sign the Honor Code, which was designed by the students and states, "As a member of the Agnes Irwin community I will promote the values of honesty and personal integrity. I will not lie, steal or cheat or tolerate this behavior in others. I will take the necessary action to defend these values." The Discipline Committee, comprising both faculty members and students, handles serious violations of the Code.

ACADEMIC FACILITIES

Agnes Irwin is located on 18 acres, with two gyms; a fitness center; a library for each division; a new Arts and Sciences Center, including a 300-seat theater; a Lower School building; and a combined Middle and Upper School building. There are seven tennis courts and three playing fields.

At Agnes Irwin, technology is delivered to the classroom in all three divisions via rolling carts of portable tablets with a networked printer. Technology is integrated into the curriculum through a variety of age-appropriate, content-specific projects and activities. All faculty members are issued tablet computers, and each classroom is equipped with a projector. The network is evaluated and updated as needed to support both the administrative and academic applications of technology throughout the School.

The three division libraries contain 30,000 volumes and provide access to laptop computers and the schoolwide wireless network. Many library reference resources are online through the AISnet portal, which is available to students from home. Each library is equipped with twenty laptop computers for student use, as well as several desktops with attached scanners.

ATHLETICS

Physical education and athletics have a strong tradition at Agnes Irwin. In the elementary years, girls have physical education four times per week, and, starting in the fifth grade, it increases to five times per week. Interscholastic competition begins in the seventh grade when the School competes in the Interacademic Athletic Association. The sports offered include basketball, crew (Upper School only), cross-country, field hockey, golf, lacrosse, soccer, softball, squash, swimming, tennis, track, and volleyball.

Those students who do not wish to participate in athletics have the option of working out in the Fitness Center as well as taking dance for their physical education requirement. About 25 percent of the girls choose this option.

EXTRACURRICULAR OPPORTUNITIES

Girls participate in concerts, dance recitals, plays, art exhibits, photography shows, and more, increasing their interest as both creators and patrons of art. Girls act, sing, design and decorate sets, and work lighting and soundboards. The School's proximity to Philadelphia enables its teachers to arrange visits to cultural events, such as art museums, concerts, and the opera.

There are numerous student-run clubs, including the yearbook, literary magazine, and school newspaper, and girls have the opportunity to start clubs of their own. In addition to long-standing favorites such as Model UN, SADD, and debate club, girls have recently started a drill team, a fencing club, and a robotics club. There are more than ninety leadership opportunities through clubs, athletic teams, and student government.

Service is an integral part of The Agnes Irwin School community. The emphasis of the program is on hands-on projects with a minimal amount of fundraising. Service activities include tutoring underserved children at urban schools, visiting senior citizens in nursing homes, learning American Sign Language, and participating in organized programs, such as Habitat for Humanity, Philadelphia Cares Day, Special Olympics, and Martin Luther King, Jr. Day of Service.

DAILY LIFE

The School day begins with homeroom at 8:05 and ends at 2:50, with seven 40-minute periods and one 70-minute period per day. Athletic teams practice and play games after school. Most games are on weekdays, although a few may be scheduled on the weekends.

SUMMER PROGRAMS

Summer Session is a seven-week summer program offering arts, athletics, and academics for boys and girls entering prekindergarten–grade 12. Academic courses for credit include Biology, Chemistry, Geometry, Greek I, Latin I, Photography I, and Physics. Enrichment courses for high school students include America on Film, SAT Prep, Pottery and Sculpture, and Journalism for Print and Web.

COSTS AND FINANCIAL AID

Tuition for the 2008–09 school year for grades 9–12 was $25,200. Additional expenses included uniforms, textbooks, and lunch (optional). Tuition is paid in two installments—60 percent in August and 40 percent in January—or families can arrange for a ten-month installment plan through Higher Education Services, with the first payment due in May.

The School is committed to making its educational opportunities available to bright, motivated, and talented girls regardless of their family's ability to pay. Agnes Irwin offered $1,850,000 in financial aid for the 2008–09 school year to 17 percent of its student body. Although financial aid is available in all grades, 50 percent of the budget was awarded to Upper School students. The awards ranged from $2000 to full tuition.

Applicants for grades 6–9 applying for financial aid are encouraged to take the Agnes Irwin scholarship exam, typically held on a Saturday in mid-November. The Carter A. Mannion '81 Athletic Scholarship is also available annually to an incoming Upper School applicant who demonstrates financial need and who is proficient in two sports or demonstrates outstanding competitive experience in one sport and who will participate in at least two athletic seasons each year. Winners of these scholarships are awarded a $500 voucher toward the cost of textbooks as well as the full amount (up to 100 percent) of financial aid for tuition as determined by the School and Student Service for Financial Aid (SSS) each year until graduation.

ADMISSIONS INFORMATION

The four main entry years are prekindergarten, kindergarten, sixth grade, and ninth grade, although students are admitted at all grade levels if space is available. For 2008–09, 83 new girls enrolled, including 14 in the ninth grade. The application process includes a parent interview, standardized testing (ISEE or SSAT), school transcripts, teacher recommendations, and a full-day student visit. Each visitor is matched with a hostess and attends her classes and activities for the day so she can better appreciate the level of course work as well as the culture of the School.

APPLICATION TIMETABLE

Applications should be submitted starting in September of the year before the student wishes to enter and should be completed by January 12. Decision letters are mailed by February 1. Those girls offered admission must secure their place in the grade by March 1. The parent or guardian signs an enrollment contract and submits it along with a $1000 nonrefundable deposit. If space becomes available after March 1, late applications as well as those on the waiting list are considered.

ADMISSIONS CORRESPONDENCE

Sally B. Keidel
Director of Enrollment Management
The Agnes Irwin School
Ithan Avenue and Conestoga Road
Rosemont, Pennsylvania 19010
Phone: 610-525-8400
E-mail: admissions@agnesirwin.org
Web site: http://www.agnesirwin.org

AMERICAN HERITAGE SCHOOL

Plantation and Delray Beach, Florida

Type: Coeducational, day, independent, nonsectarian
Grades: PK-3–grade 12
Enrollment: 2,400, Plantation campus; 1,104, Boca/Delray campus
Head of School: William Laurie, President and Founder

THE SCHOOL

American Heritage School's mission is to graduate students who are prepared in mind, body, and spirit to meet the requirements of the colleges of their choice. To this end, the School strives to offer a challenging college preparatory curriculum, opportunities for leadership, and superior programs in the arts and athletics. American Heritage is committed to providing a safe and nurturing environment for learning so that children of average to gifted intelligence may achieve their full potential to be intelligent, creative, and contributing members of society. Students receive a well-rounded education that provides opportunities for leadership and character building and extensive opportunities for growth in the arts, athletics, and new technology.

ACADEMIC PROGRAMS

The curriculum for the preprimary child is developmental and age appropriate at each level. Daily language, speech, and auditory development activities help children to listen, understand, speak, and learn effectively. The program seeks to maximize the academic potential of each child, while fostering a positive self-image and providing the skills necessary for the next level of education.

The Lower School is committed to developing a student's basic skills, helping the student master content areas, and maintaining the student's enthusiasm for learning. Students learn the fundamentals of reading, process writing, mathematics, and English through a logical progressive sequence, and they learn social studies, handwriting, spelling, science, and health, with an emphasis on the development of good study skills. In math and reading, students are grouped according to ability. Enrichment classes in computer education, art, media center, music, Spanish, Chinese, physical education, and investigative science lab are offered. Field trips, special projects and events, and assemblies supplement the work introduced in class.

Math, reading, grammar, literature, social studies, and science are the core subjects of the junior high curriculum, where critical-thinking skills become increasingly important. Writing skills are emphasized, helping students become literate and articulate thinkers and writers. Enrichment courses are an important part of the junior high curriculum, with courses rotated on a nine-week basis. Honors classes are available in all core subject areas.

At the high school level, emphasis is placed on college preparation and on higher-level thinking skills. Students are challenged by required research and speech and writing assignments in all subject areas. An extensive variety of classes in all areas of the fine arts is available. A selection of electives—from marine biology to women's literature to stagecraft—rounds out the students' schedules, allowing them to explore other interests and talents. In addition to traditional lecture and discussion, teachers supplement the text curriculum with activities, projects, and field trips that make subjects more relevant and meaningful to the students.

Honors and Advanced Placement (AP) courses are available to qualified students. Students may gain college credit as a benefit of the successful completion of AP courses, which include American government, American history, biology, calculus, chemistry, economics, English language, English literature, environmental studies, European history, French, music theory, physics, psychology, Spanish, and world history.

American Heritage School offers unique premedical, prelaw, and pre-engineering programs to qualified high school students. The programs challenge those ninth- through twelfth-grade students who have an interest in these fields of study and encourage students to consider these areas as potential career choices. The many course offerings are most often taught by working professionals in each area. In addition to course work for both programs, there are required internships that match students with professionals in their area of study.

Through the international program, in addition to an international student's regular academic classes, one to two hours of English language instruction is provided daily. Living with an American family produces more opportunity for language development and practice.

FACULTY AND ADVISERS

The students at American Heritage are served by 186 teachers, counselors, and administrators at the Plantation location and 91 teachers, counselors, and administrators at the Delray campus. Sixty-five percent hold master's or doctoral degrees. Teachers actively seek out both school-year and summer workshops to attend, and they return with creative ideas for their teaching. Faculty turnover is minimal. The faculty is also committed to the Heritage philosophy of developing good character and self-esteem as well as the reinforcement of traditional values in students. Teachers maintain close communication with parents regarding their child's progress, with frequent written progress reports, phone calls, and scheduled conference days. Classes are small, with a 17:1 student-teacher ratio.

COLLEGE ADMISSION COUNSELING

At American Heritage, the goal is to send seniors to colleges that match their goals and expectations for college life. There are 6 full-time guidance counselors in the high school, including a Director of College Placement and a Scholarship Specialist.

The college placement process begins in seventh grade with academic advising about curriculum and course selection and continues through high school with college-preparation advising. The counselors keep abreast of current admissions trends through attendance at national and local conferences and frequent contact with college admissions representatives.

The preparation for college intensifies as students in grades 9 through 12 follow a three-step program designed to help them score well on the SATs. The program includes SAT prep mini-exercises in their English and math classes. In tenth grade and above, students may take an intensive daily SAT prep class taught on campus during the regular school day. In addition, high school students participate in Kaplan Test Prep's "online tutorial" which interactively takes students through SAT preparation and test-taking strategies. It provides personalized diagnostics on student progress and is monitored by each student's English and math teachers. Students may access the program via computers at school or at home.

At this level, academic counseling gives consideration to graduation requirements and course selection, study skills and time management, leadership and club involvement, and referral to mentoring or professional tutoring, if needed. College advising is offered in the classroom on topics such as standardized test taking, the college application process, resume and essay writing, and searching for colleges and majors. The School reviews all college applications sent, writes letters of recommendation, finds scholarships for students, prepares students for college interviews, invites college admission representatives to campus, hosts a college fair, and proctors Advanced Placement (AP) exams. A guidance resource room with catalogs, videos, and guidebooks is available for students and parents.

Virtually all graduates continue their educations and are admitted to the nation's finest colleges and universities. In recent years, graduates have been admitted to such schools as Columbia, Boston College, Colgate, Cornell, Duke, Harvard, Georgetown, MIT, NYU, Pepperdine, Princeton, Rutgers, Tufts, Wake Forest, West Point, Yale, and the Universities of Connecticut, Maryland, Pennsylvania, and Southern California.

STUDENT BODY AND CONDUCT

In the Lower School, the PK-3 classes enroll about 16 students; PK-4, 17; Kindergarten, 18; grades 1 and 2, 21; grades 3 and 4, 22; and grades 5 and 6, 23. In preschool through grade six, each class has a teacher and a full-time assistant. Grades 7 through 12 in the Upper School average 17 students.

The Plantation campus has 2,400 students, with 1,170 in the Lower School and 1,230 in the Upper School. The Boca/Delray student population totals 1,104, with 557 students in the Lower School and 547 in the Upper School. The School's day population is culturally diverse, with students representing forty-three countries from around the world.

ACADEMIC FACILITIES

The Plantation campus includes a fully equipped science lab, five state-of-the-art computer rooms, and a $25-million Center for the Arts that houses a state-of-the-art 800-seat theater, a black-box theater, spacious art studios, a graphic design lab, choral and band rooms, and individual practice rooms. There are two new library/media centers, one that services the Lower School and another that meets all the technological requirements of students in the Upper School. Heritage has an excellent physical education center that includes an Olympic-sized swimming and diving facility, a gymnasium, six tennis courts, a track, four modern locker rooms, a weight-training room, and acres of well-maintained athletic fields.

The American Heritage Boca/Delray campus provides two state-of-the-art iMac computer labs, fully equipped science labs, art studios, a college guidance computer lab, a library/media center and research lab, an Olympic-sized swimming pool with eight racing lanes, a 2,600-square-foot teaching pool, a 25,000-square-foot gymnasium/auditorium, six lighted tennis courts, a football and soccer field, fully equipped weight training room, locker rooms, two well-equipped playgrounds, acres of well-maintained baseball and softball fields, practice fields for soccer and football, and beautifully landscaped grounds and courtyards.

A $20-million facility expansion is in progress.

ATHLETICS

The athletic program is an important part of the sense of community that has developed at Heritage. Parents, teachers, administrators, and students develop a special kind of camaraderie while cheering on the Patriot teams. Awards evenings are held for athletes and parents at the conclusion of each season. Heritage offers a complete competitive sports program. A "no cut" policy allows every student who wants to participate an opportunity to play on the Patriot team of his or her choice. Coaches provide high-quality instruction in all sports. Sportsmanship, team-work, recognition of effort, and thorough training and preparation are the goals toward which the School works every day. Each year, a number of student-athletes receive financial help for their college education based on their athletic ability and their performance. More importantly, however, for those who do not have the ability—or maybe the desire—to participate at the collegiate level, athletic opportunities offer a very enjoyable and memorable experience, with accomplishments and relationships that last a lifetime. American Heritage competes as a member of the Florida High School Activities Association, and the athletics programs are consistently ranked in the top ten in the state of Florida.

EXTRACURRICULAR OPPORTUNITIES

The extensive activities offered at Heritage serve several purposes. Primarily, they assist in the growth and development of students, but they also provide opportunities for leadership and excellence, which are increasingly required for college admission. Among the activities and clubs offered to high school students are the National Honor Society; Student Council; Spanish/French Honor Society; Premed, Prelaw, and Pre-engineering Clubs; the Modern Language Club; Mu Alpha Theta (math club); SADD; the computer club; yearbook; the student newspaper; thespians; marching band; orchestra; jazz band; and chorus. Lower School students can take after-school classes in art, dance, instrumental music, karate, cooking, computers, and other areas of interest. Students may also participate in Student Council, Junior Thespians, or Math Superstars.

American Heritage School provides an outstanding fine arts program to students in PK-3 through grade 12. The Center for the Arts is a beautiful, specially designed facility that enhances the arts program. Students participating in art, music, and drama programs have won awards at local, state, and national levels of competition in recent years. This recognition includes the Florida Vocal Association (superior ratings for choir, solo, and ensemble), Florida Orchestra Association (superior ratings for solo and ensemble/guitar and strings), American Choral Directors Award, and National Scholastic Art Competition (gold and silver medals).

Many students participate in enrichment and leadership programs offered in Broward County, including the National Conference for Community and Justice, Leadership Broward, Boys and Girls Clubs, Silver Knights, and the Institute for Math and Computer Science. Nationally, students have participated in Hugh O'Brian Youth Foundation, Freedoms Foundation, Presidential Classroom, and Global Young Leaders Conference. In addition, American Heritage School is home to two nonprofit organizations: Mosaic Theatre, an organization committed to promoting the dramatic arts, where students are able to work alongside professional actors, and the Center for the Arts Scholarship Foundation, a fund-raising organization that awards scholarships to talented students in the arts.

SUMMER PROGRAMS

American Heritage has provided summer fun for young campers since 1981. Summer camp provides activities that help build confidence and self-esteem. Campers enjoy the challenges and rewards of teamwork as they work and play. Through the numerous activities that are offered, campers continue to develop the socialization skills begun in school. Campers enjoy good relationships with the high school and college counselors, who serve as role models for them. American Heritage Day Camp afternoon sessions are available for students 13 years old and under.

For students who have failed a credit course in high school or have been required by their current school to attend summer school in order to pass to the next grade level, summer school is a necessity. However, many others can benefit from American Heritage's summer academic program, including preschoolers who need readiness skills to succeed in kindergarten or first grade; elementary and junior high students who need practice and development of basic skills in math, reading, and language arts; any students who perform one or two years below grade level; students for whom English is a second language; high school students who want to advance themselves academically by earning extra credits during the summer; and high school students who will soon take the SAT or ACT tests for college admission. An FCAT prep class is also offered for elementary students. More information can be obtained by contacting the American Heritage School.

COSTS AND FINANCIAL AID

In 2008–09, tuition and fees total between $14,727 for preschoolers and $18,535 for twelfth-grade students. An international program is available at additional cost for the academic school year—August through May—and includes tuition, housing, three meals a day, books, uniforms, and 2 hours a day of English language.

American Heritage offers financial aid to parents who qualify.

ADMISSIONS INFORMATION

Enrollment at American Heritage School is limited to students who are above average to gifted in intelligence and who are working at or above grade level. Math, reading, vocabulary, and IQ tests are administered and are used to determine if the student has the background and basic skills necessary to be successful. The results of these entrance exams are discussed with the parents at a conference following the testing. I-20 visas are granted to international students who are accepted. Details are available from the Director of Admissions. Students are admitted without regard to race, creed, or national origin.

For acceptance into American Heritage's international program, families must supply complete academic records from the age of 12, translated into English; two teacher letters of recommendation, translated into English; copies of the student's passport; and a completed American Heritage School application form. The American Heritage Admissions Committee reviews the student's records and determines suitable placement. Full tuition for the school year is due upon acceptance. After tuition has been received, the School issues an I-20 form, which must be taken to the U.S. Embassy in the student's country to obtain a student visa.

APPLICATION TIMETABLE

First-semester classes begin in mid-August. For information regarding specific deadlines, students should contact the Plantation campus of the American Heritage School.

ADMISSIONS CORRESPONDENCE

Attn: Admissions
American Heritage School
12200 West Broward Boulevard
Plantation, Florida 33325

Phone: 954-472-0022
E-mail: admissions@ahschool.com
Web site: http://www.ahschool.com

American Heritage School Boca/Delray
6200 Linton Boulevard
Delray Beach, Florida 33484

Phone: 561-495-7272
E-mail: admissions@mailhost.ahschoolbd.com
Web site: http://www.ahschool.com

THE AMERICAN SCHOOL IN LONDON

London, England

Type: Coeducational day college-preparatory school
Grades: PK–12: Lower School, Prekindergarten–4; Middle School, 5–8; High School, 9–12
Enrollment: School total: 1,324; High School: 455
Head of School: Mrs. Coreen R. Hester

THE SCHOOL

The American School in London (ASL), the oldest American-curriculum school in the U.K., was founded by Stephen L. Eckard in 1951 to provide an American curriculum for children of American business and government personnel on assignment in London. The School aims to provide a challenging academic program that allows graduates a wide choice of colleges and universities and the continuity of an American curriculum for students coming from and returning to American and international schools. Students of all nationalities who can meet the scholastic standards, including non-English speakers below the age of 11, are welcome to apply.

The School is situated in St. John's Wood, a residential area of London just north of Regent's Park. Underground transport and public buses are available in the neighborhood, and the School offers a door-to-door transport service. Visits to the museums, theaters, and art galleries of London are a regular part of the curriculum, and historic sites in England and Wales are easily accessible from the School. London's central location and well-connected transportation system permit easy travel for student field studies, and student trips are regularly taken in London, the U.K., and Europe.

The School is owned by the American School in London Educational Trust and is registered as a charity in the United Kingdom and as a nonprofit foundation in the United States. It is governed by a Board of Trustees with 26 full-time members from the community. The plant is owned by the School.

The School enjoys an enthusiastic response and avid support from more than 4,000 alumni and friends of ASL.

The School is accredited by the Middle States Association of Colleges and Schools and the Council of International Schools (CIS) and is a member of the National Association of Independent Schools, the European Council of International Schools, the Council for the Advancement and Support of Education, the Educational Records Bureau, and CIS.

ACADEMIC PROGRAMS

The curriculum of the High School is college preparatory. To graduate, a student must complete at least 18 credits, including 4 years of English; 3 each of social sciences and one modern language; 2 each of mathematics, science, and visual arts and/or performing arts; 1 of physical education; ½ of computer science; and ½ of health. The School recommends at least 1 additional year of modern language, science, mathematics, and fine arts. Freshmen, sophomores, and juniors must take five academics (English, modern language, history, mathematics, science) per year, and five are recommended for seniors. Elective courses are available in all subject areas. Some examples are Shakespeare, world literature, journalism, band, play production, digital imaging, psychology, photography, Japanese, human geography, and astronomy.

ASL offers the largest selection of Advanced Placement courses (nineteen courses) outside the U.S.; they include American history, European history, calculus (2), statistics, economics, computer science, biology, chemistry, physics (2), art history, French (2), Spanish (2), German, studio art, and music theory. Other courses can be taken on an independent-study basis.

Classes in basic academic courses are not usually grouped by grade level but tend toward ability grouping in each academic discipline. In modern languages, all classes are grouped by ability. The average class size is 15, and the student-teacher ratio is 11:1.

The school year is divided into two semesters. Grade reports are sent out at the end of each semester. The grading system uses letter grades of A to F. Students who receive two unsatisfactory grades (below C–) or one failing grade for any one marking period are put on academic probation.

Once a year, High School students have a three- to five-day program called Alternatives, which is an experiential learning program. Students can choose a course from among forty options, including tours, outdoor/indoor activities, travel, and community service activities.

FACULTY AND ADVISERS

The High School faculty consists of 27 men and 32 women. Most hold graduate degrees.

Coreen R. Hester became the seventh head at the American School in London in 2007. Most recently, Mrs. Hester was the head of the Hamlin School in San Francisco, California, for ten years. Prior to her appointment at Hamlin she was ASL's High School Principal, from 1995 to 1997. Early in her career, Mrs. Hester taught English at University Liggott in Grosse Point, Michigan. Later, she spent ten years at the Branson School as teacher, dean, college counselor, Assistant Head, and Interim Head of School. Mrs. Hester was also previously Director of the Western Region of Independent Educational Services. Mrs. Hester holds an A.B. in English and an A.M. in education from Stanford University.

The School hires teachers who are willing to devote the extra time required for excellence and are interested in working with the individual student, within a program that calls for imaginative instruction.

Sabbaticals can be applied for after seven years; three are awarded each year. The School encourages teacher exchanges.

COLLEGE ADMISSION COUNSELING

The High School has 3 class deans, 3 college counselors, and 1 personal counselor, who are available to students for a range of counseling services. The class deans oversee the adviser program for grades 9 through 11, and every student in grade 12 is assigned to a college counselor. A wide selection of reference materials and catalogs is constantly updated to aid students in their college choices. The college search begins with a college information session that is held midyear for the parents of juniors. A junior class meeting in February after receipt of the PSAT results establishes a schedule for seminars and individual sessions on the application process. Individual interviews are held with each student, and summer visits to selected colleges are recommended. In addition, more than 80 college admissions representatives visit the School each year. Students may take the full range of tests required for admission to colleges at the School.

The mean scores on the SAT for the class of 2008 were 641 critical reading, 654 writing, and 649 math. Ninety-five percent of the 105 seniors who graduated in 2008 enrolled in college. ASL graduates are attending Cambridge, Duke, Harvard, and Princeton, among others. In 2008, scores of 3 or higher were obtained on 86 percent of AP exams taken. Seven percent of ASL graduates were National Merit Commended Students.

STUDENT BODY AND CONDUCT

There are currently 455 students in the High School. The distribution is as follows: grade 9, 108; grade 10, 117; grade 11, 110; and grade 12, 120. There are nearly equal numbers of boys and girls in all grades. Although the majority of the students are U.S. citizens, more than fifty nationalities are represented in the student body.

The School has a well-defined code of conduct concerning such issues as drugs, alcohol, theft, and plagiarism. Serious violations, although rare, may result in suspension or expulsion.

ACADEMIC FACILITIES

The School building is of modular design and houses all three divisions. There are eighty classrooms and nine science laboratories, seven computer centers, five music rooms, five art studios, two theaters, two gymnasiums, a writing lab, a ceramics room, and two libraries containing more than 50,000 volumes, a large media center, and a recording studio. A computer network with 1,600 network outlets, a state-of-the-art high-speed server, and a high-speed Internet connection were installed in 1996, linking more than 500 computers in the building.

A renovation project began in 1999 and was completed in 2001, adding 24,000 square feet of classroom space and an additional gymnasium; ventilation and lighting were upgraded for the whole school.

ATHLETICS

The physical education program is directed toward recreational and lifetime sports, with an emphasis on fitness.

The School's varsity athletics teams compete against local British and American schools as well as American and international schools in Europe. Boys' teams and girls' teams are organized in basketball, crew, cross-country, golf, soccer, swimming, tennis, track and field, and volleyball. In addition, boys compete in baseball, rugby, and wrestling, and there are girls' teams in cheerleading, dance, field hockey, and softball.

The School's playing fields, located in nearby Canons Park, comprise 21 acres and include soccer and rugby pitches, tennis courts, and a baseball diamond. Neighborhood facilities include running tracks, tennis courts, and a swimming pool.

EXTRACURRICULAR OPPORTUNITIES

Elected officers and representatives serve on the Student Council, which conveys the interests and concerns of students to the administration and organizes social activities. The council sponsors dances, public service activities, movies, and other events. Concerts and plays are scheduled regularly. Special events include a biannual winter auction and international festival, sponsored by the Parent-Teacher Organization; a yearly alumni reception; the senior prom; and the annual music tour, which takes the student orchestra, band, madrigal singers, and choir to a European city.

Regular student activities include the yearbook; newspaper; literary magazine; drama productions; Prom Committee; Model United Nations; instrumental and choral groups; the Robotics, Writers, and Debate Clubs; Amnesty International; and Mock U.S. Senate. Volunteer groups serve in hospitals and work with elderly people and other groups in the local community.

DAILY LIFE

The school day begins at 8:05 a.m. and ends at 3:05 p.m., except on Wednesdays, which are early release days, ending at 2:10 p.m. The schedule is an eight-day rotating block schedule, with 80-minute periods divided over every two days. Because the periods rotate, classes meet at different times of the day over the course of an eight-day cycle. Lunch can be purchased in the cafeteria, which is open from 11 to 1. Snacks, sandwiches, and drinks can also be purchased on campus throughout the day. The School's open campus policy also allows students to buy their lunch at nearby establishments. Sports and club activities usually take place after school; some sports tournaments are held over weekends.

SUMMER PROGRAM

An active summer program enrolls students ranging from kindergarten through grade 8. A summer program director administers the session.

COSTS AND FINANCIAL AID

Tuition is £20,000 for grades 9–12. Financial aid is awarded on the basis of need.

ADMISSIONS INFORMATION

Applicants are considered on the basis of previous academic records, standardized test results, and recommendations from the previous school. There is a nonrefundable £100 application fee, and a £1000 tuition deposit is required upon admission. The School invites each candidate to spend a day at ASL with a student host to meet teachers and prospective classmates. The American School in London does not discriminate on the basis of race, nationality, creed, or sex.

APPLICATION TIMETABLE

Applications are accepted at any time throughout the year.

ADMISSIONS CORRESPONDENCE

Jodi Coats, Dean of Admissions
The American School in London
One Waverley Place
London NW8 0NP
England
Phone: 020-7449-1221
Fax: 020-7449-1350
Web site: http://www.asl.org

ANDREWS OSBORNE ACADEMY

Willoughby, Ohio

Type: Coeducational, independent boarding and day, college-preparatory school
Grades: Pre-K–12
Enrollment: School total: 278; Upper School: 122; Middle and Lower School: 156
Head of School: Charles J. Roman

THE SCHOOL

In a challenging and active learning environment, Andrews Osborne Academy (AOA) prepares students for college and empowers them to succeed. The Academy nurtures in each student a passion for excellence, a commitment to community, and an international perspective.

Andrews Osborne Academy offers a strong college-preparatory program that fosters individual growth, intellectual achievement, and a desire to reach one's highest potential. The Academy was created from the merger of the Andrews School, founded in 1910, and the Phillips-Osborne School, founded in 1972. Situated on 300 acres of fields, streams, woods, and trails, AOA is located 30 minutes east of downtown Cleveland and is convenient to museums and other cultural resources as well as major shopping areas.

A 12-member Board of Directors, which is composed of prominent members of the business, professional, and education community, oversees the operations of the Academy. The Head of School and his administrative staff make all decisions concerning daily student life.

Andrews Osborne Academy is accredited by the Independent Schools Association of the Central States and is approved by the Ohio State Department of Education. It holds memberships in the National Association of Independent Schools, the Secondary School Admission Test Board, the Ohio Association of Independent Schools, the Ohio Association of Secondary School Principals, Midwest Boarding Schools, The Association of Boarding Schools, the Cleveland Council of Independent Schools, the Small Boarding Schools Association, and the Association of Independent School Admission Professionals.

ACADEMIC PROGRAMS

The Andrews Osborne Academy curriculum is geared toward the student who is high average to gifted in ability and includes honors, Advanced Placement, and independent-study courses. All seniors are involved in the Senior Project Program, which exposes the students to a variety of career and community experiences during the last few weeks of their senior year. The English as a second language program serves the school's international students, with classes in ESL being required of all international students until they have scored at least 550 on the TOEFL examination.

With approximately eighty-five courses from which to choose, students in grades 9 through 12 are required to take 4 units of English; 3 units each of history, mathematics, science, and foreign language in French or Spanish; 1 unit of fine arts in art, music, or drama; 1 unit of physical education/health; and ½ unit of speech. In addition, all students must demonstrate computer literacy and acquire certification in CPR. Electives are available in all academic areas and the fine arts. The neighboring Fine Arts Association is available to students seeking private lessons in dance, art, and vocal and instrumental music.

The grading system uses designations of A to F, with pluses and minuses for finer distinctions. There are two 9-week marking periods in each semester. Small classes, averaging 10 to 15 students, and a student-teacher ratio of approximately 10:1 enable students to excel academically and grow as self-reliant individuals. Academic progress reports are sent out midway through each semester, and parents are encouraged to discuss their child's progress with his or her teachers and/or adviser at any time during the year.

Boarding students have a 2-hour study period nightly, with teachers available for assistance and tutoring. The library is open from 8 a.m. to 5 p.m., during the evening study hall, and during daytime hours over the weekend. It contains more than 13,000 volumes, including electronic and audio books. There is an online library catalog for AOA that includes selections from area schools, colleges, and libraries, including the Library of Congress. Daily newspapers include the *New York Times* and the *Wall Street Journal,* and periodicals are available in French and Spanish. There is 24-hour home and school access to major academic and international databases of newspapers, magazines, and reference works as well as a core collection in women's studies and an extensive Asian collection. The Academy library was recently renovated, with completion in fall 2007.

FACULTY AND ADVISERS

Of the 50 full-time faculty members, more than half hold advanced degrees. Each is eminently prepared for teaching and represents a rich academic background. Many faculty and staff members live on campus, and all are involved in students' lives after classes and on weekends as coaches, club advisers, weekend activity leaders, and neighbors.

Faculty and staff members are committed to the development of each student's character, intellectual potential, and well-being. All students receive extensive individual guidance on their course of study from their faculty advisers, and their progress during the year is reported regularly.

The Head of School, Mr. Chuck Roman, has more than thirty years of experience as a school administrator in the private and public school sector. Previously, Mr. Roman served as President of Lake Catholic High School in Mentor. His notable achievements in leadership include being recognized as a National Distinguished Principal and an Ohio Principal of the Year, receiving the Governor's Educational Leadership Award, being the elementary principal of two Ohio Hall of Fame Schools, and being an Educational Policy Fellow representing business and educational leaders.

COLLEGE ADMISSION COUNSELING

During the sophomore year, students and parents meet with the college counselor to begin goal setting and preparing for entrance exams. A junior spends time visiting colleges, while parents attend workshops on admission and financial assistance procedures. Seniors are busy in the fall, sending applications to the colleges of their choice.

The college counseling program is individualized as much as possible for each student and family. The counselor is consulted about the academic progress of every student and maintains an open-door policy for all so that informal discussions about colleges, majors, careers, and academic preparation can be held with family members and students from every grade. The formal selection process begins in the junior year. Workshops on various topics, such as admission, financial aid, and standardized testing, are conducted. Counselors guide each student through the entire application process. In 2008, 100 percent of the Academy's 30 graduates were accepted at institutions of higher learning. Among these colleges and universities are Bryn Mawr, Case Western Reserve, Hiram, Miami, Purdue, Savannah College of Art and Design, Smith, Sweet Briar, and Wells.

ACADEMIC FACILITIES

Academic life at Andrews Osborne Academy is centered in three buildings. The Margaret St. John Andrews Building, which was named after one of the founders of the school, houses student affairs offices, including the Dean of

Students, Residential Life Director, and Registrar; college counseling; Middle School classrooms and classrooms for English, English as a second language, and social studies courses; the school's learning specialist; and an art studio. In the Administration Building are the Head of School's office, the Office of Admission, the Academic Dean's office, the business office, the 700-seat auditorium, the dining room, the music department, foreign language classrooms, the field house, and the Upper School art studio. The Roberta M. Lee Building houses the library; the Student Center; labs for biology, chemistry, and physics; and classrooms for math.

BOARDING AND GENERAL FACILITIES

The spacious grounds provide a serene setting for resident students, who live in five Georgian Colonial houses separated by grade level. Each unit houses up to 20 students as well as 2 houseparents, who supervise the students, manage the household, and provide a pleasant family atmosphere. Each house has a kitchen, a living room, and a dining room, in addition to the students' bedrooms and the houseparents' apartments. Each dormitory also has computers, a fireplace, a piano, a television set, and laundry facilities. Students may bring their own cell phones and computers.

The Van Gorder Health Center provides modern, comfortable accommodations for students who become ill. The school nurse, who is on duty during the school day, is always on call. The school physician, who is also on call 24 hours a day, visits the Academy weekly. Medical emergencies are referred to a local hospital.

ATHLETICS

The physical education program is designed to promote physical vitality, sound health, teamwork skills, and school spirit. Students are required to take gym classes and are encouraged to participate in team sports. Fundamental skills in team and individual sports, including archery, badminton, basketball, golf, soccer, tennis, and volleyball, are emphasized. The Academy fields interscholastic teams in basketball, cross-country, lacrosse, soccer, softball, tennis, and volleyball. Andrews Osborne Academy's no-cut policy fosters participation, making it possible for all interested students to be part of a team. A state-of-the-art field house, with two full-size courts and aerobics, fitness, and weight rooms, was completed in 1999.

The equestrian center offers two full-size indoor arenas and three outdoor arenas for year-round lessons, shows, and recreational riding. There are forty-two stalls, three tack rooms, and ten grooming areas in the main building. Approximately 30 percent of the students participate in the riding program, riding one of the Academy's horses or bringing one of their own. Several students compete nationally, and an academic support system is in place for riders who frequently travel for competitions.

EXTRACURRICULAR OPPORTUNITIES

Extracurricular activities are a valuable part of school life at Andrews Osborne Academy and are open to any student who is interested in participating. Students are encouraged to participate in the wide range of organizations and activities, including choir, drama, yearbook, literary magazine, Environmental Club, Outdoors Club, International Club, Mock Trial, Art Club, Blue Key, Black Cultural Awareness Club, Chess Club, Community Service Club, Equestrian Club, Ski Club, Spirit Club, and Respecters of All Diversities Club.

The Academy frequently sponsors field trips to museums, concerts, theaters, exhibitions, and lectures to enhance the classroom learning experience. The Willoughby School of Fine Arts, which is located on the AOA campus, offers cultural programs and lessons in art, dance, drama, and instrumental music. Class trips are organized to build class unity and to provide enrichment in academic areas, including a senior trip to the Stratford Festival in Canada. Special interest trips are generally open to the upper grades and include trips to other countries, choir tours, athletic trips, and outdoor activities.

The campus provides ample space for jogging, bicycling, cross-country skiing, tennis, and horseback riding. Traditional annual events include a camping trip, a play, class trips, Parents' Weekend, and the Holiday Concert in the fall and winter. In the spring, there are the all-school musical, International Day, and Senior Farewell.

DAILY LIFE

Boarding students begin their day with breakfast in the dining room. Classes for all students begin at 8:10 a.m. and end at 3:15 p.m. After-school activities, horseback riding, clubs, and athletics follow. Boarding students have dinner at 5:30 and study hall from 7 to 9.

WEEKEND LIFE

Activities abound throughout the weekend. Boarding and day students may participate in dances and activities with nearby schools, shop, camp, ski, see a movie, or go to an amusement park. Cleveland offers a vast selection of museums, theaters, concert halls, sports events, and shopping gallerias. In addition, sports and equestrian teams take road trips to competitions.

COSTS AND FINANCIAL AID

For 2008–09, tuition was $35,600 for international students, $29,800 for seven-day boarding students, $24,250 for five-day boarding students, $16,800 for Upper School day students, $12,000 for Middle School day students, and $11,000 for Lower School day students. There are additional fees for uniforms and selected activities, including music, dance, and horseback riding lessons. A student who is accepted reserves a place by paying an enrollment deposit that is deducted from the total tuition.

Scholarships are available to qualified students entering grades 6–12, ranging from academic scholarships to those based on leadership, character, service to the school, and legacies. Financial assistance is available on the basis of need, as assessed by the Parents' Financial Statement. Payment plans are available through the Andrews Osborne Academy Business Office.

ADMISSIONS INFORMATION

AOA seeks students from diverse backgrounds, without regard to race, color, gender, creed, or national or ethnic origin. The admission decision is based on a variety of factors, the most important being the student's academic record, test scores, character references, and potential to make positive contributions to the Academy.

Candidates must take the SSAT or the ISEE entrance exam. An on-campus personal interview is required. References from guidance counselors and teachers are necessary to complete the application. A $40 application fee is required for domestic applicants ($50 for international students).

APPLICATION TIMETABLE

An initial inquiry is welcome at any time, and campus tours are available throughout the year. Students completing all required admission steps receive notification of Admission beginning March 10. Applications are then reviewed on a rolling basis when space is available.

ADMISSIONS CORRESPONDENCE

Doug Goodman, Director of Admission
Andrews Osborne Academy
38588 Mentor Avenue
Willoughby, Ohio 44094

Phone: 440-942-3606
800-753-4683 (toll free)
Fax: 440-954-5020
E-mail: admissions@andrewsosborne.org
Web site: http://www.AndrewsOsborne.org

ASHEVILLE SCHOOL

Asheville, North Carolina

Asheville School

Type: Coeducational boarding and day college-preparatory school
Grades: 9–12 (Forms III–VI)
Enrollment: 260
Head of School: Archibald R. Montgomery IV

THE SCHOOL

Asheville School was founded in 1900 by Newton M. Anderson and Charles A. Mitchell, who previously founded the University School in Cleveland, Ohio. Located on 300 wooded acres at the western edge of Asheville, the School is easily accessible by interstate highways and the nearby Asheville regional airport.

As a traditional boarding and day preparatory school, Asheville brings together motivated young men and women from across the country and around the world to form a community that is dedicated to excellence. Asheville is committed to high academic standards and seeks to encourage intellectual curiosity, sound scholarship, integrity, and service to others. Although the School is not church-affiliated, it teaches Judeo-Christian values. Nondenominational services are held on Wednesday and Friday for all students and on Sunday for boarding students.

The Mountaineering Program, a special feature of the School, is a year-round outdoor activity conducted as an integral part of the overall educational program. The mountaineering experience is available as an afternoon activity, as a project, or through many School-sponsored weekend camping trips.

The School is incorporated not-for-profit and is governed by a self-perpetuating board of 30 trustees, most of whom are alumni, parents, or parents of alumni. The endowment is approximately $38 million. The current operating budget is $10.2 million, toward which annual gifts from alumni, faculty members, and parents contribute more than $900,000.

Asheville School is accredited by the Southern Association of Colleges and Schools. It holds memberships in, among others, A Better Chance, ASSIST, the College Board, Educational Records Bureau, National Association of Independent Schools, Secondary School Admission Test Board, Southern Association of Independent Schools, Southern Association for College Admission Counseling, North Carolina Association of Independent Schools, and Council for Advancement and Support of Education.

ACADEMIC PROGRAMS

The overall student-teacher ratio is 10:1, and the average class has 12 students. Supervised evening study hall is part of the daily schedule for boarders, and extra help is available for those who want or need it. Grades are issued every eight weeks, when reports are sent to parents.

Nineteen credits are required for graduation, including 4 years of English, 3 of one foreign language, 4 of history (including 1 of U.S. history and ½ of music history), 3 of laboratory science, 4 of math (including 2 of algebra and 1 of plane geometry), and 1 credit in art. All students take five courses per year.

The curriculum includes an integrated humanities program, which incorporates literature and history with art and music for a full comprehension of the development of civilization; French, Latin, Chinese, or Spanish; algebra, geometry, precalculus, calculus, finite math, statistics, and combinatorics; biology, chemistry, and physics; and music, art, and studio art. Independent study is available. Advanced Placement (AP) courses are offered in English, history, mathematics, foreign language, science, music, and computers. All students enrolled in Advanced Placement classes take the AP exams.

FACULTY AND ADVISERS

There are 58 faculty members, 44 of whom live at the School; 17 live in the dormitories. Seventy percent of the faculty members hold graduate degrees. Each faculty member has approximately 6 advisees and writes comments to parents at the end of each marking period about each student's involvement in all areas of School life.

Archibald R. Montgomery IV, a graduate of Westminster School (1971), the University of Pennsylvania (B.A., 1975), Monterey Language School (Russian, 1976), and the University of Texas School of Law (J.D., 1982), was appointed Head of School in 2002. He began his career in education as a history teacher at St. George's School, where he also served as Director of Summer School, coach, hall parent, and chair of the History Department. He most recently served as Headmaster of Gilman School in Baltimore for nine years.

COLLEGE ADMISSION COUNSELING

Asheville's College Office employs a full-time Director of the College Office. Students are prepared for college admission by individual conferences. College visits are encouraged during the summer of the Fifth Form year, and more than 60 college admission officers from all parts of the country visit the campus each year to talk with prospective students.

From 2003 to 2007, 50 percent of Asheville School seniors scored above 600 on the verbal section of the SAT, and 50 percent scored above 600 on the math section.

Graduating seniors are continually accepted for entrance into a variety of outstanding colleges and universities throughout this country and overseas. Recent graduates are currently attending Cornell, New York University, University of the South, and the Universities of North Carolina at Chapel Hill and Pennsylvania.

STUDENT BODY AND CONDUCT

In the Third Form (ninth grade), there are 57 students; in the Fourth Form, 75 students; in the Fifth Form, 67 students; and in the Sixth Form, 61 students. Students come from twenty-six states and twelve countries.

Fundamental to the Asheville School community are the expectations of honesty, integrity, and empathy and respect for others. While it is recognized that making mistakes is a part of the learning process, certain behavior is considered serious enough, by itself or by repetition, to warrant dismissal from the School. Infractions of the rules governing conduct are dealt with at the dormitory level by hall parents and prefects or by the Conduct Council, when appropriate.

ACADEMIC FACILITIES

The main academic building, Mitchell Hall, which was built in 1903, contains classrooms, offices, and four science laboratories. The Walker Arts Center has a 380-seat auditorium and theater, an art gallery, chorale rooms, and an art studio. The Skinner Library houses 18,000 volumes, in addition to a computer lab and reading rooms for student use.

All classrooms and dorm rooms are wired for connection to the School's network. Students may bring their own computers for their dorm rooms. The network provides students and faculty members with access to e-mail and the Internet.

BOARDING AND GENERAL FACILITIES

Fifth and Sixth Formers have their own rooms, while many Third and Fourth Formers share a double room. There are three dormitories, Anderson Hall (1900), Lawrence Hall (1907), and Kehaya House (1990), with faculty apartments on each corridor.

William Spencer Boyd Memorial Chapel, Sharp Dining Hall, Tyrer Student Center, and several faculty homes are also located near the three main buildings. An infirmary staffed by 2 nurses is open 24 hours per day; a doctor is on call at all times.

ATHLETICS

Participation in one season of competitive athletics is required for all Third Formers and new Fourth Formers. Varsity and junior varsity teams compete with other independent and public schools in football, cross-country, field hockey, soccer, volleyball, basketball, swimming, wrestling, golf, tennis, track, lacrosse, and baseball. A life fitness program and equestrian, art, music, drama, dance, and mountaineering options complement interscholastic athletics. The Mountaineering Program is conducted year-round. It provides training in hiking, rock climbing, kayaking, mountain biking, camping, and caving. A ropes course and an Alpine Tower are located on campus.

The Rodgers Memorial Athletic Center, which was renovated in 2003, has facilities for basketball, volleyball, wrestling, and swimming and includes team rooms, a state-of-the-art fitness center, a training room, and conference space. Stables and the Ireland Riding Rink are maintained on the campus for equestrian studies.

EXTRACURRICULAR OPPORTUNITIES
Students are encouraged to become involved in clubs, publications, student government, and social and cultural events. The student council serves as a liaison between students and the faculty and as the nucleus of student activities. Students publish a newspaper, *The Ashnoca;* a yearbook, *The Blue and White;* and a literary magazine, *The Review.* The School has a chapel choir, a handbell choir, and a chorus. Plays are produced by the dramatic society. Other active organizations include the Mitchell Cabinet, the School's philanthropic organization; the Hoste Society, a student tour-guide association; a Christian fellowship group; and the Students for Environmental Awareness club.

DAILY LIFE
A typical academic day runs from 8 to 3:30. Included in the day is an all-School convocation or chapel as well as a midmorning break, a community-wide seated lunch, and academic class meetings. The days end earlier on Tuesdays and Fridays to allow for adviser meetings, service projects, mountaineering trips, and travel to off-campus athletic events. Saturday classes, which are held approximately every other week, begin at 9 and end at 1. Athletics are from 3:30 to 5:30, Monday through Friday. Boarding students have free time before and after the evening buffet dinner at 6. Evening study hall begins at 8. Third Formers study in a supervised group study hall. Fourth, Fifth, and Sixth Formers study in their rooms or the library.

WEEKEND LIFE
Asheville provides many cultural activities usually found only in larger cities. These include the Asheville Symphony, Community Concert Series, Asheville Art Museum, community theater, and performances by nationally known popular musicians. Dances are hosted on campus by student organizations. Students may be away from the campus on Saturday and Sunday afternoons and Saturday evening with proper permission. A grocery store is located within walking distance. Special cultural events are held on campus throughout the year. Each student may choose three weekends each semester to leave the campus, in addition to regularly scheduled holidays. In addition, "honors weekends" may be earned by students with high academic achievement.

COSTS AND FINANCIAL AID
For the 2008–09 year, tuition is $38,720 for boarding students and $22,420 for day students. There are alternative payment schedules, and tuition refund insurance is available.

Each year, Asheville is able to offer financial assistance to one third of the students because of the continuing generosity of alumni, parents, and friends of the School, including foundations. Financial aid is awarded on the basis of need. The School awarded $1.7 million in 2008. Parents seeking aid must complete the Parents' Financial Statement (the School and Student Service for Financial Aid form) by the February 1 deadline. Final decisions are made by the Financial Aid Committee; confidentiality is assured.

ADMISSIONS INFORMATION
Applicants are required to submit a completed application, a transcript from their current school, recommendations from their present English and mathematics teachers, and SSAT scores. All candidates are required to visit the campus in order to meet with faculty members, students, and admission personnel.

Since English is not taught as a second language, international applicants should have a strong command of the English language. A TOEFL score is required.

The School does not discriminate on the basis of race, creed, or ethnic background in its policies or programs.

APPLICATION TIMETABLE
Prospective students are encouraged to visit the campus while the School is in session. Most visits include a campus tour, attending a class, the admission interview, and lunch. Since regular classes are held on some Saturdays, appointments are welcomed then as well as during the week.

The deadline for Early Decision is December 10. Early Decision applications are binding; applicants who are accepted agree to enroll in Asheville School and withdraw all applications to other schools. All Early Decision applicants are notified of an admission decision by January 10. Applicants requiring financial aid may not apply for Early Decision.

The deadline for Regular Decision is February 1. All Regular Decision applicants are notified of an admission decision by March 10. A deposit and reservation agreement are due by April 10. All financial aid applicants must apply for Regular Decision.

Applications are considered after February 10 on a space-available basis only.

ADMISSIONS CORRESPONDENCE
Director of Admission
Asheville School
360 Asheville School Road
Asheville, North Carolina 28806
Phone: 828-254-6345
Fax: 828-210-6109
E-mail: admission@ashevilleschool.org
Web site: http://www.ashevilleschool.org

THE ATHENIAN SCHOOL

Danville, California

Type: Coeducational day and boarding college-preparatory school
Grades: 6–12: Middle School, 6–8; Upper School, 9–12
Enrollment: School total: 450; Upper School: 300
Head of School: Eleanor Dase, Head

THE SCHOOL

Founded in 1965 by Dyke Brown, a graduate of Yale Law School and Vice President of the Ford Foundation, Athenian has as its goal the development of each student for a life of purpose and personal fulfillment as a citizen of the world. Athenian equips graduates with a deep understanding of themselves, extraordinary skills for achievement, and the compassion to make a positive difference in the world.

With distinctive and meaningful programs, Athenian goes far beyond preparing students for outstanding colleges by making learning meaningful, exciting, and motivating. Classes average 15 to 16 students, so teachers know each student and involve them in discussion and learning. Athenian's diverse student body comes from throughout the East Bay and more than ten countries around the world. The international programs broaden students' perspectives, with opportunities across the globe for exchanges, service projects, interim trips, and conferences. Students build important skills in activities such as an airplane construction project, a championship robotics team, athletics, and art, music, chorus, and theater. All students participate in community service each year and, in grade 11, complete the Athenian Wilderness Experience. Few schools offer an experience as academically and personally enriching as Athenian's.

Most Athenian graduates gain admission to their first-choice college or university, with nearly 100 percent admitted to an outstanding array of four-year schools. Most importantly, Athenian inspires students to become lifelong learners and confident, successful adults.

Athenian's beautiful 75-acre campus of rolling hills is located 32 miles east of San Francisco at the base of Mt. Diablo. Athenian students access the cultural and educational resources of the San Francisco Bay Area via Athenian's shuttles, buses, and nearby BART stations (the Bay Area rapid transit system). Students also enjoy activities on the nearby Pacific Coast and the majestic Sierra mountains.

A nonprofit institution, Athenian is governed by a 25-member Board of Trustees. The School's operating budget was $15.3 million for 2008–09. The endowment is $5.3 million.

The Athenian School is fully accredited by the Western Association of Schools and Colleges. It is a member of the National Association of Independent Schools, the California Association of Independent Schools, the National Network of Complementary Schools, A Better Chance, Western Boarding Schools, the College Board, the National Association for College Admission Counseling, and the Round Square Conference of International Schools.

ACADEMIC PROGRAMS

Athenian's exciting broad curriculum develops analytical thinking and communication skills in all disciplines, offering a wide variety of enriching courses in English, history, math, science, fine arts, foreign language, and physical education. The ninth-grade humanities program studies major world cultures through literature, history, and art courses. The sophomore humanities program focuses on American studies in history and literature. Juniors and seniors choose enriching and varied seminars in history and literature. Athenian's mathematics program features statistics and AP statistics courses in addition to two yearlong AP calculus courses. Science features first-year and second-year courses in physics, chemistry, and biology in addition to environmental science, geology, and applied science. Modern languages offer courses through the AP level in French, Mandarin Chinese, and Spanish. Fine and performing arts feature courses in drawing, painting, sculpture, pottery, stained glass, photography, dance, musical performance, drama, theater tech, and several arts and society courses. Advanced Placement and/or honors courses are offered in all disciplines.

The academic year is divided into two semesters. The daily schedule includes six academic periods ranging from 45 to 85 minutes each. Each course meets four times a week.

Courses required for graduation are as follows: English, 4 years; laboratory science, 3 years; mathematics, 3 years; history, 3 years (including freshman humanities, American studies, and three 1-semester elective history seminars in the junior or senior year); 3 years of a foreign language; and 2.5 years of fine arts. Most students exceed these requirements. Students also fulfill graduation requirements in community service each year and must participate in the Athenian Wilderness Experience in grade 11.

Some of the electives offered are studio arts, drama workshops, instrumental ensembles, and additional courses in academic subjects. Required seminars (chosen by students) for English and history may include Shakespeare, science fiction, Russian fiction, Latin American fiction, African American studies, creative writing, or women writers. Science offers inspiring applied science, geology, and environmental science courses and extracurricular programs in airplane construction and robotics. Mathematics courses go beyond two Advanced Placement calculus courses to offer statistics and AP statistics yearlong courses.

Class size varies from 5 to 18, and the average class has 15 students. The overall student-teacher ratio is 10:1. Study for boarding students is supervised by faculty members assigned to dormitories during the evenings.

Athenian offers intermediate and advanced English learning courses to students for whom English is not the first language. ESL students take part in the in the regular curriculum for subjects other than English and history. Field trips help familiarize international students with northern California and U.S. culture.

Opportunities for independent study are provided for selected students by the academic departments. Student exchanges can be arranged either domestically or internationally. The Athenian School is a founding member of a notable consortium of international schools, The Round Square, which offers students academic exchanges, international community service opportunities, and participation in an annual international student conference. Athenian also belongs to the National Network of Complementary Schools, which arranges short-term exchanges of students across the country between member schools that have diverse strengths and resources.

Class field trips in the San Francisco Bay Area are frequent. Students may also participate in off-campus internships oriented toward community service and career exploration. Qualified seniors may take advantage of an accelerated high school program arrangement at the University of California at Berkeley.

A distinctive element of the curriculum is the Athenian Wilderness Experience, required of all students in their junior year. AWE enhances self-confidence, communication skills, and perseverance in addition to fostering an appreciation of the environment.

FACULTY AND ADVISERS

There are 55 full-time and 15 part-time faculty members, 42 of whom hold advanced degrees. Twenty-five faculty members live on-campus with their families.

Eleanor Dase, Head since 1992, graduated from the University of Michigan with a degree in mathematics. Since 1974, she has been a math teacher at Athenian; she also held responsibilities as Director of College Counseling for five years and was Assistant Head from 1987 to 1992.

The Athenian School maintains an excellent faculty by seeking the most talented people in their respective fields, by encouraging teachers to continue their education, and by providing financial support for professional growth. Enthusiasm for teaching this age group is a quality also sought in faculty members.

Faculty members perform dormitory supervision, take charge of activities several weekends a year, organize community service activities, and lead adventurous trips and activities during Interim period each spring. Each faculty member also acts as an adviser for 8 to 10 students.

COLLEGE ADMISSION COUNSELING

Two college counselors provide expert advice to students choosing colleges. College counseling starts in the junior year and includes sessions with each student and with parents, as well as preparation for the PSAT and SAT. Trips to campuses throughout the country are available. The Athenian School is visited by numerous college representatives each year.

The following is a representative list of the institutions to which graduates have been admitted: Amherst, Brown, Columbia, Cornell, Dartmouth, Duke, Evergreen State, Georgetown, Johns Hopkins, MIT, NYU, Occidental, Pomona, Princeton, Reed, Stanford, USC, Yale, and the Universities of California (all campuses), Chicago, and Pennsylvania.

STUDENT BODY AND CONDUCT

In 2008–09, there were 71 freshmen (30 boys and 41 girls), 79 sophomores (41 boys and 38 girls), 78 juniors (39 boys and 39 girls), and 72 seniors (33 boys and 39 girls). Of these 300 students, 41 (20 boys and 21 girls) were boarders and 259 (123 boys and 136 girls) were day students.

Eighty-nine percent of the students are from California, and 10 percent are international students from more than ten different countries. Forty-three percent are members of ethnic minority groups.

Living as a community—especially a community as democratic as the one at Athenian—requires cooperation, social responsibility, and a sense of having a real influence on the quality of life and the decision-making process. An informal atmosphere promotes a good rapport between students and faculty members, and faculty members help students behave with respect toward themselves, others, and the school community.

The rules encourage high ethical standards and the ability to live with others harmoniously. The use of tobacco, alcohol, and illegal drugs is prohibited. Cheating and stealing are also major rule violations.

Infractions of these rules often result either in referral by the Dean of Students to the Student Discipline Committee or expulsion. Town Meeting is the student government of the School and provides a forum for the discussion of community issues and standards.

ACADEMIC FACILITIES
Academic facilities include classrooms; a science building with four labs; a new library holding 16,000 print volumes, forty-three periodical subscriptions, and six electronic subscriptions; a new Center for the Arts with gallery, black box theater, drawing and painting, sculpture and pottery, and a dance studio; several computer labs; and the Eleanor Dase Center, for music and multipurpose space.

BOARDING AND GENERAL FACILITIES
There are two dormitories and eleven faculty homes. A number of faculty members reside in apartments or town houses on campus.

Returning students in grades 11 and 12 generally choose single rooms. The Director of the Boarding Program and dormitory parents match the new and younger students with roommates for the double rooms. Ninth graders receive support and guidance from carefully selected seniors through this all-important transition. Supervision of each dorm at the School is the responsibility of a faculty dorm head, assisted by older students who act as proctors.

Students most often arrange to spend the two-week winter and spring vacations with nearby relatives or friends, if they do not travel back to their homes. If needed, the School assists international students in finding suitable homestays during shorter vacation periods. Some trips are also provided during vacations.

The Fuller Commons Building serves as the student recreation and meeting center. The Dyke Brown Main Hall contains the kitchen, dining area, and administrative offices. The Boarding Center provides a gathering place for resident students.

The School nurse visits the dorms each day and advises what action should be taken for any students reported ill. She is available for emergencies as well as drop-in visits during scheduled hours. The School counselor is also available as a resource if needed.

ATHLETICS
Physical education, interscholastic sport, or dance is required of all students.

Athenian teams compete with other schools in the North Bay Conference of the California Interscholastic Federation. The School fields interscholastic teams in thirteen sports—seven for boys and six for girls. These are soccer, volleyball, basketball, tennis, swimming, cross-country, and baseball (for boys). There are also junior varsity teams in soccer, basketball, and girls' volleyball. Athenian's teams have won league championships in a number of sports in recent years.

Noncompetitive activities include rock-climbing, hiking, downhill and cross-country skiing, bicycling, and jazz dance.

Campus facilities include a gym, two tennis courts, a 25-meter pool, a soccer field, a second playing field, and baseball and softball diamonds.

EXTRACURRICULAR OPPORTUNITIES
The School plans occasional trips to museums, plays, the opera, concerts, art exhibits, and lectures in the Bay Area. There are also skiing trips to the Sierra Nevada and excursions to spots on the coast.

On-campus activities include the School newspaper, debate, Interweave, yearbook, and Multicultural Alliance, among many others.

Community service is required of all students. Service projects include cross-country skiing with the visually handicapped, running the scholarship auction, helping at soup kitchens in San Francisco, working with disadvantaged children or the elderly, and working on environmental projects.

DAILY LIFE
A typical day begins with breakfast between 7:30 and 8. Day students arrive in time for classes, which begin at 8:10. A hot lunch prepared at the School is served at noon. Classes end at 2:40 and are followed by sports and performing arts. Dinner is at 6. Clubs, activities, School meetings, and study occupy a portion of each day.

Faculty-supervised evening study hours are from 7:30 to 9:30, when the dormitories are kept quiet. All boarding students are in their dorms by 10:30 p.m., Sunday through Thursday, and by midnight on Friday and Saturday.

WEEKEND LIFE
Weekend activities are arranged by faculty members on duty. They may include hikes on Mt. Diablo, visits to San Francisco and Berkeley, trips to the coast or the Sierra, and an attendance of the Oregon Shakespeare Festival. Boarding students may spend weekends off campus with permission from the Dean of Students and their parents.

Day students are encouraged to participate in all activities available to boarding students and to spend the night on campus from time to time. An outdoor education program is available throughout the year.

COSTS AND FINANCIAL AID
Tuition for 2008–09 was $42,250 for boarding students and $27,520 for day students. Additional expenditures are estimated at $1000. They include such expenses as books, music lessons, field trips, and athletic uniforms. Tuition insurance and a tuition payment plan are available.

Financial aid is based on need; eligibility is determined by the School and Student Service for Financial Aid. For 2008–09, scholarship aid of nearly $1.7 million was awarded to 89 students.

ADMISSIONS INFORMATION
Admission is open to all qualified and motivated persons without regard to race, creed, or color. Athenian seeks students who will prosper in an informal, caring environment, want a rigorous academic course of studies, support Athenian's mission, and will contribute to the on-campus community. Admission is selective and based upon the applicant's intellectual ability, academic achievement, character, motivation, creativity, talents, and interests. The School seeks a student body that includes a diversity of geographical, economic, cultural, and ethnic backgrounds.

Each applicant must submit an application, including transcripts and recommendations, have a personal interview, and take an entrance examination, the ISEE, or the SSAT. ESL candidates must take the TOEFL, IELTS, or SLEP.

Priority is given to ninth graders and then to tenth graders. Admission is granted to a smaller number of eleventh graders and occasionally to a twelfth grader.

APPLICATION TIMETABLE
Initial inquiries should be made in the fall of the year preceding anticipated entrance. The School catalog and application forms are available from the Admission Office upon request. Campus visits and interviews may be arranged at any time during the academic year on weekdays between 8:30 and 3. The application deadline is January 15, and notification of admission is given no later than March 19. After this date, applications may still be received and reviewed until all places are filled.

ADMISSIONS CORRESPONDENCE
Christopher Beeson, Director of Admission
The Athenian School
2100 Mt. Diablo Scenic Boulevard
Danville, California 94506
Phone: 925-362-7223
Fax: 925-362-7228
E-mail: admission@athenian.org
Web site: http://www.athenian.org

AVON OLD FARMS SCHOOL

Avon, Connecticut

Type: Boys', boarding and day, college-preparatory school
Grades: 9–12, postgraduate year
Enrollment: 405
Head of School: Kenneth H. LaRocque, Headmaster

THE SCHOOL

Avon Old Farms (AOF), founded in 1927 by Theodate Pope Riddle (1868–1946), is a school for boys located on 990 woodland acres in the Farmington River Valley, 12 miles west of Hartford and 30 minutes from Bradley International Airport. Avon enjoys the best of both rural and suburban surroundings. In addition to campus trails and a fishing pond (used in fall and spring for fishing and in winter for skating), there are restaurants, movie theaters, retail stores, and two girls' schools nearby.

There are 405 students who bring cultural and ethnic diversity and an interesting variety of talents and skills to the school community. Avon is attuned and responsive to the unique needs and learning styles of boys and is fully committed to the development of young men as students and citizens. Avon is a community where traditions live, scholarship flourishes, and boys become men.

The physical surroundings of the School are uniquely handsome and represent Mrs. Riddle's deep appreciation for what is good and enduring about the past. The School's architecture is influenced by the English Cotswold style of building. It is inspiring for its craftsmanship, simplicity, and careful attention to detail. While the School's founder was influenced by the time-honored system of traditional English boarding schools, the approach to the education of today's boys is supportive and lively.

At Avon, education occurs not only in the classroom, but also on the playing fields, through participation in the arts, extracurricular activities, community service, and in daily campus life. Avon's core values govern day-to-day life and ensure that moral growth accompanies intellectual and personal development. Mrs. Riddle was fond of referring to her school as a "village" and, even today, the sense of community, vitality, and purpose make it a fitting term for Avon Old Farms School.

The Board of Directors numbers 24 and includes 13 alumni and 11 parents of present or former students. The School's operating budget was $16.9 million in 2008-09. Annual Giving and the Capital Campaign totaled $5.4 million in the same year. The total market value of the endowment is $33 million.

Avon Old Farms is accredited by the New England Association of Schools and Colleges and is a member of the National Association of Independent Schools, the Connecticut Association of Independent Schools, the WALKS consortium of schools, the International Boys' Schools Coalition, and the Secondary Schools Admission Test Board.

ACADEMIC PROGRAMS

The School year is divided into two semesters, and grades and comments are sent home to parents four times annually. The average class size is 12, and the student-teacher ratio is 7:1. Graduation requirements are dictated by college admissions preferences for 4 years of English, 3 of mathematics, 2 of the same foreign language, 3 of science (including biology) with intensive laboratory work, 3 of social science (including U.S. history), 1 of art, and at least 3 additional credits. Students are expected to carry a minimum of five courses per semester. Honors and Advanced Placement sections in each discipline provide additional challenge for qualified students. AP course work prepares students to take exams in at least fifteen subject areas.

Academic honors are awarded on the basis of cumulative average and range from Headmaster's List to Dean's List to Honor Roll. The Cum Laude Society recognizes students who have demonstrated outstanding scholarship by their junior or senior year. Grades are A–F; A and B are honors, D is passing.

Courses are offered in English; ancient, European, world, Asian, and U.S. history; economics; World Wars I and II; Civil War in film and fiction; criminal law and the legal process; government; moral philosophy; public speaking; biology; chemistry; physics; environmental science; physical science; geology; computer programming; algebra I and II; geometry; advanced math; precalculus and calculus; probability and statistics; and foreign language, including French, Latin, and Spanish.

Courses in the fine arts are numerous and include design, ceramics, woodworking, architecture, photography, painting and drawing, digital arts, and individualized studio courses. Music courses include chorale, jazz band, chamber music, and individual music and voice lessons.

Advanced Placement courses are offered in biology, calculus AB, calculus BC, chemistry, economics, English literature, environmental science, French language, physics C (mechanics), Spanish language, statistics, studio art-drawing portfolio, studio art-general portfolio, U.S. government and politics, and U.S. history.

FACULTY AND ADVISERS

Fifty-nine talented, energetic faculty members teach, advise, and coach Avon students. They are also directly involved in the supervision of the dorms. Avon faculty members are committed to providing the support, attention, and guidance necessary to help students—both boarding and day—meet the demands of each day. Avon strongly supports the professional development of its faculty. Currently, 85 percent of the faculty members either hold or are actively pursuing an advanced degree.

Kenneth H. LaRocque (B.A., Harvard College, 1975; M.Ed. Harvard University, 1981) was appointed Headmaster in 1998. During his twenty-seven years at Avon Old Farms, Mr. LaRocque has served in various capacities, including mathematics teacher, coach, Assistant Headmaster, Director of College Counseling, and Dean of Students. In his tenure, Avon completed an extensive strategic planning process and has initiated a comprehensive building program. The Ordway Science and Technology Center was completed in 2002, and a new woodworking/digital arts building opened in fall 2005. The 100,000-square-foot student center and athletic complex opened in fall 2006. A new performing arts center opened in spring 2007.

COLLEGE ADMISSION COUNSELING

Avon Old Farms prepares students for the college-application process through individual conferences beginning in the spring of the junior year. In February, juniors and their parents are invited to a college-planning seminar in which they are introduced to all phases of the process. A suggested list of colleges is mailed to the student and his parents in June with the recommendation that the student familiarize himself with the schools, either through personal visits or research. Meetings with the college counselors continue into the senior year. More than 130 representatives visit the campus each fall, presenting a variety of college and university programs. Both juniors and seniors attend these meetings.

The PSAT is taken once during the sophomore year and again in the fall of the junior year. The SAT is taken during the junior year and again in the senior year (opportunities are available for additional testing). The SAT Subject Tests are taken in the spring of the junior and/or senior year. The ACT is also offered. AP exams are taken in the spring of the junior and/or senior year. The math and English curriculums provide excellent preparation for this important standardized testing. In 2007–08, the mean score on the SAT was 560 verbal, 660 math, and 562 writing.

All graduates are admitted to a college or university. Among many other schools, Avon graduates are currently attending Bates, Boston College, Brown, Colby, Colgate, College of Charleston, Cornell, Dartmouth, Hamilton, Harvard, Hobart, Holy Cross, Trinity, the U.S. Coast Guard Academy, the U.S. Military Academy, the U.S. Naval Academy, William and Mary, Williams, Yale, and the Universities of Colorado, Connecticut, Delaware, Iowa, New Hampshire, Pennsylvania, and Vermont.

STUDENT BODY AND CONDUCT

Of the 405 students enrolled in 2008–09, 298 are boarding students and 107 are day students. They represent twenty-four states and sixteen other countries and present an interesting array of cultural, ethnic, and racial backgrounds. Seventy-six are freshmen (56 boarding, 20 day); 97 are sophomores (70 boarding, 27 day); 111 are juniors (81 boarding, 30 day); 105 are seniors (75 boarding, 30 day), and 16 are postgraduates (all boarding).

Avon's daily life is governed by the core values of integrity, scholarship, civility, tolerance, altruism, sportsmanship, responsibility, and self-discipline. School regulations prohibit hazing, cheating, stealing, or the use of drugs or alcohol. The violation of any of these rules requires an appearance before the Disciplinary Committee (composed of the student government president and members of the faculty and administration).

Students are expected to wear a jacket and tie to all classes, meals, and other formal occasions.

ACADEMIC FACILITIES

The Ordway Science and Technology Building opened in 2002 and offers state-of-the-art facilities for the teaching of science, math, and computer programming. Each classroom is equipped with SMART Board™ technology, which offers teachers the opportunity to add animation, audio, and video clips to their classroom presentations and also allows students access to outlines, class notes, or other materials presented by the teacher in class and posted to Avon's Web site. The building also contains a language lab (completed in 2005), two computer labs, six science labs, and four AP science labs. Most science lab stations include an IBM laptop for more precise lab work and lab reports.

Classrooms are also located on the first floors of the four quadrangle buildings and Jamerson House. The majority of these rooms contain SMART Board technology. The Baxter Library (26,000 volumes, 75 periodicals) is available to all boarding and day students throughout the day and during evening study hours.

Studio art, photography, architecture, and ceramics classes are held in the Estabrook Fine Arts Center. In fall 2005, an additional studio building opened for the digital arts program and the expanded woodworking shop.

In fall 2006, a 100,000-square-foot student center/athletic complex opened. In spring 2007, a new performing arts center opened to enhance the flourishing music and theater programs. The new facility contains a 500-seat auditorium for morning meetings, plays, and concerts as well as an entire floor of facilities exclusively for choral and instrumental music.

The entire campus is networked, and students have immediate access to the AOF Web through an Internet port in their room or computers located in various buildings on campus.

ATHLETICS

Within the last seventeen years, Avon has won more than thirty league and New England championships. Avon's athletes attend many of the nation's best Division I, II, and III collegiate programs. As a member of the Founders League, Avon's competition includes Choate, Deerfield, Hotchkiss, Kent, Loomis Chaffee, Taft, Trinity-Pawling, and Westminster. Athletic success is attributed to experienced coaches, excellent facilities, strong competition, and an emphasis on the values of teamwork, sportsmanship, and self-discipline.

In fall 2006, a new athletic complex/student center of more than 100,000 square feet opened and includes three basketball courts, one of which is a showcase court; a wrestling arena; a cardiovascular fitness center; a squash pavilion with seven international courts; team and training rooms; a full field house; spaces for social activities and parties; a bookstore; a game room; and the Hawk's Nest snack bar. In addition, the campus includes 65 acres of playing fields; an NHL-quality ice arena; Globe Foundation Tennis Center (nine courts, opened in 2003); and an all-weather, eight-lane track (opened in 2004).

A wide range of sports and team levels are available to suit the talents and abilities of all students. Students are required to play in two out of three athletic seasons. Because of the time required, involvement in dramatic productions, community service, the rock band, the newspaper, or the yearbook are considered a substitute for an athletic season. Recreational skiing and recreational golf are also athletic options.

Interscholastic team sports include baseball, basketball, cross-country, football, golf, ice hockey, lacrosse, riflery, skiing, soccer, squash, swimming, tennis, track and field, and wrestling.

EXTRACURRICULAR OPPORTUNITIES

Community service is a voluntary, active component of extracurricular activity at Avon. Projects are numerous and varied and include tutoring school children, Habitat for Humanity, Toys for Tots (a Christmas toy/clothing drive), blood drives, and weeklong community service opportunities during spring vacation.

Other clubs and organizations include the award-winning yearbook, *The Avonian* (newspaper), *Hippocrene* (literary and art journal), Creative Writing and Literary Club, Technology Club, Stock Market Club, Nimrod Club (the school's oldest club—for boys interested in the outdoors), Fly-Tying and Fishing Club, Rock Band, Art Club, Environmental Club, International Club, Ultimate Frisbee, Big Band, Math League, Chess Club, WAOF Radio, Crossfire (political debate), and Spirit Club. A musical and a dramatic production are performed each year in collaboration with students from Miss Porter's School, a nearby girls' school.

DAILY LIFE

Each day begins with breakfast, which is available from 6:40 to 7:30. The entire School meets each weekday morning for morning meeting at 7:45; twice a week, morning meeting takes the form of a simple, nondenominational chapel service at which a student or faculty member speaks to the assembled school community. Classes begin after morning meeting and continue until early afternoon. On Wednesday and Saturday afternoons, athletic contests are scheduled. An activities period held three afternoons a week allows for participation in drama, community service, or clubs and is followed by athletics. Each day, an academic enrichment hour is scheduled during which teachers are available to assist students. Two hours of supervised study hall follow in the dormitories; students may sign out to work in the library, if they prefer.

Day students are required to attend morning meeting and are welcome to remain on campus through study hall (9:45 p.m.). They are encouraged to participate in all aspects of School life, including evening meals and weekend social events, both on and off campus.

WEEKEND LIFE

Students are just minutes away from movie theaters, restaurants, and shops. Two girls' schools—Miss Porter's School and the Ethel Walker School—are nearby; students can also attend theater productions or athletic events in Hartford, 12 miles away. Dances and other social events are held almost every weekend, either on campus or at another school. The Social Activities Committee organizes amusement park trips, shuttles to movies and the mall, the annual Fall and Spring Flings (outdoor concert, barbecue, and games), skiing and snowboarding trips, and weekly Open Mic Nights, among other activities. Transportation to area churches is available every weekend.

Freshmen and sophomores are allowed four weekend leaves per semester; juniors are allowed five; and seniors are allowed six.

COSTS AND FINANCIAL AID

The annual tuition/room and board fee for the 2008–09 year was $40,850. The tuition fee for day students was $31,100. Additional fees totaled approximately $2500. For the school year 2008–09, Avon awarded $2.9 million in financial aid to 29 percent of the student population.

ADMISSIONS INFORMATION

Acceptance is based on academic achievement, motivation, and the potential for success in Avon's college-preparatory course of study. Additional consideration is given to involvement in athletics, community service, and extracurricular activities as well as personal character and standardized test results. The SSAT is required as well as a personal interview. A student application (including an essay), an official school transcript, and letters of reference (from math and English teachers and from the student's present school) are also required. In September 2008, 148 new students enrolled: 76 as freshmen, 35 as sophomores, 17 as juniors, and 20 as seniors and postgraduates.

APPLICATION TIMETABLE

A campus interview is required prior to the application deadline of February 1. The student's application, transcript, letters of recommendation, and test scores are also due by this date. All candidates are notified of their status by March 10. Accepted students must notify the school of their decision by April 10. Following that date, openings are filled on a rolling admissions basis. An online application is available at Avon's Web site, http://www.avonoldfarms.com. Avon Old Farms accepts the Admission Application Form, which is also available at the School Web site.

ADMISSIONS CORRESPONDENCE

Brendon A Welker
Director of Admissions
Avon Old Farms School
500 Old Farms Road
Avon, Connecticut 06001
Phone: 800-464-2866 (toll-free)
Fax: 860-675-6051
E-mail: admissions@avonoldfarms.com
Web site: http://www.avonoldfarms.com

THE BALDWIN SCHOOL

Bryn Mawr, Pennsylvania

Type: Girls' day college-preparatory school
Grades: PK–12: Lower School, PK–5; Middle School, 6–8; Upper School, 9–12
Enrollment: School total: 587
Head of School: Sally M. Powell

THE SCHOOL

Stressing both scope and depth in learning, the Baldwin School ultimately hopes to endow each student with the ability and enthusiasm for a life of continuing growth as a scholar, a woman, and a human being. The School strives to provide a challenging academic program in a lively, creative environment. The excellence of this program was recognized in 1984, when Baldwin was named by the U.S. Department of Education as an Exemplary Private School. Baldwin is known for its rigorous academic program, diverse student body, and genuinely committed and excellent teaching faculty.

Founded in 1888 by Florence Baldwin to prepare girls for admission to Bryn Mawr College, Baldwin expanded rapidly from its opening class of 13. It now enrolls 587 girls. Baldwin celebrated its centennial in 1988. The School has had boarding students for much of its history, but in 1972 the decision was made to phase out the boarding program. Today, day students come from throughout the Philadelphia area, including Montgomery, Chester, and Delaware counties in Pennsylvania and New Jersey and Delaware as well. The School is located 11 miles west of Philadelphia in the Main Line community of Bryn Mawr (population 8,400). Bryn Mawr College and Haverford College are within walking distance. Nearby bus and rail services provide access to the historic, cultural, and recreational resources of Philadelphia.

The Baldwin School is a nonprofit institution governed by a 30-member, self-perpetuating Board of Trustees, which meets five times a year. An active Alumnae Association maintains contact with the more than 3,600 graduates and plays a direct role in fund-raising and school events. The School has an endowment of $7.7 million. Annual Giving raised $1,016,245 last year.

The Baldwin School is accredited by the Middle States Association of Colleges and Schools and the Pennsylvania Association of Private Academic Schools. It is a member of the National Association of Independent Schools, the Association of Delaware Valley Independent Schools, the Secondary School Admission Test Board, and the Pennsylvania Association of Independent Schools.

ACADEMIC PROGRAMS

Students are expected to take 5 units of credit each year in addition to physical education. Graduation requirements include 4 units of English; 3 units of one foreign language or 2 units each of two languages; 3 units of history, 1 unit each of U.S. history, ancient history, and medieval history; 3 units of mathematics; 3 units of science; 2 units of fine arts; 1 trimester course each of speech, health, and human development; and 5 units of electives.

Among the Upper School courses offered are English I–IV and a variety of English electives; Latin I–III, Virgil, AP Latin, AP French I–V, and AP Spanish I–V; modern European history, economics, and comparative world issues; algebra I, algebra and consumer mathematics, geometry, algebra II and trigonometry, calculus, and topics in advanced mathematics; environmental science, biology I–II, chemistry I–II, and physics I–II; and art I–IV, art history, ceramics, design, architecture, photography, jewelry I–IV, theater I–III, instrumental ensemble, and chorus and handbell choir. Honors courses and independent study are available in several subjects. Baldwin also has a partnership with the Notre-Dame de Mongre School in France and the Perse School in England.

Technology is strongly supported. Students have access to more than 200 computers on campus, laptops are available for students to sign out to take home, and mobile computer labs are available for use in individual classrooms.

The average class size at Baldwin is 16, with an overall student-faculty ratio of about 7:1. Students who need extra work are recommended for either the math or writing labs, which provide supplemental work. In addition, the math lab provides enrichment for those with exceptional ability.

FACULTY AND ADVISERS

Faculty members include 73 full-time teachers and 11 part-time teachers, 75 women and 9 men. They hold eighty-nine baccalaureate and sixty-seven advanced degrees from such institutions as Curtis Institute of Music, Emory, Johns Hopkins, Pennsylvania Academy of the Fine Arts, the Sorbonne, University of Pennsylvania, and Yale. Faculty turnover is low.

Sally Powell was appointed as the seventh head of Baldwin in 2006. A native of Great Britain, she was educated in England at the Perse School for Girls and at Cambridge University where she received both her bachelor's and master's degrees. Prior to coming to Baldwin, Mrs. Powell worked at the Dwight-Englewood School in Englewood, New Jersey.

Beyond their dedication to teaching in their discipline, the Baldwin faculty members are known for their extraordinary commitment to the individual development of each girl. Many faculty members serve as advisers to individual students (with approximately 10 advisees each), grade advisers, or club advisers. Every adult in the Baldwin community is seen as a role model for the students, and faculty members are supported by the school counselor and the administration in their roles outside the classroom.

COLLEGE ADMISSION COUNSELING

The college placement process at Baldwin begins in the junior year with a College Night for students and their parents. Each girl and her parents meet with the College Adviser to define individual goals, realistic choices, and special interests as they pertain to the college admission process. There is a full-time Director of College Counseling and a part-time College Counselor.

The class of 2008 had average SAT scores of 580–730 verbal, 570–710 math, and 620–690 writing with 9 National Merit Semifinalists, and 9 National Merit Commended Students. Among the college choices for the class of 2008 were Franklin & Marshall, George Washington, Princeton, University of Pennsylvania, and Washington (St. Louis).

STUDENT BODY AND CONDUCT

In 2008–09, the School enrolled 587 girls in prekindergarten through grade 12 as follows: 17 in prekindergarten, 24 in kindergarten, 41 in grade 1, 41 in grade 2, 41 in grade 3, 39 in grade 4, 40 in grade 5, 48 in grade 6, 50 in grade 7, 40 in grade 8, 47 in grade 9, 61 in grade 10, 49 in grade 11, and 49 in grade 12. Students represented a variety of ethnic, religious, socioeconomic, cultural, and racial backgrounds. Of the total school population, 31 percent were students of color.

At Baldwin, all members of the school community are responsible for knowing the rules governing behavior, academics, and honesty. Minor infractions incur detentions (depending on the severity of the infraction), while more serious violations are heard by the Discipline Committee, which is made up of the Head of the School, the Director of the Upper School, 3 faculty members, and 4 grade-12 student senators.

ACADEMIC FACILITIES

The Baldwin campus is located on 25 acres. The Residence (1896) houses administrative offices, a reception area, an assembly room, the dining room, the kitchen, the Music Wing, the Middle School music room, an extensive arts facility (1984–86), an Early Childhood Center (1998), and a bookstore. A former resort hotel designed by Frank Furness and featuring distinctive Victorian architecture, the Residence is listed on the National Register of Historic Places. The Schoolhouse (1925, renovated 1998) contains Upper and Middle School classrooms, the library, and offices for the Head of the School as well as the Middle and Upper School directors. The Science Building (1961), expanded and renovated in 1995, provides a variety of science laboratories. A new Athletic Center was opened in November 2008. Additional school facilities include the Mrs. Cornelius Otis Skinner Dramatic Workshop, and Krumrine House (the residence of the Head of the School). The School-owned plant is valued at $31 million.

The Baldwin Library is an integral part of each student's educational experience. The librarians at Baldwin are trained teachers who work to develop in each student the ability to locate and utilize all types of print and nonprint materials, to instill an appreciation of the different kinds of literature and media, and to help each student on her way to becoming a lifelong, independent library user. The Baldwin libraries have 30,000 volumes, online database searching through the Access Pennsylvania network, and membership in the local PREP consortium for resource sharing.

ATHLETICS

At Baldwin, team sports and physical education classes provide an important opportunity for students to compete in interschool and interclass competitive settings. Girls may choose each season between playing a team sport or joining a physical education class. In many sports, teams are fielded at varsity, junior varsity, and third-team levels so that girls of every level of athletic ability may participate. Baldwin competes in a girls' interscholastic league with Agnes Irwin, Episcopal Academy, Notre Dame, Germantown Academy, Springside, and Penn Charter. Teams are fielded in basketball, crew, cross-country, dance, diving, field hockey, golf, lacrosse, soccer, softball, squash, swimming, tennis, volleyball, and winter track. Athletic facilities include one outdoor and two indoor swimming pools, three fields, five tennis courts, four international squash courts, a dance studio, a raised three-lane interior running track, a two-level fitness center, and two gymnasiums. Baldwin offers a scholar-athlete grant to students with superior academic and athletic potential and demonstrated financial need.

EXTRACURRICULAR OPPORTUNITIES

Student organizations, clubs, and activities form an important part of the Baldwin experience. Most Baldwin students participate in at least one extracurricular activity; many are involved in more. The four organizations are Student Senate, Class Officers, the Athletic Association Board, and Service League. Clubs include Lamplighters (student tour guides), Peer Counseling, SADD, the Maskers (drama), Chorus, B-Flats (a cappella group), *Roman Candle* (literary magazine), *The Hourglass* (newspaper), *The Prism* (yearbook), Debate Club, Amnesty International, Ecology Club, Football Club, Black Students' Union, French Club, and Asian Students Association.

There is also a wide range of activities and traditions that punctuate the year. These include dances, Book Fair, Pumpkin Sale, Father-Daughter Phillies Game, Athletic Association Halloween Party, IX Banner Assembly, Ring Day, Middle School Ski Trip, Café Internationale, Service Day, Alumnae Association Gift Wrap Sale, Annual Student Art Show, Marching-In Dinner, Senior Project Presentations, Alumnae Luncheon for Seniors, and Class Night.

Because of Baldwin's proximity to Philadelphia, to historic sites in Pennsylvania, and to New York City, clubs and classes frequently take part in field trips.

All of these activities constitute a vital part of the Baldwin education. Girls learn to lead as well as to be intelligent, committed members of a group. Through events sponsored by its groups, the School reaches out to the community beyond the School itself.

DAILY LIFE

The school day begins at 8:15, when students meet with advisers in homeroom to hear the daily announcements. Class periods vary in length from 42 to 75 minutes. Monday through Thursday, classes are over at 3:30; Friday classes end at 2:45. Students in grades 9 and 10 must attend study hall during a free period, while students in grades 11 and 12 have choices to make regarding free time. Girls may bring their own lunch or purchase a hot meal, salad, sandwich, or soup in the dining room. Baldwin has adopted a two-week rotating schedule that allows for club and class meetings during the school day and provides for lengthened periods for laboratory classes. There are no bells and no passing time.

Built into the weekly schedule are assemblies, a full period for meeting with advisers, and time for assignments to math or writing lab.

COSTS AND FINANCIAL AID

Tuition in grades 9–12 for the academic year 2008–09 was $24,775. Expenses such as lunch, books, lab fees, uniforms, and optional music lessons were billed separately. A tuition insurance plan is available.

For 2008–09, Baldwin awarded approximately $1.5 million in financial aid to 20 percent of the students. The number of students awarded financial aid was 120, and the average grant was $12,968. All aid is allocated according to the need analysis procedures of the School and Student Service office in Princeton, New Jersey. Renewal of all financial aid is made annually after the Financial Aid Committee has reviewed the most recent Parents' Financial Statement, tax forms, and student record for each family seeking continued assistance. Baldwin values diversity in its student body and seeks to make its education available to academically talented girls regardless of parental income level. Baldwin is committed to a policy of nondiscrimination and anti-harassment in all aspects of its members' actions and relationships on any basis, including, but not limited to, race, religion, ancestry, color, age, gender, sexual orientation, familial status, disability, veteran status, or national origin.

ADMISSIONS INFORMATION

Each year, Baldwin admits students to grades from PK–12. The School seeks girls with demonstrated academic motivation and achievement who love to learn. Individual talents and diversity of background and interests are also valued. Students are admitted on the basis of a written application, standardized test scores (WPPSI-III for prekindergarten and kindergarten, WISC-IV for grades 1–5, and SSAT or ISEE for grades 6–12), a personal interview and school visit, previous school records, two recommendations, a letter to the Head of the School, and the results of an English Placement Test (grades 6–12). Although Baldwin does not use any cutoff score on standardized tests, the Admissions Committee looks for a pattern of strong achievement in the school records. Motivation is also carefully assessed, as are the student's contributions to the previous school. There is a $50 application fee.

APPLICATION TIMETABLE

Admission inquiries should be made in the fall preceding the September of desired enrollment. Initially, parents should make an appointment to meet with the Director of Admissions and tour the School. After this visit, the application should be filed, testing should be scheduled, and the candidate should plan to come to Baldwin to visit classes. The admission deadline is February 1 for grades 2–12 and January 9 for PK, kindergarten, and grade 1. March 1 is the parents' reply date once a student has been accepted. The Baldwin admissions team strongly encourages applicants to grades 2–12 to complete their applications by early January, prior to the February 1 deadline.

ADMISSIONS CORRESPONDENCE

Sarah J. Goebel
Director of Admissions and Financial Aid
The Baldwin School
701 West Montgomery Avenue
Bryn Mawr, Pennsylvania 19010

Phone: 610-525-2700
Web site: http://www.baldwinschool.org/

THE BEEKMAN SCHOOL AND THE TUTORING SCHOOL

THE BEEKMAN SCHOOL

New York, New York

Type: Coeducational day college-preparatory and general academic school
Grades: 9–12, postgraduate year
Enrollment: 80
Head of School: George Higgins, Headmaster

THE SCHOOL

The Beekman School/The Tutoring School of New York was founded by George Matthew in 1925. The School was organized to offer a college-preparatory curriculum with the advantage of highly individualized instruction. Since no 2 students have the same abilities, learning issues, or goals, teaching is geared to the needs of the individual student. Thus, classes are limited to a maximum of 10 students in The Beekman School and a maximum of 3 students in The Tutoring School.

In addition to having small classes, The Beekman School combines a traditional academic education with a flexible yet structured approach. For instance, some students are eager to complete high school in less than four years for reasons that range from having been retained in a grade earlier in their education to feeling a natural desire to move ahead to college. If there appears (to all concerned) to be a readiness to accomplish this, the School proceeds with a program that will achieve this goal. This is done by adding one or two extra classes to the student's schedule and/or through attendance in the summer session.

In order for students to move effectively at their own pace, the School provides them with the proper level of classes in as many subjects as seems appropriate. Some students require more support to facilitate their learning in the state-mandated academic curriculum. Teachers have several periods free each day to meet with students, and there are supervised study halls each period throughout the day until 5 p.m. In addition, all homework assignments are posted on the School's Web site daily. Upon request, tutors are available through The Tutoring School.

The Tutoring School is a program within The Beekman School. This program specializes in educating students who require private or semiprivate classes. The Tutoring School teaches college-level courses as well as standard courses. Its mission is to provide a supportive environment in which students can realize their academic potential and achieve their educational goals. Generally, incoming students follow The Beekman School's college-preparatory curriculum and receive credit from The Beekman School. However, if necessary, The Tutoring School can follow any school's course syllabus, and course credit is granted by that school upon successful completion of all course work. After-school or home tutoring is available for midterm and final-exam preparation, SAT preparation, or academic support in any subject. In addition, The Tutoring School can arrange at-home schooling, if necessary.

The Beekman School is registered by the Board of Regents of the State of New York and is a member of the College Entrance Examination Board and the Educational Records Bureau.

ACADEMIC PROGRAMS

The requirements of the Board of Regents of the State of New York form the core of the college-preparatory curriculum at The Beekman School and The Tutoring School. It is strongly advised, however, that students exceed these requirements, especially in the areas of mathematics, the sciences, and humanities. In addition to the requirements, The Beekman School faculty has developed many interesting and challenging elective courses from which students may choose. Some of these are psychology, bioethics, ecology, computer animation, creative writing, modern politics, filmmaking, darkroom photography, Eastern and Western philosophy, poetry, and art. Students also participate in after-school activities, such as the literary magazine, yearbook projects, and the School's volunteer program. Students can elect to study music, music theory, voice, various musical instruments, or composition at the Turtle Bay Music School, which is a 2-block walk from The Beekman School. If 6 or more students wish to form a particular course, the administration will offer the course at The Beekman School. If 1 to 3 students wish to take a particular course, it will be offered through The Tutoring School. Otherwise, students are encouraged to take specialized elective courses at various institutions throughout the city.

If students take an elective course off campus, they must complete 48 course hours to earn a semester credit and 96 course hours to earn a full-year credit. For the college-bound student, the suggested academic high school program consists of the following courses: 4 years of English, 4 years of history (including a senior-year program that consists of a semester of U.S. government and a semester of economics), 3 years of mathematics (through algebra II/trigonometry), 3 years of science (including 1 year of a lab science), 3 years of a foreign language, 1 year of art or music, several elective courses, and 1 semester of health education and computer science.

The grading system of the School is A to D (passing) and F (failing). Sixty percent is the minimum passing grade. Midway through each quarter, an interim progress report is mailed home to any student who is earning below 70 percent in any course. Weekly updates by phone can be arranged so that parents always know the academic status of their child.

Because of the independent nature and small size of the School community, the scheduling of classes and the number of classes in which a student enrolls are flexible. Students can begin their day with the first, second, or third period. For the same reasons of independence and adaptability, the School also tries to accommodate any reasonable requests of the students for additional courses. Similarly, tutoring for study and organizational skills and remediation courses in English and math are offered through The Tutoring School.

FACULTY AND ADVISERS

There are 14 full-time members of The Beekman School faculty.

The current Headmaster, George Higgins, has been at the School since 1980, first as a teacher, then as Assistant Headmaster, before serving the School as Headmaster.

All faculty members have graduate degrees or are enrolled in a graduate degree program. In addition to teaching, faculty members also act as advisers to small groups of students. Faculty advisers review progress reports with students and hold meetings periodically to listen to student concerns and discuss upcoming events. Parent conferences are held as frequently as they are needed or requested. Twice during the school year, parents are invited to the School to attend open-house evenings, at which time they can discuss their child's progress with the teachers. When necessary, the Headmaster or classroom teacher calls parents to keep them informed of their child's homework and general behavior.

The School's offices are open to the students almost all day, every day. Students feel welcome to visit the Headmaster or the Director to talk, complain, laugh, or ask questions.

COLLEGE ADMISSION COUNSELING

Each year, approximately 95 percent of the graduating class attends college. The aim of the School's college guidance program is to find the right college for each graduating senior. Major considerations include how competitive an environment the student wants, what area of study the student is leaning toward, what size of school would be conducive to success, and where the student would like to live (i.e., city, suburb, East Coast, West Coast). In the past five years, graduates of the School have been accepted at the following colleges and universities: Bard, Boston University, Columbia, Harvard, Ithaca, NYU, Sarah Lawrence, School of Visual Arts, Smith, SUNY at Purchase, and the University of Colorado, to name a few. The Beekman School's staff and faculty members make every effort to examine not just where a student will likely be admitted but where that student will learn, grow, and feel successful for the next four years.

The senior class numbers approximately 25 students. Each student is carefully guided through the college application process, as are his or her parents. A Parents' College Evening, hosted by the School's college guidance counselor, is held each fall for the parents of seniors. It is always an informative evening for parents; the guest speaker is an administrator from the admissions office of a nearby university, who is also there to answer questions. The college guidance counselor schedules several individual appointments with all seniors in order to help them navigate the college application process.

STUDENT BODY AND CONDUCT

Each year, The Beekman School begins the fall term with approximately 70 students. Its rolling admissions policy means that the School adds members to the student body until it reaches its maximum enrollment of 80 students. The enrollment is generally evenly divided between boys and girls. All students are from the immediate tristate area of Connecticut, New Jersey, and New York and its suburbs. The success of The Beekman School's philosophy is proven by the distance students gladly travel in order to be in a school where the enrollment and class size are small, the faculty is supportive and caring, and the education is challenging yet can be paced according to the student's abilities and needs.

There is a School code of behavior that has been shaped by the students and teachers of the School. The main tenet of the code is based on the Golden Rule—"Do unto others as you would have others do unto you." The small, intimate environment makes any type of behavior problem untenable; if the code of the School is violated, there is always an appropriate response. There have been no serious discipline or behavior issues at the School; Beekman students respect their school and its philosophy and recognize the need for tolerance, compassion, and respect in this global community.

ACADEMIC FACILITIES

The School is located in an East Side Manhattan town house. There are eight classrooms; a small library; a state-of-the-art laboratory for biology, chemistry, and physics; a darkroom; a computer lab updated with the latest technology; a study hall equipped with computers; a beautifully landscaped garden; and a student lounge where students can eat lunch and socialize. Rapid Internet access is available throughout the School. Each administrator and teacher has an e-mail address, so parents and students can easily communicate with staff members.

ATHLETICS

The Beekman School meets the New York State requirements for physical education by providing a gym program at a nearby athletic facility. Students may participate in the School's program or design their own program; for example, they may wish to attend their neighborhood gym while being supervised by a private trainer, or they may decide to take dance lessons, karate lessons, or other lessons. Students must exercise for 2 hours each week. In the School's program, an instructor is provided, and students begin the year with aerobics and weight training. Activities in the gym program vary throughout the year and include swimming, volleyball, basketball, cardiovascular exercise, and track. If a student is seriously involved in an intramural activity outside the School, such as soccer or tennis, he or she may be excused from the School's sports program.

EXTRACURRICULAR OPPORTUNITIES

The School's Manhattan location gives it the opportunity to use New York City and its immediate environs as an extension of the classroom. Groups from the School attend plays, films, operas, and dance performances and visit various museums, exhibitions, historical sites, and other points of interest in and around Manhattan and as far away as Philadelphia.

In addition to day trips, the School plans several overnight trips, usually to Washington, D.C., or camping in Frost Valley. During spring break, the School plans a trip to various destinations in Europe.

Any student who wants to work on the yearbook or school literary magazine is welcome to do so, and about one third of the student body participates in one way or another. Additional after-school activities include the drama club, photography club, and film club. Upperclassmen can also take part in a community volunteer program if the desire and maturity are present.

DAILY LIFE

Students' schedules reflect their individual needs. The school day begins at 8:45 a.m. and continues until 3:50 p.m. When possible, students who have a long commuting distance are scheduled to begin classes at 9:30 or 10:15. Students with professional programs outside of school can have classes arranged for mornings or afternoons. Supervised study halls are provided throughout the day from 8:45 a.m. to 5 p.m. Lunch periods are scheduled throughout the day on a staggered basis.

SUMMER PROGRAMS

The Beekman School is in session almost year-round. In June, when the academic year is over, the School begins a three-week mini-session of intensive work for students who want or need private tutoring in a specific subject area, who need to make up work in a course for which they received an incomplete, or who exceeded the School's attendance policy (sixteen absences are allowed in a year course, and eight are allowed in a semester course).

Following the mini-session, The Beekman School operates a six-week summer session, which is attended by the School's students and by students from boarding and other private day schools who wish to accelerate in any major academic course, enrich their knowledge of a particular subject, or repeat a course. Each summer class is 90 minutes long; there are four classes each day, and the program lasts for thirty-two days. The Beekman School's summer session is approved by the New York State Education Department.

COSTS AND FINANCIAL AID

The annual tuition is $25,500, which is divided into four payments. In addition, an activity fee and an administrative fee ($250 each) are charged. All twelfth-grade students pay a senior fee of $300.

The tuition for the mini-session depends upon the individual's length of study. The tuition for the six-week summer session is $1900 per 90-minute course.

If a student wishes to take a course in The Tutoring School (average student-teacher ratio is 2:1), tuition is $7000 for each yearlong course and $3765 for each semester course. The average course load in The Tutoring School consists of four courses, for a total cost of $28,000. Activity and administration fees are included. Currently, there is no financial aid.

ADMISSIONS INFORMATION

It is a reflection of the School's philosophy that it does not use admissions tests as a means to determine a prospective student's eligibility to attend the School. The Headmaster or Director meets with each prospective student and his or her parents in an intensive interview so that all may better understand each other. Together, they try to assess whether the School would be a good match for the student. Previous school transcripts and records of testing are reviewed but are not solely used to determine a course of study. Prospective students are also welcome to observe for a half or full day so they can gain a clearer understanding of the style of the School. Informal evaluations in math and English may be administered to determine the best course placement for various students.

APPLICATION TIMETABLE

Since there are several different types of secondary schools offering many different programs, it is advisable that interviews take place during the early spring of the year prior to entry. Selecting a school in which to study and socialize is an important process, and students and their families should take the time to look closely at several schools before coming to a final decision. Occasionally, students choose a school that is not a good fit for them. Because Beekman has a rolling admissions policy, even if the traditional day program is filled, students can begin their day in the afternoon and take classes into the late afternoon or early evening. These courses are usually semiprivate and cost more than the regular Beekman tuition. The School believes that a successful secondary education is of vital importance to all young adults; its goal is to make the School available to any student who wishes to actively participate in his or her education.

ADMISSIONS CORRESPONDENCE

George Higgins, Headmaster
The Beekman School
220 East 50th Street
New York, New York 10022
Phone: 212-755-6666
Fax: 212-888-6085
E-mail: georgeh@beekmanschool.org
Web site: http://www.beekmanschool.org

BERKELEY PREPARATORY SCHOOL

Tampa, Florida

Type: Coeducational independent college-preparatory day school
Grades: PK–12: Lower Division, Prekindergarten–5; Middle Division, 6–8; Upper Division, 9–12
Enrollment: School total: approximately 1,200; Lower Division: 400; Middle Division: 300; Upper Division: 500
Head of School: Joseph A. Merluzzi, Headmaster

THE SCHOOL

The Latin words *Disciplina, Diligentia,* and *Integritas* in Berkeley's motto describe the School's mission to nurture students' intellectual, emotional, spiritual, and physical development so they can achieve their highest human potential. Episcopal in heritage, Berkeley was founded in 1960 and opened for grades 7–12 the following year. Kindergarten through grade 6 were added in 1967, and prekindergarten began in 1988. Berkeley's purpose is to enable its students to achieve academic excellence in preparation for higher education and to instill in students a strong sense of morality, ethics, and social responsibility.

Berkeley is located on a 76-acre campus in the suburban Town 'N Country area of Tampa, a location that attracts students from Hillsborough, Pinellas, and Pasco Counties and throughout the greater Tampa Bay area. Private bus transportation is available.

Berkeley is incorporated as a nonprofit institution and is governed by a 31-member Board of Trustees that includes alumni, parents of current students, and parents of alumni. The presidents of the Alumni Association and Parents' Club are also members of the board.

ACADEMIC PROGRAMS

The school year runs from the end of August to the first week of June and includes Thanksgiving, Christmas, and spring vacations. The curriculum naturally varies within each division.

In the Lower Division, the program seeks to provide appropriate, challenging learning experiences in a safe environment that reflects the academic, social, moral, and ethical values the School espouses in its philosophy. Curricular emphasis is on core subjects of reading and mathematics. An interdisciplinary approach is used in foreign language and social studies, and manipulatives are used extensively in the science and mathematics programs. Each student also receives instruction in library skills and computers.

Academic requirements in the Middle Division, where classes average 16 to 20 students, are English, English expressions, mathematics, history, foreign language, science, computers, physical education, art, drama, and music. All students in grades 6 and 7 take Latin and a choice of French, Spanish, or Chinese. Continuing grade 8 students have the option of Latin, French, Spanish, or Chinese. Every class meets five days a week and has one weekly scheduled makeup period. Extra help is available from teachers, and grades are sent to parents four times a year.

The Upper Division program, with average classes of 15 to 18 students meeting five days a week, requires students to take four or five credit courses a year, in addition to fine arts and physical education requirements. To graduate, a student must complete 22 credits, including 4 in English and 3 each in mathematics, history, science, and foreign language. Students must also complete one year of personal fitness/health and an additional year of physical education, two years of fine arts, and two electives. In addition, Berkeley students are required to take a semester of religious studies each year and complete 76 hours of community service. More than twenty Advanced Placement courses are offered.

FACULTY AND ADVISERS

There are more than 170 full-time faculty members and administrators. They hold baccalaureate, more than seventy-five graduate, and several doctoral degrees. Headmaster Joseph A. Merluzzi, who joined Berkeley in 1987, received his bachelor's degree from Western Connecticut State University and his master's degree in mathematics from Fairfield University. He came to Berkeley from the Cranbrook Kingswood School in Michigan.

In addition to teaching responsibilities, faculty members are involved in Berkeley's cocurricular programs as coaches and student activity advisers. In the Upper Division, 3 teach part-time and serve as academic grade advisers for students in ninth and tenth grades, and 3 full-time college counselors assist students in grades 11 and 12 with academic advising and the college process. Berkeley faculty members receive support for professional development opportunities, and a number have been recipients of National Endowment for the Humanities grants.

COLLEGE ADMISSION COUNSELING

Traditionally, Berkeley's entire graduating class goes on to attend college. Although Berkeley does not rank its students, more than 125 colleges visit the School each year to recruit its graduates. The mean SAT scores for the class of 2008 were 620 verbal, 628 writing, and 633 math. Berkeley's college counseling department works to assist students and their families in selecting colleges that best suit their academic, financial, and social needs.

Recent graduates are attending Boston College, Brown, Cornell, Dartmouth, Duke, Emory, Georgetown, Harvard, Johns Hopkins, Northwestern, NYU, Princeton, Stanford, Vanderbilt, Villanova, Yale, and the Universities of Florida, Miami, Michigan, North Carolina, Pennsylvania, and Virginia. Eight seniors were named National Merit Scholarship Finalists. Scholarship offers totaling more than $7 million were made to the class of 2008, and 15 percent of the graduates committed to pursuing athletic competition at the collegiate level.

STUDENT BODY AND CONDUCT

In all divisions, Berkeley students are expected to maintain high standards. Mature conduct and use of manners are expected, and an honor code outlines students' responsibilities. In exchange, students are entrusted with certain privileges, such as direct access to the administration and the opportunity to initiate School-sponsored clubs. Students wear uniforms to class.

ACADEMIC FACILITIES

The 76-acre campus is located in the Town 'N Country suburb of Tampa. It consists of classrooms, a Fine Arts Wing, a Science Wing, two libraries, computer labs, general convocation rooms, physical education fields, a 19,000-square-foot student center, a prekindergarten wing, and administrative offices for the Lower, Middle, and Upper Divisions.

The arts program was enhanced in 1997 with the addition of a 634-seat performing arts center that also includes a gallery for visual arts displays, a flex studio for both dance recitals and small drama productions, dressing rooms, and an orchestra pit.

ATHLETICS

Varsity sports for boys include baseball, basketball, crew, cross-country, diving, football, golf, lacrosse, soccer, swimming, tennis, track, weight lifting, and wrestling. Girls compete in basketball, crew, cross-country, diving, golf, soccer, softball, swimming, tennis, track, volleyball, and weight lifting. The campus has several playing fields. Upper Division teams are members of the Bay Conference, while Middle and Lower Division teams compete in the Florida West Coast League and the Youth Sports League.

Athletes use two gymnasiums, a wrestling/gymnastics room, a weight-lifting room, a rock-climbing wall, a stadium (for track meets and football and soccer games), baseball and softball diamonds, tennis courts, a ropes course, and a junior Olympic swimming pool.

Seasonal sports award banquets and a homecoming football game are scheduled annually.

EXTRACURRICULAR OPPORTUNITIES

In addition to its broad-based commitment to student organizations and clubs and its community service requirements, Berkeley offers its students a vast array of outside-the-classroom possibilities. Berkeley's Pipe and Drum Corps continues to make a significant impact in the community by performing at several special events, including the Boston St. Patrick's Day Parade and Walt Disney World. Student artwork is accepted each year into the prestigious Scarfone Gallery Art Show. An after-school Lower Division Chess Club attracts close to 50 students from kindergarten through fifth grade. Middle and Upper Division students, as well as many faculty members, participate in several international experiences, with trips to China, Costa Rica, France, Italy, Paris, and Scotland.

DAILY LIFE

Students in prekindergarten through grade 5 attend classes from 8 a.m. to 3:10 p.m. Middle and Upper Division students begin at 8 and end at 3:20. Teachers are available to assist students and offer extra help during activity periods, which are scheduled into each class day. Supervised study halls are also scheduled for some students.

SUMMER PROGRAMS

A six-week summer academic program for prekindergarten through grade 12 students is offered. Tuition ranges from $900 to $2100.

COSTS AND FINANCIAL AID

The tuition schedule for 2008–09 is as follows: $14,630 for prekindergarten–grade 5, $16,440 for grades 6–8, and $17,730 for grades 9–12. Tuition is payable in eight installments and must be paid in full by January 1. Tuition payments do not cover costs of uniforms, supplies, transportation, special event admission fees, or other expenses incurred in the ordinary course of student activities at Berkeley.

Berkeley makes all admission decisions without regard to financial status. Financial aid in the form of partial-tuition scholarships is available for families who demonstrate need. The School and Student Service for Financial Aid (SSS) guidelines are used in determining need. Berkeley may not be able to accommodate all financial aid applicants in a given year, but once a student is awarded aid, the aid continues until graduation as long as the student remains in good standing and demonstrates need. An SSS form, available from the admissions office, must be submitted annually, and Berkeley's financial aid committee determines all awards by mid-March.

Berkeley also has eleven scholarships and six partial scholarships that are available to students.

ADMISSIONS INFORMATION

In considering applicants, Berkeley evaluates a student's talent, academic skills, personal interests, motivation to learn, and desire to attend. Special consideration is given to qualified applicants who are children of faculty members or alumni or who have siblings currently attending Berkeley.

Lower Division candidates visit age-appropriate classrooms and are evaluated for placement by Berkeley teachers. Middle and Upper Division candidates are required to take the Secondary School Admissions Test (SSAT) and should register for a December or January test date. Entering juniors and seniors may submit PSAT or SAT scores in place of sitting for the SSAT.

The admission process is selective and is based on information gathered from the application form, interviews, the candidate's record, admission tests, and teacher recommendations.

Berkeley admits students of any race, color, sex, religion, and national or ethnic origin and does not discriminate on the basis of any category protected by law in the administration of its educational policies, admission policies, and scholarship, financial aid, athletic, and other School-administered programs.

APPLICATION TIMETABLE

Applications should be submitted by the fall one year prior to the student's entrance into Berkeley. Applications are considered in the order received, and decisions are made in early March. Parents are notified of their child's status as soon as possible thereafter. All applications after the initial selection process are considered on a space-available basis.

Berkeley welcomes inquiries from families throughout the year. However, because of the competitive nature of the admission process, families are encouraged to visit the campus as early as possible to become familiar with the School, its programs, and its admission procedure.

ADMISSIONS CORRESPONDENCE

Janie McIlvaine
Director of Admissions
Berkeley Preparatory School
4811 Kelly Road
Tampa, Florida 33615
Phone: 813-885-1673
Fax: 813-886-6933
E-mail: mcilvjan@berkeleyprep.org
Web site: http://www.berkeleyprep.org

BERKSHIRE SCHOOL

Sheffield, Massachusetts

BERKSHIRE SCHOOL
CELEBRATING A CENTURY

Type: Coeducational boarding and day college-preparatory school
Grades: 9–12 (Forms III–VI), postgraduate year
Enrollment: 373
Head of School: Michael J. Maher

THE SCHOOL

In 1907, Mr. and Mrs. Seaver B. Buck, graduates of Harvard and Smith respectively, rented the building of Glenny Farm at the foot of Mt. Everett and founded Berkshire School. For thirty-five years, the Bucks devoted themselves to educating young men to the values of academic excellence, physical vigor, and high personal standards. In 1969, this commitment to excellence was extended to include girls.

Berkshire School is a rigorous college-preparatory institution that has flourished for more than a century in a New England setting of extraordinary natural beauty. It is a welcoming and supportive environment where a diverse group of young men and women can develop intellectual foundations and traits of character and leadership that will permit them, in the words of the school's motto, to learn "not just for school, but for life." A medium-sized boarding school with a distinctly global character, Berkshire is home to 373 students from across the country and around the world and experienced teachers who are dedicated to their craft.

Situated at the base of Mt. Everett, the second-highest mountain in Massachusetts, Berkshire's campus spans 500 acres. It is a 75-minute drive to both Albany International Airport and Hartford's Bradley International Airport, and just over 2 hours from Boston and New York City.

Berkshire School is incorporated as a not-for-profit institution, governed by a 28-member self-perpetuating Board of Trustees. The School has an $83-million endowment. Annual operating expenses exceed $22 million. Annual Giving in 2007–08 exceeded $1.75 million. The Berkshire Chapter of the Cum Laude Society was established in 1942.

Berkshire School is accredited by the New England Association of Schools and Colleges and holds memberships in the Independent School Association of Massachusetts, the National Association of Independent Schools, the College Entrance Examination Board, the National Association for College Admission Counseling, the Secondary School Admission Test Board, and the Association of Boarding Schools.

ACADEMIC PROGRAMS

The academic program at Berkshire in many respects defines the School itself: it is formal, structured, and demanding. The program of studies centers on the five principal scholastic disciplines—English, mathematics, ancient and foreign languages (including Mandarin Chinese), the sciences, and history—and also includes extensive course offerings in philosophy and religion, computer science, and the visual and performing arts. Berkshire's Ritt Kellogg Mountain Program uses Mt. Everett as a backdrop to encourage a deeper understanding of the School's natural surroundings through curricular and extracurricular activities. Believing that the best preparation for college is the acquisition of knowledge from a variety of disciplines, Berkshire requires the following credits: 4 years of English; 3 years each of mathematics, a foreign language, and history; 2 years of science; and 1 year of the visual or performing arts. All departments provide for accelerated sections, and students are placed at a level commensurate with their skills and talent. Many students take one or more of the eighteen Advanced Placement courses offered.

Most students carry five courses. The average number of students in a class is 11, and the student-teacher ratio is 6:1. The academic year is divided into two semesters, each culminating with an assessment period. Students receive grades, teacher comments, and adviser letters twice each semester. Berkshire uses a traditional letter-grading system of A–F (D is passing).

Independent-study programs may be undertaken by Sixth Formers, with the understanding that no student may participate in more than one such project a year.

FACULTY AND ADVISERS

The Berkshire teaching faculty numbers 67, 57 of whom live on campus. Twenty-eight teachers hold a master's degree and 4 hold doctorates. Faculty members contribute to both the academic and personal development of each student. The small size of the Berkshire community permits faculty members to become involved in students' lives outside, as well as inside, the classroom. Each student is paired with a faculty adviser who provides guidance, monitors academic progress, and serves as a liaison with the student's family. Berkshire also retains the services of 4 pediatricians, a nurse practitioner, 4 registered nurses, and 2 certified athletic trainers.

Michael J. Maher was named Berkshire's fifteenth head of school in the spring of 2004. He holds a bachelor's degree in political science from the University of Vermont and a master's degree in liberal studies from Wesleyan University. Mr. Maher is in his fifth year at Berkshire; previously he held positions as administrator, teacher, and hockey coach. He and his wife, Jean, an associate director of admission and a member of the Foreign Language Department, have 3 children.

COLLEGE ADMISSION COUNSELING

College counseling at Berkshire is the responsibility of 3 full-time and 2 part-time professionals who assist students and their parents in the search for an appropriate college or university. The formal process begins in the Fifth Form, with individual conferences with the college counselors, and the opportunity to meet with some of the approximately 100 college admissions representatives who visit the campus. In May, Fifth Formers and their parents attend a weekend seminar on the college admission process. Admission strategies are discussed and specific institutions are identified for each student's consideration. During the summer, students are encouraged to visit colleges and write the first draft of their college application essay. The application process is generally completed by winter vacation in the Sixth Form year.

The 116 graduates of the class of 2008 are now attending four-year colleges or universities, including Bard, Bates, Boston College, Boston University, Colby, Colgate, Cornell, Dartmouth, Dickinson, Emory, Johns Hopkins, Kenyon, Lehigh, NYU, Northeastern, SMU, St. Lawrence, Syracuse, Union, Villanova, Williams, and the Universities of Connecticut, Massachusetts, Wisconsin and Vermont

STUDENT BODY AND CONDUCT

In the 2008–09 academic year, there were 331 boarders and 42 day students; with 2 students studying abroad in the second semester. The student body is drawn from twenty-eight states and twenty countries.

The goal of student life at Berkshire is responsible participation. Students contribute directly to the life of the school community through involvement in the Student Government, the Prefect Program, the School's Community and School Service Program, dormitory life, and various clubs and activities. Participation gives students a positive growth experience supporting the School motto of learning "not just for school, but for life." The rules at Berkshire are simple and straightforward and are consistent with the values and ideals of the School. They are designed to help students live orderly lives within an environment of mutual trust and respect.

ACADEMIC FACILITIES

Berkshire Hall, the primary academic facility built in 1930 and the centerpiece of the campus, reopened in the fall of 2008 after a full renovation. It now features larger classrooms with state-of-the-art technology, new administrative offices, a two-story atrium, and a Great Room for student study and special functions. Music facilities located in Memorial Hall include four soundproofed, air-conditioned practice rooms; a piano teaching studio; and a classroom-rehearsal space. Adjacent to Memorial Hall is the 400-seat Allen Theater. Godman House is home to several darkrooms and a digital art and electronic music studio, and deWindt Dormitory houses a visual arts studio.

The Geier Library is central to intellectual life on the campus. The library contains approximately 43,000 volumes in open stacks, an extensive reference collection in both print and electronic format, numerous periodicals, and a fine audio-visual collection. The library has wireless Internet access, as well as eighteen computers with Internet access and an online card catalog for student use. ProQuest Direct, the Expanded Academic Index ASAP, the *New York Times* full text (1994 to present), and the current ninety days' full text of 150 Northeastern newspapers, including the *Wall*

Street Journal online, keep the library fully up-to-date on breaking information.

At the Dixon Observatory, computer synchronized telescopes make it possible to view and photograph objects in the solar system and beyond. Given the combination of equipment, software, and location, Berkshire's observatory is among the best in New England.

BOARDING AND GENERAL FACILITIES

Berkshire has ten residential houses, including two girls' dormitories that were completed in the fall of 2002. Three faculty families, many with small children, generally reside in each house along with a prefect—Sixth Formers whose primary responsibility is to assist dorm parents with daily routines, such as study hall and room inspection. Dorm rooms are equipped with access to the Internet and private phone lines. There is a common room in each house, where students may relax or study. Benson Commons, the school center, features a dining hall capable of seating the entire School, a post office, the School bookstore, the Student Life office, and recreational spaces.

ATHLETICS

Berkshire enjoys a proud tradition of athletic excellence. The School provides competition in twenty-seven interscholastic sports, including baseball, basketball, crew, cross-country running, field hockey, football, golf, ice hockey, lacrosse, mountain biking, skiing, soccer, softball, squash, tennis, track and field, and volleyball. Students may also participate in the Ritt Kellogg Mountain Program, a program that utilizes Berkshire's natural environment and its proximity to the Appalachian Trail to present athletic challenges, teach leadership, and foster environmental responsibility.

In January 2009 the 117,000-square-foot Jackman L. Stewart Athletic Center opened. The facility offers two ice rinks (one Olympic-size), fourteen locker rooms, seating for 800 spectators, a 34-machine fitness center and athletic training rooms. It can also be used for indoor tennis and can accommodate all-school functions. A second athletic center features full-size courts for basketball and volleyball, four international squash courts, a climbing wall, and fitness center. Other facilities include the new Thomas H. Young Field for baseball, new softball fields, an all-weather track, a lighted football field, and two synthetic-turf fields.

EXTRACURRICULAR OPPORTUNITIES

Berkshire offers students a variety of opportunities to express their talents and passions. Students publish a newspaper, a yearbook, and a literary magazine that features student writing, art, and photography. The Ritt Kellogg Mountain Program offers backcountry skills, boatbuilding, fly fishing, hiking, kayaking, rock climbing, and winter mountaineering.

There are a number of active clubs, including the Drama Club, the International Club, the Investment Club, the Maple Syrup Program, the Philanthropy Society, and a Student Activities Committee.

Berkshire's student-run FM radio station, WBSL, operates with a power of 250 watts and is capable of reaching 10,000 listeners. Berkshire is one of the few secondary schools to hold membership in the Intercollegiate Broadcasting System and the only one affiliated with both the Associated Press wire service and its radio service.

Berkshire students pursue the arts in the classroom and in extracurricular activities. The theater program offers two plays in the fall and spring as well as a winter musical. There are three choral groups: Ursa Major, an all-school chorus; Ursa Minor, a girls' a cappella group; and Greensleeves, an all male chorus. There are two music groups: a jazz band and a chamber music ensemble. Students can also take private voice and instrumental lessons. Each season the Berkshire community looks forward to various performances, such as dance and music recitals, a jazz café, and poetry readings. Visual arts include painting, drawing, sculpture, digital art, photography, and ceramics. Students display their work in galleries in the Student Center and in Berkshire Hall.

DAILY LIFE

The first of the six class periods in a school day begins at 8 a.m., and the final class concludes at 2:45 p.m., except on Wednesday and Saturday, when the last class ends by 11:35 a.m. Berkshire follows a rotating schedule in which classes meet at different times each day.

Athletics, outdoor experiences, and art activities occupy the afternoon. Clubs often meet after dinner, before the 2-hour supervised study period that begins at 8 p.m.

The Community and School Service Program is an integral part of life at Berkshire School. Students must commit a certain number of hours toward community service, with options available on and off campus.

WEEKEND LIFE

Weekend activities are planned by a Director of Student Activities and include first-run movies, dances with live bands, and other dances hosted by DJs. There are trips to local amusement parks and theaters as well as shopping trips to Hartford and Albany. In addition, students and faculty members journey to New York and Boston to visit museums, attend theater and music productions, or take in professional sports events.

COSTS AND FINANCIAL AID

For the 2008–09 academic year, tuition was $42,450 for boarding students and $32,700 for day students. For most students, $100 a month is sufficient personal spending money. Ten percent of the tuition is paid upon enrollment, 50 percent is payable on July 1, and 40 percent is payable on November 30. Various tuition payment plans are available.

Financial aid is awarded on the basis of need to about 29 percent of the student body. The total financial aid spent in 2008–09 was $3.2 million. The School and Student Service (SSS) Parents Financial Statement and a 1040 form are required. Merit scholarships were also awarded.

ADMISSIONS INFORMATION

Berkshire adheres to the principle that in diversity there is strength and, therefore, actively seeks students from a broad range of geographic, ethnic, religious, and socioeconomic backgrounds. Admission is most frequent in the Third and Fourth Forms, and the School enrolls 12 or 13 postgraduates each year.

In order to assess the student's academic record, potential, character, and contributions to his or her school, Berkshire requires a personal interview, a transcript, test scores, and recommendations from English and mathematics teachers, along with the actual application. Candidates should have their Secondary School Admission Test (SSAT) scores forwarded to Berkshire School (school code 1612).

APPLICATION TIMETABLE

Interested families are encouraged to visit the campus in the fall or winter preceding the September in which admission is desired. Visits are arranged according to the academic schedule, Monday through Friday, from 8 a.m. to 2 p.m. and Saturday from 8 to 10:45 a.m. January 31 is the deadline for submitting applications; late applications are accepted as long as space is anticipated. Berkshire adheres to the standard notification date of March 10 and the families' reply date of April 10. Depending on availability, late applications are processed on a rolling basis. Applications for admission are available online at the School's Web site at http://www.berkshireschool.org.

ADMISSIONS CORRESPONDENCE

Andrew Bogardus, Director of Admission
Berkshire School
245 North Undermountain Road
Sheffield, Massachusetts 01257
Phone: 413-229-1003
Fax: 413-229-1016
E-mail: admission@berkshireschool.org
Web site: http://www.berkshireschool.org

BESANT HILL SCHOOL

Ojai, California

Type: Coeducational boarding and day college-preparatory school with a creative focus
Grades: 9–12
Enrollment: 105
Head of School: Mr. Paul Amadio

THE SCHOOL

Founded in 1946 by Aldous Huxley, J. Krishnamurti, Guido Ferrando, and Rosalind Rajagopal on 520 acres in the resort town of Ojai, California, this residential school community offers a vigorous college-preparatory curriculum with a cornerstone of creative expression, sustainability, and divergent thinking. Besant Hill offers thirty-three art electives, competitive athletics, travel and experiential education programs, small classes, and a 4:1 student-teacher ratio.

The School was envisioned as an educational community that would provide an atmosphere where students could develop and discover both their intellectual and creative potential and where they would learn "how to think not what to think™." This philosophy is still the core of the School today.

In addition to its fine academic and athletic programs, Besant Hill School has an active fine and performing arts program that is an integral part of the School curriculum. This signature program prepares students for a lifetime of enjoyment in the arts as well as a professional career if so desired. Music, drama, photography, studio art, digital art, and ceramics programs are all headed by experienced teachers who are also professional artists in their own crafts.

Besant Hill School holds membership in the California Association of Independent Schools, the National Association of Independent Schools, and Western Boarding Schools Association. The School is accredited by the Western Association of Schools and Colleges.

ACADEMIC PROGRAMS

The Director of Studies is responsible for the academic life of the School. The curriculum is absolutely and without exception college preparatory. Courses of study follow the University of California (UC) system and can also be determined by the individual student's future plans and interests. The average load is five academic solids, an elective, and an art.

Students also have the ability to "major" or concentrate in specific areas of interest including the arts. This allows individual students the opportunity to gravitate toward an area of passion and explore their interest on a deeper level.

Class size averages 10 students. Independent study is available for especially well-motivated students, and Advanced Placement courses are offered in calculus, English, music theory, physics, and Spanish.

Besant Hill has two academic semesters, and evaluations are sent to parents four times a year. An evening study hall is required.

Graduation requirements are as follows: English, 4 years; Science, 3 years (including 1 year of biology and 1 year of chemistry); Foreign language, 2 years of the same language; Math, 3 years (through algebra II); Social Science, 3 years (including world cultures and American (U.S.) history); Arts, 2 years (visual, theater, music) with at least one year of the same art; Fitness, 4 years; and Electives, at least 3 (one must be senior capstone).

English as a second language (ESL) is also offered. This program works to improve the development of English and oral and listening comprehension skills. Concentration on vocabulary expansion, improved pronunciation, and use of idioms aid the students in understanding and participating in class. The full-year course, which requires an additional fee, is two or three periods a day and can include ESL classes in science, social studies, U.S. history, and TOEFL preparation.

FACULTY AND ADVISERS

There are 29 teachers and administrators on the Besant Hill staff. Nineteen faculty members and administrators reside on campus, and all faculty and staff members are involved in the life of the community beyond the classroom. Of the 22 full-time teachers, half have advanced degrees, 2 of whom hold their doctorates.

COLLEGE ADMISSION COUNSELING

All students take a college-preparatory curriculum and begin their testing program with the Preliminary SAT (PSAT) in the fall of the sophomore year. They take the PSAT again as juniors, in preparation for the SAT, which they take later that same year and then again as seniors. The SAT Subject Tests are administered to those juniors and seniors for whom it is appropriate.

The School receives annual visits from college representatives. The Director of College Counseling is on campus and begins working with students in their sophomore year. In 2008, colleges or universities accepted all of the graduates. Recent graduates are attending colleges such as Bard, Beloit, Berklee School of Music, Bowdoin, Cal Arts, Chicago Institute of the Arts, Columbia, Mills, NYU, University of Washington, and various campuses of the California State University and University of California systems.

STUDENT BODY AND CONDUCT

Of the 105 students attending Besant Hill School this year, one fifth are day students and four fifths are residential. Besant Hill School seeks to instill in students a lifelong love of learning. This goal is reflected in the School motto "Aun Aprendo" ("I am still learning"). The community sets reasonable limits for its members. Elected students participate in a Disciplinary Advisory Committee, along with faculty members and administrators. The School disciplinary system works on a basis of minors and majors. Students may have occasional work crew hours or more serious disciplinary action, depending on the offense.

ACADEMIC FACILITIES

There are eleven buildings on campus. Networked computer stations are available in several buildings. Most of the campus has wireless access. The School houses a science lab, photography lab, new art studio, theater, recording studio, ceramics studio, and digital media lab. The renowned Zalk Theater houses both the drama and music departments.

BOARDING AND GENERAL FACILITIES

The Besant Hill School campus offers boarding facilities for both boys and girls. The residents are housed 2 to a room in bedrooms that contain study and storage facilities for each student. Dorm parents live in each wing of the dormitories and supervise the boarding students with the help of student prefects. Other facilities include a modern dining hall, tennis courts, volleyball courts, basketball courts, and a soccer field. Last year the School added a new baseball field facility.

ATHLETICS

Team experience and personal challenges through athletics are a valuable part of any education and are made available to every student. The School competes interscholastically in baseball, basketball, cross-country, soccer, and volleyball. Boys varsity basketball is the school's signature athletic program and the team is rated as one of the best in California.

EXTRACURRICULAR OPPORTUNITIES

The School's proximity to both the coast and the mountains provides students with a wide range of recreational activities, from surfing to rock climbing. Students can also take advantage of museums, movies, concerts, plays, skating, shopping, and bowling.

DAILY LIFE

Boarding students are responsible for cleaning their rooms and performing assigned crew jobs. Breakfast is served from 7 to 8 a.m. Academic classes are until 2:15 p.m. In the afternoon, fitness and athletics classes are offered. Dinner is at 6 p.m., followed by evening study hall.

WEEKEND LIFE

Weekends give students a chance to relax, catch up on their studies, or partake in planned activities by the Residential Life Director. Weekend trips to Los Angeles, Santa Barbara, and Ventura are frequent.

Students who have parental permission may leave the campus on open weekends, provided they are in good standing with the School.

COSTS AND FINANCIAL AID

The cost of tuition, room, and board for the 2008–09 academic year was $38,800. Day student tuition was $19,900. A book and activity fee of $1950 is required to cover the costs of books, trips, and other expenses. The ESL fee for first-year students is $6500. Participation in the School's instructional support program is $7000.

Approximately 20 percent of the School's income is given annually in scholarship and financial aid. Information on aid availability can be obtained from the Admissions Office.

ADMISSIONS INFORMATION

Students are selected on the basis of character and academic promise. Personal interviews and references are used to identify those students who are most likely to benefit from the Besant Hill School experience. Consequently, a visit to the School is strongly urged for each applicant. Acceptance is based upon records, recommendations, and a personal interview.

APPLICATION TIMETABLE

Candidates should schedule an interview with a member of the Besant Hill School admissions team, schedule a class visit, go on a tour of the School, and begin working on the Besant Hill School application for admission by fall 2009. Students should also begin requesting recommendations, transcripts, and school reports from their current school. The financial aid deadline is January 15, and the application deadline is February 22. Admissions decisions should be mailed by March 10, and new student contracts are due by April 10. Applications received after February 22 are reviewed and acted upon on a space-available basis as soon as the candidate's file is complete. After April 10, remaining spaces will be filled through a rolling admissions policy.

ADMISSIONS CORRESPONDENCE

Randy Bertin
Besant Hill School
P.O. Box 850
Ojai, California 93024

Phone: 805-646-4343 Ext. 422
800-900-0487 (toll-free)
Fax: 805-646-4371
E-mail: rbertin@besanthillschool.org
Web site: http://www.besanthillschool.org

THE BISHOP STRACHAN SCHOOL

THE BISHOP STRACHAN SCHOOL

Toronto, Ontario, Canada

Type: Girls' boarding (grades 7–12) and day (JK–12), college-preparatory school
Grades: JK–12: Junior School, JK–6; Senior School, 7–12
Head of School: Ms. Kim Gordon (Incoming Head for 2009–10 is Ms. Deryn Lavell)

THE SCHOOL

The Bishop Strachan School (BSS), Canada's oldest day and boarding school for girls, is renowned for its expertise in the particular learning needs of girls and offers a single-gender environment that helps its students achieve their best, both academically and in their life's pursuits. BSS has led the way in creating innovative learning programs that include the principle of educating the 'whole girl.' Involving girls in the arts, technology, sports, wellness, community outreach, and many other co-curricular programs empowers girls to work collaboratively, express themselves, and excel in leadership roles.

A rigorous academic curriculum coupled with a creative, nurturing, and expressive approach to education makes BSS a uniquely successful environment specifically developed to bring out the very best in each of its students.

The School is governed by a Board of Trustees and a Board of Governors, both elected bodies representing parents, alumnae, and community leaders. They duly uphold the deeply felt values of BSS that honor its tradition of excellence, its commitment to integrity and compassion, and its ambition to remain the school of choice for the world's brightest and most gifted young women and girls. Annual giving is increasing steadily, and fund-raising campaigns are well supported. With ambitious building and capital improvements nearing completion, the School remains debt free.

BSS is an accredited member of CIS, CAIS, TABS, NAIS, SSATB, and the National Coalition of Girls' Schools. Its programs are inspected and accredited by the Ministry of Education in Ontario and the Canadian Educational Standards Institute.

ACADEMIC PROGRAMS

The Junior School program (JK–6) provides sequential learning experiences that incorporate expectations for the cognitive, social, emotional, physical, and spiritual development of students, through Reggio-inspired, inquiry-based learning. The Junior School curriculum sets the standard of excellence required to ensure that students achieve the mission set out by the School. Entry years for the Junior School are JK and grade 3.

In the Senior School, all programs are offered at advanced and enriched levels. Community service, or service learning, is a part of the curriculum from grades 7 to 12. A strong emphasis is placed on the development of competent writing skills in all subject areas. Students in grades 9–12 are involved in a laptop program that fully integrates technology into the curriculum. Entry years for the Senior School (day) are grades 7 and 9. Boarders are admitted for grades 7–12.

As required by the province of Ontario for graduation, a student must obtain a total of 30 credits from grades 9–12. Compulsory credits at BSS are 4 courses in English; 1 credit in physical education; 3 credits in math (with at least 1 credit in grades 11 or 12); 1 credit in civics and career studies; 2 credits in science; 1 additional credit in science, technological education, or cooperative education; 1 Canadian history credit; 1 Canadian geography credit; 1 arts credit; 1 credit in French; 1 credit that is either an additional English, or a third language, or a social science or humanities, or Canadian and world studies, or guidance and careers education, or cooperative education; and 1 credit that is either a physical education, or the arts, or business studies, or cooperative education. The remaining 12 comprise a wide choice of electives, which include four other foreign languages, economics, law, science, and the arts.

Grading is based on the following scale: 80–100, honors (A); 70–79, very good (B); 60–69, satisfactory (C); 50–59, poor (D); and under 50, failure.

Advanced Placement exams are offered in calculus, U.S. history, microeconomics, macroeconomics, French, Spanish, chemistry, biology, statistics, computer science, English language, and English literature.

Students at the School are involved with The University of Toronto Mentorship Program and Shad Valley Enriched Science and Business Program. They can participate in various exchange programs around the world, and the School has also developed programs for experiential education in grades 8 to 10.

FACULTY AND ADVISERS

There are more than 100 faculty members representing a wide spectrum of teaching experience. All of the teaching staff members hold degrees; the majority holds additional degrees or diplomas in education, while many have higher or advanced degrees.

All staff members participate in co-curricular activities, bringing their expertise and assistance to students. Since the student body is divided into smaller units of Forms and Houses, staff members meet with their students at the beginning of each day. A Teacher-Advisor Program has been incorporated into the curriculum to provide Senior School students with additional opportunities for individualized learning and personal development.

COLLEGE ADMISSION COUNSELING

Two part-time and 3 full-time counsellors are available to assist students with personal goals, academic choices, and career planning. Visits to universities are arranged each year, and representatives from Canadian, American, and United Kingdom universities and colleges visit the School.

One hundred percent of graduating students achieve university admission, and a large number are offered places at prestigious universities in the United States and the United Kingdom, including Columbia, Cornell, Edinburgh, Georgetown, Harvard, the London School of Economics, MIT, Princeton, St. Andrews, and the University of Pennsylvania.

STUDENT BODY AND CONDUCT

Almost 80 boarders come to live at BSS from places such as Canada, the Caribbean, the Pacific Rim, Africa, the Middle East, Europe, the United States, and Mexico. Each year there are exchange students from Quebec, France, Belgium, Australia, Japan, and South Africa. Although the School has Anglican affiliations, many religions are represented in the diverse student body and faculty.

The School has an Honor Code that is clearly understood by parents and students. The underlying principle is that students are expected to conduct themselves according to legality, safety, courtesy, and consideration for others.

Student leaders, or Prefects, are elected by staff and students to represent their peers in an elected student council. There are many additional student leadership opportunities, and all students are encouraged to get involved in the life of the School and build critical leadership skills.

ACADEMIC FACILITIES

Set amid lush grounds in Toronto's prestigious Forest Hill neighborhood, the sprawling campus offers an academic atmosphere in the tradition of the finest schools around the world. Well worn stone and wood echoes with the presence of thousands of girls who have passed through these halls over that past 142 years.

In 2004, a newly built athletic wing added 90,000 square feet of learning space with modern fitness facilities, an enormous gym and dance studio. A beautiful new student centre opened in 2007, offering students healthy snacks from an environmentally conscious cafeteria and a number of study spaces that are fully equipped with Wi-Fi access. A renovated, state-of-the-art library opened in January 2009.

The 7.5 acres of living and learning space is fully appointed with outstanding facilities and technologies, including an indoor pool, a fitness centre, a 250-seat theatre, a dance studio, a Centre for Arts and Design, multi-media and film labs, and a 3-D Printer to teach girls engineering and computer-assisted design. BSS is a laptop school and has over many years, developed a unique way to fully integrate technology into the curriculum at every level.

BOARDING AND GENERAL FACILITIES

The warm and nurturing residence staff aims to make the boarding school a safe and comfortable home away from home for its students. The residence wing is part of the main school and provides easy access to all School facilities, many of which are used in the evenings for study and recreation. The residence washrooms and common rooms were renovated within the last two years, and facility upgrades and improvements are ongoing.

Supervised study occurs four times a week. Students are grouped by grade on each floor. The boarders have their own dining room, and all meals are served buffet-style with plenty of choice. Students from other countries are required to have local guardians. Each student can be contacted through her private voice mail, and all rooms are networked for e-mail and the Internet.

Though the security of BSS students is the School's top priority, it is balanced with their need to develop independence, and privileges are carefully related to age and responsibility. A staff of 11 provides excellent supervision, and the health centre has a nurse on duty daily. Five full-time staff members have housing in the residence.

ATHLETICS

Athletics play an integral role in fostering the development of the whole girl, thereby enriching the School community. The innovative program ensures exposure to a variety of physical activities and health education, encouraging the development of healthy lifestyles. The School has thirty-nine interscholastic teams. These allow almost 50 percent of the senior student body to participate each term. Teams include badminton, basketball, cross-country, field hockey, gymnastics, ice hockey, skiing, soccer, swimming, and volleyball.

EXTRACURRICULAR OPPORTUNITIES

There are seventeen student-run clubs in the School. These range from Third Wave to Amnesty International, from the Roots Club to Robotics. Meetings are usually at lunchtime. Choral, string, and instrumental groups increase the choices. Every year, there is a visiting Canadian author, and many departments invite speakers and lead field trips to local places and abroad. Debating, drama, and music provide frequent collaboration with other local private schools. The Duke of Edinburgh Award Program attracts many participants. A "crazy sports day" fosters community spirit early in the year. Each House is involved in a social service project under the direction of a prefect, and the whole School is committed to raising money for community projects at home and abroad on an ongoing basis.

Students are encouraged to participate actively through the elected residence and student council, the organization of social activities, the publication of a newspaper, and a big sister/little sister program. Social, dramatic, and athletic events are often run in conjunction with Upper Canada College, a neighbouring independent boys' school.

DAILY LIFE

The school day begins at 8:30, with students assembling in Houses and Forms. From 8:50 to 9:10 there is a full assembly of the Senior School in the chapel for a short service, presentations, and announcements. The timetable operates on a five-day cycle and four-period day ending at 3:30. Lunch is from 12:00 to 1:00; half of the lunch hour is used for recreational sport and club activities. Lunch is provided for the Junior School and the boarders; day students may purchase lunch from the cafeteria or bring a packed lunch. Extra help is available in all subjects by appointment or after school. Extramural sports are played after school.

WEEKEND LIFE

The School is close to a quaint and lively shopping area known as Forest Hill Village. Since Toronto is a safe and cosmopolitan city, students are encouraged to take advantage of its diversely enriching opportunities of theatre, museums, art galleries, concerts, sports, and cultural experiences. Staff members, with the assistance of students, organize activities for each weekend. Alternative in-residence activities are also available, and, with advance parental permission, students may visit friends or family. Special interest programs are occasionally arranged during the school week.

Students can make arrangements to attend the place of worship of their choice on weekends.

COSTS AND FINANCIAL AID

For 2009–10, the tuition fee is Can$23,550 for day students. Tuition and full boarding fees are Can$42,675. Additional costs include uniforms, laptop computers, books, field trips, and lunches (senior day girls only). A one-time nonrefundable fee of Can$5000 is charged to all students as a contribution to the existing infrastructure of the School. Private music lessons and tutoring are optional extras.

Entrance and merit scholarships are awarded to students entering grades 7 and 9 and a student who is gifted in the arts in grade 7 or 9. The Twenty-First Century scholarship is awarded to a student entering grade 9 who excels at academics, athletics, or the arts and who requires bursary assistance. These scholarships, based on an exam and a personal profile, are applied to fees and are retained as long as the student maintains a strong academic standing each year. Financial assistance is also available to qualified applicants.

ADMISSIONS INFORMATION

Admission is based on previous school reports, references, and a personal interview. Grade 7–12 applicants also take the SSAT. Students who live too far away to visit write the test at their own schools. Students applying to grades 11 and 12 and whose first language is not English must take the TOEFL. International students are asked to write math and English placement tests to help determine appropriate course placement. An application and brochure describing the School and the admission process are available on the School's Web site, www.bss.on.ca.

APPLICATION TIMETABLE

Applications may be submitted anytime, but the admissions process begins in early October for admission the following September. The entry-year application deadline is December 12, 2009. On receipt of the application, arrangements are made for a tour of the School, personal interviews with the student and parents/guardians, and assessments. The Admissions Team makes final decisions and offers places to day students at the end of February. Boarders are accepted on an ongoing basis beginning in December.

ADMISSIONS CORRESPONDENCE

The Admissions Assistant (Junior School) or
The Admissions Assistant (Senior School)
The Bishop Strachan School
298 Lonsdale Road
Toronto, Ontario M4V 1X2
Canada

Phone: 416-483-4325 Ext. 6020 (Junior) or
1220 (Senior)
Fax: 416-481-5632
E-mail: admissions@bss.on.ca
Web site: http://www.bss.on.ca

BLAIR ACADEMY

Blairstown, New Jersey

Type: Coeducational boarding and day college-preparatory school
Grades: 9–12, postgraduate year
Enrollment: 445
Head of School: T. Chandler Hardwick III

THE SCHOOL

Blair Academy is situated on 423 hilltop acres adjacent to the village of Blairstown in Warren County, one of the most scenic counties in New Jersey. The school is 10 minutes from the Appalachian Trail and the Delaware Water Gap, yet it is only 1½ hours from New York City and 2 hours from Philadelphia.

Blair was founded in 1848 by a group of prominent local merchants and clergymen headed by John Insley Blair. The school was coeducational until 1915, when it became an all-boys school. Coeducation was reinstated in 1970 with great success, and girls now comprise nearly half of the school's population. Although the day-student population is small, it is important, adding a strong dimension to the student body.

Blair maintains an enrollment of 445 students, large enough to support a broad program of studies, activities, and athletics, yet small enough so that everyone can receive ample individual help and attention. The average class size is approximately 10 students, and the programs for guidance and counseling also make for close relationships between students and members of the faculty and staff.

A Board of Trustees directs the school, and alumni are well represented on the Board. The school's endowment is estimated at approximately $71 million. Blair received $8.5 million in capital gifts for 2007–08, and its operating expenses totaled approximately $21.4 million. The Blair Fund raised more than $2 million.

Blair Academy is accredited by the Middle States Association of Colleges and Schools. Its memberships include the Cum Laude Society, New Jersey Association of Independent Schools, National Association of Principals of Schools for Girls, National Association of Independent Schools, the Association of Boarding Schools, Council for Advancement and Support of Education, and Secondary School Admission Test Board.

ACADEMIC PROGRAMS

Blair Academy's academic program follows the traditional four-year college-preparatory plan. Diploma requirements at Blair are governed by college entrance requirements, and they ensure that all students graduate with an exposure to a wide variety of disciplines.

The academic year is divided into two semesters. To graduate, a four-year student must successfully complete the following units (with each semester yielding 1.5 credits): English, 12; mathematics, 9; modern or classical language, 6; laboratory science, 6; world history, 3; U.S. history, 6; arts, 4.5; religion, 1.5; and health, 1.5. Popular course offerings include Chinese, economics, politics and government, Asian studies, Roman history, computer science, biotechnology, video production, string orchestra, and architecture. A full complement of courses is offered in the visual and performing arts. In addition, for every year a student attends Blair, he or she must complete 3 units of physical education or athletics.

Blair Academy offers a broad spectrum of courses, from the introductory level through Advanced Placement.

Individual participation is encouraged in small classroom sections. Day and evening study periods are supervised by faculty members in the dormitory. Every student is assigned a class monitor, who oversees his or her academic life at school. In addition, for the fall term, freshmen receive help from faculty members in managing study time and prioritizing academic tasks.

Blair uses a 6.0 grading system in which 2.0 is passing and 6.0 is an exceptional grade reserved for truly outstanding work.

Full reports are sent home at the end of each quarter, and interim reports are sent at any time for students who are experiencing difficulty. The full reports include grades and comments from each of the student's teachers. In addition, there are two formal reports (fall and spring) from the student's adviser and one from his or her class monitor.

FACULTY AND ADVISERS

For the 2008–09 academic year, Blair employs 78 faculty members and administrators, more than half of whom hold graduate degrees. The vast majority of faculty members and administrators live on campus, many as houseparents in the dormitories. More than two thirds also coach sports and serve as academic monitors.

T. Chandler Hardwick III was appointed the Academy's fifteenth Headmaster in 1989. A graduate of the University of North Carolina (B.A., 1975) and Middlebury College (M.A., 1983), Mr. Hardwick previously taught English and was Senior Dean at the Taft School, as well as the Director of the Taft Summer School.

Blair makes available to members of its faculty financial assistance for continuing study and enrichment, in particular through grants from the Lafayette Butler Fund, the E.E. Ford Foundation, and the James Howard and the Lillian and Samuel Tedlow funds.

COLLEGE ADMISSION COUNSELING

College counselors begin working with students and their families during the winter term of their junior year. Each student has at least four to six private meetings with a college counselor to map out the college search and application process. Counselors communicate regularly with parents to keep them informed and involved. Blair hosts on campus representatives from at least seventy colleges and universities each year.

Students from recent graduating classes are attending such colleges and universities as Brown, Colgate, Columbia, Cornell, Dartmouth, Davidson, Duke, Georgetown, Harvard, Lehigh, Middlebury, NYU, Princeton, Stanford, U.S. Military Academy, U.S. Naval Academy, the Universities of Pennsylvania and Virginia, Wellesley, Williams, and Yale.

STUDENT BODY AND CONDUCT

Blair attempts to maintain a geographically, ethnically, and socioeconomically diverse student body. For 2008–09, Blair welcomed students from twenty-two states and twenty countries. The composition of the 2008–09 student body is as follows: senior class and postgraduate year, 82 boys, 47 girls; junior class, 62 boys, 59 girls; sophomore class, 65 boys, 51 girls; and freshman class, 40 boys, 39 girls. Of the total enrollment of 445, there are 99 day and 346 boarding students.

School rules originate from and infractions are adjudicated by the Rules and Discipline Committee and the Academic Honor Committee, which are composed of students and faculty members, each elected by peers. A pamphlet, *Blair Academy School Rules, Academic Expectations, and Disciplinary Procedures,* is distributed before the opening of school, and all students and their parents are expected to be familiar with its contents.

ACADEMIC FACILITIES

At the center of the campus are the four major classroom buildings: Clinton Hall, Bogle Hall, Timken Library, and the Armstrong-Hipkins Center for the Arts. Bogle Hall, dedicated in 1989, provides laboratories and classrooms for the math and science departments and includes a state-of-the-art computer laboratory and a 150-seat auditorium. Armstrong-Hipkins Center for the Arts was dedicated in 1997. The renovated Timken Library, a state-of-the-art facility that includes classrooms and a computer center, opened in 1998. A girls' dormitory, Annie Hall, opened in fall 1999. Athletic fields and a roadway system were completed in 1997, the Romano Dining hall was completed in fall 2000, and renovation of Insley Hall was completed in 2001. Most recently, Locke Hall, East Hall, Davies Hall, and South Cottage have been renovated.

BOARDING AND GENERAL FACILITIES

Nine dormitories house boarding students. Generally, the housing philosophy has ninth and tenth graders grouped in underclass dorms, while eleventh and twelfth graders occupy the upperclass dorms. Each dormitory has its own dorm council with faculty and elected student members.

In addition to having a housemaster and dorm parents, each underclass dormitory unit has in residence senior prefects, and each student chooses a faculty member to be his or her adviser. Advisers are available to help students with personal and social growth.

A registered nurse is in charge of the infirmary (or on call) at all times, with a staff of RNs or LPNs on regular tours of duty. There are twenty beds, an examining room, and a dispensary. The home and office of the school physician are just 3 miles from the campus.

ATHLETICS

Because Blair believes that physical education is beneficial and important, all students must take part in a program of athletics or supervised recreational sports in order to be awarded a Blair diploma.

Blair fields twenty-eight competitive varsity teams in baseball, basketball, crew, cross-country, field hockey, football, golf, ice hockey, lacrosse, skiing, soccer, softball, squash, swimming, tennis, wrestling, and winter and spring track. Participation is the key to Blair's sports program, so second- and third-level teams are fielded in most sports. An extensive outdoor-skills program includes basic outdoor skills, canoeing, and kayaking.

Blair recently completed several additions to exterior sports facilities. It constructed a new all-weather turf field and ten new tennis courts. The school also added an improved track, stadium seating to accompany the turf field, and a tennis house. Furthermore, it will finish a new student activities and athletic center in November 2008. The building will house seven squash courts, a weight-lifting center, a fitness center, three basketball courts, a six-lane swimming pool, wrestling rooms, and ample locker space for students and coaches. The bookstore, "Canteen," and College Counseling offices will move to the activities portion of the new building. These new additions complement Blair's nine-hole golf course, existing fields, and a nearby ice-hockey rink.

EXTRACURRICULAR OPPORTUNITIES

The Nevett Bartow Series brings to the campus some twenty programs each year, which include such offerings as Rockapella, Solid Brass, Loudon Wainwright III, the David Grisman Quintet, Tom Chapin, Judy Collins, Arlo Guthrie, and visiting lecturers. Trips are arranged to the theater, concerts, the opera, and the ballet and to museums in New York City.

Among popular campus organizations are the Blair Academy Singers, the Blair Academy Players, the String Orchestra, the Wind Symphony and Jazz Ensemble, the Community Service and Environmental Clubs, and the Investment Club. The outdoor-skills group takes full advantage of Blair's proximity to the Delaware Water Gap and the Appalachian Trail, while the Ski Club utilizes the Pocono Mountains for daily skiing excursions. Students write for the school newspaper, compose the yearbook, and publish a literary magazine. They also work together through the International Awareness Club, Model UN, and Math Team. The Society of Skeptics, the longest continuously running high school lecture series in the country, brings countless speakers to Blair to address the student body. Service-oriented organizations, such as the Blue and White Key, encourage students to become engaged and active citizens within the Blair community.

Activity groups vary from year to year, depending on interests; they have included clubs devoted to photography, cycling, chess, recycling, electronics, and debating.

DAILY LIFE

Classes are 55 minutes long and meet four times during a six-day week. Four days per week, classes end at 3 p.m. Wednesday and Saturday are shortened days, with afternoons dedicated to athletics and drama. Extra help blocks are scheduled several times per week, and teachers are always available by appointment. All students participate in the weekly campus recycling program.

Afternoons are devoted to athletics practices and games, drama, recreational sports, or activities. Family-style dinner, a formal dining room meal, is held two to four days per week for boarding students. Blair reserves the hours from 8 to 10 p.m. for supervised room study or, for some students, monitored study hall.

WEEKEND LIFE

Closed weekends during examinations and the month of September require all boarding students to remain on campus. Otherwise, underclass students are allowed to take weekends away from the campus according to a scale based on their grade in school.

Blair provides a stimulating, engaging weekend activities program. Each weekend, teams made up of faculty members and students coordinate a comprehensive list of activities and events. Highlights include International Weekend, the midwinter formal, a taste-off between local pizzerias, and Peddie Week. Such standards as trips to area shopping malls and movies occur every weekend. Blair also takes advantage of its location to organize trips to New York City as well as hiking, camping, and canoeing excursions in the area countryside.

COSTS AND FINANCIAL AID

The annual charge for 2008–09 is $41,600 for boarders; this fee covers tuition, room and board, and ordinary infirmary care. For day students, the charge is $30,000, which covers tuition, study rooms, and meals. Additional deposits or fees are charged for the use of certain equipment, private music lessons, and extra medical services.

Financial aid is awarded on the basis of demonstrated financial need and proven personal and academic merit in accordance with procedures established by the School and Student Service for Financial Aid.

ADMISSIONS INFORMATION

Blair is interested in students who want to be a part of an independent school community and who are committed to improving their academic background.

Blair enrolls students in grades 9–11 each year and also admits a limited number of high school graduates who wish to pursue a postgraduate year of study.

In addition to a personal interview, several written components complete the formal application. To complement the school transcript and teachers' recommendations, Blair requests results from a standardized test: the SSAT for grades 9–11 and the SAT or ACT for postgraduates. Application forms must be accompanied by a nonrefundable fee of $50 ($100 for international applicants). The application deadline is February 1.

APPLICATION TIMETABLE

The initial inquiry is welcome at any time. The Admissions Office is open for interviews and tours by appointment on weekdays and some Saturdays. Applicants who complete the admissions process prior to February 1 are notified of the decision on March 10.

ADMISSIONS CORRESPONDENCE

Ryan M. Pagotto, Dean of Admissions
Blair Academy
P.O. Box 600
Blairstown, New Jersey 07825-0600
Phone: 908-362-2024
800-462-5247 (toll-free)
Fax: 908-362-7975
E-mail: admissions@blair.edu
Web site: http://www.blair.edu

BLUE RIDGE SCHOOL

St. George, Virginia

Type: Boys' boarding college-preparatory school
Grades: 9–12
Enrollment: 195
Head of School: David A. Bouton, Ph.D., Headmaster

THE SCHOOL

Blue Ridge is the right school for capable college-bound students of good character and integrity who possess tremendous, if yet untapped, potential and a positive attitude; who thrive in a small setting with a structured routine; who may benefit from learning to manage their time better and from developing more productive study habits; who are eager to be part of a supportive community that encourages them to take risks and to try new things; and who not only plan to go to college, but also want to be prepared to succeed in every aspect of their lives.

Located 18 miles northwest of Charlottesville and the University of Virginia, the School is 1½ hours from Richmond and 2 hours from Washington, D.C., allowing for frequent and easy access to the tremendous cultural resources of these historic cities. The School's scenic campus, featuring lakes, ponds, streams, and a system of trails, is situated on 800 acres on the eastern face of the Blue Ridge Mountains. Its location, 5 miles from the Appalachian Trail and Shenandoah National Park, offers a wealth of opportunities for outdoor activities both on and off campus.

Blue Ridge School was founded in 1909 as an Episcopal mission school. In 1962, the School reorganized as an independent boarding school and adopted its present mission. Although the required chapel program remains at the center of the spiritual life of the School, students of all religious backgrounds are welcomed. A nonprofit institution, Blue Ridge is governed by a national self-perpetuating Board of Trustees. The School's recorded endowment is $12 million, and strong annual giving provides funds for $1.2 million in financial aid and for support of the operating budget.

Blue Ridge School is accredited by the Southern Association of Colleges and Schools and by the Virginia Association of Independent Schools. It holds memberships in the National Association of Independent Schools, the Association of Boarding Schools, the Small Boarding School Association, the Secondary School Admission Test Board, the Council for the Advancement and Support of Education, the National Association for College Admission Counseling, the National Association of Episcopal Schools, and the National Honor Society.

ACADEMIC PROGRAMS

Blue Ridge School is college preparatory. Students are not treated as though they are in college, nor are they expected to arrive at Blue Ridge with the skills and habits of college students. When Blue Ridge students graduate, however, they are fully prepared to go on to college, as they are armed with the skills, habits, and confidence necessary to succeed.

Blue Ridge School offers a college-preparatory curriculum that is designed for young men who learn best in small classes with a supportive faculty. The academic program challenges students while also recognizing that study skills, support, and a solid academic routine are essential for success.

To graduate from Blue Ridge School, students must complete a minimum of 4 units of English; 3 units of mathematics, including 2 of algebra and 1 of geometry; 3 units of history, including 2 of U.S. history and 1 of non-U.S. history; 3 units of laboratory science, including 1 of biology and 1 of chemistry; 3 units of the same foreign language; 2 units of physical education; 1 unit of life skills; and 2 electives. Students typically take six subjects each year.

The average class size at Blue Ridge is 9 students, the maximum is 13 students, and the student-teacher ratio is 5:1. The School calendar is based on trimesters. Classroom teachers prepare written academic comments to be mailed to parents at the middle and end of each trimester. Report cards are sent home at the end of each trimester.

Classes meet Monday through Friday, with each class meeting four times per week. All students participate in evening study hall Sunday through Thursday from 8 to 10 p.m. When it comes to the students' academic success at the School, evening study hall may be considered the most important 2 hours of the day. Students study in the setting that is most suitable for them: their room, the library or computer lab, a supervised study hall, or in the Learning Center. All freshmen and new sophomores start out in a traditional, supervised study hall setting. Students who have not completed all of their homework are assigned to Homework Lab after dinner to complete the missing work.

The Fishburne Learning Center works with faculty and students to ensure that every student is provided the appropriate level of support necessary to realize his academic potential. The Director of Studies determines eligibility for such services, generally as part of the admission process, and space is limited.

FACULTY AND ADVISERS

Each student has a faculty adviser who serves as that student's surrogate parent and advocate. Because the adviser/advisee relationship is the cornerstone of both academic and residential life at the School, the adviser role is the single most important role that a faculty member has in the School community. Students meet with their adviser during a daily advisee period and sit with them at chapel and assemblies. Families communicate with the School through their son's adviser.

The professional staff consists of 35 men and 10 women. Four hold doctoral degrees and 19 have master's degrees. Faculty members are selected not only for their competencies in their academic and nonacademic fields, but also for their strong commitment to the Blue Ridge mission and to its students. Nearly all have had previous boarding school teaching experience, and their continued professional development is generously supported by the School.

David A. Bouton, a graduate of the University of Notre Dame (B.B.A., M.A.) and Virginia Commonwealth University (Ph.D.), was appointed Headmaster in 2000. From 1993 to 1999, Dr. Bouton headed Benedictine High School in Richmond, Virginia. From 1990 to 1993, he was Academic Dean at the U.S. Military War College in Carlisle, Pennsylvania, where he had served in a number of positions since 1986. Dr. Bouton's career working with young men in the U.S. Army spanned more than thirty years. He and his wife, Sheila, are the parents of 6 grown children (5 sons and 1 daughter).

COLLEGE ADMISSION COUNSELING

College counseling is an important and integral part of the School's program. Typically, 100 percent of the School's graduates go on to attend four-year colleges or universities. Blue Ridge School graduates attend a wide variety of schools. The goal of the College Counseling Office is to help students identify and gain admission to colleges and universities that offer a good fit: a place where they will be successful and fulfilled and will continue to grow. To aid in that process, the School employs a full-time college counselor. Representatives from numerous and varied colleges and universities visit Blue Ridge School to meet with students.

Members of the class of 2008 are currently attending Assumption (Thailand), Averett, Blinn, Boston College, Brevard, Catholic University, Clarkson, Davis & Elkins, Eckerd, Emory, Emory & Henry, Flagler, Hampden-Sydney, James Madison, Johnson & Wales, Longwood, Loyola Maryland, Lynn, Newcastle (UK), Pfeiffer, Randolph-Macon, Rhodes, SUNY at Albany, Syracuse, Texas Tech, Virginia Wesleyan, Wagner, Wheaton (Illinois), York, and the Universities of Illinois, Massachusetts, Mississippi, Nevada–Las Vegas, North Carolina, Notre Dame, Richmond, South Carolina, Virginia, and Wisconsin.

STUDENT BODY AND CONDUCT

All students and nearly all faculty members and administrators live on the campus, making Blue Ridge a true residential community. In 2008–09, Blue Ridge students came from twenty states, the District of Columbia, and fifteen countries. Twenty-five percent are international students, and another twenty-seven percent are students of color.

Life at Blue Ridge is guided by the Code of Conduct, which comprises the core values of the School community: being honorable and accountable, being willing to invest oneself and to try new things, persevering and maintaining a positive attitude, displaying mutual respect and tolerance, being a good citizen, and developing habits of mind, body, and spirit. Senior prefects act as the oldest brother on each of the residence halls, and as a group they serve as leaders and role models in all areas of school life. Cases involving possible honor or disciplinary infractions are heard by the Honor Council and Student-Faculty Disciplinary Committee, respectively. These boards, made up of seniors and faculty members, make recommendations to the Headmaster concerning what action should be taken. Blue Ridge maintains a traditional dress code of coat and tie attire for class.

ACADEMIC FACILITIES

A central feature of the Blue Ridge campus is the proximity of all of the buildings to one another. All classes are held in a renovated, state-of-the-art facility, including a science wing, the Fishburne Learning Center, and a technology center. The 230-seat Mayo Auditorium, the dining hall, and administrative offices are located in Loving Hall, attached to the Academic Building. Music classes, lessons and rehearsals are held in the Music Barn, and spacious art studios are located in the New York Auxiliary Student Center.

Built in 1993, the Hatcher C. Williams Library contains some 11,000 volumes. Students also have online access to the collections at the University of Virginia libraries and other regional libraries and to numerous research databases.

BOARDING AND GENERAL FACILITIES

All students live in one of two newly renovated dormitories; each hall in the dormitories is home to members of all four classes. All rooms are designed as doubles except for those occupied by prefects, and students typically have a roommate from the same class. Each hall functions as a family, and faculty members and their families who reside on each hall serve as hall parents. All halls operate under a similar set of guidelines, but, as with all families, each hall family develops its own unique personality. Among the values shared by every hall family is the importance of creating a happy, warm, and safe living environment founded on mutual respect and tolerance. Students are also expected to take care of their homes and to keep their rooms clean and organized. Students have phone and Internet connections in their rooms.

The New York Auxiliary Student Center is home to the Center Court Snack Bar, the Game Room, the Tuck Shop, and the post office. The Game Room features a large, wide-screen home-theater system; several pool, Ping Pong, and foosball tables; an air hockey table; and video games. The Tuck Shop is the School store, where students may purchase textbooks, school supplies, Blue Ridge sportswear, personal items, and other necessities. Chapel services are held in Gibson Memorial Chapel, a state and national landmark.

A ten-bed infirmary is staffed 24 hours a day by 2 nurses. The School doctor is affiliated with Martha Jefferson Hospital in Charlottesville.

ATHLETICS

All students are required to participate in the athletics program throughout the year, including at least two team sports. Teams are available at all levels so that no student is excluded, and the program emphasizes a tradition of good sportsmanship. Cross-country, football, golf, soccer, and volleyball are offered in the fall season; basketball, indoor soccer, and wrestling in the winter; and baseball, golf, lacrosse, tennis, and track and field in the spring. The Outdoor Program is offered as a team sport in each of the three seasons and competitive mountain biking is offered in the fall and spring. As alternatives to team sports, students may also participate in intramurals, drama, art, strength and conditioning, or community improvement and recycling during one of the three seasons.

The Outdoor Program is designed to give students opportunities to take full advantage of the School's unique mountain setting and location. All students, whether they are novices or accomplished outdoorsmen, are encouraged to participate. On campus, students have access to a 40-foot climbing tower; a ropes course; a zip line; an indoor bouldering room; a lake for fishing, canoeing, and kayaking; and a system of mountain trails for hiking and mountain biking. Through the Outdoor Program, students enjoy off-campus trips to go overnight camping, white-water rafting, mountain biking, skiing and snowboarding, rock climbing, and caving.

A modern athletics complex includes a gymnasium, team meeting rooms, and a laundry facility. The newly renovated field house contains four indoor tennis courts, three basketball courts, a large wrestling room, a fully equipped weight room, dressing rooms, and a training room. In addition, there are two practice fields; three game fields for football, soccer, and lacrosse; a 400-meter track; a baseball diamond with dugouts; four all-weather tennis courts; a golf driving range; and a 25-meter outdoor swimming pool. Students play golf on two local eighteen-hole courses. The School's certified athletic trainer is part of the doctoral program at the University of Virginia.

EXTRACURRICULAR OPPORTUNITIES

Blue Ridge students participate in a variety of clubs and organizations, including the Choir, the Multicultural Club, the Chess Club, the yearbook, the literary magazine, the Library Committee, the Food Committee, the Social Activities Committee, and the Boy Scouts of America Explorer Post.

Because of Blue Ridge's history as a mission school, community service has always played an important role at the School. Students have many opportunities to participate in a variety of community service projects. Students put on a musical theater production each winter as well as a major art show in the spring.

DAILY LIFE

Classes are held five days a week. Tuesdays and Fridays are half days to allow for interscholastic sports events in the afternoons. The academic day begins at 8 a.m. with assembly or chapel and ends at 3:10 p.m. All six class periods meet on Monday, Wednesday, and Thursday and last for 50 minutes. On Tuesday and Friday, only three class periods meet, lasting 75 minutes. Each day, students meet with their advisers and have the opportunity to meet with their teachers for extra help during conference period. Sports and extracurricular activities begin at 4 p.m. Dinner is served at 6 and is followed by a study hall from 8 to10 p.m. Students must be in their rooms by 10:45 p.m. and have their lights out by 11.

WEEKEND LIFE

Because Blue Ridge is a seven-day all-boarding community, weekend activities play an important role in the life of the School. Weekends generally begin after lunch on Saturday and end with study hall on Sunday evening. Saturday mornings are devoted to the Saturday Program, which has four components: residential curriculum (life skills), fine arts, community service, and outdoor programs. All students are required to participate in the Saturday Program.

The Social Activities Director, along with the students on the Social Activities Committee, develops a diverse slate of offerings, both on and off campus, every weekend. The Outdoor Program sponsors several adventurous activities each weekend. There are occasional trips to Wizards, Capitals, and Nationals games as well as to UVA soccer and lacrosse games. Every weekend, students can attend a social event at one of the BSSAC schools, a group of girls' and boys' boarding schools located throughout Virginia, Maryland, and the D.C. area. There are also weekly excursions into nearby Charlottesville for shopping, dinner, movies, paintball, ice skating, and more.

COSTS AND FINANCIAL AID

For 2008–09, tuition is $33,800. Families should also budget about $2000 a year for the student account, which covers books, school supplies, allowance, activities, and other miscellaneous expenses incurred during the year. An enrollment deposit, which is credited toward tuition, is due with the return of the Enrollment Agreement. The balance of the tuition may be paid in full by the opening of school or in two installments, in August and in December. The second option requires participation in the Tuition Refund Plan.

The School awards need-based financial aid. In 2007–08, the School awarded $1.2 million to 72 students. The School also participates in various monthly payment and loan programs.

ADMISSIONS INFORMATION

The admissions process at Blue Ridge is one of matchmaking. Blue Ridge seeks to enroll students who will be successful at the School. While the Admissions Committee considers past performance in making admissions decisions, they are primarily concerned with the candidate's potential and the likelihood that the School's program will enable the candidate to realize that potential.

Blue Ridge admits young men of good character who are committed to living according to the Blue Ridge School Code of Conduct and who, by investing themselves in the School's program and in the overall life of the School, will thrive in the Blue Ridge program. As the greatest benefit can be gained by attending Blue Ridge for at least three years, most students enter in the ninth and tenth grades. Some spaces are generally available in the eleventh grade, but it is rare for the School to admit students to the twelfth grade.

APPLICATION TIMETABLE

Initial inquiries are welcomed at any time. The most important piece of the application process is the campus visit and personal interview. Arrangements for these visits should be made early in the year prior to the desired year of entry. Visits can be scheduled on weekdays while the School is in session.

A formal application with a $50 fee ($100 for international students) should be submitted by February 15. Families are requested to reply to an acceptance by April 10. Candidates completing applications after February 15 are reviewed on a rolling admission basis.

ADMISSIONS CORRESPONDENCE

William A. Darrin III
Assistant Headmaster for Enrollment and Marketing
Blue Ridge School
St. George, Virginia 22935

Phone: 434-985-2811
Fax: 434-992-0536
E-mail: admissions@blueridgeschool.com
Web site: http://www.blueridgeschool.com

THE BOLLES SCHOOL

Jacksonville, Florida

Type: Coeducational boarding (7–12) and day (PK–12) college-preparatory school
Grades: PK–12: Lower Schools, PK–5; Middle School, 6–8; Upper School, 9–12
Enrollment: School total: 1,732; Lower Schools, 519; Middle School, 421; Upper School, 792
Head of School: John E. Trainer Jr., President and Head of School

THE SCHOOL

Bolles offers a comprehensive college-preparatory program. Bolles prepares students for the future by providing them with challenges that promote growth and development in academics, the arts, activities, and athletics. Moral development is encouraged by an emphasis on respect for self and others, volunteerism, and personal responsibility.

Bolles has served as the educational inspiration for three generations, with a strong and unshakable commitment to providing the finest preparatory education possible for each student. Located in Jacksonville, Florida, Bolles was founded in 1933 as an all-boys military school on the San Jose Campus. In 1962, the School dropped its military status; in 1971, it began admitting girls.

In 1981, the Lower School Whitehurst Campus for grades K–5 was begun. A separate campus for middle schoolers in grades 6–8 was achieved in 1991 with the acquisition of Bartram School, an independent girls' school operating since 1934 and now known as the Bolles Middle School Bartram Campus. In 1998, the Bolles Lower School Ponte Vedra Beach Campus opened its doors to serve students in pre-kindergarten through grade 5.

Today, with more than 1,700 students at four locations, Bolles is recognized as one of the finest college-preparatory institutions in the nation. All of its students are college-bound. Bolles students consistently place in the top 10 percent of Advanced Placement scores from throughout the country. The School prepares students for the future by providing them with a variety of activities and a myriad of challenges that promote growth and development in four primary areas: academics, arts, activities, and athletics. Students learn to make decisions and budget time by balancing homework, sports, extracurricular, family, and community service responsibilities.

Students from all walks of life, cultures, religions, and races learn together at Bolles, a microcosm of the world that they will inherit. The School's excellent academic and athletic offerings attracted students from sixteen countries and eight states to participate in the resident program for the 2008–09 school year. This blend of cultures and interests sets Bolles apart from other independent college-preparatory institutions in the Southeast and fosters a level of mutual respect that is crucial in learning how to meet global challenges.

The School's locations are in suburban neighborhoods. The Upper School San Jose Campus and the Lower School Whitehurst Campus occupy 52 acres on the St. Johns River. Five miles to the northeast, the Middle School Bartram Campus is set on 23 acres. The Bolles Lower School Ponte Vedra Beach Campus is located on 12 acres in Ponte Vedra Beach, east of Jacksonville.

Jacksonville, a major metropolitan area in northeast Florida, is home to the Jaguars National Football League team and many cultural associations, such as the Jacksonville Symphony, the Florida Ballet, several professional theater companies, three major museums, the Jacksonville Zoo, and several professional sports teams. Downtown Jacksonville is located approximately 35 minutes from the Jacksonville Beach area, which includes Ponte Vedra Beach, and about an hour from St. Augustine, the oldest city in the United States.

A not-for-profit institution, Bolles is governed by a self-perpetuating board of 30 trustees. The School also works with a 24-member Board of Visitors and an Alumni Board that represents more than 7,900 living graduates.

The School's operating budget is more than $30 million. The annual giving goal for 2008–09 is $1.775 million, which includes more than $1.6 million in unrestricted dollars. The School's endowment is more than $11.3 million.

The School is accredited by the Southern Association of Colleges and Schools and the Florida Council of Independent Schools and holds membership in the National Association of Independent Schools, the Council for Spiritual and Ethical Education, the Secondary School Admission Test Board, and the Southeastern Association of Boarding Schools.

ACADEMIC PROGRAMS

The Middle School curriculum includes English, government, world cultures, world geography, U.S. history, mathematics through algebra, and science. Students may select from a varied fine and performing arts program and may choose among band, chorus, drama, dance, graphics, drawing and painting, ceramics and sculpture, computers, foreign language, and language arts on a rotating basis throughout the year. Each student has an adviser, and a full-time, on-campus guidance counselor assists with decision-making skills, peer relations, and alcohol- and drug-abuse awareness.

Upper School students must earn 22 credits for graduation, with a college-certifying grade of at least C-. Specific requirements are 4 years of English; 2 of a single foreign language; 3 of social studies, including U.S. and world history; 3 of mathematics through algebra II; 3 of science, including biology and chemistry; 2 of physical education; 1 of fine arts; ½ year of life management skills; and 3½ years of additional electives. The average class size is 15 students.

Among the full-year courses are English, French, Latin, Spanish, German, Japanese, Chinese, world and U.S. history, algebra, geometry, precalculus, physical science, biology, chemistry, marine science, environmental science, band, introduction to dance, intermediate dance, upper-level dance, AP drawing, AP portfolio 2-D, AP portfolio 3-D, advanced acting, portfolio development honors, men's chorus, women's chorus, concert choir, and symphonic band. There are honors sections in English, geometry, algebra, biology, chemistry, physics, neurobiology, languages, and social studies. Courses designed to prepare students for Advanced Placement examinations are available in English, U.S. and European history, American and comparative government, languages, calculus, biology, chemistry, physics, computer science, statistics, portfolio art, and art history. A postgraduate program is available to students seeking an additional year of academics prior to entering college.

Students choose from such semester electives as foundations of studio art, drawing and painting, ceramics and sculpture, creative writing, acting, directing, production, public speaking, computer applications, AP statistics, algebra III, introduction to programming, Web site development, American government and politics, economics, human anatomy, marine science, and driver education.

Opportunities for off-campus projects sponsored directly by the School include the Outdoor Academy and the French, Spanish, and Japanese Exchange Programs.

Grades, with narrative reports from faculty advisers, are sent to parents twice each quarter.

FACULTY AND ADVISERS

Dr. John E. Trainer Jr. was appointed President and Head of School in 2001. He holds a Bachelor of Science degree in biology from Muhlenberg College in Allentown, Pennsylvania; a master's in biology from Wake Forest University in Winston-Salem, North Carolina; and a doctorate in zoology from the University of Oklahoma in Norman, Oklahoma. Dr. Trainer was selected for this position because of his strong people skills and innovative thinking and his extensive experience in working effectively with academic professionals, community leaders, executives, and legislators.

Bolles has 163 full-time faculty members and 12 part-time faculty members; there are 99 professional staff members who hold master's degrees and 11 who hold doctorates.

Each student in the Middle and Upper Schools is assigned to a faculty member, whose primary responsibility is to serve as an adviser. A minimal class load makes the adviser readily accessible to both students and parents. The School maintains an Office of Student Counseling to assist students in addressing issues that fall outside the traditional categories of academic advising.

COLLEGE ADMISSION COUNSELING

The aim of the college counseling program is to help students and their families to find college options and ultimately to find the most appropriate college choice. At the start of the second semester of the junior year, a daylong meeting is held to begin the more structured aspect of the process, and each student is assigned a college-placement adviser. An evening parent meeting provides additional information. The Williams Guidance Center offers a full range of up-to-date college reference materials, which include catalogs, videotapes, and computer search programs. In addition, approximately 100 college representatives visit the campus each year to meet with students, counselors, and parents.

In each of the past five years, 98 percent of graduates have attended four-year colleges and universities. A small number of students defer admission, and a small percentage attends two-year schools.

The middle 50 percent of scores for the last three graduating classes on the SAT Reasoning Test are 1070–1310 on a 1600 scale. The middle 50 percent of ACT scores are 22–28. Teachers in English and mathematics classes work with students in preparation for college admission testing.

STUDENT BODY AND CONDUCT

The Upper School numbers 792 students, with between 185 and 200 students in each grade. There are 85 boarding students.

There are an Honor Code and a Values Statement, and the Honor Council of Upper School students administers the Code and serves as the judiciary court for infractions against the Code. The Student Council is very active and serves as a proactive body for legislation of student privileges, organizes activities, and offers advice to the Upper School administration.

ACADEMIC FACILITIES

On the Upper School San Jose Campus, Bolles Hall houses classrooms, boys' dormitory rooms, a dining room and kitchen, offices, and three meeting rooms. Other academic buildings are Clifford G. Schultz Hall, with seventeen classrooms; the Michael Marco Science Center, which houses three science labs; the Joan W. and Martin E. Stein Computer Laboratory; the Hirsig Life Science Center; Ulmer Hall, which includes fifteen classrooms, a language lab, and two science labs; and a marine science classroom along the St. Johns River.

The Swisher Library houses the Meadow Multimedia Center, with a large-screen television, two satellite dishes, and computer labs. Other facilities include the McGehee Auditorium, which seats more than 600, and the Cindy and Jay Stein Fine Arts Center, which contains the Independent Life Music Building, the Lucy B. Gooding Art Gallery, and the Lynch Theater.

Middle School academic facilities include Murchison-Lane Hall for classrooms and administrative offices, the Art Barn, a marine science classroom along Pottsburg Creek, girls' dormitory rooms, the Pratt Library, and the Betsy Lovett Arts Center, which opened in 2007.

The Lower School Whitehurst Campus houses each grade separately in homelike classrooms set around a natural playground. The Lower School Ponte Vedra Beach Campus is a modern campus that includes an administration/classroom facility as well as the McLauchlan-Evans Building, housing classrooms, and the River Branch Building, which is the location of both the Ullmann Family Art Room and the Loeb-Lovett Family Music Room.

BOARDING AND GENERAL FACILITIES

All boarding students are housed in rooms that accommodate 2 students. Boys and girls reside on separate campuses. Students are assigned roommates based upon age and interests.

Upper School athletic facilities include Collins Stadium at the Donovan Baseball Field, Hodges Field, the Bent Tennis Complex, the Baker-Gate Petroleum Company Track Facility, and Skinner-Barco Stadium. The Davis Sports Complex includes the Huston Student Center, basketball and volleyball courts, the 25-yard Lobrano and 50-meter Uible swimming pools, the Cassidy Aquatic Fitness Center, and the Garces Diving Facility. The Agnes Cain Gymnasium features a wrestling room and athletic offices. Construction is currently underway on the Peyton Boathouse and Rice Family Crew Complex, with the Bent Student Center groundbreaking set to occur in the winter of 2009.

Among the Middle School athletic facilities are a football and soccer field, the Conroy Athletic Center, and Meninak Field, which includes Collins Baseball Stadium.

ATHLETICS

Bolles is a member of the Florida High School Athletic Association. Boys' teams compete in baseball, basketball, crew, cross-country, football, golf, lacrosse, soccer, swimming, tennis, track, volleyball, and wrestling. Girls' teams compete in basketball, cheerleading, crew, cross-country, golf, soccer, softball, swimming, tennis, track, and volleyball. Middle School boys' teams compete in baseball, basketball, crew, football, lacrosse, soccer, swimming, track, and wrestling. Middle School girls' teams compete in basketball, cheerleading, crew, soccer, softball, swimming, track, and volleyball.

EXTRACURRICULAR OPPORTUNITIES

Extracurricular activities offered include Student Government; National Honor Society; language honor societies; Amnesty International; Interact, a service club; a mentor program; three student afterschool tutoring programs; Student Advocate Council, which promotes community spirit among the students; an array of other community service opportunities; language clubs; special interest clubs; Community Service Leadership Council; Sophomore Leadership Council; class-sponsored activities; *Turris* (yearbook); *The Bugle* (newspaper); and *Perspective* (literary magazine).

DAILY LIFE

The daily schedule for the Upper School, which lasts from 8 a.m. until 3:45 p.m., includes seven 45-minute periods and "Zero Hour," a 30-minute period reserved for individual conferences and extra help. Boarders have evening study in their rooms, with faculty members available for extra help, and supervised study halls are provided for students needing more structured assistance.

WEEKEND LIFE

Resident students are strongly encouraged to take advantage of the excellent recreational facilities at Bolles. On weekends, the waterfront is open for resident students, weather permitting. In addition, regular off-campus trips are organized, as are, from time to time, special trips.

COSTS AND FINANCIAL AID

Upper School tuition costs for the 2008–09 school year were as follows: tuition, room, and meals for boarding students (grades 7–12) totaled $36,000, and tuition for day students (grades 9–12) totaled $17,350. Additional fees include $500–$750 for books, $30–$35 per gym uniform set, $375 for driver education, a one-time $500 facilities fee, and $45–$65 for the yearbook. Essential services fees for boarding students include $250 for the School clinic, $100 for emergency escrow, and an allowance of $40 per week ($1440 per school year) for students in grades 7–8, $45 per week ($1620 per school year) for students in grades 9–11, and $50 per week ($1800 per school year) for students in grade 12. Lunches and snacks are available for purchase by day students.

The School awarded over $2.9 million in financial aid for the 2008–09 academic year.

ADMISSIONS INFORMATION

The School seeks students who demonstrate the ability to meet the requirements of the college-preparatory curriculum. In addition, special talents and strengths that allow the applicant to achieve distinction within the applicant pool are desired. The ISEE or its equivalent is required of all applicants, as are a personal interview, teacher recommendations, and transcripts. There is a $45 application fee for day students and a $75 application fee for international students.

APPLICATION TIMETABLE

The Admission Office accepts applications beginning in the fall, with a rolling admission policy. Upon acceptance, the applicant must respond with a deposit of 10 percent of the total tuition and pay the facilities fee within two weeks.

ADMISSIONS CORRESPONDENCE

The Bolles School
7400 San Jose Boulevard
Jacksonville, Florida 32217
Phone: 904-256-5032
Fax: 904-739-9929
Web site: http://www.bolles.org

BRENAU ACADEMY

Gainesville, Georgia

Type: Girls' boarding and day college-preparatory school
Grades: 9–PG
Enrollment: 80
Head of School: Timothy A. Daniel

THE SCHOOL

From the day Brenau Academy opened its doors in 1928, it has been a high school committed to preparing talented young women for college educations, successful futures, and fulfilling community involvement. Brenau offers small classes, a college-preparatory curriculum, and invested teachers whose priority is to see each young woman do her best. Brenau staff members, teachers, and house directors embrace a combination of support, structure and freedom, allowing students opportunities for fun and individual growth.

The Academy's unique affiliation with Brenau University, a historic women's college with whom it shares a campus, allows students to make a confident transition into a college atmosphere. Academy students enjoy use of the university's library, athletic facility, cafeteria, and auditorium. Advanced students have the opportunity to get a head start on college by taking college courses at Brenau University, earning credits toward their college education. Brenau Academy graduates attend colleges and universities, large and small, across the nation and worldwide.

The value of a Brenau education is immeasurable. Academy graduates enter their college years with outstanding academic preparation, leadership skills, and confidence in their ability to succeed. For boarding students and day students alike, Brenau Academy opens the doors to countless exciting opportunities.

The Academy is accredited by the Southern Association of Colleges and Schools and approved by the Georgia Department of Education. It is a member of the Georgia Independent School Association, the National Association of Independent Schools, and the National Association of Boarding Schools.

ACADEMIC PROGRAMS

The Brenau Academy curriculum is designed to prepare students for college success. Brenau offers an exceptional college-preparatory program taught by a qualified and dedicated faculty. The following courses are generally pursued for graduation: English, 4 years; mathematics, 4 years; history, 3 years; science, 3 years; foreign language, 2 years; physical education, 2 years; fine arts, 1 year; and electives, 3 units. Electives available include art, drama, dance, and student publications. All students are expected to take at least five courses each term. In addition, courses are offered to advanced students, at no extra expense, in all departments of Brenau Women's College; students can earn dual credit for these courses.

Numerical grades are used at the Academy, and grades below 70 are considered failing. Progress reports are sent to parents and students every six weeks. The student's absences and teachers' comments are recorded on the report.

Classes are grouped according to course selection only. The average class has approximately 12 students, and there is an overall student-teacher ratio of 8:1. Study time is designed to assist students in developing sound study habits. Instructors are available throughout the day for individual assistance. Evening study time, monitored by residential directors, takes place in the dorm rooms, Monday through Thursday from 7:45 to 9:30, and on Sundays from 8:30 to 9:30.

Students who need extra academic help may visit with the teacher during a tutorial period built into the school day. For advanced students who need the extra challenge, the tutorial period is also of service. Teachers may require students in academic difficulty to attend help sessions during this period. Tutoring beyond what is offered at the Academy is available through the Brenau Learning Center Program.

The Brenau Academy Learning Center is designed for the college-preparatory student with a diagnosed learning difference. The student learns how to compensate for her learning differences in a highly supportive environment, including one-on-one tutoring by trained professionals in the field. Early application is recommended.

FACULTY AND ADVISERS

Timothy A. Daniel is Headmaster of the Academy, having previously served as a teacher and administrator at a number of other independent boarding and day schools, including the Grand River Academy in Ohio, Memphis University School in Tennessee, Portsmouth Abbey School in Rhode Island, University Liggett School in Michigan, Shattuck–St. Mary's School in Minnesota, and as Headmaster at the Leelanau School in Michigan. A native of Ohio, Mr. Daniel is a graduate of Deerfield Academy in Massachusetts and Northwestern University in Illinois, as well as the University of Tulsa in Oklahoma.

There are 12 teachers, 4 house directors, and 6 administrators. Most full-time instructors hold advanced degrees.

Criteria for the selection of new faculty members include strong character, sound academic preparation, demonstration of subject knowledge, teaching ability, maturity, professionalism, and, above all, a desire to teach and guide young women in high school. Faculty members serve as advisers to various student groups and as chaperones and participate in intramurals and other campus activities. Personal advising is handled primarily through the counselor, but any faculty or staff member may be sought out by a student for guidance and support.

COLLEGE ADMISSION COUNSELING

One hundred percent of Brenau Academy graduates are accepted to college each year. A guidance counselor provides assistance to all juniors and seniors as they move throughout the college selection and application process. Current information is cataloged on colleges and universities, SAT and ACT procedures, and financial aid. Recent graduates elected to attend institutions such as Boston University; Clemson; College of Charleston; Eckerd; Emory; Florida State; Furman; George Washington; Georgia Institute of Technology; Georgia State University; Indiana University; Purdue; Savannah College of Art and Design; Tulane; the University of Alabama; University of California, Berkeley; and Vanderbilt.

STUDENT BODY AND CONDUCT

Brenau Academy enrolls 80 students; 85 percent residential and 15 percent day. The 2007 student body consisted of students from ten countries and twelve states.

The Academy strives to limit enrollment to students who are mature and responsible. The Student Government Association plays an integral part in directing student life and provides leadership opportunities through the Student Council and Student Judiciary Board. The Academy provides structure and positive values for student life without excessive restriction. Brenau is not designed to serve students who have major disciplinary problems, significant learning differences, or substance dependencies. Students who enter Brenau recognize rules and regulations as necessary factors in cooperative living and welcome opportunities for mature, independent growth.

ACADEMIC FACILITIES

The two student dormitories are connected to classrooms, recreation rooms, and administrative offices. The dining hall, Victorian performing arts theater, auditorium, gymnasium, bookstore, and pool are separate facilities shared with the college. Academic facilities include spacious classrooms, a student publications office, dance studios, a $3-million library, and computer laboratories.

BOARDING AND GENERAL FACILITIES

The Academy has two major dormitories. Girls room with other students of a similar grade level. Adult female house directors reside in each dormitory; the ratio of students to house directors is 15:1. Students are assigned to rooms by the administration, but requests with regard to rooms and roommates may be submitted for consideration.

ATHLETICS

The Academy fields competitive teams in basketball, cross-country, golf, tennis, and volleyball, which compete within the Atlanta Athletic Conference. Other extra-curricular athletic activities include hiking, jogging, rafting, skiing, billiards, and swimming. Modern physical education facilities include a gymnasium, steam and sauna rooms, an exercise and weight room, an AAU-size indoor swimming pool, and a modern tennis complex.

EXTRACURRICULAR OPPORTUNITIES

In an effort to achieve its goal of providing leadership experiences and an enriching social environment, the Academy makes many extracurricular opportunities available, particularly in the fine arts. The Atlanta Symphony and the Atlanta Ballet make regular appearances at Brenau, as well as numerous local and international performing arts groups. Convocations, both formal and informal, are also regularly scheduled on campus. Community groups in drama, art, dance, and music often include Academy students. Students participate in a variety of clubs and student interest groups, including Key Club, SEA Club, Book Club, Brenau Ambassadors, and Student Government. Student journalism groups publish a yearbook, a student newspaper, and a literary magazine.

Traditional activities include a Halloween party, Christmas traditions, closed weekends, Senior Baccalaureate, and dances and activities with a local boys' academy.

Many students belong to community service and campus leadership organizations. The Key Club sponsors a Halloween party for underprivileged young girls in the community, a food drive before Thanksgiving, and a winter clothing drive. In addition, the Key Club also takes shifts ringing the Salvation Army bell during the holidays and collects for the Heart Fund. The Student Environmental Association (SEA) Club volunteers with the local Humane Society and sponsors school clean-up projects and a recycling program. An integral part in directing student life is the Student Government Association, made up of two components: the Student Council and the Judiciary Board.

Graduating seniors are honored with a year-end banquet. An Awards Night and Fine Arts Performance precedes Graduation. Seniors wear white dresses and carry red roses at Graduation—a tradition as old as the school.

DAILY LIFE

A typical day for the Brenau student begins with a 10-minute morning assembly at 7:50, followed by the first class at 8. Generally, each class lasts 50 minutes. Classroom learning experiences may extend from 8 a.m. to 7:30 p.m., depending upon a student's schedule. Lunch is in the dining room, where students may enjoy selections from a hot food line in addition to salad, soup, baked potato, and sandwich bars.

Athletic team practices and club meetings take place in the afternoon. Plenty of time is allowed for lunch and dinner, and a brief free period after dinner is followed by a 2-hour room study session. More free time is provided in the dorms before lights-out.

WEEKEND LIFE

The Academy arranges planned, supervised activities on many weekends. This activity may range from a trip to the movies and a restaurant to snow-skiing trips, trips to amusement parks in Atlanta, visits to Lake Lanier Islands, or fall hikes in the north Georgia mountains. Many of these activities are offered at no cost to students. Most weekend activities are optional to the student.

All students are required to sign in and out whenever leaving the Academy. This activity is closely monitored by the house directors.

COSTS AND FINANCIAL AID

The Brenau fee for 2008–09 is $25,400 for boarding students and $11,500 for day students. All meals are provided for boarders. Other expenses include books and supplies (approximately $500 per year), a campus technology fee ($250), and activity fees for optional weekend functions. All students pay a $2000 confirmation deposit (deducted from tuition) to secure their enrollment for the upcoming school year. Multiple payment schedules are available for the remaining balance.

Financial aid is awarded on the basis of need, as determined by the guidelines of the School and Student Service for Financial Aid.

ADMISSIONS INFORMATION

The selection of new students at Brenau is based on a comprehensive review of the previous school's transcript of grades, three letters of recommendation, and an interview with the Director of Admissions. Admission decisions are based upon a student's previous academic and behavioral record as well as their potential for success at Brenau. Because of the small enrollment at Brenau, admission is competitive and selective.

APPLICATION TIMETABLE

Initial inquiries are welcome at any time. Campus visits may be scheduled by appointment for any time during the week. Office hours are from 8:30 to 5, Monday through Friday. Applications are reviewed on a rolling basis and there are no application deadlines. Students may apply for either fall or spring enrollment. The application fee is $25 and should be submitted with the application. Notification of acceptance can typically be made within a week of completion of the application process, and parents are expected to reply to acceptances within two weeks of notification.

ADMISSIONS CORRESPONDENCE

Laura Nicholson
Director of Admissions
Brenau Academy
500 Washington Street SE
Gainesville, Georgia 30501
Phone: 770-534-6140
Fax: 770-534-6298
E-mail: lnicholson@brenau.edu
Web site: http://www.brenauacademy.org

BRENTWOOD COLLEGE SCHOOL

Mill Bay, British Columbia, Canada

Type: Coeducational boarding and day college-preparatory school
Grades: 9–12
Enrolment: 436
Head of School: Andrea M. Pennells

THE SCHOOL

Founded in 1923, Brentwood College School is a coeducational college-preparatory boarding school (grades 9–12) with a limited number of day students. Brentwood's 40-acre oceanfront campus is located close to the village of Mill Bay, 30 miles north of Victoria and 10 miles south of Duncan. Superb modern facilities for academics, athletics, and the arts, with comfortable accommodation in a pristine Vancouver Island setting, provide a remarkable boarding school environment; the proximity of Victoria provides access to numerous cultural and recreational opportunities.

While academics take priority, the Brentwood curriculum is uniquely scheduled to facilitate full student participation in diverse athletic and arts programmes. At Brentwood, there is no narrow view of education, and the School's philosophical goals are grounded in current research. Opportunities also abound for social time with friends, special events, and leadership through service. Every student has the chance to shine, each in his or her own way, and Brentwood celebrates the confidence with which graduates pursue their varied paths. Brentonians are prepared to make a living and ready to make a life. For a more comprehensive overview, students should visit Brentwood's Web site (http://www.brentwood.bc.ca).

Registered as a nonprofit association under the British Columbia Societies Act, Brentwood is guided by a Board of Governors (18 members), many of whom are alumni. The full board meets three times annually, while the Executive, Finance, and Building committees meet more frequently.

Brentwood College School is a member of the Canadian Association of Independent Schools, the Independent Schools Association of British Columbia, the Western Boarding School Association, the Association of Boarding Schools, the Boarding School Review, and the Secondary School Admission Test Board.

ACADEMIC PROGRAMS

Brentwood expects all students to achieve their personal best in the classroom in pursuit of academic excellence. Teachers' expectations are high. SMARTBoard technology supports traditional teaching to promote critical thinking; both have a place and purpose. Strong teacher-student relationships are forged through favourable class sizes and access to teachers for extra help. The average class size is 17; there are no more than 24 students per class.

The academic year, which begins in early September and ends in late June, is divided into three terms, with major vacations at Christmas (three weeks) and Spring Break (two weeks).

Each student meets regularly with a designated faculty member, who acts as an advisor for academic guidance and counselling. Academic progress is discussed with students monthly, and academic reports, showing both percentage grades and comments, are sent to parents at the end of each term.

The Brentwood curriculum includes Advanced Placement courses at the first-year university level in art history, biology, chemistry, comparative government and politics, environmental science, physics, economics, English language and literature, French, Spanish, psychology, calculus, and studio arts; this allows greater flexibility and individual choice for senior students. With a strong focus on English, mathematics, science, history, and modern languages, Brentwood has also developed unique programmes in entrepreneurship, marketing, environmental science, and global studies.

The development of skills in the arts is an important aspect of a Brentwood education. Courses offered include drawing and painting, pottery, sculpture, photography and film, drafting and design, concert choir, vocal jazz, pops orchestra, jazz band, rock band, drama, dance, musical theatre, public speaking, and debating. Every student must enrol in at least two of these courses, and some pursue as many as four. Their decisions may vary from year to year as they develop a general background of experience. Specialization is possible, particularly for students seriously interested in careers in the arts, leading to the development of the portfolios necessary to support applications to postsecondary institutions.

FACULTY AND ADVISERS

Andrea M. Pennells, Head of School, holds a Master of Arts degree from the University of Edinburgh and a Master of Education degree from the University of British Columbia. Prior to her appointment as Head, she served at Brentwood for eighteen years in successive roles as a teacher of English and English literature, Houseparent, Head of the English Department, Director of Arts, and Assistant Head of School.

The full-time faculty consists of 41 teachers (24 men and 17 women), 23 of whom live on campus. They hold forty-seven baccalaureate degrees, twelve master's degrees, and one doctorate, representing study at major universities in Canada, the United States, England, Ireland, Scotland, New Zealand, Australia, and France. Eleven part-time instructors teach visual and performing arts, and additional part-time instructors assist in coaching major sports.

COLLEGE ADMISSION COUNSELING

It is expected that all students wish to pursue postsecondary studies. University counsellors provide comprehensive advice on all major schools in North America and Europe while supervising all aspects of the application process, including registration for SATs and application for university scholarships. Brentwood's track record in postsecondary planning speaks for itself: graduates receive admission offers from the finest institutions across the globe, many with entrance scholarships. For the complete list of the universities Brentwood graduates are attending, students can visit http://www.brentwood.bc.ca/programmes/academics/where-our-graduates-go.html.

STUDENT BODY AND CONDUCT

Brentwood is home away from home for 197 boarding boys, 157 boarding girls, and 82 day students. Although more than twenty countries are typically represented on campus, most Brentonians hail from Canada and the American Pacific Northwest. A significant number are expatriate Canadians whose parents work overseas. Brentwood students are expected to demonstrate the characteristics that are fundamental to an orderly, wholesome school community: self-discipline, humour, mutual respect, humility, and consideration for others.

ACADEMIC FACILITIES

All School facilities are located on a 40-acre oceanfront campus. The Academic Centre is a modern three-story facility with SMARTBoard-equipped classrooms, an expanded library, administrative and counselling offices, an art gallery, and exhibition spaces. The classrooms are designed to form distinct teaching areas and include six fully appointed science laboratories, two computer instruction centres, an audiovisual language laboratory, and separate studios for pottery, sculpture, photography, painting, and drawing. A raked lecture theatre, which is equipped for mixed-media presentations, also serves as a recital room and recording facility. A 28,000-square-foot performing arts centre with a 431-seat theatre, dance studio, media arts room, lighting and audio control room, music facilities, and other supporting amenities is the focal point of Brentwood's performance programmes.

BOARDING AND GENERAL FACILITIES

Campus residential facilities include four Houses for boys and three for girls, all designed to accommodate 2 students per room. Each House has a recreation room, a snack kitchen, a lounge, and computer facilities. While there are washing machines in each residence, full services are provided in a central laundry facility. All residences have faculty advisors serving as houseparents, counsellors, and tutors. All meals are served in the School's dining room overlooking Mill Bay. Brentwood's Health Centre contains three examination rooms and a six-bed dormitory and isolation room in each of the boys' and girls' wings. The School doctor is regularly on call, full-time nursing service is provided, and a physiotherapist is on site on sports afternoons. Access is available to laboratory facilities in Mill Bay and hospitals in Duncan and Victoria. By arrangement, regular and specialized dental needs can be accommodated.

ATHLETICS

Brentonians value physical fitness, teamwork, and sportsmanship—and they love to compete. Through team and individual sports and outdoor pursuits, Brentwood students develop commitment, endurance, resilience, confidence, and teamwork. Rowing (crew), rugby, basketball, field hockey, volleyball, tennis, ice hockey, soccer, squash, cross-country, golf, sailing, kayaking, and hiking: Brentwood offers them all and more, from introductory to advanced. In grades 9 and 10, students are encouraged to develop a wide range of skills. Senior students may elect to specialize as training and competition become more intense.

For its size, Brentwood has produced a remarkable number of international athletes, especially in rowing, rugby, and field hockey. These include Olympic gold and silver medalists. Athletic facilities include a world-class boathouse (crew), an indoor rowing tank, sports fields, tennis courts, an outdoor basketball court, and a modern sportsplex with a gymnasium, weight rooms, and squash courts. These facilities are augmented by a sheltered oceanfront and the spectacular natural environment of Vancouver Island, British Columbia.

EXTRACURRICULAR OPPORTUNITIES

Through leadership roles, members of the grade 12 class are responsible for many aspects of daily School life. Seniors are expected to mentor younger members of the School and support the faculty in administering the daily routine. In addition, a Student Activities Council, representative of each grade level, consults and works with faculty sponsors to plan social events and special outings and to promote student involvement in community and global charities.

Parents are encouraged to visit the School at any time. Traditionally, they are loyal supporters at sports events and attend concerts and performances (Brentwood features seventeen nights of public performances), the Annual Brentwood Rowing Regatta, the Graduation Dinner and Dance, and the Closing Day Ceremonies.

DAILY LIFE

Academic classes are held between 8:15 a.m. and 1:15 p.m.; sports and arts programmes are offered on alternate afternoons in hour-long periods. Students are expected to make a minimum 2-hour commitment to their sports and arts.

A quiet, supervised study session, or "prep," is held in the residences from 7:30 to 9:30 p.m. This study time, while adequate for junior students, may need to be increased by senior students to meet their academic demands.

There is also a full School assembly at least once a week.

WEEKEND LIFE

On-campus activities include dances, concerts, showcase games, theme-based Open Houses hosted by the various residences, and other special weekend activities. Students find endless ways to relax and have fun on campus. Weekend ski trips to Mt. Washington are scheduled each Sunday during the ski season. In addition, students participate in School-sponsored excursions to Victoria for music, theatre, and other cultural events and occasionally for a meal, a movie, and some shopping.

In each of the three terms, a midterm break of five days provides most students with an opportunity to return home to visit family. In addition, Sunday leave and weekend leave may be obtained by request from the Houseparent.

COSTS AND FINANCIAL AID

For Canadian students entering all grades, tuition and boarding fees are Can$34,200. For American students entering all grades, the fees are Can$39,000; for residents of other countries, the fees are Can$43,600, payable at the time acceptance is confirmed. Canadian-based parents may elect to pay the annual fee in full before the beginning of the first term or in three installments in advance of each term. Day student tuition is Can$18,250. There is a 5 percent reduction on aggregate annual fees for siblings during their joint enrolment. Tuition insurance is required, the premium for which is waived should the entire annual fee be paid in advance. Parents are responsible for transportation costs between the student's home and the School. Arrangements for such travel, including transportation to and from the airport, are provided by the School's travel office.

Scholarship awards, based on academic standing and performance on Brentwood's scholarship examinations, are only available to new Canadian grade 9 and 10 boarding students. Financial assistance grants are needs based and are available to all new Canadian students.

ADMISSIONS INFORMATION

Students capable of succeeding in a college-preparatory programme are best suited to the School's course of studies. Admission, however, is based not only on an applicant's academic potential, but also on his or her character and willingness to participate actively in the athletics and arts programmes. In addition to taking the required entrance examination and having an admissions interview, candidates must submit previous school records and an academic and personal recommendation. Brentwood can make arrangements for the entrance test to be taken at the student's present school should distance make a campus visit impractical. The School also accepts SSAT results instead of the Brentwood entrance test. Students should visit http://www.ssat.org for online test registration and information. Students must request that SSAT test scores be sent directly to Brentwood College School by the test board, so they should designate Brentwood (#1816) as a score recipient when they register.

APPLICATION TIMETABLE

An application should be submitted as early as possible during the academic year prior to admission. The application process requires a $1000 registration fee and a $1000 deposit, which is applied to the first year's fees. The registration charges and fee deposit are refunded in full should Brentwood be unable to offer the student a place or should the applicant's family decline the offer of a place at the School.

ADMISSIONS CORRESPONDENCE

Mr. Clayton Johnston, Director of Admissions
Brentwood College School
2735 Mount Baker Road
Mill Bay, British Columbia V0R 2P1
Canada
Phone: 250-743-5521
Fax: 250-743-2911
E-mail: admissions@brentwood.bc.ca
Web site: http://www.brentwood.bc.ca

BREWSTER ACADEMY

Wolfeboro, New Hampshire

Type: Coeducational boarding and day independent college-preparatory school
Grades: 9–12, postgraduate year
Enrollment: 360
Head of School: Dr. Michael E. Cooper

THE SCHOOL

Brewster Academy was founded in 1820 and in the past decade has become known worldwide for innovation and performance in secondary education. The Brewster program, which is based on the School Design Model℠, provides students with a highly personalized education within a vigorous college-preparatory environment. The program is designed to meet students at their current level of performance and accelerate them in their mastery of skills and knowledge, ensuring that a Brewster graduate leaves the Academy prepared for the challenges of college and life after college. The Brewster program is comprehensive and multilayered and combines the best established practices in teaching, curriculum, and resources. An academic support program offers daily individual course instruction by learning-skills teachers who work with subject teachers to support and develop strategies for motivated students with high potential who have learning-style differences.

Central to the program is a philosophy that challenges and supports each student appropriately and recognizes the need for each student to pursue a sequence of four interrelated goals: the building of self-confidence by developing an individual's most effective learning style, the cultivation of responsibility and a lifelong love of learning, the development of learning skills so that students can learn for themselves in a variety of academic mediums, and the acquisition of skills and content that predict success in college.

Brewster's location on Lake Winnipesaukee, just south of the White Mountains, offers the ideal setting for outdoor activities. The 80-acre campus encompasses a half mile of the lake's southeastern shoreline, including beaches and docks. Wolfeboro is 1¾ hours from Boston and 1 hour from Manchester and Portsmouth. Nearby airports are in Manchester and Laconia.

A nonprofit corporation, the Academy is directed by the Head of School for a 25-member Board of Trustees that meets four times annually. Among the trustees are representatives of the Parents' Association, the Alumni Association, and the John Brewster Estate. The Academy's endowment is $15 million. Plant valuation is $42 million.

Brewster Academy is accredited by the New England Association of Schools and Colleges. It is a member of the Independent Schools Association of Northern New England, the National Association of Independent Schools, the Association of Boarding Schools, and the Secondary School Admission Test Board.

ACADEMIC PROGRAMS

The Brewster program is based on the School Design Model, a successful education reform model that was implemented in 1993 and has caught the attention of educators nationally and internationally. The model combines established best teaching practices with a mastery-based curriculum developed for individual learning styles, within a technology-rich environment that offers students a highly personalized education. Since its implementation, SAT scores have increased 92 points (*International Journal of Educational Reform*, April 2000), and Brewster's success has been documented in education, technology, and mainstream publications, including the *New York Times, USA Today,* and *Worth* magazine.

Learning skills receive special emphasis through academic support programs. Brewster was one of the first preparatory schools in the country with such a program, and its success has made it a model for the independent school world. In this program, students who have high potential but need additional support in their studies have their classroom instruction complemented and enhanced through active, ongoing communication among instructional support and course instructors.

Brewster offers honors-level classes in all courses and eight Advanced Placement classes. Parents receive student evaluations six times yearly and weekly interim progress reports when necessary. Students are required to follow a schedule of five courses, most of which meet five times weekly. Study hours are from 8 to 10 p.m. most nights.

A variety of fine and performing arts classes are offered—some as part of the required curriculum and others as academic enrichment classes. Offerings include studio arts, painting, drawing, pottery, photography, and drama as well as art foundation, history, and theory classes. Students who are interested in music have five ensemble choices, including HOWL (the school's award-winning eclectic chorus), Clearlakes Chorale, the Chamber Orchestra, jazz band, and the wind ensemble.

The Brewster class size averages 11. The overall student-teacher ratio is 6:1.

FACULTY AND ADVISERS

Head of School Michael E. Cooper, Ph.D., leads a faculty of 61 full-time teachers. Dr. Cooper received his doctorate in child and family studies from Syracuse University and received his M.Ed. from St. Lawrence University and his B.A. from the State University of New York.

The Academy's teachers are prepared and trained at the Brewster Summer Institute, a six-week professional development program that is designed to assist teachers in accelerating student growth. Each instructor is placed on a 9-member teaching team. Each team teaches and advises students in a single grade, allowing for constant communication and interaction. Teams meet three times weekly to discuss each student's progress and performance. The adviser serves as the major link among students, parents, teachers, and administrators.

COLLEGE ADMISSION COUNSELING

Preparing students for college may be best expressed by the extent to which they return after their first year. A recent survey showed that Brewster graduates recorded approximately 95 percent retention from their freshman to sophomore year. The national average is about 75 percent. Colleges attended by the class of 2008 include American, Boston University, Charleston (South Carolina), Colgate, Denison, Fordham, George Washington, Georgetown, Hobart and William Smith, Penn State, Princeton, St. Lawrence, University of Illinois, and Worcester Polytechnic.

College advising begins in the eleventh grade, with the college counseling dean and faculty advisers assisting juniors and seniors in selecting colleges.

STUDENT BODY AND CONDUCT

The 2008–09 student body comprises 360 students: 169 boarding boys, 111 boarding girls, 34 day boys, and 46 day girls. There were 13 postgraduates. Students came from twenty states and sixteen countries.

The Student Leadership Program fosters student involvement in the operation of the Academy. Since the Academy is central to the entire student community for most of the year, it has the responsibility to offer students the opportunity to realize and develop leadership traits. The Student Government oversees student community life and at times makes recommendations to the faculty concerning changes in rules and regulations. The Student Judicial Review Board was established to help each student develop self-discipline and personal strength. The board hears cases of student violations of school rules, clarifies the circumstances surrounding the situations, and recommends possible disciplinary actions to the Dean of Students.

ACADEMIC FACILITIES

Each grade has its own academic center, complete with classrooms, a laboratory, and student and teacher work areas. In addition to the physical work space, all students and faculty members use laptop computers, and teachers use a powerful suite of software tools to design and implement curriculum and to ensure constant communication among students, parents, and administrators. Through online portfolios, students post their work to be reviewed and evaluated by faculty members and to share with parents. Students also have online access to grades to help them evaluate their own progress.

An art center is home to pottery, photography, and visual art studios. A multi-media center features classrooms for digital photography and computer graphics, with the latest computers, software and a black box theater. A journalism and desktop publishing studio features the latest in publishing software, scanners, and digital equipment. The newly renovated Anderson Hall, with a proscenium theater and top-of-the-line acoustics and lighting, offers a first-rate performance venue for Brewster's performing arts groups.

BOARDING AND GENERAL FACILITIES

Twenty family-style dormitories (most overlooking Lake Winnipesaukee) house Brewster's boarding students. The environment is family oriented. Each dorm plans community and social activities through weekly meetings. An upperclass proctor and faculty community-life parents ensure constant communication and availability within this small setting. The Spaulding-Emerson Student Center, with a snack bar, a lounge area, and recreation facilities, is in Estabrook Hall.

ATHLETICS

All students participate in at least one season of interscholastic sports. Students also have intramural, recreational, and instructional options from which to choose when not participating in an interscholastic sport. When enrolled in an intramural, recreational, or instructional class, students can also select arts classes, providing students with a six-day athletics and arts program. Arts offerings include digital photography, drama, studio art, pottery, music, and computer graphics.

Athletic programs include baseball, basketball, crew, cross-country running, field hockey, golf, horseback riding, ice hockey (girls' and boys'), lacrosse, outdoor skills, sailing, skiing (Alpine), competitive snowboarding, soccer, softball, strength training and conditioning, student athletic training, tennis, touch football, ultimate Frisbee, wiffleball, and yoga.

The Smith Center for Athletics and Wellness opened in September 2002. This 50,000-square-foot facility features a four-lane, 200-meter indoor track; a convertible surface turf; two basketball courts; a fitness center; a rowing tank; and floor-to-ceiling netting for baseball and lacrosse practice. A climbing wall is in the Haines Climbing Barn.

Outdoor facilities include six athletic fields; nine new tennis courts, which opened in summer 2008; and a boathouse (with panoramic views of the lake and cove), which provides storage and work areas for rowing shells and "420" racing sailboats. The Outdoor Skills Program takes advantage of the White Mountain National Forest for hiking, canoeing, camping, and rock climbing.

EXTRACURRICULAR OPPORTUNITIES

Through Brewster's Leadership Program, students are responsible, under faculty guidance, for the cleanliness of dormitories and grounds, for dormitory government through floor proctors, and for school discipline set by the Student Judicial Review Board. Journalism students produce and publish the school newspaper, yearbook, and literary magazine. Other student groups include the National Honor Society, the Gold Key Society, the debate team, Interact Club, Faith Community, Brewster Big Friends, the Gay Straight Alliance, and an improv club. Each year, the drama program presents three stage productions, focusing on acting and the technical aspects of theater.

DAILY LIFE

Weekdays begin with breakfast at 7 a.m.; classes start at 8 and run 50 minutes each for eight periods. There are five periods on Wednesday and Saturday. School assemblies for information, discussions, or entertainment are held biweekly. Athletics begin after the last class. Community family-style meals are served once a week, and other meals are served cafeteria-style. Supervised evening study is from 8 to 10 p.m. Lights are out at 10:30 (11 for seniors and postgraduates).

Interscholastic athletic competitions are held Wednesday and Saturday after classes, which end at noon.

WEEKEND LIFE

Social activities include gatherings at the student center, concerts and dances, and weekend movies. Trips are planned to concerts, theaters, museums, and professional sports events around New England. Winter Carnival is at the end of January, and Family Weekends are in October and April. Coed intramural football is played in the fall. Students may be granted permission for time away on some weekends.

COSTS AND FINANCIAL AID

Tuition for 2008–09 was $40,495 for boarders and $24,450 for day students. A tuition payment plan is available. Laundry service and a drawing account for allowances are optional. Reservation deposits of $2000 for boarding, $600 for day, and $3450 for international students are applied toward books, athletics supplies, and trips.

Brewster subscribes to the School and Student Service for Financial Aid. Scholarships are granted on the basis of need. In 2008–09, 27 percent of the students received financial aid totaling $2.3 million. Under the Work Grant Program, students work in offices on campus to defray tuition charges.

ADMISSIONS INFORMATION

Candidates are evaluated based on their previous school record, interests and nonacademic accomplishments, and commitment to scholastic and social growth. References and recommendations are considered carefully. Results of the SSAT form part of the admissions review. An interview is required for both the candidate and parents. Admission is granted according to the Academy's judgment of the candidate's entire record, without regard to sex, race, religion, color, or national or ethnic origin.

APPLICATION TIMETABLE

The initial inquiry should be made as soon as a student and family begin to consider private school. A campus tour is part of the interview. Thereafter, a formal application with a $50 nonrefundable fee ($100 for international students) should be submitted. After December, transcripts and recommendations from the candidate's principal or headmaster and teachers are requested. Applicants should take the SSAT in December or January. Brewster notifies students of acceptance on March 10 and offers rolling admissions thereafter, contingent upon openings.

ADMISSIONS CORRESPONDENCE

Lynne M. Palmer, Director of Admission
Brewster Academy
80 Academy Drive
Wolfeboro, New Hampshire 03894

Phone: 603-569-7200
Fax: 603-569-7272
E-mail: admissions@brewsteracademy.org
Web site: http://www.brewsteracademy.org

BROOKS SCHOOL

North Andover, Massachusetts

Type: Coeducational boarding and day college-preparatory school
Grades: 9–12 (Forms III–VI): Middle School, Forms III and IV; Upper School, Forms V and VI
Enrollment: 361
Head of School: John R. Packard, Headmaster

THE SCHOOL

Brooks School was founded in 1926 by the Reverend Endicott Peabody, founder and headmaster of Groton School. Named for Phillips Brooks, Bishop of Massachusetts and a native of North Andover, the School opened for its first term in 1927 with Frank Davis Ashburn, a 24-year-old graduate of Yale, as headmaster. Mr. Ashburn was succeeded by H. Peter Aitken in 1973 and, in 1986, by Lawrence W. Becker. In November of 2007, Brooks named its fourth Head of School, John R. Packard.

With a broad academic curriculum, including many Advanced Placement (AP) courses, the School provides a rigorous college-preparatory program with varied opportunities for challenge. A school of great spirit and pride, Brooks is committed to addressing each student's interests through flexible schedules, close student-faculty relationships, and small class size. Although nonsectarian, Brooks has traditionally maintained a strong relationship with the Episcopal Church.

Situated on the shores of Lake Cochichewick, the 251-acre campus offers a rural setting of open land, fields, and woods, while also having ready access to the cultural, intellectual, and sports activities of Greater Boston, only 40 minutes away.

A nonprofit institution, the School is governed by a self-perpetuating 28-member Board of Trustees. The endowment is estimated at $73 million, supplemented by Annual Giving of $2 million. The School's 3,790 alumni play a continuing role in the support of the School.

The School is accredited by the New England Association of Schools and Colleges and is a member of the Cum Laude Society, the Association of Independent Schools in New England, the National Association of Independent Schools, and the Secondary School Admission Test Board.

ACADEMIC PROGRAMS

The curriculum includes offerings in art, classical languages, computer, drama, English, history, mathematics, modern languages, Chinese, music, science, and theology, together with interdisciplinary courses, such as robotics. A student's level of accomplishment, not simply the number of years of study, may determine placement in a particular subject. Considerable flexibility exists in class scheduling.

Class size averages 12 students, with an overall student-teacher ratio of 5:1. Extra help is readily available during the day and evening. The library is open every day and six evenings a week.

The minimum course load per year for students in grades 10, 11, and 12 is five major courses, or their equivalent, and one minor. A total of 80 credits, including electives, is required for a diploma. Departmental requirements are the successful completion of English every year, algebra II, one foreign language through the third-year level, two years of history, two laboratory sciences, a year of study in the arts, and tenth grade theology. Most students elect to take courses well beyond the minimum requirements.

Students may choose from a wide range of elective courses in completing the credit requirements for their diploma. Those capable of doing so are strongly encouraged to undertake the Advanced Placement work that is offered in all academic departments. Independent study is also available. Brooks is an associate member of the School Year Abroad program and runs an exchange program with schools in Kenya, Hungary, Uganda, Botswana, and Scotland. Examinations are given twice yearly, and reports are sent home at each midterm and semester's end.

FACULTY AND ADVISERS

The Brooks faculty numbers 71 members—42 men and 29 women. Fifty-four hold master's degrees, and 2 have earned Ph.D.'s.

The headmaster, John R. Packard, received a degree from Franklin and Marshall College and holds an M.A.L.S. from Wesleyan.

In what is primarily a residential community, the experience of the faculty both in and out of the classroom is essential. In part, Brooks has recognized this fact by steadily increasing salaries and benefits over recent years. There is much more to encouraging faculty members to choose to remain at Brooks than compensation, however, and much attention has been paid to overall quality-of-life considerations as well. Maintaining and improving the quality of faculty housing during these years has been a major priority, and Brooks has steadily increased its budget each year to support both personal and professional growth opportunities for the full faculty.

While annual turnover is small, in selecting its new faculty members, Brooks actively seeks men and women eager to communicate their knowledge, passion, curiosity, and talent in their various capacities as teachers, coaches, dormitory masters, and advisers. In the role of adviser, each faculty member has an overall responsibility for each student's academic and general progress. Advisers are the chief contacts between school and home. While the School assigns each new student an adviser at the beginning of the year, a student may switch at a later date if there is a better match with someone else. The considerable majority of initial adviser assignments hold until a student graduates.

COLLEGE ADMISSION COUNSELING

College counseling is handled by 3 experienced professionals: 2 codirectors and an assistant director. The counselors help students do useful research and make sound decisions through the college selection process, with the ultimate goal of finding a good match between college and graduate. The program of counseling begins in the second semester of the junior year. The active participation of both students and parents is encouraged by the School. Admission officers from a wide range of colleges come to Brooks each fall to meet with seniors.

Students take SAT Subject Tests beginning in the ninth grade, and the SAT Reasoning Test and ACT test beginning in the junior year. The College Board tests are completed in either the junior or senior year. The average critical reading score for the 2007 graduating class was 597, the average writing score was 620, and the average mathematics score was 646.

All Brooks students who wish to go directly to college gain admission. Typically, 1 or 2 postpone matriculation for a year, primarily to travel, and the College Office continues to work with them during that year. Colleges currently attended by Brooks students include Bates, Bowdoin, Brown, Colby, Colgate, Dartmouth, Duke, Georgetown, Harvard, Trinity, Wesleyan, Williams, and Yale.

STUDENT BODY AND CONDUCT

The student body is composed of 74 students in the ninth grade, 90 in the tenth grade, 97 in the eleventh grade, and 100 in the twelfth grade. Of the 162 girls and 199 boys, 250 are boarders and 111 are day students.

Over a four-year period, boarding students at Brooks have represented thirty-two states and twenty-six countries. The majority of Brooks students have traditionally come from the eastern part of the United States, but in recent years the School has experienced significant increases in enrollment from other areas. Brooks strongly believes in developing diversity in its student body, and students represent many religious, racial, and socioeconomic backgrounds.

School rules and codes of conduct are designed to maintain an orderly life for every member of the school community. Foremost in the School's expectations are respect for others and pride in oneself. Minor disciplinary matters are dealt with by the Deans of Students in conjunction with a student's faculty adviser. Violations of a major school rule are decided upon by a Discipline Committee made up of equal numbers of faculty members and students.

ACADEMIC FACILITIES

The School's thirty-eight classrooms are contained in one large building. In the fall of 2008, Brooks is scheduled to open a state-of-the-art "green" science building equipped with modern laboratories and a 130-seat lecture hall. The academic complex also houses a computer and multimedia language lab. Elsewhere on the campus are an auditorium with a well-equipped stage, a black-box theater, an art studio, and music rooms situated next to the classroom building. The Henry Luce III Library and Robert Lehman Art Center were built in 1995. These buildings combine to form the academic heart of the campus.

BOARDING AND GENERAL FACILITIES

Brooks houses its boarding students in ten recently renovated dormitories, each of which is supervised by 2, 3, or 4 faculty members. One third of the boarding students have single rooms; two thirds live in doubles. All students have their own voice mail boxes and the option to have their own phones in their rooms, and the dormitories are wired for computer network communication.

Health services are provided in the fifteen-bed Health Center, which is staffed around the clock by registered nurses. The school doctor holds clinics two mornings a week and is on call at all other times. There are two hospitals within 15 minutes of the campus. Mental health services are provided by an on-site, full-time counselor. Off-campus services are also available.

ATHLETICS

Brooks is proud of its very strong athletics tradition, which includes recent championship teams in boys' crew, cross-country, hockey, soccer, and wrestling and girls' basketball, crew, hockey, soccer, and softball. The School believes that exercise, team play, and sportsmanship are valuable parts of each student's development. Brooks endeavors to offer its sports at sufficient depth to ensure that each student is able to participate at a level that provides the greatest enjoyment. Full interscholastic schedules are played at two or three levels, including varsity, in each of the School's major sports, and there are some intramural opportunities as well.

The School completed the construction of the new athletic complex in fall 2005. The newly constructed athletic center houses three basketball courts, a wrestling center, a fitness room, and new locker rooms. The School also renovated the Danforth gymnasium into a squash and rowing center. The new athletic complex dramatically improves the already impressive outdoor facilities, which include six soccer fields, two football fields, two field-hockey fields, two lacrosse fields, two baseball fields, a softball field, two boathouses, an indoor hockey arena, and eight tennis courts. In addition, a good eighteen-hole golf course is nearby, three stables are in the immediate area, and a small ski area is within a 10-minute drive of the campus.

EXTRACURRICULAR OPPORTUNITIES

Leadership training, emphasizing student initiative and responsibility, is an important part of the School's program. One of the most exciting things about Brooks is the range of opportunities that it affords its students to explore new areas of interest outside of the classroom and to develop those areas in which they already have interest and knowledge. The list of extracurricular activities varies from year to year, depending upon the changing patterns and directions of interest in the student body. Every student is free to initiate a new organization or extracurricular activity if such a program does not already exist. Most activities have faculty advisers with both interest and experience. Activities include Art Association, Ballroom Dancing, Bible Club, Bishop's Bells, Brooks Brothers and Sisters, Brooks Improv Group (BIG), Brooks School Radio (WBSR), Chess Club, Community Service Board, Debate Club, Gay-Straight Alliance (GSA), Gentleman's Club, Golf Club, Gospel Choir, Harry Potter Club, Irish Club, International Student Club, Jazz Band, Jewish Student Organization (JSO), Math Team, Mixed A Capella, Outdoor Club, Peer Tutoring, Rugby Club, Ski Club, Steaklovers, Student Activities, Students Embracing Culture (SEC), Sushi Club, Tour Guides, Yearbook, Young Libertarians, and various singing and language-based groups.

DAILY LIFE

Major classes meet four or five times a week in 50-minute periods, from 7:50 to 3:10 on Monday, Tuesday, Thursday, and Friday and from 7:50 to about 12 noon on Wednesday and Saturday. An all-school assembly for announcements is held in the morning on Friday.

Athletics, the play production, and community service are scheduled from the end of the class day until dinner time. A family-style dinner led by the headmaster is held at 6:15 on Tuesdays and Thursdays in the fall and spring. All other meals are served cafeteria style.

A free hour from 7 to 8 p.m. is frequently used for meetings of extracurricular organizations, visiting between dormitories, or simply relaxing. Study hours run from 8 to 10 p.m. Those students who need a more supervised study environment may be required to attend a formal study hall during those hours. Freshmen begin the year in supervised study hall. All students must be in their dorm at 10, and lights-out for the ninth and tenth grades is normally at 10:30 on study nights. Late lights for added study time are granted with permission.

WEEKEND LIFE

The Student Activities Committee meets weekly to explore, plan, and arrange weekend activities. There are regularly scheduled trips off campus that take advantage of Boston's many cultural resources. On campus, there is a weekly program of major motion pictures. A lively drama program puts on an average of three productions a year, and dances are held at the School.

While the majority of Brooks students remain on campus for weekends, with parental permission a student may elect to leave campus from the time all obligations are fulfilled on Saturday until Sunday evening. Long weekends may be taken on occasion, with the express permission of each instructor of a missed class or practice. All day students are encouraged to participate in the weekend activities. Popular weekend activities include movies, themed dances, plays, indoor athletic tournaments, dorm competitions, concerts, and trips to Boston and the surrounding area.

COSTS AND FINANCIAL AID

Tuition costs for boarders for 2008–09 are $42,770; for day students, costs are $31,710. Tuition covers athletic equipment, health care, School-sponsored trips, and most other incidentals. Books are purchased separately. Tuition payment plans are available on request.

Financial aid is awarded on the basis of need to 20 percent of the student body. The grants total more than $2.1 million annually, with awards that range from $1000 to full tuition. In addition, Brooks offers a loan program.

ADMISSIONS INFORMATION

Brooks admits students on the basis of proven scholastic ability, on the promise of academic success while at Brooks, and on evidence of sound character. The School especially seeks students who are likely to make real contributions to the life at Brooks and take advantage of the opportunities offered by the School.

The most important requirements for admission are a student's essay, transcript, and recommendations from the applicant's present school. A personal interview and a visit to the School are also important parts of the admission procedure. Candidates are expected to take the SSAT, preferably in November or December. Older candidates may submit the results of the PSAT or SAT. Approximately 95 percent of any given year's new students enter into grades 9 and 10. Students may also apply for grade 11.

APPLICATION TIMETABLE

The fall prior to a candidate's prospective admission is usually the best time for a visit, which includes a student-guided tour of the School. Appointments should be made well in advance, by telephone or letter. The Admission Office hours run from 8:30 to 4:30 Monday through Friday and from 8:30 to 12 noon on Saturday.

An application for admission should be submitted along with a nonrefundable registration fee of $50 to the Admission Office by February 1. Day students and students who are applying for financial aid need to complete applications by January 15. Applicants are also encouraged to apply after that date, if necessary. In accordance with the SSAT Board acceptance and reply dates, Brooks notifies the majority of its candidates of its admission decision on March 10.

ADMISSIONS CORRESPONDENCE

Judith S. Beams
Director of Admission
Brooks School
1160 Great Pond Road
North Andover, Massachusetts 01845
Phone: 978-725-6272 or 6271
Fax: 978-725-6298
E-mail: admission@brooksschool.org
Web site: http://www.brooksschool.org

BUXTON SCHOOL

Williamstown, Massachusetts

Type: Coeducational college-preparatory boarding and day school
Grades: 9–12
Enrollment: 95
Head of School: C. William Bennett and Peter Smith, Co-Directors

THE SCHOOL

In 1928, Ellen Geer Sangster founded Buxton School as a coeducational day school in Short Hills, New Jersey. In 1947, she moved the high school to her family estate in Williamstown, Massachusetts, and formed it anew as a boarding school.

From the beginning, Buxton has been a progressive school, one devoted to innovation and change. Today, that devotion remains steadfast. At Buxton, students' pursuits help them develop the clear vision they need to comprehend the world they live in and to define their future lives. Each student's bridge to the larger world is the informed, skilled, confident self that he or she develops while at Buxton.

Buxton places great importance on the composition and character of its student body. Foremost, a young person must want to be at Buxton. In addition, Buxton seeks to enroll students who have the intelligence, motivation, creativity, and intellectual curiosity to succeed there. Prior to coming to Buxton, students have experienced positive relationships with adults as well as peers. Buxton students take a responsible and ambitious role in shaping their own lives and wish to make significant and mature social contributions. They are conscious of the importance of being useful and contributory, of serving as an asset to others, and of aiding in others' efforts to enrich the life of the group. One of the first tasks Buxton students encounter is that of developing and maintaining a sound, compassionate, stimulating environment for oneself and for the entire group.

Buxton promotes personal growth and cultivates students' abilities to understand and manage their lives. Presenting a way of life that students can come to understand and manage is of primary importance. The student body is diverse; life at the School is flexible, noninstitutional, and open to change. Opportunities often arise for collective deliberation of life's most pressing challenges. A Buxton education reflects the fundamental premise that a mature individual must be morally and actively committed, each in his or her own way, to the creation and betterment of a healthy society.

The 150-acre campus of Buxton overlooks historic Williamstown, which is located approximately 170 miles north of New York City and 150 miles west of Boston. Williams College, the Clark Art Institute, and the Massachusetts Museum of Contemporary Art (MASS MoCA) are nearby and are all exceptional resources for Buxton students.

Buxton is a nonprofit, nonsectarian institution governed by a 22-member self-perpetuating Board of Trustees. The board includes the Co-Directors, Associate Director, faculty members, alumni, parents of students and alumni, and friends of the School.

The physical plant at Buxton is valued at $6 million. The operating budget is $4 million annually. The current endowment is $1.8 million, and the Annual Fund for 2007–08 raised $259,889.

Buxton is accredited by the New England Association of Schools and Colleges and is approved by the Massachusetts Department of Education. It is a member of the Secondary School Admission Test Board, The Association of Boarding Schools, the Association of Independent Schools of New England, the National Association of Independent Schools, and the Small Boarding School Association as well as other professional organizations.

ACADEMIC PROGRAMS

Academic courses, activities, and community life are all essential parts of a Buxton education. Each offers the opportunity for unique and vital growth; therefore, each is of educational significance.

Buxton's academic curriculum is broad and demanding, offering an unusual combination of traditional subjects, courses in the arts, and electives in subjects that are usually only encountered at the college level. Students collaborate with teachers to design their course programs. Although they are advised to design a course schedule that will prepare them for higher education, students have considerable freedom of choice about what courses they take and when they take them.

Sixteen credits are required for graduation. Students must take 4 years of English and 1 year of American history. They are also counseled to complete a minimum of 3 years of mathematics, 2 years of social science, 2 years of laboratory science, and at least 2 years of a foreign language (French, Spanish, and Indonesian are offered), although 3 years are strongly recommended. Students are also encouraged to pursue courses in the arts—studio art; ceramics; black-and-white and digital photography; video production; music theory, composition, and performance; and beginning and advanced drama.

Buxton offers a range of elective courses—those offered recently include writing workshops; Coming of Age Literature; Third World Literature; Practice of Poetry; Race, Class, and Gender; Rebels, Resisters, and Revolutionaries; Africa; Cultural History of the Twentieth Century; Censorship and Media Literacy; Traditional Taoism and Western Literature; Advanced European Studies; Globalization; Radio and the Social Documentary; History of the Eugenics Movement in the U.S.; Gender Studies; Topics in Neuroscience; Calculus II; Environmental Studies; Marine Science; Geology; and Astronomy.

Buxton divides its academic year into two semesters. The School has a 5:1 student-teacher ratio, and classes average 9 students. Faculty-supervised study periods are held daily during class hours and for 2 hours in the evening. Students may be required to attend.

Each year in March, the whole School travels to a major North American city. Atlanta, Chicago, Havana, Mexico City, New Orleans, Philadelphia, San Juan, Toronto, and Washington, D.C., are among those visited in recent years. This event is of central importance in the school year, and students are involved in all aspects of planning and executing the weeklong trip. Social, economic, and political issues are the focus of project groups, and the entire Buxton community takes part in the All-School Play, which is performed several times during the trip. Upon returning to Buxton, students present their projects to the School and archive their reports.

FACULTY AND ADVISERS

There are 21 faculty members—12 men and 9 women. Five hold master's degrees. Fourteen live on campus. C. William Bennett, Director of the School since 1983, is a graduate of Williams College and has been at Buxton since 1969. In 2008, Peter Smith became Co-Director with Mr. Bennett. Mr. Smith graduated from Buxton in 1974, is a graduate of Clark University, and has been working at Buxton since 1984.

Most teaching families and teachers live at the School, interweaving their daily lives with those of the Buxton community. Along with teaching in the classroom, faculty members have advisory, leadership, administrative, and caretaking responsibilities. As advisers, faculty members are in regular contact with parents.

Compassionate adult action and reaction form the foundation of education at Buxton. Teachers seek to motivate students to engage in sincere intellectual commitment and self-evaluation. The adults are available and open to young people and are concerned with their growth in academic disciplines as well as in every other respect. Buxton faculty and staff members react to young people knowledgeably, deeply, and personally. Developing honest and caring friendships between Buxton adults and students is an educational goal in itself.

COLLEGE ADMISSION COUNSELING

Buxton faculty members counsel students as they form their college plans. Students are assigned faculty advisers in the spring of their junior year. The advisers guide students in making appropriate college choices and help students with the application process.

In recent years, Buxton graduates have attended Amherst, Bard, Bennington, Berklee School of Music, Carlton, Cornell, Dartmouth, Emory, Hampshire, Macalester, Mount Holyoke, Oberlin, Reed, Rhode Island School of Design, St. John's, Sarah Lawrence, Skidmore, Smith, Spelman, Wellesley, Williams, and the University of Chicago.

STUDENT BODY AND CONDUCT

Enrollment at Buxton averages 95 students, with an equal number of boys and girls. In 2008–09, seventeen states and the countries of Bermuda, Brazil, China, Ecuador, Japan, Mexico, the Republic of Korea, and Spain were represented among the student population.

ACADEMIC FACILITIES

The campus contains four classroom buildings (one housing science labs and a computer lab), a library with Internet-access computers and extra Ethernet ports for students' portable computers, an art studio, a ceramics studio, a darkroom, a music classroom and practice rooms, and a theater. Designated campus areas are equipped for wireless Internet access.

BOARDING AND GENERAL FACILITIES

In addition to the academic facilities, there are a number of other buildings on campus. The Main House contains a girls' dormitory, the School dining room, and administrative offices. The Gate House serves as an additional girls' dormitory; the boys' dormitory is a converted barn. The School has additional buildings for administrative offices and for faculty and staff housing. Williamstown Medical Associates provides medical services to students.

ATHLETICS

At Buxton, competitive and recreational sports programs do not merely fulfill physical education requirements; they also expose students to the challenges inherent in disciplined physical activity and different kinds of team play. Students acquire personal confidence and a sense of mastery as well as leadership skills through participation in these activities.

Competitive sports are not mandatory, but regular outdoor activity is expected of everyone. Interscholastic soccer and basketball take place on a scheduled and supervised basis. Other activities include yoga classes, biking, hiking, horseback riding, indoor soccer, intramural basketball, kayaking, martial arts, running, skating, skiing and snowboarding at a local area, sledding, softball, spring soccer, table tennis, tennis, and Ultimate Frisbee.

The campus has its own playing fields, a basketball court, a weight room, three ponds for ice skating, and a hill for sledding and skiing. Hiking trips are scheduled when there is student interest. Riding lessons can be arranged.

EXTRACURRICULAR OPPORTUNITIES

In keeping with the Buxton philosophy that all aspects of School life are valuable to the education of a student, activities play a prominent role. Students of every degree of interest and ability are urged to take part and are counted on to support the efforts of each other as co-participant, audience, or encouraging friend. All of Buxton's activities, which include art, music, drama, dance, drumming, and creative writing, are designed to foster personal expression and commitment through a combination of self-discipline, patient practice, interpersonal skill, and astute observation of life. The art studio has an extensive array of two- and three-dimensional media. Painting, drawing, figure drawing, printmaking, book arts, sculpture, metal fabrication, work with fabric or found objects, mixed media, ceramics, and black-and-white and digital photography are available. Chorus, chamber orchestra, and chamber ensembles are offered at Buxton as music activities. Drama includes acting, working on technical crews, and costuming. Each year, seniors raise funds for and produce the School yearbook, which they present as a gift to the Buxton community.

An essential part of a Buxton education is Work Program, which takes place on Tuesday afternoons and Saturday mornings. At these times, students engage in tasks such as forestry work and gardening, construction projects, office work, and cooking. Administered by volunteer students and faculty members, Work Program requires a great deal of planning, budgeting, and managing. What is done and who does it are always changing, but it is a consistent, direct challenge to everyone that Work Program can and must fill a major part of Buxton's nonprofessional needs.

The annual Fall and Spring Arts Festivals offer students' families the opportunity to share in Buxton life. Over the three days of these events, the School presents performances by the chorus, chamber orchestra, and chamber ensembles; performances of student composers' work; drama productions; and readings of students' creative writing. The School also exhibits new student artwork. Independent and joint science projects are often presented on these weekends as well. In addition, there is ample time for parent-faculty conferences.

The proximity of Williams College is particularly significant, as it provides a source of stimulation and example as well as the opportunity to occasionally attend lectures and events and use the college library. Bordering the Buxton campus is the Clark Art Institute, one of the finest small art museums in the country.

DAILY LIFE

Each day before classes, students clean their rooms and complete minor housekeeping tasks around the School. Classes begin at 8 a.m. and are held until 3 p.m., five days a week. Sports and activities are offered from 3 to 5 p.m. Students attend study hall, study on their own, or participate in rehearsals or other activities from 7 to 9 p.m. Meals are family-style, with student waiters; students attend lunch at 12:30 and dinner at 6 in the School dining room.

WEEKEND LIFE

Weekends at Buxton are considered just as important as weekdays. Students plan and organize Friday night activities, which include outdoor sports and games, dances, swimming, and theme events. On Saturday mornings, everyone in the School participates in Work Program. Students are free to go into Williamstown to buy necessities or attend a movie or cultural event on Saturday afternoons and evenings. All Saturday meals are planned and prepared by students. Sundays begin with brunch and typically are devoted to academic work. Sunday evenings feature a formal dinner and arts events or presentations concerning social issues. Students remain at Buxton on weekends except for a designated Home Weekend each semester.

Students who wish to do so may attend religious services locally.

COSTS AND FINANCIAL AID

Tuition and fees for 2008–09 were $39,500 for boarding students and $25,000 for day students. This included tickets for approved cultural events, athletics (including a ski pass), and all other School-sponsored activities.

Buxton is committed to maintaining the diversity of its student body. Approximately 40 percent receive need-based financial aid; $1 million was awarded for 2008–09.

ADMISSIONS INFORMATION

Buxton admits students into grades 9 through 11. Interested parents and prospective students may request an information packet by calling or writing the Admissions Office or through the School Web site. An on-campus interview is required, and the student's most recent SSAT or TOEFL scores should accompany the application.

APPLICATION TIMETABLE

Inquiries are welcome any time. Applications should be submitted by February 1, although they are accepted later if space is available. The application fee is $50 for U.S. students and $100 for international students.

ADMISSIONS CORRESPONDENCE

Admissions Office
Buxton School
291 South Street
Williamstown, Massachusetts 01267
Phone: 413-458-3919
Fax: 413-458-9428
E-mail: Admissions@BuxtonSchool.org
Web site: http://www.BuxtonSchool.org

CAMDEN MILITARY ACADEMY

Camden, South Carolina

Type: Boys' boarding college-preparatory military school
Grades: 7–12, PG
Enrollment: School total: 300
Head of School: Col. Eric Boland, Headmaster

THE SCHOOL

While the Camden Military Academy tradition dates back to 1892, operations on the current campus began with the 1958–59 school year. The Academy combines the traditions of three institutions—Carlisle Military School, which operated in Bamberg, South Carolina, from 1892 to 1977; Camden Academy, which was located on the current campus from 1949 to 1957; and Camden Military Academy. Camden Military Academy, which was founded by Col. James F. Risher and his son, Col. Lanning P. Risher, has operated as a nonprofit tax-exempt institution since 1974 and is governed by a self-perpetuating board of trustees.

Today, the Academy enjoys a capacity enrollment of 300 young men from around the United States and the world. The school's modern campus is located in historic Camden, South Carolina. The Academy is a fully accredited member of the Southern Association of Colleges and Schools. It holds membership in the National Association of Independent Schools, the Southern Association of Independent Schools, the Palmetto Association of Independent Schools, and the Association of Military Colleges and Schools in the United States. The Corps has been designated by the Department of the Army as a Junior Army ROTC Honor Unit with Distinction.

ACADEMIC PROGRAMS

Camden Military Academy enrolls young men in grades 7 through the postgraduate year. The academic program at the high school level (grades 9–12) is strictly college preparatory. All high school students must earn 24 units for graduation. These include 4 units of English; algebra I, geometry, and algebra II, plus a fourth math unit (precalculus and AP calculus are also available); three sciences (two of which must be lab sciences); 4½ units of history; and 3 units of a modern foreign language (all ninth graders are required to take Latin before taking a modern foreign language; French and Spanish are offered). Students must also take a course in computer literacy and in JROTC. Additional units must be earned from approved academic electives.

The academic program is structured around a traditional class day, with all students taking six classes per day as well as JROTC. All class sections are small, with typically fewer than 15 students per class. Students are apprised of their academic progress every two weeks. Those students who earn less than a C for the two-week grading period in any class are required to attend a two-week tutorial period with their teacher. In addition, a mandatory teacher-supervised study period is conducted five nights per week. All students are monitored, and assignments are checked. Students who maintain a B or better average may elect to study in the Cline Library. The library is available to other students during this time by faculty permission and is open daily to all students. The Academy encourages library use and has a full-time professional librarian available to assist in that usage.

FACULTY AND ADVISERS

Col. Eric Boland was appointed Headmaster in 2003. He has been employed by the Academy for more than twenty years. He has served as an instructor, a Tactical Officer, and the Academy's athletic director. Col. Boland earned his B.A. degree and his master's degree in secondary education from the University of South Carolina. In addition, Col. Boland holds a doctorate degree in Christian counseling from Christian Leadership University and is pursuing a doctorate degree in education from the University of South Carolina.

Lt. Col. Pat Armstrong, a West Point graduate, is the Commandant of Cadets.

The faculty consists of 24 men and 2 women.

COLLEGE ADMISSION COUNSELING

Camden Military Academy has offered only a college-preparatory curriculum for many years. More than 95 percent of Camden graduates are accepted to four-year colleges and universities. All juniors are required to take the PSAT, which is available to sophomores as well. The Academy provides students with the opportunity to take the SAT and ACT at each administration. All students are encouraged to take an SAT preparatory seminar that is offered twice each year. Students and parents work with college advisers to select the college or university best suited to each graduate. Among the colleges and universities that recent graduates have attended are The Citadel, Clemson, Emory & Henry, Georgia Tech, George Washington, Hillsdale, North Carolina State, Norwich, Ohio State, the United States Military Academy at West Point, Vanderbilt, Virginia Military Institute, Wake Forest, and the Universities of Maryland, North Carolina and South Carolina.

STUDENT BODY AND CONDUCT

Camden currently operates at a capacity of 300 boarding boys in grade 7 through the postgraduate year. Students represent seventeen states and two other countries; however, most students are from the Southeast, with the greatest concentration coming from the Carolinas.

While Camden Military Academy is a military boarding school, its strength lies in its ability to work personally with each student, meet his needs, and help him realize his potential. Because all students are seven-day boarding boys, all live by the same rules and experience daily life in the same way. Students are usually housed 2 to a room in five companies. Each company is composed of 58 to 62 young men. Each company is supervised by an adult Tactical Officer who lives on the campus with his family. He serves as the counselor, mentor, encourager, and disciplinarian for each young man in his charge. He also serves as the communications liaison with the parents. These men bring a positive dimension to the Camden experience. Their background, professional training, and personal commitment make them uniquely qualified to help one's son develop personally as well as academically. In addition, students benefit from being part of a cadet ranking structure. The organization gives each young man the opportunity to develop personal responsibility and leadership and management skills. All students are also required to participate in JROTC and attend religious services each Sunday.

ACADEMIC FACILITIES

The campus is composed of fourteen buildings. There are three academic buildings and the Cline Library dedicated to academic pursuits. Housed in these buildings are all classrooms, a computer lab, and a science lab. The Cline Library houses the school's 9,000-volume collection as well as periodicals and computer information services.

BOARDING AND GENERAL FACILITIES

The Academy's 350-seat dining hall allows for family-style meals, and the entire cadet corps eats at one time. The modern infirmary, resident nurses, and school physician meet all cadet medical needs. The gym complex houses the gym, dressing rooms, and shower facilities for all athletic teams as well as the school's band room. Each of the cadet barracks features 2- or 3-man rooms that are air-conditioned and heated and individual combination door locks.

The Carlisle House serves as the center for cadet recreational time. The Carlisle House amenities include a game room, a snack bar, a TV room, and a cadet lounge. On campus, there are three tennis courts, two athletic fields, and a state-of-the-art track complex that features one of the nation's premier running tracks.

ATHLETICS

The Academy offers thirteen different sports: baseball, basketball, bowling, cross-country, drill team, football, golf, lacrosse, rifle team, soccer, tennis, track and field, and wrestling.

EXTRACURRICULAR OPPORTUNITIES

The Academy offers a school band, Key Club, Boy Scout troop, Civil Air Patrol, FCA, and Honor Society. Cadets are also welcomed to participate in community and church-sponsored activities. In addition to these activities, the Academy offers weekly outings to area restaurants, movie theaters, and paintball. There are also trips to go white-water rafting and snow skiing and to other day and overnight activities.

DAILY LIFE

All students follow the same daily schedule. In addition to the academic day, there is drill three days per week, athletic practice, free time, and evening study period.

WEEKEND LIFE

All weekends offer both structured activities as well as free time. Inspections, a Sunday Dress Parade, all meals, and Sunday church services are required of all students. Cadets may spend their free time Saturday afternoon and Sunday afternoon in the gym, the fully equipped weight room, the student center, or in their rooms. All cadets are permitted to bring personal items such as clothes, a TV, video games, and a stereo. Use of these items is strictly monitored and permitted only during a cadet's free time. High school cadets are also permitted to go into the town of Camden on weekend afternoons for shopping, a meal, or a movie. The Academy provides all transportation; students are not permitted vehicles. Day or overnight trips are also planned during the weekends that cadets are on campus. Cadets are granted furloughs (the opportunity to stay overnight away from the campus) based on several factors. Certain furloughs are given and others must be earned. Furloughs may be earned either through merits or academic performance. All cadets have the opportunities to earn furloughs. Those who maximize their opportunities may go home about once a month.

SUMMER PROGRAMS

The Academy offers a summer academic program as well as a summer camp. Students should contact Casey Robinson, Director of Admissions, for summer program information.

COSTS AND FINANCIAL AID

The cost for a new student for the 2008–09 school year is $16,995. This includes tuition and room and board. The cost of uniforms, laundry and dry cleaning, books, and miscellaneous charges is extra. Limited financial aid is available.

ADMISSIONS INFORMATION

All applicants are examined on an individual basis. Only young men who have demonstrated a desire to enroll and are capable of undertaking college-preparatory work will be considered. An on-campus interview is required of all applicants. A catalog and DVD are available from the Admissions Office. Camden Military Academy admits students of any race, color, and national or ethnic origin. The Academy is a private, nonprofit educational institution with admission limited to young men.

APPLICATION TIMETABLE

Admission is offered on a rolling basis. Admission for the second semester is offered strictly on a space available basis. There is a $100 nonrefundable application fee.

ADMISSIONS CORRESPONDENCE

R. Casey Robinson
Director of Admissions
Camden Military Academy
520 Highway 1, North
Camden, South Carolina 29020

Phone: 803-432-6001
800-948-6291 (toll-free)
Fax: 803-425-1020
E-mail: admissions@camdenmilitary.com
Web site: http://www.camdenmilitary.com

CAMPBELL HALL (EPISCOPAL)

North Hollywood, California

Type: Coeducational day college-preparatory school
Grades: K–12: Lower School, K–6; Middle School, 7–8; Upper School, 9–12
Enrollment: School total: 1,090; Upper School: 530
Head of School: The Reverend Julian Bull, Headmaster

THE SCHOOL

Campbell Hall is an independent, K–12, coeducational, nonprofit day school affiliated with the Episcopal Church. It offers college-preparatory academic training within the perspective of the Judeo-Christian tradition. Campbell Hall was founded in 1944 by the Reverend Alexander K. Campbell as a school dedicated not only to the finest in academic education but also to the discovery of the values of a religious heritage. Campbell Hall enrolls students in kindergarten through the twelfth grade.

The school's 15-acre campus is located in a residential suburb 10 miles north of Los Angeles. Students take advantage of the school's proximity to museums, missions, historic sites, science centers, and universities.

The basic structure and operation of the school and the formulation of educational and other school policies are guided by a 20-member Board of Directors. The board is composed of community leaders, alumni, and parents of students at Campbell Hall. The Headmaster has traditionally served as a liaison between the board and the various segments of the school community.

The school's development programs include annual and capital campaigns.

Campbell Hall is accredited by the Western Association of Schools and Colleges and the California Association of Independent Schools. It holds memberships in the National Association of Independent Schools, National Association of Episcopal Schools, Episcopal Diocesan Commission on Schools, Educational Records Bureau, National Association of College Admission Counselors, Council for Advancement and Support of Education, College Board, Council for Religion in Independent Schools, and Cum Laude Society.

ACADEMIC PROGRAMS

Students must complete 7½ units in the humanities, including 4 units of the English component, 3 units of the history component, and ½ unit of senior seminar. Other requirements for graduation include 3 units of mathematics, 3 of foreign language, 3 of laboratory sciences, 2 years of physical education, 1 year of a visual or performing art, ½ year of art history, and ½ year of music history. In addition to the required courses, students must complete at least 3½ additional units chosen from electives, such as music theory, creative writing, economics, ethics, physiology, poetry, computer programming science, philosophy, psychology, and visual and performing arts. In addition, students must complete 20 hours of community service each year.

A number of special academic options attract qualified students. Nineteen Advanced Placement courses and seventeen honors courses are offered and include calculus, probability and statistics, English, French, Japanese, Latin, Spanish, European history, U.S. history, American government, geography, biology, chemistry, physics, music theory, psychology, economics, and computer science. In addition, qualified seniors may take college-level courses through the Talented High School Student Program of the California State University at Northridge, through local community colleges, and through the UCLA High School Scholars' Program.

Classes range in size from 8 or fewer students in advanced courses to 22 in some of the required courses.

The school's grading system uses percentages: 100–90 is an A; 89–80 is a B; 79–70 is a C; 69–60 is a D, and no credit is given for a grade below 59. Report cards, which are issued twice each semester, include evaluations of work habits and cooperation. At the midpoint of each quarter, students who are in academic difficulty in one or more courses are notified, as are their parents.

Each semester, students who earn all A's in all classes are eligible for the Headmaster's List; students who earn a 3.6 academic average qualify for the Honor Roll. On the basis of course history and semester grades, students may qualify for recognition by the California Scholarship Federation, and academically outstanding juniors and seniors are eligible for membership in the Cum Laude Society.

FACULTY AND ADVISERS

There are 112 full-time faculty members (73 women and 39 men); 40 hold master's degrees, and 4 have doctorates. Faculty members are encouraged to attend seminars and conferences in their fields. In addition to giving academic and social guidance to individual students, faculty advisers work closely with class officers to ensure unity and success in various class projects and social activities.

Julian Bull was appointed Headmaster in 2003. He is a graduate of Dartmouth (B.A., 1982), Boston College (M.A., 1988), and received his M.Div. from Virginia Theological Seminary in 2007. Mr. Bull was formerly Head of School at Trinity Episcopal in New Orleans, Louisiana.

COLLEGE ADMISSION COUNSELING

In October, all sophomores and juniors take the PSAT. Throughout their high school years, students receive extensive college counseling through group workshops and in-depth individual conferences with the college counseling staff members. High school families are invited to the annual Senior College Night at which the college admissions process is delineated and college-financing strategies are explained. During the fall semester, juniors and seniors have the opportunity to hear presentations from a nationwide selection of college admission officers who visit Campbell Hall.

All Campbell Hall students attend college. Graduates of the class of 2008 are attending such colleges as Barnard, Berkeley, Brandeis, Brown, Columbia, Cornell, Duke, Emory, Georgetown, Georgia Tech, Harvey Mudd, Haverford, Howard, Morehouse, Northwestern, Oberlin, Pitzer, Pomona, Rhode Island School of Design, Smith, Spelman, Stanford, Tulane, UCLA, United States Air Force Academy, USC, Vanderbilt, William & Mary, Yale, and the Universities of Chicago and Pennsylvania.

STUDENT BODY AND CONDUCT

Of the 530 boys and girls in the Upper School (grades 9–12), 136 are in the ninth grade, 132 in the tenth, 140 in the eleventh, and 127 in the twelfth. Most students live in the suburban areas of Los Angeles.

Because Campbell Hall is concerned with the formation of character traits and values that reflect a sense of responsibility as well as a concern for the needs of others, misconduct is subject to disciplinary action. Violation of school rules and regulations may result in suspension or expulsion.

ACADEMIC FACILITIES

Campus academic facilities include classroom complexes, a math-science building, seven science labs, four computer labs, the Fine Arts Building, and a theater. A 22,000-square-foot library and academic center serves as the hub for technological resources. Every classroom has computers available, including four laptop carts, networked overhead projectors, and SMART boards. Students and faculty members have e-mail accounts and can send e-mail worldwide. The Internet is available as are research tools on CD-ROM. Web pages can be reached at http://www.campbellhall.org.

ATHLETICS

There are two basic components to the athletics program. First, required physical education courses provide basic and advanced instruction for sports that are in season; and second, Campbell Hall is a member of the California Interscholastic Federation (Gold Coast Athletic Association) and field teams in baseball, basketball, cheerleading, cross-country, 11-man football, equestrian, golf, soccer, softball, tennis, track and field, and volleyball.

The school has two well-equipped gymnasiums, two tennis courts, a baseball diamond, two softball fields, and five outdoor basketball/volleyball courts.

EXTRACURRICULAR OPPORTUNITIES

The students have an active student government with elected officers representing each division of the student body. Among the student-planned events are dances, the Winter Formal, and the Halloween, Christmas, and Valentine's Day celebrations. The year's social schedule culminates in a spring prom, planned by the junior class to honor the senior class.

The environmental education program currently includes a fourth-grade trip to Sycamore Canyon, a fifth-grade trip to Leo Carrillo State Beach, and a weeklong trip to the Malibu Creek State Park for the sixth grade. At the secondary school, seventh grade students take a trip to Camp Grindling-Hilltop, eighth grade students to Camp Ocean Pines, ninth grade students to Canyon Creek, tenth grade students to El Capitan state beach, eleventh grade students to Cedar Lake, and twelfth grade students go on a senior retreat to Canyon Creek. These programs encourage the development of a passion for learning by doing, a deeper appreciation of the natural environment, and bonds of mutual respect, self-respect, and community trust.

There are also many curricular field trips and about sixty special interest groups, such as the Speech and Debate Team, Highlanders, the Cultural Awareness Club, the Spirit Club, Thespians, the Creative Writing Club, Amnesty International, Junior Statesmen of America, GSA, the Community Service Committee, and the High School Academic Honor Board.

DAILY LIFE

Monday through Thursday, there are four 80-minute academic classes that meet between 8:15 and 3:30. On Friday, each class meets for 75 minutes, between 8:15 and 2:20. Each Monday through Thursday, 40 minutes are devoted to chapel (every Monday and Thursday), advisee group meetings, or clubs. There is a 45-minute lunch break. Interspersed among the academic courses are electives that provide enrichment in the fine arts (painting, drawing, ceramics, sculpture, and photography), the performing arts (chorus, instrumental music, drama, stagecraft, and dance), sports (physical education and team sports), and computer programming. Yearbook, newspaper, and journalism are also available as curricular classes.

SUMMER PROGRAMS

The school offers a full complement of summer programs for students in kindergarten through grade 8, including summer school courses, a creative arts camp, and sports camps. Additional information may be obtained by writing to the Summer Programs Director at Campbell Hall.

COSTS AND FINANCIAL AID

Tuition for 2008–09 was $19,890 to $24,910. Additional expenses included a fee of $600; $1400 per year for books, supplies, and activities; and a student body fee of $65 per year for grades 9–12. Tuition payments may be made biannually or, at an additional charge to cover interest costs, in ten monthly installments. Students may either bring their own lunches to school or purchase them from a caterer at the school at lunchtime. Parents purchase school uniforms for their children and provide transportation.

Financial aid is available and is awarded on the basis of family need. Continuing students have priority for renewal. In 2008–09, 23 percent of Middle and Upper School students received financial aid.

ADMISSIONS INFORMATION

The school seeks students who are able to benefit from a rigorous college-preparatory curriculum and who will contribute to extracurricular as well as academic activities. The school does not discriminate against applicants on the basis of race, religion, or national or ethnic origin.

An entrance examination is required, as are recommendations from 2 teachers, a transcript from the school in which the applicant is currently enrolled, and an on-campus interview.

APPLICATION TIMETABLE

The Admissions Office is open from 8 to 4, Monday through Friday, to answer inquiries and to arrange interviews and campus visits. Applicants should file an application, accompanied by a $100 fee, by January 30 of the year entrance is desired. Most applications are submitted by December of the year preceding the desired entrance. Applicants take the Independent School Entrance Examination.

The school makes most decisions concerning new admissions by March. Parents are expected to reply to an offer of acceptance within three weeks and to pay a $2000 registration fee, which is credited toward the first semester's tuition.

ADMISSIONS CORRESPONDENCE

Alice Fleming, Director of Admissions
George White, Associate Director
Campbell Hall
4533 Laurel Canyon Boulevard
P.O. Box 4036
North Hollywood, California 91617-9985
Phone: 818-980-7280
Web site: http://www.campbellhall.org

CANTERBURY SCHOOL

New Milford, Connecticut

Type: Coeducational boarding and day college-preparatory school conducted by lay faculty and administrators
Grades: 9–12 (Forms III–VI), postgraduate year
Enrollment: 350
Head of School: Thomas J. Sheehy III, Headmaster

THE SCHOOL

Canterbury was founded in 1915 by Henry O. Havemeyer, Clarence H. Mackay, and Nelson Hume to give Roman Catholic boys the kind of college preparation offered by the best nonsectarian boarding schools. It was named for an English school established by Saint Dunstan, Archbishop of Canterbury, in the tenth century. After fifty-five years as a boys' school, Canterbury began admitting girls as day students in 1972 and as boarding students in 1973.

The hallmark of a Canterbury education is the School's willingness to accept students as they are, support them where necessary, stretch them where appropriate, and inspire them to become moral leaders in a secular world. Canterbury's spiritual tradition informs all aspects of the program, including academics, the arts, athletics, and community service, which aims to inspire in students a commitment to lifelong volunteer service.

New Milford, a western Connecticut town (population 25,000), is 45 miles from Hartford, 35 miles from New Haven, and 85 miles from New York City. Canterbury's proximity to the Berkshires, the Appalachian Trail, and the Housatonic River provides opportunities for outdoor activities, while the nearby urban areas offer concerts, plays, and other cultural events.

A nonprofit corporation, Canterbury operates under the patronage of the Archbishop of Hartford and is directed by a self-perpetuating Board of Trustees. Many of the 3,800 alumni contribute to the Annual Alumni Giving Program and actively participate in the admissions process.

Canterbury is accredited by the New England Association of Schools and Colleges and is a member of the National Association of Independent Schools, the Connecticut Association of Independent Schools, the Secondary School Admission Test Board, and the Council for Religion in Independent Schools.

ACADEMIC PROGRAMS

The academic requirements and curriculum of the School have been planned to provide preparation for entrance into colleges in the United States. For graduation, Canterbury requires 20 credits, including 4 credits in English; 3 each in foreign languages, mathematics, and history; 2 each in theology and science; and 1 in fine arts. Five major courses per semester are required of all students.

Elective courses are offered each semester; some semester courses offered in past years have been Asian studies, modern playwrights, women's studies, economics, Shakespeare, criminal justice, oceanography, anthropology, film, and theater workshop. Courses in religion are concerned with such topics as Christian doctrine, human relations, ethical living, the New Testament, and comparative religion.

Qualified students may take Advanced Placement courses in English language, English literature, AB and BC calculus, American history, European history, economics, biology, chemistry, studio arts, music theory, French language, French literature, Latin, Spanish language, Spanish literature, and statistics.

Each year is divided into five 5-week marking periods, for which students and parents receive grade reports. At the end of each semester, parents receive detailed grade reports accompanied by comments from faculty advisers. In Canterbury's grading system, D represents passing; C is a college-recommending grade; B is honors; B+, high honors; and A, highest honors.

Canterbury has a student-faculty ratio of 6:1, and the average recitation class contains 11 students. Generally, classes are grouped heterogeneously; in most subject areas, however, honors sections are offered.

Faculty members are readily available for individual assistance, as 80 percent of them live on campus. In Forms III and IV, students are required to attend supervised study halls during the school day unless they maintain an acceptable grade average.

During the spring semester, seniors with sound academic records who have been accepted at college may undertake independent-study projects. These senior projects involve students in vocational, educational, and social service programs of their choice.

Canterbury offers a program in English as a second language (ESL) to qualified students. Students in the ESL program are tested at the beginning of the year and are placed into an appropriate level of instruction. They are tested periodically to determine whether their progress warrants placement in a more advanced section. The goal of the ESL program is to channel students into the academic mainstream.

FACULTY AND ADVISERS

The full-time faculty, including administrators who teach, numbers 76. These 42 men and 34 women hold seventy-six baccalaureate degrees and forty-eight advanced degrees.

Thomas J. Sheehy III was appointed as Canterbury's fifth headmaster in December 1989 and assumed his duties in July 1990. He previously served for seven years as Headmaster of Old Westbury School of the Holy Child in New York. He is a graduate of Bowdoin College (B.A., 1969) and Pennsylvania State University (M.A., 1976). His concentrations were American history and classics, respectively. Mr. Sheehy and his wife, Betsy, live on campus with 1 of their 4 children.

Each faculty member advises a group of 6 to 8 students. The School retains a counselor, and the services of local psychologists and physicians are available. Two registered nurses supervise the infirmary, a local doctor is on call, and the facilities of the New Milford Hospital are available. A resident chaplain is appointed by the Archbishop of Hartford, or, with his permission, by the Provincial of a Catholic order.

COLLEGE ADMISSION COUNSELING

Canterbury prepares students for college through individual conferences beginning in the Fifth Form. A full-time college counselor conducts at least two conferences during the senior year. All Fourth and Fifth Formers take the PSAT in the fall and meet with the college counselor in late spring. More than 100 college admissions officers come to the School each fall for interviews and the annual college fair. The School works with each student in assembling an intelligent choice of colleges to which to apply.

Of the 110 members of Canterbury's 2008 graduating class, 100 percent were accepted by colleges. They are attending U.S. colleges and universities, including Boston College, Colby, Cornell, Dartmouth, Georgetown, Holy Cross, the U.S. Military Academy, and the Universities of Notre Dame and Pennsylvania.

STUDENT BODY AND CONDUCT

In 2008–09, 350 students were enrolled; 245 students were boarding, and 105 were day students.

Approximately two thirds of the students are from Connecticut and New York; the remainder come from eighteen other states and many other countries, including Bermuda, Canada, France, Germany, Hong Kong, Jamaica, Japan, Korea, Spain, Taiwan, and Thailand.

Students at Canterbury are expected to follow the code of conduct specifically outlined in the *Student-Parent Handbook.* Offenses are handled by the Dean of Students in most cases, but when a breach of proper conduct may lead to a student's dismissal, an ad hoc disciplinary committee composed of students and faculty members is convened to recommend a course of action to the Headmaster.

ACADEMIC FACILITIES

Nelson Hume Hall (1967) houses ten classrooms, two biology labs, a chemistry lab, a physics lab, a new science lecture room, and the 400-seat Maguire Auditorium. The Hume Music Center and classrooms were renovated in September 2008. The Old Schoolhouse (1938), which concluded a $2-million renovation in 1998, contains fifteen classrooms and seminar and tutorial rooms. Robert Markey Steele Hall (1983) houses the administrative offices, the dining room, a snack bar, a ninety-eight-seat auditorium, and the 20,000-volume David Casey Copley Library, which includes two computer rooms equipped with Macintosh and IBM computers, a study center, and an audiovisual room. Steel Hall is currently under renovation and, when completed, will include a new admission suite, new dining facilities, new administrative offices, and the library will be expanded. The Duffy Art Center is located in Duffy House. A choral facility was completed in 2001.

BOARDING AND GENERAL FACILITIES

Students and faculty members reside in Carter House (1926), Duffy House (1928), Sheehan House (1937), Ingleside House (1950), Havemeyer House (1964), Carmody House (1968), and Hickory Hearth (1985). In August 2007 South House, a new girls' dormitory, opened for 32 upper form students. Internet access is available in dormitory common areas and classrooms. The Dean of Students assigns all students to rooms, accommodating parent requests when feasible. Supplementary facilities on the campus include the Health Center, the Study Center, the snack bar, and the School store.

ATHLETICS

The School regards athletics as an integral part of student life. All students participate in one of the many sports offered. Students may compete on any of three levels in most sports. The program is designed to accommodate players of various ages, sizes, and abilities in competition with boys and girls of other western New England schools.

In September 2008 the William Higgins Aquatic Center opened. This $8-million facility houses an eight-lane Olympic-size pool built for speed and used for competitive diving. The Alumni Memorial Gymnasium houses a basketball court, wrestling rooms, squash courts, two weight rooms, a training room, an equipment room, a swimming pool, and locker room facilities. A $4-million annex was completed in 1999; additions include five international squash courts, a weight room, an aerobic/fitness room, locker rooms, and a training room. The Field House contains three courts that can be used for basketball, tennis, and volleyball. The Draddy Arena provides artificial ice for the School hockey program, local hockey leagues, and figure-skating instruction. Nine playing fields and six tennis courts offer ample space for outdoor practices.

EXTRACURRICULAR OPPORTUNITIES

The Student Government, composed of elected student and faculty representatives, forms a liaison between the student body and the administration. Senior proctors in the dormitories assist the dorm faculty.

Among the nonathletic activities are the Dramatic Society, which performs two shows a year; the monthly newspaper *(The Tabard);* the yearbook *(Cantuarian);* and the literary magazine *(Carillon).* There are also several clubs and groups in which students may participate, including Environmental Club, Outdoors Club, Women of Canterbury, Canterbury Blue, Chorale, and Admissions Tour Guides. For those interested in community service, there is work in a home for senior citizens, a swimming program for the mentally handicapped, and a children's day-care center. Eighty-five percent of Canterbury's students volunteer for community service.

Movies, dances, and field trips supplement Canterbury's regular program. On-campus events include a concert series, lectures, dramatic productions, the Spring Musical, Parents' Weekends, Homecoming, and Alumni Day.

DAILY LIFE

A student's day begins with breakfast, served from 7 to 7:45 a.m. Classes consist of seven 45-minute periods during the School day. Extra-help sessions are scheduled four mornings a week and can be scheduled at other times. The kitchen staff serves a cafeteria luncheon at noon. Following afternoon classes, athletic practices run from 3 to 5:15. A family-style dinner is served on Thursday; on the other nights of the week, a less formal cafeteria-style meal is served. There is an optional Mass each day at 5:45. Each evening, except Saturday, the students study in their rooms or in the Copley Library from 7:30 to 9:30. Faculty members in the dormitory supervise evening study hours, ensuring that students work independently. Lights are turned out at 11 p.m.

WEEKEND LIFE

The weekend begins after a student's last academic or athletics commitment on Saturday and ends at 7:30 p.m. on Sunday. Fifth and Sixth Formers are allowed two free weekends per semester. Third and Fourth Formers are allowed one weekend per semester. Third, Fourth, and Fifth Formers are allowed four Saturday overnights away from the campus; Sixth Formers are permitted six. College visits are also allowed for Sixth Formers, who are permitted two absences from school for this purpose in their Sixth Form year.

Visitors are welcome in the common rooms of the dormitories at the discretion of the dorm parents. Both boarders and day students are encouraged to take part in a variety of weekend activities on Saturday night and Sunday afternoon. Activities range from dances and movies to cultural trips and shopping ventures. Students are also given permission to walk into New Milford for a late-afternoon dinner on Saturday or to see a movie and shop on Sunday. Day students participate in all weekend activities.

COSTS AND FINANCIAL AID

In 2008–09, tuition at Canterbury was $39,000 for boarding students and $31,000 for day students. Tuition insurance and tuition payment plans are available.

In 2008, 41 percent of students received financial aid. Each scholarship is renewable yearly as the student proves he or she is deserving of aid. The criteria of the School and Student Service for Financial Aid are used to determine need, the sole basis for granting student aid.

ADMISSIONS INFORMATION

Canterbury seeks students who can compete academically at the college-preparatory level, will contribute their talents and abilities to the school community, and will participate in school activities. Applicants must submit SSAT scores, a transcript and reference from their former school, and letters of recommendation. In almost all cases, a personal interview is required. New students are accepted in all forms, with a limited number entering Form VI as postgraduates.

APPLICATION TIMETABLE

Canterbury welcomes early inquiry, in the fall if possible. Campus tours are conducted six days a week by student guides, usually on the day of the interview, Monday through Friday from 7:45 a.m. to 2 p.m. and Saturday from 7:45 a.m. to noon. A nonrefundable fee of $50 ($100 for international students) is required with the student's application, which is due by January 31. On March 10, the School notifies prospective students of acceptance; it expects parents' replies by April 10.

Applications received after January 31 will be reviewed on a rolling basis as spaces are available.

ADMISSIONS CORRESPONDENCE

Keith R. Holton, Director of Admission
Canterbury School
101 Aspetuck Avenue
New Milford, Connecticut 06776
Phone: 860-210-3832
Fax: 860-350-1120
E-mail: admissions@cbury.org
Web site: http://www.cbury.org

THE CASCADILLA SCHOOL

Ithaca, New York

Type: Coeducational boarding and day college-preparatory school
Grades: 9–12, postgraduate year
Enrollment: 60
Head of School: Patricia A. Kendall, Headmistress

THE SCHOOL

The Cascadilla School was founded in 1870 as a preparatory school for Cornell University. In 1939, it was reorganized as a nonprofit corporation under a Board of Trustees and granted an absolute charter by the Board of Regents of the State of New York.

The philosophy of education at Cascadilla is to provide a flexible, accelerated program within which each individual can achieve his or her goals in preparation for a successful college career. This learning experience emphasizes the steady development of an adult viewpoint and a mature approach to life.

The School is located in the heart of the Finger Lakes region in Ithaca, a city of 50,000 people, 20,000 of whom are college and university students. This scenic college town provides many cultural activities as well as athletics events. The School is located on the edge of the Cornell University campus, and students are encouraged to take advantage of the community's outstanding offerings, which include restaurants, shops, theater, and recreational facilities. There is direct air and bus service from New York City and other major U.S. cities.

The Cascadilla School is run by a 5-member Board of Trustees that is drawn from the business and professional community. Patricia A. Kendall is currently President of the Board and also Headmistress.

The School is privately endowed and nondenominational and has assets of approximately $1.2 million. Tuition charges provide more than 90 percent of its funding, and gifts from alumni and friends make up the remainder.

The Cascadilla School is registered with the New York State Board of Regents.

ACADEMIC PROGRAMS

The Cascadilla School offers a complete high school curriculum as well as an English as a second language program approved by the U.S. Immigration and Naturalization Service. The School's goal is to prepare students for college in an accelerated program. Full-unit high school courses are taught by the semester; the typical student completes between 7 and 8 units per year.

Twenty-three units are required for graduation, including 5 in English, 4 in social sciences, 3 in math, 3 in science, 1 in a language other than English, 1 in art and/or music, 2 in physical education, ½ in health, and 3½ in electives. All courses are taught on the New York State Regents level. In addition to taking Advanced Placement courses, seniors may enroll in actual college course work at Cornell, Ithaca College, or Tompkins Cortland Community College.

Extra help and supervised study are available in the afternoon until 5 p.m. The library and the laboratories are open until then. No evening study hall is required unless a student's academic performance falls below acceptable standards.

All class grouping is heterogeneous. Class size averages 8 students, and the student-teacher ratio is 6:1.

The Cascadilla School uses a numerical grading system that runs from 0 to 100, with 70 the minimum passing grade and 75 the start of college-recommending grades. Reports, with individual comments, are sent home monthly; more frequent reports are developed in special situations.

Certain reading and writing skills are required for entrance into English III. A three-level skills program is used for students who do not meet these requirements.

The Cascadilla School is proud to have more than seventy years of experience in providing a high-quality intensive English as a second language program. Cascadilla offers classes in reading, conversation, grammar, and writing at all levels of language ability. Students are enrolled in daily 1-hour-long classes and offered an optional elective course designed to prepare them for the Test of English as a Foreign Language (TOEFL).

Cascadilla offers three levels of study: beginning, intermediate, and advanced. Classroom instruction by teachers who are experienced in all areas of language education ensures that students make steady progress to the next level. The key to the success of Cascadilla School's ESL program is a curriculum that meets the individual needs of each student; classes average 5 students. In addition, students are assisted in their process of application to American universities and colleges.

FACULTY AND ADVISERS

The Cascadilla School has 9 full-time and 6 part-time teachers. All have bachelor's degrees, and 14 have master's degrees. The small size and personal nature of the School make every teacher an adviser. An attempt is made to make time in the school day for personal contact outside of regularly scheduled classes.

There is very little turnover in the full-time staff. The part-time staff is drawn from the Cornell and Ithaca college communities and changes as courses demand.

The Headmistress' academic background includes a B.S. degree from Syracuse University, an M.S. degree from Nazareth College, and an administrative degree in education from the State University of New York at Cortland. Mrs. Kendall brings thirty-eight years of experience in education to Cascadilla School.

COLLEGE ADMISSION COUNSELING

Planning for college begins almost as soon as a student enters Cascadilla. The School has entered a partnership with Kaplan Educational Centers, through which Cascadilla students are provided preparation for the SAT exams on campus. Kaplan tailors its SAT preparation program to meet the needs of Cascadilla students. A section of the library is devoted to college catalogs and career information. College visits are encouraged, and the School provides transportation for them. Involvement with the Cornell University community provides valuable stimulation for most Cascadilla students.

Students in the class of 2008 ranged in SAT composite math and verbal scores from 1150 to 1500. The average combined score for graduating seniors was 1150 or better. Approximately one third of the graduating seniors also took the ACT.

The School averages between 17 and 20 graduates per year. Ninety-eight percent go on to further their education, and about 98 percent attend four-year colleges. Recent graduates are attending Cornell, Emory, NYU, various SUNY colleges and universities, and the Universities of Colorado, Georgia, Illinois, and Michigan.

STUDENT BODY AND CONDUCT

The Cascadilla School attracts students from a wide geographic area. In 2008–09, students came from three states and eight other countries. The School has room for 25 boarders; day students and adult ESL students make up the rest of the School population. Seventy percent of the students are juniors, seniors, and postgraduates; unlike many private schools, Cascadilla is interested primarily in students who are planning to be at the School for one or two years. The accelerated program works best when the students have the emotional maturity to establish goals and work toward them. Most freshmen and sophomores are day students.

ACADEMIC FACILITIES

The classroom building was opened in 1880. It contains eight classrooms, a science laboratory, a language laboratory, a computer room with IBM-compatible computers, and a library of nearly 9,000 volumes.

Students who are interested in music or the visual arts may use the programs and facilities of Cornell University or Ithaca College.

BOARDING AND GENERAL FACILITIES

The two dormitories are designed to bring together the elements of a family environment, college life, and apartment living. Single and double rooms are available, each with its own refrigerator; each dormitory has a snack kitchen and a TV lounge. Supervision is provided by dorm parents, and college students also live in the dorms. The School tries to create a living environment that reinforces its academic programs.

The Cascadilla School has no formal dining facilities of its own; therefore, most students use the dorm facilities for breakfast and take the fourteen-meal option of the Cornell University Meal Plan for lunch and dinner, although a twenty-one-meal option is available. This daily exposure to the university helps them to become familiar with its programs and facilities.

ATHLETICS

Cascadilla's physical education program offers bowling, cross-country skiing, rowing, and sailboarding. Students are also encouraged to join the YMCA, which includes the weight room and aerobics, swimming, and racquetball facilities. The Cascadilla School does not have an interscholastic athletic program. Crew is offered through the Cascadilla Boat Club (a nonprofit educational organization).

EXTRACURRICULAR OPPORTUNITIES

Most extracurricular opportunities are available through the university and the community. The area is rich in cultural events that range from lectures and plays to musical performances of all types.

DAILY LIFE

Most students have 6 hours of academic course work between 9 a.m. and 4 p.m. All students and faculty members share a common lunch period. The afternoon program varies from day to day and may include physical education; special courses, such as SAT preparation through Kaplan, photography, drawing, and driver's education; and opportunities to get extra help or tutoring. After dinner, evenings typically involve study, recreation, and a movie or TV.

WEEKEND LIFE

The School sponsors movies and occasional parties. There may also be ski trips that include transportation, instruction, and rental of equipment. In addition, as is true of extracurricular activities during the week, students may take advantage of the wide range of opportunities at Cornell and other local schools and colleges.

SUMMER PROGRAMS

The Cascadilla School has offered a six-week summer session for the last seventy-six years. The program attracts both students who are interested in repeating courses and students hoping to shorten the length of time necessary to complete secondary school graduation requirements. Students are enrolled in advanced classes, repeat classes, and tutorials, as well as the driver's education course. A pamphlet is published that explains the program in detail.

COSTS AND FINANCIAL AID

Tuition, a double room, and board fees for the 2008–09 school year were $30,000. Additional charges are made for single rooms and for unusually heavy course loads.

The Cascadilla School is interested in attracting good students from all cultures and socioeconomic groups. Last year, 40 percent of the School's students received some type of financial aid or scholarship, averaging $1000 per student per semester. There are also several opportunities for part-time work at the School.

ADMISSIONS INFORMATION

The Cascadilla School is looking for students who are ready to put their high school program together and prepare for college. The SSAT is not required. The School, however, seeks students with academic potential, if not achievement. An admission interview is required for all U.S. applicants, and a $50 application fee is required of all U.S. applicants. An application fee is also required of international applicants.

The Cascadilla School admits students of any race, color, and national or ethnic origin to all the rights, privileges, programs, and activities generally accorded or made available to students at the School. It does not discriminate on the basis of race, color, or national and ethnic origin in administration of its educational policies, admissions policies, and scholarship, athletic, and other School-administered programs.

APPLICATION TIMETABLE

The Cascadilla School has a rolling admission process; however, the recommended application deadlines are January 15, June 30, and September 1, depending on the term in which a student wishes to begin. A $5000 deposit is required upon acceptance. It is strongly suggested that applications be submitted by June 1 for September entrance, as the amount of dormitory space is extremely limited.

ADMISSIONS CORRESPONDENCE

Patricia A. Kendall, Headmistress
The Cascadilla School
116 Summit Street
Ithaca, New York 14850
Phone: 607-272-3110
Fax: 607-272-0747
E-mail: admissions@cascadillaschool.org
Website: http://www.cascadillaschool.org/

CHESHIRE ACADEMY

Cheshire, Connecticut

Type: Coeducational boarding (grades 9–12 plus postgraduate year) and day (grades 6–12 plus postgraduate year) college-preparatory school
Grades: Middle School, 6–8; Upper School, 9–12; postgraduate year
Enrollment: School total: 372; Middle School: 48; Upper School: 324
Interim Heads of School: Dr. Sandra Wirth, Mr. Jay Goulart

THE SCHOOL

Cheshire Academy was founded in 1794 as the Episcopal Academy of Connecticut, a coeducational community school. While the school has gone through several phases in its history, including periods as a boys' school and military academy, Cheshire returned to coeducation in 1969 and now focuses on a student-centered, leadership-based philosophy. Academically, the school's goal is to provide a well-rounded college-preparatory education with a global perspective. The 104-acre campus is located in a small-town setting, 15 miles northwest of New Haven.

Cheshire's Middle School, for grades 6 through 8, offers day students a comprehensive curriculum, athletic options, and leadership opportunities. While maintaining a program appropriate to the ages of its students, the Middle School is an integral and vibrant part of the life of the whole school community, and students who elect to "step up" to the Upper School often become community leaders in their high school careers. Facilities shared with the Upper School include the dining commons, field house, athletic fields, library and humanities building, science and technology center, and student center.

The Upper School features both day and boarding programs for students in grade 9 through a postgraduate year. A combination of academics, athletics, the arts, community service, leadership opportunities, a diverse environment, and a strong residential life program helps students contribute to the life of the school and discover passions and talents that will shape their futures as global thinkers.

Cheshire Academy is a nonprofit corporation directed by a board of trustees, assisted by a council of overseers, who meet several times each year.

Cheshire Academy is accredited by the New England Association of Schools and Colleges and approved by the Connecticut State Board of Education. Memberships are held in the National Association of Boarding Schools, the Connecticut Association of Independent Schools, the Council for the Advancement of Secondary Education, the East Rock Institute, the Educational Records Bureau, Independent School Management, the National Association of Independent Schools, and the Secondary School Admission Test Board.

ACADEMIC PROGRAMS

Cheshire's academic program is a traditional college-preparatory curriculum. The following are required for graduation: 4 credits in English, 3 credits in mathematics, 2 credits in foreign languages, 2 credits in laboratory science, 3 credits in history (1 in U.S. history), 1 credit in art or music, 1 credit in reading, and 2 credits in electives. Most students take 4 mathematics, 3–4 foreign language, and 3 laboratory science credits.

The Roxbury Academic Support Program offers a range of services dedicated to enabling students to enhance performance. These services include identifying and communicating students' needs through regularly scheduled meetings with their classroom teachers, providing individual and group student support, coaching for writing and math, supporting the college search process, and coordinating academic coaching in specific subjects. Roxbury clearly demonstrates Cheshire Academy's understanding of the spectrum of students' learning styles and the school's commitment to discovering the potential in each student. Although Roxbury delivers an array of services, the program is best known for its individual and small-group instruction. These sessions provide the structure, support, and strategies that students with different learning styles need in a traditional school setting. Roxbury's services are designed and implemented based on the needs of the student. Roxbury sessions are supplements to the students' regular course work.

The grading system uses A to F designations with pluses and minuses. Each student also receives an effort grade, ranging from 1 to 5. The school year is divided into semesters, with examinations at the end of each semester. Term reports are sent home six times a year.

Class size averages 12. The overall student-teacher ratio is 7:1. The average course load is five academic subjects (some elective courses are ten weeks in length, while others extend for the entire year). Students may apply for honors and Advanced Placement courses as well as for independent study projects. Advanced Placement courses are available in the arts, English, history, languages, mathematics, and science.

FACULTY AND ADVISERS

The faculty and administration are composed of 86 members, including 48 women and 38 men. Fifty-four members hold master's degrees.

The Academy makes every effort to employ a diverse group of men and women who truly love to teach and who appreciate the opportunity to serve as counselors and advisers to young people. Faculty members play a vital role in all phases of the Academy, contributing their own special talents toward the goals of caring for each student and encouraging that student to grow personally and intellectually. Most faculty members serve as advisers for a group of 8 students and as liaisons between family and school.

COLLEGE ADMISSION COUNSELING

A full-time college counseling team helps students in the selection of appropriate colleges and universities. More than 150 college representatives visit the campus each year to interview interested students. In 2008, 100 percent of the graduates entered college, attending such institutions as Bates, Bentley, Boston College, Carnegie Mellon, Purdue, Smith, the University of Michigan, and Wheaton.

STUDENT BODY AND CONDUCT

In 2008–09, the student body comprised 137 boarding boys, 67 boarding girls, 62 Upper School day boys, and 58 Upper School day girls, as follows: 55 in grade 9, 78 in grade 10, 93 in grade 11, 85 in grade 12, and 13 in a postgraduate year. Boarding students represented fifteen states and twenty-one countries. The Middle School enrolled 48 day students in grades 6–8.

Discipline at Cheshire Academy provides a suitable environment for the academic and social growth of the individual and the Cheshire Academy community in general. This basic philosophy encourages the development of a sense of self-discipline and responsibility in each student. All Cheshire Academy students are expected to commit to an Honor Code that demonstrates concern for themselves and others. Offenses are handled by a faculty-student Citizenship Committee.

Student leadership groups include the Student Proctors, who are nominated by the previous year's Proctors and selected by faculty members, and the Student Council, which is composed of the 4 officers from each class plus the Proctors.

ACADEMIC FACILITIES

The Humanities Building houses classrooms for English and history classes, the Roxbury Academic Support Program, and the Cheshire Academy Library. Bronson Hall houses the music department. The John J. White '38 Science and Technology Center features eight classrooms, four laboratories, faculty offices, seminar rooms, and a 216-seat lecture hall. In addition to its athletic facilities, the Arthur N. Sheriff Field House also has classroom wings for foreign languages and the fine arts studios. The Middle School building houses classrooms and community areas for grades 6–8.

BOARDING AND GENERAL FACILITIES

The Academy has six dormitories. Most of the faculty members live on campus in dormitories or single-dwelling homes. All meals are served in the Gideon Welles Dining Commons. Breakfast and dinner are served cafeteria-style, and, at noon, the entire school gathers for lunch.

The Richmond Building Health Center is staffed by 2 nurses throughout the day. Arrangements are made for students who need to stay in the health center overnight. A local physician is on call for visits to the school when needed. Cheshire is located near several outstanding medical facilities should students need hospital care.

The Charles Harwood Student Center's features include meeting rooms for clubs, practice rooms for music and drama, a game room, a snack bar, an atrium, and the school bookstore. The top floor has a large hall designed for school dances and receptions.

ATHLETICS

The tradition of athletics is integral to the life of Cheshire Academy. With programs such as baseball, basketball, cross-country, fencing, field hockey, football, golf, lacrosse, soccer, softball, swimming, tennis, track, Ultimate Frisbee, volleyball, and wrestling, each student is encouraged to participate for a minimum of one season, although many choose to play during all three. For those who want to explore a new sport, the beginning and junior varsity teams provide a chance to acquire basic skills, make new friends, and learn about sportsmanship. Cheshire Academy's other afternoon programs introduce new interests and lifelong passions that emphasize teamwork, goal setting, and self-confidence. Cheshire's community has produced a wide range of internationally recognized athletes, musicians, actors, novelists, and playwrights.

EXTRACURRICULAR OPPORTUNITIES

Extracurricular activities are as varied as student interests and are often organized in response to student requests. The Proctors, Student Council, Peer Counselors, and the National Honor Society provide student leadership. Other organizations include the Diversity Club, Key Club, Earth Club, Chess Club, Model U.N., and two computer clubs. A literary magazine and new multimedia clubs provide practical experience in writing, editing, photography, and digital imaging.

DAILY LIFE

Classes are held five days a week—with shorter classes on Wednesday to allow for midweek athletics contests—plus several Saturdays throughout the year. The day begins with breakfast between 7 and 7:30 a.m. An extra help period runs from 7:35 to 7:55, homeroom/morning assembly is held from 8 to 8:15, and classes begin at 8:20. Classes end at 2:55 p.m., and afternoon extra help is from 3 to 3:30. Afternoon activities are from 3:30 to 5:30. Dinner is from 5:30 to 7, followed by study hall from 8 to 10. Dorm meetings are held at 10, and lights out is at 10:30 and 11.

WEEKEND LIFE

Boarding students may have weekend privileges after the first week of school, with the permission of their parents, the dormitory faculty, and the dean. Many on-campus activities are offered, and students may attend concerts, plays, and athletic contests in such cities as Boston and New York. Nearby New Haven offers many of the advantages of a university town. Day students are encouraged to participate in weekend activities.

COSTS AND FINANCIAL AID

Tuition at Cheshire Academy in 2008–09 was $41,740 for boarding students and $30,345 for day students in the Upper School. Middle School tuition was $26,250. Tuition may be paid in full before the school year begins or in two installments, one half by August 1 and the second half by December 1.

Financial aid is awarded on the basis of financial need, as determined by the School and Student Service for Financial Aid and a review by the Academy's Financial Aid Committee. Applications must be submitted each year for review. Thirty percent of the students receive financial aid. Though more than $2 million in financial aid was awarded in 2008–09, the financial aid fund is limited and applicants are urged to apply as early as possible.

ADMISSIONS INFORMATION

Cheshire Academy accepts young men and women who can contribute to, as well as benefit from, life at Cheshire. A visit to the school is required of all applicants living in the United States. Acceptance of a candidate is based on the previous school record, recommendations of teachers, and the candidate's potential, as indicated by his or her performance on standardized tests, including the ISEE or the SSAT. Applicants to the senior and postgraduate years should submit scores from the PSAT or the SAT.

APPLICATION TIMETABLE

Initial inquiries are welcome at any time. Campus tours are coordinated with the interview, from 8:30 to 2:30 on weekdays. Saturday appointments may be arranged as needed.

The Academy also has a rolling admissions policy, which begins in March. Parents are allowed one month to reply to an acceptance received by April 15. They must reply within two weeks to an acceptance received between April 15 and June 30 and within one week after June 30. If dormitory and class space are available, a well-qualified candidate may be admitted on a very selective basis after the term has begun.

ADMISSIONS CORRESPONDENCE

Jane Hanrahan
Associate Director of Admission
Cheshire Academy
Cheshire, Connecticut 06410
Phone: 203-439-7277
Fax: 203-250-7209
E-mail: jane.hanrahan@cheshireacademy.org
Web site: http://www.cheshireacademy.org

CHOATE ROSEMARY HALL

Wallingford, Connecticut

Type: Coeducational boarding and day college-preparatory school
Grades: 9–12, postgraduate year (Forms III–VI): Third Form, 9; Fourth Form, 10; Fifth Form, 11; Sixth Form, 12, postgraduate year
Enrollment: 840 on campus; 10 abroad
Head of School: Edward J. Shanahan, Ph.D., Headmaster

THE SCHOOL

Choate Rosemary Hall's rigorous academic program, through its small classes, both challenges and supports its students. This approach is the root of the school's reputation for academic excellence. At Choate, talented students and teachers from diverse backgrounds live and learn together creatively. Community spirit builds from this richness of difference in persons, cultures, and traditions to prepare students to assume leadership positions in today's global community.

The school's hope for its graduates is that they go forth from a community that valued each of them for particular talents and enthusiasms, affirmed the importance of personal integrity and a sense of self-worth, inspired and nourished joy in learning and love of truth, and provided the intellectual stimulation that generates independent thought, confident expression, and worthwhile commitments. Ideally, graduates will embody the five principles that both historically and currently capture the essence of Choate Rosemary Hall: academic excellence, character, community, physical and spiritual well-being, and giving back.

Choate Rosemary Hall was established through the merger of Rosemary Hall, a girls' school founded by Caroline Ruutz-Rees in 1890 in Wallingford, Connecticut, and The Choate School, a boys' school founded by Judge William Choate in 1896 in the same town. In 1971, the trustees of each school announced their coordination, and, in 1974, the two boards joined to form The Choate Rosemary Hall Foundation, Inc. Since 1977, the school has functioned as a single coeducational institution. The 450-acre campus is 12 miles north of New Haven, 20 miles south of Hartford, and a 2-hour drive from Boston and New York City.

The school is governed by a Board of Trustees, most of whose 30 members are alumni. The endowment is currently valued at $261 million.

Choate Rosemary Hall is accredited by the New England Association of Schools and Colleges. It holds memberships in the National Association of Independent Schools, the Connecticut Association of Independent Schools, A Better Chance, the Secondary School Admission Test Board, and the School Scholarship Service.

ACADEMIC PROGRAMS

A student's schedule for the three-term academic year is planned individually. The student chooses from more than 240 courses with the help of the academic adviser, the Dean, and college counselors. Course levels are chosen according to academic preparedness, ability, and talent in an academic area, not necessarily by age or grade level.

Students are expected to carry 15 course credits per year or five courses per term. To receive a diploma, a four-year student must have a total of 60 course credits, including 4 years of English (one course each term at Choate); algebra I, geometry, algebra II, and 14 terms in secondary school of a quantitative course; 1 year of a laboratory course in physical science, either physics or chemistry; and 1 year of a laboratory course in biology; 1 year of world history, 1 year of U.S. history, 1 term of philosophy or religion, and 1 term in contemporary global studies; 3 years (through the 300 or 350 level) of a diploma language, namely Chinese, French, Latin, or Spanish; 3 terms of athletics or 2 terms of athletics and 1 term of an alternate activity per term; and 3 terms of arts from two areas: music, visual arts, or theater.

Each of the six academic departments offers courses that prepare students for Advanced Placement work. Special features are a nationally ranked economics program; a science research program encompassing university-based lab experience; an arts concentration program; full integration of technology into the academic curriculum; a two-term creative writing seminar for qualified seniors; and the Capstone Program, an opportunity for talented seniors to explore an area of the curriculum in depth.

A number of opportunities are available for study abroad during the academic year, including immersion programs in China, France, and Spain; term-long study in Rome; and summer programs in China, France, and Spain.

The average class size is 12. Students are graded six times a year on an A–F scale; D– is the lowest passing grade. Written comments by teachers and advisers are sent home at the end of each trimester.

FACULTY AND ADVISERS

There are 64 men and 46 women on the teaching faculty, 70 percent of whom hold advanced degrees. Each serves as academic, athletic, and personal adviser to 8 to 10 students. Most also coach and are involved in extracurricular pursuits. Choate Rosemary Hall supports the same breadth in its faculty members as in its students.

Edward J. Shanahan (St. Joseph's College, 1965; M.A., Fordham University, 1968; Ph.D., University of Wisconsin, 1982), Headmaster, came to the school in 1991 after nine years as Dean of the College at Dartmouth.

COLLEGE ADMISSION COUNSELING

College counseling is facilitated by a director and 6 associates and generally begins in the winter for the Fourth Form, when students receive assistance in registering for Subject Tests. The counselors work closely with students beginning in winter of the Fifth Form year, conduct interviews with them and their parents, accompany them to college fairs, and help them prepare for formal interviews with college representatives, 200 of whom visit the campus each year. In the winter, juniors attend mock interviews held by college admissions officials who visit the school, and their parents are invited to the campus for a weekend of programs with the College Counseling Office and various university admission officers about the process of applying to college.

From 2004 through 2008, the most popular college choices included Boston University (25), Brown (29), Columbia (21), Cornell (29), Georgetown (44), George Washington (25), Harvard (25), Middlebury (21), NYU (26), Tufts (28), University of Pennsylvania (20), Washington (St. Louis) (20), and Yale (30).

STUDENT BODY AND CONDUCT

In 2008–09, the school had 610 boarders and 240 day students from forty-one states and thirty-three countries.

The Student Council, which is composed of elected members of each form, provides a forum in which students can address school-related topics and plans, and it conducts and oversees social events and community matters.

Students are expected to follow school rules. Violations of the basic honor code or major school rules, or the accumulation of a number of violations of other rules, generally lead to suspension or dismissal. Rule violations are investigated by the Judicial Committee—a committee of elected students, deans, and an appointed faculty member—which makes recommendations to the Dean of Students.

ACADEMIC FACILITIES

Most campus academic facilities are the result of generous gifts from alumni and parents. The Carl C. Icahn Center for Science (1989), a $14-million, three-story building designed by I. M. Pei, includes twenty-two classrooms and laboratories, a 150-seat auditorium, and a conservatory. Another I. M. Pei building, the Paul Mellon Arts Center (1971), houses two theaters, a recital hall, music classrooms and practice rooms, art studios, dance and film facilities, offices, and an art gallery. All academic buildings and meeting spaces are part of Choate's wireless network.

The Andrew Mellon Library, which opened in 1926, was renovated in 2003 to integrate technological innovations with traditional library resources. The collection includes more than 68,000 titles, a Web-accessible catalog and reference collection, a wireless network, more than 150 magazine subscriptions, English- and foreign-language newspapers, and thousands of reels of microfilm, videos, DVDs, and sound recordings. Additional electronic resources include a wide variety of databases and indexes that are also available via MEL—the virtual branch of the Mellon Library. Special collections include those pertaining to Adlai Stevenson '18 and John F. Kennedy '35, along with the Rare Book, Thomas Hardy, and the Haffenreffer Autograph Collections and the school's extensive archives.

The Paul Mellon Humanities Center houses a computer center and a digital video production studio. Other facilities provide a total of forty-three classrooms as well as several computer centers with 120 fully networked workstations. All student rooms have wireless access to the Internet.

BOARDING AND GENERAL FACILITIES

Resident faculty members, their families, and Sixth Form house prefects live and work with small groups of students in residential settings that house as few as 7 students or as many as 75. Larger dormitories are divided into smaller sections, with 1 faculty member advising approximately 8–10 students to ensure feelings of community and warmth. Some students live in double rooms; others choose singles. Trained student peer counselors are an intrinsic part of the support system for students. Two new dormitories that house 80 students and eight faculty families opened in fall 2008.

The Pratt Health Center is open all day every day. Registered nurses are on duty 24 hours a day; the school physician lives on campus and is always on call.

The Student Activities Center houses the School Store and Post Office and has a cyber cafe, games, large-screen TVs, and spaces for parties and dances.

ATHLETICS

There is an appropriate level of athletics for every student. Some athletes come from very competitive programs and want to hone their skills with dedicated coaches and a serious sports program. Other students take advantage of the breadth of offerings and begin a new sport at the introductory level. The physical education and athletic program emphasizes acquiring lifetime skills, shaping positive attitudes about oneself as an individual and as a contributing member of a group, and developing a sense of honesty and fair play. All students participate in class-day or after-school sports each term.

There are eighty-one varsity, JV, and third-level interscholastic teams in most sports, as well as intramural teams. The program also includes all major sports and such activities as scuba, CPR, weight training, and fitness and conditioning.

The Johnson Athletic Center includes three basketball courts, three volleyball courts, ten international squash courts, a wrestling room, team weight rooms, and a suspended 1⁄10-mile track. The Edward A. Fox '54 Fitness Pavillion contains a fully equipped fitness center, a sports medicine suite, and a dance studio as well as the school's Athletics Hall of Fame. There are twenty-two outdoor tennis courts at the Hunt Tennis Center, thirteen athletic fields, a cross-country course, hockey arena, boathouse, an Olympic-size swimming pool, and the Bruce '45 and Lueza Gelb Track (2008). Students also use a nearby golf course and a riding stable.

EXTRACURRICULAR OPPORTUNITIES

The school has more than sixty extracurricular activities, clubs, and organizations through which students may pursue special interests that range from astrophysics to conservation and from various publications to debating. Because each group requires club officers, leadership positions abound. Students are required to commit 30 hours to community service. The school's proximity to major cities provides access to cultural events, museums, and exhibits.

DAILY LIFE

Classes are held five days per week and on seven Saturdays. They are scheduled in seven 50-minute periods between 8 a.m. and 2:50 p.m. four days per week; on Wednesdays and Saturdays, classes are held in four 50-minute periods and the academic day ends at 12:30. The afternoon sports program follows. Late afternoon provides time for study or extracurricular activities, and dinner is served between 5:15 and 7:15 p.m.

Students return to their dorm by 7:30 for a 1½-hour study time but may sign out to use the library or other academic facilities. There is a break from 9 to 9:45, with final dorm check-in at 9:30. There is a second study period from 9:45 to 10:30 p.m.

WEEKEND LIFE

Weekend social and recreational events and activities, in addition to those already scheduled at the Arts Center or by student organizations, are planned for all students. Every weekend there are dances, movies, and excursions to New York, Boston, or other nearby towns and cities. There are such seasonal activities as Harvest Fest and Spring Fest, and shuttle vans provide transportation to local ski areas, shopping, theaters, and sports venues.

SUMMER PROGRAMS

The five-week summer session is designed primarily for students of day schools who are seeking enrichment of skills-oriented courses that are not offered in their home schools. Summer Programs include the Writing Project, John F. Kennedy Institute of Government, English Language Institute, and Connecticut Scholars Program (a public/private collaboration). Also offered are enrichment programs for middle school students, including a mathematics/science institute for girls who have completed grades 6–8 and the Young Writers Workshop. Classroom work is supplemented by such activities as lecture series, field trips, and sports. About 600 boys and girls attend. A five-week Arts Conservatory program is also offered, with options in theater, playwriting, and the visual arts.

The school also sponsors study trips to China, France, and Spain. Requests for information should be sent to Choate Summer Programs, 333 Christian Street, Wallingford, Connecticut 06492.

COSTS AND FINANCIAL AID

For 2008–09, the total cost for boarders was $41,520 and for day students, $31,310. Books are extra. An optional laundry service is available at an additional cost. Financial aid and loans are available for students whose families qualify. Decisions are mailed March 10. In 2008–09, 33 percent of the students received financial aid totaling $7.5 million, with the average award amounting to 65 percent of tuition.

Choate Rosemary Hall seeks students of diverse geographic, economic, social, ethnic, and racial backgrounds. The SSAT is required of applicants for grades 9 and 10 and should be taken in December if possible. The median score for ninth and tenth graders is at the 85th percentile. Most entering students test between the 80th and 99th percentiles. The PSAT/SAT is required for candidates for grades 11 and 12 and postgraduates. The TOEFL is suggested for those whose native language is not English. Applicants should be motivated achievers in their schools, attaining at least a B average on schoolwork.

For September 2008 entry, there were 1,649 final applications. The 2008–09 total enrollment of 850 included 265 new on-campus students. Students are accepted at all levels.

APPLICATION TIMETABLE

Students may submit the Pre-Interview Information Form online at the school's Web site at any time. A personal interview is required, preferably in the fall prior to the year of proposed enrollment. A final application—also submitted online—including recommendations, a transcript, and a $50 nonrefundable fee ($100 for international applicants), must be completed by January 10.

The Admission Office schedules appointments from 9 to 2, Monday through Friday, and 8 to 1 on selected Saturdays.

The Admission Committee reviews a student's records, recommendations from teachers and the principal, test results, extracurricular interests, and interview. If all materials have been completed by January 10, applicants are notified of the decision on March 10.

ADMISSIONS CORRESPONDENCE

Raymond M. Diffley III
Director of Admission
Choate Rosemary Hall
333 Christian Street
Wallingford, Connecticut 06492-3800
Phone: 203-697-2239
Fax: 203-697-2629
E-mail: admissions@choate.edu
Web site: http://www.choate.edu

CHRIST SCHOOL

Arden, North Carolina

Type: Boys' boarding and day college-preparatory school
Grades: 8–12
Enrollment: 225
Head of School: Paul M. Krieger, Headmaster

THE SCHOOL

Christ School was founded in 1900 by the Reverend and Mrs. Thomas Wetmore on the site of an old plantation called Struan. During its early years, the School educated the children of the region, but in the 1920s it evolved into an all-boys' boarding school.

Christ School is a college-preparatory school affiliated with the Episcopal Church. Its mission is to produce educated men of good character, prepared for both scholastic achievement in college and productive citizenship in adult society. The School achieves this mission through a fourfold process. First and most important, it challenges and encourages each student, in the nurturing environment of a close-knit campus, to develop academically to his maximum potential. Second, through competitive sports, student self-government, and a variety of extracurricular activities, Christ School helps each student develop his physical fitness and leadership skills and his respect for others regardless of their origins, cultures, or beliefs. Third, by involvement in the care of the campus, civic duty is learned, along with a sense of the dignity of honest labor. Finally, through religious instruction and regular participation in chapel activities, each student learns the sustaining value of faith and spiritual growth throughout his life.

Christ School is located on 500 acres of land outside the small town of Arden, in the Blue Ridge Mountains, 8 miles south of Asheville, North Carolina. The "land of the sky" abounds with lakes, golf courses, ski resorts, hiking trails, and white-water rivers. The School is located 10 minutes from the spectacular Blue Ridge Parkway, yet has easy access to cultural activities in Asheville, Atlanta, Charlotte, and Greenville.

A not-for-profit organization, the School is governed by a Board of Trustees. The 20 members meet quarterly.

All of the School's endowment, approximately $11 million, is in productive funds and is supplemented by an Annual Fund. There are approximately 2,100 living alumni who support the School both financially and through a variety of other efforts.

Christ School is accredited by the Southern Association of Independent Schools. It is a member of the National Association of Independent Schools, National Association of Episcopal Schools, North Carolina Association of Independent Schools, Secondary School Admission Test Board, College Board, and Episcopal Diocese of Western North Carolina.

ACADEMIC PROGRAMS

Preparing boys academically for college is Christ School's primary objective. The curriculum is designed to provide students with a firm foundation in both the academic subjects and the study skills they will need in college. The School's curriculum also stresses the knowledge and skills that will enable a student to become an informed and intelligent citizen of his community. The School has always believed that these objectives can best be fulfilled through a concentration in the traditional arts and sciences.

Small classes and individual attention are the keys to a boy's academic development. A structured program of independent and supervised study enables a student to better achieve his potential.

Requirements for graduation include the completion of 21 credits: English (4); mathematics (4); science (3); history (3); foreign language—Latin, French, or Spanish (2); fine arts (1); religious studies (.5); computers (.5); and electives (3). Electives include Advanced Placement courses in the arts, computer programming, English, foreign languages, history, mathematics, and science. General elective courses include choir, economics, government, history of Vietnam, journalism, marine biology, music of Western civilization, music practicum, music theory and composition, studio art I and II, and theater.

Most students carry a course load of five academic subjects, independent or supervised study, and a choice of extracurricular activities.

The average class size is 10–12 students; the student-faculty ratio is 5:1. Students are placed in classes on the basis of their achievement levels, their interests, and the requirements for graduation.

Christ School's Learning Resource Program offers academic support in English, math, and study skills within the context of a rigorous college-preparatory curriculum. The program serves those who can meet the challenges of a full academic schedule while benefiting from the program's supportive techniques.

FACULTY AND ADVISERS

The faculty consists of 43 full-time members, 23 with advanced degrees. Twenty-eight reside on campus.

Paul M. Krieger was appointed the twelfth Headmaster of Christ School in 2003. He had previously served as the school's Principal since August 2000. Before coming to Christ School, he served as Head of the Middle School at Montgomery Academy in Chester Springs, Pennsylvania. Following an extensive career in marketing, much of which was spent in the Eastern Mediterranean and the Middle East, he chose to leave the business field in 1989 for education. At the Hill School, in Pottstown, Pennsylvania, he served as Assistant Director of Development and Alumni Affairs and Assistant Director of Admissions, was Founder and Director of the Hill Sports Camp, and held the Knobloch Chair in Economics, teaching Advanced Placement courses. Mr. Krieger has a Bachelor of Arts degree from Gettysburg College and a Master of Education Leadership from Immaculata College.

The School seeks teachers who are dedicated to the spiritual, academic, and social well-being of students and who share the common interest in self-improvement that sets boys upon the path to maturity and manhood. A student's progress throughout his years at Christ School is monitored closely by the faculty. Each boy has an adviser for guidance in his academic and personal life at the School.

A strong relationship between the student and adviser is formed through meetings and frequent gatherings for meals and recreation. In addition, each new student is matched with an outstanding upperclassman as a Big Brother to further help the adjustment to boarding school life.

COLLEGE ADMISSION COUNSELING

In a student's sophomore, junior, and senior years, the Dean and College Counselor work with the student and his family to assist him in securing admission to the college most suited to his needs. In addition, college representatives visit the campus in the fall and winter to discuss college admission requirements and procedures with students.

Christ School graduated 38 seniors in 2008, all of whom were accepted at four-year colleges and universities. The School administered sixty Advanced Placement exams.

Graduates have been accepted at a variety of colleges and universities. Among them are the Air Force Academy, Art Institute of Boston, Brown, Clemson, Duke, Elon, Furman, George Washington, Georgia Tech, Macalester, Morehouse, Northeastern, Presbyterian, Rensselaer, SMU, Stanford, Wake Forest, Washington and Lee, Wheaton, William and Mary, Wofford, and the Universities of North Carolina at Chapel Hill and the South.

STUDENT BODY AND CONDUCT

Christ School has a boarding student population of 170 boarders and 55 day students. Seventeen states and eight countries are represented among the student body, and boys come from various religious backgrounds.

The responsibility for student life and conduct at Christ School is largely in the hands of the students themselves. A student council, composed of prefects appointed by the Headmaster and members elected by the various forms, makes recommendations to the Headmaster regarding discipline and other aspects of School life. Sixth Formers (twelfth graders) guide and help supervise various activities, such as house life and the self-help work program.

ACADEMIC FACILITIES

The academic facilities are housed mainly in Wetmore Hall, which contains classrooms, four science labs, a computer lab, and a music room. The Information & Media Center houses the main reading and research room, with a state-of-the-art computer center that links an in-house service with the Internet global community. The Pingree Fine Arts Auditorium was dedicated in 1992.

BOARDING AND GENERAL FACILITIES

Christ School students reside in five houses. Two boys are assigned to a room. Each house is supervised by prefects and proctors under the direction of a resident faculty master. All houses are fully equipped with computer networking capabilities. Students in grades 8 and 9 live separately from students in grades 10 through 12. A student center includes a game room, lounge, fireplace, snack shop, barbershop, bookstore, and forty-seat theater/TV room. Renovations of St. Joseph's chapel, which was built in 1907, were completed in 2006.

ATHLETICS

Physical development, sportsmanship, cooperation, and self-esteem are all fostered by organized athletics. The various levels in all team sports allow each boy to choose those activities that best meet his interests and competence.

On the School grounds are six hard-surfaced tennis courts, a football field, a baseball field, three soccer fields, an all-weather track, and a 3-acre lake that is used for kayaking, canoeing, fishing, and swimming. Indoor athletics facilities are housed in a modern field house containing a basketball court and three full-sized practice courts. The remodeled Memorial Gymnasium contains a wrestling gym, three racquetball courts, a new weight room, a training room, an equipment room, four locker rooms, and offices for coaches.

The School fields interscholastic teams in football, cross-country, soccer, basketball, wrestling, swimming, lacrosse, baseball, tennis, golf, and track. In lieu of athletics, students have the option to participate in the theater program, debate, an intramural program, or the outdoor program. An outdoor education program provides instruction and trips in white-water canoeing, climbing, hiking, camping, mountain biking, and initiatives on a low-ropes course. The outdoor program is available as an alternative to team sports.

EXTRACURRICULAR OPPORTUNITIES

Daily periods are set aside for extracurricular activities. On weekends, a wide range of planned activities is available for students to explore other interests.

The primary musical group on campus is the choir. The choir performs at chapel services and on tours outside the School.

For students who are learning to play musical instruments, private lessons in guitar, drums, keyboards, and other instruments can be arranged. The School yearbook and literary magazine provide opportunities for creative writing, photography, and art. The student newspaper is produced using the latest computer technology and appears on the School Web site. A theater program produces three plays a year, enabling students to express their talents in acting, set designing, and stage managing. The art studio contains tools and equipment for extracurricular painting, woodworking, drawing, and ceramics.

Because of the School's proximity to various winter resorts, there are many opportunities for Christ School students to ski on designated ski days and weekends.

DAILY LIFE

The Angelus bell rings at 7 a.m., and breakfast is served from 7:15 to 7:45. From 7:55 to 8:10, room inspection is held while boys complete School jobs. At 10:30, the student body comes together for chapel and assembly.

Christ School has a rotating schedule that allows for classes to meet four or five times a week. The academic day ends at 3 p.m., and boys are dismissed for sports, the outdoor program, conditioning and exercise, or theater. Dinner is served at 6.

A self-help work program, in which students do jobs to maintain the campus, is an integral part of everyday student life.

Teacher-supervised and independent study periods are held during the academic day and at night. Faculty members and advisers monitor a student's progress and make recommendations based on a boy's individual progress.

WEEKEND LIFE

Weekends offer a less structured environment that allows participation in sports, planned activities, and free time to pursue a wide variety of interests. Christ School has a student activities director to coordinate weekend and coeducational activities. Weekends provide opportunities for interscholastic athletics; white-water rafting; taking in a concert or a movie; trips to cultural events in Asheville, Atlanta, Charlotte, and Knoxville; attending professional and collegiate sporting events; shopping; dances; and course work.

COSTS AND FINANCIAL AID

For 2008–09, tuition and room and board were $36,700 for boarders and $18,630 for day students. In addition, a $400 deposit must be placed in an account to cover each boy's weekly allowance and extracurricular activities. Expenses for clothing, travel, laundry, and other needs vary considerably according to the individual and are the responsibility of each boy's parents. Tuition insurance and tuition payment plans are available.

The School aims, within its means, to ensure that no boy deemed suitable to Christ School be turned away because of financial need.

Financial aid and merit scholarships are available to qualified students. In 2008–09, the School awarded $1,295,000 in aid and scholarships.

ADMISSIONS INFORMATION

Christ School accepts students in grades 8–12. Admission policies are based on academic ability and personal qualifications. The School looks for students who can realize their full potential in a school that emphasizes the value of structure and discipline. Equally important is the ability of the potential student to fit into a small, caring community.

The School requires of candidates a campus visit, teacher recommendations, a transcript, and an application essay. The SSAT is required.

Campus visits are scheduled to suit each individual family and usually require a 3-hour commitment. This includes a tour of the campus, an appointment with the admission office, and visitation with the Headmaster.

A small number of students are accepted for the second semester. The School encourages families to set up a campus visit in the fall.

APPLICATION TIMETABLE

Application should be made as early as possible. Final decisions are made within two weeks by the admission committee after the applicant's file is complete. The majority of incoming students are determined before the end of the previous school year. There are a limited number of openings after June 1.

ADMISSIONS CORRESPONDENCE

Denis Stokes
Director of Admission
Christ School
500 Christ School Road
Arden, North Carolina 28704
Phone: 828-684-6232 Ext. 106
800-422-3212 (toll-free)
Fax: 828-684-4869
E-mail: admission@christschool.org
Web site: http://www.christschool.org

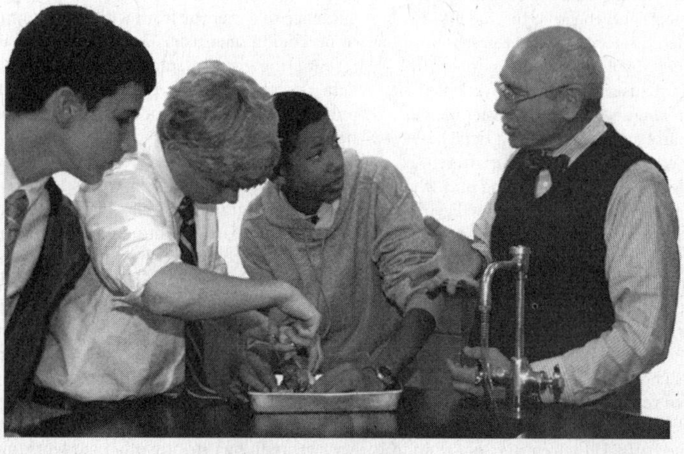

COLUMBIA GRAMMAR AND PREPARATORY SCHOOL

New York, New York

Type: Coeducational day college-preparatory school
Grades: PK–12: Grammar School, Prekindergarten–6; High School, 7–12
Enrollment: School total, 1,158; High School, 574
Head of School: Dr. Richard Soghoian, Headmaster

THE SCHOOL

Columbia Grammar was founded in 1764, just ten years after the founding of Kings College (later Columbia College) by King George II. Its original purpose was to prepare students for the rigors of Columbia College, and its earliest curriculum embraced, according to the first Headmaster, David Ogilby, "everything useful for the comfort and convenience and elegance of life, as well as everything that contributes to true happiness, both here and hereafter."

The School was incorporated as a nonprofit institution in 1941, and it joined with the Leonard School for Girls in 1956 to become coeducational. The School is governed by a Board of Trustees.

The School provides a rigorous, stimulating, and structured academic program in a warm and relatively informal atmosphere. It aims to instill in students the skills and habits of thought to enable them to benefit fully from college and at the same time to provide them with a rich and pleasurable intellectual and social experience during their school years. Music, theater, and the visual arts occupy an important place at all levels of the program. The values of tolerance of others and of responsibility for oneself and for one's community are likewise critical to the program. Decision making about one's education is gradually increased under careful guidance until, by the senior year, students are prepared for the choices facing them in college.

The School is accredited by the New York State Association of Independent Schools and the New York State Board of Regents. It maintains memberships in the National Association of Independent Schools, the New York State Association of Independent Schools, the Guild of Independent Schools of New York City, and the Independent Schools Admissions Association of Greater New York.

ACADEMIC PROGRAMS

Students in grades 7 and 8 study a core curriculum in academic subjects and the arts. In grades 9–12, they must complete a rigorous college-preparatory program of 4 years of English, 4 years of mathematics, 4 years of history, 3 years of science, 3 years of a foreign language, and a semester each of music literature and art history, plus a rich choice of electives. The goal of the English Department is to produce students who enjoy reading and who are accustomed to talking and writing intelligently about what they read. In grade 9, a full-year course addresses through literature the fundamental theme of coming of age and includes separate time for writing. In grade 10, students focus on writing clear and well-organized essays and read a selection of British and American literature. In grades 11 and 12, students choose from semester-long electives, with a major research paper each fall. Typical electives include Modernist Literature, English Literature of the Early 19th Century, Shaw and Ibsen, and the Art of Poetry. The History Department has a two-year requirement in Western civilization for grades 9 and 10 as well as a required U.S. history course in grade 11. Some electives for grades 11 and 12 include a course taught with Tufts University, economics, psychology, the Holocaust, and Latin American politics.

All students are required to take four consecutive years of high school mathematics. Computer science is required, with a number of additional electives. Science offerings include biology, chemistry, physics, Advanced Placement courses, and semester electives such as electronics, ecology, organic chemistry, genetics, human evolution, and anatomy and physiology. The foreign language department offers Chinese, French, Japanese, Latin, and Spanish. Students are free to start a second language at any point in their high school career.

Students in grades 9–12 may also choose from a wide range of offerings in the arts: studio courses in ceramics and sculpture, painting and drawing, jewelry making, and woodworking; courses in acting and photography; and participation in the chorus and instrumental ensembles.

Advanced Placement courses are offered in all the academic departments: American and European history, art history, biology, calculus AB and BC, chemistry, computer science, English, environmental science, French, government, music theory, physics, psychology, and Spanish.

Students are grouped by ability in science and mathematics. In other academic areas, students are mixed.

The student-teacher ratio is 7:1, and the average class size is 10–15. Teachers are available to work with students during their free periods, and close student-teacher relations characterize the School. Juniors and seniors can initiate tutorials in areas not covered by courses.

In the sophomore year, students who participate in the science research course choose and explore a topic of personal interest, learn to search electronic databases, read appropriate literature, define an experimental project, and seek the guidance of a mentor from within the community of practicing scientists. Their junior year is spent refining the experimental protocol and collecting data. As seniors, they present their research in public forums of scientific symposia and competitions.

The academic year is divided into two semester units, each roughly sixteen weeks long. Students receive letter grades as well as written evaluations in paragraph form at the end of each semester. Progress reports are sent in mid-semester when students are new to the School or when they are experiencing academic difficulties. Parent-teacher-student conferences take place twice a year, but parents are encouraged to meet with teachers whenever problems arise during the school year.

Students are required to perform 100 hours of service in order to graduate. Many students earn service credit by tutoring other students under the supervision of a faculty member or by helping with classes in the Grammar School. Students are encouraged to earn service credit in volunteer work outside the School, and half of their service must be done outside the School. Many have worked in local neighborhood centers tutoring and helping with day care. Others have worked for hospitals, the ASPCA, or the Central Park Conservancy or have earned service credit by working through the volunteer services of their own religious organizations.

FACULTY AND ADVISERS

The full-time High School faculty consists of 36 men and 39 women. In addition to baccalaureate degrees, faculty members also hold sixty master's degrees and two doctorates. Some faculty members hold more than one master's degree. There are also 8 part-time teachers, including 4 full-time administrators who also teach.

The Headmaster, Richard Soghoian, was appointed in 1981. He is a graduate of the University of Virginia and holds a Ph.D. in philosophy from Columbia University, where he was an International Fellow in the School of International Affairs. Prior to his appointment, Dr. Soghoian taught philosophy at the University of Denver, was Assistant Dean at Columbia College, was Director of the Graduate School at Pratt Institute, and was the Vice President for Academic Affairs at Manhattanville College in Purchase, New York.

Most full-time faculty members in the High School are assigned as advisers to a small group of students. Advisers meet daily with their students and also supervise a range of extracurricular activities.

In addition to faculty advisers, there are 4 deans in grades 9–12, one for each grade, as well as 2 student counselors and 2 college counselors.

COLLEGE ADMISSION COUNSELING

College counseling begins in the junior year, when students meet with the college counselors to discuss basic questions about the type of college in which they are interested, field of study, geographical location, and other concerns. A meeting is held for parents in February of the junior year to give them the basic outline of the college guidance program. Students are encouraged to begin visiting colleges during the spring and summer vacations before the senior year, and several Fridays are set aside during the fall of senior year for college visits. Early in the fall of the senior year, students and parents meet with the college counselors to establish a firm list of colleges to which the student can apply.

SAT mean scores for the class of 2008 were 643 verbal and 643 math. Graduates of the class of 2008 are attending the following colleges and universities: Amherst, Bard, Bates, Binghamton, Boston University, Bowdoin, Brandeis, Brown, Columbia, Connecticut College, Cornell, Davidson, Duke, Emory, Franklin and Marshall, George Washington, Guilford, Hampshire, Haverford, Indiana, Ithaca, Lehigh, LSU, McGill, Muhlenberg, NYU, Northwestern, Oberlin, Reed, Rhode Island School of Design, Skidmore, Susquehanna, Syracuse, Tufts, Tulane, Union, Vanderbilt, Washington (St. Louis), Wesleyan, Yale, and the Universities of Chicago, Michigan, Pennsylvania, Rochester, St. Andrews (Scotland), Vermont, and Virginia.

STUDENT BODY AND CONDUCT

There are currently 40 boys and 46 girls in grade 7, 36 boys and 41 girls in grade 8, 54 boys and 47 girls in grade 9, 54 boys and 46 girls in grade 10, 60 boys and 53 girls in grade 11, and 46 boys and 51 girls in grade 12. The majority of the students reside in Manhattan, but there is also representation from the other boroughs, Long Island, northern New Jersey, and Westchester. Approximately 18 percent of the students are members of minority groups, and the School has a strong commitment to the Prep for Prep program, which brings minority students into the School in the seventh grade.

The rules of conduct for the student body are set forth in the *Student Handbook* and stress consideration for others.

There is an active student government, with representatives from grades 7 to 12, which functions as the vehicle through which student discussion of School issues and policies can take place and student positions and policies can be articulated to the faculty and administration. Similarly, it becomes a forum in which the faculty and administration can raise problems and discuss areas of future planning with students. The student government plays a major role in organizing and supporting other extracurricular activities and groups.

ACADEMIC FACILITIES

The School has four separate buildings: the Grammar School's five connected brownstones on 94th Street; the original Columbia Grammar School building on 93rd Street, which contains the cafeteria, a swimming pool, a gymnasium, and two art studios; a High School building containing fifteen classrooms, three science labs, three music practice rooms, a library, a computer room, and a full-sized gymnasium; and a building, completed in 1996, containing classrooms for grades 5–7, three science rooms, and two computer rooms, plus five art studios, drama practice and performance space, and a cafeteria for grades 5–12. Another building that connects to the High School building was completed in 2001. It contains a third gym for the School, a state-of-the-art theater, and three floors of classrooms and science labs. A brownstone at 36 West 94th Street, purchased in August 2004, includes the admissions office and the development office.

ATHLETICS

The aim of the physical education program is to provide a broad range of activities that build enduring skills, provide interests for leisure time, and contribute to social adjustment and fitness. In addition to the regular physical education program, there are varsity teams in boys' baseball, basketball, golf, hockey, soccer, and tennis; girls' basketball, soccer, softball, swimming, and volleyball; and coed cross-country and track. The School makes use of the playing fields in Central Park, Randall's Island, and other city parks as well as its own swimming pool and three gymnasiums.

EXTRACURRICULAR OPPORTUNITIES

In addition to the student government (described above), club periods are scheduled in the six-day cycle to encourage student involvement in extracurricular activities (students must choose at least one), such as a literary and art magazine, the yearbook, a School paper, women's issues, a debate club, Model UN, bridge, an environmental club, and Cartoon and Comic Creation. There is also an active theater department that presents three or more productions each year, including musicals and other theatrical works.

A Moving Up Day ceremony in June brings the Preparatory School together for class jingles and an award ceremony for students in grades 7 through 12.

DAILY LIFE

The school day begins at 8 and ends at 2:55. Classes meet on a six-day cycle, with time built in for chorus and orchestra rehearsals.

COSTS AND FINANCIAL AID

Tuition and fees for grades 9 through 11 in 2008–09 are $33,190; for grade 12, they are $33,390.

The School offers two payment plans: one with a 20 percent nonrefundable deposit upon signing the contract, plus 50 percent on August 1 and 30 percent on January 1; or a ten-month payment plan, with 20 percent deposit and a 10 percent interest charge on the remaining balance, which is divided into ten equal monthly payments commencing August 1.

In 2008–09, 25 percent of the preparatory school student body receives some form of financial assistance. Awards are based strictly on need, and the average ranges from $6000 to $7000. Preference in awarding scholarships is given to students already attending the School as opposed to new applicants.

ADMISSIONS INFORMATION

The School enrolls students without discrimination on the basis of race, religion, color, or national or ethnic origin. Students are chosen for their emotional maturity, ability to work in a demanding program, talents, concern for others, and potential for growth.

The School requires the Educational Records Bureau test for admission. While the School does not have a strict cutoff point for these tests, low scores on the test may indicate that the student would have academic difficulties in the School.

APPLICATION TIMETABLE

Most students apply to the School in the fall preceding the year of entrance. Prior to an interview, students and parents are invited to special orientation meetings with the Director of the Preparatory School, teachers, and students. A tour of the School is included. Interviews are required, as are English and math teacher recommendations. Notification of acceptance for all candidates whose files are complete is on a common reply date in mid-February, and parents have until March 15 to reply.

ADMISSIONS CORRESPONDENCE

Terry Centeno, Admissions Coordinator
Columbia Grammar and Preparatory School
5 West 93rd Street
New York, New York 10025
Phone: 212-749-6200, Ext. 362
E-mail: info@cgps.org
Web site: http://www.cgps.org

COMMONWEALTH SCHOOL

Boston, Massachusetts

COMMONWEALTH SCHOOL

Type: Coeducational day college-preparatory school
Grades: 9–12
Enrollment: 154
Head of School: William Wharton, Headmaster

THE SCHOOL

The Commonwealth School was founded in 1957 by Charles Merrill, who was Headmaster until his retirement in 1981. His insistence on independence of mind and his commitment to the cause of civil rights gave the School its focus on distinction in scholarship and on activism in public affairs. Today, the School continues to build its arts, extracurricular activities, academics, sports, and sense of community on imagination and enterprise.

Commonwealth occupies a pair of extensively rebuilt town houses in the Back Bay neighborhood of Boston. Its immediate neighborhood is an urban mixture of residences, art galleries, large and small businesses, restaurants, theaters, museums, and libraries. Students can serve as teachers' assistants in Boston schools, take part in political campaigns, and engage in a wide variety of special projects in businesses, hospitals, laboratorics, and studios.

The School is a nonprofit organization whose 31-member Board of Trustees includes faculty members, alumni/ae, parents, and nonvoting student and faculty representatives. The School's endowment is $11.7 million; the operating budget for 2008–09 was approximately $6.1 million. Annual Giving in 2007–08 was just over $600,000.

The Commonwealth School is accredited by the New England Association of Independent Schools and holds memberships in the Council for the Advancement and Support of Education, the Association of Independent Schools of New England, and the National Association of Independent Schools.

ACADEMIC PROGRAMS

Commonwealth offers students exceptional training through close contact with outstanding teachers. Small classes encourage every student to speak up and be counted. The curriculum is designed to teach the essential disciplines as well as topics of interest in various fields.

Full-credit courses meet four times a week; half-credit courses meet twice. A minimum of 16 academic credits is required for graduation, including 4 in English, 3 in mathematics, 3 in a foreign language, 3 in science, and 3 in history (including U.S. history). Ninth graders are required to take a course on the city of Boston and a health and community course. All ninth and twelfth graders take courses with the Headmaster, and all students must perform 70 hours of community service before their junior year. In addition, students are required to take one course in the arts each year and to participate in two of three sports seasons.

Full-credit offerings include English 9–12, ancient history, medieval world history, U.S. history, modern European history, French 1–4, Spanish 1–4, Latin 1–4, biology 1–2, chemistry 1–2, physics 1–2, fundamentals of physics, algebra 2, geometry, intermediate algebra, introduction to calculus, theoretical and applied calculus, and economics. Half-credit subjects include an introduction to creative writing, the novel, fiction writing, modernism, short story, film, literature of the Bible, foundations of modern philosophy, film analysis, art history, constitutional law, African-American history, history of China, history of Japan, current history, Latin American history, nationalism, probability and statistics, computer programming 1–3, abstract algebra, linear algebra, biology of consciousness, chemistry 3, environmental science, structural mechanics, French 5, Spanish 5, Latin 5, and Greek 1 and 2. Music theory, jazz theory, composition, and conducting are offered. Arts courses include ceramics, chorus, chorale, orchestra, jazz band, chamber ensemble, acting, advanced dance, drawing and painting, life drawing, printmaking, artists' books, and photography.

Commonwealth does not rank its students or give prizes.

The average class size is 12. The student-teacher ratio is approximately 5:1.

FACULTY AND ADVISERS

Commonwealth has a teaching faculty of 32 teachers and administrators who also teach. Twenty-four (9 men and 15 women) are full-time and 11 are part-time. Eighty-seven percent of the full-time faculty members hold advanced degrees; 11 hold doctorates.

William D. Wharton was appointed Headmaster in 2000. A graduate of Brown University, he received his B.A. in 1979 and M.A. in 1981, both in classics. After teaching Latin for five years at the Lincoln School in Providence, Rhode Island, he joined the Commonwealth faculty in 1985 as a teacher of history, Latin, and Greek. Since then, he has also taught ancient philosophy, ethics, and world religions and has served as Faculty Trustee, College Advisor, Acting Head, and Director of Admissions. In 1988, he was awarded a Grant for Independent Study in the Humanities from the Council for Basic Education and National Endowment for the Humanities; in 1992, he was one of 38 recipients of Teacher-Scholar Grants from the NEH and DeWitt-Wallace Reader's Digest Fund, an award that funded a year's sabbatical study.

Commonwealth teachers spend most of their time out of class giving extra tutorials, conferring on essays, and meeting with advisees. Students choose their advisers. The sustained, sympathetic support of a faculty adviser for every student is an essential part of Commonwealth's program. The School also makes available the services of a consulting psychologist. Students and teachers eat lunch together, office doors are open, and informality is the rule.

The School regularly grants paid sabbatical leave to faculty members and provides funds for additional courses and degrees. Four faculty members have won summer-study grants from the National Endowment for the Humanities.

COLLEGE ADMISSION COUNSELING

A faculty member serves as College Advisor, working closely with students from the spring of their junior year on every aspect of the admissions process. All 34 graduates of the class of 2008 are attending college. The institutions they attend include Bard, Bates, Boston College, Brown, Bryn Mawr, Harvard, McGill, Middlebury, NYU, Pomona, Princeton, Reed, Smith, Tufts, University of Pennsylvania, and Wellesley.

Median SAT scores for the class of 2008 were 725 critical reading, 715 math, and 735 writing. In the classes of 2006 to 2008 (108 students), there were 51 National Merit Commended Scholars and 17 National Merit Semifinalists; 6 students were awarded National Merit Scholarships.

STUDENT BODY AND CONDUCT

Commonwealth's total enrollment is 154 students: 38 freshmen, 37 sophomores, 38 juniors, and 41 seniors. Thirty-six students (23 percent) are members of minority groups.

The School has no formal student government; issues are discussed in weekly class meetings and sometimes a weekly all-School meeting. A boy and a girl from the senior class serve as representatives of the student body on the School's Board of Trustees, and student opinion is sought both privately and publicly by the faculty and the Headmaster in shaping School policy and in making decisions. Suggestions of students with particular interests lead on occasion to the creation of new courses and activities.

ACADEMIC FACILITIES
Commonwealth's two Back Bay town houses are connected to form a single five-story building that houses classrooms; offices; a library; laboratories for physics, biology, and chemistry; a computer room; studios for art and ceramics; a darkroom; a kitchen; a student lounge; and a lunchroom that also serves as a small gymnasium, concert hall, and theater. Facilities for some productions, concerts, and sports are located in nearby churches, theaters, clubs, and colleges. The School's 6,000-volume library is supplemented by the resources of the Boston Public Library, which is two blocks away. Commonwealth is linked electronically with many of the greater Boston public libraries and provides wireless Internet access throughout the building.

ATHLETICS
Commonwealth believes that the hard work, high spirits, and competitive grit of sports give young people an essential sense of pride and vitality. Its program is designed to suit a range of interests and to teach resilience of body and mind.

Major interscholastic sports are soccer, fencing, basketball, baseball, and Ultimate Frisbee. Noncompetitive sports include dance, fitness, sailing, squash, and yoga. All sports are open to all grades and to both boys and girls.

The School has the use of a local field for soccer and of nearby courts for basketball, dance, and squash. Arrangements are made for sailing at the Community Boating Club on the Charles River, and memberships at a local YMCA are obtained for fitness instruction with a qualified personal trainer.

EXTRACURRICULAR OPPORTUNITIES
Commonwealth participates in three-week exchange programs with schools in Spain and France; financial aid for these programs is provided for students demonstrating need. Latin students are offered a trip to Italy. Each September, the entire school adjourns to a camp in Maine for a four-day weekend. There is a second all-School trip in the spring. In January, students participate in weeklong projects that range from hospital work to teaching to serving in a senator's Washington office. Seniors engage in similar, longer projects during March. A wide variety of public figures, artists, musicians, travelers, and experts in various fields perform or speak before the School at its weekly assembly. Students also participate in a debate team, Model UN, and a science olympiad.

Student publications include a literary magazine and yearbook. For many students, extra art courses are a major item of extracurricular interest. Students participate in winter and spring concerts, fall and spring plays, a dance concert, a jazz concert, and an art show. Other traditional yearly events for the Commonwealth community include a ninth-grade outing, a back-to-school night, parent-teacher conferences, museum day, impromptu day, diversity day, alumni/ae reunions in Boston and other cities, and an all-School beach day.

DAILY LIFE
The school day begins at 8:30. Class periods are normally 40 minutes long, with a 15-minute midmorning recess and 45 minutes for lunch. Refreshments are offered at recess, and a full meal is served at lunchtime. On Monday, Wednesday, and Friday, classes end at 2:40 and are followed by sports. Tuesday classes end at 3:10. On Thursday, class meetings and an assembly extend the day to 4:05.

All students take part in the jobs program, doing chores such as emptying recycling bins and dishwashing that might otherwise be done by custodial staff, and building a sense of self-reliance.

Supervised study halls are required for first-term freshmen and for students in academic difficulty. Students who would benefit from structured supervision are invited to join evening study sessions.

Students commute to Commonwealth from as far away as Framingham, Harvard, Gloucester, and Providence. A number of MBTA bus and subway lines run through Copley Square, which is two blocks from the School; Back Bay Station, with Amtrak, commuter rail, and major bus lines, is also nearby.

COSTS AND FINANCIAL AID
In 2008–09, the tuition and lunch fee was $29,070, with additional expenses of $1835. A total of more than $987,000 in scholarship aid was awarded to 53 students; awards ranged from $2600 to $30,405. A small number of student jobs are also available. A technology grant program is offered to new students who receive financial aid, enabling them to purchase new computers and printers through the School at a substantial discount.

ADMISSIONS INFORMATION
The Commonwealth School seeks boys and girls of character and intelligence, without regard to race, color, or national or ethnic origin, who are willing to work hard for a good education. The application process requires a family interview and a separate all-day School visit for the student. Applicants are asked to submit recommendations, transcripts, and Secondary School Admission Test (SSAT) scores. In 2008, the median total SSAT score for entering students was in the 94th percentile. For the ninth grade, 185 applications were received, of which 70 were accepted.

APPLICATION TIMETABLE
Initial contact with the School, preferably in the fall, can be made by telephone, mail, or e-mail. An interview with the applicant and his or her parents and a full-day visit by the applicant (both required) will be arranged. Applications for fall admission should be completed by January 2, although the School accepts new students later in the year if places remain. All supplemental materials are due February 1. Notifications are mailed on March 10, and replies must be received by April 10. Commonwealth holds open houses for prospective students and their parents in mid-October and early December. Admitted students and parents are offered a choice of three revisit days in April.

ADMISSIONS CORRESPONDENCE
Helene Carter
Director of Admissions
Commonwealth School
151 Commonwealth Avenue
Boston, Massachusetts 02116
Phone: 617-266-7525
Fax: 617-266-5769
E-mail: admissions@commschool.org
Web site: http://www.commschool.org/

CONSERVE SCHOOL

Land O'Lakes, Wisconsin

Type: Coeducational, nonsectarian boarding school
Grades: 9–12
Enrollment: 130
Head of School: Mr. Stefan Anderson, Headmaster

THE SCHOOL

Conserve School is an independent boarding high school that offers both a classical college-preparatory program tailored to academically talented students and an interdisciplinary program emphasizing wildlife, natural habitats, outdoor activities, and ecology. At Conserve School, students combine traditional subject areas with the unique areas of environmental science, technology, and outdoor recreation. The program prepares all graduates to be ethical and environmentally sensitive leaders and stewards within their career choice.

Conserve School is located in the northwoods resort community of Land O' Lakes, Wisconsin. The campus features eight lakes and borders the Sylvania Wilderness Area in Michigan's Upper Peninsula. The campus is approximately 360 miles north of Chicago and 260 miles northeast of Minneapolis. It is 38 miles north of The Rhinelander-Oneida County Airport.

Conserve School was established in 2002 as the wish of James R. Lowenstine, president and chairman of the board of Central Steel & Wire Company in Chicago. Realizing the importance of conserving northern Wisconsin's natural resources, Mr. Lowenstine bequeathed his wealth and 1,200 acres of Audubon-recognized pristine woodlands to found a school that would teach young people the importance of stewardship and ethical, environmental leadership.

Conserve School has new school status with the Independent Schools Association of the Central States (ISACS) and is on track to be accredited next year. Conserve is also a provisional member of the National Association of Independent Schools (NAIS), Midwest Boarding Schools, and the National Consortium for Specialized Secondary Schools of Mathematics, Science, and Technology.

ACADEMIC PROGRAMS

Conserve School's college-preparatory curriculum blends challenging academics, active learning, and hands-on engagement. The themes of environment, ethics, and innovation are woven throughout the educational and extracurricular program.

Graduation requirements include 4 credits of English; 3 credits each of world language, mathematics, science, and history; 2 credits of fine arts; 2½ credits of wellness and health; ½ credit of Introduction to Research Methods; and 2 elective credits.

Conserve School's curriculum has been designed with academically talented students in mind. The School offers a large number of Advanced Placement courses along with a wide variety of advanced electives. Upperclassmen are encouraged to take on independent study projects guided by a teacher-mentor. New students are given placement tests; course placement is flexible and based on the student's demonstrated capabilities.

The School's emphasis on environmental studies is reflected by the large number of unique classes focused specifically on nature and outdoor activities. These specialized courses include: Contemporary Nature Writers, Environmental Communication, Outdoor Leadership, Botanical Illustration, Limnology, Wildlife Biology, The History and Meaning of Wilderness, The Literature of Adventure, and Introduction to Forestry and Wildlife. These environmentally oriented courses are offered as part of a comprehensive college-preparatory program that includes more traditional courses such as: American Literature, U.S. History, World History, Classic Literature, Painting and Drawing, Spanish and Chinese I-V, and Advanced Composition.

FACULTY AND ADVISERS

Stefan Anderson was named Headmaster in February 2003. Stefan received his B.A. in physics at St. Olaf College and his M.S. in physics at the Massachusetts Institute of Technology. Prior to moving to Conserve School in the summer of 2001, he was the Dean of Studies for students in grades 9–12 at Breck School in Minneapolis, Minnesota.

Ninety-three percent of Conserve School teachers hold advanced degrees. Both teachers and residential interns act as surrogate parents and mentors, living in residence houses as houseparents. This model ensures students benefit from the direct involvement of mentors in every aspect of daily life.

COLLEGE ADMISSION COUNSELING

The College Resource Center is open to all students interested in learning about colleges, the college application process, and financial aid. The college counselor is available for consultation every day. The formal counseling process normally begins during the junior year and includes multiple one-on-one meetings, class meetings, and visits to selected colleges and college fairs. Students are encouraged to make well-informed choices in a timely fashion.

STUDENT BODY AND CONDUCT

Conserve School welcomes students of any race, color, or national or ethnic origin and has students with a broad range of socioeconomic backgrounds.

Students and staff members work together to live and learn in accordance with the values expressed in the Conserve School Code. This code was developed in consultation with Dr. Rushworth Kidder, founder of the Institute for Global Ethics. The Conserve School Code is built around five values: compassion, honesty, justice, respect, and responsibility. Together, these values serve the entire School as an ethical guidepost.

ACADEMIC FACILITIES

The Lowenstine Academic Building is centered on an expansive student gathering space, which features an impressive open fireplace and expansive wall of windows overlooking one of the School's eight lakes.

The Lowenstine Academic Building contains twenty-three teaching spaces with thirteen classrooms, four science laboratories, a spacious visual arts studio and photographic darkroom, a 500-seat performing arts center, a large musical ensemble room with eight private practice rooms, an electronic learning lab, a 16,000-volume library, and an impressive dining room overlooking Little Donahue Lake.

Across the campus are the Technology Center and the Green Machine, the School's own wastewater treatment facility. The Green Machine uses natural processes to treat campus wastewater before it is returned to the ground. Bacteria and plants remove contaminants from the water, making it safe and clean without the chemicals used in conventional water treatment.

BOARDING AND GENERAL FACILITIES

Each residence house contains four student wings and four houseparent apartments. Each student wing has ten individual rooms with a shared bath between every two rooms. Every wing has a large commons area with a gas fireplace, ample study and lounge space, and a small kitchenette. There are 2 houseparents assigned for every 10 students, promoting a homelike environment.

ATHLETICS

Believing that health and wellness is an important component to each student's personal development, Conserve School offers a variety of recreational sports, wellness classes, intramurals, and an interscholastic sports program as venues for athletic participation. Participants on interscholastic athletic teams have an opportunity to compete against other schools in the sports of basketball, cross-country running, golf, Nordic skiing, soccer, softball, track, and volleyball. Conserve School is a member of Wisconsin's Northern Lakes Athletic Conference. Recreational activities include a variety of individual, team, and coed sport options, focusing on the development of healthy lifetime leisure habits. Students utilize Conserve School's excellent facilities and beautiful outdoor resources to experience seasonal recreation activities such as canoeing, kayaking, hiking, biking, disc golf, cross-country skiing, snowshoeing, tobogganing, and ice-skating.

The Lowenwood Recreation Center is located on the eastern shore of Big Donahue Lake and serves as the hub for athletic and wellness activity. The facility houses a gymnasium, climbing wall, racquetball courts, dance studio, multipurpose exercise room, and a fitness center.

EXTRACURRICULAR OPPORTUNITIES

Leadership development is an important element of the Conserve School experience. Extracurricular activities provide a forum for this development as well as personal growth, socialization, and recreation. A multitude of activities in the areas of outdoor adventure, fine arts, service learning, student publications, academic interests, skills building, and personal interests are offered. Students play an important role in choosing which activities they pursue.

DAILY LIFE

At Conserve School, breakfast begins at 7 a.m. The school day runs from 8 a.m. until 3:30 p.m., with each class meeting four hours per week. Student-run all-School community meetings are held twice each week during the school day. Interscholastic athletics occur in the afternoon and on some weekends. Late afternoons and early evenings are reserved for club activities, meetings, and study time.

Individual and group study takes place each evening in the library, classrooms, conference rooms, and student residences. All students have required study hours five nights a week. Upperclassmen with an outstanding level of academic achievement may, as a privilege, be released from these regulated, supervised study hours. Students in each wing meet with their houseparents on Wednesdays for discussion and activities. Curfew is 10 p.m. Sunday through Thursday and 11 p.m. Friday and Saturday.

WEEKEND LIFE

Weekends are an opportunity for students to learn to use leisure time appropriately. The students are encouraged to become involved in the planning and organizing of group activities. On-campus activities include movies, dances, intramural sports, and club-sponsored events. The School transports students to local theaters, shopping, and places of worship. Occasionally, students travel in chaperoned groups to larger cities for cultural events. Conserve School's location provides convenient access to downhill skiing, canoeing, and kayaking venues. Opportunities for community service are also offered every weekend. Some restrictions are placed on weekend privileges, depending on a student's age, grade level, and academic standing.

COSTS AND FINANCIAL AID

Tuition and supply fees include room, board, all textbooks, lab supplies, use of a laptop computer, School-sponsored campus sports and activities, and health and wellness services.

Academic merit scholarships are awarded based upon a specific set of criteria, including grades, teacher recommendations, and test scores.

Need-based financial aid is available and is evaluated in conjunction with the School and Student Services (SSS) Division of the National Association of Independent Schools.

ADMISSIONS INFORMATION

Conserve School seeks those students whose interests and academic abilities are harmonious with Conserve School's mission. Students are expected to be capable of succeeding in a challenging academic environment and to embrace the values of compassion, honesty, justice, respect, and responsibility. Conserve School accepts above-average students, as determined by their grades and by their scores on a nationally standardized examination. To be admitted, students must score in the top 25 percent nationally. The admissions process includes a school visit, student and parent interviews, teacher and counselor recommendations, and a review of the student's previous academic history as well as standardized testing.

APPLICATION TIMETABLE

Inquiries are welcome at any time. Students are encouraged to apply early in the fall. It is encouraged that applications be sent by February 1, 2009, but they will be considered for review until June 1, as space permits.

ADMISSIONS CORRESPONDENCE

Admissions Office
Conserve School
5400 North Black Oak Lake Road
Land O'Lakes, Wisconsin 54540
Phone: 866-547-1300 Ext. 1321 (toll-free)
Fax: 715-547-1390
E-mail: admissions@conserveschool.org
Web site: http://www.ConserveSchool.org

CONVENT OF THE SACRED HEART

Greenwich, Connecticut

Type: Girls' private, independent day college-preparatory Catholic school
Grades: P–12: Lower School, Preschool–4; Middle School, 5–8; Upper School, 9–12
Enrollment: School total: 780; Upper School: 295
Head of School: Joan Magnetti, RSCJ, Headmistress

THE SCHOOL

Convent of the Sacred Heart is situated on a beautiful 110-acre wooded campus in Greenwich, Connecticut. Greenwich is a suburban town located about 30 miles from New York City and 40 minutes from New Haven. An independent, college-preparatory school for girls in preschool through grade 12, Sacred Heart was first established in New York City in 1848 and moved to Greenwich in 1945. Convent of the Sacred Heart is one of twenty-one Sacred Heart schools in the United States and part of an international network of schools that includes more than 200 schools in forty-four countries around the world.

A Sacred Heart education provides a strong academic foundation appropriate to each student's individual talents and abilities within an environment that fosters the development of her spiritual life and a strong sense of personal values. True to its international heritage, the school welcomes students and faculty members of diverse backgrounds and faiths, so that each student will grow in her understanding of different cultures and peoples. Graduates are prepared to become leaders with broad intellectual and spiritual horizons.

Convent of the Sacred Heart is a nonprofit institution governed by a 26-member Board of Trustees, which is responsible to the Society of the Sacred Heart for the implementation of the society's educational philosophy. Parents, religious, alumnae, and educators serve on the board. Sacred Heart benefits from the active involvement and strong support of its parent and alumnae organizations.

The school is accredited by the New England Association of Schools and Colleges and approved by the Connecticut State Board of Education. It is a member of the National Association of Independent Schools, the Connecticut Association of Independent Schools, the National Coalition of Girls' Schools, and the Network of Sacred Heart Schools in the United States.

ACADEMIC PROGRAMS

Sacred Heart is committed to the development of each student's intellectual, physical, spiritual, and emotional well-being. The academic program in the Upper School provides a rigorous educational foundation that enables students to become independent and creative thinkers. Students are active participants in the learning process, expanding their experience through exploration, inquiry, and discovery. Students analyze, critique, evaluate, and make important connections with the concepts they learn.

Sacred Heart's academic program is comprehensive, rigorous, and flexible. Serious study is emphasized, and the development of essential academic skills necessary for success in college and life is encouraged. College-preparatory, honors, and advanced-placement courses are offered throughout the core curriculum, which includes mathematics, science, English, history and social sciences, foreign languages, theology, and the arts. A student is afforded opportunities for exploration of her own talents and interests through special projects, study abroad, summer programs, and independent study. Emphasizing the connection between the disciplines is critical to learning at Sacred Heart. Faculty collaboration helps students in discovering and understanding the relevance of all subject areas and the importance of their learning in relationship to society and their daily lives.

A student's schedule for the three-term academic year is planned individually. The student plans her course of study with the support of her academic adviser and the Assistant Head of Upper School for Academic Life. Course levels are chosen according to academic readiness, ability, and talent in an academic area. Each student typically takes between 6 and 8 credits per school year in a combination of required courses and electives.

Graduation requirements are based on the expectations of highly selective colleges and universities; all of Sacred Heart's graduates choose to attend college. To receive a diploma, students must complete a minimum of 25 credits, although all students complete more than this minimum number. The requirements include 4 credits of English, 4 credits in theology, 3 credits in history, 3 credits in mathematics, 3 credits in a foreign language, 3 credits in science, and 2 elective credits, at least 1 of which must be in the arts. Students must also complete 2 years of physical education and a 2-year health education requirement.

All academic disciplines employ the computer as a tool for writing, research, analysis, and presentation, including the use of multimedia presentations, spreadsheets and databases for organization and analysis, and desktop publishing. The program also addresses the possibilities and responsibilities associated with the use of technology in today's society. All students in grades 7–12 use laptop computers in the classroom and anywhere else they study or work. Other students use desktop computers in the Lower School and Middle School computer laboratories.

FACULTY AND ADVISERS

High expectations and positive role models are important to the success of girls and young women. A student-faculty ratio of 6:1 and an average class size of approximately 13 students ensure the teachers know every student. Assured of the faculty's support, students are motivated to take risks through which confidence and self-discipline develop. Individual teaching styles are complemented by a common commitment to the goals and criteria of a Sacred Heart education.

Convent of the Sacred Heart has 111 faculty members, with 39 full-time and 10 part-time members teaching in the Upper School. Each serves as a personal and academic counselor to about 8 advisees, and many serve as club advisers and coaches as well. Students meet with their advisers regularly during a special advisory period. They also meet informally with faculty members at daily assemblies and weekly chapel services.

Teachers regularly participate in workshops, summer study, curriculum development, travel, and research. Approximately 73 percent of the faculty members hold advanced degrees, including 7 who have doctoral degrees. The full-time faculty has an average of fifteen years of teaching experience.

COLLEGE ADMISSION COUNSELING

The College Guidance Department at Sacred Heart believes in the importance of an individualized college process and works hard to find the best match possible for each student. An informational parent meeting in the sophomore year helps to set this tone. The Directors of College Guidance also assist sophomores with course selection, review PSAT scores, and help their student advisees plan schedules for appropriate SAT Subject Tests.

In junior year, students and parents meet with the Directors of College Guidance to identify goals and discuss expectations about college plans. The college search process is explained at an evening winter program, which features college representatives and the college counselors. Juniors also attend guidance classes that explore issues surrounding the college selection process, including identifying prospective colleges, the campus visit and interview, the college essay, and financial aid and scholarships. Students have access to a variety of college search resources, including guidebooks, Internet search engines, and an internal software program. Students are also encouraged to take advantage of opportunities to meet with the many college representatives who visit Sacred Heart in the fall.

During the senior year, each student and her parents examine the more specific details of the application process: deadlines, the submission of standardized test scores, the college essay, resumes, and financial aid. In the school's 160-year history, Sacred Heart graduates have attended many of the nation's finest colleges and universities. Recent graduates are currently attending schools such as Amherst, Boston College, Brown, Columbia, Cornell, Dartmouth, Davidson, Georgetown, Harvard, Holy Cross, Johns Hopkins, Northwestern, Notre Dame, NYU, Pennsylvania, Vanderbilt, and Yale.

STUDENT BODY AND CONDUCT

There are 780 students enrolled in preschool through grade 12, with 295 students enrolled in the Upper School. Students join the high school from more than sixty-seven different communities, coming from public, private, and parochial schools in Connecticut and New York State. The student body includes a diversity of ethnic, socioeconomic, and religious backgrounds that allows for a dynamic community with a wide range of interests, talents, and passions.

School policies and practices foster the acceptance of responsibility, self-discipline, respect for the self and others, and caring for the school and wider community. The student government, student/faculty disciplinary board, and the administration work together to establish and enforce policies and minimal rules that govern the school community.

ACADEMIC FACILITIES

Overlooking Long Island Sound, the campus consists of modern classrooms, science laboratories, an observatory, playgrounds, synthetic-turf fields, a media center, a theater, a chapel, a broadcast journalism studio, a gymnasium, a swimming pool, and a dance studio.

The media center holds a collection of 22,000 books, CD-ROM resources, online databases and encyclopedias, videos, and Internet access.

A 29,000-square-foot science center has state-of-the-art laboratories for all three divisions, art studios, special space for drama and music, classrooms, and offices. Students in the astronomy class use a computerized, 16-inch telescope with 800x magnification in a state-of-the-art observatory, as well as ten 8-inch telescopes located on an outdoor pad.

The broadcast journalism studio consists of control, editing, and recording rooms. Students learn how to operate camera, audio, lighting, and editing equipment to tell their stories. This state-of-the-art space provides students with the opportunity to practice media literacy in a meaningful, hands-on fashion.

Students studying art, environmental science, and ecology make frequent use of the school's acres of woods, trails, fields, and a working vegetable garden. The campus is further enlivened by traditions and events unique to Convent of the Sacred Heart.

ATHLETICS

The energy of the Sacred Heart community extends beyond the walls of the school buildings. The indoor competition swimming pool, tennis courts, and the synthetic and grass playing fields outside are showcases for girls accepting challenges, testing limits, and cooperating with teammates. Sacred Heart provides a full schedule of varsity and junior varsity sports, including basketball, crew, cross-country, field hockey, golf, lacrosse, soccer, softball, squash, swimming and diving, tennis, and volleyball. The teams are supported with the very best facilities and equipment, including two new synthetic-turf fields. Convent of the Sacred Heart is a member of the twelve-school Fairchester League and the Western New England Prep School Athletic Association (WNEPSAA). A certified athletic trainer services both the Middle and Upper School student-athletes.

The physical education program is designed to develop skills for a healthy and active life. Opportunities are provided for competition, excellence, and fun in a variety of activities for all students.

EXTRACURRICULAR OPPORTUNITIES

A wide range of clubs, committees, and activities provide opportunities for students to contribute to the school community, pursue their interests, and develop leadership and team skills. Students produce major theatrical productions, govern the student body through extensive collaboration with student-elected representatives, and publish their own language newspapers, school newspaper, and literary magazine. Students win awards through their participation in the Forensics/Speech and Debate Club and the Model United Nations Club. Sacred Heart students participate in local, regional, and national competitions with their peers from other schools. These programs are designed to promote self-expression, intellectual challenge, and individual leadership opportunities.

Music, dramatic readings, and gallery art shows are an important part of the Upper School experience. Diverse curricular offerings in visual arts, theater, music, and dance provide opportunities for interdisciplinary study, and core academic classes often collaborate on thematic projects with the arts departments.

Recognizing that one's own creative development emerges from exposure to the creativity of others, Sacred Heart emphasizes a balance between performance and appreciation. Guest artists, performers, and lecturers regularly visit the school. Proximity to New York City creates opportunities to investigate unlimited cultural resources, while student exhibitions and performances showcase the talents cultivated in the school's classes and studios.

The Community Service Program is also an integral part of the Upper School experience at Sacred Heart. Using age-appropriate tools, students study a wide range of issues, including racism, poverty, housing, and education. Analysis of social injustices helps the students recognize that they can use their talents to be agents of change in the world. The Community Service Program explores domestic and global issues and includes guest speakers, individual yearly projects, service trips, and retreats. While service is required for Upper School students, most exceed the required 100 hours with extra volunteer work. The Barat Foundation is a student-run philanthropic organization that awards grants to community nonprofits and teaches financial literacy to students.

The Sacred Heart Exchange Program allows students to experience different cultures in the United States and around the world. Upper School students may complete an academic exchange of two to ten weeks at another Sacred Heart school. Convent of the Sacred Heart also welcomes exchange students to its campus. Recently, Sacred Heart students have studied in California, Chicago, Houston, Miami, New Orleans, and Seattle and abroad in England, Spain, Australia, Chile, Mexico, and Nova Scotia. Upon graduating, students are given an international Sacred Heart Passport listing the Sacred Heart schools throughout the world where they are always welcome.

DAILY LIFE

The first academic period begins at 8:25 a.m. The school day includes an advisory period, assembly periods, and time for many activities and club meetings. The day concludes at 3:25. Sports and a variety of activities occur after school. Students may buy or bring their lunch. A hot lunch is provided for a yearly fee.

SUMMER PROGRAMS

Sacred Heart hosts an annual Summer Academy program for 220 boys and girls in grades 2 through 9 from low-income families. The academic program is augmented with extracurricular activities, including team sports, swimming lessons, and hands-on experience with farm animals. The Summer Science Academy is for girls who show interest and promise in science and math entering grades 6 through 9 from low-income families. The five-week program includes traditional classroom experiences as well as guided scientific activities, independent investigations, and field trips.

The Summer Humanities Academy, which began in 2002, accepts girls entering grades 7 and 8 and offers a curriculum focused on writing, literature, and art. Students refined their writing skills, enhanced their reading and analytical skills, and had hands-on experiences that allowed them to understand the distinction between and the union of art and craft. Students used computers to create a literary magazine. Artists-in-residence offered workshops in writing, dance, and music. In addition, students received swimming instruction and participated in the farm program.

COSTS AND FINANCIAL AID

An education at Sacred Heart is an investment that provides many important and valuable opportunities. Tuition for 2008–09 is $30,400 for grades 9–12. The Financial Aid Committee is committed to helping families find ways to make an education at Convent of the Sacred Heart affordable. The Financial Aid Committee works with families to determine personalized need-based assistance and financial planning. Applying for financial aid has no bearing on admission to Convent of the Sacred Heart.

ADMISSIONS INFORMATION

Sacred Heart admits students without regard to race, religion, nationality, or ethnic origin. Applicants are considered on the basis of their school records, teacher recommendations, admission test scores, class visit, and personal interview. Entrance exams are administered at the school in November and at other local independent schools throughout the fall.

Families are encouraged to attend the Saturday Open House event (in November) or Thursday morning Tour Day programs (October, November, December, and January). Every October, Sacred Heart also hosts an evening Upper School Open House for students interested in grades 9–12. Individual tours and interviews are also available.

APPLICATION TIMETABLE

All application materials and visits must be completed by February 1. Decision letters are mailed by March 1. Applications for financial aid with supporting documentation are due by February 15.

ADMISSIONS CORRESPONDENCE

Katherine Machir, Director of Admission
Convent of the Sacred Heart
1177 King Street
Greenwich, Connecticut 06831

Phone: 203-532-3534
Fax: 203-532-3301
E-mail: admission@cshgreenwich.org
Web site: http://www.cshgreenwich.org

CRANBROOK SCHOOLS

Bloomfield Hills, Michigan

Type: Coeducational day and boarding college-preparatory school
Grades: PK–12: Brookside Lower School, Prekindergarten–5; Cranbrook Kingswood Middle School, 6–8; Cranbrook Kingswood Upper School, 9–12
Enrollment: School total: 1,630; Upper School: 775; Middle School: 340; Lower School: 516
Head of School: Arlyce M. Seibert, Director of Schools

THE SCHOOL

First established in 1922, Cranbrook Schools seek to prepare young men and women from diverse backgrounds to develop intellectually, morally, and physically; to move into higher education with competence and confidence; and to appreciate the arts. The Schools also strive to instill in their students a strong sense of social responsibility and the ability to contribute in an increasingly complex world.

Its founders, George and Ellen Scripps Booth, believed that "a life without beauty is only half lived." Critics have called the 315-acre Cranbrook campus "a masterpiece of American architecture." The buildings, gardens, and fountains were designed by Finnish architect, Eliel Saarinen, and offer students an exquisite environment in which to live and learn.

The Schools are a division of Cranbrook Educational Community, which also includes Cranbrook Institute of Science (a natural history and science museum serving Michigan and the Great Lakes region) and Cranbrook Academy of Art, known worldwide for its prestigious graduate programs in fine arts and architecture as well as its Art Museum. The entire complex has been designated a National Historic Landmark.

Cranbrook offers a comprehensive college-preparatory education that commences with Brookside (PK–5), continues in Cranbrook Kingswood Middle School (6–8, separate programs for boys and girls), and culminates in the opportunity and possibility that is provided by graduation from Cranbrook Kingswood Upper School (day and boarding, 9–12).

Bloomfield Hills is a residential suburb (population 3,985) approximately 25 minutes northwest of Detroit and 5 minutes from Birmingham.

A nonprofit corporation, Cranbrook is directed by a 21-member, self-perpetuating Board of Trustees, which meets four times a year. The corporation has a $234.5 million endowment. The Schools received $7,775,000 in gifts for the fiscal year ending June 30, 2008.

Cranbrook Kingswood is accredited by the Independent Schools Association of the Central States. It is a member of the National Association of Independent Schools.

ACADEMIC PROGRAMS

The school year, from September to early June, is divided into semesters. Classes, which enroll an average of 16 students each, meet five days a week. Eight academic periods are scheduled daily. All boarding students participate in supervised evening study hours from Sunday through Thursday. Grades are sent to parents quarterly, written evaluations are given semiannually, and progress reports for new students are issued in October.

Promotion from one class level to another is contingent upon faculty recommendations and is necessary for graduation. Each student is expected to take five academic classes each semester, along with a class chosen from the fine arts, performing arts, or computer departments. In order to graduate, students must complete the following minimum unit requirements: English, 4; mathematics, 4; foreign language, 2; social science/history, 2½; science, 3; religion/philosophy, 1; and performing or fine arts, 1. (One unit is the equivalent of a full-year course.)

In addition to sixty-eight full-year courses, Cranbrook Kingswood Upper School offers seventy-six semester courses, including Anatomy, Astronomy, Eastern Religious Traditions, Ethics, Genetics, Geology, Heroes in British Literature and Film, Human Geography, Principles of Macroeconomics, Principles of Psychology, and Russia and Eastern Europe. An extensive fine and performing arts program includes basic design, drawing, painting, sculpture, metalsmithing, ceramics, weaving, photography, dance, concert band, symphony orchestra, madrigals, jazz band, mastersingers, concert choir, acting, speech, and stagecraft.

Sixteen Advanced Placement (AP) courses are available in English, foreign languages, mathematics, and social sciences. Honors courses and directed-study programs are also offered for qualified students. ESL is offered for international students who demonstrate a strong academic record and a high intermediate level of English proficiency.

The Tennessee Wilderness Expedition (modeled on Outward Bound) is available to tenth graders each March. Seniors can participate in Senior May (off-campus projects) during the spring term. A fall semester exchange program with Cranbrook Kingswood's sister school, Cranbrook Kent, in Kent, England, is available to qualified juniors and seniors.

Students are graded on an A–E scale, although some elective courses are pass/fail. Students must maintain a minimum C- average to avoid academic probation. Classes are generally grouped by ability within grade level. The student-teacher ratio is 8:1.

FACULTY AND ADVISERS

More than 70 percent of the 91 full-time Cranbrook Kingswood Upper School faculty members reside on campus; 50 are men and 41 are women; 82 percent of the Upper School faculty members hold masters or Ph.D.s in the subject area that they teach. The average tenure of a Cranbrook Schools teacher is more than fourteen years.

In selecting its faculty, Cranbrook Kingswood seeks men and women with educational and intellectual curiosity. Faculty members are encouraged to explore special interests and talents that extend beyond their academic discipline. They are continually involved in professional advancement programs—course work, conferences, and workshops, the cost of which Cranbrook Kingswood largely underwrites. All faculty members are involved in some type of extracurricular activity, and each is an adviser to an average of 8 students, helping them in all aspects of school life from course selection to peer relationships.

Arlyce M. Seibert was appointed Vice President of Cranbrook Educational Community and the Director of Schools in 1996. Mrs. Seibert joined the Upper School in 1970 and has served in many capacities in her thirty-eight years with the Schools.

COLLEGE ADMISSION COUNSELING

Four full-time counselors help students select colleges, and representatives from more than 140 colleges visit Cranbrook Kingswood each year. The selection process begins in the junior year, involving both students and parents.

Among Cranbrook Kingswood's 2008 graduates, the mean SAT scores were 631 critical reading, 638 math, and 622 writing. A total of 195 graduates are attending such colleges and universities as Amherst, Barnard, Brown, Carnegie Mellon, Columbia, Cornell, Duke, Georgetown, Harvard, Johns Hopkins, MIT, Oberlin, Princeton, Yale, and the Universities of Chicago, Michigan, and Pennsylvania.

STUDENT BODY AND CONDUCT

The 2007–08 Upper School was composed of 157 boarding boys, 250 day boys, 102 boarding girls, and 266 day girls, distributed as follows: 173 in the ninth grade, 190 in tenth, 218 in eleventh, and 194 in twelfth. Twenty-four states and twenty countries were represented. Twenty-eight percent of students identified themselves as members of minority groups, and international students made up 11 percent of the student body.

Cranbrook Kingswood's disciplinary system is designed to be educative, not punitive. Honest conduct, regular attendance, punctual completion of assignments, and thoughtful adherence to school policies and rules are the minimum commitments expected of students. A Discipline Committee, consisting of faculty members, the deans, and elected students, assumes responsibility in matters of conduct. Major offenses may result in dismissal.

Students participate in several committees that help to shape life at Cranbrook Schools, such as the Conduct Review Board, the Dormitory Council, the Athletic Committee, the Diversity Committee, the Student Leadership Task Force, and the President's Council.

ACADEMIC FACILITIES

Students have the advantage of full access to two educational campuses. Kingswood's world-famous, Saarinen-designed building is a single continuous unit that includes a library with 23,500 volumes, a gymnasium, and six separate art studios.

Cranbrook's classrooms are located around a quadrangle in Lindquist Hall (1927) and Hoey Hall (1927). Other facilities that compose the quadrangle complex are a library with more than 21,500 volumes, a dining hall, boys dormitories, and a student center. A recently renovated performing arts center and the Gordon Science Center are located adjacent to the quadrangle.

Students take shuttle buses from one campus to another according to their class schedules. Students also have access to the museums and other resources at the Cranbrook Institute of Science and the Cranbrook Art Museum.

BOARDING AND GENERAL FACILITIES
Cranbrook Kingswood maintains single-sex boarding facilities. The campus buildings are linked by a fiber-optic network and provide telephone, computer, and video access in each dormitory room, classroom, lab, and faculty and student work area. The campus is equipped with more than ninety Smartboards.

The Kingswood dormitory for girls, adjacent to Kingswood Lake, houses 102 girls. Most live in suites that contain two single or double bedrooms with adjoining bath. The dormitory has two lounges with televisions, stereo equipment, and a piano. Two kitchenettes and laundry facilities are available, in addition to a four-lane bowling alley.

At the Cranbrook campus, there are single rooms for 157 boys, who are divided according to their grade. The student activity center has a dance floor, a snack bar, a performance space, recently renovated kitchen, and a small theater for videotape recording and viewing.

Many Cranbrook Kingswood faculty members live in the dormitories with their families. Others live in faculty homes clustered throughout the grounds. Resident Advisers (senior students) live on each floor and act as confidants and helpmates to their fellow boarders.

ATHLETICS
Cranbrook Kingswood Upper School provides the opportunity for participation in eighteen interscholastic sports, including baseball, basketball, cross-country, crew, fencing, field hockey, football, golf, ice hockey, lacrosse, skiing, soccer, softball, swimming, tennis, track, volleyball, and wrestling. Recent state championships include boys' and girls' tennis, girls' golf, boys' lacrosse, and boys' and girls' hockey. Among the intramural and noncompetitive athletic activities are martial arts, modern dance, rock climbing, strength and fitness, and walking for fitness.

Athletics facilities include a football stadium, a track, fifteen outdoor tennis courts, a dance studio, an indoor ice arena, three gymnasiums, and numerous playing fields. A $12-million natatorium was completed in 1999.

EXTRACURRICULAR OPPORTUNITIES
Cranbrook Kingswood offers thirty-nine student organizations, including Model UN, forensics, ethnic clubs, dramatics, community service, and publications including a newspaper and an arts and literary publication. Other clubs meet to discuss topics as varied as politics and racial diversity.

The cultural and educational events on campus include the exhibitions, lectures, films, and concerts offered through the science and art museums, highlighted by regular planetarium and laser shows, a world-class collection of modern American and European paintings, and traveling exhibits. The spacious grounds, wooded areas, lakes and indoor and outdoor theaters provide a serene setting for cross-country skiing, biking, jogging, swimming, and canoeing, as well as the Cranbrook Music Festival, the American Artists Series, the Cranbrook Kingswood Film Program, the Symposium Series, and the Cranbrook Retreat for Writers and Artists.

DAILY LIFE
The school day is divided into eight 45-minute classes between 8 a.m. and 3:20 p.m., including lunch, Monday through Friday. After-school activities such as class meetings, extra-help sessions, and athletics follow. Dinner for boarders begins at 5:30 weekdays, followed by a study period from 8 to 10 p.m.

WEEKEND LIFE
Boarding students have an unusual opportunity to take part in urban and rural activities on the weekends. Although students may go home some weekends with parental permission, there are weekends during the year when all boarding students must stay on the campus for special activities. Shuttle buses drive students to nearby Birmingham for shopping and entertainment, and groups can go to places such as Detroit and Ann Arbor for professional sporting events and cultural activities. There are frequent weekend camping, hiking, rock climbing, and skiing trips during the year. On-campus activities include dances, concerts, exhibits, lectures, sporting events, and recent movies at the student center.

SUMMER PROGRAMS
The Cranbrook Educational Community conducts several summer programs for day and boarding students and the community at large. These include day camps, a theater school, a soccer clinic, a film-making seminar, a compensatory educational program for youngsters from low-income families, a jazz ensemble, and ice hockey, lacrosse, and tennis camps.

COSTS AND FINANCIAL AID
The 2008–09 fees were $32,900 for boarding students and $24,900 for day students. Other expenses were for books ($450), insurance ($38), and a room deposit fee ($75). A tuition-payment plan and tuition insurance are offered.

In 2008–09, 28–30 percent of the Upper School students received some amount of tuition aid, some as much as 50 percent of day or boarding tuition. Incoming boarding students may apply for one of several full-tuition merit scholarships. Aid is based on financial need, following procedures established by the School and Student Service for Financial Aid; continuation is dependent on financial need, academic performance, and positive involvement in the school community.

ADMISSIONS INFORMATION
Cranbrook admits day students in preschool through grade 12 and boarding students in grades 9 through 12. The Schools accept students without regard to race, religion, national origin, sex, or handicap. Admission is based on recommendations, past performance, a personal interview, a writing sample, and results of the SSAT or other standardized examinations. Recommended grades for entrance are A's and B's.

APPLICATION TIMETABLE
An initial inquiry is welcome at any time. Campus tours and interviews are arranged on weekdays through the admissions office. Notification of acceptance begins in February. The application fee is $25.

ADMISSIONS CORRESPONDENCE
Drew Miller
Dean of Admission and Financial Aid
Cranbrook Schools
39221 Woodward Avenue
P.O. Box 801
Bloomfield Hills, Michigan 48303-0801
Phone: 248-645-3610
Fax: 248-645-3025
E-mail: admission@cranbrook.edu
Web site: http://www.schools.cranbrook.edu

CULVER ACADEMIES

Culver, Indiana

Type: Coeducational boarding and day school
Grades: 9–12, postgraduate year
Enrollment: 795
Head of Schools: John N. Buxton

THE SCHOOLS

The Culver Academies offer a college-preparatory curriculum within a boarding school environment for boys and girls in grades 9 through 12, with select opportunities available for postgraduate study. The Academies—Culver Military Academy, founded in 1894, and Culver Girls Academy, founded in 1971—provide a coeducational academic setting, with well-developed identities, traditions, and leadership systems. In accordance with its mission statement, Culver "educates its students for leadership and responsible citizenship in society by developing and nurturing the whole individual—mind, spirit, and body—through an integrated curriculum that emphasizes the cultivation of character."

Character development is essential to the Culver mission. For more than a century, the foundation of the Culver model has been an education in the classical virtues of wisdom, courage, moderation, and justice. Given that habits of mind, spirit, and body develop over time, an education in the virtues requires understanding, self-discipline, and practice. All aspects of Culver's academic, residential, extracurricular, and athletic curricula are designed to provide students with opportunities for individual growth within a structured environment and provide opportunities for them to begin the challenging task of developing lifelong habits.

Culver Academies is located in Culver, Indiana, 2 hours east of Chicago and 2 hours north of Indianapolis. The campus is located on the north shore of Lake Maxinkuckee, and students have the opportunity to enjoy all the benefits of its location. The school community also enjoys use of the thirty-nine buildings, including the Huffington Library, one of the ten largest secondary school libraries in the country; Roberts Hall of Science; Dicke Hall of Mathematics; and Eppley Auditorium.

A 38-member Board of Trustees is the governing body of Culver. The Culver Academies endowment is valued at approximately $181 million, supplemented in 2007–08 by annual fund contributions of $5.8 million.

Culver is accredited by the North Central Association of Colleges and Schools and the Independent Schools Association of the Central States and also holds a commission from the Indiana State Department of Education. Memberships include the National Association of Independent Schools, the College Board, the Secondary School Admissions Test Board, and School and Student Service for Financial Aid. Culver is a member of the National Association of College Admission Counseling.

ACADEMIC PROGRAMS

Culver is committed to intellectual growth through participation in a demanding curriculum that prepares students for success in higher education. Culver's curriculum emphasizes critical thinking, problem solving, writing, research, artistic expression, and foreign language proficiency through innovative teaching methods and technologically rich classrooms.

The curriculum incorporates a healthy combination of project-based learning and more traditional styles of education. Culver's technology initiative—issuing students laptops and establishing a wireless campus—has expanded opportunities for newer and more creative means of teaching.

The average class size is 14 students, and Culver enjoys a 9:1 student-faculty ratio. Honors academic sections are offered in most subjects, including Advanced Placement credit in twenty-one different courses. Nineteen and a half academic units of credit are required for a Culver diploma. The following are the minimum academic unit requirements for graduation: humanities 7.5; mathematics, 3; modern and classical language, 2; science, 3; fine arts, 1; wellness, .5; leadership, .5; and electives, 2.

In addition, Culver offers comprehensive instruction in beginning, intermediate, and advanced equitation; horse training; and stable management.

The school year at Culver consists of four 8-week terms, each divided into two grading periods. The grading system uses an A to F designation. Grades are sent to parents twice each term.

FACULTY AND ADVISERS

Like the student body, Culver faculty members come from a wide range of backgrounds. Eighty-seven percent of Culver's 98 full-and part-time instructors hold a master's degree. Ten hold doctoral degrees. Culver also supports a very successful internship program with 8 first-year interns, and 3 second-year interns. In addition to teaching, faculty members supervise dorms, coach, sponsor clubs, and act as mentors. Students benefit immensely from their close contacts with Culver's outstanding educators, coaches, and mentors.

Culver seeks to hire outstanding faculty members and allows them to continue their education in their fields and to take sabbatical leaves. In addition to the regular faculty, Culver supports one of the best-established and most extensive intern programs in private education. Each year, up to a dozen highly qualified recent college graduates join the faculty for one or two years of teaching, coaching, dorm supervision, and administrative responsibilities.

John N. Buxton has served as the head of schools since 1999. Prior to coming to Culver, Buxton was the vice-rector for administration and a member of the English faculty at St. Paul's School in Concord, New Hampshire. He is a graduate of Brown University and currently a Ph.D. candidate at Boston University.

COLLEGE ADMISSION COUNSELING

Led by the Director of College Advising, Ms. Corky Miller-Strong, a full-time staff assists students in the college selection process. Nearly 100 college representatives visit Culver each year. Beginning in the junior year, weekly classes are held in college and career guidance.

One hundred percent of the seniors from the class of 2008 were accepted to four-year undergraduate programs. The list of institutions admitting Culver students included Boston College, Bryn Mawr, Chicago, Dartmouth, Davidson, Duke, Emory, Harvard, Johns Hopkins, Michigan, MIT, North Carolina at Chapel Hill, Northwestern, Notre Dame, Pennsylvania, Pomona, Princeton, Purdue, Rice, Richmond, SMU, Stanford, Texas, Vanderbilt, Washington (St. Louis), Wellesley, and Yale.

STUDENT BODY AND CONDUCT

The 2008–09 student body represented forty-one states and twenty-two countries. Enrollment was as follows: 160 freshmen, 213 sophomores, 221 juniors, and 201 seniors. There were 462 boys and 333 girls—709 boarding and 86 day students.

Students not only learn about leadership in the classroom, they also experience it. It is this experience that helps students grow intellectually, socially, and morally. The boys' leadership program is organized around its own distinctive military system. The girls' program is designed around the traditional prefect system. Through the enactment of leadership ideals that is made possible in and through these systems, students develop confidence in their abilities to complete difficult tasks as well as habits of inquiry and self-discipline.

Each student is expected to make a positive effort to perform well academically, to develop respect for self and others, to maintain an orderly personal appearance, to meet personal responsibilities punctually and thoroughly, and to live and support the Culver Honor Code, which states, "I will not lie, cheat, or steal; and I will discourage others from such actions." Student leaders have an active role in guiding and monitoring the conduct of their fellow students.

BOARDING AND GENERAL FACILITIES

The boys' and girls' dormitories typically house 2 students per room. A number of faculty members, including the faculty interns, reside in the dormitories, and all share in supervision.

Culver students, as well as faculty and staff members and their families, eat in the Lay Dining Center. Students may visit the snack bar (the Shack) or the bookstore in the Lay Student Center. Within the Student Center, there are quiet rooms for study, lounges, and a television area for socializing and relaxation. Beason Hall (for seniors only) is the site of many social occasions. The Health Center, which is staffed 24 hours a day, has fifty beds and is used by students and faculty members.

ATHLETICS

Culver's wellness-education programs are an integral part of the curriculum. Participation affords a significant opportunity for the development of the virtues associated with personal integrity. Culver's athletic, health, and residential curricula emphasize sound decision making through programs that include fitness, nutrition, and respect for the body. There are over fifty competitive sports teams supported on campus. Over 70 percent of the student body are members of one or more of these teams.

The McMillen Athletic Center contains two gymnasiums, an eight-lane pool and separate diving tank, and the athletic hall of fame. The Steinbrenner Recreation Center houses a state-of-the-art fitness center, three basketball courts, two indoor tracks, an indoor tennis court, a wrestling room, two fencing rooms, and squash and racquetball courts.

Outdoor facilities include Wilkins Baseball Field; a softball field; Oliver Field for football, boys' lacrosse, and track and field; the fifteen-court state-of-the-art Gable Tennis complex; Henderson Arena (which houses two rinks—one NHL size and one Olympic size); numerous fields for soccer, rugby, and girls' lacrosse; a nine-hole golf course; and Lake Maxinkuckee for sailing and crew.

The Vaughn Equestrian Center is one of the largest riding halls in the nation, with stables for more than 100 horses. Culver competes in polo and hunter/jumper horse shows. The Black Horse Troop, the largest mounted cavalry unit in the United States, has appeared in fourteen presidential inaugural parades, and the girls' unit, the Equestriennes, in five.

EXTRACURRICULAR OPPORTUNITIES

Students have the opportunity to join any of the forty-five clubs, six music performance groups, and four vocal performance groups during their time at Culver. The extracurricular clubs include those that are academic, social, religious, and community-service oriented.

Each year, the Culver Concert Series brings musical, drama, and dance groups from all over the world to the campus to perform. Similarly, the Montgomery Lecture Series hosts nationally recognized speakers for both formal presentations and individual classroom discussions.

DAILY LIFE

The typical daily schedule consists of four 90-minute classes, beginning at 7:50 a.m. Athletic practices are conducted from 3:45 to 5:45 p.m., followed by dinner and an activity period for club and group meetings. Evening study is adult supervised and takes place from 7:30 to 9:30. With permission and leadership privileges, students are able to study in groups and in the library during the evening study time.

WEEKEND LIFE

Students make great use of the Culver campus and its recreational facilities. Dances, picnics, and Culver-sponsored trips are regular features of campus life. Students who have permission can spend time in town on the weekends and take periodic weekend leave to go home or to a friend's home. Weekend leave is in addition to the typical holiday and vacation schedule.

Each school year, there are two Parents Weekends, one in the fall and one in the spring. During each weekend, parents are encouraged to come to the campus to spend a day with their son or daughter, attend classes, and meet teachers. Parents are also invited to attend sporting events and lectures on the college planning process and meet with the residential supervisors throughout the weekend.

COSTS AND FINANCIAL AID

The tuition for 2008–09 was $34,000. These fees included the lease of a wireless laptop computer, academic instruction, room and board, special tutorial instruction, and most medical and other services. Textbooks cost approximately $500 per year. New student uniforms require a deposit of $1000 for girls and $1850 for boys. Incidental expenses can range up to about $100 a month, depending on the student. There are additional expense requirements for horsemanship, private music lessons, and driver's training. Each payment of tuition and fees is due prior to the first day of that term. A $2000 tuition deposit is due upon acceptance.

Students are awarded grants on the basis of overall scholastic credentials and financial need, as determined by the Parent's Service for Financial Aid. In 2008–09, financial aid was awarded to 45 percent of the student body and totaled more than $7.5 million.

The Culver Academies are proud to offer four nationally-based scholarships: the Batten Scholars Program, the Duchossois Family Scholars Program, the Roberts Leadership Scholarship, and the Jud Little Scholarship. All provide full tuition, room and board, and other educational benefit awards that are renewable for three or four years while the student attends Culver. All of the scholarship programs are seeking young men and women who are extraordinary in matters of the mind, spirit, and body. The Batten Scholars Program provides 6 new freshmen or sophomores from across the country a renewable merit scholarship. The Duchossois Family Scholars Program provides 4 new freshmen or sophomores from the greater Midwest a renewable merit and need-based scholarship. This scholarship is available by invitation or nomination only. The Roberts Leadership Scholarship provides 2 new freshmen from the western United States a renewable merit and need-based scholarship. The Jud Little Scholarship has been designated for 1 new freshman or sophomore with a passion for horses and residence in rural Oklahoma. It provides a renewable merit and need-based scholarship. More information on each of these distinctive scholarships is available from the Culver Academies Admissions department.

ADMISSIONS INFORMATION

The Admissions Committee selects students who are capable of pursuing a rigorous college-preparatory program and becoming effective and responsible citizens and leaders. Culver intends that its graduates be young men and women who are capable of clear and independent judgment and are sensitive to the rights and needs of others.

Applicants for admission must submit the results of the Secondary School Admission Test (SSAT) or other approved tests as well as four teacher evaluations and current transcripts from the previous two years. Applicants are also encouraged to visit the campus for a tour and observation of classes, to complete the personal interview, and to meet with members of the Academies' community.

APPLICATION TIMETABLE

An initial inquiry is welcome at any time. However, completion of all application materials by January 15 is recommended. Campus tours are arranged in conjunction with interviews, from 9 a.m. to 4:30 p.m. on weekdays and on Saturday by appointment. These should all be arranged at least one week prior to the visit.

Applications must be accompanied by a $40 nonrefundable fee.

ADMISSIONS CORRESPONDENCE

Office of Admissions
Culver Academies
1300 Academy Road #157
Culver, Indiana 46511-1291

Phone: 800-5-CULVER (toll-free)
Fax: 574-842-8066
E-mail: admissions@culver.org
Web site: http://www.culver.org

CUSHING ACADEMY

Ashburnham, Massachusetts

Type: Coeducational boarding and day college-preparatory school
Grades: 9–12, postgraduate year
Enrollment: 442
Head of School: Dr. James Tracy, Ph.D., M.B.A.

THE SCHOOL

Cushing Academy, founded in 1865, opened as a coeducational boarding school with funds provided by Thomas Parkman Cushing. Since its founding, Cushing Academy has prepared boys and girls in grades 9 through 12 and postgraduate to be contributing members of colleges and universities and of the modern world. Students live and learn with students from over twenty-four countries and twenty-eight states in a quiet, safe, and supportive community 1 hour west of Boston. At Cushing Academy, students are prepared for the technological, political, artistic, environmental, scientific, cultural, and ethical issues already present in their lives—the big questions of this new century that frame their academics, athletics, activities, and life on campus. Cushing builds students' global awareness, helps them to fulfill their aspirations, and enables them to learn the skills they will need to succeed throughout their lives.

Cushing's 160-acre campus lies in the small, rural town of Ashburnham in north-central Massachusetts, 55 miles west of Boston and 10 miles south of the New Hampshire border. Proximity to Boston permits extensive use of the city's cultural, entertainment, and commercial resources.

The Academy is governed by a 18-member Board of Trustees, 6 of whom are alumni. The operating budget for 2008–09 was $23 million, and the endowment was estimated at $22.6 million. Total voluntary support received in 2007-08 exceeded $5 million.

Cushing is accredited by the New England Association of Schools and Colleges. The Academy is a member of the National Association of Independent Schools, the Association of Independent Schools in New England, the Secondary School Admission Test Board, and the Cum Laude Society.

ACADEMIC PROGRAMS

The hub of Cushing's academic program is the newly instituted Cushing Center for Twenty-first Century Leadership. Designed to help high-school students understand the world of today and tomorrow, meeting students at their academic level, the center brings current issues into every classroom, drives curriculum, facilitates global travel experiences, and brings a range of speakers to campus in order to deliver the world to Cushing students. The center also provides leadership and entrepreneurial opportunities on campus and coordinates the Cushing Scholars, an enrichment program for students selected on the basis of intellectual, athletic, and artistic promise, as well as leadership potential.

The Academy offers more than 150 full-year courses and seminars, including ten laboratory courses and fifteen advanced-level courses. Advanced independent study programs may be arranged through the Dean of Faculty and Academics.

Typically, Cushing Academy students carry five major courses every trimester, in addition to a required elective in the visual or performing arts. To satisfy Cushing's diploma requirements, students must earn a total of 18 credits distributed as follows: English, 4; mathematics, 4; foreign language, 2; history and social science, 2; science, 2; and fine arts, ⅓ per year at Cushing. The remaining requirements may be filled by choosing from numerous electives, including ethics, creative writing, ecology, marine biology, economics, comparative religions, global diplomacy, and leadership.

All teachers are available in their classrooms during a daily extra-help period. Informal tutoring may also take place after dinner or during free time.

The Academy offers a structured academic support program staffed by 6 educational specialists who work with students on a variety of strategies to assist them with their academic programs. Students who enroll in the academic support program, either through the admissions process or who are identified as needing additional support after they arrive at Cushing, take one or more courses with the academic support specialists, concurrent with their other classes, for an additional fee. With students from twenty-nine countries, Cushing also has a thriving international community. Students entering Cushing in need of English as a second language enroll in the ESL program for one or more years and then transition into the standard academic offerings.

The academic year is divided into three terms of twelve, ten, and nine weeks in length. Cumulative final exams are given at the end of fall and spring terms in all academic courses. Evaluations are sent home six times each year. Letters warning of academic difficulty are written at the discretion of the Academic Dean.

Cushing uses a letter grading system that follows a 4.0 scale; 1.2 is passing, 3.3–3.6 is honors, and 3.7 and above is high honors. Class placement is determined by demonstrated ability and past performance in each subject area. The average class size is 12 students. The student-teacher ratio is approximately 8:1. On weeknights from 8 to 10 p.m., students work quietly in their rooms during supervised study hall.

FACULTY AND ADVISERS

In 2008–09, the faculty and administration consisted of 92 full-time teachers and administrators—45 women and 47 men, of whom 52 had master's degrees, and 7 had earned their Ph.D.'s. Seventy percent of faculty members live on campus, and all faculty members are involved in the daily life of students beyond the classroom experience. Each teacher is responsible for the academic, social, extracurricular, and dorm life for 5 to 7 student advisees.

The Headmaster, Dr. James Tracy, came to Cushing in 2006. He received an M.A. from the University of Massachusetts, a Ph.D. from Stanford University, and an M.B.A. from Boston University.

COLLEGE ADMISSION COUNSELING

Staffed by 5 experienced professionals, the Cushing Academy College Counseling Office is a resource available to all students and parents. The counseling process begins when a student enters the school, at which time a comprehensive College Counseling Guide is presented to each student and his or her parents. Cushing believes in engaging the students at all levels and that the college advising process should focus on each student's particular needs, aspirations, and abilities. The goal is to provide students and parents with information that will help all to feel knowledgeable, confident, and calm as they move through this exciting time.

Group meetings are held regularly for each of the various grade levels on such topics as summer activities, college research, campus visits, athletic recruitment, interviews, financial aid, applications, and standardized tests. Workshops for parents are presented during Parent Weekends in the fall and spring. During the winter and spring trimesters, juniors meet individually with a member of the college counseling staff to establish a prospective list of colleges. The following fall, a new round of group meetings and individual interviews take place to aid the seniors in completing their applications to universities of responsible choice.

Standardized tests, including the SAT and the ACT, are administered on-site at Cushing throughout the year, beginning with the PSAT in October. Individual tutoring and group test preparation is available for an additional fee.

The College Counseling Office utilizes Naviance, a Web-based counseling tool and database that aids the students and the office in the research process as well as in the organization and management of the application process. In addition, a library of college counseling books, course catalogs, viewbooks, DVDs, and other college materials are available in the College Counseling Office.

College enrollments for the class of 2008 included Boston College, Boston University, Bowdoin, Brown, Cornell, College of the Holy Cross, Dartmouth, George Washington, Hofstra, Parsons School of Design, Purdue, Syracuse, University of Virginia, Vanderbilt, and Wellesley. Admission representatives from over eighty colleges and universities visit the Cushing Academy campus each fall to meet with the students and college counseling staff.

STUDENT BODY AND CONDUCT

The 2008–09 student body consisted of 38 boys and 18 girls in the freshman class; 60 boys and 61 girls in the sophomore class; 71 boys and 50 girls in the junior class; 67 boys and 56 girls in the senior class; and 20 boys and 1 girl in the postgraduate class.

Of these 442 students, 369 were boarders. Students were predominantly from Massachusetts (146) and other parts of New England (52), as well as from New York (15), Florida (10), and Georgia (9), and Texas (9). Twenty-eight states and Puerto Rico, as well as twenty-nine other countries, ranging from Indonesia to Germany, were represented. Of the total enrollment, 6 percent were African American.

Students play an active role in school governance through their participation in the school's thriving student organizations, such as student proctors, class officers, student-faculty senate, and tour guides, and through participation in the school's discipline committee process. Through these and other organizations, students influence decision making at the school and serve as leaders for the community.

ACADEMIC FACILITIES

The center of school life is the Main Building, which contains offices, classrooms, and the school's Cowell

Chapel. Also in the Main Building is the Fisher-Watkins Library, which is well equipped for research and informal reading. The Joseph R. Curry Academic Center, which houses mathematics, the sciences, and the performing arts, opened in January 2005. This state-of-the-art facility of more than 56,000 square feet includes instructional laboratories, studios, student project rooms, and seminar space. The English building houses seven newly renovated classrooms. The Emily Fisher Landau Center for the Visual Arts has both studio and gallery space for students to create and display professional-quality work in a variety of media, including fused and stained glass, silver, ceramics, photography, painting, and sculpture. Academy students have been invited to display their works in galleries in both Santa Fe and New York.

The Cushing Network, a campuswide computer network, may be accessed from more than 500 locations throughout the school, including all classrooms and dormitory rooms; all academic areas of the school are equipped with wireless technology. CushNet and Penguin, the school's intranet systems, allow students to send e-mail, join bulletin-board discussions for many classes, communicate with teachers and friends, follow campus happenings, monitor homework and submit assignments. SmartBoard technology is available in all classrooms.

BOARDING AND GENERAL FACILITIES

The Academy houses more than 350 students in seven dormitories and six student-faculty houses that vary in capacity from 3 to 81 students each. Almost all rooms are doubles, and returning students select rooms through a room-draw system that favors seniority. New students are assigned rooms by the Co-Directors of Admission and the Student Life Office. The ratio of faculty to students in the dormitories is generally 1:12.

Cushing's dining facility houses a student center on the lower level, which includes a recreational area, snack bar, bookstore, and post office. Formal family-style dinners are served once a month.

ATHLETICS

In the belief that physical fitness and agility enrich both the individual and the community, Cushing's renowned athletic program is designed to involve everyone in physical endeavors. There are boys' interscholastic teams in baseball, basketball, cross-country, football, golf, ice hockey, lacrosse, skiing, soccer, tennis, and track; girls compete in basketball, cross-country, field hockey, ice hockey, lacrosse, skiing, soccer, softball, tennis, track, and volleyball. Organized recreational sports include aerobics, dance, figure skating, riding, skiing, tennis, volleyball, and weight lifting.

The Heslin Gymnasium contains four locker rooms, the John Biggs Jr. Memorial Fitness Center, a training room, and a basketball court. There are also six playing fields and six tennis courts. In addition to year-round ice skating, the Theodore Iorio Ice Arena offers boys' and girls' locker rooms, work-out facilities, a multipurpose function room, snack bar, and pro shop.

EXTRACURRICULAR OPPORTUNITIES

In addition to their commitments in the classroom and on the playing fields, Cushing students take advantage of the many opportunities to join or start up clubs and to organize campus events. Always based on student interest, clubs in recent years have included Open Doors, International Club, Environmental Club, Cushing Academy Music Association, Literary Magazine, and Book Club. Students are also involved in coordinating campus events.

Cushing's proximity to Boston enables students to have access to the city's cultural resources—ballet, opera, theater, symphony, and museums—and regular trips to take advantage of these opportunities are scheduled throughout the year. Students interested in exploring opportunities in business, the arts, law, or other fields can also pursue internships with Boston-area professionals.

DAILY LIFE

The Monday-through-Friday schedule, which begins with classes at 8 a.m., provides time for an extra-help period, activities, and athletics before evening study hall at 8 p.m. Lights-out is at 10:30 p.m. for underclassmen and 11 for seniors and postgraduates. Classes are 40 minutes long on Mondays and Fridays and 55 minutes long on Tuesdays, Wednesdays, and Thursdays. Courses, activities, and athletics are all centrally scheduled to avoid unnecessary conflicts. Saturday morning classes are held from 8 a.m. to noon once per term. On weekdays, the hours from 3 to 5 p.m. are reserved for athletics, arts, and activities; interscholastic competitions occur on Wednesday, Friday (occasionally), and Saturday.

WEEKEND LIFE

On a typical weekend at the Academy, students enjoy many off-campus trips with faculty chaperones. Movies are shown on campus each weekend, while dances and concerts are often scheduled in the evening. Students are permitted to spend a limited number of weekends off campus, but on any given weekend 70 to 75 percent of the boarding population chooses to remain at school. Five weekends throughout the school year are restricted, meaning students may not sign out to leave campus, in an effort to foster community spirit. These include the first weekend of the year, as well as the weeks just prior to exams.

SUMMER PROGRAMS

During the five-week summer session, Cushing offers a unique boarding school experience for girls and boys ages 12–18 from throughout the United States and around the world. The program features Prep for Success for middle school students, regular and advanced college-preparatory courses for high school students, intensive art, and extensive English as a second language instruction. Each program is combined with interesting artistic and athletic electives as well as exciting excursions throughout New England. For further information, students should contact Margaret Lee, Director of Summer Programs.

COSTS AND FINANCIAL AID

Tuition and required fees for 2008–09 were $42,000 for boarding students and $30,600 for day students. There were optional fees for skiing, music lessons, and fine arts materials. A $4200 nonrefundable enrollment deposit is credited toward the balance due; half of the remaining total is due on July 1 and the balance on December 1.

In 2008–09, 26 percent of the student body received $2.9 million in financial aid. Funds are awarded on the basis of need as demonstrated by established criteria of the School and Student Service for Financial Aid. Financial aid is renewed annually, subject to continued need and availability of funds.

ADMISSIONS INFORMATION

Cushing Academy seeks students are interested in taking an active role in promoting their own academic and social growth. Cushing values strong character, motivation, diversity, and strength in extracurricular activities. Candidates are evaluated based on school performance, SSAT, PSAT, SAT, ACT, TOEFL, or other tests, and a personal interview. If travel is too difficult, international applicants may request an interview by telephone.

APPLICATION TIMETABLE

Initial inquiries are welcome at any time, and application materials including the school's viewbook are provided upon request. Interviews and campus tours are scheduled Monday through Friday and some Saturdays.

Completed applications should be submitted, along with the $50 nonrefundable application fee ($100 for international students), by February 1. Applications may be submitted after February1, and will be acted on after March 10, subject to the availability of spaces in the classes. Decisions are mailed out on March 10 for students submitting applications by the deadline, and for others on a rolling basis as space permits.

ADMISSIONS CORRESPONDENCE

Deborah Gustafson, Co-Director of Admission
Adam Payne, Co-Director of Admission
Cushing Academy
39 School Street
P.O. Box 8000
Ashburnham, Massachusetts 01430
Phone: 978-827-7300
Fax: 978-827-6253
E-mail: admission@cushing.org
Web site: http://www.cushing.org

DANA HALL SCHOOL

Wellesley, Massachusetts

Type: Girls' boarding (9–12) and day college-preparatory school
Grades: 6–12: Middle School, 6–8; Upper School, 9–12
Enrollment: School total: 500; Upper School: 370; Middle School: 130
Head of School: Caroline Erisman P11

THE SCHOOL

Founded in 1881 as a preparatory school for Wellesley College, Dana Hall today sends its graduates to a variety of colleges and universities in the United States and abroad. In addition to maintaining its traditional focus on academic preparation for college, Dana Hall provides young women with opportunities to develop intellectual abilities, self-knowledge, and a sense of community in an atmosphere of women that is enriched by the diversity among its students and faculty members. Dana Hall's belief is that education should be a continuous process of personal challenges directed toward the individual's effective participation in a changing world. The School strives to provide a composite of learning through intellectually rigorous programs and independent study, through the sharing of common purposes and responsibilities for the School community, and through involvement in the world beyond the campus.

Dana Hall is located 12 miles west of Boston, offering the cultural and academic advantages of the city as well as its own attractive suburban campus. A 24-member Board of Trustees is the governing body; currently, it is composed of 17 women and 7 men. Ten members are Dana Hall graduates.

Dana Hall is accredited by the New England Association of Schools and Colleges and is a member of the Secondary School Admission Test Board, the Educational Records Bureau, the National Association of Independent Schools, the Independent School Association of Massachusetts, the Association of Independent School Admission Professionals, A Better Chance, the National Coalition of Girls' Schools, and The Association of Boarding Schools.

ACADEMIC PROGRAMS

Students must complete 18 academic credits in grades 9–12, including the following requirements: English, 4; foreign language, through third level of the same language; mathematics, 3; science and social studies, 5 combined; laboratory science, minimum 2; social studies, minimum 2 (including 1 credit in U.S. history and 1 credit in area studies); computer science, ½; performing arts, ½; visual arts, ½.; fitness/athletics, 1 (earned as ¼ yearly); community service, 20 hours (must be completed in grade 10).

Dana Hall's academic philosophy expects students to reach beyond the School's minimum requirements and to develop independence in the pursuit of learning. The School also emphasizes the links between study and experience through dynamic, interactive classroom teaching; special programs; guest lecturers; field trips; and independent projects.

Students interested in pursuing independent study in a particular area may do so under the guidance of an adviser from the corresponding academic department. Off-campus internship experiences are arranged through the Community Service Program. School Year Abroad (SYA) is a yearlong program recognized by Dana Hall for the valuable educational experience it provides its students. Students may choose to study abroad in China, France, Italy, or Spain. Students live with a host family and attend classes for the academic year. There is also an opportunity to participate in a six-week exchange program with the Ruyton Girls' School in Melbourne, Australia, or St. Mary's Anglican Girls' School in Perth, Australia, and an opportunity to be part of the Rocky Mountain Institute in Leadville, Colorado. Other travel opportunities are available through spring break trips, led by faculty members, throughout the United States and to Costa Rica, France, Italy, Spain, and South Africa.

The average class at Dana has 12 students; the student-faculty ratio is 9:1. Grades and comments are sent out to parents three times per year. Students meet with their advisers twice as a group and once each week on an individual basis to discuss academic progress and overall well-being.

FACULTY AND ADVISERS

Dana Hall employs 64 full-time teachers, all of whom are active in advising and counseling students. Sixty-six faculty members have degrees beyond the bachelor's level, and 33 members of the faculty and staff reside on the campus. In addition, there are 6 house directors and 6 house assistants who help supervise the nonacademic life of the residential students.

Ms. Caroline Erisman was appointed Dana Hall's tenth Head of School, effective July 2008. Ms. Erisman is a graduate of Wellesley College and holds a master's degree from Columbia University's Teachers College and a juris doctorate degree from New York University School of Law. Prior to becoming Head of School at Dana Hall, she was Associate Head of School at the Hewitt School in New York City from 2001–08. She also held the position of Director of College Counseling from 1996–2002 and taught English and Latin in the Middle and Upper Schools at Hewitt. She has also taught at Rye Country Day School, New York, and the Town School, New York City.

COLLEGE ADMISSION COUNSELING

Beginning in the junior year, all students meet weekly with one of the college counselors as part of the Forum Program. Group discussions concerning preparation for the senior year, leadership, and social responsibility are part of the program. In addition, such topics as self-evaluation, decision-making, testing, and the college admission process are discussed. The college counselor meets with individual students and parents by appointment throughout the junior and senior years and plans a special college day for juniors and their parents each spring. Students also meet with any of the 120 college representatives who visit the Dana Hall campus annually. In addition, the college counselor plans special programs addressing issues involved in the college application and selection process for parents and students throughout the year. Seniors are encouraged to apply to colleges and universities with varying degrees of selectivity and to consider choices in terms of their own performance and goals.

The diversity of the students at Dana Hall is reflected in the variety of their college choices. In the past three years, graduates have attended more than 100 colleges and universities worldwide. The following colleges are representative of the larger number of colleges chosen by the Dana Hall graduates in the class of 2008: Boston University, Brown, Colorado College, Lehigh, Santa Clara, Smith, Tufts, and Wellesley.

STUDENT BODY AND CONDUCT

Of the 370 students enrolled in the Upper School at Dana Hall, 145 are boarding students and 225 are day students. Each class size varies, with 85 in grade 9, 99 in grade 10, 98 in grade 11, and 88 in grade 12. Although a majority of the students come from New England, eleven states and seventeen countries are represented, including Bermuda, China, Ecuador, Germany, Hong Kong, Japan, Korea, Mexico, the Philippines, Rwanda, Saudi Arabia, Spain, Taiwan, Thailand, and the United Kingdom.

Student Council considers the overall life of the School and provides proactive solutions through proposals and open forums to issues in the community. Student Council meets weekly, and members include the Dean of Students, the All-School Co-Presidents, and 2 elected students from each grade (1 boarding and 1 day student).

ACADEMIC FACILITIES

There are four main academic buildings: the Classroom Building, the Dana Hall School of Music, Wayside Resource Center, and the Middle School Building. Among the facilities of the Classroom Building and Middle School Building, there are four computer centers, Waldo Assembly Hall, a fully wired lecture hall, the art gallery, and two art studios. The Wayside Student Center houses the language lab, the math lab, the writing lab, the offices of the Learning Specialist, and the School Psychologist. Bardwell Auditorium, located on Cameron Street, is home to Dana Hall's Performing Arts Department. Although the campus is fairly spread out, the Helen Temple Cook Library, the Shipley Athletic Center, and the Dining Center bring students together during the day.

The Helen Temple Cooke Library offers students and faculty members a collection of more than 32,000 items (books, audiobooks, videos, CDs, DVDs), 175 print periodical subscriptions (including seven daily and two weekly newspapers), a pamphlet file, two digital pianos, two photocopiers, a media production facility, and the Dana Hall School Archives. The library catalog, a full array of databases and e-books, 20,000 full-text online periodicals, course pathfinders, and additional information about the library can be accessed through the library resource page. The library is fully automated and is a member of several shared library systems that provide access to the resources of hundreds of libraries statewide. There are eighteen desktop computers and nineteen laptops available for student use, and wireless Internet access throughout the library enables laptop users to access a wide variety of applications. There is a fireplace in the periodical room, which is a great place to read and study. In addition to instruction in the use of traditional research tools, the library staff also offers training in audiovisual technology and educates students in media literacy.

BOARDING AND GENERAL FACILITIES

Girls reside in six dormitories, which range in character from a contemporary four-building complex to houses. The Johnston dormitories are the largest units, with up to 25 girls in each unit. Girls in the ninth and tenth grades are the primary residents of the Johnstons. Each of the Johnstons connects via an underground tunnel system, which also houses laundry facilities and the ceramics studio. In each of the house dorms are 14–25 girls in grades 11 and 12. Each dormitory is supervised by a set of house directors and a house assistant. A student proctor aids in house supervision.

Beveridge Hall, an attractive Greco-Roman-style building in the center of campus, is the location of the Development, Business, College Counseling, and Admission and Financial Aid offices. The remaining administrative offices—Academic Affairs, Student

Activities, and Residential Life—are located in the Classroom Building. The corridor connecting the Dining Center to Beveridge Hall contains darkroom facilities and a photography gallery.

The Dana Hall School campus also includes the Shipley Center, a state-of-the-art athletic, health, and wellness facility. Three buildings in one—health center, athletic and fitness center, and student activity center—the facility meets the needs of students and faculty members during the school day as well as after school and on the weekends. *Athletic Business Magazine* honored the Shipley Center as one of the top 10 cutting-edge buildings in the country and presented the School with a 2006 Facility of Merit Award. The campus also includes a riding center featuring a brand new large barn complete with forty-five stalls.

ATHLETICS

Dana Hall's athletic/fitness program is designed to meet the varying needs of students, as each student is required to participate in physical education each trimester. Students may elect to play on interscholastic teams at the varsity and junior varsity levels. Competitive teams include basketball, cross-country, equestrian, fencing, field hockey, golf, ice hockey, lacrosse, soccer, softball, squash, swimming, tennis, and volleyball. Fitness and physical education classes are available, which introduce all aspects of fitness including cardiovascular fitness, nutrition, weight training, and stretching exercises, or offer a chance to play in a variety of cardiovascular or sports-related activities, such as aqua aerobics, yoga, self-defense, strength and conditioning, rock climbing, and Ultimate Frisbee. The physical education requirement can also be satisfied through the dance program or riding program.

The Shipley Center for Athletics, Health & Wellness is a 93,000-square-foot facility that opened in fall 2005 and houses a 21,000-square-foot gymnasium with two NCAA regulation-size basketball courts; a three-lane, suspended indoor track; a 25-yard six-lane swimming pool; a 465-sqaure-foot, custom-designed climbing wall; a squash center composed of four squash courts; a fencing studio equipped with six built-in fencing strips; a weight and fitness room; a Health Center; a student hub; and a dance studio.

The Dana Hall Riding School includes a new, state-of-the-art barn featuring forty-five spacious stalls that allow all horses to be housed in one location, two heated indoor wash stalls, and a safe and clean environment for horses and riders. In addition, the Riding Center has two indoor arenas and a large outdoor ring. The facility also includes six turnout paddocks, two of which are on grass. Rounding out the campus are four athletic fields for fall and spring games.

EXTRACURRICULAR OPPORTUNITIES

Extracurricular activities are viewed as an important part of student life. Participation in the various activities enables students to develop interests, determine individual strengths, and encounter the outside community. Students may choose from a variety of opportunities, including athletic teams, musical groups, a literary society, language clubs, student publications, student government, the activities committee, and service clubs. Also available are Blue Key, Drama, International Student Club, People Recognizing Injustices in Need of Thoughtful Solutions (PRINTS), Sisters Honoring All Diasporas and Enlightening the Community (SHADES), Bridge, Environmental Club, Green Team, Outdoors Club, and Peer Education. These activities are open to any student who wishes to join.

DAILY LIFE

On weekdays, the morning begins at 8 a.m. with either an adviser meeting (twice a week) or an all-school assembly (three times a week). Classes meet five days a week on a modular block schedule from 8:20 a.m. until 3:30 (Monday, Tuesday, and Thursday) or until 2:05 p.m. (Wednesday and Friday). Incorporated into the academic day on Mondays, Wednesdays, and Fridays is a conference/study period, a time during which all students and teachers are free. This is a valuable opportunity for students to talk with their teachers about concepts covered in class, review class notes, begin their homework, ask for feedback on an assignment, prepare for a test, or work on group projects. Students may also make arrangements to meet with their teachers during common free periods. Sports practices and games take place after the academic day. Assemblies, conference seminars, and special programs, such as the Wannamaker Lecture Series, may be scheduled in the evening.

WEEKEND LIFE

The boarding program at Dana Hall prepares young women for adulthood as they learn the skills necessary for continued growth and development of character. All Upper School students (grades 9 through 12) have the opportunity to take advantage of the boarding program. Although the day students commute from the surrounding communities, boarders come not only from New England but also from across the country and around the world.

Students live in one of six dormitories on the campus, which are supervised by house directors, house assistants, and student proctors. To strengthen the community, all faculty members have a dorm affiliation. The affiliate program brings the community together for overnights, cookouts, outings into Boston, and late-night snacks.

Social opportunities are also an important aspect of Upper School life. Students work with the Activities Coordinator to create a variety of weekend activities to be enjoyed by boarders and day students alike. Opportunities range from movies, concerts, plays, dances on campus, and sporting events in Boston to ski trips or Six Flags New England. There are a number of independent boys' schools and coed schools in the area with which the School collaborates on social events, community service projects, and drama productions.

COSTS AND FINANCIAL AID

In 2008–09, Upper School tuition was $33,981 for day students and $44,904 for boarding students.

No one should hesitate to apply for admission to Dana Hall solely because of an inability to meet costs. Financial aid is awarded on the basis of need, as determined by the School, with the assistance of the need assessment of the School and Student Service for Financial Aid and a family's 1040 income tax form. In 2008–09, more than $2.8 million in financial aid grants were awarded on the basis of need.

ADMISSIONS INFORMATION

Candidates for admission are often concerned about how applicants are evaluated. At Dana Hall, the first considerations are a student's academic ability and intellectual curiosity, as reflected by her school record and recommendations. Dana Hall is also interested in a student's spirit, motivation, character, and ability to work with others.

All candidates must take the ISEE or the SSAT. International students must take the TOEFL. Test results are very helpful in determining patterns of strengths or weaknesses, but Dana Hall does not have a test cutoff–point below which applicants are refused consideration.

In addition to test scores and school records, students must submit two teacher recommendations. A personal interview is required for each applicant. However, if a student cannot travel to the campus, a phone interview can be arranged.

APPLICATION TIMETABLE

Completed applications should be submitted, along with the application fee, by February 1 for March 10 notification. Applications may be submitted after February and will be acted on as the files are completed, subject to the availability of places in the class.

ADMISSIONS CORRESPONDENCE

Wendy Sibert Secor, P13, 15
Director of Admission and Financial Aid
Dana Hall School
45 Dana Road
Wellesley, Massachusetts 02482
Phone: 781-235-3010
Fax: 781-239-1383
E-mail: admission@danahall.org
Web site: http://www.danahall.org

DARLINGTON SCHOOL

Rome, Georgia

Type: Coeducational, college-preparatory boarding and day school
Grades: Pre-K–12 and postgraduate: Lower School, pre-K–5; Middle School, 6–8; Upper School, 9–12; Upper School boarding, 9–12; postgraduate year
Enrollment: School total: 898 Upper School: 506
Head of School: Thomas C. Whitworth III, Headmaster

THE SCHOOL

Darlington School offers motivated students rigorous academics, numerous fine arts opportunities, and a competitive athletics program in a nurturing environment. Named after a teacher, Darlington was founded in 1905 as a boys' school by students of Joseph James Darlington, who believed in academic excellence, insisted upon honest and diligent effort, and stressed development of character directed to the service of God and humankind. These fundamental principles, which put the student-teacher relationship at the forefront of everything the School does, have carried Darlington through a century of changes, including the addition of a boarding division in 1923, the establishment of coeducation in 1973, and an emphasis on technology throughout the curriculum in the 1990s.

Stretching for more than 400 acres, Darlington's beautiful campus is nestled around a small lake in the foothills of the Appalachian Mountains in Rome, Georgia, a community of 93,000. Home to Berry, Georgia Highlands, Coosa Valley Technical, and Shorter Colleges and the medical hub of northwest Georgia, Rome is a little more than an hour's drive from Atlanta and Chattanooga, Tennessee.

Under the governance of a 36-member Board of Trustees composed of alumni, parents, and grandparents, Darlington operates on a $ 22.2-million budget, with more than $1.5 million coming from Annual Giving and another $ 2.3 million generated from a $4.8-million endowment fund.

Darlington, a nonprofit organization, is dually accredited by the Southern Association of Colleges and Schools and the Southern Association of Independent Schools. In addition, Darlington holds membership in the National Association of Independent Schools as well as other professional organizations.

ACADEMIC PROGRAMS

The academic year, divided into trimesters, begins in late August and ends in late May, with extended breaks at Thanksgiving, Christmas, and spring. Classes, held five days a week, are scheduled in eight 45-minute rotating periods between 8 a.m. and 3:30 p.m. A 1-hour period for athletics, fitness, fine arts, and other activities follows the class day for residential students. The schedule allows students to maintain five or more academic subjects, electives, and extracurricular activities throughout the day. The average class size is 14, with a 13:1 student/teacher ratio. Extra help is available every morning in classroom sessions before school. The School's Learning Center is designed to support and enhance the academic experience of all students, while directly serving students who have documented learning differences. Resident students have a supervised study hall of 2 hours each evening in their rooms. Grades are available online continuously for students and parents. Parents receive daily e-mail notification of updates. Teacher comments and conduct reports are also available on the Web site.

To graduate from the Upper School, a student must complete 22 credits, including 4 years of English, 2 of a single world language, 3 of history, 3 of mathematics, 3 of science, 1 of information technology, 1 of fine arts, 2 electives, 1 of fitness, and 2 of health/wellness. Beginning with the class of 2010, 3 years of world language will be required for graduation.

Darlington offers a wide range of courses. English 1–4 covers grammar, composition, literary criticism, and American, British, and world literature. Language department offerings include French 1–5 and Spanish 1–5. The history department offers full-year courses in ancient world history, modern world history, U.S. history, and government/economics, and electives in world religions. Math department courses include algebra 1–3, geometry, precalculus, statistics, and calculus. Courses in the science department consist of biology, chemistry, organic chemistry, physics, environmental science, Georgia natural history, and anatomy. The fine arts department offers art 1–4, drama 1–2, musical theater, humanities, music appreciation, music theory, cinema, chorale, concert choir, instrumental music, wind ensemble, percussion methods, orchestra, and steel drum band. Information technology and communications offerings include introduction to computers, computers and robotics, advanced Web design, video production 1–2, graphic design, and computer science. Additional courses include health/wellness, and fitness.

Honors courses are available in most subjects. Twenty-two Advanced Placement courses are offered in English language, English literature, European history, U.S. history, world history, macroeconomics/microeconomics, psychology, calculus (AB), calculus (BC), statistics, French, Spanish, Spanish language, Spanish literature, chemistry, biology, physics B, physics C, environmental science, computers, studio art, art history, and music theory. In 2008, 157 Darlington students took a total of 307 AP exams. In 2007, Darlington had 20 AP Scholars, 9 AP Scholars with Honors, 11 AP Scholars with Distinction, and 3 AP National Scholars, for a total of 43 AP Scholars.

FACULTY AND ADVISERS

Darlington takes great pride in hiring faculty members who are passionate about the subjects they teach and who have a devout interest in working with young people. Of the 85 teachers and administrators in the Upper School, 47 live on campus. All hold baccalaureate degrees, and more than half have advanced degrees. It is a common occurrence for teachers and students to work on English papers, figure out math problems, and practice foreign languages after school hours.

In July 2005, Thomas C. Whitworth III became Darlington's seventh President. With more than twenty-five years of administrative experience, Whitworth served as founding Headmaster of Flint Hill School in Oakton, Virginia, from 1989 to 2005. He has served as Assistant Headmaster and Academic Dean at St. Stephen's School in Alexandria, Virginia; Headmaster at Frederica Academy on St. Simon's Island, Georgia; and Assistant Headmaster and Upper School Director at Sea Pines Academy on Hilton Head Island, South Carolina. Whitworth holds a Bachelor of Arts degree in journalism from the University of North Carolina at Chapel Hill and a Master of Education in secondary education and supervision and English from The Citadel.

Every Darlington student is assigned an academic adviser and is in an advisee group of about 8 students. These groups meet at the beginning of each day and occasionally go out to dinner or meet at the adviser's home. The adviser may also meet with advisees on an individual basis to discuss academic performance and other issues. The adviser is considered the parents' primary contact at the School, whether the concern is academic or personal. The advisory program is under the direction of the School's full-time personal counselor and the Director of Student Life.

COLLEGE ADMISSION COUNSELING

All Darlington graduates go to college and are systematically counseled by the Dean of College Guidance, the Associate Dean of College Guidance, and a team of 12 college advisers.

The 114 graduates in the class of 2008 were accepted at 131 colleges and universities and attended sixty different colleges in twenty states and France.

Of the class of 2008, 52 members were offered 108 academic, athletic, and special achievement scholarships valued at more than $4.6 million. More than 90 representatives from colleges and universities throughout the nation visit the campus each year to talk with the students.

STUDENT BODY AND CONDUCT

Darlington operates on the philosophy that a diverse student body gives its students a realistic perspective of the real world. Darlington typically enrolls students from twenty states and thirty countries, with most students coming from the Southeast. For the 2008–09 school year, the student population was composed of students from thirty-six countries and nineteen states. The 183 resident students (evenly divided between boys and girls) make up approximately 40 percent of the student body in the Upper School.

The close ratio of resident and day students allows the two groups many excellent opportunities to influence one another. Students may request to be assigned a Rome Parent. Rome Parents are usually parents of a current day student, who take on the responsibility of making sure their resident student feels at home at Darlington and in Rome. They often open their homes to their "adopted" students, inviting them over for dinner or to spend a weekend. A number of resident families assert that this program is a significant reason for choosing Darlington.

The School has a long-standing tradition of strong student leadership. The House Senate helps to formulate and implement School policy and spirit, the Honor Council helps maintain honesty and integrity, and the "Y" Cabinet generates spiritual life at the School. Darlington expects its students to be good citizens, with major disciplinary infractions turned over to a discipline committee composed of students and faculty members.

ACADEMIC FACILITIES

The Upper School buildings, grouped around a lake, are all wired for Internet access and house nearly 100 courtesy terminals and lab computers. Darlington's 17,000-square-foot, fully automated McCallie Kennedy Library is the focal point of the campus. The library is complemented by Kawamura Science Center, a 10,000-square-foot facility, which ensures students frequent laboratory work. Four other classroom buildings provide space for the English, history, math, world language, and fine arts departments as well as computer labs and the student publications center. The entire of the campus is wireless.

BOARDING AND GENERAL FACILITIES

Six houses, three for boys and three for girls, each accommodating roughly 35 resident students and 45 day students, are supervised by 6 heads of house and resident faculty members. Through the support of student prefects (leaders), school life is mediated through the houses. Every house has a common room where students may watch TV or movies and socialize. A snack bar is open during the day. An infirmary, which is staffed seven days a week, is centrally located. All resident rooms have T1 Internet access; all students are assigned e-mail addresses.

ATHLETICS

Darlington's athletics program offers something for everyone, and all students are encouraged to participate in one or more of the School's many sports offerings. Varsity boys' competition is offered in baseball, basketball, cross-country, football, golf, lacrosse, soccer, swimming and diving, tennis, track, crew, and wrestling. Varsity sports for girls comprise basketball, cheerleading, competition cheerleading, cross-country, golf, lacrosse, soccer, softball, swimming and diving, tennis, track, crew, and volleyball. During the last five years, state championships have been won in cross-country (boys and girls), tennis (boys and girls), and track (girls). There are also junior varsity and freshman teams in many sports. Lifetime Fitness offers students not participating in a competitive sport a variety of noncompetitive activities, such as aerobics, baseball, basketball, beach volleyball, dodge ball, fitness, Frisbee, golf, running, soccer, swimming, and tennis.

Athletic facilities include a 96,000-square-foot athletic center that houses a performance arena, field house, wrestling room, weight room, aerobics room, indoor track, and indoor swimming pool. There is also a twelve-court tennis complex, a track and stadium, and eight playing fields.

EXTRACURRICULAR OPPORTUNITIES

The Darlington Players stages three drama productions each year, with students having numerous opportunities to direct, act, produce, and build sets. The Scholar Bowl team competes successfully in tournaments throughout the state. The chorale and concert choir present traditional seasonal concerts and frequently represent the School at civic and School-related events.

Darlington students produce four student publications (newspaper, yearbook, literary magazine, and video). Five hands-on classes are offered as electives: graphic design, creative writing, desktop publishing, Web authoring, and video production. Darlington's student publications lab has eighteen PC computers, two flatbed scanners, and a color printer.

DAILY LIFE

Breakfast is served until 8 a.m., and school begins with advisee meetings at 8 and coach classes at 8:07 for those needing additional assistance. Classes, which rotate through an eight-period-per-day schedule, begin at 8:30 and last until 3:30 p.m., with a 35-minute assembly, chapel service, or break in the morning and a 45-minute lunch break. After-school activities follow the school day (3:55–4:45), after which students are free until dinner (5:45). Study hall lasts from 7:30 to 9:30, and lights out follows at 11.

WEEKEND LIFE

Every weekend, activities are offered on campus, including movies, games, tournaments, dances, cookouts, and talent shows. Among the off-campus activities are excursions to Atlanta and Chattanooga shopping malls, amusement parks, athletic contests, and cultural events.

Other activities are scheduled over vacations, from skiing trips in Utah or to travel in Costa Rica or England.

SUMMER PROGRAMS

Darlington School offers a variety of one-week overnight experiences in June and July and the Summer Scholar's Program, a program that merges academic enrichment and hands-on experience for highly motivated students. Campers entering the sixth through ninth grades live in residential houses and enjoy Darlington's many athletic and academic facilities. Tennis and several outside-sponsored sports camps are available. Interested students should visit the School's Web site or call the School for more information.

COSTS AND FINANCIAL AID

Tuition for 2008–09 was $35,700 for boarding students and $15,800 for day students. There was an additional charge of $2500 for ESL. Other expenses included textbooks, school supplies, and spending money. The School has a number of different payment plans and a discount for early payment.

Darlington awards more than $1.5 million annually in financial aid to 20 percent of its students on the basis of need. Twenty-eight percent of boarding students receive financial aid. All families applying for financial aid must complete the forms for the School and for the National Association of Independent Schools Student Service for Financial Aid.

ADMISSIONS INFORMATION

The student body is made up of students with diverse talents and interests and from various socioeconomic levels. Darlington is interested in boys and girls of average to superior ability who are committed to making the most of their academic and personal potential. Students in grades 9–12 as well as those seeking a postgraduate experience may apply, although the School prefers applicants at the freshman and sophomore levels. Day students may enter grades pre-K–12.

Applicants must submit SSAT scores, a transcript, and teacher recommendations and have an interview on campus. Applicants may take admission tests when they visit the campus or at home.

Darlington School does not discriminate on the basis of race, color, or national or ethnic origin in the administration of its educational or admissions policies.

APPLICATION TIMETABLE

Initial inquiries are welcome at any time. Interviews are conducted between 9 and 5, Monday through Friday. Campus tours are organized during the school day and on Saturday by appointment. There is a testing fee of $50 ($75 for international students). To be considered in the first round of application decisions, students are advised to apply by March 1. Notification of acceptance is usually given within a month of receipt of complete application materials.

ADMISSIONS CORRESPONDENCE

Stormy S. Johnson, Director of Admission
Darlington School
1014 Cave Spring Road
Rome, Georgia 30161-4700
Phone: 706-235-6051
800-36-TIGER (toll-free)
Fax: 706-232-3600
E-mail: admission@darlingtonschool.org
Web site: http://www.darlingtonschool.org

DARROW SCHOOL

New Lebanon, New York

Type: Coeducational boarding and day college-preparatory school
Grades: 9–12, postgraduate year
Enrollment: 98
Head of School: Nancy M. Wolf

THE SCHOOL

Darrow School, which is located along the New York–Massachusetts border, offers a hands-on college-preparatory curriculum and is supplemented by active, experiential learning within a structured, supportive environment. Small classes, stimulating and friendly faculty members, individual advisers, supervised study, and a strong tutorial program ensure that each student receives individual attention.

In its educational philosophy, Darrow has historically emphasized active learning and the belief that education is not limited to the classroom. Current pedagogical theory supports that longtime tradition, and the School continually seeks to incorporate new methods and technologies that enhance its development as a community for learning.

As an outgrowth of the Shaker motto, "Hands to Work, Hearts to God," the School sets aside Wednesday morning to foster the dignity of labor and cooperative effort. All members of the community—administrators, teachers, and students—participate in such projects and tasks as wood chopping, making apple cider and maple syrup, recycling, gardening, woodworking, and Habitat for Humanity. The purpose is to encourage self-confidence, awareness of nature, and community involvement.

Darrow School is accredited by the Middle States Association of Colleges and Schools. It is a member of the National Association of Independent Schools, the New York State Association of Independent Schools, the Association of Boarding Schools, and the Secondary School Admission Test Board.

Darrow was founded in 1932 by a group of Shaker, community, and educational leaders, including the headmasters of Deerfield, Taft, and Hotchkiss. Situated in the Berkshire Mountains on the site of the Mt. Lebanon Shaker Village, Darrow is a designated National Historic Landmark.

The School occupies 365 acres adjoining the Pittsfield State Forest on the western slope of Mount Lebanon. On the campus are three playing fields, two tennis courts, extensive hiking paths, and a cross-country ski trail as well as ponds, sheep pastures, orchards, marshlands, and an expansive forest. Darrow is located 25 miles east of Albany, New York; 9 miles west of Pittsfield, Massachusetts; 150 miles north of New York City; and 150 miles west of Boston.

ACADEMIC PROGRAMS

Darrow seeks to challenge each student through an active, hands-on curriculum that contributes to the development of essential learning skills. Classes are small, averaging 9 students, and the overall student-teacher ratio is 4:1.

Darrow follows a semester system, with a unique eight-day Spring Term after the fourth quarter. The daily schedule includes half days on Wednesday and Saturday and follows a unique, modified block program comprising class blocks of 45 to 65 minutes.

Darrow's evaluation system reflects a variety of assessment tools, from traditional tests to oral or PowerPoint presentations, and portfolios. Academic and effort grades are given, along with extensive teacher and adviser comments, including dorm parent observations on residential life. Grade reports are sent home four times per year. Advisers are also in direct contact with parents regularly to report on their advisees' progress.

Central to Darrow's academic structure is the tutorial program. This program is designed to motivate and enable students to produce higher-quality work through a process of feedback and frequent assessment of their skills as learners, writers, and problem solvers. The program also allows Darrow students to learn how to deal effectively with increasing academic challenges. Tutors and students meet during the class day at least two times per week. Throughout the year, information about each student's learning style and needs is garnered from teachers' observations, testing, grades, and narrative reports, contributing to the ongoing refinement of each student's individually designed tutorial program.

Extra help is also available outside of the tutorial program. Darrow considers asking for extra help a sign of strength, not weakness, and faculty members make time each day for formal and informal sessions and study halls.

As a responsible citizen of the Hudson River Watershed, Darrow promotes environmentally responsible lifestyles by explicitly linking the concept of environmental sustainability throughout the curriculum and the community.

Graduation requirements include the successful completion of 20 credits, including 4 credits of English, 3 credits of social studies, 3 credits of mathematics, 3 credits of science, 2 credits of language, 2 credits of arts, 1 credit of physical education, ½ credit of health, and 1½ additional elective credits. Students typically take five academic courses per term.

FACULTY AND ADVISERS

Darrow has 31 full-time faculty members (17 men and 14 women). All hold bachelor's degrees, and 15 have graduate degrees. Nearly all faculty members, including 11 with families, reside on campus. Most serve as dorm parents in dormitories.

Head of School Nancy M. Wolf is the tenth Head at Darrow and the first woman to hold this position, which she began in July 2001. Her career in independent education started in 1970, when she was Darrow's first full-time female faculty member, during the School's transition to coeducation. Since then, she has gained a range of expertise at a select group of independent schools, including twenty-eight years as a classroom teacher and experience in nearly every administrative capacity. Mrs. Wolf has served as Math Chair and Middle and Upper School Head at Severn School in Maryland, Dean of Students at Lawrenceville School in New Jersey, and, most recently, Director of Development and Assistant Head for Advancement and Operations at Oldfields School in Maryland, where she worked for thirteen years. Mrs. Wolf earned a B.A. in mathematics (cum laude) from Ithaca College and an M.Ed. in administration and supervision from Loyola College in Baltimore. She and her husband, Robert, live on the Darrow campus.

COLLEGE ADMISSION COUNSELING

The curriculum at Darrow is college preparatory, and active steps are taken to provide guidance in the college placement process. A full-time college counselor offers individual instruction, recommendations, and advice to students to aid them in their college search and maintains a well-equipped library of college catalogs. Starting early in the eleventh grade, juniors are provided with an overview of the college selection process and are helped to formulate opinions and direction as the year progresses. Seniors work on an individual basis with the Director of College Counseling to determine the most appropriate colleges at which to apply. Faculty members prepare detailed letters of recommendation for each senior. The SAT remains an important tool in the selection process for many colleges and universities and is administered on campus during May of the junior year and November of the senior year. Because the selection process itself constantly evolves, parents are also educated and assisted throughout the entire process.

In 2008, the majority of the graduating seniors went on to college. Among the colleges and universities that accepted Darrow students are Alfred, the Art Institute of Boston, Bates, Colgate, Connecticut College, Fashion Institute of Technology, Howard, Mount Holyoke, Northeastern, Sarah Lawrence, Trinity College, and the University of Vermont.

STUDENT BODY AND CONDUCT

In 2008–09, 98 students were enrolled in grades 9–12, 77 boarding students and 21 day students. There are 60 boys and 38 girls. Thirteen states and seven countries are represented by the student body.

A strong student leadership program offers students the opportunity to learn the value of leadership and the importance of knowing how to develop a responsible leadership style. Students have several avenues by which they can pursue these goals.

The student government is composed of 12 members, including the student body president, class presidents, and dorm and day student representatives. A member of the faculty serves as an adviser. The purpose of the student government is to provide the School with an organized student group that works to serve the needs of the Darrow community and to aid the student body president in his or her role of student leader. In addition to student government positions, students serve in leadership positions as prefects and resident assistants. Prefects work with faculty advisers, and each is primarily concerned with activities or services in one area of student life, such as the library, computers, admissions, or student activities. The resident assistants work with dorm parents and help with check-in and other supervisory responsibilities. Darrow also has a Discipline Committee, composed of both students and faculty members, which meets when a serious disciplinary infraction must be addressed.

ACADEMIC FACILITIES

There are twenty-four buildings on the Darrow campus; twenty-one are original Shaker structures. Wickersham houses the administrative offices, classrooms, and one of three computer labs.

The Joline Arts Center opened for student use in September 2002. The 12,000-square-foot building provides studio and lab spaces for a broad range of fine arts programming and areas for seminars and presentations. Included are classrooms specifically designed for painting, drawing, ceramics, photography (wet and digital), and woodworking. In addition, there are extensive studio space for private work and individual projects and a public exhibition gallery for the display of student, faculty, alumni, and guest works.

Darrow's $1.8-million Samson Environmental Center cleans the School's wastewater and provides unique, hands-on learning opportunities to Darrow students and others of all ages who are interested in the process. The centerpiece of the facility is the Living Machine, an ecological wastewater treatment system that transforms the wastewater from dormitories, academic buildings, and the dining hall into clean water that is released into the Hudson River Watershed. In October 2003, Darrow secured a grant from the New York State Energy Research and Development Authority to install photovoltaic panels, which now provide partial power to the center. Adjacent to the Samson Environmental Center is the science building, which houses four laboratories and faculty offices.

The gymnasium, theater, fitness center, student center, and dining hall are in the Dairy Barn, which was built on the site of the original Shaker dairy barn.

The Second Meeting House, which was built in 1824 and remodeled in 1962, houses the library, which contains more than 15,000 volumes. A computer network links the library to other libraries in the greater Albany area and to the Web site. Darrow Net, a campuswide intranet program, connects all classroom and science lab computers.

BOARDING AND GENERAL FACILITIES

Darrow's dormitories are Shaker structures that have been adapted to provide comfortable, spacious accommodations for both students and faculty members. The capacity of each dorm ranges from 12 to 28 students, with 4 faculty dorm parents. Most dorm rooms are doubles, eight of the larger rooms serve as triples, and there are also a few single rooms available.

The on-campus health services clinic is staffed by 2 nurses, and hospital facilities are 15 minutes away. A full-time School counselor offers support for students on campus.

A School Store and newly remodeled Student Center are also available.

ATHLETICS

Darrow maintains a wide-ranging sports program with emphasis on inclusion. The School wants students to be actively involved, not simply watching. A number of life sports and several competitive sports are available for boys and girls. Baseball, basketball, cross-country, fitness, lacrosse, outdoor education, skiing, snowboarding, soccer, softball, tennis, and Ultimate Frisbee are offered. All students are required to participate in afternoon activities, including at least one team sport each year.

Darrow's athletic program focuses on athletic skills, sportsmanship, physical fitness, and teamwork.

EXTRACURRICULAR OPPORTUNITIES

Students at Darrow have a range of cocurricular opportunities available to them. Theater is a highly popular endeavor, with three major productions each year. A student-organized coffeehouse allows students and faculty members to share their talents in music and poetry. Additional activities include design and production of the yearbook, an independent-study music program, or other activities, such as a literary magazine, initiated and driven by student interest.

DAILY LIFE

Darrow's daily schedule reflects its structured approach to academic life. Days are planned to provide not only variety but also the predictability necessary to allow students to plan ahead and achieve.

Breakfast is served starting at 7 a.m., and the academic day begins at 8. There are six periods—five academic periods and a conference period. Sports begin at 3:30, and dinner is served at 5:30. A daily School meeting for all students and faculty members, where announcements and commendations are shared, occurs each morning. The Friday morning meeting is reserved as time for quiet, personal contemplation and sharing of thoughts.

WEEKEND LIFE

A number of student activities, including both on- and off-campus events, are planned for weekends. Sports, movies, dances, coffeehouses, and trips to theaters and special events off campus occur throughout the year. Students also go to Albany or Pittsfield for shopping and Saturday dinner. Day trips to New York City and Boston are occasionally scheduled.

Students may take weekends off campus with parental permission. Special annual events include Family Weekend in the fall, winter, and spring.

COSTS AND FINANCIAL AID

For the 2008–09 school year, boarding student tuition is $41,200 and day student tuition is $23,600. Other expenses include $1500 for books and personal items. Tutorial costs are $3900 or $7800, depending on frequency.

Darrow provides financial assistance to 38 percent of its student body. Financial aid is determined by need and the availability of funds. Candidates who require aid should discuss their needs at the time of their interview and are required to fill out the Parents' Financial Statement and mail it to the School and Student Service in Princeton, New Jersey.

ADMISSIONS INFORMATION

Darrow encourages applications from students who want a successful and rewarding educational experience, who need structure and support, and who are willing to take advantage of the School's exciting and hands-on academic and cocurricular program.

Students are admitted to grades 9 through postgraduate. Applicants must submit recommendations from a math teacher, an English teacher, and a guidance counselor; school transcripts; a personal essay; and a parent essay. A personal interview is required.

APPLICATION TIMETABLE

Decisions are made on a rolling basis. Some midyear or immediate enrollments may be considered. Enrollment decisions are made by the Admission Committee, which is composed of the Head of School, the Director of Studies, the Dean of Students, 2 faculty members, and the Director of Admission.

ADMISSIONS CORRESPONDENCE

Jamie Hicks-Furgang
Director of Admission
Darrow School
110 Darrow Road
New Lebanon, New York 12125
Phone: 518-794-6000
Fax: 518-794-7065
E-mail: hicksj@darrowschool.org
Web site: http://www.darrowschool.org

DEERFIELD ACADEMY

Deerfield, Massachusetts

Type: Coeducational boarding and day college-preparatory school
Grades: 9–12, postgraduate year
Enrollment: 600
Head of School: Dr. Margarita O'Byrne Curtis

THE SCHOOL

Since its founding in 1797, Deerfield Academy has provided a unique and challenging opportunity for young people. Deerfield Academy is a vibrant learning community nurturing high standards of scholarship, citizenship, and personal responsibility. Through a demanding liberal arts curriculum, extensive cocurricular program, and supportive residential environment, Deerfield encourages each student to develop an inquisitive and creative mind, sound body, strong moral character, and commitment to service. The setting of the campus, which is rich in tradition and beauty, inspires reflection, study and play, the cultivation of friendships, and the growth of a defining community spirit.

The school's 280-acre campus is located in the center of historic Deerfield, a restored Colonial village in rural western Massachusetts, 90 miles from Boston and 55 miles from Hartford. Only 20 minutes south is the five-college area that includes Amherst, Smith, Mount Holyoke, and Hampshire Colleges and the University of Massachusetts, providing rich cultural and intellectual resources.

A 26-member Board of Trustees is the Academy's governing body. The endowment is valued at approximately $363 million. In 2007–08, operating expenses totaled $42.9 million, capital gifts amounted to $15.6 million, and Annual Giving was $5.7 million, with 48 percent of the 10,690 alumni participating.

Deerfield is accredited by the New England Association of Schools and Colleges. It is a member of the National Association of Independent Schools, the Independent School Association of Massachusetts, and the Secondary School Admission Test Board.

ACADEMIC PROGRAMS

Deerfield's curriculum is designed to enable its students to assume active and intelligent roles in the world community. Courses and teaching methods are aimed at developing logical and imaginative thinking, systematic approaches to problem solving, clear and correct expression in writing and speech, and the confidence to pursue creatively one's interests and talents. Students take five courses per trimester. Their schedules are planned individually in consultation with advisers and the Academic Dean.

Graduation requirements include English, 4 years; mathematics, 3 years; foreign language, 3 years of a language (Arabic, Chinese, French, Greek, Latin, or Spanish); history, 2 years (including 1 year of U.S. history); laboratory science, 2 years; fine arts, two terms; and philosophy and religious studies, one term. All sophomores take a one-term course in health issues. In addition, all new students take a required course in library skills. Advanced Placement (AP) courses are offered in seven subject areas. Last year, 265 students sat for 523 AP exams. Ninety percent of the tests received qualifying scores of 3 or better. Independent study is offered in all departments.

During the spring term, seniors may engage in off-campus alternate-studies projects, ranging from working in a local hospital to serving as an intern for a member of Congress. Juniors may spend half of their year at the Maine Coast Semester, which combines regular classes with studies of environmental issues; at the Mountain School in Vermont; or at a boarding school in South Africa, Botswana, or Kenya. Sophomores and juniors may spend a semester at the Island School on Eleuthera in the Bahamas. The Swiss Semester in Zermatt is a program that gives sophomores an opportunity to study geology, European history, and foreign language at the foot of the Matterhorn. Deerfield participates in the School Year Abroad program in China, France, Italy, Spain, and India, which is available for juniors and seniors. Students may also choose one of seven exchange programs, including programs in Australia, Hong Kong, Japan, and New Zealand. Summer opportunities are available in China, El Salvador, France, Greece, Italy, Peru, Spain, and Uruguay.

The average class size is 12. The overall faculty-student ratio is 1:5. Placement in AP courses, honors sections, and accelerated courses is based upon preparedness, ability, and interest. All students have study hours Sunday through Thursday evenings.

The school year is divided into three 11-week terms. Grades are sent at the end of each term and at midterm. In the fall and spring, the student's academic adviser prepares a formal written report, commenting extensively on the student's academic performance, attitude, work habits, dormitory life, and participation in athletics and cocurricular activities and as a citizen of the school.

Grading is based on a numerical scale of 0 to 100; 60 is passing. The honor roll is made up of students with minimum averages of 87, and the high honor roll recognizes students with averages of 93 and above. Students in academic difficulty are reviewed by the Academic Standing Committee at the end of each term. Teachers are available during evenings, weekends, and free periods to assist students individually. In addition, the Study Center provides assistance in all academic areas each evening. Students can also get help from the Study Skills Coordinator.

FACULTY AND ADVISERS

The high quality of Deerfield's faculty is the school's greatest endowment. The faculty consists of 118 full- and part-time members (49 women and 69 men); 70 percent hold advanced degrees. Ninety percent reside on campus or live in the village of Deerfield. All faculty members act as advisers to students, coach sports, head tables in the dining hall, and serve on various committees. Teachers receive summer grants and time away from the Academy for advanced study, travel, and exchange teaching.

Dr. Margarita O'Byrne Curtis was appointed Head of School in July 2006. She earned her B.A. from Tulane, her B.S. from Mankato State, and a doctorate in romance languages and literature from Harvard.

COLLEGE ADMISSION COUNSELING

College advising is coordinated by 4 college advisers. Beginning in their junior year, all students attend small-group discussions that help them make informed decisions about college. In mid-winter, every junior is assigned to an individual college adviser, who further develops, with parental consultation, a list of prospective colleges. In the fall of the senior year, college advisers assist students in narrowing their college choices and in making the most effective presentation of their strengths. During the fall, representatives of approximately 135 colleges visit the Academy for presentations and interviews.

Normally, sophomores and juniors take the PSAT in October. Juniors take the SAT Reasoning Test in January; SAT Subject Tests in December, May, and June; and Advanced Placement (AP) tests in May. Seniors, whenever advisable, take the SAT in the fall and additional AP tests later in the year. The midrange of SAT scores for the class of 2008 was 600–700 critical reading, 620–720 math, and 620–720 writing.

Of the 198 graduates in 2008, 182 are attending college; 16 students deferred admission to college for a year. Colleges attended by 4 or more students are 9 at Georgetown and Harvard; 8 at Brown, Trinity, and Yale; 7 at Bucknell and Middlebury; 6 at Dartmouth; 5 at Colgate and Cornell; and 4 at Boston College, Bowdoin, Colby, and Hamilton.

STUDENT BODY AND CONDUCT

In fall 2008, Deerfield enrolled 600 students: 293 girls and 307 boys. There were 85 boarders and 16 day students in the ninth grade, 140 boarders and 18 day students in the tenth grade, 145 boarders and 22 day students in the eleventh grade, and 150 boarders and 24 day students in the twelfth grade (including 24 postgraduates). Recognizing that diversity enriches the school, the Academy seeks to foster an appreciation of difference. To that end, international students made up 11 percent of the student body, and those from minority groups made up 25 percent. Deerfield students came from thirty-four states and twenty-four countries.

In all communities, a healthy tension exists between the need for individuality and the need for common values and standards. A community's shared values define the place, giving it a distinct sense of itself. In all facets of school life, Deerfield strives to teach that honesty, tolerance, compassion, and responsibility are essential to the well-being of the individual, the school, and society. Deerfield Academy is a residential community in which students learn to conduct themselves according to high standards of citizenship. Expectations for students are clear, and the response to misbehavior is timely and as supportive as possible of the students involved.

ACADEMIC FACILITIES

Deerfield's campus has eighty-one buildings. The Frank L. Boyden Library has a collection of more than 85,000 books, periodicals, and films. Most of the library's collection is accessible via a fully integrated online catalog. The Koch Center, a new, state-of-the-art 80,000-square-foot center for science, mathematics, and technology, includes a new planetarium; thirty classroom and laboratory spaces, including dedicated spaces for independent research; a 225-seat auditorium; the Star Terrace; and a central atrium.The Memorial Building contains the main auditorium, Hilson Gallery, Russell Gallery, the student-run FM radio station, art studios, a black-box theater, a dance facility, and music recital and practice rooms.

BOARDING AND GENERAL FACILITIES

There are seventeen dormitories. Faculty members live in apartments attached to each dorm corridor and maintain a close, supportive relationship with students. Two senior proctors also live on the freshman and sophomore corridors. Eighty percent of the boarding students have single rooms.

The fifteen-bed health center, Dewey House, is staffed full-time by a physician and registered nurses.

ATHLETICS

Participation in sports—at the student's level of ability—is the athletic program's central focus. The Academy fields interscholastic teams in baseball, basketball, crew, cross-country, field hockey, football, golf, ice hockey, lacrosse, skiing, soccer, softball, squash, swimming, tennis, track, volleyball, water polo, and wrestling. Supervised recreational activities include aerobics, cycling, dance, skiing, squash, strength training, tennis, and an outdoor skills program.

Deerfield's gymnasium complex contains three basketball courts; a wrestling arena; an indoor hockey rink; a fitness center; the Dewey Squash Center, a 16,000-square-foot facility housing ten international squash courts and tournament seating; and the largest preparatory school natatorium in New England, which includes an indoor, eight-lane, 25-yard pool with a separate diving well. Ninety acres of playing fields include three football fields, twelve soccer/lacrosse fields, three field hockey fields, eighteen tennis courts, a major-league-quality baseball field, a softball field, paddle tennis courts, a new boathouse and crew facility, and a new eight-lane track. Two synthetic turf fields were added in the summer of 2008.

EXTRACURRICULAR OPPORTUNITIES

Deerfield students and faculty members are extraordinarily productive in the performing and visual arts. Musical groups include wind ensemble, chamber music, jazz ensemble, brass choir, madrigal singers, a cappella groups, and the Academy Chorus. Many opportunities exist for acting as well. In addition to the three major theater productions each year, plays and scenes are also performed by advanced acting classes. Students who are interested in dance may explore modern, jazz, and ballet, with the opportunity to perform all three terms.

Cocurricular organizations include WGAJ-FM, Peer Counselors, the Diversity Task Force, Amnesty International, and debate, photography, and political clubs. Outing groups offer opportunities to ski, rock climb, and bike on weekends. Publications include an award-winning campus newspaper, the yearbook, and literary publications.

Students provide service as tutors, dormitory proctors, tour guides, and waiters in the dining hall. Students serve responsibly on various standing and ad hoc administrative committees and play an especially important role on the disciplinary committee. Students are also involved in various community service projects. The Community Service program encourages Deerfield students and faculty members to broaden their perspectives by sharing with and learning from people of different ages, abilities, cultures, and economic backgrounds. Ongoing projects include mentoring at nearby schools, volunteering in shelters and day-care centers, tutoring, organic farming and on-campus recycling, visiting nursing homes, and sponsoring Red Cross blood drives. Some students also serve as Big Brothers or Big Sisters to local youth.

DAILY LIFE

Students normally take five courses each term, and each course meets four times per week. The length of a class period ranges from 45 to 70 minutes. Classes begin at 8:30 and end at 3, except on Wednesday, when classes end at 12:30 and are followed by cocurricular activities. Classes do not meet on Saturdays. One morning a week, students and faculty members gather together for a school meeting, and students and faculty members attend seven family-style meals per week. All sports and drama activities take place after classes. Clubs and cocurricular groups meet between dinner and study hours or on weekends.

Students study in their dormitory rooms between 7:45 and 9:45 p.m., Sunday through Thursday. They may also study in the library, perform laboratory experiments, or seek help from a faculty member or the student tutoring service. During the school week, the curfew for freshmen and sophomores is 7:45 p.m.; for juniors and seniors, it is 9:45 p.m.

WEEKEND LIFE

In addition to athletic events on Saturday afternoon, there are films, theatrical productions, and musical performances. Social activities, sponsored by the Student Activities Committee and chaperoned by faculty members, include coffeehouses, talent shows, concerts, and dances. Deerfield's rural setting and extensive athletic facilities are ideal for recreational hiking, rock climbing, skiing, swimming, ice skating, and other activities.

The Academy Events Committee plans and sponsors weekend events throughout the school year. The Robert Crow Lecture Series brings to the Academy leaders in politics, government, education, science, and journalism. Students attend concerts and film series. Art exhibitions and numerous dramatic productions provide recognition for promising young artists, photographers, and actors. Students also have access to cultural programs in the five-college area.

Freshmen may take two weekends off campus in the fall term and three each in the winter and spring terms; sophomores may take two weekends in fall, three in winter, and an unlimited number in spring; juniors and seniors in good standing may take unlimited weekends. On weekends, the curfew for freshmen and sophomores is at 10:30 p.m. on Friday and 11 on Saturday. For juniors and seniors, Friday curfew is at 11; Saturday curfew is at 11:30.

COSTS AND FINANCIAL AID

For 2008–09, the cost for boarding students was $39,275; for day students, it was $28,200. Additional fees were $1815 for books, infirmary, and technology. Parents are asked to maintain a drawing account of $75 for their child's personal expenses. Tuition is payable in two installments—on August 1 and December 1. A $1500 deposit (credited to the August tuition bill) is due within four weeks of the student's acceptance by Deerfield.

Deerfield awards financial aid to 36 percent of its students. Grant aid totals $6.1 million for the current academic year; grants, based on demonstrated need and procedures established by the School and Student Service for Financial Aid, range from $2500 to full tuition.

ADMISSIONS INFORMATION

Deerfield maintains rigorous academic standards and seeks a diverse student body—geographically, socially, ethnically, and racially. Selection is based upon academic ability and performance, character and maturity, and promise as a positive community citizen. The Admission Committee closely examines candidates' teacher and school recommendations, standardized test scores, and personal essays.

The SSAT or ISEE is required of applicants for grades 9 and 10 and should be taken during an applicant's current academic year. The SSAT, ISEE, or PSAT is required for eleventh-grade applicants, and the SAT or ACT is required for twelfth-grade and postgraduate candidates. The TOEFL may be taken in place of the aforementioned tests by students for whom English is not their first language.

Deerfield Academy does not discriminate on the basis of race, color, creed, handicap, sexual orientation, or national or ethnic origin in its admissions policies or financial aid programs.

APPLICATION TIMETABLE

Applicants normally visit the Academy in the year prior to the proposed date of entrance. Campus tours and interviews are conducted from 8:30 a.m. to 2:20 p.m. on Monday, Tuesday, Thursday, and Friday; from 8 to 11:45 on Wednesday; and at 9, 10, and 11 on Saturday. Weekdays are preferable. The applicant is sent formal application papers during the fall. The completed application—including teacher recommendations, the school transcript, and essays—should be postmarked no later than January 15. Applicants receive notification of the admission decision on March 10. The candidate reply date is April 10.

ADMISSIONS CORRESPONDENCE

Patricia L. Gimbel
Dean of Admission and Financial Aid
Deerfield Academy
Deerfield, Massachusetts 01342

Phone: 413-774-1400
E-mail: admission@deerfield.edu
Web site: http://www.deerfield.edu

DELBARTON SCHOOL

Morristown, New Jersey

Type: Boys' day college-preparatory school
Grades: 7–12: Middle School, 7–8; Upper School, 9–12
Enrollment: School total: 539; Upper School: 477
Head of School: Br. Paul Diveny, O.S.B., Headmaster

THE SCHOOL

Delbarton School was established in 1939 by the Benedictine monks of Saint Mary's Abbey as an independent boarding and day school. Now a day school, Delbarton is located on a 400-acre woodland campus 3 miles west of historic Morristown and 30 miles west of New York City. Adjacent to the campus is Jockey Hollow, a national historic park.

Delbarton School seeks to enroll boys of good character who have demonstrated scholastic achievement and the capacity for further growth. The faculty strives to support each boy's efforts toward intellectual development and to reinforce his commitment to help build a community of responsible individuals. The faculty encourages each boy to become an independent seeker of information, not a passive recipient, and to assume responsibility for gaining both knowledge and judgment that will strengthen his contribution to the life of the School and his later contribution to society. While the School offers much, it also seeks boys who are willing to give much and who are eager to understand as well as to be understood.

The School is governed by the 8-member Board of Trustees of the Order of Saint Benedict of New Jersey, located at Saint Mary's Abbey in Morristown. Delbarton's 2008–09 annual operating expenses totaled $17.2 million. It has an endowment of $20.9 million. This includes annual fund-raising support from 48 percent of the alumni.

Delbarton School is accredited by the Middle States Association of Colleges and Schools and approved by the Department of Education of the State of New Jersey. It is a member of the National Association of Independent Schools, the New Jersey Association of Independent Schools, the Council for Advancement and Support of Education, the National Catholic Educational Association, and the New Jersey State Interscholastic Athletic Association.

ACADEMIC PROGRAMS

The academic program in the Upper School is college preparatory. The course of study offers preparation in all major academic subjects and a number of electives. The studies are intended to help a boy shape a thought and a sentence, speak clearly about ideas and effectively about feelings, and suspend judgment until all the facts are known. Course work, on the whole, is intensive and involves about 20 hours of outside preparation each week. The curriculum contains both a core of required subjects that are fundamental to a liberal education and various elective courses that are designed to meet the individual interests of the boys. Instruction is given in all areas that are necessary for gaining admission to liberal arts or technical institutions of higher learning.

The school year is divided into three academic terms. In each term, every boy must take five major courses, physical education, and religious studies. The specific departmental requirements in grades 9 through 12 are English (4 years), mathematics (4 years), foreign language (3 years), science (3 years), history (3 years), religious studies (2 terms in each of 4 years), physical education and health (4 years), fine arts (1 major course, 1 term of art, and 1 term of music), and computer technology (2 terms). For qualified boys in the junior and senior years, all departments offer Advanced Placement courses, and it is also possible in certain instances to pursue work through independent study or to study at neighboring colleges.

The grading system uses 4 to 0 (failing) designations with pluses and minuses. Advisory reports are sent to parents in the middle of each term as well as at the end of the three terms. Parents are also contacted when a student has received an academic warning or is placed on probation. The average class size is 15, and the student-teacher ratio is about 7:1, which fosters close student-faculty relations.

FACULTY AND ADVISERS

In 2008–09 the faculty consisted of 13 Benedictine monks and 72 lay teachers. All are full-time members, with 56 holding advanced degrees.

Br. Paul Diveny, O.S.B., became Headmaster in July 2007. Br. Paul received his B.A. from the Catholic University of America in 1975; his diploma in Monastic Studies from the Pontificio Ateneo Sant'Anselmo in Rome, Italy in 1982; and his M.A. in German from Middlebury College in 1987. He has served the School previously as a teacher of Latin, German, ancient history, and religious studies, and as Assistant Headmaster.

The teaching tradition of the School has called upon faculty members to serve as coaches, counselors, or administrators. A genuine interest in the development of people leads the faculty to be involved in many student activities. Every boy is assigned to a guidance counselor, who advises in the selection of courses that meet School and college requirements as well as personal interests. Individual conferences are regularly arranged to discuss academic and personal development. The counselor also contacts the boy's parents when it seems advisable.

COLLEGE ADMISSION COUNSELING

Preparation for college begins when a boy enters Delbarton. The PSAT is given to everyone in the tenth and eleventh grades. Guidance for admission to college is directed by the senior class counselor. This process generally begins in the fall of the junior year, when the junior class counselor meets with each boy to help clarify his goals and interests. Many college admissions officers visit the School annually for conferences. Every effort is made to direct each boy toward an institution that will challenge his abilities and satisfy his interests.

The mean SAT verbal and math score for the class of 2008 was 1325. More than 25 percent of the young men in the classes of 2005, 2006, 2007, and 2008 have been named National Merit Scholars, Semifinalists, or Commended Students. In addition, 85 percent of the members of the class of 2008 were enrolled in at least one AP course.

All of the graduates of the classes of 2005, 2006, 2007, and 2008 went on to college, with 5 or more attending such schools as Boston College, Columbia, Cornell, Dartmouth, Duke, Georgetown, Harvard, Holy Cross, Johns Hopkins, Middlebury, Notre Dame, Princeton, the U.S. Naval Academy, Villanova, Williams, Yale, and the Universities of, Pennsylvania and Virginia.

STUDENT BODY AND CONDUCT

The 2008–09 Upper School student body consisted of 118 ninth graders, 116 tenth graders, 120 eleventh graders, and 123 twelfth graders. The Middle School has 32 seventh and 30 eighth graders. All of the students are from New Jersey, particularly the counties of Morris, Essex, Somerset, Union, Bergen, Hunterdon, Passaic, and Sussex.

Regulations, academic and social, are relatively few. The School eschews the manipulative, the coercive, the negative, or the merely punitive approach to discipline. The basic understanding underlying the School's regulations is that each boy, entering with others in a common educational enterprise, shares responsibility with his fellow students and with faculty members for developing and maintaining standards that contribute to the welfare of the entire School community. Moreover, shared responsibility is essential to the growth of the community; at the same time, much of an individual boy's growth, the increase in his capacity for self-renewal, his sense of belonging, and his sense of identity spring from his eagerness and willingness to contribute to the life of the School. Each class has a moderator, who is available for advice and assistance. The moderator works closely with the boys, assisting them in their progress.

ACADEMIC FACILITIES

The physical facilities include two classroom buildings, a fine arts center, a science pavilion, a greenhouse, the church, and the dining hall. Academic facilities include thirty-four classrooms, six science laboratories, art and music studios, a language laboratory, and a library of more than 20,000 volumes. The five computer laboratories consist of 250 workstations in a networked system. Also, the music department provides twelve personal computers for the advanced study of music and composition.

ATHLETICS

Sports at the School are an integral part of student life. The School holds the traditional belief that much can be learned about cooperation, competition, and character through participating in sports. Almost 80 percent of the boys participate on one or more interscholastic athletics teams. Varsity sports offered in the fall term are football, soccer, and cross-country; in the winter term, basketball, wrestling, track, hockey, squash, bowling, and swimming (in an off-campus pool); and in the spring, baseball, track, lacrosse, tennis, and golf. In most of these sports, there are junior varsity, freshman, and Middle School teams. Some intramural sports are available, depending upon interest, every year.

The facilities consist of two gymnasiums, eight athletics fields, six tennis courts, and an outdoor pool for swimming during warm weather. Students who join the golf team are able to play at nearby golf clubs.

EXTRACURRICULAR OPPORTUNITIES

The School provides opportunities for individual development outside the classroom as well as within. The faculty encourages the boys to express their intellectual, cultural, social, and recreational interests through a variety of activities and events. For example, fine arts at Delbarton are available both within and outside the curriculum. Studio hours accommodate boys after school, and students visit galleries and museums. In the music department, vocal and instrumental instruction is available. Performing ensembles include an orchestra, band, and chorus and smaller vocal and instrumental ensembles. Under the aegis of the Abbey Players, drama productions are staged three times a year, involving boys in a wide variety of experiences.

Other activities include Deaneries (student support groups promoting School unity and spirit), the *Courier* (the School newspaper), the *Archway* (the yearbook), *Schola Cantorum* (a vocal ensemble), the Abbey Orchestra, and the Model UN, Mock Trial, Speech and Debate, Junior Statesmen, Art, History, Chess, Cycling, Stock Exchange, and Future Business Leaders clubs. In addition, faculty moderators of the Ski Club regularly organize and chaperone trips during School vacations.

To expose students to other cultures and to enhance their understanding of the world, faculty members have organized trips to Europe, Africa, and Latin America. The Campus Ministry office is active in sponsoring several outreach programs that lead boys to an awareness of the needs of others and the means to answer calls for help. The outreach programs include community soup kitchens, Big Brothers of America, Adopt-a-Grandparent, Basketball Clinic for exceptional children, and a program in which volunteers travel to Appalachia during break to contribute various services to the poor of that area.

Students' imagination and initiative are also given opportunities for expression through Student Council committees and assemblies. The students are also offered School-sponsored trips to cultural and recreational events at area colleges and in nearby cities.

DAILY LIFE

Classes begin at 8:15 a.m. and end at 2:34 p.m. The average number of classes per day for each student is six. Two classes are an hour long, while the remainder are 40 minutes each. The School operates on a six-day cycle, and each class meets five days per cycle. Physical education classes are held during the school day. After classes, students are involved in athletics and the arts. Clubs and organizations also meet after school, while many meet at night.

COSTS AND FINANCIAL AID

Charges at Delbarton for the 2008–09 academic year were $24,975. These are comprehensive fees that include a daily hot lunch as well as library and athletics fees. The only other major expenses are the bookstore bill and transportation, the cost of which varies. Optional expenses may arise for such items as the yearbook, music lessons, or trips.

Because of the School's endowment and generous alumni and parent support, a financial aid program enables many boys to attend the School. All awards are based on financial need, as determined by the criteria set by the School and Student Service for Financial Aid. No academic or athletics scholarships are awarded. Financial aid is granted to boys in grades 7 through 12. This year, the School was able to grant $1.3 million to students.

ADMISSIONS INFORMATION

Delbarton School selects students whose academic achievement and personal promise indicate that they are likely to become positive members of the community. The object of the admissions procedure is for the School and prospective student to learn as much as possible about each other. Admission is based on the candidate's overall qualifications, without regard to race, color, religion, or national or ethnic origin.

The typical applicant takes one of the four entrance tests administered by the School in October, November, and December. Candidates are considered on the basis of their transcript, recommendations, test results, and personal interview in addition to the formal application. In 2008–09, 337 students were tested for entrance in grades 7 and 9; of these, 139 were accepted. Ninety-seven percent of the students who were accepted for the seventh grade were enrolled; 82 percent of those accepted for the ninth grade were enrolled. Delbarton does not admit postgraduate students or students who are entering the twelfth grade.

APPLICATION TIMETABLE

The School welcomes inquiries at any time during the year. Students who apply are invited to spend a day at Delbarton attending classes with a School host. Interested applicants should arrange this day visit through the Admissions Office. Tours of the campus are generally given in conjunction with interviews, from 9 a.m. to noon on Saturdays in the fall, or by special arrangement. The formal application for admission must be accompanied by a nonrefundable fee of $65. Application fee waivers are available upon request.

It is advisable to initiate the admissions process in the early fall. Acceptance notifications for applicants to grades 7 and 9 are made by the end of January. Applicants to all remaining grades, as well as students placed in a waitpool, are given acceptance notification as late as June. Parents are expected to reply to acceptances two to three weeks after notification. A refundable deposit is also required. Application for financial aid should be made as early as possible; the committee hopes to notify financial aid applicants by the middle of March.

ADMISSIONS CORRESPONDENCE

Dr. David Donovan
Dean of Admissions
Delbarton School
Morristown, New Jersey 07960
Phone: 973-538-3231 Ext. 3019
Fax: 973-538-8836
E-mail: admissions@delbarton.org
Web site: http://www.delbarton.org/admissions

THE DELPHIAN SCHOOL™

Sheridan, Oregon

Type: Coeducational, boarding and day, college-preparatory school
Grades: K–12
Enrollment: School total: 277; Upper School: 190
Head of School: Rosemary Didear, Headmistress

THE SCHOOL

Established in 1976, the Delphian School began as the dream of a small group of educators to build an innovative learning environment. Dr. Alan Larson, the Founding Headmaster of the School, and several of his colleagues dedicated themselves to the goal of reversing the downward-trending standards in education. The legacy of these founding staff members is a school that provides young people with a rich academic background, a strong sense of ethics, and a broad range of abilities to successfully launch them into higher education, a career, and life.

As the founding school in a network of seven schools around the country, the Delphian School employs an educational philosophy acknowledged by parents and educators alike as a breakthrough in its innovation and workability. This methodology, developed more than forty years ago by renowned American author and educator L. Ron Hubbard, gives students the tools to study independently and attain high academic standards. Parents and students often acknowledge these methods as the source of the program's effectiveness and the Delphian students' enthusiasm for learning.

The School cultivates the concept that students should take increasing responsibility for their studies, their school, their environment, and their fellow man. All students participate in activities that develop these abilities. For example, students have the opportunity to enter into apprenticeships with professionals in the local community—choosing from a wide variety of professions, such as journalism, computer graphics, photography, medicine, law, the arts, and more. They also take an active role in community service, which might involve working on projects with the local Chamber of Commerce or tutoring in nearby schools. Student committees are responsible for the planning and execution of weekend activities that include ski trips, dances, camping, etc. In these activities, Delphi students are continually asked to make the connection between themselves, their education, and the rest of the world.

The Delphian School is located on 800 acres overlooking the beautiful Willamette Valley. Ideally positioned near Oregon's coastal mountains and an hour southwest of Portland, the campus provides a serene backdrop for learning and intermingling with students from all over the world.

Delphi is nonsectarian and welcomes students of all religions. The Delphian School is a member of the Oregon Federation of Independent Schools, is registered with the Oregon Department of Education as a private school, and is a candidate member of the Pacific Northwest Association of Independent Schools. The Delphian School is authorized under Federal law to enroll nonimmigrant, alien students and is licensed to use Applied Scholastics™ educational services.

ACADEMIC PROGRAMS

Delphi's approach to learning differs dramatically from other schools. The School's basic assumptions are that within every individual is an innate desire to learn, that the process of learning should be an inherently pleasurable experience, and that the only reason a student feels otherwise is because there is something not understood. That "something" could be a word, a concept, or an action or it could just be, "How does this apply to me?" The study methods employed at the School help students to identify basic barriers that prevent them from understanding and give students the knowledge and ability to break through these barriers to find true comprehension.

Each arriving student is given diagnostic testing from which an individual program based on their interests, strengths, and weaknesses is designed to meet specified requirements for completion of each level of the program. Instructors work closely with students and keep track of their progress daily. By applying the study methods learned, students progress at their optimum pace—learning extremely rapidly when they can and taking the time to work through more difficult subjects when they need to. The time spent studying any particular subject may vary from student to student. However, all students are expected to move quickly while achieving full understanding of what they study, and they do not move on until they can demonstrate that they have done so. Practical application of the studied material is emphasized, and students spend a great deal of time outside the classroom applying what they have learned.

The Delphi Program™ curriculum is comprehensive, covering a wide spectrum of cultural, scientific, and social subjects. More than 300 courses have been designed to directly support the School's approach to learning. Reading, writing, and mathematics are taken to a full mastery. Delphi students read scores of books per year from a reading list that includes children's classics and culminates in an advanced literature program of authors as diverse as Plato, de Tocqueville, and Voltaire. Structured to gradually improve ability, this program gives students a true love of reading and an exposure to a wide range of philosophic ideas.

Numeracy is the mathematical equivalent of literacy and includes the fluent use of numbers and numerical concepts. Students achieve numeracy through daily math study and practical application, augmented by drilling on tailor-made, proprietary computer programs at the lower levels and progressing up to trigonometry and calculus.

The richness of the Delphi Program has its full impact once the basics are in good shape. In addition to a full round of traditional core academic subjects, students receive training in practical areas such as communication, manners, computers, nutrition, and organization. Ethics, logic, and research—often considered advanced topics—are not only offered but are begun early on. At Delphi these subjects are set in the framework of application to everyday life, allowing students to gain judgment as to their value.

FACULTY AND ADVISERS

There are 99 staff members at Delphi, including 57 full- and part-time teachers and 42 additional staff members who instruct, provide dorm supervision, coach, and generally advise students outside of the classroom in the afternoons and evenings. In addition to their academic backgrounds, all faculty members have been trained in the study methods of L. Ron Hubbard and have a broad range of practical and professional experience. All faculty and staff members have been chosen to work closely with students, and most live on campus with their families.

COLLEGE ADMISSION COUNSELING

The Delphian School helps students find and apply to colleges to enable them to accomplish their life and career goals. The college-counseling process begins in the sophomore year in coordination with the parents. The School has a career center, which is fully stocked with catalogs, pamphlets and computers for researching careers and colleges. PSAT, SAT, and ACT preparation is available as well as assistance in obtaining financial aid.

Delphi graduates have gained acceptance to a variety of distinguished colleges and universities, such as Berkeley, Berklee College of Music, Georgetown, Harvard School of Business, Harvey Mudd, MIT, NYU, Ohio State (Honors College), Pepperdine, Stanford, and the Universities of Chicago, Michigan, Oregon, and Southern California. Interested students may contact the School or visit http://www.Delphian.org for a complete list of these colleges and universities.

STUDENT BODY AND CONDUCT

The student body is quite diverse; currently enrolled students come from twenty-two states and ten other countries.

The School assumes that students enroll at Delphi with aims of achieving scholastic competence and receiving strong college or career preparation. The School, therefore, expects a high level of integrity, purpose, responsibility, and initiative from its students. The student rules are a guide to proper conduct; serious infractions may result in suspension or dismissal.

The Student Council works with the faculty and students to establish and maintain the ethical agreements that govern the community.

ACADEMIC FACILITIES

Most facilities are located in the 110,000-square-foot main building. The structure houses dormitories, classrooms, a chemistry and biology laboratory, a theater, a 10,000-volume library, music practice rooms, a career center, a woodshop, an audiovisual lab, a computer lab, and art, ceramics, and photography studios.

BOARDING AND GENERAL FACILITIES

The dining room overlooks the oak and fir forest to the north. A dormitory offers a panoramic view of the Willamette Valley. There are also student lounges, a recreation room, a laundromat, and a snack bar. Campus housing for faculty and staff members is on campus. A Medical Liaison provides liaison for students to health-care practitioners in the area; emergency services are available in neighboring towns.

ATHLETICS

Varsity sports for boys are baseball, basketball, soccer, and tennis; girls compete in basketball, softball, and volleyball. All of these sports are also played intramurally. Noncompetitive sports include skiing, hiking, biking, snowboarding, yoga, and tennis with lighted courts. A gymnasium houses a weight-lifting and gymnastics room as well as facilities for basketball, volleyball, and racquetball.

EXTRACURRICULAR OPPORTUNITIES

The student recreation room is an informal meeting place for students in the evenings and on weekends. There are regularly scheduled dances and activities on campus. Other weekend activities include trips to Portland and Salem for shopping, movies, concerts, sports, and cultural events as well as trips to ocean beaches, to Ashland for the Shakespearean Festival, to the Cascade Range for hiking, and to Mount Hood and Mount Bachelor for skiing and snowboarding.

Traditional annual events include Alumni Weekend, All-School Halloween Festival, Winter Bazaar and Music Festival, Sweetheart's Ball, Spring Bazaar and Music Festival, Parents' Weekend, the prom, and Commencement.

DAILY LIFE

The regular school day for Upper School students is divided into three parts. From 8:30 a.m. to 3 p.m., there is classroom work with additional practical projects and seminars that cover such areas as foreign language, advanced math, science, literature, business, and current events as well as the English as a Second Language (ESL) program for international students. From 3:25 to 6 p.m., students participate in afternoon activities, including physical education, music, ceramics, computers, photography, team practice, and art.

Middle School students have similar schedules. Classroom work is from 8:30 a.m. to 1:50 p.m. Afternoon activities are from 2:10 to 5:10. The remainder of the day is spent with student activities, free time, helping with various responsibilities on campus, and study halls.

WEEKEND LIFE

The Student Councils in the Upper School and Middle School organize weekend activities and other special events for their respective schools under faculty guidance. Students publish a yearbook, and there are clubs for students with such interests as music, audio/visual, singing, drama, archery, chess, and computers. All students age 9 and older spend 50 minutes each day in the Student Service program, helping in such places as the kitchen, library, computer center, Lower School, or building maintenance. Special community service projects are organized throughout the year, wherein students in the Middle and Upper Schools contribute to their community by such activities as tutoring local students, visiting retirement homes, and helping in the cleanup of beaches, parks, and business areas.

SUMMER PROGRAMS

Summer at Delphi™ is a program of four to six weeks that offers challenging study and recreational opportunities for some 300 students from all over the world. Students pursue advanced work, strengthen weak areas, or take part in the extensive ESL program. There is also a computer study program for beginning, intermediate, and advanced students.

The first thing a student learns at Delphi's summer camp is how to study. Thus prepared, students have access to a curriculum of more than 250 courses. In addition to the academics, students participate in a wide range of outdoor sports and activities and attend seminars and workshops or supervised study in the evenings. Overnight camping and river rafting trips are some of the activities planned for the weekends.

Students age 8 and older may enroll in the boarding program. More information is available from the Admissions Office.

COSTS AND FINANCIAL AID

The Delphian School offers many different programs (day school, seven-day boarding, five-day boarding, English as a Second Language, and summer boarding and day programs); each has its own price structure. Interested families should contact the Admissions Office to request a price sheet. Tuition payment plans and financial aid are available.

ADMISSIONS INFORMATION

Students are admitted to the Delphian School on the basis of their previous academic records, results of any available standardized testing, and personal interviews. The Delphian School does not discriminate on the basis of race, religion, or national or ethnic background. Boarders must be at least 8 years of age. Day students may enroll at 5 years of age.

APPLICATION TIMETABLE

Although most students enroll in September, the highly individualized nature of the Delphi program allows qualified students to enroll at other times during the school year, space permitting. Priority is given to those eligible students first completing the full application procedure. Tuition, room, and board are prorated according to the date of enrollment.

ADMISSIONS CORRESPONDENCE

Donetta Phelps, Director of Admissions
The Delphian School
20950 Southwest Rock Creek Road
Sheridan, Oregon 97378
Phone: 800-626-6610 (toll-free)
503-843-3521 (outside the U.S.)
Fax: 503-843-4158
E-mail: info@delphian.org
Web site: http://www.delphian.org
http://www.summeratdelphi.org
http://www.eslatdelphi.org

THE DERRYFIELD SCHOOL

Manchester, New Hampshire

Type: Coeducational, college-preparatory day school
Grades: Grades 6–12
Enrollment: Total: 385; Middle School: 123; Upper School: 262
Head of School: Craig N. Sellers, Head of School

THE SCHOOL

The Derryfield School, an independent, coeducational, college-preparatory day school in Manchester, New Hampshire, was founded by a group of local citizens in 1964 to provide an outstanding secondary education for local students who want to live at home.

Derryfield strives to guide a student's academic growth through the acquisition of sound study habits and the development of analytical, independent thinking skills—as well as to foster each child's social, emotional, and ethical growth.

Derryfield is governed by a 20-member Board of Trustees and, in addition to tuition, is supported financially through annual giving and an endowment fund that currently totals more than $4.5 million.

Derryfield is accredited by the New England Association of Schools and Colleges and is a member of the National Association of Independent Schools (NAIS), the Association of Independent Schools of New England (AISNE), and the Independent Schools Association of Northern New England (ISANNE).

ACADEMIC PROGRAMS

Derryfield's challenging academic program combines a seriousness of purpose with a sense of spirit. A core college-preparatory curriculum is enhanced by more than seventy elective classes and independent learning opportunities.

Students entering Derryfield in the Middle School participate in a curriculum that provides a firm background in skills and basic discipline areas in preparation for Upper School courses. All students in grades 6, 7, and 8 take English, mathematics, science, history, and a foreign language. In addition, all Middle School students participate in drama, music, wellness, physical education, and art.

Students entering the Upper School (grades 9–12) plan their course of study in the context of graduation requirements, college plans, and interests. A total of 18 academic credits is required with the following departmental distribution: 4 credits in English, 2 credits in history (including U.S. history), 3 credits in mathematics, 3 credits in a foreign language, 2⅓ credits in science, 1 credit in visual and performing arts, and participation in either the alternative sports program or a team sport two seasons per year. Each student carries a minimum of five courses each term. The academic year consists of three terms.

The Independent Senior Project is an option for seniors during the final six weeks of the spring term. The project allows students to explore their interests and to gain practical experience outside of the classroom.

FACULTY AND ADVISERS

The Derryfield faculty consists of 55 members (29 men and 26 women). Master's degrees are held by 27 members and Ph.D.'s are held by 3 members. Twenty-three faculty members have taught at Derryfield for ten or more years, and annual faculty turnover is low. The student-faculty ratio is 8:1.

Faculty members are hired on the basis of a high level of expertise in their academic areas as well as enthusiasm to contribute to the overall success of their students and the School. In addition to their classroom obligations, faculty members advise approximately 8 students, coach Derryfield's athletic and academic teams, advise student activities, and make themselves available to counsel students in other areas of student life.

COLLEGE ADMISSION COUNSELING

Two dedicated college counselors begin working with students in February of their junior year. College counseling is an active process that includes group seminars and individual meetings with students and their families. More than 50 college representatives visit Derryfield each year.

The average SAT scores for the class of 2008 were 625 in critical reading, 630 in math, and 637 in the writing section. Fifty-three students graduated in 2008, with 100 percent of the class going to college. A sampling of the colleges and universities currently attended by 2 or more Derryfield graduates includes Bates, Boston College, Carnegie Mellon, Colby, Connecticut College, Emory, George Washington, Hamilton, Harvard, Holy Cross, Lehigh, Middlebury, Rensselaer Polytechnic, Smith, Trinity, Tufts, Tulane, Vassar, Wellesley, Wesleyan, and the Universities of California (Berkeley and San Diego), New Hampshire, Pennsylvania, and Vermont.

STUDENT BODY AND CONDUCT

Of the 385 students enrolled at The Derryfield School, 123 students attend the Middle School program and 262 students attend the Upper School program. Students come from forty local communities.

Violations of School rules are handled by the Discipline Committee, which consists of elected students and faculty members who evaluate discipline issues and make recommendations to the Head of School.

ACADEMIC FACILITIES

Derryfield's academic facilities include classroom buildings with five fully equipped science laboratories, a technology center with workstations and laptops, a 95-seat multimedia lyceum, a 17,000-volume library with a large subscription database, two art studios, a photography darkroom, an art gallery, and a 400-seat performing arts center. Outdoor classroom facilities include several miles of cross-country trails, high and low ropes courses, a ravine, and many acres of woods. A turf field, a full-sized gymnasium, weight-training area, and trainer's room are also valuable learning sites for courses in physical education and health and wellness.

ATHLETICS

"A healthy mind in a healthy body" defined the Greek ideal and is the concept at the core of Derryfield's physical education, health and wellness, and athletics philosophy.

All Middle Schoolers (grades 6–8) take physical education and health and wellness. Seventh and eighth graders also have competitive athletic requirements. Middle School athletics include baseball, basketball, cross-country running, field hockey, ice hockey (eighth graders only), lacrosse, Nordic and alpine skiing, snowboarding, soccer, softball, and tennis.

In the Upper School (grades 9–12), two levels of competitive sports teams (junior varsity and varsity), as well as some alternative physical activities (e.g., yoga, weight training), are offered. Upper School athletics include baseball, basketball, crew, cross-country running, field hockey, golf, ice hockey, lacrosse, Nordic and alpine skiing, snowboarding, soccer, softball, and tennis. With the intent of honoring areas of physical interest that the School does not offer on site, the School allows students to request that an independent physical activity be a replacement for one of the two required seasons.

Derryfield is a member of the New Hampshire Interscholastic Athletic Association, and, by nature of its smaller size, assumes the category of a Class S school. Derryfield currently has the most athletic offerings of any Class S school in New Hampshire and has garnered more than twenty state championships in the last ten years.

EXTRACURRICULAR OPPORTUNITIES

Derryfield's commitment to the arts is evident. High school students perform two large-scale drama productions each year, while seventh and eighth graders take part in their own musical. Each sixth grade drama class produces its own junior musical. Instrumental ensembles that include classical, jazz, and orchestral instruments are active in both the Middle and Upper School. There are vocal groups in both schools, and Upper School students may audition for a select chorus. All musicians participate in two concerts per year and frequently in talent shows and assemblies. Each year students are encouraged to audition for the New Hampshire All-State Chorus and Band. Visual art students regularly submit materials to the New Hampshire Student Artist Awards and the Boston Globe Scholastic Art Awards, and they also help organize or display their own work in Derryfield's art gallery openings.

In each of the two schools, Middle and Upper, students participate in more than a dozen student-organized clubs. Choices include School Council, Conservation Club, Art Klub, Gay/Straight Alliance, Cartooning Club, and Outing Club, among others. Derryfield also offers competitive clubs, including the math and debate teams, Granite State Challenge, and Model United Nations. Students publish newspapers, literary magazines, and a yearbook.

Field trips, organized through classes or clubs, include regular visits to New York City, Boston, and Manchester museums, theaters, courtrooms, and outdoor areas of interest. Each year, different faculty members lead groups of students on cultural or service-learning outings. Recent trips have been led to China and France.

In its dedication to local and global communities, Derryfield's Key Club actively partners with more than a dozen organizations, including the New Hampshire Food Bank, Heifer International, New Horizons Soup Kitchen, Boys and Girls Club, and local immigrant relocation programs.

Breakthrough Manchester (formerly Summerbridge Manchester), a year-round, tuition-free academic program, is also an important part of The Derryfield School. Breakthrough offers motivated students from Manchester's public elementary schools the opportunity to learn from outstanding high school and college students. Several Derryfield faculty members work as mentor teachers, while a large number of Derryfield students teach for Breakthrough.

Traditional Derryfield events and celebrations include Founders' Day, Winter Carnival, Grandparents' Day, Head's Holiday, Country Fair, Moose Revue talent show, and the Prom.

DAILY LIFE

Because Derryfield students come from approximately forty different surrounding towns, the School itself becomes a hub for learning, playing, serving, and socializing.

A full Derryfield School day begins at 7:55 a.m. and ends between 2:15 and 3:15 p.m. (depending on the grade level). Departure times vary, depending on a student's level of involvement in extracurricular activities or a student's desire to obtain extra help from a teacher, use the library, or attend study hall.

Homeroom gatherings occur three mornings per week, and advisories meet twice per week. The Tuesday and Thursday class schedules allow time for an activities period, during which clubs meet. A 30-minute all-school assembly takes place each Monday morning. The class schedule is a seven-period, seven-"day," rotating schedule.

SUMMER PROGRAMS

Derryfield offers several summer camps, including drama, tennis, and girls' field hockey.

COSTS AND FINANCIAL AID

Tuition and fees for 2008–09 were $22,750. In addition to the Financial Aid Program, which offers direct grants, the School offers installment payment options.

The Financial Aid Program is designed to make a Derryfield education accessible to qualified students who could not otherwise afford the cost of attending. On average, Derryfield provides financial assistance to 17 percent of the student body, with awards that vary from 5 to 95 percent of tuition. Derryfield awards more than $1 million in financial aid grants annually.

ADMISSIONS INFORMATION

The Admission Committee considers applications from students entering grades 6 through 12. Although the largest number of students enters in grades 6, 7, and 9, spaces are often available in other grades as well.

Applicants are required to complete an on-campus interview and a written application. The SSAT is required for all applications to grades 6 through 9. Applicants to grade 10, 11, and 12 have the option to submit their PSAT or SAT scores.

APPLICATION TIMETABLE

The priority deadline for applications is February 2. Tours and interviews are offered through the Admission Office. There is a $50 preliminary application fee for applicants.

Notification of acceptance is mailed on March 10, and families are expected to reply by April 10.

ADMISSIONS CORRESPONDENCE

Admission Office
The Derryfield School
2108 River Road
Manchester, New Hampshire 03104-1396

Phone: 603-669-4524
Fax: 603-641-9521
E-mail: admission@derryfield.org
Web site: http://www.derryfield.org

THE DOANE STUART SCHOOL

Albany, New York

THE DOANE STUART SCHOOL

Type: Coeducational, interfaith, day college-preparatory school
Grades: N–12 (Lower School, N–4; Middle School, 5–8; Upper School, 9–12)
Enrollment: 280 (110 Upper School, 170 Middle and Lower Schools)
Head of School: Richard D. Enemark, Ph.D., Headmaster

THE SCHOOL

The Doane Stuart School is a coeducational, nursery through grade 12 day school, welcoming students of all faiths. As the nation's only successfully merged Protestant-Catholic school, Doane Stuart stands as a unique model for interfaith education in America. Founded in 1975, Doane Stuart was created from the merger of the Roman Catholic Kenwood Academy of the Sacred Heart (founded in 1852) and the Episcopal St. Agnes School (founded in 1870).

The mission of Doane Stuart is education. In a college-preparatory context, where the joy of discovery is valued, Doane Stuart emphasizes serious study, educates to social responsibility, and lays the foundation for a strong faith. With 270 students, N–12, Doane Stuart is small by intent and small by design, claiming a premier college-preparatory program and unique partnerships with many organizations in its home community and beyond—including Lagan College in Belfast (the first integrated school in Northern Ireland, welcoming both Protestant and Catholic students), the University at Albany (the region's largest university), the Albany College of Pharmacy (affording Doane Stuart students premedical and prepharmacological study and research), and the Albany Institute of History and Art.

Doane Stuart is a member in good standing of the National Association of Independent Schools (NAIS). It is governed by an independent Board of Trustees with 15 members and has an annual operating budget of more than $3 million and an endowment of approximately $1 million. Doane Stuart is fully and successfully accredited by the New York State Association of Independent Schools and is a member in good standing of the National Association of Episcopal Schools.

ACADEMIC PROGRAMS

Doane Stuart has a student-teacher ratio of 7:1 and an average class size of 14. Doane Stuart's standard Upper School course of study includes 4 years of English, 3–4 years of math, 3–4 years of science, 4 years of history, 3–4 years of foreign language, 4 years of comparative religion, 4 years of physical education, three to four elective courses (which may include fine and performing arts classes), and 25 hours per year of community service. Doane Stuart students have regular access to and classes in newly renovated, state-of-the-art science laboratories and a learning technology center.

Any junior or senior who has completed a course for which there is an AP exam may take that examination to receive college credit for his or her high school work. Doane Stuart students may pursue independent study or take courses through the School's distinct partnership with the University at Albany for high school or college credit. Students also receive exceptional preparation for such standardized tests as the SAT and SAT Subject Tests.

Doane Stuart uses a standard 4.0 grading scale; honors are earned with an average of 3.25 or higher, and high honors are earned with an average of 3.7 or higher. Upper School students work within a quarterly structure each year, while Middle and Lower School students are graded on a trimester basis. Report cards are issued at the end of each grading period, with interim or midquarter reports (as applicable) issued between report cards.

Each Doane Stuart Upper School student is assigned an adult mentor, who helps his or her assigned students to manage successfully the academic, social, and emotional rigors of the Upper School years.

FACULTY AND ADVISERS

Doane Stuart has 38 faculty members (15 men, 23 women); more than 60 percent have advanced degrees. Each Upper School faculty member serves as a mentor for 5 to 10 students and may also serve as an adviser or coach for clubs, activities, and athletic teams. Doane Stuart has a Campus Ministry Team made up of faculty members from all three divisions, who coordinate interfaith chapel services and help facilitate community service opportunities. The School encourages and finances continuing professional development among its teachers and has offered sabbaticals to senior faculty members.

Doane Stuart has been headed by Dr. Richard D. Enemark since 1998. Dr. Enemark received his A.B. from Colgate University (where he was elected to Phi Beta Kappa) in 1972, his M.A. from the University of Vermont in 1978, his M.Phil. from Columbia University in 1983, and his Ph.D. in English and comparative literature, with highest distinction, from Columbia in 1986. Beginning his teaching career in the 1970s at Burke Mountain Academy in Vermont (where he was Director of Studies and now serves on its Board of Trustees as Co-Chair of the Governance Committee), Dr. Enemark has served on the boards of other independent schools and agencies, including the Eaglebrook School in Deerfield, Massachusetts.

COLLEGE ADMISSION COUNSELING

Doane Stuart's Director of College Counseling provides expert direction and oversight of the college placement process, which begins in earnest during the freshman year, although college awareness offerings are provided to students throughout their Middle School and Lower School years as well. Each Upper School student and his or her parents meet, one-on-one, with the Director for a minimum of two sessions before the senior year. More than 75 college admissions officers visit the School annually, while Doane Stuart staff members take students on regular visits to colleges throughout the region and beyond.

Doane Stuart students have median SAT scores more than 20 percent higher than the national average. The School's students have been admitted to some of the most prestigious colleges and universities in the country. Of the School's graduates, 100 percent are admitted to the nation's most selective colleges, and each graduate receives an average of $80,000 in merit-based college scholarships.

STUDENT BODY AND CONDUCT

Doane Stuart's Upper School has 110 students, while the Lower and Middle Schools combined have 170 students, split nearly 50:50 between boys and girls. Approximately 10 percent of the School's students are from minority communities, and another 2–5 percent each year are exchange students from international programs, including the School's unique exchange with Lagan College in Belfast. Doane Stuart students are primarily from the eight counties surrounding Albany, from as far south as the Berkshires to as far north as Saratoga Springs, with busing provided from Saratoga, Columbia, and Greene Counties. Campus safety and behavior policies are provided to students each year via School handbooks for each division.

ACADEMIC FACILITIES

Doane Stuart is among the largest independent school properties in northeastern New York, with 80 acres of forest, formal gardens, and playing fields. Doane Stuart's academic facilities include a historically significant nineteenth-century administrative and Upper School building, outlying structures designed by A. J. Davis, an architecturally significant Gothic-Revival chapel, a newly dedicated outdoor chapel and classroom, and a main academic building built in 1966, housing classrooms, laboratories, a Lower School library, and an Upper School learning technology center.

ATHLETICS

Doane Stuart's Upper School teams compete in the Central Hudson Valley League. Doane Stuart encourages all of its students to participate in the School's athletic programs, which include basketball, cross-country, soccer, and track and field in the Middle School and basketball, crew, cross-country, fencing, soccer, softball, tennis, and track and field in the Upper School. Doane Stuart's campus includes an acclaimed cross-country course, outdoor tennis and basketball courts, two soccer fields, a softball field, two indoor gym facilities, a swimming pool, and two new, state-of-the-art playgrounds.

EXTRACURRICULAR OPPORTUNITIES

Every Doane Stuart Middle and Upper School student participates in one or more of the School's extracurricular offerings. Programs include varsity and junior varsity athletics, drama and theater productions, community service beyond required levels (25 hours per year), the School magazine, the School newspaper, photography club, outdoor club, student government, National Honor Society, and independent study or internships at one of Doane Stuart's exclusive partner organizations, including the University at Albany, the Albany Institute of History and Art, the Albany College of Pharmacy, and Lagan College in Belfast, Northern Ireland.

DAILY LIFE

A typical day consists of seven 45-minute class periods, a 50-minute lunch and activities period, and a 15-minute morning meeting period, which is used for division gatherings, all-School meetings, or chapels. School begins at 8:20 a.m. and ends at 3:20 p.m., Monday through Thursday, and 2:35 p.m. on Friday, when extracurricular activities begin. Before- and after-school programs are available for Lower and Middle School students.

COSTS AND FINANCIAL AID

For the 2008–09 school year, tuition ranged from $11,100 in nursery to $18,850 in grade 12. Extra charges include lab fees, field trips, music lessons, lunch, books (if not available from within parents' home school districts), and special tutoring. Doane Stuart offers a generous financial aid program for qualified students whose families have demonstrated financial need; more than 40 percent of Doane Stuart students received some form of financial aid in 2007–08. Financing and payment plans are available.

ADMISSIONS INFORMATION

Admission to Doane Stuart is selective. The School seeks and welcomes talented students from all backgrounds and from all faiths, expecting that new students will contribute to the School community as much as they benefit from it.

APPLICATION TIMETABLE

Due to the competitive nature of Doane Stuart's admission process, prospective families are encouraged to begin the application process in the fall before the year that their student enrolls in the School. The admission process includes tours, classroom visits, tests, letters of recommendation, transcripts, and screening reviews by the Admission Committee. Waiting lists are implemented as soon as class sizes reach expected levels.

ADMISSIONS CORRESPONDENCE

Michael P. Green, Director of Admission
The Doane Stuart School
799 South Pearl Street
Albany, New York 12202
Phone: 518-465-5222 Ext. 241
Fax: 518-465-5230
E-mail: admissions@doanestuart.org
Web site: http://www.doanestuart.org

DUBLIN SCHOOL

Dublin, New Hampshire

Type: Coeducational boarding and day college-preparatory school
Grades: 9–12
Enrollment: 123
Head of School: Bradford Bates, Interim Headmaster

THE SCHOOL

Dublin School was founded in 1935 by Paul and Nancy Lehmann, who sought to create an institution that would provide a demanding college-preparatory education tempered by a high degree of personal attention and a strong sense of community. Since its founding, Dublin has sought to help each student develop intellectually, physically, socially, and morally. To accomplish this, the School provides a rigorous academic program in which students gain self-confidence from success, are prepared for the demands of college, and learn the importance of teamwork. In addition to learning the responsibilities of academic independence, students receive a diverse experience that requires participation in community service, athletics, internships, and a school work program.

The School is located in southwestern New Hampshire, 1¾ hours from Boston and 4 hours from New York City. The village of Dublin, largely residential, has about 1,400 year-round residents. The Monadnock region is rich in artistic, cultural, and intellectual activities. Situated on more than 300 wooded acres, Dublin School's campus is conducive to a host of outdoor activities. Dublin Lake is within walking distance of campus and is available for canoeing, swimming, and sailing. Mount Monadnock, the second most frequently climbed mountain in the world, is accessible and explored often by Dublin students throughout the year.

The School is governed by a self-perpetuating Board of Trustees. Recent support has made it possible to construct Hoyt-Horner Dorm and 14,000-square-foot Whitney Gymnasium, which houses multipurpose facilities for Dublin's athletic program. In addition to a full-size basketball court and the Athletic Director's office, the building also houses a weight-training and conditioning room. The fully equipped Von Mertens Woodworking Shop was constructed by students and faculty members a few years ago.

Dublin School is accredited by the New England Association of Schools and Colleges and approved by the state of New Hampshire Department of Education. It is a member of the National Association of Independent Schools, the Independent Schools Association of Northern New England, the National Association of College Admission Counselors, the Secondary School Admission Test Board, the Small Boarding Schools Association, and the Network of Complementary Schools.

ACADEMIC PROGRAMS

The School believes that the best preparation for a demanding college environment is exposure to a variety of subjects and disciplines. Students must take a minimum of 4 credits of English; 7 credits in the disciplines of mathematics and science; 6 credits in the disciplines of history and foreign languages (including at least 2 credits in one language); 2 credits in the arts; 1 credit in elective courses in English, mathematics, history, science, foreign languages, or the arts; and .3 credits in computer literacy. (Graduation requires 20.3 credits.) An Honors Diploma requires 8 credits in mathematics and science and 7 credits in history and foreign language or 2 credits each in two different foreign languages, with a minimum of 3 credits in one language. In addition, a student seeking Honors designation must maintain a minimum GPA of 3.0 for the junior and senior years. Honors courses are weighted. Elective courses are offered in diverse areas, including marine science, American Sign Language, photography, and psychology. A senior exhibition of mastery is also available to interested students.

The teacher-student ratio is 1:5; classes average 5 to 12 students each. Dublin's classes permit a great deal of individualized instruction, which is one of the hallmarks of the School. Courses that are designed to prepare students for Advanced Placement exams are available in English, history, foreign languages, biology, and mathematics.

The academic program is enhanced by the Humanities Program, which is designed to involve the community in the exploration of contemporary issues. Artists, speakers, craftspersons, and professionals from all over the world come to the campus to share their talents and experience in this all-School activity. Themes, chosen by presenters, students, and faculty members each year, have included gender issues, storytelling, environmental awareness, and local history.

The Learning Skills Program is designed for students who are intellectually capable but who lack academic achievement. This program includes students with learning differences and those who are experiencing general academic difficulties related to a diagnosed learning disability. Students who struggle with specific areas, including reading, written expression, mathematics, or organizational skills, are typical candidates for this program. The Learning Skills Program is not an alternate curriculum; it is a structured support system for the student mainstreamed in Dublin School's curriculum.

Grades are mailed to parents during the middle, and at the end of the trimester, grades are accompanied by teacher comments and a letter from the adviser. Each student receives not only a letter grade but also an effort grade in each class. Parents may also elect for their child to be part of the Evening Study Assistance Program. This program places a small number of students in a structured academic environment under the guidance of one of the Learning Skills Program's instructors. The program allows students to meet academic challenges and complete nightly homework assignments on their own and to receive attention when they are not able to find solutions to academic questions.

FACULTY AND ADVISERS

The heart of Dublin School is its faculty members, who are deeply involved in student life and have invested in the success of each student. In addition to strong academic backgrounds, faculty members have a deep commitment to working with students and to helping them develop academically and personally. There are 31 full-time faculty members, 15 of whom hold advanced degrees. Faculty members are required to participate in ongoing professional development and are evaluated yearly by the Headmaster and the Academic Dean.

Faculty members and administrators coach athletic teams or advise special interest groups. Each faculty member and administrator also acts as an adviser to no more than 5 students, interacting with them on a daily basis. Twenty faculty members and their families live on campus. Students also have access to a resident full-time nurse, an athletic trainer, a counselor, and a learning skills specialist.

COLLEGE ADMISSION COUNSELING

Dublin School's college guidance office is staffed by a full-time director who provides the information needed to help students evaluate their options and to guide through the college admission process.

During the junior year, students are given a College Assessment Form to complete and share with their parents. Students also attend a college fair and meet with college admission representatives. By the end of their junior year, students have taken their PSAT and SAT. Some juniors take their SAT Subject Tests as well. Counselors assist students and their parents in developing a list of appropriate colleges. Juniors are encouraged to begin visiting colleges of their choice during the March vacation and the summer of the junior year. Informal meetings with parents are held during the school year to discuss topics such as admissions, financial aid, and other aspects of the college admission process.

In their senior year, students have additional opportunities to take the SAT Subject Tests as well as Advanced Placement tests. Recent college choices include Bates, Bentley, Boston University, Bowdoin, Brandeis, Clarkson, Colby, Colgate, Cornell, Dartmouth, Dickinson, Evergreen, Goucher, Hamilton, Holy Cross, Ithaca, Mt. Holyoke, NYU, Pitzer, Smith, St. Lawrence, Skidmore, Stanford, Swarthmore, Tufts, Union, Wellesley, Wentworth, Wesleyan, Williams, and the Universities of California, Colorado, Illinois at Urbana-Champaign, Maine, Massachusetts, New Hampshire, Oregon, and Vermont. Dublin School students are accepted to their first-choice college 90 percent of the time.

STUDENT BODY AND CONDUCT

The student body is a remarkably heterogeneous group, coming from eight countries and seventeen states. Students come from both rural and inner-city environments. This diversity enriches the life of the School and ensures a community in which students of widely differing backgrounds and interests can feel at home. There are 98 boarding students (65 boys and 33 girls) and 25 day students (11 boys and 14 girls).

ACADEMIC FACILITIES

Classes at Dublin are held in a number of facilities around campus, including the School House, Science Building, Arts Building, Art Studio, the Evans Library, or outside. Specialized facilities include three science labs, a computer technology center, language lab, recording studio, recital hall, theater, darkroom, the arts studio, and an audiovisual resource center. The Evans Library houses a 13,000-volume collection, provides electronic research capabilities, and is part of the interlibrary loan system of New Hampshire.

BOARDING AND GENERAL FACILITIES

There are seven dormitories on campus. Most student rooms are doubles, and the dorms house 8–24 students. One or 2 faculty members and their families live in each dormitory. Each dorm also has a resident student proctor who assists with the dormitory's operation. One of the living facilities, Lehmann House, also houses the dining hall, the day student locker area, the school store, and the student center.

ATHLETICS

Dublin's athletic program aims to instill in students a love of exercise and a commitment to good sportsmanship. Students are required to participate in the athletic program and play interscholastic sports.

The School recognizes that there are different ways of enjoying and experiencing achievement in athletics and offers a variety of competitive and recreational sports. Dublin competes interscholastically in soccer, basketball, cross-country, equestrian, lacrosse, sailing, skiing, snowboarding, and tennis. Recreational offerings include crew, sailing, tennis, and weightlifting.

In addition to the recently completed Whitney Gymnasium, the School has two large playing fields, six tennis courts, a trainer's room, a fitness room, several kilometers of cross-country running and ski trails, and an outdoor skating facility. The sailing and crew programs are conducted on Dublin Lake.

EXTRACURRICULAR OPPORTUNITIES

Academics are just part of the overall program at Dublin School, and students are offered a wide variety of extracurricular options. These include "Dubliners," the School's choral group; dance; music lessons; the use of compact disc recording equipment; a jazz/rock band; and the option of being a part of two major theater productions each year. Other extracurricular options include student government, Amnesty International, Oxfam America, the yearbook, and student coffeehouses.

Dublin's proximity to Boston as well as other major cities presents students with a wide variety of cultural and entertainment opportunities. Recent student excursions have included trips to a renaissance fair, the historic towns of Salem and Plymouth, museums in Boston, the annual Scottish Highland Games, and Boston Cultural Day.

Students are also involved in a mandatory community service program. They teach dance at local preschool and afterschool programs; host a Halloween party for Dublin Elementary School children; clear trails at nearby state forests or on town land; serve as big brothers and sisters at the local elementary school; and help staff charity booths at local fairs. Together, Dublin students donate more than 1,000 hours of community service to local charities/organizations during the school year.

DAILY LIFE

The student work program embodies the founders' belief in the importance of shared responsibilities. Student jobs include kitchen duty, cleaning buildings, emptying dormitory trash, sweeping hallways, and cleaning bathrooms. These jobs are assigned on a rotating basis and are supervised by proctors and faculty members. The academic day consists of seven periods and a daily school meeting, followed by athletics, dinner, and evening study hours from 8 to 10 p.m. Boarding students are expected to be in their dorms and day students off campus by 10 p.m.

WEEKEND LIFE

On Saturday morning, students and faculty members participate in Work Gang. Projects have included clearing trails, stacking wood, designing and planting gardens, major cleaning projects, and painting. Students also work off campus to earn credit for community service.

On Saturday afternoon, students participate in athletic competitions against other area independent schools, both on campus and away. Students who are not competing usually support friends on teams, work on class projects, relax, and spend time with friends.

Students have the chance to participate in a range of recreational offerings. Many make the most of the School's setting by enjoying Dublin Lake, climbing Mount Monadnock, and walking other area trails. There are also movies on and off campus and trips to local restaurants and shopping locations. Special events, such as an annual "all-night" shopping trip to L. L. Bean in Maine, excursions to Boston, hiking trips, museum trips, professional games, and concerts occur as well.

Three times each year, an entire weekend is devoted to family activities. Parents' Weekend in the fall provides an opportunity for parents to visit faculty members, each other, and their children's friends and to see athletic events and the results of student projects. In February, Dublin hosts Winterfest, a day of winter-related activities for students, siblings, parents, faculty members, and the local community. The third major weekend event of the year is Mayfair, an annual celebration of the arts and preparation for graduation.

COSTS AND FINANCIAL AID

In 2008–09, tuition, room, and board were $41,150; day students' expenses were $25,000. There are additional fees for the Learning Skills Program, the Evening Study Assistance Program, English as a Second Language, laboratory fees, some athletic offerings, and the ski/snowboarding program.

For the 2008–09 academic year, 31 percent of the student body received financial aid, with a total disbursement of $1 million. To apply for financial aid, families need to contact the School's Financial Aid Officer, fill out a Parent's Financial Aid Statement, and provide financial information to both the Financial Aid Officer and the School and Student Service for Financial Aid in Princeton, New Jersey.

ADMISSIONS INFORMATION

Dublin School seeks students who have the ability and motivation to excel in a challenging college-preparatory curriculum, who have strong character, who are enthusiastic about becoming a student at Dublin School, and who are willing to become involved in the life of the School and to work for the common good of all students. In evaluating each candidate for admission, the Admission Committee is guided by the applicant's transcript, application essay, interview, and teachers' recommendations. Applicants are encouraged to visit the campus for a tour and interview. Class visits can also be arranged and are hosted by a student tour guide.

APPLICATION TIMETABLE

Candidates for admission are encouraged to apply by January 31. Although applications are considered after that date, students who have completed the application process by January 31 are notified regarding their acceptance by March 10. They then have until April 10 to accept or decline the School's offer. The application fee is $50, due when the application is presented to the School. Candidates who apply after January 31 are notified as soon as a decision has been reached. The Admission Office is open from 8 a.m. to 4 p.m., Monday through Friday. Interviews are scheduled during regular school hours; if necessary, special arrangements can be made to schedule a tour and interview.

ADMISSIONS CORRESPONDENCE

Sheila Bogan, Director of Admission
Dublin School
18 Lehmann Way
P.O. Box 522
Dublin, New Hampshire 03444-0522

Phone: 603-563-1235
Fax: 603-563-8671
E-mail: admission@dublinschool.org
Web site: http://www.dublinschool.org

THE DWIGHT SCHOOL

New York, New York

Type: Coeducational international college-preparatory day school
Grades: Nursery–12: Woodside Preschool, ages 2–5; Timothy House, K–5; Bentley House, 6–8; Franklin House, 9–10; Anglo House, 11–12
Enrollment: 470 (Preschool: 120)
Head of School: Stephen H. Spahn, Chancellor

THE SCHOOL

The Dwight School, which was founded in 1872, became the first school in the U.S. to offer the three International Baccalaureate (I.B.) programs, grades nursery–12. The School's motto is "every student has a spark of genius." The School's mission is to develop each student's unique capabilities. It seeks to integrate mind, body, and spirit. The program incorporates academic excellence and a commitment to educate a diverse student population in leadership and responsibility to others. The School's structured environment places emphasis on integrating the latest educational research into a traditional curriculum.

The Dwight spirit is communicated through weekly advisory meetings, Honor Council, peer leaders, house community programs, and monthly whole-school assemblies. Dwight students aim to become confident, self-motivated, disciplined, knowledgeable, and open-minded inquirers as well as caring, principled, and responsible citizens. Dwight cofounded the Institute for Civic Leadership in order to construct a school model for civic leadership, continuing the tradition of graduates Mayor Fiorello LaGuardia, Robert Moses, Walter Lippmann, Governor Herbert Lehman, and Secretary of the Treasury Henry Morganthau. Every student is immersed in a program of civic responsibility.

Dwight is accredited by the International Baccalaureate Organization, the Council of International Schools, and the Middle States Association of Colleges and Schools. Graduating students enter leading universities in the United States and abroad.

ACADEMIC PROGRAMS

The school year of thirty-eight weeks lasts from September to June. Dwight utilizes a trimester system. Grades are sent to parents three times a year, and scheduled conferences between parents and teachers are held two times per year. All students in grades 6 through 11 meet in small weekly advisory groups. These complement house meetings.

The Dwight School's average student-teacher ratio of 10:1 allows for small classes in the Lower, Middle, and Upper Schools.

The School is organized into four houses, each with a Dean, and a nursery school, Woodside Preschool for children ages 2–5. Woodside Preschool focuses on the development of the whole child. Through structured inquiry and play, children are challenged to think, learn, and discover in a caring and nurturing environment. Spanish, Chinese, music, art, and P.E. are taught by specialist teachers. Timothy House (K–5) became the first I.B. Primary Years Program in the U.S. in 1998. Students master traditional math, reading, and writing skills and are immersed in 6 units of inquiry in geography, humanities, and science. Students study Spanish or French, as well as Chinese, starting in kindergarten. Small classes allow each child to reach his or her full intellectual, physical, and social potential. More than fifteen after-school offerings extend the normal drama, music, art, foreign language, technology, and sports programs.

Problem solving utilizes multiple approaches and solutions. The faculty members strive to awaken the sense of wonder that makes learning significant and lifelong.

The Primary Years Program transitions into the I.B. Middle Years Program offerings in Bentley House (grades 6–8). All students study the major academic disciplines, and they also learn technology, environmental studies, civics, community activities, and health and social education across all academic disciplines. After school, there are teams, clubs, and activities that extend a student's passion. Trips to Australia, England, France, Peru, Kenya, Mexico, India, and China are another aspect of the Dwight international experience. Students are offered a highly structured curriculum with challenging interdisciplinary units. A comprehensive study skills program is integrated into all course work. Emphasis is placed on the study of grammar and composition. Essay writing is required across the curriculum. By sixth and seventh grades, students are introduced to departmentalization.

The Upper School presents a classical core of academic subjects that incorporate community service, social education, goal setting, environmental awareness, and a knowledge of human achievement and potential. In the junior year, students enroll in the International Baccalaureate Diploma Program. The I.B. Diploma can give up to one year's credit at U.S. colleges and is an acceptable entrance standard for major international universities. Students may choose to take individual I.B. courses instead of the full program and thus earn advanced-placement credit.

Franklin House (grades 9 and 10) and Anglo House (grades 11 and 12) place special emphasis on the I.B. Diploma Program. All students in grade 10 work on a personal project of their selection, under the steady hand of an adviser. All students study I.B. subjects with the expectation that many will complete the full Baccalaureate by grade 12. Rich course offerings from theater, art, and music extend to unique programs in design technology, environmental studies, and microeconomics and business management.

All educational programs help students to reach world-class standards. The Enrichment Work Program is offered to grades K–12 in order to go beyond the standard curriculum. Students may read additional books, study art history, and be introduced to advanced studies of science and mathematics.

Mother Tongue Instruction is available to students to maintain mastery of their native language. Students study Arabic, Chinese, Dutch, French, German, Hebrew, Hindi, Italian, Japanese, Russian, and Spanish. English as an alternate language (EAL) is provided for students who have not achieved the necessary level of competency in English.

The Quest Department provides a limited number of individualized mentoring programs for students of high academic ability. These students need to enhance their skills in one particular academic discipline in order to succeed in a rigorous academic setting. Quest students operate in the traditional class setting and execute a full academic program. Quest mentors observe students in classes and consult with their teachers on an ongoing basis. There is frequent communication with parents.

A student exchange program exists with Woodside Park International School in London. The Dwight School also enjoys a rich tradition of athletic excellence. In recent years, the School has won national championships in fencing and local or state championships in basketball, track, tennis, and cross-country.

FACULTY AND ADVISERS

Stephen H. Spahn became the Headmaster in 1967 and Chancellor in 1993. Mr. Spahn received a B.A. from Dartmouth (1963) and the equivalent of an M.A. from Oxford, and he finished course work for a Ph.D. at Columbia. He was an all-American basketball player, an International Fellow, a member of Phi Beta Kappa, a Senior Fellow, and a Woodrow Wilson Fellow. He has served as Project Officer with the Special Fund of the United Nations and helped to conduct the first health survey of Nepal. Currently, he is a trustee of the Institute for Civic Leadership, the International Baccalaureate Fund, and the Rubin Museum of Himalayan Art.

The Dean of Community Life, Evan Flamenbaum, is responsible for the health and well-being of every student. He chairs a team of professionals who work with families and students in order to navigate the passage to adulthood. The team is made up of the school health-care provider, a certified guidance counselor, a health teacher, and an experienced psychologist. The Dean runs a study-skills program for new students in June to allow for a smooth transition into Dwight.

A highly talented faculty reflects and models the qualities of leadership, scholarship, character, and service. All participate in mentoring and professional development programs.

The School is organized into six departments under the educational leadership of Anthony Foster, who has been a member of the Dwight faculty for more than twenty years. As Assistant Headmaster, Mr. Foster has created a balance of classical and innovative curricula. Master teachers are always available to discuss individual programs and concerns.

COLLEGE ADMISSION COUNSELING

Dwight has a comprehensive college guidance program under the Directors of College Guidance, Mrs. Susheila Mani, Mrs. Ryna Bab, and Mr. Arthur Samuels. The program involves parents, students, college admissions officers, and financial aid consultants. Dwight's success in placing students in colleges demonstrates the effectiveness of the program.

The first phase begins with ninth-, tenth-, and eleventh-grade meetings. The guidance team introduces parents and students to the college process—the options, the requirements, and the many considerations involved in selecting the best school for each child.

In the junior year, the team meets with each student to help select courses, to schedule and prepare for college testing, and to discuss individual talents and concerns. A college priority list is then personally tailored to fit each student's needs.

In the senior year, students meet with college representatives who visit Dwight to discuss the academic offerings of their schools and to answer student questions. Dialogue continues with parents, students, and admissions officers until the process is complete.

For the past two years, scores on the verbal and math portions of the SAT have ranged from 500 to 800, and SAT Subject Test scores have ranged from 520 to 800.

Dwight graduates attend Barnard, Bowdoin, Brown, Carnegie Mellon, Colgate, Columbia, Cornell, Dartmouth, Duke, Emory, Georgetown, Harvard, Lehigh, Middlebury, Mount Holyoke, Northwestern, NYU, Oberlin, Princeton, Skidmore, Smith, Stanford, Syracuse, Tufts, Tulane, Vassar, Wellesley, Yale, and the Universities of California, Michigan, Pennsylvania, Vermont, Virginia, and Wisconsin. Students have also recently attended Bocconi, Hebrew University, McGill, Oxford, Queen's University, St. Andrews, the Sorbonne, and the Universities of Brussels, Edinburgh, London, Milan, Rome, and Toronto.

STUDENT BODY AND CONDUCT

The enrollment at the Dwight School is 120 in the preschool, 200 in grades K–8, and 270 in grades 9–12. Two thirds of the students are from New York City.

ACADEMIC FACILITIES

The Dwight School recently completed construction of new Upper and Lower School libraries; a large common meeting space, the Quad; a state-of-the-art Middle School laboratory; and additional classrooms. The School also acquired the adjoining brownstone, which will be used to house, among others, science labs, an expanded film and technology center, and multipurpose athletic space.

The Dwight School originally occupied three buildings—a five-story structure built in 1912, two brownstones that were converted for School use in 1968 and enlarged in 1983, and an expanded gym that was added in 1993. Together, the buildings provide thirty-seven classrooms, four new science laboratories, a 17,000-volume Upper and Lower School library, two computer centers, a theater, two art rooms, and two gyms. The Lower School was recently expanded and refurbished. Woodside Preschool is situated in brand-new, state-of-the-art facilities. The campus consists of eleven bright classrooms, two indoor gyms, and a playroom. Each class is equipped with a computer and library area. For outdoor play, children enjoy a playground a few feet away in Riverside Park. In addition, a new science lab, library, and theater were constructed in 2006.

ATHLETICS

The importance of a sound body to complement a sound mind is integral to the Dwight School's philosophy. Athletes are introduced to the best techniques of physical and mental development produced in both the East and West. The School has two gymnasiums and utilizes several local athletic facilities.

The Dwight School has a history of outstanding scholar-athletes. The Dwight School has had national championships in fencing and tennis. State championships have been won in boys' and girls' basketball. Other teams include baseball, cross-country, golf (developmental), soccer, tennis, and track.

EXTRACURRICULAR OPPORTUNITIES

The Dwight Conservatory includes a chorus, a jazz ensemble, a classical string group, and a select choir (by audition). Individual instrumental and voice lessons are available. Students are active in the Interschool Orchestra. Twelve performances for the Middle and Upper Schools are held annually.

The drama program has among its four productions a musical. The dance team completed a fourth successful year. Students in all grades participate in annual art festivals. Students recently performed at the Edinburgh Fringe Festival. The Art Department has three annual exhibitions. A staff of professional artists and an internationally recognized photographer take students every week to galleries and museums.

An active Parents' Association runs numerous events, including a gala benefit. The student government and honor council provide students with firsthand experience in the democratic process by giving them a formal voice in School affairs.

Numerous publications are produced at all grade levels; the School believes in the concept of writing for publications as a necessary part of every student's education.

The Dwight School believes that student awareness of and participation in the surrounding community is essential. The Community Action Service (CAS) program is incorporated into the curriculum, with independent work required of all students. CAS has established relationships with a wide variety of community organizations. This program helps run a soup kitchen for the homeless, provides toys for hospitalized children, and organizes parties at local hospitals. Recently, the School won the Hagoort Award, which is given to a school whose community service project was deemed best in this hemisphere by the International Baccalaureate North American Office.

The Model United Nations Association sends students to university-run General Assembly competitions. The mock trial team is consistently among the best in the region. Dwight is a cofounder of the Institute for Civic Leadership, a nonprofit organization dedicated to training future leaders for public service. Student leaders help to organize conferences at the American Museum of Natural History and the United Nations. The institute seeks to be a model for other schools. A strong peer leaders program is the foundation stone of the program. Dwight is piloting an online service leadership curriculum to nurture the next generation of positive change agents.

The School sponsors trips to England, France, Peru, India, Kenya, China, and Australia, which provides students with an opportunity to experience another culture while performing community service for an extended period of time. The Contemporary Arts Society offers trips to New York City's museums, theaters, and other places of interest.

The Junior Passport Program at the preschool offers a wide range of extracurricular activities for students ages 3 to 5—including music, art, drama, sports, and language immersion. In addition, the Woodside Clubhouse provides an extended day program and more informal after-school activities. The Passport Program offers students in grades K–4 a rich developmental sports program in tennis, swimming, soccer, gymnastics, basketball, and fencing. The Middle School Ambassadors Program, for grades 5–6, has an early-morning training program and intramural competition. After school, students participate in fencing, track, cross-country, volleyball, soccer, basketball, student council, art, music, choir, and drama. The Dean of the Middle School, a former Ivy League basketball and soccer player, oversees each student's pastoral care.

DAILY LIFE

The academic schedule, from 8 to 3, includes eight 45-minute class periods. After classes, students remain for extracurricular activities, library work, conferences with faculty members, supervised study, sports, and advanced seminars. Grades K–6 are offered an extensive after-school program, including swimming, karate, music, in-line skating, art, fencing, and tennis.

The school year, from early September to June, is divided into three terms and includes an orientation period, a Thanksgiving recess, winter and spring vacations, a midwinter holiday, and several long weekends.

COSTS AND FINANCIAL AID

The 2008–09 tuition ranged from $29,900 to $32,200 plus fees for books and activities. Financial aid is granted on the basis of need and academic promise. A separate charge is made for Quest. The Dwight School Foundation provides scholarships to students with financial need.

ADMISSIONS INFORMATION

The Dwight School seeks to enroll students who are interested in and can benefit from a classical and challenging innovative academic program. New sections have been added in kindergarten and sixth, seventh, and ninth grades. Applicants must take an Educational Records Bureau admissions test (http://www.erbtest.org), submit a transcript from the previous school, and have a personal interview. Other arrangements may be made for students residing in other parts of the country and abroad. A letter of recommendation from a person who knows the student well must be included to supplement the file. This should be sent directly to the Admissions Department.

The Dwight School is able to issue I-20 immigration forms for international applicants. Students residing abroad who cannot visit the School for an interview must send the following materials along with the application: an official school transcript, a sample of writing in English, a teacher recommendation, and standardized test results. International applicants can arrange a videoconference interview.

APPLICATION TIMETABLE

Students are notified after all admissions information has been received by the School.

ADMISSIONS CORRESPONDENCE

Chris Allen
Director of Admissions, Nursery–PreK
Woodside Preschool
140 Riverside Boulevard
New York, New York 10069
Phone: 212-362-2350

Alicia Janiak
Director of Admissions, Grades K–8
Marina Bernstein
Director of Admissions, Grades 9–12
The Dwight School
291 Central Park West
New York, New York 10024
Phone: 212-724-7524

For a brochure and application:

Alyson Rosenthal, Associate Director of Admissions
The Dwight School
291 Central Park West
New York, New York 10024
Phone: 212-724-7524
Fax: 212-724-2539
E-mail: admissions@dwight.edu
Web site: http://www.dwight.edu

ECOLE D'HUMANITÉ

Hasliberg-Goldern, Switzerland

Type: Coeducational, international, college-preparatory, boarding school
Grades: Ungraded, ages 12–19 in American program, K–Matura in Swiss/German Program
Enrollment: 144 (45 in American Program)

THE SCHOOL

The founders of the Ecole d'Humanité, Paul and Edith Geheeb, first established a school in Germany in 1910, which achieved international recognition as a successful experiment in progressive education. During the Nazi period, the Geheebs emigrated to Switzerland and rebuilt their school. Barely surviving through the lean war years, the Geheebs held on to their humanitarian vision, taking in as many refugee children as they could, helping them to rediscover faith in humankind.

In 1956, Natalie Lüthi-Peterson, founder of the Lüthi-Peterson Camps for International Understanding, created the American High School Program at the School. The American Program runs parallel to and is intertwined with the Swiss Program, thus giving English-speaking and German-speaking students a unique opportunity to experience firsthand one another's customs, language, and school culture while still pursuing their own country-specific academic goals.

The philosophy of the Ecole d'Humanité continues to emphasize education of the person as a whole—a balance between artistic, athletic, and rigorous academic programs. The School stresses humanistic values and responsible community living. Students live in the midst of spectacular natural surroundings and are not inundated by television, advertising, and constant appeals to consumerism. The School's commitment to working together rather than competing with one another extends from the classroom through the "Ecole families" (residential groups) to all aspects of School life.

The Ecole d'Humanité is located in the mountain village of Hasliberg-Goldern in the heart of the Swiss Alps, just off the rail line between Lucerne and Interlaken. The campus includes twelve buildings where students and faculty members live and work together, plus nine buildings in the village with additional living space. The mountains provide an ideal setting for outdoor activities such as rock climbing, skiing/snowboarding, ski touring, and hiking.

The Ecole d'Humanité is accredited by the Department of Youth and Education of Bern and the Commission on International and Trans-Regional Accreditation (CITA) and is a member of the Swiss Group of International Schools (SGIS) and the Verein der Deutsche Landerziehungsheime. The School is an authorized SAT and AP testing site.

ACADEMIC PROGRAMS

The academic program is designed to encourage in-depth learning, true understanding, and intrinsic motivation. To this end, students choose their own courses, receive individual feedback rather than letter grades, and study only three academic subjects per trimester. To counterbalance this intensive academic program, they devote their afternoons to art, music, sports, and handwork, selecting from some eighty possible courses. Students learn to determine the most effective learning methods for themselves and to organize a balanced schedule. Classes are taught in both English and German.

A student takes the same three academic courses every day from Monday through Saturday. Those wishing to concentrate in a particular area may do so as long as university requirements and career plans are considered. Older students occasionally work independently if they have proved their ability to work on their own and have a project that meets with faculty approval. Juniors and seniors write a major research paper on a chosen subject in order to learn the techniques of note-taking, outlining, and citation and the self-discipline of long-term independent study.

A graduating student must have at least 4 years of English, 3 years of mathematics, 2–3 years of foreign language, 2–3 years of laboratory science, 1 year of social science, 1 year of history, and 1 year of humanities. Arts, sports, and music courses are required throughout the student's academic career.

Small classes (the student-teacher ratio is 5:1) allow individual instruction and encourage students' active participation. Pupils are grouped according to ability and interest rather than by age categories. Class periods of 55 to 75 minutes allow for depth and varied approaches to the subject matter. Neither grades nor final examinations are given, though quizzes, oral presentations, and papers are common. Teachers communicate regularly with the students about their work and evaluate each one's performance every six weeks in a special "blue book." Students also evaluate themselves, which is essential if they are to see their education as primarily their own responsibility. Parents receive a full report on their child's academic and social development at the end of the child's first and final terms, based on the blue book entries and staff conferences. Interim reports can be requested as needed.

Students who have mastered the prerequisite materials and techniques and who demonstrate high levels of responsibility and motivation may take AP courses and exams, which are regularly offered in a variety of subjects. Students who study in the American Program but who wish to attend universities outside of the English-speaking world have the chance to earn the AP International Diploma (APID).

FACULTY AND ADVISERS

Thirty-four full-time teachers and teacher/administrators and 2 part-time teachers live on campus. Additional teachers are engaged part-time as needed for instruction of specialty courses such as musical instruments, ski touring, and mountain climbing. The teachers also serve as "family heads" who are responsible for the general well-being of the children in their family group. This regular contact engenders positive student-teacher relationships. Teachers also serve as academic advisers, conferring with students about their individual goals, counseling them as they choose their courses, and following their progress throughout their time at the school.

Ashley Curtis will become the director of the American Program and co-director of the school in summer 2009. He was a teacher at the Ecole from 1988 to 2003, and has also taught at schools in Massachusetts and in Italy. He earned B.A. and M.A.R. degrees at Yale University. Kathleen Hennessy, who has directed the American Program since 1995, will serve as interim director until 2009.

Teachers are passionate about both academic and nonacademic pursuits, and so offer sports, music, arts, and crafts courses as well as courses in their academic disciplines. The success of a student's experience at the Ecole d'Humanité depends so much on the quality of the staff that great care is taken to hire individuals who are dedicated, well-rounded, and energetic as well as highly qualified in their academic fields. Faculty members are offered continuing education in the use of Dr. Ruth Cohn's Theme-Centered Interaction, a humanistic method for furthering effective and cooperative group work, which corresponds closely to the educational philosophy of the School.

COLLEGE ADMISSION COUNSELING

The Dean of Academics meets with juniors to review college aspirations and to plan a college-visiting tour, using catalogs and online resources. Each senior meets weekly with a college adviser to complete college applications. The Ecole is an official College Board Testing Center, and students take the SAT Reasoning and Subject tests, as well as any AP exams they have chosen, right on campus. American colleges and other colleges around the world readily accept students who have had a thorough U.S. high school education combined with the experience of living abroad. Recent graduates have attended Bard, Boston University, Brown, Colorado College, Dartmouth, Earlham, Georgetown, Guilford, Ithaca, Middlebury, Oberlin, Quest, Vassar, and the Universities of California at Santa Cruz, Chicago, Richmond, Sheffield (England), and Vienna (Austria).

STUDENT BODY AND CONDUCT

The student body for 2007–08 was 139—70 boys and 69 girls. Eighteen were day students. More than 90 percent of the students were in the grade 6–12 age group. About 50 percent of the students came from Switzerland and the rest from twenty-one other countries. About 14 percent of the student body was non-Caucasian; 25 percent received financial assistance.

Although this is a school with a demanding academic program, it is also a living community. Students take charge of such important tasks as organizing job rotations and managing committees that run the library, entertainment programs, and fire brigade. Some students are active in the student council or involved in peer counseling. Everyone participates in weekly community meetings, chaired by a student, in which individual and community concerns can be addressed.

ACADEMIC FACILITIES

Twelve buildings are used for academic purposes. Besides regular classrooms, they house three science laboratories; a workshop each for wood, pottery, metal, silver smithy, and studio art; a flexible performance space/assembly hall; seven instrumental practice rooms; a computer room; a kitchen for general use; and an audiovisual room. The library houses more than 22,000 volumes in German, English, and French and subscribes to several German and English periodicals.

BOARDING AND GENERAL FACILITIES

Students live in family groups of 2 faculty members and from 4 to 12 boys and girls of varying ages. Each family lives together in one of the School houses and eats together in the common dining room. Each Wednesday night is devoted to a family activity, such as playing games, cooking, or working on a project. Nearly all students have double rooms. Living with a mixed group including both sexes and various ages and cultures helps everyone to see beyond stereotypes and to appreciate individual differences. Students from distant lands usually go home for the long winter and spring vacations or may be invited to stay with friends or relatives. When this is not available, the School helps to make other arrangements for them.

A trained professional assists the family heads in administering to common illnesses and ailments. A physician visits once a week. There are 2 teachers trained in psychology to consult with students as needed or to make special arrangements outside the School. There is also a psychotherapist who works closely with the School.

ATHLETICS

The Alps provide a stunning natural setting for outdoor sports, which include hiking, skiing, rock climbing, ski touring, and, occasionally, mountain biking and kayaking. In the fall and spring trimesters the entire School breaks into small groups for four- and six-day hiking trips. In winter, students have the opportunity to ski almost every day at the Meiringen-Hasliberg ski area, which extends right down to the School. The School also offers team sports such as basketball, soccer, and volleyball. Students and faculty members often organize intramural competitions on weekends. The School has its own playing field and basketball and volleyball courts as well as access to the local gymnasium. A swimming pool and a riding stable are located in a nearby village.

EXTRACURRICULAR OPPORTUNITIES

A rich and broad palette of "Afternoon Courses" provides a balance to the intensive academic work in the three morning hours. Students may choose to take up to three afternoon classes per day, four days a week. Theater, music (instrument, ensemble, singing), dance, painting, blacksmithing, jewelry-making, pottery, weaving, printmaking, archery, carpentry, cooking, and stonecarving are regularly among the more than eighty courses that student can choose from at the beginning of each trimester.

The school year officially begins with the Blueberry Hike, when everyone goes up the mountain to gather blueberries. In the middle of the fall trimester, an "Intensive Week" allows students to devote an entire week, morning and afternoon, to a single project. In keeping with local culture, in late fall the School begins to bustle with preparations for the Nicholasfest, the Christmas play, and the 'Heinzelmännchen (Secret Santa) Week.' In winter a humorous Fasnacht (Mardi Gras) festival is prepared, as is the annual Shakespeare production. A summer festival concludes the year with theater, musical, and other performances as well as exhibitions from the many handwork courses. Student theater, musical, and dance performances are presented throughout the year.

Each student has a daily cleaning task and participates weekly in community service. Students may get involved in other activities as well, such as the student council, the stage and lighting group, or the group that cares for the School's donkeys.

DAILY LIFE

Wake-up is at 6:30 a.m., with breakfast at 7:10. All meals are eaten in family groups in the common dining hall and are served and washed up by students. The first morning course begins at 8:05. The nonacademic courses take place Monday through Thursday between 2:30 and 6:15, following lunch and siesta. After dinner, there is free time until the evening Quiet Hour. Family Evening is on Wednesday. The School gathers for a community meeting on Friday afternoon and singing on Saturday morning.

WEEKEND LIFE

The weekend officially lasts from Saturday at midday until Sunday dinner. Students and teachers alike organize activities for the weekend, including sports events, coffeehouses, films, and biweekly disco and folk-dance evenings. Students and/or teachers present an "Andacht" on Sunday evenings, which is generally a reflection on ethical, philosophical, or social issues. Older students may visit the nearby town, and all are free to explore the surrounding natural wonders. In winter, many students spend at least part of the weekend skiing or snowboarding.

COSTS AND FINANCIAL AID

Tuition is dependent on the current exchange rate. The tuition for the academic year 2008–09 was SF 43,000. Tuition is payable in one payment, in three payments (one per term), or in ten (monthly) installments. A Scholarship Committee reviews applications for financial aid.

ADMISSIONS INFORMATION

The Admissions Committee seeks students who are eager to challenge themselves academically, to discover and develop their own individual passions, and to participate in a simple and ecologically sound community life without the distractions of excessive electronic entertainment. All applicants who live in or near Switzerland must visit the School for an interview and tour that offer the opportunity to meet students and faculty members. Applicants who live farther away can request an interview by telephone or with someone familiar with the School in their area. The English program requires two letters of recommendation and school records.

APPLICATION TIMETABLE

Applications are accepted on a rolling basis. Applications received by May 15 have the best chance of acceptance.

ADMISSIONS CORRESPONDENCE

Kathleen Hennessy, Director, English-speaking Program
Frédéric Bächtold, Director, German-speaking Program
Ecole d'Humanité
CH-6085 Hasliberg-Goldern
Switzerland

Phone: +41-33-972-92-92
Fax: +41-33-972-92-11
E-mail: admissions@ecole.ch
Web site: http://www.ecole.ch

EMMA WILLARD SCHOOL

Troy, New York

Type: Girls' boarding and day college-preparatory school
Grades: 9–12, postgraduate year
Enrollment: 310
Head of School: Trudy E. Hall

THE SCHOOL

In 1814, Emma Hart Willard founded the school that now bears her name, making it the oldest institution for the higher education of young women in the United States. Her belief in women's intellectual capabilities, a radical idea for the time, is the cornerstone of a curriculum that has challenged Emma Willard students for nearly 200 years.

The exceptionally beautiful 137-acre campus has forty-three buildings. Emma Willard School is located on the edge of the city of Troy, 7 miles from Albany, at the crossroads of the Berkshires, the Adirondacks, and the Catskills.

The 28-member Board of Trustees includes 17 alumnae, 4 parents, and 1 faculty member. An operating budget of $18 million is supported in part through a $104-million endowment and Annual Giving that exceeds $1.6 million.

Emma Willard School is accredited by the New York State Association of Independent Schools and by the New York State Board of Regents. It is a member of the National Association of Independent Schools, the New York State Association of Independent Schools, the Cum Laude Society, and the National Coalition of Girls Schools.

ACADEMIC PROGRAMS

The Emma Willard curriculum develops those abilities and qualities of mind that are essential to the successful woman. The rigorous college-preparatory curriculum ensures a strong foundation in all major academic areas in addition to extensive exposure to the arts. Emma Willard celebrates leadership, rewards successes, offers appropriate support, and reminds girls of the limitless possibilities the world presents an educated woman.

Each student's faculty adviser helps her plan her courses in coordination with the Director of College Counseling and the Dean of Curriculum and Programs. Graduation requirements include a minimum of 4 years of English; 3 years of mathematics, history, and foreign language; 2 years of lab science (including biology and chemistry); and 2 years of visual and performing arts. All students are required to participate in the Elizabeth Cady Stanton Service Program and the Emma Willard Seminar Program, as well as in physical education.

The School offers more than 130 courses, including Advanced Placement (AP) preparation in all academic departments, including arts and computer science. A student who wishes to study subjects beyond the curriculum offerings may arrange individualized tutorials with faculty supervision.

All underclass women are assigned to a daily supervised study hall during the fall term; students in good academic standing are excused from this study hall at the end of the term. There is a 2-hour evening study period Sunday through Thursday for all boarding students all year. Students may be assigned by their advisers to a supervised evening study hall. The library is open 15 hours a day, seven days a week. At least one professional librarian is on duty 66 hours a week.

Emma Willard students may take courses for credit at nearby universities. In addition, the School is a member of the National Network of Complementary Schools, which offers students an opportunity to pursue special programs on an exchange basis. Practicum, Emma Willard's independent study program, provides opportunities to earn credit and explore a career interest through hands-on experience in many industries, organizations, and professions. Recent Practicum projects have focused on broadcasting, publishing, microbiology, veterinary medicine, law, environmental engineering, photojournalism, advertising, government, and architecture. Vacation trips abroad, as well as work with Habitat for Humanity, are undertaken by students with faculty chaperones each year; groups have traveled to Austria, Belize, England, Ethiopia, France, Germany, Greece, Ireland, Italy, Russia, and Spain.

The grading system uses letter grades with plus and minus notations. A few courses are graded Credit/No Credit. Grades and comments are issued to parents and students at midterm and at the end of each semester.

FACULTY AND ADVISERS

The faculty numbers 66 (53 full-time and 13 part-time); 75.8 percent are women and 24.2 percent are men. The student-faculty ratio is 5:1. Fifty faculty members reside on campus. Ninety-three faculty members, administrators, and residence staff members hold sixty-four advanced degrees, including four Ph.D.'s, four J.D.'s, and sixty-two master's, earned at such colleges and universities as Amherst, Boston College, Boston University, Brown, Bryn Mawr, Columbia, Dartmouth, Duke, Fairleigh Dickinson, Harvard, Macalester, Manhattanville, Massachusetts College of Liberal Arts, Middlebury, Mount Holyoke, Northeastern, NYU, Oxford, Princeton, Rensselaer, Russell Sage, Smith, St. Lawrence, Saint Rose, SUNY at Albany, Swarthmore, UCLA, Vassar, Wellesley, Wesleyan, Williams, and Yale.

Trudy E. Hall was appointed Head of School in 1999. She holds a B.S. from St. Lawrence University, an M.Ed. from Harvard University, and an M.A.L.S. from Duke University.

In selecting its teachers, Emma Willard looks for adults who are dedicated to enriching the lives of young people in and out of the classroom. The School has a full-time Director of Faculty Development. Faculty development grants are available to those who wish to pursue advanced degrees or enrich their current areas of study and to those who wish to develop new courses. Sabbaticals and travel funds are available to all faculty members. Most dormitory staff members are full-time residence personnel and do not teach. All faculty members act as advisers to 4–6 students each. Faculty members chaperone weekend activities, sit on School committees, and advise student organizations. Annual faculty turnover is typically less than 10 percent.

COLLEGE ADMISSION COUNSELING

Formal college counseling begins in the junior year. The Director of College Counseling supervises all college placement testing (the PSAT, the SAT, and Subject Tests), coordinates visits to Emma Willard by college admissions officers, assists students in planning college visits, and writes a comprehensive recommendation for each senior, based on the student's academic record and teachers' written evaluations.

Ninety-one students in the class of 2008 have enrolled in sixty-two colleges and universities, including Amherst, Bates, Boston University, Brown, Carnegie Mellon, Colorado College, Connecticut College, Cornell, Dartmouth, Emory, Franklin and Marshall, Grinnell, Hamilton, Haverford, Hobart and William Smith Colleges, MIT, Mount Holyoke, NYU, Northwestern, Oberlin, Pomona, Rensselaer, Rhode Island School of Design, Skidmore, Swarthmore, Syracuse, Trinity, Tufts, Tulane, University of Edinburgh, University of Glasgow, University of Illinois, University of Miami, University of Pennsylvania, University of Rochester, University of St. Andrews, University of Vermont, Vanderbilt, Vassar, Villanova, Wake Forest, Wellesley and Yale. The average SAT scores for the class of 2008 were 1951: 644 (critical reading), 642 (math), and 665 (writing).

STUDENT BODY AND CONDUCT

In 2008–09, Emma Willard had 218 boarding and 92 day students, as follows: grade 9, 63; grade 10, 84; grade 11, 73; and grade 12, 90. Students came from twenty-six states and twenty-one foreign countries; 17 percent are students of color.

The School seeks to enroll girls who are responsible and mature enough not to require rigid structure, but all are expected to abide by the fundamental rules that govern major issues of discipline.

Uniforms are not required, but students are expected to meet standards of neatness and cleanliness in dress code during the academic day or in the dormitories. Dress for plays, concerts, and academic convocations is more formal.

ACADEMIC FACILITIES

The oldest buildings, of Tudor Gothic design, include the Alumnae Chapel and Slocum Hall, which contains classrooms, offices, Kiggins Hall, the main auditorium, a lab theater, and a dance studio. The Hunter Science Center, an addition to Weaver Hall, opened in 1996. Hunter includes computer equipment integrated with revolutionary fractal laboratories. Completing the main quadrangle is the art, music, and library complex designed by Edward Larabee Barnes and constructed from 1967 to 1971. Other campus buildings house an additional auditorium and dance studio, ten music practice rooms, twenty-one grand pianos, six science laboratories, an audiovisual center, two photography darkrooms, a microcomputer center, and a weaving studio.

The William Moore Dietel Library holds more than 32,000 volumes and seventy-seven periodical subscriptions. Twenty-one online databases with full text augment the journal collection. Microfilm and microfiche readers and reader-printers are available for student use. The collection also includes hundreds of CDs, a sizable art and architecture slide collection, and the School archives, which include nineteenth-century photographs and manuscripts and some medieval manuscripts.

BOARDING AND GENERAL FACILITIES

Students reside in three connected dormitories, Sage, Hypen, and Kellas. Sophomores, juniors, and seniors live together on various halls; ninth grade students live together on the same hall. There are single rooms, doubles, and suites. Eleven professional residential faculty members supervise student life in the dormitories. A team of faculty affiliates, student proctors, and peer educators shares in dormitory responsibilities. Day students are assigned to residence halls to facilitate their integration into the residential program.

In 2004, the School embarked on a $32-million "adaptive reuse" project of the first and garden levels of the residence halls to create new community spaces. The design included a new state-of-the-art dining hall, student center, student study lounge, e-café, admissions suite, and student services offices. The project was completed in fall 2007. Other campus buildings include a variety of on-campus faculty residences.

ATHLETICS

Emma Willard encourages students to combine lifetime sports with competition; students can fulfill the physical activities requirement through team sports, individual sports, or dance. Emma Willard teams compete in a league with other local schools, both public and private, in basketball, crew, cross-country, field hockey, lacrosse, soccer, softball, swimming, tennis, track, and volleyball. Recreational activities include cross-country skiing, dance, skating, swimming, tennis, volleyball, weight conditioning, and yoga. In addition to the Mott Gymnasium, which includes two indoor tennis courts and full facilities for basketball, volleyball, and fitness training, facilities include six outdoor tennis courts, three large playing fields, and an all-weather 400-meter track. In 1998, the Helen S. Cheel Aquatics and Fitness Center opened with a competition-size swimming pool and state-of-the-art fitness equipment.

EXTRACURRICULAR OPPORTUNITIES

The Serving and Shaping Her World Speakers Series and the 175th Anniversary Speakers Series bring prominent individuals to campus for lectures, classroom interaction, and residencies. Recent speakers have included Poet Laureate Billy Collins; playwrights Wendy Wasserstein and Shirley Lauro; award-winning author Maxine Hong Kingston; mathematician and author Edward Burger; Russian poet Yevgeny Yevtushenko; National Public Radio reporter Linda Wertheimer; Herbert Hauptman, Nobel laureate in mathematics; and award-winning novelist Tobias Wolff. The EWS arts calendar features an impressive array of renowned chamber groups, dance companies, artists, and exhibitions.

The surrounding region offers performances at the historic Troy Music Hall, the Saratoga Performing Arts Center, and Tanglewood; events at the Empire State Performing Arts Center in Albany; ethnic festivals; sports events; theater; and activities at nearby colleges and universities. The School sponsors a world-class chamber music series and all students are required to attend at least two cultural events each term.

Among the twenty-three clubs and organizations are the Outing Club, Student Organization for Animal Rights (SOAR), EMMA Green (environmental group), Quiz Team, Foreign and American Student Organization, Black and Hispanic Awareness, Phila (charitable service club), and various singing groups. There are also three student publications: *Triangle,* the arts and literary magazine; *The Clock,* the School newspaper; and *Gargoyle,* the yearbook. Through Interact, girls may serve the community in volunteer projects such as Big Brothers/Big Sisters. Traditions include the opening-of-school Academic Convocation, fall and spring Senior Dinners, Holiday Eventide, Revels, the surprise holiday Principal's Playday, May Day, and the Flame Ceremony.

DAILY LIFE

Classes are held Monday through Friday from 8 to 3:30, in time blocks of 50-minute and 75-minute periods. On Wednesdays, students and teachers gather to participate in schoolwide academic programs, such as the Elizabeth Cady Stanton Community Service Program and the Serving and Shaping Her World Speakers Series. A mid-morning all-school meeting is held three times a week. Team sports, choir, some dance classes, and drama rehearsals meet after 3:30. Dinner is served from 5:30 to 7 p.m., and quiet study hours are 7:30 to 9:30. All students must be on their floor by 10:30 and in their rooms by 11 p.m.

WEEKEND LIFE

An extensive Weekend Activities Program is developed and coordinated by a full-time staff member of Student Affairs. The Emma Willard campus is at the crossroads of New England, the Adirondacks, the Catskills, and the Berkshires. This location gives students an exciting array of cultural and recreational venues. Weekend activities include sports events, dances with boys' schools, dinner in the Capital District, movies both on and off campus, and trips to Boston, New York, and Montreal. Generally, 75 to 80 percent of the boarders remain on campus during the weekend, and day students are encouraged to participate in weekend activities. Transportation to area events and places of worship is provided upon request.

COSTS AND FINANCIAL AID

Tuition, room, and board in 2008–09 were $38,400. Day student tuition was $25,000. A Smart-Card fee of $600 for boarding students in grades 9–11 ($650 for seniors) and $400 for day students in grades 9–11 ($450 for seniors) covers testing, field trips, and other class-related expenses. A technology fee of $750 per year is required to cover all technology services, including the use of the computer and access to all of the services available over the wired and wireless networks. Emma Willard requires all new students in grades 9 and 10 to use a Toshiba Portege m400 tablet PC as their regular computer. The tablet PC comes bundled with a combo drive that reads and writes CDs and reads DVDs, assorted software, extended warranty, and insurance. The Office of Information Services carries the responsibility of maintaining the computer until the student graduates or leaves the School.

Families purchase text books directly from the School's online vendor. The average cost of books per year is $500. Special-fee courses include private music lessons, ballet, skiing, and horseback riding. A $1500 deposit is required to confirm enrollment; School fees are billed in July and December, and families may elect to pay 60 percent in August, with the remainder due in January. Families who wish to make monthly tuition payments may do so through the School's ten-month installment plan.

The School is committed to maintaining the diversity of its student body and allocated more than $3.2 million in financial aid to 48 percent of the student body during 2008–09. Aid is awarded on the basis of academic promise and family financial need, as determined by the parents' financial statement of the School and Student Service for Financial Aid. Applications for financial aid must be submitted by February 1. As long as a student is in good standing and family circumstances warrant continued assistance, grants are renewed from year to year.

ADMISSIONS INFORMATION

Emma Willard seeks students of above-average to superior academic ability who are self-motivated, responsible, interested in learning, and involved in activities outside the classroom. All candidates for admission must submit an application, a personal essay, transcripts, three recommendations, and the results of the SSAT. Students for whom English is not their first language should submit the results of the TOEFL in lieu of the SSAT. An interview is strongly encouraged. Applicants for the postgraduate year should submit SAT scores.

APPLICATION TIMETABLE

Initial inquiries are welcome at any time. Campus visits include tours for parents and daughters, interviews, a class visit, and frequently a meal. On weekdays, office hours are 8:30 a.m. to 4:30 p.m. Appointments may be made at any time of year, but October through April visits are strongly recommended. Open house programs are scheduled on Columbus Day, Veterans Day, and Martin Luther King's birthday.

The application fee of $50 ($100 for international students) is nonrefundable. The application deadline is February 1. Prospective students and their parents are notified of the Admission Committee's decision in March. Applications received after that time are accepted on a space-available basis.

ADMISSIONS CORRESPONDENCE

Director of Enrollment
Emma Willard School
285 Pawling Avenue
Troy, New York 12180

Phone: 518-833-1320
Fax: 518-833-1805
E-mail: admissions@emmawillard.org
Web site: http://www.emmawillard.org

EPISCOPAL HIGH SCHOOL

Alexandria, Virginia

Type: Coeducational boarding college-preparatory school
Grades: 9–12
Enrollment: 435
Head of School: F. Robertson Hershey

THE SCHOOL

Founded in 1839 as the first high school in the state of Virginia, Episcopal High School (EHS) is a coeducational boarding school of 430 students, with talented and motivated students from more than thirty states and twenty countries. Located 10 minutes from Washington, D.C., Episcopal is distinguished by its dynamic and rigorous academic program and strong sense of community.

Episcopal is dedicated to educating boys and girls who, as responsible citizens of the world, are prepared to lead lives of honor, courage, and compassion. The School emphasizes the intellectual, spiritual, physical, and moral development of every student through rigorous academics, daily athletics, regularly scheduled chapel services, and extensive activities and community service programs. The School's most enduring tradition is its Honor Code, one of the oldest among secondary schools in the nation and a tradition that remains a central part of community life.

Episcopal's 130-acre campus in Alexandria, Virginia, is just 10 minutes from the vast educational, cultural, and governmental resources of Washington, D.C., and teachers use the nation's capital as a second campus. Alexandria, which is situated on the Potomac River in northern Virginia, offers a spectrum of cultural, social, historical, and educational events.

Episcopal is a nonprofit corporation governed by a 30-member Board of Trustees, most of whom are alumni. The School's endowment is $150 million, and the plant is valued at more than $150 million. In 2006–07, contributions to the annual giving program totaled $2.7 million, and total gifts reached $10 million. The 4,700 living alumni, current and past parents, and the advisory council all lend their support to the School's mission.

Episcopal High School is accredited by the Southern Association of Colleges and Schools and the Virginia Association of Independent Schools. It holds membership in the National Association of Independent Schools, the National Association of Episcopal Schools, the Association of Boarding Schools, the Association of Independent Schools of Greater Washington, and the Cum Laude Society.

ACADEMIC PROGRAMS

EHS is committed to providing a liberal arts education in which students learn to think independently, analyze, and reason. The college-preparatory curriculum offers 134 courses, including forty honors and Advanced Placement (AP) courses. A minimum of 23 credits is required for graduation, including English (4), mathematics (3 or 3½), foreign language (2 or 3), social studies (2), laboratory sciences and physical education (2 each), and theology and fine arts (1 each). The passing grade is 65; a grade of 90 or better constitutes honors-level work.

In classes, students are grouped into regular, honors, and AP sections of about 12 students each according to their ability and familiarity with the subject matter. Tutorial sessions are available six periods each week, and evening study hours ensure a quiet study environment. Parents receive grades quarterly, which are accompanied by teachers' and advisers' comments.

Episcopal's Washington Program enhances classroom learning with weekly trips to museums, galleries, plays, concerts, and government agencies in Washington, D.C., and meetings with national leaders and experts in a variety of professions. In addition, the entire school attends each presidential inauguration. Qualified seniors take part in a one-month internship in which they work in such places as Capitol Hill, banks, hospitals, social service organizations, government agencies, media companies, and law firms.

As part of the foreign language program, students may take part in summer study trips to Austria, France, Spain, and Italy. Students also have the option of studying in China, France, Italy, or Spain as part of the School Year Abroad program, and qualified seniors may take a postgraduate year in Great Britain as part of the English-Speaking Union program. In addition, Episcopal offers a semester-long cultural exchange with St. Leonard's School in St. Andrews, Scotland.

FACULTY AND ADVISERS

Nearly 90 percent of the full-time faculty of 80 men and women live on campus with their families and are available to teach and guide students while promoting community.

Rob Hershey, who was appointed Headmaster in 1998, was previously Headmaster at his alma mater, the Collegiate School in Richmond, and at Durham Academy. He received his B.A. from Williams College and his M.Ed. from the University of Virginia.

Faculty members are chosen for their interest in and dedication to young people and for their proficiency in teaching their subject area. As teachers, coaches, dorm parents, counselors, and good friends, they support and direct students' growth. Nearly all serve as advisers. Each is responsible for the academic and social progress of 6 to 8 advisees, and each maintains close contact with parents.

COLLEGE ADMISSION COUNSELING

Students are encouraged to start thinking about college as early as possible. Formal college counseling begins in the winter of the junior year, when students meet with a college counselor to begin considering appropriate colleges and to become familiar with the application process. More than 175 colleges take part in Episcopal's annual College Fair, and representatives from about eighty-five schools conduct on-campus interviews. The 104 graduates of the class of 2007 are attending fifty-seven colleges and universities, including Brown, Davidson, Duke, Middlebury, Northwestern, Vanderbilt, Washington and Lee, Williams, and the Universities of North Carolina, Pennsylvania, and Virginia.

STUDENT BODY AND CONDUCT

Approximately 120 new students enroll each year. The student body represents more than thirty states, the District of Columbia, and twenty other countries.

Episcopal's Honor Code is an essential part of community life and is strongly supported by the faculty and students. The Honor Code is overseen by an Honor Committee of 8 students and 4 faculty members. The code asserts that students will not lie, cheat, or steal. Out of genuine concern for and responsibility to those who do, students are asked to report violators to the Honor Committee. Students whose values and conduct prove to be irreconcilable with the Honor Code are asked to leave.

The student body is led by student monitors, who are nominated to the Headmaster by faculty members and students. Monitors are responsible for discipline and orderliness in the day-to-day life of the School. A student-elected Dorm Council offers additional leadership opportunities.

ACADEMIC FACILITIES

Episcopal's academic facilities include seven buildings. The Baker Science Center opened in fall 2005. A two-story, 34,000-square-foot building, it features state-of-the-art laboratories for biology, chemistry, physics, and environmental science. Special features include a beautiful glass rotunda, greenhouse, science library, and auditorium with video and computer equipment to enhance any teaching situation. As a LEED Certified Green Building, the Science Center sets a new standard for energy-efficient design on campus, and this environmentally sound building enables students to explore the world of science while simultaneously becoming stewards of their environment.

Since 2003, the Ainslie Arts Center has provided a magnificent setting for Episcopal's arts program. It features a digital photography studio, MIDI lab and 24-channel digital recording studio, and professional and student galleries, along with painting, drawing, ceramics, and dance studios, plus a 540-seat auditorium and black-box theater. The David H. March Library houses more than 33,000 books, videos, and CDs; 160 periodicals; twelve newspapers, microforms, and CD-ROMs; and access to seven online commercial databases and a national interlibrary loan network via OCLC.

EHS requires all students to own a laptop specified by the Technology Department. Student desks in all classrooms are wired with both power outlets and data drops, allowing any classroom to be used as a computer lab. Each classroom has a monitor for the display of both video and data. All dorm rooms are also equipped with Internet connections. EHS provides access to the Internet via a T1 line for research and recreational purposes.

BOARDING AND GENERAL FACILITIES

Residential facilities include seven dormitories. Most have double rooms, although there are a few singles and triples, and all feature common rooms and laundry facilities. A faculty member, often with a family, lives in an apartment or town house attached to each dormitory. Together with the senior monitors who also live on each dormitory floor, they help foster a comfortable, relaxed atmosphere.

Students attend services in Patrick Henry Callaway Chapel. Health services are provided at McAllister Health Center, a twelve-bed facility that is staffed by a registered nurse 24 hours a day, seven days a week. The Medical Director, who is also the school physician, is available to see patients during weekdays and is on call during evenings and weekends. Alexandria Hospital, just two blocks away, offers outstanding emergency, inpatient, and outpatient services.

Other residential facilities include Laird Dining Room, where buffet- and family-style meals are served; Blackford Hall, the main coed student lounge with a snack bar, a vending area, the student post office and mailboxes, a big-screen projection unit for Friday night movies, and a jukebox; two other coed lounges, each equipped differently; and fifty-nine faculty residences.

ATHLETICS

The athletics program promotes physical fitness and good sportsmanship while instilling a healthy respect for regular exercise and competition. The School offers fifty-four athletic options per year, including forty-four teams in fifteen sports. These include junior, junior varsity, and varsity teams in many sports. Episcopal offers baseball, basketball, crew, cross-country, dance, field hockey, football, golf, lacrosse, soccer, squash, tennis, track, volleyball, and wrestling as well as aerobics, cross-training, and weight training during some seasons. Boys' teams participate in the Interstate Athletic Conference, and girls' teams take part in the Independent School League. Episcopal's teams play a full schedule with other independent schools in Maryland, Pennsylvania, Virginia, and Washington, D.C.

Episcopal's outstanding athletics facilities include Hummel Bowl, a 2,800-seat stadium; Flippin Field House, with three tennis courts, three basketball courts, a 200-yard track, and a batting cage; Centennial Gymnasium, which has a basketball court and fitness center; seven playing fields; Goodman Squash Center, which houses five squash courts; Cooper Dawson Baseball International Diamond on Bryant Athletic Field; a wrestling cage; twelve all-weather tennis courts; an outdoor swimming pool; and Hoxton Track, a six-lane, 400-meter outdoor track. In summer 2006, two new FieldTurf fields were installed, enabling teams to practice and compete in the face of inclement weather.

EXTRACURRICULAR OPPORTUNITIES

The School makes maximum use of the opportunities of the Washington metropolitan area, and students are also encouraged to participate in and support on-campus activities with equal vigor. The School presents at least three plays each year, one of which is a musical. Four School publications—a yearbook, a newspaper, and two literary magazines—offer opportunities for students to display their creative literary skills. Other extracurricular opportunities include three boys' and girls' a cappella groups, art, campus choir, pep band, community service council, e-club (the varsity athletic club), environmental club, investment club, jazz ensemble, Latin club, model UN, outdoor club, performing arts group, pythonian society (student tutors), quiz bowl, spectrum (diversity group), student health awareness committee, student rock bands, student vestry, tour guides, Web publications, and youth in philanthropy, plus a varied activities program that involves students in athletics, cultural, historic, outdoor, and social activities throughout the Washington area. The School regularly provides tickets for performances at the Kennedy Center and other major theaters and concert halls in and near Washington. Qualified students may audition for the Mount Vernon Youth Symphony, which rehearses weekly at Episcopal, and the American Youth Philharmonic Orchestra.

DAILY LIFE

A buffet breakfast at 7:15 a.m. begins the day. Before the beginning of classes at 8 a.m. students put their rooms in order and participate in a work program that helps maintain the School. Four 45-minute periods precede required chapel on most days at 11:30 a.m. Chapel is followed by a seated lunch, three more class periods, and an afternoon athletics period. Students then attend dinner, which is followed by a 1-hour activities period in which students may relax or take part in extracurricular activities and clubs. The remainder of the evening is spent in study period until lights-out (10:15 p.m. for freshmen, 11 p.m. for sophomores and juniors, and 11:30 p.m. for seniors). During the evening study period, qualified students may study in their rooms, the library, or other approved study areas, while others report to supervised study hall.

All students attend chapel services three times a week and bimonthly Sunday services. Students who wish to participate more fully in the religious life of the School take part in the student vestry and a variety of community service programs. Students of other faiths are provided opportunities to attend services of their choosing in the Alexandria community.

WEEKEND LIFE

The School endeavors to make weekend life relaxing and productive. Activities include on-campus movies, dances, concerts, trips to Old Town Alexandria, and sports events in Washington, D.C. Faculty members regularly take students skiing, camping, hiking, and biking. The School provides tickets for performances at the Kennedy Center and other major theaters and for professional sports events.

COSTS AND FINANCIAL AID

The comprehensive fee for the 2008–09 session is $40,875. Tuition is payable in one, two, or nine installments.

Financial aid is awarded annually to those families whose need has been demonstrated through the School and Student Service for Financial Aid in Princeton, New Jersey. For the year 2007–08, scholarship funds of $3.3 million were allocated to 30 percent of the student body. Several job opportunities enable students to supplement their personal spending money.

ADMISSIONS INFORMATION

Episcopal enrolls students with proven academic ability, strong character, and an interest in contributing significantly to the EHS community.

Typically, 110–130 new students enroll each year. In most years, fewer than 40 percent of applicants are offered admission. The majority enroll in the ninth or tenth grade; a few enter in the eleventh. In special cases, a student may be admitted for his or her senior year. There are no postgraduates.

The formal application includes a personal application, recommendations from current teachers, an official school record, and a personal interview. Applicants to grades 9 and 10 are required to take the SSAT; applicants to grades 11 and 12 may submit PSAT or SAT scores.

APPLICATION TIMETABLE

Students who complete their applications ($50 fee) by January 31 are notified on March 10. Late applicants are considered on a rolling basis if space becomes available.

A personal interview and a visit to the campus are part of the admission process. Interviews and campus tours should be scheduled for class days. Classroom visits can be arranged. If a campus visit is not possible, the Admissions Office tries to coordinate other arrangements.

ADMISSIONS CORRESPONDENCE

Emily M. Atkinson, Director of Admissions
Episcopal High School
1200 North Quaker Lane
Alexandria, Virginia 22302
Phone: 703-933-4062
877-933-4347 (toll-free)
Fax: 703-933-3016
E-mail: admissions@episcopalhighschool.org
Web site: http://www.episcopalhighschool.org

FOUNTAIN VALLEY SCHOOL OF COLORADO

Colorado Springs, Colorado

Type: Coeducational boarding and day college-preparatory school
Grades: 9–12
Enrollment: 250
Head of School: Craig W. Larimer Jr. '69, Headmaster

THE SCHOOL

Fountain Valley School of Colorado (FVS) was established in 1929 and was opened the following year led by a group of visionary men and women who were philanthropists, statesmen, scientists, entrepreneurs, and educators. Many had personal and professional ties to the East; all shared the conviction that the Eastern independent school tradition of academic excellence, progressive ideals, self-reliance, and intellectual curiosity would thrive in the expansiveness of the Rocky Mountain West. John Dewey, the notable American educational reformer, was on the first Board of Trustees, and his grandson graduated with the class of 1940.

The School's mission remains unchanged: FVS is dedicated to providing a rigorous college-preparatory curriculum in academics, athletics, and the arts. The community endeavors to foster a lifelong love of challenge and learning in an environment of diversity and mutual respect and to prepare adolescents to become individuals who are open-minded, curious, courageous, self-reliant, and compassionate.

The School is situated at the base of Pikes Peak on the former Bradley Ranch on 1,100 acres of rolling prairie in southeastern Colorado Springs. The School's 40-acre Mountain Campus is located 115 miles west of the main campus, in the San Isabel National Forest.

Fountain Valley School of Colorado is a nonprofit corporation governed by a 23-member Board of Trustees, 15 of whom are alumni. The School's endowment is valued at more than $30 million. In 2007–08, annual giving was $1,142,607. More than 2,600 alumni maintain contact with FVS, and many are actively involved. In June 2005, more than 600 alumni returned to campus to celebrate the School's seventy-fifth anniversary. In 2003, FVS completed a $24-million capital campaign, the largest in Colorado independent-school history.

FVS is accredited by the Colorado State Board of Education and the Association of Colorado Independent Schools and holds memberships in the National Association of Independent Schools, the Secondary School Admission Test Board, the College Board, the Association of Boarding Schools, the Council for Advancement and Support of Education, the Colorado High School Activities Association, and the Cum Laude Society.

ACADEMIC PROGRAMS

Fountain Valley's academic program is rigorous and comprehensive, offering honors and Advanced Placement courses in all disciplines and providing a flexible approach to placing students in courses appropriate to their abilities. More than 70 courses were offered by seven departments in the 2008–09 year.

The school year is divided into two semesters; major semester courses receive ½ credit. Twenty credits in major courses are required for graduation (most seniors graduate with more than 22 credits), with the following minimum departmental expectations: 4 credits of English; completion of the third-year level of one foreign language (French, Mandarin Chinese, or Spanish); 3 credits of high school mathematics, with the minimum successful completion of algebra II, 3 credits of science (including 1 credit of biology); 3½ credits of history (including 1 credit of Western civilization, 1 credit of global studies, and 1 credit of U.S. history); 1 credit of visual and performing arts; ½ credit of computer skills; ½ credit of human development; and 4 credits of physical education. Most students take one minor and five major courses per semester. In addition, English as a second language (ESL) is offered at the intermediate and advanced levels. Qualified seniors, with the approval of the Curriculum Committee, design Independent Study Projects to supplement their advanced studies. All seniors participate in the Senior Seminar, a weeklong service project culminating their FVS education. New as of 2007–08 is a required Freshman Transitions course, which seeks to help students adjust to life at FVS.

The Western Immersion Program (WIP) is a signature interdisciplinary program for all FVS sophomores. Weaving together the disciplines of literature, history, science, and art, WIP explores how the Western landscape shaped the people, history, and culture of the region.

The student-teacher ratio is 6:1, and the average class size is 12 students. The small classes allow for personal attention and provide an intimate learning environment characterized by mutual respect and active participation.

Grades (letters A through E) are given at midterm and at the conclusion of each semester. Written comments are provided for each course at the fall midterm for all new students and at the end of the term for all students.

FACULTY AND ADVISERS

FVS has 40 total teaching faculty, with 35 teaching full-time. Seventy percent of faculty members hold advanced degrees; 30 live on campus, with 13 in residence halls; 34 are advisers, and 25 are coaches.

Fountain Valley's seventh headmaster, Craig W. Larimer Jr. '69, assumed the leadership of the School in 2007. He graduated from Pomona College and earned his M.A. from Johns Hopkins School of Advanced International Studies. Prior to his appointment as Headmaster, Larimer served for five years as president of the FVS Board of Trustees, where he coauthored the School's current Strategic Plan. Professionally, he worked for twenty-two years in international capital markets with the First National Bank of Chicago and Bank One. Larimer began his career in government, where he served in the U.S. Treasury Department's office at the U.S. Embassy in London as well as the Office of International Monetary Affairs in Washington, D.C.

Because all faculty members share responsibility for the residential and cocurricular programs at the School, Fountain Valley seeks to recruit teachers with personal idealism, a genuine respect for students, and high professional competence. An endowment and annually budgeted funds ensure continued faculty professional development.

COLLEGE ADMISSION COUNSELING

Students begin to prepare for college in their first year at Fountain Valley through course choice and careful planning with the Academic Dean. Formal college counseling starts in the junior year. Sessions are planned to help students understand the complexities of the college application process and learn about the range of colleges offering programs in which they are interested.

Each fall, Fountain Valley holds a college fair to give juniors and seniors an opportunity to talk with representatives from approximately 140 colleges and universities. Students gather firsthand information from the Director of College Counseling, college Web sites and other college Internet resources, an extensive library of college catalogs and media, and a workbook designed to help them with the college application process.

FVS has a detailed section on its own Web site devoted to college counseling. The section includes information on college programs, summer programs and scholarships, financial aid, and detailed Web listings to help the college-bound student.

The Director of College Counseling begins working with individual students and small groups during the junior year. She creates an individual list of college possibilities for each junior tailored to their expressed interests and needs. She continues to work closely with each senior in refining his or her college plans.

The classes of 2006 through 2008 had an SAT range of scores (middle 50 percent) of critical reading, 520–650; math, 530–680; and writing, 520–645. From 2006 through 2008, FVS graduates were admitted to 241 four-year colleges and universities.

STUDENT BODY AND CONDUCT

In 2008–09 the School's enrollment is 156 boarding students and 94 day students from twenty-seven states and thirteen countries.

The School works to create and maintain an environment for learning in which goodwill and mutual trust exist among all members of the campus community. At the same time, it adheres to the belief that every strong community must have a clear set of standards and defined values for all its members to uphold. If a student is found to be involved in a serious disciplinary matter, the case is heard by an honor council composed of elected student representatives and faculty members. The council considers all facets of each case and recommends a course of action to the Headmaster.

A Community Council chaired by the president of the student body provides a forum in which any members of the School community can make recommendations regarding the operation of the School.

ACADEMIC FACILITIES

The majority of classes are conducted in the Froelicher Academic Building, which includes a state-of-the-art science annex and two computer labs (including one outfitted with new iMacs in the summer of 2008). There are also clusters of computers in other parts of campus that students can use, including in the library and the Learning Center.

The William Thayer Tutt Art Center (Art Barn) houses art, jewelry, and ceramics studios; an art gallery; a photo laboratory; and production rooms for the School's publications. The John B. Hawley, Jr. Library has forty-one study carrels, two seminar rooms, and a film editing and projection room. The library has an online catalog of more than 25,000 volumes and a collection of periodicals on microfilm.

The FVS Learning Center offers important education support for students, parents, and teachers. Students who need help with study skills, personal organization, time management, or test anxiety can meet with a trained staff member individually or in small groups.

Students who need continued, regular support for their learning issues can be enrolled by their parents in the Learning Assistance Program. There is an additional charge for the program, and enrollment is limited.

BOARDING AND GENERAL FACILITIES

In 2001, the School completed a three-year, $16-million residence hall renovation and construction master plan. Fountain Valley School's four residence halls include ten individual houses where 160 students and 13 houseparent families live. Spacious double and triple bedrooms, common rooms, a kitchen, dining area, bathrooms, laundry facilities, and a computer lab are laid out in floor plans unique to each house.

The Hacienda, Fountain Valley's original ranch house, has dining facilities for 300, private dining rooms for meetings, and a living room for meetings and quiet conversation. The dining room was renovated in 2008 to provide a better atmosphere and a wider selection of menu choices for students and faculty. The Chase Stone Infirmary is a recently renovated ten-bed facility with a nurse on call at all times.

The Frautschi Campus Center was completed in 1990 and has a student-operated snack bar, a campus bookstore, a post office, lounge and recreation facilities, a faculty lounge, a multimedia viewing room, and a meeting space.

The Lewis Perry Jr. Chapel, which is currently being expanded to accommodate the School's increased student population, houses weekly All-School meetings, concerts, and other regular activities. The Performing Arts Center contains a small black-box type theater that houses the School's three yearly productions.

ATHLETICS

Fountain Valley believes strongly in the value of sports for building physical fitness, self-confidence, and character. Most students fulfill their requirement by participating in a variety of interscholastic sports, including basketball, climbing, cross-country, golf, ice hockey, lacrosse, soccer, tennis, track, and volleyball for boys and basketball, climbing, cross-country, field hockey, lacrosse, soccer, swimming, tennis, track, and volleyball for girls.

Students may also earn physical education credit for horseback riding, skiing, snowboarding, and outdoor education. The School provides suitable levels of competition for students of varying abilities. FVS offers a comprehensive horsemanship program that provides diverse training in both English and Western riding. Riding facilities include the largest outdoor arena in the Colorado Springs area, a covered arena, a gymkhana field, a barn, stables, and more than 1,000 acres of open prairie. In 2007, the English riding team earned the national title at the IEA championships. A new state-of-the-art indoor riding facility that includes stables, tack rooms, offices, and classroom space is scheduled to open by the end of 2008.

The Penrose Sports Center includes a gymnasium, two squash courts, a newly renovated (2008) strength and conditioning facility, and a five-lane, 25-yard indoor swimming pool. FVS athletic fields are some of the finest in Colorado for soccer, field hockey, and lacrosse. Also, the School's first-ever outdoor track is scheduled for completion by the end of 2008, just in time for the 2009 track season. Nine tennis courts and a climbing wall complete the facilities.

EXTRACURRICULAR OPPORTUNITIES

Extracurricular activities vary from season to season. Students can perform in three major drama productions annually, including a winter musical. Guest speakers and artists regularly visit the campus for formal presentations and lectures. There are three student publications (newspaper, poetry book, and yearbook) and about twenty student activity clubs.

Special annual events include gymkhanas in which a riding team from Fountain Valley competes with teams from local riding clubs, Earth Day, Mountain Bike Weekend, Ski Weekend, Stupid Night Out, and Unity Day.

During Interim, traditional classes are suspended, and students participate in a variety of on- and off-campus programs. Recent Interims have included learning about French culture while in Paris, discovering southern culture and the blues in Memphis, kayaking in Georgia, and connecting with American musical theater in New York. Freshman Interim introduces students to the central premise of Interim—learning by doing. Organized in small groups, Freshman Interim focuses on the history of Colorado by exploring subjects such as ranching, Colorado wildlife, Native American heritage, Hispanic heritage, and pioneer heritage.

DAILY LIFE

Classes meet five days per week in six 50-minute sessions between 8 and 3. Afternoon activities (athletics or theater) are scheduled from 3:15 to 5:30. One period is used for student-adviser and All-School meetings. Students and teachers generally have at least one free period daily.

Dinner is at 5:30, and study hours run from 7 to 8 p.m. and 8:30 to 10 p.m. All boarding students are expected to observe study hours, although seniors in good academic standing may be excused in the spring of their senior year.

Day students are expected to be on campus before their first commitment and to remain until 5:30 p.m. on weekdays. Day students may stay overnight in a residence hall with permission from the houseparent and the student's parents.

WEEKEND LIFE

Weekends are time for relaxation and taking advantage of campus resources and a host of opportunities in the surrounding mountain region.

Student and faculty teams sponsor recreational activities throughout the weekend. Events include mountain climbing, skiing, and pack trips, often based at the Mountain Campus; excursions to Colorado Springs and Denver for movies, theater, concerts, dinner, and shopping; and dances, barbecues, movies, and athletics on campus.

Students with parental permission may request a weekend away from the campus. Many students visit friends or relatives or are invited to another student's home.

COSTS AND FINANCIAL AID

In 2008–09, tuition is $38,100 for boarding students; the cost (including all meals and bus transportation) for day students is $20,670. A book fee of $1060 covers textbooks, art supplies, lab fees, and one yearbook.

Interim, a required weeklong experiential learning opportunity, varies in cost according to the student's choice of trip. There are also fees for optional activities such as music lessons, horseback riding, and horse boarding. Tuition insurance and a tuition payment plan are available.

In 2007–08, 33 percent of students received approximately $1.65 million in merit- and need-based financial aid. Fountain Valley School adheres to the principles of good practice in its need-based aid distribution as part of the National Association of Independent Schools. All first-round applicants for ninth and tenth grade are considered for merit scholarships through the School's Summit Scholarship program.

ADMISSIONS INFORMATION

Students are admitted without regard to race, religion, or nationality. Fountain Valley School of Colorado seeks students who have the potential to benefit from a rigorous academic program and contribute to the School community. Students are admitted in grades 9 through 11 (in some cases grade 12) on the basis of previous school records, three academic recommendations, results of the Secondary School Admission Test (SSAT), an essay, and a personal interview.

APPLICATION TIMETABLE

Fountain Valley subscribes to the March 10 notification date endorsed by the SSAT Board. The application deadline is February 1. Applications are processed after that date if openings remain. The application fee is $50 for applicants residing in the United States and $100 for applicants living outside the United States.

ADMISSIONS CORRESPONDENCE

Randy Roach, Director of Admission and Financial Aid
Fountain Valley School of Colorado
6155 Fountain Valley School Road
Colorado Springs, Colorado 80911

Phone: 719-390-7035 Ext. 251
Fax: 719-390-7762
E-mail: admission@fvs.edu
Web site: http://www.fvs.edu

FOXCROFT ACADEMY

Dover-Foxcroft, Maine

Type: Coeducational, boarding and day, college-preparatory
Grades: 9–12
Enrollment: 418
Head of School: Raymond P. Webb, Ph.D.

THE SCHOOL

Foxcroft Academy (FA), located in Dover-Foxcroft, Maine, was established as a private college-preparatory school on January 30, 1823, and as such, is one of the oldest private schools in America. Today Foxcroft Academy serves a diverse coed population of 418 day and boarding students in grades 9–12.

Foxcroft Academy is situated in north central Maine, providing opportunities for whitewater rafting, skiing, snowboarding, swimming, hiking, biking, ice skating, and snowmobiling. It is 80 miles from the Atlantic Ocean, Acadia National Park, and Bar Harbor; 10 miles from the mountains and lakes of northern Maine; and 3–4 hours from Portland and Boston.

Foxcroft Academy is a member of the National Association of Independent Schools and the Independent School Association of Northern New England and is accredited by the New England Association of Schools and Colleges.

ACADEMIC PROGRAMS

The Academy offers a challenging college-preparatory curriculum, with 142 course offerings, including thirty-two honors courses and eight Advanced Placement courses.

Foxcroft Academy's math and science programs exceed national standards and utilize state-of-the-art technology. Students in Foxcroft Academy's well-known humanities program understand the culture of an era through a study of its history, literature, art, and music. The foreign language program includes four levels of French, Latin, Spanish, and Chinese.

In addition to the traditional core academic offerings, students may take courses in music composition, Web design, art history, economics, computer-assisted drawing, personal finance, vocational subjects, and ethics. Foxcroft Academy offers a comprehensive ESL program for the international student who is planning for a university education. Students receive individual testing before placement at one of three levels of ESL, including ESL Writing.

Music education at Foxcroft Academy is more than learning to sing or play an instrument. Music is a science, a mental discipline, and an art. Students are able to participate in a variety of programs and courses of study, including orchestra and chamber ensemble, band, jazz ensemble, select choir, and percussion ensemble. Art education takes place in the Ebersteen Art Center, where students are engaged in everything from the study of art history to pottery and jewelry making.

FACULTY AND ADVISERS

Foxcroft Academy has 61 staff members, including 42 faculty members, and a student-faculty ratio of 16:1. The nurturing as well as engaging style of faculty members stimulates a student's growth, both intellectually and socially. Each student meets weekly with his or her faculty adviser. In addition, faculty members are available before school, after school, and during structured evening study sessions for additional academic support. About 40 percent of the faculty members coach at least one sport.

COLLEGE ADMISSION COUNSELING

Foxcroft Academy provides intensive college admission counseling beginning in a student's sophomore year. Universities often visit the Academy's campus for information and interview sessions. SAT and TOEFL prep workshops are also offered throughout the school year. Counseling staff members work with students individually during each step of the college application process.

A long list of illustrious names testifies to the success Foxcroft Academy graduates have achieved in various fields, including law and medicine. One such graduate was Dr. Mary Chandler Lowell, class of 1881, who to this date is the only known woman anywhere in the world to have earned the degrees of Doctor of Medicine, Bachelor of Law, and Doctor of Jurisprudence. Foxcroft graduates have gone on to such prestigious institutions as Boston College, Bowdoin, Colby, Cornell, Dartmouth, Georgia Tech, Harvard, Middlebury, Northeastern, NYU, Purdue, Worcester Polytechnic Institute, and Yale.

STUDENT BODY AND CONDUCT

There is no typical student at the Academy; for more than 185 years, FA's democratic tradition has welcomed students from the widest array of backgrounds. Today, Foxcroft Academy has an enrollment of 418 day and boarding students from sixteen Maine communities and twelve countries. International students represent about 15 percent of the student body. The average class size is 16.

ACADEMIC FACILITIES

The Oakes Academic Building sits in the center of campus and is adjoined by the Muriel Philpot Watson Library, the gymnasium, and the music and English wing. In addition, the Ebersteen Art Center, the Packard Center for Admissions and Development, and the industrial arts building populate the campus.

BOARDING AND GENERAL FACILITIES

Foxcroft Academy's campus is located on 120 acres of fields, forest, and red brick buildings, nestled along the Piscataquis River and not far from Mount Katahdin and Acadia National Park. The beautiful New England village setting of Dover-Foxcroft ensures a safe and nurturing learning experience.

Students are currently housed in two new dormitories, completed in 2008, and a third is under construction, scheduled for completion in spring 2009. The $7-million dormitory that will open in 2009 will house 48 students and provide six individual faculty family apartment units. All dorms have wireless Internet access, secured entrances, laundry facilities, study areas, and other modern conveniences. On school nights, study hours take place after 7 p.m., with lights out by 11:30. All meals are served in the dining hall and the Pride Student Center. A few students can be placed with host families upon request.

ATHLETICS

Foxcroft Academy's commitment to excellence extends beyond the classroom to the athletic playing fields, where the school has a long and proud tradition. The Academy has seven athletic fields, including Oakes stadium, which includes its football field and an eight-lane all-weather track and field complex. In recent years, the Academy's wrestling, football, baseball, field hockey, and cross-country teams have won multiple state and regional championships.

Along with winning championships, the classic ideal of the sound mind in the sound body remains the guiding principle of athletics at Foxcroft. There are nearly thirty interscholastic teams, both girls' and boys'. All students have an opportunity to try out for any sport they wish. In sports like football, soccer, swimming, track, cross-country, tennis, and ice hockey, everyone makes the team at either a varsity or junior varsity level. Programs like basketball, field hockey, and baseball carry a limited squad, but even here, most students who try out make the team.

EXTRACURRICULAR OPPORTUNITIES

Foxcroft provides a rich environment—one that is intellectually challenging in and out of the classroom. The Academy offers more than twenty clubs and student organizations, including the Latin Club, the Key Club, the Asian Culture Club, the French Club, the Drama Club, and a student-run newspaper. Students also have an opportunity to do volunteer work with a variety of organizations in town. Students can serve as mentors to elementary school children or help at a nursing home, the food bank, local churches, or the YMCA.

DAILY LIFE

Classes are held Monday through Friday from 8 a.m. to 3 p.m. Structured study sessions are available from 6:30 p.m. to 8:30 p.m. Foxcroft does not have Saturday classes.

WEEKEND LIFE

On Friday nights, many interscholastic sports teams have their games, and everyone cheers for the FA Ponies. Saturdays are often spent shopping at the mall, snowboarding at Squaw Mountain, taking a shopping trip to outlet stores in Freeport, or swimming at the local YMCA. Spring and early fall provide opportunities to go to Portland, Acadia National Park, Bar Harbor, and participate in water sports on Sebec Lake. An annual trip to New York City, Boston, or Washington, D.C., is scheduled for all boarding students.

Student Council also sponsors dances, concerts, and movies on campus throughout the year. Foxcroft Academy encourages students to attend a few cultural events each semester. On-campus choices include the regionally recognized fall musical, usually a well-known Broadway show such as *Hello, Dolly!* or *Fiddler on the Roof,* and a fall or spring music concert. Students might also choose to attend a performance at the Maine Center for the Arts at the University of Maine or see a movie at the local theater.

SUMMER PROGRAMS

Each spring or summer, Foxcroft Academy students can travel abroad to France, Spain, Greece, England, or other countries around the world. Available to all students, this annual trip is sponsored by the Academy's International Club.

COSTS AND FINANCIAL AID

Foxcroft Academy's tuition rate is one of the lowest in New England among competitive college-preparatory schools. Room, board, and tuition for residential students total $31,800 for the 2009–10 school year. Day students pay $10,800 in tuition. All Academy-sponsored financial aid is need-based only. The Financial Aid Committee accepts letters of request, which should explain in detail the reason financial aid is requested. Supporting documents may be requested. All financial aid information is kept in strict confidence. The committee notifies the accepted candidate within two weeks after receiving a letter of request. The candidate must make a decision on acceptance of the financial aid award within two weeks after notification.

ADMISSIONS INFORMATION

Foxcroft Academy seeks students whose academic ability, motivation, and personal integrity will contribute to the school community. The ideal FA student is one who has a willingness to contribute to and gain from the rigorous college-preparatory program offerings. Admission is based upon the candidate's academic record, application essay, teacher and counselor recommendations, and standardized testing such as the SSAT, PSAT, SLEP, TOEFL, or CAT. A $50 processing fee is required at the time of application. An interview is required for admission, and a campus visit is strongly suggested, but not required. Phone interviews are acceptable and can be arranged once all application materials have been received.

Foxcroft Academy does not discriminate on the basis of race, color, religion, sex, national origin, or physical or mental disability in the administration of its educational, admissions, or financial aid policies. All students enjoy the same rights and privileges and participate in all academic, athletic, and social programs generally available to the student body.

APPLICATION TIMETABLE

Admission is ongoing throughout the school year and summer; however, interested students are encouraged to apply prior to April 1. Most admission decisions are made within two weeks of the interview.

ADMISSIONS CORRESPONDENCE

John J. Brennan, Associate Head of Admissions
Foxcroft Academy
975 West Main Street
Dover-Foxcroft, Maine 04426

Phone: 207-564-8664
Fax: 207-564-8394
E-mail: jay.brennan@foxcroftacademy.org
Web site: http://www.foxcroftacademy.org

FOXCROFT SCHOOL

Middleburg, Virginia

Type: Girls' boarding and day college-preparatory school
Grades: 9–12
Enrollment: 185
Head of School: Mary Louise Leipheimer

THE SCHOOL

Foxcroft School offers a strong college-preparatory program in a challenging and supportive academic atmosphere. Charlotte Haxall Noland founded the School in 1914 and remained Director until her retirement in 1955. Miss Charlotte, as she was called by the students, valued determination, courage, and character. She sought to establish a school that would instill in its graduates high purpose, leadership, integrity, and understanding. Faculty members and students at Foxcroft continue to strive for this goal.

Located in the shadow of the Blue Ridge Mountains, Foxcroft is about an hour by car from Washington, D.C. Five hundred acres of orchards, fields, trails, and streams provide a backdrop and resource for campus life, while the proximity of Washington, D.C., enables the School community to take advantage of museums, theaters, concerts, and the halls of government.

In 1937, Foxcroft was incorporated as a nonprofit institution. The 21 members of the Board of Trustees meet three times annually. The School plant is valued at $43 million, and the endowment is $25,657,922. There are approximately 2,922 graduates in the Alumnae Association and 8 alumnae on the Board of Trustees.

Foxcroft is accredited by the Virginia Association of Independent Schools and is a member of the National Association of Independent Schools, the National Association of Principals of Schools for Girls, the Council for Advancement and Support of Education, the Secondary School Admission Test Board, the Association of Boarding Schools, and the National Coalition of Girls' Schools.

ACADEMIC PROGRAMS

The minimum requirement for graduation is the successful completion of 18 academic units plus 4 years of physical education. A unit is the equivalent of a single full-year course. The Foxcroft school year is divided into two semesters; each course of one semester's length counts as ½ unit.

The minimum course requirements must be distributed as follows: English, 4 units; foreign language, 3 units; history, 3 units; mathematics, 3 units; science, 3 units; and fine arts, 1.5 units. To qualify for sequential courses beyond minimum requirements, a student must have a grade of at least 70 in the course that is the prerequisite.

The School is small, but its program is large. With ninety-four course offerings, Foxcroft's curriculum meets the needs of students' varying interests and abilities and offers a very wide variety of electives, ranging from discrete mathematics to lab techniques in molecular biology, from Southern gothic literature to history of the Middle East.

Advanced Placement courses are available in American history, Spanish, French, English, mathematics (AB and BC calculus), biology, physics, chemistry, macroeconomics, human geography, and U.S. government.

Classes meet according to a rotating schedule that allows for flexibility in class times and lengths depending on individual course needs. A student–teaching faculty ratio of 6:1 leads to close contact between students and teachers and prevents any student from going unnoticed. Similarly, regular review of students' progress during faculty meetings ensures that each student receives individualized attention. The Learning Center and Math Lab offer students the opportunity to improve their study skills, to develop strategies for learning, to find special support when they encounter academic difficulty, and to take increasing responsibility for their own learning.

Sunday through Thursday, students are in study hall from 7:30 to 9:45 p.m. They may study in their dormitory rooms or in the library; in both places, a student leader and a faculty member are present to maintain a quiet, focused atmosphere and to offer extra help.

The Foxcroft academic program is further enriched by the following special cocurricular events: Interim Term, which offers two weeks of seminars, events, speakers, and off-campus trips, during which the whole community pauses to explore a topic of current interest; the Goodyear Fellowship Program, which brings to Foxcroft each year a person distinguished in the arts, humanities, science, or public affairs to speak and conduct seminars with students (past speakers have included Barbara Walters, David McCullough, Andrei Codrescu, Maya Angelou, Aimee Mullins, Doris Kearns Goodwin and physicist Lisa Randall); the Niblack Lecture Series, which bring a variety of literary, performing, and fine artists, artisans, and designers to Foxcroft to share their work and experience while engaging the School in the creative process; and an annual two-day Bergan Poetry Festival sponsored by the English Department sponsors, during which published poets read from their work, lead workshops, and judge a student reading competition.

FACULTY AND ADVISERS

Foxcroft capitalizes on the fact that nearly 80 percent of the faculty and administration live on campus. The faculty members and their families are the hub of a caring community. A large part of the responsibility for counseling and advising students rests with the faculty members. Each girl has a faculty adviser in addition to her housemother.

Mary Louise Leipheimer, appointed Head in 1989, graduated from Indiana University of Pennsylvania with a B.S. in English. She has served as both a faculty member and an administrator since 1967.

Foxcroft has 48 full-time faculty members and administrators. Thirty-eight teachers and administrators live on the campus, 22 of them with their families. They hold forty-three baccalaureate and twenty-two advanced degrees from such institutions as Colgate, Denison, Duke, Georgetown, Harvard, Indiana, Middlebury, Princeton, Skidmore, Vanderbilt, William and Mary, and the Universities of Maryland, North Carolina at Chapel Hill, South Carolina, and Virginia.

COLLEGE ADMISSION COUNSELING

During their eleventh-grade year, students meet formally with the College Counselor to begin discussing their college plans. They receive guidance on course selection, extracurricular activities, and PSAT preparation. All sophomores and juniors take the PSAT in October. Approximately fifty colleges send representatives to Foxcroft for information sessions each fall. Both juniors and seniors are encouraged to attend meetings with the colleges that are of interest to them. With the help of the College Counselor, each student begins compiling a list of colleges to research in the winter of her junior year, although the College Counselor is available to assist students and families who wish to begin the search earlier. Throughout the college admission process, the College Counseling Office provides information and workshops on topics such as evaluating colleges, writing application essays, visiting college campuses, interviewing, and preparing for standardized testing.

All Foxcroft students attend college after graduation, although a small number choose to participate in an internship or study-abroad program during an interim year with the consent of their colleges. Students in the class of 2008 matriculated at fifty-three different colleges and universities. Acceptances were received from a wide range of schools, including Boston University, Charleston (South Carolina), Duke, James Madison, Johns Hopkins, NYU, Sewanee: The University of the South, Swarthmore, Syracuse, Tulane, USC, Washington and Lee, William and Mary, and the Universities of Colorado at Boulder, Michigan, and Virginia.

STUDENT BODY AND CONDUCT

For the 2008–09 school year, Foxcroft enrolled 32 students in grade 9, 52 students in grade 10, 57 students in grade 11, and 44 students in grade 12. There were 140 boarders and 45 day students, representing twelve different countries and twenty two states, plus the District of Columbia.

Student leaders and members of the faculty and administration share in the governing of the School, including the enforcement of rules and the handling of offenses. The School Council is composed of student, faculty, and administration representatives who act as a clearinghouse for new policies. Students serve on the Student and Judicial Councils.

ACADEMIC FACILITIES

The Schoolhouse has fourteen classrooms, a studio art wing, two music labs, science laboratories, lab preparation rooms, two photography darkrooms, and an auditorium. A science wing contains three laboratory classrooms, a science library, a computer room, an animal and plant room, and facilities for permanent specimen collections.

The Currier Library contains nearly 50,000 books and bound periodicals as well as information in fourteen other formats, including DVD, videocassette, microfiche, CD, and slides. Within the three-story facility are two computer labs with e-mail and Internet access, an AV/listening room, eighty-five study carrels, a classroom, comfortable student study nooks, and the Foxcroft archives. The electronic, Web-based catalog serves as a gateway to thousands of resources, both physical and electronic, including several online research databases.

The Duncan Read Observatory houses a 10-inch reflecting telescope, a tracking system, a Newtonian

Cassegrain reflecting telescope, two 8-inch Celestron telescopes, and accessories for astrophotography and solar observing.

BOARDING AND GENERAL FACILITIES

Students at Foxcroft live in five dormitories. In addition to having a full-time housemother, each dormitory has 2 seniors as student leaders and counselors and 2 or 3 juniors to assist them. Usually 3 students share a room, in which each girl has a desk, bureau, and closet. From 2 to 4 girls share a full bath. Each dorm has a living room, dedicated sleeping areas, and kitchen and laundry facilities.

The restored Brick House, dating from the 1700s, holds the main dining hall—large enough for the whole School to have a formal sit-down lunch twice a week—and cafeteria and kitchen facilities. The Activities Building contains the gymnasium, a weight room, cardiofitness room, student lounge, snack bar, student kitchen, dance studio offices, and locker rooms. A major expansion and renovation, including a double-box gym floor, additional team rooms, and student center, among other enhancements, is under construction. The outdoor swimming pool (1987) is open for recreational use in the early fall and spring.

ATHLETICS

Every student is required to take part in some form of athletics throughout the year. Dance and riding are offered each term; physical education classes in such varied activities as kickboxing, core conditioning, and yoga are offered in the winter.

The interscholastic sports program includes basketball, cross-country, field hockey, golf, lacrosse, riding, soccer, softball, swimming, tennis, and volleyball. All but riding teams compete in the all-Virginia Delaney Athletic Conference and against other schools in Virginia, Maryland, and Washington, D.C. In addition, every student is a member of the Fox or Hound spirit/intramural teams and has an opportunity to enjoy the experience of being part of a team. The riding teams compete in the Tristate Equitation League and various intrascholastic and open eventing and jumping competitions.

The athletic facilities consist of a dance studio, a gymnasium, four playing fields (one with a softball diamond), eight tennis courts, three riding rings (one indoors), and three jump courses adjacent to the campus buildings. Current construction will add a double-box gym, an indoor running track, a rock-climbing wall, and additional fitness workout facilities.

McConnell Stables and Indoor Ring allow riding throughout the school year for students who range from beginners to advanced riders. Approximately 30 percent of the students participate in the riding program, riding one of the School's 30 horses or boarding their own.

With 500 acres of trails, streams, fields, and woods, as well as an active outdoors club, many opportunities exist for hiking, camping, and exploring.

EXTRACURRICULAR OPPORTUNITIES

Foxcroft has many clubs and student organizations, including Activities Committee, Art Club, Art History, Astronomy, Athletic Association, Blue Planet Society (environment and recycling), CAPS tour guides, Chinese Language and Culture, Community Service, Cooking Club, Current Events and Debate , Fox-Hound, International Club, Outing Club, Special Friends (visiting senior citizens), and a Christian Fellowship. There are three singing groups: Octet, Afternoon Delights, and Soggie Cheerios. Student publications include *Chimera* (literary magazine) and *Tally-Ho!* (yearbook).

Foxcroft also has a Leadership Program with more than fifty formal leadership positions available. This program is designed to offer every student the opportunity to become a leader. Students seeking these positions are required to obtain peer and adviser references, submit essays outlining their strengths and weaknesses, and present speeches. Once Foxcroft leaders are elected, they must attend a leadership retreat and complete specialized training to learn trust-building skills and conflict-resolution techniques.

Foxcroft has an active community service program that expects each student to give back in some way to the School and to the larger community. Students and teachers work together on a projects several times during the year. Projects have included collecting clothing for an abused women's organization, walking for breast cancer research, and working for an animal shelter. Throughout the year, community service opportunities exist on campus and at a nursing home, hospital, and humane foundation. In addition, the junior class organizes a major walkathon held each spring; the 2008 walk raised $30,000 for the Christopher and Dane Reeve Foundation.

DAILY LIFE

Classes meet five days a week according to a rotating schedule. Each academic day begins at 8 a.m. after breakfast and has six or seven periods. Morning Meeting, a student-run, all-School assembly, meets midmorning three times a week, and athletics take place daily before dinner. Study hall runs from 7:30 to 9:45 p.m., and lights-out is at 10:30 for freshmen and 11 for upperclassmen.

WEEKEND LIFE

Foxcroft's Director of Activities works closely with the students in the Activities Club to plan on- and off-campus activities. On-campus activities range from a movie and snack bar night to Battles of the Dorms. Examples of off-campus activities include trips to the theater and the mall, dances or mixers at other schools, sporting events, Kings Dominion, and skiing or rafting trips.

Foxcroft is located 4 miles from Middleburg, and students may shop and eat in town on the weekends or arrange a ride with a faculty member if they need to do something in town during the week. Middleburg offers a variety of restaurants, quaint shopping, a supermarket, and a pharmacy.

Day and overnight permissions allow students to take advantage of extended weekend trips to Washington, D.C.; Richmond; Williamsburg; and other cities to enjoy the many cultural and recreational opportunities available in and around Virginia.

COSTS AND FINANCIAL AID

The boarding tuition for the 2008–09 school year was $40,950; day tuition was $30,712. Textbooks and supplies cost approximately $500 to $600. Optional riding lessons were offered for $850 per term (three terms per year).

In 2008–09, 24 percent of students received financial assistance. This assistance is awarded according to financial need as determined by the School and Student Service for Financial Aid. For 2008–09, Foxcroft awarded grants totaling approximately $1,257,953. Foxcroft offers two merit scholarships, a variety of payment plans, and a generous Middle Income Loan Program.

ADMISSIONS INFORMATION

Foxcroft looks for motivated young women, able to succeed in a college-preparatory program and eager to participate in all aspects of school life.

Admission decisions are based on a personal interview; recommendations from teachers, counselors, or a principal; previous academic achievement; a writing sample; and SSAT scores. Foxcroft admits students of any race, color, or national or ethnic origin to all the programs and activities generally made available to students at the School.

APPLICATION TIMETABLE

An initial inquiry is welcome anytime. Campus tours are usually given right before the interview and are best scheduled Monday, Wednesday, or Friday between 9:30 and 2:30 when school is in session. A number of Admission Day Festivals are offered throughout the year to provide prospective students with an opportunity to visit classes, spend the day with current students, and interview.

The application deadline is February 15, and admissions decisions are mailed March 10. Students who are accepted have until April 10 to notify the School of their decision. Should spaces remain, candidates accepted after April 10 have fifteen days to reply.

ADMISSIONS CORRESPONDENCE

Erica L. Ohanesian, Director of Admission
Foxcroft School
P.O. Box 5555
Middleburg, Virginia 20118-5555
Phone: 540-687-5555
800-858-2364 (toll-free, U.S.)
Fax: 540-687-3627
E-mail: admissions@foxcroft.org
Web site: http://www.foxcroft.org

FRYEBURG ACADEMY

Fryeburg, Maine

Type: Coeducational boarding and day college-preparatory school
Grades: 9–PG
Enrollment: 683
Head of School: Daniel G. Lee Jr., Headmaster

THE SCHOOL

Fryeburg Academy, founded in 1792, is a boarding and day school serving students in grades 9–12 and a postgraduate year.

Recognizing that young people of varying aptitudes, interests, and abilities must be prepared to meet the challenges of the world, Fryeburg offers a challenging yet flexible curriculum. Fryeburg is accredited by the New England Association of Schools and Colleges and approved by the Maine Department of Education. It holds membership in the National Association of Independent Schools, the College Board, the Maine Secondary Schools Association, and the Independent School Association of Northern New England.

The Academy is governed by a 15-member self-perpetuating Board of Trustees and has an endowment of $8 million.

ACADEMIC PROGRAMS

Fryeburg Academy offers a comprehensive curriculum with more than 100 course offerings, including Advanced Placement, honors, and college-preparatory curriculum as well as four levels of English for Speakers of Other Languages (ESOL). A minimum of 19 credits is required for graduation; these must include the following courses: English (4 Carnegie units), history (3 units, including 1 unit of U.S. history), science (3 units), mathematics (3 units), fine arts (1 unit), and computer proficiency. Students are given some latitude in selecting the remaining credits. They must carry at least five academic subjects each semester, but most elect to carry six. Remedial and developmental reading programs are available for students who need them.

Classes range in size from 8 to 20 students; the average class size is 15. Supervised study hours are held from 7:30 to 9:30 p.m., Sunday through Thursday.

The Academy operates on a two-semester system. Reports are sent to parents every six weeks. Letter grades are given for achievement and numerical grades for effort.

FACULTY AND ADVISERS

The faculty consists of 65 full-time and 2 part-time instructors. Of the full-time instructors, 30 are men and 37 are women. The administration consists of 15 members, 3 of whom teach part-time. Faculty members are available for extra help in the dormitories on a daily rotating schedule and every day in school. All serve as advisers to the student body.

COLLEGE ADMISSION COUNSELING

The College Placement Office helps students prepare for their postsecondary education. Six experienced guidance counselors serve as advisers in this area. Visits by college representatives to the Academy campus are open to interested juniors and seniors.

In 2008, 83 percent of the graduating students were accepted by postsecondary institutions. Recent graduates enrolled at Babson, Bates, Boston University, Colby, Dartmouth, Harvard, Northeastern, St. Lawrence, and the Universities of Maine, Massachusetts, New Hampshire, and Vermont.

STUDENT BODY AND CONDUCT

There are 683 students enrolled. Of these students, 548 are day students and 135 are boarding students. For the 2008–09 academic year, Academy students represented ten states and twenty countries. The senior class numbers 197.

There are 110 international students representing countries such as China, Denmark, Germany, Japan, Korea, Nepal, Russia, Spain, Sweden, and Vietnam.

Most disciplinary problems are handled by the judicial board, which is made up of students and faculty members, meets as needed, and acts on reports presented to the faculty. A student who violates the rules is referred to this committee.

ACADEMIC FACILITIES

The brick and frame buildings on campus represent several periods of construction. The main building is a large brick structure with administrative offices and two classroom wings. A newer wing includes the Mattson Student Union and the LaCasce Dining Hall.

Separate buildings contain the foreign language department, the music studio, special services, and the industrial arts shop. Newer buildings include the Eastman Science Center, which was completed in 1996; the Bion Cram Library, completed in 2003; and a 48,500-square-foot athletic complex opened in June 2007. Construction on a 400-seat performing arts center began in August 2007, with completion scheduled for January 2009.

BOARDING AND GENERAL FACILITIES

Four dormitories, all of brick construction, have a capacity of 135 students, 2 to a room, and contain two apartments for resident faculty members. In addition to the dormitories and academic buildings, the campus has an infirmary, maintenance buildings, athletic fields, tennis courts, and ten faculty homes.

ATHLETICS

All students are encouraged to participate in a sport or outside activity.

Because of the Academy's location, winter sports are popular, particularly skiing, ice hockey, and snowboarding. Baseball, basketball, cheerleading, cross-country, field hockey, football, golf, ice hockey, lacrosse, skiing, soccer, softball, tennis, track, and wrestling are offered as team sports. Interscholastic teams compete with both private and public schools in the area.

Converse Fields, which occupy much of the central portion of the 34-acre campus, include football, soccer, and field hockey fields and a ¼-mile track. The Manoriti Memorial Baseball Field and two tennis courts are adjacent to the dormitories. An excellent cross-country skiing course is located within a mile of the campus. Daily access to some of the best East Coast skiing and snowboarding facilities, such as Cranmore, Waterville Valley, Shawnee Peak, and Bretton Woods, is provided for both the recreational and the competitive ski enthusiast.

EXTRACURRICULAR OPPORTUNITIES

Clubs and activities are organized around current student interests. The extracurricular program includes drama, yearbook, school newspaper, environmental club, outdoor club, community service club, student ambassadors, international club, a chapter of the National Honor Society, math team, Interact (the junior branch of

Rotary), and photography club as well as Latin, French, and Spanish clubs.

DAILY LIFE

Each class runs for 45 minutes, and there are seven periods a day. Classes rotate on a six-day schedule. The learning center is open for all students every period. There are no classes on weekends or holidays. A cafeteria-style lunch is served at midday. Full breakfast and dinner are served to boarders; brunch and dinner are served on weekends and holidays. All students participate in an afternoon activity.

WEEKEND LIFE

Boarding students are provided with several weekend activities both on and off campus. Field trips to Boston, Massachusetts, and Portland, Maine, are scheduled to access cultural and other fun events that are limited only by student interest. On-campus activities include sports contests, dances, and special events such as Homecoming and Winter Carnival. Transportation is provided to the Mount Washington Valley ski resorts on most days during the week as well as on weekends and holidays.

COSTS AND FINANCIAL AID

In 2008–09, the cost of tuition, room, and board for the seven-day boarding program is $35,500; a five-day boarding rate of $28,250 is also available. Day student tuition is $17,750.

Financial aid is available to full-time students on the basis of need. In 2008–09, 51 students received financial aid.

ADMISSIONS INFORMATION

Fryeburg Academy selects its students without regard to race, color, creed, or national origin. The Admissions Committee selects students on the basis of an evaluation of their character and their capacity to benefit from the school's varied educational program. An in-person or phone interview is required of all applicants. The Admissions Office is open by appointment Monday through Friday to interested students and their families.

APPLICATION TIMETABLE

The Admissions Office accepts applications throughout the year on a space-available basis. Families are encouraged to apply by February 1.

ADMISSIONS CORRESPONDENCE

Office of Admission
Fryeburg Academy
745 Main Street
Fryeburg, Maine 04037
Phone: 207-935-2013
877-935-2013 (toll-free)
Fax: 207-935-4292
E-mail: admissions@fryeburgacademy.org
Web site: http://www.fryeburgacademy.org

GEORGE SCHOOL

Newtown, Pennsylvania

GEORGE SCHOOL

Type: Coeducational Friends boarding and day college-preparatory school
Grades: 9–12
Enrollment: 520
Head of School: Nancy Starmer, Head of School

THE SCHOOL

Established in 1893 by the Religious Society of Friends, George School is committed to cultivating respect for differences by affirming the Light of God in everyone and to meeting the intellectual, social, and developmental needs of students.

A coeducational boarding and day school of 520 students in grades 9–12, George School was among the first secondary schools in the nation to establish foreign student exchanges, a campus co-op program, international work camps and service projects, and tuition assistance programs for families in need of financial aid. Quaker values, such as equality, social justice, and respect for others create a diverse community where academics, sports, arts, and service learning share emphasis.

Situated in historic Newtown, Pennsylvania, the 265-acre campus is conveniently located within 30 miles of the cultural centers of Princeton, New Jersey, and Philadelphia and 70 miles of New York City.

George School is under the governance of the 27-member George School Committee, the majority of whom are members of the Religious Society of Friends (Quakers); other members include 1 parent, 2 faculty members, and 2 student representatives. The School's endowment is $77.2 million.

ACADEMIC PROGRAMS

George School offers a comprehensive college-preparatory curriculum designed to prepare students for a lifetime of learning.

Every four-year George School student is expected to satisfactorily complete the following requirements: 4 years of English, 3 years of history (including U.S. history), 3 years of math, 3 years of science, third-year proficiency in a foreign language, 3 years of the arts, 4 years of physical education or sports, 4years of co-op, and 1.5 years of religion and health classes. Also required are 65 hours of community service.

Full-year courses are offered in English literature and composition, American literature, world literature, Chinese I-II, French I–V, Latin I–V, Spanish I–V, global interdependence, world history, U.S. history, Middle Eastern history, economics, Asian history, European history, African American history, twentieth-century history, physical science, chemistry, biology, physics, environmental science, computer programming and robotics, algebra I, algebra II, geometry, statistics, precalculus, and calculus. The yearlong arts courses include arts foundations, painting and drawing, photography, video production, woodworking, ceramics, orchestra, music seminar, theater arts, stagecraft, dance, and chorale.

George School's diverse curriculum includes Advanced Placement (AP) courses in English, history, mathematics, sciences, foreign languages, and arts as well as English as a second language (ESL) courses in English, history, and science. In addition, the school offers the International Baccalaureate (IB) Diploma Program. The IB Program is a rigorous two-year course of study in six subjects. Students who successfully complete the program graduate with an additional diploma that is recognized by universities across the country and world. Ninety-three percent of George School IB Diploma candidates have succeeded in earning the IB Diploma over the last ten years, compared to the international average of 85 percent.

The school year is divided into three terms. Comprehensive grade reports, with teacher and adviser comments and letter grades (A–F), are sent to parents four times a year.

The student-teacher ratio is 7:1, and the average class size is 14 students. All students are required to attend meeting for worship on Tuesdays or Thursdays; boarders and day students staying on campus must also attend on Sunday mornings.

Students are required to participate in a cooperative work program each year to promote a personal and financial commitment to the School. International and domestic work camps and service projects are available to juniors and seniors during their two-week spring break and the summer. George School has recently sponsored projects to Arizona, coastal Louisiana and Mississippi, Costa Rica, France, India, Massachusetts, Nicaragua, South Africa, South Korea, Vietnam, and Washington, D.C.

FACULTY AND ADVISERS

Appointed in 2000, Nancy Starmer is the School's seventh Head of School. Before coming to George School, she served as Principal of the Upper School at Milton Academy. During the 1999–2000 academic year, she spent her sabbatical studying issues of diversity and community as a visiting scholar at the Wellesley Centers for Women and as a visiting practitioner at Harvard Graduate School of Education. After graduating from the College of Wooster in 1970, she received a Master's in Education at Boston University.

Of the 84 faculty members, 78 have advanced degrees. Almost 30 percent of the faculty members are Quakers and 19 percent are of members of minority groups. Most faculty members reside on campus and interact with students on a full-time basis.

The adviser system is an important and effective program at George School. Advisers offer academic guidance and serve as confidants, counselors, and friends. Each adviser has approximately 8 advisees and serves as the liaison between parents and the School. Students meet with advisers daily.

Faculty members are eligible for a sabbatical after seven years of service and school chairs, fellowships, and grants after three. A faculty enrichment fund helps cover faculty expenses for professional development whenever possible and appropriate.

COLLEGE ADMISSION COUNSELING

Three college counselors work with juniors and seniors and their parents as they explore educational and career options. From the class of 2007, 132 students matriculate at eighty-five colleges and universities in the United States and 5 attend universities abroad. Over the past five years, 10 or more graduates have attended each of the following colleges and universities: Boston University, Carnegie Mellon, Franklin & Marshall, Guilford, Ithaca, Northeastern, NYU, Oberlin, Penn State, Temple, Ursinus, and the Universities of Chicago, Pennsylvania, and Pittsburgh.

The college counselors encourage students to meet with them often, visit colleges, and attend meetings on campus with college admissions officers.

STUDENT BODY AND CONDUCT

In 2007–08, George School enrolled 292 boarders and 228 day students, including 272 girls and 248 boys. Students came from twenty-two states and twenty-seven countries. Of the total enrollment, 21 percent were members of minority groups, and Friends made up 16.5 percent of the student body.

The School's various committees include student members, providing them an opportunity to both shape and influence School policies. All decisions are reached by Quaker consensus, not majority rule. Individuals who do not abide by major School rules are considered by the Discipline Committee, which is made up of faculty members and students and makes decisions in conjunction with the deans and advisers. Minor infractions are handled by the deans. Each student is expected to accept the responsibilities inherent in George School's close-knit community.

ACADEMIC FACILITIES

There are five major academic buildings on campus. Bancroft, Retford, Hallowell Arts Center, and the Spruance-Alden Science Center house the English, mathematics, history, language, arts, and science departments; Walton Center is a 600-seat theater-auditorium with two stages, five practice rooms, a dance studio, and classroom facilities for music and drama.

The meetinghouse, originally built in Philadelphia in the 1700s, was dismantled, moved to George School, and reconstructed in 1974. It is used for Quaker meeting for worship, religion classes, and community functions. McFeely Library has an excellent collection of books (20,000 volumes), audio and video sources, electronic and hard-copy periodicals, and a broad range of scholarly online reference resources. Thirty-five computers are available for students, all with full access to the Internet. Instruction in library use and research techniques is provided. The campus is fully wired for network access, including student residential rooms. Most academic buildings, including the library, have wireless network access.

BOARDING AND GENERAL FACILITIES

Students are housed according to grade level in single-sex residence halls. There are three boys' dormitories: Campbell (ninth), Orton (tenth), and Drayton (eleventh and twelfth). The girls' dorms consist of Westwood (ninth) and three sections of Main. West Main houses sophomore girls, while juniors and seniors live in both Central and East Main. Faculty members reside in the dorms in faculty apartments, and senior prefects live alongside students on each floor.

Marshall Center, the student activities center, houses the bookstore, the post office, a snack bar, a coffeehouse, day-student lounges and lockers, and offices for the deans and the student activities director.

The Student Health Center has a nurse practitioner and registered nurses available 24 hours a day, seven days a week. A physician and two counselors are on call at all times.

ATHLETICS

The George School physical education program offers a combination of physical education classes and interscholastic team sports, emphasizing involvement and cooperation.

Interscholastic team sports include baseball, basketball, cheerleading, cross-country, equestrian, field hockey, football, golf, lacrosse, soccer, softball, swimming, tennis, track, volleyball, and wrestling. Physical education classes include aerobics, coed intramurals, equestrian, floor hockey/soccer, instructional swimming, lifeguard training, lifetime sports, net sports, personal fitness, Ultimate Frisbee, volleyball, and yoga.

Worth Sports Center houses an eight-lane, 25-meter pool as well as facilities for indoor tennis, volleyball, and basketball. The Alumni Gym houses a basketball court, wrestling room, and weight training facilities. In addition, there are fourteen outdoor tennis courts, ten athletic fields, stables and two riding rings, a ¼-mile running track, and a cross-country course.

EXTRACURRICULAR OPPORTUNITIES

George School students are encouraged to get involved in campus organizations and to start their own interest groups that influence the quality of life of the community. Current student clubs include Amnesty International, Ceramics Club, Community Chorus, Goldfish in Java (coffeehouse music group), Model United Nations, Open Doors (gay-straight alliance), Outdoor Club, PAWS (Pets are Worth Supporting), the R&B Step Team, Students Against Drunk Driving, TERRA (Sierra Student Coalition), and Women's Issues Now.

The *Curious George,* the School's student newspaper, *Opus* (the yearbook), and *Argo* (a literary magazine) provide opportunities for creativity and self-expression. To support the needs of students from rich cultural and religious traditions, George School sponsors Havurah (Jewish culture), Latin American Student Organization, LOGOS (a Christian interest group), Pacific Rim Organization, Samosa (South Asian student society), UMOJA (culture, heritage, and ethnicity of African descendants), and Young Friends (Quaker support group).

With their adviser's permission, students interested in providing leadership to the community may apply to participate in the Discipline Committee, Diversity Steering Committee, Drug and Alcohol Coordinating Committee, George School Committee, Peer Group, Prefects, Student Council, and Students Associated for Greater Empathy (SAGE). Founded in 1971, SAGE is a student-run organization of peer counselors who are trained to address social and emotional issues common to teenagers.

DAILY LIFE

The academic day begins at 8 a.m. and ends at 3:30 p.m., except on Tuesdays and Fridays, when classes end at 2:35 p.m. Breakfast is available from 7:15 to 8 and lunch from 11 to 1. Both are served cafeteria-style. During the academic week, dinner is served between 5:30 and 6:30 p.m. A special period is set aside from 10 to 10:40 a.m. for an all-School assembly with guest speakers on Mondays and Fridays and for meeting for worship on Tuesdays and Thursdays. There are six classes each day of either 50 or 105 minutes. All students meet with their advisers in a group setting for 10 minutes every weekday morning at 8:50.

The majority of sports activities take place between 3:30 and 5:30. Clubs and committee meetings generally occur after dinner and before study hall. Study hall is scheduled between 7:30 and 9:30 p.m.; students may choose to study in their dormitory rooms or the library. They may also be assigned to a supervised study hall. All students must check into their dormitories at 10 p.m. on school nights.

WEEKEND LIFE

Under the guidance of the Director of Student Activities, weekends are organized around themes and sponsored by student organizations or faculty members. Past weekend themes included Amnesty, Outdoor Challenge, Open Doors, Pacific Rim Organization, Freedom from Chemical Dependency, Harvest, Live Music, Spring Fling, and Parents/Sibling/Alumni weekends.

Easily accessible by foot, Newtown offers a movie theater, clothing stores, shopping centers, coffee shops, and restaurants. Philadelphia and its cultural and entertainment opportunities are often a part of the weekend activities and field trips. A weekend shuttle is available to the local train station in Trenton, New Jersey.

Boarding students are free to leave campus on weekends or visit day students' homes with proper permission and parental consent. Day students are encouraged to stay overnight in the dorms for weekend activities.

COSTS AND FINANCIAL AID

The 2008–09 annual day student cost of $29,300 covered tuition, meals, activities, infirmary costs, and laboratory fees. The boarding cost of $39,600 covered room, board, tuition, activities, infirmary costs, laundry, and laboratory fees.

Students buy textbooks—new or used—at the School bookstore. Books and incidentals for the year usually cost between $500 and $750. Required athletic equipment and clothes might cost students up to $200 each year. An initial deposit of 10 percent of tuition is required upon enrollment.

Grants and loans for scholarship assistance are awarded according to need and are based on national standards established by the School and Student Service for Financial Aid. Four $15,000 merit-based Anderson scholarships are awarded annually to students who embody the principles of social involvement, respect for others, and a commitment to academic excellence. Forty-five percent of the students received $5.1 million in financial aid. The average award was $22,310.

ADMISSIONS INFORMATION

George School seeks students with a high degree of academic interest and intellectual curiosity who are open to new experiences and friendships. The Admission Committee seeks a student body diverse in race, creed, and economic and social background, with some preference given to Quakers and children of alumni. The committee takes into consideration the previous school record, recommendations, writing samples, the interview, and SSAT results.

APPLICATION TIMETABLE

Inquiries are always welcome. The Admissions Office is open from 8 to 4, Monday through Friday. Student-guided tours and admissions interviews are conducted at 9, 10:45, and 1:15 daily. The application fee is $50 for domestic applicants and $75 for international applicants.

Day students should apply no later than January 15; boarding students are advised to apply before February 15. Admissions decisions are announced beginning March 10, and applicants must reply by April 10. After April, the Admissions Committee meets weekly to make decisions on a space-available basis.

ADMISSIONS CORRESPONDENCE

Director of Admission
Box 4460
George School
Newtown, Pennsylvania 18940
Phone: 215-579-6547
Fax: 215-579-6549
E-mail: admission@georgeschool.org
Web site: http://www.georgeschool.org

GEORGE STEVENS ACADEMY

Blue Hill, Maine

Type: Coeducational boarding and day college-preparatory school
Grades: 9–12
Enrollment: 307
Head of School: John Greene, Headmaster

THE SCHOOL

George Stevens Academy (GSA) was founded in 1803 as Blue Hill Academy. The first students, men and women from nearby towns, were taught by a preceptor and 2 teachers, and their courses of study included Greek, Latin, and navigation. The Academy flourished under the guardianship of the Congregational Church, but in 1832, George Stevens, the first non-Congregationalist to become a member of the Board of Trustees, offered money and land to the Academy on the condition that it become an equal-opportunity institution. When the Board refused, he donated 150 acres of land to build another school, the George Stevens Academy. In 1943, the two schools finally merged into Blue Hill–George Stevens Academy.

Today, GSA consists of 20 acres, including administrative buildings and athletic fields, plus another 500 acres for future development. The mission of the Academy is to create a caring and dynamic community that educates and encourages students to reach their highest potential through a wide array of challenging academic and extracurricular programs. It is committed to academic excellence, creative thinking, and artistic expression and offers diverse opportunities for self-discovery that enable and require students to make responsible choices. The governing body includes the Headmaster, the Assistant Head of School, the Academic Dean, the Dean of Students, and a 20-person Board of Trustees, on which many GSA alumni sit.

Academically, students from GSA rank among the best in the state, with many graduates attending the top universities and colleges in the U.S. In music, the Jazz Band and the Jazz Combo have won state championships for the past six years, bringing home six first-place trophies and six MVP awards. For more than eighteen years, the Jazz Band has placed in the top three spots at the State Competition. GSA's Jazz Combo, Musiquarium, won fourth place at the 2005 Berklee College of Music Jazz Festival in Boston. In athletics, in 2006, GSA had a cross-country runner who was the Eastern Maine Champion. The girls' varsity soccer team also won the Eastern Maine Championship in 2006. In 2005, students earned a state championship in sailing and the Eastern Maine Championship in baseball. In 2004, GSA won two state championships in baseball and tennis and the Eastern Maine Championship in girls' soccer.

GSA is accredited by the New England Association of Schools and Colleges (NEAS&C) and the Maine Department of Educational and Cultural Services. GSA is also a member of the College Board, the Secondary School Admission Test Board (SSATB), and the Independent Schools Association of Northern New England.

ACADEMIC PROGRAMS

The academic year is divided into two semesters: September through December and January through June. In order to graduate, students must earn a total of 22 academic credits, including 4 English credits, 3 math credits, 3 science credits, 3 social science credits, 1 physical education credit, 1 fine arts credit, ½ credit in health, and 6½ elective credits. All students are required to carry a minimum of 5 credits each semester. Juniors and seniors may also participate in a two-week Independent Study and Internship Program. Seniors must fulfill a senior debate requirement in order to graduate. Every June, seniors debate one another on a wide range of topics, from current events to legal issues. Public speaking, research, cooperation with partners and team members, synthesizing an informed argument, and self-expression are important elements of the debate process. The debate is a logical culmination of the high school language arts experience and gives students an opportunity to study, in depth, a topic of their choice.

In order to accommodate different learning styles and abilities, GSA offers a varied curriculum at three different levels: skills, college-prep (CP4), and honors. Seven AP courses are also available. Honors and AP courses challenge students to pursue subjects deeply, intensively, and rigorously. The foreign language program includes French, Spanish, and German. Some of the more unique courses at GSA are human geography, earthworks, boat building, marine science, Maine environment, forensics, jazz, chamber music for strings, photography, psychology, lab geometry, and advanced applications of finite math. A state-certified special education teacher is available to support students with special needs who are taking the majority of their courses in regular classes.

GSA offers a comprehensive ESL program for international students at three levels: beginner, intermediate, and advanced. Students are tested prior to placement in one of the levels. ESL courses focus on developing conversational and writing skills as well as the language necessary for regular subject classes. Special emphasis is also placed on preparing students for the TOEFL exam and entry into U.S. colleges and universities.

An Alternative Course Contract (ACC) provides an opportunity for a student to take a course not offered in the regular curriculum. A student, in consultation with the Office of Faculty and Student Services and a member of the GSA faculty, may design the curriculum and write a course proposal that includes a description of the course, goals, and objectives and the amount of credit to be earned. An Alternative Course Contract may be taken on a pass/fail basis or for a numerical grade. Alternative Course Contracts are usually taken in addition to the required 5 academic credits. The Head of School must pre-approve all Alternative Course Contracts.

FACULTY AND ADVISERS

There are 31 teachers at the Academy; more than half of the instructors have advanced degrees. The faculty is composed almost equally of men and women. GSA faculty members are skilled, caring educators who are actively involved in students' lives. Each full-time faculty member serves as an adviser for up to 15 students to assist them in their academic, social, and emotional development. They help students set educational goals and develop the skills necessary to accomplish them. In addition, advisers assist students through the college-admission process, including the coordination of college aptitude tests and the various aspects of applying to college. Faculty members are also involved in advising student clubs and coaching athletics.

John Greene has a B.A. from Colby College and has also studied at Boston University, the University of Maine, and the U.S. Army German Language School in Nuremburg, Germany. Mr. Greene has been a teacher and coach and has also held the positions of athletic director, assistant headmaster, and headmaster during a forty-year period at GSA. In addition, he has served in the U.S. Army and worked for the First National Bank of Boston. He has served on four accreditation teams for the New England Association of Schools and Colleges and served on the local school board for eight years.

COLLEGE ADMISSION COUNSELING

The Office of Faculty and Student Services meets with students on an individual and group basis to discuss and map out students' future plans, explore and refine individual goals, and organize a time-management system for the college application process. There is a dedicated college counselor specifically for international students who guides students through the college selection and application process. This counselor also helps arrange for students to take the SAT, ACT, or TOEFL exams. The Academy hosts a number of college admissions representatives and financial aid workshops every year. About 81 percent of students who graduate from the Academy attend postsecondary institutions. Within Maine, recent graduates have attended Bates, Bowdoin, Colby, and the Universities of Maine and Southern Maine. Recent graduates are attending such colleges and universities as Berklee College of Music, Cornell, Dartmouth, Harvard, NYU, Penn State, RPI, Smith, Stanford, Yale, the University of Virginia, and the U.S. Naval Academy.

STUDENT BODY AND CONDUCT

In the 2008–09 academic year, the Academy enrolled a total of 307 students: 133 boys and 174 girls. In grade 9, there were 25 boys and 40 girls; grade 10, 34 boys and 48 girls; grade 11, 43 boys and 45 girls; and grade 12, 31 boys and 41 girls. The majority of students come from Blue Hill and the surrounding towns. The socioeconomic range is wide; students have parents in occupations ranging from lobstermen and mill workers to lawyers and doctors. In fall 2008, GSA admitted 27 international students from China, Finland, Italy, Korea, Spain, Thailand, and Vietnam,.

Students participate in the management of the school through the Student Council, which provides leadership, school service, a forum for student voice, and channels for student involvement. Students' rights and responsibilities are outlined in the school handbook, and both students and faculty members are expected to maintain an atmosphere of respect and encouragement for learning, take responsibility for their actions, foster a safe and caring atmosphere, use courteous and appropriate language, abide by the highest standards of honesty, and remain chemically free. GSA's administrators and faculty members are responsible for discipline.

ACADEMIC FACILITIES
GSA's campus is located in the heart of Blue Hill and currently consists of four main buildings plus two residence halls. The Academy's library contains a collection of more than 8,000 items for research and recreational reading. Materials are offered in a variety of formats, including books, magazines, microfiche, videotapes, and CD-ROMs. The library also includes seven computers with Internet access. In addition, there are thirty laptops in two mobile units for student use as well as sixteen computers in the campus computer lab. The entire campus is wireless, and every teacher has an in-class computer. Students also have access to the Blue Hill Library, which has more than 39,000 items, and the MERI Center for Marine Studies.

BOARDING AND GENERAL FACILITIES
GSA has two residential options for international students: home stay and boarding. The Host Family Program provides international students with the opportunity to live with a family in the community. Students become a member of that family for the school year and may spend time with their host family after school, on weekends, and during vacations. This offers students the chance to practice English intensively while experiencing life in an American household. GSA also has one recently renovated and one new residence hall. The girls' residence houses 8 students, and the boys' dormitory holds 16. Each building also houses full-time dorm parents who provide constant supervision for the students. GSA's residential facilities are a reflection of the school's overall aim to provide students with a comfortable environment in a warm, caring community.

ATHLETICS
GSA participates in twelve interscholastic sports throughout the year, including baseball, basketball, golf, indoor and outdoor track, sailing, soccer, tennis, and wrestling. Games and practice times take place after school during the week and sometimes in the morning on weekends. In order to play, students must be enrolled in five full-credit courses at the Academy and maintain good academic standing. Other requirements include a parents consent form, a yearly physical examination, an emergency medical card completed and on file in the Athletic Office, and attendance at a preseason meeting. In addition to a gymnasium, GSA also has extensive athletic fields where teams play baseball, soccer, and softball.

EXTRACURRICULAR OPPORTUNITIES
There are more than twenty-five clubs and activities for students at GSA. Some of the clubs include Amnesty International, Chamber Music Ensemble, Chess Team, Drama Club, Environmental Action Club, French Club, International Cooking Club, Jazz Band, Jazz Combo, Literary Magazine, Math Team, Model United Nations, National Honor Society, Outing Club, Spanish Club, Student Council, and Yearbook.

GSA sponsors an annual Arts Festival, a three-day event that celebrates arts in all its forms and allows students to show parents and friends their special accomplishments. Every year, students can take part in three days of studio-based learning at Haystack Mountain School of Crafts, which attracts some of the finest craftspeople in the nation. The Academy also offers numerous opportunities to participate in sports, performing arts, community service, and other interests.

DAILY LIFE
The school day begins at 8 a.m. and ends at 2:35 p.m., with a 15-minute break at 9:20 and a 45-minute lunch beginning at 12:15. The Academy runs on an eight-period schedule. Each eight-period cycle lasts two days. Each day is divided into four periods, which are 75 minutes in length. Students may spend one of these periods in a study hall, and juniors and seniors may have the opportunity to explore an academic or vocational interest through a self-designed, two-week course of study.

WEEKEND LIFE
Students can spend their weekends in the Blue Hill Peninsula, which is known for its traditional, coastal fishing and boatbuilding history. More recently, it has become a haven for writers, painters, sculptors, and musicians. The village of Blue Hill offers shops, art galleries, pottery studios, and restaurants. Throughout the year, there are opportunities to attend or participate in classical, jazz, steel drum, and choral concerts. The Blue Hill Library hosts Friday movie nights. Students can walk along the beach, hike up Blue Hill Mountain, go canoeing and kayaking, take a bike ride through blueberry fields, kick a soccer ball in the park, and browse local shops and bookstores. In the winter, there are plenty of chances for ice-skating, cross-country skiing, and downhill skiing. Chaperoned weekend trips may include shopping, movies, or bowling in nearby Ellsworth or Bangor; visits to Acadia National Park and Bar Harbor; whale watching; and cultural visits to Portland and Boston. Blue Hill is an hour's drive from Acadia National Park or the Camden Snow Bowl, 3 hours from Portland or Sugarloaf Mountain, and 5 hours from Boston.

COSTS AND FINANCIAL AID
The Academy admits almost any student from Blue Hill or a neighboring town that does not have its own high school as well as international students and students from nonsupporting towns who are open to new challenges and experiences. The homestay tuition of $29,500 per year includes tuition, the stipend for host families, book rental, and most regular school activities. The boarding tuition is $32,500 and includes tuition, room and board, book rental, and most regular school activities. Participation in the English as a second language course costs $1500 per semester. Students requiring health insurance must pay $600 per year, and all students are required to pay a $500 general deposit for emergency expenses.

ADMISSIONS INFORMATION
George Stevens Academy admits students of any race, religion, gender, national origin, or sexual orientation to the rights, privileges, programs, and activities available to students at the school. GSA does not discriminate in the administration of its educational policies, admissions policies, or any other programs administered by the school. Admission is based on the candidate's transcript, application essay, recommendations, and, when possible, PSAT, SSAT, TOEFL, or SLEP scores. GSA's Admissions Committee carefully screens all applicants to determine their level of maturity, academic competency, and ability to function successfully in the GSA community.

APPLICATION TIMETABLE
A $50 nonrefundable processing fee is required at the time of application. A campus visit and interview are highly recommended for all applicants. Telephone interviews are arranged for candidates who are unable to visit. GSA has a rolling admissions policy, which means that applications are accepted throughout the school year and summer. However, candidates are encouraged to complete the application process by April 15. An admissions decision is made within three weeks of receipt of the application.

ADMISSIONS CORRESPONDENCE
Sheryl Stearns
International Program Director
George Stevens Academy
23 Union Street
Blue Hill, Maine 04614
Phone: 207-374-2808 Ext. 134
Fax: 207-374-2982
E-mail: s.stearns@georgestevens.org
Web site: http://www.georgestevensacademy.org

GILL ST. BERNARD'S SCHOOL

Gladstone, New Jersey

Type: Coed college-preparatory day school
Grades: Pre-K–12
Enrollment: 680
Head of School: Sidney A. Rowell, Headmaster

THE SCHOOL

Located on 72 breathtaking acres in central New Jersey, Gill St. Bernard's School (GSB) is an independent, nonsectarian college-preparatory day school for students in prekindergarten through grade 12. GSB teaches students to become engaged, thoughtful learners and responsible citizens and leaders in their communities, the nation, and the world. The School strives to foster academic and extracurricular excellence in every student inside and outside the classroom. In all aspects of life, GSB values integrity, compassion, and respect for others.

The School is the result of the merger of two Somerset Hills institutions, St. Bernard's School for boys in Gladstone and the Gill School for girls in Bernardsville. Today, the collegiate-style setting includes three separate divisions—a Lower, a Middle, and an Upper School—located on 72 acres that span the Somerset–Morris County line between the Borough of Peapack-Gladstone and Chester Township. GSB offers each student a meaningful academic program and solid preparation for college study, supported by the School's extraordinary sense of community and the students' respect for one another. Students participate broadly in athletic, community service, and extracurricular options. They benefit from the dedication of a talented, highly qualified faculty, a global learning perspective, a cutting-edge research program, and Unit Study experiences. GSB students graduate as well-spoken, goal-oriented people who find success in higher education and who are able to think critically and analytically, act with integrity and compassion, and embrace their role as responsible citizens of the world.

ACADEMIC PROGRAMS

GSB offers an excellent curriculum with small classes and dedicated teachers and advisers. Honors and Advanced Placement courses are available, and a broad range of athletic and other extracurricular offerings enhance the curriculum at all levels.

The Lower School is divided into the early childhood years (prekindergarten and kindergarten) and the elementary years (grades 1–4). The goal of the early childhood program is to instill in each child a sense that learning is exciting and that he or she has the ability to achieve academic and personal success. The early childhood curriculum provides a balanced day, including structured academic work periods, adequate developmental play, and a variety of music and art experiences. Small classes allow teachers the opportunity to closely monitor their students' academic and personal progress. During the elementary years, a traditional academic program and skill development are the primary concerns. An integrated curriculum encourages each child to become an independent learner, develop thinking skills, and enjoy learning. Social problem-solving skills, such as cooperation and building positive relationships with peers and adults, are emphasized.

The Middle School curriculum is designed to build confidence and competence. Class sizes average 15 students, encouraging interaction between teachers and students. By the time they leave Middle School, students are well grounded in the academic skills necessary to succeed in the increasingly rigorous Upper School program and have developed a positive sense of who they are and what they can accomplish.

The goal of Gill St. Bernard's Upper School is to prepare students for academic success in college and create a strong desire for lifelong learning. Students have ample opportunity to participate in the rich and varied college-preparatory curriculum, with Advanced Placement sections in eleven subject areas and numerous honors-level courses in each department. Students are encouraged to select courses that are rigorous and enable them to pursue specific areas of interest in addition to building an academic record of achievement in the traditional college-preparatory curriculum.

The GSB Scholars Program is designed to challenge the highest-achieving and most intellectually curious Upper School students. GSB Scholars are expected to be school leaders in a full range of School activities. During the school year, Scholars assume several distinct roles and responsibilities and participate in activities designed solely for the GSB Scholars Program. They attend cultural events and other learning opportunities, such as theatrical performances and museum visits. Scholars also act as tutors for other GSB students and define an area of academic interest that culminates in a senior thesis project. Scholars enter the program in ninth grade; status is renewed annually. Membership in the program includes a $5000 annual merit scholarship.

FACULTY AND ADVISERS

There are 93 faculty members and administrators; 64 percent of the Upper School faculty members have advanced degrees, as do 54 percent of the Middle School and 34 percent of the Lower School instructors. GSB's 9:1 student-teacher ratio results in an average class size of 14 to 16 students, promoting student participation and learning. When teachers know students well, high academic expectations and success result.

COLLEGE ADMISSION COUNSELING

Gill St. Bernard's School is a college-preparatory school, sending 100 percent of its graduating seniors to college. The philosophy of the GSB college guidance program is to find the right school for every student by offering personalized attention to each student and family. The School has an impressive record for admission of its students to many of the most competitive colleges and universities in the country. In addition to 100 percent acceptance of 2008 seniors into colleges of their choice, other notable honors include a National Achievement Finalist, National Merit Commended Students, Edward Bloustein Distinguished Scholars, and the New Jersey Independent School Athletic Association Male Scholar Athlete of the Year.

STUDENT BODY AND CONDUCT

GSB attracts students from a 40-mile radius, who have diverse ethnic, socioeconomic, religious, and geographic backgrounds representing eleven New Jersey counties.

ACADEMIC FACILITIES

The campus is composed of sixteen buildings in Somerset and Morris Counties in central New Jersey. The collegiate-style setting includes separate Lower, Middle, and Upper School buildings; a gymnasium; an athletic center; a theater/art gallery; a woodshop; art studios; and various administrative buildings. Other sports facilities include five all-weather tennis courts, indoor and outdoor tracks, two full-size basketball courts, and professional soccer and ball fields.

ATHLETICS

In the spirit of healthy competition, athletes at all levels are expected to strive to win, as a winning tradition is one measurement of success and can invigorate an entire community. GSB recognizes, however, that success is not exclusively a function of winning, and all student athletes work toward team goals and conduct themselves with honor, integrity, and sportsmanship at all times. It is a philosophy and approach that complements the educational process, mission, and overall environment of Gill St. Bernard's School. GSB fields teams in baseball, basketball, cross-country, fencing, golf, ice hockey, soccer, softball, track and field, and tennis. The School is a member of the New Jersey State Interscholastic Athletic Association (NJSIAA) and the New Jersey Independent Schools Athletic Association (NJISAA). In recent years, GSB has won several conference titles and state championships.

EXTRACURRICULAR OPPORTUNITIES

Most students at GSB participate broadly in extracurricular offerings. In this way, new interests can be cultivated, new talents developed, and new friends made. A wide variety of extracurricular activities is available for Middle and Upper School students in the areas of the arts, community service, student government, academics, and sports. In grades 9–11, students are required to participate in at least one activity each year; nearly all continue in their senior year.

DAILY LIFE

The school day is from 8:15 to 3, Monday through Friday. Each student is issued a copy of the class schedule in September. The prekindergarten program includes a choice of five half days, three half days and two full days, or five full days. Kindergarten is a full-day program that runs five days a week. GSB offers an extended-day program of supervised play, special activities, and homework for students in kindergarten through the fourth grade. Supervised study hall is available until 5:30 for Middle School students. Extracurricular activities and team sports meet from 3:30 to 5:15.

SUMMER PROGRAMS

GSB has a full slate of summer programs for children of all ages—camps, academic programs, and sports. Two summer camps are offered for children ages 4–14. Mega-Fun Camp runs the last two weeks of June, and Hi-Hills Camp has eight-, six-, and four-week sessions; both camps offer an extended-day option. A variety of other summer programs are available.

COSTS AND FINANCIAL AID

Tuition ranges between $13,600 for the five-half-days-a-week prekindergarten program to $25,700 for students in grades 9–12. Tuition covers lunch and student accident insurance. A $100 fee is charged to all Lower School students to help cover the cost of workbooks and textbooks supplied by the School. A $250 to $350 fee is charged to all Middle and Upper School students to help cover the costs of some trips, yearbooks, and orientation programs. Purchases made at the School store, books for Middle and Upper School students, athletic equipment, special field trips, and other expenses are billed on a monthly basis as they occur. More information is available online.

Financial aid is awarded on an annual basis to qualified students grades 7 through 12 and is based on information provided by the parents and the School and Student Service for Financial Aid (SSS). Financial aid applications are mailed to families who request them and are typically mailed in early December. The Parent Financial Statement (PFS) should be completed and mailed to SSS by February 1. A copy of the parents' tax returns and a copy of all form W2s should be submitted to the Admission Office by March 1. GSB also offers the Key Education Resources monthly payment plan. The plan enables families to make tuition payments in monthly installments without interest charges.

ADMISSIONS INFORMATION

The admission process provides the School with an opportunity to get to know each child and helps parents and applicants learn about Gill St. Bernard's School. GSB seeks motivated, intellectually capable students who are eager to learn and take advantage of the many opportunities the School offers. Before applying, a student must make a day visit to the GSB classrooms, and a parent or guardian must visit the campus and complete an interview by an admission associate. Applicants must submit the completed application, the $75 application fee, an official school transcript of grades (including standardized test scores), and recommendations from current teachers. In addition, for grades 5–12, a writing sample (an essay done at home on an assigned topic) and a completed student questionnaire are required.

APPLICATION TIMETABLE

Interviews, tours, and student visits begin in mid- to late September. The application deadline for grades 5–12 is January 26, whereas applications for grades pre-K–4 are due February 2. Admission decisions are mailed around February 26 for grades pre-K–4 and in early March for grades 5–12.

ADMISSIONS CORRESPONDENCE

Karen Loder, M.Ed., Director of Admission and Financial Assistance
Gill St. Bernard's School
St. Bernard's Road
Gladstone, New Jersey 07934
Phone: 908-234-1611 Ext. 245
E-mail: kloder@gsbschool.org
Web site: http://www.gsbschool.org/

GOULD ACADEMY

GouldAcademy

Bethel, Maine

Type: Coeducational boarding and day college-preparatory school
Grades: 9–12, postgraduate year
Enrollment: 244
Head of School: Daniel A. Kunkle

THE SCHOOL

Founded in 1836, Gould Academy is a coeducational boarding school small enough to know each student well and large enough to provide appropriate levels of challenge and support to the individual within a rigorous college preparatory curriculum. Gould graduates consistently go on to find success at college and in life after college.

Gould believes that the seven-day boarding school is the ideal environment for inspiring a love of ideas and learning while developing social and intellectual confidence in each individual. By exposing students to all the benefits of a liberal arts education, Gould strives to develop leaders who are physically and morally sound, intellectually curious, and tempered by experience.

A small student-teacher ratio allows for students to know and develop adult relationships with teachers who challenge and support them to achieve their individual academic best while pursuing their passions. Gould's Academic Skills Program provides additional support to students with an identified learning difference or those who could benefit from improved study habits.

Gould's location at the eastern edge of the White Mountains fosters an appreciation for the outdoors, while the Academy's aggressive integration of technology prepares students for lives in an increasingly complex global society. Gould students benefit from the growing cultural and artistic offerings spurred by Bethel's growth as a close neighbor of Sunday River Ski Resort, one of the Northeast's largest ski destinations only 6 miles from the campus.

The Gould campus is 1.5 hours northwest of Portland and 3.5 hours north of Boston by car. Chartered buses carry students between the school and both the Portland International Jetport and Boston's Logan International Airport.

The Academy is governed by 29 trustees, 12 of whom are Gould graduates. The physical plant is valued at $43 million, and the school's endowment is $13.3 million. In 2007–08, the annual fund raised more than $600,000 in contributions from parents, friends, and an alumni body of 4,500.

Gould Academy is accredited by the New England Association of Schools and Colleges. It is a member of the Association of Boarding Schools, the National Association of Independent Schools, the Association of Independent Schools in New England, the Independent Schools Association of Northern New England, the Secondary Schools Admission Test Board, and the Educational Records Bureau.

ACADEMIC PROGRAMS

Gould's primary academic objective is to prepare academically motivated students for college and help them become independent-minded, ethical citizens who will lead lives of purpose, action, excellence, and compassion in a dynamic world. The academic program is designed to meet students where they are and challenge them to achieve their full potential. Three values at the heart of any Gould endeavor are the energy to try, willingness to risk, and capacity to persevere. All courses stress writing, analysis, and problem solving, and certain departments concentrate on research and oral presentation. All new students in grades 11 and 12 must enroll in an expository writing course in their first trimester.

To graduate, a Gould student must earn at least 18 credits and satisfy departmental requirements, including 4 years of English, 3 years of mathematics, 3 years of history, 3 years of a foreign language, and 2 years of laboratory science. These requirements broaden students intellectually and prepare them for the most rigorous colleges.

Departments offer elective courses designed to give breadth and allow students to pursue a subject in depth in the junior and senior years. Electives range from art courses like Design, Printmaking, and Silversmithing to science courses like Environmental Science, Astronomy, and Advanced Placement (AP) Electricity and Magnetism. English electives such as Creative Writing and Native American Story provide work in literary analysis, while trimester courses in robotics, networking, and the Linux operating system expose students to leading-edge technologies.

At Gould, an average class has 10 students. The grading system is numerical; 60 is passing, 85–91 is Honors, and 92 and above is High Honors. Grades and teachers' comments are sent home six times a year and are also available to parents at all times via private login on the school's Web site. Gould participates in the National Honor Society.

Advanced Placement courses are offered in every core subject area, with an average of seven AP courses available at any time. A wide variety of honors courses are also available. Students who wish to do in-depth work in a discipline may pursue an independent study program in lieu of a fifth course. Upper-level foreign language students participate in international travel as a supplement to their course work.

For the last twenty years, the Four Point Program has served as an integral aspect of the Gould educational experience, providing a unique experiential learning opportunity for each class every March. Ninth graders travel abroad to experience homestays in countries such as Germany, Hungary, and China. Sophomores remain on campus immersed in projects that expand their understanding of community, arts, and the local environment. In what is one of the most anticipated Gould experiences, juniors spend eight days hiking, snowshoeing, and camping in the nearby, snow-covered White Mountains. Bolstered by their previous Four Point experiences, seniors create their own projects off campus that reflect their academic or personal interests or professional goals.

FACULTY AND ADVISERS

Of the 44 members of the faculty, 2 have doctorates and 20 hold master's degrees. Twenty-one are men and 23 are women.

Daniel A. Kunkle was appointed Head of School in 2001 and resides on campus with his wife. Mr. Kunkle received his B.A. from Brown University and holds an M.Ed. from Harvard University. Prior to coming to Gould, Mr. Kunkle spent ten years as Head of the Midland School in Los Olivos, California, where he also taught mathematics and physics. He was at Mercersburg Academy in Pennsylvania for thirteen years, where he served as a mathematics teacher, dormitory head, and Academic Dean.

Gould selects teachers who have a genuine interest in young people and have special talents that they wish to share with community members. Every faculty member also serves as a member of the residential faculty, as a coach, or as an adviser.

COLLEGE ADMISSION COUNSELING

For Gould students, college preparation begins with the selection of their very first classes, which paves the way for their entire academic curriculum. Gould's wide variety of course offerings allows students to explore diverse fields and discover their individual passions, intellectual interests, and academic talents.

College Counselors at Gould use their substantial knowledge about specific colleges and programs to ensure that students are optimally connected. The college counseling process at Gould Academy is a four-year partnership, beginning when students enter in the ninth grade.

Throughout the year, the college counselors offer workshops on athletic recruiting, interviewing, college essay writing, and making college visits. Gould also holds parent meetings during each of the three Parents' Weekends, with an entire program each spring devoted to the college search and application process.

Schools Gould students find to be a good fit include Bates, Berkeley, Colorado at Boulder, Colorado College, Dartmouth, Emory, Lewis and Clark, MIT, Rhode Island School of Design, St. Lawrence, Tufts, and University of Vermont.

STUDENT BODY AND CONDUCT

For 2008–09, 50 ninth graders, 59 sophomores, 71 juniors, 65 seniors, and 3 postgraduates were enrolled. This included 181 boarding students and 67 day students. While 40 percent are from Maine, students come from all over the United States and the world, with twelve different countries represented. Gould enrolls students from various socioeconomic backgrounds.

Gould has a clear disciplinary code, and students understand that major rule infractions, including drinking and use of any form of illegal drugs, are grounds for dismissal. Tobacco is not permitted, and the health staff runs educational programs on smoking and smokeless tobacco each year. Gould prefers to encourage discussions of the issues that face young people today, from AIDS and drugs to other problems of human interaction.

ACADEMIC FACILITIES

All classrooms except those for art, music, science, and drama are located in Hanscom Hall, which houses a library of 13,000 volumes, a darkroom for black-and-white photography, and twenty classrooms. The McLaughlin Science Center houses state-of-the-art laboratories, prep rooms, a science library, a greenhouse, and a lecture auditorium that seats sixty people. A widely distributed switched network hosts powerful workstations and connects all school buildings, including dormitories, where each dorm resident has a network port available.

The Art Cottage houses extensive facilities for working in a wide variety of mediums, many of which are uncommon at the high school level. The pottery resources include fifteen wheels, a glaze room, a bisque kiln, a 60-cubic-foot car kiln, and a wood-fired kiln. There are separate studios for printmaking, painting and design, photography (color and black and white), silversmithing, and blacksmithing. The James B. Owen Gallery displays five shows each year, including one by students and four by professionals; recent displays of work by Subhankar Banerjee, Peter Spadone '73, Jamie Wyeth, and Andrew Wyeth as well as local artisans contribute to the gallery's growing reputation.

Drama, music, and dance classes are held in the Bingham Auditorium complex, which includes a 500-seat theater with a professional stage, lighting board, practice space for instrumental and vocal music, and a musical instrument digital interface (MIDI) lab where students learn about arranging, sound synthesis, and remixing, while producing their own musical compositions and videos.

BOARDING AND GENERAL FACILITIES

Boarding students are housed in three dormitories. Gehring Hall houses 68 girls in double rooms. Holden Hall houses 50 boys in double and single rooms. Davidson Hall, which accommodates 66 boys, is arranged in suites of three rooms shared by 4 students each. Each dormitory has laundry facilities.

Registered nurses supervise the eight-bed health center. Doctors are on call through the local health center.

ATHLETICS

The Gould athletic program guarantees each student the opportunity to aim for excellence, face challenge, and build self-confidence. The talented coaching staff, most of whom are full-time faculty members, work diligently to provide a program focused on the enhancement of Gould student leadership, teamwork, commitment, positive communication, and sportsmanship. In addition, Gould offers a wide variety of wellness and wilderness programs that promote lifetime fitness and health.

All students must be on an interscholastic team or participate in other organized activities each season; one team sport is required per year for ninth graders and sophomores, while juniors and seniors must be involved in at least one trimester of a competitive sport or a wellness program.

Each team sport maintains a full competitive schedule with schools throughout the state and region. Interscholastic basketball, cycling, cross-country, equestrian, golf, lacrosse, mountain biking, running, skateboarding, skiing, snowboarding, soccer, and tennis are available for both boys and girls. Field hockey and softball are additional options for girls, and baseball is available for boys.

Gould is proud to offer the finest competitive ski and snowboarding program in the Northeast, which includes world-class training opportunities in competitive alpine and Nordic skiing, snowboarding, freeride, freestyle, and ski instructing and ski patrol certification. The Gould Academy Competition Center is located slopeside at Sunday River Ski Resort and serves as the winter home for Gould's Competitive On-Snow Program.

Farnsworth Field House contains two indoor tennis courts, a fitness center, a training room, a basketball court, an indoor skate park, a ropes course, a trampoline for USSA members, a team room for "chalk talks," and full locker room facilities. There are five outdoor fields, a synthetic turf field, six all-weather tennis courts, and 40 kilometers of groomed cross-country ski trails on the campus.

EXTRACURRICULAR OPPORTUNITIES

The theater department presents three major productions each year. The fall and winter productions are both full-scale events that range from Shakespeare to contemporary. The spring musical includes a full pit ensemble. The student choral group performs numbers from Bach to rock several times each year. Students may also join the band or a smaller jazz or brass ensemble. Private vocal and instrumental lessons are arranged according to students' schedules and abilities.

Throughout the year, faculty members run outdoor excursions on weekends, including hikes, canoeing, fly-fishing, rock climbing, and backcountry skiing in Tuckerman's Ravine.

As part of its On-Snow Program, Gould is one of the only schools in the country to offer a National Ski Patrol certification course. Students also take part in the "Rug Rats" ski instruction program, where they work with elementary and middle school students from the Bethel area.

The Farm and Forest program offers students hands-on agriculture and forestry experience. Members compete in woodsmen's competitions, tap trees to make maple syrup, and plant an organic vegetable garden. In addition, they help tend the sheep, goats, chickens, pigs, and draft horses that live in the Gould Academy barn.

Gould has a number of service-based clubs including Reach Out and the Interact Club (part of Rotary International). Students involved in Blue Key help out the Admissions Office, and those in Gold Key assist Gould's Development Office. Other clubs and activities include a literary magazine, peer tutoring, many academic clubs, and *The Herald*, a student-run yearbook overseen by a faculty sponsor. New clubs are formed each year based on student interest.

DAILY LIFE

The class day begins with a community assembly in the auditorium at 7:45. Classes are 90 minutes in length allowing in-depth inquiry in the humanities and social sciences and laboratory sessions in science courses. On Wednesdays, classes end at lunch for an extended sports and activities period in the afternoon. Classes are held on occasional Saturday mornings throughout the year. Athletics and other physical activities are scheduled every weekday afternoon. There is supervised study time every school night from 7 to 9; appropriate homework is assigned based on the course and grade level. Typically, students can expect 30 to 60 minutes of homework for each class. The academic schedule changes during the winter trimester to increase the time outside during the daylight hours.

WEEKEND LIFE

Weekend activities on campus include movies, concerts, dances, and coffeehouses. Many faculty members have get-togethers in their homes. There are frequent trips into the mountains for hiking, canoeing, or snowshoeing. Each weekend there is at least one off-campus trip to a nearby city for shopping and movies. Several special excursions are made to larger urban centers, such as Boston, New York City, and Quebec City. All students may spend a limited number of weekends off campus, but most remain on campus each weekend. All students are required to remain on campus during occasional "closed" weekends.

SUMMER PROGRAMS

Gould Academy hosts the Bethel Camp for the Arts, two different soccer camps, and dry-land training camps for on-snow competitors.

COSTS AND FINANCIAL AID

Boarding student tuition for the 2008–09 school year was $41,500. Day student tuition was $24,500. Bookstore charges amount to approximately $800 a year.

Forty percent of the students receive financial aid, which totaled more than $1.42 million for the 2007–08 school year. Financial aid is offered to qualified students based on financial need. Information regarding financial aid may be obtained from the Admissions Office.

ADMISSIONS INFORMATION

Admission to Gould is selective. The school looks for students who are likely to benefit from what the school offers and who will actively contribute to the life of the Gould community.

As guidelines for admission, the school uses those characteristics that have in the past led students to be most successful at Gould. They include a solid record of academic achievement, the potential for continued academic success, an interest in learning from the school's environment and extracurricular activities, sound moral character emphasizing honesty and caring for others, vitality, a developing self-confidence, and the potential for leadership. The school also considers a thoughtful, well-written application and the applicant's personal statement.

Gould recommends that all applicants take the SSAT. Parents are urged to bring candidates for an interview while school is in session, although visitors are welcome throughout the year. The admissions office can suggest accommodations in the Bethel vicinity and can arrange for lift tickets for skiers at Sunday River Ski Resort, 6 miles from campus.

APPLICATION TIMETABLE

As a member of the Secondary School Admission Test Board, Gould abides by the acceptance and response dates established by that organization. Students should apply by February 1 to be considered in the regular admissions process and are notified of the school's decision on March 10. Candidates have until April 10 to reply. After that date, a rolling admissions plan is in effect, and parents are notified of the decision as soon as the file is complete. There is a $30 application fee for residents of the U.S.; $60 for those living abroad.

ADMISSIONS CORRESPONDENCE

Todd Ormiston, Director of Admissions
Gould Academy
P.O. Box 860
Bethel, Maine 04217
Phone: 207-824-7777
Fax: 207-824-2926
E-mail: admissions@gouldacademy.org
Web site: http://www.gouldacademy.org

GRIGGS UNIVERSITY AND GRIGGS INTERNATIONAL ACADEMY

Silver Spring, Maryland

Type: Christian distance education school
Grades: Preschool–college
Enrollment: 1,878
Head of School: Dr. Donald R. Sahly, President

THE SCHOOL

At the beginning of the twentieth century, correspondence education was increasing in popularity within the United States. An educator by the name of Frederick Griggs envisioned educating people around the world. Within the context of the Seventh-day Adventist school system, his vision took shape in 1909 with the establishment of the Fireside Correspondence School. The goal was to provide the benefits of an education to those who were unable to attend traditional schools. Within two years, the Fireside Correspondence School offered eleven secondary and nine college courses. By 1916, its students represented nearly every state and province in the U.S. and Canada, as well as ten other countries. The Fireside Correspondence School was later renamed Home Study Institute (HSI); the name was subsequently changed to Home Study International.

In 1990, the HSI Board of Directors assigned names to its three academic divisions; thus, Home Study Elementary School, Home Study High School, and Griggs University became part of HSI's terminology. In 1991, Griggs University began offering college degrees.

In recent years, the home-school movement has exploded, but the term "home school" has taken on special meaning for school districts and families who design their own school programs. Pressure from overseas affiliations drove the HSI Board of Directors to reexamine the school's name and determine something that better reflected the mission and operation of HSI. In 2005, the board voted to change the name of the organization to Griggs University (GU) and Griggs International Academy (GIA).

Since 1909, more than a quarter of a million people have studied with Griggs University and Griggs International Academy. Griggs plays a unique and vital role in the educational development of students of all ages in all parts of the world. People from all walks of life have discovered that the quiet conditions of private correspondence study help develop self-reliance, independent thinking, and responsibility. From its humble beginnings in a one-room office, Griggs has grown into a worldwide school that maintains high scholastic standards and utilizes the services of qualified professionals in all phases of its operation, yet Griggs maintains a personal touch in its student-teacher relationships.

In addition, GU/GIA also helps fill in the educational gaps in private traditional schools with programs such as the Alternative Program for Learning Enrichment (APLE), which helps small private schools augment their course offerings.

Griggs International Academy is regionally accredited by the Southern Association of Colleges and Schools (SACS) Commissions on Elementary, Middle, and Secondary Schools and the Middle States Association of Colleges and Schools (MSA) Commission on Elementary Schools. Griggs is also accredited by the Commission on International and Trans-Regional Accreditation (CITA), the Accrediting Commission of the Distance Education and Training Council (DETC), and the Accrediting Association of Seventh-day Adventist Schools, Colleges, and Universities (AAA). GIA is approved by the Maryland State Department of Education for Kindergarten, Elementary, and High School.

ACADEMIC PROGRAMS

GIA offers both a basic high school diploma and a college-preparatory diploma. The basic diploma requires 21 Carnegie units, which must include 4 units of English, 3 units of math, 3 units of social studies (one of which must be American history), 2 units of science, and 4 units of Bible study (students may be excused from the Bible requirement if their personal convictions and familial belief systems so dictate). One half-credit is given toward a Griggs diploma for a student who has taken driver's education.

The college-preparatory diploma requires 24 units, including those listed for the basic diploma plus an additional unit in science and 2 units of a language.

Each Griggs International Academy course comes equipped with a "teacher on paper"—the course study guide. The study guide includes all learning objectives, instructional sections, reading assignments, supplemental information, self-diagnostic tools, and lessons/submissions. The student also receives a full set of supplies, including a textbook and, sometimes, cassettes, CDs, lab equipment, and reading supplements. Experienced teachers are assigned to each course to provide positive, individual interaction with students. Students may be given phone numbers or e-mail addresses for the teachers of individual courses.

For most courses, two examinations are required each semester—a midterm and a semester examination. All examinations must be supervised by a school or community official (such as a teacher or registrar) or by a responsible adult who is not related to the student. If a student is enrolled in another school while taking GIA courses, the examinations should be taken under the direction of that school's registrar or testing department. Final grades are issued as A, B, C, D, or F. At the high school level, pluses and minuses (e.g., B+ and B–) are also used.

Because GIA's high school program offers year-round registration and self-paced instruction, students may adapt their class schedules to meet learning needs. The structure of the instructional materials engenders self-discipline and motivation as well as academic excellence.

Since July 2003, Griggs International Academy has been offering high school courses online. Available courses are listed on the Griggs Web site.

FACULTY AND ADVISERS

The writers for GIA courses are exceptional professionals in their specialties, and most hold degrees at the master's or doctoral level. The courses are intellectually stimulating and designed to foster academic excellence. Griggs has 1 full-time and 62 part-time faculty members. In addition, 18 full-time nonteaching professionals provide assistance to students and teachers. Of Griggs' 63 teachers (25 women and 38 men), 45 have advanced degrees.

Dr. Alayne Thorpe, the vice president for education, has been with Griggs University and International Academy since 1980. Dr. Thorpe has taught in the Maryland state public school system and at the University of Maryland. She has served as a master teacher, a curriculum supervisor, and a writing consultant. Dr. Thorpe holds a Ph.D. from the University of Maryland.

Faculty members are chosen on the basis of their expertise in their disciplines and their ability to counsel, advise, and instruct an international, multicultural student body.

COLLEGE ADMISSION COUNSELING

Graduates of GIA attend colleges and universities throughout the world. The Advisory Teacher, the Registrar, the Associate Vice President for Education, and the Vice President for Education provide guidance counseling and college placement information to all interested students.

STUDENT BODY AND CONDUCT

Griggs International Academy's elementary and high school enrollment is approximately 2,000 students in grades kindergarten through 12. Because Griggs is not limited to a traditional school year, enrollment figures may shift slightly from month to month as new students enroll and others finish their programs. Griggs also provides opportunities for supplementing and augmenting programs for students attending traditional secondary schools.

In 2005–06, the GIA student body consisted of students from every state in the United States as well as thirty other countries.

DAILY LIFE

GIA students progress at their own speed. This allows most students to finish the study portion of their day early. The rest of the day is available to reinforce what is being learned or to expand upon one's studies. The student is not held back by a classroom of other students who learn at various levels.

Full-time Griggs students can enjoy intramural sports groups and have extra time to use the library, museums, and other learning centers near their homes.

On average, full-time students spend 4 to 5 hours a day on their studies.

COSTS AND FINANCIAL AID

GIA offers two options (grades K–8)—the Accredited Plan and the Non-Accredited Plan.

The Accredited Plan is state approved and includes tuition, textbooks and study guides, daily lesson plans, exams, teacher assistance, grading services, record keeping, report cards, and transcript services. The 2008–09 prices for all subjects for one full year (the nonrefundable shipping/handling fee and $10 enrollment fee) are preschool, $79; kindergarten, $294; grade 1, $981; grade 2, $963; grade 3, $1071; grade 4, $985; grade 5, $1129; and grade 6, $1040.

The junior high program (grades 7 and 8) allows for more immediate interaction between parent and student. The prices for the four core courses, including shipping and an $80 enrollment fee, are $1008 for grade 7 and $1018 for grade 8 in 2008–09.

The 2008–09 high school tuition prices are $196 per semester per course plus the cost of supplies, an $80 enrollment fee, and shipping. An additional technology fee of $35 per semester applies for all online courses. College tuition is $295 per semester hour plus the cost of supplies, an $80 enrollment fee, and shipping.

The Non-Accredited Plan (K–8 only) is for those who do not choose to use Griggs International Academy's teaching, grading, advising, or record-keeping services. However, this plan does offer guides/activity sheets/tests (no answer keys for tests) and placement advising for the student if necessary. Prices for the Non-Accredited Plan are substantially lower. Financial aid is not available. All prices are subject to change July 1 of each year. For the 2008–09 school year, costs are preschool, $79; kindergarten, $188; grade 1, $717; grade 2, $666; grade 3, $769; grade 4, $696; grade 5, $806; and grade 6, $735.

ADMISSIONS INFORMATION

Griggs accepts applications for admission at any time. Applications/enrollments can now be completed online through the Griggs Web site.

ADMISSIONS CORRESPONDENCE

Joan Wilson, Director of Admissions/Registrar
Griggs University and Griggs International Academy
12501 Old Columbia Pike
Silver Spring, Maryland 20904
Phone: 301-680-6570
800-782-4769 (toll-free; enrollment inquiries only)
E-mail: enrollmentservices@griggs.edu
Web site: http://www.griggs.edu

GROTON SCHOOL

Groton, Massachusetts

Type: Coeducational boarding and day college-preparatory school
Grades: 8–12: Lower School, Forms II and III; Upper School, Forms IV–VI
Enrollment: School total: 358; Upper School: 247
Head of School: Richard B. Commons, Headmaster

THE SCHOOL

Groton was founded in 1884 by the Reverend Endicott Peabody as a school whose aims were the intellectual, moral, and physical development of its students in preparation not only for college but also for "the active work of life." While the means of achieving these aims have changed, the aims themselves continue to govern a Groton education, and many of the original practices of the School have become valued traditions.

While Groton does not hold as its exclusive goal the preparation of students for college, it does offer a curriculum that prepares students for the most demanding of college environments. Groton is by design a small school, enabling the School community to gather together daily and to develop close personal relationships. As students adjust to life at Groton, they come to appreciate less the emblems of success and more the personal qualities of peers and faculty members. A notable characteristic of Groton is the expectation of leadership. All students are expected to grow into positions of leadership in the School, and, traditionally, every member of the Sixth Form has been a prefect of the School, with particular responsibilities in almost every aspect of School life.

The School is 40 miles northwest of Boston and a little more than a mile from the town of Groton. Its location permits the students the freedom of country life along with the accessibility of Boston and its museums, plays, concerts, and sports events. The 390-acre campus includes fields and woodlands as well as the academic buildings and dormitories that are grouped around the lawn of the Circle.

A not-for-profit corporation, Groton is governed by a 25-member Board of Trustees. The endowment is currently valued at more than $290 million and is supplemented by an Annual Fund that totaled more than $2.5 million last year. This generous support comes from parents, friends, and an alumni body of more than 3,500.

Groton is accredited by the New England Association of Schools and Colleges and is affiliated with the National Association of Independent Schools, the Independent School Association of Massachusetts, the Council for Religion in Independent Schools, and the Secondary School Admission Test Board.

ACADEMIC PROGRAMS

The Groton curriculum is predicated on the belief that certain qualities are of major importance: to be able to reason carefully and logically and to think imaginatively and sensitively, to have a command of precise and articulate communication, to be able to compute accurately and reason quantitatively, to have a grasp of scientific approaches to problem solving, to be able to identify and develop creative talents, and to acquire an understanding of the cultural, social, scientific, and political background of Western and non-Western civilizations. Students in the Second, Third, and Fourth Forms are, therefore, introduced to a wide variety of courses that draw on interests and capabilities that might otherwise be unchallenged. Older students have choices among elective courses, independent studies, off-campus projects, and concentrations in specific areas of interest.

Minimum graduation requirements include a Lower School and an Upper School science course; English, through expository writing in the Sixth Form year; mathematics, through trigonometry; American history and European history; biblical studies and ethics; a Lower and an Upper School arts course; and three years through the end of Fifth Form in either French, Greek, Latin, or Spanish. Students joining Groton in eighth or ninth grade take two years of Latin in addition to their modern language.

At Groton, an average class contains between 10 and 14 students. The mathematics and language courses are sectioned on the basis of interest and ability, and Advanced Placement courses are offered in every discipline. The minimum course load for Upper Schoolers is 5 credits each term; most students take 6 or 6½. The grading system is numerical, with 60 being a passing grade and 85 or above, honors. Grades, along with teachers' comments and a letter from the faculty adviser, are sent home three times a year.

FACULTY AND ADVISERS

The Groton teaching faculty consists of 84 full- and part-time members (35 women and 49 men). The Headmaster, who was appointed in 2003, is a graduate of the University of Virginia and Stanford University (M.A.) and holds an M.A. from Middlebury College's Bread Loaf School of English.

In selecting its faculty, Groton looks for individuals who are excited by their subject, who enjoy working with adolescents, who involve themselves in the nonacademic life of a residential school, and who have lively interests of their own. Every faculty member at Groton fills a variety of roles, taking on responsibilities in the classroom, in the dormitory, on the athletics field, in various activities, and as an adviser to students. An adviser assumes a major role in communication with the parents and is the resident expert on his or her advisees. Faculty benefits at Groton include financial support for continuing education and a ten-year sabbatical program.

COLLEGE ADMISSION COUNSELING

College advising is the responsibility of 3 members of the faculty, who assist students and their families in determining what kind of environment and options the students are seeking for their college years. The median SAT scores for the class of 2008 were 690 on the critical reading, 670 on the mathematics, and 700 on the writing sections. The 82 members of the class of 2007 are attending forty different colleges and universities. The most popular are Georgetown (5), Harvard (4), Tufts (4), Brown (3), Carnegie Mellon (3), and Columbia (3).

STUDENT BODY AND CONDUCT

In 2008–09, Groton's enrollment numbered 358 students, of whom 184 were boys and 174 were girls. Of the 358 students, 291 were boarders and 67 were day students. Students from twenty-eight states and fourteen other countries enrolled. The student body represents diversity in both geographic and socioeconomic backgrounds.

At Groton, the breaking of major School rules (lying, cheating, stealing, or using or possessing drugs or alcohol) is a serious matter and may lead to dismissal. Disciplinary action is not taken, however, without the advice of the Discipline Committee (composed of students and faculty members), which considers all circumstances. Beyond rules and regulations, the School expects all its students to offer both courtesy and respect to other students and to teachers, staff members, and their families. This expectation is one of the most important characteristics of Groton.

ACADEMIC FACILITIES

The academic heart of the School is the Schoolhouse, where most of the classrooms, the science laboratories, the woodworking shop, music rehearsal studios and performance halls, and administrative offices are found. Adjacent to the Schoolhouse is the Dillon Center for the Visual Arts, which houses ceramics, painting, sculpture, and drawing studios as well as multimedia and gallery space. The library contains approximately 60,000 volumes; 150 periodical subscriptions, including publications in French, German, and Spanish; and a rare-book collection. Local, national, and international newspapers are received daily. The library's microfilm, microfiche, and CD-ROM material and ProQuest and other Internet databases are used for periodical research.

BOARDING AND GENERAL FACILITIES

Groton houses its 291 boarding students in seventeen dormitories, all of which have been completely renovated in the last ten years. The Upper School dormitories have single, double, and some triple rooms and house from 14 to 23 students each, with a faculty member or faculty family living in the dormitory. Each dormitory's common room, which comprises a large and comfortable living room and kitchenette, adjoins the faculty residence. Student rooms are equipped with voice and intranet hookups. Use of the Internet is available in dorm rooms and common room spaces as well as in public computer space. A wireless laptop program was initiated in 2003. There is a central dining hall where faculty members and students sit down together for dinner three times a week. Other meals are more informal and are served buffet-style. Adjacent to the dining hall is the School Center, which has a snack bar, a dance floor, the student radio station, a game room, and a television-viewing room.

ATHLETICS

Sports are an essential part of the curriculum at Groton, and the School follows an "athletics for all" philosophy. It holds that, through sports, much can be learned about cooperation, competition, and character and that every student, regardless of ability, should have the opportunity to participate. Groton fields interscholastic teams in baseball, basketball, crew, cross-country running, field hockey, football, ice hockey, lacrosse, soccer, squash, and tennis. Intramural and recreational sports include canoeing, figure skating, fives, recreational and cross-country skiing, running, soccer, softball, squash, swimming, tennis, and weight training.

Not far from the buildings on the Circle are the School's eight playing fields and Athletic Center. In 1998, the School completed the construction of a new Athletic Center, which houses twelve international squash courts, twelve outdoor and eight indoor tennis courts, three basketball courts, an indoor track, two hockey rinks, an indoor pool, a dance studio, and a fitness center as well as locker rooms and a training facility for athletic rehabilitation. The Bingham Boathouse is on the Nashua River, which flows by the campus on its western boundary.

EXTRACURRICULAR OPPORTUNITIES

A lecture series brings to Groton on numerous occasions speakers of distinction in politics, government, science, art, education, and other fields. There is also a concert series that brings to the campus various individuals and groups with special talents in the performing arts. In addition, proximity to Boston and Cambridge provides opportunities to attend concerts, lectures, plays, and sports events.

An elected Student Congress represents all Forms and dormitories, and students serve on the Discipline Committee, the Student Activities Committee, and a number of other student-faculty committees. Sixth Formers assume major responsibilities in the dormitories, the dining hall, the library, the School Center, and the work program, through which all students share responsibility for cleaning and other routine chores on campus. Students do volunteer work in the local public schools, at a local day care center and institution for retarded children, and in a nearby regional hospital, among others. Other activities include bell ringing, chess, orchestra, jazz band, choral and instrumental groups, dramatics, debating, a minority awareness society, literary magazines, a newspaper, a student vestry, and the yearbook.

DAILY LIFE

Classes at Groton meet six days a week and are 40-, 60-, or 80-minute periods, with a shortened day on Wednesday and Saturday. Four days a week, the School gathers for a morning chapel service, whose centerpiece is a chapel talk given by a student and at other times by the Chaplain, the Headmaster, a member of the faculty, or a visiting speaker. While no attempt is made to indoctrinate students in any particular religious faith, the School does maintain that religious faith is as important to human life as other areas of concern.

Athletics are scheduled at the end of the class day and before dinner time. The evening hours are for study, with Second, Third, and Fourth Formers having a supervised study period. All students check in at their dormitories by 10 p.m.

WEEKEND LIFE

Weekend activities at Groton are planned by a student-faculty Social Activities Committee. In addition to interscholastic sports, these activities include coffeehouse entertainment, regular Saturday night dances, and special events such as casino night, games, and dorm competitions. Saturday afternoon and Sunday are also times for excursions to Boston or to the mountains. Each term includes a long weekend (Friday noon to Monday evening), and, if desired, a student may take two additional weekend leaves in each of the three terms. Day students participate fully in the life at Groton, whether on weekends or in evening activities during the week.

COSTS AND FINANCIAL AID

Tuition at Groton for 2008–09 was $44,350 for boarders and $33,260 for day students. This fee covers instruction, residence, routine infirmary care, athletics, use of laboratories and studios, and admission to all athletic events, plays, lectures, and concerts held at the School. Additional costs that are not included are personal expenses, such as laundry, books, rental of sports equipment, and travel. The charges for the year are due and payable in two equal installments in August and January. Monthly payment plans, tuition-refund insurance, and accident and sickness insurance are available.

The School aims to accept students on their own qualifications, without regard to their families' financial situation. Accordingly, no student should be deterred from applying out of concern for the family's ability to pay. Financial aid grants are based on the guidelines established by the School and Student Service for Financial Aid. In 2008–09, approximately 37 percent of the students received aid that totaled more than $4.5 million.

ADMISSIONS INFORMATION

Groton accepts applications for Forms II–V (eighth through eleventh grades). Though it would be difficult to define admission policies in quantifiable terms, the School clearly favors students with plentiful spirit, significant academic ability, a willingness to participate fully in the School community, outstanding special talents, and interesting backgrounds.

Applicants must submit a school record, a writing sample, three recommendations, and the results of the SSAT. In addition, all candidates are expected to have a personal interview with a member of the admission staff or a representative of the School. Approximately 1 out of 4 applicants is offered admission.

APPLICATION TIMETABLE

The initial inquiry and a preliminary application and application fee of $50 ($100 for international students) are welcome at any time. Visits to the campus should be made during the months of September through January prior to the anticipated year of entrance. Appointments should be made by e-mail, mail or, preferably, telephone well in advance of the intended visit. The Admission Office schedules visits between the hours of 8:30 a.m. and 1:30 p.m. on weekdays and from 8 to 10:30 a.m. on Saturday. Because applications should be completed by January 15, the SSAT should be taken in November, December, or January. With the exception of late applicants (those whose applications are completed after January 15), all applicants are mailed notification letters on March 10, and parents are expected to reply by April 10.

ADMISSIONS CORRESPONDENCE

Mr. Ian Gracey
Director of Admission
Groton School
P.O. Box 991
Groton, Massachusetts 01450
Phone: 978-448-7510
Fax: 978-448-9623
E-mail: admission_office@groton.org
Web site: http://www.groton.org

THE GUNNERY

Washington, Connecticut

THE GUNNERY
MR. GUNN'S SCHOOL ESTABLISHED 1850

Type: Coeducational boarding and day college-preparatory school
Grades: 9–12, postgraduate year
Enrollment: 300
Head of School: Susan G. Graham

THE SCHOOL

In 1850, Frederick Gunn fulfilled a lifelong dream by establishing a school for boys and girls in his home of Washington, Connecticut. In this setting, he and his wife sought to develop each student's intellect, character, and values. In 1911, The Gunnery became a school for boys, but it returned to coeducation in 1977.

More than 157 years after its founding, the school's goal remains the same: the education of each student to his or her highest potential in an atmosphere of academic excellence, competitive athletics, and strong, nonsectarian moral guidance. Students are responsible for promoting their own intellectual, physical, and social development and contributing to the well-being of others. The Gunnery's special character and strength result from the unique manner in which faculty members both challenge and support students in preparing them for the demands of college and later life.

The 220-acre campus borders the village green of Washington, a small, historic town in the foothills of the Berkshires in western Connecticut. By car, The Gunnery is about an hour from New Haven and Hartford, 2 hours from New York, and 3 hours from Boston.

A nonprofit corporation, The Gunnery is directed by a 22-member, self-perpetuating Board of Trustees. The school's physical plant is valued at $30 million. The endowment is $21 million and was supplemented in 2005–06 by $1 million from the Annual Giving Program.

The Gunnery is accredited by the New England Association of Schools and Colleges and is approved by the Connecticut Association of Independent Schools and the Connecticut State Department of Education. It is a member of the National Association of Independent Schools, the Secondary School Admission Test Board, A Better Chance, and the Cum Laude Society.

ACADEMIC PROGRAMS

The curriculum reflects the school's commitment to a liberal arts education as the most appropriate vehicle for developing intellectual curiosity and the basic skills of communication and inquiry. The Gunnery aims to prepare students both for the rigors of college study and for lifetime learning. Students generally carry five courses for each of the three terms, which are approximately ten weeks in length. To graduate, students must complete 4 years of English, 3 years of mathematics, 3 years of laboratory sciences, 3 years of one foreign language, 3 years of history, and two terms of art. Additional noncredit requirements include one term of ethics in the sophomore year and one term of public speaking in the junior year.

The curriculum is unusually varied; Advanced Placement courses and many electives are offered in all disciplines. In the spring term, seniors may apply for independent-study projects by submitting formal, written proposals. During independent-study projects, some seniors leave the campus to work full-time; others remain on campus, retaining a partial academic schedule while researching a project or working in the community. In both cases, a student designs his or her own project, works closely with a faculty adviser, and submits a written final report.

Faculty-supervised study hall is held in central locations for all students who have not yet achieved Academic Merit status. Academic Merit students may observe monitored study hall in their dormitory rooms. Study hall is held from 7:30 to 9:30 each night except Saturday; supervised study halls are also held during each class period. Classes, which average 14 students in size, provide a seminar atmosphere, allowing for maximum student-teacher interaction. In certain disciplines, students are grouped by ability.

The grading system uses the designations of distinction, high honors, honors, high pass, pass, low pass, and no credit to reflect a student's achievement in a course. Six grade reports, containing detailed written comments, are issued during the year.

Through the School Year Abroad program, students may earn a full year of credit by spending their junior or senior year studying, living with a family, and traveling in France or Spain. One or two juniors are selected each year through The Gunnery/SAGE program to spend half the academic year at a prestigious boarding school in northern India. The study culminates with six weeks of supervised travel throughout India before returning to The Gunnery in mid-January to finish the year.

FACULTY AND ADVISERS

There are 55 faculty members (29 men and 26 women). They hold thirty-one advanced degrees. Forty faculty members live on campus, 27 of them in dormitories.

In 1991, Susan G. Graham was appointed the tenth Head of School. She holds a B.S. in English and library science from Kent State University and an M.S. in counseling from Fordham University. Mrs. Graham came to The Gunnery from the Masters School in Dobbs Ferry, New York, where she served as Assistant Head for six years. Prior to that time, she worked as Dean of Students and as an English teacher there. Mrs. Graham has also taught at Lake Forest Academy and the Columbus School for Girls.

When hiring new teachers, the school carefully looks for individuals who are enthusiastic about teaching and working in a variety of roles with young people. Most faculty members live on campus, coach, and lead activities. Each student works closely with a faculty adviser, who serves as a mentor throughout the student's years at The Gunnery.

COLLEGE ADMISSION COUNSELING

Careful and extensive college counseling, beginning in the winter of a student's junior year, is conducted by 1 full-time and 1 part-time college counselor. Each student's academic record, test scores, extracurricular activities, and personal promise are all evaluated at that time, and a preliminary list of colleges is drawn up by the student in conference with his or her parents and the college adviser. Juniors and seniors are encouraged to talk with college representatives who visit the campus every autumn. Students also conduct research, visit campuses, and attend college fairs. By the end of the junior year, their options are refined; in the senior year, each student files applications to approximately seven colleges, generally no later than January 1.

The 84 graduates of the class of 2007 are enrolled at many fine colleges and universities, including Barnard, Colby, Colgate, Trinity (Hartford), the U. S. Naval Academy, and the University of Pennsylvania.

STUDENT BODY AND CONDUCT

In 2007–08, there were 192 boys and 106 girls (213 boarders and 85 day students) in grades 9–12, with 44 in grade 9, 85 in grade 10, 83 in grade 11, and 86 in grade 12 (including 11 postgraduates). They come from twenty-three states and sixteen other countries.

In keeping with the school's tradition of sharing responsibility, students are given opportunities to become school leaders. The student body is led by 6 elected senior prefects, who serve as liaisons with the faculty and Head of School. Selected students serve as residential assistants, working closely with dorm parents in running each dormitory and in supervising evening study halls. Students are also instrumental in implementing The Gunnery's work program and such organizations as the Red and Gray tour guides and the Student Activities Committee. Also, faculty members and students serve together on the Disciplinary Committee.

The Gunnery has clearly defined rules by which each student is expected to abide for the benefit of all. A first violation of a major school rule usually results in the student being placed on probation; a second violation may result in dismissal.

ACADEMIC FACILITIES

The Tisch Family Library has 15,000 volumes, subscriptions to seventy-five periodicals, computers for student use, and ample space for study. Recently renovated Brinsmade has four classrooms and the Schoolhouse has sixteen. The Science Building contains three laboratories, two classrooms, a lecture hall, a computer center, and a study area. The art studio and darkroom are in Memorial Hall. The Emerson Performing Arts Center has music practice and performance facilities. The Gunnery has a strong information technology program that prepares students for college and beyond. A state-of-the-art wireless network and computer facilities that include two large labs and a well-equipped library complement a schoolwide laptop program for those who wish to participate. For all students, there is ample availability of school computers, and both Internet and voice mail access are available at central locations on campus.

BOARDING AND GENERAL FACILITIES

Nine dormitories house from 12 to 48 students each. In most cases, students are grouped by class. Each dormitory, with primarily single or double student rooms, also houses faculty members and their families. The Teddy House, completed in the fall of 2007, is the newest addition to The Gunnery campus. The dormitory was donated in loving memory of Teddy Ebersol, who was tragically killed in a plane crash during his freshman year at The Gunnery. Teddy House is now home to 22 freshman boys.

ATHLETICS

The Gunnery views required athletics as an important part of the overall development to be promoted in each student. Nearly all sports involve team participation and competition with other schools. Fall offerings include crew, cross-country, field hockey, football, and soccer. Winter offerings include basketball, ice hockey, and wrestling for boys and basketball, ice hockey, and volleyball for girls. Spring offerings include baseball, crew, golf, lacrosse, softball, and tennis.

Participation in the athletics program is mandatory. Community service, an arts option, the ski program, outdoor club, and the Independent Study Program are available alternatives for eleventh and twelfth graders for one term only.

The Ogden D. Miller Memorial Athletic Center includes two full-sized gymnasiums, the fully equipped Noto Fitness Center, a weight room, a wrestling room, and locker and shower facilities. The Linen Ice Rink was renovated and enclosed in 1996. The newly restored Haddick Field House provides additional locker, shower, and storage areas. There are four clay and four hard tennis courts, a new boathouse on Lake Waramaug, four athletic fields, and a cross-country course. In addition, students have access to the 2,000-acre Steep Rock Reservation and The Gunnery's Neergard Woods, 70 acres of woodlands, where the school cabin is located.

EXTRACURRICULAR OPPORTUNITIES

Students are strongly encouraged to participate in extracurricular activities. There are three student publications: *The Gunnery News, The Red and Gray* (the school yearbook), and *Stray Shot* (the literary magazine). Two major dramatic productions, one of which is a musical, are held annually, and there are opportunities in both vocal and instrumental music. Student organizations include Amnesty International and the One World, computer, international, photography, Ultimate Frisbee, and UN clubs. Members of the Community Council and student tutors help their peers with personal and academic problems. More than 50 students volunteer to serve as campus tour guides for admissions and other visitors.

DAILY LIFE

Classes are held six days a week; Wednesday and Saturday classes are held in the mornings only, followed by sports competitions in the afternoons. Monday through Saturday, breakfast is served from 7:15 to 8:15, followed by participation in the campus job program (a commitment of approximately 20 minutes each week), dormitory jobs, and room cleanup. Seven 45-minute class periods begin at 8:30 and end at 3. Each class meets four times per week; two meetings each week are double periods. Lunch is served daily at 12:30; Tuesday and Friday lunches are formal, family-style meals at tables headed by students' advisers.

The Gunnery community comes together for an all-school meeting every Monday and Thursday morning for special programs or general announcements. Sports practices take place daily between 3 and 5:30, and dinner begins at 5:30. Study hall is from 7:30 to 9:30, and students must be in their dormitories at 10.

WEEKEND LIFE

Because the school values community spirit, students are required to remain on campus during a number of weekends each term. On the remaining weekends, they are allowed to go home or visit a friend after Saturday classes and sports. Sunday on campus is a leisure day until dinner, which is followed by study hall. A late-morning brunch is served, and students are free to worship at area churches if they wish.

A four-day weekend falls near the middle of each term. The school closes during these long weekends, and all students must leave the campus. The Gunnery is also closed during Thanksgiving recess, winter vacation, and spring break.

The Student Activities Committee plans many activities, including movies, dances, concerts on campus and at other schools, and open houses in faculty members' homes. Also offered are trips off campus to New York City, local shopping centers, sports events, and ski areas. The Metropolitan Opera in New York is a perennial favorite.

COSTS AND FINANCIAL AID

Tuition for 2008–09 is $42,000 for boarders and $31,400 for day students. Tuition is paid in two installments, on July 15 and December 1. A registration fee of 10 percent of the tuition is credited toward the first tuition payment. Additional costs (books, dress code items, school supplies, laundry, personal items) amount to about $1800.

The Gunnery is committed to enrolling a diverse student body. Approximately $2.4 million in financial aid has been awarded to 44 percent of the student body for 2007–08. Most awards are made on the basis of financial need, although a small number of merit scholarships are also available each year. To apply for need-based financial aid, a family should file the School and Student Service for Financial Aid (SSSFA) application, which the Admissions Office can provide after November 1. Financial aid applications are due February 10.

ADMISSIONS INFORMATION

When considering applicants for The Gunnery, the Admissions Committee considers academic aptitude and achievement, character, and extracurricular abilities and interests. The school selects applicants who can be served well by its programs and who will, in turn, enhance the community. The Gunnery seeks active and involved students with a strong desire to excel academically and to participate in sports and other activities.

Most new students enter in grade 9 or 10. A few eleventh graders are admitted, and, on occasion, a highly qualified twelfth grader is accepted. Approximately 12 postgraduates also enroll each year.

An admissions decision is based on a student's academic record, a guidance counselor or adviser recommendation, two teacher references, a written application, a student writing sample, and SSAT, PSAT, or SAT scores. Applicants for grades 9 through 11 should take the SSAT, and twelfth grade and postgraduate candidates are asked to submit SAT scores. A personal interview with a member of the admissions staff is required. The Gunnery also has an active network of parent and trustee volunteers who answer questions for prospective families.

APPLICATION TIMETABLE

An inquiry is welcome at any time. Campus tours and interviews can be arranged by contacting the Admissions Office in advance. Appointments are scheduled from 8:15 a.m. to 2:15 p.m. Monday, Tuesday, Thursday, and Friday and from 8:30 to 11 on Wednesday and Saturday. Applicants whose files are successfully completed by January 31 are notified of their acceptance on March 10, and students are expected to reply by April 10. After March 10, applications are considered until all places are filled.

ADMISSIONS CORRESPONDENCE

Shannon M. Baudo
Director of Admissions
The Gunnery
99 Green Hill Road
Washington, Connecticut 06793

Phone: 860-868-7334
Fax: 860-868-1614
E-mail: admissions@gunnery.org
Web site: http://www.gunnery.org

HACKLEY SCHOOL

Tarrytown, New York

Type: Coeducational day college-preparatory school with five-day boarding available (grades 9–12)
Grades: K–12: Lower School, Kindergarten–4; Middle School, 5–8; Upper School, 9–12
Enrollment: School total: 836; Upper School: 383
Head of School: Walter C. Johnson, Headmaster

THE SCHOOL

Hackley School, founded in 1899 by Mrs. Caleb Brewster Hackley, is a nonsectarian, coeducational, college-preparatory school, enrolling day students in kindergarten through the twelfth grade and five-day boarding students in the ninth through the twelfth grades. Hackley challenges students to grow in character, scholarship, and accomplishment; to offer unreserved effort; and to learn from the community's varying perspectives and backgrounds.

For more than a century, Hackley School has welcomed all with the words carved over the entry: "Enter Here to Be and Find a Friend." The warmth of the Hackley community enables both challenge and nurture, giving students the means to set high personal goals and attain them. Supporting student achievement in rigorous academics, arts, athletics, and community service, Hackley honors student commitment and strength of character. A Hackley education prepares students and alumni to think and act with care and effectiveness both in college and in their broader communities.

At Hackley, students encounter a challenging academic curriculum, with teachers and peers who inspire students to work hard. The students do more than master content. They learn how to think. Hackley believes that "character" is the whole that should not be sacrificed to "thinking" as one of the parts. Individuals doing things at exceptionally high levels earn respect at Hackley, but such accomplishment is not the sole or preeminent definition of success. Academic brilliance, athletic prowess, musical genius, and artistic accomplishment are admired, but the student who has truly learned what it means "to be and find a friend," who has shared commitment through every aspect of school life, will have his or her peers' deepest respect.

Hackley's sense of community is expressed by the school motto: *Iuncti Iuvamus,* or "United we help one another." This unity, however, is not the unity of people who look and think alike. Hackley strives to be an inclusive community that provides the emotional security fundamental to education. All students need to feel wanted and cared for, and to feel fully a part of the community regardless of their differing economic backgrounds, gender, national origin, physical appearance, and capacity, political views, race, religion, and sexual orientation. Hackley benefits from such diversity and celebrates the cognitive stimulation that comes from a community where people feel safe in sharing their differing experiences and perspectives and are able to disagree, challenge, and argue.

Hackley is located in Tarrytown, New York, in the heart of the scenic Hudson River Valley, and 25 miles north of Manhattan. The School is reached easily by bus, car, or train.

Hackley is governed by a 20-member Board of Trustees. The annual operating budget is $26.7 million; the School's endowment portfolio is valued at about $29.1 million. The Hackley Annual Fund raises more than $2 million in operating support from parents, grandparents, alumni, and friends each year. The Hackley Parents Association enhances school life through volunteer activities and fund-raising.

Hackley is registered by the New York State Board of Regents. It holds memberships in the National Association of Independent Schools, the College Board, the National Association for College Admission Counseling, and the New York State Association of Independent Schools.

ACADEMIC PROGRAMS

The school year is divided into semesters. There are breaks for Thanksgiving and winter and spring vacations. Class sizes average 2 to 8 students in seminars and 15–16 students in Lower, Middle, and Upper Schools. There are supervised study halls throughout the day for students in the fifth through the twelfth grades. Five-day boarding students also have supervised evening study. Teachers provide extra help as necessary; long-term tutoring is offered for an hourly fee. Grades are issued and sent to parents four times yearly, with interim reports issued as required.

Kindergarten through the third grade curriculum emphasizes reading and oral and written expression. Beginning in the third grade, students write weekly and begin to work on research papers. The mathematics program teaches the logical structure of the number system and fosters dexterity in computation. Also included in the program are history, science, art, music, computers, and physical education. Spanish is introduced in the third grade. The Director of the Lower School is Ronald DelMoro.

The curriculum for the fourth grade and the Middle School (fifth through eighth grades) includes English, which focuses on grammar, oral expression, literary analysis, and expository and creative writing; American, ancient, and world history and Asian civilizations; mathematics, emphasizing the four basic operations and probability, graphing, statistics and prealgebra, algebra I, and geometry; science, including the physical world, life science, chemistry, and biology; art; drama; and music. All Middle School students are required to take a computer curriculum and health education. At the sixth grade level, they may begin the study of Latin, Chinese, or French or continue Spanish. Alona Scott is the Director of the Middle School.

To graduate, Upper School students must complete 4 years of English; 3 years of a foreign language, American history to 1900, and twentieth-century world history; mathematics through algebra II and trigonometry; 3 years of science, including a laboratory course; and 1 year of performing or visual arts. The Upper School puts a major emphasis on writing. At least twenty additional essays are assigned during a weekly period dedicated to composition during the academic year.

The Upper School offers Advanced Placement courses in twenty-one subjects. Other courses include Shakespeare, creative writing, electronic publishing (print- and Web-based), economics, modern European history, government and politics, Chinese, Italian, computer science, ecology, biology, organic chemistry, chemistry, advanced physics, marine biology, calculus, finite math, statistics, music theory, jazz improvisation, art history, studio art, advanced ceramics, photography, computer graphics, 3-D sculpture and design, and architecture and design. The Director of the Upper School is Andrew King.

FACULTY AND ADVISERS

Walter C. Johnson was appointed Headmaster in February 1995. He graduated summa cum laude from Amherst (B.A., 1974) and earned master's degrees in literature and educational administration from the University of Pennsylvania and Teachers College, Columbia University, respectively. Mr. Johnson has had educational and administrative experience at Trinity School and Collegiate School in New York City and at the American School in London.

Faculty members, including assistants and administrators who teach, number 132; 108 hold graduate degrees and 58 reside on the campus.

Each student in both the Middle School and the Upper School has an academic adviser who provides extensive course counseling for the current year as well as advice for planning a course of study for the student's entire Hackley career. Other student support services include a full-time nurse, 3 full-time psychologists, and 1 full-time learning specialist.

COLLEGE ADMISSION COUNSELING

The College Counseling office is staffed by 3 experienced professionals. In the past four years, the following colleges and universities have enrolled the greatest number of Hackley graduates: Colgate, Columbia, Cornell, George Washington, Harvard, Pennsylvania, Trinity (Hartford), Tufts, and Yale.

STUDENT BODY AND CONDUCT

In 2008–09, the School enrolled 404 day boys, 407 day girls, 11 boarding boys, and 14 boarding girls, as follows: 209 in grades K–4, 244 in grades 5–8, and 383 in grades 9–12. Students come from ninety-eight communities throughout New York, New Jersey, and Connecticut. Twenty-seven percent of students are African American/black, Asian, and/or Latino/a.

Hackley's philosophy challenges students to put forth their best academic effort, to maintain high standards of personal behavior, and to dress according to a dress code outlined on the School's Web site.

ACADEMIC FACILITIES

Hackley uses technology to provide resources, access information, and enhance critical-thinking skills in support of its mission. This is accomplished two ways: direct computer instruction and technological support in all academic areas. The greater focus is on the latter area since Hackley does not teach computer use as an end unto itself but rather as a supplement to its curriculum.

Three Computer Coordinators provide academic support to each of the three divisions, and the Director of Technology coordinates all of the academic initiatives of this team. Constantly reviewing the program, this team is responsible for instructing students and supporting faculty members in technology integration.

The Hackley computer network, both wired and wireless campuswide, includes direct Internet access in every classroom. In the Lower School, there are a computer lab and workstations in every classroom. The Middle and Upper Schools have two and three computer labs respectively, and classrooms in all divisions are outfitted with built-in LCD projectors and Smart Boards. In addition, available sets of wireless laptops allow for setting up any classroom as a mini lab, and Upper School students can also check out laptops for individual use.

A strong professional development program allows teachers to make informed decisions about technology enhancements to their courses. Faculty education work is supported by the availability of laptops through the faculty laptop loan program. This professional development work drives curricular integration. Working cooperatively with the Computer Coordinators, faculty members can use their expertise in their subject areas to determine appropriate integration of technology into the courses they teach. Research in every subject area at some point includes an Internet component. Every academic area now engages the use of technology from guided Internet research to formal application use, such as Geometer's Sketchpad in mathematics, Rosetta Stone in foreign languages, and computer-based measurements in physics labs.

The second academic component, direct computer use instruction, falls into three categories: computer applications, electronic publishing, and computer science. Hackley School believes the spark for any use of technology must come from a curricular-based decision-making process. Through improving technological infrastructure, professional development, and curricular application, academic technology gains greater use each year. The Director of Technology is Joseph E. Dioguardi III.

The Hackley libraries support the K–12 curriculum, serving as resource centers for the students and teachers. The Lower School library houses more than 8,000 titles, and the Middle/Upper School library has more than 10,000 print titles and over 400 DVDs. Other nonprint resources available to the community include a variety of databases and e-Books. The Head Librarian is Laura Pearle.

BOARDING AND GENERAL FACILITIES

The Hackley School that Mrs. Caleb Brewster Hackley created in 1899 was a seven-day, all boys' boarding school. In the early 1970s, as young women were admitted to Hackley and boarding became a five-day program, the School's mission nonetheless retained commitment to the character and qualities of its tradition. The boarding program is still a vital part of the School's culture and philosophy of education. Hackley expects students to be good citizens and to develop character as well as academic skills and knowledge. The five-day boarding program is at the heart of this commitment to character, helping to shape the culture captured by the carving over Hackley's entrance, "Enter Here To Be and Find a Friend," and ensuring that the Hilltop is alive and full of activity 24 hours a day.

Six faculty members supervise single-gender halls, each with their own common room and laundry facility. There is also a coed common space where students can play Foosball or watch TV. Teachers live throughout the students' living space to ensure close contact with every student. They and other faculty members who live on campus are available to help students with questions of an academic or personal nature. Today's boarding structure creates a positive intimate living environment where students are able to grow emotionally, academically, and socially. Boarding makes it easy to participate in evening activities, including sports practice, drama rehearsals, music performances, and community service. Boarders come from Manhattan, the Bronx, and communities in upstate New York, New Jersey, and Connecticut.

The School, situated on a 285-acre woodland campus, with stone and half-timbered buildings of English Tudor style, overlooks the Hudson River. Additional facilities available to students include the Performing Arts Center; the Music Institute (a conservatory); the fifth through twelfth grade science building; the Athletics and Physical Education Center; the kindergarten through fourth grade Kathleen Allen Lower School; Saperstein Middle School for the fifth through eighth grades; an infirmary; playgrounds; a 3.2-mile hiking and cross-country nature trail; a high-ropes course; a photography studio; six tennis courts; four international squash courts; an indoor swimming pool; arts studios; a football and track and field facility; and field hockey, softball, soccer, lacrosse, and baseball fields.

ATHLETICS

Hackley competes within the Ivy, New York Metro, and NYSAIS Interscholastic Leagues and public and parochial schools. Girls' sports include basketball, cross-country, field hockey, golf, indoor track, lacrosse, soccer, softball, squash, swimming, tennis, and track and field. Boys' sports include baseball, basketball, cross-country, fencing, football, golf, indoor track, lacrosse, soccer, squash, swimming, tennis, track and field, and wrestling. Coed sports include fencing. Physical education courses also include nonteam activities such as working out in the fitness center and hiking. Swimming is required in kindergarten through the sixth grade.

Hackley athletic teams have accumulated much recognition for their success and sportsmanship over the years. Since 1990, teams have won league championships in football, boys' and girls' soccer, field hockey, girls' basketball, boys' and girls' lacrosse, swimming, track and field, baseball, and softball. Since 1982, 21 students have received All-American accolades. Hackley has had many undefeated teams and is the home of many championships in sports sponsored by the New York State Association of Independent Schools, the Ivy League, and the New York Metropolitan Lacrosse Association Tournament.

EXTRACURRICULAR OPPORTUNITIES

The Community Council, composed of student and faculty representatives from grades 5 through 12, organizes nearly fifty student academic, cultural, performance, and service organizations. In addition to sixty-one athletic teams, a variety of physical education classes are offered. Dedicated to building a sense that lives are more valuable when connected to a community in need, Hackley's community service program begins in kindergarten through the fourth grade, with a focus on building local awareness and then spreads its vision to the world. As students grow, the program asks them to become more actively and independently involved. Middle School students initiate their own projects and learn the ideals of compassion by working directly with the people they help support through the Helping Hands program. The Upper School program is completely student driven. All ideas, projects, and inspiration come from the student body, with the guidance of the Upper School community service coordinator.

Lower school students typically visit the Union Church of Pocantico to see the Chagall and Matisse windows studied in art classes. Other trips go to the Metropolitan Opera, the Bronx Zoo, and the Botanical Gardens. Middle School students typically visit Canada to supplement French language courses and travel annually to Boston and Washington, D.C. Upper School students can take part in the Casten Travel Program, which provides travel grants for teachers to design and lead three trips per year. Trips have included the Galapagos Islands, China, Italy, Greece, Belize, Peru, Russia, England, Spain, Vietnam, and New Orleans (for Habitat for Humanity). In addition, Hackley plans frequent trips to New York City, with visits to the Metropolitan Opera, Federal Reserve, American Museum of Natural History, Metropolitan Museum of Art, Adelson Gallery, and Lincoln Center. Students take in Broadway shows, participate in AIDS Walk New York, and visit monthly to help the homeless.

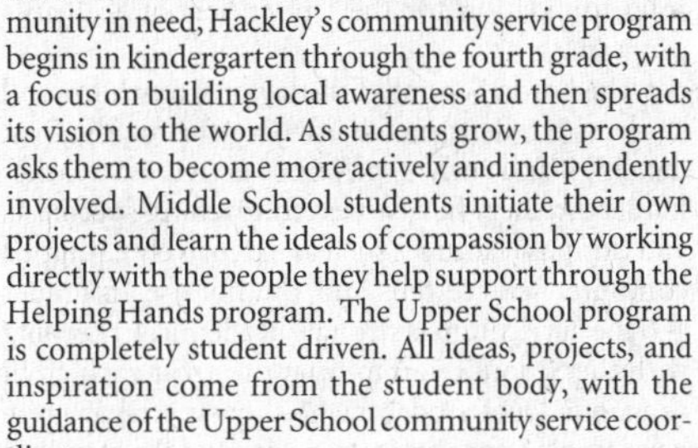

DAILY LIFE

Middle and Upper School classes are scheduled in a seven-day rotation, allowing ample community time and study time in each division and a variety of classes that range in time from 40 to 70 minutes. The day begins at 8:05 for fifth through eighth grades and ends at 2:45 for fifth and sixth graders and 4:30 for seventh and eighth graders. All classes and activities are included within the school day. Upper School students attend classes from 8:05 until 3:05. Sports rehearsals, clubs, and committees meet after school.

A typical day for Lower School students, beginning at 8:05 and ending at 2:40, includes academic classes, recess, gym and lunch. The classes are scheduled in a five-day rotation. There is an after-school program available for grades K–6. Buses for day students depart at 2:45 for grades K–6 and 4:45 for grades 7–12.

Hackley's five-day boarding program provides students in grades 9 through 12 with the advantages of both a traditional boarding school and weekends at home with their families. Resident faculty members, living on the boarding corridor, provide personal attention, structure, and a supportive and friendly family atmosphere.

SUMMER PROGRAMS

Hackley offers a variety of summer athletic programs.

COSTS AND FINANCIAL AID

In 2008–09, tuition ranges from $27,600 for kindergarten to $31,600 for grade 12. The boarding charge is $9700. Tuition includes lunch but not the cost of Middle and Upper School books. In the current year, a total of $3 million in financial aid was awarded to 122 students on the basis of demonstrated need. Low-interest loans, an installment payment plan, and tuition insurance are also available.

ADMISSIONS INFORMATION

Hackley seeks students of diverse backgrounds who demonstrate quickness of intellect and resourcefulness in problem solving, tempered by curiosity and love of truth. Students are admitted on the basis of a personal interview and written essay, a campus visit, one to two teacher recommendations, an academic transcript, ERB scores for grades 2, 3, and 4, and ISEE or SSAT scores for Middle and Upper Schools. Students should visit the School's Web site for grade-specific requirements.

APPLICATION TIMETABLE

The application deadline is December 15. Early submission of the online application is strongly encouraged.

ADMISSIONS CORRESPONDENCE

Julie S. Core, Director of Admissions, Grades K–6
Christopher T. McColl, Director of Admissions, Grades 7–12
Hackley School
293 Benedict Avenue
Tarrytown, New York 10591
Phone: 914-366-2642
Fax: 914-366-2636
E-mail: admissions@hackleyschool.org
Web site: http://www.hackleyschool.org

THE HARKER SCHOOL

San Jose, California

HARKER
Est. 1893 · K-12 College Prep

Type: Coeducational day college-preparatory school
Grades: K–12: Lower School, Kindergarten–5; Middle School, 6–8; Upper School, 9–12
Enrollment: School total: 1,720; Lower School: 580; Middle School: 460; Upper School: 680
Head of School: Christopher Nikoloff

THE SCHOOL

The origins of The Harker School belong in the city of Palo Alto where two schools, Manzanita Hall and Miss Harker's School, were established in 1893 to provide incoming Stanford University students with the finest college-preparatory education available.

Harker's three campuses are located minutes from each other in the heart of California's famed Silicon Valley. The campuses are well maintained, beautifully landscaped, and secured with an emphasis on student safety. The Upper School campus is 16 acres, the Middle School campus is 40 acres, and the Lower School campus is 10 acres. The Harker Upper School opened in 1998 and graduated its first senior class in 2002.

Harker's suburban San Jose location attracts day students from surrounding communities, such as Los Gatos, Saratoga, Cupertino, Los Altos, and Fremont.

Harker operates as a nonprofit organization, governed by a board of directors composed of business leaders, educators, and parents. With strong support from parent volunteers, the School's Annual Fund raised more than $1 million during the 2006–07 school year. Funds are used to enhance programs such as computer science and fine arts.

Harker is accredited by the Western Association of Schools and Colleges and is a member of the California Association of Independent Schools.

ACADEMIC PROGRAMS

The Harker School is a coeducational day school for students in kindergarten through grade 12. Harker students are highly motivated, creative young people who come from families with strong commitments to educational values. The exceptional faculty, caring and qualified support staff, and modern, safe campuses give students a definite advantage in becoming top achievers. For example, students consistently score among the highest percentiles in nationally normed achievement tests. Each year, an impressive number of seventh-grade students qualify for academic recognition as Johns Hopkins University Scholars by scoring above 500 on the SAT. Small class sizes, with an average of 16 students, enable teachers to form flexible ability groupings so that children's needs are constantly evaluated and met.

The Upper School curriculum offers a full array of academic courses, from introductory-level to Advanced Placement and honors-level courses in every discipline, from sciences and math to English, foreign language, and the fine arts. The Upper School offers a complete athletic program for boys and girls as well as a full extracurricular program, including yearbook, performing arts, newspaper, and debate.

The use of technology in teaching is an important facet of the academic program, and every student takes a year of technology as a graduation requirement. A unique aspect of the program is Harker's requirement that every student have Internet access at home. The Internet is utilized for academic research through the Harker Library's online periodical databases and access to faculty help after school hours. Grades 6–12 are also required to have a personal laptop that is linked to the School's wireless network. A Middle School laptop program was implemented in fall 2007.

Graduation requirements include 4 years of English, third-year proficiency in a foreign language (French, Spanish, Japanese, or Latin), 3 years of science (physics, chemistry, and biology), 3 years of mathematics (with a strong recommendation to take 4 years), 3 years of history, 2 years of physical education, 1 year of fine arts, and 1 semester of computer science.

The Lower and Middle Schools' solid curriculum in both the core subjects of math and language arts and the enriching opportunities with specialists in science, expository writing, Spanish, French, Japanese, computer science, physical education, art, music, dance, and drama provides a solid foundation for the Upper School academic program.

The Lower School's full-day program allows all students ample time for learning through games, dancing, and other physical activities. Harker kindergarteners have access to teaching specialists and campus resources such as extensively equipped computer science labs and the library. In grades 1–5 the curriculum is strongly academic. In keeping with the School's commitment to treat each child as an individual, students who show special promise have ample opportunity to go beyond the standard curriculum through Harker's advanced placement grouping. Study-travel trips to Marin Headlands and California's Gold Country add field experience to the academic science offerings.

Harker's Middle School program offers students a safe and trusting atmosphere in which to grow through the challenging times of early adolescence. Special courses aid students in gaining a sense of self-worth, dealing with anxiety, understanding the risks of substance abuse, and learning about other major health issues. Student performances, field trips, art exhibitions, and assembly presentations enliven the School atmosphere. Study-travel trips to Yosemite, the Grand Canyon, and Washington, D.C., are meaningful Middle School experiences.

FACULTY AND ADVISERS

The Harker faculty is composed of 186 professionals. They hold twenty-one doctoral degrees and ninety master's degrees. Christopher Nikoloff, Head of School, earned his B.A. in English literature and his M.A.T. in education at Boston University. Faculty members serve as advisers to students on a daily basis. Many participate in after-school athletics and academic and arts enrichment activities. Continuing education is facilitated with monthly meetings and individual incentives for professional growth. Harker seeks highly qualified candidates who reflect the School's commitment to academic excellence and diversity.

COLLEGE ADMISSION COUNSELING

Harker is a college-preparatory school whose rigorous curriculum prepares students for top universities. Four college counselors provide extensive guidance to students and parents in the junior and senior years regarding preparation for college admission. Over the four years of high school, there are parent workshops, family interviews, individual student interviews, classes for students, visits from college representatives, and special speakers from college admission offices.

STUDENT BODY AND CONDUCT

During the 2008–09 academic year, there were 1,720 students enrolled in kindergarten through grade 12. The student body reflects the dynamic and diverse Bay Area population, and the international programs further prepare the students as global citizens.

Harker Lower and Middle School students are required to wear uniforms. Upper School students adhere to a dress code. Students are expected to comply with rules defined in the *Student/Parent Handbook.* Good citizenship, along with academic and athletic achievement, is frequently rewarded. Discipline rests primarily with the faculty.

With leadership from its Student Council, the entire School communicates its views on codes and policies and works on community service projects. Students participate in a variety of leadership opportunities, spirit commission, and service volunteer programs.

ACADEMIC FACILITIES

Harker's strong sense of community ties three campuses into one school, while allowing children close contact with their peers. The Lower, Middle, and Upper School campuses are within 3 miles of each other. Modern, extensively equipped facilities such as computer and science labs and art and dance studios provide enhanced learning opportunities for students at all grade levels. A new state-of-the-art Science & Technology Center was scheduled to open in September 2008.

The library system has 28,500 volumes among the three campuses. Each campus has its own library facility, staffed by full-time professional librarians, and equipped with electronic encyclopedias and CD-ROM information access systems. With an extensive online periodical library, students have access to a wide variety of databases from such publishers as Gale, Oxford University Press, Grove, Encyclopedia Britannica, and others. The School's computer science laboratories are constantly updated with the latest technologies in hardware and software. In addition, computers and CD-ROM capabilities are located in each classroom.

Harker has extensive student support services. The full-time staff includes licensed school counselors, college counselors, registered school nurses, certified lifeguards, and a professional chef.

ATHLETICS

Students of all ability levels are encouraged to participate in the School's extensive athletics program. Baseball, basketball, cross-country, football, golf, soccer, softball, tennis, track, and volleyball are popular Upper School sports. Combined athletic facilities include two competition-sized pools, eight tennis courts, three wood-floored gymnasiums, a new lighted football/soccer field with synthetic turf, and expansive playing fields.

EXTRACURRICULAR OPPORTUNITIES

While the basic goal is to prepare students for future schooling by introducing them to a large body of knowledge, the focus on academics is balanced with numerous opportunities for personal development, including school spirit, sports and arts activities, and community service projects. Students take an active role in their school community, including planning school dances and rallies and participation in more than forty clubs. Harker's proximity to San Francisco makes frequent field trips to major cultural attractions and performances possible for students at all grade levels.

DAILY LIFE

Students can arrive on campus as early as 7 a.m. The school day begins and ends at staggered times between 8 a.m. and 3:30 p.m. The campus closes at 6 p.m. Supervised after-school recreation and athletics programs are available to all students at no additional cost. A professional chef supervises food service on all campuses, providing nutritious lunch selections of hot meals, fresh fruits, salad bars, and vegetarian options.

SUMMER PROGRAMS

Harker Summer Programs offers an intriguing variety of activities for boys and girls ages 4½ to 18. For students in grades K–8, day camp choices offer academic enrichment combined with sports, recreation, and computer science for a total of eight weeks. Field trips to local natural and cultural attractions such as Santa Cruz beaches, local redwood forests, and San Francisco are a popular aspect of the program. Harker's Summer Institute for students in grades 9–12 runs for 6 weeks during the summer. Students attend academic credit courses to hone existing skills or learn new topics. Offerings have included the Summer Conservatory program of music, theater, and dance; Speech and Debate Camp; rigorous math and science courses; and an enrichment courses in expository writing, Spanish, and PSAT/SAT. Annual enrollment is approximately 1,300. Enrollment in Harker's academic program is not required. Harker Summer Programs is accredited by the American Camping Association and the Western Association of Independent Camps. Further information can be obtained by contacting Summer Programs Director Kelly Espinosa at the Harker School office.

COSTS AND FINANCIAL AID

For the 2008–09 school year, tuition ranged from \$21,910 to \$32,250. A \$1000 to \$1100 lunch fee was added to tuition for Middle and Upper Schools. Estimated extra costs are as follows: \$400 to \$550 plus lunch fee for Lower School and \$700 to \$850 for Middle and Upper School students. A nonrefundable \$700 new Lower and Middle School student fee and an enrollment deposit of \$2500 for students are due within seven days of acceptance. The balance is due by July 1. Financial aid based on need is available.

ADMISSIONS INFORMATION

Harker seeks a diversified student body that reflects a range of backgrounds, aptitudes, and interests. Students performing at average to above-average levels are considered for acceptance. Student motivation and the ability to adjust comfortably to a close-knit and congenial educational community are also important factors. The specific criteria used in admissions are entrance exams, school records, character evaluations by a teacher or principal, and extracurricular experiences.

APPLICATION TIMETABLE

An initial inquiry is welcome at any time, and students should visit the Web site for School and application information. Potential students and their families are encouraged to attend an open house or schedule a visit because there is no better way to appreciate Harker's warmth and vitality. A visit may be arranged by contacting the School offices, which are open from 8 a.m. to 5 p.m.

ADMISSIONS CORRESPONDENCE

Ms. Nan Nielsen
Director of Admission and Financial Aid
The Harker School, Saratoga Campus

Lower School (K–5)
4300 Bucknall Road
San Jose, California 95130
Phone: 408-871-4600
Fax: 408-871-4320

Middle School (6–8)
3800 Blackford Avenue
San Jose, California 95117
Phone: 408-248-2510
Fax: 408-248-2502

Upper School (9–12)
500 Saratoga Avenue
San Jose, California 95129
Phone: 408-249-2510
Fax: 408-984-2325
E-mail: admissions@harker.org
Web site: http://www.harker.org

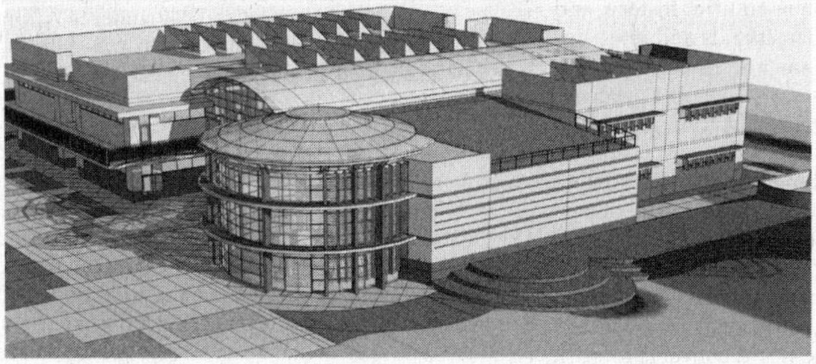

HAWAI'I PREPARATORY ACADEMY

Kamuela, Hawaii

Type: Coeducational boarding and day college-preparatory school
Grades: K–12, PG: Lower School, K–5; Middle School, 6–8; Upper School, 9–12, PG
Enrollment: School total: 575; Upper School: 336
Head of School: Mr. Lindsay Barnes Jr., Headmaster

THE SCHOOL

Founded in 1949, Hawai'i Preparatory Academy (HPA) is one of the premier independent, coeducational, college-preparatory boarding and day schools in the Pacific Region, offering a full range of academic and extracurricular opportunities for 575 students in grades K–12. The school is located on two campuses encompassing 228 acres in the heart of world-famous Parker Ranch on the Island of Hawaii. HPA offers a boarding option for students in grades 6–12 and draws its diverse student body from the Hawaiian Islands, sixteen other states and U.S. territories, and twelve other countries.

Students pursue an ambitious, well-rounded course of studies in small classes taught by dedicated, highly professional faculty members using the latest in educational technology. The challenging academic curriculum takes advantage of Hawaii's geographic and social setting to give students a strong sense of Hawaii and its culture. The marine science program, in collaboration with NOAA, National Marine Fisheries Service, Pacific Islands Fisheries Science Center, offers unrivaled encounters with the island's remarkable ocean environment. Partnerships with its high-tech neighbors, such as the Mauna Loa Observatory, enable participation in real-world, cutting-edge research.

The school is fully accredited by the Western Association of Schools and Colleges and is a member of twelve educational organizations, including the Council for the Advancement and Support of Education, College Entrance Examination Board, Cum Laude Society, Western Boarding Schools Association, Hawaii Association of Independent Schools, and National Association of Independent Schools.

The mission of the Academy is to provide exceptional learning opportunities and a diverse community honoring the traditions of Hawaii. To fulfill the mission, the school offers a full range of educational opportunities for all grades; ensures a diverse student mix; educates, challenges, and develops all students to reach beyond their perceived level of ability; nurtures a strong sense of community based on acceptance, mutual respect, compassion, and service to others; models humane values and responsible behavior; respects the unique culture, history, and environment of the Hawaiian Islands and gives students a strong sense of Hawaii and its culture; helps students better themselves each day; and produces leaders who are committed to family, community, and the environment.

Opportunity is the hallmark of the HPA Experience. At HPA, students have opportunities to participate in a range of "big-school" programs in a small-school setting while meeting and making lifelong friendships with peers from around the world. There is a special synergy at HPA, a place where youngsters and adults from around the world converge to work toward common goals and reach for unlimited levels of excellence and fulfillment, with exceptional support from remarkable faculty members for whom teaching is not just a career, but a lifestyle.

ACADEMIC PROGRAMS

Hawai'i Preparatory Academy expects each of its students to pursue a rigorous course of studies. Students work to their potential to achieve strong basic skills and gain a broad knowledge in the humanities, arts, and sciences.

Students who attend HPA after they have received a high school diploma from another school are classified as postgraduates (PG). For these students, HPA supplements their secondary school education before they continue on to college. In a PG year, students may take more advanced courses to improve their chances of getting into the college or university of their choice. International PG students are expected to be completely fluent in English.

Success in college largely is dependent on three things that students acquire in their high school years: skills, knowledge, and attitude. HPA works hard to make these three areas solid pillars upon which to build further education.

A total of 22 credits is required for graduation. This includes 4 years of English, 3 years of history, 3 years of mathematics, 3 years of science, 3 years of modern languages, 3 years of fine arts, and 3 years of elective courses (including 1 semester of technology).

The school's philosophy is to encourage students to challenge themselves by taking an appropriate number of Advanced Placement (AP) courses. Most of the AP courses require specific prerequisites or minimum GPAs for entrance. Only students in grades 11 and 12 are eligible to enroll in AP classes. HPA offers students the following Advanced Placement courses: art history, biology, calculus AB, calculus BC, chemistry, English language, English literature, European history, Japanese, physics B, psychology, Spanish, statistics, studio art, U.S. history, and world history.

The average class size is 12–13 students. The school year is divided into two terms, from August to December and from January through May. Grades and written reports are sent to parents four times per year.

FACULTY AND ADVISERS

There are 74 faculty members (31 men and 43 women), including teaching administrators, for grades K–12 and PG. About two thirds of the faculty members hold advanced degrees, including four doctoral degrees. Twenty-eight Upper and Middle School faculty members live in the residence halls or in school housing. Each resident faculty member supervises between 6 and 20 students. All Upper School faculty members teach, coach, share supervisory duties, and act as advisers to boarders and day students. A librarian and registered nurses also are on the staff. A psychologist is available on an as-needed basis.

COLLEGE ADMISSION COUNSELING

Full-time college counselors have developed a unique style of college counseling that adapts the best practices of the profession to create a program that reflects the students, environment, and philosophy of the HPA school community. Although the process of selecting and applying to college can be a very stressful experience for many people, HPA works hard to help students and families make the college application process rewarding and enjoyable. The College Counseling Center maintains a relaxed and welcoming atmosphere and is recognized as a favorite place for students to spend their free periods.

As part of the college-preparatory education, HPA provides a comprehensive college-counseling curriculum to help students and parents navigate the college application and selection process. As soon as students enter HPA, they are exposed to the early steps of the college-planning process: self-reflection, academic planning, standardized testing, goal setting, and college research. As upperclassmen, they work individually with the college counseling team to find appropriate college matches, work on applications, and discuss ideas about their future.

Through professional guidance, and excellent resources, HPA has consistently supported able students in gaining admittance into the nation's most selective colleges and universities.

For the graduating class of 2008, students earned admission to such prestigious schools as Berkeley, Boston College, Boston University, Colorado College, Cornell, Davidson, Emory, NYU, and the University of California, Davis. Although it is admirable to strive for admission at such schools, HPA keeps this goal secondary to the idea of finding the right match and being conscious of the student's own well-being.

STUDENT BODY AND CONDUCT

For the 2008–09 academic year, there were 575 total students in grades K–12, including 145 boarders and 191 day students at the Upper School and 24 boarders and 98 day students at the Middle School. Forty-one international Upper and Middle School students attend the Institute of English Studies.

Students come from the Hawaiian Islands, sixteen other states and U.S. territories, and twelve countries. The student body reflects the multiracial and diversified ethnic background of the Pacific Basin. About 41 percent of students are of non-Caucasian descent.

HPA believes that a primary goal of education is the development of character. Beyond academic commitments, students are assigned a number of responsibilities that support the daily operation of a boarding school. Elected senior student representatives, teachers, and a member of the administration meet with the student and adviser to determine the degree of discipline appropriate for violations of major rules.

ACADEMIC FACILITIES

Academic facilities on the Upper Campus include twenty-two classrooms, the Kono Institute of English Studies, Castle Lecture Hall, the Science and Technology Center, and Davenport Music Center and rehearsal rooms. Other academic facilities include the Gates Performing Arts Center, the Dyer Memorial Library, the Gerry Clark Art Center, the Davies Chapel, and a 4,100-square-foot student union. An energy lab—to engage students in the design, construction, and evaluation of renewable energy solutions—is currently under construction and is expected to be completed in January 2010.

Middle School students use two computer laboratories equipped with Macintosh computers and a projection system. Two mobile wireless lab carts equipped with Macintosh laptop computers also are available. The library is equipped with ten Macintosh computers, a projection system, and SMART Board. All of the Middle School classrooms are equipped with xvga projectors and screens, and many of the classrooms have SMART Boards installed.

Upper School students use three computer laboratories equipped with Macintosh computers and a projection system. Macintosh computers also are available in all dorm common areas and in the Upper School library and College Counseling Center. Most classrooms are equipped with xvga projectors and screens, and selected classrooms have SMART Boards.

Wireless access is available in all classrooms and in the dorm commons areas. All dorm rooms also have wired Ethernet access. Filtered Internet access is provided through two enterprise-level connections: one for the dorm areas and one for the rest of the campus.

BOARDING AND GENERAL FACILITIES

For many students, the boarding program at Hawai'i Preparatory Academy is central to the HPA experience. The ability to live with students from Hawai'i—and from around the world—gives each student the chance to be a part of a community of motivated students and dedicated teachers. Connections made between students develop into lifelong friendships and foster a feeling of 'ohana (family).

The Upper Campus' three dorms are separated by gender. Most students live in double rooms, but there are single rooms as well. Students are encouraged to room with someone whose native language is different from their own. This provides a unique opportunity to learn about another culture firsthand. All rooms have high-speed Internet access, and common areas in all dormitories include computers, table games, and fireplaces.

The HPA experience is enhanced by the presence of senior prefects who assist the dorm parents and act as big brothers and sisters to the younger students. Students benefit from the availability of their teachers in the dorms and develop important relationships with their dorm parents because of the multiple connections in the classroom, on the playing field, and in the dorm halls. The small average number of students per dorm parent (8:1) means that dorm parents can focus on each student individually to help ensure a successful HPA experience.

The Residential Lifestyle is an overall "life of wellness" as HPA provides a safe, healthy, and rewarding learning and living environment. The teachers, school counselor, administration, and director of residential life work together to build a community of high standards regarding social conduct and personal integrity. A formal Boarding Curriculum addressing the many ways to build a healthy and enriching community is implemented daily.

The Middle School can accommodate 34 boarders, and they share spacious bedrooms and bathrooms. Six students share a hall or suite, and each area has a Residential Faculty person who guides students in healthy daily living. The campus has Security most hours of the day and at night. A trained nursing staff visits the campus each weekday morning, and nurses are on call as needed.

ATHLETICS

In addition to HPA's rigorous academic curriculum, sports and activities are a vital part of the day. All Upper School students participate in co-curricular activities. A daily 2-hour period after the academic day offers students the opportunity to participate in interscholastic and intramural sports. Although HPA teams have earned many state and league titles, the emphasis is on participation.

HPA is part of the Big Island Interscholastic Federation (BIIF). Junior varsity and varsity teams compete against other teams on the island and in the state. Students must maintain at least a C grade point average to compete at the junior varsity and varsity levels. The sports term is divided into twelve-week trimesters. Each season, students are required to select a sport or activity.

Castle Gymnasium houses a basketball/volleyball court, a wrestling room, locker rooms, athletic training room, and equipment and drying rooms. The 2,000-square-foot Nakamaru Fitness Center is equipped with both exercise machines and free weights. Other sports facilities include Dowsett Swimming Pool, the indoor Rutgers Tennis Center, a cross-country course, a track, a tack room, and football, baseball, soccer, softball, and polo fields.

EXTRACURRICULAR OPPORTUNITIES

HPA encourages the pursuit of extracurricular interests. Student organizations and activities include the Beatles Club, Bodysurfing Association, Chapel Committee, Bible study, dance, Environmental Club, Go Green Club, Hawaiian Club, Ka Makani Flyers, Kawaihae Transitional Housing Club, literary magazine, Make a Wish Foundation of HPA, Marine Expeditions, Math League, North Hawaii Youth Coalition, Paper Brigade (recycling club), peer tutoring, Philosophy Club, Photography Club, Red Cross Youth Group, Robotics Club, School of Rock (rock band), Skate Club, Speech/Debate Club, Student Ambassadors, Student Council (government), Students Against Destructive Decisions, and vocal ensemble. Students may also participate in service activities throughout the community.

Student retreats each fall and various off-campus trips during the year focus on the special culture of Hawaii and HPA. The school emphasizes intraclass cooperation with schoolwide competitions among classes during Fall Games and Olympics (held in March), celebrates its diversity during International Students Week in February, and teaches risk taking and self-expression when the Upper School classes participate in a festival and celebration that embraces Hawaiian language and culture.

DAILY LIFE

Upper School students attend classes five days a week: Monday through Friday from 8 a.m. to 2:45 p.m. Enrichment classes—some optional and some required—are offered on various Saturdays during the year. Class meeting times vary during the week. The daily schedule provides structure for students with opportunities for interaction between students and dorm faculty/dorm parents. After classes end, the typical boarding student schedule may include afternoon sports and activities, free time, dinner, supervised study hall, dorm chores, free time, and mandatory lights out.

WEEKEND LIFE

Students may participate in diverse, engaging, and fun activities organized by staff members and students. A wide range of activities is available to students on and off campus and take advantage of the cultural, social, and vast natural opportunities available on the island. In addition, every Wednesday and weekend, there are regular van shuttles to the local town Waimea (Kamuela), where there are grocery stores, restaurants, and shops. There is a regular weekend van to one of the top-rated beaches in the U.S. and regular trips to Kona or Hilo for movies or shopping at the larger department stores. Formal dinners are held once a month, offering an opportunity to dress up and dine in style.

SUMMER PROGRAM

The HPA Summer Session, established in 1974, offers enrichment and unique study opportunities in English, science, and culture for boarding students and a limited number of day students entering grades 6–12. The program, which enrolls boys and girls from throughout the world, runs for four weeks, from mid-June to mid-July. Summer Session offers new and prospective HPA students an excellent introduction to the school's program and instructors. Many students return every summer to take advantage of the outstanding program and staff and to meet students from around the world.

Students attend classes Monday through Friday from 8 a.m. to 3 p.m., followed by sports until 5 p.m. A 1-hour study hall follows the buffet dinner, and the day ends with a dorm activity and lights out. Weekend excursions are planned according to student interest and may include trips to state and national parks, such as Volcanoes National Park; ocean kayaking; snorkeling; and hiking. Optional sports include instruction in horseback riding, scuba certification, and tennis.

COSTS AND FINANCIAL AID

Tuition for the 2008–09 school year was $36,150 for boarders in grades 9–12 and PG, $38,500 for boarders in grades 6–8, and $18,250 for day students (grades 9–12). Books, supplies, testing costs, and incidental fees add about $500. A reservation deposit of $2500 for boarders and $1000 for day students is required upon acceptance. The remainder of the tuition is due on July 15. Tuition payment plans and student accident and health insurance are available. Tuition increases annually. Tuition for the 2009–10 academic year will be announced in March 2009.

Hawai'i Preparatory Academy is committed to helping as many families as possible find the financial resources to afford an HPA education. In 2008–09, HPA granted $1.6 million in financial aid according to need, based on the national standards of the School and Student Service for Financial Aid. About 28 percent of the student body receives financial aid.

ADMISSIONS INFORMATION

Hawai'i Preparatory Academy seeks boys and girls of good character who have demonstrated sound scholastic ability, show promise of future accomplishment, and who will bring to the school a wide range of interests, abilities, and talents. The school does not discriminate in violation of the law on the basis of race, gender, religion, color, creed, sexual orientation, age, physical challenge, national origin, or any other characteristic in the administration of its educational and admissions policies, financial aid programs, athletics, or other school-administered programs and activities.

The priority application deadline for the 2009–10 academic year is February 1, 2009. Late applications are accepted and considered if vacancies are available after the regular decision deadline. Candidates are requested to submit an application, a written essay, an official school transcript, teacher references, and the results of the SSAT, ISEE, or other standardized test. An interview, either on campus or with an alumnus in the candidate's area, is required.

APPLICATION TIMETABLE

Inquiries and interviews are welcome throughout the school year. The Office of Admission is open Monday through Friday from 8 to 4, Hawaii Standard Time.

ADMISSIONS CORRESPONDENCE

Mr. Joshua D. Clark, Director of Admission
Stephanie Rutgers, Associate Director of Admission
Hawai'i Preparatory Academy
65-1692 Kohala Mountain Road
Kamuela, Hawaii 96743-8476

Phone: 808-881-4321
Fax: 808-881-4003
E-mail: admissions@hpa.edu
Web site: http://www.hpa.edu

HEBRON ACADEMY

Hebron, Maine

Type: Coeducational boarding and day college-preparatory
Grades: 6–12 and PG
Enrollment: 244; Upper School: 209
Head of School: John J. King

THE SCHOOL

Founded in 1804, Hebron Academy inspires and guides students to reach their highest potential in mind, body, and spirit. Hebron's 1,500-acre campus is an academic village, a place where students can enjoy modern facilities for research and study as well as an incomparable setting for environmental study and outdoor activities. Hebron is 6 miles from the towns of Norway and South Paris and 16 miles from the larger cities of Auburn and Lewiston. The Academy is an hour's drive from Portland and 2½ hours from Boston.

Hebron Academy is accredited by the New England Association of Schools and Colleges. Hebron is a member of the National Association of Independent Schools, the College Board, the Secondary School Admission Test Board, and the Cum Laude Society.

ACADEMIC PROGRAMS

Learning and teaching at Hebron are in the active voice. Students work in a variety of contexts to develop and understand the process of inquiry and investigation. The curriculum is organized within traditional academic departments; however, learning also becomes integrated in interdisciplinary electives emphasizing ethics and humanities, mathematics, and technology.

Graduates of Hebron Academy have taken at least five classes each year and successfully completed 18 credits, including English (4 years), mathematics (3 years), language (2 years of the same language), laboratory science (2 years, including biology), history (2 years, including U.S. history), and, for four-year students, fine arts (1 year) and computer studies (1 term). Advanced Placement courses are available in seven subject areas as are honors sections in English, mathematics, and history. More than twenty electives are offered, including human anatomy and physiology, environmental ethics, world religions, international relations, and photography. Programs for students with mild learning disabilities or English as a second language serve 24 students each.

The academic day is organized by a rotating schedule of seven periods of 45 minutes each. Students are grouped by interest and ability, with an average class size of 12. The faculty-student ratio is 1:7. Grades are reported on a 4-point scale, with 3.0 (B) or better required for inclusion on Honor Roll and 2.3 (C+) or better to be exempt from supervised study hours. The academic year is divided into trimesters, with major exams given in the fall and spring. Advisers provide grade and progress reports for parents seven times a year, after two weeks of school and thereafter at the midpoint and close of each trimester.

Study hall is held between 8 and 10 p.m., Sunday through Thursday. Hupper Library and the Academy's computer center are available every weekday from 8 a.m. to 4 p.m. and again from 6:30 to 8:30 p.m.

FACULTY AND ADVISERS

Hebron's teachers represent a wonderfully diverse and talented resource. Each faculty member is the adviser for 4 to 7 students, and virtually all coach or supervise activities. Twenty faculty members have been at Hebron for ten years or more. Above all, the Hebron faculty members are a community and family of people—caring, inquiring, nurturing people invested in the lives and growth of young adults.

John J. King leads Hebron Academy as the Head of School. Mr. King's fifteen years of teaching, coaching, and administration at two independent schools as well as ten years' experience as a communications executive makes him well suited to lead Hebron into its third century.

COLLEGE ADMISSION COUNSELING

Throughout a student's experience but especially during the junior and senior years, Hebron's 2 college counselors ensure that each student receives the individual attention to move confidently through the admissions process and gain admission to a college or university thoughtfully selected to be appropriate for each student's needs, goals, and talents. More than 75 college representatives visit the Hebron campus each year and students regularly attend college fairs.

In 2008 the median verbal SAT score was 530 and the median math SAT score was 544. Among the colleges and universities currently attended by Hebron graduates are Boston College, Boston University, Bowdoin, Colby, Columbia, Cornell, Dartmouth, McGill, Purdue, Tufts, Wellesley, Wheaton, Williams, and the Universities of Maine and Miami.

STUDENT BODY AND CONDUCT

There are 209 Upper School students enrolled, 125 boarding and 84 day. There are 143 boys and 66 girls in grades 9–PG. In addition, there are 35 students in Hebron's Middle School.

With students from twenty-two states and twelve countries, Hebron becomes an international community within a New England village. Most students choose Hebron because of its balance of excellent academics, competitive athletics, outdoor opportunities, and strong sense of community.

The Dean of Students, together with the student proctor group, is responsible for setting the tone of the school. Ordinary disciplinary matters are handled directly by the Dean, while major infractions are referred to a committee of student proctors and faculty members.

ACADEMIC FACILITIES

Hebron's buildings surround a spacious open area known as the Bowl. The focus of academic life is Sturtevant Hall (1894), listed on the National Register of Historic Places, which accommodates classrooms and offices. Flanking Sturtevant Hall are Treat Science Hall, which houses classrooms, laboratories, the technology center, and the greenhouse, and Hupper Library, the center for a 16,500-volume circulating collection, reference and periodical collections, archives, and an art gallery. Overall, there are twenty-eight classrooms on campus, plus two lecture halls, five art studios, a dark room, a music recital room and private practice rooms, and an outdoor center and classroom.

BOARDING AND GENERAL FACILITIES

Students are housed in double and some single rooms in three dormitories on campus. Junior and senior boys live in the central dormitory, Sturtevant Home, which also houses the Fine Arts Center, school dining services, and the health center. Freshman and sophomore boys reside across the Bowl in Atwood Dormitory. All girls live in Halford Hall, which also houses the Leyden Student Center. All dormitories have common rooms and are supervised by resident faculty members and student proctors.

The Leyden Student Center includes a snack bar and school store as well as a game room and TV lounge.

Hebron's Health Center is staffed by 3 registered nurses; the school physicians hold office hours twice weekly and are available in case of emergency. The school also retains a psychiatrist.

ATHLETICS

Hebron's athletic facilities include a 58,000-square-foot athletic complex, which opened in November 2008, housing indoor basketball courts; tennis courts; squash courts; dance studio; fitness center; climbing wall; an elevated running track; practice facilities for baseball, softball, and lacrosse; and other amenities. In addition, the academy has an indoor ice arena, six playing fields, two diamonds, an all-weather track, six outdoor tennis courts; and a 1,500-acre wilderness track with running, mountain biking and Nordic skiing trails.

Hebron fields twenty-eight varsity and junior varsity teams in fourteen interscholastic sports and seven activities. There is a place for everyone in the program; all students participate in athletics. The program serves athletes who seek a high level of competition and those who enjoy the opportunity to participate actively or try a new sport. At all levels, athletics at Hebron fosters enjoyment of physical activity and ethical competition, personal goal-setting and development, and the appreciation of working with a group to achieve common goals.

Interscholastic boys' and girls' team sports include basketball, cross-country, golf, ice hockey, lacrosse, mountain biking, Alpine skiing, running, snowboarding, soccer, tennis, and track and field. Additional sports for boys are baseball and football; for girls, field hockey and softball. Noncompetitive coeducational activities include drama, outdoor skills, physical conditioning, and yearbook. Hebron teams participate in the Maine Independent School League and the New England Prep School Athletic Conference.

EXTRACURRICULAR OPPORTUNITIES

Life at Hebron is varied and active; students supplement their academic and athletics experiences with social, service, cultural, and physical activities. Campus groups abound. Student Government, the student proctors, Green Key guides, Young Women's Group, and Diversity Committee shape the life of the community.

Fine arts opportunities are equally vital. Student groups produce the *Spectator* yearbook and the *Etchings* art and literary magazine. The drama group, a cappella group, community orchestra and chorus, and the string ensemble practice and perform throughout the year, and some performers are selected for the Maine All-State orchestra and chorus.

Hockey players teach local youngsters to skate. The Community Service Group works for service programs in surrounding communities as volunteers in food pantries, foundations, and convalescent homes. The Outing Club maintains a local hiking trail and offers hiking, canoeing, whitewater kayaking, snowshoeing, and rock-climbing trips throughout the year.

On weekends, students may participate in activities at the Leyden Center or go on trips to Auburn, Portland, or Boston for dining, seeing movies, or shopping. Winter Carnival and Casino Night are a midwinter extravaganza of games, a dance, and wacky intramural competition. Senior Prom comes in late April, and the seniors conclude the year with an overnight rafting trip in northern Maine.

DAILY LIFE

Hebron's school day begins with a morning meeting of the whole community. Seven 45-minute periods compose the day, with a midmorning break and a time for lunch. Athletics and activities occur from 3:30 to 5:30 p.m. Wednesdays throughout the year and Fridays during the winter are abbreviated to five periods ending at 12:30 p.m. to facilitate athletic competitions and trips. Saturday classes are conducted seven times each year and follow an abbreviated schedule. Regular evening study hall for all students is scheduled from 8 to 10 p.m., and check-in is at 10:30 p.m.

WEEKEND LIFE

Weekend life includes regular and special events. A faculty coordinator ensures a full calendar of activities and trips for each weekend and helps students to plan and arrange transportation for spontaneous trips beyond the regularly scheduled activities. Special activities are also scheduled, often according to the season. Trips to regional fairs, professional sports, or ski resorts are planned.

Students may sign out for weekend permissions as long as they are in good standing and have met athletic or academic obligations. Day students and boarders participate equally in planning weekends at Hebron.

COSTS AND FINANCIAL AID

Tuition and room and board for boarding students in 2008–09 were $41,975. Upper School day student tuition was $23,250. Middle School tuition was $19,100. Transportation, books, music lessons, CEEB testing, and weekend activities are additional. A nonrefundable deposit is required of all students upon enrollment to reserve a place in the class.

Forty-five percent of students received need-based financial aid in 2008–09.

ADMISSIONS INFORMATION

Hebron seeks students who have strong character and are motivated to acquire good preparation for college. Candidates are selected based upon academic records, interviews, recommendations, and test scores. New boarding and day students are admitted in all four classes, and postgraduates are assimilated into the senior class.

The SSAT is requested for ninth and tenth grade applicants. An interview and campus visit are encouraged for all applicants. Applicants for the postgraduate year are required to have had a college-preparatory program throughout high school.

Hebron Academy reaffirms its long-standing policy of nondiscriminatory admission of students on the basis of race, color, national or ethnic origin, religion, sex, marital or parental status, or handicap.

APPLICATION TIMETABLE

The application deadline is February 1. Inquiries, visits, interviews, and applications are welcome at any time throughout the year; however, most students apply for fall admission during the late fall or winter of the prior school year. Applications received after February 1 are considered as long as there is space.

ADMISSIONS CORRESPONDENCE

Office of Admission
Hebron Academy
P.O. Box 309
Hebron, Maine 04238
Phone: 207-966-5225
888-432-7664 (toll-free, U.S. only)
Fax: 207-966-1111
E-mail: admissions@hebronacademy.org
Web site: http://www.hebronacademy.org

HIGH MOWING SCHOOL

Wilton, New Hampshire

Type: Coeducational boarding and day college-preparatory Waldorf school
Grades: 9–12
Enrollment: 117
Head of School: Patrice Pinette, Faculty Chair

THE SCHOOL

Beulah Hepburn Emmet (1890–1978) founded High Mowing School in 1942 as a boarding and day school that offers Waldorf education to high school students. One of more than 900 Waldorf schools worldwide, High Mowing is the only one in North America to have a boarding program.

Waldorf schools work with the educational principles of Rudolf Steiner (1861–1925), the Austrian educator, scientist, and philosopher. The Waldorf curriculum seeks to build a balance in the human capacities of intellect, imagination, and will. This balance is achieved through the combination of stimulating academic studies, challenging activities in the arts, and the development of physical and practical skills.

The School's 125-acre campus is situated on a wooded hilltop approximately 2 miles from the center of Wilton (population 3,000) in the Mount Monadnock region of southern New Hampshire. It is 12 miles from both Nashua and Peterborough, 18 miles from Manchester, and 55 miles from Boston.

Trustees named a Faculty Council to oversee day-to-day operations of the School, such as faculty development, programming, students and parents, the community, and the administration.

A nonprofit corporation, the School has a 20-member Board of Trustees, which includes 6 faculty members. The board meets four times a year. There are 2,225 graduates. The School's physical plant is valued at $8 million, and the value of the endowment is $1 million.

High Mowing School is accredited by the New England Association of Schools and Colleges and approved by the Department of Education of the State of New Hampshire. It holds memberships in the National Association of Independent Schools, the Independent Schools Association of Northern New England, the Association of Independent Schools of New England, the Secondary Schools Admission Test Board, and the Association of Waldorf Schools of North America.

ACADEMIC PROGRAMS

High Mowing awards diplomas to students who have earned 82 units. (A unit is roughly equivalent to 30 to 40 classroom hours.) Specific academic requirements include 16 units in English, 12 in social sciences, 10 in mathematics, 14 in science, and 4 in a foreign language. In addition, 16 units of studio and performing arts, 6 units of physical education, 15 hours of community service, and 4 units for Projects Block are required. A successful completion of a senior research paper and presentation is also required.

Courses in literature, history, mathematics, and science are taught in blocks of concentrated study. There are eight blocks in the year, each block meeting for 1¾ hours each day for three to five weeks. The goal is to build a balance between the objective and the subjective aspects of experience. The content of each subject is presented at the time it will best meet the needs of the developing adolescent during the four high school years. Therefore, members of each class attend their block together.

The block courses offered for freshmen include creation myths, drama, modern history, drawing upon the book of nature, art history, anatomy and physiology, organic chemistry, and projects block. For sophomores, block courses include Greek drama, *The Odyssey*, ancient history, meteorology, embryology, chemistry: acids and bases, surveying and math, and projects block. For juniors, block courses include Dante, Shakespeare, *Parcival*, projective geometry, botany, medieval renaissance history, atoms and electrons, and projects block. For seniors, block courses include Man and Nature, Faust, drama, world religions, modern art history, Russian studies, physics: optics, and projects block.

English, humanities, mathematics, foreign languages, the arts, digital arts, and science laboratories are offered in track classes. These courses include English skills, French, German, Spanish, American history, economics, algebra, geometry, trigonometry, precalculus, calculus, computer science, digital arts, environmental ethics, government, seminars in philosophy and literature, The Way of the Naturalist, digital arts, filmmaking, eurythmy, painting, drawing, weaving, batik, pottery, choral and instrumental music, and drama. Driver's education and English as a second language (ESL) are also available.

Track classes have an enrollment that ranges from 8 to 15 students. Faculty members are available for extra help and organizational or math tutoring can be arranged for an additional charge. The school year, which runs from September to June, is divided into three terms. Marks, with written comments, are sent to parents three times annually. The School uses grades of A, B, C, D, F (failing), and P (pass).

The annual Projects Block allows two weeks for students, with faculty members, to pursue their studies and interests outside the regular classroom.

FACULTY AND ADVISERS

There are 40 full- and part-time faculty and staff members at High Mowing School; more than 40 percent have advanced degrees. Fifteen faculty members, including 4 dormitory counselors, live on campus.

The School chooses faculty members who have been trained in Waldorf education as well as those who have expressed interest in doing so. They also must have the ability to relate well to adolescents and be experts in their respective fields. The faculty-student ratio is about 1:4. All faculty members are assigned to individual students as advisers.

COLLEGE ADMISSION COUNSELING

College counseling is done by a faculty college counselor. Juniors take the SAT, and formal college counseling begins in spring of the junior year. The counselor advises students individually, helping them to select the colleges or other options that best meet their special needs and abilities. The counselor also assists the students in arranging to take appropriate tests and to visit college campuses.

The majority of the students go to college immediately; others take a year off for travel or other pursuits. Recent graduates are enrolled in the following schools, programs, colleges, and universities: Alfred; American Academy of Dramatic Arts; Antioch College; Art Institute of Boston; Bennington; Boston University; California of Pennsylvania; California State Channel Island; California State, East Bay; California State, San Marcos; Carleton (Ottawa); Castleton State; College of the Atlantic; College of Wooster; Colorado College; Connecticut College; Curry; Dalhousie; Earlham; Eckerd; École de Cirque de Québec; Eugene Lange (New School); Fisher; Franklin Pierce; Goucher; Green Mountain; Guilford; Hampshire; Hendrix; Hollins; Johnson & Wales; Johnson State; Keene State; Landmark; Laval; Lesley; Lyme Academy College of Fine Arts; Lyndon State; Maharishi International; Manhattan; Marietta; Marlboro; Mount Allison; Mount Holyoke; New England; New England School of Communications; New Hampshire Institute of Art; Newbury; North Carolina School of the Arts; Occidental; Plymouth State; Prescott; Providence; Queen's at Kingston; Rensselaer, RIT, Roger Williams, Ryerson, San Jose State, Savannah College of Art and Design; Sierra Nevada; Simmons; St. Olaf; Suffolk; Suffolk (Madrid); Transylvania; Trent; Tulane; Warren Wilson; Wells; Wentworth Institute of Technology; Wheaton; Wheelock; Whitman; Whittier; and the Universities of California, Santa Barbara; Colorado at Denver; King's College (Canada); Maine; New Hampshire; North Carolina at Greensboro; and Tampa.

STUDENT BODY AND CONDUCT

In 2008–09, the School had an enrollment of 113 students: 57 boarding students and 56 day students. There were 20 freshmen, 24 sophomores, 34 juniors, and 35 seniors. Students came from seventeen different states and seven other countries.

Both faculty members and students are strongly committed to responsible behavior. Mutual support of ideas concerning the best ways people can live and work together is an important aspect of the High Mowing community experience.

ACADEMIC FACILITIES

In fall 2003, the Dr. Bruce Bairstow Science and Technology Building, a beautiful steel-and-wood, post-and-beam classroom building, opened, offering two science labs, a small auditorium, a classroom, a recording studio, an assembly room, and state-of-the-art facilities in the digital arts classroom.

The architecture on the High Mowing campus reflects the School's New England surroundings. The Main Building, which was originally a barn built in 1787 and converted to a school building in 1942, was recently renovated and will re-open in spring 2008. It includes two classrooms, a large assembly room, and a eurythmy studio. The Library Building includes four classrooms and a library housing 10,000 volumes. The lower level of the boys' dormitory includes three large art studios for painting, drawing, batik, weaving, and pottery. The lower level of the girls' dormitory includes an art studio and a darkroom.

In 1990, facilities were developed for the Naturalist Program, including a traditional longhouse built by students. The gymnasium includes a basketball court and weight room.

BOARDING AND GENERAL FACILITIES

The Main Building contains the dining room, the main meeting room, offices, a student sitting room, and a humanities classroom. Both the boys' and girls' dorms include recreational and laundry facilities. The four professional Dorm counselors have apartments in the dormitories (two per dorm). There are double and single rooms. Students are assigned rooms by the dorm counselors. Room assignments may be changed during the year, if necessary.

Campus facilities include faculty housing units, the chapel, a library and classroom building, and a science and technology building as well as a maintenance center, kiln shed, well house, tool shed, and recycling center.

Nearly all faculty and staff members are qualified to administer first aid. Monadnock Community Hospital in Peterborough and Milford Medical Center in Milford are nearby.

ATHLETICS

The High Mowing School athletics program is an integral component of the High Mowing School experience. The program is a means for every student to honor a true sense of teamwork, respect for self and others, and fair play and is a practical means for honoring its own physical self, health, and well-being.

In that the School believes its athletics program, together with its academics and arts programs, serves as the optimal vehicle for the healthy growth of the students and community, it is the goal that every student participates in High Mowing School's athletic program with enthusiasm, direction, and discipline. Interscholastic team sports include soccer, basketball, Ultimate Frisbee, girls' lacrosse, and boys' baseball. A variety of coed intramural sports is also offered. Both classroom and team experiences at High Mowing School teach that it is the substance of relationships between people that is the most important aspect of everyday lives.

EXTRACURRICULAR OPPORTUNITIES

The student government consists of the Student Council, which is composed of representatives from each class. Students and faculty members comprise the Standards Committee, which oversees the upholding of the School's standards. A Dorm Council of students and faculty members helps to plan dorm activities. In addition, each class has activities for which it is responsible. For example, the junior class works on the Halloween Party and the prom.

Students are active in social and environmental reform through the Cabin for Peace and Justice.

There are many opportunities for drama and musical performances (Jazz Band, several ensemble groups, and singing groups), and there are opportunities to attend performances in the community and in Boston. Each year, a trip is made to New York City to attend a performance at the Metropolitan Opera. There are frequent exhibitions of student and faculty artwork as well as museum trips. The art studios are open for students to work in after school. In addition, guest lecturers and performers are invited to the School.

Students in the Naturalist Program are involved in activities beyond the school day. For example, there are camping trips and treks in the White Mountains on certain weekends throughout the year.

School traditions include celebrations of several holidays. Annual events include Class Orientation Trips, Parents' Weekend, the Halloween Party, Yule Festival and many other holiday events, the prom, and Alumni Weekend. Coffee Houses, in which students and faculty members perform for each other, are held four times a year.

DAILY LIFE

The daily schedule begins at 8 a.m. with a short assembly that includes roll call and a School verse. From 12 to 12:45 p.m., a lunch of mostly natural and organic food, including meat, vegetarian, and non-dairy foods, is served. Block classes meet every day from 8:15 to 10 a.m.; track classes meet from 10:20 a.m. to 3:15 p.m., followed by cleanup, in which everyone is involved, and the afternoon program from 3:45 to 4:30 p.m. In the winter months, skiing is available every weekday during the afternoon and on the weekends. From 4:30 to 6 p.m., students may return to the art studios or have free time. Following dinner, supervised study periods for boarding students are scheduled from 7 to 9 p.m., Monday through Thursday. Boarding students must be in their dormitory by 10 p.m.Added additional p.m. designations throughout this paragraph for the sake of consistency

WEEKEND LIFE

On-campus weekend activities include plays, dances, coffeehouses, movies, and concerts. Students may also attend off-campus plays and concerts or go shopping, camping, and skiing in the area. There is an active trekking program in the fall, winter, and spring. Students also make visits to Boston for special cultural events or for field trips to museums and sites of particular interest. With permission, individual students may leave the campus on weekends. Day students also participate in most weekend activities.

COSTS AND FINANCIAL AID

Tuition for boarding students was $38,900 in 2008–09. Day student tuition was $24,400. Additional charges for supplies and activities amounted to $1000. Tuition payments are due upon enrollment (10 percent), on August 1 (40 percent), and on December 10 (50 percent), unless special arrangements are made with the business office.

In 2008–09, High Mowing students received approximately $500,000 in financial aid. Aid is awarded on the basis of need and is given in the form of grants.

ADMISSIONS INFORMATION

High Mowing School looks for students who are bright and open, with curiosity and imagination, as well as a willingness to contribute actively in the classroom and to community life. Applicants are admitted in grades 9, 10, and 11 for the boarding and day programs. The admissions decision is based on an interview, previous school records, and recommendations.

APPLICATION TIMETABLE

Candidates for fall enrollment who complete applications by February 15 have their admissions decision sent to them on March 10. Applications for admission received after mid-February are welcome and are considered on a space-available basis. Students are occasionally enrolled at midyear if vacancies exist. There is a $50 application fee for US applicants and $100 for international applicants.

ADMISSIONS CORRESPONDENCE

Patricia MeissnerDirector of Admissions
High Mowing School
222 Isaac Frye Highway
Wilton, New Hampshire 03086

Phone: 603-654-2391 Ext.109
Fax: 603-654-6588
E-mail: admission@highmowing.org
Web site: http://www.highmowing.org

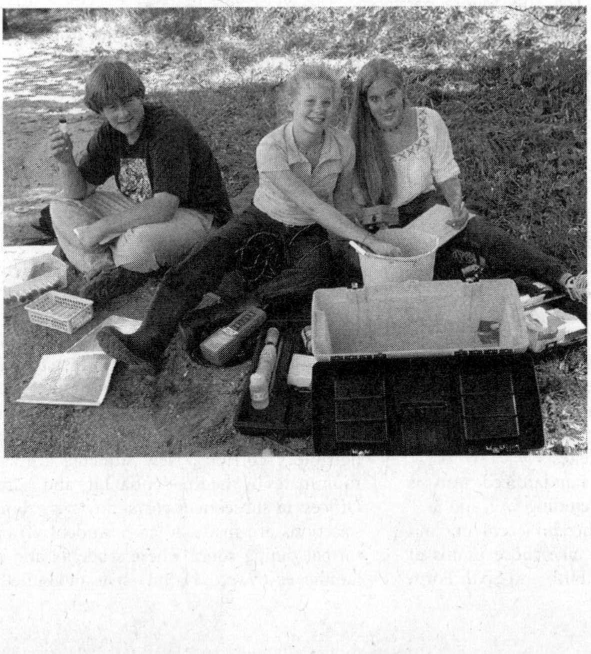

THE HILL SCHOOL

Pottstown, Pennsylvania

The Hill School

Type: Coeducational boarding and day college-preparatory school
Grades: 9–12 (Forms III–VI)
Enrollment: 496
Head of School: David R. Dougherty, Headmaster

THE SCHOOL

The Hill School was founded in 1851 by Matthew Meigs, and the Meigs family was instrumental in guiding the course of the School for three generations. In 1920, ownership was transferred to the alumni, who now operate the School as a not-for-profit institution through a 28-member Board of Trustees. In 1998, the School began admitting young women and became a coeducational institution.

The Hill School continues to emphasize both structure and guidance in the quest for academic excellence. The School's mission is to prepare students well for college, careers, and life. The Hill also strives to instill an awareness of accountability for all decisions and to teach those standards of personal conduct that are expected throughout life.

The Hill's 200-acre campus in Pottstown is located 37 miles northwest of Philadelphia and 15 miles from Valley Forge National Park. Because of its Middle Atlantic location, students at The Hill can take advantage of a balanced climate, including warm autumn weather and a winter season that makes possible such activities as skiing in the nearby Pocono Mountains.

The School's endowment is $135 million. The amount of Annual Giving for 2007–08 was more than $2 million, with approximately 30 percent of the living alumni participating.

The Hill School is accredited by the Middle States Association of Colleges and Schools and is a member of the Secondary School Admission Test Board and the National Association of Independent Schools.

ACADEMIC PROGRAMS

The Hill School's principal academic goal is to instill in each student the capacity and desire to learn. The School maintains a student-faculty ratio of approximately 7:1 and an average class size of 12 students.

Sixteen academic credits in grades 9 through 12 are required to earn a diploma, and the distribution of courses includes no fewer than four in English (4 years), three in mathematics (algebra I, geometry, and algebra II), three in one foreign language (or two in each of two languages), two in history, two in laboratory science (biology, chemistry, or physics), and a course in the arts as well as one in theology or philosophy. Foreign language offerings include 6 years of Latin, 5 years of Spanish and French, and 4 years of Chinese, German, and Greek. Courses offered within the Department of History include world history, European history, and U.S. history; U.S. Civil War, World War II, and Vietnam history; Islamic, Latin American, and Native American civilizations; economics; and other electives. Department of Mathematics offerings include algebra I and II, geometry, precalculus, functions and discrete math, calculus, graph theory, and advanced topics. Science courses include 2 years of biology, 2 years of chemistry, 2 years of physics, and 2 years of computer science as well as environmental science, astronomy, human physiology, kinesiology, and psychology.

Academic reports are sent home at the conclusion of each of the three terms. Comments from instructors, the hall parent, and the academic adviser are mailed to parents after the fall and spring terms. Students have seven-day-a-week access to the teaching faculty, nearly all of whom live on campus; many faculty members live in the residence halls as dormitory parents. The School library is open 12 hours each school day as well as weekends.

FACULTY AND ADVISERS

The 58 men and 39 women on the faculty hold ninety-three baccalaureate, fifty-five master's, and seven doctoral degrees from many major universities in the United States and abroad. Ninety-eight percent of faculty members live on campus with their families.

David R. Dougherty was appointed Headmaster in 1993. He received a B.A. in English from Washington and Lee University in 1968. He earned an M.A. in English from Georgetown University and a master's in literature from Middlebury College's Bread Loaf School of English at Lincoln College, Oxford. Prior to becoming The Hill's tenth Headmaster, Mr. Dougherty had been Headmaster of North Cross School in Roanoke, Virginia, since 1987. From 1982 to 1987, he was Assistant Headmaster of Episcopal High School in Alexandria, Virginia. He began his teaching career at Episcopal High School in 1968.

COLLEGE ADMISSION COUNSELING

For more than 155 years, the Hill School has prepared students for outstanding colleges and universities throughout the United States. The College Advising Office, staffed by 5 individuals, is devoted exclusively to helping students select appropriate colleges and universities and to helping them plan and prepare college admission materials.

Each year, more than 100 college and university representatives visit The Hill to present information about their institutions. Interested students are invited to attend these sessions, and Sixth Form students may schedule formal interviews with college representatives. During the Fifth Form year, students participate in a college forum class, which addresses the college application process. Topics covered include decision making, career interest identification, essay writing, interview techniques, methods of quality assessment, and SAT practice tests.

A complete range of standardized tests is administered on campus, including SAT and SAT Subject Tests, ACT, Advanced Placement, and TOEFL; students generally take those exams at regular intervals during the Fifth and Sixth Form years. The middle 50 percent ranges on the SAT for the class of 2008 were 560 670 critical reading, 570–680 math, and 580–690 writing.

Recent graduates are attending such colleges and universities as Bucknell, Colgate, Cornell, Dickinson, George Washington, Georgetown, Harvard, Princeton, Tufts, the United States Naval Academy, Wellesley, William and Mary, Yale, and the Universities of Pennsylvania, Richmond, St. Andrews (Scotland), and the South.

STUDENT BODY AND CONDUCT

In the Third Form, there are 66 boarding and 38 day students; in the Fourth Form, there are 90 boarding and 48 day students; in the Fifth Form, there are 87 boarding and 34 day students; and in the Sixth Form, there are 133 students. Students come from thirty states and fourteen other countries. Sixty-nine percent of the students come from Middle Atlantic states, with the rest of the students coming in equal measure from New England, the Southeast, and Midwestern and Western states. Twenty-five percent of Hill's student body is multicultural.

In 1997, the Hill School students and faculty members adopted a student-initiated Honor Code to promote an environment of mutual trust and respect and to uphold the School's principles of trust, honor, and integrity in all intellectual, athletic, and social pursuits. Most disciplinary matters are handled by either the Discipline Committee or Honor Council, depending on the nature of the offense. Both groups consist of students and faculty members who have been chosen by their peers.

ACADEMIC FACILITIES

The Hill School's fifty-five academic buildings include the 40,000-volume John P. Ryan Library, the Alumni Chapel, Harry Elkins Widener Memorial Science Building, Theodore N. Danforth Computer Center, the 31,000-square-foot Center for the Arts, the $12-million Academic and Student Center, and the McIlvain Multimedia Learning Classroom, a state-of-the-art, twenty-four-computer digital language lab.

BOARDING AND GENERAL FACILITIES

The Hill School's eleven major dormitory structures are divided into residential units that most often house 12 students and one faculty family. Housing has been designed for 2 students per dormitory room. Two selected Sixth Form prefects, who share some supervisory responsibilities with the residential faculty family, live on each dormitory corridor. New students are assigned roommates by the Residential Life and Admission Offices; in subsequent years, however, roommate selections are made by each student. There is a formal dining room where students and faculty families enjoy seated family-style and buffet meals.

The Student Health Service is staffed by full-time registered nurses and 2 physicians who are on call around the clock.

ATHLETICS

Athletics are an integral part of The Hill's educational offering. A program of twenty-eight sports enables each student to compete and develop expertise in the sports of their choice.

The athletic facilities at The Hill include a 34,000-square-foot field house and seven squash courts, a gymnasium complex, four basketball courts, a six-lane swimming pool, and a fitness center that includes twenty cardiovascular machines, Body Masters strength training equipment, and free weights. Additional structures include a brand-new 92-foot by 200-foot collegiate-sized indoor ice-hockey arena and a wrestling room. The Hill shares an eighteen-hole golf course and owns eleven tennis courts and 90 acres of playing fields for baseball, cross-country, field hockey, football, lacrosse, and soccer.

EXTRACURRICULAR OPPORTUNITIES

Students at The Hill are involved in many pursuits that take them well beyond the classroom and frequently beyond the campus itself. The students publish a newspaper, a literary magazine, and a yearbook. Students fulfill a community service requirement, which includes a written reflection, and also initiate a variety of community-wide service projects. For students interested in music, there are several instrumental and vocal groups, including the Hilltones and Hilltrebles (a cappella groups), jazz band, orchestra, men's glee club, women's chorus, and more. Other student organizations include the Hill Athletic Association, Student Government Association, Ellis Theatre Guild, and numerous clubs that reflect special interests.

The Hill School Humanities Fund provides students with tickets and transportation to hear the Philadelphia Orchestra and makes possible other cultural excursions as well. In addition, numerous on-campus lectures, concerts, plays, and exhibits are scheduled to stimulate and enrich students' cultural life.

DAILY LIFE

Classes are held six days a week, with a mid-morning chapel service on Monday and Thursday. A full academic day is divided into eight 40-minute periods, beginning at 7:55 a.m. and ending at 3:10 p.m. Wednesday and Saturday classes meet in the morning only. Athletic practice takes place between 3:45 and 5:45 p.m. Additional help with faculty members can be scheduled during free periods and in the evening. Student organizations meet after dinner. Evening study hours are supervised by faculty members and prefects.

Every Hill student "gives back" to the School by completing specifically assigned jobs within the School community several times each week for approximately 40 minutes each session.

WEEKEND LIFE

The Student Activities Office organizes weekend activities for Hill students. Off-campus activities include trips to movie theaters and malls, sporting events, amusement parks, outdoor activities (skiing, snow tubing, paintball), and excursions to Baltimore, Philadelphia, the Jersey shore, New York City, and Washington, D.C. Special on-campus events include concerts, dances, karaoke night, outdoor movie nights, the International Food Fair, and Spring Fling, where student participate in schoolwide volleyball competitions and rock climbing, listen to live bands, and more.

COSTS AND FINANCIAL AID

The annual charge for boarding students in 2008–09 is $42,000. This fee covers instruction, board, room, concerts, lectures, movies, athletic contests, services of the School physician and nurses at daily dispensaries, and athletic equipment on an issue basis. It also includes subscriptions for the newspaper and the literary magazine. There is an optional laundry service for an additional fee.

The day student tuition in 2008–09 is $29,000, which includes lunch for every day except Sunday. All day students are required to board for one year.

Financial aid is awarded to students whose parents are unable to meet the full cost of tuition. Aid is granted without regard to race, color, or ethnic origin. Financial aid grants are based on the guidelines established by the School and Student Service for Financial Aid. Grants are renewed annually; parents must submit the School and Student Service for Financial Aid form each year. For 2008–09, approximately $4 million was awarded. Applications for financial aid should be submitted by December 15.

ADMISSIONS INFORMATION

The Hill School seeks to enroll students who show academic promise, intellectual curiosity, and strong character. The School encourages applications from students who demonstrate involvement in the arts, athletics, and community service. The following credentials are required for admission: a formal application; a writing sample; a transcript of grades; results from the SSAT, PSAT, or SAT; a letter of recommendation from the school counselor and English and mathematics teachers; and an interview.

APPLICATION TIMETABLE

During the year preceding the applicant's proposed entrance, a formal application for admission should be filed, accompanied by a nonrefundable application fee of $50 ($100 for international students). January 31 is the deadline for consideration in the first round; late applications are considered on a space-available basis.

Families are encouraged to visit The Hill during the school term to meet members of the faculty and student body. An appointment should be made in advance.

ADMISSIONS CORRESPONDENCE

Thomas Eccleston IV, '87
Director of Admission and Enrollment
Management
The Hill School
717 East High Street
Pottstown, Pennsylvania 19464
Phone: 610-326-1000
Fax: 610-705-1753
E-mail: admission@thehill.org
Web site: http://www.thehill.org

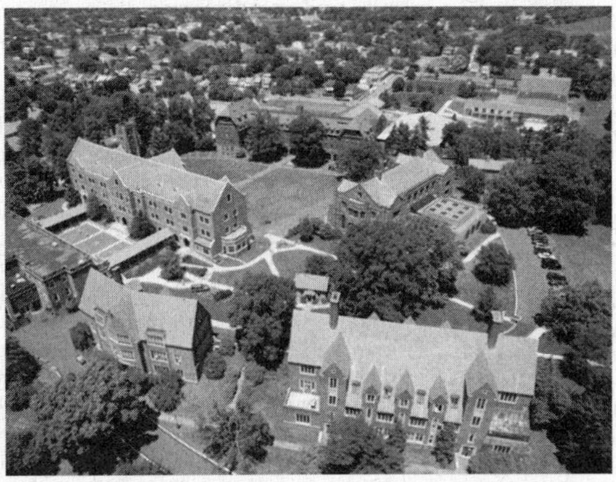

THE HOCKADAY SCHOOL

Dallas, Texas

Type: Girls' day college-preparatory (Prekindergarten to grade 12) and boarding (grades 8–12) school
Grades: Prekindergarten–12: Lower School, Prekindergarten–4; Middle School, 5–8; Upper School, 9–12 (Forms I–IV)
Enrollment: School total: 1,040
Head of School: Jeanne P. Whitman, Eugene McDermott Headmistress

THE SCHOOL

The Hockaday School, founded in 1913, provides a nationally recognized college-preparatory education for bright girls of strong potential who may be expected to assume positions of responsibility and leadership in a rapidly changing world. Ela Hockaday dedicated herself to giving each girl a foundation for living based on scholarship, character, courtesy, and athletics—the traditional Four Cornerstones that remain the dominant influence in the School's educational philosophy.

Hockaday's campus extends across more than 100 acres of open fields and wooded creeks in residential northwest Dallas. The School's contemporary architectural setting features an academic quadrangle built to provide views of exterior gardens and landscaped terraces. The science center and Clements Lecture Hall opened in 1983, the Ashley Priddy Lower School Building in 1984, the Biggs Dining Room and Whittenburg Dining Terrace in 1985, the Fine Arts Wing in 1987, the Lower School addition in 2001, the Liza Lee Academic Research Center in 2002, the renovated Middle and Upper Schools in 2005, and the renovated Clements Lecture Hall in 2007.

A Board of Trustees is the governing body. The School's endowment is more than $100 million, and the operating income is supplemented by Annual Fund giving of $1.7 million. The Alumnae Association, with more than 7,000 graduates and former students, contributes significantly to the ongoing programs of the School.

The Hockaday School is accredited by the Independent Schools Association of the Southwest. It holds membership in the National Association of Independent Schools, the National Association of Principals of Schools for Girls, the College Board, the National Association for College Admission Counseling, the Educational Records Bureau, the National Coalition of Girls' Schools, and the Secondary School Admission Test Board.

ACADEMIC PROGRAMS

Students are exposed to a rigorous academic curriculum that offers core educational subjects as well as unique offerings in technology, the arts, and leadership and personal development. Graduation requirements (in years) include English, 4; mathematics, 3; history, 2.5; foreign language, 2; laboratory science, 3; fine arts, 1.5; physical education and health, 4; and academic electives from any department, 2, plus basic proficiency in computer usage. Hockaday offers 121 courses, including many honors courses. Advanced Placement courses are offered in eighteen subjects, including English, modern European history, U.S. history, AB and BC calculus, statistics, physics, chemistry, biology, studio art, Latin, French, Spanish, computer science, and economics. For some selected courses, Hockaday has a cooperative program with St. Mark's School of Texas, a boys' school in Dallas. Private lessons are available in cello, flute, guitar, piano, violin, and voice.

A one-year English as a second language (ESL) program is offered to students on intermediate and advanced levels. Intensive language training in writing, reading, listening, and speaking skills is the focus of the program. Students may continue at Hockaday after the first year, following acceptance into the regular academic program. International students with intermediate or advanced English proficiency may study at Hockaday. Along with these special classes, students may study math, science, fine arts, and other courses in the mainstream curriculum. First-year students travel to Washington, D.C., and the Texas Hill Country.

Class sizes average 14 students, with an overall student-teacher ratio of 10:1.

The grading system in grades 7–12 uses A to F designations with pluses and minuses. Reports are sent to parents at the end of each quarter period. High achievement in the Upper School is recognized by inclusion on the Headmistress's List and by initiation into a number of honor societies, including the Cum Laude Society.

Each student receives careful counseling throughout her Hockaday career. Academic counseling begins even in the admissions process and continues under the supervision of the counseling office, which coordinates the faculty adviser system and general counseling program. Each student has an interested, concerned faculty adviser to assist her with academic or personal matters on a daily basis.

FACULTY AND ADVISERS

The Hockaday faculty is represented by accomplished individuals, most of whom have advanced degrees, with 6 holding Ph.D.'s.

Hockaday's teachers are chosen for depth of knowledge in their fields of specialization, personal integrity, and the ability to facilitate the progress of individual students. Many are successful writers, lecturers, artists, musicians, photographers, or composers; many regularly assist colleagues in other schools by giving workshops and lectures. Summer study grants are awarded to faculty members to encourage both research and professional development.

Ms. Jeanne P. Whitman, the Eugene McDermott Headmistress, is a magna cum laude graduate of Wake Forest University. She earned her master's degree in English from the University of Virginia and a second master's degree in business from Wake Forest University.

COLLEGE ADMISSION COUNSELING

The college counselors work directly with Upper School students in their college planning. Each student participates with her parents in conferences with the counselor concerning applications and final selection.

For the middle 50 percent of the class of 2007, SAT scores ranged from 620 to 730 in critical reading, 640 to 720 in math, and 630 to 730 in writing. In the class of 2008, there are 23 National Merit finalists and 20 National Merit commendees, three National Achievement Scholars, three National Hispanic Recognition Scholars, Two National Hispanic Honorable Mention finalists, and one Gates Scholar. One hundred percent of the class was accepted to university. They matriculated at sixty different colleges and universities, including Columbia, Dartmouth, Harvard, Johns Hopkins, MIT, NYU, Princeton, Rhodes, Rice, SMU, Stanford, USC, Vanderbilt, Vassar, Wake Forest, Yale, and the Universities of North Carolina, St. Andrews (Scotland), and Texas at Austin.

STUDENT BODY AND CONDUCT

The student body is composed of 1,040 girls (73 of whom board) from seven states and ten countries outside of the United States. The Upper School is composed of 443 students, the Middle School 308 students, and the Lower School 277 students. Thirty-three percent of the girls are members of minority groups.

The Upper School Student Council and the Honor Council exert strong, active, and responsible leadership in student affairs. In addition to planning activities, allocating funds, and serving as a forum for student concerns, these councils promote and exemplify the School's written Honor Code.

Students are expected to abide by the guidelines set forth in the Upper School manual. Disciplinary measures rest primarily with the Head of the Upper School and the Headmistress.

ACADEMIC FACILITIES

The campus includes sixteen buildings. The Liza Lee Academic Research Center is 52,000-square-feet and hosts two expansive libraries, several computer labs, breakout rooms, and a versatile hall that doubles as a lecture facility and audiovisual theater. In the academic area are classrooms; laboratories for languages, computers, and reading; and a study center. The campus is fully wireless, and Middle and Upper School classrooms are equipped with SMART Board™ technology for use in conjunction with students' laptops, required for every girl in grades 6–12. The Fine Arts facilities include a 600-seat auditorium, instrumental and voice studios, practice rooms, a painting studio, ceramics facilities with outdoor kilns, a photography laboratory, printmaking facilities, and an electronic music studio. The Science Center contains a recently renovated lecture hall, study lounges, classrooms, ten major laboratories, a computer lab, and a greenhouse. The Wellness Center includes the 5,000-square-foot Hill Family Fitness Center, an 1,800-square-foot aerobics room with state-of-the-art aerobic and resistance equipment, and athletic training facilities fully equipped for the treatment of sports-related injuries.

BOARDING AND GENERAL FACILITIES

Accommodations for boarding students are comfortable dormitories, updated study areas, and lounges. Girls of similar grades are normally housed on a separate hall, each with its own lounge, kitchen, large-screen plasma television, DTR, and laundry room. Other facilities include an aerobics center, two computer rooms (IBM and Macintosh), and an exercise equipment room. An additional common lounge is also updated with a large-screen television, kitchen and fireplace, and overlooks an outdoor swimming pool and tennis courts. Two students share a room, and each hall contains a small suite for the adult counselor in charge. The dormitories are closed for Thanksgiving, Christmas, and spring vacations.

An infirmary is located on the ground floor of the dormitory area, with a registered nurse on duty at all times and the School doctor on call. Campus security is maintained 24 hours a day.

The Wellness Center features an aerobics center, a fitness testing area, a trainer's facility, and the Hill Fitness Center, a 4,000-square-foot facility offering aerobic, resistance, and circuit training equipment.

ATHLETICS

Athletic facilities include two gymnasiums housing basketball courts (convertible to volleyball and indoor tennis courts), a climbing wall, two racquetball courts, a swimming pool, and a dance studio. On the grounds are six athletic fields, a softball complex, an all-weather track, a tennis center with ten courts and seating for 90, and 100 acres of open space. Interscholastic sports include basketball, crew, cross-country, fencing, field hockey, golf, lacrosse, soccer, softball, swimming and diving, tennis, track, and volleyball.

EXTRACURRICULAR OPPORTUNITIES

Thirty-three special interest organizations and honor societies, plus eight elected boards, including Student Council, the Athletic Board, and the Fine Arts Board, augment the academic and sports programs. Upper School interest groups that meet weekly are concerned with a wide variety of areas, changing from year to year according to student and faculty choices. To encourage student creativity, the Upper School sponsors a literary and journalistic magazine, a newspaper, and the Hockaday yearbook. These publications are edited by students with the guidance of faculty advisers.

Service to the School and its surrounding community is an important part of a girl's life at Hockaday. Each Upper School student is required to contribute a minimum of 15 volunteer hours per year in service to the wider community.

DAILY LIFE

Upper School classes begin at 8 a.m. and end at 3:45 p.m. Monday through Friday. The daily schedule provides time for academic help sessions and club meetings.

Varsity sports meet after the close of the regular school day. Residence students have a 2-hour required study time, Sunday through Thursday nights.

WEEKEND LIFE

Off-campus activities each weekend enable residence students to take advantage of the many cultural and recreational resources in the Dallas–Fort Worth area. Faculty members are frequently involved in boarding activities, as are families of the Hockaday Parents Association, who sponsor girls who are new to Hockaday and include them in family activities. Each residence student is matched with a local Dallas family through the Host Family Program. The host families offer local support for the girls and encourage their participation in social activities outside of school.

SUMMER PROGRAMS

A six-week coed academic summer session is offered for day and boarding students. Students may attend three- or six-week sessions beginning in June and July. Summer boarding is limited to girls ages 12–17. Programs in language immersion, math and science enrichment, computers, sports, SAT preparation, study skills, English, creative writing, and arts/theater are offered. Academic courses focus on enrichment opportunities. English as a second language, an international program lasting three weeks, begins in July. Information on the summer session is available in late spring. Applications are accepted until all spaces are filled, although students are encouraged to apply early to ensure their preferred course selection.

COSTS AND FINANCIAL AID

In 2008–09, tuition for Upper School day students averaged $21,526. For resident students, costs were approximately $39,624 for tuition, room, and board. Additional expenses for both day and resident students include, among others, those for books and uniforms. A deposit of $1000 is due with the signed enrollment contract, and the balance of tuition and fees is due by July 1 prior to entrance in August. Partial payment for room and board for resident students is also made at this time. The room and board balance for resident students is payable by December 1 following entrance in August.

The Hockaday Financial Aid Program offers assistance based on financial need. Parents of all applicants for financial aid must provide financial information as required by the Financial Aid Committee. More than $2.2 million was awarded to students in 2008–09. Details of the programs are available from the Admission Office.

ADMISSIONS INFORMATION

Applicants to Hockaday's Upper School are considered on the basis of their previous academic records, results of aptitude and achievement testing, teacher and head of school evaluations, and, in most cases, a personal interview. There is no discrimination because of race, creed, or nationality. Because the School requires a student to attend the School for at least two years to be eligible for graduation, new students are not normally admitted to the senior class. In order to qualify for admission and have a successful experience at Hockaday, a girl needs to possess a strong potential and desire to learn.

APPLICATION TIMETABLE

Initial inquiries are welcome at any time, and applications are received continuously. There is a nonrefundable application fee for both day-student and boarding-student applications. Entrance tests are scheduled in December, January, and February and periodically throughout the spring and summer. Campus tours are available at convenient times during the year. Notification of the admission decision is made approximately six weeks after the testing. Parents are expected to reply to an offer of admission within two weeks.

ADMISSIONS CORRESPONDENCE

Jen Liggitt, Director of Admission
The Hockaday School
11600 Welch Road
Dallas, Texas 75229-2999

Phone: 214-363-6311
Fax: 214-265-1649
E-mail: admissions@mail.hockaday.org
Web site: http://www.hockaday.org

HOLDERNESS SCHOOL

HOLDERNESS

Plymouth, New Hampshire

Type: Coeducational boarding and day college-preparatory school
Grades: 9–12
Enrollment: 280
Head of School: R. Phillip Peck

THE SCHOOL

Holderness School was founded in 1879 by a group of Episcopal clergymen who sought "to combine the highest degree of excellence in instruction and care-taking with the lowest possible rate for tuition and board." For 129 years, this charge has been carried out by extraordinarily dedicated and capable men and women, and the reputation of the School continues to prosper.

The geographical setting has been significant in shaping both the attitudes and the types of programs at Holderness. Much of the 600-acre campus is wooded, and its proximity to the White Mountain National Forest leads to a natural emphasis on the outdoors. Plymouth, a college town of 8,500, is ¾ mile away, and Logan Airport in Boston can be reached by car in less than 2 hours.

Holderness is governed by a self-perpetuating Board of Trustees, of which the Bishop of New Hampshire is an ex officio member. Annual expenses are met through tuition, endowment, and Annual Giving. The endowment currently totals more than $40 million. Additional funds were contributed by friends of the School.

Holderness School is accredited by the New England Association of Schools and Colleges and is a member of the Secondary School Admission Test Board, the Cum Laude Society, the National Association of Independent Schools, the Association of Independent Schools of New England, and the Independent Schools Association of Northern New England.

ACADEMIC PROGRAMS

The Holderness curriculum includes 4 years of English; AP composition and AP literature; public speaking; mathematics through AP calculus and AP statistics; Web programming; foreign languages through AP French, Spanish, and Latin; chemistry, honors chemistry; physics, honors physics; biology, AP environmental science, AP biology, human anatomy and physiology, and biotechnology; ancient, modern European, AP European, contemporary world, U.S., and AP U.S. history; cold war, economics, AP art history, women's history, and global crises: instability and extremism in the post–cold war world; music, music theory and composition, AP music theory and composition, and black music in twentieth-century America; drawing, sculpture, painting, photography, ceramics, woodworking, media studies and video production, and printmaking; and ethics and religion. Advanced Placement courses are offered in eleven of the fourteen test areas.

A minimum of 48 credits is required for graduation: English, 12 credits; mathematics, 9 credits; foreign language, 6 credits; history, 6 credits; science, 6 credits; and electives, 9 credits. Most students take more than the minimum requirements in science, foreign language, and mathematics.

Students are strongly encouraged to seek individual instruction whenever necessary. The student-faculty ratio is 6:1, and Holderness believes that the best education is available when there are extensive opportunities for contact between student and teacher.

Through a grant provided by the McCulloch family, each senior who has met all academic requirements has a chance to participate in a project that involves on- or off-campus study.

FACULTY AND ADVISERS

There are 44 full-time faculty members (29 men, 15 women). Ph.D.'s are held by 3 members and master's degrees are held by 26 members. All but 12 members reside in School housing, and 27 faculty members or couples supervise dormitory floors or houses.

Each faculty member is the adviser for the students in his or her dormitory, and most faculty members coach School sports. The Service Committee; the yearbook; the literary magazine and the newspaper; presentations in art, music, and drama; various clubs; study hall; evening library hours; and weekend activities are all under faculty supervision. With faculty help, a full-time librarian and a part-time assistant keep the library open 14 hours every day.

The Head of School, R. Phillip Peck, was inducted in 2001 after teaching, coaching, and dorm parenting at Holderness School for seventeen years. A former Olympic and World Cup ski coach, Peck was an adjunct lead instructor in Columbia's Klingenstein summer program from 1992 to 2001. He earned a B.A. at Dartmouth College and an M.A. at Columbia University, where his is currently pursuing his Ed.D.

COLLEGE ADMISSION COUNSELING

College counseling begins in February of the junior year. A counselor meets with students individually and encourages them to think about the colleges they should visit. Spring and summer tours are suggested. Admissions officers from colleges and universities visit the campus during the school year and hold college meetings, which interested students are encouraged to attend. In the spring, parents and students are invited to attend a college fair of more than 200 colleges and universities. In addition, the School has hosted the admission directors from Williams College, Colby College, and the University of New Hampshire to speak to current parents on a panel discussion over Parents Weekend.

Eighty students graduated in 2008, and 100 percent were college bound. Among the colleges and universities currently attended by 2 or more Holderness graduates are Amherst, Bates, Boston College, Bowdoin, Brown, Colby, Colgate, Colorado College, Connecticut College, Cornell, Dartmouth, Gettysburg, Hamilton, Hobart and William Smith, Lewis & Clark, Middlebury, St. Lawrence, Whitman, Williams, and the Universities of Colorado, Connecticut, New Hampshire, Richmond, and Vermont.

STUDENT BODY AND CONDUCT

There are 280 students enrolled: 28 boys and 21 girls in grade 9, 41 boys and 29 girls in grade 10, 44 boys and 36 girls in grade 11, and 47 boys and 34 girls in grade 12.

The Holderness community is built around a strong system of student government that has been in operation for fifty-three years. The School president, vice president, and student leaders are elected on a schoolwide ballot and, with faculty support, are responsible for day-to-day life at the School. The goal of student government at Holderness is to generate in each student a genuine feeling of responsibility for the community and to develop capable leadership within the student body.

Each member of the community has a daily job. Students work in the kitchen, on the School grounds, in the buildings, on the trails, and at other School facilities. The jobs usually take less than 30 minutes each day.

Holderness is an Episcopal school that maintains respect for all faith traditions. There are two required all-school services each week. The first opens the week on Monday morning, and the second is on Thursday evening before a family-style dinner. Voluntary services are offered on the other mornings of the week as well as an optional Sunday night Eucharist. The student body is interdenominational. Opportunities for worship in other denominations and faiths are supported by the staff and school.

ACADEMIC FACILITIES

There are twenty-nine school buildings. Academic facilities include the Hagerman Center, a math and science building. Computer facilities are also housed there, along with a 325-seat auditorium. Other classes are held in the Schoolhouse and Carpenter Arts Center. A video-sound-light studio stocked with video equipment and cameras is open for serious students of photography and recording. This professional facility was made possible by the Jennie R. Donaldson Trust.

The Alfond Library has more than 16,000 volumes, more than 50 periodicals and newspapers, a large collection of reference works, videos, and microform files and readers. It also houses two computer labs.

BOARDING AND GENERAL FACILITIES

There are nine boys' dormitories that accommodate 4 to 36 students each; most rooms are doubles. On the South Campus, adjacent to the dining hall, there is a semicircle of seven houses, each with accommodations for 8 to 16 girls. On the girls' side, Holderness has achieved an 8:1 ratio of students to faculty residents in all of the dormitories, and the School is moving toward that same ratio on the boys' side. The students have a lounge of their own, a snack bar, and a game room.

There is a health center, including an infirmary, in which the School physician holds daily visiting hours, and a registered nurse is in attendance. Students who are too sick to stay at the School are taken to Speare Memorial Hospital in Plymouth, just a few minutes away.

ATHLETICS

Holderness' highly competitive and rigorous sports program promotes fair play and sportsmanship. New students are required to play a fall sport in their first year. Ninth and tenth graders are required to participate in a competitive sport all three terms each academic year; eleventh and twelfth graders, two terms—as they may elect noncompetitive activities in place of one season of a competitive sport. Students may choose to pursue an interest in the arts on a per season basis, limited to one season per year. For example, students may choose to take one of the Art Department's offerings, or they may request to use the afternoon for such activities as preparing a portfolio or practicing a musical instrument.

Boys' and girls' team sports include basketball; cross-country running; cycling; golf; hockey; lacrosse; Nordic, Alpine, freestyle, and free-ride skiing; snowboarding; soccer; and tennis. Other boys' sports are baseball and football, while girls may choose field hockey and/or softball. Holderness also offers a rock-climbing club in the fall and spring and dance and an equestrian club in the spring.

The Gallop Athletic Center houses basketball and squash courts, a training room with state-of-the-art equipment, and a ski-tuning room with storage lockers.

Other facilities include a gymnasium; ten playing fields, including a turf field for soccer and lacrosse; ten tennis courts; a 10-kilometer cross-country trail, with 5 kilometers lit by lamps; a covered artificial-ice rink; and 600 acres of backyard wilderness. An eighteen-hole golf course is 3 miles away.

EXTRACURRICULAR OPPORTUNITIES

Life at Holderness is varied and energetic. The range of extracurricular activities is wide. The drama group presents three major productions a year. The School offers a chorus, a band, and a group specializing in vocal music. Lessons are available in guitar, piano, strings, brass, percussion, and woodwinds, and students are encouraged to try out for the New Hampshire All-State Chorus and the Granite State Youth Orchestra. The School's art and photography programs are very strong and enjoy a high level of student participation. A video/sound light studio enables students to become acquainted with the professional equipment and techniques involved in video tape recording, sound recording using a synthesizer, and still photography. Students publish a newspaper, a literary magazine, and a yearbook.

Various outdoor activities sponsored by the Holderness School Outing Club include biking, camping, canoeing, hiking, fishing, rock climbing, and winter climbing.

Every March for the past thirty years, the eleventh-grade class has snowshoed or skied away from school on Out Back, a ten-day wilderness program with Outward Bound features and philosophy. While the junior class is participating in Out Back, the two lower classes are immersed in Artward Bound, an intensive program in the arts that includes classes in art, drama, writing, and music, with evening programs ranging from movies and mime to readings by poets. An alternative to Artward Bound for sophomores is renovating houses for Habitat for Humanity. The twelfth grade spends the same period in Senior Colloquium, a rigorous seminar. Recent themes have included public speaking, writing for publication, production of paper, French cooking, classic American movies, and canoe building.

DAILY LIFE

Classes are held six days a week. Wednesday and Saturday are half days, to allow for interscholastic sports events in the afternoons. Classes begin at 8 a.m. and end at 3 p.m. during the fall and spring terms. There are five or six classes a day, each either 45 or 75 minutes long. Sports and extracurricular activities are from 3:30 to 5:30. During the winter term, classes run from 8 a.m. to 12:30 p.m.; the activity period is from 1 to 4; and class time follows and lasts until 5:30. Dinner is served at 6 p.m. and is followed by study hall from 7:30 to 9:30. Dorm check-in is at 10 p.m. for underclass students and at 10:30 for seniors.

WEEKEND LIFE

Weekend life at Holderness is planned by rotating faculty members and student leaders and varies with the seasons to some extent, but there are some constants. Movies are shown at the School every Saturday night, and students may walk to Plymouth, where there are shops and restaurants. Informal dances are held regularly at the School all year long. Sports events are held on Saturday afternoons.

Though there are many planned activities on Sunday, there is also the opportunity for students to organize their own free time. Day students are encouraged to participate in weekend events and social life.

COSTS AND FINANCIAL AID

Tuition for boarding students is $40,700, with additional expenses of books ($125–$200) and laundry ($120–$550). Day tuition is $24,190. Lessons for students participating in the band are free. There are separate charges for individual music lessons, driver's education, and participation in the U.S. Ski or Snowboarding Association program.

Tuition may be paid in full in July or in two installments in July and November. The latter method requires participation in the Tuition Refund Insurance Plan.

Financial aid grants are awarded in excess of $2.4 million, and over 40 percent of the students are currently receiving financial assistance.

ADMISSIONS INFORMATION

Holderness looks for boys and girls who are able to benefit from the challenge Holderness offers and who are willing to take an active part in the life of the School. Holderness seeks students of demonstrated scholastic ability who will be likely to achieve in a number of areas.

The most important requirements for admission are a student transcript and letters of recommendation from the applicant's present school. Applicants are strongly urged to visit the School for a tour of the campus and a personal interview. Candidates are expected to take the SSAT, preferably in December, for admission the following September. Most applications each year are for grades 9 and 10, although Holderness will accept a few students in grades 11 and 12.

APPLICATION TIMETABLE

Inquiries about the School or requests for a catalog are welcome anytime. Interested students and their parents are invited to make an appointment for a student-led tour of the School and an interview with an admissions officer. It is strongly recommended that this visit be made at a time when school is in session. The Admissions Office schedules appointments from 8:15 a.m. to 2:15 p.m. on Monday, Tuesday, Thursday, and Friday and from 8:15 to 10:45 a.m. on Wednesday and Saturday. During the winter term, appointments are scheduled for mornings, Monday through Saturday. In addition to application and personal forms, recommendations from math and English teachers and an extracurricular source will be requested. Grades for the entire first half of the school year, the results of any testing by the home school, SSAT scores, and a $50 fee complete the application.

Applications completed by February 1 have priority over those arriving later. Decisions on all applications received by February 1 are mailed on the mid-March date established by the National Association of Independent Schools. Parental confirmation of acceptance, plus a 10 percent reservation deposit for boarding and day students, is expected as soon as possible but not later than April 10. Financial aid awards are mailed out with acceptances.

For those students unable to meet the February 1 deadline, the Admissions Committee will review credentials after mid-April. If there should be openings then, or during the summer, late applicants will be notified.

ADMISSIONS CORRESPONDENCE

Nancy Dalley, Admissions Administrator
Holderness School
Plymouth, New Hampshire 03264
Phone: 603-536-1747
Fax: 603-536-2125
E-mail: admissions@holderness.org
Web site: http://www.holderness.org

HOOSAC SCHOOL

Hoosick, New York

Type: Coeducational boarding college-preparatory school
Grades: 8–12, postgraduate year
Enrollment: 113
Head of School: Richard J. Lomuscio, Headmaster

THE SCHOOL

Hoosac is an independent coeducational boarding school. Founded in 1889, the School still follows many of the traditions for which it is well known—for example, the nation's first student work program, in which students participate in the maintenance of their environment, and the Boar's Head and Yule Log Christmas Celebration, in which Burgess Meredith ('26) performed as a student.

Hoosac School is well suited to students who are academically motivated and are seeking a small-school environment. Hoosac also serves those who have not lived up to their potential in larger school settings, students with mild learning differences, and students who have talent but have received poor training through the years.

Hoosick is a rural community located 30 miles northeast of Albany, New York; 7 miles west of Bennington, Vermont; and 13 miles northwest of Williamstown, Massachusetts. The name of the town, like that of the School, is one of several spellings of a Native American word meaning "Place of the Owl."

Hoosac's setting amid 350 acres of fields and woods at the head of the Taconic Valley allows for a variety of outdoor activities, and the proximity of Williams College and Rensselaer Polytechnic Institute and the larger centers of Albany and Troy provides access to a wide range of cultural and educational opportunities.

Hoosac follows the Episcopal tradition in the short chapel services offered several times a week.

The School is operated by the Headmaster for an independent, self-perpetuating Board of Trustees. The plant is valued at $15 million.

Hoosac is accredited by the Middle States Association of Colleges and Schools and chartered by the New York State Board of Regents. It is a member of the National Association of Independent Schools, the Secondary School Admission Test Board, the National Association of Episcopal Schools, and the New York State Association of Independent Schools.

ACADEMIC PROGRAMS

The student-faculty ratio of 5:1 ensures that classes are kept small and that students receive a great deal of individual attention. One-to-one tutorials, independent study, and Advanced Placement courses are all available.

The curriculum consists of English I–IV, French I–II, ancient and modern European history, global studies, U.S. history, early American history, algebra I and II, geometry, precalculus, biology, chemistry, physics, psychology, earth science, computer literacy, art, photography, drama, music, film appreciation, criminology, fashion design, dance, and health. Advanced Placement courses are offered in calculus, U.S. history, and English.

In addition, the Oasis Program provides individual instruction to students with mild learning problems, relying on tutorials to establish healthy patterns of self-reliance.

Graduation requirements include the following: 4 years of English, 3 of science, 3 of mathematics, 3 of history and social studies (including 1 of U.S. history), 2 of a foreign language, 1 of a lab science, 1 of health, 1 of ethics, 1 of computers, and 1 trimester each of music, drama, and art. A three-year ESL program is available for international students.

Hoosac uses "Mastery Teaching." The concept of mastery education is older than the one-room schoolhouse where it was practiced; only the name is new. Mastery is an approach commonly used in every walk of life except formal education. For example, a person who wants to learn how to play tennis would not say, "I have 40 minutes to learn to serve. If I cannot do it in this time, I will never play tennis." Learning to serve a tennis ball well may take time. Therefore, a person would keep practicing until he or she mastered it. As in tennis, many things in life require time and repetition to learn. Given enough time and exposure, most people can master most things. Given enough exposure and support, students can learn almost anything.

Mastery uses testing as part of the instructional process. Each test reveals what a student does not know. On the basis of this, he or she is redirected and retaught in the weak areas. Each test, therefore, is a review of a student's knowledge for the purpose of reteaching. For example, a student takes a test, which is corrected and returned in class. The student is then retaught the information that they did not understand and tested again. Students also get extra help outside of class.

Mastery is an old and proven technique. It is used all over the United States, and it is a successful approach for most students. It allows the student to develop self-confidence and self-reliance.

FACULTY AND ADVISERS

Hoosac's Headmaster is Richard J. Lomuscio. Mr. Lomuscio is a graduate of NYU. He has been a newspaper editor and taught in both public and private schools. Mr. Lomuscio has served Hoosac for thirty-four years in many capacities—teacher of math, French, science, history, and English; housemaster; coach; college counselor; Director of Athletics; Director of Studies; Dean; and Headmaster.

The faculty numbers 24, of whom 8 are women. Faculty members live on campus. They and their families participate fully in all activities.

The School's adviser system is one more example of the individual attention given to students. The system provides the structure and support students need to be successful. A faculty member is responsible for up to 8 advisees, whom he or she sees at least twice a week—once in a private meeting and once in a group meeting. Advisers receive biweekly reports on each student from the student's teachers so that any changes or problems that arise can be handled quickly. Parents also play a significant role in this system; they can monitor their child's progress by keeping in close contact with his or her adviser.

COLLEGE ADMISSION COUNSELING

College counseling, supervised by the Headmaster, begins in the junior year, and students visit colleges during the summer and fall. Admissions officers from many colleges and universities visit Hoosac.

In the last several years, graduates have been accepted to Bennington, Boston College, Boston University, Bowdoin, Clarkson, Connecticut College, Drexel, Hamilton, Hartwick, Manhattanville, Northeastern, NYU, Penn State, Rensselaer, St. Lawrence, Syracuse, Trinity (Hartford), Vassar, Vanderbilt, Washington and Jefferson, Wheaton, and the Universities of Hartford, New Hampshire, Southern California, and Vermont.

STUDENT BODY AND CONDUCT

Hoosac enrolls 113 boarding boys and girls. Most students come from the northeastern United States; others are from Georgia, Virginia, Pennsylvania, Idaho, California, Texas, and Florida and from several other countries.

Students are represented in school affairs through a traditional prefect system and play major leadership roles in important areas of school life. The kitchen and dining hall are supervised by student stewards. All class bells are rung by a student bell ringer, and the coaches are helped by student assistants. The work program is supervised by student proctors, as are the dormitory facilities. The faculty and administration offer careful guidance in order to strengthen the lessons of leadership and responsibility.

Minor infractions of Hoosac's rules and regulations result in an obligation to donate work for the benefit of the School community; more serious infractions of the regulations can result in suspension, and very serious cases can lead to dismissal. Possession or use of illegal drugs results in automatic expulsion from school, even for a first offense.

ACADEMIC FACILITIES

Tibbits Hall, built in 1828 and remodeled in 1860, is a freestone Gothic castle containing offices, classrooms, a dormitory, and faculty apartments. Wood Hall contains the School's library, a faculty apartment, and a dormitory area. Crosby Arts Center provides facilities for theater, art, music, and dance.

Other buildings include Memorial Dining Hall (1963), which houses a spacious dining area and student lounge as well as classrooms. Blake Hall (1969) is the science building and includes classrooms, laboratories, a darkroom, a lecture hall, and an observatory equipped with two telescopes.

BOARDING AND GENERAL FACILITIES

Lewisohn and Dudley houses are small dormitories. Whitcomb Hall houses the chapel, a dormitory, and a faculty residence.

Several more recent buildings complete the campus. Pitt Mason Hall (1967) is the largest of the dormitories, housing 30 students; it includes apartments for three faculty families. Lavino House (1969) also serves as a dormitory. The Edith McCullough House (1990) holds 8 students and a faculty family, as does Cannon House, built in 1970.

About half the dormitory rooms are doubles and the rest are singles. At least one faculty family lives in every dormitory.

ATHLETICS

Every student is required to participate in athletics or an athletics alternative during the afternoon. The School fields teams at the varsity level in soccer, ice hockey, lacrosse, basketball, tennis, baseball, and volleyball and offers skiing and flag football as intramural sports. Modern dance and fitness classes are also available. Hoosac's teams participate in league competition.

Campus sports facilities include three soccer fields, one baseball diamond, a skating pond, 6 miles of cross-country running and skiing trails, and tennis courts. Students can also fish in nearby trout streams and hike and camp in Tibbits Forest. The School's sports complex includes a gymnasium, a locker and shower area, and a swimming pool. Hoosac has a ski slope on campus as well.

EXTRACURRICULAR OPPORTUNITIES

Because the student body is small, individual interests and casual groups, rather than formal clubs, are emphasized. Extracurricular activities include student publications, academic clubs, music, and art. The students present theatrical productions and participate annually in the century-old Boar's Head and Yule Log Christmas Celebration.

The Student Activities Committee works with a faculty member to provide weekend opportunities. Informal organized activities include hiking, camping, horseback riding, fishing, skiing, and skating. Traditional events for the School community include two Parents' Weekends. There is a banquet with a speaker every Friday evening.

A driver's education course is offered, as is a Red Cross lifeguarding course.

DAILY LIFE

Breakfast is served at 7:20 a.m. Chapel is at 8, followed by a Schoolwide meeting. Classes run from 8:35 to 2:50; there is a break at noon for a family-style sit-down lunch. Sports take place in the afternoon after classes. Dinner is at 6, followed each evening by a required study period. Lights-out is at 10:30.

Classes meet six days a week for 45 minutes each period; Wednesday and Saturday are half days to leave time for special activities and free time.

WEEKEND LIFE

Dances, concerts, lectures, and other special activities are planned with local schools, such as Emma Willard, Stoneleigh-Burnham, Miss Hall's, and Doane Stuart. On Saturday evenings, students go to movies or the mall in Pittsfield, Albany, and Saratoga or at the School or participate in other leisure-time activities. They may also attend musical, theatrical, and educational programs at local colleges, particularly Williams and Rensselaer in Troy.

Following brunch on Sunday, students explore the woodlands, climb, hike, fish, or ski on campus or at nearby resort areas. One long weekend is scheduled during each trimester, and students may take additional weekend leaves.

COSTS AND FINANCIAL AID

Boarding tuition for 2008–09 was approximately $31,300. Hoosac, which subscribes to the School and Student Service for Financial Aid, grants financial aid on the basis of demonstrated need. Approximately 30 percent of the students receive aid totaling more than $500,000 per year.

ADMISSIONS INFORMATION

New students are accepted at all grade levels on the basis of previous academic records and a personal interview. The first step for interested students and their families is to request a catalog and application and schedule a visit to the campus.

APPLICATION TIMETABLE

Candidates are encouraged to apply by March 15, although applications are considered at any time during the year as long as there are spaces available.

ADMISSIONS CORRESPONDENCE

Dean S. Foster, Assistant Headmaster
Hoosac School
Hoosick, New York 12089
Phone: 800-822-0159 (toll-free)
Fax: 518-686-3370
E-mail: info@hoosac.com
Web site: http://www.hoosac.com

Photo by Gabriel Amadeus Cooney

Photo by Gabriel Amadeus Cooney

THE HOTCHKISS SCHOOL

Lakeville, Connecticut

Type: Coeducational boarding and day college-preparatory school
Grades: 9–12 (Prep, Lower Middle, Upper Middle, Senior), postgraduate year
Enrollment: 590
Head of School: Malcolm McKenzie

THE SCHOOL

The Hotchkiss School was founded by Maria Bissell Hotchkiss in 1891 at the urging of President Timothy Dwight of Yale. The School was established to prepare young men in the basic skills of the classical curriculum then in vogue so that they might go on to attend Yale. The Hotchkiss tradition of academic excellence prevails today but with a much broader scope of course offerings and within a coeducational community.

A small-school community with a large-school diversity, Hotchkiss strives to develop in students a lifelong love of learning, responsible citizenship, and personal integrity. The Hotchkiss School's Statement of Goals and Purposes is as follows: The School is a community based on trust, mutual respect, and compassion, and it holds all members of the community accountable for upholding these values. The School is committed to mastery of learning skills, development of intellectual curiosity, excellence, and creativity in all disciplines, and enthusiastic participation in athletics and other school activities. The School encourages students to develop clarity of thought, confidence and facility in expressing ideas, and artistic and aesthetic sensitivity. In and out of the classroom, all members of the community are expected to subject their views and actions to critical examination and to accept responsibility for them. The School hopes that graduates will leave Hotchkiss with a commitment to environmental stewardship and service to others and with a greater understanding of themselves and of their roles in a global society.

The village of Lakeville is in the Township of Salisbury, a community of 3,700 people in rural northwestern Connecticut. The School is situated on 810 acres of hills and woodlands bordering on two lakes. The campus is 2 hours from New York City; 1½ hours from Hartford, Connecticut; and 3 hours from Boston.

The Hotchkiss School is a nonprofit corporation governed by a 25-member Board of Trustees. The School's endowment is currently valued at $383,000,000. In celebration of the School's centennial, a $100-million capital campaign was completed, allowing for enhancement of academic programs and renovation and enlargement of campus facilities. In addition to the $10-million renovation of the science building, the School has enlarged and remodeled the athletic facilities, raised increased funding for financial assistance, completed a $20-million state-of-the-art music facility, and completed construction on two new dormitories. The Annual Fund generates more than $3 million for the yearly operating budget. The Hotchkiss Alumni Association maintains contact with more than 8,550 alumni, many of whom provide substantial financial support and are active in student recruiting activities.

The School is accredited by the New England Association of Schools and Colleges and the Connecticut Association of Independent Schools. It holds membership in the National Association of Independent Schools, the National Association of Principals of Schools for Girls, and the Council for Advancement and Support of Education.

ACADEMIC PROGRAMS

The curriculum at Hotchkiss has evolved over the years from a classical, formal, and prescriptive set of courses with limited sectioning to an increasingly diverse but interwoven learning opportunity, offering a choice of 227 separate courses, some of them interdisciplinary and many offered as seminars. Classes begin in September and end in June, with time off for Thanksgiving Break, Winter Break, and Spring Break.

Seventeen courses, including 4 years of English; 3 years of mathematics; 3 years of one language; 1 year of American history; 1 year of art, including art, dànce, drama, music, or photography; and 1 year of biology, chemistry, or physics, are required of four-year students for graduation. Advanced Placement courses are available in many subject areas. Incoming students are given placement exams to determine the level at which they should begin their studies.

Students carry an average of five courses per semester. The average class size is 12. The School uses a letter grading system, and reports are sent to parents four times a year, or more often if the situation warrants it. Faculty members provide extra help in and out of the classroom setting and student tutors are available to help their peers. In addition, a comprehensive study skills program supports students who find some difficulty with an intensive academic program.

Qualified upperclass students may participate in a School Year Abroad program in China, France, India, Italy, or Spain; the Maine Coast Semester program; the Rocky Mountain Semester program; or the CityTerm program at the Masters School. They also may participate in student exchanges with Round Square schools and may apply through the English-Speaking Union for a postgraduate year of study at an English boarding school.

FACULTY AND ADVISERS

In 2008–09, the Hotchkiss faculty consisted of 153 faculty members and administrators. Of the 150 faculty members, 90 hold advanced degrees, including eleven doctorates.

Hotchkiss seeks a diverse and experienced faculty dedicated not only to teaching academic courses but also to aiding the full personal growth of each student. In addition to their teaching and administrative responsibilities, they are dormitory parents, academic advisers, and coaches.

COLLEGE ADMISSION COUNSELING

Hotchkiss seeks to provide each student with the advice, support, and information necessary to make appropriate choices for future education. Three advisors guide students through the selection of colleges and the application process. More than 100 college representatives visit the School each year to conduct group meetings or interviews with students. Ten or more graduates of the past four classes, 2005–2008, attend the following schools: Boston University, Bowdoin, Brown, Colgate, Cornell, Dartmouth, Georgetown, George Washington, Harvard, Johns Hopkins, Middlebury, NYU, Princeton, Trinity College (Connecticut), University of Pennsylvania, Vanderbilt, Williams, and Yale.

STUDENT BODY AND CONDUCT

The enrollment for 2008–09 consisted of 590 students, 542 of whom were boarding students, (290 girls and 300 boys). Students came from thirty-nine states and thirty-two other countries. International students constituted 17 percent, and students who were members of minority groups accounted for 36 percent of the student body.

The day-to-day life at Hotchkiss is governed by several important principles: concern for others, respect for all members of the community, and understanding and adherence to the rules as stated in the Hotchkiss School Handbook. The actions and attitudes of each student at Hotchkiss should be governed by concern for others, with the rules serving as guidelines for expected behavior. Composed of students and faculty members, the Hotchkiss Discipline Committee reviews reports of possible infractions of School rules and in each case makes recommendations for action to the Head of School.

ACADEMIC FACILITIES

A great advantage of the Hotchkiss campus is the centralization of the academic facilities. Handsomely renovated and significantly enlarged in 1995, the Main Building is the hub of campus life. Main Building has wings accommodating the student center, chapel, auditorium, and dining hall; two computer labs; the Cullman Art Center; the Tremaine Art Gallery, dance studio, and black-box theater; and the Edsel Ford Library, which holds a collection of more than 80,000 volumes. In fall 2005, a new wing of the Main Building was completed, which houses the School's state-of-the-art music and art facilities. All classes other than those in science are held in the Main Building. The recently renovated Griswold Science Building has a full range of laboratories and areas for independent study, extensive photographic facilities, a weather station, and a radio station with full broadcasting capabilities.

BOARDING AND GENERAL FACILITIES

Hotchkiss has twelve dormitories. About three quarters of the students reside in single rooms on corridors organized by class, averaging 15 students per corridor. Faculty members and senior proctors reside on each corridor and provide extensive supervision and guidance.

The School has one dining hall, a student center with a snack bar, a bookstore that carries a full line of supplies, and a number of areas for informal gatherings. The fully equipped, recently renovated Wieler Infirmary on campus is open 24 hours a day and the Sharon Hospital is 7 miles down the road.

ATHLETICS

The athletics program is one of the School's great strengths and a major source of its spirit. All students participate in the program every season, and they pursue an activity of their choice at a level to suit their abilities.

The School prides itself on its ability to compete equally with other New England secondary schools. Hotchkiss also regularly takes part in annual coeducational New England championship meets in cross-country, field hockey, football, swimming, squash, track, volleyball, water polo, and boys' wrestling.

The School's athletic facilities are superb. A 212,000-square-foot athletic and fitness center opened in 2002. The Hotchkiss community now enjoys a second indoor ice rink, a field house with three basketball/volleyball courts and an elevated track, an expanded wrestling/multipurpose room, eight international-style squash courts, and a ten-lane swimming facility with a separate diving well. Other existing athletic facilities include a nine-hole golf course, a 400-meter all-weather track, a regulation baseball field, two football fields, four field hockey fields, five soccer/lacrosse fields, two paddle tennis courts, and twenty all-weather and three indoor tennis courts as well as a lakefront with a boathouse.

EXTRACURRICULAR OPPORTUNITIES

The location of the Hotchkiss School allows for many extracurricular opportunities on campus, in the local community, and in various locations beyond the town of Lakeville. Among the most active organizations are the Hotchkiss Dramatic Association, which schedules three major productions per year and presents as many as twelve student plays; the music department, which sponsors and encourages a wide range of informal musical groups; and the various student publications.

The community service club, the St. Luke's Society, is involved in volunteer community affairs, including tutoring the handicapped, helping the aging, working in the Sharon Hospital, and working with the local volunteer ambulance service. Hotchkiss is a campus chapter member of Habitat for Humanity. Hotchkiss also has a School service program, whereby each student is expected to perform service within the School community for at least one semester each year.

DAILY LIFE

Classes are held six days a week, with Wednesdays and Saturdays as half days to accommodate interscholastic athletic competitions. A typical day begins with breakfast served cafeteria style between 7 and 8:30 a.m. The first period begins at 8, with 45-minute class periods thereafter. Students eat lunch during their free noontime period. Classes end at 3:10 p.m., and sports begin at 3:30. The dining hall is open for dinner between 5:30 and 7. Evening study times are set for ninth and tenth graders between 8 and 10.

WEEKEND LIFE

Students are permitted to take weekends away from the campus, but most choose to remain at the School and join the variety of activities taking place. The standard weekend events include sports competitions, movies, dances, concerts, and other scheduled activities. As students move from the lower classes to the senior year, they are permitted more weekends away from campus.

COSTS AND FINANCIAL AID

Tuition for 2008–09 was $42,000 for boarding students and $34,250 for day students. Tuition payments are due twice yearly, at the start of each semester.

Hotchkiss offered more than $6 million in scholarships for the 2008–09 school year. In 2008–09, 34 percent of enrolled students received some level of financial assistance. Awards are made to families on the basis of family financial need, as determined by the School and Student Service for Financial Aid in Princeton, New Jersey. Those who do not qualify for direct assistance or who need additional assistance above the amount awarded may apply for loans.

ADMISSIONS INFORMATION

The School seeks to enroll students of good will and strong character who will be examples of integrity and decency. The School seeks students who provide evidence of academic ability and intellectual curiosity. Hotchkiss students should be prepared for and are expected to take advantage of the academic and cocurricular opportunities available at the School. The School aims to attract students from among the most accomplished and promising young people of diverse backgrounds, experiences, and expectations.

Applicants must complete a formal application of admission, which includes a writing sample and applicant project as well as recommendations from three teachers and an official school record. Applicants to the ninth, tenth, and eleventh grades are also required to submit results of the SSAT or ISEE. Applicants to the senior or postgraduate year are required to submit scores from the PSAT or SAT. An interview is a required part of the admission process.

APPLICATION TIMETABLE

Initial inquiries are welcome at any time. Visits to the campus include a student-led tour and an interview with a member of the admission committee. It is strongly recommended that candidates and their parents visit when the School is in session. If this is impossible, an interview may be arranged at the School or elsewhere through the Office of Admission.

A final application and a $50 nonrefundable application fee ($100 for international applications) must be submitted by January 15. Hotchkiss notifies candidates and their families of admission decisions by March 10, with a reply date of April 10.

ADMISSIONS CORRESPONDENCE

Rachael N. Beare
Dean of Admission and Financial Aid
The Hotchkiss School
P.O. Box 800
Lakeville, Connecticut 06039
Phone: 860-435-3102
Fax: 860-435-0042
E-mail: admission@hotchkiss.org
Web site: http://www.hotchkiss.org

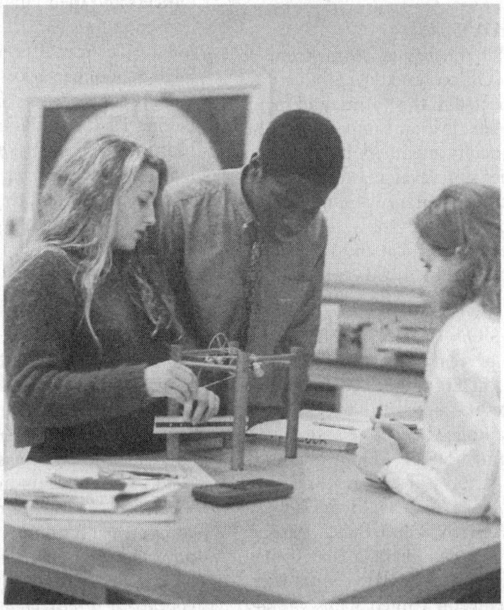

HOWE MILITARY SCHOOL

Howe, Indiana

Type: Coeducational, boarding college-preparatory and military school
Grades: 5–12: Junior High, 5–8; High School, 9–12
Enrollment: School total: 153; High School: 115
Head of School: Dr. Duane VanOrden, Superintendent

THE SCHOOL

Howe Military School is a private, college-preparatory boarding school for boys and girls in grades 5 through 12. Located in northeastern Indiana, the village of Howe (population 500) is midway between LaGrange, Indiana, and Sturgis, Michigan. Accessible via the Indiana Toll Road (Interstate 80/90), the School is an hour from South Bend, Indiana; 3 hours from Indianapolis, Chicago, and Detroit; and 5 hours from Cincinnati.

The School was established in 1884 as the result of a bequest to the Episcopal Church by the Honorable John Badlam Howe. The military program was instituted in 1895, and since 1920, the School has had a Junior ROTC Honor Unit with Distinction sponsored by the Department of the Army.

Howe Military School seeks to provide a balanced education that affords opportunities for college preparation through academics, physical development through athletics, leadership through the military program, and spiritual development through Christian worship and service. Howe maintains its historic affiliation with the Episcopal Church, but welcomes young people of all faiths.

A nonprofit institution, Howe is governed by a self-perpetuating Board of Trustees, 20 in number, which meets quarterly. Included on the board are the Bishop of the Episcopal Diocese of Northern Indiana (its head), the Superintendent, parents, and alumni. The Alumni Association, which represents the more than 3,100 living graduates, elects the 2 alumni board members.

Howe Military School is accredited by the State of Indiana, the North Central Association of Colleges and Schools, and the Independent Schools Association of the Central States. Howe has memberships in the Association of Military Colleges and Schools of the United States, the Council for Advancement and Support of Education, the National Association of Independent Schools, and the Association of Boarding Schools (TABS).

ACADEMIC PROGRAMS

The School year, from mid-August to late May, is divided into semesters, with Thanksgiving, Christmas, and Spring Break vacations. Classes, which have a maximum enrollment of 16, meet five days a week.

The average class size is 8 to 10 students. Cadets receive extra help from teachers during the daily after-school extra-help period. To encourage academic growth, each cadet is assigned a Potential Achievement Rating (PAR), based on objective test results, teacher ratings, and a self-evaluation. The cadet is expected to attain and maintain this goal, which is revised periodically to reflect changes in performance. Grades are sent to parents every six weeks (three weeks for Lower School students).

Computers are integrated into classes, with a computer for every teacher and two full labs, one of which is a multimedia lab. All are networked into each High School barracks room, where each cadet also has his or her own leased computer. All High School cadets are required to lease a personal computer through a third-party vendor.

To graduate, High School cadets must complete 21 academic units, including 4 of English; 3 of mathematics, including algebra I and geometry; 3 of science; 3 of social studies, including United States history and government; 2 of the same foreign language; 1 of computer science; 1½ of health/physical education; and 1–4 years of Leadership Excellence Training. The additional units are taken in elective courses. The High School curriculum includes full-year courses in English I–IV, algebra I–II, geometry, college algebra/trigonometry, calculus, French I–III, German I–III, Spanish I–IV, biology, advanced biology, chemistry, physical science, physics, environmental science, U.S. history, world history, accounting I–II, band, choir, and woods I–II. Semester courses are offered in computer programming, computer graphics, keyboarding, multimedia graphics, health (substance-abuse prevention included), electricity, power mechanics, biochemistry, organic chemistry, economics, Christian ethics (required), and sociology.

Military training for the younger cadets consists of drill, "the manual of arms, the school of the soldier, and other instructions contributing to the precision and poise of the individual and the esprit de corps of the group." High School courses cover a variety of topics, such as drill, hygiene, first aid, weapons safety, land navigation, military history, and the U.S. Constitution.

FACULTY AND ADVISERS

The full-time faculty consists of 26 men and 9 women. Six Tactical Officers and their families live in apartments connected to the dorms, and many of the faculty members live on campus or in the village of Howe. Faculty members hold sixteen baccalaureate degrees and eleven master's degrees. Faculty benefits include insurance and retirement plans, payment for advanced study, and Social Security. One retired army officer and 1 noncommissioned officer conduct the JROTC program.

COLLEGE ADMISSION COUNSELING

Annually, nearly 95 percent of Howe graduates go on to higher education. From the 2008 graduating class, 90 percent were accepted to the schools of their choosing and enrolled in colleges and universities across the United States. Recent graduates are attending such schools of higher learning as DePauw, Kenyon, Loyola Chicago, Miami (Ohio), Michigan State, Norwich, Ohio State, Purdue, Rose Hulman, St. Mary's, Spelman, the United States Air Force Academy, the United States Merchant Marine Academy, the United States Military Academy, the United States Naval Academy, Valparaiso, Virginia Military Institute, Wooster, and the Universities of Arizona, Chicago, Illinois, Indiana, Indianapolis, Miami, Michigan, Tampa, and Washington.

STUDENT BODY AND CONDUCT

Most of the students come from Illinois, Indiana, Michigan, and Ohio. The School also accepts students from all fifty states and around the world.

The Corps of Cadets is governed by the rules and regulations of the School. It is also expected to live up to the Cadet's Personal Code of Honor, which states: "I will not lie, steal or cheat, nor tolerate among us anyone who does." The School motto is "Faith and honor."

ACADEMIC FACILITIES

Classes are held in the Memorial Academic Building and annex, which together provide twenty classrooms and four science laboratories. The main biology lab was completely remodeled in 1996. Junior High classes are held in White Hall. The Grace Libey Library contains 14,000 volumes and three reference computers with CD-ROM capability; limited Internet access is available in the library. Other School buildings are Bouton Auditorium, the Industrial Arts Building, St. James Chapel, All Saints' Chapel, Memorial Gym, the Quartermaster Store, and Herrick Administration Building.

BOARDING AND GENERAL FACILITIES

Junior High cadets reside in the Frank M. Little Barracks, which provides quarters for 2 Tactical Officers and their families. High School cadets are housed in four barracks that also provide quarters for the Tactical Officers and their families. Each High School barracks room allows one computer per student. Cadets eat in the Major Merritt Dining Hall; in addition, cadets may visit the Fr. Jennings Canteen/Recreational Center. The Doctors Wade Infirmary has thirty beds divided into two wards for boys and girls. The infirmary is staffed day and night by Parkview Hospital.

ATHLETICS

The 150-acre campus includes a 50-acre athletics complex, sports fields, and six tennis courts. Indoor athletics facilities are located in the gymnasium, which provides a wrestling room, a basketball court, and a weight room that was totally refurbished in 1999. An indoor swimming pool is adjacent to the gymnasium and was renovated in 2000. Varsity teams in baseball, basketball, golf, soccer, tennis, track, girls' volleyball, and wrestling compete with those of other independent and public high schools. There are intramural teams in basketball, swimming, tennis, touch football, and volleyball. Junior High cadets participate in basketball, cross-country, golf, soccer, track, and wrestling.

EXTRACURRICULAR OPPORTUNITIES

Many extracurricular activities reflect the military nature of the School. Among the cadet organizations are the Rangers, the Hussars (drill team), the rifle team, VHC (the lettermen's club), the Old Guard (cadets in attendance four or more years), and the Color Guard.

Cadets may join the staff of the School newspaper and the yearbook. Cadets may participate in the Howe Military School radio station, WHWE-FM, where they put together shows and perform other aspects of managing a radio station. They may also participate in Howe's chapter of the National Forensic League or the National Thespians. Qualified cadets are elected to the Cum Laude Society. Cadets who consistently earn a 3.5 GPA are entered in the Alpha Delta Tau Society. Musical groups include the marching band, the concert band, and the chapel choir. Cadets of all ages may receive acolyte training and participate regularly in chapel services.

DAILY LIFE

A typical day begins with First Call at 6 a.m. and First Mess from 7 to 7:45. Regular academic classes begin at 8 and continue until 3 p.m., with a break for lunch from 11:40 until 12:15. For those who need or want it, an extra-help period immediately follows classes, from 3 until 3:35. Athletics begin at 4 and continue until 5:30. At 6:05, the Cadets form up for the ceremony to lower the flag (Retreat). From 6:15 until 6:30 on Monday, Tuesday, Thursday, and Friday evenings, there is a prayer service in one of the chapels. Third Mess begins at 6:35. Evening study hall runs from 7:30 until 9:15. Junior High taps is at 9:30, at 10 for underclassmen, and at 11 for seniors.

WEEKEND LIFE

Cadets have free time on Friday evenings and Saturday and Sunday afternoons, for a half hour each evening, and for brief periods during the School day. Social activities include movies, occasional professional entertainment, three sock hops and two formal dances each year, numerous club dinners, a trip to Cedar Point, mall shopping, and theater productions. Among the traditional annual events are a Family Picnic, Founders' Day, Boar's Head Dinner, family weekend in February, Alumni Weekend, and Mother's Day Weekend. Field trips are arranged to such places as nearby zoos, the Football Hall of Fame, Greenfield Village, the Henry Ford Museum, Cedar Point Amusement Park, Chicago museums, and professional sporting events.

COSTS AND FINANCIAL AID

It is understood that once a cadet is enrolled, he or she remains for the entire academic year or, in cases of late enrollment, for the balance of the year. The overall cost for the 2008–09 year was $25,000 plus a computer fee of $300 for High School cadets. The School does not provide health and accident insurance, so this should be taken care of by the parents.

Transportation to and from School during vacation periods and on open weekends is over and above the estimated cost. A cadet should be provided with a weekly allowance or spending money; the School recommends a moderate amount.

There are some additional charges according to the cadet's interests, such as fees for band instrument rental or private music lessons.

There are three payment plans available. The Basic Payment Plan requires full payment of $25,000 by the enrollment date. The Deferred Payment Plan and the Monthly Payment Plan are available at costs of $400 and $600, respectively. The Deferred Payment Plan requires 60 percent of the total cost to be paid at registration, with the remaining 40 percent due on or before December 10. The Monthly Payment Plan requires payment in ten installments. These program payments are due commencing March 10 and ending December 10. This plan may be selected during any month, by issuing payment for months missed and continuing payment through December 10. Parents who are interested in a tuition loan or further information should call the Admissions Office.

The School has a limited amount of scholarship funds available through endowments from friends of Howe. These funds are awarded on the basis of academic ability and performance, conduct, general attitude, and family financial need. Parents wishing to apply for scholarship funds should contact the Director of Admissions for a Financial Aid Application Form.

ADMISSIONS INFORMATION

Howe seeks boys and girls of good character who have the ability to do college-preparatory work. Howe Military School is neither a correctional facility nor a therapeutic school. Howe is a traditional, private, college-preparatory boarding school. Howe's military orientation is not intended to prepare students for the military service. The military program is used to teach Howe's students self-discipline, focus, organization, and authority. Cadets are accepted in grades 5–12 on the basis of admission test results, school records, and three school references. Admission tests are administered at Howe at the time of the campus visit; if candidates cannot take the tests at the School, they may arrange to do so under supervision at a more convenient location. There is a $100 application fee.

APPLICATION TIMETABLE

Initial inquiries are welcome at any time. Campus tours are arranged, in conjunction with interviews and Howe's admissions test, from 8 to 4:30 EST on weekdays and by appointment only on weekends.

ADMISSIONS CORRESPONDENCE

Dr. Brent Smith, Director of Admissions
Howe Military School
P.O. Box 240
Howe, Indiana 46746
Phone: 260-562-2131 Ext. 221
888-GO-2-HOWE (toll-free)
Fax: 260-562-3678
E-mail: admissions@howemilitary.com
Web site: http://www.howemilitary.com

THE HUN SCHOOL OF PRINCETON

Princeton, New Jersey

Type: Coeducational boarding (grades 9–PG) and day (grades 6–12) college-preparatory school
Grades: 6–PG: Middle School, 6–8; Upper School, 9–12, postgraduate year
Enrollment: School total: 596; Upper School: 505
Head of School: Mr. Jonathan Brougham, Headmaster

THE SCHOOL

The Hun School of Princeton was established as the Princeton Math School in 1914 by Dr. John Gale Hun, an assistant professor of mathematics at Princeton University. The School expanded its curriculum and facilities as colleges implemented higher standards of admission. In 1925, The Hun School moved to its present location, a 45-acre campus in Princeton's residential western section. The School was incorporated under the direction of a board of trustees in 1944. Today, the board consists of 33 members.

Students enjoy the advantages of a town that is home to one of the greatest universities in the country and yet preserves the flavor of a small community. The School is within walking distance of Princeton University, and New York and Philadelphia are both about an hour away by train, bus, or car.

The Hun School is dedicated to providing a strong college-preparatory program that leads to informed college choices. A full range of athletics and activities supplement a strong curriculum designed to stimulate critical thinking and analysis and to inspire curiosity. Competent, caring faculty members work closely with students to promote excellence and self-esteem in an environment of high but fair expectations. The faculty and curriculum are responsive to individual learning styles and interests. The total program is committed to the development of solid scholarship and sound character in an environment dedicated to timeless values: honor, service, perseverance, responsibility, compassion, respect, and leadership.

The Hun School enjoys strong support from parents, trustees, alumni, faculty and staff members, foundations, and friends of the School. Through this support, the School recently completed major additions to the library, dining hall, and academic building and has recently built a new athletic complex.

The Hun School is accredited by the Middle States Association of Colleges and Schools and approved by the Department of Education of the state of New Jersey. It is a member of the College Board, National Association of Independent Schools, the Association of Boarding Schools, National Association for College Admission Counseling, Council for Advancement and Support of Education, Cum Laude Society, and National Association for Foreign Student Affairs.

ACADEMIC PROGRAMS

The Hun School requires 19½ units for graduation, including 4 in English, 3 in mathematics, 3 in history, 3 in laboratory science, 2 in foreign language, and ½ in fine arts. Students may choose from more than ninety-five courses, including government, economics, the arts, and public speaking. Foreign language study includes French, Latin, and Spanish.

Upper School offerings also include independent study, honors, accelerated, and Advanced Placement courses. Hun has one of the oldest international student programs in the country and an Academic Learning Skills Program for students with mild learning differences.

The grading system uses numerals; 60 is the minimum passing grade. The academic year is divided into eighteen-week semesters, each containing two marking periods. Term examinations are given at the end of each semester, and academic reports are issued to parents four times a year. Written progress reports are also issued three or more times annually.

Classes average 14 students each. Five is the average number of courses taken each term. During the day, some students may have a free period available for study; in the evening, boarding students study in their rooms or in the library. For academic reasons, some students may be assigned to a supervised study hall during the school day. Students may also use their free time in the Writing and Study Strategies Centers. There is a period scheduled at the end of each day when all faculty members are available to meet students individually or in small groups to review, clarify, or expand classroom learning.

FACULTY AND ADVISERS

The faculty consists of 59 men and 47 women, all of whom serve full-time. More than half of The Hun School faculty members hold master's or doctoral degrees. Thirty of the faculty members live on campus. They have an average of twelve years of teaching experience. Faculty turnover is low.

Headmaster Jonathan Brougham was appointed in 2008. A graduate of Williams College, Mr. Brougham holds a juris doctorate from Columbia University School of Law and a master's degree in educational administration from Columbia's Klingenstein Center. He most recently served as the head of the Upper School at Collegiate School in Richmond, Virginia. Mr. Brougham will serve his first year as headmaster in the 2009–10 academic year.

The School supports the professional development of the staff by providing grants for graduate study and by encouraging the faculty to participate in workshops and conferences. Faculty members coach, counsel, and supervise extracurricular activities in addition to teaching.

COLLEGE ADMISSION COUNSELING

The College Counseling Office arranges group and individual meetings with students, starting in the sophomore year. By the senior year, regular individual meetings are conducted that center on the selection of institutions that meet the academic and extracurricular interests of the students. All students are encouraged to visit colleges, attend college fairs, and meet with the representatives of more than 200 institutions that visit The Hun School annually.

During the spring semester, the School, in conjunction with other local independent schools, hosts a college fair, inviting representatives from more than 300 colleges and universities to the Princeton area. The Hun School also sponsors a special evening program in the fall of the junior year and again in the fall of the senior year to explain the college selection process. In the past, the programs have featured college directors of admission, Educational Testing Service representatives, and financial aid experts. In the summer sessions, The Hun School also conducts briefings on preparing for the SAT.

In 2008, 130 graduates entered college. Former Hun School students attend Boston College, Colgate, Dartmouth, Duke, Florida State, Harvard, Penn State, Princeton, Rutgers, Stanford, Tufts, Wellesley, Yale, the Universities of Notre Dame and Pennsylvania, and others.

STUDENT BODY AND CONDUCT

The composition of the Upper School is as follows: 115 students in grade 9, 121 in grade 10, 141 in grade 11, 116 in grade 12, and 14 postgraduates. Although the largest group of students comes from New Jersey, New York, and Pennsylvania, seventeen states and fourteen countries are represented; about 10 percent of the students are from other countries.

Each member of the School community is expected to be responsible, self-disciplined, and concerned for the welfare of all. The Hun School has an Honor Code, and, through School agencies, students have a voice in the determination and enforcement of rules. The Discipline Committee, with voting student representation, makes recommendations to the Headmaster. The Honor Council, composed of students and faculty members, hears cases relating to the Honor Code and makes recommendations to the Headmaster, teachers, and students.

ACADEMIC FACILITIES

The Chesebro Academic Center and the Buck Activities Center, the two academic buildings, contain thirty-two classrooms, six science laboratories, three computer centers (thirty-six stations), photography darkrooms, an art studio, a ceramics and sculpture studio with a potter's wheel and kiln, and a music studio. Other academic facilities include a renovated 50,000-volume library with more than 45 online and CD-ROM databases, a greenhouse, a vocal music room, a wet laboratory, an aquarium, project rooms, and television and radio broadcast studios.

BOARDING AND GENERAL FACILITIES

Boys at The Hun School live in two dorms, one of which is for older students, and girls reside in a third dorm. All dorms are supervised by resident faculty members and student proctors. The dorms have lounges equipped with televisions and cooking facilities. Resident faculty families and students eat together in the centrally located dining hall. A bookstore and clinic are available on campus. The Student Activities Center houses a snack bar and a game room.

ATHLETICS

Every student can find a niche in the variety of individual and team sports offered at The Hun School at freshman, junior varsity, and varsity interscholastic levels and on intramural teams. The primary aims of the coaching staff are to teach individual skills, to develop leadership and teamwork on the field, and to instill the concept of fair play. Cross-country, golf, fencing teams, swimming, and track and field are open to boys and girls on a competitive basis. In addition, boys compete in baseball, basketball, crew, football, ice hockey, lacrosse, soccer, tennis, and wrestling. Girls compete in basketball, crew, field hockey, lacrosse, soccer, softball, and tennis.

Coeducational intramural programs are offered in dance, seasonal sports, water polo, weight lifting, and other exercises promoting physical fitness.

The School's new athletic facility includes a gymnasium, a health and fitness center, eight tennis courts, a cross-country course, six playing fields (including an artificial turf field), and a 400-meter all-weather track.

EXTRACURRICULAR OPPORTUNITIES

Through extracurricular activities, students may pursue special interests and develop social as well as personal skills. Clubs and other student activities, often organized around curricular and career interests, are under the direction of faculty advisers. Resident and day students work on the student newspaper, *The Mall,* and the yearbook, *Edgerstounian,* and take part in annual plays, dance performances, bands, photography, foreign-language dinners, regional math and national science competitions, student elections, and campus dances. Students also run various snack concessions at sporting events.

In response to student interest, the School arranges excursions to Broadway shows, the Metropolitan Opera, historic landmarks, or professional sports events in New York and Philadelphia.

All Upper School students must fulfill a community service requirement. They may serve as volunteers at local medical facilities, participate in programs such as Habitat for Humanity, or give of their time and effort to The Hun School community.

DAILY LIFE

Classes for the Upper School commence at 8 a.m. and end at 2:33 p.m. Classes are 43 minutes long, except labs, which are 88 minutes. There are no Saturday classes. The academic day includes lunch and an extra-help or activity period, which ends at 3:15 p.m. Upper School athletics continue from 3:30 until 5:30. Day students share in all activities.

WEEKEND LIFE

Weekends at The Hun School involve a broad range of activities. On campus, students participate in athletic and theatrical events, visit with faculty members in a relaxed atmosphere, and have full use of the School's facilities. Taking advantage of the Princeton location, students spend time watching Ivy League sporting events or visiting McCarter Theatre. Trips to Philadelphia and New York City are also popular, allowing for shopping, sightseeing, and enjoying the latest Broadway plays. The nearby Pocono Mountain range area offers outdoor activities, such as skiing, whitewater rafting, and paintballing. Student input is essential to planning, and there is always something to do.

SUMMER PROGRAMS

Noncredit enrichment courses and credit courses for make up or acceleration are offered during a five-week summer session starting in early July. The courses are open to anyone, and about 100 students attend. About 10 members of the School's regular faculty teach. Study skills and the development of good work habits are integral parts of the program. Classes are offered in English, mathematics, foreign languages, history, and SAT preparation.

A Day Camp for students aged 6–12 is also held at the School. Sessions run from two to five weeks. A theater arts program, dance workshops, and the International Student Program, which provides ESL classes and cultural trips, are also offered.

COSTS AND FINANCIAL AID

Day student tuition for 2008–09 was $28,390. Boarding student tuition was $41,670. There were additional fees for the Academic Learning Skills Program ($15,725) and the English as a Second Language Program ($8950) and a health fee for all residents ($390). Between $390 and $590 should be budgeted for Upper School books, whereas Middle School students should expect to spend between $250 and $300. The School recommends a weekly allowance of between $30 and $40. At the time of contract signing, a $1000 tuition deposit is required. Commercial laundry service for resident students is available for an additional fee.

A student with a strong record who is seriously interested in the opportunities offered at The Hun School should not be deterred from applying because of financial considerations. Financial aid, which is expended mainly from the School's operating budget, is granted by the School's Financial Aid Committee on the basis of need as determined by the School and Student Service (SSS). Because student aid resources are limited, they are distributed in the most careful and equitable manner possible. Approximately 25 percent of the students receive $2 million in financial aid on the basis of need. Application forms for financial aid may be obtained from the Admissions Office.

ADMISSIONS INFORMATION

Individuals who are motivated, able to do college-preparatory work, and who exhibit promise of being well-adjusted and responsible campus citizens are encouraged to apply to The Hun School. All candidates must complete and return an application to the Admissions Office. Also required are three confidential teacher and guidance counselor recommendations and a school transcript, complete with any available test data and related commentary. An interview at the School is highly recommended.

All applicants take the Secondary School Admission Test, administered by the Secondary School Admission Test Board. The entrance difficulty level at The Hun School is considered moderately difficult. Admission is determined by the applicant's previous record, entrance tests, and potential for college matriculation. Of the 559 students who applied for grades 6–PG in a recent year, 281 were accepted and 164 enrolled.

The Hun School does not discriminate against applicants or students on the basis of race, religion, sex, color, or national or ethnic origin.

The School welcomes all applications. Because of campus layout and the age and design of some buildings, however, The Hun School may not be suitable for certain handicapped students. Wherever possible, the School will attempt to accommodate handicapped applicants in accordance with each applicant's needs and the School's ability to serve the student within the scope of its overall educational program and goals.

APPLICATION TIMETABLE

Inquiries are welcome at all times. The deadline for the first round of admissions decisions is January 31. Admission after that time is on a rolling basis. Students and their families are welcome to visit the School, meet the admissions staff, and tour the campus. The preferred times to visit the School are between 9 a.m. and 2 p.m. on weekdays when school is in session.

New applicants are notified of acceptance on a continuous basis from March 10 through August. The Parents' Reply Date is normally April 10, but it can be later, depending upon when the applicant is accepted.

ADMISSIONS CORRESPONDENCE

P. Terence Beach, Director of Admissions
The Hun School of Princeton
176 Edgerstoune Road
Princeton, New Jersey 08540

Phone: 609-921-7600 Ext. 4954
E-mail: admiss@hunschool.org
Web site: http://www.hunschool.org

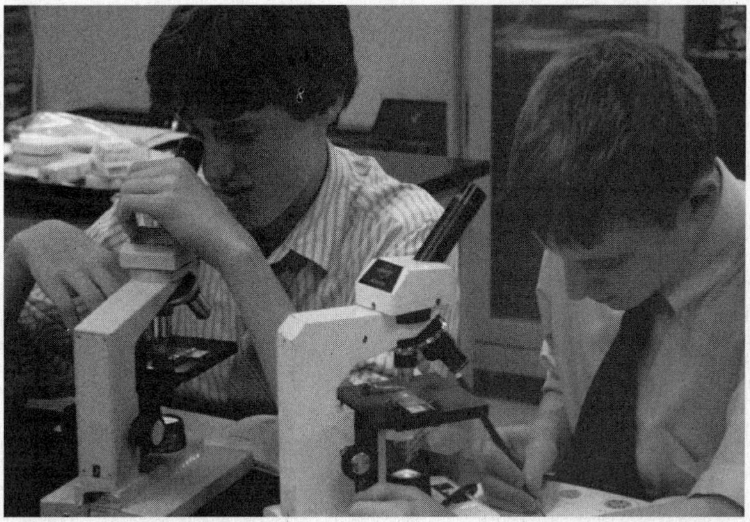

HYDE SCHOOLS

Bath, Maine
Woodstock, Connecticut

Type: Coeducational boarding and day college-preparatory schools
Grades: Bath campus, 9–PG; Woodstock campus, 9–PG
Enrollment: Total, 332; Bath campus, 151; Woodstock campus, 181
Heads of Schools: Bath campus, Donald McMillan; Woodstock campus, Laura D. Gauld

THE SCHOOL

Educator Joseph Gauld founded Hyde School in 1966 in deliberate reaction to a system of education he believed had become overly preoccupied with students' abilities and insufficiently focused on their character.

For over forty years, Hyde has been developing its program in accordance with a simple premise: "Let us value attitude over aptitude, effort over ability, and character over talent." The program has evolved to focus on three emphases: character development, family renewal, and college preparation. Character development is fully integrated into School life. Family renewal results from real parent participation. Parents are not here to support the work of the faculty; they are here to develop their own character. Hyde has established a parallel curriculum for students and parents. This family-student partnership has, in fact, become the trademark of Hyde. More than 95 percent of Hyde's graduates attend four-year colleges.

The Bath campus has 145 acres of meadowland and forest that provide an inspiring background for athletics and outdoor challenges, as well as daily campus life. Bath's heritage as an important shipbuilding port provides an interesting historical environment. Bath is located on the Maine coast, just 40 minutes from Portland and 2½ hours from Boston.

A second boarding campus opened in the summer of 1996 in Woodstock, Connecticut, located in the northeastern corner of the state, 1 hour from Boston and Hartford and ½ hour from Providence, Rhode Island. Located near five cities, Providence, Rhode Island; Worcester, Massachusetts; Boston, Massachusetts; Hartford, Connecticut; and New Haven, Connecticut, the Woodstock campus offers extensive cultural and historical opportunities. Hyde owns and operates a fully staffed wilderness education program located in Eustis, Maine, on 600 acres at Flagstaff Lake. Both Hyde campuses utilize this property for outdoor challenges.

Hyde is governed by a self-perpetuating Board of Governors, which meets regularly.

The School plant at Bath is valued at $35 million, and the facilities at Woodstock are valued at $41 million. Annual operating expenses are approximately $15.5 million.

Both campuses are accredited by the New England Association of Schools and Colleges, Inc. (NEASC), and the school at Bath is a member of the National Association of Independent Schools (NAIS), the Maine Association of Independent Schools, and the Independent School Association of Northern New England. Hyde's Woodstock campus is a member of the National Association of Independent Schools (NAIS) and the Connecticut Association of Independent Schools.

ACADEMIC PROGRAMS

The academic curriculum at Hyde is designed to help a student think critically about the world and examine his or her moral and physical development. Emphasis is placed on critical writing and the discipline of mathematics as fundamental tools for each student's academic growth. Creative focus in the areas of science, history, and foreign language impresses upon the student the importance of breadth as well as depth of knowledge. Special emphasis is placed in the classroom on the ties between the academic program and character development.

Advanced students may choose from a variety of courses, such as physics, advanced biology, AP composition, AP U.S. history, and AP calculus. A high level of faculty involvement creates an academic atmosphere that combines challenge, diversity, individuality, and support.

Perhaps the most important aspect of Hyde's academic curriculum is the emphasis placed upon effort and growth. A student receives separate evaluations each term for effort and achievement. The final grade reflects a factoring of the year's effort and achievement grades. Students at all class levels are closely supervised academically and receive special help and independent study as needed.

The academic program is divided into trimesters. Grade reports are released three times a year. Vacations are scheduled at Thanksgiving, at Christmas, and in the early spring.

The Hyde graduate has taken four years of English, three years of history, three years of mathematics, three years of science (two of which must be lab courses), and two years of foreign language, plus electives in the areas of art, computer science, and performing arts.

Senior responsibilities include tutoring, serving as mentors for students, attending faculty meetings, proctoring, and meeting with faculty candidates.

The student-faculty ratio is 5:1. The average class size is between 10 and 16. Grades are determined on a 100-point scale; 65 is a passing grade. In the evening, there is a 2-hour study hall; the privilege of independent study must be earned.

FACULTY AND ADVISERS

The Bath campus faculty consists of 8 women and 17 men; 9 hold advanced degrees. There are 10 Hyde alumni and alumni parents on the faculty. The Woodstock campus faculty consists of 10 women and 16 men; 10 hold advanced degrees. There are 13 alumni and alumni parents on the faculty. Nearly all of Hyde's faculty members live on campus and are responsible for counseling and supervision in the dormitories. All serve as advisers to students and their families and share coaching, performing arts, and community action responsibilities.

Donald McMillan, Head of School of the Bath campus, received an A.B. from Bowdoin College in 1983, an M.Ed. from Harvard Graduate School of Education in 1996, and an M.A. from Antioch Graduate School of New England in 2005. He has worked for over twenty years as a teacher, coach, and administrator at both Hyde School boarding campuses and the Hyde Public Charter School in Washington, D.C.

Laura D. Gauld '76, Head of School of the Woodstock campus, was an undergraduate at Beloit College and University of Southern Maine, studying early American history. In 1998, Laura established The Biggest Job Program, which evolved into the book *The Biggest Job We'll Ever Have* (Scribner, 2002). Her efforts to affect the parenting culture in this country have been recognized through such honors as Maine's Mother-of-the-Year Award and the 2005 Maine Media Women President's Award.

COLLEGE ADMISSION COUNSELING

Hyde's graduates traditionally attend four-year colleges. The College Counseling Office works closely with each junior and senior in planning postsecondary study. The office maintains an extensive library of college and university admissions materials and uses software programs to help students choose colleges that will best further their growth.

College applications are supervised and processed by the office. At least three faculty recommendations, the student's personal statement, an academic transcript, College Board scores, and an explanation of Hyde's curriculum accompany applications.

In the class of 2007, 53 students graduated from the Bath campus, with 51 attending colleges and universities, including Colgate, McGill, Notre Dame, Mt. Holyoke, Reed, and Rochester Institute of Technology. On the Woodstock campus, 47 members of the class of 2007 graduated, with 44 attending such colleges and universities as Berkeley, Colgate, Dickinson, NYU, Pitzer, and Skidmore.

STUDENT BODY AND CONDUCT

In 2007–08 on the Bath campus, there were 8 students in grade 9, 19 in grade 10, 55 in grade 11, 42 in grade 12, and 5 post grads. On the Woodstock campus, there were 10 students in grade 9, 28 in grade 10, 74 in grade 11, 54 in grade 12, and 3 post grads. Between both campuses, twenty-seven states were represented in the student body, as were Bermuda, Canada, China, England, Japan, Korea, Nigeria, Rwanda, and Spain.

Students and faculty members share in maintaining discipline. A traditional student government does not exist at Hyde; instead, the entire student body establishes and maintains the ethics that govern the community. These ethics encourage individuals to live by conscience rather than rules.

ACADEMIC FACILITIES

On the Bath campus, The Mansion houses faculty offices, a computer lab, a darkroom, the College Counseling Office, the Family Education Office, and administrative offices. A new academic wing and library were completed in early 2007 (8,600 volumes and Internet access to the News Bank Curriculum Resource and facts.com). It also contains a media room. Additional classrooms are located in The Mansion, its annex, and in the Carriage House; and a renovated barn serves as a spacious art studio. Students have access to Bath's Patten Free Library, and responsible students may conduct research at the Hawthorne-Longfellow Library at nearby Bowdoin College. The Student Union houses facilities for the School's performing arts program, the bookstore, mailroom, and a dining hall.

On the Woodstock campus, the Cultural Center contains a 1,100-seat state-of-the-art theater, classrooms, a lecture hall and science labs, a computer lab, and administrative offices. The Student Center houses classrooms, the student coffee house, the dining hall, and the bookstore. Annhurst Hall, which was recently renovated, contains a new library, the media center, classrooms, the College Counseling Office, the admissions office, and the Family Learning Center. Westhaver Hall houses classrooms and administrative offices, as well as dormitory rooms. In 2008 a state-of-the-art track and field complex was completed. The field turf athletic surface is permanently lined for soccer, football, and men's and women's lacrosse. The six-lane urethane track has an eight-line sprint and hurdle space, pole vault, high jump, long and triple jump, and discus and shot put areas.

BOARDING AND GENERAL FACILITIES

On the Bath campus, seven dormitories provide the living quarters for boarding students. Five dorms have been built since the School was established. Each dorm has faculty members in residence, and older students share in dormitory responsibilities. A health center is located on campus, and 1 full-time and 3 part-time nurses are employed. A student union was built to accommodate community activities and rehearsal and stage space for the performing arts program. The Family Renewal Center provides conference rooms and dormitories for family weekends and retreats. Some recent additions include a new dining room, a weight-lifting room, a student activities barn, and a 600-seat theater.

On the Woodstock campus, two large three- and four-story dormitory buildings house boarding students; one is for boys and one is for girls. Each dorm has faculty members in residence. Additional faculty housing was completed in late 2006. A health center is located in Warren Hall and is staffed by nurses. The Cultural Center is a 1,100-seat state-of-the-art facility, providing optimal space for the performing arts curriculum, as well as for the local community's cultural events. Annhurst Hall was recently renovated to house a new library, a computer lab, classrooms, and administrative offices; it also provides housing for families participating in retreats and family weekends.

ATHLETICS

All Hyde students participate in interscholastic athletics regardless of their experience or skill level. Students learn the value of competitive sports and share the accomplishment of a genuine team effort.

On the Bath campus, a modern field house, playing fields, and a locker-room center at the track and field complex offer excellent facilities for a successful athletics program; a major renovation and expansion of the field house and construction of a new student center and health facility was completed in spring 2006. A new academic building was also completed in the spring of 2007; the focal point is the Chan Wheeler Library. On the Woodstock campus, the Krebs' Family Gymnasium was constructed in 1998–99 with new basketball courts, fitness and training rooms, wrestling rooms, and athletic offices. New athletic fields have been built as well, and a new outdoor track complex was completed in 2007.

Hyde boys compete in basketball, crew (Bath), cross-country running, cross-country skiing (Bath), football, lacrosse, soccer, tennis, track, and wrestling. Hyde girls compete in basketball, crew (Bath), cross-country running, cross-country skiing (Bath), lacrosse, soccer, tennis, and track. The Woodstock campus also has martial arts.

EXTRACURRICULAR OPPORTUNITIES

Some activities that are traditionally regarded as extracurricular are conducted at Hyde on a co-curricular basis. These activities include the performing arts, community action, and outdoor education.

The community action program enables Hyde students to serve as volunteers in area nursing homes, local elementary schools, the animal shelter, and other community projects.

The performing arts program involves all Hyde students and faculty members in the research, development, and choreography of a musical presentation. In addition, everyone participates at the performing level, either singing, dancing, or acting. Hyde also has formal instruction in music, drama, and dance.

Outdoor education activities include wilderness trips to explore the rivers, mountains, and coastline of Maine, the majority of which are conducted at Hyde's 600-acre property in northern Maine near Sugarloaf ski area. The addition of high- and low-ropes courses on both the Bath and Woodstock campuses provides group and individual challenges for students, faculty members, parents, and alumni.

Hyde offers many opportunities for students to pursue interests beyond the scope of the usual academic program. The visual arts program offers an opportunity for students to be involved with sculpture, pottery, ceramics, art history, film, painting, sketching, and photography.

Students are encouraged to contribute to various publications created on both campuses.

DAILY LIFE

Breakfast is served at 7 a.m. After daily jobs for all students, classes begin at 8 and continue until 2:45 p.m. Sports practices are conducted after the academic day and are followed by dinner at 6. Evening study hall is from 7:30 to 9:30. Wednesday and Saturday afternoons are reserved for interscholastic sports competition.

WEEKEND LIFE

Weekends provide an opportunity for students to relax and interact on a social level. On Sunday mornings, brunch is served. Activities organized by students may include dances, movies, coffeehouses, camping, and trips into town and the surrounding cities. All facilities are open to students during their free time, and the School provides time and transportation for attendance at religious, civic, and social functions in the area. Day students are encouraged to participate in weekend activities.

SUMMER PROGRAMS

The Summer Challenge Program is an opportunity for students to experience a character-based educational program, as well as an orientation for students interested in developing their character and leadership and for new students who will attend during the following regular school year. Most students begin their Hyde education with this program. There are two 4-week programs in the summer. The curriculum addresses excellence through individual and group challenges in academics, athletics, performing arts, and outdoor education.

COSTS AND FINANCIAL AID

For 2008–09, the cost of tuition, room, and board was $41,500 for boarding students; day school tuition was $23,950. The Summer Challenge Programs cost $4800 per four-week session.

Hyde offers a financial aid program and grants-in-aid based on need. In 2008–09, a total of $1,500,000 was awarded to students on both campuses. Hyde attempts to offer its varied educational programs to as many students as possible. Inquiries about financial aid should be addressed to the Admission Office.

ADMISSIONS INFORMATION

Hyde School seeks to enroll students who have the character, potential, and enthusiasm to challenge and develop themselves within the School's diverse curriculum. While consideration is given to a candidate's past performance, the admissions process concentrates on the prospective student's hopes and desires for the future.

The SSAT is not required but is recommended. Evaluation of past academic performance is important, but acceptance is based on effort and potential, not on grades. A student should have the interest and capacity for a college career.

An in-depth family interview is the main criterion for admission and must be scheduled with the Admissions Office.

Hyde School does not discriminate on the basis of sex, handicap, race, creed, color, or national or ethnic origin. A family's income must be considered in determining financial aid allocations, but it does not have a bearing on admissions status.

APPLICATION TIMETABLE

The Admissions Office has a March 1 deadline and then operates on a rolling basis and interviews candidates throughout the balance of the year. Families of prospective students should contact the Admissions Office in order to discuss an appointment for an interview. Candidates can expect notification of the Admissions Committee's decision within two weeks after the interview. Interviews for the Summer Challenge Programs are completed by June 20.

ADMISSIONS CORRESPONDENCE

Gene Devlin, Director of Admission
Hyde School at Bath
616 High Street
Bath, Maine 04530-5002
Phone: 207-443-7101
E-mail: bath.admissions@hyde.edu
Web site: http://www.hyde.edu

or

Jason Warnick, Director of Admission
Hyde School at Woodstock
P.O. Box 237
Woodstock, Connecticut 06281-0237
Phone: 860-963-4736
E-mail: woodstock.admissions@hyde.edu
Web site: http://www.hyde.edu

IDYLLWILD ARTS ACADEMY

Idyllwild, California

Type: Coeducational boarding and day college-preparatory school emphasizing the performing and visual arts
Grades: 9–12, postgraduate year
Enrollment: 264
Head of School: William M. Lowman, President

THE SCHOOL

The Idyllwild Arts Academy is a boarding and day academy offering preprofessional arts training and academic preparation for colleges and conservatories to boys and girls in grades 9 through 12 and to those taking a postgraduate year.

Dr. Max Krone and Beatrice Krone founded the Idyllwild Arts Foundation in 1946 and established the Academy as a summer program in 1950. The Academy opened for 100 students that year. The summer program, which reached an enrollment of more than 2,000 children and adults as it developed, was the Academy's focus for much of its history.

The Idyllwild Arts Academy seeks to prepare students for further education, for advanced arts studies, and for adult life as contributing, productive members of society. The Academy believes in an education of high quality that places demands on both faculty members and students, who in turn must be committed to the good of the school community.

The Academy is situated on 206 acres at an elevation of more than 5,000 feet in the San Jacinto Mountains. Strawberry Creek borders the campus, which is surrounded by more than 20,000 acres of protected forest and parkland. The village of Idyllwild, a community of 2,500 year-round residents, is a center for wilderness enthusiasts, who use the hundreds of miles of trails for hiking and mountain biking and the nearby lakes and creeks for boating and fishing. Idyllwild is about 100 miles from San Diego and 125 miles from Los Angeles. Its location near the junction of Routes 74 and 243 makes it accessible from all directions over freeway and highway routes. Motels, inns, campgrounds, and bed-and-breakfast facilities are available for visitors.

The Idyllwild Arts Foundation, which administers the Academy, is a nonprofit corporation governed by a 50-member self-perpetuating Board of Trustees. The trustees elect 16 of their members to a Board of Governors, which meets as often as necessary to conduct the foundation's affairs.

The Idyllwild Arts Academy is accredited by the Western Association of Schools and Colleges and is a member of the Secondary School Admission Test Board, Western Boarding Schools, NAFSA: Association of International Educators, the Network of Performing and Visual Arts Schools, the National Association of Independent Schools, California Association of Independent Schools, and the Federation of American and International Schools.

ACADEMIC PROGRAMS

In order to stimulate young people intellectually and to advance their knowledge in all areas, the Arts Academy provides an exciting and challenging academic program. In accordance with the thesis that artistically inclined young people tend to learn best by experiencing and doing rather than by simply reading or listening to information, the Academy's program of studies is designed to motivate students to think for themselves and to use disciplined inquiry to explore concepts in the various domains of knowledge.

Upon graduation, Arts Academy students have met or exceeded the admission requirements of the University of California System and are prepared to enter selective colleges, universities, and conservatories across the nation. Students must complete 17 academic units in addition to their arts curriculum. The academic units must include 4 units of English, 3 of mathematics, 2 of foreign language, 2 of laboratory sciences, 3 of social studies, 2 of physical education, and 1 of academic electives. In addition, students must meet the Academy's requirement for computer literacy. Postgraduates engage in a one-year intensive program in academics and the arts.

Students choose a major and plan individual schedules with faculty members and the Dean of the Arts and Dean of Academics. Placement in arts courses is by level of ability and experience; students then advance according to their performance. Areas of study include creative writing, music (including classical and jazz), dance, acting, theatrical production and design, musical theater, moving pictures, interdisciplinary arts, and the visual arts. Each program incorporates courses in four categories: theory, history, and fundamentals of the form; creation, production, presentation, or performance; specialized master classes and private instruction; and field trips to arts communities of southern California to observe professionals at work.

Among the regular courses offered are tap, ballet, modern dance, pointe, jazz, men's class, pas de deux, and dance composition; music fundamentals, introduction to music literature, ear training/sight singing, music theory, music history, voice class, chamber music, orchestra, class piano, piano proficiency, accompaniment, and repertoire class; acting, voice and diction, musical theater, technical theater, drama history and literature, movement, playwriting, directing, and stage design; drawing and painting, art history, ceramics, sculpture, design and aesthetics, computer graphics illustration, and photography; and creative writing I and II, individual critique, and visiting artist workshops.

The academic year is divided into two semesters. Teachers are available to provide extra help in both the academic and the arts programs. Grades are issued and sent to parents four times a year.

FACULTY AND ADVISERS

William M. Lowman, a graduate of the University of Redlands (A.B.), is President of both the Arts Academy and the Idyllwild Arts Foundation. A recipient of the Nevada Governor's Arts Award, Mr. Lowman founded the Nevada School for the Arts.

The full-time faculty, including administrators who teach, numbers 35 members. All have distinguished themselves as teachers and professional artists. They hold baccalaureate and graduate degrees from such institutions as California Institute of the Arts, Catawba, DePaul, Harvard, Juilliard, New England Conservatory of Music, Oberlin, Royal College of Music (London), San Francisco Conservatory of Music, Stanford, UCLA, USC, Yale, and the Universities of California, Santa Cruz, New Mexico, and Texas at Austin. Private instructors are appointed on a part-time or short-term basis to meet special needs. Prominent performing artists are scheduled to be in residence at various times during the academic year to conduct master classes and give performance examples.

COLLEGE ADMISSION COUNSELING

College guidance for students is provided by their advisers and one full-time college counselor. Students take the SAT and ACT and receive coaching on auditions and portfolio presentation.

More than 95 percent of Arts Academy graduates have gone on to attend a wide range of colleges and conservatories, including Art Center College of Design, Berkeley, Boston Conservatory, California Institute of the Arts, Carnegie Mellon, Cornish College of the Arts, Curtis Institute, Harvard, Indiana University, Juilliard, New England Conservatory, NYU (Tisch School of the Arts, Steinhardt School of Education, Gallatin School of Individualized Study, College of General Studies, and the College of Arts and Science), Oberlin College Conservatory of Music, Peabody Conservatory of Music, Rice, Sarah Lawrence, Stanford, UCLA, USC, Yale, and the Universities of California at San Diego and Santa Cruz, Hartford (Hartt School of Music), and Michigan.

Other graduates of the Arts Academy have gone directly to positions with institutions such as the San Francisco Ballet, BalletMet, and Circle Repertory Company.

STUDENT BODY AND CONDUCT

In 2008–09, the Academy enrolled 167 girls and 97 boys. The student body represents twenty-seven states and twenty-one other countries.

The Dean of Students is responsible for students' residential life. The Judicial Committee, comprising 2 faculty members, 1 dorm parent, and 3 students, works in cooperation with the Dean of Students to oversee the rules and regulations instituted by the Academy. There is no formal dress code.

ACADEMIC FACILITIES

The campus of the Idyllwild Arts Academy is designed to be in harmony with its forested surroundings. Lecture halls, science laboratories, classrooms, art and dance studios, and three theaters are among the many campus facilities that enable Arts Academy students to live, study, practice, and perform in this special high school environment. The Bruce Ryan soundstage opened in 2002 for students in the moving pictures (film and video) major. Nelson Hall, a new dining facility, opened in May 2006.

The Max and Bee Krone Library, a state-of-the-art multimedia center, opened in 2000. It includes a museum, a 6,000-volume music library, 6,564 books, and a computer graphics lab.

The Idyllwild Arts Foundation Theater, seating 300 people, is ideal for concerts, recitals, and mainstage plays.

Three dance facilities, complete with barres, mirrors, and resilient flooring, are in constant use throughout the year.

Music facilities include excellent recital and performance areas as well as practice rooms and several studios for ensemble rehearsals.

Studios for painting and drawing, design, sculpture, and photography are located near the center of the campus. A large ceramics studio has separate facilities for throwing on the wheel and hand building. A variety of kilns, including raku, Anagama, salt, gas, and wood, are available for student use.

Parks Exhibition Center, which opened in 2002, provides a spacious, well-lighted facility where students, faculty members, and guest exhibitors show their work.

BOARDING AND GENERAL FACILITIES

For most of the nine-month academic year, the dormitories are home to the Academy's boarding students. They share double rooms in four modern, comfortable dormitories supervised by faculty members and dorm parents. The close-knit family atmosphere provides a strong base of support for the artistic, academic, and social life of the students.

A registered nurse is available at all times, and a physician in Idyllwild is on call. Emergency medical care is available at nearby hospitals.

ATHLETICS

Owing to the type of curriculum offered at the Arts Academy, the physical education program tends to be more creative than typical standardized course offerings. Physical education courses are intended to inspire a lifelong commitment to fitness.

Although students are required to complete 2 years of physical education, including one semester of health education, it is recommended that they take a physical education course each semester they are enrolled.

Health education serves to promote a knowledge of nutrition and weight control as well as an understanding of stress in work and recreation, substance abuse, family issues, sexuality and relationships, and values in the decision-making process.

Idyllwild's current Physical Education facility includes a swimming pool, small gym with Universal weights and cardio equipment, a tennis court, and a playing field.

EXTRACURRICULAR OPPORTUNITIES

Extracurricular activities are planned by the student government and Student Services personnel. All students and faculty members are invited to make suggestions for these activities. Students sometimes go off campus for skiing, skating, and rock climbing and for trips to concerts, art museums, dance performances, theater productions, conferences, sports events, and beaches. Students who sign up for an off-campus trip are charged according to the cost of that particular event, including the costs of transportation, food consumed away from school, and entrance fees/tickets.

Students are also encouraged to become involved in student publications, including the yearbook, the literary magazine, and the photography magazine.

DAILY LIFE

Academic classes begin at 8 a.m. and are held Monday through Saturday mornings. Arts classes are held in the afternoons, Monday through Friday, until dinner at 6:30. Evenings from 7 to 10 are set aside for rehearsals, study halls, and studio time.

WEEKEND LIFE

On weekend field trips, students enjoy the outstanding cultural attractions of Los Angeles and San Diego—museums, theaters, art galleries, and concert halls—and the many world-famous recreational areas nearby, including Disneyland, Knott's Berry Farm, Magic Mountain, Sea World, and the San Diego Zoo. In addition, southern California offers a wide variety of world-class sports attractions. The Arts Academy seeks to offer its students both the renewing serenity of the mountains and the bright lights and cultural stimulation of the city—the best of two worlds.

SUMMER PROGRAMS

The Summer Arts Program offers a wide variety of courses ranging in length from a weekend to two weeks for students of all ages. These include a Children's Arts Center, Creative Writing and Poetry (for junior high and high school students and adults), Native American arts, and comprehensive offerings in dance, music, theater and musical theater, and the visual arts. Steven Fraider is the Vice President and Director of the Summer Program.

COSTS AND FINANCIAL AID

For the 2008–09 school year, boarding tuition was $44,900 and day tuition was $28,950. The Academy subscribes to the School and Student Service for Financial Aid and awards more than $3 million in financial aid annually on the basis of talent and financial need. A tuition payment plan is available.

ADMISSIONS INFORMATION

The Idyllwild Arts Academy seeks dedicated, motivated, and talented students. Students are admitted in grades 9 through 12 and for a postgraduate year on the basis of academic transcripts, recommendations, a personal interview, and a demonstration of potential in the performing or visual arts through audition or portfolio.

APPLICATION TIMETABLE

Application deadlines begin February 1, and applicants are accepted until quotas are filled in each major. Students may be admitted at midyear, if space is available. The priority deadline for financial aid is February 1. The application fee is $50.

ADMISSIONS CORRESPONDENCE

Karen R. Porter, Dean of Admission and
Financial Aid
Academy Admission Office
Idyllwild Arts Academy
52500 Temecula Road
P.O. Box 38
Idyllwild, California 92549-0038

Phone: 951-659-2171 Ext. 2223
Fax: 951-659-2058
E-mail: admission@idyllwildarts.org
Web site: http://www.idyllwildarts.org

KENT PLACE SCHOOL

Summit, New Jersey

Type: Girls' day college-preparatory school
Grades: N–12: Primary School, N–5; Middle School, 6–8; Upper School, 9–12
Enrollment: School total: 647; Upper School: 263; Middle School: 137; Primary School: 247
Head of School: Susan C. Bosland

THE SCHOOL

Since 1894, Kent Place School has provided a superior education for girls in a structured environment that combines tradition and innovative approaches to teaching. An independent, nonsectarian, college-preparatory day school, Kent Place's threefold mission is to provide a well-rounded curriculum in a caring atmosphere, to educate students who demonstrate scholastic and creative potential, and to encourage contributions to and success in an academically rigorous environment. The School's commitment to excellence encourages each student to achieve her maximum potential while developing a love of learning, respect for self and others in a multicultural community, self-discipline, confidence, and responsibility. Kent Place also strives to strengthen each girl's moral awareness, to prepare young women for leadership roles, and to work in partnership with parents to develop individual potential through a variety of intellectual, physical, and creative experiences and opportunities.

The School is located on a 26-acre campus in suburban Summit, New Jersey. Within easy access of New York City, Kent Place offers field trips to museums, concerts, the theater, and points of cultural and historic interest.

Kent Place is a nonprofit organization governed by a 27-member board of trustees.

Kent Place is accredited by the Middle States Association of Colleges and Schools, the New Jersey Association of Independent Schools (NJAIS), and the Council for the Advancement and Support of Education (CASE). Its memberships include the National Coalition of Girls' Schools, the National Association of Independent Schools, the New Jersey Association of Independent Schools, the Secondary School Admission Test Board, the College Board, and the Educational Records Bureau.

ACADEMIC PROGRAMS

A Kent Place education provides a solid foundation for lifelong learning. Because of its commitment to single-sex education, Kent Place is able to focus exclusively on how girls learn and to encourage its students to explore learning opportunities that they may be inclined to avoid in a coeducational setting.

The Kent Place Primary School focuses on creativity, fun, and imagination and encourages children to grow, take risks, and ask questions. Students are introduced to the larger world around them through an interdisciplinary curriculum that is enhanced and reinforced by the use of technology. Kent Place challenges the girls to stretch the boundaries of their own self-knowledge, as the School draws upon their natural curiosity, inquisitiveness, and sense of discovery to instill a love of learning.

Middle School girls are provided with an environment in which they can explore and grow. Classroom learning is rigorous, interactive, and collaborative, and girls are permitted to forge an individual approach to the learning process. Enthusiasm for science, mathematics, and technology is fostered through the academic program.

Kent Place's rigorous Upper School academic curriculum challenges all students and ensures that each gains the critical skills, knowledge, and experiences that she needs to be a successful college student and constructive member of society. Ninth through twelfth graders are immersed in the humanities, sciences, mathematics, and the fine and performing arts. Innovative teaching strategies bring speakers into the classroom and send students out of the School to gain real-world experiences. Girls who are so inspired may pursue a topic beyond the regular academic curriculum with the assistance of a faculty adviser. Academic credit is granted for such independent study. Kent Place graduates enter the world prepared for what lies ahead, equipped with the ability to question, analyze, and think abstractly while feeling confident in their own talents and abilities and comfortable with the larger world around them.

All Upper School students are required to take five courses a trimester; four of the five must be core courses. Courses are 1 credit per term, 3 credits for a full year. Total credits required for graduation are 60, including English, 13; mathematics, 9; foreign language, 6–9; history, 9; science, 9; fine arts, 6; and electives, 5–9. Noncredit requirements are physical education for all four years and women's studies (one trimester in grade 10). Electives include such classes as contemporary history, economics, environmental science, physics for calculus students, advanced drama, biomedical issues, etymologies, photography, Web page design, and computer programming.

FACULTY AND ADVISERS

The School maintains a distinguished faculty and staff of more than 100 members that both challenges and nurtures its students. Seventy-eight percent of the faculty members have advanced degrees. Susan C. Bosland, who was appointed Head of School in 1999, holds a Bachelor of Arts degree from Denison University and a Master of Arts in educational administration from Teachers College, Columbia University.

COLLEGE ADMISSION COUNSELING

College advising begins upon a girl's enrollment in the Upper School. Course selections are reviewed yearly to ensure that every student completes the requirements needed for college admission. With the goal of helping each young woman find the most appropriate college based on her individual talents, the college advisers work individually with students and parents to develop a list of schools that best matches the interests of the student.

Kent Place is proud of the high quality and range of colleges chosen by its graduates, which in the last two years have included Barnard, Boston College, Brown, Columbia, Cornell, Dartmouth, Duke, Georgetown, Harvard, Middlebury, Northwestern, Princeton, the University of Pennsylvania, and Yale.

STUDENT BODY AND CONDUCT

The students of Kent Place represent more than seventy communities.

ACADEMIC FACILITIES

The Kent Place campus features a blend of historic and modern facilities. The School House, now the Upper School, was built in 1913, and the field house was constructed in 1985. The Primary Building was opened in 1993, and a dining hall was erected in 1995. Additional facilities include a 280-seat theater with an adjacent dance studio and art gallery, two art centers, music practice rooms, a recital room, computer centers, two libraries, two playing fields, and five tennis courts.

ATHLETICS

Kent Place School provides a competitive athletic program for students who choose to participate in interscholastic sports. Kent Place is a member of the Mountain Valley Conference and competes against a variety of private and public schools. Kent Place teams participate in Union County tournaments, New Jersey State Interscholastic Athletic Association (NJSIAA) state tournaments, and New Jersey Independent School Athletic Association (NJISAA) state tournaments. Student-athletes are encouraged to compete in team sports to develop physical capabilities, self-discipline, confidence, sportsmanship, and personal character. Participation in competitive sports is not required; most girls, however, choose to take part in some way, whether as athletes, team managers, or fans. A number of Kent Place athletes have gone on to compete in intercollegiate sports at all levels of college programs in a variety of sports.

Girls compete at the junior varsity or varsity level in cross-country, field hockey, soccer, tennis, and volleyball in the fall; basketball, indoor track, and swimming in the winter; and golf, lacrosse, outdoor track, and softball in the spring. Squash is also offered as a club sport.

Physical education is a requirement at Kent Place School. Students participate in physical education six times in a ten-day cycle. The program provides enjoyment of activity while fulfilling the needs for fitness, social interaction, and knowledge of sports and exercise. When a student competes in a competitive interscholastic sport, Chamber Dancers, Dance Ensemble, or independent athletic study, the physical education department waives the physical education requirement for the trimester.

EXTRACURRICULAR OPPORTUNITIES

Each year, Kent Place's gallery program brings professional art shows to campus, through which exhibiting artists work with students. Students host their own annual art shows. Drama, dance, and music are featured throughout the curriculum, and students in all grades perform enthusiastically.

Middle School girls take part in community service programs and extracurricular activities that include Key Club, Outreach (a community service committee), the Social Committee, Student Council, dramatic productions, instrumental ensemble groups, the Minisingers, a forensics club, and several miniclubs. Middle School student publications include *The Log,* a literary magazine; *Reflections,* a foreign language publication; *Soundings,* the eighth grade yearbook; and a Middle School newsletter, *Catamaran.*

Extracurricular opportunities for Upper School girls abound. Student leadership groups include the Athletic Association, the Judiciary, the Senate, the Social Committee, and Student Affairs. Upper School publications feature the *Ballast,* the Upper School newspaper; *Cargoes,* the Upper School yearbook; *Dichos,* a foreign language magazine; and *Windward,* the literary magazine. Arts activities include the Chamber Dancers, Chamber Singers, chorale, Dance Ensemble, dramatic productions, instrumental ensemble, and the Kent Place Singers. Other clubs are the Ambassadors, Amnesty International, the Black Cultural Association, Environmental Club, Junior States, Green Key, and Voices.

Community service is not a required part of the Kent Place Upper School curriculum, but more than 95 percent of the students pursue such opportunities. Students serve on first aid squads, in hospitals, and at soup kitchens and battered women's shelters; bring food to the homeless; tutor disadvantaged children; coach physically challenged swimmers; and collect nonperishables for area food banks.

DAILY LIFE

The school day begins at 8:15 and ends at 3:10. Sports continue after school until 5:30–6 p.m.

COSTS AND FINANCIAL AID

Tuition for Kent Place School for the 2008–09 school year was as follows: nursery school, $9450; prekindergarten, $15,885; kindergarten, $21,555; primary grades 1–5, $23,565; middle and upper grades 6–12, $28,125. Tuition includes lunch for grades 1–12. After the initial deposit, which varies by grade, all fees are due in two installments, one on August 1 and one on February 1. The School offers a discount for tuitions paid in full by August 1. Other fees include a $200 publication fee for grades 9–12, a $50 publication fee for grades 6–8, a $185 activities fee for grades 9–12, a $125 activities fee for grades 6–8, and book fees, which range from approximately $175 for the Primary School to $625 for the Upper School.

All families are encouraged to consider Kent Place regardless of their economic circumstances. Financial aid is awarded yearly in the form of grants. The School uses the recommendations of the School and Student Service for Financial Aid as guidelines to determine financial need.

ADMISSIONS INFORMATION

Kent Place seeks motivated young women without regard to race, religion, color, or national origin and welcomes inquiries and applications from girls of strong character, academic promise, and purpose. Admission is contingent on previous school records, written recommendations, a student application, the results of an entrance exam (SSAT or ISEE), and a personal on-campus visit and interview.

APPLICATION TIMETABLE

A $70 application fee must be submitted with the application for admission. The application for admission must be received no later than January 9. Applicants who have completed all application requirements by February 1 are given first consideration by the Admission Committee. Applications completed after February 1 are reviewed on a rolling admission basis. Kent Place notifies candidates and their families of admission decisions in March.

ADMISSIONS CORRESPONDENCE

Nancy J. Humick, Director of Admission and Financial Aid
Kent Place School
42 Norwood Avenue
Summit, New Jersey 07902-0308
Phone: 908-273-0900 Ext. 254
Fax: 908-273-9390
E-mail: admission@kentplace.org
Web site: http://www.kentplace.org

KENT SCHOOL

Kent, Connecticut

Type: Coeducational boarding and day college-preparatory Episcopal school
Grades: 9–12, PG (Forms III–VI)
Enrollment: 550
Head of School: Rev. Richardson W. Schell, Headmaster and Rector

THE SCHOOL

The Rev. Frederick H. Sill, whose vision of education centered on simplicity of life, self-reliance, and directness of purpose, established Kent School in 1906. From its beginning, Father Sill intended the School to be a place in which boys not only learned academics and athletics to prepare them for college and professional life but also learned the value of physical labor.

After a half century as a school for boys, Kent became coeducational and today is a community of learning that is dedicated to helping boys and girls develop their abilities and increase their knowledge. The School prepares students for college studies and beyond through a program that includes academics, athletics, chapel, daily work, and extracurricular activities.

The School has a strong, long-standing affiliation with the Episcopal Church and is committed to understanding and transmitting the values of the Judeo-Christian tradition. It is also committed to seeking truth in all its forms and welcomes students from all religious backgrounds.

Kent School is in the small town of Kent, Connecticut, which is about 90 miles north of New York City and 50 miles west of Hartford.

The School is governed by a 30-member Board of Trustees that, together with the Headmaster and Rector, oversees the operation of the School. Kent School's endowment is currently valued at $73.5 million. Combined giving by alumni, parents, grandparents, and friends in 2007–08 was the second-highest Annual Fund total in the history of Kent School.

Kent School is accredited by the New England Association of Schools and Colleges and is approved by the Connecticut State Department of Education. It holds memberships in the National Association of Independent Schools, the National Association of Episcopal Schools, the Connecticut Association of Independent Schools, and the Council for Advancement and Support of Education.

ACADEMIC PROGRAMS

Kent offers a strong college-preparatory program, with courses from basic to advanced levels in the liberal arts. A normal course load is five courses per term. To graduate, a student must complete English through the Sixth Form year; mathematics through algebra II and trigonometry or through the Fifth Form year (whichever comes first); three years of one foreign language; two yearlong laboratory sciences; two years of history, one of which must be U.S. history; and two term courses in theology. There are also required term courses in art and music.

One further course is required for Third Formers. This course, Third Form Seminar, is designed to help students make a smooth transition into the academic life at Kent School and focuses on the development of sound study habits. The course teaches the skills of time management, listening, reading, note taking, study methods, and test taking.

Course placement is based on ability and prior experience rather than on age or grade level; students are encouraged to progress to a high level as rapidly as possible. Small class size ensures that all students become well known by their teachers and have ample opportunities to participate fully in discussions and other class activities. Students get a chance to demonstrate their mastery of the subject, confront new ideas, and hone their skills every day.

Working at the appropriate level through the flexible placement system, a student at Kent can complete a thorough course of study for college preparation. The more able students have opportunities to work at the college level in the Advanced Placement program. Kent offers twenty-nine AP courses in every discipline, including computer science.

The student-faculty ratio is 8:1; the average class size is 12. Grades range from a high of 6.0 to a passing low of 2.0; 1.0 is failure. Grade reports are submitted every five weeks; written comments are given in all courses at the end of each term after term exams and at the end of each five-week period in courses in which a failure occurs.

FACULTY AND ADVISERS

Of the 75 teaching faculty members, 57 percent are women; 82 percent have earned advanced degrees. Five faculty members hold doctorates. Faculty members have an average of sixteen years of teaching experience. Thirty faculty members live in the dorms on campus, and 57 also serve as coaches.

Because education at Kent goes far beyond the classroom, faculty members are chosen not only for their academic ability but also for their willingness to provide support to and participate with the students in the full life of the School. Every student has a faculty adviser, and each adviser works with about 8 students. Advisory periods are scheduled twice a week.

The Rev. Richardson W. Schell assumed duties as Headmaster and Rector of Kent School in 1981. Father Schell is a graduate of Kent School, Harvard, and Yale Divinity School. Previously, he served as a parish priest in Chicago (1976–80) and as Chaplain of Kent School (1980–81).

COLLEGE ADMISSION COUNSELING

From February of the Fifth Form year through the spring of the Sixth Form year, girls and boys work closely with the Office of College Guidance. More than 100 college representatives visit Kent each year. All Fourth and Fifth Form students take the PSAT. The SAT is offered in both the Fifth and Sixth Form years, along with SAT Subject Tests in all major disciplines. Of the 175 graduates of the class of 2008, 100 percent entered college; 104 matriculated at the most competitive and highly competitive schools, including Bates, Berkeley, Boston College, Boston University, Columbia, Cornell, Dartmouth, George Washington, Georgia Tech, NYU, Parsons, Rensselaer, Southern Methodist, Syracuse, U.S. Military Academy, U.S. Naval Academy, and the Universities of Pennsylvania, South California, and Virginia.

STUDENT BODY AND CONDUCT

In 2008–09, there were 75 students in grade 9 (10 day and 65 boarding), 140 in grade 10 (12 day, 128 boarding), 164 in grade 11(17 day, 147 boarding), and 171 in grade 12 and PG (11 day and 160 boarding). About half of the School's students were from the Northeast section of the United States; the rest came from all parts of the country and the world, including thirty-two states and thirty countries.

The Sixth Form prefects (5 boys and 5 girls) are appointed by the Headmaster to work closely with the dormitory masters in supervising the dormitories. Together with elected representatives from each form, these prefects comprise the Student Council. Boys and girls are represented equally on the Student Council, which serves as a forum for discussion of School life and makes recommendations to the Headmaster.

ACADEMIC FACILITIES

The Schoolhouse, Dickinson Science Center, and Gifford T. Foley '65 Hall are the center of academic life on the campus. The John Gray Park '28 Library has 57,000 volumes, and extensive periodical, microfilm, and computer databases are listed on the Kent School Web page. The library is open from 8 a.m. to 10 p.m. daily. The Fairleigh S. Dickinson Jr. Science Center houses chemistry, physics, biology, and genetics labs; a lecture hall; and a greenhouse. The entire campus, dormitory rooms, classrooms, and faculty member offices have direct Internet and e-mail access through Kent's own World Wide Web server. All students are expected to take full advantage of notebook computers in their classes and during study time. Students play important roles in training and support of computer users. The Graham D. Mattison '22 Auditorium is fully equipped for play productions, movies, and concerts and also houses the music studios. The Bruce Robinson Field '81 Dormitory houses the art studios.

BOARDING AND GENERAL FACILITIES

Boys live in three dormitories, which house from 40 to 120 students each. Girls live in three dormitories, which house from 40 to 98 students each. Several faculty members live in each of the dorms. Learning to live with students from a diversity of backgrounds is central to the Kent experience. Students live in double rooms and may change roommates twice a year if they wish.

ATHLETICS

Boys' sports include ballet, baseball, basketball, crew, cross-country running, football, golf, ice hockey, jazz dance, lacrosse, modern dance, riding, soccer, squash, swimming, and tennis. Girls' sports include ballet, basketball, crew, cross-country running, field hockey, fitness, golf, ice hockey, jazz dance, lacrosse, modern dance, riding, soccer, softball, squash, tennis, and swimming.

The Magowan Field House contains two basketball courts; the Brainard Squash Courts (three); a six-lane, 25-yard swimming pool with spectator stands; a newly renovated fitness center; and locker rooms. A separate building contains four indoor tennis courts. Other facilities include the Kent School Riding Stables, an enclosed ice rink, six soccer and lacrosse fields, two field-hockey fields, three baseball diamonds, and thirteen outdoor tennis courts. The Benjamin Waring Partridge Rowing Center opened in 2005. Crews now have this state-of-the-art facility throughout the entire academic year, in addition to 4½ miles of rowing water on the Housatonic River. There are lights for evening football games.

EXTRACURRICULAR OPPORTUNITIES

Kent encourages students to initiate clubs whenever there is sufficient interest; recent popular organizations have included a debating club, a varsity math team, Habitat for Humanity, and a culture club. The Art, Spanish, French, and German Clubs meet informally and sponsor trips and other events. Publications include the *Kent News;* the *Cauldron,* the student literary production; and the *Kent Yearbook.* Volunteer groups work at local rest homes. Students also train to assist the town's volunteer fire department. Instruction is offered in any band or orchestral instrument, and there are Dixieland and jazz bands, a concert band, an orchestra, chamber groups, the choir, the Kentones, the Kentettes, the Chamber Choir, and brass, string, and wind ensembles. Students produce at least three major plays each year.

DAILY LIFE

Each student's day begins with voluntary breakfast, which is followed by jobs. The academic day runs from 8 to 3, except on Wednesdays and Saturdays, when it ends at noon. Classes are 45 minutes long. Although meals generally are served buffet-style, there are family-style dinners on Thursdays. Athletics practices follow the class day. Study conditions are maintained throughout the campus from 7:30 to 9:30 p.m. Third and Fourth Formers are checked in at 10:30; Fifth and Sixth Formers, at 11. Late lights may be requested. Students are free to study on campus where they please if they use the freedom responsibly.

Attendance at chapel is required of all students on Tuesdays and Thursdays. Voluntary Eucharists are held on Mondays.

WEEKEND LIFE

Saturdays are considered school days until noon and are protected as such by a small day-student population and by a policy that limits students to five weekends (Friday afternoon to Sunday evening) or ten overnights (Saturday afternoon to Sunday evening) away from Kent. These weekends do not include the fall and spring Parent Weekends. Permission from both parents and the School is required for all weekend absences. Most students take fewer weekends a year because they do not want to miss athletics, Saturday night dances and movies, and special concerts and lectures. Friday evening services are provided for Jewish and Muslim students and faculty members, and Sunday Mass is offered in town for Roman Catholics as well as for Mormon students; all other students attend an Episcopal Eucharist on Sunday morning at St. Joseph's Chapel. School-sponsored trips to concerts, plays, and museums in New Haven and New York City occur each term.

SUMMER PROGRAMS

Kent School offers a summer program in creative writing.

COSTS AND FINANCIAL AID

The 2008–09 charges were $42,000 for boarding students and $33,000 for day students. There are annual fees of $1245 that cover infirmary care, publications, activities, and technology. There is an additional fee of $100 for international students. A prescribed dress code applies to girls and boys for all School appointments. Approximately $2500 is necessary for such personal expenses as books, supplies, laboratory and art fees, special medicine or X-rays, and laundry. Students have debit cards for personal expenses.

For the 2008–09 school year, 34 percent of students received financial aid, with a total financial aid budget of $6 million. Kent's financial aid is awarded on the basis of demonstrated need. However, as a result of its limited budget, the School each year has more families who qualify for assistance than it is able to fund.

ADMISSIONS INFORMATION

Kent students come from diverse cultural, economic, and geographical backgrounds, and the School does not discriminate on the basis of race, color, creed, or national origin. Kent is demanding of students in academic, athletic, extracurricular, and social areas and seeks students who have a high level of energy and are ready to participate fully in all aspects of the School community.

All candidates are required to take the SSAT. International students must also take the TOEFL. Personal interviews are required, and a tour of the campus is recommended. Tours and interviews take about 2 hours.

APPLICATION TIMETABLE

Candidates and parents are encouraged to visit Kent from 8 to 2 on Mondays, Tuesdays, Thursdays, and Fridays or from 9 to noon on Wednesdays and Saturdays. Although a few places may be available for highly qualified candidates who apply after the March 10 notification date, candidates are strongly advised to submit applications during the fall of the year prior to intended entry and to complete their files by January 15. The application fee is $65. The fee for international students is $120 (U.S. dollars). Families have one month following receipt of an offer of admission to accept the offer.

ADMISSIONS CORRESPONDENCE

Kathryn F. Sullivan
Director of Admissions
Kent School
Kent, Connecticut 06757
Phone: 860-927-6111
800-538-5368 (toll-free)
Fax: 860-927-6109
E-mail: admissions@kent-school.edu
Web site: http://www.kent-school.edu

KENTS HILL SCHOOL

Kents Hill, Maine

Type: Coeducational boarding and day college-preparatory school
Grades: 9–12, postgraduate year
Enrollment: 228
Head of School: Rist Bonnefond

THE SCHOOL

Kents Hill School, one of the oldest coeducational boarding schools in the country, was founded by Luther Sampson and chartered in 1824. The 400-acre campus is on the summit of a high, rolling hill that overlooks the valleys and lakes of the Belgrade region in Maine. Located within easy reach of Colby, Bates, and Bowdoin colleges, Kents Hill is located 1 hour north of Portland, Maine, and 3 hours north of Boston, Massachusetts.

A comprehensive college-preparatory school, Kents Hill School prepares students to become lifelong learners and leaders who make a principled difference in the world.

The School is governed by a self-perpetuating 30-member Board of Trustees, which meets four times a year. The School's physical plant is valued at $19.9 million and operates with a $4.5-million endowment. In the last eight years, the School has renovated Davis Hall and built three new buildings: the $7-million Alfond Athletics Center; Reed Hall, a new girls' residence hall; and the Chip Williams Woodworking Studio. In October 2008, the School dedicated the Harold Alfond Athletics Fields, a 200,000-square-foot set of turf fields, the largest turf complex in New England. In spring 2009, the School will open the Performing Arts Center at Newton Hall, and construction on a new Learning Center is scheduled to begin during the summer of 2009.

The School is accredited by the New England Association of Schools and Colleges. It holds memberships in the Cum Laude Society, the National Association of Independent Schools, the College Board, the New England Association of College Admissions Counseling, the Secondary School Admission Test Board, the Independent Schools Association of Northern New England, the Council for the Advancement and Support of Education, the Council for Religion in Independent Schools, and the Association of Boarding Schools.

ACADEMIC PROGRAMS

Kents Hill School offers more than 100 college preparatory courses. Thirteen Advanced Placement courses are offered, and there are honors classes in every department. The School was one of twelve schools in the nation to receive the Siemens Foundation Award for Advanced Placement programs in science and math in 2003, and in 2007, a teacher received the prestigious Harvard Singer Prize for Excellence in Secondary School Teaching, one of three awarded in the country.

Eighteen credits are required to earn a diploma, including 4 credits in English, 3 in history (1 of which must be in U.S. history), 3 in mathematics, 3 in science (including two lab courses), and a minimum of one course each in environmental studies, performing arts, visual arts, and health. Students must also complete at least 2 years of the same foreign language (unless this requirement is waived by the Director of the Learning Center). Advanced Placement courses are offered in English, U.S. history, European history, calculus AB, computer science, biology, chemistry, physics, environmental studies, statistics, and studio art (Drawing, 2D, and 3D). A comprehensive English as a Second Language (ESL) program is offered to international students. The Waters Learning Skills Center provides motivated students with mild or moderate learning differences with one- or two-on-one tutoring. The Learning Skills Program teaches students to develop strategies that maximize their learning strengths. The Visual Arts department is particularly strong in ceramics, woodworking, graphic design, filmmaking, and photography. The Performing Arts Department was added in 2002 and offers classes in acting, stage management, and playwriting.

Classes range in size from 5 to 16 students. The academic year is divided into trimesters, with major exams given twice a year. The open-stack library and research room are available for use every weekday from 8 a.m. to 3 p.m. and again from 7 to 10 p.m. Five computer labs throughout the campus provide ongoing access to computers for all students. All residence hall rooms and the Student Union are wired for Internet access.

FACULTY AND ADVISERS

Most of the 42 faculty members live on campus and are readily available to assist students who are in need of extra help. Seventeen of the faculty members hold master's degrees or higher, with 4 more working toward their master's degrees. Faculty members serve a variety of roles as teachers, coaches, advisers, and residence hall parents.

Rist Bonnefond, appointed Headmaster in 1990, is a graduate of Phillips Exeter Academy and Cornell University (B.A., 1971). He has also done graduate work at the University of Rhode Island. Before his appointment, Mr. Bonnefond was Director of College Guidance at the Loomis Chaffee School in Windsor, Connecticut.

COLLEGE ADMISSION COUNSELING

The College Counseling Office begins working with students in their junior year, starting with the Junior Seminar in the fall of the junior year. The College Counseling Office continues to work closely with juniors and seniors to help with the college and university selection, the application and admissions processes, and the mechanics of interviewing. Representatives from approximately sixty colleges and universities from all over the country and overseas visit Kents Hill each fall to present information to students regarding a variety of college choices and options.

All sophomores and juniors take the PSAT in the fall. Juniors take the SAT and SAT Subject Tests as necessary in the spring. Seniors take the SAT and SAT Subject Tests in the fall and additional Advanced Placement tests in the spring. ACT and TOEFL testing are also arranged.

Recent graduates have been admitted to colleges and universities such as Bates, Boston University, Bowdoin, Brown, Colby, Colgate, Dickinson, Fordham, George Washington, Hamilton, Haverford, Hobart, Mount Holyoke, Rensselaer, Rhodes, Richmond, St. Lawrence, Skidmore, Smith, Syracuse, Tufts, U.S. Military and Naval Academies, Villanova, Wesleyan, Wheaton, and the Universities of Illinois at Urbana-Champaign and Michigan.

STUDENT BODY AND CONDUCT

In 2008–09 there are 228 students—25 percent day students and 75 percent boarders.

Students come to Kents Hill from twenty states and eighteen other countries. Most students choose Kents Hill because of the small classes, the close relationship between faculty members and students, the family atmosphere, and the opportunities afforded students in the community and throughout the world through the programs.

Expectations for student behavior are very high. Any student who cannot abide by firm policies concerning attendance and social mores on campus will be subject to disciplinary action and possible dismissal.

ACADEMIC FACILITIES

More than twenty classrooms are housed in four academic buildings: Bearce Hall, Ricker Hall, the Williams Woodworking Studio, and Dunn Science Building, which includes an observatory. The Mathematics and Modern Language Departments are also found in Dunn. Sampson Hall houses the Bass Art Center and the Cochrane Library. Ricker Hall houses the English Department and the Performing Arts Department, which will move to the Performing Arts Center at Newton Hall in spring 2009. Bearce Hall is the location of the School offices, the Social Studies Department, the School Bank, Deering Chapel, and several classrooms. The Cochrane Library contains 14,000 volumes, two study rooms, microfilm machines, and the Isaacson '69 Computer Center.

BOARDING AND GENERAL FACILITIES

Students are housed in five residence halls. All residence halls are supervised by resident faculty members, who are assisted by appointed student proctors.

Returning students have their choice of rooms and roommates. New students are assigned rooms by the Dean of Students.

The School maintains a school store, a snack bar and game room, and a well-equipped student health center. A local physician makes regular calls and is available in case of emergency, although the School is in proximity to a major medical center.

Masterman Student Union, built in 1971, contains a large, modern dining room that is used for activities as well as for meals. The building also contains the kitchen, the Husky Den snack bar, the College Counseling Center, and comfortable lounges; it serves as the social center of the campus.

ATHLETICS

Kents Hill strongly believes that participation in athletics plays a key role in the development of well-rounded individuals. The School offers a wide range of sports designed to challenge students individually and as part of a team. Interscholastic sports include Alpine skiing (with an on-campus alpine racing and snowboarding center), baseball, basketball, cross-country, field hockey, football, golf, ice hockey, lacrosse, mountain biking, snowboarding, soccer, softball, and tennis. The Outing Club, Nordic Ski Club, and an equestrian program are also offered.

The Alfond Athletics Center houses two basketball courts, an ice rink, a fitness center, and dressing and training rooms. The School also has six competitive playing fields, including two turf fields, and on-campus Alpine skiing and snowboarding facilities at the Liz Cross Mellen Lodge. The Alpine training center is lighted for night skiing and snowboarding. Natural snowfall is supplemented by state-of-the-art snowmaking and grooming. The School also has 14 kilometers of groomed cross-country ski trails for skiing and snowshoeing.

EXTRACURRICULAR OPPORTUNITIES

Students may become involved in the yearbook, newspaper, literary magazine, photography, Student Council, Kents Hill Singers, Drama Club, Environmental Club, Outing Club, Chess Club, Current Affairs Club, and Amnesty International. Students participate in a schoolwide community service program.

Student leadership activities include serving on the Student Council as campus tour guides, as proctors, as peer counselors, and as student ambassadors for international students.

DAILY LIFE

Each class meets three times per week for 45 minutes and one time per week for 75 minutes. The school day begins at 8 a.m. and ends at 3 p.m., with 45 minutes for lunch. On Wednesday, classes end at 12:40 p.m. Study hall is held between 8 and 10 p.m., Sunday through Thursday.

WEEKEND LIFE

With faculty members on duty each weekend, it is possible for the School to schedule a variety of weekend activities while providing the necessary supervision. Kents Hill School offers fishing, canoeing, backpacking, camping, and rock-climbing. Trips to nearby Augusta, Portland, Freeport, and Waterville supplement such on-campus activities as movies, dances, and concerts. Trips are also scheduled during the winter to the nearby ski areas of Sugarloaf and Sunday River. The student union and the athletics center are open on the weekends, and a variety of on-campus activities are offered each weekend.

COSTS AND FINANCIAL AID

The tuition, room, and board costs for boarding students in 2008–09 are $41,200. Tuition for day students was $22,900. Expenses for transportation for vacations, books and supplies, and tutorial assistance are additional. A $3000 deposit is required following acceptance or reenrollment to reserve a place. Tuition payment is due by August 1 unless a payment plan is arranged. The payment plans require purchase of a tuition insurance plan.

Approximately 43 percent of students receive financial assistance. All financial aid awards and loans are based on need.

ADMISSIONS INFORMATION

Kents Hill School admits students, regardless of race, creed, or national origin, on the basis of a willingness to become an active school participant, motivation to succeed, and the ability to do the work. Students are admitted to any of the four grades or to the postgraduate year.

The SSAT is recommended for applicants to grades 9, 10, and 11, and the SAT is recommended for applicants to grade 12 and the postgraduate year. An interview on campus is required, unless waived by the Director of Admissions.

APPLICATION TIMETABLE

The School recommends that applications be submitted by February 15. However, inquiries and applications are welcome throughout the school year, and interviews can be arranged at any time. An application is considered as long as space is available. A $50 fee must accompany each application.

ADMISSIONS CORRESPONDENCE

Ms. Amy Smucker, Director of Admissions
Kents Hill School
P.O. Box 257
Kents Hill, Maine 04349-0257
Phone: 207-685-4914
Fax: 207-685-9529
E-mail: info@kentshill.org
Web site: http://www.kentshill.org

KIMBALL UNION ACADEMY

Meriden, New Hampshire

KIMBALL UNION ACADEMY

Type: Coeducational boarding and day college-preparatory school
Grades: 9–12, postgraduate year
Enrollment: 350
Head of School: Michael J. Schafer

THE SCHOOL

Founded in 1813, Kimball Union Academy (KUA) is the fifteenth-oldest boarding school in the country. Kimball Union's unique location in the Upper Connecticut River Valley and its proximity to Dartmouth College have long made it the preferred choice for both boarding and day students seeking an educational experience that develops the whole person as scholar, athlete, artist, and global citizen. The Academy's mission is to "discover with each student the path to academic mastery, to creativity, and to responsibility." Kimball Union offers its students an education that balances a challenging, dynamic curriculum with excellent programs in athletics and the arts.

Located in Meriden, New Hampshire, the Academy's 1,300-acre rural campus is 2 hours via major highways from Boston, Massachusetts, and Hartford, Connecticut. Nearby bus, train, and plane terminals link the area directly with Boston, New York City, and Manchester, New Hampshire.

The Academy is governed by a 21-member Board of Trustees. The school's physical plant is valued in excess of $40 million, and the school is supported by a $19.1-million endowment. The 2007–08 annual fund campaign, which was generously supported by alumni and parents, raised more than $1 million.

ACADEMIC PROGRAMS

The Kimball Union curriculum includes 4 years of English; mathematics through BC calculus; world history, European history, Chinese history, U.S. history, anthropology, human geography, American government; biology, chemistry, physics for sustainability, environmental and wildlife sciences; and language courses in French, Spanish, and Latin, from beginning through Advanced Placement, and beginning levels of Mandarin Chinese.

Electives are offered in history, English, math, and the sciences. There is an extensive arts program, with electives in music, dance, theater, and the visual arts, including pottery and photography. Nineteen Advanced Placement courses are offered for qualified students in English, mathematics, four sciences, history (world and U.S., human geography), music theory, studio art, and art history as well as three languages.

Students must obtain a minimum of 19 credits for graduation (most four-year students complete 22 to 24 credits), including 4 credits of English, 3 of mathematics, 3 of history, 3 of a foreign language, 2 of science, and 1 of the arts. The normal academic load is five to six courses per trimester.

The average class size is 12 students. With a student-faculty ratio of 6:1, faculty members are able to give individual attention through appointments and regular office hours. During the evening study period, students study in their rooms under the supervision of faculty members and student proctors. The Freshman Orientation and Learning Strategies (FOALS) Program is a required course that explores a variety of material throughout the first trimester, including learning styles, technology and library resources, study skills and techniques, and writing skill development. Freshmen are in specially supervised study halls; as students move up through the school, they are progressively given more responsibility for the use of their own time.

There is a letter system for course grades, with effort evaluated on a numerical scale. Grades and teachers' comments are sent to parents three times a year, and students receive periodic interim reports during the year. A grade point average of at least 3.0, with no grade below a B-, qualifies for the honor roll. A student with a GPA of 2.0 or below and/or low effort grades is considered in academic difficulty and is given special attention.

The Academy's curriculum is traditional at its core, but teaching methods include problem-solving techniques and cooperative learning. Both the English and the language departments have peer tutoring labs. Writing Across the Curriculum is a schoolwide initiative. There is an exciting environmental science program, which not only includes classes at several levels, including AP, but also integrates environmental science into other disciplines through a shared philosophy about the importance of the environment. An 800-acre tract on nearby Snow Mountain provides an environmental classroom.

FACULTY AND ADVISERS

The Kimball Union faculty consists of 53 full-time teachers, most of whom hold advanced degrees.

Michael J. Schafer, who was appointed Head of School in 2003, is a graduate of Colby College and holds an M.Ed. from Harvard University. He previously served as Assistant Head of School at Middlesex School. His teaching career began at Cushing Academy. Moving on to Belmont Hill School, he served as a Spanish teacher, college adviser, and coach.

Faculty members at Kimball Union fill many roles: teachers, advisers, coaches, and house parents. All but a few faculty members live on campus. Faculty members each advise about 6 students, for whom they oversee academic work and scheduling.

COLLEGE ADMISSION COUNSELING

The college selection process begins in the junior year, when each student is assigned to a college adviser. A college information weekend for parents of juniors is held in the spring.

In the College Advising resource room, juniors and seniors can use various sources of information, including catalogs and computer software, in making their college selections. Computer software and Internet access are available for applications, and college representatives visit the school regularly throughout the fall.

An SAT preparation course is available to all juniors in the spring and all seniors in the fall preceding the administration of the test. Kimball Union's SAT scores are higher than the national averages. Students also have the opportunity to take the ACT Assessment on campus.

The graduates of the class of 2008 are attending such colleges and universities as Boston College, Bowdoin, Carnegie Mellon, Clarkson, Columbia, Connecticut College, Cornell, Dartmouth, Drew, George Washington, Johns Hopkins, Lehigh, Middlebury, Occidental, Purdue, St. Lawrence, Swarthmore, Vanderbilt, Wesleyan, and the Universities of Colorado, New Hampshire, Rhode Island, and Vermont.

STUDENT BODY AND CONDUCT

For 2008, Kimball Union enrolled 341 students: 198 boys and 143 girls. There were 46 students in the ninth grade, 73 in the tenth grade, 103 in the eleventh grade, and 119 in the twelfth grade and the postgraduate year; 108 were day students. Although the majority of students are from New England, students come to the Academy from eighteen states and nineteen different countries.

Kimball Union Academy has an Honor Code intended to reflect its core values, support its mission, and guide the behavior of its community. In establishing its policies on conduct, Kimball Union considers it a priority to teach its students concern for others. Violations of major school rules are reviewed individually by a disciplinary committee of peers and faculty members, which makes a recommendation to the Head of School. Violations of minor rules are normally handled by a faculty member.

ACADEMIC FACILITIES

The original Academy building is Baxter Hall, which houses the humanities classrooms. Fitch Science Hall, for math and the sciences, has been entirely renovated, and the E. E. Just Center provides a magnificent home for the environmental science and human geography programs. There are three major computer labs and a language lab, and each academic department has an individual computer minilab.

The historic Kimball Barn houses Kimball Union's woodworking program. The Flickinger Arts Center is a spacious home for all of the arts. It contains a 400-seat, fully equipped theater; a dance studio; a darkroom; music rooms; practice rooms; separate ceramics, painting, and drawing studios; and an art gallery as well as a state-of-the-art computer lab/recording studio.

The Coffin Library contains 20,000 volumes, more than 100 periodicals, a large video/DVD/audio book library of more than 1,500 titles, a considerable microfiche collection, and computer stations featuring online resources.

BOARDING AND GENERAL FACILITIES

Kimball Union operates nine residences, ranging in size from 5 to 50 students. The variety in residence size gives students the opportunity to choose the environment that suits them best. There is a faculty member living on each floor of the larger halls and in each of the smaller houses. At least 60 percent of the students live in single rooms, with the rest in double rooms.

There is a health center staffed by registered nurses, and the Dartmouth Hitchcock Medical Center is a 15-minute drive away. The spacious and comfortable Dining Commons and new, adjacent Campus Center are the center of daily life at Kimball Union, providing space for dining and informal gathering; included here are Student Life Offices and student activity rooms and areas for performances, a media viewing lounge, computer terminals, day student lockers, the Campus Store and café, the faculty lounge, and outdoor terraces and seating areas.

ATHLETICS

The athletic program at KUA seeks to complement what the students are learning in the classroom and is vital to the life of a boarding school. KUA successfully competes in a variety of interscholastic sports. Sports and athletic offerings include baseball, basketball, cross-country, cycling, equestrian, field hockey, fitness training, hockey, lacrosse, mountain biking, mountain football, rugby, skiing, soccer, softball, and a wilderness program.

In order to promote good health and ensure that all students have the opportunity to experience a team sport or activity, every student is required to participate in two group activities per year. Kimball Union offers teams at different levels, so there is a team appropriate for every student who wants to play.

Athletic facilities center on the Whittemore Athletic Center, which includes the Akerstrom Ice Arena. Kimball Union's new state-of-the-art lower fields complex includes a lighted artificial-turf field. There are also playing fields for soccer and/or lacrosse; a football field; baseball and softball diamonds; two basketball courts; an all-weather track; an ice-hockey arena, with indoor turf in the off-season; two weight rooms; and a swimming pool. The Miller Student Center houses a fully equipped fitness center. Cross-country running and ski trails cut across portions of the campus and through surrounding woods. The Alpine Ski Team trains alongside the Dartmouth Ski Team at the Dartmouth Skiway. Freestyle and snowboard teams train just 15 minutes away.

EXTRACURRICULAR OPPORTUNITIES

The Arts Center runs a cultural events series of concerts and gallery openings. There are at least three lavishly produced student shows in the theater each year, and the Concordians (an a cappella group), Rock and Jazz Band, and Dance Ensemble perform seasonally.

Student leadership is extremely active at Kimball Union, and there are many opportunities for students to participate. There is an elected student government, and the president runs all-school meetings. Community service activities are planned through a standing committee, and weekly community dinners are sponsored by a group called the Penny Fellowship. The Academy has a fire squad that provides essential support to the Meriden Volunteer Fire Department. There is an active diversity program called Relay, and there are an Environmental Club and many other clubs and organizations.

Traditional events and celebrations include the Wildcat Challenge, class trips, Winter Carnival, the International Festival, Senior Girls' Tea, the Junior/Senior Spring Formal, and parents' weekends.

DAILY LIFE

Classes are scheduled Monday through Saturday (some Saturdays are set aside for alternative programming), with half days on Wednesdays and Saturdays to accommodate sports events. The daily schedule includes seven periods. All-school meetings take place twice a week. Scheduled community times and adviser/advisee lunches occur throughout the year.

Sports and activities meet every day for 2 hours in the afternoon, except on Wednesdays and Saturdays, when games take place. A modified winter schedule accommodates winter sports.

There is a dedicated period at the end of the day for performing arts and activities, enabling students to attend without scheduling conflicts. Dinner, which is served at 6 p.m., is family-style or formal on one day and cafeteria-style on six. The evening study hall is from 8 to 10, and students must check into their dorms by 7:45. Freshman through senior evening schedules are adjusted appropriately for age.

WEEKEND LIFE

Kimball Union is committed to providing students with a rich residential life program. Weekend activities are many and varied. Saturday evening events include trips to dinner or the movies, on-campus movies, and dances, while on Sundays there are regular shopping trips to town; trips to major ski areas, to Boston, and to concerts and sports events at Dartmouth; and outdoor activities such as apple-picking and hiking. Most day students spend a large part of the weekend on campus.

Apart from scheduled campus weekends, students may go home or, with their parents' permission, visit friends after their last obligation on Saturday. They must return to the campus by 7:30 p.m. on Sunday.

COSTS AND FINANCIAL AID

Tuition for the 2008–09 school year at Kimball Union was $42,500 for boarders and $27,500 for day students. For boarders, the fee includes room, board, use of all facilities, and admission to plays, lectures, and concerts held on campus. Charges beyond the basic fee include those for books, athletic store purchases, the musical, and transportation. An initial deposit of 10 percent of tuition is requested upon confirmation of enrollment, with the balance due on August 1 and January 1. Loan plans and tuition-refund insurance are available.

Kimball Union accepts students without regard to their ability to pay and then attempts to present the family with a financial aid package to make attendance possible. Kimball Union awards financial aid based strictly on financial need as determined by the School and Student Service for Financial Aid of Princeton, New Jersey. This year, 33 percent of all Kimball Union students received a total of $2.3 million in financial aid.

ADMISSIONS INFORMATION

Kimball Union seeks students who want to grow and contribute as students and individuals within its family-oriented community. Typically, successful candidates have strong academic backgrounds, extracurricular interests in arts and athletics, or the willingness to stretch and try new things. The Admissions Committee views as most important the student's academic achievement as well as recommendations from current teachers and the personal interview. The majority of Kimball Union students enter in either the ninth or tenth grade.

APPLICATION TIMETABLE

Candidates for admission are required to visit the campus for a student-guided tour and an interview. The Admissions Office schedules appointments Monday through Saturday morning. Applications should be accompanied by standardized test scores (SSAT, PSAT, SAT, TOEFL), an academic transcript, a parent statement, three recommendations, and a $40 fee ($75 for international applicants). The application must be received by February 1 in order for the applicant to be notified of a decision on March 10. Students are requested to reply to an acceptance by April 10. Admissions continue on a rolling basis after April 10.

ADMISSIONS CORRESPONDENCE

Rich Ryerson, Interim Admissions Director
Kimball Union Academy
Meriden, New Hampshire 03770

Phone: 603-469-2100
Fax: 603-469-2041
E-mail: admissions@kua.org
Web site: http://www.kua.org

LAKE FOREST ACADEMY

Lake Forest, Illinois

Type: Coeducational boarding and day college-preparatory school
Grades: 9–12
Enrollment: 390
Head of School: John Strudwick

THE SCHOOL

Lake Forest Academy (LFA) is located on a 150-acre campus on Chicago's North Shore, 35 miles from the Loop and 5 miles from Lake Michigan.

Lake Forest Academy was founded in 1857 by a group of Chicago businessmen as an independent, all-boys college-preparatory school. In 1869, the Young Ladies' Seminary at Ferry Hall was established as an independent girls' school in Lake Forest. LFA has been coeducational since 1974, when the school merged with Ferry Hall. The LFA campus, which was originally contiguous to the Lake Forest College grounds, moved to its current location, the former J. Ogden Armour estate, in 1948 after a fire destroyed the Academy buildings. Lake Forest Academy is governed by a board of trustees and accredited by the Independent Schools Association of the Central States, the National Association of Independent Schools, and the State of Illinois.

Lake Forest Academy strives to embody in its practices and to cultivate in its students excellence of character, scholarship, citizenship, and responsibility. Character encompasses respect for others and their beliefs, dedication to honesty in every sphere of life, realization of moral clarity and conviction, and pursuit of virtue and value in life. Scholarship encompasses acquisition of knowledge, development of critical thinking, enthusiasm for discovery and learning, and exercise of a powerful imagination. Citizenship encompasses appreciation of diversity and multiculturalism, involvement in the LFA community, participation in service to others, and commitment to global awareness and understanding. Responsibility encompasses development of self-reliance, ability to seek guidance, dedication to cooperation and teamwork, and action based upon informed decisions.

LFA is a mission-driven, college-preparatory school of between 380 and 400 students, with approximately equal numbers of boarding and day students. The school is respected for the exceptional quality and diversity of its student and faculty communities, who are drawn from across the globe, as well as for the depth and breadth of its academic and extracurricular programs. LFA is recognized as a liberal arts school that, in addition to academic excellence, develops character and changes its students' lives through the efforts of great faculty members and their commitment to outstanding teaching. Finally, LFA is committed to a high-caliber physical plant with state-of-the-art facilities for both program and residential needs and to a healthy financial position to secure the ongoing success of the school and its vision.

The school is committed to providing the kind of education that enables students to accomplish their ultimate goals. It is a community that provides the support and caring needed to develop confidence and strong values and where learning is a constant adventure. It has created an atmosphere that builds character and fosters respect for individuality.

The endowment is currently valued at $25.8 million, and revenue is supplemented by more than $1.8 million raised through the Annual Academy Fund. Many of Lake Forest Academy's alumni and parents contribute significantly to the fund to support student programs, scholarships, and operating expenses.

ACADEMIC PROGRAMS

Students are required to carry at least five courses each semester. Diploma requirements include English, 4 years; mathematics, 3 years; and fine arts, 2 years. Students are required to complete 3 years in two disciplines chosen from history, science, and foreign language and 2 years in the other. Two additional credits are required for graduation. Requirements are adjusted for students entering after the ninth grade.

Elective courses are offered in all subjects. In addition, 24 Advanced Placement courses are offered, including art, biology, calculus (AB and BC), chemistry, Chinese, computer science, economics (micro and macro), English, environmental science, French, government, history (world, European, and U.S.), Latin, music, physics, Spanish, and statistics.

The average class size is under 12, and the student-teacher ratio is 7:1. Freshmen have a proctored study hall during some of their free periods. Sophomores, juniors, and seniors with a sufficient GPA may be granted honor-study privileges. The school library is open during the school day and in the evening. An interlibrary loan system gives students access to more than 2 million volumes.

The grading system uses an A to F scale, with pluses and minuses. Examinations are held twice a year, with grades and teachers' comments sent to parents four times a year, after each interim and at the end of each semester.

FACULTY AND ADVISERS

The teaching faculty is composed of 52 percent men and 48 percent women; 72 percent of the faculty members have advanced degrees, and 82 percent live on campus. These teachers are responsible for counseling and supervision in the dormitories and are available to give extra help during evenings and weekends to all students. Faculty members also serve as advisers to students, meeting with them and communicating with their parents on a regular basis. In addition to teaching, faculty members are responsible for extracurricular activities, usually coaching or club sponsorship.

The Head of School is Dr. John Strudwick, who was appointed in 2001 after a seventeen-year career at Phillips Academy in Andover, Massachusetts.

COLLEGE ADMISSION COUNSELING

Four college counselors work with students to guide them through the college selection process. Students take the PSAT in tenth grade and again in eleventh. Students take the SAT in the spring of the junior year as well as in the fall of the senior year. Students' SAT verbal, writing, and mathematics scores range from the 500s to 800. Representatives of more than 150 colleges visit the campus in the fall of each year. Counselors work very closely with students from the spring of the junior year through the senior year to help them with the decision-making process.

Recent graduates currently attend such institutions as Brown, Carnegie Mellon, Columbia, Cornell, Emory, George Washington, Harvard, Northwestern, Pomona, Princeton, Tufts, the University of Pennsylvania, Williams, and Yale as well as many other outstanding colleges and universities.

STUDENT BODY AND CONDUCT

The student body is divided evenly, with 50 percent boarding and 50 percent day students, as well as approximately equal numbers of boys and girls. Reflecting the school's diversity, students come to Lake Forest Academy from seventeen states and twenty-three other countries. International students make up 25 percent of the student body. Thirty-seven percent of the students are members of minority groups, including African and African-American, Asian and Asian-American, and Hispanic students.

Students are expected to behave according to prescribed standards. Violations of school rules are handled by the Dean of Students and the Discipline Committee, a group composed of students and faculty members.

LFA also has a Student Council that comprises the all-school president plus the class president and 3 representatives from each grade. The council plans activities, allocates funds, makes recommendations to the Dean of Students Office, and serves as a forum for students' concerns.

ACADEMIC FACILITIES

The Corbin Academic Center is the hub of academic life, with its classrooms, science labs, language lab, and student center. Reid Hall houses the library, the English department, most administrative offices, and the Admission Office. Hutchinson Commons is the school's dining hall and sits adjacent to New Hall, which holds the Campus Store, Student Seminar classroom, and some offices. The $5.5-million Cressey Center for the Arts was completed in 2001 and houses the 430-seat professional proscenium theater, performing and fine arts studios, digital media lab, photo darkrooms, and display galleries.

BOARDING AND GENERAL FACILITIES

Four single-sex dormitories constitute the living quarters for boarding students. Two students share each room, and every dormitory has a common room for informal gatherings. Each dorm has faculty members in residence. An infirmary is located on the campus. All students must leave the campus for the Thanksgiving, winter, and spring vacations.

ATHLETICS

Students at all ability levels are required to participate in athletics in order to experience team involvement and competition. Interscholastic sports for the boys include baseball, basketball, cross-country, football, golf, ice hockey, soccer, swimming, tennis, track, volleyball, and wrestling. Girls' teams include basketball, cheerleading, cross-country, field hockey, golf, ice hockey, soccer, softball, swimming, tennis, track, and volleyball. In addition, the physical education program offers opportunities to participate in dance, aerobics, squash, weight training, yoga, water polo, and various intramural sports.

Glore Memorial Gymnasium has a pool, a basketball court, a wrestling room, locker rooms, and a trainer's room. The campus has football, soccer, baseball, softball, and field hockey fields, as well as an outdoor track, an indoor ice arena, practice fields, and four tennis courts. A fitness center, which opened in spring 2004, offers weight machines, free weights, cardio machines, and on-site fitness and weight-lifting experts.

EXTRACURRICULAR OPPORTUNITIES

The proximity of Lake Forest Academy to Chicago provides a wide variety of opportunities for students to participate in cultural events. Trips are made to many of the major theatrical and musical productions that come to Chicago as well as to museums, exhibits, and sports events. Seasonal weekend trips include skiing, camping, biking, and sailing on Lake Michigan. Transportation is provided to nearby shopping centers, where students may shop, eat, or see a movie.

Other activities on campus include Model UN, Harvard Model Congress, and working on the staffs of the yearbook, newspaper, and literary magazine. Many students are involved in various clubs (math club, Interact, bridge club) as well as service-learning activities. Traditional annual events include Homecoming, International Fair, Prom, Winter Formal, Ra Weekend, Move-up Day, and many theatrical productions.

DAILY LIFE

Classes are held from 8:30 a.m. to 3 p.m. Time is set aside each week for club and class meetings and assemblies. Student-adviser meetings are held two times per week. The school also meets as a group during morning meeting twice per week. Students have a 2-hour supervised study hall in the dormitory Sunday through Thursday nights from 8 to 10.

COSTS AND FINANCIAL AID

Tuition for 2008–09 was $28,500 for day students and $38,500 for boarding students. Books cost approximately $800 for the year, and there are additional fees for music lessons. For boarding students, an allowance of $25 to $30 per week is recommended for snacks and toiletries. An initial deposit is due with the signed Enrollment Contract. There are various payment plan options available to families.

LFA offers need-based financial aid. In 2008–09, students received more than $2.8 million in financial aid. Financial aid is reviewed on a yearly basis. Parents must submit their most recent federal income tax returns and the Parents' Financial Statement (PFS) to the School and Student Service for Financial Aid (SSS) in Princeton, New Jersey, annually.

ADMISSIONS INFORMATION

All applicants to Lake Forest Academy are considered by the Admission Committee on the basis of their academic record, a personal interview, teacher and school recommendations, and the result of their SSAT (or equivalent). Lake Forest Academy admits students of any race, nationality, religion, or ethnic background to all rights, privileges, programs, and activities generally accorded or made available to students. The school does not discriminate on the basis of race in the administration of its educational policies, admission policies, scholarship programs, or school-administered programs.

Applicants take the SSAT (or equivalent test). Approximately 40 percent of all applicants are accepted for admission.

APPLICATION TIMETABLE

Lake Forest Academy's application deadline is January 31. Families who plan to apply for financial aid should note that the financial aid application deadline is January 15. Early submission of materials is strongly encouraged. Waiting lists form as soon as a class is fully enrolled. In addition to taking the SSAT, students must file an application and transcript release form with a $50 application fee, submit personal and teachers' recommendations, and have an interview. Decisions are mailed in late February along with financial aid award letters. Applications submitted after the deadline are considered on a rolling admission basis, depending on available space. The Admission Office is open Monday through Friday from 8 to 4 (Central time) throughout the year. Tours and interviews are scheduled by appointment only.

ADMISSIONS CORRESPONDENCE

Loring Kinder Strudwick
Dean of Admission
Lake Forest Academy
1500 West Kennedy Road
Lake Forest, Illinois 60045

Phone: 847-615-3267
Fax: 847-295-8149
E-mail: lstrudwick@lfanet.org
Web site: http://www.lfanet.org

LAWRENCE ACADEMY

Groton, Massachusetts

Type: Coeducational boarding and day nondenominational college-preparatory school
Grades: 9–12
Enrollment: 396
Head of School: D. Scott Wiggins

THE SCHOOL

Founded in 1793, Lawrence Academy is nestled in the rolling hills of a classic New England town. Lawrence's excellent academic reputation is built upon more than 200 years of tradition and furthered by signature programs, such as the Ninth Grade Program, Winterim, and the Independent Immersion Program.

Lawrence Academy's 100-acre campus is located 31 miles northwest of Boston. Easily accessible by public transportation and major highways, it is close enough to several urban centers for students to take advantage of a variety of social, cultural, and recreational offerings, and it is far enough removed for all to enjoy the save and quiet character of the New England countryside.

The Academy is a nonprofit corporation directed by a self-perpetuating Board of Trustees, which meets three times yearly. Endowment in productive funds totals $16 million, and the school plant is valued at $50 million. The 2006–07 Annual Fund raised a total of $840,000. The Alumni Council represents 4,000 graduates and assists the school in fund-raising, recruiting, and long-range planning. The Parents Association works closely with faculty members on a variety of projects.

Lawrence Academy is accredited by the New England Association of Schools and Colleges and is a member of the National Association of Independent Schools, the Association of Independent Schools of New England, the Secondary School Admission Test Board, the Principals of Girls Independent Schools, and the Council for Advancement and Support of Education.

ACADEMIC PROGRAMS

Lawrence Academy distinguishes itself through a student-centered curriculum and a series of signature programs. A student-centered classroom is characterized by teachers designing exercises that give students opportunities to practice the thinking skills that will allow them to arrive at their own interpretations, develop their own points of view, and learn the facts within the context of a meaningful question or problem.

The Ninth Grade Program (NGP) is the foundation of the rigorous college-preparatory curriculum. The NGP offers a new approach to interdisciplinary learning that provides the first step in preparing students to become responsible for their own learning and capable of thinking for themselves. Together with mastery of subject matter, the primary purpose of the NGP is to develop the intellectual skills essential for successful advanced work in English, history, science, and the arts. In addition to the NGP curriculum, students study math and a foreign language commensurate with their ability.

In the tenth grade, the team-taught Combined Studies Course integrates history and English around the skills established in the NGP. Sophomores generally study chemistry and continue on in mathematics, a foreign language, and the arts. As juniors and seniors, students develop more sophisticated critical-thinking abilities in all their studies and learn to support their conclusions through well-reasoned papers, oral presentations, and group discussions. Extensive elective offerings in history, science, English, dance, music, visual art, and theater help students develop their own viewpoint. Qualified students may enroll in honors-level or Advanced Placement courses, as well as apply to study independently for one academic term or the full year.

Winterim is a two-week intensive study program with a focus on experiential learning. Typical Winterim projects include backpacking through the rainforest in Costa Rica; trekking through the Gallivare region of Sweden; sea kayaking and sea turtle tagging in Baja, Mexico; working at a farmhouse restoration project in Soma, Japan; quilting; rock climbing; artisan bread making; and humanitarian work in the Dominican Republic.

The Independent Immersion Program (IIP) creates unique academic programs that include intensive independent studies with on- and off-campus professionals, internships, and traditional course work for students with a demonstrated passion in an area of academic study.

The English as a Second Language program (ESL) provides international students with strong academic preparation for college and careers. In class, students focus on mastering reading, writing, speaking, and listening comprehension.

The average class size is 12; the overall student-teacher ratio is 7:1. Class enrollments are determined on the basis of students' abilities, needs, and interests. Most students take five courses each term. Instruction is provided in small classes and through seminars, independent study, and individual instruction. Extra help is available in all subjects. Supervised study is provided for students in academic difficulty. The library, computer rooms, laboratories, and studios for independent study are open from 8 a.m. to 10 p.m.

To graduate, students must complete 18 credits and their Winterim courses. Minimum credit requirements are English, 4; mathematics, 3; foreign language, 2; history, 2 (3 for ninth graders); science, 2 (including 1 of biology); and arts, 2.

Letter grades (A to F) are awarded. Standards for high honors–honors and minimum acceptable performance are set by the faculty. Progress reports from each teacher, including performance and effort marks, are given to students and advisers weekly; parents are sent midterm and term grades six times a year and adviser letters three times a year.

FACULTY AND ADVISERS

The full-time faculty consists of 41 men and 34 women. They hold seventy-five baccalaureates, forty-eight master's degrees, and two doctoral degrees. Thirty-five faculty members and their families live on campus.

D. Scott Wiggins became Head of School in 2003. He is a graduate of Boston University (B.A., 1977) and Arizona State University College of Law (J.D., 1988). Mr. Wiggins worked as an associate attorney and as an assistant district attorney in Chester County, Pennsylvania. Mr. Wiggins' experience in independent schools includes Athletic Director at The Fessenden School, Director of Admissions at Fountain Valley School, and, most recently, Upper School Head at Metairie Park Country Day School in New Orleans.

Most faculty members coach, supervise dormitory and student activities, and act as advisers. Guidance services are provided by a full-time counselor, the dean of students, and faculty members. A faculty intervention team and a sophomore sexuality program are additional guidance services. Lawrence seeks diversity within its faculty and supports professional growth opportunities during the school year as well as in the summer.

COLLEGE ADMISSION COUNSELING

College counseling procedures begin in the junior year with individual conferences. Each student spends considerable time with one of the 4 college counselors, and a list of possible colleges is developed. Juniors are encouraged to read a variety of college publications and to visit schools during spring break and the summer prior to their senior year. Parents are involved in the process from the beginning.

Application procedures begin early in the senior year after each student, his or her parents, and one of the college counselors have discussed thoroughly that student's interests, abilities, academic credentials, and other related criteria. Consistent with the Academy's policy of diversity among students and faculty, Lawrence graduates have matriculated at a wide range of colleges in recent years.

The middle 50 percent of the most recent class scored between 510 and 610 on the verbal SAT, between 510 and 650 on the quantitative. and between 510 and 630 on the writing portion. Ninety-eight percent of all graduates enter college the fall following graduation, and virtually all have entered college within two years of graduation.

STUDENT BODY AND CONDUCT

Lawrence has 210 boys and 186 girls. Grade distribution is as follows: 79 in grade 9, 108 in grade 10, 108 in grade 11, and 101 in grade 12. Day students come from nearby towns in Massachusetts and New Hampshire. Boarders are from fourteen states and fifteen other countries.

Students play a responsible role in governing themselves and participate on a variety of policy-making and advisory committees related to curriculum and campus life. An active student government provides formalized procedures for student involvement in the decision-making process, and a proctor system enables students to provide support, structure, and leadership in dormitories. School rules are described and defined in the *Omnibus Lucet.*

ACADEMIC FACILITIES

The new Ansin Academic Building (2004) houses state-of-the-art classrooms and science laboratories. Classrooms with computers are equipped with seven workstations with PCs and a teacher workstation, an HP printer, and access to the Ethernet network. In addition, students may independently use three more rooms that contain computers with Internet and e-mail access and online resources similar to those in the library. The Ferguson Building houses a new 500-seat theater and the library, with 20,000 volumes, fifty-two periodical subscriptions, and computers with educational software, online resources, CD-ROM databases, Internet access, an automated card catalog, an art gallery, the theater, and the college office. The Williams Art Center includes a recital hall, black box theater, Steinway grand piano, several music practice rooms, two ensemble rehearsal rooms, a professional recording studio, a photography lab, a music technology lab, a digital media lab, visual arts studios, and a radio station.

BOARDING AND GENERAL FACILITIES

Students live in ten dormitories, seven of which are Colonial homes that date from 1793 to 1839. A new dormitory was opened in fall 2003. All dormitories are networked for wireless Internet access from rooms. Students generally are assigned to double rooms, but a few singles are available. There are three school nurses in the expanded health center, and 2 doctors are on call. A 102-bed hospital is 4 miles from campus.

ATHLETICS

The Academy competes in the Independent School League (ISL). Lawrence supports a varied athletics program in which all students are required to participate. In the fall this includes football, boys' and girls' soccer, boys' and girls' cross-country, and field hockey. In the winter, Lawrence competes in boys' and girls' basketball and ice hockey, wrestling, and volleyball; in the spring, in baseball and golf, boys' and girls' lacrosse and tennis, and softball. Outdoor programs, offered in the fall and spring term, include rock climbing, hiking, camping, bicycling, cross-country skiing, and snowshoeing. Dance and theater are offered every term. An intramural program develops skills in a variety of sports.

The Academy's facilities include the new Shumway athletic fields. In addition, the Stone Athletic Center has locker rooms for boys and girls, visitors, and officials as well as a weight room, Nautilus equipment, a training room, a wrestling room, offices, a meeting room, and a large gymnasium with two basketball courts, a climbing wall, and a volleyball court on a wood floor. The athletics department also utilizes 14 acres of playing fields, eight newly renovated outdoor tennis courts, and a newly renovated, covered artificial-ice skating rink.

EXTRACURRICULAR OPPORTUNITIES

At least three student dramatic productions and dance, music, and visual art performances are presented in the school's newly expanded 500-seat theater or black box theater each year.

Student organizations include Amnesty International, the Cultural Coffeehouse Series, SADD, and Multi-Cultural Alliance clubs. Students interested in music have opportunities to join the chorus, concert choir, SLACS, stage band, and the brass, wind, string, and jazz ensembles. Additional organizations include the Athletic Council, Faculty-Student Senate, Health Committee, and the staffs of the yearbook, school newspaper, and literary magazine.

DAILY LIFE

The daily schedule begins with an optional breakfast, followed by adviser-advisee meetings or all-school meetings at 7:45. Classes meet from 8 a.m. until 3:30 p.m. three days a week and until 2 p.m. twice a week, with a special class period three times a week with extra time for first-year language students, full choral and instrumental group rehearsals, extra help, and class or extracurricular meetings. Four to six academic periods of varying lengths are scheduled daily; each class meets four times a week on a rotating basis. A hot meal, a deli selection, and a salad bar are offered at noon. From 3:30 to 5:30 p.m., students participate in athletics. After dinner in the dining hall, residents have ample time for academic work and socializing. The hours 8–10 p.m. are study hours on campus, and a supervised study hall is provided for students who need it.

WEEKEND LIFE

Saturdays provide opportunities for a variety of extracurricular, social, and academic activities (including SAT preparation and driver education) and for athletics competition and outdoor program trips. Opportunities for off-campus activities with faculty chaperones are announced during the week, and students are urged to participate. Trips to Boston, beaches, sporting events, dances, skiing, and continual activities are planned by a full-time director of weekend activities. With parental permission, boarding students may leave campus most weekends if all school commitments have been met and the adviser's and dormmaster's approval have been obtained.

COSTS AND FINANCIAL AID

In 2008–09, tuition was $44,200 for boarding students and $33,900 for day students. Additional expenses for books, class trips, art fees, and school and athletic supplies range from $150 to $400 per term. Transportation for boarders and optional expenses for tutoring or music lessons are extra. A 10 percent tuition deposit is due in May; half the remaining total is due on August 1 and the rest on December 1. A tuition payment plan is also available.

Approximately 30 percent of the student body receives $2.6 million in scholarships and loans each year. Lawrence subscribes to the School and Student Service for Financial Aid and grants aid on the basis of need. Candidates indicating an interest in financial aid on the application form receive a Parents' Financial Statement from the Academy.

ADMISSIONS INFORMATION

Lawrence Academy seeks talented and motivated college-bound students who will contribute to the community as well as benefit from it. New students are accepted in all grades except grade 12, unless applying to the Independent Immersion Program. An interview, SSAT, PSAT, SAT or TOEFL scores, transcripts, and academic references are required.

APPLICATION TIMETABLE

An application packet, which contains pertinent information with step-by-step procedures, and the school catalog are provided on request. Candidates for fall entrance should apply the preceding fall. February 1 is the deadline for consideration for domestic boarding applicants in the first round, and January 15 is the deadline for consideration for domestic day applicants and for international applicants in the first round; late applications are considered if vacancies exist. Acceptances are mailed by March 10. The Parents' reply date is April 10. There is a nonrefundable $50 application fee (international application fee is $100).

Candidates should contact the Admissions Office (8 a.m.–4 p.m., Monday–Friday) to arrange for a visit. If the distance is too great, an attempt will be made to arrange a telephone interview or an interview with a nearby parent or alumnus.

ADMISSIONS CORRESPONDENCE

Tony Hawgood, Director of Admissions
Admissions Office
Lawrence Academy
P.O. Box 992
Groton, Massachusetts 01450-0992
Phone: 978-448-6535
Fax: 978-448-9208
E-mail: admiss@lacademy.edu
Web site: http://www.lacademy.edu

THE LAWRENCEVILLE SCHOOL

Lawrenceville, New Jersey

Type: Coeducational boarding and day college-preparatory school
Grades: 9–PG (Forms II–V): Lower School, Form II; Circle/Crescent Level, Forms III–IV; Fifth Form
Enrollment: 798
Head of School: Elizabeth A. Duffy, Head Master

THE SCHOOL

The Lawrenceville School was established in 1810 as an academy by the pastor of the village church, whose elders had sons to educate. By 1885, the physical plant was greatly enlarged, the present House System adopted, and the enrollment expanded. Lawrenceville, a small historic town, is 55 miles from New York City and 40 miles from Philadelphia.

In 1987, Lawrenceville became coeducational, enrolling girls at all grade levels. Girls account for 45 percent of the student population.

The mission of the Lawrenceville School is to inspire and educate promising young people from diverse backgrounds for responsible leadership, personal fulfillment, and enthusiastic participation in the world. Through its unique House system, collaborative Harkness approach to teaching and learning, close mentoring relationships, and extensive cocurricular opportunities, Lawrenceville helps students develop high standards of character and scholarship, a passion for learning, an appreciation for diversity, a global perspective, and strong commitments to personal, community, and environmental responsibility.

Twenty-five of the 32 members of the Board of Trustees are alumni of Lawrenceville. The School endowment is more than $300 million, and the 2007–08 operating expenses totaled more than $50 million. Fiscal year-end gifts for 2007–08 amounted to more than $21.3 million. Of this, the Annual Fund contributed some $5.7 million, with 42 percent of the almost 11,500 solicitable alumni participating.

Lawrenceville is accredited by the Middle States Association of Colleges and Schools and is a member of the Secondary School Admission Test Board, the National Association of Independent Schools, the New Jersey Association of Independent Schools, and the Council for Religion in Independent Schools.

ACADEMIC PROGRAMS

In fall 2006, after an eighteen-month curriculum review, the School adopted new graduation requirements, beginning with the class of 2011. They are designed to ensure that students receive a strong foundation in all disciplines during their first two years at the School that can be built on in the upper forms. The new requirements meet NCAA standards and are aligned with the standard requirements for college admissions, simplifying academic advising. The new requirements for entering Second Formers (the class of 2012) are arts, 3 terms; English, 9 terms; history, 6 terms; humanities–English, 3 terms; humanities–cultural studies, 3 terms; interdisciplinary, 2 terms; language, through Unit 9*; mathematics, through advanced algebra or precalculus*; religion and philosophy, 2 terms; and science, 9 terms*. (Students may opt to finish their course work in one of the areas marked with an asterisk.) Students are required to give at least 40 hours of community service before they graduate.

Lawrenceville offers approximately 280 courses plus twenty-seven laboratory courses. Electives include law as literature, bioethics, Spanish, theater, and history of China.

Individual participation is encouraged in small classroom sections averaging 12 students. Classes are grouped randomly except for the honors sections and are taught around a large oval table called the Harkness Table. Evening study periods, held in the houses, are supervised by the Housemaster, the Assistant Housemaster, or an Associate Housemaster.

Students with a particular interest in exploring new fields or in testing themselves against the challenge of a job may apply for Independent Study, off-campus projects, or the Term Abroad Program (France, Spain, and the Bahamas). Driver's education is available.

Lawrenceville uses a letter grading system (A–F) in which D– is passing and B+ qualifies for honors.

The school year is divided into three 10-week terms. Full reports are sent home at the end of each term, with interim reports at midterm. The full reports include comments and grades from each of a student's teachers indicating his or her accomplishments, efforts, and attitudes. Less formal progress reports are also written by teachers throughout the term as needed. Students in academic difficulty are placed on academic review, which entails close supervision and additional communication with parents.

FACULTY AND ADVISERS

Of the 151 faculty members, 140 are full-time. Ninety-six faculty members hold master's degrees, and 19 hold doctorates. Most reside on the campus, and many serve as residential housemasters, coaches, and club advisers.

Elizabeth A. Duffy was appointed the twelfth Head Master of the Lawrenceville School in 2003. Ms. Duffy graduated magna cum laude from Princeton University in 1988 with an A.B. in molecular biology. In 1993, she received an M.B.A. from the Graduate School of Business at Stanford University and an A.M. in administration and policy analysis from the School of Education there. She has spent her entire career working with educators at all levels.

Faculty members take advantage of the School's policy of providing financial help for continuing education. They have summers free, and each year 3 or 4 faculty members take a trimester off with full pay to pursue scholarly activities. All are active in advising and counseling students.

COLLEGE ADMISSION COUNSELING

The goal of the College Counseling Office is to educate students and families about the nuances of college admissions, advise students about a range of interesting college options that best suit their individual needs, and support and encourage students as they complete the application process.

Lawrenceville's experienced college counselors provide timely advice to families and help students present their abilities, talents, and experiences to the colleges in the most appropriate manner. Families and students receive information through newsletters, classwide meetings, and parent weekend programming. They also have access to a detailed Blackboard-based college counseling program via the Web, which gives them unlimited access to relevant topics on college admission and links to important sources of information and support, as well as overall advice on selecting and applying to college. These resources are designed to ensure that students and their families are well prepared to embrace the college counseling process when students are officially assigned to individual counselors in the middle of their Fourth Form year. Over the course of their junior and senior years, all students engage in a series of college-related standardized testing, a self-reflective process, college visits, on-campus college fairs, visits and/or interviews with more than 150 colleges, and individual meetings with college counselors to discuss their goals and aspirations.

The class of 2008's median SAT scores were 660 verbal, 680 math, and 670 writing. Two hundred thirty-six students graduated from Lawrenceville in 2008. Between 2005 and 2007, the twenty colleges most attended by Lawrenceville students were Princeton, 44; Georgetown, 29; Vanderbilt, 25; Columbia, 23; Duke, 23; Harvard, 23; Cornell, 22; NYU, 22; USC, 20; Pennsylvania, 16; North Carolina at Chapel Hill, 15; Brown, 14; George Washington, 12; Trinity (Hartford), 12; Yale, 12; Virginia, 11; Boston College, 10; Stanford, 9; William & Mary, 9; and, tied with 8 students each, Bucknell, Colgate, Dartmouth, Delaware, Richmond, St. Andrews (Scotland), and the U.S. Naval Academy.

STUDENT BODY AND CONDUCT

For 2007–08, there are 798 students, 253 of whom are day students. There are 147 students in the Second Form, 208 students in the Third Form, 208 students in the Fourth Form, and 235 students (including postgraduates) in the Fifth Form. Students come from forty states and thirty countries. Most boarders are from New Jersey, New York, Pennsylvania, California, Illinois, Georgia, Connecticut, Virginia, Texas, Massachusetts, Florida, and North Carolina.

Lawrenceville expects its students to achieve good records and develop self-control, systematic study habits, and a clear sense of responsibility. The School has a high regard for energy, initiative, a positive attitude, and active cooperation. Students accepting this premise have no trouble following the basic regulations.

The School separates disciplinary action into three categories. They are, in decreasing order of severity, the breaking of a rule for which dismissal from school is a possible consequence, general misbehavior deemed inappropriate by the School community, and house-related offenses that reflect a lack of cooperation in the day-to-day working of the house. A student-faculty committee makes recommendations to the Head Master in regard to disciplinary action for offenses in the first category.

The student body elects 5 governing officers from among students in the Fifth Form, and each house elects its own Student Council.

ACADEMIC FACILITIES

There are thirty-four major buildings on Lawrenceville's 700-acre campus, including the Bunn Library (with space for 100,000 volumes), which opened in 1996. The Bunn Library offers sophisticated computer research facilities, a state-of-the-art electronic classroom, and greatly expanded study areas. A 56,000-square-foot science building opened in spring 1998, a visual arts center opened in fall 1998, a history center reopened in fall 1999, and a music center opened in fall 2000.

Lawrenceville's computer network links all academic and administrative buildings. All Lawrenceville students have network ports in their dorm rooms.

BOARDING AND GENERAL FACILITIES

Lawrenceville's most distinguishing feature is its House System. In each of the nineteen houses, the housemaster maintains close contact with the residents. House athletics teams compete intramurally, and house identity is maintained through separate dining rooms in the Dining Center for the underformers. This distinctive system provides a small social environment in which each student's contribution is important and measurable.

At Lawrenceville, the ninth graders live in four Lower School Houses; the tenth and eleventh graders live in ten Circle Houses, six for boys and four for girls; and the seniors live in five Fifth Form Houses and eat as a class in the Abbott Dining Hall. Five residential houses for girls opened in 1987.

Services in Edith Memorial Chapel are nondenominational. The McGraw Infirmary has a full-time resident physician and a round-the-clock nursing staff.

ATHLETICS

Because many physical, social, and moral values can be instilled through the disciplines and demands of team sports, competitive athletics at both the interscholastic and house levels are the core of the physical education program. There are interscholastic teams in baseball, basketball, crew, cross-country, fencing, field hockey, football, golf, ice hockey, indoor and outdoor track, lacrosse, soccer, softball, squash, swimming, tennis, volleyball, water polo, and wrestling. Dance, karate, outdoor programs, and yoga add to the physical fitness offerings at Lawrenceville. An extensive lifetime sports program is offered, as are a variety of intramural sports among the houses, including 8-man tackle football for boys' Circle Houses.

The Edward J. Lavino Field House is an unusually fine one for a secondary school. The main arena area has been completely refinished with a synthetic surface and includes a permanent banked 200-meter track and three tennis/basketball/volleyball courts. The arena can also be used for rainy-day indoor practice. Two additional hardwood basketball courts, a six-lane swimming pool, a wrestling room, two fitness centers with full-time strength and conditioning coaches, and a training/wellness facility are housed in the wings of the building. A new squash court facility, hosting ten new internationally zoned courts, opened in 2003.

Lawrenceville has fourteen interscholastic athletics fields (including two lighted artificial-surface playing fields), a golf course, sixteen outdoor tennis courts, a quarter-mile all-weather track, an indoor ice-hockey rink, a state-of-the-art ropes course, and a crew boathouse.

EXTRACURRICULAR OPPORTUNITIES

Lawrenceville offers students numerous opportunities for extracurricular activities. Students can choose from more than 100 organizations in debating, drama, music (the Lawrenceville Orchestra, the Lawrenceville Chorus, Jazz Ensemble, and Lawrentians), art, history, religion, science, language, photography, and video. The largest single student enterprise is the Periwig Club, whose dramas, comedies, and musicals attract more than a third of the students. Publications include *The Lawrence*, the *Lit*, and the *Olla Pod* (yearbook). Exhibits occur throughout the year. Several lecture programs bring to the campus authoritative speakers and artists from many fields. Student clubs have their own guest lecturers.

There is a required Community Service Program, in which students may serve as tutors, elementary school study center supervisors, directors of sports, and group activity counselors. The School sponsors organized educational and cultural trips to New York City and Washington, D.C.

Annual events include Parents' Weekend in the fall, Parents' Winter Gathering, and Alumni Weekend in the spring.

DAILY LIFE

Lawrenceville classes are generally 55 minutes per session—science classes and advanced classes in other disciplines also have one double period each week. Classes meet for half days on Wednesdays and Saturdays. Students engage in sports in the afternoon; most clubs and groups meet in the evening. Students take lunch at their adviser's table on Mondays.

WEEKEND LIFE

The School's location provides numerous opportunities for social, cultural, and entertainment activities. Regular weekends begin after the last class on Saturday. Students may go out for dinner with responsible adults. Drama and musical performances are often held on weekends, as are major sports events, mixers, and dances. Day students are welcome at all of these.

COSTS AND FINANCIAL AID

The annual charges for 2008–09 are $42,320 for boarding students and $35,290 for day students.

Through the generosity of alumni, friends, and foundations, approximately $8 million in funds are available to provide scholarships and financial assistance to qualified students. Currently, 28 percent of the student body receives assistance. Awards are made on the basis of character, ability, past performance, and future promise. Amounts are based solely on need, range from $1000 to the full annual cost, and are determined by procedures established by the School and Student Service for Financial Aid.

ADMISSIONS INFORMATION

All students who enter must be able to meet the academic standards. Lawrenceville also looks for students who possess the potential to become vitally interested members of the student body—students who make individual contributions.

Selection is based on all-around qualifications without regard to race, creed, or national origin. Character, seriousness of purpose, and future promise as well as past performance, the recommendation of a headmaster or principal, and the results of the SSAT are all taken into consideration by the Admission Committee.

For fall 2008, there were 1,860 formal applications for grades 9 through 12, of which 379 were accepted, and 245 enrolled in the following grades: grade 9,149; grade 10, 62; grade 11, 8; and grade 12, 27 (including postgraduates).

Required for admission is the formal application, which includes a written essay, a transcript of the applicant's school record, and a letter of recommendation from the head of the current school, plus three reference letters, SSAT or ISEE and/or TOEFL scores, and an on-campus interview.

APPLICATION TIMETABLE

Campus interviews are conducted throughout the week from 9 to 2 Monday, Tuesday, Thursday, and Friday. Applicants can also interview on Wednesdays between 9 and 10:30 and on Saturdays from 8:30 to10:30. Interviews are not conducted on Saturday during the summer months.

The application deadline is January 31 for boarding students and January 15 for day students, at which times three teacher recommendations, student transcripts, SSAT scores, and the head-of-school recommendation must be submitted. All campus interviews should also be completed by this date.

The notification date is March 10, and parents reply by April 10.

ADMISSIONS CORRESPONDENCE

Dean of Admission
The Lawrenceville School
2500 Main Street
P.O. Box 6008
Lawrenceville, New Jersey 08648
Phone: 609-895-2030
800-735-2030 (toll-free outside New Jersey)
Fax: 609-895-2217
E-mail: admissions@lawrenceville.org
Web site: http://www.lawrenceville.org

LEYSIN AMERICAN SCHOOL IN SWITZERLAND

Leysin, Switzerland

Type: Coeducational boarding college-preparatory school
Grades: 8–12, postgraduate year
Enrollment: 380
Head of School: Dr. K. Steven Ott, Executive Director; Dr. Marc-Frédéric Ott, Associate Executive Director; Mr. Vladimir Kuskovski, Headmaster

THE SCHOOL

As an international university-preparatory high school committed to excellence, the Leysin American School in Switzerland (LAS) educates students to respect people of other cultures and to be responsible, productive, and ethical citizens with the skills to think creatively, reason critically, and communicate effectively. This is achieved because students live in a family-like global community with high standards. LAS offers both an International Baccalaureate (I.B.) program and a U.S. high school curriculum. LAS teachers are highly qualified, dedicated international educators.

The School is located in Leysin, an alpine resort above Lake Geneva. About 90 minutes from the Geneva International Airport, Leysin is easily accessible by car or train. The magnificent beauty, serenity, and healthy environment of Leysin are enhanced by the cultural wealth of Europe and unlimited opportunities for outdoor enjoyment.

LAS strives to foster a harmonious community of young people who represent more than fifty-five nationalities. By living and learning together, students develop into "citizens of the world" with an appreciation for other cultures and languages. LAS provides a challenging college-preparatory program within a supportive framework. Many students take IB certificate courses; a limited number pursue the International Baccalaureate Diploma. Virtually all students continue their studies in excellent universities in the U.S., Canada, Europe, and Asia.

The Leysin American School was founded in 1960 by Mr. and Mrs. Fred C. Ott and graduated its first class in 1961. It was solely owned and operated by the Ott family until June 2005. Today, the Foundation for the Advancement of International Education is the majority owner of the Leysin American School, but the School continues under the family's leadership. It is governed by a 5-person Foundation Board under the chairmanship of Dr. K. Steven Ott.

A new Junior High program, grades 8 and 9, will begin in the 2009–10 school year. These two grade levels will run independently from the rest of the school, providing a separate environment for these students. Following in the existing boarding school structure, teachers who work in the Junior High section will also be living in dormitories with the Junior High students, as well as working with them after classes for their extracurricular activities. Part of the Junior High curriculum is the Advisory class, which consists of 10–13 students who are the same age but of different nationality. This class is used for mentoring, building international understanding, and tending to social events such as celebrating birthdays, enjoying pizza, seeing a movie, or participating in other fun activities.

LAS is accredited by the Council of International Schools, the Middle States Association of Colleges and Schools, and the Department of Swiss Private Education. LAS holds membership in the Swiss Group of International Schools, Advanced Placement, the College Board, and the International Baccalaureate organization. In 1999, LAS became the first high school worldwide to be certified ISO 9001 by the Swiss Association of Quality and Management Systems (SQS).

ACADEMIC PROGRAMS

The school year is divided into two semesters. The first extends from late August to mid-December and the second from January to early June. The grading system is based upon a standard A to F, 4-point scale. LAS was the first school outside of the United States to provide PowerSchool Internet access to parents interested in communicating directly with teachers, administrators, and students. PowerSchool provides real-time information for students and parents and includes complete grade access, attendance records, discipline and health information, financial accounts, and the daily School bulletin.

Students follow a demanding college-preparatory curriculum, including International Baccalaureate study. AP calculus AB and BC are also offered.

The college-preparatory curriculum meets admission requirements for colleges and universities in the U.S. and Canada. The high school diploma is granted on the basis of the following criteria: a minimum of two semesters of LAS residency, including the two semesters of the final year, and completion of a minimum of 24 credits, which include 4 credits in English, 3 in social studies, 3 in modern languages, 3 in sciences, 3 in mathematics, 2 in creative arts, 1 in senior humanities, 1 in physical education, 1 in computer studies, and 3 electives. ESL students must earn 7 ESL course credits, which thus fulfills the English and modern languages requirements.

The International Baccalaureate, a challenging program that is open to qualified students, can be followed during the last two years of high school. Students take courses leading to external exams in six areas (three higher level and three standard level); enroll in the Theory of Knowledge (TOK) course; write an extended essay; and participate in creativity, action, and service requirements. The IB Diploma is recognized by universities throughout the world and, in some cases, allows up to one year of advanced standing in U.S. universities. IB graduates are also awarded the U.S. high school diploma.

All students are encouraged to take a full range of courses to enrich their education. LAS offers electives such as visual arts, band, choir, drama, photography, private piano lessons, yearbook, additional modern languages, social studies electives, and computer science studies. The average class size is 14 students. The academic staff–student ratio is 1:7. Students take seven courses per semester.

The annual educational travel program includes two cultural excursions that are designed to acquaint students with the history and culture of Switzerland and major European cities. The students travel in small groups to various regions and submit a cultural report.

FACULTY AND ADVISERS

LAS has 75 faculty members and administrators. Ninety percent are from countries whose native language is English, and more than 70 percent hold advanced degrees. The School is firmly committed to its *in loco parentis* philosophy. Faculty members reside on campus, taking on a strong parenting role for the students. They share in dormitory and study-period supervision, sponsor sports and recreational activities, and supervise excursions.

Faculty members also serve as sponsors for Faculty Families, which play an important role in providing a caring, family-oriented environment for students. Two faculty members "adopt" 10–15 students of different nationalities and ages and serve as personal/academic advisers, guiding students through all aspects of boarding school life. Families meet regularly during the week and join in activities and excursions on weekends.

Dr. K. Steven Ott was appointed Executive Director of the School in 1982. He served in numerous capacities at LAS from 1970 to 1977, at which point he was appointed professor and charged with curriculum development at the newly founded King Faisal University in Saudi Arabia. He earned his B.S., M.S., and Ph.D. degrees at Stanford University.

Dr. Marc Frédéric Ott was appointed Director of External Relations in 2005 and Associate Executive Director in 2007. He earned his master's degree in teaching business, economics, and accounting at the University of St. Gallen, Switzerland. He holds a doctorate in education (Ed.D.) from Teachers College, Columbia University.

COLLEGE ADMISSION COUNSELING

A full-time college counselor and 2 assistant counselors give advice and guidance to students as they prepare for admission to universities. Current college materials and online resources are available in the College Counseling Office. Students have many opportunities to meet college admissions officers from American and European campuses. On average, 35 school representatives visit LAS each year.

LAS is a regional testing center for the SAT and SAT Subject Tests and ACT tests. TOEFL examinations are taken online and are organized through the School's English as a second language department. Graduating students continue their education in leading U.S. and Canadian universities such as Bates, Boston University, Cornell, Dartmouth, Duke, Harvard, McGill, Stanford, U.S. Air Force Academy, and Yale.

International placements include the Federal Institute of Technology (Switzerland), Cambridge and King's College (England), Keio University (Tokyo), and the Universities of Bremen (Germany), Durham (England), and St. Andrew's (Scotland).

STUDENT BODY AND CONDUCT

In 2007–08, 360 students were enrolled from fifty-five countries. Just over 30 percent were U.S. passport holders, many of whom had families living abroad. Some of the other countries represented included Brazil, Germany, Japan, Kazakhstan, Mexico, Mongolia, Norway, Russia, Saudi Arabia, Spain, and Taiwan. Approximately one third of the student body was enrolled in LAS's English as a second language program.

The LAS publications explain community standards and behavioral expectations. LAS fosters a sense of responsibility for the School community and the individual, with honesty, respect, and fairness as key concepts. Both on and off campus, LAS is a nonsmoking school at all times. LAS has a zero-tolerance policy on drug use and related activities and imposes testing.

ACADEMIC FACILITIES

The LAS campus offers excellent facilities in every academic area. There are two main academic complexes and five additional residential halls. The Savoy Complex has thirty classrooms, administrative offices, and an Information and Technology Center that includes a teaching lab and an additional lab of thirty computers. There is a modern and spacious library with 20,000 volumes, a CD-ROM online data bank, and Internet access. The Savoy also houses the dining room; health center; Visual Arts Center, which includes a darkroom for photography; a ceramics studio; and a beautiful painting studio with terraces overlooking the Rhone Valley. There is also a modern theater (The Black Box), a music room with recording technology, and two new art galleries. Athletic facilities, next to the Savoy, feature a gymnasium, a squash court, a fitness center, and a dance studio.

The Beau Site houses the Science Center, with four labs and a lecture hall. The Admissions Office and the primary reception area are located in Beau Site. Students can relax in the student center (the Red Frog), and dance in the Valley View multipurpose hall, which is frequently the LAS Disco. The Vermont Complex, which is located directly between the Savoy and the Beau Site, includes a bookstore, activities and travel offices, and the math chalet with six classrooms.

The Beau Réveil facility, which was renovated in 2005, houses the six classes of the modern languages department, offices, and a computer language lab. The language lab features twenty computers with networked online Auralog TeLL me More® language software in French, German, and ESL.

Beginning in 2007, LAS began a green project to upgrade the heating facilities in all campus dormitories. The 500,000 Swiss franc project includes installing solar panels on all dormitories supported by clean-burning natural gas boilers. Two of the seven planned buildings have already been completed.

BOARDING AND GENERAL FACILITIES

The LAS campus blends into the friendly, picturesque village of Leysin. From every building there is a spectacular view of the Alps.

Residence halls are the key to the well being and positive functioning of the School community. Students and teachers have rooms and apartments, respectively, in electronic-key-controlled-entry residence halls. The newly installed key system ensures a secure environment. The constant adult presence of teachers and their families creates a homelike atmosphere. Students have comfortable rooms, sharing them with 1 or 2 roommates of different nationalities. Every room has a private toilet and shower. Students enjoy wireless Internet access from anywhere on campus and have their own personal LAS cell phone. Every dormitory has recreation/TV rooms, community kitchens, and laundry facilities.

ATHLETICS

Sports and physical education are an integral part of the balanced program, which is designed to develop lifelong skills and to promote health and vitality, teamwork, and school spirit. During the fall and spring terms, students devote at least one afternoon per week to instructional sports. Team sports include basketball, cross-country, soccer, swimming, tennis, and volleyball. Individual sports include aerobics, hiking, horseback riding, ice skating, mountain biking, rock climbing, swimming, and weight lifting.

LAS uses its own gymnasium as well as two local sports centers. Facilities include a full-size skating rink, 25-meter indoor swimming pool, gymnasium, indoor and outdoor tennis courts, soccer field, indoor squash courts, two indoor climbing walls, fitness center, exercise room, and cross-country running track.

Beginning in January, students enjoy two afternoons a week during the winter term participating in winter sports in and around the alpine village of Leysin. Skiing and snowboarding, as well as ice skating and snowshoeing, are offered. The ski resorts of Leysin and Les Mosses, which are connected by a short bus link, offer unlimited access to 110 kilometers of downhill trails. In addition, there are more than 20 kilometers of cross-country trails right at LAS's front door. Professionally trained members of the Swiss Ski School provide lessons.

EXTRACURRICULAR OPPORTUNITIES

LAS provides many leadership opportunities through Student Council, National Honor Society, Model UN, and dormitory/student life committees. There are several groups that are active in global awareness projects, including Habitat for Humanity. Students attend concerts, visit museums, go to plays, and enjoy festivals, fairs, and special events.

Three major LAS-sponsored excursions introduce Europe's wealth of culture and history. The first, September Weekend, is a three-day outing organized by Faculty Families. Swiss Cultural Excursions acquaint students with the host country, with small groups traveling to a variety of destinations. Seniors and postgraduate (PG) students participate in a separate trip to Rome, Florence, or Venice as part of their Theory of Knowledge course. The five-day European Cultural Excursions introduce the historic and cultural richness of neighboring countries. Typical destinations are Budapest, Istanbul, Munich, Paris, Prague, Salzburg, and Vienna. Students may join one of the humanitarian trips to Hungary, Poland, and Romania. Seniors have the choice of a humanitarian trip or a special senior trip, with typical destinations being Madrid and Kiev.

DAILY LIFE

Classes are held five days a week from 8 a.m. to 3:30 p.m., followed by sports and activities or free time. Faculty Families meet once a week within the school day. There is one weekly assembly for all students and faculty members. Monitored study time is held in the students' rooms from 7:30 to 10, Sunday through Thursday evenings. The library, computer labs, and music and art studios are open throughout the day.

WEEKEND LIFE

Weekends offer many options, including sports tournaments; trips to Lausanne, Geneva, and other nearby cities; Faculty Family excursions; and special outings. There are regular hiking and biking trips sponsored by the faculty. Students may go to the village after classes and on weekends. Friday and Saturday evenings, students may attend the local cinema, School-sponsored dances, sports events, or cultural activities.

SUMMER PROGRAMS

Summer in Switzerland (SIS) is LAS's well-established summer academic enrichment, recreation, and travel program. Boys and girls from more than forty-five countries participate in one of three programs: Alpine Adventure for ages 9–12, Alpine Exploration for ages 13–15, and Alpine Challenge for ages 16–19. All three programs offer challenging academic/language courses, a choice of excursions, creative arts, and exciting sports—all in the spectacular setting of the Swiss Alps.

SIS provides courses that are appropriate to the age group served, including French (in native French-speaking Leysin), Spanish, English literature, math, computer studies, and SAT/ACT preparation. Students may be able to earn high school credit in certain subjects, including French, English, and math.

The creative arts program offers theater, music, and art. The theater program schedules two productions in one 3-week session. Musicians and visual artists develop individual skills in their chosen instrument or discipline.

In the mornings, students attend classes, while the afternoons are devoted to sports activities and excursions. Choices include tennis, soccer, skating, paragliding, and alpine activities such as climbing, hiking, and rafting. Weekend excursions permit students to explore cities such as Geneva, Lausanne, Lucerne, Zermatt, and Montreux, as well as Paris and Milan for the Alpine Challenge participants.

SIS also offers three specialized programs for 13- to 19-year-olds. Theatre International enables students to focus on their theatrical skills and credits in an international setting. The intensive Outdoor Leadership Adventure program allows students to explore the beauty of the Swiss Alps while learning to lead others and work as part of a close-knit group. The SAT-prep program allows students to prepare for the SAT and ACT in an intensive three-week program sponsored by StudyWorks, Inc.

There are two 3-week sessions, beginning in late June and ending in early August. Optional faculty-supervised weeklong excursions within Switzerland or to another European destination, such as England, France, Italy, or Germany, are also offered for Alpine Exploration and Alpine Challenge students.

COSTS AND FINANCIAL AID

In 2008–09, enrollment, tuition, room, and board fees are SF 64,000 for the full school year. Fees cover all regular instruction and laboratory fees, book charges, dormitory facilities, full board, LAS health plan (accident and health insurances and use of health center), residence permit, three major LAS-sponsored excursions, weekend activities, social events, spring prom, and a sports/ski pass with ski/snowboard lessons.

Parents establish a personal account for disbursement of weekly pocket money and extra expenses. Financial aid is available. Families living or transferring overseas and receiving educational allowances from their employers may apply for the LAS Corporate Plan based on company policy.

ADMISSIONS INFORMATION

Students who demonstrate good character and academic potential may apply for admission. LAS requires a school transcript, three recommendations, personal essay, and completed application form. An interview is recommended. Applicants are notified without delay regarding acceptance status. LAS encourages prospective students to visit the campus.

APPLICATION TIMETABLE

LAS encourages candidates to apply between late fall and early spring but accepts applications on a rolling admissions basis beginning in January before the school year begins, space permitting.

ADMISSIONS CORRESPONDENCE

Admissions Office
Leysin American School
CH-1854 Leysin
Switzerland

Phone: 41-24-493-3777 (Swiss)
603-431-7654 (U.S.)
888-642-4142 (toll-free within the U.S.)
Fax: 41-24-494-1585 (Swiss)
E-mail: admissions@las.ch
Web site: http://www.las.ch

LINDEN HALL

Lititz, Pennsylvania

Type: Girls' boarding and day college-preparatory school
Grades: 6–12, postgraduate year
Enrollment: 165

THE SCHOOL

Established in 1746, Linden Hall is a college-preparatory day and boarding school for grades 6–12, located in the historic town of Lititz, Pennsylvania. Linden Hall is the oldest girls' boarding school in the United States and continues to dedicate itself to excellence in the education of young women.

Linden Hall provides a rigorous and multi-faceted college-preparatory experience. Here, each student is nurtured and inspired to reach her highest personal potential. Linden Hall's community values scholarly achievement, character development, cultural awareness, and physical wellness as it strives to prepare young women to assume the leadership roles of their generation.

The school is located on 47 acres and is two blocks from the square of Lititz, Pennsylvania, a safe and charming town of 8,000 located between Harrisburg and Philadelphia. The campus is within 2 to 3 hours of Baltimore; Washington, D.C.; and New York City. An airport, train station, and turnpike are nearby.

Linden Hall is accredited by the Middle States Association of Colleges and Schools and approved by the Pennsylvania Department of Education. It is a member of the National Association of Independent Schools, the Secondary School Admission Test Board, the National Coalition of Girls' Schools, the Pennsylvania Association of Independent Schools, Advancement for Delaware Valley Schools, the Parents League of New York, the Association of Boarding Schools, and the Small Boarding School Association.

ACADEMIC PROGRAMS

Linden Hall's SAT and Advanced Placement (AP) exam scores place it among the top girls' schools in the United States. Its average SAT score of 1806 is significantly above the national norm of 1511. In addition, Linden Hall's average score of 4.0 on AP exams is substantially above the national average of 2.9, with 90 percent of Linden Hall students earning college-qualifying AP scores of 3, 4, or 5.

Linden Hall is dedicated to providing multiple levels of curricular sophistication to ensure that students are appropriately challenged by a course of study designed for each individual girl. The rigorous curriculum offers college-preparatory, honors, and college-level (Advanced Placement) classes, with schedules customized for each student. Writing skills are emphasized, with a required class in composition. There is focused, in-class preparation for SAT Subject Tests in at least four subject areas that can include math 1 or 2, American history, biology, Spanish, and French. Linden Hall offers a twenty-first-century technology program, including electronic whiteboards (Smartboards), graphing calculators, and computer-based science equipment. Individualized college counseling is available to all students.

Just recently, Linden Hall launched its Advanced Scholars Program (ASP). The Advanced Scholars Program is a curriculum designed for talented and motivated Upper School (grades 9–12) students who wish to challenge themselves with advanced study. Certainly, Linden Hall's entire academic program is college-preparatory; however, ASP is an option designed for those students capable of and interested in the pursuit of honors and college-level work while in secondary school. The details of ASP can be found on the Linden Hall Web site (http://www.lindenhall.org).

Tutoring for supplemental instruction is available. There is also an English as a second language (ESL) course of study for international students who wish to develop fluency and proficiency in the English language.

The average class size at Linden Hall is 9 to 11 students, one of the smallest class sizes in the nation. The grading system uses A to F (failing) with pluses and minuses. Reports are sent home six times a year. The school year is divided into trimesters.

The academic day has seven 48-minute periods, time for academic help each afternoon, a class meeting period, physical activities/sports/riding, and an extracurricular activity period. A faculty-supervised study hall takes place for 2 hours each evening during the academic week.

FACULTY AND ADVISERS

Linden Hall employs 25 full-time and 5 part-time teaching faculty members. Many of the faculty members live on campus, either in the dormitories or in faculty apartments adjacent to the dorms. Faculty and staff members provide students with the support and encouragement to help each young woman develop her interests and talents. Each girl also has an adviser who attends the girls' activities, monitors their academic progress, and serves as a friend and mentor. A weekly meeting keeps all faculty and staff members immediately informed of any student's status, both in school and in the dorms.

COLLEGE ADMISSION COUNSELING

Linden Hall provides a comprehensive and supportive College Counseling Program. One-on-one guidance aids students in identifying the colleges best matched to their academic potential and personal interests, while detailed supervision optimizes the college application process. An assessment program unique to Linden Hall, including College Board and ACT tests, develops essential academic skills in grades 7–12. Students also complete a yearlong, rigorous SAT preparation course in grade 11. Linden Hall's thorough and personal college counseling approach results in 100 percent acceptance to some of the nation's finest schools.

Among the colleges attended by recent Linden Hall graduates are Bryn Mawr, Bucknell, Carnegie Mellon, George Washington, Kenyon, MIT, NYU, Rensselaer, Smith, Spelman, and the Universities of Chicago and Michigan.

STUDENT BODY AND CONDUCT

For the 2008–09 academic year, the student body was made up of 130 boarding students and 35 day students, with approximately 110 students in the Upper School and 55 students in the Middle School. Students came from eleven states and ten countries.

Guidelines for student conduct are defined in the parent, student, and dormitory handbooks. An Honor Code Committee, composed of faculty members and students, recommends the appropriate disciplinary action to the Headmaster when a major infraction occurs. There is an active Student Council.

ACADEMIC FACILITIES

Stengel Hall houses both the Middle and Upper Schools as well as the administrative offices and two computer labs. The Frueauff Library contains more than 12,000 volumes and belongs to Power Library PA, with access to EBSCOhost, Gale Publications, and Schribners. The Carr Arts Center, a multipurpose room, is located on the first floor of the Mary Dixon Chapel. Linden Hall recently opened its newly constructed sports and fitness center on the campus. This center includes a new dance studio, a fitness center, and a regulation-size gymnasium. A new visual and performing arts center features a theater, a gallery, and the art and photography departments. Recent renovations were made to the science facilities, complete with state-of-the-art classrooms and labs.

BOARDING AND GENERAL FACILITIES

The Byron K. Horne Dormitory, divided into four separate dormitory areas, has double rooms for 84 students. There are laundry facilities in each dormitory, and every student has Internet access in her room. The remaining double rooms are located in the Annex, which is the dorm connected to Horne Dormitory. Five student lounges are each equipped with a television, a DVD player, game stations, computers, and a microwave. An indoor pool is located in the lower level of the Annex, and testing rooms are located on the third floor. The school infirmary is also located in the Annex. A full-time school nurse holds regular infirmary hours.

ATHLETICS

Linden Hall is a member of the Pennsylvania Interscholastic Athletic Association (PIAA). At Linden Hall, participation in the athletic program is a vital part of a student's education. Students are encouraged to participate in any sport for which they have an aptitude or an interest. These sports, both intramural and interscholastic, include tennis, volleyball, riding, soccer, basketball, lacrosse, field hockey, track, cross-country, and softball. Students may participate in the following nonvarsity physical activities: aerobics, swimming, dance, Pilates, kickboxing, yoga, weight training, and conditioning.

Linden Hall's championship riding program is designed to meet the needs of riders from recreational beginners to advanced competitors. The focus of instruction is hunter/jumper and equitation based.

Linden Hall's riding team competes in the Interscholastic Equitation Association; five horse shows are hosted on campus each year. The Linden Hall Equestrian Team has held the titles of Zone II Regional Champion and IEA National Qualifying Team for the past two years.

EXTRACURRICULAR OPPORTUNITIES

In addition to riding and other athletics, students are urged to become active in a wide variety of extracurricular activities, including Linden Hall Chorus, quiz bowl, handbell choir, HOBY, *The Echo* (the oldest continuously published secondary school literary magazine in the United States), the Middle School newsletter, swimming, yearbook, student council, dance, and drama. Three drama productions are performed each year, the chorus performs regularly in the community, and art and photographic works are exhibited continuously and are submitted to and recognized in national competitions.

Linden Hall takes advantage of its proximity to urban centers. Day trips are arranged for the students to explore the history and culture of New York City, Philadelphia, Baltimore, and Washington, D.C. During fall and spring breaks, chaperoned trips are offered to other U.S. destinations and to Europe. All travel is designed to enhance the students' studies and experience at Linden Hall.

DAILY LIFE

Breakfast is served from 7 to 7:45; classes begin at 8 a.m. A nondenominational chapel is held once a week during the academic day. School assemblies are held three times per week to provide an opportunity for announcements and for student public speaking. Lunch is scheduled for all students and faculty members at noon. There are extended periods for labs weekly. There is an Academic Help period at the end of each day, which allows students to independently seek help from a teacher or adviser. Athletics and other extracurriculars follow Academic Help each afternoon.

Breakfast, lunch, and dinner are served cafeteria-style. Students are required to attend a study hall under faculty supervision each evening from 7:30 to 9:30.

WEEKEND LIFE

Faculty members work in rotating teams to plan, supervise, and provide transportation for various weekend activities that are offered at Linden Hall. Cultural activities may include the theater, a musical or dance concert, or a trip to a museum. Other weekend activities may include hikes, skiing, dances, rafting, videos, shopping, or day trips to Philadelphia, Baltimore's Inner Harbor, New York City, or Washington, D.C. If students choose to attend church or synagogue, transportation is provided. Day students are encouraged to participate in any or all of the weekend activities.

SUMMER PROGRAMS

Residential riding camps for students of all levels are offered each summer. An ESL camp is offered for international students with various levels of English proficiency, providing them with an opportunity to improve their English in the classroom and to experience American culture through various field trips and activities.

COSTS AND FINANCIAL AID

Yearly tuition, room, and board for the 2008–09 school year were $37,590 for five-day boarders and $39,990 for seven-day boarders. Day student tuition costs were $16,990. Additional required fees and deposits for books, technology, and the Parents' Association amount to approximately $1650. Other expenses include the purchase of uniforms, student allowance, and fees for optional programs such as riding, music lessons, and tutoring. A nonrefundable deposit of $2000 is due at the time of enrollment. Tuition is payable in full or in installments.

Linden Hall offers both need-based financial aid and merit scholarships. The school is enormously proud of its instructional program and is committed to making excellence in education available to more families. Official application for financial aid must be made through School and Student Service (SSS). Early application is encouraged.

With a mission statement that calls for preparing "young women to assume the leadership roles of their generation," Linden Hall offers two scholarship programs (Merit and Headmaster) aimed at students of strong academic potential and accomplishment. No formal application is needed for either of these scholarships.

ADMISSIONS INFORMATION

Admission to Linden Hall is dependent on the strength of the application. The school seeks young women of average to above-average ability, with good character and a strong desire to work hard to achieve their personal goals and potential. Race, color, creed, and nationality are not considered, nor is the ability to pay. The school welcomes young women who demonstrate a willingness to better themselves through academic and social involvement, contribute in a positive way to the school community, and work closely with their peers and teachers to reach their personal goals. In selecting students for admission, Linden Hall places great importance on the personal interview. Every application is reviewed by an admission committee. The school also requires academic transcripts, SSAT test scores, and teacher recommendations.

APPLICATION TIMETABLE

The first-round application deadline is February 1, with admission consideration on a space-available basis thereafter. The application must be accompanied by the nonrefundable fee of $45 ($100 for international students). For maximum financial aid benefits, application should be made by February 1 or as early as possible.

ADMISSIONS CORRESPONDENCE

Kate R. Rill
Director of Admission
Linden Hall
212 East Main Street
Lititz, Pennsylvania 17543
Phone: 717-626-8512
800-258-5778 (toll-free)
Fax: 717-627-1384
E-mail: admissions@lindenhall.org
Web site: http://www.lindenhall.org

THE LOOMIS CHAFFEE SCHOOL

LoomisChaffee

Windsor, Connecticut

Type: Coeducational boarding and day college-preparatory school
Grades: 9–12, postgraduate year
Enrollment: 710
Head of School: Sheila Culbert, Head of School

THE SCHOOL

The precursor of The Loomis Chaffee School, The Loomis Institute, was chartered in 1874 in Windsor, Connecticut and the doors opened in 1914 as a coeducational boarding and day school. The School's founders were 4 Loomis brothers and their sister, who united their considerable estates to found an institution for secondary education. The School was built on the site of the Loomis family homestead at the confluence of the Farmington and Connecticut rivers.

The charter, unusual for the time, stipulated that the institute should offer a vocational as well as college-preparatory curriculum, not discriminate against staff or students because of their religious or political beliefs, and offer "free and gratuitous education" as far as the endowment would permit.

In order to emphasize the education of young women, the girls' division moved to another part of Windsor in 1926, becoming The Chaffee School, with the boys' school becoming The Loomis School. The two schools were reunited in 1972 and became The Loomis Chaffee School.

In keeping with the vision of the founders, the School strives to develop independence of mind, sensitivity to others, a capacity for hard work, and strong values.

The 300-acre campus is 6 miles from Hartford, 45 miles from New Haven, 110 miles from New York, and 100 miles from Boston.

The School is governed by a Board of Trustees, the majority of who are alumni. The physical plant is valued at $115 million and the endowment at approximately $200 million.

The School is accredited by the New England Association of Schools and Colleges and is approved by the Connecticut Education Association and the Connecticut Department of Education. It is a member of A Better Chance, the Albert G. Oliver program, Prep 9, the Cum Laude Society, the National Association of Independent Schools, and the Secondary School Admission Test Board.

ACADEMIC PROGRAMS

The highly diverse and rigorous curriculum comprises nearly 200 courses and is designed not only to prepare students for college admission but also to provide skills, instill curiosity, and encourage a love of books and ideas. Instruction in the freshman and sophomore years concentrates on basic skills of communication and computation, preparing students for the wider program of electives available in the junior and senior years.

Subject requirements are 4 years of English, 3 years of mathematics, third-level proficiency in one foreign language, 2 years of history (1 year at the freshman-sophomore level and 1 year of U.S. history), 2 years of laboratory science (1 of which must be biology), 3 terms of the arts, and 2 terms of philosophy and religion. Students must earn 16 credits in grades 9–12; most earn 19 or 20.

Independent study for academic credit is available in each discipline. Students are also encouraged to undertake extradepartmental, off-campus projects. Advanced-level and Advanced Placement courses are available in all areas of study. All students and faculty members also participate in a work program.

Through the School Year Abroad program, students may earn a full year of credit by spending their junior or senior year abroad in France, India, Italy, Spain, or China, studying, living with a family, and traveling. Loomis Chaffee students may also participate in the Mountain School Program in Vershire, VT, living and studying for half a year on a 300-acre farm. Students may also participate in CITY Term, a semester-long, interdisciplinary urban studies program.

The school year is divided into three terms. The daily schedule operates within an eleven-day cycle, and Saturday classes are held every other week. The average class size is 12, and the student-faculty ratio is 5:1. The ratio of boarders to on-campus faculty members is 4:1.

The grading system uses traditional letter grades of A to F with pluses and minuses; D is passing. Grades are given at midterm and at the end of each term. An adviser works closely with each student.

Study conditions are maintained in each dormitory on class nights from 7:45 to 9:45 p.m. and resumed at 10:30 p.m.; a supervised study hall is also held during the day.

FACULTY AND ADVISERS

There are 150 faculty members (50 percent men and 50 percent women); 112 hold advanced degrees, including eight doctorates.

Loomis Chaffee believes that faculty members must be dedicated to the task of educating the whole student, as classroom teaching, coaching, dormitory supervising, advising, and working with various campus clubs and organizations are all part of the job. Professional growth is encouraged through sabbatical leaves, travel and summer-study grants, and endowed chairs.

Sheila Culbert became the seventh Head of The Loomis Chaffee School in July 2008 after nineteen years at Dartmouth College where she taught history and worked in various administrative capacities, including as senior assistant to the president of the college and interim vice president for communications. She earned a B.Ed. from the University of Nottingham, U.K., and an M.A. and a Ph.D. in history and American Studies from Indiana University.

COLLEGE ADMISSION COUNSELING

Four full-time college counselors provide expert advice in helping students choose colleges. College counseling starts in the junior year and continues in the senior year until a student is accepted at college. Grades, test scores, extracurricular activities, and personal interests are used as guides to help juniors make tentative decisions about colleges.

All juniors take the PSAT in the fall and the SAT in the following spring and again in the senior year. In 2008, the middle 50 percent ranges of the SAT scores were 570–700 (critical reading) and 570–700 (math).

Of the class of 2008, 77 percent were admitted to colleges and universities deemed most competitive or highly competitive by *Barron's Profiles of American Colleges.* In the last five years (2004–08), the following numbers of students were accepted at these representative colleges and universities: Amherst (22), Boston College (60), Brown (22), Columbia (26), Cornell (42), Dartmouth (12), Emory (27), Harvard (8), Middlebury (22), Princeton (5), Smith (20), Stanford (5), Washington (St. Louis) (32), Wellesley (8), Wesleyan (20), Williams (15), Yale (14), and the Universities of Chicago (13) and Pennsylvania (27).

STUDENT BODY AND CONDUCT

In 2008–09, Loomis Chaffee had students from thirty states and fifteen countries. There were 714 students, including 400 boarding and 314 day students, representing many different racial, religious, and economic backgrounds.

The immediate purpose of Loomis Chaffee's rules and regulations is to promote order, mutual respect, and academic excellence. The long-range goal is to prepare students for their roles in society. School policy fosters increased responsibility as students mature and advance from class to class.

Students take an active leadership role through the Student Council and the prefect system, serve on the Disciplinary and Curriculum committees, and sit as representatives on the Board of Trustees.

ACADEMIC FACILITIES

The Katharine Brush Library contains 60,000 volumes; more than 42,000 e-books; access to over 10,000 periodicals and scholarly journals; 4 major newspapers, with access to 65 current full-text newspapers and 12 historical newspapers; 1,500 videos; 2,000 CDs; an extensive microfilm collection; 50 subscription databases; eighteen public computers; and full electronic reference and information services.

The Richmond Art Center was completed in 1992. Housing printmaking, drawing, painting, and ceramics studios, the center also includes a fourteen-station black-and white-darkroom, a color darkroom, an extensive video production facility, two exhibition galleries, a fully equipped computer graphics center, and an art history lecture hall.

The first half of a two-year $16 million modernization of the School's science center opened in September 2008. Separate classroom and laboratory spaces were replaced with eight combined lab/classrooms that support the Science Department's active-learning pedagogy. The Clark Center for Science and Mathematics also features a renovated lecture auditorium, a robotics lab, a planetarium, a computer lab, student project rooms, faculty offices and, once completed in September 2009, eleven new high-tech mathematics classrooms fitted with overhead projectors for use with graphing calculators and whiteboards on three walls.

Altogether the School has sixty-one teaching spaces in six buildings, and more than 100 computer stations are available to students and faculty across the campus. Additional academic facilities include Founders and Chaffee halls (with thirty-four classrooms), eight music practice rooms, a dance studio, and the Norris Ely Orchard Theatre.

BOARDING AND GENERAL FACILITIES

The School has ten dormitories, which make up the Grubbs and Rockefeller quadrangles. Each dormitory houses 30 to 40 students and 3 or 4 faculty members and their families. There are 5 additional faculty members associated with each dorm. Acting both as personal and academic counselors, faculty members maintain close contact with students through small advisory groups. The members of a dormitory function as a group; they compete in informal athletic contests, share dining tables, and plan social activities.

A multimillion-dollar student center includes a snack bar, a game room, an enlarged school store, and an outdoor amphitheater. The bookstore and snack bar are open to students during the class day. The School also has a well-staffed health center.

ATHLETICS

All students are required to participate in interscholastic, intramural or daytime athletic programs. Coaching responsibilities are shared by 8 Athletic Department members, including 3 athletic trainers, and many faculty members. Interscholastic sports include baseball, basketball, cross-country, field hockey, football, golf, hockey, lacrosse, skiing, soccer, softball, squash, swimming/diving, tennis, track, volleyball, water polo, and wrestling. Intramural sports include basketball, cycling, hockey, soccer, softball, tennis, and volleyball. Also available are aerobics, aquatics, cross-country skiing, ice-skating, modern dance, and physical fitness programs.

Facilities include a double gymnasium and two other gymnasia, supporting basketball and volleyball courts; a fitness center and a weight room, totaling 6,300 square feet; a 25-meter, six-lane swimming pool; an enclosed hockey rink; a 400-meter, eight-lane, all-weather track; eight international squash courts; seventeen tennis courts; a 3.1 mile cross-country course; a synthetic turf field; two baseball diamonds; two softball diamonds; seventeen fields for football, soccer, lacrosse and field hockey; and a golf practice driving range, putting green and sand trap.

EXTRACURRICULAR OPPORTUNITIES

There are myriad extracurricular opportunities. Many students volunteer their time in the local communities through the Community Service Program and the Service Club.

There are 3 student publications: the student newspaper, the yearbook, and a literary magazine. The School also has its own separate theater building, and approximately 125 students are involved on-stage or behind the scenes in three major annual productions.

The chorus, chamber singers, orchestra, concert band, jazz band, and small-group ensembles provide opportunities for the musically inclined, as well as academic credit.

There are many clubs that suit a wide variety of special interests, including the debate society; the computer club; an outing club; and PRISM, a club that promotes multicultural awareness. The Student Activities Committee organizes social and cultural programs. Students may also elect to serve as tour guides.

DAILY LIFE

The class day runs from 8:10 to 3:10. Students generally take five subjects per term, each of which meets eight times in an eleven-day cycle. Some class periods are short (45 minutes), and some are longer (70–90 minutes) to allow more focused work in a discipline as well as laboratory work, projects, group work, research, and class trips. The School is committed to employing a wide variety of pedagogical techniques to reach students of all learning styles. Classes end at lunchtime on Wednesdays and alternate Saturdays to allow time for interscholastic games. The School meets as a community several times per month for all-School meetings and convocations.

WEEKEND LIFE

Weekends are an important part of School life. Sports contests, dances, coffeehouses, concerts, theatrical and musical performances, and movies are held. Dormitories often plan their own cookouts and excursions. Faculty-chaperoned trips are frequently arranged. Bicycling, hiking, rock-climbing, windsurfing, and boating are popular in the fall and spring. The School owns 104 acres of woodland in East Hartland, Connecticut.

COSTS AND FINANCIAL AID

Tuition, room, and board for 2008–09 were $41,200; tuition for day students was $31,100. This was paid in two installments on August 1 and January 1. For new students, a registration fee is held as a deposit, with half returned on January 1 and the other half at the conclusion of the school year.

Financial aid is available for students who complete the School and Student Service for Financial Aid form and demonstrate need. In 2007–08, more than $6 million in financial aid was allocated to 30 percent of the students.

ADMISSIONS INFORMATION

The School seeks boys and girls of sound character and much promise, whose previous record, character, and potential indicate that they can contribute to, as well as benefit from, life at Loomis Chaffee. The School considers the previous school record, recommendations by teachers and friends, a candidate's potential as judged during the interview, and performance on standardized tests.

Each applicant must submit an application, have a personal interview, and take the SSAT. Candidates who have completed their junior year or beyond are expected to take either the PSAT or the SAT.

For the 2008–09 school year, 1,200 students applied for 240 places. The median SSAT score of those accepted was in the 77th percentile, and 64 percent of all students entered in the ninth or tenth grade. Ten to 20 postgraduate students matriculate each year also.

APPLICATION TIMETABLE

Contacting the Admission Office begins the admission process. Complete sets of application materials are sent to those who have made a formal inquiry. Campus tours and interviews are conducted from 8 a.m. to 2:30 p.m. on Monday, Tuesday, Thursday, and Friday and from 8 a.m. to noon on Wednesday and alternating Saturdays. Appointments should be made well in advance. The application deadline is January 15; students applying after this date are considered on a rolling admission basis, according to the availability of space.

Notices of admission are mailed on March 10. Students are not required to confirm the admission until April 10.

ADMISSIONS CORRESPONDENCE

Thomas D. Southworth, Director of Admission
The Loomis Chaffee School
4 Batchelder Road
Windsor, Connecticut 06095
Phone: 860-687-6400
Fax: 860-298-8756
E-mail: admission@loomis.org
Web site: http://www.loomischaffee.org

THE LOWELL WHITEMAN SCHOOL

Steamboat Springs, Colorado

THE LOWELL WHITEMAN SCHOOL

Type: Coeducational boarding and day college-preparatory school
Grades: 9–12
Enrollment: 97
Head of School: Walter H. Daub, Headmaster

THE SCHOOL

The Lowell Whiteman School was founded in 1957 by Lowell Whiteman, who wished to provide a traditional and structured college-preparatory school in an informal western setting that also ensured an international exposure for all students and faculty members. Having celebrated its fiftieth anniversary, the Lowell Whiteman School continues to emphasize this unique combination of educational opportunities.

The School's location on the western slope of the Continental Divide contributes much to its atmosphere. All-School outings and camping trips into the mountain, river, and desert country of Colorado and Utah provide varied Western outdoor experiences. Informal dress and culture at Lowell Whiteman balance a conservative and structured academic curriculum. Whiteman's 190-acre campus lies 5 miles north of the ski-resort and ranching town of Steamboat Springs and 160 miles northwest of Denver. Easy access has been provided in recent years by the establishment of a 45-minute airplane flight between Steamboat Springs and Denver that departs several times a day. Direct flights to Steamboat Springs are available during the ski season from Atlanta, Chicago, Dallas, Denver, Houston, Los Angeles, Minneapolis, Salt Lake City, St. Louis, and San Francisco.

An annual international trip has been a feature of education at Lowell Whiteman since the School's inception. Every spring, faculty members and all students (except those in the competitive ski/snowboarding program) travel in small groups to a wide variety of other countries chosen for that year.

A nonprofit corporation, The Lowell Whiteman School is governed by a Board of Trustees that meets three times annually. Operating expenses of $2.3 million are covered by tuition. Capital campaigns are supported by faculty members, current and former parents, alumni, friends, and foundations.

The Lowell Whiteman School is accredited by the Association of Colorado Independent Schools and the Colorado State Board of Education. It is a member of the National Association of Independent Schools, the Association of Boarding Schools, and the Western Boarding Schools Association.

ACADEMIC PROGRAMS

The Lowell Whiteman School requires a minimum of 18 credits for graduation. These credits can be completed in four years. Students must take five subjects each year, and they may take up to six. The minimum graduation requirements are as follows: 4 credits of English (students must take English every year), 3 credits of math, 3 credits of social studies, 2 credits of a foreign language, 2 credits of science, 1 credit of art, and 1 credit of computers. Varied advanced-placement courses are offered. Credit is given for physical education through the ski/snowboarding and activities programs, and participation is required.

Daily and evening supervised study halls are held for all students. Those who achieve Honors distinction may opt to study outside of the proctored study halls.

The average class size at Lowell Whiteman is 8 students. The student-teacher ratio is approximately 6:1. Those periods when a student does not have a class are spent in a study hall. Evening study hall is also required on Sunday through Thursday nights.

The school year is divided into trimesters. The first trimester ends with final exams before Thanksgiving break, and the second runs from November to February. The final trimester runs from February through March and then resumes after intersession in May. Final exams and graduation occur in early June. The trimester grades are used to determine the Dean's and Honor's lists. The Lowell Whiteman School uses a numerical grading scale from 0 to 100.

The spring intersession provides an opportunity for Lowell Whiteman students to travel abroad. With the exception of competitive skiers and snowboarders, all LWS students participate in the annual international trip. In the months prior to the trip, a minicourse in the language, geography, and culture of the country to be visited is required of the students. Although regular classes are not continued during the international travel, students study the culture of the country and participate in community service projects. In recent years, students have visited Bhutan, Chile, China, Costa Rica, Ecuador, the Galapagos Islands, the Himalayas of Nepal, Indonesia, Mongolia, Samoa, South Africa, Vietnam, and much of Western Europe.

Intersession also provides an opportunity for competitive winter athletes to make up classwork that was missed because of heavy competition schedules and training during the winter. Students drop two classes during the winter competition season. The same course work is then covered during four weeks of intensive classes during Intersession. This schedule ensures that winter athletes do not compromise their education by pursuing their ski/snowboard ambitions.

FACULTY AND ADVISERS

There are 18 full-time and 6 part-time faculty members; 44 percent of the faculty members hold advanced degrees. Dorm parents do not teach but serve as advisers. Three fellows assist the dorm parents.

Walter H. Daub was appointed Headmaster in 1998. Before coming to Lowell Whiteman, Mr. Daub served the Albuquerque Academy for seventeen years in the positions of Upper School Head, Assistant Head, and Academic Dean. He received a B.A. in philosophy from Hamilton College and an M.A. in English from the University of Delaware. In 1986, he was presented with an Exemplary Teacher Award by President Reagan.

COLLEGE ADMISSION COUNSELING

Students participate in a step-by-step process of researching colleges, visiting campuses, and applying to institutions appropriate to their needs and abilities. Serious exploration begins in a student's junior year.

In the class of 2008, 18 graduating seniors who applied to four-year colleges and universities were accepted. Recent graduates are currently enrolled at Bates, Boston University, Bowdoin, Colorado College, Cornell, Dartmouth, Fort Lewis, Harvard, McGill, Middlebury, Mount Holyoke, New England, NYU, Reed, St. Lawrence, Stanford, Texas A&M, Tulane, and the Universities of California, Colorado, Denver, Montana, Texas, Utah, Vermont, Washington, and Wyoming.

All seniors and juniors take the SAT and the ACT. Median SAT scores for the classes of 2008 and 2009 were 560 Critical Reading, 570 Math, and 550 Writing. Advanced Placement examinations are administered in May of each year.

STUDENT BODY AND CONDUCT

In 2008–09, there were 12 freshmen, 21 sophomores, 27 juniors, and 37 seniors; about 45 percent of the students are girls.

The largest numbers of boarders come from Colorado; smaller numbers of students come from Alaska, Arizona, California, Idaho, Kentucky, Massachusetts, Michigan, Minnesota, Montana, Nevada, New Mexico, New York, Oregon, South Carolina, Texas, Virginia, Washington, Wisconsin, and Wyoming. Canada, England, Germany, Finland, and United Arab Emirates are also represented. Each year, the enrollment includes some international and minority students.

The Lowell Whiteman School's rules are written by the faculty and administered by the Dean of Students and the disciplinary committee, which includes both faculty members and students. A point system is used as a guideline to determine the seriousness of an offense; accumulation of 125 points by a student results in dismissal.

ACADEMIC FACILITIES

The classroom buildings have nine classrooms and a variety of project labs, including a computer lab, a life science laboratory, and a physical science laboratory. They also house the 3,000-volume library, a new language lab, computers with software, periodicals, and a darkroom. Art classes are held in a studio adjacent to the classroom building. Study halls are held in the School's 125-seat lecture hall/theater. An improved library, updated for twenty-first-century technologies and standards, including state-of-the-art Internet access, was renovated four years ago.

BOARDING AND GENERAL FACILITIES

There are three dormitories. The girls' dorm houses a maximum of 25 girls; rooms vary in size and accommodate 2–3 girls. The freshman and sophomore boys' dorm houses a maximum of 15 boys; most rooms accommodate 2–3 boys, with two single rooms. The junior and senior boys' dorm houses a maximum of 20 boys; most rooms are doubles, but some are singles. Each dorm has at least 2 live-in dorm parents who supervise the activities and hours of its occupants.

The School has a student store to provide many of the items required for everyday life.

ATHLETICS

Because of The Lowell Whiteman School's Rocky Mountain environment, athletics are centered on the activities one would expect to do in the mountains. Students may choose from the following: Alpine and Nordic skiing, freestyle skiing and snowboarding, backpacking, camping, canoeing, kayaking, hockey, horseback riding, ice-skating, mountain biking, rock climbing, soccer, tennis, cross-country, volleyball, softball, and basketball. There are an on-campus gymnasium, an athletic field, a climbing wall, and a skateboard ramp.

There are opportunities for competition in most high school sports. Those students capable of skiing or snowboarding at a high competitive level are eligible to train with and compete for the renowned Steamboat Springs Winter Sports Club at the USSA and USASA levels. Introductory competitive programs are also available. The Steamboat Springs Winter Sports Club was awarded the United States Ski Association Club of the Year Award in 2004. Sixteen alumni of the LWS Ski and Ride Program have gone on to compete in the Olympics and the XGames.

EXTRACURRICULAR OPPORTUNITIES

Opportunities include concerts in town, music, painting, pottery, photography, camping, backpacking, the School yearbook committee, dances, and community service. Whiteman's drama program presents theater performances for the student body and parents during Parents' Weekend in February.

In order to take advantage of especially fine weather, classes are canceled one day each autumn for treks to mountain lakes and other picturesque areas. Students also participate in three camping trips in the fall.

During the winter months, students have daily opportunities to take advantage of the world-class Steamboat Springs Ski Area and its surrounding facilities. When the famous deep snows arrive in Steamboat, two days are set aside to enjoy the superb powder skiing. In the winter, skiing and snowboarding constitute credits in physical education, and students may ski and ride as often as six times per week.

DAILY LIFE

Daily life at The Lowell Whiteman School is structured but allows for some flexibility. A typical weekday begins with breakfast at 7:15 a.m., followed by seven 45-minute classes, lunch, and afternoon activities from 3 to 5. Dinner is at 6:15, followed by a supervised study hall from 7:30 to 9:30. Students on the Dean's List are not required to attend this study hall but are expected to study on their own. There are 45 minutes of free time before students return to their dormitories by 10:15. Lights are out by 11.

Students are expected to contribute to the care of community facilities and dormitories. Therefore, participation in some community tasks is required.

WEEKEND LIFE

Students have considerable time to themselves from Friday evening to Sunday afternoon, provided that they have done their work during the week. Juniors and seniors may take trips on their own with parental and faculty permission. Freshmen and sophomores have more restrictions. The School also offers a variety of faculty-sponsored outings on weekends during the fall term to such places as the Mt. Zirkel Wilderness Area, the Flat Tops Wilderness Area, Browns Park, and Colorado National Monument. Students often go to movies in town on Friday and Saturday nights.

Students have the opportunity to attend church services in Steamboat Springs on Sunday.

COSTS AND FINANCIAL AID

Tuition with room and board for 2007–08 was $32,250. Day student tuition was $17,350. The annual international trip (transportation and room and board) was $3600. For 2007–08, trips to Senegal, Sikkim India, Argentina, Mongolia, and South Africa were arranged. The total of the other costs, including books and a season ski pass to the local ski area, should not exceed $2000 annually; a miscellaneous student account is billed three times a year. Tuition is due on July 15, minus the $3000 tuition deposit due by May 1. International trip costs are assessed and payable on December 15. The School recommends that an additional $20–$25 per week be allotted for spending money for each boarding student.

In 2007–08, approximately 30 percent of the students received need-based financial aid. Tuition installment schedules can be arranged, and exceptional academic and athletic student achievement is eligible for merit scholarship consideration.

ADMISSIONS INFORMATION

Applications are due in the Admission Office by March 15, with notifications mailed by April 1. If space remains after April 1, applications are considered on a rolling basis. A personal interview and a campus visit are normally required, although distance has exempted some applicants.

APPLICATION TIMETABLE

Applications and visits are encouraged throughout the year. The personal interview may be scheduled anytime, but an interview on campus during the school year, when classes are in session, is preferred. An off-campus interview is possible in some situations. Office hours are 9 to 5 during the school year and during the summer. A $40 application fee is required.

ADMISSIONS CORRESPONDENCE

Jared Olson
Director of Admission
The Lowell Whiteman School
42605 County Road 36
Steamboat Springs, Colorado 80487
Phone: 970-879-1350 Ext. 15
Fax: 970-879-0506
E-mail: olsonj@lws.edu
Web site: http://www.lws.edu/admissions

LYNDON INSTITUTE

Lyndon Center, Vermont

Type: College preparatory and general academic coeducational day and boarding school
Grades: 9–12
Enrollment: 620
Head of School: Richard D. Hilton, Headmaster

THE SCHOOL

Lyndon Institute (LI) was founded in 1867 in the tradition of the New England academy. The Institute still shows the effects of the shaping hand of T. N. Vail, founder of AT&T, who served as president of LI in the early 1900s and was responsible for considerable growth in its programs and facilities.

An accomplished faculty that includes published authors, noted artists, college faculty members, and others active in their professional fields provides a challenging, comprehensive educational program in a picturesque Vermont village setting. Lyndon students enjoy personal attention from the faculty members, genuine respect for their individuality and unique talents, a truly inclusive environment, and outstanding preparation for their choices of colleges and careers.

Lyndon Institute consists of three campuses on 150 acres centered on the village green of historic Lyndon Center, Vermont, along the banks of the Passumpsic River. Academic buildings surround a tree-lined common marked by the village church's steeple and the Institute's bell tower. It is a safe, supportive community of exceptional beauty. In addition, the school owns Binney Woods, a 360-acre preserve on nearby Burke Mountain. LI is located 10 miles north of St. Johnsbury on Interstate 91. Boston and Hartford are 3–4 hours away by car. Burlington, Vermont, and Montreal are only 2 hours from the campus. Airline service to Burlington; Manchester, New Hampshire; or Boston, Massachusetts, provides easy access. Burke Mountain Ski Area is 7 miles away. Stowe and Jay Peak Ski Areas are within an hour's drive. The school is 1 mile from Lyndon State College (LSC). The two institutions have been historically linked from the time of their founding, and together they form a unique cultural setting in Vermont's beautiful Northeast Kingdom.

LI is governed by a 27-member board of trustees, who are elected from a group of 150 corporators. The board meets four times per year. Each trustee sits on one of five standing committees. The school's operating budget is $10.1 million; parents, friends, and an active alumni group raise about $250,000 in annual support. The endowment is $7 million.

Lyndon Institute is accredited by the New England Association of Schools and Colleges and approved by the Vermont Department of Education. Memberships include the Independent School Association of Northern New England, the Vermont Independent School Association, the Secondary School Admission Test Board, and The Association of Boarding Schools.

ACADEMIC PROGRAMS

Lyndon Institute is a comprehensive secondary school offering college-preparatory and fine arts programs of study as well as business, information, and technical education areas. Twenty-two credits are required for graduation, with the following distribution: English, 4 credits; social studies, 3 credits; mathematics, 3 credits; science, 3 credits; fine arts, 1 credit; health and physical education, 2½ credits; and electives, 4½ credits.

Other course offerings include French, 4 years; Japanese, 4 years; Latin, 4 years; Spanish, 4 years; band and chorus, 4 years; art and theater, 4 years; advanced math, 2 years; algebra, 3 years; geometry, 1 year; trigonometry, 1 year; biology, 2 years; chemistry, 2 years; physics, 1 year; computer science, 7 courses; technology, 14 courses; drafting, 5 courses, including computer-aided design; word processing, 3 courses; and office technology, 3 courses. Honors courses are offered in English literature, advanced senior composition, advanced senior literature (classics), algebra 1 and 2, calculus 1 and 2, geometry, world geography, U.S. history, contemporary U.S. history, world civilizations, biology, chemistry, and advanced art. LI offers Advanced Placement courses in English composition, chemistry, European history, calculus A/B and B/C, and studio art. Students are required to take five courses or the credit equivalent each year but are encouraged to take up to seven courses each year.

The fine arts program allows students to take a series of courses within the fine arts concentration, which includes concert band, jazz band, improvisation, music theory, chorus, select chorus, art, art 4, advanced art, book arts, painting, printmaking, design, 2-D and 3-D art, photography, dance, jazz dance, lyrical ballet, four years of acting, and theater production.

With special permission, students may take courses at Lyndon State College and receive academic credit from both LI and LSC. Advanced students may also pursue independent study with a faculty sponsor. Students have access to the library from 7:30 a.m. to 4:30 p.m. each day and from 7 to 9 p.m. in the evening. Research is also conducted from many classrooms using the computer network and library computer search features.

Classes are grouped on the basis of ability. The student-teacher ratio is 10:1, with an average class size of 16. The grading system ranges from A to F and is calculated on a 4-point scale: A, 4.0; B, 3.0; C, 2.0; D, 1.0; and F, 0.0. The academic year is divided into two semesters consisting of two quarters each. Exchange trips are available during vacation times, and many opportunities for class travel are offered throughout the year.

FACULTY AND ADVISERS

There are 63 full-time and part-time faculty members at Lyndon Institute (33 men and 30 women). Thirty-one percent have earned a master's degree or higher.

Richard D. Hilton was appointed Headmaster in 1999. He holds a B.A. in English from Notre Dame and a master's degree from Villanova. Prior to coming to Lyndon Institute, Mr. Hilton was at the Hill School in Pottstown, Pennsylvania, where he worked for twenty years, holding a variety of positions, most recently Assistant Headmaster for Academics.

New faculty members are selected on the basis of academic quality and experience within their academic discipline, any special skills that may enhance the school's environment, and individual pursuit of academic excellence. The school has a very stable faculty employment rate. All faculty members participate in extracurricular activities, serving as coaches or advisers to clubs and activities, and act as advisers to students.

COLLEGE ADMISSION COUNSELING

College planning is accomplished through individual and small-group counseling beginning in the freshman year. Two full-time counselors work in concert with students and families to develop postsecondary plans. In a student's junior year, counselors from the Student Services Office help with coordinating college applications and essay writing. Students use computer software and other informational tools to aid in their searches and career planning.

Representatives from more than thirty colleges visit Lyndon Institute annually. LI cosponsors the Northeast Kingdom College Night program each spring with representatives from more than 100 colleges and universities in attendance.

In the last two years, 75 percent of LI graduates have pursued postsecondary options. Within Vermont, graduates have attended Middlebury, Norwich, Saint Michael's, and colleges in the Vermont State College System, including Lyndon State, Vermont Tech, and the University of Vermont. Outside Vermont, students have attended Boston College, Boston University, Brown, Clarkson, Cornell, Dartmouth, Harvard, McGill, Northeastern, Purdue, Rensselaer, Smith, St. Lawrence, Ursinus, Virginia Commonwealth, Washington State, and the Universities of Illinois, Maine, Massachusetts, Michigan, New Hampshire, and Washington.

STUDENT BODY AND CONDUCT

The total enrollment is 620 students, who come from the surrounding communities in Vermont and New Hampshire and from countries around the globe. The school implemented a boarding program in 2003–04, which had 85 students in grades 9–12 in the 2008–09 school year. Countries represented in the international program in the last five years include Afghanistan, China, Germany, Japan, Kazakhstan, Korea, Mexico, Pakistan, Spain, Sweden, and Taiwan.

The Code of Conduct is established by the faculty members, the administration, and the Board of Trustees and is based on common courtesy, mutual respect, and socially acceptable behavior.

Student involvement is vested in each class's elected officials and the Student Council. These officials are elected at the beginning of each year. As each student is a valued member of the community, the Headmaster is available to all students at any time.

ACADEMIC FACILITIES

Lyndon Institute comprises three campuses that surround Lewis Field, which is used for football and track. The Darling Campus consists of the Main Building (1922), containing ten classrooms, four science labs, a small performing arts space, administrative offices, and a multilevel media center (currently under renovations); Pierce Hall (1978), containing seven classrooms, a computer lab, and a 250-seat cafeteria; Alumni Wing, which houses a 550-seat gymnasium and a 650-seat auditorium; and Lewis Field, home to the Vikings' championship football and track and field programs. In addition, the Town House, which the school leases from the town of Lyndon, is an historic building used for dance and small drama practices and performances.

The Harris Campus consists of five main buildings, including the school's health center; Prescott House, where health is taught; Daniels Hall (1997), which houses the math department; Brown Business Center (renovated in 1993), which houses business and information technology classrooms; Harris Building (renovated in 1999), which has English classrooms and a weight-training facility; Sanborn Hall (1988), which provides locker rooms, athletic training facilities, and a full-size auxiliary gymnasium; and Bean Cottage, which serves as a dormitory. The Harris Campus also includes a softball field.

The Vail Campus comprises eleven buildings, eight of which house technology classrooms, laboratories, and workshops, including a fully networked computer-aided design (CAD) lab and drafting studio, a newly dedicated art center (2003), and four residence dormitories. The Vail Campus also includes the Forrest Field complex, where Lyndon Institute's football, soccer, field hockey, and baseball teams practice and compete. The Institute also uses Binney Woods, a 360-acre nature preserve located on Burke Mountain, for study and recreation.

BOARDING AND GENERAL FACILITIES

The residential facilities are housed in Mathewson House, Campbell House, Buschman House, Collison Cottage, and the Tavern Dormitory on the Vail Campus and Bean Cottage on the Harris Campus. The six dormitories can accommodate 80 students in single or double rooms and 13 resident dorm parents. After-school and weekend activities center on the residence areas, the gymnasiums, and the Pierce dining hall.

ATHLETICS

All students are urged to supplement their classroom experience by participating in interscholastic competition. In the 2008–09 school year, roughly 45 percent of the student body participated in the fall sports program. Lyndon Institute participates in the Vermont Principal's Association in Division II for baseball, basketball, cross-country running, cross-country skiing, football, golf, ice hockey, soccer, and track and field; and in Division III for field hockey. Interscholastic athletics are held on the varsity, junior varsity, and freshman levels (when appropriate). Cheerleading is also offered, as are volleyball (as a club sport) and lifetime fitness activities. Facilities include Alumni Gym, Sanborn Hall, Lewis Field, Brown Field, Forrest Fields, and the Harris weight-training facility. Ice hockey athletes practice and play at the Fenton Chester Ice Arena, which is adjacent to the school. Alpine and Nordic ski teams train and race at Burke Mountain Ski Area, which is 7 miles from the campus. The golf team practices at nearby St. Johnsbury Country Club's championship golf course. The baseball team plays at the LSC field. In the last five years, LI teams have won state championships in baseball, cross-country running, golf, Nordic skiing, softball, and track.

EXTRACURRICULAR OPPORTUNITIES

Student clubs and organizations run the gamut of student interests. Organizations include Student Council, National Honor Society, Future Business Leaders of America, and USA Skills/Vocational Industrial Clubs of America. Students may join the jazz ensemble; choral and drama groups; French, Latin, and Spanish clubs; the forensics team, and the scholars bowl team. The award-winning *Janus* magazine, an art and literature magazine that has won All-New England honors in the annual Boston University competition in four of the five years it was submitted; the *Viking Voice*, LI's student newspaper; *Cynosure*, the yearbook; and the Writers Workshop offer students writing, editing, and desktop publishing opportunities. Other clubs include the chess club, volunteer club, and SADD (Students Against Destructive Decisions).

The French and Spanish clubs organize trips abroad in alternating years. Students can take advantage of the cultural events and concerts at LSC, the Catamount Film and Arts Center in St. Johnsbury, and the Hopkins Center at Dartmouth College, which is only an hour away. The Music, Dance, and Art Departments offer students opportunities to work and perform with guest artists-in-residence. In addition to dances, plays, concerts, and athletics events, Spirit Week and Winter Carnival are two schoolwide events that engage the entire student body. Kingdom Trails offers a network of trails in the region for mountain biking in the summer and fall, and cross-country skiing and snowshoeing in the winter. Numerous field trips throughout Vermont, New England, and Canada are offered throughout the year. LI also hosts the statewide Kingdom Awards in literature, and in 2004, it hosted the first annual Vermont Dance Festival, which it has continued to host in each subsequent year.

DAILY LIFE

Classes begin each day at 7:55 a.m. and end at 2:30 p.m. There are seven class periods of 45 minutes each. Faculty members remain in their classrooms until 3 p.m. to assist students. Activities are scheduled at 3 p.m. or later to allow students additional time to meet with faculty members as needed. The library is open from 7:30 to 4:30 during the day and from 7 to 9 during the evening.

WEEKEND LIFE

Weekends in the Northeast Kingdom are always an adventure. Many interscholastic events take place on Saturday. Trips are scheduled to nearby ski areas and to the urban centers of Burlington; Hanover, New Hampshire; and Montreal. Catamount Film and Arts Center in St. Johnsbury always has a special event or series in the area, and some of these are scheduled at LI and Lyndon State College. Students in good standing and with advance permission have the option to spend the weekend with a host family in the area or to travel home.

SUMMER PROGRAMS

Lyndon Institute sponsors day camps for football, basketball, and soccer in late July and August.

COSTS AND FINANCIAL AID

Tuition for boarding students for 2009–10 is $33,400. A deposit of $2000 is due by May 31 to reserve a place. The Institute works with parents to arrange alternative payment schedules when needed.

Financial aid is based on need as determined by the School's Financial Aid Committee. Financial aid consists of both grants and loans. Special talent scholarships in music and art may be available.

ADMISSIONS INFORMATION

Acceptance to Lyndon Institute is based on academic performance and potential, school citizenship, and motivation. The SSAT is required for domestic students. The TOEFL or SLEP is required for international students whose native language is not English. A minimum score of 46 on the SLEP is necessary for acceptance.

Lyndon Institute admits students of any race, color, or national or ethnic origin to all the rights, privileges, programs, and activities generally accorded or made available to students at the school. LI does not discriminate on the basis of race, color, or national or ethnic origin in the administration of its educational policies, admission policies, scholarships, and loan programs or athletics and other school-administered programs.

APPLICATION TIMETABLE

Inquiries are welcome at any time. An interview is strongly suggested. Interviews and tours are scheduled between 10 and 2 Monday through Friday. Weekend appointments are available by special arrangement. Admissions decisions are made on a rolling basis. Since the boarding program is limited in enrollment, early application (by March 31) is recommended.

ADMISSIONS CORRESPONDENCE

Mary B. Thomas
Assistant Head for Admissions
Lyndon Institute
P.O. Box 127
Lyndon Center, Vermont 05850-0127
Phone: 802-626-5232
Fax: 802-626-6138
E-mail: admissions@lyndon.institute.org
Web site: http://www.lyndoninstitute.org

THE MACDUFFIE SCHOOL

Springfield, Massachusetts

Type: Coeducational boarding (9–12) and day college-preparatory school
Grades: 6–12: Middle School, 6–8; Upper School, 9–12
Enrollment: School total, 215; Upper School, 170
Head of School: Kathryn P. Gibson

THE SCHOOL

The MacDuffie School was founded in 1890 by Dr. John MacDuffie, a Harvard alumnus, and his wife Abby, a member of Radcliffe's first graduating class, to provide "a fine education" for girls preparing for college. Today, MacDuffie continues its commitment to academic excellence in preparing both boys and girls for college and for life. The School emphasizes the development of the individual within a supportive community that recognizes and welcomes diversity.

The MacDuffie campus occupies 14 acres in a historic residential area. Downtown Springfield is within walking distance of the School and offers access to the city's cultural resources, including museums, a theater, a symphony orchestra, a large public library, and a civic center. Local colleges, including Amherst, Hampshire, Mount Holyoke, Smith, and the University of Massachusetts, provide further intellectual and cultural opportunities.

MacDuffie is 25 miles from Hartford, Connecticut, and 20 miles from Bradley International Airport. Boston is 90 miles from Springfield, and New York City is 150 miles away; both cities are accessible by bus, rail, and air transportation.

A nonprofit institution, MacDuffie is governed by a 21-member Board of Trustees. Many of the more than 3,300 alumni assist with recruitment efforts and provide support through the Annual Fund.

The MacDuffie School is accredited by the New England Association of Schools and Colleges. It holds memberships in the National Association of Independent Schools, the Council for Advancement and Support of Education, and the Secondary School Admission Test Board.

ACADEMIC PROGRAMS

A defining principle of MacDuffie's academic program is that learning is an ongoing and intrinsic part of life. Students explore intellectual and artistic possibilities, debate differences of opinion, question assumptions, and take the kind of risks that help them to grow into informed, involved, articulate, and self-confident adults.

Middle School students benefit from an integrated curriculum that combines the study of English, history, math, science, Latin, and modern foreign languages, along with performing and visual arts and physical education. Multicultural themes provide an appreciation of varied cultural backgrounds. Students develop learning skills such as critical thinking and creative problem solving as well as computer use, effective study habits, and the art of test taking. The goal for the sixth, seventh, and eighth graders is to become confident and articulate learners ready for the challenges of the Upper School.

Upper School students choose from a solid core curriculum and have the chance to broaden their horizons through a variety of electives. To graduate, students must complete a minimum of 18 academic credits in grades 9–12 plus physical education. One credit equals one full year of work. The required credits include English, 4; mathematics, 3; U.S. history plus one other history course, 2; science, 2 (laboratory science); foreign language, 2 (with at least 3 credits of one language recommended); performing or visual arts, 1; and electives, 4. Students may study five years of French or Spanish as well as four years of Latin. English as a second language courses are available at the intermediate and advanced levels. Students must take at least four academic courses each year.

Electives may include astronomy, film studies, journalism, meteorology, peace studies, SAT review, twentieth-century conflict, and Western philosophy. Arts electives include acting, communications, dance and choreography, vocal and instrumental music, and a variety of visual arts, such as design, illustration, and photography.

Honors and Advanced Placement (AP) courses are available. In a typical year, more than half of the senior class and several underclass students take AP examinations in such subjects as English, French, Spanish, U.S. history, calculus, chemistry, and statistics. Independent study is also available.

The average class size is about 11 students, and the student-teacher ratio is 6:1. There are faculty-supervised study halls during the school day and regularly scheduled extra-help sessions after school without charge. The school year is divided into semesters. Examinations take place at the end of the first semester and at the end of the year. Students receive letter grades and teacher and adviser comments four times a year. Progress reports are provided as necessary during the school year.

FACULTY AND ADVISERS

Kathryn P. Gibson was appointed Head of School in 1999. She is a graduate of Vassar College (A.B., magna cum laude) and Columbia University (M.A.). Prior to coming to MacDuffie, Mrs. Gibson served as the Associate Director of Development at Springfield College and as a regional officer at the National Endowment for the Humanities in Washington, D.C.

There are 34 full-time faculty members. Seventy-one percent of the faculty members hold advanced degrees. Faculty members serve as academic advisers to an average of 6 students, overseeing their progress throughout the year. Faculty members also advise student organizations, organize class activities, and coach sports teams. Several staff and faculty members live on campus as do the Head of School's family and the families that host students in the Ames Hill boarding program.

COLLEGE ADMISSION COUNSELING

The Director of College Counseling guides students through the college selection and application process. Individual and group meetings are held frequently with students and their parents beginning in the junior year. More than 60 college representatives visit the campus each year to meet with interested students.

The mean SAT scores of last year's graduates were 561 verbal, 602 math, and 557 writing. An SAT preparation course is offered to juniors and seniors.

One hundred percent of the members of the class of 2008 were accepted to 124 different colleges and universities. Ninety-seven percent are attending four-year colleges and universities, including Boston University, George Washington, Massachusetts Amherst, and Wheaton.

STUDENT BODY AND CONDUCT

The total Upper School enrollment is 170, and the Middle School enrollment is 45; there are 126 girls and 89 boys. Of the total, 45 are boarding students. Day students reside in Springfield and nearby Massachusetts and northern Connecticut towns. Boarding students currently come from China, Germany, Hong Kong, Jamaica, Kazakhstan, Korea, Brazil, Spain, Japan, Taiwan, Vietnam, Ethiopia, and Russia.

ACADEMIC FACILITIES

School life revolves around Rutenber Hall, named for Ralph D. Rutenber, the Headmaster from 1941 to 1972. It houses the classrooms, science laboratories, the Holly Fisher Computer Laboratory, the Sadowsky Family Library, the Sally Fenelon-Young Auditorium, the Jostrom Multimedia Room, and the Guided Study Room. The dance, music, theater, and visual arts departments are located in the Arts Center.

BOARDING AND GENERAL FACILITIES

MacDuffie's innovative approach to cultural exchange is known as the Ames Hill Boarding Program. It combines the best of a homestay experience with a small boarding school program. Girls and boys from the United States and around the world live on campus with faculty families in five gracious homes named Castle, Caswell, Lemire, Tifft, and Young Houses. From the time students arrive, they share in the daily life of a family and of the larger School community.

Other facilities on campus include the dining room in South Hall; the student lounge, Finn's Bin; Young House, the admissions and administrative offices; and Wallace Hall, development offices and where several faculty and staff members reside. A hospital is located 1 mile from campus.

ATHLETICS

The School encourages but does not require involvement in athletics. The emphasis is on individual challenge and competing as part of a team. Interscholastic teams for girls include basketball, field hockey, lacrosse, softball, tennis, and volleyball. Boys' teams include baseball, basketball, soccer, and tennis. Coed teams include cross-country and junior varsity and varsity soccer. Activities offered as part of the physical education program include those listed above plus archery, badminton, and dance. The School participates in private-school sports clinics and playdays (all-star games and tournaments) in field hockey, lacrosse, tennis, and volleyball.

Athletic facilities include Downing Gymnasium, athletic fields, and tennis courts. Local facilities for bowling, swimming, skiing, gymnastics, hockey, ice skating, and horseback riding are available for recreational purposes.

EXTRACURRICULAR OPPORTUNITIES

A wide variety of clubs and activities offers students the opportunity to get involved and share interests. Student Admission Representatives (STARS), Dance Ensemble, Student Cultural Alliance, Ibero-Hispanic Club, Drama Club, Jazz Ensemble, Mathletes, STOP (Student/Teacher Organization for Peace), MacDuffie Singers, Chess Club, and Key Club are just a few of the choices. Students publish a yearbook, *The Magnolia;* a newspaper, *The Magnet;* and a literary magazine, *The Unicorn.* The Student Council plans activities for the School community and offers leadership opportunities. Students also volunteer as tutors in local schools.

Traditional annual events include Mountain Day, Parents' Back to School Night, Grandparents' Day, Winter Carnival, Diversity Day, School plays and performances, International Meals, and activities sponsored by the Parents' Association.

DAILY LIFE

MacDuffie's school day begins with an all-School assembly at 8:15. Classes meet five days a week until 3:15 p.m. every day except Wednesday, when the school day ends at 1:50. There are eight class periods in the school day. Supervised study periods may be scheduled during the day. Ames Hill students have an evening study period as well. An activity period is scheduled during the school day for clubs to meet, while sports and other club activities take place after school or on weekends.

Students and faculty members eat lunch together in the dining room in South Hall. Ames Hill students and their MacDuffie families prepare and eat breakfast and dinner in their homes on campus.

WEEKEND LIFE

Weekend activities for boarding students may include going to the movies or restaurants, on shopping trips, to concerts, plays, sporting events, or dances held at MacDuffie and at other nearby schools.

Supervised day or weekend trips are planned to such places as Boston, New York City, and Washington, D.C.

COSTS AND FINANCIAL AID

In 2008–09, tuition for day students was $15,150 in grade 6, $17,150 in grade 7, and $19,150 in grade 8. Tuition for day students in grades 9–12 was $21,200. Tuition, room, board, and an activities fee for Ames Hill Boarding Program students were $37,150. Payment plans are available. Financial assistance is given in the form of need-based aid and scholarships for tuition only. Merit scholarships are available for incoming freshmen.

ADMISSIONS INFORMATION

MacDuffie seeks a diverse, college-bound student body and has a policy of admitting students without regard to race, color, national or ethnic origin, or sexual orientation. The School considers recommendations, results of the SSAT, and previous school records in the selection of applicants. An interview is required and a visit is strongly encouraged. The Admissions Office is open Monday through Friday from 8:30 to 4:30, but appointments for interviews and visits can be arranged in the evening or on weekends as well.

APPLICATION TIMETABLE

Although there is no closing date for applications, candidates for September entrance should apply during the previous winter or early spring. If space is available, students may enroll at the beginning of the second semester in January. There is a $50 application fee; for boarding students, the application fee is $100.

ADMISSIONS CORRESPONDENCE

Linda Keating
Director of Admissions and Financial Aid
The MacDuffie School
One Ames Hill Drive
Springfield, Massachusetts 01105
Phone: 413-734-4971 Ext. 140
Fax: 413-734-6693
E-mail: lkeating@macduffie.com

MAINE CENTRAL INSTITUTE

Pittsfield, Maine

Type: Coeducational boarding and day college-preparatory and comprehensive curriculum
Grades: 9–12, postgraduate year
Enrollment: 480
Head of School: Christopher Hopkins

THE SCHOOL

Founded in 1866 by Free Will Baptists, Maine Central Institute (MCI) retains the inventive spirit and philosophy of its founders but no longer has a formal affiliation with the church. During the school's pioneer years, MCI served as a feeder school to Bates College in nearby Lewiston, Maine. Although adhering to upstanding and traditional educational values, MCI is progressive and broad-minded, pledging to provide a comprehensive college-preparatory education to a multicultural student body diverse in talents, abilities, and interests.

MCI regards each student as an individual with individual needs and aspirations. In keeping with its belief in individuality, MCI strives to foster an overall environment of mutual respect, cooperation, and tolerance among all of its members and with the surrounding community. In a safe and caring atmosphere, students are encouraged to develop a moral and social consciousness, self-esteem, and social responsibility and to become globally aware, lifelong learners.

The rural town of Pittsfield (population 4,500) is nestled in between the Atlantic Ocean and the mountains of western Maine. The region of central Maine provides prime opportunities for hiking, skiing, biking, fishing, skating, and snowmobiling. The campus is within walking distance of local eateries, recreational parks, shopping, hiking trials, and a movie theater.

Maine Central Institute is accredited by the New England Association of Schools and Colleges and approved by the State of Maine Department of Education. MCI is also a member of the College Board and the National Association of Independent Schools.

ACADEMIC PROGRAMS

MCI offers a rigorous comprehensive curriculum to accommodate various learning styles and academic abilities. MCI fosters the intellectual curiosities of its student body by offering accelerated and advanced placement courses in all core subject areas.

For grades 9–12, 20 credits are required for graduation. Students must successfully complete units in English (4), mathematics (4), social studies (3, including U.S. history), science (4), physical education (1), fine arts (1), computer science (½), and health (½). Students are required to take the equivalent of at least 5 units each semester.

MCI's math and science programs exceed national standards and utilize state-of-the-art technology and academic facilities. Students in MCI's well-known humanities program understand the culture of an era through a study of its history, literature, and art. The Institute has an award-winning music program.

The foreign language program includes four levels of French and Spanish. In addition to the traditional offerings, students may take courses in psychology, music composition, the Internet, sociology, child development, computer-assisted drawing, personal finance, vocational subjects, and philosophy.

MCI offers a structured ESL program for the international student who is planning for a university education. Students receive individual testing before placement at one of three levels of ESL. The extensive ESL program includes American history for international students and carefully structured math classes that focus on the development of math language skills.

FACULTY AND ADVISERS

The 2007–08 faculty consisted of 42 full-time members. Twenty-six percent of the faculty and staff members reside on campus, while the remainder live in nearby towns such as Newport, Waterville, and Bangor.

Faculty members are selected on the basis of three main criteria. They must possess a strong subject-matter background, the ability to relate to students, and an educational philosophy consistent with that of the institution and its mission. Faculty members are also expected to become actively involved in coaching, supervising dormitories, advising, counseling, and student affairs.

COLLEGE ADMISSION COUNSELING

A guidance team of 4 professionals is available for students. Counselors are responsible primarily for helping students with postsecondary placement and academic program planning. Approximately 75 college admissions representatives visit MCI's campus annually. Career counseling is also an integral part of the guidance department. Financial aid workshops for seniors, postgraduates, and their parents are offered. Preparation for the SAT and ACT is offered within the math and English curricula.

MCI has a strong history of placing students in postsecondary school. Schools attended by recent graduates include Bates, Boston University, Colby, Cornell, Emerson, Emory, George Mason, Gettysburg, Hofstra, Husson, Maine Maritime Academy, Michigan State, Muhlenberg, Northeastern, Syracuse, Tufts, Worcester Polytechnic, and the Universities of Connecticut, Maine, New England, New Hampshire, and Rhode Island.

STUDENT BODY AND CONDUCT

The 2008–09 enrollment of 480 includes 354 day students and 126 boarding students. Students came to MCI from seven states and seventeen countries.

Students at MCI are expected to be good citizens and are held responsible for their behavior. The rules that provide the structure for the school community are written in the student handbook. Disciplinary issues are the responsibility of the administration, the faculty, and the residence hall staff.

ACADEMIC FACILITIES

There are sixteen buildings housed on the 23-acre campus. Visitors are greeted upon entrance with the stoic simplicity of the campus with its brick-front buildings and the historic bell tower of Founder's Hall.

The Math and Science Center is a 23,000-square-foot recent addition to MCI, including fourteen instructional spaces, two computer classrooms, and a botany area. More than 210 computers are available for student use campuswide, many of which have Internet and e-mail access. The 12,000-volume Powell Memorial Library has a computerized card catalogue as well as Internet access. The Pittsfield Public Library is also available for school use.

BOARDING AND GENERAL FACILITIES

Boarding students reside in single-sex residence halls on campus, supervised by resident faculty and staff members. Each residence hall has its own recreation room and laundry facilities. MCI celebrated the opening in fall 2007 of an Honors Dormitory, converted from a home owned by the school to reward the highest-achieving residential students. Construction of the Donna Leavitt Furman Student Center was a second notable addition to the MCI campus in 2007. It is home to the dining hall, student lounge, and garden sitting area, including a performance stage, food court, garden benches, and game room.

Weymouth Hall houses the Student Services Center, consisting of the student union, snack machines, the Wellness Center, and the school bookstore.

MCI offers a unique Host Family Program. Participating students are paired with a family from the community that makes the student a part of its family for the school year. Students may spend time with their host family on weekends, after school, and during vacations, if so desired.

ATHLETICS

MCI believes that athletics not only provide a wholesome outlet for youthful energies but also help students apply and further develop their skills in various sports. The school strives to furnish opportunities for participation by students of all abilities by offering JV, varsity, and club-level sports.

There are seventeen sports teams for boys and girls, including football, field hockey, soccer, basketball, golf, skiing, softball, track, wrestling, cheering, rifle, baseball, and tennis.

Wright Gymnasium and Parks Gymnasium are multiple-use athletic facilities, and each contains a weight room and locker facilities. Located on the main campus are a football field, a practice field, a ¼-mile track, two tennis courts, and a rifle range. Manson Park has fields for soccer, field hockey, baseball, and softball as well as three tennis courts. The school has the use of a local golf course and ski areas for competitive teams and recreation.

EXTRACURRICULAR OPPORTUNITIES

MCI students may choose from among more than thirty campus organizations, which represent some of the following interests: drama production; foreign languages and travel to places such as Spain, England, and Russia; chess; hiking; weight lifting; Future Problem Solvers; Key Club, which is the school's community service organization; computer science; and public speaking. Students may participate in Student Council; MCI's strong, award-winning music program includes concert band, concert choir, chamber choir, vocal jazz ensemble, instrumental jazz ensemble, jazz combo, percussion ensemble, and pep band; and the Math Team and the Science Olympiad, which compete locally and statewide.

Bossov Ballet Theatre offers MCI students a unique opportunity to study classical ballet as part of the academic curriculum. Ballet classes are taught by Andrei Bossov, a world-renowned teacher who previously taught at the Vaganova Academy in Saint Petersburg, Russia. The program consists of a preprofessional-level syllabus that prepares students for a professional ballet career.

DAILY LIFE

The school day begins at 7:40 and ends at 2:36, with a 42-minute lunch break beginning at 11:30. Classes run from Monday through Friday, with dinner served from 5 to 6:30 p.m.

Sunday through Thursday, there is a mandatory supervised study hall from 7 to 8:30 p.m. for all boarding students.

WEEKEND LIFE

Supervised weekend activities include trips to Canada, Boston, the nearby capital of Augusta, the city of Portland, historic ports, lighthouses and coastal towns along the Atlantic shoreline, and cultural and athletic events both on and off campus. Activities such as whale watching, whitewater rafting, and skiing at Sugarloaf Resort are also offered. With parental permission, students are allowed to go home on weekends or visit the home of their host family.

COSTS AND FINANCIAL AID

The 2008–09 tuition, room, and board are $33,500 for boarding students, and tuition is $10,000 for private day students. The cost for ESL support is $2500 for the first class and $1500 for each additional class. The nonrefundable deposit of $2000 is due within two weeks of an offer of admission. A variety of payment plans are available.

Financial aid is awarded on a need basis, determined by information shown on the Parents' Confidential Statement and any additional financial information that is requested.

ADMISSIONS INFORMATION

MCI's Admissions Committee screens all applicants to determine their compatibility with MCI's philosophy that students should assume a mature responsibility for their own education. No entrance tests are required, but an on-campus interview with each student and his or her parents is strongly recommended. School transcripts and results of standardized tests are used to determine academic ability and appropriate academic placement in classes in accordance with the student's individual needs, abilities, and interests.

Maine Central Institute does not discriminate on the basis of race, sex, age, sexual preference, disability, religion, or national or ethnic origin in the administration of its educational and admission policies, financial aid programs, and athletic or other school-administered programs and activities.

APPLICATION TIMETABLE

Inquiries and applications are welcome at any time; however, applying by June 1 is recommended. Visits may be scheduled at any time during the year but are most effective when school is in session. Tours and interviews can be arranged by calling the Admissions Office, which is open Monday through Friday from 8 to 4:30. A nonrefundable application fee of $50 is required.

ADMISSIONS CORRESPONDENCE

Clint M. Williams, Director of Admission
Maine Central Institute
295 Main Street
Pittsfield, Maine 04967
Phone: 207-487-2282
Fax: 207-487-3512
E-mail: cwilliams@mci-school.org
Web site: http://www.mci-school.org

MAINE SCHOOL OF SCIENCE AND MATHEMATICS

Limestone, Maine

MSSM
THE MAINE SCHOOL OF SCIENCE AND MATHEMATICS
www.mssm.org

Type: Coeducational boarding school
Grades: 10–12
Enrollment: 120
Head of School: Walt Warner, Executive Director

THE SCHOOL

The Maine School of Science and Mathematics (MSSM) is a public, residential magnet school serving talented sophomore, junior, and senior high school students from across the state. MSSM was created by the 116th Maine Legislature in 1995 as the state's first charter school and is a member of the National Consortium of Specialized Secondary Schools of Science, Mathematics, and Technology. A residential community committed to the pursuit of academic excellence, MSSM provides an extensive curriculum in science, mathematics, technology, and the arts and humanities. The challenging curriculum and stimulating environment create an ongoing learning experience, with students working, studying, and socializing with classmates who share similar interests and goals. In addition to the yearly high school curriculum, the School provides students with the opportunity to participate in specialized learning where students participate in internships, research projects, or attend on-campus seminar-style classes.

The administration, faculty, staff, and Board of Trustees of MSSM are committed to providing academic excellence to enhance previous knowledge and to prepare students for future studies. The opportunity to attend MSSM is a privilege, and each student can make the most of this experience by being dedicated to the academic and residential programs. Graduates of MSSM have experienced a well-defined curriculum based upon academic standards fostering both academic discipline and honesty.

The Maine School of Science and Mathematics is located in a rural area of northern Aroostook County, Maine (approximately 5 hours north of Portland). All students live in residence to fully participate in this scholastic program of excellence with students who share similar interests. The nurturing of this educational community—the integration of the academic and residential components—is crucial to success at MSSM. Students are responsible for taking advantage of the academic and extracurricular pursuits and for supporting community members in both their academic and personal development.

ACADEMIC PROGRAMS

An MSSM education prepares young people for future studies and for life. At MSSM, students learn the importance of time management, organization, and inquisitiveness while being a positive contributor to a community. Students learn to live and grow with others who may be very different from themselves. They learn the importance of honesty, dedication, and hard work. An MSSM education is truly one that prepares the whole student for life. The academic program at MSSM is well defined and demanding. Courses challenge students to achieve their potential and excel. There are several levels of mathematics and science courses that meet individual students' needs and abilities. While these classes are well known for their high quality, the humanities and social science courses also provide students with a challenge that fosters their overall development. Students may choose from a variety of English, foreign language, and social science courses. Through MSSM classes, students gain valuable skills to help them succeed in college. Students must enroll in at least four courses per semester. Among these courses, mathematics, laboratory sciences, and English are mandatory. Each student is also required to participate in recreation and work service every semester. The January Term (or J Term) is an intensive two-week session that follows the fall semester in which each student selects one area of study. Experiences range from traditional classroom settings to trips and job shadows. During J Term, students focus on a particular area of interest and broaden their experiences.

FACULTY AND ADVISERS

The average class size is 16 students, which means there is a great deal of faculty-student interaction. In addition to imparting knowledge, teachers at MSSM often take the extra step for students, whether this means having a pizza party while watching Shakespeare after class or simply being available for assistance with a difficult homework problem or perplexing lab write-up. The faculty members at MSSM are all specialists in their fields, enthusiastic about disseminating information and challenging students to explore the world. Faculty members work with students outside the classroom and take an active interest in each student. The advisory program is another means of close interaction. Each MSSM student is assigned an academic adviser, who meets with the student regularly to devise the student's schedule and review the student's progress. The academic adviser, serving as the student's advocate, oversees and helps the student handle any difficulties that may arise.

COLLEGE ADMISSION COUNSELING

As a specialized secondary school, one of MSSM's primary goals is to prepare students for college. The College Counseling Office plays an integral role by assisting students in finding the most appropriate college matches through a combination of personal meetings and small seminar courses that begin in the spring of the junior year. College planning, standardized testing, and college financial aid information are all organized through the College Counseling Office and available for both students and parents. The Director of College Counseling provides individualized exploration and planning throughout the process. Recent graduates have gone on to such schools as Carnegie Mellon University, Maine Maritime Academy, Massachusetts Institute of Technology, Rensselaer Polytechnic Institute, the University of Maine, and Worcester Polytechnic Institute.

STUDENT BODY AND CONDUCT

The School is small (approximately 150 students each year); its size makes it possible for students to know everyone. Furthermore, the low student-faculty ratio allows instructors to forge friendships with students. Without the distance between instructor and student, there is more dialogue and a better mutual understanding, helping students produce exemplary work. Students are also very close, and living in the dormitory environment not only helps prepare students for college life but also teaches tolerance, mediation, and compromise.

ACADEMIC FACILITIES

MSSM shares facilities with the Limestone Community School, which serves 325 students in grades K–12.

BOARDING AND GENERAL FACILITIES

MSSM has one large dorm that serves both boys and girls. The dorm is divided into four separate wings; within each are two to three small community lounges. The wings are connected by two large common areas where students of both genders can socialize. Students have access to a full kitchen, where they are often seen cooking and baking. A connecting gym offers games such as pool and table tennis and several practice rooms for music. Two centrally located laundry rooms comfortably meet the needs of students. Through job assignments, students help maintain the common areas and facilities.

ATHLETICS

Sports are available in the spring, fall, and winter. Athletic teams are competitive, with several teams and individual athletes qualifying for regional- and state-level competition each season. Students are encouraged to participate in a sport to help round out their total experience at MSSM. During the fall season, MSSM joins forces with the Limestone Community School to provide boys' and girls' soccer, boys' and girls' cross-country, and boys' golf. The winter months offer boys' and girls' basketball, boys' and girls' volleyball, cheerleading, and a competitive swim team. Spring sports include baseball, softball, track and field, and tennis.

EXTRACURRICULAR OPPORTUNITIES

The diversity of student interests encourages participation in a variety of clubs and activities, most of which are student-driven and supported by faculty members. Current clubs include A Cappella, the Key Club, ACM, Math Competition, Boffer, Model UN, the Cooking Club, the Prom Committee, the Dorm Council, the Science Team, the Environmental Club, the Student Senate, and Ensemble Band. Throughout the year, students enjoy holiday activities, semiformals, prom, theater performances, local cultural events, and special holiday dinners.

DAILY LIFE

Quiet hours begin Sunday at 7 p.m. and remain in effect until Friday afternoon at 4. Structured study hours are from 7:30 p.m. through 9:30 p.m. Sunday through Thursday.

WEEKEND LIFE

The weekends are more relaxed; resident students can interact with faculty members in a more casual, family-style setting. Faculty members are responsible for weekend supervision and check-in and assist in providing student activities such as family game nights and other relaxing and enjoyable times that students would experience if they lived at home. Students can visit the local mall, go hiking and skiing, and attend concerts and cultural events at the nearby Caribou Performing Arts Center. They have access to the area's amenities, including an ice-skating arena, a world-class cross-country skiing facility, and a rock-climbing wall in Presque Isle.

SUMMER PROGRAMS

The MSSM mission is advanced through its outreach programs, including distance education, summer programs, and workshops for students and teachers throughout the state. Every summer, MSSM welcomes more than 300 students in grades 5–9 to participate in the Summer X program. Its offerings challenge the mind and develop interests in math, science, and technology in a variety of ways, satisfying intellectual curiosity and an adventurous spirit. Academic classes offered include Robotics Challenge, Physics of Ballistics, and Real Life CSI. Through summer outreach programs, students develop the skills to be lifelong learners and leaders. When not in class, a variety of recreational activities are offered, enhancing the summer camp atmosphere.

COSTS AND FINANCIAL AID

Maine residents pay for room and board only, which was $6400 in 2007–08. For all other students, the cost was $23,500 per year in 2007–08. For financial aid consideration, families should complete a financial aid application using the National Association of Independent Schools (NAIS) process, available online at https://sss.ets.org/. Financial aid applications should be completed by July 1.

ADMISSIONS INFORMATION

Admission to MSSM is highly competitive. In addition to their academic ability, students are selected on the basis of maturity, motivation, and their ability to contribute positively to the residential environment. Students must submit the completed application, personal essays, official SAT scores, three letters of recommendation, the completed Guidance Counselor's Recommendation Form, and an official transcript. All applicants are required to visit the campus, at which time a personal interview is conducted with an MSSM faculty member and a current MSSM student.

APPLICATION TIMETABLE

The majority of prospective parents and students enjoy Open Houses and/or Visiting Day tours. Students who visit during an Open House can attend morning classes of their choice, while parents get to learn more about MSSM. Prospective parents and students may visit the campus by calling the Admissions Office and scheduling a private visit outside of the Open House/Visiting Day time frame.

Applications are given priority review three times annually—December 15, February 15, and April 15. Applications received after priority review dates are considered only on a rolling basis and as openings become available.

ADMISSIONS CORRESPONDENCE

Miss Pamela Perkins, Director of Admissions
Maine School of Science and Mathematics
95 High Street
Limestone, Maine 04750
Phone: 207-325-3303
Fax: 207-325-3340
E-mail: mssm@mssm.org
Web site: http://www.mssm.org/

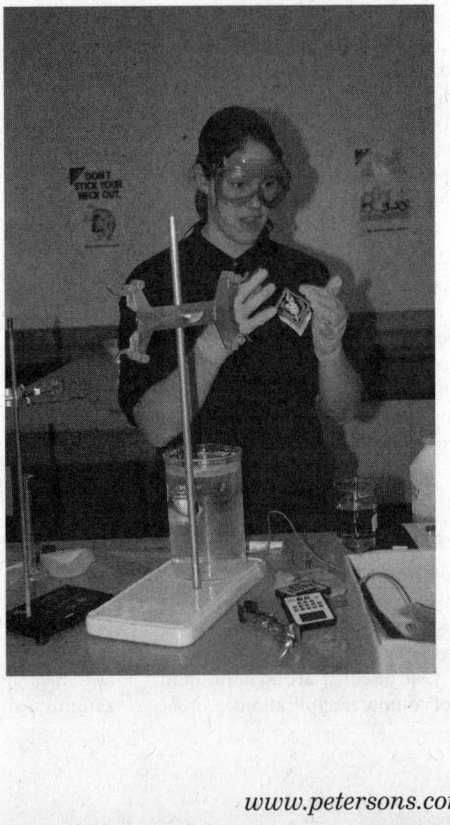

MARIANAPOLIS PREPARATORY SCHOOL

Thompson, Connecticut

Type: Coeducational boarding and day Roman Catholic college-preparatory school
Grades: 9–12, postgraduate year
Enrollment: 325
Head of School: Marilyn S. Ebbitt, Headmistress

THE SCHOOL

Located on a 250-acre arboretum, Marianapolis Preparatory School prides itself on its sense of community and academia. Founded in 1926, Marianapolis is situated in the heart of Connecticut's antique district. The School is 1 hour from Boston, 45 minutes from Hartford and Providence, and 3 hours from New York City.

The School's 325 students, representing twenty countries, contribute to an enriching academic and cultural experience. Athletics and Advanced Placement (AP) courses abound, with thirteen AP courses offered and more than thirty clubs and sports to choose from. Many courses are also offered at the honors level.

Marianapolis Preparatory School's aim and purpose is to encourage scholarship and mature character, develop analytical and critical-thinking skills, build communication and problem-solving skills, promote a love of learning and the highest standards of academic achievement, foster aesthetic sensitivity and creativity, encourage the classical ideal of *mens sana in corpore sano* (a sound mind and body), enable students to appreciate the value of cultural diversity, nurture active and intelligent citizenship in the world, and affirm Catholic principles through ethical and moral values.

Marianapolis is a Catholic school that is inclusive of all faiths. In every student, Marianapolis fosters a commitment to compassionate values, which can be felt in the School's genuine dedication to service—service to the world community, the local community, fellow students, and oneself. This commitment to fundamental values helps to develop the confidence, inner purpose, and well-being that are important building blocks in life.

Marianapolis Preparatory School is accredited by the New England Association of Schools and Colleges and is a member of the Connecticut Association of Independent Schools, the Secondary School Admission Test Board, and the Catholic Boarding School Association. Marianapolis is also registered and approved as an independent secondary school by the Department of Education of the state of Connecticut.

ACADEMIC PROGRAMS

To achieve a Marianapolis diploma, all students are required to fulfill 4 years of English, 3 years of math, 3 years of history, 3 years of lab science, 3 years of foreign language, six semesters of theology, 1 year of either art or music, and one semester of computer applications.

Advanced Placement courses are offered in American history, art and music theory, biology, calculus AB and BC, chemistry, English literature, European history, government, physics, psychology, and Spanish.

Reporting of grades occurs four times a year, once at the end of each academic quarter. Full academic grades, teacher comments, and adviser comments are written at the end of the first and third marking periods. At the end of the second and fourth marking periods, academic grades and adviser comments are written; course comments are required only for those students who have earned below a C- in any course. In addition, every student who is new to Marianapolis receives an interim progress report after the first four weeks of classes.

FACULTY AND ADVISERS

The faculty consists of 42 members, who serve as educators, advisers, coaches, and mentors.

Marilyn S. Ebbitt was named Headmistress in 2001. She holds an A.B. from Marquette University and an M.S. from Georgetown University and has been an educator for more than thirty years.

COLLEGE ADMISSION COUNSELING

During their junior and senior years, students are given a college guide complete with the essentials of the application process. Students meet with the College Placement Director to investigate various college possibilities, and they can also practice their college interview. Dozens of college representatives visit during the school year to meet with interested students. Juniors and seniors are also encouraged to visit college campuses throughout the year.

Assistance is offered at all stages of the college placement process, including the formation of realistic expectations, filling out application forms, and understanding financial aid procedures.

All of the 2007 graduates were accepted into colleges. Recent graduates are attending such colleges and universities as Boston College, Brown, Carnegie Mellon, Cornell, Dartmouth, George Washington, Georgetown, Hamilton, Holy Cross, Notre Dame, NYU, Purdue, RIT, the U.S. Naval Academy, William and Mary, and the Universities of Chicago, Connecticut, and Virginia.

BOARDING AND GENERAL FACILITIES

Marianapolis has four dormitories located on campus, all supervised by live-in faculty members. Bayer House, White House, and St. Albert's Hall are restored historic mansions that house boarding girls. A new girls' residence hall will open in fall 2008. Recreational lounges within the various halls offer a combination of wireless Internet access, television, board games, air hockey, and table tennis. Laundry facilities are located in each of the dormitories.

St. John's Hall houses boarding boys and has a capacity of 85 students. Boys have the use of two recreational lounges with wireless Internet access, television, a Foosball table, table tennis, and a billiards table. A student store sells snacks and other items.

The dormitories are closed during the Thanksgiving, Christmas, and spring recesses. Arrangements with local families are provided for international students who, because of distance, cannot travel home during vacations.

A laundry service with dry cleaning is available at an extra charge for students wishing to enroll in the program.

ATHLETICS

At Marianapolis, athletics are an integral part of the School's mission to nurture the mind, body, and spirit of each student. The athletic program is seen as an extension of the values and ideals developed in the academic classroom and reflects the School's underlying philosophy. Interscholastic sports at various skill levels enable students to practice and understand the values of teamwork, commitment, and sportsmanship as well as to develop a positive work ethic. Sports provide students the opportunity to learn how to work with others for a common goal and how to gain confidence in their own abilities. All students are required to participate in a minimum of two interscholastic sports.

Athletic offerings include cross-country, volleyball, and soccer in the fall; basketball and wrestling in the winter; and baseball, softball, golf, lacrosse, tennis, Ultimate Frisbee, and track in the spring.

EXTRACURRICULAR OPPORTUNITIES

Various extracurricular clubs and activities are offered throughout the school year, depending upon the needs and interests of the students. Clubs and activities include music appreciation, Amnesty International, computer, debate, math center, writing center, yearbook, science quiz bowl, peer leadership, drama, chorus, band, Ski Club, Student Government, and Student Council. Traditional events each year include the Annual Rake Day, Sports Day,

Spirit Week, Breakfast with Santa, Halloween Dress-Down Day, and Mardi Gras. All events involve students in spirit-building activities.

DAILY LIFE

School begins each weekday with a small-group advisory at 8 a.m., and the academic day concludes at 2:45 p.m. There are five 1-hour periods each day. Classes meet on a rotating schedule. Club meetings and extra help sessions are scheduled during a half-hour period each day. Athletic practices are scheduled after school from 3:30 to 5:15.

Boarding students are served three meals daily in the dining room and have required night study hours from 7 to 9 p.m. Depending on their individual academic achievement, as determined by their GPA, students are placed in an appropriate study-hall environment. Students with a GPA of 95 percent or higher earn the right to study independently. Students with a GPA of at least 85 percent are permitted to study in their dormitory rooms, and students with a GPA under 85 percent have structured study hall, which is supervised by faculty members in the academic building. After study, students have free time to enjoy their friends, call home, or surf the Web with wireless Internet access. Lights-out is at 11 p.m. in the dormitories.

WEEKEND LIFE

While most students enjoy taking part in events planned on campus, boarding students are also offered a variety of activities on the weekends. Friday night and Saturday activities can range from trips to Boston or Providence to a night at the movies. School dances are sponsored by various clubs and classes each month. On Sundays, students are required to attend Mass in the chapel, followed by brunch. Off-campus activities extend into Sunday; however, study hours are enforced on Sunday evenings.

COSTS AND FINANCIAL AID

Tuition for the 2008–09 academic year is $10,695 for day students and $31,875 for boarding students. Boarding tuition for the ESL program is $36,625. Tuition covers all expenses except textbooks, supplies, and medical insurance for boarding students. There is also a nominal technology fee. Financial aid is available, and all families are encouraged to complete a financial aid form. The financial aid application deadline is March 1.

ADMISSIONS INFORMATION

Marianapolis Preparatory School seeks qualified applicants of average and above-average academic ability. The School does not discriminate on the basis of race, creed, gender, nationality, or disability. Applicants are considered on the basis of previous school transcripts, recommendations from teachers and school officials, results of the entrance examination, and a personal interview.

Marianapolis has the approval of the Department of State, Washington, D.C., for the admission of immigrant students under the Immigration Act of 1924.

APPLICATION TIMETABLE

Initial inquiries are welcome at any time, and campus visits are encouraged. The first round of boarding school applications is due March 1; after that date, applications are accepted on a rolling-admissions basis. An application fee must accompany the completed application.

ADMISSIONS CORRESPONDENCE

Daniel Harrop
Director of Admissions
Marianapolis Preparatory School
P.O. Box 304
Thompson, Connecticut 06277
Phone: 860-923-9565
Fax: 860-923-3730
E-mail: dharrop@marianapolis.org
Web site: http://www.marianapolis.org

THE MARVELWOOD SCHOOL

Kent, Connecticut

Type: Coeducational boarding and day college-preparatory school
Grades: 9–12, PG
Enrollment: 165
Head of School: Scott E. Pottbecker

THE SCHOOL

A Marvelwood education is characterized by intensive personal attention to the individual student. Marvelwood is passionate about providing an educational environment that nurtures academic and personal growth and awakens the potential that resides in each of its students. The School strives always to be a place where each child is known, valued, and treated with respect.

Honors and Advanced Placement courses, English Language Learners (ELL), private Strategies and Math Tutorial Programs, and a dedication to experiential education enable Marvelwood to serve a diverse student body with a wide range of learning styles. The School's experienced and dedicated faculty is committed to each student's success and delivers a superior educational program attuned to individual strengths and weaknesses. Nonacademic programs, including weekly community service, visual and performing arts electives, an impressive slate of interscholastic and noncompetitive sports offerings, and a variety of leadership opportunities, increase the potential for engagement and success outside the classroom. In every way, the structure of the School is thoughtfully designed to support college-bound students in their efforts to achieve positive intellectual, social, personal, and moral growth.

Marvelwood is located in the foothills of the Berkshire Mountains, just 55 miles from Hartford, 80 miles from New York City, and 150 miles from Boston. The 83-acre campus sits atop Skiff Mountain and is surrounded by protected lands that are available for the School's use. Field study and outdoor recreational activities, including hiking, rock climbing, canoeing, skiing, and snowboarding, are integral parts of school life.

The School is governed by the Board of Trustees, which is composed mainly of alumni and parents of current or past students. The School's budget is $5 million. Each year, the Annual Fund raises upward of $150,000. Capital funds are sought continually to enlarge the School's endowment and expand and improve the School's facilities. Improvements and renovations are ongoing throughout the campus, including the dining hall, dormitories, library, and a new athletic center.

Marvelwood is accredited by the New England Association of Schools and Colleges and is a member of the National Association of Independent Schools and the Connecticut Association of Independent Schools.

ACADEMIC PROGRAMS

Currently, a minimum of 24 academic and arts credits are required for graduation, in the following distribution: 4 credits of English, 4 credits of math, 3–4 credits of history, 3–4 credits of science, 2–4 credits of foreign language, and 2–3 credits in the arts. A full-year course is awarded 1 credit. Certain students may be exempted from required foreign language courses. The School has an expanded arts program, with course work in drawing and painting, creative writing, ceramics, design, photography, film, drama, and journalism. Participation in athletics is also required each term; a full year's credit in sports is a graduation requirement.

The overall student-teacher ratio is 4:1. Class sizes range from 5 to 14 students, with an average size between 8 and 10. During the freshman and sophomore years, there are two levels of academic difficulty. During the junior and senior years, the School offers three academic levels. Eight AP classes are currently offered.

Classes at Marvelwood operate on a modified block schedule. Each student is involved in course work for the entire academic day. Study halls are held in the afternoon as needed and in the evening. During the evening, each dormitory's study hall is supervised by 2 faculty members.

Report cards are issued every three weeks and include separate grades in academic achievement and effort. At the end of the fall, winter, and spring terms, comprehensive reports with comments from the student's teachers, coach, and adviser and the Head of School are sent to parents. Students also complete a self-evaluation and meet with their adviser at the end of each trimester to discuss this evaluation, the reports, and goals for the following term.

Approximately 40 percent of the student body is enrolled in the Strategies Program, a one-on-one daily tutorial program in which students are paired with teachers who can best serve their needs. A Math Tutorial Program is also offered. Some learning disabilities may be supported through the Strategies Program, although Marvelwood cannot accommodate students with severe learning difficulties or serious dyslexic conditions. Strategies teachers develop a curriculum for each student and monitor all aspects of their students' academic progress, making sure expectations are being met and ensuring that appropriate accommodations are in place. The effectiveness of the program is fostered by the strong partnership that exists between Strategies and classroom teachers.

The Sebring-Vaughn Learning and Language Lab features assistive technology including Kurzweil 3000, a text-to-speech program; Dragon Naturally Speaking, a speech-to-text program; and Report Writer, for assistance with expressive language weaknesses, as well as Recordings for the Blind and Dyslexic CD players for listening to audio books.

Marvelwood's English Language Learners program is designed to help international students gain fluency in all areas of language: speaking, listening, reading, and writing. These skills are essential for the students to succeed in the mainstream program.

New students are tested prior to enrollment to determine placement within one of three ELL levels. Placement of students is determined by three factors: the Secondary Level English Proficiency Test (SLEP), an essay written in a controlled setting, and a face-to-face interview with the ELL department chairperson. All courses offer a small class size and are ELL-centered, utilizing an approach that includes pair work, group work, and oral presentations.

Marvelwood offers a comprehensive, three-level ELL program. ELL I is an intensive English program designed to accommodate students with elementary to moderate levels of English proficiency. Courses include reading and vocabulary, writing and grammar, life science (a content-based course that reflects learning in the mainstream classroom), and world view (a content-based course that offers a combination of geography, history, current events, and cultures in the United States).

ELL II is for intermediate to high intermediate learners, and courses include literature, academic writing, and U.S. history.

ELL III is a supplemental support class that meets once a day for students who need additional English language instruction alongside their academic course work in the mainstream program.

The mainstream program is for students with TOEFL scores of 75 or higher who participate fully in the mainstream academic program.

FACULTY AND ADVISERS

Marvelwood currently employs 35 full-time teachers and 6 part-time faculty members. Of these, 20 are men and 21 are women. Sixteen hold master's degrees and 2 hold Ph.D.'s.

The current Head of School, Scott E. Pottbecker, was appointed Marvelwood's fifth Headmaster in 2005. Previously, he had been the Assistant Head of School and Chief Financial Officer at Forman School in Litchfield, Connecticut. Mr. Pottbecker has held administrative and teaching roles in boarding schools for more than fifteen years. He is a graduate of the University of Connecticut and holds a master's degree in public administration from the University of Hartford. Mr. Pottbecker and his wife, Amy, have 4 children. The family resides in the Headmaster's house on the Marvelwood campus.

Marvelwood's faculty members have had anywhere from one to twenty-five years of experience in private school education. All faculty members and most administrators assume duties in all School areas, including teaching, dorm supervision, coaching, and advising. Every faculty member advises 4 to 5 students, oversees their progress, and communicates with their parents.

COLLEGE ADMISSION COUNSELING

Preparation for college placement begins in the junior year. This extensive and prescriptive process emphasizes individual attention for students and their families. Attention is given to helping students fine-tune their writing skills, thus enabling them to write their best college essay. The comprehensive Naviance program is used by students, parents, and college counselors to facilitate and track the application process.

The Director of College Counseling and his assistant meet with students to guide them in selecting colleges that answer their personal needs and interests. Future career choices are also explored. Students and parents fill out questionnaires that assist counselors in identifying appropriate colleges. Students have the opportunity to hear about colleges from representatives who visit during the year. During the summer before the senior year, students and parents are encouraged to visit those colleges in which they are interested.

SAT score averages for the class of 2008 were 458 reading, 451 math, and 440 writing. Of the 41 students in the class of 2008, 38 matriculated in colleges and universities. Colleges and universities recently attended include Boston University, Hobart and William Smith, Massachusetts Amherst, NYU, Ohio State, Penn State, Purdue, Rutgers, SUNY at Albany, Syracuse, Ursinus, and Wheaton.

STUDENT BODY AND CONDUCT

Of the 165 students at Marvelwood, 105 are boarding boys, 49 are boarding girls, 9 are day boys, and 2 are day girls. There are 29 freshmen, 42 sophomores, 47 juniors, and 47 seniors. Students come from fourteen states and twelve countries.

Students at Marvelwood are expected to observe basic community principles. Core values of honesty, responsibility, service to others, and respect for oneself and one's community are the foundations that guide all aspects of school life.

Disciplinary offenses are handled by a faculty Disciplinary Committee. A recommendation is then passed on to the Headmaster, who makes the final decision. Violation of major School rules or consistent disregard for general community principles can lead to suspension or expulsion. Any recommendation of expulsion is reviewed by the Headmaster.

A Student Council is elected by the student body and provides input regarding School life. Its members also help organize special events.

ACADEMIC FACILITIES

Classes are held in the main schoolhouse in fifteen classrooms, including two up-to-date science labs. The Bodkin Library, with a total collection size of 9,000 volumes, offers titles in classic and current fiction as well as a focus on nonfiction titles to support the curriculum. Periodicals include more than fifty magazines, weekly local newspapers, and a daily subscription to the *New York Times.* Resources available include ten computers for class or individual use, a media center with smart board and DVD capability, and an archive center established in 2007. The library is in the process of converting to a digital card catalog, using open-source software. When complete, the collection may be searched from any location through a link on the School's Web site.

The original gymnasium building houses the performing arts department, including a large stage, classrooms, practice space for drama productions, and fully equipped music rooms for instruction and practice.

BOARDING AND GENERAL FACILITIES

Marvelwood's comfortable dormitories are supervised by faculty members who have apartments in each of the buildings. Each dormitory houses students from all grade levels. With only a few exceptions, roommates are of the same grade level or age. During School vacations, the School does not provide dormitory facilities. Students who cannot go home may arrange to spend time with another student who lives in the area.

ATHLETICS

Marvelwood believes that participation in athletics is an important part of a student's growth. Students participate in sports in lieu of gym classes. One full year's credit in sports is required of students during each year of their enrollment at Marvelwood. Marvelwood competes with other schools at the varsity and junior varsity levels. In the fall, teams are fielded in cross-country (coed), soccer (boys' and girls'), and volleyball (girls'); in the winter, in basketball (boys' and girls'), downhill skiing (coed), and wrestling (boys'); and in the spring, in lacrosse (boys' and girls'), softball (girls'), tennis (boys' and girls'), golf (coed), and Ultimate Frisbee (coed).

In addition to the competitive team and individual sports, there are also recreational activities, such as the Wilderness Ways program, featuring hiking and wilderness skills. A professionally constructed low-ropes course on campus is incorporated into many outdoor training and team-building activities. Other noncompetitive offerings include mountain biking and rock climbing in the fall, yoga and skiing and snowboarding at nearby Mohawk Mountain in the winter, and white-water canoeing on local rivers and lakes in the spring.

The School has five playing fields, eight tennis courts, and two gymnasiums. The Ann D. Scott Athletic Center opened in October 2007 and features a full-size regulation basketball court, two practice courts, a wrestling room, dance studio, multipurpose room, locker rooms, and a fully equipped fitness and weight room.

EXTRACURRICULAR OPPORTUNITIES

Marvelwood believes that interest and participation in extracurricular activities are important parts of every student's life. Such activities include yearbook, drama, chorus, a cappella, band, instrumental ensembles, private music lessons, photography, chess, Cultural and Social Awareness Club, student government, admissions tour guide, driver's education, literary magazine, creative writing, and peer mediation. Each year, the Marvelwood Players present two theatrical productions: a play in the fall and a musical, featuring a live pit orchestra, in the spring.

A special part of students' education at Marvelwood is participation in the School's Community Service Program. Each Wednesday, students are transported off campus to volunteer at a wide variety of placements, including day-care centers, elementary schools, nursing homes, soup kitchens, nature conservancies, animal shelters, local farms, and Habitat for Humanity. On-campus placements include the school newspaper, *Mouth of the Mountain;* an Amnesty International group; a puppet troupe that performs at area elementary schools; and an extensive recycling program. Marvelwood's program receives strong local recognition and was recently given an award by the governor of Connecticut. Students may also volunteer to participate in overnight trips to New York City to work with the Youth Service Opportunities Project (YSOP) organization.

DAILY LIFE

The academic program runs from September through June, with vacations for Thanksgiving, Christmas, and spring break in March as well as long weekend breaks in the fall and winter. The school day begins at 7:45 a.m. with breakfast, and classes start at 8:30. At 10 a.m. there is a daily meeting period for an all-school meeting twice a week and adviser and class meetings once a week each. Classes are over at 2:40, and sports practice begins at 3 p.m. Dinner is at 6 p.m., and evening study hall, supervised by faculty members, runs from 7:30 to 9:15. Bedtime lights-out is staggered by grade. Community Service takes place on Wednesday mornings. On Wednesday afternoons, there are games or other sports activities. On Saturdays, three classes are held in the morning, followed by athletics in the afternoon. Sunday is a more relaxed day during which students attend a 10:30 brunch, followed by a free afternoon. The Sunday evening schedule is similar to that on the weekdays, with dinner followed by a dorm clean-up and study hall.

WEEKEND LIFE

Marvelwood's rural campus provides opportunities for numerous outdoor activities on weekends. These include camping trips, hikes, bicycling trips, fishing, ice skating, snowboarding, and Nordic and alpine skiing. On Saturday evenings, students have a choice of movies, off-campus trips, plays, concerts, or other special events. Weekend activities are supervised by faculty members. Occasionally, students attend dances at other schools. Skiing at nearby Mohawk Mountain also provides an opportunity for social interaction with students from other schools. Day students are welcome to participate in weekend activities and may stay overnight at the School with appropriate permission. Attendance at religious services is not required, but transportation to services is available for those who wish to attend.

SUMMER PROGRAMS

The Marvelwood Summer Program features classes for credit or enrichment, SAT and TOEFL preparation, ELL, and a choice of two intense extracurricular seminars: Leadership or Theater. The four-week Marvelwood Summer Program recognizes that each student walks a unique path toward success, one that is not always easily recognized in traditional teaching environments. Small classes, an experienced faculty, and a dedication to each student's individual success distinguish Marvelwood's Summer Program and provide a solid foundation for academic success. The Leadership Seminar features rock climbing, white-water canoeing and kayaking, hiking, and peer mediation. In the Drama Seminar, participants study all aspects of theater production, culminating in a performance for the public. Cultural immersion and homestay opportunities are available for international students following the Summer Program.

COSTS AND FINANCIAL AID

In 2008–09, the cost of tuition, room, and board was $41,500. Tuition insurance was $2780. Day student tuition was $25,250, with a tuition insurance cost of $1692. The cost of the daily one-on-one Strategies or Math Tutorial Programs is $7300 per year, billed separately by trimester as needed. A tuition deposit of $3000 is due within thirty days of acceptance. The first major payment is due on July 1, with the remainder due on December 1.

Need-based financial aid is available. Parents must file a Parents' Financial Statement with the School and Student Service for Financial Aid in Princeton, New Jersey. Forms are available through the Admissions Office or online at https://sss.ets.org/. Approximately 24 percent of Marvelwood's students receive financial aid. In 2008–09, more than $500,000 was awarded.

ADMISSIONS INFORMATION

To be considered for admission, applicants must file an application, visit the campus for an interview, provide a transcript from their current school, and submit three letters of recommendation. SSAT scores or results from other standardized tests may be submitted but are not required. Prior to scheduling a campus visit, submission of a competed application is requested.

Marvelwood seeks students interested in a superior education, personal growth, and excellence through an educational program attuned to each student's particular strengths and weaknesses. Students enter Marvelwood in the ninth, tenth, or eleventh grade. Occasionally, a student may enter as a senior or postgraduate student.

APPLICATION TIMETABLE

Inquiries are welcome Monday through Friday throughout the year. Campus tours and interviews are conducted when school is in session and can be arranged by calling the Admissions Office. Interviews may be scheduled for Monday, Tuesday, Thursday, or Friday. Files must be complete by February 1, including a nonrefundable fee of $50 ($100 for international applicants), and students are notified of the Admissions Committee's decision by early March. Following that deadline, the School operates on a rolling admission basis, as space provides.

ADMISSIONS CORRESPONDENCE

Katherine Almquist
The Marvelwood School
P.O. Box 3001
Kent, Connecticut 06757-3001

Phone: 860-927-0047
Fax: 860-927-0021
E-mail: admissions@marvelwood.org
Web site: http://www.marvelwood.org

MARYMOUNT SCHOOL

New York, New York

Type: Girls' independent college-preparatory Catholic day school
Grades: N–12: Lower School, Nursery–3; Middle School, 4–7; Upper School, 8–12
Enrollment: School total: 565; Upper School: 225
Head of School: Concepcion R. Alvar

THE SCHOOL

Marymount School is an independent Catholic day school that educates girls in a tradition of academic excellence and moral values. The School promotes in each student a respect for her own unique abilities and provides a foundation for exploring and acting on questions of integrity and ethical decision making. Founded by Mother Joseph Butler in 1926 as part of a worldwide network of schools directed by the Religious of the Sacred Heart of Mary, Marymount remains faithful to its mission "to educate young women who question, risk, and grow; young women who care, serve, and lead; young women prepared to challenge, shape, and change the world." Committed to its Catholic heritage, the School welcomes and values the religious diversity of its student body and seeks to give all students a deeper understanding of the role of the spiritual in life. The School also has an active social service program and integrates social justice and human rights into the curriculum.

Marymount occupies three adjoining landmark Beaux Arts mansions, located on Fifth Avenue's historic Museum Mile, and a fourth mansion at 2 East 82nd Street. The Metropolitan Museum of Art and Central Park, both located directly across the street from the School, provide resources that are integral to the School's academic and extracurricular programs. As part of the humanities curriculum, students visit the museum regularly, as often as twice a week in the Upper School. Central Park is used for science and physical education classes as well as extracurricular activities. Other city sites, such as the United Nations, the Tenement Museum, Ellis Island, the New York Zoological Society, the American Museum of Natural History, the Rose Planetarium, the Frick and Guggenheim Museums, and El Museo Del Barrio are also frequent extensions of the classroom.

Since 1969, the School has been independently incorporated under the direction of a 30-member Board of Trustees made up of parents, alumnae, educators, and members of the founding order. The School benefits from a strong Parents' Association; an active Alumnae Association; the involvement of parents, alumnae, and student volunteers; and a successful Annual Giving Program.

Marymount is chartered by the New York State Board of Regents and accredited by the New York State Association of Independent Schools. The School holds membership in the National Association of Independent Schools (NAIS), the New York State Association of Independent Schools, the Independent Schools Admissions Association of Greater New York, the National Catholic Education Association, the National Coalition of Girls' Schools (NCGS), and the Educational Records Bureau.

ACADEMIC PROGRAMS

Emphasizing classic disciplines and scientific inquiry, the challenging college-preparatory curriculum provides students with the skills necessary to succeed in competitive colleges and in life beyond the classroom. Through its rigorous academic program and its focus on the education of young women, Marymount seeks to instill in its students self-confidence, leadership ability, a risk-taking spirit, and a love of learning.

Technology is part of the DNA of the School. The commitment to twenty-first century learning and the STEM initiative (science, technology, engineering, and mathematics for girls) is reflected in its curriculum, which fully integrates information and communication technologies into all subject areas. Students have access to wired and wireless desktop and laptop computers throughout the School. Upper School students and staff members have individual e-mail accounts and use computers to carry out research, create presentations, publish work, communicate, and demonstrate ideas and concepts. All students learn a wide variety of authoring tools to create and publish digital media, including academic Web sites, podcasts, digital video, images, and interactive simulations. Via e-mail, videoconferencing, blogging, and the Marymount Web site, students collaborate on projects with other Marymount Schools and with students and researchers from around the globe.

Staying at the forefront of educational technology extends beyond the actual investment in laptops, smartboards, software, and networks, however. To realize gains and to maintain its cutting-edge reputation for excellence by NAIS and NCGS, the School offers two weeks of technology seminars every summer for the faculty and other NAIS-school faculty members. In addition, a faculty fellowship program within Marymount supports the development of award-winning curriculum/technology integration projects.

High school graduation requirements include satisfactory completion of 4 years of English, 3 years of history, 3 years of math, 3 years of laboratory science, 3 years of one foreign language, 4 years of religious studies, 4 years of physical education, 1 year of studio art, 1 year of formal computer/technology instruction (although technology is integrated throughout the curriculum), 6 semesters of health/guidance, and 1 semester of speech. These requirements are structured to provide a broad, solid base of knowledge while sharpening problem-solving and research skills and promoting critical and creative thinking.

The School offers strong honors and Advanced Placement programs. Electives include AP art history, economics, classical Greek, music history, history of theater, two AP studio art courses, studies in Africa, studies in South America, Middle Eastern studies, and modern-China studies. Hybrid online courses offered include atmospheric science, multimedia applications, and programming languages. In senior English, students choose from seminars that cover topics from Shakespeare's history plays to modern Irish literature to the literature of African American and Asian American women writers. Most students elect to take a fourth year of math, which includes AP calculus and AP statistics, and a fourth year of science, which includes AP biology, AP chemistry, AP physics C, and advanced physics with calculus applications. The science program connects with and utilizes the research of numerous institutions, including the New York Academy of Sciences and Princeton University.

A leader in science and technological education, Marymount is also committed to the study of humanities. All Class IX students take part in the Integrated Humanities Program, an interdisciplinary curriculum that focuses on history, literature, art history, the major world religions, and art in the study of ancient world civilizations. Classes are held at the Metropolitan Museum of Art at least once a week. The program includes a World Civilizations Festival and a collaborative project involving creation of a virtual museum on the Web site.

The Visual Arts Department offers studio art, sculpture, AP 2-D design, and AP drawing. The performing arts program includes the school chorus, a chamber choir, music history courses, the history of theater, and speech and interpretive readings.

The Religious Studies Program includes Hebrew scriptures, the New Testament, ethics, social justice, the social encyclicals of the Catholic Church, comparative religions, and world issues. With a focus on moral and ethical decision making, students analyze social systemic issues and immerse themselves in the community through numerous service projects. The Catholic-Jewish Initiative provides students with a deeper understanding of the Judeo-Christian tradition. This program includes Holocaust studies and a trip to the National Holocaust Museum in Washington, D.C.

During the last four weeks of the academic year, seniors participate in an off-campus internship to gain significant exposure to a specific career of interest. Students have interned at hospitals, research laboratories, law firms, financial organizations, theaters, schools, nonprofit organizations, and corporations. They also attend a career day, with visiting alumnae as guest speakers. A financial literacy curriculum beginning in kindergarten culminates in a Senior Finance Day, which helps prepare them for the financial challenges of college and life.

As members of a worldwide network of schools, students may opt to spend the second semester of their sophomore year at a Marymount International School in London or Rome. In addition, students have participated in exchanges with the Santa Fe Indian School in New Mexico and Chiba Higashi School in Japan, as well as American Field Service summer immersion programs around the globe. Annual faculty-led spring and summer trips extend the curriculum. Recent trips that link to academic subjects have included the Galapagos Islands, the theater and literature of London and Strafford-upon-Avon, and the cities, countryside, language, and culture of Italy, France, and Spain. Recent School-sponsored service trips have focused on work with disabled orphans in Jamaica (2007) and building homes in New Orleans (2008). Marymount Singers enjoys an annual concert tour in Europe every spring. They have performed in churches and concert halls in Rome, Florence, Bologna, Paris, Avignon, Beziers, Prague, and Vienna.

Upper School students are formally evaluated four times a year, using an A–F grading system. The evaluation process includes written reports and parent/student/teacher conferences.

The Middle School curriculum welcomes the diverse interests of young adolescents and is structured to channel their energy and natural love of learning. The integrated core curriculum gradually increases in the degree of departmentalization at each grade level, and challenging learning activities and flexible groupings in main subject areas ensure that the students achieve their full potential. Foreign language study begins in Class IV, when students choose a four-year sequence of either French or Spanish. In addition, they study Latin in Classes VI and VII. The Middle School years culminate in a study tour to France and Spain that increases the students' knowledge of language, culture, architecture, and history. A Class VII robotics class provides students with the opportunity to learn basic and advanced programming, problem solving, and analytic skills in both computer science and physical science. Regular visits to the Metropolitan Museum of Art and laptop computers, which are accessible to every student, are effectively integrated and enhance all aspects of the curriculum.

Twice weekly speech classes prepare the girls for drama presentations reflective of their social studies and literature curriculum: *Revolutionary Voices, Greek Mythology, Canterbury Tales,* and a performance of scenes from a Shakespearean play. Uptown Broadway, an extracurricular option offered in the fall and spring, allows the students to participate in a full-scale musical. The entire Middle School celebrates music and voice at their annual spring concert.

The Lower School provides child-centered, creative learning within a challenging, structured environment. The Lower School curriculum focuses on the acquisition of foundational skills, often through an interdisciplinary approach. Programs engage students in the exciting process of learning about themselves, their surroundings, and the larger world. A hands-on science program, an emphasis on technology integration, a study of robotics in Class III, a popular Lower School chorus, and an extensive afterschool program are some highlights of the Lower School.

FACULTY AND ADVISERS

There are 90 full-time and 8 part-time faculty members, allowing for a 6:1 student-teacher ratio. Seventy-one percent of the faculty members hold master's degrees, and 6 percent hold doctoral degrees. In Nursery through Class I, each class has a head teacher and at least one assistant teacher. Classes II and III have two co-head teachers in each classroom. Curriculum leaders in both math and language arts ensure that all students are challenged and/or supported in these subjects. In the Middle School, students make the transition from having homeroom teachers to having advisers. In Classes IV and V, each class has two homeroom teachers. In Classes V–XII, each student has a homeroom teacher and an adviser, usually one of her teachers, who follows her academic progress and provides guidance and support. Technology integrators, museum integrators, a school nurse, learning resource specialists, a writer-in-residence, a school counselor, and a school psychologist work with students throughout the School.

Concepcion Alvar was appointed Headmistress in 2004 after thirteen years as the Director of Admissions and three years as a head teacher. She also served as the Director and Supervisor of Marymount Summer for sixteen years. Mrs. Alvar holds a B.S. from Maryknoll College (Philippines) and an M.A. from Columbia University, Teachers College.

COLLEGE ADMISSION COUNSELING

Under the guidance of the Director of College Counseling, the formal college counseling program begins during the junior year. In the second semester, two College Nights are held for students and parents. Individual counseling throughout the semester directs each student to those colleges that best match her achievements and aspirations. Students participate in weekly sessions to learn about general requirements for college admission, the application process, and the SAT testing process. During the fall of their senior year, students continue the weekly sessions, focusing on essay writing, admissions interviews, and financial aid applications.

Graduates from recent classes are attending the following colleges and universities: Amherst, Barnard, Boston College, Boston University, Bowdoin, Brown, Columbia, Connecticut, Cornell, Dartmouth, Davidson, Duke, Fairfield, Fordham, George Washington, Georgetown, Harvard, Holy Cross, Kenyon, Middlebury, NYU, Oberlin, Princeton, Skidmore, Smith, Trinity, Tufts, Vanderbilt, Villanova, Wake Forest, Wellesley, Wesleyan, Wheaton, Williams, Yale, and the Universities of Notre Dame, Pennsylvania, and St. Andrew's, Scotland.

STUDENT BODY AND CONDUCT

Marymount's enrollment is 565 students in Nursery through Class XII, with 225 girls in the Upper School. Most students reside in New York City; however, Upper School students also commute from Long Island, Staten Island, New Jersey, and Westchester. Students wear uniforms, except on special days; participate in athletic and extracurricular activities; and attend weekly chapel services and annual class retreats.

Marymount fosters active participation by the students in their own education and in the life of the School community. Students seek out leadership and volunteer opportunities, serving as advocates for one another through peer assistance, peer mentoring, Retreat Team, and Big Sister/Little Sister programs within the School. Student government and campus ministry provide social and service opportunities that enable students to broaden their perspectives, sharpen public-speaking skills, and form lasting friendships.

Teachers and administrators encourage each student to respect herself and others and to be responsible members of the community. While there are relatively few rules, those that exist are consistently enforced to promote freedom and growth for the individual and the entire School community.

ACADEMIC FACILITIES

The Beaux Arts mansions provide spacious rooms for the Nursery–Class XII educational program. Facilities include wired and wireless smart classrooms, a networked library complex, five state-of-the-art science laboratories, three computer centers, a math laboratory, an art suite, a chapel, a language lab, a music lab, an auditorium, a courtyard playground, a gymnasium, and the Middle School multipurpose Commons.

ATHLETICS

The athletic program promotes good health, physical fitness, coordination, skill development, confidence, and a spirit of competition and collaboration through its physical education classes, the electives program for Classes X–XII, and individual and team sports.

Marymount provides a full schedule for varsity and junior varsity sports, as well as Middle School teams at the V/VI and VII–VIII class levels. In the Middle School, students stay two days per week for an afterschool sports program. The junior varsity and varsity teams compete within the Athletic Association of Independent Schools League (AAIS) in badminton, basketball, cross-country, fencing, field hockey, lacrosse, soccer, softball, swimming, tennis, track and field, winter track, and volleyball. In the 2005–06 school year, junior varsity soccer, varsity basketball, and varsity softball teams all won or shared AAIS titles.

In addition to its gymnasium, Marymount uses the facilities at the Harlem Armory, Riverbank State Park, and Roberto Clemente State Park. Central Park, Randalls Island, and Van Cortland Park are preferred sites for field sports. Tennisport, Riverbank State Park, and Flushing Meadows are competitive sites for the tennis and swim teams. Additional athletic facilities are used throughout New York City.

EXTRACURRICULAR OPPORTUNITIES

A wide range of clubs and activities complement the academic program and provide students with the opportunity to contribute to the School community, pursue their individual interests, and develop communication, cooperation, and leadership skills. Activities offered include Amnesty International, art club, campus ministry, chamber choir, cultural awareness, digital photography, drama, environmental awareness, film club, finance club, forensics team, Mathletes, Marymount Singers, Mock Trial (2006 state champions), Model United Nations, National Honor Society, philosophy club, Science Bowl, Science Olympiad, set design/tech crew, student government, the New York Medical College Club, and women's issues. Student publications include a yearbook (*Marifia*), a newspaper (*Joritan*), and an award-winning literary/arts journal (*Muse*). A wide range of Friday noontime clubs in the Middle School includes Student Council, Italian, Latin, French, altar servers, handbells, environmental science, art, drama, handwork, and the literary magazine, *Chez Nous.*

Each year, the Upper School presents two dramatic productions, including a musical; produces either a Bias Awareness Day or Harambee Night during Black History Month; sponsors an Art Festival Week; and participates in numerous community service projects, local and national competitions, and conferences with other schools.

The Vincent A. Lisanti Speakers Series brings people of stature and high achievement to the School, including former poet laureate Billy Collins, athlete Tegla Laroupe, author Jhumpa Lahiri, bioethicist Ronald Green, nanotechnologist Dr. Susan Arney, African American painter Philomena Williamson, feminist Gloria Steinem, and Sr. Helen Prejean, author of *Dead Man Walking.*

Students have the opportunity to interact with boys from neighboring schools through exchange days, drama productions, community service projects, coffee houses, walkathons, and other student-run social activities.

DAILY LIFE

Upper School classes are held from 8:20 a.m. to 3:30 p.m. on Monday, Tuesday, and Thursday. To accommodate electives, extracurricular activities, and team sports, classes end at 2:45 p.m. on Wednesdays and Fridays. Class periods are each 45 minutes in length and typically meet nine out of ten days in a two-week cycle, with a double period each week in each course. Students meet daily with their advisory group, gather with the entire Upper School every Friday for assembly, and frequently meet individually with their classroom teachers. After classes have ended, most students remain for sports, extracurricular activities, and/or independent study.

COSTS AND FINANCIAL AID

The average tuition for the 2008–09 academic year is $31,668 for Classes K–XII. In February, parents are required to make a deposit of $5000, which is credited toward the November tuition. The Key Education Resources Payment Plan is available.

More than $1.8 million in financial aid was awarded in 2007–08 to students of outstanding academic promise after need was established by School and Student Services. Twenty percent of Marymount students receive financial aid.

ADMISSIONS INFORMATION

As a college-preparatory school, Marymount aims to enroll young women of academic promise and sound character who are seeking a challenging educational environment and multiple opportunities for learning outside the classroom. Educational Records Bureau tests, school records, and interviews are used in selecting students.

The School admits students of any race, color, or national or ethnic origin to all the rights, privileges, programs, and activities generally accorded or made available to students at the School and does not discriminate on these bases in the administration of its educational policies, admissions policies, scholarship or loan programs, or athletic or other School-administered programs.

APPLICATION TIMETABLE

Interested students are encouraged to contact the Admissions Office as early as possible in the fall for admission the following year. The application deadline is November 30, but may be changed at the discretion of the Director of Admissions. Notification of admissions decisions is sent during February and March, according to the dates established by the Independent School Admissions Association of Greater New York.

ADMISSIONS CORRESPONDENCE

Lillian Issa
Director of Admissions
Marymount School
1026 Fifth Avenue
New York, New York 10028

Phone: 212-744-4486
Fax: 212-744-0163 (general)
212-744-0716 (admissions)
E-mail: Admissions@marymount.k12.ny.us
Web site: http://www.marymount.k12.ny.us

MASSANUTTEN MILITARY ACADEMY

Woodstock, Virginia

Type: Coeducational boarding college-preparatory school with an Army JROTC program
Grades: 7–12, postgraduate year
Enrollment: School total: 216; Upper School: 182; Middle School: 34
Head of School: Col. Roy F. Zinser, President

THE SCHOOL

Massanutten Military Academy's (MMA) mission is to provide every cadet with an academic, character, leadership, and physical education of excellence, which ensures his or her development and readiness for college, leadership, and citizenship. The mission is established on the founding motto of the Academy, "Non nobis solum" ("Not for ourselves alone"), and based on the principles of Courage, Purity, and Industry.

Massanutten's cadets are young men and women who desire advanced preparation for college within a structured, military environment. Established in 1899, the Academy adopted a military program in 1917. Today, the military structure plays a crucial role in the education of every cadet by creating a stable environment that is conducive to learning.

Situated on 40 acres in the small 250-year-old town of Woodstock, Virginia, in the heart of the Shenandoah Valley, the Academy is only 90 minutes from downtown Washington, D.C., and 2 hours from Baltimore, Maryland.

Massanutten's maximum enrollment is 224 cadets, 160 male and 64 female, enrolled in grades 7–12 and one year of postgraduate study. Massanutten provides both boarding and day cadet programs. The corps of cadets is diverse, with cadets from many countries and more than twenty states. This diversity is one of Massanutten's greatest strengths.

Massanutten Military Academy is accredited by the Southern Association of Colleges and Schools (SACS) and the Virginia Association of Independent Schools (VAIS). MMA is a member of the National Honor Society, the Association of Military Colleges and Schools of the United States (AMCSUS), and The Association of Boarding Schools (TABS).

ACADEMIC PROGRAMS

At Massanutten, the small average class size of 9 students per class enables faculty members and cadets to develop close positive relationships that foster greater success in the classroom. A daily tutorial period offers cadets the opportunity to return to their teachers for additional instruction. A mandatory, supervised evening study period is held each class night. Individual tutoring is available through a separate contract. The Academy library and computer labs are open during the afternoon and evening study periods and during the weekends for research or computer use. Each cadet is assigned a faculty mentor team that keeps parents informed of progress throughout the year by telephone, e-mail, and mail.

Massanutten offers three diploma options. The advanced college-preparatory diploma may include, in addition to the Academy's transcript, a transcript of courses taken through Shenandoah University. The college-preparatory diploma is the standard Academy diploma, which requires the cadet to earn the necessary course credits in preparation for attendance at a major college or university. The international diploma is for young men and women from other countries.

The Middle School program concentrates on developing academic skills and knowledge necessary for the cadet's success in high school. In addition to the four core subjects, cadets are required to take art, health, physical education, and critical reading. Advanced eighth graders may take high school–level courses, such as a foreign language or algebra I.

The Commandant's Department has the primary responsibility for the character, discipline, and leadership education of the Corps of Cadets and cadet life outside of the classroom. The Commandant of Cadets directs 15 dorm supervisors called CDOs (Cadet Development Officers) as well as 3 deputy commandants, the quartermaster, the tailor, a barber, the nurses, and dining hall personnel.

The Army Junior ROTC Program at Massanutten consistently has earned the Army's highest designation of Honor Unit with Distinction, which means it is one of the best programs in the nation. The mission of the JROTC program is to motivate each cadet to be a better citizen. JROTC's objectives include having each cadet develop an appreciation of the ethical values and principles that underlie good citizenship, including integrity, acceptance of responsibility, and a respect for constituted authority. JROTC cadets are under no obligation to enter the military. The completion of one or more years of JROTC may provide cadets with college-level ROTC credit. The fact that MMA earned the Honor Unit with Distinction designation allows the Academy to nominate selected, qualified cadets to the service academies. In addition, the JROTC Department assists cadets in competing for ROTC scholarships to major universities.

Grades are issued based on the percentage of points available versus points earned: A+=98–100, A=93–97, A-=90–92, B+=87–89, B=83–86, B-=80–82, C+=77–79, C=73–76, C-=70–72, D=65–69. A portion of the grade is earned from each of class participation (10 percent), homework (20 percent), quizzes (20 percent), tests (20 percent), and two semester exams (15 percent each).

Along with the superb college preparatory academic program, the Academy provides every cadet with character and leadership education and development. Each Sunday morning cadets are required to attend a religious service in Woodstock or an on-campus religious service or a nonreligious character development class. Since many religious denominations are represented in the town of Woodstock, cadets may travel the few blocks to the church of their choice or remain on campus for a nondenominational service.

FACULTY AND ADVISERS

Massanutten's faculty consists of 29 full-time and 6 part-time teachers. Of this number, almost 40 percent hold bachelor's degrees and 30 percent are working to complete master's degrees. In addition, there are 3 full-time JROTC Army Instructors. Faculty members are hired based on their education, experience, passion, and ability to teach their assigned subjects. Faculty members take advantage of many continuing education programs, including those offered by George Mason, James Madison, and Shenandoah Universities.

Colonel Roy F. Zinser, President, received his bachelor's degree in business administration from The Citadel and holds master's degrees in business administration, in strategic policy, and in international relations. He served for more than twenty-nine years as an active-duty Army leader. He has been a leader in military secondary education for eleven years and is committed to the education and success of young people.

COLLEGE ADMISSION COUNSELING

Cadets begin receiving guidance in college selection in their junior year. The process continues until the cadets have chosen and been accepted at the college they plan to attend. The task of guiding students toward college placement is overseen by the Academic Dean. Cadets take the PSAT once during their junior year in preparation for the SAT. Cadets take the SAT once in their junior year and at least twice during their senior year. For the last five years, 100 percent of MMA's graduates were accepted to colleges or universities, including Case Western Reserve, The Citadel, George Washington, James Madison, Mary Baldwin, the United States Air Force Academy, the United States Military Academy, the United States Naval Academy, Virginia Commonwealth, Virginia Military Institute, Virginia Tech, and the University of Pennsylvania.

STUDENT BODY AND CONDUCT

Massanutten's maximum enrollment is 224 cadets. Currently, there are 4 cadets in the seventh grade, 18 in the eighth grade, 35 in the ninth grade, 43 in the tenth grade, 44 in the eleventh grade, 43 in the twelfth grade, and 15 postgraduates.

About 10 percent of the cadets are international students and represent seven other countries. The remaining cadets represent more than twenty states and every region of the United States.

The *Cadet Handbook* provides each cadet with the guidelines for life at the Academy, including each cadet's duties and responsibilities and the Academy's rules and regulations. Cadets are required to adhere to the strict guidelines of behavior established in the *Cadet Handbook*. The handbook also outlines the Cadet Honor Code, which states, "A cadet will not lie, cheat or steal nor tolerate those who do."

The corps of cadets is organized into a battalion with six companies. Cadets who lead the corps have earned rank by demonstrating leadership potential, academic success, strong character, and athletic or extracurricular performance.

ACADEMIC FACILITIES

The academic facilities include twenty-two classrooms, three science laboratories, a band room, and an art studio. All of the classrooms were renovated in 2005 and 2006 and are configured to hold only twelve to fifteen desks. In addition, there are five computer labs used to teach keyboarding and computer courses, support the teaching of foreign languages and other courses, produce the school yearbook, and teach the SAT/PSAT/ACT preparatory courses. The computer labs are open with adult supervision at designated times for cadets to check e-mail or complete academic research assignments. Every teacher has a laptop computer with wireless capabilities as well as digital projectors, interactive smart white boards, and student feedback devices to enrich the educational process. The Academy implements all available technology to enhance teaching and learning.

Lantz Hall contains a 300-seat auditorium and laboratory classrooms for biology, chemistry, and physics.

BOARDING AND GENERAL FACILITIES

Male cadets are housed in Benchoff, Harrison, and Lantz Halls. Generally, two cadets of the same age and grade level are assigned to a room. All of the Academy's dorms were renovated in 2005 and 2006 and provide cadets with first-class living conditions. Each dorm is equipped with security cameras, and an adult is awake and on duty whenever there are cadets present.

Female cadets are housed in Rosedrey Warehime Dormitory, which was built in 1988 and is fully air-conditioned. The building can house 64 female cadets in double or single rooms. A woman dormitory supervisor is awake and on duty whenever females are in the dorm. The building is protected by an alarm system as well as security cameras. Warehime Dorm provides the girls with a brand-new laundry room, a kitchen, a specially designed gymnasium, a television lounge, and a computer lab.

The Infirmary was recently renovated and is centrally located. A nurse is on duty between 6 a.m. and 10 p.m. every day and on call during the night. Local physicians are available to provide cadets with needed medical care. Shenandoah Memorial Hospital is located less than a half mile from the Academy, and there are numerous medical specialists in the community.

ATHLETICS

Physical fitness is a vital part of the educational program at Massanutten. Its goals are to teach the cadets character, leadership, good sportsmanship, teamwork, and an appreciation of regular exercise. All cadets are required to play on competitive athletic teams or participate in the Academy's physical development programs throughout the year. Varsity and junior varsity athletics are offered to both male and female cadets in grades 9 to 12. Postgraduates may participate on sports teams but may not compete in conference events. The sports program includes air pistol, air rifle, baseball, basketball, cheerleading, cross-country, drill team, field hockey, football, golf, lacrosse, master fitness, Raiders, rifle, rugby, soccer, softball, swimming, tennis, track and field, volleyball, and wrestling. Many Massanutten athletes have succeeded on college and professional teams. In 2003, Massanutten launched a Postgraduate Basketball Program for men. The team has competed against other college-prep teams as well as junior college and college junior varsity teams and has succeeded in having more than 40 players earn full four-year college scholarships.

The Academy's athletics facilities include a football field and stadium with seating for more than 1,000 spectators, a 440-yard track, a 30,000-square-foot gymnasium, three state-of-the-art weight rooms, an indoor swimming pool, three new tennis courts, a new baseball field, a new softball field, two outdoor basketball courts, an on-campus cross-country course, four practice fields, an indoor rifle range, and an indoor pistol range.

EXTRACURRICULAR OPPORTUNITIES

Cadets may participate in a variety of extracurricular clubs, including Boy Scout Troop 1899, a Civil War reenactment squad, the national and junior national honor societies, the Rotary Interact Club, and a scuba club. These clubs take full advantage of the Shenandoah Valley and nearby state and national parks. The Academy sponsors a very active Rotary Interact community service program.

Cadets who remain on the campus for the weekend are required to attend either an on-campus religious service or nonreligious character-development class each Sunday morning. Since many religious denominations are represented in the town of Woodstock, cadets may travel the few blocks to the church of their choice or remain on campus for a nondenominational service.

DAILY LIFE

Cadets wake up at 6 a.m. Monday through Friday, and breakfast is served from 6:15 to 7:15. Cadets clean their rooms and participate in a room and uniform inspection from 7:15 until 8. Seven 45-minute classes begin at 8. Lunch is served at 12. Classes end at 3, and special academic assistance period is held until 3:45. All students must report to their chosen sport by 4. Dinner is served at 6. Students are required to be in their rooms by 8 for a 90-minute supervised study session. Lights-out is at 10.

WEEKEND LIFE

Cadets in good standing with the Academy may enjoy the many options available to them on the weekends. Downtown Woodstock is only a 5-minute walk from the campus. Cadets can see a movie at the theater, eat at one of the restaurants, go bowling, or shop in one of the stores. Off-campus trips offered to cadets include amusement parks, water parks, paintball, local caverns, music or dramatic productions, professional or college athletic events, and visits to attractions in Washington, D.C., or Baltimore. Seasonal activities include paintball exercises, horseback riding, golfing, camping, fishing, white-water rafting, indoor water parks, and snow skiing.

On-campus activities include the use of the new Cadet Activities Center, the company dorm lounges with TV and video games, and planned events each weekend, such as swimming, outdoor court sports, dances, athletic competitions, and other group activities.

SUMMER PROGRAMS

Massanutten operates one of the nation's only summer programs with full military structure; it occurs in late June and July. The emphasis is on academic success as well as character, leadership, and athletic development. This is supported by the traditional military structure that provides cadets with the opportunity to learn discipline (doing what is right even when no one is watching), responsibility, and respect. In addition, the Academy offers the nation's only summer JROTC program, from which cadets may earn a full high school credit for JROTC in just five weeks. Enrollment in the regular school year is not required for participation in the summer program.

COSTS AND FINANCIAL AID

The 2008–09 new student tuition is $24,664. This includes tuition, seven-day room and board, initial issue and rental of uniforms, laundry, haircuts, technology, and basic infirmary needs. Because of Massanutten's rolling admissions policy, the tuition is prorated based on the date of entry. If applying for admission after September 30, prospective students or parents should inquire about the tuition for the remainder of the year.

Financial aid, tuition credits, and scholarships are available. All awards are assessed and granted on an annual basis.

ADMISSIONS INFORMATION

Students who are accepted to Massanutten must show a determination and willingness to comply with a structured program and must be average to above-average students. The parents or guardians of the cadets must also be willing to comply with and support the Academy's rules and policies.

APPLICATION TIMETABLE

Massanutten Military Academy operates on a rolling admissions, space-available basis. Inquiries are always welcome. All applicants must complete an application form and forward transcripts to the Admissions Office; an academic achievement test may be required. A campus tour and interview are strongly recommended and can be scheduled on weekdays or weekends to accommodate those interested in giving their son or daughter the opportunity to attend MMA.

ADMISSIONS CORRESPONDENCE

Murali Sinnathamby, Director of Admissions
Massanutten Military Academy
614 South Main Street
Woodstock, Virginia 22664

Phone: 540-459-2167 Ext. 262
877-466-6222 (toll-free)
Fax: 540-459-5421
E-mail: admissions@militaryschool.com
Web site: http://www.militaryschool.com

THE MASTERS SCHOOL

Dobbs Ferry, New York

Type: Coeducational boarding (grades 9–12) and day (grades 5–12) college-preparatory school
Grades: 5–12: Middle School, 5–8; Upper School, 9–12
Enrollment: School total: 560; Upper School: 410
Head of School: Dr. Maureen Fonseca

THE SCHOOL

The Masters School, founded in 1877 as a school for girls by Eliza Bailey Masters and her sister, Sallie, became coeducational in 1996. The Masters School offers an all-girls Middle School as well as a parallel all-boys Middle School. The Upper School (grades 9–12) provides a coeducational framework utilizing the Harkness Table method of teaching, which features an oval table in each classroom around which students and teacher actively engage in learning. The Harkness Table approach encourages significant student participation, cooperation, and collaboration.

Dobbs Ferry, a town of some importance during the Revolutionary War, lies on the east bank of the Hudson River in culture-rich Westchester County, 20 miles north of New York City, 100 miles southwest of Hartford, and 200 miles southwest of Boston. The proximity of these and other major cities of the Northeast enables the School to use them as valuable resources in the implementation of its curriculum and activities.

The Masters School is committed to an educational experience that not only prepares students for college but also instills the joy of learning as an end in itself.

The 22 members of the Board of Trustees include graduates, parents of present and former students, and friends of the School. The School's endowment is approximately $27 million. Annual Giving totaled more than $1.45 million for 2006–07; 23 percent of the 4,650 living alumnae participated. Last year's operating expenses were $20.4 million.

The Masters School is accredited by the Middle States Association of Colleges and Schools and is a member of the National Association of Independent Schools, the New York State Association of Independent Schools, and the Federation of American and International Schools.

ACADEMIC PROGRAMS

A Middle School for girls (grades 5–8) and a parallel Middle School for boys (grades 5–8) both offer a curriculum that includes English, math, science, history, Latin, Chinese, art, and music. All students participate in physical education, music, and art programs for the entire year. Everett "Doc" Wilson is Head of the Middle Schools.

All students at The Masters School follow an academic year that is divided into two semesters. Students in grades 9–12 choose some courses that span the year and others that last for only part of the year. The Masters School's basic requirements ensure that every student masters the fundamental skills and concepts in all the major disciplines. Accordingly, courses are required in the following disciplines: English, 4 years; mathematics, 3 years; foreign language, 3 years; science, 2 years; and history, 3 years. Additional requirements include a 1-year minor course in world religions, 3 trimesters of fine arts, 1 trimester of speech, 2 of health, and 4 years of physical education.

The Masters School offers 121 courses, including Advanced Placement in all departments. In addition to the regular course offerings, independent studies are often arranged with individual faculty members by students who wish to pursue a special topic in depth or from an interdisciplinary perspective not offered as part of the standard curriculum. Additional courses may be developed to reflect the current interests of faculty and students.

The visual and performing arts are a featured component of the total curriculum. Arts courses as well as performances and exhibitions abound.

Many subjects are offered on two or three levels, differing in pace, content, and depth of coverage. The average class size is 12 with a student-faculty ratio of 6:1.

CITYterm, a highly selective, interdisciplinary urban studies program, was initiated in 1996. CITYterm is an innovative semester-long program that draws upon the resources of New York City in its academic and experiential curriculum. CITYterm is based on The Masters School campus and accepts applications from its own students and juniors and seniors from the program's national consortium of public and private schools.

The Masters School uses a numerical grading system with 60 as passing and 83 qualifying for honors. The School operates on the semester system. Parents receive grades and comments from teachers and dorm directors at the end of each term and an initial report within the first months of the fall term. Teachers are available for conferences at specified times during the academic day and also by appointment.

FACULTY AND ADVISERS

The Masters School faculty, approximately 57 percent of whose members reside on campus, includes 80 full-time and 10 part-time teachers; they hold four doctoral degrees and fifty-two master's degrees.

Dr. Maureen Fonseca was appointed Head of School in 2000. Dr. Fonseca holds a B.A. from Vassar and a Ph.D. in French literature from Fordham. Prior to her appointment, Dr. Fonseca was the Founding Head of St. Philips Academy in Newark, New Jersey.

Many faculty members take advantage of opportunities given to them for professional advancement through the sabbatical program and the financing of continuing educational programs. All faculty members are involved in advising students, and several also serve as dormitory directors in addition to their classroom duties. Each student has a faculty adviser. The staff includes professional health and guidance personnel.

COLLEGE ADMISSION COUNSELING

In the junior year, each student has individual and group conferences with college counseling personnel. This program is augmented by on-campus interviews with college representatives as well as college-visiting weekends during the senior year. Juniors take the PSAT in the fall. The SAT critical reading and math scores ranged last year from the mid-500s to just under 800. Ninety students took 150 Advanced Placement exams and 83 percent scored 3 or better.

In 2007, 100 students graduated and are now attending such colleges and universities as Columbia, Cornell, George Washington, Harvard, NYU, Oberlin, Wesleyan, Yale, and the Universities of Vermont and Wisconsin.

STUDENT BODY AND CONDUCT

In 2007–08, 40 percent of the Upper School students at The Masters School were boarders, and 60 percent were day students. There are 150 students enrolled in the Middle School in grades 5–8. While the majority of the students reside in the northeastern United States, fifteen states and sixteen countries are represented.

The Masters School is committed to a curriculum that allows students to develop their individual talents and abilities. Four principles are basic to life at the School: integrity, consideration, cooperation, and responsibility. Disciplinary problems are handled by the Dorm Council or, in serious matters, by the Disciplinary Committee, which is composed of an equal number of adults and students. The Community Government is operated by the students and functions according to the School's constitution.

ACADEMIC FACILITIES

Masters Hall, the main academic and administration building, houses all disciplines with the exception of science, physical education, and music. Departments have their own commons, which contain faculty offices as well as reference materials and study areas. The Pittsburgh Library, containing 25,000 volumes, is located on the main floor. A Computer Research Center within the library provides state-of-the-art computer research stations. This networked system incorporates access to library materials and CD-ROM resources. Access to e-mail, the Internet, and community information is also provided on each computer research station. The Claudia Boettcher Theater has a seating capacity of 450 and adjoins the spacious visual arts studio. Strayer Hall houses the physical education and music departments. Morris Hall, the science and technology facility, opened in 2004.

BOARDING AND GENERAL FACILITIES

There are six dorms on campus, some accommodating students in adjoining single rooms and others in double rooms. All dorms contain student lounges, kitchens, faculty apartments, and dorm directors' apartments used for informal gatherings throughout the year. Over the vacation periods, students from other countries often visit the homes of their American classmates or take School-sponsored trips in the United States and abroad.

A student recreation center and private meeting rooms are located in the Cameron Mann Dining Hall. The Health Center has a full-time nurse, a nonresident physician, and immediate access to medical facilities in Westchester County and New York City.

ATHLETICS

The Masters School considers physical education to be an integral part of each student's experience at the School, not only for physical well-being but also for the development of the social and moral values of fair play and sportsmanship. For girls, there are teams in basketball, cross-country, fencing, field hockey, golf, lacrosse, soccer, softball, tennis, Ultimate Frisbee, and volleyball. Sports for boys include baseball, basketball, cross-country, fencing, golf, lacrosse, soccer, tennis, and Ultimate Frisbee.

The School has field hockey, lacrosse, and soccer fields and has added additional fields to accommodate boys' baseball and soccer. Other athletic facilities include nine tennis courts, a large three-bay gymnasium, a fencing room, and an expansive weight-training and conditioning room.

The School has a dance studio and an excellent dance program. Students may elect dance classes for physical education credit or they may audition for various levels of technique-oriented classes. Experienced dancers may audition for Muse Dance Company, which performs throughout the year.

EXTRACURRICULAR OPPORTUNITIES

The Masters School offers a full program of extracurricular activities, with more than thirty organizations from which a student can choose. These include clubs in the performing arts, languages, and mathematics, the literary publications, and athletics. Many of these groups take advantage of the proximity of New York City by attending concerts, dance performances, plays, and various other events.

Special programs bring outstanding lecturers, artists, and performers from many fields to the School. Community service groups include Gold Key and Masters Interested in Sharing and Helping (MISH). A well-organized Community Service Program ensures every student of the opportunity to help others through volunteer work at hospitals, children's homes, schools, and other community organizations.

Different groups within the School traditionally organize special annual events. The Senior Halloween Party, the Sophomore Fair, the International Club's Model UN, and the Glee Club's Candlelight Service are among the high points of the year.

DAILY LIFE

Most school days begin with a student-led all-school gathering at 8 a.m., followed by class periods ranging from 55 to 110 minutes in length. The cocurricular program begins at 3:30. Students can choose from a variety of activities, including athletics, theater, community service, and arts offerings. Evening study hours for boarding students run from 8 to 10 p.m.

The Student Activities Center is open throughout the day for Ping-Pong, pool, Foosball, air hockey, and big-screen TV. The dining hall has extended hours for breakfast, lunch, and dinner and offers a variety of delicious options at each meal.

WEEKEND LIFE

There are many opportunities for on- and off-campus activities during the weekends, with frequent trips to New York City; hiking, canoeing, skiing, and camping outings; and attendance at college or professional games. The Social Activities Committee plans dances, trips, and informal events with several other schools. In addition, there are numerous concerts, plays, and recitals at the School and in the surrounding community. All activities are open to nonresidents, and they can arrange to spend the night in the dorms after a late-night function. There are numerous open weekends during the year, and any student in good social and academic standing may leave campus during those times after having obtained parental permission.

COSTS AND FINANCIAL AID

Charges for 2008–09 are $42,000 for residents (grades 9–12) and $30,250 (which includes lunch) for nonresidents in the Upper School; Middle School nonresidents pay $29,250. Books and supplies are estimated at $650. Art is required of all students, with studio and lab fees ranging from $50 to $325 per year. An initial deposit of $2000 is required with the Enrollment Agreement, and tuition installments are due July 31 and November 30.

Twenty-seven percent of the student body currently receives financial aid based on need. Grants range from $2200 to $42,000. The total financial aid budget was $3.2 million in 2007–08. The Masters School also offers a payment plan to help families spread tuition costs over a period of time.

ADMISSIONS INFORMATION

The Masters School seeks students who not only show academic promise but also possess those characteristics that indicate they will be vital and contributing members of the School community. Students are selected without regard to race, creed, or national origin. An application form (including a short essay), the application fee, an official school transcript covering at least the last two years, two teacher recommendations, and results from the SSAT or ISEE are required of all applicants for grades 5–12. Applicants whose first language is not English must take the TOEFL as well as the SSAT (if available in their country).

APPLICATION TIMETABLE

It is suggested that a formal application with the $50 fee ($100 for international students) be sent as early as possible. Tour and interview dates should be scheduled during school hours while the School is in session. All applicants should plan to visit the campus. Students wishing to be considered in the first round of decisions should submit all admission materials by January 5 for all day applicants and February 5 for all boarding applicants. All other applications are reviewed on a space-available basis. Applications are accepted as long as places are available. Admission Office hours are from 8 a.m. to 4 p.m. during the week.

ADMISSIONS CORRESPONDENCE

Office of Admission
The Masters School
49 Clinton Avenue
Dobbs Ferry, New York 10522
Phone: 914-479-6420
Fax: 914-693-7295
E-mail: admission@themastersschool.com
Web site: http://www.themastersschool.com

THE MCCALLIE SCHOOL

Chattanooga, Tennessee

McCALLIE
HONOR TRUTH DUTY

Type: Boys' boarding (9–12) and day (6–12) college-preparatory school
Grades: 6–12: Middle School, 6–8; Upper School, 9–12
Enrollment: School total: 910; Upper School: 650; Middle School: 260
Head of School: Dr. R. Kirk Walker, Headmaster

THE SCHOOL

McCallie School, located in Chattanooga, Tennessee, was founded in 1905 and today is recognized as a preeminent college-preparatory school. It accepts young men with above-average to exceptional academic abilities, and those students matriculate at some of the best colleges and universities in the nation. In recent years, McCallie has been recognized for its innovative educational programs and its overall standards of excellence. The *Atlanta Journal/Constitution* has called McCallie "one of the leading secondary educational institutions in the United States." McCallie's alumni are leaders in business, politics, art, science, and religion.

McCallie's purpose is to prepare students for entrance into and successful academic work at college. McCallie stresses high academic standards and believes that challenging work best develops useful intellectual ability. Although not affiliated with any religious organization, McCallie supports the spiritual growth of its students and believes that response to the Christian gospel builds a strong moral foundation and a sense of civic and social duty. The School teaches and values personal integrity, intellectual honesty, and a strong work ethic. McCallie promotes the development of leadership skills and the ability to be both a self-confident individual and a dynamic member of a community.

McCallie's campus comprises 110 acres on Missionary Ridge, the site of a major battle during the Civil War, and is located 3 miles east of downtown Chattanooga. A major expansion program over the past few years has extended the campus southward and doubled the number of athletic fields available to students.

McCallie's endowment is $65 million, with an annual operating budget of about $24 million. The Annual Sustaining Fund drive raises about $2.5 million a year, and McCallie recently completed a $125-million capital campaign.

McCallie is an all-boys school that believes that the educational, physical, and social needs of many secondary school students can best be met in a single-sex educational environment. To complement its single-gender commitment, McCallie has a coordinate program with Girls' Preparatory School (GPS) in Chattanooga. McCallie and GPS students participate in a wide variety of afternoon and weekend social activities.

McCallie is accredited by the Southern Association of Colleges and Schools and is a member of the National Association of Independent Schools, the Southern Association of Independent Schools, the Tennessee Association of Independent Schools, the International Coalition of Boys Schools, the Independent Schools Innovation Consortium, the Secondary School Admission Test Board, the Educational Records Bureau, and the Council for the Advancement and Support of Education.

ACADEMIC PROGRAMS

McCallie's academic program centers on a strong core curriculum of math, science, English, foreign language, and history. Students are required to earn course credits distributed as follows: 4 English credits, 3 math credits, 3 science credits, 3 foreign language credits in the same language, 3 history credits, 1 Bible credit, 1 fine arts credit, ¼ public speaking credit, ¼ human development credit, and 1½ to 2 elective credits. Electives are offered in all core disciplines and in music, computer science, economics, writing, and world religions.

Foreign languages offered by McCallie include Spanish, French, Latin, ancient Greek, and Mandarin. German is available through independent study.

McCallie offers eighteen Advanced Placement courses, and nearly half the members of every graduating class receive college placement or credit for AP courses taken at McCallie.

Classes, grouped by age and ability, average 14 students. The academic year consists of two 18-week semesters. Each day consists of a seven-period rotating schedule, with each class meeting four times a week. At the teacher's discretion, students can be required to attend special "backwork" sessions during the school day.

The School offers an extensive academic support system to students. Among its many resources are the Caldwell Writing Center, several computer labs, and the Learning Center, where academic counselors and tutors are available throughout the day to assist students. The Upper and Middle School libraries have subscriptions to 30 online databases and house more than 32,000 volumes.

McCallie's academic offerings include travel and study-abroad programs.

FACULTY AND ADVISERS

McCallie has 104 full-time faculty members, 12 part-time faculty members, 4 full-time academic counselors, and numerous adjunct faculty members and tutors. More than half of the faculty members have advanced degrees in their disciplines. Nearly half of the faculty and staff members live on campus, in either dormitories or nearby houses.

When a student enrolls at McCallie, he is assigned an Academic Adviser, who follows his academic and extracurricular achievement throughout the year and provides feedback to his parents. The Academic Dean, the Dean of Students, the Dean of Residential Life, the guidance counselors, and other administrators also act as advisers. In the dormitories, selected seniors act as Resident Advisers to underclassmen.

McCallie has five endowed chairs on its faculty: the Sen. Howard Baker Jr. Chair of American History, the Sherrill Chair of Bible, the Caldwell Chair of Composition, the Alumni Chair of Mathematics, and the Caldwell Chair of Christian Ethics.

COLLEGE ADMISSION COUNSELING

A principal part of McCallie's mission is to help students identify, gain admission to, and successfully graduate from the college or university that is best for them. A full-time college guidance staff, made up of 3 counselors and an administrative assistant, works with sophomores, juniors, and seniors in a comprehensive guidance program. They hold several individual sessions with each student, at least one session with the student and his parents, and numerous seminars and group sessions.

Students are encouraged to use the college admissions process to explore their specific goals and tastes. The School makes a distinction between gaining admission to the most competitive colleges and gaining admission to the college that is best for the individual student. More than 125 colleges and universities send representatives to McCallie and GPS each year to talk personally to students.

STUDENT BODY AND CONDUCT

Boarding students in the 2007–08 student body came from twenty-five different states and five other countries. The largest student groups are from Georgia, North Carolina, Tennessee, Kentucky, Alabama, and South Carolina. Minority enrollment is approximately 15 percent.

A central part of the School's culture is its Honor Code. All students are held to this code, which proclaims that lying, cheating, and stealing are unacceptable for a McCallie student. The code also stipulates that McCallie students are trusted by their teachers and administrators to tell the truth in all circumstances. The code is structured to encourage a life of honor and integrity and to establish a McCallie student as one whose word is his bond, whose work is always his own, and around whom the property of others is safe. Every student is required to sign his name to the Honor Pledge on all written schoolwork: "On my honor I have neither given nor received aid on this test (or work, examination, etc.)." The Student Senate, a group elected by the students, administers the Honor Code.

ACADEMIC FACILITIES

McCallie's campus consists of a dozen major buildings and several smaller structures. The main academic building is the Robert L. Maclellan Academic Center, which rises five stories on the ridge. This building houses the library, the Burns Learning Center, the Brock Humanities Center, the McIlwaine Mathematics Center, the Chapin Science Center, and the Caldwell Writing Center. Other buildings related to the academic program include the Hunter Arts Center; the McCallie Chapel, where the music department is located; Tate Hall; and Caldwell Hall, the administration building.

All academic buildings and all dormitories have fiber-optic connections with Internet access. Numerous computer centers are located throughout the academic facilities, with students having access to more than 125 PCs. In addition, McCallie has Ethernet ports and a wireless network in strategic locations.

BOARDING AND GENERAL FACILITIES

Boarding students live in five different dormitories located adjacent to the academic quadrangle. Most of the dorm rooms are doubles, and soft-drink machines, washing machines, and student lounges are available in all dorms.

In 1999, McCallie opened McDonald Hall, which houses boys in grades 6–8. In the winter of the 2003–04 school year, the School opened a new dining facility, and in 2007 it opened Pressley Hall, a state-of-the-art residence for boarding students and faculty members.

ATHLETICS

In addition to its academic program, McCallie is committed to the physical development of its students. The School participates in fourteen varsity sports (baseball, basketball, bowling, cross-country, football, golf, lacrosse, rock climbing, rowing, soccer, swimming, tennis, track, and wrestling).

In recent years, the School has expanded its athletic program to make more opportunities available to students who do not wish to compete on the varsity level. An elaborate intramural program offers such opportunities as judo, karate, fencing, and juggling as well as nonvarsity competition in traditional sports.

Over the last few years, McCallie has expanded its athletic offerings. It was the first school in the state, and among the first in the South, to offer interscholastic competition in sports such as crew, lacrosse, and Ultimate Frisbee.

In 1993, McCallie opened the 180,000-square-foot Sports and Activities Center, which has been recognized as one of the finest high school athletic facilities in the nation. The facility contains five performance courts, a 25-yard-by-25-meter indoor pool, a wrestling room, a 9,000-square-foot weight room managed by a full-time strength and conditioning coach, an indoor track, a racquetball court, and a climbing gym. It also contains a large Student Center, complete with a snack bar, pool and Ping-Pong tables, televisions, a movie room, and a video arcade.

Other athletic facilities include the 4,000-seat Spears Stadium with a six-lane track, the outdoor swimming area (known as McCallie Lake), six intramural fields, a tennis center with two indoor and twelve outdoor courts, three baseball fields, and a soccer field.

EXTRACURRICULAR OPPORTUNITIES

Students participate in many musical and drama presentations throughout the year. These include five plays a year, one musical play, and two musical concerts. Several of these are performed in McCallie's new black-box theater. Formal music groups include the Men's Glee Club, Handbells, the Pep Band, the Jazz Ensemble, the McCallie and GPS Select Chorus, the Honors Orchestra, and the Wind Ensemble. McCallie's instrumental department practices in a newly renovated facility with professionally calibrated acoustics. The Hunter Gallery includes the artwork of McCallie students in its periodically updated displays.

An organized effort by the faculty introduces students to cultural activities in the surrounding community. Students also contribute to charitable organizations in the Chattanooga area, where they lend a hand and learn the importance of service. The senior class annually builds a Habitat for Humanity house.

During School breaks and in the summers, students are offered a variety of travel opportunities. Annual trips include skiing in the Rockies, diving in the Caribbean, backpacking in the Appalachians, and travel/study trips to such places as France, Japan, Italy, and Costa Rica.

DAILY LIFE

As an achievement-oriented work ethic school, McCallie believes that a boy matures best when he is challenged and busy. From the time they wake until lights out, students stay busy. For boarding students, the day begins at 7 a.m. with a full breakfast that is served in the cafeteria. Classes begin at 8, and each of the seven periods of the day lasts 50 minutes. If a student has a free period, he can study in the library, the Learning Center, or the Writing Center, or he can relax in the Student Center.

All students attend assembly once a week and chapel three days a week, at midmorning. Chapel services consist of nondenominational talks by students, faculty members, or guest speakers. Lunch is served from 11 a.m. to 1:30 p.m. and includes a variety of choices, including several entrées, a deli bar, a salad bar, a pasta bar, and a hamburger and pizza area. Academic classes end at 3, and students then attend athletics, drama, or music practice or work on student publications. These activities conclude at 5:15, at which time day students leave the campus. Dinner is served from 5:30 to 6:45, and the period from 7:30 to 9:30 is set aside for study. McCallie also serves a "fourth meal," which runs from 9:30 to 10:30 on weeknights. Lights out is at 10:45 for freshmen and is later by 30-minute intervals for each grade.

WEEKEND LIFE

With a full-time Activities Director, McCallie offers boarders one of the most extensive activities programs in the nation. Throughout the school year, students take advantage of more than 125 opportunities, ranging from trips to major sporting events and concerts to off-the-wall activities, such as paintball or cosmic bowling. At least one group goes to events and attractions in Atlanta, Nashville, Knoxville, Charlotte, or other major southeastern cities virtually every weekend. Likewise, the Outdoor Program takes advantage of the mountains and rivers near Chattanooga. Groups go backpacking, skiing, fly fishing, sailing, rock climbing, canoeing, and kayaking.

On-campus activities include frequent concerts by some of the most up-and-coming bands in the country. In addition, weekend interdorm competitions are frequent and include football, softball, basketball, sand volleyball, and battleball tournaments.

Boarding students are required to attend Sunday worship services of their choice. Student-led services are often held on campus, and McCallie buses transport students to off-campus churches, temples, mosques, and other places of worship.

SUMMER PROGRAMS

McCallie offers an action-oriented sports camp for boys ages 9–14. This boarding program emphasizes fun and team participation regardless of athletic ability. McCallie also offers a residential lacrosse camp for boys ages 11–15. The toll-free telephone number for summer activity information is 800-MSC-CAMP.

COSTS AND FINANCIAL AID

Boarding charges for 2008–09, including tuition, room, board, and activities, are $35,760. Day tuition is $18,900.

McCallie offers approximately $2 million in need-based financial aid annually. A full-time Director of Financial Aid assists families in applying for tuition assistance.

In 1998–99, McCallie introduced the McCallie Honors Scholarship. This endowed program offers approximately twenty merit-based scholarships each year to boys who display leadership both inside and outside the classroom.

ADMISSIONS INFORMATION

McCallie is interested in students who possess outstanding character as well as the ability and desire to meet competitive academic standards. A student's extracurricular interests and abilities are also considered in the admission process. Ideal McCallie applicants must be willing to give of themselves to benefit others in the community.

The Admission Committee uses parent statements, transcripts, SSAT scores, a personal interview, and teacher recommendations to assess the qualities of each prospective student. A majority of new boarding students enroll in the ninth and tenth grades. Outstanding candidates for grades 11 and 12 are also considered.

APPLICATION TIMETABLE

All interested students are encouraged to contact the Office of Admission to schedule a campus visit. McCallie hosts several Visitors Days in the fall to enable prospective students and their parents to see the School in session. Applications are due by January 1 for Honors Scholarship candidates. All other applications for admission must be submitted by February 1. Students applying after February 1 are considered on a rolling basis, according to the availability of space.

ADMISSIONS CORRESPONDENCE

Troy Kemp
Dean of Admission and Financial Aid
The McCallie School
500 Dodds Avenue
Chattanooga, Tennessee 37404
Phone: 423-624-8300
800-234-2163 (toll-free)
Fax: 423-493-5426
E-mail: admission@mccallie.org
Web site: http://go.mccallie.org
http://www.mccallie.org

MIDDLESEX SCHOOL

Concord, Massachusetts

Type: Coeducational, boarding and day, nondenominational college-preparatory school
Grades: 9–12
Enrollment: 344
Head of School: Kathleen C. Giles, Head

THE SCHOOL

Since opening in 1901 as a nonsectarian boarding school, Middlesex School has continued to fulfill the mission of founder Frederick Winsor to "find the promise" in every student. Through a century of challenge and change, Middlesex has always dedicated itself to developing the whole individual, nurturing personal and intellectual growth, as well as inculcating a sense of purpose and responsibility. Accordingly, Middlesex has defined itself as a college-preparatory school in the most holistic sense—an environment in which teaching and learning only begin in the classroom and extend to the playing fields, theaters, art studios, music halls, and dormitories.

Over the years, Middlesex has deliberately remained a small school, enabling deeper relationships within the community and promoting opportunities for supported exploration and discovery. Middlesex's strength lies in its intimacy and its intensity; students are known, appreciated, and respected.

The historic town of Concord, Massachusetts, is an ideal setting for the intellectual activity that characterizes the Middlesex School community. Concord's Old Manse—whose former residents include Nathaniel Hawthorne and Ralph Waldo Emerson—and the Old North Bridge, site of the "shot heard 'round the world," are just a few miles from the School's 350-acre woodland campus. With the cultural enticements of Boston and Cambridge only 20 miles away, Middlesex students take advantage of the richness and variety of metropolitan life while living in a picturesque, secure rural setting.

A nonprofit institution, Middlesex School is governed by a self-perpetuating, 30-member Board of Trustees. The endowment is estimated at $110 million, supplemented by the Annual Fund, which raised $3.2 million in 2007–08.

Middlesex is accredited by the New England Association of Schools and Colleges.

ACADEMIC PROGRAMS

In its wide range of curricular offerings, from mathematics to the natural, physical, and social sciences to the humanities and the arts, Middlesex emphasizes the value of critical thinking as the cornerstone of effective learning. The School also recognizes the value of the "verbal classroom," in which students are encouraged to join and take a leadership role in the lively classroom discussions.

Freshmen and sophomores enroll in 5½ courses per semester; juniors and seniors typically take 5. Departmental requirements include 8 semesters of English, mathematics through trigonometry and analytic geometry, a foreign language through the third-year level, 2 years of laboratory science, 1 year of American history, a semester of European history, and ½-credit courses in the arts (freshmen and sophomores only). Students also participate in the Middlesex Writing Program, which includes three years of cross-disciplinary, increasingly sophisticated work. At the program's core is the Sophomore Writing Workshop, a weekly session intended to cover essential skills and techniques of analytical writing. In addition, juniors and seniors are required to distribute their courses among the four divisions of the curriculum: eight in the humanities, five in the natural sciences, three in the social sciences, and one in the arts, with three unrestricted. The School's curriculum guide includes 170 courses, with electives ranging from Vietnam and the 1960s to Mandarin Chinese and from Vector Calculus to DNA: Biotechnology and Analysis.

The School also offers college-level preparation, with twenty-five Advanced Placement courses. In May 2008, 208 students took 502 Advanced Placement tests. Middlesex offers opportunities for students to push their own limits, with the chance to go beyond the Advanced Placement level in formal classes and faculty-student tutorials. Middlesex encourages seniors to define their own Independent Study Projects, which in recent years have included taking courses such as individualized architectural studies, microprocessor design, and modern fiction from Africa, Ireland, and China.

International programs give students the opportunity to practice their language skills and experience other parts of the world. Middlesex offers overseas immersion programs in French, Spanish, and Chinese. Teachers lead summer trips to such destinations as the northern coast of Spain, France, Ecuador, Argentina, Beijing, Hong Kong, and Mexico.

Student performance is evaluated with numerical grades and comments. Courses are administered on a semester or yearlong basis.

The average class size is 11; the student-faculty ratio is 5:1. Informal, drop-in-style extra help is always available from individual teachers. Formal tutoring is available at additional cost.

FACULTY AND ADVISERS

Middlesex faculty members encourage learning in the classroom and in all facets of residential life. Not only are teaching faculty members accomplished scholars, artists, and athletes in their own right—with nearly 70 percent holding advanced degrees—but they are also dedicated educators, athletic coaches, advisers, and dorm parents.

Most of Middlesex's 82 faculty members live on campus, many in student dormitories. The accessibility and chance for friendship that their constant presence on campus affords help faculty members gain a thorough knowledge of each student's strengths, weaknesses, interests, and goals. The integration of students and faculty in a residential setting also fosters a sense of community and shared purpose.

Middlesex faculty members are integrated into their students' experiences at every level. Students at Middlesex choose their own adviser to assist with course selection and provide support and counsel on other concerns.

In 2003, Kathleen C. Giles (B.A., Harvard College; J.D., Harvard Law School) became the fifth Head of Middlesex School. In addition to her myriad duties as head of school, Mrs. Giles teaches freshman English and is a parent of two current Middlesex students.

COLLEGE ADMISSION COUNSELING

Beginning in the early fall of the junior year, two full-time Directors of College Counseling work closely with each student to help him or her make sound judgments about college interests at each step of the application process. The Directors meet frequently with parents as well as with students. More than 80 college representatives visit Middlesex to meet with students each fall.

The median scores on the SAT for Middlesex's class of 2008 were 670 verbal, 670 math, and 690 writing.

The members of the class of 2008 are attending sixty-one colleges and universities. The top five choices for the class were Georgetown, Brown, Boston College, Tufts, and Colby, respectively.

STUDENT BODY AND CONDUCT

Middlesex's 344 girls and boys, over 70 percent of whom live on campus, are a talented and eclectic group representing twenty-four states and thirteen countries. There is a balanced ratio of girls to boys, and students of color constitute 22 percent of the student body.

Middlesex's commitment to high individual and collective achievement hinges on the honesty and high moral and intellectual standards of all members of the School community. A Discipline Committee consisting of faculty members and students deals with infractions of major School rules. Students gain experience with responsibility, leadership, and consequential decision making through involvement with student government, the proctor system, the Peer Support Group, student-faculty committees on discipline and admissions, and a range of extracurricular clubs and organizations.

ACADEMIC FACILITIES

Most classes and administrative activities take place in Eliot Hall, one of the eight Georgian brick buildings that surround an oval green known as "The Circle." The new Clay Centennial Center opened in fall 2003; it includes lab/classrooms, math classrooms, an observatory with a research-grade 18-inch Centurion telescope and seven smaller rooftop telescopes, a project room to support independent study, and a student lounge. With its extensive studio space, large main stage, and small teaching theater, the Cornelius Ayer Wood '13 Theatre Arts Center has served as a model for a number of secondary schools. The Warburg Library supports student research with 41,000 carefully selected volumes, nearly 100 periodical subscriptions, 100 audiobooks, 20 online databases, and 1,500 DVDs and videos. The Warburg Library has its own wide area network (WAN) that includes the online card catalog as well as access to the Internet, CD-ROM multimedia information, and word processing software.

Technology and computers play a significant role in the lives of the students and faculty members at Middlesex. Two state-of-the-art technology centers contain multimedia computers and full Internet access. Middlesex also has converted the majority of its classrooms into SMART classrooms. Each of these classrooms has a teacher station with multimedia capabilities and an interactive SMART Board. In addition, some classrooms also have lab computers for the study of mathematics, computer science, modern languages, science, and economics. All dormitory rooms have access to the School's academic and library networks, the Internet, and e-mail.

BOARDING AND GENERAL FACILITIES

Residential life at Middlesex takes place in the nine dormitories on campus. Proctors, senior leaders selected by the faculty and students, live on each floor in order to be available for all students. Middlesex students enjoy vertical housing, in which all classes live together, allowing for role modeling by upper classmen and greater integration among the classes. Seventy-five percent of rooms on campus are singles, yet most students will live in a double or triple at some point in their Middlesex career. Two to three faculty families live in every Middlesex house and oversee the activities of the 24–30 resident students, while nonresident faculty members provide additional support. The formal and informal interactions in the houses between students, faculty members, and families create an environment that promotes close personal relationships and balanced lives.

The firm of famed landscape architect Frederick Law Olmsted designed Middlesex's beautiful campus. Beyond the dormitories, the academic facilities, and the athletic center, the simple, dignified chapel provides the campus its stately center and a community meeting place. Four of the dormitories, the athletic center, and the chapel were all recently renovated. The dining hall includes a student center complete with snack bar, game rooms, and lounge area. The health center is affiliated with Emerson Hospital, which is located less than 5 miles from the campus.

ATHLETICS

For most students, athletics are a vital part of their Middlesex experience, offering a welcome balance to their academic work. In addition to the recognition of the importance of exercise and fitness, the School seeks to teach its students a love of fair play, the benefits of teamwork, and respect for their opponents—lessons that enable them to better know themselves and meet the challenges of the world.

Ninth- and tenth-grade students participate in three seasons of team sports. Students in the upper classes are required to participate in one or two seasons, although many choose to continue their involvement beyond this requirement. Interscholastic competition is available at all levels for boys and girls in cross-country running, soccer, Alpine skiing, basketball, ice hockey, squash, lacrosse, crew, golf, and tennis. Boys also participate in football, wrestling, and baseball; girls play field hockey in the fall and softball in the spring.

The Atkins Athletic Center houses the School's basketball and indoor practice facilities, with team and officials' rooms as well as two basketball courts. Athletic facilities include a recently expanded fitness center, a dance studio, eight international squash courts, an indoor hockey rink that converts to indoor tennis courts, eight outdoor tennis courts, and a wrestling arena. Middlesex enjoys some of the best playing fields in the Independent School League, including two new turf fields. The campus also includes a boathouse and a ½-mile rowing course.

EXTRACURRICULAR OPPORTUNITIES

From a multicultural student alliance to student government to community outreach and an award-winning Model United Nations delegation, extracurricular endeavors flourish at Middlesex because of the energy and commitment students and faculty members bring to them. The School encourages an "if we don't have it, start it" approach to extracurricular activities, which allows the program to remain as lively and creative as the students involved.

More than a third of the student body participates each year in two full-length dramatic productions, a one-act-play festival, and Green Rooms. The music program attracts nearly half of the student body, either in one of four different singing groups, the jazz orchestra, the chamber ensemble, a variety of bands, or private studio voice or instrument lessons.

In 1990, the School implemented a campuswide community service program, which now engages many students in invigorating, socially responsible projects. In addition to voluntary weekly community service opportunities, the entire Middlesex community gathers annually to complete community service projects around the Boston area. Middlesex seeks to expand the process of learning beyond the classroom and athletic field to include an understanding of the value and importance of service to others.

One of the School's oldest traditions requires that every senior carve a wooden plaque. The week before graduation, each plaque is mounted on the walls in the corridors of the School buildings. Dating back to the School's first graduates, the plaques bear witness to the unique impression that each student has made in the academic, athletic, or cultural life of the School.

DAILY LIFE

Classes meet four or five times a week in 40-minute periods, from 8 a.m. to 3 p.m. on Monday, Tuesday, Thursday, and Friday; 8 to 12:10 on Wednesday; and 8 to 11:25 on Saturday. All-School assemblies on Tuesday and Saturday set aside time for announcements, student group meetings, and presentations by distinguished visiting speakers. Wednesday morning chapel provides a more intimate and serene gathering place in which students and faculty members give talks on issues of ethical and personal significance and engage the School in group singing and quiet reflection.

Athletic practices follow the end of classes at 3:15 each day. Most interscholastic competition takes place on Wednesday and Saturday afternoons.

Breakfast (7:15 to 8:30), lunch (11:30 to 12:45), and dinner (5:30 to 6:45) are served each day in Ware Hall. Dinner is followed by either free time or club meetings. During the regular evening study period, which runs from 7:30 until 9:30, students are required to be in the dormitory or the Warburg Library. On Monday through Thursday, freshman and sophomore students must be checked into their dormitories by 7:30 p.m. (10 for sophomores during the spring semester), juniors by 10:15, and seniors by 10:30 p.m. On Friday, all students are free at 9; check-in for juniors, sophomores, and freshmen is at 10:15 and seniors, 10:30 p.m. All students are required to be in their dorms by 11 p.m. on Saturdays. On Sundays, check-in for juniors and seniors is at 10 p.m. Freshmen and sophomores must be in their rooms by 10:30 on weeknights, and at that time freshmen must have their lights out. Occasional requests for a half-hour of "late lights" may be made to the faculty member on duty. Day students participate in all activities and may remain on campus until 10:15 p.m.

WEEKEND LIFE

The Student Activities Committee, a joint student-faculty venture, plans exciting events for students on nonschool days, such as dances, parties, weekend movies, and live music performances. Major dramatic and musical presentations in the theater arts center draw full houses of students, parents, and visitors. The proximity of Cambridge and Boston provides an almost inexhaustible supply of interesting off-campus cultural options for students and faculty members. Four weekends during the school year are designated campus weekends when all boarding students stay on campus. Four weekends are long weekends and open for all boarders to travel off-campus. Of the remaining weekends, ninth graders may choose to leave the campus four weekends a semester; sophomores, five weekends; and juniors and seniors, six weekends.

Most of the weekend activities enjoyed by boarding and day students are informal. Many students use the School's extensive woodlands for hiking, running, biking, and cross-country skiing. The School's athletic facilities are open for spirited student and faculty competition. In the winter, students skate in the rink and on the pond. On weekends, students are active in the woodworking, metal-welding, ceramics, and photography studios and in the music rooms.

COSTS AND FINANCIAL AID

The fee for tuition and residence for 2008–09 is $42,820. Day student tuition, which includes breakfast, lunch, and dinner, is $34,250. These charges were payable in two installments, the first due July 1 and the second, December 1. When a student enrolls, a deposit is required to hold the place. Essential additional costs, such as books and laboratory and studio fees, are estimated at $1200.

As Middlesex continues to seek talented students who represent the widest possible geographic, social, ethnic, and economic range, the financial aid budget increases with the availability of School funds. In 2008–09, Middlesex will administer $3.45 million to 106 students based on demonstrated need. Students can earn extra money through Middlesex Student Services, which employs students in various jobs on campus.

ADMISSIONS INFORMATION

Middlesex seeks to enroll motivated students who demonstrate academic promise, a willingness to take risks, curiosity, imagination, maturity, and concern for others. The School looks for applicants eager to contribute to the shared life of the community and to take advantage of the School's many opportunities. The admissions committee closely evaluates intellectual curiosity and the ability to meet the demands of the School's academic program. In addition, Middlesex is committed to enrolling students from a wide range of cultural, racial, and socioeconomic backgrounds from across the United States and around the world.

All students at Middlesex are admitted based on their academic merit and personal credentials. Prospective students submit four recommendations, a transcript, and SSAT scores with their application. A campus visit and personal interview are strongly recommended. In 2008, Middlesex had 931 applicants for 108 openings; 78 students entered grade 9, 23 joined grade 10, and 6 entered grade 11.

APPLICATION TIMETABLE

Families are encouraged to visit Middlesex between 9 and 3 on weekdays (between 9 and 12 on Wednesday and Saturday) in the fall preceding the year in which they would like to see their children matriculate. The completed application is due on January 15 for day students and January 31 for boarding students. A $50 application fee must accompany the application. For applicants residing outside the United States, the fee is $100. Appointments for campus tours and interviews should be made well in advance. Admissions decisions are mailed on March 10, and the last date for acceptance of an offer of admission is April 10.

ADMISSIONS CORRESPONDENCE

Douglas C. Price, Director of Admissions
Middlesex School
1400 Lowell Road
P.O. Box 9122
Concord, Massachusetts 01742-9122
Phone: 978-371-6524
Fax: 978-402-1400
E-mail: admissions@mxschool.edu
Web site: http://www.mxschool.edu

MILLBROOK SCHOOL

Millbrook, New York

Type: Coeducational boarding and day college-preparatory school
Grades: 9–12 (Forms III–VI)
Enrollment: 258
Head of School: Drew Casertano, Headmaster

THE SCHOOL

Millbrook is a co-educational boarding and day school, which offers a rigorous college-preparatory curriculum that integrates academics, service, athletics, and leadership. Excellent teaching and close, stimulating relationships between students and their teachers have been the School's hallmark since its founding by Edward Pulling in 1931. Under Mr. Pulling's thirty-four-year tenure, Millbrook also became known for its strong commitment to a community service program on campus in which all students contribute to the daily functioning of the School. Students operate their own store, bank, recycling program, and zoo—to name but a few of the many services. These qualities remain firmly in place in the Millbrook of today, as well as the decision to remain a size where every student can be needed and known.

Originally a school for boys, Millbrook first admitted girls as day students in 1971 and then as boarding students in 1975. The current boy-girl ratio is 55:45. In keeping with the founder's vision, Millbrook's goal is to promote in every student the intellectual, emotional, spiritual, and physical growth that will lead to a life both individually satisfying and valuable to the greater society.

As the student body is diverse, so are the reasons for each individual's choice of Millbrook. For many, the appeal is the ideal size combined with the strength of the academic program and the fact that all students have a meaningful role in the community. The AZA-accredited Trevor Zoo, with such auxiliary features as a forest canopy walkway, a wetlands sanctuary, and a center for the captive breeding of endangered species and for the recovery of sick and injured animals, draws students with related interests. Community service is also of interest as it offers a student the opportunity to have a significant, positive impact on the daily lives of others in the School. For the athlete, there is the promise of active, frequent team participation that in much larger schools might be available only to a limited number. For the arts enthusiast, there is ample opportunity to study, exhibit, and perform.

The campus of 800 acres is located in the rolling hills of Dutchess County, New York—90 miles north of New York City, 20 miles northeast of Poughkeepsie, and 8 miles from the Connecticut border. Woods, fields, streams, and ponds are the dominant features of the land, all central to the natural science and recreational interests of many Millbrook students and faculty members.

The School is incorporated not-for-profit and is governed by a self-perpetuating Board of Trustees, many of whom are alumni. Millbrook has an endowment of $22 million and is not encumbered by long-term debts. Annual contributions from the Board of Trustees, parents, and the 2,400 alumni generally total in excess of $5 million. These funds are used to make up the difference between tuition income and per-student expense, as well as to support capital projects and the growth of the endowment.

Millbrook School is accredited by the New York State Association of Independent Schools and the Board of Regents of the State University of New York. Institutional memberships include the Cum Laude Society, the Secondary School Admission Test Board, the National Association of Independent Schools, the New York State Association of Independent Schools, the Association of Boarding Schools, the Council for Advancement and Support of Education, and A Better Chance.

ACADEMIC PROGRAMS

Millbrook offers a traditional college-preparatory curriculum, which is rigorous, varied, and comprehensive. It features a variety of honors and AP courses, electives, and independent study opportunities and is supplemented by field trips and forums with guest speakers. Every aspect of the curriculum is intended to embrace five core values: curiosity, respect, integrity, stewardship of the natural world, and service to others. All students participate in a weeklong intersession in which they explore interests outside the classroom or off campus. Juniors of strong academic standing may apply to study overseas through the School Year Abroad Program (SYA) or take a semester away at a program sanctioned by the School. Seniors are required to produce a Culminating Experience project in the spring term and present it to the student body. All students carry a minimum of five major academic subjects throughout each year. The minimum graduation requirements are 4 years of English, 3 of mathematics, 3 of one foreign language, 2 laboratory sciences (of which one must be biology), and 1 year of fine arts. The history/social science requirement varies with the grade level at which the student enters, but all students must take U.S. history. Extensive reading and writing are the essence of the broadly based Millbrook curriculum. Students' academic achievement is recognized at the end of each semester by placement on the High Honor Roll, Honor Roll, and Effort List. In addition, each year a limited number of seniors who have demonstrated academic excellence and intellectual leadership are elected to the Cum Laude Society.

The arts are a full partner in Millbrook's overall program. The $8.5 million, 34,000 square-foot Holbrook Arts Center is home to an exceptional arts faculty and 80 percent of the student body who elect to take an art class each term.

A rich and varied curricula in music, the visual arts, dance, and drama is enhanced by many opportunities for performance and exhibition. Student art exhibits, as well as those of visiting artists, are presented throughout the year in the Warner Gallery. The Arts Department presents three to four plays each year, including a musical, a dramatic production, and a series of one-act plays. Students also perform in approximately six arts nights, which are evenings of dance, music, and acting.

The academic year is divided into two semesters. Students receive indicator grades at the mid-term and grades and comments at the end of each semester.

FACULTY AND ADVISERS

In the tradition begun by Edward Pulling, Millbrook attracts and maintains teachers who share a passion for their disciplines, a commitment to and belief in the power of education, and a desire to involve themselves deeply in the lives of young people. The 2008 faculty consists of 60 members who have the ability to teach in a variety of roles and encourage their students to be curious, involved, active learners. All hold a bachelor's degree, 26 hold a master's degree, and 2 hold a doctoral degree.

In addition to their teaching responsibilities, faculty members serve as coaches to teams and extracurricular activities, advisers to 2–6 students, dorm parents, and community service advisers. The majority live on campus, and many occupy dorm housing.

Drew Casertano was appointed Headmaster of Millbrook in 1990. He is a graduate of the Choate School and Amherst College and holds an Ed.M. from Harvard University. Prior to his appointment at Millbrook, Mr. Casertano served as a teacher, coach, dorm parent, and the Director of Admission and Financial Aid over the course of his ten-year tenure at the Loomis Chaffee School in Windsor, Connecticut.

COLLEGE ADMISSION COUNSELING

Virtually all Millbrook graduates continue their formal education on the college level. The College Counseling Office works closely with students, parents, and faculty advisers to help ensure strong and appropriate placement. Mean SAT scores for the class of 2008 were 583 critical reading, 589 math, and 577 writing.

The graduates of the class of 2008 entered colleges and universities that include Bowdoin, Colby, Colorado College, Colgate, Cornell, Denison, Elon, Gettysburg, Hobart and William Smith, Northwestern, St. Lawrence, Skidmore, Trinity, Union, Vassar, and the Universities of Chicago, Pennsylvania, St. Andrew's, and Scotland.

STUDENT BODY AND CONDUCT

Of 258 students, 203 are boarders and 55 are day students; 139 are boys, 119 are girls. They come from nineteen states and nine other countries and are distributed among grades as follows: Form III, 47; Form IV, 72; Form V, 78; and Form VI, 61. Of the student body, 12 percent are students of color and 10 percent are international. Students for whom English is not their primary language must enter with fairly well-developed English language skills.

In keeping with Millbrook's motto, *Non Sibi Sed Cunctis,* and its commitment to student involvement, students take an active role in the School's leadership and creating School culture. The Student Council officers run School assemblies that are held three times a week and meet with the Headmaster on a weekly basis to discuss student issues. Dorm leaders, appointed by the faculty, provide leadership and guidance in the dormitories. In addition, there is an active group of trained Peer Counselors who work with the Director of Counseling in providing support for fellow students. Prefects, seniors who are elected by the student body, also provide leadership on campus and serve with faculty members on the Discipline Committee, which makes recommendations to the Headmaster in response to major student disciplinary infractions. In addition, there are leadership opportunities for students in their respective community service activities.

It is the School's expectation that Millbrook students conduct themselves in a way that is consistent with the character, values, and mission of the School. Behavior that is determined to be detrimental to the School or unbecoming to a Millbrook student is met with serious consequences. The disciplinary system, led by the Dean of Students, is educational in nature. In most instances when a student admits to a first violation of a major school rule in a given year, the resources of the School and family are mobilized to hold the student accountable and to afford him or her the opportunity to learn from his or her mistake. There are times, however, when the School recognizes that there are limits to its ability to assist an individual's growth, and one violation of a major School rule may result in expulsion. In all cases, the discipline system is intended to be a process of accountability, reflection, reparation, and change.

ACADEMIC FACILITIES

The thirty classrooms are distributed in several buildings. The Schoolhouse contains classrooms for the humanities, administrative offices, a computer center, and an 18,000-volume library that is equipped with an online public access catalog. The Flagler Memorial Chapel serves as a meeting space for the entire School community and also contains several classrooms. The $8.5 million, 34,000-square-foot Holbrook Arts Center, completed in 2001, houses the 325-seat Chelsea Morrison Theater, the Warner Art Gallery, several classrooms and studios (2-dimensional, dance, and ceramics), a state-of-the-art digital and print photography complex with a dark room, a music suite (a recital/lecture hall and four practice rooms), and department offices. Construction of a $12 million, 25,000-square-foot math and science center was completed in winter 2008. This LEED-certified building (Leadership in Energy and Environmental Design) contains four science laboratories, five math classrooms, a technology center, and faculty offices in addition to a detached greenhouse and exhibit spaces for the School's extensive biological and geological collections. Additional laboratory space is located in the 6-acre Trevor Zoo. The Harris-Kenan Foreign Language Center, completed in fall 2008, features three classrooms, a seminar room, a lounge area for students, and offices for teachers in that department.

BOARDING AND GENERAL FACILITIES

Seven dormitories of varying capacities house Millbrook students in single; double; and, in some cases, triple rooms. Students in grades 10–12 are housed together; ninth graders are housed separately. Each dorm has a staff of 4 faculty members and 2–4 student dorm leaders and peer counselors, who assist the faculty members in maintaining the high quality of dormitory life. Dormitories are closed during long weekends and major School vacations. Students have access to e-mail and the Internet in the dormitories and classroom buildings through a wireless network.

Most meals are served buffet-style in the dining room, with the exception of a formal family-style meal once a week. The latter is preceded by a Chapel Talk, traditionally given by students on a topic of their choice.

The Barn is home to Millbrook's student center, which includes lounges and game areas, the School store, a snack bar, and the college counseling office. Three full-time RNs staff a fully equipped health center, and a physician makes regular visits to the campus and is on call at all times. The health center also utilizes the resources of the nearby Sharon (Connecticut) Hospital, an excellent medical facility.

ATHLETICS

Millbrook has a long history of strong, competitive athletics with a high standard of sportsmanship. Millbrook's teams are well-coached and compete squarely with larger schools. The School's athletic program boasts a state-of-the-art $9 million, 86,000-square-foot sports complex. The Bradford and Cheryl Mills Athletic Center contains an indoor hockey rink that converts into four indoor tennis courts in the off-season, a basketball court, four international squash courts with a gallery for viewing, and a training room and fitness center. Nine playing fields, a 3.2-mile cross-country trail, and a stable for student-owned horses complete Millbrook's athletic facilities.

Students are required to play a sport at least two of the three athletic seasons. Interscholastic teams include those for baseball (boys), basketball, cross-country, field hockey (girls), golf, ice hockey, lacrosse, skiing, soccer, softball (girls), squash, and tennis. Varying team levels ensure a place for all, from beginners to accomplished athletes. Non-team offerings include horseback riding, dance, weight training/conditioning, and racquet sports. Options in lieu of a sport are theater, Improv, zoo squad, and outdoor skills.

EXTRACURRICULAR OPPORTUNITIES

Traditional clubs are largely incorporated within the framework of community service. Student interests are served, as are the needs of the School community, through work in one of the many community services, including the zoo, library, observatory, store, bank, post office, outreach activities, recycling, and student tutors. Other offerings outside of community service include Model UN, Environmental Council, Jazz Ensemble, Millbrook Singers, Improv, the newspaper and literary magazines, the yearbook, and tour guides.

DAILY LIFE

The academic day runs from 8 a.m.–3 p.m. on Mondays, Tuesdays, Thursdays, and Fridays and 8:15 a.m.–12:15 p.m. on Wednesdays and Saturdays. Each class meets for three 45-minute periods and one 90-minute period a week. The entire school convenes four times a week for an all-school assembly and four times a week for community service work. On Mondays, Thursdays, and Fridays, a class period is dedicated to extra help. Athletic practices take place each afternoon. On Wednesdays and Saturdays, classes meet in the morning only; sports teams compete against other schools in the afternoon.

WEEKEND LIFE

Films, dances, concerts, trips to museums, professional sports events, Broadway shows, sleeping, studying, fishing, hiking, bicycling, playing an instrument, working on an art project, watching television, listening to music, tramping the hills with camera in hand, skiing, riding, and more combine to make each weekend as active or as quiet as each individual prefers. Students with parental permission may leave campus on open weekends after their last Saturday commitment, but an energetic and creative Activities Committee plans a full array of activities and outings on and off campus.

Day students have access to all School programs and activities, are encouraged to be full participants in the life of the School, and have bed space within the dormitories.

COSTS AND FINANCIAL AID

The 2008–09 charge for boarders was $41,400; for day students, $30,100. Extra costs, such as activity and athletics fees, books, allowances, athletic equipment, linen, and insurance, added approximately $1000 to the base fee for boarders, slightly less for day students.

Financial aid is awarded on the basis of a family's demonstrated need and within the confines of the School's available financial resources. In determining its awards, Millbrook consults the information provided by families to the School and Student Services for Financial Aid. For the 2008–09 year, 25 percent of the student body shared grants totaling $1.9 million.

ADMISSIONS INFORMATION

Millbrook enrolls young men and women whose tested abilities range from average to superior, who are able to work in a school that makes considerable academic demands without being highly pressured, who are willing to participate actively in learning, and who are willing to share their talents with others through extracurricular activities and community service. As part of the application process, taking the SSAT is required. For the last several years, SSAT scores for incoming Form III and Form IV students have ranged from the low 30s to the high 90s. Mean scores for both groups have hovered at the 60th percentile mark. No candidate is denied or offered a place solely on the basis of a particular test score.

Many factors are considered in making admissions decisions. Academic and testing information, teachers' recommendations, extracurricular involvement, and a host of intangibles are evaluated carefully as part of the admissions process. For entrance in fall 2008, 483 applications for admission were completed; 229 applicants were accepted, and 97 new students were enrolled.

APPLICATION TIMETABLE

Inquiries are welcomed at any time; interviews are welcomed and the application deadline is January 31. Admissions decisions are made and announced March 10 and on a rolling basis thereafter. It is to the advantage of the candidate and the family to visit Millbrook during the academic year. The admissions office welcomes visitors by appointment Monday, Tuesday, Thursday, and Friday between 8:15 a.m. and 2:15 p.m. and on Wednesday and Saturday mornings.

ADMISSIONS CORRESPONDENCE

Cynthia S. McWilliams
Director of Admissions
Millbrook School
131 Millbrook School Road
Millbrook, New York 12545

Phone: 845-677-8261
Fax: 845-677-1265
E-mail: admissions@millbrook.org
Web site: http://www.millbrook.org

THE MILLER SCHOOL OF ALBEMARLE

Charlottesville, Virginia

MILLER SCHOOL

Type: Coeducational boarding and day college-preparatory school
Grades: 8–12, postgraduate year
Enrollment: 150
Head of School: Winn Price, Headmaster

THE SCHOOL

Samuel Miller, a native of Albemarle County, had long dreamed of establishing a school near his birthplace. Although he was born into poverty, Mr. Miller had a successful, industrious life and left a large legacy to finance the establishment of The Miller School of Albemarle after his death in 1869.

Miller School is built on the democratic premise that all children can become self-reliant and contributing members of society. The School features a college-preparatory curriculum, an extensive service program, and a range of athletic options. In a fee-based system, Miller School offers a Study Skills (SS) program and individual tutoring.

Miller School's unique approach is to develop the mind, hands, and heart of each student in a structured, disciplined, and safe environment.

On the School's 1,600 acres in the foothills of the Blue Ridge Mountains are wooded areas, farmland, orchards, and a large reservoir. The main campus has lawns, a pond, sports facilities, and a swimming pool. There is also a 12-acre lake for swimming, fishing, and canoeing. The campus is located 15 miles west of Charlottesville, Virginia, and about 120 miles southwest of Washington, D.C. The School's setting is ideally suited to the pursuit of outdoor recreational interests, yet its proximity to Charlottesville and the University of Virginia, as well as to the Shenandoah Valley, provides easy access to extracurricular academic and cultural activities.

A nonprofit organization, the School is governed by a 15-member Board of Trustees. The annual operating budget is approximately $2.7 million, with total assets well in excess of $20 million.

The Alumni Association, representing the School's 1,000 living alumni, meets monthly, and its members conduct social and fund-raising events.

Miller School is accredited by the Virginia Association of Independent Schools. It is approved by the Virginia Board of Education and holds membership in the National Association of Independent Schools, the Association of Boarding Schools, the Association for the Advancement of Sustainability in Higher Education, Independent School Management, and the Institute for Global Ethics.

ACADEMIC PROGRAMS

Miller School's traditional college-preparatory curriculum requires 23 credits for graduation. The high school academic program includes 4 years of English, 4 years of history, 3 years of science, 3 years of a foreign language (French, Spanish, or Latin), 3 years of mathematics (through at least algebra II), and 2 years of arts, whether it be studio art, drama, music, photography, or woodworking. Qualified students may take Advanced Placement courses in a variety of disciplines.

Grade 8 builds into the Upper School (grades 9–12) program and offers a strong grounding in the foundational subjects of English (including spelling, grammar, and vocabulary building), mathematics, social studies, science, foreign language, and the arts.

Miller's Study Skills program is staffed to provide qualified assessments of learning needs. While it is not a special-needs program, students placed in SS meet in a small group on a daily basis, at which time qualified staff members address these study skills and organizational needs. SAT prep courses and ESL courses are also offered.

Each afternoon, students are involved in a variety of athletic programs. After dinner, required evening study halls are overseen every school night by a team of faculty members, who give needed help. There are also help sessions with available faculty members between the end of classes and the start of athletics for students in need of extra help.

FACULTY AND ADVISERS

In addition to the Headmaster, there are 53 faculty and professional staff members, 27 women and 26 men. In addition to baccalaureates, 26 hold advanced degrees, with faculty members hailing from such schools as Auburn; Bates; College of William and Mary; Columbia; Dartmouth; Denison; Denis Diderot (Paris); Florida State; Georgetown; Hofstra; Indiana; James Madison; Laval (Quebec); LIU, C.W. Post; Mary Baldwin; Mary Washington; Metropolitana (Caracas); Pacific; UCLA; Virginia Commonwealth; Virginia Tech; William and Mary; Xavier; and the Universities of Colorado, North Carolina at Chapel Hill, Pennsylvania, Richmond, and Virginia.

Miller School employs teachers who are dedicated to working with the whole child in a boarding school program. Faculty benefits include Social Security, health and dental insurance, a retirement plan, and housing and meals. The proximity to the University of Virginia and three other colleges allows faculty members to pursue advanced degrees on a part-time basis.

Each student is assigned a faculty adviser, and students sit with their adviser at lunch and meet together frequently.

Walter W. "Winn" Price III, was appointed twelfth Headmaster of Miller School in 2008. A graduate of the U.S. Naval Academy and the U.S. Naval War College, he holds a master's degree in business administration from Harvard University.

COLLEGE ADMISSION COUNSELING

The college placement process is overseen by the Director of College Placement, who works closely with each student to develop a college admissions plan. This plan includes identifying particular strengths and interests of the student, reviewing his or her academic program and performance, ensuring that appropriate standardized testing takes place, building a college search strategy and application list, and helping the student through the college application process. The goal of this process is to help students and parents find a good fit for a successful collegiate career.

The average combined SAT score for the class of 2008 was 1671 (out of a possible 2400). In 1998 through 2008, 100 percent of the seniors who sought college admission were accepted at, among other schools, American, Catholic, Christopher Newport, Colgate, Dartmouth, Dickinson, Duke, Fordham, Hampden-Sydney, Harvard, James Madison, Johns Hopkins, Johnson and Wales, New Mexico Tech, Old Dominion, Penn State, Purdue, Providence, Roanoke, Seton Hall, Smith, Stanford, Union, VMI, Virginia Tech, William and Mary (including a Monroe Scholar), Yale, and the Universities of North Carolina at Chapel Hill, Pennsylvania, Richmond, Virginia (including a Jefferson Scholar), and Wisconsin–Madison.

STUDENT BODY AND CONDUCT

The key word for students at Miller School is involvement. The School's educational mission is best served by keeping total enrollment and individual classes small and personal. The practical effect on the student body is that all students participate fully in the life of the School, and significant leadership roles exist for interested students in all areas of School life and work. The residential program is run by a director who is assisted by appointed student leaders. The Honor Committee and Disciplinary Review Board are made up of a mix of students and faculty members.

The general student body is composed of approximately 150 students distributed over grades 8–12, with a 6:1 student-faculty ratio and an average class size of 10. Currently, ten states and fourteen countries are represented in the student body, with approximately 25 percent of the student population belonging to minority groups.

A unique aspect of Miller School is the Service Program, which is an integral part of the overall experience. Miller School was founded on the notion of community service, and today's students are an important part of that historical legacy. On alternate Wednesday afternoons, students spend 2 hours involved in their service activity. At the beginning of the school year, students choose one of a number of options in which they can participate through the year. Examples of service activities include students traveling to Charlottesville to visit nursing homes or volunteer at the SPCA, visiting area elementary schools to serve as reading tutors, archiving documents and items from Miller School's historic past for preservation and study, maintaining outdoor trails on the 1,600-acre campus, working on the yearbook or newspaper, building or repairing needed campus items in the woodshop, and working with the local Parks and Recreation Department.

ACADEMIC FACILITIES

The collegiate Victorian-style buildings of Miller School have been designated National Historic Landmarks. Old Main (1878) houses classrooms, the library, the Chapel, the Dining Hall, the Flannagan Technology Center, and administrative offices. There is also a fully equipped technology teaching lab adjoining the Flannagan Technology Center. Located in the Arts Building (1882) are the newly renovated, state-of-the-art woodshop, art studio, darkroom and photography classroom, and music room. The Science Building (1885) provides science classrooms and laboratories. The library contains more than 8,000 volumes, receives forty-five magazines and several newspapers, and has computer access to local libraries as well as the University of Virginia library. The library has both print and online reference resources and Internet access. Audiovisual equipment and computers are available for classroom and student use. Each student receives an e-mail account during Orientation.

BOARDING AND GENERAL FACILITIES

Boys reside in large dorm rooms in Old Main, with 2 to 4 boys per room. The School's dining room and chapel are also located in Old Main. The girls reside in one of two dorms. The newly renovated Haden-Hart Hall houses eighth and ninth grade girls who share a room with one other roommate, and Wayland Hall has single rooms for girls in the tenth to twelfth grades. Both dorms offer comfortable lounges, laundry facilities, a large meeting room, and computer labs.

In 2000–01, the top floor of Old Main was renovated to include two additional classrooms and a spacious lounge with breathtaking views of the Blue Ridge Mountains and western Albemarle County. The lounge is used for student and faculty meetings of various types as well as special activities and gatherings.

Two registered nurses, one of whom is also a degreed psychological counselor, staff the health clinic and infirmary. A local doctor makes visits to the school when the need arises for the purpose of diagnosing and treating students. A family medical practice, a dentist, and a rescue squad are within 5 miles of the School, and there are three nationally ranked hospitals within 15 miles.

ATHLETICS

Miller School offers a program of interscholastic competition designed to accommodate varied skill levels and teach the important principles of good sportsmanship and cooperation. Facilities include five athletic fields; a fully equipped gymnasium with a weight room, wrestling room, and training room; a swimming pool; basketball and tennis courts; a lake; and miles of scenic cross-country trails in the surrounding hillsides.

All students participate in sports or drama during the year's three athletic seasons. Miller provides an excellent opportunity for all students to become involved in varsity and junior varsity athletics. Interscholastic sports include baseball, basketball, cross-country, girls' volleyball, golf, horseback riding, lacrosse, soccer, tennis, and wrestling. Strength and conditioning is an option for one season each year, and drama is available as an alternate choice in the fall and winter seasons.

EXTRACURRICULAR OPPORTUNITIES

Students' extracurricular programs are limited only by their imagination and interests. The School offers a wide variety of faculty-sponsored activities, ranging from the nationwide Youth Leadership Initiative and the Student Government Association to paintball and skiing. Students may attend an array of off-campus activities, including dances, concerts, professional sports, collegiate sports, readings, and plays. Several clubs exist through the efforts of students and faculty members alike and include the Book Club, Chess Club, Salsa Dancing Club, International Club, Key Club, National Honor Society, Outdoors Club, Poetry Club, and many others.

DAILY LIFE

Classes begin at 7:45 a.m. and run for 50 minutes each, with all classes meeting daily, Monday through Friday. Students and faculty and staff members meet in the chapel every morning for announcements and special presentations. Service days (alternate Wednesdays) are shortened class days, with the afternoons devoted to service-group programs and projects. Dinner is at 6 p.m., and evening study hall is from 7:30–9:30 on Sunday through Thursday evenings, with a ten minute break in the middle.

COSTS AND FINANCIAL AID

In 2008–09, the cost of tuition was $33,000 for seven-day boarding students, $29,750 for five-day boarding students, $38,650 for international students, and $14,350 for day students. A variety of tuition-payment plans are available.

Parents wishing to apply for financial aid should contact the School by mid-February for aid for the following school year. Awards are based foremost on demonstrated financial need, with merit being a secondary criterion. Recipients must reapply for aid yearly. In 2008–09, students received more than $726,000 in financial aid, with an average award of $12,691 to boarding students and $7007 to day students.

ADMISSIONS INFORMATION

Miller School's academic program is designed for students of good character with average to superior ability. Miller School does not discriminate on the basis of race, color, sex, nationality, religion, or ethnic origin in the administration of its educational policies, scholarship programs, or athletic or other school-related programs.

A complete application includes: the application and fee, the Applicant Questionnaire, the Parent/Guardian Questionnaire, letters of recommendation from math and English teachers, a copy of the student's transcript or report card, standardized test scores, and a copy of the student's birth certificate or passport. An on-campus interview is required, except for out-of-state and international applicants; however, it is highly recommended for all. The application fee is $50 ($100 for international applicants).

APPLICATION TIMETABLE

Inquiries and visits are welcome year-round. Applicants who wish to be notified of the admission decision in early March must complete the application by February 20. Applications are welcome after February 20 and are reviewed on a rolling basis. In such cases, applicants are notified of the admissions decision shortly after the application process has been completed. Campus tours and interviews are generally available Monday through Friday. Arrangements can be made through the Admissions Office on weekdays from 8:30 a.m. to 5 p.m.

ADMISSIONS CORRESPONDENCE

Jay Reeves
Director of Admissions
The Miller School of Albemarle
Charlottesville, Virginia 22903-9328

Phone: 434-823-4805
Fax: 434-205-5007
Web site: http://www.millerschool.org

MILTON ACADEMY

Milton, Massachusetts

MILTON ACADEMY

Type: Coeducational boarding and day college-preparatory school
Grades: K–12: Lower School, Kindergarten–5; Middle School, 6–8; Upper School, 9–12
Enrollment: School total: 1000; Upper School: 680
Head of School: Todd B. Bland (as of July 1, 2008)

THE SCHOOL

The Academy received its charter in 1798 under the Massachusetts land-grant policy. It bequeathed to the school a responsibility to "open the way for all the people to a higher order of education than the common schools can supply." Milton's motto, "Dare to be true," not only states a core value, it describes Milton's culture. Milton fosters intellectual inquiry and encourages initiative and the open exchange of ideas. Teaching and learning at Milton are active processes that recognize the intelligence, talents, and potential of each member of the Academy.

For more than 200 years, Milton has developed confident, independent thinkers in an intimate, friendly setting where students and faculty members understand that the life of the mind is the pulse of the school. A gifted and dedicated faculty motivates a diverse student body, providing students with the structure to learn and the support to take risks. The faculty's teaching expertise and passion for scholarship generates extraordinary growth in students who learn to expect the most of themselves. The Milton community connects purposefully with world issues. Students graduate with a clear sense of themselves, their world, and how to contribute.

From Milton Academy's suburban 125-acre campus, 8 miles south of Boston in the town of Milton (population 26,000), students and faculty members access the vast cultural resources of Boston and Cambridge. Minutes from campus is the Blue Hills Reservation, 6,000 wooded acres of hiking trails and ski slopes.

Milton Academy is a nonprofit organization with a self-perpetuating Board of Trustees. Its endowment is $190 million as of June 2008.

Milton Academy is accredited by the New England Association of Schools and Colleges and holds memberships in the National Association of Independent Schools, the Cum Laude Society, and the Association of Independent Schools in New England.

ACADEMIC PROGRAMS

Milton students and faculty members are motivated participants in the world of ideas, concepts, and values. Milton's curriculum provides rigorous preparation for college and includes more than 172 courses in nine academic departments. For students entering Milton in the ninth grade, a minimum of 18 credits are required for graduation. This includes 4 years of English, 2 years of history (including U.S. and modern world history), 2 years of science, 1 year of an arts course, and successful completion of algebra II, geometry, and a level III foreign language course. Noncredit requirements include current events/public speaking, physical education, a ninth-grade arts course (music/drama/visual arts), and a four-year affective education curriculum that includes health, values, social awareness, and senior transitions.

Electives are offered in all academic areas. Examples of electives include computer programming, comparative government, performing literature, Spanish film and social change, advanced architecture, philosophy and literature, choreography, film and video production, psychology, engineering, nuclear physics, issues in environmental science, creative writing, music theory, observational astronomy, and marine biology. Students may petition to take independent study courses, and Advanced Placement courses leading to college credit are offered in most subject areas.

In January, seniors submit a proposal for a five-week spring independent project, on or off campus. Senior projects give students the opportunity to pursue in-depth interests stemming from their work at Milton.

The typical class size is 14 students, and the overall student-teacher ratio is 5:1. Nightly 2-hour study periods in the houses are supervised for boarding students.

Faculty members are available for individual help throughout the day and in the houses at night. Students seeking assistance with assignments or help with specific skills, organization, and/or time management visit the Academic Skills Center, which is staffed throughout the day.

The school year, which is divided into two semesters, runs from early September to early June with an examination period at the end of January. Students typically take five courses per semester. Students earn letter grades from E (failure) through A+, and comments prepared by each student's teachers and adviser are sent to parents three times a year in November, February, and June.

All academic buildings and residential houses are part of a campuswide computer network. MiltONline, the Academy's e-mail and conferencing system, allows students to join conference discussions for many classes and extracurricular activities, communicate with faculty members and friends, and submit assignments. Students have access to the Milton Intranet as well as the Internet.

Class II students (eleventh graders) may apply to spend either the fall or spring semester at the Mountain School Program of Milton Academy (an interdisciplinary academic program set on a working 300-acre farm in Vermont); at CITYterm at the Master's School in Dobbs Ferry, New York; or at the Maine Coast Semester at Chewonki. Through School Year Abroad, Milton provides opportunities in Spain, France, Italy, and China. Milton also offers six- to eight-week exchange programs with schools in Spain, France, and China.

FACULTY AND ADVISERS

The deep commitment of a learned and experienced group of teachers is Milton's greatest treasure. Teaching in Classes IV-I (grades 9–12) are 139 full-time faculty members, 75 percent of whom hold advanced degrees (Ph.D. and master's degrees). Eighty percent of faculty members live on campus.

In addition to teaching, faculty members also serve as house parents and coaches, as well as advisers to student clubs, organizations, publications, and activities. Each faculty member is an adviser to a group of 6 to 8 students and supports the students' emotional, social, and academic well-being at Milton.

COLLEGE ADMISSION COUNSELING

Four college counselors work one-on-one with students, beginning in their Class II (eleventh grade) year, in a highly personal and effective approach toward the college admissions process.

For the classes of 2006–2008, the top college choices were Harvard (34), Brown (22), University of Pennsylvania (18), George Washington (16), Wesleyan (16), Yale (16), Cornell (14), Tufts (14), Colby (13), and Georgetown (12).

STUDENT BODY AND CONDUCT

Of the 680 students in the Upper School, 50 percent are boys and 50 percent are girls; 50 percent are boarding students and 50 percent are day students. Forty percent of Milton's enrolled students are students of color. Eighteen percent of the boarding students are international, coming from twenty countries across the globe. Thirty-three percent of Milton students receive financial aid, and the average grants account for 75 percent of tuition.

All Upper School students from Classes IV-I (grades 9–12) participate in the Self-Governing Association, led by 2 elected student representatives, 1 senior girl and 1 senior boy. Elected class representatives serve with faculty members on the Discipline Committee, which recommends to the Head of School appropriate responses when infractions of major school rules occur. Rules at Milton Academy foster the cohesion and morale of the community and enhance education by upholding standards of conduct developed by generations of students and faculty members.

ACADEMIC FACILITIES

Among the prominent buildings on the Milton campus are three primarily academic buildings; Warren Hall (English), Wigglesworth Hall (history), and Ware Hall (math and foreign languages); the Kellner Performing Arts Center, with a 350-seat teaching theater, a studio theater, dressing rooms, scene shop, practice rooms, orchestral rehearsal room, dance studio, and speech/debate room; the Athletic and Convocation Center, opened in 1998, including a hockey rink, a fitness center, three basketball courts, and an indoor track; the Williams Squash Courts; the Ayer Observatory; and Apthorp Chapel. Construction on the Pritzker Science Center was scheduled to begin November 8, 2008.

Cox Library contains more than 46,000 volumes, more than 150 periodicals with back issues on microfilm, and a newspaper collection dating back to 1704. It also provides CD-ROM sources, Internet access and online search capabilities. Within Cox Library is one of several computer laboratories.

BOARDING AND GENERAL FACILITIES

Milton Academy students live in one of eight single-sex houses ranging in size from 31 to 48 students; four for boys and four for girls. Single rooms house one third of the students, while the other two thirds of the students reside in double rooms. Milton houses include all four classes as well as faculty members' families. Students spend all their Milton years in one house, experiencing a family-at-school context for developing close relationships with valued adults, learning about responsibility to the community, taking leadership roles with peers, and sharing social and cultural traditions. All rooms are networked, and each student has an e-mail account, a telephone line, and voicemail. School computers are available for student use in the house common rooms.

The Health and Counseling Center and the Academic Skills Center, as well as house parents in each residential house, class deans, and the office of the school chaplain, are available to meet students' needs.

ATHLETICS

Milton believes that teamwork, sportsmanship, and the pursuit of excellence are important values and that regular vigorous exercise is a foundation of good health. Milton offers a comprehensive athletic program that includes physical education classes and a range of intramural and interscholastic sports geared to the needs and interests of every student.

The school's offerings in interscholastic sports are Alpine skiing, baseball, basketball, cross-country, field hockey, football, golf, ice hockey, lacrosse, sailing, soccer, softball, squash, swimming and diving, tennis, track, volleyball, and wrestling.

Intramural offerings include the outdoor program, Pilates, self-defense, soccer, squash, strength and conditioning, tennis, Ultimate Frisbee, and yoga.

Sports facilities include four athletic buildings, an ice hockey rink and fitness center, two indoor climbing walls, twelve playing fields, seventeen tennis courts, seven international squash courts, an all-weather track, a cross-country course, and a ropes course.

EXTRACURRICULAR OPPORTUNITIES

The breadth of extracurricular opportunities means that every student finds a niche—a comfortable place to develop new skills, take on leadership, show commitment, make friends, and have fun. Clubs and organizations include cultural groups such as the Asian Society, Latino Association, Onyx, and Common Ground (an umbrella organization for the various groups); the Arts Board; Dance Workshop; the Outdoor Club; the Chinese, French, and Spanish clubs; the debate, math, and speech teams; and Students for Gender Equality. There are twelve student publications, among them *The Asian, La Voz, MAGUS/MABUS, Mille Tonnes, Milton Measure, Milton Paper,* and the yearbook. Music programs include the chamber singers, the gospel choir, the glee club, the orchestra, improvisational jazz combos, four a cappella groups. The performing arts are an important part of the extracurricular offerings at Milton. Main stage theater productions, studio theater productions, play readings, and speech and debate team are a few of the available opportunities. Milton stages ten major theater productions each year, including a Class IV (ninth grade) play, student directed one-act plays, a dance concert, and a biennial musical. Service opportunities include the audio-visual crew, community service, Lorax (environmental group), Orange and Blue Key (admission tour guides and leaders), and the Public Issues Board.

DAILY LIFE

The academic day runs from 8 a.m. to 2:55 p.m., except on Wednesday, when classes end at 1:15. There are no classes on Saturday or Sunday. Cafeteria-style lunch is served from 11 a.m. to 1:30 p.m., and students eat during a free period within that time. The students' activities period is from 3 to 3:30 p.m. Athletics and extracurricular activities take place from 3:30 to 5:30 p.m. Family-style dinner is at 6 p.m., and the evening study period runs from 7:30 to 9:30 p.m. Lights-out time depends on the grade level of each student.

WEEKEND LIFE

Interscholastic games are held on Wednesday, Friday, and Saturday afternoons. Social activities on Friday and Saturday evenings are planned by the Student Activities Association. Day students join boarders every weekend for events such as dances with live or recorded music, classic and new films, concerts, plays, drama readings, dormitory open houses, and trips to professional sports events, arts events, or local museums.

Prior to leaving campus, students must check their plans with house parents, who must approve their whereabouts and any overnight plans.

SUMMER PROGRAMS

Milton Academy's summer programs develop, schedule, and supervise a wide range of offerings that connect with the school's mission. These programs include professional development opportunities for teachers, academic and recreational activities for students, and corporate and community-related events. In addition to hosting many outside programs, the Academy runs Sports Plus and Milton Academy Summer Hockey camps, as well as E-Cast Computer/Science School, all for students, along with the Cultural Diversity Institute and the Boarding Staff Conference for teachers from across the country.

COSTS AND FINANCIAL AID

For the 2008–09 academic year, tuition is $40,395 for boarding students and $33,150 for day students.

Milton seeks to enroll the most qualified applicants regardless of their financial circumstances. To that end, more than $6.1 million was provided in financial aid to students in the 2008–09 school year. All financial aid at Milton is awarded on the basis of need. In addition to the program of direct grants, the school offers installment payment options and two low-interest loan programs.

ADMISSIONS INFORMATION

Milton Academy seeks students who are able, energetic, intellectually curious, and have strong values and a willingness to grow. Applicants must submit the Secondary School Admission Test (SSAT) scores (students applying for eleventh grade may submit PSAT or SAT scores if applicable). All applicants must also submit a preliminary application, school transcript, teacher recommendations, parental statement, and two essays. An interview, on or off campus, is also required.

APPLICATION TIMETABLE

The deadline for applying is January 15. Notification letters are sent out on March 10; the reply date is April 10. There is a $50 application fee for U.S. applicants and a $100 fee for international applicants.

ADMISSIONS CORRESPONDENCE

Paul Rebuck, Dean of Admission
Milton Academy
170 Centre Street
Milton, Massachusetts 02186
Phone: 617-898-2227
Fax: 617-898-1701
E-mail: admissions@milton.edu
Web site: http://www.milton.edu

MISS HALL'S SCHOOL

Pittsfield, Massachusetts

Type: Girls' boarding and day college-preparatory school
Grades: 9–12
Enrollment: 190
Head of School: Jeannie K. Norris

THE SCHOOL

Founded in 1898 by Mira Hinsdale Hall, Miss Hall's School was one of the first girls' boarding schools established in New England. A graduate of Smith College, Mira Hall understood the advantages to girls of having a place of their own in which to learn and grow. During her forty-year tenure, she created a learning environment based on respect for the individual student, stimulating teaching, competitive spirit, intelligent supervision, and personal warmth. More than 100 years later, the School continues to educate young women and guide them toward success and fulfillment in their academic, professional, and personal endeavors.

The School's mission is grounded in a strong belief in the benefits of an all-girl educational environment. Since its founding, Miss Hall's School has remained convinced that the best learning and surest growth—in and out of the classroom—occur in a single-sex, small-school environment. The trustees, faculty members, and alumnae of the School are determined to preserve a family-style atmosphere wherein a girl can mature surely and gracefully into a bright, confident, self-reliant young woman.

Surrounded by wooded hills and New England villages, the School takes full advantage of its location in Berkshire County in western Massachusetts. The beauty of the 80-acre campus is captured in the vibrant autumns, snowy winters, colorful springs, and lush, green summers. With its rich history and natural beauty, the area has long attracted a wide array of artists, dancers, and musicians. Thousands of visitors travel to the Berkshires every year to attend festivals and special events and to visit historical sites, museums, and performing arts centers. The Clark Art Institute, *The Mount*, Tanglewood, Jacob's Pillow, Williamstown Theatre Festival, Shakespeare & Company, Hancock Shaker Village, the Norman Rockwell Museum, and the Massachusetts Museum of Contemporary Art are among the most popular attractions. The campus is just a 5-minute drive from the center of Pittsfield, a well-populated city that offers all the amenities associated with a tourist region.

A nonprofit corporation, Miss Hall's School is governed by a 26-member Board of Trustees. An active Alumnae Association of more than 3,000 members works with the administration, faculty members, and friends of Miss Hall's to ensure that the School continues to succeed in its fund-raising and recruiting efforts. Accredited by the New England Association of Schools and Colleges, Miss Hall's School is a long-standing member of the Secondary School Admission Test Board, the National Association of Independent Schools, and the National Coalition of Girls' Schools.

ACADEMIC PROGRAMS

Miss Hall's School augments a sophisticated college-preparatory curriculum with two innovative, nationally acclaimed programs. Through Horizons, girls work off campus to hone communication and problem-solving skills, refine ethical positions, and strengthen financial literacy. Through PAaLS, girls design programs around the themes of "voice" and leadership.

The Miss Hall's School college-preparatory academic program includes full offerings in math, science, history, English, foreign languages, English as a second language, the arts, and athletics. Each student must take at least five courses per term and graduate with a minimum of 18 credits. Within this framework, considerable care is taken to provide students with appropriate challenges. For many students, this means acceleration into the honors and Advanced Placement courses offered in all disciplines. An average class size of 11 and a student-teacher ratio of 7:1 ensure that each student receives the individual attention and encouragement that are vital to her success.

Graduation requirements are as follows: 4 years of English; 3 years of history, including United States history; 3 years of a foreign language; 3 years of mathematics, including algebra I and II and geometry; 3 years of science; a minimum of 2 additional elective credits; successful completion of *Horizons;* and two terms each year of athletics.

To fulfill their elective credit requirements, many students choose to enroll in courses in the Miss Hall's Expressive Arts Department. The seasoned expressive arts faculty members, drawing from their own experiences as professional artists and performers, enthusiastically promote the students' aesthetic, creative, academic, and intellectual growth. Expressive arts students also develop a thorough understanding of women's significant contributions to the art world, both historically and in the present day.

Not everything girls need to learn about the world and themselves can be learned in the classroom. Each Thursday throughout the school year, all students participate in *Horizons.* This unique experiential learning program allows students to gain new skills, explore areas of interest for college majors and careers, increase financial literacy, and learn the value of service. By graduation, each girl has volunteered in her community, written a sophisticated resume, developed interview skills, and completed an individual professional internship. *Horizons* work sites include Berkshire Medical Center, Norman Rockwell Museum, Merrill Lynch, American Red Cross, Sacred Heart School, Pittsfield Community Television, Congressman John Olver's office, Sabic Plastics, Canyon Ranch, Cranwell Resort, and many more.

FACULTY AND ADVISERS

Of the 56 Miss Hall's faculty members, 30 hold advanced degrees and 18 live on campus. Using their unique talents to serve the School in multiple capacities, faculty members act as academic instructors, class advisers, club facilitators, coaches, and dorm residents. Each Miss Hall's student also has the opportunity to select a faculty adviser, who is available to her for both academic and personal guidance.

Appointed the Head of School in 1996, Jeannie K. Norris continues to guide Miss Hall's through an exciting period of growth and campus expansion. A graduate of Pittsburg State University (B.M.Ed.) and Temple University (M.M.), she has previously served as Director of Admission and Financial Aid and Assistant Head of Enrollment at the Madeira School. With twenty-four years of teaching and administrative experience in all-girls independent schools, Norris arrived well prepared for the challenges of her position. Among her greatest achievements is the success of the Centennial Campaign, which was launched in 1998 to raise funds for the construction of new campus facilities.

COLLEGE ADMISSION COUNSELING

Preparation for college begins when a girl enrolls at Miss Hall's. Formal meetings occur in the junior year, when the student and her college counselor begin to talk about her goals and accomplishments and examine the possibilities for her college experience. The college counseling staff continues to offer guidance and support to each student throughout her junior and senior years as she refines her list, visits college campuses, takes the SAT and ACT tests, completes the college application process, and decides among her acceptances.

Recent Miss Hall's graduates have gone on to attend schools such as Barnard; Boston University; Chicago Art Institute; Colby; Cornell; Dartmouth; Georgetown; George Washington; Harvard; Lehigh; Middlebury; Northeastern; NYU; Smith; Williams College; Wellesley; Yale; the Universities of Massachusetts, Southern California, Virginia, and Wisconsin; and many other fine schools.

STUDENT BODY AND CONDUCT

With an enrollment of 190 students, Miss Hall's is able to maintain a small-school environment in which every girl is recognized for unique talents and encouraged to explore all of her interests. The 140 boarding students and 50 day students represent a broad spectrum of cultural and socioeconomic backgrounds, creating a valuable diversity within the student body. Of the currently enrolled students, 23 percent are students of color, 25 percent are international, and 47 percent receive financial assistance from the School. Geographically, they represent twenty states and twenty-two countries.

At Miss Hall's, each student is encouraged to try new activities, test out her leadership ability, and play an active role in the life of the School. As athletics team captains, Student Council representatives, class officers, club presidents, and musical ensemble leaders, girls gain valuable leadership experience that will help them grow into confident and capable young women. They are also given the serious responsibility of electing student representatives to serve on the School's two disciplinary committees, the Judicial Committee, and the Student-Faculty Advisory Committee.

ACADEMIC FACILITIES

The Main Building is a 90,000-square-foot, Georgian-style building that houses classrooms, laboratories, choral and instrumental music rehearsal space, administrative offices, Humes Euston Hall Library, the Melissa Leonhardt Academic Skills Center, and the Pamela Humphrey Firman Technology Center. Other campus resources include the Anne Meyer Cross Athletic Center, Ara West Grinnell Teaching Greenhouse, Elizabeth Gatchell Klein Arts Center, and Jessie P. Quick Ski Chalet.

The Humes Euston Hall Library, a 7,200-square-foot addition extending from the Main Building, opened in 2001. It incorporates spaces for electronic and traditional research and the Gustafson Family Lending Library. Study carrels and a periodical room designed around the Joseph Buerger Fireplace Alcove provide additional places for study and reading, while enclosed seminar rooms offer space for group work.

The Klein Arts Center also opened in 2001. This 14,000-square-foot building contains a flexible-space theater with dressing rooms, costume and prop-storage rooms, and a design workshop. Spacious dance, art, ceramics, and photography studios are housed in this impressive building.

BOARDING AND GENERAL FACILITIES

In addition to all of the resources listed above, the Main Building also houses underclass student dormitory rooms, faculty apartments, the Dining Room, the Health Center, and several living rooms and lounges. The senior dormitory, Witherspoon Hall, is located just a few yards from the Main Building.

ATHLETICS

In the 18,720-square-foot Cross Athletic Center, students enjoy the Thatcher Family Gymnasium for basketball and volleyball competitions, the Humphrey Family Aerobics and Fitness rooms, team rooms, lockers and showers, and Wilderness Program facilities.

Miss Hall's requires each student to participate in an athletic activity of her choice each term, including at least one team sport per year. Athletics teach girls valuable skills, enhance self-discipline, encourage confidence, and provide leadership opportunities. The wide variety of athletic offerings includes varsity and junior varsity sports as well as noncompetitive and recreational activities. In the fall term, students choose among crew, cross-country, field hockey, movement and dance, recreational tennis, soccer, and the Wilderness Program. Winter term offerings include aerobics, basketball, both competitive and recreational skiing, fitness, snowboarding, and volleyball. During the spring term, students participate in crew, fitness, lacrosse, movement and dance, softball, tennis, or the Wilderness Program.

EXTRACURRICULAR OPPORTUNITIES

With clubs and organizations to match every interest, it is easy to get involved at Miss Hall's School. The Student Council, the Social Committee, the Athletic Association, the Judicial Committee, and the Student-Faculty Advisory Committee provide excellent leadership opportunities, while the Essence Diversity Club, the Environmental Club, the Art Club, the French Club, the Latin Club, the Spanish Club, Students for a Free Tibet, and the International Student Alliance bring together students with common interests and goals. The *Hallways* student newspaper, *Hallmark* yearbook, and *Sol* literary magazine provide ample opportunities for aspiring artists and journalists. In addition to taking private lessons on campus, musicians and vocalists can choose from several performance groups, such as Grace Notes, the School's stellar a cappella singing group; Vocal Ensemble; Merrie Melodies, a student-faculty vocal group; and various instrumental ensembles. Two major theater productions each year showcase the talent, commitment, and enthusiasm of the School's actors and technical crew members.

DAILY LIFE

Academic classes are held five days a week for 50-minute periods, beginning at 8 a.m. On Mondays and Fridays, all members of the Miss Hall's community gather at Morning Meeting to share important announcements, updates on School-related issues, and reflections on global current events. Athletics take place between 3:45 and 5:15 p.m., after which students are free to relax, chat with friends, get started on their homework, and head to the Dining Room for dinner. Various club meetings, rehearsals, and tutorials are held in the evening, followed by a 7:30 to 9:30 p.m. quiet study-hall period.

WEEKEND LIFE

The Miss Hall's campus is a lively place on the weekends. While students do have the option of returning home for an occasional weekend, most girls remain on campus in order to participate in the wide variety of social and recreational activities arranged by the School's student-run Social Committee. Day students are also involved during the weekend, often arranging a Friday or Saturday overnight stay with a boarding friend.

Weekend activities include interscholastic dances and social events, volunteer and community service opportunities, trips to Boston and New York, pick-up sports, movie trips, shopping excursions, and theater, music, and dance performances held at nearby professional venues and colleges.

COSTS AND FINANCIAL AID

Tuition for the 2008–09 school year is $41,800 for boarding students and $25,850 for day students. Strongly committed to providing need-based financial aid for deserving candidates, Miss Hall's awarded more than $2 million in financial aid to 47 percent of the School's 2007–08 student population.

ADMISSIONS INFORMATION

Miss Hall's welcomes applications from girls who have the intellectual capacity and academic commitment necessary to meet the challenges of a demanding college-preparatory curriculum. The School also values extracurricular involvement, a spirit of curiosity, a willingness to explore new interests, and evidence of good citizenship.

Application materials are provided by the Admission Office upon a student's request for information about the School. In order to be considered for admission to Miss Hall's, each applicant must submit a completed student questionnaire and essay, three letters of recommendation, a completed parent form, school transcripts from the past two years, and a Secondary School Admission Test score report. Each applicant is also required to schedule an interview with a member of the admission staff. While telephone interviews can be arranged, Miss Hall's School strongly encourages prospective students to visit the campus for a tour and an interview. There is a $40 application fee ($75 for international students) for each submitted application.

APPLICATION TIMETABLE

Prospective students may choose to submit an early decision application by January 1, in which case they are notified of their admission status by January 15. Students who choose to submit their applications by the regular deadline of February 15 are notified of their admission status by March 10. Applications submitted after February 15 are considered on a rolling basis, as space permits.

ADMISSIONS CORRESPONDENCE

Kimberly B. Boland, '94
Director of Admission
Miss Hall's School
492 Holmes Road
Pittsfield, Massachusetts 01201
Phone: 800-233-5614 (toll-free)
Fax: 413-448-2994
E-mail: info@misshalls.org
Web site: http://www.misshalls.org

MISS PORTER'S SCHOOL

Farmington, Connecticut

Type: Girls' boarding and day college-preparatory school
Grades: 9–12
Enrollment: 330
Head of School: Katherine Gladstone Windsor

THE SCHOOL

Located in the center of Farmington, Connecticut, Porter's is a college-preparatory boarding and day school for girls in grades 9 through 12. Founded in 1843 by lifelong scholar and educator, Sarah Porter, the School's innovative, rigorous, well-rounded approach to education prepares girls to expand their minds and grow into socially engaged, confident young women. With 330 students hailing from twenty-two states and twenty countries, Porter's provides a diverse high school experience that helps young women become local and global leaders of the future.

A respected leader in preparing young women for college, Porter's demanding curriculum, collaborative environment, and supportive community distinguishes it as one of the nation's finest boarding schools. Porter's mission statement sets high expectations for students: "We challenge our students to become informed, bold, responsible, and ethical global citizens. We expect our graduates to shape a changing world."

The teaching faculty serves as educators, advisers, coaches, and mentors—developing close relationships with their students as they accept this challenge. All graduates earn acceptance into four-year colleges and universities.

Porter's location allows students to enjoy the charm of Farmington, while providing easy access to Hartford, New York, and Boston for social, cultural, and academic events. The picturesque, 50-acre campus is close to village stores and within a short walk of the Farmington River.

The School's governing board is composed of 35 trustees, both men and women, 27 of whom are alumnae. The Annual Fund Program provides 11 percent of the operating budget each year.

Porter's is accredited by the New England Association of Schools and Colleges. It is a member of the National Coalition of Girls' Schools, the Association of Boarding Schools, the Connecticut Association of Independent Schools, the National Association of Independent Schools, the Council for Advancement and Support of Education, and the Cum Laude Society.

ACADEMIC PROGRAMS

Porter's academic program prepares girls for college and beyond by emphasizing oral and written communication, critical thinking, research skills, and leadership development through the rigorous study of mathematics, foreign languages, science, history, English, and visual and performing arts.

During the fall and spring semesters, 112 courses are offered. To graduate, each student must have a total of 36 semester units, including 8 units of English, 6 units of a foreign language, 5 units of history, algebra I, intermediate or advanced algebra, geometry, 6 units of science, 2 units in the arts (visual art, music, theater, dance, art history, or photography), 1 unit in computers, and a ½ unit in ethical leadership. Students also must complete 20 hours of community service and 80 hours of an experiential education project (often an internship). They must participate in one of a variety of team sports offered, for a minimum of two seasons, and in athletics-based classes during the other seasons.

Advanced Placement examination preparation is available in art history, biology, calculus AB, calculus BC, chemistry, Chinese language and culture, computer science A, English language and composition, English literature, European history, French language, French literature, Latin literature, Latin: Vergil, macroeconomics, microeconomics, music theory, physics B, psychology, Spanish language, Spanish literature, statistics, studio art: drawing, and U.S. history.

Porter's average class size is 11 students. Honors courses are available for exceptional students. All ninth grade boarding students attend a required study hall each evening, while upper class boarding students observe quiet hours from 7:30 to 9:30 p.m. Grades, based on the letter system, and comments are provided four times a year. Adviser and house faculty comments are mailed at the end of each semester.

Qualified students may participate in independent projects and are encouraged to investigate career opportunities in carefully selected internships across the country. Juniors may choose to spend either their fall or their spring semester in the Maine Coast Semester or the Rocky Mountain Semester, or they may elect to participate in the School Year Abroad in France, Spain, China, India, or Italy.

FACULTY AND ADVISERS

Katherine Gladstone Windsor began as Head of School in 2008 and brings to Porter's a passion for education, a belief in the importance of educating girls for leadership, and wide-ranging experience with independent schools.

Before coming to Porter's, Ms. Windsor was the head of The Sage School, a coeducational day school for academically gifted students. Previously, Ms. Windsor held several positions at Sandy Spring Friends School, a coeducational boarding school, serving as head of residential life, department head/director of the Ninth Grade Program, women's athletic director and coach, history teacher, and director of the Summer Friends Camp Program. She also served as the site director for the residential program for exceptionally gifted students at the Center for Talented Youth Program at Johns Hopkins University.

Ms. Windsor has a B.A. in English from the University of Rochester and an M.A. in Leadership in Teaching from the College of Notre Dame in Baltimore, a women's institution. Currently, she is enrolled in the Mid-Career Doctoral Program in Educational Leadership at the University of Pennsylvania, which addresses the ongoing transformation of public and private educational organizations from a leadership perspective.

There are 55 teaching faculty members. Of these, 62 percent have advanced degrees. The School seeks teachers who are committed both to their own academic discipline and to the intellectual and personal development of young women. Faculty members participate fully in boarding school life, also serving as student advisers, coaches, and club advisers. House directors supervise dormitories, getting to know students individually and serving as parental influences. Each student has her own adviser, who helps her manage her academic program and is in frequent contact with her parents as well as with her teachers, coaches, and house director.

Summer sabbaticals for study and travel are available to faculty members who have served at the School for at least seven years. Assistance also is offered in financing graduate study.

COLLEGE PLACEMENT

The Director and Assistant Director of College Counseling help students plan their educational futures. Responsibility for handling college applications falls ultimately on the student, but the School offers strong support and counsels parents and students from the beginning to the end of the process. Beginning in February of the students' junior year, the college counselors meet with the students in small groups. They also confer with girls individually, helping each to understand her unique situation. When each girl leaves for spring vacation, she takes with her a recommended college list and is urged to visit at least one campus during that break.

Before June, students usually have decided on which colleges to visit during the summer. A comprehensive letter is sent to parents outlining each girl's choices, with assessments by the college counselor of the student's chances for admission. During the fall, more than 120 college representatives visit the School to meet with interested girls. During Parents' Weekend in October, the college counselor holds individual conferences with parents of seniors.

For the class of 2008, the middle 50 percent of SAT scores were 550–670 on the verbal portion, 570–670 on the mathematics portion, and 580–670 on the writing component. In 2008, students took 223 Advanced Placement tests. Twenty-three percent of the students achieved a score of 5, 33 percent achieved a score of 4, and 85 percent achieved a score of 3 or higher.

The class of 2008 had 80 graduates. The majority of graduates elected liberal arts programs, but a small number selected specialized curricula—fine arts, architecture, engineering, and business. Boston University, Brown, George Washington, Johns Hopkins, NYU, Princeton, Smith, and the U.S. Military Academy at West Point are just a few examples of the colleges and universities Porter's graduates currently are attending.

STUDENT BODY AND CONDUCT

In 2008–09, the student distribution by grade is grade 9, 75; grade 10, 88; grade 11, 86; and grade 12, 81. The current total of 330 students includes 215 boarding students and 115 day students from twenty-two states and twenty countries.

The goal of developing self-discipline and concern for others underlies student conduct rules. Each girl is expected to abide by School rules and adhere to the following Honor Code: As a student and member of the Miss Porter's School community, I promise to uphold the tradition of honesty and fairness that this community has taught since 1843. I will be truthful. I will be respectful of others, their property, and their opinions. I promise to foster these values in the community.

An important facet of the School's structure is the student government. The Student Council serves as the judiciary board in cases of rule infractions. When rules are broken, judicial decisions are made by the council and are subject to review by the head of school.

ACADEMIC FACILITIES

History and English classes meet in the Hamilton Building. The Ann Whitney Olin Center for the Arts and Sciences houses classrooms with state-of-the-art equipment and technology for the instruction of math, science, and computer technology, including Mac and PC labs. Art studios for photography, ceramics, painting, sculpture, printmaking, and jewelry making and a computer lab for graphic design are also located in Olin. Theater classes convene in the Barbara Lang Hacker '29 Theater. Dance classes are held in the recently renovated Dance Barn. Music classes meet in The KLG. The M. Burch Tracy Ford Library offers a number of amenities to support education and research, including an extensive book collection, fully wired classroom computers, conference rooms, and tranquil study spaces. Interlibrary loan networking supports the research curriculum. The Leila Dilworth Jones '44 Memorial holds a state-of-the-art language laboratory and classrooms for foreign language instruction.

BOARDING AND GENERAL FACILITIES

Nine dormitories, most of which were formerly private homes, are supervised by house directors. House directors are usually young couples with children, and they provide students a real sense of parental influence and family life. In five of the dormitories, students from grades 9 through 11 live together; two dormitories are reserved for ninth graders, and two are reserved for seniors.

The recently renovated dining room and administrative offices are located in Main, which also houses the Daisy Café, a student gathering place. The Ivy–The Shop at Miss Porter's School is Porter's on-campus store. The Student Health Center is staffed 24 hours a day by registered nurses. A physician makes regular visits and is on call 24 hours a day.

ATHLETICS

Porter's believes in maintaining a healthy balance between intellectual activity and physical exercise; each student participates daily on a team or in a sports class. The School is the only girls' school that belongs to the highly competitive Founders League. Interscholastic sports are badminton, basketball, crew, cross-country, equestrian, field hockey, golf, lacrosse, soccer, softball, skiing, squash, swimming and diving, tennis, track and field, Ultimate Frisbee, and volleyball. An extensive number of playing fields and seven DecoTurf tennis courts are available. An athletics/recreation center contains two gyms, an indoor track, a climbing wall, a fitness center, and basketball and volleyball courts. An additional athletic facility with an eight-lane pool and eight international squash courts opened in September 2007. A new boathouse for crew sits on the Farmington River. Equestrian and skiing participants use nearby facilities.

EXTRACURRICULAR OPPORTUNITIES

Endowments bring concerts, speakers, drama productions, and poets to the campus. There are many weekend activities both on and off the campus. Membership in campus clubs is open to any student who wishes to participate; most students belong to at least one extracurricular group. Among the organizations are *Salmagundy* (student newspaper); *Daeges Eage* (yearbook); *Chautauqua* (expository writing); *Haggis Baggis* (creative writing); Archives (school history), several singing groups; Debate Team; Concordia (social service); Model UN, Dance Workshop, Players Mandolin Performance Troupe, and *Watu Wazuri* (multicultural organization). Students also operate their own radio station, which broadcasts to the School community. Theater, dance, vocal, and instrumental performances are staged several times a year. Annual events include Parents' Weekend, Grandparents' Day, Reunion Weekend, and Graduation.

DAILY LIFE

Classes, held Monday through Friday, begin at 7:45 a.m., following breakfast. Each class is 50 minutes long. Lunch is served from 11:30 to 1:30. Sports begin at 3:45. Morning meetings are held two times a week, and the entire School community gathers regularly for assemblies and convocations. Club meetings take place during Clubs Period once a week and before or after the 5:30 dinner hour. Study hours begin at 7:30 and end at 9:30. Students may study in the dormitories, in the library, or in monitored study halls.

WEEKEND LIFE

Each weekend, a variety of activities are offered, ranging from dances, movies, and trips to plays, special dinners, and concerts. During closed weekends, students remain on the campus, except for day trips. On open weekends, girls may, with permission from home, leave school for the weekend, but many girls remain at school and participate in the wide variety of activities. Day students are encouraged to take part in all weekend activities. About half of a semester's weekends are open.

Coeducational events are held frequently on campus and at other schools, including concerts, dances, and community service activities. Churches and synagogues are located nearby.

COSTS AND FINANCIAL AID

The cost of tuition, room, and board in 2008–09 was $41,100. Day student tuition was $31,850. A health center fee and an activities fee are additional charges for both day students and boarders. Books and private music or athletic lessons are extra.

For the 2008–09 school year, financial aid totaling $3.6 million was awarded to approximately 40 percent of the students. Scholarship aid is given on the basis of merit and need, as demonstrated by the School and Student Service form, available from the Admission Office. In addition, the Admission Office requires a copy of the family's most recent federal income tax form 1040 as well as W-2 wage statements. Financial aid decisions are announced at the time of the admission decisions and are renewable each year if the student demonstrates continued need and meets academic standards.

ADMISSIONS INFORMATION

Admission is based on school records, aptitude and achievement, character, citizenship, and potential. A personal interview is required. The Secondary School Admission Test (SSAT) or ISEE should be taken in November, December, or January preceding the September in which a student wishes to enter. International students must also take the TOEFL if English is not their first language. Students may apply for entrance in grade 9, 10, 11, or 12. The School encourages able students to apply, without regard to race, color, creed, national or ethnic origin, or socioeconomic background.

APPLICATION TIMETABLE

Applicants are urged to contact the Admission Office to arrange for a tour, a visit to class, and an interview. The office is open Monday through Friday from 8:30 to 4:30. Most interviews and tours take place in the fall, but they may be scheduled year-round. The application, including recommendations, SSAT scores, and a $50 nonrefundable fee ($100 for international applicants), must be completed by January 15. Candidates are notified by March 10 of the admission committee's decision, and families must reply by April 10. If openings are available after April 10, interested families are encouraged to complete the application process.

ADMISSIONS CORRESPONDENCE

Deborah W. Haskins
Office of Admission
Miss Porter's School
Farmington, Connecticut 06032
Phone: 860-409-3530 (admission)
860-409-3500 (general)
Fax: 860-409-3531
E-mail: admission@missporters.org
Web site: http://www.porters.org

MONTCLAIR COLLEGE PREPARATORY SCHOOL

Van Nuys, California

Type: Coeducational boarding and day college-preparatory school
Grades: 6–12: Lower School, 6–8; Upper School, 9–12
Enrollment: School total: 300; Upper School: 240
Head of School: Dr. Mike McDonnell, Director

THE SCHOOL

Montclair College Preparatory School is the oldest independent coeducational school in the San Fernando Valley. The School is divided into an Upper School (grades 9–12) and a Lower School (grades 6, 7, and 8), which share the same campus. It is conveniently located near the Roscoe exit of the San Diego freeway.

Montclair was founded in 1956 by Dr. Vernon E. Simpson. The School was established to provide solid academic training to prepare students to enter college or university. Limited boarding facilities are available.

A nonprofit organization, Montclair is governed by a Board of Directors and faculty academic advisement and standards committees that work together to maintain the high caliber of academics and to provide appropriate social, athletic, and cultural outlets for the student body.

Montclair College Preparatory School is fully accredited by the Western Association of Schools and Colleges and is a member of the California Scholarship Federation, the College Board, the National Association of Secondary School Principals, and the National Honor Society.

ACADEMIC PROGRAMS

Requirements for graduation include 4 years of English (including a full year of senior composition); 3 years of a foreign language; 3 years of laboratory sciences (beginning in the ninth grade); 4 years of math; 1 year of computer science, U.S. history, economics, psychology, and government; and 1 year of fine arts. Elective courses complete the 21-unit total.

Montclair also offers strong Advanced Placement courses. Recent students have achieved scores of 3 or better on the Advanced Placement Program tests in English language and composition, Spanish language, U.S. history, economics (microeconomics and macroeconomics), biology, European history, calculus (AB and BC), and U.S. government.

The Upper School offers many electives, such as film production, statistics, speech and debate, humanities (art and music theory), drama, and art. Students in all grade levels are able to take advantage of the School's new visual and performing arts center. All students are required to take physical education, and many participate in the athletics program.

FACULTY AND ADVISERS

Faculty members are selected for their commitment to strong academic instruction as well as their superior academic backgrounds and personal enthusiasm for the School. In addition to teaching, they act as class advisers, coaches, and club sponsors. There are 40 full-time and 8 part-time instructors. Faculty members hold forty-two baccalaureate degrees, twenty-eight master's degrees, and three doctoral degrees. Faculty members belong to a number of professional associations.

COLLEGE ADMISSION COUNSELING

College counseling begins in the tenth-grade guidance classes and continues in the junior year with a College Counseling Night for parents and students. At this meeting, all aspects of college entrance are discussed, including application procedures, requirements, and the differences among schools. The counseling office maintains a file of college catalogs from every major college in the country and provides application forms and scholarship applications.

During the senior year, field trips are taken to both public and private colleges and universities. College representatives are also invited to speak on the campus to interested students.

Recent Montclair graduates have been admitted to Amherst, Brown, Colgate, Harvard, MIT, Oxford, Princeton, Stanford, Swarthmore, USC, Wellesley, and Yale as well as to all campuses of the University of California and California State University.

STUDENT BODY AND CONDUCT

Student government activities are held frequently. There are class officers as well as Associated Student Body officers. The Student Council meets weekly and sets the pace of outside student activities. A Student Court also convenes regularly.

ACADEMIC FACILITIES

The 5-acre campus includes the main classroom building, which was erected in 1970. There are thirty-three classrooms, including four science laboratories. In 1975, the Leslie H. Green Auditorium was constructed. It serves as both auditorium and gymnasium and is used for drama and theatrical productions. The library contains 7,500 volumes and subscribes to twenty periodicals. The Annex, across the street from the main campus, contains the new visual and performing arts center, an amphitheater, and a multimedia center. Nine classrooms were added in 1990, along with an additional two in 2002. In 2005, construction was completed on a state-of-the-art technology center, administrative offices, and a conference room.

ATHLETICS

Montclair is a competitive school, both in academics and in athletics. The sports program emphasizes fair play and sportsmanship. The coaching staff stresses skills and teamwork rather than individual performance. All students in grades 6 through 9 are required to participate in daily physical education classes. Students in grades 11 and 12 are encouraged to participate in extracurricular sports.

Coeducational sports are tennis, track, and volleyball. Girls' teams are available in basketball, soccer, softball, and volleyball. Boys' teams are fielded in baseball, basketball, football, and soccer. Montclair also fields teams in golf.

Athletics facilities include a fully equipped gym, which was constructed in 1975. The building houses offices for the athletics directors, locker rooms, and a weight-training room. The campus includes a recently renovated, all-purpose, artificial-turf recreational field for physical education and team practice; regular games are held at local public school facilities as well as at facilities that are either owned or leased by the School. The School recently completed a state-of-the-art baseball field located just a few minutes from the campus.

The School is a member of the California Interscholastic Federation (CIF). The football team won the league championship for seven of the last eleven years and was CIF champion in 1990. The basketball team won the league championship for six of the last twelve years and was State Division V champion in 1995. The baseball team won the league championship for nine years and won the CIF championship in 1979, 1981, 1982, 1983, 1990, and 1991.

EXTRACURRICULAR OPPORTUNITIES

Life at Montclair is varied and energetic. An active drama club stages several productions each year. There are cheerleading squads and a pep squad. A newspaper is published by the journalism class, and another group assembles the yearbook. There are campus clubs in science, languages, and photography. A Ski Club conducts trips to nearby resorts on weekends and during the semester break. In addition, the School offers trips to Greece, Italy, France, the Galapagos Islands, and Washington, D.C.

Montclair provides a well-balanced social program. Major social events include Homecoming, Spirit Week, and the Junior-Senior Prom. Other social events are held by each grade level under the guidance of the administration.

DAILY LIFE

Classes begin at 8 a.m. There are three periods of instruction prior to a 15-minute nutrition break at 10:30. Three more periods of instruction follow before the 1:15 lunch break. The cocurricular classes then begin, and all students have an elective or study hall or participate in sports from 1:45 until dismissal at 2:30.

SUMMER PROGRAMS

A six-week summer program offers remedial and review work in English, math, study skills, and languages. Interested students from any school may enroll. The summer school runs from early July to mid-August. The School also sponsors a summer course in marine biology. Summer camps are available for students who are interested in football, baseball, and basketball. Further information may be obtained from the Director of Athletics at the School address. The price of the summer athletics camps varies from sport to sport.

COSTS AND FINANCIAL AID

Tuition for the 2008–09 school year is $15,000 (grade 6, $12,000). Textbooks and tuition insurance are an additional $1000 per year. International students' room and board, books, and activity fee are an additional $18,900. A deposit is required upon acceptance of admission. The balance may be paid in one or two payments (September 1 and January 1) or on a monthly basis.

A limited amount of financial aid is available and is awarded on the basis of need.

ADMISSIONS INFORMATION

A 3-hour in-house entrance exam or the ISEE is required. In addition, applicants must provide one personal reference, two teacher references, and a transcript. All factors are considered before a student is accepted.

APPLICATION TIMETABLE

Inquiries are welcome at any time. Application forms are sent on request, and, after the completed form and a $100 application fee are received, the applicant is advised of the date for the entrance examination. Each decision concerning admission is made after the applicant has submitted all the necessary forms and taken the entrance exam. Interested students are advised to apply before April 1 if they wish to enter the School the following September.

ADMISSIONS CORRESPONDENCE

Director of Admissions
Montclair College Preparatory School
8071 Sepulveda Boulevard
Van Nuys, California 91402
Phone: 818-787-5290
Fax: 818-786-3382
Web site: http://www.montclairprep.net

MORAVIAN ACADEMY

Bethlehem, Pennsylvania

Type: Day college-preparatory school
Grades: PK–12: Lower School, prekindergarten–5; Middle School, 6–8; Upper School, 9–12
Enrollment: School total: 814; Upper School: 287
Head of School: George N. King Jr., Headmaster

THE SCHOOL

Moravian Academy (MA) traces its origin back to 1742 and the Moravians who settled Bethlehem. Guided by the wisdom of John Amos Comenius, Moravian bishop and renowned educator, the Moravian Church established schools in every community in which it settled. Moravian Academy became incorporated in 1971 when Moravian Seminary for Girls and Moravian Preparatory School were merged. The school has two campuses: the Lower–Middle School campus in the historic downtown area of Bethlehem and the Upper School campus on a 120-acre estate 6 miles to the east. The school is within minutes of three major hospitals, and medical services are easily available.

For more than 260 years, Moravian Academy has encouraged sound innovations to meet contemporary challenges while recognizing the permanence of basic human values. The school seeks to promote young people's full development in mind, body, and spirit by fostering a love for learning, respect for others, joy in participation and service, and skill in decision making. Preparation for college occurs in an atmosphere characterized by an appreciation for the individual.

Moravian Academy is governed by a Board of Trustees. Six members are representatives of the Moravian Church. The school is valued at $31.2 million, of which $11.5 million is endowment. Annual Giving in 2007–08 was $568,000, and the operating expenses for that year were $13.2 million.

Moravian Academy is accredited by the Middle States Association of Colleges and Schools and the Pennsylvania Association of Independent Schools. The school is a member of the National Association of Independent Schools, the Association of Delaware Valley Independent Schools, the College Board, the Council for Spiritual and Ethical Education, the School and Student Service for Financial Aid, and the Secondary School Admission Test Board.

Moravian Academy does not discriminate on the basis of race, nationality, sex, sexual orientation, religious affiliation, or ethnic origin in the administration of its educational and admission policies, financial aid awards, and athletic or other school-administered programs. Applicants who are disabled (or applicants' family members who are disabled) and require any type of accommodation during the application process, or at any other time, are encouraged to identify themselves and indicate what type of accommodation is needed.

ACADEMIC PROGRAMS

Students are required to carry five major courses per year. Minimum graduation requirements include English, 4 credits; mathematics, 3 credits; lab sciences, 3 credits; foreign language, 3 credits; social studies, 3 credits; fine arts, 1 credit; and physical education and health. All students must successfully complete a semester course in world religions or ethics. Community service is an integral part of the curriculum. Electives are offered in many areas, such as drama, advanced chemistry, calculus, economics, art, history, and Chinese and Japanese language. Moravian Academy offers Advanced Placement courses, numerous honors courses, and honors independent study. The Academy also participates in a high school scholars program that enables highly qualified students to take college courses at no cost. The overall student-faculty ratio is about 9:1, with classes ranging from 10 to 18 students.

Supervised study halls are held regularly during the school day. Grades in most courses are A–F; D is a passing grade. However, a C- is required to advance to the next level. Reports are sent to parents, and parent-conference opportunities are scheduled in the fall semester. Faculty and staff members are available for additional conferences whenever necessary. Examinations are held at the end of each seventeen-week semester in all major subjects. In the senior year, final examinations are given in May to allow seniors time for a two-week Post Term Experience before graduation.

FACULTY AND ADVISERS

The Upper School has 37 full-time and 6 part-time faculty members. Eighty-four percent of the full-time Upper School faculty members have advanced degrees. Several faculty members have degrees in counseling in addition to other subjects, and the entire faculty shares in counseling through the Faculty Advisor Program.

George N. King Jr. was appointed Headmaster in 2007. He previously served as the Head of the Wooster School in Danbury, Connecticut. Mr. King received his B.A. from Murray State University and his M.A. from the New England Conservatory of Music.

COLLEGE ADMISSION COUNSELING

The Director of Academic Counseling begins group work in college guidance in the eleventh grade. Tenth graders take the PSAT as practice and repeat it the following year. College Night is held annually for juniors and their parents. Juniors meet weekly in small groups for college counseling during the second semester and have an individual family conference in the spring. They take the PSAT, SAT Reasoning Test, and SAT Subject Tests. Some students also elect to take the ACT in their junior or senior year. Seniors meet twice weekly in small groups during the first semester for additional guidance and are guided through the college application process. They take the SAT Reasoning Test and Subject Tests again, if necessary. In recent years, approximately 80 to 85 percent of the junior and senior classes take at least one Advanced Placement course and earn a score of 3 or higher.

Average SAT scores of 2008 graduates were 624 verbal, 622 math, and 627 writing. Graduates of 2008 are attending Boston University, Cornell, Dartmouth, Drexel, Elizabethtown, Lehigh, Temple, University of Pennsylvania, and Yale. Some students participate in travel abroad or Rotary international exchange programs before attending college.

STUDENT BODY AND CONDUCT

The Upper School in 2008–09 had 131 boys and 157 girls. The school understands the value of diversity in the educational setting. In all divisions, students and faculty members from a variety of ethnic, cultural, religious, and socioeconomic backgrounds carry on this commitment. Through classroom activities, nondenominational chapel services discussing many faiths, and active engagement with each other, students at Moravian Academy are encouraged to appreciate one another's individuality.

Students enjoy the small classes and the opportunity for participation in sports and other activities. Students are expected to wear clothing that is neat and appropriate for school. Denim is not permitted during the school day, and a school uniform is required for members of performing groups. Students participate actively in a Student Council. Serious matters of discipline come before a faculty-student discipline committee.

ACADEMIC FACILITIES

Snyder House, Walter Hall, and the Heath Science Complex hold the classrooms, studios, and laboratories (chemistry, physics, biology, and computer). In September 2007, the Academy dedicated the new Van S. Merle-Smith Woodworking Studio. All of the library's resources are integrated with the instructional program to intensify and individualize the educational experience. The Richard and Lorraine Fuisz Library contains 8,500 volumes and fifty-two periodicals and features an enhanced CD-ROM reference center network that supports a strong interlibrary-loan program. There are dedicated computer labs, additional computers in the library, portable wireless labs, and a computer in every classroom. SMARTboards are used in all divisions to enhance the learning process. The Couch Fine Arts Center houses the studio arts department. A 350-seat auditorium enhances the music and theater programs. There are seven colleges in the area.

ATHLETICS

A strong athletics program meets the guidelines of the school's philosophy that a person must be nurtured in body, as well as in mind and spirit, and that respect for others and participation are important goals. A large gymnasium, eight athletics fields, and six tennis courts provide the school with facilities for varsity and junior varsity teams in boys' lacrosse and baseball; girls' field hockey; boys' and girls' basketball, cross-country, soccer, swimming, and tennis; coeducational golf;

and a girls' varsity team in softball. Students also have the opportunity to participate in football, track, and wrestling in co-operative programs with a local school. A gymnasium that includes a weight room complements the physical education facilities in Walter Hall. An outdoor recreational pool is available for special student functions as well as the Academy's summer day camp program for younger children.

All students have the chance to take part in team sports—and many of them do. In any given athletic season, more than one third of the Upper School student body participates in after-school athletics at the Academy.

There are golf courses in the Lehigh Valley, along with an indoor rock-climbing facility, a bicycle velodrome, and indoor stables. Many students belong to the ski club during the winter.

EXTRACURRICULAR OPPORTUNITIES

Moravian Academy's activity program provides opportunities for varied interests and talents. Included are service projects, outdoor education, International Club, *Legacy* (yearbook), the newspaper, Model Congress, Model UN, PJAS, Scholastic Scrimmage, and a variety of activities that change in response to student interests. A fine arts series combines music, art, drama, and dance. The annual Country Fair gives students an opportunity to work with the Parents' Association to create a family fun day for the school and Lehigh Valley community. Rooted in Moravian tradition, a strong appreciation of music has continued. There are several student musical groups, including chorale, MA Chamber Singers, handbell choirs, and instrumental ensembles. A highlight of the year is the Christmas Vespers Service.

DAILY LIFE

A typical school day begins at 8 a.m., and classes run until 3:15 p.m. on Monday, Tuesday, Wednesday, and Friday. On Thursday, classes conclude at 2:45. The average length of class periods is about 40 minutes. Students usually take six classes a day.

A weekly nondenominational chapel service is held on Thursday mornings. On Monday, Tuesday, Wednesday, and Friday, there is a period for class or school meetings.

COSTS AND FINANCIAL AID

Tuition is $19,380. There is an additional dining fee for students. An initial deposit of $1000 is required upon acceptance, and the remainder of the fee is to be paid in two installments, unless other arrangements are made. An additional fee for tuition insurance is recommended for all new students.

Financial aid is available, and the school uses the recommendation of the School and Student Service for Financial Aid. Once a student has been accepted for admission, aid is determined and renewed or awarded on the basis of demonstrated financial need. Aid is received by approximately 17 percent of Upper School students.

ADMISSIONS INFORMATION

Students are admitted in grades 9–11. Each applicant is carefully considered. Students who demonstrate an ability and willingness to handle a rigorous academic program, as well as such qualities as intellectual curiosity, responsibility, creativity, and cooperation, are encouraged to apply. Scores on tests administered by the school are also used in the admission process. In addition, school records, recommendations, and a personal interview are required. Admissions are usually completed by May, but there are sometimes openings available after that time.

APPLICATION TIMETABLE

Inquiries are welcome at any time. The Admission Office makes arrangements for tours and classroom visits during the school week. If necessary, other arrangements for tours can be made. The application fee is $65. Test dates are scheduled on specified Saturday mornings from January through March. Notifications are sent after February 15, and families are asked to respond within two weeks.

ADMISSIONS CORRESPONDENCE

Daniel J. Axford
Director of Admissions, Upper School
Moravian Academy
4313 Green Pond Road
Bethlehem, Pennsylvania 18020
Phone: 610-691-1600
Web site: http://www.moravianacademy.org

MORRISTOWN–BEARD SCHOOL

Morristown, New Jersey

Type: Coeducational day college-preparatory school
Grades: 6–12
Enrollment: School total: 538; Upper School: 392
Head of School: Dr. Alex D. Curtis

THE SCHOOL

The Morristown-Beard School (MBS) was established in 1971 by the merger of the Morristown School (for boys) and the Beard School (for girls), both of which were founded in 1891. Three Harvard University graduates founded the Morristown School as a preparatory school for their alma mater. While the Beard School originated as a kindergarten, it continued to add grade levels and courses for girls who wanted to attend college. In 1903, the first graduate of the Beard School matriculated to Vassar College, thus establishing a standard for future graduates.

The Morristown-Beard School is located in Morristown, a historic town in northern New Jersey. Its location 25 miles west of New York City allows frequent field trips to experience the cultural and educational benefits of Manhattan. Situated on a 22-acre campus of rolling lawns and shady trees, the pristine campus reflects the heritage and beauty befitting a school on the National Registry of Historic Places.

The purpose of the School as an academic institution is to challenge and support a range of learners, with a particular emphasis on preparation for rigorous college study. The School's goal is to guide students to appreciate the life of the mind and to become creative, thoughtful, and caring individuals who possess a sense of awareness of and a responsibility for the needs, concerns, and dignity of others.

A 24-member Board of Trustees governs the School. The School endowment is more than $10 million.

Morristown-Beard School is accredited by the Middle States Association of Colleges and Schools and approved by the New Jersey State Department of Education. It is affiliated with the National Association of Independent Schools, the New Jersey Association of Independent Schools, the Educational Records Bureau, the Advanced Placement Program of the College Board, the Council for Advancement and Support of Education, the School Consortium of New Jersey, the National Association of Principals of Schools for Girls, and the National Association of College Admission Counselors.

ACADEMIC PROGRAMS

The academic year is divided into two 16-week terms. Communication is very important, so teachers send frequent reports to parents. Full grade and comment reports are provided at the end of each 8-week period, and interim reports are provided at the middle of each quarter, with additional progress reports sent as needed. Parent/adviser conferences are held twice annually. A letter grading system is used.

The Middle School (grades 6–8) is housed in one building, where an interdisciplinary approach to academics is accompanied by individual attention and an emphasis on character building. In addition, Middle School students enjoy numerous sports and extracurricular activities that are designed to supplement and enhance the classroom experience. The major objectives in the Middle School are teaching students how to learn, challenge themselves, and appreciate an environment that is supportive of others. The Middle School core curriculum includes language arts, social studies, math, science, and world languages. Reading for challenge and enrichment is emphasized, and technology is incorporated into teaching strategies.

The Upper School daily schedule is a modified block schedule, whereby each class meets three times per week for extended periods. Extra help is readily available and is integrated into the daily schedule. In each subject, students are placed in one of three academic levels according to their aptitude and achievement. Staff learning specialists are available to provide assistance.

To graduate from the Upper School, students must complete a minimum of 4 years of English; 3 years each of history, science, mathematics, and foreign language; and additional requirements in fine arts, the senior project, community service, and health and physical education. Nearly 130 course offerings are available in the Upper School, including English; Spanish, French, and Latin; early modern world history, United States history, the twentieth century, African studies, and constitutional law; algebra, geometry, statistics, precalculus, and calculus; biology, chemistry, and physics; and art, engineering drawing, architecture, theater, choir, dance, and jazz.

One-term minicourses include creative writing, a writing workshop, and speech; computer programming; photography and printmaking; art history; and studies of Africa, Asia, Russia, and the Middle East.

The School regularly offers thirteen Advanced Placement courses: English, European history, American history, calculus AB, calculus BC, statistics, biology, chemistry, physics, studio art, French, Spanish, and Latin. An Honors Program is offered in English, French, Spanish, history, algebra, geometry, trigonometry, precalculus, chemistry, and biology. Qualified juniors and seniors may undertake independent study.

Six full-credit courses plus physical education are required each term. A typical course load includes English, math, history, science, foreign language, and physical education. Most students elect to add one or two full-credit courses or minicourses.

Independent studies are available to juniors and seniors with the approval of the Head of the Upper School. During the last three weeks of May, seniors complete their Advanced Placement and final exams and then engage in independent-study projects.

MBS is an active member in the American Field Service student exchange program, with at least 1 international student in attendance each year. The School offers many and varied educational field trips throughout the year, including two-week intensive language programs in France and Spain.

The average class size at Morristown-Beard is 12, and the ratio of students to faculty members is 7:1.

The Morristown-Beard School academic schedule comprises thirty-two weeks of instruction, divided into semesters. The schedule provides for long winter and spring vacations. Final examinations are held in June.

FACULTY AND ADVISERS

The faculty consists of 90 full-time and 3 part-time teachers. Fifty-three hold master's degrees and 13 hold doctoral degrees.

Dr. Alex D. Curtis was appointed Head of School in 2004. Previously, he was the Director of Admission and Financial Aid at Princeton Day School. He holds a bachelor's degree from Swarthmore College and a doctoral degree in art history from Princeton University. Dr. Curtis has taught art history and Latin and has coached rugby. He is currently teaching an advanced senior seminar on Baroque art.

At Morristown-Beard, faculty and staff members are dedicated to supporting and challenging each student. Virtually every faculty member meets the student in some capacity in addition to that of a classroom teacher: on the playing field or stage, as an adviser for various activities, and especially in the role of counselor to between 10 and 12 students.

COLLEGE ADMISSION COUNSELING

Virtually every graduate of Morristown-Beard continues his or her education at a highly selective college. Students begin the personalized college application process in eleventh grade with individual counseling and group information sessions. Parents, students, advisers, and college counselors work closely together throughout the process. Admissions officers from more than 100 colleges and universities visit Morristown-Beard annually to interview juniors and seniors.

Members of the class of 2008 are attending sixty-four different colleges, including Bucknell, Boston College, Bryn Mawr, Dartmouth, Franklin and Marshall, Fordham, George Washington, Johns Hopkins, NYU, Rutgers, Syracuse, Skidmore, and Wesleyan.

STUDENT BODY AND CONDUCT

In 2008–09, the School enrolled 536 day students in grades 6–12 as follows: grade 6, 42; grade 7, 52; grade 8, 52; grade 9, 99; grade 10, 96; grade 11, 103; and grade 12, 94. Students come from seventy-eight different communities in central and northern New Jersey.

The Morristown-Beard School expects students to respect academic achievement, to be aware of differences, and to be thoughtful toward others. As a community, MBS lives by five core values: compassion, courage, integrity, respect, and responsibility. The School admires students who exhibit creative thought and intellect and who believe in serving the community at large. The School operates on the basis of honor, both inside and outside the classroom. In addition, the School insists that students appreciate a reasonable but clearly defined dress code. There is an active Student Government Association that works closely with the faculty and administration toward common goals.

ACADEMIC FACILITIES

The Morristown-Beard School campus consists of ten buildings. Grant Hall houses the English and World Language Departments. Newly renovated Headmaster's Cottage houses the Alumni and Development Office. Beard Hall houses the History Department and administrative offices. South Wing, also newly renovated, is home to Visual Arts and the learning center. Wilke Hall houses two vocal and instrumental music classrooms and a 100-seat black-box theater. The science building houses six classrooms and labs and the dining hall. The new Middle School building was completed in September 2008, and the performing arts center is projected to be finished early in 2009.

The Anderson Library, which was completed in 2001, is home to 14,500 volumes, more than fifty printed periodicals, and many online databases, including full-text newspapers and periodicals. The library is connected to the campuswide network and the Internet. In addition, MBS participates in Jerseycat, a state-wide interlibrary loan program to provide students and faculty members with additional research and reference materials. Morristown-Beard library resources are supplemented by the School Loan Program of the Morris County Library, which is located adjacent to the campus.

ATHLETICS

Morristown-Beard School believes that students learn the value of commitment, teamwork, and sportsmanship through their participation in athletics. Every student has the opportunity to be actively involved on teams. The Middle School athletic program emphasizes skill acquisition and participation. In the Upper School, most sports have both varsity and junior varsity squads. The boys' teams include baseball, basketball, cross-country, football, golf, ice hockey, lacrosse, soccer, swimming, tennis, and track. Girls' teams compete with other schools in basketball, field hockey, lacrosse, soccer, softball, swimming, tennis, track, and volleyball. In 2005, two new FieldTurf athletic fields were installed, along with a state-of-the-art track. There is a third, natural-grass athletic field for baseball and soccer on the campus. The William E. Simon Athletic Center and the William W. Rooke Family Pool were dedicated in 1986.

EXTRACURRICULAR OPPORTUNITIES

Involvement in extracurricular activities is a key element in a student's total development and therefore is greatly encouraged at Morristown-Beard. Students participate in student government, the School newspaper *(Crimson Sun)*, the yearbook *(Salmagundi)*, an art/literary magazine *(Mariah)*, various instrumental music ensembles, and chorus; astronomy, chess, computer, drama, photography, and skiing clubs; and local chapters of the Cum Laude Society, American Field Service, and National Junior Honor Society. There are also School-sponsored trips to educational and cultural events in the area and in nearby cities. Opportunities for student travel are available during spring and summer vacations.

While participation in community service is a requirement, most students exceed the minimum number of hours by assisting the community in a variety of programs, some of which include assisting children in after-school programs, visiting nursing homes and veterans' hospitals, participating in Habitat for Humanity, and sponsoring Special Olympics programs on campus.

Class dances, an Upper School prom, a foreign language fair, and a fine arts festival that is shared with a consortium of schools are among the social activities. Special events include several dramatic productions, including musical theater and choral and band concerts, and drug and alcohol awareness programs, varied assembly presentations, and a parent/student athletics awards dinner.

DAILY LIFE

Classes are held from 8:05 a.m. to 3:15 p.m., Monday through Friday, on a modified block schedule. Students have a half-hour lunch period. Study halls, extra help, and activities periods are incorporated into the schedule. Sports competition follows the academic day.

COSTS AND FINANCIAL AID

In 2008–09, Upper School tuition was a comprehensive fee of $27,320.

Financial aid is available to all qualified students. Amounts granted are based on financial need. In 2008–09, over $1 million in aid was given to 60 students (11 percent of the student body), with awards ranging from $5000 to full tuition.

ADMISSIONS INFORMATION

Admission decisions are based on recommendations, grade reports, interviews, test results, effort, potential for future achievement, and seriousness of academic curiosity. Applicants must submit a formal application, which includes a family information sheet, parent and student questionnaires, transcripts, and four letters of recommendation. In addition, each student must complete an interview with an admission officer and submit test scores from the ISEE or SSAT. MBS administers the ISEE monthly from October to May. All applicants are considered without regard to race, creed, color, or ethnic or national origin.

APPLICATION TIMETABLE

Morristown-Beard School offers an early deadline in December and a regular deadline in February. It is recommended that applications for each deadline be completed as early as possible, since places in various grades are limited. Information sessions, interviews, and campus tours are available Monday through Friday by calling the Admissions Office. Financial aid information may also be received by calling the office. Admissions decisions are made independent of financial aid considerations. Initial inquiries are welcome at any time of the year.

ADMISSIONS CORRESPONDENCE

Mrs. Tracey Wetmore
Director of Admission
Morristown-Beard School
70 Whippany Road
Morristown, New Jersey 07960
Phone: 973-539-3032
Fax: 973-539-1590
Web site: http://www.mobeard.org

MOUNT SAINT MARY ACADEMY

Watchung, New Jersey

Type: Girls' day college-preparatory Roman Catholic school
Grades: 9–12
Enrollment: 394
Head of School: Sr. Lisa D. Gambacorto, Ed.S., Directress

THE SCHOOL

Mount Saint Mary Academy proudly celebrated its Centennial Year. Since 1908, the Academy has maintained a tradition of excellence in the education of young women. With this tradition as its valuable asset and a moving force, the institution has embarked upon a new path to ready itself for a promising future. In 2001, state-of-the-art science laboratories and science and math classrooms greeted students as they began the school year. Several months later, the student center/cafeteria and school bookstore were completed in the newly renovated lower corridor of the Saint Joseph's building. Last year, a majestic athletic facility was added to the spacious campus. A turf soccer field, a six-lane track, and bleacher seating for 600 are among the notable features.

The Mount was founded by the Sisters of Mercy of New Jersey and opened with 77 students. A fire destroyed the main building in 1911, but the school reopened in the following year and has grown steadily to its present enrollment of 381. The school's philosophy encompasses a view of human life as "a journey of people in evolution toward a final destiny which is knowable through faith and attainable through free choice." The Academy stresses the importance of having a skilled and caring faculty work with small classes within an environment in which personal integrity and moral values are nourished. All students take courses in religion each year.

The campus is situated on a ridge of the Watchung Mountains, overlooking surrounding suburban towns and the skyline of New York City, which is 23 miles to the east. Students and teachers take advantage of the many cultural and recreational offerings in the city and area.

The school, a sponsored work of the Sisters of Mercy, is a nonprofit organization governed by a Board of Trustees. Its Alumnae Association, composed of about 4,300 graduates, provides support for a number of school functions.

In 1984–85, Mount Saint Mary Academy was one of sixty-five private schools in the United States to receive the Council for American Private Education's Exemplary Private School Recognition Project award for being a "model for the nation." In a congratulatory letter, Governor Kean of New Jersey stated, "I hope that we can guarantee all of New Jersey's young people the opportunity to receive the kind of education your school provides."

Mount Saint Mary Academy is accredited by the Middle States Association of Colleges and Schools and holds membership in the National Association of Independent Schools, the New Jersey Association of Independent Schools, the National Catholic Educational Association, and the College Board. A ten-year Middle States Association special report was completed utilizing the Accreditation for Growth format. Mount Saint Mary Academy received highly complimentary evaluations in all areas of its study.

ACADEMIC PROGRAMS

To graduate, a student must complete 4 years of English, 4 of religion, 3 of history (2 of U.S. history), 3 of a foreign language, 3 of mathematics, 3 of science, 1 of art/music, 4 of physical education and health, and various elective courses. The school recommends that students complete 4 years each of foreign language, mathematics, and science.

Among the class offerings are English I–IV, playwriting, journalism, public speaking, and acting for the stage; American history I and II, various history electives, world civilizations, psychology, and economics; religion I–III, World Religions, Prayer, Living and Dying: A Catholic Perspective, Women's Spirituality, and directed study; algebra I and II, geometry, trigonometry, precalculus, discrete math/statistics, and calculus; Visual Basic 6.0, Technology Today, Microsoft Publisher, Microsoft FrontPage, and PowerPoint; biology I and II, chemistry, physics, and global science; Latin I and II, Italian I–IV, and Spanish I–IV; physical education, health I–IV, and driver's education; basic drawing, studio art, art history, painting and mixed media, and 3-D design; and music theory I and II, advanced music theory, music appreciation, music of the U.S. and the world, chorale, instrumental program, bell choir, jazz study, classical, chamber ensemble, and private lessons (available in voice and most instruments).

Honors sections are available for all English and mathematics classes as well as for the following special topics: chemistry, biology, physics, American history I and II, Cicero, Virgil, Latin II, Spanish II–IV, and Italian II and III. Advanced Placement courses are also offered in the following areas: English literature, English language and composition, Spanish, calculus, physics, biology, history, and psychology. Students take part in such competitions as the JETS-TEAMS (Junior Engineering & Technical Society–Tests of Engineering and Math/Science), Mock Trial, Odyssey of the Mind, PRISM (Project for Research in Science and Math), Fed Challenge, and Euro Challenge.

The academic year, divided into trimesters, begins in early September and extends to early June, with vacations at Christmas, spring break, and Easter. Classes are held five days a week. The average class has 20 students. Grades are issued to students three times a year. Parents and students are able to view grades via participation in NET-Classroom.

FACULTY AND ADVISERS

The faculty and staff consist of 52 lay teachers and 9 Sisters of Mercy. More than 60 percent of the faculty members have advanced degrees.

Sister Lisa Gambacorto, R.S.M., a graduate of Georgian Court College (B.A.) with certification in social studies education (K–12), was appointed Directress in 2000. She holds M.A. degrees from Seton Hall University in both counseling psychology and educational administration. Sister Lisa also has certification in student personnel services and is a nationally certified psychologist and a New Jersey–licensed marriage and family therapist. She has taught on the elementary, secondary, and college levels and, in addition, holds an Ed.S. from Seton Hall University.

The administrative team also consists of three Assistant Directresses whose special areas of concern include faculty, curriculum, and student activities.

The Campus Minister and a group of peer ministers work together to create a Christian atmosphere at the school. They are responsible for retreat planning, social concerns, and peer counseling, among other things. Through the ministers' efforts, faculty members and students are made aware of their responsibility to others and are encouraged to participate in a variety of service and ministry programs. The curriculum includes a community service requirement on all grade levels.

The services of a School Psychologist are available to students experiencing any adjustment difficulty. Individual sessions, family sessions, seminars for life development, and workshops for parents are some of the many services provided through student assistance. A Peer Mediator group also functions on campus to help students in need.

COLLEGE ADMISSION COUNSELING

The Director of Student Personnel Services and the School Counselors at Mount Saint Mary Academy become well acquainted with their students since each maintains the same counselees over a period of four years. Individual and group conferences are held to assist students and their parents in determining the best college and career choices. Students can meet individually with college representatives who visit the school or participate in a series of mini college fairs conducted during school hours. The Academy's guidance department has recently instituted the use of the Naviance program for all levels.

Students also receive valuable college and scholarship information during the course of their College Skills classes, which are taught for one trimester during the junior and senior years.

SAT scores are consistently higher than New Jersey and national averages in both the verbal and math sections. Of the 79 graduates of the class of 2008, 1 was a National Merit Semifinalist, 3 were National Merit Commended Scholars, 6 were Edward J. Bloustein Distinguished Scholars, and 1 was a National Achievement Scholar. The class achieved 100 percent college acceptance, at institutions such as Barnard, Boston College, Duke, Georgetown, George Washington, Harvard, NYU, Princeton, and the University of Pennsylvania. They were awarded more than $7.5 million in scholarships and grants.

STUDENT BODY AND CONDUCT

In 2008–09, 394 girls were enrolled. Students came from sixty-eight towns within a 35-mile radius. Van transportation is available from most areas. Students are predominately Roman Catholic, but many other faiths are also represented.

Each girl receives a copy of the *Student Planner Handbook,* which outlines what is expected of her. It is her responsibility to respect the rights of others and to maintain a high regard for truth, honesty, and integrity. The Dean of Discipline reviews any infractions of the code. There is also a dress code, which requires girls to wear attractive uniforms, one for winter and another for warm weather.

ACADEMIC FACILITIES

The Mount building, a three-story structure of rough-cut Washington Valley stone, serves as the residence of the Sisters of Mercy and also contains classrooms, the computer center, the music rooms, the English-History Resource Center, and a parlor for recitals. It is connected by an arcade to Gabriel Hall (1912), a structure of similar design containing classrooms and math and science classrooms and labs. In addition, its top floors serve as a residence hall for retired Sisters of Mercy, who are a valuable resource in the life of the school community. St. Joseph Hall (1960) has a 15,000-volume technology-equipped library, classrooms, a TV studio, and an art studio. The new cafeteria, kitchen, student center, and school store are also in this building.

The school has a student infirmary. A nurse is on duty full-time during the school day. A local hospital is less than 15 minutes away.

Immaculate Conception Chapel (1954) seats 500. Beneath the chapel is Mercy Hall, used for social functions. Other buildings on the campus are the House of Prayer and McAuley Hall, which houses the McAuley School for Exceptional Children and an infirmary and retirement home for the Sisters of Mercy.

ATHLETICS

The athletics program emphasizes the development of sound health, sportsmanship, and the enjoyment and discipline of team play. The Mount is a member of the Skylands Conference and the New Jersey State Interscholastic Athletic Association (NJSIAA). Varsity teams compete in basketball, cheerleading, cross-country, field hockey, lacrosse, soccer, softball, swimming, tennis, track, and volleyball. Dance and archery are part of the physical education program; skiing and golf can be pursued as extracurricular activities, according to student interest.

Athletics facilities on campus include six tennis courts, a field for hockey and softball, and the Mother Mary Patrick McCallion Gymnasium. A turf soccer and track facility has just been added to the campus.

EXTRACURRICULAR OPPORTUNITIES

Students elect class officers and members of a Student Council, which organizes activities and promotes student initiative and self-government. Among the other regular student activity groups are the yearbook, newspaper, and literary magazine; National Honor Society; Cum Laude Society; language clubs; United Cultures Club; drama club; forensics; library and guidance aides; and health careers and arts and crafts groups. Other activities include the Mock Trial Team; the Model UN; the Academic Team; the Science League; Music Ministry; the naturalist, chess, computer, and poetry clubs; and others, according to student interest.

The school hosts monthly dances, and students participate in social exchanges with nearby Catholic boys' schools. The many varied experiences available include trips to theaters, museums, Lincoln Center, the United Nations, Philadelphia, and Washington, D.C.

Each year, the Academy sponsors a European trip, which is open to all students.

DAILY LIFE

The school day begins with classes from 7:55 to 2:40. Both hot and cold luncheons are served during three lunch periods. Extracurricular activities follow the regular school day, and vans leave the Mount after 3:30 p.m., allowing students time for involvement on campus.

COSTS AND FINANCIAL AID

Tuition and fees for the 2008–09 year were $16,100. Transportation, which is not included in the fees, ranged in cost from $3400 to $3800, depending on distance. Most townships reimburse parents for $700 of the cost if they do not actually provide the transportation. Bus and van service is available to most areas from which students commute.

Financial aid is available to parents who qualify by filing the Parents' Financial Statement with the School and Student Service for Financial Aid in Princeton, New Jersey. Scholarship aid and tuition grants totaling approximately $175,000 were awarded for the 2008–09 school year. Scholarships and grants for academic excellence are awarded to incoming freshmen based upon scores on the Scholarship/Entrance Test, which is given in November.

ADMISSIONS INFORMATION

Mount Saint Mary Academy seeks students of average to above-average ability without regard to race, color, creed, or ethnic background. Admission decisions are based on entrance examination scores, transcripts of the previous three years, two letters of recommendation, and a personal interview.

New students are accepted into grades 9, 10, and 11.

APPLICATION TIMETABLE

Inquiries are welcome at any time, and prospective students are urged to spend a day at the school. An Open House is held in October, and the entrance test is given in November; additional testing is done by individual appointment. There are fees of $50 for the application and $35 for testing. Brochures are available from the Admissions Office, and appointments for interviews and tours can be made by calling that office.

ADMISSIONS CORRESPONDENCE

Donna V. Toryak, Director of Admissions
Mount Saint Mary Academy
1645 Highway 22 at Terrill Road
Watchung, New Jersey 07069
Phone: 908-757-0108 Ext. 4506
Fax: 908-756-8085
E-mail: dtoryak@mountsaintmary.org
Web site: http://www.mountsaintmary.org

MUNICH INTERNATIONAL SCHOOL

Starnberg, Germany

MUNICH INTERNATIONAL SCHOOL

Type: Coeducational day college-preparatory school
Grades: PK–12: Junior School, Early Childhood (ages 4 and 5)–grade 4; Middle School, grades 5–8; Senior School, grades 9–12
Enrollment: School total: 1,314; Junior School: 475, Middle School: 435, Senior School: 404
Head of School: Dr. Mary Seppala

THE SCHOOL

Munich International School (MIS) is a nonprofit coeducational primary and secondary day school that serves students from early childhood (ages 4 and 5) through grade 12, with English as the language of instruction. A total of 1,314 students who represent about fifty countries and nationalities attend MIS. Students are accepted without regard to race, creed, nationality, or religion. The 26-acre MIS campus lies in an environmentally protected area of woodlands and farmland near scenic Lake Starnberg, some 20 kilometres (12 miles) south of Munich. School buses serve the cities of Munich and Starnberg and the surrounding region.

Founded in 1966, the School serves the international community in and around Munich, Germany, as well as those from the local community who wish to take advantage of the unique MIS educational experience. As an exemplary English language International Baccalaureate (I.B.) World School, MIS inspires students to be interculturally aware and achieve their potential within a stimulating and caring learning environment. The curriculum follows the frameworks of the I.B. Primary Years Programme (IBPYP) and the I.B. Middle Years Programme (IBMYP), which culminate in the final two years with the International Baccalaureate Diploma (IBDP) or the American high school diploma.

MIS regards the acquisition of knowledge, concepts, and skills as essential. They are seen as part of a broad and significant process of personal development toward independence, understanding, and tolerance. Learning is a lifelong process, and students are encouraged to cultivate a respect for learning and the ability and wisdom to use it well. Furthermore, since the School is an international and multicultural community, it seeks to develop in young people an active and lasting commitment to international cooperation.

All parents whose children attend MIS constitute the membership of the MIS Association, a tax-exempt, nonprofit organisation that elects a Board of Directors from its membership to operate the School in accordance with its Articles of Association.

Munich International School is fully accredited by the Council of International Schools (CIS) and the New England Association of Schools and Colleges (NEASC) and is approved by the German and Bavarian Educational Authorities.

ACADEMIC PROGRAMME

The academic programme throughout the School covers English language and literature, mathematics, humanities (including history, business and management, economics, geography, and social studies), sciences (including biology, chemistry, and physics), foreign languages, computer science, the fine arts, and film studies.

In the belief that students best benefit from the experience of living in Germany if they are able to communicate effectively and take part in local culture, MIS offers German language instruction to all students in early childhood classes through grade 12. Furthermore, comprehensive instruction in English as a second language (ESL) is offered to serve students who come to MIS with minimal or no English language skills. In the Senior School, however, English language competence is required.

The School programme is designed so that all students have the opportunity to pursue studies in the fine arts (art, music, drama, and film studies) and computing, athletic, and recreational skills.

The Junior School (early childhood–grade 4) follows the curriculum of the IBPYP, which emphasises an inquiry-based approach to learning across all core academic subjects. The children are taught in self-contained classes in a nurturing environment. The early childhood classes prepare the students for successful entry to grade 1.

The Middle School (grades 5–8) provides a caring, stable environment with a balance of challenging academic studies and opportunities for curricular and extracurricular skill development. The curriculum conforms to the frameworks of the IBMYP in grades 6, 7, and 8. The IBMYP is now also part of the curriculum in grades 9 and 10. Studies emphasise the development of thinking skills that involve moral reasoning, aesthetic judgement, and the use of scientific method. The Middle School is committed to providing students with the knowledge, learning strategies, and study skills necessary for the demanding Senior School programme. Food technology and ethics are introduced in grade 6, and French and Spanish are offered as electives from grade 6 onwards. Additional programmes that focus on health, design and technology, social skills, and the importance of the environment are also provided.

The academic programme of the Senior School (grades 9–12) is designed to prepare students for higher education, reflecting the aspirations and priorities of MIS parents. The guidance counselor especially encourages career planning to make students aware of the education and skills necessary to pursue lifetime goals. The academic programme culminates in grades 11 and 12, with studies leading to a full International Baccalaureate Diploma or an American high school diploma.

FACULTY AND ADVISERS

The Head of School, Dr. Mary Seppala, has taught in and administered schools for thirty-four years in the United States and abroad. At MIS, more than 150 teachers from some seventeen nations are part of this broad international experience, coming from such countries as Australia, Canada, France, Germany, Great Britain, Ireland, Kenya, Nigeria, the Netherlands, New Zealand, Sri Lanka, and the United States. The faculty members are fully qualified; many have taught overseas and hold advanced degrees.

COLLEGE ADMISSION COUNSELING

Students have the opportunity to prepare and sit for the American PSAT, SAT, and ACT—tests normally needed for U.S. college entrance. About 90 percent of MIS graduates continue their education at universities and colleges in the world, including Brown, Cambridge, Harvard, the London School of Economics, MIT, Oxford, Princeton, Yale, and the Universities of Munich (Germany), Melbourne (Australia), and Waseda (Japan), to cite some recent examples.

STUDENT BODY AND CONDUCT

The strong MIS community of students, teachers, and parents works together. MIS teachers and administrators understand the uncertainties and complexities that accompany a student's transition from one country to another and from one school to another, as well as the normal challenges of growing up. A coordinated support system across the School consists of homeroom teachers, grade coordinators, year coordinators, year advisers, IBPYP/IBMYP/IB coordinators, and a guidance counselor.

ACADEMIC FACILITIES

The Junior School is housed in a strikingly new and adjoining modern facility, with spacious, light-filled classrooms that radiate from a central multipurpose activity area. There are rooms for computing, German, ESL, learning support, art, and music classes as well as a large, well-equipped library. The Health Office and the School cafeteria, which serves hot meals, are also located in this building.

The Middle School meets in a modern building on campus. The architectural concept maximises the use of windows, allowing students to feel close to the natural beauty of the campus. In addition to the spacious classrooms, there are two science laboratories, a computer laboratory, and a multipurpose auditorium as well as rooms for ESL, academic support, music, and food technology.

The Senior School combines a new building and a traditional Bavarian-style building. Multipurpose classrooms are enhanced by five science laboratories, music and computer rooms, and a library.

The recent completion of building construction provides additional classrooms, a student lounge, larger libraries, a performing arts center, and an additional gymnasium.

Stately Schloss Buchhof, an original manor house of the area that dates back to 1875, has been renovated to house the Middle and Senior School fine arts departments as well as the administrative offices of the School.

ATHLETICS

Sports activities, which play an important role at MIS, are conducted for all ages after school and during weekends. Soccer, skiing, volleyball, basketball, track and field, tennis, cross-country, and softball are the main sports offered. Tennis courts, several sports fields, and a well-equipped triple gymnasium are available on campus.

The School competes in several ISST tournaments and participates in local leagues and events under the auspices of a School-sponsored sports club. Middle and Senior School teams represent MIS at various international school competitions across Europe.

EXTRACURRICULAR OPPORTUNITIES

In order to take advantage of the experience of living in Germany and Europe, there is a wide range of half- or full-day field trips at all school levels. There are overnight trips for the Middle and Senior School, when teachers and students travel both within Germany and beyond for educational and cultural experiences.

Students may select from a variety of activities in the fine arts, ranging from painting, drawing, and ceramics to handicrafts, drama, and dance. There are several School choirs, bands, and an orchestra. Private instrumental instruction is available. A number of student drama productions are performed throughout the year. Senior and Middle School students participate in the International School Theatre Festival, the Speech and Debate Team, and several international school tournaments. Students in grades 11 and 12 have a weekly period set aside for recreational sports and service activities. They may take part in the Business@School and Model United Nations programmes.

Each year, a group of 8 to 10 students travels to Tanzania to visit project sites funded by donations from the MIS community. The travelling students present their findings at special assemblies held in each division of the School.

An active Parent-Teacher Organisation (PTO) operates as a voluntary support group for the School and fellow parents. The PTO organises a wide range of activities throughout the year, including a Ski Swap, Winterfest, and, in the spring, Frühlingsfest. During the winter, more than 300 students, parents, and teachers take part in Ski Saturdays.

DAILY LIFE

The school year begins at the end of August and ends in late June. It is interspersed with short vacations, usually a week at the beginning of November, two weeks at Christmas, a Ski Week, and two weeks for Spring Break.

The school day starts at 9:10 a.m.; it ends at 3:15 p.m. for Junior School students and 4 p.m. for Middle and Senior School students. Buses organised by the School and serving most areas in and around Munich provide transportation for nearly 80 percent of the students.

SUMMER PROGRAMMES

A two-week daytime sports programme at the beginning of July includes a week of camping in the Dolomite Mountains in northern Italy.

COSTS AND FINANCIAL AID

In the school year 2008–09, tuition is €12,340–€12,490 for pre-reception–grade 5, €14,080–€14,450 for grades 6–8, and €15,400–€15,500 for grades 9–12. There is also an entrance fee of €4800 per child upon initial admission and an additional €1500 per child in each of the following two school years.

ADMISSIONS INFORMATION

Applicants are advised that the School does not have the facilities to serve the educational needs of students who have mental, emotional, or physical handicaps or severe learning disabilities. The School does not have boarding facilities.

APPLICATION TIMETABLE

Interested students are required to submit a completed MIS application packet. Following submission of all required documentation, applicants are screened. Based on the School's judgment of the suitability of the educational programme for the prospective student and on space availability, applicants are admitted throughout the year. Earliest acceptance of application material is six months prior to attendance and/or January of that particular year. A nonrefundable application fee is paid in advance of admission decisions being made.

ADMISSIONS CORRESPONDENCE

Admissions Office
Munich International School
Schloss Buchhof
D-82319 Starnberg
Germany

Phone: 49-8151-366-120
Fax: 49-8151-366-129
E-mail: admissions@mis-munich.de
Web site: http://www.mis-munich.de

NEW HAMPTON SCHOOL

New Hampton, New Hampshire

Type: Coeducational, boarding and day, college-preparatory
Grades: 9–12, postgraduate year
Enrollment: 310
Head of School: Andrew Menke

THE SCHOOL

Founded in 1821, New Hampton School (NHS) prepares students for life-long learning through self-discovery, authentic relationships, civic responsibility, and global citizenship.

New Hampton School's values ground the School community and its programs, initiatives, and distinctive culture by: promoting and engaging students in purposeful self-exploration that models and encourages healthy risk-taking in the context of personal growth; being committed to social equality and personal respect among all members of the School and extended communities; honoring and validating diversity of all learners in the NHS community, thereby promoting understanding of the unique gifts each student possesses; and celebrating a genuine approach to campus living where individuals are respected for who they are and what they contribute to the School and extended communities.

Within about an hour's drive of the campus are Dartmouth College, Plymouth State University, and the University of New Hampshire. Boston, Massachusetts, is 1½ hours to the south. In addition, Lake Winnipesaukee, Newfound Lake, and the foothills of New Hampshire's White Mountains are within 10 miles of the campus.

New Hampton School is accredited by the New England Association of Schools and Colleges. The School is a member of the National Association of Independent Schools, the New England Association of College Admission Officers, the National Association of College Admission Officers, the Independent Schools Association of Northern New England, and the Cum Laude Society.

ACADEMIC PROGRAMS

New Hampton's academic requirements ensure a proper distribution of courses in the basic core subjects: English, math, science, history, foreign language, and the arts. Twenty credits are recommended for a diploma; 18 are required, of which 16 must be in core subjects. At least 1 credit of visual and performing arts is required.

Program development is flexible in all courses and reflects a student's proficiency. Students are encouraged to explore New Hampton's extensive academic electives, particularly in their junior and senior years. (For a list of specific electives, interested candidates and their parents should write for a course catalog.)

The average New Hampton class size is 10 students, and the overall student-teacher ratio is 5:1. Advanced Placement (AP) courses allow students to progress to college-level studies in science, computer science, math, languages, English, history, and art. The Cum Laude Society recognizes outstanding academic achievement.

New Hampton School offers an extensive array of academic supports to students. Accommodation plans are provided for students with documented learning differences. Language waivers are granted to students with recent psycho-educational or neuropsychological testing that supports granting the waiver. Students who receive a waiver are encouraged to take a language on a pass/fail basis. An advanced reading class is offered at all levels. Individual tutorial is offered at all grade levels and utilizes the students' ongoing assignments as the basis for teaching academic strategies. Group tutorial is offered for juniors, seniors, and postgraduate students. Small group classes (maximum of 6 students) are offered in English I, II, and III; world geography and civilizations, U.S. history, algebra II, and geometry. Instruction in these classes is individualized, and academic skills are explicitly taught in addition to the curriculum content. Additional charges apply to all services except the advanced reading class.

An English Support Program is provided for all international students at New Hampton. English Support (ES) classes include International Literature (Advanced ESL), American Culture (ESL U.S. history), and Advanced Academic Support (tutorial). These classes not only develop students' reading, writing, speaking (pronunciation), and listening skills, but help them to understand the new culture in which they are living. At the same time students are taking one or more ES classes, they are also taking mainstream courses such as science, math, and art electives. The English Support Program works with mainstream teachers, dorm parents, and coaches to provide extra support for international students.

New Hampton is a candidate school to offer the International Baccalaureate (IB) Diploma Programme. This curriculum of study is recognized worldwide for its outstanding interdisciplinary approach to education.

FACULTY AND ADVISERS

Seventy-two faculty members, 31 of whom hold advanced degrees, dedicate themselves to specific aspects of New Hampton School life.

Each student is assigned an adviser, who becomes his or her academic counselor and personal confidant. Other faculty duties include teaching, managing, supervising activities, and advising students on the spectrum of teenage life concerns.

COLLEGE ADMISSION COUNSELING

Students may seek advice from one of the School's college advisers. Students are strongly encouraged to research colleges and arrange visits to those of interest. Many college representatives visit New Hampton School throughout the academic year.

The SAT and ACT are administered several times each year on campus. New Hampton School students have a wide range of SAT results; the median scores are 500 verbal and 530 math.

Graduating seniors and postgraduates matriculate into colleges that are appropriate for their abilities. Recent graduates are attending American, Babson, Boston College, Boston University, Bucknell, Carnegie Mellon, Colby, Connecticut College, Cornell, Dartmouth, Duke, Endicott, Holy Cross, Johns Hopkins, Keene State, Lafayette, Lehigh, Lewis and Clark, Merrimack, Middlebury, MIT, Mount Holyoke, Northeastern, Plymouth State, St. Anselm, St. Lawrence, Skidmore, Springfield, Swarthmore, Tulane, the United State Air Force Academy, the United States Naval Academy, Wake Forest, Worcester Polytechnic, and the Universities of Colorado, Massachusetts, New Hampshire, North Carolina, Pennsylvania, and Vermont.

STUDENT BODY AND CONDUCT

In 2008–09, New Hampton had 310 students; 70 day students and 240 boarders. Varying religious, racial, and socioeconomic backgrounds add to the well-rounded cultural atmosphere. Students come from twenty-six states and sixteen nations (international students compose 14 percent of the student body).

New Hampton is a structured school with a carefully thought-through system of rules and governance. Community decision making is central to the New Hampton experience. Regular all-community meetings provide students and faculty members with opportunities to work alongside each other to shape and set standards. Throughout the discipline code, New Hampton holds the highest standards of moral, interpersonal, and community decorum and behavior.

ACADEMIC FACILITIES

The School buildings are a blend of Federal architecture, New England Colonial style, and modern design. The Academic Research Center (1997) houses a 25,000-stack library and serves as the technology hub of the campus with more than fifty computers (including three film-editing stations), 300 data ports, and a master classroom. The third floor contains classrooms and houses the College Advising Office. The T. Holmes Moore Center (1987), part of the Arts and Athletic Center, is home to a 360-seat theater; the Milne Campus Center and adjoining outdoor patio; art classrooms, studios, and gallery; a music center, which includes a state-of-the-art digital recording studio; and photography labs. Three other classic brick buildings house the foreign language, science, and humanities classrooms. The Gordon Nash Town Library also offers ready access to 40,000 volumes, more than 150 periodicals, eight daily newspapers, and excellent research facilities.

The new Pilalas Center for Math and Science is scheduled to open in fall 2009. This 31,000-square-foot, $9-million building project will integrate classrooms with laboratories and allow students hands-on experimentation. SmartBoards and digital projectors will be built into classroom and laboratory spaces.

BOARDING AND GENERAL FACILITIES

There are fourteen dormitories, ranging in capacity from 7 to 30 students. Single-room availability depends on several circumstances, such as individual living needs. Each dormitory is supervised by specific faculty members, which results in a more efficient and personal system of student accountability.

ATHLETICS

New Hampton School believes that a regular program of physical and extracurricular activities is an integral part of a student's education. New Hampton's objective is to offer an appropriate level of instruction in team sports and extracurricular programs to all students so they may discover in themselves, and in association with their peers, the enjoyment and challenge of athletic endeavors and other activities.

There are many athletic offerings at NHS, including alpine racing, baseball, basketball, cross-country, cycling, equestrian, field hockey, football, golf, ice hockey, kayaking, lacrosse, mountain biking, outdoor adventure, rock climbing, snowboarding, soccer, softball, tennis, volleyball, and weight training.

The School's athletic facilities include nine tennis courts, 5 miles of cross-country trails, a covered ice rink, five athletic fields, a baseball diamond, three indoor basketball courts, one outdoor basketball court, and a climbing wall. The Frederick Smith Gymnasium building contains a comprehensive weight-training and cardiovascular facility, a training room, and locker rooms. Burleigh Mountain provides 120 acres of walking and cross-country skiing trails.

New Hampton School's new state-of-the-art, illuminated, multipurpose athletic field was installed in fall 2007. This synthetic turf field will be the setting for field hockey, football, lacrosse, and soccer programs. New Hampton School supports some of the finest athletic facilities in New Hampshire.

EXTRACURRICULAR OPPORTUNITIES

The visual and performing arts programs offer a variety of opportunities for students. The visual arts program includes drawing, painting, printmaking, sculpture, graphic design, and both film and digital photography. Classes range from introductory level to Advanced Placement for college credit. Students may display work in the Galletly Gallery on campus and submit work to several off-campus exhibits, including the Scholastic Art Awards.

Each year, New Hampton students may participate in more than twenty-five performing arts productions and presentations. Performances include main stage theater productions, student produced plays, touring productions, children's shows, dance, and musical performances. The School's arts resources include a digital recording studio, a portable film studio, a film/graphics lab with industry-standard Adobe Creative Suite 3 and Final Cut Pro, rehearsal halls, practice rooms, the McEvoy Theater, photography labs, art studios, and the Galletly Gallery.

Opportunities abound for participation in activities that encompass academic goals, cultural growth, and recreational interests. All students are encouraged to participate in at least one extracurricular activity.

Participation is required in the School's various community service projects. These projects include volunteer work at the local fire department, an elderly housing facility, the community elementary school, and a local home for underprivileged teenagers.

The Student Activities Director schedules weekly visits by lecturers and artists and arranges trips to Boston and nearby cities for sports, cultural, and "just for fun" events.

Other extracurricular activities include the tour guide Key Club, a photography club, the *Belfry* yearbook, the *Manitou* newspaper, the literary magazine, Student Council, and Student Activity Council.

DAILY LIFE

During the fall and spring terms, students attend classes Monday through Saturday. Classes begin at 7:45 a.m. and end at 2:55 p.m., except on Wednesday and Saturday, when classes end at noon to allow for interscholastic sports competition. During the winter term, the schedule is adjusted to allow skiers to be on the slopes by 2 p.m. Students are expected to attend all classes and meet all commitments.

WEEKEND LIFE

Many events for day and boarding students take place on the weekends. Activities might include movies, bowling, ski trips, excursions to Boston, shopping trips, plays, concerts, and intramural games. With parental permission, students may leave the campus on weekends.

SUMMER PROGRAMS

Summer programs are available at New Hampton School; more information can be found online at http://www.newhampton.org/summer/ or by phone at 603-677-3476.

COSTS AND FINANCIAL AID

Tuition for 2008–09 was $40,500 for boarding students and $24,000 for day students. A nonrefundable $3000 deposit is required. Extra costs include a $300 General Deposit, refundable upon graduation, $500 Registration Fee, and $275 Student Fee. Various co-curricular programs, such as equestrian, ski, snowboarding, golf, and personal music lessons, also have associated fees. Students may purchase debit cards to operate laundry machines on campus, and a contracted laundry service is available at an additional cost. Student debit accounts are used for allowance and for purchases at the campus store, the New Hampton Country Store, and the Crum Center Snack Bar. Various school charges, such as the Student Fee, books, transportation, and yearbook, are also expensed to this account.

Need-based financial aid is available to support a diverse student body. Though there is never enough funding available to supply full need, $2,075,000 was awarded for School Year 2007, the majority of which was funded from operations. Financial aid information and application forms may be obtained from the Admission Office.

ADMISSIONS INFORMATION

Admission to New Hampton is based on an evaluation of the prospective student's capacity to do college-preparatory work. The committee also evaluates each candidate's overall level of citizenship, sense of purpose, and potential to be a leader in New Hampton's community. Prior school records, test scores (SSAT, PSAT, and SAT), recommendations, and interviews are carefully considered by the Admission Committee. A personal interview is required.

APPLICATION TIMETABLE

Campus tours and interviews are arranged Monday through Friday from 8:45 a.m. to 1:30 p.m. Parents should contact the Admission Office to arrange an interview.

Applications must be sent with a nonrefundable $50 fee ($75 for international students). The first-round application deadline is February 1. Admission decisions are mailed on March 10. Applications completed after February 1 are considered on a rolling admission basis, contingent upon available space.

ADMISSIONS CORRESPONDENCE

Suzanne Buck
Director of Admission
New Hampton School
70 Main Street
New Hampton, New Hampshire 03256

Phone: 603-677-3401
Fax: 603-677-3481
E-mail: admissions@newhampton.org
Web site: http://www.newhampton.org

THE NEWMAN SCHOOL

Boston, Massachusetts

Type: Coeducational day college-preparatory school
Grades: 9–12, postgraduate year
Enrollment: 240
Head of School: J. Harry Lynch, Headmaster

THE SCHOOL

The Newman School provides a diverse student body with a college-preparatory, liberal arts education based on Judeo-Christian values, intellectual rigor, and trust, guided by the spirit and philosophy of John Henry Cardinal Newman. Located in the heart of Boston's historic Back Bay district, the Newman School, near Copley Square and the Prudential Center, is convenient to railroad stations, bus terminals, and MBTA stations. Newman's motto "let heart speak to heart" establishes the tone for each day, encouraging students to form mature and stimulating relationships with teachers and peers and to recognize their individual gifts.

The Newman School, which was named in honor of John Henry Cardinal Newman, was founded in 1945 by Dr. J. Harry Lynch to provide a year of college-preparatory work. Since then, the Newman School has grown into a four-year high school. Classes are offered in fall, winter, and summer sessions, enabling students to attend the School year-round, if desired. Intensive instruction for international students is also available.

Newman is incorporated as a not-for-profit organization and directed by a self-perpetuating 10-member Board of Trustees, which meets quarterly and includes several alumni.

The Newman School is approved by the Boston School Committee and the Department of Education of the Commonwealth of Massachusetts and is accredited by the New England Association of Schools and Colleges. The School holds membership in the Association of Independent Schools of New England (AISNE), the National Association of Secondary School Principals, the Massachusetts Secondary School Principals Association, the National Association of College Admission Counselors, and the Secondary School Admission Test Board. It is approved by the U.S. Immigration and Naturalization Service for the teaching of international students.

ACADEMIC PROGRAMS

Transfer credit may be accepted for high school work completed in other schools; however, diploma candidates must take a minimum of 6 credits at Newman. To graduate, a student must complete 22 credits as follows: 4 English; 3 social studies (including U.S. history); 4 mathematics; 3 laboratory science; 2 foreign language; 1 fine/applied arts; 1 computer science; and 4 electives.

The Newman School offers students a traditional, liberal arts education in preparation for the academic demands of college. Based on the philosophy of Cardinal John Henry Newman, the curriculum provides students with the opportunity to connect their education to their personal development. Students are challenged to reach their potential as they strive toward academic excellence, social consciousness, and responsibility within the context of high expectations and consistent standards. Through an interdisciplinary approach to teaching and learning, students begin to make important connections in their learning and take an active role in the learning process. The curriculum includes diverse elective options and AP courses, including English, Spanish, French, calculus, biology, history, and language and composition as well as university course enrollment.

Grade reports are issued every four weeks. A tutorial program is available for students who fall behind in their studies, and long-term tutoring may be arranged for an additional fee.

The International Student Adviser and the School's Guidance Department aid students from other countries who are preparing for entrance to American colleges and universities. Intermediate and advanced English courses for international students are offered in an intensive program of six classes per day for sixteen weeks in the fall and spring semesters and ten weeks in the summer session. Special attention is given to preparing for the Test of English as a Foreign Language and for College Board tests.

FACULTY AND ADVISERS

J. Harry Lynch, the Headmaster, is a graduate of the College of the Holy Cross (B.A., 1974) and Northeastern University (M.B.A., 1976). He has been Headmaster of Newman since 1985.

The faculty includes 22 full-time teachers and 2 part-time teachers. These 9 men and 13 women hold twenty-two baccalaureate degrees, thirteen master's degrees, and one doctorate.

Members of the faculty are available each day to give students extra help with their course work.

COLLEGE ADMISSION COUNSELING

The College and Career Reference Area provides students with information regarding college admissions and the employment outlook in various fields.

An average graduating class has approximately 65 students, of whom more than 95 percent attend four-year colleges and universities. Recent graduates from Newman have been accepted to the following four-year colleges and universities, among others: American, Assumption, Babson, Bates, Boston College, Boston University, California Institute of Technology, Clark, Columbia, Emerson, Fairfield, Georgetown, Grinnell, Harvard, Holy Cross, MIT, Oberlin, Regis, St. Anselm, Smith, Stonehill, Tufts, Tulane, the U.S. Air Force Academy, Vassar, Wellesley, Wheaton, Worcester Polytechnic, and the Universities of Connecticut, Delaware, Maryland, Massachusetts, Miami, New Hampshire, and Rhode Island.

STUDENT BODY AND CONDUCT

The Newman School enrolls approximately 240 day students ranging from 14 to 19 years of age. About 50 of them are out-of-town residents who are temporarily living in Boston. Current and recent students have come from California, Connecticut, Florida, Illinois, Massachusetts, New Hampshire, New Jersey, New York, Ohio, Austria, France, Germany, Greece, India, Iran, Ireland, Italy, Japan, Korea, the People's Republic of China, Poland, Russia, Saudi Arabia, Thailand, Spain, Vietnam, the West Indies, and several Central and South American countries.

Admission to and continuance in the Newman School is to be regarded as a privilege and not a right; the Board of Trustees requires the withdrawal of any student for disciplinary or scholastic reasons that it deems sufficiently grave to warrant such action. The board is the final judge in matters of admission and retention of students. Each student has the responsibility of being thoroughly informed at all times concerning the regulations and requirements of Newman; these are outlined in the School brochure and student handbook.

ACADEMIC FACILITIES

The School plant consists of two nineteenth-century town houses located on Marlborough Street that contain libraries, laboratories, classrooms, and offices. Both buildings are wireless-network accessible. The School does not maintain boarding facilities but does assist out-of-town students in finding homestay families.

ATHLETICS

The School competes interscholastically with other independent schools in sports such as boys' and girls' basketball and soccer, girls' softball, and boys' baseball and cross-country. Intramural sports, which include competitive cheerleading, crew, flag football, rugby, sailing, and tennis, are available according to student interest but may not be available each term.

EXTRACURRICULAR OPPORTUNITIES

Extracurricular activities that are available each year include a yearbook and a newspaper *(247)*. There are drama, dance, student government, community services, peer leadership, robotics, photography, film, recreation and outing, and science clubs, as well as chorus, ensembles, and bands that perform throughout the year. Other activities may be organized based on student interest. The School has sponsored study-abroad as well as student exchange programs with Spain, Italy, and Colombia.

DAILY LIFE

The academic year is divided into two 18-week sessions beginning in September and January and a ten-week session beginning in June. The school day starts at 8:15 and ends by 2:40. Classes are held five days a week; to permit completion of a year's work in one fall or spring session, many courses meet for two periods each day.

The summer session incorporates the same amount of work in extended class periods. Thus, summer students may earn a full year's credit for courses not previously taken.

SUMMER PROGRAMS

Newman students may continue their studies during the summer session, receiving academic credit for regular high school courses. In addition, refresher and makeup courses are offered for students from other schools who need to correct deficiencies. International students may attend the Newman School's summer program to work on their English skills and to experience many aspects of American culture within the city of Boston.

COSTS AND FINANCIAL AID

Day tuition was estimated at $13,200 to $22,000 for the 2008–09 school year, depending on the individual schedule. Additional expenses include books (approximately $300 per semester). Estimated living expenses for out-of-town students were $9400 for the 2008–09 school year.

Entering ninth graders may be given scholarships, depending on the result of the entrance examinations. The School awarded $75,000 in scholarship aid for 2008–09. Financial aid is also available.

ADMISSIONS INFORMATION

Applicants are accepted for enrollment in September, January, and June. Transcripts of any previous high school work, a personal interview, and a character reference letter from the previous school are all part of the requirements to determine acceptance. Applicants must also take a placement test that is administered at the School.

It has always been the policy of the Newman School to admit students without distinction as to race, color, creed, sex, age, ethnic background, or national origin.

APPLICATION TIMETABLE

Candidates for admission should file an application on the required form at the earliest feasible date preceding the session in which they wish to enroll. There is a $40 application fee for American students and a $300 application and processing fee for international students.

ADMISSIONS CORRESPONDENCE

Mrs. Patricia Lynch, Ph.D.
Director of Admissions
The Newman School
247 Marlborough Street
Boston, Massachusetts 02116
Phone: 617-267-4530
Fax: 617-267-7070
E-mail: @newmanboston.org
Web site: http://www.newmanboston.org

NEW YORK MILITARY ACADEMY

Cornwall-on-Hudson, New York

Type: Coeducational, college-preparatory, military boarding and day school
Grades: 7–12, PG: Middle School, 7–8; Upper School, 9–PG
Enrollment: 166
Head of School: Capt. Robert D. Watts, Superintendent, USN (Ret.)

THE ACADEMY

Founded in 1889 by Col. Charles J. Wright, New York Military Academy (NYMA) prepares young people for success through competitive academic, athletic, character, and leadership development programs geared to set them apart for excellence in higher education and future endeavors. NYMA is a coeducational, nondenominational, independent, college-preparatory school for students in grades 7–PG from around the world. The 165-acre campus is located in Cornwall-on-Hudson, in historic Orange County, New York, just 65 miles north of New York City.

The structured and disciplined approach to learning provides for small classes, tutorial assistance, and 100 percent of the graduates entering the college or university of their choice. Participation in JROTC (Junior Reserve Officer Training Corps) and character and leadership development instills a higher level of self-discipline in the cadets while enhancing overall performance through organizational structure, accountability, responsibility, and good citizenship. Outstanding performance by the Corps of Cadets has earned the Academy the highest designation awarded by the Department of the Army, "Honor Unit with Distinction". This designation allows NYMA the opportunity to directly nominate qualified seniors for admission into the United States Service Academies.

Accredited by the Middle States Association of Schools and Colleges, NYMA is also a member of the National Association of Independent Schools, The Association of Boarding Schools, New York State Association of Independent Schools, and the Association of Military Colleges and Schools of the United States.

ACADEMIC PROGRAMS

NYMA cadets are required to achieve more than the minimal graduation requirements set forth by New York State. The Academy requires a cadet to successfully complete 4 years of history, 4 years of English, 3 years of high school math, 3–4 years of science, 3–4 years of a foreign language, computer studies, JROTC (4 years recommended, minimum 2 years), art or music, health, and 3.5 electives. These requirements both meet and exceed New York State's required curriculum. Community service is a must, and all seniors must complete 50 hours of volunteer work prior to graduation. An adequate number of computers are available for cadet use. JROTC is taught by military instructors and is required of all cadets in grades 9–PG. The curriculum promotes and assists cadets in developing the self-discipline, confidence, sound morals, and high self-esteem needed to become effective and responsible citizens. English as a second language (ESL) is available to non-English-speaking students. International and ESL applicants are required to submit the results of the TOEFL or SLEP test. A minimum score of 450 is necessary for international students to complete the high school curriculum in four years. The academic curriculum and the challenge of maintaining physical fitness enable each cadet to achieve strength of mind and spirit.

FACULTY AND ADVISERS

The Academy's faculty is composed of 11 men and 10 women members, who either presently hold an advanced degree or are undertaking advanced studies. The faculty members fulfill duties outside the classroom as mentors and coaches and assist with cadet activities on the weekend. Due to their many duties and responsibilities to the Corps, faculty members are offered campus housing. The Commandant and his staff oversee cadet life and provide for the cadet military code of conduct that governs all cadets at NYMA.

Capt. Robert D. Watts was appointed the thirteenth Superintendent in May 2005. Prior to his position at NYMA he served as the Head of the Defense Equal Opportunity Management Institute at Patrick Air force Base in Florida. Capt. Watts is a 1973 graduate of the United States Naval Academy at Annapolis and earned his Master of Science degree in national resource strategy in 1997 from the Industrial College of Armed Forces in Washington, D.C. Throughout his distinguished naval career he has trained more than 300 aviation personnel, managed 113 helicopters and 120 fixed-wing aircraft, and directed more than 1500 military and government employees. He has been awarded the Legion of Merit (three), Defense Meritorious Service Medal, Meritorious Service Medal (two), Navy Commendation Medal (two), Navy Achievement Medal, and various theater and service medals. Capt. Watts is an accomplished leader and decision maker. He is a mentor who creates professional environments that deliver optimal results. He has demonstrated success in the training and education of tomorrow's leaders and experience in building character.

COLLEGE ADMISSION COUNSELING

College selection and placement are a collective effort on the part of the Dean of Academics, mentor, and Guidance Counselor at New York Military Academy. During the junior year, cadets begin to sort through colleges and universities based upon area of study, number of students, and geographic location. SAT preparation, essay writing, and interview techniques are available to all junior and senior cadets.

Qualified NYMA seniors may be accepted to the U.S. Military Academy at West Point as well as other U.S. Service Academies. Other graduating seniors select colleges that are non-military, while others seek colleges offering an ROTC program. College placements for the class of 2008 include Arizona State, Babson, Drexel, Penn State, RIT, Rutgers, SUNY at Albany, SUNY at Binghamton, SUNY College at Geneseo, University of Maryland, the U.S. Military Academy Prep School, and the U.S. Naval Academy Prep School, to name a few.

STUDENT BODY AND CONDUCT

The Corps of Cadets, comprises students from fourteen states and twelve countries.

Through instruction in JROTC, cadets learn the proper decorum and appropriate behaviors. All cadets in grades 9–12 have the opportunity to advance in rank based upon their personal deportment, academic achievement, and participation in athletics. Top performers within the Corps are invited to attend Leadership Development School (LDS) during the month of August to compete for key leadership positions for the upcoming school year. The newly selected Cadet Cadre shares the responsibility of ensuring the Corps of Cadets adheres to the Academy's rules and regulations as set forth in the *Cadet Manual.* The Cadet First Captain is responsible and accountable to the Superintendent and Commandant for the overall performance of the Corps of Cadets.

ACADEMIC FACILITIES

Scarborough Hall, built in 1963, houses math and science classrooms for grades 7–PG, the auditorium, Booth Library, and the Brunetti Computer Center. The main Academic Building, as it is known, was constructed in 1912 and features newly renovated classrooms for JROTC, humanities, and computer courses for grades 7–PG, plus administrative offices. Also within the main building is Davis Chapel, which is adorned with magnificent stained glass windows and is available to the cadets for church services on Sundays. The chapel also serves as the setting for many prestigious ceremonies throughout the year. The Cadet Activities Center is home to the Cadet Canteen and Recreation Center as well as the Academy Band.

BOARDING AND GENERAL FACILITIES

Dickinson Hall and Jones Barracks are the boys' dormitories for grades 10–PG, while Dingley Hall houses cadets in grades 7, 8, and 9. Pattillo Hall, the girls' dormitory, sits just below Jones Barracks. Advances in technology allow all dorm rooms to be equipped with computer connections (with access to e-mail and the Internet). Since computers run off the Academy's main server, individual modems are not required. Pattillo Hall also houses an indoor pool, a fitness center, and an indoor rifle range. Toward the top of the Quad, adjacent to the Academic Building, is Curie Dining Hall. The dining hall staff prepares highly nutritious, well-balanced meals served cafeteria-style. Brunch and dinner are served to the cadets on Sundays.

ATHLETICS

All cadets must participate in interscholastic sports. A wide variety of interscholastic athletics are offered at the modified, varsity, or junior varsity levels. Boys' sports include baseball, basketball, football, ice hockey, lacrosse, soccer, and wrestling. Girls' sports include basketball, soccer, softball, and volleyball. Several of the varsity sports are coed and include cross-country, golf, rifle, swimming, tennis, and track and field. Raiders, an outdoor program, and Drill Team are conducted by JROTC. D Troop, as the equestrian program is referred to, is held at a local stable. Throughout the parade season, these cadets have the opportunity to perform in several parades as a mounted unit. Cadets have the opportunity to ski, ice skate, or snowboard at nearby West Point.

Athletic facilities include the Alumni Gymnasium and Olympic-size pool, the Munday Wrestling Room, and the Heilbrunn Training Room. Outdoor basketball courts, nine tennis courts, an outdoor pool, and soccer, football, lacrosse, baseball, and softball fields complete the athletic facilities.

EXTRACURRICULAR OPPORTUNITIES

Cadets may compete for membership in the National Honor Society or volunteer to participate in chorus, marching band, drama club, and the Boy Scouts or yearbook committee. Over the years, the marching band has been fortunate to participate in parades abroad. The Corps of Cadets participates in the Columbus Day Parade in New York City as well as in the Memorial Day Parade in Cornwall-on-Hudson.

DAILY LIFE

Structure sets the pace for daily life at NYMA. The cadets adhere to a strict schedule, allowing for a minimum of free time. The daily regimen requires cadets to be up at 6 a.m. and attend classes from 8 a.m. to 3 p.m.; participate in athletics for 2 hours, four afternoons per week; and attend supervised evening study hall from 7:30 to 9:30. Tutorials are held daily during the academic day and evening study period. Cadets may be required to attend mandatory study hall and tutorials, as directed.

WEEKEND LIFE

Trips are planned to local malls and movie theaters, Great Adventure, athletic events, New York City, and other points of interest. Dances are held throughout the year.

COSTS AND FINANCIAL AID

In 2008–09, new cadet tuition and fees totaled $31,900; new international cadet tuition and fees totaled $35,200. Additional fees, applied where indicated, are the art fee, the laboratory science fee, the commencement fee, haircuts (for boys), textbooks, and the equestrian program. Financial aid is available and awarded on an annual basis.

ADMISSIONS INFORMATION

NYMA admits young men and women into its college-preparatory program without regard to race, religion, color, or ethnic origin. Prospective cadets should be average to above average in academic ability and able to express their desire to undertake this commitment regardless of how demanding it may become. Recommendations from prior schools, complete academic transcripts, and a personal interview are required. Interviews may be scheduled Monday through Friday mornings. Admissions open house events are held throughout the year.

APPLICATION TIMETABLE

Applicants in grades 7–PG will be considered for admission to the Academy in September, and those in grades 7–11 can also be considered for midyear enrollment in late January. The application for admission should be completed and returned to the admissions department, with the application fee, as soon as possible.

ADMISSIONS CORRESPONDENCE

Maureen T. Kelly
Director of Admissions
New York Military Academy
78 Academy Avenue
Cornwall-on-Hudson, New York 12520
Phone: 888-ASK-NYMA (toll-free)
Fax: 845-534-7699
E-mail: admissions@nyma.org
Web site: http://www.nyma.org

NORTHFIELD MOUNT HERMON SCHOOL

Northfield, Massachusetts

Type: Coeducational boarding and day college-preparatory school
Grades: 9–12, postgraduate year
Enrollment: 620
Head of School: Thomas K. Sturtevant

THE SCHOOL

Northfield Mount Hermon School (NMH) offers a unique educational program, diverse and talented people, a values-oriented experience, and extensive resources. Focus, opportunity, individual attention, and values form the academic program. The School believes these are the elements that awaken in students a love of learning and that inspire them to lead purposeful lives.

Students focus their minds and energy by taking three major courses each semester in extended periods, for a total of six college-prep courses per year. These courses are complemented by enrichment minor courses. A special ninth-grade orientation and program provides foundation. NMH offers an extensive choice of courses, sports teams, performing arts groups, club activities, and study-abroad options. Cutting-edge technology enhances learning in and out of the classroom; students are required to bring a computer.

Individualized attention is ensured through the Moody system of advising, which matches teachers with advisee groups of about 7 students, small class size, college counseling, and a teacher-student ratio of 1:7. NMH also challenges its students to examine their values and to develop a sense of commitment. Every student participates in the School's work program 4 hours per week, and 200 students volunteer each term in outreach activities. Multifaith beliefs are examined in religious studies courses, at school meetings, and in spiritual life groups that are supported by the faculty.

NMH began as two schools: the Northfield Seminary for Young Ladies, which opened in 1879, and the Mount Hermon School for Boys, which began in 1881. Both schools were founded by Dwight Lyman Moody, who wanted to provide an excellent secondary education for young people regardless of race, religion, and economic circumstances. In 1971, the schools became a single coeducational institution.

In January 2004, the NMH Board of Trustees decided to reduce the size of the student body and become a one-campus school as of September 2005. The School is located on the Gill campus, which encompasses about 2,000 acres on the wooded banks of the Connecticut River in western Massachusetts, near the borders of Vermont and New Hampshire. Brattleboro, Vermont, is 13 miles north, and Greenfield, Massachusetts, is located 14 miles to the south. New York is 3½ hours south via I-91 and I-95; Boston is 2 hours east on Route 2 or the Massachusetts Turnpike. Bradley International Airport, which serves Hartford and Springfield, is 1¼ hours south via I-91.

The 27-member Board of Trustees, which includes many alumni, is the governing body of the School. The endowment in productive funds has a market value of $148 million. Contributions received from approximately 25,000 alumni are the predominant force in NMH's fund-raising efforts.

Northfield Mount Hermon has been designated an exemplary school by the U.S. Department of Education, is accredited by the New England Association of Schools and Colleges, and is a member of the Independent School Association of Massachusetts, the National Association of Independent Schools, and the Educational Records Bureau.

ACADEMIC PROGRAMS

A Northfield Mount Hermon education begins and ends with the individual; every student is expected to take the most rigorous course load in which he or she can succeed. Each faculty adviser works with about 7 students, and they help students select challenging courses appropriate to their individual needs. More than 200 courses are offered, including Chinese, environmental science, Arabic, multivariable calculus, and Russian. Additional courses are offered in English, mathematics, classics, French, Spanish, religious studies, the visual arts, theater, music, dance, and physical education. Advanced Placement opportunities are offered in twenty-three subject areas, and there are eleven study-abroad options. The ninth-grade curriculum includes a health course that focuses on age-appropriate health, wellness, and life skills and afternoon writing and history courses to improve academic preparedness. Ninth graders are required to participate in one term of interscholastic athletics.

All NMH students participate weekly in a work program designed to teach responsibility and the dignity of labor through a variety of jobs, which may include working in the student houses, the language labs, the library, the School farm, or the dining service.

The Center for International Education offered study abroad in 2007–08 in Brazil, Costa Rica, France, Greece, Uruguay, and New Zealand.

Ninth and tenth graders participate in humanities courses, which are planned collaboratively by teachers from different disciplines and have a thematic focus.

The typical class consists of 14 students, and the student-teacher ratio is about 7:1. Reports and comments are sent to parents twice each term.

One academic credit is earned by the successful completion of a major course. Twenty-two credits are required to graduate. Students also enroll in minor courses. Participation in minor courses and activities is measured in units. A student must take 4 credits of English, 2 credits of math, 2 credits of a foreign language (successful completion of a second-level course in a foreign language), 2 credits of science (1 credit of a lab), and 2 credits of history and social science (1 credit of U.S. history). The arts requirement depends on the length of the student's attendance at the School. Students are required to take courses in religious studies, physical education, or athletics each year and to participate satisfactorily in the work program.

FACULTY AND ADVISERS

For 2008–09, there were 91 full-time teaching faculty members. Of the full faculty, 62 percent hold advanced degrees. Faculty members coach, advise, and live in the dorms.

Head of School Thomas K. Sturtevant previously taught at St. Andrew's School in Delaware and was Upper School Principal at Friends Academy in New York.

COLLEGE ADMISSION COUNSELING

NMH places special emphasis on college counseling. College counselors, in conjunction with each student's adviser, guide students through the entire college search process, including the taking of standardized tests. Members of the college counseling office have worked on the admission staffs of selective colleges and universities, such as Columbia and Smith. Each year more than 160 college admission officers visit the School. Colleges and universities at which Northfield Mount Hermon students were accepted in the last five years include, among others, Amherst, Brown, Columbia, Cornell, Georgetown, Harvard, Johns Hopkins, Macalester, MIT, Middlebury, Oberlin, Stanford, the U.S. Naval Academy, Wesleyan, Williams, Yale, and the University of Pennsylvania.

STUDENT BODY AND CONDUCT

Total enrollment for 2008–09 was 612, with 480 boarding students and 132 day students. Students come from twenty-eight states and twenty-four countries. International students make up about 19 percent of the total student body.

All members of the NMH community are required to abide by the school's standards, policies, and procedures. Students must agree to conduct themselves according to the highest standards of integrity in all areas of School life and to treat others with honesty, civility, and respect.

ACADEMIC FACILITIES

A large array of facilities is available to students. The online library system includes an advanced media center and information commons area and houses more than 70,000 print and nonprint materials, which are indexed by an online catalog. The entire campus, including student rooms, is wired to a high-speed network. Students bring their own computers, and they can access their personalized virtual desktop through their computer, any computer on campus, or any Internet-connected computer in the world. State-of-the-art digital language labs opened in spring 2004.

The Rhodes Arts Center is a three-story home for music, dance, theater, and visual arts. The 63,000-square-foot building, which supports study, practice, and studio time, offers ample professional and teaching gallery and performance spaces and was completed in fall 2008. The Raymond Hall, with superb acoustics and a state-of-the-art audio and video recording booth, a recital hall and an instrumental rehearsal hall, a harpsichord, fourteen grand pianos and five uprights, an electronic music lab with recording capabilities and small studio, six teaching studios, ten practice rooms, a percussion room, a chapel with an Andover tracker pipe organ, and a world music classroom with a collection of musical instruments from all over the world maximize learning and afford superb performance opportunities in the music program, which presents more than twenty performances a year. A dance performance space with sprung floor that doubles as a black box theater, and a separate dance studio, also with sprung floor, offer the two dance companies and many dance classes excellent practice and performing space for their five concerts each year. An end stage theater, with orchestra pit and full technical support, as well as advanced lighting and recording, supports four major productions a year. NMH maintains a black-and-white darkroom and studios for printmaking, design, drawing, digital graphics, photography, video production, ceramics, and painting.

BOARDING AND GENERAL FACILITIES

The School encompasses privately maintained country roads, ponds, a watershed and reservoir, and a working farm with a maple sugar house.

The Blake Student Center houses a full snack bar and grill, meeting rooms, lounges, and game rooms.

Faculty members and their families live with students in the student houses. Alumni Hall, the dining hall, is centrally located.

O'Connor Health Center is an accredited hospital with 24-hour service. The medical staff includes a resident physician, 2 full-time psychologists, nurses, and an X-ray technician.

ATHLETICS

Boys' sports include alpine and Nordic skiing, baseball, basketball, crew, cross-country running, football, ice hockey, lacrosse, soccer, swimming and diving, tennis, track, Ultimate Frisbee, volleyball, water polo, and wrestling. Girls' sports include alpine and Nordic skiing, basketball, crew, cross-country running, field and ice hockey, gymnastics, lacrosse, water polo, soccer, softball, swimming, tennis, track, and volleyball. Golf is a coeducational sport. In addition, there are physical education opportunities in swimming and lifesaving, dance, conditioning, outdoor education, and more.

Two gymnasiums with a swimming pool and newly renovated fitness center, eleven playing fields, and twelve outdoor and three indoor tennis courts are available at NMH; as are a covered hockey rink, thirteen playing fields including two new turf fields, a track, a nine-hole golf course, indoor and outdoor batting cages, a boathouse and dock, and miles of cross-country and ski trails. Athletic facilities are scheduled for renovation and expansion.

EXTRACURRICULAR OPPORTUNITIES

Students develop many interests through the various clubs at NMH. Groups include an international students association, a literary magazine, affinity groups, and a debate club. Students interested in communications publish an award-winning school newspaper, an art and literary magazine, and a yearbook, and they operate a campus radio station.

Music plays an important part in School life and draws continual support from alumni and friends. There are numerous musical groups, including several choirs, orchestras, and a concert band. Musicians and singers perform in about fifty events each year, including two major traditional concerts: Christmas Vespers and the Concert of Sacred Music. Classes and individual instruction are offered in voice and musical instruments.

DAILY LIFE

Classes meet five days a week. A typical routine consists of major academic courses in the morning; lunch, major or minor classes, study time, and sports in the afternoon; dinner, rehearsal, and free time in the evening; and 2 hours of supervised study from 8 to 10 p.m. Campus work jobs are part of the daily schedule.

WEEKEND LIFE

The student activities office organizes an extensive array of weekend programming. Each weekend, films are shown in the campus theaters. In addition, students may attend dances, concerts, coffeehouse gatherings, and theater productions. Other weekend options include day trips to Boston and other locations as well as hiking, mountain biking, snowboarding, and skiing.

SUMMER PROGRAMS

The Northfield Mount Hermon School offers several summer programs for motivated students in grades 7 through 12 and postgraduates. A five-week on-campus program provides academic-enrichment courses (both credit and noncredit).

The faculty includes teachers from NMH and other secondary schools, as well as teaching interns. Greg Leeds is the director of NMH Summer Session.

COSTS AND FINANCIAL AID

Boarding student tuition for the academic year 2008–09 was $41,700; day tuition was $29,300, plus fees.

The financial aid program awarded approximately $6.8 million in direct grants and loans to more than 44 percent of the student body for 2008–09.

ADMISSIONS INFORMATION

Students who demonstrate good character and academic potential may apply for admission to any class. Depending on the grade of entry, students must submit the results of one of the following standardized tests: SSAT, ISEE, CTP, PSAT, SAT, or ACT. An interview is required of any family living within 200 miles of Northfield Mount Hermon School. While the School recognizes that distance may preclude a visit to the School for those living further away, it encourages an on-campus visit as an important part of the admission process.

APPLICATION TIMETABLE

Students completing applications by February 1 are notified of an admission decision by March 10, and parents or guardians are expected to reply by April 10. Applications submitted after March 10 are considered as long as spaces remain available.

ADMISSIONS CORRESPONDENCE

Director of Admission
Northfield Mount Hermon School
One Lamplighter Way
Mount Hermon, Massachusetts 01354

Phone: 413-498-3227
Fax: 413-498-3152
E-mail: admission@nmhschool.org
Web site: http://www.nmhschool.org

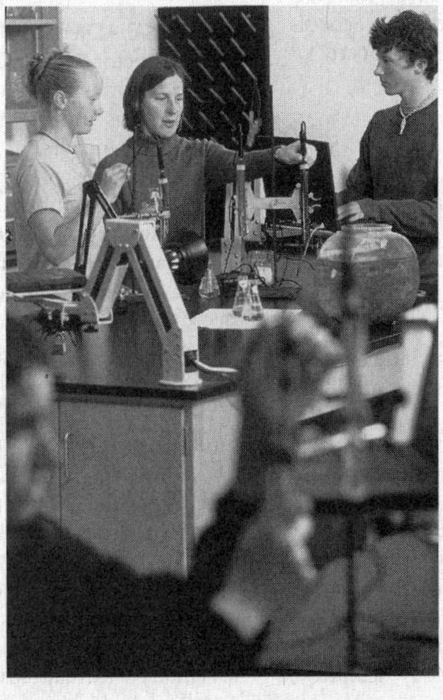

NORTHWOOD SCHOOL

Lake Placid, New York

Type: Independent, coeducational, college-preparatory boarding and day school
Grades: 9–12, postgraduate
Enrollment: 175
Head of School: Edward M. Good

THE SCHOOL

Founded in 1905, Northwood is located in the heart of the Adirondack Mountains in Lake Placid, a small village that twice hosted the Winter Olympics (1932 and 1980). It is also the home of the Lake Placid Center for the Arts; consequently, the area offers unique outdoor, athletic, and cultural opportunities. The School is 2 hours from Montreal, Ontario, Canada; Albany, New York; and Burlington, Vermont. The 85-acre campus is nestled in the heart of the village and at the base of Cobble Mountain. The Adirondack Mountains surround the village and are a beautiful backdrop for the School.

Northwood is dedicated to sound scholarship in a diverse environment. It endeavors to stimulate intellectual curiosity in its students and encourages them to learn for themselves through the guidance of its faculty and the examples set by all in the Northwood community. In addition to its academic rigor, the School also stresses responsibility to self and community, asking students to discuss and establish core values, respect different perspectives, and contribute to both the School and its surroundings through various student activities and required community services.

Northwood has a wide variety of athletic opportunities, in both competitive team sports and intense outdoor experiences. All students are asked to challenge themselves and display their talents through concerts and theater productions, presentation of darkroom and studio work in art shows and the annual Artsfest, and writing for the School newspaper and literary magazine. Informed by their active lives, Northwood students are independent young men and women who are prepared to lead and achieve in college.

Northwood School is accredited by the New York State Association of Independent Schools (NYSAIS) and the New York State Board of Regents.

ACADEMIC PROGRAMS

Graduation requirements include 19½ units in the following areas: English (4 years), social science (3 years), U.S. history (1 year), science (3 years), mathematics (3 years), language (2 years), fine arts (1 year), and health (½ year). The required number of courses per year is five.

Advanced Placement courses include biology, calculus, English literature, statistics, and U.S. history.

Honors courses include algebra II, biology, chemistry, English III, physics, precalculus, and U.S. history.

Elective courses include art exploration, art history, anthropology, ceramics, constitutional law, drama, drawing and painting I and II, economics, ethics, fiber arts, geology, government, Great Issues, instrumental ensemble, Irish history, photography, political geography, psychology, sculpture, and steel drums.

The average class size is 9, and the overall student-teacher ratio is 6:1. In the evening, students who struggle with a particular course are assigned supervised study hall. Study hall conditions are in effect for room study Monday through Thursday evenings from 7 to 9 p.m. Ample time is given to all students for laboratory work and library study. Lectures and workshops are scheduled on a regular basis with nearby colleges (St. Lawrence and Middlebury, for example). Trips are scheduled to museums and art centers in Ottawa, Ontario, and other cities near the School.

Many opportunities are available for trips to other countries, especially for the language department. The English as a second language (ESL) program is designed for nonnative English speakers. Usually, less than 10 percent of the student body is involved in ESL.

The grading system is based on letter grades from A to F. Academic reports go home to parents and to advisers four times per year.

FACULTY AND ADVISERS

There are 30 full-time faculty members, 20 of whom reside on campus. Thirteen of the 30 faculty members have master's degrees (currently, 2 faculty members are pursuing master's degrees). Mr. Edward M. Good, the Headmaster, comes from thirty years of experience in education. He holds a bachelor's degree from Bowdoin, a master's degree from Brown, and a CAGS from the University of Massachusetts. Mr. Good has been at Northwood since 1996. He teaches one current events course. Faculty turnover is very low at Northwood. Faculty members serve as advisers to students, with whom they meet periodically. The adviser communicates any problems to the parents.

COLLEGE ADMISSION COUNSELING

The Director of College Guidance is Jeffrey Edwards. Mr. Edwards works with each senior on a regular basis until the student is accepted by a college or university. He assists students and parents with the college application process. Three other faculty members also assist with the college application process. The average verbal SAT score is 553, and the average math SAT score is 582.

Of last year's 54 graduates, 95 percent were accepted and enrolled at four-year colleges or universities. Last year, Northwood seniors chose to attend schools such as Bates, Brown, Clarkson, Colgate, Cornell, McGill, Norwich, Queens, Skidmore, St. Lawrence, and Wesleyan.

STUDENT BODY AND CONDUCT

Northwood has 175 students. Of these, 145 are boarders and 30 are day students. The boy-to-girl ratio is 2:1. Fifteen percent of the student population is international, coming from countries such as Brazil, Canada, China, England, France, Germany, Korea, Mexico, Norway, Poland, Scotland, and Spain.

ACADEMIC FACILITIES

Northwood has twelve classrooms, a lecture hall, a fine arts studio, four science laboratories, a theater, and a library. The library is student friendly and provides many resources for both academic and personal growth.

The fine arts department has been renovated to provide a photography studio, a fiber arts room, and first-rate painting and drawing facilities as well as a pottery studio. The dining room, kitchen, and administrative offices were remodeled in the summer of 2002.

BOARDING AND GENERAL FACILITIES

Residential facilities include one main-building dormitory for boys, separated on three floors. A girls' dorm is located away from the main building.

The Student Center is complete with pool tables and video games, as well as vending machines and a separate television lounge. The bookstore and student mailboxes are also located in the student lounge area.

A state-of-the-art fitness center has been built, complete with all new fitness/weight machines, an indoor climbing wall, a racquetball/squash court, and an aerobics dance floor.

Four outdoor tennis courts, three soccer/lacrosse fields, and an outdoor adventure cabin and lean-to make up the outside facilities for athletics. Northwood also has two indoor tennis courts to complete the on-campus facilities. The School uses the Olympic Center for all figure skating and hockey practices and home games.

ATHLETICS

True to the credo on its seal, "Power Through Health and Knowledge," Northwood has a wide variety of athletics opportunities in both competitive team sports and intense outdoor experiences through the Outdoor Adventure Program. A full-time athletics trainer resides on campus.

Girls' sports include Alpine/Nordic skiing, crew, cycling, figure skating, freestyle skiing, golf, ice hockey, lacrosse, soccer, and tennis. Boys' sports include Alpine/Nordic skiing, crew, cycling, freestyle skiing, golf, ice hockey, lacrosse, soccer, and tennis. Coed athletics offerings include canoeing, conditioning, four-season camping, hiking, kayaking, orienteering, rock/ice climbing, telemarking/backcountry skiing, and wilderness first aid.

Northwood also has access to other Olympic facilities for sports such as bobsledding, luge, ski jumping, and speed skating.

EXTRACURRICULAR OPPORTUNITIES

There are various extracurricular activities at Northwood. The yearbook is created mostly by upperclass students. The literary magazine focuses on publishing student works and entering literary accomplishments in local writing competitions. The newly formed student-faculty steel drums band performs both on campus and for the community. Trips to nearby cities for cultural or sporting events are frequent. Students are encouraged to join one of the many on-campus clubs or groups, such as the French club or the food committee.

Learning at Northwood School happens in many ways and on many levels. One of the most significant lessons students learn is their responsibility to the greater community. Over the years, students have adopted many service projects as expressions of this sense of responsibility. They run blood drives for the Red Cross, maintain several miles of cross-country ski and hiking trails, and organize annual fundraisers for the Myelin Project and breast cancer research. Students work one-on-one as athletes' assistants for the Special Olympics winter events, and they offer a certified group of search-and-rescue volunteers to help the New York State forest rangers.

Northwood School's faculty members and students are ever mindful of their obligation to serve beyond the boundaries of their campus.

DAILY LIFE

Breakfast starts at 6:50 a.m. and finishes at 7:20. Students attend class from 7:45 until 2:30 p.m., Monday through Friday. A two-week rotating academic schedule incorporates a work program, daily School meeting, and lunch within the 40-minute class periods. Friday evenings are often used for outside presentations and lectures.

Sports and activities meet each afternoon from 3 to 4:30 p.m. After dinner there is a supervised 2-hour study hall.

During the winter schedule, classes, which normally take place after lunch, are moved to 4:15 p.m. to allow skiers and other winter athletes to train at appropriate times.

WEEKEND LIFE

Weekends are full of diverse events. There are trips to Montreal for hockey or baseball games and trips to nearby colleges, such as Middlebury College or St. Lawrence University. The movie theater, bowling alley, and Main Street shopping in town or in nearby cities are popular weekend activities. Friday evenings often include on-campus activities and visiting musical groups as well as talent night and trivia night. A weekend might also include an overnight camping trip or snowshoeing to a cabin in the woods. Students and faculty members together enjoy planning weekend events at Northwood.

SUMMER PROGRAMS

The Northwood School campus is home to the Lake Placid Soccer Center, the Can/Am Hockey camp, and various cultural programs that make Lake Placid their home in the summer.

COSTS AND FINANCIAL AID

The 2008–09 tuition for boarding students was $38,350. Day student tuition was $20,975. There is an additional fee of $1000 for international students, and $1500 for those needing ESL.

Fifty percent of Northwood School students receive financial assistance.

ADMISSIONS INFORMATION

Northwood School accepts students on a rolling admissions basis. Upon receipt of the application and all required admissions material, the admissions committee meets to discuss acceptance. Admission to Northwood School is based upon evaluation of the applicant's academic record and aptitude test results received from his or her present school. Each candidate is required to take the Secondary School Admission Test, which is published by the Educational Testing Service, Princeton, New Jersey, and is administered numerous times each year at various centers. Northwood may designate other testing according to need. A short essay exercise is required of all candidates who visit the campus.

APPLICATION TIMETABLE

Persons interested can call, write, or visit the School's Web site for information. The Web site has much information and pictures of the facilities and students. Prospective students can download an application from the admissions page of the Web site.

ADMISSIONS CORRESPONDENCE

Timothy Weaver
Director of Admissions and Financial Aid
Northwood School
P.O. Box 1070
Lake Placid, New York 12946
Phone: 518-523-3357
E-mail: admissions@northwoodschool.com
Web site: http://www.northwoodschool.com

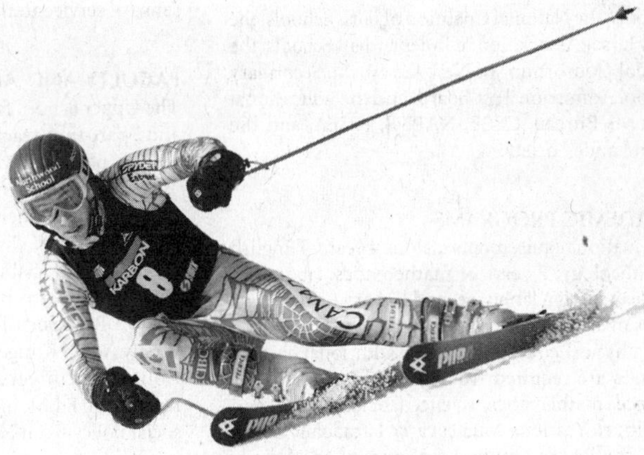

OAK KNOLL SCHOOL OF THE HOLY CHILD

Summit, New Jersey

Type: Girls' day college-preparatory religious school (coeducational in Lower School); a member of the Holy Child Network of Schools
Grades: K–12: Lower School, K–6; Upper School, 7–12
Enrollment: School total: 556; Upper School: 313
Head of School: Timothy J. Saburn

THE SCHOOL

Oak Knoll School of the Holy Child, founded in 1924, is an independent Roman Catholic day school for boys and girls in grades K–6 and for young women only in grades 7–12. Located on an 11-acre campus in Summit, New Jersey, the School enjoys the cultural and historic resources of the metropolitan New York area. An additional 14 acres in nearby Chatham Township, New Jersey, was recently developed into state-of-the-art athletic fields.

Operated by the Sisters of the Holy Child Jesus, Oak Knoll helps each student develop to his or her fullest potential in an environment that fosters the growth of the whole child. The curriculum is designed to engage students' interests and challenge their abilities. The School aims to infuse young people not only with knowledge but also with the spiritual, aesthetic, and moral values that will prepare them for a life of achievement, service, and fulfillment.

Oak Knoll is governed by a 20-member Board of Trustees. The 2008–09 operating budget was $17.3 million, and the 2007–08 Annual Giving campaign raised $1,200,000. The School's endowment is approximately $9.5 million.

Oak Knoll is accredited by the Middle States Association of Colleges and Schools and the New Jersey State Department of Education. It is a member of the National Association of Independent Schools, the National Coalition of Girls Schools, the New Jersey Association of Independent Schools, the School Consortium of New Jersey, the Secondary School Admission Test Board, and the Educational Records Bureau, CSEE, NAPSG, NCEA, and the Cum Laude Society.

ACADEMIC PROGRAMS

Graduation requirements include 4 years of English and theology; 3 years of mathematics, laboratory science, foreign language, and history (including 2 years of world history and 1 year of U.S. history); and physical education. Three additional elective courses are required from offerings in computer science, mathematics, science, social studies, and studio art. Yearlong courses carry 1 academic credit; 27.5 credits are required for graduation. A cycle program, which includes art, music, computer, and dance, is required for grades 9 and 10.

An accelerated program in mathematics begins in the seventh grade. In addition, an honors option is available in most subjects, and there are Advanced Placement studies in biology, calculus AB, calculus BC, chemistry, computer science, English language, English literature, European history, French, physics, Spanish, studio art, U.S. history, and world history, for a total of fourteen. Given the intensity of AP courses, students apply for these courses and must sit for the AP exams.

The program of studies lists nearly 100 courses for grades 7–12. Latin is a requirement in grades 7 and 8 and a course offering in grades 9, 11, and 12. Italian I and II Honors was introduced in the 2007–08 school year as a college-level course for seniors who excel in languages. The widest variety of electives is open to juniors and seniors; Honors Pre-engineering—The Infinity Project was added for them in 2007–08. This innovative course allows students to learn how engineers create, design, and test the technologies and devices of the twenty-first century using their math, science, and creative skills. Report cards with letter grades are issued after each trimester, and exams are scheduled at the end of the year.

Each year, the School inducts students into the Cum Laude Society as well as the French, Spanish, and Science honor societies. Oak Knoll is a wireless campus and is in the fifth year of an individual laptop program for grades 9 through 12. Grades 7 and 8 have individual laptops available for each class.

The average class size is 15 students. With a 1:8 faculty-student ratio, the School is noted for what its Middle States Association's evaluation cited as "the personal devotion of the administration and faculty to the students. This pleasant rapport among the members of the School community and the evident responsiveness on the part of the students are perfectly in accord with the School's concept of the importance of the individual, the formation of Christian community, and the development of a sense of service to the larger world community."

FACULTY AND ADVISERS

The Upper School faculty has 55 full-time teachers and 2 part-time teachers, 7 of whom are men. More than 64 percent have advanced degrees.

Faculty members serve as homeroom teachers, advisers, and moderators for a variety of extracurricular activities, clubs, and student organizations.

Timothy J. Saburn, the Head of School, was appointed by the Board of Trustees in 2005. He holds a Bachelor of Arts from St. Lawrence University, was a Klingenstein Summer Fellow within Columbia University's Teachers College, and received an Ed.M. in administration, planning, and social policy from Harvard University.

COLLEGE ADMISSION COUNSELING

College guidance begins in the sophomore year under the direction of the College Counselor. In the tenth grade, students take the PSAT/NMSQT for the first time. Students attend college fairs in the metropolitan New York area, and college admissions representatives visit the School. Each September, the junior class takes a three-day college trip to the Boston, Philadelphia, Virginia, or Washington, D.C., area; the trip includes visiting numerous colleges, attending information sessions, and touring the campuses. A PSAT prep course is offered to the entire junior class on five fall weekends. The PSAT is administered to the sophomore and junior classes. One hundred percent of graduates enter four-year colleges or universities.

In the College Counseling Office, two counselors work directly with the senior and junior classes in weekly guidance classes as well as in individual meetings with both the student and her parents or guardians. Guidance classes are held for grades 7 through 12 and focus on academic and social issues, personal and group values, community building, course selection, and individual college planning. In addition to the college counselors, two Deans, a guidance counselor, and a consulting psychologist all work together to support the students in their academic pursuits and to support the guidance and college programs.

Oak Knoll graduates are accepted at highly competitive colleges and universities. The 62 members of the class of 2008 are now attending numerous institutions, including Boston College, Brown, Bucknell, Colby, Colgate, Columbia, Cornell, Dartmouth, Duke, Fairfield, George Washington, Georgetown, Hamilton, Hobart, Holy Cross, Lehigh, Pepperdine, Princeton, Stanford, UCLA, Villanova, Wake Forest, Yale, and the Universities of Pennsylvania, Richmond, and Virginia.

STUDENT BODY AND CONDUCT

The Upper School enrolls 313 girls in grades 7–12, drawing its diverse student body from nearly seventy communities in the suburban Summit area.

A Code of Conduct outlines the rules and regulations of the School, which are designed to facilitate the partnership of faculty members and students in a community. It is the responsibility of each student to think of others, to respect their rights, and to manifest behavior that results from inner convictions and a high regard for truth, honesty, and integrity. A Conduct Review Committee made up of administrators, teachers, and students advises the two Deans in cases of major disciplinary infractions.

The dress code requires the wearing of a school uniform while on campus.

ACADEMIC FACILITIES

Oak Knoll is situated on a wooded hill in a residential suburban neighborhood. Grace Hall provides administrative and faculty offices, six classrooms, a chapel, and a creative arts center with media, music, and art studios and a photography darkroom.

Connelly Hall includes a library, a performing arts center, a dining hall, three science laboratories, nine classrooms, a computer center, a senior class lounge, a publications room, and faculty and administrative offices.

The Tisdall Hall complex houses the gymnasium; the weight training room; the dance studio; the offices of the school nurse, athletic director, athletic trainer, and the physical education staff; and two classrooms.

The Hope Memorial Library offers computerized information services and a book collection of 11,000 volumes. Additional materials are available through an interlibrary loan system.

ATHLETICS

Oak Knoll School of the Holy Child is committed to a strong athletic program that balances physical fitness with a personal commitment to good sportsmanship, which is reflected in gym classes, on the playing fields, and in individual competition. Team spirit in competitive play teaches skills in cooperative effort, and lifelong lessons are learned in victory and defeat. Involvement in the extracurricular sports program is optional.

Oak Knoll athletic memberships include the Mountain Valley Conference (MVC, conference level), the Union County Interscholastic Athletic Conference (UCIAC, county level), the New Jersey State Interscholastic Athletic Association (NJSIAA, state level), the New Jersey Independent School Athletic Association (NJISAA, preps), the New Jersey Catholic Track Conference (NJCTC), and the North Jersey Girls Golf League (NJGGL). Oak Knoll's 14 acres of athletic fields and its field house are located a short distance away in Chatham Township. A newly renovated turf field was recently completed in Summit.

Young women in grades 9–12 compete on twenty teams at the varsity and junior varsity level. Fall sports are cross-country, field hockey, soccer, tennis, and volleyball. The winter season offers basketball, fencing, indoor track, and swimming. In spring, girls compete on golf, lacrosse, outdoor track, and softball teams. During fall 2007, Oak Knoll School's field hockey team earned various athletic titles, including Mountain Valley Conference championship, Union County championship, NJSIAA Sectional Title, and NJSIAA-Group 1 championship. Winter 2008 championships included Fencing NJISAA and the NJSIAA District championship. In spring 2008, athletic titles in lacrosse included the Mountain Valley Conference championship and the NJISAA championship.

Students in grades 7 and 8 experience interscholastic competition in cross-country and field hockey in the fall, basketball in the winter, and lacrosse and softball in the spring. Spring tennis, as a noncompetitive program, is also offered. Oak Knoll also competes annually in the cross-country and tennis events sponsored through the New Jersey Middle School Consortium.

EXTRACURRICULAR OPPORTUNITIES

Student activities and organizations appeal to a variety of interests and talents. An active Student Council provides leadership opportunities and directs the life of the School in five areas: academic, athletic, campus ministry, creative arts, and social. Student fund-raising for particular charities is also done through the Student Council each year. Students publish a yearbook, newspaper, a newsletter in both French and Spanish, and an award-winning literary magazine, in addition to the writers' roundtables. In the creative arts, students can join the Jesters (a drama group), the Dancers, the Ensemble (and other various choral music groups), a Chamber Orchestra, and the photography club.

Other extracurricular activities include Mock Trial, Junior Great Books, Senior Peer Leaders and Peer Mentors, forensics, "Operation Smile," Junior Statesmen, book and film clubs, tour guides, the competitions of the New Jersey Science and Math Leagues, The Society of Black Scholars, and Shades. Seventh and eighth graders actively participate in the New Jersey Middle School Consortium.

"Culture Vultures" draws students interested in experiencing opera, ballet, Broadway musicals, drama, and concerts in both New Jersey and New York. There is an annual musical theater production and dance concert. The Concert Choirs are featured in the Christmas and Spring Concerts.

An integral part of Holy Child education is its emphasis on service to others. Students in grades 7–12 keep service portfolios. All students participate in annual service days, during which the entire School travels to a variety of sites to volunteer. Service projects organized by the School include Bridges runs, tutoring programs for inner-city children, Operation Smile, and a clowning ministry that visits hospitals and makes monthly trips to a regional food bank. Ongoing outreach programs support a variety of local and national charities.

DAILY LIFE

The School runs on a six-day-cycle schedule, with the day beginning at 8:10 a.m. and ending at 3:05 p.m.; classes are 45-minute periods.

Oak Knoll students arrive at school via various methods. Many students utilize New Jersey Transit buses and trains. Oak Knoll provides a shuttle bus that runs to and from the Summit train station—both in the morning and after school—for a fee. Many families carpool. In the 2008–09 school year, Oak Knoll began offering private transportation routes in New Jersey's Bergen, Essex, and Morris counties for a fee.

Hot/cold lunch is served daily in the School dining hall and is included in the tuition.

COSTS AND FINANCIAL AID

Tuition for the 2008–09 academic year was $27,600 for grades 7–12. Included in the tuition is the cost of a hot lunch program. There are additional expenses for a laptop, uniforms, transportation for contracted van service, and a book fee. Some suburban school districts provide bus service to Oak Knoll; others provide reimbursement for part of the transportation cost. A contract with a tuition deposit is due by early March. Monthly payments can be arranged through Key Tuition Payment Plans.

Financial aid is available to parents who qualify by filing the Parents' Financial Statement with the School and Student Service for Financial Aid in Princeton, New Jersey. For the 2008–09 school year, tuition grants of $1,200,000 were awarded; the grants ranged from $1000 to $23,000.

ADMISSIONS INFORMATION

Oak Knoll Upper School seeks young women of promise, those who are achievement oriented, and those who have the potential to succeed in a challenging college-preparatory program. The School does not discriminate on the basis of race, creed, or national origin in the administration of its educational policies, financial aid program, or athletic or other School-administered programs.

Seventh and ninth grades are the primary entry grades for the Upper School. Applicants for grades 7 and 9 are required to take the ISEE test, which is administered at Oak Knoll on two test dates, one in November and one in December. Transcripts of report cards and standardized test records and two current teacher recommendations must be forwarded from the sending school. Applicants are also asked to bring a graded paper with them at the time of their visit. An application, $50 fee, an interview at Oak Knoll, and a day spent visiting classes are also required. Applications for eighth and tenth grades may be accepted on a limited basis. Openings in these grades, if any, are based on attrition.

APPLICATION TIMETABLE

Inquiries are always welcome. Open Houses usually occur in October and November. Interviews and visiting days run from November through January. An early application date of December 10 was introduced during 2006–07 to assist families whose search is focused on Catholic schools with earlier notification dates. The January 28 deadline for the entire admissions process remains in place. These decisions are mailed in mid-February. After this date, applications and visits are handled on a rolling-admission basis. Interviews and visits are conducted by appointment only. Admissions office hours are 8 a.m. to 5 p.m. during the academic year or 9 a.m. to 4 p.m., Monday through Thursday, during the summer.

ADMISSIONS CORRESPONDENCE

Suzanne Kimm Lewis, Admissions Director
Oak Knoll School of the Holy Child
44 Blackburn Road
Summit, New Jersey 07901

Phone: 908-522-8109
Fax: 908-277-1838
E-mail: admissions@oakknoll.org
Web site: http://www.oakknoll.org

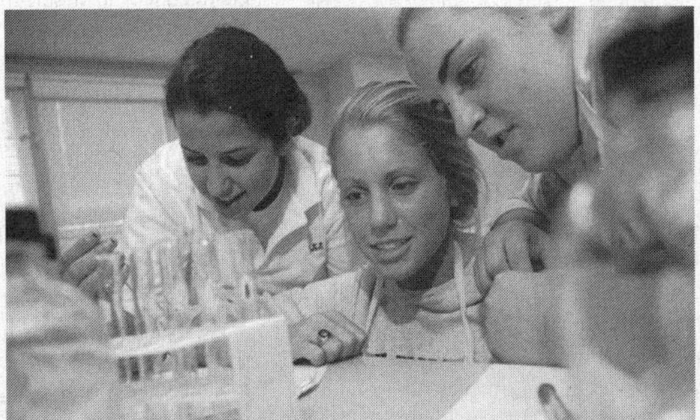

OAK RIDGE MILITARY ACADEMY

Oak Ridge, North Carolina

Type: Coeducational boarding and day college-preparatory and military school
Grades: 6–12
Enrollment: 157
Head of School: Col. Roy W. Berwick, Ph.D., President

THE SCHOOL

Oak Ridge Military Academy is a coeducational college-preparatory school that enrolls students in grades 6–12. The 101-acre campus, a National and State Historic District, is located on the Piedmont plateau, about 15 miles from Greensboro, Winston-Salem, and High Point, North Carolina. The campus is 6 miles north of the Piedmont Triad International Airport and is situated at the crossroads of State Highways 68 and 150.

The school was founded in 1852 as the Oak Ridge Institute by community leaders seeking to offer a superior college-preparatory education to students in the region. In 1899, Oak Ridge became the first school in North Carolina to be accredited by the Southern Association of Colleges and Schools. A Junior Reserve Officers' Training Corps (JROTC) unit was established at the school in 1926. The Academy began enrolling women in 1971, and the present name was adopted ten years later. In 1991, the North Carolina General Assembly designated Oak Ridge Military Academy "The Official Military Academy of North Carolina."

Oak Ridge Military Academy's mission is to offer, within a military structure, a college-preparatory curriculum that develops well-rounded young men and women who are equipped to succeed in college and have the self-discipline, integrity, and leadership skills necessary to reach their potential in life.

The Academy is a nonprofit institution owned by the Oak Ridge Foundation, Inc. It is accredited by the Southern Association of Colleges and Schools and holds membership in the Association of Military Colleges and Schools and the National Association of Independent Schools as well as in other associations.

ACADEMIC PROGRAMS

The academic year, divided into semesters, begins in August and extends to the end of May, with vacations of one week in October, a Thanksgiving break in November, two weeks at Christmas, one week in February, and a week over Easter in the spring. Classes meet five days a week and are scheduled in seven academic periods. The average class has 15 students.

Special provisions within the curriculum are made for the gifted and talented. Extra academic help is offered (or may be required) during Help Classes, which are scheduled after the last class period every day. Academic reports are maintained online through Edline.

The Academy offers two diplomas: the Advanced College diploma and the College Preparation diploma. To graduate with the Advanced College diploma, a cadet must complete 28 units of credit, including 4 in English, 4 in history/social studies, 4 in Leadership Education Training (LET) in the U.S. Army JROTC program, 4 in mathematics, 4 in science, 3 in a foreign language, 2 in electives, ½ in health, ½ in physical education, 1 in writing, ½ in computer studies, and ½ in SAT preparation.

To graduate with the College Preparation diploma, a cadet must complete 24 units of credit, including 4 in English, 4 in Leadership Education Training in the U.S. Army JROTC program, 3 in history/social studies, 4 in mathematics, 3 in science, 2 in a foreign language, 1 in electives, ½ in health, ½ in physical education, 1 in writing, ½ in computer studies, and ½ in SAT preparation.

The curriculum includes a full range of the traditional academic subjects, from introductory courses in math, language arts, science, and social studies through fourth-year French, German, and Spanish. On-campus college-level courses are offered in English and history. English as a second language is available for international students.

FACULTY AND ADVISERS

Col. Roy W. Berwick, Ph.D., is a retired soldier. While on active duty, he served in the Military Police Corps in every leadership position, from squad leader to battalion executive officer, and at every staff level, from battalion to Department of the Army. In addition, he served in the Judge Advocate General's Corps as a lawyer. Upon retirement from the U.S. Army in 1993, he entered private education as the Senior Army Instructor at Oak Ridge Military Academy and has worked in the field as Commandant of Cadets, St. John's Northwestern Military Academy; President, Millersburg Military Institute; and Vice President and Academic Dean, Massanutten Military Academy. In July 2005, he returned to Oak Ridge Military Academy as President. He resides on campus with his family and the family cats, Raggs and Harper.

The full-time faculty consists of 12 men and 14 women. Eleven faculty and staff members live on campus. Many of the faculty members hold master's degrees. There are 4 part-time instructors. Faculty members serve as study hall supervisors, coaches, and advisers for classes and organizations. They are encouraged to pursue advanced degrees at several local universities and to attend conferences and seminars related to their professional development.

An infirmary on campus is staffed by qualified medical personnel. Full medical services are available at hospitals in Greensboro and Winston-Salem.

COLLEGE ADMISSION COUNSELING

All juniors and seniors take the SAT. A college counselor maintains a collection of college catalogs and scholarship information and actively monitors the placement process as well as the application process. Faculty and staff members, including the President, also assist in the process of college placement. For the past twelve years, 100 percent of the Academy's graduates have been accepted to a college or service academy.

STUDENT BODY AND CONDUCT

In 2007–08, there were 119 boys and 38 girls enrolled. Thirty two were day students and 125 boarded. Most students come from North Carolina. Others were from twenty-five states and twenty-one other countries.

The Corps of Cadets is organized as a brigade that comprises two battalions. First Battalion consists of Band Company, Headquarters Company, Alpha Company, and Bravo Company. Second Battalion consists of Charlie Company, Delta Company, and Echo Company. The Commandant of Cadets places cadets in companies based on age, grade, and leadership abilities. A cadet's rank and position within the Corps is determined by his or her academic and military performance, participation in activities, and demonstrated leadership potential. All cadets are required to adhere to the policies outlined in the *Oak Ridge Military Academy Cadet Regulations Handbook* and the Cadet Honor Code and Creed.

ACADEMIC FACILITIES

A 31,000-square-foot classroom building was constructed in 2001 and includes a state-of-the-art science laboratory. The Alumni Building houses the administrative offices, the Oak Ridge Military Academy Archives, and the Ragsdale Memorial Library. The library is a sophisticated twenty-first century learning environment offering a wide range of print resources (more than 9,000 volumes) and electronic resources that prepare students to be productive, responsible citizens in a changing global society. The library subscribes to more than 20 periodicals and has nineteen networked computers that provide high-speed Internet access and access to several different online databases that students and faculty members can use to meet their individual educational, emotional, and recreational needs.

BOARDING AND GENERAL FACILITIES

The Cadet Dining Hall, where all meals are provided by a professional food service, is adjacent to the Cadet Lounge. A Cadet Store offers necessities. Cadets live 2 to a room in the four dormitories, Holt Hall, Whitaker Hall, Armfield Hall, and Caesar Cone Hall. All the dormitories have at least one apartment in which a staff or faculty member resides.

The Colonel Bonner Field House is the primary athletic facility. King Gymnasium is used for indoor sports. The swimming pool was built as an addition in 1934, and the whole building was remodeled in 1992. Three athletic fields, one paintball course, a challenge course, two rifle ranges, and three tennis courts are among the athletic resources. Other facilities include Linville Chapel and the Linville Infirmary.

ATHLETICS

Men's and women's teams compete against private and public schools in baseball, basketball, cross-country, golf, 8-man football, soccer, swimming, tennis, track and field, volleyball, and wrestling. The rifle and drill teams compete on a national level. Middle School students may compete for positions on junior varsity and varsity teams. Every student has the opportunity to participate in a cocurricular activity, including paintball, rappelling, and the obstacle course. Oak Ridge is a member of the Triad Athletic Conference and the North Carolina Independent Schools Athletic Association.

EXTRACURRICULAR OPPORTUNITIES

Students may participate in community service activities, clubs, leadership opportunities, and other pursuits. Among the extracurricular options are the production of the yearbook and *The Oak Leaf,* and a scouting program. Cadets are invited to take part in the Governor's Page Program, the Military Band Festival, and state and national drill competitions.

Scheduled social events include the Junior Ring Dance (junior prom) and the Military Ball (senior prom). A full range of activities is planned for every weekend. Traditional events scheduled on the school calendar include Homecoming, Parents' Days, Alumni Day, Academic Awards Day, Annual Sports Banquet, and Mother's Day.

DAILY LIFE

The student day begins with reveille at 6:30 a.m. Seven academic periods are scheduled from 8:30 to 3:45. Teachers remain in their classrooms from 3:15 to 3:45 to offer additional help. During the afternoon activity period from 4 to 6, cadets participate in extracurricular activities, character development, chapel assembly, and drill practice. Athletic practice for interscholastic sports is held between 4 and 6. Retreat is held at 6 each evening, and dinner is at 6:30. Call to quarters (mandatory study period) is from 7:30 to 9 p.m. Taps (lights-out) is at 10.

WEEKEND LIFE

Weekend activities for boarding students are closely supervised and include recreational and athletic activities designed to provide a change from the scheduled routine of the week. Off-campus trips are generally scheduled on Saturday and include travel to cultural events, athletic activities, and outdoor recreational areas as well as regular trips to a local enclosed shopping mall. Students may attend religious services of their choice. Chapel is mandatory for those remaining on campus.

COSTS AND FINANCIAL AID

In 2008–09, the cost of tuition for a seven-day boarding student is $21,490; for a five-day boarding student, $18,590; and $9690 for day students. Additional fees are books, mandatory accident insurance, medication dispensing fee, international student processing fee, activity fee, and class ring (juniors only). Haircuts, laundry, and dry cleaning are included in the price of tuition. There is a one-time uniform fee of $1980 ($1500 for day students) for first-year cadets. Limited financial aid is available.

ADMISSIONS INFORMATION

Oak Ridge Military Academy seeks students of average to above-average academic ability who have the motivation to succeed in a college-preparatory environment. It maintains a nondiscriminatory admission policy. New students are accepted in grades 6–12. Admission is based upon a vote of the Admissions Committee, based on a student's grades, behavior, and participation. A personal interview is not required but is recommended.

APPLICATION TIMETABLE

Applications, with a fee of $100, should be submitted as early as possible, preferably in the spring to qualify for fall enrollment. Students may be accepted at any time during the year.

ADMISSIONS CORRESPONDENCE

Dr. Jad Davis, Ph.D.
Director of Admissions
Oak Ridge Military Academy
2317 Oak Ridge Road
Oak Ridge, North Carolina 27310
Phone: 336-643-4131 Ext. 131
Fax: 336-643-1797
E-mail: jdavis@ormila.com
Web site: http://www.oakridgemilitary.com

OAKWOOD FRIENDS SCHOOL

Poughkeepsie, New York

Type: Coeducational boarding (grades 9–12) and day (grades 6–12) college-preparatory school
Grades: 6–12
Enrollment: 176
Head of School: Peter F. Baily

THE SCHOOL

Oakwood Friends School, guided by Quaker principles, educates and strengthens young people for lives of conscience, compassion, and accomplishment. Students experience a challenging curriculum within a diverse community, dedicated to nurturing the spirit, the scholar, the artist, and the athlete in each person. Oakwood Friends is the only school under the care of the New York Yearly Meeting of the Religious Society of Friends. Oakwood dates to 1796, when it was known as the School of Nine Partners in Millbrook, New York. It later moved to Union Springs, New York, where it became known as Oakwood. Oakwood Friends settled into its present campus in 1920 and continues to elicit "that of God in every person" in its rigorous educational setting where academic preparation is based on primary texts and hands-on learning, and where the focus on developing intellectual skills and habits maintains respect for the mind and imagination of students.

The School is located on 63 acres in the Hudson Valley with a view of the Shawangunk Mountains—a major rock-climbing area—75 miles north of New York City.

At least 13 members of the Board of Managers, which includes 7 trustees, are Quakers appointed by the New York Yearly Meeting of the Religious Society of Friends to oversee the School, which is a nonprofit corporation. Five other board members are nominated by the Alumni Association, and 5 members-at-large are nominated by the board itself. Operating expenses for 2007–08 were $4.5 million. The endowment was $3 million.

Oakwood Friends School is accredited by the New York State Association of Independent Schools and chartered by the New York State Board of Regents. It is a member of the National Association of Independent Schools, the Friends Council on Education, the Association of Boarding Schools, and the Small Boarding Schools Association.

ACADEMIC PROGRAMS

The school year is divided into three 11-week trimesters. In the progressively challenging college-preparatory curriculum, students are placed according to their ability in mathematics and foreign language, and they progress to college freshman-level courses in the senior program.

Minimum requirements for the diploma include 4 years of English; 4 years of history; 3 years of a foreign language; 3 years of mathematics; 3 years of science (including 2 lab courses); 1⅓ years of the arts (theater, visual arts, or music); one-term courses in Quakerism, computer literacy, and health; 4 years of team/life sports; and a community-service program each year.

A unified senior program is the final requirement for graduation. It begins with a camping trip to start the yearlong process of personal and group goal setting, which continues through weekly advisory group meetings. The intellectual focus of the program is provided by challenging interdisciplinary courses that involve considerable writing and critical reading of a variety of texts. Those courses include Cultural Anthropology, Genocide Studies, Globalization, Existentialism, and Revolutions. After completing their end-of-year final exams, seniors embark on a short trip together that allows them several days to reflect on their experience at Oakwood and enjoy one another's company before they part ways. The senior year culminates in a final, week-long community service project

Advanced Placement courses are offered in English language, English literature, French, Spanish, calculus AB, calculus BC, chemistry, and biology. Elective courses include Introduction to Robotics and Engineering Applications, Greek Philosophy, Asian Religion, Creative Writing, Writing for College, Chaos Theory and Fractal Geometry, Play Writing, Photography, Drama Tech, Fashion Art and Design, Music Theory, History of Jazz, and Advanced Scene Study.

Twenty percent of the School's students are from abroad, with most receiving some ESL support. Students who have mild, documented learning differences receive support in a regularly scheduled two-to-one class through the Academic Support Center, where instruction is geared toward skills enhancement (reading, writing, math, study skills, and organization) and subject-matter support.

Boarding students are required to study in the dorms for 2 hours, Monday through Thursday nights, under the supervision of dorm parents and student proctors. Students achieving independent status (IS) standing are exempt from the supervised study hall and may study independently.

By arrangement, Oakwood Friends students may take courses at nearby colleges and have access to the Vassar College library collection. Independent or accelerated study may be arranged for students in good standing.

Students are assigned grades in academic and nonacademic subjects. A scale of A, B, C, D, and F is employed. Grades and reports are given to parents six times a year.

FACULTY AND ADVISERS

There are 30 full-time teachers, 10 part-time instructors, and 8 administrators. Of these, most live at the School. They hold thirty-seven baccalaureate and twenty-two advanced degrees, including doctorates and doctor of medicine, from such colleges and universities as Adelphi; Alvan Ikoku; Brooklyn; Brown; Bryn Mawr; Bucknell; Central Michigan; Colgate; Columbia; Cornell; Drew; Dutchess Community College; Earlham; Fashion Institute of Technology; Gallaudet; Georgetown; Harvard; Imo State; Manhattanville; Marist; Middlebury; Nasson; NYU; Ohio State; Ohio Wesleyan; Parson's; St. John's; St. Lawrence; St. Luke's School of Education at Exeter University; St. Michael's; Scarritt; Siena; Smith; SUNY at Albany, Brockport, Buffalo, Cortland, Fredonia, Geneseo, New Paltz, and Potsdam; Tufts; Tulane; Universidad de Chile; Universidad de Moron Buenos Aires; Universite Lumiere-Lyon; Vassar; Wesleyan; William and Mary; and the Universities of Alabama, Chicago, Delaware, Denver, Illinois, Michigan, New Mexico, Portsmouth (England), and Tennessee.

Peter F. Baily, appointed Head of School in July 2000, is a graduate of Earlham College, Nasson College (B.A., M.E.), and Bryn Mawr College (M.A.). Prior to his last position as Interim Head of School of the Quaker School at Horsham, Mr. Baily served seven years as Head of School at Oak Lane Day School in Blue Bell, Pennsylvania.

Oakwood Friends' primary criteria for selecting faculty members are their academic background, teaching experience, and agreement with the School's philosophy, as well as the capacity to relate to students in ways that enhance intellectual, personal, and social growth.

Professional growth opportunities are available to faculty members. All faculty members serve as student advisers, and many supervise activities or coach.

COLLEGE ADMISSION COUNSELING

The college counseling program is designed to make all students aware of the multitude of postsecondary options and the academic preparation required to achieve their goals. The goal of the program is to educate and counsel students and families to help them make choices that reflect the interests, abilities, and needs of each student. The college counseling program includes parent and student programs, local college visits, a quarterly newsletter that informs parents and students about timely topics, trips to college fairs, financial aid education, a regularly updated College Resource Room that is available to all students and families, individual meetings with parents and students, and visits from approximately fifty college representatives. The College Counselor works closely with the Senior Class Advisors to guide seniors and their parents through the college application process in the fall of the senior year and continues to advise students as they sort through financial aid and admission offers.

One hundred percent of Oakwood's graduates continue on to colleges and universities. Graduates of the class of 2008 are attending Carleton, Clark, Drew, Dutchess Community College, Fordham, George Washington, Goucher, Hampshire, Hobart and William Smith, Ithaca, Manhattanville, Penn State, Rensselaer, RIT, Art Institute of Chicago, SUNY at Purchase, Syracuse, Worcester Polytechnic, and the University of Wisconsin.

STUDENT BODY AND CONDUCT

Oakwood Friends' enrollment includes 61 day boys, 44 day girls, 39 boarding boys, and 32 boarding girls. There are 5 in grade 6, 10 in grade 7, 14 in grade 8, 41 in grade 9, 41 in grade 10, 39 in grade 11, and 26 in grade 12. Seventy-five percent are from New York State, 5 percent are from five other states, and 20 percent are from four other countries. Twenty percent are members of minority groups.

The Student/Parent Handbook offers guidelines of conduct for the entire Oakwood Friends community. A fall orientation program facilitates the development of strong community standards. When necessary, disciplinary responses are student-centered in nature. While addressing the actions of students, disciplinary responses allow the opportunity for individual growth and education. A Judicial Committee of students and faculty members considers violations of rules and recommends action to the Head of School.

ACADEMIC FACILITIES

Main Building houses administrative offices, the meeting room, four classrooms, the art room, the ceramics studio, student lounge and work room, college counselor's office, Academic Support Center, and the infirmary. Stokes and Crowley classroom buildings contain Middle School classrooms, a computer lab, library, and lounge. The Turner Math and Science Building, with state-of-the-art Biology, Chemistry, and Physics laboratories, houses the Upper School math and science programs. Lane Auditorium houses performing arts facilities that include a music room with recording equipment, instrument practice rooms, and a black box theater. A photography classroom and dark room support the arts department. Collins Library, completed in 1990, contains 12,000 volumes, microform materials, five classrooms, and two computer laboratories with Intel-based systems. Connor Gymnasium has a basketball court, locker rooms, and a weight room. Campus facilities include athletic fields for baseball, soccer, softball, and Ultimate Frisbee, as well as six tennis courts.

BOARDING AND GENERAL FACILITIES

Boarding students are housed in two dormitories, Reagan Dormitory for seniors and Craig Dormitory for grades 9–11. Two dorm parents reside in Reagan and 4 reside in Craig. Student proctors, chosen by dorm parents, work closely with the dorm parents to nurture and support the general morale of their dormitory community. All students leave the campus during long breaks; some stay for extended weekends.

ATHLETICS

Oakwood Friends participates in the Western New England Preparatory School Athletic Association and the Hudson Valley Athletic League. All students must participate in some sport or physical education activity each term. Students are required to play on one of the School's interscholastic sports teams each year. Team sports include baseball, basketball, cross-country, soccer, softball, swimming, tennis, Ultimate Frisbee, and volleyball. During the other two trimesters, students not wishing to play on sports teams must participate in a noncompetitive life sport. Life sports include martial arts, bowling, fitness training, running, table tennis, the Spring musical production, and yoga. Independent life sports may be completed off-campus and must be arranged with the approval of the Athletic Director.

Connor Gymnasium houses a full basketball court, a weight-lifting room, and locker rooms. Facilities include six outdoor tennis courts, a baseball diamond, three soccer fields, and a cross-country course.

EXTRACURRICULAR OPPORTUNITIES

The theater department produces three main stage productions each year: a drama, a comedy, and a musical. All students and faculty members engage in two all-school Workshare Days each year. Student organizations include No Sweat/Peace Club, an environmental club, Model United Nations, Academic Worldquest, The New Orleans Club, and Student Government. Students and faculty members work together through Friends, Judicial, Nominating and Academic Committees. Students have opportunities to participate in choral and instrumental groups as well as periodic cabaret and "open mic" events. Students can assist in the production of the yearbook or share their written and art work through *Lumen,* a collection of students' creative works published each term.

DAILY LIFE

Breakfast is served for boarders from 7:15 a.m.to 7:45 a.m. At 8 a.m., the full community of students, faculty and administration join for Collection, where important information regarding the day and upcoming events is shared. Five class periods extend from 8:15 a.m. to 3:20 p.m., with three breaks, one for lunch and two for other purposes, which might include opportunities to study or meet with teachers for extra help, Community Meeting, Meeting for Worship, or additional instructional time for students enrolled in Advanced Placement classes. Team and life sports extend from 3:30 p.m. to 5 p.m. Dinner is served for boarding students from 6 p.m. to 6:45 p.m. Boarders have free time until study hall, which runs from 7:30 p.m. to 9:30 p.m. Ninth and tenth graders check in after study hall at 10 p.m. and turn their lights out at 10:30 p.m. Eleventh graders check in at 10:30 p.m. and have lights-out at 11 p.m.

Community Meeting, held once weekly, allows opportunities for students to showcase work they have done in a class, time to discuss community concerns, and a forum for outside speakers to share their work or perspective on a topic of interest to Oakwood's students. Meeting for Worship, also held weekly, provides a time for students and faculty members to center themselves spiritually. A time of silent reflection, it is most often unprogrammed; occasionally, the community is offered queries or statements upon which to reflect.

WEEKEND LIFE

Every weekend, the Dean of Residential Life and staff members on duty provide a program of activities. Many events are special to the season, such as hiking, sledding, or tubing, and occasional trips to see a play or a museum in New York City are organized. Students may also attend local fairs, such as the Renaissance Fair. Weekends are also a time to catch up on sleep, go to nearby shopping centers, or get ahead on assignments. Nearby colleges and the city of Poughkeepsie provide a number of cultural opportunities.

COSTS AND FINANCIAL AID

The 2008–09 tuition, including room and board, is $36,740 for seven-day boarders and $31,917 for five-day boarders. Day student tuition is $21,195 for grades 9–12 and $18,302 for grades 6–8. There is a charge of $767 per term for those students enrolled in Focused Instruction and an annual charge of $5430 for those enrolled in the Academic Support Center. International students pay an International Student Advisor Fee of $1902 per year. Fees for extra tutoring and instrumental lessons are billed directly to parents.

An initial, nonrefundable tuition deposit of 5 percent of the cost of attendance is required within two weeks of contract receipt.

Financial aid is available on the basis of need. Financial applications are processed through the School and Student Service for Financial Aid. Parents must also submit their IRS 1040 form to the School. In 2007–08, more than $650,000 was awarded in financial aid to 37 percent of the student body.

ADMISSIONS INFORMATION

Students enter in grades 6 through 11, and a few are considered for grade 12.

Oakwood Friends seeks students who are intellectually curious, academically motivated, and willing to engage actively and constructively in the School community. Admissions decisions are based on previous school records, three letters of recommendation (math, English, and personal), and an on-campus interview. A nonrefundable $40 application fee is required with the student application form.

APPLICATION TIMETABLE

Applications are reviewed on a continuing basis. Applications received after April 1 will be considered if space remains. Applicants are notified of a decision within two weeks of the completion of their files. Students requiring financial aid are encouraged to apply for admission as early as possible and to follow immediately with an application for financial aid.

ADMISSIONS CORRESPONDENCE

Susan Masciale-Lynch
Director of Admissions
Oakwood Friends School
22 Spackenkill Road
Poughkeepsie, New York 12603
Phone: 845-462-4200
800-843-3341 (toll-free)
Fax: 845-462-4251
E-mail: admissions@oakwoodfriends.org
Web site: http://www.oakwoodfriends.org

OJAI VALLEY SCHOOL

Ojai, California

Type: Coeducational boarding and day secondary- and college-preparatory school
Grades: Pre-K–12: Lower School, Pre-Kindergarten–8; Upper School, 9–12
Enrollment: School total: 325; Upper School: 125; Lower School: 200
Heads of School: Michael Hall-Mounsey, Headmaster (Lower School); Carl S. Cooper, Headmaster (Upper School)

THE SCHOOL

Ojai Valley School originated in 1911 as The Bristol School. In 1923, Headmaster Edward Yeomans built a new campus for students in grades 3 through 8 and changed the school name to Ojai Valley School. At that time, the School occupied 14 acres near the city of Ojai. Mr. Yeomans felt that the environment of the campus would "stimulate the interests of the children in a spontaneous way." The high school was built in 1961, following the acquisition of a separate 195-acre campus in the east end of the Ojai Valley. Today, the Lower School offers programs for students in prekindergarten–grade 8, and the Upper School for students in grades 9–12.

The primary objective of Ojai Valley School is to provide a traditional education in a safe and supportive environment. The complete program stresses the importance of the well-rounded individual and encompasses athletics, horsemanship, camping, art, music, and a variety of electives, activities, and field trips. The School offers a challenging curriculum for motivated students with special attention given to study skills, positive values, and character development.

Ojai Valley School is a tax-exempt, nonprofit organization governed by a 10-member volunteer Board of Trustees. Alumni, parents of current and former students, and friends generously support the Annual Giving campaign.

The city of Ojai (population 8,000) is a rural resort community bordered by the Los Padres National Forest. It is located 70 miles north of Los Angeles, 30 miles southeast of Santa Barbara, and 15 miles inland from the coastal city of Ventura.

Ojai Valley School is accredited by the Western Association of Schools and Colleges and is a member of the National Association of Independent Schools, California Association of Independent Schools, Secondary School Admission Test Board, NAIS Boarding Schools, Council for Advancement and Support of Education, National Association of College and University Business Officers, Interscholastic Equestrian League, American Camping Association, Western Association of Independent Camps, and Western Boarding Schools Association.

ACADEMIC PROGRAMS

In the primary and elementary program (pre-Kindergarten–grade 5), a sequential curriculum emphasizing the fundamental skills in math, reading, language arts, the sciences, and social studies is supplemented with art, music, computer training, sports, horseback riding, and other outdoor activities.

The Middle School curriculum (grades 6–8) stresses fundamental skills as well as conceptual learning. Classes reflect a strongly integrated curriculum of writing, literature, math, social studies, science, and foreign language. Middle School students also receive instruction in music, art, and computers. A daily physical education program consists of sports, horseback riding, and other outdoor activities, including fall and spring camping trips.

Graduation requirements for students in the Upper School (grades 9–12) include 4 years of English, 3 years of a foreign language, 3 years of history, 3 years of mathematics, 2 years of laboratory science, 1 year of fine arts, and 1 additional year of credit from any of the five academic solids. Advanced Placement courses are available in English, French, Spanish, biology, chemistry, computer science, environmental science, math, psychology, and studio art. Upper School students carry an average load of five courses per term.

The School seeks to provide a wide range of electives that represent the diverse interests and needs of the student body in any given year. Among the electives that have been offered at both campuses in recent years are drama, chorus, computers, study skills, ceramics, photography, painting, yearbook, and music.

Class size ranges from 7 to 15 students and averages 12 students. Most faculty members reside on campus and are easily accessible for individual tutoring sessions. A student's academic and social progress is reviewed at weekly faculty meetings.

There are four grading periods during the year. Students are given both letter grades (A–F) and effort grades (1–4). Teachers' and resident counselors' comments are also included.

FACULTY AND ADVISERS

Of the 55 full-time and part-time faculty members currently employed at the combined campuses, 22 teach at the Upper School. Eight of the Upper School faculty members have advanced degrees.

Each campus has its own headmaster. The Headmaster of the Lower School is Michael Hall-Mounsey, who received degrees from St. Paul's College, Bristol University, and King Alfred's College, Winchester, England. He completed his M.Ed. degree at California Lutheran University. The Headmaster of the Upper School, Carl S. Cooper, received a bachelor's degree from California State University, Northridge, and a master's degree in education from California Lutheran University. Cooper is a graduate of Ojai Valley School.

Academic guidance is coordinated by the Director of Studies at each campus. Students are assigned faculty advisers who meet with their advisees on a weekly basis. As leaders of camping trips and weekend activity trips, faculty members interact with students outside of the school environment.

COLLEGE ADMISSION COUNSELING

College counseling begins in the sophomore year and continues through the student's senior year. Care is taken to ensure appropriate placement of each graduate. Approximately 45 representatives from various colleges and universities visit the campus each fall.

All graduates go on to college. Recent graduates enrolled at Berkeley, Boston University, California State Polytechnic (San Luis Obispo and Pomona), Caltech, Cornell, Embry-Riddle, George Washington, Johns Hopkins, Loyola Marymount, Miami (Ohio), Michigan State, Mount Holyoke, NYU, Pepperdine, Pitzer, Purdue, Sarah Lawrence, UCLA, USC, and the Universities of California (Irvine, Santa Barbara, Riverside, and San Diego), Massachusetts Amherst, and Michigan.

STUDENT BODY AND CONDUCT

Ojai Valley School attracts students from around the world. In 2008–09, seventeen countries and six states were represented in the student body. There were 125 students enrolled in the Upper School, 100 residents and 25 day students. Ojai Valley School can accommodate equal numbers of boys and girls, and traditionally there has been an even split between the sexes.

Ojai Valley School seeks to give students an environment where they can learn to accept responsibility for themselves and their own education. This goal is reflected in the School's motto, "Integrity." The School has high expectations and standards, and there are specific guidelines regarding a student's responsibility for personal, social, and academic commitments. Major offenses, which can result in dismissal without tuition refund, include the use and possession of illegal drugs and alcohol, absence from school without official permission, dishonesty and other violations of integrity, and sexual misconduct. The policy on such offenses is strictly enforced.

Student prefects help oversee school activities and take a leadership role in all aspects of campus life.

ACADEMIC FACILITIES

Lower School facilities include six self-contained elementary school classrooms, five junior high school classrooms, an ESL classroom, a library, a fully equipped science lab, a technology center consisting of a four-station state-of-the-art computer room and language lab, and a new performing arts center. Each classroom is equipped with its own computer.

Upper School facilities support the high school program. Wallace Burr Hall houses eight air-conditioned high school classrooms, a library, computer lab, science lab, tutoring room, and science technology center. Fine arts and photography facilities and a ceramics/pottery room are housed in a separate art studio.

BOARDING AND GENERAL FACILITIES

The Lower School campus offers boarding facilities for both girls and boys. Reed Hall, which houses boarding girls, is directly across from a ten-bed infirmary staffed by two full-time nurses. Frost Hall has accommodations for boarding boys. It also houses the kitchen, dining hall, and administrative offices.

In addition, Lower School facilities include 5 acres devoted to the equestrian program, 2 acres of playing fields, baseball and soccer fields, a 25-meter heated pool and swim center, lighted tennis and basketball courts, an art and ceramics studio, and a separate elementary and middle school playground and fitness structure.

Upper School boys are housed in three dormitories, each of which also includes faculty apartments. Grace Smith Hobson House provides air-conditioned living quarters for boarding girls. Each girl has a roommate. The girls' dormitory provides a large living room with a fireplace and kitchen area. All Upper School dorms have laundry facilities. Students and faculty members eat their meals together in the dining hall, which is located near the boys' dormitory.

The Headmaster of the Upper School and half of the faculty members reside on the high school campus.

A large outdoor amphitheater is used for school assemblies, drama productions, guest lectures, and graduation ceremonies. A high and low ropes challenge course is used to develop self-confidence and team cooperation.

A student center, which consists of a swimming pool, lockers for boys and girls, and a barbecue area, is used for a multitude of activities.

ATHLETICS

Teams compete interscholastically in baseball, basketball, cross-country, equestrian, football, golf, lacrosse, soccer, tennis, track, and volleyball. Noncompetitive and intramural offerings include aerobics, cycling and mountain biking, fitness programs, golf, karate, rappelling, skating, skiing, surfing, swimming, walking, weight training, and yoga.

EXTRACURRICULAR OPPORTUNITIES

There are several extracurricular activities from which students may select. Students participate in drama, chorus, yearbook, mountain-biking, mountaineering, and a variety of clubs. New clubs and activities are added each year according to student interest. Community service programs include trips to Oaxaca, Mexico; peer tutoring; visiting nursing homes; Habitat for Humanity; and the Surfriders Foundation.

DAILY LIFE

A typical day begins with breakfast at 7. Students clean their room and dorm area before going to an optional morning tutorial at 8. Classes begin at 8:30. The academic day ends at 2:45, with the exception of Wednesday, when interscholastic sports contests are played in the afternoons. Sports practices and co-curricular activities are offered between 3:15 and 4:45. Students are transported to town for shopping and leisure on Saturday mornings. Dinner is at 6, followed by study hall from 7:30 to 9:30. The amount of time allowed for socializing and lights-out are dependent on a student's grade and academic standing.

WEEKEND LIFE

During the week, students are expected to work hard on their studies. Weekends give students a chance to play equally hard. Students and faculty members together organize activities on and off campus. Weekend trips to visit landmarks and attend cultural events and concerts in Los Angeles, Santa Barbara, and Ventura are frequent. Camping trips are a key part of student life. Recent destinations have included Yosemite, Morro Bay, Canyonlands, Arches National Park, Zion National Park, the Sierra Nevada mountain range, Mammoth Lakes, and Death Valley, as well as local beaches and wilderness areas.

Students may, with parental permission, leave campus provided that their absence does not conflict with school-related commitments.

SUMMER PROGRAMS

One of the few boarding schools in the West to operate year-round, Ojai Valley School hosts a variety of safe, purposeful, and fun summer programs.

In operation since 1943, Ojai Valley Summer School and Camp offers programs to students in prekindergarten through grade 12. Sessions are offered in two-week, four-week, or six-week increments geared for students who want to preview difficult classes, take enrichment courses, earn credit toward high school graduation requirements, and take advantage of the range of recreational and camping opportunities. Afternoon and evening enrichment activities include most of the offerings available during the academic year. Many OVS faculty members are part of the summer staff. Study for Success, a course on study skills and the psychology of self-esteem, is one of the more popular courses. English as a second language is available for international students.

Britannia Soccer Camp, with coaches from Great Britain, is held during the first week of August at the Lower School.

Many international students ages 10 to 18 attend the August English Language Camp. This 2-week program offers intensive English instruction with teachers and peer tutors in the morning, recreational activities in the afternoon, and day and weeklong trips to Southern California theme parks.

COSTS AND FINANCIAL AID

The cost of tuition, room, and seven-day boarding for the 2008–09 academic year was $34,400 for grades 3–5 and $40,850 for grades 6–12. Five-day boarding is also available for students in grades 3–8. Day student tuition ranged from $12,825 to $18,590, depending on the grade.

About $250,000 in aid is given annually on the basis of need. Information on aid availability and affordability options can be obtained from the Admission Office.

ADMISSIONS INFORMATION

The School seeks applicants who are committed to their personal, social, and academic growth. Parents and prospective students should call the Admission Office to receive a current catalog, which contains admission instructions and application forms.

The following items are taken into consideration before an admission decision is made: the student's transcript, SSAT scores, teacher recommendations, and a personal interview. For international students, TOEFL scores are also required. Each applicant's potential for success and desire for involvement in the program are given careful consideration.

Ojai Valley School does not discriminate on the basis of sex, race, color, creed, or national or ethnic origin. The School welcomes a geographically and ethnically diverse student body.

APPLICATION TIMETABLE

The application deadline is February 1. The Lower School enrolls students during the academic year on a space-available basis. The Upper School also has a rolling admission policy.

ADMISSIONS CORRESPONDENCE

Tracy Wilson, Director of Admission
Ojai Valley School
723 El Paseo Road
Ojai, California 93023
Phone: 805-646-1423
Fax: 805-646-0362
E-mail: tracy_wilson@ovs.org
Web site: http://www.ovs.org

OLDFIELDS SCHOOL

Glencoe, Maryland

Type: Girls' boarding and day college-preparatory school
Grades: 8–12, PG
Enrollment: 120
Head of School: Taylor Smith

THE SCHOOL

Oldfields was founded in 1867 by Mrs. John Sears McCulloch and has continued to reflect her desire to provide young women with the opportunity to make the most of their academic and personal potential. The goal of Oldfields is to provide a familylike environment in which students can best develop intellectually, ethically, and socially by learning the values of self-discipline and self-respect.

The 230-acre campus is located in the country, 25 miles north of Baltimore, with convenient access to the cultural and recreational activities there as well as in Washington and Philadelphia.

Oldfields is governed by a self-perpetuating Board of Trustees made up of alumnae and parents of current and past students. The current endowment is $12 million. In 2006–07, 20 percent of the alumnae, 72 percent of the parents of current students, 100 percent of the Trustees, and 65 percent of faculty members participated in the Annual Giving campaign.

Oldfields is accredited by the Middle States Association of Colleges and Schools and holds memberships in the Educational Records Bureau, the American Council on Education, the National Association of Independent Schools, the Association of Boarding Schools, the Association of Independent Maryland Schools, and the Council for Religion in Independent Schools.

ACADEMIC PROGRAMS

Oldfields is committed to focusing on what matters most: each girl's success. Oldfields provides each student with the college-preparatory course of study most appropriate to her needs and interests.

Honors-level courses are available to students who show outstanding potential in particular disciplines and prepare students for Advanced Placement exams. Everyone at Oldfields is committed to the idea that every student learns differently and that, by understanding and working with the students' strengths, students can be led to academic success.

Nineteen credits are required for graduation. Students must take 4 years of English, 3 years of mathematics, 2 years of laboratory science, 3 years of a foreign language, 3 years of history (including 1 year of American and 1 year of world history), 1 year of fine arts, and physical education (each trimester). In addition, students are required to take classes in health and computer proficiency.

Oldfields faculty members prefer the curricular flexibility of an honors course while they also prepare students for advanced national exams; although the AP designation does not appear on transcripts, Advanced Placement exams were taken by students in Honors Studio Art, Honors French, Honors Spanish, Honors Biology, Honors Calculus AB, Honors Calculus BC, Honors English 11, Honors English 12, and Honors U.S. History.

Qualified seniors may undertake an independent study in any academic discipline. Students are required to carry at least five courses each term.

Students in each grade level at Oldfields participate in the Seminar Series. In the ninth grade, the Seminar Series focuses on study skills and time management; tenth grade, financial literacy; eleventh grade, the college search and admission process; and twelfth grade and postgraduate students, leadership.

The average class size is 12 students. The student-teacher ratio is 6:1.

Underclass students have room study, supervised by dormitory parents, from 7:45 to 9:30 p.m. Monday through Thursday and quiet hours on Sunday evenings. Any student needing more closely supervised study is required to attend all daytime and evening study halls under faculty supervision in the library.

The school year is divided into three trimesters, with final exams or projects given at the end of each term. Grades and comprehensive comments from faculty members and advisers are each sent home three times a year. Numerical grades are assigned. The academic and social progress of each student is reviewed at weekly faculty meetings.

During May Program, a two-week-long session, students may study abroad, participate in other off-campus experiences, or choose from a variety of on-campus programs offered in a wide array of academic disciplines. From 2006 to 2008, students traveled to Peru, Costa Rica, New Mexico, the Southern states to follow the civil rights movement, and to New Orleans with Habitat for Humanity to help build new homes. On campus, students learned to plan and run a horse show and about French cuisine. Some traveled to Middle East embassies in Washington, D.C., to learn more about the different cultures and religions in that region of the world. Several seniors created independent projects with the permission of the Director of Studies.

FACULTY AND ADVISERS

There are 23 full-time and 4 part-time faculty members, 5 of whom are men. Forty-three percent of the faculty members hold advanced degrees. Seventy-five percent of the full-time faculty members live on campus and serve as dormitory parents in one of the six dormitories.

Taylor A. Smith, appointed Head of Oldfields in 2008, holds a Bachelor of Arts degree from Wesleyan University and a Master of Education degree from Loyola College.

COLLEGE ADMISSION COUNSELING

During her junior year, each student and her parents receive the *Oldfields College Guidebook,* which outlines the step-by-step procedures for pursuing college admission. Group counseling and aptitude testing begin in the fall of the junior year. Sophomores take the PSAT, and juniors and seniors take part in the SAT and ACT programs. The college counselor coordinates on-campus visits of more than 60 college representatives as well as College Fair evenings and direct communication with colleges to which girls are applying.

Each year, Ivy League institutions, as well as large and small colleges and universities located around the country, are represented. Oldfields' commitment to academic diversity is reflected in the diversity of the colleges the students attend. Among the colleges and universities attended by recent graduates are the College of Charleston, Gettysburg, Howard, Miami (Ohio), Rhode Island School of Design, and the Universities of Colorado, Georgia, Massachusetts, Pennsylvania, and Virginia.

STUDENT BODY AND CONDUCT

Oldfields has 80 boarding and 30 day students. The School size is limited to 190 girls in order to maintain its familylike atmosphere. Seventy percent of the girls are boarding students. In 2007–08, the student body represented fourteen states and eleven countries, including Germany, Korea, Mexico, Nigeria, Bermuda, China, and the United Kingdom.

The Student Judiciary Board and Academic Judiciary Board, made up of 2 elected students and 2 faculty members each, help to formulate and implement School policy.

ACADEMIC FACILITIES

The academic center—composed of Caesar Rodney Hall, Hook Day Hall, and the fine arts wing—houses the School's library, five science labs, classrooms, academic offices, four fine arts studios, and an art gallery. Across the quadrangle from Hook Day Hall is New House, which houses the David Niven Theatre, a music wing, and the photography resource room and photography labs as well as additional classrooms. All academic areas are fully wired for Internet access in order to support the School's 100 percent integrated laptop computer program.

BOARDING AND GENERAL FACILITIES

The six campus dormitories house girls of all grade levels as well as dormitory parents. Faculty dorm parents, aided by resident advisers, supervise the dorms.

During Thanksgiving, winter, and spring breaks, the School is closed and all students go home or, in the case of students who live far from school, to the home of a schoolmate.

ATHLETICS

All students are encouraged to participate in athletics suited to their various interests and ability levels. A variety of competitive and noncompetitive sports are offered on various levels. Field hockey, basketball, lacrosse, and soccer are played on the varsity, junior varsity, and squad III levels. Varsity and junior varsity teams are offered in badminton, tennis, and volleyball, and varsity teams are offered in cross-country and softball. Riding teams compete with other teams throughout the Middle Atlantic states at the varsity and junior varsity levels. Dance classes (ballet, pointe, tap, modern, and jazz) and aerobics classes are also offered each afternoon. The student body and faculty are divided into the Green and White teams, which compete throughout the year in many sports and other spirited activities.

Campus facilities for athletics include four playing fields, five all-weather tennis courts, an outdoor swimming pool, and a gymnasium with an indoor court for badminton, basketball, and volleyball. The gym also houses a dance studio and a weight-training/fitness room with Nautilus and fitness equipment. The riding facilities include an indoor riding arena, two outdoor show rings, and miles of trails along the Gunpowder River. In addition, the School has a thirty-two-box stall barn, seven double-fenced paddocks, two heated wash stalls, and two well-equipped tack rooms. There are more than thirty well-schooled horses available for students to ride, and a varying number of girls bring their own horses each year. Riders can participate in local and regional shows, compete at horse trials, attend on- and off-campus clinics, and fox hunt and trail ride on weekends. There are three levels of competitive riding; in past years, approximately 30 percent of the students rode to fulfill their physical education requirement.

EXTRACURRICULAR OPPORTUNITIES

A regular program of lectures, workshops, concerts, and movies is offered on campus, along with trips off campus to local and regional areas of interest. Plays, concerts, and dances with nearby boys' schools, as well as ski weekends and hiking trips, are scheduled regularly. Student-run clubs include the Student Council, Global Awareness, FOCUS, Gold Key, Dubious Dozen, Images, Environmental Awareness, Outing, Art, and Black Awareness clubs.

Traditional events include Parents' Weekend in the fall, Alumnae Weekend in the spring, the Garden Party, the Annual Awards Banquet, drama and music presentations, the holiday party, Green and White Night, and graduation.

Many students do volunteer work in community organizations. Regular trips are made to Baltimore, where students work with Our Daily Bread, a soup kitchen, and Kid's Place, a shelter for women and children. Girls often participate in awareness-raising events such as Race for the Cure and the Walk for the Homeless, as well.

DAILY LIFE

Classes meet in a combination of 80-minute periods, with students typically taking a six-course load. Clubs and interest groups meet daily after academic classes, a time set aside for these activities.

WEEKEND LIFE

A regular program of lectures, workshops, concerts, and movies is offered on campus, along with trips off campus to local and regional areas of interest. Plays, concerts, and dances with nearby boys' schools, as well as ski weekends and hiking trips, are also scheduled regularly. Weekends offer Oldfields students special opportunities for further enrichment and enable them to enjoy a faculty-student relationship outside of the classroom. All cocurricular events are planned by the Director of Student Activities and chaperoned by the faculty. Because of the School's proximity to Baltimore, Philadelphia, and Washington, D.C., students can attend events and programs in these cities. Theater, concert, and museum trips are scheduled, along with shopping and sports events. Current movies are shown on campus each Friday and Saturday night, and rafting trips, impromptu cookouts, restaurant trips, and faculty dinners supplement the weekend activities.

Certain weekend, day, and overnight privileges are extended to all students with parental permission. Students may participate in as many faculty-chaperoned events as they wish. Day students are included in all aspects of boarding school life and are encouraged to participate in extracurricular programs. Frequently, day students spend overnights and weekends at school.

COSTS AND FINANCIAL AID

The comprehensive fee for 2008–09 is $40,475 for seven-day boarders, $35,800 for five-day boarders, and $25,075 for day students. Additional expenses include textbooks, school supplies, and a laptop computer. Optional expenses include photography, music, and riding lessons. A registration fee of $3500 for boarders and $2000 for day students, applicable toward the comprehensive fee, is required with the signed entrance contract. Sixty percent of the balance of the cost is due by July 15 and the remainder by November 15.

Financial aid grants and loans are available on the basis of need and a student's commitment to the academic and ethical values of Oldfields. Thirty-three percent of the students were awarded aid in excess of $1.2 million for 2008–09. All families applying for financial aid must complete the form from the School and Student Service for Financial Aid and submit their tax forms from the last two years.

ADMISSIONS INFORMATION

The student body is made up of students with diverse talents and interests from various socioeconomic backgrounds. Oldfields is interested in girls of average to superior ability who are committed to making the most of their academic and personal potential.

Applicants must submit a personal essay, standardized test scores, a transcript, two teacher recommendations, and a principal's recommendation and have an interview on campus. International students are required to submit a written essay and results from the TOEFL to determine their English proficiency level. Telephone interviews are required when visits are not possible.

Oldfields School does not discriminate on the basis of race, color, or national or ethnic origin in the administration of its educational policies, admissions policies, faculty recruitment policies, scholarship or loan programs, sports, or other School-administered programs.

APPLICATION TIMETABLE

An application fee of $50 (domestic) or $125 (international) must accompany the application. Oldfields School has a priority deadline for the admission application of February 1. Those students who submit their completed application on or before February 1 are given preference in the admission process. The School continues to accept applications after that, if space is available. Decisions are sent on March 1 to day student applicants and March 10 to boarding student applicants. Families are expected to reply no later than April 10.

ADMISSIONS CORRESPONDENCE

Dr. Parnell Hagerman, Associate Head of School
Oldfields School
1500 Glencoe Road
P.O. Box 697
Glencoe, Maryland 21152-0697
Phone: 410-472-4800
Fax: 410-472-6839
E-mail: admissions@oldfieldsschool.org
Web site: http://www.oldfieldsschool.org

OLNEY FRIENDS SCHOOL

Barnesville, Ohio

Type: Coeducational boarding and day college-preparatory school
Grades: 9–12
Enrollment: 61
Head of School: Richard F. Sidwell

THE SCHOOL

Olney Friends School offers a value-centered, college-directed, interactive curriculum that promotes the concepts and practice of sustainability. Founded in 1837 by the Religious Society of Friends, the School is reorganized as an independent Quaker high school that strives to create a diverse and globally representative student body. Students and staff members celebrate intellectual vigor, provoke questions of conscience, and nurture skills of living in community. The program of stimulating academics, spiritual exploration, service to others, and useful work prepares students for the challenges they are likely to face in college and beyond.

Olney Friends School embraces two community rules: Be truthful; harm no one. These values reflect the Quaker principle of "that of God in all of us." The School community solves conflicts creatively and nonviolently, embraces differences, and strives to be a place where no one slips through the cracks; its small size and rural setting ensure that each person is known.

Although the concept of 'green' schools may be new to the education field, Olney's sustainability program is founded on 170 years of Quaker practice. Self-reliance and conservation, the use of local resources and service to community, and taking a stand on issues that affect the world have always been a part of education at Olney. The historic main building was originally built with bricks made from clay dug from the hillside and fired on site by students and the staff. This 350-acre campus in the Appalachian foothills of Southeastern Ohio includes cultivated fields and pastures, a hardwood forest preserve, orchards, and organic gardens. Lovely Livezy Lake hosts fishing, boating, swimming, and skating as well as providing a lab for aquatic studies. A dedicated Sustainability Coordinator brings research and management experience to integrating the 'green' program into Olney's curriculum and community life.

The governing body of Olney Friends School is an independent board of 12 members from the parent, alumni, Quaker, and professional communities. Alumni are generous with their time and support.

Olney Friends School is accredited by and is a member of the Independent Schools Association of the Central States and is chartered by the Ohio State Department of Education. Olney Friends School holds memberships in the Ohio Association of Independent Schools, Midwest Boarding Schools, the School Scholarship Service, the Friends Council on Education, the Association of Boarding Schools, and the National Association of Independent Schools.

ACADEMIC PROGRAMS

Olney Friends School's college-preparatory curriculum emphasizes integrated content and skills development. Each student spends 80 minutes per day in humanities, an integrated course that uses the disciplines of English and history to deepen understanding of major historical themes. The School's math and science programs are linked, so mathematical skill progresses as scientific depth increases. Spanish language and literature courses focus on conversation and cultural exploration. Religion courses are offered in world religions, Quakerism, Biblical studies, and meditation.

The humanities sequence begins in the modern world and then focuses on more specific areas of study. Ninth graders explore concepts of identity and world citizenship. Tenth graders undertake a study of the American experience. In the eleventh grade, students move into ancient civilizations, and in twelfth grade they study modern European history. Math courses are offered in algebra, geometry, algebra II, pre-calculus, and calculus. The science sequence begins with an introduction to the laws of the universe in ninth-grade conceptual physics. Students then take chemistry and biology. Upper-level students choose between environmental science and advanced physics. Spanish is available in levels I–V and includes literature and cultural studies in each class.

Advanced Placement credit classes include English literature, physics, calculus, biology, and Spanish. Academic electives rotate and are offered in a wide variety of subjects, including media studies, environmental history, chaos theory, and astronomy. Fine and performing arts options include ceramics, drawing and painting, photography, woodcarving, theater, and instrumental and vocal ensembles. Students may take short explorative courses or follow a sequence designed to develop a particular talent. Some individual music lessons are offered for credit on a variety of instruments at no additional tuition charge.

The student-teacher ratio is 4:1; class sizes range from 4 to 20. The school year is divided into four quarters. Students receive grade reports and narrative commentary for each class at the end of each quarter.

FACULTY AND ADVISERS

Classes are taught by a classroom faculty of 17 members: 9 women and 8 men. Most faculty members live on campus, either in apartments in the dormitories or in School-owned houses and apartments.

All students are assigned an adviser to help with academic or social issues as well as to maintain contact with students' parents. Advisory groups pair up for peer support, informal discussion, and to plan schoolwide activities.

COLLEGE ADMISSION COUNSELING

Every student is accepted to a four-year college before graduation from Olney Friends School. The college counselor meets with students individually and in small groups throughout their academic careers. Students also receive assistance with applications, testing, and arranging college visits. The college resource room houses college-selection resources, test-preparation materials, and a designated computer for research and practice tests. Students are encouraged to visit colleges throughout the year. Several times each year, representatives from colleges around the country come to Olney Friends School for "college lunches."

STUDENT BODY AND CONDUCT

Olney Friends School's 2008–09 opening enrollment was 61 students: 31 girls and 30 boys. Students came from sixteen states, ranging from Arizona to New York, and from nine other countries: Bulgaria, China, Congo, Ecuador, Ethiopia, Korea, Rwanda, Saudi Arabia, and Vietnam.

To create a structured family atmosphere, Olney Friends School has rules that are necessary to community well-being and academic success. Students play a contributory role in making decisions for the School. Students take on leadership roles while practicing the art of responsible decision making. A Discipline Committee composed of 3 faculty members and 3 students meets to discern best consequences for student rule infractions. Students also participate as class delegates and on Self-Government, Co-Curricular, Outdoor Education, Spiritual Life, and Admissions Advisory Committees.

ACADEMIC FACILITIES

The main building, referred to as "the Main," houses academic classrooms, science laboratories, a multimedia computer classroom, a library, a gymnasium, the college room, an art room, faculty offices, kitchen and dining facilities, the School store, and the School bank. Adjacent buildings house the music department, ceramics studio, and wood shop. Other facilities include boat and bike storage, the barns, and the greenhouse.

BOARDING AND GENERAL FACILITIES

Student residences include boys' and girls' dormitories. Each dormitory has a meeting space, a full kitchen, coin-operated laundry facilities, and a recreation room. There are three faculty apartments in each dormitory. Also located on campus are four faculty and staff homes, a guest house, and an infirmary. The School nurse is on campus each day and is on call as needed. Barnesville Hospital provides emergency services if necessary.

Dormitory life is coordinated by a dorm staff made up of faculty members and students. Each dorm has students who plan dorm activities and supervise the general upkeep of the dorm.

ATHLETICS

At Olney Friends School, everyone is a participant rather than a spectator. Since the School is small, everyone has a chance to learn new skills and join one of the teams. The soccer and basketball teams excel in competitions with local schools. Cooperative gymnastics, cross-country, cycling, field hockey, folk dancing, softball, tennis, Ultimate Frisbee, volleyball, walking and running, and other sports are played competitively or taken for fun and health.

EXTRACURRICULAR OPPORTUNITIES

The Dean of Students coordinates the co-curricular program, including advising, dorm life, student activities, sports, theater, clubs, and other aspects of social and community life. Activities are focused on helping students develop their ability to live in a community respectfully and truthfully. Community expectations and rules require every person to think about their health and safety and the health and safety of others in the community.

The Olney Friends School work program provides an opportunity for all students and staff members to become invested in the physical and aesthetic maintenance of the community. Students spend about 20 minutes each day on chores, rotating between cleaning the dormitories or the Main, washing dishes, or working in the barn, garden, or greenhouse.

Regularly scheduled classes and activities are put aside for community service learning projects five days each year. Students give cultural presentations at local schools; help out at local charities, senior homes, or museums; and participate in trail restoration and environmental protection projects. Olney also invites the community to the campus for special performances and educational symposiums.

Olney's outdoor education program focuses on fun, environmental awareness, and skill building. The School's location in the Appalachian foothills offers a wide variety of hiking and biking trails, scenic rivers for canoeing, and nature preserves for lessons on minimum-impact camping techniques.

DAILY LIFE

Each morning, students and faculty members gather around the kitchen table for optional breakfast between 7 and 7:45 a.m. The school day begins and ends with the entire community meeting together for a brief period of silent reflection called Collection. Each student uses this time in their own way: to collect their thoughts, meditate, or pray in their traditions of choice. Classes begin at 8:20, following Collection, and end at 4:20. There are seven 40-minute academic blocks each day and two meeting blocks. Meeting blocks are used for committee or class meetings, Student Self-Government, and advisories. Sports teams meet between 4:40 and 6. From 7 to 8:30 each evening, all students have study hall. Students who have demonstrated their academic responsibility may study in a location of their choice, while students who need more structure work in quiet rooms in the Main with faculty supervision. Tutoring, small-group work, and study workshops can also happen during this time. After evening Collection, students have free time until they check into the dorms for the night.

In addition to morning and evening Collections each day, longer times of worship are held midweek and on Sunday mornings. Quaker principles or queries are often approached creatively with silent art making, music, or shared reflections. Students may also choose to attend other religious services by arrangement.

WEEKEND LIFE

Weekends are relaxed but provide a variety of options for activities. Most students stay on campus during weekends. Movies, concerts, biking, camping, bowling, trips to nearby cities, games, sporting events, and traditional Olney events are often on the agenda. There is also time for quiet walks around the campus or trips to town with friends.

On most weekends, students may choose to take weekends or overnights away from the School if they have met their obligations and have parental permission.

COSTS AND FINANCIAL AID

The 2008–09 annual boarding cost of $26,100 covered room, board, tuition, and fees. The day student tuition of $13,500 covered tuition, fees, and breakfast and lunch five days a week. An initial deposit of $500 is required upon enrollment and is applied to tuition. Families usually plan on an additional $700–$800 for books, trips, and personal expenses.

Grants for scholarship assistance are awarded according to need and availability of funds. More than half of the students receive financial aid.

ADMISSIONS INFORMATION

Students who do well at Olney Friends School are those who are looking for a challenging college-preparatory education in a caring community in which they can learn to take responsibility for their own academic, social, and spiritual growth. The goal is a student body that is diverse in race, culture, and economic background. The School promotes acceptance of individual differences in a community that values integrity, tolerance, and compassion.

APPLICATION TIMETABLE

The Admissions Office encourages a weekday campus visit during the academic year prior to fall enrollment. Visits may be arranged through the Admissions Office. Phone interviews can be arranged for international students. A nonrefundable application fee of $50 ($200 international) should be submitted with the application forms. Applications and financial aid information may be downloaded from the Web site, or students may request a complete application and information packet from the Admissions Office.

Applications are due February 1 for the first round of admissions and financial aid awards. Students are admitted on a rolling basis after that time, as openings permit. On a space-available basis, Olney does accept ninth to eleventh grade students for the second semester, which begins mid-January. School transcripts, test results, an admissions interview, ESL assessment results for international students, and recommendations are taken into consideration in the admissions process. One of the most important factors, however, is a student's motivation and desire to engage in an Olney Education. Alumnae and current students are always eager to share their experiences with students considering Olney.

ADMISSIONS CORRESPONDENCE

Ela J. Robertson
Director of Admissions
Olney Friends School
61830 Sandy Ridge Road
Barnesville, Ohio 43713

Phone: 740-425-3655 Ext. 206, 207
800-303-4291 (toll-free)
Fax: 740-425-3202
E-mail: admissions@olneyfriends.org
ela@olneyfriends.org
Web site: http://www.olneyfriends.org

OREGON EPISCOPAL SCHOOL

Portland, Oregon

OES
OREGON EPISCOPAL SCHOOL
1869

Type: Coeducational boarding and day college-preparatory school
Grades: PK–12: Lower School, Prekindergarten–5; Middle School, 6–8; Upper School, 9–12
Enrollment: School total: 839; Upper School: 305
Head of School: Dr. Matthew H. Hanly

THE SCHOOL

Oregon Episcopal School provides an excellent college-preparatory education in proximity to the cultural scene of Portland, Oregon, and the mountains and seacoast of the Pacific Northwest. The 60 residential students live in an intimate dormitory setting with boarders from 13 countries in a program that stresses academics, service, and global awareness. Instructors work closely with students in humanities classes and in an award-winning, research-based science program. Fencing enthusiasts can train at the world-class, on-campus salon where Olympics coach Ed Korfanty prepares Olympic medalists.

Oregon Episcopal School (OES) was founded in 1869 as a girls' school called St. Helens Hall and in 1965 Bishop Dagwell Hall, a companion school for boys, was added. The two schools merged and became Oregon Episcopal School in 1972.

OES is located just beyond the west hills of Portland on a 59-acre wooded campus. Students enjoy the outdoor beauty of the region and the cultural and educational resources of Oregon's largest city. Beyond the city, the Oregon coast and the Cascade Range are just an hour and a half away.

Governed by a 19-member Board of Trustees, OES operates a physical plant valued at $25 million with an annual budget of $19 million. Endowment funds total $21 million. Parents, faculty, alumni, and friends supported the OES Fund with contributions of more than $701,000 in unrestricted gifts last year.

OES is accredited by the Northwest Association of Schools and Colleges and the Pacific Northwest Association of Independent Schools. The School is a member of the Oregon Federation of Independent Schools, the Pacific Northwest Association of Independent Schools, the National Association of Independent Schools, the National Association of Episcopal Schools, the Association of Boarding Schools, the Western Boarding Schools Association, the Council for Advancement and Support of Education, and the Secondary School Admission Test Board.

ACADEMIC PROGRAMS

The Upper School academic program is based on the School's conviction that learning how to learn is central to real education. Students do not just read summaries in textbooks, they analyze original source documents. They do not just memorize what should happen as the result of a science laboratory experiment; they conduct independent research and perform the experiments. Precise composition is expected in laboratory reports as well as in English and history essays. Careful, analytical reading is as much a part of mathematics as it is of foreign language study. Problem solving occurs in art as well as in math and science. The academic demands are rigorous, but the "stretching" pays dividends that last a lifetime.

Classes are small. With sections averaging 14 students and a student-faculty ratio of 7:1, personal contact between students and teachers happens naturally.

The school year has forty weeks and is divided into two semesters. Grade reports and adviser comments are issued four times a year; additional reports are written if warranted. Parents' conference days are scheduled each fall and spring, but the faculty encourages additional conferences whenever the need arises.

In order to be eligible for an OES diploma, a student must earn at least 20½ credits from departmental offerings in computer science, English, fine arts, foreign language, history, mathematics, performing arts, science, religion, physical education, health, and history. Specific requirements include English, 4 credits; mathematics, 3 credits; fine arts, 2 credits; foreign language, 2 credits in one language; history, 2 credits; science, 2 credits; religion, 1 credit; computer science, ½ credit; physical education and health, 2½ credits; and electives, 1 credit.

Students are expected to take at least five yearlong courses as well as two electives annually. Beyond courses required for graduation, electives are offered in each academic discipline and include statistics, marine ecology, technology and society, and numerous art, music, drama, and physical education courses. Students are also expected to complete College Decisions for Juniors (a program on college selection) and the Senior Discovery Program (a one-week career exploration) and to participate in the School's Service Learning Program and Winterim (elective enrichment courses and trips). Service Learning helps build a strong sense of community as students work together helping others. Each sophomore, junior, and senior is expected to contribute 40 hours a year. Students also receive credit for regular off-campus community service.

FACULTY AND ADVISERS

Of the 59 Upper School instructors, 45 have advanced degrees, including seven Ph.D.'s. There are 31 men (including 1 Episcopal clergyman) and 28 women on the faculty. Twelve faculty and staff members live on the campus—6 with their families. The Dean of Residential Life and 11 dorm parents live in the dormitory complex. OES has two endowed faculty chairs: the Winningstad Chair in Physical Science and the Gerlinger Chair in Mathematics.

Matthew H. Hanly, Head of School, is well known in educational circles and has more than twenty-five years of experience as a teacher and school administrator. Mr. Hanly is a graduate of Bowdoin College (A.B. in mathematics and Romance languages) and Harvard University (M.Ed. in counseling and consulting psychology) and is a Klingenstein Visiting Fellow.

The Upper School administrative team, working with the Head of Upper School, coordinates the OES advisory programs. All are available for student and parent conferences. Each student works with an academic adviser, who assists with course selection and reviews grade reports each time they are issued. All of the faculty members are involved in student extracurricular activities.

COLLEGE ADMISSION COUNSELING

The college counselors begin working individually with students during their junior year and introduce them to the college selection procedure through the College Decisions program, which is part of the beginning-of-the-year junior trip. In the fall, juniors are encouraged to take advantage of the more than 80 college representatives who visit the campus each year, and in the spring individual family conferences are held. The counselors help students and their parents establish priorities and gather information, and encourage them to visit colleges that are a good match.

OES does not rank its students, and grades are not weighted. A junior year grade distribution sheet is available. As part of the application materials sent to colleges, the college counselors write comprehensive secondary school reports for each student.

Virtually all of the School's graduating seniors attend college. Recent graduates have attended Boston University, Bryn Mawr, Carnegie Mellon, Columbia, Cornell, Harvard, Macalester, Middlebury, MIT, Northwestern, NYU, Oberlin, Occidental, Pomona, Princeton, Reed, RIT, Scripps, Smith, Stanford, Wellesley, Whitman, Yale, and the Universities of Chicago and San Francisco.

STUDENT BODY AND CONDUCT

In 2007–08, the Upper School had 305 students, half boys and half girls. Fifty-five were boarders who represented five states and twelve other countries, and 245 were day students. The day students come from the Portland-Vancouver area and participate with boarding students in all school activities.

The Student Council includes a representative from each class as well as student body officers and serves as a forum for student concerns. The responsibility for discipline is shared by the Faculty/Student Discipline Committee, advisers, and the Head of the Upper School.

ACADEMIC FACILITIES

The newly renovated main Upper School building houses administrative offices, classrooms, a computer lab, and the Upper School Library. The Great Hall provides students with space for meetings and casual visiting and doubles as a theater for fall, winter, and spring drama productions. The Drinkward Center for Math, Science, and Technology houses several science labs and classrooms as well as two computer labs. The Episcopal Parish Church of St. John the Baptist provides additional space for weekly chapel, concerts, and lectures on campus. The visual arts building contains a ceramics studio, four large multipurpose art studios, and computer-aided design, film/video, and photography facilities. A 15-acre educational wetland serves as an on-campus natural field study laboratory.

BOARDING AND GENERAL FACILITIES

Campus residents form a close-knit community. Twelve dorm parents, including the Dean of Residential Life, live on the campus.

Two spacious dormitories house resident students and their dorm parents. There are three lounges with fireplaces, table games, two televisions, and two pianos. All students have accounts on the computer network and have wireless access to the Internet. Computers are available in the library, the International Student Center, and the three computer labs.

All student rooms are for double occupancy, although seniors generally have singles. Each dorm has washing machines and dryers for student use. Meals are served in the nearby dining hall. The School health center is located in the residence complex.

The campus is closed during Thanksgiving, Christmas, Memorial Day, and spring vacations. Boarding students either return to their homes or spend the holiday with guardians, friends, relatives, or host families. Students from abroad must have guardians in the United States, preferably in the Pacific Northwest, who act as surrogate parents during the school year.

ATHLETICS

Eighty percent of the Upper School students at OES play at least one competitive sport. Sports offered to both boys and girls include soccer, basketball, fencing, skiing, cross-country, lacrosse, track, and tennis; volleyball is also offered for girls. The athletic program offers all students the opportunity to participate on a team and in meaningful physical activity. The program actively promotes the health and safety of the participants and provides an opportunity for growth through individual and team participation. OES operates on a no-cut policy; there is a team for every level of experience and skill.

The School has a regulation-size gymnasium, three soccer fields, four outdoor tennis courts, and a 400-meter all-weather track. SPARC, a 43,000-square-foot athletics facility, features indoor tennis and racquetball courts, a fencing facility, a basketball/volleyball court, and practice space.

EXTRACURRICULAR OPPORTUNITIES

The yearbook, *Art-Lit* (an annual featuring students' writing and art), and the student newspaper, *Blophish*, provide opportunities for publication. The choir, the Jazz Band, the Orchestra, and thrice-yearly drama productions offer experiences in the performing arts.

Other activities include Student Council, calligraphy, photography, driver's education, stagecraft, and a cappella. OES also offers many outdoor/experiential education opportunities.

DAILY LIFE

The school day begins at 8 a.m. Three times a week, students assemble for Upper School gatherings or class meetings. There are seven 47-minute class periods on Monday, Wednesday, and Friday and three or four 65-minute classes on Tuesday and Thursday. During the day, students usually have one free period in which to study, meet individually with instructors, or socialize. All Upper School students gather weekly in the Church of St. John the Baptist for chapel. Interscholastic teams practice and compete at 2:50 p.m. when classes are over.

Breakfast is served to boarding students from 7:15 to 7:45 a.m. At lunch, all students choose among four options—salad bar, sandwich bar, hot entrée, or specialty bar—each of which has a vegetarian option. Salad, bread, dessert, and an assortment of drinks are available for all. Weeknight dinners for boarding students, from 6 to 6:30 p.m., include two hot options, one vegetarian, as well as a salad bar, bread, and dessert. Study hours are from 7:30 to 9:30 p.m. Sunday through Thursday. On weeknights, all boarding freshmen, sophomores, and juniors must be in the dorm by 10:30 and in their rooms by 11; on weekends, freshmen and sophomores are expected to be in by 11, and juniors and seniors by midnight. On Saturday and Sunday mornings, boarders have breakfast at 8, brunch or lunch at 11:30, and dinner at 6.

WEEKEND LIFE

OES offers a wide range of weekend activities throughout the year specifically for resident students: trips around Portland, outdoor programs, a film series, dances, speakers and performing artists, and observances of holidays, birthdays, and other special occasions. OES is close to shopping centers, restaurants, and a bus line. With parental permission, boarders may leave the campus in pairs on most weekends.

COSTS AND FINANCIAL AID

Tuition, fees, and board costs in 2007–08 were $36,870 for resident students. Tuition for day students was $20,300, including fees and lunch costs. A yearly international fee of $1200 is required of students whose parents live outside the United States. Tuition and fees are due by August 1. The School also offers installment and insurance plans. The school provides $780,000 in need-based financial aid.

ADMISSIONS INFORMATION

Admission is based on academic performance, recommendations, and standardized test scores. The SSAT is recommended. OES administers achievement and/or aptitude tests if sufficient information is not available from previous schools. The testing is scheduled as needed. OES also asks prospective students to write a short personal essay.

APPLICATION TIMETABLE

Initial inquiries are welcome year-round, but the application deadline for the fall semester is February 1. There is a $75 application fee ($100 for international students), and early application is recommended. The School conducts campus tours and interviews by appointment. Prospective applicants are asked to visit on a school day in order to see the School in full operation. Contracts are issued in March. The School continues to accept applications, issuing contracts after that date only if space permits.

ADMISSIONS CORRESPONDENCE

David Lowell, Director of Admissions
Oregon Episcopal School
6300 Southwest Nicol Road
Portland, Oregon 97223
Phone: 503-768-3115
Fax: 503-768-3140
E-mail: admit@oes.edu
Web site: http://www.oes.edu

OVERSEAS FAMILY SCHOOL

Singapore

Type: Coeducational day college-preparatory school
Grades: PK–12: Prekindergarten; Kindergarten, K1–K2; Elementary School, 1–5; Middle School, 6–8; High School, 9–12
Enrollment: School total: 3,500; Middle and High Schools: 1,650
Head of School: Dr. Bhim P. Mozoomdar

THE SCHOOL

Overseas Family School (OFS), which was founded in 1991 for overseas families living in Singapore, provides classes from kindergarten through high school. The International Baccalaureate (I.B.) curriculum is taught throughout the entire school, and English is the primary medium of instruction. The School curriculum is designed to prepare an international student body to enter colleges and universities in the country of their choice, including Australia, Canada, India, Japan, Korea, the United States, and Singapore, as well as institutions throughout Europe.

The students of the School represent more than seventy different nationalities. The School has an international faculty that includes members from twenty-four different countries, with experience and training in a variety of educational systems. The School places an emphasis on high academic standards measured against the personal potential of each student.

Educational growth occurs in a supportive atmosphere where students work cooperatively to achieve their school goals and where self-discipline and self-respect are the basic guidelines for behavior. The School environment cultivates a flexible approach to problem solving and the development of higher-thinking skills. All aspects of a student's schooling are seen as important and interdependent.

An appreciation and respect for cultural diversity are valued, and a "worldwide family" approach to the School curriculum helps students overcome any biased attitudes toward other cultures. Active participation in the learning process and in community service inspires each student to become a lifelong learner and responsible world citizen who is prepared for the challenges of the future.

The Overseas Family School offers a specialized Study Preparation Program (SPP) for students for whom English is a second or other language (ESOL). Students make international friendships in specialized programs such as SPP as well as through the academic program, extracurricular activities, and sports.

The School is located near Orchard Road and the center of Singapore. It is easily accessible from all parts of the island republic by public transportation. School buses with safety belts in each seat bring children to school from every district in Singapore.

The Overseas Family School is authorized by the International Baccalaureate Organization (IBO), Geneva; is accredited by the Western Association of Schools and Colleges (WASC) in California, U.S.A.; and is registered with the Singapore Ministry of Education.

ACADEMIC PROGRAMS

The International Baccalaureate curriculum is taught throughout the entire school, from kindergarten to high school. Upon entry into the Overseas Family School, students' English proficiency is assessed. Secondary students needing further preparation in English join the Study Preparation Program, which offers a full range of specially developed classes in most academic subjects, including English, science, mathematics, humanities, and computers. SPP students join the regular program for nonacademic classes and extracurricular activities. When students in the SPP have reached the appropriate level of English, they transfer to regular classes.

Kindergarten and Elementary School (grades 1–5) students follow the International Baccalaureate Primary Years Program (PYP), an inquiry-based approach to teaching and learning. Individual attention and regular assessment by experienced teachers prepare young students for secondary school or reentry into their national systems.

Kindergarten students (ages 3–5) develop social skills as well as the foundation for academic learning. Young children learn through play in a rich and stimulating school environment.

Students in the Middle School (grades 6–8) follow the International Baccalaureate Middle Years Program (MYP), which prepares students for the demanding requirements of a high school curriculum.

High School students in grades 9 and 10 study the final two years of the five-year International Baccalaureate Middle Years Program. In addition to the MYP, many grade 9 and 10 students also study for the British-based International General Certificate of Secondary Education (IGCSE). Assessment of the IGCSE program is by external examination, whereas in the MYP, students' work is internally assessed and then moderated by the I.B. to ensure it meets their rigorous international standards.

The thorough preparation received by students in grades 9 and 10 facilitates their studies in grades 11 and 12 to graduate with an OFS High School Graduation Diploma. Students are awarded the High School diploma either through the prestigious and demanding I.B. Diploma Program or through completion of all the internal credit requirements and standards set by the School. Regular assessment and counseling help monitor and evaluate student progress and provide frequent academic feedback to teachers, students, and parents.

A comprehensive language program offers students in all grades the opportunity to study another language. All students in grades 1–10 who are not in the SPP program are expected to study another major international language other than English. The School currently offers French, German, Japanese, Mandarin, and Spanish.

FACULTY AND ADVISERS

All 302 faculty members have required teacher training and certificates; approximately one quarter have master's degrees. Eighty-nine of the faculty members are men and 213 are women. Time is allocated for support classes, and pastoral care is provided by home-based teachers and 2 academic advisers. The principals and academic advisers maintain an open-door policy for students and parents.

COLLEGE ADMISSION COUNSELING

Academic advisers assist senior students in college placement but start emphasizing college counseling early in the secondary programs. Group counseling scheduled for the second semester provides needed information to senior students. Tenth-grade students may choose to take the PSAT. Eleventh-grade students meet a number of college representatives to discuss college requirements, application procedures, reference building, and college selection criteria. SAT- and ACT-preparation workshops are presented before major testing dates. Small-group presentations and individual counseling sessions assist senior-year students with final college placement arrangements.

STUDENT BODY AND CONDUCT

A significant feature of the Overseas Family School is that no one nationality dominates the School. The top 10 nationality groups in the 2008 school year are India (549), Korea (449), Britain (242), the United States (240), Japan (192), Norway (167), Denmark (154), Australia (138), Indonesia (98), and Sweden (94). The remainder of the student body represented a total of sixty other nationalities.

ACADEMIC FACILITIES

The Overseas Family School campus is situated on 12 acres, with twelve buildings clustered around its sports facilities. Old trees and greenery create a pleasant and inviting learning environment.

The School has 165 classrooms, nine science labs, seven computer labs, five art studios, six music rooms, two drama room/theaterettes, and an auditorium. The five School libraries have a collection of more than 35,000 volumes controlled by the Winnebago computer software system. The libraries have a collection of Proquest Periodical Database facilities. All classrooms are equipped with two Apple iMacs with e-mail and Internet facilities. All rooms are air conditioned, carpeted, linked by a campuswide computer network, and equipped with appropriate audiovisual equipment and learning resources.

ATHLETICS

The Overseas Family School provides an extensive sports program and participates in interschool competition in badminton, cricket, rugby, soccer, softball, tennis, and volleyball. Many of these events take place at the School, or students travel by bus to other venues.

The School has five shaded basketball and netball courts, a school hall, a playing field with two soccer pitches, and one tennis court. A junior pool is provided for kindergarten and elementary students, and secondary school students utilize a newly constructed swimming pool.

EXTRACURRICULAR OPPORTUNITIES

A large number of extracurricular activities are offered during the school day as well as after school and on weekends. These activities continually vary according to student request and faculty offerings. All students must choose one activity and may change their selection each quarter. Each member of the faculty is involved in at least one sport, cultural, special interest, or academic activity. Popular extracurricular activities include chess club, soccer skills, table tennis, aerobics, tae kwon do, karate, jewelry making, basketball, drama, choral music, calligraphy and crafts, Scouts, Guides, Brownies, and community service.

DAILY LIFE

The school day begins at 9 a.m. and ends at 3:30 p.m., when the buses are scheduled to take students home. All students have a morning or afternoon break of approximately 15 minutes and a lunch break of 60 minutes. The school days for grades 1–12 are divided into five 1-hour periods. Meals and snacks may be purchased from the School canteen at break and lunch time. Many students bring packed lunches from home. They enjoy different taste sensations by sharing their lunches with their friends from other nations.

The School maintains a closed campus; therefore, students need written permission from parents and/or their principal before they may leave the School compound during the school day.

COSTS AND FINANCIAL AID

In 2008–09, tuition fees per semester are as follows (in Singapore dollars): PK, $6000; K1–K2, $9000; grades 1–5, $10,000; grades 6–8, $11,000; and grades 9–12, $12,500. There is an additional fee of $1000 for those students who enroll in the ESOL-SPP program. There are two semesters per year.

ADMISSIONS INFORMATION

Overseas Family School serves the educational needs of diplomatic, business, and professional families of the international community. The School admits students of every race, nationality, and ethnic origin and accordingly runs a strictly secular program.

APPLICATION TIMETABLE

Applications for admission are welcome throughout the year, because the School recognizes that many families have no control over the timing of their posting to Singapore.

The application is made on the School's standard application form, with two recent passport photographs and the latest copies of previous school reports. When the School registrar advises the family that a place is available, a refundable deposit equivalent to one semester's tuition fee reserves the place for that student, and the School proceeds to provide the resources necessary for the proposed start date. Tuition fees are payable on commencement and before the start of each semester.

Families are encouraged to visit the School as often as they wish to assess whether their children are happy and successful there.

ADMISSIONS CORRESPONDENCE

Mrs. Soma Mathews, Registrar
Overseas Family School
25F Paterson Road
Singapore 238515
Republic of Singapore
Phone: 65-6738-0211
Fax: 65-6733-8825
E-mail: soma@ofs.edu.sg
Web site: http://www.ofs.edu.sg

THE OXFORD ACADEMY

Westbrook, Connecticut

Type: Boys' boarding college-preparatory school whose mission is to provide young men with a successful educational experience through one-to-one instruction
Grades: 9–12, postgraduate year
Enrollment: 48
Head of School: Philip H. Davis, Headmaster

THE SCHOOL

The Oxford Academy was founded in 1906 by Dr. Joseph M. Weidberg, who was appalled by the seeming lack of interest on the part of traditional schools in educating young men with good potential who were experiencing academic problems. He knew that some young men who do not always do well in a classroom situation can achieve acceptable, and sometimes extraordinary, academic success when given individualized attention.

After investigating different types of pedagogy, Dr. Weidberg decided to use the Socratic method of teaching. He taught his students by questioning them and stimulating them to know themselves, to think, to understand, to use initiative, and to express themselves. The school continues to do this for young men between the ages of 14 and 20 who have experienced learning difficulties in a traditional school setting. A special feature of the school is that all teaching is one-to-one—1 teacher to 1 student per class.

The school, originally located in Pleasantville, New Jersey, was destroyed by fire in 1971 and moved to a 12-acre site in Westbrook, Connecticut, along the state's shoreline. Since then, campus improvements include the Corthouts Gymnasium, Hoskins Hall, and a recreation hall as well as an academic wing built in 1999. In addition, two playing fields were developed and three tennis courts completed.

Westbrook is a 5-minute drive from Old Saybrook, which has Amtrak train service from Boston and New York, each approximately 2 hours away. Bradley International Airport, in Hartford, is an hour from the school.

The school's physical plant is valued at $3.7 million.

The Oxford Academy is accredited by the New England Association of Schools and Colleges and approved by the Connecticut Department of Education. It is a member of the Connecticut Association of Independent Schools and the National Association of Independent Schools and is an associate member of the International Council of Schools.

ACADEMIC PROGRAMS

Because of its pedagogical approach, unique among boarding schools, the Oxford Academy admits students whenever there is an opening, and a boy begins his course of studies at the point dictated by his academic needs, which are determined after extensive testing. A curriculum is planned to compensate for each student's deficiencies, taking into account his individual academic needs and psychological makeup. The curriculum is geared to high school and postgraduate students and consists of courses in the five traditional academic subject areas: English, mathematics, science, social studies, and foreign languages. In addition, courses in developmental reading and mathematics, language arts, studio art, English as a second language, and other curricular areas of need can be incorporated into a boy's program.

Although the vast majority of students follow a college-preparatory curriculum, provision is made for a course of study leading to a general high school diploma. Many types of developmental learning disabilities can be addressed, but boys with severe learning disabilities are not accepted. A boy must have at least average intelligence in order to be admitted.

Every week, each student's program is evaluated, and grades for achievement and effort are handed in to the Dean of Studies. Standardized testing is used periodically to evaluate a boy's progress, and sufficient help is given to enable students to take the ACT, SAT, and TOEFL in order to make the transition from the Academy to a traditional preparatory school or to college.

FACULTY AND ADVISERS

In 2008–09, the faculty consists of 19 full-time and 3 part-time members; 10 hold master's degrees. Teachers at the Oxford Academy receive special instruction and supervision in one-to-one pedagogy from the Headmaster and the Dean of Studies.

The Headmaster, Philip H. Davis, has a B.A. from Middlebury College and an M.A.L.S. from Wesleyan University.

Most faculty members live on campus and thus are in constant contact with the boys to advise them not only on academic matters but also on personal and social problems.

COLLEGE ADMISSION COUNSELING

The Academy offers individual help in college placement. A quarter of the school population normally stays at the Academy for up to twelve months before seeking placement in a traditional preparatory school. The remaining students, who tend to stay at the Academy for less than three years, are usually college bound. Educational consultants are kept abreast of a student's progress and thus are in a good position to evaluate college needs after a year or two at the Oxford Academy.

Graduating seniors were accepted by the following colleges and universities in 2007: Fordham, Green Mountain, Skidmore, Suffolk, and the University of Colorado.

STUDENT BODY AND CONDUCT

The Oxford Academy has a limited number of places. Forty-eight students is the maximum number that can be accommodated with the present facilities and staff. In September 2007, the ages of the students ranged from 14 to 19, and they came from twelve states and five other countries. These boys and their parents were attracted to the Academy because of its individualized instruction and the cultural and geographical diversity of the student body, which enhances the general educational atmosphere.

Each student is required to commit himself to the program in writing before he is accepted. By this commitment, he tells the school and his parents that he is willing to work hard and to obey the rules and regulations of the Academy.

If students do not conduct themselves in a gentlemanly fashion and with good intentions after having been given a chance to succeed, they are asked to leave. It is understood that the basic regulation at the Oxford Academy is consideration for one's peers and for the adult community.

ACADEMIC FACILITIES

The main academic building, Knight Hall, named after a former Headmaster, is more than 6,500 square feet and includes offices, classrooms, a general reference library, and a state-of-the-art computer facility as well as an art studio and a darkroom. There is also a science laboratory, with a greenhouse, fully equipped for general science, biology, chemistry, and physics. The Westbrook Public Library is located directly across from the Academy.

Hoskins Hall, named in honor of an Oxford teacher who was at the school for thirty-eight years, houses three additional classrooms.

BOARDING AND GENERAL FACILITIES

The Academy has two dormitory buildings, each with facilities for 24 students. Resident faculty members live in each dormitory building with the students. Most rooms are double occupancy, and there is a common bathroom for each dormitory. One dormitory houses the dining room. Hill House, an eighteenth-century Colonial building, contains business offices, a reception center, and the admissions office. Next door is the nineteenth-century Post

House, which houses faculty members. The Headmaster's residence, built in 1800, is located on the western property line next to the skating pond, which adjoins the beach area on Long Island Sound. Completing the plant is a former barn, which has been converted into a recreation center for the students.

ATHLETICS

Oxford's daily sports program aims neither to attract students nor to discourage them. Students come to Oxford for what it can do for them academically. The athletics program is designed to provide the physical activity necessary to maintain each student at his physical and psychological best. The Academy has limited interscholastic competition, usually in basketball, softball, soccer, and tennis. All other sports and games—golf, karate, paintball, and bowling—are played on either an intramural or individual basis.

Corthouts Gymnasium was built in 1983. The foyer to the gymnasium and a weight room are located in Hoskins Hall.

EXTRACURRICULAR OPPORTUNITIES

A darkroom is available for students interested in photography. In addition to participating in the interscholastic sports program, students enjoy swimming, skiing, golf, and riding near the school. Occasional field trips are sponsored.

DAILY LIFE

Breakfast is served from 7 to 7:55 a.m., and classes begin at 8. Classes end at 3 and are followed by a scheduled athletic period. Dinner is served at 6, and the evening study period runs from 7:30 to 8:45. Lights-out is at 11 p.m.

WEEKEND LIFE

Because of the location of the Oxford Academy, students are able to take advantage of cultural events in New Haven and Hartford. Often, weekend day trips are planned to Boston and New York.

Students who have met their academic and social obligations may leave the campus after testing on Saturday, with parental permission, and return by 7 p.m. on Sunday.

SUMMER PROGRAMS

In the summer, Oxford runs a program that offers the same type of work as its winter session. The program is intended primarily for students enrolled in the regular program who would like to accelerate their studies, but the Academy does accept students for the summer session only.

COSTS AND FINANCIAL AID

Tuition for the 2008–09 school year was $50,456. A security deposit of $1000 for domestic students and $2000 for international students is required. Additional expenses may include those for testing ($400), laundry, books, and field trips.

ADMISSIONS INFORMATION

Admission to the Oxford Academy is selective. The school accepts young men between the ages of 14 and 20 who have yet to realize their academic potential, wish to make up for lost time, or are international students seeking entrance into American colleges and universities. The Oxford Academy does not discriminate on the basis of race, color, or creed. The admissions policy excludes youngsters of below-normal intelligence and students who are emotionally disturbed in the medical sense. As Oxford is not a therapeutic facility, other schools are recommended to students with severe learning disabilities or significant behavioral issues.

APPLICATION TIMETABLE

Application for admission to Oxford can be made at any time. A student begins his program the day he arrives, since he is in a class by himself. The limited number of spaces may necessitate waiting one or two months before the student begins, but the school has rolling admissions procedures. No student is accepted until all previous school records have been received and he and his parents have had an interview at the school. Exceptions have been made for international students who cannot travel to the United States but who have been interviewed by parents of former students or by alumni in their home countries.

ADMISSIONS CORRESPONDENCE

Mr. Philip H. Davis
Headmaster
The Oxford Academy
1393 Boston Post Road
Westbrook, Connecticut 06498
Phone: 860-399-6247
Fax: 860-399-6805
E-mail: admissions@oxfordacademy.net
Web site: http://www.oxfordacademy.net

Philip H. Davis, Headmaster.

PARK TUDOR SCHOOL

Indianapolis, Indiana

Exceptional Educators. Extraordinary Opportunities.

Type: Coeducational day college-preparatory school
Grades: Junior Kindergarten–12: Hilbert Early Education Center, Junior–Senior Kindergarten; Lower School, 1–5; Middle School, 6–8; Upper School, 9–12
Enrollment: School total: 982; Upper School: 426
Head of School: Douglas S. Jennings

THE SCHOOL

Park Tudor School was established in 1970 by a merger of Tudor Hall School for girls and Park School for boys. The Reverend James Cumming Smith and Miss Fredonia Allen founded Tudor Hall School in 1902. The Reverend Smith, formerly pastor of Tabernacle Presbyterian Church, served as the School's first Dean. Park School began in 1914 as the Brooks School for Boys. When the School moved in 1920, the name was changed to Park School because the new campus was near the Thomas Taggart Park. Both schools were founded to provide the kind of education offered by Eastern preparatory schools of the era.

Continuing the tradition established by its predecessors, Park Tudor School today offers a vigorous program in English composition and literature, laboratory science, mathematics, foreign languages, history, art, music, speech, and drama. Special interest clubs and an extensive program of athletics and physical education complement the academic program.

Park Tudor School is governed by a 22-member Board of Directors. Annual giving averages $900,000. Active alumni, mothers', fathers', athletic, and multicultural associations support the School's scholarship program.

Park Tudor School is accredited by the Independent Schools Association of the Central States and holds a continuous commission from the Indiana Department of Public Instruction. The School is a member of the National Association of Independent Schools, the College Board, the Educational Records Bureau, the Indiana Non-Public Education Association, the Council for Advancement and Support of Education, and the Secondary School Admission Test Board.

ACADEMIC PROGRAMS

The Hilbert Early Education Center provides junior and senior kindergarten students (ages 3–6) with a varied, active environment in which young learners can move and choose freely among activities, materials, and learning options. The junior kindergarten program is designed for children ages 3–5, and the senior kindergarten program is for ages 5 and 6. Both JK and SK are full-day programs. Activities include an integrated Spanish program beginning at age 3, computer instruction, art, music, books, science, math, and gym. Lower School (1–5) provides children with a program in reading, language arts, social studies, mathematics, science, music, art, and Spanish. An After-School Program is available from the time of dismissal until 6 p.m. for Park Tudor families. In the Middle School (6–8), students must take English, geography, U.S. history, mathematics, science, etymology, and physical education. Latin, French, Spanish, music, art, drama, and algebra are offered as electives.

Upper School students must earn 40 credits to qualify for a diploma. At least 32 credits must be earned and distributed as follows: English, 8 credits; foreign languages, 4 credits; mathematics, 6 credits; fine arts, 2 credits; science, 6 credits; social studies, 6 credits; and speech, 1 credit. Students must also complete 3 semesters of physical education and 1 semester of health.

Elective courses include government, economics, ethics, sociology, computer science, statistics, calculus, advanced chemistry, advanced physics, advanced biology, art history, film history, journalism, military history, music theory, music history, theater history, graphic design, photography, Latin, classical Greek, French, Spanish, etymology, and creative writing. Most courses at the twelfth-grade level offer college-level instruction, and students regularly take Advanced Placement tests in English, French, Spanish, German, art history, chemistry, biology, American history, mathematics, and music theory. The School offers twenty Advanced Placement courses and a rigorous Global Scholars program, Park Tudor's version of the International Baccalaureate, for highly able and motivated juniors and seniors.

The student-faculty ratio in the Upper School is roughly 9:1. During the 2008–09 academic year, the average class size was 14 students.

Grades—on an A-to-F scale with pluses and minuses—are issued after each quarter, but mid-quarter comments are prepared for students who require encouragement or a warning. All quarter grade reports carry full written comments on student progress. Grade reports are mailed to parents, and copies are given to students in conference with their adviser. At the end of each semester, the administration reviews the progress of each student and advises the family if marked improvement is necessary. All teachers are available for additional help during a conference period at the end of the school day.

FACULTY AND ADVISERS

Of the 158 teaching faculty members, 60 percent hold master's degrees in their fields, and 20 percent of Upper School teachers hold Ph.D.'s. The School encourages faculty members to continue their education and assists with the costs of tuition for graduate courses and short-term seminars and workshops. Sabbaticals or fortnight study leaves are available.

Although all faculty members are involved in informal counseling, academic and personal counseling are primary responsibilities of the student's adviser and the Coordinator of Counseling Services.

Douglas S. Jennings is the School's fourth Head of School. He received his B.A. degree from Lafayette College and M.A. degrees from Montclair State College and Columbia University.

COLLEGE ADMISSION COUNSELING

The Director of Guidance and Counseling assists students in selecting and applying to colleges. Almost 100 colleges and universities send representatives to the campus each year, and students are encouraged to visit colleges in which they have a particular interest. For the class of 2008, mean scores on the SAT were 627 critical reading, 617 math, and 620 writing.

The 100 graduates of the class of 2008 were accepted by colleges and universities across the country. Their final choices included Bowdoin, DePauw, Emory, Indiana, Purdue, and Vanderbilt.

STUDENT BODY AND CONDUCT

There are 354 students in the Hilbert Early Education Center and the Lower School and 202 in the Middle School. There are currently 54 boys and 50 girls in grade 9, 55 boys and 53 girls in grade 10, 54 boys and 55 girls in grade 11, and 58 boys and 47 girls in grade 12. Nearly all the students come from metropolitan Indianapolis, but a few students commute from neighboring towns. Each year the School hosts 1 or 2 students sponsored by American Secondary Schools for International Students and Teachers.

Rules are deliberately kept simple and few in number because the School's philosophy hinges on the concept that a strong school is one in which individuals respect the rights of others and recognize their responsibility to the School community of which they are a part. A dress code is in force schoolwide. There is an honor code in the Upper School.

Parent and student participation in School activities is a tradition at Park Tudor School. There are Student Councils in the Lower, Middle, and Upper Schools.

ACADEMIC FACILITIES

The School is located in the 55-acre Lilly Orchard, a gift to the School from the late Josiah K. Lilly and the late Eli Lilly. Six major buildings, constructed of Indiana limestone, are set among the trees and rolling hills.

The Jane Holton Upper School Building (1970; expanded and renovated in 2000) houses classrooms, four laboratories, a computer lab, central administrative offices, a lecture hall, and a 17,000-volume library. The Ruth Lilly Science Center (1989) contains four labs, a computer lab, and a science resource center. The Frederic M. Ayres Jr. Auditorium and Fine Arts Building (1976; expanded and renovated in 2000) has classrooms; music rehearsal rooms; teaching studios; a music library; studios for art, photography, ceramics, and dance; and a 425-seat auditorium. The Middle School Building (1988) has eleven classrooms, a library, and a computer lab. The Lower School Building (1967) and Hilbert Early Education Center (1997) contain twenty-five classrooms, a 17,000-volume library, and a computer lab. The Hilbert Early Education Center (1997) houses classes for junior kindergarten and senior kindergarten. Clowes Commons (1967) provides dining, seminar, and reception facilities. The Head of School's home is on campus, and Foster Hall (1927) provides a small conference and reception center. The athletic facilities (1967, 1970, 1992) house three gyms, a fitness deck, a suspended running track, and seven athletic fields, including an artificial-turf football field.

ATHLETICS

Practically every student in the Upper School is involved in the athletics and physical education program. Park Tudor fields varsity teams for boys in baseball, basketball, crew, cross-country, football, golf, hockey, lacrosse, soccer, swimming, tennis, track, and wrestling, and varsity teams for girls in basketball, crew, cross-country, golf, lacrosse, soccer, softball, swimming, tennis, track, and volleyball. Junior varsity teams also compete in many of these sports.

The facilities include three gymnasiums, a room for free-weight lifting, a fitness deck, locker and shower facilities, and offices. There are also seven playing fields, including one with artificial turf, twelve tennis courts, a track, and an exceptionally fine cross-country course.

EXTRACURRICULAR OPPORTUNITIES

In addition to athletics and the fine arts programs, the School sponsors a wide variety of extracurricular activities. Students are encouraged to enter into the life of the School and to pursue and develop their individual interests.

New activities groups are formed whenever there is sufficient interest, while certain clubs are always included in the program. Organizations and activities include Thespians, *Chronicle* (yearbook), and *Artisan* (literary magazine); foreign language, international, science, and service clubs; and the student councils and Model UN.

DAILY LIFE

The school day extends from 8 until 3. Classes are 40 minutes long; some science classes have double periods once or twice a week. Most sports and extracurricular activities meet after the end of the school day. Except for students who are having academic difficulties, no study halls are assigned for Upper School students.

SUMMER PROGRAMS

Park Tudor School offers a nine-week summer session for youngsters ages 3 and up. Courses are offered for academic credit and for enrichment. The School also is host to soccer and basketball camps.

COSTS AND FINANCIAL AID

Tuition for the 2008–09 academic year was $16,570 for grades 6–12. This fee covered instruction, testing, and some additional activities fees. Books and lunches are extra. Tuition for senior kindergarten–grade 5 was $15,639; junior kindergarten tuition (full-day program) was $13,300. Additional fees vary by grade level.

Park Tudor School encourages qualified students, regardless of economic background, to consider the opportunity of attending. The primary basis for making grants and loans is financial need; other factors considered are academic promise and potential contributions to School life. The fact that an applicant may need financial assistance is not considered when his or her qualifications for admission are reviewed.

Thirty-eight percent received financial aid for the 2008–09 school year; the average grant was half tuition, and the total value of the grants was more than $2.5 million. The School subscribes to the School and Student Service for Financial Aid.

ADMISSIONS INFORMATION

Park Tudor School selects students for admission on the basis of intellectual aptitude, sound character, and motivation. Qualified candidates are accepted at all grade levels, depending on vacancies. Admission to grade 12 is rare and occurs only when the applicant's record is exceptionally strong. Applicants are chosen without regard to race, religion, or color.

All applicants are required to take the Independent School Entrance Exam.

The admissions record for 2008–09 for grades 9–12 was as follows: 112 applied and 52 enrolled.

APPLICATION TIMETABLE

Initial inquiries are welcome at any time. Although applications are accepted as long as there are openings at a particular grade level, candidates have the best chance for admission if their applications are submitted by mid-December for grades 9–12 and mid-January for junior kindergarten–grade 8.

Open Houses are held in October/November, and tours of the campus may be arranged at any time. Prospective parents are invited to observe classes during "See Us in Action" events from November through January, and prospective Middle and Upper School students spend a day at school observing classes. Entrance examinations are given at regular intervals, usually starting in November. The Admissions Committee informs the family of its decision in February and March. Families ordinarily have two weeks to decide whether they will accept the offer of admission.

ADMISSIONS CORRESPONDENCE

David Amstutz, Director of Admissions
Park Tudor School
7200 North College Avenue
Indianapolis, Indiana 46240-3016
Phone: 317-415-2777
Fax: 317-254-2714
E-mail: damstutz@parktudor.org
Web site: http://www.parktudor.org

PEDDIE SCHOOL

Hightstown, New Jersey

PEDDIE SCHOOL

Type: Coeducational boarding and day college-preparatory school
Grades: 9–12, postgraduate year
Enrollment: 527
Head of School: John F. Green, Head

THE SCHOOL

Peddie School is recognized as one of the nation's finest boarding schools. Noted for its distinctive programs in academics, athletics, the arts, and residential life, Peddie provides a rigorous academic experience, mixing tradition with innovation while focusing on the education of the whole child. Peddie's faculty encourages and inspires bright and enthusiastic students to reach for new levels of achievement in a uniquely friendly, supportive, and diverse community.

Peddie was established in 1864 under the auspices of the Hightstown Baptist Church. A year later it was chartered by the state legislature as the New Jersey Classical and Scientific Institute. In 1872, it was renamed to honor a benefactor, the Honorable Thomas B. Peddie. In the early 1900s it became a boys' school, but in 1970, it returned to coeducation, enrolling boarding and day girls. Although Peddie is no longer church related, its historical religious affiliation is still reflected in its twice-weekly required nondenominational chapel services.

A beautiful 230-acre campus encompasses Peddie Lake and woodlands as well as extensive athletics facilities, including an eighteen-hole golf course. Peddie's location and size are both significant. As a midsized boarding school, Peddie is able to provide impressive educational resources to its students without sacrificing the personalized attention of smaller schools. In addition, Peddie is situated in the village of Hightstown, New Jersey, just east of Princeton and midway between New York City and Philadelphia, providing students with a peaceful environment only an hour from the cultural assets of these two cities.

The School, which is nonprofit, is directed by a board of 35 trustees. The endowment totals $280 million. The value of the physical plant is $116 million. Operating expenses for 2007–08 totaled $26 million, and Annual Giving for the same period was $2 million.

Peddie School is accredited by the Middle States Association of Colleges and Schools and is a member of the Secondary School Admission Test Board, the National Association of Independent Schools, and the New Jersey Association of Independent Schools.

ACADEMIC PROGRAMS

All students receive a laptop computer as part of their tuition. The academic year is divided into three terms. In the first two terms, students study a rigorous core curriculum that is designed to provide a well-balanced liberal education. During the third term, most students have the opportunity to choose electives of particular interest. Qualified students are given the opportunity to enter honors programs.

In order to graduate, a student must earn a total of 47 term units. Specific area requirements are English, 11; mathematics, 8; foreign language, 6; history, 6; science, 6; and fine arts, 5.

Although teachers employ a variety of methods and techniques, the emphasis is placed on interactive learning, and students are expected to play an active role in their classes. To accommodate this approach, the average class size at Peddie is 12.

Advanced Placement courses are offered in a variety of areas: biology, chemistry, environmental science, physics, psychology, European history, U.S. history, French, Spanish, Latin, Chinese, calculus, statistics, computers, music theory, art history, and studio art. An Independent Study Program provides students with the opportunity to study a specialized subject in great depth; seniors may participate in off-campus projects during the spring term.

Students receive grades six times a year, at the middle and end of each academic term. Grade reports are also mailed to parents on six occasions, and extensive teacher comments are produced three times a year.

FACULTY AND ADVISERS

John F. Green was appointed Head in 2001. A graduate of Wesleyan (B.A.) and Harvard (M.Ed.), Mr. Green was Dean of Faculty at St. Paul's School, where he was also Director of Admission, Senior College Adviser, and head of the history department. Previously, he taught at Western Reserve Academy and the Fessenden School.

The faculty consists of 85 full-time teachers, of whom 50 are men and 35 are women, and 21 administrators. Faculty members have a median of nineteen years of teaching experience. All actively advise and counsel students. Ninety percent of the faculty members reside on campus. The faculty holds eighty-five baccalaureate and seventy-two graduate degrees (85 percent), representing study at seventy colleges and universities.

COLLEGE ADMISSION COUNSELING

A college guidance staff helps to counsel students and direct them to colleges that are suitable for their needs and capabilities. The college counseling process begins in the junior year, when all students are expected to take the PSAT, ACT, and SAT. Many college representatives meet with seniors and interested juniors each fall for interviews. Students are encouraged to make their college visits during the spring vacation of the junior year and the summer.

In 2008, all 135 graduates continued on to colleges and universities. Over the past five years, the most popular schools have been Boston College, Carnegie Mellon, Cornell, George Washington, Georgetown, the University of Pennsylvania, and the U.S. Naval Academy.

STUDENT BODY AND CONDUCT

Peddie enrolls 527 students—181 boarding boys, 162 boarding girls, 87 day boys, and 97 day girls—as follows: 129 in grade 9, 128 in grade 10, 137 in grade 11, and 133 in grade 12, including postgraduates. The students, who range from 13 to 19 years of age, represent twenty-three states and U.S. territories and twenty-one countries. Day students come from Hightstown and nearby communities—principally Cranbury, West Windsor, Hamilton, Allentown, and Princeton.

The Student Council consists of elected representatives from all residence halls and day student groups. The council organizes social activities and proposes changes to the Student-Faculty Senate, which has equal representation from faculty members and students.

ACADEMIC FACILITIES

Annenberg Hall houses twenty-three classrooms, conference rooms, a computer center, and the Annenberg Library, which holds more than 30,000 volumes and has a campuswide computer network that links directly with similar networks at the Princeton University library, as well as campuswide e-mail and full access to the Internet. Students can access the library services from any residence room, home, and anywhere they have access to the Internet. September 2006 marked the opening of the exciting Caspersen History House, featuring "tech pods" in every classroom, student work rooms and lounge areas, and a 120-seat auditorium. Only a year earlier, in 2005, the extraordinary Walter and Leonore Annenberg Science Center opened, with eleven state-of-the-art laboratory classrooms equipped with multimedia stations, DVD players, ceiling projectors, electronic white boards, special project rooms for long-term experimentation, interactive science displays, a DNA laboratory, and a two-story greenhouse. The Swig Arts Center houses an art gallery, three painting and drawing studios, independent studio space for all advanced studio art students, three music practice rooms, a student art gallery, a state-of-the-art photography laboratory, a video imaging center, three classrooms, a large choral and instrumental performance room, an electronic music composing room, and many private studios. All Peddie academic buildings have full wireless access to the Peddie network and the Internet.

BOARDING AND GENERAL FACILITIES

Boarding students reside in fourteen residence halls, the smallest of which houses 8 students and the largest, 34 students. All residence halls are supervised by resident faculty members, and almost all the rooms are doubles. The Caspersen Campus Center contains a dining hall, student lounges and recreation rooms, the Peddie Grille snack bar, and the college counseling office. Also on campus are the Geiger-Reeves Theater; the Hensle Health Center; Ayer Memorial Chapel; the headmaster's home; the Yu Child Care Center, which is available to the children of faculty members; and twenty-five faculty residences.

ATHLETICS

Peddie is fortunate to have one of the best-equipped facilities for athletics of any preparatory school in the country. The Athletic and Physical Education Department offers a very competitive interscholastic program of twenty-seven sports, a comprehensive physical education program emphasizing lifetime sports, and a variety of intramural activities. All students are required to participate on an interscholastic team or in one of the elective physical education activities after school.

The Athletic Center houses a swimming pool and separate diving tank, three basketball/volleyball/tennis courts surrounded by an indoor Mondo surface track, a wrestling room, an indoor soccer and lacrosse turf facility, a 2,000-square-foot fitness center with state-of-the-art equipment, a training room, locker rooms, a kitchen, and offices. Outdoor facilities include fourteen tennis courts, eight multi-purpose fields, a softball field, an Olympic-caliber ¼-mile all-weather track with Mondo track surface, a football field, three baseball diamonds, and the eighteen-hole Peddie School Golf Club.

Peddie is a member of the New Jersey Independent Schools Athletic Association (NJISAA). Traditional rivals include Blair Academy, the Lawrenceville School, the Hill School, Mercersburg Academy, and the Hun School of Princeton.

EXTRACURRICULAR OPPORTUNITIES

Students are actively involved in a wide range of activities. A theater is used for dramatics, speaking contests, lectures, and films. Students produce a monthly news publication, a literary magazine, and a yearbook. Musical organizations include a chorus and three select singing groups, an orchestra, a jazz band, and several smaller ensembles. The annual Spring Arts Festival in April focuses attention on student work in art and music and brings guest artists to the campus. There are many clubs, including those that involve students in photography, astronomy, drama, arts, chess, foreign languages, creative writing, debate, the stock market, Model UN, and social service. Students can also participate in Outward Bound–type activities through the Outing Club, as well as a two-week spring bicycle trip, traveling historic back-country roads in the Mid-Atlantic states. Summer travel, supervised by Peddie faculty members, includes trips to France, Spain, or China, with local family homestays and country tours.

DAILY LIFE

Classes meet six days a week; Wednesday and Saturday are half days. A typical daily schedule includes classes between 8 a.m. and 3 p.m. Sports are scheduled from 3:30 to 5:30. In the evening, boarders have approximately 2 hours of supervised study.

WEEKEND LIFE

A student's life at Peddie is distinguished by full, varied, and challenging involvement—academic, athletic, and social. Students actively contribute to the Peddie community in the residence halls, in the close relationships between day students and boarders, and in their extracurricular activities. The same close relationships exist between the students and their teachers and residence hall supervisors. Trips to Princeton, New York, and Philadelphia are frequent, and while weekend activities keep the students entertained and the campus active and full, boarding students have the opportunity to return home periodically between vacations. The School also allows day leaves on weekends as well as frequent Saturday overnights for boarding students. Both of these privileges are based on maintaining a good citizenship record and are allowed only with specific written parental instructions.

Typical weekend events on campus are dances, concerts, movies, residence parties, and Drama Club performances. The Outing Club schedules periodic trips to such sites as the Poconos and the Delaware River. Traditional annual events include Christmas Vespers, the Geiger-Reeves Speaking Contest, Parents Day, and Alumni Day.

COSTS AND FINANCIAL AID

Charges at Peddie in 2008–09 were $39,900 for boarders and $30,200 for day students. Peddie does not charge a health center fee, tech fee, or student activity fee, and each student is provided with a laptop computer at no extra cost. Other expenses are for books ($500), insurance ($30), sports equipment ($45), allowances for boarders ($350), and travel. There are additional fees for professional tutoring, piano or organ lessons, driver education, and the photography course. A tuition payment plan is offered.

Approximately 40 percent of the students received financial aid from Peddie's $5 million annual budget; the average financial aid award was $19,000. Grants are based on need, using input from the School and Student Service for Financial Aid, academic potential, and good citizenship. A limited amount of aid is awarded through competitive academic merit scholarships. Need-based low-interest student loans are also available.

ADMISSIONS INFORMATION

Peddie seeks students who demonstrate a willingness to apply themselves to their schoolwork and who appreciate the value of a broad academic and social experience. New students, including a limited number of high school graduates, are admitted to grades 9 through 12 and the postgraduate year. Most students enter in the ninth grade. For fall 2008, 1,257 applications were received and 330 were accepted. New students entering in fall 2008 were as follows: 129 ninth graders, 25 tenth graders, 15 eleventh graders, and 10 postgraduates.

Applicants must submit an academic transcript, teachers' recommendations, and scores from the SSAT, ISEE, or College Board aptitude tests. An interview on campus or with an alumni representative is also required. International applicants must demonstrate basic proficiency in English. They also should have been following a curriculum of continuous course work in mathematics and their native language (e.g., grammar, literature).

APPLICATION TIMETABLE

The application deadline is January 15 for notification on March 10. There is a $50 application fee ($125 for international students). An initial inquiry is welcome at any time. Campus interviews and tours are conducted during the school year from 9 a.m. to 3 p.m., Monday through Friday, and from 9 a.m. to noon on Saturday. During the summer, interviews are limited to weekdays only.

ADMISSIONS CORRESPONDENCE

Raymond H. Cabot, Director of Admission
Peddie School
South Main Street
P.O. Box A
Hightstown, New Jersey 08520
Phone: 609-490-7501
Fax: 609-944-7901
E-mail: admission@peddie.org
Web site: http://www.peddie.org

THE PENNINGTON SCHOOL

Pennington, New Jersey

Type: Coeducational day and boarding college-preparatory school
Grades: 6–12: Middle School, 6–8; Upper School, 9–12
Enrollment: School total: 478; Upper School: 387
Head of School: Stephanie G. Townsend, Head of School

THE SCHOOL

The Pennington School was founded in 1838 by the Southern New Jersey Conference of the United Methodist Church, making it one of the oldest Methodist secondary schools in the nation. Established as the Methodist Episcopal Male Seminary, the School became known as The Pennington School in 1926. From 1854 to 1910, Pennington was coeducational but reverted to being a boys' school in 1910, remaining so until 1972, when it again welcomed both girls and boys.

Pennington is committed to educating the whole person—mind, body, and spirit—by taking the uniqueness of the individual student into consideration.

The 54-acre campus is strategically located in a suburban setting just 60 miles from New York City, 40 miles from Philadelphia, and within 8 miles of Trenton and Princeton. This makes it convenient for cultural and educational field trips.

The governing body is a 36-member Board of Trustees. The 2007–08 budget was $14.7 million, and the endowment was $25 million. Total giving by faculty, alumni, and friends in 2006–07 was $2.25 million.

The Pennington School is accredited by the Middle States Association of Colleges and Schools and approved by the New Jersey State Department of Education. It is a member of the National Association of Independent Schools, the New Jersey Association of Independent Schools, and the Secondary School Admission Test Board. Pennington is affiliated with the University Senate and the Board of Higher Education and Ministry of the United Methodist Church.

ACADEMIC PROGRAMS

Pennington's objectives are to offer a challenging academic program and to nurture the moral development of its students, helping them to acquire the kind of stable maturity that contributes to success in college and in life.

Middle School students concentrate on five major subject areas: math, English, social studies, science, and foreign language. All students rotate through a series of exploratory courses during the year, including art/drama, music, health, technology, writing workshop, and ethics.

Students in the Upper School usually take six classes per day. The minimum number of credits necessary for graduation is 20. Requirements include the following: English, 4; mathematics, 3; history, 3; science, 3; foreign language, 2; religion, 1; art, 1; health, 1; technology, ½; and public speaking, ¼. Honors and Advanced Placement courses are offered in all disciplines.

The student-teacher ratio is 9:1, and the average class size is 13, with a maximum of 18 students in any one class. A 2-hour evening study period for boarders is supervised. The School library is open during the day and for 3 hours each evening.

The School uses the semester system, but, with midterm evaluations, there are four marking periods. Parent-teacher-student conferences are held twice a year. Individual conferences are arranged as required.

Official grades are issued at the conclusion of each semester. Pennington uses a letter grading system in which D– (60) is the passing grade and C– (70) the minimum grade for a course to count toward graduation requirements.

The Pennington School has two unique programs: a Center for Learning, limited to 42 academically talented students with language-based learning disabilities, and an International Student Program offering ESL.

FACULTY AND ADVISERS

The faculty consists of 47 men and 52 women, including 8 administrators. Forty-nine live on campus. The faculty holds thirty five baccalaureate, sixty master's, and four doctoral degrees. Faculty members serve as advisers for 6 to 8 students. Other counseling is available from trained counselors. Teachers also serve as hall parents, providing the basis for yet another kind of close relationship.

Stephanie (Penny) Townsend, appointed Head of School in 2006, earned her bachelor's degree from the University of Connecticut and her master's degree from Middlebury College. Before coming to Pennington, she taught Spanish at Northfield Mount Hermon School in Massachusetts and at the Taft School in Connecticut. Most recently, Townsend served as the Dean of Faculty at the Taft School.

COLLEGE ADMISSION COUNSELING

College counseling is the responsibility of trained counselors who coordinate all aspects of the college planning and placement process, including the taking of PSAT, SAT, TOEFL, and Advanced Placement tests. Representatives from almost 200 colleges visit Pennington to meet with students. Juniors and seniors meet individually with their college counselors and attend a College Ahead Program, during which a panel of returning graduates share their college experiences. Juniors attend special college programs, including two spring on-campus college fairs.

In 2007, 99 graduates attended a college or university. Among the schools they are attending are American, Barnard, Boston College, Boston University, Brown, Georgetown, Muhlenberg, Parsons School of Design, Princeton, Rutgers, Villanova, and the University of Pennsylvania.

STUDENT BODY AND CONDUCT

There are 97 students in grade 9, 97 in grade 10, 100 in grade 11, and 93 in grade 12. In grades six through twelve, 42 students are in the Center for Learning program, and 40 students are in the International Student Program. The ratio of girls to boys in the Upper School is approximately 4:5, and boarding to day is 1:3. Students represent nine states and come from sixteen other countries—Canada, China, Germany, Great Britain, France, Guatemala, Italy, Kenya, Liberia, Nigeria, Russia, Saint Kitts and Nevis, South Africa, South Korea, Taiwan, and Thailand. Thirteen percent of the students belong to minority groups.

There is a Student Council, elected by the student body, and a Boarding Council. Students are expected to follow the rules defined in the *Student Handbook*. Violations may be dealt with by the Behavior Review Board, which is made up of students and faculty members.

During class hours, Upper School boys must wear dress shirts and ties, slacks, and dress shoes; girls must wear dresses or wear slacks or skirts with blouses or sweaters. Middle School students wear Pennington polo shirts and khakis. Monday dinner and certain programs call for jackets and ties for boys and dresses or skirts and blouses for girls. The dress code permits jeans, T-shirts, and sneakers to be worn by students after class hours and on weekends but not during class time.

ACADEMIC FACILITIES

The centers of academic activities are Stainton Hall, a classroom/administration building; the Campus Center, containing art and music studios, a theater, foreign language classrooms, and the Student Center; Meckler Library, which contains the academic book collection, online databases, and the Computer Center; and Old Main, which houses classrooms and five residence halls.

BOARDING AND GENERAL FACILITIES

There are two additional dormitories containing another five residence halls: Becher Hall, a one-story residence with ten student rooms and two faculty apartments, and Buck Hall, containing four halls with double rooms and private bathrooms. There are eight faculty apartments in this building. The School has an attractive dining facility and a health center, with 2 registered nurses in residence. Boarding facilities close for the Christmas and spring holidays and for Thanksgiving, so all students must leave the campus during those vacation periods.

ATHLETICS

The Pennington School believes that the lessons learned through athletics involvement are valuable ones. Thus, every student is expected to participate in a team or individual sport that fits his or her own ability level. Although Pennington's athletics teams are very successful and frequently win state championships, the emphasis is on participation, collective effort, sportsmanship, and personal growth. All students must participate in at least one sport per year. Boarders must take three terms of activities. When boarding students are not involved in a sport, they must be involved in other extracurricular activities.

The sports available for boys and girls in grades 9 to 12 are basketball, cheerleading, cross-country, golf, lacrosse, soccer, swimming, tennis, track and field, and club water polo. In addition, field hockey and softball are available for girls, and baseball, football, and ice hockey are offered for boys.

In addition to a gymnasium/swimming pool complex, Pennington has five tennis courts, 30 acres of playing fields, and an all-weather-surface track.

EXTRACURRICULAR OPPORTUNITIES

Life at Pennington is more than classrooms, laboratories, and the library, essential as these are. Opportunities exist for participation in a wide range of extracurricular activities.

Apart from the athletics program, there are many clubs and organizations that students may join. These include three drama productions a year, the Pennington Singers, Mock Trial, Peer Leadership, National Honor Society, Photography Club, International Club, International Thespian Society, Model United Nations, Pennington Sports News, Brazilian Ju-Jitsu, Youth Service Fellowship, Campus Guides, United People of Many Colors, jazz ensemble, chamber ensemble, Junior Proctors, foreign language clubs, and staffs of the yearbook, newspaper, and literary annual, which contains creative writing of students and faculty members. All students are encouraged to do community service during the year. Students do volunteer work for hospitals and charitable organizations in Pennington, Princeton, and Trenton.

A student activities program provides for social events such as dances, ski trips, movies, theater presentations, and visits to area places of interest.

Life at Pennington also includes a spiritual component, and all students are required to attend an interfaith weekly chapel service.

DAILY LIFE

The day's activities begin at 8 a.m. and conclude at 2:45. There is an activities period on Fridays and a bimonthly assembly on Wednesdays. There are two lunch periods. A half-hour extra help conference period follows the class day. Sports practice takes place from 3:15 to 5:15, and dinner follows at 5:30. A monitored study period for boarders from 7:30 to 9:30 completes the day. Lights are out at 10:30 p.m. on weekdays.

WEEKEND LIFE

Day students and boarders are encouraged to participate in weekend activities. These include functions on campus as well as trips off campus to attend plays, museums, festivals, and professional sports contests. The library, swimming pool, and gymnasium are open on weekends. Transportation is also provided to shopping centers, where students may shop, eat, or see a movie.

COSTS AND FINANCIAL AID

The 2008–09 charges were $26,500 for day students, $39,400 for boarding students, $11,250–$14,200 for the Center for Learning classes, and $2310 for each English as a second language course. Additional costs are a $50 application fee, a book deposit of $500 or $600, and an activity fee of $145 or $275. There are special fees for private music lessons and tutoring. An allowance of $15 to $25 per week is recommended for spending money for residential students.

When an enrollment contract is signed, a nonrefundable deposit of 10 percent of tuition for day students and boarders is required to hold a space for the student; it is applied toward the year's tuition. The remainder of the tuition may be paid in installments of one half on August 1 and the remaining half on November 1, or tuition may be paid through a ten-month payment plan. Enrollment in school tuition insurance is required.

Financial aid is based on demonstrated need, except for two competitive merit scholarships. Parents applying for aid must submit the Parents' Financial Statement to the School and Student Service for Financial Aid. Financial aid is granted on an annual basis. Nineteen percent of the students received more than $1.4 million in aid for the 2008–09 school year.

ADMISSIONS INFORMATION

Pennington seeks students who have strong academic ability, as demonstrated on the SSAT, good character, and a record of good citizenship. The School does not discriminate on the basis of race, color, religion, gender, or national or ethnic origin in the administration of its admission or educational policies or the financial aid, athletic, or other School-administered programs.

Approximately 37 percent of the applicants are accepted for admission. In 2008, 48 new students were enrolled in the ninth grade, 14 in the tenth grade, and 4 in the eleventh grade.

APPLICATION TIMETABLE

Students should begin the application process for Pennington early in the fall. The School uses a March 10 notification date, an April 10 reply date, and then rolling admissions as space is available. Students who wish to be considered in March should have all materials and the $50 application fee submitted and the interview completed by February 1. The Admission Office is open throughout the year for interviews and tours of the campus from 8:30 to 2, Monday through Friday, by appointment.

ADMISSIONS CORRESPONDENCE

Mark Saunders
Director of Admissions and Financial Aid
The Pennington School
Pennington, New Jersey 08534
Phone: 609-737-6128
Fax: 609-730-1405
E-mail: admiss@pennington.org
Web site: http://www.pennington.org

PHILLIPS ACADEMY

Andover, Massachusetts

Type: Coeducational boarding and day college-preparatory school
Grades: 9–12, postgraduate year
Enrollment: 1,105
Head of School: Barbara L. Chase

THE SCHOOL

Phillips Academy was founded by Samuel Phillips during the Revolutionary War for the purpose of "enlarging the minds and forming the morals" of "youth from every quarter." A sister school, Abbot Academy, which was an all-girls school, was founded in 1828. In 1973, the schools merged to create a distinctive coeducational institution that combined the best of both traditions. Still committed to the education of mind and heart and dedicated anew to serving "youth from every quarter" in a truly multicultural community, Phillips Academy (often called Andover) today includes 1,105 young men and women from forty-six states and thirty-four countries. On a splendid 500-acre campus, under the tutelage of a gifted faculty, these students strive for academic excellence and moral decisiveness. The class of 2009 had 38 National Merit Semifinalists and 5 National Achievement Semifinalists.

The school is located on a hilltop in the town of Andover, Massachusetts, 21 miles north of Boston and less than an hour's drive from some of the loveliest beaches and mountains in New England. On the school's campus are a 125-acre bird sanctuary and two exceptional museums, the Addison Gallery of American Art and the Robert S. Peabody Museum of Archaeology.

The Academy's governing body is a 19-member Board of Trustees. The school has an endowment of approximately $820 million, as of May 2008.

Phillips Academy is accredited by the New England Association of Schools and Colleges. It is a member of the National Association of Independent Schools and the Secondary School Admission Test Board.

ACADEMIC PROGRAMS

Andover's curriculum encompasses 300 courses in eighteen academic departments. In all of these departments, courses are offered beyond the college entrance level and also at a variety of entry levels in order to respond sensitively to a student's incoming level of preparation.

Requirements vary according to the level at which a student enters the curriculum. In general, students receive extensive instruction in English, math, foreign language, history, and science as well as exposure to the arts, religion and philosophy, and physical education. An academic adviser guides a student throughout his or her career.

The grading is 0 (failure) through 6 (high honors). Grades are sent to parents after each of the three terms that make up the school year; comments are sent in the fall and spring. The average number of students in a classroom is 13; the overall student-teacher ratio is 5:1. Most students take five courses each term. Faculty members are available for individual help daily during the conference period and in the evenings; math study hall is open three nights a week.

Andover's Residential Education curriculum offers programs that address health and human issues. The Graham House Counseling Center offers psychological counseling, study skills courses, and student tutorial services. The school's Office of Community and Multicultural Development provides counseling and support services and sponsors workshops, lectures, and educational programs.

Several special complementary programs are also available. Qualified students may join the School Year Abroad program in China, France, Italy, and Spain. In addition, advanced language students may attend a local school in Göttingen, Germany; Burgos, Spain; Antibes, France; Kyoto, Japan; Santo Domingo, Dominican Republic; Salamanca, Spain; and Yokohama, Japan.

FACULTY AND ADVISERS

Andover has 223 faculty members who hold, among them, 162 Ph.D. and master's degrees and are as devoted to their students as they are passionate about their fields of expertise. Faculty members serve as students' coaches, house counselors, and advisers in addition to being classroom teachers. Roughly 95 percent of the faculty lives on campus. Turnover among faculty members at Andover is low.

The Head of School, Barbara L. Chase, came to Andover from Bryn Mawr School in 1994. She has an A.B. from Brown University and an M.L.A. from Johns Hopkins University.

COLLEGE ADMISSION COUNSELING

Each Andover upper and new senior is assigned to one of the school's six college counselors who sees him or her through the college admission process. Parents are enlisted from the outset as partners in this and receive a quarterly newsletter from the College Counseling Office.

Roughly 150 college representatives visit the Andover campus each year. The mean SAT score for the 2008 graduates was 684 for critical reading, 700 for math, and 692 for writing. The class of 2008 matriculated at 99 colleges and universities, with 8 or more Andover graduates attending each of the following schools: Yale (16), Stanford (15), Princeton (13), University of Pennsylvania (13), Georgetown (10), Harvard (9), Columbia (8), and Duke (8).

STUDENT BODY AND CONDUCT

In 2008–09, 543 boys and 562 girls from forty-six states and thirty-four countries were enrolled at Andover. Among these students, 806 were boarders and 299 were day students; 330 were seniors, 271 were upper-middlers, 296 were lower-middlers, and 208 were juniors. Forty-two percent of Andover's students received financial aid, 37 percent were members of minority groups, and 7 percent were international students.

Rules at Andover have a dual purpose: to preserve an atmosphere in which learning can take place and to teach students that individual freedom can be achieved only through due consideration for others. When a rule infraction involves discipline rather than counseling, the discipline is handled at the cluster level and involves the cluster dean, the house counselor, and other faculty and student representatives. Major offenses may result in dismissal.

ACADEMIC FACILITIES

Among Andover's 160 buildings are such significant academic buildings as Samuel Phillips Hall (history and language classrooms and the first all-digital language lab facility in the country), Morse Hall (mathematics), Bullfinch Hall (English and the debating room), Pearson Hall (classics), Graves Hall (music center), George Washington Hall (student center, drama laboratory, and 400-seat theater), and the Elson Art Center. The state-of-the-art Gelby Science Center opened in 2004. The Addison Gallery of American Art, with its collection of 12,000 works by such artists as Winslow Homer, Edward Hopper, Georgia O'Keefe, Jackson Pollack, and Andrew Wyeth, and the Robert S. Peabody Museum of Archaeology, which houses one of the country's outstanding collections of Native American artifacts, are used extensively by students for classes and exhibitions.

Other academic facilities include extensive rehearsal and performance space for music, an astronomy observatory, ten science laboratories, a greenhouse, and a radio station. The Oliver Wendell Holmes Library contains Andover's main collection of 120,000 volumes, subscribes to 260 current and foreign language serials, and contains an extensive retrospective periodical collection in microform. Also in the library is the Academic Computing Center, with more than ninety computers and printers. The library is a service-oriented teaching library, open for students and faculty members more than 85 hours each week.

BOARDING AND GENERAL FACILITIES

Andover has forty-three dormitories housing from 4 to 42 students; the large dorms have several faculty families in residence. One third of boarding students live in single rooms; two thirds live in large double rooms. Currently, network access is available to all students through the dormitories and through public Technology Learning Centers (TLCs) with more than 120 computers. Every student is provided with an e-mail account, a private telephone line, and a personal voice mailbox. Seniors, uppers, and lowers live together in dormitories; juniors all live together in dorms with special study hours, visiting hours, and lights-out policies.

All Andover students and faculty members are assigned to one of the school's five clusters. At the heart of Andover's residential life and school spirit, clusters function as small schools within the school and provide the context for students' academic advising, disciplinary proceedings, personal counseling, intramural sports, weekday social functions, and Blue Key (school spirit) events.

ATHLETICS

At Andover, to play is the thing. Competitive athletics are available in all major sports at the varsity, subvarsity, and intramural levels; for students who are not interested in competitive sports, the school offers an exciting range of athletic alternatives, including dance, aerobics, yoga, kayaking, swim instruction, Search and Rescue, and many others. All lowers take one challenge-based physical education course for one term. All students participate in daily afternoon athletics and fitness activities. The athletic facilities include eighteen playing fields and eighteen tennis courts; the Sorota Track; the Borden, Memorial, and Abbot gymnasiums, with swimming and diving pools, two basketball and eight squash courts, two dance studios, a wrestling room, and a fitness center; an indoor track; two hockey rinks; a lighted varsity stadium; and a boathouse on the Merrimack River.

EXTRACURRICULAR OPPORTUNITIES

The school has four orchestras, four choral groups, several small singing groups, a Concert Band and Jazz Band, and more than forty student-run clubs, among them several literary and political magazines, a weekly newspaper, a radio station, the debate and math teams, and several drama and dance groups.

More than 700 students take part every year in the school's extensive Community Service Program. By helping others, students fulfill the mandate of Andover's motto, *non sibi,* meaning not for oneself.

DAILY LIFE

Students normally meet in four or five courses per day in 45-minute periods. Classes begin at 8 a.m. and end at 2:45 p.m., followed by athletics. There are double-block periods of 75 minutes on Wednesday and Thursday. In most courses, students meet for one double period each week. This schedule provides opportunities for creative teaching and learning.

On Wednesday mornings and three Saturday mornings in both the fall and spring, classes are held, and interscholastic sports or community service are scheduled for the afternoon. All-school meetings are held once a week. Faculty-student conference periods are held three mornings a week. Extracurricular activities normally take place after dinner, and official study hours begin at 8 p.m.

WEEKEND LIFE

Dances, concerts, dramatic productions, movies, exhibits at the museums, or special cultural events are offered on campus every weekend. Students may leave campus if their parents have given them permission. Public transportation enables students to take advantage of cultural and sporting events in nearby Boston.

SUMMER PROGRAMS

The Phillips Academy Summer Session is a five-week, intensive academic program and precollege experience of both innovative and traditional courses and focused college counseling. It offers the Lower School Institute with interdisciplinary curricula for rising eighth graders. Also held on campus in the summer is the $(MS)^2$ Program—Math and Science for Minority Students—an intensive three-summer math and science enrichment program for talented and economically disadvantaged African American, Latino, and Native American public high school students. For information, those who are interested should write to the directors of these programs at Phillips Academy.

COSTS AND FINANCIAL AID

Tuition for 2008–09 was $39,100 for boarding students and $30,500 for day students. Tuition covers instruction, room, board, and admission to authorized athletic and social events but does not include textbooks, tutoring, special instruction in music or some athletics, medical expenses, some art materials, or incidentals. To reserve a place, new students pay a deposit of $2000; the tuition less that deposit is billed in two equal amounts, although additional financing options are available through the Andover Plan.

Andover is committed to admitting an economically diverse student body and awards financial aid on a basis of demonstrated need from a financial aid budget of $14.6 million. Forty-two percent of Andover's students received financial aid.

ADMISSIONS INFORMATION

Andover is especially interested in accepting students with sound character and strong academic achievement who demonstrate independence, maturity, and concern for others. Valuing diversity in its student body, the school seeks to bring together a community from all parts of the country and from many nations.

Applicants for grades 9–11 must submit the results of the Secondary School Admission Test or the Independent School Entrance Exam; candidates for grade 12 and the postgraduate year must submit scores from either the PSAT or SAT. In 2008, Andover received 2,852 preliminary applications and 2,386 final applications and offered admission to 457 students.

APPLICATION TIMETABLE

Andover welcomes initial inquiries at any time. Tours and interviews are conducted on campus from 8:45 until 2 on Monday, Tuesday, and Friday; from 10:15 until 2 on Thursday; and from 8:45 until 11:15 on Wednesday and some Saturdays. Applicants for admission to the ninth, tenth, and eleventh grades must submit the results of either the November, December, or January Secondary School Admission Test or the Independent School Entrance Exam. Senior-class and postgraduate-year applicants must submit the results of their SAT or PSAT. Students taking later tests are considered late applicants.

For those who cannot visit the campus, interviews are also conducted elsewhere by admission representatives. The application deadline is January 15 for day students and February 1 for boarding students; the application fee is $40 for domestic candidates and $60 for international candidates. Notification of acceptance is mailed on March 10, and a reply is required by April 10.

ADMISSIONS CORRESPONDENCE

Admission Office
Phillips Academy
Andover, Massachusetts 01810

Phone: 978-749-4050
Fax: 978-749-4068
E-mail: admissions@andover.edu
Web site: http://www.andover.edu

PHILLIPS EXETER ACADEMY

Exeter, New Hampshire

Type: Coeducational boarding and day college-preparatory school
Grades: 9–12, postgraduate year
Enrollment: 1,043
Head of School: Tyler C. Tingley, Principal

THE SCHOOL

Phillips Exeter Academy was founded in 1781 by John and Elizabeth Phillips. In their deed of gift, they made clear their belief in the need to link goodness with knowledge. Exeter remains a school committed to academic excellence, and the faculty members work closely with students to help them develop lifelong habits of industry and intellectual curiosity. The Academy is also committed to fostering an awareness of an individual's responsibilities toward others. *Non sibi*, "not for oneself," is the motto of the Academy.

Exeter is well known for originating Harkness teaching, whereby 12 students and a teacher join together around an oval Harkness Table. The teacher is a facilitator rather than a leader, and the learning style encourages everyone in a class to think independently, to express oneself articulately, and to understand the beliefs and viewpoints of others. As the physical table itself implies, learning at Exeter is a cooperative enterprise in which the students and instructor work together as partners. This philosophy is key to life outside the classrooms as well. The Academy strives to encourage connectedness in all areas of community life.

The Academy is located in the center of Exeter, New Hampshire, a historic town 20 minutes from the Atlantic Ocean and an hour north of Boston. Students have convenient access to charming shops, restaurants, cafés, and a movie theater, all of which are within walking distance of the campus. With its proximity to the ocean, classes in science and the environment are able to make field trips to the New Hampshire seacoast to study wetlands and wildlife. Exeter is also near enough to the White Mountains for easy access to hiking and skiing.

A 20-member Board of Trustees is the Academy's governing body. The Academy's endowment, currently valued at approximately $1 billion, is supplemented by an annual fund of about $12.5 million and recent noncampaign capital gifts of about $45 million. More than 20,000 graduates are members of the general alumni association and contribute significantly to the support of the Academy.

Phillips Exeter Academy is accredited by the New England Association of Schools and Colleges. It is a member of the Cum Laude Society, the Independent Schools Association of Northern New England, the National Association of Independent Schools, and the Secondary School Admission Test Board.

ACADEMIC PROGRAMS

Exeter offers a rich curriculum with more than 450 courses, including opportunities to study college-level material well beyond the Advanced Placement level. The Harkness Table is central to both the Exeter classroom and the Exeter curriculum. Though teaching and learning look different in the various disciplines and levels of study, they have in common the ideal of active, participatory, student-centered learning that values imparting to students not just a given course's content but also the skills required to become their own and each other's teachers.

The Academy's customary college-preparatory curriculum includes comprehensive instruction in English, foreign language (classical or modern), history, mathematics, and science. Other requirements include art, drama, or music; religion; health and human development; and junior studies for all entering ninth graders. Graduation requirements vary depending on a student's grade upon entry. The academic year consists of three terms.

Academic work is graded using A–E (failing) designations with pluses and minuses. Grades and teacher comments are sent to parents following each trimester.

In most cases, students are assigned to the Harkness-style classes on a random basis. Class size averages 12 students, and the student-teacher ratio is 5:1. The standard course load is five courses per term.

Exeter's international and domestic off-campus study programs offer students many distinct opportunities. Qualified eleventh and twelfth graders may undertake a year of foreign language and cultural immersion through the School Year Abroad program in China, France, Italy, or Spain. Other international study programs include a term in China, England, France, Germany, Ireland, Mexico, and Russia and summer programs in France, Japan, Mexico, Spain, and Taiwan. Two domestic off-campus study programs round out the offerings: one term of study at the working farm of the Milton Mountain School in Vermont and a spring term in Exeter's Washington Intern Program.

FACULTY AND ADVISERS

Exeter faculty members are passionate about Harkness teaching and sharing their scholarly enthusiasm with students. They see themselves as counselors as well as teachers, and their interests and talents extend beyond their academic disciplines. Faculty advisers live in the dorms with their advisees and are available for academic advice and any other concerns a student may have. Faculty members also participate in the Academy's physical education program and advise student-run extracurricular activities. Annual faculty turnover is low. The faculty plays a vital role in the operation of the Academy, sharing responsibility for admissions, financial aid, discipline, and curriculum.

COLLEGE ADMISSION COUNSELING

A full-time college counseling staff helps students in the selection of postsecondary institutions. More than 200 college representatives visit the Academy each year. The average SAT scores for 2007 graduates were 691 critical reading, 706 math, and 688 writing. Ninety-nine percent of the members of the class of 2007 went on to college (a total of 119 institutions). In 2007, schools where 5 or more students matriculated were Carnegie Mellon (5), Columbia (9), Cornell (8), Dartmouth (11), Duke (5), Georgetown (11), Harvard (17), Johns Hopkins (6), MIT (5), McGill (6), Middlebury (5), NYU (13), Princeton (10), Stanford (9), Trinity College (5), Tufts (12), the University of Chicago (5), the University of Pennsylvania (9), Wellesley (5), and Yale (8).

STUDENT BODY AND CONDUCT

When John and Elizabeth Phillips founded Phillips Exeter Academy, they stressed the importance of bringing together "youth from every quarter." In 2008–09, 516 boys and 527 girls from forty-three states, the District of Columbia, the U.S. Virgin Islands, and twenty-nine other countries attended Phillips Exeter Academy. The student body consisted of the following: ninth grade, 94 boys and 106 girls; tenth grade, 120 boys and 121 girls; eleventh grade, 133 boys and 153 girls; and twelfth grade and postgraduate year, 169 boys and 147 girls. Of these totals, 840 students boarded and 203 were day students.

Principles rather than rules are the basis for the Academy's discipline policy. The Academy acts on the assumptions that its students enter the school with a serious purpose and that their conscience and good sense are a sufficient guide to behavior. Student representatives help define and enforce essential regulations, and they hold four nonvoting seats on the Discipline Committee. Major offenses may result in the student being required to withdraw or being placed on probationary status.

ACADEMIC FACILITIES

An attractive campus of Georgian and modern buildings spreads over 471 acres. Central to campus life is the Academy's Class of 1945 Library. The award-winning structure was designed by Louis I. Kahn and is the largest secondary school library in the world in both size and number of volumes. Exeter's performing arts facilities are state-of-the-art and include the Frederick R. Mayer Art Center, the Lamont Gallery, the Fisher Theater, and the Forrestal-Bowld Music Center. Phillips Hall houses classrooms for English and modern languages, a language media room, the Daniel Webster Debating Room, and a small theater. The Academy Building houses classrooms for mathematics, history, religion, classical languages, and anthropology; a computer lab; photography labs; the P. Phillips Foundation Anthropology Museum; and the Assembly Hall, where an all-school assembly takes place three times weekly. The new Phelps Academy Center is designed to be the hub of student life and the campus crossroads. The first floor houses the Grill, the Post Office, and a large lounge with leather chairs and a working fireplace. The second floor consists of the Student Activities Office, the Day Student Lounge, and Club Central. The below-ground floor hosts a large kitchen with an adjoining TV room, a game room, three music practice rooms, and the student-run radio station, WPEA. The Grainger Observatory has two domes with telescopes, a classroom, an observation deck, and a chart room. The multidenominational Phillips Church is the center of religious worship at Exeter, where students from eleven of the world's religions gather to express their faith.

Science classes are taught in the $38-million, award-winning Phelps Science Center, which opened in fall 2001, bringing together two exciting pedagogies: experiential, hands-on learning and the discussion-based Harkness method. The building has many distinguishing features, including a complete humpback whale skeleton hanging in its rear atrium and a 900-gallon tropical aquarium in the lobby. The building is divided into four classroom wings serving physics, chemistry, biology, and a shared space for interdisciplinary work. There are a total of twenty classroom labs and four common labs; each classroom features its own Harkness table and state-of-the-art audiovisual system. Among the other special features found in the Phelps Science Center are a marine biology table, a teaching garden with seven different habitats, an outdoor classroom, a rotating turntable and Dickensen runway in the physics area, and 16 feet of fume hood in the chemistry area. The building also contains the 300-seat Grainger Auditorium and the Peter Durham '85 Computer Science Lab.

BOARDING AND GENERAL FACILITIES

The Harkness spirit of collaborative learning extends to Exeter's twenty-nine centrally located residences. Twenty dormitories accommodate 30 to 60 students each, and nine smaller houses board 10 to 20 students. Each residence is supervised by faculty members who serve as advisers to students and ensure that an adult is always available for assistance and counsel. Many teachers, some with their spouse and children, live in dormitory apartments and share their family lives with students. All residences have common areas for relaxation and recreation, and—depending on the residence—amenities include televisions, Ping-Pong and pool tables, kitchenettes, and laundry facilities. All rooms are equipped with individual phone, voice mail, and Internet connections.

The Lamont Health Center provides comprehensive health care 24 hours a day. The center is staffed by a Board-certified pediatrician, a nurse practitioner, registered nurses, counselors, athletic trainers, a nutritionist, and a health educator, who are available for any health concern.

Two dining halls serve the Exeter community, providing balanced, healthy meals with a wide range of choice. The Grill is a legendary spot for getting together with friends between classes, for study breaks, and for hearing bands on the weekends.

ATHLETICS

The Academy was founded on the belief that it is important to develop a sound body as well as a sound mind. More than 200 years later, the commitment remains. The Academy promotes good health and fitness by teaching skills in diverse physical activities ranging from bicycling to wrestling. There are four levels of participation available to students: competitive and intramural teams, fitness, and the ninth-grade physical education program. Exeter offers thirty-three different sports from instructional to varsity level. Nine full-time physical education instructors are assisted by more than 90 faculty members, who serve as coaches at all levels and provide another opportunity for interaction among teachers and students.

The Love Gymnasium contains two indoor hockey rinks, three basketball courts, ten squash courts, a training room, a weight room, and an eight-lane swimming pool. The Thompson Gymnasium houses an indoor track, a wrestling room, a dance studio, two basketball courts, and a pool. Outdoor sports facilities include nineteen tennis courts, the 5,000-seat lighted Phelps Stadium, the 400-meter all-weather Lovshin track, 33 acres of playing fields, and more than 4 miles of cross-country trails. Exeter's Saltonstall Boathouse houses twenty-four shells, eight ergometers, and locker rooms for the boys' and girls' teams.

EXTRACURRICULAR OPPORTUNITIES

Nearly 100 student-run clubs meet regularly and offer every student the chance to become involved. While students take primary responsibility for organizing activities, faculty advisers meet regularly with club members and provide guidance and resources. Choices include art and performance clubs; academic, athletic, and game clubs; math, science, and computer clubs; language, cultural, and religious organizations; student publications; service organizations; and political clubs.

Exeter maintains a close connection to the local community through the student-run Exeter Social Services Organization (ESSO), which links the Academy's volunteer resources with local organizations and institutions such as schools and hospitals.

DAILY LIFE

Central to community life at Exeter is the Assembly Program. The entire Academy community gathers three times a week for programs featuring student groups, renowned speakers, alumni, and other special guests.

Classes are held five days a week and on some Saturdays; Wednesdays and Saturdays are half days. On full days, which run from 8 to 6, four class periods are held before lunch and four after lunch. Two class periods are reserved for athletics on Monday, Tuesday, Thursday, and Friday, while interscholastic contests are scheduled on either Wednesday or Saturday afternoons. Three mornings a week, there is a 30-minute all-school assembly. Student organizations meet after dinner, which is offered from 5 to 7 p.m. Evening study hours run from 8 until 10:30. Light fare is available in both dining halls from 7 a.m. until 7 p.m. Day students are fully integrated into all aspects of Academy life.

WEEKEND LIFE

Current-year events include coffeehouses, dances, films, casino and games nights, cookouts, and hiking and ski trips. Regular shuttles are available to Portsmouth and Boston. The student-run Weekend Activities Committee works closely with the Student Activities Office to schedule, plan, and implement the calendar of weekend events both on and off campus.

SUMMER PROGRAMS

The Summer School at Exeter, begun in 1919, enrolled nearly 700 boys and girls from forty states and thirty-six countries in 2007. Able high school students come to enrich their academic programs, to improve in particular subjects, to enjoy the challenge of rigorous college-preparatory courses, or to have an independent school experience. More than 100 faculty members from Exeter, other schools, and other countries participate in the program. Although the Academy gives no credit, students may make arrangements with their own schools for validation of their summer work. Further information may be obtained by writing to the Director of the Summer School.

COSTS AND FINANCIAL AID

In 2008–09, tuition was $37,960 for boarding students and $29,330 for day students. These figures included most services, all meals, and admission to on-campus concerts, plays, and athletic events but excluded the cost of books and incidentals. Optional expenses were incurred for health care, private music instruction, some art materials, and off-campus programs. To reserve a place, new students pay an initial deposit of $1700, $1500 of which is applied to the first year's tuition and $200 of which is refunded when the student departs the Academy.

In 2008–09, Exeter provided more than $15 million in financial aid grants to 50 percent of the student body. Grants are awarded on the basis of financial need, as indicated by the guidelines of the School and Student Service for Financial Aid. In addition, more than $100,000 is allocated annually to financial aid recipients for expenses related to travel, books, clothing, and athletic equipment. Since its founding, the Academy has used its resources to supplement what a family contributes toward an Exeter education.

In 2008–09, Exeter embarked on a financial aid initiative that has enabled the children of families whose income is $75,000 or less to attend the Academy for free. For each family in that economic category that completes the financial aid process and whose child is admitted to Exeter, there will be no charge for tuition, fees, or books and other academic supplies. The cost of a new computer will also be included in the financial aid award.

ADMISSIONS INFORMATION

Phillips Exeter Academy seeks to enroll students who combine proven academic ability and intellectual curiosity with decency and good character. Exeter wants young people who welcome the challenges and opportunities provided by a strong academic program within a diverse community. Students come from a wide range of racial, geographic, socioeconomic, ethnic, religious, and cultural backgrounds. Because what happens in the classrooms and dorms and on the stages and playing fields depends to an unusual degree upon student engagement with other students and adults, candidates are sought who demonstrate interest and involvement with others. Above all, the Academy looks for students who have the capacity to grow and who are likely to thrive at Exeter, whether they enter as four-year, three-year, two-year, or one-year students.

The SSAT is required of applicants for grades 9 or 10. The SSAT or the PSAT is required of applicants for grade 11. Senior-class and postgraduate applicants must submit results of the PSAT and the SAT, respectively. TOEFL scores are required of all applicants for whom English is not the primary language. In addition, applicants are required to have a personal interview with a member of the admissions staff or an Academy representative. Approximately 1 out of 5 students is accepted each year.

APPLICATION TIMETABLE

Interested students and their families are encouraged to visit Exeter. Campus tours and interviews are scheduled from 8 a.m. to 4 p.m. Monday through Friday and from 8 a.m. to noon on Saturday.

All application materials must be received by January 15; completed forms must be accompanied by a nonrefundable $50 fee for U.S. residents or a $100 fee for non-U.S. residents. Notification of acceptance is mailed on March 10, and families are expected to reply by April 10.

ADMISSIONS CORRESPONDENCE

Michael Gary
Director of Admissions
Phillips Exeter Academy
20 Main Street
Exeter, New Hampshire 03833-2460

Phone: 603-777-3437
Fax: 603-777-4399
E-mail: admit@exeter.edu
Web site: http://www.exeter.edu

POMFRET SCHOOL

Pomfret, Connecticut

Type: Coeducational boarding and day college-preparatory school
Grades: 9–12 (Forms III–VI) and PG
Enrollment: 354
Head of School: Bradford Hastings, Headmaster

THE SCHOOL

Prospective families find 354 students and 75 faculty members learning and living together on a 500-acre campus situated in the charming northeastern corner of Connecticut. Pomfret's campus is an oasis, with boutique shopping, movie theaters, malls, and Connecticut's premier antique district all close by. Pomfret School is just 50 minutes from Providence, 50 minutes from Hartford, a little over an hour from Boston, and 3 hours from New York City. Interesting and challenging academics (thirty-seven AP and honors courses and independent projects offered in all disciplines) combined with competitive athletics (fourteen varsity teams, with five recent New England championships) and exciting opportunities in the creative arts continue the 113-year tradition of educational excellence that defines Pomfret School. In addition to its excellent academic programs, Pomfret is particularly well-known for its strong community atmosphere, which helps students develop as good citizens. Students form close relationships with their advisers and other faculty members, all of whom are devoted to guiding students in the classroom, on the playing fields, and in the art studios.

The School is governed by a Board of Trustees, most of whose 27 active members are alumni, current parents, or parents of alumni. The physical plant is valued at $53 million, and the endowment is in excess of $42 million. In 2007–08, more than $1.6 million was donated to the Annual Giving fund; 86 percent of current parents participated.

Pomfret School is accredited by the New England Association of Schools and Colleges and is approved by the Connecticut State Department of Education. Its memberships include the Connecticut Association of Independent Schools, the Headmasters' Association, the National Association of Independent Schools, the Secondary School Admission Test Board, A Better Chance (ABC), and the Cum Laude Society.

ACADEMIC PROGRAMS

Pomfret School offers a traditional college-preparatory curriculum that stresses the fundamentals. Emphasis is placed on reading, writing, math, foreign languages, science, history, and computer competence. The minimum academic requirements for graduation include 4 years of English, 3 years of mathematics through the junior year and through algebra II, a foreign language through the third level, 3 years of history, 3 years of science (physics, chemistry, and biology, taken in that sequence), 1 trimester of religion, and 1 trimester of social issues. The school year is divided into trimesters, with exams in November, March, and June.

Pomfret School recognizes the value of imaginative and creative development and offers a particularly strong arts program. Students are required to enroll in an art course in two of three terms each year they attend Pomfret. Creative arts courses are offered in music, theater, painting, sculpture, film, dance, creative writing, photography, painting, drawing, and digital arts. The religion requirement may be met through such electives as Faith and Imagination and World Religions. Pomfret encourages its students to participate in community service. Options include tutoring, assisting youth groups, hospital projects, blood drives, and environmental activities.

The average class size is 11 students, and the faculty-student ratio is 1:6. The grading system uses letter grades of A to E. Grades are given twice during each trimester, and teacher comments accompany grades four times per year. A faculty adviser works closely with a group of 5 to 7 students.

FACULTY AND ADVISERS

There are 75 faculty members (44 men and 31 women), 57 of whom teach; 65 are full-time, 40 have earned master's degrees, and 3 hold doctorates. Most faculty members have advisees and live on the campus. The average length of teaching experience is eleven years.

Pomfret employs teachers who engender enthusiasm for learning. The job of any faculty member goes beyond the classroom to include coaching, advising, and, usually, running a dormitory. Pomfret believes it is at the forefront in providing for the professional growth of its faculty members. Leaves with full pay plus travel stipends during sabbaticals enable faculty members to study in an academic area of their choice. Summer study and travel grants are also available.

Bradford Hastings became Headmaster in 1993, after serving as Assistant Headmaster at Deerfield Academy. He is a graduate of Pomfret and was on the faculty from 1972 to 1978. Mr. Hastings served on Pomfret's Board of Trustees from 1985 to 1992. His master's degree in education is from Harvard University.

COLLEGE ADMISSION COUNSELING

College placement starts with college counseling, a process that begins at Pomfret during the sophomore year and continues as a refining and defining process until graduation. At all times, it is thought of as an effort that fosters individual social maturity, academic growth, and a deeper commitment to School activities.

All juniors take the PSAT in the fall and the SAT and SAT Subject Tests in the winter and spring.

A complete portrait of each individual's life at Pomfret—social, academic, and extracurricular—and a personal understanding of each student's aspirations enable the college counseling office to provide very close personal attention.

Pomfret's graduates have chosen to attend such prestigious colleges and universities as Amherst, Columbia, Dartmouth, Duke, and Yale.

STUDENT BODY AND CONDUCT

Pomfret currently has 264 boarding and 90 day students. There are 59 in the Third Form (grade 9), 83 in the Fourth Form (grade 10), 115 in the Fifth Form (grade 11), 88 in the Sixth Form (grade 12), and 9 in the postgraduate program. The students come from twenty-six states and thirteen countries. Fourteen percent of students classify themselves as members of minority groups.

Participation in the student government enables students to assume active leadership roles within the School. A president (a Sixth Former) chairs the government, which is made up of elected representatives from each Form and from the faculty.

Students at Pomfret are expected to follow the School rules outlined in the student handbook. Any infraction of these rules leads to an appearance before the Discipline Committee, which is composed of both students and faculty members and is chaired by the Dean of Students. The committee makes recommendations on discipline to the Headmaster.

ACADEMIC FACILITIES

The School is located on 500 acres, which consist of thirteen playing fields, rolling hills, and woodlands. The principal school buildings are grouped in the middle of the campus. The new athletic and student center, which opened in 2004, houses a two-floor student center, study room, snack bar, student radio station, student publications office, and bookstore. It also includes eight international-size squash courts, a wrestling room, a fitness center, locker rooms, an athletic trainer's facility, a trophy room, and offices for the Athletic Director and Director of Student Activities. In addition to the new athletic and student center, Pomfret recently opened a new ice-hockey rink, boathouse, and outdoor tennis center.

The School House contains history and foreign language classrooms, administrative offices, and the recently renovated music center. It is flanked on one side by four brick dormitories and on the other by Hard Auditorium, the center for dramatic and musical productions.

Nearby is the Monell Science Building, with laboratories for biology, chemistry, and physics as well as lecture rooms furnished with video equipment. The Centennial Building (1996) houses all mathematics and English classes as well as two- and three-dimensional art studios, metal and wood shops, and a 125-seat state-of-the-art theater.

The du Pont Library completes the current academic buildings. Along with its 22,000 volumes and the Technology Center, the library provides students with Internet access, a fully automated catalog and circulation system, and more than a dozen online subscription databases that cover a broad spectrum of disciplines with full-text and print capability. In addition, materials from outside the library are available through interlibrary loan.

Other nearby buildings include a dance studio and the Main House, which contains the dining hall, mail room, School store, and health center, which is staffed by 3 registered nurses. The School physician is at the health center in the mornings. Clark Memorial Chapel also occupies a central location on campus.

BOARDING AND GENERAL FACILITIES

Pomfret students are housed in nine dormitories on campus. Four converted homes, four large brick dormitories, and the recently renovated Pyne Hall serve as student residences. A wireless campus connects all Pomfret dormitory rooms, classrooms, faculty apartments, and offices, permitting computer and telephone networking throughout the campus as well as access to e-mail and the Internet in each dorm room. Most students are assigned to double rooms, though some returning students can choose to live in single rooms. All dorms are supervised by live-in faculty dorm parents, each of whom supervises between 7 and 14 students on his or her floor.

ATHLETICS

Athletics at Pomfret are an integral part of the educational experience, and all students are expected to participate each season at the level that is most challenging to them. Coaching responsibilities are shared by most faculty members. In addition, the School employs an athletics trainer.

The goal of the athletics program is to field competitive teams that exhibit discipline, the desire to excel, and pride in themselves and the School.

A varied interscholastic program is offered throughout the academic year. It includes cross-country, field hockey, football, soccer, and volleyball in the fall; basketball, ice hockey, squash, and wrestling in the winter; and baseball, crew, golf, lacrosse, softball, and tennis in the spring. In addition, aerobics, community service, dance, drama, and outdoor education are offered as athletic alternatives.

Pomfret has a new, fully equipped, 3,000-square-foot fitness center. Under faculty supervision, students are able to supplement their work on the playing field with a complete resistance training or aerobic program.

Students may opt to undertake an independent project for a given season rather than engage in sports. The 2006–07 faculty-sponsored independent projects included Ecosystem Relationships in Tropical Rainforests and Their Preservation, Advanced Compact Disk Design, and Sports Journalism.

EXTRACURRICULAR OPPORTUNITIES

Pomfret encourages student participation in a wide range of extracurricular activities. The *Pontefract* (newspaper), *Griffin* (yearbook), and *Manuscripts* (magazine) enjoy good student leadership and participation. An active theater program presents six plays and numerous theater projects each year, including musical productions (staged each spring). Auditions are open to students, faculty members, and local artists.

DAILY LIFE

Classes are scheduled in eight 50-minute periods from 8 to 3:15. Sports practices are scheduled in the afternoons from 3:45 to 5:45. The class day ends at 12:25 p.m. on Wednesdays and at 11:30 a.m. on class Saturdays. Evening study hours are 8 to 10 p.m., Sunday through Friday. Students study in their rooms. Lights-out is at 10:30 for Third and Fourth Formers and at 11 for Fifth and Sixth Formers.

The academic year, which is divided into trimesters, begins in early September and ends in early June, with vacations scheduled for one week at Thanksgiving, two weeks at Christmas, and three weeks in March.

WEEKEND LIFE

Most students prefer to remain at school on the weekends to enjoy time with friends and take advantage of the planned activities. On Saturday afternoons, there are interscholastic athletics contests. Students appreciate the local area, which combines rural beauty with elegant shopping and café dining. They also enjoy Sunday trips to Boston, Vermont ski slopes, and area shopping malls and movie theaters, as well as canoeing and biking excursions. Indoor and outdoor movie nights, concerts, and other special events on campus at Pomfret School are always popular.

The student lounge, tuck shop, indoor tennis courts, squash courts, and gymnasium are open and available seven days a week. On Sundays, students are invited but not required to attend a chapel service or a local church service. Brunch is served at 10. The weekend officially ends on Sunday before dinner. There are regular study hours on Sunday evening in preparation for Monday classes.

COSTS AND FINANCIAL AID

In 2008–09, tuition was $42,900 for boarding students and $26,750 for day students. Costs for textbooks, stationery, athletics equipment, laundry, and dry cleaning are charged separately through a student debit account. For families who qualify, $2.5 million in need-based financial aid is available.

ADMISSIONS INFORMATION

Pomfret seeks students whose past achievement indicates that they could benefit from and contribute to life at the School. Pomfret gives prime consideration to those applicants who possess academic ability, interest in the arts and/or athletics, and a willingness to become involved in and supportive of the Pomfret School community.

Each applicant must submit an application, come to Pomfret for an interview (preferably when school is in session), and take the SSAT by January 15. Notification to prospective students is made on March 10.

Pomfret School admits students of any race, color, creed, handicap, gender, sexual orientation, or national origin to all the rights, privileges, programs, and activities generally accorded or made available to students at the School. The School does not discriminate on the basis of race, color, creed, handicap, gender, sexual orientation, age, or national origin in the administration of its educational policies, admission policies, financial aid, or other programs administered by the School.

APPLICATION TIMETABLE

Initial inquiries are welcome at any time, and tours and interviews can be arranged by calling the Admissions Office. Office hours are 8 to 4 Monday through Friday and 8 to noon on class Saturdays. School catalogs and applications can be obtained from the Admissions Office.

Pomfret adheres to the Parents' Reply Date of April 10. Thus, a place that has been offered on March 10 is reserved until April 10. Late applications (those to which it is not possible to reply by March 10) are accepted and acted upon as soon as possible and as enrollment permits.

ADMISSIONS CORRESPONDENCE

Erik C. Bertelsen
Assistant Head for Admissions and Enrollment
Pomfret School
398 Pomfret Street
P.O. Box 128
Pomfret, Connecticut 06258-0128
Phone: 860-963-6120
Fax: 860-963-2042
E-mail: admission@pomfretschool.org
Web site: http://www.pomfretschool.org

PORTSMOUTH ABBEY SCHOOL

Portsmouth, Rhode Island

Type: Coeducational boarding and day college-preparatory school
Grades: 9–12 (Forms III–VI)
Enrollment: 359
Head of School: Dr. James M. De Vecchi, Headmaster

THE SCHOOL

Portsmouth Abbey School was founded by Benedictine monks of the English Congregation in 1926. Unique among American boarding schools, Portsmouth Abbey School has created a community rooted in the ideals of the Catholic tradition and the high scholastic standards practiced by the Benedictine community since the sixth century.

The School offers the many attractions one expects to find at a leading boarding school: a challenging college-preparatory program, talented and compassionate teachers, an international student body, fine facilities, a busy and lively student life, and a supportive residential environment.

The aim of Portsmouth Abbey School today, as it has been since Father John Hugh Diman founded it in 1926, is to help students to grow in knowledge and grace. The School seeks to embody those ideals and qualities that lie at the heart of the 1,500-year-old Benedictine tradition: reverence for God and man, respect for learning and order, and an appreciation of the shared experience of community life.

The School property covers 500 acres on Narragansett Bay. The location of the Abbey, which is set in a rural-suburban town, is convenient to the cultural and recreational centers of Newport (10 miles), Providence (28 miles), Boston (65 miles), and New York (190 miles). Throughout the year, students enjoy trips to athletics events, whale-watching out of Boston, and symphony and theatrical performances in Providence and Boston.

The governing body of the School is a 28-member Board of Regents. It is made up of laypersons and members of the monastic community. The total endowment is currently valued at approximately $35 million.

Portsmouth Abbey School is accredited by the New England Association of Schools and Colleges and is a member of the National Association of Independent Schools, the Association of Boarding Schools, and the Cum Laude Society.

ACADEMIC PROGRAMS

The program of studies offers young men and women of academic potential a solid foundation in the liberal arts. The School believes that these disciplines best foster the development of the skills that are fundamental to all learning: the ability to read with understanding, to reason clearly, and to express oneself with precision.

Students carry six full courses plus religion. To be eligible for the diploma, a student must pass a course in Christian doctrine each year and complete a minimum of 20 college entrance units, including 4 in English, 3 in a foreign language, 3 in mathematics, 2 in a laboratory science, 1 in art/music, 1 in U.S. history, and 1 in European history or humanities. The remaining units may be obtained in any course offered for credit, including courses in art, music, photography, history, science, political science, economics, computer science, Chinese, French, Latin, Greek, and Spanish.

A wide variety of noncredit courses—play production, public speaking, chorus, and chamber music—are offered. Sixth Formers are encouraged to design independent-study programs. Twenty Advanced Placement courses are available.

Students are grouped by their level of achievement and ability in mathematics, language, and the sciences. The average class size is 13 students, and the student-faculty ratio is 7:1. A science building, a computer center, a library, and an arts center are open afternoons and evenings as well as on weekends. Faculty members are available for extra help during daily conference periods and supervised study hours.

A student's progress is carefully monitored by an adviser, the houseparent, and deans. Reports are mailed home six times per year. The median grade is 80 percent, and the passing grade is 60 percent. A learning specialist can assist students in their study, reading, and writing skills and in developing a time-management program.

FACULTY AND ADVISERS

There are 87 faculty members, including 13 Benedictine monks. Fifty advanced degrees, including seven doctorates, are held by faculty members. The majority of faculty members live on the campus.

The Right Reverend Dom Caedmon Holmes is Abbot and Head of the School's Governing Body. Dr. James M. De Vecchi is the Headmaster. He earned an undergraduate degree from Saint Francis College and master's and doctoral degrees in mathematics from the University of New Hampshire. Dr. De Vecchi joined the faculty in 1973 and has served in many capacities, including Mathematics Department Head, Registrar, Academic Dean, and Associate Headmaster.

Portsmouth Abbey's monastic community acts as a point of stability for the School. All new faculty members appointed each year are chosen because they are distinguished in their academic field and embrace the School's mission.

COLLEGE ADMISSION COUNSELING

Students are assigned to college counselors when they enter Portsmouth Abbey and are encouraged to meet with a counselor anytime they have questions. The formal process begins with a seminar for Fifth Formers and parents in early winter. Fifth Formers meet individually with their counselors during the spring and begin the research that will result in a college list. Counselors assist students in planning visits to college campuses and scheduling meetings with over 90 college representatives who visit the campus during the fall or spring. College counselors meet frequently with Sixth Formers, assisting with all aspects of the process.

Ninety-nine percent of the class of 2008 entered four-year colleges, including Boston College, Duke, Emory, Fordham, Georgetown, Harvard, Holy Cross, Johns Hopkins, Notre Dame, Union, the U.S. Naval Academy, and West Point Academy.

STUDENT BODY AND CONDUCT

Supported by the presence and example of the resident Benedictine community, the traditional ideas of Christian living and learning are intended to inform every part of School life and to guide the policies and practices of the community and its members. The School welcomes students from diverse backgrounds while encouraging an appreciation for the Catholic faith. Portsmouth thus aspires to develop informed and open-minded leaders educated in the Christian tradition.

Good judgment, common sense, and consideration for others are primary guidelines for behavior in the School community. A serious breach of School rules is referred to the Discipline Committee, which is composed of students and faculty members. The Student Council is a forum for student concerns.

In 2008–09, Portsmouth Abbey School enrolled 359 students. They came from twenty-three states, the District of Columbia, and sixteen countries. More than 10 percent of the students are members of minority groups.

ACADEMIC FACILITIES

Surrounding the quadrangle are the Burden Classroom Building, the Science Building, and the Cortazzo Administration Building, which houses the Auditorium. Other buildings include the St. Thomas More Library, the McGuire Fine Arts Center, the Squash/Fitness Center, and a Victorian manor house designed by Richard Upjohn in 1864. The School's St. Thomas More Library contains a 38,000-item collection and a computerized catalog, online computers, and seminar rooms. There are more than 18,000 additional monastery items cataloged for student use and about 20,000 additional volumes housed in the monastery library.

BOARDING AND GENERAL FACILITIES

Portsmouth offers its students a structured environment built on a schedule of shared daily activities—classes, athletics, clubs, and social life—and of regular community worship. The eight Houses each contain 20 to 40 students and provide the student with a familial base, a greater amount of attention, and an identity within the School. Within each House, there are 3 houseparents and a monk from the monastery is appointed to serve as spiritual leader of the dormitory. Such a support system proves ideal for teaching students the intrinsic values of education: compassion and morality.

Members of the Third Form (ninth grade) are housed in the same dorm; other dorms house students of mixed ages. Students in the lower forms usually share double rooms; seniors and some juniors elect singles.

Students from other countries or distant locations are welcome to spend long weekends, as well as other relatively short vacations, on campus. However, the School encourages students to take advantage of such breaks in the academic routine.

Additional School facilities include the Nesbitt Infirmary, the Stillman Dining Hall, and the Abbey Church of St. Gregory the Great. The majority of buildings on campus are of redwood and fieldstone and were designed by Pietro Belluschi, formerly Dean of Architecture at MIT. Also, there is a wind turbine and solar home.

ATHLETICS

Portsmouth has an extensive athletics program. All students must participate in athletics as part of their education and personal development. Dispensation for special projects is sometimes permitted for a season, and students with physical handicaps or injuries are asked to help in the training room or serve as team managers.

The School has varsity and junior varsity teams. Sports offered include baseball, basketball, cross-country, field hockey, football, golf, ice hockey, lacrosse, sailing, soccer, softball, squash, swimming, tennis, and track and field. A state-of-the-art fitness center includes eight squash courts. There are also six tennis courts; a six-lane, all-weather running track; an indoor ice-hockey rink; two basketball courts; and ten outdoor playing fields. The golf team practices at the Carnegie Abbey Golf Course, a privately owned eighteen-hole championship Scottish links golf course located on campus.

EXTRACURRICULAR OPPORTUNITIES

Outside the classroom, students are encouraged to become involved in the betterment of the Portsmouth Abbey School community at large. Among the forty clubs and organized activities offered at Portsmouth Abbey School are the School radio station, fishing club, rocketry club, theater group, Abbey Singers, Model United Nations, community service, debate club, cultural awareness group, School newspaper, yearbook, literary magazine, and equestrian program.

The School also sponsors the Dom Luke Childs lecture series, and trips to cultural, social, and sports events in the Providence and Boston areas.

DAILY LIFE

Classes begin at 8:15 and end at 2:50. On Wednesdays and Saturdays, the academic day is shortened to accommodate travel to athletics contests. Athletics are usually scheduled from 3:30 to 5:30, but there are variations in the times depending on the team and season. There are buffet dinners five nights a week and formal meals twice weekly in the fall and spring terms. After dinner, there is free time for activities, followed by evening study from 7:30 to 9:30. Lights-out is from 10:30 to 11:30, depending on the Form. Jackets and ties for boys and blazers for girls are required for classes, assemblies, and church services.

WEEKEND LIFE

The Student Council, the Social Committee, Houses, and individual classes plan a variety of social activities both on and off campus. The Social Committee, under the supervision of the Assistant Headmaster for Student Life, coordinates dances and other social events and sponsors the Christmas semiformal and the Spring Prom. Form and House parties and trips to athletics events, movie theaters, malls, and concerts are other planned weekend activities.

Students may receive permission to leave the campus on Saturday and Sunday afternoon for Newport. In addition to scheduled School vacations, students may take a limited number of Saturday overnights. Day students are integrated with Houses and are encouraged to participate in evening and weekend activities. Their families often host students who come to Portsmouth from a distance.

SUMMER PROGRAMS

Portsmouth has operated a summer session since 1943. The Portsmouth Abbey Summer Program provides rising seventh through tenth graders with a month full of new friends, fun experiences, and academic skills, all while living on the School's campus along the shores of Narragansett Bay in Rhode Island. The 2009 Summer Program is scheduled Sunday, June 28 to Saturday, July 25.

Beyond traditional courses that emphasize reading, writing, and public speaking, students may participate in hands-on enrichment activities, including environmental and marine sciences and plein-air painting. Whether in seminars, exploring marine environments, or trying new painting techniques, students explore subjects with experienced Portsmouth Abbey faculty members. The aim of the Summer Program is to help students discover the joy of learning, both in the classroom and through fun enrichment activities.

Additional activities include sailing, visits to area beaches, and day trips to nearby Boston, Martha's Vineyard, and amusement parks.

Tuition for the Summer Program is $5400 and includes room, board, textbooks, and all activities and trips. There is a reduced tuition rate for the children of alumni and for day students. Interested students should contact Mr. Peter O'Connor, Director of the Summer Program, at 401-643-1225, or via e-mail at summer@portsmouthabbey.org.

COSTS AND FINANCIAL AID

For the 2008–09 academic year, the charge for tuition, room, and board was $41,150. Day student tuition was $28,150. Additional costs for books, laboratory and studio fees, athletics equipment, allowances, and social events were about $1000. Fees are payable in full on August 1 or in two installments. Tuition insurance and tuition payment plans are available.

Portsmouth has an extensive financial aid program; 35 percent of the student body received more than $2.7 million. Awards are made on the basis of need and academic performance. Financial aid is renewed on a yearly basis; parents must submit the School and Student Service for Financial Aid form each year. Portsmouth also offers the Reverend Hugh Diman Scholarship to a boarding student who is entering Form III; this is a full merit scholarship that covers the cost of tuition, room and board. In addition, Portsmouth designates up to 10 highly qualified applicants each year as recipients of a Merit Scholarship that is renewable annually.

ADMISSIONS INFORMATION

Candidates are accepted on the basis of their personal and academic qualifications, without discrimination as to race, color, or creed. Recommendations from a student's headmaster and teachers, the school record, and test scores are all given serious consideration by the Admission Committee. A personal interview is required.

Applicants must take the SSAT. The median SSAT score for entering ninth graders is around the 70th percentile, but grades and recommendations are more significant factors in the admission decision. Portsmouth Abbey School accepts new students in the Third, Fourth, and Fifth Forms. Occasionally a well-qualified student will be accepted into the Sixth Form. The School accepts midyear applications if a vacancy occurs.

APPLICATION TIMETABLE

Portsmouth Abbey School is a member of the Secondary School Admission Test Board and subscribes to the March 10 notification date and the April 10 reply date. Parents are encouraged to visit the campus in the fall prior to the year of entry. Applications should be postmarked by January 31. There is a $50 application fee for U.S. citizens and a $75 application fee for international students.

ADMISSIONS CORRESPONDENCE

Mrs. Meghan Fonts
Director of Admissions
Portsmouth Abbey School
Portsmouth, Rhode Island 02871
Phone: 401-643-1248
Fax: 401-643-1355
E-mail: admissions@portsmouthabbey.org
Web site: http://www.portsmouthabbey.org

PROFESSIONAL CHILDREN'S SCHOOL

New York, New York

Type: Coeducational day college-preparatory school
Grades: 6–12: Middle School, 6–8; High School, 9–12
Enrollment: School total: 181; Middle School: 34; High School: 147
Head of School: Dr. James Dawson

THE SCHOOL

Professional Children's School (PCS), located near Lincoln Center in New York City, is a coeducational day school for students in grades 6–12. Now in its ninety-fourth year, PCS offers an academic, college-preparatory education to students who are professional actors, dancers, models, or musicians; who are preparing for careers in the performing arts or sports; or who desire an environment supportive of the arts.

When Professional Children's School was founded in 1914, all the students were performing on stage as actors, dancers, jugglers, musicians, comedians, and singers. The need for young actors to have formal schooling was recognized by Mrs. Franklin W. Robinson and Deaconess Jane Harris Hall, the founders of PCS, when they discovered 5 young actors backstage playing poker instead of studying. Since the early 1900s, the composition of the student body has been broadened to reflect the development of film and television, the growth of classical and modern dance, and the importance of training for Olympic sports.

PCS is dedicated to educating its students so they are qualified to pursue any profession in which they are interested. A rigorous liberal arts program ensures that students can choose from a number of career options. While the arts are an integral part of the curriculum, students pursue professional training at such well-known schools and institutions as the Juilliard School of Music, School of American Ballet, Dance Theatre of Harlem, and Skating Club of New York. Support for artistic interest is reflected in a concentrated and flexible schedule that allows time for practice, rehearsals, and auditions.

Self-reliance is stressed. Students are given responsibility for the effective use of time to complete their work and meet their professional commitments. Scheduling and assignments often reflect a high degree of individualization.

The School is governed by a 25-member Board of Trustees. The School's endowment is valued at $2.7 million, supplemented by Annual Giving of $1.6 million during fiscal 2007–08.

Professional Children's School is accredited by the New York State Education Department and the Middle States Association of Colleges and Schools and is registered by the New York State Board of Regents. The School is affiliated with the National Association of Independent Schools, New York State Association of Independent Schools, Guild of Independent Schools in New York, Headmistresses Association of the East, National Association of Principals of Schools for Girls, School and Student Service for Financial Aid, and Council for Advancement and Support of Education.

ACADEMIC PROGRAMS

Eighteen credits are required for graduation, not including 1 in physical education. Students usually carry 5 credits a year and may carry more, depending on their professional schedules. Requirements include 4 credits in English, 3.5 credits in history (global studies, U.S. history, and a history elective), 2 credits in a foreign language (French or Spanish), 2 credits in math, 2 credits in science, 1 credit in the arts, and ½ credit in health. In addition, students must select a three-year sequence in a foreign language, mathematics, or science.

Electives are offered in all academic areas, including the arts. Examples of electives are literature and film, constitutional law, printmaking, and dramatics workshop. Seniors may also take for credit approved courses at a nearby university.

The High School also offers English as a second language, history, and mathematics courses for international students.

The school year is divided into two semesters and four marking periods. Class size ranges from 10 to 22, with an overall student-teacher ratio of about 8:1.

A special offering at PCS is the guided study program. Students who miss school for professional reasons (whether the absence is due to a morning rehearsal or a six-week theatrical tour) are provided with assignments to be completed during the time away from the classroom.

FACULTY AND ADVISERS

The 25 full-time faculty members hold five doctorates, twenty-three master's degrees, and twenty-five bachelor's degrees.

Dr. James Dawson was appointed Head of School in 1995. He is a graduate of the State University of New York at Albany (B.S., biology, 1977; Ph.D., behavior, 1982). Prior to his appointment at Professional Children's School, Dr. Dawson had been the Head of Upper School at the Spence School since 1988. He has taught at the middle- and upper-school levels as well as at the university level since 1977.

Professional Children's School seeks faculty members who are knowledgeable in and supportive of the performing arts, who can instill academic excellence in students, and who are flexible in their teaching methodology. Faculty members are encouraged to pursue advanced degrees; compensation for relevant in-service training is offered. A grade adviser is assigned to students for academic and personal counseling. A college guidance counselor works with juniors, seniors, and alumni who are formulating college plans. In addition, all faculty members are available to counsel students. A consulting psychologist meets regularly with the faculty and is available for referrals.

COLLEGE ADMISSION COUNSELING

Professional Children's School provides college counseling for juniors, seniors, and recent graduates of the School. About 75 percent of the senior class attend college directly after graduation. Of the remaining students, many enroll in college after pursuing careers or training, for several years, in the performing arts. Counseling, offered by the College Advisor, begins in the eleventh grade and extends through the time of college acceptance.

Members of the class of 2008 are attending Boston University, Duke, Fordham, Juilliard, the Manhattan School of Music, NYU, and Stamford College.

STUDENT BODY AND CONDUCT

Of the 147 students enrolled in the High School, 42 are seniors; 48, juniors; 36, sophomores; and 21, freshmen. There are 49 boys and 121 girls enrolled in the School. The professional composition of the High School is as follows: 60 dancers, 37 musicians, 14 actors, 4 models, 21 athletes, 7 singers, 1 fine artist, 1 arts-affiliated student, and 1 student studying robotics.

There is a wide geographical distribution within the student body: twenty-two states and ten other countries are represented. International students and students who are members of minority groups make up 36 percent of the student enrollment. An even distribution of socioeconomic groups is represented.

Orderly, respectful conduct is expected. Rules, as described in the student handbook, are established with the safety and well-being of the students in mind.

ACADEMIC FACILITIES

Professional Children's School is housed in an eight-story classroom building with an adjacent play yard. Eighteen classrooms, two science laboratories, a music room, an art studio, a drama room, an auditorium, a cafeteria, and a gymnasium are located in the building. (The School serves both a hot lunch and a cold buffet daily.)

The library contains 10,000 volumes and a collection of CDs and DVDs, as well as audio-visual equipment and resources. There are fifty computers and four SMART boards for instructional use.

ATHLETICS

Physical education is required at PCS. Students meet the requirement either through the School's athletics program or through regularly scheduled classes at approved dance, ice-skating, or gymnastics schools. Physical education classes are focused on volleyball, basketball, movement, and calisthenics.

EXTRACURRICULAR OPPORTUNITIES

Because PCS students are so actively involved with professional organizations outside the School, extracurricular opportunities are limited to those activities initiated through joint student-faculty efforts. A yearbook and school newspaper are published annually, a drama production is staged twice a year, and students perform for each other and parents on a regular basis. An outdoor Field Day, an annual benefit, and excursions to New York City performing arts productions are also offered.

DAILY LIFE

Class hours extend from 8 to 2:45. Teachers are available from 8 until 3:15; time before and after class hours is used for extra help and makeup tests. The school day has a combination of 40-, 50-, and 100-minute class periods.

COSTS AND FINANCIAL AID

High School tuition for 2008–09 ranged from $28,250 for ninth graders to $31,000 for incoming seniors. Fees, primarily for books, are set at $512; additional costs include a graduation fee and supply costs for selected courses. Tuition payment plans offer billing one or two times during the year as well as a ten-month payment plan through Sallie Mae. A $2000 deposit, credited to the last payment, is required when the contract is signed.

Thirty-four percent of the student body received partial tuition aid. Awards are based on financial and professional need. The 2008–09 tuition aid budget was set at $672,000.

ADMISSIONS INFORMATION

It is the admissions policy of the School not to discriminate on the basis of sex, race, color, religion, or national origin. Candidates for admission are evaluated on their academic preparation (transcript and testing required), an interview, and professional need.

The High School admits students into grades 9–12. The School prides itself on accommodating motivated young people who may be involved in some outside activity that might interfere with classroom attendance during regular school hours.

The faculty at PCS is strongly committed to a four-year education for high school students. Seniors with extra credits who have a legitimate professional need may be able to arrange a part-time program or graduate in January.

A careful screening process ensures that all students who complete the application process have a clear understanding of and desire for PCS's unique educational opportunities. From 145 applications received for 2008–09, 95 students were accepted and 60 enrolled. Twenty-one were enrolled in the Middle School and 39 in the High School.

APPLICATION TIMETABLE

Applications are accepted throughout the school year. Admission openings occur in September and January. Upon receipt of the application and a $50 application fee, an appointment for an interview is arranged. Families are notified of the Admissions Committee's decision by letter and, in most cases, by telephone.

ADMISSIONS CORRESPONDENCE

Sherrie Hinkle, Director of Admissions
Professional Children's School
132 West 60th Street
New York, New York 10023
Phone: 212-582-3116
Fax: 212-307-6542
E-mail: hinkle@pcs-nyc.org
Web site: http://www.pcs-nyc.org

THE PUTNEY SCHOOL

Putney, Vermont

Type: Coeducational boarding and day college-preparatory school
Grades: 9-12, postgraduate year in the visual arts
Enrollment: 226
Head of School: Emily H. Jones, Director

THE SCHOOL

The Putney School, one of the first independent coeducational boarding schools in America, was founded in 1935 by Carmelita Hinton, a pioneering progressive educator who believed that students learn best by doing—both in and out of the classroom. Putney has continued to be an educational community where experiences are broad, expectations are high, and friendships are close. It is a school where energetic and thoughtful young people engage in a variety of educational experiences, learn self-reliance, and begin to develop their potential.

Putney has a great "density of purpose." The School embraces most of the traditionally progressive goals: education is about creating good citizens and should be an engine for social betterment, it should foster personal initiative and adaptability, and it must engage the whole child, not just the academic child. The School also has some goals that are particular to Putney. Putney aims to make school life a more real, less sheltered, less self-centered venture; to make the arts part of everyday life; and to teach stewardship of the land both by the way School participants live and in a curriculum designed for that purpose.

Putney is located on a 500-acre farm in southeastern Vermont, off Interstate 91. It is 10 miles from Brattleboro, 115 miles from Boston, and 215 miles from New York City. The School draws students from all over the United States and the world.

The Putney School is governed by a 30-member Board of Trustees that includes 2 members of the faculty, 2 students, and a number of alumni. The School's 4,000 alumni members play an important role in the support of the School.

Putney is accredited by the New England Association of Schools and Colleges and holds membership in the National Association of Independent Schools, the Association of Boarding Schools, and the Council for the Advancement and Support of Education.

ACADEMIC PROGRAMS

At Putney, academic achievement is important. Students carry five college-preparatory academic courses during all four years. The aim of the academic program is to motivate students to ask significant questions, read carefully, listen to the ideas of others, write persuasively, and think independently and critically. A typical class meets four to five times per week and has 9 to 15 students. The teacher-student ratio is about 1:9.

A graduating senior will have taken at least 4 years of English, 3 years of mathematics, 3 years of a foreign language, 3 years of a laboratory science, 2½ years of history, 1 year of the arts, and seven semester-long electives. Electives include advanced calculus, molecular biology, comparative religions, philosophy, choral/instrumental music, music theory, drama, painting/drawing, sculpture, ceramics, fiber arts, and photography. Seniors choose from among several history courses and have English electives in the spring.

The academic year is divided into two semesters. Written progress reports are sent regularly to students and parents. Students receive scores and comments rather than grades on tests and papers. Grades are recorded with the Academic Dean every three to four weeks and kept for internal purposes; they are provided to students in the junior year to help them in college planning.

Just after winter vacation and at the close of the spring term, ten-day periods are designated as Project Weeks. During these periods, the student undertakes two projects of his or her design: one relating to academic work and the other relating to an evening activity or nonacademic work. Each project is approved and supervised by a qualified adult. Project Week offers students an opportunity to achieve and demonstrate mastery of a subject or skill and usually culminates with a program in which students can present, display, or perform their work for others and for parents.

Seniors have an opportunity to participate in Work Term, a five-week period in the spring. During this period, they can pursue off-campus work-study projects. In the past, students have worked in schools, political organizations, laboratories, clinics, rural redevelopment offices, and the office of a U.S. senator.

FACULTY AND ADVISERS

Including administrators who teach, there are 35 full-time and 4 part-time faculty members. Additional adjunct faculty members give instruction in instrumental music and selected evening activities. The whole staff of more than 80 interacts closely with the students.

Emily H. Jones, appointed Director in 2007, received an A.B. from Harvard University and an M.A. from Yale University. Before coming to The Putney School, Emily was the head of the Upper School at the Catlin Gabel School in Portland, Oregon.

In selecting its faculty, Putney seeks men and women who enthusiastically devote themselves to a wide variety of tasks, who are extremely well qualified academically, and who relish the company of young people.

COLLEGE ADMISSION COUNSELING

The College Counselor starts working with students in the junior year and encourages all to investigate and visit suitable colleges. Many college representatives come to Putney to speak with seniors in the fall.

During the past three years, Putney graduates have attended such colleges as Amherst, Barnard, Bowdoin, Columbia, Dartmouth, Duke, Georgetown, Hampshire, Harvard, NYU, Reed, Rhode Island School of Design, Sarah Lawrence, Smith, Swarthmore, Trinity College of Vermont, the University of Chicago, Wesleyan, Williams, and Yale.

STUDENT BODY AND CONDUCT

The student body in 2007–08 numbered 226: 102 boys and 124 girls; 164 boarding students and 62 day students. They came from twenty-three states and fourteen countries. Approximately 14 percent were students of color, and 19 percent were international students.

The School government involves representatives from the faculty, staff, and student body. At any given time, about one third of the student body is involved in School or dormitory government through membership on various committees, such as the Work Committee, the Educational Programming Committee, and the Standards Committee.

ACADEMIC FACILITIES

Five large buildings house classrooms, laboratories, studios, music rooms, and the assembly hall. The library has more than 26,000 titles and subscribes to more than 100 periodicals and newsletters. Biology students have the use of two greenhouses and can perform field studies on the campus's 500 acres. All academic buildings and dormitories are equipped with high-speed wireless Internet. Laptops are available for student and classroom use in the Instructional Technology Center.

The Michael S. Currier Center, which houses a dance studio, music practice rooms, a MIDI Lab, a digital film editing lab, an assembly hall, gallery space, and a meditation room, opened in 2004.

BOARDING AND GENERAL FACILITIES

There are nine dormitories accommodating from 9 to 30 students each. In addition to the regular dorms, there are five student cabins, each occupied by two students, usually seniors, who have earned the privilege. The cabins were built by students and are heated with wood that was cut and split by students. Both old and new students may request their choice of dorm, room, and roommates. When assigning rooms, the School takes into consideration what is known of each student's personality and interests. Double rooms are more numerous than singles. All dorms have common rooms with refrigerators, microwaves, and free laundry facilities. Students and faculty and staff members eat together in the School's dining hall. Four nights per week, dinners are served family-style.

The School also enlists the services of 3 full-time nurses (1 lives on campus), an on-call physician, and a psychologist who is available to provide assessment and support for students and adults in the community. The counselor also makes outside referrals to therapists when necessary.

ATHLETICS

Putney seeks to promote in each student a lifelong love of the outdoors through organized work and sports programs that are designed to develop the student's skills in a variety of outdoor activities. These programs are offered four times per week, except team sports, which are scheduled six times per week.

Competition with other schools is scheduled for the major team sports: basketball, crew, cross-country running, cross-country skiing, lacrosse, soccer, and Ultimate Frisbee. Other recreational sports and activities include Alpine skiing and snowboarding, cross-country skiing, cycling, dance, fencing, hiking, horseback riding, mountain biking, snowshoeing, and yoga.

Everyone at Putney has an opportunity to engage in recreational or competitive skiing on the School's 40 kilometers of groomed ski trails. The cross-country teams have placed consistently high in New England meets. Several Putney students and graduates have skied for the United States in the Winter Olympics and on national ski teams.

In place of sports, students may fulfill the afternoon activity requirement with supervised work in the garden, on the farm, or on the School's woods crew.

EXTRACURRICULAR OPPORTUNITIES

In the spring, groups of faculty and staff members and students take a week on camping trips around Vermont. Students may choose among biking, hiking, rock-climbing, canoeing, horseback riding, kayaking, or service trips.

In the fall, the whole school prepares for Harvest Festival, when parents, alumni, and a great many friends of the School visit Putney.

Choral and instrumental concerts, dance and drama performances, and exhibits of student work in the arts and crafts contribute to the winter holiday and graduation festivities.

Students are required to take part in two evening activities each week. Offerings include African drumming, blacksmithing, orchestra, dance, drama, drawing, filmmaking, jazz ensemble, jewelry making, knitting, painting, photography, madrigals, sculpting, stained glass, string quartet, weaving, Web design, and woodworking. In addition, students may opt to work on the literary magazine and yearbook and take part in School Council meetings.

Putney has 500 acres of farmland, pasture, sugarbush, and woodland. During their time at the School, all students participate in the Work Program, rotating through a variety of duties in the barn, milk house, kitchen, forest, garden, and other sites on campus. In many ways, the community is self-sustaining. It produces many of the vegetables and essentially all of the milk, yogurt, cheddar cheese, maple syrup, and eggs used by the kitchen. Firewood is cut on School land, and much of the lumber used in maintenance and construction is cut and milled on campus.

DAILY LIFE

The academic day begins at 7:45 and ends at 3, with breaks for "milk lunch," daily assembly, and lunch. For 40 minutes on Thursday morning, students and faculty members gather for Sing. Wednesdays are half days, and Saturday classes are held from 8 to 12:15.

Afternoon activities, sports, and jobs are scheduled from 3:10 to 4:50 four days each week (six days for participants in team sports). Jobs may include community service projects in Putney or Brattleboro.

Dinner is served at 6. From 7:30 to 9, students attend evening activities (two nights per week) or study (five nights per week) either in the dormitory or library study halls. All students must be in their dormitories by 10 p.m.

WEEKEND LIFE

The Putney weekend proper is brief—from midday on Saturday to 7 p.m. on Sunday. Students may, with parental and School permission, be away over Saturday night, but most elect to remain at the School for an evening of movies, dancing, or other planned activities.

Transportation is available to nearby Brattleboro for shopping on Saturday afternoon and movies on Saturday night. There are also weekend overnight camping trips as well as expeditions to museums, plays, conferences, lectures, concerts, and fairs. A few times each semester, Sunday Night Meetings allow the community to gather to hear outside speakers who come to campus to discuss ethical and societal issues.

COSTS AND FINANCIAL AID

Tuition at Putney for 2008–09 was $41,100 for boarding students and $26,900 for day students. Expenses for books, supplies, lab fees, and incidentals were between $1500 and $2000.

Tuition is payable in semiannual payments or in ten monthly installments. A deposit of 10 percent of tuition for both boarding and day students is required to hold the student's place. In addition, Putney is affiliated with several extended-payment and loan plans that families can use to help finance the student's education.

To make Putney accessible to young people of diverse economic backgrounds, a strong program of financial aid is offered through need-based grants. Forty-four percent of the student body received aid in 2007–08. Financial aid forms are due January 1 and may be obtained by calling the Admission Office.

ADMISSIONS INFORMATION

Putney seeks bright and motivated young people of widely diverse interests. The admission process requires an interview, essays to be completed by the applicant, and a completed parent form. In addition, recommendations from 2 teachers and a guidance counselor or principal and an official school transcript should be sent directly from the student's school. Students are also required to submit scores from the Secondary School Admission Test (SSAT). Applicants applying for grades 11 or 12 may submit PSAT scores in lieu of SSAT scores.

APPLICATION TIMETABLE

There is no formal deadline for applications. Students who apply by January 15 are notified by March 10, and parents are expected to reply by April 10. Thereafter, applications are reviewed on a rolling basis, pending available space. Families also applying for financial aid must complete the financial aid application by January 1 and the application for admission by January 15.

Prospective applicants are urged to visit, preferably on a school day, so they have the opportunity to tour the campus, talk with students and teachers, and visit a class, followed by a personal interview. Applicants should call for an appointment.

There is an application fee of $40. For international applicants, the fee is $75. The Admission Office remains open from 8:30 to 4:30 Monday through Friday throughout the year.

ADMISSIONS CORRESPONDENCE

Rick Cowan
Director of Admission
The Putney School
Putney, Vermont 05346
Phone: 802-387-6219 (Admission Office)
802-387-5566 (Reception)
Fax: 802-387-6278
E-mail: admission@putneyschool.org
Web site: http://www.putneyschool.org

RABUN GAP–NACOOCHEE SCHOOL

Rabun Gap, Georgia

Type: Coeducational boarding and day college-preparatory school
Grades: 6–12: Middle School, 6–8; Upper School, 9–12
Enrollment: School total: 355; Upper School: 266
Head of School: John D. Marshall

THE SCHOOL

Rabun Gap–Nacoochee School (RGNS) was formed by the 1927 merger of Rabun Gap Industrial School, founded in 1905, and Nacoochee Institute, founded in 1903, under the leadership of Harvard graduate Andrew J. Ritchie. The School enrolls students from fifteen states and fourteen countries.

Rabun Gap–Nacoochee School offers a competitive college-preparatory program enrolling boarding students in grades 7 through 12 and day students in grades 6 through 12. The School has a covenant relationship with the Presbyterian Church (USA), hosting ecumenical chapel services twice weekly, and an active community service program assisting local charities and agencies. The School is characterized by small groups (in classes, in dorms, and with advisers) that encourage individual growth and the development of close relationships among peers, teachers, and staff members. At Rabun Gap, students are provided with opportunities to maximize their academic performance and personal development.

Rabun Gap–Nacoochee School is accredited by the Southern Association of Colleges and Schools and by the Southern Association of Independent Schools. It holds memberships in the National Association of Independent Schools, the Southern Association of Independent Schools, the Association of Boarding Schools, the Southeastern Association of Boarding Schools, the Georgia Independent School Association, the Secondary School Admission Test Board, and the Educational Records Bureau.

ACADEMIC PROGRAMS

The Rabun Gap curriculum challenges each student and prepares him or her for the college experience. Small classes, ranging in size from 7 to 17 students, promote teacher-student interaction and better peer discussions. Rabun Gap utilizes an alphabetical grading system, and progress reports are sent home to parents twice each semester. Each student has an adviser to ensure that he or she has consistent academic and personal support.

Graduation requirements include 4 units of English, 3 units of history, 4 units of mathematics, 3 units of science (including two laboratory courses), 3 units of Spanish or French, 2 units of fine arts, 1 unit of physical and health education, 1 unit of Bible history, and up to 5 units of electives. Seniors are encouraged to conduct and complete a Senior Project.

The regular curriculum offers 4 years of English, creative writing, journalism, and public speaking; 4 years of mathematics; physical science, environmental science, biology, chemistry, physics, and human anatomy and physiology; ancient history, modern world history, U.S. history, Bible history, economics, and government; 4 years of French and Spanish; 3 years of visual art; 2 years of drama, dance, chorus, Gap Singers, wind ensemble, and music preparation; 2 years of woodworking; and mechanical drawing.

In addition to regular and honors-level courses, Rabun Gap offers Advanced Placement courses in studio art, art history, music theory, biology, chemistry, physics, environmental science, psychology, calculus, English, European history, government, French, Spanish, and U.S. history.

Rabun Gap–Nacoochee School offers an English as a second language (ESL) program for international students who require additional help with English prior to being placed in regular classes. The multinational mix of students encourages the exchange of ideas and cultural traditions and is a vital element of the cultural education and global awareness of the Rabun Gap student.

FACULTY AND ADVISERS

There are 78 faculty and administration members; 52 live on campus. All members of the faculty and administration hold baccalaureate degrees; 43 hold advanced degrees.

John D. Marshall was appointed Head of School in 2004. Mr. Marshall holds a B.A. in history from the University of North Carolina at Chapel Hill and an M.B.A. from Duke University.

COLLEGE ADMISSION COUNSELING

Rabun Gap provides an excellent counseling program that is designed to help each student select the college or university best suited to his or her needs. College testing begins in the sophomore and junior years with the administering of the PSAT, followed by the SAT in the spring of the junior year and fall of the senior year; students are also encouraged to take the ACT. Students begin their college search during the junior year and apply to colleges during the fall of the senior year.

Colleges where recent graduates have enrolled include Agnes Scott, American University of Paris, Auburn, Berea, Brigham Young, Brown, The Citadel, Clemson, College of Charleston, Davidson, Duke, Embry-Riddle, Emerson, Emory, Florida Institute of Technology, Florida State, Furman, Georgetown, Georgia Southern, Georgia Tech, Gettysburg, Guilford, Kenyon, Johns Hopkins, Mary Baldwin, Mercer, Morehouse, Ohio State, Presbyterian, Princeton, Rhodes, Tufts, the U.S. Naval Academy, Vanderbilt, Virginia Tech, Washington and Lee, Wofford, Yale, and the Universities of Alabama, Colorado, Florida, Georgia, Michigan, Mississippi, North Carolina, Oregon, South Carolina, Pennsylvania, and Tennessee. Typically, 100 percent of the graduating seniors attend the college or university of their choice.

STUDENT BODY AND CONDUCT

For the 2008–09 school year, Rabun Gap–Nacoochee School enrolled students from fifteen states and twelve countries in grades 6 through 12. The 2008–09 enrollment was 355; approximately 50 percent of the students are girls and 50 percent are boys, and 53 percent are boarding students.

The majority of the students come from Georgia, North Carolina, South Carolina, and Florida. Other states represented are Arizona, California, Delaware, Kentucky, Louisiana, Maryland, New Jersey, New Mexico, New York, Tennessee, and Virginia. International students come from China, Germany, Hungary, Jamaica, Korea, Malaysia, Mexico, Rwanda, Saudi Arabia, Taiwan, the Turks and Caicos Islands, and Venezuela. Rabun Gap admits students who meet academic and conduct standards without regard to race, color, gender, or national or ethnic origin.

Rules are in place to ensure the safety of all students. Students are held accountable for their own conduct and the conduct of their peers. Student prefects assist administrators and dorm parents with the legislation and administration of discipline. In addition to rules for daily living, Rabun Gap students follow an honor code in all phases of their school life.

ACADEMIC FACILITIES

Hodgson Hall contains classrooms for the Upper School, the chapel, the computer center, and School offices. The Morris Brown Science Center houses science classrooms and laboratories along with the Louise M. Gallant Herbarium. The Middle School is located in two restored homes just a short walk from the Upper School. The Industrial Arts Building houses both woodworking and metalworking machinery.

Two facilities were opened in January 2002. The library offers enhanced academic resources for students and is an integral part of the School's education, providing students with materials for research and pleasure reading. Included within the spacious two-story facility are a computer lab, a professional library, small group-study rooms, and a periodical reading area. The library houses a print and nonprint collection of 14,000 books and videos, which are searchable through a computerized catalog and circulation system. The library has sixty-five periodicals and newspapers and a leasing system of bestselling books from Baker and Taylor Book Publishers. The Arts and Technology Building offers state-of-the-art performing and visual arts classrooms, a dance studio, a technology center, a black-box theater, and a 620-seat auditorium.

Administrative offices, the Head of School's office, and the campus bookstore, along with the Student Center, are located in the Woodruff Memorial Administrative Building.

BOARDING AND GENERAL FACILITIES

The main campus occupies approximately 200 of the 1,400 acres owned by the School. The balance of the property consists of a working farm and forest, including a 20-acre recreational lake.

There are seven dormitories—three each for boys and girls in grades 7 through 11. Jane Hall, a suite-style dormitory for twelfth-grade students, was formally dedicated on June 6, 2003. Most rooms are double occupancy, and a member of the residential faculty staffs each dorm. These faculty members have no other duties at the School and serve as a resource to the students in their dorms. Student prefects assist with residential life, including evening study hall and other leadership duties.

Students and faculty members take their meals in the Addie Corn Ritchie Dining Hall, located in the middle of central campus.

ATHLETICS

The interscholastic athletics program helps foster teamwork, the improvement of physical skills, leadership, and school spirit. Coaches are also teachers; this interaction between coaches and team members helps build relationships between teachers and students in a setting outside the classroom. Competitive sports include baseball, basketball, cross-country, golf, soccer, softball, swimming, tennis, track and field, and volleyball. Rabun Gap teams maintain a distinguished record in both achievement and sportsmanship. RGNS also offers a middle school football program, which seeks to help young adolescent boys learn the fundamental skills of football, cooperative teamwork, and leadership.

EXTRACURRICULAR OPPORTUNITIES

Rabun Gap takes advantage of its location by planning a full schedule of extracurricular outdoor activities. During the spring and fall, the outdoors club goes hiking, camping, white-water rafting, or mountain biking. During the winter months, students take ski trips to nearby Georgia and Carolina slopes. The School's extensive campus provides numerous opportunities for fishing, hiking, and rock climbing.

At Rabun Gap, clubs provide students with numerous educational and recreational activities. Service clubs, such as the Beta Club and the Diversity Club, offer students leadership opportunities and provide valuable services to the School and community. The Art Guild, astronomy club, environmental club, language clubs, science club, student newspaper, literary magazine, and yearbook afford learning opportunities outside of the classroom. In addition, students may choose to join recreational clubs.

DAILY LIFE

The typical student day, following academic periods, includes athletics, student work responsibilities, and other activities. Chapel services are held on Thursdays and Sundays.

Open time is available after dinner for socializing at the Student Center or relaxing in the dormitories. On Sunday through Thursday evenings, dorm faculty members and prefects supervise a mandatory 2-hour study period for boarding students.

WEEKEND LIFE

On weekends, a variety of on-campus and off-campus activities are offered, including dances, sports events, hiking, camping trips, miniature golf, bowling, and skating as well as trips to malls, concerts, amusement parks, and movies. Boarding students attend chapel every Sunday. With proper parental and administrative permission, boarding students may go home or stay with friends from school on certain "open" weekends throughout the year.

COSTS AND FINANCIAL AID

Tuition for 2008–09 was $15,220 for day students, $33,700 for domestic boarding students, and $38,850 for international students. A nonrefundable enrollment fee of $500 for day students, $1000 for domestic boarding students, and $4000 for international students is due at the time the contract is submitted. The nonrefundable enrollment fee is part of the tuition costs and is credited to the student's tuition account. Books and uniforms are not part of the tuition.

The School offers payment plans by year, by semester, and by month. Financial aid is provided on the basis of need. In order to be considered for financial aid, families must complete the Parents' Financial Statement (PFS) and mail it to the School and Student Service for Financial Aid (SSS). The School uses the SSS report as a guide when making final decisions regarding the amount of aid awarded. Merit-based scholarships are also available for outstanding students.

ADMISSIONS INFORMATION

Rabun Gap seeks motivated students of good moral character who possess the skills necessary to compete in a college-preparatory environment. Candidates for admission are evaluated through school transcripts, references, on-campus interviews, and standardized testing. The School requires all applicants to take either the ISEE or the SSAT.

APPLICATION TIMETABLE

The application process begins in the fall of the year preceding entry and continues until classes are full. The Admission Office recommends initiating the process as early as possible. The School's first notification date is during the first week of March and then on a rolling basis. In addition, some applicants are admitted for the January term. Application packets are available through the Admission Office; online inquiries may be made and applications are available on the School's Web site at http://www.rabungap.org.

ADMISSIONS CORRESPONDENCE

Adele Yermack
Director of Admission and Financial Aid
Rabun Gap–Nacoochee School
339 Nacoochee Drive
Rabun Gap, Georgia 30568
Phone: 706-746-7467
800-543-7467 (toll-free)
Fax: 706-746-2594
Web site: http://www.rabungap.org

RANNEY SCHOOL

Tinton Falls, New Jersey

Type: Coeducational college-preparatory day school
Grades: BG (3 years old)–grade 12: Lower School, BG–Grade 5; Middle School, Grades 6–8; Upper School, Grades 9–12
Enrollment: School total: 815
Head of School: Lawrence S. Sykoff, Ed.D.

THE SCHOOL

Ranney School was founded in 1960 by Russell G. Ranney for the purpose of fostering high academic achievement. A former Associate Director of the New York University Reading Institute, Mr. Ranney was a firm believer in the three R's. A 17-member Board of Trustees, plus the Head of School, supervises the School's operation on its campus of more than 60 acres in a residential neighborhood located approximately 60 miles south of New York City.

The purpose of Ranney School is to prepare its students for college and to encourage them to become independent and self-reliant young adults. The School believes a well-prepared student is one who is inquisitive, knows how to acquire knowledge, and exercises sound judgment and common sense in all matters.

The Board of Trustees is the School's governing body. During 2006–07, annual giving totaled $225,000; annual operating expenses average $15 million.

Ranney School alumni number approximately 1,400; an Alumni Council oversees alumni activities.

Ranney School is accredited by the Middle States Association of Colleges and Schools. The School maintains active membership in the National Association of Independent Schools (NAIS), the New Jersey Association of Independent Schools (NJAIS), the Council for Advancement and Support of Education (CASE), the Educational Records Bureau (ERB), and the National Association for College Admission Counseling (NACAC).

ACADEMIC PROGRAMS

The Lower School (beginners (age 3) through grade 5) curriculum is designed to stimulate a child's natural love of learning. Goals are set forth in a program consistent with the early stages of child development. The primary goal is to maximize the growth of each individual. The curriculum remains rooted in the development of language arts. Course time is allotted to vocabulary building, spelling, grammar usage, reading, and the development of writing skills. Strong programs in mathematics, science, social studies, instrumental music, and computer education complement these courses. Students are also introduced to studies in the fine arts, music, and foreign languages. Aquatics and physical education complete the course of study. Teaching strategies include cooperative learning, interdisciplinary arrangements, and individual attention.

The Middle School (grades 6 through 8) curriculum is designed to provide a special community in which students can grow, learn about themselves, develop personal and group values, and prepare for the challenges of higher learning, particularly within the Ranney Upper School. The comprehensive English and mathematics programs initiated in the Lower School continue through the middle years, along with additional concentrations in science, history, and foreign languages, including a foundation in Latin. Courses in computer fundamentals, art, music, drama, word processing, physical education, and aquatics are part of the total curriculum. To provide flexibility in instruction, some classes in math, history, and foreign languages are arranged to cover the curriculum over a two-year period.

The Upper School (grades 9 through 12) graduation requirements include a minimum of 20 academic credits, plus 4 units in health and physical education. All students are expected to take 5 full credits of course work each year. Specific requirements include English (4 credits), foreign language (3 credits), history (3 credits, 1 of which must be American history), mathematics (3 credits), science (2 credits with lab, including biology and either chemistry or physics), art (1 credit), and physical education (4 credits). In addition to required courses, a number of single-semester and full-year electives are available to sophomores, juniors, and seniors. The Upper School curriculum also offers many honors and college-level Advanced Placement (AP) courses. Nineteen AP units are available to students who are capable of accelerated study.

Ranney utilizes the letter grade system (A through F). The school year consists of two semesters and four marking periods, with grades and written evaluations being sent home at the end of the first and third marking periods. Report cards with grades only are sent at the end of each semester. Midterm exams are given in January and final exams in June.

FACULTY AND ADVISERS

There are 96 full-time faculty members, plus 4 part-time instructors. Thirty-four faculty members have master's degrees or higher. Each Middle and Upper School faculty member serves as an adviser to an average of 6 to 8 students. Ranney faculty members are accomplished and recognized professionals whose contributions to the growth and status of their calling often extend outside the School community.

Dr. Lawrence S. Sykoff was appointed Headmaster in June 1993. He holds degrees from the University of San Diego (Ed.D. and M.Ed.) and Baruch College of Business Administration of the City University of New York (B.B.A.).

COLLEGE ADMISSION COUNSELING

The College Guidance Office assists in planning family visits to colleges. It schedules visits with college admission representatives, many of whom visit Ranney each year to interview prospective students. Juniors attend various college fairs to gather information about colleges throughout the country.

Early in the sophomore year, students take the PSATs. In the junior year, group and individual meetings with students and parents are held to assist in the college selection process. During the summer prior to their senior year, students meet with the Director of College Guidance to formulate a list of college choices and devise a plan of action for the senior year. As the application process reaches its peak in the fall of that year, students receive individual help and encouragement. All seniors receive assistance from the Director of College Guidance in writing college essays and preparing their final applications.

The mean SAT scores for 2007 graduates were 600 critical reading, 620 writing, and 630 math.

The senior class of 2007 achieved 100 percent college acceptance at schools such as Boston University, Cornell, Georgetown, Middlebury, NYU, Princeton, Tufts, and Yale.

STUDENT BODY AND CONDUCT

The 2007–08 student body consisted of 815 students, as follows: 191 boys and 201 girls in the Lower School, 106 boys and 76 girls in the Middle School, and 108 boys and 133 girls in the Upper School.

Ranney's families represent many different countries, including China, India, Japan, and Russia. The School sponsors an International Week of Celebration each year in all three divisions.

A Judicial Board handles routine disciplinary issues in the Upper School. The board consists of 2 faculty members and 2 students and is chaired by the Dean of Students. Recommendations are given to the Principal and the Headmaster for review and decision.

ACADEMIC FACILITIES

The Lower School is composed of three buildings and has its own computer lab, resource room, and library. Each classroom is equipped with two computers, and all computers are connected to the network and the Internet. The Middle School and Upper School are housed in Ranney's modern and high-tech academic complex. The facility offers thirty-three classrooms, state-of-the-art biology and chemistry laboratories, a foreign language laboratory, a college guidance center, a modern library, student assembly areas, 300 computers, and a unique Distance Learning Center. The entire building is wired for the Internet. In addition, the Middle and Upper Schools have their own dining hall.

ATHLETICS

Ranney School encourages students to participate in sports and views athletics as an important part of the educational program. All students are eligible to participate regardless of ability. The middle and upper divisions field teams in soccer, cross-country, tennis, basketball, swimming, baseball, softball, golf, and lacrosse. Ranney competes against other accredited public and private schools in the area and maintains active membership in the New Jersey Prep Conference. Interscholastic competition begins in the sixth grade. The School has two gymnasiums, a 25-meter indoor swimming pool, new tennis courts, two baseball fields, and brand-new athletic facilities, including a synthetic turf field and a state-of-the-art track. In addition there is a new fitness center with a certified athletic trainer on duty.

EXTRACURRICULAR OPPORTUNITIES

The Lower School offers a variety of extracurricular and after-school activities for grades 2 through 5, including computers, art instruction, creative writing, chorus, band, cooking, swimming, and other sports.

Both the Middle and Upper Schools have a broad selection of student organizations in which to participate. Both schools have a student council, foreign language clubs, and excellent forensics teams. Students in grades 6 through 9 are eligible to join the Science Olympiad Team, which travels to Rider University for participation in the New Jersey State Science Olympiad.

The Upper School has an active chapter of the National Honor Society. Students can also participate in Mock Trial, math, chess, and academic bowl teams. Chorus and drama clubs offer students an opportunity to perform for friends, parents, and peers. Publications include *Horizons* (the School's award-winning yearbook), *The Torch,* and *RSVP (Ranney School Verse & Prose),* which showcases the talents of Ranney's young artists and authors.

Throughout the year, the Ranney School Fine Arts Department and Thespian Troupe present art exhibitions, music recitals, and two major drama productions. Traditional events include Spirit Day/Homecoming, International Week, Halloween Parade, Grandparents' Thanksgiving Feast, Parents' Day Tea, and Lower, Middle, and Upper School Carnivals (fund-raisers). Field trips, both interstate and intrastate, offer cultural exposure outside the Ranney campus for students in the middle and upper divisions.

DAILY LIFE

The typical school day consists of six 45-minute academic periods and one 60-minute period, with a 10-minute break between second and third periods, plus a lunch period. Assemblies are held throughout the year. Each week, grades 6–12 meet with their advisers for approximately 20 minutes during an adviser period. School begins at 8:25 a.m. and ends at 3:25 p.m. The cafeteria serves hot and cold lunches. Bus transportation is available to most students.

SUMMER PROGRAMS

Students can enroll for six weeks to take enhancement and/or credit courses in several academic subject areas. Most courses are taught by Ranney School faculty members. In addition, an eight-, six-, or four-week summer day camp program is available for boys and girls ages 3 through 13. Ranney-in-the-Summer is fully accredited by the American Camping Association.

COSTS AND FINANCIAL AID

Tuition for 2008–09 ranged from $10,550 to $23,210. Extras include books (Lower School: $150–$450; Middle School: $300–$600; Upper School: $550–$850) and transportation ($3800–$4100). Parents of students in grades pre-K through 12 are required to purchase a $1000 bond, which is redeemed when the child either graduates or leaves Ranney School.

Ranney School is committed to awarding financial aid to those students who demonstrate a financial need. Families who feel that a need for assistance exists are encouraged to apply. The Financial Aid Committee of the Board of Trustees bases financial aid decisions on the formula provided by the School and Student Service for Financial Aid (SSS) in Princeton, New Jersey. The Financial Aid Committee diligently reviews each application in order to distribute available funds equitably. All applications are held in strict confidence. Each student applying for aid must be in good standing in all aspects of student life. Parents must complete the SSS financial aid form annually and should send it to Princeton as early as possible. Inquiries should be directed to the Associate Head for Admissions and Marketing.

Parents can arrange to pay the tuition over a ten-month period through the Knight Tuition Payment Plan. An enrollment deposit must be paid directly to the School upon registration.

Applications are also available through the Business Office for a Knight Tuition Plan Achiever Loan, which has a ten-year repayment term.

ADMISSIONS INFORMATION

Standardized placement tests are administered on an individual or small-group basis. Transferring students should forward a completed application and appropriate school records to the Admission Office prior to the scheduled date of the placement exam. All candidates must complete an interview with appropriate members of the Admission Committee. Ranney School does not discriminate on the basis of sex, race, religion, ethnic origin, or disabilities in the administration of its education, hiring, and admission policies; financial aid program; and athletic or other School-administered programs.

APPLICATION TIMETABLE

Ranney School does not stipulate a formal application deadline, but it strongly recommends that parents contact the Admission Office during the fall to enroll for the next academic year. There is a $75 application fee.

ADMISSIONS CORRESPONDENCE

Heather Rudisi, Associate Head for Admissions and Marketing
Ranney School
235 Hope Road
Tinton Falls, New Jersey 07724
Phone: 732-542-4777 Ext. 107
Fax: 732-460-1078
E-mail: hrudisi@ranneyschool.com
Web site: http://www.ranneyschool.org

RIVERSIDE MILITARY ACADEMY

Gainesville, Georgia

RIVERSIDE MILITARY ACADEMY

Type: Boys' boarding and day college-preparatory academy within a military structure
Grades: 7–12
Enrollment: 350
Head of School: Col. Guy S. Gardner, USAF (Ret.), Superintendent

THE SCHOOL

At Riverside Military Academy—an all-boys boarding and day school serving grades 7–12—cadets benefit from a structured educational setting with dedicated teachers and role models, outstanding athletics, and leadership development opportunities. Riverside is focused on educating and equipping young men with the knowledge, skills, and values that establish a foundation for success in college and in life.

Riverside's 206-acre campus is located in Gainesville, Georgia, bordering Lake Lanier in the foothills of the Blue Ridge Mountains. The moderate climate features pleasant seasonal changes in weather and allows for year-round outdoor recreation. Gainesville is a suburban community, conveniently located 1 hour northeast of Atlanta's Hartsfield-Jackson International Airport. Gainesville offers easy connections to I-85, I-75, and Amtrak rail service.

Riverside Military Academy's distinctive educational approach challenges young men to set goals and reach their full potential—academically and personally. With its single-gender educational setting, the Academy focuses on the unique learning styles and developmental needs of boys. Small classes and active learning strategies are designed to engage boys' interest and help them develop the skills needed for success in college and in life. Riverside's safe, structured environment provides a positive atmosphere that values diversity of interests and cultural backgrounds and helps cadets become self-confident leaders and responsible citizens.

Riverside Military Academy teaches time-honored values and character traits—manners, pride, honor, scholarship, and personal integrity—that help cadets become young men of distinction in today's society. Riverside Military Academy works in close partnership with each student's family to achieve their educational goals. This partnership is enriched and strengthened by Riverside's weekend leave program, which allows boarding cadets in good standing to spend most weekends at home with their families and friends.

Riverside is jointly accredited by the Southern Association of Colleges and Schools and the Southern Association of Independent Schools. In addition, Riverside is a member of the National Association of Independent Schools, the Association of Military Colleges and Schools in the United States, the Association of Boarding Schools, and the Georgia Independent Schools Association, among others.

Cadets in grades 9–12 participate in Riverside's JROTC program, which is affiliated with the United States Army and has earned the designation of Honor Unit with Distinction for over fifty consecutive years. The JROTC program focuses on citizenship, leadership, fitness, and health; it does not require future military service.

Riverside Military Academy is a nonprofit, tax-exempt corporation governed by a self-perpetuating board of trustees.

An interactive CD-ROM about Riverside Military Academy is available upon request, and a video is also available on the Academy's Web site www.cadet.com.

ACADEMIC PROGRAMS

Riverside Military Academy's structured educational environment and active learning approach are designed to engage boys in learning and help motivate them to reach their academic potential. Riverside's college-preparatory academics combine small classes (the average class size is 10 cadets), one-on-one tutoring, a caring and experienced faculty, and the integration of study skills into the core curriculum. To provide regular and frequent feedback about each cadet's progress, weekly academic reports are available to parents via the Internet.

The academic year, which is divided into two semesters, begins in mid-August. The calendar includes one vacation week at Thanksgiving, two vacation weeks at Christmas, and one week in the spring. The Academy also offers a five-week summer academic program for review or new credit courses.

The curriculum includes classes in algebra, American history, American literature, art, biology, calculus, chemistry, computer science, current events, economics, English, government/civics, journalism, military science, music, physics, Spanish, speech, trigonometry, world history, world literature, and writing. Twenty-four credits are required for graduation, including 18 from the following areas: English, foreign language, mathematics, science, and social studies. Honors and Advanced Placement classes are offered in English, foreign language, history, mathematics, and science.

Riverside maintains supervised study hours each evening Sunday through Thursday. During this time, faculty members and peer tutors are available to assist cadets with homework.

FACULTY AND ADVISERS

There are more than 45 full-time teachers on the faculty, many of whom have advanced degrees. Faculty members are chosen on the basis of their academic credentials, personality, and ability to work successfully with boys in a wide variety of endeavors. Many teachers also serve as coaches or club sponsors.

There is a full-time nursing staff on duty around the clock in the campus infirmary, and a physician visits the infirmary several times a week to see patients. Cadets also have access to spiritual and mental health counseling through either the Academy's chaplain or counselor.

Each area of the dormitory is staffed with 2 adult supervisors who serve as teacher-adviser-counselor (TAC) officers. These gentlemen serve as role models and leaders in all areas of cadet life outside the classroom.

COLLEGE ADMISSION COUNSELING

Riverside Military Academy has a dedicated college counseling center through which cadets are able to research college options and receive support with the application and scholarship process. For the past nine years, Riverside has maintained a 100 percent college acceptance rate.

In addition to a wide array of state and private universities, graduates attend some of the country's premier colleges, including Auburn, Brown, the Citadel, Clemson, Florida State, Furman, Georgia, Georgia Tech, Johns Hopkins, North Carolina State, Penn State, Syracuse, Texas A&M, Tulane, the United States Military Academy, the United States Naval Academy, Vanderbilt, and others. Many Riverside graduates earn full scholarships to the college of their choice.

STUDENT BODY AND CONDUCT

The student body is organized into a Corps of Cadets, which represents about twenty states and fifteen countries each year. The Corps is composed of a cadet battalion staff and four individual companies, with cadet leaders responsible for the daily nonacademic activities of each company. The Corps receives adult supervision and guidance from the office of the commandant and the TAC officers in their companies. Every cadet has an opportunity to earn a leadership position. Each cadet is expected to be familiar with and to govern himself according to the *Code Book of Cadet Rules and Regulations.*

A system of merits and demerits offers strong incentives to cadets for good and courteous conduct and academic achievement.

ACADEMIC FACILITIES

In 2004, Riverside completed a $90-million construction program to renovate the campus and build state-of-the-art academic, residential, and athletic facilities. Today, the Riverside campus rivals that of many small colleges. Riverside's primary academic facility, Elkin Hall, features bright classrooms, extensive science laboratories, language labs, a computerized algebra lab, Riverside's exclusive Center for Student Success, and the College Counseling Center.

Riverside's Lanier Hall houses the computer science department and the military science department.

The newest addition to Riverside's academic facilities is the Sandy Beaver Center for Teaching and Learning, which houses a new library and reading room, art and photography classrooms, instrumental and choral rehearsal rooms, and a 790-seat theater. The center also includes an area for on-campus faculty and professional staff development.

BOARDING AND GENERAL FACILITIES

Cadets are housed 2 to a room in new dormitories that are part of a quadrangle complex that includes an infirmary and a post office. Each room is equipped with a computer with e-mail, Internet capability, and current software applications. The dormitories have television lounges and recreation rooms in each company area. TAC officers in each company area fulfill the role of dorm parents, providing positive leadership and mentoring to help cadets achieve academic and personal success.

In the cadet grill, cadets may purchase refreshments, play billiards or table tennis, watch television, or participate in other activities. A barbershop and a cadet store are also available. Riverside's stately dining hall accommodates the entire Corps for each meal and is the site of many special events.

ATHLETICS

Riverside's award-winning athletic program encourages all cadets to participate in activities that promote teamwork and physical fitness. Through physical education classes, team sports, or intramural activities, each cadet devotes an average of 2 hours each day to athletic activities. Riverside competes interscholastically in baseball, basketball, cross-country, football, golf, lacrosse, military drill, riflery, soccer, swimming, tennis, track, and wrestling.

Riverside's facilities include baseball, football, lacrosse, and soccer fields; an Olympic-size natatorium; tennis courts; indoor and outdoor basketball courts; a waterfront area on Lake Lanier; and a 45,000-square-foot field house with an indoor track. The football complex features NFL-size lockers, a film room, and a physical therapy/athletic training room. Curtis Hall, the Academy's new gymnasium complex, features a 6,000-square-foot weight-training room with customized equipment and an indoor rifle range.

EXTRACURRICULAR OPPORTUNITIES

Social events, off-campus trips, entertainment programs, dances, publications, movies, and honor and leadership groups are an integral part of Riverside's program to ensure that cadets can pursue interests that are essential to well-rounded development. Excellent musical, drill, and performing organizations, including a marching band, provide opportunities for training and participation. Riverside cadets produce two publications: the campus newspaper, *The Talon,* and the yearbook, *The Bayonet.* Some of the other club activities in which cadets may participate are Boy Scouts, Fellowship of Christian Athletes, the Horton Society, National Honor Society, Rangers/Raiders, Academic Bowl team, and chorus.

DAILY LIFE

The class day consists of eight periods that accommodate the typical assignment of five subjects, plus military science and advisement. After school, cadets participate in team sports or general athletics, followed by dinner. There is sufficient free time for relaxation, correspondence, independent study, and socializing. All cadets participate in a 2-hour supervised study period each Sunday through Thursday evening. The Corps of Cadets gathers weekly for character education assemblies and twice each week for military drill and ceremony exercises. Wednesday afternoons are traditionally reserved for clubs, cadet training, and other meetings.

WEEKEND LIFE

On most weekends, boarding cadets who are in good standing may leave the campus to visit their families and friends. Weekend leaves depend on parental permission and the accumulation of merits—a means of linking privilege to academic achievement and good behavior.

For those who remain on the campus during the weekend, Saturday and Sunday afternoons are times for relaxation, recreation, and activities on a sign-out basis. Social events and recreation are provided on campus. In addition, the campus activities director schedules regular off-campus excursions and high-adventure recreation.

Interdenominational chapel services are held on Sunday mornings. Alternatively, cadets may choose to attend one of many church services in the community. Periodically, the Corps conducts formal military-style parades. Families are encouraged to visit the campus for these special events.

SUMMER PROGRAMS

Riverside offers a five-week summer academic program called SOAR (Summer Opportunity and Academic Review). This program helps cadets earn academic credit toward high school graduation or review essential academic skills. The program is structured to give young men a holistic educational experience, including academics, character development, and athletics.

Riverside also offers several boarding and day camps each summer, including a High Adventure Camp, a Young Cadet Camp, and sport-specific athletics camps.

COSTS AND FINANCIAL AID

Riverside's tuition for the 2008–09 school year of $27,500 included room and board, books, athletic fees, haircuts, on-campus athletic events, and other incidental expenses. Day cadet tuition was $16,500. There is an additional uniform fee of $2350 for all new cadets. Cadets incur additional fees for laundry, technology, the administration of daily medications or vitamin supplements, and transportation to individual medical appointments or the airport.

Tuition discounts are available for early tuition payment or for families with 2 or more brothers enrolled.

ADMISSIONS INFORMATION

Riverside Military Academy seeks boys of high moral character and academic potential who are willing to set and attain worthy goals. Applicants are admitted on the basis of school transcripts and letters of recommendation. All prospective cadets are required to visit the Academy for an interview with admissions counselors. Application forms can be found on the Academy's Web site.

APPLICATION TIMETABLE

Riverside accepts admission inquiries year-round for enrollment during various academic terms.

ADMISSIONS CORRESPONDENCE

Director of Admissions
Riverside Military Academy
2001 Riverside Drive
Gainesville, Georgia 30501

Phone: 770-532-6251 Ext. 2119
800-GO-CADET (toll-free)
Web site: http://www.cadet.com

ROWLAND HALL–ST. MARK'S SCHOOL

Salt Lake City, Utah

Type: Coeducational day college-preparatory school
Grades: Pre-K–12; Preschool, 2-year-olds through kindergarten; Lower School, 1–5; Middle School, 6–8; Upper School, 9–12
Enrollment: School total: 987; Beginning School: 151; Lower School: 327; Middle School: 225; Upper School: 284
Head of School: Alan C. Sparrow

THE SCHOOL

Rowland Hall–St. Mark's School (RHSM) is Utah's oldest coeducational college-preparatory day school. In 1964, Rowland Hall (a girls' boarding and day school established in 1880) and St. Mark's (a boys' day school dating back to pre–Utah statehood) merged to become a coeducational, college-preparatory day and boarding school, housed on a block in the historic Avenues neighborhood of downtown Salt Lake City.

RHSM is committed to offering its students a broad liberal arts education with English, social studies, mathematics, science, and foreign languages at the core of its academic program. Equally important are the arts and athletics. RHSM encourages students to love learning, appreciate the arts, and strive for healthy lifestyles.

Rowland Hall–St. Mark's School is governed by a self-perpetuating Board of Trustees. The School's 2007–08 operating budget is $16.4 million. The endowment is approximately $3.3 million. Tuition alone does not cover the cost of each child's education. An active Annual Giving effort further supplements the budget. This effort was supported by 100 percent of the faculty, 74 percent of parents, and a large number of grandparents, alumni, and friends of the School.

RHSM is accredited by the Pacific Northwest Association of Independent Schools, the Northwest Association of Schools and Colleges, the National Association for the Education of Young Children, and the Utah Department of Education. The School is a member of the National Association of Independent Schools, the Pacific Northwest Association of Independent Schools, the National Association of Episcopal Schools, and the Utah High School Activities Association.

ACADEMIC PROGRAMS

Rowland Hall–St. Mark's builds its curriculum around a solid core of academic courses and an array of elective and specialty choices. Class size averages 14; the student-teacher ratio is 10:1.

Requirements for graduation are as follows: 4 years of English; 3 years of mathematics (2 years above algebra I); 3 years of social studies; 2 years of laboratory science (1 life science, 1 physical science); 2 years of one foreign language (Spanish, Latin, or French), four trimesters of fine arts; two trimesters of health; one trimester of computer science; one trimester of world religions; one trimester of ethics, one trimester of an activity (e.g., debate, yearbook); and 2⅔ years of physical education. The minimum total credits for graduation is 24.

Beginning in kindergarten, computers are regularly used in all core curriculum areas as well as art, music, chess, and other specialty and elective classes. A major financial commitment by the RHSM's parent body, beginning in 1995, resulted in the availability of state-of-the-art computer hardware and software for all RHSM students, faculty members, and administration. Computers are available for student use in computer centers, classrooms, and libraries. RHSM's high school is a laptop school, with all faculty and students working together on Apple laptop computers.

RHSM's Beginning School is a fertile learning ground and builds a strong foundation for the elementary years. Lower School students concentrate on an integrated curriculum in reading, mathematics, science, the arts, social studies, and world cultures. RHSM takes a balanced approach to literacy in its first- and second-grade reading and writing curriculum. Language arts curriculum used through the elementary years reinforces basic reading and writing skills, bolsters proficiency in written and oral communication, and continues to make the most of the campus's literature-rich environment. Specialty and elective classes enrich the core curriculum through music, drama, the visual arts, chess, computer science, science, environmental activities, and community service projects.

During the exciting years of early adolescence, Middle School students at Rowland Hall–St. Mark's are fortunate to have programs specifically designed to meet their changing needs and developing talents. With courses in language arts, social studies, mathematics, science, computers, and foreign languages, students benefit from small, lively classes with high academic expectations. Close support is offered through the advisory program.

The Upper School mixes a challenging academic schedule with sports, the arts, community service, and social activities. RHSM students achieve a solid academic grounding through a strong liberal arts curriculum with numerous electives and are well prepared for entrance into selective colleges and universities across the country. Approximately 90 percent of the high school student body enrolls in Advanced Placement classes, and, historically, all of the graduating seniors enter college.

Upper School subjects offered are algebra, American history, American literature, art history, band, biology, calculus, ceramics, chemistry, chorus, computer graphics, computer science, creative writing, dance, debate, economics, English, English literature, environmental science, ethics, European history, French, geology, geometry, health, history, journalism, Latin, math applications, music theory, photography, physical education, physics, political science, psychology, Spanish, statistics, studio art, sustainability, theater/drama, trigonometry, world history, and world religion. Advanced Placement preparation in eighteen test areas, honors sections, independent study, study at local colleges for college credit, and study abroad are all available.

Parent conferences are scheduled twice a year, and parents are encouraged to confer with teachers at other times as well.

FACULTY AND ADVISERS

Of the 113 faculty members, 89 are full-time, 51 hold master's degrees, and 6 hold doctorates. The Upper School total full-time faculty is 29. Alan C. Sparrow was appointed headmaster of Rowland Hall–St. Mark's in 1992. He received his Bachelor of Arts degree from Brown University and a Master of Arts and a Master of Science from the University of Rochester. In addition to teaching duties, faculty members serve as athletic coaches, and each teacher acts as an adviser to approximately 10 students. RHSM has made a significant financial commitment to support faculty members' continuing education and professional development.

COLLEGE ADMISSION COUNSELING

Seventy-nine students graduated in 2008 and all plan to attend college. Institutions enrolling more than 1 member of the class of 2008 include Chapman, Lewis & Clark, Occidental, St. Olaf, Seattle, USC, Utah, Western Washington, Westminster (Pennsylvania), Whitman, and the Universities of Denver, Puget Sound, and Utah. Five members of the class of 2008 were National Merit Scholarship Program winners.

The middle 50 percent SAT Critical Reading score range for the class of 2008 was 540–640. The middle 50 percent SAT Math score range for the class of 2008 was 530–670. The middle 50 percent SAT Writing score range for the class of 2008 was 540–640. The middle 50 percent ACT Composite score range for the class of 2008 was 23–28. The average GPA for the class of 2008 was 3.55.

STUDENT BODY AND CONDUCT

There are 284 students in RHSM's Upper School. Grade 9: 28 girls, 33 boys; Grade 10: 29 girls, 44 boys; Grade 11: 36 girls, 36 boys; Grade 12: 40 girls, 38 boys.

Every student who enters RHSM' Middle or Upper Schools is asked to declare acceptance of the responsibility to uphold ethical, honest standards in their academic life by signing a copy of the Academic Honor Code. When a student is suspected of violating the Academic Honor Code, a disciplinary committee is convened to propose a course of action. All RHSM students are expected to show respect for themselves, for other people, for the School environment, and for public property.

ACADEMIC FACILITIES

For more than 121 years, RHSM's historic, 2-acre downtown Salt Lake City Avenues campus housed the School's youngest students through grade 5. In December 2002, RHSM's Preschool and Lower School moved to a new 9-acre campus on the east side of Salt Lake City. The new Beginning School facility, the two-story Lower School/administrative building, the chapel, the library, the gymnasium and the dining hall/fine arts building—surrounded by courtyards and green fields, gardens and playgrounds—creates a residential, rather than an institutional, educational environment for the youngest students. The new gymnasium comfortably accommodates home basketball games and large nonathletic events. A regulation-sized basketball court, with additional room for bleachers to seat more than 400, plus boys' and girls' locker rooms, make the gym an ideal setting for Middle and Upper School practices and games. Lower School students use this facility for daily, year-round physical education classes.

The Middle School and Upper School are located on the Lincoln Street Campus, approximately ¼ mile from the McCarthey Campus on Guardsman Way.

Sixth through eighth graders enjoy the light and spacious environment of a new Middle School completed in 1994. It adjoins the Upper School facility, formerly a public junior high school, acquired and renovated in the 1980s. A state-of-the-art performance and assembly center, the Larimer Center for the Performing Arts, was built on the Lincoln Street campus in 1992. Science, math, and computer labs contain the latest available innovations in computer hardware and software. A library, gymnasium, playing fields, computer labs, and fine arts studios offer Middle and Upper School students many learning opportunities outside the classroom.

ATHLETICS

Physical education classes and activities throughout all grades stress the importance of lifetime fitness and taking responsibility for healthy life choices.

RHSM, a member of Region XIV of the Utah High School Activities Association, was designated Utah's 2A Sports School of the Year for 2007–08. The School offers the following interscholastic athletic activities at the High School level: fall—girls' soccer, tennis, and volleyball; boys' golf; and girls' and boys' cross-country running and swimming; winter—girls' and boys' basketball and swimming; spring—boys' baseball, soccer, and tennis; girls' golf and softball; and girls' and boys' track (middle distance running only). The School has an Athletic Director, an Assistant Athletic Director, 4 full-time PE instructors, 12 full-time coaches, 18 part-time coaches, and 2 part-time sport trainers.

Established in 1982, Rowmark Ski Academy is one of the country's top ski racing programs for young, elite Alpine ski racers. Approximately 25 high school-aged student-athletes from around the United States and other countries participate in rigorous ski training and RHSM course work for a diploma. Students from out of town live with host families. Todd Brickson is the director. For more information, students should visit the Academy's Web site at http://www.rowmark.org.

EXTRACURRICULAR OPPORTUNITIES

Students are encouraged to participate in the School's rich array of extracurricular activities each year. At the Lower School opportunities for enrichment in the visual arts, music, drama, cooking, science, community service, athletics, journalism, computer science, and chess are offered through the Extended Day Program. In the Middle School, students may choose to join the yearbook staff and participate in Dance Company, debate, mock trial, chorus, band, Mathcounts, the newspaper staff, literary magazine, and intramural and interscholastic athletic teams.

In the Upper School, student government is an important part of the extracurricular program. The Student Council serves as a channel for school communication, a voice in decision making, and a sponsor of social activities and community service. RHSM Upper School students may also become involved in National Honor Society; Rotary Interact Club; Pep Club; Dance Company; Amnesty International; the yearbook or newspaper staff; jazz band; debate team; the Spanish, French, or Latin Clubs; Community Service Council; or the literary magazine staff.

DAILY LIFE

Students in Beginning School full-day programs and Lower School grades begin their school day at 8:30 and classes end at 3:15. Middle School students begin their day at 8:15 and are released at 3:40. Several extracurricular activities are planned beginning at 7:30 a.m. before class and also after the school day ends.

Upper School period 1 starts at 8:15 and classes continue through 3:40. There are nine 42-minute periods. All competitive athletic teams' practices and games, some performing arts and fine arts classes, and other student activity classes occur in the last block of the day. Each morning, there is a 20-minute period for assemblies, student-teacher consultation time, or class meetings.

SUMMER PROGRAMS

RHSM established a summer program in 1983. Academic courses (remediation, enrichment, advancement), sports, and computer instruction programs are offered and held on the Lincoln Street campus for RHSM Upper School students and high school students from other schools. Approximately 40 students enroll. An additional fee is charged for Summer School programs. RHSM also conducts a summer day camp, SummerWorks, for children of preschool and elementary school ages.

COSTS AND FINANCIAL AID

The cost of tuition for full-day programs for the 2008–09 school year range from $11,630 (full-day, 4–Pre-K) to $15,775 (grade 12). A bundled billing fee of approximately $700 per year covers laboratory and other expenses for Middle and Upper School students. School lunch program and transportation are available for an additional fee.

Rowland Hall–St. Mark's School offers financial aid to applicants whose families demonstrate financial need in grades 1 through 12. The financial aid application deadline is March 1. Approximately 18 percent of the student body currently receives some degree of financial aid. Financial aid decisions are made in the spring for the following year. For the 2007–08 school year, grants totaling more than $1.3 million were made to students in amounts ranging from $1000 to $15,775.

ADMISSIONS INFORMATION

Rowland Hall–St. Mark's School does not discriminate on the basis of race, religion, color, national or ethnic origin, sexual orientation, or gender in the administration of any of its programs. The admissions committee seeks motivated students who will be challenged by academic excellence and will thrive in an atmosphere of respect and concern for the individual.

Applicants are required to submit an application, applicant questionnaire (grades 6 through 12), copies of school records, a current transcript or report card, and two teacher recommendations. It is also recommended that the applicant visit the School and complete a personal interview. Standardized tests are administered to applicants for grades 6 through 12. Individual assessments are required for those children applying to 2–Pre-K to fifth grade. Previous testing information may also be required. If the child is of preschool age and has not attended school, recommendations are required from persons who know the applicant well and who have seen them in social situations.

APPLICATION TIMETABLE

Inquiries are welcomed year-round. Tours and interviews are given Monday through Friday by appointment. Two admission open house events are offered in the fall and in January. Admissions applications are accepted on a rolling basis for the current year when space is available. The application deadline is March 1 for fall admission for the following year. A $50 nonrefundable fee is due with the application.

ADMISSIONS CORRESPONDENCE

Beginning School and Lower School (2–Pre-K–grade 5)
Kathy Gundersen, Director of Admissions
Rowland Hall–St. Mark's School
720 Guardsman Way
Salt Lake City, Utah 84108
Phone: 801-355-7485
Fax: 801-363-5521
E-mail: kathygundersen@rhsm.org

Middle School and Upper School (grade 6–12)
Karen Hyde, Director of Admissions
Rowland Hall–St. Mark's School
843 South Lincoln Street
Salt Lake City, Utah 84102
Phone: 801-355-7494
Fax: 801-355-0474
E-mail: karenhyde@rhsm.org
Web site: http://www.rhsm.org

RYE COUNTRY DAY SCHOOL

Rye, New York

Type: Coeducational day college-preparatory school
Grades: P–12: Lower School, Prekindergarten–4; Middle School, 5–8; Upper School, 9–12
Enrollment: School total: 873; Upper School: 385
Head of School: Scott A. Nelson, Headmaster

THE SCHOOL

Founded in 1869, Rye Country Day School (RCDS) is entering its 139th year. Reflecting and reaffirming the School's purposes, the mission statement states, "Rye Country Day School is a coeducational, college-preparatory school dedicated to providing students from Pre-Kindergarten through Grade Twelve with an excellent education using both traditional and innovative approaches. In a nurturing and supportive environment, we offer a challenging program that stimulates individuals to achieve their maximum potential through academic, athletic, creative, and social endeavors. We value diversity, expect moral responsibility, and promote strength of character within a respectful school community. Our goal is to foster a lifelong passion for knowledge, understanding, and service."

The 26-acre campus is located in Rye at the junction of routes I-95 and I-287, one block from the train station. The School's location, 25 miles from Manhattan, provides easy access to both New York City and to a suburban setting with ample playing fields and open spaces. Through frequent field trips, internships, and community service projects, the School takes considerable advantage of the cultural opportunities in the New York metropolitan area.

A nonprofit, nonsectarian institution, Rye Country Day is governed by a 23-member Board of Trustees that includes parents and alumni. The annual operating budget is $23 million, and the physical plant assets have a book value in excess of $48 million. Annual gifts from parents, alumni, and friends amount to more than $2.9 million. The endowment of the School is valued at more than $22 million.

Rye Country Day School is accredited by the Middle States Association of Colleges and Schools and the New York State Association of Independent Schools and is chartered and registered by the New York State Board of Regents. It is a member of the National Association of Independent Schools, the New York State Association of Independent Schools, the Educational Records Bureau, the College Board, and the National Association for College Admission Counseling.

ACADEMIC PROGRAMS

Leading to the college-preparatory program of the Upper School, the program in the Middle School (grades 5–8) emphasizes the development of skills and the acquisition of information needed for success at the secondary school level by exposing students to a wide range of opportunities. The academic program is fully departmentalized. Spanish or French is offered to all students in grades 2–5. Starting in grade 6 students may choose Latin or Mandarin Chinese or continue with Spanish or French. The math, foreign language, and writing programs lead directly into the Upper School curriculum. Programs in art, music (vocal and instrumental), computer use, and dramatics are offered in all grades. Students in kindergarten through grade 6 are scheduled for sports for 45 to 75 minutes daily, and a full interscholastic sports program is available to both boys and girls in grades 7 and 8 and in the Upper School.

Sixteen courses are required for Upper School graduation, including 4 years of English, 3 years of mathematics, 3 years of one foreign language, 2 years of science, and 2 years of history. Students entering the School by grade 9 must complete ½ unit in art and music survey, and ½ unit in the arts. Seniors must successfully complete an off-campus June-term community service program. In addition, seniors must satisfactorily complete 1 unit in the senior humanities seminar. Students are expected to carry five academic courses per year.

Full-year courses and semester electives in English include English 9, 10, and 11; major American writers; English literature; and creative writing. Required mathematics courses are algebra I, algebra II and trigonometry, and geometry. Regular course work extends through calculus BC, and tutorials are available for more advanced students. Yearlong courses in science are environmental science, biology, chemistry, and physics. Science courses are laboratory based. The computer department offers beginning and advanced programming, software applications courses, desktop publishing, and independent study opportunities.

The modern language department offers five years of Mandarin Chinese, French, and Spanish, and the classics department teaches five years of Latin. History courses include world civilizations, U.S. history, government, and modern European history. Semester electives in the humanities include philosophy, psychology, government, economics, and the twentieth century.

In the arts, full-year courses in studio art, art history, and music theory are available. Participation in the Concert Choir and Wind Ensemble earns students full academic credit. Semester courses in drawing, printmaking, sculpture, graphic design, ceramics, and photography are available. The drama department offers electives in technique, history, oral presentation, and technical theater.

Advanced Placement courses leading to the AP examinations are offered in biology, psychology, environmental science, chemistry, physics, statistics, calculus, English, government, U.S. and modern European history, French, Spanish, Latin, music theory, art, and computer science. Honors sections are scheduled in tenth- and eleventh-grade English, math, physics, biology, and chemistry and in foreign languages at all levels. Independent study is available in grades 11 and 12 in all disciplines.

The student-teacher ratio is 8:1, and the average class size in the Upper School is 12. Extra help is provided for students as needed.

The year is divided into two semesters. Examinations are given in March. Grades are scaled from A to F and are given four times a year. Written comments accompany grades at the end of each quarter.

Academic classes travel to New York City and other areas to supplement classroom work. Although not a graduation requirement, all students are involved in community service programs. Semester class projects as well as individual experiences involve work with local charities and schools, YMCA, Habitat for Humanity, Midnight Run, United Cerebral Palsy, Big Brother-Big Sister, Doctors Without Borders, and AmeriCares.

FACULTY AND ADVISERS

The Upper School faculty consists of 65 full-time teachers—35 men and 30 women, the large majority of whom hold at least one advanced degree. The average length of service is eight years, and annual faculty turnover averages fewer than 6 teachers.

Scott A. Nelson became Headmaster in 1993. He holds a B.A. from Brown University and an M.A. from Fordham University. Prior to his appointment at Rye, he served as Upper School Director both at the Marlborough School in Los Angeles and at the Hackley School in Tarrytown, New York. Mr. Nelson and his family reside on campus.

Nearly all faculty members in the Middle and Upper Schools serve as advisers for 5 to 12 students each. In addition to helping students select courses, faculty advisers monitor the students' progress in all areas of school life and provide ongoing support. The advisers also meet with students' parents at various times throughout the year.

Rye Country Day seeks faculty members who are effective teachers in their field and who, by virtue of their sincere interest in the students' overall well-being, will further the broad goals of the School's philosophy. The School supports the continuing education of its faculty through grants and summer sabbaticals totaling more than $300,000 a year.

COLLEGE ADMISSION COUNSELING

The college selection process is supervised by a full-time Director of College Counseling and an Associate Director. Advising is done in groups and on an individual basis, with the staff meeting with both students and their families. More than 150 college representatives visit the campus each year.

The 94 graduates of the class of 2008 enrolled in fifty-nine colleges and universities, including Amherst, Brown, Columbia, Cornell, Dartmouth, Duke, Georgetown, Harvard, Johns Hopkins, Middlebury, Northwestern, Notre Dame, Pennsylvania, Vanderbilt, Wake Forest, Wesleyan, Williams, and Yale.

STUDENT BODY AND CONDUCT

The Upper School enrollment for 2008–09 totaled 385: 197 boys and 188 girls. There were 98 students in grade 9, 96 in grade 10, 98 in grade 11, and 93 in grade 12. Members of minority groups represented 23 percent of the student body in grades 5–12. Students came from more than forty different school districts in Westchester and Fairfield Counties as well as New York City. Students holding citizenship in fourteen countries are enrolled.

While School regulations are few, the School consciously and directly emphasizes a cooperative, responsible, and healthy community life. The Student Council plays a major role in administering School organizations and activities. Minor disciplinary problems are handled by the division Principal or Grade Level Dean; more serious matters in the Upper School may be brought before the Disciplinary Committee. There is student representation on the Academic Affairs and other major committees.

ACADEMIC FACILITIES

The main academic facility is the Mary Struthers Pinkham Building. Classes are also held in the Edward B. Dunn Performing Arts Center and in the Main Building. Specific facilities include five science labs, a two-room Upper School computer center, seven music rehearsal and practice rooms, a two-story art studio, a darkroom, and a dance studio.

Opened in 1984, the Klingenstein Library contains more than 30,000 volumes, with circulation and collection management fully automated. Additional resources include significant periodical and reference materials available via direct online services and the Internet, CD-ROM, a substantial videotape collection, and other audiovisual and microfiche materials.

Significant improvements have been made to the interior campus areas over the last several years. The Edward B. Dunn Performing Arts Center, a $5-million facility containing a 400-seat theater-auditorium and classroom spaces for vocal music, instrumental music, and general use, was opened in 1990. A separate dance facility is adjacent. The School continues a consistent program of technological progress. Laptop computers are required of all students in grades 7 to 12 and are used extensively throughout the curriculum. Access to the School network and the Internet is via a wireless network. In total, there are approximately 600 networked computers on campus, which play a continually increasing role in curricular and general campus life.

ATHLETICS

Rye's athletics program centers on interscholastic competition, with teams in most sports on both varsity and junior varsity levels. Representative varsity sports are baseball, basketball, cross-country, fencing, field hockey, football, golf, ice hockey, lacrosse, sailing, soccer, softball, squash, tennis, and wrestling. Approximately 70 percent of the students participate in team sports. The physical education department offers classes in aerobic dancing, CPR, ice skating, kickboxing, squash, tennis, and weight training. Athletics facilities include ample field space, two gymnasiums, and the Gerald N. LaGrange Fieldhouse (with an indoor ice rink/tennis courts, and locker facilities). In 2000, the Scott A. Nelson Athletic Center opened adjacent to the field house, housing two basketball courts, four squash courts, fitness facilities, and locker rooms. In the fall 2007, RCDS completed the construction of a state-of-the-art artificial turf field to be used by the entire school community.

EXTRACURRICULAR OPPORTUNITIES

More than thirty-five extracurricular activities are available. Students can choose vocal music (Concert Choir, Madrigal Singers, and solfeggio classes) and instrumental music (Wind Ensemble, Concert Band, and Jazz Band). Many of these offerings have curricular status. The performance groups give local concerts and occasionally travel to perform at schools and universities here and abroad. In addition, 10 professional instructors offer private instrumental and voice lessons during and after the school day. The drama department presents major productions three times a year. Recent productions have included *The Laramie Project, South Pacific, Dark of the Moon, The Mystery of Edwin Drood, Macbeth, The Pajama Game, The Arabian Nights,* and *Anything Goes.*

Student publications include a yearbook, newspaper, literary magazine, and public affairs journal, each of which is composed using student publications desktop publishing facilities. The School's Web site (http://www.ryecountryday.org) is an ever-changing location for student- and staff-provided information on and perspectives of the School. Students participate in Model Congress programs on campus and at other schools and colleges. The School has a dynamic community service program that embodies the RCDS motto: "Not for self, but for service." Students also participate in many other activities and School organizations, including foreign language, mock trial, debate, theater, sports, and computer clubs.

DAILY LIFE

Beginning each day at 8:05, the Upper School utilizes a six-day schedule cycle. Most courses meet five of the six days, with one or two longer, 70-minute periods per cycle. The day includes an activity/meeting period and two lunch periods as well as seven class periods. Class periods end at 2:50, and team sport practices and games begin at 3:30. Breakfast and lunch may be purchased in the school dining room; seniors may have lunch off campus. Study halls are required for grade 9.

SUMMER PROGRAMS

The Rye Country Day Summer School enrolls approximately 200 students—grades 6 to post-graduate—in remedial, enrichment, and advanced-standing courses. New York State Regents exams are given in appropriate subjects. The program is six weeks long and runs on a five-period schedule from 8 a.m. to noon, Monday through Friday. Tuition averages $1200 per course. A brochure is available after April 1 from the Director of the Summer School or on the School's Web site.

In addition to the Summer School, Rye conducts a summer program, ACTION, for students in grades 6–8 from nearby Westchester communities. Fifty students from minority groups enroll in a four-week program that emphasizes academic enrichment in the areas of writing, math, and computer use.

COSTS AND FINANCIAL AID

Tuition for grade 9 for 2008–09 was $28,900. Additional charges are made for textbooks, lunches, sports, field trips, and private music lessons, as appropriate.

Tuition aid is available on a need basis. For 2008–09, 122 students received a total of more than $3.2 million in aid. All aid applications are processed through the School and Student Service for Financial Aid.

ADMISSIONS INFORMATION

Students are accepted in all grades. In 2008–09, 23 new students enrolled in the ninth grade, 8 in the tenth grade, 4 in the eleventh grade, and 1 in the twelfth grade. Academic readiness is a prerequisite; a diversity of skills and interests, as well as general academic aptitude, is eagerly sought. The School seeks and enrolls students of all backgrounds; a diverse student body is an important part of the School's educational environment.

Required in the admissions process are the results of the Educational Records Bureau's ISEE or the Secondary School Admission Test (SSAT); the student's school record; and school and faculty recommendations. A visit to the campus and an interview are also required.

APPLICATION TIMETABLE

Inquiries are welcome throughout the year. Interviews and tours of the campus begin in late September. To be considered in initial admissions decisions, applicants must fully complete the Application by December 15. All other parts of the Application Folder (transcripts, testing, recommendation forms, etc.) are due by January 15. Candidates whose Application Folders are complete by that date are notified by approximately February 15. Applications received after February 1 are evaluated on a rolling basis.

ADMISSIONS CORRESPONDENCE

Matthew J. M. Suzuki, Director of Admissions
Rye Country Day School
Cedar Street
Rye, New York 10580-2034
Phone: 914-925-4513
Fax: 914-921-2147
E-mail: matt_suzuki@ryecountryday.org
Web site: http://www.ryecountryday.org

ST. ANDREW'S SCHOOL

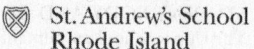

St. Andrew's School
Rhode Island

Barrington, Rhode Island

Type: Coeducational boarding and day college-preparatory school
Grades: 3–12: Lower School, 3–5; Middle School, 6–8; Upper School and Boarding, 9–12
Enrollment: School total: 223; Upper School: 165
Head of School: John D. Martin

THE SCHOOL

St. Andrew's School is a coeducational boarding and day school for students in grades 3–12, with the boarding program starting in the ninth grade. The School is located on a 100-acre campus 1 mile from the center of Barrington (population 16,000), a suburban community 10 miles southeast of Providence on Narragansett Bay. The campus contains open space and woodlands. Its proximity to Providence and Newport, as well as Boston, offers a wide variety of cultural opportunities for students.

St. Andrew's School was founded in 1893 by Rev. William Merrick Chapin as a school for homeless boys. From these simple beginnings through its years as a working farm school to its present role as a coeducational boarding and day college preparatory school, St. Andrew's steadfastly maintains the same sense of purpose and concern for the individual. The curriculum is designed primarily to prepare students for college, with emphasis on helping them to develop stronger academic skills, study habits, and self-esteem.

St. Andrew's was named an "Exemplary School" by the nationally recognized Schools Attuned program. Every St. Andrew's teacher is trained to teach using a multisensory approach for the different ways students may learn. St. Andrew's students find that when they get to college, they are well prepared to handle the course work because they have a true understanding of how they learn and an awareness of the tools they need to achieve their best.

St. Andrew's School is a nonsectarian, nonprofit corporation. A Board of Trustees governs the School; this 21-member board meets five times a year. The School's physical plant is valued at approximately $23 million. The School's endowment is currently valued at more than $19 million.

St. Andrew's is accredited by the New England Association of Schools and Colleges. It is a member of the National Association of Independent Schools, the Association of Independent Schools in New England, and the Independent Schools Association of Rhode Island.

ACADEMIC PROGRAMS

St. Andrew's School believes that every student can find success in the classroom. With a 5:1 student-teacher ratio, the average class size at St. Andrew's is 10 students. Small classes, along with twice-daily adviser meetings, help to ensure that no student is overlooked. The homelike community, nurturing environment, and hands-on approach to learning and teaching help maintain close student-teacher relationships.

To graduate from the Upper School, a student must complete 26 credits: 24 academic credits and 2 credits in physical education. Students are expected to take course work in English, math, science, social studies, and physical education each year. Preparation in a foreign language is also highly recommended. Students may only have one study hall in their schedule. Seniors must pass the equivalent of five full-credit courses in order to graduate. Specific minimum requirements for Upper School students are 4 credits in English, 3 credits in social studies (including 1 in U.S. history), 3 credits in mathematics, 3 credits in science (including 2 in a lab science), 2 credits in physical education, 1 credit in art, and 10 elective credits. An English as a Second Language (ESL) Program is provided for international students. The School's computer network, which is available to all students, provides Internet access from all classrooms, dorm rooms, and offices.

The School's Resource Program (certified by the state of Rhode Island) for students with mild language-based learning disabilities is taught by certified special education teachers. All students enrolled in the Resource Program take a mainstreamed college-preparatory course of study. An Individual Education Plan (IEP) identifies which language remediation skills need to be addressed. Resource teachers work collaboratively with regular classroom teachers to develop and integrate school study skills (time management, test-taking, outlining, etc.) into the existing Upper School curriculum. Middle School students receive their remediation skills during their regular language arts classes. An IEP identifies which language remediation skills need to be addressed in the Resource class. Additional programs include Focus (extra support and monitoring for attention difficulties), speech/language therapy, and the Wilson Reading System.

The school year runs on a semester basis. Students are evaluated frequently by their teachers so that each student's progress is monitored closely throughout the year. Each advisee meets twice a day with his or her adviser to discuss issues pertaining to the student's academic progress and his or her involvement in the School community. Advisers communicate with families every three weeks by phone or e-mail.

FACULTY AND ADVISERS

The full-time faculty numbers 48, with 21 men and 27 women. Twenty-three reside on campus, 11 with their families. All full-time faculty members serve as advisers. John D. Martin was appointed Head of School on July 1, 1996, and has an extensive background in independent schools, including teaching and administrative positions at Sewickley Academy, Peddie School, and Tabor Academy. He holds a Master of Divinity degree from Yale University, a Master of Education degree from American International College, and a Bachelor of Arts degree from Tufts University.

COLLEGE ADMISSION COUNSELING

More than 97 percent of St. Andrew's graduates enter four-year colleges, two-year colleges, or technical schools upon graduation each year. Goal setting, short- and long-term planning, and informal discussions about careers and postsecondary plans are ongoing between students and advisers from the moment a student enters the Upper School. Formal college counseling begins in the tenth grade. The college counselor works with students and their parents to assist in determining the best steps for each student. The advisers and other faculty members assist the college counselor in assessing each student's options. PSATs are given in the fall of sophomore year and again at the start of junior year. SATs should be taken during the junior and senior years. College representatives visit the campus throughout the year to meet with interested students.

St. Andrew's graduates have attended the following colleges and universities in the last three years: Boston College, Bryant, Emmanuel, Emory, George Washington, Iona, Ithaca, New England College, Parsons School of Design, Providence, Purdue, Randolph-Macon, Rhode Island College, Roger Williams, Savannah College of Art and Design, Simmons, Syracuse, and the Universities of Illinois, Louisville, Maine, Massachusetts, Minnesota, Rhode Island, Vermont, and Wisconsin.

STUDENT BODY AND CONDUCT

The School enrolls both boarding and day students. Approximately one third of the Upper School population boards. Approximately 25 percent of the School's population is enrolled in the Lower and Middle Schools, and less than 40 percent of the School's population participates in the Resource/Focus Programs.

Over the years, St. Andrew's School has attracted boarding students from all corners of the United States and other countries, including China, Germany, India, Israel, Jamaica, Japan, South Korea, and Taiwan.

Each student receives a copy of the *Parent and Student Handbook,* which defines expectations for students within the community. Difficulties, if they arise, are handled according to degree; minor issues are handled by teachers and dorm parents, while major offenses are handled by the Director of Student Life in conjunction with a joint student-faculty disciplinary committee. Faculty advisers play a major role in working with students to help them understand the expectations of them as members of the community.

ACADEMIC FACILITIES

Stone Academic Center (1988) houses fifteen classrooms, a newly renovated resource wing with five classrooms for instruction, a computer lab, academic offices, and a faculty workroom. It is also the site of a new library, which features study carrels, meeting rooms, and computer workstations. Hardy Hall (1898) was renovated in 2008 and houses the Middle School (6–8) and new Lower School (3–5). The building's small classrooms are designed for interactive learning in groups of 5 to 12 students. The George M. Sage Gymnasium (2001) and the Karl P. Jones Gymnasium (1965) each house a full-size gymnasium and locker room facilities. The Annie Lee Steele Adams Memorial Student Service Center (1997) houses the Health Center, classrooms, and additional office space. The David A. Brown '52 Science Center houses four science labs, two regular classrooms, and the office of the College Placement Counselor. The Norman E. and Dorothy R. McCulloch Center for the Arts (2004) houses a 287-seat theater, two visual art classrooms, a ceramics lab, a music room with practice rooms, a black-box/theater classroom, a computer graphics lab, and storage and scene construction facilities for drama productions.

BOARDING AND GENERAL FACILITIES

Upper School girls live in Cady House (1969). Upper School boys live in Bill's House (1970), Perry Hall (1927), and Coleman House (circa 1795). Girls are all assigned to single rooms, while boys are assigned to single or double rooms. Each dormitory is supervised by faculty dorm parents, who are aided by the Director of Student Life. Each dorm has a common room, laundry facilities, access to a kitchen area, and ample storage space. Gardiner Hall (1926) houses the Herbert W. Spink Dining Room and the Headmaster's dining room. McVickar Hall (1913) contains the Admissions office, the Headmaster's office, the Development and Communications department, and reception area. Peck Hall (circa 1895) contains the Business office. Clark Hall (1899), houses the Student Center, offering students variety, entertainment, and relaxation. The second floor provides faculty housing.

Coleman House and the Rectory, the Headmaster's house, are late-eighteenth-century buildings that were acquired by the School from two local estates. Both buildings are said to have been stops for travelers on the Underground Railroad. The Rectory has a "hidden" back staircase and room.

ATHLETICS

Upper School students participate in athletics at the completion of each class day. St. Andrew's fields varsity teams in boys' and girls' basketball, cross-country, golf, lacrosse, soccer, and tennis. Intramural sports programs are also offered and include fitness training, weight training, ultimate Frisbee, biking, lawn games, and Project Adventure Ropes Course.

EXTRACURRICULAR OPPORTUNITIES

Because of the School's proximity to Providence, Newport, and Boston, myriad cultural and recreational activities are available. Students may take advantage of museums, movies, concerts, plays, rock climbing, skating, bowling, skiing, and professional and collegiate sporting events. Among the on-campus extracurricular activities are theater, photography, debate club, and yearbook. The St. Andrew's Parent Association (SAPA) organizes a wide variety of social activities for students throughout the year, from dances to laser tag to paintball to barbecues on the Quad.

DAILY LIFE

Boarders generally rise at about 7 each morning. Boarding students are responsible for making their beds, cleaning their rooms, and performing other assorted dorm chores. Breakfast is served at 7:30 and is a favorite gathering spot for day and boarding students alike. Students assemble for Morning Meeting at 8 and then meet in their advising groups. Classes begin at 8:30. Adviser meetings are held again at the end of the day. Activities and athletics begin at 3:00 and run until approximately 4:00. Students may leave the campus between athletics and dinner if they are in good standing in the community. Dinner is at 5:30, and evening study hall is from 7:30 to 9:30. All study halls are proctored by faculty members, who are able to provide extra academic assistance if needed. During study hall, the library is open for those students who need to conduct research.

The Student Center is open on weekdays from 11 a.m. to 1 p.m.. On weekends, the center is open all day Saturday and at other times depending on activities both on and off campus.

WEEKEND LIFE

Weekend activities are planned by the Director of Student Life, with student and faculty input. Students choose from an array of on- and off-campus activities, including sporting events, concerts, movies, plays, hayrides, open gymnasium, bicycle riding, skiing, attending performances by special guests on campus, dances, skating, festivals and fairs, hiking, and shopping. Visits to nearby cities and other places of interest are also offered. Boarders may leave for the weekend, with parental permission, either to go home or to visit a day student's family. Each weekend, about 75 percent of the boarding community remains on campus.

COSTS AND FINANCIAL AID

Tuition for a boarder in 2008–09 is $39,500; for a day student, it is $25,800. Additional costs for the Resource and Focus Programs are $9900. The yearly book fee is about $400. Parents of a boarding student should plan to set up an account in the on-campus bank for weekly allowance needs. The amount varies from family to family and student to student.

Approximately 40 percent of the student body received financial aid for the 2008–09 academic year, with more than $1 million offered in grants and loans. Financial aid is based solely on need. St. Andrew's School is affiliated with the School and Student Service for Financial Aid in Princeton, New Jersey, and works in conjunction with this organization to provide an objective and fair basis for awarding financial aid. All required information is due to the School by February 13. Final awards are determined by the School's Financial Aid Committee.

ADMISSIONS INFORMATION

In order to assess the match between student and school and to plan an appropriate academic program, the School requires a tour, a personal interview, an application with a fee of $50 ($100 for international students), a school transcript covering the last three years, three teacher recommendations, and standardized test scores. For applicants to the Resource Program, an educational evaluation and a psychological evaluation (both within eighteen months of potential enrollment) and a current Individualized Education Plan (if applicable) are required. A student applying to the Focus Program must establish a history of attention difficulties and supply the School with a medical diagnosis from a physician and appropriate testing results. International students must also submit results from an SLEP or TOEFL evaluation.

APPLICATION TIMETABLE

Parents and prospective students are encouraged to contact the Admissions Office for information during the fall semester. Because the School considers a visit to the campus and a personal interview with the candidate to be such a critical part of the admissions process, it asks that all families call for an appointment. It is best to visit the School during the fall if considering enrollment for the following September, although the School welcomes campus visitors throughout the year.

St. Andrew's School does not discriminate on the basis of race, creed, gender, or handicap in the administration of policies, practices, and procedures.

Applications are due by January 30. Students are notified of acceptance by March 10, and the School holds a place for accepted students until April 10. Depending on available space, rolling admission may be offered thereafter. A nonrefundable deposit of $1000 is due when students agree to attend and is credited toward tuition.

ADMISSIONS CORRESPONDENCE

R. Scott Telford
Director of Admissions
St. Andrew's School
63 Federal Road
Barrington, Rhode Island 02806

Phone: 401-246-1230
Fax: 401-246-0510
E-mail: inquiry@standrews-ri.org
Web site: http://www.standrews-ri.org

ST. ANNE'S–BELFIELD SCHOOL

Charlottesville, Virginia

Type: Coeducational five- and seven-day boarding and day college-preparatory school
Grades: P–12: Lower School, Preschool–4; Middle School, 5–8; Upper School, 9–12
Enrollment: School total: 841; Upper School: 333
Head of School: David S. Lourie, Head of School

THE SCHOOL

St. Anne's–Belfield School was formed in 1970 by the merger of St. Anne's School, a girls' boarding school founded in 1910, with the Belfield School, a coeducational elementary school established in 1955. The School is located near the University of Virginia on two campuses that total almost 50 acres. All students attend a weekly nonsectarian chapel service. The School offers a day program for boys and girls in preschool through grade 12 and five- and seven-day boarding programs for boys and girls in grades 9–12.

St. Anne's–Belfield is incorporated not-for-profit under a self-perpetuating Board of Trustees. Assets include a $16.8-million plant and an endowment of more than $4.3 million. Annual Giving for 2007–08 was $1,051,568.

St. Anne's–Belfield is accredited by the Virginia Association of Independent Schools. Its memberships include the Cum Laude Society, the Council for Advancement and Support of Education, the National Association of Independent Schools, and the National Association of Episcopal Schools.

ACADEMIC PROGRAMS

In agreement with the School's philosophy that both a breadth and depth of knowledge are essential for true growth, all students at St. Anne's–Belfield are encouraged to attain excellence in a variety of subjects. The requirements for graduation are 8 semesters of English, 6 of mathematics, 6 of history and government, 6 of laboratory science, 6 of one foreign language, 2 of religion, 2 of fine arts, 60 hours of community service, and the successful completion of the freshman seminar.

Freshmen, sophomores, juniors, and seniors are required to take five academic courses each semester. A significant number of students elect to carry six academic courses. The School offers honors courses in physics and chemistry and Advanced Placement (AP) courses in English, calculus, European and U.S. history, physics, chemistry, biology, Latin, French language, French literature, environmental science, Spanish language, and statistics.

The School's calendar is arranged on a trimester system. Interim reports are given each trimester, and more frequent comments are provided when deemed advisable. All teachers are available for extra help five mornings a week during office hours, and every student in grades 7–12 has an adviser. The average class size is 13 students; the overall student-faculty ratio is 8:1.

St. Anne's–Belfield offers a three-day SAT preparation course to all juniors. This course reviews basic math and English skills and acquaints students with the principles of good test taking.

All students in grades 9–12 are involved in the School's Community Service Program, which is designed to develop in students an awareness of their responsibilities to the School and the community and to broaden their education by encouraging involvement with those in need.

The School offers an ESL program to students in grades 9–10. These students, many of whom participate in a seven-day boarding program, take ESL courses that are designed to prepare them to be mainstreamed into the college-preparatory program by the eleventh grade. The School employs an ESL director and a teaching staff who oversee their academic progress as well as a dorm counselor who plans and supervises their weekend activities. There is no additional fee for ESL students. At present, thirteen countries are represented in the ESL program.

FACULTY AND ADVISERS

The St. Anne's–Belfield faculty and administration consists of 105 full- and part-time members. In the Upper School, 80 percent of the faculty members hold graduate degrees. In selecting its faculty, the School seeks people with scholarly commitment and enthusiasm who are willing to view themselves as counselors as well as teachers. Upper School faculty members serve as advisers to groups of 10 to 12 students. The adviser is responsible for guiding a student's overall academic and social progress and serves as an important link between parents and the School.

Mr. David S. Lourie, recently appointed Head of School, earned his undergraduate degree at Yale University and his graduate degree at Columbia University. Mr. Lourie was Head of School at Midland School in Los Olivos, California. He was formerly Head Teacher at Terrace Community School and Director of Admissions and teacher at Tampa Preparatory School, both in Tampa, Florida.

COLLEGE ADMISSION COUNSELING

The principal counselor in the college selection process is the Director of College Counseling, who, along with her assistants, works personally with the students, parents, and college admissions officers. The Director of College Counseling helps students in the ninth through twelfth grades in selecting a suitable yet rigorous college-preparatory curriculum and arranges for a variety of SAT preparation programs. The median combined SAT score for the class of 2008 was 1790. Ninety-two percent of students taking AP exams scored 3 or higher.

Recent graduates of St. Anne's–Belfield are currently attending a variety of colleges and universities, including Brown, Columbia, Dartmouth, Duke, Harvard, Johns Hopkins, Rhode Island School of Design, Vanderbilt, Wake Forest, Washington and Lee, William and Mary, Williams, Yale, and the Universities of Colorado, North Carolina, and Virginia.

STUDENT BODY AND CONDUCT

Central to the School's philosophy of promoting personal integrity is the Honor Code. The code states simply: A student is not to lie, cheat, or steal. It is the intention of the Honor Code to create and preserve an environment in which honorable behavior is the standard for all conduct. It is a system in which each case is judged individually and a student is assumed to have acted honorably unless it has been proven otherwise. The Honor Code is a student tradition. It remains the responsibility of the students to ensure that honorable behavior is encouraged and nurtured and that dishonorable behavior is not tolerated. A student Honor Council is responsible for investigating possible honor violations and recommending appropriate measures to the Head of School.

The honor system is a method of student self-government and is separated from School discipline, which is primarily the responsibility of the faculty and administration. While the Head of School may, at his discretion, refer a discipline case to the Disciplinary Committee for investigation and recommendation, all final decisions involving disciplinary or honor violations are made by the Head of School. The Disciplinary Committee is appointed by the Head of School and comprises both students and faculty members.

ACADEMIC FACILITIES

Upper School classes are held primarily in Randolph Hall, which includes twenty-three classrooms, a 340-seat chapel/auditorium, a student union, and a library with more than 10,000 volumes and various audiovisual, CD-ROM, and Internet capabilities. The Fine Arts Center houses all art, drama, and music classes. It contains a ceramics studio, a studio for two-dimensional art, a drama studio, a veranda for stone carving, and music practice rooms in addition to space for all extracurricular activities. All Upper School science facilities are housed in a 38,045-square-foot academic building. The science wing of this building includes four laboratories, three classrooms, and a computer center with two IBM computer labs with Internet access. The lower level of this building houses the new Digital Media Center, which includes photography labs and a recording studio.

BOARDING AND GENERAL FACILITIES

The Lee-DuVal Building houses administrative offices as well as the renovated dining hall and boarding facilities. Students in the five-day boarding program live on campus during the academic week but are able to enjoy home life on the weekends. The students leave campus Friday afternoon or Saturday morning and return to the dorms either Sunday night or Monday morning. The seven-day boarders use their time on the weekends for study, leisure, and planned activities. Residential facilities include separate halls for the girls and boys and a shared lounge and study room. Two of the 5 dormitory parents are faculty members. Day faculty members also join residential students for dinner on a regular basis.

Enrollment is intentionally limited to 51 students in an effort to maintain the program's family atmosphere.

ATHLETICS

St. Anne's–Belfield offers an interscholastic athletics program for boys and girls. Boys' teams include football and soccer in the fall, basketball in the winter, and lacrosse, tennis, baseball, and golf in the spring. Offerings for the girls include field hockey, tennis, and volleyball in the fall; basketball in the winter; and lacrosse, soccer, and softball in the spring. In addition, a coeducational cross-country team is offered in the fall; indoor track, squash, and swimming in the winter; and outdoor track in the spring. Conditioning is offered all three seasons.

The philosophy of the program stresses participation, regardless of a student's previous experience or level of talent. The School's goal is to have each student participate in the interscholastic program during at least one season per year. More than 85 percent of the students participate in team sports.

St. Anne's–Belfield has two gymnasiums, a field house, a weight-training facility, a wrestling room, six tennis courts, six playing fields, and a practice field.

EXTRACURRICULAR OPPORTUNITIES

The extracurricular activities and organizations at St. Anne's–Belfield School enrich and supplement the students' academic experience. Traditions foster a sense of community and provide a historic continuity for the School. Upper School traditions include the Winter Ball, Senior Easter Egg Hunt, Prom, Class Night, Thanksgiving dinner, Thanksgiving Chapel, and Madame Day.

Clubs give students with a common interest an opportunity to meet in groups in order to expand that interest. The Upper School offers the Latin Club, International Relations Club, Environmental Club, Model OAS, Gold Key Society (student guides), Spanish Club, Mathematics Club, Transcendental Society, Student-Faculty Senate, Student Government, Martial Arts Movie Club, Art Forum, Academic Team, Amnesty International, Habitat for Humanity, and Ski Club.

Publications include *Saintly Speaking,* the School newspaper; *Saints and Sinners,* the yearbook; and *Oasis,* the literary magazine.

DAILY LIFE

Classes are held five days a week: from 8 to 3:30 Monday, Wednesday, and Thursday; from 8 to 2:40 Tuesday; and from 8 to 1:45 Friday. All academic classes are held on Tuesday and Friday but are of slightly shorter length so athletics can be scheduled at that time. Sports practices run from 3:45 to 5:45 throughout the week.

Boarders eat breakfast at 7:15 and dinner at 6:30. In the evening, supervised study hours for boarders are from 7:30 to 9:30.

SUMMER PROGRAMS

St. Anne's–Belfield School offers a wide range of coeducational summer programs for students in preschool through grade 8. Enrollment is open to students from St. Anne's–Belfield School and other schools. Middle School offerings include classes in reading and writing, math, and an SAT preparatory course. Also offered are a Summer Camp for students in grades 1–5, lacrosse camps for boys and girls, a boys' and girls' basketball camp, a girls' field hockey camp, and soccer camps for girls and boys. The 2008 summer session begins June 16, 2008.

COSTS AND FINANCIAL AID

Tuition for 2007–08 ranged from $16,400 in the fifth grade to $18,950 in the twelfth grade. Five-day boarding students paid an additional $12,750; seven-day boarding students paid an additional $21,750. Tuition may be paid in full on or before July 31, in two equal payments that are due on July 31 and December 31 (with a $200 service charge), or in eleven equal payments from July 31 to May 31 (with a $600 service charge). A prepayment of $1000 is required to reserve a place for day students, and there is a prepayment of $1500 for five-day boarding students and $2500 for seven-day boarding students.

Financial aid for tuition charges is available. The School subscribes to the School and Student Service for Financial Aid and uses its need assessment as a major factor in determining awards. A tuition loan program augments the system of financial aid. About 33 percent of the student body receives some form of financial assistance.

ADMISSIONS INFORMATION

In an individualized admission process, St. Anne's–Belfield School seeks to enroll inquisitive, enthusiastic, and conscientious students who will bring their own special talents, energy, and skills to the School community. The goal is to enroll students who will both benefit from and contribute to the School's offerings and who will feel successful in the process. St. Anne's–Belfield does not discriminate on the basis of race, color, sex, disability, nationality, or ethnic origin in the administration of its educational policies, admission policies, scholarship and loan programs, and athletics and other School-administered programs.

All applicants and families are encouraged to visit the campus to discuss the School program and the applicant's candidacy with a member of the admissions staff. The first formal step in applying for admission is to complete an application and send it with the application fee to the Admissions Office. SSAT scores, a transcript, two teacher recommendations (from current math and English teachers), administrative recommendation, and an interview are required.

APPLICATION TIMETABLE

Preliminary application should be made in the year prior to the academic year in which the applicant wishes to be admitted. The first round of admission ends February 20, 2008. The second round of admission is considered in late spring. The day application fee is $30. The boarding application fee is $50. Campus interviews and tours are conducted throughout the school year. The SSAT must be taken before a candidate is considered for admission to grades 7–12. SSAT scores should be sent to St. Anne's–Belfield School. Applicants should also request the forwarding of a transcript from their current school and should ask their current teachers of mathematics and English to submit letters of recommendation to the Admissions Office. In addition, all students must supply immunization records before admittance.

ADMISSIONS CORRESPONDENCE

Bo Perriello, Director of Admissions, grades 5–12
St. Anne's–Belfield School
2132 Ivy Road
Charlottesville, Virginia 22903
Phone: 434-296-5106
Fax: 434-979-1486
E-mail: bperriello@stab.org
Web site: http://www.stab.org

ST. GEORGE'S SCHOOL

Newport, Rhode Island

Type: Coeducational boarding and day college-preparatory school
Grades: 9–12 (Forms III–VI)
Enrollment: 348
Head of School: Eric F. Peterson

THE SCHOOL

St. George's was founded in 1896 by the Reverend John B. Diman as a college-preparatory school; in 1901, the School moved to its present site. The 230-acre campus sits atop a promontory overlooking the Atlantic Ocean, the Sakonnet River, and the city of Newport.

St. George's is committed to the development of each student's potential. The course of study challenges students to strive for academic excellence. High standards and expectations are the norm, and the faculty is committed to assisting students in their pursuit of scholarship. The academic and extracurricular opportunities have the common goal of helping students become more effective, competent, and concerned people, dedicated to making a positive contribution in life.

Since its founding, St. George's has enjoyed a close relationship with the Episcopal Church and continues to foster the spiritual and moral development of students of every religious persuasion. In 1972, the School became coeducational.

Located 2½ miles from Newport, 35 miles from Providence, and about 70 miles south of Boston, the School encourages students and faculty members to explore the many cultural and athletic events in those cities. The School also takes advantage of its proximity to the ocean. It has developed a wide range of programs that investigate the marine environment and draw attention to ocean-related issues. Through a combination of formal academic training and exposure to superb recreational opportunities, these programs help students appreciate the interrelationship between humankind and the ocean.

St. George's is a nonprofit institution governed by a 37-member Board of Trustees. The endowment is currently $110 million and is supplemented by an annual fund that raised more than $2.1 million in 2007–08, ample testimony to the generosity and commitment of the 4,900 living alumni and of the parents, grandparents, and friends of the School.

St. George's School is accredited by the New England Association of Schools and Colleges. The School is affiliated with the National Association of Independent Schools, the Independent School Association of Massachusetts, the Council for Religion in Independent Schools, the Secondary School Admission Test Board, and the Association of Boarding Schools.

ACADEMIC PROGRAMS

A student's course of study begins by emphasizing the mastery of fundamentals and later broadens to offer numerous elective courses. While all entering students have a strong record of academic achievement at their previous schools, relatively few have had substantial experience in planning their course of study. Consequently, careful counseling by the Dean of Academic Affairs and by faculty advisers and the college advisers ensures that both new and returning students are able to make intelligent course selections.

Graduation requirements include English, 4 years; mathematics, 3 years (algebra I, algebra II, and geometry); laboratory sciences, 2 years; U.S. history, 1 year; Bible and theology, 1 year (for students entering after the ninth grade, ½ year); and art or music, ½ year. All students are required to complete a modern or classical language through the third level.

Advanced Placement courses are offered in twenty-two subject areas, including art, computers, economics, English, history, language, mathematics, music, and science. Students took 360 Advanced Placement exams. On 78 percent of those exams, students achieved scores of 3, 4, or 5.

Courses for grades 9 and 10 generally meet for four 50-minute class periods per week and require about the same amount of time for preparation. Courses for grades 11 and 12 usually require less classroom time and more time for assignment preparation. Because classes are small (typically 10 to 12 students), emphasis is placed on conscientious preparation and on willingness to participate in discussion. Most students carry five full courses each semester. Grades accompanied by faculty comments and a letter from the faculty adviser are sent home three times a year.

The Off-Campus Program is predicated on the belief that students benefit from an opportunity to apply their learning to problems and questions of concern that lie outside the School community. Students initiate, plan, and evaluate these projects with the aid of the program director.

St. George's offers its students an exceptional opportunity in oceanography aboard the School-owned Research Vessel *Geronimo,* which operates year-round in coastal and offshore waters between the gulf of Maine and the northern Caribbean. There are three 6-week research cruises during the school year, and students who sail aboard *Geronimo* receive full academic credit.

FACULTY AND ADVISERS

The faculty consists of 78 full- and part-time members (39 women and 39 men). Most of the faculty members (85 percent) live on or within walking distance of the campus and, in addition to their teaching responsibilities, serve as dormitory supervisors, as advisers to individual students and extracurricular organizations, and as coaches.

Eric F. Peterson was appointed Head of School in 2004. He holds a Bachelor of Arts degree from Dartmouth College and a Juris Doctor degree from Northwestern University. For the five years prior to his appointment at St. George's, he served as the Upper School head and assistant head of school, English teacher, and coach at Forsyth Country Day School.

Generous funding is available to faculty members who wish to pursue sabbaticals, summer study, travel, and advanced degrees.

COLLEGE ADMISSION COUNSELING

St. George's students plan for college with the help of 3 college advisers, whose overriding concerns are to acquaint students with the range of options appropriate for their abilities and interests and to support them throughout their decision making.

Through individual conferences at the midpoint of the Fifth Form year, students begin the process of identifying a group of colleges and universities for investigation. Parents are involved in college planning through Fifth Form Parents' Weekend, an annual event combining formal presentations on college selection and college life by admission officers and family conferences with the college advisers.

Students are urged to visit college campuses during the summer months to interview with admission officers and see facilities. A second round of individual conferences in the fall helps Sixth Formers decide the final shape of their college lists. During an average fall, 100 colleges send representatives to St. George's, and Sixth Formers are encouraged to attend these presentations.

In conjunction with their counseling duties, the advisers work with students in selecting academic programs, registering for standardized testing, and planning summer work or study experiences. In both the Fifth and Sixth Form years, the college advisers sponsor workshops to prepare students for the SAT, college interviews, and writing application essays. Every year, college admission personnel conduct mock admission committee workshops. Other representatives conduct an essay-writing workshop for students. In addition, the college advisers routinely visit college campuses and participate in regional and national admission counseling programs to enhance their professional skills.

Since its founding, the School has prepared students for the country's leading colleges and universities. The graduates of the class of 2008 are attending such colleges and universities as Amherst, Columbia, Connecticut College, Cornell, Duke, Georgetown, Harvard, Smith, Stanford, the University of Pennsylvania, and the U.S. Naval Academy.

STUDENT BODY AND CONDUCT

In 2008–09, St. George's had 348 students (164 boys and 184 girls). Of the 348 students, 82 percent were boarding students. Generally, there are 68 students in grade 9 and approximately 90 students in each of the other three grades. St. George's makes every effort to attract a student body that is diverse in geographic, economic, and racial backgrounds as well as in interests and talents. Students come from twenty-seven states and fifteen countries.

St. George's believes that one of the most significant aspects of a residential school is the interaction within the school community—the students and faculty and staff members. Rules and expectations support the principle that disciplined living leads to a sense of real freedom. Major infractions or repeated minor infractions may lead to dismissal.

ACADEMIC FACILITIES

The Schoolhouse, which contains twenty-one classrooms, is the center of campus activity during the academic day. A $6.5-million Center for the Visual and Performing Arts was completed in September 1999. In addition to a 400-seat theater, the center contains new classrooms and studios for architecture, ceramics, dance, music, painting and drawing, photography, welding, and woodworking. Other facilities include the Dupont Science Building, which houses six well-equipped laboratories with adjoining classrooms and a new technology center, and the Smiley-Sturtevant Observatory. The Nathaniel P. Hill Memorial Library houses approximately 27,000 volumes, which include nonfiction and fiction collections, 2,500 reference titles, and an audiovisual collection. The library also subscribes to a number of electronic databases and e-books, including Jstor, Biography Resource Center, and ProQuest Historical Newspapers. The library is a member of the Ocean State Libraries consortium, Nelinet, and the Online Computer Library Center (OCLC). Librarians teach information literacy classes and provide reference services for the community.

Each dormitory room is wired for access to computing, the Internet, e-mail, and voice mail. During their first year, students complete a required computer literacy course.

BOARDING AND GENERAL FACILITIES

Boarding students live in fourteen dormitories. Most entering ninth graders live in single rooms. Returning students select the type of accommodations they prefer. Some dormitories are equipped with kitchenettes. Older students are appointed as dormitory prefects and assist the faculty in supervision.

In 2002, St. George's completed a $6-million building program to provide for two new dormitories, four faculty homes, and significant improvements to other living areas. At St. George's, 70 percent of the dormitory rooms are single rooms and 30 percent are double rooms.

In 2004, St. George's completed a new campus center. The facility houses a recreation center with a game room, a grill, and spaces for dances and special events.

ATHLETICS

Because the essential mission of the School is to educate young people in mind, body, and spirit, the afternoon program is an integral part of the St. George's curriculum, and participation is required of all. As is the case with the academic program, students plan carefully with the help of advisers the activities in which they participate in each of the three seasons. Opportunities range from interscholastic athletics to the performing arts to community service and special projects, all of which share the common goal of enabling students to expand their horizons, to test themselves, and to learn important lessons about teamwork, volunteerism, sportsmanship, competition, collaboration, and creativity.

St. George's fields forty-eight interscholastic teams: in the fall, cross-country, field hockey, football, and soccer; in the winter, basketball, ice hockey, squash, and swimming; and in the spring, baseball, lacrosse, sailing, softball, tennis, and track. In addition, there are various recreational and intramural offerings.

Facilities for athletics include a new rim-flow indoor swimming pool, new twin ice-hockey rinks, and a recently completed field house, which houses four indoor tennis courts, four basketball courts, and a fully equipped weight-training facility. There are ten outdoor tennis courts, a new all-weather track, and numerous game and practice fields. The School maintains its own fleet of 420s for sailing. A squash facility housing eight international courts was completed in 1996.

EXTRACURRICULAR OPPORTUNITIES

The creativity, imagination, and diverse talents of the student body are given full expression in the almost limitless array of extracurricular organizations, including the School newspaper, yearbook, literary magazine, St. George's Cultural Society, debate club, women's forum, entertainment committee, drama club, music guild, choir, vestry, and St. George's dance troupe.

The student council takes a strong lead in identifying new directions for the School. The joint faculty-student Disciplinary Committee works closely with the Dean of Students and the Head of School. Student advisers welcome newcomers and serve as experienced friends.

There is a strong commitment to community service. Each term, students volunteer to work in various agencies and institutions. Each summer, 15 students act as volunteer counselors at Camp Ramleh, which provides a camp experience for children from disadvantaged backgrounds.

DAILY LIFE

The first class period is at 8 a.m. each day (8:30 on Thursdays), and the last class ends at 2:55 p.m., except on Wednesdays and Saturdays, which are half days. A typical academic day consists of four or five classes. Free periods provide time for class preparation, research projects, music lessons, and other individual pursuits. Four days a week, there is a school assembly advisory or form meetings before lunch. Sports practices are generally scheduled between 3:15 and 5:15. After dinner, an hour is set aside for extracurricular activities and visiting speakers. Evening study runs from 8 to 10. Attendance at chapel on Thursday is required. The Head of School sometimes presides over these services, but most are conducted by student and faculty volunteers. The central worship service of St. George's is on either Tuesdays or Sundays and is conducted by the chaplains. Music is provided by the choir and organist-choirmaster. Attendance at this service or at a service in Newport is required.

COSTS AND FINANCIAL AID

The tuition for 2008–09 was $41,000 for boarders and $28,000 for day students. Additional expenses include books, laundry, and travel. Students may cash checks at the Business Office on weekdays and also arrange travel plans and obtain tickets.

Financial aid awards are based on the guidelines established by the School and Student Service for Financial Aid. There is substantial aid available to qualified students. For 2008–09, St. George's awarded grants and loans in excess of $2.7 million to approximately 30 percent of the student body.

ADMISSIONS INFORMATION

Applicants submit a complete school record, including two teacher evaluations, a writing sample, and the results of standardized testing. Students are required to take the Secondary School Admission Test (SSAT). When appropriate, candidates for grades 11 and 12 submit PSAT, SAT, or TOEFL scores in place of the SSAT. All candidates are expected to visit St. George's or, in exceptional situations, meet with a local representative.

The Admission Committee consists of 6 experienced staff members. In selecting students, the committee gives preference to candidates with strong records of achievement who have demonstrated a depth of interest in some area beyond the classroom.

APPLICATION TIMETABLE

A formal application and the $50 fee ($100 for international students) should be filed by February 1 in order to guarantee a decision on March 10, the notification date for applicants. In place of St. George's own application, candidates may choose to submit the Boarding School Common Application Form, which can be downloaded from the Internet at http://www.schools.com. Interviews are scheduled beginning at 8:30 a.m., Monday through Friday, and beginning at 8 a.m. on Saturdays. Appointments for an interview and a tour of the campus should be made well in advance, preferably by telephone.

ADMISSIONS CORRESPONDENCE

Jim Hamilton, Director of Admission
St. George's School
372 Purgatory Road
Middletown, Rhode Island 02842-5984

Phone: 401-842-6600
Fax: 401-842-6696
E-mail: admissions_office@stgeorges.edu
Web site: http://www.stgeorges.edu

ST. GREGORY COLLEGE PREPARATORY SCHOOL

Tucson, Arizona

St. Gregory
COLLEGE PREPARATORY SCHOOL
Character • Scholarship • Leadership

Type: Coeducational day college-preparatory school
Grades: 6–12: Middle School, 6–8; Upper School, 9–12
Enrollment: School total: 320; Upper School: 170; Middle School: 150
Head of School: William Creeden

THE SCHOOL

St. Gregory is an independent, coeducational, college-preparatory day school. It is not a parochial school. It is nonsectarian and nondenominational in its admissions, curricular, and extracurricular policies and practices. The principal purpose of the School, which has grown from a first-year enrollment of 48 students to its present size of 320, is to provide a first-rate college-preparatory education for students of all social, ethnic, and economic segments of the greater Tucson community.

The School is governed by a 20-member Board of Trustees, which, during the twenty-eight years of the School's existence, has developed a campus with a capital value of $14 million and has attained the level of $350,000 in annual giving.

St. Gregory is accredited by the Independent Schools Association of the Southwest as a College Preparatory School (one of six in the state of Arizona). Professional memberships are held in the National Association of Independent Schools and the Educational Records Bureau.

ACADEMIC PROGRAMS

The standard academic load is six courses per semester, one of which may be performance or production based. The average class size is 15. The teacher-student ratio is 1:10.

Twenty-four academic credits are required for graduation, of which the following 17 are prescribed: English, 4 years; foreign language, 3 consecutive years of one language; mathematics, 3 years; laboratory science, 3 years; history, 3 years; and fine arts, 1 year.

Advanced Placement courses are offered in English, calculus, chemistry, biology, physics (C), U.S. government, U.S. history, European history, Spanish, French, Latin, studio art, and music theory. In AP classes, the grades are weighted .5.

In those rare but welcome instances in which a student's exceptional academic skills outrun the School's curriculum, independent studies are designed, or the student may take courses for credit at the University of Arizona.

During grades 6–11, students participate in a challenge course curriculum designed to enhance communication, strategic thinking, trust, leadership, and group dynamics within an enjoyable yet intensive structured program. In the spring of their junior year, students are invited to apply to be trained and serve as Peer Leaders during their senior year. This group of seniors participates in an extensive training program to learn the hard and soft skills necessary for facilitating students through St. Gregory's challenge course programs and faculty- and student-run programs for students in grades 6–11.

FACULTY AND ADVISERS

St. Gregory's teaching faculty has 39 members. Sixty percent have master's degrees, and 3 hold doctorates.

Mr. William Creeden, Headmaster, earned his B.S. from the Wharton School of the University of Pennsylvania and his M.S. in educational administration also from the University of Pennsylvania. He completed his formal education at Penn in 1985 with Advanced Studies in Leadership and Administration.

Each student is assigned to a homeroom adviser. Academic advisory functions are retained by the Headmaster and key administrative staff members.

COLLEGE ADMISSION COUNSELING

The School's college placement philosophy is that the best college or university for a student is one where the student can feel at home and, in addition, is challenged and stimulated intellectually, offered varied social and personal experiences, and prepared for the next step in life. The college counseling program is directed toward helping students identify the schools that suit them in these ways, supporting the application process, and aiding in confronting the challenges of college affordability.

The college planning program begins in the freshman year, when students are advised on the relationship between their selection of courses and their admissibility to college. The college counselor holds a meeting with parents of freshmen and sophomores once each year to describe the college counseling program and respond to any concerns they may have.

In the fall of the junior year, the college counselor meets with students and their parents, outlining in detail the School-guided process for selecting and applying to colleges. Families receive information on the reference resources that are available in the College Counseling Center, in the form of college catalogs, directories, CD-ROMs, and Internet resources. The importance of having good grades, a challenging course selection, and sustained extracurricular activity is stressed for those students whose objective is admission to the more competitive colleges. Juniors and seniors are encouraged to visit colleges and universities to which they are considering applying.

Juniors and their parents regularly meet with the college counselor throughout the year. Juniors take the SAT and/or ACT tests during the last months of the academic year, as well as the appropriate SAT Subject Tests.

A weeklong class in writing the college essay is offered to rising seniors just before the fall semester begins. Seniors review their final lists of selected colleges with their counselor early in the fall and begin the actual application process. A highlight of the process is College Day, in mid-October, when admissions representatives from more than 100 colleges gather on the St. Gregory campus. In addition, more than 40 individual college representatives offer on-campus information sessions for St. Gregory students throughout the fall.

The colleges and universities that members of the class of 2008 are attending include Boston University, British Columbia, Brown, Caltech, Clark, Colombia College, Creighton, Lewis & Clark, Loyola Chicago, Maryland Institute College of Art, MIT, Mills, Northeastern, School of the Museum of Fine Arts, Suffolk, Wellesley, USC, and the Universities of Arizona (including the Honors Program), Colorado at Boulder, Denver, Kansas, Montana, North Carolina at Chapel Hill, Pennsylvania, Puget Sound, San Diego, Santa Clara, and Seattle.

STUDENT BODY AND CONDUCT

Currently, there are 150 students in the Middle School, grades 6–8. There are 50 students in grade 6 in three sections and 45 to 55 students in grades 7 and 8 in four sections. There are 170 students in the Upper School, grades 9–12, with a goal of 45 to 55 in each class.

The School operates under four guiding principles: respect, responsibility, honesty, and safety in making decisions. An Honor Committee made up of students and faculty members assists the Dean of Students, division heads, and headmaster in violations of academic integrity policies and occasionally in disciplinary matters.

ACADEMIC FACILITIES

The principal buildings on the St. Gregory campus include two administration buildings, a library, a Middle School classroom building, the gymnasium El Mirador (for standard indoor sports such as basketball and volleyball, with seating for 400), the 400-seat Performing Arts Center, and four classroom buildings.

The theater features a gallery space for displaying student art, a thrust and side stage, and state-of-the-art lighting and sound systems. Classrooms for choral work and theater production and shop space for stage construction and storage are included in this building.

Housed in Zeskind Hall, the Upper School administration building, is a dining facility for 300. A full kitchen provides an extensive variety of fresh food for students and faculty and staff members throughout the day. Students may purchase meal cards for daily lunches and snacks.

The Humanities building houses the Fine Arts and Foreign Language Departments as well as the drama classroom. There are four classrooms, an art studio, a band room, and music practice rooms.

Two buildings house the sciences and the English and math classrooms. State-of-the-art laboratories and classrooms are featured in these buildings, as well as storage, offices, a computer lab, a college counseling center, and a publications lab. The science labs include a greenhouse and space for long-term student experiments. The English office building also includes space for an outdoor education/student government office.

The refurbished Marshall building houses the library, a dance studio, a digital photography classroom, history classrooms, offices, and computer labs.

The Louise Marshall Library houses more than 7,000 books, fifty periodicals and newspapers, and database access to 150 more journals. The facility includes a computer lab, study carrels, and an audiovisual library for student and faculty use. The computerized library is also connected to the University of Arizona library and the Pima County Public Library System. The School's librarian, who holds a master's degree in library science, sees her task as preparing students for college-level research.

ATHLETICS

The School believes that participation in athletics is instrumental in helping students mature. In addition to promoting the objective of achieving physical fitness, the School makes an effort to develop the important skills of self-discipline, sportsmanship, and teamwork.

Interscholastic offerings are boys' soccer, boys' and girls' cross-country and swimming, girls' golf and volleyball in the fall; girls' soccer and boys' and girls' basketball in the winter; and baseball, golf, softball, boys' volleyball, and boys' and girls' tennis in the spring.

Athletics facilities include playing fields for soccer, baseball, and softball; an indoor gym for volleyball and basketball; and two outdoor basketball courts. The School uses the tennis courts and swimming pool at nearby Fort Lowell Park. Housed in the gym is an athletic training center that features aerobic, free-weight, and variable-resistant equipment.

EXTRACURRICULAR OPPORTUNITIES

Students are able to participate in a wide variety of extracurricular activities, and virtually 100 percent of the School is involved in the arts, publications, athletics, or other activities. A student may choose to work on the newspaper, yearbook, or literary magazine. Popular club activities include Outdoor Action, French Club, and Astronomy Club, providing students with social and leadership opportunities. Extracurricular arts activities include theatrical productions, string ensemble, and a yearly musical production.

Outdoor clubs sponsor day hiking experiences in the local area as well as extended backpacking experiences during school breaks.

Students have many opportunities to meet the community service requirement by serving the Tucson community. Working as hospital volunteers or nursing home aides, serving in a crisis nursery, or participating in political internships—all of these opportunities and more are available to the St. Gregory student. The School encourages and facilitates community service as an important element of the school years, and a certain number of community service hours are required at each grade level.

DAILY LIFE

A block schedule provides for each of eight periods to meet every other day for 75 minutes. Interscholastic sports and other activities follow in the afternoon.

SUMMER PROGRAMS

The School conducts summer enrichment programs that vary from two to six weeks in length. Sixth- through eleventh-grade students may choose from several basketball camps. Popular summer travel courses for Upper School students have included marine biology (with significant study time in the Gulf of California), tropical ecology (with study in the Galapagos), and Spanish (studied in Spain or Central America), among others. In alternate years, there is a travel and study program in France for students in grades 9–11, a trip to Italy for Middle School students, and a trip to Italy for Upper School students.

COSTS AND FINANCIAL AID

Tuition for the 2008–09 school year is $15,300 for grades 9–12 and $14,300 for grades 6–8. Additional costs include lunches purchased in the dining hall and books.

Need-based financial aid is offered. Approximately 25 percent of the students received some share of the $775,000 in financial assistance budgeted by the board and augmented by state of Arizona tax credit donations.

ADMISSIONS INFORMATION

Qualification for admission is determined by the Admissions Committee on the basis of the applicant's scores on an admissions test, a transcript from the previous school, teachers' evaluations, a writing sample, and an interview.

APPLICATION TIMETABLE

Tours of the campus and visits to classes may be requested for any day the School is in regular session. Requests for visits, interview appointments, and admission materials may be made by telephone, by e-mail, or in writing. The deadline for applications is February 6, 2009, and applicants are notified of admission by the end of February. The application/testing fee is $45. The financial aid application deadline is March 6. St. Gregory considers late applications, depending on space in the class.

ADMISSIONS CORRESPONDENCE

Debby Kennedy
St. Gregory College Preparatory School
3231 North Craycroft
Tucson, Arizona 85712

Phone: 520-327-6395
Fax: 520-327-8276
E-mail: admissions@stgregoryschool.org
Web site: http://www.stgregoryschool.org

SAINT JAMES SCHOOL

St. James, Maryland

Type: Coeducational boarding and day college-preparatory school
Grades: 8–12
Enrollment: 225
Head of School: The Reverend Dr. D. Stuart Dunnan, Headmaster

THE SCHOOL

Saint James School is the oldest Episcopal boarding school founded on the English model in the United States. Founded by Bishop William Whittingham in 1842, the School originally included a preparatory school and college. In the years following the Civil War, the college was eliminated, and Saint James evolved toward its present shape. Located in a rural setting, the Georgian-style campus of Saint James sits on 900 acres of farmland containing a natural spring, fields, and streams. The campus lies 5 miles southwest of Hagerstown and is approximately 65 miles from both Baltimore and Washington, D.C. The region offers many cultural and historic points of interest, including the C&O Canal, Harpers Ferry, and Antietam and Gettysburg Battlefields. The faculty members and students enjoy the cultural resources of the Baltimore-Washington metropolitan area on regular field trips.

Throughout its history, Saint James has remained committed to the precepts of sound mind and body, emphasizing the spiritual, intellectual, physical, and moral development of each student through challenging academics, daily athletics, extensive activities, and community service. At the start of each academic day, the entire School gathers for Chapel, providing an opportunity for thought and reflection for faculty members and students of all faith traditions. Simultaneously challenged and supported, Saint James students study a traditional core curriculum, which provides a solid foundation for strong academic achievement at the collegiate level.

Saint James is governed by a self-perpetuating Board of Trustees. The School's operating budget is $7.8 million per year. The endowment is approximately $21 million. An active Annual Giving program is supported by better than 50 percent of the alumni.

Saint James School is accredited by the Middle States Association of Colleges and Schools and the Maryland State Department of Education. It is a member of the National Association of Independent Schools, Association of Independent Maryland Schools, Cum Laude Society, Association of Independent Schools of Greater Washington, Council for Advancement and Support of Education, and National Association of Episcopal Schools.

ACADEMIC PROGRAMS

Small classes and a student-teacher ratio of 7:1 provide an optimal learning environment at Saint James. The core curriculum encompasses courses in English, history, mathematics, science, foreign languages, art, music, and religion, with electives available to upperclassmen. Advanced Placement courses are offered in all major academic areas. Eighteen academic credits, each worth a full-year course, are required to earn a diploma, and the distribution of courses includes no fewer than English (4), history (3), mathematics (3), science (3), foreign language (3), and art/music (1). Students generally take five courses each year.

The school year is divided into three terms; examinations are given in November, March, and May. Reports and comments are sent to parents in October and at the end of each term. Students receive additional reports at the end of each six-week marking period.

FACULTY AND ADVISERS

The faculty members at Saint James are highly-talented, deeply dedicated educators with the strongest possible commitment to each student's success. The School has 33 faculty men and women; 52 percent have advanced degrees.

The Reverend Dr. D. Stuart Dunnan was appointed Headmaster in 1992. He graduated from St. Albans School and Harvard University (A.B., A.M.). He received his B.A. in theology from Christ Church of Oxford University and was awarded a certificate in Anglican studies from General Theological Seminary in New York. At Oxford, he received his M.A. and completed his D.Phil. Father Dunnan was also a member of the theology faculty of Oxford University, where he served as a research fellow and chaplain at Lincoln College.

In addition to their teaching duties, faculty members coach students in athletics and the arts, live in the dormitories, and eat with students in the dining hall. All faculty members act as advisers to 7 students, supporting and directing their academic and personal growth and achievement.

COLLEGE ADMISSION COUNSELING

As a private college-preparatory institution, Saint James School believes each student and parent ultimately invests in a high-quality education, which will lead to appropriate college placement. Each year, Saint James places 100 percent of its graduating seniors in college. The Director of College Counseling has designed a college search program, which allows students the opportunity to pursue a wide range of colleges. Saint James students begin this process in the fall of the tenth grade. The School's personalized approach incorporates college admission officers, teachers, students, and parents working together to ensure every senior gets the most from his or her college search process. In addition, admission representatives from more than forty colleges and universities visit the Saint James campus annually to recruit students.

During the past four years, graduates have matriculated at the following colleges: Amherst; Boston College; Boston University; Bucknell; Davidson; Dickinson; Furman; Georgetown; George Washington; Harvard; Johns Hopkins Peabody Conservatory; McGill; Princeton; Rice; Stanford; United States Air Force, Military, and Naval Academies; Vanderbilt; Wake Forest; Wellesley; and the Universities of California, Maryland, North Carolina, Pennsylvania, the South (Sewanee), and Virginia.

STUDENT BODY AND CONDUCT

In 2008–09, 225 students were enrolled in grades 8–12, 57 of whom were day students. The majority of students come from Maryland, Pennsylvania, Virginia, West Virginia, the District of Columbia, and a number of other states throughout the country. In addition, 10 percent of the student body comes from fifteen different countries.

A student's character is of fundamental importance at Saint James, and because of this, the School strives to foster a sense of personal and group responsibility and a high standard of honor in each student. The Honor Code (a pledge not to lie, cheat, or steal) expects each student to respect other people and their property. Furthermore, the use of alcohol and nonprescription drugs is strictly prohibited, as is the use of tobacco in any form. The Honor Council and the Disciplinary Committee, comprised largely of students, review instances of dishonor and misconduct and recommend appropriate dispositions to the Headmaster.

The Prefect Council, made up of 10 seniors elected by the students and the faculty, upholds the traditions of Saint James and assists faculty members and the Headmaster in the day-to-day operations of the School. Of this group, 1 member is elected Senior Prefect and he or she leads the Prefects in their work.

The Student Activities Committee consists of 2 prefects, both appointed by the Senior Prefect, and up to 7 underformers as selected by the Committee at the beginning of the year. The Committee serves to advise the Dean of Students and the Prefect Council on matters relating to student activities and student morale. It also organizes activities such as dances and special programs.

ACADEMIC FACILITIES

A quadrangle on the east side of campus is anchored by the John E. Owens Library, containing nearly 20,000 volumes, with the School Archives, science laboratories, and classrooms located downstairs. Powell Hall, the main academic building, contains classrooms and newly renovated science laboratories. The Bowman-Byron Fine Arts Center has a 270-seat auditorium, art studios, and stagecraft and music rooms.

BOARDING AND GENERAL FACILITIES

Claggett Hall is the main boys' dormitory, housing boys in Forms IV–VI (grades 10–12), with each form grouped together by floor. Onderdonk Dormitory is for the younger boys in Form II (grade 8) and Mattingly Hall is for boys in Form III (grade 9). A common room with a TV, DVD player, and computers can be found on every hall. The Gertrude Steele Coors Hall houses girls in Forms II–IV, and Holloway House, the new girls' dormitory, is for girls in Forms IV–VI. Faculty members who have apartments within the dormitory and student prefects supervise each dormitory. Faculty houses also surround the perimeter of the campus. A new dining hall provides seated and buffet meals for students and faculty members. Kemp Hall, housing the Detweiler Student Center, the School bookstore, and a snack bar, offers an opportunity for students to socialize together informally.

The Saint James Chapel provides for daily services. A guild of student sacristans, a student vestry, and the Chapel Choir assist and direct worship in the Chapel. The Laidlaw Infirmary houses a full-time nurse, an athletic trainer, and the office of the School Chaplain.

ATHLETICS

By requiring daily participation in the athletic program, the School seeks to enhance each student's confidence by simultaneously challenging and supporting each individual. On the field and in the field house, students develop principles of teamwork and sportsmanship and learn to stretch themselves so that they may achieve beyond their own expectations. These lessons are invaluable preparation for the challenges of life.

A program of sixteen interscholastic sports for boys and girls is offered at Saint James, and the teams play schools of similar size in the Washington-Baltimore metropolitan area. The sports available to boys include baseball, basketball, cross-country, football, golf, lacrosse, soccer, tennis, weight training, and wrestling. The sports available to girls include basketball, dance, field hockey, lacrosse, soccer, indoor soccer, softball, tennis, volleyball, and weight training.

The Alumni Hall Athletic Center contains two wrestling rooms, locker room facilities, and a field house with three basketball courts that can be converted to tennis and volleyball courts. The Fitness Center houses a state-of-the-art weight room and dance studios. Seven athletic fields and a twelve-court tennis pavilion are also located on School grounds. In the winter, students can ski at Whitetail Ski Resort, 25 miles north of the campus.

EXTRACURRICULAR OPPORTUNITIES

Students are encouraged to participate in the School's diverse extracurricular activities each year. Saint James students may become involved in *The Bai Yuka* (yearbook), *Jacobite* (newspaper), Vestry, Sacristan's Guild, Choir, Lay Readers, Multi-Cultural Club, Photography Club, Ushers' Guild, Historical Society, Delta Society (math and science), Irving Society (literary), *Syrinx* (literary magazine), and the Mummers' Society (drama). In addition, there is a student tutoring group, which offers assistance to students needing additional academic support, and the Maroon Key Society, which provides tour guides for prospective students, their families, and other guests of the School. One of the strengths of the activities program is its flexibility. If a group of students has a particular interest and finds a faculty member willing to act as sponsor, the School will support new activities whenever possible.

During the school year, Saint James students hold and attend dances/mixers with other schools. A block of tickets for symphony performances in the local community is a regular offering, and additional performances at theaters in Washington and Baltimore are attended frequently.

DAILY LIFE

Breakfast for boarding students is at 7:15. Day students arrive by 8, at which time the School meets for chapel. The academic day begins at 8:15 with the students following a seven-period day. Two extra-help periods are offered on Tuesdays and Thursdays. Faculty members are available at this time to help students who need assistance. An athletic period follows the academic day from 3:45 until 5:45, and all students participate. Dinner is served at 6:30. The majority of meals are sit-down, family-style meals, with a faculty member heading each table.

The nightly study hall period runs from 7:30 to 9:30 for all boarding students. Lights-out is between 10:30 and 11, depending on the Form.

WEEKEND LIFE

A variety of activities on campus and in the metropolitan area can be found. Regular activities include mixers, dances, movies, and concerts, and these are augmented by field trips, informal outings, and sporting and cultural events in Washington and Baltimore. During the winter, skiing is a regular weekend event.

All activities are coordinated by the Dean of Students and the Student Activities Committee, who solicit suggestions from the student body. Saint James is affiliated with twenty boarding schools in the Baltimore–Washington, D.C., region that coordinate various social activities throughout the year. Transportation is provided by the School, and these events are supervised by faculty members.

COSTS AND FINANCIAL AID

The comprehensive fee for the 2008–09 school year is $33,000 for boarding students and $22,000 for day students. A nonrefundable 10 percent deposit is required by April 10 for new students. Tuition is payable in one, two, or ten installments.

Financial aid grants, based on need and renewed annually, are given in March for the following academic year, provided the requisite financial aid forms are returned to the Admission Office by February 10. For the 2008–09 year, $1.5 million in financial aid was awarded to 30 percent of the students in amounts ranging from $3000 to $28,000.

ADMISSIONS INFORMATION

Saint James School accepts students without regard to race, sex, color, religion, or ethnic origin and has a diverse student body. It seeks girls and boys of good character who have the drive and curiosity to make the most of their talents and who wish to participate fully in the life of the School. Students are admitted in grades 8 through 11 on the basis of a completed application, teacher and guidance counselor recommendations, academic transcript, and the results of the SSAT, PSAT, or SAT.

APPLICATION TIMETABLE

Inquiries are welcome all year. The application deadline is January 31, and admission decisions are mailed March 10. Students have until April 10 to notify Saint James of their decision. After January 31, applications are welcomed and considered on a space-available basis.

A personal interview and visit to campus are part of the admission requirements. Appointments must be made in advance, and are scheduled between 8 a.m. and 3 p.m., Monday through Friday.

ADMISSIONS CORRESPONDENCE

Lawrence Jensen, Director of Admissions
Saint James School
St. James, Maryland 21781
Phone: 301-733-9330
Fax: 301-739-1310
E-mail: admissions@stjames.edu
Web site: http://www.stjames.edu

ST. JOHNSBURY ACADEMY

St. Johnsbury, Vermont

Type: Coeducational boarding and day college-preparatory, technical, and fine arts school
Grades: 9–12, postgraduate year
Enrollment: Approximately 1,000
Head of School: Thomas W. Lovett, Headmaster

THE SCHOOL

St. Johnsbury Academy is a coeducational boarding and day school enrolling students in grades 9–12 and a postgraduate year. The Academy was founded in 1842 by the Fairbanks family, local residents and manufacturers, to provide "intellectual, moral, and religious training for their own children and the children of the community." Since its founding, the Academy has enrolled boarding students while also serving day students from St. Johnsbury and surrounding towns. For the school year 2008–09, international boarding students represent twenty-four countries and territories, including the first ever from Kazakhstan and Oman. Domestic boarding students are from fifteen states and territories. Day students travel from forty-nine Vermont and northern New Hampshire towns.

Each Academy student is expected to meet four school-wide standards: becoming an accomplished communicator, problem-solver, citizen, and scholar. These standards describe what is expected from each student to know, be able to do, and be like by the time they graduate. The Academy's curriculum, which offers college-preparatory, business, art, and technical courses, is designed to meet the needs of students with varied interests and abilities.

A nonprofit institution, the Academy is governed by a self-perpetuating 21-member Board of Trustees, many of whom are alumni. The operating budget for 2007–08 was $23 million. Approximately 85 percent of this amount is funded directly through tuition revenue, with the balance provided through Annual Giving, endowment, and various other programs. Of the 11,750 living graduates, 9 percent contributed to the Annual Fund last year. The school-owned facilities are valued at $60 million. In addition, endowment funds total $17 million.

The Academy is fully accredited by the New England Association of Schools and Colleges and approved by the Vermont State Department of Education. It is a member of the National Association of Independent Schools, the Independent Schools Association of Northern New England, and the Vermont Independent Schools Association. In addition, the Academy is a member of the College Board and has been designated by that body as an examination center.

The town of St. Johnsbury (population 8,000) was recently named by *National Geographic Adventure Magazine* as the number 1 small town for adventure. St. Johnsbury is situated in the scenic Northeast Kingdom of Vermont, which offers opportunities for skiing, canoeing, camping, and hiking; is a center for the state's maple sugar industry; and provides students with access to the educational and cultural resources of Dartmouth College, the University of Vermont, and Lyndon State College. St. Johnsbury is 180 miles north of Boston, 330 miles north of New York City, and 150 miles south of Montreal. Served by local and interstate buses, it is easily reached via Interstates 91 and 93. There are international airports in Burlington, Vermont and Manchester, New Hampshire, and the school provides transportation to and from the airports during school vacations.

ACADEMIC PROGRAMS

The school year, from late August to early June, is divided into two 18-week semesters and includes Thanksgiving, holiday, winter, and spring recesses. Core classes, which have an average size of 12 students, meet five days a week. Some electives meet every other day.

The Academy introduced a new class schedule in the fall of 2008. The new five-block schedule of 70-minute blocks (previously four 80-minute blocks) offers specific benefits. First, students who are enrolled in the performing arts (dance, music, theater) or academic support programs (ESL, Guided Studies, Study Skills) will have more time during the school day. Second, all underclassmen (Grades 9 and 10) not in the above-named courses will be assigned to a study block, adding structured study to their day. Upperclassmen (Grades 11 and 12) will be able to have a free block, adding additional flexibility to obtain enrichment.

To meet the various learning needs of students, the Academy remains committed to a student-centered approach to teaching, recognizing that each individual learning style of every student must be determined and then the delivery of instruction is adapted to maximize his or her performance.

In combination with the smaller class size and more time for conferences, the Academy has established the Center for Academic Improvement and Enrichment. The Center provides individualized support in areas of difficulty or enrichment in areas of strength or interest.

Evening study support and classroom accommodations are arranged as necessary. Freshmen participate in a study skills program. Individual tutorials can be arranged. Grades are sent to parents at the close of each term; interim reports are issued if a student is experiencing difficulty. Each student has a faculty adviser who provides guidance in establishing and achieving personal and educational goals. Remedial courses are offered in all academic areas at no additional cost.

To graduate, students must complete 26 credits. One semester of course work provides 1 credit. Specific requirements are 4 credits in English and 3 credits each in social science, mathematics, and science. All students carry four full courses each semester, with the opportunity to add a fifth course as described above (ESL, performing arts, or students enrolled in learning support programs).

The Academy offers an extensive, four-level English as a Second Language (ESL) program. The ESL program addresses the needs of individual students through a series of ESL, English, and social studies courses that are directed at the specific needs of the nonnative speaker.

St. Johnsbury Academy's extensive curriculum is designed to provide maximum flexibility so that a student may elect a course of study that meets his or her needs. The comprehensive curriculum includes 219 courses, including twenty-one Advanced Placement courses. Other courses are offered at basic, standard, and accelerated levels. Eleven in-depth technical programs, four accelerated engineering courses, five languages, and thirty-seven arts courses round out the curriculum. Many technical courses have been individualized, allowing students to learn technical skills while they prepare for college admission.

FACULTY AND ADVISERS

The faculty numbers 115—65 men and 50 women. They hold 102 bachelor's degrees and eighty-one graduate degrees, representing study at more than ninety colleges and universities. Twenty-six faculty members live on the campus.

Thomas W. Lovett was appointed Headmaster in 2001. He is a graduate of Providence College (B.A.) and Brown University (M.A.). Mr. Lovett has been a member of the English faculty and has served as Acting Academic Dean, English Department Chair, and Director of the Advanced Placement Institute. He has also coached football and baseball and has been a dormitory head.

COLLEGE ADMISSION COUNSELING

The Director of the Guidance Office and 5 counselors help students complete their college applications. The members of the Guidance Office have more than seventy-four years of collective experience in course selection guidance and the college application process. Advising for entry to college starts early in the junior year, just before the PSAT is taken. For the 2007–08 school year, admissions representatives from over seventy colleges visited the Academy campus to meet with students. Groups of students attend college fairs that are held in the area. The Guidance Office maintains an extensive reference library of college catalogs and other material to help students make their selections.

In 2008, 90 percent of the Academy's 267 graduates chose to continue their education. The colleges and universities they are attending include Carnegie Mellon, Duke, Emory, Middlebury, Rochester Institute of Technology, Smith, Syracuse, Tufts, the United Sates Air Force Academy, and the Universities of Connecticut, Notre Dame, Pennsylvania, Vermont, Wheaton, and Wisconsin.

STUDENT BODY AND CONDUCT

In 2007–08, St. Johnsbury Academy had 764 day and 233 boarding students, as follows: 205 in grade 9, 253 in grade 10, 265 in grade 11, and 267 (including 7 postgraduates) in grade 12. Boarders come from nineteen states and twenty-one countries.

Discipline is handled on an individual basis; the school attempts in all cases to maintain a firm, fair, and flexible policy.

The Student Council gives students a voice in school policy. The council helps the administration by offering advice on student attitudes toward current rules and regulations and suggesting possible changes and revisions.

ACADEMIC FACILITIES

Carl Ranger Hall, the English and writing center, houses thirteen classrooms and the department's writing lab, which contains twenty-five PCs. Colby Hall is the main administration building, with offices and twenty classrooms. Severance Hall contains the Resident Life Office and eight math classrooms. Streeter Hall, home to the STeM lab (science and technology departments, including a pre-engineering lab), opened in 2006.

In addition to these state-of-the-art academic facilities, Streeter Hall includes the dining hall, Common Ground Café, television studio, and a 450-seat outdoor amphitheater. Fuller Hall contains an 800-seat theater and dressing rooms. Newell Hall provides the foreign language department with extensive facilities for instruction, including two Tandberg computerized language-learning systems. The Charles Hosmer Morse Center for the Arts provides extraordinary facilities, consisting of six fine arts studios and an art gallery, a print and photography studio, two music performance studios with five practice rooms, a dance studio, and a 200-seat black-box theater.

The Mayo Center provides space for the Grace Stuart Orcutt Library (20,000 volumes), a student lounge, and the Colwell Center for Global Understanding. The nearby St. Johnsbury Athenaeum provides students with access to an additional 45,000 volumes.

BOARDING AND GENERAL FACILITIES

The Academy has eight dormitories housing 186 students. Faculty members reside in each dorm. The student-faculty ratio in the dorms is 5:1. Boarding students care for their own rooms.

A school nurse is available on campus at all times, and emergency services are available at nearby Northeastern Vermont Regional Hospital.

During vacation periods when dormitories are closed, arrangements are made for those students who are unable to return home to travel with an Academy group or to stay with a local family.

ATHLETICS

Varsity and junior varsity teams for boys are organized in baseball, basketball, football, lacrosse, soccer, and wrestling; there are also freshman teams in football, basketball, and soccer. Girls' varsity and junior varsity teams are formed in basketball, lacrosse, soccer, softball, and field hockey. There are also interscholastic competition in cross-country, golf, ice hockey, tennis, track and field, and Ultimate Frisbee for boys and golf, gymnastics, lacrosse, tennis, track and field, and Ultimate Frisbee for girls. Nordic and Alpine skiing are offered on a coeducational basis. In addition, intramural sports are offered throughout the year. Tennis, skiing, golf, hiking, canoeing, riding, mountain climbing, and camping are among the recreational sports and activities available.

Alumni Memorial Gymnasium contains the basketball court, seating for 1,250, and locker rooms. The Academy's field house contains three multipurpose tennis, volleyball, and basketball courts; a 1/12-mile indoor track; and a 25-yard, 6-lane indoor swimming pool. The building also provides locker rooms, team rooms, areas for hydrotherapy and wrestling, and a weight room with a Universal Gym, nine Nautilus stations, and extensive free-weight and aerobics equipment. A 400-meter all-weather track was completed in 1996.

EXTRACURRICULAR OPPORTUNITIES

The Student Council, which is composed of elected representatives of each class, meets weekly to advise the administration on matters of student concern and to organize student activities.

Students publish a yearbook *(The Lamp)* and a newspaper *(The Student)*. Qualified students are invited to join the National Honor Society. Other extracurricular organizations include the Academy Theatre, Scholars Bowl, and Lyceum, a book discussion group. Among the more than sixty clubs and activities are cheerleading, band, chorus, FBLA, martial arts, math, mountain biking, photography, recycling, wilderness, science, audio-visual, computer, naturalist, and chess clubs. The International Club provides several opportunities each year for travel abroad.

DAILY LIFE

Breakfast is served at 7:15 on weekday mornings. The academic day begins with Chapel, an all-school assembly, at 8. Classes begin at 8:15 and run until 3:10. Following classes, there is a conference period, during which all faculty members are available to students for additional help. Extracurricular activities are scheduled between 3:30 and 5; dinner is at 5:30. Proctored study hall is held from 7:30 to 9; honor students are exempted from the mandatory study period. The library is open in the evening, Monday through Thursday. The quiet hours in the dormitory extend until 10:30 p.m.

WEEKEND LIFE

Brunch and dinner are served on weekends. Dances, films, concerts, plays, and sports events are typical weekend activities. Transportation is provided to area ski resorts (Burke Mountain) as well as other destinations, including Boston, Montreal, and Burlington. With parental and school permission, students may leave the campus on weekends.

SUMMER PROGRAMS

St. Johnsbury Academy offers an English as a Second Language Summer Program, which is designed to provide intensive training in spoken language, listening comprehension, reading, and writing. A unique aspect of the Academy ESL Summer Program is the homestay family; each student lives with an American family during the entire six weeks of the program. During the day, the program retains the rigorous structure and numerous activities found in a high-quality boarding school. Thus, the students enjoy the advantages of a structured academic and extracurricular program combined with the benefits of living with an American family.

COSTS AND FINANCIAL AID

In 2008–09, tuition and boarding fees are $38,500, and day tuition is $12,980. Personal expenses for boarders totaled approximately $1800 per year.

Approximately $500,000 in financial aid is awarded annually to qualified students on the basis of need.

ADMISSIONS INFORMATION

St. Johnsbury Academy seeks to enroll students of good character who are interested in rigorous college preparation or who are serious about preparation for a vocation or trade. Candidates are accepted in all grades and occasionally for a postgraduate year, but most enter in grade 9 or 10. Admission is based on previous school records, references, a personal interview, and standardized test scores.

APPLICATION TIMETABLE

Applications are accepted throughout the year. Applying during the winter or spring prior to the anticipated fall entrance is recommended. There is a $20 application fee. Admissions are handled by the Director of Admission.

ADMISSIONS CORRESPONDENCE

Mary Ann Gessner, Director of Admission
St. Johnsbury Academy
1000 Main Street
St. Johnsbury, Vermont 05819
Phone: 802-751-2130
Fax: 802-748-5463
E-mail: admissions@stjacademy.org
Web site: http://www.stjohnsburyacademy.org

SAINT JOHN'S PREPARATORY SCHOOL

Collegeville, Minnesota

SAINT JOHN'S PREP
SAINT JOHN'S PREPARATORY SCHOOL
Your World Awaits

Type: Catholic/Benedictine, co-educational, day and boarding, college-preparatory school for students in grades 7–12; boarding options begin in grade 9.
Grades: 7–12, postgraduate
Enrollment: 338
Head of School: Father Timothy Backous, O.S.B.

THE SCHOOL

The Benedictine monks have been educating young people and preserving the culture of Western civilization since the sixth century. Saint John's Preparatory School is a continuation of that 1,500-year-old educational system and lifestyle. During the mid-1800s, German and Irish pioneers began to settle the Minnesota territory. Saint John's was founded to minister to those early Minnesotans. Since 1857, Saint John's Prep has continuously served students from Minnesota as well as from other parts of the country and the world. The School continues to celebrate the enduring quality of education in the Benedictine tradition.

Saint John's is set on a 2,700-acre campus of woods and lakes in central Minnesota. Located on the same campus are a major university (Saint John's University), a publishing house, the largest Benedictine monastery in the world, an ecumenical and cultural research center, and the Hill Monastic Museum and Manuscript Library.

Academic excellence and spiritual growth are the pillars on which the School stands. Students learn alongside goal-directed peers from across the United States and abroad, all of whom are challenged to reach their highest potential in an environment that prepares them for college and a lifetime of learning. Students follow a college-preparatory curriculum, which often includes a wide variety of college courses. In addition to learning in the classroom, Saint John's Prep students learn to live with others, examine individual values and aspirations, and seek God.

Saint John's is located 12 miles west of St. Cloud. Cited as one of the fastest-growing metropolitan areas in Minnesota, St. Cloud and the surrounding suburbs have a current population of 165,000. Saint John's is located off Interstate 94, a 1½-hour drive west from Minneapolis–St. Paul.

Saint John's Prep is accredited by the Independent Schools Association of the Central States and the North Central Association (ISACS). Memberships include the Minnesota Catholic Conference, the National Association of Independent Schools, the National Catholic Educational Association, and the Midwest Boarding Schools Association.

ACADEMIC PROGRAMS

Saint John's Prep follows a traditional liberal arts curriculum. A minimum of 22.5 full-year credits are required for graduation, among which the following must be included (waivers and exemptions are granted by the Academic Dean): English, 8 semesters; math, 6 semesters; fine arts, a minimum of 4 semesters; modern language, 6 semesters of one language or the equivalent; science, 6 semesters; social studies, 8 semesters; health, 1 semester; and theology, 5 semesters. Graduation requirements are met through a combination of required and elective courses. Independent study is also available. Courses for college credit in Spanish, German, English, math, science, and dozens of other subjects are available for qualified students through the School, Saint John's University, or the College of Saint Benedict.

Students take five or more classes per semester. They may also take courses at Saint John's University on the same campus and at the nearby College of Saint Benedict. Graduates of Saint John's Prep can complete a B.A. degree in three years with careful planning.

New international students are given an assessment of their English language skills as they arrive in the fall to determine their need for English as a Second Language classes and what level best fits their need.

A year-long study-abroad program at Melk, Austria is offered to juniors, seniors, and Prep graduates. This program, which began in 1966, is one of the oldest high school level exchange programs in the United States. It features a full academic curriculum enriched by travel throughout Europe. A month-long study-abroad program to Segovia, Spain, is also offered in the summer.

The postgraduate program offers students the flexibility to design a course of study that best meets their needs and interests. Students may take all of their courses at the Prep School or take up to three courses each semester at Saint John's University. Credits earned at Saint John's University and the College of Saint Benedict can be transferred elsewhere when the student enrolls in college.

The grading system uses A–F designations with pluses and minuses. Student progress reports are available on the School's Web site with parent access codes, and formal grade reports come out at the end of each semester. The system allows careful monitoring of students' progress throughout the semester. Parent-teacher conferences are held twice a year, and parents are invited to arrange an appointment with teachers and staff members whenever they are concerned about their son's or daughter's academic or social progress. Supervised study time during the school day is required, the amount varying according to a student's grade point average. Boarding students also have evening study hall.

FACULTY AND ADVISERS

In 2008–09, the faculty consisted of 20 men and 13 women. Twenty-six have earned a master's degree. Nearly all faculty members contribute to the quality of life through coaching, advising, counseling, and helping with musical, dramatic, and other special events. The faculty members are assisted by college students—paraprofessionals studying education—who work as tutors for students having academic difficulty.

Father Timothy Backous, O.S.B., was appointed Head of School in July 2006. Father Tim is a graduate of Saint John's University (B.A., 1976) and earned his master's and doctoral degrees from Accademia Alfonsiana in Rome, Italy. Prior to his appointment at Saint John's Prep, Father Tim taught English and served as the English Department Chair at Saint John's University, as well as serving as Director of Campus Ministry for nine years.

COLLEGE ADMISSION COUNSELING

The School employs a college placement counselor and maintains an office with a complete collection of catalogs of colleges and universities in the United States as well as handbooks and brochures. Many college admissions representatives visit the Prep School each year, and seniors' trips to various schools are arranged through the counseling office. Ninety-eight percent of all Prep graduates pursue education at institutions of higher learning. Recent graduates are attending Babson, Boston College, Caltech, Carleton, the College of Saint Benedict, Harvard, Lewis and Clark, Macalester, Saint John's, Stanford, Wellesley, and the Universities of Minnesota and Wisconsin—and more than 100 other schools in the past five years. A complete list of colleges and universities offering admission to the graduates of Saint John's Prep in recent years can be found at http://www.sjprep.net.

STUDENT BODY AND CONDUCT

The enrollment on campus for 2008–09 included freshmen, 26 boys and 19 girls; sophomores, 28 boys and 41 girls; juniors, 49 boys and 32 girls; seniors, 37 boys and 25 girls; and postgraduates, 2 boys. Of these, 8 were studying in Austria. There were 79 students enrolled in the Middle School.

About 35 percent of the Upper School students board. Through the English Second Language Program and the Study Abroad Program, Saint John's Prep maintains an international position. This year, there are international students from twelve countries living on campus. U.S. boarders come from states across the country, including California, Florida, Iowa, Nebraska, New Jersey, North Dakota, North Carolina, South Dakota, Texas, Washington, and Wyoming, as well as Minnesota. Day students come from fourteen local school districts. Approximately 50 percent of the students are not Catholic.

Students of Saint John's Preparatory School have common expectations and rights that deserve mutual support. These expectations and rights include physical safety, honesty, protection of physical and mental health, and an orderly environment in which to pursue the goals that bring Saint John's together as a school community.

In order to protect the rights of all members of the Prep community and to establish and maintain an orderly environment for the pursuit of goals that are consonant with the philosophy of the School, rules have been established and are published in the student handbook. Disciplinary action for major offenses is carried out by the Dean of Students. Consequences for major offenses might include community service, work details, fines, in-school suspension, home suspension, probation, and/or dismissal.

ACADEMIC FACILITIES

In November 2007, the School concluded its five-year, $15-million capital campaign with more than $18.3 million raised. A portion of the money raised was dedicated to the construction of a 22,600-square-foot expansion, which houses the entire middle school and provides additional area for the school's extensive music program. The expansion was completed in August 2008. In addition, a portion of the capital campaign funds assists in increasing both financial aid dollars awarded and the financial aid endowment. The campaign continues the School's aggressive goal to reach a desired level of salary and benefits for teachers.

Many educational facilities are shared by the Prep School and Saint John's University, including the Alcuin Library, which houses more than 250,000 volumes, microfilms, and videotapes. A technology link to the University's computer system provides Prep students and faculty members with individual e-mail accounts, access to the Internet, and numerous online databases and software programs.

BOARDING AND GENERAL FACILITIES

At Saint John's Prep, being in residence is viewed as much more than living in a room on campus. It brings young people together from around the world to create an exciting community accented with cultural diversity and friendships. Resident students have a peer group that values study. They also have adults who know from their own experience what study entails and what college requires of the student. Prep boarding boys are housed on the Prep School campus. The residential program for girls is offered through the cooperation of the nearby College of Saint Benedict. The College of Saint Benedict, located 4 miles away in the small town of St. Joseph, Minnesota, is a premier liberal arts college for women, operating a coordinated program with Saint John's University. Each freshman student shares a room, and upper-level students are assigned single rooms on a seniority basis.

Students have five dining facilities to choose from, including one at the School, two on the Saint John's University campus and two on the College of Saint Benedict's campus. Medical attention is available at the Health Center. A doctor is available each day for appointments, and a pharmacy is located on campus. The St. Cloud Hospital is located about 20 minutes away.

Other facilities, shared by the University and the Prep School, include the Saint John's Abbey Church, the Stephen B. Humphrey Auditorium, and the Warner Palaestra, which houses an indoor track, indoor tennis courts, racquetball courts, a climbing wall, and an Olympic-size swimming pool.

ATHLETICS

At Saint John's Prep, a variety of formal and informal athletics programs provide not only an outlet for adolescent energy but also an opportunity to learn the fundamentals of teamwork and community building. On the informal level, biking, cross-country skiing, and hiking are available on campus. Ski trips are organized throughout the winter by the resident staff. Ping-Pong, racquetball, swimming, and tennis are also popular.

Saint John's Prep is a member of the Prairie Conference, fielding varsity teams for boys in baseball and football; for girls in gymnastics, softball, and swimming; and for boys and girls in basketball, cross-country running, cross-country skiing, hockey, soccer, tennis, and track and field.

EXTRACURRICULAR OPPORTUNITIES

Weekly movies, college sports, cultural events, and pickup games are regular parts of student life at Saint John's Prep. The Convocation Series brings guest artists and lecturers to the School.

Several musical organizations, including the band and chorus, string ensembles, jazz band, and other clubs are open to students. Instrumental and vocal music lessons are offered at the School. The theater department produces three plays each year, with one having a travel component. Speech, *Prep World* (the student yearbook), Knowledge Bowl, student government, Mock Trial, Campus Ministry, Peer Ministry, National Honor Society, Film Club, World Club, Spanish Club, and German Club are other extracurricular activities.

DAILY LIFE

Classes are held five days each week. The school day begins at 8 a.m. and ends at 3:10 p.m. Class periods are 42 minutes long. Intramural sports, driver's education, and other activities take place after school. Once each week an All-School Convocation or Mass takes place. Boarding students must study in the residence hall from 8 to 10 p.m., Sunday through Thursday.

WEEKEND LIFE

For boarding students, permission to spend an evening off campus is granted at the discretion of the Dean of Students. Students may spend weekends at their own or another student's home. At least one school-sponsored social event is held each month. There are three-, four-, or five-day Home Weekends scheduled regularly throughout the school year. The Residence Hall Life Committee plans other weekend activities, such as tournaments, bonfires, ski trips, and special dinners, in addition to regular weekend bus trips to movie theaters and shopping areas.

SUMMER PROGRAMS

A variety of weeklong summer camps are available. Summer Leadership Camps for boys and girls ages 10–15 are located at Prep during the summer. The Leadership Camp aims to instill a sense of personal responsibility in each camper. Small-group discussions and a variety of athletics, swimming, canoeing, wall climbing, and crafts are included. German Camp, Art Camp, and Theater/Circus Camps are conducted as well. Additional information about all camps is available by calling Saint John's Prep School.

COSTS AND FINANCIAL AID

The comprehensive fee for the 2008–09 school year was $6384 for grades 7 and 8, $12,739 for Upper School day students, $25,757 for five-day boarders, $28,918 for seven-day boarders, and $33,320 for international students. This included, where applicable, room, board, tuition, fees for activities, books, and room deposit. Seniors pay a small extra fee for graduation. Tuition payments may be made in one payment prior to the start of the school year, through semester payments, or through monthly payments, which may be made in eleven installments.

Financial aid is available and is granted on the basis of need, as assessed by the Financial Aid Office through its financial aid form (Parents' Financial Statement). The School also offers merit-based scholarships for qualified students. In 2008–09, 57 percent of the U.S. students received financial aid. Each award includes a combination of a scholarship or grant and a work-study.

ADMISSIONS INFORMATION

Saint John's Prep admits students whom the Committee on Admission judges to have the intellectual capacity, character, and ability to do well in their studies, benefit their fellow students by the quality of their personal lives, and give promise of distinction in community service and leadership.

Students applying for admission must submit an application form and fee, a transcript of previous work, and two letters of recommendation using the School's form. They must take an entrance exam—the Differential Aptitude Test (DAT). Minimum expectations are a 2.0 GPA (C average) and a score in the 60th percentile or higher on the DAT. A campus visit with an interview is normally required. Approximately 100 new students are admitted each year.

APPLICATION TIMETABLE

Inquiries are welcome at any time. Campus visits are arranged to suit the family's convenience. Normal office hours are 8 to 4:30, Monday through Friday. Visits may be arranged by calling for an appointment. Students may also visit during Discovery Days, held from October through April. The application fee is $30 for U.S. students or $100 for international students. The entrance exam can be taken during the campus visit. Applications are considered up to the desired date of entrance, with preference given for early registration. After parents accept an offer of admission for their children, they are requested to submit a $500 deposit to reserve a room in the residence hall; for day students, a $200 deposit is required.

ADMISSIONS CORRESPONDENCE

Bryan Backes, Director of Admissions
Saint John's Preparatory School
Collegeville, Minnesota 56321

Phone: 320-363-3321
800-525-7737 (toll-free)
Fax: 320-363-3322
E-mail: admitprep@csbsju.edu
Web site: http://www.sjprep.net

ST. MARGARET'S SCHOOL

Tappahannock, Virginia

Type: Girls' boarding and day Episcopal college-preparatory school
Grades: 8–12
Enrollment: 151
Head of School: Margaret R. Broad, Head of School

THE SCHOOL

St. Margaret's School is an Episcopal college-preparatory boarding and day school enrolling girls in grades 8 through 12. Located 45 miles northeast of Richmond in historic Tidewater Virginia, the School's picturesque 51-acre campus provides an ideal setting for academic work. Set on the banks of the Rappahannock River, St. Margaret's enjoys the recreational and educational opportunities made available by a riverfront campus while benefiting from the nearby cultural centers of Washington, D.C., and Richmond and Williamsburg, Virginia.

Founded in 1921 by the Episcopal Diocese of Virginia, St. Margaret's prepares girls for an increasingly complex and international world by supplementing a college-preparatory education with interdisciplinary seminars, town meetings, independent studies, and travel programs.

St. Margaret's is recognized as a leader among boarding schools in character and life skills education. Through a formal cocurriculum, experienced staff members and outside experts lead girls through age-appropriate explorations of identity and relationships, healthy lifestyles, and decision making.

A nonprofit institution with more than 2,000 alumnae, St. Margaret's School is governed by a Board of Governors that includes alumnae and parents. The endowment is currently valued at $5.7 million. The School plant is valued at more than $18 million.

St. Margaret's is accredited by the Southern Association of Colleges and Schools and the Virginia Association of Independent Schools. It holds membership in the National Association of Independent Schools, the National Association of Episcopal Schools, the Virginia Association of Independent Schools, the National Coalition of Girls' Schools, and a variety of other educational organizations.

St. Margaret's also is a member of the Queen Margaret of Scotland Girls' Schools Association (QMSGSA), a group of thirteen schools in nine countries, which provides opportunities for cross-cultural programs. The School offers exchanges with the St. Margaret's Schools in Berwick, Australia; and Wellington, New Zealand, for selected sophomores and juniors, respectively.

ACADEMIC PROGRAMS

All St. Margaret's students must earn at least 21 credits en route to their diplomas. Each student carries a minimum of five academic courses.

Eighth graders may elect a variety of courses and can earn some high school credit. Algebra I and the first year of a foreign language qualify.

St. Margaret's is committed to providing solid college preparation. The 21 required credits are distributed in the following nine academic areas: English, 4 credits; foreign language, 2–3 credits; mathematics (algebra I, algebra II, and geometry), 3 credits; laboratory science (chemistry and biology), 2 credits; history (world history, U.S. history, and government), 3 credits; religious studies, 1 credit; fine arts, 1 credit; health, ½ credit; and electives (psychology, foreign policy, photography, pottery, journalism, and study skills), 2 or more credits. In addition, students must demonstrate computer proficiency and participate in physical activity twice weekly. St. Margaret's defines a credit as the completion of one year of secondary-level course work or its equivalent.

Within these areas, students can select from more than seventy courses, including English 8; introduction to literature and composition; introduction to world literature and composition; American literature; British literature; college reading and writing; Honors English; Advanced Placement English; history 8; geography; world history I and II; U.S. history and government; great books; current events; foreign policy; the twentieth century; personal finance; prealgebra; algebra I, II, and III; geometry; precalculus; calculus; Advanced Placement calculus; science 8; conceptual physics; chemistry; anatomy and physiology; ecology; biology; physics; Advanced Placement biology; French I–V; Advanced Placement French; Latin I–V; Spanish I–V; introduction to the New Testament; introduction to the Old Testament; comparative religion; health/physical education 8; health; driver education; art history; mixed media; fashion design; photography; drawing I, II, and III; painting I, II, and III; watercolors; mosaics; ceramics; Treble Choir; vocal ensemble; music history; drama history; piano; low-intermediate ESL; high-intermediate ESL; advanced ESL; ESL–U.S. history; ESL–science; and ESL–American culture.

To enhance academic success, St. Margaret's provides supervised, structured study time each school day and in the evening. Daytime study halls, supervised by faculty members, are for all students except those on the honor roll and seniors with in-room study privileges. The evening study period is from 7:30 to 9:30, Sunday through Thursday, and, depending on academic standing, may take place in study hall or in the student's dormitory room. Students working on special projects are encouraged to make use of the library or the computer lab or to study with another student.

Academic standing is evaluated every five weeks. Students whose performance indicates a need for additional support are assigned to math lab, writing lab, or special study halls.

The grading system uses A to F designations with pluses and minuses. Reports are sent to parents at the midpoint and end of each trimester.

To provide as many opportunities as possible for a well-rounded education, St. Margaret's offers a two-week minimester program. Every February, faculty teams teach intensive, seminar-style courses that encourage creative inquiry, experiential learning, and an exploration of cross-curricular themes.

During this time, most seniors participate in an independent off-campus project to explore a potential career or field of study. In addition, study trips are offered each year. Recent destinations include China, Greece, Peru, Spain, Morocco, and the Bahamas.

FACULTY AND ADVISERS

Appointed Head of School in 1989, Margaret R. Broad is a graduate of Denison University (B.A., 1970) and the University of Virginia (M.A., 1988). Prior to becoming Head, she served as Academic Dean for two years, Head of the Foreign Language Department for eight years, and a French teacher for nine years.

Each student has a faculty adviser, who provides guidance in academic as well as resident life. The School aims to know each girl well and work with her to develop her special talents to the fullest. The faculty-student ratio is 1:6, and 75 percent of the staff members are in residence. There are 32 faculty members.

COLLEGE ADMISSION COUNSELING

St. Margaret's prepares all of its students to succeed as undergraduates in a college or university setting. All new St. Margaret's students entering eighth, ninth, and tenth grades take a trimester-long credit course in study skills. The course teaches, reinforces, and develops appropriate and consistent techniques and habits.

Throughout their junior and senior years, students work with the college counselor to explore college options and complete applications. St. Margaret's publishes an annual college handbook that provides extensive information about the college search, application, and selection process.

College representatives visit St. Margaret's throughout the year, and juniors attend the Richmond Independent Schools' College Fair to meet with representatives from a diverse array of colleges and universities. Many juniors also elect to take the Next Steps minimester course that provides SAT preparation, college application workshops, and visits to multiple college campuses. Students access extensive college information and manage their applications using the online Naviance program. The Naviance Family Connection site allows students and parents access to St. Margaret's specific college counseling information from anywhere in the world.

Each year, freshmen, sophomores, and juniors take the PSAT, and juniors and seniors take the SAT. SAT Subject Tests are also offered, and qualified students may take Advanced Placement tests. In 2007, 4 students were named AP scholars, 2 were awarded the distinction of National Merit Commended Scholars, and 1 was named a National Merit Semifinalist. The class of 2007 graduated 28 students who are attending such institutions as Colorado State University, George Washington University, New York University, Parsons: The New School of Design, Washington and Lee, and Wofford College.Auburn, James Madison, Virginia Tech, William and Mary, and the Universities of Texas at Austin and Virginia.

STUDENT BODY AND CONDUCT

In 2008–09, the School enrolled 151 students, 112 of whom were boarding students. The student body represents seventeen states, the District of Columbia, and ten countries. Although St. Margaret's is an Episcopal school, students of all faiths are enrolled, welcomed, and valued.

It is the School's belief that stressing honor, trust, and high principles builds not only a better school but also a better world. Students abide by an honor code and clearly structured system of rules; they are accountable for their actions. Many students share in the leadership of the school community as prefects, peer leaders, school and class officers, and honor council members. Increasing maturity is accompanied by increasing privileges and responsibility.

ACADEMIC FACILITIES

St. Margaret's Hall (1820), the central building, contains administrative offices, classrooms, the chapel, an art center, and a music center. The Viola Woolfolk Learning Center (1991) contains the library, study hall, and classrooms. The library houses a collection of approximately 9,000 books, fifty current periodicals, extensive reference materials, a variety of audiovisual media, and access to more than 30 online research databases. Additional classrooms are located in the Cottage (1923). The Community/Technology Center (1999) houses science classrooms; chemistry, physics, and biology labs; computer labs; and a spacious dining hall that overlooks the Rappahannock River.

BOARDING AND GENERAL FACILITIES

Students live in air-conditioned dormitories with resident dorm parents on each floor. In 2005, the School opened a 24-student dormitory that includes three faculty-member residences. The School fully renovated its largest dormitory in 2002. Meals are served buffet-style in the School dining room overlooking the Rappahannock River. Student rooms are wired for personal telephones and Internet and Intranet connections. Each student has her own e-mail account. A swimming pool, tennis courts, and a fitness room provide after-class recreation.

Two nurses staff the infirmary, and a doctor is on call. There is a hospital in Tappahannock.

ATHLETICS

Athletics and physical education are an integral part of St. Margaret's overall program, a challenge to each girl to grow in physical well-being and to be the best she can be. In 2006, the School opened its fall athletic season on new playing fields, developed on 42 acres of land 5 minutes from the campus.

About two thirds of the students participate on athletic teams. St. Margaret's teams do well because the students understand teamwork and team spirit. Students may try out for cross-country, field hockey, tennis, and volleyball in the fall; basketball, swimming, and track in the winter; and crew, golf, soccer, softball, and lacrosse in the spring.

In addition to team sports, plenty of other activities are designed for solo performers, such as aerobics, dance, golf, horseback riding, running, walking, and yoga.

To promote sportsmanship, school spirit, teamwork, and friendly competition, every student is a member of either the Blue or Grey team. Contests between these intramural teams are held throughout the year.

EXTRACURRICULAR OPPORTUNITIES

Students must participate in an after-school activity each trimester and are encouraged to try something they have not done before. The following clubs, societies, and outside organizations are active at St. Margaret's: activities committee, art club, Basic Needs (service club), *The Channel* (newspaper)*, *The Current* (yearbook)*, ensemble*, Treble Choir*, the honor council*, National Honor Society*, peer leaders*, poetry club, Quill & Scroll*, Soulful Voices (gospel music)*, student ambassador society*, Student Government Association*, *The Tides* (literary magazine), and Guild of Sacristans. (An asterisk denotes that students must be elected, appointed, or invited to join.)

St. Margaret's has a community service requirement of 12 hours per year that students often exceed. In addition to established programs such as Habitat for Humanity, students participate in projects ranging from work with children in educational, athletic, and recreational programs to community beautification projects.

DAILY LIFE

The daily schedule begins with breakfast at 7, followed by chapel or announcements at 7:50. Classes are held from 8:20 until 3:30 and are followed by athletics and activities. Dinner is at 5:30, study hall runs from 7:30 to 9:30, and lights-out is at 10:45.

Each week consists of three 7-period days, one 3-period day, and one 4-period day. The three- and four-period days, which have 75-minute periods, allow for flexible and varied class activities. The Teachers Available period occurs after classes four days a week. At this time, all teachers are in their classrooms and are available to provide extra help.

WEEKEND LIFE

On weekends, students have time for special interest programs, cultural trips, or social activities. To help students discover lifetime leisure interests, the School requires them to participate in at least one cultural or outdoor activity each trimester. For example, girls can enjoy themselves in museums in the nation's capital, take an overnight sailing trip on the Chesapeake Bay, or attend plays in Richmond. Students at St. Margaret's experience all that the area has to offer.

A varied calendar provides the opportunity for dances and social gatherings at other Virginia schools such as Christchurch School, Episcopal High School, Woodberry Forest School, and Virginia Episcopal School. St. Margaret's is a member of the Boarding Schools Social Activities Committee, which plans social events for Virginia and Maryland boarding schools.

Students are allowed off campus five weekend nights per trimester in addition to major vacations. Juniors and seniors are granted additional time to visit colleges. Parental permission is required for all off-campus weekends.

COSTS AND FINANCIAL AID

For 2009–10, tuition for boarding students is $40,000; tuition for day students is $16,000. Boarding students must pay a $2000 deposit to cover charges for supplies, special testing programs, weekend trips, and other incidental expenses. Day students pay a deposit of $1000. Additional charges are made for musical instruction and ESL.

The School subscribes to the School and Student Service for Financial Aid. In 2007, financial aid was awarded to approximately 30 percent of the student body on the basis of need and academic standing.

ADMISSIONS INFORMATION

St. Margaret's School seeks students who can benefit from and contribute to the School community. The School actively admits students without regard to race, color, creed, or national or ethnic origin. Candidates are accepted in all grades on the basis of recognized potential and achievement, completion of the SSAT, the applicant's extracurricular activities, and the recommendations of 2 teachers and 1 personal acquaintance. An interview on campus is required.

APPLICATION TIMETABLE

Although St. Margaret's conducts rolling admissions, prospective students are urged to apply in the winter. If vacancies exist, applications may be considered throughout the summer.

ADMISSIONS CORRESPONDENCE

Director of Admission
St. Margaret's School
Tappahannock, Virginia 22560
Phone: 804-443-3357
Fax: 804-443-6781
E-mail: admit@sms.org
Web site: http://www.sms.org

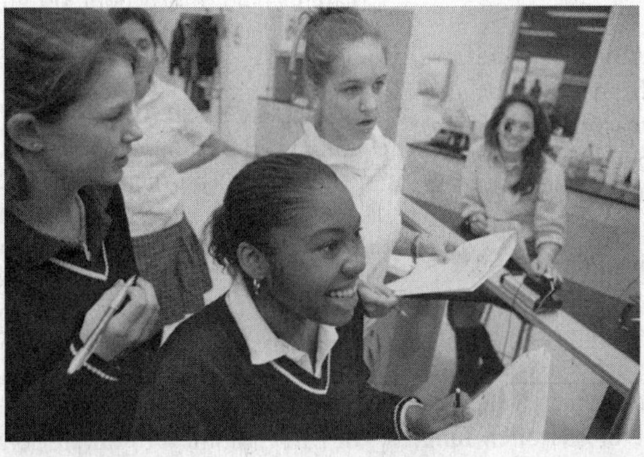

ST. MARK'S SCHOOL OF TEXAS

Dallas, Texas

Type: Boys' day college-preparatory school
Grades: 1–12: Lower School, 1–4; Middle School, 5–8; Upper School, 9–12
Enrollment: School total: 843; Upper School: 366
Head of School: Arnold E. Holtberg, Headmaster

THE SCHOOL

St. Mark's is the descendant of three former Dallas boys' schools: Terrill School (1906–1944), Texas Country Day School (1933–1950), and Cathedral School (1944–1950). St. Mark's was organized in 1950 on the Preston Road campus of Texas Country Day School (TCD) when the Cathedral School merged with TCD. The campus is located on 43 acres in the residential area of North Dallas.

St. Mark's college-preparatory program fosters intellectual, academic, and artistic excellence in young men and encourages development of the strengths in each boy's character and personality. Toward these ends, St. Mark's offers a broad range of intellectual, artistic, and athletic opportunities for its students. Challenging studies in the sciences, arts, and humanities form the basis of a St. Mark's education. Teachers work to instill an enthusiasm for learning, encourage independent and critical judgment, and demonstrate the methods for making sound inquiries and for effective communications. St. Mark's aims to prepare young men to assume leadership and responsibility in a competitive and changing world.

St. Mark's Lower School (grades 1–4) is housed in a single building and has approximately 25 faculty members. The program offers diverse learning activities, including academic instruction in Spanish language and culture, language arts, mathematics, science, and social studies; regular instruction in the arts (visual arts, music, creative dramatics); and a developmental physical education program that teaches fundamental skills at a level geared to the age and abilities of the child.

St. Mark's School of Texas is accredited by the Independent Schools Association of the Southwest. Its memberships include the National Association of Independent Schools, the Cum Laude Society, the International Boys' School Coalition, and the College Board.

ACADEMIC PROGRAMS

The academic program in the Upper School is designed to satisfy the most exacting requirements for admission to colleges and universities across the country, but it is more broadly defined by the School and the faculty as preparation for personal independence, enlightenment, and maturity.

There are required courses, Advanced Placement courses, and many electives available. Graduation requirements are 4 years of English, 3 years of a foreign language, 3 years of mathematics, 4 years of physical education or athletics, 3 years of social studies, 3 years of a laboratory science, 1 year in fine arts, a senior exhibition, and 15 hours of community service each Upper School year. Each student takes five classes per year, and some students, with the permission of the Head of the Upper School, may take more.

The individual teaching sections average about 15 students. In most classes, the students are randomly grouped; the notable exceptions are in honors and Advanced Placement courses.

The School operates on a trimester system. Hence, grade reports are given three times a year and are mailed home to the parents with written comments. Interim reports are also written to help ensure adequate reporting to the parents. Parents are encouraged to communicate at any time with their son's adviser. Only final grades in Upper School classes are recorded for transcript purposes.

FACULTY AND ADVISERS

For the academic year 2008–09, the faculty consists of 121 full-time members; 76 hold master's degrees, and 9 have earned doctoral degrees.

The Headmaster, Arnold E. Holtberg, graduated cum laude from Princeton University in 1970 with a baccalaureate degree in sociology. He also received an M.A. degree in pastoral care and counseling in 1976 from the Lutheran Theological Seminary in Philadelphia, Pennsylvania.

The School seeks to employ faculty members who are willing to give an unusual amount of time to the School. One of the strengths and challenges of a faculty member at St. Mark's is that he or she often functions in several roles within the School.

COLLEGE ADMISSION COUNSELING

The Director of College Counseling and staff members coordinate college planning and counseling. All Upper School students are encouraged to attend the College Previews, held in September, and are welcome to utilize the college office. Several required college conferences are scheduled with students and parents, beginning in the junior year. The SAT mean scores for the class of 2008 were critical reading, 681; math, 710; and writing, 688. St. Mark's graduates are attending major universities throughout the country, including Brown, Carnegie Mellon, Dartmouth, Duke, Emory, Georgetown, Harvard, Johns Hopkins, Princeton, Stanford, Yale, and the Universities of Chicago, Pennsylvania, and Texas at Austin.

STUDENT BODY AND CONDUCT

In 2008–09, there are 98 boys in grade 9, 85 in grade 10, 95 in grade 11, and 88 in grade 12. Since St. Mark's is a day school, almost all of the boys come from the Dallas area. Approximately 33 percent of the students are members of minority groups.

While the rules that govern the School are published by the School, these rules or guidelines provide only a part of the criteria that determine student behavior. Students are also encouraged to take responsibility for their own actions, with the guidance of the faculty and class sponsors. A faculty- and student-led Discipline Council deals with some disciplinary problems.

Each boy has a faculty adviser who is available for personal counseling and advice and is responsible for reporting to the parents and the School on the student's overall performance.

ACADEMIC FACILITIES

Among the campus buildings are Centennial Hall and the Hoffman Center, both new facilities for fall 2008; the Green-McDermott Science and Mathematics Center; the Cecil and Ida Green Library; Nearburg Hall; the H. Ben Decherd Center for the Arts; the St. Mark's Chapel; Thomas O. Hicks Family Athletic Center; Mullen Family Fitness Center; Wirt Davis Hall; the A. Earl Cullum, Jr., Alumni Commons; and the Athletic Center, which includes the

Morris G. Spencer Gymnasium and the Ralph B. Rogers Natatorium. The Cecil and Ida Green Library seats 230 and houses 41,000 volumes, 4,000 microfilm reels, and twelve networked Pentium computers for research and Internet access, including 26 online subscription databases. Three professional librarians and a technical assistant staff the library. The School has an integrated campuswide technology network that includes video projection systems in more than 90 percent of the classrooms and numerous labs and access to extensive advanced information systems.

ATHLETICS

Every boy at St. Mark's is required to participate daily in some form of athletics. Upper School boys may select either the physical education program or one of the sports teams.

In physical education, the School is concerned with students' neuromuscular and cardiovascular development, as well as their development of an appreciation of physical fitness, through the specialty classes and intramural program.

The School provides many levels of interscholastic team sports to fit the needs of each student. There are sixteen different sports that are available to Middle and Upper School students, including baseball, basketball, crew, cross-country, cheerleading, fencing, football, golf, lacrosse, soccer, swimming, tennis, track and field, volleyball, water polo, and wrestling. For the 2007–08 school year, St. Mark's was awarded the Athletic Director's trophy for the best overall boys' athletic program in the Southwest Preparatory Conference.

EXTRACURRICULAR OPPORTUNITIES

Students at St. Mark's are encouraged to do more than excel in their academic subjects. A boy has the opportunity to participate in speech and debate, the Student Council, the mathematics team, the robotics team, the School's yearbook and newspaper, drama activities, the environmental club, the letterman's club, the Cum Laude Society, the Lion and Sword Society, the tutorial program, the astronomy club, the School's literary magazine, and many other activities.

DAILY LIFE

The school day begins at 8 a.m. for all boys and ends at 3:45 p.m. for grades 9–12. Most of the classes, except science and fine arts, last 45 minutes. Sports and extracurricular activities for grades 9–12 are from 3:55 to 6 p.m.

COSTS AND FINANCIAL AID

In 2008–09, tuition, including textbooks and supplies, lunches, and fees, is $22,874 for grade 9, $22,489 for grades 10 and 11, and $25,186 for grade 12. At the time of enrollment, a deposit of $1000 is due with the signed enrollment contract, and the balance of the tuition is due by July 1 prior to entrance in August.

The awarding of financial aid is based upon the student's financial need. Approximately 17 percent of the students receive financial aid. Parents are expected to furnish all of the financial information, as requested by the financial aid committee. Specific details are available from the Office of Admission.

ADMISSIONS INFORMATION

Applicants receive information about the School upon request or at the School's Web site at http://www.smtexas.org. Parents are asked to file an application, obtain a teacher's recommendation, and send a transcript of the applicant's prior work. Applicants take general aptitude, reading comprehension, vocabulary, and mathematics tests. A writing sample and on-campus interviews are also required. The application fee is $50 for grade 1 and $125 for grades 2–12.

APPLICATION TIMETABLE

Inquiries are welcome at any time. Group tours and individual tours are recommended. Applications should be submitted by December for grade 1 and by November for grades 2 through 4. Applications for grades 5 through 12 are due in January. Testing and interviewing are completed in February, and decision letters are mailed in mid-March for grades 1–12.

ADMISSIONS CORRESPONDENCE

David Baker
Director of Admission
St. Mark's School of Texas
10600 Preston Road
Dallas, Texas 75230-4000
Phone: 214-346-8700
Fax: 214-346-8701
E-mail: admission@smtexas.org
Web site: http://www.smtexas.org

SAINT MARY'S HALL

San Antonio, Texas

Type: Coeducational, nondenominational college-preparatory day school
Grades: P–12: Montessori Preschool/Kindergarten; Lower School, 1–5; Middle School, 6–8; Upper School, 9–12
Enrollment: School total: 960; Upper School, 330; Middle School, 217; Lower School, 273; Montessori Preschool/Kindergarten, 141
Head of School: Bob Windham, Head of School

THE SCHOOL

Saint Mary's Hall, a coeducational college-preparatory school, was founded in 1879 by the Right Reverend Robert Woodward Barnwell Elliott, the first bishop of the Protestant Episcopal Diocese of West Texas. In 1925, the school became a nonparochial independent school and was placed under the direction of a 25-member Board of Trustees.

Saint Mary's Hall has been at its present San Antonio location since 1968. The school is on a 60-acre wooded campus in a northeast suburb, just 3 miles east of the International Airport and within 15 minutes of downtown. The buildings of yellow Mexican brick were designed by architect O'Neil Ford in a style that features bright airy classrooms, open courtyards, and graceful Spanish arcades. The architecture blends harmoniously with the suburban setting.

The school has an endowment of $38 million and a physical plant valued at $44 million. The Alumni Association maintains contact with more than 3,200 alumni throughout the world.

The Lower School is composed of a Montessori program for ages 3 to 5, a kindergarten program, and a Lower School for Forms 1 through 5. The Montessori program follows the educational philosophy developed by Dr. Maria Montessori, which calls for an environment devoted to the young child's emotional, intellectual and physical self. Children learn to develop their sensory perceptions, acquire basic reading ability, and master simple arithmetic.

In the Lower School, the curriculum stresses language arts, mathematics, social studies, and science skills. An accelerated and enriched program provides special opportunities for advanced work. The program is designed to foster the development of critical, creative, and productive thinking. Physical education, music, art, computer science, drama, and Spanish are all part of the curriculum.

Saint Mary's Hall offers an extended care program from 7 a.m. to 6 p.m. for children in the Lower School.

The Middle School program provides a challenging curriculum with advanced courses in math and foreign language, as well as fine art classes, organized sports, clubs, a student senate, and a peer counseling program. The rigorous academics combined with a friendly environment create a well-balanced approach to education, including academic, creative, physical, and character-building activities.

Saint Mary's Hall is accredited by the Independent Schools Association of the Southwest and holds membership in Cum Laude Society, National Honor Society, College Board, Secondary School Admission Test Board, Educational Records Bureau, National Association of Independent Schools, National Association of College Admission Counseling, and American Montessori Society.

ACADEMIC PROGRAMS

The Saint Mary's Hall college-preparatory curriculum places strong emphasis on writing, researching, and analytical thinking.

Students must complete 26 credits to graduate. Requirements consist of English, 4; mathematics, 3; history, 3½; foreign language, 3; science, 3; physical education/athletics, 2; fine arts, 2; electives, 4½; and additional fine arts or physical education/athletics, 1.

Honors courses are offered in English, drama, foreign language, math, history, and science. Advanced Placement (AP) courses are offered in art history, biology, calculus AB, calculus BC, chemistry, computer science A, computer science AB, drawing, English language, English literature, environmental science, European history, French language, Latin Vergil, Latin literature, physics C, Spanish literature, Spanish language, statistics, studio art (drawing, 2-D, sculpture, 3-D), and U.S. government. In 2006, 484 AP examinations were given. Seventy-nine percent of the students were awarded scores of 3 or above, which qualifies for credit hours at most colleges and universities.

The school year of thirty-six weeks is divided into two semesters, the first ending before Christmas vacation and the second at the end of May. Each day is divided into seven 45-minute class periods and two conference periods. Students are expected to carry five solid academic subjects and one elective each semester and may choose the elective from courses offered in every department.

Private instrumental music lessons are available for additional fees. Tutors in all disciplines also are available privately and are paid for by parents.

FACULTY AND ADVISERS

The Upper School faculty includes 41 full-time members and 9 part-time members.

The Upper School has a strong advisory program, with each faculty member having 12 advisees. The adviser provides both personal and academic support and is the student's advocate in all matters.

Bob Windham, Head of School, attended Texas A&M University for his undergraduate degree. He received his master's degree in educational administration from the University of Houston. Bob Windham was formerly Headmaster at Trinity Valley School in Fort Worth, Texas. He has more than thirty years of experience in the public school setting as a teacher, coach, principal, and associate superintendent. Daily academic leadership is provided by Jonathan Eades, Assistant Head of School and Head of Upper School; Sam Hamilton, Head of Middle School; and Suzanne Todd, Head of Lower School.

COLLEGE ADMISSION COUNSELING

Preparation for college or university entrance begins in Form 9, when students are assisted in designing four-year curriculum plans that will best prepare them for college. Juniors and seniors participate in monthly college counseling sessions designed to identify career goals and academic interests. Every year, more than 75 college representatives visit the campus. Saint Mary's Hall hosts its own selective college fair, and students are prepared, through individual conferences, to select the colleges that best suit them.

The PSAT is required in the sophomore and junior years, and the SAT is taken in both the junior and senior years. Students are encouraged to include SAT preparation courses in their college-preparatory curriculum.

Mean SAT scores for the graduating class of 2007 were 637 verbal and 631 math, for a combined score of 1268. Members of the class of 2007 were accepted at Cornell, Davidson, Duke, Georgetown, George Washington, Harvard, Northwestern, Princeton, Southern Methodist, Stanford, Texas A&M, Texas at Austin, Texas Christian, Trinity, the United States Naval Academy, Vanderbilt, and Yale.

STUDENT BODY AND CONDUCT

In 2008–09, the Upper School had 98 freshmen (49 boys and 49 girls), 73 sophomores (37 boys and 36 girls), 83 juniors (39 boys and 44 girls), and 76 seniors (41 boys and 35 girls).

The Student Council works closely with the administration in planning activities for the student body and providing opportunities for the expression of student opinion. The Honor Council, comprising students and faculty members, recommends disciplinary measures for students who break school rules.

ACADEMIC FACILITIES

Educational facilities include a lecture hall with stage and projection room; three computer laboratories; thirteen science laboratories; two art studios; two libraries with more than 20,000 volumes; a fine arts instructional center, including studios for instrumental and choral music, photography, and theater; Lower School and Middle School buildings and additions; a dance building; more than seventy smart boards; an eight-lane track; and a 500-seat theater/chapel.

ATHLETICS

Competitive sports play an important part in the overall development of students, are open to all, and include baseball, basketball, cross-country, golf, lacrosse, soccer, softball, tennis, track, and volleyball. Varsity teams compete in the Southwest Preparatory Conference, which includes private school teams from Texas and Oklahoma. They also compete against local public schools. Athletics facilities include seven lighted tennis courts; a weight room; a swimming pool; three playing fields for soccer, softball, and baseball; an NCAA-regulation, lighted athletic complex; and two fully equipped gymnasiums.

EXTRACURRICULAR OPPORTUNITIES

Saint Mary's Hall strongly encourages students to develop their creative talents and leadership potential through extracurricular activities. The drama department produces two major plays each year, and the dance and choral music departments present a major cooperative production each year. The choral and instrumental music groups give regular performances, as do musically gifted piano and classical guitar students. The school sponsors the publication of a yearbook and a literary magazine. There also are language and special interest clubs.

DAILY LIFE

Classes begin at 8 a.m. and end at 3:10 p.m. There are eight class periods and an announcement time for the students and faculty members each school day. In addition, there is time reserved for chapel once a week and as a meeting period for students and teachers on other days. Sports and extracurricular activities take place after school.

COSTS AND FINANCIAL AID

In 2008–09, tuition for the Upper School students was $18,175. Additional costs are for uniforms and books (estimated at $1000).

A deposit of 10 percent of tuition is due with the signed enrollment agreement. The remainder of the fees must be paid by July 1 for entrance in the fall semester. Arrangements may be made to pay the tuition in two installments, the second due December 1. There also is a ten-month payment plan that may be arranged through the Business Office.

Financial aid is available for students. It is based on need and is awarded according to an evaluation prepared by the Saint Mary's Hall Grant Committee and review of the School and Student Service for Financial Aid application. Aid is awarded in the form of grants in amounts that depend on the availability of funds.

Merit scholarship funds also are available. The Campbell Academic Scholarship Program awards four full-tuition scholarships to outstanding students entering Form 9.

ADMISSIONS INFORMATION

An application for admission includes recommendations, past school records, an admission interview, standardized test results, and an application fee.

APPLICATION TIMETABLE

All highly interested applicants are encouraged to apply to Saint Mary's Hall by February 15. Complete applications received by February 15 receive priority consideration for admission into Saint Mary's Hall. Applications filed after the February 15 are considered on a space-available basis.

Visits to Saint Mary's Hall are welcome at any time during the year.

ADMISSIONS CORRESPONDENCE

Amy Anderson
Director of Admission
Saint Mary's Hall
9401 Starcrest Drive
San Antonio, Texas 78217

Phone: 210-483-9234
Fax: 210-655-5211
E-mail: admissions@smhall.org
Web site: http://www.smhall.org

ST. MARY'S PREPARATORY SCHOOL

Orchard Lake, Michigan

Type: Boys' boarding and day college-preparatory Catholic school
Grades: 9–12
Enrollment: 500
Head of School: James Glowacki, Headmaster

THE SCHOOL

Founded in Detroit in 1885 along with SS. Cyril and Methodius Seminary and St. Mary's College, St. Mary's Preparatory provides an education in the Catholic tradition for boys in grades 9–12. The School's founder, Fr. Joseph Dabrowski, wanted a complete educational complex for Polish immigrants interested in the priesthood. His aspiration has developed into a thriving community of three distinct schools on one campus. The present site for the schools is a beautiful 125-acre campus on the east shore of one of the state's largest lakes, Orchard Lake. The campus consists of twenty-one buildings, nine of which were present when the School moved to the site of the former Michigan Military Academy in 1909. Located in a largely affluent, suburban area 1 hour from Detroit and 10 minutes from Pontiac, St. Mary's offers a diverse, affordable, high-quality education, rich in personal contact and Catholic values, to students from Michigan, other parts of the United States, and the world.

The School is an incorporated, not-for-profit institution and is administered by a Board of Trustees. An active Moms & Dads Club and an Athletic Booster Club keep parents involved in School activities.

The emphasis at St. Mary's is on the individual student so that each student's needs are considered on a personal basis. The administration, teachers, and coaches work to develop each individual's talents and abilities at his own pace and in his own way. The average class size of 18 students allows teachers to understand the needs of their students and to teach to those needs in a style that stresses dialogue, not lecture. Counseling, tutoring, and supervised study are all available, but it is the personal contact and understanding directed toward each student that produces results.

ACADEMIC PROGRAMS

St. Mary's has designed an academic program that meets the basic entrance requirements for any college curriculum. Along with required courses, however, students, parents, and guidance counselors work together to determine an appropriate elective schedule. St. Mary's encourages students to create a program that addresses their individual interests and needs. Requirements for graduation are 4 years of theology and English; 3 years of mathematics, science, and social studies; 2 years of foreign language; and a semester each of computer programming, computer applications, physical education, health, fine arts, and speech. Students are required to fulfill 28 credits for graduation.

Seniors and selected juniors may take classes at Madonna University–Orchard Lake Center, which is conveniently located on the same campus. These students earn college credit directly, with no need to take an Advanced Placement exam. St. Mary's students have graduated with more than 30 college credits.

Although students need not be Catholic to attend St. Mary's, all students are educated in the Catholic tradition. This tradition includes 4 years of theology in the classroom as well as attendance at Mass twice weekly. Students are also required to perform a certain amount of community service as determined by the theology department. In addition, students may attend class retreats, and the School Chaplain and many campus priests make their time available to students.

The scholastic year is divided into two semesters and each semester into three marking periods. Parents are advised of grades through report cards that are mailed at the end of each six-week marking period. Deficiency reports are mailed three weeks into each marking period to the parents of any student who is doing poorly in a subject. In addition, frequent, informal contact between parents and faculty members is provided to keep parents involved in their son's progress.

The grading scale at St. Mary's ranges from A+ to E. Passing grades are A+ to D–, which corresponds with a 4.0 scale of 4.3 to 0.7 and a percentage scale of 100 to 70 percent. Students transferring to St. Mary's from another school meet with the Counselor to determine which grades are transferable and which requirements need to be completed.

FACULTY AND ADVISERS

Mr. James Glowacki, a 1985 graduate of St. Mary's Preparatory, was named Headmaster in 1999. Mr. Glowacki earned both a B.A. and an M.A. from Wayne State University and served as the head of the English department at St. Mary's before his current appointment.

St. Mary's maintains an established and capable faculty and staff that consists of 49 teachers and several administrators. The faculty is very active in the lives of students through coaching, clubs, tutoring, and School activities.

COLLEGE ADMISSION COUNSELING

A full-time guidance counselor assists students in selecting colleges and universities. Many college representatives visit St. Mary's during the year and are given the opportunity to speak to the students in groups and individually. Seniors are given frequent, personalized guidance.

Traditionally, 99 percent of St. Mary's graduates are accepted to four-year colleges and universities each year. Recent graduates have attended colleges across the United States and in several other countries, including Brown, Carnegie Mellon, Columbia, Holy Cross, Kettering (formerly GMI), Loyola of Chicago, Michigan State, Notre Dame, Tufts, the United States Military Academy, Yale, and the Universities of Michigan, Pennsylvania, and Virginia.

STUDENT BODY AND CONDUCT

The 2008–09 student body consisted of 113 freshmen, 122 sophomores, 140 juniors, and 125 seniors. There were 65 boarding students representing several states and countries.

Students are guided in their attitude and conduct by St. Mary's *Parent/Student Handbook.* The Code of Conduct is based on Christian values, which must be part of the external actions of each student. The goal of the student code is to aid students in developing self-discipline. These rules apply to all students at School functions on or off campus, as participants or spectators, or when using School-sponsored transportation. The Headmaster, Dean of Students, and Dean of Resident Students determine the appropriate action to be taken for any offense against the Code of Conduct. Actions include a detention to be served after school hours, a Saturday detention to be served for 5 hours on Saturday morning, suspension, and expulsion for the most serious offenses. Most discipline is handled without formal action by the teachers. Dorm discipline also includes work crews that take care of the maintenance tasks in the dormitory.

Students follow a dress code during classes and in the chapel. On Wednesdays and Fridays, all students wear the School uniform. In addition to the regular dress code, the uniform is required for special School functions and during off-campus School-sponsored trips and consists of a blue blazer with the School crest and a School tie.

At the conclusion of the academic year, the administration reviews each student's academic and social performance. Students are invited to return to St. Mary's on a yearly basis. A positive attitude toward oneself and one's neighbor is a requirement at St. Mary's Prep.

ACADEMIC FACILITIES

The School is situated on a 125-acre campus, 70 acres of which are developed. Facilities include a three-story residence dormitory; two gymnasiums; a crew house; the campus dining commons; Shrine Chapel; the Classroom Building; the Science Center; the Alumni Library, with a $5-million addition containing more than 75,000 volumes; the Prep Library, located in the residence dormitory; and the $5-million St. Mary's Athletic Complex, including an ice arena, an indoor track, a weight room, a wrestling room, and concessions. The campus has a lake shoreline of 1 mile, with two docks and a swimming area.

BOARDING AND GENERAL FACILITIES

St. Mary's Prep houses students in a modern, three-story dormitory. The dormitory is under the direction of the Dean of Resident Students, and Prefects are assigned to each floor to provide direction and assistance. Students share rooms with a roommate of the same grade level. Seniors may have single rooms if available. Each room is furnished with a bed, desk, bookshelves, dressers, and sinks. Bathroom facilities are located between every two rooms.

The dormitory contains a library and a recreation hall. The library gives boarding students access to computer facilities, while the recreation hall has a big-screen television, pool tables, and other entertainment. Other facilities include two gymnasiums, the campus dining commons, and Shrine Chapel.

ATHLETICS

Although all students participate in the physical education program at St. Mary's, interscholastic sports are not a requirement. An estimated 80 percent of students participate in varsity, junior varsity, and freshman athletics. The programs available include baseball, basketball, cross-country, football, golf, hockey, lacrosse, rowing, skiing, soccer, track and field, and wrestling.

The School's athletic facilities are quite extensive and include an ice arena, which includes an indoor track, a weight room, and a wrestling room. The campus also has two gymnasiums, a crew house, two football fields, two baseball diamonds, a track, lacrosse and soccer fields, tennis courts, and many outdoor basketball courts as well as Orchard Lake, which is often used for swimming, windsurfing, fishing, ice skating, and cross-country skiing.

Athletics programs are under the direction of the Athletic Director. Interscholastic and intramural activities are coached by members of the faculty and staff as well as a staff of part-time coaches. Competitions are held against schools of similar or larger size. St. Mary's takes great pride in its tradition of competing at a level much higher than its size would indicate.

EXTRACURRICULAR OPPORTUNITIES

St. Mary's makes a serious attempt to provide for the interests of its students. Social exchanges are conducted with local schools, and field trips to places of cultural and historic interest are sponsored by various student classes or the Classmasters. Student organizations include Student Council, which sponsors a variety of activities; an Eco-club; choir; band; robotics; youth ministry; forensics; debate; Key Club (social service); SADD; *The Eaglet,* the School yearbook; and a monthly newsletter. In addition, clubs and other organizations are formed each year based on student interest and have included the Chess and Gaming Club, the Ski Club, the Bowling Club, and others.

DAILY LIFE

Students rise at 6:45 a.m., with breakfast served until 7:30. Classes begin at 7:45 on Monday, Tuesday, and Thursday. On Wednesday and Friday, Mass is celebrated at 7:45, and classes begin promptly afterward. There are seven class periods daily, and the schedule is adjusted so that they end at 2:45 each day. After classes end, athletics activities fill the time until 5:30, when dinner is served. A supervised evening study period is held from 7 to 9. Following the study period is an activity period that usually involves intramurals, open-gym time for weight lifting or playing basketball, movies in the dorm, free time to use the recreation hall, and other activities. The Dean of Resident Students occasionally rearranges the evening schedule to accommodate such events as the Dorm Olympics, cookouts, or movie nights. Lights-out is between 10:30 and 11:30, depending on the class.

WEEKEND LIFE

The schedule is varied on weekends, with students having free time to attend various social or cultural events or to take care of their personal needs.

With the permission of their parents and the Dean of Resident Students, students may go home after class on Friday and return by 9 p.m. on Sunday night. The Dean of Resident Students or his assistant coordinates recreational and social activities for students during the weekend.

COSTS AND FINANCIAL AID

The 2008–09 costs for tuition, room, board, and supervision were $9550 for day students, $18,800 for five-day boarding students, $22,100 for seven-day boarding students, and $25,100 for international students. Books and fees cost approximately $500. The initial deposit, which is nonrefundable and due at registration, is $1000 and is applied to tuition. The balance may be paid before the beginning of the school year or in monthly installments.

Financial aid is available. Parents must apply through the School and Student Service for Financial Aid; awards are based on need. Forms may be obtained through the Dean of Admissions.

ADMISSIONS INFORMATION

Admission to St. Mary's Preparatory School is based on a personal interview with the Dean of Admissions; a transcript from the student's previous school; and recommendations from the principal, an English teacher, and a science or mathematics teacher. Also required are a health report, a photograph, and a $35 nonrefundable application fee. Whenever possible, SSAT or Catholic High School Placement Test results should be submitted. St. Mary's does not discriminate on the basis of race, color, creed, or national or ethnic origin in the administration of its educational policies, admissions policies, or athletics or other School-administered programs.

APPLICATION TIMETABLE

Inquiries are welcome at any time. Students are accepted for the fall semester (August) and the spring semester (January).

A personal interview with the Headmaster or Dean of Admissions is required. Parents are urged to visit St. Mary's with their son during the school term to meet members of the faculty and the students. International students should apply well in advance of the start of the new semester to comply with immigration regulations for obtaining the F-1 student visa.

ADMISSIONS CORRESPONDENCE

Leonard Karschnia
Assistant Headmaster and Dean of Admissions
St. Mary's Preparatory School
3535 Indian Trail
Orchard Lake, Michigan 48324
Phone: 248-683-0532
Fax: 248-683-1740
E-mail: admissions@stmarysprep.com
Web site: http://www.stmarysprep.com

ST. PAUL'S SCHOOL

Concord, New Hampshire

Type: Coeducational boarding college-preparatory school
Grades: 9–12 (Forms III–VI)
Enrollment: 533
Head of School: William R. Matthews Jr., Rector

THE SCHOOL

St. Paul's School (SPS) was founded in 1856 by Dr. George Cheyne Shattuck of Boston, who gave his country home, just west of Concord, New Hampshire, as a campus for the new school. St. Paul's School now encompasses 2,000 acres of woodlands, open fields, and ponds. From the beginning, the School has had an association with the Episcopal Church. Today, St. Paul's School community members come from varied faiths and many backgrounds.

St. Paul's School is committed to academic excellence and is deeply concerned with the quality of the life of its School family. The hallmarks of a successful community—trust, friendship, understanding, honest dialogue, and honorable behavior—have long been valued and continue to be priorities. Among its students, the School promotes the idea of "Freedom with responsibility."

St. Paul's actively seeks students who have the abilities, talent, and capacity to contribute to the community and who have the energy, enthusiasm, and desire to take full advantage of the School's resources.

As an all-boarding school, St. Paul's hopes to inspire and cultivate in its students an understanding of how communities work and a willingness to make the personal sacrifices needed to sustain a community and serve those in it. The character of the School's students is as important as their intellect. Goodness outweighs knowledge in the School's scale of values, or, more precisely, the St. Paul's School community pursues knowledge for the sake of goodness.

The School's tradition and heritage are Anglican, an expression of Christianity grounded in scripture, tradition, and reason that is open to and affirming of other religions. While St. Paul's School represents the Episcopal Church, its understanding of the depth of religious experience and spirituality is not confined to any one church or faith. The School strives to be inclusive of all faith groups and recognizes that an important part of its understanding and self-identity comes from the tradition and beliefs known as religious faith. Four mornings each week, the School gathers to begin the day in the chapel, where services may include a student or faculty member speech or a student musical performance by an a cappella singing group or a string ensemble. It is a time for the entire community to join together and reflect on the events of the day in a way that enhances personal spirituality and provides a perspective for all aspects of learning.

ACADEMIC PROGRAMS

The curriculum encompasses core courses in five academic divisions: the humanities, languages, mathematics, sciences, and the arts. An innovative and student-centered residential life course is taught in each house.

The Humanities Program integrates English, history, and religious studies in a required course curriculum for students in the Third, Fourth, and Fifth Forms. Also incorporating aspects of art history, philosophy, and music, these courses involve students in an engaging interplay of imagination and intellect. This allows students to cross over the boundaries between traditional disciplines by viewing the human experience as a whole. In particular, the humanities curriculum emphasizes analytical thinking, intellectual curiosity, research, and writing by using the resources and information systems of Ohrstrom Library, technologically sophisticated classrooms, and the Internet.

The humanities curriculum offers a different focus within its three-year required program: Self, Society, and Culture (Third Form); The American Experience (Fourth Form); and European Studies from the Renaissance to the First World War (Fifth Form). Students in the Sixth Form engage in studies that build on the core curriculum. They select numerous elective courses, many of which focus on non-Western themes, religious studies, and contemporary issues.

Students generally take five courses each term, including an appropriate distribution among the humanities, mathematics, science, technology, languages, and arts. All students receive instruction in the use of computers, which are available in residential houses and academic buildings; a fiber-optics network connects all School buildings.

There are exceptional opportunities for language study in the Fifth and Sixth Forms through School Year Abroad, the Classical Honors Program, and the School's programs in Spain, France, Italy (Rome), Greece, Chile, India, Japan, Germany, Ghana, Chile, England, Sweden, and Denmark.

Sixth Form students may take part in the Independent Study Program, engaging in projects that may be academic, creative, vocational, social service–oriented, or experiential in nature.

FACULTY AND ADVISERS

All 110 full-time faculty members and their families live on the School grounds with the students, teach them in the classroom and laboratory, instruct them in the arts, coach them in athletics, and act as advisers. Faculty members are dedicated to the ideals of St. Paul's School, knowing that what they provide for students on the playing fields, at the boat docks, during meals, and in the houses is every bit as important as the lessons students learn in the classrooms.

COLLEGE ADMISSION COUNSELING

College admissions advisers supervise college applications and related matters. About sixty-five colleges and universities send representatives to the School each year to talk with interested students. St. Paul's School students are accepted annually into all the country's major universities. Over the last five years, the colleges most attended by SPS graduates have been Brown, Columbia, Georgetown, Harvard, Princeton, Stanford, Yale, and the University of Pennsylvania.

STUDENT BODY AND CONDUCT

In 2008–09, the Third Form (ninth grade) numbered 48 girls and 54 boys; Fourth Form (tenth grade), 72 girls and 77 boys; Fifth Form (eleventh grade), 75 girls and 66 boys; and Sixth Form (twelfth grade), 71 girls and 70 boys. All were boarding students and represented thirty-five states and twenty-three countries.

The Residential Life curriculum, taught during bi-monthly meetings in the residence houses, is designed to foster the development and refinement of life skills and the spirit of working cooperatively within a community. The meetings serve to further the physical, intellectual, emotional, and spiritual development and well-being of students as they assume increasing responsibilities as young adults in the School community and the world.

ACADEMIC FACILITIES

The School's academic buildings include the Schoolhouse, with classrooms arranged in round-table format and with a comprehensive audiovisual language teaching center; Payson Laboratory; Moore Mathematics Building, which houses a computer-based teaching laboratory; separate buildings for drama, dance, and music; the Art Center in Hargate, which contains studios, photographic darkrooms, and a gallery for the visual arts; and Ohrstrom Library, with more than 65,000 volumes, 225 periodicals, and numerous online databases.

BOARDING AND GENERAL FACILITIES

The School has eighteen residence houses, with 20–36 students in each. In most houses, there are 3 resident faculty members. Faculty members not living in houses are associated with them as advisers.

Clark House, the health center, is staffed by three shifts of registered nurses and a medical director, who is the resident physician.

The Samuel Freeman Student Center features a student lounge and a snack bar. The center is open during the day and evening.

Daily chapel is viewed as a binding force in the life of the School, and the magnificent Chapel of St. Peter and St. Paul is at the center of the grounds. In addition to required morning chapel four times each week at the beginning of the day, as well as on several Sundays and evenings during the year, there are voluntary evening Compline, Taize, and Sunday and weekday Eucharist services. Student involvement and participation in these services is eagerly sought and encouraged. Students also are able to explore and receive baptism, confirmation, and reception into the Episcopal Church.

ATHLETICS

Athletics is an integral part of the holistic mission of St. Paul's School. Through interscholastic and intramural sports, as well as instructional activities, the athletic program fosters the development of the mind, body, and spirit. The School strives to provide a safe environment in which the values of teamwork, sportsmanship, respect, and humility are taught through healthy human interaction and competition. Moreover, the School is committed to promoting a student's appreciation for athletics and wellness beyond St. Paul's School.

All students must participate in athletic programs each term through their Fourth Form year. Students are required to fill three more terms, with two or three in their Fifth Form and/or a floating term to be taken at their discretion in their Fifth or Sixth Form year.

There are interscholastic schedules in twenty-eight programs: Alpine skiing, basketball, crew, cross-country, ice hockey, lacrosse, Nordic skiing, soccer, squash, tennis, and track and field for boys and girls; field hockey, softball, and volleyball for girls; and baseball, football, and wrestling for boys. The School also offers instructional programs such as fitness, golf, squash, and tennis. In addition, the School has strong club programs in crew, ice hockey, and soccer.

A state-of-the-art athletic and fitness center is equipped with two hardwood courts to accommodate fall volleyball and winter basketball; ergometer, free weight, and cardiovascular rooms with an office to ensure supervision; an athletic training room to treat and nurture students in times of injury, rehabilitation, and prevention; a climbing wall; two-mat wrestling rooms with adequate spectator space that can be converted to a multipurpose room for off-season activities such as yoga, tai chi, and aerobics; classroom space in which teams and groups can meet; an eight-lane, 25-yard pool to support community recreation and wellness and to aid in injury prevention and rehabilitation, provide a lifelong activity option for fitness, and maximize future program flexibility; a renovated cage facility with a new artificial turf floor and a three-lane indoor track; offices to support athletic department faculty and staff members for administration of programs and supervision of facilities; locker rooms to accommodate visiting interscholastic teams (while having the capacity and potential for multi-purpose use); common area/entry space to welcome all visitors to the building and to showcase the School's athletic heritage and achievements; and faculty/staff locker rooms to support all adult members of the community in a healthy lifestyle.

EXTRACURRICULAR OPPORTUNITIES

A variety of activities are available; most of them take place in the late afternoon after athletics and are organized entirely by students. Some activities, such as the Debate Team, are highly structured and require intense activity. Others, such as the Bridge and Chess Clubs, meet occasionally and are informal.

The Pelican, the students' award-winning newspaper, appears approximately eight times a year and offers experience in journalism and photography. The *Horae Scholasticae*, the literary and art magazine published five times a year, encourages writers, poets, and artists, as does *The Mayflower*, published jointly by St. Paul's School and Eton College (U.K.).

Drama activities take place on the stage of Memorial Hall, in the black box experimental theater of the New Space, and often in house common rooms. Each year, the Third Form presents a Shakespeare play. In the winter, the different houses participate in the Fiske Cup plays, a lively inter-house one-act play competition open to all.

Musical groups, both instrumental and vocal, perform regularly in chapel, in the Concord area, on Parents Day, and at graduation. Groups include the Concert Band, Jazz Band, Chamber Orchestra, Chorus, Gospel Choir, Madrigal Singers, Deli Line, Mad Hatters, B-List, and T-Tones.

The St. Paul's School Ballet Company provides students with the opportunity to study classical and modern works and to perform before audiences from within and outside the School. Graduates of the program have gone on to dance professionally with major companies, including the Chicago City Ballet, the Royal Ballet of Flanders, and the New York City Ballet.

International societies and language clubs offer opportunities outside the classroom for pleasure and further development of skills.

Seasonal activities, such as fly-fishing, ice skating, in-line skating, mountain biking, boating on trout-stocked streams and ponds, and cross-country skiing on miles of forest trails provide a recreational change of pace.

DAILY LIFE

After breakfast, a regular day includes chapel at 8 a.m., an event that presents a rich variety of programs with a religious component embracing all faiths. Thereafter, classes continue until 2:30 p.m., except Wednesday and Saturday, when they end at 12:25. A cafeteria lunch is served for 2 hours, allowing students and faculty members to enjoy a leisurely meal and conversation with friends. Athletics occupy during a 2-hour period in mid-afternoon. Dinner follows, with the School in a formal assigned seating arrangement two evenings per week.

Within the six days of the academic week, a student's class meetings are distributed so that a student generally has three or four classes per day, some of which are of 90-minute duration. During evening study, from after dinner until about 10, students study alone or with one another in their rooms, in the library, in a proctored study hall, or in the classroom buildings.

WEEKEND LIFE

A student committee arranges and coordinates a comprehensive schedule of social, cultural, and entertainment activities for the weekend enjoyment of the community. These may include student drama and musical performances; films, dances, and special events sponsored by a Form, a house, or a club; and presentations by an individual or group from outside the School.

Saturday night Open House at the Rectory is a regular and long-established tradition where students gather in the Rector's home for food, games, and fellowship. Trips away from the School range from attending music and drama performances in Concord, Boston, or New York City to hikes to the top of Mount Washington with the Outing Club.

Short or long weekends may, with parental and School permission, be taken from time to time by students whose performance is satisfactory and whose absence will not interrupt their School responsibilities. On certain weekends designated as "closed," all students are expected to be in residence.

COSTS AND FINANCIAL AID

The charge for tuition and residence for the year 2008–09 was $41,300, which is payable in one, two, or ten installments. In addition to tuition, families should anticipate variable expenses for books and academic supplies; travel to and from the School; laundry service; $875 in fees for student health, publications, and technology; spending money; and medical insurance if current coverage is not adequate.

The School supports one of the most robust financial aid programs available at the secondary school level. For the 2008–09 school year, St. Paul's School awarded approximately $6.1 million of financial aid to 177 students, or 34 percent of the student body. Grants ranged from $1200 to approximately $41,300. Practically speaking, every St. Paul's School student receives financial aid from the School's endowment because the cost of educating each student far exceeds the full tuition. The majority of aid is awarded based on demonstrated need. In general, admitted students whose family income is less than $80,000 may attend free.

Interested families should contact the Director of Financial Aid. Applicants must submit the Parents' Financial Statement to School and Student Services in Princeton, New Jersey, and supporting documentation to St. Paul's School.

ADMISSIONS INFORMATION

Candidates compete with many others for admission into St. Paul's School. Students who have demonstrated intellectual ability, motivation, and curiosity are most likely to be among those admitted. However, the School is also interested in a candidate's strength of character, leadership ability, and athletic and artistic talents.

New students are enrolled only in September and generally in the Third and Fourth Form years; a few students are admitted in the Fifth Form. All candidates are required to take the SSAT or the ISEE if the SSAT is not available.

Personal interviews are required. Parents are urged to bring candidates to visit the School in the fall or winter of the school year prior to the September in which the student wishes to enroll. It is suggested that candidates and their families visit in the morning and plan on spending approximately 2 hours at the School. During the visit, parents and candidates talk with a member of the admissions staff and have a student-guided tour of the facilities and grounds.

APPLICATION TIMETABLE

Candidates should register and file the $50 fee by December of the year preceding enrollment. Candidates applying from abroad must pay a $100 application fee. The application, interview, and accompanying forms must be completed and returned to the Admissions Office by January 15. St. Paul's School notifies candidates and their families of admissions decisions on March 10. Parents are expected to notify the School of their decision by April 10.

During the academic year, visitors are encouraged to come to the School on weekdays or on Saturdays until noon. The School welcomes visitors in the summer months, when the Admissions Office is open from 9 a.m. to 4 p.m., Monday through Friday. Candidates or their parents should arrange an appointment at least three weeks before a proposed visit.

ADMISSIONS CORRESPONDENCE

Jada Hebra
Director of Admissions
St. Paul's School
325 Pleasant Street
Concord, New Hampshire 03301-2591
Phone: 603-229-4700
Fax: 603-229-4772
E-mail: admissions@sps.edu
Web site: http://www.sps.edu

ST. STANISLAUS COLLEGE

Bay St. Louis, Mississippi

Type: Boys' day and resident college-preparatory school
Grades: 6–12: Middle School, 6–8; Upper School, 9–12
Enrollment: School total: 430
Head of School: Brother Ronald Hingle, SC, President

THE SCHOOL

St. Stanislaus College (SSC), which was founded in 1854, is an independent Catholic school located on the Mississippi Gulf Coast 50 miles east of New Orleans. Operated by the Brothers of the Sacred Heart, the school specializes in building character and helping young men in grades 6–12 develop to their full potential and become happy, self-confident, well-educated adults.

The mission of St. Stanislaus, a Catholic residency and day school for young men, is to teach Gospel values and to nurture the total development of each student according to the charism of the Brothers of the Sacred Heart. The school fosters character formation and integrates faith development within a curriculum that is primarily college preparatory. As an integral part of its mission, St. Stanislaus maintains a residency program that offers students opportunities for educational success and personal growth within a disciplined and structured environment.

St. Stanislaus is one of the largest Catholic resident high school for boys in the United States. Since boarding has been a central component and a mainstay of the school, to live at SSC is to experience the richness of a tradition of 150 years. Even fourth- and fifth-generation students have benefited from this rich tradition. Resident students come from diverse backgrounds and cultures, with eleven countries and twelve states currently represented. Over the years, students from fifty-two countries and forty-two states have profited from the rich education and character building offered by St. Stanislaus. This diversity promotes a heightened awareness of each student's value and provides opportunities for appreciation of other cultures and for lasting friendships with students from other countries.

In 1870, St. Stanislaus was recognized by the state of Mississippi as a college; however, by 1923 the curriculum became college preparatory. Since 1923, the school has been known as St. Stanislaus College and is incorporated under that name. The school is governed by a 10-member board of directors; its annual operating budget is $6 million, with an endowment of $8 million.

St. Stanislaus is accredited by the Mississippi State Department of Education, the Southern Association of Colleges and Schools, and the Mississippi High School Activities Association. It holds membership in the Catholic Boarding Schools Association, the National Catholic Education Association, and the Association for Supervision and Curriculum Development.

ACADEMIC PROGRAMS

The school's strong core curriculum includes 4 units each of religion, English, history, science, and mathematics; 2 units of foreign language; 1 unit of art; 1 unit of computer education; and 1 unit of health and physical fitness. Electives are available in language arts, art, band, business, computer science, social studies, science, physical education, and foreign languages. Honors classes and advanced-placement classes are also offered. The grading system uses A through F during four 9-week marking periods, with academic progress reports issued twice each nine weeks. After-school and evening tutoring are available.

FACULTY AND ADVISERS

The school's 36 faculty members, the 10 residency staff members, and the 5 Brothers of the Sacred Heart who are active in the educational process exemplify the educational values of the Brothers of the Sacred Heart. More than 44 percent of the faculty and resident staff members possess a master's degree or higher.

COLLEGE ADMISSION COUNSELING

Ninety-eight percent of the graduating seniors attend college. The curriculum at St. Stanislaus is geared specifically toward preparation for college, and formal college guidance begins in the junior year, with each student expected to take either the ACT or the SAT. The application process for college admissions begins in August of the senior year.

Students from the most recent graduating classes have received scholarships from such institutions as Boston University; Charleston; Christian Brothers; CUNY–Hunter; Dartmouth; Florida State; George Washington; Harvard; Johnson & Wales; Kansas Wesleyan; LSU; Loyola; Mercer; Merchant Marine Academy; Millsaps; Mississippi State; NYU; Northwestern; Notre Dame; Oxford; Penn State; Princeton; Rhodes; Santa Clara; Spring Hill; Texas A&M; Tulane; the U.S. Air Force, Military, and Naval Academies; and the Universities of Chicago, Florida, Miami, Mississippi, Pennsylvania, South Florida, and Virginia. Of the 98 percent of the seniors who go on to university study, 80 percent receive academic and/or athletic scholarships.

STUDENT BODY AND CONDUCT

St. Stanislaus enrolls 430 students, of whom 100 are resident students.

The student body is expected to adhere to a carefully delineated code of conduct that specifies the rules and regulations of the institution. The Dean of Students is responsible for maintaining student discipline. A dress code mandates that a Stanislaus shirt and designated khaki pants be worn to class. On special occasions, a white dress shirt and tie are worn. The dress code excludes jeans, shorts, and sports shoes as classroom wear.

ACADEMIC FACILITIES

The main classroom and administrative building (constructed in 1971) was enlarged significantly in 1991. The Kleinpeter-Gibbens Memorial Library houses a diverse subject-area collection and reference library and a fiction collection that covers all genres of literature. The periodicals collection provides a bridge to the curriculum, and the newspaper subscriptions enhance the cultural diversity present at St. Stanislaus. The computerized card catalog is available on the World Wide Web, and the library Web page gives students remote access to programs, including Grolier Multimedia Encyclopedias, Popular Science Online, Student Resource Center Gold/Gala Reference Collection, and many other online resources. The librarian teaches library skills and supervises Internet use on the Internet workstations.

BOARDING AND GENERAL FACILITIES

St. Stanislaus overlooks the Gulf of Mexico, with 30 acres of campus extending from the beach into the town of Bay St. Louis. The Brother Aurelian Dormitory (1968) houses the resident students and dorm staff members. This building is fully air conditioned; rooms with private baths house 2 or 3 students.

The swimming pool (1970), three lighted tennis courts, basketball courts, playing fields, the Brother Peter Memorial Gymnasium (1977), the Fitness Center (2002), and the Brother Romuald, SC Instrumental and Vocal Music Building (2007) complete the front campus. At the back campus, the Brother Philip Memorial Stadium includes a football field surrounded by a 400-meter all-weather track, soccer fields, a field house, and a baseball field and concession stand.

The new Instrumental and Vocal Music Building (band hall) houses a rehearsal hall, practice rooms, a library room, equipment storage, and offices. The band hall provides the SSC music and vocal programs ample space for group or individual rehearsal.

An experienced Director of Residency directs the resident staff of 10 men and women. The staff devotes full time to the care and development of the resident students. Through in-service programs and staff workshops, the prefects are trained to become effective counselors, guides, mentors, and friends. The residency curriculum is designed to nurture the development of sound study habits, self-discipline, and a Christian appreciation of others. Structured study periods with tutoring assistance constantly encourage the young men to reach their potential.

ATHLETICS

The SSC mascot, adopted in the 1920s when football and baseball became popular at SSC, is the Rock-A-Chaw. This is the Native American name for a sticker burr indigenous to the sandy soil of south Mississippi. Playing fields were primitive and replete with the tenacious and painful rock-a-chaws. Unwary opponents on the playing field usually went home with hundreds of the burrs clinging to their uniforms and pricking their skin.

The school community has long encouraged student participation in both interscholastic and intramural athletics. As a member of Division 8-4A of the Mississippi High School Activities Association, SSC athletes have garnered a number of titles: the football team captured the district title in 2004; the basketball team won the district title in 2003 and 2004; the soccer team won the 4-A State Championship in 2003 and 2004; district honors went to the track, golf, and tennis teams in 2004 and 2005; the swimming team captured second place in the state in 2004; and the sailing team, after winning the Sugar Bowl Regatta, was invited to the National Regatta at Annapolis is 2004. Colonel Felix "Doc" Blanchard, '42, donated his Heisman, Maxwell, and Sullivan Trophies to SSC.

Interscholastic competition includes baseball, basketball, cross-country, football, golf, sailing, soccer, swimming, tennis, track and field, and powerlifting. Each sport fields junior high, junior varsity, and varsity teams. Athletes are encouraged to join the Fellowship of Christian Athletes.

EXTRACURRICULAR OPPORTUNITIES

SSC provides a variety of clubs and organizations appealing to students. The Student Council, the Key Club, and the Student Ministry Program provide opportunities for leadership in various phases of student life. Students who qualify are invited to join the honor organizations: the National Junior Honor Society and the National Honor Society. Other clubs and activities appealing to student interests are band, Drama Club, Fellowship of Christian Athletes, Fishing Club, Literary Magazine, Magic Club, Math Club, newspaper, Outdoor Club, Radio Club, robotics, SCUBA Club, Varsity Quiz Bowl, and Youth Legislature. The Christmas and spring band concerts, spring drama productions, and beach barbecues, together with frequent dances, complement student activities.

The SSC band, drum line, and flag corps perform at football games and community functions and also present Christmas and spring concerts. Annually, the band and drum line participate in local parades.

Students from the neighboring girls' school participate in the swimming team, the band, the flag corps, and cheerleading.

DAILY LIFE

All resident students rise for breakfast at 7 a.m. Class begins at 8:30 and ends at 3:30 p.m. Lunch is one of the eight 50-minute periods of the school day. Classes meet on a daily basis, Monday through Friday. Athletics or other extracurricular activities occupy most students' afternoons. The first study period for resident students is 5:15 to 6:15 p.m. Resident students dine at 6:15. The second study period begins at 8 p.m. and is preceded by prayer. 10 p.m. is lights out for the younger students; older students retire at 10:30.

WEEKEND LIFE

Weekend activities for those who remain on campus are organized with the students' educational, spiritual, social, and recreational needs in mind. International students are encouraged to spend the weekend with domestic students. Attendance at Sunday Eucharist is required. A regular prayer schedule is the backdrop of each day's schedule.

COSTS AND FINANCIAL AID

The 2008–09 total for tuition and fees for resident students was $19,325 ($24,225 for international students), plus a $725 registration fee after May 15 ($800 for international students). Day school tuition was $5170, with a $375 registration fee after May 15. There is an application fee of $100, which is applied to the registration upon acceptance.

ADMISSIONS INFORMATION

The school's administrators choose carefully from the broad range of applicants who seek admission to St. Stanislaus College. The school does not discriminate on the basis of race, color, national or ethnic origin, or handicap.

The following criteria are used to admit prospective students: the student's overall school record, the recommendation of former teachers or principals, and an interview with each applicant and his parents. Consideration is given to sons of alumni and younger brothers of alumni and students presently in school. For resident students, an application form with the application fee, an unofficial copy of the transcript, recommendations from school officials, and a personal interview are required.

APPLICATION TIMETABLE

Inquiries are always welcome, and interviews and tours can be scheduled at any time during the year. March and April are the normal registration periods for resident students for the following year. Brochures and application materials may be obtained from the Admissions Office. Office hours are from 8 to 4. Students may request material and information by e-mailing or calling the Admissions Office.

ADMISSIONS CORRESPONDENCE

Director of Admissions
St. Stanislaus College
304 South Beach Boulevard
Bay St. Louis, Mississippi 39520
Phone: 228-467-9057 Ext. 226
Fax: 228-466-2972
E-mail: admissions@ststan.com
Web site: http://www.ststan.com

ST. STEPHEN'S EPISCOPAL SCHOOL

Austin, Texas

Type: Coeducational boarding and day college-preparatory
Grades: 6–12: Middle School, 6–8; Upper School, 9–12
Enrollment: School total: 663; Middle School: 191; Upper School: 472
Head of School: Robert Kirkpatrick

THE SCHOOL

St. Stephen's Episcopal School was opened in 1950 in response to the need for a top-quality boarding school in Texas. The Rt. Rev. John E. Hines, then Bishop Coadjutor of the Diocese of Texas and later Presiding Bishop of the Episcopal Church, chose the Austin area for the School so as to be near the University of Texas and the seat of state government. The founding vision called for the creation of a caring, diverse, Christian community with rigorous academic standards that nurtures moral growth and values the potential and dignity of every human being. The School was the first coeducational boarding school in the Episcopal Church and one of the first racially integrated boarding schools in the South. The 370-acre campus is nestled in the rolling, wooded hill country, 8 miles west of downtown Austin.

St. Stephen's Episcopal School is accredited by the Texas Education Agency and the Independent Schools Association of the Southwest. It is a member of the National Association of Independent Schools, the National Association of Episcopal Schools, the Western Boarding Schools Association, and the Cum Laude Society.

ACADEMIC PROGRAMS

St. Stephen's challenges motivated students to live intelligently, creatively, and humanely as contributing members of society. The School develops the whole person by providing rigorous academic preparation, stimulating physical activities, and rich opportunities in the fine arts.

Students are required to take the following courses: English: 4-year sequence—no advanced classes are offered; however, many seniors elect to take the AP examination in Literature and Composition.

History: 3-year sequence—no advanced classes are offered in the required sequence; electives offered to juniors and seniors include the Social Science Seminars and Advanced European History.

Mathematics: 3-year requirement—an advanced track is offered beginning with geometry; three levels of calculus are offered, including AB and BC; elective courses offered include Advanced Statistics, Computer Science, Multivariable Analysis, and Statistics & Selected Topics in Mathematics.

Foreign Language: 3-year requirement—advanced levels are offered through Latin V, Spanish VII, and French VII; and a 4-year sequence is offered in Chinese.

Science: 3-year lab science requirement (Biology I, Chemistry I, Physics I)—electives offered include Astrophysics, Environmental Science, Geology, and Robotics; advanced electives are offered in biology, chemistry, and physics.

Theology: A senior course is required, constituting a full academic discipline stressing critical spirituality and theological reasoning.

Fine Arts: 1-year requirement—full-credit courses offered include Advanced Acting, Dramatic Literature, History of Music, and Visual Studies; advanced electives are offered in art history, music theory, and visual studies.

As of the 2008–09 school year, St. Stephens does not offer any courses labeled Advanced Placement. The School is an AP test site, and students may sit for as many AP exams as they wish. In 2008, 103 students took 165 AP exams, earning grades of 3 or higher on 90 percent of the tests.

Science students engage in independent research, field research experiences throughout Texas, science courses rarely found in high schools, and mentorship options with researchers in local laboratories. In collaboration with the Nature Conservancy of Texas, a West Texas field station has been established in the Davis Mountains.

There are three theater productions per year, including a musical and a student-directed one-act play. The Theater Focus Program inspires student artists through the study of theater and its place in society. In addition to a core of rigorous academic classes, the curriculum includes acting, directing, musical theater, and Spartan Studios technical theater. Each student takes private or small-group lessons in acting, dance, and voice.

St. Stephen's offers a wide variety of elective courses, including many that prepare students to sit for the Advanced Placement exams. In 2008, 103 students took 165 AP examinations, making grades of 3 or higher on 90 percent of the tests.

The school year is divided into three terms. The grading system is based on marks of honors, very good, good, passing, unsatisfactory, and seriously failing. Advisers report grades to their advisees and confer with them and their parents whenever necessary.

Class size averages 16 students. The student-teacher ratio is 8:1.

St. Stephen's is an international community with students from twenty countries. The School offers an Intensive English Program (IEP) for international students that includes an interdisciplinary course, supplemental activities, and advising. There is an extended orientation for new IEP students. St. Stephen's has an annual exchange program for tenth-grade boys with St. Andrew's Boys' High School, Osaka, Japan, and for tenth-grade girls with St. Margaret's School in Tokyo, Japan.

FACULTY AND ADVISERS

There are 67 full-time and 4 part-time faculty members. Of that number, 50 hold advanced degrees. Many faculty members live on campus and supervise boarding students.

The School encourages and provides financial support for faculty professional development. Teachers serve as advisers to students and meet with them during a daily advisory period. They know their advisees well and offer special help, such as planning study programs tailored to individual interests and academic needs, making sure each advisee understands the responsibilities of school routine, and keeping parents informed about their child's activities and academic progress.

COLLEGE ADMISSION COUNSELING

At St. Stephen's, the process of college planning is student centered but supported by the College Counseling Office. Individual college conferences are available to all Upper School students, with a required sequence of conferences in the junior and senior years that are crucial to the planning process. Counselors who oversee the progress of a class through the students' last two years encourage communication from families and prepare information for transmission to colleges.

The PSAT is given to all tenth and eleventh graders. The mean SAT scores for the class of 2008 were 619 critical reading, 644 math, and 626 writing. Admission representatives from the country's top colleges and universities visit the School each year to recruit students. Of the class of 2008, 24 percent received national academic recognition; there were 10 National Merit Semifinalists and 14 National Merit Commended Students, and 2 National Hispanic Scholars.

All 116 graduates of the class of 2008 went on to four-year colleges; 80 percent of the class went to colleges outside of Texas. Two or more graduates enrolled at the following schools: Berkeley, Boston University, Columbia, George Washington, Texas at Austin, and Wesleyan.

STUDENT BODY AND CONDUCT

St. Stephen's enrolls a total of 472 students in the Upper School as follows: 162 boarding boys and girls and 310 day boys and girls. There are 191 students enrolled in the Middle School, including 6 boarders. Most boarding students come from Texas, but there are also students from ten other states. International students come from twenty-two countries, including China, Germany, Greece, Jamaica, Japan, Mexico, Saudi Arabia, Swaziland, and Thailand. Members of minority groups (not including international students) account for 26 percent of the student population.

The rules at St. Stephen's are the guidelines to maturity, self-respect, and independence. A committee of elected students and faculty members reviews disciplinary cases and recommends action to the Head of School.

ACADEMIC FACILITIES

Academic classrooms for the Upper School are located in several classroom buildings surrounding the chapel. The new Temple Academic Center has fourteen classrooms, a multipurpose room, and an outdoor courtyard. Each room has amazing views of the hill country and the naturally landscaped campus. Nearby, the new Aragona Commons offers study space, tutor and testing rooms, and faculty offices. There are 135 computers available on campus for student use in the library, study areas, and in the foreign language, teaching, and project labs. The campus features fast, efficient connection to the Internet through a fiber-optic network in all of the academic buildings and dorms. Wireless access is also available across campus. The Science Department is housed in Hines Hall, which has seven modern labs. The observatory features one of the largest refracting telescopes in Texas and is used for astrophysics and other classes.

Becker Library has 16,000 volumes, three banks of computers that link students to a local area network, a library of CD-ROM materials, and several online databases. The library also houses an extensive audiovisual collection, ninety periodicals, microfiche, and a collection of rare books.

The Helm Fine Arts Center includes a 400-seat theater, an eighty-seat recital hall, visual arts studios, a darkroom, an art gallery, a kiln, and teaching/practice studios.

A recent expansion to the Middle School building created four new classrooms, an art room, two science labs, three common areas, two outdoor classrooms, and restrooms. The existing Middle School facility was renovated and includes classrooms, tutoring rooms, computer labs, an additional science lab, and conference areas.

BOARDING AND GENERAL FACILITIES

St. Stephen's has six boys' and four girls' dormitory buildings. All boarding students have senior proctors in charge of their hallways. A majority of the rooms are doubles. New boarding boys and girls are assigned roommates; returning students may request their roommate. Faculty members and their families live in or next to the dormitories. The student-faculty ratio in the dorms is about 3:1.

An eight-bed infirmary is located near the dormitory complex, and a registered nurse is on duty 24 hours a day. An Austin practitioner serves as the School doctor. In addition, 4 psychologists and counselors serve the St. Stephen's community.

ATHLETICS

St. Stephen's requires that students in the Upper School participate in at least one interscholastic sport through their sophomore year and take part in physical education classes when not participating in a sport. St. Stephen's provides a full range of traditional varsity sports, including baseball, basketball, crew, cross-country, football, field hockey, golf, lacrosse, soccer, swimming, tennis, track and field, and volleyball. The program also provides alternative activities for students to fulfill the athletic requirement, including caving, dance, mountain biking, triathlon, and rock-climbing on St. Stephen's indoor climbing wall. St. Stephen's competes in games and tournaments with schools from the Southwestern Preparatory Conference, which ranges from Houston to Oklahoma City.

St. Stephen's also offers two intensive year-round programs for soccer and tennis athletes interested in continuing their participation on the collegiate level.

The Tennis Academy offers intensive training to sectionally, nationally, and internationally ranked players who aspire to join teams at the NCAA Division I and Division III levels. Private lessons and daily team practice are led by experienced coaches who travel with the players to tournaments. Summers include tennis camps and additional tournament travel.

The Soccer Academy has a highly qualified coaching staff directed by full-time UEFA-licensed coaches. Players participate in a highly competitive thirty-game winter high school season. In addition to individualized training sessions at the School, soccer players participate with Division I Austin clubs in the fall and spring.

Facilities include soccer fields, modern gymnasiums with weight and conditioning rooms, a spacious dance studio, six athletic fields, an all-weather six-lane UIL track, a cross-country running trail, a sand volleyball court, and a swimming pool. A tennis facility features twelve lighted hard-surface courts and two lighted clay courts.

EXTRACURRICULAR OPPORTUNITIES

St. Stephen's, which encourages community service at home and abroad, recently launched service programs in Haiti, El Salvador, and Nicaragua.

Closer to home in central Texas, St. Stephen's Upper School students performed more than 5,500 hours of community service at nonprofit organizations and agencies in 2007–08. Other activities include the Madrigals (an a cappella group); the St. Stephen's Choir; literary journal; the student-run, fully digital yearbook; the student newspaper; Amnesty International; the Mu Alpha Theta math honor society; the computer club; Model U.N., the recycling club, and the Fine Arts Council. Breakthrough gives students a chance to participate in an educational outreach mentorship program with low-income children in Austin. The Peer Assistance Group enables St. Stephen's students to affirm and support one another, and Peer Tutoring matches student tutors with other students seeking help with academic subjects. In Mock Trial, an attorney helps students develop legal skills and understanding while they alternately play the roles of prosecutors or the defense. FACES is a support and discussion group that focuses on multicultural issues.

The Devil's Canyon Wilderness Program (DCWP) takes students climbing, caving, cycling, surfing, and backpacking throughout the United States and Mexico. The goals include fostering leadership skills and personal growth, as well as teaching students to be safe and responsible in the wilderness.

DAILY LIFE

Students meet daily with their advisers before gathering in the chapel. There are eight periods in the academic day, including one or more study times.

Varsity teams and a number of extracurricular activity groups meet from 3:45 to 6 p.m., five days a week. Six nights a week, dinner is cafeteria style, and on Wednesday it is a family-style meal. There is a designated study period each evening from 8 until 10 p.m.

WEEKEND LIFE

Student life on weekends is enhanced by a full program of activities, such as trips to movies, malls, sporting events, drama productions, and concerts. Out-of-town trips include amusement parks, theaters, sporting events, and museums. For on-campus activities, the student center is always open for movies, pool, games, television, and relaxation. The campus gyms and swimming pool are also open. Dances and other special events are planned throughout the year.

Boarding students are allowed one 3-day weekend and up to six overnights per term. To spend the weekend at a friend's house or engage in other off-campus weekend activities, the student must have parental permission. On other weekends students may sign out to go off campus for the day or evening, but again they must have their parents' approval, and they must return to campus at a predetermined time. Day students are invited to take part in campus activities and frequently invite boarders to their homes. In addition, a host family program provides a home away from home for out-of-state students.

SUMMER PROGRAMS

St. Stephen's offers opportunities to study and travel abroad in language-immersion, academic, cultural exchange, and community service programs. In summer 2008, St. Stephen's students and faculty members visited León, Spain, for a language-immersion program and did service work in Haiti, Nicaragua, and El Salvador. Plans for students during spring break 2009 include trips to Austria, China, Germany, Haiti, Italy, and New York City.

COSTS AND FINANCIAL AID

Charges for 2008–09 were as follows: tuition (grades 6–8), $18,690; tuition (grades 9–12), $20,260; boarding supplement, $15,220; day food service, $980; boarding food service, $1930; new student facility use fee, $1000; returning student facility use fee, $100. Students pay for books separately.

In support of diversity, St. Stephen's awarded more than $1.7 million in need-based financial assistance to 13 percent of the student body in 2008–09. The average financial award was $19,381. Eligibility is based on need and determined by criteria established by the School and Student Service for Financial Aid of Princeton, New Jersey. The priority deadline to apply for financial aid is February 1.

ADMISSIONS INFORMATION

St. Stephen's seeks students of above-average ability and motivation. The School does not discriminate on the basis of race, national and ethnic origin, creed, gender, gender expression, or sexual orientation. Boarding and day students are accepted in each class annually. Applicants are considered on the basis of Independent School Entrance Exam (ISEE) or Secondary Schools Admission Test (SSAT) scores, recommendations and academic records from previous schools, candidate and parent questionnaires, and an interview.

APPLICATION TIMETABLE

The application deadline for the first round of admission decisions is February 1. Applicants and their parents are responsible for submitting all application materials—student and parent questionnaires, teacher and personal recommendations, entrance exam results, and the student interview—by the deadline.

After the February 1 deadline, applications are considered on a rolling admission basis. When all spaces are filled, qualified candidates are placed in the wait pool.

ADMISSIONS CORRESPONDENCE

Lawrence Sampleton, Director of Admission
St. Stephen's Episcopal School
2900 Bunny Run
Austin, Texas 78746
Phone: 512-327-1213 Ext. 210
Fax: 512-327-6771
E-mail: admission@sstx.org
Web site: http://www.sstx.org

SAINT THOMAS MORE SCHOOL

Oakdale, Connecticut

Type: Boys' boarding college-preparatory school
Grades: 8–12, postgraduate year
Enrollment: 210
Head of School: James F. Hanrahan Jr., Headmaster

THE SCHOOL

Saint Thomas More School was founded in 1962 by James F. Hanrahan to assist boys who have the ability to succeed but who have not yet shown their potential through academic achievement. The intellectual, moral, physical, and social development of each student is the focus of the School's educational design.

The goal of Saint Thomas More School is to prepare young men for college. The School believes that with the proper supervision, encouragement, and guidance from a dedicated faculty and with an environment that fosters self-discipline and responsibility, students will develop the skills that are essential to a successful college career and a fulfilled life. Faculty members work on an individual basis with students to develop strong study habits and to foster a desire to succeed. It is the School's hope that its students will establish a record of success, build confidence through achievement, and embrace those fundamental Christian principles that enrich and dignify the human spirit.

The School is situated on 100 acres of Connecticut's most beautiful countryside, bordering Gardner Lake, the largest natural lake in the eastern part of the state. While the campus and its immediate surroundings provide a rural atmosphere that is conducive to study and reflection, as well as to sports and outdoor recreation, the benefits of historic Connecticut and the cultural events of Hartford, New Haven, and Providence can be enjoyed only a short distance from the campus. Although Saint Thomas More School is a Catholic school, boys of all faiths are welcome. The School is a nonprofit organization directed by a Board of Trustees composed of civic leaders, educators, alumni, and prominent businesspeople.

Saint Thomas More School is accredited by the New England Association of Schools and Colleges and is a member of the Connecticut Association of Independent Schools, the National Association of Independent Schools, the National Catholic Educational Association, and the NAFSA Association of International Educators.

ACADEMIC PROGRAMS

The academic requirements and curriculum have been designed to provide preparation for entrance into any U.S. college or university. All courses offered are academic in nature, and each student is required to take at least five courses per year. A total of 16 academic credits is required for graduation, including 4 in English, 3 in college-preparatory mathematics, 2 in science, 2 in foreign languages, 1 in religion, 1 in fine arts, and 1 in U.S. history. Several elective courses are available. In recent years, these have included computer science, political science, presidential politics, art history, economics, and academic writing. In addition, SAT-prep courses and driver's education are offered. All Catholic students are required to take a course in theology each year. The theology courses deal with the problems of personal responsibility, morality, ethics, and tradition.

Along with the normal study of content, all courses emphasize the development of study and organizational skills, such as note-taking techniques, outlining skills, and reading and vocabulary development.

The English as a second language (ESL) program offers two levels of instruction to students from other countries. In addition, TOEFL preparation is given.

The School year is divided into the traditional four marking periods. Midway through each marking period, progress reports are given to students who are not reaching their potential. These students are assigned to additional study sessions. After each marking period, parents receive report cards giving the student's numerical average, a grade for effort, and a written comment from each teacher regarding the progress of the student. Midterm examinations are administered after the return from Christmas vacation. A final examination is required before credit is awarded.

The student-faculty ratio is 8:1, and the average class size is between 13 and 16 students. At the end of the class day, all teachers are available in their classrooms for a 30-minute extra-help session.

Essential to the Saint Thomas More experience is the mandatory evening study hall from 7:30 to 9:30, with quiet time until 10:15 and lights out at 10:30. During this time, students study in their dormitory rooms under the close supervision of members of the faculty, who give individual assistance and help students to budget their study time.

FACULTY AND ADVISERS

The faculty is composed of 31 lay teachers of various denominations and 1 full-time member who is a Roman Catholic priest. All hold bachelor's degrees, and most either hold advanced degrees or are involved in graduate studies at one of the many nearby universities.

James F. Hanrahan Jr., son of the founder and Headmaster Emeritus, is a native of Oakdale, Connecticut. He holds a B.S. in mathematics from Fairfield University and an M.Ed. in educational administration from Boston College. His teaching experience began in 1976 at Saint Thomas More School, where he taught math, physics, and computers as well as coached various athletic teams. Since that time, he has held the positions of Business Manager and Assistant Headmaster. He was appointed Headmaster in 1997. Mr. Hanrahan lives on campus with his wife, Gina, and their daughters, Shannon and Casey.

All faculty members are appointed as advisers to a small group of students. In addition, faculty members direct and supervise all activities, including the evening study hall. The advisers also report each student's social progress to his parents at the end of each term.

COLLEGE ADMISSION COUNSELING

The placement of students in college is a thoughtful procedure. Beginning in the junior year, conferences with students and parents help direct each student toward the colleges and universities that best suit his needs. A college placement officer helps each student develop a list of six to eight colleges that he can investigate further, often through visits during School vacations and on weekends.

For the class of 2008, the average verbal score of students taking the SAT was 500 and the average math score was 520.

Nearly all graduates of the class of 2008 are currently enrolled in various colleges and universities throughout the country, including Assumption, Babson, Boston College, Boston University, Clark, C.W. Post, Fairfield, Northeastern, Rider, Saint Michael's, Seton Hall, Southern Connecticut State, Villanova, and the Universities of Colorado, Connecticut, Massachusetts, New Haven, Tampa, Texas, and Wisconsin.

STUDENT BODY AND CONDUCT

The School enrolls 210 boys, all of whom are boarding. There are 15 students in grade 8, 24 in grade 9, 40 in grade 10, 50 in grade 11, 55 in grade 12, and 26 postgraduates. Approximately 60 percent come from Connecticut, New Jersey, New York, Massachusetts, Rhode Island, New Hampshire, and Pennsylvania. An additional 20 percent come from southern and midwestern states, including Virginia, Florida, Ohio, Illinois, Texas, and Wisconsin. Approximately 30 percent of the student body is made up of students from such places as China, Japan, Korea, Mexico, Puerto Rico, Russia, Spain, and Taiwan.

Expectations of student behavior are carefully explained in the *Student Handbook* and during the several orientation meetings that are held during Opening Weekend. All students are held strictly accountable to these expectations, which are based on Christian principles of community living. Minor disciplinary measures are handled by faculty members, while serious offenses are referred to the Dean of Students. When dismissal from the School is a possible disciplinary procedure, the Dean of Students meets with the student and his adviser and submits a recommendation of procedure to the Headmaster.

ACADEMIC FACILITIES

Classes are conducted in four buildings. Saint Benedict's Hall has twelve classrooms and two administrative offices. The Loyola Building has eight classrooms. The Aquinas Building houses a chemistry/physics lab, a biology lab, and administrative offices. The library, containing more than

8,500 volumes, online computers, and a microfiche collection, is located on the first floor of the Saint Edmund's dormitory. This building also contains four classrooms, two computer centers, and a language laboratory. An art cabin is also located on the property for art appreciation and history courses, with additional space for individual expression. The administration building includes conference rooms, the student mailroom, and all administrative offices.

BOARDING AND GENERAL FACILITIES

Students and several faculty members are housed in Saint Benedict's, Saint Edmund's, and Kennedy dorms. Most dormitory rooms are designed for double occupancy, and room assignments are made by the Dean of Students. Students may request room changes at designated times.

Other facilities include the dining hall (overlooking Gardner Lake), a health office, and the Charles Hanrahan Memorial Gymnasium, which houses locker rooms; a basketball court; a weight room; student recreation areas, including a big-screen television with DVD; and pool and Ping-Pong tables. A boathouse, which houses crew boats, sailboats, canoes, and rowboats, is located on the waterfront. Our Lady's Chapel, situated on the lake shore, was dedicated in 1997. The Canisius Building, located near the entry of the campus, houses the Admissions Office.

ATHLETICS

Athletics are an integral part of the School; all students are required to participate in a sport. Interscholastic sports, which are offered on several levels to accommodate varying abilities and ages, are baseball, basketball, cross-country, football, golf, ice hockey, lacrosse, sailing, soccer, tennis, and track and field. Intramural activities include basketball, martial arts, physical conditioning, sailing, skiing/snowboarding, softball, swimming, and weight lifting. The athletics facilities include the gymnasium, an outdoor skating pond, a quarter-mile track, a football field, two soccer fields, two baseball diamonds, two all-purpose fields, and 4,000 feet of lakefront, with swimming, boating, sailing, and fishing areas.

EXTRACURRICULAR OPPORTUNITIES

The School's location allows students to pursue a wide range of cultural and recreational activities. Proximity to Hartford, New Haven, and Providence, as well as to many colleges and universities, gives students the opportunity to attend collegiate and professional sports events, concerts, shows, and plays.

On campus, students may become involved in the production of the yearbook. Other activities include the Big Brothers Program, the Ambassadors Club, and driver's education. The National Honor Society participates in a variety of public service projects.

The Student Council, the formal student government organization, is composed of elected officials representing the various residence halls and classes and organizes social events and provides leadership in the dormitories. Meetings are held to plan assemblies and activities and to discuss items of importance to the student body.

DAILY LIFE

Breakfast, which is served from 7:20 to 8, begins the day. After dorm cleanup and room inspection, which run from 8:05 to 8:20, the class day begins. There are seven 45-minute periods until 2 (six classes and one lunch period). Daily help is conducted from 2 to 2:30. Clubs meet from 3:30 to 4:30. Athletics begin at 3:30 and last until 5. Dinner is served from 5 to 6:15. The evening study hall is from 7:30 to 9:30. Lights-out is at 10:30.

WEEKEND LIFE

Because the academic week begins on Sunday evening at 7:30 and ends on Friday afternoon at 2:17, students are permitted to go home any weekend as long as their studies and deportment are in good standing, but they must be back on campus by 7 on Sunday evening. Approximately one third of the students leave the campus on any given weekend.

Students remaining on campus for the weekend may become involved in any number of activities. All recreational facilities are available to students and faculty members throughout the weekend. Regularly scheduled trips into town to movie theaters are available each Saturday evening. Other activities include dances with neighboring girls' schools, shows of all types at the Hartford Civic Center, collegiate and professional sports events, and concerts.

SUMMER PROGRAMS

Saint Thomas More School offers an all-boys, five-week Summer Academic Camp. Courses are offered for credit, makeup, or enrichment for students in grades 7–12. The faculty is composed of the School's regular staff. The average attendance is 100. Classes are conducted until 12:05 p.m., recreational activities are from 1 to 7, and study hall runs from 7:15 to 9:45. The all-inclusive cost for 2008 is $5495. For more information, applicants should visit the School Web site at http://www.stmct.org or call 860-823-3861.

COSTS AND FINANCIAL AID

The annual cost for 2008–09 is $34,900 for domestic students and $38,400 for international students. Costs include tuition, room, board, books, athletic clothing, and laundry.

Each year, approximately 20 percent of the students receive financial assistance, which is offered to qualified students based on need.

ADMISSIONS INFORMATION

Saint Thomas More School requires that applicants have a personal interview with the Director of Admissions and requires a transcript of academic work, the Otis-Lennon Test, a writing sample, two teacher's recommendations, and a guidance counselor's recommendation. The results of standardized tests are helpful, if available. The School seeks students who will be positive, contributing members of the student body and who will benefit from the special experience the School has to offer. The School admits boys throughout the school year, provided that there is space available in the grade in which entrance is sought.

APPLICATION TIMETABLE

Parents interested in Saint Thomas More School should write or call the Admissions Office to make an appointment for an interview. Interviews and tours are conducted from 8:30 to 2, Monday through Friday, by appointment. Saturday morning appointments are also available. Applications are accepted on a continuous basis, but early application is recommended to guarantee enrollment. Prospective students are notified of acceptance.

ADMISSIONS CORRESPONDENCE

Office of Admissions
Saint Thomas More School
45 Cottage Road
Oakdale, Connecticut 06370

Phone: 860-823-3861
Fax: 860-823-3863
E-mail: triordan@stmct.org

ST. TIMOTHY'S SCHOOL

Stevenson, Maryland

Type: Girls' boarding and day college-preparatory school
Grades: 9–12
Enrollment: 154
Head of School: Randy S. Stevens

THE SCHOOL

St. Timothy's School was founded in Catonsville, Maryland, in 1882 by the Misses Sally and Polly Carter. In 1951, it moved to its present 145-acre site in Stevenson, just 15 minutes from the center of Baltimore, a city that serves as an extension of the campus. After merging with Hannah More Academy in 1974, St. Tim's holds the oldest Episcopal girls school charter in the United States. The School's educational philosophy is to educate the whole person and to prepare students to make contributions to a changing and challenging world. St. Timothy's curriculum is based upon the International Baccalaureate (IB) program, which is one of the most advanced curricula today for preparing students for the varied challenges they will confront throughout their lives.

A 20-member Board of Trustees is the School's governing body. There is an active Alumnae Board of Governors, and there are several alumnae branches in the United States and one in Great Britain. The endowment is $10.5 million, and it is supplemented each year by the Annual Fund, which receives in excess of $950,000. The St. Timothy's–Hannah More Alumnae Association has approximately 3,300 members.

St. Timothy's School is accredited by the Middle States Association of Colleges and Schools, and it is a member of the National Association of Independent Schools, the Association of Independent Maryland Schools, the National Association of Episcopal Schools, the Federation of American and International Schools, and the National Coalition of Girls' Schools. St. Tim's is an IB World School.

ACADEMIC PROGRAMS

St. Timothy's School is an all-girls boarding school in Maryland focusing exclusively on a rigorous, college-preparatory, ninth- through twelfth-grade program. The IB curriculum prepares students to gain acceptance into prestigious colleges and universities around the world. It allows practice of the cognitive tools needed for success in an increasingly interconnected, global world. The School also offers an English as a second language (ESL) program for international students. The ESL program has an intermediate and an advanced level, and ESL students typically assimilate into the standard curriculum after one or two years. All classes are small, averaging from 10 to 12 students. To better prepare students for success with the IB Diploma Program, St. Timothy's has designed a tailored curriculum for the ninth and tenth grades. The International General Certificate of Secondary Education (IGSCE), a pre-International Baccalaureate program designed by Cambridge University, provides a broad study program that draws from three areas of knowledge: languages, sciences, and mathematics. The curriculum equips students with a balanced mix of practical experience and theoretical concepts and is specifically tailored to meet the needs of students with different levels of ability.

Diploma Program students (eleventh and twelfth grades) are required to select one subject from each of the following subject groups: English; world languages; history, individuals, and societies; experimental sciences; mathematics; and arts or elective. At least three, but not more than four, subjects are taken at a higher level; the others are taken at the standard level. Students must also complete a theory of knowledge course, the extended essay, and creativity, action, and service.

All students must take the PSAT/NMSQT and the SAT. Students elect to take the Subject Tests of the College Board in their junior and senior years.

The faculty-student ratio is 1:5. There is required study hall Sunday through Thursday evenings. Exams are given at the end of each trimester. Parents receive comments and grades at regular intervals throughout the year.

FACULTY AND ADVISERS

For the 2007–08 academic year, there were 38 full-time and 7 part-time members of the faculty. Twenty-one faculty members hold advanced degrees. Approximately 64 percent of the faculty members live on campus with their families. Faculty members also serve as dorm parents, advisers, and coaches. Faculty members have 3 to 5 advisees and meet with them weekly during the advisory period.

COLLEGE ADMISSION COUNSELING

Graduates of St. Timothy's School are accepted by highly selective colleges and universities both here and abroad. Because the School is small, the list of colleges St. Timothy's girls attend varies enormously from year to year. The School's College Counseling Office hosts selective colleges and universities to visit the campus during the course of the academic year. Each year, St. Timothy's School holds a special presentation for parents about the college admissions process. The office provides advice and assistance with all phases of the admission and selection process, and 100 percent of the girls attend college. All students take the SAT.

The colleges attended by recent graduates include Bennington, Boston University, Bowdoin, Cornell, Duke, Georgetown, Haverford, Princeton, Stanford, Wake Forest, Washington (St. Louis), Wesleyan, and the Universities of Chicago, Pennsylvania, and Virginia.

STUDENT BODY AND CONDUCT

St. Timothy's School recognizes that no education is complete without regard to the development of each student's values. Honor, trust, truth, and kindness form the basis upon which this community has been built. The Honor Code at St. Tim's is important to the students: they have been responsible for developing it and administering it, and it is held in high regard by students and faculty members alike. At St. Tim's, compassion and disciplined understanding is not only the goal but also the process of education itself.

The Student Government, with representation from all areas of the School, works as an advisory board to the Head of School. It makes recommendations to the administration and takes responsibility for the everyday life of the School. Members serve on the Honor Council and the Disciplinary Committee, along with the faculty.

ACADEMIC FACILITIES

The campus has twenty-three buildings, including two dormitories; the Hannah More Performing Arts Center, with a 350-seat theater; a new, state-of-the-art athletic center; playing fields and tennis courts; a barn with indoor and outdoor riding rings; a classroom building complete with state-of-the-art technology in the classrooms and library; computer labs; and a chapel, as well as faculty homes and an administrative building. The Ella R. Watkins Library has more than 22,000 volumes and computerized catalog search capabilities that link the School with the public library system. Other facilities include a Visual Arts Center for both two- and three-dimensional studies, including photography and digital imaging, and three science labs for biology, chemistry, and physics. The entire campus is networked, and St. Tim's integrates computer use in its curriculum. There are computer labs in both dorms as well as the academic building.

BOARDING AND GENERAL FACILITIES

Approximately 60 percent of this year's students are boarders. Students room together by class. Both dorms were recently renovated with new furniture, paint, and carpet. There are 2- and 3-girl rooms. Faculty members live in each dormitory, and each dormitory has both formal and informal living rooms. The newly renovated recreation room in Heath House is equipped with a big-screen television and a full kitchen. There is a fully equipped health center and a registered nurse on call at all times.

ATHLETICS

A state-of-the-art athletic complex opened in 2003. It includes a basketball gymnasium, fitness center, training room, home and away team locker rooms, faculty locker rooms, and a classroom.

All girls participate in the athletic program each season. The year is divided into three seasons for sports, and girls are required to join a team sport for two seasons each year. In the fall term, field hockey, soccer, tennis, and volleyball are offered. In the winter, girls may choose basketball, ice hockey, indoor soccer, or squash. In the spring, badminton, golf, lacrosse, and softball are available. Dance and horseback riding are offered year-round. In addition, the Duke of Edinburgh Young America's Challenge is a yearlong commitment that meets St. Timothy's athletic requirement and provides students with a fun, challenging opportunity for personal achievement.

The athletic facilities include playing fields for soccer, lacrosse, and field hockey; six all-weather tennis courts; an outdoor recreational swimming pool; and nature and cross-country jogging trails. The Hamilton-Ireland Riding Center has twenty-four stalls, two tack rooms, double-fenced turnout paddocks, and both indoor and outdoor arenas. St. Tim's owns between 15 and 20 horses at any one time.

EXTRACURRICULAR OPPORTUNITIES

St. Timothy's School is located in the Maryland countryside, just 15 minutes from downtown Baltimore and 1 hour from Washington, D.C. Students enjoy the city's cultural activities, museums, theaters, historic sites, and research facilities.

The on-campus activities allow students to pursue areas of special interest. Some of the popular choices are Drama Club, choir, the a cappella singing group Salut in the Morning!, *Moongate* (a literary magazine), *Steward* (yearbook), Environmental Action Club, Social Activities Committee, Black Awareness Club, International Club, and Challenge 20/20, to name a few. The Social Services Club provides volunteer opportunities in the community. There are two major theatrical performances on campus each year as well as dance performances and piano and voice recitals.

DAILY LIFE

A typical day for a boarding student at St. Tim's begins at 7:15 a.m. with breakfast. Classes begin at 8 and 8:30 and end at around 3:30 p.m., with family-style seated lunch four days each week. The afternoon includes sports, study hall, and extracurricular activities. The student self-government, the prefects, clubs, and classes all have scheduled times and days to meet. Buffet dinner begins at 6 p.m. One night each week, there is a formal dinner. All students have required study hall in the evenings from 7:30 to 9:30 p.m., and the academic building and study halls remain open until 10 p.m. Girls must be in their dormitory rooms by 10:30 p.m. on weekdays.

WEEKEND LIFE

St. Tim's is committed to retaining the special qualities that distinguish a boarding school from a day school, and the extracurricular program offers a full component of weekend activities. The program is planned by the Dean of Students along with a student committee. A schedule listing all the opportunities for the weekend is posted each week. Many off-campus activities in the Baltimore and Washington area are planned. Trips to the theater, concerts, museums, and movies; hiking; dances and parties; shopping trips; and horse shows and other sports events are a few of the more popular offerings. The School is also a member of the Boarding Schools Social Activities Committee (BSSAC), which plans social events for boys' and girls' boarding schools in Maryland and Virginia. Recent BSSAC events have included a boat cruise on the Potomac River and mixers at various schools. The day girls are invited to take part in all aspects of the extracurricular program, and many choose to spend an occasional night or weekend on campus. Boarders may take weekends to go home or visit friends.

COSTS AND FINANCIAL AID

Tuition for boarding students in 2008–09 is $41,000. Day student tuition is $24,200. Several payment plans are available to fit each family's needs.

Financial aid is granted on the basis of a candidate's financial need. About one third of the students received financial aid through grants and/or loans. In addition, several merit awards are available.

ADMISSIONS INFORMATION

Girls are admitted without regard to religion, race, color, or national origin. In making admissions decisions, the School considers the applicant's school transcript, recommendations from the adviser and teachers, standardized test scores (SSAT or ISEE), interview, extracurricular involvement, and application essay. Most students enter in the ninth or tenth grade.

APPLICATION TIMETABLE

An initial inquiry is welcome at any time. Campus visits include a tour and an interview and may include a classroom visit. Visitors are welcome between 8:30 a.m. and 2 p.m. when school is in session.

Applications for all students should be complete by February 10. Day student notifications are mailed March 1; boarding student notifications are mailed March 10. However, there is early notification for boarding students for whom St. Tim's is their only choice. These applications must be completed no later than January 10, with notification on February 1. St. Tim's accepts applications on a rolling basis after the March notifications, dependent upon space available.

Applicants should complete and submit the application form with a $45 application fee. Recommendations are required from the student's principal or adviser and her math and English teachers. Parents are asked to complete a parent statement.

ADMISSIONS CORRESPONDENCE

Patrick Finn
Director of Admissions and Assistant Head of School
St. Timothy's School
8400 Greenspring Avenue
Stevenson, Maryland 21153
Phone: 410-486-7401
Fax: 410-486-1167
E-mail: admis@stt.org
Web site: http://www.stt.org

SALEM ACADEMY

Winston-Salem, North Carolina

Type: Girls' boarding and day college-preparatory school
Grades: 9–12
Enrollment: 176
Head of School: Karl Sjolund

THE SCHOOL

Founded in 1772 by Moravian settlers, Salem Academy has been in continuous operation for more than 236 years. Initially a day school, it added boarding facilities in 1802. During the 1860s, college-level courses were added, and Salem College was chartered in 1866. In 1930, the Academy and college were separated; both institutions remained on the original campus.

Throughout its history, Salem Academy has maintained its original commitment to the education of women. It endeavors to provide "a thorough preparation for a continuing education and a fulfilling personal life, a spiritual and ethical climate in all phases of school life, and a program promoting mental and physical well-being." While the Academy retains its affiliation with the Moravian Church, students of various religious backgrounds are enrolled.

The 64-acre campus, which is shared with Salem College, adjoins the restored eighteenth-century Moravian village of Old Salem. The Academy's grounds encompass lawns and wooded areas as well as hockey fields, a softball field, an archery range, and twelve tennis courts.

Winston-Salem (population 200,000) is located in the Piedmont region of the state, approximately 90 miles from both Charlotte and Raleigh. It is served by two airports and Interstate Highways 40, 77, and 85. A nationally recognized cultural and arts center, the city has a symphony, the Little Theater, art galleries, and four colleges—North Carolina School of the Arts, Wake Forest University, Winston-Salem State University, and Salem College—that provide cultural and educational opportunities for Academy students.

A nonprofit institution, Salem Academy is governed by a 30-member Board of Trustees, which serves as a common board for the school and Salem College. Board members are chosen by the Moravian Church, the Alumnae Association, and other organizations. Many graduates lend it financial support and refer prospective students. The endowment is approximately $8.3 million. Operating expenses were $6.5 million for 2008–09. Annual Giving contributed $420,000 for the same year. The Academy plant is valued at $5 million.

Salem Academy is accredited by the Southern Association of Colleges and Schools and the Southern Association of Independent Schools. It holds membership in the National Association of Independent Schools, the North Carolina Association of Independent Schools, the National Coalition of Girls Schools, the National Association of College Admission Counselors, the College Board, and the Secondary School Admission Test Board.

ACADEMIC PROGRAMS

The school year is divided into two academic terms and a 2½-week miniterm in January. There are two long weekends as well as vacations at Thanksgiving and Christmas and in the spring.

To graduate, a student must earn 20 academic credits, including English, 4 credits; mathematics, 4; science, 3; history, 3; and a modern foreign language, 2. Mandatory noncredit courses are health in grade 9, religion in grade 11 or 12, and physical education in grades 9, 10, and 11. One fine arts course is required from art, drama, or music.

The curriculum includes English composition and literature I, English II, Seminar English II, English III, Seminar English III, English IV: The 20th Century, English IV: Banned Books, English IV: Hot Buttons, AP English IV, ESL English, French I–III, AP French language, Spanish I–II, honors Spanish II, Spanish III, AP Spanish language, Latin I–II, AP Latin Poetry—Vergil, non-Western cultures, honors non-Western cultures, European history, U.S. history, AP U.S. history, economics, political science, AP world history, decorative arts, the South, algebra I–II, honors algebra II, geometry, discrete mathematics, precalculus, AP calculus AB, AP calculus BC, AP statistics, biology, environmental science, chemistry, AP chemistry, physics, AP biology, biblical narratives, world religions, studio art, theater, and choral and vocal instruction. Private lessons are available in piano, organ, harp, woodwind, classical guitar, harpsichord, and brass and percussion instruments. Juniors and seniors have the opportunity to take courses for credit at Salem College.

The miniterm gives each student an opportunity to choose her own educational experience. Programs both on and off campus provide a variety of ways for students to pursue interests. A school-sponsored trip is offered each year to such places as Costa Rica, the Galapagos Islands, Germany, and Italy. Internships and independent studies in teaching, music, medicine, banking, and other fields may be pursued under faculty supervision. In on-campus classes, teachers conduct intensive reviews and tutorials, introduce special topics not covered within the course outline, and assign and supervise independent projects.

There are 10 students in an average class. The student-faculty ratio is 7:1. Conference periods provide opportunity for individual help, and Salem College students are available to tutor. The January miniterm also offers a concentrated tutorial program. Grades are discussed with the student and sent to parents every six weeks.

FACULTY AND ADVISERS

The full-time faculty numbers 22 members. They hold twenty-two baccalaureate degrees and thirteen master's degrees. Six faculty and staff members and 3 house counselors supervise the dormitories.

Faculty members are chosen for their solid academic training, their willingness to care for and advise students, and their talents in outside areas that can benefit the community. Each faculty and staff member advises approximately 6 students, serves as an adviser to classes or organizations, serves on school committees, and chaperones school-sponsored activities.

Karl Sjolund holds a bachelor's degree from Virginia Military Institute and a master's degree from Columbia University.

COLLEGE ADMISSION COUNSELING

The full-time College Counselor begins advising students in their freshman and sophomore years. In the second semester of the junior year, the counselor meets with each student on a one-to-one basis to discuss her college interests and to review the general admissions process. In their senior year, the students again meet individually with the College Counselor for advice on writing college applications and essays and on interviewing techniques. The counselor helps the students meet all testing deadlines and arranges their transportation. In addition, more than 50 college representatives visit Salem each year to interview interested students.

The school provides access to SAT review classes. The SAT mean score for the class of 2008 was 1893 out of 2400. In the 2007–08 school year, 84 students took a total of 127 Advanced Placement exams; 84 percent received scores making them eligible for college credit.

Members of the classes of 2005 through 2008 are attending such colleges as Boston College, Brown, Cornell, Dartmouth, Davidson, Duke, NYU, the Universities of North Carolina and Virginia, Wake Forest, and Yale.

STUDENT BODY AND CONDUCT

In 2008–09, Salem Academy had 85 boarding girls and 91 day girls, 14 to 18 years of age, as follows: 38 in grade 9, 42 in grade 10, 51 in grade 11, and 45 in grade 12. Students came from twelve states and six other countries. Salem welcomes students from diverse economic, racial, and geographic backgrounds.

The development of self-discipline and consideration for others is the primary concern that underlies the goals for student behavior at Salem Academy. In keeping with this philosophy, Salem operates under an honor system. The student government, which is composed of two elected bodies—the Honor Cabinet and the Student Council—is based on Salem's honor tradition. The Honor Cabinet advises and guides students by providing constructive counsel and leadership, and it may recommend disciplinary actions. The Honor Cabinet comprises elected student representatives and 2 faculty advisers.

ACADEMIC FACILITIES

Six connected buildings constitute the self-contained portion of the Academy's facilities. The main building (1930) houses administrative offices, and Weaver Building (1956) contains the library, the art studio, and the admissions office. Critz Hall (1971) houses classrooms, language and science laboratories, and faculty offices. Hodges Hall (1971) contains a music studio and library, an auditorium, and a small meditation chapel. In addition, the school shares with Salem College the Dale H. Gramley Library, the Salem Fine Arts Center, a student Commons Building, and a gymnasium and indoor swimming pool.

BOARDING AND GENERAL FACILITIES

Boarding girls live in Hodges, McMichael, Shaffner, and Bahnson residence halls. Most rooms are doubles. Seniors and some juniors live in the new wing, in which groups of 4 girls share a suite with a connecting bath.

In addition to an elected student hall representative, an adult dormitory counselor resides on each hall. New students are assigned roommates and rooms by the Dean of Students; returning students choose roommates and participate in a room lottery in the spring. Laundry and storage areas are provided, and the main building also contains reception rooms and a snack area. Weaver Building contains the dining room and school kitchen.

The Academy shares the services of physicians and a full-time infirmary staff with Salem College. The Baptist Hospital, Forsyth Memorial Hospital, and Bowman-Gray School of Medicine are nearby.

ATHLETICS

Salem believes that an active and healthy body is important to a girl's overall academic and social performance. In addition, the wholesome competition inherent in team sports is important for each girl's development.

Varsity teams in cross-country, golf, softball, swimming, and track and varsity and junior varsity teams in basketball, field hockey, soccer, tennis, and volleyball compete with other schools in the Triad Athletic Conference of the NCISAA. Salem also has an equestrian program. The Student Life and Fitness Center, which is shared with Salem College, houses the gymnasium and pool.

EXTRACURRICULAR OPPORTUNITIES

Students are given many opportunities to develop interests outside the classroom. They publish a newspaper, a yearbook, and a literary-art magazine. The Drama Club stages two major productions a year, and the Glee Club performs on and off campus. Visual arts students exhibit and compete on campus and in the community and state. Other student organizations include the Fellowship Council, which sponsors parties, campus activities, and community service projects. Traditional annual events include Opening Assembly, Ring Banquet, Smoosh Cake Banquet, Parents' Weekend, Alumnae Day, Senior Vespers, Honors Banquets, and Recognition and Graduation Exercises.

DAILY LIFE

Classes meet five days a week. A typical school day includes six academic class periods, a cookie break, and an assembly period. Language and science laboratories, study halls, music, studio art, and physical education are scheduled during two afternoon class periods. Boarding students have supervised study in the evening.

WEEKEND LIFE

On the weekends, the Student Activities Director plans local trips to the theater, opera, concerts, and local sporting events. Also scheduled are outdoor activities such as white-water rafting, canoeing, hiking, camping, and snow skiing in the nearby mountains. Dances and other social events are planned with various boys' schools.

With written parental approval, boarding students in grade 12 may have unlimited overnight permissions on weekends; students in grades 9–11 are limited to between twelve and eighteen overnights per year. Three times a month, boarding students are expected to attend church or synagogue.

COSTS AND FINANCIAL AID

In 2008–09, room and board were $33,800; day student tuition was $17,000, including lunches. Additional expenses were books ($450), an activities fee ($125), and music lessons.

The Academy awards scholarships on the basis of financial need. Sixty-six students received aid totaling approximately $1 million for the 2008–09 school year. Parents who wish their daughters to be considered for financial aid should request a School and Student Service for Financial Aid form from the Admissions Office.

All applicants are automatically considered for merit-based scholarships. The Salem Academy Sisters Merit Scholarship competition offers incoming ninth- and tenth-grade boarders an opportunity for a full merit scholarship. Nomination and Scholarship profile forms can be requested from the Admissions Office or found on the Salem Academy Web site.

ADMISSIONS INFORMATION

Salem Academy enrolls motivated students who have integrity, a positive attitude, and the desire and motivation to give their best in all phases of school life. New students are admitted in grades 9–11 and occasionally in grade 12. Candidates must submit a transcript, academic and personal recommendations, and the results of the Secondary School Admission Test (SSAT). An interview is also required.

APPLICATION TIMETABLE

Students interested in Salem Academy should contact the Admissions Office to obtain a catalog and to arrange for an interview and tour. Special visiting days are scheduled throughout the year, but students and parents may call for an interview during the work week. Students are encouraged to spend a night in the dormitory when they visit.

An application may be filed at any time during the year for the following fall. However, priority consideration is given to early applicants. As soon as the admissions folder is complete, it is sent to the admissions committee. The applicant is notified of the committee's decision promptly. Parents must notify Salem of their decision within two weeks. Later applications are acted upon as soon as they are completed, and qualified applicants are awarded enrollment on a space-available basis.

ADMISSIONS CORRESPONDENCE

Lucia Uldrick
Director of Admissions and Financial Aid
Salem Academy
500 East Salem Avenue
Winston-Salem, North Carolina 27101
Phone: 336-721-2643
877-407-2536 (toll-free)
Fax: 336-721-2696
E-mail: academy@salem.edu
Web site: http://www.salemacademy.com

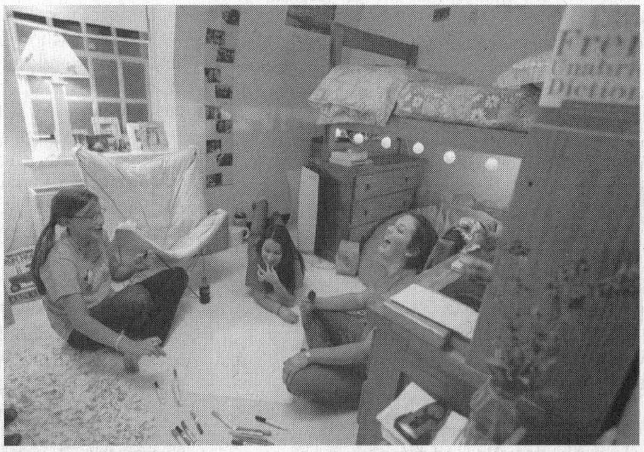

SALISBURY SCHOOL

Salisbury, Connecticut

Type: Boys' boarding and day college-preparatory school
Grades: 9–PG (Forms III–VI, postgraduate year)
Enrollment: 295
Head of School: Chisholm S. Chandler, Headmaster

THE SCHOOL

The Rev. Dr. George E. Quaile founded Salisbury School in 1901 after serving as Headmaster of St. Austin's School on Staten Island in New York from 1894 to 1901. After his death in 1934, Rev. Dr. Quaile was succeeded by his son, Emerson B. Quaile, whose untimely death in 1942 led to the hiring of the Rev. George D. Langdon. With the blessing of the Board of Trustees, Rev. Langdon initiated the School's first modern expansion program. After Rev. Langdon's retirement in 1965, growth continued under his successor, the Rev. Edwin M. Ward. Upon Rev. Ward's departure in 1981, the Rev. Peter W. Sipple was appointed Salisbury's fifth Headmaster. Mr. Richard T. Flood Jr. was appointed Salisbury's sixth Headmaster in 1998. Under his leadership, the School completed a $40-million capital campaign in conjunction with its centennial in 2001. As part of the campaign, all classroom spaces and the library were completely reconstructed. In 2002, Chisholm S. Chandler was selected as the School's seventh Headmaster.

The Wachtmeister Mathematics and Science Building and the Harris Science Center opened in 1999, and the 65,000-square-foot Centennial Library and Humanities Building opened in 2001. In addition, the Miles P. H. Seifert '53 Theater, the Ruger Family Visual Arts Center, and the Tremaine Gallery complete a total renovation of the School's arts facilities. The Chapel Building contains the Field Music Center, which offers space for the School's music program and includes a new music technology lab. It includes practice rooms for piano, band, and choral rehearsals. Recent additions to campus include Ward House, a dormitory housing 44 students and six faculty families (fall 2004), four single-family faculty homes (fall 2006), Wachtmeister Turf Field (fall 2007), and a new boathouse (spring 2008). A state-of-the-art athletic center is currently under construction and is set to open in fall 2009.

Salisbury is an accredited college-preparatory school for approximately 295 boys from ninth through twelfth grades. Some boys are accepted for a postgraduate year. (By tradition, Salisbury refers to ninth grade as Third Form, tenth grade as Fourth Form, eleventh grade as Fifth Form, and twelfth grade as Sixth Form.) The majority of students are boarders, while about 7 percent are day students from the surrounding area.

The School is set on a hilltop surrounded by nearly 700 acres of extensive woodlands, fields, streams, and lakefront in the foothills of the Berkshire Mountains. The campus is bordered by the Appalachian Trail to the west and the Twin Lakes to the north. Salisbury is only 1 hour from Hartford, 2 hours from New York City, and 3 hours from Boston.

The mission of Salisbury School is to instill within each student the self-confidence needed to develop intellectually, morally, and physically in an environment of personal guidance and small-group instruction. The School seeks to encourage each young man to find satisfaction and take pride in his accomplishments inside and outside the classroom and to build a sense of self-worth as he formulates goals for the future. The Salisbury School community is distinguished by a quality of life that promotes religious faith, trust, service, respect, and friendship in relationships among faculty members and students within a framework of traditional values.

Salisbury School is accredited by the New England Association of Schools and Colleges. It is a member of the National Association of Independent Schools, the Connecticut Association of Independent Schools, the Secondary School Admission Test Board, the College Board, and the Cum Laude Society.

ACADEMIC PROGRAMS

For the diploma, the following requirements must be met: English every trimester; history (ancient history in the Third Form, world history in the Fourth Form, U.S. history in the Fifth or Sixth Form); mathematics for 3 years (algebra I, geometry, and algebra II); a single foreign language for 3 years or 2 years each of two foreign languages; a laboratory science for 2 years (Fourth Formers must take at least one of their two required science courses at Salisbury); philosophy and religion for 1 full year; and art for two trimesters. Extensive participation in drama or music (instrumental or choral) may also fulfill the art requirement, even though they are not academic courses. The student must pass all courses in the Sixth Form year.

Letter grades are issued to each student and his adviser every five weeks. Every trimester, grades are sent to parents with written comments from each of the student's teachers and his adviser. Exams are given in late November and late May.

The average class size is 12, and the student-teacher ratio is 5:1. Classes are held six days a week; each class meets for 45 minutes five times a week and for 75 minutes once a week.

There is a strong support system for students at Salisbury. Teachers are available to give extra help, and private tutoring is available to students in the Learning Center. There is a fee for this service.

Salisbury School is committed to technological development and to furthering its implementation in all academic disciplines. To that end, a campuswide computer network was completed in 1996. Significant attention has also been directed recently to expanding the performing arts at Salisbury and to enhancement of environmental studies (e.g., forestry, geology, freshwater ecology). In addition, Salisbury offers an Entrepreneurial Studies Program for qualified students.

FACULTY AND ADVISERS

The Salisbury School faculty and administration consist of 67 members. Thirty-one members hold a master's or higher degree.

Chisholm S. Chandler, the School's current Headmaster, attended the Hotchkiss School, Brown University (B.A.), and Harvard University (M.Ed.). During his seventeen years at Salisbury, Mr. Chandler has served in a variety of capacities, including Director of Admissions, Director of College Advising, and Assistant Headmaster for External Affairs. He has also served as a dorm parent, coach, and adviser.

The School community is close-knit and supportive. The majority of faculty members live on campus, coach, and supervise extracurricular activities.

Advising is at the core of Salisbury's dedication to its students and guarantees that each student will receive the personal attention he requires. Throughout the year, the adviser is the link between the student, his teachers, and his family.

School-funded projects include taking courses toward advanced degrees, traveling, and attending workshops and conferences relevant to one's teaching. A sabbatical program, instituted in 1984, and a newly created Summer Travel Fund offer faculty members professional development opportunities.

COLLEGE ADMISSION COUNSELING

Beginning in his Fifth Form (junior) year, each student meets regularly with a college adviser. Careful attention is given to selecting colleges that best suit the student's interests and abilities. Parents may also meet with the college advising staff whenever possible. College representatives visit the campus throughout the year, and students may have interviews at the School.

Eighty percent of Salisbury's graduates are accepted to their first- or second-choice college or university. Since 2000, graduates have enrolled in such institutions as Boston College, Colgate University, Hobart and William Smith Colleges, St. Lawrence University, Trinity College, Union College, and the University of Vermont.

STUDENT BODY AND CONDUCT

The 2008–09 student body was composed of 295 boys in grades 9–12, as follows: Form III, 50; Form IV, 75; Form V, 85; and Form VI, 85. Of this number, 20 are day students. The students come from twenty-four states and twelve other countries. The School seeks a diversity of backgrounds and interests.

The School believes that students play a vital role in leadership; thus, the Student Council works closely with the Headmaster and the faculty members. Student committees deal with honor and citizenship matters and advise the Headmaster. The breaking of major School rules is punished by suspension or dismissal.

ACADEMIC FACILITIES

The Main Building contains the Admissions Office, administrative offices, and dining hall. Academic facilities are centered in the Wachtmeister Mathematics and Science Building and the Centennial Library and Humanities Building, which contains 25,000 volumes and more than 120 periodicals. Arts facilities include the Miles P. H. Seifert '53 Theater, the Tremaine Gallery, and the Ruger Family Visual Arts Center. The Chapel Building contains the Field Music Center, which offers newly renovated space for music rehearsals and piano, band, and choral practice as well as a music technology lab.

BOARDING AND GENERAL FACILITIES

There are ten dormitories with faculty apartments. Single, double, and a few triple rooms are available.

Returning students select their own rooms through a lottery, while new students are assigned rooms. Students live according to classes, with seniors in each dormitory serving as prefects. The remodeled Belin Lodge, the School's student center, offers a fully stocked snack bar, large-screen TVs, pool and Ping-Pong tables, and a space for special events. Salisbury School provides phone service, voice mail, access to the campus computer network, and Internet services to every student's room.

A modern Health Center contains private and semiprivate rooms, a doctor's office, and faculty apartments. A full-time M.D. and 2 full-time athletic trainers are in residence on the campus.

ATHLETICS

Every student at Salisbury is expected to participate in the afternoon athletics program each season. The School offers a wide range of choices to students of every age and every level of athletic ability. Some students choose to take on team managerial roles.

In almost all of the following interscholastic sports, there are two or three teams: varsity, junior varsity, and thirds. In the fall, cross-country, football, and soccer are offered; in the winter, Alpine skiing, basketball, hockey, squash, and wrestling are offered; and, in the spring, baseball, crew, golf, lacrosse, sailing, and tennis are offered. There are approximately thirty-three interscholastic teams in a given year.

Recreational athletic offerings include basketball, biking, hockey, paddle tennis, rock climbing, sailing, skiing, snowboarding, soccer, tennis, volleyball, and wilderness.

The Myers Gymnasium contains locker rooms, a training room, a basketball court, a wrestling room, various team rooms, locker rooms and showers, rooms for the ski team, international squash courts, and a fitness center. Other facilities for sports include fields for football, soccer, baseball, and lacrosse; eight outdoor tennis courts; two heated platform tennis courts; a lake; and miles of cross-country trails. The Class of 2002 Dome houses three indoor tennis courts and provides another indoor recreational space. A new boathouse was opened for student use in spring 2008 and a state-of-the-art 106,000-square-foot athletic center is currently under construction and will be opened in fall 2009.

EXTRACURRICULAR OPPORTUNITIES

Salisbury's proximity to Boston, New York, and Hartford enables the School to sponsor trips off campus. In addition, the School brings speakers and entertainers to the campus. Other extracurricular activities available during free time include a variety of community service programs as well as Gospel Choir, Guitar/Jazz Ensemble, Music Technology, Dramatic Society, Radio Station, *The Cupola* (newspaper), *The Pillar* (yearbook), *The Quill* (literary magazine), Debating Club, International Club, Key Society, Peer Counselors, Math and Science Clubs, and driver education.

DAILY LIFE

Classes are held six days a week; Wednesday and Saturday are half-days, with athletic contests taking place in the afternoons. Breakfast is served from 7 to 8:30 a.m. Classes run from 8 until 3 p.m. The class day also includes a midmorning recess and an activities period. Athletic practice takes place from 3:30 until 5:30, and dinner is from 5:30 to 7. Study hall takes place from 7:30 to 9:30 p.m., and all students must be in their dormitories by 10:15. Sunday is free until dinner at 5:30. Day students eat meals at school and are invited to participate in dorm activities.

WEEKEND LIFE

After classes and sports events on Saturday, students may go into town, visit day students' homes, or remain on campus. Dances with nearby schools (Miss Porter's, Ethel Walker, Emma Willard, Westover, and Miss Hall's) are held frequently either on campus or at other schools. Transportation is provided to concerts off campus, ski areas, shopping malls, and local movie theaters. Faculty "teams" provide supervision for these trips.

Students may take weekends off campus on a limited basis. Weekends begin Saturday afternoon and end Sunday evening.

SUMMER PROGRAMS

The Salisbury Summer School of Academic Enrichment was founded in 1946 on the belief that a student's ability to understand and use the written word determines, to a substantial degree, his academic achievement. It is the purpose of the summer school to offer intensive training in reading, writing, and study skills. This training is determined by individual needs and is conducted in a supportive and friendly environment.

Enrollment in the summer school is limited to 105 boys and girls. These students come from private and public schools across the country. Reading instruction is conducted by teachers of varied experience with sound training in this specialized field. Classes in the summer program are small; the program has a student-teacher ratio of 4:1. The school includes an extensive recreational program.

The courses offered include reading and study skills, word skills, composition, creative writing, and mathematics.

The Summer School is under the direction of Ralph J. Menconi.

COSTS AND FINANCIAL AID

Tuition for the 2008–09 academic year was $41,700 for boarding students and $31,700 for day students. These amounts do not include incidental expenses, books, and other fees that can total an additional $700–$1000. Tutoring in the Learning Center, driver's education, and music lessons are available at extra cost. A deposit is due at the time of enrollment, with further payments due in August and December. An initial deposit of $750 is held in escrow until the student leaves Salisbury.

During the 2008–09 academic year, approximately 30 percent of the students received financial aid, with grants that totaled more than $2.5 million. The School uses the School and Student Service for Financial Aid in Princeton, New Jersey.

ADMISSIONS INFORMATION

The Admissions Committee seeks to accept students who have demonstrated the ability to do college-preparatory work and who can be active participants in all phases of community life.

Applicants for grades 9 through 11 should take the SSAT. The majority of students enter in grades 9 and 10, while a few twelfth graders and postgraduates are accepted. A personal interview is required.

APPLICATION TIMETABLE

An initial inquiry is welcome at any time. Campus tours are arranged when the interview appointment is made. The ideal time to visit is Monday through Friday from 9 a.m. to 2 p.m. and Saturday from 9 to 11 a.m., when classes are in session. The Admissions Office is open until 4:30 p.m. Applications should be received before February 1, although late applications may be considered after that time. The application should be accompanied by a nonrefundable fee of $50 ($100 for international students). Notification of acceptance is made by March 10, and parents are expected to reply by April 10.

ADMISSIONS CORRESPONDENCE

Peter B. Gilbert
Director of Admissions and Financial Aid
Salisbury School
Salisbury, Connecticut 06068
Phone: 860-435-5700
Fax: 860-435-5750
E-mail: admissions@salisburyschool.org
Web site: http://www.salisburyschool.org

SANDY SPRING FRIENDS SCHOOL

Sandy Spring, Maryland

Type: Coeducational day and five- and seven-day boarding college-preparatory school
Grades: PK–12: Lower School, PK–5; Middle School 6–8; Upper School 9–12
Enrollment: School total: 571; Lower School: 179; Middle School: 141; Upper School: 251
Head of School: Kenneth W. Smith

THE SCHOOL

Sandy Spring Friends School (SSFS) was founded by Brook Moore in 1961 under the care of the Sandy Spring Monthly Meeting of Friends. The School provides a college-preparatory liberal arts curriculum for students of varying ethnic, economic, and religious backgrounds. It is situated on a 140-acre campus that contains woodlands, a pond and stream, walking and biking paths, and playing fields. Sandy Spring is in Montgomery County and is located approximately 35 minutes from both Washington, D.C., and Baltimore.

As a Quaker school, Sandy Spring Friends School shares the Quaker concern for the unique worth of the individual. Qualities of sensitivity, inventiveness, persistence, and humor are valued, along with intellectual traits. The School's goal is to help each student develop a sense of personal integrity while growing academically and learning to be a responsible member of the community. The School offers a diverse liberal arts curriculum, with courses ranging from basic college-preparatory to Advanced Placement courses. Performing and fine arts courses and athletics are an important part of the curriculum.

The 26-member Board of Trustees includes appointments by the Baltimore Yearly Meeting, the Sandy Spring Monthly Meeting, and the Sandy Spring Friends School. The 2008–09 budget exceeded $14 million, with a growing endowment program that began in 1989.

The School is accredited by the Association of Independent Maryland Schools and approved by the State of Maryland Department of Education. It is a member of the National Association of Independent Schools, the Association of Independent Maryland Schools, the Association of Independent Schools of Greater Washington, the Association of Boarding Schools, the Friends Council on Education, the Secondary School Admission Test Board, the Education Records Bureau, A Better Chance, the National Association for College Admission Counseling, the Black Student Fund, the Potomac and Chesapeake Association of College Admissions Counselors, and the College Board.

ACADEMIC PROGRAMS

The curriculum at Sandy Spring Friends School is intended to prepare students not only for entering college but also for being valuable citizens of the world. It stresses the challenge of Quaker values, academic excellence, and personal growth in an environment that stresses personal responsibility. The school year, from early September to early June, includes Thanksgiving, winter, and spring vacations. A typical daily schedule includes six academic periods, jobs, lunch, an electives period, and sports. The school day is from 8 to 3:20, with sports and activities after school. Boarding students are required to attend dinner at 6 and study hall from 7:30 to 9:30 p.m. The average class size is 14, with a faculty-student ratio of 1:8.

Meeting for Worship is required once a week for Lower School children and twice a week for Middle and Upper School students.

The required academic load for an Upper School student is six courses. To graduate, students must earn 24 credits, including English, 4; foreign language, 3; history, 3 (including United States history); mathematics, 3; science, 3; fine arts, 3; and electives, 3. Additional requirements are participating in a physical activity two times per year, passing a semester course on Quakerism, and community service. Advanced Placement courses are available in English, Spanish, French, history, math, art, and science. The ESL program is open to students in grades 9–12; currently, 31 students are enrolled.

Intersession week in the spring gives Upper School students an opportunity to participate in off-campus activities that supplement the standard curriculum. Projects have included trips to countries such as Belize, Brazil, France, Greece, Italy, Korea, Senegal, and Turkey after intensive study; community service projects in Georgia, Maryland, New York, North Carolina, Tennessee, Virginia, and Washington, D.C.; intensive arts workshops in modern dance, improvisational theater, spinning and weaving, and other arts; and numerous opportunities for outdoor exploration by foot, bike, and boat.

The School operates on a semester schedule, and the grading systems vary by division according to the developmental needs of the students in the age group. The Lower School works within the framework of parent and teacher conferences with extensive comments; the Middle and Upper Schools use letter grades, with additional comments and parent-teacher conferences as appropriate.

FACULTY AND ADVISERS

There are 67 full-time and 7 part-time teachers and administrators who teach. Seventeen live on campus, 6 with their families. Twenty-eight faculty members hold advanced degrees.

Kenneth W. Smith, who was appointed Head of School in 1996, is a graduate of Trinity University (B.S.), Princeton Theological Seminary (M.Div., Th.M.), and Southern Methodist University (D.Min.). Prior to assuming his current position, Ken Smith worked at Friends School of Baltimore as Middle School Head and at the Pine Crest School of Ft. Lauderdale as Assistant to the Headmaster and Vice President.

Sandy Spring faculty members share a variety of nonacademic duties, including supervising student activities, proctoring the dorms, and advising students. The School encourages and supports faculty members in the pursuit of educational interests by providing funding and by supporting a professional development committee of the School.

Middle and Upper School students have a strong adviser-advisee relationship that is based on developing a mutual trust and respect. It provides parents with a personal contact when they have questions or concerns about their child's progress.

COLLEGE ADMISSION COUNSELING

Active college planning begins in the junior year with individual meetings with the College Guidance Director to discuss plans and to identify colleges of interest. Parents and students attend special College Night Programs that include information regarding common admission and application for financial aid procedures. A catalog library and a computer search program are available to students. Also, many college representatives make personal visits to students each year. The School's goal is to match the student with the right school.

Ninety-eight percent of the class of 2008 entered college. They are attending institutions such as American, Boston Conservatory, Dartmouth, Dickinson, Earlham, Emerson, Georgia Tech, Haverford, Johns Hopkins, Penn State, St. Mary's (Maryland), Tufts, Xavier, and the Universities of Delaware, Maryland, Pittsburgh, St. Andrews (U.K.), Vermont, Virginia, and Washington.

STUDENT BODY AND CONDUCT

In 2008–09, the Upper School enrolled 251 students, 126 boys and 125 girls, as follows: 51 in grade 9, 76 in grade 10, 57 in grade 11, and 67 in grade 12. The boarding program enrolled 49 students from the mid-Atlantic region and nine countries. Thirteen percent are members of the Religious Society of Friends, and 37 percent are students of color. International students represent 16 percent of the Upper School student body.

The Torch Committee, the student government organization, includes day and boarding students as well as faculty and administration representatives. The committee, operating by consensus, considers student concerns and makes recommendations to faculty committees and to the administration. A student member of Torch is invited to attend faculty and business meetings and meetings of the Board of Trustees.

ACADEMIC FACILITIES

The School's physical plant, which is valued at more than $41 million, includes a science center, an expanded Lower School, a new Middle School building, a dormitory and dining hall, three major classroom buildings and an administration building, a new performing arts center with a fine arts wing, a new athletic complex, and Yarnall Hall, a $1.75-million resource center that houses a 20,000-volume library, a gymnasium, and an observatory. Computers are integrated into many aspects of the curriculum. Every division of the School is equipped with its own computer lab, and every classroom includes at least one computer and is wired for network and Internet access. The School's library includes computers for online research through the public library system, subscription to online reference tools, and the Internet. A fiber-optic backbone connects the network, and a T1 line connects the Internet and e-mail accounts to students and faculty members.

BOARDING AND GENERAL FACILITIES

All of the boarding students live with their roommates in one 2-story dormitory. Boys and girls each have a separate floor. Community life for boarders includes regular dorm meetings (with decisions reached by consensus), committee-style sponsored activities, family-style dinners with resident staff members, and visits to the homes of day student friends. The dorm staff members (6½ adults for 49 boarders in 2008–09) all reside in either apartments or town houses located in or near the Westview dormitory.

The School nurse assists with the appropriate care for students who may become ill. The School's infirmary is open during the school day.

ATHLETICS

Interscholastic sports and a strong physical education program are all a part of what keeps students active and healthy. The Upper School offers interscholastic sports, including baseball, basketball, cross-country, golf, lacrosse, soccer, softball, tennis, track and field, and volleyball. Other activities are weight lifting, outdoor exploration, and Ultimate Frisbee.

The athletic facilities include a new complex with a 9,000-square-foot gymnasium, a fully equipped fitness center, and state-of-the-art training and locker room facilities. The 140-acre campus includes four soccer and lacrosse fields and a 5-kilometer cross-country course.

EXTRACURRICULAR OPPORTUNITIES

Getting involved is made easy at Sandy Spring Friends by a weekly activities period that allows students to participate in clubs such as Amnesty International (now in its tenth year at SSFS), the Multicultural Club, the International Student Club, the Open Door Club, the ski club (eight weeks of Friday-night skiing plus other trips), the chess club, and the outdoor exploration club. The yearbook and the literary magazine are also popular activities for students.

The purpose of the Community Service Program at Sandy Spring Friends School is to respond to the needs of others and to enrich the School community and the lives of its members. Every student at the School is expected to perform community service as a requirement for graduation. The programs are extremely diverse in order to allow for individual interests to be pursued.

DAILY LIFE

Breakfast for the boarding community begins at 7. Classes begin at 8 and end at 3:20. Advisory and tutorial periods occur once a week, Meeting for Worship occurs two times each week, and a "jobs" period is scheduled daily for dorm students. Lunch is served cafeteria-style daily.

Athletics take place between 3:30 and 5:30, and dinner is served family-style at 6. Dorm meetings or activity groups frequently meet before the study hours, which begin nightly at 7:30, Sunday through Thursday.

WEEKEND LIFE

Weekends at the School are relaxed. Activities, which are frequently designed by both students and faculty members, have included adventures such as day trips into Washington, D.C., for a museum visit, a march on the Mall, lunch at Planet Hollywood and a show at the Kennedy Center, or shopping in Georgetown. In addition, the students have visited Baltimore's Inner Harbor, Harper's Ferry, and various hot spots around the School. While boarding students are not required to stay at the School on weekends, all students can choose the weekend activities in which they wish to participate (day students and five-day boarders are charged an appropriate fee for the off-campus activities). One third of the weekends during the school year include on-campus activities such as School dances; student performances in theater, music, and modern dance; art shows; and special concerts and symposiums in the areas of science and the arts.

COSTS AND FINANCIAL AID

In 2008–09, tuition ranged from $18,600 to $22,100 in the Lower School, $22,250 in the Middle School, and $24,400 in the Upper School. Boarding tuition was $34,900 for five days and $42,900 for seven days. A hot lunch is provided beginning in the first grade. Additional costs include an incidental account for the School store, student allowances, laboratory fees, and art supplies.

Sandy Spring Friends School offers financial aid on the basis of need. The financial aid decisions for applications submitted by January 15 are made by mid-March for the following year. Thirty-one percent of the students received financial aid for the 2008–09 school year. The average award was $24,700 for boarders and $13,000 for day students in the Upper School.

ADMISSIONS INFORMATION

Sandy Spring Friends School actively seeks a diverse, capable, and enthusiastic community of students. The admissions process allows prospective students and their families to become familiar with as many aspects of the School as possible. New students enter at all grade levels as space permits.

APPLICATION TIMETABLE

Inquiries are welcome at any time. The Admissions Office is open from 8 a.m. to 4:30 p.m., Monday through Friday. Application forms are due by January 15. The application process must be completed by February 1 to ensure first-round consideration. Applications received after January 15 are reviewed as space permits.

ADMISSIONS CORRESPONDENCE

Kent Beck, Upper School Admissions
Sandy Spring Friends School
16923 Norwood Road
Sandy Spring, Maryland 20860-1199
Phone: 301-774-7455 Ext. 203
Fax: 301-924-1115
E-mail: admissions@ssfs.org
Web site: http://www.ssfs.org

SEISEN INTERNATIONAL SCHOOL

Tokyo, Japan

Type: Girls' Catholic day college-preparatory school with a coeducational Montessori Kindergarten
Grades: K–12: Montessori Kindergarten; Elementary School, 1–6; Middle School, 7–8; High School, 9–12
Enrollment: School total: 710; High School: 174
Head of School: Sr. Concesa Martin, School Head

THE SCHOOL

Seisen International School began in 1949 as a kindergarten with only 4 American children. When the School moved to Gotanda in 1962, it enrolled 70 students and started a first-grade program as well. By 1970, the School included nine grades; in 1973, when Seisen moved to its present location, its curriculum was extended to include twelve grades. The School has an enrollment of more than 700 students representing approximately sixty nationalities.

Seisen is operated by the Handmaids of the Sacred Heart of Jesus under the auspices of the Seisen Jogakuin Educational Foundation. The order was founded in 1877 by St. Rafaela Maria Porras to dedicate its efforts to educational activities. As a Catholic school with a Christian atmosphere in which students of all races, nationalities, and creeds can thrive, Seisen has high expectations for the students' character development, particularly in respect, compassion, and international understanding.

Seisen offers a Montessori Kindergarten, which is designed to take full advantage of young children's self-motivation and their sensitivity to their environment. In this program, the teacher observes each child's interests and needs and offers the stimulation and guidance that will enable him or her to experience the excitement of learning by choice. The Montessori equipment helps in the development of concentration, coordination, good working habits, and basic skills according to each child's capacities and in a noncompetitive atmosphere.

Seisen's Elementary School strives to create a Christian environment that welcomes and respects children of all nationalities and faiths. Seisen, an authorized International Baccalaureate Primary Years Programme (PYP) school, follows the PYP model in elementary school, grades 1–6. The Primary Years Programme is a transdisciplinary program of international education designed to foster the development of the whole child and encourage students to be inquirers and critical thinkers.

PYP focuses on the development of the whole child, touching hearts and minds. In addition to academics, PYP encompasses social, physical, emotional, and cultural aspects of learning. PYP strives to give children a strong foundation in all the major areas of knowledge: social studies, science, language, the arts, math, and personal, social, and physical education (PSPE). The heart of the PYP program is grounded in the use of inquiry to foster knowledge and skills. Through the inquiry process, teachers and students work together in a PYP classroom to create an environment that encourages the inquiry process. The goal is to enable students to gain essential knowledge and skills and to engage in responsible action.

The High School program prepares young women to face the challenges of a global society with excellent academic preparation, a strong program of athletics, advanced preparation in the visual and performing arts, and an emphasis on community service. From the time the International Baccalaureate Program was adopted at Seisen in 1988, Seisen students have consistently scored higher than the worldwide I.B. mean each year.

Seisen is accredited by the New England Association of Schools and Colleges, the Council of International Schools, and the Japanese Ministry of Education. The School is also a member of the Japan Council of Overseas Schools, the Kanto Plains Association of Secondary School Principals, and the East Asia Regional Council of Overseas Schools.

The School is located in Tokyo's largest residential area, Setagaya-ku. It is easily accessible from downtown Tokyo and surrounding cities by public transportation. Seisen also operates ten school buses, which cover different routes throughout Tokyo.

ACADEMIC PROGRAMS

Seisen requires that students earn 22 credits in grades 9 through 12. Graduation requirements are as follows: English, 4 credits; social sciences, 4 credits; mathematics, 3 credits; science, 3 credits; foreign language, 3 credits; religion, 1 credit; physical education, 1 credit; and academic electives, 3 credits. Academic electives in the senior year include art, music, math, history, foreign language, and an introduction to Montessori teachings. Other electives are yearbook, journalism, survival Japanese, computer graphics, choir, drama, 2-D art, and pottery. In grades 9 and 10, students are required to take a performing/visual arts block, drama, music, pottery, or 2-D art. The Personal Social Health Education course is also a requirement at the ninth and tenth grade levels. Special instruction in English as a second language is available.

Class size varies according to subject. The grading system uses letter grades (A to F) for all subjects. Reports are sent to parents at the end of each quarter.

Students are grouped heterogeneously, except in mathematics, in which there are regular, honors, and accelerated groups. The average course load is five or six classes in academic subjects and one elective. The library is open during the school day and before and after school.

To fully serve the needs of a university-bound, international student body, Seisen offers a program of studies in grades 11 and 12 that can culminate in either a full International Baccalaureate diploma or certificates in individual subjects. These attainments are recognized for admission by over 2,000 universities in more than seventy countries, including many American colleges that accept the I.B. for advanced standing. The I.B. diploma is considered equivalent to most European university entrance requirements.

The following are administered in the School: PSAT/NMSQT, SAT and SAT Subject Tests, selected IGCSE, the Iowa Test of Basic Skills, and the Iowa Test of Educational Development.

FACULTY AND ADVISERS

The faculty consists of 68 full-time members, of whom 52 are women. Approximately 55 percent of the faculty members hold a master's degree or higher.

The administration and faculty members endeavor to educate the students in academic areas and to foster their spiritual and emotional growth. Teachers are involved in counseling and advising students. The personal counselor helps students with life strategies, and teachers assist through the homeroom and teacher adviser system.

COLLEGE ADMISSION COUNSELING

The college advisers help students in college selection and career orientation. Many college representatives visit the School each year, and some Seisen graduates return to give juniors and seniors information about various colleges.

During the junior year, all students take the PSAT and SAT. The SAT middle 50 percent range of scores for last year's graduates was 480–620 for verbal, 570–690 for mathematics, and 520–630 for writing.

Virtually all Seisen graduates move on to higher education. A representative list of schools in which Seisen graduates have been matriculated in the past three years includes Bennington, Boston University, Brown, Carleton, Central St. Martins College of Art and Design, Chapman, Clark, Columbia, Cornell, Duke, Elon, George Washington, Ithaca, Lewis & Clark, Liverpool John Moores University,

London School of Economics, McGill, NYU, Parsons, Pepperdine, Plattsburgh State, Royal Veterinary College, School of the Art Institute of Chicago, Stanford, Sophia (Tokyo), UCLA, USC, Waseda (Tokyo), York, and the Universities of British Columbia; California, San Diego; California, Santa Barbara; Glasgow; Hawaii at Manoa; Kansas; Miami (Florida); Pennsylvania; Toronto; and Washington (Seattle).

STUDENT BODY AND CONDUCT

The 2008–09 student body includes 50 in the ninth grade, 44 in the tenth, 46 in the eleventh, and 34 in the twelfth. The largest percentage of students are from the United States, Korea, the United Kingdom, India, and Japan, but nationalities from all over the world are represented.

ACADEMIC FACILITIES

In addition to classrooms, the School has a chapel, three science laboratories, a computer center, a music room, two art rooms, a media center, a gymnasium, two tennis courts, playgrounds, and a cafeteria.

The School's libraries together have a collection of more than 20,000 volumes and subscribe to sixty periodicals and three newspapers. The High School library houses a multimedia center, two color printers, ten computer workstations, and ten laptops. Students are able to access the library homepage as well as various online references and databases from outside the School.

ATHLETICS

In addition to the physical education program, Seisen offers badminton, basketball, cross-country, soccer, swimming, tennis, track and field, and volleyball. Basketball, tennis, and volleyball are offered at varsity and junior varsity levels.

EXTRACURRICULAR OPPORTUNITIES

As a member of the Kanto Plains Association of Secondary School Principals, Seisen is active in various competitions (debate, speech, Brain Bowl, Math Field Day). There are vocal and instrumental groups, a choir, and a drama group. Other organizations and activities include the National Honor Society, the Student Council, student publications, Alleluia Club, Bell Choir, Booster Club, Model United Nations (MUN), social service groups, and the Girls' Athletic Association (GAA).

Seisen After School Activities (SASA), which are offered to elementary school students, include sports, art, computer graphics, music, science, and language classes.

DAILY LIFE

Students have eight 40-minute classes, which include study halls and activity periods. The School cafeteria serves hot lunches, but students may choose to bring their own lunch from home. Classes begin at 8:20 a.m. and end at 3:20 p.m. There are no Saturday classes. Students are encouraged to participate in competitive sports and other activities after school.

SUMMER PROGRAMS

A three-week program of remedial studies is offered in June. Enrichment programs and sports are offered on a limited basis.

COSTS AND FINANCIAL AID

School fees are quoted in Japanese yen. For the 2008–09 school year, the High School tuition is 1.94 million yen. Transportation and lunches are available at additional cost. A registration fee of 300,000 yen and a land and building development fee of 400,000 yen are payable when a student registers.

ADMISSIONS INFORMATION

Seisen International School serves the needs of diplomatic, business, and professional families of the international community. It also provides education for Japanese children who have lived abroad and wish to continue their education in English.

A completed application form and Confidential Counselor Recommendation, transcripts from the school(s) previously attended, and payment of the application fee are required of all applicants in the initial process of admission. An interview with the respective principal or the School Head of Seisen International School and an entrance examination are required in the final phase of the admission process.

APPLICATION TIMETABLE

Applications are welcome at any time. Parents and prospective students are encouraged to visit the School.

ADMISSIONS CORRESPONDENCE

Sr. Concesa Martin, School Head
Seisen International School
12-15, Yoga 1-chome
Setagaya-ku
Tokyo
Japan 158-0097
Phone: 81-3-3704-2661
Fax: 81-3-3701-1033
E-mail: sisadmissions@seisen.com
Web site: http://www.seisen.com

THE SHIPLEY SCHOOL

Bryn Mawr, Pennsylvania

Type: Coeducational, day, college-preparatory school
Grades: P–12: Lower School, Prekindergarten–5; Middle School, 6–8; Upper School, 9–12
Enrollment: School total: 879; Upper School: 340
Head of School: Dr. Steven Piltch

THE SCHOOL

The Shipley School, a coeducational, college preparatory day school, was founded in 1894 by the Misses Hannah, Elizabeth, and Katherine Shipley to prepare girls for Bryn Mawr College. While boys were first enrolled in 1972, the School now has 879 students (453 boys and 426 girls).

The Upper and Lower Schools are located on landscaped campuses (36 acres) one block apart near the SEPTA Railroad station and directly opposite the Bryn Mawr College campus. Bryn Mawr is a suburban community 12 miles west of Philadelphia, and Shipley is one of the closest schools to the SEPTA trains.

While Shipley places the greatest emphasis on education of the mind, it is also concerned with the moral and emotional needs of its students and is dedicated to developing in each one a love of learning and a compassionate participation in the world. Through a strong college-preparatory curriculum in the humanities and sciences, the School encourages curiosity, creativity, and respect for intellectual effort. Shipley upholds and promotes moral integrity, a sense of personal achievement and worth, and concern for others at school and in the larger community.

A nonprofit institution, Shipley is governed by a 29-member Board of Trustees, which consists of 13 men and 16 women. An active Alumni Association represents the more than 5,100 living graduates.

The School plant is valued at $60.4 million. The School endowment is estimated at $16.3 million.

The Shipley School is accredited by the Pennsylvania Association of Private Academic Schools and the Middle States Association of Colleges and Schools and is a member of the Secondary School Admission Test Board, the National Association of Independent Schools, and the Pennsylvania Association of Independent Schools.

ACADEMIC PROGRAMS

To graduate, a student must complete at least 16 credits in grades 9–12, including 4 years of English; 3 years of mathematics, including algebra II; 3 years of a foreign language; 2 years of history, including U.S. history; 2 years of science; and 1 year of computer science. Most graduates have many more credits than the minimum. Students in grade 9 are also required to take art and music, and all Upper School students must take a seminar in health and perform 40 hours of community service.

Yearlong courses include American Studies, computer science, economics, English, French, history, Latin, mathematics, music, philosophy, science, Spanish, and studio art. Advanced Placement–level courses are available in English, studio art (drawing and 2-D design), history of art, U.S. history, European history, Latin Vergil and Latin literature, French language, Spanish language, biology, chemistry, physics C (Mech.), calculus AB, calculus BC, computer science A, music theory, and statistics. By special arrangement, seniors may take courses at Bryn Mawr College. Electives include Chinese/Japanese history, Russia and Contemporary Europe, American Studies, economics, and new courses on globalization and Middle Eastern history.

The school year is divided into quarters and semesters, and most students carry five subjects per term. Most classes are homogeneously grouped, particularly mathematics and foreign languages. There are 15 or 16 students in an average class. Students in grades 9–10 attend supervised study halls during free periods. The overall student-teacher ratio is 8:1.

Grades are discussed with the student by his or her academic adviser and then sent to parents four times a year. Reports have letter grades with comments written by individual faculty members. Extra help is often available from faculty members.

Independent service projects are required of seniors after the completion of their final exams in mid-May.

During spring and summer vacations, various departments offer study-travel trips, some with homestays. In the past few years, students have traveled to France, Panama, and Italy. "City Term" in New York City and the Island School are open to upperclassmen.

FACULTY AND ADVISERS

The Upper School faculty consists of 48 teachers (42 full-time and 6 part-time), including 23 men and 25 women. Six administrators who teach are part of the faculty as well. Sixty-three percent of teachers and administrators who teach hold advanced degrees.

The Head of School, Dr. Steven Piltch, was appointed in 1992. A graduate of Williams College, Dr. Piltch has received two master's degrees in education from Harvard University, one in counseling and consulting psychology and the other in secondary and middle school administration. In 1991, he received a Doctor of Education degree from Harvard in administration, planning, and social policy.

All members of the faculty and administration are active in advising and counseling students. Many of them coach. With funds generated by a foundation and the School, faculty members are encouraged to continue their education during summer vacation.

Two nurses are on duty at the health centers, a physician is on call, and 3 consultants are at the School several days per week.

COLLEGE ADMISSION COUNSELING

Beginning in the eleventh grade, 3 college guidance counselors and an assistant work closely with students, helping them individually throughout the college-selection process. The counselors also meet once a week with small groups of their advisees during both their junior and senior years. College admissions officers from across the country come to the School each fall to conduct interviews, and students are assisted in making plans to visit colleges themselves. Virtually all graduates attend four-year colleges and universities. A representative list of institutions attended includes Amherst, Bates, Bowdoin, Brown, Bucknell, Carnegie Mellon, Columbia, Cornell, Dickinson, Drexel, Duke, Franklin and Marshall, George Washington, Hamilton, Harvard, Lehigh, Middlebury, Mount Holyoke, Muhlenberg, NYU, Penn State, Princeton, Swarthmore, Syracuse, Trinity (Connecticut), Tufts, Ursinus, Villanova, Wesleyan, Williams, Yale, and the Universities of Colorado, Delaware, Michigan, Pennsylvania, Pittsburgh, Vermont, Virginia, and Wisconsin.

STUDENT BODY AND CONDUCT

In grades 9 through 12, there are 340 students. In these grades, there are 172 boys and 168 girls.

Students come from fifty-five towns and cities in the greater Philadelphia area. Members of minority groups represent 15 percent of the total enrollment.

The Shipley School Government consists of the Executive Council, which discusses and implements decisions, and the Judicial Board, which handles all serious disciplinary matters. In addition, there is an Athletic Association, an Arts Association, a Students' Organization for Service, and a Community Life Organization.

ACADEMIC FACILITIES

Two wings of the main Upper School building house classrooms, the Snyder Science Center, art studios, music rooms, the library, the gymnasium, and renovated computer facilities, college counseling offices, and student and faculty lounges. Administrative offices, the dining rooms, and the kitchen are also housed in the main building. The new Lower School opened in 2001; another Lower School gym was added in 2002. The School added two new turf fields in 2006.

ATHLETICS

All students are members of the Athletic Association and are members of the Blue or Green teams, which reflect the school colors. Vital to the successful development of the whole student is the belief that important physical, social, and moral values are learned through the experience of team sports and a rigorous physical education program. Cross-country, crew, field hockey, soccer, lacrosse, tennis, baseball, golf, and softball are the fall and spring varsity activities. In winter, basketball, squash, swimming, and volleyball are options. Games are scheduled with schools in suburban Philadelphia.

The Yarnall Gymnasium has two basketball courts with stands; the same area converts easily for volleyball, badminton, gymnastics, and indoor tennis. On the lower level, there are coaches' offices, locker rooms, and a fitness center. Some games and practices also take place in the new Lower School Gym.

The Fuller fields include a separate soccer field and a hockey field, adjacent to six tennis courts. Three additional athletics fields, 2 miles away, are reached by bus. Several of the school's fields have recently been converted to safer, synthetic turf.

EXTRACURRICULAR OPPORTUNITIES

Shipley offers students a variety of extracurricular activities, such as *The Beacon,* the school newspaper; *Tempora Praeterita,* the yearbook; and *The Compass,* the literary and art magazine; selective singing groups, the Madrigals and Madriguys; the Upper School Choir, an All-School Choir; instrumental and jazz ensembles; the School Orchestra; Computer Club; Model UN; Environmental Awareness; It's Mathematical (an interscholastic math team); jewelry and photography; Students United for Racial Equality (SURE); Amnesty International; SAT Prep; the award-winning horticultural group (the Sprouts); and the Yearbook Committee. Students also volunteer to help the Admissions Office, tutor inner-city children, rehabilitate urban housing, and work in local hospitals and nursing homes through the Students' Organization for Service (SOS). Participation in the community service program is required, including a service project at the end of the senior year.

Annual events include parents' evenings, Parents' Weekend, "Shipley Today" and "Shipley on Saturday," open houses for parents of prospective students, Alumni Weekend, and annual academic, character, and sports award assemblies. The Social Committee plans many on-campus activities and organizes exchange events with nearby schools. Dances and other social events, including Super Saturday, an annual charity fundraiser, are scheduled on weekends. In addition, students can be in downtown Philadelphia in 20 minutes; there they can attend cultural and recreational events.

DAILY LIFE

Classes are 40 or 80 minutes long and run from 8:30 a.m. to 3:15 p.m. A hot meal and salad bar are available for lunch daily. Prepaid school lunches are required in the Middle and Upper Schools. There are nine academic periods per day. The day includes "office hours," when all students are free to meet with teachers individually. Most students have at least one free period (a study hall for grades 9 and 10) everyday.

SUMMER PROGRAMS

Shipley also hosts a Summer Enrichment Camp for boys and girls ages 6–14, with a focus on sports and the arts, cooking classes, and sports clinics in soccer, lacrosse, and basketball. A transitional program for urban youth is also cosponsored by Shipley in July every summer with the Young Scholars Fund of Philadelphia. This program is for students who have completed grade 7 or 8 and are interested in applying to independent school for grade 9. It involves four weeks of classes in English, mathematics, and science and is taught by Shipley teachers.

COSTS AND FINANCIAL AID

The 2008–09 tuition for Upper School students is $26,500. Other expenses (books, lab fees, testing, athletic fees, and trips) vary from $500 to $1000, not including lunches. The lunches cost $795 per year. Tuition insurance and a tuition payment plan are offered.

More than 20 percent of students receive need-based financial aid. Grants are made possible through the generosity of certain foundations, endowment income, and the Annual Giving campaign. Grants are based on financial need and are determined by procedures established by the School and Student Service for Financial Aid. Recipients are chosen for their ability, character, past performance, and promise. Awards range from $1000 to $26,000 and total more than $3.1 million per year. All families are expected to contribute to their children's educational expenses. The Centennial Scholarship Exam, given each January, provides endowed scholarships to incoming ninth graders based on need and merit (as judged by the exam). Winners receive more than 100 percent of demonstrated financial need for four years.

ADMISSIONS INFORMATION

Shipley seeks responsible, self-directed students of above-average to superior ability who enjoy learning. New students are admitted at all grade levels. An interview, the School's placement testing, and reports from previous schools are required of all applicants. Students must also submit results of the SSAT, the ISEE, or the Wechsler Intelligence Scale for Children (WISC–IV). For entrance to the Upper School in the 2007–08 academic year, there were 122 applicants. Of these, 48 were accepted, and 27 new students enrolled in the following grades: grade 9, 18; grade 10, 3; grade 11, 5, and grade 12, 1.

APPLICATION TIMETABLE

The Admissions Office is open year-round. Campus interviews and tours are possible throughout the week during the school year from 8:30 a.m. to 4:30 p.m.

While there is no closing date for applications, candidates are encouraged to submit a formal application during the fall of the year before prospective enrollment. To be considered in the first round of decisions, applications must be completed by January 15 for entrance the following September. The application fee is $60. A student should register for the next available SSAT or ISEE or arrange to take the WISC–IV with an accredited tester before January 1. Transcripts and recommendations should be secured after the first marking period and mailed to the Director of Admissions. The first acceptances are announced at the end of January. Shipley expects a response from students accepted in this first round by March 1.

After February 1, the Shipley School works on a rolling admissions system whereby admissions decisions are announced when all necessary information has been compiled and reviewed by the Admissions Committee. Parents are expected to reply to an offer of admission within two weeks of notification. An applicant who is waiting to hear from other schools with later acceptance dates should inform the Admissions Office of the situation.

ADMISSIONS CORRESPONDENCE

Gregory W. Coleman, Director of Admissions
The Shipley School
814 Yarrow Street
Bryn Mawr, Pennsylvania 19010-3598
Phone: 610-525-4300 Ext. 4118
Fax: 610-525-5082
E-mail: admit@shipleyschool.org
Web site: http://www.shipleyschool.org

SHORECREST PREPARATORY SCHOOL

St. Petersburg, Florida

Type: Coeducational day college-preparatory school
Grades: P–12: Prekindergarten, 3- and 4-year-olds; Lower Division K–4; Middle Division, 5–8; Upper Division, 9–12
Enrollment: School total: 967; Upper Division: 274; Middle Division: 291; Lower Division: 304; Pre-K: 71
Head of School: Michael A. Murphy

THE SCHOOL

Shorecrest Preparatory School, the oldest independent day school in Florida, was founded in 1923 as a coeducational proprietary school. Situated on 28 tree-shaded acres in northeast St. Petersburg, Shorecrest attracts academically able students from the Tampa Bay area. Originally founded to meet the educational needs of winter visitors from the North, the School was expanded in the 1940s and 1950s to offer an education of high quality to the growing number of permanent residents. In 1973, the Upper Division was added, and in 1975 Shorecrest became a not-for-profit independent institution. The Shorecrest curriculum extends from the Early Childhood Program, which enrolls 3- and 4-year-olds, to grade 12. In the upper grades, the curriculum is designed to meet the many needs of college-bound students.

Shorecrest has a child-centered approach to education, reflecting the belief that teachers and administrators should work with understanding and patience toward the fullest development of each child. The School's philosophy is that the educational development of each student is a joint venture in which the student, faculty members, and parents share responsibility. Parents are encouraged and expected to share any concerns they might have regarding their child's education with his or her teachers. The learning environment at the School is challenging yet nurturing. Students are expected to meet high standards so that they can experience the satisfaction of academic accomplishment. The School community is supportive, united by a common respect for the contributions and rights of each student and each teacher. Administrators and faculty members work together to strengthen the student's sense of self-respect and respect for others. New students are impressed by the friendliness that pervades Shorecrest and find that they become assimilated into the student body quickly and easily.

The School is governed by a board of 25 trustees who are elected by the current board to serve on a rotating basis. Alumni participate in many key operations of the School community, including service activities and development.

Shorecrest is accredited by the Southern Association of Colleges and Schools, the Florida Council of Independent Schools, and the Florida Kindergarten Council. It is a member of the College Board, the Cum Laude Society, the School and Student Service for Financial Aid, the National Association of Independent Schools, the Southern Association of Independent Schools, the Bay Area Association of Independent Schools, Tampa Bay Independent Secondary Schools, the National Association for College Admission Counseling, the Southern Association for College Admission Counseling, the Secondary School Admission Test Board, the Educational Records Bureau, and the Florida High School Activities Association.

ACADEMIC PROGRAMS

Academics are the core of the Shorecrest Preparatory School experience, and the School offers a strong college-preparatory curriculum. Students are expected to demonstrate competence in literature, writing, foreign language, history, mathematics, science, and the arts. The School has committed substantial resources to the creation of state-of-the-art technology facilities. Through its integration in the curriculum, experience in the use of technology is available to all students.

The Early Childhood Center (for 3- and 4-year-olds) provides an integrated, experiential approach to learning. Hands-on activities that are developmentally and individually appropriate promote growth in all areas of the students' development.

The kindergarten through grade 4 program emphasizes the development of a well-balanced student. The integrated reading–language arts curriculum stresses oral and written communication, reading comprehension, and vocabulary development. The mathematics curriculum focuses on developing an understanding of mathematical concepts and number sense, providing opportunities to apply higher-level critical-thinking and problem-solving skills. Science and social studies offer concrete experiences through discovery and investigation. Classroom computers, along with access to a full computer lab, enable technology to become a vehicle for enhancing all curriculum areas. Spanish, art, music, and physical education enrich the K–4 education.

The Middle Division years (grades 5 through 8) are a period of transition when academic, social, and emotional development occurs. A challenging academic curriculum emphasizes literature, writing, higher-level mathematics, science, and social studies. World languages, physical education, and arts courses form an integral part of the curriculum. Technology is emphasized at every grade level. An advisory program, along with the Student Council, service learning, and other clubs, offer leadership and skill-building opportunities that complement the overall Middle Division program.

At the secondary level, the curriculum is designed to meet—and often exceed—the course requirements for admission to the most competitive colleges and universities. For graduation, students are required to complete a minimum of 4 years each of English and mathematics; 3 years each of a foreign language, history, and science; and 1 year each of physical education and fine arts. Honors courses are offered in algebra, geometry, precalculus, calculus, biology, chemistry, English, French, Spanish, and political science. For academically able students who wish to take Advanced Placement (AP) examinations to qualify for college credit, the following courses are offered: English Language and Composition, English Literature, French Language, French Literature, Spanish Language, Calculus AB/BC, Biology, Chemistry, Physics, Computer Science, U.S. History, European History, World History, Economics, Psychology, Art History, Studio Art (Portfolio), and Music Theory. In 2008, 117 students took 269 Advanced Placement exams, and 90 percent earned college-level credit based on their scores.

FACULTY AND ADVISERS

The 2008–09 Shorecrest faculty numbered 101 members. While all of the faculty members are college graduates, more than half hold master's degrees and 4 hold doctoral degrees.

COLLEGE ADMISSION COUNSELING

The College Counseling staff begins working with students in the college selection process at the beginning of the junior year. The college counseling program incorporates all aspects of the research, preparation, and application process. Numerous individual conferences are supplemented by such events as a Parent and Student Workshop and a comprehensive Junior Seminar. College representatives visit Shorecrest throughout the year to meet with juniors and seniors.

One hundred percent of Shorecrest graduates attend four-year colleges and universities. A representative list of where recent graduates have matriculated include Amherst, Brown, Colgate, Columbia, Connecticut College, Cornell, Dartmouth, Duke, Emory, Florida State, Georgetown, Harvard, Julliard, Lehigh, MIT, Northwestern, Notre Dame, Princeton, Tufts, Tulane, the U.S. Military Academy, the U.S. Naval Academy, Vanderbilt, Wake Forest, Washington and Lee, William and Mary, Yale, and the Universities of Florida, Miami (Florida), and Pennsylvania.

STUDENT BODY AND CONDUCT

For the 2008–09 school year, there were 274 Upper Division students: 127 boys and 147 girls. The student body represents a diversity of ethnic and economic backgrounds.

The School fosters a sense of community among students, faculty members, and parents. School rules and regulations are set forth in the *Student/Parent Handbook* and stress the importance of the partnership between the School and the parents. Students and faculty and staff members adhere to an Honor Pledge. Students are expected to conduct themselves in a way that promotes self-respect, tolerance of others' differences, and a sense of responsibility for the greater school community. Character education is an integral part of the Shorecrest curriculum throughout all grade levels. Believing that an education is not complete without opportunities to serve others, the School offers a broad range of community service experiences, such as opportunities to work with young children, the elderly, the homeless, and the disabled.

ACADEMIC FACILITIES

Academic facilities include sixty-five classrooms, three science labs, twelve computer labs, three language labs, and an early childhood center. The

Sci-Tech Center houses biology, chemistry, and physics laboratories and two fully equipped computer classrooms. A 615-seat, state-of-the-art theater, a gymnasium, a student center, and a Library Media Center are shared by the Upper, Middle, and Lower Divisions. A newly constructed high school facility opened in 2008. All classrooms are wireless and contain 42" flat screens. The visual art center contains a digital film lab and art patio with an outdoor kiln. A closed-circuit TV system is the center of the broadcasting and communications curriculum, where students are encouraged to produce content and enhance their public speaking skills.

ATHLETICS

Physical education classes emphasize the importance of physical fitness, the improvement of basic skills, and the development of self-esteem, sportsmanship, and a sense of team spirit. In addition, all students take a required health class.

The School has a varied and competitive athletics program. Boys may choose from baseball, basketball, cross-country, football, golf, soccer, swimming, tennis, and track. Girls compete in basketball, cheerleading, cross-country, golf, soccer, softball, swimming, tennis, track, and volleyball. The School is proud of its record of achievement in winning district and state championships. Shorecrest has ranked in past years in the top five among the 165 Florida schools in the I-A competitive division by the Florida Athletic Coaches Association for the overall quality of its athletics programs. In addition, Shorecrest has won the Class 2A Sportsmanship Award for the state of Florida several times.

Sports facilities include a football–soccer field with stands and lights, a practice field, indoor and outdoor basketball courts, a baseball diamond, a softball diamond, two weight rooms, and an eight-lane, all-weather track. The swim team uses the North Shore Pool, the tennis team plays at The Racquet Club, and the golf team plays at Feather Sound Country Club.

EXTRACURRICULAR OPPORTUNITIES

A wide variety of cocurricular and extracurricular activities are designed to match the varied interests of the students.

The Student Council provides a forum for the discussion of all issues concerning school government and serves as the liaison between the student body and the administration. The council, which meets weekly, also plans and sponsors numerous special social, recreational, and educational events throughout the year.

Learning through serving others is a crucial part of a Shorecrest education. Service Learning extends beyond community service or volunteerism; it connects students' academic learning with serving the community's needs and vice versa. At Shorecrest, Service Learning is a valuable tool for student civic engagement and the development of student leaders. It provides an arena where students can stand out beyond the classroom, the athletic fields, or on center stage. Ongoing partnerships with local organizations allow students to select an area of focus for their service activities and become advocates for the organizations and the causes they serve. Shorecrest Service Partners include American Cancer Society, Big Brothers/Big Sisters, Florida Holocaust Museum, Habitat for Humanity, Hospice, Ronald McDonald House, SPCA, St. Petersburg Free Clinic/Food Bank, and the YWCA.

Numerous academic honor societies and clubs give students the opportunity—through field trips, special projects, and contests—to extend their interest beyond the classroom.

Shorecrest is especially proud of its student publications: *Crestviews,* the yearbook; and *The Chronicle,* the newspaper, which has won the Florida Scholastic Press Association's First Place Award for student journalism, an award for excellence from the Southern Interscholastic Press Association, and a Medalist Award from Columbia University. Shorecrest students have the professional assistance of the Poynter Institute and use the Institute's facilities in the production of the newspaper. Students who work on these publications are eligible for election into Quill and Scroll, an international honor society for high school journalists.

Shorecrest presents a fall play and a spring musical production each year. All students are invited to participate. Students with a particular interest in drama may be elected to membership in the Thespian Society.

Shorecrest also has chapters of the National Honor Society and Cum Laude Society.

DAILY LIFE

School hours are from 7:45 to 3. There are eight academic periods, a lunch period, and an advisory/community meeting each day.

Shorecrest believes that leadership ability resides in all students, and, through the Leadership Development program, all students are encouraged to become engaged citizens and leaders in society. The ninth grade focus is on ethical decision making and public speaking, the tenth grade focus is on leadership, the eleventh grade focus is on service and mentoring, and the twelfth grade focus is on life skills.

COSTS AND FINANCIAL AID

The tuition for the Upper Division for the 2008–09 session was $16,315. Payment may be made monthly or in one or two payments. The cost of books and other fees increases the total by approximately $500.

A total of $850,000 is available for financial aid. Awards are made in accordance with principles established by the School and Student Service for Financial Aid. The Dewar Tuition Refund Plan is available to parents who want tuition payment insurance.

ADMISSIONS INFORMATION

Admissions decisions for grades 5 through 12 are based on previous academic records, teacher recommendations from the current school, standardized test scores, a personal interview, and results of an admissions test. Candidates should also submit a graded writing sample. In making decisions, the Admissions Committee places priority on the applicant's ability to successfully meet the academic expectations of the School's demanding college-preparatory curriculum. From among those who meet these criteria, the committee endeavors to choose those students who will benefit most from attending Shorecrest and who will contribute most to making the School an interesting, enjoyable, and productive community. Shorecrest strives to be an inclusive society, and students are admitted without regard to race, creed, or national origin.

APPLICATION TIMETABLE

Applications are received and processed at any time of the year, but candidates are advised to submit their application by mid-January to ensure consideration for the limited number of places available for the following session. Prospective students may schedule visits to the campus at their convenience, and they are encouraged to spend an entire day at Shorecrest, visiting in appropriate classes and becoming acquainted with students.

ADMISSIONS CORRESPONDENCE

Diana Craig, Director of Admissions
Shorecrest Preparatory School
5101 First Street, NE
St. Petersburg, Florida 33703-3099

Phone: 727-456-7511
Fax: 727-527-4191
E-mail: admissions@shorecrest.org
Web site: http://www.shorecrest.org

SOLEBURY SCHOOL

New Hope, Pennsylvania

Type: Coeducational, boarding and day, college-preparatory school
Grades: 7–12: Middle School, 7–8; Upper School, 9–12
Enrollment: School total: 220; Upper School: 194
Head of School: Thomas G. Wilschutz

THE SCHOOL

Solebury School was founded in 1925 by four teachers whose vision was to create an environment that fostered close connections between teachers and pupils, where there would be a respectful exchange of opinions and ideas and where students would be well prepared for both college and life. This educational philosophy of Solebury's founders continues today. Solebury School's mission is to offer a challenging academic curriculum and an environment of educational excellence that prepares students for success in college and beyond. The Solebury community strongly values academic and intellectual challenge, creative and independent thinking, mutual respect between students and teachers, deep respect for each individual, and diversity.

The School is located in beautiful Bucks County, Pennsylvania, and enjoys a rural setting on more than 90 acres not far from the banks of the Delaware River. It is 65 miles from New York City and 35 miles from Philadelphia.

Solebury is a nonprofit school and is directed by a board of 28 trustees that includes 15 alumni.

Solebury School is accredited by the Middle States Association of Colleges and Schools. It is a member of the National Association of Independent Schools, Pennsylvania Association of Independent Schools, the Association of Boarding Schools, the Independent School Teachers' Association, Secondary School Admission Test Board, School and Student Services for Financial Aid, National Association of Foreign Student Advisors, Association of Delaware Valley Independent Schools, and Council for Advancement and Support of Education.

ACADEMIC PROGRAMS

Students at Solebury are required to carry a minimum academic load of 9 credits per trimester. At least 109 credits are required for graduation, including 24 credits in English, 18 in a foreign language, 18 in mathematics, 12 in science (including conceptual physics and biology), 12 in social science (including U.S. history), 6 in the arts (two full years), 1 in computer science, 1 in health, electives, 10 hours each year of community service, and three trimesters each year of a sport or activity.

About 100 electives are offered, as well as opportunity for independent study. These rigorous college-level courses are presented throughout all the disciplines: English, math, science, social studies, languages, arts, and English as a second language (ESL). Included in these electives are Advanced Placement and honors courses. Typical of some of these electives are Applied Science: Forensics; Global Warming; Mathematics of Archaeology: Digging for Math; The Arab World and the West: Migration of People and Ideas; Media, Economics, & Justice; Major Playwrights of the Elizabethan Age; Logic, Rhetoric, and Debate (mock trial); and Music Skills: Application and Interpretation.

Middle School courses prepare students for high school work in the disciplines and include English, foreign language: Spanish and French 1A and 1B, pre-algebra, social studies, science, and the Introduction to the Arts Program. Middle School students who qualify may take advanced courses in math, foreign language, and the arts.

In addition to local field trips throughout the year, there are a variety of experiences for students to participate in during the longer school breaks, including tours of Canada, France, and Costa Rica. Each year, teachers have the opportunity to design new trips, depending upon interest and availability.

Solebury's curriculum each year is highlighted by an academic theme intended to give teachers and students common experiences and to promote interdisciplinary learning. This year, the theme was Migration.

Class size averages 11 students. Independent study is available for especially well motivated students, and credit can be earned for special projects. Annual senior projects focus on areas of special interest and may include apprenticeships with craftsmen, community service groups, or businesses and other organizations.

Solebury has three academic trimesters. Comprehensive grade reports with teacher comments are sent to parents three times per year.

A Learning Skills Program assists 29 students who have learning differences in the basic language areas. This program is for students who possess average to above-average intelligence and need to strengthen their reading, writing, and language-related skills. Classes use multisensory Orton and Wilson models to teach phonological processing. Students also work on organization, study skills, and oral communication.

For international students, English as a second language (ESL) programs are offered during the full year and in summer. With small classes of 8 students, Solebury's goal is to help students develop their speaking, listening, reading, and writing skills. Classes are also offered to prepare students for the TOEFL. In addition, the School assists them individually in college advising and placement. Solebury's main objective is to prepare students for entrance into American colleges or universities with little or no ESL support.

FACULTY AND ADVISERS

On July 1, 2008, Thomas G. Wilschutz became Solebury School's eighth Head of School. Tom comes to Solebury School from Laurel School of Cleveland, Ohio, where he had been Assistant Head for three years and, before that, Director of Admissions and Financial Aid for twelve years. In the early 1990s, he served as Associate Director of Admissions at both Kent State University and Michigan State University.

From 1994–2004, Wilschutz was the Managing Director of The Streetsboro Community Theatre, a publicly funded, community-based theater, where he was responsible for all of the technical and business aspects of the theater's operation. Also, from 2000 to the present, he was a founder and principal of College Solutions, a consulting group that offers college admissions counseling services to urban public school students in Cleveland.

Wilschutz has a Bachelor of Arts in history and philosophy from the University of Iowa and an M.A. in European history from Michigan State University, and he has completed the course work for his Ph.D. in British history from Michigan State.

There are 55 teachers and administrators on Solebury's staff, 27 of whom hold advanced degrees. Twenty-four faculty members and administrators reside on campus, and all faculty and staff members are involved in the life of the community beyond the classroom.

The adviser system is an essential part of the life of the School, nurturing an informal relationship between teachers and students that supplements the roles filled by each in the classroom. Advisers meet weekly with their students and are the personal contacts for parents when they have questions or concerns about their child's progress. Although each new student is assigned an adviser temporarily, all students select their own advisers.

COLLEGE ADMISSION COUNSELING

The Director of College Counseling, administrators, and the faculty advisers for juniors and seniors support each student in the college-search process. Computer-assisted research, career information, and a college catalog library are maintained for student use. In addition, college representatives visit the Solebury campus yearly to speak to interested students. To assist students and parents with the completion of applications, essays, and financial aid forms, the College Counselor holds meetings with both students and parents throughout the year. Current students are also invited to meet with recent graduates as they share their college experiences. It is recommended that sophomores and juniors take the PSATs, and juniors and seniors the SATs, and international students the TOEFL. Preparation for these tests is offered in-house through workshops and classes.

Forty-nine seniors graduated in June 2008. Graduates were admitted to a wide range of schools, including Brown, Colgate, Fordham, Fashion Institute of Technology, George Washington, Johnson and Wales, NYU, Pepperdine, and Rhode Island School of Design.

STUDENT BODY AND CONDUCT

Of the 220 students in grades 7–12 in 2008–09, the breakdown was as follows: 38 boarding boys, 28 boarding girls, 81 day boys, and 73 day girls. There were 13 students in grade 7, 13 in grade 8, 40 in grade 9, 47 in grade 10, 46 in grade 11, and 60 in grade 12. Students came from Pennsylvania, New Jersey, and five other states as well as Canada, China, Germany, Jamaica, Japan, South Korea, Taiwan, Tunisia, and Vietnam.

The community sets reasonable limits for its members. The students participate with the faculty members in many areas of decision making. Students are represented on the Judiciary Committee, which makes recommendations on all serious matters of discipline. Students are also represented on the Academic Committee and the Community Council.

ACADEMIC FACILITIES

The $3-million Abbe Science Center, which opened in 2002, includes four state-of-the-art science labs, four math classrooms, and a greenhouse. The Penney International Center, opened in 2003, has five classrooms and a study lounge with eight computer stations, and a computerized active board.

The Founders Library contains 13,000 items and is a member of Access Pennsylvania, including P.O.W.E.R. Library. In addition, the library subscribes to a number of online databases, the complete list of which can be found on the library page under Academics at http://www.solebury.org. The library and the adjacent multimedia room, which is equipped with a large-screen video projection system, video-audio editing equipment, and computers for student use, form the reference and research hub for the Solebury community. The campus network has direct high-speed Internet access through a T-1 line, and all the classrooms and dormitory rooms are wired. There are 168 computers campuswide. The student-computer ratio is 2:1. The Art Center facilities are housed downstairs and include studios for painting, drawing, ceramics, and graphics and a darkroom for photography, which includes six enlarger stations.

Classrooms for English, social studies, foreign language, and the Learning Skills Program are located in a number of other buildings on the campus.

BOARDING AND GENERAL FACILITIES

Boarding is offered to students in grades 9 through 12. Returning students select their roommates, while new students are assigned roommates through a carefully designed questionnaire. Holmquist House, the girls' 28-bed dormitory, houses two girls to a room and is supervised by two dormitory parents. Walter Lamb Hall, the boys' 40-bed dormitory, includes two-bedroom suites and baths for four boys and is supervised by four dorm parents. The School nurse is an RN and pediatric nurse practitioner. The School uses the local services of the Phillips Barber Health Center in Lambertville, New Jersey, when students need to see a physician.

Other buildings include the Farm House, for administration, and Boyd Dining Hall, where meals are served cafeteria-style to students, faculty members, and faculty families. The Carriage House houses offices, the music room, and the infirmary. The refurbished barn contains a 100-seat black box theater, a lounge and lockers for day students, a student café and recreation room, and offices for the deans. Six new faculty homes were completed in 2002.

ATHLETICS

The new $7.5-million John D. Brown Athletic Center, opened December 2007, includes a 22,000-square-foot gymnasium, 400-meter track and playing field, site work, and 7,000-square-foot maintenance building. At Solebury, everyone is required to participate in some form of exercise: team sports or activities. On-campus facilities include the new gymnasium, fitness center and weight room, wrestling/dance room, 6-lane running track, four playing fields, four tennis courts, an outdoor swimming pool, and a cross-country course. In addition, the School has the use of local stables that are 1½ miles from the campus.

Interscholastic programs are available for boys in baseball, basketball, cross-country, soccer, tennis, track, and wrestling and for girls in basketball, cross-country, field hockey, lacrosse, soccer, softball, tennis, and track. In addition to competitive sports, Solebury offers aerobics, biking, dance, golf, horseback riding, rock climbing, a walking club, weight training, and a variety of recreational sports, according to the interests of the students.

EXTRACURRICULAR OPPORTUNITIES

A calendar listing the various activities is posted. Solebury's proximity to New York, Philadelphia, and Princeton allows for day trips to sports events, concerts, Broadway plays, and museums. Plays, dances, films, festivals, concerts, and the Annual Creative Thinkers Series are scheduled on campus. An eight-day Annual Arts Festival is a major highlight each spring.

Groups and activities of special interest are organized by students and teachers and have included publishing a yearbook *(Enthymion)*, newspaper *(The Scribe)*, and literary magazine *(SLAM)*; singing in the chorus and playing in the instrumental ensemble; and participating in the video club and the theater tech club. Other interests include conversation partners, the environmental club, AIDS awareness group, book club, diversity club, Amnesty International, and a Spanish club.

Solebury asks that its high school students participate in 10 hours of community service yearly as a graduation requirement. Middle School students are required to complete 5 hours per year. Many opportunities, local and international, are available.

Students have many opportunities to become involved in leadership positions in the community. Certain elected and appointed positions, including Community Council, dormitory proctors, judiciary committee reps, academic committee reps, peer leading, peer tutoring, and Sherpa (the admission tour guides), carry a formal commitment to the School's well-being.

DAILY LIFE

The academic day starts at 8 a.m. and continues until 3:30 p.m. Once a week, students have work jobs for 20 minutes. Conference time is available on Tuesdays from 12:55 to 1:25 p.m. In addition, teachers post additional office hours for conferences on other days each week. Breakfast is from 7 to 7:45, lunch (over two periods) is from 11:30 to 12:50, and dinner is from 5:45 to 6:15. Sports and activities are from 3:30 to 5:30, three days a week for noncompetitive sports and five days a week for competitive sports. On Sunday through Thursday, there is a required supervised evening study hall from 7:15 to 9; students who meet special criteria are entitled to study in their dormitories. Students must be in their dorms by 10:30, with lights out by 11. Seniors can have lights out at midnight.

WEEKEND LIFE

Both boarding and day students are welcome to participate in weekend activities. Activities are planned by the faculty members on duty and the students. Off-campus trips to New York City, Philadelphia, and Baltimore's Inner Harbor are offered. The New Hope area is also full of many recreational opportunities. Students often go into town or to nearby malls to shop and see movies. On-campus activities include School-sponsored dances and coffeehouses. Bonfires, roller skating, and evening games are just a few of the activities offered, as well as the diversity movie series. Boarding students who have parental permission may visit day students' homes on the weekends. A shuttle is available to and from the train station in Trenton, New Jersey, on Fridays and Sundays.

SUMMER PROGRAMS

Solebury offers a summer day camp for younger children. Basketball and soccer programs and a swim club are offered for all ages. An ESL program is offered for six weeks in July and August. Brochures for programs may be obtained by writing the School.

COSTS AND FINANCIAL AID

Tuition for the 2008–09 school year was $38,500 for boarding students and $25,650 for day students. Middle School day students paid $22,950. Additional tuition for the Learning Skills Program was $10,150. The additional fee for English as a second language was $9600. Additional costs are a $50 application fee ($100 for international students) and a $900 deposit for incidental expenses, which include books, school supplies, certain laboratory and art supplies, and medical expenses. Within two weeks of a student's acceptance to the full-year program, an advance deposit of 10 percent of the net annual fee must accompany the enrollment contract to reserve a place in the School. The 2009 ESL Summer Program fee is $8440.

Solebury has always had a generous scholarship program. Offered annually are the Trustees' Merit Scholarships, with awards ranging from $2500 to $10,000. For 2008–09, 36 percent of the students received partial financial aid that totaled $1,500,000. Awards are based on financial need as determined by the School and Student Service for Financial Aid.

ADMISSIONS INFORMATION

Admission decisions are based on the candidate's potential for academic success at Solebury as well as his or her possible contributions to the School community. These characteristics are identified by a personal interview, transcripts from previous schools, and recommendations. Admission to Solebury School is open to all qualified candidates, without regard to race, sex, or national or ethnic origin.

APPLICATION TIMETABLE

Inquiries are always welcome. Candidates are strongly encouraged to visit the School for a tour and interview. The Admission Office is open Monday through Friday. Candidates who apply before January 15 are notified the week of March 10. Applications should be submitted prior to January 15 for day students and prior to February 1 for boarding students; those applications submitted after that time are considered if vacancies exist.

ADMISSIONS CORRESPONDENCE

Director of Admission
Solebury School
6832 Phillips Mill Road
New Hope, Pennsylvania 18938-9682

Phone: 215-862-5261
Fax: 215-862-3366
E-mail: admissions@solebury.org
Web site: http://www.solebury.org

SOUNDVIEW PREPARATORY SCHOOL

Yorktown Heights, New York

Type: Coeducational day college-preparatory school
Grades: Middle School, 6–8; Upper School, 9–12
Enrollment: Total, 73; Middle School, 13; Upper School, 60
Head of School: W. Glyn Hearn, Headmaster

THE SCHOOL

Soundview Preparatory School, a coeducational, college-preparatory school for grades 6 through 12, was founded in 1989 on the belief that the best environment for students is one where classes are small, teachers know the learning style and interests of each student, and an atmosphere of mutual trust prevails. At Soundview, students and teachers work in close collaboration in classes with an average size of 7 students.

The School's mission is to provide a college-preparatory education in a supportive and non-competitive environment that requires rigorous application to academics, instills respect for ethical values, and fosters self-confidence by helping each student feel recognized and valued. Soundview empowers students to develop their potential and reach their own goals in a setting that promotes respect for others and a sense of community.

Soundview Prep opened its doors with 13 students in the spring of 1989. In the spring of 1998, having outgrown its original quarters in Pocantico Hills, New York, the School moved to a larger facility in Mount Kisco, New York. On January 14, 2008, Soundview moved to its first permanent home, a 13.8-acre campus in Yorktown Heights, New York. New York City, only an hour away, provides a wealth of cultural opportunities for Soundview students to explore on class trips.

The School is governed by an 11-member Board of Trustees. The current operating budget is $2 million. In 2006–07, Soundview raised a gross total amount of $322,000 through the Annual Fund, major gifts to the New Site Fund, and fund-raising events, from parents, alumni families, grandparents, friends, foundations, and corporations.

Soundview is chartered by the New York State Board of Regents and is accredited by the New York State Association of Independent Schools. The School is a member of the National Association of Independent Schools, the Education Records Bureau, and the Council for Advancement and Support of Education.

ACADEMIC PROGRAMS

Soundview provides a rigorous academic program to ensure that students not only develop the skills and acquire the knowledge needed for college work but also have the opportunity to pursue their own personal goals.

The academic day is carefully structured but informal, with nurture a crucial ingredient. Soundview's student-teacher ratio of 4:1 guarantees that students are monitored closely and receive the support they need. At the same time, the School provides advanced courses for students who wish to go beyond the high school level or take a subject that is not usually offered, allowing students to soar academically and truly develop their potential.

The Middle School curriculum is designed to establish a foundation of knowledge and skills in each academic discipline, strong comprehension and communication skills, good work habits and study skills, confidence in using technology, and creativity in the arts.

The Upper School curriculum provides a traditional college-preparatory education in academics and the arts. In addition to the core subjects—English, history, math, and science—Soundview offers four languages (Latin, French, Spanish, and Italian), studio art, and electives such as history of philosophy, drama, history of art, psychology, government, economics, creative and expository writing, genetics and forensics, and anatomy and physiology.

AP courses are made available according to students' abilities and interests. Recently, AP courses have been offered in calculus, biology, physics, English, U.S. history, European history, government, art, French, and Spanish.

Academic requirements for graduation are 4 years each of English and history, 3 years each of math and science, 3 years of one foreign language or 2 years each of two different languages, 1 year of art, and ½ year of health.

Computer technology at Soundview is integrated into the curriculum. Teachers post assignments on the School's Web site, and students upload completed work into teachers' folders. The School is wired for wireless technology and has a well-equipped computer lab.

The School's annual two-week trips abroad (to Argentina, Russia, China, and Greece over the last few years) offer students experience with other cultures. Upper and Lower School trips to Washington, D.C., Boston, and other destinations in the U.S. provide hands-on learning in history and government.

Every two years, the School sponsors a community service trip to Nicaragua to build houses with the organization Bridges to Community.

The school year is divided into two semesters, with letter grades sent out at the end of each. Individual conferences with parents, students, faculty members, and the Headmaster are arranged throughout the year.

Students take the Educational Records Bureau (ERB) standardized tests every year for use by the School in monitoring each student's progress.

FACULTY AND ADVISERS

The faculty consists of 18 teachers (15 women and 3 men); the majority hold advanced degrees. One teacher is part-time; the rest, full-time. Turnover is low, with an average of two replacements per year.

Each teacher serves as adviser to up to 5 students. Most faculty members supervise a club or publication or coach an athletic team.

W. Glyn Hearn has served as Headmaster since the School was founded in 1989. He obtained his B.A. in English at the University of Texas at Austin and his M.A. in American literature at Texas Tech University. He spent twelve years at the Awty International School of Houston, Texas, where he served as Principal of the Lower, Middle, and Upper Schools and Head of the American Section, before becoming Assistant Headmaster and then Headmaster of the American Renaissance School in Westchester County in 1987.

COLLEGE ADMISSION COUNSELING

College placement at Soundview is directed by Carol Gill, president of Carol Gill Associates and one of the nation's leading college counseling experts. The process starts early on, when eighth, ninth, and tenth graders plan and refine a course sequence that is appropriate for a competitive college. In the junior year, students and their parents begin meeting with Ms. Gill to discuss the college application process, develop lists of colleges, and plan college visits. The meetings continue through the senior year to complete applications.

Because of the School's small size, the faculty and staff members know each student well and are able to assist students in selecting colleges that are the right match for them. The Headmaster writes a personal recommendation for each senior.

College acceptances in recent years include Allegheny, Bard, Bates, Brandeis, Brown, Carnegie Mellon, Clark, College of Wooster, Columbia, Dickinson, Earlham, Gettysburg, Goucher, Hampshire, Hartwick, Manhattanville, Muhlenberg, NYU, Oberlin, Rhode Island School of Design, Sarah Lawrence, School of Visual Arts, SUNY, Syracuse, Vassar, Wheaton, and the Universities of Hartford, Oregon, and Vermont.

STUDENT BODY AND CONDUCT

Soundview reflects the diversity—ethnic, religious, and economic—of American society. The 52 boys and 21 girls come from Westchester, Fairfield, Putnam, and Rockland Counties and New York City. Approximately 14 percent of the student body are members of minority groups.

Respect for ethical values such as kindness, honesty, and respect for others are paramount at Soundview, where individual responsibility and a sense of community are stressed.

The School's disciplinary structure is informal, since it is based on the assumption that students attending the School desire to be there and are therefore willing to adhere to a code of conduct that demonstrates awareness that the community is based upon a shared sense of purpose and commitment. Despite the cordiality of its atmosphere, Soundview is quite strict in its expectations of behavior. The result of this policy is a remarkably cooperative, considerate group of students who value each other and who appreciate their teachers.

Attire appropriate for a school is expected of all students, although there is no formal dress code.

ACADEMIC FACILITIES

Soundview's new campus consists of 13.8 rustic acres with an historic main house, numerous outbuildings, a large pond, meadows, and woods, all in the heart of the village of Yorktown Heights, New York. The main house, the former Underhill mansion built by Yorktown's leading family in the eighteenth and nineteenth centuries, contain classrooms, administrative offices, the computer lab, and meeting rooms. A large barn houses the science lab, art studios, additional classrooms, and a cafeteria-meeting hall, while a third building is home to the Middle School. A fourth building provides another large meeting space, while a small former chapel is used seasonally for drama rehearsals. Woodland paths and footbridges lead across streams and around the property.

ATHLETICS

Physical education and sports at Soundview offer students the opportunity to develop leadership and teamwork skills as well as to excel in individual sports. Students participate on coed soccer, boys' basketball, girls' basketball, and Ultimate Frisbee teams. Depending upon student interest in a given year, other sports, such as softball and baseball, are also offered. Any student who wishes to play is accepted, regardless of ability.

Golf and ski clubs offer opportunities for noncompetitive sports. For physical education, students complete the Presidential Physical Fitness Challenge, play intramural sports, work out on exercise equipment, figure skate at a local ice rink, and participate in martial arts classes.

Soundview's home gym is the Brewster Sports Center, a 60,000-square-foot, state-of-the-art multisport center on a 10-acre site 20 minutes from the School. The facility includes a 176-foot by 90-foot indoor soccer field, a regulation outdoor soccer field, three large indoor basketball courts, and exercise equipment.

EXTRACURRICULAR OPPORTUNITIES

Soundview offers a wide range of clubs and activities, with additional choices added each year by students themselves.

Drama is important at Soundview. Students perform at School functions, attend plays on Broadway, and meet backstage with theater professionals. The Language Club sponsors schoolwide activities such as Cultural Heritage Week, which features speakers and banquets, and organizes trips at home and an annual trip abroad. The Student Action Club involves itself in human rights, poverty, justice, and the environment; in 2003–04, members raised money to build a school in Pakistan and sponsor a student there. Model UN focuses on political and government issues.

Other activities students are likely to sign up for include yearbook, literary magazine, student newspaper, Film Club, Chess Club, Meditation Club, Political Club, Student Action, Ethnic Food Club, Cheerleading Squad, photography, Outdoor Club, Ski Club, and Middle School Math Club.

Major annual functions at Soundview include the Back-to-School Picnic; the Spring Gala, a dinner and fund-raiser for the Soundview community; the Talent Show, which involves every student in the School; Texas Day, a lighthearted event featuring spoofs on American history and the Headmaster's home state; a June Book Fair; and the Graduation Dinner, an evening for Soundview parents to honor the graduating class.

DAILY LIFE

The school day begins at 8:20 a.m. with Morning Meeting, when the entire student body, faculty, and staff assemble to hear announcements about ongoing activities, listen to presentations by clubs, and discuss the day's national and international news. The Headmaster encourages students to express their views and helps them to assess events that are unfolding in the world around them.

Classes begin at 8:40 and end at 3:20 p.m. There are seven academic periods of 50 minutes each, with 50 minutes for lunch.

SUMMER PROGRAMS

Soundview offers a small summer school with classes that vary each year. A typical offering includes English, writing, math, history, a science, and a language. Some 12 to 15 students from Soundview take courses to skip ahead in a given subject or fulfill a requirement. In summer 2008, Soundview plans to offer a language institute for children, teenagers, and adults, with three weeks of classes in Japanese, Mandarin, French, Italian, Latin, and Spanish.

COSTS AND FINANCIAL AID

Tuition and fees for 2008–09 are $31,000 for Middle School, $32,000 for ninth through the eleventh grades, and $32,300 for twelfth grade. (Fees include gym, books, art and lab fees, ERB exams, and literary publications.)

In 2007–08, the School provided a total of $220,000 in financial aid to 15 percent of the student body.

ADMISSIONS INFORMATION

Soundview operates on a rolling admissions policy, with students accepted throughout the year in all grades except twelfth. Families of prospective students meet with the Admissions Director, after which the student spends a day at the School. The SSAT is not required, but portions of the ERB standardized examination are administered (unless the applicant provides the School with sufficient, current test data).

Students of all backgrounds are welcomed. The academic program is demanding, but the School's small size allows it to work with each individual student in order to develop strategies for success.

APPLICATION TIMETABLE

Soundview accepts applications on a rolling basis throughout the year. The application fee is $50.

ADMISSIONS CORRESPONDENCE

Mary E. Ivanyi
Director of Admissions and Assistant Head
Soundview Preparatory School
370 Underhill Road
Yorktown Heights, New York 10598
Phone: 914-962-2780
E-mail: info@soundviewprep.org
Web site: http://www.soundviewprep.org

SOUTH KENT SCHOOL

South Kent, Connecticut

Type: Boys' boarding college-preparatory school
Grades: 9–12 and PG (Forms III–VI)
Enrollment: 151
Head of School: Andrew J. Vadnais

THE SCHOOL

South Kent School, founded in 1923, offered young men the opportunity to develop their potential in an environment that fostered "simplicity of life, self-reliance, and directness of purpose." Committed to its original goal, the School has proven successful over the years with several types of students. First, South Kent is an excellent school for bright and imaginative students who do well academically. Second, it is a school where a student who is bright but has yet to achieve his academic potential can gain needed focus through a comprehensive study skills program beginning in grade 9. Third, for students who are motivated to learn but have had difficulties in their current school, South Kent offers, through its Academic Resource Center, the personal attention and guidance that they need to succeed. Finally, South Kent is an excellent choice for all students who recognize the advantages provided by a small boarding school. The prefect, dorm supervisor, and Jobs Programs allow students to develop and apply their potential for leadership. Opportunities to lead are found in every aspect of school life—in the dorms, in the classrooms, in activities, and on the sports fields.

Guided by Christian principles and nurtured by an abiding respect for the worth of each person, South Kent School is a community in which young men are challenged to take responsibility for their lives. They develop, through a variety of activities, a true sense of themselves and their potential.

South Kent School is set on a hillside in the midst of 350 acres of School property. The boys have access to all of this property, which includes miles of trails for running and mountain biking, two ponds for skating and fishing, high open fields, wooded areas, and countless old stone walls. Wildlife is plentiful, and the change of seasons is arresting and inspirational.

South Kent's operating expenses for 2007–08 were $5.5 million. The endowment is currently $6 million. Thirty-eight percent of South Kent's alumni participated in last year's annual giving, which amounted to $894,000. A self-perpetuating Board of Trustees, which may not exceed 25 members, governs the School.

South Kent is accredited by the New England Association of Schools and Colleges and holds memberships in the Cum Laude Society, National Association of Independent Schools, National Association of Episcopal Schools, Secondary School Admission Test Board, Connecticut Association of Independent Schools, and National Association for College Admission Counseling.

ACADEMIC PROGRAMS

South Kent is committed to academic excellence, and all of its students pursue postsecondary study. It provides a traditional college-preparatory program and offers some Advanced Placement courses. Graduates join the larger world with the tools and skills to accept life's challenges. In the academic curriculum, South Kent values perseverance, self-awareness, risk taking, goal setting, and self-advocacy. Essential skills instruction and practice begin in Forms III and IV (grades 9 and 10).

South Kent School's Form Program is an integrated, interdisciplinary programs that builds and reinforces strong academic and community skills, thereby nurturing self-confidence and initiative in the boys. The goal of the lower forms is to produce motivated and inquisitive students equipped to be lifelong learners. Each form program is staffed by a 5-person faculty team. In the Third Form, these faculty members come from the English, history, and science departments; the Fourth Form team combines the disciplines of English, history, and art. Using an inquiry or problem-based approach, the Form Program teachers encourage students to become independent thinkers by teaching them to master the techniques of learning. The faculty teams meet biweekly to discuss curriculum, teaching strategies, and the progress of each boy.

In the Fifth and Sixth Forms, students face a more traditional classroom program, guided once again by faculty teams that oversee their academic and social progress through the upper forms. Students exercise their skills of organization, time management, and articulate communication in all of their upper-level courses. South Kent's academic program is designed to provide a broad education in English, mathematics, languages, sciences, history, and the arts and to prepare students for a successful and energetic college career. Academic requirements for graduation include 4 credits in English, 3 credits in mathematics, 2 credits in a foreign language (special considerations are provided to learning-difference students), 2 credits in laboratory science, 1 credit in U.S. history, and 2 credits in art. A student must earn a minimum of 18 credits between the beginning of the ninth grade and the end of the twelfth grade. The average student program comprises five courses per term.

FACULTY AND ADVISERS

South Kent has 34 full-time faculty members and administrators. Thirty-nine percent of the faculty members have advanced degrees. The 22 men and 12 women average seventeen years of service in education. All but 3 of the full-time teachers live on campus, many in dormitories as dorm parents.

Each student has a faculty member assigned as his adviser. A student meets with his adviser at least once a week to discuss academic progress. The size of the school, however, ensures faculty members the opportunity to have conversations with advisees almost every day.

Headmaster Andrew J. Vadnais was appointed in 2003. He received his B.A. from Williams College and his M.A. from University of Delaware. Andrew has taught at the School since 1998. His wife, Nancy Lyon, is the Fourth Form Dean and a history teacher.

COLLEGE ADMISSION COUNSELING

College counseling begins formally in the Fifth Form with individual conferences and group meetings. Kenneth Brown, Director of College Counseling, works closely with each student and family to identify the colleges that best suit the student's individual interests. Every attempt is made to place students in colleges that will challenge them and where they will succeed. A computerized search is an integral part of the advising process and contributes to the diversity of schools students attend. The Internet is used to further research individual colleges, file financial aid applications, and, in some cases, apply online. About 50 college and university representatives visit South Kent each year to discuss opportunities for students.

South Kent enjoys a 99 percent college placement rate. Students generally apply to no more than five schools. Among the colleges and universities attended by recent graduates are Colgate, Emory, Hobart and William Smith, Kenyon, Lafayette, Northwestern University, Purdue, School of Visual Arts, Trinity College, Tufts University, University of Maryland, University of Virginia, and the Universities of Connecticut, Vermont, and Wisconsin–Madison.

STUDENT BODY AND CONDUCT

During the 2007–08 school year, the Sixth Form had 58 students, the Fifth Form had 42 students, the Fourth Form had 29 students, and the Third Form had 22 students. South Kent has students from seventeen states and thirteen other countries, including Bermuda, Canada, Great Britain, Japan, Korea, Montenegro, Nigeria, Senegal, Serbia, Singapore, Sweden, Taiwan, and Ukraine.

Members of the Sixth Form play an important role in the daily running of the School. Led by elected prefects, Sixth Form students work with faculty members to supervise the daily Jobs Program; they help monitor evening study periods in the dormitories, freeing resident faculty members to provide individualized attention in the form of extra help sessions to those students who need it. The prefects work closely with the Headmaster, meeting weekly to discuss School issues. Students' efforts are evaluated weekly; they receive Effort Ratings in the areas of academics, athletics, dormitory life, and the Jobs Program.

ACADEMIC FACILITIES

The Schoolhouse, Wittenberg Science Building, Bringhurst Complex, and the Noble and Elizabeth Richards Academic Center are at the center of academic life. Other academic buildings include the art studios and the Martin Henry Library. The Schoolhouse houses two floors of classrooms, an assembly hall, and a multimedia center. Close by, art studios have potter's wheels, kilns, and an etching press as well as facilities for drawing, painting, sculpture, and work in batik, copper enamel, and linoleum-block prints. There is a darkroom available for photography classes as well as for general student and faculty use. The Henry Library houses 20,000 volumes. The Wittenberg Science Building has three laboratories and two classrooms. Computer stations are available to students in the Henry Library, the Wittenberg Science Building, Bringhurst Complex, and Schoolhouse. Students are permitted their own personal computers in their rooms.

BOARDING AND GENERAL FACILITIES

Approximately 90 percent of South Kent students are boarders. Most of the Third, Fourth, and Fifth Formers live in double rooms; Sixth Formers may opt for singles, doubles, or triples. There are eight dormitories of varying sizes, housing from 8 to 20 students. St. Michael's Chapel is the spiritual center of the School. Services are available seven days a week; with required attendance at four. Most students take advantage of the opportunity to read at one of these services sometime in their South Kent career. Voluntary communion services are held two mornings a week before breakfast. The Old Building houses the administrative offices, the Admissions Office, the mail room, a common room, and the dining hall. The School bookstore and athletics store are located in the lower level of the Old Building. The health clinic is staffed by 2 nurses; the School doctor sees students three days a week on campus.

ATHLETICS

South Kent competes interscholastically in basketball, crew, cross-country, football, golf, hockey, lacrosse, soccer, tennis, and Ultimate Frisbee. The golf team matches are played at the Bull's Bridge Golf Club, which was designed by Tom Fazio. Both varsity and junior varsity–level teams compete in games against other schools. Participation in sports is required of all students. There is an opportunity for every student, regardless of ability, to play on a competitive team with a challenging schedule. Athletics facilities include an enclosed ice rink; a gymnasium; a climbing wall; a weight room; football, soccer, and lacrosse fields; six all-weather tennis courts; a new athletic facility that has an open-air basketball court and a roller hockey rink; and a lake with three boathouses for the crew program.

EXTRACURRICULAR OPPORTUNITIES

Two activity periods a week are used for chorus and drama rehearsals, music lessons, or media club publications work. On weekends, there are dances and play days with neighboring schools. The student body is divided into two teams, Cardinals and Blacks, and competitions are held in informal sports events such as volleyball, softball, and Ultimate Frisbee. Students are encouraged to generate ideas for activities on their own; in the past, they have organized weekend trips to adventure parks, rural fairs, New York City museums, Broadway plays, professional sports events, and air shows. The location of the School offers a wide variety of outdoor pursuits, including camping, canoeing, cycling, hiking, rock climbing, and skiing.

DAILY LIFE

The daily schedule is determined by the day of the week. The school day begins with a healthy breakfast at 7 Monday through Saturday, ensuring that more students eat a healthy breakfast to fuel their day. Classes are held six days a week, with half days on Wednesdays and Saturdays, when afternoon interscholastic sports contests take place. The 20–25 minutes a day devoted to jobs are scheduled either after breakfast, or immediately after lunch. During these periods, the classrooms, labs, chapel, library, offices, clinic, athletic buildings, and dining room are cleaned by students; dishwashing and some grounds work are assigned as well. Every student takes part in the Jobs Program, with the Sixth Formers working along with the underformers as well as supervising them. An all-school assembly precedes classes every morning. A family-style sit-down lunch is served six days a week and is followed by afternoon classes and sports.

Evening activities at South Kent also vary according to the day of the week. On Monday, chapel precedes formal dinner at 6:30. Formal dinner offers a time to reflect on the day, with members of the faculty joining students at assigned tables. Dinners for the remainder of the week are buffet style. Following the dinner hour, boys have time to meet with their advisers, attend club meetings and rehearsals, or relax before formal study time, which lasts from 8 until 9:45, five nights a week. During evening study hall, students may receive help from faculty proctors in tackling the day's assignments.

WEEKEND LIFE

Weekends at South Kent offer a wide variety of social events. Activities include dances with nearby girls' schools and trips to the movies, the mall, minor-league ballparks, and local restaurants. Visiting musicians and lecturers come to the campus several times a year for entertainment and enrichment. The area around Kent abounds with art galleries, musical performances, local theater productions, and small museums. With New York City and Boston just a few hours away, students can explore these cities and support their respective professional athletic teams. An Activities Committee made up of students and faculty members ensures that there is always a variety of outings offered.

COSTS AND FINANCIAL AID

Charges for the 2008–09 academic year were $40,500 for boarding students and $26,000 for day students. Costs of books, supplies, and personal sports equipment are charged separately. A yearly allowance of $1000–$1400 for those costs is recommended. Financial aid is available and is awarded on the basis of need as recommended by the School and Student Service for Financial Aid.

ADMISSIONS INFORMATION

Although affiliated with the Episcopal Church, South Kent welcomes students of all faiths. Seventy-five percent of all students enter the Third or Fourth Forms (ninth or tenth grades); 20 percent come in the Fifth Form, and a limited few for a postgraduate year.

Participation in and contribution to all parts of school life are essential to a student's success. The program challenges the student to immerse himself in the life of the community. Admissions decisions are based both on academic ability and potential for success as well as nonacademic interests and achievements. Candidates must submit an application, a writing sample, a counselor recommendation, and a complete transcript, including teacher recommendations. In addition, applicants are required to have a personal interview at the School and take the SSAT, when possible. Candidates for the Student Learning Services Program must submit necessary documentation as requested by South Kent School.

APPLICATION TIMETABLE

South Kent adheres to the March 1 deadline for applications. Following the March deadline, the School operates on a rolling admissions basis; initial inquiries are welcome at any time. Interviews and tours can be arranged by writing to or calling the Admissions Office. Office hours are 8 to 4:30, Monday through Friday. Application forms and school brochures can be obtained from the Admissions Office. There is an application fee of $50 for those living in the United States and $100 for those living abroad. The first notices of acceptance for the following September are sent out in early March. After this initial date, applicants are notified of acceptance three weeks after the application process has been completed.

ADMISSIONS CORRESPONDENCE

Richard A. Brande
Director of Admissions and Financial Aid
South Kent School
40 Bull's Bridge Road
South Kent, Connecticut 06785

Phone: 860-927-3539 Ext. 201
Fax: 860-927-0024
E-mail: admissions@southkentschool.net
Web site: http://www.southkentschool.org

SOUTHWESTERN ACADEMY

San Marino, California
Beaver Creek Ranch, Arizona

Type: Coeducational boarding and day college-preparatory and general academic school
Grades: San Marino: 6–12, postgraduate year; Beaver Creek: 9–12, postgraduate year
Enrollment: San Marino, 140; Beaver Creek, 45
Head of School: Kenneth R. Veronda, Headmaster

THE SCHOOL

Southwestern Academy offers achievement-based, departmentalized, and supportively structured classes limited to 9 to 12 students. Small classes allow for individualized attention in a noncompetitive environment. Southwestern was founded by Maurice Veronda in 1924 as a college-preparatory program "for capable students who could do better" in small, supportive classes. While maintaining that commitment, Southwestern Academy includes U.S. and international students with strong academic abilities who are eager to learn and strengthen English-language skills as well as pursue a general scholastic program in a small, supportive school structure. Southwestern Academy is accredited by the Western Association of Schools and Colleges (WASC).

Southwestern Academy offers students the opportunity to study at either of two distinctly different and beautiful campuses. The San Marino, California, campus is situated in a historic orange grove area near Pasadena. The Arizona campus, which is known as Beaver Creek Ranch, is located deep in a red-rock canyon in northern Arizona. Students may attend either campus and, if space permits, may divide the academic year between the two.

The San Marino campus occupies 8 acres in a residential suburb 10 miles from downtown Los Angeles and immediately south of Pasadena, home to the renowned Tournament of Roses Parade. The Beaver Creek campus is a 180-acre ranch located 100 miles north of Phoenix, 12 miles from the resort community of Sedona, and 45 miles south of Flagstaff. Although the program and philosophies are the same at both campuses, each offers a very different learning environment. Students at the California campus draw on the offerings of the urban setting. Students studying at the Beaver Creek Ranch campus enjoy a living and learning environment that takes full advantage of the rich cultural, scenic, and environmentally significant region.

A mix of U.S. and international students from several countries offers a unique blend of cultural, social, and educational opportunities for all. Every effort is made to enroll a well-balanced student body that represents the rich ethnic diversity of U.S. citizens and students from around the world. The student body consists of college-bound students who prefer a small, personalized education; above-average students who have the potential to become excellent academic achievers in the right learning environment; and average students who, with a supportive structure, can achieve academic success.

Southwestern Academy is incorporated as a not-for-profit organization. Operating expenses are approximately $4.2 million per annum and are met by tuition (92 percent) and grants and annual giving (8 percent). The Academy has no indebtedness.

ACADEMIC PROGRAMS

Middle school students are placed in classes based on individual achievement levels. High school classes are divided by grade level, and students are assigned based on ability and achievement.

High school graduation requirements are based on University of California requirements and include completion of a minimum of 200 academic credits plus 40 credit hours of physical education. The academic term is mid-September through mid-June, with a summer quarter offered at both campuses. Requirements include 4 years of English, 3 years of mathematics, 2 years of a foreign language, 2 years of laboratory sciences, and 1 year each of U.S. history and world cultures, plus one semester of U.S. government and economics and 2 years of visual/performing arts. Proficiency exams in English, mathematics, and computer literacy, as well as community service hours, are also required for graduation.

A typical semester of course work includes six classes plus physical education. Advanced Placement classes are available in English, history, language, math, and science. Review and remedial classes are made available to students who need additional instruction. International students are offered three levels of classes in English as a second language (ESL), including an introductory class, to prepare them to enter and succeed in other academic areas.

Teachers are available daily during a midafternoon study period to work individually with students and meet with parents. There is no extra charge for this tutoring. Boarding students are required to attend a monitored evening study hall, where additional teacher assistance is available.

Student achievement is recognized with a grading system that ranges from A to F. Progress letters are sent monthly to parents and report cards are sent quarterly. The minimum college-recommending grade upon completion of academic requirements is C.

While studying at the Beaver Creek Ranch campus, students attend classes on a block schedule, Monday through Thursday. Each Friday, students participate in educational, project-oriented, and assignment-based field trips. Experiential learning allows students to apply knowledge from the classroom. It also supports an integrated academic element that links core subject areas in a practical, applied manner, promoting understanding and retention of key concepts.

FACULTY AND ADVISERS

Headmaster Kenneth Veronda was born at the San Marino campus that his father founded. Mr. Veronda attended classes at Southwestern, graduated, and completed undergraduate and graduate work in American history and foreign relations at Stanford University. The majority of 31 faculty members, 22 in California and 9 in Arizona, hold advanced degrees in their subject areas. Each teacher serves as a faculty adviser to a few students and meets with them individually throughout the school year. On-campus college and career counselors are also available to meet with and assist students in making post–high school graduation plans.

COLLEGE ADMISSION COUNSELING

The college counselors closely monitor the advisement and placement needs of each student. Beginning in the ninth grade, every effort is made to assist students in researching a variety of colleges and universities that match their interests and academic achievement levels. Students are provided a college planning handbook that offers helpful hints and suggestions regarding college application processes. A variety of college representatives are invited annually to visit each campus and meet with students.

Approximately 35 students graduate each year from Southwestern Academy. Almost all enter a U.S. college or university. Some choose to attend a local two-year community college before transferring to a four-year college or university. In recent years, Southwestern Academy graduates have been accepted to the following schools: American; Arizona State; Art Center College of Design; Azusa Pacific; Boston University; Brown; Butler; California State, Fullerton, Monterey Bay, and Northridge; California State Polytechnic, Pomona; Columbia; Hampton; Howard; Loyola; Marymount; Menlo College; Mills; Occidental; Oregon State; Parsons; Penn State; Pepperdine; Pitzer; Temple; USC, Whittier; Woodbury; Wooster; Xavier; and the Universities of California, La Verne, Nevada, New Orleans, the Pacific, San Diego, San Francisco, and Washington (Seattle).

ACADEMIC FACILITIES

The San Marino campus includes seven buildings encircling a large multisport athletic field. Lincoln Hall, the main academic building, houses morning assembly and study hall, ten classrooms, science and computer labs, and the library. Pioneer Hall includes several classrooms, a kitchen, dining rooms, and business offices. A separate building is home to large music and art studios and an additional science classroom and lab.

Newly renovated classrooms, a learning resource center, and the dormitories blend into the picturesque setting along Beaver Creek.

BOARDING AND GENERAL FACILITIES

Four dormitory halls are located on the San Marino campus. Each is designed to accommodate up to 20 boys in double and single rooms. Two off-campus dormitories (located within a mile) house a total of 32 girls. Dorm parents live in apartments adjoining each hall.

At Beaver Creek, seven stone cottages encircle the main campus area and provide faculty/staff housing. Four recently renovated residence halls accommodate up to 56 students. The Beaver Creek

Ranch campus includes recreation rooms, a gymnasium, several large activity fields, and an indoor, solar-heated swimming pool.

ATHLETICS

Gyms and playing fields are available to all students at both campuses, where sports opportunities exist for physical education requirements and recreation. As a member of federated leagues in California and Arizona, Southwestern Academy fields teams at both campuses in all major sports except tackle football. Athletic events are held in late afternoon, following the regular school day.

EXTRACURRICULAR OPPORTUNITIES

Southwestern offers a wide range of cocurricular and extracurricular activities and opportunities, including art, drama, music, journalism, student government, and student clubs. Current clubs include chess, Interact, International, the Southwestern Arts Society, Southwestern Environmental Associates, and tennis. Frequent class trips to southern California and northern Arizona places of interest, such as tide pools, museums, archaeological sites, art galleries, and live theater, are great learning experiences for students at both campuses.

DAILY LIFE

Boarding students begin each school day with a breakfast buffet at 7:30. Following breakfast, day and boarding students meet for a required assembly at 8:10, with classes following from 8:30 to 2:45. Required study halls and optional clubs and athletic events are held between 2:50 and 4:30. Dinner is served at 6 and is followed by a monitored study hall lasting until 8. Lights out is at 10:30 for middle school students and 11 for high schoolers.

WEEKEND LIFE

Students in good standing may leave the campus, with permission, during any weekend. Many students take advantage of the planned activities that are arranged for them, including theater performances, shopping at the malls and Old Town Pasadena, barbecues, beach parties, and movies. Visits are planned to Disneyland, Magic Mountain, and Big Surf, and the other attractions of the two-state areas are a part of the social program at Southwestern Academy. Day students are welcome to attend all weekend activities if space permits.

SUMMER PROGRAMS

Summer school sessions are offered at both campuses. Both offer intensive yet enjoyable individualized classes in English and other subjects, plus educational and recreational trips to interesting places in southern California and northern Arizona.

The summer program in San Marino is an excellent opportunity for domestic students to catch up, if needed, or to move ahead academically in order to take more advanced courses before graduation. For non-English-speaking international students, the summer session can provide an entire semester of the appropriate ESL level necessary to successfully complete a college-preparatory curriculum.

Summer sessions at Beaver Creek Ranch combine review and enrichment courses with experiential learning and high-adventure activities in classwork, camp-type activities, and travel in northern Arizona. ESL is offered at the Beaver Creek campus during the summer.

COSTS AND FINANCIAL AID

Tuition for the 2008–09 U.S. boarding student was $36,500. International student tuition was $36,750. The cost for a day student (U.S. citizens and permanent residents only) was $14,900. An incidental account containing $2000 for boarding students or $1000 for day students is required of all students to cover expenses such as books, school supplies, physical education uniforms, and discretionary spending money. Payment is due in advance unless other arrangements are made with the business office.

Financial aid is awarded based on financial need. More than $730,000 was awarded in 2007–08.

ADMISSIONS INFORMATION

Southwestern Academy admits students of any race, color, national and ethnic origin, creed, or sex. A completed application packet is required, followed by a personal on-campus interview with students and parents. A daylong visit to classes (and an overnight for prospective boarding students) is strongly encouraged for prospective students already living in the U.S. Interviews with prospective international students and parents are scheduled by the international admissions director and do not require a campus visit.

Each campus offers exceptional learning opportunities. Prospective students are encouraged to seriously consider both campuses and apply to the one that seems better suited to them.

Admission materials and other information can be downloaded from the Southwestern Academy Web site. It can also be obtained by contacting the Office of Admissions.

APPLICATION TIMETABLE

Admission offers are made throughout the year, as space permits. Appointments are required for interviews and campus tours at both locations. The admissions office for both campus locations is located in San Marino. Students should write or call the San Marino office for information on either campus.

ADMISSIONS CORRESPONDENCE

Office of Admissions
Southwestern Academy
2800 Monterey Road
San Marino, California 91108

Phone: 626-799-5010 Ext. 5
Fax: 626-799-0407
E-mail: admissions@southwesternacademy.edu
Web site: http://www.southwesternacademy.edu

SQUAW VALLEY ACADEMY

Olympic Valley, California

SQUAW VALLEY ACADEMY

Type: Coeducational international boarding school
Grades: 6–12
Enrollment: 100
Head of School: Donald Rees, Headmaster and Founder

THE SCHOOL

Squaw Valley Academy (SVA) was founded in 1978 to offer a combination of project-based learning, outdoor education, and sports opportunities in the scenic California High Sierra. Many SVA students are highly capable but may not be highly motivated, and they need the structure provided by small class sizes, evening study halls, and daily skiing and snowboarding as a reward for academic achievement. She or he must have an interest in pursuing winter snow sports. SVA offers strong preparation for college as its central focus and many outdoor sports and activities as a catalyst for personal growth and achievement.

Located 200 miles east of San Francisco and 45 miles west of Reno, SVA sits at the foot of Squaw Valley ski area, site of the 1960 Winter Olympics. At an elevation of 6,200 feet in a beautiful alpine setting, SVA offers easy access to Lake Tahoe and nearby forests, mountains, lakes, and rivers. Squaw Valley Academy is located within the small residential community of Olympic Valley, with commercial centers easily accessible 5 miles south in Tahoe City and 10 miles north in historic Truckee.

SVA's mission statement is as follows: "We challenge with rigorous academics; we support with consistent behavioral standards; we train in life-long sports; we provide outdoor adventure; and we foster self-esteem through real accomplishment."

Squaw Valley Academy is fully accredited by the Western Association of Schools and Colleges.

ACADEMIC PROGRAMS

The Squaw Valley Academy college-preparatory curriculum focuses on hands-on, project-based learning to keep students engaged throughout the course. All core academic courses are approved by the University of California. The curriculum includes two weeklong Outdoor Education trips that allow students to participate in athletics and academics in an outdoor setting.

Class size and the student body remain small to allow individual attention in the classroom and the dormitory. The average class size is 9 students. All boarding students are required to attend a supervised 2-hour study hall Sunday–Thursday. Honors students earn the privilege to study in their dormitory rooms.

The Squaw Valley Academy's school year is composed of two semesters. Students entering the school after September may transfer credits from their former school.

To graduate, students must complete 4 years of English, 4 years of social studies (including U.S. history and American government), 3 years of mathematics, 3 years of laboratory science, 3 years of a foreign language, 4 years of physical education, and sufficient electives each year to complete the normal five- or six-course academic load. Independent study is offered, and tutorial assistance is available to students with special needs. Transfer students at upper levels may apply for waivers in areas in which their backgrounds are deficient.

English course offerings include basic grammar and composition, American literature, British and world literature, and literary analysis. Science courses are taught as laboratory courses and include chemistry, biology, physics, and physical sciences. World history, U.S. history, world geography, U.S. government, and economics are among the social studies courses. Mathematics courses extend from algebra through calculus. Spanish is the primary foreign language taught at SVA, although French and Japanese may be offered based on student interest. Electives are offered in music, studio art, photography, publications, drama, psychology, outdoor leadership, and computer literacy and programming.

Advanced Placement classes can be available in calculus, English literature and composition, chemistry, physics, Spanish, U.S. history, and other courses based on student interest and skill level. AP courses may be offered on alternate years, depending on enrollment.

Students receive letter grades, A–F. Grades are issued four times per year. Written comments supplement all grade reports. Teachers' comments identify specific strengths and weaknesses in each subject area, indicate the quality of a student's effort, and offer encouragement and structure for improvement. Grades are based on labs, quizzes, papers, hands-on projects, tests, class participation, and a 2-hour final examination. Students earn the privilege of daily participation in athletics such as skiing and snowboarding by keeping effort and grades up to standard.

Extra tutoring and academic guidance, as needed, are available, especially for underachieving or newly arrived students.

SVA is an international school and offers an immersion academic program for international students. Incoming students should have functional English-language skills. International students' class schedules are determined according to their English-language abilities. International students make up about 15 percent of the student population.

FACULTY AND ADVISERS

Typically, full-time teachers have a teaching credential and/or two years of previous experience in the classroom. All faculty members are assigned advisees, and many of the staff members serve as athletic coaches and dormitory parents. Most faculty members are on duty as campus supervisors one day each week and one weekend per month.

Faculty advisers mentor and guide students to become responsible, mature members of the school community and to help them develop the strong study skills that are necessary for academic success. There is an ongoing, respectful relationship between parents and advisers, and contact is frequent concerning academic, behavioral, and social matters.

SVA teachers have experience and professional competence, high personal standards and integrity, interest in athletics and outdoor adventure, and a genuine respect for their students' learning and growth.

Headmaster Donald Rees founded SVA and continues to be involved in daily activities, including student tutoring. He graduated from the University of California, Santa Barbara, with a degree in history. Mr. Rees has taught at the Polytechnic School in Pasadena, The American School in Switzerland, and Laguna Blanca School in Santa Barbara. He is the founding Executive Director of the Yosemite Institute in Yosemite Valley, the Headlands Institute near San Francisco, and Squaw Valley Academy.

COLLEGE ADMISSION COUNSELING

SVA is proud of its 100 percent college acceptance rate for all graduates. Most seniors are accepted into one or more of their top three college or university choices.

College counseling and guidance begins early in a student's junior year. Juniors take the PSAT in the fall and the SAT and/or ACT in the spring. SVA advises juniors about the nature of different colleges and encourages students to have summer interviews at the colleges that meet their interests and needs. SAT prep courses are offered and often required.

Individual guidance is given to each senior, who again takes the SAT and SAT Subject Tests. College representatives visit the school throughout the school year. Seniors receive step-by-step guidance regarding the college application process. While final responsibility for college applications lies with the student and parents, the school makes every effort to help students gain acceptance at colleges of their choice.

Virtually all SVA graduates go on to four-year colleges and universities. Acceptances include California state universities, Colby, Colorado College, Dartmouth, Middlebury, Notre Dame, Sarah Lawrence, U.S. Naval Academy, University of California campuses, and University of Colorado at Boulder.

STUDENT BODY AND CONDUCT

The school has approximately 100 coed students in grades 6–12. Students come from all over the country and the world, as SVA is authorized by the U.S. government to accept international students.

Students are expected to assume personal accountability for their behavior and self-discipline, yet the school recognizes that young men and women respond best to a positive structure. School rules and principles of conduct are clearly stated in the *Student/Parent Handbook*, and students are expected to follow the letter and spirit of these guidelines to help foster a community of mutual trust and respect. Students are assigned daily work jobs as an important part of learning responsibility, accountability, and pride in themselves and the school. Dormitory rooms are regularly inspected for tidiness and cleanliness. Violation of rules or failure to perform assigned chores may result in the loss of privileges.

Squaw Valley Academy was the first school in the U.S. to administer random and for-cause drug tests. Students are tested for five types of drugs, including marijuana. Students are tested throughout the year to help ensure a clean, safe campus.

ACADEMIC FACILITIES

The main building houses various classrooms, faculty and administrative offices, and kitchen-dining facilities. The campus also includes a fully equipped science laboratory, music equipment, an art studio, and a photographic darkroom.

BOARDING AND GENERAL FACILITIES

There are two well-built, separate dormitories for boys and girls, with common areas, locker rooms, and classrooms in each building. The first three-story boys' dormitory was built in 1984, and the latest girls' dorm was built in 1997. Each room has a private bath and usually 2–3 students to a room.

Dormitories have live-in house parents, usually teachers. An alarm system is set each evening at curfew, deterring students from leaving their dormitory rooms at night. The campus also has locker rooms and other storage for ski/snowboard and bicycle equipment.

Nearby athletic facilities include a professional-size FieldTurf soccer field, indoor rock-climbing walls, mountain biking and hiking trails, world-class skiing and snowboarding resorts, and kayaking and river rafting opportunities.

A fully staffed medical clinic is located 2 miles from the school and serves the local area during the winter season. A full-service hospital is 10 miles away in Truckee.

ATHLETICS

In the fall, students choose a variety of individual or team sports: interscholastic soccer, rock climbing, mountain biking, yoga, skateboarding, and weight training and conditioning.

During the winter months, the academic schedule provides time each day for students to ski or snowboard—provided grades are up to standard—at Squaw Valley USA, which is located within 2 miles of the campus. Most students are recreational skiers and snowboarders. Advanced athletes may train and compete with the Squaw Valley USA Ski Team or at Alpine Meadows.

During the spring, SVA students return to sport activities similar to the fall schedule. Activities include rock climbing, soccer, golf, tennis, volleyball, basketball, fly-fishing, kayaking, and swimming. These activities depend on student and staff interest, weather, a willingness to share extra costs, and facilities and equipment.

EXTRACURRICULAR OPPORTUNITIES

The Student Council provides a forum for all members of the community to have a voice in school affairs and activities. All students are required to complete 10–15 hours of community service or service-learning. The goal and spirit of the school's community service program is to provide each student with the lifelong experience of helping those who are less fortunate than themselves and giving unselfishly to the local community or environment. Educational day trips are organized periodically to provide a supplement to academic classes. Students may enroll in a service-learning elective and plan a long-term, academic-based service project.

All students participate in the school's two-week-long Outdoor Education Program. Students learn leadership, team building, outdoor skills, and experience personal growth through such diverse endeavors as backpacking, rafting, kayaking, mountaineering, backcountry skiing/snowboarding, rock climbing, fly-fishing, and other activities. Supervised by SVA teachers and dormitory staff members, these trips take the curriculum into the outdoors. Past trips include marine life studies while sea kayaking at Point Reyes National Seashore, snow survival skills while snowboarding at Mammoth Mountain, and ecology and natural history while mountain biking in the Redwood National Forest.

DAILY LIFE

A typical school day in the fall or spring begins with breakfast at 8 a.m., with classes starting at the close of breakfast. Students enroll in six courses, and physical education or team sports take place for 1 to 3 hours during the day. Free time is available until dinner at 5:30 p.m., followed by evening chores and a teacher-supervised evening study hall. Day students participate in school athletics and sports activities and are welcome to remain on campus for meals and evening study hall.

During the winter season, schedules are modified to allow for daily skiing and snowboarding.

WEEKEND LIFE

On-campus activities, recreational and adventure outings, theater, movies, music/concerts, cultural activities, shopping, and sporting events are scheduled on many weekends.

A regular meal schedule is followed on Saturday; on Sunday, a brunch is served, with dinner at the regular time. Parents often visit on weekends to take advantage of the many activities in the Tahoe-Reno area. Students may visit home if work is complete and they are in good behavioral standing.

SUMMER PROGRAMS

Summer school offers the opportunity to earn credits for one semester in three weeks or one year in six weeks. Students participate in academic classes in the morning and outdoor activities at Lake Tahoe in the afternoon.

COSTS AND FINANCIAL AID

Boarding tuition for the 2008–09 school year for U.S. students was $36,675, with additional costs of a ski pass at Squaw Valley USA and Outdoor Education trips. Summer school boarding tuition for 2009 for U.S. students is $4608 per three-week session. Students should attend SVA for at least one term before applying for financial aid.

ADMISSIONS INFORMATION

Admission centers on an applicant's ability to perform college-preparatory work, to participate fully in the school's outdoor athletic programs, and to remain drug- and alcohol-free. The school is effective with bright, active, and motivated students as well as with bright and active underachievers. The decision to accept a candidate is based on a personal interview, teacher and counselor recommendations, a school transcript, a completed application, and diagnostic testing.

APPLICATION TIMETABLE

Inquiries are welcome at any time, and a student may be accepted at any time during the academic year. Prospective students and their parents should visit on a school day to receive a firsthand view of the program and to meet faculty members and students. An interview is conducted at that time, and diagnostic testing may be given. A nonrefundable U.S. student application fee of $100 must accompany the application. Notification of admission varies with the date of application.

ADMISSIONS CORRESPONDENCE

Squaw Valley Academy
235 Squaw Valley Road
P.O. Box 2667
Olympic Valley, California 96146
Phone: 530-583-9393
Fax: 530-581-1111
E-mail: enroll@sva.org
Web site: http://www.sva.org

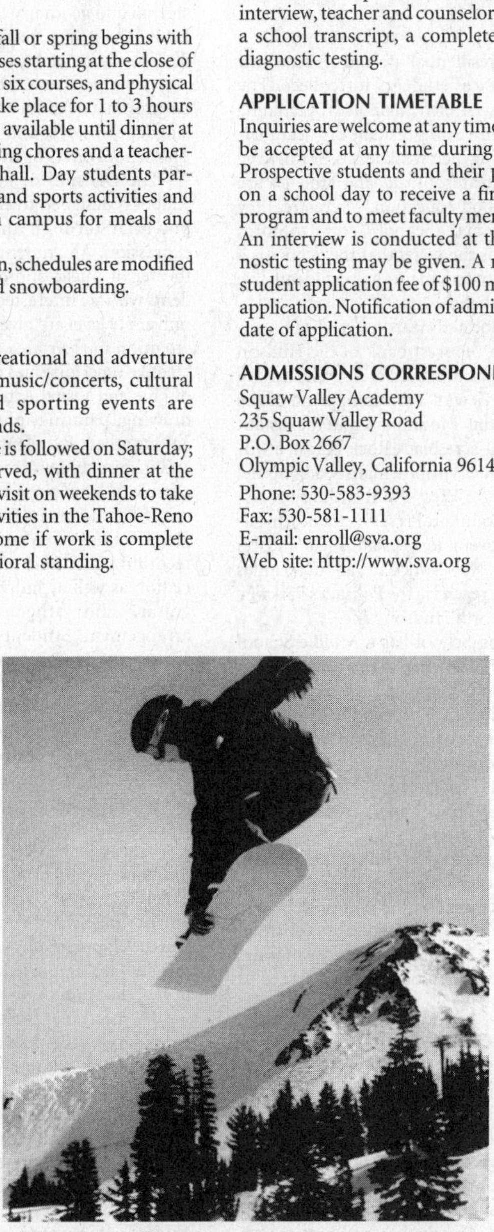

THE STORM KING SCHOOL

Cornwall-on-Hudson, New York

Type: Coeducational boarding and day college-preparatory school
Grades: 8–12, postgraduate year
Enrollment: 132
Head of School: Helen Stevens Chinitz

THE SCHOOL

The Storm King School was founded in 1867 as a college-preparatory school by the Reverend Louis P. Ledoux. In 1928, it was chartered by the Board of Regents of the State University of New York as a nonprofit institution governed by a self-perpetuating 18-member Board of Trustees. The School has an endowment of $1 million and an active Annual Giving campaign.

The Storm King School seeks to provide a caring, structured residential life and an academic program that prepares students for college. The School helps students stretch themselves by building upon their strengths while realistically acknowledging and addressing their weaknesses. Storm King believes that art, theater, music, and athletics are components of a good education. Therefore, they are a part of daily life at the School. Central to Storm King's philosophy is the belief that the School is a learning community striving to help students live as productive members.

The School is located near the crest of Storm King Mountain on the west bank of the Hudson River. The 40-acre campus offers a serene setting and a magnificent view of a sweeping bend of the river, the Shawangunk Mountains, and the distant Catskills. The 4,000-acre Black Rock Forest, a wilderness preserved by environmentalists, adjoins the campus to the south; West Point Military reservation and Bear Mountain Preserve are nearby, as are the estates of several long-established Hudson Highlands families. New York City, about 50 miles away, is within easy reach via the Palisades Parkway or via the Metro-North Hudson Line.

The Storm King School has a Middle School program for grade 8. The focus of this program is to help students develop and retain a sense of responsibility and individuality. The Middle School curriculum offers the basic core courses as well as technology, physical education, and performing and visual arts. Students are allowed to be creative and self-exploring while fulfilling an educationally intensive program.

The School is accredited by the Middle States Association of Colleges and Schools. It is a member of the Cum Laude Society, the National Honor Society, the New York State Association of Independent Schools, the National Association of Independent Schools, and the College Board.

ACADEMIC PROGRAMS

College preparation is a goal of the Storm King School; therefore, the School emphasizes the development of present skills and talents as the best way to prepare for the future. The School seeks to discover and extend what a student has learned and to identify and develop what he or she has not. The curriculum focuses on skill development as well as content knowledge. The English and history programs stress reading and writing skills and include both required and elective courses; offerings range from creative writing to the British novel and from contemporary world history to psychology and economics. To graduate, a student must also complete a course in public speaking.

The School believes that all students can improve their mathematical skills and reasoning ability. The flexible curriculum encourages students to remedy any past deficiencies in mathematics and to move forward. Courses range from algebra and geometry to advanced-placement calculus. The science program includes a basic foundations course, biology, chemistry, physics, ecology, and other electives. The foreign language program ensures that all students become familiar with the language, history, and culture of other countries. The School offers Spanish and Mandarin Chinese.

The Division of the Arts at the Storm King School is designed to encourage students' creative potential through the exploration of artistic expression. All students are required to take one theater or music and one visual arts course. Students who are interested in pursuing the arts on the university level are given advanced, individualized attention in their area of interest to develop their creative repertoire and portfolios. The Department of Fine and Visual Arts offers courses in ceramics, drawing, painting, photography, and sculpture, among others. Excellent faculty members encourage and inspire students to create works of art that far exceed students' personal expectations. These works are then shown in public art exhibitions. The Department of Music offers chorus, digital recording and studio production, and music appreciation as well as individual instruction in piano, guitar, and other instruments by special arrangement. Students learn performance techniques and are prepared for public recitals. The Dance Department offers instruction in classical ballet, tap, jazz, and modern dance. Dance students also present their work in public recitals. The Department of Theatre Arts offers performance, stage craft, theater history, theater appreciation, and courses in design and production. Students apply classroom instruction in rehearsals and production work through the two or three Storm King Theatre Ensemble productions, on which the entire division collaborates. Arts education and training at the Storm King School enhance a student's education and development through academic courses in the arts and are supported by opportunities for practical application in every creative area.

The Learning Center (TLC) helps selected students develop the skills and self-confidence that are essential for academic independence. Services include personalized/group reinforcement and assistance in the classroom setting. TLC works collaboratively with teachers in order to plan instruction that is directly related to classroom curriculum. This approach supplements the teaching skills of the classroom teachers and provides the student with a chance to link skills learned in TLC with knowledge gained from the classroom. The Learning Center focuses on building current strengths that students may not be aware of while improving academics and organization. Study skills work includes note-taking, outlining, researching, test taking, and time management.

In 2004, the Storm King School inaugurated a school within a school called the Mountain Center, using the same curriculum as the Upper School. This program is designed for above-average students who have an Individual Education Plan (IEP) or the equivalent developed to address the need for different learning styles. The program does not accept students who have significant emotional or behavioral problems. The Mountain Center presents core subjects (English, math, science, social studies) in a 5:1 ratio setting. The center uses a variety of methods that are appropriate to the needs of each student to accomplish the desired outcome.

To graduate, a student must complete 25 credits. The requirements include 4 years each of English and social studies, 3 years of mathematics, 3 years of science, 2–3 years or the equivalent of a foreign language, a minimum of 1 year each in the visual and performing arts, and a credit in health.

The grading system uses a numeric system. An effort grade is also given. These grades are sent to parents four times a year, but, for guidance purposes, progress reports are sent out in the middle of each marking period.

FACULTY AND ADVISERS

The boarding school teacher must not only have a genuine enthusiasm for the subject matter he or she teaches but must also relate well to the middle school and high school student. Ninety percent of the faculty members live on campus—either in the dormitories or in campus housing—and are available for extra help, especially in the evening. All faculty members are active in advising and counseling students and provide a critical link between the family and the School. Of the 30 full-time and 6 part-time faculty members, 24 hold advanced degrees. The School provides funds for continuing education.

Helen Stevens Chinitz was appointed the fifteenth Head of School in July 2004. She is the first woman head of the Storm King School.

COLLEGE ADMISSION COUNSELING

Guidance is a continuing process that takes place throughout a student's entire stay at Storm King and quite often even after graduation. College guidance begins in the sophomore year. In group meetings, students and their advisers discuss what lies ahead; individual conferences take place frequently and often include parents. There are many "right" colleges for each student. In recent years, 2 or more graduates have attended the following colleges, among others: Bennington, Boston University, Bucknell, Emerson, George Washington, Hamilton, Iona, Northeastern, NYU, NYU-SVA, Parsons, Pratt, Roger Williams, Skidmore, Smith, several campuses of the State University of New York, Syracuse, Tufts, Virginia Tech, and the Universities of Colorado, Hartford, Illinois at Urbana-

Champaign, Massachusetts, Miami, Southern California, and Vermont. In the past year, a class of 37 students attracted $1.1 million in scholarships and aid.

STUDENT BODY AND CONDUCT

The Storm King School student body represents a wide spectrum of socioeconomic backgrounds from fourteen states and seven other countries. The student body includes 79 boarding and 53 day students. About 50 new students enroll annually.

A disciplinary committee and the Head of School determine consequences for disciplinary infractions. Major offenses may result in withdrawal. Student and faculty groups are consulted in policy formation. Students are expected to be supportive of School policies and to take an active and positive part in the School's programs and activities.

ACADEMIC FACILITIES

Stillman Hall contains mathematics and science classrooms, laboratories, a greenhouse, a darkroom, and department offices. Dyar Hall provides humanities classrooms. The Ogden Library is a split-level learning center with study carrels, an audio-visual room, and the Computer Center, which is equipped with seventeen microcomputer workstations. The Walter Reade, Jr. Theatre was dedicated in 1984. The Cobb-Matthiessen Astronomy Observatory was dedicated in 1990. The Allison Vladimir Art Center, a converted carriage house, is a beautiful facility with a spectacular view of the Black Rock wilderness area. The center was dedicated in 1994.

BOARDING AND GENERAL FACILITIES

Students, teachers, and faculty families reside in Highmount Hall, McConnell Hall, Dempsey Hall, and Cottage. Most of the rooms are doubles, but there are several singles available. The Student Commons contains lounges, a video room, music practice studios, modern kitchen and dining room facilities, and a recently remodeled Student Center for informal recreation. The health center is on the ground floor of Stillman Hall. An admissions/development complex opened in 1992. Also on campus are several faculty residences; the Administration Building, the second floor of which has a faculty apartment; and Spy Rock House, the Headmaster's residence. New faculty residences were completed in December 2003.

ATHLETICS

Athletics at Storm King include recreational and competitive activities as well as a physical education program that is part of the course curriculum.

Each student must participate in an approved activity in each of the three sport seasons and in a competitive sport in one of the three seasons each year.

The gymnasium provides a basketball court, weight-lifting and fitness equipment, a dance studio, and locker and shower facilities. There are interscholastic teams for boys in basketball, cross-country, lacrosse, soccer, tennis, wrestling, and Ultimate Frisbee and for girls in basketball, cross-country, soccer, softball, tennis, Ultimate Frisbee, and volleyball. Coed volleyball is also offered as an interscholastic team sport. The recreational alternatives include martial arts, skiing, tennis, golf, and weight lifting. The Wilderness Program takes advantage of the School's physical setting, adjacent to the Black Rock Forest Wilderness Preserve, offering outdoor-skill activities that stress the leave-no-trace wilderness ethic.

EXTRACURRICULAR OPPORTUNITIES

The Student Activities Committee oversees many extracurricular activities. Among the student activities are the yearbook, photography, art, the literary journal, the Environmental Club, and several dramatics productions. A work program involves students in routine chores on campus. Learning service opportunities are available on and off campus.

DAILY LIFE

Classes are 45 minutes long and meet five times a week. The day begins with breakfast from 7:15 to 7:50, followed by a morning meeting and classes, which end at 3:45. This is followed by required activities from 4 to 5:30. Sit-down dinners alternate with buffet-style meals. A 2-hour supervised study period, either in the dorm or in the library, and some free time cap off the evening. The day ends at 10 p.m.

WEEKEND LIFE

The School's location provides various opportunities for social, cultural, and entertainment activities. Students may attend theater performances and concerts in New York City. The activities director and a student committee plan weekend activities, such as movies, dances, intramural athletics, hikes, skiing, horseback riding, visits to museums, and trips to special events and points of interest in the Northeast and as far south as Washington, D.C. The School plans an international trip each year; most recently, students have visited Mexico, Great Britain, and Italy. Students may go home any weekend after their obligations have been met.

COSTS AND FINANCIAL AID

For 2008–09, costs for Upper School boarding students totaled $35,950; for Upper School day students, costs totaled $19,950. Costs for Mountain Center boarding students totaled $41,200; costs for Mountain Center day students totaled $25,950. Costs for books, insurance, and laundry are additional. Students have to pay for transportation to and from the School. The School banks an account for a student, from which spending money may be drawn.

Financial assistance totaling about $321,000 is awarded annually in the form of grants and loans, according to guidelines determined by the School and Student Service for Financial Aid, to about 27 percent of the student body.

ADMISSIONS INFORMATION

The School accepts students in grades 8 through 12 as well as some postgraduates. Selections are made without regard to race, creed, or national origin and are based upon the applicant's promise of success and past record. An interview at the School is highly desirable. The School also offers prospective students the opportunity to participate in the student-for-a-day program to help them feel more comfortable and to enable them to learn about the School directly from their peers. The Director of Admission recommends candidates for consideration to the Faculty Admissions Committee.

APPLICATION TIMETABLE

Initial inquiries are welcome at any time, and campus interviews can be arranged from 8:30 to 3:30 during the week. A nonrefundable $85 fee must accompany the application. Acceptance notifications are sent as soon as all information is complete and the Admissions Committee makes a decision.

ADMISSIONS CORRESPONDENCE

David Flynn
Director of Admissions
The Storm King School
314 Mountain Road
Cornwall-on-Hudson, New York 12520-1899
Phone: 845-534-7892
800-225-9144 (toll-free)
Fax: 845-534-4128
E-mail: admissions@sks.org
Web site: http://www.sks.org

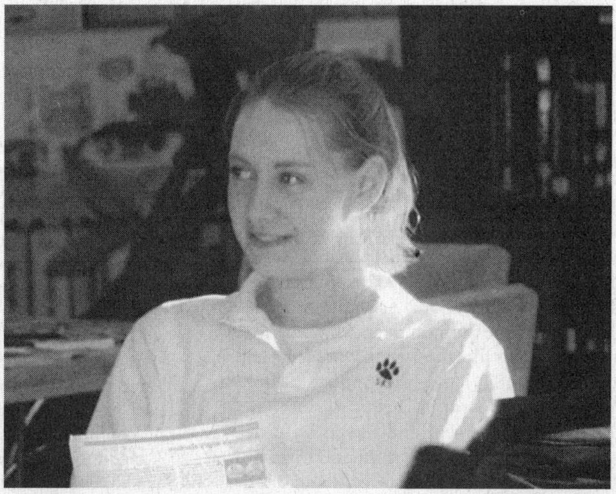

SUFFIELD ACADEMY

Suffield, Connecticut

Type: Coeducational boarding and day college-preparatory school
Grades: 9–12, postgraduate year
Enrollment: 413
Head of School: Charles Cahn III, Headmaster

THE SCHOOL

Challenge, structure, and support characterize Suffield Academy. A rigorous college-preparatory program in academics is supported by each student's ownership of a laptop computer, beautiful new facilities for music and the visual and performing arts, and extracurricular and athletic programs that round out each student's education. The school has a tradition of academic and athletic excellence and a deep sense of community spirit.

Founded as the Connecticut Literary Institution in 1833, the school became coeducational in 1843 and provided a traditional education for 100 years as both a private academy and the town's only public high school. It took the name of Suffield Academy in 1916 and after World War II became a fully independent boarding and day school for boys. In 1974, Suffield Academy returned to coeducation.

Suffield's strength lies in the personal concern and support shown for each student. The school emphasizes small classes and a structured academic program. In this setting, faculty members encourage students to take an active role in their education and to seek creative insights and solutions.

Each student is challenged intellectually, ethically, and physically to make the best use of his or her talents while developing a sound system of personal and social values.

The Academy's beautiful 350-acre campus is located in the historic residential town of Suffield, Connecticut, a community of 15,000 people located in a region that offers excellent opportunities for bicycling and hiking. Concerts, museums, theaters, and other city offerings are easily accessible in Springfield, Massachusetts, 10 miles north of Suffield, and Hartford, Connecticut, 17 miles to the south. New York is 135 miles to the south, and Boston is 90 miles to the northeast. Bradley International Airport is 5 miles from the campus.

A nonprofit institution, Suffield is governed by a self-perpetuating 24-member Board of Trustees. It has an endowment of $28 million. Annual Giving from alumni and alumnae, parents, and friends exceeds $1 million. The annual budget is more than $13 million.

Suffield is accredited by the New England Association of Schools and Colleges. It is a member of or is affiliated with each of the following organizations: the Connecticut Association of Independent Schools, the National Association of Independent Schools, the Cum Laude Society, American Secondary Schools for International Students and Teachers (ASSIST), the Secondary School Admission Test Board, A Better Chance, the Council for Advancement and Support of Education, Hartford Area Boarding Schools, Hartford Youth Scholarship Foundation, the Alumni Presidents Council, Secondary School Research Programs, and the WALKS Foundation.

ACADEMIC PROGRAMS

Suffield offers a college-preparatory curriculum that is grounded in the liberal arts. The academic program stresses acquiring the fundamental skills and knowledge needed to succeed in a variety of academic disciplines and in college. With careful guidance, students select a program of study designed to meet special interests and needs.

The school year is divided into three terms. Classes are held six days a week but end at noon on Wednesday and at 11 a.m. on Saturday, when athletics contests are scheduled in the afternoon. Classes average 10 students, and each class meets four times per week (two 45-minute periods and two extended 70-minute periods). Teachers are available for extra help on an individual basis. Students also have the support of faculty advisers and a walk-in counseling office. The student-faculty ratio is 7:1.

The Suffield Computer Initiative has enabled the school to integrate the use of technology into its traditional liberal arts curriculum. Each student possesses a laptop computer, and the dorm rooms are wired for Internet and phone use. The campus is wireless.

The Suffield Leadership Scholar Program offers partial scholarships to students who demonstrate the potential to be leaders at Suffield, in college, and in their careers. This program is an outgrowth of the excellent leadership development opportunities already available. A 40-acre leadership training site opened in June 2000. The Suffield Leadership Initiative is a unique program that is designed to teach ways of thinking and develop skills, traits, and habits that enhance each student's leadership qualities.

Students may choose from course offerings in the visual arts (painting, sculpture, woodworking, architecture, computer graphics, and more) or the performing arts (instrument ensembles, choral groups, dance, and private instruction in voice or instrument) to satisfy the requirement of a year's study in the arts.

The Academic Support Office provides resources for students who have different learning styles or challenges, as shown by their prior academic evaluation. The Director of Academic Support meets regularly with each student to create strategies that will sharpen their focus and strengthen their academic performance in the classroom. The Director also works with faculty members to communicate specific student needs so that Academy teachers are better able to meet the needs of students who have a broad range of learning styles.

Freshmen and sophomores carry five or six full-credit courses; juniors and seniors carry four, five, or six. To graduate, a student must demonstrate computer literacy and complete a total of 20⅓ credits, including 4 credits in English; 4 in leadership classes; 3 in mathematics; 2 in history, including 1 in U.S. history; 2 in Latin or a modern language; 2 in science, including 1 in a laboratory science; 2 in technology portfolios; 1 in the arts; ⅓ in religion; and the balance in electives.

All major departments offer honors-level courses. Advanced Placement courses are offered in computer science, English, foreign languages, history, math, and science. Interest in a course may lead to individual work with a teacher. In the senior year, students may select an independent study project for credit.

Grades, based on a minimum passing grade of D-, are recorded every five weeks. Effort also plays a significant part in the grading system. Academic reports from teachers (including grade, effort rating, and detailed comments), along with an evaluation from the adviser, are sent to parents at the end of each term and at the first midterm.

Ample time is provided for uninterrupted study, both during the day and in the evening. All boarding students study in their rooms, in the library, or in the computer lab in the evening from 8 to 10. Unsatisfactory effort necessitates attendance at supervised study halls during the day and evening until the student's effort improves.

FACULTY AND ADVISERS

There are 85 dedicated men and women on the faculty at Suffield Academy, 58 of whom have or are working toward graduate degrees. With few exceptions, faculty members and their families live on campus and all serve as advisers, coaches, dormitory parents, activity supervisors, and trip leaders. They engage in training programs and workshops as well as graduate programs leading to advanced degrees and professional expertise in their academic discipline.

Charles Cahn III was appointed headmaster on June 30, 2003. A native of Baltimore, Maryland, Charlie graduated from the Gilman School, received his bachelor's degree from the University of Michigan, and earned a master's degree in liberal studies at Wesleyan University. He also pursued graduate studies at Oxford University. Charlie came to Suffield in 1992 to teach in the English department. He also coached the boys' varsity lacrosse team and was a dorm parent in a girls' dorm. In 1996, Charlie took on the role of director of admissions, a position he retained until being named assistant headmaster in 1999. Charlie then served as associate headmaster for three years, overseeing the day-to-day affairs of the school.

Suffield is above all a caring school, and its faculty members reflect this attitude. All faculty members serve as advisers, with an average advisee group of 5 students. Students select their advisers, meet with them on a regular basis, and confer with them when needed. Two traditional annual events, Parents' Day in the fall and Spring Parents' Weekend, feature parental conferences with teachers and advisers that enable parents to share the results of their son's or daughter's experience at Suffield. Advisers are available to meet with parents and teachers as needed concerning a student's progress.

COLLEGE ADMISSION COUNSELING

Suffield's College Counseling Office provides a comprehensive program. Preparatory testing begins in the sophomore year, and meetings between students and their college counselors begin in the spring of the junior year. Representatives of more than 100 colleges visit the school annually, and students are encouraged to visit colleges.

In 2008, graduates enrolled in seventy-nine colleges and universities, including Amherst, Cornell, Emory, Georgetown, Johns Hopkins, NYU, Syracuse, Tufts, and Williams.

STUDENT BODY AND CONDUCT

The student community of 2008–09 had an enrollment of 413 students; 153 were boarding boys, 112 were boarding girls, 70 were day boys, and 78 were day girls. Students came from eighteen states and twenty-six other countries. A wealth of understanding and enrichment is fostered through this diversity of cultural backgrounds.

Although all students are encouraged to become constructively involved in the extracurricular life of the school, class representatives contribute to the decision-making process through participation in the Student Council and Discipline Committee. Cooperation and consideration of the rights of others are important factors in the decision-making process of each student. Each student holds at least one leadership position as part of the school's four-year leadership program.

The School Work Program and off-campus Community Service Program are vital parts of Suffield Academy life, promoting pride in the school and respect for other people. Everyone in the Suffield community performs a daily job that contributes to the general well-being of the school. A number of seniors and faculty members oversee this program.

ACADEMIC FACILITIES

The school occupies twenty major buildings, including Memorial Building, the main classroom building that houses a computer resource center with a multimedia classroom, desktop publishing center, printing stations, and a repair facility; the Alfred E. Holcomb science building, with four newly-renovated laboratories, a lecture room, and a weather satellite tracking system; and the 20,000-volume S. Kent Legare Library with a multimedia center, Tisch Auditorium, and computer resources that include fifty-five Internet drop sites located throughout the library. The Jeanice H. Seaverns Performing Arts Center and Guttag Music Center include a 200-seat theater, an art gallery, a set design studio and scene shop, a recording studio, practice rooms, and space for Suffield's dance and choral programs. The Emily Hall Tremaine Visual Arts Center features a multipurpose art studio, ceramics studio, graphics lab, photography lab, library office, and gallery. Nondenominational chapel services are held once a week in the town's Second Baptist Church. Centurion Hall, an academic building that houses classrooms for history, leadership, and math courses, opened in September 2002. The new wellness center opened in fall 2007, and renovations in the music and performing arts center were completed in winter 2008.

BOARDING AND GENERAL FACILITIES

Twelve dormitories provide double rooms for 260 students. All dorm rooms are wired for both telephone and Internet use. Five new cottage-style dorms opened in September 1998. The newest cottage-style dorm opened in 2007. Fuller and Spencer Halls are larger dormitories housing 46 and 50 students, respectively. There are also four homes, each shared by between 6 and 12 students. All dormitories have faculty residents, including families, and student proctors.

The downstairs part of Brewster Hall contains the school dining room, the kitchen, and the student union with lounge, TV room, game room, snack area, bookstore, and post office. Other buildings are the Fuller Hall administration building and the historic Gay Mansion, the official residence of the Headmaster.

ATHLETICS

With more than thirty-five interscholastic teams, as well as various other athletics options, all students participate in sports on a level of competition that matches individual experience and ability. Athletics at Suffield stress good sportsmanship, acquisition of skills, and leadership development. The Sherman Perry Gymnasium houses a Nautilus center, trainers' room, four international squash courts, and facilities for basketball, wrestling, volleyball, swimming, and riflery. The campus includes a football field, five soccer fields, two baseball diamonds and a softball diamond, ten tennis courts, a hockey field, three lacrosse fields, a sand volleyball pit, and an all-weather track. Facilities for skiing and golf are available nearby. Fitness programs, outdoor programs, team management, volunteer service, or play production may be undertaken in lieu of interscholastic sports. A state-of-the-art fitness center opened in December 2003. The artificial turf field was completed in fall 2007, and Tisch Field house, with four international squash courts and two basketball courts with a multipurpose floor, is scheduled for completion in winter 2009.

EXTRACURRICULAR OPPORTUNITIES

Suffield believes that every student should become constructively involved in the life of the school outside of the classroom. In addition to weekly chapel and a varied program of assemblies, both required, the school sponsors visiting artists and professionals who share experiences with the student body that often provoke new interests.

Students may choose from more than twenty-five activities, including concert and theater series, bicycling, bands, the yearbook, drama productions, the school newspaper, photography, chess, horseback riding, community service, and computers. Suffield Outdoor Leadership Opportunities (S.O.L.O.) maintains an active program, including rock-climbing, caving, backpacking, hiking, canoeing, camping, and other seasonal activities. The school opened an outdoor leadership center in 2000 with a rock climbing wall and high and low ropes courses. Suffield's location gives students access to plays, concerts, and museums in two major cities.

DAILY LIFE

Classes begin at 8 a.m. and conclude at 3:05 p.m. on Monday, Tuesday, Thursday, and Friday. Athletics follow the end of the academic day. Only morning classes are scheduled on Wednesday and Saturday; the afternoons are reserved for interscholastic athletics contests. Most clubs meet after dinner.

WEEKEND LIFE

The Student Union was expanded, redesigned, and renovated in 1992. The Weekend Activities and Film committees, as well as the Student Union Board of Governors, use this facility as the center of social life at the school.

On-campus weekend activities include dances, live entertainment, films, plays, and special events, such as Chill on the Hill and Luau. Off-campus options include movies, ski and shopping trips, indoor tennis, and activities sponsored by the Weekend Committee.

Boarding students in good standing may, with parental permission, take an unlimited number of weekends. Rapport between day and boarding students is close, with day students sharing campus activities and many boarding students visiting day students' homes on weekends.

COSTS AND FINANCIAL AID

Charges for 2008–09 were $41,500 for boarders and $29,500 for day students. Additional expenses included books and supplies ($400–$600), spending money ($20/week), laundry, and travel. The required, subsidized computer purchase ranges in cost from $750 to $1800.

For 2008–09, 133 need-based scholarships with a total value of more than $3,132,000 were awarded.

ADMISSIONS INFORMATION

The Admissions Committee seeks students who are committed to serious study and who have a sense of purpose, a good previous record both academically and personally, and supportive recommendations from persons who know the student well. Admissions requirements include the application form with a written essay; an academic transcript from the current school; letters of recommendation from the student's guidance counselor or placement officer, English and mathematics teachers, and a third teacher of the student's choice; and SSAT, SAT, PSAT, or WISC results. TOEFL is required from students for whom English is not their spoken language.

APPLICATION TIMETABLE

When classes are in session, campus interviews and tours are conducted daily from 8 a.m. to 2 p.m., (8 to 10 a.m. on Wednesday and Saturday). Prospective students are encouraged to visit the campus.

Applications are due January 15 and should be accompanied by a $50 fee for domestic applicants; and a $100 fee for international applicants. The mailing of acceptances is March 10, and students are asked to reply by April 10.

ADMISSIONS CORRESPONDENCE

Terry Breault
Director of Admissions and Financial Aid
Suffield Academy
185 North Main Street
Suffield, Connecticut 06078
Phone: 860-386-4440
Fax: 860-668-2966
E-mail: saadmit@suffieldacademy.org
Web site: http://www.suffieldacademy.org

THE TAFT SCHOOL

Watertown, Connecticut

Type: Coeducational boarding and day college-preparatory
Grades: 9–PG: Lower School, 9–10; Upper School, 11–12, postgraduate year
Enrollment: 577
Head of School: William R. MacMullen, Headmaster

THE SCHOOL

The Taft School was established in 1890 as a boys' preparatory school and became coeducational in 1971. Horace Dutton Taft, brother of President and Chief Justice William Howard Taft, was the School's founder and its Headmaster for forty-six years. Because he had faith in humankind's uniqueness and educability for high purpose, his was to be a nondenominational school in which boys would receive physical, mental, moral, and spiritual training for leadership and constructive citizenship. He stressed the opportunity that is open to all individuals, and particularly to Taft students, to make a democratic society work.

The focal point of the School's educational philosophy is still on the wholeness of the student—on the essential interdependence of personal and intellectual growth. Known for its close faculty-student relationships, Taft emphasizes individual development through participation in vigorous artistic, athletic, and extracurricular programs. Eighty-three percent of the seniors take Advanced Placement courses and are involved in at least three extracurricular organizations.

The 220-acre campus is located 30 miles from New Haven, 35 miles from Hartford, 90 miles from New York City, and 120 miles from Boston.

Since 1927, The Taft School has been governed by a Board of Trustees. The physical plant is valued at more than $165 million, and the endowment is nearly $190 million. In 2007–08, $3.4 million was raised in Annual Giving, with a 40 percent rate of participation from the alumni body of more than 7,992.

Taft is accredited by the New England Association of Schools and Colleges. Its memberships include the Connecticut Association of Independent Schools, the Cum Laude Society, the National Association of Independent Schools, the Secondary School Admission Test Board, the Educational Records Bureau, the Association of Boarding Schools, and the College Board.

ACADEMIC PROGRAMS

Taft's liberal arts education prepares its students in a community devoted to creating lifelong learners, thoughtful citizens, and caring people. The School offers more than 200 courses, each worth 1 unit, in each of two semesters. Subject requirements are 8 semesters of English, foreign language study through the third year of a language (though students may elect an additional language), mathematics through algebra II/trigonometry, 4 semesters of history or social science, 4 units of laboratory science, and 1 to 3 units of arts. Most students exceed these course requirements. Thirty-six semester units are required for graduation. In grades 9 and 10, the minimum course load is five academic subjects; in grades 11 and 12, the requirement is four major subjects, though many students carry five. Electives, honors, and Advanced Placement courses are offered in all major areas of study.

The School encourages students to express themselves clearly, purposefully, and creatively in all of their academic endeavors as well as in their arts education. The arts at Taft are incorporated into the regular academic program as well as through extracurricular and informal involvement. Visual arts, theatrical and dance classes and productions, and musical instruction and performance are offered to all students, who must fulfill the School's arts requirement for graduation.

Achievement grades are numerical, on a scale of 40 to 100. Students who earn at least an 87 grade point average are on the honor roll, while 93 merits high honors. Students also receive letter grades from A to D for each course. Most classes range in size from 10 to 16 students, and the student-faculty ratio is 5:1. Taft closely monitors the progress of all students, with teachers submitting achievement and effort grades approximately every three weeks. The faculty meets seven times each academic year to discuss how individual students are faring. Complete grades and teachers' reports are mailed home four times per year.

The opportunity for independent study at Taft has been part of the academic offerings for decades. Interested and qualified students may work individually with faculty members in any field for academic credit in a self-designed course of study. The Senior Project and Independent Project programs give students the chance to pursue intellectual or artistic passions not necessarily within traditional academic parameters. Finally all students are required to complete a Senior Research Thesis in a topic of their choosing during the winter of their senior year.

FACULTY AND ADVISERS

Of the 93 teaching faculty members, 66 have earned master's degrees and 6 hold a doctorate. The full-time teaching faculty numbers 65 (39 men and 26 women), and the part-time teaching faculty numbers 28; 80 percent live on campus. The turnover of the faculty is estimated at 10 to 15 percent a year.

Members of the faculty are selected for their ability to instill enthusiasm for learning, for other inspirational qualities, and for excellence in teaching both in and out of the classroom. Taft promotes professional growth through sabbatical leaves, travel and summer study grants, teaching fellowships, and endowed chairs. Each student chooses his or her adviser at the outset of each year and then works closely with that faculty member for the duration of the year.

William R. MacMullen, Taft's fifth Headmaster, joined the faculty in 1983 upon graduating from Yale University; he earned an M.A. degree in English from Middlebury College. Mr. MacMullen was appointed Headmaster in 2001.

COLLEGE ADMISSION COUNSELING

From January of the eleventh-grade year through the spring of the twelfth-grade year, students work closely with the college counselors. Parents are consulted in group and individual conferences and informed about the college admissions process and students' progress.

All eleventh graders take the PSAT in the fall and the SAT the following winter and again in the senior year. The average SAT scores for the class of 2008 were 641 verbal and 644 math. SAT Subject Tests are offered in all major subjects.

Representatives from more than 130 colleges come to Taft each year to meet with seniors and juniors. The 162 graduates of the class of 2008 are attending ninety-two colleges, with 4 or more at Amherst, Bowdoin, Carnegie Mellon, Connecticut College, Cornell, George Washington, University of Pennsylvania, St. Lawrence, Trinity, and Wake Forest.

STUDENT BODY AND CONDUCT

In 2008–09, Taft had students from thirty-three states and twenty-eight countries. The 577 students included 467 boarding students and 110 day students, 271 girls and 306 boys. Thirty-five percent of the students are from public schools, 51 percent from private schools, and 14 percent from schools outside the United States. Taft prides itself on the geographic, ethnic, and economic diversity of its student body.

One out of every 7 students serves at some time in the elected student government. The president of the student body directs the honor system. A joint faculty-student Discipline Committee handles all major violations by recommending appropriate action to the Headmaster. Because Taft students are assumed to be responsible, serious, disciplined, and hardworking, the honor system guides them in all social and academic matters.

ACADEMIC FACILITIES

The center of the academic community is the Benjamin M. Belcher Learning Center, including the Library Reading Room and the Hulbert Taft Jr. Library. The library's collection includes more than 58,000 books, sound recordings, videocassettes, and DVDs, as well as an outstanding newspaper collection dating from 1704 to the present. The library's subscriptions to electronic databases provide access to full-text articles and documents from thousands of periodicals. Interlibrary loan service is offered to both students and faculty. The three-story building includes an auditorium, conference rooms, small study rooms, a computer/teaching lab, forty networked computers, and the Archives.

The Lady Ivy Kwok Wu Science and Mathematics Center, opened in 1997, contains 45,000 square feet of state-of-the-art teaching and learning space. The Charles Phelps Taft and Horace Dutton Taft buildings contain an additional thirty-five classrooms as well as Bingham Auditorium, a 595-seat theater equipped with facilities for play production, movies, and concerts.

The Arts/Humanities Center, completed in 1985, contains classrooms, faculty offices, a computer center and digital imaging studio, a student union, and facilities for teaching theater, music, dance, photography, pottery, sculpture, batik, and printmaking. The arts facilities feature an experimental theater that seats 250 people, a large dance studio, special practice rooms for the several concert bands and singing groups, an electronic music studio, and art rooms designed for work in clay, printmaking, and fabric design. Many smaller rooms are used for individual work in the arts. The student union contains a snack bar and spaces where students can socialize and relax.

The Modern Language Learning and Resource Center opened in 1992. Its Sony Virtuoso-equipped carrels provide digital facilities for the learning of modern languages. The center is linked to satellites to receive news broadcasts and programs from other countries.

BOARDING AND GENERAL FACILITIES

Taft students live in twelve dormitory units. Most students have a roommate, although single rooms are available. The five girls' dormitories have their own common rooms and laundry facilities. The boys live in self-contained groups on each of the corridors of Charles Phelps Taft and Horace Dutton Taft halls and in one smaller dormitory. Student rooms are equipped with Ethernet data parts and telephone connections. The student union is centrally located, and there are lounge areas in the dormitories. The campus is covered by a wireless network.

Teachers' apartments are located among student rooms. The closeness of the central cluster of dormitory units along with the presence of faculty members establishes a strong and positive sense of community.

ATHLETICS

The Taft athletics program is sufficiently broad and varied to encourage both the physical and the psychological growth of all students. At both interscholastic and intramural levels, emphasis is placed on developing good sportsmanship, cooperation, confidence, competitiveness, and self-discipline.

Varsity and junior varsity interscholastic teams are organized in football, field hockey, wrestling, baseball, and softball; boys' and girls' soccer, cross-country, ice hockey, basketball, squash, ski racing, track, lacrosse, tennis, golf, and crew; and girls' volleyball. Lower School teams compete interscholastically in boys' basketball, ice hockey, and tennis; boys' and girls' soccer, lacrosse, and crew; and field hockey. Intramural sports are offered in soccer, golf, squash, and boys' and girls' tennis, Ultimate Frisbee, basketball, and ice hockey. Exercise programs are offered in horseback riding, aerobics, weight training, running and rock climbing, dance, and outdoor leadership.

Taft's newest athletic facility, a synthetic "field turf," was completed in 2007. Currently, Taft teams play field hockey, lacrosse, and soccer on the turf. Other facilities include an ice hockey arena containing an international-sized ice surface with seating for 600 spectators, a second hockey rink, an eighteen-hole golf course, twelve outdoor tennis courts, sixteen playing fields, and an all-weather, six-lane, 400-meter track. The Paul and Edith Cruikshank indoor facility houses boys' and girls' locker rooms, three international glass-backed squash courts, a wrestling room, a large up-to-date athletic trainer's area, equipment rooms, eight visiting team rooms, a state-of-the-art wood-surfaced floor for two basketball courts, three volleyball courts, and a climbing wall. A newer indoor athletics facility opened in 1993. It houses four indoor tennis courts, two basketball courts, a three-lane running track (8.5 laps to a mile), an exercise center that was renovated in 2007 with twenty Paramount and Precor machines, computerized bikes, StairMasters, ellipticals, treadmills, and free weights area, five international squash courts, a video projection room, meeting and function rooms, and the Athletic Department offices.

EXTRACURRICULAR OPPORTUNITIES

More than forty clubs and organizations are open to Taft students; opportunities range from the radio and computer clubs to filmmaking and photography. The major student publications are the *Annual,* Taft's yearbook; the *Papyrus,* the student newspaper; and *Red, Inc.,* a literary magazine. *Masque and Dagger* and *Taft Improv* theater groups present several plays each term to the student body and the community.

The School brings writers, poets, and artists to the campus; speakers often come to address individual classes. Popular films are screened weekly as well. Many students are involved in daily volunteer community service as well as weekend service projects.

DAILY LIFE

On Monday through Saturday, the school day begins at 7:50 a.m. There are seven class periods, one of which is used for lunch, and four or five for regular classes; the others may be used for study, music practice, art, or a conference session with a teacher. Required sports practice or volunteer service follows the class day. On Wednesday and Saturday, because of interscholastic games, classes are finished at lunchtime.

On two weekday mornings, the School assembles for School Meeting, at which a faculty member, student, or guest speaker presents a brief program and assembly on Wednesdays and Saturdays. On two weekday evenings, students share in a formal seated dinner with faculty members and their families. Various organizations and faculty-student committees often meet after dinner, but study, individually or with the help of an instructor, usually lasts 3 to 4 hours. Boarding students (except seniors) have a 2-hour required room-study period each evening.

WEEKEND LIFE

After Saturday classes, students are free to go out to dinner; on some weekends they may spend the night away from Taft, provided that permission has been received from their parents and authorized by the Dean of Students. Most students choose to remain on campus for the weekend. The entertainment ranges from movies to dances to plays. In addition, there are often School-sponsored trips to plays and concerts in New York, New Haven, or Hartford. Day students are encouraged to join in all weekend activities. On Sundays, students may get up for a local church service or sleep until brunch is served.

SUMMER PROGRAMS

Taft offers a five-week coeducational summer program for boarding as well as day students. The courses, given for enrichment purposes and not for credit, include English, mathematics, history, languages, and science.

COSTS AND FINANCIAL AID

In 2008–09, charges for boarding students were $41,300 and for day students, $30,700. There is a technology fee of $500 for boarding students, $150 for day students. An enrollment deposit of $4100 for boarding students and $3000 for day students is payable on May 15. Scholarship and loan funds were available in the amount of $5.6 million. Of the 577 students at Taft in 2008–09, 196 received some form of financial assistance, ranging from a $1000 scholarship and low-interest student loan to a full $41,300 scholarship. Financial assistance is awarded to students on the basis of financial need, as evidenced through the School and Student Service for Financial Aid form.

ADMISSIONS INFORMATION

Taft is interested in candidates as people—not just as scholars. The School seeks girls and boys who are curious, who will become involved, and who will commit themselves to a high standard of intellectual and personal growth. Because of the rigorous academic demands at the Taft School, the Admissions Committee finds that students with A and B averages who are involvement oriented and come highly recommended are usually the most successful candidates.

All candidates except prospective seniors are required to take the SSAT, preferably in December or January. The minimum percentile score accepted is generally 50. Most entering students test between the 75th and 99th percentiles. Candidates for the senior class are expected to take the PSAT and SAT. All candidates are urged to have an on-campus interview with a member of the admissions staff.

APPLICATION TIMETABLE

Admissions Office interviews may be scheduled Monday through Saturday. On Wednesdays and Saturdays, appointments are available in the morning only. Inquiries are welcome at any time. Appointments for interviews and tours should be made well in advance. The application deadline is January 15, and the application fee is $50; the fee for students living outside the U.S. is $100. Candidates are notified of the decision on March 10, and the Parents' Reply Date is April 10.

ADMISSIONS CORRESPONDENCE

Mr. Peter Frew
Director of Admissions
The Taft School
Watertown, Connecticut 06795
Phone: 860-945-7700
Fax: 860-945-7808
E-mail: admissions@taftschool.org
Web site: http://www.taftschool.org

TALLULAH FALLS SCHOOL

Tallulah Falls, Georgia

Type: Coeducational day and boarding college-preparatory
Enrollment: 140

THE SCHOOL

Tallulah Falls School is an independent, coeducational day and boarding school currently serving 140 students in grades 6–12. Tallulah Falls is located in the northeast Georgia mountains, approximately 90 miles from Atlanta.

Founded in 1909 by the Georgia Federation of Women's Clubs, the School and the Federation have deep roots in the history of secondary education in Georgia. Tallulah Falls School continues to provide opportunities for intellectual challenge, physical participation, and personal growth to students from the local area as well as to students from across the state of Georgia, around the nation, and throughout the world.

For all of the students, the Tallulah Falls experience is centered on community and characterized by personal attention in a nurturing environment. Classes are small, with an average of 10–12 students per class. The community consists of students and members of the faculty, staff, and administration who are committed to promoting an atmosphere of respect and encouragement that is conducive to learning and living.

Academically, students find fulfillment and challenge at Tallulah Falls. The quality of the academic program and the success of its students as scholars and citizens form the foundation on which the School is built. A broad and ambitious curriculum, engaging teaching methods, and an emphasis on student involvement in the classroom all contribute to the mental development and educational achievement that students realize as they prepare for college and for life.

Students find themselves immersed in an atmosphere that not only fosters academic excellence, but also encourages an appreciation for nature and the preservation of natural resources. Tallulah Gorge State Park, with its interpretive education center, hiking trails, and scenic vistas, is a neighbor of the School in the town of Tallulah Falls. Hiking, camping, cycling, whitewater rafting, horseback riding, and snow skiing offer students the opportunity to experience the wonders of nature. For those who prefer the sophistication and energy of the city, there are supervised weekend excursions into metro Atlanta that allow students to enjoy the best of the Southeast's premier cultural attractions, athletic events, and extensive shopping and dining.

Tallulah Falls School is accredited by the Southern Association of Colleges and Schools and the Southern Association of Independent Schools. It holds membership in the Georgia Independent School Association, the Georgia High School Association, the National Association of Secondary School Principals, the Secondary School Admission Test Board, The Association of Boarding Schools, the National Association of Independent Schools and the Small Boarding School Association.

ACADEMIC PROGRAMS

The curriculum at Tallulah Falls School has been designed to meet the needs of college bound students, from the average to the academically gifted.

Twenty-two credits are required for graduation, which include 4 years of English, 4 years of math, 3 units of science, 3 years of social studies, 2 years of foreign language, and 1 year of physical education.

The 12:1 student-teacher ratio ensures that students receive personal attention from each of their teachers. Tallulah Falls School operates on a six-period day. A 45-minute tutorial is held daily after sixth period to provide additional assistance. A mandatory, staff-supervised study hall is held on Sunday through Thursday evenings in the dormitories. Additional study time is assigned to all students needing academic assistance.

The school year, which begins in mid-August and ends in late May, is divided into two semesters. Grades are reported every nine weeks. Tallulah Falls School uses a traditional numeric grading scale, with no credit given for grades below C. Students whose semester grade point averages (GPAs) are at least 4.0, 3.5, or 3.0 (on a 4.0 scale) qualify for academic honor rolls. Students who fail to maintain an overall GPA of 2.0 and students who fail two or more subjects in a semester are placed on academic probation and are subject to dismissal unless grades improve during the following grading period.

FACULTY AND ADVISERS

Teaching at Tallulah Falls School is a highly personal commitment to helping young people succeed as scholars and citizens. Of the 24 teachers on staff, approximately 75 percent hold one or more advanced degrees. Faculty members serve in a multiplicity of roles, including teacher, adviser, mentor, coach, and sponsor.

The Advisory Program at Tallulah Falls School is an integral part of the educational process. Each member of the faculty serves as an adviser to a small group of students that meets once a day during the academic year. The primary purpose of these groups is to serve as an additional support service within which students can discuss personal and academic concerns. Together, these groups plan service projects and experiential learning activities and discuss developmentally appropriate issues.

COLLEGE ADMISSION COUNSELING

The School counselor assumes the primary role in assisting students and their families with college selection, applications, and scholarships. Students are encouraged to begin focusing on career interests and future plans early in their high school careers.

Tallulah Falls School offers many research tools, including texts and computer-based programs, for students to use in selecting colleges, universities, technical schools, and scholarships. Juniors, seniors, and interested parents have the opportunity to attend the annual PROBE Fair, a meeting with representatives of colleges and technical schools, military personnel, and the Georgia Student Finance Authority. In addition, representatives of colleges and technical schools make campus visits throughout the year.

Students take the PSAT in the fall of their freshman and sophomore years. Juniors and seniors take the SAT in the fall. For college admission purposes, students are encouraged to take either the SAT or the ACT in their senior year as well. Several college admission test–preparation workshops are offered to students, as is an individualized computerized tutorial program.

Of the 2007–08 graduates, 100 percent were accepted to postsecondary schools. Of those students who are attending college, many have received academic scholarships. Representative colleges and universities at which Tallulah Falls School graduates have been accepted include the Art Institute of Atlanta, Auburn, Berry, Brevard College, Brewton Parker, Dartmouth, Duke, Emmanuel, Emory, Fort Valley State, Gainesville, Georgia Southern, Georgia State, Georgia Tech, Howard, Kennesaw State, Mercer, Michigan State, North Carolina State, North Georgia, Ohio State, Penn State, Piedmont, Presbyterian College, Reinhardt College, Southern Polytechnic State, Vanderbilt, Wesleyan College, Winthrop, Valdosta State, and the Universities of Georgia, Illinois, Indiana, and Virginia.

STUDENT BODY AND CONDUCT

Tallulah Falls School seeks to enroll a student body that is diverse geographically, socially, academically, culturally, and economically. The School believes that diversity acts as a positive influence as it reflects the global community, with all students learning from the others' unique backgrounds and experiences.

The purpose of the Honor Code is to promote high ideals of personal honor and integrity. Tallulah Falls School students are expected not to lie, steal, cheat, plagiarize, or assist others in these actions. The Honor Code is modeled and enforced by the Honor Council, an autonomous organization of 5 students and an adviser appointed to review honor violations. For all other disciplinary infractions, a demerit system is utilized. The demerit system is outlined in the Student/Parent Handbook and is administered by all members of the Tallulah Falls School staff, faculty, and administration. Serious disciplinary infractions may be referred to the Disciplinary Committee for review.

ACADEMIC FACILITIES

Highlighting the historical significance of Tallulah Falls School, the original School property has been placed on the National Historic Register. The School has grown from two buildings and 5 acres of land at its inception to twenty-two buildings and approximately 500 acres of land today, 120 acres of which have been developed to form the current School campus. The physical plant is valued in excess of $17 million, excluding land values.

Most classrooms are located in the H. R. and C. R. Cannon Academic Building, which won a special award for its design from the American Institute of Architects. The academic building also includes the Briggs Computer Laboratory, two ultramodern science labs, and the Passie Fenton Ottley Library, which houses approximately 14,000 volumes. Music and physical education classrooms are located in the Young Matrons' Circle Building, a multipurpose fine arts facility that includes a 300-seat theater, offices, a gymnasium, practice rooms, and classrooms. The theater is a focal point for assemblies, invited lecturers, visiting artists, student performances, and School-sponsored community activities.

BOARDING AND GENERAL FACILITIES

Students are housed in two 2-story dormitories—Fitzpatrick Hall for boys and Westmoreland Hall for girls. Each dormitory is staffed by 3 to 4 full-time dormitory supervisors who are assisted by student life assistants. These students are campus leaders who serve as role models for students. They are selected based on leadership, scholarship, and interviews.

The dormitory rooms are designed for double occupancy. Roommate assignments are based on student preferences whenever possible, and students are allowed to change roommates at designated times each year if they wish. Free laundry facilities are available to students in each dormitory, or students may choose to use the School laundry service, which is included in the tuition. In each dormitory, students have access to lounge areas with televisions, exercise equipment, and other recreational activities. Students also have access to the Lettie Pate Evans Student Center after school hours, on weekends, and during recreation periods.

The School infirmary is operated by a registered nurse during regular school hours. After hours, student health needs are closely monitored by dormitory supervisors.

ATHLETICS

A member of the Georgia High School Association, Tallulah Falls School competes with other independent schools and public schools in baseball, basketball, cross-country, soccer, tennis, track and field, and volleyball. All students are encouraged to participate in sports, either through membership on varsity teams, enrollment in physical education classes, or participation in the School's voluntary intramural program, which includes activities such as basketball, soccer, softball, and volleyball. Each year, all students participate in Field Day, during which students are divided into four teams and compete for a full day in a wide range of athletic events and activities. During recreation periods, students have access to the gymnasium, athletic fields, and tennis courts.

EXTRACURRICULAR OPPORTUNITIES

Participation in cocurricular activities is an integral part of the overall boarding school experience. An elected Student Council is responsible for planning weekend trips and activities and also coordinates student service opportunities and community service projects.

Nonathletic competition is available to students in such areas as writing, spelling, mathematics, foreign language, word processing, geography bee, and vocal solo. An active School chorus performs regularly. Talented art students enter several competitions each year, including the School Art Symposium, sponsored by the University of Georgia. Students with writing and design skills produce *Retrospect*, the School yearbook.

Teachers and staff members sponsor a wide range of clubs for students, including the Astronomy Club, Debate Team, Outdoor Club, Fishing Club, Chess Club, and Gourmet Cooking Club. The National Honor Society chapter is very active and has won five first-place awards at the NHS State Convention.

In 1989, a group of Tallulah Falls School students and faculty members entered the National Aeronautics and Space Administration's (NASA) Orbiter-Naming Program, a nationwide contest designed to name the space shuttle built to replace *Challenger*. NASA chose the Tallulah Falls entry as the national secondary school winner, and the name *Endeavour* continues to be a source of pride for the School and the nation.

DAILY LIFE

The school day begins with a buffet-style breakfast served from 7 to 7:30, which is mandatory for all students except seniors. Classes begin at 8:10 and end at 3:15 daily, with a break of approximately 40 minutes for lunch. During the academic day, students wear School uniforms. During certain portions of the year, all boarding students participate in the School's work program. Work program assignments vary from working in the kitchen to general cleaning of their dorms and other buildings on the campus. Regardless of the job, students learn the value of hard work and the importance of cooperation in maintaining the beauty and integrity of the Tallulah Falls School community. Dinner is served around 6 p.m. and is followed by recreation. Students report to the dormitories at 7:45 for study time. Study time is held on Sunday through Thursday evenings from 8 until 9:30. Lights-out for underclassmen is at 10; senior lights-out is at 11.

WEEKEND LIFE

The Boarding Director works closely with students to plan trips and events for each weekend. Weekend activities include dances, movies, and special events on campus; trips to college and professional sports events; nature-related pursuits, including hiking, horseback riding, rafting, and kayaking; and cultural activities, including art exhibits, museums, and theater performances off campus.

All students are required to go home for long weekends or vacations approximately eight times during the school year, including Thanksgiving, Christmas, winter break, spring break, and four long weekends. Students are permitted weekend leaves on other weekends as requested by parents.

COSTS AND FINANCIAL AID

For the 2008–09 academic year, boarding costs are $19,000 for Georgia residents and $21,000 for out-of-state students who board seven days per week. The five-day boarding cost is $14,500, and the international student tuition is $25,000. Day student costs are $8000 for middle school and $8500 for high school. These amounts include tuition and textbook rental for all students. Included in the boarding tuition are some activities. A mandatory ESL and orientation week for new international students is held prior to the beginning of the academic year in August. Interested students should inquire concerning the current cost. Additional charges may include weekend activities, uniform purchases, school supplies, and long-weekend fees. Incidental charges are billed monthly throughout

Financial assistance is awarded on the basis of need, as determined by a Financial Aid Committee. This year, the School awarded more than $1 million in student assistance.

ADMISSIONS INFORMATION

The Admissions Committee at Tallulah Falls School believes that certain criteria are essential to the ultimate success of a student seeking admission. First and foremost, the School selects students who are motivated to succeed academically, physically, socially, and spiritually, who are pursuing college preparation. A student demonstrates the desire to achieve through a personal essay, prior school performance, and a formal interview with a member of the Admission Office. A student must be eligible to return to his or her previous educational institution and show performance at or above grade level. These criteria are evaluated based on the student's applications, official school transcripts, teacher and principal recommendations, standardized test scores, and parent questionnaires.

APPLICATION TIMETABLE

For fall enrollment, applications should be submitted by February 15. Applicants seeking January admission should submit applications by November 15. A $30 fee ($75 for international students) should accompany the application. Applicant files are only considered by the Admissions Committee when they are complete and all parts of the application have been received.

ADMISSIONS CORRESPONDENCE

Admissions
Tallulah Falls School
P.O. Box 249
Tallulah Falls, Georgia 30573

Phone: 706-754-0400
Fax: 706-754-5757
E-mail: admissions@tallulahfalls.org
Web site: http://www.tallulahfalls.org

TASIS THE AMERICAN SCHOOL IN ENGLAND

Thorpe, Surrey, England

TASIS

Type: Coeducational boarding and day college-preparatory school
Grades: Nursery–13: Nursery; Lower School, Nursery–5; Middle School, 6–8; Upper School, 9–13
Enrollment: School total: 750; Upper School: 370
Head of School: Dr. James A. Doran, Headmaster

THE SCHOOL

TASIS England was founded in 1976 by Mrs. M. Crist Fleming as a branch of The American School in Switzerland (TASIS), which she established in 1956. The 43-acre campus is set in a country village in the Thames valley, only 18 miles from central London and 6 miles from Heathrow Airport.

The School offers a traditional, college-preparatory program. While academics are emphasized, sports, extracurricular activities, cultural excursions, and weekend trips ensure the balanced education of the whole student. The program takes full advantage of its location and the opportunities that England and Europe offer as extensions to classroom learning. The TASIS Schools and Summer Programs are owned and fully controlled by the TASIS Foundation, a Swiss, independent, not-for-profit educational foundation, registered in Delémont, Switzerland.

TASIS England is an IB World School; is accredited by the Council of International Schools (CIS) and the New England Association of Schools and Colleges (NEASC); and is a member of the National Association of Independent Schools (NAIS) and The Association of Boarding Schools (TABS). It was inspected by the British Office for Standards in Education (Ofsted) in November 2008, and it received high ratings for its academic, arts, athletics, and extracurricular programs; student care; and facilities.

ACADEMIC PROGRAMS

The upper school encompasses grades 9 to 13. The minimum requirements for graduation from the upper school are 4 years of English, 3 years of history (including U.S. history at the eleventh- or twelfth-grade level), a third-level proficiency in a foreign language, 3 years of mathematics (through algebra II), three laboratory sciences (including a biological and a physical science), and 1 year of fine arts. All seniors are required to take a full-year humanities course. Students who have attended TASIS England for three years or more are expected to complete 21 credits. A normal course load consists of six courses per year. Advanced Placement courses are offered for qualified students and include art history, biology, calculus, chemistry, computer science, economics, English, environmental science, French, government and politics, history, music theory, physics, statistics, and Spanish.

TASIS also offers the International Baccalaureate (IB) diploma. Students may apply to this program for their final two years at TASIS, and successful IB diploma candidates can earn both the IB diploma and the TASIS England high school diploma. Entry into the IB Program is made in consultation between the School, student, and family and is open to highly motivated students with strong academic, time management, and study skills.

The average class size is 15, with a teacher-student ratio of 1:8. The aim is to provide an intimate learning environment that can challenge a young person to realize his or her full potential. The Advisor Program enhances this aspect of a TASIS education, as the advisers are charged with the social and academic well-being of each advisee.

A student's day is fully structured. Participation in supervised evening study hall for boarding students is a requirement for all but those who have earned the privilege of independent study in their rooms.

The academic year is divided into two semesters, ending in January and June, respectively. Grades and comments are mailed home to parents four times a year at mid-semester and end-of-semester breaks, together with a summary report from the adviser. The grading system uses A to F, indicating achievement levels, and 1 to 5 as a measure of a student's attitude and application to his or her work.

An educational travel program during the October break is required for all boarding students and is included in the tuition. Past trips have included such destinations as Austria, France, Germany, Greece, Hungary, Italy, Poland, Romania, Russia, Spain, and Switzerland. These school trips are also an option for day students.

FACULTY AND ADVISERS

Dr. James A. Doran was appointed as headmaster of TASIS in 2005. He holds a doctorate in curriculum and instruction as well as degrees in education and educational administration. A seasoned administrator who has worked in international schools for more than twenty-five years, Dr. Doran has led schools and taught in Panama, Singapore, Tokyo, Manila, Jeddah, and Tunis. He was also Executive Director at Stetson University—Celebration Campus in Florida, where, in addition to his administrative responsibilities, he taught graduate-level courses in educational leadership, research, communications, and school finance.

The faculty represents one of the School's strongest assets. Its members are a group of dedicated professionals with a true sense of vocation. Duties are not limited to teaching but encompass the responsibilities of advisors, sports coaches, dorm parents, community service aides, and trip chaperones. There are 123 full-time faculty members—43 men and 80 women—and 5 part-time teachers. Approximately half of them have advanced degrees and 19 live on campus. In addition, music specialists visit the School for private instruction by arrangement.

COLLEGE ADMISSION COUNSELING

TASIS England employs 4 college counselors. They meet individually with students in their junior and senior years to discuss academic programs, careers, and college plans. Support programs include student seminars, career day, transition workshops, and a case study night. The counselors maintain a reference library of college catalogs, videos, and computer software and familiarize students with the range of opportunities available to them. The counselors coordinate visits to the School by college admissions officers from universities in the United States and Europe and administer the college admissions testing program. TASIS England is a test center for the PSAT, ACT, and SAT for juniors and seniors and all Advanced Placement examinations.

TASIS students are accepted by universities around the world and have recently attended such schools as Boston University, Brown, Bryn Mawr, Cambridge (U.K.), Connecticut College, Cornell, Dartmouth, Duke, Durham (U.K.), Georgetown, George Washington, Imperial College of London (U.K.), London School of Economics (U.K.), Northwestern, Notre Dame, Princeton, Rhode Island School of Design, Rice, SMU, Stanford, Tufts, University College London, Waseda (Japan), Yale, and the Universities of Pennsylvania and St. Andrews (U.K.). TASIS believes that students should be encouraged to think deeply about the purposes of higher education, about the intangible benefits of genuine intellectual activity, and about the range of philosophical options offered by educational institutions. The major responsibility for college choices lies with each student, but the School provides as much advice and support as possible.

STUDENT BODY AND CONDUCT

For the 2008-09 academic year, there were 370 students in the upper school (grades 9–13): 80 seniors, 110 juniors, 100 sophomores, and 80 freshmen. Overall, the ratio of boys to girls in each grade level is close to 1:1. In some cases, the parents of boarding students are expatriates undertaking assignments overseas, in such locations as Saudi Arabia, Africa, Europe, and various parts of the British Isles. The student body is culturally diverse, with 54 percent of the students in the upper school representing over fifty different countries. In the lower school, there are 230 children, and the middle school (grades 6–8) has 150 students

The *Student Handbook* clearly identifies the accepted codes of conduct within the School community. A uniform is required for upper school students. Lower and middle school students wear white and navy blue. An infraction of a major school rule is dealt with by the upper school administration with the Disciplinary Advisory Board. TASIS England reserves the right to dismiss at any time a student who has proved to be an unsatisfactory member of the school community, even though there may have been no infraction of a specific rule.

In the upper school, the Student Council is made up of representatives from all grade levels and is the vehicle of student government. Prefects, as student leaders, carry special responsibilities in dormitory and general school life.

ACADEMIC FACILITIES

Two large Georgian mansions and purpose-built classrooms are the focal points of the campus. There are computer and science laboratories, a library for each school division, art studios, a darkroom, music rooms, a state-of-the-art language laboratory, a new health center, two multipurpose gymnasiums, a fitness center, two drama/dance studios, and a 350-seat theater. TASIS England has embarked on a ten-year master plan to enhance all campus facilities.

BOARDING AND GENERAL FACILITIES

Boarding students (grades 9–13) are accommodated in dormitories supervised by a faculty resident and assisted by prefects. Each unit holds 13–15 students, usually in 2-, 3-, or 4-person rooms, which are located in parts of the main buildings as well as in the adjacent cottages, such as Renalds Herne, Tudor House, Orchard, and Shepherd's Cottage. The Boarding Program is coordinated by two staff members, both of whom are experienced in providing boarding care and serving the needs of young people.

ATHLETICS

An awareness of physical fitness, the discipline of training the body as well as the mind, and the spirit of competition are viewed as important elements in a student's education at TASIS England. All upper school students participate in the afternoon sports/activities program, which operates on a three-term basis, reflecting seasonal sports. The minimum requirement is participation for two afternoons a week.

Varsity sports include basketball, cross-country, soccer, tennis, and volleyball as well as boys' teams in rugby and baseball and a girls' team in softball. Other recreational sports include badminton, horseback riding, squash, lacrosse, golf, swimming, and a conditioning program.

There are four large playing fields on campus, six all-weather tennis courts, two gymnasiums, and a fitness center that offers a complete weight-training circuit and a wide variety of cardiovascular machines. The nearby Egham Sports Center offers fine supplementary facilities.

Besides participating in local sports events, the School competes in International Schools Sports Tournaments (ISSTs) with other international schools throughout Europe and the Middle East.

EXTRACURRICULAR OPPORTUNITIES

England's capital city, London, only 18 miles away, provides an unrivaled opportunity for students to enjoy such pleasures as theater, opera, concerts, art galleries, and museums. Through course-related study or School-chaperoned trips, in the evenings and on weekends, students are regularly encouraged to participate in as many educational experiences as possible.

On-campus activities include drama productions, choir, the School newspaper, Model UN, the Duke of Edinburgh Award Program, and the yearbook committee as well as School dances and movies.

A committee composed of students and teachers jointly coordinates and plans on-campus and off-campus recreational activities, including day trips (sightseeing, for example) and weekends away. Traditionally, the International Festival, Christmas Dinner Dance, Spring Prom, and May Fair are the highlights of the year.

The Community Service Program aims to help each student to develop skills outside the classroom, leading to a sense of involvement and greater responsibility for others. The commitment involves approximately 1 hour a week; students serve the School community by helping in the library or tutoring younger children, and they serve the local community by visiting homes for the elderly and disabled, participating in conservation projects, and raising funds for local charities. Special summer projects are also available.

DAILY LIFE

Classes commence at 8:25 daily and end at 3:15. In the Upper School, there are four 80-minute periods with a lunch break on Monday through Thursday. Fridays consist of eight 40-minute periods with a lunch break. Each upper school class meets three times a week, allowing a structured advisory and tutorial period during the day. Sports/activities time is between 3:30 and 5 p.m. each day, except Fridays. An upper school meeting is regularly scheduled for Wednesdays. No classes are held on Saturday or Sunday.

WEEKEND LIFE

Day students as well as boarders participate freely in organized social events on the weekends. These can include trips to the theater and concerts, the ballet, and professional sports events. The Activities Coordinator and Student Council members collaborate to develop a wide variety of activities. Day trips are organized to such destinations as Stratford-upon-Avon, Salisbury, Cambridge, Oxford, Canterbury, and Bath in the U.K., Lille in France, and a weekend trip to Christmas markets in Germany.

Excursions are chaperoned by a member of the faculty.

SUMMER PROGRAMS

During the summer, seven-week credit-based academic courses are offered in such subjects as math, English literature and composition, and international business, as well as enrichment courses such as the ShakespeareXperience, theater in London, study skills, English as a second language, film production, movie animation, and art. Some 370 students regularly participate from schools in the United States and from international schools all over the world. Faculty members from one or more TASIS schools constitute the majority of the summer administration, while qualified teachers and counselors from the United States and around the world make up the remaining summer faculty. Weekend travel is included in the program.

In addition to the courses in England, TASIS offers a variety of summer programs in France, Spain, and Switzerland to students from all over the world. From intensive study of painting, photography, and architecture at Les Tapies in the Ardèche to learning Spanish in Salamanca or French at Chateaux d'Oex in Switzerland, TASIS summer courses enrich the talents, skills, and interests of its participants.

COSTS AND FINANCIAL AID

In 2008–09, tuition and fees for day students were £5500–£17,500 per annum. Optional expenses, including costs for music lessons and horseback riding, are by private arrangement. Boarding fees, including tuition and costs for the October Travel Week were £26,750. Costs for the October Travel Week are included in the boarding fees. A recommended personal allowance is £50 per week.

There is a one-time-only Development Fund Fee of approximately £750 per student for on-campus building projects and an enrollment deposit of £1000 for day students and £2000 for boarders. The balance of fees becomes payable for each semester by July 1 and December 1.

Students are invited to apply for financial aid, which is granted on the basis of merit, need, and available funds. Early application for financial help is recommended. Each year the School awards approximately £250,000 in financial aid.

ADMISSIONS INFORMATION

Applications for admission are considered by the Admissions Committee upon receipt of a completed application form together with the application fee, three teachers' recommendations, and a transcript. Standardized test scores are requested, and a student questionnaire is required. An interview is recommended unless distance is a prohibiting factor. A decision is reached on the basis of a student's academic and social acceptability to the TASIS England School community. A student's nationality, religion, ethnic background, and gender play no part in the committee's decision, although availability of space in a certain dormitory (all are grouped by gender) is sometimes a limiting factor.

APPLICATION TIMETABLE

Applications are processed throughout the year. Visitors are welcome on campus at any time of the year. An interview by prior arrangement, even on very short notice, is recommended. It is preferable for visitors to choose days when school is in session in order to appreciate the working atmosphere of the community.

While early applications are encouraged, there is no final deadline, since a rolling admissions policy exists. Acceptances are made with the provision that students complete their current year in good standing. There is an application fee of £95.

ADMISSIONS CORRESPONDENCE

Bronwyn Thorburn-Riseley
Director of Admissions
TASIS The American School in England
Coldharbour Lane
Thorpe, Nr Egham
Surrey TW20 8TE
England

Phone: 44-1932-565252
Fax: 44-1932-564644
E-mail: ukadmissions@tasis.com

The TASIS Schools
2640 Wisconsin Avenue, NW
Washington, D.C. 20007

Phone: 202-965-5800
Fax: 202-965-5816
E-mail: usadmissions@tasis.com
Web site: http://www.tasis.com

TASIS THE AMERICAN SCHOOL IN SWITZERLAND

Montagnola-Lugano, Switzerland

Type: Coeducational boarding and day college-preparatory school
Grades: Pre-K–12, PG: Elementary School, pre-K–6; Middle School, 7–8; High School, 9–12, postgraduate year
Enrollment: School total: 561; High School: 329; Middle School: 61; Elementary School: 171
Head of School: Michael Ulku-Steiner, Headmaster

THE SCHOOL

TASIS The American School in Switzerland was founded in 1956 by Mrs. M. Crist Fleming to offer a strong American college-preparatory education in a European setting. TASIS was the first American boarding school to be established in Europe. Over time, it has become a school for students from more than fifty countries seeking an American independent school experience. The International Baccalaureate (IB) Program is also offered within this setting.

The objective of the School is to foster both the vital enthusiasm for learning and those habits that are essential to a full realization of each student's moral and intellectual potential. The curriculum gives special emphasis to the achievements of the Western heritage, many elements of which are easily accessible from the School's location. By providing an international dimension to education, the School stresses the need for young people to mature with confidence and competence in an increasingly interrelated world.

The beautiful campus is in the village of Montagnola, overlooking the city and the lake of Lugano, nestled among the southernmost of the Swiss Alps in the Italian-speaking canton of Ticino. Ideally situated in the heart of Europe, the School makes the most of its location by introducing students to European cultures and languages through extensive travel programs.

The TASIS Foundation, a not-for-profit Swiss foundation, owns the School. The TASIS Foundation also has a school near London and offers summer programs in England, Spain, and Italy as well as Switzerland. Alumni provide enthusiastic support for the School's activities and participate in annual reunions.

TASIS is accredited by the Council of International Schools (CIS) and the New England Association of Schools and Colleges (NEASC). The School is a member of the National Association of Independent Schools and the Swiss Group of International Schools.

ACADEMIC PROGRAMS

The minimum requirements for graduation from the high school college-preparatory program are 4 years of English, 3 years of history (including European and U.S. history), a third-year proficiency in a modern foreign language, 3 years of mathematics (through algebra II), 3 years of laboratory science (including physical and biological sciences), and 1 year of fine arts, plus senior humanities, sports/physical education, and community service requirements. Students must satisfactorily complete a minimum of 19 credits. Students are required to enroll in a minimum of five full-credit courses per year or the equivalent. A normal course load for students consists of six courses.

TASIS has an extensive EAL program, the goals of which are fluency in oral and written academic English and competence in a high school curriculum leading to the TASIS college-preparatory diploma.

TASIS offers a diverse and challenging curriculum, including the Advanced Placement Program (AP), the International Baccalaureate Diploma, and a wide range of required and elective courses. In 2008, 53 students were involved in the Advanced Placement Program, and ninety AP exams were taken in ten subject areas. Students may also select from among the range of International Baccalaureate courses, earning either certificates or the full diploma. In 2008, 79 students took 353 IB exams.

The average class size is 12; the teacher-student ratio is 1:6. The student's day is fully structured, including time for academics, sports and activities, meals and socializing, and supervised evening study hours. The grading system uses A to F for performance and assigns effort grades of 1 to 5, reflecting students' attitudes and application to their work. The academic year is divided into two semesters; grades and comment reports are sent home to parents five times a year.

The postgraduate year presents an additional opportunity to high school graduates who wish to spend an interim year in Europe before going on to college. Each postgraduate student can design a tailor-made course of study with the assistance and approval of the Academic Dean that enables him or her to explore and develop new interests, strengthen academic weaknesses, or concentrate in areas of strength or particular interest. The program includes course-related, in-program travel.

FACULTY AND ADVISERS

The faculty represents one of the School's strongest assets. Its members are a group of dedicated professionals who are enthusiastic about working with young people. Seventy-two percent of the faculty members have advanced degrees. There are 61 full-time teaching administrators and faculty members, of whom 31 are women and 30 are men. Twenty-two faculty members live on campus; the rest live nearby and participate in most campus activities. In addition to teaching, faculty members act as advisers, sports coaches, trip chaperones, and dormitory residents and help to create a warm, familylike atmosphere.

COLLEGE ADMISSION COUNSELING

The School employs 2 full-time college counselors, who meet with students individually and in groups during their junior and senior years. The college counseling office maintains an up-to-date reference library of college catalogs so that students can familiarize themselves with the wide variety of opportunities that are open to them. As a counseling resource, the School provides a small computer lab for college research. Many college admissions officers from universities in the United States and Europe visit the School and speak to students. TASIS is a testing center for the PSAT, SAT, SAT Subject Tests, ACT, TOEFL, and all AP and IB examinations.

Graduates are attending such colleges and universities as Redding and Nottingham Universities in the United Kingdom and such U.S. colleges and universities as Boston University, Colorado College, George Washington, Notre Dame, Stanford, and Tufts.

STUDENT BODY AND CONDUCT

The total student enrollment of 561 consists of 171 elementary day students, 273 middle and high school boarding students, and 117 middle and high school day students. They come from more than forty countries; 20 percent are American.

Each student is honor bound to abide by the rules, as defined in the *Student Handbook.* The Student-Faculty Review Board deals with infractions of School rules, with more serious offenses being handled by the School administration and Governing Board.

The students at TASIS bear a serious responsibility to conduct themselves not only in a way that does credit to them, to their School, and to their country of origin, but also in a way that is consistent with the high standards set by the citizens of the European countries they visit. For this reason, TASIS has established reasonable but definitive standards of behavior, attitude, and appearance for all of its students. The School reserves the right to ask any student to withdraw for failure to maintain these standards.

ACADEMIC FACILITIES

The historic and architecturally interesting seventeenth-century Villa De Nobili was the original building of the School and houses the dining hall and dormitories. An extension houses the administration and the School's science laboratories. Hadsall House contains classrooms and dormitories. Villa Monticello contains modern classrooms and the computer center and computer language lab. Villa Aurora contains classrooms and a theater, and the fine arts are housed in Ca'Gioia. Additional classes are held in the dormitories of Scuderia, Belvedere, and Casa del Sole. Additional dormitories are found in Panorama, Casa Norma, Balmelli, and Giani. Coach House has classrooms and photography studios. The School's Palestra houses a sports complex containing a gymnasium, a fitness center, a dance studio, locker rooms, a recreation lounge, and music rooms. The School recently completed the new 22,000-volume Mary Christ Fleming library, and a new theater and dormitory are scheduled for completion in 2009 and 2010 respectively. The newly renovated Casa Focolare houses Elementary School students from prekindergarten to second grade.

BOARDING AND GENERAL FACILITIES

There are twelve dormitories on campus, housing from as few as 6 to as many as 43 students. All dormitories have faculty supervision. Rooms accommodate from 2 to 4 students each. Although School facilities are closed during winter and spring vacations, optional faculty-chaperoned trips are offered for students who are unable to return home.

Two recreation centers and a snack bar serve as focal points for student social activities. Two fully qualified nurses are in residence.

ATHLETICS

Students are required to participate in either a varsity sport three days a week or recreational sports after classes. TASIS offers such recreational sports as soccer, basketball, fitness training, mountain biking, volleyball, rugby, tennis, track and field, squash, swimming, rock climbing, and aerobics. Horseback riding and tennis are available at an extra cost. On weekends, students often go on hiking and mountain-climbing trips in the Swiss Alps during the fall and spring and go skiing during the winter season. During the one-week ski term in Crans-Montana or Verbier, every student takes lessons in downhill or cross-country skiing or snowboarding. The Fleming Cup Ski Race is held during the Crans-Montana term.

Varsity sports give students the opportunity to compete against many schools in Switzerland and other countries and to take part in tournaments sponsored by the Swiss Group of International Schools. Varsity sports include rugby, soccer, volleyball, basketball, tennis, and track and field.

Facilities include a playing field, a gym, and an outdoor basketball/volleyball area. The newly constructed sports complex includes a gymnasium with seating for up to 400 spectators, a dance studio, a fitness center, changing rooms, and a student commons lounge.

EXTRACURRICULAR OPPORTUNITIES

The School's location in central Europe offers a wide range of cultural opportunities. Trips to concerts, art galleries, and museums in Lugano, Locarno, and Milan extend education beyond the classroom. All students participate in in-program travel, which consists of a four-day, faculty-chaperoned trip in the fall and a seven-day, faculty-chaperoned trip in the spring to such cities as Athens, Barcelona, Florence, Madrid, Munich, Nice, Paris, Prague, Rome, Venice, and Vienna.

On-campus activities include drama productions, choir, Model UN and Model Congress, the Environmental Club, Student Council and peer helping, tutoring programs, the yearbook, the literary magazine, and numerous community service opportunities, such as ACA (Assisting Children with AIDS), Habitat for Humanity, and the summer service trip to Africa. Parents Weekend, the Christmas Dinner Dance, the Lugano Boat Dinner Dance, the Spring Prom, and the Arts Festival are major School social events.

DAILY LIFE

Classes commence at 8 a.m. and follow a rotating schedule. Classes meet from 50 to 65 minutes. There is a weekly all-School assembly, and students meet with their advisers every day. Sports and activities take place after school until 5:30 p.m. Meals are self-service except for Wednesday evening, when students share a formal dinner with their adviser. Evening study hours are from 7 until 10.

WEEKEND LIFE

Both day and boarding students are encouraged to participate in organized social events on weekends, including such options as mountain-climbing and camping trips to scenic areas in Switzerland, shopping trips to open-air markets in northern Italy, and sightseeing excursions to Zurich, Milan, Venice, or Florence. On-campus events include talent shows, coffeehouses, films, and discotheque dances.

On weekends, students have Lugano town privileges if they have no School commitments and are in good academic and social standing. All excursions beyond Lugano are chaperoned by a member of the faculty, except those for seniors and some juniors, who, with parental permission, enjoy the privilege of independent travel in groups of 2 or more.

SUMMER PROGRAMS

The TASIS Summer Language Program offers three- and four-week sessions of intensive French, Italian, and English as a second language at beginning, intermediate, and advanced levels of instruction for students ages 14–18. Art history, drawing and painting, and digital photography are also offered. Approximately 350 students attend each session, a small number of whom are TASIS full-year students seeking credit or enrichment. The experienced staff is drawn from TASIS and other schools, and there are visiting faculty members as well. Sports, social activities, and excursions are parts of the program. Students also have the opportunity to participate in the AC Milan Junior soccer camp, under the supervision of AC Milan coaches.

The TASIS French Language Program, which is located in the French-speaking canton of Vaud, offers a five-week full-academic-credit course as well as a four-week session for students ages 11–17 who wish to improve their language skills or develop fluency.

TASIS also offers two sessions of summer camp language programs in French, Italian, and English for younger students. The Château des Enfants Program is for children ages 4–10, and the Middle School Program is for children ages 11–13.

COSTS AND FINANCIAL AID

The all-inclusive tuition fee is CHF 65,000; the enrollment deposit is CHF 3,500. This includes all fees that are necessary for attendance—room, board, tuition, eleven days of in-program travel, ski term, textbooks, laundry, and activities and lab fees. A weekly personal allowance of CHF 50–80 is recommended. Seventy percent of the tuition is due by July 1 and the remainder by November 15.

Students are invited to apply for financial aid, which is granted on the basis of merit, need, and the student's ability to contribute to the School community.

ADMISSIONS INFORMATION

All applicants are considered on the basis of previous academic records, three teachers' evaluations, and a personal statement. The SSAT is recommended, and the SLEP test is required for students whose native language is not English. TASIS does not discriminate on the basis of race, color, nationality, or ethnic origin in its admissions policies and practices.

Application for entrance is recommended only for those students with sufficient academic interest and motivation to benefit from the program. The School accepts students from pre-K to grade 12 and at the postgraduate level.

APPLICATION TIMETABLE

TASIS The American School in Switzerland has a rolling admissions policy and considers applications throughout the year. Applicants are encouraged to make an appointment to visit the campus. Within ten days of receipt of a completed application, the CHF 300 application fee, an official transcript from the previous school, and three teachers' evaluations, the Admissions Committee notifies the parents of its decision.

ADMISSIONS CORRESPONDENCE

Mr. William E. Eichner, Director of Admissions
TASIS The American School in Switzerland
CH-6926 Montagnola-Lugano
Switzerland

Phone: 41-91-960-5151
Fax: 41-91-993-2979
E-mail: admissions@tasis.ch
Web site: http://www.tasis.com

or

The TASIS Schools
1640 Wisconsin Avenue, NW
Washington, D.C. 20007

Phone: 202-965-5800
Fax: 202-965-5816
E-mail: usadmissions@tasis.com

THOMAS JEFFERSON SCHOOL

St. Louis, Missouri

Type: Coeducational boarding and day college-preparatory school
Grades: 7–12
Enrollment: 78
Head of School: William C. Rowe

THE SCHOOL

Thomas Jefferson School was founded in 1946. It has received national attention for its academic excellence and its teacher-trustee system, the two guiding ideas of the founders. It became coeducational in 1971. The campus is a 20-acre estate in Sunset Hills, a suburb 15 miles southwest of downtown St. Louis.

The School's mission is to give its students the strongest possible academic background, responsibility for their own learning, a concern for other people, and the resources to live happily as adults and become active contributors to society. Many of the School's unusual features, such as the daily schedule, are outgrowths of this mission.

The School is unique in its business organization. A majority of the members of its Board of Trustees must be teachers in the School; moreover, no one may teach full-time for more than five years without becoming a trustee. The Headmaster and the other teacher-trustees make up the administration of the School, with the exception of the Director of Development, who is not a faculty member. This structure gives teachers a greater stake in the School and a breadth of experience that produces better teaching.

Thomas Jefferson School is a member of the National Association of Independent Schools, the Association of Boarding Schools, the Independent Schools Association of the Central States, Midwest Boarding Schools, the School and Student Service for Financial Aid, and the Educational Records Bureau.

ACADEMIC PROGRAMS

Thomas Jefferson offers a challenging approach to learning, with the emphasis on the student's own efforts. Classes are short, and the teachers seldom lecture; instead, everyone is called on to answer questions and generate discussion. During afternoon and evening study time, the students have a good deal of freedom in choosing when and where to do their homework, with help readily available.

Seventh and eighth graders take English, mathematics, science, social studies, and Latin. In the ninth through twelfth grades, students take 4 years of English; 4 years of mathematics through calculus; 2 years of Greek (ninth and tenth grades); 2 years of Italian or French (tenth and eleventh); at least 2 years of science, including an AP course; and at least 2 years of history, including AP American history. Electives include more language and science courses and European history. Advanced Placement exams are a standard part of the courses in American history, European history, calculus, biology, advanced French, junior and senior English, physics, and chemistry. The faculty members also help students work toward AP exams in Latin, government, computer science, and studio art.

The English curriculum gives students intensive training in grammar, vocabulary, and writing skills. They also read and discuss a great deal of literature, including recognized classics (Shakespeare, the Bible, and epics), time-tested authors (Austen, Dickens, Dostoyevsky, Fitzgerald, Manzoni, Melville, and Shaw), and more recent major authors, such as Amy Tan, Ralph Ellison, and Chaim Potok.

A special feature is the study of classical Greek, which contributes to intellectual development (including concrete benefits such as enhanced vocabulary) and cultural background. This subject, in which the School is a national leader, continues to stir curiosity and ambition. A number of graduates continue to study it in college; others do so independently or later in life.

The average class size is 10, and the overall student-teacher ratio is 6:1. During the day, teachers are accessible to everyone and are ready to help; one teacher is on duty each evening and visits the students' rooms to assist with homework. There are no study halls except for younger new students and for those in academic difficulty.

The grading system uses letter grades of A, B, C, D, and E. An average of B– is Honors. To remain in good standing, a student must have no more than one D in any marking period; students in their first year, however, are allowed extra time to adjust. One-hour examinations are given at the end of the first and third quarters (October and April), and 2- to 3-hour examinations are given at midyear and at the end of the year (January and June). Following each exam period, a student's adviser sends the parents a letter discussing the student's progress and giving the latest grades and teachers' comments.

The unusually long Christmas and spring vacations (about one month each) give students an opportunity to unwind, spend time with their families, and do independent work for extra credit.

FACULTY AND ADVISERS

The faculty consists of 7 women and 6 men, including the Headmaster. Faculty members hold thirteen baccalaureate degrees, nine master's degrees, and one law degree.

William C. Rowe became the third Head of School in the summer of 2000, succeeding Lawrence Morgan. Mr. Rowe attended Thomas Jefferson School and Wesleyan University (A.B., 1967) and holds a master's degree from Washington University.

All faculty members are expected to continue educating themselves by regular reading, both within and outside the subject areas they teach. They meet periodically to report on their reading and to discuss it.

Currently, 5 of the 13 faculty members live on the campus. Each teacher, whether resident or not, has several duties besides teaching, such as athletics supervision, evening study help, and advising students. Teachers meet with each of their advisees regularly to check the student's grades and to keep in touch with his or her personal development. The School also has two Residential Assistants who live on the campus.

COLLEGE ADMISSION COUNSELING

The Headmaster visits a number of colleges each year; he and other faculty members help students decide where to apply. Guidance is provided throughout the application process, and great care is taken in writing recommendations.

In sixty-two years, the School has had 549 graduates; all have gone to college—most to well-known, selective institutions. Among the colleges and universities attended by Thomas Jefferson graduates in the past eight years are Boston University (3), Brown (2), Caltech (2), Carnegie Mellon (1), Carleton (1), Claremont-McKenna (1), Columbia (2), Duke (3), Emory (2), Harvard (1), Haverford (3), Johns Hopkins (2), Lake Forest (2), Northwestern (6), Pitzer (2), Pomona (3), Reed (3), Rensselaer (2), Rhodes (4), Smith (2), Stanford (1), Swarthmore (2), Vanderbilt (3), Washington (St. Louis) (7), Wesleyan (3), and the Universities of Missouri–Columbia (3) and Chicago (3).

Ten-year medians for the SAT are 710 critical reading and 670 math.

STUDENT BODY AND CONDUCT

In 2007–08, the School had 78 students (42 boarding, 36 day) enrolled as follows: seventh grade, 9; eighth grade, 8; ninth grade, 12; tenth grade, 18; eleventh grade, 17; and twelfth grade, 14. Most students come from the region between the Appalachians and the Great Plains. Approximately 29 percent are international students from various countries (ESL instruction is available, although some knowledge of English is required for admission). Most grades have girls and boys in about equal numbers.

A Student Council, whose members are elected twice a year, brings student concerns before the faculty and helps maintain a healthy, studious atmosphere. Collectively, the council has one vote in faculty meetings on any decision concerning student life.

Demerits are given for misconduct, lateness, and other routine matters; a student who receives too many demerits in one week has to do chores around the campus on Saturday. Students may appeal any demerits, even those given by the Headmaster, before a Student Appeals Court.

ACADEMIC FACILITIES

The Main Building, a former residence, provides a comfortable, homelike setting for classes and meals; it also contains teachers' offices, the business office, the library, computer terminals, and an art gallery. Sayers Hall, next to the Main Building, provides science laboratories, classrooms, and a library/computer annex. In 2008, the School opened a new art facility and built an addition onto the gymnasium.

BOARDING AND GENERAL FACILITIES

Boarders live in the Gables—a smaller building from the original estate—and in five modern one-story houses, built in 1960, plus one additional, similar house added in 1994. Each house has four double rooms; each room has an outside entrance, a private bath, large windows, wall-to-wall carpeting, and air conditioning. The houses were designed to provide quiet, privacy, and independence. Normally, 2 boarding students share a room with 1 or 2 day students. All dorm rooms provide phone and Internet access.

ATHLETICS

Thomas Jefferson School athletics are meant to help students relax, stay healthy and in good condition, and study better. Outdoor sports include tennis (five courts), soccer, and sometimes running, walking, cycling, or ice-skating at a nearby rink; indoor sports are volleyball and basketball (in the gymnasium) and sometimes aerobics. Athletics are required on Monday, Tuesday, Thursday, and Friday afternoons. There is competition with other local schools in basketball, soccer, and volleyball.

EXTRACURRICULAR OPPORTUNITIES

St. Louis has a wealth of resources in art, music, and theater, as well as an excellent zoo, a science museum, and a botanical garden. The faculty members keep the students informed and help provide them with transportation and tickets whenever possible. Teachers often take classes on field trips or invite students out informally. In recent years, groups have gone to the Ozarks for camping, to the Mississippi River to see bald eagles, and to many symphony concerts, ballets, and plays. Students also attend movies, sports events, and rock concerts.

Volunteer service is encouraged, and the School helps students find opportunities and use them. All students must plan and complete a required amount of voluntary community service before they graduate. Students are encouraged to pursue their own interests, such as music lessons, and the School helps make arrangements. A piano and a darkroom are available. Sometimes students organize and carry through a major project, such as producing the School yearbook (since 1981) or the student newspaper (since 1984).

DAILY LIFE

A school day begins with the 7:45 rising bell and breakfast at 8. Between 8:30 and 1:10, there are eight class periods of 35 minutes each, including lunch. In grades 10 through 11, students attend each of their four classes (grades 7 through 9 attend five classes) every day. Seniors, who have longer assignments, attend each class only four days a week. After lunch, a student may have a science lab, a language lab, or other supplementary academic work. Then they have an hour of athletics, perhaps a meeting with their adviser or study help from another teacher, and some independent time in which they are expected to start their homework for the next day. Supper is at 5:45, and evenings are devoted to study. On Wednesday and Friday afternoons, there are fine arts classes in such subjects as drawing, photography, ceramics, and art and music appreciation, and students may leave the campus for nearby shopping centers. Day students are on campus from about 8:30 to 5.

WEEKEND LIFE

Weekends are leisure time. As long as students are in good standing academically, they have considerable freedom and may leave the campus for movies, shopping, dates, and overnights. Older students may keep cars on campus at the discretion of the faculty. The sports facilities are available for weekend use. Dances are organized periodically by the Student Council.

SUMMER PROGRAMS

Thomas Jefferson has no summer school, but there have often been summer trips to Europe, led by the Headmaster. The size of the party has varied from 2 to 10 or more students, plus adults. Thomas Jefferson groups have stayed at the same pensione in Florence for more than thirty years.

COSTS AND FINANCIAL AID

Charges for 2008–09 were $33,900 for full boarding, $32,000 for weekday boarding, and $20,250 for day students. This includes room plus all meals for boarders and all lunches for day students. The School estimates that $2000 covers books, school supplies, and other expenses related to School activities. Optional off-campus activities such as music lessons (and the necessary transportation) cost extra.

A $2000 deposit, nonrefundable but credited to tuition, is required when a student enrolls. The balance of the tuition is paid through Sallie Mae's Tuition Pay program.

Financial aid is available, based on a student's need. About one fourth of the student body currently receives some financial aid; the total amount awarded is about $530,000. An applicant's family must file a statement with the School and Student Service, and this information is used in judging need. Many middle-income families receive some assistance.

ADMISSIONS INFORMATION

The School looks for signs of native intelligence, liveliness, energy, ambition, and curiosity. Good grades and high test scores are important considerations but not always the deciding ones. The School gives its own 2-hour battery of entrance tests; as an alternative, a candidate may submit the results of the Secondary School Admission Test (SSAT) or the Independent School Entrance Examination (ISEE). International students and others living abroad follow different procedures. About two thirds of those who complete the application process are accepted.

APPLICATION TIMETABLE

Inquiries and applications are welcome at any time. When an application (mailed with the catalog) comes in, the School writes or telephones the family to arrange a visit for testing and the interview. Prospective students usually spend a day at the School visiting classes, having lunch, and taking the tests. Acceptances are sent out in early March, although parents can be notified by January 1 if they inform the Director of Admissions that their child is applying for early decision. Any remaining places are filled by a rolling admissions system. Parents should reply within two weeks of acceptance. There is a $40 fee for domestic applications ($100 for international applications).

ADMISSIONS CORRESPONDENCE

Marie De Jesus, Director of Admissions
Thomas Jefferson School
4100 South Lindbergh Boulevard
St. Louis, Missouri 63127

Phone: 314-843-4151
Fax: 314-843-3527
E-mail: admissions@tjs.org
Web site: http://www.tjs.org

TILTON SCHOOL

Tilton, New Hampshire

Type: Coeducational boarding and day college-preparatory
Grades: 9–12, postgraduate year
Enrollment: 260
Head of School: James R. Clements

THE SCHOOL

Tilton School challenges students to embrace and navigate a world marked by diversity and change. Through the quality of human relationships, Tilton School's faculty cultivates in its students the curiosity, the skills, the knowledge and understanding, the character, and the integrity requisite for the passionate pursuit of lifelong personal success and service.

Tilton School values people. Students, faculty, staff, parents, and alumni are the cornerstones of the School. Students are at the center of the Tilton Experience, and Tilton enrolls young men and women capable of both contributing to and benefiting from the School. Tilton is committed to recruiting and supporting faculty and staff members who are dedicated, through both education and example, to the School's mission. Tilton seeks and expects a genuine partnership with parents, working together to challenge and support the students. While encouraging the alumni to be active in their School's life, there is also a commitment to honor them and their historic relationship to the School.

Tilton School values education—the active pursuit of knowledge and the growth of intellectual curiosity. The rigorous academic program is designed to prepare graduates to be successful college students and contributing members of society. Various pathways to learning are supported; the acquisition of genuine understanding is the goal. Tilton is committed to the principle that all students can excel. Through a broad range of learning experiences, students develop problem-solving skills and self-confidence while becoming independent and critical thinkers.

Tilton School values community and believes that the well-being of the whole community is founded on the fundamental principle of respect. The current moral, ethical, spiritual, cultural, and ecological dilemmas are explored. By doing so, a just and healthy School community and wider world are promoted.

Tilton School values commitment. All members of the School have a duty to commit themselves to learning, building a respectful community, and supporting the well-being of the School to the extent each is capable.

A nonprofit corporation, Tilton is governed by the Head of School and a 24-member Board of Trustees. Annual expenses of $8.8 million are met through tuition, endowment, and annual giving. The endowment currently totals $16 million. More than 5,200 living alumni have a beneficial impact on fund raising, with pledges and gifts to the School of more than $3 million annually for both annual and restricted purposes.

Tilton School is accredited by the New England Association of Schools and Colleges and is a member of the National Association of Independent Schools, the Independent Schools Association of Northern New England, the Cum Laude Society, the National Honor Society, the Secondary School Admission Test Board, and the Council for Religion in Independent Schools.

ACADEMIC PROGRAMS

Tilton's academic program offers a traditional college-preparatory curriculum framed within a twenty-first century skills-based program, supporting the student's intellectual maturation and encouraging the development of academic and personal competencies. The School seeks to produce students who have a genuine interest in intellectual pursuits, to teach students self-discipline, and to reinforce in students the sound moral and ethical judgment that are needed to successfully navigate the complex and changing world of the twenty-first century.

The school year is divided into two semesters. During each term, students at Tilton take a minimum of five full-credit courses. Required credits include English, mathematics, foreign language, fine arts, laboratory science, and social studies (history), for a total of 18.

Interdisciplinary standards in the five essential domains of Critical Thinking, Communication, Creativity, Community, and Character are the cornerstones of the curriculum.

The program of study for ninth grade students is a team-taught integrated program (FIRST) emphasizing a strong academic foundation and supportive intellectual, personal, and social development.

Additional grade-level programs are designed from Grade 10 through Grades 11, 12, and the postgraduate (PG) Year to support student growth and development in a purposefully designed developmental program. At the end of the tenth grade year, and prior to graduation, all students must provide evidence of learning that meets benchmark curriculum standards through participation in performance assessment programs, the Gateway Program (Grade 10), and the Capstone Program (Graduating class).

The average class size is 12 students, and the student-teacher ratio is 5:1. Evening study hall is supervised. Evening study hours are designed to allow for availability of resources and a quiet, uninterrupted study atmosphere where reinforcement of learned skills can be emphasized under direct supervision by faculty members. Academic focus is the primary purpose of evening study hall, which provides a balance of structure and self-directed study.

At Tilton School, student learning is assessed by measuring demonstrated performance of learned skills and knowledge against specific standards developed for grade levels, departments, and specific courses that have been structured within the school's twenty-first century skills-curriculum framework, with reference to national and state standards for specific academic disciplines. Within this system, letter grades mean the following; A = significantly exceeds the standard; B = exceeds the standard; C = meets the standard; D= does not yet meet the standard.

The Learning Center serves approximately 30 percent of the students, complementing their regular academic instruction by identifying individual needs and helping to devise strategies that enable them to achieve academic success. The center provides specialized instructional support for students whose academic progress is limited by deficiencies in basic skills or study habits, or by distinct learning-style differences. A 1:1 SAT tutorial is also offered through the center.

The English as a Second Language Program serves students who need intermediate and advanced English language support skills.

FACULTY AND ADVISERS

Tilton's faculty consists of 44 members (28 men and 16 women). All of the faculty members hold bachelor's degrees, and there are fifteen advanced degrees, including two Ph.D.'s. Most members of the faculty and administration live on campus with their families.

Faculty members must have not only a high level of expertise in their academic areas but also an enthusiastic commitment to students' interests and student life. In addition to dormitory and afternoon coaching and activity duties, most faculty members have 6 to 8 student advisees. The adviser is responsible for monitoring academic progress and for counseling in other areas of school life.

James R. Clements, appointed Head of School in 1998, is a graduate of the University of New Hampshire (B.A., 1972; M.B.A., 1998). Prior to joining Tilton, Mr. Clements spent twenty-one years at the Chapel Hill–Chauncy Hall School in Waltham, Massachusetts, most recently as Head of School from 1993–98.

COLLEGE ADMISSION COUNSELING

Three full-time counselors guide students in the selection of colleges and coordinate the application process, beginning in the junior year. Approximately 60 college admissions officers visit the School each year to talk with groups of students or to interview individual students.

Members of the class of 2005–08 were accepted at numerous colleges and universities, including Bowdoin, Boston University, Carnegie Mellon, Clarkson, Colby, Hobart and William Smith, Notre Dame, Syracuse, Union, Wesleyan, and the Universities of Massachusetts, New Hampshire, and Vermont.

STUDENT BODY AND CONDUCT

In 2008–09, Tilton enrolled 260 students—79 percent were boarders and 21 percent were day students. There were 167 boys and 93 girls. Tilton students represent many racial, religious, and socioeconomic backgrounds; approximately 67 percent come from New England, 14 percent come from other parts of the United States, and 19 percent come from other parts of the world.

Expectations at Tilton are high and are thoroughly communicated. Although the immediate goal of School rules and regulations is to promote order, mutual respect, and academic excellence, this structure serves, in the long range, to prepare students for productive and responsible roles in a changing society. At Tilton, there is a basic faith in young people. Guided by the attitude that students can learn and want to learn, faculty members are eager to inspire commitment, pride, and responsibility in their students.

ACADEMIC FACILITIES

Plimpton Hall houses twelve classrooms, three science laboratories, and other facilities, including the Computer Center and bookstore. Eight more classrooms are contained in Pfeiffer Hall and the lower level of the chapel. Pfeiffer Hall houses the Learning Center. The Helene Grant Daly Art Center provides excellent facilities for art classes, including ceramics, computer graphics, studio art, printmaking, sculpture, silk-screening, and photography. The Lucien Hunt Memorial Library contains approximately 17,500 volumes, including subscriptions to forty periodicals, four newspapers, and an online periodical index and encyclopedias. The library features ten computers, reading and conference rooms, and extensive facilities for research. Drama and musical productions are performed in the theater in Hamilton Hall.

A brand new facility connects Plimpton Hall to the west side of campus, creating the academic quad Tilton has long envisioned. The new 38,000-square-foot academic building includes a new Learning Center, wireless technology and SMART Boards throughout, state-of-the-art math and science classrooms/labs, a 100-seat lecture hall, a greenhouse, and foreign language labs and classrooms.

The Tilton campus is connected by a fiber-optic backbone that supports an Ethernet 10Base-T network. All classrooms and dormitories are wired and connected to the network, as is the library. Two CD-ROM towers service the network as well as an e-mail program. The network is serviced through a Novell parent package. All students have their own account, accessible through a password. The network supports Microsoft Works in the PC environment as well as the Macintosh environment. There are three labs—one has twelve Compaq EVO D300V machines, the second contains six Power Macintosh 6100/60 machines, and the third, in the School's library, contains ten Compaqs. The Macintosh lab is set up to support electronic music classes and computer art courses. An Internet link is available for student use in the library, PC lab, and dorm rooms with prearrangement.

BOARDING AND GENERAL FACILITIES

Six dormitories, each housing 18 to 48 students and 1 to 4 faculty members and their families, are located on campus. Students live in double or single rooms. Returning students may state their preference for room assignments. Students whose homes are a long distance from Tilton may visit with friends or family during vacations.

The new 15,000-square-foot dormitory houses 20 students and includes three faculty apartments. Highlights of the new facility include a two-story common room, a group study room, suite-style rooms (two double rooms that share a common bathroom), a recreation room, a laundry area, and storage space.

The school store, MARC Student Center, and the snack bar are open at various times of the day and evening. There is a six-bed health center, licensed as a hospital, with a resident nurse and a doctor on call.

ATHLETICS

The School believes that people of all ages perform best when they are active and healthy and that organized sports promote physical development, physical courage, self-discipline, and a sense of team spirit. All students must participate in an afternoon activity. Students must play at least one sport each year to fulfill their annual +5 Program requirements.

Each year, approximately twenty-five different teams are formed. Boys' sports include baseball, basketball, football, ice hockey, lacrosse, soccer, tennis, and wrestling. Girls' sports are basketball, field hockey, ice hockey, lacrosse, soccer, softball, and tennis. Coed sports include Alpine skiing, cross-country running, golf, and snowboarding.

Facilities include 25 acres of outstanding playing fields, 3 miles of cross-country trails, three tennis courts, a gymnasium, a field house with an indoor ice rink, and an outdoor swimming pool. The golf team uses a nearby eighteen-hole course.

EXTRACURRICULAR OPPORTUNITIES

Tilton's +5 Program, distinctive among independent secondary schools, requires that all students involve themselves in five areas of nonacademic campus life: art and culture, team athletics, outdoor experiences, community services, and leadership roles. These learning experiences enhance self-confidence and self-esteem.

By structuring extracurricular activities, the School broadens students' interests, enables them to develop skills that enhance their self-worth, and provides enjoyment during their free time. Faculty members' commitment to excellence and their guidance encourage and reassure students who may be doubtful of their abilities. As a result, strong relationships develop, and students and teachers work together more effectively in the classroom. Students choose afternoon activities in athletics, performing arts, and the outdoors.

Offerings in art and culture include drama, musical theater, tech crew, ceramics, graphic design, photography, and chorus.

Throughout the school year, there are opportunities to participate in outdoor trips for canoeing, mountain biking, Alpine skiing, fishing, rock climbing, hiking, snowshoeing, or cross-country skiing.

Community service opportunities are available both on campus and in the Tilton community. This division of the +5 Program encourages students to commit themselves to helping others. Other projects include helping at a soup kitchen; reading to patients at the New Hampshire Veterans' Home; tutoring local children; raising funds for UNICEF, Oxfam, and Toys for Tots; and teaching in a learn-to-skate program for young children.

Leadership may be the most important of the five areas. Experience as a dorm proctor, work-program supervisor, Student Council officer, editor, or team captain offers a rigorous challenge.

Movies, plays, lectures, and concerts are regular events on campus, while trips to museums and theaters in Boston are regular off-campus activities.

DAILY LIFE

Class periods are approximately 45 minutes long, with each class meeting once a week for a double period. Mid-morning each day, there is a meeting either with advisee groups, special committees, or the entire School at School Meeting, which is held two times per week. Conference period and work programs are also part of daily life. The conference period is an opportunity to meet teachers for extra help or to make an appointment to meet a teacher later in the evening for more extensive work.

After classes, everyone participates in after-school programs. Wednesday and Saturday schedules are half days, which allows time for athletic competitions and program activities.

WEEKEND LIFE

Faculty and staff teams plan all weekend activities with student support. Saturday events include sports competitions, movies, dances, concerts, and trips to shopping areas and movie theaters. The gym, field house, student center, and art center are periodically open both Saturday and Sunday. Sunday is for scheduled activities, both on and off the campus. Day students are invited to participate and are active in weekend life.

COSTS AND FINANCIAL AID

For 2008–09, tuition, room, and board cost $40,750; tuition for day students was $23,750. Additional expenses, such as those for books and laundry, range from $600 to $1000. Private music or voice lessons, skiing, snowboarding, learning center sessions, and ESL classes are charged separately. Tuition may be paid in full in mid-July, or families can take advantage of one of Tilton's payment plan options.

Thirty-eight percent of the students receive financial aid in the form of direct grants and/or loans. For 2008–09, more than $2 million in aid was granted. Applications for aid, which should be made before February 15, are reviewed separately from admission decisions.

ADMISSIONS INFORMATION

The Admissions Committee seeks to admit students who will benefit from and contribute to Tilton and those of diverse backgrounds and individual personal strengths. Students with various academic abilities who seek to challenge themselves and take advantage of Tilton's programs within and outside the classroom are excellent candidates for admission. Candidates for the ninth and tenth grades should take the SSAT and have the results sent to Tilton. Eleventh and twelfth graders and postgraduates should take the PSAT or SAT. The most important application requirements for admission are the student's school transcript and current teacher recommendations. All prospective students are expected to visit the School and interview with the Admission Office. Students may enter at all grade levels; entry in the eleventh or twelfth grade or the postgraduate year is more competitive.

APPLICATION TIMETABLE

Initial inquiries are welcome at any time but are recommended before the late spring prior to the year in which admission is sought. Ideally, applications (accompanied by a $50 application fee) should be filed by February 1. The Admission Office is open for interviews on weekdays and on selected Saturday mornings. It is best to plan a visit while school is in session.

Admission decisions are made on a rolling basis after March 10. The School adheres to the Parents' Reply Date of April 10. A nonrefundable deposit is required to hold a place at Tilton and is applied to tuition for the year.

ADMISSIONS CORRESPONDENCE

Beth Skoglund
Director of Admissions
Tilton School
Tilton, New Hampshire 03276

Phone: 603-286-1733
Fax: 603-286-1705
E-mail: admissions@tiltonschool.org
Web site: http://www.tiltonschool.org

TRINITY–PAWLING SCHOOL

Pawling, New York

Type: Boys' boarding (9–PG) and day (7–PG) college-preparatory school
Grades: 7–12, postgraduate year
Enrollment: 330
Head of School: Archibald A. Smith III, Headmaster

THE SCHOOL

The Pawling School was founded in 1907 by Dr. Frederick Gamage. In 1946, it was renamed Trinity-Pawling School in recognition of its ties with Trinity School of New York City. In 1978, Trinity-Pawling School became a separate educational and corporate entity. Trinity-Pawling's Episcopal background is reflected in daily chapel services and course offerings in religion, ethics, and psychology. On weekends, boarding students attend services in the School chapel, at a Roman Catholic church, or at a synagogue.

The School is located 68 miles north of New York City along the Connecticut border; regular train service is available from Grand Central Station to Pawling (population 5,000). The campus, set on 140 acres of rolling hills, is just over an hour's drive from New York's major airports. On vacations, the School transports students to and from the airports and train stations.

It is Trinity-Pawling's belief that an appreciation of one's own worth can best be discovered by experiencing the worth of others, by understanding the value of one's relationship with others, and by acquiring a sense of self-confidence that comes through living and working competently at the level of one's own potential. Trinity-Pawling respects and recognizes the differences in individuals and the different processes required to achieve their educational potential.

The School is governed by a self-perpetuating 26-member Board of Trustees. The School raises more than $1 million in Annual Giving, in part from its more than 4,000 alumni. The School's endowment exceeds $29 million, and its operating budget for 2008–09 is more than $10 million.

Trinity-Pawling is accredited by the New York State Association of Independent Schools and chartered by the New York State Board of Regents. It is a member of the National Association of Independent Schools, the Secondary School Admission Test Board, the New York State Association of Independent Schools (NYSAIS), and the National Association of Episcopal Schools.

ACADEMIC PROGRAMS

To graduate from Trinity-Pawling, a student must obtain a minimum of 112 credits. A full-year course is worth 6 credits, and a term course (trimester) is worth 2 credits. If a student enters after grade 9, his school record is evaluated and translated into Trinity-Pawling's system.

The total number of required credits is 102, distributed as follows: 24 credits in English; 18 credits in mathematics; 18 credits in a laboratory science; 18 credits in social studies; 12 credits in a foreign language; 6 credits in fine, performing, or manual arts (music, art, drafting, or drama); 4 credits in religion or philosophy; and 2 credits in health. Elective courses must be taken to make up the additional 10 credits. Advanced Placement courses are offered in English, U.S. history, European history, chemistry, physics, biology, mathematics, computer science, Latin, French, and Spanish. No credit is given for physical education courses since they are required by New York State law.

Students carry a minimum of five courses per term. Evening study periods, held in student residences, are supervised by dorm masters. Students with academic difficulty have a formally supervised study hall. Teachers are available to give students extra help at any time that is agreeable to both. Reports are posted online for parents three times per term. Trinity-Pawling uses a number grading system (0–100) in which 60 is passing, 80 qualifies for honors, and 85 qualifies for high honors.

In addition to academic grades, the School utilizes a unique effort system to rank students based on overall effort in many aspects of School life, including academics, athletics, clubs, and dormitory life. A student's privileges are then tied to his overall effort ranking. This program is designed to work in conjunction with the School's philosophy of encouraging each student to work toward his own personal potential.

The Language Program, open to a maximum of 40 students, is initiated in the ninth and tenth grades. A modification of the Orton-Gillingham method, it strives to retrain students with developmental dyslexia. First-year students work in pairs with tutors. In addition, they take a skills-oriented language arts course. Phonetics, sequencing ideas, handwriting, memorization, and other language skills are emphasized. The second-year student is placed in an analytical writing class in addition to a skills-level English class. All students in the program also take basic history, mathematics, and science courses. The program's goal is to enable students to complete Trinity-Pawling's regular college-preparatory curriculum. Students in the program are not required to take a foreign language but may elect to do so.

FACULTY AND ADVISERS

There are 55 full-time members of the faculty, all of whom reside on the campus. Members of the teaching faculty hold fifty-five baccalaureate and thirty-five graduate degrees. All participate in counseling and advising students. The School actively supports advanced study for its teachers during summers and other holidays.

Archibald A. Smith III was appointed Headmaster in 1990, after having served at Trinity-Pawling as a chemistry teacher, Director of College Placement, and Assistant Headmaster at various times since 1975. He is a graduate of St. John's School in Houston, Texas; Trinity College (Hartford) (B.S., 1972); and Wesleyan University (M.S., 1980). His career also includes teaching at the Northwood School in Lake Placid, New York. Mr. Smith is the past president of the New York State Association of Independent Schools and a member of the Accreditation Council of NYSAIS. He is a trustee of Dutchess Day School, a trustee of the International Boys School Coalition, a trustee of the Parents' League of New York, and is a member of the Headmasters Association.

COLLEGE ADMISSION COUNSELING

Trinity-Pawling's Director of College Counseling works closely with other administrators and faculty members to advise and aid students and their families with college placement. Individual meetings and group workshops are held on a regular basis, and more than 80 college representatives visit the campus each fall for presentations and interviews. More than 95 percent of the class of 2008 gained admission to their first- or second-choice college.

All of the 2008 graduates earned college or university acceptances. Among those they attend are Boston College, Clarkson, Colby, Colgate, College of Charleston, Columbia, Connecticut College, Fordham, Georgetown, Hobart and William Smith, Lehigh, Sacred Heart, Saint Michael's (Vermont), Syracuse, Trinity, Wesleyan, and the Universities of Illinois at Urbana-Champaign, Maryland, North Carolina, and Toledo.

STUDENT BODY AND CONDUCT

Boarding students number 240, and day students number 90. Students come from twenty-nine states and thirteen countries. Students from minority groups make up 18 percent of the total enrollment. Students who choose Trinity-Pawling tend to desire a reasonably structured community that is dedicated to individual growth. A strong academic program in harmony with fine athletics and activities programs brings the School together. The School seeks students who want to actively pursue their academic and social development in a caring atmosphere.

Major violations of community rules are handled by a Faculty-Student Disciplinary Committee, which makes recommendations to the Headmaster. Less serious breaches are handled by the Dean of Students and others.

The Student-Faculty Senate is composed of School prefects and elected student and faculty representatives. The senate works to develop self-government, plans School activities, and fosters a bond between the students and the faculty. It consists of six committees, each with a responsibility for specific areas of School life.

ACADEMIC FACILITIES

The Dann Building (1964) and the Science and Technology Center (2002) house classrooms and science and computer labs. The Art Building, completed in 2004, houses the fine arts, theater, and music programs. This building contains a theater that is used for student productions, lectures, and visiting professional performances. The library features an online catalog, more than 28,000 volumes, and available computers. It is located in the historic Cluett Building, which also contains administrative offices and the student center.

BOARDING AND GENERAL FACILITIES

Students reside in single or double rooms in eighteen dormitory units located in eight buildings, including Starr Hall (1984), Starr East (1987), and Cluett (renovated 1995). Each is under the supervision of 1 or more faculty members aided by senior proctors. Students are allowed to choose roommates, and, whenever possible, housing choice is granted. Students are grouped in housing units according to grade level. A student's dorm master is usually his adviser, so a strong personal relationship often develops. Trinity-Pawling stresses the value of close student-faculty relationships.

Students enjoy a School store and snack bar that are open daily. The Scully Dining Hall is currently under construction and will be completed for the opening of the 2009 academic year. Medical services are provided by the Health Center, staffed by a resident nurse and a doctor who makes daily visits. Several hospitals serve the area. Trinity-Pawling is within walking distance of the village of Pawling.

ATHLETICS

Trinity-Pawling is a member of the New England Private School Athletic Conference and the Founders League, which affords it the opportunity to play schools in New England, such as Avon, Choate, Hotchkiss, Kent, Loomis Chaffee, Salisbury, Taft, and Westminster. Because the School believes that athletics and physical development are key ingredients in a student's growth, all students are required to participate in the program during the school year. Three or four levels of teams are formed in each interscholastic sport, including baseball, basketball, cross-country, football, golf, hockey, lacrosse, soccer, squash, tennis, track and field, and wrestling. Also offered at both the interscholastic and intramural levels are running, skiing, and weight training.

The Carleton Gymnasium contains a 50-foot by 90-foot basketball court with two cross courts for practice. The lower floor and wing contain weight-training rooms, five international squash courts, and locker rooms. There are also six soccer fields, a new stadium, football fields, baseball fields, an all-weather track, twelve tennis courts, three lacrosse fields, ponds for skating and fishing, the McGraw wrestling pavilion, and the enclosed Tirrell Hockey Rink, which underwent a $1 million renovation in 2007.

EXTRACURRICULAR OPPORTUNITIES

Each student is encouraged to participate in one or more of the twenty-four activities offered on the campus. These activities are often initiated and directed by the students with the guidance of an interested faculty adviser. Among the offerings are the student newspaper, Model United Nations, the Minority Student Union, the yearbook, the choir, the photography club, the dramatic club, the chess club, the computer club, the fishing club, foreign language clubs, jazz groups, and the outing club. Trinity-Pawling encourages student initiative in starting new activities.

The School sponsors regular trips to nearby areas of educational and cultural interest, including museums and theaters in New York City. Annual events include Parents' Weekend, Junior Parents' Weekend, and several alumni functions. The concert series, offering five concerts annually, brings a rich variety of musical talent to the campus during the school year.

Each student participates in the work program that emphasizes the School's policy of self-responsibility and economy of operation. Boys assist with parts of the routine maintenance work throughout the buildings and on the grounds.

DAILY LIFE

At 8 a.m., four mornings a week, a brief community chapel service is held for all students. Classes are scheduled from 8:20 until 2:40 four days a week and until noon on Wednesdays and Saturdays. Wednesday and Saturday afternoons are reserved for interscholastic sports events. Athletic practices take place in the afternoon, while most extracurricular activities are scheduled in the evening. Lunches are generally served cafeteria-style, dinners sit-down family-style. Students are required to study from 7:30 to 9:30 in their rooms, the library, or the study hall, depending upon their academic status.

WEEKEND LIFE

Dances, plays, concerts, trips to New York City, and informal activities are planned for weekends. The Student-Faculty Senate organizes and plans many of the weekend activities. Social activities are also arranged with girls' schools in the area. Weekend leaves from the School are based upon a group rating, which encompasses a student's record in academic effort and achievement, general citizenship, and dormitory life. In general, as the group rating increases, so do the amount and nature of privileges. Students are evaluated twice per term.

COSTS AND FINANCIAL AID

Charges for 2008–09 were $41,250 for boarding students, $29,150 for day students in ninth through twelfth grade, and $20,150 for day students in seventh and eighth grade. Extra expenses total approximately $2000 per year. The Language Program is an additional $4900–$7000 per year, depending on the grade. A tuition payment plan and tuition insurance are available.

Thirty-five percent of the students receive a total of over $2 million in financial aid each year. Trinity-Pawling subscribes to the School and Student Service for Financial Aid and grants aid on the basis of need.

ADMISSIONS INFORMATION

Trinity-Pawling seeks the well-rounded student who will both gain from and give to the School. New students are accepted in all grades; a limited number are accepted for the postgraduate year. Selection is based upon all-around qualifications without regard to race, color, creed, or national origin. Candidates must submit a complete transcript plus two or three teachers' recommendations, have a personal interview at the School, and take the SSAT. Candidates for the Language Retraining Program are asked to have completed a Wechsler Test (WISC-R).

In 2008, there were 385 applicants, of whom 250 were accepted and 130 enrolled.

APPLICATION TIMETABLE

Initial inquiries are welcome at any time. Campus tours and interviews (allow 1½–2 hours) can be arranged by appointment, Monday through Friday, 8:30–1:30, and on Saturday, 8:30–11. All candidates must have an interview. The completed forms must be accompanied by a nonrefundable fee of $40 ($100 for international students).

Fall is the usual time for applying, and notification of acceptance begins in early March. Parents are expected to reply to acceptances one month after notification.

ADMISSIONS CORRESPONDENCE

MacGregor Robinson
Director of Admission
Trinity-Pawling School
Pawling, New York 12564
Phone: 845-855-4825
Fax: 845-855-4827
E-mail: kdefonce@trinitypawling.org
Web site: http://www.trinitypawling.org

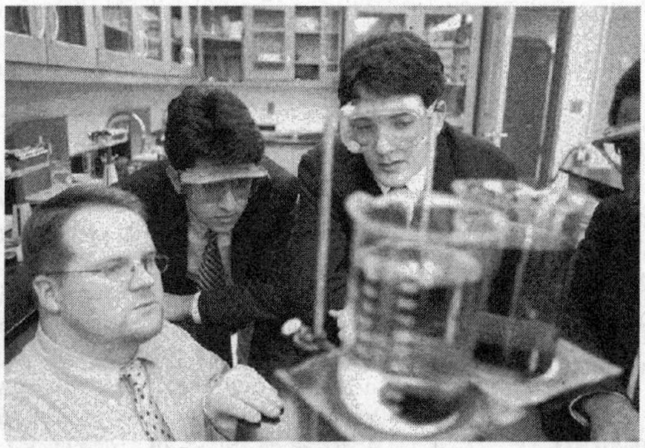

THE UNITED WORLD COLLEGE–USA

Montezuma, New Mexico

UNITED WORLD COLLEGES

Type: Coeducational boarding college-preparatory school
Grades: 11–12 (International Baccalaureate Diploma Program)
Enrollment: 200
Head of School: Lisa Darling, President

THE SCHOOL

The United World College–USA (UWC–USA) is one of thirteen worldwide secondary schools affiliated with the International Board of the United World Colleges (UWC), whose central office is in London. Other UWC schools are located in Bosnia and Herzegovina, Canada, Costa Rica, Hong Kong, India, Italy, the Netherlands, Norway, Singapore, Swaziland, Venezuela, and Wales. The term "college" is used in the British sense, meaning the last two years of schooling before entry into a university. UWCs host some of the brightest, most motivated, and most engaging students from around the world. The principal goal of the United World College schools is to make education a force to unite people, nations, and cultures for peace and a sustainable future.

The admission office of the UWC–USA is responsible for the selection of all U.S. students for all the UWCs. Fifty U.S. students are selected each year, and all are awarded Davis Scholarships, which cover full tuition, room, and board at a United World College. Additional need-based assistance is available for pocket money, travel, and insurance to all students who qualify

The UWC schools offer students from all socioeconomic, religious, political, and geographic backgrounds the opportunity to live, study, and work together in an intensive two-year course of study. The academic program prepares students for the International Baccalaureate (I.B.) exams.

Graduates traditionally enter the finest universities in the world, and students who receive I.B. diplomas may qualify for advanced standing at U.S. colleges and universities.

UWC–USA is near the Pecos Wilderness in the Sangre de Cristo mountain range. It is a 70-mile drive from Santa Fe and 130 miles from Albuquerque. The campus is located on the site of the restored Montezuma Hotel, a century-old resort hotel developed by the Santa Fe Railroad Company. The building is officially known as the Davis International Center, while informally it has been known as "The Castle" for three generations. Visitors are attracted by the area's climate, nearby hot springs and historic sites, and its proximity to the southern Rocky Mountains.

UWC–USA is accredited by the Independent Schools Association of the Southwest (ISAS) and the International Baccalaureate Organisation (IBO) and is approved by the state of New Mexico.

ACADEMIC PROGRAMS

To earn the I.B. diploma, students must successfully complete six subjects discussed below. Of these, three are taken at the Higher Level, typically 4 hours of class work each week; the other three are taken at the Standard Level, usually 3 hours per week. Courses last two years.

Group 1, or Language A, is the language in which the student is most fluent. Students study the literature associated with the language as well as world literature in translation. English, Spanish, and French are currently taught, and help is also provided for those who wish to prepare for exams in other languages. Group 2, or Language B, is a second language, chosen from English, Spanish, and French. Group 3, Society and Individuals, includes economics, social anthropology, European history, and geography. Group 4, Science, includes biology, environmental systems and society, chemistry, and physics. In Group 5, Mathematics, a variety of courses are offered to meet the needs and interests of each student. For Group 6, students may choose art, music, theater arts, or a second subject from Group 2, 3, or 4. In addition, every student takes Theory of Knowledge, an interdisciplinary course that enables students to critically examine their academic experiences at the School and to reflect on the knowledge they are acquiring.

Students are required to undertake original research and write an extended essay of 4,000 words. This project offers the opportunity to investigate a topic of special interest and acquaints students with the type of independent research and writing skills expected at a university.

FACULTY AND ADVISERS

There are 26 full-time faculty members and 4 part-time faculty members. Eighteen hold master's degrees, and 8 have doctorates from both U.S. and international universities. Twenty-six teachers and administrators live on campus. All faculty members act as academic advisers and involve themselves in activities as participants or leaders. Some faculty members are resident tutors and dormitory supervisors.

COLLEGE ADMISSION COUNSELING

The University Advisor counsels students on college preparation, selection, and application. An extensive library of references and guides is available to students. Each year more than 100 American colleges and universities make on-campus presentations and offer interviews to interested students. Students are engaged in an active college advising program.

Graduates matriculate at some of the world's most selective universities. In recent years, approximately 20 percent of UWC–USA alumni have matriculated at Ivy League colleges. Many graduates attend universities across the world as well, including Cambridge, the London School of Economics, and St. Andrews in the U.K.; McGill and Trent in Canada; and national and private universities of more than thirty other countries.

STUDENT BODY AND CONDUCT

About 200 students are enrolled each year at the United World College–USA, with 100 in each class of the two-year program. There are about 150 international students and 50 U.S. students. Approximately eighty countries are represented each year. About 90 percent of the students receive considerable scholarship support.

There is a written code of conduct. The vice president, dean of students, and resident tutors handle disciplinary matters.

ACADEMIC FACILITIES

The Castle houses classrooms, offices, two dormitories, the dining hall, and the student center. The Old Stone Hotel houses classrooms, faculty and administrative offices, and the library. Various other buildings house science labs and classrooms, a technology center, a language lab and classrooms, an art studio, and music rooms. Other facilities include an auditorium with a stage and the Dwan Light Sanctuary, a nondenominational chapel.

The library has five study areas; contains 18,000 volumes, several encyclopedias, and other reference materials; and subscribes to sixty-seven magazines and thirteen newspapers. Students also have access to online reference services.

BOARDING AND GENERAL FACILITIES

There are six dormitories, each housing from 24 to 40 students. Students share rooms and have access to a common room with a kitchen as well as computer and study rooms. Men and women live in separate dorms. Resident tutors check on all students every night. Two nearby physicians are on 24-hour call. A registered nurse runs the infirmary and treats minor ailments.

ATHLETICS

The Edith Lansing Field House opened in 2002. It contains an indoor multipurpose gymnasium, weight room, dance studio, and squash and racquetball courts. There are also a small indoor pool, several playing fields, and outdoor tennis and basketball courts.

The campus is surrounded by forest and nature trails. There is a skating pond nearby and easy access to hiking, biking, running, and rock climbing. There are no interscholastic sports, but there is an active informal intramural program of basketball, volleyball, and soccer.

EXTRACURRICULAR OPPORTUNITIES

All students are expected to participate actively in the cocurricular programs.

The wilderness program, which promotes fitness and develops teamwork and leadership, consists of environmental studies, navigation, wilderness first aid, and search and rescue. Students who are part of the school's search and rescue team assist when called for emergency searches in the northern New Mexico wilderness areas.

Community service programs promote interaction with the local community. Service can involve working with the elderly, being a peer educator in the local high schools, working in the sustainable agriculture program, or helping on construction projects like adobe church renovation.

There is an active Wellness Program in which students make presentations about health-related topics to peers and to local schools as a community service. An active Cross-cultural and Spirituality Program offers meditation, yoga, guest speakers, and student presentations on religious and cultural topics. The Bartos Institute for the Constructive Engagement of Conflict has generated an extensive Global Issues and Conflict Resolution training program.

Among the other extracurricular activities offered are programs and discussions on world affairs, an on-campus film series, weekend expeditions in conjunction with the wilderness program, cultural activities, drama, photography, choir, and instrumental groups. Students attend cultural events in Albuquerque and Santa Fe.

Students plan and present national days—celebrations of their country's and region's heritage—with traditional foods, music and dance programs, and games.

DAILY LIFE

Six and a half hours a day, Monday through Friday, are devoted to academics. There are no scheduled classes on weekends. Most school days run from 8:30 to 2:30, with breaks, lunch, services, and activities scheduled into the day. Dinner is served from 6 to 7, and activities and studying take up most of the evening hours. During the 3-hour activity period in the afternoon, students are involved in sports, community service, or wilderness activities.

WEEKEND LIFE

On weekends, students participate in activities on and off campus. Off-campus activities include camping trips, ski trips, excursions, and trips to Santa Fe, Taos, or Albuquerque. Students may leave the campus on weekends with their parents' permission.

COSTS AND FINANCIAL AID

All accepted U.S. students are awarded Davis Scholarships. The Davis Scholars competition is a national scholarship program for U.S. students. Davis Scholars receive merit scholarships covering tuition, room, and board for two years of study at a UWC school. The Davis Scholar awards are made possible through major funding to the endowment of the United World College by donors Shelby and Gale Davis. "Our contribution is intended to prepare a growing cadre of young Americans for global opportunities in the twenty-first century," says Mr. Davis, founder and CEO of Davis Selected Advisors, a major mutual fund and money management firm.

Families seeking consideration for additional need-based assistance, such as for travel and pocket money, should contact the Office of Admissions to request a Parent Financial Statement form after their child has been accepted.

ADMISSIONS INFORMATION

All U.S. students apply to the UWCs through the U.S. selection process outlined at the admission section of the Web site (http://www.uwc-usa.org). Students are admitted on the basis of merit. Davis Scholars are academically motivated and also have personal attributes of responsibility, motivation, perseverance to follow through in both academic and nonacademic areas, and a tolerance and openness toward different attitudes and customs.

A candidate entering the Davis Scholar competition completes a written application and submits academic transcripts and test scores. Standardized test scores may be from any one of the following tests: PLAN, PSAT, SAT, or ACT. Written recommendations from a teacher, an activity adviser, and a school guidance counselor are also required. The online application and all forms can be accessed on the admission section of the Web site.

Candidates are judged on academic record, test scores, recommendations, character, and commitment to serving others. Davis Scholars are U.S. citizens or permanent residents and must be either 16 or 17 by September 1 of the year they intend to enroll in a UWC.

Students from abroad are selected by approved national selection committees. The United World Colleges adhere to the principle that the admission of students and the employment of teachers should be conducted irrespective of race, nationality, religion, and political background.

APPLICATION TIMETABLE

Completed applications for the Davis Scholars competition must be received by early January. After the January deadline, a group of finalists are selected to advance to an interview process in March. Notifications of the results of the selection process are sent out in mid-April.

ADMISSIONS CORRESPONDENCE

Tim Smith, Director of Admission and University Advising
UWC–USA
P.O. Box 248
Montezuma, New Mexico 87731
Phone: 505-454-4245
Fax: 505-454-4294
E-mail: admission@uwc.usa.org
Web site: http://www.uwc-usa.org

VALLEY FORGE MILITARY ACADEMY & COLLEGE

Wayne, Pennsylvania

VALLEY FORGE MILITARY ACADEMY

Type: Boys' college-preparatory and coeducational transfer college military boarding school
Grades: 7–PG: Middle School, 7–8; Upper School, 9–PG
Enrollment: 565
Head of School: Charles A. McGeorge, President

THE SCHOOL

The 120-acre campus of Valley Forge Military Academy includes a boys' boarding preparatory high school and a coeducational transfer college, located 15 miles west of Philadelphia. The mission of Valley Forge is to educate individuals to be fully prepared to meet their responsibilities, alert in mind, sound in body, and considerate of others and to have a high sense of duty, honor, loyalty, and courage. Valley Forge fosters these goals through a comprehensive system that is built on the five cornerstones of academic excellence, character development, personal motivation, physical development, and leadership.

The Academy is accredited by the Middle States Association of Colleges and Schools. It holds memberships in the Association of Military Colleges and Schools of the United States, the Council for Religion in Independent Schools, the Boarding School Headmasters' Association, the International Boys School Coalition (IBSC), and the National Association of Independent Schools. The U.S. Department of the Army designates Valley Forge as an honor unit with distinction.

ACADEMIC PROGRAMS

Valley Forge seeks to educate and develop students for college entrance, career success, and responsible citizenship. A challenging curriculum, dedicated faculty members, small classes, individual attention, and faculty-supervised evening study hall provide cadets with an environment conducive to attaining academic success. The acquisition of knowledge, the development of skills, and the shaping of attitudes are emphasized to enable cadets to excel academically and to inspire them to pursue education throughout life.

The school year extends from late August to early June and is divided into two semesters; each has two marking periods. At the end of each marking period, grades are sent to parents. Unsatisfactory grades result in special afternoon help and extra study hall, with biweekly evaluations forwarded to parents. Evening study hall is required of all students. Cadets are placed in one of three college-preparatory curricula—honors, intermediate, or standard—according to aptitude level or achievement. The grading system uses A to F with pluses and minuses. Class periods (eight per day) normally cover 45 minutes each, with double periods for laboratory courses. Twenty and a half credits are required for graduation, distributed as follows: English, 4; mathematics, 4; social studies, 3 (1 of which must be U.S. history); foreign language, 2; science, 2; laboratory science, 1; and electives, 4.5.

The average Academy class size is 13; the student-teacher ratio is approximately 10:1. Opportunities for independent study, off-campus field trips, and enrollment in courses at Valley Forge Military College are available to eligible cadets.

FACULTY AND ADVISERS

There are 52 full-time and 13 part-time teachers at the Academy. Thirty-one members hold master's degrees; currently, 2 have doctorates.

Charles A. McGeorge, President, is a graduate of Boston University. He earned a Master of Science degree in the dynamics of organizations from the University of Pennsylvania. He holds a certificate in advanced management from Northwestern University's Kellogg School of Business.

Experienced teachers, dedicated to educating young men, are selected primarily for their professional ability and concern for young people. Faculty members perform additional duties as athletic coaches, study hall supervisors, and advisers for extracurricular activities. Ongoing professional development is strongly encouraged.

COLLEGE ADMISSION COUNSELING

The Guidance Department has 4 full-time counselors and gives continual assistance and counseling to each cadet. The department follows each cadet's academic progress and keeps in close contact with parents. College orientation and parent involvement begin during the second semester of the junior year and continue throughout the cadet's residence. College orientation sessions cover college selection, nomination to service academies, financial aid, the Army ROTC program, and contacts with college placement representatives. College test requirements are reviewed, and cadets are counseled in college application preparation and interview procedures. Ninety-nine percent of the class of 2008 went on to college, with the greatest representation at Embry-Riddle, Penn State University Park, Purdue, the U.S. Air Force Academy, the U.S. Naval Academy, and Villanova.

STUDENT BODY AND CONDUCT

The 2008–09 Upper School student body was composed of 350 boarding cadets. The student body is diverse, and this year cadets came from thirty-three states and thirty-one countries. Eight percent were African American, 11 percent were Hispanic, 13 percent were Asian/Pacific Islanders, and 13 percent were international students.

The military structure of Valley Forge provides extraordinary opportunities for students to develop and exercise their leadership abilities in a safe environment. The Valley Forge experience is designed to foster the development of individual responsibility, self-discipline, and sound leadership skills by providing opportunities for the practical application of leadership theories in positions of increasing responsibility.

The Corps of Cadets is a self-administering body organized in eight company units along military lines, with a cadet officer and noncommissioned officer organization for cadet control and administration. Cadet leadership and positive peer encouragement within this structured setting result in a brotherhood and camaraderie among cadets. Through their student representatives, cadets cooperate with the administration in enforcing regulations regarding student conduct. A Student Advisory Council represents the cadets in the school administration. The Dean's Council meets regularly to discuss aspects of academic life.

Character development and personal motivation are integral parts of the Valley Forge experience. The character development program includes weekly chapel and vesper services and monthly character development seminars that are facilitated by peer/faculty teams. Valley Forge emphasizes time-proven standards of conduct, ethical behavior, integrity, spiritual values, and service to community and country. It also motivates young men to strive for excellence, both as individuals and as members of an organization, in all areas of endeavor. Motivation is encouraged through positive competition, recognition, loyalty, teamwork, organizational pride, and the establishment of personal goals.

ACADEMIC FACILITIES

Shannon Hall is the principal academic building. In addition to classrooms, it includes biology, chemistry, and physics laboratories; a computer complex; and the military science department. The Friedman Auditorium, adjacent to Shannon Hall, serves as a large study hall, a conference and instructional center, and a center for SAT and other testing procedures. The May H. Baker Library provides more than 70,000 books, 500 video titles, more than 60 periodical subscriptions, and more than 30 subscriptions to online research resources. To integrate library resources into the curriculum, the library faculty collaborates with the classroom faculty in implementing information literacy instruction in two fully networked computer classrooms and two seminar rooms. The educational psychologists of the Cadet Achievement Center, housed in the library, counsel and advise cadets concerning learning and personal issues.

A fiber-optic, Internet-capable network connects all classrooms, laboratories, and library and dormitory rooms on the campus.

BOARDING AND GENERAL FACILITIES

Cadets are housed by their military companies in individual dormitories, 2 cadets to a room, under the supervision of adult Tactical Officers and their cadet leaders. Cadets eat together in the Regimental Mess. The Health Center has a resident physician and a 24-hour staff; special consultants are always available. The Alumni Chapel of St. Cornelius the Centurion seats 1,500. The service is nondenominational but Christian in format, and services are available for all faiths. Mellon Hall provides a parents' reception room, a ballroom, piano and instrument practice rooms, a photography laboratory, a 10-point rifle and pistol range, and meeting rooms. Other facilities include the student center, the cadet laundry, the tailor shop, and the Cadet

Store. Price Athletic Center and Trainer Hall house three full-size and six intermediate-size basketball courts, a five-lane swimming pool, locker rooms, weight rooms, meeting rooms, administrative offices, and the L. Maitland Blank Hall of Fame. Also on campus are six athletic fields, nine outdoor tennis courts, an outdoor Olympic-size swimming pool, the cavalry stables, and the Mellon Polo Pavilion.

ATHLETICS

Athletics and physical well-being are important elements in a Valley Forge education. The aim of the program is to develop all-around fitness, alertness, character, esprit de corps, leadership, courage, competitive spirit, and genuine desire for physical and mental achievement. There is competition at three levels: varsity, junior varsity, and intramural. To have every cadet on a team is the constant goal. Sports opportunities include baseball, basketball, cross-country, equestrian jumping, football, golf, lacrosse, riflery, rugby, soccer, swimming, tennis, track, and wrestling.

Valley Forge has a strong athletic tradition. Since 1986, the VFMA&C football program has sent more than 140 cadets to Division I schools on full football scholarships. Seven VF alumni currently play in the NFL. One alumnus currently plays for a major league baseball team. In 2003, the equestrian show jumping team participated in the Junior Olympics.

EXTRACURRICULAR OPPORTUNITIES

Clubs, honor societies, publications, intramurals, the Regimental Choir, the Anthony Wayne Legion Guard, and some thirty-five other organizations (forensic, literary, language, science, and Boy Scouts, to name a few) attract about 75 percent of the Corps. Publications include the *Legionnaire* (the newspaper) and *Crossed Sabers* (the yearbook).

Outside lecturers visit the Academy regularly. The band and choir travel widely and have performed at the Kennedy Center, Carnegie Hall, Westminster Abbey, Lincoln Center, and the White House and have participated in inaugural events for several U.S. presidents. Various cadet units assist local communities in parades, community events, and horse shows. Cadets participate in various public service activities in the surrounding communities; several cadet groups pay regular visits during the year to local children's homes, centers for the disabled, and nursing homes. Important traditional events are Parents' and Grandparents' Weekend, Regimental Mounted Parades, Dunaway Oratorical Contest, and frequent band and choir concerts.

DAILY LIFE

Classes (45 minutes each) are held five days a week from 7:30 a.m. to 3:30 p.m. The average number of classes per student is six in an eight-period day. An extra instruction period is available after the last class period. Athletics and other activities are held between 3 and 5:45 p.m. daily. Evening study hours extend from 7:30 to 9:30 p.m. Taps sounds at 10 p.m. Monday afternoon is reserved for drill, company meetings, and special activities, such as the ropes course and rappelling.

WEEKEND LIFE

Special or afternoon leaves as well as overnight and weekend privileges may be earned. Ample opportunities exist for cadets to take advantage of the cultural and entertainment opportunities in the Philadelphia area. Cadets desiring to stay at school can use all facilities and attend movies on Friday and Saturday nights in the student center. The cadets frequently enjoy mixers, formal dances, plays, band concerts, special sports events, and polo matches with students from neighboring schools. All events are chaperoned by faculty members.

Gold and Silver Star cadets are those who have earned academic achievement. They are granted trips into town on Wednesday afternoons and evenings. On Friday, Saturday, and Sunday, those not restricted for academic or other reasons may visit town after their last duty until early evening. Periodically during the year, weekend leaves are authorized for the entire corps; other times there are special weekend leaves for Gold and Silver Star honor students. The leaves help reinforce positive peer pressure to excel in both academics and leadership tasks. Following chapel and Regimental Parade on Sunday, cadets may leave the grounds on special dinner leave with their parents or other authorized adults.

SUMMER PROGRAMS

A four-week residential summer camp is available for young men ages 8–16. A day camp is available for young men and women ages 6–16. These programs provide them with the very best in recreational and educational opportunities.

COSTS AND FINANCIAL AID

The annual charge for 2008–09 was $33,176. This charge included tuition, room and board, uniforms, and all other fees. There is an optional charge for private music lessons, developmental reading, and driver's education. Health center stays for each period of more than 24 hours' duration are also an additional expense. A nonrefundable application fee of $100 is required with an application. At the time of acceptance, a $1000 validation fee is required.

In 2008–09, approximately 40 percent of the students received financial aid totaling more than $1 million. Merit-based scholarships are offered for academic excellence and performance in athletics, the band, and the choir. Through the generosity of many friends of Valley Forge, some special and endowed scholarships, with varying need and/or merit-based criteria, are available.

ADMISSIONS INFORMATION

Admission is based on academic aptitude as measured by the Otis-Lennon Mental Ability Test and/or the SSAT, information pertaining to grade level, personal character and scholastic references, and the recommendation of the Admissions Counselor based on a personal interview with the applicant. Applicants must present evidence of being capable of meeting the demands of a college-preparatory curriculum.

The admission policies of Valley Forge Military Academy & College are nondiscriminatory with respect to race, color, creed, and national or ethnic origin and are in compliance with federal laws.

APPLICATION TIMETABLE

Inquiries are always welcome. Those seeking further information are invited to attend periodic Sunday Campus Visitations; everyone is encouraged to contact the admissions office to make an appointment to visit the campus. New cadets are enrolled in late August, and limited openings also exist for January, or midyear, entry. While there is no application deadline, it is recommended that applications be submitted three months before the desired entry date.

ADMISSIONS CORRESPONDENCE

Dean of Admissions
Valley Forge Military Academy & College
Wayne, Pennsylvania 19087-3695

Phone: 610-989-1300
800-234-VFMA (toll-free)
Fax: 610-688-1545
E-mail: admissions@vfmac.edu
Web site: http://www.vfmac.edu

VERMONT ACADEMY

Saxtons River, Vermont

Type: Coeducational, boarding and day, college-preparatory school
Grades: 9–12, postgraduate year
Enrollment: 210
Head of School: James C. Mooney, Headmaster

THE SCHOOL

Founded in 1876 as a coeducational, college-preparatory boarding and day school, Vermont Academy has always been a leader in the field of education. The 500-acre campus, nestled in the foothills of the Green Mountains, is the ideal location to discover individual talents and develop the creative problem-solving, communication, and leadership skills needed for success in college and in life.

Vermont Academy's dedicated faculty members provide inspiration and personal attention, teaching the students to ask the questions, rather than merely get the right answer.

Vermont Academy's students represent a diverse community, bringing their open-mindedness and cultural pride to share with each other. In this global educational village, they study the world within the place-based curriculum, using Vermont as a microcosm for resolving environmental, political, and social issues.

The Academy's students are active participants with generous spirits, always striving for their personal best as they support their peers to do the same. They are of solid character, respectful of themselves and others, embracing a strong work ethic and compassion for those around them. They may be scholars, athletes, or artists when they arrive, yet, when they graduate, they are all three. They develop into confident and independent lifelong learners, offering creative problem solving and leadership to make a difference in the world.

A nonprofit and nondenominational institution, Vermont Academy is directed by a 25-member Board of Trustees, 12 of whom are alumni. The school endowment is $7.5 million, with more than $630,000 in annual gifts from alumni, parents, and friends. The Academy recently completed a $24.5-million campaign that has allowed it to add many new features, including a 350-seat state-of-the-art theater, a Winter Snow Park, a new 20-student girls' dormitory, a renovated boys' dorm, a professional dance studio, and a renovated hockey rink, gym, and fitness center.

Vermont Academy is accredited by the New England Association of Schools and Colleges. Its memberships include the Cum Laude Society, National Honor Society, the Independent Schools Association of Northern New England, the National Association of Independent Schools, the Council for Advancement and Support of Education, and the Vermont Independent Schools Association.

ACADEMIC PROGRAMS

Vermont Academy's rigorous academic program is designed for students who want a challenging college-preparatory curriculum with a wide range of departmental and creative electives. The average class has 11 students, and the overall student-teacher ratio is 7:1. Most students take five courses each semester and earn 20–24 credits by graduation. This includes 4 credits in English, 4 in math, 3 in a second language, 3 in history, 4 in science, and 2 or more in visual or performing arts, computer science, or other electives.

Vermont Academy offers advanced-level honors courses in all departments to challenge highly motivated students. The science department offers astronomy, organic biochemistry, advanced biology, environmental studies, environmental science, ecology, kinesiology, and advanced physics. The Conflict Resolution class participates in a national essay contest, and for the past three years, members of the class have been cited as state winners. Independent study is offered in all academic departments to help students develop complex projects and portfolios to accompany their college applications.

A Learning Skills program is offered to students who require help in developing basic study skills and compensatory techniques. Six full-time instructors meet with students in 1- or 2-person tutorials from one to four times per week. The course is noncredit and entails an extra fee. For students with certified learning disabilities in the language areas, a Basic Spanish course is offered, followed by Spanish 1, to meet the two-year foreign language requirement.

Vermont Academy offers an English language program for international students who have some verbal proficiency in the English language. Courses include English as a Second Language (ESL), English for International Students (EIS), and a sheltered course entitled American History for International Students, which fulfills the U.S. history graduation requirement. A TOEFL preparation tutorial is available, and a minimum score of 500 on the TOEFL is required for students to qualify for a Vermont Academy diploma.

In addition to one or two study blocks available to students during the academic day, an evening study time is held in the supervised dormitories from 8 to 9:30 p.m. In addition, teachers regularly hold evening study seminars for group work and AP tutorials. Students receive effort marks every two weeks, based on their participation and preparedness in their classes. The effort marks determine student privileges. Each student's progress is discussed by faculty members following the issuance of effort marks. If a student is not progressing, a Student Action Plan is written and reviewed with the student and his/her parents. This has proven to be an effective tool for a student's success.

In addition, letter grades and written comments are reported at the end of each quarter. Interim reports are sent to parents of students who are experiencing academic difficulties.

FACULTY AND ADVISERS

Vermont Academy's faculty consists of 48 members; 15 hold master's degrees, and 2 hold doctorates.

James C. Mooney was appointed Headmaster in 1993. He received his B.A. in history from Yale University in 1978 and a master's degree in education administration from Stanford University in 1984.

More than 85 percent of faculty members and their families live on campus with the students and are accessible to students throughout the day and evening, creating opportunities for individual attention and greater communication. All other faculty members live nearby and are at school at least one evening a week to help supervise dormitories.

Each student has a faculty adviser who assists with academic planning and personal development. Each adviser has approximately 6 advisees, and meets with those advisees three times a week. The adviser is the student's on-campus advocate and the liaison between the student and teachers, as well as parents and teachers. The adviser monitors the progress of each advisee, helping to design a plan for academic success.

COLLEGE ADMISSION COUNSELING

Counseling for college placement begins in the spring of a student's sophomore year. Meetings with the college counselors continue through the spring of the senior year. With few exceptions, Vermont Academy graduates attend four-year colleges or universities, choosing the ones that best suit their abilities, interests, and objectives. Approximately 90 percent of the students get into their first- or second-choice college. Students take the SAT, SAT Subject Tests, ACT, and various Advanced Placement tests. An intensive SAT preparation course is available for all juniors and seniors. In addition, Advanced Placement test preparation is offered on a tutorial basis in any subject that is part of the curriculum.

The following is a partial list of colleges and universities where the Vermont Academy graduates have been accepted in the past five years: Barnard, Bates, Brown, Colby, Dartmouth, Dickinson, Georgetown, Gettysburg, Guilford, Harvard, Lake Forest, Lehigh, Middlebury, Mount Holyoke, NYU, Quinnipiac, Rhode Island School of Design, St. Lawrence, St. Michael's, Simmons, Syracuse, U.S. Naval Academy, Williams, and the Universities of California, Colorado, Massachusetts, New Hampshire, and Vermont.

STUDENT BODY AND CONDUCT

The 2008–09 student body is composed of 156 boarding and 54 day students from thirty states and twelve countries (international students make up 29 percent of the student body). The majority of students come from California, Connecticut, Florida, Illinois, Massachusetts, New Hampshire, New York, Pennsylvania, and Vermont. International countries represented are Australia, Bahamas, Brazil, Canada, China (Hong Kong), England, Germany, Korea, Mexico, Russia, Spain, and Ukraine. Forty percent of the student body is female.

Residential life is an integral part of Vermont Academy's curriculum. Community living requires certain personal obligations and restrictions that are designed to promote a healthy, safe, and comfortable atmosphere and to enhance the learning environment. Vermont Academy places a strong emphasis on mutual respect, self-discipline, and concern for others as central components of its program. High expectations exist for the entire community.

A committee of faculty members and students has written an Honor Code for the Vermont Academy community. The core values of honesty, trust, respect, and responsibility are expected of all members of the community. At the beginning of the school year, students and faculty members sign a book pledging their commitment to the Honor Code.

The Vermont Academy Student Association (VASA) is the students' governing body. It includes representatives from all classes and meets weekly with a member of the Dean of Students' office to consider issues of interest. The meetings are open to the entire school.

Students facing major disciplinary action appear before a standards committee consisting of students and faculty members. Final action is taken by the Headmaster on the recommendation of this committee.

ACADEMIC FACILITIES

The Academy has a Tablet PC program with wireless Internet access throughout the campus, including dormitories, as well as full-time T1 access with an Internet-connected Windows XP Pro network with Windows XP Pro workstations for all computers. The Tablets are an outstanding educational tool for communication, organization (with GoBinder software), note taking, and retrieving and completing assignments.

Each department has a classroom projector for use with the Tablet. Students can purchase or rent Tablet PCs through the Academy's Technology Department. In addition, there are a number of desktop computers for student use in the library and most classrooms as well as in a small computer lab.

Most classes are held in Fuller and Alumni Halls, with art, music, theater, and filmmaking classes conducted in nearby buildings. The average class size is 11, and in most classes, students and teachers sit around tables to facilitate stimulating discussion. Students are expected to be prepared and participate in the sharing of knowledge.

The Tillinghast Library contains 14,000 volumes, periodicals, study carrels, fifteen computers, the College Counseling office, and the Learning Skills Center. The library is open to students throughout the day and evening, as well as on weekends.

In fall 2006, the new 350-seat state-of-the-art theater opened. Twice-weekly morning meetings, speakers, and performers have graced the stage of this magnificent structure. Other arts facilities include a large music room for choral and band rehearsals, five soundproof practice rooms, and a recording studio; three well-lit art studios; a pottery studio with six potters' wheels and a large gas-reduction kiln; two darkrooms for black-and-white photo developing; a new, fully equipped filmmaking studio; and a professional dance studio.

BOARDING AND GENERAL FACILITIES

Students reside in dormitories (three for boys, six for girls) ranging from 6 to 60 students in capacity. Most dorm rooms are doubles, although there are some single rooms available. Faculty members and their families live in each dorm. All dorms have free laundry facilities and most have common rooms as well. Roommate assignments are based on many factors, including interests, lifestyle habits, and personality.

Shepardson Center contains a large dining hall, a student study area, the Student Lounge, a school store, and the VA Café. Students can study, relax, and socialize as well as snack on healthy food from 7 a.m. until 10 p.m.

ATHLETICS

Excellent coaching, enthusiastic spirit, and outstanding facilities combine to make able competitors of the Vermont Academy teams. The athletic programs support Vermont Academy's belief in developing the whole student (head, hand, and heart) by focusing on teamwork and sportsmanship, self-discipline to acquire and apply specific athletic skills and strategies, appreciation for being fit, and having fun.

During the three seasons of the school year, students are required to earn either 3 team-activity credits or 2 team-activity credits and 1 nonteam-activity credit. Team activities include eighteen different sports. In the fall, cross-country running, field hockey, football, horseback riding, mountain biking, outdoor challenge, soccer, team manager, and theater are offered. During the winter, students participate in basketball, dance, ice hockey, skiing (cross-country, downhill, freestyle, and jumping), snowboarding, team manager, and theater. Spring activities include baseball, golf, lacrosse, rock climbing, softball, tennis, team manager, theater, and track.

Athletic facilities include the newly renovated Lucy Athletic Complex, with an outstanding basketball court and climbing wall as well as new locker rooms, fitness center, dance studio, and training room; the enclosed Michael Choukas Skating Rink with an artificial ice-making system; the Winter Snow Park, with three ski jumps, a modest alpine run, a terrain park, and 20 kilometers of cross-country trails as well as a lift, lights, and grooming equipment; the Chivers Ski and Outdoor Education Center, which includes 1,600 square feet for waxing, sharpening, and storage; seven beautifully maintained playing and practice fields, with a ¼-mile track; and six tennis courts. Ascutney, Bromley, Killington, Magic Mountain, Okemo, and Stratton ski areas are nearby.

EXTRACURRICULAR OPPORTUNITIES

Several afternoon activities are available for students during one of the three seasons they are in school. These include athletic training/weight room management, community service, cycling, photography, silversmithing, and yoga.

Other opportunities include yearbook, literary magazine, jazz band, vocal ensemble, private music lessons, the fall musical and other theater productions, cabarets, coffee houses, and dance performances. In addition, speakers and concert performances are brought to campus at least once a month to enrich the students' experience.

Students are also involved in Vermont Academy's community service program. Possibilities include mentoring and sports clinics with local elementary schools; helping at the soup kitchen, nursing homes, the historical society, and day care center; raking leaves and shoveling snow for the elderly neighbors; and helping the local community as stewards of the environment.

DAILY LIFE

In the fall and spring, the class day begins at 7:45 a.m. with adviser meetings. Classes are held until 3:15 p.m. on Monday, Tuesday, Thursday, and Friday and until noon on Wednesday and Saturday. The winter schedule is slightly altered to accommodate snow-sports teams. A modified dress code is required for classrooms, with more formal dress and assigned seating two evenings a week for Formal Dinner.

Sports and activities are scheduled from 3:45 to 5:45 p.m. Interscholastic competition with other boarding schools is scheduled on Wednesday and Saturday afternoons.

For boarding students, dinner is at 6:30 on weekday evenings and study hours are from 8 to 9:30 p.m. Everyone is back in their dorms at 10, and lights out is at 10:30. Each week, there are two formal dinners with assigned seating and required formal dress.

WEEKEND LIFE

There is always something to do on the weekends. Activities are varied to provide students with a change of pace, the opportunity to participate in sports and activities, and a chance to relax and enjoy the New England area. A committee of students and faculty members plan the activities, which can include movies, plays, concerts, or dances on Saturday evenings either at school or nearby, as well as trips to Boston, Burlington, Northhampton, New York, and nearby ski areas.

COSTS AND FINANCIAL AID

The tuition for 2008–09 was $41,500 for boarding students and $24,000 for day students. A deposit of $4000 for boarding students and $2000 for day students is required and is credited toward tuition. Scholarships are available to families demonstrating financial need. More than $1.8 million is awarded each year to approximately 30 percent of the student body. A financial aid committee reviews these awards annually.

ADMISSIONS INFORMATION

Admission to Vermont Academy is made on the basis of academic achievement or potential; character; athletic, creative, and leadership interests; and previous record. Taken into consideration are a candidate's school record, recommendations from current teachers, and standardized test results (e.g., SSAT, PSAT, SAT, ACT, SLEP, TOEFL, and others). A student essay, a graded writing sample, a parent profile (of the student), and an on-campus interview are required. For 2008–09, there were 378 applications, of which 251 were accepted and 106 students enrolled. Selection is based on all-around qualifications without regard to race, creed, religion, gender, sexual orientation, or national or ethnic origin.

APPLICATION TIMETABLE

Arrangements should be made early in the school year for a tour of the campus and a personal interview with a member of the admissions staff. The Admissions Office is open Monday through Friday from 8:30 to 4:30 and Saturday mornings. A formal application with a $50 fee ($100 for international students) should be submitted. Students should register early in the fall to take one of the standardized tests. The application deadline is February 1, with rolling admissions thereafter, if space is available.

ADMISSIONS CORRESPONDENCE

Admissions Office
Vermont Academy
10 Long Walk
Saxtons River, Vermont 05154

Phone: 802-869-6229
800-560-1876 (toll-free in the U.S.)
E-mail: admissions@vermontacademy.org
Web site: http://www.vermontacademy.org

VIEWPOINT SCHOOL

Calabasas, California

Type: Coeducational day college-preparatory school
Grades: K–12: Primary School, Kindergarten–2; Lower School, 3–5; Middle School, 6–8; Upper School, 9–12
Enrollment: School total: 1,210; Upper School: 485
Head of School: Dr. Robert J. Dworkoski

THE SCHOOL

Founded in 1961, Viewpoint School offers an enriched college-preparatory program in a nurturing and wholesome environment. Located at the western end of the San Fernando Valley, Viewpoint is nestled in the foothills of the Santa Monica Mountains on a campus of 25 acres, with scenic vistas, open spaces, and heritage oak trees. Downtown Los Angeles, with its museums, libraries, and cultural attractions, is only 25 miles away.

The School's mission is to help children develop a love of learning and those qualities that provide them with strength and direction for a lifetime. Viewpoint recognizes the uniqueness of each child and is committed to the identification, preservation, and development of that individuality. Viewpoint School respects and teaches the wisdom and traditions of the world's cultures and faiths. While students are encouraged to pursue an accelerated academic program appropriate for each student's level, Viewpoint also stresses citizenship, moral and ethical development, and good deportment.

Within this environment, students learn to value the differences among individuals and to appreciate the unique contributions each person adds to the School's diverse community. Weekly assemblies, foreign trips, and community service encourage such development. Student participation is high in all areas of school life, and the nurturing atmosphere encourages healthy relationships between students and faculty members.

Viewpoint School is a nonprofit institution governed by a self-perpetuating Board of Trustees and is fully accredited by the California Association of Independent Schools and the Western Association of Schools and Colleges. Viewpoint holds memberships in the National Association of Independent Schools, the *Cum Laude* Society, the Educational Records Bureau, the Independent School Alliance for Minority Affairs, the National Association for College Admission Counseling, the National Association of Principals of Schools for Girls, A Better Chance, the National Association of Secondary School Principals, and the Council for Advancement and Support of Education.

ACADEMIC PROGRAMS

Viewpoint organizes itself into four divisions, each with its own Head of School and distinct geographic identity on the School's 25-acre parcel of land. The Primary School encompasses Kindergarten through second grade; Lower School, grades 3 through 5; Middle School, grades 6 through 8; and Upper School, grades 9 through 12.

The academic program at Viewpoint School emphasizes the traditional disciplines at all levels and provides a rich curriculum in the arts, music, foreign language, computer science, and athletics.

The academic year, divided into semesters, begins in early September and extends to early June, with vacations of two weeks in the winter and spring. Middle and Upper School students follow a six-day rotation schedule that includes periods of varying lengths. Class sizes, on average, range from 18 to 22 students; The School sends grades to parents four times a year and provides four additional interim reports for parents of students whose grades are C+ or below. Teachers also write annual comments for every student in each class.

To graduate, an Upper School student must complete four years of English; 3½ years of history, including United States history and American government; three years of mathematics, laboratory science, and a single foreign language; two sequential semesters of an art in the same discipline; the technology and human development course; eight seasons of physical education; and 45 hours of community service.

Students choose from a wide variety of electives that match their unique interests and abilities. In the Upper School, elective choices may include such offerings as women's voices in literature, Shakespeare Project, neuroscience, nutrition, oceanography, contemporary short fiction, the novel of Africa, poetry of the Romantic period, creative writing, statistics and probability, modern Latin American history, contemporary politics, humanities, abnormal psychology, computer science (animation, programming, artificial intelligence, and robotics), speech, drama, history of theater, music theory, chorus, instrumental music (jazz, strings, and winds), art history, ceramics, sculpture, photography, filmmaking, and video production.

Middle School students may also choose from a range of electives that include exciting opportunities for the study of musical instruments, voice, acting, dance, film, photography, art and sculpture, chess, stock market analysis, newspaper, and literary magazine. Students in the Middle and Upper Schools also benefit from the Laptop Program in which students receive laptop computers for use in the classrooms.

In the Primary and Lower Schools, all children take seven enrichment classes: daily sports, a library class, art, music, a foreign language, a lab science, and computers.

The School offers twenty-nine Advanced Placement (AP) courses in the following disciplines: biology, calculus AB, calculus BC, chemistry, Chinese language, comparative government, computer science, English language, English literature, environmental science, European history, French language, French literature, Latin emphasizing Virgil, Latin literature, music theory, physics B, physics C (mechanics), physics C (electricity and magnetism), psychology, Spanish language, Spanish literature, statistics, studio art (general or drawing), studio art (3-D design), U.S. history, and world history.

In spring 2008, 187 students sat for 453 examinations in twenty-nine subject areas, with 92 percent receiving scores of 3 or above, 76 percent receiving scores of 4 or 5, and 42 percent receiving scores of 5. Viewpoint's participation in APs in May 2008 was 13 percent for tenth grade, 56 percent for eleventh grade, and 73 percent for twelfth grade. The classes of 2006 and 2007 had 16 AP National Scholars, 71 AP Scholars with Distinction, 32 AP Scholars with Honors, and 52 AP Scholars.

FACULTY AND ADVISERS

The faculty consists of 154 full-time and several part-time teachers, including administrators with teaching responsibilities. The faculty members and administrators hold 144 baccalaureate and forty-eight advanced degrees, including six Ph.D.'s, from colleges and universities located in the United States and in several other countries. Diverse in age, background, and experience, the men and women of Viewpoint's faculty are selected for their academic expertise, for the enthusiasm and energy they bring to their teaching, and for their enjoyment of working with young people. Recently, several faculty members received awards from the National Endowment for the Humanities, the Council for Basic Education, the National Science Foundation, the Klingenstein Summer Institute, and the Fulbright Scholarship Program.

Dr. Robert J. Dworkoski was appointed Headmaster in 1986. He is a graduate of George Washington University (B.A., 1968), New York University (A.M., 1971), and Columbia University (M.A., 1972; Ph.D., 1979, European history). Prior to his appointment, Dr. Dworkoski taught history at Brooklyn College in New York and was Department Chairman of Social Studies at Woodmere Academy in New York. From 1980 to 1986, Dr. Dworkoski was the Head of Upper School at the Harvard School in Los Angeles. A Fulbright scholar in Europe in 1983 and a recipient of a grant from the National Endowment for the Humanities in 1993, Dr. Dworkoski has been active in the California Association of Independent Schools and the National Association of Independent Schools and sits on the Board of the Will Geer Theatricum Botanicum.

COLLEGE ADMISSION COUNSELING

Working closely with parents and students, the college counseling staff clarifies the complicated process of college admission and achieves 100 percent placement of students in four-year colleges. By completing the minimum requirements for graduation, Viewpoint students exceed the basic requirements for entrance to the campuses of the University of California and to the most selective universities in the country. Graduates from the class of 2008 achieved mean SAT scores of 642 Critical Reading, 654 Math, and 660 Writing.

Recent Viewpoint graduates are currently attending such colleges and universities as American, Barnard, Boston University, Brandeis, Brown, Carnegie Mellon, Cornell, Dartmouth, Duke, Georgetown, George Washington, Harvard, Johns Hopkins, Loyola Marymount, MIT, NYU, Oxford, Pepperdine, Princeton, Stanford, Tufts, Tulane, Vassar, Yale, all campuses of the University of California, and the Universities of Pennsylvania and Southern California.

STUDENT BODY AND CONDUCT

The 2008–09 enrollment totaled 1,210 students, with 200 students in kindergarten through grade 2, 200 students in grades 3 through 5, 325 students in grades 6 through 8, and 485 students in grades 9 through 12. Students come to Viewpoint from the San Fernando and Conejo Valleys, Malibu, Topanga, Pacific Palisades, and other neighboring communities. They represent a rich variety of ethnic, religious, socioeconomic, cultural, and linguistic backgrounds; fifteen languages are spoken in the homes of the School's families. The School hosts foreign exchanges with other countries, including China, England, France, Germany, Japan, Russia, and Spain. All Viewpoint students benefit from a teaching and learning environment that is enriched by these diverse perspectives, talents, and interests.

Students in kindergarten through grade 8 wear uniforms. Upper School students follow a dress code.

ACADEMIC FACILITIES

The School provides each division with separate library facilities, academic classrooms, art and music studios, science laboratories, and computer laboratories with extensive access to the Internet. The 41,000-square-foot Gates Academic Center houses Upper School students with state-of-the-art classrooms; technology centers, and laboratories. It also includes music, performing arts, and dance studios, which are used by children in all grades. The Ahmanson Foundation Black Box Theater and the 400-seat Carlson Family Theater provide a spacious environment for the School's numerous annual dances, drama, and musical productions at all grade levels. The combined libraries of all divisions contain approximately 20,000 volumes and offer CD-ROM access to the Los Angeles County's library collection, the Los Angeles Times Network, and ProQuest magazine collection. Additional facilities include ECOLET, an outdoor natural science laboratory and classroom for field studies on campus.

ATHLETICS

All students participate in physical education, and 80 percent of Middle and Upper School students are involved in team sports. Upper School students compete interscholastically in baseball, basketball, cheerleading, cross-country, equestrian events, fencing, football, golf, soccer, softball, swimming, tennis, and volleyball. Outdoor education and dance (modern, jazz, tap, and ballet) are also available. The sports facilities on the 25-acre campus include two athletic fields, including the Ring Family Field stadium; two regulation-size swimming pools; the Rasmussen Family Pavilion for athletics; outdoor basketball courts; batting cages; a weight-training facility; locker rooms for athletics; and playgrounds for children in the elementary grades.

EXTRACURRICULAR OPPORTUNITIES

Viewpoint students are involved in a variety of social and extracurricular activities. They include the yearbook, newspaper, literary journal, the student council, speech and debate competitions, theatrical and musical productions, foreign language presentations, and honor societies. Student clubs include mock trial, rocketry, Model UN, Junior States of America, Amnesty International, astronomy, science fiction, film, Spanish, Chinese, community service honor society, flight simulator, poetry, Cum Laude society, multicultural, surfing, newspaper, animal rights, fashion design, magic, and chess.

Viewpoint is one of the first two schools in the United States to offer the Duke of Edinburgh International Award Program. Founded by HRH, The Duke of Edinburgh in 1956, the International Award is an exciting self-development program that is available to young people worldwide, equipping them with life skills to make a difference to themselves, their communities, and their world. To earn this award, students and their advisers at Viewpoint designed a set of personal goals in four different areas: Service to Others, Adventurous Journey, Practical or Vocational Life Skills, and Physical Recreation. There are three levels of the award: Bronze requires a minimum of six months of participation, Silver requires a minimum participation of twelve months, and Gold requires at least eighteen months of participation. Students must complete all of their goals to earn awards.

Viewpoint offers formal and informal dances, domestic and international trips, and foreign exchange programs with secondary schools in several countries. The opportunity to travel abroad, exchange ideas with students in other parts of the world, and improve foreign language skills currently includes such locations as England, France; Spain, Germany, China, Italy, and Costa Rica and has in the past included Japan and Russia. Each spring, ninth and tenth graders join the Voyage of Discovery, a nine-day tour of the historic sites of the East Coast. Other annual trips include an East Coast tour of college campuses.

Outdoor Education trips provide students with additional opportunities for growth and learning. Astrocamp, in Idyllwild, is the site for the three-day retreat for fifth graders. Sixth graders camp in the mountains for three days, seventh graders travel to Catalina Island to explore marine biology, and eighth graders spend four days working through team-building activities in the wilderness. To ease the transition from Middle to Upper School, ninth graders travel to Camp Surf, located near San Diego, to study the ecosystem of California's coastline. These trips give students the opportunity to strengthen friendships and to make new friends while enjoying outdoor activities.

The community of the School extends to include parents, grandparents, alumni, and friends who are invited to the campus for a variety of special events, including Great Pumpkin Day, Open House, Homecoming, the annual Benefit, assemblies, alumni reunions, sporting events, and musical and dramatic productions.

DAILY LIFE

Students travel to and from school by the bus system or by car pool. The academic day for a kindergartner starts at 8 a.m. and ends at 2 p.m., while students in grades 1 through 5 begin at 8 and end at 3:15. Middle and Upper School students begin their day at 8 a.m. and conclude at 2:45 p.m. with an Academic Assistance period from 2:45 to 3:15, where they can meet informally with their teachers to go over topics discussed in class and to get questions answered. Students may elect to stay after school to study in the library; participate in sports, clubs, and other extracurricular activities; or work on a computer program.

SUMMER PROGRAMS

Viewpoint offers an exciting summer camp opportunity, Camp Roadrunner, along with an optional academic summer program for students entering the Primary and Lower Schools. For the athletically inclined, Viewpoint also sponsors basketball, baseball, volleyball, swimming, dance, and theater camps each summer.

COSTS AND FINANCIAL AID

Tuition for the 2008–09 academic year was $20,200 for kindergarten through grade 2, $20,850 for grades 3–5, $22,250 for grades 6–8, and $23,750 for grades 9–12. General fees were $570 for kindergarten through grade 5 and $515 for grades 6–12. There is a one-time new-family fee of $1500. In addition, students in grades 6–12 purchase textbooks from the School. Tuition payment and insurance plans are available.

Financial aid is available in cases of demonstrated need.

ADMISSIONS INFORMATION

Viewpoint attracts highly motivated, academically talented students with diverse backgrounds, interests, and abilities. Admission is very selective and is based on an interview of parents and child, a review of entrance examinations, recommendations, and transcripts from previous schools. International students must demonstrate a strong command of English.

The School is committed to diversity in its student body. The School's Minority Admission Program (MAP) provides scholarships to academically able members of minority groups from families with financial need. The program works with various community organizations, local schools, and churches to identify and to recruit talented and promising students.

APPLICATION TIMETABLE

Inquiries are welcome at any time. Families should submit an application and accompanying fee to the Admission Office no later than January 10 for the subsequent academic year. Later applications are considered if openings are available.

ADMISSIONS CORRESPONDENCE

Laurel Baker Tew, Director of Admission
Viewpoint School
23620 Mulholland Highway
Calabasas, California 91302

Phone: 818-340-2901
Fax: 818-591-0834
E-mail: info@viewpoint.org
Web site: http://www.viewpoint.org

VILLANOVA PREPARATORY SCHOOL

Ojai, California

VILLANOVA
PREPARATORY SCHOOL

Type: Coeducational, Catholic boarding and day college-preparatory school
Grades: 9–12
Enrollment: 325
Head of School: Anthony J. Sabatino

THE SCHOOL

Villanova Preparatory School was founded in 1924 as a Catholic school in the Augustinian tradition. Villanova is a college preparatory, coeducational, day and boarding school where cultural, ethnic, and socioeconomic diversity are welcomed and embraced. The School was established in 1924 in response to a growing demand for a Catholic boys' boarding school in southern California. The Augustinian Order was invited by the Most Reverend John Cantwell, then Bishop of Los Angeles, to found and staff the proposed school. Since most of the requests had come from Ventura County, that area was selected as the general locality, and the Ojai Valley was chosen as the specific site.

After forty-six years as an all-boys boarding and day school, Villanova opened its doors in 1970 to girl day students. The School became fully coed in 1987 when it began accepting girl boarding students.

Located in the Ojai Valley, the 127-acre campus provides a naturally beautiful setting, with mountains complementing the Spanish mission–style architecture of the School. The Ojai Valley is home to approximately 29,000, including the city of Ojai's residents, which number 8,000. Ojai is 12 miles from Ventura beaches and 35 miles from Santa Barbara. Los Angeles is 90 miles southeast of the School. The Ojai Valley provides easy access to year-round outdoor activities in a safe, small-town setting, while still providing access to educational and cultural activities available in Los Angeles and Santa Barbara.

In the Augustinian tradition, Villanova Preparatory School's mission is to graduate mature young adults of diverse backgrounds who express to the world the qualities of unity, truth, and love. The School provides a rigorous college-preparatory curriculum, including AP and Honors courses. Reflecting the Augustinian values of unity, truth, and love, Villanova fosters the growth of the whole student, in mind, body, and heart. A broad array of activities, clubs, and sports are available, providing ample opportunity for students to pursue varied interests. Community service is required. Graduates are well rounded and prepared to succeed in competitive universities and to lead moral, active, and healthy lives.

A nonprofit institution, Villanova is owned by the Priests and Brothers of the Western Province of the Order of St. Augustine in the United States and is governed by a Board of Trustees composed of both lay and religious members and the Head of School.

The School is accredited by the Western Association of Schools and Colleges and the Western Catholic Education Association. In addition, Villanova is approved by the California State Department of Education and by the U.S. Department of Justice Immigration and Naturalization Service. The School holds memberships in the National Catholic Educational Association, the Augustinian Secondary Education Association, the Catholic Boarding Schools Association, the Association of American Boarding Schools, the Council for Religion in Independent Schools, and the Secondary School Admission Test Board.

ACADEMIC PROGRAMS

Through a challenging college-prep program, religious studies courses, community service, athletics, fine arts, clubs, and activities, Villanova fosters the intellectual, physical, emotional, and spiritual growth of each student. Ideally, Villanova's graduates are leaders, effective communicators, educated in Christian values, self-directed lifelong learners, critical and conceptual thinkers, and aware of social and global issues. To graduate, students complete a minimum of 27 units of required and elective courses including: 4 units of English; 1 unit of fine arts; 3 units of Japanese, Latin, or Spanish; 1 unit of physical education/health; 3 units of social studies; 3 units of science; 4 units of religion, and 4 elective units. In addition to this core curriculum, students may choose from electives in all disciplines. Examples include drama, choral ensemble, advanced visual arts, film studies, communications, publications, photography, psychology, and sociology. Advanced Placement preparation is offered in math, English, foreign language, and social studies. The average class size is 16 students, with a student-faculty ratio of 10:1.

A program in English as a second language (ESL) serves students whose language skills are not sufficient to allow them to participate fully in regular courses. For students whose English skills are not yet strong enough for a full college-preparatory course load, the School offers a comprehensive English Immersion with Support (EIS) Program. Depending on their previous course work and English proficiency, students enter the program at either ninth or tenth grade and are immersed in regular classes for credit and cross-curricular support classes. The program is designed to develop students' skills in reading, writing, speaking, and listening.

Letter grades are issued quarterly. Advanced Placement and honors courses receive weighted grades. Semester grades are an average of the quarter grades and the grades on semester examinations. Written progress reports are prepared at midquarter and are distributed at parent-teacher conferences and by electronic mail.

All students receive tutoring assistance upon request from teachers at the end of classes each day. Resident students have mandatory supervised study periods each evening, Sunday through Thursday.

FACULTY AND ADVISERS

The School has 41 faculty members, 3 of whom are from the Augustinian Order and 2 are members of the Sisters of the Holy Cross. Eighty-eight percent of the faculty members have either advanced degrees or bachelor's degrees with enrollment in a master's or credential program. Five additional staff members work full-time with the boarding program. There is a full-time nurse on duty during class days as well as a full-time resource director, a full-time college counselor, a full-time guidance counselor, and two full-time academic counselors.

School president Reverend Gregory Heidenblut, O.S.A. entered the seminary in 1968 in Monroe, Michigan, and attended St. Gregory's Seminary (Pontifical College Josephinum) in Cincinnati, Ohio. He earned a master's degree in educational leadership from the University of San Diego, a master's degree in divinity from the Washington Theological Union and a master's degree in management from National University in San Diego. He was ordained a priest of the Augustinian Order in 2004 and became Villanova's president in 2008.

COLLEGE ADMISSION COUNSELING

College guidance is under the direction of the Director of College Counseling, with assistance from members of the administration and faculty. Information, college catalogs, career guidance, and assistance in completing applications and financial aid forms are available from the Director of College Counseling. The average SAT score for the class of 2008 was 1721.

Students have the opportunity to meet with college representatives who visit the School. They are also encouraged to visit college campuses during their junior and senior years. Information regarding college admission is presented to parents in general evening sessions and individually by appointment.

One hundred percent of graduates continue their education beyond high school. Some of the colleges and universities admitting members of the classes of 2005 through 2008 include American; Berkeley; California Polytechnic, San Luis Obispo; California State Polytechnic, Pomona; Catholic University; Claremont McKenna; Cornell; Drexel; Embry-Riddle; Emerson; Emory; Georgetown; Gonzaga; Loyola Marymount; Marquette; Notre Dame; Northwestern; NYU; Pepperdine; Pitzer; SMU; Syracuse; Tufts; USC, Villanova; Whitman; and the Universities of Arizona; California, Davis, Los Angeles, Riverside, San Diego, Santa Barbara, and Santa Cruz; Chicago; Colorado; Illinois; Indiana; Michigan; Oregon; Pennsylvania; San Diego; Stanford; Vermont; and Wisconsin.

STUDENT BODY AND CONDUCT

In 2008–09, Villanova's enrollment of 315 included 88 freshmen, 82 sophomores, 71 juniors, and 72 seniors. Currently, there is approximately the same number of boys as girls. There are 225 day students and 90 resident students. Students come from the United States and twelve other countries. Fifty-five percent of the day student body comes from the Ojai Valley. The School seeks to enroll a geographically, ethnically, and socioeconomically diverse student body.

In order to create an environment of Christian living where young people are free to achieve their potential academically, spiritually, and socially, Villanova maintains a disciplinary system that stresses each student's responsibility for self-discipline and for respecting the rights of others. The basic premise at the School is that students behave in a way that facilitates learning and represents the values of the School in a community-based environment.

ACADEMIC FACILITIES

The Villanova campus consists of ten buildings that house seventeen classrooms, art and choral rooms, a theater, science laboratories, an audiovisual center, counseling offices, an administration building, an outdoor amphitheater, and state-of-the-art athletic facilities. The Keller Library is located in Cantwell Hall and functions as an academic resource center.

A main computer lab houses more than twenty-five Macintosh computers, and computer labs are available in the library and the dorms. Wireless Internet access is available on campus.

BOARDING AND GENERAL FACILITIES

Boarding students are challenged to become active members of the Villanova community and are required to participate in clubs, activities, performing arts, or athletics in order to experience a complete Villanova education. Villanova's two residence halls house 30 girls and 65 boys. Both halls are divided into two dorms. Each dorm plans its own activities and special events and elects its own dorm representative. Each residence hall is equipped with laundry facilities, telephone stations, wireless Internet, and a comfortable TV/VCR lounge. All girls in Glynn Hall have roommates, and most boys in Cantwell Hall have roommates. Single-room priority in Cantwell Hall begins with fourth-year seniors.

ATHLETICS

The purpose of the athletic program at Villanova is to promote camaraderie, discipline, self-confidence, and leadership as well as physical fitness.

Villanova is a member of the Tri-County Athletic Association (TCAA), which includes a combination of Catholic and public schools in Ventura and Santa Barbara counties. The TCAA is a member of the California Interscholastic Federation (CIF). Interscholastic offerings include baseball, basketball, football, golf, soccer, softball, surfing, swimming, tennis, volleyball, water polo, and track and field.

Athletics facilities include the softball diamond, Ferrari Field (baseball), tennis courts, a football/soccer field, beach volleyball courts, a gymnasium, a swimming pool, and a cross-country course. There are golf courses and riding stables near the campus.

EXTRACURRICULAR OPPORTUNITIES

Students need not be artistic or athletic standouts to participate in the variety of extracurricular activities and clubs available on campus. They need only to be committed and dedicated. More than twenty clubs and activities are available, including the Mock Trial Team, Chess Club, Film Club, California Scholarship Federation, Drama Club, Film Club, National Honor Society, Rotary Interact, *Hogar Infantil*, Student Diplomats, Recycling Club, Art Club, Campus Ministry, Galloping Ghosts Spirit Club, Project Africa, and Red Cross.

The Christian Service Program at Villanova exists to provide the students with the opportunity to put into practice the command of Jesus to "love one another as I have loved you." Through a program of practical service to the people in and around the School community, students proudly give more than 6,000 hours each year. Another tangible result of this schoolwide program is the building of the student-volunteer's self-image and self-worth. The annual food drive at Thanksgiving and the fund drive at Easter are traditional components of the School's community service program.

Students are provided with opportunities for out-of-classroom faith experiences that foster the growth of a person-centered, Christian community within the School. Each student attends their specific class retreat. Villanova retreats consist of discussions and activities directed towards helping students grow in their own self-understanding and in their relationship with God and their family. In addition, students are given opportunities to open new channels of communication and understanding with faculty and staff members and fellow students, thereby fostering community.

Throughout the year, the Associated Student Body sponsors dances, a beach day, lunchtime intramurals, roller-skating, a ski trip, and trips to plays, special films, and amusement parks. The highlight of the fall semester is Wildcat Day, an all-school event that is a tradition at Villanova and introduces the freshmen to the Augustinian core values of the School.

DAILY LIFE

The class day begins at 7:50 a.m. On most days, Villanova students have seven class periods of 48 minutes each, and on block days, the students have three or four classes of 80 minutes each; the class day ends at 2:50 p.m.

After school, resident students may seek extra help with their studies, return to their room, or participate in sports or other extracurricular activities. They may be allowed off-campus time but must return to the dormitory by 5:30 p.m. Dinner at 6 is followed by a brief recreation period. The study period begins at 7 and continues, with a break, until 10. Lights-out times start at 10:30 p.m. and vary depending on the grade level of each student.

There are no classes on Saturday, but sports teams frequently compete on that day.

WEEKEND LIFE

On the weekends, students participate in activities and sports, visit family and friends, meet students from other schools, and enjoy the Ventura, Santa Barbara, and Los Angeles metropolitan areas. Villanova provides activities every weekend, including dances, day hikes, on-campus movies, beach trips, group outings to plays or concerts, and visits to cultural and educational sites.

COSTS AND FINANCIAL AID

For 2008–09, the tuition for day students was $13,300. The tuition, room, and board for resident students were $39,000 for the year. ESL students are required to pay an additional fee varying between $2500 and $5000 depending on the student's needs. Boarding students pay a nonrefundable deposit of $3000. The annual cost for textbooks ranges from $300 to $750.

Villanova is committed to serving students from every economic background. More than 40 percent of students attending Villanova receive financial support from the School. To apply for financial aid, students must submit an application to the School Scholarship Service. Though Villanova works to assist every qualified student, the School cannot guarantee that every student applying for aid will receive it. Several scholarships, grants, and awards are available, including merit scholarships that are based on results of the High School Placement Test (HSPT) given in January at Villanova; Fr. Howard Grants, which are awarded to Catholic students based on nomination by parish priests; Fr. Glynn Awards, which are awarded to deserving Catholic students; President's Awards, which are awarded to Catholic students who show exceptional leadership qualities in their parish and community; and Clare Booth Luce Scholarships, which are awarded to female students who excel in math and science and demonstrate financial need.

ADMISSIONS INFORMATION

Villanova Preparatory School admits students of any race, color, racial or ethnic origin and does not discriminate in the administration of its educational policies, scholarship and loan programs, and athletics and other School-administered programs.

Applicants must demonstrate the potential for academic success in a college-preparatory curriculum. Admission to the ninth grade normally depends on High School Placement Test (HSPT) or Secondary School Admission Test (SSAT) scores, middle school grades, teacher recommendations, and a required on-campus interview. Admission at the tenth-grade level or above is determined on the basis of performance on the SSAT and grades earned in college-preparatory course work.

APPLICATION TIMETABLE

Appointments should be made in order to visit or tour the campus. Open house days are held in November and January.

For students applying for admission to the ninth grade in the fall, Villanova administers the SSAT the first Saturday in December and the HSPT the last Saturday in January. Students should register for both tests prior to the test dates. Students should register for the SSAT online at http://www.ssat.org and for the HSPT on line at www.villanovaprep.org/admissions/admissions.php. The School office is open Monday through Friday from 8 a.m. to 4 p.m.

Tours for resident students should be scheduled in the fall or early winter. Students interested in becoming day students should attend one of the open house events. Applications should be filed in the fall or early winter.

ADMISSIONS CORRESPONDENCE

Villanova Preparatory School
12096 Ventura Avenue
Ojai, California 93023

Phone: 805-646-1464
Fax: 805-646-4430
Web site: http://www.villanovaprep.org

Office of Admission
Sarah Angell
Dean of Resident Students
E-mail: sangell@villanovaprep.org

Irene Snively, Admission Support
E-mail: isnively@villanovaprep.org

Michelle Kolbeck, Admission Assistant
E-mail: E-mail: admissions@villanovaprep.org

VIRGINIA EPISCOPAL SCHOOL

Lynchburg, Virginia

Type: Coeducational, boarding and day, college-preparatory school
Grades: 9–12
Enrollment: 209
Head of School: Dr. Phillip L. Hadley, Headmaster

THE SCHOOL

Virginia Episcopal School (VES) was founded in 1916 by the Reverend Dr. Robert Carter Jett, who served as the School's first Headmaster and, later, as the first Bishop of the Diocese of Southwestern Virginia. The mission of the School is to provide rigorous academic training and vigorous individual attention in a spiritual and ethical environment.

The School is located on a beautiful 160-acre campus in Lynchburg, Virginia. Because Lynchburg is the location of several institutions of higher learning and an active Fine Arts Center, numerous cultural opportunities are available to students. The Blue Ridge Parkway and the Appalachian Trail are also nearby.

VES is governed by a 25-member Board of Trustees composed of alumni, parents, parents of alumni, college and university administrators, and friends of the School. In addition, the Bishop of the Diocese of Southwestern Virginia serves as a permanent member of the board. The School is on sound financial footing, and approximately 12 percent of the yearly operating income is provided through gifts from its various constituencies. During the 2007–08 session, alumni, parents, and friends contributed $752,000 unrestricted and $141,000 restricted to the Annual Giving Program. The School's endowment surpassed the $20 million threshold. VES has both an active Alumni Association and a Parents Association, whose members assist the School in its fund-raising and recruiting endeavors.

Virginia Episcopal School holds memberships in the National Association of Independent Schools, the Virginia Association of Independent Schools, the Cum Laude Society, the College Board, the Secondary School Admission Test Board, and the National Association of Episcopal Schools.

ACADEMIC PROGRAMS

Essentially directed toward the liberal arts and the humanities, the curriculum is structured and rigorous. It emphasizes study skills and offers sound preparation for college. To qualify for graduation, students must earn 18⅓ acceptable credits and take at least five courses per trimester. Specifically, they must gain credit for 4 years of English, 3 years of mathematics through algebra II/trigonometry, 2 years of one foreign language, 2 years of history, 2 years of laboratory science, 1 year of fine arts, ⅔ of a year of religion, ⅓ of a year of computer applications, and ⅓ of a year of life issues. Each student must also participate in the athletics program and complete 30 hours of community service each school year. Several departments, including computer science, music, art, English, history, science, mathematics, music, and foreign languages, offer Advanced Placement courses.

Students in grade 9 take part in the 9th Grade Initiative Program. This distinctive program is designed to foster personal development in each of four dimensions: intellect, character, citizenship, and wellness. Because classes rarely contain more than 12 students, the School is able to challenge superior students as well as give the proper amount of support and encouragement to those experiencing difficulties because of a weakness in background. A student's particular course load is determined jointly by the adviser, the student, and the Director of Studies. Each student also has a faculty adviser who gives regular progress reports to parents. Grades and comments are mailed every six weeks, and the School encourages parent-teacher conferences.

Because the academic program is rigorous, students are required to do a great deal of work outside of class. To help them meet this academic obligation, the School provides 2½ to 3½ hours of scheduled study time each day. All students attend a supervised study hall at night. Others study for the full 2-hour period in their rooms or in the library. Faculty members residing in the dormitories ensure that an atmosphere conducive to study prevails during the study hours, 7:30–9:30 p.m. Sunday through Thursday.

FACULTY AND ADVISERS

The School has 46 full-time faculty members and administrators who teach. More than half of these individuals hold master's degrees.

The Headmaster is Dr. Phillip L. Hadley. He is completing his eleventh year at VES. Dr. Hadley's most recent position has been as head of St. Mary's Hall in San Antonio, Texas. He has previously served in a variety of teaching and administrative posts at St. Stephen's School in Austin, Texas, the Brookstone School in Columbus, Georgia, and the Bishop's School in La Jolla, California. Dr. Hadley received a Bachelor of Science degree in mathematics and a master's degree in Spanish literature from Ohio University, and holds a Ph.D. in Latin American history from the University of Texas.

The School seeks teachers who possess a keen interest in their fields as well as a sincere commitment to young people. Almost every faculty member serves as an adviser, coach, club sponsor, and study hall or dormitory supervisor.

VES encourages its teachers to pursue additional education for themselves. The School will underwrite much of the cost for more schooling as well as for attendance at professional conferences and seminars.

COLLEGE PLACEMENT

The college counseling program seeks to challenge students to make college decisions that reflect self-awareness, knowledge of institutions, ambition, and realistic selections. The Directors of College Counseling encourage students to begin this important process early in the junior year. The college counselors and the faculty advisers for juniors and seniors are available to aid each student in the college search. In addition, representatives from more than fifty colleges and universities visit VES annually.

The range of SAT scores for the middle 50 percent of the class of 2006 were 1050–1240. The graduates, numbering 62, enrolled in forty-one colleges and universities, including Carnegie-Mellon, Johns Hopkins, Middlebury, Rhodes, Richmond in London, Tulane, Virginia Tech, Yale, and the Universities of Alabama, Colorado at Bolder, Georgia, Mississippi, North Carolina at Chapel Hill, North Carolina at Wilmington, South Carolina, and Virginia.

STUDENT BODY AND CONDUCT

In the 2008–09 session, the ninth grade contained 43 students (20 boarding, 23 day), the tenth grade had 56 (32 boarding, 24 day), the eleventh grade had 76 (55 boarding, 21 day), and the twelfth grade had 87 (57 boarding, 30 day). In 2008–09, 103 girls, including 65 boarders, were enrolled. The majority of boarders came from North Carolina, Virginia, South Carolina, Texas, and West Virginia.

At the heart of all relationships among faculty, students, and staff is the Honor Code, which underscores the importance of mutual trust, respect, and concern. Through this code, all students pledge that they will not cheat, lie, or steal, and they accept the obligation of reporting to a member of the Student Honor Committee any violation they may observe.

Most instances of misconduct relating to academics, discipline, or honor merit a second chance; any involvement whatsoever with illegal drugs, however, results in dismissal, and VES reserves the right to ask students to leave if their values are not consistent with those of the School.

Each spring a select group of juniors is chosen by the Headmaster (after nominations by faculty and students) to serve as counselors during their senior year. The counselors advise and counsel new and old students and actively work to guide underclassmen and to tighten the already strong sense of School community. At least 1 counselor lives on each dormitory floor.

ACADEMIC FACILITIES

The major academic facility is Jett Hall, which contains several classrooms, an auditorium, a writing lab, administrative offices, and living space for students and faculty members. Other buildings containing classrooms are Pendleton Hall; Randolph Hall; Banks-Gannaway, which houses a 16,000-volume library; and the Zimmer Science and Activity Center. The Center offers state-of-the-art laboratories; an audiovisual hall; lecture, seminar, and multimedia rooms; faculty offices; and a computer center equipped with IBM-compatible Pentium personal computers with color monitors, laser printers, and scanners. Wireless connections are available throughout the campus.

BOARDING AND GENERAL FACILITIES

Boarders live in seven dormitories. Most students live in double rooms. New students are assigned roommates, while returning students are generally allowed to choose their own. The teachers in residence in the dormitories, along with the student counselors, are responsible for overseeing all dormitory activities. Each dorm room is equipped with two Internet connections and one phone jack.

ATHLETICS

The VES athletics program seeks to have every student fully realize his or her physical potential, achieve a sense of pride, and meet the challenges contained within interscholastic competition. Whether a student is experienced in a given sport or not, there is a place for everyone on a VES team.

Students must earn a given number of athletics credits as part of their graduation requirements. These may be earned as a player, manager, or student trainer. The credit system does allow time for alternative activities such as aerobics, drama, music, dance, riding, and community service, but it is demanding enough to expect each student to take an active role in the interscholastic aspect of the School.

Thirty-two teams at different levels compete wearing the garnet and white of the Bishops throughout the course of one year at VES. Sports available to boys are baseball, basketball, cross-country, football, golf, indoor soccer, indoor track, lacrosse, soccer, swimming, tennis, track, and wrestling. For the girls, basketball, cross-country, field hockey, golf, indoor track, lacrosse, soccer, swimming, tennis, track, and volleyball are offered.

There are seven playing fields for the field sports, two baseball fields, and an outdoor track. Indoor facilities are housed within two buildings: Barksdale-King Gymnasium and Van Every Fieldhouse. Barksdale-King features a wooden basketball/volleyball court, a wrestling room, an athletic training room, and locker and shower facilities. The 30,000-square-foot Van Every Fieldhouse holds a wooden basketball/volleyball court, two versaturf basketball/soccer courts, a versaturf track with field event space, and a batting cage.

EXTRACURRICULAR OPPORTUNITIES

All students are encouraged to participate in clubs, publications, and debates. At least two days a week, time is scheduled for gatherings of many of these organizations.

Popular activities include the yearbook *(The Vestige)*; the Alpha Order, whose members work with prospective students and their parents; and the Outdoor Club, whose faculty sponsors organize hiking and camping trips. Other extracurricular opportunities include science, art, drama, and photography.

DAILY LIFE

Students are involved in a variety of activities from the breakfast until the conclusion of study hall at 9:30 p.m. A buffet breakfast is served from 7:15 until 7:45. On Wednesday, a required 20- to 30-minute chapel service is held at 9:30. On Monday, Tuesday, Thursday, and Friday, all faculty members and students meet in Langhorne Memorial Chapel for announcements. Monday through Thursday, a six-period class day begins at 8 a.m. and ends at 3:05 p.m. All meals during the week are required and are served buffet-style. On Friday, classes end at 1 p.m. so that sports contests may take place. A student taking the normal load of five courses has one daily supervised study period.

Students are involved in sports practices or games each afternoon from approximately 3:30 to 5:30. Supper ends at 7:00, and study hall begins at 7:30 and concludes at 9:30 p.m. The students are free to sign out to the Student Center to be with friends and get something to eat from 9:30-10 p.m. Students are expected to be in their dormitories at 10 p.m. during the academic week.

WEEKEND LIFE

The Activities Committee meets regularly with the full-time Activities Coordinator to plan the School's social calendar, which includes several concerts hosted by VES, class trips to Washington and other cities, Casino Night, in-school concerts by vocal groups or bluegrass bands, and ski trips.

The School provides a bus so that students can go into Lynchburg on Friday and Saturday evenings. Students frequently attend dances and mixers at nearby schools. The School's on-campus coffeehouse opens every Friday and Saturday evening for the students' enjoyment.

COSTS AND FINANCIAL AID

Tuition and room and board for 2008–09 were $33,500. Total expenses for boarders, including an activities fee, books, and technology fees were about $36,000. Total expenses for day students were $18,000. There are several different payment plans that the School has developed. The business office is willing to work with families in an effort to make VES affordable.

Financial assistance in the form of grants is available to financially needy students as determined by the VES Financial Aid Committee. In September 2008, 21 percent of the students were receiving more than $860,000 in merit- and need-based aid.

ADMISSIONS INFORMATION

VES seeks able students from a variety of backgrounds. Candidates must submit an application, respond to a questionnaire, and take the SSAT if possible. The Admissions Committee's decision is based on a review of these materials plus an official transcript, teachers' recommendations, and personal references. Candidates must visit the campus for a tour and a one-on-one conference with an admission director. The most important considerations in an applicant's candidacy are an ability to be successful in the School environment, a willingness to get involved, and a desire to put his or her ability into action. Each year, 90 to 100 new students, most of them entering as ninth or tenth graders, are selected from an applicant pool of 250 or more.

APPLICATION TIMETABLE

The Admission Committee begins reviewing completed applications on February 1 and continues interviewing qualified applicants throughout the spring and summer months. The admission office is open Monday through Friday from 8 a.m. to 4 p.m. and on some Saturdays throughout the school year. We accept applications for enrollment on a rolling basis throughout the year.

ADMISSIONS CORRESPONDENCE

Katherine Saunders
Director of Admission
Virginia Episcopal School
400 VES Road, P.O. Box 408
Lynchburg, Virginia 24505
Phone: 434-385-3605
Fax: 434-385-3603
E-mail: admissions@ves.org
Web site: http://www.ves.org

WALNUT HILL SCHOOL

Natick, Massachusetts

Type: Coeducational boarding and day school for the arts and academics
Grades: 9–12
Enrollment: approximately 300
Head of School: Eileen Soskin

THE SCHOOL

The mission of Walnut Hill is to educate talented, accomplished, and intellectually engaged young artists from all over the world. The School does so in a diverse, humane, and ethical community. Walnut Hill is internationally recognized for its program of training in the arts accompanied by a rigorous academic curriculum. Students concentrate in ballet, writing and publishing, music, theater, or visual art. Founded in 1893, Walnut Hill is a boarding and day school for grades 9–12, located 17 miles west of Boston in Natick, Massachusetts. The beautiful, tree-covered, 45-acre campus is within 25 minutes of Boston—a major academic and cultural center. The School has a long tradition of outstanding placement with students being offered admission to top-ranked universities, colleges, conservatories, ballet and dance companies, and institutes throughout the United States and Europe.

Walnut Hill is the only high school in the nation affiliated with a major conservatory of music. The New England Conservatory of Music (NEC) at Walnut Hill is a joint program that offers students access to conservatory-level instruction while still in high school. Because of the School's proximity to Boston, students in all arts concentrations have access to a great cultural center. Students have the opportunity to attend performances by the Boston Symphony Orchestra, the Boston Lyric Opera, the Boston Ballet, the American Repertory Theater, and the Huntington Theater as well as Broadway shows on tour. Art students have access to the collections of the Museum of Fine Art, the Gardner Museum, the Institute of Contemporary Art, and Harvard's Fogg Museum and other university public collections. Throughout the year, the writing program invites many guest authors to campus for workshops and readings with students.

Passion is a word often heard at Walnut Hill. The School attracts dedicated and focused students from around the world to study in an environment that is challenging and supportive. People at the School are devoted to demonstrating respect and compassion and actively pursuing learning, with an emphasis on the development of the whole student.

Walnut Hill is accredited by the New England Association of Schools and Colleges.

ACADEMIC PROGRAMS

The academic curriculum is designed to prepare students for admission to highly selective colleges and universities. The curriculum builds critical-thinking skills that serve students well throughout life. A well-rounded program of mathematics, science, literature, languages, and history provide a strong liberal arts foundation. Walnut Hill is a member in good standing of the Cum Laude Society.

Advanced course work is offered in biology, calculus, chemistry, English, French, Spanish, and physics. Nearly 40 percent of the members of the class of 2008 had taken either calculus or advanced calculus before graduation. English as a second language is offered from the beginning to the advanced level.

Academic requirements for graduation include 4 years of English, 3 years of mathematics, 2 years of laboratory science, 2 consecutive years of a modern world language, and 2 years of history, one of which must be United States history. Typically, a student takes two academic courses per semester. Semester-long courses, each meeting for longer instructional periods, are equal to one full year of study. Successful completion of each academic semester-long course earns an academic credit toward the graduation requirement.

Ballet study at Walnut Hill develops strength and flexibility through a pure classical technique. Students have daily classes in ballet technique, men's technique, variations, pointe, character, modern, jazz, and Pilates, all taught by teachers of the highest standard. Performance opportunities are an important part of the preprofessional curriculum and training necessary for company placement. Throughout the year, lecture on important topics such as nutrition, injury prevention, costuming, stage lighting, and choreography supplement the curriculum. Prior to taking teaching positions at Walnut Hill, the ballet faculty members have enjoyed successful performance careers with major companies. Because of their personal experience, the instructors are prepared to assist students as they move forward in their own careers.

In writing and publishing, the curriculum is designed to help students acquire and refine the power of language through the practice of their craft so that they may best communicate their thoughts and feelings with both clarity and originality. Class sizes are very small and allow for effective critique and exploration of ideas. Students are exposed to the work of professional writers through frequent guests who share their work and speak about the craft of writing. Recent visiting writers have included John Irving, Derek Wolcott, Susan Kenny, David Budhill, David Updike, Christopher Tilghman, and Perri Klass.

In music, the curriculum is designed to provide students with an intensive level of instruction. Students study chamber music, music theory, music history, ear training, solfege, and chorus daily at Walnut Hill. Students also participate in a weekly master class with noted conductor Benjamin Zander, artistic director of the program. Through the NEC at Walnut Hill program, students participate in an orchestra at the Conservatory. Private teaching is offered by faculty members from New England Conservatory and Boston University, members of the Boston Symphony, and other noted professional musicians in greater Boston.

In theater, the curriculum is designed to develop skilled and disciplined young actors. The theater concentration includes acting and musical theater, combining rigorous training of the mind, body, and voice, forming a solid technique and approach to the craft. Advanced acting courses combine scene study analysis and synthesis, analysis of dramatic literature, theater history, and performance. In addition to actor training, students also develop an understanding and appreciation of design and production. All theater students are expected to complement their work with courses in dance and private voice lessons.

In visual art, the curriculum is designed to expose students to a professional studio environment. Working closely with faculty members, students develop a personal artistic language while continually improving on skills such as drawing, painting, sculpture, printmaking, and photography. Students receive 10 to 15 hours of studio instruction each week. Within each studio course, they are introduced to a variety of techniques particular to that individual medium. Through this process, students continually acquire, and improve upon, fundamental skills and concepts central to all visual art: composition, form, light, color, line, shape, and texture.

FACULTY AND ADVISERS

There are 44 teaching faculty members at Walnut Hill School. The 6:1 student-faculty ratio allows for close relationships between teacher and student. Faculty members at Walnut Hill are hired for demonstrated talent in teaching their discipline and for their commitment to students. Eighty-four percent of the faculty members have earned advanced degrees. They are graduates of colleges such as Brown, Cornell, Eastman, Harvard, Michigan, Middlebury, Northwestern, Smith, Swarthmore, Tufts, Yale, and the University of Virginia.

In addition to full-time faculty members, adjunct artist teachers are drawn from local organizations such as the Boston Symphony Orchestra, the School of the Museum of Fine Arts, and the New England Conservatory.

COLLEGE ADMISSION COUNSELING

The School has a full-time counseling staff who work with junior and senior students and their families throughout the college process. During the fall term, more than eighty colleges visit the Walnut Hill campus to meet with students. In the class of 2006, seniors were offered admission to a wide range of schools, including the Art Institute of Chicago, Bennington, Brown, Carnegie-Mellon, the Cleveland Institute of Music, Curtis, Juilliard, the New England Conservatory, Northwestern, NYU, Oberlin, Pratt, Princeton, Rhode Island School of Design, Rice, Smith, Swarthmore, and the University of Michigan.

STUDENT BODY AND CONDUCT

The 2008–09 enrollment was 295 (240 boarding, 55 day) as follows: grade 9, 43; grade 10, 70; grade 11, 84; and grade 12, 98. Walnut Hill is a diverse community, with 16 percent of the students identifying themselves as members of a minority group and 32 percent as international. There are students from thirty-one states and fifteen different countries.

Walnut Hill provides an open and supportive environment in which students may balance their self-expression with community expectations. The School community relies upon respect, honesty, vision, flexibility, and understanding. It believes that students are responsible for their own actions and that by setting forth a common code of conduct, students can best understand the expectations and responsibilities while at the School.

Student participation in the governing of the School is an important aspect of a Walnut Hill education. Students find direct expression in the election of student officers to the Community Council.

ACADEMIC FACILITIES

The Academic and Technology Center was opened in September 2002, with a state-of-the-art computer center and new biology and chemistry laboratories. The Creative Writing Center is housed within the Academic and Technology Center. The Joe Keefe Library has been recently renovated and has high-speed Internet connection and a music listening room. The Music Department is housed in Highland Hall, which includes faculty offices, classrooms, Amelia Avery Hall Choral Room, and twenty-one soundproof practice rooms. The Music Department holds performances in the eighty-seat Boswell Recital Hall. In addition to on-campus facilities, music students have access to the library at New England Conservatory; the orchestra performs at NEC's Jordan Hall. The Visual Art Department is housed in the Dartley Center for the Arts, which includes faculty offices, drawing and painting studios, a printmaking studio, a digital media lab, ceramics and sculpture studios, a kiln room, and private studio space for seniors. A state-of-the-art photography lab is also available. Visual art shows are displayed in Pooke Gallery in Highland Hall. The Ballet Department is housed in the Dance Center at Walnut Hill, with five large studios, offices, dressing rooms, and a costume shop. The Theater Department is housed in the Jane Oxford Keiter Performing Arts Center, which includes the Stephanie Bonnell Perrin Theater, a black box theater, a green room, design and production facilities, a costume room and lab, and classrooms.

BOARDING AND GENERAL FACILITIES

The School's Campus Center includes a dining hall, bookstore, offices of the Dean of Students, a conference room, lockers for day students, a mailroom, and a large social space with a fireplace and wide-screen television. Boarding students live in one of eight residence halls. All dorms have wireless Internet access and a common living room for residents. Each hall sustains a warm and friendly atmosphere, and each hall has resident dorm parents. The health facility on campus is operated throughout the day by the nursing staff. Emergency services are available close to campus.

ATHLETICS

Walnut Hill does not participate in competitive school athletics. However, a new fitness facility, which includes two movement studios, provides students with a variety of classes and equipment such as stair climbers, stationary bikes, and weights. The campus is beautiful, and many students enjoy playing Frisbee, playing soccer, and running. Yoga classes are regularly available. There is also an outdoor pool.

WEEKEND LIFE

The School's Activities Director keeps an extensive schedule of after-school events. Regular dances, movies, parties, and social gatherings are held on campus. The town of Natick is located 5 minutes from the campus. Students frequent the coffee shops, the town green, and Russ's Diner. Students also take part in the numerous cultural opportunities available in Boston. Natick is connected to Boston by commuter rail. With parental permission, students are able to enjoy the rich offerings of the city on the weekend. In addition, music students spend Saturday afternoon at New England Conservatory in orchestra or chamber music.

SUMMER PROGRAMS

Walnut Hill offers summer programs in ballet, creative writing, theater, and opera. The ballet and theater programs offer intensive training with performance opportunities, while the other two programs incorporate a European travel component. Admission to these programs is selective. In the summer, there are approximately 350 students on campus.

COSTS AND FINANCIAL AID

Tuition for the 2008–09 school year was $42,000 for boarders and $32,800 for day students. There were additional program fees varying from $1000 to $3000, depending on the program. ESL courses, if needed, are available at an additional cost. Approximately 50 percent of Walnut Hill students receive some form of financial assistance. Families are required to file a Parents' Financial Statement (PFS) to establish need, as well as submit recent tax forms. International students are not typically considered for assistance.

ADMISSIONS INFORMATION

Walnut Hill seeks applications from students who have demonstrated passion for and commitment to the arts and have a solid academic background. Each application is reviewed thoroughly, with attention paid to the individual strengths of the students. Admission is highly selective and based on a combination of audition/portfolio review, academic review, and personal qualities. It is recommended that students interview and audition on campus. Students are only admitted to a single arts concentration.

APPLICATION TIMETABLE

To be included in the primary applicant pool, students must complete their application by the deadline of February 1.

ADMISSIONS CORRESPONDENCE

Lorie K. Komlyn, Dean for Admission and Placement
Walnut Hill School
12 Highland Street
Natick, Massachusetts 01760-2199
Phone: 508-650-5020
Fax: 508-655-3726
E-mail: admissions@walnuthillarts.org
Web site: http://www.walnuthillarts.org

WASATCH ACADEMY

Mount Pleasant, Utah

Type: Coeducational boarding and day college-preparatory school
Grades: 9–12
Enrollment: 200
Head of School: Joseph R. Loftin

THE SCHOOL

Past swerving mountain roads, farms, and undulating fields, Wasatch Academy is located in the exact geographical center of Utah. Wasatch's location has inherently affected the institution and students alike, ultimately imbuing the community with a distinguishing spirit. The Academy provides an intimate academic experience and places attention on each individual student.

Though Wasatch Academy was founded in 1875 with a Presbyterian affiliation, the school currently holds no ties to any religious communities. A commitment to spiritual and moral growth, which includes weekly nonsectarian chapel meetings and ethics courses, has, however, endured since the school's founding.

The campus is a National Historic Site and is ensconced deep into the Sanpete Valley. The school has long been an integral part of the Mount Pleasant City community, a city with a population of 2,700. Wasatch is 60 miles from Provo, Utah, and 95 miles from Salt Lake City, Utah, home of the 2002 Winter Olympics. The Academy is close to six national parks and internationally renowned ski resorts.

Wasatch is a member of the Council for Spiritual and Ethical Education, the National Association of Independent Schools (NAIS), the Association of Boarding Schools (TABS), the Western Boarding Schools Association (WBSA), the Secondary School Admission Test Board (SSATB), the Council for Advancement and Support of Education (CASE), and the National Association for College Admission Counseling. Governed by a 16-member Board of Trustees composed of parents, alumni, and professional leaders from across the country and Native American nations, the Academy is a registered, nonprofit organization and is accredited by the Northwest Association of Schools and Colleges and the Pacific Northwest Association of Independent Schools.

ACADEMIC PROGRAMS

Wasatch Academy's broad curriculum offers a wide spectrum of academic opportunities, including Advanced Placement (AP) classes, Learning Support (to fill in educational gaps), and traditional honors courses. Course offerings include electives in English, history, philosophy, and art history. Students are able to enroll in the many offered performing and visual arts courses, field-based and laboratory sciences, and English as a second language.

Wasatch is committed to teaching all students how to succeed independently with self-discipline, time-management, and learning strategies. A Learning Strategies course is taught with a student-teacher ratio of 4:1 and focuses on the above-mentioned aspects of successful academic accomplishment; this course is geared toward students who need additional learning support. Exceptional students may follow an honors curriculum and earn an honors diploma. Wasatch offers three levels of ESL instruction: beginning, intermediate, and advanced.

The average class has 10 students, and all classes are limited to 18 students. Twenty-four credits are required for a diploma, including the following specific distributions: 4 English credits, 3 math credits, 3 history and social science credits, 3 science credits, 2 foreign language credits (3 for honors), 2 fine arts credits, and elective credits.

Parents and students may view up-to-the-minute grade updates via the Internet through the Academy's *PowerSchool.* Parents also receive written grade reports six times a year; reports of unsatisfactory work are issued every two weeks.

Students complete homework assignments during a study hall period held in the dormitories. They may also go to their classrooms to receive additional academic support from their instructors during the study hall each evening.

FACULTY AND ADVISERS

The faculty and administration consist of 51 members. All faculty members are required to carry at least a bachelor's degree, and together, they hold eighteen master's degrees and one Ph.D. The student-teacher ratio is 10:1.

Every faculty member provides mentoring to approximately 5 students through the advising system. Advisee groups meet twice per week, often over dinner or dessert. Formal dinners for advisee groups encourage the development of social poise and etiquette and create a stronger sense of community.

The majority of faculty members reside in faculty housing along the perimeter of the main Wasatch quadrangle. Full-time faculty members and residential life staff members are certified and trained in Dr. Melvin Levine's *Schools Attuned* methodologies.

Joseph R. Loftin has been a member of the faculty since 1986 and was appointed Head of School in 1988. He holds degrees from Utah State University and the University of Texas and completed the Klingenstein Fellowship at Columbia University.

COLLEGE ADMISSION COUNSELING

Wasatch has a strong tradition of college placement. The college counseling office works with students to maintain a schedule of deadlines for standardized testing, scholarship competitions, and financial aid paperwork. One-on-one counseling sessions give all students an opportunity to plan college visits, refine essays, and complete applications. Wasatch also transports students to various regional college fairs and college interview sessions.

Recent graduates have matriculated to such colleges and universities as Carnegie Mellon, Emory, Gonzaga, Grinnell, Harvard, Mount Holyoke, Northwestern, NYU, the United States Military Academy at West Point, and the Universities of California, Pennsylvania (Wharton), Oregon, Utah, and Washington.

STUDENT BODY AND CONDUCT

Wasatch Academy is arguably situated in the most diverse location in Utah. Students come from across the U.S. and abroad, representing more than twenty states and twenty-two countries. Currently, 32 percent of the student body hails from abroad. Among the countries represented are China, Ethiopia, Germany, India, Jamaica, Kenya, Nepal, Rwanda, Switzerland, and Tibet.

Whether they are from urban, suburban, or rural environments, Wasatch students are fully immersed into a positive, comprehensive, and academically inclined community. Student success and benefit is attributed to the motivated environment of the school.

Student prefects assist in establishing standards of behavior on and off campus, particularly in the residence halls. Student conduct is rewarded with a citizenship-level system.

ACADEMIC FACILITIES

Wasatch's facilities are nearly as diverse as the student body. Some buildings are more than a century old, while others are recently constructed. The entire campus is networked through a high-speed wireless network.

Three buildings hold academic classrooms. The 12,000-square-foot Mathematics and Science Building houses four science labs, math classrooms, and computer centers. The Craighead School Building houses the humanities and language classrooms, the library, the auditorium, and administrative offices. The library is a member of the Utah University Interlibrary System, which makes state library and college collections available to students. The Hansen Music and Art Center provides eight music practice rooms as well as three art studios for photography, pottery, general arts, jewelry making, and oil painting. The Academy also offers a Tech Support service for student use. The new Technology Center will provide Wasatch Academy students with classes in desktop publishing, Web design, film and video editing, broadcasting, Linux, and (eventually) programming. Laptops are required.

BOARDING AND GENERAL FACILITIES

Students reside in six dormitories, separated by gender and age. Students have one roommate. All rooms are equipped with Ethernet and wireless Internet connections. Dormitories are equipped with cooking and laundry facilities, television lounges, and storage rooms. Each dormitory is managed by a full-time "dorm parent" whose sole responsibility is the care of the dorm residents and the dorm.

Students and faculty members alike share meals in the newly constructed Student Center, a $3.1-million addition to the campus. The Student

Center provides a recreation area, a lounge, a bookstore, a cafeteria, and a snack shop.

Other facilities include two athletic centers, playing fields, tennis courts, a rock-climbing room, a dance studio, a skate park, a mountain cabin and snowboarding/ski park, a health center, a chapel, a museum, and indoor and outdoor equestrian facilities.

ATHLETICS

Varsity sport offerings include boys' and girls' basketball, cross-country, equine science, fencing, golf, skiing, snowboarding, soccer, tennis, and track. Girls may also choose from volleyball and cheerleading. Boys are offered baseball in the fall. Other athletic opportunities include mountain biking, rock climbing, skateboarding, dance, and fly fishing.

EXTRACURRICULAR OPPORTUNITIES

Extracurricular opportunities include, but are not limited to, community service, SAT prep, computer tech support, hiking, yoga, drama, painting, photography, choir, instrumental music, yearbook, Literary Magazine, snowboarding, paintball outings, dancing, orienteering, Student Ambassadors, National Honor Society, debate, Students for a Free Tibet, and Amnesty International.

Wasatch's Literary Magazine is the winner of thirteen consecutive first-place awards from the Association of Scholastic Periodicals. The debate team competes at the international level of competition and frequently qualifies students for the world championships. A number of Wasatch snowboarders annually qualify for the national competition.

DAILY LIFE

Breakfast begins at 7:45 a.m. The community meets for assembly or chapel once a week. Classes officially begin at 9 a.m. Each student takes three academic classes (out of a student's six total courses) per day, two before lunch and one after. When the academic classes conclude, students are allotted two periods for athletics or extracurricular pursuits. The dinner hour begins at 5:30, 30 minutes after the conclusion of the sports and extracurricular period. Study halls are held in the dormitories between 7:30 and 9:30 p.m. "Lights-out" is either 10:30 or 11 p.m., depending on the student's year of school. The schedule, while providing free time, assumes students have to devote additional time to studying outside of the mandatory study hall hours.

WEEKEND LIFE

Wasatch offers a variety of weekend trips off campus; the costs of nearly all trips are included in tuition expenses. Regular outdoor offerings include camping, hiking, and mountain-biking trips. Other trips in the past have included excursions to Salt Lake City for cultural or sporting events, snowboarding, shopping, movie-going, and musical performances. Ski and snowboarding trips are offered every weekend from Thanksgiving until early April.

SUMMER PROGRAMS

Interested students should visit the Academy's Web site (http://www.wacad.org) and click on "Summer Programs" for more information. Summer sessions are six weeks in length. Students may earn up 2.5 academic credits toward high school graduation.

COSTS AND FINANCIAL AID

Tuition for the 2008–09 academic year was $37,500 for seven-day boarding students, $34,500 for five-day boarding students, and $21,400 for day students. Tuition for international students was $42,500 for the year. This includes a nonrefundable deposit of $3500. For students who begin their studies during the spring semester, tuition was $22,500 for domestic students and $25,500 for international students. A family must also make deposits for weekly student allowances and bookstore purchases. Optional expenses include private music lessons, private dance lessons, art materials, ski passes, and Learning Strategies.

Wasatch awards financial aid to 40 percent of its student body. Aid is granted according to need, as calculated by the School and Student Service for Financial Aid (SSS). Returning students may earn merit and effort scholarships. Wasatch also offers special payment plans and loans in order to help families manage their educational investment.

ADMISSIONS INFORMATION

Students and parents who are interested in Wasatch should contact the Office of Admissions to receive admission materials and an application.

Wasatch seeks motivated and socially responsible students. While a record of success is ideal, the Academy also gives admission consideration to an applicant who may have extenuating circumstances but shows an ambition for improvement and dedication. Ninth grade is the traditional secondary-level entrance grade.

A candidate is reviewed on the basis of school transcripts, three teacher recommendations, a personal interview, and aptitude, intelligence, and SSAT scores; TOEFL scores are required for international applicants. Wasatch Academy does not discriminate on the basis of sex, color, creed, or national or ethnic heritage.

APPLICATION TIMETABLE

Students and parents are encouraged to request admission information throughout the year. However, most applications for fall enrollment are submitted in the spring. Families are notified of admission decisions within two weeks after completing a campus visit and interview. Wasatch traditionally reserves spaces for some students to enroll in January for the second semester.

ADMISSIONS CORRESPONDENCE

Office of Admissions
Wasatch Academy
120 South 100 West
Mount Pleasant, Utah 84647
Phone: 435-462-1400
Fax: 435-462-1450
E-mail: admissions@wacad.org
Web site: http://www.wacad.org

WASHINGTON ACADEMY

East Machias, Maine

Type: Coeducational boarding and day college-preparatory school; business studies and vocational training available
Grades: 9–12
Enrollment: 438
Head of School: Judson L. McBrine III, Head of School

THE SCHOOL

As one of the oldest academies in Maine, Washington Academy (WA) has been meeting the educational needs of students in grades 9–12 since the school's charter was signed by John Hancock in 1792.

Originally a feeder school for Bowdoin College in the early 1900s, the Academy has maintained an emphasis on academics and success for the individual. Taking into account each student's differences, the Academy strives to create opportunities that equip students socially and intellectually for their future endeavors. The curriculum is geared toward college preparation, but it is also flexible enough for the student who seeks a quality education that includes business and technology education and vocational studies. Emphasis is placed on the performing and visual arts, math and sciences, and involvement in the community.

The Academy's 55-acre campus is located in a safe, rural community in coastal Downeast Maine. The location enhances the nurturing environment created by a low student-teacher ratio, individualized attention, and a welcoming community. Just 2 miles from the Atlantic Ocean, the area also provides excellent recreational opportunities, including kayaking, sailing, fishing, hiking, and nature walks.

The school is governed by a 15-member, self-perpetuating Board of Trustees. An active Alumni Association supports the school's Development Office in annual giving and alumni relations. Washington Academy is accredited by the New England Association of Schools and Colleges and approved by the Maine Department of Education.

ACADEMIC PROGRAMS

The Academy offers a challenging and comprehensive curriculum to meet the needs of students of varying academic abilities. Courses range from training opportunities in boat building to Advanced Placement and Honors courses in many disciplines. More than 100 courses are offered, with class sizes ranging from 2 to 20. The average class size is 16 and the student-teacher ratio is 11:1.

Twenty (20) credits are required for graduation. Required credits include 4 credits in English; 3 credits in science, including 1 credit in biology or coastal studies/environmental science and 1 credit in chemistry or physical science; 3 credits in math; 3 credits in social studies, including 1 credit in U.S. history and 1 credit in world history or AP European history; ½ credit in health; 1 credit in physical education; 1 credit in fine arts; and 1 credit in adviser/advisee.

Students are given latitude in selecting electives, which include many fine arts courses, such as advanced digital photography, music composition, and concert chorus. Other electives include eight Advanced Placement courses, foreign languages (Spanish, French, Chinese, and Latin), coastal ecology, and internships, including an exploratory course in health occupations at a local hospital. Students must carry at least five subjects but most opt to carry six or seven.

The curriculum includes English as a second language (ESL). Students are provided with beginning, intermediate, and advanced ESL, as well as courses in American culture and history. International students are integrated into classes within the regular curriculum. A one-on-one personal learning lab is available to students needing help with standard curriculum courses, as well as support labs in English and math.

The Academy operates on a two-semester system. Reports with grades and comments are sent to parents every four weeks.

FACULTY AND ADVISERS

The faculty consists of 41 full-time instructors and 12 administrators. Faculty members are available after school and during prep periods for academic assistance. The faculty provides co-curricular activities during and after school.

The Academy operates an adviser/advisee program that mentors students through their four years of high school. Each faculty member oversees a group of 9 to 12 students from the time they are freshmen through graduation. Groups meet daily to monitor student progress, discuss concerns, and facilitate character development and career planning. New students are paired with a peer proctor during their first few weeks at the Academy.

Judson L. McBrine III, a graduate of the University of Maine (B.S., 1990) and University of Maine Graduate School (M.Ed., 1996), was appointed Head of School in 1997. In 2006, he received his Certificate of Advanced Studies in educational leadership. Mr. McBrine had formerly been the Assistant Head of School at Washington Academy, as well as a history, health, and physical education teacher in a number of Maine schools. In 2007, McBrine was named the state of Maine's Principal of the Year. He is married to Paula McBrine, and they have two sons, Jacob and Landon.

COLLEGE ADMISSION COUNSELING

The Guidance Office assists students in preparing for their postsecondary education and career objectives. A full-time college placement counselor who assists the guidance counselor in researching colleges, admissions and financial aid applications, and scholarship opportunities joined the staff in 2004. Visits by college representatives to the Academy are open to interested juniors and seniors.

In recent years, on average, 85 percent of the graduating class has applied and been accepted to colleges or universities. Recent graduates have been accepted at American, Bates, Bowdoin, Boston University, Bryant, Dartmouth, Ithaca, Maine Maritime Academy, Middlebury, Roger Williams, Vassar, Worcester Polytechnic Institute, and the University of Maine.

STUDENT BODY AND CONDUCT

The student enrollment at Washington Academy for 2008–09 was 438. There were 241 boys and 197 girls in grades 9–12. Of these students, 335 were day students, and 103 were residential boarding students. The residential students represented sixteen different countries, including Bermuda, Chile, China, Czech Republic, Germany, Italy, Jamaica, Japan, Korea, Philippines, Spain, Taiwan, Thailand, Ukraine, the U.S., and Vietnam.

Disciplinary problems are handled by the Dean of Students, in cooperation with the Head of School, and in accordance with established policies. Policies are clearly defined in the *Student Handbook*. School policies emphasize the acceptance of responsibility, personal integrity, and zero tolerance for harassment.

ACADEMIC FACILITIES

The Academy is located on a 55-acre campus with eight buildings. Four of the buildings serve as the academic facilities. The original Academy Building, built in 1823 and renovated most recently in 1994, houses foreign languages, special education, and mathematics. The Alumni Building is the main facility for administrative offices and classrooms. Renovated in the early 1970s and again in 1994, the building is also home to three science labs, an art studio, cafeteria, and the Larson Library.

The library holds 10,000 volumes and is fully automated. Using the library's seven computers and services provided by the University of Maine System, students may access a suite of shared databases and journal articles.

The Gardner Gymnasium has two courts with tiered seating and a seating capacity of 1,100, a weight room, and a training room. It also contains music classrooms, practice rooms, and a computer lab for music composition. Gardner Gym hosts volleyball and basketball games, assemblies, concerts and music programs, the junior prom, graduation, and other special events.

The Industrial Technology Building houses the Marine Trades Program, Industrial Arts, and Computer Networking and Repair. The facility has computerized numerical cutting equipment, a professional paint booth, fiberglass boat building resources, and a CAD/drafting lab.

The Academy's computer resources include a campuswide network with both wired and wireless capabilities. Students are encouraged to bring their own laptops. For students who do not have their own laptops, the library houses desktops as well as twenty laptops for student use. Desktop computers are also located in the study hall for access during study periods and within individual classrooms. For classroom use led by a teacher, the Academy hosts a ten-station technology lab for digital media technology, a ten-station marine trades drafting lab, a ten-station remedial math lab, and fifteen laptops available for classroom use in the Old Academy building.

Students and parents alike particularly appreciate the Academy's student management system. Grades, attendance, and discipline are all entered in daily and are immediately available over a secure network to both students and parents with Internet access. For those parents without Internet access, the Academy still provides traditional progress reports and report cards.

During fall 2008, a new Point of Sale system (POS) school lunch program was implemented. This POS is a Web-based application that allows parents to view lunch balances and detailed records of a student's purchases within the past 30 days, and parents can use a credit card to place money into the school account if they prefer not sending in cash or checks.

BOARDING AND GENERAL FACILITIES

Washington Academy currently operates three boarding facilities. The newest dormitory opened in December 2006 and houses 46 boys. The Larson dormitory houses up to 12 boys, with 2 students in each room. The Edwin and Linnie Cates dormitory, with its recent sixteen-bed addition, has the capacity to house 32 girls. Internet and cable access is available in all rooms. The Academy employs dorm parents to supervise the facilities. There are dorm parents living in each dorm with 24-hour supervision on the weekends. Breakfast, lunch, and dinner are provided each day at the school cafeteria. Weekend and after-school activities are coordinated, including transportation, by the Director of Residential Life.

The Academy also operates an active Host Home Placement Program for both boys and girls. Families in the program have been carefully screened and matched with incoming students.

ATHLETICS

The Academy promotes sports and activities as an integral part of the educational process. Team sports include baseball, basketball, cheerleading, cross-country, football, golf, soccer, softball, swimming, tennis, volleyball, and wrestling. The Academy competes with both private and public schools in the area. The Academy has competed in many eastern Maine and state championships. Due to the rural setting, the community is very involved in the Academy's athletic program. The amount of support and pride from fans is tremendous and has been more evident with the addition of a lighted soccer field in 2006, allowing for more community attendance during evening hours.

Athletic fields occupy the rear portion of the campus and consist of soccer, baseball, and softball fields. The Academy has a wooded cross-country trail that covers blueberry fields and ascends a notoriously difficult hill. Outdoor basketball courts are located behind the rear parking lot.

EXTRACURRICULAR OPPORTUNITIES

Students are encouraged to get involved in clubs and activities and to start their own groups that can benefit the overall student body. The Academy offers more than thirty clubs, including, but not limited to, National Honor Society, Robotics, Student Council, Envirothon, Yearbook Committee, JMG Career Association, chess, yoga, ski outings, and a championship math team.

The *Silver Quill* (literary magazine), the *Student's Voice* (newspaper), and the yearbook provide opportunities for artistic and written self-expression.

The WA Players, the Academy's theater troupe, produces a fall show for the community and competes in spring competitions, often placing within the top three to five in the state. Musicians are given opportunities to learn and demonstrate musical talents through jazz band, pep band, choruses, all-state auditions, music festivals, steel drum band, and guitar class.

DAILY LIFE

The Academy's daily schedule consists of a seven-period day, with each period running for 43 minutes. Classes begin at 7:53 a.m. and conclude at 2:13 p.m. No classes are held on weekends and holidays. Drama, music, and sports practices are held after school.

WEEKEND LIFE

Boarding students are provided with many supervised weekend activities. Weekend trips to Bar Harbor, Acadia National Park (1 hour away); Boston (6 hours away); and Canada (½ hour away) provide access to cultural and recreational events. Skiing, whale watching, and hiking on the bold coast are all within walking and driving distances. Residential students are provided with memberships to the local University's Life Long Learning Center (3 miles away), which includes an Olympic size pool, a weight room, racquetball courts, a gym, and cardiovascular equipment. Karate, dance, music, and horseback lessons are all available within a couple miles of the school.

On-campus activities often include athletic competitions, concerts, plays, and special events, such as the winter arts festival and Junior Prom.

COSTS AND FINANCIAL AID

The cost of tuition, room, and board for the 2009–10 school year is $32,500. Costs for ESL support are $2500 for the first class and $2000 for each additional class. An enrollment deposit of $3000 is due within thirty days of acceptance. Most parents set up accounts for weekly spending and extra expenses through a local bank or bank card.

Scholarships are based upon academic achievement, extracurricular involvement, and financial need. The Scholarship Committee determines financial awards. All submitted information is confidential.

ADMISSIONS INFORMATION

Washington Academy seeks students who are likely to both benefit from and positively contribute to the school and its student body. Entrance tests are not required; however TOEFL or SLEP scores are required for international students to determine placement for ESL courses. Admission decisions are made by an Admissions Committee after reviewing information on the candidate's academic ability, achievements, and other interests.

Washington Academy does not discriminate on the basis of race, religion, sex, national origin, or disability. The school is committed to ensuring all enrolled students are provided with equal social and academic opportunity.

APPLICATION TIMETABLE

The Admissions Office accepts applications throughout the year but strongly encourages fall applicants to send all forms and supporting documents to the Admissions Office by April 1. Parents are notified of the committee's decision on a rolling basis. The school encourages both campus interviews and visits at anytime (by appointment). The school is open from 7:30 a.m. until 4 p.m. Students may make an initial inquiry of the school through an online admission form. There is a $50 application fee.

ADMISSIONS CORRESPONDENCE

Kim Gardner
Admissions Coordinator
Washington Academy
66 Cutler Road
P.O. Box 190
East Machias, Maine 04630
Phone: 207-255-8301 Ext. 207
Fax: 207-255-8303
E-mail: admissions@washingtonacademy.org
Web site: http://www.washingtonacademy.org

THE WEBB SCHOOL

Bell Buckle, Tennessee

Type: Coeducational boarding and day college-preparatory school
Grades: 6–12, postgraduate year
Enrollment: 302
Head of School: Albert Cauz

THE SCHOOL

The Webb School offers an exceptional college-preparatory experience. At Webb, students can be athletes and artists, courage is developed with wisdom, and personal integrity goes hand in hand with academic success. Most importantly, the lives of Webb students are enriched in the School's close-knit, familylike environment. The School was founded in 1870 by noted Chapel Hill scholar William R. "Old Sawney" Webb. It is Tennessee's oldest continuously operating college-preparatory boarding school and the South's leading producer of Rhodes scholars. Proven hallmarks of Webb's formula for success include a structured liberal arts program, individual attention, and an emphasis on honor.

Webb's 150-acre campus lies among the beautiful, rolling hills of middle Tennessee. This rural setting enhances its learning and living environment, keeping students free from distractions while fostering the development of close relationships among students.

Webb has a $22-million endowment, an active 43-member Board of Trustees, and more than 3,200 loyal alumni to provide a lasting framework for the School's continued growth. Webb's parents are also very involved as members of Webb's Parents' Association.

The Webb School is a charter member of the Southern Association of Colleges and Schools and continues to be accredited by that organization. It also holds membership in the National Association of Independent Schools, the Southern Association of Independent Schools, the Tennessee Association of Independent Schools, the Council for Religion in Independent Schools, the Secondary School Admission Test Board, and the College Board.

ACADEMIC PROGRAMS

The Webb School academic program is a traditional college-preparatory liberal arts curriculum offered in a structured environment that is conducive to the development of good academic habits. School is in session from late August to early June. Webb classes, which meet five days a week, have an average size of 12 students.

Webb offers both a standard college-preparatory diploma track and a more rigorous Honors Diploma. The standard program requires a minimum of 4 years of English; 3 years of mathematics (algebra I and II, geometry); 2 years of the same foreign language (French, Spanish, Latin, or German), with 3 years recommended and 4–5 years offered; 2 years of history, including American history; 2 years of laboratory science (biology and integrated science); semester courses in Issues in Democracy, computer literacy, psychology, speech, drama, ethics, and the fine arts; and at least six full-year electives.

The Honors Diploma program increases the mathematics requirement to 4 years, foreign language to 3 years, history to 3 years, and laboratory science to 3 years. Participation in this program requires that a student undertake a minimum of two honors or Advanced Placement courses each year and receive no grade lower than 70.

Webb has a unique fine arts requirement that asks each student to take one semester of art each year. Half of this requirement must be performance based, including visual art, music, or drama.

The School requires that boarding students study for 2 hours in the evening five days a week. This study time is supervised by dormitory personnel. Students whose academic performance is deficient are assigned to study halls for their unscheduled periods during the day. Extra help is available from faculty members during a period that is set aside for that purpose at the end of each academic day.

Each student has a faculty adviser, who guides the student and acts as a liaison between the parents and the School. Parents are kept informed through regular written progress reports that are sent to them at least once every three weeks and through academic monitoring reports as required.

Whereas inadequate performance may result in increased restrictions, good academic performance yields privileges. Students on the honor roll are exempt from required study hours and may earn personal holidays away from school.

The required reading program at Webb ensures that students read widely above and beyond the assigned readings required in English classes. Books are selected from a list approved by the English faculty. This program is required of students in both the regular and the summer sessions. All Webb students are also required to declaim—recite a memorized passage before the assembled School—once a year. This program, which was instituted by Sawney Webb, is designed to teach poise in public speaking.

FACULTY AND ADVISERS

Webb's faculty members are its pride and joy. Teachers approach their work with a great passion for their subject as well as a sincere interest in educating the whole student. Because of this commitment, they spend a great deal of time outside the classroom with their students and essentially become like family to the children while they deeply delve into their academic interests and their creative and intellectual pursuits.

The Webb School has 44 teaching faculty members. All hold bachelor's degrees, and 43 percent hold advanced degrees. Many faculty members reside in the dormitories or in houses on campus.

Albert Cauz was appointed Head of School in 2005. He serves as Webb's tenth Head in more than 135 years. He received a B.A. from Boston College and an M.A. from Middlebury. Mr. Cauz brings more than twenty years of experience in independent boarding schools, including serving most recently as Abbot Residential Dean at Phillips Academy, Andover.

COLLEGE ADMISSION COUNSELING

College counseling is offered to juniors and seniors, and representatives from many colleges and universities visit the campus each year. Webb's recent graduates have gone on to further study at institutions that include Auburn, Boston College, Brown, Colby, Dartmouth, Davidson, Duke, Emory, Harvard, MIT, Northwestern, Princeton, Rhodes, Transylvania, Tulane, Vanderbilt, Yale, and the Universities of Michigan, Mississippi, North Carolina, Pennsylvania, the South, Tennessee, and Virginia.

STUDENT BODY AND CONDUCT

In 2008–09, there were 44 boarding boys, 107 day boys, 47 boarding girls, and 104 day girls enrolled. The students, who come from various economic and social backgrounds, represent fifteen states and eight other countries.

An Honor Code that has been part of the School's program since its founding is administered by an Honor Council consisting of representatives from each grade.

ACADEMIC FACILITIES

Academic facilities consist of the main classroom building, which is called the Big Room; four smaller classroom buildings; a reading laboratory; a computer room with twenty personal computers; and the 22,000-volume William W. Bond Library. In addition, the School has a state-of-the-art computer and science building.

BOARDING AND GENERAL FACILITIES

Boarding students live in one of four residential dormitories. Each building includes a common room, where students can socialize, watch movies, or grab a quick snack after study hours. Faculty members live in each dorm to help ensure the academic and social success of each resident. Student prefects (leaders) help faculty members by providing positive peer support. Each dorm includes a wireless Internet connection, and all students are assigned an e-mail address. An infirmary is located on campus for health concerns.

Webb's campus also includes three buildings on the National Register of Historic Places: the Old Library, the Son Will Admissions Building, and the Junior Room, which was erected in 1886 and is now open to the public as a museum. Also located on the campus are a bookstore, a student commons, and seventeen faculty residences. The 25,000-square-foot Barton Athletic Complex opened in 2002. It houses an indoor walking track, three basketball courts, a dance studio, and a weight room. The School's new Lundin Fine Arts Center provides space for a choir and string ensemble and a piano lab as well as areas for two- and three-dimensional art.

ATHLETICS

The athletic program includes interscholastic competition for both boys and girls in soccer, volleyball, basketball, golf, baseball, lacrosse, softball, tennis, trap, and cross-country. An extensive outdoor education program includes white-water rafting, high- and low-ropes courses, rock climbing, spelunking, rappelling, hiking, mountain biking, and camping.

Athletics facilities on campus include two gymnasiums, five playing fields, five tennis courts, three outdoor education courses, and a trap and skeet range.

EXTRACURRICULAR OPPORTUNITIES

Student organizations include the Trap and Skeet Club, Fly Fishing Club, Student Council, Mock Trial, the student newspaper and yearbook, Interact (a community service club), the student orientation committee, Habitat for Humanity, Diversity Club, Young Democrats, Young Republicans, and the student activities committee. At least two major dramatic productions are performed each year by the Webb School players.

Outerlimits uses the outdoors to teach students teamwork and self-confidence as they overcome obstacles on high- and low-ropes courses. Each year, up to 8 students are selected for WILD, a three-year program that uses an array of challenging outdoor activities to foster character development and leadership skills.

DAILY LIFE

A typical day begins at 8 a.m. and ends at 3:30 p.m. It includes seven academic periods, a chapel service, and a lunch period. An optional tutorial period is held each day after the last class period. Afternoon activities programs begin at 3:45 and end by 5:45.

WEEKEND LIFE

Dances and movies are scheduled at the School. Weekend activities are organized both on and off campus each weekend by the School's activities director. There are also trips to Nashville and Murfreesboro for dinner, shopping, movies, concerts, and cultural and sports events. Athletic teams also offer numerous on-campus events. The Outerlimits program offers more than twenty weekend trips each year that feature white-water rafting, rock climbing, hiking, and camping.

COSTS AND FINANCIAL AID

Room, board, and tuition for the 2008–09 academic year were $33,600. Day student tuition was $14,100.

Scholarships are granted to students on the basis of need. Thirty-four percent of the student body received more than $920,000 in financial aid in 2008–09. The School also offers a Webb Legacy Scholarship and the newly announced Webb School Honors Scholarship. The Honors Scholarship offers two full boarding merit scholarships. The deadline for applying for the scholarship is February 16.

ADMISSIONS INFORMATION

The Webb School seeks students who desire the challenge of academic excellence in a traditional liberal arts program that emphasizes honor. The School expects students to be contributing members of the School community, have an understanding of the importance of honor and personal integrity, and possess the capability and desire to pursue a college-preparatory curriculum. With these prerequisites, Webb accepts students without regard to race, creed, or national or ethnic origin.

APPLICATION TIMETABLE

Inquiries concerning fall or midyear admission are welcome at any time. Campus tours and interviews are available by appointment year-round. Students are encouraged to visit when school is in session. Office hours are from 8 a.m. to 4:30 p.m., Monday through Friday. Applications are processed continuously. There is an application fee of $35 ($50 for international students).

ADMISSIONS CORRESPONDENCE

Julie Harris, Director of Admissions
The Webb School
Highway 82 Sawney Webb Road
Bell Buckle, Tennessee 37020
Phone: 931-389-6003
888-SEE-WEBB (toll-free)
Fax: 931-389-6657
E-mail: admissions@webbschool.com
Web site: http://www.thewebbschool.com

WESTERN RESERVE ACADEMY

Hudson, Ohio

Type: Coeducational, boarding and day, college-preparatory
Grades: 9–12, postgraduate year
Enrollment: 370
Head of School: Christopher D. Burner, Headmaster

THE SCHOOL

Founded in 1826 as a preparatory school for Western Reserve College, Western Reserve Academy inherited its present campus in Hudson when the college moved to Cleveland in 1882 to eventually become Case Western Reserve University. In 1916, the Academy was greatly aided by a handsome endowment given by James W. Ellsworth. The school's endowment ranks among the top boarding/day, independent secondary schools in the United States.

Reserve is a traditional college-preparatory school that is committed to maintaining academic excellence and to offering its students a well-rounded program so that they may develop into interesting, knowledgeable, and sensitive adults. The academic part of the day is not overly structured, but an atmosphere of academic seriousness prevails. Close relationships among the adults and students are an essential and natural part of daily life.

Hudson lies between Cleveland (30 minutes away) and Akron (25 minutes away), just off the Ohio Turnpike. The main part of the Reserve campus is located one block from downtown Hudson, but most of its 190 acres extend into the surrounding countryside. Thus, outdoor activities are as much a part of life at Reserve as are those kinds of activities associated with major urban areas. Concerts (classical and otherwise), drama, art museums, outdoor activities, and cinema are a functional part of a student's life at the school.

Western Reserve Academy is governed by a board of 30 trustees who supervise the school's $114-million endowment. The annual budget of more than $15.5 million is fortified by the interest from that endowment as well as by funds from an Annual Giving Program. Parent organizations such as the Dad's Club and the Pioneer Women are actively involved in campus events as well. Approximately $3.6 million is allocated for financial aid, providing an opportunity for students who otherwise would be unable to attend.

Western Reserve Academy is accredited by the Independent Schools Association of the Central States. It is a member of the National Association of Independent Schools, the Secondary School Admission Test Board, the School and Student Service for Financial Aid, the Committee on Boarding Schools, the Midwest Boarding Schools, the Association of Boarding Schools, and the Ohio Association of Independent Schools.

ACADEMIC PROGRAMS

Western Reserve Academy offers a spirited four-year academic program of the highest caliber; students typically find it challenging. Structured beginning-level courses prepare younger students for what lies ahead in their final two years: opportunities to take advanced work in computer programming and Advanced Placement (AP) courses in English, Latin, French, Spanish, German, U.S. history, European history, art history, biology, physics, chemistry, computer science, statistics, calculus, and economics, as well as the opportunity to take several courses for college credit through a special School College Articulation Program (SCAP) in conjunction with Kenyon College. Each student graduates with at least 21 credits, which are earned in the following configuration: 4 credits of English, 3 of mathematics, 3 of a foreign language, 3 of a lab science, 2½ of history (including U.S. history), 1 of fine arts and a Senior Seminar, and ½ each of health and ethics and athletics, with the remaining credits in electives.

For upperclass students, the AP and SCAP courses may be supplemented by independent study. Upperclass students may also participate in the School Year Abroad program.

On the average, students take approximately 5 credits per year, in schedules arranged with their faculty advisers. The classes are small, with an average size of 12, although classes for advanced-level courses are typically smaller in size. There are no formal opportunities for remedial studies in any academic discipline.

To a great extent, students determine the use of their free periods during the academic day on an individual basis; there are no supervised study halls except during the evenings. At that time, students typically study in their dormitory rooms, although they may study in the library or in open classrooms or labs, depending on their specific needs.

Advisers work closely with students and parents to determine academic programs, daily schedules, preparation for final exams, and the need for extra help.

FACULTY AND ADVISERS

Western Reserve Academy has 69 full- and part-time faculty members, of whom all but a few live on campus in school houses or in apartments in dormitories. Many administrators teach at least one course. All faculty members have a bachelor's degree, and 60 percent have advanced degrees; 5 have doctorates.

Only the third alumnus to serve as Headmaster since the school's founding in 1826, Christopher D. Burner, '80, was appointed in 2008 and is a graduate of Franklin & Marshall College (B.A.), Dartmouth College (M.A.L.S), and Harvard University (M.Ed.). Mr. Burner has taught at Western Reserve Academy on two separate occasions. During his first term (1986) at Reserve, Mr. Burner served as the Assistant Dean of Students, taught Latin, and coached varsity wrestling, football, and lacrosse. He also held faculty positions at Saint James School in Maryland and Westminster School in Connecticut. After returning to Reserve (1992), Mr. Burner served as the Director of Admission and most recently as the Dean of Faculty and Administration, in addition to teaching Latin and coaching.

The average faculty member has been at Western Reserve Academy for more than twelve years. Typically, it is the younger teachers moving on to graduate, law, or medical school who leave the staff. Almost all teachers coach a sport, serve evening duty in dormitories, supervise an activity, and advise students. Mandatory on-campus housing and meals (morning and evening meals are available for all faculty families) constitute part of each teacher's salary. A sabbatical program and summer study grants are also a part of faculty benefits.

COLLEGE ADMISSION COUNSELING

College placement is handled by the College Adviser, who consults with students and their families during the junior and senior years. The school report on each student is prepared by the Faculty Guidance Committee, which is chaired by the College Adviser. Naturally, college visits are encouraged, but each year Reserve is visited by more than 85 representatives from colleges. The College Guidance Office keeps on file an extensive selection of college catalogs and other admission information.

Of the Academy's graduates, 100 percent attend colleges or universities each year. SAT averages have remained very high. Recent graduates are attending such institutions as Case Western Reserve, Georgetown, Harvard, Miami (Ohio), Middlebury, Northwestern, Princeton, Stanford, the U.S. Naval Academy, Vanderbilt, Yale, and the Universities of Chicago and Pennsylvania.

STUDENT BODY AND CONDUCT

Two thirds of all students are boarders, and slightly more than half are boys. Students at Reserve come from many parts of this country and the world. The Academy is dedicated to creating and maintaining a healthy and pluralistic composition in its student body. Currently, 28 percent of the students represent minority groups (African American, Hispanic American, and Asian American).

Discipline and student conduct are handled by the Student Affairs Committee, which is made up of junior and senior class officers and selected faculty members in equal proportions and is chaired by the Dean of Students, with the final arbiter being the Headmaster. Student government officers, dorm prefects, and various other student leaders contribute their views in most matters of student conduct and general rule determination, although the school behavior and dress code is generally considered conservative.

ACADEMIC FACILITIES

Almost every building at Reserve has an academic function, but there are seven principal academic buildings: Seymour Hall, the chapel, Hayden Hall, Wilson Hall, Knight Fine Arts Center, Metcalf Center, and the John D. Ong Library. The seven buildings house classrooms, labs, music practice rooms, a lecture hall, a recital hall, dance rooms, a student lounge, woodworking and metalworking shops, a photography studio, a computer center, art studios, a publications room, administrative offices, and the school library of 45,000 volumes. The Wilson Hall Science Center was completely renovated in 2001.

Visually dominating the campus is the chapel, modeled, as were most of the buildings, on the architectural style of Yale College. Some of the buildings, such as the Loomis Observatory (circa 1838), are more than 100 years old.

BOARDING AND GENERAL FACILITIES

Western Reserve Academy has nine dormitories and one large dining hall for its boarding students. Monday through Thursday, evening meals are served family-style, as are lunches on Tuesday and Thursday. Lunches Monday, Wednesday, and Friday are buffet-style. Students can also purchase items at the bookstore, or they can sign out to eat at one of Hudson's many restaurants. Most boys' dorm rooms are doubles, with some triples, and a few single rooms are available. Girls have dorms with doubles and a few singles. There are laundry facilities in five dorms.

The new school Health Center is state-of-the-art and has a dispensary, examination and waiting rooms, and six sick-bay rooms. A nurse is on duty during the day and on call at night unless needed for a student who is restricted to the Health Center overnight. The school doctor visits the campus every weekday to examine and talk to students.

The Student Center, which is located in the lower level of Ellsworth Hall, contains the Green Key snack bar, booths for eating and talking, a wide-screen television, and Ping-Pong, pool, and video games. Next door are the radio station and one of the publications rooms.

ATHLETICS

Western Reserve Academy emphasizes athletic competition and believes student participation in team sports is an essential part of the daily program. There are two or three levels of interschool competition for boys and girls in tennis, basketball, ice hockey, diving, swimming, cross-country, track, golf, lacrosse, soccer, football, wrestling, baseball, riflery, volleyball, softball, and field hockey. Reserve is a member of the Interstate Prep School League.

The Academy's athletics facilities include a ProTurf stadium with a six-lane all-weather track, a competition swimming pool and separate diving well with 3- and 1-meter boards, a state-of-the-art fitness center with Nautilus equipment, two football fields, four soccer/lacrosse fields, a 3.1-mile cross-country course, two field-hockey fields, a wrestling arena, and twelve all-weather tennis courts. An indoor athletic complex features a 45,000-square-foot field house housing a 200-meter indoor track, varsity and four practice basketball courts, and a complete training facility.

EXTRACURRICULAR OPPORTUNITIES

Aside from participating in the Student Council, student publications, and services already mentioned, students may join a diverse and changing group of clubs and organizations: photography, debate, chess, REACH (a community service club), Green Key (the student center), skiing, drama, Green Action Committee, Culinary Club, and WWRA (the school radio station). The school social committee, an extension of the Student Council, organizes dances and weekend activities on campus as well as in Cleveland and Akron.

DAILY LIFE

The class day at Reserve begins at 8 a.m. There are six 55-minute periods each day. From 3:30 to 5:45, all students participate in athletics. Dinner begins at 6:30 p.m., and study halls in dorms are from 8 until 10. Classes meet on Saturday from 8 a.m. until noon.

WEEKEND LIFE

All students may sign out for weekend leave for most weekends. Leaves begin about noon on Saturday and extend until study hours begin on Sunday evening. Less than one fourth of the students leave the campus on a given weekend.

A variety of activities are presented to the student body (for both day and boarding students) Saturday and Sunday afternoons.

The Academy is located in a thriving geographic area. Nestled in the quaint village of Hudson, Reserve is within easy walking distance of attractive shops, restaurants, and community activities. Beyond Hudson, Cleveland and Akron offer major cultural events. The world-famous Cleveland Orchestra, the Rock and Roll Hall of Fame, E. J. Thomas Hall, Playhouse Square, the Ohio Ballet, the Cleveland Institute of Art, and the Museum of Natural History are easily accessible. Weekend programs also include downhill skiing at nearby slopes, concerts, off-campus movies, trips to the Gateway Sports Complex to see professional athletics teams, and outdoor activities at the nearby Cuyahoga Valley National Recreation Area. The Academy's proximity to Case Western Reserve, Hiram, Kent State, Oberlin, and the University of Akron makes the resources of these colleges and universities available as well.

SUMMER PROGRAMS

Western Reserve Academy hosts numerous summer programs. Among them are sports camps for lacrosse, field hockey, soccer, basketball, swimming, and diving. New programs will be added during the summer of 2009.

COSTS AND FINANCIAL AID

Fees for 2008–09 were $37,900 for boarders and $27,000 for day students. Extra fees of about $600 covered books and other incidental expenses. Payments are made in three installments: July, September, and December. Reserve uses the Knight Tuition Payment Plan and the Dewar Tuition Refund Plan.

For 2008–09, more than $3.6 million in financial aid was awarded to 34 percent of Reserve's students. In addition to awards made on the basis of family need (as established by the School and Student Service for Financial Aid), merit scholarships are also available. The average award was $17,298 for day students and $27,792 for boarders.

ADMISSIONS INFORMATION

Western Reserve Academy admits students of any race, sex, color, disability, or national or ethnic origin to all rights, privileges, programs, and activities generally accorded or made available to students at the Academy. It does not discriminate on the basis of race, sex, color, disability, or national or ethnic origin in the administration of its educational policies, admissions policies, scholarship and loan programs, and athletics or other school-administered programs.

Reserve requires that all applicants submit SSAT, ISEE, or SAT scores and recommendations from 2 current teachers. Applicants average in the top three deciles on the SSAT and have achieved A's and B's at their previous schools. Most students enter in grade 9 or 10. Reserve admits approximately 100 freshmen per year.

APPLICATION TIMETABLE

Most inquiries are made in the fall, with applications ($25 fee for students within the United States and $150 for international students) completed by January 15 (day students, December 15). Applicants and their families should have a campus tour and an interview. After an application is submitted, it is reviewed by the Faculty Admission Committee; families are notified after March 10 (day students, January 10) and are usually allowed four weeks to notify the school of their intentions.

ADMISSIONS CORRESPONDENCE

Laura Hudak
Admission Office
Western Reserve Academy
Hudson, Ohio 44236
Phone: 330-650-9717
800-784-3776 (toll-free)
Fax: 330-650-5858
E-mail: admission@wra.net
Web site: http://www.wra.net

WESTMINSTER SCHOOL

Simsbury, Connecticut

Type: Coeducational boarding and day college-preparatory school
Grades: 9–12 (Forms III–VI)
Enrollment: 385
Head of School: W. Graham Cole Jr., Headmaster

THE SCHOOL

Founded in 1888 by William Lee Cushing, Westminster School was first located in Dobbs Ferry, New York. At the turn of the century, the School was moved to its present location in Simsbury, Connecticut. Westminster began admitting girls in 1971 and now has an equal number of boys and girls.

Westminster is a school with a strong sense of identity and tradition. Members of the School community recognize the importance of duties and obligations, not only to other people, but to one's own aptitudes, strengths, and opportunities as well. There is a sense of the importance of trust and of living up to one's responsibilities, and there is agreement on the importance of living cheerfully within the limits a society sets and of respecting its ceremonies and symbols. These agreements support a coherent social pattern with opportunities for many different kinds of people.

Westminster is situated on 230 acres of wooded plateau overlooking the scenic Farmington River valley, 13 miles northwest of Hartford. It is 20 minutes from Bradley International Airport and a little more than a 2-hour drive from New York and Boston.

A 30-member Board of Trustees is the governing body. Westminster's current endowment is valued at $88 million. In 2007–08, the School received $2.4 million in Annual Giving and $8.6 million in capital gifts.

Westminster is accredited by the New England Association of Schools and Colleges. It has memberships in the National Association of Independent Schools, the Connecticut Association of Independent Schools, the Secondary School Admission Test Board, the Educational Records Bureau, and the Council for Religion in Independent Schools.

ACADEMIC PROGRAMS

Westminster offers a liberal arts curriculum that emphasizes balance and depth. Eighteen credits are required for graduation; however, the vast majority of students accumulate 20 or more credits. The minimum department requirements for graduation include 4 credits of English, 3 credits of mathematics, 2 credits of laboratory science, 2 credits of Latin or a modern foreign language, 2 credits of history (including 1 credit in U.S. history at the Fifth- or Sixth-Form level), and 1 credit in the creative arts.

Each of the academic departments offers Advanced Placement (AP) courses. The English program culminates with a final trimester of electives, which have included Frost and Cummings, the American Dream, Children's Literature, Modern Literature, and Modern Drama. Three trimester electives are offered for Sixth Formers in creative writing. Students can continue mathematics course work through AP calculus, AP computers, and AP statistics. Latin, French, and Spanish are offered through the AP level, with tutorials available for sixth-year study. Chinese was added to the curriculum for the 2008–09 academic year. The history department provides advanced courses in twentieth-century American history and ethical philosophy as well as AP courses in economics, United States history, comparative government, modern European history, and art history. In addition to the basic courses in biology, chemistry, physics, astronomy, and geology, students can choose from AP courses in chemistry, physics, biology, and environmental science. Creative arts offerings include introductory and advanced art courses, a broad range of music and theater courses, and a noteworthy architecture program that begins with engineering drawing and leads to architecture II.

Independent-study programs may be undertaken by Fifth and Sixth Formers in lieu of athletics in any trimester, with the understanding that no student may participate in more than one such project a year.

A teacher acts as an adviser for each student. Advisers monitor both the academic progress and the social adjustment of their students, meeting regularly with them and maintaining communication with their families.

The School is on the trimester system. Students normally carry five courses per year. The grading system is numerical—60 is needed to pass and 85 to achieve honors. In order to earn promotion (and in the Sixth Form, a diploma), students must successfully complete at least four major courses and achieve a minimum general average of 70. At the end of each trimester, students' parents and advisers receive grades and teacher comments; at each mid-trimester, interim grades are provided. In addition to receiving these fixed evaluations, students, parents, and advisers are alerted to any problems that might arise. The average class size is 12 students, and the student-faculty ratio is 5:1.

FACULTY AND ADVISERS

Of the 85 faculty members at Westminster, 45 are men and 40 are women. Master's degrees are held by 58 of the 85, and 3 members have completed their Ph.D. degrees. The average tenure of faculty members at Westminster is twelve years (seventeen years in teaching). Virtually all live on campus, either in a dormitory or in one of the twenty-four houses on the campus.

Faculty turnover is minimal each year, and new members are selected for their dedication to teaching young men and women and for their versatility, richness of background, and professional preparation. Faculty members have access to an endowed fund that is intended for professional improvement in such areas as advanced study and traveling.

W. Graham Cole Jr. is Westminster's seventh Headmaster. He graduated Phi Beta Kappa from Williams College in 1966 and received his M.A. in history from Columbia University. Mr. Cole is in his sixteenth year at Westminster, following a twenty-year tenure at the Lawrenceville School.

COLLEGE ADMISSION COUNSELING

Three college guidance counselors work closely with students and their parents throughout the college application process. Students begin the process by taking the PSAT in the fall of the junior year, followed in the winter by an on-campus College Day, which exposes them and their parents to all aspects of the college application process. In the spring and continuing through the following year, students and parents schedule frequent individual conferences with their college guidance counselor. Students take the SAT and the SAT Subject Tests in the spring of the junior year and again in the fall of the senior year. In 2007–08, the average scores on the SAT were 604 verbal and 616 mathematics.

Westminster sends all of its graduates to four-year colleges or universities. Colleges and universities attended by the class of 2008 include Amherst, Boston College, Bowdoin, Brown, Colby, Cornell, Duke, Middlebury, Notre Dame, Tufts, Williams, and the Universities of Michigan, Pennsylvania, and Virginia.

STUDENT BODY AND CONDUCT

In 2008–09, Westminster's student body was composed as follows: Third Form, 36 boys and 30 girls; Fourth Form, 53 boys and 52 girls; Fifth Form, 60 boys and 50 girls; and Sixth Form, 56 boys and 48 girls. Of the total of 385 students, 144 were boarding boys, 71 were day boys, 110 were boarding girls, and 60 were day girls. Students came from twenty-six states and twenty other countries. About as many students came from independent schools as from public schools.

Seniors assume responsibility in the dorms, extracurricular programs, and work squad program. They inherit responsibilities and privileges that make them the leaders of the student body. The members of the Student Council are elected from every grade but are led by a board of prefects chosen from the senior class. Students and faculty members work together on ad hoc and standing committees to determine and enforce disciplinary standards.

Westminster believes that by entering into the life of a coherent and purposeful community, students are able to develop a point of view that makes sense of the opportunities and obstacles they face. To this end, Westminster inspires young men and women of promise to cultivate a passion for learning, to explore and develop their talents in a balanced program, to reach well beyond the ordinary, to live with character and intelligence, and to commit to a life of service beyond oneself.

ACADEMIC FACILITIES

Baxter Academic Center is the hub of academic life. It contains twenty-six classrooms; six science laboratories; computer facilities that include an equipped classroom, a working laboratory, and science computers; a greenhouse facility equipped with aquariums and terrariums; a spacious library containing more than 24,000 volumes; an auditorium; and a bookstore. Students taking astronomy make use of the School's astronomical observatory, which features a computer-guided 14-inch telescope. The Centennial Performing Arts Center has a theater that seats 400, a dance studio, and rooms for music courses, private music lessons, and practice sessions. There are also studios and classrooms for art and architecture. The School's new LEED-certified 85,000-square-foot academic center is scheduled to be ready for the 2009–10 academic year.

BOARDING AND GENERAL FACILITIES

There are six dormitories, all of which underwent complete renovations in 1996, as well as one dorm that opened for use in that same year. All dorm rooms and dorm study spaces have wireless computer access to the local campus network as well as the Internet. Computers are provided in the common study spaces of each dorm. Every student receives a phone number that rings to a phone in the student's room or to a voice mail system. Each student normally has a roommate, but there are singles available for upperclass students. Corridors have between 10 and 15 students, and a faculty member and his or her family reside on each corridor. In addition, each floor has at least 2 Sixth Formers who help in supervising the underclass students.

Students spend some of their free time in the School's bookstore or student center. The bookstore, the Martlet's Nest, sells school and personal supplies and has a small café. The Timken Student Center, which was originally built by students and faculty members, has recently undergone a complete renovation. The student center contains a snack bar, an extension of the School's bookstore, a game room, and a lounge that is equipped with networked computers.. The School also has a well-equipped and fully staffed infirmary.

ATHLETICS

Westminster considers athletics to be part of the School's curriculum and requires participation by every student. The School fields fifty-two teams in sixteen different sports: cross-country, field hockey, football, and soccer in the fall; basketball, hockey, paddle tennis, squash, and swimming and diving in the winter; and baseball, golf, lacrosse, softball, tennis, and track in the spring.

Westminster's athletic facilities include 30 acres of playing fields, a 400-meter synthetic track, two clay and twelve all-weather tennis courts, twelve squash courts, two weight-training rooms, two paddle tennis courts, two full-sized basketball courts, a hockey rink, a swimming pool, locker room facilities, and two athletic training rooms.

In 2004, Westminster completed an $11-million, state-of-the-art athletic complex that includes an indoor pool, a fitness center, and a health and counseling center. The facility houses an eight-lane, 25-yard pool complete with locker rooms, an overnight health complex, and a 4,500-square-foot fitness center with the latest fitness equipment. The building is the second of four major additions to an already significant athletic complex.

EXTRACURRICULAR OPPORTUNITIES

Westminster students have an opportunity to become involved in a variety of extracurricular activities, and students are encouraged to participate in at least one.

Activities vary from year to year according to interest, time, and student initiative. Those of an ongoing nature include the school newspaper, the *Martlet* (a creative arts magazine), and the yearbook; theater, with both acting and technical work; three choral groups; a jazz ensemble; instrumental and voice lessons; chapel services, which are conducted almost entirely by students and faculty members; and social service groups, such as a group that visits a local convalescent home each week. Clubs include the Environmental Awareness Group and the Debate and Women's Issues Clubs. Off-campus activities, including trips into Hartford to see performances by the Hartford Stage Company and games at the Civic Center, take place whenever appropriate.

DAILY LIFE

Classes are held six days a week, with half days on Wednesday and Saturday. An optional buffet breakfast is offered from 7:15 to 8:30 a.m. on each school day. Classes begin at 8 and run until 2:30 on Monday, Tuesday, Thursday, and Friday and until 11:40 on the other days. Students have one or two study periods during an average day.

Each class is 40 or 60 minutes long, and all major courses meet ten times in two weeks. A cafeteria-style lunch is served for 2 hours each day. Students perform assigned work squad tasks sometime during the day, either at 2:30 after classes, during a free period, or during the evening, amounting to a contribution of about 1½ hours per week. A required afternoon commitment is scheduled for approximately 1½ hours. Chapel is mandatory for all students on Tuesday and Friday at midmorning.

On Monday, Tuesday, and Thursday, dinner is a formal sit-down meal at which students dine with the faculty members and their families. Following these meals, Sixth Formers join faculty members for coffee and tea in the Hinman Reading Room. All other nights, dinner is served cafeteria-style. Study period is held from 7:30 to 9:15 p.m. Students study in their own rooms or the Baxter Academic Center or work in the computer labs.

WEEKEND LIFE

After classes on Saturday, most students are involved in athletics; those who are not support the various teams by attending the games. There are always a couple of events planned by the Student Activities Committee for Saturday evenings. Typical activities include on- and off-campus dances and movies, skating parties, visits to coffeehouses, and trips into Hartford to attend plays or sports events.

Students are allotted a certain number of overnights or weekends, ensuring that there is a critical mass of students on campus every weekend. This keeps the community vibrant and active seven days a week. Day students are encouraged to participate in all activities, both during the school week and on the weekend. Students who want some time off campus to eat at one of the dozen restaurants, buy clothes or groceries, or browse can easily walk into the town of Simsbury.

COSTS AND FINANCIAL AID

Tuition at Westminster for 2008–09 was $41,700 for boarding students and $31,100 for day students. Students can expect approximately $1500 in additional expenses, which include such items as books, school supplies, dry cleaning, laundry, and personal needs. New students are expected to pay an initial deposit of $4000 by April 10. The balance is payable in equal installments on July 15 and December 1.

For the 2008–09 school year, approximately $3.5 million in need-based financial assistance was awarded to approximately 30 percent of the students. Financial aid is reviewed each year, and all families applying for assistance must submit the Parents' Financial Statement to the School and Student Service for Financial Aid in Princeton, New Jersey.

ADMISSIONS INFORMATION

Students are admitted to Westminster on the basis of their ability to contribute to the School community and, in a general sense, to society beyond Westminster. The admissions committee seeks students who show a willingness and enthusiasm to grow, to become involved, to work cheerfully with others, and to meet new challenges. Experience has shown that a record of accomplishment, whether in or out of the classroom, is the best evidence that a student has the potential, the will, and the imagination needed to do more things well at Westminster.

Requirements for admission include a personal interview, recommendations from English and math teachers, a school transcript, writing samples, and the results of the SSAT. The admissions committee considers each of these requirements an essential factor in establishing a complete profile of a candidate.

Most students come to Westminster as Third or Fourth Formers (grades 9 or 10), but the School accepts some students each year for grade 11 and for a postgraduate year.

APPLICATION TIMETABLE

An initial inquiry is welcome at any time. Scheduled visits are available from 8 a.m. to 1:45 p.m. on Monday, Tuesday, Thursday, and Friday and from 8 to 11 on Wednesday and Saturday. The application deadline is January 15. Fees are $75 for domestic applications, $150 for international. Candidates with all credentials on file by the deadline are notified of a decision on March 10; students are expected to reply to acceptances by April 10.

ADMISSIONS CORRESPONDENCE

Jon C. Deveaux, Director of Admissions
Westminster School
Simsbury, Connecticut 06070

Phone: 860-408-3060
Fax: 860-408-3042
E-mail: admit@westminster-school.org
Web site: http://www.westminster-school.org

WEST NOTTINGHAM ACADEMY

Colora, Maryland

Type: Coeducational boarding and day college-preparatory school
Grades: 9–12, postgraduate year
Enrollment: 135
Head of School: Dr. D. John Watson

THE SCHOOL

The oldest boarding school in America, West Nottingham Academy (WNA) was founded in 1744 on the principle that an excellent and inclusive education is vital to the future. That belief and knowledge is the Academy's heritage and philosophy. Students discover a school where everyone is respected and listened to and where every student is encouraged to participate in, and be a part of, an energetic and caring community.

The 120-acre campus includes 20 acres of woodland. The broad lawns are dotted by an unusual variety of trees. Located about an hour from Baltimore and Philadelphia, the Academy enjoys a quiet, rural setting and supplements its overall program with the regular use of the recreational and cultural resources of the Baltimore-Philadelphia area.

West Nottingham Academy is accredited by the Middle States Association of Colleges and Schools and by the Maryland State Department of Education. The Academy is a member of the National Association of Independent Schools, the Association of Independent Maryland Schools, the Association of Delaware Valley Independent Schools, the Small Boarding School Association, and the Association of Boarding Schools.

ACADEMIC PROGRAMS

West Nottingham Academy's rigorous, college-preparatory academic program and educational philosophy are rooted in a commitment to inspire curiosity while helping students develop critical-thinking skills. Rather than serving as a mere funnel for information, its student-centered and experiential approach enables the Academy to cultivate a lifelong passion for learning that is fulfilling for the individual and valuable to society.

WNA's newly developed master schedule offers many benefits, including more structured advisory time between faculty and students and changes to various courses to address pedagogical needs. For example, it reshapes the lab science sequence to allow for deeper hands-on learning and greatly enhances the English curriculum, providing increased academic support during the freshman and sophomore years while augmenting standard course loads for juniors and seniors.

All courses of study are regularly reviewed by the Academic Committee for Excellence (ACE), chaired by the Academic Dean. This committee works to ensure that WNA's academic program remains vital and reflects the educational demands of the twenty-first century.

The academic year is divided into trimesters and includes a Thanksgiving recess as well as winter and spring vacations. Classes are held from 8 to 3 five days a week.

An average class has 10 students; the student-teacher ratio is 7:1. All teachers are available for extra help during daily academic assistance periods, which students may attend voluntarily or by faculty request. Boarding students have a supervised 2-hour study period Sunday through Thursday evening. Parents are sent grades and comments eight times per year, with interim reports issued for students experiencing academic difficulty.

Of the 84 credits required for graduation, 22 must be in literature and composition and 12 each in history, mathematics, sciences, and foreign language. In addition, 8 credits are required in fine arts and 2 each in computer science, health, and religious thought/ethics.

Courses offered are English literature 1–4 and English composition 1–4; French 1–4 and Spanish 1–4; world history, United States history, European history, ancient history, international relations, psychology, and religious thought/ethics; algebra 1–2, geometry, pre-calculus, and calculus; biology, chemistry, physics, computer science, and polymers; and drawing, painting, clay, photography, sculpture, performing arts, acting, survey of Western art, and health. Honors-level study is offered in most subject areas.

FACULTY AND ADVISERS

D. John Watson, Ph.D., became Head of School in 2002. Previously, Dr. Watson was Assistant Head and Director of the CASCLE program at Cheshire Academy and held positions at the Peddie School and Darrow School. He holds a degree from Northern Michigan University and earned M.A. and Ph.D. degrees in music composition and theory at the University of Minnesota.

There are 47 members of the administrative and teaching faculty, 29 men and 18 women. More than half have earned master's degrees or beyond; 3 hold doctorates. Among their representative colleges and universities are Columbia, Dartmouth, Delaware, Emory, Guilford, Haverford, Johns Hopkins, Loyola, Millersville, Muhlenberg, Penn State, St. Andrews (Scotland), St. John's College, Smith, SUNY, Towson State, Vanderbilt, Virginia Tech, Washington College, West Virginia, and the Universities of Alaska, Colorado, Connecticut, Kentucky, Maine, Maryland, Michigan, and Pennsylvania.

On-campus nursing and counseling services are available during academic hours and in the early evening. Complete hospital services are available in two nearby towns.

Faculty members serve as advisers to students. They also actively participate in student clubs, accompany students on field trips and weekend outings, and share dormitory life with them. Many faculty members serve as coaches, and all are available to students for informal counseling, extra academic help, and companionship.

The Academy employs teachers who are not only proficient in and passionate about their subject areas but also committed to sharing their lives with the students in a caring and supportive community. Teachers listen to students, one of the characteristics that define the Academy.

COLLEGE ADMISSION COUNSELING

College counseling begins upon enrollment at the Academy and is completed upon acceptance of a college's offer of admission. The Academy provides families and students with timely, accurate information and sound counsel; individualized assistance is provided to all students. No question goes unanswered and no student is overlooked.

A sampling of college acceptances from the class of 2008 includes Brandeis, Case Western Reserve, Dickinson, Franklin & Marshall, Ithaca, James Madison, Michigan State, Neumann College, Quinnipiac, Radford, SUNY at Albany, and the Universities of Delaware, Maryland, and Texas.

Recent college acceptances include the Art Institute of Chicago, Babson, Bucknell, Colby, Delaware College of Art and Design, Dickinson, Elon, Guilford, Hofstra, Ithaca, James Madison, Oberlin, Penn State, Rollins, St. John's, Seton Hall, Smith, Syracuse, USC, York College, and the Universities of Connecticut, Maryland, Pittsburgh, Vermont, and Wisconsin.

STUDENT BODY AND CONDUCT

West Nottingham has 140 students across four grades and a postgraduate program.

The Academy's enrollment is drawn from all socioeconomic levels and averages 60 percent boys, 40 percent girls, and 30 percent day students. Twelve percent are members of minority groups. Most of the boarding students come from Delaware, Maryland, New Jersey, Pennsylvania, Virginia, and Washington, D.C., but there are representatives from Colorado, Florida, Ohio, and Texas. International students come from China, Ethiopia, Germany, Japan, Nigeria, Russia, South Korea, Taiwan, and Thailand.

The Student Government Association provides leadership in making the Academy understood by the student body and responsive to students' needs and in identifying areas of concern to students. A Residential Life Committee identifies problems in residential life and seeks solutions that encourage cooperation among students and faculty members who live in dormitories.

The Academy considers honesty as the first rule of the school. The Dean of Students and a faculty-student committee monitor school rules and student behavior. Advisers advocate for students and stay in touch with their families to keep them informed.

ACADEMIC FACILITIES

The Patricia A. Bathon Science Center is home to three state-of-the-art science labs and classroom spaces. Recently renovated, the academic center of the campus is Finley Hall, which was built in memory of the Academy's founder, Rev. Samuel Finley. It houses twenty classrooms and a writing lab. The Slaybaugh Old Academy building is used for drama performances, student variety shows, and other presentations during the school year. Magraw Hall, a 1930 structure that was refurbished in 2000, houses the library, computer lab, art studio, music room, high-technology presentation room, academic program offices, and Office of Admission.

Faculty members and students regard the entire campus as an extension of the academic facilities. Classes occasionally meet in faculty homes. The trees on the Academy's grounds come from all over the world, providing an unusual opportunity for botanical study.

BOARDING AND GENERAL FACILITIES

The 120-acre campus includes 20 acres of woodland; football, field hockey, and soccer fields; and baseball and softball diamonds. Indoor athletic facilities are housed in Ware Field House. The C. Herbert Foutz Center is the focal point of the Academy's student activity. It houses the Frank D. Brown Dining Room, the Hallock Student Union, and administrative offices.

East Dorm and West Dorm (1998) house 22 girls and 22 boys, respectively. Other dormitories are Rush House for boys and Rowland for girls. Recent campus improvements (summer 2007) include renovation and expansion of Rush House and the construction of Durigg Plaza, an outdoor meeting space for students and visitors. Renovation and expansion of Rowland is scheduled for summer 2008. The oldest building on campus is Gayley House (circa 1700), which serves as the Head of School's residence. Bechtel House, Hilltop House, and Log Cabin provide additional faculty housing. The Academy-owned physical plant is valued at $12.6 million.

ATHLETICS

All students participate in sports. There are interscholastic teams in baseball, basketball, cross-country, field hockey, football, golf, lacrosse, power lifting, soccer, tennis, track and field, volleyball, and wrestling; noncompetitive activities include conditioning, weight lifting (off season), horseback riding, and outdoor activities.

Athletic facilities include the Ware Field House, which contains the basketball court and weight-lifting equipment. In addition, there are fields for baseball, football, hockey, lacrosse, and soccer. Two athletic fields were debuted in 2001. Academy students have access to nearby riding stables and golf courses. The emphasis in the sports program includes not only competition but also cooperation and mutual reliance, which are important in the school community. No student gets cut from a team. Students who do not know how to play a sport are taught.

EXTRACURRICULAR OPPORTUNITIES

The Student Government Association provides a forum for matters of student concern. The Student Dormitory Council identifies issues in residential life and seeks solutions.

Club activity varies according to student interest, but all students are encouraged to take part in the activity program. Activities include the yearbook, skiing, and the Computer, Library, Riding, and Varsity Clubs. Qualified students are invited to join the National Honor Society.

Weekend activities include outings to Baltimore; Philadelphia; Wilmington; Washington, D.C.; and the surrounding area. Traditional events and activities include homecoming, parents' weekend, homecoming and winter formal dances, theater productions, and prom.

DAILY LIFE

Students begin each school day by meeting with their adviser in an assigned homeroom to hear announcements and touch base. There are four classes in the morning and four in the afternoon. At midmorning, there is a half hour of academic assistance, during which students may see their teachers for additional help.

The remainder of the afternoon is devoted to athletics and activities, in which all students must participate. From the time dinner is over until study hall, students are free to enjoy the campus, use the game room in the Student Union, watch television, or relax with friends.

Students attend a 2-hour study hall each evening, Sunday through Thursday. Students who are performing well academically are allowed to study in their dorm room, with supervision by a faculty member who has been assigned to the dorm. In the supervised study hall, students are in a classroom setting, with a faculty member present at all times. They may move out of the supervised study hall when their grades attain an acceptable level. Students may utilize additional study time at the end of the regular study hall. A detailed description of a typical day at WNA is also available at the school's Web site.

WEEKEND LIFE

Each Saturday and Sunday features a late-morning brunch. Cultural events are frequently held on campus. All students are invited to participate in on-campus activities, including movies, small concerts, variety shows, open gym time, and games, as well as off-campus options, such as trips to the museums in Philadelphia, local shopping malls, and the Smithsonian Institution in Washington, D.C.; snow skiing, college and professional sports, equestrian events, canoeing, sailing, and white-water rafting; and dances, concerts, movies, and amusement parks.

Ware Field House is also available on weekends for basketball, volleyball, and other sports.

COSTS AND FINANCIAL AID

In 2007–08, the cost of room, board, and tuition for students enrolling in the boarding program was $34,900; tuition for day students was $18,100. There are additional charges for the Chesapeake Learning Center and the English as a second language (ESL) program.

In addition to these costs, a $1200 student account covers expenses for books, room/key deposits, lab fees, and emergencies. A checking account may be established with a local bank.

All financial aid is awarded on the basis of demonstrated need. The Academy is proud of its effort to assist the sons and daughters of families who otherwise could not attend. Students should contact the Admission Office for more information.

WNA is also proud to offer the Hallock Scholarships (in honor of decorated war hero Richard Hallock, '37) to qualified foreign-service and career military families. Students should visit the Web site and contact the Admission Office for more information.

ADMISSIONS INFORMATION

The admission decision is based on various criteria, including grades, test scores, recommendations, and an interview, with a focus on the student's experiences, interests, abilities, and willingness to be a positive member of the school community.

Students should note that West Nottingham places great emphasis on the student interview. The most important criteria for the Academy are the student's sincere willingness to embrace the opportunities available, a true desire to become an active and responsible participant in one's own academic and social development, and to prepare for college with serious hard work and effort. On the school's seal are the words "Nihil sine labore"–nothing without work.

APPLICATION TIMETABLE

West Nottingham maintains a rolling schedule. However, although inquiries are welcome throughout the year, admission has in recent years become increasingly competitive, so families are strongly encouraged to begin the application process as early as possible. The Academy's admissions office is open weekdays from 8 to 4. Meetings with families may also be scheduled on Saturday morning. An interview is required.

ADMISSIONS CORRESPONDENCE

Mr. Jesse Roberts
Director of Admission
West Nottingham Academy
1079 Firetower Road
Colora, Maryland 21917-1599
Phone: 410-658-9279
410-658-5556
Fax: 410-658-9264
E-mail: jroberts@wna.org
Web site: http://www.wna.org

WESTOVER SCHOOL

Middlebury, Connecticut

100 YEARS OF INSPIRING WOMEN

Type: Girls' boarding and day college-preparatory school
Grades: 9–12
Enrollment: 199
Head of School: Ann S. Pollina

THE SCHOOL

Westover, founded in 1909, is a selective boarding and day school of 200 girls, grades 9–12, located in a classic New England town near New York City. Westover School prepares its students to meet the academic and social challenges of the world's top colleges.

The Westover community is ethnically, geographically, and socioeconomically diverse. Westover offers excellent college placement, and its students demonstrate outstanding success in twenty-one AP programs.

Westover's Mission Statement is: To provide an environment that inspires the intellectual, artist, athlete, and philosopher in each student. Westover challenges young women to think independently, to embrace diversity, and to grow intellectually and spiritually. Westover encourages in each student integrity, responsibility, and commitment to community.

The School's operating expenses are $10.6 million; parents, friends, and a base of 3,451 alumnae raised $1,400,911 for the 2007–08 Annual Fund. The School's endowment is $42 million.

The School is accredited by the New England Association of Schools and Colleges and approved by the state of Connecticut. Memberships include the National Association of Independent Schools, the National Coalition of Girls' Schools, the Connecticut Association of Independent Schools, and the College Board.

ACADEMIC PROGRAMS

The purpose of the academic program is to develop the student's capacity for thought, to provide a sound background of knowledge of the physical world and of the School's cultural heritage, and to cultivate creativity. A minimum of 18 credits is required for graduation, including 4 in English, 3 in mathematics, 3 in languages, 2⅓ in history, 2⅓ in science, and 2 in the arts. Computer literacy and community service are required. Twenty-one AP courses are offered. Some requirements may be modified for entering juniors.

There are numerous English trimester electives for eleventh- and twelfth-grade students—for example, Contemporary Poetry; Dante's Vision; Fantastic and Possible Futures (Film and Fiction); Inner and Outer Nature; Genesis, Job, and the Gospels; Poetics and the Iliad; Romantic Poetry; Shakespeare: Comedy, Tragedy, and Romance; Tolstoy; and Truth, Beauty, Justice. Advanced Placement courses are offered in art, art history, biology, calculus, chemistry, computer science, English, environmental science, European history, French, Spanish, statistics, Latin, music, physics, U.S. history, and U.S. government. In May 2007, 76 students took a total of 138 Advanced Placement tests in eighteen different areas; 96 percent received grades of 3 or better, with 68 percent receiving a 4 or 5.

The arts requirement may be fulfilled not only by numerous studio art, art history, and music courses but also by advanced trimester courses in dance and theater arts.

Three special programs enhance the curriculum at Westover. For talented musicians, there is a joint program with the Manhattan School of Music Pre-College Division. For qualified girls who hold a strong interest in science and engineering, Westover offers the Women in Science and Engineering (WISE) program, which is a joint program with Rensselaer Polytechnic Institute. For the preprofessional dancer, there is a joint program with Brass City Ballet of Middlebury.

Westover School provides an advanced English as a second language program for international students who are otherwise highly qualified but who require assistance in improving their English skills.

The average class size is 11 students, and the student-teacher ratio is approximately 8:1. The full class load is five courses. Conference periods, during which teachers are available in their classrooms, are part of the weekly schedule. All of these elements in the School's academic program enhance a close student-faculty rapport. Freshmen and sophomore boarders attend a required study hall, 7–9 p.m., Monday through Thursday, with quiet conditions prevailing throughout the School. The grading system is numerical: 60 is the passing grade. Students are notified of their academic progress four times a year: in October and at the end of each trimester in November, March, and June. Seniors who have completed their required courses may seek approval for a special independent project.

FACULTY AND ADVISERS

There are 30 full-time and 18 part-time teaching faculty members. All have bachelor's degrees, 21 have master's degrees, and 1 holds a Ph.D. The majority of the teaching faculty members live in School-owned housing. Dorm parents live in apartments on the nine residential student corridors. All members of the faculty are encouraged to seek professional development, and funds are available to do so.

Ann Pollina, who holds a B.A. (Fordham University) and an M.A. (New York University), came to Westover in 1972 as an instructor in mathematics. She has since served the School as Head of the Mathematics Department and Dean of Faculty and was appointed Head of School in 1997. She has been involved in numerous research projects involving how best to instruct girls in math and science and has published several articles on gender equity in the classroom and how to teach girls math.

While returning students may choose advisers, each new student is assigned a classroom teacher as an adviser to assist with academic and personal issues and to help in the planning of an academic program. Faculty members serve as advisers to the numerous student organizations. The Dean of Students, class advisers, and a day-student adviser coordinate and supplement the resources for advising students.

COLLEGE ADMISSION COUNSELING

Through group and individual conferences beginning in the eleventh grade, a college adviser guides students in selecting colleges. The School's approach to college placement is thorough and systematic. Parents as well as students are involved. On the SAT, the middle 50 percent of critical reading scores was 520–640, the middle 50 percent of math scores was 530–650, and the middle 50 percent of writing scores was 570–670. The middle 50 percent of ACT scores was 24–30. The English, math, and science departments review material for the ACT, SAT, and SAT Subject Tests; other departments provide reviews for Subject Tests as needed.

Among a wide array of colleges and universities, Westover students from the last three graduating classes have attended Barnard, Boston College, Carnegie Mellon, Columbia, Connecticut College, Cornell, Dartmouth, Emory, Franklin and Marshall, Georgetown, Harvard, Howard, Johns Hopkins, Middlebury, Northwestern, Swarthmore, Tufts, University of Chicago, Vassar, and Wheaton.

STUDENT BODY AND CONDUCT

The total enrollment of 199 young women includes 119 boarders and 80 day students. Eighteen states and nineteen countries are represented in the student body. Slightly more than half of the students come from public and parochial schools, and the rest come from independent schools.

Student leadership is vested in class officers and officers of other organizations. Student opinion and influence are also expressed through representation on the Faculty-Student Senate as well as the Discipline Committee, in which faculty members consult with student senior officers before recommending penalties to the Head of School for serious infractions of the rules. Junior and senior proctors live on corridors with students and work with them as friends and advisers.

ACADEMIC FACILITIES

The Main Building, organized around a central, garden-like quadrangle, is the single greatest influence on the School's character and ethos. Housing most of the classrooms and administrative offices, the Chapel, the Dining Hall, and all of the dormitory spaces, the Main Building and its unique architecture foster and shape a close and unified community. Red Hall, for example, is large enough to seat the entire school on its soft crimson carpet during Morning Assembly and is often used as a rehearsal or performance space and a venue for special presentations. Yet its lamp-lit tables are also a favorite spot for study or for meeting with teachers and tutors. The Chapel's superb acoustics make it a perfect space for rehearsing the 70-voice Glee Club, but it is also an intimate practice space for a single violinist. During the weekly chapel service on Thursday morning, the same space comfortably holds the entire School community.

Satellite buildings augment the quality and scope of already existent programs originally housed in the versatile Main Building. Among these are various visual arts spaces that house drawing, painting, and sculpture classes; the Whittaker Library and Science Building; the Fuller Athletic Center; and the Louise Bulkley Dillingham Performing Arts Center. All of these facilities—old and new—mirror and support the School's philosophy. These structures inspire pride, ambition, independence, and excellence.

BOARDING AND GENERAL FACILITIES

All boarding students live in the various wings of the Main Building, which also houses the dining room and the chapel. Most students are assigned to spacious double rooms. There is a dorm parent on corridor for approximately every 14 girls. There is a Health Center staffed by a physician's assistant and registered nurses.

ATHLETICS

Westover's athletic program provides unique opportunities regardless of previous experience. Westover offers a wide variety of sports ranging in levels of competition from highly competitive varsity teams to noncompetitive individual endeavors such as rock climbing. These varied offerings allow for the development of athletic abilities and social skills while fostering a healthful way of life.

The Fuller Athletic Center, houses a full-length basketball court, four volleyball courts, a multi-level indoor-climbing wall, a fitness center, four international squash courts, and a multipurpose room for yoga, aerobics, and meetings.

Westover is a member of the New England Prep School League and the Western New England Prep School Athletic Association (WNEPSAA). Some of the schools from WNEPSAA that Westover plays are Gunnery, Kingswood-Oxford, Kent, Miss Hall's, Miss Porter's, Taft, and Westminster.

Westover also participates in the Connecticut Independent School Athletic Conference (CISAC) in basketball, field hockey, lacrosse, soccer, softball, and tennis. Some of the CISAC schools include Chase Collegiate, Ethel Walker's, Hamden Hall, and Williams.

EXTRACURRICULAR OPPORTUNITIES

There are numerous clubs and organizations that support interests in the environment, social services, arts, languages, and writing. Three School publications and the Glee Club involve large numbers of students. Many students and other members of the Westover community take part in all aspects of the production of a musical. The West and Over teams—the underclass spirit teams—each devise, direct, and perform musical entertainment every spring. Opportunities for community service are provided by the School and may also develop through students' initiatives.

Classes often make trips to New York, Boston, New Haven, and other cultural centers to visit museums or to see theater productions, operas, or ballets.

DAILY LIFE

Weekday breakfasts are at 7 a.m., followed by morning assembly at 7:45 and then classes of 40 minutes' duration that continue on most days until 1:20 p.m. Glee Club meets three days per week. Arts programs follow, as do intramural and team sports and drama rehearsals. Dinner is at 6, followed by study hall, which is required for freshmen and sophomore boarders. Lights-out for these younger students is at 10:30, with progressively later hours for older students. Seniors have no required lights-out. All students attend an interdenominational chapel program once a week.

WEEKEND LIFE

A more relaxed schedule with many options is followed on the weekends. There are later hours for breakfast and lights-out. Many students participate in an arts program on Saturday mornings, while those on sports teams may have interscholastic competitions on Saturday afternoons. A calendar issued each week lists numerous activities, which include trips to New York, New Haven, or Boston; to performances or sports events; to other schools for dances; and to stores. Occasional festive dinners are followed by cultural or entertainment programs. There are also programs and dances on campus. An all-student Social Committee works with a faculty member to ensure that the activities are varied and interesting and that Westover students have ample opportunities to meet students from other schools. To preserve the community aspects of life, alternate weekends are closed—there are no leaves for boarders except in special circumstances.

Day students are welcomed at all scheduled events, have their own adviser and day-student head, and have lounges and lockers on corridors with boarding students.

COSTS AND FINANCIAL AID

Costs for the 2008–09 academic year were $39,900 for boarding students and $28,000 for day students.

Financial aid is based on need and involves both grants and loans. Families applying for aid must submit the Parents' Financial Statement to the School and Student Service for Financial Aid in Princeton, New Jersey. For 2008–09, grants totaling $2,370,190 were distributed to approximately half of the student body. Grants range from $5000 to full tuition. Three types of special scholarships are awarded. Daughters of teachers can apply for the Mandeville Scholarship, which provides financial assistance during a student's time at Westover. Talented musicians are eligible to receive an award that provides them with funding for Westover's joint program with the Manhattan School of Music Pre-College Division in New York City. There is also a scholarship for students from Maine.

ADMISSIONS INFORMATION

Acceptance to Westover is based on school performance, academic potential, motivation, and character. The SSAT is required; the TOEFL is required for students whose native language is not English.

Westover School admits girls of any race, color, or national or ethnic origin to all the rights, privileges, programs, and activities generally accorded or made available to students at the School. It does not discriminate on the basis of race, color, or national or ethnic origin in the administration of its educational policies, admissions policies, scholarship and loan programs, or athletic and other School-administered programs.

APPLICATION TIMETABLE

Inquiries are always welcome. An on-campus interview, required of all candidates, should be scheduled Monday through Friday between 8 a.m. and 12 noon. The application deadline is February 1 for receipt of all materials. Admissions decisions are mailed on March 10. Applications completed after that date are considered on a rolling basis for available spaces.

ADMISSIONS CORRESPONDENCE

Admissions Office
Westover School
Box 847
1237 Whittemore Road
Middlebury, Connecticut 06762-0847

Phone: 203-577-4521
Fax: 203-577-4588
E-mail: admission@westoverschool.org
Web site: http://www.westoverschool.org

THE WHITE MOUNTAIN SCHOOL

Bethlehem, New Hampshire

Type: Coeducational boarding and day college-preparatory school
Grades: 9–12, postgraduate year
Enrollment: 100
Head of School: Brian Morgan

THE SCHOOL

Founded in 1886 as Saint Mary's School, The White Mountain School is an independent boarding and day school dedicated to preparing young people for college studies and life beyond formal academics. Through challenging course work and innovative instruction, students learn to think critically and creatively and are encouraged to own their education and become responsible, independent young adults. The student-faculty ratio is 4:1, with an average class size of 9. Local and international community service, sustainability, performing and fine arts, and outdoor sports and experiences are integral parts of the School's program.

In 1935, the School was moved from its Concord, New Hampshire, campus to Bethlehem. The move north, adjacent to the spectacular 600,000-acre White Mountain National Forest, was made to offer students an opportunity to live in and among things that were much greater than themselves, to help them form perspective, and to give them a sense of appreciation for the natural environment. The School changed its name from St. Mary's-in-the-Mountains to The White Mountain School (WMS) in 1972 to better reflect its commitment to a balanced college-preparatory program with the hands-on, student-focused, interactive learning experiences available in a mountain setting. While the School maintains its affiliation with the Episcopal Church, it welcomes students from diverse backgrounds and all religious traditions.

The 250-acre campus is easily accessible from I-93 and is a beautiful drive from the Hartford (3½ hours), Boston (2½ hours), and Manchester (2 hours) airports.

Governed by a 16-member Board of Trustees, The White Mountain School is fully accredited by the New England Association of Schools and Colleges (NEASC). It is a member of the National Association of Independent Schools (NAIS), the Independent School Association of Northern New England (ISANNE), the Association of Boarding Schools (TABS), the National Association of Episcopal Schools (NAES), the Council for Advancement and Support of Education (CASE), the Association of Experiential Education (AEE), and the American Mountain Guides Association (AMGA).

ACADEMIC PROGRAMS

The White Mountain School is dedicated to offering a student-focused, college-preparatory curriculum. White Mountain education is designed with small, collaborative classes that allow students to be actively involved in their own learning.

Students are well prepared for higher education through a challenging core curriculum and an array of upper-level electives. The extensive curriculum includes opportunities for students to take Advanced Placement exams in select disciplines, honors programs by department, and student-designed independent study and/or senior projects.

Classes are discussion-based, and teachers use a variety of approaches to engage and motivate students. Students engage in authentic learning—learning that matters outside the walls of the classroom. They conduct hands-on research, write APA-formatted research papers, create screen-cast tutorials for peers, and present findings at local town meetings. In short, students learn not just for a grade or credit but to add value to the world. Small classes mean teachers touch base with every student every day; faculty members challenge and support students at an individual level. WMS teachers create an atmosphere that emphasizes interdisciplinary learning and enlivens academic study.

Students participate in special Saturday project block classes throughout the year. Each class has one designated Saturday morning class each semester. This substantial block of time (about 3–3.5 hours) is set aside for innovative projects, such as collaborative projects, interdisciplinary explorations, hands-on learning, and field trips. Typically, students have six Saturday project blocks each semester.

Outside the classroom, White Mountain offers students special opportunities to learn and develop. Through Community Service Odysseys and Outdoor Learning Expeditions (OLE), students explore the world around them, put theoretical understanding into action, and gain confidence to face challenges and overcome obstacles. Students gain new perspective and appreciation for different cultures, the environment, and their place within the world. An educational component is built into each trip, bringing classroom instruction to life. Recent trips have included studies of Fresh Water Ecology; Search and Rescue in Mahoosuc Notch, Adirondack Climbing History, Literature and the Land, and Winter Ecology; building projects with Habitat for Humanity; and opportunities to participate in community service projects in Peru, Nicaragua, and the Dominican Republic. The WMS experience empowers students to make a positive difference in the community and the world and challenges them to create a life of meaning.

To graduate, students must earn 20 academic credits, including a minimum of 4 credits in English, 3 credits in history and human values, 3 credits in mathematics, 2 credits in science, 2 credits in world language, 1 credit in the arts, and 1 credit in sustainability studies. Independent study courses are an option for qualified students. Classes are consistently small, with an average of 9 students per class. Parents receive grade reports and teacher comments six times per year. Advisers maintain close contact with students and parents to ensure that students receive both the challenge and support they need.

In addition, The White Mountain School offers a Learning Assistance Program (LAP) for some students. The Learning Assistance Program provides additional tutorial and/or remedial help for students who have met academic challenges and are prepared for a rigorous college-preparatory curriculum. While keeping students and parents involved with weekly progress reports, this program is designed to give each student the tools needed to become involved learners as well as to understand their own strengths, weaknesses, and distinct learning styles. English as a second language (ESL) is also offered to international students.

FACULTY AND ADVISERS

Individual attention is a basic part of the White Mountain approach to education. Students and faculty members are on a first name basis, living and learning in a community of respect. Most faculty members live on campus, and all faculty members interact with students on multiple levels. Students know the faculty as dorm parents, coaches, outdoors enthusiasts, and participants in weekend activities and other extracurricular clubs and programs, as well as inspirational teachers. Every student has a faculty adviser who serves as the primary contact for parents. Many faculty members hold advanced degrees as well as a variety of additional certifications.

COLLEGE ADMISSION COUNSELING

The college counselor works extensively with each junior and senior to explore educational options. Ninety-nine percent of White Mountain graduates normally attend college within the first year after graduation. Recent WMS graduates have attended colleges and universities that include Boston University, Bryn Mawr, Carnegie Mellon, Colorado College, Cornell, Dartmouth, Emerson, Hampshire, Ithaca, Lewis & Clark, Loyola University, Mount Holyoke, Northeastern, Oberlin, Pratt, Sarah Lawrence, Smith, Swarthmore, and Syracuse.

STUDENT BODY AND CONDUCT

The White Mountain School enrolls approximately 100 students from around the country and the world. Students come from varying geographical, cultural, and economic backgrounds; have diverse personal strengths; and contribute a variety of interests and talents to the School community. Students who attend The White Mountain School value academic challenges and individual attention.

The White Mountain School believes that each member of the community is important and shares the responsibility for the well-being of the School. The *Community Handbook* outlines expectations to help provide structure for personal support, academic success, and boundaries for safety. Through the Student-Faculty Citizenship Committee, students participate in the disciplinary process of the School.

Student Council and the Student Social Committee serve as forums for student ideas. They also make recommendations to the administration regarding school policies, curriculum, activities, and other aspects of community life. Opportunities are provided for responsible leadership, individual initiative, and group decision making. Recently, students in the junior class helped design a senior humanities course.

In addition, all students share in community responsibilities. Students participate in on-campus service through the Work Jobs Program and the farm and forest crew. Duties include being on kitchen crew, recycling, or helping in the library. In addition to their campus jobs, all students have rotating work assignments in their respective dormitories.

ACADEMIC FACILITIES

The Main Building houses the classroom wing, multimedia center, learning labs, and extensive art studios that include a photo lab and ceramics, drawing, and printmaking rooms. More than 7,000 volumes, an online catalog, several online databases, and interlibrary loan with Dartmouth College and the University of New Hampshire are available to students through the School library. The Fred Steele Science Center is equipped with SMART Board interactive whiteboards and state-of-the-art labs, which allow for a wide range of hands-on projects.

BOARDING AND GENERAL FACILITIES

The School's clapboard and fieldstone dormitories are equipped with common rooms and wireless Internet access. All dorm rooms contain beautiful light oak furniture (XL twin bed with four drawers, wardrobe with drawers, and a desk with a hutch) for each student.

Most rooms are doubles. A student center is located in the Main Building, providing a central location for students to gather and relax. There are several faculty apartments in each dormitory, along with six multifamily houses on the campus.

A School farm, including a student-built post and beam shed; a chicken house with 30 egg-laying hens; a vegetable and fruit garden; and composting bins are integral parts of the School kitchen, the farm and forest crew, and the award-winning Sustainability Program.

A state-of-the-art 3,000-square-foot indoor climbing wall is part of an indoor sports center outfitted with Nautilus equipment, free weights, aerobic equipment, and a running track. In addition, two athletic fields and an extensive trail system are part of the 250-acre property, with an additional 150 acres available for the School's use.

The School Health Services office is staffed by a registered nurse and an emergency medical technician (EMT). Around-the-clock emergency services at Littleton Hospital are available within 7 miles of the campus.

ATHLETICS

Students can choose from a variety of recreational and interscholastic sports. White Mountain offers men's and women's lacrosse and soccer as well as extensive opportunities in skiing/snowboarding, rock climbing, white-water paddling, hiking, and mountain biking.

The White Mountain School's rock-climbing program is the first high school program, public or private, to earn accreditation from the American Mountain Guides Association. The focus of the outdoor education program is skill building. Students who choose to pursue outdoor sports learn the technical aspects of their activity and such important topics as minimum-impact travel, first aid, navigation, orienteering, trip planning, and natural history. Team building and leadership are important components of the program. A primary goal is that students develop skills in the outdoors that they can use throughout their lives.

During the winter sports term, students choose among outdoor recreational ski/snowboard options that include Nordic skiing, backcountry skiing, alpine skiing, and snowboarding and indoor activities such as theater, fitness, dance, and yoga. Students interested in competitive winter sports may join the freestyle teams or race with the prestigious Franconia Ski Club.

EXTRACURRICULAR OPPORTUNITIES

Extracurricular opportunities vary from year to year depending upon the interests of the student body and faculty. The yearbook, *The Pendulum*, is designed and produced by students. Students interested in the performing arts are given the opportunity to perform in chorus, theater productions, and informal coffee houses. With a focus on international song and dance, a strong cultural events' series brings professional performers and artists to the School. Occasionally, during vacations or the summer, The White Mountain School offers special trips with an outdoor, service, or academic focus.

Community service is a strong part of The White Mountain School and gives students the opportunity to experience firsthand involvement with their larger world community. Many White Mountain students go beyond the graduation requirement for service projects. The School has received local, state, and national recognition for its Community Service Program. Most recently, the National Association of Independent Schools (NAIS) awarded White Mountain the 2007 Leading Edge Award for Global Sustainability.

DAILY LIFE

Breakfast begins at 7 a.m. A student-led all-school Morning Meeting at 7:35 brings the community together for announcements. Morning Meeting gives the community time to check in and get ready for classes. It is followed by "Morning Reading," an activity presented by one or more members of the faculty or student body. Intended to be something inspirational to get the day off to a good start, Morning Reading may include reading personal or reflective writing, sharing a video of a recent trip, engaging in Morning Sing, learning a new dance, or playing a team-building game.

Classes begin at 8 a.m. The academic day is based on a rotating block schedule. Each class meets four times per week, with one long block weekly to allow student project work, films, outdoor activities, or labs to take place without interruption. After classes, all students participate in afternoon sports or activities. Dinner is served at 6 p.m. Supervised study time is set aside for all students from 7:30 to 9:30 p.m., Sundays through Thursdays. The library and computer labs are open for student use during study hall. For freshmen and sophomores, "lights out" is at 10:30 p.m.; for juniors and seniors, "lights out" is at 11 p.m.

WEEKEND LIFE

Activities are planned by faculty and students and include dances, intramural games, board game nights, bonfires, cider making, theater rehearsals, and art workshops. Studios in the art wing are usually open. Trips are made to Dartmouth College, Boston, Portland, Burlington, or Montreal for a variety of cultural and sporting events. Students can also go to nearby Littleton to shop, have lunch, or attend the movies. On weekends, transportation is provided to take students to optional religious services. There is a network of trails on campus available for hiking, running, biking, and cross-country skiing. Students are permitted to take weekends or overnights away from campus if they have parental permission and all academic and community responsibilities have been met.

COSTS AND FINANCIAL AID

Tuition and room and board for 2008–09 were $41,100. Day student tuition was $20,000. A student expense account is required in the amount of $1500 ($1000 for day students). The Learning Assistance Program and the ESL Program each have additional, separate tuition fees.

Approximately 50 percent of the students receive financial aid. Eligibility is based on need as established by the School and Student Service for Financial Aid. Academic achievement, citizenship, and future promise are also taken into consideration when awards are made.

In keeping with the tradition of the School, an Episcopal Woman's Scholarship is offered to a deserving young woman. Please contact the School for more information regarding WMS scholarship applications and deadlines.

ADMISSIONS INFORMATION

The White Mountain School seeks to admit students who wish to challenge themselves and to enrich and broaden their educational experience by becoming involved in the academic, co-curricular, creative, and personal opportunities at White Mountain. Admissions candidates should have above average to high ability and the intellectual curiosity and motivation needed to perform college-preparatory work. Students come from varying geographical, cultural, and economic backgrounds; have diverse personal strengths; and contribute a variety of interests and talents to the School community.

To complete the application process, the student needs to submit the application form and fee, references, a writing sample, and an official transcript of school records. The SSAT is requested. Admissions staff members look forward to meeting and getting to know prospective students and their families through the campus visit and interview. Admission candidates are expected to visit the campus, but phone (or Skype, msn) interviews may be arranged for overseas candidates.

APPLICATION TIMETABLE

For March 10 notification, completed applications and the application fee should be submitted by February 1. Applications submitted after February 1 are reviewed and considered on a rolling admissions basis and are subject to the availability of spaces in the class. Students generally enroll in September, and a small number of students may enroll in January if there are spaces available.

ADMISSIONS CORRESPONDENCE

Joanna Evans
Director of Admissions and Financial Aid
The White Mountain School
371 West Farm Road
Bethlehem, New Hampshire 03574
Phone: 603-444-2928
800-545-7813 (toll free within the U.S. only)
Fax: 603-444-5568
E-mail: admissions@whitemountain.org
Web site: http://www.whitemountain.org

THE WILLISTON NORTHAMPTON SCHOOL

Easthampton, Massachusetts

Type: Coeducational boarding and day college-preparatory school
Grades: 7–PG: Middle School, 7–8; Upper School, 9–12, postgraduate year
Enrollment: School total: 550; Upper School: 460
Head of School: Brian R. Wright, Headmaster

THE SCHOOL

Named in 1991 by the U.S. Department of Education as an Exemplary Secondary School as part of its Blue Ribbon Schools Program, Williston Northampton has a long history of excellence.

Williston Seminary was founded in 1841 by Samuel and Emily Williston. Initially coeducational, Williston Seminary later became a college-preparatory school for boys. The Willistons amassed a great fortune from the production of cloth-covered buttons and the manufacture of rubber webbing and thread. They also supported the local colleges both financially and personally.

Eighty-three years later, in 1924, Sarah B. Whitaker and Dorothy M. Bement founded the academic Northampton School for Girls.

In 1971, the two schools merged to form Williston Northampton, a coeducational school offering a strong secondary education to prepare interested students for the rigorous academic programs of colleges today and the demands and complexities in life afterward.

The School is located on 100 acres in the heart of the Pioneer Valley a few miles from the base of Mount Tom, 85 miles west of Boston, and 150 miles north of New York. Within a 15-mile radius are Smith, Mount Holyoke, Hampshire, and Amherst colleges and the University of Massachusetts.

A self-perpetuating 25-member Board of Trustees governs the School, which is a nonprofit institution. The current endowment is estimated at $40 million. The School's alumni body of 8,000 contributed more than $1 million in Annual Giving last year.

Williston Northampton is accredited by the New England Association of Schools and Colleges and is affiliated with the National Association of Independent Schools, the Association of Independent Schools of New England, the College Board, the School and College Conference on English, the Art Association of New England Preparatory Schools, and the Council for Advancement and Support of Education.

ACADEMIC PROGRAMS

A strong and varied academic program is the heart of the School. To strengthen, expand, and encourage students' skills and interests in the essential disciplines are the goals of the program. Care is taken to place each student in the courses and sections most appropriate to his or her abilities. A student may enroll in Honors English while working in an average section of math. Small classes of 10 to 15, which enable instructors to know each student's abilities, and the flexibility of the program make it possible for the School to structure the best program for every student.

The faculty also feels strongly that it is important for each student to experience as many academic and creative disciplines as possible so that, before having to make decisions concerning career goals, he or she will have sampled many alternatives. Therefore, Williston Northampton expects each of its students not only to satisfy the minimum basic requirements of 4 years of English, 3 years of math, 2 of science, 2 of a foreign language, and 2 in the social sciences but also to select two semester courses from the area of fine arts and one semester course from the area of religious and philosophical studies. Sixteen AP classes are offered every year. Qualified students may elect to complete extra work in consultation with the teacher to prepare to take the Advanced Placement exam in two additional subject areas. In 2007, Williston students took 183 AP subject tests. Of the tests taken, 59.6 percent received scores of either a 4 or a 5, allowing the students to receive college course credit at most elite universities and colleges around the world. In addition, 84.7 percent of the tests were scored a 3 or above, which also gives the students course credit at many leading institutions both nationally and internationally.

Most students choose to complete work beyond the basic requirements established by each department. In order to graduate, a student at Williston Northampton must have earned 19 academic credits (a one-year course equals 1 credit) in grades 9–12 and must pass all courses taken during the senior year. Diploma requirements also include regular participation in the athletics program, satisfactory completion of the Senior Project for those who elect to do one, enrollment at Williston Northampton throughout the senior year, and satisfactory citizenship.

The passing and college-recommending grade at Williston Northampton is 60. Students attaining honor grades are recognized at the end of each term. The highest honor is election to the Cum Laude Society.

FACULTY AND ADVISERS

The Williston Northampton School teaching faculty numbers 86 full-time members—45 men and 41 women. Fifty-five hold master's degrees, and 4 have earned Ph.D.'s. Thirty live in dorms. The School has established programs and staff members to counsel students about academic work, personal problems, class functions, and future educational goals and opportunities. Each boarding student has a faculty adviser who is also a dorm parent and may be easily consulted on academic or personal matters. The Dean of Students, Chaplain, and Academic Dean can be consulted as the need arises. All students are encouraged to participate in a series of health workshops directed by the Health Services staff, which focuses on issues of health and personal decision making. The School also employs the services of professional counselors for those who find they require additional personal counseling.

Brian R. Wright was appointed Headmaster in 1999. Dr. Wright graduated magna cum laude and Phi Beta Kappa from Occidental College and earned his master's degree and doctorate in politics from Princeton University. He was Principal at Windward Preparatory School in Kailua, Hawaii; Head of Lower School at The Wardlaw-Hartridge School in New Jersey; Director of the Upper School at Packer Collegiate Institute in Brooklyn; Headmaster at The Birch Wathen School in New York; and Head at the Potomac School in McLean, Virginia, from 1992 until his appointment at Williston Northampton.

COLLEGE ADMISSION COUNSELING

A thorough college counseling program is provided for each student making postsecondary educational plans. Three full-time counselors and one part-time counselor coordinate the program. From the beginning, the counseling process draws in both parents and students to establish a dialogue between the School and the family. During the junior year, the counselor and members of the faculty meet with students to acquaint them with standardized test taking, financial aid, roles and functions of college officials, and campus lifestyles.

Of the 143 members of the class of 2008, 100 percent are attending a college or university. Two or more graduates are attending Art Institute of Boston, Babson, Bates, Bentley, Boston College, Boston University, Colby, Connecticut College, Cornell, Elon, Endicott, High Point, Johns Hopkins, Lehigh, Merrimack, Muhlenberg, Northeastern, Occidental, Quinnipiac, St. Lawrence, and the Universities of Hartford, Miami (Florida), New Hampshire, Rhode Island, and Vermont.

STUDENT BODY AND CONDUCT

Most students enter Williston during the freshman or sophomore year. In 2007–08, grade 9 had 70 members (35 boys, 35 girls), of whom 34were day students. Grade 10 had 120 members (59 boys, 61 girls), of whom 50 were day students. Grade 11 had 123 members (64 boys, 59 girls), of whom 46 were day students. Grade 12 had 127members (62 boys, 65 girls), of whom 50 were day students. There were 20 postgraduate students. Fifteen percent of the students are members of minority groups. Students came from twenty-four states and twenty-three countries.

The regulations of the School have evolved from experience and lengthy discussion. They provide clear-cut guidelines for everyone living in the School community. It is expected that both the spirit and the letter of these regulations as described in the *Student Handbook,* which is sent to every enrolling student and is also available upon request, will be followed.

Students who are reported to have violated School rules and regulations meet with the Discipline Committee, made up of faculty and student representatives. The committee's decisions and recommendations are reviewed by the Headmaster, who makes the final decision in disciplinary matters.

ACADEMIC FACILITIES

The campus is located on approximately 100 acres. The School's thirty-eight buildings include the Reed Campus Center, the science building, the theater, the Schoolhouse, the library, the chapel, and the Middle School building. The Williston Theatre reopened in 1995 after suffering fire damage in 1994. The internal renovation of the Schoolhouse (the major classroom building) was completed in 1984. Renovations to the old gymnasium to create a new Campus Center that includes music and fine arts classrooms were completed in 1996. The Technology and Student Publications Center, the Science Tech Lab, the library, and the math floor house four student computer labs.

BOARDING AND GENERAL FACILITIES

The buildings on campus include the Headmaster's home, the administration buildings, the chapel, the dining hall, six dormitories with facilities for 25 to 50 students, five residence houses with boarding facilities for 8 to 12 students, and faculty homes. Ford Hall, which houses 50 boys, received a million-dollar renovation in 1999, adding sun-splashed common rooms and other enhancements. All dorm rooms are wired into the campus computer network and have voice mail.

Each housing unit is supervised by resident faculty houseparents to create an environment conducive to academic achievement and a warm and pleasant home atmosphere.

ATHLETICS

Sports are an integral part of Williston Northampton life, whether interscholastic or recreational. The School requires that each student be involved in the athletics program in each of the three sports seasons. The athletics department instills the principles of fair play, good sportsmanship, teamwork, and respect for rules and authority. Most of the academic faculty members also coach team sports, and the Director of Athletics oversees the program.

In general, seventh to tenth graders participate in the basic athletics program, while older students have additional options. Interscholastic teams for girls include crew, cross-country, field hockey, soccer, and volleyball in the fall; basketball, ice hockey, skiing, squash, swimming and diving, and wrestling in the winter; and crew, golf, lacrosse, softball, tennis, track, and water polo in the spring. For these periods, boys may elect crew, cross-country, football, soccer, or water polo; basketball, ice hockey, skiing, squash, swimming and diving, or wrestling; and baseball, crew, golf, lacrosse, tennis, or track. Horseback riding at a nearby stable and modern dance are available every season. Fitness training, aerobics, and volleyball are choices open to upperclass students.

Excellent facilities and equipment are available. An athletic center contains two basketball courts, a six-lane pool with a diving well, five squash courts, a weight room and fitness center, and a wrestling room. Other facilities include a lighted, synthetic-surface football/lacrosse field, a dance studio, an indoor skating facility, twelve new tennis courts, a new (as of 2007), all- weather running track with a synthetic surface field within it, more than 30 acres of playing fields, and a 3.4-mile cross-country course. In addition, there are several golf courses in the Easthampton area.

EXTRACURRICULAR OPPORTUNITIES

The countryside offers excellent climbing, biking, and skiing opportunities, and the proximity of five colleges provides a culturally rich environment of fine museums, libraries, and theater programs as well. The cities of Northampton and Springfield, Massachusetts, and Hartford, Connecticut, are near enough so that concerts and activities there are as readily available as those at the colleges.

DAILY LIFE

The academic day runs from 8 a.m. until 1:50 or 2:50 p.m. on Monday, Tuesday, Thursday, and Friday and until 12 noon on Wednesday. Classes are held every other Saturday morning as well. Students take five courses in a six-period schedule, with classes lasting 50 or 70 minutes, depending on the day. All-School assemblies for announcements and special presentations are held once each week. Sports are scheduled from the end of the class day until dinnertime. Except for theme-based formal dinners, most meals are served buffet-style. A free period from 6:40 to 8 is frequently used for meetings of extracurricular organizations, library work, theater or music rehearsals, visiting between dormitories, or simply relaxing. Supervised evening study hours run from 8 to 10 p.m. All students are checked into the dorms at 10 by the dorm faculty.

WEEKEND LIFE

While the vast majority of students remain on campus, weekends at home or at the home of a friend are permitted with parental approval after all school obligations have been met. The Student Activities Director and the students on the Activity Committee organize a variety of weekly activities, and students may take advantage of the events listed in the Five-College Calendar. Students travel off campus for such programs as college and professional athletics contests, films, concerts, plays, dance performances, and rock concerts and to go skiing in Vermont. The many on-campus activities include dances and coffeehouse entertainment, talent shows, lectures by invited speakers, and a film series.

SUMMER PROGRAMS

During the summer, the School offers an intensive four-week Spanish program in Mexico, as well hosting many outside camps, which offer theater, music, and athletics on the campus.

COSTS AND FINANCIAL AID

Tuition for boarders for 2008–09 was $42,000; for day students, it was $29,500. Additional expenses include books, insurance, laundry, and other incidental expenses. Tuition payment and insurance plans are recommended upon request.

Financial aid is awarded on the basis of need to approximately 40 percent of the student body. The grants totaled $4.3 million for 2007–08.

ADMISSIONS INFORMATION

Williston Northampton seeks students who are interested in their own education and who can show solid academic performance. Students should also be positive, involved, caring contributors to life at the School. Admission is based upon an evaluation of these traits, a personal interview, and satisfactory scores on the SSAT. For 2007–08, 166 new students were enrolled in the Upper School.

APPLICATION TIMETABLE

The fall or winter prior to a candidate's prospective admission is usually the best time for a visit, which includes a student-guided tour of the School and an interview. The Admission Office is open Monday through Friday, from 8 a.m. to 4:30 p.m., and on some Saturday mornings.

An application for admission should be submitted by February 1 along with a nonrefundable fee of $40. Beginning July 1, 2008, the application fee will change to $50 for students who reside within the United States and $100 for international students. The School abides by the March 10 notification date. After that date, a rolling admission plan is in effect.

ADMISSIONS CORRESPONDENCE

Ann C. Pickrell, Director of Admission
The Williston Northampton School
19 Payson Avenue
Easthampton, Massachusetts 01027
Phone: 413-529-3241
Fax: 413-527-9494
E-mail: admissions@williston.com
Web site: http://www.williston.com

THE WINCHENDON SCHOOL

Winchendon, Massachusetts

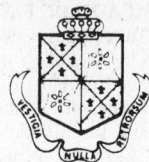

Type: Coeducational boarding and day college-preparatory school
Grades: 8–12, postgraduate year
Enrollment: 243
Head of School: John A. Kerney, Headmaster

THE SCHOOL

The Winchendon School was founded in 1926 in Dexter, Maine, by Lloyd H. Hatch, whose purpose was "to create a structured and traditional atmosphere for students of good ability who may not yet have reached their potential, where they may grow academically, physically, socially, and spiritually." The School was later located in Newport, Rhode Island, before moving to Winchendon in 1961. Girls were first admitted in 1973. The environment of the School remains structured, and rules are enforced sensibly. The educational philosophy of the School is conservative. Students work hard and are held accountable for their actions. The curriculum is traditional and is designed to prepare students of average to above-average ability to be successful in college, yet it is also flexible. Skills deficiencies, learning gaps, and mild learning disabilities are remediated. Strengths are challenged, and interests are developed.

Located in north-central Massachusetts in the foothills of the Monadnock Mountains, the 350-acre campus is 20 miles from Keene, New Hampshire; 35 miles from Worcester; and 65 miles from Boston. The region is noted for its skiing facilities and for its many lakes. Proximity to Boston makes that city's cultural, entertainment, educational, and commercial resources readily available.

A nonprofit institution, the School is governed by a 17-member Board of Trustees. Most of the trustees are alumni, parents of students, and parents of alumni. The operating budget for 2008–09 exceeded $9 million. The value of the physical plant and equipment has been assessed at $25 million. The endowment is valued $20 million.

The Winchendon School is accredited by the New England Association of Schools and Colleges. It holds memberships in the Association of Independent Schools of New England, the National Association of Independent Schools, the National Honor Society, the Orton Society, and the Association of Boarding Schools.

ACADEMIC PROGRAMS

Although the School seeks to prepare its students for college-level study, the academic program is intended to provide a valuable educational experience in its own right. By using small classes, a personalized teaching approach, and a flexible structure of guidance and support, the School endeavors to create and stimulate students' interest in learning and to teach them that they are the most valuable contributors to their own education.

On the basis of its experience and capabilities in evaluating student progress and its careful analysis of all pertinent data on each student, the School makes decisions concerning each student's grade level, credit status, course requirements, and assignments.

Eighteen units, including 4 of English, 4 of mathematics, 3 of social studies (including 1 of U.S. history), and 2 of laboratory sciences, are required for graduation. A unit is equal to one year of completed course work. French, Spanish, and Latin are offered but are not required.

Students attend classes generally ranging in size from 3 to 7 students each. Math and English classes are usually limited to 6 students each. Such class size allows for individualization. Learning differences can be acknowledged, needs can be addressed, and abilities can be challenged.

The grading system—the traditional A, B, C, D (supplemented by pluses and minuses), and F—is used to give constant guidance and reinforcement to the student. Each student is graded daily in each course. These daily grade slips are distributed each night to a boarding student's dorm parent, who then reviews the grades with the student during the 2-hour evening study period. Reports are mailed to parents each week so that they are equally aware of their child's progress. Although academic achievement is rewarded with Honor Roll status and privileges, effort in academic, athletic, and community service endeavors is also encouraged and rewarded.

Remediation of academic deficiencies and the teaching of study skills are done within the context of each course. Instructors are trained to develop the process of learning along with the content of their courses. This mainstream approach is extremely effective, since the study skills are immediately made relevant to the material of the course.

Tutorial assistance is available daily to assist students having difficulty with particular assignments or concepts.

FACULTY AND ADVISERS

Each member of the staff is a trained, caring, and dedicated teacher who can work well with students who need an individualized approach to education. In 2008–09, the teaching staff consisted of 40 men and women. All of the dormitory parenting and athletics coaching are done by the academic staff.

John A. Kerney was appointed headmaster in 2008. Mr. Kerney earned his B.A. in Art History from Middlebury College. After a twenty-year career in business, John's family tradition of working in private school education led him to return to secondary school, first at Gould Academy as Associate Head of School, and then at Winchendon as the school's sixth headmaster. His global interests have him eagerly reading anything by Thomas Friedman and getting his evening laugh with the news from The Daily Show. Any day on the water whether he is sailing, kayaking or just catching a fabulous ocean sunset is a great day for John. His environmental sensibilities can be noted as he frequently chooses to walk, bike or skateboard his way around the Winchendon campus. John and Marilyn live on campus in Homewood. Their children, Alex and Sara, are attending Colorado College and Connecticut College respectively. One day soon he hopes to return to teaching a class on global issues. John is on the move all day from his office to morning meeting to sporting events where he is one of most ardent Winchendon fans.

COLLEGE ADMISSION COUNSELING

The college counselors, working closely with parents and staff, assist all students in selecting appropriate colleges. Representatives of various colleges visit the School, and there is a comprehensive collection of college catalogs and videos in the College Placement Office.

Close to 100 percent of the class of 2008 are attending colleges and universities that include Bentley, Boston University, Butler, Clark, Clarkson, Colby, Connecticut College, Curry, George Washington, Gettysburg, Hamilton, Harvard, Hobart, Hofstra, Johnson & Wales, Northeastern, Notre Dame, Parsons School of Design, Providence, RIT, Rutgers, Seton Hall, St. Lawrence, St. John's, Syracuse, Temple, Tufts, West Point, Wheaton, Worcester Polytechnic, and the Universities of Maine, Massachusetts, New Hampshire, Pennsylvania, and Vermont.

STUDENT BODY AND CONDUCT

In 2008-09, the student body consisted of 180 boys and 63 girls. Twenty-three of them are day students; 178 are boarding students; and 42 students are in home stays. Students come from fourteen states and twenty countries.

Because Winchendon is a close-knit community of young people and adults, there is a need for certain rules and policies. Acts and attitudes that interfere with the educational process, that encroach on the privacy or sensitivities of others, or that violate School policies are not permitted. Rules governing conduct at Winchendon are based upon traditional values and standards of behavior. Two examples of such standards are the dress code, which requires a tie and jacket for boys and comparable dress for girls during classes and some evening meals; and the rule prohibiting tobacco use.

The Student Council, with representatives from each class, meets as the Advisory Council to the Headmaster. Students also serve on the Student-Faculty Judicial Board as Dormitory Proctors and on various committees.

ACADEMIC FACILITIES

The Winchendon School campus is highly centralized. The academic buildings contain a library (15,000 volumes), four laboratories, and forty seminar-size classrooms. There is also an academic wing on Ford Hall.

The Computer Center contains twenty Dell computers. The Art Center has facilities for graphic arts, photography, and ceramics. The Performing

Arts Center houses facilities for dance, instrumental music, vocal music, and drama.

BOARDING AND GENERAL FACILITIES

Once a resort hotel, Ford Hall contains administrative offices, lounges, dining facilities, faculty apartments, and student living quarters. Merrell Hall, which houses boys, is a modern dormitory with a lounge and two faculty apartments. A girls' dormitory was added in 1988. A new Dining Hall and Student Center were completed in 2001.

Student rooms, furnished with draperies and wall-to-wall carpeting, are designed for comfort and privacy. There are as many double rooms as single rooms. Nearly all rooms have direct access to baths and showers. A store and a snack bar are located in the student center area.

There are 2 day nurses in the School's infirmary, and a hospital is located in a neighboring town. The School also arranges for the services of a consulting clinical psychologist and a psychotherapist to be available to students.

ATHLETICS

By requiring participation in athletics, the School seeks not only to provide the proper level of physical activity for each student but also to foster physical fitness, fair play, and selfless contribution to group endeavors. Interscholastic and club sports include alpine and cross-country skiing, baseball, basketball, cross-country running, golf, horseback riding, ice hockey, lacrosse, soccer, softball, swimming, tennis, volleyball, and weight lifting.

A new gymnasium was completed in 1990. It houses two full courts for basketball, one for volleyball, an indoor soccer area, and facilities for weight lifting and aerobic dance. There is also a complete athletics training room. A new ice arena opened in 2007.

Winchendon owns an eighteen-hole golf course designed by Donald Ross, several tennis courts, and an outdoor swimming pool.

EXTRACURRICULAR OPPORTUNITIES

As a small school, Winchendon provides exceptional opportunities for many students to participate in extracurricular activities, including student government, the yearbook *(Vestigia)*, the newspaper *(Progress)*, the literary magazine *(Impressions)*, and the camera, computer, chess, drama, and outing clubs. The School has also initiated a Cultural Affairs Program, which introduces students to activities and events—chiefly in Boston—that entertain people from all over the world.

Annual campus events include the Alumni Homecoming, Parents' Weekends in October and April, and Commencement Weekend.

DAILY LIFE

The typical daily schedule starts with breakfast at 7, room inspection at 7:30, and classes starting at 7:50. There is a midmorning all-school meeting at 10, and classes resume until lunchtime. After lunch there is a daily conference or help period, which is followed by the athletics period. Dinner is served at 5:30, and required supervised study runs from 7 to 9.

WEEKEND LIFE

A student who has met all of his or her School obligations may leave the campus on weekends with parental approval. There are many weekend activities on the campus, in nearby cities and towns, and on local college campuses. These include sports events, concerts, plays, and other cultural events as well as frequent trips to Boston and major New England ski areas and camping sites.

COSTS AND FINANCIAL AID

Tuition, room, and board for 2008–09 was $40,500; tuition for day students was $24,200. Additional fees are charged for music lessons and driver's education. Tuition payments are due twice yearly, in August and October.

Approximately 23 percent of the students receive financial aid, which is awarded on the basis of need and merit. For 2008–09, aid totaling $1.8 million was awarded.

ADMISSIONS INFORMATION

Winchendon accepts students of various abilities on the basis of their individual promise, avoiding stereotyped qualifications and standardized bases of judgment. A weak school record does not disqualify an applicant who shows good character and a potential for achievement in higher education.

Applicants for admission to any grade may submit recent Wechsler intelligence test (WISC or WAIS) scores and subtest scores. Postgraduate applicants should submit PSAT or SAT results as well. The SSAT is not required.

APPLICATION TIMETABLE

Initial inquiries are welcome at any time. Visits to the campus include a tour and an interview with the Director of Admissions. Applicants are encouraged to visit while the School is in session; if this is impossible, other arrangements can be made by the Admissions Office.

Interviews are scheduled between 8 and 4, Monday through Friday, and on Saturdays and Sundays.

Decisions on all applications are made from early February until all spaces are filled.

The nonrefundable application fee is $50 ($100 for international students). The initial deposit, required to reserve a place at Winchendon, is 10 percent of the base tuition.

ADMISSIONS CORRESPONDENCE

Ellyn Baldini, Director of Admissions
The Winchendon School
172 Ash Street
Winchendon, Massachusetts 01475
Phone: 978-297-4476
800-622-1119 (toll-free)
Fax: 978-297-0911
E-mail: admissions@winchendon.org
Web site: http://www.winchendon.org

WINDWARD SCHOOL

Los Angeles, California

Type: Coeducational day college-preparatory school
Grades: 7–12; Middle School 7–8; Upper School 9–12
Enrollment: 475
Head of School: Thomas W. Gilder

THE SCHOOL

Windward School, which was founded in 1971 through the determined efforts of Shirley Windward, a well-known educator and writer, is a self-governing independent school on the west side of Los Angeles. From its founding, Windward aimed to be a bulwark of academic excellence and personal integrity, whose character could be summed up by its motto, which is found across the entrance to the School: responsible, caring, ethical, well-informed, prepared.

Through its small classes, Windward's rigorous academic program both challenges and buoys its students. This two-fold approach of rigor and support is the root of the School's well-earned reputation for academic excellence. The School's hope for its graduates is that they go forth from a school that prized each of them for their individual gifts, helped them recognize the significance of personal integrity and community service, enlivened their joy in learning, and provided the intellectual liveliness that produces independent thought, self-assured expression, and rewarding life endeavors.

A not-for-profit corporation, Windward is governed by a 21-member Board of Trustees and an administrative team centered by the Head of School. The Western Association of Schools and Colleges accredits Windward. The School holds membership in the National Association of Independent Schools, the Independent School Alliance for Minority Affairs, A Better Chance, Independent School Management, the Educational Records Bureau, and the California Association of Independent Schools.

ACADEMIC PROGRAMS

The energetic character of Windward's academic program is set forth on the belief that certain qualities are of primary importance. These include the ability to reason with care and logic and think outside the box, communicate well orally, compute accurately and reason quantitatively, master scientific approaches to problem solving, identify and develop aesthetic talents, and complement strong academic preparation with the development of ethics, character, and well-developed people skills.

At Windward, classes contain a maximum of 17 students. In academic areas, courses are sectioned on the basis of interest and ability, and Advanced Placement courses are offered in every discipline. The minimum course load for students in grades 7–10 is six. Students in grades 11–12 may opt for an alteration of this pattern, though approval of the grade-level deans is required, and students are actively encouraged to take six or seven classes.

In the Upper School, minimum course requirements are one English course each year through grade 12, one history course each year through grade 12 (seniors who wish to take two courses in another discipline may petition to waive the grade 12 history requirement), one mathematics course each year through grade 11, one science course each year through grade 10, one science course in either grade 11 or grade 12 (this must include one year of laboratory science), completion of Level III in one foreign language or completion of Level II in each of two foreign languages (continuation of foreign language through grade 11 is required), one arts course each year through grade 10, and one physical education course each year through grade 10 (students in grades 9 and 10 who compete in an interscholastic team sport are excused from physical education during that sport's season).

Community service has long been at the heart of the Windward tradition. Beginning in Middle School, service learning is a core component of the program, and in the Upper School, all students are required to complete two separate and extensive community service projects prior to graduation.

Windward maintains a sister school relationship with two schools in Spain and France. Students are able to attend a sister school for a three-week academic exchange once they have mastered an appropriate level of linguistic fluency. Generally, the schools exchange 15 to 20 students at a time. The culminating academic experience of a Windward education is the School's annual senior trip for one week at the School's expense. This "classroom in the field" is the capstone of six years of work and allows for an appropriate opportunity to say goodbye to one another.

FACULTY AND ADVISERS

The Windward faculty consists of 75 full- and part-time members (37 women and 38 men). Seventy-three percent have advanced degrees, with 11 possessing doctorates. Thomas W. Gilder, Head of School, was appointed in 1987.

In selecting its faculty members, Windward looks for individuals who enjoy the art of teaching, who are enthusiastic about working with adolescents, who will involve themselves in the nonacademic life of the School, and who have lively personal interests of their own. Every faculty member at Windward is an integral component in the life of the School. Faculty benefits at Windward are generous on all accounts and include financial support for continuing education and the funding of faculty-generated betterment opportunities.

COLLEGE ADMISSION COUNSELING

Windward places the utmost importance upon each senior having options from which to choose. Increasingly drawn toward the top colleges in the nation, students in the last several graduating classes chose between such diverse opportunities as Brown, Colby, Columbia, Emory, Harvard, Kenyon, Princeton, the Rhode Island School of Design, Rice, Stanford, the University of California at Berkeley, the University of Pennsylvania, Vassar, Washington University (St. Louis), Wesleyan, and Yale. College counseling begins in earnest in the fall of eleventh grade, when grade-level deans and the college counseling staff meet with students and families to map out strategies and provide advice for Subject Tests. Students are helped to prepare for interviews with college representatives, more than 100 of whom visit the School. The School offers close guidance in the application processes, essay writing, and the developmental challenge of separation from family, friends, and Windward School.

STUDENT BODY AND CONDUCT

Windward has 475 students in grades 7–12. The average class size is 17 students, allowing teachers to offer individualized attention.

The student government is directed by a group of 20 prefects, selected on the basis of community respect, personal integrity, and the ability to positively affect the life in the community. By working closely with the adults at Windward, acting as intermediaries, organizing School activities, and leading by example, the prefects help to set the tone of the School. Of primary importance is the cultivation of respect and consideration for others and their property, the enhancement of relationships between faculty members and students, and the general well-being of the student body. The prefects are expected to respect Windward's standards in their personal conduct and in the way in which they lead others.

At Windward, the breaking of major School rules (lying, cheating, stealing, or using or possessing drugs or alcohol) is a pressing matter and typically leads to dismissal. A committee headed by the appropriate division-level Dean of Students handles disciplinary matters and refers matters to the appropriate division head for final consideration. Beyond rules and regulations, however, the School's deeply ingrained code of honor expects all students to offer both civility and compassion to other students and to teachers, staff members, and their own families. In fact, this expectation is one of the defining characteristics of Windward School.

Under the oversight of the Head of School, the Middle and Upper School Directors oversee the successful operation of the School and ensure that appropriate procedures are in place for students to enjoy their Windward experience and to be safe in the knowledge that discipline is expected of all community members.

ACADEMIC FACILITIES

Windward moved to its present 9-acre site in 1982, envisioning then the pastoral campus with which today's Windward students are familiar. As the School's programs have expanded, new facilities have been added to the campus. In 2002, the School constructed a ten-room classroom building, the Lewis Jackson Memorial Sports Center, the Student Pavilion, the Arts Center, and renovated the playing fields. Currently under construction is a new library/learning center with performing arts studios and broadcast production center and a science/math center, scheduled to open in the spring of 2009.

ATHLETICS

There is a suitable level of athletics for every student. Some students seek out competitive accomplishment in one sport through years of participation, while others take advantage of Windward's breadth of offerings to begin new sports at the introductory level. The physical education and athletic programs emphasize acquiring lifetime skills, shaping confident attitudes about oneself as an individual and a contributing member of a group, and developing along the way a true sense of integrity and fairness.

There are junior varsity and varsity offerings in most sports, including football, soccer, lacrosse, baseball, cross-country, tennis, volleyball, basketball, and golf.

The Lewis Jackson Memorial Sports Center houses a weight training facility, meeting space, and trophy room display, while the gymnasium offers basketball and volleyball courts. The beauty of the playing fields, which are built to university and professional specifications, offers all participating students a chance to play at their best.

EXTRACURRICULAR OPPORTUNITIES

An array of extracurricular opportunities is available to students through period eight activity programs. Period eight is a block of scheduled time that is set aside twice a week for clubs, study hall, and other activities that provide extracurricular opportunities for Upper School students. Students choose from a wide variety of activities that include robotics, debate, yoga, ceramics, chorus, the yearbook, the newspaper, junior senate, and comedy sports. Students are encouraged to participate and to explore interests that support the development of talents and strengths that are not just limited to academic success.

DAILY LIFE

Beginning at 8 each morning and ending at 3 p.m., both Middle and Upper Schools utilize a five-day schedule cycle. Monday mornings offer an all-School meeting for both Middle and Upper School students and faculty members, and there is a morning nutrition period five days a week. Seniors may take lunch off campus.

COSTS AND FINANCIAL AID

Tuition for 2008–09 was $29,995. The School's philosophy is to avoid extra charges for sports, field trips, or other activities offered through the School. Approximately 12 percent of the students at the School receive need-based scholarship opportunities.

ADMISSIONS INFORMATION

In every year, more students wish to become members of the Windward community than can be admitted. The admissions office works diligently to ensure that students who are accepted offer positive contributions to the community and succeed in Windward's challenging academic environment. The School seeks qualified students of diverse economic, social, ethnic, and racial backgrounds. The ISEE, grades, recommendations from the previous school, and an interview with Windward admissions personnel are required for all applicants. Openings exist traditionally for grades 7 and 9, although students may apply for grades 8 and 10 with permission of the admissions office. Applicants to Windward should all possess admirable strengths of character, be positive contributors to school and community, and attain high grades at their present schools.

APPLICATION TIMETABLE

Inquiries are welcome throughout the year, though the deadline for application for the following year is in December. Interviews and tours of the campus begin as soon as all faculty and staff members have returned in September.

ADMISSIONS CORRESPONDENCE

Sharon Pearline
Director of Admission
Windward School
11350 Palms Boulevard
Los Angeles, California 90066

Phone: 310-391-7127
Fax: 310-397-5655
Web site: http://www.windwardschool.org

WOODBERRY FOREST SCHOOL

Woodberry Forest, Virginia

Type: Boys' boarding college-preparatory school
Grades: 9–12 (Forms III–VI)
Enrollment: 398
Head of School: Dr. Dennis M. Campbell, Headmaster

THE SCHOOL

Standing Together, We Stand Apart. These words describe Woodberry Forest School, which stands together as a community of students, faculty and staff members, parents, and generations of distinguished alumni. The School stands apart in its commitment to higher expectations—academic and moral—that are all too rare in schools today. The Woodberry community stands together in its belief that an all-male, all-boarding environment allows students to focus on, above all, an outstanding educational experience. The School also stands together in the sense that every Woodberry student is expected to use his talents to meet the challenges the School offers. Thus Woodberry students develop the work ethic and perseverance that enable them to stand apart in everything they do.

Woodberry was founded in 1889 by Robert Stringfellow Walker to educate his 6 sons. At the time of Captain Walker's death in 1914, the School had grown in size and influence to become one of the foremost independent schools in the South. Captain Walker was succeeded by his son J. Carter Walker, who served as headmaster for fifty-one years. Under his leadership, the School's reputation grew.

Today Woodberry is one of the nation's leading boarding schools.

Woodberry emphasizes strong academic preparation for college. Just as important, the School community fosters an atmosphere of civility and cooperation. Woodberry maintains no formal church ties, but all students attend nonsectarian services each Sunday evening in St. Andrew's Chapel.

Woodberry Forest is located in a rural setting in central Virginia within easy driving distance of Charlottesville, Richmond, and Washington, D.C. The bucolic 1,200-acre campus has sweeping views of the Blue Ridge Mountains.

Woodberry Forest is an incorporated not-for-profit under a self-perpetuating 21-member board of trustees. Assets include a beautiful physical plant and a $237-million endowment. Annual Giving in 2007–08 totaled $2.7 million. Sixty-seven percent of the current parents and 55 percent of the alumni made gifts to the annual campaign.

Woodberry Forest is accredited by the Virginia Association of Independent Schools and by the Southern Association of Colleges and Schools. Its memberships include the Cum Laude Society and the National Association of Independent Schools.

ACADEMIC PROGRAMS

Woodberry's four-year, college-preparatory curriculum requires the following courses for graduation: English, 4 credits; mathematics, 3 credits; foreign language, 3 credits; history, 3 credits; laboratory science, 3 credits; art and music, 1 credit; and religion, 3 credits. The curriculum contains twenty- three college-level courses, and honors-level sections are taught in most disciplines each year (instead of freshman, sophomore, junior, and senior, Woodberry uses Third Form, Fourth Form, Fifth Form, and Sixth Form, as in the British model of education).

The average class size is 10 students; the overall student-faculty ratio is 4:1. Woodberry uses a 4-point grading scale for passing grades (A–D); no credit is given for a failed course. Academic reports are issued six times a year, at the midterm and end of each eleven-week trimester. All teachers are available for consultation during the day and in the evenings.

Woodberry offers an expansive program of outdoor education and leadership development. The Fourth Form Leadership Program brings all Fourth Form (tenth grade) students together, giving them tools to aid in personal growth. The first part of this program is a four-day Outward Bound course in the mountains of North Carolina. Each Fourth Form class has the opportunity to take this trip.

The School offers a number of opportunities for overseas study. Advanced language students may study under Woodberry Forest teachers in Central America, China, France, Scotland, and Spain. Summer study is also available in Oxford University in England, and, in a special Spring Break program, in South Africa.

FACULTY AND ADVISERS

Woodberry's full-time faculty is composed of 86 men and women who live on campus. Seventy percent of faculty members hold advanced degrees, including seven doctorates. In selecting its faculty members, Woodberry seeks people with both a scholarly and enthusiastic commitment to their discipline as well as a desire to serve as supervisors on dorm, coaches of sports, sponsors of activities, and advisers to a group of students. The adviser, who is responsible for guiding a student's overall academic and social progress, serves as an important link between parents and the School. Woodberry provides financial help for continuing education and periodically grants sabbaticals to senior faculty members.

Dennis M. Campbell has a B.A. and Ph.D. from Duke University and a B.D. from Yale University. He served as dean of the Divinity School at Duke for fifteen years before being appointed headmaster of Woodberry Forest in 1997. A noted lecturer and author, Dr. Campbell has written many articles and four books on ethics and theology.

COLLEGE ADMISSION COUNSELING

Beginning in tenth grade, a full-time college counselor advises students in selecting colleges and coordinates the visits of college representatives. The mean SAT scores for the class of 2008 were Critical Reading 603, Math 627, and Writing 617; 100 percent of graduates were accepted at four-year colleges and universities. The 101 graduates of the class of 2008 have been accepted at forty-eight colleges and universities, including Brown, Columbia, Cornell, Davidson, Duke, Princeton, Rice, Vanderbilt, Wake Forest, Washington and Lee, Williams, and the Universities of North Carolina and Virginia.

STUDENT BODY AND CONDUCT

In 2008–09, the Third Form was composed of 90 students; the Fourth Form, 102; the Fifth Form, 106; and the Sixth Form, 100. Students from thirty-one states (plus the District of Columbia) and eight countries were enrolled. The School welcomes students from a range of economic and racial backgrounds.

Fundamental to student life at Woodberry Forest is the honor system, which rests on the conviction that students want to be honorable and have the right to be trusted. In order to have this right, no student may lie, cheat, or steal. This must be understood by anyone thinking about entering the school. The honor system is a method of student self-government distinct from faculty-administered school discipline. The prefects are a small group of sixth formers appointed by the headmaster on the basis of student and faculty nominations to maintain and nurture the honor system. Student Council representatives are elected to canvass student opinion and make recommendations on disciplinary policy and other practical matters of student life.

ACADEMIC FACILITIES

Armfield Hall houses the foreign language department, a multiuse lecture hall, and a third computer center. The Reynolds Computer Center serves as the hub for the campuswide network. Anderson Hall contains classrooms for English and history; the Gray Math-Science building contains complete laboratory facilities, a computer center, two greenhouses, and the Slane Lecture Hall. Hanes Hall houses the Belk Audio-Visual Center, a computer center, and the William H. White Jr. Library, a wireless facility that contains 33,500 volumes, ninety-four periodical subscriptions, and twenty-eight online databases that are accessible across the campus. The J. Carter Walker Fine Arts Center features a 525-seat theater, prop shops, darkrooms, a small art gallery, School publications offices, and nine studios for music, painting, drawing, sculpture, ceramics, and woodworking.

BOARDING AND GENERAL FACILITIES

The Walker Building is the main school facility, housing administrative offices, the Reynolds Family Dining Room, post office, student store and recreation rooms, and dormitory rooms for about 160 boys on five halls. There are seven smaller dormitories: Turner, Taylor, Dowd-Finch, Dowd House,

House D, Terry House, and Griffin House. Most students reside in double rooms, but there are a limited number of single and triple rooms. Resident medical staff members work in the Memorial Infirmary.

ATHLETICS

There are few ways of teaching the meaning of responsibility, respect, honesty, and loyalty quite like sports at Woodberry Forest, where athletic activities are an integral component of school life.

The athletics program provides opportunities for students to compete on a wide variety of teams at all levels. Ninety percent of the student body participates in athletics each season. Woodberry offers thirteen interscholastic athletic programs and thirty-eight teams, more than at most schools.

The student-athletes are supported by one of the finest prep-school athletic complexes in the nation. Woodberry has recently constructed Johnson Stadium for its football and lacrosse programs; two synthetic turf fields; a nine-court, climate-controlled squash pavilion; and an eight-lane, NCAA-quality track and Bermuda grass field. These additions complement the School's other outstanding facilities. The Harry Barbee, Jr. Center features a 200-meter indoor track, three basketball courts, a racquetball court, three additional squash courts, and a six-lane swimming pool with diving board.

Adjacent to L. W. Dick Gymnasium, in which most of the School's basketball games are played, is Reily Wrestling Center, featuring two full mats, and the Glover Center, which houses a state-of-the-art fitness facility. Woodberry also has a regulation nine-hole golf course designed by Donald Ross, seven additional full-sized playing fields, two baseball fields, fourteen tennis courts, and an outdoor pool. Woodberry hosts the state cross-country meet on its challenging course each year.

EXTRACURRICULAR OPPORTUNITIES

The more than twenty organizations at Woodberry include the Choir; the Dozen, an a cappella vocal group; an academic team; a cycling team; and the Rod and Gun Club (with an automatic trap and skeet range). The Drama Department stages three major productions a year; smaller productions take place three times a year in the Black Box Theatre. The Rapidan outdoor program is highlighted by a 50-foot alpine tower for climbing and team-building activities. School publications include the *Fir Tree* (yearbook), *Oracle* (newspaper), *Talon* (literary magazine), and Voice (leadership journal).

The Artists and Speakers Series as well as the Fitzpatrick Lectures bring distinguished speakers and performers to the campus on a regular basis. Recent performances on campus have included the Kronos Quartet, Step Africa, and the Canadian Brass. Throughout the year, cultural and entertainment trips to Washington, Richmond, and Charlottesville are arranged in conjunction with other schools.

Each student is required to complete 60 hours of community service by graduation, and the Chapel Council and Service Committee enable students to participate in service projects in the local community.

DAILY LIFE

Classes are held six days a week—from 8 to 3:15 on Monday, Wednesday, and Thursday (seven 45-minute periods), from 8 to 12 on Tuesday and Friday (five periods), and from 8 to 11 on Saturday (four periods). A student normally has a balance between light and heavy class days, with a maximum of five classes on the latter. Athletics practices run from 3:45 to 5:30, with contests scheduled for Tuesday and Friday and an occasional Saturday. Evening study hours are from 7:45 to 10 Sunday through Friday. Club activities are scheduled for Thursday evenings and cultural programs for Friday evenings.

WEEKEND LIFE

Woodberry hosts mixers and dances with area girls' schools throughout the year. The School also sponsors frequent weekend trips to plays, concerts, and sports events in Charlottesville, Washington, and Richmond. Students are frequently given the option of attending mixers at area schools.

Sixth formers are allowed five overnight weekends per trimester, beginning after classes Saturday to 6 p.m. Sunday. Fifth formers are allowed four overnight weekends per trimester; fourth formers, three; and third formers, two. Students may combine two overnights and take a long weekend from Friday to Sunday. Weekend requests must be approved by the student's adviser, and parental permission is also necessary.

SUMMER PROGRAMS

The School offers boys ages 10-16 basketball and lacrosse camps, as well as a sports camp that has been in operation since 1967.

COSTS AND FINANCIAL AID

Charges for 2008–09 were $38,900, which covered tuition, room and board, and activities. A deposit of $3000 to reserve a place is payable by April 10. The deposit is not refundable but is applied toward the basic fee.

A substantial financial aid budget is providing tuition assistance totaling $3.8 million for approximately one third of the student body. Scholarships ranging from partial assistance to full cost are awarded on the basis of financial need, as indicated by the guidelines of the School and Student Service for Financial Aid. A tuition loan program augments the system of financial aid.

ADMISSIONS INFORMATION

Admission to Woodberry Forest is open to all students regardless of race, creed, or national origin. Acceptance of any candidate is based on academic capability, character, and extracurricular interests. The Admissions Committee uses teachers' recommendations, an applicant questionnaire, a transcript of grades, SSAT scores, and a personal interview at the School to assess the qualifications of every candidate. Woodberry accepts a majority of its students into the ninth and tenth grades. Students with outstanding qualifications, however, are admitted into the eleventh grade.

In an average year, between 30 and 45 percent of the students who apply are accepted.

APPLICATION TIMETABLE

Preliminary application should be made a year prior to the year in which the applicant wishes to be admitted. In September, the final application forms are mailed to those indicating interest for the following fall. Campus interviews are conducted throughout the year from 8:30 to 1 on weekdays and from 8:30 to 10:15 on Saturday. All applicants are requested to take the SSAT on one of the November, December, or January test dates. By February 1, the candidate's folder should be complete if he is to be considered for admission. A small number of places are left open for late applicants.

ADMISSIONS CORRESPONDENCE

Office of Admissions
Woodberry Forest School
Woodberry Forest , Virginia 22989
Phone: 540-672-6023
888-798-9371 (toll-free)

WOODLANDS ACADEMY OF THE SACRED HEART

Lake Forest, Illinois

Type: Girls' boarding and day college-preparatory school
Grades: 9–12
Enrollment: 171
Head of School: Gerald J. Grossman

THE SCHOOL

Woodlands Academy of the Sacred Heart is a college-preparatory boarding and day school for girls in grades 9 through 12. It is conducted by the Religious of the Sacred Heart, an order founded in 1800 by Madeleine Sophie Barat, which now operates more than 200 educational institutions throughout the world. Woodlands Academy has been located in Lake Forest, Illinois, for 150 years.

At Woodlands, students encounter what generations of young women have since 1858—an educational experience that is rigorous academically, supportive personally, and uniquely empowering of individual talents. Sacred Heart education "emphasizes serious study, educates to social responsibility, and lays the foundation of a strong faith." In relating this purpose to its own programs, Woodlands strives to educate the whole person, providing a value-based environment that supports rigorous intellectual training and opportunities for emotional, religious, and social growth. The enrollment includes girls of diverse religious backgrounds, and non-Catholic students are encouraged to pursue their own faiths.

Woodlands Academy is located near Chicago and all its rich and varied cultural offerings. Many colleges and universities are located nearby, and activities for students that take advantage of these opportunities are planned frequently.

The school is a nonprofit institution under the direction of a Board of Trustees. In 2007–08, $1,610,046 was received from the Academy's Annual Giving Program. Woodlands Academy of the Sacred Heart is fully accredited by the North Central Association of Colleges and Schools and the National Association of Independent Schools.

ACADEMIC PROGRAMS

The school year is divided into quarters. Classes are held five days a week. Each girl is expected to carry five major subjects a year; well-qualified students are permitted to carry six. The minimum graduation requirements include 4 credits in English, 3 credits in history, 3 credits in religion, 3 credits in mathematics, 3 credits in foreign language, 3 credits in science, and 1½ credits in fine arts. Physical education is required for 3½ years. A sampling of the courses available includes such diverse offerings as British literature, speech, acting, ceramics, chorus, painting and drawing, photography, French, Latin, Spanish, psychology, sociology, comparative government, political theories, math functions, computer literacy, Christian ethics, peace and justice, physics, anatomy, and driver's education. Advanced Placement courses are offered in sixteen courses and eleven subjects. These include art, biology, calculus AB, English literature, European history, French language, French literature, Latin literature, music theory, Spanish language, statistics, and U.S. history.

Junior and senior girls may receive college credit for selected freshman classes at Lake Forest College. All Sacred Heart schools participate in an exchange program that enables girls to attend affiliated schools in the United States and, upon arrangement, in Austria, England, France, and other countries in which Sacred Heart schools are located.

Woodlands Academy offers an English as a second language program to meet the needs of international students who want to graduate from an American high school and then enter an American college or university or want to attend an American high school in order to learn spoken and written English. Students recently enrolled in this program have come from Brazil, Canada, Egypt, Germany, Hong Kong, Indonesia, Japan, Korea, Mexico, and Saudi Arabia. The core program includes courses in grammar, composition, American literature, reading, and vocabulary development. Students are placed according to their level of English ability, which is determined through testing. In addition, students take courses in mathematics, science, religion, history, fine arts, and physical education.

The average class is 13 students, and the ratio of students to full-time faculty members is approximately 8:1. In many courses, class sections are organized on the basis of ability and level of skill development. Assignments average 30–40 minutes per subject each day. Parents receive progress reports every five weeks. Students are given preparation for the American College Testing Program and College Board examinations; international students take the Test of English as a Foreign Language (TOEFL).

FACULTY AND ADVISERS

The faculty consists of 20 full-time teachers, the majority of whom hold advanced degrees, including doctorates.

In selecting faculty members, the administration seeks men and women who are interested in the goals and standards of the school, who can instill an intellectual curiosity and enthusiasm in students in more than a teacher-student situation, and who are willing to share their personal as well as scholarly talents.

The advisory system is an important feature of life at Woodlands Academy. Each student is a member of an advisory group that meets daily. These groups average 12 students and give each one of them an experience of personal growth within the framework of a small, stable peer group. The adviser is a counselor as well as a teacher and serves a student and her family as a resource person in all areas of school life.

COLLEGE ADMISSION COUNSELING

A full-time college counselor is on campus to help students arrange to take tests, fill out applications, and apply for scholarships and to assist them in finding the information they need to select colleges. Representatives from approximately 100 colleges visited Woodlands last year, both on an individual basis and as part of the school's annual College Day, which is held in November.

In 2008, 100 percent of the Academy's graduates entered a variety of colleges and universities. Woodlands graduates are attending Boston College, Brown, Carnegie Mellon, DePaul, Emory, Fairfield, Georgetown, Harvard, Holy Cross, John Carroll, Northwestern, Notre Dame, NYU, Princeton, Providence, St. Mary's (Notre Dame), Skidmore, Syracuse, Tufts, Tulane, Washington (St. Louis), Yale, and the Universities of Chicago, Colorado, Illinois, Michigan, Southern California, and Wisconsin.

STUDENT BODY AND CONDUCT

In 2008–09, the Academy had 35 boarders and 136 day students in grades 9–12. Day students live in the nearby North Shore suburbs and surrounding areas. Resident students come from Barrington, Chicago, Oakbrook, and Hinsdale as well as the surrounding states of Indiana, Michigan, and Wisconsin. International students represent China, Hong Kong, Japan, Korea, Mexico, and Thailand.

Students are given a handbook setting out policies of the school, and their behavior is expected to comply with the rules. Violations are dealt with by the Head of School, the Dean of Students, and the Director of Resident Students. Students influence decisions concerning school life through the Woodlands Academy Council of Representatives.

ACADEMIC FACILITIES

Garden courtyards are surrounded by learning centers that house classrooms, laboratories, a small theater, three media and resource centers, art and ceramics studios (including a kiln), a darkroom, a journalism workshop, and faculty offices.

Since its opening in 1999, the Reynolds Technology Center has become vitally important to school life at all levels. The state-of-the-art facility contains a computer lab, technology classroom, publications room, and offices for technology staff members, featuring high-end computers, scanners, and a CD-ROM tower. The results are impressive: Woodlands has one full Internet computer for every 5 students. The center has also enabled faculty members to integrate more cutting-edge technology into classroom instruction and curriculum development. Using this new equipment, students are learning to complete assignments using complex software such as computer-based probes and graphing calculators.

BOARDING AND GENERAL FACILITIES

The campus is situated on rolling, heavily wooded grounds. Connected brick wings form a three-level complex that is dominated by a distinctive chapel, noted for its glass, copper, and brick design. The facilities include lounges, dining rooms, a kitchen, a canteen and student center, offices, an infirmary, and dormitories with rooms for resident students.

Dormitories consist of four halls, with private as well as double and triple rooms. New students are assigned roommates by the director, with consideration given to students' preferences as shown on a student questionnaire; returning students may choose their own roommates. Two or three houseparents are on duty; each staff member is interested in and concerned about each student. Permission for off-campus activities is prearranged by parents. School dormitories are closed during the two-week Christmas and Easter vacations as well as during Thanksgiving weekend, but arrangements for housing can be made.

ATHLETICS

Students are required to earn 3½ years of credit within the instructional physical education or sports program. Organized teams in field hockey, basketball, tennis, volleyball, soccer, and softball compete in local and regional leagues. Participation on varsity and junior varsity teams, as well as in intramural activities, is encouraged.

The campus has tennis courts, athletic fields, and a gymnasium.

EXTRACURRICULAR OPPORTUNITIES

Off-campus field trips are made to cultural events, the theater, exhibits, concerts, museums, and programs at nearby colleges or in downtown Chicago. Staff members are available to chaperone the students. Special on-campus programs with guest lecturers or performances are sponsored by the school. On-campus student programs held each year include a Fine Arts Festival in the spring, choral performances, and several dramatic productions. Traditional events, such as Ring Ceremony, May-Crowning, Father-Daughter Breakfast, and Conges (surprise holidays), are also scheduled each year.

Students may serve on the newspaper, literary magazine, or yearbook staff or participate in the chorus, the Girls Athletic Association, and the art, photography, French, Spanish, media, science, and international clubs. There are several more clubs to choose from, and new organizations are formed each year.

Girls can take part in student government either by representing their class as officers or by becoming involved in the Woodlands Academy Council of Representatives (WACOR). A council of elected officers, WACOR promotes student involvement in the school and the community (along with the dance and tradition committees) and has a say in decisions that concern school life. Its officers comprise a Council Board. The Resident Community Council (RCC), an organization for boarding students only, also promotes student interest in school affairs and arranges special events in the residence halls, including a talent-variety show, a faculty dinner, birthday parties, and programs for international students. The RCC also sponsors a newspaper for resident students and does fund-raising.

DAILY LIFE

The class day begins with a homeroom period at 8:15 a.m. and ends with dismissal at 3:15 p.m. Lunch is served at 11:30 and includes a variety of choices, including several hot entrees, a deli bar, a salad bar, a pasta bar, and a pizza area, along with a variety of fresh fruits and desserts. The daily schedule consists of nine 40-minute periods. On Friday, there is an activity period before lunch, which provides time for Masses, special assemblies, and club meetings. Students attend Chapel every Wednesday, and school lets out at 2:30 that day. Sports events, socials, dances, and other activities are held after school hours. Boarding students have leisure time after classes and in the evening after a required study hall from 6:30 to 8:30.

WEEKEND LIFE

Boarders visit friends on weekends, while others remain on campus, where they assist in the planning of recreational activities, some of which are shared with other schools. Shows, games, special events, and trips to restaurants are among the selections available on weekends. Exercise and physical fitness activities are popular, and the nearby shores of Lake Michigan offer opportunities for running and bicycling.

COSTS AND FINANCIAL AID

The 2008–09 tuition and fees were as follows: $39,515 for boarding students and $20,770 for day students. Optional expenses are private lessons or tutoring; special programs, such as the English as a second language program or the Learning program; and bus service. The girls wear an attractive sweater and skirt uniform, which is an additional expense; however, because the clothes are worn for several years, the expense is incurred primarily in the first year.

Many members of the student body receive financial aid, which is awarded on the basis of need. Parents must submit the Parents' Financial Statement, prepared by the School and Student Service for Financial Aid in Princeton, New Jersey.

Woodlands Academy awards four-year merit scholarships on a competitive basis.

ADMISSIONS INFORMATION

Applicants to Woodlands Academy are considered on the basis of their application, previous school records, teachers' and personal recommendations, and a personal interview. Entrance or placement tests are given at the school in January. The Admissions Committee interviews prospective students and makes decisions on selection. Students of any race or ethnic origin are welcome. Woodlands seeks students striving for an excellent education—girls who recognize their self-worth and who seek to cultivate their intellectual and spiritual needs to become informed, intelligent, and enlightened young women.

APPLICATION TIMETABLE

Inquiries are welcome at any time. Tours can be arranged through the Admissions Office, from 8:30 to 4 on weekdays. Applications are accepted at any time, but admission cannot be granted after the semester has begun; a late applicant is required to wait until the next semester to enroll in classes. The completed application and necessary information should be accompanied by a $50 nonrefundable application fee. Upon notification of admission, a student's family is expected to reply, and an enrollment contract is then sent out to accepting students.

ADMISSIONS CORRESPONDENCE

Director of Admission
Woodlands Academy of the Sacred Heart
Lake Forest, Illinois 60045
Phone: 847-234-4300
Fax: 847-234-4348
E-mail: admissions@woodlandsacademy.org
Web site: http://www.woodlandsacademy.org

WOODSIDE PRIORY SCHOOL

Portola Valley, California

Type: Coeducational day and boarding college-preparatory school
Grades: 6–12
Enrollment: 350
Head of School: Timothy J. Molak, Headmaster

THE SCHOOL

Woodside Priory School is a Catholic, Benedictine coeducational college-preparatory school. Core values of spirituality, community, integrity, and individuality are practiced daily in Priory School life. The Priory combines its 60-acre campus with a rigorous and balanced college-preparatory curriculum, a 10:1 student-teacher ratio, and a full complement of athletics and extracurricular activities. Founded in 1957 by Hungarian Benedictine monks, the Priory is associated with Saint Anselm College and Abbey in New Hampshire.

The Priory is located within a 35-minute drive of San Francisco and San Jose on the San Francisco Peninsula. It is also within an hour's drive of the Pacific Ocean and the recreational areas of Santa Cruz and Monterey. The facilities of Stanford University are 4 miles east. The area is served by three international airports and is 15 minutes from the Caltrain station in Menlo Park.

The governing body of the School is the Board of Directors. Operating expenses for 2008 were $11 million, with $2 million in Annual Giving.

The Priory received a six-year accreditation by the Western Association of Schools and Colleges in 2006. It is a member of the National Association of Independent Schools, the College Board, the National Catholic Education Association, and the Association of Boarding Schools, among other professional educational organizations.

ACADEMIC PROGRAMS

The curriculum seeks to educate well-rounded individuals who are prepared for success in college and life. The educational program and the School's sense of community take their character from the tradition of Benedictine education, which spans fifteen centuries. The school year consists of two semesters, with students carrying seven courses each semester. High school graduation requirements include 8 semesters of English literature, 1 semester of expository writing lab, 8 semesters of social studies, 6 semesters of mathematics, 6 semesters of lab sciences, 6 semesters of language (Spanish, Japanese, Mandarin, or French), 6 semesters of theology, 2 semesters of health and physical education, 2 semesters of humanities, 1 semester of computer science, and 2 semesters of fine arts/drama/music.

Eighteen Advanced Placement courses were offered in 2008–09 in art portfolio, biology, calculus (AB and BC), chemistry, economics, English, environmental science, French, government and politics, music, physics, Spanish language, Spanish literature, statistics, and U.S. history, among others. Eighteen elective courses are offered in the sophomore, junior, and senior years. Honors courses are offered in the sophomore through senior years in English, mathematics, modern languages, and social studies. Students who achieve at a higher level in mathematics are placed according to their skills. Students may take course work through local colleges and universities. Close, personal faculty attention as a result of small class settings allows student's progress to be monitored and facilitates effective communication among parents, students, and teachers.

Students must maintain at least a 2.0 GPA (on a 4.0 scale) and achieve a passing grade of at least 60 percent in each course to remain in the School. Letter grades range from A through F. Student progress may be monitored by parents and students on a daily basis via the Internet. In addition, parents receive notification of student academic progress on a regular basis.

Students participate in cultural events and field trips that enhance the academic program. They make visits to the San Francisco Symphony and art and science museums; participate in the Washington, D.C., Model United Nations Program; and take field trips to the Monterey Bay Aquarium, the Exploratorium, the Stanford Linear Accelerator Center, and the NASA–Ames Research Center. Speakers on the campus have included Senator William Bradley, anthropologist Jane Goodall, former Secretary of Defense William Perry, filmmaker Jerry Zucker, and Ambassador Shirley Temple Black.

A four-year service-learning program is an integral part of High School academics, requiring 80 hours of community service for High School graduation. High School students work with children, young adults, the infirm, and the elderly as well as homeless and displaced persons. Middle School students work with faculty members on specific community projects and service programs. An active retreat program in each grade complements the academic program for personal and spiritual growth as well as community building.

FACULTY AND ADVISERS

Timothy J. Molak (M.A., Saint Mary's University, and M.A., Saint Thomas University) is Head of School. He was appointed Head of School following eight years as the Priory's Dean of Students. Before his appointment as Dean in 1990, he was the Academic Dean at Bishop Kelly High School.

With a team of 7 administrators, the Head of School works with a faculty of 50 men and women. Most faculty members hold advanced degrees, and 3 have doctorates.

Faculty members are chosen on the basis of their qualifications, teaching experience, and willingness to participate actively in the community life of the School. Faculty members participate in counseling, coaching, and moderating activities. A monastic community of 5 and eighteen faculty families live on campus.

COLLEGE ADMISSION COUNSELING

Juniors and seniors begin the college application process early in the fall of each year in group sessions, and each student receives individual counseling. Visits from college representatives provide information for students. The College Guidance Center maintains an up-to-date library of catalogs, CDs, viewbooks, and videos for student research. A full-time College Counselor directs the College Guidance program.

Sophomores and juniors take the PSAT as well as the SAT in the spring and again in the fall of their senior year. Mean SAT scores of Priory students are significantly above national and state averages. Priory students annually earn AP scholar awards, University of California Regents scholarships, and a variety of individual college merit awards. In the class of 2007, 24 percent of the class achieved finalist, semifinalist, commended, or Hispanic Nationalist scholar status by the College Board. For the May 2007 AP exams, 90 percent of the students taking the exams scored 3, 4, or 5; 75 percent scored a 4 or 5.

Priory graduates continue their undergraduate and graduate educations at colleges and universities throughout the world, including Boston College, Brown, Claremont-McKenna, California State Polytechnic, Cornell, Dartmouth, Duke, Georgetown, Harvard, Johns Hopkins, MIT, Notre Dame, NYU, Northwestern, Princeton, Reed, Santa Clara, Stanford, Syracuse, Wellesley, Williams, and Yale, as well as the Universities of Chicago, San Francisco, Southern California, and Wisconsin and the University of California campuses at Berkeley, Davis, Irvine, Los Angeles, Riverside, San Diego, Santa Barbara, and Santa Cruz.

STUDENT BODY AND CONDUCT

One third of the students are enrolled in the Middle School and two thirds are enrolled in the High School. The Priory is internationally and culturally diverse, as more than twenty-five countries are represented in the student body and faculty.

The Priory attempts to foster Christian values in each student. Honesty and a respect for others are the primary objectives of the School's mission.

ACADEMIC FACILITIES

Facilities include Founders Hall, a fine arts studio, the chapel, and twenty-three classrooms. The Briggs Science Center houses full laboratories for biology, chemistry, physics, an electron microscope, and computer studies. Each lab has four Internet-connected PCs. The 18,000-volume Panonhalma Library and Technology Center contains twenty-four computer stations that are connected to the Internet. The Priory is a totally wireless campus. There are more than 150 computer workstations throughout the campus. Computer technology is integrated into every academic department. Opened in September 2007, the $15-million Center for the Performing Arts at the Priory includes a 400-seat state-of-the-art theater, a black-box theater for improvisational drama, and a choir/orchestra building, which includes a sound-mixing lab.

BOARDING AND GENERAL FACILITIES

The boarding program fosters Christian social living within a highly structured environment. Two dormitories provide living space for 50 boarders and 6 adult Resident Advisors. In addition, the Boarding Program is also supported by 16 resident faculty members who live on campus. Students share a double room. Each dormitory has its own recreational area. September 2006 marked the opening of the new Student Center, which is available for day as well as boarding students.

A seven-day boarding program is open to students in grades 9–12. While boarders have the option to go home for the weekends, recreation opportunities are provided for students who wish to remain on campus. The dormitories are closed during the summer vacation and the major vacation periods of the school year. International students must have a local guardian.

Generally, boarders enter in the freshman year. Transfers to the program in the sophomore and junior years are considered on a space-available basis.

ATHLETICS

Enrollment in the physical and health education curriculum is required of each student. A coed interscholastic sports program provides an opportunity for all students to compete in baseball, basketball, cross-country, golf, lacrosse, soccer, swimming, tennis, track, and volleyball. Facilities include a 10,000-square-foot gymnasium, a 25-meter heated pool, three soccer fields, two baseball diamonds, four tennis courts, and two outdoor basketball courts.

The Priory is a member of the Peninsula Private School Athletic League and participates with other independent schools in sixteen interscholastic teams. Athletic teams are available for Middle School and High School students.

EXTRACURRICULAR OPPORTUNITIES

Clubs and organizations play a significant role in student life. Activities include yearbook, school newspaper, drama, photography, ski, electronics, science, robotics, and computer clubs. Annual family events include the Family Picnic, which opens the school year.

DAILY LIFE

Breakfast for boarding and day students is served from 7:30 to 8:15. Day students and boarders begin classes at 8:30 and end at 3:30. The academic day consists of seven classes. Class periods are on a rotating schedule and are 75 minutes long. A hot lunch and a salad bar are provided for all students.

Dinner for boarders is served at 6 p.m. Evening study periods are held Sunday through Thursday from 7 to 9:30 p.m.

WEEKEND LIFE

The Dean of Students and Director of Residential Life coordinate with the student government, Dormitory Council, and various clubs in planning activities on and off campus for both day students and boarders. Dances are regularly held on campus and students are invited to dances sponsored by area schools.

The Priory is situated in an area of unsurpassed cultural and recreational opportunities. Communities in and around the San Francisco Bay Area and nearby Stanford University offer events throughout the year that are enjoyed by students and faculty members. The Ski Club organizes trips to Lake Tahoe. Professional football, basketball, hockey, and baseball teams are within minutes of the Priory. The School sponsors weekend trips to the Santa Cruz Beach Boardwalk, the Sierras, and nearby state and national parks.

COSTS AND FINANCIAL AID

Tuition is the cost of the academic program and general expenses, such as daily hot lunch, student government, athletics, assemblies, the yearbook, and other student publications. The tuition noted for boarders includes room and board for students enrolled in the Priory's boarding school for the academic year. For the 2007–08 school year, tuition was $28,050 for day students and $38,950 for boarders. Books are extra.

At registration, a $3500 deposit for boarders or a $1500 deposit for day students is required to ensure placement. This is a nonrefundable deposit applied to tuition. A tuition assistance program is available, and currently 22 percent of the students share more than $1.5 million in financial aid. Families wishing to apply for financial aid should contact the Admissions Office. Tuition and fees are normally paid in installments in July and December. The Priory also offers a ten-month payment plan as well as a commercial loan program for tuition.

ADMISSIONS INFORMATION

Admission is based upon the applicant's school record, standardized test (ISEE, SSAT, or STS/HSPE) results, two recommendations from teachers, and the evaluation of the student by his or her principal or adviser. There is a $75 application fee.

Students are admitted into the sixth through eleventh grades each year. There are no senior (twelfth-grade) transfers.

Applicants to the High School must take the SSAT, ISEE, or STS/HSPE. The median SSAT score for entering students is above the 80th percentile. However, grades and recommendations are more significant factors in admission decisions. The TOEFL is required for international students whose first language is not English, with a minimum score of 525 to 550 on the paper-based test or 70 to 80 on the Internet-based test.

The Priory seeks to admit students who are motivated learners, desiring a well-rounded college-preparatory education. The Priory is determined to provide the student with the support, opportunities, and environment necessary to meet his or her educational goals. Candidates are accepted on the basis of their personal and academic qualifications without discrimination as to race, color, or creed.

APPLICATION TIMETABLE

For admission to the 2009–10 academic year, application materials must be filed with the Priory by mid-January 2009. Candidates meeting this date are the first considered by the Admissions Committee, and notification of the committee's action is mailed on March 15, 2009. Students making application after this date are notified within two weeks after all admission forms have been received, pending available space in the class. Applicants are required to spend a class day at the Priory; an appointment may be made with the Director of Admissions. Families interested in taking a tour may do so by attending an Open House in the fall. If attendance at an Open House is not possible, a personal tour can be arranged through the Admissions Office. A school tour and an interview usually take an hour; comfortable attire and walking shoes are suggested for the visit. A downloadable admissions application is available on the Priory Web site.

ADMISSIONS CORRESPONDENCE

Al Zappelli, Director of Admissions and Financial Aid
Founders Hall
Woodside Priory School
302 Portola Road
Portola Valley, California 94028-7897
Phone: 650-851-8223
Fax: 650-851-2839
E-mail: prioryadmissions@yahoo.com
Web site: http://www.PrioryCA.org

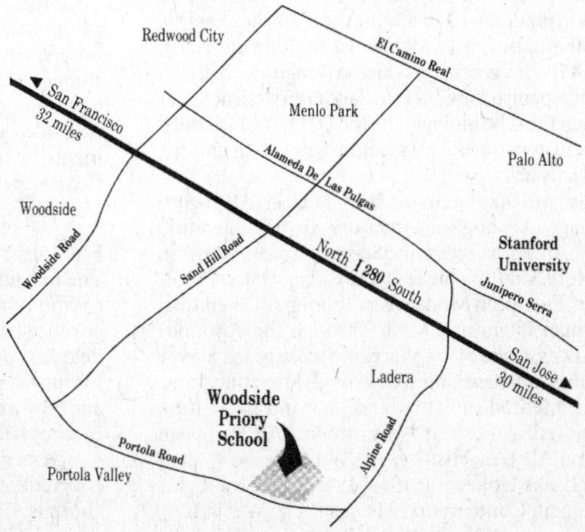

WORCESTER ACADEMY

Worcester, Massachusetts

ACHIEVE THE HONORABLE

Type: Coeducational day and boarding college-preparatory school
Grades: 6–12, postgraduate year
Enrollment: 658
Head of School: Dexter Morse

THE SCHOOL

Since 1834, Worcester Academy has been creating life-changing experiences for students, faculty members, families, and the community. It is a place where hard-working students are engaged, empowered, and equipped to truly "achieve the honorable," now and throughout their entire lives.

In an authentic, unpretentious culture where there is no place for elitism, Worcester Academy thoughtfully blends challenge and care—meeting students where they are in life, then helping them to understand both who they are and what they have to contribute. At the end of the day, perhaps the Academy's greatest accomplishment is that its graduates are better prepared for college, and for life, because of the real world experiences they have had with it.

The school, which moved to its present site in 1869, is only a 10-minute walk from the center of Worcester, home to many excellent colleges, various libraries, museums, science centers, a large number of industries, and a nationally known civic center. The main campus is a 12-acre tract on which buildings surround a central area of open lawns and shade trees. The campus includes three classroom buildings, four dormitories, a gymnasium, the Warner Memorial Theater, and the student center. In 2008, Kingsley Hall, which houses English and math classrooms and the science laboratories, underwent a $5.8-million renovation to create state-of-the-art facilities.

The school is a nonprofit corporation under the direction of a self-perpetuating Board of Trustees with up to 35 members. The endowment is valued at approximately $38 million. Annual Fund giving for the most recent academic year amounted to approximately $847,000.

Worcester Academy is accredited by the New England Association of Schools and Colleges and is affiliated with the National Association of Independent Schools, the Secondary School Admission Test Board, the Association of Independent Schools in New England, the National Association for College Admission Counseling, and the Cum Laude Society.

ACADEMIC PROGRAMS

A traditional college-preparatory curriculum is offered. To graduate, a student must earn a minimum of 18 credits in grades 9–12, including the following: English, 4; mathematics, 3 (which must include algebra I, algebra II, and geometry); foreign language, 2 (Latin, French, Spanish, or Chinese); laboratory science, 2 (1 of which must be biology); history, 2 (1 of which must be U.S. history); arts, 1⅓ (studio art, music, or drama); and electives.

Electives may be chosen from English (AP English Language, AP English Literature, British Literature Survey, American Literature Survey, African American Literature, Crafting the Essay, Creative Writing, Short Fiction, European Modernism, Immigrant Literature, Dystopian Literature, Myth Through the Postmodernist Lens, Code of the Warrior, Shakespeare: Survey by Genre, Japanese Culture Through Literature, Journalism, Method of Satire, and Law and Literature), history (AP American Government, AP European History, AP U.S. History, AP World History, Economics, The Holocaust: 1935–1945, The Civil Rights Movement, Contemporary Issues I: The War in Iraq, Contemporary Issues II: Globalization, Contemporary Issues III: Poverty in America, The Sixties Experience, World War II in Europe, World War II in the Pacific, Thinking Like a Social Scientist, Introduction to Ethics, and Science and Religion), mathematics (Precalculus, AP Calculus AB and BC, Multivariable Calculus, and Statistics–Level I Honors), science (AP Biology, AP Chemistry, AP Physics, AP Environmental Science, Human Anatomy and Physiology, Comparative Anatomy and Physiology, Marine Science, Introduction to Geology, and Introduction to Forensic Science), technology (AP Computer Science, Video and Multimedia Design, Multimedia and Web Design, Introduction to CAD, and Introduction to Photoshop), and the visual and performing arts (AP Studio Art, Ceramics, New Media Art, Sculpture, Mixed Media, Architecture, Printmaking, 2-D Design, 3-D Design, Instrumental Ensemble, Choral Ensemble, Music Theory, AP Music Theory, Acting, Costume Design, East Meets West, Stagecraft, Porter in Performance, and Shakespeare in Hollywood).

Students are required to carry a minimum of five courses plus health and wellness (noncredit) in their freshman and sophomore years. Students must also fulfill an off-campus community service requirement. Special programs exist for international students.

Recent students have earned Advanced Placement credit in English Language, English Literature, Spanish Language, French Language, Biology, Chemistry, Physics, Environmental Science, Calculus AB and BC, Computer Science, U.S. History, European History, World History, and Government and Politics. Honors sections, accelerated programs, and independent study are available.

Classes in mathematics (grades 9–12), English (grades 9–11), history (grades 10–12), and science (grades 9–12) are homogeneously grouped. Class size is approximately 15 students.

The new library has study carrels and books and periodicals for general reading, research, and reference. Thirty-two computers are available for student use in the library. The librarians make every effort to help students make use of the facility.

Students receive an excellent preparatory education. There are refurbished biology, geology, physics, chemistry, and biochemistry laboratories with completely modern equipment.

Each student is provided with an adviser, with whom he or she meets once a week to review academic progress. Advisers are given a biweekly update by each student's teacher, and these reports may be accessed by parents on the Academy's Web site. The school year is divided into trimesters. Grades and written comments by teachers are sent home three times a year. Parents may request meetings with teachers or advisers at any time.

FACULTY AND ADVISERS

The full-time faculty is composed of 103 teachers, all of whom hold baccalaureate degrees. Fifty-four hold advanced degrees, including five doctorates, three law degrees, one medical degree, and one Master of Divinity degree. Forty-five faculty members are women and 58 are men. Twenty-nine faculty members live on campus with their families.

Dexter Morse, appointed Head of School in 1997, is a graduate of Phillips Academy in Andover, Massachusetts; Bowdoin College (A.B., 1962); and the University of Vermont (M.Ed., 1967). Mr. Morse previously served as Head of the Upper School at Phoenix Country Day School.

In selecting its faculty, the Academy looks first for classroom teaching ability. All members of the faculty are also responsible for extracurricular activities, and those living on campus are also dorm masters.

COLLEGE ADMISSION COUNSELING

The College Counselor assists students in the college application process and aids them in gaining admission to, and entering, colleges suited to their needs and ambitions. It is the school's goal that each student be able to select from among several colleges extending offers of admission.

The process of college counseling at the Academy follows a general pattern. In the spring, individual conferences for each junior are scheduled to discuss college plans, and the junior class attends a college fair in Boston to obtain information about colleges throughout the country. During the summer before their senior year, students are urged to write to colleges for literature, study college publications, and visit the colleges to which they intend to apply. In the fall of the senior year, individual conferences with the College Counselor are held to discuss final application procedures and to examine each student's goals and abilities in relation to the programs at the colleges to which he or she is applying.

The college counseling office holds individual conferences to discuss colleges; welcomes college representatives, who conduct individual interviews or small informational sessions; maintains a large collection of college catalogs; provides transcripts for applications; writes statements about each student to supplement the factual information given in the transcript; gives advice on financial aid; and helps students in all areas of the college admission process.

The ranges of SAT scores in the middle 50 percent for the classes of 2003 to 2008 were 570–690 verbal and 570–700 math. Verbal scores do not include those of international students. The middle 50 percent of ACT scores were 24–29.

The SAT Reasoning Test, SAT Subject Tests, and the ACT are administered throughout the year by the college counseling office, which advises students on the appropriate testing program to highlight their strengths and satisfy the requirements of colleges. International students are registered for the TOEFL during their junior and senior years.

All of the 147 seniors who graduated in 2008 proceeded immediately to higher education. Worcester Academy graduates are enrolled at eighty-eight different colleges, including Amherst, Bates, Bentley, Boston College, Boston University, Bowdoin, Brandeis, Carnegie Mellon, Dartmouth, Emory, George Washington, Georgetown, Georgia Tech, Hobart and William Smith, Lehigh, Middlebury, Northwestern, Purdue, Rice, Skidmore, Trinity, Tufts, Union, Wheaton, and the Universities of Chicago, Michigan, and Vermont.

STUDENT BODY AND CONDUCT

The 2008–09 student enrollment is distributed as follows: sixth grade, 21 boys and 22 girls; seventh grade, 33 boys and 18 girls; eighth grade, 31 boys and 36 girls; ninth grade, 52 boys and 50 girls; tenth grade, 65 boys and 55 girls; eleventh grade, 67 boys and 61 girls; twelfth grade, 61 boys and 61 girls; and postgraduate year, 24 boys and 1 girl. There are 513 day students and 145 boarding students. Students came from sixteen states and eleven countries.

Students are expected to follow the rules and behave in a socially mature and responsible manner, which includes respecting the rights and property of others. The Head of School has final authority over all disciplinary matters and has the right to dismiss any student.

ACADEMIC FACILITIES

Walker Hall houses administrative offices, classrooms, the Information Services Center (containing twelve computers for student use), the Walker Hall Gallery, the Andes Performing Arts Center, and the newly refurbished art studio. Rader Hall, which opened in 2001, is a beautiful, state-of-the-art four-story academic building that adds eleven new classrooms and a two-story library. Kingsley Hall, completely renovated in 2008, houses English and math classrooms and nine science laboratories. The newly renovated Warner Theater houses the music department and is used for plays, recitals, movies, and assemblies. The Megaron is a building that is also used for social events. The Kellner Student Center opened in 1991. This facility houses recreation rooms, club rooms, the general office, and the school store. Six Worcester Academy buildings are included on the National Register of Historic Places.

BOARDING AND GENERAL FACILITIES

Dexter Hall and Davol Hall are boys' dormitories, and Heydon Hall and Stoddard Hall are girls' dormitories. In addition, Stoddard Hall also houses the infirmary. All rooms are singles or doubles. All dormitories have faculty members as dorm masters. During vacation, the dormitories are closed.

The full-time infirmary staff, including 2 nurse practitioners, is aided by a physician who visits the school twice a week. The Academy has 24-hour access to Worcester Medical Center and a family health service facility. In addition, there are 2 school counselors on campus.

ATHLETICS

Every student is required to participate in some form of physical education or sports. This year, there were forty-six interscholastic sports teams, playing the following sports: baseball, basketball, crew, cross-country, field hockey, football, golf, hockey, lacrosse, skiing, soccer, softball, swimming, tennis, track, volleyball, water polo, and wrestling.

Worcester Academy has a rich athletic tradition. Its alumni include many college, professional, and Olympic competitors. The boys' varsity teams compete against the Class A prep schools of New England as well as several college junior varsity teams. Girls and underclassmen compete against other independent schools.

The Daniels Gymnasium houses a swimming pool, two basketball courts, a track, a wrestling room, a weight room, a sports store, a training room, and a varsity club room. Gaskill Field, completely renovated in 1994, is an 11-acre facility with tennis courts; a track; soccer, football, and baseball fields; and a field house. The New Balance Fields, a 37-acre tract about 4 miles from the campus, were completed in fall 2001 and provide additional baseball and softball diamonds and fields for soccer, lacrosse, and field hockey.

EXTRACURRICULAR OPPORTUNITIES

The Academy offers more than thirty clubs, which the students are encouraged to join. Some examples of clubs are Academy Singers, Ambassadors, Amnesty International, Art Club, Big Brother/Big Sister, Book Club, Dance Club, Debate, Dexter Prize Speaking, Drama Club, Environmental Club, Foreign Language, Gay-Straight Alliance, Habitat for Humanity, Investment Club, Jazz Combo, Jimmy Fund, Law, Math Teams, Model UN, Multicultural, Multimedia, Physics, Robotics, SADD, Varsity Club, and World Cultures. Students also publish a yearbook, the school newspaper, and a literary magazine. All students are required to participate in an after-school activity (sports, drama, clubs, etc.) in at least two of the trimesters.

There are assemblies at which lecturers and performers appear. Traditional events include Homecoming, Winter Carnival, and Alumni Day. There are dances, concerts, plays, and movies throughout the year.

Located in Worcester, a city of 170,000 residents, 1 hour west of Boston, the Academy is distinctive because of its urban location. The Academy's easy access to many museums, concert halls, libraries, shopping malls, and a nationally known civic center provides its students with a number of recreational opportunities.

DAILY LIFE

Classes for Upper School students begin daily at 7:45 and end at 3:15 on Monday, Tuesday, and Thursday. On Wednesday classes end at 1:35, and on Friday classes end at 2:30. Class periods are 49 minutes long. On Wednesday afternoons and on Saturdays, there are athletic contests. Extracurricular activities and sports practices are held from 3:30 to 6 p.m. For boarders, breakfast begins at 7 and dinner begins at 6:15. Lunch is served to the entire campus from 11:30 to 1:30. On Sunday through Thursday evenings, there is a 2-hour required supervised study hall from 7:45 to 9:45 in the dormitories. Students have free time until 10:30, when they must be back in their rooms.

WEEKEND LIFE

Friday and Saturday nights are free nights, and activities are planned and chaperoned by the faculty. A typical weekend offers two or three activities, which might be dances, movies, concerts, or field trips to points of interest. Students may also sign out to leave the campus.

COSTS AND FINANCIAL AID

Tuition for the 2008–09 academic year was $22,640 for day students in grades 6–8 and $23,910 for grades 9–12 (costs include lunch), $37,790 for five-day boarders, and $42,290 for seven-day boarders. Tuition refund insurance is required on some payment plans. Health insurance and tuition payment plans are available. International students pay $3500 to cover infirmary services, activities, health insurance, TOEFL testing, and immigration support.

All financial aid is awarded on the basis of need. The Parents' Financial Statement must be filed with the School and Student Service for Financial Aid in Princeton, New Jersey. For 2007–08, scholarships amounted to approximately $3 million, including $9000 allocated to a student work program.

ADMISSIONS INFORMATION

The Academy admits each student on the basis of his or her transcript of grades, letters of recommendation, standardized test scores, and personal interview. Only college-bound students are admitted. Since each student is considered on the basis of individual college goals, no fixed grade level is required for admission. The Admission Committee evaluates candidates for admission, paying close attention to past performance as well as personal qualities. The campus visit is an important aspect of the admission process, since it gives the candidate a chance to learn a great deal about the school and to see it in operation.

Worcester Academy subscribes fully to all federal and state legislation prohibiting discrimination of any sort against applicants, students, or faculty or staff members for reasons of race, sex, religion, or national origin.

APPLICATION TIMETABLE

Worcester Academy invites inquiries at any time of the year. Campus visits may be arranged Monday through Friday. The priority deadline for applying for admission is January 15; after that date, applications are reviewed on a space-available basis. Notification of acceptance is mailed on March 10. The application fee is $50 for U.S. applicants and $125 for international applicants.

ADMISSIONS CORRESPONDENCE

Susanne C. Carpenter
Director of Admission and Financial Aid
Worcester Academy
81 Providence Street
Worcester, Massachusetts 01604

Phone: 508-754-5302
Fax: 508-752-2382
E-mail: admission@worcesteracademy.org
Web site: http://www.worcesteracademy.org

WYOMING SEMINARY COLLEGE PREPARATORY SCHOOL

WYOMING SEMINARY
founded 1844

Kingston, Pennsylvania

Type: Coeducational boarding (grades 9–12) and day college-preparatory school
Grades: PK–PG: Lower School, PK–8; Upper School, 9–12, postgraduate year
Enrollment: School total: 782; Upper School: 445
Head of School: Kip P. Nygren, President

THE SCHOOL

Located in the Wyoming Valley of northeastern Pennsylvania, Wyoming Seminary is a coeducational college-preparatory school enrolling day students in preschool (age 3) through grade 12 and boarding students in grades 9–12 and a postgraduate year. The Lower School campus is located in Forty Fort, approximately 3 miles from the Upper School campus. Kingston, a suburb of historic Wilkes-Barre, lies along the banks of the Susquehanna River. Kingston is a 2-hour drive from New York City, 2 hours from Philadelphia, and 25 minutes from the Wilkes-Barre/Scranton International Airport, which is served by major airlines.

Wyoming Seminary was founded in 1844 by leaders of the Methodist church to "prepare students for the active duties of life—for a course of professional or collegiate studies or any degree of collegiate advancement." Today, Wyoming Seminary students and teachers challenge themselves and each other to reach their academic and personal goals. Students learn to manage their time, write and speak clearly and effectively, study efficiently, and continue learning for college and life.

Five colleges, the Kirby Center for the Performing Arts, the Northeastern Pennsylvania Philharmonic, the Everhart Museum, Steamtown National Historic Park, the Wachovia Arena, and area theater, music groups, and lecture series provide cultural opportunities. Skiing, biking, hiking, whitewater rafting in nearby state parks, the Philadelphia Yankees AAA farm club games, and the Wilkes-Barre/Scranton Penguins AHL games are popular weekend activities.

Wyoming Seminary is directed by a 44-member Board of Trustees. Endowment is valued at more than $50 million, of which approximately 40 percent is used for scholarship purposes. Wyoming Seminary is accredited by the Middle States Association of Colleges and Schools, approved by the University Senate of the United Methodist Church, and a member of the National Association of Methodist Schools and Colleges, the Pennsylvania Association of Independent Schools, the Boarding Schools Association of the Philadelphia Area, the Association of Boarding Schools, the National Association of Independent Schools, the Secondary School Admission Test Board, the Council for Religion in Independent Schools, the College Board, and the National Association of College Admission Counselors.

ACADEMIC PROGRAMS

Wyoming Seminary prides itself on its high standards of academic excellence and its competitive spirit. Seminary offers more than 160 college preparatory courses, from the fundamental to the advanced, including twenty-six Advanced Placement courses in all major disciplines. Classes meet five days per week and have an average of 13 students. Advanced classes are much smaller. The student-teacher ratio is 10:1.

To be awarded a Wyoming Seminary diploma, a student must accumulate a minimum of 19.33 credits; students earn .33 credits for a term course or 1 credit for a full-year course. Specific requirements are English, 4 credits; mathematics, 3 credits; foreign language, 3 credits; history/social science, 3 credits; laboratory science, 3 credits; physical education, 4 credits; health, .33 credit; religion .33 credit; music history, .33 credit; art history, .33 credit; public speaking, .33 credit; and computer science, .33 credit. The trimester system increases the number of possible choices.

Qualified students may enroll in advanced courses at nearby Wilkes University or King's College. With faculty approval, juniors, seniors, and postgraduates may pursue independent-study programs or a school exchange abroad for one or more terms. Seniors and postgraduates have opportunities to further investigate areas of interest through internships in local businesses and professional offices.

Wyoming Seminary enrolls between 15 and 20 postgraduate students each year. All are qualified to enter college directly from their previous schools but choose to spend a year at a college-prep school to improve their college options. They take advanced courses previously unavailable to them and strengthen their skills in areas such as math or writing. Working with Seminary's postgraduate coordinator, these students enroll in two courses designed to meet their needs: The Postgraduate Experience seminar and Postgraduate English. Other than these two requirements, they have great flexibility to choose among Wyoming Seminary's multifaceted curriculum.

An ESL program is also offered for international students.

FACULTY AND ADVISERS

The teaching faculty at the Upper School includes 34 women and 42 men; 12 percent hold doctoral degrees and 58 percent hold master's degrees from a variety of colleges and universities. There are 45 women and 9 men at the Lower School; 43 percent hold master's degrees. Two thirds of the faculty members live on the campus; this gives students an opportunity to consult with their teachers beyond the usual school day.

Kip P. Nygren, appointed eleventh President of Wyoming Seminary in 2007, is a graduate of the United States Military Academy (B.S.), Stanford University (two M.S. degrees), and Georgia Institute of Technology (Ph.D. in engineering).

COLLEGE ADMISSION COUNSELING

Beginning in the sophomore year, students receive highly personalized counseling, which continues until they select a college or university that suits their interests, abilities, and needs. Virtually all graduates of Wyoming Seminary pursue their education in a four-year program. Most graduates are accepted by at least one highly competitive or most competitive college.

Members of the class of 2008 are enrolled at such colleges and universities as Amherst, Bucknell, Carnegie Mellon, Dickinson, Georgetown, Lafayette, Lehigh, NYU, Northwestern, Penn State, Skidmore, Smith, the United States Naval Academy, University of Wisconsin, and Yale.

STUDENT BODY AND CONDUCT

The current enrollment in the Upper School is 445. This includes 98 boarding boys, 89 boarding girls, 130 day boys, and 128 day girls. The students are from eleven states and twenty-three countries, including Canada, Croatia, Germany, Japan, Spain, and Thailand.

The Wyoming Seminary student body is governed by a legislative assembly, made up of students and members of the faculty and administration, which is responsible for many nonacademic aspects of campus life. Within the government are four standing committees: spirit, activities, assemblies and programs, and finance.

The Dean of Upper School monitors the conduct of the student body, and, depending on the seriousness of the offense, either the Dean or a disciplinary committee determines the penalty.

ACADEMIC FACILITIES

Wyoming Seminary (Upper School) occupies a 22-acre main campus that includes traditional ivy-covered nineteenth-century buildings as well as more modern facilities. Nesbitt Hall contains science laboratories, arts studios, and a dance studio. Sprague Hall includes a new addition with state-of-the-art classrooms, a conference room, computer facilities, a bookstore, and administrative offices. The Kirby Library was completely redesigned and outfitted in 2008 and is housed in the Stettler Learning Resources Center. The Carpenter Athletic Center and Pettebone Dickson Student Center cater to athletics and student clubs. Great Hall offers performance and classroom space for the performing arts department.

BOARDING AND GENERAL FACILITIES

Boarding students live in four dormitories. Swetland, Darte, and Fleck Halls are interconnected to form one unit. Girls are housed in Swetland and Fleck and freshman and sophomore boys in Darte. Junior, senior, and postgraduate boys live in Carpenter Hall. Within each dormitory are computers for individual use and lounge areas where students can gather and relax.

E-mail accounts exist for each boarding student and are also available for day students. Wireless Internet access is available throughout the campus.

ATHLETICS

More than 75 percent of Wyoming Seminary students take part in interscholastic sports. Twenty varsity teams compete in more than 200 contests each year. Girls compete in basketball, cross-country, field hockey, golf, ice hockey, lacrosse, soccer, softball, swimming, and tennis. Boys participate in baseball, basketball, cross-country, football, golf, ice hockey, lacrosse, soccer, swimming, tennis, and wrestling. The Carpenter Athletic Center, with its swimming pool, two gymnasiums, and a new weight room, provides accommodations for both varsity and intramural sports. New in 2006 were the completely renovated wrestling room and the first-ever artificial turf field for lacrosse and field hockey.

EXTRACURRICULAR OPPORTUNITIES

Whether it is athletics or music, creative writing or drama, students easily find their niche. Student activities include Peer Group, *The Wyoming* (yearbook), *The Opinator* (newspaper), *Pandemonium* (literary magazine), Dance, International Club, "W" Club, Blue Key, Model United Nations, Environmental Club, Social and Gender Issues Club, Ski Club, and others. Involvement in community service is required by the EXCOLO program.

The Buckingham Performing Arts Center houses a 460-seat auditorium with a dramatics practice area and a scenery construction shop, giving students the chance to become involved in every aspect of the theater. Three drama productions are performed each year. Orchestra and vocal performances take place in the Great Hall. Musical organizations include the 100-voice Chorale; the Madrigal Singers, a select group of 28 who toured Asia in March of 2006; orchestra, jazz, and string ensembles; and a handbell choir. Music practice rooms, rehearsal studios, and a listening center give musicians a special place to perform and work. Private instruction is available in instrumental music and voice.

DAILY LIFE

A typical academic day at Seminary begins at 8 a.m. and includes four class periods in the morning followed by lunch and three classes in the afternoon in addition to weekly school meetings. Each class period is approximately 45 minutes long. A conference period is scheduled at the end of the day, giving students the opportunity to meet with teachers or advisers for extra help. During the hours between class and dinner, students participate in extracurricular activities or athletics. Family-style dinner is served in the dining hall for all boarding students and faculty families. Boarding students study in their rooms or the library from 7:30 to 9:50 p.m., Sunday through Thursday.

WEEKEND LIFE

The weekend schedules provide plenty of social activity. Along with movies, sports events, dances, and plays are white-water rafting, mountain biking, weekend ski trips, outdoor cookouts and concerts, and trips to New York and Philadelphia. Wilkes-Barre gives students additional cultural and social events to attend, and it has a great variety of restaurants and shops.

COSTS AND FINANCIAL AID

In 2008–09, Upper School tuition was $38,000 for boarding students and $19,200 for day students. Additional expenses include allowances, books, athletic clothing, a graduation fee of $60, and travel.

Financial aid is available to students who qualify on the basis of need, academic performance, and citizenship. More than $6 million in aid is awarded to about 44 percent of all students.

ADMISSIONS INFORMATION

To be accepted at Wyoming Seminary, a student must demonstrate strong character and the ability to do college-preparatory work. Applicants for grades 9, 10, and 11 must take the SSAT. A limited number of seniors and postgraduates are accepted each year, and they are asked to submit College Board scores. Each applicant is evaluated on the basis of his or her application, recommendations, and school transcripts. An interview is not required but is strongly recommended.

APPLICATION TIMETABLE

Inquiries and applications are welcome the year round. The school encourages applicants to schedule an on-campus interview. There is a charge of $75 to cover processing expenses.

ADMISSIONS CORRESPONDENCE

John R. Eidam, Dean of Admission
or
Anne Lew, Director of Admission
Wyoming Seminary
201 North Sprague Avenue
Kingston, Pennsylvania 18704-3593
Phone: 570-270-2160
877-996-7361 (toll-free)
Fax: 570-270-2191 or 2198
E-mail: admission@wyomingseminary.org
Web site: http://www.wyomingseminary.org

YORK PREPARATORY SCHOOL

New York, New York

Type: Coeducational day college-preparatory school
Grades: 6–12: Lower School, 6–8; Upper School, 9–12
Enrollment: School total: 340
Head of School: Ronald P. Stewart, Headmaster

THE SCHOOL

York Prep is a college-preparatory school where contemporary methods enliven a strong, academically challenging, traditional curriculum. In a city known for its diversity of private schools, York Prep has developed a unique program that leads students to their highest potential. The School's approach emphasizes independent thought, builds confidence, and sends graduates on to the finest colleges and universities. York Prep believes that success breeds success. At York, every student finds opportunities to flourish. Excellence in academics, arts, or sports creates self-confidence that enhances all aspects of life, both in and out of the classroom.

York Prep was established in 1969 by its current Headmaster, Ronald P. Stewart, and his wife, Jayme Stewart, Director of College Guidance. Situated on West 68th Street between Columbus Avenue and Central Park West, the School is well served by public transportation. Consequently, it attracts students from all over the metropolitan area. The School's programs take full advantage of the prime location, with regular visits to museums, parks, and theaters, all of which are easily accessible.

York Prep is approved by the New York State Board of Regents and accredited by the Middle States Association of Colleges and Schools.

ACADEMIC PROGRAMS

The curriculum is designed to develop the superior academic skills necessary for future success. Close attention to each student's needs ensures that progress toward personal excellence is carefully guided.

Students must complete 20 credits for graduation: 4 in English, 4 in math, 4 in science, 4 in history, a minimum of 3 in foreign language, 1 in art or music, ½ in health, and ½ in community service.

Eleventh and twelfth graders choose from a number of course offerings in every subject area. In addition to selecting one course from each required category, a student must choose an elective from a variety of options that range from the creative and performing arts to the analytical sciences. Students are required to carry at least five major subjects a year plus physical education.

York Prep pioneered the requirement of community service for graduation from high school. The School requires 100 hours of structured and supervised community service with a final end-of-year paper. York Prep is in close contact with the charitable agencies where its students serve the community.

Independent study courses and Advanced Placement courses are offered. When it is appropriate, students may graduate early or enroll at local colleges for specific classes.

Classes at York are small—the average class has 15 students. There are close student-teacher relations and an advisory system. All students meet with their adviser every morning during a "house" period. Each student's academic and social progress is carefully monitored by the teachers, advisers, and deans of the Upper and Lower Schools. The deans, in turn, keep the Headmaster and the Principal informed at weekly meetings. In addition, the Headmaster and Principal maintain close relationships with the students by teaching courses and are readily available to students and parents alike. At the close of each day, there is a period when students may go to faculty members or advisers for help.

Parents are kept informed of a student's progress through individual reports posted on "Edline," a component of the York Prep Web site, every Friday. Each family signs in with a unique password and can see their child's progress in all academic subjects. The annual Curriculum Night, in which parents become students for an evening by attending their child's truncated classes, provides a good overview of the course work and the faculty members. Parent involvement is encouraged, and there is an active Parents' Association.

FACULTY AND ADVISERS

York Prep is proud of having maintained a stable faculty of outstanding and dedicated individuals. New teachers join the staff periodically, creating a nice balance between youth and experience.

There are 62 full-time faculty members, including 2 college guidance counselors, 11 reading and learning specialists, 2 computer specialists, and a librarian.

Mr. Ronald P. Stewart, the founding Headmaster, is a graduate of Oxford University (B.A., 1965; M.A., 1966; B.C.L., 1968), where he also taught.

COLLEGE ADMISSION COUNSELING

York Prep has a notable college guidance program. Mrs. Jayme Stewart, the Director of College Guidance, is well known for her expertise, experience, and authorship of *How to Get into the College of Your Choice.* She meets with all tenth graders to outline the program and then meets individually with eleventh graders and their parents. The students begin working on their college essays in eleventh grade. Extensive meetings continue through the twelfth grade on an individual basis.

One hundred percent of York Prep's graduating students attend college. The ultimate aim of the college guidance program is the placement of each student in the college best suited to him or her. More than 85 percent of York Prep graduates are accepted to, attend, and finish at one of their first-choice college. Graduates are currently attending schools that include Barnard, Berkeley, Bowdoin, Colgate, Columbia, Cornell, Franklin and Marshall, Hamilton, Harvard, Hobart, Pennsylvania, Skidmore, Vassar, Wesley, and the University of Michigan. Numerous college representatives visit the School regularly to meet with interested students.

STUDENT BODY AND CONDUCT

There are 340 students enrolled at York Prep. York Prep students reside in all five boroughs of New York City as well as Long Island, northern New Jersey, and Westchester County. The School has a student code of conduct and a dress code. The elected student council is also an integral part of life at York Prep.

ACADEMIC FACILITIES

Located steps from Central Park at 40 West 68th Street, York Prep is a seven-story granite building housing two modern science laboratories, state-of-the-art computer equipment, performance and art studios, and a sprung hardwood gymnasium with weight and locker room facilities. The classrooms are spacious and airy, carpeted, and climate controlled. All classrooms have computers and audiovisual (AV) projectors. A T1 line provides high-speed Internet access for the whole School and enables students to e-mail their teachers and review homework assignments. In addition, all classrooms are linked to the School's in-house television channel, WYRK, over which daily announcements are aired. The building is wheelchair accessible and is located near Lincoln Center on a safe and lovely tree-lined street.

ATHLETICS

All students are required to take courses in physical education and health each year. A varied and extensive program and after-school selection offer students the opportunity to participate in competitive, noncompetitive, team, and individual sports. York Prep is a playing member of several athletics leagues.

EXTRACURRICULAR OPPORTUNITIES

The Student Council organizes regular social events and trips. The School provides a wide range of extracurricular activities, including a mock trial law team, golf, roller hockey, and a drama club.

DAILY LIFE

The School day begins at 8:40 with a 10-minute house period. Academic classes of 42-minute duration begin at 8:56. There is a midmorning break at 10:24. Lunch period is from 12:08 to 12:53, Mondays through Thursdays, and classes end at 3:12. Following dismissal, teachers are available for extra help. During this time, clubs and sports teams also meet. On Fridays the school day ends at 1:35.

SUMMER PROGRAMS

The School provides workshops during the summer, both in study skills and in academic courses, most of which are set up on an individual tutorial basis. In addition, the athletic department provides summer sports camps.

COSTS AND FINANCIAL AID

Tuition for the 2007–08 academic year ranged from $31,500 to $32,100. More than 40 percent of the student body receives some financial assistance. During the previous year, $750,000 was offered in financial aid.

ADMISSIONS INFORMATION

The School seeks to enroll students of above-average intelligence with the will and ability to complete college-preparatory work. Students are accepted on the basis of their applications, ISEE test scores, writing samples, and interviews.

APPLICATION TIMETABLE

The School conforms to the notification guidelines established by the Independent Schools Admissions Association of Greater New York. Subsequent applications are processed on a rolling admissions basis. Requests for financial aid should be made at the time of application for entrance.

ADMISSIONS CORRESPONDENCE

Elizabeth Norton, Director of Enrollment
Lisa Smith, Director of Admissions
Jacqueline Leber, Director of Admissions
York Preparatory School
40 West 68th Street
New York, New York 10023
Phone: 212-362-0400
Fax: 212-362-7424
E-mail: admissions@yorkprep.org
Web site: http://www.yorkprep.org

Special Needs Schools

THE ACADEMY AT SISTERS

PO Box 5986
Bend, Oregon 97708-5986

Head of School: Stephanie Alvstad

General Information Girls' boarding general academic school; primarily serves underachievers and individuals with emotional and behavioral problems. Grades 7–12. Founded: 1994. Setting: rural. Students are housed in single-sex rooms. 20-acre campus. Approved or accredited by CITA (Commission on International and Trans-Regional Accreditation), Northwest Association of Schools and Colleges, and Oregon Department of Education. Upper school faculty-student ratio: 1:12.
Upper School Student Profile 100% of students are boarding students.
Faculty School total: 5. In upper school: 1 man, 4 women; 4 have advanced degrees.
Special Academic Programs Honors section; independent study; remedial reading and/or remedial writing; remedial math.
Student Life Upper grades have uniform requirement, honor system. Discipline rests primarily with faculty.
Summer Programs Remediation programs offered; held on campus; accepts girls; not open to students from other schools. 40 students usually enrolled. 2009 schedule: June 15 to August 14.
Tuition and Aid Guaranteed tuition plan. Tuition installment plan (monthly payment plans, individually arranged payment plans). TERI Loans, AchieverLoans (Key Education Resources), prepGATE Loans available.
Admissions Deadline for receipt of application materials: none. Application fee required: $1000. Interview required.
Athletics Intramural: aerobics, aerobics/dance, aquatics, backpacking, badminton, climbing, cooperative games, dance, equestrian sports, fitness, fitness walking, hiking/backpacking, horseback riding, jogging, martial arts, modern dance, outdoor activities, physical fitness, project adventure, rock climbing, skiing (cross-country), skiing (downhill), snowboarding, snowshoeing, soccer, volleyball, walking, wall climbing, yoga. 2 PE instructors.
Computers Computers are regularly used in all academic classes. Computer resources include on-campus library services, Internet access, Internet filtering or blocking technology.
Contact Mr. Guy Leguyonne. 541-389-2748. Fax: 541-389-2897. E-mail: gleguyonne@academyatsisters.org. Web site: www.academyatsisters.org/.

ACADEMY AT SWIFT RIVER

151 South Street
Cummington, Massachusetts 01026

Head of School: Dr. Frank Bartolomeo

General Information Coeducational boarding college-preparatory and arts school; primarily serves individuals with Attention Deficit Disorder, individuals with emotional and behavioral problems, and dyslexic students. Grades 9–12. Founded: 1997. Setting: rural. Nearest major city is Northampton. Students are housed in single-sex dormitories. 630-acre campus. 5 buildings on campus. Approved or accredited by CITA (Commission on International and Trans-Regional Accreditation), European Council of International Schools, and Massachusetts Department of Education. Candidate for accreditation by New England Association of Schools and Colleges. Member of Secondary School Admission Test Board. Total enrollment: 100. Upper school average class size: 8. Upper school faculty-student ratio: 1:8.
Upper School Student Profile Grade 9: 26 students (15 boys, 11 girls); Grade 10: 28 students (18 boys, 10 girls); Grade 11: 28 students (17 boys, 11 girls); Grade 12: 18 students (12 boys, 6 girls). 100% of students are boarding students. 4% are state residents. 30 states are represented in upper school student body. 4% are international students. International students from Bermuda, Canada, Guatemala, Spain, Switzerland, and Turkey; 6 other countries represented in student body.
Faculty School total: 14. In upper school: 9 men, 2 women; 5 have advanced degrees.
Subjects Offered Addiction, adolescent issues, algebra, American history, American literature, art, biology, calculus, career and personal planning, career/college preparation, character education, chemistry, civics, college counseling, college placement, communication skills, community service, composition, computers, conflict resolution, current events, death and loss, decision making skills, ecology, environmental systems, English, English composition, English literature, environmental science, experiential education, fitness, geography, geometry, government/civics, health, health and wellness, history, independent study, integrated arts, interpersonal skills, lab science, life management skills, literature, martial arts, mathematics, nature study, nutrition, peer counseling, personal development, physical education, physics, pre-algebra, pre-calculus, reading/study skills, relationships, SAT/ACT preparation, science, social science, social studies, Spanish, U.S. government, weight training, world geography, world history.
Graduation Requirements Arts and fine arts (art, music, dance, drama), English, health and wellness, history, lab science, language, mathematics, physical education (includes health), completion of individualized therapeutic program. Community service is required.
Special Academic Programs Honors section; accelerated programs; independent study; study at local college for college credit; academic accommodation for the artistically talented; programs in English, mathematics, general development for dyslexic students.
College Admission Counseling 33 students graduated in 2008; 29 went to college, including Clark University; Drexel University; Ithaca College; Sarah Lawrence College; Skidmore College; Syracuse University. Other: 3 had other specific plans.
Student Life Upper grades have specified standards of dress, student council, honor system. Discipline rests primarily with faculty.
Tuition and Aid 7-day tuition and room/board: $78,720. Tuition installment plan (monthly payment plans, individually arranged payment plans, prepaid tuition discount). Middle-income loans, Sallie Mae Loans, Clark Custom Educational Loans, AchieverLoans (Key Education Resources) available. In 2008–09, 10% of upper-school students received aid.
Admissions Traditional secondary-level entrance grade is 11. Battery of testing done through outside agency, Rorschach or Thematic Apperception Test, Wechsler Intelligence Scale for Children or WISC/Woodcock-Johnson required. Deadline for receipt of application materials: none. No application fee required.
Athletics Interscholastic: basketball (boys), lacrosse (g); coed interscholastic: soccer; coed intramural: aerobics, aerobics/dance, alpine skiing, backpacking, baseball, basketball, bicycling, bowling, canoeing/kayaking, climbing, combined training, cooperative games, cross-country running, dance, field hockey, fishing, fitness, fitness walking, flag football, fly fishing, Frisbee, golf, hiking/backpacking, horseback riding, in-line skating, independent competitive sports, indoor soccer, jogging, kayaking, lacrosse, martial arts, mountain biking, outdoor activities, paddle tennis, physical fitness, physical training, rafting, rock climbing, ropes courses, running, skiing (cross-country), skiing (downhill), snowboarding, snowshoeing, soccer, softball, swimming and diving, table tennis, tennis, ultimate Frisbee, volleyball, walking, wall climbing, weight lifting, weight training, whiffle ball, yoga. 1 PE instructor.
Computers Computers are regularly used in English, foreign language, history, science classes. Computer network features include on-campus library services, Internet access, Internet filtering or blocking technology. Students grades are available online.
Contact Rhonda J. Papallo, Director of Admissions and Student Support Services. 800-258-1770 Ext. 102. Fax: 413-634-5300. E-mail: rpapallo@swiftriver.com. Web site: www.swiftriver.com.

ALPINE ACADEMY

1280 Whispering Horse Drive
Erda, Utah 84074

Head of School: Janet Mulitalo

General Information Girls' boarding college-preparatory, general academic, arts, vocational, bilingual studies, and Equestrian; Consumer Sciences school; primarily serves underachievers, students with learning disabilities, individuals with Attention Deficit Disorder, individuals with emotional and behavioral problems, and dyslexic students. Grades 7–12. Founded: 2001. Setting: rural. Nearest major city is Salt Lake City. Students are housed in single-sex dormitories. 35-acre campus. 8 buildings on campus. Approved or accredited by Northwest Association of Accredited Schools and Utah Department of Education. Total enrollment: 50. Upper school average class size: 8. Upper school faculty-student ratio: 1:4.
Upper School Student Profile Grade 8: 8 students (8 girls); Grade 9: 8 students (8 girls); Grade 10: 10 students (10 girls); Grade 11: 12 students (12 girls); Grade 12: 12 students (12 girls). 100% of students are boarding students. 2% are state residents. 12 states are represented in upper school student body.
Faculty School total: 11. In upper school: 1 man, 10 women; 1 has an advanced degree.
Subjects Offered Art, basic skills, debate, drama, English, equine studies, health, history, journalism, life skills, mathematics, physical education, science.
Graduation Requirements Graduation is therapeutically indicated rather than academically.
Special Academic Programs Accelerated programs; independent study; study at local college for college credit; academic accommodation for the gifted; remedial reading and/or remedial writing; remedial math; special instructional classes for blind students.
College Admission Counseling 8 students graduated in 2008; 5 went to college. Other: 3 went to work.
Student Life Upper grades have specified standards of dress. Discipline rests primarily with faculty.
Summer Programs Remediation, enrichment, advancement, sports, art/fine arts programs offered; session focuses on making up or getting ahead on credits toward graduation; held on campus; accepts girls; not open to students from other schools. 45 students usually enrolled. 2009 schedule: May 5 to July 18. Application deadline: April 5.
Tuition and Aid Guaranteed tuition plan. Need-based scholarship grants available. In 2008–09, 2% of upper-school students received aid.
Admissions Traditional secondary-level entrance grade is 10. Psychoeducational evaluation required. Deadline for receipt of application materials: none. No application fee required.
Athletics Interscholastic: aerobics, aerobics/dance, basketball, climbing, cooperative games, dance, equestrian sports, fitness, fitness walking, hiking/backpacking, horseback riding, outdoor activities, physical fitness, physical training, rock climbing, running, soccer, softball, strength & conditioning, volleyball, walking, wall climbing, weight lifting, weight training, yoga; intramural: soccer. 1 PE instructor.

Computers Computers are regularly used in English, history, writing classes. Computer resources include Internet filtering or blocking technology. Computer access in designated common areas is available to students. Students grades are available online.
Contact Christian Egan, Admissions Director. 800-244-1113. Fax: 435-843-5416. E-mail: cegan@youthvillage.org. Web site: www.alpineacademy.org.

AMERICAN ACADEMY

12200 West Broward Boulevard
Plantation, Florida 33325
Head of School: William R. Laurie

General Information Coeducational day college-preparatory and arts school; primarily serves underachievers, students with learning disabilities, individuals with Attention Deficit Disorder, dyslexic students, and slow learners, and those with lowered self esteem and confidence. Grades 1–12. Founded: 1965. Setting: suburban. Nearest major city is Fort Lauderdale. 40-acre campus. 9 buildings on campus. Approved or accredited by Association of Independent Schools of Florida, Southern Association of Colleges and Schools, and Florida Department of Education. Total enrollment: 403. Upper school average class size: 14. Upper school faculty-student ratio: 1:12.
Upper School Student Profile Grade 6: 34 students (30 boys, 4 girls); Grade 7: 53 students (45 boys, 8 girls); Grade 8: 35 students (22 boys, 13 girls); Grade 9: 38 students (25 boys, 13 girls); Grade 10: 45 students (33 boys, 12 girls); Grade 11: 52 students (39 boys, 13 girls); Grade 12: 60 students (46 boys, 14 girls).
Faculty School total: 37. In upper school: 4 men, 19 women; 18 have advanced degrees.
Subjects Offered Algebra, American history, American literature, anatomy, art, band, biology, business mathematics, ceramics, chemistry, chorus, community service, computer graphics, computer science, creative writing, drafting, drama, drawing, earth science, English, English literature, environmental science, fine arts, French, geometry, health, jazz, mathematics, music appreciation, oceanography, orchestra, photography, physical education, physical science, science, sculpture, Spanish, theater, vocal music, weight training, word processing, world geography, world history, world literature, writing, yearbook.
Graduation Requirements 20th century history, arts and fine arts (art, music, dance, drama), computer science, English, mathematics, physical education (includes health), science, social studies (includes history), must be accepted to a college, 120 Community Service hours over 4 years of high school. Community service is required.
Special Academic Programs Honors section; independent study; academic accommodation for the gifted, the musically talented, and the artistically talented; remedial reading and/or remedial writing; remedial math; programs in English, mathematics, general development for dyslexic students; ESL (6 students enrolled).
College Admission Counseling 53 students graduated in 2008; all went to college, including Broward Community College; Florida Atlantic University; Lynn University; Nova Southeastern University; Palm Beach Community College.
Student Life Upper grades have uniform requirement, student council. Discipline rests primarily with faculty.
Summer Programs Remediation, enrichment, advancement, ESL, art/fine arts, computer instruction programs offered; session focuses on remediation and make-up courses; held on campus; accepts boys and girls; open to students from other schools. 400 students usually enrolled. 2009 schedule: June 8 to August 7. Application deadline: none.
Tuition and Aid Day student tuition: $22,586–$26,061. Tuition installment plan (monthly payment plans, semester payment plan, annual payment plan). Tuition reduction for siblings, need-based scholarship grants available. In 2008–09, 42% of upper-school students received aid. Total amount of financial aid awarded in 2008–09: $1,042,945.
Admissions Traditional secondary-level entrance grade is 9. Psychoeducational evaluation, SAT and Slosson Intelligence required. Deadline for receipt of application materials: none. Application fee required: $100. On-campus interview required.
Athletics Interscholastic: baseball (boys), basketball (b,g), cheering (g), cross-country running (b,g), dance (g), dance squad (g), diving (b,g), football (b), golf (b,g), lacrosse (b), roller hockey (b), soccer (b,g), softball (g), swimming and diving (b,g), tennis (b,g), track and field (b,g), volleyball (b,g), weight lifting (b), weight training (b,g), winter soccer (b,g), wrestling (b). 7 PE instructors, 4 coaches.
Computers Computers are regularly used in graphic arts, literary magazine, newspaper, Web site design, word processing, writing, yearbook classes. Computer network features include on-campus library services, online commercial services, Internet access, Internet filtering or blocking technology, Questia. Student e-mail accounts and computer access in designated common areas are available to students. Students grades are available online. The school has a published electronic and media policy.
Contact William R. Laurie, President. 954-472-0022. Fax: 954-472-3088. Web site: www.ahschool.com.

ARROWSMITH SCHOOL

245 St. Clair Avenue West
Toronto, Ontario M4V 1R3, Canada
Head of School: Ms. Barbara Arrowsmith Young

General Information Coeducational day school; primarily serves underachievers, students with learning disabilities, and dyslexic students. Ungraded, ages 6–20. Founded: 1980. Setting: urban. 1 building on campus. Approved or accredited by Ontario Ministry of Education and Ontario Department of Education. Language of instruction: English. Total enrollment: 75. Upper school average class size: 20. Upper school faculty-student ratio: 1:8.
Faculty School total: 8. In upper school: 1 man, 3 women.
Special Academic Programs Remedial reading and/or remedial writing; remedial math; programs in English, mathematics for dyslexic students.
College Admission Counseling 5 students graduated in 2008; 4 went to college, including University of Toronto; York University. Other: 1 went to work.
Student Life Upper grades have specified standards of dress. Discipline rests equally with students and faculty.
Tuition and Aid Day student tuition: CAN$17,000. Tuition installment plan (monthly payment plans).
Admissions Traditional secondary-level entrance age is 14. For fall 2008, 20 students applied for upper-level admission, 20 were accepted, 20 enrolled. Achievement tests, Differential Aptitude Test, Oral and Written Language Scales, Otis-Lennon Mental Ability Test, Raven (Aptitude Test); school's own exam, Reading for Understanding, school's own test, Wide Range Achievement Test, WISC/Woodcock-Johnson or writing sample required. Deadline for receipt of application materials: none. No application fee required. Interview required.
Computers Computer resources include Internet access.
Contact Ms. Annette Goodman, Director of Admissions. 800-963-4904. Fax: 416-963-5017. E-mail: agoodman@arrowsmithprogram.ca. Web site: www.arrowsmithschool.org.

ARTHUR MORGAN SCHOOL

60 AMS Circle
Burnsville, North Carolina 28714
Head of School: Lisa Schultz

General Information Coeducational boarding and day college-preparatory, general academic, arts, and service learning; outdoor experiential learning school. Grades 7–9. Founded: 1962. Setting: rural. Nearest major city is Asheville. Students are housed in boarding homes. 100-acre campus. 7 buildings on campus. Approved or accredited by North Carolina Department of Non-Public Schools and North Carolina Department of Education. Member of Small Boarding School Association. Endowment: $1 million. Total enrollment: 20. Upper school average class size: 9. Upper school faculty-student ratio: 1:3.
Upper School Student Profile Grade 7: 10 students (6 boys, 4 girls); Grade 8: 12 students (8 boys, 4 girls); Grade 9: 4 students (2 boys, 2 girls). 50% of students are boarding students. 73% are state residents. 7 states are represented in upper school student body.
Faculty School total: 12. In upper school: 5 men, 6 women; 1 has an advanced degree; 11 reside on campus.
Subjects Offered 3-dimensional art, 3-dimensional design, acting, ADL skills, adolescent issues, African American history, African American studies, African history, agriculture, agroecology, algebra, alternative physical education, American culture, American government, American history, American literature, American minority experience, American studies, anatomy, ancient/medieval philosophy, animal behavior, animal husbandry, anthropology, art, arts and crafts, astronomy, athletics, audio visual/media, audition methods, auto body, auto mechanics, auto shop, backpacking, baseball, biology, bookbinding, botany, career education, career education internship, carpentry, ceramics, character education, chemistry, civics, civil rights, clayworking, communication skills, community garden, community service, comparative cultures, comparative politics, composition, computer skills, computers, conflict resolution, conservation, constitutional history of U.S., consumer education, crafts, creative arts, creative dance, creative drama, creative thinking, creative writing, critical thinking, culinary arts, current events, dance, debate, decision making, decision making skills, democracy in America, design, drama, drama performance, dramatic arts, drawing, earth science, ecology, English, English composition, English literature, entrepreneurship, ethical decision making, ethics, ethics and responsibility, evolution, experiential education, expressive arts, fabric arts, family and consumer science, family and consumer sciences, family life, family living, family studies, fiber arts, first aid, fitness, food and nutrition, foreign language, forestry, gardening, gender issues, general science, geography, geology, geometry, global issues, global studies, grammar, guitar, health and wellness, health education, high adventure outdoor program, history, horticulture, human rights, human sexuality, humanities, independent living, integrated math, interpersonal skills, jewelry making, journalism, language arts, leadership and service, leadership skills, life issues, mathematics, media studies, medieval/Renaissance history, meditation, mentorship program, metalworking, music, mythology, Native American studies, natural history, natural resources management, nature study, North Carolina history, oil painting, organic gardening, outdoor education, painting, peace and justice, peace education, peace studies, peer counseling, permaculture, personal growth, photo shop, photography, physical

education, physics, piano, playwriting, poetry, politics, pottery, practical living, printmaking, probability and statistics, reading/study skills, relationships, sex education, shop, social justice, social sciences, social skills, social studies, socioeconomic problems, Spanish, sports, stained glass, study skills, swimming, travel, values and decisions, Vietnam War, visual and performing arts, visual arts, weaving, wilderness studies, wilderness/outdoor program, woodworking, work experience, writing, yearbook, yoga.

Graduation Requirements Annual 18-day field service learning trip, annual 3-, 6- and 8-day outdoor education trips.

College Admission Counseling 7 students graduated in 2008; they went to Carolina Friends School; George School; The Meeting School; Westtown School.

Student Life Upper grades have honor system. Discipline rests primarily with faculty.

Tuition and Aid Day student tuition: $11,000; 5-day tuition and room/board: $21,000; 7-day tuition and room/board: $21,000. Tuition installment plan (40% by 8/15, 60% by Dec. 15; monthly payment 10% interest; full payment by 8/15- 2% discount). Need-based scholarship grants, individually negotiated barter arrangements may be made available. In 2008–09, 60% of upper-school students received aid. Total amount of financial aid awarded in 2008–09: $92,469.

Admissions Traditional secondary-level entrance grade is 7. For fall 2008, 17 students applied for upper-level admission, 15 were accepted, 14 enrolled. Deadline for receipt of application materials: none. Application fee required: $35. On-campus interview required.

Athletics Coed Interscholastic: soccer; coed intramural: aquatics, backpacking, bicycling, billiards, blading, canoeing/kayaking, climbing, cooperative games, cross-country running, dance, fishing, Frisbee, hiking/backpacking, jogging, mountain biking, outdoor activities, rafting, running, skateboarding, soccer, swimming and diving, ultimate Frisbee, wilderness, winter walking, wrestling, yoga.

Computers Computers are regularly used in writing classes. Computer resources include supervised student access to computers for Web research, word processing, spreadsheet. Computer access in designated common areas is available to students.

Contact Lisa Schultz, Admissions Coordinator. 828-675-4262. Fax: 828-675-0003. E-mail: admissions@arthurmorganschool.org. Web site: www.arthurmorganschool.org.

ASSETS SCHOOL

One Ohana Nui Way
Honolulu, Hawaii 96818

Head of School: Mr. Paul Singer

General Information Coeducational day college-preparatory school; primarily serves students with learning disabilities, individuals with Attention Deficit Disorder, dyslexic students, and gifted/talented students. Grades K–12. Founded: 1955. Setting: urban. 3-acre campus. 7 buildings on campus. Approved or accredited by The Hawaii Council of Private Schools, Western Association of Schools and Colleges, and Hawaii Department of Education. Member of National Association of Independent Schools. Endowment: $665,826. Total enrollment: 357. Upper school average class size: 7. Upper school faculty-student ratio: 1:7.

Upper School Student Profile Grade 9: 26 students (21 boys, 5 girls); Grade 10: 23 students (15 boys, 8 girls); Grade 11: 27 students (19 boys, 8 girls); Grade 12: 24 students (20 boys, 4 girls).

Faculty School total: 74. In upper school: 9 men, 12 women; 18 have advanced degrees.

Subjects Offered Algebra, American history, art, biology, British literature, business skills, calculus, calculus-AP, chemistry, computer science, consumer education, creative writing, current events, earth science, economics, English, English-AP, fine arts, fitness, general science, geometry, government/civics, health, humanities, independent study, integrated science, Japanese, keyboarding, literature, marine biology, marine science, mathematics, music, music appreciation, philosophy, physical education, physics, pre-calculus, psychology, sign language, social studies, Spanish, statistics, theater, trigonometry, women's health, woodworking, word processing, world history, world literature.

Graduation Requirements Arts and fine arts (art, music, dance, drama), biology, business skills (includes word processing), computer science, English, foreign language, mathematics, physical education (includes health), science, social studies (includes history), study skills, participation in mentorship program in 10th-12th grades.

Special Academic Programs Academic accommodation for the gifted; remedial reading and/or remedial writing; remedial math; programs in English, mathematics, general development for dyslexic students.

College Admission Counseling 24 students graduated in 2008; 22 went to college, including Chaminade University of Honolulu; Hawai'i Pacific University; Oregon State University; University of Hawaii at Manoa. Other: 2 went to work.

Student Life Upper grades have specified standards of dress, student council. Discipline rests primarily with faculty.

Summer Programs Advancement programs offered; session focuses on Learning Strategies for students in the 9th and 10th grades; held on campus; accepts boys and girls; not open to students from other schools. 20 students usually enrolled. 2009 schedule: June 11 to July 15. Application deadline: none.

Tuition and Aid Day student tuition: $19,900. Tuition installment plan (monthly payment plans, semester payment plan). Need-based scholarship grants, partial tuition remission for children of staff available. In 2008–09, 31% of upper-school students received aid. Total amount of financial aid awarded in 2008–09: $164,000.

Admissions Traditional secondary-level entrance grade is 9. For fall 2008, 14 students applied for upper-level admission, 10 were accepted, 10 enrolled. WISC III or other aptitude measures; standardized achievement test required. Deadline for receipt of application materials: none. Application fee required: $75. Interview required.

Athletics Interscholastic: baseball (boys), basketball (b,g), bowling (b,g), canoeing/kayaking (b,g), cheering (g), cross-country running (b,g), diving (b,g), football (b,g), golf (b,g), gymnastics (g), judo (b,g), kayaking (b,g), sailing (b,g), soccer (b,g), softball (g), swimming and diving (b,g), tennis (b,g), track and field (b,g), volleyball (b,g), water polo (b,g), wrestling (b,g); intramural: basketball (b,g), volleyball (b,g); coed intramural: basketball, dance, flag football, golf, juggling, jump rope, kickball, Newcombe ball, soccer, softball, tai chi, touch football, ultimate Frisbee, unicycling, volleyball, whiffle ball, yoga. 1 PE instructor.

Computers Computers are regularly used in English, mathematics, science classes. Computer network features include on-campus library services, Internet access, assistive technology for learning differences.

Contact Ms. Sandi Tadaki, Director of Admissions. 808-423-1356. Fax: 808-422-1920. E-mail: stadaki@assets-school.net. Web site: www.assets-school.net.

BREHM PREPARATORY SCHOOL

1245 East Grand Avenue
Carbondale, Illinois 62901

Head of School: Mr. Richard G. Collins, PhD

General Information Coeducational boarding and day college-preparatory and general academic school; primarily serves students with learning disabilities, individuals with Attention Deficit Disorder, dyslexic students, and language-based learning differences. Grades 6–PG. Founded: 1982. Setting: small town. Nearest major city is St. Louis, MO. Students are housed in single-sex dormitories. 80-acre campus. 13 buildings on campus. Approved or accredited by Independent Schools Association of the Central States, North Central Association of Colleges and Schools, and Illinois Department of Education. Member of National Association of Independent Schools. Total enrollment: 97. Upper school average class size: 8. Upper school faculty-student ratio: 1:4.

Upper School Student Profile Grade 9: 10 students (7 boys, 3 girls); Grade 10: 23 students (18 boys, 5 girls); Grade 11: 23 students (17 boys, 6 girls); Grade 12: 27 students (20 boys, 7 girls); Postgraduate: 5 students (1 boy, 4 girls). 97% of students are boarding students. 18% are state residents. 31 states are represented in upper school student body. 9% are international students. International students from Belgium, Cameroon, Canada, India, Nigeria, and Saudi Arabia.

Faculty School total: 26. In upper school: 9 men, 17 women; 15 have advanced degrees.

Subjects Offered ACT preparation, algebra, American history, art, biology, calculus, chemistry, computer science, computer skills, consumer education, creative writing, current events, earth science, economics, English, environmental science, geometry, government/civics, keyboarding, learning cognition, mathematics, photography, physical education, psychology, reading/study skills, science, social studies, sociology, speech, trigonometry, weight training, world history, writing skills.

Graduation Requirements Computer science, consumer education, English, government, learning cognition, mathematics, physical education (includes health), science, social studies (includes history).

Special Academic Programs Study at local college for college credit; academic accommodation for the gifted; remedial reading and/or remedial writing; remedial math; programs in English, mathematics, general development for dyslexic students.

College Admission Counseling 24 students graduated in 2008; they went to John A. Logan College; New England College; Southern Illinois University Edwardsville. Other: 4 entered a postgraduate year. Median composite ACT: 17. 7% scored over 26 on composite ACT.

Student Life Upper grades have specified standards of dress, student council, honor system. Discipline rests equally with students and faculty.

Tuition and Aid Day student tuition: $34,500; 7-day tuition and room/board: $56,280.

Admissions Traditional secondary-level entrance grade is 9. For fall 2008, 67 students applied for upper-level admission, 56 were accepted, 48 enrolled. Wechsler Individual Achievement Test, WISC or WAIS, Woodcock-Johnson and writing sample required. Deadline for receipt of application materials: none. Application fee required: $75. On-campus interview required.

Athletics Interscholastic: basketball (boys, girls); coed interscholastic: soccer; coed intramural: aerobics, basketball, billiards, bowling, dance, fishing, flag football, hiking/backpacking, horseback riding, outdoor skills, paint ball, physical fitness, soccer, softball, strength & conditioning. 1 PE instructor, 1 coach.

Computers Computers are regularly used in all academic, desktop publishing, graphic arts, graphic design, keyboarding, learning cognition, photography, yearbook classes. Computer network features include Internet access, wireless campus network, Internet filtering or blocking technology. Student e-mail accounts are available to students. The school has a published electronic and media policy.

Contact Mrs. Heather Brady, Administrative Assistant of Admissions. 618-457-0371 Ext. 1304. Fax: 618-549-2329. E-mail: hbrady@brehm.org. Web site: www.brehm.org.

ANNOUNCEMENT FROM THE SCHOOL This is Brehm's third year with a one-to-one laptop program, which assigns a laptop equipped with all the latest assistive technology to each student. Also on hand at Brehm is an Educational Technologist who instructs students on how to utilize this technology, based on the individual needs of the students.

See Close-Up on page 1086.

BRIDGES ACADEMY

3921 Laurel Canyon Boulevard
Studio City, California 91604

Head of School: Carl Sabatino

General Information Coeducational day college-preparatory, arts, technology, and music, drama, talent development school; primarily serves gifted students with non-verbal learning differences. Grades 6–12. Founded: 1994. Setting: suburban. Nearest major city is Los Angeles. 4-acre campus. 3 buildings on campus. Approved or accredited by California Association of Independent Schools, Western Association of Schools and Colleges, and California Department of Education. Total enrollment: 100. Upper school average class size: 9. Upper school faculty-student ratio: 1:9.

Upper School Student Profile Grade 9: 17 students (16 boys, 1 girl); Grade 10: 14 students (12 boys, 2 girls); Grade 11: 16 students (13 boys, 3 girls); Grade 12: 15 students (14 boys, 1 girl).

Faculty School total: 15. In upper school: 7 men, 8 women; 3 have advanced degrees.

Subjects Offered 20th century history, algebra, American government, American literature, anatomy and physiology, art, biology, calculus, chemistry, drama, economics, European history, European literature, film, genetics, geometry, Japanese, modern European history, non-Western literature, physics, pre-calculus, senior project, Spanish, statistics, study skills, technology, U.S. history, world history.

Graduation Requirements Economics, English, foreign language, government, history, mathematics, performing arts, science, senior seminar, visual arts.

Special Academic Programs Honors section; academic accommodation for the gifted.

College Admission Counseling 14 students graduated in 2008; 11 went to college, including California State University, Northridge; The University of Arizona; University of California, San Diego. Other: 3 had other specific plans. 58% scored over 600 on SAT critical reading, 24% scored over 600 on SAT math.

Student Life Upper grades have student council. Discipline rests primarily with faculty.

Summer Programs Enrichment, art/fine arts, computer instruction programs offered; session focuses on enrichment; held on campus; accepts boys and girls; open to students from other schools. 2009 schedule: June 1 to July 31. Application deadline: none.

Tuition and Aid Day student tuition: $28,400. Tuition installment plan (Insured Tuition Payment Plan, monthly payment plans). Need-based scholarship grants available. In 2008–09, 8% of upper-school students received aid. Total amount of financial aid awarded in 2008–09: $200,000.

Admissions For fall 2008, 17 students applied for upper-level admission, 11 were accepted, 9 enrolled. Deadline for receipt of application materials: March 1. Application fee required: $150. On-campus interview required.

Athletics Coed Interscholastic: basketball, cross-country running. 2 PE instructors, 1 coach.

Computers Computers are regularly used in all classes. Computer network features include Internet access, wireless campus network. Campus intranet and student e-mail accounts are available to students.

Contact Doug Lenzini, Director of Admissions. 818-506-1091. Fax: 818-506-8094. E-mail: doug@bridges.edu. Web site: www.bridges.edu.

BROMLEY BROOK SCHOOL

2595 Depot Street
PO Box 2328
Manchester Center, Vermont 05255

Head of School: Laura Mack

General Information Girls' boarding college-preparatory and arts school; primarily serves students with learning disabilities, individuals with Attention Deficit Disorder, individuals with emotional and behavioral problems, and dyslexic students. Grades 9–12. Founded: 2004. Setting: small town. Nearest major city is Albany, NY. Students are housed in single-sex dormitories. 6-acre campus. 1 building on campus. Approved or accredited by European Council of International Schools and Vermont Department of Education. Candidate for accreditation by New England Association of Schools and Colleges. Total enrollment: 80. Upper school average class size: 8. Upper school faculty-student ratio: 1:6.

Upper School Student Profile Grade 9: 16 students (16 girls); Grade 10: 20 students (20 girls); Grade 11: 24 students (24 girls); Grade 12: 20 students (20 girls). 100% of students are boarding students. 1% are state residents. 25 states are represented in upper school student body. 2% are international students. International students from Bermuda and Canada.

Faculty School total: 11. In upper school: 4 men, 7 women; 6 have advanced degrees.

Subjects Offered 1½ elective credits, acting, advanced studio art-AP, algebra, alternative physical education, American history, American literature, ancient world history, art, arts and crafts, audio visual/media, biology, business mathematics, calculus, calligraphy, career/college preparation, ceramics, character education, chemistry, chorus, college counseling, community service, composition, computer graphics, conflict resolution, consumer mathematics, cultural geography, dance, digital photography, drama, drawing, earth science, English, English composition, English literature, environmental science, European history, fashion, French, geography, geometry, government, health, internship, lab science, mythology, painting, photography, physical fitness, physics, piano, portfolio art, pottery, pre-algebra, pre-calculus, psychology, SAT preparation, Spanish, sports, studio art, U.S. history, video, voice, world history, yoga.

Graduation Requirements Algebra, American history, American literature, chemistry, composition, English, English literature, environmental science, geometry, history, pre-algebra, pre-calculus, science, social sciences, trigonometry, U.S. history, U.S. literature.

Special Academic Programs Programs in English, mathematics for dyslexic students.

College Admission Counseling 18 students graduated in 2008; 15 went to college. Other: 2 went to work, 1 entered a postgraduate year.

Student Life Upper grades have uniform requirement, student council, honor system. Discipline rests equally with students and faculty.

Tuition and Aid 7-day tuition and room/board: $71,900. Tuition installment plan (Clark Custom Education Loans, prepGate Loans, Key Bank Loans).

Admissions Traditional secondary-level entrance grade is 11. Individual IQ, MAT WISC III, psychoeducational evaluation, SSAT or WISC III, Wechsler Individual Achievement Test, Wechsler Intelligence Scale for Children, WISC-III and Woodcock-Johnson or WISC/Woodcock-Johnson required. Deadline for receipt of application materials: none. Application fee required: $2500. Interview recommended.

Athletics Interscholastic: basketball, lacrosse, soccer, softball; intramural: alpine skiing, bowling, cross-country running, dance, equestrian sports, fitness, fitness walking, flag football, Frisbee, hiking/backpacking, horseback riding, ice skating, jogging, skiing (downhill), snowboarding, tennis, volleyball. 1 coach.

Computers Computers are regularly used in college planning, English, French, geography, graphic design, history, psychology, science, Spanish, video film production classes. Computer resources include Internet access, Internet filtering or blocking technology. Computer access in designated common areas is available to students. The school has a published electronic and media policy.

Contact Beth Bove, Admissions Director. 802-362-9966 Ext. 107. Fax: 802-362-5539. E-mail: bbove@bromleybrook.com. Web site: www.bromleybrook.com/.

See Close-Up on page 1088.

CEDAR RIDGE ACADEMY

RR 1, Box 1477
Roosevelt, Utah 84066

Head of School: Robert A. Nielson

General Information Coeducational boarding college-preparatory, general academic, and arts school; primarily serves underachievers, students with learning disabilities, individuals with Attention Deficit Disorder, individuals with emotional and behavioral problems, and dyslexic students. Grades 9–12. Founded: 1996. Setting: rural. Nearest major city is Salt Lake City. Students are housed in single-sex dormitories. 100-acre campus. 8 buildings on campus. Approved or accredited by Northwest Association of Accredited Schools, Northwest Association of Schools and Colleges, and Utah Department of Education. Upper school average class size: 10. Upper school faculty-student ratio: 1:9.

Upper School Student Profile Grade 9: 8 students (4 boys, 4 girls); Grade 10: 5 students (2 boys, 3 girls); Grade 11: 12 students (7 boys, 5 girls); Grade 12: 5 students (5 boys). 100% of students are boarding students. 1% are state residents. 16 states are represented in upper school student body. 1% are international students. International students from Puerto Rico.

Faculty School total: 7. In upper school: 5 men, 1 woman; 2 have advanced degrees; 2 reside on campus.

Subjects Offered 1½ elective credits, 20th century American writers, 20th century history, 20th century world history, ACT preparation, algebra, American government, American history, American literature, ancient world history, art, art appreciation, biology, British literature, business mathematics, career and personal planning, career/college preparation, ceramics, character education, computer keyboarding, computer literacy, consumer mathematics, drawing, electives, English, geometry, government/civics, health education, independent living, language arts, life management skills, martial arts, peer counseling, personal fitness, physics, pre-algebra, pre-calculus, psychology, SAT/ACT preparation, Shakespeare, studio art.

Graduation Requirements 20th century history, 20th century world history, algebra, American government, American history, ancient world history, art appreciation, biology, British literature, computer literacy, consumer economics, earth systems analysis, English, environmental science, geometry, government, health, keyboarding, life management skills, martial arts, reading/study skills, U.S. history, visual arts, world history, writing.

Special Academic Programs Accelerated programs; remedial reading and/or remedial writing; remedial math.

College Admission Counseling 14 students graduated in 2008; 13 went to college, including The University of Texas at Arlington. Other: 1 went to work. Median composite ACT: 23. 22% scored over 26 on composite ACT.
Student Life Upper grades have specified standards of dress, student council, honor system. Discipline rests primarily with faculty.
Summer Programs Remediation, advancement programs offered; session focuses on credit recovery; held on campus; accepts boys and girls; not open to students from other schools. 50 students usually enrolled. 2009 schedule: June 1 to August 31.
Tuition and Aid 7-day tuition and room/board: $37,800. Guaranteed tuition plan. Tuition installment plan (monthly payment plans). Tuition reduction for siblings, need-based scholarship grants available. In 2008–09, 15% of upper-school students received aid. Total amount of financial aid awarded in 2008–09: $45,000.
Admissions Traditional secondary-level entrance grade is 11. For fall 2008, 53 students applied for upper-level admission, 50 were accepted, 48 enrolled. Application fee required: $500.
Athletics Intramural: basketball (boys), volleyball (g); coed intramural: aerobics/dance, physical training, softball. 3 athletic trainers.
Computers Computers are regularly used in English, keyboarding, Spanish, word processing classes. Computer resources include Internet access. Student e-mail accounts and computer access in designated common areas are available to students.
Contact Shirley Page, Receptionist. 435-353-4498 Ext. 100. Fax: 435-353-4898. E-mail: staff@cedaridge.net. Web site: www.cedaridge.net.

CHATHAM ACADEMY

4 Oglethorpe Professional Boulevard
Savannah, Georgia 31406

Head of School: Mrs. Carolyn M. Hannaford

General Information Coeducational day college-preparatory, general academic, and technology school; primarily serves underachievers, students with learning disabilities, individuals with Attention Deficit Disorder, dyslexic students, and different learning styles. Grades 1–12. Founded: 1978. Setting: suburban. 5-acre campus. 1 building on campus. Approved or accredited by Georgia Independent School Association, Southern Association of Colleges and Schools, and Georgia Department of Education. Endowment: $100,000. Total enrollment: 99. Upper school average class size: 10. Upper school faculty-student ratio: 1:10.
Upper School Student Profile Grade 9: 20 students (14 boys, 6 girls); Grade 10: 9 students (6 boys, 3 girls); Grade 11: 8 students (4 boys, 4 girls); Grade 12: 8 students (5 boys, 3 girls).
Faculty School total: 18. In upper school: 3 men, 5 women; 6 have advanced degrees.
Subjects Offered Algebra, American history, American literature, art, biology, earth science, economics, English, English literature, expository writing, French, geology, geometry, government/civics, grammar, history, keyboarding, mathematics, physical education, physical science, reading, SAT/ACT preparation, science, social studies, world history, world literature, writing.
Graduation Requirements Algebra, American government, American history, biology, British literature, chemistry, civics, composition, consumer economics, earth science, economics, electives, English, English composition, English literature, foreign language, French, grammar, marine biology, mathematics, physical education (includes health), physical science, reading/study skills, science, social studies (includes history), U.S. history.
Special Academic Programs Independent study; study at local college for college credit; remedial reading and/or remedial writing; remedial math; programs in English, mathematics, general development for dyslexic students.
College Admission Counseling 8 students graduated in 2008; 5 went to college. Other: 3 went to work.
Student Life Upper grades have uniform requirement, student council, honor system. Discipline rests primarily with faculty.
Tuition and Aid Day student tuition: $13,500. Tuition installment plan (monthly payment plans, individually arranged payment plans). Tuition reduction for siblings, need-based scholarship grants, Georgia Special Needs Scholarship available. In 2008–09, 33% of upper-school students received aid. Total amount of financial aid awarded in 2008–09: $50,000.
Admissions Achievement tests, Individual IQ, Achievement and behavior rating scale, school's own test, Stanford Binet, Wechsler Individual Achievement Test, Wechsler Intelligence Scale for Children III, WISC or WAIS, WISC-R, Woodcock-Johnson Revised Achievement Test or writing sample required. Deadline for receipt of application materials: none. Application fee required: $50. Interview required.
Athletics Interscholastic: flag football (boys, girls), football (b); intramural: football (b), soccer (b,g); coed interscholastic: basketball, fitness, flag football; coed intramural: canoeing/kayaking, cheering, cooperative games, fitness, fitness walking, flag football, football, jump rope, kickball, Newcombe ball, outdoor activities, outdoor recreation, paddle tennis, physical training, soccer, whiffle ball. 2 PE instructors, 2 coaches.
Computers Computer network features include Internet access. The school has a published electronic and media policy.
Contact Mrs. Carolyn M. Hannaford, Principal. 912-354-4047. Fax: 912-354-4633. E-mail: channaford@chathamacademy.com. Web site: www.chathamacademy.com.

CHELSEA SCHOOL

711 Pershing Avenue
Silver Spring, Maryland 20910

Head of School: Anothony R. Messina Jr.

General Information Coeducational day college-preparatory, general academic, arts, bilingual studies, technology, and science and math school; primarily serves students with learning disabilities, individuals with Attention Deficit Disorder, and dyslexic students. Grades 5–12. Founded: 1976. Setting: suburban. 10-acre campus. 3 buildings on campus. Approved or accredited by Maryland Department of Education. Total enrollment: 76. Upper school average class size: 8. Upper school faculty-student ratio: 1:8.
Upper School Student Profile Grade 6: 3 students (1 boy, 2 girls); Grade 7: 6 students (5 boys, 1 girl); Grade 8: 5 students (3 boys, 2 girls); Grade 9: 9 students (7 boys, 2 girls); Grade 10: 18 students (16 boys, 2 girls); Grade 11: 15 students (14 boys, 1 girl); Grade 12: 20 students (13 boys, 7 girls).
Faculty School total: 29. In upper school: 11 men, 7 women.
Subjects Offered Algebra, American history, American literature, art, biology, calculus, career/college preparation, chemistry, community service, composition, computer graphics, computer technologies, computers, conceptual physics, earth and space science, earth science, English, English literature, environmental science, foreign language, geometry, health, health and wellness, independent study, information technology, math review, music, personal fitness, physical education, physics, pre-algebra, pre-calculus, reading, reading/study skills, remedial study skills, science, social skills, Spanish, state government, U.S. government, U.S. history, U.S. literature, wellness.
Graduation Requirements 20th century world history, algebra, American government, American history, art, biology, career/college preparation, chemistry, earth science, electives, English, English composition, English literature, general math, geometry, health and wellness, physical education (includes health), pre-algebra, Spanish, U.S. history.
Special Academic Programs Remedial reading and/or remedial writing; remedial math; programs in English, mathematics, general development for dyslexic students.
College Admission Counseling 18 students graduated in 2008; 16 went to college, including Macalester College. Other: 1 had other specific plans.
Student Life Upper grades have student council. Discipline rests primarily with faculty.
Summer Programs Remediation, enrichment, computer instruction programs offered; session focuses on remediation; held on campus; accepts boys and girls; not open to students from other schools. 30 students usually enrolled. 2009 schedule: July to August. Application deadline: none.
Tuition and Aid Day student tuition: $35,610. Tuition installment plan (individually arranged payment plans). Need-based scholarship grants available. In 2008–09, 13% of upper-school students received aid.
Admissions Traditional secondary-level entrance grade is 9. Academic Profile Tests, Wechsler Individual Achievement Test, Wide Range Achievement Test, WISC III or other aptitude measures; standardized achievement test, WISC or WAIS, WISC-R or Woodcock-Johnson required. Deadline for receipt of application materials: none. Application fee required: $50. On-campus interview required.
Athletics Interscholastic: basketball (boys, girls), flagball (b); coed interscholastic: soccer, softball, track and field. 1 PE instructor.
Computers Computer network features include on-campus library services, Internet access, wireless campus network, Internet filtering or blocking technology. Campus intranet, student e-mail accounts, and computer access in designated common areas are available to students. The school has a published electronic and media policy.
Contact Debbie Lourie, Director of Admissions. 301-585-1430 Ext. 303. Fax: 301-585-0245. E-mail: dlourie@chelseaschool.edu. Web site: www.chelseaschool.edu.

CHEROKEE CREEK BOYS SCHOOL

198 Cooper Road
Westminster, South Carolina 29693

Head of School: David LePere

General Information Boys' boarding general academic, arts, bilingual studies, environmental studies, and experiential education school; primarily serves underachievers, students with learning disabilities, individuals with Attention Deficit Disorder, individuals with emotional and behavioral problems, dyslexic students, and Mild learning disabilities. Grades 5–9. Founded: 2002. Setting: rural. Nearest major city is Atlanta, GA. Students are housed in single-sex dormitories. 77-acre campus. 2 buildings on campus. Approved or accredited by Southern Association of Colleges and Schools. Total enrollment: 36. Upper school average class size: 12. Upper school faculty-student ratio: 1:6.
Upper School Student Profile Grade 6: 2 students (2 boys); Grade 7: 8 students (8 boys); Grade 8: 14 students (14 boys); Grade 9: 12 students (12 boys). 100% of students are boarding students. 1% are state residents. 14 states are represented in upper school student body. 1% are international students.
Faculty School total: 8. In upper school: 6 men, 2 women; 3 have advanced degrees.
Graduation Requirements Completion of emotional growth program, meet therapeutic and academic goals, readiness to return home or transition to traditional boarding school.

Special Academic Programs Independent study; remedial reading and/or remedial writing; remedial math; programs in English, mathematics, general development for dyslexic students.
College Admission Counseling 26 students graduated in 2008.
Student Life Upper grades have specified standards of dress, honor system. Discipline rests primarily with faculty.
Tuition and Aid 7-day tuition and room/board: $73,200. Tuition installment plan (individually arranged payment plans). Need-based scholarship grants available. In 2008–09, 1% of upper-school students received aid.
Admissions For fall 2008, 42 students applied for upper-level admission, 30 were accepted, 22 enrolled. Battery of testing done through outside agency and psychoeducational evaluation required. Deadline for receipt of application materials: none. Application fee required: $2000. Interview recommended.
Athletics Interscholastic: backpacking, badminton, baseball, basketball, billiards, bowling, canoeing/kayaking, climbing, fishing, flag football, fly fishing, Frisbee, hiking/backpacking, horseback riding, in-line skating, kayaking, martial arts, mountain biking, outdoor activities, paddle tennis, paddling, physical fitness, rafting, ropes courses, soccer, swimming and diving, table tennis, tennis, touch football, ultimate Frisbee, volleyball, walking, wilderness survival, winter soccer; intramural: basketball, soccer. 2 PE instructors, 4 coaches, 2 athletic trainers.
Computers Computers are regularly used in mathematics classes. Computer resources include Internet access, Internet filtering or blocking technology. The school has a published electronic and media policy.
Contact Betsy Deane, Admissions Director. 864-710-8183. Fax: 866-399-1869. E-mail: bdeane@cherokeecreek.net. Web site: www.cherokeecreek.net.

CHERRY GULCH

PO Box 678
Emmett, Idaho 83617
Head of School: Andrew D Sapp, PhD

General Information Boys' boarding college-preparatory, general academic, arts, business, and technology school; primarily serves underachievers, students with learning disabilities, individuals with Attention Deficit Disorder, individuals with emotional and behavioral problems, and dyslexic students. Grades 5–9. Founded: 2004. Setting: rural. Nearest major city is Boise. Students are housed in single-sex dormitories. 220-acre campus. 2 buildings on campus. Approved or accredited by Northwest Association of Accredited Schools and Idaho Department of Education. Upper school average class size: 8. Upper school faculty-student ratio: 1:4.
Upper School Student Profile Grade 6: 4 students (4 boys); Grade 7: 8 students (8 boys); Grade 8: 12 students (12 boys); Grade 9: 1 student (1 boy). 100% of students are boarding students. 14 states are represented in upper school student body. 8% are international students. International students from Canada; 1 other country represented in student body.
Faculty School total: 3. In upper school: 3 men; 2 have advanced degrees; all reside on campus.
Subjects Offered ADL skills, algebra, American history, art, biology, character education, civics, communication skills, community garden, community service, composition, computer applications, computer programming, conflict resolution, culinary arts, death and loss, earth science, English, English composition, English literature, equine management, ethical decision making, ethics and responsibility, filmmaking, gardening, geometry, government/civics, grammar, independent study, Internet research, language and composition, language arts, leadership skills, life science, literature, martial arts, mathematics, organic gardening, outdoor education, peer counseling, personal and social education, personal development, personal growth, physical education, physical science, pre-algebra, psychology, reading, reading/study skills, relationships, social studies, student government, technology/design, U.S. government, U.S. history, U.S. literature, Web site design, wilderness camping, world history, world literature, writing fundamentals, writing skills.
Graduation Requirements An emotional growth curriculum and levels program must be completed in order to graduate with full honors.
Special Academic Programs Independent study; academic accommodation for the gifted; remedial reading and/or remedial writing; remedial math; programs in English, mathematics, general development for dyslexic students.
College Admission Counseling 10 students graduated in 2008.
Student Life Upper grades have specified standards of dress, student council. Discipline rests primarily with faculty.
Summer Programs Enrichment, advancement, sports, art/fine arts, rigorous outdoor training, computer instruction programs offered; session focuses on academics and emotional and psychological growth; held on campus; accepts boys; not open to students from other schools. 25 students usually enrolled.
Tuition and Aid 7-day tuition and room/board: $97,940. Guaranteed tuition plan. Tuition installment plan (monthly payment plans). Tuition reduction for siblings available. In 2008–09, 10% of upper-school students received aid.
Admissions Deadline for receipt of application materials: none. No application fee required. Interview recommended.
Athletics Intramural: alpine skiing, aquatics, archery, backpacking, baseball, basketball, bowling, boxing, broomball, canoeing/kayaking, climbing, combined training, cooperative games, cross-country running, equestrian sports, fishing, fitness, fly fishing, Frisbee, golf, hiking/backpacking, horseback riding, ice skating, indoor soccer, jogging, judo, kayaking, kickball, lacrosse, mountaineering, nordic skiing, outdoor activities, paint ball, physical fitness, rafting, rappelling, rock climbing, rodeo, ropes courses, running, skiing (cross-country), skiing (downhill), snowboarding, snowshoeing, soccer, strength & conditioning, swimming and diving, tennis, touch football, ultimate Frisbee, wallyball. 15 PE instructors.
Computers Computers are regularly used in all academic, business applications, computer applications, research skills classes. Computer resources include Internet access, Internet filtering or blocking technology.
Contact Andrew D Sapp, PhD, Founder. 208-365-3473 Ext. 502. Fax: 208-365-7235. E-mail: info@cherrygulch.org. Web site: www.cherrygulch.org.

COMMUNITY HIGH SCHOOL

1135 Teaneck Road
Teaneck, New Jersey 07666
Head of School: Dennis Cohen

General Information Coeducational day college-preparatory school; primarily serves students with learning disabilities, individuals with Attention Deficit Disorder, and dyslexic students. Ungraded, ages 14–19. Founded: 1968. Setting: suburban. Nearest major city is Hackensack. 1 building on campus. Approved or accredited by New Jersey Association of Independent Schools, New York Department of Education, and New Jersey Department of Education. Total enrollment: 185.
Subjects Offered Algebra, American history, American literature, art, biology, business, calculus, chemistry, computer science, creative writing, drama, driver education, English, English literature, European history, expository writing, fine arts, geography, geometry, government/civics, grammar, history, journalism, mathematics, music, photography, physical education, physics, psychology, science, social science, social studies, sociology, Spanish, speech, study skills, theater, trigonometry, writing.
Graduation Requirements Arts and fine arts (art, music, dance, drama), English, mathematics, physical education (includes health), science, social science, social studies (includes history).
Special Academic Programs Remedial reading and/or remedial writing; remedial math; programs in English, mathematics, general development for dyslexic students.
College Admission Counseling 45 students graduated in 2008.
Student Life Upper grades have specified standards of dress. Discipline rests primarily with faculty.
Tuition and Aid Day student tuition: $38,437.
Admissions Traditional secondary-level entrance grade is 9. For fall 2008, 190 students applied for upper-level admission, 54 were accepted, 50 enrolled. Deadline for receipt of application materials: none. Application fee required: $65. On-campus interview required.
Athletics Interscholastic: baseball (boys), basketball (b), soccer (b), softball (g); intramural: baseball (b), basketball (b,g), softball (g), table tennis (b,g), track and field (b,g), volleyball (b,g). 4 PE instructors, 8 coaches.
Computers Computers are regularly used in all academic classes. Computer network features include online commercial services, voice recognition systems. The school has a published electronic and media policy.
Contact Toby Braunstein, Director of Education. 201-862-1796. Fax: 201-862-1791. E-mail: tbraunstein@communityhighschool.org.

THE CRAIG SCHOOL

10 Tower Hill Road
Mountain Lakes, New Jersey 07046
Head of School: Mr. David Dennen Blanchard

General Information Coeducational day college-preparatory and general academic school; primarily serves underachievers, students with learning disabilities, individuals with Attention Deficit Disorder, and dyslexic students. Grades 3–12. Founded: 1980. Setting: suburban. Nearest major city is Lincoln Park. 1-acre campus. 2 buildings on campus. Approved or accredited by Middle States Association of Colleges and Schools, New Jersey Association of Independent Schools, and New Jersey Department of Education. Total enrollment: 153. Upper school average class size: 8. Upper school faculty-student ratio: 1:6.
Upper School Student Profile Grade 9: 11 students (9 boys, 2 girls); Grade 10: 13 students (13 boys); Grade 11: 12 students (8 boys, 4 girls); Grade 12: 10 students (9 boys, 1 girl).
Faculty School total: 45. In upper school: 9 men, 8 women; 4 have advanced degrees.
Subjects Offered Algebra, American history, art education, biology, business, character education, chemistry, creative writing, current events, earth science, geometry, health education, literature, performing arts, physical education, physics, psychology, public speaking, SAT preparation, short story, Spanish, U.S. history, world history, writing fundamentals, writing workshop.
Graduation Requirements Arts and fine arts (art, music, dance, drama), electives, English, language, mathematics, physical education (includes health), science, social studies (includes history). Community service is required.
Special Academic Programs Remedial reading and/or remedial writing; programs in English, mathematics, general development for dyslexic students.
College Admission Counseling 22 students graduated in 2008; 19 went to college. Other: 1 went to work, 1 entered a postgraduate year, 1 had other specific plans.
Student Life Upper grades have specified standards of dress, student council. Discipline rests primarily with faculty.

Tuition and Aid Day student tuition: $29,300. Tuition installment plan (monthly payment plans). Tuition reduction for siblings available.
Admissions Traditional secondary-level entrance grade is 9. For fall 2008, 30 students applied for upper-level admission, 11 were accepted, 6 enrolled. Psychoeducational evaluation or WISC/Woodcock-Johnson required. Deadline for receipt of application materials: none. Application fee required: $50. Interview required.
Athletics Coed Interscholastic: cross-country running; coed intramural: basketball, bowling, cross-country running. 1 PE instructor.
Computers Computers are regularly used in all classes. Computer resources include Internet access, wireless campus network. The school has a published electronic and media policy.
Contact Julie Sage Day, Director of Advancement. 973-334-1295. Fax: 973-334-1299. E-mail: jday@craigschool.org. Web site: www.craigschool.org/.

ANNOUNCEMENT FROM THE SCHOOL Founded in 1980, The Craig School is an independent college-prepartory school for students of average or above-average ability who have diagnosed language-based learning differences or difficulty succeeding in the traditional classroom. The School is located on two campuses: grades 3–8 are in Mountain Lakes, New Jersey, and grades 9–12 are in Lincoln Park, New Jersey. Over the past 27 years, the School has promoted a solid educational program based on the most recent and effective multisensory classroom techniques, assistive technology, social skills curricula, and organizational methods. Certified special education teachers and professionals provide individualized instruction in classes of 8 or fewer in a safe, nurturing learning environment with small, structured classrooms, positive student-teacher interaction, and strong ties to parents. Over the years, Craig School has adopted many Orton Gillingham programs to address difficulties in decoding, reading comprehension, fluency, and written expression. A hallmark of a Craig education is the integration and application of effective teaching strategies across subject areas. For example, the speech therapist shares approaches with the reading teachers; note-taking skills are coordinated by language arts, science, and social studies teachers; and vocabulary acquisition and organizational methods are reinforced within all departments. All classrooms are equipped with desktop or wireless laptop computers that provide specialized software to assist with reading comprehension, the writing process, and computational fluency. The liberal arts curriculum at the upper school is integrated, interdisciplinary, and project-based and is designed to prepare students for college or other postsecondary experiences. The program focuses on developing solid written language skills, strategies for content acquisition and retention, and the social, behavioral, and self-advocacy skills essential for success in the extended community. Students may participate in a rich variety of social and athletic opportunities, including competitive team and intramural sports, after-school activities, and cultural arts trips.

CRAWFORD DAY SCHOOL

825 Crawford Parkway
Portsmouth, Virginia 23704

Head of School: Mr. Jeffrey R. Gray

General Information Coeducational day general academic school; primarily serves underachievers, students with learning disabilities, individuals with Attention Deficit Disorder, individuals with emotional and behavioral problems, and Autism Spectrum Disorders (high functioning, Asperger's Syndrome), developmental delay, mental retardation (mild). Grades K–12. Founded: 1989. Setting: urban. 1 building on campus. Approved or accredited by Virginia Department of Education. Total enrollment: 25. Upper school average class size: 7. Upper school faculty-student ratio: 1:4.
Upper School Student Profile Grade 6: 1 student (1 boy); Grade 7: 2 students (1 boy, 1 girl); Grade 8: 4 students (2 boys, 2 girls); Grade 9: 4 students (4 boys); Grade 10: 1 student (1 boy); Grade 11: 7 students (4 boys, 3 girls); Grade 12: 3 students (3 boys).
Faculty School total: 5. In upper school: 2 men, 1 woman.
Graduation Requirements Graduation requirements are those of the public school district that is responsible for the student.
College Admission Counseling 1 student graduated in 2008. Other: 1 went to work.
Student Life Upper grades have uniform requirement. Discipline rests primarily with faculty.
Summer Programs Enrichment programs offered; session focuses on maintenance of behavioral goals; held on campus; accepts boys and girls; open to students from other schools. 45 students usually enrolled. 2009 schedule: June 20 to August 18. Application deadline: June 5.
Tuition and Aid Tuition is paid by the sending city, county or state. available.
Admissions Deadline for receipt of application materials: none. No application fee required. Interview required.
Athletics 1 PE instructor.
Computers Computers are regularly used in all academic classes. Computer network features include Internet access, Internet filtering or blocking technology, educational programs online. Computer access in designated common areas is available to students.
Contact Mr. Jeffrey R. Gray, Director. 757-391-6675. Fax: 757-391-6651. Web site: www.firsthomecareweb.com.

CROSS CREEK PROGRAMS

150 North State Street
LaVerkin, Utah 84745

Head of School: Karr Farnsworth

General Information Coeducational boarding college-preparatory, general academic, arts, and business school; primarily serves underachievers, students with learning disabilities, individuals with Attention Deficit Disorder, and individuals with emotional and behavioral problems. Grades 7–12. Founded: 1987. Setting: small town. Nearest major city is St. George. Students are housed in single-sex dormitories. 5-acre campus. 4 buildings on campus. Approved or accredited by Northwest Association of Accredited Schools, Northwest Association of Schools and Colleges, and Utah Department of Education. Total enrollment: 200. Upper school average class size: 18. Upper school faculty-student ratio: 1:15.
Upper School Student Profile Grade 9: 45 students (20 boys, 25 girls); Grade 10: 37 students (12 boys, 25 girls); Grade 11: 58 students (32 boys, 26 girls); Grade 12: 30 students (15 boys, 15 girls). 100% of students are boarding students. 1% are state residents. 42 states are represented in upper school student body. International students from Canada and Mexico.
Faculty School total: 17. In upper school: 7 men, 8 women; 3 have advanced degrees.
Subjects Offered 20th century American writers, 20th century world history, advanced chemistry, advanced math, algebra, American government, American history, American literature, art, art appreciation, art history, athletic training, athletics, baseball, basketball, biology, business, business applications, business technology, calculus, career/college preparation, careers, chemistry, child development, choir, chorus, computer applications, computer keyboarding, computer technologies, consumer mathematics, drawing, early childhood, earth science, electives, English, English composition, English literature, fitness, food and nutrition, general math, general science, geography, geometry, government, health, health education, honors algebra, honors English, honors geometry, honors U.S. history, honors world history, human biology, intro to computers, introduction to theater, keyboarding, language and composition, language arts, mathematics, parenting, pre-algebra, pre-calculus, projective geometry, psychology, reading/study skills, SAT preparation, SAT/ACT preparation, science, Spanish, sports, state history, U.S. government, U.S. history, world civilizations, world cultures.
Graduation Requirements 20th century world history, American government, American history, arts and fine arts (art, music, dance, drama), business skills (includes word processing), business technology, computer keyboarding, English, geography, mathematics, physical education (includes health), science, social science, social studies (includes history), senior project (including 90 hours of community or school service).
Special Academic Programs Honors section; accelerated programs; independent study; study at local college for college credit; remedial reading and/or remedial writing; remedial math; programs in English, mathematics, general development for dyslexic students.
College Admission Counseling 80 students graduated in 2008; 73 went to college, including DePaul University; Loyola Marymount University; Oregon State University; Southern Utah University; University of California, Los Angeles; University of Colorado Denver. Other: 5 went to work, 2 entered military service. Median SAT critical reading: 483, median SAT math: 506, median SAT writing: 531, median combined SAT: 1520, median composite ACT: 21.
Student Life Upper grades have uniform requirement, student council, honor system. Discipline rests primarily with faculty.
Tuition and Aid 7-day tuition and room/board: $53,880. Guaranteed tuition plan. Tuition installment plan (monthly payment plans, discount for one year paid in-advance tuition). Tuition reduction for siblings, middle-income loans, Wells Fargo, Health One, First Again available.
Admissions Traditional secondary-level entrance grade is 10. Deadline for receipt of application materials: none. No application fee required. Interview required.
Athletics Interscholastic: backpacking (boys, girls), baseball (b,g), basketball (b,g), bowling (b,g), cooperative games (b,g), cross-country running (b,g), danceline (b,g), fitness (b,g), fitness walking (b,g), hiking/backpacking (b,g), outdoor activities (b,g), physical fitness (b,g), physical training (b,g), running (b,g), softball (b,g), strength & conditioning (b,g), track and field (b,g), volleyball (b,g), walking (b,g), water skiing (b,g), winter walking (b,g); intramural: basketball (b,g), cross-country running (b,g), track and field (b,g); coed interscholastic: baseball, softball. 1 PE instructor, 4 coaches.
Computers Computers are regularly used in business, career education, college planning, computer applications, economics, English, foreign language, geography, health, history, mathematics, reading, science classes. Computer resources include on-campus library services, Internet access.
Contact Kami Farnsworth, Admissions Representative. 800-514-7438. Fax: 435-635-2331. E-mail: kami@crosscreekprograms.com. Web site: www.crosscreekprograms.com.

CROSSROADS

400 Earhart Street
Medford, Oregon 97501

Head of School: Greg Huston

General Information Coeducational day general academic and arts school; primarily serves underachievers, students with learning disabilities, individuals with Attention Deficit Disorder, and individuals with emotional and behavioral problems. Grades 7–12. Founded: 1987. Setting: suburban. 1-acre campus. 1 building on campus. Approved or accredited by Northwest Association of Accredited Schools, Northwest Association of Schools and Colleges, and Oregon Department of Education. Upper school average class size: 10. Upper school faculty-student ratio: 1:6.
Faculty School total: 3. In upper school: 2 men, 1 woman; 2 have advanced degrees.
Subjects Offered Algebra, American history, biology, child development, economics, English, fine arts, geometry, government, grammar, health, keyboarding, literature, mathematics, newspaper, physical education, physical science, pre-algebra, science, social science, social studies, world geography, world history.
Graduation Requirements Arts and fine arts (art, music, dance, drama), foreign language, mathematics, religion (includes Bible studies and theology), science, social science, social studies (includes history).
Special Academic Programs Remedial reading and/or remedial writing; remedial math; programs in English, mathematics for dyslexic students.
Student Life Discipline rests primarily with faculty.
Admissions No application fee required.
Athletics 1 PE instructor.
Computers Computers are regularly used in career education, writing fundamentals classes. Computer network features include on-campus library services, online commercial services, Internet access, Internet filtering or blocking technology, PLATO educational software. Campus intranet and computer access in designated common areas are available to students. The school has a published electronic and media policy.
Contact Cori Thye-Couch, Administrative Assistant. 541-770-1270. Fax: 541-858-4016. E-mail: cthyecouch@community-works.org.

CROTCHED MOUNTAIN REHABILITATION CENTER SCHOOL

1 Verney Drive
Greenfield, New Hampshire 03047

Head of School: Bill Cossaboon

General Information Coeducational boarding and day arts, vocational, and technology school; primarily serves underachievers, students with learning disabilities, individuals with Attention Deficit Disorder, individuals with emotional and behavioral problems, dyslexic students, and students with multiple disabilities. Ungraded, ages 6–22. Founded: 1936. Setting: rural. Students are housed in group home, apartments. Approved or accredited by European Council of International Schools, New England Association of Schools and Colleges, and New Hampshire Department of Education. Endowment: $32 million. Upper school average class size: 6.
Faculty School total: 25. In upper school: 1 resides on campus.
Subjects Offered Art, computers, desktop publishing, English, health, history, home economics, horticulture, mathematics, music, physical education, science, technology, vocational arts.
Graduation Requirements Arts and fine arts (art, music, dance, drama), business skills (includes word processing), computer science, English, mathematics, physical education (includes health), science, social science, social studies (includes history).
Special Academic Programs Remedial reading and/or remedial writing; remedial math; special instructional classes for deaf students, blind students.
Summer Programs Session focuses on preventing regression in students' performance; held on campus; accepts boys and girls. 108 students usually enrolled. 2009 schedule: July 5 to August 27. Application deadline: none.
Tuition and Aid Funding from local districts and other agencies available.
Admissions Deadline for receipt of application materials: none. No application fee required. Interview recommended.
Athletics Coed Intramural: Special Olympics, swimming and diving. 2 PE instructors.
Computers Computers are regularly used in art, English, history, mathematics, music, science classes. Computer resources include Internet access.
Contact Archie Campbell, Director of Admissions. 603-547-3311 Ext. 1894. Fax: 603-547-3232. E-mail: archibald.campbell@crotchedmountain.org.

DALLAS ACADEMY

950 Tiffany Way
Dallas, Texas 75218

Head of School: JIm Richardson

General Information Coeducational day college-preparatory, general academic, arts, and technology school; primarily serves students with learning disabilities, individuals with Attention Deficit Disorder, dyslexic students, and Asperger's Syndrome. Grades 1–12. Founded: 1965. Setting: suburban. 2-acre campus. 2 buildings on campus. Approved or accredited by Southern Association of Colleges and Schools and Texas Education Agency. Endowment: $250,000. Total enrollment: 177. Upper school average class size: 10. Upper school faculty-student ratio: 1:6.
Upper School Student Profile Grade 9: 22 students (12 boys, 10 girls); Grade 10: 24 students (22 boys, 2 girls); Grade 11: 24 students (17 boys, 7 girls); Grade 12: 22 students (16 boys, 6 girls).
Faculty School total: 27. In upper school: 4 men, 12 women; 5 have advanced degrees.
Subjects Offered Algebra, American history, art, computer science, computers, drawing, economics, English, fine arts, geography, government/civics, health, history, literature, mathematics, music, photography, physical education, physical science, pottery, science, social science, social studies, Spanish, speech, woodworking, world history, writing skills, yearbook.
Graduation Requirements Arts and fine arts (art, music, dance, drama), computer science, English, foreign language, mathematics, physical education (includes health), science, social science, social studies (includes history), 4 hours of community service per semester.
Special Academic Programs Study at local college for college credit; remedial reading and/or remedial writing; remedial math; programs in English, mathematics, general development for dyslexic students.
College Admission Counseling 21 students graduated in 2008; 16 went to college, including Lon Morris College; Oklahoma State University; Richland College; Texas A&M University; The University of Texas at Austin; University of the Ozarks. Other: 5 went to work.
Student Life Upper grades have uniform requirement, student council. Discipline rests primarily with faculty.
Summer Programs Remediation, enrichment programs offered; held on campus; accepts boys and girls; not open to students from other schools. 8 students usually enrolled.
Tuition and Aid Day student tuition: $15,000. Tuition installment plan (semester payment plan). Need-based scholarship grants available. In 2008–09, 20% of upper-school students received aid. Total amount of financial aid awarded in 2008–09: $60,000.
Admissions Traditional secondary-level entrance grade is 9. Admissions testing and WRAT required. Deadline for receipt of application materials: none. No application fee required. On-campus interview required.
Athletics Interscholastic: baseball (boys), basketball (b,g), cheering (g), cross-country running (b,g), football (b), golf (b), soccer (b,g), track and field (b,g), volleyball (g); intramural: tennis (g); coed interscholastic: soccer. 1 PE instructor, 5 coaches, 1 athletic trainer.
Computers Computers are regularly used in English, geography, history, library, SAT preparation, science, typing, writing, yearbook classes. Computer network features include on-campus library services, online commercial services, Internet access, Internet filtering or blocking technology. Students grades are available online. The school has a published electronic and media policy.
Contact Jim Richardson, Headmaster. 214-324-1481. Fax: 214-327-8537. E-mail: jrichardson@dallas-academy.com. Web site: www.dallas-academy.com.

DELAWARE VALLEY FRIENDS SCHOOL

19 East Central Avenue
Paoli, Pennsylvania 19301-1345

Head of School: Katherine A. Schantz

General Information Coeducational day college-preparatory, arts, technology, and Reading school, affiliated with Society of Friends; primarily serves students with learning disabilities, individuals with Attention Deficit Disorder, and dyslexic students. Grades 7–12. Founded: 1986. Setting: suburban. Nearest major city is Philadelphia. 8-acre campus. 1 building on campus. Approved or accredited by Pennsylvania Association of Independent Schools. Endowment: $2.4 million. Total enrollment: 205. Upper school average class size: 9. Upper school faculty-student ratio: 1:5.
Upper School Student Profile Grade 9: 32 students (22 boys, 10 girls); Grade 10: 52 students (35 boys, 17 girls); Grade 11: 47 students (25 boys, 22 girls); Grade 12: 34 students (16 boys, 18 girls). 6% of students are members of Society of Friends.
Faculty School total: 49. In upper school: 24 men, 25 women; 29 have advanced degrees.
Subjects Offered 20th century world history, algebra, American history, Asian studies, biology, calculus, chemistry, crafts, first aid, geometry, human development, language arts, photography, physical education, physics, pre-calculus, printmaking, Spanish, studio art, trigonometry, world history.
Graduation Requirements Arts and fine arts (art, music, dance, drama), English, lab science, language arts, mathematics, physical education (includes health), senior internship, social studies (includes history), at least one Adventure Based Learning (A.B.L.E.) course. Community service is required.
Special Academic Programs Remedial reading and/or remedial writing; remedial math; programs in English, mathematics, general development for dyslexic students.
College Admission Counseling 35 students graduated in 2008; 31 went to college, including Drew University. Other: 2 went to work, 1 entered a postgraduate year, 1 had other specific plans.
Student Life Upper grades have specified standards of dress, student council. Discipline rests primarily with faculty. Attendance at religious services is required.

Summer Programs Remediation, enrichment, art/fine arts programs offered; session focuses on individualized reading skills/writing tutoring using Orton-Gillingham methods; held on campus; accepts boys and girls; open to students from other schools. 50 students usually enrolled. 2009 schedule: June 29 to July 31. Application deadline: none.
Tuition and Aid Day student tuition: $33,000. Tuition installment plan (monthly payment plans, 2-payment plan (66% due May 1, 34% due January 1)). Tuition reduction for siblings, need-based scholarship grants available. In 2008–09, 23% of upper-school students received aid. Total amount of financial aid awarded in 2008–09: $490,425.
Admissions Traditional secondary-level entrance grade is 9. For fall 2008, 65 students applied for upper-level admission, 37 were accepted, 29 enrolled. Psychoeducational evaluation and WISC or WAIS required. Deadline for receipt of application materials: none. Application fee required: $100. On-campus interview required.
Athletics Interscholastic: basketball (boys, girls), cross-country running (b,g), Frisbee (b), lacrosse (b,g), soccer (b,g); coed interscholastic: Frisbee, golf, soccer, tennis, ultimate Frisbee; coed intramural: backpacking, bicycling, hiking/backpacking, rock climbing, sailing, skiing (cross-country). 2 PE instructors, 5 coaches.
Computers Computers are regularly used in all classes. Computer network features include Internet access, Internet filtering or blocking technology, adaptive technologies, homework site. Student e-mail accounts are available to students. The school has a published electronic and media policy.
Contact Kathryn W. Wynn, Associate Admissions Director. 610-640-4150 Ext. 2160. Fax: 610-560-4336. E-mail: wynnk@fc.dvfs.org. Web site: www.dvfs.org.

DENVER ACADEMY

4400 East Iliff Avenue
Denver, Colorado 80222
Head of School: Kevin Smith

General Information Coeducational day college-preparatory, general academic, arts, vocational, and technology school; primarily serves underachievers, students with learning disabilities, individuals with Attention Deficit Disorder, dyslexic students, and unique learning styles. Grades 1–12. Founded: 1972. Setting: urban. 22-acre campus. 19 buildings on campus. Approved or accredited by Association of Colorado Independent Schools and Colorado Department of Education. Member of National Association of Independent Schools. Endowment: $1 million. Total enrollment: 439. Upper school average class size: 12. Upper school faculty-student ratio: 1:6.
Upper School Student Profile Grade 9: 44 students (37 boys, 7 girls); Grade 10: 68 students (47 boys, 21 girls); Grade 11: 60 students (52 boys, 8 girls); Grade 12: 80 students (53 boys, 27 girls).
Faculty School total: 86. In upper school: 26 men, 23 women; 6 have advanced degrees.
Subjects Offered ACT preparation, adolescent issues, algebra, American history, American literature, anatomy, art, art history, arts, baseball, basic skills, basketball, biology, botany, business, calculus, ceramics, chemistry, comparative cultures, computer applications, computer graphics, computer math, computer processing, computer programming, computer science, computer skills, creative writing, drama, dramatic arts, earth science, English, English literature, environmental science, ethics, European history, film, filmmaking, fine arts, geography, geometry, government/civics, grammar, health, history, life skills, mathematics, music, philosophy, photography, physical education, physics, physiology, psychology, science, social science, social studies, Spanish, speech, theater, trigonometry, values and decisions, world history, world literature, writing, yearbook.
Graduation Requirements Arts and fine arts (art, music, dance, drama), English, mathematics, physical education (includes health), science, social science, social studies (includes history).
Special Academic Programs Independent study; academic accommodation for the gifted; remedial reading and/or remedial writing; remedial math; programs in English, mathematics, general development for dyslexic students.
College Admission Counseling 57 students graduated in 2008; 52 went to college, including Fort Lewis College; Metropolitan State College of Denver; University of Colorado Denver; University of Northern Colorado. Other: 1 entered military service, 4 had other specific plans. Median composite ACT: 21. 10% scored over 26 on composite ACT.
Student Life Upper grades have specified standards of dress, student council, honor system. Discipline rests equally with students and faculty.
Summer Programs Remediation, enrichment, advancement, art/fine arts, rigorous outdoor training, computer instruction programs offered; session focuses on academics, remediation, and summer fun camp; held both on and off campus; held at various locations around the city and the Rocky Mountains; accepts boys and girls; open to students from other schools. 75 students usually enrolled. 2009 schedule: June to July. Application deadline: June.
Tuition and Aid Day student tuition: $21,675. Tuition installment plan (monthly payment plans). Tuition reduction for siblings, need-based scholarship grants available. In 2008–09, 26% of upper-school students received aid.
Admissions For fall 2008, 39 students applied for upper-level admission, 32 were accepted, 29 enrolled. WISC/Woodcock-Johnson required. Deadline for receipt of application materials: none. Application fee required: $75. On-campus interview required.
Athletics Interscholastic: baseball (boys), basketball (b,g), cross-country running (b,g), golf (b), soccer (b,g), volleyball (g); intramural: volleyball (g); coed interscholastic: cheering, physical fitness, physical training; coed intramural: backpacking, basketball, boxing, canoeing/kayaking, climbing, cooperative games, fishing, flag football, golf, indoor hockey, indoor soccer, indoor track, jump rope, mountaineering, outdoor activities, rafting, rock climbing, skiing (downhill), soccer, swimming and diving, track and field, wall climbing. 7 PE instructors, 7 coaches.
Computers Computers are regularly used in basic skills, career exploration, career technology, college planning, drawing and design, English, foreign language, independent study, introduction to technology, mathematics, media arts, media production, media services, multimedia, music, occupational education, SAT preparation, science, writing fundamentals, yearbook classes. Computer network features include on-campus library services, online commercial services, Internet access, wireless campus network, Internet filtering or blocking technology. Student e-mail accounts and computer access in designated common areas are available to students. Students grades are available online. The school has a published electronic and media policy.
Contact Janet Woolley, Director of Admissions. 303-777-5161. Fax: 303-777-5893. E-mail: jwoolley@denveracademy.org. Web site: www.denveracademy.org.

EAGLE HILL SCHOOL

45 Glenville Road
Greenwich, Connecticut 06831
Head of School: Dr. Mark J. Griffin

General Information Coeducational boarding college-preparatory, arts, and technology school; primarily serves students with learning disabilities, dyslexic students, and language-based learning disabilities. Grades 1–9. Founded: 1975. Setting: suburban. Nearest major city is New York, NY. Students are housed in single-sex by floor dormitories. 20-acre campus. 21 buildings on campus. Approved or accredited by Connecticut Association of Independent Schools and Connecticut Department of Education. Member of Secondary School Admission Test Board. Endowment: $18 million. Total enrollment: 230. Upper school average class size: 6. Upper school faculty-student ratio: 1:4.
Upper School Student Profile Grade 6: 45 students (45 boys); Grade 7: 45 students (45 boys); Grade 8: 45 students (45 boys); Grade 9: 25 students (25 boys). 30% of students are boarding students. 50% are state residents. 4 states are represented in upper school student body.
Faculty School total: 76. In upper school: 15 men, 20 women; 33 have advanced degrees; 35 reside on campus.
Subjects Offered Art, English, health, history, mathematics, music, physical education, science, technology.
Graduation Requirements Arts and fine arts (art, music, dance, drama), computer science, English, mathematics, physical education (includes health), science, social science, social studies (includes history), study skills.
Special Academic Programs Remedial reading and/or remedial writing; remedial math; programs in English, mathematics, general development for dyslexic students.
College Admission Counseling 53 students graduated in 2008; they went to Purnell School; Rumsey Hall School; The Forman School; The Harvey School.
Student Life Upper grades have specified standards of dress, student council, honor system. Discipline rests primarily with faculty.
Tuition and Aid Day student tuition: $48,200; 5-day tuition and room/board: $51,350. Tuition installment plan (Academic Management Services Plan, monthly payment plans, individually arranged payment plans). Need-based scholarship grants available. In 2008–09, 20% of upper-school students received aid. Total amount of financial aid awarded in 2008–09: $1,500,000.
Admissions For fall 2008, 75 students applied for upper-level admission, 43 were accepted, 40 enrolled. Psychoeducational evaluation and Wechsler Intelligence Scale for Children III required. Deadline for receipt of application materials: none. Application fee required: $50. On-campus interview required.
Athletics Interscholastic: baseball, basketball (g), cheering (g), field hockey (g), lacrosse; intramural: aerobics (g), aerobics/dance (g), aerobics/Nautilus, flag football, football, lacrosse (g); coed interscholastic: basketball, cross-country running, ice hockey; coed intramural: basketball, bicycling, billiards, canoeing/kayaking, dance, fitness, fitness walking, floor hockey, Frisbee, golf, gymnastics, ice skating, jogging, judo, martial arts, outdoor activities, outdoor education, outdoor recreation, physical fitness, physical training, volleyball, yoga. 1 PE instructor, 1 athletic trainer.
Computers Computers are regularly used in English, history, mathematics, science classes. Computer network features include on-campus library services, online commercial services, Internet access, wireless campus network, Internet filtering or blocking technology, digital lab, iMovie, Active Boards, intranet. The school has a published electronic and media policy.
Contact Rayma-Joan Griffin, Director of Admissions. 203-622-9240. Fax: 203-622-0914. E-mail: r.griffin@eaglehill.org. Web site: www.eaglehillschool.org.

ANNOUNCEMENT FROM THE SCHOOL Eagle Hill School is a coeducational day and five-day residential program serving children ages 6–16 with average to above-average intellectual potential with diagnosed learning disabilities. Academic programs are individually designed to meet the specific learning needs of students with learning difficulties to help the child develop the skills and strategies necessary to work to his or her potential in a more traditional learning environment. Eagle Hill School is located 35 miles northeast of New York City. The 20-acre suburban campus has six classroom buildings, a dormitory, and state-of-the-art technology in all buildings. A 10,000-volume library, a gymnasium, and playing fields complement the classrooms. Eagle Hill is accredited by the CAIS and the state Department of Special Education in Connecticut as a school for children with language-based learning disabilities. In addition to the intense remedial program, Eagle Hill offers a full extracurricular program, including interscholastic and intramural sports, art, music, an on-campus radio station, community service, an active student council, and a yearbook club.

EAGLE HILL SCHOOL

PO Box 116
242 Old Petersham Road
Hardwick, Massachusetts 01037

Head of School: Peter J. McDonald

General Information Coeducational boarding and day college-preparatory and arts school; primarily serves students with learning disabilities, individuals with Attention Deficit Disorder, dyslexic students, and non-verbal learning disabilities. Grades 8–12. Founded: 1967. Setting: small town. Nearest major city is Worcester. Students are housed in single-sex dormitories. 175-acre campus. 14 buildings on campus. Approved or accredited by Association of Independent Schools in New England, Massachusetts Office of Child Care Services, New England Association of Schools and Colleges, and The Association of Boarding Schools. Member of National Association of Independent Schools and Secondary School Admission Test Board. Endowment: $5 million. Total enrollment: 158. Upper school average class size: 5. Upper school faculty-student ratio: 1:4.

Upper School Student Profile Grade 9: 33 students (22 boys, 11 girls); Grade 10: 38 students (21 boys, 17 girls); Grade 11: 38 students (22 boys, 16 girls); Grade 12: 38 students (24 boys, 14 girls). 90% of students are boarding students. 33% are state residents. 26 states are represented in upper school student body. 5% are international students. International students from Bermuda, Canada, France, Kuwait, Saudi Arabia, and United Kingdom; 1 other country represented in student body.

Faculty School total: 44. In upper school: 19 men, 22 women; 30 have advanced degrees; 17 reside on campus.

Subjects Offered 20th century history, acting, advanced math, algebra, American foreign policy, American government, American literature, anatomy and physiology, art, arts and crafts, biology, botany, British literature, calculus, career/college preparation, cell biology, ceramics, chemistry, chorus, college counseling, communication skills, composition, computer graphics, computer keyboarding, conceptual physics, contemporary issues, creative writing, culinary arts, current events, desktop publishing, drama, dramatic arts, earth science, English, English composition, English literature, environmental science, expository writing, film appreciation, film studies, filmmaking, food and nutrition, foreign policy, forensic science, French, gender issues, general science, geography, geometry, government/civics, graphic arts, graphics, guidance, health, history, history of rock and roll, Holocaust studies, Internet research, interpersonal skills, lab science, language development, Latin, leadership training, life management skills, literary magazine, mathematics, mentorship program, multicultural literature, music appreciation, music history, music theory, newspaper, outdoor education, participation in sports, peer counseling, personal finance, personal fitness, philosophy, photography, physical education, physical science, physics, poetry, pragmatics, pre-algebra, pre-calculus, printmaking, psychology, publishing, reading, relationships, Russian, SAT/ACT preparation, science, sculpture, set design, Shakespeare, silk screening, social science, social skills, social studies, speech therapy, technology, theater arts, U.S. history, video and animation, video film production, visual and performing arts, visual arts, Web site design, women in literature, women's literature, woodworking, world history, world literature, world wide web design, writing, zoology.

Graduation Requirements Art, college counseling, computer science, electives, history, literature, mathematics, physical education (includes health), science, writing. Community service is required.

Special Academic Programs Honors section; academic accommodation for the gifted, the musically talented, and the artistically talented; remedial reading and/or remedial writing; remedial math; programs in English, mathematics, general development for dyslexic students.

College Admission Counseling 40 students graduated in 2008; all went to college, including American University; Brandeis University; Curry College; Mount Holyoke College; Suffolk University; University of Denver. Mean composite ACT: 30.

Student Life Upper grades have specified standards of dress, student council, honor system. Discipline rests primarily with faculty.

Summer Programs Remediation, enrichment, advancement, sports, art/fine arts, computer instruction programs offered; session focuses on academics and recreation; held on campus; accepts boys and girls; open to students from other schools. 74 students usually enrolled. 2009 schedule: June 29 to July 31. Application deadline: none.

Tuition and Aid Day student tuition: $36,586; 7-day tuition and room/board: $51,692. Tuition installment plan (Key Tuition Payment Plan).

Admissions Traditional secondary-level entrance grade is 9. For fall 2008, 212 students applied for upper-level admission, 54 were accepted, 40 enrolled. Achievement tests, WISC/Woodcock-Johnson and writing sample required. Deadline for receipt of application materials: none. Application fee required: $75. On-campus interview required.

Athletics Interscholastic: basketball (boys, girls), softball (b,g); intramural: aerobics/dance (g), dance (g), yoga (g); coed interscholastic: cross-country running, golf, lacrosse, soccer, tennis, wrestling; coed intramural: aerobics, aerobics/Nautilus, alpine skiing, basketball, bicycling, fencing, fitness, fitness walking, floor hockey, Frisbee, ice skating, jogging, mountain biking, Nautilus, outdoor adventure, physical training, roller blading, roller skating, running, skiing (cross-country), skiing (downhill), snowboarding, snowshoeing, swimming and diving, touch football, weight lifting. 1 PE instructor.

Computers Computers are regularly used in college planning, creative writing, desktop publishing, English, foreign language, graphic arts, keyboarding, mathematics, music, music technology, newspaper, photojournalism, programming, research skills, theater arts, video film production, Web site design, writing, yearbook classes. Computer network features include on-campus library services, Internet access, wireless campus network, Internet filtering or blocking technology. Student e-mail accounts are available to students. Students grades are available online.

Contact Dana M. Harbert, Director of Admission. 413-477-6000. Fax: 413-477-6837. E-mail: admission@ehs1.org. Web site: www.ehs1.org.

See Close-Up on page 1090.

EAGLE HILL-SOUTHPORT

214 Main Street
Southport, Connecticut 06890

Head of School: Leonard Tavormina

General Information Coeducational day arts school; primarily serves underachievers, students with learning disabilities, individuals with Attention Deficit Disorder, and dyslexic students. Ungraded, ages 7–16. Founded: 1985. Setting: small town. Nearest major city is Bridgeport. 2-acre campus. 1 building on campus. Approved or accredited by Connecticut Association of Independent Schools and Connecticut Department of Education. Member of National Association of Independent Schools. Endowment: $6.5 million. Total enrollment: 112. Upper school average class size: 5. Upper school faculty-student ratio: 1:4.

Faculty School total: 28. In upper school: 8 men, 20 women; 20 have advanced degrees.

Subjects Offered Algebra, art, biology, computer skills, creative writing, earth science, English, grammar, history, literature, mathematics, physical education, reading, social studies, writing.

Special Academic Programs Remedial reading and/or remedial writing; remedial math; programs in English, mathematics, general development for dyslexic students.

Student Life Upper grades have uniform requirement, student council. Discipline rests primarily with faculty.

Summer Programs Remediation programs offered; session focuses on academic skills reinforcement; held on campus; accepts boys and girls; open to students from other schools. 92 students usually enrolled. 2009 schedule: June 29 to July 31. Application deadline: none.

Tuition and Aid Day student tuition: $37,600. Tuition installment plan (monthly payment plans, individually arranged payment plans). Need-based scholarship grants available. In 2008–09, 3% of upper-school students received aid. Total amount of financial aid awarded in 2008–09: $82,200.

Admissions Wechsler Intelligence Scale for Children required. Deadline for receipt of application materials: none. Application fee required: $75. On-campus interview required.

Athletics Interscholastic: cheering (girls); intramural: cheering (g); coed interscholastic: baseball, basketball, cross-country running, fishing, fitness, physical fitness, soccer, tennis; coed intramural: baseball, basketball, soccer.

Computers Computers are regularly used in English, mathematics, writing classes. Computer resources include Internet access.

Contact Carolyn Lavender, Director of Admissions. 203-254-2044. Fax: 203-255-4052. E-mail: info@eaglehillsouthport.org. Web site: www.eaglehillsouthport.org.

THE EDUCATION CENTER

4080 Old Canton Road
Jackson, Mississippi 39216

Head of School: Lynn T. Macon

General Information Coeducational day college-preparatory and general academic school; primarily serves students with learning disabilities, individuals with Attention Deficit Disorder, individuals with emotional and behavioral problems, and dyslexic

students. Grades 1–12. Founded: 1964. Setting: urban. 5-acre campus. 2 buildings on campus. Approved or accredited by National Independent Private Schools Association, Southern Association of Colleges and Schools, Southern Association of Independent Schools, and Mississippi Department of Education. Total enrollment: 170. Upper school average class size: 10. Upper school faculty-student ratio: 1:9.
Upper School Student Profile Grade 9: 22 students (13 boys, 9 girls); Grade 10: 31 students (17 boys, 14 girls); Grade 11: 33 students (17 boys, 16 girls); Grade 12: 39 students (18 boys, 21 girls).
Faculty School total: 17. In upper school: 5 men, 11 women; 6 have advanced degrees.
Subjects Offered ACT preparation, advanced math, algebra, American government, American history, American literature, American studies, ancient history, art, art appreciation, biology, British literature, British literature (honors), business applications, business mathematics, character education, chemistry, computer applications, creative writing, economics, English, environmental science, French, health, health and wellness, honors algebra, honors English, honors geometry, human anatomy, keyboarding, mathematics, music appreciation, physical science, physics, pre-algebra, pre-calculus, psychology, sociology, Spanish, state government, U.S. history, world geography, world history, world literature, writing skills.
Graduation Requirements Algebra, American history, American literature, anatomy and physiology, art, biology, British literature, chemistry, computer applications, economics, English, geography, geometry, health, languages, mathematics, social studies (includes history).
Special Academic Programs Advanced Placement exam preparation; honors section; accelerated programs; independent study; study at local college for college credit; academic accommodation for the gifted, the musically talented, and the artistically talented; remedial reading and/or remedial writing; remedial math; programs in English, mathematics for dyslexic students; special instructional classes for deaf students.
College Admission Counseling 65 students graduated in 2008; 58 went to college, including Hinds Community College; Millsaps College; Mississippi College; Mississippi State University; University of Mississippi; University of Southern Mississippi. Other: 2 went to work, 5 entered military service. Mean composite ACT: 20. 15% scored over 26 on composite ACT.
Student Life Upper grades have uniform requirement, student council. Discipline rests primarily with faculty.
Summer Programs Remediation, enrichment, advancement, computer instruction programs offered; held on campus; accepts boys and girls; open to students from other schools. 250 students usually enrolled. 2009 schedule: June 2 to July 31. Application deadline: none.
Tuition and Aid Day student tuition: $6000. Tuition installment plan (monthly payment plans, individually arranged payment plans). Need-based scholarship grants available.
Admissions Traditional secondary-level entrance grade is 9. Otis-Lennon School Ability Test or TerraNova required. Deadline for receipt of application materials: none. No application fee required. On-campus interview required.
Athletics 1 PE instructor.
Computers Computers are regularly used in computer applications, creative writing, English, French, history, independent study, keyboarding, word processing classes. Computer network features include Internet access, Internet filtering or blocking technology. Computer access in designated common areas is available to students. The school has a published electronic and media policy.
Contact Lynn T. Macon, Principal. 601-982-2812 Ext. 224. Fax: 601-982-2827. E-mail: edcenter@bellsouth.net. Web site: www.educationcenterschool.com.

ELAN SCHOOL

PO Box 578
Poland, Maine 04274
Head of School: Ms. Sharon Terry

General Information Coeducational boarding college-preparatory and general academic school; primarily serves underachievers, students with learning disabilities, individuals with Attention Deficit Disorder, and individuals with emotional and behavioral problems. Grades 7–12. Founded: 1970. Setting: rural. Nearest major city is Portland. Students are housed in single-sex dormitories. 32-acre campus. Approved or accredited by Massachusetts Department of Education and Maine Department of Education. Total enrollment: 62. Upper school average class size: 9. Upper school faculty-student ratio: 1:6.
Upper School Student Profile Grade 9: 5 students (4 boys, 1 girl); Grade 10: 9 students (8 boys, 1 girl); Grade 11: 19 students (14 boys, 5 girls); Grade 12: 29 students (18 boys, 11 girls). 100% of students are boarding students. 5% are state residents. 12 states are represented in upper school student body. 3% are international students. International students from Canada.
Faculty School total: 12. In upper school: 8 men, 3 women; 6 have advanced degrees.
Subjects Offered 20th century history, advanced math, algebra, American Civil War, American history, American literature, anthropology, applied arts, art history, astronomy, biology, calculus, chemistry, composition, computer tools, creative writing, critical thinking, earth science, economics, English, English literature, fine arts, French, geography, geometry, government/civics, health, history, life skills, mathematics, military history, organic chemistry, physical education, physical science, physics, pre-algebra, pre-calculus, research seminar, science, social studies, Spanish, statistics, trigonometry, world history.
Graduation Requirements American history, arts and fine arts (art, music, dance, drama), computer literacy, English, foreign language, mathematics, physical education (includes health), science, social studies (includes history).
Special Academic Programs Accelerated programs; independent study; study at local college for college credit; academic accommodation for the gifted; remedial reading and/or remedial writing; remedial math; programs in English, mathematics, general development for dyslexic students.
College Admission Counseling 38 students graduated in 2008; 32 went to college, including Colby College; Curry College; Earlham College; Hofstra University; Saint Anselm College; Salve Regina University. Other: 3 went to work, 2 entered military service, 1 entered a postgraduate year.
Student Life Upper grades have specified standards of dress, honor system. Discipline rests equally with students and faculty.
Summer Programs Remediation, enrichment, advancement, sports, art/fine arts, computer instruction programs offered; session focuses on enrichment and remediation; held on campus; accepts boys and girls; not open to students from other schools. 80 students usually enrolled. 2009 schedule: June 15 to August 6.
Tuition and Aid 7-day tuition and room/board: $54,961. Tuition installment plan (monthly payment plans). Clark Behavioral Health Loans available.
Admissions Traditional secondary-level entrance grade is 10. For fall 2008, 39 students applied for upper-level admission, 32 were accepted, 32 enrolled. Achievement tests, Individual IQ, Achievement and behavior rating scale, psychoeducational evaluation, Rorschach or Thematic Apperception Test, Wechsler Individual Achievement Test, Wechsler Intelligence Scale for Children III, Wide Range Achievement Test, WISC-R, Woodcock-Johnson or WRAT required. Deadline for receipt of application materials: none. No application fee required. Interview recommended.
Athletics Interscholastic: basketball (boys, girls), cross-country running (b,g), track and field (b,g); intramural: aquatics (b,g), baseball (b,g), basketball (b,g), bicycling (b,g), track and field (b,g); coed interscholastic: golf; coed intramural: alpine skiing, bowling, canoeing/kayaking, cross-country running, figure skating, fishing, fitness, fitness walking, Frisbee, golf, hiking/backpacking, horseback riding, ice skating, jogging, kickball, nordic skiing, outdoor activities, outdoor recreation, paddle tennis, physical fitness, racquetball, rafting, roller blading, roller skating, ropes courses, running, sailing, skiing (cross-country), skiing (downhill), snowboarding, soccer, softball, strength & conditioning, swimming and diving, table tennis, telemark skiing, ultimate Frisbee, volleyball, walking, wallyball, water skiing. 1 PE instructor, 3 coaches.
Computers Computers are regularly used in English, history, life skills classes. Computer resources include Internet access, Internet filtering or blocking technology.
Contact Ms. Connie E. Kimball, Admissions Director. 207-998-4666 Ext. 122. Fax: 207-998-4660. E-mail: info@elanschool.com. Web site: www.elanschool.com.

See Close-Up on page 1092.

ELVES CHILD DEVELOPMENT CENTRE

10825 142nd Street
Edmonton, Alberta T5N 3Y7, Canada
Head of School: Barb Tymchak Olafson

General Information Coeducational boarding and day and distance learning Modified Alberta Education currriculum school; primarily serves underachievers, students with learning disabilities, individuals with Attention Deficit Disorder, individuals with emotional and behavioral problems, The Elves special Needs Society serves individuals ages 2½ to 20. Our students are classified as having severe, and disabilities requiring an individualized program plan. Ungraded, ages 2–20. Distance learning grade X. Founded: 1973. Setting: urban. 3 buildings on campus. Approved or accredited by Association of Independent Schools and Colleges of Alberta. Language of instruction: English. Total enrollment: 123. Upper school average class size: 8. Upper school faculty-student ratio: 1:3.
Upper School Student Profile 100% are province residents. 1 province is represented in upper school student body.
Faculty School total: 15. In upper school: 1 man, 14 women; 2 have advanced degrees.
Graduation Requirements Elves students have severe disabilities can not be assessed by standardized testing. Students graduate to alternative to work day programs.
Special Academic Programs Remedial math; special instructional classes for deaf students, blind students, all students are classified as having severe disabilities, including physical and cognitve delays; ESL (3 students enrolled).
Student Life Discipline rests primarily with faculty.
Admissions Traditional secondary-level entrance age is 14. For fall 2008, 1 student applied for upper-level admission, 1 was accepted. No application fee required. Interview required.
Computers Computer resources include augmentative communication. The school has a published electronic and media policy.
Contact Angela Vardy, Social Worker. 780-454-5310. Fax: 780-454-5310. E-mail: elvessoc@telusplanet.net.

EXCEL ACADEMY, INC.

116 West Church Street
Newark, Ohio 43055

Head of School: Marlene Jacob

General Information Coeducational day college-preparatory, general academic, and technology school; primarily serves underachievers, students with learning disabilities, individuals with Attention Deficit Disorder, individuals with emotional and behavioral problems, dyslexic students, and autism. Grades K–12. Founded: 1991. Setting: urban. 1-acre campus. 1 building on campus. Approved or accredited by Ohio Department of Education. Total enrollment: 150. Upper school average class size: 10. Upper school faculty-student ratio: 1:3.

Faculty School total: 54. In upper school: 5 men, 3 women; 2 have advanced degrees.

Subjects Offered Accounting, algebra, American government, American history, American literature, art, art appreciation, arts, astronomy, biology, biology-AP, business mathematics, calculus-AP, chemistry, chemistry-AP, composition, composition-AP, discrete math, drama, drawing, English, English literature-AP, environmental science, fine arts, French, geometry, health, humanities, journalism, Latin, literature, mathematics, music appreciation, painting, physical education, physics, pre-calculus, psychology, religion, science, social science, social studies, sociology, Spanish, speech, studio art, theology, women's literature, word processing, world history, writing.

Graduation Requirements Arts and fine arts (art, music, dance, drama), English, foreign language, mathematics, physical education (includes health), religion (includes Bible studies and theology), science, social science, social studies (includes history).

Special Academic Programs Study at local college for college credit; remedial reading and/or remedial writing; remedial math; programs in English, mathematics, general development for dyslexic students.

College Admission Counseling 11 students graduated in 2008; 2 went to college. Other: 1 entered military service.

Student Life Upper grades have uniform requirement. Discipline rests primarily with faculty.

Summer Programs Remediation, computer instruction programs offered; held on campus; accepts boys and girls; open to students from other schools. 10 students usually enrolled. 2009 schedule: June 15 to August 14.

Tuition and Aid Tuition installment plan (2-payment plan). IEP with their local school district where the district pays tuition available.

Admissions Deadline for receipt of application materials: none. No application fee required. On-campus interview required.

Athletics Interscholastic: basketball (boys), cheering (g), flag football (b), volleyball (g), wrestling (b). 2 PE instructors.

Computers Computers are regularly used in English, mathematics, science classes. Computer network features include Internet access, wireless campus network, Internet filtering or blocking technology.

Contact Mrs. Jessica Bolen, Director of Pupil Services. 740-323-1102 Ext. 32. Fax: 740-349-5834. E-mail: jbolen@laca.org.

FAIRHILL SCHOOL

16150 Preston Road
Dallas, Texas 75248

Head of School: Ms. Jane Sego

General Information Coeducational day college-preparatory, arts, and technology school; primarily serves students with learning disabilities, individuals with Attention Deficit Disorder, and dyslexic students. Grades 1–12. Founded: 1971. Setting: suburban. 16-acre campus. 2 buildings on campus. Approved or accredited by Southern Association of Colleges and Schools and Texas Department of Education. Endowment: $3 million. Total enrollment: 240. Upper school average class size: 12. Upper school faculty-student ratio: 1:12.

Upper School Student Profile Grade 9: 23 students (14 boys, 9 girls); Grade 10: 25 students (18 boys, 7 girls); Grade 11: 23 students (19 boys, 4 girls); Grade 12: 18 students (12 boys, 6 girls).

Faculty School total: 32. In upper school: 6 men, 10 women; 4 have advanced degrees.

Subjects Offered American history, American literature, art, biology, British literature, chemistry, computer science, economics, English, government, health, journalism, mathematics, music, performing arts, physical education, physical science, physics, psychology, reading, Spanish, speech, study skills, world geography.

Graduation Requirements Arts and fine arts (art, music, dance, drama), computer science, English, mathematics, physical education (includes health), science, social studies (includes history), 60 hours of volunteer service for seniors.

Special Academic Programs Honors section; remedial reading and/or remedial writing; remedial math; programs in English, mathematics, general development for dyslexic students.

College Admission Counseling 24 students graduated in 2008; 22 went to college, including Collin County Community College District; Dallas County Community College District; Southern Methodist University; St. Edward's University; Texas Tech University. Other: 1 went to work, 1 entered military service.

Student Life Upper grades have uniform requirement, student council. Discipline rests primarily with faculty.

Summer Programs Remediation, computer instruction programs offered; session focuses on academics; held on campus; accepts boys and girls; open to students from other schools. 50 students usually enrolled. 2009 schedule: June 1 to June 26. Application deadline: none.

Tuition and Aid Day student tuition: $13,900. Need-based scholarship grants available. In 2008–09, 6% of upper-school students received aid. Total amount of financial aid awarded in 2008–09: $50,000.

Admissions Traditional secondary-level entrance grade is 9. Psychoeducational evaluation required. Deadline for receipt of application materials: none. Application fee required: $100. Interview required.

Athletics Interscholastic: baseball (boys), basketball (b,g), cheering (b,g), golf (b,g), soccer (b,g), tennis (b,g), volleyball (g); intramural: cheering (b,g), jump rope (b,g); coed interscholastic: cheering, golf, soccer, tennis. 3 coaches.

Computers Computers are regularly used in college planning, English, technology, yearbook classes. Computer network features include on-campus library services, Internet access, wireless campus network, Internet filtering or blocking technology. The school has a published electronic and media policy.

Contact Mrs. Melinda Cameron, Head of Upper School. 972-233-1026. Fax: 972-233-8205. E-mail: mcameron@fairhill.org. Web site: www.fairhill.org.

THE FAMILY FOUNDATION SCHOOL

431 Chapel Hill Road
Hancock, New York 13783

Head of School: Mr. Emmanuel A. Argiros

General Information Coeducational boarding college-preparatory, arts, religious studies, and character education school, affiliated with Christian faith, Jewish faith; primarily serves underachievers, individuals with Attention Deficit Disorder, individuals with emotional and behavioral problems, and alcohol and drug abuse. Grades 6–12. Founded: 1987. Setting: rural. Nearest major city is Binghamton. Students are housed in single-sex dormitories. 158-acre campus. 18 buildings on campus. Approved or accredited by Joint Commission on Accreditation of Healthcare Organizations, Middle States Association of Colleges and Schools, and New York State Board of Regents. Total enrollment: 245. Upper school average class size: 12. Upper school faculty-student ratio: 1:8.

Upper School Student Profile Grade 8: 3 students (3 boys); Grade 9: 36 students (20 boys, 16 girls); Grade 10: 57 students (35 boys, 22 girls); Grade 11: 70 students (39 boys, 31 girls); Grade 12: 79 students (54 boys, 25 girls). 100% of students are boarding students. 20% are state residents. 21 states are represented in upper school student body. 3% are international students. International students from Canada, Germany, Panama, Russian Federation, and United Kingdom. 97% of students are Christian, Jewish.

Faculty School total: 44. In upper school: 27 men, 17 women; 14 have advanced degrees; 14 reside on campus.

Subjects Offered Advanced chemistry, algebra, American government, American history, analysis and differential calculus, ancient world history, applied music, art, Bible studies, biology, British literature, character education, chemistry, choir, chorus, college writing, community service, dance, debate, drama, earth science, economics, English, family living, geometry, global studies, government, health and safety, health education, Jewish studies, journalism, modern dance, mythology, photography, physical education, physics, pre-calculus, religious education, Russian, sociology, Spanish, tap dance, trigonometry, woodworking, work-study, world history, yearbook.

Graduation Requirements Character education, English, foreign language, life skills, mathematics, physical education (includes health), science, social studies (includes history), New York State Board of Regents requirements, Completion of character education program.

Special Academic Programs Study at local college for college credit; remedial reading and/or remedial writing.

College Admission Counseling 83 students graduated in 2008; 77 went to college, including George Mason University; Grand Valley State University; Hofstra University; Marywood University; Montclair State University; University of Mary Washington. Other: 6 had other specific plans. Mean SAT critical reading: 519, mean SAT math: 638, mean SAT writing: 520, mean combined SAT: 1660.

Student Life Upper grades have specified standards of dress, student council, honor system. Discipline rests equally with students and faculty. Attendance at religious services is required.

Tuition and Aid 7-day tuition and room/board: $61,920. Tuition installment plan (monthly payment plans). Need-based scholarship grants, paying campus jobs available. In 2008–09, 15% of upper-school students received aid. Total amount of financial aid awarded in 2008–09: $560,000.

Admissions Traditional secondary-level entrance grade is 10. Math Placement Exam required. Deadline for receipt of application materials: none. No application fee required. On-campus interview required.

Athletics Interscholastic: basketball (boys, girls), soccer (b,g), softball (g); intramural: basketball (b,g), lacrosse (b), strength & conditioning (b,g); coed interscholastic: cheering, dance, golf; coed intramural: aerobics/dance, ballet, basketball, fishing, fitness, fitness walking, flag football, fly fishing, Frisbee, hiking/backpacking, horseback riding, horseshoes, ice skating, outdoor activities, outdoors, running, soccer, softball, tennis, ultimate Frisbee, volleyball, weight training. 4 PE instructors, 8 coaches.

Computers Computers are regularly used in English, history, journalism, science, Spanish, yearbook classes. Computer network features include on-campus library services, online commercial services, Internet access, wireless campus network, Internet filtering or blocking technology. Computer access in designated common areas is available to students.
Contact Mr. Jeff Brain, Acting Director of Admissions. 845-887-5213 Ext. 499. Fax: 845-887-4939. E-mail: jbrain@thefamilyschool.com. Web site: www.thefamilyschool.com.

See Close-Up on page 1094.

FOOTHILLS ACADEMY

745 37th Street NW
Calgary, Alberta T2N 4T1, Canada
Head of School: Mr. G. M. Bullivant

General Information Coeducational day technology school; primarily serves underachievers, students with learning disabilities, individuals with Attention Deficit Disorder, and dyslexic students. Grades 1–12. Founded: 1979. Setting: urban. 7-acre campus. 1 building on campus. Approved or accredited by Association of Independent Schools and Colleges of Alberta and Alberta Department of Education. Language of instruction: English. Endowment: CAN$3 million. Total enrollment: 195. Upper school average class size: 12. Upper school faculty-student ratio: 1:12.
Upper School Student Profile Grade 9: 29 students (22 boys, 7 girls); Grade 10: 24 students (17 boys, 7 girls); Grade 11: 27 students (22 boys, 5 girls); Grade 12: 21 students (19 boys, 2 girls).
Faculty School total: 40. In upper school: 10 men, 15 women; 6 have advanced degrees.
Subjects Offered Algebra, animation, art, athletics, basic skills, biology, calculus, career and personal planning, career education, chemistry, college admission preparation, college awareness, college planning, community service, computer animation, computer applications, computer education, computer keyboarding, computer literacy, computer multimedia, computer skills, conflict resolution, consumer mathematics, decision making skills, digital photography, drama, drama performance, dramatic arts, electives, English composition, English literature, environmental studies, expository writing, food and nutrition, grammar, health education, information processing, Internet research, interpersonal skills, keyboarding/computer, language arts, leadership, leadership and service, learning strategies, library research, library skills, mathematics, mechanics of writing, oral communications, painting, personal and social education, photography, physical fitness, poetry, reading, reading/study skills, remedial study skills, research and reference, research skills, science, Shakespeare, short story, social skills, social studies, speech therapy, study skills, technological applications, track and field, writing skills.
Graduation Requirements Athletics, career and personal planning, English, English composition, English literature, expository writing, grammar, keyboarding/computer, language arts, learning strategies, mathematics, mechanics of writing, physical fitness, reading/study skills, research skills, science, social studies (includes history), study skills, Alberta Education Standards.
Special Academic Programs Remedial reading and/or remedial writing; remedial math; programs in English, mathematics for dyslexic students.
College Admission Counseling 20 students graduated in 2008; 14 went to college, including Macalester College; Mount Allison University; The University of Winnipeg; University of Calgary; University of Victoria. Other: 6 went to work.
Student Life Upper grades have specified standards of dress, student council, honor system. Discipline rests primarily with faculty.
Summer Programs Remediation, enrichment programs offered; session focuses on remedial reading, language, organization skills; held on campus; accepts boys and girls; open to students from other schools. 50 students usually enrolled. 2009 schedule: July 6 to August 21. Application deadline: June 30.
Tuition and Aid Day student tuition: CAN$12,220. Guaranteed tuition plan. Tuition installment plan (The Tuition Plan, monthly payment plans, individually arranged payment plans). Bursaries, need-based scholarship grants available. In 2008–09, 60% of upper-school students received aid. Total amount of financial aid awarded in 2008–09: CAN$500,000.
Admissions Traditional secondary-level entrance grade is 9. For fall 2008, 40 students applied for upper-level admission, 14 were accepted, 14 enrolled. Achievement tests, CTBS, Stanford Achievement Test, any other standardized test, math, reading, and mental ability tests, Wechsler Intelligence Scale for Children, Woodcock Language Proficiency Test, WRAT or writing sample required. Deadline for receipt of application materials: June 30. Application fee required: CAN$50. On-campus interview required.
Athletics Interscholastic: badminton (boys, girls), basketball (b,g); intramural: badminton (g), basketball (b,g), football (b); coed interscholastic: cross-country running, golf, indoor track & field, tennis, track and field, volleyball; coed intramural: badminton, ball hockey, baseball, cooperative games, cross-country running, curling, fitness, flag football, floor hockey, gymnastics, handball, in-line skating, indoor soccer, indoor track & field, jogging, kickball, life saving, outdoor activities, outdoor education, physical fitness, physical training, roller blading, running, skiing (downhill), snowboarding, soccer, softball, strength & conditioning, tennis, touch football, track and field, volleyball, walking, weight lifting, weight training, wilderness, wrestling. 1 PE instructor, 10 coaches, 2 athletic trainers.
Computers Computers are regularly used in all academic, animation, basic skills, career education, career exploration, computer applications, creative writing, desktop publishing, keyboarding, library skills, mentorship program, research skills, social studies, Web site design, word processing, writing, yearbook classes. Computer network features include on-campus library services, online commercial services, Internet access, wireless campus network, Internet filtering or blocking technology.
Contact Ms. A. Rose, Student Applications. 403-270-9400. Fax: 403-270-9438. E-mail: arose@foothillsacademy.org. Web site: www.foothillsacademy.org.

THE FORMAN SCHOOL

12 Norfolk Road
PO Box 80
Litchfield, Connecticut 06759
Head of School: Adam K. Man

General Information Coeducational boarding and day college-preparatory, arts, and technology school; primarily serves students with learning disabilities, individuals with Attention Deficit Disorder, and dyslexic students. Grades 9–12. Founded: 1930. Setting: small town. Nearest major city is Hartford. Students are housed in single-sex dormitories. 100-acre campus. 30 buildings on campus. Approved or accredited by New England Association of Schools and Colleges and The Association of Boarding Schools. Member of National Association of Independent Schools and Secondary School Admission Test Board. Endowment: $50 million. Total enrollment: 182. Upper school average class size: 11. Upper school faculty-student ratio: 1:3.
Upper School Student Profile Grade 9: 27 students (21 boys, 6 girls); Grade 10: 49 students (36 boys, 13 girls); Grade 11: 59 students (36 boys, 23 girls); Grade 12: 46 students (25 boys, 21 girls). 87% of students are boarding students. 33% are state residents. 26 states are represented in upper school student body. 13% are international students. International students from Bermuda, Canada, Canada, Dominican Republic, Hong Kong, and Jamaica; 2 other countries represented in student body.
Faculty School total: 65. In upper school: 26 men, 39 women; 33 have advanced degrees; 33 reside on campus.
Subjects Offered Algebra, American history, American literature, art, art history, biology, calculus, ceramics, chemistry, computer science, creative writing, driver education, ecology, English, English literature, environmental science, European history, expository writing, fine arts, French, geography, geometry, grammar, history, history-AP, Holocaust seminar, human development, mathematics, music, photography, physical education, physics, psychology, science, social science, social studies, Spanish, trigonometry, world history, world literature, writing.
Graduation Requirements Arts and fine arts (art, music, dance, drama), English, mathematics, physical education (includes health), science, social science, social studies (includes history).
Special Academic Programs Advanced Placement exam preparation; honors section; programs in English, mathematics, general development for dyslexic students; ESL.
College Admission Counseling 41 students graduated in 2008; all went to college, including Hofstra University; Lynn University; The University of Arizona. Mean SAT critical reading: 439, mean SAT math: 411, mean composite ACT: 22. 1% scored over 600 on SAT critical reading, 1% scored over 600 on SAT math, .5% scored over 26 on composite ACT.
Student Life Upper grades have specified standards of dress, student council, honor system. Discipline rests primarily with faculty.
Tuition and Aid Day student tuition: $43,500; 7-day tuition and room/board: $53,000. Tuition installment plan (The Tuition Plan, Key Tuition Payment Plan, self-funded tuition, refund plan, Key Tuition Payment Plan). Need-based scholarship grants available. In 2008–09, 20% of upper-school students received aid. Total amount of financial aid awarded in 2008–09: $849,000.
Admissions Traditional secondary-level entrance grade is 9. For fall 2008, 254 students applied for upper-level admission, 92 were accepted, 64 enrolled. WISC-III and Woodcock-Johnson required. Deadline for receipt of application materials: none. Application fee required: $50. Interview required.
Athletics Interscholastic: baseball (boys), basketball (b,g), golf (b), ice hockey (b,g), lacrosse (b), soccer (b,g), softball (g), tennis (b,g), volleyball (g), wrestling (b); intramural: blading (g); coed interscholastic: alpine skiing, cross-country running, football, kayaking, skiing (downhill), swimming and diving; coed intramural: bicycling, dance, equestrian sports, golf, horseback riding, kayaking, modern dance, outdoor education, outdoor skills, rock climbing, skateboarding, skiing (cross-country), skiing (downhill), snowboarding, squash, tennis, weight lifting, weight training, yoga. 1 athletic trainer.
Computers Computers are regularly used in English, foreign language, mathematics, music, science, writing classes. Computer network features include Internet access, Internet filtering or blocking technology. Student e-mail accounts are available to students. The school has a published electronic and media policy.
Contact Beth A. Rainey, Director of Admissions. 860-567-1803. Fax: 860-567-3501. E-mail: admissions@formanschool.org. Web site: www.formanschool.org.

See Close-Up on page 1096.

FRANKLIN ACADEMY

106 River Road
East Haddam, Connecticut 06423

Head of School: A. Frederick Weissbach

General Information Coeducational boarding and day college-preparatory school; primarily serves Nonverbal Learning Differences (NLD) and Asperger's Syndrome. Grades 9–PG. Founded: 2000. Setting: rural. Nearest major city is Hartford. Students are housed in single-sex by floor dormitories and single-sex dormitories. 75-acre campus. 18 buildings on campus. Approved or accredited by New England Association of Schools and Colleges and Connecticut Department of Education. Total enrollment: 81. Upper school average class size: 8. Upper school faculty-student ratio: 1:3.

Upper School Student Profile Grade 9: 15 students (9 boys, 6 girls); Grade 10: 15 students (11 boys, 4 girls); Grade 11: 27 students (20 boys, 7 girls); Grade 12: 23 students (16 boys, 7 girls); Postgraduate: 1 student (1 boy). 90% of students are boarding students. 18% are state residents. 22 states are represented in upper school student body. 2% are international students.

Faculty School total: 40. In upper school: 14 men, 20 women; 16 have advanced degrees; 20 reside on campus.

Special Academic Programs Term-away projects; study abroad; academic accommodation for the gifted; remedial math.

College Admission Counseling 20 students graduated in 2008; 17 went to college. Other: 1 went to work, 1 entered military service, 1 entered a postgraduate year. 28% scored over 600 on SAT critical reading, 17% scored over 600 on SAT math, 22% scored over 600 on SAT writing, 22% scored over 1800 on combined SAT.

Student Life Upper grades have student council, honor system. Discipline rests equally with students and faculty.

Summer Programs Enrichment programs offered; session focuses on social skills, special interest areas; held on campus; accepts boys and girls; open to students from other schools. 60 students usually enrolled. 2009 schedule: July 1 to July 29. Application deadline: May 15.

Tuition and Aid Day student tuition: $56,500; 7-day tuition and room/board: $69,800. Tuition installment plan (monthly payment plans, individually arranged payment plans).

Admissions Traditional secondary-level entrance grade is 9. Achievement tests, psychoeducational evaluation, Wechsler Intelligence Scale for Children and writing sample required. Deadline for receipt of application materials: none. Application fee required: $75. On-campus interview required.

Athletics Coed Intramural: aerobics/dance, aquatics, basketball, bicycling, bowling, canoeing/kayaking, climbing, cooperative games, dance, fishing, fitness, fitness walking, Frisbee, golf, horseback riding, kayaking, martial arts, mountain biking, paint ball, physical fitness, physical training, scuba diving, soccer, softball, swimming and diving, tai chi, tennis, ultimate Frisbee, walking, yoga.

Computers Computers are regularly used in all classes. Computer network features include on-campus library services, Internet access, wireless campus network, Internet filtering or blocking technology. Campus intranet, student e-mail accounts, and computer access in designated common areas are available to students.

Contact Cynthia L. Pope, Director of Admissions. 860-873-2700. Fax: 860-873-9345. E-mail: cindy@fa-ct.org. Web site: www.fa-ct.org.

FRASER ACADEMY

2294 West 10th Avenue
Vancouver, British Columbia V6K 2H8, Canada

Head of School: Mrs. Maureen Steltman

General Information Coeducational day college-preparatory, general academic, arts, technology, and BC Ministry of Education curriculum school; primarily serves students with learning disabilities and dyslexic students. Grades 1–12. Founded: 1982. Setting: urban. 1 building on campus. Approved or accredited by Canadian Association of Independent Schools and British Columbia Department of Education. Language of instruction: English. Total enrollment: 199. Upper school average class size: 8. Upper school faculty-student ratio: 1:3.

Upper School Student Profile Grade 6: 17 students (11 boys, 6 girls); Grade 7: 27 students (20 boys, 7 girls); Grade 8: 17 students (12 boys, 5 girls); Grade 9: 30 students (17 boys, 13 girls); Grade 10: 25 students (17 boys, 8 girls); Grade 11: 28 students (20 boys, 8 girls); Grade 12: 19 students (16 boys, 3 girls).

Faculty School total: 70. In upper school: 6 have advanced degrees.

Graduation Requirements British Columbia Ministry of Education requirements.

Special Academic Programs Programs in English, mathematics, general development for dyslexic students; special instructional classes for Orton Gillingham Tutoring program.

College Admission Counseling 19 students graduated in 2008. Other: 3 had other specific plans.

Student Life Upper grades have uniform requirement, honor system. Discipline rests primarily with faculty.

Tuition and Aid Day student tuition: CAN$22,145. Tuition installment plan (quarterly payment plan). Tuition reduction for siblings, bursaries available.

Admissions Traditional secondary-level entrance grade is 8. For fall 2008, 25 students applied for upper-level admission, 21 were accepted, 21 enrolled. Academic Profile Tests required. Deadline for receipt of application materials: none. Application fee required: CAN$250. Interview required.

Athletics Interscholastic: volleyball (girls); intramural: volleyball (g); coed interscholastic: alpine skiing, basketball, canoeing/kayaking, cross-country running, field hockey, flag football, kickball, martial arts, outdoor activities, outdoor education, physical fitness, running, skiing (downhill), snowboarding, soccer, softball, track and field; coed intramural: alpine skiing, ball hockey, basketball, bicycling, climbing, cross-country running, martial arts, mountain biking, rock climbing, running, scuba diving, skiing (downhill), snowboarding, soccer, softball, track and field, wall climbing. 1 PE instructor.

Computers Computers are regularly used in all academic classes. Computer network features include Internet access, Internet filtering or blocking technology, various learning disabilities/dyslexic-specific software.

Contact Ms. Brooke Ellison, Executive Assistant and Admissions Coordinator. 604-736-5575 Ext. 222. Fax: 604-736-5578. E-mail: bellison@fraseracademy.ca. Web site: www.fraser-academy.bc.ca.

THE FROSTIG SCHOOL

971 North Altadena Drive
Pasadena, California 91107

Head of School: Ms. Tobey Shaw

General Information Coeducational day arts, vocational, and technology school; primarily serves underachievers, students with learning disabilities, individuals with Attention Deficit Disorder, and dyslexic students. Grades 1–12. Founded: 1951. Setting: suburban. Nearest major city is Los Angeles. 2-acre campus. 1 building on campus. Approved or accredited by National Association of Private Schools for Exceptional Children, Western Association of Schools and Colleges, and California Department of Education. Endowment: $3 million. Total enrollment: 120. Upper school average class size: 12. Upper school faculty-student ratio: 1:6.

Faculty School total: 25. In upper school: 3 men, 4 women; 4 have advanced degrees.

Special Academic Programs Remedial reading and/or remedial writing; remedial math; programs in English, mathematics, general development for dyslexic students.

College Admission Counseling 9 students graduated in 2008; 6 went to college, including Glendale Community College; Moorpark College; Pasadena City College; Santa Monica College. Other: 1 went to work, 2 had other specific plans.

Student Life Upper grades have specified standards of dress, student council. Discipline rests primarily with faculty.

Summer Programs Remediation programs offered; session focuses on maintaining skills obtained during the regular term, work experience for high school students; held on campus; accepts boys and girls; not open to students from other schools. 36 students usually enrolled. 2009 schedule: July 6 to August 14.

Tuition and Aid Day student tuition: $25,000. Tuition installment plan (monthly payment plans, individually arranged payment plans). Need-based scholarship grants available. Total amount of financial aid awarded in 2008–09: $50,000.

Admissions Traditional secondary-level entrance grade is 9. For fall 2008, 2 students applied for upper-level admission, 2 were accepted, 2 enrolled. Admissions testing required. Deadline for receipt of application materials: none. Application fee required: $100. On-campus interview required.

Athletics Coed Interscholastic: basketball, flag football, softball, touch football. 1 PE instructor, 2 coaches.

Computers Computers are regularly used in art, basic skills, career education, career exploration, college planning, computer applications, creative writing, current events, English, geography, health, history, keyboarding, lab/keyboard, library, library skills, life skills, mathematics, media, music, occupational education, photography, psychology, reading, remedial study skills, research skills, science, social sciences, social studies, study skills, technology, video film production, Web site design, word processing, writing, writing fundamentals, yearbook classes. Computer network features include on-campus library services, Internet access, assistive technology services.

Contact Ms. Joan Ferry-Scott, Admissions Coordinator. 626-791-1255. Fax: 626-798-1801. E-mail: admissions@frostig.org. Web site: www.frostig.org.

GABLES ACADEMY

811 Gordon Street
Stone Mountain, Georgia 30083

Head of School: Dr. James D. Meffen III

General Information Coeducational boarding and day college-preparatory, general academic, arts, vocational, bilingual studies, and technology school; primarily serves underachievers, students with learning disabilities, individuals with Attention Deficit Disorder, dyslexic students, Students with Tourette's Syndrome, Asperger's Syndrome, MTBI, High Functioning Autism, and Bi-Polar Disorder. Boarding grades 7–12, day grades 4–12. Founded: 1961. Setting: small town. Nearest major city is Atlanta. Students are housed in single-sex dormitories. 7-acre campus. 5 buildings on campus. Approved or accredited by National Association of Private Schools for Exceptional Children and Georgia Department of Education. Total enrollment: 12. Upper school average class size: 6. Upper school faculty-student ratio: 1:6.

Upper School Student Profile Grade 6: 1 student (1 boy); Grade 7: 1 student (1 boy); Grade 8: 1 student (1 boy); Grade 9: 3 students (3 boys); Grade 10: 3 students (2 boys,

1 girl); Grade 11: 2 students (1 boy, 1 girl); Grade 12: 1 student (1 boy). 10% of students are boarding students. 90% are state residents. 3 states are represented in upper school student body.

Faculty School total: 5. In upper school: 3 men, 2 women; 3 reside on campus.

Subjects Offered Acting, adolescent issues, algebra, American history, American literature, anatomy, art, arts, basic skills, biology, calculus, career and personal planning, ceramics, chemistry, choir, community service, computer applications, computer keyboarding, computer science, computer skills, CPR, creative arts, creative writing, drama performance, dramatic arts, ecology, English, English literature, fine arts, geometry, history, home economics, horticulture, instrumental music, journalism, mathematics, newspaper, personal development, photography, physical education, playwriting, science, social science, social studies, Spanish, typing, world history, writing, yearbook.

Graduation Requirements 1½ elective credits, arts and fine arts (art, music, dance, drama), English, foreign language, mathematics, physical education (includes health), science, social studies (includes history), world history. Community service is required.

Special Academic Programs Accelerated programs; independent study; study at local college for college credit; academic accommodation for the gifted; remedial reading and/or remedial writing; remedial math; programs in English, mathematics, general development for dyslexic students; special instructional classes for deaf students, blind students; ESL.

College Admission Counseling 3 students graduated in 2008; all went to college, including Georgia Perimeter College; Georgia State University.

Student Life Upper grades have uniform requirement, student council. Discipline rests equally with students and faculty.

Summer Programs Remediation, enrichment, advancement, ESL, sports, art/fine arts, computer instruction programs offered; session focuses on remediation and credit recovery; held both on and off campus; held at various locations chosen for experiential education programs designed specifically for each summer; accepts boys and girls; open to students from other schools. 25 students usually enrolled. 2009 schedule: June 8 to July 17. Application deadline: May 18.

Tuition and Aid Day student tuition: $17,500; 7-day tuition and room/board: $46,900. Tuition installment plan (Key Tuition Payment Plan, individually arranged payment plans). Tuition reduction for siblings available.

Admissions Traditional secondary-level entrance grade is 9. For fall 2008, 12 students applied for upper-level admission, 5 were accepted, 5 enrolled. Comprehensive educational evaluation or psychoeducational evaluation required. Deadline for receipt of application materials: none. Application fee required: $100. On-campus interview required.

Athletics Interscholastic: baseball (boys), basketball (b), cheering (g), cross-country running (b,g), football (b), gatorball (b), independent competitive sports (b,g), physical fitness (b,g), physical training (b,g), soccer (b,g), softball (b,g), strength & conditioning (b,g), touch football (b,g), track and field (b,g), volleyball (b,g), yoga (b,g); intramural: flag football (b), gatorball (b), skateboarding (b), weight lifting (b); coed interscholastic: basketball, cross-country running, kickball, martial arts, soccer, softball, strength & conditioning, tennis, touch football, track and field, volleyball, yoga; coed intramural: backpacking, badminton, bowling, canoeing/kayaking, climbing, cooperative games, fishing, fitness, Frisbee, hiking/backpacking, jump rope, outdoor activities, physical fitness, rafting, rappelling, rock climbing, roller skating, ropes courses, running, skiing (downhill), snowboarding, softball, strength & conditioning, swimming and diving, table tennis, ultimate Frisbee, volleyball. 1 PE instructor, 1 coach.

Computers Computers are regularly used in all academic, yearbook classes. Computer network features include online commercial services, Internet access, wireless campus network, Internet filtering or blocking technology. Computer access in designated common areas is available to students.

Contact Ms. Katrina Locklear, Administrative Assistant. 770-465-7500 Ext. 10. Fax: 770-465-7700. E-mail: admin@gablesacademy.com. Web site: www.gablesacademy.com.

See Close-Up on page 1098.

GATEWAY SCHOOL

2570 NW Green Oaks Boulevard
Arlington, Texas 76012

Head of School: Mrs. Harriet R. Walber

General Information Coeducational day college-preparatory, general academic, arts, and technology school; primarily serves underachievers, students with learning disabilities, individuals with Attention Deficit Disorder, and dyslexic students. Grades 5–12. Founded: 1980. Setting: urban. 7-acre campus. 1 building on campus. Approved or accredited by Southern Association of Colleges and Schools, Southern Association of Independent Schools, Texas Education Agency, and Texas Department of Education. Total enrollment: 34. Upper school average class size: 10. Upper school faculty-student ratio: 1:8.

Upper School Student Profile Grade 9: 8 students (6 boys, 2 girls); Grade 10: 5 students (4 boys, 1 girl); Grade 11: 8 students (7 boys, 1 girl); Grade 12: 3 students (3 boys).

Faculty School total: 6. In upper school: 1 man, 5 women; 5 have advanced degrees.

Subjects Offered Algebra, American literature, art, biology, British literature, career planning, chemistry, college awareness, college counseling, community service, composition, computer education, computer keyboarding, computer literacy, computer science, computer skills, developmental math, drama, earth science, economics, English, English composition, English literature, environmental science, geometry, government, government/civics, grammar, health, health education, history, intro to computers, introduction to theater, journalism, language arts, literature, mathematics, music, music performance, music theater, newspaper, physical education, pre-algebra, reading, reading/study skills, science, social studies, Spanish, speech, state history, theater, U.S. government, U.S. history, word processing, world history, world literature, writing, writing workshop, yearbook.

Graduation Requirements Computer science, English, mathematics, physical education (includes health), science, social studies (includes history), Spanish. Community service is required.

Special Academic Programs Independent study; study at local college for college credit; remedial reading and/or remedial writing; remedial math; programs in English, mathematics, general development for dyslexic students.

College Admission Counseling 2 students graduated in 2008; all went to college, including Lon Morris College; Texas Wesleyan University.

Student Life Upper grades have uniform requirement, student council. Discipline rests primarily with faculty.

Tuition and Aid Day student tuition: $10,800. Guaranteed tuition plan. Merit scholarship grants, need-based scholarship grants available. In 2008–09, 15% of upper-school students received aid.

Admissions Traditional secondary-level entrance grade is 9. School's own test, Wechsler Intelligence Scale for Children and Woodcock-Johnson required. Deadline for receipt of application materials: none. Application fee required: $150. On-campus interview required.

Athletics Interscholastic: basketball (boys, girls), golf (g); intramural: basketball (b,g), bowling (b,g), golf (b,g), jogging (b,g); coed interscholastic: fitness walking, golf, jogging, scuba diving, tennis, triathlon; coed intramural: bowling. 1 PE instructor, 1 coach.

Computers Computers are regularly used in basic skills, English, mathematics, science classes. Computer network features include Internet access.

Contact Harriet R. Walber, Executive Director. 817-226-6222. Fax: 817-226-6225. E-mail: walberhr@aol.com. Web site: www.gatewayschool.com.

GLEN EDEN SCHOOL

8665 Barnard Street
Vancouver, British Columbia V6P 5G6, Canada

Head of School: Dr. Rick Brennan

General Information Coeducational day school; primarily serves underachievers, students with learning disabilities, individuals with Attention Deficit Disorder, individuals with emotional and behavioral problems, and Autism Spectrum Disorders. Grades K–12. Founded: 1976. Setting: urban. 1 building on campus. Approved or accredited by British Columbia Department of Education. Language of instruction: English. Upper school average class size: 4. Upper school faculty-student ratio: 1:5.

Faculty School total: 7. In upper school: 3 men, 1 woman; 2 have advanced degrees.

Special Academic Programs Remedial reading and/or remedial writing; remedial math.

Summer Programs Remediation programs offered; session focuses on outreach/group dynamics; held on campus; accepts boys and girls; not open to students from other schools. 20 students usually enrolled. 2009 schedule: July 1 to August 31. Application deadline: June 1.

Tuition and Aid Bursaries available. In 2008–09, 5% of upper-school students received aid. Total amount of financial aid awarded in 2008–09: CAN$30,000.

Admissions Deadline for receipt of application materials: none. Application fee required. Interview required.

Computers Computers are regularly used in journalism classes. Computer resources include Internet access.

Contact Dr. Rick Brennan, Director. 604-267-0394. Fax: 604-267-0544. E-mail: glenedenschool@gleneden.org.

THE GLENHOLME SCHOOL

81 Sabbaday Lane
Washington, Connecticut 06793

Head of School: Maryann Campbell

General Information Coeducational boarding and day and distance learning college-preparatory, arts, vocational, technology, social skills, and study skills school; primarily serves underachievers, students with learning disabilities, individuals with Attention Deficit Disorder, individuals with emotional and behavioral problems, Asperger's Syndrome, school anxieties, and social skills training, problem solving/critical thinking skills. Grades 5–12. Distance learning grades 11–PG. Founded: 1968. Setting: rural. Nearest major city is Hartford. Students are housed in single-sex dormitories. 105-acre campus. 30 buildings on campus. Approved or accredited by Connecticut Association of Independent Schools, Connecticut Department of Children and Families, Council of Accreditation and School Improvement, Massachusetts Department of Education, National Association of Private Schools for Exceptional

Children, New England Association of Schools and Colleges, New Jersey Department of Education, New York Department of Education, US Department of State, and Connecticut Department of Education. Member of National Association of Independent Schools. Endowment: $50,000. Total enrollment: 105. Upper school average class size: 12. Upper school faculty-student ratio: 1:12.

Upper School Student Profile 95% of students are boarding students. 10% are state residents. 12 states are represented in upper school student body. 8% are international students. International students from Bermuda, Canada, Hong Kong, Mexico, Panama, and Switzerland; 1 other country represented in student body.

Faculty School total: 25. In upper school: 6 men, 19 women; 20 have advanced degrees.

Subjects Offered ADL skills, adolescent issues, aerobics, algebra, art, basketball, biology, career and personal planning, career education, career exploration, career/college preparation, character education, chemistry, choral music, chorus, college admission preparation, college planning, communication skills, community service, computer animation, computer applications, computer art, computer education, computer graphics, computer keyboarding, computer literacy, computer skills, creative arts, creative dance, creative drama, creative thinking, creative writing, culinary arts, dance, decision making skills, digital photography, drama, drama performance, earth science, English, equine management, ESL, fine arts, geometry, graphic arts, guidance, health, health and wellness, health education, Internet research, interpersonal skills, library, life skills, mathematics, media arts, moral and social development, music, participation in sports, performing arts, personal fitness, photography, physical education, piano, play production, radio broadcasting, SAT preparation, science, social science, Spanish, theater, U.S. history, video and animation, world history, writing, yearbook.

Special Academic Programs Academic accommodation for the gifted; remedial reading and/or remedial writing; remedial math; programs in English, mathematics, general development for dyslexic students; ESL (3 students enrolled).

College Admission Counseling 16 students graduated in 2008; 14 went to college, including American University; Mitchell College; University of Colorado at Boulder; University of Hartford; Westchester Community College; Western Connecticut State University. Other: 1 entered a postgraduate year, 1 had other specific plans.

Student Life Upper grades have uniform requirement, student council, honor system. Discipline rests primarily with faculty.

Summer Programs Remediation, enrichment, ESL, sports, art/fine arts, computer instruction programs offered; session focuses on social development and education; held on campus; accepts boys and girls; open to students from other schools. 95 students usually enrolled. 2009 schedule: July 7 to August 23. Application deadline: May.

Tuition and Aid Tuition installment plan (Key Tuition Payment Plan). Local and state board of education funding available.

Admissions For fall 2008, 250 students applied for upper-level admission, 55 were accepted, 45 enrolled. Individual IQ, Achievement and behavior rating scale or psychoeducational evaluation required. Deadline for receipt of application materials: none. Application fee required: $150. On-campus interview required.

Athletics Interscholastic: basketball (boys, girls), softball (b,g), volleyball (g); intramural: aquatics (b,g), baseball (b,g), basketball (b,g), cheering (g), fishing (b,g), floor hockey (b,g), hiking/backpacking (b,g), skiing (cross-country) (b,g), skiing (downhill) (b,g), snowboarding (b,g), snowshoeing (b,g), softball (b,g), swimming and diving (b,g), tennis (b,g), ultimate Frisbee (b,g), volleyball (g), weight training (b,g); coed interscholastic: soccer; coed intramural: aerobics, aerobics/Nautilus, artistic gym, cooperative games, dance, dressage, equestrian sports, fitness, fitness walking, flag football, Frisbee, golf, horseback riding, ice skating, jogging, kickball, modern dance, Newcombe ball, outdoor activities, outdoor recreation, paddle tennis, physical fitness, physical training, roller blading, ropes courses, skiing (cross-country), skiing (downhill), snowboarding, soccer, softball, strength & conditioning, tennis, ultimate Frisbee, volleyball, walking, wall climbing, weight training. 1 PE instructor, 2 coaches, 1 athletic trainer.

Computers Computers are regularly used in all academic classes. Computer network features include on-campus library services, Internet access, wireless campus network, Internet filtering or blocking technology, distance learning, Web CAM parent communications. Campus intranet, student e-mail accounts, and computer access in designated common areas are available to students. Students grades are available online. The school has a published electronic and media policy.

Contact Stephanie Skrok, Admissions Associate. 860-868-7377 Ext. 285. Fax: 860-868-7413. E-mail: sskrok@devereux.org. Web site: www.theglenholmeschool.org.

ANNOUNCEMENT FROM THE SCHOOL The Glenholme School, a Devereux Center, is an exceptional learning environment and boarding school for young people with special needs. Set on over 100 acres in Washington, Connecticut, Glenholme is ideal for students, ages 11–21, with varying levels of academic, social, and emotional development, as the School's philosophy is that the development of the whole student contributes to academic success. The Glenhome program, which utilizes the Glenholme Motivational Management Approach, is built on the use of positive behavior supports, individualized instruction, stimulating classes, and a curriculum that emphasizes character development and applying creative approaches to problem solving to engage the student and foster self development. Glenholme's academic program emphasizes a low student-teacher ratio and a full curriculum including sports, fine arts, and extracurricular activities such as the equestrian program and culinary arts, as well as a college preparatory syllabus. Glenholme's year-round design prepares students for continued education in traditional learning environments, such as day schools and boarding schools, as well as higher learning opportunities in colleges and universities. As a center of the Devereux Foundation, The Glenholme School has been in existence since 1968 and has a rich legacy of education, care, and commitment to young people with special needs.

THE GOW SCHOOL

PO Box 85
South Wales, New York 14139-9778

Head of School: Mr. M. Bradley Rogers Jr.

General Information Boys' boarding college-preparatory, arts, technology, and reconstructive language school; primarily serves students with learning disabilities, individuals with Attention Deficit Disorder, dyslexic students, and language-based learning disabilities. Grades 7–PG. Founded: 1926. Setting: rural. Nearest major city is Buffalo. Students are housed in single-sex dormitories. 100-acre campus. 22 buildings on campus. Approved or accredited by New York State Association of Independent Schools, New York State Board of Regents, and The Association of Boarding Schools. Member of National Association of Independent Schools. Endowment: $8 million. Total enrollment: 142. Upper school average class size: 5. Upper school faculty-student ratio: 1:4.

Upper School Student Profile Grade 7: 6 students (6 boys); Grade 8: 12 students (12 boys); Grade 9: 29 students (29 boys); Grade 10: 35 students (35 boys); Grade 11: 37 students (37 boys); Grade 12: 23 students (23 boys). 100% of students are boarding students. 20% are state residents. 28 states are represented in upper school student body. 14% are international students. International students from Bermuda, Canada, Cayman Islands, Hong Kong, Japan, and Oman; 14 other countries represented in student body.

Faculty School total: 35. In upper school: 27 men, 7 women; 27 have advanced degrees; 29 reside on campus.

Subjects Offered Algebra, American history, American literature, art, biology, business, business applications, business skills, calculus, ceramics, chemistry, computer applications, computer keyboarding, computer literacy, computer programming, computer science, drama, earth science, economics, English, English literature, European history, expository writing, fine arts, geology, geometry, grammar, health, journalism, mathematics, metalworking, music, physics, reading, reconstructive language, robotics, science, social studies, theater, trigonometry, typing, world history, yearbook.

Graduation Requirements Arts and fine arts (art, music, dance, drama), business skills (includes word processing), English, mathematics, reconstructive language, research seminar, robotics, science, senior humanities, senior seminar, social studies (includes history). Community service is required.

Special Academic Programs Independent study; study at local college for college credit; academic accommodation for the musically talented; remedial reading and/or remedial writing; remedial math; programs in English, mathematics, general development for dyslexic students.

College Admission Counseling 23 students graduated in 2008; all went to college, including Lynn University; Savannah College of Art and Design; St. Lawrence University. Median SAT critical reading: 410, median SAT math: 460, median SAT writing: 400, median combined SAT: 1230, median composite ACT: 21. 5% scored over 600 on SAT critical reading, 19% scored over 600 on SAT math.

Student Life Upper grades have specified standards of dress, student council. Discipline rests primarily with faculty.

Summer Programs Remediation, enrichment, advancement, sports, art/fine arts, rigorous outdoor training, computer instruction programs offered; session focuses on remediation and course work; held both on and off campus; held at camping sites and city venues; accepts boys and girls; open to students from other schools. 100 students usually enrolled. 2009 schedule: June 28 to July 31. Application deadline: none.

Tuition and Aid 7-day tuition and room/board: $51,625. Tuition installment plan (FACTS Tuition Payment Plan, monthly payment plans, individually arranged payment plans). Need-based scholarship grants available. In 2008–09, 37% of upper-school students received aid. Total amount of financial aid awarded in 2008–09: $550,000.

Admissions Traditional secondary-level entrance grade is 9. For fall 2008, 46 students applied for upper-level admission, 37 were accepted, 32 enrolled. Cognitive Abilities Test, Wechsler Intelligence Scale for Children, Woodcock-Johnson or Woodcock-Johnson Revised Achievement Test required. Deadline for receipt of application materials: none. Application fee required: $100. On-campus interview required.

Athletics Interscholastic: basketball, crew, cross-country running, lacrosse, rowing, soccer, squash, swimming and diving, tennis, wrestling; intramural: alpine skiing, aquatics, backpacking, badminton, basketball, bicycling, bowling, climbing, cross-country running, fitness, fitness walking, flag football, floor hockey, freestyle skiing, Frisbee, golf, handball, hiking/backpacking, ice hockey, in-line skating, indoor soccer, jogging, jump rope, lacrosse, martial arts, mountain biking, Nautilus, nordic skiing, outdoor education, paint ball, physical fitness, physical training, power lifting, racquetball, rappelling, riflery, rock climbing, roller blading, roller hockey, ropes courses, skateboarding, skiing (cross-country), skiing (downhill), snowboarding, soccer, softball, squash, street hockey, strength & conditioning, swimming and diving, tennis, touch football, volleyball, walking, wall climbing, weight lifting, weight training, whiffle ball. 25 coaches.

Computers Computers are regularly used in all classes. Computer network features include on-campus library services, online commercial services, Internet access, Internet filtering or blocking technology, scanners, digital photography, voice recognition. Student e-mail accounts are available to students. The school has a published electronic and media policy.

Contact Mr. Robert Garcia, Director of Admission. 716-652-3450. Fax: 716-687-2003. E-mail: admissions@gow.org. Web site: www.gow.org.

See Close-Up on page 1100.

GROVE SCHOOL

175 Copse Road
PO Box 646
Madison, Connecticut 06443

Head of School: Mr. Richard L. Chorney

General Information Coeducational boarding and day college-preparatory, general academic, arts, technology, Drama, and Music school; primarily serves students with learning disabilities, individuals with Attention Deficit Disorder, dyslexic students, depression, ADHD, Bipolar Disorder, Tourette's Syndrome, PTSD, and Asperger's Syndrome, Executive Functioning Disorder, Obsessive-Compulsive Disorder, and other neuropsychiatric disorders. Grades 7–PG. Founded: 1934. Setting: small town. Nearest major city is New Haven. Students are housed in single-sex dormitories. 92-acre campus. 18 buildings on campus. Approved or accredited by Connecticut Department of Children and Families and Connecticut Department of Education. Total enrollment: 99. Upper school average class size: 6. Upper school faculty-student ratio: 1:3.

Upper School Student Profile Grade 9: 15 students (11 boys, 4 girls); Grade 10: 17 students (9 boys, 8 girls); Grade 11: 23 students (10 boys, 13 girls); Grade 12: 33 students (19 boys, 14 girls); Postgraduate: 6 students (5 boys, 1 girl). 100% of students are boarding students. 19% are state residents. 16 states are represented in upper school student body. 7% are international students. International students from Bermuda, France, and Mozambique; 3 other countries represented in student body.

Faculty School total: 34. In upper school: 15 men, 18 women; 15 have advanced degrees; 24 reside on campus.

Subjects Offered ADL skills, algebra, American literature, art, biology, calculus, chemistry, computer science, creative writing, earth science, English, English literature, fine arts, geometry, health, history, marine biology, mathematics, music, physical education, psychology, science, social science, social studies, Spanish, world history, world literature, writing.

Graduation Requirements Algebra, arts and fine arts (art, music, dance, drama), biology, electives, English, English literature, mathematics, physical education (includes health), science, social science, social studies (includes history).

Special Academic Programs Independent study; academic accommodation for the gifted and the artistically talented; remedial reading and/or remedial writing; remedial math; programs in English, mathematics, general development for dyslexic students; special instructional classes for deaf students, blind students.

College Admission Counseling 28 students graduated in 2008; 25 went to college, including Curry College; Mitchell College; New England College; Ohio Wesleyan University; University of Connecticut; Virginia Commonwealth University. Other: 2 went to work, 1 entered a postgraduate year. 28% scored over 600 on SAT critical reading, 28% scored over 600 on SAT math, 22% scored over 600 on SAT writing, 17% scored over 1800 on combined SAT.

Student Life Upper grades have specified standards of dress, student council, honor system. Discipline rests primarily with faculty.

Summer Programs Remediation, enrichment, advancement, sports, art/fine arts, rigorous outdoor training, computer instruction programs offered; session focuses on academic courses for enhancement and obtaining necessary credits; held both on and off campus; held at U.S. Virgin Islands and other countries; accepts boys and girls; not open to students from other schools. 99 students usually enrolled. 2009 schedule: July 8 to August 15. Application deadline: none.

Tuition and Aid Day student tuition: $72,500; 7-day tuition and room/board: $93,600. Tuition installment plan (monthly payment plans).

Admissions Battery of testing done through outside agency, WISC or WAIS or WRAT required. Deadline for receipt of application materials: none. Application fee required: $200. On-campus interview required.

Athletics Intramural: aquatics (boys, girls), backpacking (b,g), ballet (g), modern dance (g), swimming and diving (b,g); coed interscholastic: baseball, basketball, ice hockey, soccer, tennis; coed intramural: aquatics, backpacking, badminton, baseball, basketball, bicycling, blading, bowling, canoeing/kayaking, cross-country running, dance, equestrian sports, fishing, fitness, fitness walking, floor hockey, freestyle skiing, golf, gymnastics, hiking/backpacking, horseback riding, ice hockey, ice skating, kayaking, martial arts, mountain biking, mountaineering, Nautilus, outdoor activities, physical fitness, physical training, rafting, rock climbing, roller skating, ropes courses, sailing, skiing (downhill), snowboarding, soccer, strength & conditioning, swimming and diving, table tennis, tai chi, tennis, ultimate Frisbee, walking, wall climbing, weight lifting, weight training. 2 PE instructors, 3 coaches.

Computers Computers are regularly used in computer applications, independent study, journalism, media arts, SAT preparation classes. Computer resources include Internet access, Internet filtering or blocking technology, Naviance Program. The school has a published electronic and media policy.

Contact Mr. Peter J. Chorney, Executive Director. 203-245-2778. Fax: 203-245-6098. E-mail: peter@groveschool.org. Web site: www.groveschool.org.

ANNOUNCEMENT FROM THE SCHOOL Grove School has opened two off-campus Transition Houses for 8 of its postgraduate young men and women who are currently attending local colleges and/or working part-time. This program is designed to give them increased independence while still maintaining the benefits of our campus on an as-needed basis. Students work on heightened self-management and social skills, as well as increasing their competencies in the activities of daily living. The Houses opened in February and August of 2008.

See Close-Up on page 1102.

GUILFORD DAY SCHOOL

3310 Horse Pen Creek Road
Greensboro, North Carolina 27410

Head of School: Mrs. Laura Mlatac

General Information Coeducational day college-preparatory, arts, and technology school; primarily serves students with learning disabilities, individuals with Attention Deficit Disorder, and dyslexic students. Grades 1–12. Founded: 1987. Setting: suburban. Nearest major city is Greensboro/Winston-Salem. 40-acre campus. 3 buildings on campus. Approved or accredited by Southern Association of Colleges and Schools, Southern Association of Independent Schools, and North Carolina Department of Education. Endowment: $1 million. Total enrollment: 136. Upper school average class size: 8. Upper school faculty-student ratio: 1:8.

Upper School Student Profile Grade 9: 17 students (11 boys, 6 girls); Grade 10: 11 students (10 boys, 1 girl); Grade 11: 10 students (7 boys, 3 girls); Grade 12: 17 students (13 boys, 4 girls).

Faculty School total: 30. In upper school: 3 men, 6 women; 5 have advanced degrees.

Subjects Offered Algebra, American history, art, basic skills, biology, career and personal planning, career exploration, chemistry, civics, college counseling, drama, earth science, economics, English, environmental science, geometry, health, journalism, life management skills, political systems, pre-algebra, pre-calculus, reading, reading/study skills, Spanish, world history, world history-AP, yearbook.

Graduation Requirements Algebra, American history, biology, earth science, economics, English, environmental science, geometry, physical education (includes health), Spanish, world history, 8th Grade End-of-Grade Test, 20th percentile score on Standardized Reading Test, North Carolina Computer Competency Test.

Special Academic Programs Study at local college for college credit; remedial reading and/or remedial writing; remedial math; programs in English, mathematics, general development for dyslexic students.

College Admission Counseling 11 students graduated in 2008; all went to college, including Brevard College; Elon University; Guilford College; Peace College; St. Andrews Presbyterian College; The University of North Carolina at Greensboro. Median SAT critical reading: 510, median SAT math: 420, median SAT writing: 480. Mean combined SAT: 1458. 12% scored over 600 on SAT critical reading, 12% scored over 600 on SAT math, 12% scored over 600 on SAT writing.

Student Life Upper grades have student council, honor system. Discipline rests primarily with faculty.

Summer Programs Remediation, advancement, computer instruction programs offered; session focuses on Courses for credit; held on campus; accepts boys and girls; open to students from other schools. 25 students usually enrolled. 2009 schedule: June 18 to August 3. Application deadline: June 4.

Tuition and Aid Day student tuition: $15,007. Tuition installment plan (Insured Tuition Payment Plan, monthly payment plans, individually arranged payment plans). Need-based scholarship grants available. In 2008–09, 12% of upper-school students received aid. Total amount of financial aid awarded in 2008–09: $31,800.

Admissions Traditional secondary-level entrance grade is 9. For fall 2008, 9 students applied for upper-level admission, 8 were accepted, 8 enrolled. WISC/Woodcock-Johnson required. Deadline for receipt of application materials: none. Application fee required: $75. On-campus interview required.

Athletics Interscholastic: cheering (girls); coed interscholastic: basketball, cross-country running, flag football, golf, soccer, tennis, volleyball; coed intramural: tennis. 1 PE instructor, 7 coaches.

Computers Computers are regularly used in all classes. Computer network features include on-campus library services, Internet access, Internet filtering or blocking technology. The school has a published electronic and media policy.

Contact Ms. Tim Montgomery, Assistant Head and Director of Admissions. 336-282-7044. Fax: 336-282-2048. E-mail: tim@guilfordday.org. Web site: www.guilfordday.org.

HIDDEN LAKE ACADEMY

830 Hidden Lake Road
Dahlonega, Georgia 30533

Head of School: Mr. Joe Stapp

General Information Coeducational boarding college-preparatory, arts, and Executive Functioning Skills school; primarily serves students with learning disabilities, individuals with Attention Deficit Disorder, individuals with emotional and behavioral problems, dyslexic students, and Oppositional Defiant Disorder. Grades 7–PG. Founded: 1994. Setting: rural. Nearest major city is Atlanta. Students are housed in single-sex dormitories. 210-acre campus. 16 buildings on campus. Approved or accredited by Georgia Accrediting Commission, Georgia Association of Private Schools for Exceptional Children, Georgia Independent School Association, Southern Association of Colleges and Schools, and Southern Association of Independent Schools. Member of National Association of Independent Schools and Secondary School Admission Test Board. Total enrollment: 130. Upper school average class size: 9. Upper school faculty-student ratio: 1:9.

Upper School Student Profile 100% of students are boarding students. 25% are state residents. 20 states are represented in upper school student body. 8% are international students. International students from Costa Rica, Mexico, United States, and Venezuela.

Faculty School total: 12. In upper school: 6 men, 1 woman; 5 have advanced degrees; all reside on campus.

Subjects Offered ACT preparation, algebra, American history, ancient world history, art, biology, calculus, chemistry, drama, earth science, ecology, economics, electives, English, environmental science, environmental studies, fine arts, geography, geometry, government/civics, history, mathematics, performing arts, photojournalism, physical education, physical science, physics, SAT preparation, science, social science, social studies, Spanish, trigonometry, U.S. history, visual arts, world history.

Graduation Requirements Arts and fine arts (art, music, dance, drama), English, foreign language, mathematics, physical education (includes health), science, social science, family dynamics, interpersonal relationships, social dynamics.

Special Academic Programs Honors section; independent study; academic accommodation for the gifted and the artistically talented; remedial reading and/or remedial writing; remedial math; programs in English, mathematics, general development for dyslexic students.

College Admission Counseling 18 students graduated in 2008; 9 went to college, including Brevard College; Lynn University; The College at Brockport, State University of New York; Warren Wilson College; Wingate University. Other: 2 entered a postgraduate year. Median SAT critical reading: 460, median SAT math: 430, median SAT writing: 440, median combined SAT: 1330, median composite ACT: 21. 34% scored over 600 on SAT critical reading, 6.8% scored over 600 on SAT math, 2.9% scored over 600 on SAT writing, 10% scored over 1800 on combined SAT, 14.3% scored over 26 on composite ACT.

Student Life Upper grades have uniform requirement, student council, honor system. Discipline rests primarily with faculty.

Summer Programs Remediation, enrichment, art/fine arts programs offered; held on campus; accepts boys and girls; not open to students from other schools. 60 students usually enrolled. 2009 schedule: June to August.

Tuition and Aid 7-day tuition and room/board: $71,400. Guaranteed tuition plan. Tuition installment plan (monthly payment plans, individually arranged payment plans, extended payment plans). Tuition reduction for siblings, need-based scholarship grants available. In 2008–09, 25% of upper-school students received aid.

Admissions Traditional secondary-level entrance grade is 10. Achievement tests, psychoeducational evaluation or WISC III or other aptitude measures; standardized achievement test required. Deadline for receipt of application materials: none. No application fee required. Interview recommended.

Athletics Interscholastic: baseball (boys), basketball (b,g), cross-country running (b,g), soccer (b,g), softball (g), tennis (b,g), track and field (b,g), volleyball (g), wrestling (b); intramural: aquatics (b,g), flag football (b), rock climbing (b,g), swimming and diving (b,g); coed interscholastic: cheering, golf; coed intramural: aerobics, aerobics/dance, aerobics/Nautilus, backpacking, basketball, billiards, canoeing/kayaking, climbing, combined training, cooperative games, cross-country running, dance squad, equestrian sports, fishing, fitness, fitness walking, floor hockey, Frisbee, hiking/backpacking, horseback riding, horseshoes, jogging, kickball, mountaineering, outdoor activities, physical fitness, rappelling, rock climbing, ropes courses, running, softball, strength & conditioning, table tennis, tennis, ultimate Frisbee, volleyball, walking, wall climbing, weight lifting, whiffle ball, wilderness, wilderness survival, yoga. 5 coaches.

Computers Computer network features include on-campus library services, Internet access, Internet filtering or blocking technology. Campus intranet is available to students.

Contact Mr. Jeffrey S Holloway, Director of Admissions. 706-864-4730. Fax: 706-864-9109. E-mail: jeffh@hiddenlakeacademy.com. Web site: www.hiddenlakeacademy.com.

THE HILL CENTER, DURHAM ACADEMY

3200 Pickett Road
Durham, North Carolina 27705

Head of School: Dr. Sharon Maskel

General Information Coeducational day college-preparatory school; primarily serves underachievers, students with learning disabilities, individuals with Attention Deficit Disorder, and dyslexic students. Grades K–12. Founded: 1977. Setting: small town. 5-acre campus. 1 building on campus. Approved or accredited by National Association of Private Schools for Exceptional Children, North Carolina Association of Independent Schools, Southern Association of Colleges and Schools, Southern Association of Independent Schools, and North Carolina Department of Education. Member of National Association of Independent Schools. Endowment: $3.5 million. Total enrollment: 164. Upper school average class size: 4. Upper school faculty-student ratio: 1:4.

Upper School Student Profile Grade 9: 20 students (11 boys, 9 girls); Grade 10: 17 students (9 boys, 8 girls); Grade 11: 22 students (11 boys, 11 girls); Grade 12: 30 students (12 boys, 18 girls).

Faculty School total: 30. In upper school: 1 man, 10 women; 8 have advanced degrees.

Subjects Offered Algebra, American literature, calculus, English, English literature, expository writing, geometry, grammar, mathematics, mechanics of writing, pre-algebra, pre-calculus, Spanish, writing.

Graduation Requirements Graduation requirements are determined by the student's home-based school.

Special Academic Programs Remedial reading and/or remedial writing; remedial math; programs in English, mathematics, general development for dyslexic students.

College Admission Counseling 27 students graduated in 2008; 24 went to college, including Elon University; Hampden-Sydney College; The George Washington University; The University of North Carolina at Asheville; The University of North Carolina at Greensboro. Other: 2 went to work, 1 entered a postgraduate year. Median SAT critical reading: 520, median SAT math: 500, median SAT writing: 530. 4% scored over 600 on SAT critical reading, 5% scored over 600 on SAT math.

Student Life Upper grades have student council. Discipline rests primarily with faculty.

Tuition and Aid Day student tuition: $15,800. Guaranteed tuition plan. Tuition installment plan (The Tuition Plan, Key Tuition Payment Plan, monthly payment plans, The Tuition Refund Plan). Need-based scholarship grants available. In 2008–09, 14% of upper-school students received aid. Total amount of financial aid awarded in 2008–09: $70,100.

Admissions Traditional secondary-level entrance grade is 9. For fall 2008, 29 students applied for upper-level admission, 25 were accepted, 21 enrolled. WISC-III and Woodcock-Johnson required. Deadline for receipt of application materials: March 15. Application fee required: $50. On-campus interview required.

Computers Computers are regularly used in English, foreign language, mathematics, writing classes. Computer network features include Internet access. Campus intranet is available to students.

Contact Ms. Wendy Speir, Director of Admissions. 919-489-7464 Ext. 725. Fax: 919-489-7466. E-mail: wspeir@hillcenter.org. Web site: www.hillcenter.org.

HILLCREST SCHOOL

3510 North A Street
Building C
Midland, Texas 79705

Head of School: Mrs. Betty Noble Starnes

General Information Coeducational day college-preparatory, general academic, and technology school; primarily serves students with learning disabilities, individuals with Attention Deficit Disorder, and dyslexic students. Grades 1–12. Founded: 1993. Setting: urban. 2-acre campus. 1 building on campus. Approved or accredited by Southern Association of Colleges and Schools, Texas Education Agency, and Texas Department of Education. Endowment: $300,000. Total enrollment: 39. Upper school average class size: 10. Upper school faculty-student ratio: 1:10.

Upper School Student Profile Grade 9: 6 students (6 boys); Grade 10: 6 students (4 boys, 2 girls); Grade 11: 3 students (3 boys); Grade 12: 6 students (4 boys, 2 girls).

Faculty School total: 10. In upper school: 8 women; 1 has an advanced degree.

Graduation Requirements Computers, electives, English, history, mathematics, physical education (includes health), science, senior methods course.

Special Academic Programs Accelerated programs; independent study; remedial reading and/or remedial writing; remedial math; programs in English, mathematics, general development for dyslexic students.

College Admission Counseling 4 students graduated in 2008; 3 went to college. Other: 1 went to work.

Student Life Upper grades have uniform requirement. Discipline rests primarily with faculty.

Tuition and Aid Day student tuition: $7700. Tuition reduction for siblings, need-based scholarship grants available. In 2008–09, 25% of upper-school students received aid. Total amount of financial aid awarded in 2008–09: $21,000.

Admissions Traditional secondary-level entrance grade is 9. For fall 2008, 6 students applied for upper-level admission, 3 were accepted, 3 enrolled. Deadline for receipt of application materials: none. Application fee required: $100. Interview required.

Athletics Coed Intramural: badminton, baseball, basketball, fitness, flag football, football, jump rope, kickball, outdoor activities, outdoor education, physical fitness, soccer, track and field, volleyball.
Computers Computers are regularly used in all classes. Computer network features include on-campus library services, Internet access, Internet filtering or blocking technology. The school has a published electronic and media policy.
Contact Mrs. Sharel Sims, Program Coordinator. 915-570-7444. Fax: 915-570-7361. Web site: www.hillcrestschool.org.

THE HILL TOP PREPARATORY SCHOOL

737 South Ithan Avenue
Rosemont, Pennsylvania 19010

Head of School: Mr. Thomas W. Needham

General Information Coeducational day college-preparatory, arts, and technology school; primarily serves students with learning disabilities and individuals with Attention Deficit Disorder. Grades 6–12. Founded: 1971. Setting: suburban. Nearest major city is Philadelphia. 25-acre campus. 4 buildings on campus. Approved or accredited by Middle States Association of Colleges and Schools, Pennsylvania Association of Independent Schools, and Pennsylvania Department of Education. Member of National Association of Independent Schools. Total enrollment: 79. Upper school average class size: 6. Upper school faculty-student ratio: 1:4.
Upper School Student Profile Grade 9: 16 students (13 boys, 3 girls); Grade 10: 24 students (18 boys, 6 girls); Grade 11: 9 students (8 boys, 1 girl); Grade 12: 12 students (11 boys, 1 girl).
Faculty School total: 27. In upper school: 6 men, 6 women.
Subjects Offered Algebra, American history, American literature, art, biology, ceramics, chemistry, civics, college counseling, computer keyboarding, computer math, computer science, computers, creative writing, drama, earth science, economics, electives, English, English literature, environmental science, European history, geography, geometry, government/civics, grammar, health, history, journalism, mathematics, media studies, music appreciation, Native American studies, photography, physical education, physics, psychology, public speaking, science, senior project, social studies, study skills, theater, trigonometry, U.S. history, woodworking, world cultures, world history, writing.
Graduation Requirements Business skills (includes word processing), computer science, English, mathematics, physical education (includes health), science, senior project, social science, social studies (includes history), study skills.
Special Academic Programs Independent study; study at local college for college credit; academic accommodation for the gifted and the artistically talented; remedial reading and/or remedial writing; remedial math; programs in English, mathematics, general development for dyslexic students.
College Admission Counseling 12 students graduated in 2008; all went to college, including Albright College; Gwynedd-Mercy College; Mitchell College; University of Pittsburgh. Median SAT critical reading: 520, median SAT math: 470, median SAT writing: 510, median combined SAT: 1500.
Student Life Upper grades have specified standards of dress, student council, honor system. Discipline rests primarily with faculty.
Summer Programs Remediation, enrichment programs offered; session focuses on remediation, enrichment, and recreation; held on campus; accepts boys and girls; open to students from other schools. 30 students usually enrolled. 2009 schedule: June 22 to July 31. Application deadline: none.
Tuition and Aid Day student tuition: $36,600. Tuition installment plan (monthly payment plans, payment in full, 60% due June 1 and 40% due December 1, monthly payments over 10 months). Tuition reduction for siblings, need-based scholarship grants available. In 2008–09, 18% of upper-school students received aid. Total amount of financial aid awarded in 2008–09: $69,400.
Admissions Traditional secondary-level entrance grade is 10. For fall 2008, 23 students applied for upper-level admission, 13 were accepted, 4 enrolled. Achievement tests, psychoeducational evaluation, Rorschach or Thematic Apperception Test, WISC or WAIS and WISC/Woodcock-Johnson required. Deadline for receipt of application materials: none. Application fee required: $75. On-campus interview required.
Athletics Interscholastic: baseball (boys), basketball (b,g), cross-country running (b,g), soccer (b,g), softball (g), tennis (b,g), volleyball (b,g), wrestling (b,g); intramural: skiing (downhill) (b,g), soccer (b,g), softball (b,g), tennis (b,g), volleyball (b,g), weight lifting (b,g); coed interscholastic: baseball, basketball, cross-country running, golf, soccer, softball, tennis, track and field, volleyball, wrestling; coed intramural: aerobics/Nautilus, badminton, ball hockey, basketball, climbing, combined training, cooperative games, Cosom hockey, fitness, flag football, floor hockey, Frisbee, indoor hockey, indoor soccer, Newcombe ball, outdoor adventure, paint ball, physical fitness, physical training, pillo polo, rock climbing, skiing (downhill), snowboarding, soccer, softball, strength & conditioning, team handball, tennis, touch football, ultimate Frisbee, volleyball, weight lifting. 2 PE instructors, 5 coaches.
Computers Computers are regularly used in English, mathematics, science, study skills classes. Computer network features include on-campus library services, Internet access, wireless campus network, Internet filtering or blocking technology, one-to-one student and faculty laptop initiative, online student information system, ACTIV-Boards, projectors and audio in all classrooms. Campus intranet, student e-mail accounts, and computer access in designated common areas are available to students. Students grades are available online.
Contact Ms. Cindy Falcone, Assistant Headmaster. 610-527-3230 Ext. 697. Fax: 610-527-7683. E-mail: cfalcone@hilltopprep.org. Web site: www.hilltopprep.org.

HUMANEX ACADEMY

2700 South Zuni Street
Englewood, Colorado 80110

Head of School: Ms. Tracy Wagers

General Information Coeducational boarding and day and distance learning college-preparatory, general academic, and arts school; primarily serves underachievers, students with learning disabilities, individuals with Attention Deficit Disorder, individuals with emotional and behavioral problems, dyslexic students, and Aspergers Disorder, High Functioning Autism. Grades 7–12. Distance learning grade X. Founded: 1983. Setting: suburban. Nearest major city is Denver. 1-acre campus. 1 building on campus. Approved or accredited by North Central Association of Colleges and Schools and Colorado Department of Education. Endowment: $10,000. Total enrollment: 63. Upper school average class size: 7. Upper school faculty-student ratio: 1:7.
Upper School Student Profile Grade 7: 3 students (3 boys); Grade 8: 4 students (2 boys, 2 girls); Grade 9: 10 students (7 boys, 3 girls); Grade 10: 10 students (10 boys); Grade 11: 10 students (6 boys, 4 girls); Grade 12: 26 students (19 boys, 7 girls).
Faculty School total: 11. In upper school: 5 men, 6 women; 8 have advanced degrees.
Subjects Offered 1½ elective credits, 1968, 20th century American writers, 20th century history, 20th century physics, 20th century world history, 3-dimensional art, 3-dimensional design, ACT preparation, addiction, ADL skills, adolescent issues, advanced biology, advanced math, advanced studio art-AP, advanced TOEFL/grammar, aerobics, American Civil War, American culture, American democracy, American foreign policy, American government, American history, American legal systems, American literature, American politics in film, anatomy, anatomy and physiology, ancient world history, animal behavior, animation, anthropology, art, art appreciation, art history, arts and crafts, athletic training, athletics, biology, British literature, calculus, career and personal planning, career exploration, cartooning, cartooning/animation, chemistry, civics, civics/free enterprise, Civil War, civil war history, college counseling, college placement, comedy, composition, computer art, computer graphics, conflict resolution, consumer mathematics, creative writing, critical thinking, current events, drawing, English, English literature, epic literature, evolution, existentialism, expository writing, film, film and literature, fitness, foreign language, general, general math, general science, geography, geology, geometry, government, government/civics, grammar, graphic arts, graphic design, great books, Greek drama, guitar, Harlem Renaissance, health, health education, history, Holocaust, honors algebra, honors English, honors geometry, honors U.S. history, honors world history, human anatomy, human biology, human sexuality, illustration, independent living, keyboarding, keyboarding/computer, language, language arts, language structure, languages, literacy, literary genres, literary magazine, literature, mathematics, media literacy, military history, newspaper, non-Western literature, North American literature, novel, novels, nutrition, peer counseling, philosophy, physical fitness, physics, physiology, play/screen writing, poetry, politics, pottery, pre-algebra, pre-calculus, psychology, public speaking, reading, reading/study skills, remedial study skills, remedial/makeup course work, research, research skills, research techniques, SAT preparation, SAT/ACT preparation, science, science fiction, sculpture, sexuality, Shakespeare, short story, speech, speech and debate, sports, statistics, U.S. government, U.S. government and politics, U.S. history, U.S. literature, Vietnam history, Vietnam War, weight fitness, weight training, weightlifting, Western civilization, Western literature, world geography, world governments, world history.
Special Academic Programs Honors section; academic accommodation for the gifted; remedial reading and/or remedial writing; remedial math; programs in English, mathematics, general development for dyslexic students; special instructional classes for deaf students, blind students, all classes.
College Admission Counseling 13 students graduated in 2008; 10 went to college, including Colorado School of Mines; Colorado State University; Fort Lewis College; University of Colorado at Boulder; University of Denver; University of Northern Colorado. Other: 3 went to work. Median composite ACT: 24. 33% scored over 26 on composite ACT.
Student Life Upper grades have specified standards of dress, student council. Discipline rests equally with students and faculty.
Summer Programs Remediation, advancement programs offered; session focuses on academics; held on campus; accepts boys and girls. 30 students usually enrolled. 2009 schedule: June 1 to June 19. Application deadline: June 1.
Tuition and Aid Day student tuition: $16,900. Guaranteed tuition plan. Tuition installment plan (FACTS Tuition Payment Plan). Tuition reduction for siblings, need-based scholarship grants, middle-income loans, paying campus jobs, Sallie Mae available. In 2008–09, 13% of upper-school students received aid. Total amount of financial aid awarded in 2008–09: $35,000.
Admissions Traditional secondary-level entrance grade is 10. Deadline for receipt of application materials: none. Application fee required: $350. On-campus interview required.
Athletics Coed Intramural: aerobics, ball hockey, basketball, bocce, bowling, cooperative games, fitness, flag football, Frisbee, handball, kickball, physical training, power lifting, ultimate Frisbee, weight lifting, weight training. 1 PE instructor.
Computers Computers are regularly used in art, English, health, history, literacy, mathematics, philosophy, psychology, reading, research skills, social studies, Spanish,

speech, study skills, writing, writing, writing fundamentals classes. Computer resources include on-campus library services, online commercial services, Internet access, Internet filtering or blocking technology. Campus intranet is available to students. Students grades are available online. The school has a published electronic and media policy.
Contact 303-783-0137. Fax: 303-783-5901. Web site: www.humanexacademy.com.

THE JANUS SCHOOL

205 Lefever Road
Mount Joy, Pennsylvania 17552

Head of School: Mrs. Deborah Kost

General Information Coeducational day college-preparatory, general academic, vocational, technology, Assistive Technology, Transition Skills/Internship Program, and Socialization and Communication Skills, Study Skills school; primarily serves underachievers, students with learning disabilities, individuals with Attention Deficit Disorder, dyslexic students, and Asperger's Syndrome. Grades 1–12. Founded: 1991. Setting: small town. Nearest major city is Harrisburg. 40-acre campus. 1 building on campus. Approved or accredited by Middle States Association of Colleges and Schools and Pennsylvania Department of Education. Member of National Association of Independent Schools. Total enrollment: 64. Upper school average class size: 8. Upper school faculty-student ratio: 1:4.
Upper School Student Profile Grade 9: 7 students (3 boys, 4 girls); Grade 10: 17 students (15 boys, 2 girls); Grade 11: 3 students (3 boys); Grade 12: 7 students (4 boys, 3 girls).
Faculty School total: 20. In upper school: 5 men, 9 women; 11 have advanced degrees.
Subjects Offered Acting, advertising design, agriculture, algebra, American government, American history, art, botany, career education internship, career planning, ceramics, chemistry, Chesapeake Bay studies, civics, computer keyboarding, computer literacy, drama, ecology, English, English composition, environmental education, European history, general science, global issues, government, grammar, history, human biology, human development, improvisation, introduction to literature, introduction to theater, journalism, language and composition, language arts, language development, math applications, math methods, math review, mathematics, personal development, personal finance, personal growth, physical education, physical fitness, physical science, physics, pre-algebra, psychology, public speaking, reading, reading/study skills, remedial/makeup course work, SAT preparation, science, science project, senior internship, Shakespeare, short story, social studies, society and culture, speech therapy, vocational skills, world geography.
Special Academic Programs Remedial reading and/or remedial writing; remedial math; programs in English, mathematics, general development for dyslexic students.
College Admission Counseling 6 students graduated in 2008; 4 went to college, including Millersville University of Pennsylvania. Other: 2 went to work.
Student Life Upper grades have specified standards of dress, student council. Discipline rests primarily with faculty.
Summer Programs Remediation, enrichment programs offered; session focuses on core skill remediation (language arts, math, study skills); held on campus; accepts boys and girls; open to students from other schools. 20 students usually enrolled. 2009 schedule: June 22 to July 31. Application deadline: May 1.
Tuition and Aid Day student tuition: $23,500. Tuition installment plan (Academic Management Services Plan, monthly payment plans, individually arranged payment plans). Tuition reduction for siblings, need-based scholarship grants available. In 2008–09, 35% of upper-school students received aid. Total amount of financial aid awarded in 2008–09: $75,000.
Admissions Traditional secondary-level entrance grade is 10. Deadline for receipt of application materials: none. Application fee required: $50. On-campus interview required.
Athletics 1 PE instructor.
Computers Computers are regularly used in all classes. Computer resources include on-campus library services, Internet access, wireless campus network, Internet filtering or blocking technology, Kurzweil Voice, Smartboard, Reading Pens, Laptops, Alphasmarts, Voice-Activated Software, Inspiration Visual Organizing Software. Students grades are available online. The school has a published electronic and media policy.
Contact Mrs. Robin R. Payne, Director of Admission. 717-653-0025 Ext. 106. Fax: 717-653-0696. E-mail: rpayne@thejanusschool.org. Web site: www.thejanusschool.org.

THE JOHN DEWEY ACADEMY

389 Main Street
Great Barrington, Massachusetts 01230

Head of School: Dr. Thomas E. Bratter

General Information Coeducational boarding college-preparatory and arts school; primarily serves underachievers, students with learning disabilities, individuals with Attention Deficit Disorder, individuals with emotional and behavioral problems, and gifted, underachieving, self-destructive adolescents. Grades 10–PG. Founded: 1985. Setting: small town. Nearest major city is Hartford, CT. Students are housed in single-sex by floor dormitories. 90-acre campus. 3 buildings on campus. Approved or accredited by New England Association of Schools and Colleges and Massachusetts Department of Education. Member of Secondary School Admission Test Board. Total enrollment: 30. Upper school average class size: 6. Upper school faculty-student ratio: 1:3.
Upper School Student Profile Grade 10: 4 students (3 boys, 1 girl); Grade 11: 20 students (10 boys, 10 girls); Grade 12: 6 students (4 boys, 2 girls). 100% of students are boarding students. 5% are state residents. 11 states are represented in upper school student body. 10% are international students. International students from Bangladesh, Canada, and Mongolia.
Faculty School total: 10. In upper school: 5 men, 5 women; 9 have advanced degrees; 1 resides on campus.
Subjects Offered Adolescent issues, algebra, American literature, art, art history, biology, calculus, chemistry, creative writing, drama, English, English literature, environmental science, ethics, European history, fine arts, French, geometry, government/civics, grammar, health, history, Italian, moral reasoning, philosophy, physical education, physics, psychology, sociology, Spanish, statistics, theater, trigonometry, world history, world literature, writing.
Graduation Requirements American history, arts and fine arts (art, music, dance, drama), biology, English, English literature, European history, foreign language, leadership skills, literature, mathematics, moral reasoning, physical education (includes health), science, social studies (includes history), moral leadership qualities.
Special Academic Programs Honors section; accelerated programs; independent study; study at local college for college credit; academic accommodation for the gifted and the artistically talented; remedial reading and/or remedial writing; remedial math; programs in general development for dyslexic students.
College Admission Counseling 10 students graduated in 2008; all went to college, including Brandeis University; Brown University; Columbia University; Oberlin College; Skidmore College; University of Chicago. 95% scored over 600 on SAT critical reading, 95% scored over 600 on SAT math, 95% scored over 600 on SAT writing, 95% scored over 1800 on combined SAT.
Student Life Upper grades have specified standards of dress, student council, honor system. Discipline rests equally with students and faculty.
Summer Programs Session focuses on continuing college preparatory program; held on campus; accepts boys and girls; not open to students from other schools. 30 students usually enrolled.
Tuition and Aid 7-day tuition and room/board: $84,000. Tuition installment plan (monthly payment plans, individually arranged payment plans). Need-based scholarship grants available. In 2008–09, 25% of upper-school students received aid.
Admissions Traditional secondary-level entrance grade is 10. Deadline for receipt of application materials: none. No application fee required. On-campus interview required.
Computers Computer resources include Internet access. Computer access in designated common areas is available to students.
Contact Dr. Thomas E. Bratter, President. 413-528-9800. Fax: 413-528-5662. E-mail: tbratter@jda.org. Web site: www.jda.org.

See Close-Up on page 1104.

THE KARAFIN SCHOOL

40-1 Radio Circle
PO Box 277
Mount Kisco, New York 10549

Head of School: Bart A. Donow, PhD

General Information Coeducational day college-preparatory and general academic school; primarily serves underachievers, students with learning disabilities, individuals with Attention Deficit Disorder, individuals with emotional and behavioral problems, emotionally disabled students, and Tourette's Syndrome. Grades 8–12. Founded: 1958. Setting: suburban. Nearest major city is New York. 1 building on campus. Approved or accredited by New York Department of Education. Total enrollment: 82. Upper school average class size: 6. Upper school faculty-student ratio: 1:6.
Upper School Student Profile Grade 9: 19 students (10 boys, 9 girls); Grade 10: 21 students (8 boys, 13 girls); Grade 11: 21 students (8 boys, 13 girls); Grade 12: 15 students (7 boys, 8 girls).
Faculty School total: 25. In upper school: 8 men, 16 women; 23 have advanced degrees.
Subjects Offered Algebra, American history, American literature, art, art history, arts, biology, business, business skills, calculus, chemistry, computer math, computer programming, computer science, creative writing, earth science, ecology, economics, English, English literature, environmental science, European history, expository writing, fine arts, French, geography, geology, geometry, government/civics, grammar, history of ideas, history of science, Italian, Latin, mathematics, music, photography, physical education, physics, psychology, science, social science, social studies, sociology, Spanish, speech, trigonometry, typing, world history, world literature, writing, zoology.
Graduation Requirements Arts and fine arts (art, music, dance, drama), business skills (includes word processing), computer science, English, foreign language, mathematics, physical education (includes health), science, social science, social studies (includes history).

Special Academic Programs Independent study; academic accommodation for the gifted, the musically talented, and the artistically talented; remedial reading and/or remedial writing; remedial math; programs in English, mathematics, general development for dyslexic students; special instructional classes for deaf students.
College Admission Counseling 14 students graduated in 2008; 10 went to college, including Iona College; John Jay College of Criminal Justice of the City University of New York; Manhattanville College; University at Albany, State University of New York; Western Connecticut State University. Other: 4 went to work. Mean SAT critical reading: 500, mean SAT math: 550.
Student Life Upper grades have student council. Discipline rests primarily with faculty.
Tuition and Aid Day student tuition: $27,860. Tuition installment plan (monthly payment plans).
Admissions Traditional secondary-level entrance grade is 9. For fall 2008, 600 students applied for upper-level admission, 100 were accepted, 35 enrolled. Deadline for receipt of application materials: none. No application fee required. On-campus interview required.
Athletics Coed Intramural: aerobics, aerobics/dance, archery, badminton, ball hockey, baseball, basketball, billiards, bowling, cooperative games, fitness, fitness walking, floor hockey, football, Frisbee, golf, gymnastics, jump rope, kickball, paddle tennis, physical fitness, physical training, pillo polo, power lifting, project adventure, racquetball, soccer, strength & conditioning, table tennis, team handball, tennis, touch football, volleyball, weight lifting, whiffle ball, wrestling. 1 PE instructor.
Computers Computers are regularly used in all academic classes. Computer resources include Internet access, Internet filtering or blocking technology. The school has a published electronic and media policy.
Contact Bart A. Donow, PhD, Director. 914-666-9211. Fax: 914-666-9868. E-mail: karafin@optonline.net. Web site: www.karafinschool.com.

KILDONAN SCHOOL

425 Morse Hill Road
Amenia, New York 12501

Head of School: Benjamin N. Powers

General Information Coeducational boarding and day college-preparatory, general academic, arts, and technology school; primarily serves dyslexic students and Language-based learning differences. Boarding grades 7–PG, day grades 2–PG. Founded: 1969. Setting: rural. Nearest major city is New York. Students are housed in single-sex dormitories. 325-acre campus. 19 buildings on campus. Approved or accredited by Academy of Orton-Gillingham Practitioners and Educators, New York State Association of Independent Schools, The Association of Boarding Schools, and New York Department of Education. Member of National Association of Independent Schools and Secondary School Admission Test Board. Endowment: $579,300. Total enrollment: 108. Upper school average class size: 6. Upper school faculty-student ratio: 1:6.
Upper School Student Profile Grade 10: 19 students (13 boys, 6 girls); Grade 11: 19 students (14 boys, 5 girls); Grade 12: 8 students (5 boys, 3 girls). 61% of students are boarding students. 37% are state residents. 15 states are represented in upper school student body. 6% are international students. International students from Bermuda, Brazil, Canada, Philippines, and Puerto Rico; 1 other country represented in student body.
Faculty School total: 56. In upper school: 26 men, 28 women; 11 have advanced degrees; 46 reside on campus.
Subjects Offered Algebra, American history, American literature, anthropology, art, art history, biology, botany, business skills, calculus, ceramics, chemistry, computer programming, computer science, creative writing, earth science, ecology, economics, English, English literature, environmental science, European history, expository writing, fine arts, geography, geology, geometry, government/civics, grammar, health, history, mathematics, photography, physical education, physics, science, social studies, trigonometry, typing, world history, world literature, zoology.
Graduation Requirements Arts and fine arts (art, music, dance, drama), English, mathematics, physical education (includes health), science, social studies (includes history).
Special Academic Programs Independent study; remedial reading and/or remedial writing; programs in English, mathematics, general development for dyslexic students.
College Admission Counseling 18 students graduated in 2008; 17 went to college, including Curry College; Mitchell College; Xavier University. Other: 1 went to work.
Student Life Upper grades have specified standards of dress, student council, honor system. Discipline rests primarily with faculty.
Summer Programs Remediation, art/fine arts, computer instruction programs offered; session focuses on intensive academic tutoring for students with dyslexia; exciting, fun summer camp activities; held on campus; accepts boys and girls; open to students from other schools. 85 students usually enrolled. 2009 schedule: June 26 to August 7.
Tuition and Aid Day student tuition: $37,000; 5-day tuition and room/board: $49,250; 7-day tuition and room/board: $51,500. Tuition installment plan (Tuition Management Systems). Need-based scholarship grants available. In 2008–09, 35% of upper-school students received aid. Total amount of financial aid awarded in 2008–09: $135,000.
Admissions Traditional secondary-level entrance grade is 9. Wechsler Individual Achievement Test, WISC or WAIS, WISC/Woodcock-Johnson or Woodcock-Johnson Revised Achievement Test required. Deadline for receipt of application materials: none. Application fee required: $50. On-campus interview required.
Athletics Interscholastic: aerobics (girls), dance (g), fitness (g); intramural: basketball (b,g); coed interscholastic: archery, bicycling, canoeing/kayaking, cross-country running, equestrian sports, fitness walking, flag football, golf, hiking/backpacking, horseback riding, lacrosse, martial arts, mountain biking, outdoor activities, paddle tennis, physical fitness, rock climbing, sailing, skiing (cross-country), skiing (downhill), snowboarding, softball, strength & conditioning, swimming and diving, table tennis, tennis, touch football, walking, water skiing, weight lifting, weight training, yoga; coed intramural: basketball, bicycling, cross-country running, equestrian sports, golf, lacrosse, paddle tennis, skiing (cross-country), skiing (downhill).
Computers Computers are regularly used in English, mathematics, multimedia classes. Computer network features include on-campus library services, Internet access, wireless campus network. Student e-mail accounts are available to students.
Contact Marcie Wistar, Associate Director of Admissions. 845-373-2012. Fax: 845-373-2004. E-mail: info@kildonanadmissions.org.

ANNOUNCEMENT FROM THE SCHOOL Kildonan was founded in 1969 in response to an urgent need for a school for intelligent students with learning difficulties arising from dyslexia. The academic program is unique in that it revolves around intensive and daily one-on-one Orton-Gillingham tutoring for each student. Courses in mathematics, history, literature, and science are designed to meet the learning style of dyslexic students. Enhanced confidence is achieved via participation in such activities as the arts, athletics, and community life.

See Close-Up on page 1106.

KING GEORGE SCHOOL

2684 King George Farm Road
Sutton, Vermont 05867

Head of School: Dr. David Hans

General Information Coeducational boarding college-preparatory, arts, personal development, and emotional growth school; primarily serves underachievers, students with learning disabilities, individuals with Attention Deficit Disorder, individuals with emotional and behavioral problems, and dyslexic students. Grades 9–12. Founded: 1998. Setting: rural. Nearest major city is St. Johnsbury. Students are housed in single-sex dormitories. 330-acre campus. 12 buildings on campus. Approved or accredited by Vermont Department of Education. Candidate for accreditation by New England Association of Schools and Colleges. Total enrollment: 60. Upper school average class size: 8. Upper school faculty-student ratio: 1:3.
Upper School Student Profile 100% of students are boarding students. 5% are state residents. 25 states are represented in upper school student body. 5% are international students. International students from Saudi Arabia and United Kingdom; 3 other countries represented in student body.
Faculty School total: 16. In upper school: 5 men, 6 women; 6 have advanced degrees; 5 reside on campus.
Subjects Offered Acting, algebra, American literature, ballet, biology, British literature, ceramics, chemistry, chorus, civics, communication skills, composition, creative writing, culinary arts, dance, dance performance, drama, drama performance, drawing, earth science, English, French, geometry, guitar, health and wellness, instrumental music, introduction to theater, jazz dance, jewelry making, modern dance, music performance, outdoor education, painting, performing arts, personal growth, photography, physics, play production, portfolio art, pre-algebra, SAT/ACT preparation, social science, social skills, Spanish, speech, stagecraft, studio art, study skills, transition mathematics, U.S. history, visual and performing arts, world history.
Graduation Requirements Arts, English, foreign language, mathematics, physical education (includes health), science, social studies (includes history), wellness.
Special Academic Programs International Baccalaureate program; independent study; study abroad; academic accommodation for the gifted, the musically talented, and the artistically talented; remedial reading and/or remedial writing; remedial math; programs in general development for dyslexic students.
College Admission Counseling 41 students graduated in 2008; 28 went to college, including Rhode Island School of Design. Other: 1 went to work, 1 had other specific plans. Median SAT critical reading: 600, median SAT math: 630, median composite ACT: 26. 50% scored over 600 on SAT critical reading, 50% scored over 600 on SAT math, 50% scored over 26 on composite ACT.
Student Life Upper grades have specified standards of dress, student council, honor system. Discipline rests primarily with faculty.
Summer Programs Enrichment, advancement, art/fine arts programs offered; held both on and off campus; held at various mountain, coastal, and wilderness areas and museums; accepts boys and girls; open to students from other schools. 45 students usually enrolled. 2009 schedule: April 17 to August 24. Application deadline: March 27.

Tuition and Aid Tuition installment plan (Key Tuition Payment Plan, monthly payment plans, individually arranged payment plans). Tuition reduction for siblings, need-based loans, middle-income loans available. In 2008–09, 5% of upper-school students received aid.
Admissions Traditional secondary-level entrance grade is 10. For fall 2008, 150 students applied for upper-level admission, 55 were accepted, 45 enrolled. Achievement/Aptitude/Writing, Individual IQ, Achievement and behavior rating scale, Wechsler Individual Achievement Test, Wechsler Intelligence Scale for Children, Wechsler Intelligence Scale for Children III, Wide Range Achievement Test or writing sample required. Deadline for receipt of application materials: none. No application fee required. Interview recommended.
Athletics Coed Interscholastic: aerobics, aerobics/dance, aerobics/Nautilus, alpine skiing, backpacking, climbing, cross-country running, dance, equestrian sports, fitness, hiking/backpacking, horseback riding, independent competitive sports, indoor soccer, jogging, martial arts, mountain biking, mountaineering, nordic skiing, outdoor activities, physical fitness, rock climbing, running, skateboarding, skiing (cross-country), skiing (downhill), snowboarding, snowshoeing, soccer, ultimate Frisbee, walking; coed intramural: basketball, broomball, canoeing/kayaking, dance, fishing, hiking/backpacking, ice hockey, ice skating, modern dance, mountain biking, outdoor adventure, outdoor education, physical fitness, skiing (cross-country), skiing (downhill), snowboarding, snowshoeing, telemark skiing, ultimate Frisbee. 1 PE instructor, 2 coaches, 1 athletic trainer.
Computers Computers are regularly used in all academic classes. Computer resources include wireless campus network, Internet filtering or blocking technology.
Contact Mr. Jeremy McGeorge, Admissions Director. 800-218-5122 Ext. 106. Fax: 802-467-1041. E-mail: jmcgeorge.kgs@gmail.com. Web site: www.kinggeorgeschool.com.

KINGSHILL SCHOOL

RR 1, Box 6125
Kingshill
St. Croix, Virgin Islands 00850
Head of School: Mrs. Janie M. Koopmans

General Information Coeducational day college-preparatory, general academic, arts, vocational, and technology school; primarily serves underachievers, students with learning disabilities, individuals with Attention Deficit Disorder, dyslexic students, cerebral palsy, and Asperger's syndrome. Grades 7–12. Founded: 1997. Setting: rural. Nearest major city is Christiansted, U.S. Virgin Islands. 6-acre campus. 2 buildings on campus. Approved or accredited by Virgin Islands Department of Education. Candidate for accreditation by Middle States Association of Colleges and Schools. Total enrollment: 26. Upper school average class size: 6. Upper school faculty-student ratio: 1:4.
Upper School Student Profile Grade 7: 5 students (3 boys, 2 girls); Grade 8: 6 students (5 boys, 1 girl); Grade 9: 4 students (3 boys, 1 girl); Grade 10: 6 students (4 boys, 2 girls); Grade 12: 5 students (3 boys, 2 girls).
Faculty School total: 8. In upper school: 2 men, 6 women; 3 have advanced degrees.
Subjects Offered Algebra, American government, American history, American literature, ancient world history, applied arts, architecture, art appreciation, arts appreciation, athletics, auto mechanics, biology, bowling, career exploration, career planning, career/college preparation, Caribbean history, chemistry, civics, college admission preparation, college counseling, community service, composition, computer skills, computer technologies, consumer mathematics, current events, earth science, electives, English, English literature, entrepreneurship, environmental science, geography, geometry, health, health education, history of the Americas, keyboarding, language-AP, learning lab, learning strategies, marine biology, math applications, music appreciation, physical education, pre-algebra, remedial/makeup course work, SAT preparation, scuba diving, Spanish, world geography, world history.
Graduation Requirements Algebra, American government, American history, art history, biology, Caribbean history, chemistry, health, physical science, Spanish, transition mathematics, world civilizations, world history, world literature.
Special Academic Programs Accelerated programs; independent study; study at local college for college credit; remedial reading and/or remedial writing; remedial math; programs in English, mathematics, general development for dyslexic students.
College Admission Counseling 5 students graduated in 2008; 2 went to college. Other: 1 went to work, 1 entered a postgraduate year, 1 had other specific plans. Median SAT critical reading: 420, median SAT math: 420.
Student Life Upper grades have honor system. Discipline rests equally with students and faculty.
Tuition and Aid Day student tuition: $9000. Tuition installment plan (monthly payment plans, individually arranged payment plans). Tuition reduction for siblings, merit scholarship grants, need-based scholarship grants, paying campus jobs available. In 2008–09, 67% of upper-school students received aid; total upper-school merit-scholarship money awarded: $9000. Total amount of financial aid awarded in 2008–09: $9000.
Admissions Traditional secondary-level entrance grade is 10. For fall 2008, 28 students applied for upper-level admission, 12 were accepted, 10 enrolled. WISC or WAIS, Woodcock-Johnson Educational Evaluation, WISC III or WRAT required. Deadline for receipt of application materials: none. No application fee required. Interview required.
Athletics Intramural: football (boys); coed intramural: aerobics/dance, baseball, basketball, bowling, canoeing/kayaking, cooperative games, fitness walking, flag football, Frisbee, hiking/backpacking, horseback riding, independent competitive sports, kayaking, outdoor activities, physical fitness, scuba diving, Special Olympics, surfing, swimming and diving, table tennis, touch football, volleyball, walking. 1 PE instructor.
Computers Computers are regularly used in all academic, computer applications classes. Computer network features include Internet access, wireless campus network, Internet filtering or blocking technology. Computer access in designated common areas is available to students. The school has a published electronic and media policy.
Contact Mrs. Janie M. Koopmans, Director. 340-778-6564. Fax: 340-778-0520. E-mail: kingshillschool@gmail.com.

LA CHEIM SCHOOL

1413 F Street
Portable 1
Antioch, California 94509
Head of School: Ms. Sue Herrera

General Information Coeducational day general academic and vocational school; primarily serves underachievers, students with learning disabilities, individuals with Attention Deficit Disorder, and individuals with emotional and behavioral problems. Grades 1–12. Founded: 1974. Setting: suburban. 2 buildings on campus. Approved or accredited by Western Association of Schools and Colleges and California Department of Education. Total enrollment: 20. Upper school average class size: 10. Upper school faculty-student ratio: 1:4.
Upper School Student Profile Grade 6: 1 student (1 boy); Grade 7: 2 students (2 boys); Grade 8: 8 students (6 boys, 2 girls); Grade 9: 3 students (3 boys); Grade 10: 3 students (2 boys, 1 girl); Grade 11: 1 student (1 girl); Grade 12: 2 students (2 girls).
Faculty School total: 5. In upper school: 1 man, 1 woman.
Subjects Offered Adolescent issues, American government, American history, art, basic skills, biology, economics, grammar, health, language arts, life science, life skills, mathematics, physical education, physical science, science, social studies, vocational skills, world history, writing skills.
Special Academic Programs Remedial reading and/or remedial writing; remedial math.
Student Life Upper grades have specified standards of dress. Discipline rests primarily with faculty.
Summer Programs Remediation, enrichment programs offered; session focuses on continue education and mental health services; held on campus; accepts boys and girls; not open to students from other schools. 20 students usually enrolled. 2009 schedule: June 18 to July 31.
Tuition and Aid Tuition installment plan (expenses covered by referring district and county agencies with no cost to parents).
Admissions Traditional secondary-level entrance grade is 10. Deadline for receipt of application materials: none. No application fee required. On-campus interview required.
Athletics Intramural: basketball (boys, girls), flag football (b,g).
Computers Computers are regularly used in all academic classes. Computer resources include Internet access.
Contact Ms. Sue Herrera, Director. 925-777-1133. Fax: 925-777-9933. E-mail: sue@lacheim.org. Web site: www.lacheim.org/schools/index.htm.

LANDMARK EAST SCHOOL

708 Main Street
Wolfville, Nova Scotia B4P 1G4, Canada
Head of School: Timothy F. Moore

General Information Coeducational boarding and day college-preparatory school; primarily serves students with learning disabilities, individuals with Attention Deficit Disorder, and dyslexic students. Grades 6–12. Founded: 1979. Setting: small town. Nearest major city is Halifax, Canada. Students are housed in single-sex dormitories. 5-acre campus. 9 buildings on campus. Approved or accredited by Canadian Association of Independent Schools and Nova Scotia Department of Education. Language of instruction: English. Total enrollment: 65. Upper school average class size: 8. Upper school faculty-student ratio: 1:2.
Upper School Student Profile Grade 10: 10 students (7 boys, 3 girls); Grade 11: 11 students (6 boys, 5 girls); Grade 12: 20 students (18 boys, 2 girls). 80% of students are boarding students. 30% are province residents. 12 provinces are represented in upper school student body. 30% are international students. International students from Australia, Bahamas, Barbados, Bermuda, Bolivia, and United States; 3 other countries represented in student body.
Faculty School total: 39. In upper school: 10 men, 14 women; 2 have advanced degrees; 9 reside on campus.
Subjects Offered Art, biology, career and personal planning, chemistry, computer science, drama, economics, English, entrepreneurship, geography, geology, history, integrated science, law, mathematics, physics, strategies for success.
Special Academic Programs Remedial reading and/or remedial writing; remedial math; programs in English, mathematics, general development for dyslexic students.

College Admission Counseling 7 students graduated in 2008; 6 went to college, including Acadia University. Other: 1 went to work.
Student Life Upper grades have uniform requirement, student council, honor system. Discipline rests primarily with faculty.
Tuition and Aid Day student tuition: CAN$26,900; 5-day tuition and room/board: CAN$35,500; 7-day tuition and room/board: CAN$38,700. Need-based scholarship grants, prepGATE Loans (American students), Benecaid student loans (Canadian students), Globex Foreign Exchange (International students) available. In 2008–09, 25% of upper-school students received aid. Total amount of financial aid awarded in 2008–09: CAN$100,000.
Admissions Traditional secondary-level entrance grade is 10. Achievement tests and psychoeducational evaluation required. Deadline for receipt of application materials: none. Application fee required: CAN$50. On-campus interview required.
Athletics Coed Interscholastic: aerobics, alpine skiing, aquatics, archery, badminton, basketball, bicycling, cross-country running, curling, dance, equestrian sports, fitness, gymnastics, ice skating, lacrosse, running, skiing (cross-country), skiing (downhill), snowboarding, soccer, softball, squash, swimming and diving, tennis, track and field, volleyball, weight training; coed intramural: aquatics, ball hockey, basketball, billiards, bowling, cooperative games, fitness, ice skating, indoor soccer, running, strength & conditioning, table tennis, weight training. 8 PE instructors.
Computers Computers are regularly used in art, English, mathematics, science classes. Computer resources include on-campus library services, Internet access.
Contact Janet Cooper, Administrative Assistant. 902-542-2237. Fax: 902-542-4147. E-mail: jcooper@landmarkeast.org. Web site: www.landmarkeast.org.

LANDMARK SCHOOL

PO Box 227
429 Hale Street
Prides Crossing, Massachusetts 01965-0227
Head of School: Robert J. Broudo

General Information Coeducational boarding and day college-preparatory, general academic, and language arts tutorial, skill-based curriculum school; primarily serves students with learning disabilities, dyslexic students, and language-based learning disabilities. Boarding grades 8–12, day grades 2–12. Founded: 1971. Setting: suburban. Nearest major city is Boston. Students are housed in single-sex dormitories. 50-acre campus. 22 buildings on campus. Approved or accredited by Association of Independent Schools in New England, Massachusetts Office of Child Care Services, National Association of Private Schools for Exceptional Children, New England Association of Schools and Colleges, The Association of Boarding Schools, and Massachusetts Department of Education. Member of National Association of Independent Schools. Endowment: $10 million. Total enrollment: 446. Upper school average class size: 7. Upper school faculty-student ratio: 1:3.
Upper School Student Profile Grade 8: 1 student (1 boy); Grade 9: 63 students (37 boys, 26 girls); Grade 10: 69 students (44 boys, 25 girls); Grade 11: 84 students (58 boys, 26 girls); Grade 12: 82 students (59 boys, 23 girls). 54% of students are boarding students. 71% are state residents. 22 states are represented in upper school student body. 2% are international students. International students from Israel, Lebanon, Mexico, Netherlands, Saudi Arabia, and United Kingdom; 6 other countries represented in student body.
Faculty School total: 222. In upper school: 77 men, 135 women; 139 have advanced degrees; 43 reside on campus.
Subjects Offered Advanced math, algebra, American government, American history, American literature, American sign language, anthropology, art, auto mechanics, basketball, biology, boat building, British literature, calculus, calculus-AP, chemistry, chorus, communications, composition, computer programming, computer science, consumer mathematics, creative thinking, creative writing, cultural geography, dance, drama, early childhood, environmental science, expressive arts, film and literature, filmmaking, geometry, grammar, instrumental music, integrated math, language and composition, language arts, literature, marine science, modern world history, multimedia design, newspaper, oral communications, oral expression, peer counseling, photography, physical education, physical science, physics, physiology-anatomy, portfolio art, pragmatics, pre-algebra, pre-calculus, psychology, public speaking, radio broadcasting, reading, reading/study skills, senior thesis, sociology, stage and body movement, study skills, technical theater, technology, television, U.S. history, visual literacy, weightlifting, women's health, woodworking, world history, yearbook.
Graduation Requirements English, mathematics, physical education (includes health), science, social studies (includes history), Landmark School Competency Tests, minimum grade equivalents on standardized tests in reading and reading comprehension.
Special Academic Programs Study at local college for college credit; remedial reading and/or remedial writing; remedial math; programs in English, mathematics, general development for dyslexic students; special instructional classes for deaf students.
College Admission Counseling 73 students graduated in 2008; 67 went to college, including Curry College; Lynn University; New England College; Suffolk University; University of Denver. Other: 1 entered a postgraduate year, 5 had other specific plans. Mean SAT critical reading: 447, mean SAT math: 425.
Student Life Upper grades have specified standards of dress, student council. Discipline rests primarily with faculty.
Summer Programs Remediation programs offered; session focuses on academic remediation and study skills; held both on and off campus; held at two campuses, HS: July 5—July 31, 2009, and Elementary & Middle: June 29—August 7, 2009; accepts boys and girls; open to students from other schools. 140 students usually enrolled. 2009 schedule: July 5 to July 31. Application deadline: May 15.
Tuition and Aid Day student tuition: $35,975–$42,525; 7-day tuition and room/board: $50,100–$56,650. Tuition installment plan (Key Tuition Payment Plan). Need-based scholarship grants, paying campus jobs, community and staff grants available. In 2008–09, 5% of upper-school students received aid. Total amount of financial aid awarded in 2008–09: $362,041.
Admissions For fall 2008, 322 students applied for upper-level admission, 127 were accepted, 100 enrolled. Achievement tests, psychoeducational evaluation and WISC or WAIS required. Deadline for receipt of application materials: none. Application fee required: $150. On-campus interview required.
Athletics Interscholastic: baseball (boys), basketball (b,g), dance (g), lacrosse (b,g), soccer (b,g), tennis (b,g), wrestling (b); intramural: basketball (b,g), floor hockey (b), volleyball (b,g); coed interscholastic: cross-country running, golf, swimming and diving, track and field; coed intramural: ropes courses, skateboarding, skiing (downhill). 5 PE instructors, 1 athletic trainer.
Computers Computers are regularly used in all academic, programming, publishing, technology, yearbook classes. Computer network features include on-campus library services, Internet access, wireless campus network, Internet filtering or blocking technology. Student e-mail accounts are available to students. The school has a published electronic and media policy.
Contact Carol Bedrosian, Admission Liaison. 978-236-3420. Fax: 978-927-7268. E-mail: cbedrosian@landmarkschool.org. Web site: www.landmarkschool.org.

ANNOUNCEMENT FROM THE SCHOOL Established in 1977, the Landmark School Outreach Program provides professional development programs and publications that offer practical and effective research-based strategies to help children learn. Offerings include teaching guides, a series on "Understanding Language-Based Learning Disabilities," a Professional Development Institute held each summer at Landmark School, on-site consultation and programs in schools, and online seminars through LOOP, the Landmark Outreach Online Program. Programs and publications are based on applied educational research, Landmark's "Six Teaching Principles," and innovative instruction of students at Landmark School. For more information about programming and publications, visit www.landmarkoutreach.org or call 978-236-3216.

See Close-Up on page 1108.

THE LAUREATE ACADEMY

100 Villa Maria Place
Winnipeg, Manitoba R3V 1A9, Canada
Head of School: Mr. Gregory D. Jones

General Information Coeducational day college-preparatory school; primarily serves students with learning disabilities, individuals with Attention Deficit Disorder, and dyslexic students. Grades 1–12. Founded: 1987. Setting: suburban. 10-acre campus. 1 building on campus. Approved or accredited by Manitoba Department of Education. Language of instruction: English. Total enrollment: 95. Upper school average class size: 10. Upper school faculty-student ratio: 1:5.
Faculty School total: 12. In upper school: 4 men, 4 women; 3 have advanced degrees.
Graduation Requirements Algebra, Ancient Greek, biology, Canadian geography, Canadian history, chemistry, communication skills, composition, computer skills, English, English literature, geometry, life issues, mathematics, physical education (includes health), physics, public speaking, science, social studies (includes history), writing, Department of Manitoba Education requirements, university preparatory study. Community service is required.
Special Academic Programs Academic accommodation for the gifted; remedial reading and/or remedial writing; remedial math; programs in English, mathematics for dyslexic students.
College Admission Counseling 9 students graduated in 2008; 7 went to college, including The University of Winnipeg; University of Manitoba. Other: 2 went to work.
Student Life Upper grades have specified standards of dress, student council, honor system. Discipline rests primarily with faculty.
Summer Programs Remediation programs offered; session focuses on remedial reading; held on campus; accepts boys and girls; open to students from other schools. 8 students usually enrolled. 2009 schedule: July 6 to August 21. Application deadline: June 1.
Tuition and Aid Day student tuition: CAN$15,800. Tuition installment plan (monthly payment plans, quarterly payment plan). Tuition reduction for siblings, bursaries, merit scholarship grants available. In 2008–09, 23% of upper-school students received aid; total upper-school merit-scholarship money awarded: CAN$750. Total amount of financial aid awarded in 2008–09: CAN$35,000.
Admissions Traditional secondary-level entrance grade is 9. For fall 2008, 13 students applied for upper-level admission, 8 were accepted, 7 enrolled. WISC-III and

Woodcock-Johnson required. Deadline for receipt of application materials: none. Application fee required: CAN$75. Interview required.

Athletics Interscholastic: basketball (boys), volleyball (b); intramural: badminton (b), ball hockey (b), basketball (b); coed interscholastic: badminton, cross-country running, soccer, track and field, volleyball; coed intramural: aerobics, alpine skiing, badminton, ball hockey, basketball, broomball, combined training, cooperative games, fitness, flag football, floor hockey, Frisbee, golf, outdoor activities, outdoor education, outdoor recreation, physical fitness, physical training, running, skiing (downhill), snowboarding, soccer, softball, strength & conditioning, table tennis, touch football, track and field, ultimate Frisbee, volleyball, weight lifting, weight training. 3 PE instructors, 3 coaches.

Computers Computers are regularly used in career education, career exploration, computer applications, creative writing, English, mathematics, research skills, science, social studies, writing, yearbook classes. Computer network features include Internet access, Internet filtering or blocking technology. Student e-mail accounts are available to students.

Contact Mrs. Dora Lawrie, Admissions Coordinator. 204-831-7107. Fax: 204-885-3217. E-mail: dlawrie@laureateslanding.ca. Web site: www.laureateacademy.com.

LAWRENCE SCHOOL

Upper School
10036 Olde Eight Road
Sagamore Hills, Ohio 44067

Head of School: Mr. Lou Salza

General Information Coeducational day college-preparatory school; primarily serves students with learning disabilities, individuals with Attention Deficit Disorder, and dyslexic students. Grades 1–12. Founded: 1969. Setting: small town. Nearest major city is Cleveland. 47-acre campus. 1 building on campus. Approved or accredited by Independent Schools Association of the Central States, North Central Association of Colleges and Schools, Ohio Association of Independent Schools, and Ohio Department of Education. Endowment: $2 million. Total enrollment: 299. Upper school average class size: 11. Upper school faculty-student ratio: 1:11.

Faculty School total: 34. In upper school: 11 men, 22 women; 9 have advanced degrees.

Subjects Offered 20th century history, accounting, Advanced Placement courses, algebra, American history, American sign language, anatomy, art, astronomy, biology, calculus, choir, chorus, college counseling, computer applications, consumer economics, creative writing, debate, drama, earth science, economics, English, English composition, forensics, geography, geometry, global studies, government, graphic arts, graphic design, health, integrated math, journalism, keyboarding/computer, language arts, Latin, law, life science, life skills, mathematics, meteorology, military history, music, mythology, painting, physical education, physical science, physics, physics-AP, poetry, pre-algebra, psychology, research skills, sign language, society, politics and law, sociology, Spanish, speech, speech communications, The 20th Century, U.S. history, U.S. history-AP, video, video communication, Web site design, weight training, world geography, world history, yearbook.

Graduation Requirements Independent study project for seniors, community service hours.

Special Academic Programs Advanced Placement exam preparation; honors section; independent study; remedial reading and/or remedial writing; remedial math; programs in English, mathematics, general development for dyslexic students.

College Admission Counseling 26 students graduated in 2008; 22 went to college, including Bowling Green State University; Denison University; Drexel University; Mount Union College; Ohio University; Valparaiso University. Other: 2 went to work, 2 entered a postgraduate year.

Student Life Upper grades have specified standards of dress, student council. Discipline rests primarily with faculty.

Summer Programs Remediation, enrichment, advancement, sports, art/fine arts, computer instruction programs offered; session focuses on academic remediation, course credits; held on campus; accepts boys and girls; open to students from other schools. 40 students usually enrolled. 2009 schedule: June 16 to July 11. Application deadline: May 1.

Tuition and Aid Day student tuition: $16,800–$18,000. Tuition installment plan (FACTS Tuition Payment Plan, monthly payment plans, individually arranged payment plans). Need-based scholarship grants available. In 2008–09, 25% of upper-school students received aid. Total amount of financial aid awarded in 2008–09: $352,300.

Admissions Traditional secondary-level entrance grade is 9. For fall 2008, 74 students applied for upper-level admission, 61 were accepted, 55 enrolled. Admissions testing required. Deadline for receipt of application materials: none. Application fee required: $100. Interview required.

Athletics Interscholastic: baseball (boys), basketball (b,g), cross-country running (b,g), volleyball (g); intramural: volleyball (g), wrestling (b); coed interscholastic: golf, soccer, track and field; coed intramural: badminton, bowling, cooperative games, fishing, flag football, floor hockey, outdoor activities, physical fitness, physical training, running, skiing (downhill), snowboarding, strength & conditioning, team handball, tennis, ultimate Frisbee, volleyball, walking, whiffle ball, yoga. 1 PE instructor, 1 coach.

Computers Computers are regularly used in all classes. Computer network features include on-campus library services, Internet access, wireless campus network, Internet filtering or blocking technology, one-to-one notebook laptop program for grades 9 to 12, laptop program for grades 7-8. Students grades are available online. The school has a published electronic and media policy.

Contact Mrs. Janet Robinson, Admissions Assistant. 440-526-0717. Fax: 440-526-0595. E-mail: jrobinson@lawrenceschool.org.

LITTLE KESWICK SCHOOL

PO Box 24
Keswick, Virginia 22947

Head of School: Marc J. Columbus

General Information Boys' boarding arts school; primarily serves underachievers, students with learning disabilities, individuals with Attention Deficit Disorder, individuals with emotional and behavioral problems, and dyslexic students. Founded: 1963. Setting: small town. Nearest major city is Washington, DC. Students are housed in single-sex dormitories. 30-acre campus. 10 buildings on campus. Approved or accredited by Virginia Association of Independent Specialized Education Facilities and Virginia Department of Education. Total enrollment: 33. Upper school average class size: 7. Upper school faculty-student ratio: 1:4.

Upper School Student Profile 100% of students are boarding students. 12% are state residents. 18 states are represented in upper school student body. 6% are international students.

Faculty School total: 6. In upper school: 2 men, 4 women; 4 have advanced degrees; 2 reside on campus.

Subjects Offered Algebra, American history, biology, computer applications, earth science, English, geography, government/civics, health, industrial arts, mathematics, physical education, practical arts, social studies, world history.

Student Life Upper grades have specified standards of dress, student council. Discipline rests primarily with faculty.

Summer Programs Remediation, enrichment, sports, art/fine arts, rigorous outdoor training, computer instruction programs offered; session focuses on remediation and therapy; held on campus; accepts boys; open to students from other schools. 33 students usually enrolled. 2009 schedule: July 5 to August 7. Application deadline: none.

Tuition and Aid 7-day tuition and room/board: $92,840. Need-based scholarship grants available. In 2008–09, 3% of upper-school students received aid. Total amount of financial aid awarded in 2008–09: $20,000.

Admissions WISC-III and Woodcock-Johnson required. Deadline for receipt of application materials: none. Application fee required: $350. On-campus interview required.

Athletics Interscholastic: basketball (boys), combined training (b), soccer (b); intramural: basketball (b), climbing (b), cross-country running (b), equestrian sports (b), fishing (b), fitness (b), gymnastics (b), hiking/backpacking (b), horseback riding (b), lacrosse (b), outdoor activities (b), soccer (b), softball (b), swimming and diving (b), volleyball (b). 1 PE instructor, 2 coaches.

Computers Computer resources include Internet access. Computer access in designated common areas is available to students.

Contact Terry Columbus, Director. 434-295-0457 Ext. 14. Fax: 434-977-1892. E-mail: tcolumbus@littlekeswickschool.net. Web site: www.littlekeswickschool.net.

ANNOUNCEMENT FROM THE SCHOOL Little Keswick School is a therapeutic boarding school with a strong special education program that serves 33 boys with significant learning, emotional, or behavioral difficulties. The School's warm, nurturing approach in a highly structured environment enables students to return home, or to a less restrictive boarding school, generally within two to three years. Little Keswick School is currently celebrating forty-five years of service to children. A beautiful new academic and residential building opened in July of 2008.

LOGOS SCHOOL

9137 Old Bonhomme Road
St. Louis, Missouri 63132

Head of School: David C. Thomas, PhD

General Information Coeducational day college-preparatory, general academic, and arts school; primarily serves underachievers, students with learning disabilities, individuals with Attention Deficit Disorder, individuals with emotional and behavioral problems, dyslexic students, and depression, Bipolar Disorder, anxiety disorders, and Asperger's Syndrome. Grades 6–12. Founded: 1970. Setting: suburban. 4-acre campus. 1 building on campus. Approved or accredited by Independent Schools Association of the Central States, Missouri Independent School Association, North Central Association of Colleges and Schools, and Missouri Department of Education. Member of National Association of Independent Schools. Total enrollment: 151. Upper school average class size: 6. Upper school faculty-student ratio: 1:6.

Upper School Student Profile Grade 6: 5 students (4 boys, 1 girl); Grade 7: 7 students (4 boys, 3 girls); Grade 8: 10 students (8 boys, 2 girls); Grade 9: 29 students

(22 boys, 7 girls); Grade 10: 46 students (39 boys, 7 girls); Grade 11: 34 students (23 boys, 11 girls); Grade 12: 20 students (8 boys, 12 girls).
Faculty School total: 25. In upper school: 12 men, 11 women; 4 have advanced degrees.
Subjects Offered Algebra, American history, American literature, anatomy, art, biology, calculus, chemistry, community service, computer science, crafts, creative writing, current events, drama, earth science, economics, English, English literature, environmental science, expository writing, fine arts, geography, geology, geometry, government/civics, history, journalism, mathematics, physical education, physics, physiology, psychology, science, social science, social studies, Spanish, trigonometry, world history, world literature, writing.
Graduation Requirements Arts and fine arts (art, music, dance, drama), computer science, English, mathematics, physical education (includes health), science, social science, social studies (includes history), 120 hours of community service.
Special Academic Programs Honors section; accelerated programs; study at local college for college credit; academic accommodation for the artistically talented; remedial reading and/or remedial writing; remedial math; programs in general development for dyslexic students.
College Admission Counseling 32 students graduated in 2008; they went to St. Louis Community College at Florissant Valley; St. Louis Community College at Meramec; University of Missouri–Columbia; University of Missouri–St. Louis; Webster University. Median composite ACT: 27.
Student Life Discipline rests primarily with faculty.
Tuition and Aid Day student tuition: $22,420. Need-based scholarship grants available. In 2008–09, 33% of upper-school students received aid. Total amount of financial aid awarded in 2008–09: $100,000.
Admissions Deadline for receipt of application materials: none. Application fee required: $235. On-campus interview required.
Athletics Interscholastic: baseball (boys), basketball (b,g), soccer (b), volleyball (g). 1 PE instructor, 4 coaches.
Computers Computers are regularly used in art, English, mathematics, science classes. Computer network features include Internet access, Microsoft Office Products.
Contact Stephanie J. Kolker, Director of Admissions. 314-997-7002 Ext. 116. Fax: 314-997-6848 Ext. 116. E-mail: Skolker@logosschool.org. Web site: www.logosschool.org.

MAPLEBROOK SCHOOL

5142 Route 22
Amenia, New York 12501

Head of School: Donna M. Konkolics

General Information Coeducational boarding and day general academic, vocational, and technology school; primarily serves underachievers, students with learning disabilities, individuals with Attention Deficit Disorder, and low average cognitive ability (minimum I.Q.—70). Ungraded, ages 11–18. Founded: 1945. Setting: small town. Nearest major city is Poughkeepsie. Students are housed in single-sex dormitories. 90-acre campus. 20 buildings on campus. Approved or accredited by Middle States Association of Colleges and Schools, National Association of Private Schools for Exceptional Children, New York Department of Education, New York State Association of Independent Schools, New York State Board of Regents, and US Department of State. Member of National Association of Independent Schools. Endowment: $1 million. Total enrollment: 77. Upper school average class size: 6. Upper school faculty-student ratio: 1:8.
Upper School Student Profile 98% of students are boarding students. 12% are state residents. 25 states are represented in upper school student body. 11% are international students. International students from Barbados, Bermuda, Israel, Mexico, Senegal, and United Kingdom; 5 other countries represented in student body.
Faculty School total: 55. In upper school: 14 men, 13 women; 27 have advanced degrees; 37 reside on campus.
Subjects Offered Algebra, American history, art, biology, business skills, computer science, consumer mathematics, creative writing, drama, driver education, earth science, English, geography, global studies, government/civics, health, home economics, industrial arts, integrated mathematics, keyboarding, mathematics, music, occupational education, performing arts, photography, physical education, physical science, science, social skills, speech, theater, world history, writing.
Graduation Requirements Career and personal planning, computer science, English, mathematics, physical education (includes health), science, social science, social skills, social studies (includes history), attendance at Maplebrook School for a minimum of 2 years.
Special Academic Programs Study at local college for college credit; remedial reading and/or remedial writing; remedial math; programs in English, mathematics, general development for dyslexic students.
College Admission Counseling 16 students graduated in 2007; 2 went to college, including Dutchess Community College; Mitchell College. Other: 1 went to work, 13 entered a postgraduate year.
Student Life Upper grades have specified standards of dress, student council, honor system. Discipline rests primarily with faculty.
Tuition and Aid Day student tuition: $31,350; 5-day tuition and room/board: $44,200; 7-day tuition and room/board: $48,700. Tuition installment plan (Key Tuition Payment Plan, individually arranged payment plans, Tuition Management Systems Plan, Sallie Mae Loans). Merit scholarship grants, need-based scholarship grants, need-based loans, paying campus jobs, minority and cultural diversity scholarships, day-student scholarships available. In 2007–08, 18% of upper-school students received aid. Total amount of financial aid awarded in 2007–08: $150,000.
Admissions Traditional secondary-level entrance age is 14. For fall 2007, 244 students applied for upper-level admission, 97 were accepted, 31 enrolled. Achievement tests, Bender Gestalt, TerraNova, Test of Achievement and Proficiency or WISC or WAIS required. Deadline for receipt of application materials: none. No application fee required. Interview required.
Athletics Interscholastic: basketball (boys, girls), cheering (g), field hockey (g); coed interscholastic: cooperative games, cross-country running, equestrian sports, fitness, freestyle skiing, horseback riding, running, skiing (cross-country), skiing (downhill), soccer, softball, swimming and diving, tennis, track and field, weight lifting, weight training; coed intramural: aerobics/dance, alpine skiing, basketball, bicycling, bowling, cooperative games, cricket, dance, figure skating, fitness, fitness walking, flag football, floor hockey, freestyle skiing, golf, hiking/backpacking, horseback riding, ice skating, indoor hockey, martial arts, outdoor education, outdoor recreation, roller blading, skiing (cross-country), skiing (downhill), soccer, softball, Special Olympics, swimming and diving, table tennis, tennis, volleyball, weight lifting, weight training, wrestling. 1 PE instructor, 12 coaches.
Computers Computers are regularly used in all academic classes. Computer network features include on-campus library services, Internet access, wireless campus network, Internet filtering or blocking technology. Campus intranet, student e-mail accounts, and computer access in designated common areas are available to students. The school has a published electronic and media policy.
Contact Jennifer L. Scully, Dean of Admissions. 845-373-8191. Fax: 845-373-7029. E-mail: admissions@maplebrookschool.org. Web site: www.maplebrookschool.org.

ANNOUNCEMENT FROM THE SCHOOL Maplebrook School serves students with a primary diagnosis of a learning disability. The mission of Maplebrook School is to provide high-quality academic programs for the youngster who is considered a slow learner or who may exhibit a learning disorder. Through small group and individualized instruction, the student will be assisted in reaching his or her academic, social, vocational, and physical potential.

MONTANA ACADEMY

9705 Lost Prairie Road
Marion, Montana 59925

Head of School: Dr. John Alson McKinnon

General Information Coeducational boarding arts and vocational school; primarily serves underachievers, students with learning disabilities, individuals with Attention Deficit Disorder, and individuals with emotional and behavioral problems. Ungraded, ages 14–18. Founded: 1997. Setting: rural. Nearest major city is Kalispell. Students are housed in single-sex dormitories. 300-acre campus. 8 buildings on campus. Approved or accredited by Joint Commission on Accreditation of Healthcare Organizations, Northwest Association of Accredited Schools, and Northwest Association of Schools and Colleges. Total enrollment: 70. Upper school average class size: 12. Upper school faculty-student ratio: 1:2.
Upper School Student Profile 100% of students are boarding students. 2% are state residents. 15 states are represented in upper school student body. 2% are international students.
Faculty School total: 9. In upper school: 4 men, 4 women; 8 have advanced degrees; 6 reside on campus.
Subjects Offered Algebra, American government, American history, American literature, art, biology, botany, British literature, construction, creative writing, culinary arts, current events, English, field ecology, geometry, health science, literature, mathematics, music, outdoor education, physical science, political science, pre-calculus, reading, reading/study skills, remedial study skills, research skills, SAT preparation, social studies, speech communications, substance abuse, U.S. government and politics, work experience, world history, world literature, world wide web design, writing, writing fundamentals, zoology.
Graduation Requirements Completion of emotional growth program.
Special Academic Programs Advanced Placement exam preparation; honors section; independent study; study at local college for college credit; academic accommodation for the gifted; remedial reading and/or remedial writing.
College Admission Counseling 45 students graduated in 2008; 32 went to college, including American University; Goucher College; Lewis & Clark College; Portland State University; The George Washington University; The Ohio State University. Other: 1 went to work, 2 entered a postgraduate year, 10 had other specific plans.
Student Life Upper grades have specified standards of dress, student council, honor system. Discipline rests primarily with faculty.
Tuition and Aid 7-day tuition and room/board: $70,000. Guaranteed tuition plan. Tuition installment plan (monthly payment plans). Financial aid available to upper-school students. In 2008–09, 8% of upper-school students received aid. Total amount of financial aid awarded in 2008–09: $40,000.

Admissions Traditional secondary-level entrance age is 14. Psychoeducational evaluation, Rorschach or Thematic Apperception Test, WISC-R or WISC-III or Woodcock-Johnson required. Deadline for receipt of application materials: none. Application fee required: $1000.
Athletics Interscholastic: soccer (boys, girls); coed interscholastic: cross-country running; coed intramural: aerobics, alpine skiing, backpacking, baseball, basketball, bicycling, canoeing/kayaking, climbing, cooperative games, cross-country running, dance, dressage, equestrian sports, fitness, fitness walking, flag football, fly fishing, hiking/backpacking, horseback riding, ice hockey, ice skating, mountain biking, nordic skiing, outdoor activities, physical fitness, rafting, rappelling, rock climbing, ropes courses, running, skiing (cross-country), skiing (downhill), snowboarding, snowshoeing, soccer, softball, swimming and diving, volleyball, walking, weight training, wilderness survival, winter walking, yoga.
Computers Computers are regularly used in research skills classes. Computer resources include Internet access.
Contact Mrs. Rosemary Eileen McKinnon, Director of Admissions. 406-755-3149. Fax: 406-755-3150. E-mail: rosemarym@montanaacademy.com. Web site: www.montanaacademy.com.

MOUNT BACHELOR ACADEMY

33051 NE Ochoco Highway
Prineville, Oregon 97754
Head of School: Sharon Bitz

General Information Coeducational boarding college-preparatory and arts school; primarily serves underachievers, students with learning disabilities, individuals with Attention Deficit Disorder, individuals with emotional and behavioral problems, and dyslexic students. Grades 9–12. Founded: 1988. Setting: rural. Nearest major city is Bend. Students are housed in single-sex dormitories. 32-acre campus. 41 buildings on campus. Approved or accredited by Northwest Association of Schools and Colleges and Oregon Department of Education. Total enrollment: 101. Upper school average class size: 8. Upper school faculty-student ratio: 1:4.
Upper School Student Profile 100% of students are boarding students. 5% are state residents. 23 states are represented in upper school student body. 1% are international students. International students from Canada and Panama.
Faculty School total: 16. In upper school: 9 men, 7 women; 8 have advanced degrees; 1 resides on campus.
Subjects Offered Addiction, adolescent issues, advanced chemistry, algebra, American government, American literature, art, biology, British literature, calculus, career and personal planning, chemistry, civics, civil war history, communication skills, community service, consumer mathematics, current events, developmental math, earth science, English, English composition, English literature, environmental science, experiential education, foreign language, fractal geometry, geography, geometry, history, independent study, literature, mathematics, personal growth, physical education, physical fitness, physical science, physics, poetry, political science, pre-algebra, pre-calculus, reading/study skills, remedial/makeup course work, research and reference, SAT preparation, Shakespeare, social skills, social studies, Spanish, U.S. history, values and decisions.
Graduation Requirements Completion of emotional growth program.
Special Academic Programs Independent study; study at local college for college credit; study abroad; academic accommodation for the gifted; remedial reading and/or remedial writing; remedial math; programs in general development for dyslexic students.
College Admission Counseling Colleges students went to include Central Oregon Community College; Florida State University; Marymount College, Palos Verdes, California; University of Colorado at Boulder.
Student Life Upper grades have specified standards of dress, honor system. Discipline rests primarily with faculty.
Tuition and Aid 7-day tuition and room/board: $76,800. Tuition installment plan (monthly payment plans).
Admissions Traditional secondary-level entrance grade is 10. Deadline for receipt of application materials: none. No application fee required. Interview recommended.
Athletics Interscholastic: basketball (boys, girls); intramural: aerobics (g), aerobics/dance (g); coed interscholastic: cross-country running; coed intramural: alpine skiing, aquatics, backpacking, basketball, bowling, canoeing/kayaking, climbing, cross-country running, fitness, Frisbee, hiking/backpacking, indoor soccer, kayaking, mountaineering, outdoor activities. 2 PE instructors, 3 coaches.
Computers Computer network features include Internet access, Internet filtering or blocking technology, computer access in classrooms is available to students.
Contact Admissions Department. 888-416-3665. Fax: 541-416-3675. E-mail: info@mtba.com. Web site: www.mtba.com.

See Close-Up on page 1110.

NEW HORIZON YOUTH MINISTRIES

1002 South 350 East
Marion, Indiana 46953
Head of School: Dr. Charles P. Redwine

General Information Coeducational boarding and day college-preparatory, general academic, vocational, religious studies, and bilingual studies school, affiliated with Christian faith, Evangelical faith; primarily serves underachievers, students with learning disabilities, individuals with Attention Deficit Disorder, individuals with emotional and behavioral problems, dyslexic students, and Attention Deficit Hyperactivity Disorder. Grades 7–12. Founded: 1983. Setting: rural. Nearest major city is Indianapolis. Students are housed in single-sex dormitories. 180-acre campus. 11 buildings on campus. Approved or accredited by Association of Christian Schools International, North Central Association of Colleges and Schools, and Indiana Department of Education. Total enrollment: 26. Upper school average class size: 6. Upper school faculty-student ratio: 1:4.
Upper School Student Profile Grade 9: 5 students (1 boy, 4 girls); Grade 10: 4 students (1 boy, 3 girls); Grade 11: 10 students (6 boys, 4 girls); Grade 12: 7 students (5 boys, 2 girls). 85% of students are boarding students. 15% are state residents. 19 states are represented in upper school student body. 85% of students are Christian, members of Evangelical faith.
Faculty School total: 7. In upper school: 2 men, 4 women; 2 have advanced degrees; 2 reside on campus.
Subjects Offered Addiction, adolescent issues, algebra, American government, American literature, Bible studies, biology, Christian education, Christian ethics, Christian scripture, Christianity, decision making skills, economics, English, English composition, ethics, ethics and responsibility, general math, geography, geometry, government, grammar, health, history, math applications, pre-algebra, science, social studies, U.S. history, wilderness studies, world history.
Graduation Requirements Computer keyboarding, economics, English, foreign language, government, life management skills, mathematics, physical education (includes health), religious studies, science, social studies (includes history), U.S. history, world geography, world history, Indiana State graduation requirements, group problem solving.
Special Academic Programs Accelerated programs; study at local college for college credit; study abroad; academic accommodation for the gifted, the musically talented, and the artistically talented.
College Admission Counseling 2 students graduated in 2008; 1 went to college, including Indiana Wesleyan University. Other: 1 entered military service. Median SAT critical reading: 600, median SAT math: 630, median SAT writing: 570.
Student Life Upper grades have uniform requirement, honor system. Discipline rests equally with students and faculty. Attendance at religious services is required.
Summer Programs Remediation, sports, rigorous outdoor training programs offered; session focuses on wilderness training; held off campus; held at Canada; accepts boys and girls; open to students from other schools. 40 students usually enrolled. 2009 schedule: May 31 to August 9. Application deadline: none.
Tuition and Aid 7-day tuition and room/board: $6200. Guaranteed tuition plan. Tuition installment plan (monthly payment plans). Tuition reduction for siblings, need-based scholarship grants available. In 2008–09, 86% of upper-school students received aid. Total amount of financial aid awarded in 2008–09: $710,106.
Admissions Traditional secondary-level entrance grade is 10. Deadline for receipt of application materials: none. No application fee required.
Athletics Intramural: aerobics (boys, girls), aerobics/dance (g), backpacking (b,g), basketball (b,g), canoeing/kayaking (b,g), climbing (b,g), combined training (b,g), cooperative games (b,g), drill team (g), fitness (b,g), fitness walking (g), flag football (b), Frisbee (b,g), gatorball (b,g), hiking/backpacking (b,g), indoor track & field (b,g), kickball (b,g), outdoor activities (b,g), physical fitness (b,g), physical training (b,g), ropes courses (b,g), soccer (b,g), softball (b,g), strength & conditioning (b,g), team handball (b,g), track and field (b,g), ultimate Frisbee (b,g), volleyball (b,g), walking (b,g), weight lifting (b,g), weight training (b,g), whiffle ball (b,g), wilderness (b,g), wilderness survival (b,g); coed intramural: outdoor activities, physical fitness, ropes courses, soccer, wilderness. 1 PE instructor.
Computers Computer network features include on-campus library services, Internet access, wireless campus network, Internet filtering or blocking technology. Students grades are available online. The school has a published electronic and media policy.
Contact Monica Bush, Registrar. 800-333-4009 Ext. 109. Fax: 765-662-1407. E-mail: admissions@nhym.org. Web site: www.nhym.org.

NEW SUMMIT SCHOOL

PO Box 12347
Jackson, Mississippi 39216
Head of School: Dr. Nancy Boyll

General Information Coeducational day college-preparatory and general academic school; primarily serves underachievers, students with learning disabilities, individuals with Attention Deficit Disorder, individuals with emotional and behavioral problems, and dyslexic students. Grades K–12. Founded: 1996. Setting: suburban. 3-acre campus. 4 buildings on campus. Approved or accredited by Southern Association of Colleges and Schools and Mississippi Department of Education. Total enrollment: 94. Upper school average class size: 8. Upper school faculty-student ratio: 1:10.
Faculty School total: 9. In upper school: 1 man, 8 women; 8 have advanced degrees.
Subjects Offered Adolescent issues, algebra, American literature, ancient world history, applied arts, art, biology, business education, career and personal planning, career/college preparation, chemistry, computer applications, computer keyboarding, consumer mathematics, developmental language skills, developmental math, drama, earth science, economics, English, English composition, English literature, family and consumer science, foreign language, general science, geography, geometry, guidance,

health, history, Internet, interpersonal skills, language arts, life issues, literature, math methods, math review, mathematics, occupational education, pre-algebra, psychology, public speaking, remedial study skills, remedial/makeup course work, science, sociology, Spanish, speech, state government, state history, U.S. government, U.S. history, world geography, world history, writing.
Graduation Requirements Arts and fine arts (art, music, dance, drama), computers, electives, English, health, mathematics, science, social studies (includes history).
Special Academic Programs Remedial reading and/or remedial writing; remedial math.
College Admission Counseling 18 students graduated in 2008; 14 went to college, including Hinds Community College; Holmes Community College. Other: 2 went to work, 1 entered military service, 1 had other specific plans. Median composite ACT: 17. 2% scored over 26 on composite ACT.
Student Life Upper grades have uniform requirement, student council, honor system. Discipline rests primarily with faculty.
Summer Programs Enrichment, advancement programs offered; session focuses on academics; held on campus; accepts boys and girls; open to students from other schools. 85 students usually enrolled. 2009 schedule: June 5 to July 16.
Tuition and Aid Day student tuition: $7200. Tuition installment plan (individually arranged payment plans). Tuition reduction for siblings available. In 2008–09, 2% of upper-school students received aid.
Admissions Traditional secondary-level entrance grade is 10. For fall 2008, 12 students applied for upper-level admission, 12 were accepted, 12 enrolled. Grade equivalent tests required. Deadline for receipt of application materials: none. No application fee required. On-campus interview required.
Athletics Coed Interscholastic: Frisbee, kickball, outdoor recreation, running, soccer, softball; coed intramural: aerobics, badminton, fitness, fitness walking, flag football, Frisbee, physical fitness, volleyball, walking, whiffle ball. 1 PE instructor.
Computers Computers are regularly used in desktop publishing, keyboarding, mathematics, media arts, reading, video film production, yearbook classes. Computer network features include Internet access, Internet filtering or blocking technology. Student e-mail accounts are available to students.
Contact Ms. Marilyn W. McGregor, Director of Counseling/Admissions. 601-982-7827. Fax: 601-982-0080. E-mail: mmcgregor@newsummitschool.com.

NEW WAY LEARNING ACADEMY

1300 North 77th Street
Scottsdale, Arizona 85257

Head of School: Dawn T. Gutierrez

General Information Coeducational day college-preparatory, general academic, vocational, technology, and Reading and Language Therapy school; primarily serves students with learning disabilities, individuals with Attention Deficit Disorder, dyslexic students, and speech and language delays. Grades K–12. Founded: 1968. Setting: suburban. Nearest major city is Phoenix. 2-acre campus. 3 buildings on campus. Approved or accredited by Arizona Association of Independent Schools and Arizona Department of Education. Candidate for accreditation by North Central Association of Colleges and Schools. Total enrollment: 119. Upper school average class size: 10. Upper school faculty-student ratio: 1:7.
Upper School Student Profile Grade 7: 17 students (14 boys, 3 girls); Grade 8: 14 students (10 boys, 4 girls); Grade 9: 13 students (9 boys, 4 girls); Grade 10: 11 students (9 boys, 2 girls); Grade 11: 9 students (3 boys, 6 girls); Grade 12: 8 students (3 boys, 5 girls).
Faculty School total: 37. In upper school: 2 men, 8 women; 7 have advanced degrees.
Special Academic Programs Independent study; study at local college for college credit; academic accommodation for the gifted; remedial reading and/or remedial writing; remedial math; programs in English, mathematics, general development for dyslexic students.
College Admission Counseling 8 students graduated in 2008; 4 went to college, including Arizona State University; Northern Arizona University; Southern Illinois University Edwardsville. Other: 2 went to work, 1 entered military service, 1 had other specific plans.
Student Life Upper grades have specified standards of dress, student council. Discipline rests primarily with faculty.
Summer Programs Remediation, enrichment, computer instruction programs offered; session focuses on remediation of reading, writing, mathematics and language skills, review and study skills; held on campus; accepts boys and girls; open to students from other schools. 30 students usually enrolled. 2009 schedule: June 8 to July 10. Application deadline: May 15.
Tuition and Aid Day student tuition: $18,750. Tuition installment plan (monthly payment plans, individually arranged payment plans). Need-based scholarship grants available. In 2008–09, 12% of upper-school students received aid. Total amount of financial aid awarded in 2008–09: $40,000.
Admissions Traditional secondary-level entrance grade is 9. For fall 2008, 17 students applied for upper-level admission, 12 were accepted, 10 enrolled. WISC/Woodcock-Johnson required. Deadline for receipt of application materials: none. Application fee required: $100. On-campus interview required.
Athletics Interscholastic: basketball (boys, girls); coed interscholastic: flag football, track and field. 1 PE instructor.
Computers Computers are regularly used in all academic, career exploration classes. Computer network features include on-campus library services, Internet access, wireless campus network, Internet filtering or blocking technology. Campus intranet and computer access in designated common areas are available to students. Students grades are available online. The school has a published electronic and media policy.
Contact Denise Collier, Admissions Assistant. 480-946-9112 Ext. 101. Fax: 480-946-2657. E-mail: denise@newwayacademy.org. Web site: www.newwayacademy.org.

NORTHWEST ACADEMY

PO Box 370
Naples, Idaho 83847

Head of School: Adam McLain, Psy.D.

General Information Coeducational boarding college-preparatory, general academic, Substance Abuse, and Character Development school; primarily serves underachievers, students with learning disabilities, individuals with Attention Deficit Disorder, individuals with emotional and behavioral problems, and dyslexic students. Grades 11–12. Founded: 1994. Setting: rural. Nearest major city is Spokane, WA. Students are housed in single-sex dormitories. 214-acre campus. Approved or accredited by Northwest Association of Schools and Colleges. Total enrollment: 25. Upper school average class size: 9. Upper school faculty-student ratio: 1:3.
Upper School Student Profile Grade 11: 7 students (5 boys, 2 girls); Grade 12: 18 students (15 boys, 3 girls). 100% of students are boarding students. 15 states are represented in upper school student body.
Faculty School total: 10. In upper school: 7 men, 3 women; 4 have advanced degrees.
Subjects Offered Economics, English, foreign language, health, humanities, mathematics, physical education, science, speech, U.S. history.
Graduation Requirements Economics, English, foreign language, humanities, mathematics, physical education (includes health), science, social studies (includes history), speech, Theory and Practice of Life Skills, Personal Fitness.
Special Academic Programs Honors section; accelerated programs; independent study; study at local college for college credit; academic accommodation for the musically talented; remedial reading and/or remedial writing; remedial math; programs in English, mathematics, general development for dyslexic students; special instructional classes for Theory and Practice of Life Skills.
College Admission Counseling 11 students graduated in 2008; 10 went to college, including Berklee College of Music; Pace University; Saint Louis University; The University of Tennessee at Chattanooga; Xavier University. Other: 1 went to work.
Student Life Upper grades have specified standards of dress, student council, honor system. Discipline rests equally with students and faculty.
Tuition and Aid 7-day tuition and room/board: $6300. Tuition installment plan (monthly payment plans, individually arranged payment plans). Tuition reduction for siblings, need-based scholarship grants available. In 2008–09, 10% of upper-school students received aid.
Admissions Traditional secondary-level entrance grade is 11. Deadline for receipt of application materials: none. No application fee required.
Athletics Coed Intramural: aerobics, alpine skiing, backpacking, baseball, basketball, bicycling, canoeing/kayaking, climbing, fishing, flag football, Frisbee, hiking/backpacking, horseback riding, nordic skiing, outdoor activities, physical training, project adventure, rock climbing, ropes courses, skiing (cross-country), skiing (downhill), snowboarding, snowshoeing, soccer, softball, swimming and diving, volleyball, wall climbing, weight lifting, weight training, yoga. 1 PE instructor.
Computers Computers are regularly used in all academic classes. Computer network features include on-campus library services, Internet access, wireless campus network, Internet filtering or blocking technology. Campus intranet and computer access in designated common areas are available to students. The school has a published electronic and media policy.
Contact Brandi Elliott, Director of Admissions and Marketing. 877-882-0980. Fax: 208-267-3232. E-mail: brandi.elliott@uhsinc.com. Web site: nwacademy.net.

OAK CREEK RANCH SCHOOL

PO Box 4329
West Sedona, Arizona 86340-4329

Head of School: Mr. David Wick Jr.

General Information Coeducational boarding college-preparatory, general academic, technology, and experiential learning school; primarily serves underachievers, students with learning disabilities, individuals with Attention Deficit Disorder, and dyslexic students. Grades 6–12. Founded: 1972. Setting: rural. Nearest major city is Phoenix. Students are housed in single-sex dormitories. 17-acre campus. 21 buildings on campus. Approved or accredited by Arizona Association of Independent Schools, National Independent Private Schools Association, North Central Association of Colleges and Schools, and Arizona Department of Education. Total enrollment: 83. Upper school average class size: 8. Upper school faculty-student ratio: 1:8.
Upper School Student Profile Grade 9: 15 students (8 boys, 7 girls); Grade 10: 15 students (12 boys, 3 girls); Grade 11: 23 students (15 boys, 8 girls); Grade 12: 20 students (14 boys, 6 girls). 100% of students are boarding students. 20% are state residents. 16 states are represented in upper school student body. 5% are international students. International students from Canada, India, Japan, and Mexico; 1 other country represented in student body.

Faculty School total: 13. In upper school: 9 men, 3 women; 10 have advanced degrees; 2 reside on campus.
Subjects Offered Advanced math, algebra, American literature, art, biology, chemistry, computer applications, computer information systems, computer multimedia, computer skills, earth science, economics, English, English literature, geography, geometry, government/civics, history, mathematics, physical education, physics, pre-algebra, reading, science, social science, social studies, Spanish, U.S. history, word processing, world history.
Graduation Requirements Computer science, electives, English, foreign language, mathematics, science, social studies (includes history).
Special Academic Programs Accelerated programs; remedial reading and/or remedial writing; remedial math; programs in English, mathematics, general development for dyslexic students.
College Admission Counseling 21 students graduated in 2008; 19 went to college, including Arizona State University; Northern Arizona University. Other: 1 went to work, 1 entered military service. Median SAT critical reading: 520, median SAT math: 500.
Student Life Upper grades have specified standards of dress, student council, honor system. Discipline rests primarily with faculty.
Summer Programs Remediation, enrichment, advancement, computer instruction programs offered; session focuses on academics; held both on and off campus; held at scenic locations in California, New Mexico, Colorado, and Arizona; accepts boys and girls; open to students from other schools. 35 students usually enrolled. 2009 schedule: June 7 to August 1. Application deadline: none.
Tuition and Aid 7-day tuition and room/board: $36,500. Guaranteed tuition plan. Tuition reduction for siblings, need-based scholarship grants, Wells Fargo Bank K-12 Private Student Loans available. In 2008–09, 10% of upper-school students received aid. Total amount of financial aid awarded in 2008–09: $36,500.
Admissions Traditional secondary-level entrance grade is 10. Deadline for receipt of application materials: none. Application fee required: $400. Interview recommended.
Athletics Interscholastic: basketball (boys, girls), flag football (b), volleyball (g); intramural: cheering (g), flag football (b), football (b); coed interscholastic: golf, soccer, softball; coed intramural: backpacking, badminton, bicycling, billiards, bowling, climbing, cross-country running, equestrian sports, fishing, fitness walking, fly fishing, freestyle skiing, golf, hiking/backpacking, horseback riding, horseshoes, ice skating, jump rope, kickball, mountain biking, Nautilus, outdoor activities, paddle tennis, paint ball, physical fitness, physical training, rafting, riflery, rock climbing, roller blading, ropes courses, running, skateboarding, skiing (downhill), snowboarding, softball, strength & conditioning, swimming and diving, table tennis, tennis, track and field, volleyball, walking, wall climbing, water polo, weight lifting, weight training, whiffle ball, wilderness, yoga. 1 PE instructor, 2 coaches.
Computers Computers are regularly used in English, foreign language, information technology, mathematics, multimedia, photography, photojournalism, science, word processing classes. Computer network features include on-campus library services, Internet access, wireless campus network, Internet filtering or blocking technology, Electric Library (research service), Website instruction and hosting (students only). Student e-mail accounts and computer access in designated common areas are available to students. Students grades are available online. The school has a published electronic and media policy.
Contact Mr. David Wick Jr., Headmaster. 928-634-5571. Fax: 928-634-4915. E-mail: dwick@ocrs.com. Web site: www.ocrs.com.

ANNOUNCEMENT FROM THE SCHOOL For 36 years, Oak Creek Ranch School has been helping undermotivated students and teens with ADD/ADHD realize their true potential. Oak Creek Ranch School offers a caring and structured environment, small classes (fewer than 10 per class), individualized programs, and a focus on leadership and character development. Activities include mountain biking, hiking, competitive sports, and horseback riding. The campus is located on 17 wooded acres fronting Oak Creek near the beautiful red rocks of Sedona, Arizona. Oak Creek Ranch School is a college-preparatory, NCA-accredited, coeducational boarding school for grades 7–12 (ages 12–19).

See Close-Up on page 1112.

OAKLAND SCHOOL

Boyd Tavern
Keswick, Virginia 22947
Head of School: Ms. Carol Williams

General Information Coeducational boarding and day general academic school; primarily serves underachievers, students with learning disabilities, dyslexic students, processing difficulties, and organizational challenges. Grades 2–9. Founded: 1950. Setting: rural. Nearest major city is Richmond. Students are housed in single-sex dormitories. 450-acre campus. 25 buildings on campus. Approved or accredited by Virginia Association of Independent Specialized Education Facilities and Virginia Department of Education. Upper school average class size: 5. Upper school faculty-student ratio: 1:5.
Faculty School total: 17. In upper school: 4 men, 13 women; 8 have advanced degrees.
Subjects Offered Algebra, American history, earth science, English, expository writing, geometry, grammar, health, keyboarding, life science, mathematics, physical education, physical science, remedial study skills, study skills, world history.
Graduation Requirements Skills must be at or above grade/ability level.
Special Academic Programs Remedial reading and/or remedial writing; remedial math; programs in English, mathematics for dyslexic students.
Student Life Upper grades have specified standards of dress, student council. Discipline rests primarily with faculty.
Summer Programs Remediation, sports, art/fine arts, computer instruction programs offered; session focuses on academics; held on campus; accepts boys and girls; open to students from other schools. 135 students usually enrolled. 2009 schedule: June 29 to August 5.
Tuition and Aid Day student tuition: $24,000; 7-day tuition and room/board: $41,000. Tuition installment plan (SMART Tuition Payment Plan, individually arranged payment plans). Need-based scholarship grants available. In 2008–09, 10% of upper-school students received aid.
Admissions Wechsler Intelligence Scale for Children III required. Deadline for receipt of application materials: none. No application fee required. On-campus interview required.
Athletics Interscholastic: basketball (boys, girls), cheering (g); intramural: yoga (g); coed interscholastic: soccer; coed intramural: archery, basketball, bicycling, billiards, cooperative games, equestrian sports, fishing, fitness, Frisbee, golf, hiking/backpacking, horseback riding, in-line skating, indoor soccer, kickball, lacrosse, mountain biking, outdoor activities, outdoor recreation, outdoors, paddle tennis, physical fitness, roller blading, roller skating, skateboarding, soccer, softball, swimming and diving, table tennis, tennis. 1 PE instructor.
Computers Computers are regularly used in English classes.
Contact Ms. Carol Williams, Director. 434-293-9059. Fax: 434-296-8930. E-mail: information@oaklandschool.net. Web site: www.oaklandschool.net.

THE PENIKESE ISLAND SCHOOL

Box 161
Woods Hole, Massachusetts 02543
Head of School: Toby T. Lineaweaver

General Information Boys' boarding general academic and vocational school; primarily serves underachievers, students with learning disabilities, individuals with Attention Deficit Disorder, individuals with emotional and behavioral problems, dyslexic students, and substance abuse problems, family issues, court involvement. Ungraded, ages 15–18. Founded: 1973. Setting: rural. Nearest major city is Hyannis. Students are housed in single-sex dormitories. 75-acre campus. 4 buildings on campus. Approved or accredited by Massachusetts Department of Education and Massachusetts Department of Education. Endowment: $150,000. Total enrollment: 9. Upper school average class size: 4. Upper school faculty-student ratio: 1:2.
Upper School Student Profile Grade 8: 1 student (1 boy); Grade 9: 3 students (3 boys); Grade 10: 3 students (3 boys); Grade 11: 2 students (2 boys). 100% of students are boarding students. 100% are state residents. 1 state is represented in upper school student body.
Faculty School total: 17. In upper school: 12 men, 5 women; 4 have advanced degrees; 4 reside on campus.
Graduation Requirements Students must successfully complete 9 home pass visits which involve behavioral contracts conforming to treatment program goals and expectations.
Special Academic Programs Remedial reading and/or remedial writing; remedial math; programs in English, mathematics, general development for dyslexic students.
Student Life Discipline rests primarily with faculty.
Tuition and Aid 7-day tuition and room/board: $123,390. Tuition installment plan (monthly payment plans, individually arranged payment plans).
Admissions Traditional secondary-level entrance age is 15. Deadline for receipt of application materials: none. No application fee required. Interview required.
Athletics Intramural: aquatics, baseball, basketball, billiards, cooperative games, cross-country running, fishing, fitness, flag football, Frisbee, jogging, outdoor activities, physical fitness, physical training, sailing, soccer, strength & conditioning, swimming and diving, table tennis, tai chi, touch football, volleyball, walking, weight lifting, weight training, wilderness, yoga. 2 athletic trainers.
Contact Pam Brighton, Clinical Director. 508-548-7276 Ext. 205. Fax: 508-457-9580. E-mail: pbrighton@penikese.org. Web site: www.penikese.org.

PINEHURST SCHOOL

10 Seymour Avenue
St. Catharines, Ontario L2P 1A4, Canada
Head of School: Mr. Dave Bird

General Information Coeducational boarding college-preparatory, arts, business, and technology school; primarily serves students with learning disabilities, individuals with Attention Deficit Disorder, and individuals with emotional and behavioral problems. Grades 7–12. Founded: 2000. Setting: urban. Students are housed in single-sex by floor dormitories. 5-acre campus. 2 buildings on campus. Approved or accredited by Ontario Ministry of Education and Virginia Association of Independent

Specialized Education Facilities. Language of instruction: English. Total enrollment: 30. Upper school average class size: 6. Upper school faculty-student ratio: 1:10.
Upper School Student Profile Grade 7: 1 student (1 boy); Grade 9: 2 students (2 boys); Grade 10: 11 students (10 boys, 1 girl); Grade 11: 6 students (6 boys); Grade 12: 10 students (7 boys, 3 girls). 100% of students are boarding students. 90% are province residents. 2 provinces are represented in upper school student body. 10% are international students. International students from Bahamas, Bermuda, and United States.
Faculty School total: 7. In upper school: 2 men, 3 women; 1 has an advanced degree.
Graduation Requirements 20th century world history, art, business applications, Canadian geography, English, French, geography, health education, history, math applications, mathematics, outdoor education, science.
Special Academic Programs Honors section; accelerated programs; independent study; remedial reading and/or remedial writing; remedial math.
College Admission Counseling 2 students graduated in 2008.
Student Life Upper grades have uniform requirement, student council, honor system. Discipline rests primarily with faculty.
Tuition and Aid 7-day tuition and room/board: CAN$32,000. Tuition installment plan (monthly payment plans).
Admissions Traditional secondary-level entrance grade is 11. For fall 2008, 7 students applied for upper-level admission, 7 were accepted, 7 enrolled. Deadline for receipt of application materials: none. No application fee required. On-campus interview required.
Athletics Coed Intramural: alpine skiing, aquatics, archery, backpacking, badminton, ball hockey, baseball, basketball, bicycling, billiards, blading, bocce, bowling, canoeing/kayaking, climbing, cooperative games, cricket, croquet, curling, field hockey, fishing, fitness, flag football, floor hockey, football, golf, hiking/backpacking, hockey, ice hockey, ice skating, in-line skating, indoor hockey, indoor soccer, kayaking, mountain biking, outdoor activities, paddling, physical fitness, physical training, rock climbing, roller blading, ropes courses, scuba diving, skateboarding, skiing (cross-country), skiing (downhill), snowboarding, snowshoeing, soccer, softball, street hockey, strength & conditioning, swimming and diving, table tennis, touch football, volleyball, walking, wall climbing, weight lifting, weight training, wilderness, wilderness survival, wildernessways, winter soccer, winter walking, yoga. 1 PE instructor, 1 coach, 1 athletic trainer.
Computers Computers are regularly used in all classes. Computer network features include on-campus library services, Internet access, wireless campus network, Internet filtering or blocking technology. Student e-mail accounts are available to students.
Contact Mrs. Donna MacDonald, Admissions/Office Coordinator. 905-641-0993. Fax: 905-641-0399. E-mail: pinedonna@sympatico.ca. Web site: www.pinehurst.on.ca.

PINE RIDGE SCHOOL

9505 Williston Road
Williston, Vermont 05495
Head of School: Dana Blackhurst
General Information Coeducational boarding and day college-preparatory, general academic, and remedial school; primarily serves underachievers, students with learning disabilities, dyslexic students, and language-based learning differences. Ungraded, ages 13–18. Founded: 1968. Setting: rural. Nearest major city is Burlington. Students are housed in single-sex dormitories. 130-acre campus. 15 buildings on campus. Approved or accredited by Academy of Orton-Gillingham Practitioners and Educators, Association of Independent Schools in New England, Massachusetts Department of Education, New England Association of Schools and Colleges, and The Association of Boarding Schools. Total enrollment: 98. Upper school average class size: 6. Upper school faculty-student ratio: 1:2.
Upper School Student Profile 98% of students are boarding students. 2% are state residents. 6 states are represented in upper school student body.
Faculty School total: 17. In upper school: 2 men, 6 women; 6 have advanced degrees; 6 reside on campus.
Subjects Offered Acting, art, basketball, English, expository writing, fitness, geography, history, library skills, mathematics, music, reading, reading/study skills, remedial study skills, remedial/makeup course work, research skills, Roman civilization, social skills, social studies, speech origins of English, sports, student publications, study skills, U.S. history, weight fitness, world history.
Graduation Requirements English, history, mathematics, physical education (includes health), science, social education, social science.
Special Academic Programs Study at local college for college credit; remedial reading and/or remedial writing; remedial math; programs in English, mathematics, general development for dyslexic students.
College Admission Counseling 34 students graduated in 2008; 19 went to college, including Landmark College; Mitchell College; New England College. Other: 2 went to work, 7 entered a postgraduate year, 6 had other specific plans.
Student Life Upper grades have specified standards of dress, honor system. Discipline rests primarily with faculty.
Tuition and Aid Day student tuition: $42,000; 7-day tuition and room/board: $56,000. Scholarship available for Vermont residents available.
Admissions Traditional secondary-level entrance grade is 9. Traditional secondary-level entrance age is 14. For fall 2008, 32 students applied for upper-level admission, 6 were accepted, 2 enrolled. Wechsler Intelligence Scale for Children and Woodcock-Johnson required. Deadline for receipt of application materials: none. Application fee required: $150. On-campus interview required.
Athletics Interscholastic: basketball (boys, girls), bowling (b), unicycling (b), weight training (b); intramural: figure skating (b,g), lacrosse (b); coed interscholastic: bowling, cross-country running, jogging, running, skiing (downhill), snowboarding, snowshoeing, soccer, softball, tennis, ultimate Frisbee; coed intramural: alpine skiing, canoeing/kayaking, cheering, climbing, cooperative games, fitness, floor hockey, golf, hiking/backpacking, ice skating, indoor soccer, mountaineering, Nautilus, nordic skiing, outdoor activities, physical fitness, rock climbing, ropes courses, skiing (downhill), snowshoeing, swimming and diving, weight lifting, wilderness survival, yoga. 1 PE instructor, 3 coaches.
Computers Computers are regularly used in English, mathematics, science, social studies classes. Computer network features include on-campus library services, Internet access, wireless campus network, Internet filtering or blocking technology. Student e-mail accounts and computer access in designated common areas are available to students. The school has a published electronic and media policy.
Contact John Thomas, Director of Admission. 802-434-6932. Fax: 802-434-5512. E-mail: admissions@pineridgeschool.com. Web site: www.pineridgeschool.com.

ANNOUNCEMENT FROM THE SCHOOL Pine Ridge School was founded in 1968 to meet the needs of students with dyslexia, language-based learning disabilities, and nonverbal learning disabilities. The academic program utilizes an Orton-Gillingham philosophy in the classes and an individualized, daily one-on-one tutorial. Students participate in athletics, arts, and a variety of community service activities.

See Close-Up on page 1114.

PURNELL SCHOOL

51 Pottersville Road
PO Box 500
Pottersville, New Jersey 07979
Head of School: Ms. Ayanna Hill-Gill
General Information Girls' boarding and day college-preparatory, general academic, and arts school; primarily serves students with learning disabilities, individuals with Attention Deficit Disorder, and dyslexic students. Grades 9–12. Founded: 1963. Setting: rural. Nearest major city is New York, NY. Students are housed in single-sex dormitories. 83-acre campus. 23 buildings on campus. Approved or accredited by Middle States Association of Colleges and Schools, New Jersey Association of Independent Schools, The Association of Boarding Schools, and New Jersey Department of Education. Member of National Association of Independent Schools and Secondary School Admission Test Board. Endowment: $5 million. Total enrollment: 123. Upper school average class size: 11. Upper school faculty-student ratio: 1:8.
Upper School Student Profile Grade 9: 30 students (30 girls); Grade 10: 35 students (35 girls); Grade 11: 29 students (29 girls); Grade 12: 29 students (29 girls). 92% of students are boarding students. 47% are state residents. 19 states are represented in upper school student body. 13% are international students. International students from Bermuda, Bolivia, China, El Salvador, Republic of Korea, and Taiwan; 2 other countries represented in student body.
Faculty School total: 25. In upper school: 5 men, 19 women; 15 have advanced degrees; 22 reside on campus.
Subjects Offered Algebra, American history, American literature, anatomy, art, art history, biology, botany, calculus, ceramics, chemistry, creative writing, dance, drama, earth science, ecology, English, English literature, environmental science, fashion, fine arts, French, geography, geometry, government/civics, health, history, mathematics, music, photography, physical education, science, Shakespeare, social science, social studies, Spanish, speech, statistics, theater, trigonometry, women's studies, world history, world literature, writing.
Graduation Requirements Art history, arts and fine arts (art, music, dance, drama), English, foreign language, history, mathematics, performing arts, physical education (includes health), science, study abroad, Project Exploration.
Special Academic Programs Independent study; study abroad; programs in English, mathematics, general development for dyslexic students; ESL (7 students enrolled).
College Admission Counseling 37 students graduated in 2008; 36 went to college, including Boston College; Goucher College; Hampshire College; Lynn University; Mitchell College; Penn State University Park. Other: 1 went to work.
Student Life Upper grades have uniform requirement, student council. Discipline rests primarily with faculty.
Tuition and Aid Day student tuition: $38,484; 5-day tuition and room/board: $43,964; 7-day tuition and room/board: $45,711. Tuition installment plan (Academic Management Services Plan, Key Tuition Payment Plan, monthly payment plans, individually arranged payment plans). Need-based scholarship grants, prepGATE Loans available. In 2008–09, 18% of upper-school students received aid. Total amount of financial aid awarded in 2008–09: $500,000.
Admissions Traditional secondary-level entrance grade is 9. For fall 2008, 165 students applied for upper-level admission, 76 were accepted, 53 enrolled. Deadline for receipt of application materials: none. Application fee required: $50. Interview required.

Athletics Interscholastic: basketball, dance, dance team, lacrosse, soccer, softball, tennis, volleyball; intramural: aerobics, aerobics/dance, aerobics/Nautilus, ballet, equestrian sports, fitness, golf, horseback riding, jogging, modern dance, outdoor adventure, physical training, self defense, strength & conditioning, weight training, yoga. 1 PE instructor, 5 coaches.
Computers Computers are regularly used in English, foreign language, history, mathematics, science classes. Computer network features include on-campus library services, Internet access, wireless campus network, Internet filtering or blocking technology. Student e-mail accounts are available to students. The school has a published electronic and media policy.
Contact Ms. Lisa Bauch, Associate Director of Admission. 908-439-2154. Fax: 908-439-4088. E-mail: lbauch@purnell.org. Web site: www.purnell.org.

ANNOUNCEMENT FROM THE SCHOOL Purnell gives young women the gift of discovering what they are truly great at doing by recognizing different learning styles and tailoring programs to enable every student to realize her potential. Purnell offers small classes, extensive studio and performing arts, technology-rich curricula, and competitive and noncompetitive athletic offerings. At Purnell, everyone experiences success and the confidence that comes with it.

See Close-Up on page 1116.

RIVERVIEW SCHOOL

551 Route 6A
East Sandwich, Massachusetts 02537

Head of School: Mrs. Maureen B. Brenner

General Information Coeducational boarding and day arts and technology school; primarily serves underachievers, students with learning disabilities, individuals with Attention Deficit Disorder, and adolescents and young adults with complex language, learning and cognitive disabilities. Grades 6–12. Founded: 1957. Setting: rural. Nearest major city is Boston. Students are housed in single-sex dormitories. 16-acre campus. 20 buildings on campus. Approved or accredited by Association of Independent Schools in New England, Massachusetts Office of Child Care Services, National Association of Private Schools for Exceptional Children, New England Association of Schools and Colleges, and Massachusetts Department of Education. Member of National Association of Independent Schools. Endowment: $4.7 million. Total enrollment: 95. Upper school average class size: 8. Upper school faculty-student ratio: 1:8.
Upper School Student Profile Grade 9: 11 students (7 boys, 4 girls); Grade 10: 20 students (14 boys, 6 girls); Grade 11: 20 students (12 boys, 8 girls); Grade 12: 31 students (12 boys, 19 girls). 90% of students are boarding students. 37% are state residents. 23 states are represented in upper school student body. 4% are international students. International students from Canada, Mongolia, Puerto Rico, and United Kingdom.
Faculty School total: 34. In upper school: 10 men, 23 women; 20 have advanced degrees.
Subjects Offered Art, computer skills, drama, graphic arts, history, industrial arts, language arts, mathematics, music appreciation, physical education, reading, science, sexuality, social skills, social studies, speech therapy, writing.
Special Academic Programs Remedial reading and/or remedial writing; remedial math; programs in English, mathematics for dyslexic students.
College Admission Counseling 31 students graduated in 2008. Other: 26 entered a postgraduate year, 5 had other specific plans.
Student Life Upper grades have specified standards of dress, student council. Discipline rests primarily with faculty.
Summer Programs Remediation, enrichment, sports, art/fine arts, computer instruction programs offered; session focuses on reading, language arts, math, computers, fitness, art, sports; held on campus; accepts boys and girls; open to students from other schools. 72 students usually enrolled. 2009 schedule: July 6 to August 8. Application deadline: none.
Tuition and Aid Day student tuition: $36,966; 7-day tuition and room/board: $65,498. Tuition installment plan (initial deposit upon acceptance, 3-installment payment plan (July, August, and November)). Need-based scholarship grants, middle-income loans available. In 2008–09, 10% of upper-school students received aid. Total amount of financial aid awarded in 2008–09: $156,000.
Admissions Traditional secondary-level entrance grade is 9. For fall 2008, 233 students applied for upper-level admission, 73 were accepted, 50 enrolled. Achievement tests, comprehensive educational evaluation, Individual IQ, Achievement and behavior rating scale, psychoeducational evaluation, WISC or WAIS, Woodcock-Johnson or writing sample required. Deadline for receipt of application materials: none. Application fee required: $75. On-campus interview required.
Athletics Interscholastic: baseball (boys), basketball (b), soccer (b), swimming and diving (b,g), tennis (b,g), track and field (b,g); intramural: bowling (b,g), fitness (b,g), jogging (b,g), jump rope (b,g), running (b,g); coed interscholastic: basketball, cross-country running, soccer, swimming and diving, tennis, track and field; coed intramural: aerobics/Nautilus, basketball, bowling, fitness, jogging, jump rope, Nautilus, physical fitness, project adventure, running, soccer, softball, yoga. 2 PE instructors, 2 coaches, 3 athletic trainers.
Computers Computers are regularly used in all academic classes. Computer network features include Internet access, Internet filtering or blocking technology, digital photography, scanners, PowerPoint presentations, Smartboards, Kurzweil, Dragon Naturally Speaking, Mimio, Lexia, Ultra Key, Type to Learn. Computer access in designated common areas is available to students. The school has a published electronic and media policy.
Contact Ms. Monica Lindo, Admissions Assistant. 508-888-0489 Ext. 206. Fax: 508-833-7001. E-mail: admissions@riverviewschool.org. Web site: www.riverviewschool.org.

ROBERT LOUIS STEVENSON SCHOOL

24 West 74th Street
New York, New York 10023

Head of School: B. H. Henrichsen

General Information Coeducational day college-preparatory school; primarily serves underachievers, students with learning disabilities, individuals with Attention Deficit Disorder, individuals with emotional and behavioral problems, and dyslexic students. Grades 7–PG. Founded: 1908. Setting: urban. 1 building on campus. Approved or accredited by New York State Association of Independent Schools and New York Department of Education. Member of National Association of Independent Schools. Total enrollment: 81. Upper school average class size: 9. Upper school faculty-student ratio: 1:5.
Upper School Student Profile Grade 8: 5 students (4 boys, 1 girl); Grade 9: 13 students (10 boys, 3 girls); Grade 10: 18 students (14 boys, 4 girls); Grade 11: 20 students (15 boys, 5 girls); Grade 12: 23 students (17 boys, 6 girls).
Faculty School total: 14. In upper school: 6 men, 7 women; 8 have advanced degrees.
Subjects Offered Algebra, American history, American literature, anatomy, ancient history, ancient world history, art, biology, ceramics, chemistry, computer literacy, computer science, creative writing, current history, drama, earth and space science, earth science, English, English literature, environmental science, European civilization, European history, expository writing, film appreciation, geometry, government/civics, grammar, health, history, history of ideas, mathematics, philosophy, physical education, physics, physiology, poetry, political science, political thought, pre-algebra, pre-calculus, psychology, robotics, science, senior project, sex education, Shakespeare, social science, social studies, theater, trigonometry, world literature, writing.
Graduation Requirements Computer literacy, English, mathematics, physical education (includes health), science, social science, social studies (includes history), portfolio of work demonstrating readiness to graduate.
Special Academic Programs Accelerated programs; independent study; academic accommodation for the gifted; remedial reading and/or remedial writing; remedial math; programs in English, mathematics, general development for dyslexic students.
College Admission Counseling 17 students graduated in 2008; 16 went to college, including City University of New York System; Pace University; State University of New York System. Other: 1 went to work.
Student Life Upper grades have student council. Discipline rests primarily with faculty.
Summer Programs Remediation, enrichment, advancement programs offered; session focuses on tutorial work; held on campus; accepts boys and girls; open to students from other schools. 18 students usually enrolled. 2009 schedule: June 29 to July 29. Application deadline: June 22.
Tuition and Aid Day student tuition: $42,000. Tuition installment plan (individually arranged payment plans). Need-based scholarship grants, need-based loans available. In 2008–09, 4% of upper-school students received aid. Total amount of financial aid awarded in 2008–09: $12,000.
Admissions Traditional secondary-level entrance grade is 9. For fall 2008, 68 students applied for upper-level admission, 47 were accepted, 42 enrolled. Psychoeducational evaluation required. Deadline for receipt of application materials: none. No application fee required. On-campus interview required.
Athletics Coed Interscholastic: basketball, bowling, cross-country running, fitness, floor hockey, jogging, soccer, softball, yoga; coed intramural: aerobics, ball hockey, basketball, bicycling, blading, bowling, cooperative games, fitness, flag football, floor hockey, jogging, judo, juggling, martial arts, physical fitness, physical training, soccer, softball, strength & conditioning, table tennis, tennis, touch football, volleyball, weight lifting, weight training, yoga. 1 PE instructor.
Computers Computers are regularly used in art, English, history, science, technology classes. Computer resources include Internet access, wireless campus network, Internet filtering or blocking technology. The school has a published electronic and media policy.
Contact B. H. Henrichsen, Headmaster. 212-787-6400. Fax: 212-873-1872. Web site: www.stevenson-school.org.

ANNOUNCEMENT FROM THE SCHOOL Stevenson's program for bright underachieving adolescents provides a challenging academic program combined with extensive support services. Advisers help students cope with academic, social, and emotional issues. Learning-disabled students receive help individually and in small groups. Very small classes offer individualized instruction and attention to organizational and study skills.

ST. CHRISTOPHER ACADEMY

4141-41st Ave. SW
Seattle, Washington 98116
Head of School: Darlene Jevne

General Information Coeducational day arts, business, religious studies, bilingual studies, and technology school; primarily serves underachievers, students with learning disabilities, individuals with Attention Deficit Disorder, and dyslexic students. Grades 9–12. Founded: 1982. Setting: suburban. 1 building on campus. Approved or accredited by Association of Independent Schools of Greater Washington, Pacific Northwest Association of Independent Schools, and Washington Department of Education. Member of European Council of International Schools. Total enrollment: 20. Upper school average class size: 10.
Special Academic Programs Programs in English, mathematics, general development for dyslexic students.
Student Life Upper grades have specified standards of dress, student council, honor system.
Tuition and Aid Day student tuition: $15,000. Guaranteed tuition plan.
Admissions Deadline for receipt of application materials: April 1. Application fee required: $350. Interview required.
Athletics 3 PE instructors, 15 coaches.
Computers Computer resources include on-campus library services, Internet access. Campus intranet is available to students. Students grades are available online.
Contact Dena Reindel, Assistant to the Director. 206-246-9751. Fax: 206-937-6781. E-mail: dreindel@seattlelutheran.org. Web site: www.stchristopheracademy.com.

SHEILA MORRISON SCHOOL

8058 Concession 8
RR # 2
Utopia, Ontario L0M 1T0, Canada
Head of School: Adm. Scott Morrison

General Information Coeducational boarding and day college-preparatory and general academic school; primarily serves underachievers, students with learning disabilities, individuals with Attention Deficit Disorder, individuals with emotional and behavioral problems, dyslexic students, and Obsessive Compulsive Disorder. Grades 4–12. Founded: 1976. Setting: rural. Nearest major city is Toronto, Canada. Students are housed in coed dormitories. 30-acre campus. 6 buildings on campus. Approved or accredited by Ontario Ministry of Education and Ontario Department of Education. Language of instruction: English. Total enrollment: 26. Upper school faculty-student ratio: 1:3.
Upper School Student Profile Grade 9: 4 students (2 boys, 2 girls); Grade 10: 4 students (4 boys); Grade 11: 5 students (1 boy, 4 girls); Grade 12: 8 students (6 boys, 2 girls). 90% of students are boarding students. 80% are province residents. 6 provinces are represented in upper school student body. 20% are international students. International students from Bolivia, China, Hong Kong, Turkey, and United States.
Faculty School total: 4. In upper school: 3 men, 1 woman; 1 has an advanced degree; 2 reside on campus.
Subjects Offered Accounting, biology, business, Canadian history, careers, chemistry, civics, computers, economics, English, ESL, family living, geography, health, history, learning strategies, mathematics, physical education, physics, public speaking, science, world civilizations.
Graduation Requirements Ontario Secondary School Diploma requirements.
Special Academic Programs Accelerated programs; remedial reading and/or remedial writing; remedial math; programs in English, mathematics, general development for dyslexic students; special instructional classes for students with poor motor skills, motivational issues; ESL (1 student enrolled).
College Admission Counseling 2 students graduated in 2008; all went to college.
Student Life Upper grades have uniform requirement, honor system. Discipline rests primarily with faculty.
Tuition and Aid Day student tuition: CAN$14,000; 5-day tuition and room/board: CAN$30,000; 7-day tuition and room/board: CAN$30,000. Tuition installment plan (individually arranged payment plans).
Admissions Traditional secondary-level entrance grade is 9. Deadline for receipt of application materials: none. No application fee required. On-campus interview recommended.
Athletics Coed Interscholastic: alpine skiing, archery, backpacking, ball hockey, baseball, basketball, bicycling, billiards, blading, bowling, canoeing/kayaking, combined training, cooperative games, cross-country running, field hockey, fishing, fitness, fitness walking, flag football, football, freestyle skiing, Frisbee, golf, hiking/backpacking, hockey, horseback riding, ice hockey, ice skating, independent competitive sports, jogging, martial arts, nordic skiing, outdoor activities, paint ball, physical fitness, physical training, rafting, rock climbing, ropes courses, running, self defense, skiing (cross-country), skiing (downhill), snowboarding, soccer, softball, squash, swimming and diving, table tennis, tennis, touch football, walking, wildernessways. 1 PE instructor.
Computers Computers are regularly used in English, geography, history, mathematics, science classes. Computer resources include LAN computer service. Campus intranet is available to students.
Contact Adm. Scott Morrison, Headmaster. 705-424-1110. Fax: 705-424-7068. E-mail: admissions@sheilamorrisonschool.com. Web site: www.sheilamorrisonschool.com.

SHELTON SCHOOL AND EVALUATION CENTER

15720 Hillcrest Road
Dallas, Texas 75248
Head of School: Suzanne Stell

General Information Coeducational day college-preparatory and general academic school; primarily serves students with learning disabilities, individuals with Attention Deficit Disorder, and dyslexic students. Grades PS–12. Founded: 1976. Setting: suburban. 1-acre campus. 1 building on campus. Approved or accredited by Independent Schools Association of the Southwest and Southern Association of Independent Schools. Endowment: $4.7 million. Total enrollment: 862. Upper school average class size: 8. Upper school faculty-student ratio: 1:8.
Upper School Student Profile Grade 9: 61 students (36 boys, 25 girls); Grade 10: 63 students (44 boys, 19 girls); Grade 11: 58 students (31 boys, 27 girls); Grade 12: 56 students (38 boys, 18 girls).
Faculty School total: 163. In upper school: 16 men, 28 women; 23 have advanced degrees.
Graduation Requirements Arts and fine arts (art, music, dance, drama), computers, English, ethics, foreign language, mathematics, physical education (includes health), reading, science, social studies (includes history), speech.
Special Academic Programs Programs in English, mathematics, general development for dyslexic students.
College Admission Counseling 46 students graduated in 2008; 44 went to college, including Oklahoma State University; Southern Methodist University; Texas Christian University; University of Arkansas; University of Denver; University of North Texas. Other: 2 had other specific plans.
Student Life Upper grades have uniform requirement, student council, honor system. Discipline rests primarily with faculty.
Summer Programs Enrichment programs offered; session focuses on enrichment; held on campus; accepts boys and girls; open to students from other schools. 39 students usually enrolled. 2009 schedule: June 29 to July 23. Application deadline: May 12.
Tuition and Aid Tuition installment plan (Insured Tuition Payment Plan, Key Tuition Payment Plan). Need-based scholarship grants available. In 2008–09, 9% of upper-school students received aid. Total amount of financial aid awarded in 2008–09: $485,732.
Admissions Traditional secondary-level entrance grade is 9. WISC/Woodcock-Johnson required. Deadline for receipt of application materials: none. No application fee required. Interview required.
Athletics Interscholastic: baseball (boys), basketball (b,g), cheering (g), cross-country running (b,g), football (b), golf (b,g), softball (g), tennis (b,g), track and field (b,g), volleyball (g). 5 PE instructors, 10 coaches.
Computers Computers are regularly used in English, foreign language, information technology, lab/keyboard, library, research skills, SAT preparation, video film production classes. Computer network features include on-campus library services, Internet access, wireless campus network, Internet filtering or blocking technology. Campus intranet and student e-mail accounts are available to students. Students grades are available online. The school has a published electronic and media policy.
Contact Diann Slaton, Director of Admission. 972-774-1772. Fax: 972-991-3977. E-mail: dslaton@shelton.org. Web site: www.shelton.org.

SKY RANCH FOR BOYS, INC.

10100 Sky Ranch Place
Sky Ranch, South Dakota 57724
Head of School: Gene Pribyl

General Information Boys' boarding school; primarily serves underachievers, students with learning disabilities, individuals with Attention Deficit Disorder, and individuals with emotional and behavioral problems. Founded: 1960. Setting: rural. Nearest major city is Rapid City. Students are housed in single-sex dormitories. 3,000-acre campus. 12 buildings on campus. Approved or accredited by South Dakota Department of Education. Total enrollment: 32. Upper school average class size: 10. Upper school faculty-student ratio: 1:6.
Upper School Student Profile Grade 6: 5 students (5 boys); Grade 7: 5 students (5 boys); Grade 8: 5 students (5 boys); Grade 9: 5 students (5 boys); Grade 10: 6 students (6 boys); Grade 11: 6 students (6 boys). 100% of students are boarding students. 50% are state residents. 5 states are represented in upper school student body.
Faculty School total: 6. In upper school: 3 men, 3 women; 2 have advanced degrees.
Student Life Upper grades have specified standards of dress. Discipline rests primarily with faculty.
Summer Programs Remediation programs offered; held on campus; accepts boys; not open to students from other schools. 32 students usually enrolled. 2009 schedule: June 1 to August 20.

Admissions Traditional secondary-level entrance grade is 10. For fall 2008, 45 students applied for upper-level admission, 20 were accepted, 14 enrolled. No application fee required.
Athletics Interscholastic: basketball, billiards, fishing, flag football, horseback riding, in-line skating, outdoor activities, outdoor recreation, paddle tennis, physical fitness, roller blading, running, skateboarding, softball, strength & conditioning, table tennis, touch football, volleyball, walking, weight lifting, whiffle ball. 1 PE instructor, 1 coach.
Contact Jodi Duttenhefer, LSW, MS, Executive Director. 605-797-4422. Fax: 605-797-4425. E-mail: jduttenhefer@skyranchforboys.com. Web site: www.skyranchforboys.com.

SMITH SCHOOL

131 West 86 Street
New York, New York 10024

Head of School: Karen Smith

General Information Coeducational day college-preparatory school; primarily serves students with learning disabilities, individuals with Attention Deficit Disorder, and depression or anxiety disorders; emotional and/or motivational issues. Grades 7–12. Founded: 1990. Setting: urban. 1 building on campus. Approved or accredited by New York State Board of Regents. Total enrollment: 55. Upper school average class size: 4. Upper school faculty-student ratio: 1:4.
Upper School Student Profile Grade 8: 8 students (5 boys, 3 girls); Grade 9: 11 students (7 boys, 4 girls); Grade 10: 13 students (8 boys, 5 girls); Grade 11: 10 students (7 boys, 3 girls); Grade 12: 13 students (8 boys, 5 girls).
Faculty School total: 10. In upper school: 6 men, 4 women; 9 have advanced degrees.
Subjects Offered Algebra, art, biology, calculus, chemistry, computer skills, earth science, ecology, English, European history, film, French, geometry, government, lab science, life science, philosophy, physical science, physics, pre-calculus, remedial study skills, SAT preparation, Spanish, trigonometry, U.S. history, world history.
Graduation Requirements Algebra, American history, art, biology, chemistry, conceptual physics, earth science, English, environmental science, European history, geometry, government, languages, physical education (includes health), physical science, pre-algebra, pre-calculus, trigonometry, world history, community service/25 hours per year.
Special Academic Programs Accelerated programs; independent study; remedial reading and/or remedial writing; remedial math.
College Admission Counseling 8 students graduated in 2008. Median SAT critical reading: 600, median SAT math: 620, median SAT writing: 620, median combined SAT: 600. 50% scored over 600 on SAT critical reading, 40% scored over 600 on SAT math, 50% scored over 600 on SAT writing, 50% scored over 1800 on combined SAT.
Student Life Upper grades have student council, honor system. Discipline rests primarily with faculty.
Summer Programs Remediation, enrichment, advancement, computer instruction programs offered; session focuses on academic courses for enrichment, remediation, or credit; held on campus; accepts boys and girls; open to students from other schools. 25 students usually enrolled. 2009 schedule: June 15 to August 19. Application deadline: June 1.
Tuition and Aid Day student tuition: $26,000–$29,500. Tuition installment plan (monthly payment plans, individually arranged payment plans, quarterly payment plan). Tuition reduction for siblings available.
Admissions Traditional secondary-level entrance grade is 9. For fall 2008, 32 students applied for upper-level admission, 24 were accepted, 20 enrolled. Comprehensive educational evaluation, psychoeducational evaluation, school placement exam, Wide Range Achievement Test or writing sample required. Deadline for receipt of application materials: none. Application fee required: $50. On-campus interview required.
Athletics Coed Interscholastic: aerobics, aerobics/dance, basketball, flag football, kickball, martial arts, physical fitness, running, soccer, tai chi, volleyball, yoga; coed intramural: physical fitness. 2 PE instructors, 2 coaches.
Computers Computers are regularly used in English, history, research skills, study skills, writing, yearbook classes. Computer resources include Internet access. Computer access in designated common areas is available to students. The school has a published electronic and media policy.
Contact Cristina Martinez, Admissions Director. 212-879-6317. Fax: 212-879-0962. E-mail: cmartinez@smithschool.net.

ANNOUNCEMENT FROM THE SCHOOL The Smith School offers a unique learning environment that enables students to achieve their academic goals and develop a sense of self-esteem. Students benefit from the small classroom settings while receiving emotional and academic support from a highly qualified team of educators. The faculty is experienced and resourceful in using multisensory teaching methods and individual learning styles to create a challenging classroom environment.

SORENSON'S RANCH SCHOOL

PO Box 440219
Koosharem, Utah 84744

Head of School: Shane Sorenson

General Information Coeducational boarding college-preparatory, general academic, arts, and vocational school; primarily serves underachievers, students with learning disabilities, individuals with Attention Deficit Disorder, and individuals with emotional and behavioral problems. Grades 7–12. Founded: 1982. Setting: rural. Nearest major city is Salt Lake City. Students are housed in single-sex dormitories. 10-acre campus. 16 buildings on campus. Approved or accredited by Northwest Association of Accredited Schools, Northwest Association of Schools and Colleges, and Utah Department of Education. Total enrollment: 75. Upper school average class size: 12. Upper school faculty-student ratio: 1:7.
Upper School Student Profile Grade 7: 1 student (1 boy); Grade 8: 3 students (1 boy, 2 girls); Grade 9: 18 students (10 boys, 8 girls); Grade 10: 15 students (8 boys, 7 girls); Grade 11: 23 students (12 boys, 11 girls); Grade 12: 15 students (9 boys, 6 girls). 100% of students are boarding students. 3% are state residents. 18 states are represented in upper school student body.
Faculty School total: 14. In upper school: 10 men, 4 women; 4 have advanced degrees.
Subjects Offered Animal husbandry, art, biology, chemistry, computer science, economics, English, home economics, life skills, mathematics, metalworking, physical education, physics, science, social studies, Spanish, woodworking.
Graduation Requirements Computer science, English, mathematics, physical education (includes health), science, social studies (includes history).
Special Academic Programs Accelerated programs; independent study; remedial reading and/or remedial writing; remedial math.
College Admission Counseling 40 students graduated in 2008; 15 went to college, including Brigham Young University; California State University, Sacramento; Southern Utah University; Texas Tech University. Other: 14 went to work, 3 entered military service, 3 entered a postgraduate year, 5 had other specific plans. Median SAT critical reading: 430, median SAT math: 420, median SAT writing: 440, median combined SAT: 1300, median composite ACT: 21. 1% scored over 600 on SAT critical reading, 1% scored over 600 on SAT math, 1% scored over 600 on SAT writing, 1% scored over 1800 on combined SAT, 1% scored over 26 on composite ACT.
Student Life Upper grades have specified standards of dress, student council. Discipline rests primarily with faculty.
Summer Programs Remediation, sports, art/fine arts, computer instruction programs offered; session focuses on recreational therapy, academics; held on campus; accepts boys and girls; not open to students from other schools. 75 students usually enrolled. Application deadline: none.
Tuition and Aid 7-day tuition and room/board: $66,000. Guaranteed tuition plan. Tuition installment plan (Key Tuition Payment Plan, monthly payment plans). Tuition reduction for siblings available. In 2008–09, 5% of upper-school students received aid. Total amount of financial aid awarded in 2008–09: $20,000.
Admissions Deadline for receipt of application materials: none. No application fee required.
Athletics Interscholastic: aerobics/dance (girls); intramural: aerobics (g), aerobics/dance (g), aquatics (b,g), backpacking (b,g), badminton (b), baseball (b), basketball (b,g), bicycling (b,g), billiards (b,g), bocce (b,g), bowling (b,g), cooperative games (b,g), equestrian sports (b,g), fishing (b,g), fitness (b,g), flag football (b), floor hockey (b), football (b), golf (b,g), hiking/backpacking (b,g), horseback riding (b,g), ice skating (b,g), indoor hockey (b), mountain biking (b,g), mountaineering (b,g), outdoor activities (b,g), outdoor education (b,g), physical fitness (b,g), physical training (b,g), roller skating (b,g), ropes courses (b,g), skiing (downhill) (b,g), snowboarding (b,g), soccer (b,g), softball (b,g), strength & conditioning (b,g), swimming and diving (b,g), table tennis (b,g), touch football (b), volleyball (b,g), walking (b,g), weight training (b,g), whiffle ball (b), wilderness (b,g), wildernessways (b,g), wrestling (b). 1 PE instructor.
Computers Computers are regularly used in English, keyboarding, library classes. Computer network features include on-campus library services, online commercial services. Students grades are available online.
Contact Mr. Layne Bagley, Director of Admissions. 435-638-7318 Ext. 155. Fax: 435-638-7582. E-mail: layneb@sorensonsranch.com. Web site: www.sorensonsranch.com.

SPRING RIDGE ACADEMY

13690 South Burton Road
Spring Valley, Arizona 86333

Head of School: Jean B. Courtney

General Information Girls' boarding college-preparatory and arts school; primarily serves individuals with Attention Deficit Disorder and individuals with emotional and behavioral problems. Grades 9–12. Founded: 1997. Setting: rural. Nearest major city is Phoenix. Students are housed in single-sex dormitories. 27-acre campus. 7 buildings on campus. Approved or accredited by North Central Association of Colleges and Schools and Arizona Department of Education. Total enrollment: 70. Upper school average class size: 10. Upper school faculty-student ratio: 1:8.

Upper School Student Profile Grade 9: 5 students (5 girls); Grade 10: 21 students (21 girls); Grade 11: 28 students (28 girls); Grade 12: 16 students (16 girls). 100% of students are boarding students. 2% are state residents. 19 states are represented in upper school student body.
Faculty School total: 9. In upper school: 3 men, 6 women; 5 have advanced degrees.
Subjects Offered 3-dimensional art, advanced chemistry, advanced math, algebra, art, art history, biology, chemistry, clayworking, computer applications, dance, dance performance, drama, ecology, economics, English, French, geology, geometry, health, journalism, photography, physical education, pre-calculus, Spanish, U.S. government, U.S. history, women's studies, world history.
Graduation Requirements Advanced math, algebra, American literature, arts, biology, chemistry, dance, economics, English, foreign language, geometry, life management skills, physical education (includes health), physical fitness, U.S. government, U.S. history, world history.
Special Academic Programs Accelerated programs; independent study; remedial reading and/or remedial writing; remedial math.
College Admission Counseling 28 students graduated in 2008; all went to college, including The Boston Conservatory.
Student Life Upper grades have uniform requirement, student council, honor system. Discipline rests primarily with faculty.
Summer Programs Remediation, enrichment, advancement, sports, art/fine arts, computer instruction programs offered; session focuses on semester courses; held on campus; accepts girls; not open to students from other schools. 64 students usually enrolled. 2009 schedule: June 4 to July 27. Application deadline: none.
Tuition and Aid 7-day tuition and room/board: $72,000. Guaranteed tuition plan. Tuition installment plan (monthly payment plans).
Admissions Traditional secondary-level entrance grade is 10. Psychoeducational evaluation and WISC/Woodcock-Johnson required. Deadline for receipt of application materials: none. No application fee required.
Athletics Interscholastic: basketball, soccer, softball, volleyball; intramural: aerobics/dance, basketball, cooperative games, dance, fitness, fitness walking, flag football, hiking/backpacking, jogging, modern dance, physical fitness, physical training, running, soccer, softball, strength & conditioning, track and field, volleyball, walking, weight training, yoga. 1 PE instructor.
Computers Computers are regularly used in computer applications classes. Computer resources include on-campus library services.
Contact Susan Coatney, Assistant Director of Admission. 928-632-4602 Ext. 116. Fax: 928-632-7661. E-mail: admissions@springridgeacademy.com. Web site: www.springridgeacademy.com.

STANBRIDGE ACADEMY

515 East Poplar Avenue
San Mateo, California 94401

Head of School: Mrs. Marilyn Lynch

General Information Coeducational day general academic school; primarily serves underachievers and students with learning disabilities. Grades K–12. Founded: 1982. Setting: suburban. Nearest major city is San Francisco. 1-acre campus. 1 building on campus. Approved or accredited by Western Association of Schools and Colleges. Total enrollment: 104. Upper school average class size: 8. Upper school faculty-student ratio: 1:8.
Upper School Student Profile Grade 6: 6 students (5 boys, 1 girl); Grade 7: 10 students (9 boys, 1 girl); Grade 8: 13 students (11 boys, 2 girls); Grade 9: 14 students (6 boys, 8 girls); Grade 10: 13 students (9 boys, 4 girls); Grade 11: 12 students (8 boys, 4 girls); Grade 12: 12 students (8 boys, 4 girls).
Faculty School total: 30. In upper school: 5 men, 6 women; 6 have advanced degrees.
Subjects Offered Algebra, American government, biology, career/college preparation, ceramics, college planning, English, English literature, experiential education, general math, geography, geometry, health education, mathematics, physical education, physics, pragmatics, pre-algebra, pre-calculus, probability and statistics, science, social science, Spanish, U.S. history, world cultures, world history, yearbook.
Graduation Requirements Algebra, American government, biology, English, English composition, English literature, experiential education, foreign language, geometry, health and wellness, physical education (includes health), physical science, physics, trigonometry, U.S. history, visual and performing arts, world cultures.
Special Academic Programs Independent study; remedial reading and/or remedial writing; remedial math.
College Admission Counseling 9 students graduated in 2008; 8 went to college, including Academy of Art University; California State University, Sacramento; College of San Mateo. Other: 1 went to work.
Student Life Upper grades have specified standards of dress, student council, honor system. Discipline rests primarily with faculty.
Summer Programs Enrichment programs offered; held on campus; accepts boys and girls; not open to students from other schools. 35 students usually enrolled. 2009 schedule: June 21 to July 31. Application deadline: June 20.
Tuition and Aid Day student tuition: $27,500. Guaranteed tuition plan. Tuition installment plan (monthly payment plans). Need-based scholarship grants available. In 2008–09, 10% of upper-school students received aid. Total amount of financial aid awarded in 2008–09: $80,000.
Admissions Traditional secondary-level entrance grade is 9. For fall 2008, 8 students applied for upper-level admission, 8 were accepted, 8 enrolled. Psychoeducational evaluation or SSAT required. Deadline for receipt of application materials: none. Application fee required: $300. On-campus interview required.
Athletics Coed Intramural: aerobics, badminton, basketball, climbing, cooperative games, cross-country running, dance, fitness walking, flag football, Frisbee, jogging, kickball, outdoor education, outdoor skills, physical fitness, physical training, soccer, strength & conditioning, table tennis, touch football, track and field, volleyball, walking. 3 PE instructors.
Computers Computers are regularly used in yearbook classes. Computer network features include on-campus library services, wireless campus network, Internet filtering or blocking technology. Campus intranet and computer access in designated common areas are available to students. Students grades are available online. The school has a published electronic and media policy.
Contact Ms. Susan Coyne, Administrative Assistant. 650-375-5860. Fax: 650-375-5861. E-mail: scoyne@stanbridgeacademy.org. Web site: www.stanbridgeacademy.org.

STONE MOUNTAIN SCHOOL

126 Camp Elliott Road
Black Mountain, North Carolina 28711

Head of School: Susan Hardy

General Information Boys' boarding arts and vocational school; primarily serves underachievers, students with learning disabilities, individuals with Attention Deficit Disorder, individuals with emotional and behavioral problems, dyslexic students, NLD, and Aspergers. Grades 6–12. Founded: 1990. Setting: rural. Nearest major city is Asheville. Students are housed in single-sex dormitories. 100-acre campus. 19 buildings on campus. Approved or accredited by European Council of International Schools, North Carolina Department of Exceptional Children, Southern Association of Colleges and Schools, and North Carolina Department of Education. Total enrollment: 58. Upper school average class size: 5. Upper school faculty-student ratio: 1:4.
Upper School Student Profile Grade 9: 17 students (17 boys); Grade 10: 14 students (14 boys); Grade 11: 6 students (6 boys); Grade 12: 2 students (2 boys). 100% of students are boarding students. 10% are state residents. 24 states are represented in upper school student body. 3% are international students. International students from Canada; 3 other countries represented in student body.
Faculty School total: 11. In upper school: 8 men, 3 women; 3 have advanced degrees.
Subjects Offered 1½ elective credits, algebra, art, biology, earth science, English, family studies, geography, geometry, government/civics, history, keyboarding, mathematics, natural resources management, physical education, physical science, pre-algebra, science, social studies, Spanish, U.S. history, world history.
Graduation Requirements English, mathematics, physical education (includes health), science, social studies (includes history).
Special Academic Programs Academic accommodation for the gifted; remedial reading and/or remedial writing; remedial math; programs in English, mathematics, general development for dyslexic students.
College Admission Counseling 3 students graduated in 2008; 2 went to college. Other: 1 went to work.
Student Life Upper grades have specified standards of dress, student council. Discipline rests primarily with faculty.
Summer Programs Remediation, rigorous outdoor training programs offered; session focuses on remediation; held on campus; accepts boys; not open to students from other schools. 12 students usually enrolled. 2009 schedule: June 10 to July 24. Application deadline: none.
Tuition and Aid 7-day tuition and room/board: $70,000. Tuition installment plan (monthly payment plans). Need-based loans, middle-income loans available. In 2008–09, 40% of upper-school students received aid.
Admissions Traditional secondary-level entrance grade is 9. Achievement tests and Wechsler Intelligence Scale for Children III required. Deadline for receipt of application materials: none. No application fee required. Interview recommended.
Athletics Interscholastic: backpacking, canoeing/kayaking, climbing, fencing, fishing, fly fishing, Frisbee, hiking/backpacking, kayaking, mountain biking, mountaineering, outdoor activities, paddling, physical fitness, rafting, rappelling, rock climbing, ropes courses, skiing (downhill), snowboarding, soccer, swimming and diving, ultimate Frisbee, volleyball, wall climbing, wilderness, wilderness survival; intramural: baseball, basketball, bicycling, billiards, crew, football, paddle tennis, sailing, skiing (downhill), soccer, swimming and diving, table tennis, track and field, volleyball.
Computers Computers are regularly used in English, history, mathematics, science classes. Computer network features include Internet access, wireless campus network, Internet filtering or blocking technology. The school has a published electronic and media policy.
Contact Shannon Wheat, Admissions Coordinator. 828-669-8639. Fax: 888-218-5262. E-mail: swheat@stonemountainschool.com. Web site: www.stonemountainschool.com.

SUMMIT PREPARATORY SCHOOL

1605 Danielson Road
Kalispell, Montana 59901

Head of School: Rick Johnson, MSW

General Information Coeducational boarding college-preparatory, arts, and General college preparatory school; primarily serves students with learning disabilities, individuals with Attention Deficit Disorder, individuals with emotional and behavioral problems, college-bound students with depression, anxiety, family conflict, and substance abuse, adoption issues, trauma, ADHD, mild learning disabilities. Grades 9–12. Founded: 2003. Setting: rural. Students are housed in single-sex dormitories. 540-acre campus. 4 buildings on campus. Approved or accredited by Northwest Association of Accredited Schools, Pacific Northwest Association of Independent Schools, and Montana Department of Education. Total enrollment: 50. Upper school average class size: 10. Upper school faculty-student ratio: 1:5.

Upper School Student Profile Grade 9: 5 students (3 boys, 2 girls); Grade 10: 12 students (7 boys, 5 girls); Grade 11: 18 students (10 boys, 8 girls); Grade 12: 15 students (9 boys, 6 girls). 100% of students are boarding students. 1% are state residents. 25 states are represented in upper school student body.

Faculty School total: 9. In upper school: 7 men, 2 women; 1 has an advanced degree.

Subjects Offered Accounting, algebra, American history, American literature, anatomy and physiology, art, astronomy, basketball, biology, British literature, calculus, ceramics, chemistry, choral music, composition, computer applications, drama, drawing, earth science, fitness, geometry, global studies, government, guitar, healthful living, interpersonal skills, journalism, painting, physical education, physics, poetry, portfolio art, pre-algebra, pre-calculus, SAT/ACT preparation, science fiction, sculpture, Shakespeare, Spanish, speech and debate, studio art, substance abuse, swimming, trigonometry, U.S. government, weight training, wilderness camping, world history, wrestling.

Graduation Requirements Electives, English, government, history, mathematics, physical fitness, science, Completion of therapeutic program, which includes individual, group and family therapy, and follows the student through a series of four therapeutic stages.

Special Academic Programs Accelerated programs; independent study; study at local college for college credit; academic accommodation for the gifted; remedial math.

College Admission Counseling Colleges students went to include Mississippi State University; New York University; Savannah College of Art and Design; The Ohio State University; The University of Montana; University of California, Berkeley.

Student Life Upper grades have specified standards of dress, student council. Discipline rests primarily with faculty.

Tuition and Aid 7-day tuition and room/board: $79,800. Tuition installment plan (monthly payment plans, individually arranged payment plans). Need-based scholarship grants available. In 2008–09, 15% of upper-school students received aid. Total amount of financial aid awarded in 2008–09: $100,000.

Admissions Individual IQ, Achievement and behavior rating scale, psychoeducational evaluation, Rorschach or Thematic Apperception Test or WISC or WAIS required. Deadline for receipt of application materials: none. No application fee required. Interview required.

Athletics Interscholastic: aerobics (boys, girls), alpine skiing (b,g), aquatics (b,g), backpacking (b,g), basketball (b,g), billiards (b,g), bowling (b,g), canoeing/kayaking (b,g), climbing (b,g), cooperative games (b,g), cross-country running (b,g), fishing (b,g), fitness (b,g), floor hockey (b,g), fly fishing (b,g), Frisbee (b,g), golf (b,g), hiking/backpacking (b,g), horseback riding (b,g), ice skating (b,g), indoor soccer (b,g), indoor track (b,g), martial arts (b,g), mountaineering (b,g), nordic skiing (b,g), outdoor activities (b,g), physical training (b,g), rafting (b,g), rock climbing (b,g), roller blading (b,g), roller skating (b,g), ropes courses (b,g), running (b,g), skiing (cross-country) (b,g), skiing (downhill) (b,g), snowboarding (b,g), snowshoeing (b,g), soccer (b,g), strength & conditioning (b,g), swimming and diving (b,g), ultimate Frisbee (b,g), volleyball (b,g), walking (b,g), wall climbing (b,g), water polo (b,g), water volleyball (b,g), weight lifting (b,g), weight training (b,g), winter walking (b,g), yoga (b,g); intramural: basketball (b,g), indoor soccer (b,g), outdoor skills (b,g), soccer (b,g), wrestling (b); coed interscholastic: bicycling, bowling, indoor soccer, mountain biking; coed intramural: bicycling, indoor soccer, mountain biking, outdoor skills. 1 PE instructor.

Computers Computers are regularly used in business, computer applications, creative writing, word processing, writing classes. Computer resources include Internet filtering or blocking technology, supervised access only to Internet.

Contact Judy Heleva, M.A., Admissions Counselor. 406-758-8113. Fax: 406-758-8150. E-mail: jheleva@summitprepschool.org. Web site: www.summitprepschool.org.

SUNRISE ACADEMY

65 North 1150 West
Hurricane, Utah 84737

Head of School: Joel Beckstrand

General Information Girls' boarding college-preparatory and general academic school; primarily serves underachievers, students with learning disabilities, individuals with Attention Deficit Disorder, and individuals with emotional and behavioral problems. Grades 7–12. Founded: 2000. Setting: small town. Nearest major city is St. George. Students are housed in single-sex dormitories. 2-acre campus. 1 building on campus. Approved or accredited by European Council of International Schools and Utah Department of Education. Total enrollment: 32. Upper school average class size: 10. Upper school faculty-student ratio: 1:10.

Faculty School total: 3. In upper school: 1 man, 2 women; all have advanced degrees.

Subjects Offered 20th century physics, 20th century world history, ACT preparation, advanced math, algebra, American government, American history, American literature, American studies, anatomy, art, biology, calculus, career/college preparation, chemistry, civil rights, CPR, crafts, creative writing, dance, decision making, decision making skills, drama, drama performance, English, equine studies, ethics, family life, family living, first aid, foods, general science, government, government/civics, health education, healthful living, history, human anatomy, human biology, human sexuality, independent living, leadership skills, leadership training, learning cognition, mathematics, nutrition, outdoor education, personal growth, physics, physics-AP, pre-algebra, pre-calculus, SAT/ACT preparation, science, social skills, social studies, society and culture, sociology, Spanish, swimming, trigonometry, U.S. government, volleyball, writing fundamentals, writing skills, yoga.

Graduation Requirements Therapeutic advancement and personal accountability.

Student Life Upper grades have specified standards of dress, honor system. Discipline rests equally with students and faculty.

Tuition and Aid Guaranteed tuition plan. Tuition installment plan (The Tuition Plan, individually arranged payment plans).

Admissions Psychoeducational evaluation required. Deadline for receipt of application materials: none. No application fee required.

Athletics Interscholastic: aerobics/dance, aquatics, backpacking, bicycling, bowling, cooperative games, dance, equestrian sports, fitness walking, hiking/backpacking, horseback riding, jogging, outdoor activities, rappelling, running, swimming and diving, walking, yoga. 1 PE instructor, 1 coach, 2 athletic trainers.

Contact Heather Black, Office Manager. 435-635-1185. Fax: 435-635-1187. E-mail: heatherb@sunrisertc.com. Web site: www.sunrisertc.com/.

TIMBER RIDGE SCHOOL

1463 New Hope Road
Cross Junction, Virginia 22625

Head of School: Dr. John J. Lamanna, EdD

General Information Boys' boarding vocational and technology school; primarily serves underachievers, students with learning disabilities, individuals with Attention Deficit Disorder, and individuals with emotional and behavioral problems. Grades 6–12. Founded: 1969. Setting: rural. Nearest major city is Washington, DC. Students are housed in single-sex dormitories. 250-acre campus. 21 buildings on campus. Approved or accredited by National Commission of Accreditation of Special Education Services, Southern Association of Colleges and Schools, Virginia Association of Independent Specialized Education Facilities, and Virginia Department of Education. Total enrollment: 85. Upper school average class size: 9. Upper school faculty-student ratio: 1:10.

Upper School Student Profile Grade 9: 29 students (29 boys); Grade 10: 18 students (18 boys); Grade 11: 11 students (11 boys); Grade 12: 6 students (6 boys). 100% of students are boarding students. 50% are state residents. 2 states are represented in upper school student body.

Faculty School total: 12. In upper school: 9 men, 3 women; 3 have advanced degrees.

Subjects Offered Agriculture, algebra, biology, carpentry, chemistry, computer-aided design, earth science, English, geometry, health, journalism, keyboarding, library studies, physical education, U.S. government, unified math, Virginia government, woodworking, word processing, work experience, world geography, world history.

Graduation Requirements Arts and fine arts (art, music, dance, drama), English, mathematics, physical education (includes health), science, social science, social studies (includes history).

Special Academic Programs Independent study; study at local college for college credit; remedial reading and/or remedial writing; remedial math; programs in English, mathematics for dyslexic students.

College Admission Counseling 17 students graduated in 2008; 4 went to college. Other: 6 went to work, 3 entered a postgraduate year, 3 had other specific plans.

Student Life Upper grades have specified standards of dress, student council. Discipline rests primarily with faculty.

Summer Programs Remediation programs offered; held on campus; accepts boys; not open to students from other schools.

Admissions Traditional secondary-level entrance grade is 9. For fall 2008, 122 students applied for upper-level admission, 56 were accepted, 42 enrolled. Comprehensive educational evaluation or Woodcock-Johnson Revised Achievement Test required. Deadline for receipt of application materials: none. No application fee required. Interview required.

Athletics Interscholastic: basketball (boys), football (b), soccer (b), wrestling (b); intramural: basketball (b), football (b), soccer (b). 1 PE instructor.

Computers Computers are regularly used in computer applications, library studies, mathematics classes. Computer network features include on-campus library services, Internet access, wireless campus network, Internet filtering or blocking technology. Student e-mail accounts and computer access in designated common areas are available to students. The school has a published electronic and media policy.

Contact Mr. Philip E. Arlotta, Director of Admissions. 877-877-3025 Ext. 1123. Fax: 540-888-4511. E-mail: arlotta@trschool.org. Web site: www.timber-ridge-school.org.

TRIDENT ACADEMY

1455 Wakendaw Road
Mt. Pleasant, South Carolina 29464

Head of School: Joe Ferber Jr.

General Information Coeducational boarding and day college-preparatory, general academic, arts, technology, and Drama, Community Service school; primarily serves underachievers, students with learning disabilities, individuals with Attention Deficit Disorder, dyslexic students, Central Auditory Processing Disorder, dyscalculia, dysgraphia, and non-verbal learning disorders. Boarding grades 9–12, day grades K–PG. Founded: 1972. Setting: suburban. Nearest major city is Charleston. 11-acre campus. 2 buildings on campus. Approved or accredited by Academy of Orton-Gillingham Practitioners and Educators, South Carolina Independent School Association, Southern Association of Colleges and Schools, and Southern Association of Independent Schools. Member of National Association of Independent Schools. Endowment: $1 million. Total enrollment: 90. Upper school average class size: 9. Upper school faculty-student ratio: 1:4.

Upper School Student Profile Grade 9: 8 students (6 boys, 2 girls); Grade 10: 6 students (5 boys, 1 girl); Grade 11: 5 students (3 boys, 2 girls); Grade 12: 6 students (6 boys).

Faculty School total: 30. In upper school: 3 men, 12 women; 12 have advanced degrees.

Subjects Offered Algebra, American history, American literature, art, astronomy, athletics, basketball, biology, business, business mathematics, calculus, career and personal planning, career/college preparation, cheerleading, chemistry, college admission preparation, college counseling, college placement, community service, composition, computer art, computer graphics, computer science, consumer mathematics, creative writing, drama, drama performance, earth science, economics, English, English literature, European history, geography, geometry, government/civics, grammar, guidance, health, history, journalism, language arts, language development, language enhancement and development, library, life science, marine biology, mathematics, music, newspaper, physical education, physics, poetry, pre-algebra, probability and statistics, psychology, reading/study skills, research skills, science, service learning/internship, Shakespeare, social skills, social studies, Spanish, speech therapy, sports, statistics and probability, student government, student publications, study skills, tennis, typing, writing fundamentals, writing skills, writing workshop, yearbook.

Graduation Requirements Computer science, English, foreign language, mathematics, physical education (includes health), science, social studies (includes history).

Special Academic Programs Remedial reading and/or remedial writing; remedial math; programs in English, mathematics, general development for dyslexic students.

College Admission Counseling 11 students graduated in 2008; all went to college, including Anderson University; College of Charleston; Landmark College; Marshall University; The Citadel, The Military College of South Carolina; Trident Technical College.

Student Life Upper grades have specified standards of dress, student council, honor system. Discipline rests primarily with faculty.

Summer Programs Remediation programs offered; session focuses on remediation; held on campus; accepts boys and girls; open to students from other schools. 35 students usually enrolled. 2009 schedule: June to July. Application deadline: none.

Tuition and Aid Day student tuition: $20,050–$22,950. Tuition installment plan (Key Tuition Payment Plan, monthly payment plans). Merit scholarship grants, need-based scholarship grants available. In 2008–09, 21% of upper-school students received aid; total upper-school merit-scholarship money awarded: $3500. Total amount of financial aid awarded in 2008–09: $32,000.

Admissions Traditional secondary-level entrance grade is 9. For fall 2008, 9 students applied for upper-level admission, 6 were accepted, 6 enrolled. Individual IQ, Achievement and behavior rating scale, psychoeducational evaluation and WISC III or other aptitude measures; standardized achievement test required. Deadline for receipt of application materials: none. Application fee required: $150. On-campus interview required.

Athletics Interscholastic: cheering (girls), volleyball (g); coed interscholastic: basketball, cooperative games, golf, soccer, tennis, weight lifting; coed intramural: gymnastics, martial arts, physical training, self defense. 1 PE instructor, 3 athletic trainers.

Computers Computers are regularly used in all academic, library science, library skills, newspaper, SAT preparation, word processing, writing, yearbook classes. Computer network features include on-campus library services, online commercial services, Internet access, wireless campus network, Internet filtering or blocking technology. Computer access in designated common areas is available to students. Students grades are available online. The school has a published electronic and media policy.

Contact Betsy A. Fanning, Associate Head of School. 843-884-7046. Fax: 843-881-8320. E-mail: bfanning@tridentacademy.com. Web site: www.tridentacademy.com.

ANNOUNCEMENT FROM THE SCHOOL Trident Academy serves children in grades K5–12 with average to above-average intelligence who have diagnosed learning differences and are free from emotional disturbance. The overall teacher-student ratio is 1:4. Multisensory teaching is used in a structured, individualized environment. Accreditations include SAIS, SACS, SCISA, and the Academy of Orton-Gillingham Practitioners and Educators. Trident Academy: "Empowering Creative Learners."

VALLEY VIEW SCHOOL

91 Oakham Road
PO Box 338
North Brookfield, Massachusetts 01535

Head of School: Dr. Philip G. Spiva

General Information Boys' boarding college-preparatory, general academic, and arts school; primarily serves underachievers, students with learning disabilities, individuals with Attention Deficit Disorder, individuals with emotional and behavioral problems, and difficulty socially adjusting to family and surroundings. Grades 5–12. Founded: 1970. Setting: rural. Nearest major city is Worcester. Students are housed in single-sex dormitories. 215-acre campus. 9 buildings on campus. Approved or accredited by Massachusetts Office of Child Care Services. Endowment: $450,000. Total enrollment: 56. Upper school average class size: 6. Upper school faculty-student ratio: 1:6.

Upper School Student Profile 100% of students are boarding students. 5% are state residents. 25 states are represented in upper school student body. 8% are international students. International students from Canada and Mexico; 2 other countries represented in student body.

Faculty School total: 12. In upper school: 9 men, 3 women; 4 have advanced degrees; 2 reside on campus.

Subjects Offered Algebra, American literature, anatomy, art, biology, British literature, chemistry, civics, composition, computer math, computer programming, computer science, creative writing, drama, drama performance, drama workshop, dramatic arts, drawing, drawing and design, driver education, Dutch, early childhood, earth and space science, earth science, earth systems analysis, East Asian history, East European studies, Eastern religion and philosophy, Eastern world civilizations, Easterner in the West, ecology, ecology, environmental systems, economics, economics and history, economics-AP, education, Egyptian history, electives, electronic imagery, electronic music, electronic publishing, electronic research, electronics, emergency medicine, emerging technology, engineering, English, English as a foreign language, English composition, English language and composition-AP, English language-AP, English literature, English literature and composition-AP, English literature-AP, English-AP, English/composition-AP, ensembles, entomology, entrepreneurship, environmental education, environmental geography, environmental science, environmental science-AP, environmental studies, environmental systems, epic literature, equestrian sports, equine management, equine science, equine studies, equitation, ESL, essential learning systems, ethical decision making, ethics, ethics and responsibility, ethnic literature, ethnic studies, ethology, etymology, European civilization, European history, European history-AP, general science, geography, geometry, government, grammar, health, history, life science, literature, mathematics, music, physical education, physical science, science, social studies, Spanish, study skills, theater, typing, U.S. history, Western civilization, world history, world literature, writing, zoology.

Graduation Requirements English, mathematics, physical education (includes health), science, social studies (includes history).

Special Academic Programs Remedial reading and/or remedial writing; remedial math.

College Admission Counseling 20 students graduated in 2008. Other: 15 had other specific plans.

Student Life Upper grades have specified standards of dress, honor system. Discipline rests primarily with faculty.

Tuition and Aid 7-day tuition and room/board: $60,300. Tuition installment plan (quarterly payment plan).

Admissions Deadline for receipt of application materials: March. No application fee required. On-campus interview required.

Athletics Interscholastic: basketball, cross-country running, golf, lacrosse, soccer, softball, tennis, ultimate Frisbee; intramural: alpine skiing, archery, backpacking, baseball, basketball, bicycling, billiards, blading, bowling, canoeing/kayaking, fishing, fitness, flag football, floor hockey, Frisbee, golf, hiking/backpacking, ice skating, in-line skating, mountain biking, outdoor recreation, riflery, rock climbing, roller blading, skateboarding, skiing (cross-country), skiing (downhill), snowboarding, softball, street hockey, swimming and diving, table tennis, touch football, ultimate Frisbee, volleyball, wall climbing, weight lifting, whiffle ball. 1 PE instructor.

Computers Computers are regularly used in English, mathematics, science classes. Computer network features include Internet access. Student e-mail accounts are available to students.

Contact Dr. Philip G. Spiva, Director. 508-867-6505. E-mail: valview@aol.com. Web site: www.valleyviewschool.org.

See Close-Up on page 1118.

THE VANGUARD SCHOOL

22000 Highway 27
Lake Wales, Florida 33859-6858

Head of School: Dr. Cathy Wooley-Brown, PhD

General Information Coeducational boarding and day and distance learning college-preparatory and general academic school; primarily serves underachievers, students with learning disabilities, individuals with Attention Deficit Disorder, dyslexic students, Non-verbal Learning Disabilities, and Higher functioning Asperger's Syndrome. Grades 6–PG. Distance learning grades 9–PG. Founded: 1966. Setting: small town. Nearest major city is Orlando. Students are housed in coed dormitories, single-sex dormitories, and honors dorm. 75-acre campus. 13 buildings on campus. Approved or accredited by Florida Council of Independent Schools, Southern Association of Colleges and Schools, The Association of Boarding Schools, and Florida Department of Education. Member of National Association of Independent Schools and Secondary School Admission Test Board. Endowment: $3.8 million. Total enrollment: 130. Upper school average class size: 10. Upper school faculty-student ratio: 1:10.

Upper School Student Profile Grade 9: 22 students (19 boys, 3 girls); Grade 10: 23 students (19 boys, 4 girls); Grade 11: 37 students (21 boys, 16 girls); Grade 12: 34 students (25 boys, 9 girls); Grade 13: 2 students (2 boys). 80% of students are boarding students. 40% are state residents. 18 states are represented in upper school student body. 28% are international students. International students from Bahamas, Bermuda, Cayman Islands, Jamaica, Republic of Korea, and Turks and Caicos Islands; 17 other countries represented in student body.

Faculty School total: 22. In upper school: 9 men, 9 women; 6 have advanced degrees.

Subjects Offered Algebra, American history, art, biology, chemistry, computer math, computer science, construction, creative writing, driver education, earth science, economics, English, English literature, environmental science, fine arts, geometry, government, government/civics, grammar, history, industrial arts, journalism, life management skills, mathematics, physical education, physical science, reading, science, social studies, study skills, world history, world literature.

Graduation Requirements Arts and fine arts (art, music, dance, drama), biology, career exploration, computer science, economics, English, government, life management skills, literature, mathematics, physical education (includes health), reading, science, social studies (includes history), participation in a leadership seminar.

Special Academic Programs Honors section; accelerated programs; study at local college for college credit; remedial reading and/or remedial writing; remedial math; programs in English, mathematics, general development for dyslexic students.

College Admission Counseling 31 students graduated in 2008; 20 went to college, including Florida International University; Hofstra University; Johnson & Wales University; Lynn University; The University of Texas at San Antonio; Valencia Community College. Other: 2 went to work, 2 entered military service, 5 entered a postgraduate year, 2 had other specific plans.

Student Life Upper grades have specified standards of dress, student council, honor system. Discipline rests equally with students and faculty.

Tuition and Aid Day student tuition: $22,500; 7-day tuition and room/board: $41,500. Tuition installment plan (monthly payment plans, individually arranged payment plans). Need-based scholarship grants available. In 2008–09, 23% of upper-school students received aid. Total amount of financial aid awarded in 2008–09: $374,700.

Admissions Traditional secondary-level entrance grade is 9. For fall 2008, 107 students applied for upper-level admission, 56 were accepted, 44 enrolled. Wechsler Intelligence Scale for Children required. Deadline for receipt of application materials: none. Application fee required: $100. Interview required.

Athletics Interscholastic: basketball (boys, girls), cheering (g), football (b), golf (b), running (b,g), soccer (b), tennis (b), track and field (b,g), volleyball (g), weight lifting (b); intramural: basketball (b,g), flag football (b,g), floor hockey (b,g); coed interscholastic: aquatics, cross-country running, golf, soccer, tennis; coed intramural: aerobics/dance, basketball, bowling, canoeing/kayaking, fishing, fitness, fitness walking, golf, physical fitness, scuba diving, skateboarding, soccer, swimming and diving, walking, weight lifting, weight training, yoga. 5 PE instructors, 5 coaches.

Computers Computers are regularly used in all classes. Computer resources include on-campus library services, online commercial services, Internet access, wireless campus network, Internet filtering or blocking technology. Computer access in designated common areas is available to students. Students grades are available online. The school has a published electronic and media policy.

Contact Melanie Anderson, Director of Admissions. 863-676-6091. Fax: 863-676-8297. E-mail: vanadmin@vanguardschool.org. Web site: www.vanguardschool.org.

See Close-Up on page 1120.

WEDIKO SCHOOL AND TREATMENT PROGRAM

11 Bobcat Boulevard
Windsor, New Hampshire 03244

Head of School: Harry Parad

General Information Boys' boarding and day general academic, vocational, multi-sensory instruction, and skill acquisition school; primarily serves underachievers, students with learning disabilities, individuals with Attention Deficit Disorder, individuals with emotional and behavioral problems, dyslexic students, and Asperger's Syndrome, developmental delays, mood disorders, attachment issues, and high risk adoptions. Founded: 1989. Setting: rural. Nearest major city is Boston, MA. Students are housed in single-sex dormitories. 450-acre campus. 35 buildings on campus. Approved or accredited by New Hampshire Department of Education. Total enrollment: 40. Upper school average class size: 7. Upper school faculty-student ratio: 1:2.

Upper School Student Profile 80% of students are boarding students. 75% are state residents. 6 states are represented in upper school student body.

Faculty School total: 44. In upper school: 10 men, 12 women; 7 have advanced degrees; 33 reside on campus.

Subjects Offered Algebra, arts, geometry, music, physical education, reading, science, social skills, social studies, therapeutic horseback riding, trigonometry, writing.

Graduation Requirements Graduation requirements determined by student's home school.

Special Academic Programs Remedial reading and/or remedial writing; remedial math; programs in English, mathematics, general development for dyslexic students; special instructional classes for children struggling with emotional issues.

College Admission Counseling 3 students graduated in 2008; 1 went to college. Other: 1 went to work, 1 entered a postgraduate year.

Student Life Upper grades have specified standards of dress. Discipline rests primarily with faculty.

Summer Programs Remediation, sports, art/fine arts, computer instruction programs offered; session focuses on maintaining grade levels, improving social competency; held on campus; accepts boys and girls; open to students from other schools. 140 students usually enrolled. 2009 schedule: July 5 to August 18. Application deadline: none.

Tuition and Aid Day student tuition: $50,079; 5-day tuition and room/board: $102,203; 7-day tuition and room/board: $102,203. Tuition installment plan (individually arranged payment plans). Tuition paid privately or by city, school district, or state education funds available.

Admissions For fall 2008, 17 students applied for upper-level admission, 12 were accepted, 12 enrolled. Deadline for receipt of application materials: none. No application fee required. Interview required.

Athletics Interscholastic: basketball (boys); intramural: aerobics/Nautilus (b), alpine skiing (b), aquatics (b), archery (b), ball hockey (b), baseball (b), basketball (b), bicycling (b), billiards (b), canoeing/kayaking (b), climbing (b), cooperative games (b), equestrian sports (b), fishing (b), floor hockey (b), gymnastics (b), hiking/backpacking (b), horseback riding (b), ice skating (b), indoor soccer (b), kayaking (b), kickball (b), mountain biking (b), outdoor education (b), outdoor recreation (b), outdoors (b), paddling (b), physical fitness (b), rock climbing (b), skiing (cross-country) (b), skiing (downhill) (b), snowshoeing (b), soccer (b), softball (b), swimming and diving (b), touch football (b), wall climbing (b), weight lifting (b), weight training (b), wilderness (b). 1 PE instructor, 2 coaches.

Computers Computers are regularly used in English classes. Computer network features include Internet access, Internet filtering or blocking technology.

Contact Marianne Hammond, Administrative Coordinator. 603-478-5236 Ext. 203. Fax: 603-478-2049. E-mail: mhammond@wediko-nh.org. Web site: www.wediko.org.

WILLOW HILL SCHOOL

98 Haynes Road
Sudbury, Massachusetts 01776

Head of School: Dr. Rhonda Taft-Farrell

General Information Coeducational day college-preparatory, arts, technology, and visual and performing arts school; primarily serves underachievers, students with learning disabilities, individuals with Attention Deficit Disorder, dyslexic students, non-verbal learning disabilities, and Asperger's Syndrome. Grades 6–12. Founded: 1970. Setting: suburban. Nearest major city is Boston. 26-acre campus. 4 buildings on campus. Approved or accredited by Massachusetts Department of Education and New England Association of Schools and Colleges. Member of National Association of Independent Schools and Secondary School Admission Test Board. Total enrollment: 60. Upper school average class size: 8. Upper school faculty-student ratio: 1:4.

Upper School Student Profile Grade 9: 9 students (7 boys, 2 girls); Grade 10: 11 students (8 boys, 3 girls); Grade 11: 9 students (7 boys, 2 girls); Grade 12: 6 students (6 boys).

Faculty School total: 20. In upper school: 9 men, 7 women; 16 have advanced degrees.

Subjects Offered 20th century world history, algebra, American government, American history, American literature, art, biology, career/college preparation, chemistry, computer science, computer technologies, conceptual physics, consumer mathematics, creative writing, decision making skills, drama, dramatic arts, earth science, English composition, English literature, geography, geometry, grammar, integrated science, keyboarding/computer, library studies, life science, mathematics, outdoor education, physical education, physical science, pragmatics, pre-algebra, pre-calculus, science, senior composition, social studies, study skills, technology, U.S. history, U.S. literature, world history, World War II.

Graduation Requirements Art, computer keyboarding, drama, English composition, literature, mathematics, physical education (includes health), science, social

studies (includes history), wilderness/outdoor program, Students must pass the Massachusetts Comprehensive Assessment System (MCAS), a state mandated competency requirement.
Special Academic Programs Independent study; study at local college for college credit; academic accommodation for the artistically talented; remedial reading and/or remedial writing; remedial math; programs in English, mathematics, general development for dyslexic students.
College Admission Counseling 7 students graduated in 2008; 6 went to college, including Anna Maria College; Hartwick College; Mount Ida College; Regis College; The Art Institute of Boston at Lesley University. Other: 1 went to work.
Student Life Discipline rests primarily with faculty.
Tuition and Aid Day student tuition: $46,423. Tuition installment plan (Academic Management Services Plan). PrepGATE Loans available.
Admissions Traditional secondary-level entrance grade is 9. For fall 2008, 69 students applied for upper-level admission, 17 were accepted, 11 enrolled. Comprehensive educational evaluation and WISC or WAIS required. Deadline for receipt of application materials: none. No application fee required. On-campus interview required.
Athletics Coed Interscholastic: basketball, soccer, track and field; coed intramural: backpacking, basketball, bicycling, canoeing/kayaking, climbing, cooperative games, croquet, cross-country running, floor hockey, Frisbee, hiking/backpacking, horseshoes, kayaking, lacrosse, martial arts, mountain biking, outdoor activities, outdoor education, rock climbing, snowshoeing, soccer, track and field, volleyball, wall climbing. 1 PE instructor.
Computers Computers are regularly used in all academic, art, keyboarding, library science, technology classes. Computer network features include on-campus library services, Internet access, wireless campus network. The school has a published electronic and media policy.
Contact Ann Marie Reen, Director of Admissions. 978-443-2581. Fax: 978-443-7560. E-mail: amreen@willowhillschool.org. Web site: www.willowhillschool.org.

WINSTON PREPARATORY SCHOOL

126 West 17th Street
New York, New York 10011
Head of School: Mr. William DeHaven

General Information Coeducational day college-preparatory and arts school; primarily serves underachievers, students with learning disabilities, individuals with Attention Deficit Disorder, and dyslexic students. Grades 6–12. Founded: 1981. Setting: urban. 1 building on campus. Approved or accredited by New York State Association of Independent Schools. Member of National Association of Independent Schools. Total enrollment: 240. Upper school average class size: 11. Upper school faculty-student ratio: 1:3.
Upper School Student Profile Grade 9: 40 students (30 boys, 10 girls); Grade 10: 38 students (20 boys, 18 girls); Grade 11: 43 students (27 boys, 16 girls); Grade 12: 21 students (15 boys, 6 girls).
Faculty School total: 77. In upper school: 28 men, 49 women; 63 have advanced degrees.
Subjects Offered Accounting, algebra, American history, American literature, art, biology, chemistry, community service, creative writing, drama, earth science, ecology, environmental systems, economics and history, English, English literature, European history, expository writing, fine arts, geography, geometry, government/civics, grammar, health, history, mathematics, music, physical education, physics, science, social skills, social studies, speech, theater, trigonometry, U.S. history, world history, world literature, writing.
Graduation Requirements Arts and fine arts (art, music, dance, drama), English, history, mathematics, physical education (includes health), science. Community service is required.
Special Academic Programs Honors section; remedial reading and/or remedial writing; remedial math; programs in English, mathematics, general development for dyslexic students.
College Admission Counseling 36 students graduated in 2008; 33 went to college. Other: 3 went to work.
Student Life Upper grades have specified standards of dress, student council. Discipline rests primarily with faculty.
Summer Programs Remediation, enrichment, art/fine arts programs offered; session focuses on reading, writing, and mathematics skills development; held on campus; accepts boys and girls; open to students from other schools. 60 students usually enrolled. 2009 schedule: June 30 to July 25. Application deadline: none.
Tuition and Aid Day student tuition: $47,500. Tuition installment plan (monthly payment plans, individually arranged payment plans). Need-based scholarship grants available. In 2008–09, 20% of upper-school students received aid.
Admissions Achievement tests, battery of testing done through outside agency and Wechsler Intelligence Scale for Children required. Deadline for receipt of application materials: none. Application fee required: $70. On-campus interview required.
Athletics Interscholastic: basketball (boys, girls), soccer (b), softball (b); intramural: basketball (b,g); coed interscholastic: cross-country running, golf, track and field; coed intramural: physical fitness, physical training, walking, yoga. 3 PE instructors, 3 coaches.
Computers Computers are regularly used in art, English, history, mathematics, science classes. Computer network features include Internet access, wireless campus network.
Contact Ms. Courtney DeHoff, Director of Admissions. 646-638-2705 Ext. 634. Fax: 646-839-5457. E-mail: cdehoff@winstonprep.edu.

ANNOUNCEMENT FROM THE SCHOOL Winston Prep is a highly individualized and responsive setting for high-potential middle and high school students with learning differences, such as language-based learning difficulties, nonverbal learning difficulties, and attention deficit problems. The Winston Prep program is designed to challenge each student's strengths while developing the essentials of reading, writing, mathematics, organization, and study skills. Independence is at the core of Winston's philosophy. To this end, individualization and the rich curricular experience happen in a climate of unwavering focus on maximizing independence and self-reliance. Each individualized educational program is based upon a continuously modified understanding of each student's dynamic learning profile that evolves as the student progresses and matures. Within the curriculum, skills are taught explicitly and directly, including 45 minutes of daily instruction in writing, literature, and language skills and 60 minutes in mathematics, through grade 12. Small classes of 8 to 12 students help to create a comfortable learning environment and facilitate the individualization of course work. In addition to classes, students participate in a daily one-to-one instructional period called Focus, designed to serve as the diagnostic, instructional, and mentoring centerpiece of their experience. Education does not end with academics at Winston. Fostering the social and emotional growth of the students is considered an essential part of development and is addressed throughout the School experience. Current enrollment is 240. Art, drama, gym, and a variety of challenging enrichment choices are offered within the school day and during a newly expanded after-school program. Interscholastic athletic programs are also available after school. At the high school level, students with appropriate levels of skill mastery may participate in an academic honors program and in college courses. A majority of Winston Prep's graduates continue their education at the college level.

THE WINSTON SCHOOL

5707 Royal Lane
Dallas, Texas 75229
Head of School: Dr. Polly Peterson

General Information Coeducational day college-preparatory, arts, technology, and science school; primarily serves students with learning disabilities, individuals with Attention Deficit Disorder, and dyslexic students. Grades 1–12. Founded: 1975. Setting: suburban. 4-acre campus. 2 buildings on campus. Approved or accredited by Independent Schools Association of the Southwest and Texas Department of Education. Member of National Association of Independent Schools. Endowment: $4.8 million. Total enrollment: 205. Upper school average class size: 9. Upper school faculty-student ratio: 1:5.
Upper School Student Profile Grade 9: 26 students (18 boys, 8 girls); Grade 10: 26 students (20 boys, 6 girls); Grade 11: 28 students (24 boys, 4 girls); Grade 12: 30 students (21 boys, 9 girls).
Faculty School total: 37. In upper school: 17 men, 5 women; 11 have advanced degrees.
Subjects Offered 3-dimensional art, algebra, American history, American literature, archaeology, astronomy, athletics, biology, career/college preparation, ceramics, cheerleading, chemistry, computer science, drama, economics, engineering, English, English literature, film, fine arts, foreign language, geometry, government/civics, grammar, health, journalism, keyboarding/computer, Latin, photography, physical education, physics, poetry, pre-calculus, SAT/ACT preparation, Spanish, speech, student government, technical theater, theater, trigonometry, world history, world literature, writing, yoga.
Graduation Requirements Computer science, English, foreign language, mathematics, physical education (includes health), science, social science, social studies (includes history).
Special Academic Programs Accelerated programs; independent study; study at local college for college credit; remedial reading and/or remedial writing; remedial math; programs in English, mathematics, general development for dyslexic students.
College Admission Counseling 19 students graduated in 2008; 18 went to college, including Lynn University; Savannah College of Art and Design; Stephen F. Austin State University; Texas A&M University; Texas Tech University; University of North Texas. Other: 1 had other specific plans. Mean SAT critical reading: 547, mean SAT math: 510, mean SAT writing: 530, mean combined SAT: 1587, mean composite ACT: 22.
Student Life Upper grades have specified standards of dress, student council. Discipline rests primarily with faculty.
Summer Programs Remediation, enrichment, advancement, sports, art/fine arts, computer instruction programs offered; session focuses on earning academic credit; held on campus; accepts boys and girls; open to students from other schools. 80 students usually enrolled. 2009 schedule: June 2 to July 3.

Tuition and Aid Day student tuition: $23,500–$24,000. Tuition installment plan (Insured Tuition Payment Plan, FACTS Tuition Payment Plan, monthly payment plans). Need-based scholarship grants available. In 2008–09, 21% of upper-school students received aid. Total amount of financial aid awarded in 2008–09: $233,150.
Admissions Traditional secondary-level entrance grade is 9. For fall 2008, 28 students applied for upper-level admission, 17 were accepted, 15 enrolled. Psychoeducational evaluation required. Deadline for receipt of application materials: none. Application fee required: $150. On-campus interview required.
Athletics Interscholastic: baseball (boys), basketball (b,g), cheering (g), fitness (b,g), flag football (b), football (b), indoor soccer (g), softball (g), volleyball (g), winter soccer (b,g); coed interscholastic: fitness, golf, independent competitive sports, outdoor education, physical fitness, soccer, strength & conditioning, tennis, weight training, yoga. 2 PE instructors, 2 coaches.
Computers Computers are regularly used in all academic classes. Computer resources include on-campus library services, online commercial services, Internet access, wireless campus network, Internet filtering or blocking technology. Students grades are available online. The school has a published electronic and media policy.
Contact Amy C. Smith, Director of Admission. 214-691-6950. Fax: 214-691-1509. E-mail: amy_smith@winston-school.org. Web site: www.winston-school.org.

ANNOUNCEMENT FROM THE SCHOOL Founded in 1975, The Winston School is a coeducational, college-preparatory school enrolling *bright students who learn differently*®. Students are of average to superior intelligence in grades 1–12, with a diagnosed learning difference and/or ADHD. Based on diagnostic testing and ongoing monitoring, faculty and staff members formulate individualized academic programs that inspire students' self-confidence and self-reliance with full parental involvement. The Winston School is accredited by the Independent School Association of the Southwest and is a member of the National Association of Independent Schools. Visit www.winston-school.org.

THE WINSTON SCHOOL SAN ANTONIO

8565 Ewing Halsell Drive
San Antonio, Texas 78229

Head of School: Dr. Charles J. Karulak

General Information Coeducational day college-preparatory, general academic, arts, and technology school; primarily serves students with learning disabilities, individuals with Attention Deficit Disorder, and dyslexic students. Grades K–12. Founded: 1985. Setting: urban. 16-acre campus. 2 buildings on campus. Approved or accredited by Independent Schools Association of the Southwest, Southern Association of Colleges and Schools, and Texas Education Agency. Total enrollment: 203. Upper school average class size: 10. Upper school faculty-student ratio: 1:10.
Upper School Student Profile Grade 9: 22 students (5 boys, 17 girls); Grade 10: 21 students (11 boys, 10 girls); Grade 11: 25 students (6 boys, 19 girls); Grade 12: 14 students (4 boys, 10 girls).
Faculty School total: 27. In upper school: 7 men, 8 women; 6 have advanced degrees.
Subjects Offered Algebra, American history, anatomy and physiology, art, athletics, basketball, biology, calculus, chemistry, college counseling, college planning, community service, computer graphics, computer literacy, computer multimedia, economics, English, English composition, English literature, environmental science, geography, geometry, government, graphic design, health, health education, journalism, multimedia, music, photography, physical education, physical science, physics, pre-calculus, reading, Spanish, speech, world geography, world history, yearbook.
Graduation Requirements Arts and fine arts (art, music, dance, drama), computer science, English, foreign language, history, mathematics, physical education (includes health), science, social science, 20 hours of community service per year.
Special Academic Programs Independent study; study at local college for college credit; programs in English, mathematics, general development for dyslexic students.
College Admission Counseling 19 students graduated in 2008; 16 went to college, including San Antonio College; Schreiner University; The University of Texas at San Antonio; University of the Incarnate Word. Other: 2 went to work, 1 entered military service.
Student Life Upper grades have uniform requirement, student council, honor system. Discipline rests primarily with faculty.
Summer Programs Remediation, advancement, sports, computer instruction programs offered; session focuses on high school classes for credit; held on campus; accepts boys and girls; open to students from other schools. 50 students usually enrolled. 2009 schedule: June 15 to July 10. Application deadline: May 30.
Tuition and Aid Day student tuition: $14,500. Tuition installment plan (individually arranged payment plans). Need-based scholarship grants available. In 2008–09, 25% of upper-school students received aid.
Admissions Traditional secondary-level entrance grade is 9. For fall 2008, 17 students applied for upper-level admission, 15 were accepted, 14 enrolled. Individual IQ, Achievement and behavior rating scale and WISC or WAIS required. Deadline for receipt of application materials: none. Application fee required: $100. On-campus interview required.
Athletics Interscholastic: baseball (boys), basketball (b,g), cheering (g), football (b), softball (g), strength & conditioning (b), volleyball (g); coed interscholastic: baseball, cross-country running, golf, track and field; coed intramural: cheering, golf, outdoor education, physical fitness, physical training, tennis, track and field. 2 PE instructors.
Computers Computers are regularly used in all academic classes. Computer network features include on-campus library services, Internet access, wireless campus network, Internet filtering or blocking technology. Students grades are available online. The school has a published electronic and media policy.
Contact Ms. Julie A. Saboe, Director of Admissions. 210-615-6544. Fax: 210-615-6627. E-mail: saboe@winston-sa.org. Web site: www.winston-sa.org.

BREHM PREPARATORY SCHOOL

Carbondale, Illinois

Type: Coeducational boarding and day school for students with complex learning disabilities and attention deficit disorder
Grades: 6–12, postgraduate studies; ages 11–21
Enrollment: Boarding capacity limited to 96 on campus
Head of School: Dr. Richard G. Collins, Executive Director

THE SCHOOL

Founded in 1982, Brehm Preparatory School is the only boarding school in the Midwest specifically designed to meet the academic, social, and emotional needs of students with complex learning disabilities and attention deficit disorder. Brehm's mission—to empower such students to recognize and optimize their full potential—is accomplished both through a family environment where individual needs are addressed by a focused holistic program and through the partnership developed among the staff, students, parents, board of directors, and surrounding community. Awarded the prestigious U.S. Department of Education Blue Ribbon School of Excellence honor in 1993, Brehm places a high value on student empowerment, integrity, active problem solving, ongoing communication, continuous staff and program development, and financial stability.

Brehm's 80-acre campus is located in Carbondale, a town of 27,000 in southern Illinois. Carbondale, easily reached from the major cities of St. Louis, Chicago, and Paducah, is best known as the home of Southern Illinois University. The University offers the Brehm student access to theatrical productions, sports events, concerts, and museums. Giant City State Park, the Shawnee National Forest, and many lakes provide abundant recreational areas.

A not-for-profit corporation, Brehm is governed by a board of directors that works actively with parents, faculty and staff members, and community residents to develop plans to maintain high-quality programs and increase community involvement.

Brehm is a member of the National Association of Independent Schools (NAIS) and the National Association of Private Schools for Exceptional Children (NAPSEC). Brehm is accredited by the North Central Association of Colleges and Schools and the Independent Schools Association of Central States.

ACADEMIC PROGRAMS

A full range of course work required for junior and senior high school graduation is offered in the areas of laboratory sciences, the humanities, visual arts, mathematics, microcomputers, and physical education. The maximum class size is 8 to 10 students in content-area classes, and teaching incorporates hands-on, multisensory instruction geared to meet each student's needs while allowing him or her to function as part of a group. Learning cognition classes focus on teaching students how they learn and which strategies they need to use to be successful. Maximum class size in learning cognition classes is 5 students.

Brehm recognizes that the student with learning disabilities and attention deficit disorder is affected across interrelated academic, social, and emotional areas and is in need of simultaneous, integrated interaction within a systematically constructed environment. Brehm therefore emphasizes a holistic approach toward educating students with these complex needs, integrating all three concerns to enhance both the cognitive and the personal development of each student. Brehm's comprehensive services thus include not only instruction in core academic areas, remedial services, and guidance in compensatory strategies for skill-deficit areas but also social and life skills development, recreational therapy, cultural enrichment, career counseling, and prevocational exploration. Instruction in Orton-Gillingham, Lindamood-Bell, and the Wilson Reading Program is available, as is individual and group language therapy. Individual psychological counseling is available on an as-needed contractual basis.

The Brehm environment proactively acknowledges that new behaviors are taught when the academic, social, and emotional needs of each student are addressed in this manner. As the student demonstrates a new behavior leading to success in each area, this success provides motivation for greater changes. Acquisition of communication skills, language development, and empowered learning translate to success in all areas of development.

Assessment, parent input, teacher observation, and analysis of language deficits by a speech pathologist result in the development of an individualized program for each student. Each student receives instruction and counseling about the nature of his or her unique learning difference and learning style.

Each student's strengths and weaknesses are regularly evaluated. Using a holistic team approach, teachers meet weekly to review students, assessing standardized as well as individual testing and teacher reports. Emphasis is placed on the strengths of the individual, while introducing strategy intervention and skill building.

Brehm's postsecondary transition program OPTIONS is designed for high school graduates who need to further develop academic, organizational, or social skills. Depending on individual needs, the program provides some remediation, acquisition of learning strategies, study skills training, academic enhancement, and social skills training. College and/or career assessment are explored through John A. Logan College and Community Internship Programs.

FACULTY AND ADVISERS

One of Brehm's main objectives is to meet each student's unique needs through the provision of high-quality, individualized services delivered by highly trained, experienced, and certified staff members. Toward that end, Brehm employs certified learning disabilities instructors, certified content instructors, and 6 full-time speech and language pathologists. The majority of staff members have master's degrees in their educational field. Brehm's academic staff averages more than ten years of professional experience. All are committed, enthusiastic professionals dedicated to the success of each student.

Teachers at Brehm are involved in decision making. They serve on curriculum committees and participate in the formulation of discipline policies and in program evaluation. Through ongoing meetings, staff members evaluate the curriculum and recommend and implement changes.

COLLEGE ADMISSION COUNSELING

College entrance exam preparation and administration as well as college exploration and application counseling are provided. Also important at Brehm is the development of self-advocacy skills. These skills help students to search out their best possible postgraduation placements and to work to make these placements successful and also enable students to effectively communicate learning needs to prospective admissions directors or future employers.

Brehm graduates, bolstered by the School's commitment to and belief in their success, can currently be found at colleges, junior colleges, and vocational-technical schools around the country. Alumni have graduated from colleges and technical schools, and many are working as teachers and coaches, in the social services, and as businessmen and businesswomen. Brehm alumni can also be found in master's and Ph.D. programs throughout the country.

STUDENT BODY AND CONDUCT

Boarding enrollment at Brehm is 96 (18 boys per dorm, 18 girls per dorm, 6 girls in an Honor Dorm).

Brehm students operate under a residential tier system that rewards students who demonstrate responsibility with increased individual privileges, including free time and off-campus hours. Responsibility for personal living space and general dormitory maintenance falls to each student.

Brehm encourages student financial planning through an allowance and banking arrangement. The School acts as the student's banker through an account opened on the student's allowance, which is provided by parents.

Students are not permitted to have cars, motorcycles, or televisions on campus.

ACADEMIC FACILITIES

Brehm's campus contains three classroom buildings designed specifically to meet the needs of the program and its students. Microcomputers are used extensively in instruction. The proximity of Southern Illinois University and John A. Logan College and access to the Internet provide opportunities for library research as well as college credit and noncredit academic experiences.

BOARDING AND GENERAL FACILITIES

A family-style living environment is designed to foster independence and responsibility. Brehm's five dormitories are designed and built much like apartment buildings, each with nine bedrooms housing 2 or 3 students per room. Each dorm has its own kitchen with ample hours for occasional meals and snacks, a lounge area with cable television, and a laundry facility for student use. A new dining hall provides lunch and dinner.

Each dormitory is supervised by 2 dorm parents who supervise, teach, coach, counsel, console, facilitate, and regulate as needed. Emphasis is placed on group living, socialization, and development of appropriate study behaviors.

Postsecondary students in the OPTIONS program reside in supervised off-campus apartments near Southern Illinois University.

ATHLETICS

Brehm's physical education program takes place at the new Student Activity Center, which includes a full gymnasium and workout room. The campus features additional grounds for baseball, football, volleyball, soccer, and other outside games.

EXTRACURRICULAR OPPORTUNITIES

Brehm's recreation program is structured on a daily basis (1½ hours per day) and weekends. Students have the flexibility to plan individual activities and participate in scheduled group events. Clubs include but are not limited to art, dance, drama, ecology, fitness programming, gymnastics, horseback riding, karate, music lessons, and tennis. Through this program, Brehm works toward expanding student interest in hobbies and recreational involvement, enhancing social skill development, furthering group interaction and leadership skills, increasing time-management skills, facilitating community integration, and supporting students in their transition from Brehm to adult life. Recreational activities are supervised by skilled recreation staff members.

DAILY LIFE

Academic classes are held from 8 a.m. to 3:35 p.m. Monday through Friday. A regular school day includes seven periods of classroom instruction followed by a supervised study period Sunday through Thursday evening.

Students are also involved in two weekly Social Skills Training sessions, which are held in individual dorms and in Campus Forum. Sessions focus on communication, listening, problem solving, and interpersonal social skills. Students explore how their learning differences may impact them in their social environment and develop strategies to overcome such issues.

WEEKEND LIFE

Students are encouraged to enjoy the southern Illinois area, "The Land between the Rivers," known for its almost unlimited access to outdoor recreational activities. A regional shopping mall as well as many small specialty shops are located in Carbondale. Numerous churches and a synagogue representing all major faiths and denominations are found in the area. Regularly scheduled transportation is provided for student activities around town and for the many weekend field trips to area activities and events. Student interests determine weekend activities.

COSTS AND FINANCIAL AID

Tuition for the 2008–09 school year was $56,280 for boarding students and $34,500 for day students. A nonrefundable $5000 deposit, applied toward tuition, is due at the time of acceptance. Upon enrollment, the remaining tuition balance is required.

Payment for the special services provided by Brehm Preparatory School may in many circumstances be considered by the Internal Revenue Service as a deductible expense, depending on individual circumstances. Parents are encouraged to consult with their tax consultants for further information about tuition deductibility.

ADMISSIONS INFORMATION

A current (not more than two years old) assessment of intelligence (Wechsler Scale, complete with subscores) and academic achievement data (the Woodcock-Johnson Psycho-Educational Batteries, Cognitive and Achievement, with Summary Scores pages) must be submitted with the application, along with a complete language evaluation and other information pertinent to assessing the applicant's educational needs, such as previous standardized testing or school records and any medical reports containing information necessary for the student's well-being.

As a prerequisite to acceptance and enrollment, each prospective student must have a complete psychoeducational evaluation and a primary diagnosis of a specific learning difference and/or attention deficit disorder.

APPLICATION TIMETABLE

Upon receipt of the application, which must be accompanied by a $75 fee, the Admissions Committee reviews all forms and records and determines the appropriateness of the Brehm program for the student. If it is determined that Brehm and the student are a suitable match, the Director of Admissions invites the student and his or her parent(s)/guardian(s) for a campus visit. Interviews with administration and staff members are conducted at the time of this visit, as is a campus tour. An offer for admission is made by the Admissions Committee if it is determined that Brehm can meet both the educational and boarding needs of the applicant. Acceptance is confirmed by the receipt of a nonrefundable $5000 deposit.

ADMISSIONS CORRESPONDENCE

Donna E. Collins
Director of Admissions
Brehm Preparatory School
1245 East Grand Avenue
Carbondale, Illinois 62901
Phone: 618-457-0371
Fax: 618-549-2329
E-mail: admissionsinfo@brehm.org
Web site: http://www.brehm.org

BROMLEY BROOK SCHOOL

Manchester Center, Vermont

BROMLEY BROOK SCHOOL

Type: Girls' boarding school
Grades: Grades 9–12 (ages 13–18)
Enrollment: 75
Head of School: Laura Mack, Executive Director

THE SCHOOL

Bromley Brook School is an intentionally small, traditional all-girls boarding school that teaches each student to recognize her own individual needs and to use her self-awareness to achieve more than she thought possible. Now in its fourth year, Bromley enrolls students in grades 9–12 who may have difficulties in traditional school settings due to issues such as low self-esteem, family problems, and social pressures.

Located in the Green Mountains of southwestern Vermont, Bromley Brook is not just a school that enrolls girls—it is a place designed specifically for girls. The School takes the time-honored traditions of all-girl boarding schools and enhances them with professional mentoring, leadership training, and strong family involvement. Bromley Brook's mission is to educate girls who know they are capable of more but do not yet have the strength of character to confidently pursue their passion. Struggling socially, emotionally, and academically, these girls dream of what is possible but have no voice to make it happen.

The School gives these girls the skills and confidence they need to find their voices and fully express themselves personally, artistically, and academically. In collaboration with parents, teachers, counselors, and the students themselves, the School assesses each girl to design an academic program that best meets her learning style and individual needs. As a result, Bromley Brook's students are well-prepared to succeed in college and beyond.

The academic program is designed to address each student's individual needs and interests in preparation for success in college and throughout their lives. On-site faculty members provide oversight to the development and implementation of the Individualized Learning Plan and serve as the primary liaisons between the School and the families. In addition, a registered nurse, master's-level clinicians, and a consulting psychiatrist are available. All students receive individual, group, and family therapy.

Bromley Brook believes in the need for girls to be girls and that each young woman is a unique, beautiful individual with special talents that only she can offer the world. The School helps each girl find a way to share her unique self with the world around her. Its in-depth curriculum promotes personal exploration, social skills refinement, and emotional resilience and provides the necessary balance for girls to pursue their academic goals.

Bromley Brook's methodology is based on creating a caring, supportive classroom environment. It believes that when students experience the classroom as a place where there is a sense of belonging and where everyone is valued and respected, they tend to participate more fully in and outside the classroom. The School's community service and service learning projects enable girls to gain greater social connections with others and promote empathy, awareness, and responsibility—factors that often bring about real changes in their own relationships with families, peers, and the community at large.

Bromley Brook School is a Recognized Independent School in the Department of Education in the state of Vermont and accredited by the Commission on International Trans-Regional Accreditation (CITA). The curriculum is approved by the state, facilitating appropriate credit transfer to other schools across the country. High school diplomas are recognized by the state of Vermont.

ACADEMIC PROGRAMS

The Bromley Brook School's curriculum is based on research and experience. It incorporates four elements that are essential to creating future success and cultivating personal leadership: character-building life exposure, a high level of self-knowledge, personal connection with the world around them, and an excellent mentoring and educational experience.

The course of study, a college-preparatory academic curriculum, emphasizes science, math, and computer technology—all taught in a female-friendly environment. Bromley Brook students learn to excel in fields traditionally underrepresented by women.

To graduate, a student must complete 4 credits of English, 3 credits of science, 3 credits of mathematics (must include algebra II), 3.5 credits of social studies, 1.5 credits of physical education, 1 credit of health education, and 9 credits of electives, for a total of 25 credits. Grades are given on a 4.0 scale. Bromley Brook School does not rank its students.

When a student enters the School, there is an ongoing period of assessment that results in an Individualized Learning Plan designed to meet her specific academic and social/emotional needs. Faculty members and therapists use and continually update this learning plan to support a student's success in and outside of the classroom. For example, an auditory-learning style means that a student absorbs knowledge best through lecture and discussion; visual learners grasp material through reading and film, and kinesthetic learners prefers a hands-on approach in their classes. Some students use a combination of learning styles.

Regular tutoring sessions and daily study periods provide a student with the discipline necessary to reach her academic goals. Instructional techniques include experiential, collaborative, cooperative, mastery, thematic, service learning, cognitive coaching, scaffolding, and instructional technology. In addition, there are classes in health, sexuality, and nutrition education. Girls are also encouraged to express themselves through the arts of drawing, painting, pottery, photography, chorus, music instruction, and writing; sharing family traditions and ceremony; meditation, visualization, and relaxation exercises; and maintaining a guided journal.

FACULTY AND ADVISERS

Bromley Brook's faculty members are the heart of its program. All hold advanced degrees, and all are deeply committed to the students' well-being and advancement. There are 49 staff members at the School, including 12 teachers; 8 therapists, including a clinical director; a consulting psychiatrist, a full-time nurse, and a community life director. Therapists play a significant role in the daily life of the School. Students have the opportunity to meet with their counselor for a weekly session, in addition to participating in one or two weekly therapy groups that focus on their individual concerns. In addition, teachers and staff members often schedule family meetings and conference calls as therapeutically recommended through the student's therapist.

Each dorm wing is assigned an adult supervisor, community life coaches, and overnight coaches to maintain safety and monitor behavior in the dorms.

Laura Mack, M.S., is the School's Executive Director. She has more than thirty years of experience in education and has spent many years in curriculum development and academic directorship. She is particularly passionate about helping girls find their own voice and has incorporated this passion into the academic curriculum at Bromley Brook. A former professional actress, Laura Mack also shares her love of theater and acting with the girls.

COLLEGE ADMISSION COUNSELING

Students who have attended Bromley Brook have continued their education at a number of prep schools, including Banff School, Culver Academy, Marvelwood School, Purnell School, and Stoneleigh-Burnham School.

The challenging college-preparatory program prepares girls to continue their education at leading colleges and universities. Graduates are currently attending the following colleges and universities: Adelphi, Auburn, Drexel, Fordham, Hunter, Northeastern, Quinnipiac, Saint Michael's, Savannah College of Art, and Syracuse.

STUDENT BODY AND CONDUCT

Bromley Brook enrolls approximately 75 girls each year between the ages of 13 and 18. They are expected to follow the guidelines of the School, including wearing the school uniform and taking part in school activities. Students are able to work with faculty members, counselors, and parents to design their own curriculum to meet their individual interests.

ACADEMIC FACILITIES

Students spend their classroom and study time in the School's chemistry and biology labs, an art room, and a computer lab—all located in one wing of the School. A recreation room, dining hall, and study hall are adjacent to this wing of the building.

BOARDING AND GENERAL FACILITIES

Bromley Brook's modern facility, designed by a renowned architect, is ideally suited to its purpose—from its science and computer labs to its art studio and ball fields, students have the opportunity to explore and expand on their various talents in a nurturing and well-conceived environment.

The student dormitories are found on two wings of the Bromley Brook School. Each dorm room consists of a bedroom and bathroom that is shared among 3 or 4 girls. Each student is responsible for keeping her surroundings and personal belongings orderly. The dorms are organized so that they form a wing of approximately 32 students, with a common area at the end of the hall.

ATHLETICS

Competitive interscholastic teams include basketball, lacrosse, and soccer. Intramural and recreational sports include volleyball, softball, skiing, snowboarding, yoga, Tai Chi, self defense, hip hop dance, and horseback riding.

EXTRACURRICULAR OPPORTUNITIES

Outside the classroom, students take part in a number of enrichment activities, such as piano and voice lessons, acting classes, culinary arts, community service, knitting club, and student government. They attend individual, group, and family counseling as well as personal seminars to develop increased emotional intelligence.

DAILY LIFE

Each day starts with academic classes that are based on each girl's Individualized Learning Plan. The evenings are devoted to studying or other activities of the student's choosing, including visual arts, music instruction, and relaxation exercises. Throughout the day, students may also take part in tutoring sessions with faculty members. Students are able to have home visits during the winter, spring, and summer breaks, as well as open weekends consistent with appropriate use of the program.

WEEKEND LIFE

Weekend activities include intensive art seminars, guest speakers, outdoor recreation (skiing, hiking, or sports), community service projects, and personal quiet time. Students also have the opportunity to provide suggestions for things they would like to do in the evenings and during the weekend. Vermont provides a number of recreational opportunities, including swimming, hiking, and berry picking in the summer; and skating, snow shoeing, and skiing in the winter.

SUMMER PROGRAMS

Bromley Brook School is in session all year long, consisting of three 4-month semesters.

COSTS AND FINANCIAL AID

The tuition of $6100 per month covers normal, daily boarding and educational expenses. The enrollment fee of $2500 includes textbooks, uniforms, and basic assessments. These costs do not include medications and medical treatment, travel expenses, or recreational spending money for trips and outings. Student loans are available at low interest rates and can be deferred for up to twelve months.

ADMISSIONS INFORMATION

The School seeks high school aged girls who are bright and capable but struggling to meet social and academic expectations due to unrealistic internal and external pressures. Some typical behaviors of students include depression, anxiety, confusion, social isolation, conflicts with family, and academic underachievement. Girls are generally ages 13–18 and have expressed a desire to go to college. The minimum FSIQ score is 95, but they may also exhibit difficulties in reading, written/oral language, or organizational and study skills. Students are generally expected to stay at the School for twelve months or longer. The School anticipates that a student needs approximately three full four-month semesters to complete the core curriculum requirements.

APPLICATION TIMETABLE

Applications may be completed and submitted online at the Bromley Brook Web site. Bromley Brook has a rolling admissions policy, so prospective students can enter the School at any point in the year. For additional information, parents should contact an admissions counselor at 866-537-2702 (toll-free).

ADMISSIONS CORRESPONDENCE

Beth Bove
Admissions Director
Bromley Brook School
2595 Depot Street
P.O. Box 2328
Manchester Center, Vermont 05255-2328
Phone: 802-362-9966 Ext. 107
866-537-2702 (toll-free)
Fax: 802-362-5539
E-mail: info@bromleybrook.com
Web site: http://www.bromleybrook.com

EAGLE HILL SCHOOL

Hardwick, Massachusetts

Type: Coeducational college-preparatory boarding school for adolescents with learning differences, including specific learning disabilities and/or ADD
Grades: 8–12
Enrollment: 150
Head of School: Dr. P. J. McDonald, Headmaster

THE SCHOOL

Established in 1967, Eagle Hill School is a private college-preparatory boarding school located in Hardwick, Massachusetts. The School's program is designed to address the academic and social needs of students with learning differences, including specific learning (dis-)abilities (LD) and/or attention deficit disorder (ADD). Serving a coeducational population of 150 young men and women, Eagle Hill School has long been recognized for its ability to remediate academic and social deficits while continuing to develop strengths. It is the School's philosophy that every student should be given the opportunity to realize success. The faculty members at Eagle Hill School truly understand the numerous challenges that face today's youth. Academic, peer, and societal demands are only a few of the hurdles that students must address on their respective paths through adolescence.

Eagle Hill School is a not-for-profit organization. It is governed by a Board of Trustees, representing alumni, parents, and prominent community members. Eagle Hill School has an exceptionally strong record of meeting the needs of LD and ADD students. Transforming years of educational frustration and deterioration into academic success and achievement has become the rule rather than the exception. The formula for attaining this goal is not left to chance.

ACADEMIC PROGRAMS

The philosophy of Eagle Hill School is to provide an individualized program of study. The Individual Education Plan (IEP) is used to define measurable objectives and provide a working plan for academic and personal growth. Each student's skill levels are determined by the review of test results, psychoeducational evaluation, previous IEPs, and a full battery of diagnostic testing performed at Eagle Hill School by the education department. The student-teacher ratio of 5:1 creates a small-class environment in which students work at their own pace with individual attention and support. These factors combine to provide an educational atmosphere that is conducive to success. The attention is focused on the individual and his or her needs.

The seven-period school day consists of two periods of English language arts and one period each of math, science, history, and one or more elective classes. Electives include Basics of Filmmaking, Culinary Arts, Graphic Arts, Latin, Spanish, French, Russian language and culture, forensic science, fundamentals of music theory, Performing Arts Seminar, Prehistory of Rock, Philosophy, Psychology, Studio Art, Technical Theater Internship, Technology, Woodshop, and Zoology. Pragmatics classes stress verbal and nonverbal communication skills, as well as student leadership opportunities. Class groupings are homogeneous by age and skill level.

A fundamental component of academic growth is the need to be sufficiently challenged in the classroom. The Eagle Hill School curriculum combines process writing, metacognitive strategies, and multisensory teaching with the proven practices of a traditional curriculum. The curriculum ranges from pre-algebra and writing workshop and reading classes to advanced mathematics, literature seminar, and critical thinking. Students work together on similar goals and objectives, creating a comfortable learning environment.

The IEP establishes a baseline to measure improvement of skills. The evaluation of objectives from September through June offers a reliable and accurate depiction of a student's skills and progress. Beyond its use as an educational yardstick, the IEP is also an effective motivator. When students can visualize and understand clear objectives, they surpass everyone's expectations.

FACULTY AND ADVISERS

Eagle Hill School employs 80 full-time faculty members, including teachers, administrators, and resident counselors. The student-faculty ratio in the classroom is 5: 1. The cornerstone of Eagle Hill School's success is its faculty, whose members' unconditional commitment, in combination with continuous training, has made it one of the finest. Teachers and resident counselors commonly offer extra help, insightful advice, or even a shoulder to lean on during the evening hours. Dedicated, motivated, and professional are only a few of the adjectives used by students and parents to describe the faculty members. Their investment in each student's life has made Eagle Hill School an environment conducive to learning and thriving.

Eagle Hill School recruits nationally, seeking individuals who possess the qualities and characteristics of exceptional educators. These committed faculty members are experienced, certified, and dedicated to excellence in a highly challenging environment.

COLLEGE ADMISSION COUNSELING

Eagle Hill School's college-preparatory program provides a full range of services designed to assist students in selecting the right environment for postsecondary education. Approximately 96 percent of graduates are accepted into colleges and universities prior to graduation. Eagle Hill School administers the ACT tests proctored and untimed to assist LD and ADD students. Preparation courses and practice tests are also offered. Graduates currently attend colleges and universities that include Adelphi, American, Clark, Curry, Franklin Pierce, George Washington, Goucher, Hampshire, Hofstra, Ithaca, Johnson and Wales, Lesley, Mitchell, Mount Holyoke, Mount Ida, Muhlenberg, Roger Williams, Sacred Heart, Wheaton, Worcester Polytechnic Institute, and the Universities of Arizona, Denver, Hartford, and Massachusetts.

STUDENT BODY AND CONDUCT

Eagle Hill School enrolls 150 students, grades 8–12, in a coeducational environment with approximately a 3:2 boys-to-girls ratio. The current student population represents twenty-four states and seven countries. All students have been diagnosed with a learning disability and/or attention deficit disorder and range from average to above-average on diagnostic evaluations. Student behavior is governed by a code of student conduct, with emphasis placed upon personal development and individual responsibility. The expectations for student conduct are high.

ACADEMIC FACILITIES

Eagle Hill School is located on the eastern edge of the Quabbin Reservoir and encompasses 165 acres. Sixteen buildings, tennis courts, soccer fields, a softball diamond, a gymnasium and fitness center, and a swimming pool occupy the grounds. The Richardson Academic Center, which was completed in October 2005, brings together the majority of Eagle Hill's academic resources under one roof. These include forty-eight classrooms, five computer labs, six state-of-the-art science labs, a library, and culinary arts.

The center is also the new home for Eagle Hill's curriculum library and professional resources, a faculty library and common room, and a multiuse conference and professional development center. At the heart of the complex is a suite of college-counseling and guidance offices, a student art gallery, and the campus bookstore.

The Cultural Center at Eagle Hill, which opened in the fall of 2008, provides a venue for learning, creating, exhibiting, performing, and enjoying art. A $15-million facility, it features two theaters; art galleries; visual art and graphics classrooms and studios; a music classroom and recording studio; a woodshop; and a function hall. Students are involved in producing and promoting professional musical and theatrical programs through theater arts and arts management intern programs.

BOARDING AND GENERAL FACILITIES

Students are housed in three residential buildings. The two resident halls for underclassmen accommodate 2 students per room and approximately 18 students per building. Upperclassmen live in the state-of-the-art Harmsworth Hall. This facility features single rooms and multiple spacious lounges. Every student's room is equipped with Internet and telephone access. All residential buildings house full-time, live-in resident counselors who are primarily responsible for developing and maintaining a positive, community-based living environment.

ATHLETICS

Designed to complement the educational programs, athletics at Eagle Hill School are an integral part of the total development of each student. Teamwork and good sportsmanship are only two of the lifelong lessons that students learn as part of their participation in the athletic program. Beyond sports' self-esteem value, the exertion of energy serves as a positive release.

Eagle Hill School offers the interscholastic sports of basketball, cross-country golf, lacrosse, running, soccer, softball, tennis, and wrestling. Varsity and junior varsity teams compete against many area schools. Students who do not wish to compete on a sports team during a given semester participate in an independent aerobic activity of their choosing, including basketball, biking, kickboxing, rollerblading, running, skateboarding, tennis, and walking.

Facilities at Eagle Hill include a gymnasium and fitness center, an outdoor swimming pool, an adventure ropes course, and a new outdoor athletic complex, which includes two soccer fields, four tennis courts, a basketball court, a softball diamond, and a walking track.

EXTRACURRICULAR OPPORTUNITIES

Eagle Hill School offers a wide variety of clubs and activities. During the evening hours, students may participate in a formal club program or a variety of leisure activities. A sampling of clubs and activities available in the evening includes biking, tennis, outdoor/indoor basketball, guitar, weight training, student government, fencing, chess, swimming (seasonal), literary magazine, school newspaper, environmental society, radio broadcasting, world cultures, adopt-a-grandparent, and off-campus trips. Students may choose from many different options based on individual interests. Students may also choose to relax or play a game of billiards in the Student Activity Center.

DAILY LIFE

The class day at Eagle Hill School begins at 8:30 and finishes at 3:15, followed by a 30-minute period reserved for extra help. At 3:45, the sports and aerobics programs round out the day, with dinner starting at 5:30. Students eat meals in the dining hall, conversing with faculty members. From 6:30 to 8, all students participate in mandatory study halls, which are held on each dorm floor. Resident counselors and classroom teachers provide supervision and assistance. Beginning at 8, students have an hour of free time to spend relaxing with friends or participating in clubs. A wide variety of on- and off-campus activities are offered at this time. Campus curfew is in effect at 9 for those students who have not earned Pioneer Privilege. Bedtime is determined by age and dormitory.

WEEKEND LIFE

Eagle Hill School employs a full-time Director of Weekend Services, whose sole responsibility is to plan activities for Friday evening through Sunday evening. Weekend activities occur on and off campus, taking advantage of all that New England has to offer. On campus, the Student Activity Center has billiards, a wide-screen TV and VCR/DVD, and a stereo system. The Athletic Center is open, complete with a full health and fitness center and a basketball court. All off-campus trips are supervised, and they are designed for the interest of the adolescent. Student participation in planning events is encouraged and solicited. During the winter months, students enjoy skiing, snowboarding, and sledding at local mountains in Massachusetts and Vermont. Those who do not choose this type of activity can participate in other options, including in-line skating, laser tag, paintball, visits to New York and Boston, and trips to movies, theaters, and sporting events. In warmer weather, students can enjoy the outdoors in many ways, including camping, hiking, deep-sea fishing, whale watching, white-water rafting, and visits to amusement and water parks.

SUMMER PROGRAMS

Eagle Hill School offers a five-week summer session for those students who need programmatic continuity, time to make the transition into the fall program, and/or prevention of skill regression. The summer session limits its enrollment to 75 students, with an emphasis on promoting a camp-like atmosphere. The program offers an eight-period class day. Four classes concentrate on reading, writing, math, and pragmatics, while the remaining four classes are designed to foster community dynamics and build self-esteem. Those classes include swimming, adventure ropes, art, woodshop, graphic arts, culinary arts, fly fishing, photography, and computers, among other subjects.

Following the class day, students enjoy a variety of afternoon activities that rotate on a daily basis. These activities may include swimming, fishing, arts and crafts, billiards, hiking, football, kickball, adventure ropes, and a wide variety of other offerings. Each evening, students participate in a club of their choice. Clubs are scheduled Monday through Thursday and do not rotate. Clubs are designed to have educational value but also incorporate fun.

Summer weekends provide the same level of structure as in the fall program but offer a wider choice of outdoor activities, given the New England summer weather. Weekend programming includes hiking, camping, amusement parks, water parks, beach trips, whale watching, deep-sea fishing, and white-water rafting.

The Eagle Hill School summer population is made up of three main groups. One group of the summer students is currently enrolled in the academic-year program as well and needs the continuity of the summer program to maintain skill levels. The second group consists of new or returning students who come just for the summer session and the academic boost it provides before returning to their home placements. The third group consists of new students who will make the transition to the academic-year program the following fall. For them, the summer session is a time of acclimation and preparation for the upcoming school year. They learn the routine, get to know the faculty members, meet some of their peers, and learn how to navigate campus life. When they return to Eagle Hill School in September to face increased academic expectations, their transition tends to be much smoother. In essence, attending the summer session reduces the anxiety and the unknown of a new situation.

The Eagle Hill Summer College program is designed for recent Eagle Hill graduates and Eagle Hill students entering their senior year. The program provides an opportunity for these students to acquire college credits, test their independence, and develop greater self-advocacy skills before they officially enter college. For five weeks, students live on the Eagle Hill campus and take two courses at a local college.

COSTS AND FINANCIAL AID

Academic-year tuition, room, and board were $51,692 for the 2008–09 academic year. Student bank funds for an allowance, activities, and other expenses total $3700. A room deposit of $7500 is required on enrollment. Summer tuition, room, and board for 2009 are $7266 plus student bank funds totaling $800.

ADMISSIONS INFORMATION

Eagle Hill School admits students of any race, color, sexual orientation, religion, or national and ethnic origin to all of the rights, privileges, programs, and activities generally accorded or made available to students at the school. It does not discriminate on the basis of race, color, religion, sexual orientation, or national and ethnic origin in the administration of its educational policies, admission policies, athletic programs, or any other school-administered programs.

The admission procedures for both the school year and the summer programs are identical. Eagle Hill School has designed the following convenient guidelines to assist applicants in making sure their applications are processed expediently. Applications are accepted throughout the year, and qualified applicants may join the program during any semester, space permitting.

Prior to the interview process, applicants should submit a current psychoeducational evaluation to the admission department. This evaluation should include a cognitive assessment (WISC-IV) and academic achievement testing (e.g., WJ-R, WIAT), educational assessments, pertinent school records, teacher evaluations, a writing sample, IEPs, clinical evaluations, standardized testing, and official high school transcripts with school seal and signature of registrar. Following a review of the submitted records, an admission officer contacts applicants to schedule a mutually convenient time for an interview. Parents/guardians are notified of admission decisions. Should further information be needed, an admission representative contacts applicants immediately.

APPLICATION TIMETABLE

Inquiries are welcome at any time. Typically, interviews are scheduled Monday through Friday during the school year. While there is no application deadline, parents are advised to begin the admission process as soon as possible. Typically, early decisions are made in November, with two additional rounds of decisions in January and March. Once Eagle Hill School is at capacity, candidates who qualify for admission are placed in a waiting pool. Midyear enrollments are based on space availability. Admission to the summer program is rolling.

ADMISSIONS CORRESPONDENCE

Admission Office
Eagle Hill School
242 Old Petersham Road
P.O. Box 116
Hardwick, Massachusetts 01037

Phone: 413-477-6000
Fax: 413-477-6837
E-mail: admission@ehs1.org
Web site: http://www.ehs1.org

ELAN SCHOOL

Poland, Maine

Type: Coeducational boarding college-preparatory and general academic school for adolescents with emotional, behavioral, or adjustment problems
Grades: 8–12
Enrollment: 62
Head of School: Sharon Terry, Executive Director

THE SCHOOL

Elan School is a carefully conceptualized, caringly administered residential community. Founded in 1970, it continues to be independently owned and operated. At its inception, it was designed as a facility that would help adolescents permanently change attitudes and life patterns, teaching them to function effectively in the mainstream of life. Elan's program has been modified a bit over the years, but the philosophy remains the same: "Elan's purpose is not to change an ill-behaved child into a well-behaved child; but rather to return home a responsible young adult." Students are admitted at any time year-round and stay an average of twenty-seven months. The 32-acre campus is in a rural community 20 minutes from Lewiston and 40 minutes from Portland.

The program is based on the principle that behavior cannot be changed by simply eliminating negative actions. The adolescent must not only stop antisocial acts but must also learn a new way of doing things. Elan is a closely knit, highly structured community that simulates society. Students living the house are in charge of its operation under the supervision of direct-care staff members. There is a job hierarchy designed to instill self-respect and teach personal responsibility, honesty, consideration for others, self-control, and patience. A work ethic is stressed throughout the program, and each promotion results in new privileges and increased status. If students fail to perform with initiative, they participate in additional group and individual sessions. If this is not successful, they are demoted; this teaches them to function under adversity and to deal with failure, disappointment, and disagreement. They learn that occasionally failing is part of life, that they can start again and succeed, and that the development of resilience is fundamental to success. Peer pressure and support teaches and enforces constructive behavior. Students learn that they must earn what they want and that they must give to receive.

The peer-oriented social structure is vital to the Elan concept. Students learn to take direction, accept criticism without taking it personally, criticize constructively, give orders reasonably, and care for and work with others; they also learn that self-esteem is not purely dependent on the acceptance of others.

Students manifest significant improvements in interpersonal relations at Elan. Psychodynamic problems are dealt with at Elan, usually in group sessions. The exercises teach sensitivity to the needs and problems of others and foster getting in touch with feelings, understanding what touches off feelings, and controlling the acts engendered by them. Elan brings acting-out behavior into dynamic group sessions, where the goals are getting along with peers and learning how to deal with inner stresses and strains.

Elan is licensed by the Maine Department of Education as a special-purpose, private school. Elan is a member of National Association of Therapeutic Schools and Massachusetts Association of Approved Private Schools, and it is approved by Immigration and Naturalization Services.

ACADEMIC PROGRAMS

Elan offers a fully approved junior high, high school, and special education program. Those students planning to continue their education in postsecondary schools are challenged through upper-level courses, while those who need intensive remediation are helped to acquire skills necessary to cope in the working world, as well as open doors to postsecondary education and training. Elan's credit requirements for issuing State of Maine high school diplomas is 4 English, 3 science (including 1 lab), 3 math, 3 history (including U.S. history), 1 fine arts (humanities, theater, music), 1 physical education, health, and electives (such as organic chemistry, physics, Spanish, French, personal finance, and others) to total 24 credits.

Students follow a block schedule in which they take three courses per semester and earn 1 full credit in each subject. A student may earn up to 6 credits during the regular school year plus the required studies in life skills and physical education. Foreign languages are offered but are not required. Students are provided the opportunity to work in independent study programs under faculty supervision to augment their course of studies, if needed. Elan's curriculum reflects the needs of the student body and the expertise of its faculty members.

School during evening hours allows students to work through behaviors that interfere with concentration and learning during the day; students thereby arrive in class better prepared to focus.

Class size is kept small (maximum 14 students, optimum 10 students), and students are grouped by ability and course requirements. Supervised study halls and weekly grades help eliminate end-of-quarter "surprises." The passing grade is 65, and honors grades are recognized by the entire School. Each quarter, the student receives written comments from each teacher as well as numerical grades. Elan's program also includes an eight-week summer session featuring remedial work, enhancement courses, and electives. Students earn a half credit in each of the two subjects taken during summer school.

FACULTY AND ADVISERS

Faculty members at Elan are certified in their subject specialty and/or special education. Weekly faculty meetings allow continuous collaboration, brainstorming, and curriculum development. Most teachers either have earned or are working toward advanced degrees. Various professions are represented among the teaching staff, including a professional musician, a retired Army officer, a private business owner, a writer, and a psychologist.

Elan's Superintendent, Frank McDermott, was appointed to that position in July 2004. He has been Elan's Director of Education since 2000 and the Principal since 1998. He spent thirty-five years in public education, the last twenty-six as an Assistant Superintendent and Superintendent of Schools in Maine. Frank has been recognized both nationally and locally for leadership in Quality Principles application in education and the use of technology to transform schools. Mr. McDermott has a master's degree in educational administration and a Certificate of Advanced Studies in administration from the University of Maine.

Dr. Mary Waters, Elan's Special Education Coordinator, joined in August 2005. She received her master's degrees in exceptionality and administration from the University of Maine in 1975 and 1980 respectively and a doctorate in educational leadership from Nova University in 1990. Prior to joining Elan, Meg worked as a classroom teacher, special education teacher, and, for the past thirty years, as Coordinator of Special Services in Raymond, Maine. Her extensive background and varied experiences in education in both national and statewide organizations and initiatives allows her to serve as a resource providing support to the faculty, staff, and families to enhance student learning.

COLLEGE ADMISSION COUNSELING

Elan is a closed SAT testing site. Students go on to two- and four-year colleges as well as to a variety of vocational programs and schools. More than 300 schools, colleges, and universities throughout the country have accepted Elan graduates during its nearly forty year history. Seventy-five percent of graduates continue their education. The remainder may enter the workforce or join the armed services, but several of these students have long-range goals that include furthering their education. Elan has 2 part-time college counselors to assist students with the college admissions process.

Johnna Mulligan graduated from Bates College in Lewiston, Maine, with a B.A. in psychology. She also received a M.Ed. from the University of Southern Maine and a M.A. in counseling psychology, with a focus on school counseling, from Vermont College. Johnna has taught French at a local high school for seven years and spent the last two years as a school counselor at the same school. Johnna has worked at Elan for the past 2½ years assisting students with the college research and application process.

Carrie Mrowka has a B.A. in psychology from the University of Maine and an M.S. in counseling, with a focus in school counseling, from the University of Southern Maine. Her past employment includes service as regional director for an internship program for both high school and college students. Since 2003, she has been a school counselor at a local public high school. Carrie has been working with Elan students since fall 2007.

STUDENT BODY AND CONDUCT

Currently, there are 9 students in grade 9, 12 students in grade 10, 17 students in grade 11, and 24 students in grade 12. Students who are members of minority groups make up 20 percent of the student body; 68 percent of the students are boys.

ACADEMIC FACILITIES

Elan has a central library located in the School House as well as a house library consisting of fiction and nonfiction. The computer lab is used by students to develop computer literacy. Teachers also use the lab as part of their course work with the students.

BOARDING AND GENERAL FACILITIES

Students reside in a coeducational house. The house is self-contained and is set up to simulate a real home with a kitchen, dining room, and living room with a big screen television with surround sound. Meals are prepared in the main kitchen at Elan by two chefs and are served family style to the students. Dormitory rooms may have from 2 to 8 students. The School operates year-round, and all students live on campus, even during major holidays. Academic classes are not held during standard public school vacation times.

Elan has an on-site medical clinic where routine medical care is provided. Elan's Medical Director is a practicing emergency physician with more than twenty years' experience, He is routinely on-site, treating students one day a week, or more often when needed. He performs initial physical exams, which include a lab workup, for all new admissions. He reviews the previous week's activities and is always available for telephone consultation. Elan's medical assistant handles day-to-day health problems in consultation with the physician when necessary. If specialty care is required and cannot wait for a home visit, treatment is conducted at local specialists' offices.

Clothing is usually informal, but there are occasions when dress clothes are appropriate.

ATHLETICS

Elan has a certified physical education instructor. In season, an active schedule of intramural sports allows students to enjoy friendly competition. Special trips are organized weekly during the summer for hiking on Maine's Calendar Islands, sailing, and deep-sea fishing. Additional trips are scheduled for other recreational opportunities, including bowling, canoeing, hiking, ice skating, downhill and cross-country skiing, snow tubing, whale watching, swimming, and white-water rafting

Elan currently has girls' and boys' cross-country track teams (the varsity boys won the Class D State Championship in 1997, 1999, and 2004 and were runners-up in 1998 and 2000 and the MAISAD State Championship in 2005; the junior varsity boys won the Class D State Championship in 1997, 1998, and 1999; the girls won the Class D State Championship in 2000, 2001, 2002, and 2003); boys' and girls' basketball teams (the boys' team won the Maine Principals' Association Sportsmanship of the Year Award in 1998 and the MAISAD Sportsmanship of the Year Award in 2004); a boys' golf team; and boys' and girls' track teams (the boys won the Class C State Championship in 1998), all of which compete against other area private and public schools. Elan has produced several championship teams in the MAISAD (both the boys' and girls' teams won the MAISAD Basketball Championships in 2001) and regional divisions, as well as two all-American racewalkers, who were ranked among the top 10 nationally. Peter Rowe, the cross-country and track and field coach, was named Coach of the Year in 1997, 1998, and 1999.

The School's location on Upper Range Pond affords a waterfront program of leisure swimming (supervised by a qualified lifeguard) and canoeing. In recreational activities, Elan stresses teamwork and sportsmanship. Healthy peer interaction, a cornerstone of the program, is a goal in athletics as well as in all other aspects of the program.

EXTRACURRICULAR OPPORTUNITIES

Videos are shown every week. Concerts, festivals, local fairs, exhibits, sports events, and trips out to dinner, the movies, art museums, planetariums, aquariums, and the theater are organized regularly for students who have earned the privilege. Most entertainment trips are to Portland, where professional hockey and baseball teams are among the attractions. Other trips may be to attend area football games, amusement parks, or places of historical or cultural interest. Trips to various state parks are organized during the summer months. In addition to the regular recreational trips, house trips include canoeing, white-water rafting, snow tubing, whale watching, roller skating, and bowling.

Elan students participate in an annual campuswide talent show. Students showcase their creative side by playing musical instruments, performing comedy skits or variety acts, singing, reading poetry, or participating in other performing arts. Winter and Spring Carnivals are also held; students participate in a variety of competitions, including tug-of-war, volleyball, basketball, relay races, and other athletic competitions. Students also participate in an annual "End of Summer" field day. Students are awarded tickets that are redeemed for various events, such as lawn bowling, a sherpa walk (which is part of the ropes course), a beanbag toss, a dunk tank, and other fun-filled activities.

DAILY LIFE

Weekday schedules begin at 8 with showers, cleaning dorm rooms, and breakfast; from 10 to 4:30 is a rotation of job functioning, physical education, group and individual sessions, and other events necessary to maintain balanced structure. Lunch is at noon, dinner is at 4:30, and school is from 6 to 10:30 p.m. Students return to their dorm rooms around 11 p.m.; lights-out is half an hour after students return to their dorm rooms.

WEEKEND LIFE

Elan is a demanding place. Students are busy weekdays with group sessions, house functioning, and school. Elan recognizes the need for change of pace, so weekends and holidays are less structured. Students may sleep until 11 a.m. and have brunch at 1 p.m. The rest of the day is usually spent in recreational activities. Elan School is nonsectarian.

SUMMER PROGRAMS

Elan's eight-week summer program is a continuation of the regular school year, except for a change in class times. (Summer program classes run from 7 to 10 p.m.) The curriculum focuses on remedial work tailored to current needs and on special electives. Full use is made of Maine's natural resources and points of interest.

COSTS AND FINANCIAL AID

The rate for the 2008–09 school year is $54,960.60, billed monthly at $4580.05. Components of the annual cost are tuition, $21,490.88; supportive services, $19,172.72; and board and care, $14,295.74. The daily rate is $150.58. Each student's personal account for sundries and entertainment (Student Bank) averages $125 per month and is billed separately.

No financial aid is provided by the Elan School directly; however, students not funded privately may be eligible through special education, social services, or combinations of the above. Certain Elan fees may be deductible for federal income tax purposes as medical care expenses incurred on behalf of a dependent. Families should visit http://www.frcd.org (Family Resource Center on Disabilities) for more information. For private loan information, families should visit http://www.ClarkBHF.com.

If the student is privately funded, due on the date of admission are the balance of the present month (if paid after the fifteenth, the following month's fees must also be paid) plus a three-month prepayment or Performance Deposit (which is applied to the final three months of the program). A $200 deposit for the Student Bank is also required; this is always the parents' responsibility.

ADMISSIONS INFORMATION

Elan accepts referrals from parents/legal guardians, school districts, government agencies, therapists, educational consultants, psychologists, psychiatrists, and anyone with a personal or professional interest in the student. A current psychological evaluation and educational records are reviewed by the Admissions Committee, along with Elan's Admissions Application. Questions of appropriateness are resolved via phone; occasionally, an interview is required. If criteria are met, the referral source is notified—first by phone, and then in writing; funding is verified (if privately placed, Elan's Financial Statement is required); and details of admission are finalized. By the date of admission, school transcripts, birth certificate, immunization records, medical authorizations, health insurance information, and applicable legal documents are required. In order to maximize understanding of Elan's program, parents receive a comprehensive tour before admission (or at the time of admission in emergency placements). The tour includes a visit through the house (escorted by an Elan student) and meetings with personnel from the Admissions, Education, and Medical Departments.

The successful candidate must have at least an average IQ, good reality testing, the ability to develop socialization skills, no history of violent crimes, and must not require continued psychotropic medications, as Elan does not utilize them (although there may be a history of medication). Mild to moderate learning disabilities and acting-out behavior are acceptable. Applicants not considered for admission are those with a major mental illness or cognitive deficits or who are actively violent, need continued psychotropic medications, have a physical condition requiring dietetic restriction or constant medical attention, or are non-English-speaking.

APPLICATION TIMETABLE

Inquiries and admissions occur year-round. Unless an interview is necessary, admissions decisions are usually made within three to four working days. Interviews, tours, and admissions are conducted weekdays (excluding legal holidays), by appointment only. Except for emergency situations, admissions are scheduled for Monday through Thursday during regular business hours. Due to Elan's rolling admissions policy, there are always students graduating from the School; therefore, if there is a waiting list, it is usually short.

ADMISSIONS CORRESPONDENCE

Connie Kimball, Admissions Director
Elan School
P.O. Box 578
Poland, Maine 04274-0578
Phone: 207-998-4666
Fax: 207-998-4660
E-mail: info@elanschool.com
Web site: http://www.elanschool.com

THE FAMILY FOUNDATION SCHOOL

Hancock, New York

Type: Therapeutic, college-preparatory boarding school offering an integrated program of academics, therapeutic counseling, and 12-Step living to at-risk teens, ages 12–18
Grades: 6–12
Enrollment: 250
Head of School: Emmanuel Argiros, President

THE SCHOOL

Founded in 1987, The Family Foundation School (high school and separate middle school) serves at-risk teens who struggle with a variety of behavioral, emotional, and learning difficulties and/or substance abuse. Its students have gotten into trouble at home, at school, and sometimes with the law. Most are underachievers with considerable potential for academic success.

While the School sets unique academic and emotional growth goals for each student based on individual circumstances, all students are expected to meet the fundamental goals of The Family Foundation School: to maximize their academic potential in completing a challenging curriculum by developing the concentration, study skills, and love of learning that will serve them in college and beyond; to develop themselves spiritually and emotionally while acquiring new coping strategies based on the 12-Step program of recovery; and to grow and mature psychologically, using individual and group counseling to deal with the problem behaviors and developmental issues that brought them to the School. The School monitors progress toward these goals with a formal assessment process for each student that looks at his or her academic performance, therapeutic progress, and peer interaction.

The Family Foundation School program is accredited by the Joint Commission.

ACADEMIC PROGRAMS

The Family Foundation School has a well-earned reputation for the best academics of any residential program for at-risk teens. It offers a college-preparatory curriculum, is registered with the New York State Board of Regents and accredited by the Middle States Association of Colleges and Schools, and insists on high-academic and extracurricular achievement from all students.

FFS students produce above-average SAT scores, and the School has had 100 percent of its graduates accepted to postsecondary institutions, which is particularly impressive considering the many students who are enrolled with little hope of finishing high school.

Courses for high school and middle school include math through calculus; earth science, biology, chemistry, and physics; four years of Spanish and standard four-year sequences in history and English. Several college courses conducted by qualified college instructors are offered on campus, allowing some students to stay and strengthen the changes they have made with no loss of educational opportunity.

Classes are small, averaging 12 students each, with an overall student-teacher ratio of 8:1. Peer tutoring and study groups operate for all classes, and teachers are always available to work one-on-one with students who need extra help.

In addition to the academic requirements, students must successfully complete the prescribed living skills and character education curriculum in order to graduate. It is this critical component that instills the honesty, unselfishness, and work ethic that distinguish Family Foundation School graduates.

The School runs two 25-week semesters, which allows for the enrollment of new students year-round and provides them with special attention while they adjust. It also gives students extra review time for finals, the Regents exams, and the SAT and ACT. The School's high academic standards are reflected in its higher-than-average passing grade of 75 percent.

FACULTY AND ADVISERS

Many faculty members possess not only the teaching credentials but the recovery history that uniquely qualifies them to teach at-risk teens, reaching and relating to them where others might fail. All teachers are knowledgeable of the 12 Steps, ever mindful of their students' backgrounds and unique emotional circumstances, and ready to inject program principles into the curriculum wherever helpful and appropriate.

Six faculty members have Ph.D.'s, and many have master's degrees in their fields. Notable faculty members include children's author Jan Cheripko in the School's English department.

The counseling department, under the direction of a licensed clinical social worker (LCSW-R), a consulting psychiatrist, and clinical psychologist, conducts diagnostic evaluations, crisis intervention, and short-term individual counseling for students, along with daily and weekly group counseling. This year, one of the School's master's-level clinicians received certification as a Clinical Trauma Specialist, with others scheduled for certification in 2009.

Each student receives the immediate and ongoing personal attention of a staff mentor or "sponsor." The primary function of the sponsor is to counsel and coach and to guide the student's observations and self-reflection going through the 12 Steps. Sponsors usually become the ones students approach with problems, and the bond that forms between them is integral to the student's recovery.

COLLEGE ADMISSION COUNSELING

FFS students take the PSAT in October of their junior year, and they take the SAT the following May and in October of their senior year. Students who wish to may take the ACT as well. Students are sometimes required to take SAT Subject Tests, which the School also uses for evaluating proficiencies in certain areas.

The School's Vice President for Academic Affairs and academic coordinators work with students throughout the year in the college selection and application process. The School also facilitates college visits for students and their parents.

Graduation ceremonies take place in both June and December. Over the past six years, 100 percent of FFS graduates have been accepted to postsecondary institutions: 85 percent to four-year colleges or universities and 15 percent to community colleges or professional schools, such as the Culinary Institute of America and the Fashion Institute of Technology. Family Foundation School alumni have gone on to Brandeis, Grinnell, NYU, Rutgers, Purdue, St. John's, Temple, U.S. Naval Academy, Wake Forest, and the Universities of Virginia and Wisconsin.

STUDENT BODY AND CONDUCT

Each of the 250 students enrolled in The Family Foundation School struggles emotionally and behaviorally with such problems as depression, anxiety, difficulty in relating to parents and other family members, ADHD, ODD (Oppositional Defiant Disorder), self-injury, or eating disorder.

The nurturing, therapeutic environment of the School, coupled with high academic and extracurricular expectations and support, enable students to work through their problems while progressing through middle school and high school. The overwhelming majority of them recover, become responsible for themselves and considerate of others, grow in self-respect and self-esteem, and develop a spiritual life. Most notably, they are able to mend relations with their families, receive a diploma, and go off to college.

The numerous rules and requirements for the School's at-risk population have evolved over time, and many were originally suggested and refined by students themselves after considering what works and does not work to help them recover. Those who abide by the rules enjoy everything the School has to offer: its many activities, family outings, weekend movies, treats, phone calls and visits home. Those who excel are given extra privileges, responsibilities, and opportunities to develop leadership skills. Consequences for infractions, also suggested by the students, can involve extra work, extra supervision, and restriction of privileges.

Rules and consequences are reviewed regularly to make sure they are applied therapeutically and are still serving their intended purposes: to teach self-discipline, respect for self, and consideration for others and thus help students make positive changes in a safe and supportive environment.

ACADEMIC FACILITIES

The main building on the School's 150-acre mountaintop campus houses twelve classrooms, a regulation-sized gymnasium, a full stage for dramatic and choral productions, two science labs, a fine arts studio, and administrative, guidance, and counseling offices. Classrooms for middle school students are located in a separate building, as is the school library, which contains more than 11,000 volumes and is part of New York State's interlibrary loan system. Other facilities include a choral- and dance-rehearsal building and a woodcarving shop. All buildings are wired for T-1 Internet connection, and all eleventh- and twelfth-grade students are provided with a personal laptop computer.

BOARDING AND GENERAL FACILITIES

Since its inception, The Family Foundation School has used the structure of the family to define the relationship between staff members and students, believing that families are the bedrock of society and that their primary responsibility is to teach the values and lessons needed to live meaningful, productive lives.

To help promote the personal growth of students in its care, the School is divided into eight separate "families" of about 30 students and 15–20 staff members each. Each family has a boys' and girls' dormitory and a comfortable living and dining room suite for meals, socializing, and studying—located in the three-story "House," along with the central kitchen. The School's interdenominational chapel overlooks the campus, and the entire campus overlooks the Upper Delaware River National Scenic Park.

A new multifamily boys' dormitory was completed in 2004, and a similar unit for girls is scheduled for completion in June 2009. A separate facility houses the School store, a fully equipped laundry, and a hair-cutting salon.

ATHLETICS

The School's interscholastic sports program consists of boys' and girls' basketball, boys' and girls' soccer, coed golf, girls' softball, and a coed cheerleading squad. The boys' basketball and soccer teams have been particularly strong over the years, and both have been recent state Class D, Section IX champions.

Students are required to participate in physical education during the school day, and most participate in intramural sports on the weekends. The School has a growing program for outdoor enthusiasts including hiking, gardening, fly-fishing, and even dog training as well as its own Boy Scout troop and Venturing crew. New to the School this year are horseback riding and tennis.

EXTRACURRICULAR OPPORTUNITIES

FFS is widely known for its comprehensive programs in art (drawing, painting, and woodcarving), music (dance, chorus, and show choir), drama, journalism, and debate. Students routinely bring back armloads of trophies from the annual North American Music Festival, Columbia journalism awards for both the school newspaper and yearbook, and national honors for the debate team.

DAILY LIFE

The weekday begins with morning chapel service for all students, conducted by Jewish, Catholic, Methodist, and Episcopalian spiritual leaders on a rotating schedule, giving students an opportunity to pray and meditate with members of other faiths. Breakfast is followed by academic classes until noon. Lunch includes time for families to review progress and offer guidance to those experiencing behavioral and academic difficulties. Staff members and students actively engage in this important hour of sharing their experience, strength, and hope.

Afternoon classes conclude at 4 p.m. and are followed by extracurricular activities for 2 hours. Studying resumes after dinner until 8 p.m., when students begin evening chores. The day concludes with prayer and meditation in the families until 8:45, when students retire to their dorms.

WEEKEND LIFE

Saturdays are given to chores, study halls, support groups, and free time for gym or outdoor activities. Saturday evenings are generally spent playing games and watching movies. Sunday activities include various church services, arts and crafts classes, barbecues, intramural sports tournaments, and 12-Step meetings.

Individual families frequently spend the weekend off campus visiting such spots as the Gettysburg Battlefield, Plymouth Rock, Hershey Park, and Amish country; enjoying Broadway plays, ballets, and concerts; or bowling, skating, go-carting, and snow tubing.

COSTS AND FINANCIAL AID

Tuition, room, and board cost $5160 per month. There are no application or orientation fees. A $4600 enrollment fee is due on admission and is applied to the last month's tuition, room, and board on successful completion of the program. Personal needs and special activities, including educational field trips and SAT-prep courses, may add $500 to $2500 per year.

Some or all of the tuition costs may be paid by the student's home school district. Rules vary from state to state, and parents are advised to consult their attorney. The School also participates in the Key Bank Achiever Loan program (http://www.key.com/educate) and has scholarship money reserved for students who have been at FFS for at least a year and are progressing in the program.

ADMISSIONS INFORMATION

The Family Foundation School admits students on a year-round basis. Parents are asked to complete the Application for Admission (available by mail or online at http://www.thefamilyschool.com. Once it is reviewed, a half-day, on-site interview and tour is scheduled for the parents. It is important to note that prospective students are NOT interviewed prior to enrollment. If the School and parents agree that the student would benefit from the program, an enrollment date can be set.

APPLICATION TIMETABLE

Inquiries are welcome at any time. The decision to accept a student can be made immediately following the parents' on-site interview and tour of the campus. In most cases, and especially for families in crises, enrollment can take place immediately thereafter.

ADMISSIONS CORRESPONDENCE

Jeff Brain, Acting Director of Admissions
The Family Foundation School
431 Chapel Hill Road
Hancock, New York 13783

Phone: 845-887-5213
Fax: 845-887-4939
E-mail: jbrain@thefamilyschool.com
Web site: http://www.thefamilyschool.com

THE FORMAN SCHOOL

Litchfield, Connecticut

Type: Coeducational boarding and day college-preparatory school for students with learning differences
Grades: 9–12
Enrollment: 182
Head of School: Adam K. Man

THE SCHOOL

The Forman School was founded in 1930 by John and Julie Forman as a school for young boys who would benefit from close personal attention. An upper school was added in 1935. Forman became coeducational in 1942.

Forman is dedicated to helping students with learning differences achieve academic excellence. Students learn to recognize their own merit and potential and develop an appreciation for challenges as opportunities. Forman nurtures personal growth and love of learning in a caring, supportive environment. A Forman education provides opportunities for achievement and service to others.

Forman is a place where students "fit"—often for the first time in their lives. That is because Forman helps students realize that even though their brains process information differently, they are really the same as everyone else. For students, this is the difference that matters most of all.

Litchfield is a small, rural town located in the hills of northwestern Connecticut, offering an abundance of opportunities for sightseeing, recreation, shopping, dining, and cultural activities. It is famous for its historic sites and monuments and for the White Memorial Foundation, an environmental education center and nature museum. Litchfield is 30 miles from Hartford and approximately 100 miles from Boston and New York City. The School campus occupies 100 acres. The property encompasses fields, trout streams, and ponds, with numerous hiking trails. This setting provides the Forman student with many opportunities to pursue nature-oriented interests, as well as cultural, sports, and intellectual activities in the greater Hartford area.

Forman is accredited by the New England Association of Schools and Colleges and is approved by the Connecticut State Department of Education. It is a member of the National Association of Independent Schools, the Connecticut Association of Independent Schools, the National Honor Society, the International Dyslexia Association, the Secondary School Admission Test Board, and the New England Association of College Admissions Counselors. The School is also a member of the International Association of Outdoor Recreation and Education.

The Forman School is a nonprofit corporation governed by a self-perpetuating Board of Trustees that meets four times a year. The School has an annual operating budget of $9.5 million. The School plant is valued at $19 million. The Annual Fund raises more than $300,000 yearly.

ACADEMIC PROGRAMS

Academic work at Forman is designed to prepare students for success in college. Courses are broad in focus, giving students a solid background upon which to build. Skills are taught so that students will be able to handle the rigor of the college curriculum. Learning Center teachers provide direct, explicit instruction in reading, writing, study, and self-advocacy skills. Teachers work together to provide an optimal learning experience for Forman students.

To graduate, students must earn a minimum of 20 credits, including the following: English, 4; Thinking and Writing for College, 2; history (including U.S. history), 3; mathematics, 3; science (including two laboratory courses, one of which must be biology I), 3; and art, 1.

The curriculum includes English: Introduction to Literature, Journeys of Discovery, The American Experience, Explorations in Literature, and Thinking and Writing for College; history: modern European, early American, modern American, Model United Nations, and screening American history; foreign languages: French, Spanish, and American Sign Language; science: ecology, biology, environmental (which includes rain forest research in Costa Rica), chemistry, physics, psychology, and Human Wellness; math: math fundamentals, consumer math, algebra I, algebra II, geometry, statistics, precalculus, calculus, and functions, statistics, and trigonometry; computer science; and arts: advanced portfolio, photography, ceramics, robotics, video, theater arts and production, music composition I and II, music theory, and design I, II, and III. The average class size is 12 students, and the student-teacher ratio is 3:1.

The Learning Center offers students remedial instruction and strategies while they pursue a college-preparatory curriculum. Each student in the program spends five days a week with a trained specialist. The work focuses on skill acquisition, strategic instruction, and compensatory techniques to aid in developing learning skills. Instruction is designed to work with a student's strengths while helping to improve weak skill areas. The structured program includes critical language and study-skills instruction and self-advocacy in educational settings. The learning specialist works with the student's classroom teachers to establish a close, supportive learning environment.

Grades are given for effort as well as for achievement. Grades are available every three weeks for students. Detailed reports are mailed to parents three times a year.

The school year is made up of three 11-week terms, with examinations given at the end of the fall, winter, and spring terms.

FACULTY AND ADVISERS

There are 68 full-time faculty members and administrators who teach; one half live on campus. More than 60 percent of the faculty members hold advanced degrees.

Adam K. Man was appointed Head of School in 2008. He is a graduate of Bard College at Simon's Rock and received a master's degree in education, including certification in special education, from the University of New Hampshire. Mr. Man comes to Forman from St. Timothy's School in Stevenson, Maryland, where he was the Academic Dean.

COLLEGE ADMISSION COUNSELING

Forman has a full-time college counselor. College representatives visit the campus every fall. Students begin college planning in their junior year and receive assistance in finding colleges to match their grades, test scores, interests, and needs. Students also undertake college visits in their senior year.

In 2008, 40 of Forman's 42 graduates went on to college. They are attending such colleges and universities as Fairfield, Hofstra, Lynn, Morehouse, Ohio Wesleyan, and Roger Williams.

STUDENT BODY AND CONDUCT

In 2008–09, the Forman School had 182 students: 155 boarding and 27 day, 119 boys and 63 girls. There were 27 ninth graders, 49 tenth graders, 59 eleventh graders, and 47 twelfth graders. Boarding students come from twenty-seven states and seven countries.

Student committees motivate community growth and provide input to the School. There is an elected student government. Students learn to serve by participating in the School's Job Program.

The School has a judicial system composed of both faculty members and students. The School strongly maintains its code of conduct. Alcohol and illegal drugs are strictly forbidden, and their possession or use is cause for immediate dismissal. All students must undergo a drug screening prior to starting the school year.

ACADEMIC FACILITIES

The Thomas D. Williams Academic Center and Johnson Arts Center constitute the primary classrooms, along with the newly renovated Carpenter Hall, which houses the Barbara Chace Library, Computer Lab, and the Learning Center. The library and computer lab are equipped with wireless technology and state-of-the-art equipment.

BOARDING AND GENERAL FACILITIES

There are twelve dormitories on campus that are all fully wired for phones and Internet access. Three out of the twelve dormitories and a student center that includes a student lounge, snack bar, game room, and bookstore were built in the 1990s. In 2002, a dormitory and a fully equipped fitness center were built. In summer 2006, Henderson House, which houses the Offices of the Head of School, Admissions, and Alumni/Development and the Business Office, was completely renovated. The Olson Outdoor Education Center, which was built in 2006, is the home of the Outdoor Wilderness Program and woodworking and boatbuilding.

ATHLETICS

Students are required to participate each afternoon throughout the year in Forman's after-class program. The program includes activities ranging from competitive sports to theater arts. The after-class program provides for social interaction, teamwork, caring for others, leadership opportunities, and, in many cases, physical activity. Most programs meet from 3:30 to 5:30 p.m. Monday through Saturday; however, due to special needs, some activities meet during evenings. Fall offerings include cross-country, football, soccer, and volleyball. Winter offerings include Alpine racing, basketball, girls' and boys' ice hockey, recreational skiing, snowboarding, and wrestling. Spring offerings include baseball, golf, lacrosse, softball, and tennis. Community service, Outdoor Leadership Skills, and theater arts are offered all year.

Outdoor Leadership Skills is offered as an after-class program and includes canoeing, kayaking, hiking, fishing, boat-building, rock climbing, and weekend camping. A wilderness skills program is also offered throughout the year. The fitness program is offered during the winter term.

Forman has four playing fields, six outdoor tennis courts, two indoor tennis courts, a fitness center, and an 18,000-square-foot gymnasium. There is also an indoor skateboarding facility.

EXTRACURRICULAR OPPORTUNITIES

Students are encouraged to become involved with the yearbook, student government, the student leader program, and the ambassador program.

The Forman Ensemble Players of the drama department present three productions during the school year. The Gallery at the Johnson Arts Center features the work of Forman visual arts students and visiting artists. Special events include Parents' Weekend, Alumni Weekend, the Charity Benefit, the Strawberry Festival, the Junior-Senior Prom, and a winter carnival.

DAILY LIFE

Classes are held six days a week, beginning at 8:45 a.m. on Monday, Tuesday, Thursday, and Friday and 9:30 a.m. on Wednesday and Saturday. The school day ends at 3 p.m. on Monday, Tuesday, Thursday, and Friday. Wednesday and Saturday classes end at 12:10. On Monday and Friday, the School comes together for morning assembly. A typical day includes breakfast, classes, lunch, sports from 3:30 to 5:30, dinner, and study hall from 7:30 to 9.

WEEKEND LIFE

The Student Activities Committee plans many activities, including movies, dances, trips to local shopping malls, plays and professional sporting events, and museum tours. Students may also go on trips for fishing, skiing, canoeing, hiking, and other chaperoned activities. A Community Life Program is integrated into the daily routine of the School, with a focus designed to draw students into discussions of topics that are currently relevant to their world, such as conflict, social interaction, and health.

COSTS AND FINANCIAL AID

For 2008–09, tuition charges were $53,000 for boarding students and $43,500 for day students. This cost included learning center instruction and study hall tutors. The Forman School requires a Tuition Refund Plan at a cost of $1600 for boarding students and $1300 for day students. Financial aid is available to students based solely on financial need. Parents send their financial statement form to the School and Student Service (SSS) in Pittsburgh, Pennsylvania. The Forman School's Financial Aid Committee makes a final determination as to the award.

ADMISSIONS INFORMATION

Forman admits students into grades 9–12 and PG. The Admissions Committee looks for students of good character with average to above-average cognitive ability. Prior to completing the application packet, the committee requires a psychological evaluation, current within two to three years, which includes a cognitive and an educational evaluation, and an Individual Educational Plan, if available. After review of the evaluations, the Admissions Committee requests an application; a parent and student questionnaire; English, math, and principal/counselor recommendations; a preliminary health form; and school transcripts. The application process also includes a School tour and personal interview.

APPLICATION TIMETABLE

Students are encouraged to apply in the late fall and winter of the year prior to matriculation. There is no application deadline. Inquiries are welcome at any time, and campus tours and interviews are scheduled through the Admissions Office from 8 a.m. to 4 p.m. Monday through Friday.

Admissions decisions are made on a rolling basis as space permits. The application fee is $50.

ADMISSIONS CORRESPONDENCE

Beth A. Rainey, Director of Admissions
The Forman School
12 Norfolk Road
P.O. Box 80
Litchfield, Connecticut 06759-0080

Phone: 860-567-1802
Fax: 860-567-3501
E-mail: admissions@formanschool.org
Web site: http://www.formanschool.org

GABLES ACADEMY

Stone Mountain, Georgia

Type: Coeducational day and boarding special needs school
Grades: 4–12; Elementary School, 4–6; Middle School, 7–8; Upper School, 9–12; postgraduate year
Enrollment: Total: 24
Head of School: James D. Meffen III, Headmaster/President

THE SCHOOL

Gables Academy was founded in 1961 by Dr. James D. Meffen and has been providing life-changing experiences for students ever since. The Academy was formed to address the needs of bright students who could not learn to read like other students their age. The program has matured into a semi-clinical, highly individualized course of excellence. Academics are addressed along with the socialization problems neglected during previous educational experiences. Gables Academy is dedicated to providing a college-prep curriculum as guided by the state of Georgia Department of Education. Vocations are also encouraged and supported.

Nestled in the shadow of historic Stone Mountain, the school's campus is minutes from downtown Atlanta. It is an ideal learning environment for creative, "differently abled" learners. The campus is situated in a rustic wooded setting with a picturesque lake. Because of its rustic campus tucked away in the Village of Stone Mountain, it is a "close in, yet worlds away" setting. Students at Gables Academy are immersed in the best of both worlds. From the best of city living, such as museums, music, art, dance, and theater, to outdoor experiences, like climbing Stone Mountain, horseback riding, fishing, and backpacking—both worlds are at their door.

Gables Academy is a nonprofit independent school governed by a Board of Trustees. The school's current annual operating budget is $500,000. The alumni association, along with grants writing, corporate giving, and fund-raising events, provide many volunteer opportunities for parents and the community.

Gables Academy is fully accredited and maintains memberships in a variety of professional associations. The school maintains membership in the Georgia Association of Private Schools for Exceptional Children (GAPSEC), Learning Disabilities Association of America (LDA), Children and Adults with Attention-Deficit/Hyperactivity Disorder (CHADD), National Association of Private Special Education Centers (NAPSEC), the International Dyslexia Association (IDA), and other relevant organizations.

ACADEMIC PROGRAMS

Gables Academy believes in educating the whole person. For this reason, the school is always reaching out to meet the individual needs of diverse children. The Gables program is designed to meet two specific needs. One emphasis is that of basic skills in reading, writing, and mathematics, stressing the necessary academic requisites for success in academic, vocational, or career pursuits. The second approach tends to the needs of the child or adolescent who has mastered the basic skills but appears unmotivated to learn in a typical learning environment.

Specialized corrective instruction is necessary to compensate for specific learning differences. The emphasis for the child or adolescent is to strengthen the basic skill areas through increased proficiency of learning. These goals are accomplished through teaching to the student's strengths in an overall 6:1 pupil-teacher ratio. Each student receives both individualized corrective or remedial instruction along with larger group instruction.

The fundamentals of reading, writing, and arithmetic are stressed. The state's college-preparatory upper-school curriculum mandates 22 credits for high school graduation. This includes 4 years of English, 4 years of mathematics, 3 years of science, 3 years of social studies, 2 years of foreign language, 1 year of physical education, 1 combined year of computer/fine arts, and 4 years of electives (photography, art, reading, music, drama, etc.). Vocational diplomas have different emphases and stress post–high school tech school and/or employment. Generally, high school students take six courses, with ¼ credit four times per year equaling 6 total credits per nine-month school year.

Gables believes in the restorative, healing, and challenging powers of the fine arts. Students are encouraged to participate in visual arts classes (painting, drawing, working with clay), the performing arts program (creative dramatics and improvisational classes), and literary arts such as poetry, fiction, playwriting, and journal keeping. Special arrangements can be made for students to study on a more concentrated basis, off campus, with professional artists and musicians. Sessions with art, music, and drama therapists can be arranged.

Elementary and middle school students similarly undertake six classes per day as prescribed by the state of Georgia. Students in the elementary school are appropriately grouped in a self-contained classroom. The self-contained classroom plays a very important part in removing fears and insecurities developed by traumatic experiences in more harsh environments. By remaining in a familiar, safe environment, Gables' youngest students settle into a nurturing, consistent, and happy family-style classroom home. Reading specialists are a regular part of their classroom experience. Teachers for elementary school are professional certified educators. Gables assists its youngest students in reaching developmental milestones by using a multisensory approach that is both challenging and nonthreatening. Along with their academic activities, elementary students participate in regular physical education/recess activities as well as art classes and creative dramatics games.

Middle school students are gracefully ushered through a time that frequently becomes a traumatic breakdown between middle and high school. With the introduction of small classes, appropriate homework, classes that change from period to period, and available counseling that supports the student's fragile self-concept, healthy development is afforded the young adolescent. The curriculum for middle school students incorporates experiential activities, physical education, recreation, visual arts classes, and extracurricular participation in creative drama classes.

Boarding/resident students have supervised time each evening for homework. Computer use and library and Internet research skills are important areas of emphasis since they are so important for a successful college experience. A fully equipped computer lab with high-speed Internet access and educational programs serves the students and teachers. Students are encouraged and assisted in reaching out for enriching experiences in diverse areas. These may be areas such as music, photography, art, drama, and foreign language. Weekly progress reports are mailed home. Each student is "staffed" with parent participation during the course of the school year. A staffing is similar to the IEP process in a public school setting.

Progress reports are sent to parents biweekly. The traditional "A–F" letter grading system is the norm at Gables Academy; it focuses on effort as well as achievement. Each high school class has a final test after which report cards are mailed home. Marking periods are nine weeks long. There are numerous opportunities for independent study, off-campus projects, field trips, and more. All classes are remedial in nature. A multisensory approach is incorporated into all classes.

FACULTY AND ADVISERS

Core faculty members possess certifications, advanced training, degrees, and experience with children having learning differences. Full-time and support staff receive regular updates in their training. A variety of licensed professionals from the community are used for any consulting and psychotherapy/counseling needed. All teaching staff members meet accreditation standards. Staff members who are enthusiastic and energetic and have a heart for service to children are sought. Teaching staff members further their education through attendance at school-subsidized conferences and in-service workshops.

Teachers participate with students in activities such as camping, theater, hiking, backpacking, team and individual sports, museum visits, and arts.

James Meffen III, the school's Headmaster, is an exceptionally qualified reading specialist. He has a B.A. degree in psychology from Hispanic International University, an M.S.Ed. degree in reading from the University of Miami, and a doctoral degree in teaching. Dr. Meffen is the son of the school's founder and, as such, has been associated with Gables Academy since its inception in 1961. He has been directly employed by the school for more than two decades, qualifying him as one of the highest-caliber special needs school heads in the nation.

COLLEGE ADMISSION COUNSELING

Every effort is made to guide seniors and postgraduates to actively explore opportunities in regular college classes or vocational-technical course work on a joint enrollment basis. The joint effort with local colleges and technical schools provides counseling, course selection, career and goal orientation, and academic support to specific academic needs. Juniors and seniors are prepared throughout the school year for various tests. This may include the SAT, ACT, ASVAB, and others. Students at Gables Academy, when appropriately diagnosed, are able to take the SAT in an untimed setting. All high school students are counseled in career education, helping them to set realistic goals for post–high school.

STUDENT BODY AND CONDUCT

Day students come from the greater metropolitan Atlanta area and surrounding towns. Typically, 20 percent of the students are boarding students. Most resident students come from the Eastern Seaboard, while others have come from as far away as Kuala Lumpur. The student body is governed by a student/parent handbook and a peer review board overseen by staff members. Every effort is made to settle all disputes in house.

Gables Academy is proud of its ethnic diversity. The school has a well-rounded population of African American, Latin, Asian, and Anglo students. International (ESL) students are proactively sought. Gables Academy's English as second language (ESL) program utilizes the research-based educational technique of immersion, and international faculty and staff members welcome ESL students, helping them feel right at home.

ACADEMIC FACILITIES

Gables Academy currently operates six classrooms and has three offices, totaling 4,500 square feet. A fully equipped computer lab with high-speed Internet access and educational programs serves the students and teachers. There are adjacent athletic fields for soccer, football, softball, and other outdoor activities.

BOARDING AND GENERAL FACILITIES

The resident experience is home-style living. There are 2 to 4 students per room, with a dresser, bed, and closet space provided. Boys reside in a six-bedroom/two-bath residential building. Girls are housed in a homelike environment separate from the boys. Students are required to leave campus for long holidays and three-day weekends. Resident status is available for students needing additional life skills and/or supports for their first year or two of college and/or work experience after high school. This allows the student to continue maturing and to cultivate the independence needed to function outside the family home.

Common areas for leisure activities are provided, and the school has a "Pavilion" for outdoor picnicking, gatherings, and shelter from the sun on exceptionally warm days. Resident students regularly visit Stone Mountain Village for small gift shopping, trinkets, and the diverse interests provided in specialty shops. Fishing, weight lifting, basketball, paint ball, and, of course, video gaming are activities many of the resident students choose to pursue for relaxation and free time.

ATHLETICS

Gables Academy participates in the Atlanta Athletic Conference. Competitive, supervised, and refereed activities are available in flag football, basketball, softball, tennis, soccer, golf, wrestling, swimming, and other sports. Good sportsmanship is encouraged and supported by the school and its staff. A minimum "C" average is required to remain eligible for interscholastic competition. Playing fields adjoining school property along with a local gymnasium are used for these activities when played at home.

In addition to regular conventional physical education activities, each student participates in an outdoor challenge program that develops self-confidence and coordination along with problem-solving skills. These problem-solving skills elicit the appropriate social interactions necessary for success in today's society.

EXTRACURRICULAR OPPORTUNITIES

Enrichment activities available to students are rafting, hiking, camping, backpacking, professional baseball, basketball, football, fishing, theater, music, arts, Ping-Pong, African drumming, and more. Students may participate in student government, chess and backgammon clubs, newspaper/journalism clubs, and the school Annual (yearbook) preparation committee. Community service is an expected part of life for junior and senior high school students.

DAILY LIFE

The school day begins at 8:45 a.m. and runs until 3 p.m. Monday through Thursday and 1:05 on Friday. There is a 15-minute homeroom Tuesday through Friday mornings to start the day. An opening exercise program takes place every Monday morning during this same time. There are five 50-minute classes and an 80-minute sixth period Monday through Thursday for special electives and physical education at the end of each day. Lunch is 30 minutes.

WEEKEND LIFE

On the weekends, boarding students watch movies and take part in religious activities, clean their rooms and wash their clothes, fish, and take trips to malls, nearby towns, and the YMCA. Swimming, canoeing, and hiking are all part of their experience.

SUMMER PROGRAMS

Gables Academy offers a full curriculum of summer school classes in which students in high school can make up lost credits. Younger students in middle and elementary school typically work to advance their basic skills.

Gables Summer Camp dovetails with the Summer School program and offers all the excitement and adventure expected of any good camp. Campers participate in on- and off-campus adventures. These include sports, wilderness adventures, hiking, swimming, boating, arts and crafts, and cultural activities. Located less than a mile from Georgia's famous Stone Mountain Park, Gables is even more accessible to summertime adventure with its campers.

COSTS AND FINANCIAL AID

In 2008-09, fees for day students are $17,500. Fees for resident students are $46,900 and include allowance awarded through the school for performance of assigned daily chores around the school and/or resident home. Limited financial aid is occasionally available on a need basis for day students only. Detailed financial disclosures are necessary. Various payment plans are available.

ADMISSIONS INFORMATION

Gables Academy is a nonprofit independent school admitting students without regard to race, color, creed, or national origin. The special needs students served at the school are average or above average in intellectual ability with various learning differences. Judeo-Christian values are adhered to with open consideration for all faiths. School records are solicited, and parent and child must interview with admissions personnel. Most students are prescreened through prior submission of requested materials and upon interview completion may enroll.

APPLICATION TIMETABLE

Gables Academy holds entrance interviews year-round, with ongoing admission throughout the school year. Standard admission dates around marking periods are encouraged.

ADMISSIONS CORRESPONDENCE

Dr. James D. Meffen III, Headmaster/President
Gables Academy
811 Gordon Street
Stone Mountain, Georgia 30083

Phone: 770-465-7500
877-465-7500 (toll-free)
Fax: 770-465-7700
E-mail: info@gablesacademy.com
Web site: http://www.gablesacademy.com/

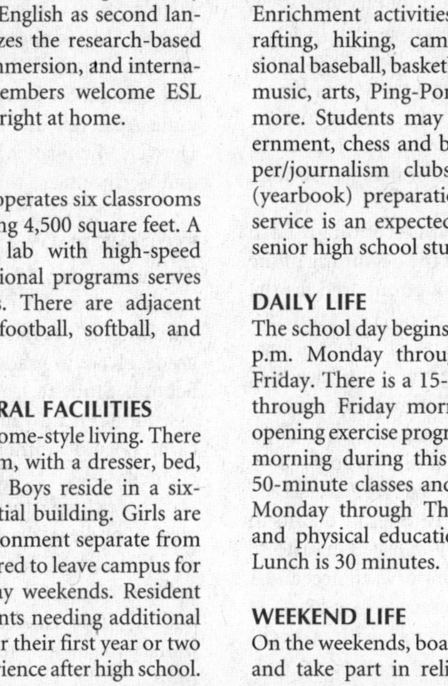

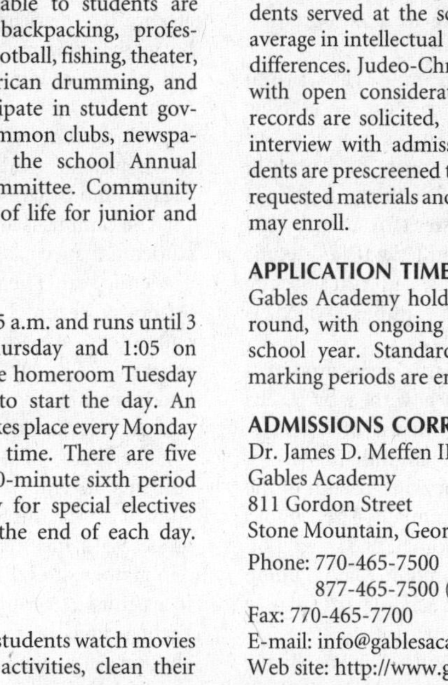

THE GOW SCHOOL

South Wales, New York

Type: Boys' boarding college-preparatory school for young men with dyslexia/language-based learning differences
Grades: 7–PG: Middle School, 7–9; Upper School, 10–12, postgraduate year
Enrollment: School total: 148; Upper School: 108
Head of School: M. Bradley Rogers, Jr., Headmaster

THE SCHOOL

The Gow School was founded in 1926 by Peter Gow, a teacher who wanted to develop better methods for teaching young men who were experiencing scholastic failure. His work and the research of others led to the establishment of a program for students who have at least average general ability but have a developmental disability in one or more phases of language use. Reconstructive Language (RL) training, reading, writing, and other aspects of language development are stressed throughout the Gow School's college-preparatory curriculum.

There are a wide variety of extracurricular, leadership, and athletic opportunities to aid students' development outside the classroom. Attendance at weekly worship services is required; students either attend local services of their choice or participate in a nonsectarian Meeting on campus.

The School is located in South Wales, a rural community in the western portion of New York, approximately 30 miles southeast of Buffalo and 100 miles south of Toronto, Ontario. Hilly woodlands, thirty buildings (including the Headmaster's residence and twelve faculty houses), athletic fields, tennis courts, mountain bike trails, and a ski slope are located on the 100-acre campus, which is traversed by a stream.

The Gow School, which was incorporated not-for-profit in 1975, is governed by a self-perpetuating 23-member Board of Trustees. The board, composed of alumni, parents of alumni, parents of students, and friends of the School, meets three times annually. The School's plant is valued at approximately $14 million and the endowment is $8 million. Many alumni, parents, and friends of the School participate in the Annual Giving Program.

The School is permanently chartered by the New York State Board of Regents and accredited by the New York State Association of Independent Schools. It holds a membership in the National Association of Independent Schools and the International Dyslexia Association.

ACADEMIC PROGRAMS

The school year, which is divided into semesters, extends from early September to late May. Detailed written reports are sent to parents at the end of each marking period and semester. There is also an adviser program, with teachers serving as advisers for 3 to 6 students. Adviser reports are issued to parents four times a year.

Classes, which range in size from 3 to 6, meet six days a week. Generally, a student takes five academic courses in addition to one full-credit Reconstructive Language (RL) course. Each student's program is individualized. RL instruction, a multisensory approach emphasizing phonetics, involves training in deriving meaning from reading, in vocabulary extension, and in oral and written expression. In mathematics, a multisensory manipulative approach stressing concept understanding along with daily drill is used. Throughout the curriculum, instruction begins with the most basic operations and proceeds to more advanced concepts. Daily oral and written work is assigned as a means of promoting accurate and immediate recall.

The traditional college-preparatory curriculum includes advanced biology, algebra I, algebra II, American perspectives, art, biology, business seminar, calculus, chemistry, computer literacy, computer programming, developmental math, earth science, economics, English, geometry, global studies I and II, music, physics, prealgebra, precalculus, robotics, theater, and U.S. history.

The campus is awash with technology. Each student is issued a laptop at the beginning of the academic year. The laptop is configured for the School wi-fi and LAN servers. The students' computers are loaded with assistive technology software (Kurzweil, Dragon Naturally Speaking, and Inspiration) to aid in their reading, writing, and organization of their notes.

The course of study is designed to prepare students to enter college. To graduate, each student must complete 21½ academic credits in grades 9–12, including 4 in English, 3 in history, 3 in mathematics, 2 in laboratory science, and 1 in art/music. Computer literacy, which involves keyboarding, word processing (with a spell-checker), and using database programs, spreadsheets, and presentation software; Upper School health; and an outdoor camping program are all requirements for graduation.

FACULTY AND ADVISERS

The faculty consists of 35 full-time members and 2 part-time members. Twenty-nine faculty members and the Headmaster live in the dormitories or in other campus housing. Members of the faculty hold nineteen baccalaureate degrees, twenty-five master's degrees, and one doctoral degree.

M. Bradley Rogers Jr. was elected Headmaster in 2004. He holds a B.A. degree from the University of Dayton (Ohio) and a master's degree from Johns Hopkins University. He and Mrs. Rogers and their 4 sons reside on the campus.

COLLEGE ADMISSION COUNSELING

The Director of College Counseling begins discussions with students and parents in the junior year. Seniors can leave the campus for college visits. A large collection of college catalogs, videos, and computer search programs is available in the College Advising Center. Most seniors take the ACT and/or SAT in a nonstandard format.

Among the colleges and universities entered by recent graduates are Bates, Centre, Cornell, Davis & Elkins, Denison, Elon, Gannon, Hobart and William Smith Colleges, Long Beach State, Loyola New Orleans, Marshall, Mount St. Joseph, Muskingum, New England, Northeastern, Regis, RIT, Savannah College of Art and Design, St. Lawrence, Syracuse, West Virginia Wesleyan, and the Universities of Arizona, Denver, Michigan, Missouri–Kansas City, Utah, and Vermont.

STUDENT BODY AND CONDUCT

The School enrolls students from twenty-eight states and sixteen countries. The 2007–08 enrollment, by grade, was 33 in grade 12, 29 in grade 11, 42 in grade 10, and 44 in the Middle School. Student leadership includes resident assistants, headwaiters, Crimson Key Club campus guides, Interact Club, and the student council.

The School does not tolerate the use of alcohol or illegal drugs. The *Student and Parents Handbook* describes the School's no-tolerance policies regarding alcohol and illegal drug use and all other rules and regulations. All disciplinary problems are handled on an individual basis.

ACADEMIC FACILITIES

The Main Building (1926) houses classrooms, the Health Care Center, the Development Office, the Business Office, and the Govian Bookstore. In February 2005, the renovations to the George Reid Arts Center were completed. It houses the Simms Family Theatre, a ceramics studio, a painting and drawing studio, a music room, a digital lab, and the applied technology workshop for the BattleBot IQ program. The Isaac Arnold Library Building (1979) is a reference and study library with 8,000 volumes and ten online computers. In addition, the building contains seven classrooms, administrative offices, and the College Advising Center. In 2006, the School converted the Wolbach water treatment facility to the Wolbach science lab.

Orton Hall (1987) houses an all-student study hall, the Constantine Computer Center, fourteen classrooms, and the physics/chemistry laboratory.

BOARDING AND GENERAL FACILITIES

Students and dorm families reside in Green Cottage (1926); Templeton Dormitory (1961); Ellis House (1956); Cornwall House (1926); Whitcomb House (1984); and Warner House (1999), which houses 16 students and two faculty families. All of the student dormitory rooms have telephones, Internet access, and cable television. The summer of 2008 saw the ground breaking for the new 28,000-square-foot dining hall that is scheduled for completion in September 2009.

In addition to the Health Care Center, which is staffed by 7 nurses, a local doctor serves as the School physician, and Buffalo hospitals are approximately 30 minutes away. Emergency services are provided by a local rescue facility a short distance from the School.

ATHLETICS

Athletics and participation in sports are vital parts of the School's program. Interscholastic teams are organized in basketball, crew, cross-country running, lacrosse, soccer, squash, tennis, and wrestling. The School teams compete with nearby public and other independent schools. Other programs, such as intramurals, skiing, snowboarding, and weight training, are available. The outdoor education program also has a low- and high-ropes course and an indoor and outdoor climbing wall.

The Gow Center (2002) accommodates many of the athletic and recreational needs of the Gow students and faculty members. It houses an indoor multipurpose space for tennis (two courts), soccer, and lacrosse practices as well as intramurals; hardwood basketball courts; three international squash courts; and a 3,000-square-foot fitness center. The building also includes an ample student union, three locker rooms, and two classrooms.

EXTRACURRICULAR OPPORTUNITIES

Extracurricular activities vary from year to year. Typical activities are the yearbook, student newspaper, theater, chess, music, in-line skating, skateboarding, and mountain biking. All students are encouraged to participate in drama activities, including the production of at least one play and one musical production each year. A Fall Weekend is scheduled in early October for parents and students. All students are required to participate in a community service program.

DAILY LIFE

The weekday schedule begins with wake-up and room inspection, breakfast, and house jobs between 6:50 and 8:10 a.m. Classes, an all-school assembly, supervised study, lunch, a tutorial period, and athletics are scheduled from 8 a.m. until 6 p.m. Following dinner six days each week, all students have approximately 2 hours of supervised study and a reading period before returning to their dorms. Faculty members provide assistance during these study periods, although some students work more independently in their dorm rooms if they meet certain academic standards.

WEEKEND LIFE

There are dances and social activities scheduled throughout the year. Girls from various local schools attend. Each Saturday evening, boys have dates or take a bus to a local mall to shop and see a movie. The Director of Student Activities oversees the selection of a variety of area events for Gow students to attend with faculty supervision. These have included symphony and rock concerts, theater, plays and musicals, auto shows, ethnic festivals, paintball, NHL hockey games, and NFL football games. During each semester, certain weekends are designated for students to go home or visit with a local family. Special trips and activities are planned for those who remain on campus.

COSTS AND FINANCIAL AID

Tuition, room, and board are $46,250 for the 2008–09 school year. Books, supplies, and allowances total approximately $1800.

Tuition loans and scholarships are available on a limited basis. The $4600 enrollment deposit is applied to the first year's tuition.

ADMISSIONS INFORMATION

Gow admits young men capable of traditional, intensive college-preparatory work who need specific Reconstructive Language and mathematics training. Gow is not equipped to educate those with severe physical handicaps, below-average intelligence, or serious emotional or behavioral problems. Diagnostic testing, school records, recommendations, and a personal interview are required for admission. In addition, specific skill testing to determine class placement is mandatory at the School. The testing and the interview usually require one day to complete. New students are admitted to all grades; late enrollment is possible if vacancies exist.

APPLICATION TIMETABLE

Students are interviewed throughout the year. Parents are encouraged to begin the process as early as possible by making inquiry, forwarding to the School all testing and academic records, and setting up an admissions appointment. The application fee is $100.

ADMISSIONS CORRESPONDENCE

Director of Admissions
The Gow School
P.O. Box 85
South Wales, New York 14139
Phone: 716-652-3450
Fax: 716-687-2003
E-mail: admissions@gow.org
Web site: http://www.gow.org

GROVE SCHOOL

Madison, Connecticut

Type: Coeducational boarding college-preparatory and general academic school within a therapeutic milieu
Grades: 6–PG: Middle School, 6–8; Upper School, 9–12, postgraduate year
Enrollment: School total: 105; Upper School: 80
Head of School: Richard L. Chorney, President and CEO; Peter J. Chorney, Executive Director

THE SCHOOL

Grove School was founded in 1934. The academic program is based on the "educateur" (teacher-counselor) live-in model. The academic program has 6 Mentor Teachers and Content Facilitators for added support to school administrators and teachers. They assist their peers in a collegial way to insure that there is veteran support for newer teachers. These teachers do not live in the dorms but do have a place in residential life—particularly with activities that are educational in nature, such as homework, tutoring, and extracurricular activities. Grove is a therapeutic boarding school with strong clinical support and an academic program that emphasizes supportive education. All teachers are involved in residential life and activities. Classes are small and oriented to the individual. Tutoring and remediation are readily available and geared to address the best way for a student to learn.

The School is located on 90 acres of beautifully wooded land in Madison, Connecticut (population 18,719), a New England shoreline community 20 miles north of New Haven and 50 miles south of Hartford. The School is about 1 mile from the beaches of the Long Island Sound.

Grove School is a proprietary corporation with an Advisory Board composed of 12 individuals with varied backgrounds, including many noted professionals in the fields of medicine and education. The School is funded in its entirety by monies generated from tuition.

Grove School is approved by the Connecticut State Department of Education and licensed by the Connecticut State Department of Children and Families (DCF). Grove is an affiliate of the World Federation for Mental Health. The School is also a member of the National Association of Therapeutic Schools and Programs (NATSAP) and the American Academy of Child and Adolescent Psychiatry (AACAP). Grove School is also a founding member of the Independent Small Programs Alliance (ISPA).

ACADEMIC PROGRAMS

Grove School's program is designed to meet the academic and therapeutic needs of adolescent boys and girls between the ages of 11 and 18 who have average or above-average intelligence but who need opportunities to increase their social skills at school, at home, or with peers.

The general philosophy of Grove School is based on a supportive, psychoeducational approach delivered through academic programming in a holistic milieu. Both therapeutic and academic plans are determined to meet the needs of each child. Students who successfully complete academic requirements for the high school grades, 9 through 12, as established by the state of Connecticut and Grove School, are awarded a high school diploma.

In order to qualify for a high school diploma, all students must complete the following courses: 4 years of English; 2 years of U.S. history; 2 years of mathematics; 2 years of science, 1 of which must be biology; and 4 years of physical education (unless excused for medical reasons). Additional elective courses in the arts, sciences, and humanities may be selected by the student with the advice of his or her administrative adviser and the Principal, to bring the total academic units required for graduation to 21.

Students are placed in classes based on their academic level, age, and social-emotional development. The student-teacher ratio is about 4:1. There is a supervised 1½-hour evening study period in the dorms. Students in need of extra help spend additional time in a supervised after-school study hall.

Grades and performance reports are sent home monthly. Remedial assistance and additional tutoring are readily available.

The School offers a twelve-month program with four vacation periods, each of about two weeks' duration. Intensive, individualized work is carried on during the summer months as well as during the regular academic year. The therapeutic and academic work of the summer session is accompanied by extensive activities. A minimum stay of two years is generally required in order to take full advantage of the Grove program.

FACULTY AND ADVISERS

The School's faculty numbers 36 full-time members (men and women in equal numbers). Most teachers are Connecticut certified in a content area, including many in special education. There are also assistant teachers and part-time instructors, who expand students' experience and activities with music lessons (a variety of instruments), the arts (videography, ceramics, and stained-glass craft), and sports (including swimming, snow skiing, tennis, and fitness training). These offerings are changed from time to time.

Twenty-five percent of the teachers have advanced degrees, and about half of the others are actively pursuing higher education in the Grove School/Southern Connecticut State University–sponsored master's program in special education.

In addition to teachers, Grove School has 12 clinicians on staff—5 psychiatrists, 2 psychologists, 2 LCSWs, and 3 LMFTs. All students are seen twice a week in individual psychotherapy. All students and staff members meet daily (after dinner) in large-group community meetings that are generally conducted by the Executive Director or Assistant Director(s). Students also meet weekly in group counseling sessions of up to 8 students with a therapist and an administrator.

The President and CEO, Richard L. Chorney, has an M.S. degree in special education from Southern Connecticut State University and a B.A. in psychology from Bard College. He also has a certificate in psychiatric administration from the University of Wisconsin. He has more than forty years' experience in Residential Treatment and Therapeutic Boarding Schools. Members of the Executive Group and the Residential Administrators also serve as Administrative Advisors to the students.

The Executive Director, Peter Chorney, graduated from Bucknell University with a B.A. in psychology and school psychology and has his M.S. in special education from Southern Connecticut State University. He has been a part of Grove School since he was a teenager, as he grew up next door to the campus. As Executive Director, he manages many different aspects of the program, including hiring, recruitment of staff members, and overall campus supervision and management. He is also the baseball coach and student council adviser. He has worked at Grove for more than fifteen years in various capacities.

COLLEGE ADMISSION COUNSELING

Juniors and seniors prepare for the SAT early in the year through various practice exercises and an SAT preparation program. Senior English classes include the preparation of a college essay. The students' adviser and the School Principal help students select appropriate colleges. Parents and therapists are included in the college selection process.

Special testing procedures such as untimed administration of the SAT or large-type tests are arranged when appropriate for learning-disabled students.

Recent Grove graduates are attending Case Western Reserve, Curry, Drew, Lynn, Manhattanville, Simmons, Suffolk, and the University of Connecticut. This year's graduates plan to attend the Art Institute of Chicago, Castleton State, Hofstra, Ohio Wesleyan, and Virginia Commonwealth, among others.

STUDENT BODY AND CONDUCT

There are 25 students in the Middle School and 80 in the Upper School as well as postgraduate students. The population of the School represents twenty states and several countries. International students and members of minority groups are encouraged to seek admission.

The School's code of conduct is clearly explained to all students. Much importance is attached to the relationships students establish with staff members and one another. All issues are discussed and worked through with the child's therapist and with other adults who are connected to the student. Privileges are earned, and there is a clear hierarchy of responsibilities that lead to the granting of privileges. Students help one another as peer assists, and older students often tutor younger students. The Student Council is advised and guided by the Executive Director.

ACADEMIC FACILITIES

Two main School buildings house the majority of the Upper and Middle School classes. The Redlich Building contains the Computer Program Resource Center; the Upper School houses the art program for fine and graphic arts and ceramics, the science laboratories, and the Middle School classrooms. The Pavilion doubles as the Student Union.

BOARDING AND GENERAL FACILITIES

Students live in twelve cottages and dorms that hold from 5 to 10 youngsters and 2 faculty members each. There are seven spaces for transitioning students who have earned additional responsibility and live more independently. Most rooms are doubles. Post-graduate students have an opportunity to live in off-campus housing.

There is a Health Center on the campus, where registered nurses take care of students' medical needs and concerns and refer patients to local physicians and dentists as appropriate. The nurses also maintain close contact with families concerning medical and dental issues.

ATHLETICS

The School offers a complete, noncompetitive coed sports program that emphasizes participation, the benefits of physical activity in the development of a healthy body, and the social benefits derived from games and play. There are opportunities to take part in off-campus sports activities that include biking, bowling, camping trips, canoeing, fishing, golf, hiking, horseback riding, rafting, rock climbing, sailing, skiing, snorkeling, and waterskiing. There are also competitive teams in baseball, basketball, and soccer as well as intramural basketball and ice hockey. Individual interests in specific activities such as tennis, racquetball, weight training, kick-boxing, and golf may be pursued on an individual basis.

In addition to its gymnasium, Grove maintains a baseball and soccer field. The Madison beaches on the Long Island Sound can be used for water sports.

EXTRACURRICULAR OPPORTUNITIES

Grove students regularly attend local plays, concerts, and movies. Frequent trips are made to New York City and Boston to pursue both cultural and sports interests. All students are expected to involve themselves in at least one of the extracurricular or athletic activities. After school and on evenings and weekends, a variety of regularly scheduled activities are offered, including ceramics, drawing and painting, stained-glass craft, videography, work-maintenance projects, culinary arts (cooking and baking), drama, creative writing (newspaper and yearbook), and journalism. Filmmaking, musical instruction, gardening and horticulture, sculpture, and model making, as well as a variety of scientific interests, are offered. Yoga, aerobics, dance, and gymnastics are also available.

A yearly parents' day is held in the spring, and six parent education seminars are held throughout the year. A holiday program is presented in December. A graduation ceremony for students, staff members, and parents of graduates takes place in August. A sailing and/or international-travel program takes students and staff members to the Caribbean and other countries. The focus is on art, adventure, science, history, and the sea. Other international trips with historical, artistic, or cultural goals are also a significant part of the School's program. Some are "service" based.

DAILY LIFE

Students awaken at 7 a.m. and have breakfast at 8. A brief community meeting takes place every morning after breakfast. Students have Homeroom at 8:45. Classes start at 8:50. There are six 50-minute periods, ending at 2:40, and Homeroom until 2:50. The lunch period is from 12:19 to 12:49. Classes begin again at 12:54 p.m. Activity periods are from 3 to 4:45 and from 6:00 to 7:30. Supper is from 5 to 5:45. Study hall runs from 7:30 to 9. All students are expected to be in their dorms by 7:30, unless they are attending a supervised activity.

WEEKEND LIFE

Weekend programs are planned regularly with the weekend on-duty Residential Administrators and the staff members on duty. Most students are at Grove on any given weekend, so a wide array of events is planned. Movies are shown on and off campus, and there are trips to theaters, sports events, and other activities. Trips to amusement parks, camping, and rafting are popular warm-weather activities. Snow skiing, cross-country skiing, skating, and sledding occur regularly during the winter.

SUMMER PROGRAMS

The Grove summer program carries on the regular activities of the year. All students attend school. There is added emphasis, however, on individual tutoring and remediation. Large-group activities, using the outdoors and the advantages of the Northeast, are promoted. Favored excursions include visits to amusement parks and fairs as well as sailing lessons, deep-sea fishing, and camping trips. Summer is a very active and enjoyable time at Grove.

COSTS AND FINANCIAL AID

The cost of tuition (education, room, board, and clinical services) for the 2008–09 year is $93,600. Tuition is subject to change. Three months' tuition must be paid in advance, on admission. Billing thereafter is on a monthly basis, in advance. There is a one-time application fee of $200, which is non-refundable.

A $1000 deposit is also required to complete the admission process. This sum remains as a revolving fund to cover certain incidental expenses and is to be replenished monthly, depending on expenses incurred during the preceding month.

Incidental expenses include, but are not limited to, transportation, medical and dental fees, clothing purchases, school supplies, laundry, special instruction, and special recreational events (including international travel, skiing, and the Caribbean sailing program).

ADMISSIONS INFORMATION

Grove encourages inquiries and referrals from parents, therapists, educational consultants, and school representatives. Requirements include an interview and School tour with parents and the student. Appointments for interviews must be made in advance. Referral materials, including but not limited to educational transcripts and summaries, and a recent psychological, psychoeducational, and/or psychiatric assessment should be sent to the Director of Admissions after a preliminary referral call requesting information.

Grove School does not discriminate on the basis of race, sex, color, creed, or national origin in its admissions policies. Admission is determined by the Admissions Committee.

APPLICATION TIMETABLE

Initial inquiries are welcome at any time. Interviews and tours are conducted from 9 to 2, Monday through Friday. Application may be made at any time during the school year and the summer. Grove has an open, rolling admissions policy. Parents are advised of the admissions decision shortly after the interview.

ADMISSIONS CORRESPONDENCE

Director of Admissions
Grove School
175 Copse Road
P.O. Box 646
Madison, Connecticut 06443
Phone: 203-245-2778
Fax: 203-245-6098
E-mail: info@GroveSchool.org
Web site: http://www.GroveSchool.org

THE JOHN DEWEY ACADEMY

Great Barrington, Massachusetts

Type: Coeducational, year-round, college-preparatory, residential therapeutic school
Grades: 10–12, postgraduate year
Enrollment: 35
Head of School: Dr. Thomas Edward Bratter, President

THE SCHOOL

Founded in 1985 by Dr. Thomas Edward Bratter, the John Dewey Academy offers intensive, individualized instruction that stimulates academic excellence and moral integrity. The John Dewey Academy is accredited by the New England Association of Schools and Colleges. This proprietary program devotes its efforts to the dual goals of academic excellence and emotional growth.

The John Dewey Academy is a residential, college-preparatory, therapeutic high school for 35 gifted and formerly alienated students who range in age from 16 to 21 and who have engaged in self-destructive behavior. Although misdiagnosed as unmotivated, they are, in fact, unconvinced. In the absence of fulfillment of affective, intellectual, and creative needs, often the gifted act out against an environment they feel is sterile and hostile. The common presenting problem for these students is a negative attitude. They are demoralized because they have compromised (and in extreme cases have seemingly destroyed) future educational, professional, and social options. Traditional educational and psychotherapeutic approaches do not work with this difficult-to-convince-and-motivate group of adolescents.

The vast majority of students arrive at JDA after multiple attempts to help them have failed. These efforts in the past of more conventional mental health practitioners generally include the prescription of a variety of psychotropic medications, none of which have been effective in the slide into dysfunction. Presenting symptoms include self-medication with alcohol, prescription drugs, or illegal drugs; promiscuity; depression and suicidal ideation and attempts; anxiety; self-mutilation; eating disorders; withdrawal into the Internet or other electronic media; anger and defiance; and deceit, including stealing, lying, or cheating. By creating constant crises with their dangerous behaviors and performing dangerous acts, students have demonstrated they need a structured, safe, and supportive residential treatment environment to help them control and curtail self-destructive behavior.

In 1902, Dewey identified three kinds of growth pragmatic learning must address—intellectual, emotional, and moral. The John Dewey Academy achieves this ambitious mandate with a two-pronged approach. First, the school promotes intellectual growth by equipping students with the written and verbal communications skills necessary to succeed. They teach the student how to become an active learner; think conceptually, constructively, critically, and creatively and communicate their beliefs logically and persuasively; achieve written, verbal, and computational proficiency; problem solve; appreciate intellectual, cultural, and aesthetic achievement; and use, rather than continue to abuse, superior intellectual and creative potential. The school's second aim is to nurture the moral, psychological, and spiritual development of students.

These adolescents have trapped themselves in a no-win labyrinth in which the negative self-fulfilling prophecy imprisons them. Failing begets failure, rejecting begets rejection, betraying begets betrayal—producing the intense pain of demoralization. These adolescents are on a collision course that may result in permanent damage to their lives.

Dewey students are admitted on the basis of an interview regardless of standardized test scores, academic performance, and psychiatric reports. The school understands that such historical data are often not reflective of a student's true potential. When the students are placed in the unrelenting and uncompromising environment of John Dewey, they achieve the greatness of which they are capable.

At JDA, students often complain about feeling stressed. Expectations for academic achievement and moral integrity escalate as students improve. The school rejects mediocrity and demands excellence, both academically and morally. Only those who are ready to commit to improve by working diligently should apply. Caring confrontation by their peers forces students to accept responsibility for their behavior; thus, the stage is set for deep and lasting change.

JDA teaches the adolescent to accept responsibility for attitudes and acts; develop a positive concept of self and a proactive philosophy of life; take control by becoming independent; trust and be trusted, respect and be respected, help and be helped, and love and be loved; regain self-respect by making reasonable, responsible, and realistic decisions; and contribute to the betterment of the community.

The treatment orientation is confrontation. The presenting problem, reduced to its lowest common denominator for Dewey students is that they possess toxic and often antisocial attitudes. Self-destructive behavior is symptomatic. The ultimate treatment goal is to nurture the psychological, moral, and spiritual growth of each student by creating conditions conducive to (re)regaining self-respect and personal integrity. Each adolescent is encouraged to establish a positive identity. In group work, teenagers relate to and learn from peers, learning how to establish positive and reciprocal relationships with family and adults. The group not only demands that the member accepts responsibility for stupid and self-destructive behavior but also helps the youth resolve problems. "Alone you can do it, but you can't do it alone" describes this potent psychotherapeutic principle that all self-help approaches, such as Alcoholics Anonymous, utilize.

Confrontation psychotherapy demands growth and improvement. Such growth sets up a cycle of positive reinforcement that leads to further and deeper changes/maturation in the individual. Confrontation forces the student to take control of his or her life. When the student's behavior becomes congruent with a positive value system, self-respect is a realistically attainable goal. Confrontation, though often painful, becomes a caring, creative, and constructive intervention to maximize change. Thus, the process virtually ensures future personal, educational, professional, and social success in the students who graduate from JDA. The primary treatment goal is to help the student (re)gain self-respect.

Group work is the primary method employed, which is supplemented by individual and family therapy. There are at least three 2-hour groups per week. There is also a weekly men's and women's group. Each night, students participate in a 1-hour self-help group. In groups, students can relate to and identify with their peers, who offer insight and suggestions that provide the catalytic conditions necessary for self-exploration and change. Each student has a primary counselor who discusses personal and family problems.

Eight times throughout the year, parents participate in therapeutic weekends at the school: first, a group in which parents can introduce themselves and discuss their concerns regarding their child; second, family-group meetings with the primary clinician; and third, a mothers' and a fathers' group where discussion focuses on role-related problems. A sibling group meets as well to help both the JDA student and his or her sibling(s) repair their relationships.

The John Dewey Academy rejects claims by psychopharmacologists and neuropsychiatrists that these students' problems are caused by metabolic disorders, genetic imbalances, and cellular deficiencies. The Academy believes that the feelings of depression (which are reality based), pain, shame, inadequacy, and fear that overwhelm adolescents are caused by conscious dysfunctional, dishonest, destructive decisions not biological aberrations. The Academy believes that the assumption that people have biochemical defects ignores the impact of toxic acts and attitudes. When asked, students can provide realistic reasons why they are depressed and are consumed by self-contempt. There is no pill that teaches self-respect or cures noxious narcissism, deceit, or antisocial attitudes. The school eschews the use of all psychotropic medications at John Dewey. JDA is a drug-free environment.

ACADEMIC PROGRAMS

The quality and breadth of academics distinguishes the John Dewey Academy from other special-purpose schools.The curriculum is designed to stimulate and inspire active learning and the development of critical-thinking skills. This learning approach helps students define the synergetic relationship between themselves and society by gaining an awareness and appreciation of science, mathematics, history, social sciences, language, and the arts. Advanced math and science courses, such as advanced calculus, linear algebra, and advanced physics, are offered. The school offers French, Italian, Spanish, and Latin. Students can study philosophy and psychology as well as multidisciplinary offerings in the social sciences. Students can take an independent study course in a subject of interest to them. Students can earn honors credits by designing individualized projects. Class size ranges from 1 to 8 students.

To graduate, students need to complete a minimum number of credits, including English (4), social studies (4), mathematics (3), science (3), foreign language (2), creative arts (1), physical education (2), and electives (4), but they are expected to be carrying a full course load of at least six courses until they graduate. Opportunities are available to take advanced courses at local colleges. There are two 18-week semesters and one 11-week summer program.

The John Dewey Academy is generally a two- to three-year program, depending on academic performance and attitude. Individualized programs for PG students can include taking college courses, serving as a congressional intern, and participating in other types of community activities.

FACULTY AND ADVISERS

There are 9 full-time faculty members, augmented by 4 part-time members. Faculty members possess B.A. degrees from Columbia, St. John's (Annapolis), the School of Visual Arts, Tulane, and the Universities of Michigan and Wisconsin. Faculty members have M.A. degrees from Columbia, New School for Social Research, Oxford, and SUNY. They have doctorates from Columbia Teachers College, NYU, Stanford, and SUNY. More than half of the faculty members have doctorates in their academic disciplines and college teaching experience. One third of the faculty are members of Phi Beta Kappa. One faculty member is a Rhodes Scholar.

In addition to demonstrated academic competence, the faculty members promote self-discovery, self-reliance, and respect for oneself and others.

Dr. Thomas Bratter, a graduate of Columbia College, received his master's degrees and his doctorate in counseling psychology from Columbia University, Teachers College. Dr. Bratter created and directed six community-based programs in Westchester County, New York. He maintained an independent practice of psychotherapy in Scarsdale, where he worked with adolescents and their families. He founded the John Dewey Academy, because he felt there were no rigorous academic programs that addressed the psychosocial-educational needs of gifted adolescents requiring a residential setting. Dr. Bratter has written more than 150 articles about individual, group, and family treatment for at-risk adolescents. He has coauthored four books: *The Reality Therapy Reader, How to Survive Your Adolescent's Adolescence, Alcoholism and Substance Abuse: Strategies for Intervention,* and *Smart Choices.*

COLLEGE ADMISSION COUNSELING

Most students enter the John Dewey Academy with mediocre grades and inconsistent academic records. Many function more than one grade level below their chronological age, so they need intensive, individualized instruction to remedy educational deficits.

Since the first class graduated in 1987, 100 percent of graduates have attended college. Similar to elite U.S. prep schools, this academy judges itself by the reputations of the colleges that admit the graduates. Seventy percent attend some of the most selective fifty colleges in the United States. Dewey students compete successfully against the brightest and the best for admission to top colleges and universities.

JDA graduates excel when they reach the university setting. A third have made the dean's list at Barnard, Bates, Carleton, Columbia (College and University) Connecticut College, Cornell, George Washington, Georgetown, Hobart and William Smith, Holy Cross, Mount Holyoke, NYU, Oberlin, Ohio Wesleyan, Rensselaer, Rochester, Skidmore, Spelman, Syracuse, Trinity, Tufts, Union (New York), Vassar, Wellesley, Williams, and the Universities of Chicago, Hartford, Massachusetts, and Oregon. Seventy percent graduate from college in four years; a small percentage require longer to complete college.

After graduation from college, less than one fifth of the Academy's graduates feel the need for psychotherapy or psychopharmacology. The John Dewey Academy believes that teaching students that their behavior has consequences serves the students well in later life. The records of graduates, therefore, are indistinguishable from those of the most prestigious and elite prep schools in the country. More importantly, graduates are productive and honorable members of society.

STUDENT BODY AND CONDUCT

The Honor Code is regarded as sacrosanct. Each student must agree to abide by an Honor Code that enhances the learning environment and the quality of residential life. Any violation of this contract can result in expulsion. Students assume responsibilities for the maintenance and management of the school, including the complete running of the kitchen, including food ordering, cooking, and cleaning. There are also student academic advisers and tutors.

Students play active roles in formulating and implementing school policies. The President retains the right to make the final determination but remains accountable to the students, staff, and parents. Students learn about leadership by often being deliberately placed in situations in which they need to render their opinions and act decisively.

Positive peer pressure encourages individual empowerment and the acceptance of responsibility for behavior; thus, staff supervision is advisory rather than authoritative. Students gain status and tangible privileges when they convince the faculty that they are responsible and productive.

ACADEMIC FACILITIES

Completed in 1887 at a cost of $2.3 million and modernized eighty years later, Searles Castle was designed by Sanford White and is listed in the National Register of Historic Places. The forty-five rooms are used for classrooms, offices, and living space. Located in an oak-paneled room, the library houses 13,000 volumes.

BOARDING AND GENERAL FACILITIES

Students live on grounds, with most rooms doubles, and a maximum of 4 students residing in the largest rooms.

ATHLETICS

The John Dewey Academy has no competitive teams. Leisure-time fitness activities are emphasized, including hiking, jogging, skating, skiing, swimming, and tennis. The 40-acre campus can accommodate various team sports, such as soccer and basketball. There are tennis and basketball courts on the property as well as a small indoor gym facility with machines and free weights.

EXTRACURRICULAR OPPORTUNITIES

Students assume the responsibility to govern the John Dewey Academy. There are four teams—business, academic, kitchen, and maintenance—that provide students with pragmatic opportunities to learn how to work and develop their leadership abilities in real-world situations. Internships in a variety of community-based agencies can be arranged to augment students' learning.

DAILY LIFE

The school day begins at 8 a.m. and adheres to a college model of class scheduling. From 7 until 9 nightly, students study either individually or in small groups. There is a 3-hour Saturday study hall. Curfew is at 11:30 p.m., except on Friday and Saturday nights, when students can stay up until 1 a.m.

WEEKEND LIFE

After a Saturday morning study hall, students have no classes until Monday, and they may go into town. As a destination resort, the Berkshires region has many cultural and recreational opportunities, including classical music, theater, ballet, and lectures. During the summer, there is hiking and camping; in the winter, skiing is available 3 miles away. Those students with cars can transport peers to local movies and concerts.

COSTS AND FINANCIAL AID

The fifty-two-weeks' tuition is approximately $84,000 in 2008–09. The Academy is not a licensed residential treatment center; however, insurance companies generally reimburse a portion of the cost of a therapeutic program. School districts in Connecticut, Indiana, Maryland, Massachusetts, New Hampshire, New York, and Pennsylvania have reimbursed parents for tuition. Financial aid is limited.

ADMISSIONS INFORMATION

The interview is the most important determinant in the admissions process; it reveals the prospective student's current attitude and potential. Persuading the Academy that the applicant has redeeming intellectual virtues and personal qualities remains the task of the adolescent, not the family or the referral source. The candidate can plead his or her case during the mandatory on-campus interview and is expected to specifically answer the questions "Why should the John Dewey Academy admit me?" and "What am I prepared to contribute to the community?" After admission, students undergo a probationary period. Assuming the student wants to remain and the clinical staff approves, a majority vote by the community determines full admission into the community. Acceptance is not automatic. Only those students who are able to handle rejection and are willing to work toward becoming strong, stable, and socially sophisticated should apply.

APPLICATION TIMETABLE

The Academy accepts students at any time, depending on space and scheduling considerations. For further information or to set up an interview, students should contact Dr. Lisa Sinsheimer at 917-597-7814 or via e-mail at lisa@sinsheimer.net.

ADMISSIONS CORRESPONDENCE

Dr. Thomas E. Bratter, President
Dr. Kenneth Steiner, Dean
The John Dewey Academy
389 Main Street
Great Barrington, Massachusetts 01230
Phone: 413-528-9800
Fax: 413-528-5662
E-mail: tbratter@jda.org
Web site: http://www.jda.org

KILDONAN SCHOOL

Amenia, New York

Type: Coeducational boarding and day college-preparatory and general academic school for students with dyslexia
Grades: 2–12, postgraduate year
Enrollment: 130
Head of School: Benjamin N. Powers, Headmaster

THE SCHOOL

The Kildonan School was founded in 1969 by Diana Hanbury King to serve the needs of students with dyslexia of average to above-average intelligence. The School's threefold mission remains consistent. Kildonan strives to remediate skills in reading, writing, and spelling; provide intellectually stimulating subject matter courses in mathematics, literature, science, and social studies; and foster confidence and self-esteem.

A residential setting free from distractions is most effective in providing a unified program that is consistent with the needs of the student. Each student's day is carefully planned to include a variety of experiences designed to diminish anxiety while building confidence in mental and physical capabilities.

Central to the success of the School is a faculty committed to its philosophy and willing to work hard to implement its goals and ideals. A faculty member's respect for each student as an individual is combined with a willingness to demand the best from each student. A teacher shows regard for a student by refusing to accept any but the student's best efforts.

The School was originally established on a rented campus in Bucks County, Pennsylvania. In 1980, it acquired its own campus in Amenia, New York. The School can now accommodate more than 100 boarding students in a spacious rural setting 90 miles north of New York City; 30 miles northeast of Poughkeepsie, New York; and 55 miles west of Hartford, Connecticut. Located on a hillside, the 325-acre campus is made up of woodlands, fields, and a pond.

The Kildonan School is a nonprofit corporation, governed by a self-perpetuating Board of Trustees. The board is composed primarily of parents of alumni and meets three times a year.

The physical plant is valued at approximately $14 million. Alumni, parents, relatives, and friends of the School support the Annual Giving Fund.

The Kildonan School holds a permanent charter from the New York State Board of Regents. It is accredited by the New York State Association of Independent Schools and holds membership in the National Association of Independent Schools.

ACADEMIC PROGRAMS

The academic program is unique in that it revolves around the intensive, daily, one-to-one Orton-Gillingham tutoring for each student. The language-training instructor is responsible for devising a sequential learning program in language skills in accordance with Dr. Samuel T. Orton's principles and his belief that "such disorders should respond to specific training if we become sufficiently keen in our diagnosis and if we prove ourselves clever enough to devise the proper training methods to meet the needs of each particular case." Orton-Gillingham tutoring is multisensory, direct, and effective. The tutorial setting makes it possible to tailor the teaching to the unique learning style of each individual. The instructor is also responsible for inculcating orderly study habits; students are held accountable for daily independent reading and writing assigned to reinforce the skills taught during the tutorial. Students learn to work through periods of frustration and even temporary failure. Ultimately, the goal is for students to become independent learners.

Subject matter courses in mathematics, history, literature, and science are designed to meet the learning style of dyslexic students. Visual, auditory, and kinesthetic presentations supplement textbooks. Class size is small; courses stimulate thinking and provide opportunities for creativity. The approach to mathematics is closely aligned with language training both in its logical, sequential approach and its daily assignments. Reading and writing demands are reduced or removed entirely from other content courses while the student is building reading and writing skills in the tutorial. Classes are structured to ensure that success is possible even for the student with minimal literacy skills.

Enhanced confidence is achieved through activities, such as the arts, athletics, and community life. Involvement in extracurricular activities that capitalize on the innate strengths of the dyslexic student often leads to lifelong interests. Leadership and service opportunities provide additional means for personal and social growth. Students become confident, experience greater success, and gain the courage to invest increasing effort in their personal and academic achievement.

Kildonan believes that learning best occurs in a structured, safe, and caring environment, which Kildonan provides in both its academic and student-life programs.

All students leave equipped with the best preparation available for the next stage of their academic development, and, of equal importance, with an appreciation for the strengths of the dyslexic mind. While most students are expected to graduate from high school and enter college or other postsecondary programs, the more severely dyslexic students achieve functional mastery of the language.

Minimum requirements for graduation are as follows: 4 units each of English, social studies, and mathematics; 3 units in science; 1 unit in art; 2 units in physical education; and elective courses that bring the total up to at least 22 units.

FACULTY AND ADVISERS

There are 59 faculty members—24 men and 35 women. Of the total, 1 has a doctorate, 9 have master's degrees, and 48 have bachelor's degrees. There are also 4 Fellow of the Academy of Orton-Gillingham Practitioners and Educators on staff.

Headmaster Benjamin Powers is working toward a Master of Arts in language education from Indiana University. He holds a B.A. in Russian/French from LaSalle University and has a Certificate from the University of Paris Sorbonne IV in French studies. He has been Assistant Head of School, Head of the History Department, and a Language Training Tutor at the Kildonan School, as well as Director of the summer program, Dunnnabeck at Kildonan.

The Academic Dean is Dr. Robert A. Lane. Dr. Lane received his doctorate in learning dis/Abilities from Teachers College at Columbia University. As an instructor in Columbia's Department of Curriculum and Teaching, he taught graduate-level courses in the Learning dis/Abilities Program, coordinated the student-teaching program, and was Clinical Supervisor at the Center for Educational and Psychological Services. His career in education began at Kildonan, where he taught literature and language training and supervised a dormitory from 1992 to 1995. Before returning to Kildonan, Dr. Lane also was a Diagnostic Clinician and Educational Consultant at a private clinic in Connecticut.

COLLEGE ADMISSION COUNSELING

College placement is a collaborative effort by the student, parents, the college adviser, the Academic Dean, and the Headmaster. About 95 percent of each graduating class continues in schools and colleges throughout the country. During the past five years, Kildonan students have continued their education at, among others, the following schools and colleges: Adelphi, American International, Boston University, Curry, Elon, Florida Technical, George

Mason, Landmark College, Lynn University, Marshall, Muskingum, New England College, Rhode Island School of Design, RIT, SUNY at Alfred, Syracuse, Wesleyan College (Georgia), and the University of West Virginia.

STUDENT BODY AND CONDUCT

Kildonan enrolls both national and international students with learning differences arising from dyslexia.

The School does not tolerate harassment or the use of alcohol or illegal drugs. Disciplinary problems are handled on an individual basis.

ACADEMIC FACILITIES

The Schoolhouse contains ten classrooms, including a science laboratory; a computer center; development, administrative, and business offices; study halls; tutoring rooms; and an auditorium. An elementary school classroom building contains seven classrooms, thirteen tutoring rooms, and a community gathering area. The Francis St. John Library has seven tutoring rooms, two classrooms, and two large study areas. The Simon Art Studios contain two classrooms, art and ceramics studios, a printmaking studio, and a darkroom. Other academic buildings house eight tutoring rooms and an assistive technology lab. There are also two stables and a well-equipped woodworking facility on the campus. A new athletic center opened in September 2008.

BOARDING AND GENERAL FACILITIES

There are three student residences on campus. The main boys' residence hall houses 62 students, and the girls' residence houses 28. The School has a fully equipped infirmary with full-time nursing coverage, and local physicians serve as the School doctors. Sharon Hospital (Connecticut) is approximately 5 miles away.

ATHLETICS

Athletics is an integral part of the Kildonan School curriculum. Each day students participate in an after-school sport that provides instruction and activities to help students develop the knowledge, motivation, and insights needed to maintain their physical fitness level throughout their lives. There is also a highly successful, long-standing ski program that culminates with a weeklong ski trip to Killington, Vermont.

The athletic program has two levels of focus: to provide a healthy, structured environment for the development of interscholastic athletic competition and to provide a program for the development of a wide range of intramural activities.

Sporting and fitness activities include intramural and interscholastic sports, such as basketball, biking, golf, hiking, horseback riding, lacrosse, skiing, soccer, softball, tennis, and weight training. Kildonan is a member of the New England Preparatory School Athletic Association.

DAILY LIFE

The weekday schedule begins with morning wake-up, room inspection, and breakfast followed by a morning assembly. Classes, sports, and supervised study are scheduled between 8:15 a.m. and 4:45 p.m. Evening study halls vary depending on grade from 1½ to 2 hours on weekdays and from 2 to 3 hours on weekends. Students participate in a community curriculum program that involves small-group, topic-based discussions.

Wednesday afternoons from 2 to 3:15 p.m. students participate in a community service project of their choosing, which may include trail clearing, building, painting, gardening, computers, cooking for the elderly, or running the bookstore.

WEEKEND LIFE

While weekend activities differ from those on academic days, the School is dedicated to the same supervision and structure. The weekend begins with small group dinners in faculty members' apartments. Often, off-campus trips are planned. These may include bowling, miniature golf, movies, biking, skiing, and whitewater rafting. Occasionally students purchase tickets for professional sporting events or theater for Saturday night. Students also enjoy movies on campus or dinner out with their dorm masters. Pickup sports are also popular pastimes. Some students choose an excursion or attend church, some watch an in-house video, and some write letters or play music.

SUMMER PROGRAMS

Dunnabeck at Kildonan is a six-week summer program that was established in 1955 to meet the needs of normal, intelligent boys and girls failing or underachieving in their academic work because of specific difficulty in reading, writing, or spelling. Over the years, hundreds of students have returned from their summer of intensive work at Dunnabeck to find success in school, often for the first time.

The founder and Director Emeritus of Dunnabeck, Diana Hanbury King, was educated in England and Canada. She holds a B.A. Hons. degree from the University of London and an M.A. from George Washington University. She has taught at the Ruzawi School in Rhodesia; at Sidwell Friends School in Washington, D.C.; and at the Potomac School in Virginia. Mrs. King was the 1990 recipient of the Samuel T. Orton Award, the highest honor bestowed by the International Dyslexia Association. Publications include *Writing Skills, Writing Skills Teacher's Manual, Keyboarding Skills, Cursive Writing Skills,* and *English Isn't Crazy.*

Dunnabeck can accommodate 85 boys and girls, ranging in age from 8 to 16. Great care is taken to ensure that the younger campers receive sufficient attention. A number of activities are planned just for this group. They remain under the careful supervision of the counselor and the health center staff. Older students follow a schedule that allows for longer periods of study and for more intensive and challenging forms of recreation such as backpacking, canoeing, windsurfing, and waterskiing.

COSTS AND FINANCIAL AID

Tuition for the 2008–09 school year was $51,500 for boarding students, $49,250 for five-day boarding students, $37,000 for day students, and $29,800 for elementary students. There is an additional activity fee of $900 for all middle- and upper-school students.

Tuition for the 2009 Dunnabeck Program is $9500 for boarding students, $7200 for full-day students, and $4800 for half-day students.

ADMISSIONS INFORMATION

Parents interested in enrolling their son or daughter should fill out the preliminary application form and send it to the School, together with all available records of educational and psychological testing as well as a transcript. As soon as the material is received, the family is invited for an interview. Acceptance at Kildonan is not competitive; students are selected on the basis of their ability to benefit from the program.

APPLICATION TIMETABLE

It is in the student's best interest to plan entrance for September, though some are admitted in January and a few at other times throughout the year as space becomes available.

ADMISSIONS CORRESPONDENCE

Marcie Wistar
Associate Director of Admissions
Kildonan School
425 Morse Hill Road
Amenia, New York 12501
Phone: 845-373-2013
Fax: 845-373-2004
E-mail: info@kildonanadmissions.org
Web site: http://www.kildonan.org

LANDMARK SCHOOL

Prides Crossing, Massachusetts

Type: Coeducational boarding and day college-preparatory and general academic school for students with language-based learning disabilities, such as dyslexia
Grades: Grades 2–12
Enrollment: 455
Head of School: Robert J. Broudo, M.Ed.

THE SCHOOL

Landmark School was founded in 1971 by Dr. Charles "Chad" Drake with the goal of educating students whose reading, writing, spelling, and mathematical skills did not match their thinking and problem-solving capacities. Most call these children dyslexic or learning disabled. Chad saw their promise, and called them bright and capable. Landmark opened its doors with 40 students and a small group of teachers on one campus in Prides Crossing, Massachusetts. Since then, Landmark has grown to 455 students on two North Shore campuses and a faculty and staff of more than 300. Today Landmark is recognized as a pioneer in the field of language-based learning disabilities.

Landmark is a coeducational boarding and day school offering a full range of customized programs for students in grades 2 to 12. With a college-preparatory high school, a middle school, and an elementary school, Landmark is one of the most comprehensive schools serving students with language-based learning disabilities in the United States. Landmark individualizes instruction for each student, emphasizing the development of language and learning skills, and cultivates a uniquely supportive and structured living and learning environment.

Landmark offers day and residential programs and enrolls students from across the United States and around the world. The School accepts bright students who have been diagnosed with a language-based learning disability, such as dyslexia. Successful candidates should be emotionally healthy and motivated to learn but need remedial help with reading, writing, spelling, listening, and speaking, as well as mathematics.

Landmark teachers are committed to the success of every student. The faculty is at the core of the School's innovative, effective program of remediation. Landmark's teaching principles and practices are based on more than thirty-five years of front-line experience. Practical, classroom-tested methods are influenced by the latest research on human intelligence, cognitive development, and learning disabilities.

With a 1:3 teacher-student ratio, teaching at Landmark is concentrated and dynamic. Teachers, tutors, and case managers meet and share information about students every morning. The entire team is focused on the progress of each student.

Landmark School is located on Boston's North Shore, overlooking the ocean, in an area rich in historic sites and recreational opportunities. The high school and administration offices are located in the Prides Crossing section of Beverly, Massachusetts, just 25 miles north of Boston. The elementary–middle school campus is 3 miles to the northeast, nestled in the woods on an estate in Manchester-by-the-Sea.

Landmark is a nonprofit, nonsectarian educational organization. It is governed by a 26-member Board of Trustees. The School's operating expenses for 2007–08 were $23 million. Contributions and grants totaled $2.04 million.

Landmark is accredited by the New England Association of Schools and Colleges. It is a member of the Massachusetts Association of 766 Approved Private Schools, the National Association of Independent Schools, and the Association of Independent Schools of New England and is approved as a school for children with language-based learning disabilities by the Division of Special Education of the State Department of Education in the Commonwealth of Massachusetts. It is licensed as a residential facility by the Massachusetts Office of Child Care Services.

ACADEMIC PROGRAMS

The key to Landmark's successful model is the daily one-to-one tutorial. Students meet and work closely with one tutor for the entire year. A customized tutorial curriculum is designed to remediate specific language needs, which may encompass decoding, fluency, phonological awareness, written composition, and organizational skills. The tutorial has a distinct curriculum and provides a personal connection between the student and teacher.

At Landmark high school, preparation for college and beyond is the goal of the program. Focus is placed on skill acquisition and achievement; an individualized program is designed for each student. The curriculum addresses the spectrum of student needs. Based on their unique abilities and skill levels, students are assigned to a schedule of courses.

The curriculum is designed to teach the students to become independent learners. Individual assessments are made continually to determine the appropriate approach of remediation.

Core subjects are math, social studies, science, language arts, oral expression, study skills, and electives. Computer technology is integrated across the entire curriculum.

For students who need intensive help with oral and written communication, Landmark offers courses in expressive language skills. Rigorous remediation is provided through an integrated curriculum to reinforce the relationship between listening, speaking, reading, and writing. Landmark teachers receive supervision from certified speech-language pathologists.

When students progress within one year of grade level, their case manager may consider transitioning them to a more advanced level of course work. The pace is likely to be a bit faster and the classes slightly larger (8–12 students). For some students, the daily one-to-one tutorial is replaced by a study skills class. Mathematics is assigned based on skill level.

The elementary school program, for ages 7 to 10 (grades 2–5), is a self-contained model in which children are assigned to a small group of less than 8 students and matched with a key teacher for their academic day. Every child receives a daily individual language arts tutorial specifically attuned to diagnosed needs in the areas of reading, spelling, writing, and handwriting. The group stays together for the remaining classes: language arts, oral expression/literature, social studies, and science. Math classes are grouped separately according to each student's needs. Enrichment and elective offerings include arts and crafts, music, physical education, woodworking, computers, and small-engine repair.

The middle school program serves students ages 10–14 (grades 6–8), and each student receives a daily individual language arts tutorial as well as a schedule of small-group classes (4–8 students) consisting of language arts, math, science, social studies, auditory/oral expression, literature, and study skills. Computer competencies and keyboarding skills are incorporated into the class schedule, and electives (physical education, art, computer graphics, woodworking, and small-engine repair) complete the daily schedule.

FACULTY AND ADVISERS

Landmark employs 280 educational personnel made up of teaching faculty members, case managers, supervisors, and department heads. More than 65 percent hold advanced degrees.

In addition to teaching, staff members support the residential team after school hours and on weekends.

Through the Landmark School Outreach Program, faculty members present graduate courses and workshops at schools and conferences nationwide. Faculty members have published books on teaching study skills, writing, and mathematics. A professional development institute and lectures are presented each summer on the Landmark campus.

COLLEGE ADMISSION COUNSELING

Landmark's Guidance Department works with juniors and seniors. Counselors meet individually with seniors to help them select a successful path to the future and specifically work with preparing applications, interviewing, and completing the SAT, with accommodations as needed. College representatives come to Landmark, and students visit colleges.

Ninety-five percent of graduates from the class of 2006 are attending college. Of alumni from the classes of 2002–06, 92 percent attended college. While 99 percent of graduates attain jobs after college, many also pursue postgraduate and vocational programs. Landmark alumni attend colleges and universities including Boston College, Colby-Sawyer, Lynn, Syracuse, Texas A&M, and the Universities of Denver, Massachusetts, and New Hampshire.

STUDENT BODY AND CONDUCT

The 2007–08 student body had 455 students. The high school had 314 students; 134 day students (96 boys and 38 girls) and 180 boarding students (115 boys and 65 girls). The elementary–middle school had 141 day students. Students came from twenty-three states and ten other countries. Approximately 19 percent of the students were members of a minority group.

Landmark provides a safe and positive environment for its students, teaching respect, honesty, and commitment. Programs are structured to help students acquire and improve academic and social skills. The Dean of Students and a Standards Committee composed of faculty and staff members address individual conduct issues as needed.

The Student Council, which is elected by all grade levels and includes dormitory representatives, helps plan community service activities, parties, dances, lectures, and trips.

ACADEMIC FACILITIES

Landmark's high school campus is located in an estate setting on 30 acres that overlook the Atlantic Ocean. The Alexander Academic Center contains a library containing 8,000 volumes, a newly renovated dining room, a tutorial center, anda radio station, WLMK. Classes are conducted in Governor's Landing Academic Center, Prep Building, Classroom Building, Computer Center, and Early Literacy Tutorial Center. Science labs, the health center, and a girls' dormitory are in Bain Hall. Performing arts, visual arts, woodshop/boat building, auto shop, the gymnasium, Collins Athletic Field, and Tot Spot Childcare Center are all located on the upper campus.

Lopardo Center contains boys' living space and the student center. Student residences are Williston Hall and Woodside Hall (both girls' dorms), Porter House, Buchan House, and the Campus Cottage.

The elementary and middle school (EMS) campus has a main building with classrooms, a newly renovated dining hall, a meeting room, a library, and offices. Three additional buildings house the tutorial center, art center, woodworking shop, small-engine shop, gymnasium, and more classrooms.

BOARDING AND GENERAL FACILITIES

Landmark has a fully staffed Residential Life Program that provides a round-the-clock living and teaching environment. Students learn how to manage their schoolwork, support their friends and roommates, and enjoy a wide range of planned activities, outings, and social events. The program incorporates a structured-level-based system that gives students the opportunity to earn privileges as they demonstrate their developing abilities in time management, organization, and peer mediation and to consistently manage their responsibilities.

ATHLETICS

Fitness, health, competition, and recreation are all part of Landmark's athletic program. Students are encouraged to stay active and healthy. Eighty percent of Landmark high school students participate in organized team sports, and 95 percent of Landmark coaches are teachers at Landmark. Landmark competes in the Eastern Independent League and the Independent Girls Conference. Students may join twenty-six sports teams and intramural programs as part of middle and high school life.

Landmark offers varsity and junior varsity baseball, basketball, cross-country, golf, lacrosse, soccer, swimming, tennis, and wrestling. Intramural programs include basketball, dodgeball, floor hockey, and volleyball. Supervised recreational clubs and activities typically include downhill skiing, mountain biking, skateboarding, and weight training.

EXTRACURRICULAR OPPORTUNITIES

In addition to intramural sports, the School also offers student council, radio broadcasting, confidence courses, gay/straight alliance, auto mechanics, visual arts, and the performing arts. Support of the greater community is encouraged; Landmark students have completed thousands of community service hours to support local and national charities.

DAILY LIFE

Classes are held Monday through Friday from 8 a.m. to 2:50 p.m., with seven 45-minute classes. After-school activities are encouraged. On weeknights, high school boarding students are required to attend a supervised study hall.

WEEKEND LIFE

Landmark's Residential Life Program emphasizes responsibility, respect, and independence. Students enjoy a great range of planned activities, outings, and social events, including movies, cultural trips, and skiing. Home visits are arranged individually on request. Transportation to attend religious services is provided.

SUMMER PROGRAMS

Summers at Landmark offer a six-week program of learning and fun in a supportive environment for grades 1 to 12 (boarding 8 to 12). The program combines intensive academic skill development with recreational activities and exploration along Boston's North Shore. Landmark faculty members provide a customized program designed to improve reading, writing, spelling, and composition skills for each student. Full- and half-day academic programs feature daily one-to-one tutorials and small classes that can be combined with recreational or hands-on activities that foster personal growth. Choices vary by grade and age but have included marine science, kayaking, adventure ropes, musical theater, and practical arts such as woodworking and small engines. Admission criteria are similar to the academic year programs.

COSTS AND FINANCIAL AID

The 2008–09 tuition for the academic program for day students is $42,525 and $56,650 for boarding students. The Prep day program cost is $35,975, and the boarding cost is $50,100. Enrollment deposits ranging from $6700 to $9000, depending on the program, are due on acceptance. Half of the balance of the tuition is due July 1, and the remainder by December 1. Parents have the option of a ten-month payment plan.

More than 50 percent of Landmark's students receive financial aid through various agencies, mainly local departments of education.

ADMISSIONS INFORMATION

Landmark programs are designed for students with average to above-average intellectual ability; well-developed thinking, problem-solving, and comprehension skills; difficulty decoding, spelling, and writing; difficulty processing language; and no apparent primary emotional, social, or behavioral issues. Prior to admission, Landmark must receive a diagnostic evaluation as well as educational and medical records.

APPLICATION TIMETABLE

Landmark accepts applications and admits students throughout the year as space permits. Early application for summer programs is recommended.

Students who meet admission criteria are invited to visit Landmark with at least one parent or guardian. The half-day visit includes an interview, individual testing, tour, discussion of test results, and a decision regarding acceptance.

A fee of $150 must accompany the application form.

ADMISSIONS CORRESPONDENCE

Carolyn Orsini Nelson, Director of Admission
Landmark School
P.O. Box 227
Prides Crossing, Massachusetts 01965-0227
Phone: 978-236-3000
Fax: 978-927-7268
E-mail: admission@landmarkschool.org
Web site: http://www.landmarkschool.org

MOUNT BACHELOR ACADEMY

Prineville, Oregon

Type: Coeducational boarding school offering college-preparatory course work for students with behavioral or motivational difficulties
Grades: Ages 14–17.5
Enrollment: 113
Head of School: Sharon Bitz

THE SCHOOL

Mount Bachelor Academy, founded in 1988, provides a well-rounded, college-preparatory, academic, and emotional growth curriculum designed for children who may have academic, behavioral, emotional, or motivational problems. The fourteen- to sixteen-month integrated curriculum at Mount Bachelor Academy encourages increased self-awareness in students, builds their self-esteem, and develops their problem-solving and decision-making skills through experiential learning.

Students are in group counseling sessions two times a week. In these sessions, students learn to deal with situational living issues as well as personal issues. In a highly structured yet nurturing peer environment, students learn to address issues that have prevented them from achieving academic and personal success.

Mount Bachelor Academy's highly skilled teaching faculty and staff members are experienced in working with children who may have displayed behavior that is symptomatic of low self-esteem and poor self-concept.

A strong addictions recovery program serves students with substance abuse issues through NA/AA-style meetings, addictions classes, and processing groups run by certified drug and alcohol counselors.

Mount Bachelor Academy is fully accredited by the Pacific Northwest Association of Independent Schools and the Northwest Association of Schools and Colleges. The Academy is also a member of the Aspen Education Group.

ACADEMIC PROGRAMS

Mount Bachelor Academy provides a high school college-preparatory academic curriculum that incorporates both classroom and individual tutoring experiences. Each student participates in dynamic field trips that supplement their traditional course work. In addition, interpersonal skill building is emphasized, and the students' desire for learning is fostered.

Strong emphasis is placed on each student's learning style. Students meet with the school's special education director on site to do a learning styles assessment and develop an individual learning plan that addresses each student's learning needs, whether LD issues, a need for challenge and academic acceleration, or both.

Many classes employ experiential hands-on techniques that keep the subject material exciting and interesting for students.

The development of caring, personal teacher-student relationships helps the faculty members to know how to better motivate their students. Mount Bachelor Academy carefully selects experienced teachers who have enthusiasm both for their respective discipline and for working with adolescents. Teachers are involved with student activities and counseling outside the classroom.

FACULTY AND ADVISERS

Mount Bachelor Academy has a student-faculty ratio of 4:1. Teaching faculty members and counseling staff members are involved in an on-site training program that augments their prior professional training and education.

All students are assigned to a mentor who guides them as they progress through the emotional growth component of the curriculum. The mentor also communicates on a regular basis with the students' families.

COLLEGE ADMISSION COUNSELING

Mount Bachelor Academy offers an SAT preparatory class for juniors and seniors. Once this class is completed, students take the SAT in preparation for college.

The Academy's college counselor helps students make application to the colleges of their choice. Approximately 85 percent of graduates matriculate into and continue their education at a four-year college or university.

STUDENT BODY AND CONDUCT

The student population consists of boys and girls from all over the United States, Canada, and some other countries. A strong, positive peer culture is the core of Mount Bachelor Academy's curriculum.

Students serve as dorm leaders, proctors, aides, and tutors. They utilize school forums for both conflict resolution and peer support.

ACADEMIC FACILITIES

Mount Bachelor Academy is located about an hour east of Bend, Oregon, in the Ochoco National Forest. The school offers students the opportunity to learn and grow in a beautiful forest setting, far from the pressures and influences of the urban areas of today.

Facilities include classrooms, a library, computers in classrooms and the library, a dining room, a living/social area, an art center, a gymnasium, a weight room, a climbing wall, a ropes course, hiking trails, an outdoor swimming pool, and twenty-two dorms.

BOARDING AND GENERAL FACILITIES

Mount Bachelor Academy students live in comfortable dorms that house 4 to 5 students each. The dorms are student-proctored, with staff oversight. The students work together to share daily and weekly housekeeping responsibilities.

The setting of the dorms engenders a safe environment where strong and reliable friendships are built. Staff and faculty members are part of evening student life, contributing to a warm family atmosphere.

ATHLETICS

All students participate in a variety of physical activities both on and off campus, including basketball, climbing, cross-country skiing, dance, disc golf, downhill skiing, hiking, running, snowboarding, soccer, swimming, and volleyball.

Mount Bachelor Academy also competes with other area schools and teams. In addition, all students participate in wilderness challenges with their peer group in the form of backpacking, climbing, camping, and skiing.

EXTRACURRICULAR OPPORTUNITIES

Students enjoy extracurricular opportunities that include study trips to the Oregon Shakespeare Festival and political science excursions to Presidential Classroom in Washington, D.C. There are also visits to college and university activities within the state of Oregon. In addition, there are ongoing field trips that utilize state parks and facilities.

Traditional holidays, such as Thanksgiving, Hanukkah, Christmas, Easter, Passover, and Martin Luther King Day, in addition to events unique to the school (Summer Olympics and community service days), are observed every year.

DAILY LIFE

Each student's day begins with dorm and campus housekeeping, followed by a busy academic schedule.

Tutoring and school forums take place in the late afternoons. Evenings are dedicated to study sessions and activity and social time.

WEEKEND LIFE

Saturdays and Sundays are busy on-campus project and physical activity times. Sunday brunch is followed by a host of eventful field trips or recreational activities.

COSTS AND FINANCIAL AID

Tuition, room and board, and therapeutic costs amount to $6400 per month.

Additional one-time enrollment fees include an application, interview, and alumni services fee of $8600; a student supply pack of $482; and a wilderness clothing fee of approximately $350, depending on the season. All fees are subject to change.

ADMISSIONS INFORMATION

Applications are accepted for boys and girls, ages 14 to 17.5. A full battery of psychoeducational evaluations and academic records are required as part of the enrollment process.

If a student's evaluations are incomplete, nonexistent, or more than a year old, Mount Bachelor Academy's consulting psychologist can administer the necessary tests, for an additional fee.

Children are selected to attend Mount Bachelor Academy on the basis of their ability to integrate with the school environment and their ability to receive the maximum benefit from the combined academic and emotional growth curriculum.

A parent interview is required.

APPLICATION TIMETABLE

Admission inquiries are welcome at any time. Parents are encouraged to schedule a tour of the campus in order to meet faculty members, staff members, and students.

Depending on their individual circumstances, students may be enrolled as soon as the application process and interview are completed.

ADMISSIONS CORRESPONDENCE

Admission Department
Mount Bachelor Academy
33051 NE Ochoco Highway
Prineville, Oregon 97754

Phone: 800-462-3404 (toll-free)
Fax: 541-462-3430
Web site: http://www.mtba.com

OAK CREEK RANCH SCHOOL

West Sedona, Arizona

Type: Coeducational boarding school with general and college-preparatory programs for ADD/ADHD students and undermotivated teens
Grades: 7–12, postgraduate (ages 12–19)
Enrollment: School total: 80–90
Head of School: David Wick Jr., Headmaster

THE SCHOOL

For thirty-six years, Oak Creek Ranch School has been helping undermotivated teens and students with ADD/ADHD realize their true potential. The School offers individualized programs, small classes, and a highly experienced faculty. Programs are designed to help teens achieve their academic goals while gaining valuable social and interpersonal skills. The School's Leadership and Character Development program teaches students the importance of integrity, responsibility, and commitment to others.

The 17-acre campus is located on the banks of Oak Creek, near beautiful Sedona, Arizona. The rural setting, temperate climate, and adjacent Coconino National Forest provide an ideal setting for students to enjoy outdoor activities both on and off the campus. The School is located 100 miles north of Phoenix, Arizona.

Oak Creek Ranch School was established in 1972 by David Wick, Sr. and is fully accredited by the North Central Association of Colleges and Schools.

ACADEMIC PROGRAMS

Students must complete 22 credits to graduate, including classes in art, computer science, physical education, English, mathematics, science, and social studies. Foreign languages are also offered.

The School's academic program is specifically designed to meet the needs of teens with ADD/ADHD and other learning challenges. Therefore, class sizes are limited to less than 10 students per class, which allows the School's faculty to work with each student, individually.

The faculty utilizes the following proven methodologies to address the ADD/ADHD student's special needs: A predictable routine and structure; Clear expectations that are communicated frequently; Immediate and explicit feedback; Cooperative learning activities; Accommodation of the individual learning style while focusing on developing additional learning skills; Breaking down tasks into sub-tasks and sub-skills and arranging tasks hierarchically; Using performance incentives; Teaching compensatory strategies (calculator skills, keyboarding, spell check, mnemonic devices, verbal rehearsal); Devoting adequate time in class to teach the basic skills of listening, note-taking, preparing for tests, and taking tests.

The school year is divided into semesters. However, students may enroll throughout the year.

FACULTY AND ADVISERS

The School's faculty includes the Headmaster, Principal, Dean of Students, Director of Residential Life, 13 certified teachers, and a college guidance counselor. The majority of the faculty members have advanced degrees.

COLLEGE ADMISSION COUNSELING

The School provides career counseling and college placement advice and assistance to all students.

Students enrolled in the college-preparatory program are encouraged to take the SAT in January of their eleventh- and twelfth-grade years. Preparation for the SAT and/or ACT is provided through special sessions and tutoring. SAT and ACT tests are administered through Northern Arizona University in Flagstaff.

Ninety percent of OCRS graduates from last year continued their education. Recent graduates have attended the following universities and other fine schools: Arizona State; Brooks Institute, DePaul, The Illinois Institute of Art, Marymount College, Northern Arizona, Ohio State, Purdue, Texas Tech, UCLA, University of the Pacific, and the Universities of Denver and Nevada, Las Vegas.

STUDENT BODY AND CONDUCT

The School enrolls approximately 80–90 students from throughout the U.S., Europe, Asia, Canada, and Mexico.

Campus life is relaxed and informal. Most students dress in casual attire for classes. More formal dress is required for special events, such as proms and graduation.

The School has a Student Council, which is made up of students elected from each class. This group helps new students adjust to the School's social and academic environment, assists dormitory supervisors, and helps plan special events.

The School uses positive reinforcement to develop leadership and character. The Leadership and Character Development Program teaches students the importance of living a life that demonstrates integrity, responsibility, loyalty, respect for self, and consideration for others. All faculty and staff members administer the program universally. Students are required to participate in one outdoor adventure program per semester, which may include white-water rafting, overnight camping in the mountains, canoeing, or hiking in the Grand Canyon. Through this program, students gain valuable life experiences that help them discover their own strengths while learning how they may contribute to the success of others.

ACADEMIC FACILITIES

The main building houses administrative offices and classrooms. The School has an art building with its own kiln, a separate science lab, and three classroom buildings. A fully equipped Macintosh computer lab provides students with an opportunity to learn Web site design, video production, and graphic design. A separate PC lab is used to teach the proper use of office productivity programs, including Microsoft Word, PowerPoint, and Excel. The library's PCs are available for students to prepare homework, practice skills, and utilize Internet resources.

BOARDING AND GENERAL FACILITIES

The campus has seventeen buildings, including the dormitories, classrooms, and recreational buildings. Other facilities include a pool, tennis court, basketball court, low-ropes course, and skateboard park. The School also has an equestrian center that offers instruction in Western and English riding. Students are encouraged to enter local competitions and gymkhanas.

A supervisor in residence monitors each dormitory. All residences are centrally heated and cooled. Each dormitory contains smoke and/or fire alarm systems that have been approved by the Arizona State Fire Marshal and the state health department. A registered nurse is on duty in the School's health center.

ATHLETICS

Physical education is an important component of the curriculum. All students must attend a physical activity of their choice for 1 hour, four days a week. Interscholastic competitive sports include baseball, golf (at some of the most beautiful Sedona courses), flag football, soccer, and volleyball. In 2008, the flag football team won the state championship in their division, and the girls' volleyball team took second place.

EXTRACURRICULAR OPPORTUNITIES

The School offers mountain biking, hiking, backpacking, horseback riding (arena and trail rides), skateboarding, rock climbing, weight lifting, tennis, swimming, golf, and fishing. Other popular recreational activities include paintball games, overnight camping, white-water rafting, snowboarding/skiing, and trips to water parks, the Grand Canyon, concerts, and other special events in Phoenix, Flagstaff, Prescott, and Tucson.

DAILY LIFE

Students rise at 7:30 a.m., and breakfast is served between 8 and 9. Classes begin at 9 and continue until 3:30 p.m., with breaks for snacks and lunch. Physical education begins at 4 and lasts until 5. Dinner is served from 5 to 6, and evening activities last from 6 to 9 p.m. Students must be in their dorms at 9, with lights-out at 10 p.m. on school nights.

WEEKEND LIFE

Weekend activities may include concerts in Phoenix, snowboarding in Flagstaff, hiking the Grand Canyon, camping and horseback riding in the scenic areas of northern Arizona, mountain biking along the red rocks of Sedona, shopping, movies, sporting events, paintball, water parks, and fairs and festivals.

With parental permission, students may sign up for overnight trips to the Grand Canyon, Oak Creek Canyon, camping in the Arizona mountains, tours of local Native American historical sites, and surrounding area lakes. During the winter months, snowboarding and skiing are available at the local ski facilities outside Flagstaff. Off-campus trips and other functions are supervised by residential staff and/or teaching faculty members. The School provides transportation to all off-campus activities, including religious services. All students are encouraged to attend the religious service of their choice.

SUMMER PROGRAMS

The School offers three 4-week summer school sessions for credit or personal enrichment. Students may earn ½ credit in each of two subjects during one session. Classes are held in the morning, with study periods early in the afternoon. For the remainder of the day, students participate in a variety of recreational activities on and off campus. Wilderness Literature and other experiential learning classes are offered during summer school. Transportation is provided to and from the Sky Harbor Airport in Phoenix.

COSTS AND FINANCIAL AID

Tuition, room, board, transportation fees, and all other expenses for the 2008–09 school year were $37,000. There is a $400 enrollment fee for new students. A $1000 revolving internal account fund is required for personal student expenditures such as weekly allowances, medical expenses, and special activity fees. The balance in the internal account is refunded within sixty days of the close of the school year. Horses can be boarded for an additional monthly fee.

Student loans are available through Wells Fargo Bank. The School also offers a payment plan for qualified applicants.

Summer School tuition for 2008 is $4150 for a four-week program. There is a $400 application fee for new students.

ADMISSIONS INFORMATION

Information about the admissions process may be obtained through the School's admissions office. Please contact David Wick Jr. at dwick@ocrs.com. Personal visits are welcomed and encouraged. New students are accepted after a personal interview and review of their academic and social/behavioral records by the School's admissions department.

Applicants must submit a completed application form and health report. An application form may be requested through the admissions office or downloaded from the School's Web site.

APPLICATION TIMETABLE

Inquiries and enrollments are accepted throughout the year. Applications for fall enrollment should be made in the spring or summer to ensure that space is available. Visits are always welcome. Interested students should call the admissions department to schedule an appointment.

ADMISSIONS CORRESPONDENCE

David Wick Jr., Headmaster
Oak Creek Ranch School
P.O. Box 4329
West Sedona, Arizona 86340-4329
Phone: 928-634-5571
877-554-OCRS (6277) (toll-free)
Fax: 928-634-4915
E-mail: dwick@ocrs.com
Web site: http://www.ocrs.com

PINE RIDGE SCHOOL

Williston, Vermont

Pine Ridge School

Type: Coeducational boarding and day college-preparatory and general academic school for students with learning differences, namely dyslexia, specific language-based learning differences, and nonverbal learning disabilities
Grades: Ungraded, ages 13–18
Enrollment: Approximately 50
Head of School: Dana K. Blackhurst

THE SCHOOL

Pine Ridge School was founded in 1968 to meet the needs of students ages 13 to 18 of average to above-average intelligence who have learning differences—namely, dyslexia, specific language-based learning disabilities, and nonverbal learning disabilities. The School recognizes that this student population possesses unique strengths, weaknesses, and learning styles, and every member of the faculty is committed to its mission to provide "an educational community that is committed to empowering students with dyslexia and other language-based learning differences to define and achieve success throughout their lives."

Students are provided with a highly structured, safe, supportive, and success-oriented environment where classes are small and opportunities for teacher-student interactions are frequent. The Orton-Gillingham approach is integrated throughout all major components of the program—academic, remedial, residential/social, and athletic/recreational—to address all aspects of this student population's education and growth. In addition, essential skills for lifelong success—organization, time management, and self-advocacy—are taught and measured across all settings.

Located at the foot of Vermont's Green Mountains, the Pine Ridge School campus encompasses 150 acres of rolling hills, forest, and athletic fields. While the setting is rural, the School is only 8 miles from Burlington, the state's largest city and home to multiple colleges, including the University of Vermont. Recent studies have ranked Vermont as one of the two safest states, and Burlington, culturally rich beyond its size, is regularly listed as one of America's best places to live.

Pine Ridge School is a nonprofit corporation governed by a Board of Trustees representing parents, educators, and prominent community members. The School is accredited by the New England Association of Schools and Colleges and the Vermont Department of Education as a private secondary school with diploma-granting privileges and is approved for special education funding by the Vermont State Board of Education. The School's instructional offerings, including the student summer program, are approved by the Academy of Orton-Gillingham Practitioners and Educators; in addition, the School's teacher-training program is accredited by the Academy. Pine Ridge is a member of the Vermont Principals' Association, the International Dyslexia Association, the Independent School Association of Northern New England, and the Vermont Independent School Association.

ACADEMIC PROGRAMS

The Orton-Gillingham approach—pioneered by the neuropsychiatrist/pathologist Samuel Orton and the educator/psychologist Anna Gillingham—is validated by the tenets of current research as "best practice" for teaching children with language-processing challenges. The integration of this comprehensive, holistic approach into the Pine Ridge School program is nowhere more apparent than in the academic and remedial components, where Orton-Gillingham-trained faculty members emphasize diagnostic and prescriptive teaching, beginning at the most fundamental levels and focusing on the needs of the individual learner. Instruction is language-based, multisensory, structured, sequential, cumulative, cognitive, and dynamic.

Academic subjects include English, math, social studies, computer skills, health, physical education, art, and science. At the beginning of each school year, new students receive class placements based on their entrance assessments, psycho-educational profiles, and past school histories. Returning students are placed on the basis of previous year-end testing and faculty recommendations. Students are able to work at their own pace in order to master the skills they need to be successful; they learn to apply the skills of reading, composition, problem solving, and studying to their academic courses as they develop these skills in the remedial program component. The Pine Ridge academic experience allows students to build self-confidence and develop positive attitudes about learning, while mastering basic subject matter upon which more complex knowledge can be built.

The foundation for academics at the Pine Ridge School—the remedial component—is designed to improve students' language skills through three subcomponents: a daily one-to-one tutorial, a proctored study hall, and communications strategies integrated into all aspects of the program.

The 60-minute tutorial is a time of intensive interaction between the remedial language specialist (RLS) and the student; the primary goal is to develop the student's language skills in listening, speaking, reading, and writing. The RLS continually assesses the student in the four major skill areas while also providing sufficient instruction, drill, and practice to establish new concepts and enable the student to perform new skills independently. The tutorial is highly individualized: each student works to remedy the specific language skills that impede his/her acquisition, interpretation, expression, or application of verbal information, based on his or her diagnostic tests. The student develops skills in phonemic awareness, word attack and decoding, and cursive handwriting; he/she also learns the history of English, spelling rules, morphology, and other aspects of language—with the goal of making language processes "automatic."

FACULTY AND ADVISERS

The Pine Ridge School professionally trained faculty includes teachers, remedial language specialists (RLS), and residential instructors. The student-faculty ratio is approximately 2.5:1. All staff members possess Orton-Gillingham training. Most of the School's RLS are Academy of Orton-Gillingham Practitioners and Educators–credentialed. The faculty is integrated so that the residential instructors are also content teachers, tutors, and coaches. This provides consistency and structure for the student body.

Head of School Dana K. Blackhurst is a nationally recognized educator and authority in the field of dyslexia. He has been long affiliated with the International Dyslexia Association and has served on its board of directors as well as on numerous other educational advisory boards, including the Marshall University Help Program board of directors, the South Carolina–based Child's Haven board, and the board of directors for the Andre Agassi Preparatory Charter School.

An educator since 1983, Blackhurst has received numerous teaching honors, including the Educator Award–Carolina Branch of the IDA (2002), South Carolina Middle School Teacher of the Year (1990–91), P. Buckley Moss Teacher Award for national outstanding educator in learning disabilities (runner-up), and congressional proclamation as "Outstanding Educator" in South Carolina.

As an administrator, Blackhurst has held leadership roles with several prominent schools for students with learning differences. Most recently, he was Executive Director of the Center for Innovative Learning at the Carroll School in Lincoln, Massachusetts, where he also taught social studies. From 1991–2005, he served as Head of Camperdown Academy in Greenville, South Carolina. Previously, Blackhurst held positions with the Kildonan School in Amenia, New York; the Jemicy School in Baltimore, Maryland; and the Sandhills School in Columbia, South Carolina.

Jean Foss, Director of Clinical Teaching and Research, received her M.Ed. from the University of Vermont. A member of the faculty at Pine Ridge School since 1968, she is a past president of the New England Branch of the International Dyslexia Association, a Founding Fellow and first Vice President of the Academy of Orton-Gillingham Practitioners and Educators, and an adjunct faculty member at St. Michael's College. Ms. Foss is a nationally recognized author and lecturer on the remediation of dyslexia and nonverbal learning disabilities.

COLLEGE ADMISSION COUNSELING

Pine Ridge School is dedicated to helping students develop skills and interests for life outside of and after secondary school.

The School's College Placement Office helps students prepare and arrange for precollege visits and aptitude testing and develop skills such as filling out applications, interviewing, and resume writing. Pine Ridge offers extended-time versions of the PSAT, SAT, and ACT on campus.

On average, 75 percent of the students who graduate from Pine Ridge School enroll in postsecondary educational settings, including colleges, universities, and technical centers, such as Adelphi; Berkshire; Curry; Marist; Marshall; Marymount; Mount Holyoke; Mount Ida; SUNY Brockport, Cobleskill, Farmington, and Purchase; Vincennes; Whittier; and the Universities of Denver, Hartford, San Francisco, and Nevada.

STUDENT BODY AND CONDUCT

Pine Ridge enrolls students from a broad spectrum of national and international towns and cities. The School fosters a strong sense of community between staff members and students, emphasizing respect, academics, and individual responsibility and accountability.

The School's expectations for student conduct, including academic integrity, are high; school guidelines for behavior, accountability, and discipline are outlined in the student handbook. The School does not tolerate harassment, hazing, or the use of alcohol, tobacco, or illegal drugs. The dress code is informal, with some restrictions. Students are expected to care for their rooms and share in the rotating tasks in the dorm.

ACADEMIC FACILITIES

The Pine Ridge School campus includes the Hopwood Academic Building, built in 1985 and home to the School's classrooms, computer lab, art and music room, and library; a new digital media lab; two buildings devoted to tutorial areas; and a fourth building housing science labs and greenhouses.

Physical education classes take place in the Duerr Activity Center, built in 2001, and the newly operated Wellness Center. Other facilities include a student recreational center/cafeteria, a health center, and administrative and business offices.

BOARDING AND GENERAL FACILITIES

Pine Ridge School strongly encourages students to live on campus. Currently, there are two girls' dorms and two boys' dorms. The School also offers residential options in two new living and learning centers that feature full kitchens and a large community dining area. All dormitories are equipped with a refrigerator, microwave, and a common area with a television and DVD/VCR.

ATHLETICS

Pine Ridge School has a varied athletic program that emphasizes skill development, team spirit, cooperation, personal satisfaction, and success. Students are required to take physical education courses, including a health class, as part of the academic program. Activities include individual sports, such as track, archery, tennis, badminton, and bowling and team sports, including basketball, soccer, and softball. Plans for an on-campus weight-training facility are underway. Many Pine Ridge students participate interscholastically in soccer, basketball, tennis, and softball.

EXTRACURRICULAR OPPORTUNITIES

Pine Ridge School offers extracurricular activities after school, in the evenings, and on weekends through its Residential Life and Electives components. The Residential Life component focuses on activities that promote self-awareness and advocacy, interpersonal communication, self-management, personal organization, tolerance, and diversity. Residential Life and Electives activities include digital media, drama, cooking, school newspaper, yearbook, art, music, and horticulture as well as opportunities for civic involvement and volunteerism in partnership with the Town of Williston Recycling Program, Vermont Green Up Day, American Heart Association, United Way, Muscular Dystrophy Association, and Special Olympics.

Special social events are scheduled throughout the year, including a Halloween party, December holiday party, winter carnival, sports banquet, Head's Day, and a prom

DAILY LIFE

The academic day begins in homeroom at 8:15 a.m. and ends at 2:50 p.m. Electives curriculum or extra academic help is offered from 3:15–5:30, and dinner is served at 6 p.m. A mandatory proctored study hall takes place from 7–9 p.m., residential life activities and free time are offered from 9–10 p.m. Students are required to return to their dormitories at 10 p.m.

WEEKEND LIFE

Students are offered a variety of recreational and cultural activities on weekends. The School's proximity to the city of Burlington provides many opportunities for such activities as concerts, plays, movies, college and semiprofessional sports, shopping, skating, hiking, bicycling, and mountain biking. Students can visit historic sites or sightsee both locally and in major cities such as Montreal or Boston. School trips to nearby ski areas—including Bolton Valley, Sugarbush, and Stowe—are a highlight of winter weekends.

On campus, the student recreational center offers flat-screen TV/DVD, pool and foosball tables, and other games/activities.

COSTS AND FINANCIAL AID

Academic-year tuition, room, and board were $56,035 for the 2008–09 academic year for residential students; the tuition cost for day students was $42,130. The new Vermont Scholarship, available to qualifying Vermont-based applicants, can reduce the day student's tuition to $28,250. Each student maintains an individual bank account for personal needs and activities. A portion of the student body receives financial assistance from their local school districts and/or from their state's department of education.

ADMISSIONS INFORMATION

Pine Ridge accepts students of average to above-average intelligence who have a primary diagnosis of a language-based variance without significant emotional or behavioral issues. The Pine Ridge School is not a therapeutic school. Admissions requires a completed admissions application, student questionnaire, a current (within three years) psycho-educational evaluation that includes a Weschler Intelligence Profile, a transcript; and any other relevant reports from counselors or evaluators who have worked with the student. Prospective students and their families may visit the School informally Monday through Friday, from 9 a.m. to 3 p.m., by making an appointment with the Admissions Office. Applicants who are being considered for acceptance are asked to make a formal visit, at which time placement testing and personal interviews are conducted.

APPLICATION TIMETABLE

Pine Ridge has a rolling admissions process. Students may be accepted into the School at any time through the end of the first semester (i.e., late January), provided a vacancy exists. Applicants seeking September admission are urged to apply before June. Admissions to the summer school are rolling.

ADMISSIONS CORRESPONDENCE

John Thomas
Director of Admissions
Pine Ridge School
9505 Williston Road
Williston, Vermont 05495

Phone: 802-434-6932
Fax: 802-434-5512
E-mail: admissions@pineridgeschool.com
Web site: http://www.pineridgeschool.com

PURNELL SCHOOL

Pottersville, New Jersey

Type: Girls' boarding and day general academic and college-preparatory school
Grades: 9–12
Enrollment: 125
Head of School: Ayanna Hill-Gill

THE SCHOOL

Since 1965, Purnell has educated young women, who, for a variety of reasons, have needed an individualized, personal setting in which to best develop academically and socially. The 83-acre farm that is now the Purnell campus was chosen by the founders, Mr. and Mrs. Lyttleton B. P. Gould Jr., and is in the village of Pottersville, with the rolling hills of northwestern New Jersey as a backdrop and the cultural opportunities of New York City just an hour away. The core of the campus, a 20-acre area, is composed of the main administrative building; a complex housing the dining hall and three dormitories; a studio arts center with ceramics, photography, and painting labs; a performing arts center with a theater and music practice rooms; faculty housing; a health center; an athletic center with a gymnasium, dance studio, weight and workout room, and a yoga and pilates room; tennis courts; and athletic fields.

Purnell is a boarding school with an emphasis on developing the whole person in a single-sex environment. A close community of learners, Purnell celebrates differences and seeks out that which is unique in each girl. The School prides itself on its feeling of family and the close personal attention promised to every girl. Meals in the dining hall are served with family-style seating, and celebrations and banquets are held throughout the year.

The educational program is designed to engage a variety of learning styles with appropriate challenge and support for a wide range of abilities. Purnell is intentionally small so that each student holds a place of individual importance in the group, no matter what her background. The curriculum prepares all girls for the university or college that is most appropriate for her. As a school that is centered on learning rather than academic competition, students are not ranked. Each student is able to find the path that best serves her needs and goals.

Purnell's Board of Trustees is composed of 18 members, many of whom are alumnae or past parents. The Head of School serves as an ex-officio member. The School depends on tuition, Annual Giving, Capital Campaigns, and Endowment income to support its budget that is annually in excess of $5.5 million. The endowment is approximately $6.2 million.

Purnell is accredited by the Middle States Association of Colleges and Schools and the New Jersey Association of Independent Schools and is a member of the National Association of Independent Schools, the National Association of Principals of Schools for Girls, the National Coalition of Girls' Schools, and the Alumni Presidents' Council.

ACADEMIC PROGRAMS

The academic program at Purnell is designed as a hands-on, integrated approach. It stresses teaching girls in the ways that allow them to flourish, as made evident by national educational research. In addition to understanding what works well for girls, faculty members are trained and certified in Mel Levine's "All Kinds of Minds" program as well as the Kansas University Strategic Instruction Model (SIM) program, which places the emphasis on structuring a learning environment that is dynamic, engaging, and student-centered. With a traditional university and college preparatory course sequence, students are prepared in English, history, mathematics, science, foreign language, athletics, and performing and studio arts. Students are encouraged to participate in as challenging a course sequence as possible. Students are supported by Purnell's Affinities Program, which is a four-year curriculum for developing students' strengths.

Class size ranges from 8 to 15 students. Purnell has many programs that differentiate it from other girls' schools. The Learning and Enrichment Center is integrated into the total program so that teachers are continually trained by the Learning Specialists on ways to make accommodations for different learners within the classroom. There is time built into each day for students to seek one-on-one help with their teachers. This time does not conflict with athletics or extracurricular events. A supervised study hall also occurs in the evening for students. An SAT preparation course is offered at an additional cost.

International students are welcomed into the curriculum and offered opportunities to improve their English through the School's immersion program. Purnell is flexible in their requirements for foreign language, depending on the circumstance.

The performing and studio arts programs have always attracted creative minds to Purnell. The dance troupe, acting ensemble, handbell choir, and singing group have consistently been of top quality and have often led to careers in these fields. The studio arts program at Purnell is extraordinary given the size of the School. Purnell not only attracts students who already understand their artistic talent, but regularly helps a girl discover unknown talents.

An exceptional feature of Purnell's curriculum is Project Exploration, a 2½-week period set aside in February and March for experiential learning. During this time, students explore a particular topic in depth. The approach to the topic is hands-on and project-oriented. Options have included digital filmmaking, a community service offering, and participation in the School musical. Eleventh graders interested in attending an art school after graduation may use this time to prepare their portfolios. Seniors and juniors may have the opportunity to study abroad for two weeks in a Spanish- or French-speaking country, with Purnell faculty members serving as trip leaders. Students live with host families, attend a language institute, and travel to cultural and historic sites. Other trip options have included volunteering at an animal sanctuary in Utah (open to tenth grade students as well), or at an orphanage in Africa. Students must also complete a two-week internship during the summer before their senior year, pursuing career interests of their choice. Seniors then use this internship experience in a specially designed program to prepare them for their college experiences.

Seniors are required to take a public speaking course, which culminates with a speech delivered to the entire school regarding their experiences during their four years of high school and how they have grown.

FACULTY AND ADVISERS

Purnell seeks teachers who are not only highly qualified in their fields (more than half of the faculty members hold advanced degrees) but also sensitive, compassionate, and enthusiastic people, willing to give of themselves and committed to the philosophy of the School. There are 25 full-time faculty members, most of whom reside on campus. They also serve as dorm parents, committee and publication advisers, coaches, and advisers to 2 to 5 students each. Students meet individually with their adviser, an adult friend and advocate, once a week.

Ayanna Hill-Gill, affectionately known as Yanni, enters her fourteenth year at Purnell School. Throughout her tenure, she has performed many jobs, such as science teacher, dorm parent, Dean of Students, and Associate ZHead of School. In July 2007, she assumed the role as the sixth Head of School to oversee the daily operations of the School. Anyanna holds a B.S. in Biology and an M.A. in organizational leadership from Teachers College, Columbia University. In 2003, she was a Klingenstein Fellow where she took a one-year sabbatical to complete a graduate degree and focus on private school leadership. In 2006, Ayanna was awarded an E. E. Ford fellowship to NAIS' Aspiring Heads Program'.

Purnell has established a fund to further faculty professional growth, particularly in the study of the learning process. All faculty members attend extensive professional development workshops at the beginning and end of each school year.

Purnell's Laura McCord-Grauer Center for Excellence in Teaching Center provides training and support for new and experienced teachers across the country, and creates a space where international dialogues can take place on curriculum and teaching. Through the Center, Purnell seeks to provide the highest quality of professional development for each member of its faculty, while reaching out to educators at secondary schools, universities, and colleges around the country.

COLLEGE ADMISSION COUNSELING

The Director of College Counseling works closely with students and their parents in individual and group sessions to guide choices for each student's future. Most Purnell students choose to continue their education immediately after leaving Purnell, their choices including two- and four-year liberal arts institutions and art schools. Colleges chosen in the last three years include Alfred, American, Boston College, Bowdoin, Drew, Eckerd, Elmira, George Washington, Georgetown, Gettysburg, Guilford, Hampshire, Ithaca, Lynchburg, Lynn University, Marymount Manhattan College, Marshall, Michigan State, Muhlenberg, NYU, Parsons, Penn State, Philadelphia University, Purdue, Rhode Island School of Design, Roanoke College, Rutgers, St. Joseph's University, Savannah College of Art and Design, Temple, Washington College, Wentworth Institute of Technology, and the Universities of Arizona, Denver, Hartford, Minnesota, and Vermont.

STUDENT BODY AND CONDUCT

Approximately 125 girls make up the student body, hailing from nineteen states and seven other countries. In 2008, the most popular feeder states included California, Connecticut, Georgia, Illinois, Maryland, Massachusetts, New Jersey, New York, North Carolina, Ohio, Pennsylvania, and Virginia. International students represent Bermuda, Bolivia, China, El Salvador, Korea, Netherlands Antilles, Taiwan, and the Virgin Islands.

The guidelines of the School—use of common sense, consideration of others, and truthful relationships with all—encourage each girl to assume responsibility for the community's well-being. Breaches of this trust are dealt with on an individual basis, but the possession or use of alcohol and/or illegal drugs in school is not tolerated and results in suspension or expulsion.

Students regularly evaluate programs, courses, and School procedures. There are many opportunities for leadership in School government, classes, sports, and activities. Senior Peer Leaders meet with peer groups throughout a student's first year at Purnell and facilitate weekly peer groups for new students.

ACADEMIC FACILITIES

The original Colonial residence of the farm-estate contains the office of the Head of School and other administrative offices. The Stringfellow Library/Media Center, a large converted barn, houses the Learning and Enrichment Center, library, computer center, and classroom wing containing teachers' offices and several smaller classrooms. The adjoining Gardner Building contains the science lab, larger classrooms, and the E. E. Ford Computer Lab. Attached to the library and classroom complex is the Johnson Art Center, an airy, fully equipped facility, where courses including oil, acrylic, and watercolor painting; pen and ink; fashion design; photography; ceramics; and drawing are held. Independent course study opportunities and portfolio preparation studies are also offered.

Purnell's Carney Center for Performing Arts is a professionally equipped 200-seat theater. Students are encouraged to use the facility in a number of capacities, whether they are participating in one of the performing groups, working backstage and in the sound booth as a "techie," or taking private music lessons. Professional performers from the New York metropolitan area are frequently brought to Purnell.

BOARDING AND GENERAL FACILITIES

Three dormitories along one side of the residential quadrangle provide living quarters, with some single, numerous double, and a few triple rooms and quads for students. Dorm parents, who live in apartments attached to the dormitories on every floor, are available and supportive. They work with the Director of Residential Life on the School's residential life curriculum. Student floor leaders are responsible for the smooth running of the dorms. Each dorm has a common room with a TV/DVD, laundry facilities, and a storage room. Each dorm room is wired for personal phones, the School intranet, and the Internet. The student-run Student Café and Student Store are also located in the dorm complex.

Baker Dining Hall provides gracious dining facilities as well as a place to study and socialize. The dormitory and dining hall complexes are connected, allowing students to pass safely from activity to activity in the evening.

The Deborah Gordon Nothstine Health Center is adjacent to the dormitories, housing the School nurse as well as the Director of Advising and Counseling. Facilities include an examination room and several sick rooms for students.

ATHLETICS

Purnell is committed to guiding students toward lifelong personal health, and every student is required to participate in interscholastic or individual sports four days a week. Competitive offerings include basketball, dance 1, lacrosse, soccer, softball, tennis, and volleyball. Noncompetitive activities include aerobics, dance 2, golf, horseback riding, a personal fitness course, and yoga.

The 22,000-square-foot Moran Athletic Center includes a gymnasium with basketball, volleyball, and indoor tennis courts. The athletic center also has a weight room with athletic equipment, a circuit training room, and a state-of-the-art dance studio. A gallery the length of the building is used to display student and faculty artwork.

Three playing fields and five all-weather tennis courts constitute the School's outdoor athletic facilities. Horseback riding is available fall through spring at the nearby Tranquility Farm.

EXTRACURRICULAR OPPORTUNITIES

Frequent field trips are taken to art and science museums, recital halls, cultural centers, and theaters in New York City, Philadelphia, and Princeton. On E. B. Osborn Artists-in-Residence Weekend, professional visual and performing artists lead workshops.

Most students participate twice a week in the activities program, selecting from options such as Art Activity, Greens Environmental Group, Roots and Shoots Community Service, Voices Diversity Group, as well as yearlong activities for the yearbook and performing groups. There are three performing groups for which students may audition: Dance Synthesis (a jazz and modern dance ensemble), Shoots & Strawberries (an a cappella singing group), and Adlibbers (an acting troupe with a rotating cast that produces a one-act play each term). Private instrumental and vocal lessons are also available, with the option of collaborating on a student ensemble.

DAILY LIFE

Classes are held Monday through Friday. The academic day starts with class, dorm, or all-School meetings at 8 a.m., followed by breakfast. Classes begin at 9 a.m. and continue until 2:40, with a buffet-style lunch from 12:45 to 1:15 p.m. The daily schedule is on a two-week cycle, with classes meeting for 75 minutes to facilitate cooperative learning, science labs, research, and studio work. The afternoon consists of extra help, guided study, activities, and sports, with dinner at 6 p.m. Study hours take place from 7:30 to 9, with dorm activities from 9 to 10 p.m. Lights-out for ninth, tenth, and eleventh graders is 11 p.m.; seniors are encouraged to use good judgment.

WEEKEND LIFE

The Director of Residential Life plans an array of weekend activities every week. Faculty members participate fully in such activities, which include excursions to New York or Philadelphia for cultural, sports, and shopping trips; dances and sports events with boys' schools; hiking, biking, and ski trips; and crafts, movies, games, and other events on campus. About half of all weekends are "open," with students who have met their responsibilities free to leave Friday afternoon if they choose; "campus" weekends often include all-School activities as well as free time.

COSTS AND FINANCIAL AID

The combined fee for tuition, room, and board for 2008–09 is $45,711 for seven-day boarding and $43,964 for five-day boarding; day students paid $38,484. Costs for uniforms, books, and laundry averaged $1000. Such expenses as riding and music lessons, some weekend activities, and transportation are extra. Several financing options are available.

Typically, 23 percent of the students receive financial aid. In 2008–09, students received awards totaling approximately $500,000. Financial aid is awarded based on need, with significant awards going to families with middle-level income.

ADMISSIONS INFORMATION

A personal interview is required along with a completed application in order for an applicant to be considered for admission. SSAT scores or other relevant educational testing results should be available, but they are not primary factors in decisions about admission to the School. Neither race nor religious faith is considered in accepting candidates.

APPLICATION TIMETABLE

Purnell has a rolling admission plan, and a candidate's file is presented to the Admission Committee after the personal interview has been completed and all paperwork has been submitted. Parents and the candidate are notified in writing of the action taken. Parents are required to reply within one month of acceptance.

ADMISSIONS CORRESPONDENCE

Nicole Moon
Director of Admission and Financial Aid
Purnell School
Pottersville, New Jersey 07979
Phone: 908-439-2154
Fax: 908-439-4088
E-mail: info@purnell.org
Web site: http://www.purnell.org

VALLEY VIEW SCHOOL

North Brookfield, Massachusetts

Type: Boarding school for boys with moderate special needs
Grades: 5–12
Enrollment: 56
Head of School: Philip G. Spiva, Ph.D., Director

THE SCHOOL

Valley View is a private residential guidance school providing a therapeutic educational environment for 56 boys between the ages of 11 and 16 who are having difficulty getting along with their families, the world around them, and themselves. These are generally bright and healthy youngsters who differ in family and geographic backgrounds but who share the experience of functioning below their academic and social potential.

Located 1½ miles from North Brookfield, in rural central Massachusetts, Valley View is situated on a 215-acre site that was once used for farming. The School provides a relaxed yet structured environment for boys who are not able to adjust to living with their families or to life in a traditional boarding school.

The Valley View School was founded in 1970 by its present director, Dr. Philip G. Spiva, a clinical psychologist. Typical Valley View students may be boys who challenge authority to the point of psychologically intimidating their parents; others have difficulty in channeling their physical energy in meaningful ways; and a few may appear overly lethargic, bored, or depressed. The majority have had difficulty in traditional schools and, although bright, have a history of attention deficit disorder (ADD), are oppositional, and are a source of frustration to their families. Many lack an awareness of the effect that their behavior has upon others and often seem to "not get it." Although Valley View can help many boys, it is not equipped to educate overtly psychotic adolescents or alienated "streetwise" boys with histories of antisocial behavior or drug-related problems.

Dr. Spiva developed a school based on the model of a therapeutic environment for boys who show good potential but are having difficulty adjusting to the world around them. The primary objectives of the School are to provide youngsters with the skills they need to function effectively, to help them to like themselves better, and to help them achieve a higher level of success. Valley View provides a structured program that stresses a wide range of success-oriented experiences and offers the quality of interaction and instruction necessary for each boy to develop a better feeling about himself. Through this program, the School promotes self-confidence and the ability to interact with others in a more meaningful way. Boys mature socially as they gain an increased awareness of themselves and the world around them.

The School is incorporated as a nonprofit organization and is governed by a 9-member Board of Directors. It has an annual operating budget of approximately $2.7 million. Proceeds of the annual capital improvement drive assist in the development of new physical resources.

Valley View School is authorized under federal law to enroll nonimmigrant alien students.

ACADEMIC PROGRAMS

Traditional classroom methods and practices have generally frustrated rather than encouraged students who go to Valley View. These boys have been characterized as "learning disabled," "unmotivated," "hyperactive," or "disruptive" in the classroom setting. With a maximum of 56 students in the School and an average of 6 in each class, Valley View School can provide intensive remedial instruction. Classes focus on the development and strengthening of skills in basic subjects, including language arts, mathematics, social and physical sciences, physical education, history, and art. An extensive computer facility has recently been installed that integrates current technology into the entire academic curriculum.

Students who have learning difficulties in specific areas and need additional assistance may receive remedial help both from their teachers as well as from computer-aided programs. To motivate students to develop more effective study skills and habits, a study hour is required Sunday through Thursday nights.

In addition to the usual academic curriculum, music lessons are available for a variety of instruments, and boys may participate in the School's drama program.

Travel in the United States and abroad provides special intellectual challenges. Valley View students have taken a number of weeklong study tours of Washington, D.C., and Gettysburg and have visited such countries as India, Israel, the People's Republic of China, Russia, South Africa, and Vietnam.

Boys receive academic credit for all course work that is successfully completed, permitting them to progress at a normal pace. Valley View credits are transferable to more traditional public or private schools. Comprehensive quarterly reports, sent to families, address social and emotional adjustment as well as academic progress in all areas.

Valley View offers a year-round program, and boys are accepted only on that basis. The program from September to June parallels a traditional two-semester academic year, while the summer program is a combination of academic, remedial, and special-interest courses balanced with outdoor recreation.

A minimum enrollment period of two to three years is required for successful completion of the program. A student can earn a recognized high school diploma from Valley View School; however, diplomas are infrequently conferred, since most students continue their education in a standard public or private secondary school. Approximately 65 percent of departing students receive counseling to help them transfer to a more traditional boarding school.

FACULTY AND ADVISERS

Valley View's staff numbers 50. Of these, two thirds are either classroom teachers or counselors who supervise a range of activities during evenings and weekends. Responsibility for the direction of the program is shared by an administrative council of 8 senior staff members.

Philip G. Spiva, the founder and Director of Valley View School, holds a doctorate in psychology from the University of Oklahoma, is a diplomate in clinical psychology of the American Board of Professional Psychology, and is a fellow of the Academy of Clinical Psychology. He has had more than thirty years of experience in the residential treatment of emotionally maladjusted children and adolescents. He has served on the Board of Directors of the National Association of Private Schools for Exceptional Children and the American Association of Children's Residential Centers.

Eric T. Bulger, Valley View School's Associate Director, earned his Master of Social Work degree from Boston College and has worked with adolescents in residential care for sixteen years. He works closely with the director, facilitating admission interviews, and communicates extensively with parents. In addition, he closely coordinates the activities of the academic program with the Educational Coordinator, who is a certified teacher with twenty-nine years of experience, and the Program Coordinator, who has a degree in psychology and twenty-five years of experience working directly with adolescents.

There are 11 full-time academic teachers, all with appropriate degrees in their subject matter. Seventeen counselors, most of whom hold a college degree, supervise the program on evenings and weekends. This includes an extensive range of physical and recreational activities. In addition, three clinical psychologists spend a number of days at the School to see boys in individual therapy sessions. Two Board-certified psychiatrists also make regularly scheduled consultation visits to monitor psychopharmacological issues when appropriate.

COLLEGE ADMISSION COUNSELING

Most alumni complete their secondary education at a more traditional school before they contemplate advanced education. If a family wishes to send their son to a private boarding school when he is ready to leave Valley View, help in selecting an appropriate school, usually one with a "counseling attitude," is provided. The majority of Valley View graduates have ultimately gone on to college after completion of their secondary education.

STUDENT BODY AND CONDUCT

Because of the need for a high level of individual attention, the student population is limited to 56 boys, who come from throughout the United States as well as a number of other countries. Although the average age at the time of enrollment is 13, boys at Valley View range in age from 11 to 16.

The School expects students to behave in an appropriate manner. Because, by nature of their difficulties, they often fall short of this expectation, the program is designed so that boys are held accountable for their actions and are expected to assume responsibility for obtaining rewards. All boys must work for their spending money through a point-earning system that is translated into cash used for activities. Parents are asked not to subsidize activities unless they have received approval from the School administration.

Although the expectations for student conduct are based on a standard of reasonableness and are not overly rigid, there is a dress code that applies during classes and at Sunday brunch. There is a high level of open and honest interaction among students, the faculty, and the administration regarding problems and issues that arise. Since it is the policy of the School to accept only those students who have a high probability of benefiting from the Valley View experience, there are very few expulsions.

ACADEMIC FACILITIES

The academic complex consists of two classroom buildings and a gymnasium. Classrooms include a computer lab that is part of an extensive campus network, a science laboratory with eight work stations designed to accommodate upper-level courses, and a creative arts studio that promotes expression in a variety of areas, including painting, sculpting, and ceramics. The gymnasium has a full-court playing surface and a locker room as well as a fully equipped weightlifting and aerobic center.

BOARDING AND GENERAL FACILITIES

The main building, a completely remodeled structure consisting of a farmhouse, a carriage house, and a barn, houses 25 students comfortably in single, double, and triple dormitory rooms. A dining room accommodates School assemblies, and a recently added stage enhances a very active dramatic arts program.

Separated from the main building are three other self-contained dormitories, which house 9 to 12 students. All of the dormitories have lounge areas for reading, watching television, and other quiet activities. They are also connected to the computer network so students have access to the central file server throughout the evening and weekend.

ATHLETICS

All students are expected to take physical education classes as a component of the program. Boys are also required to participate each year in at least one varsity or junior varsity team that competes against local schools. A full-court gymnasium and adjoining athletics field provide attractive facilities for basketball, soccer, softball, lacrosse, and volleyball. In addition, there are numerous opportunities for individual sports, such as golf, skiing, snowboarding, and tennis.

EXTRACURRICULAR OPPORTUNITIES

The activity program plays a crucial role in the overall philosophy of the School, because it offers students a wide variety of success-oriented experiences. Because most of the boys who come to Valley View feel that they are—and indeed they have been—failures in some critical areas of their adjustment, their experience of success is fun and gratifying, yet challenging.

A reasonably strenuous outdoor program includes camping, rock climbing, bike trips, canoeing, and hiking. There is ample opportunity for more relaxing activities, such as photography, playing a musical instrument, painting and drawing, and fishing. Field trips are held throughout the year to various educational centers, museums, and historic sites.

DAILY LIFE

During the school year, the seven 40-minute classes begin at 8:20 and end at 2:30. Classes in traditional academic courses are held in the morning, while afternoon classes include science and math lab courses and physical education. A compulsory study hour is held Sunday evening through Thursday evening. Although certain periods of the day are free, the overall program is quite structured.

WEEKEND LIFE

During the academic year, a brunch is held each Sunday, followed by an assembly on a variety of informative subjects for student interest and enjoyment. Students also take trips away from the School, including overnight camping trips. Many activities are offered during the weekend, and all boys must elect a certain number of these options. Weekends are also most convenient for parents' visits with their sons.

SUMMER PROGRAMS

Because Valley View School has a twelve-month school year, the summer program is a component of the overall program. Classes held during July and August are somewhat less formal than those held from September through June, including summer reading and remedial programs and a number of high-interest courses, such as Art, Astronomy, Birds 101, Chess, Geology, History and Science of Baseball, Life in the Middle Ages, Litera'Tours, and the Local History of Quaboag Plantation. They are balanced equally with recreational activities.

COSTS AND FINANCIAL AID

Valley View School bases its fee on the actual operating cost of $60,300 ($15,075 per quarter) for a twelve-month program. Under some conditions, financial assistance may be available through programs administered by certain states. Valley View School, however, is not able to offer scholarship assistance.

ADMISSIONS INFORMATION

The majority of new students begin their experience in the summer, which provides the staff with an opportunity to thoughtfully plan their academic program. However, if space is available, a student may begin his program in September or at another time during the year. Valley View accepts qualified students without regard to race, religion, or ethnic origin.

Inquiries should be made to the Director or his associate. If, on the basis of the initial review, the applicant appears to be an appropriate candidate, a formal application for admission is requested, along with clinical summaries from professionals who are familiar with the applicant. All prospective students and their families are expected to visit the School.

APPLICATION TIMETABLE

Applications for admission are considered at any time during the year for vacancies that occur primarily in early July or September. If space is not available at the time of application, a boy may be placed on a waiting list at his family's request. If sufficient information has been submitted, parents are generally notified about acceptance when they visit the School for the personal interview.

ADMISSIONS CORRESPONDENCE

Philip G. Spiva, Ph.D., Director
Valley View School
P.O. Box 338, Oakham Road
North Brookfield, Massachusetts 01535
Phone: 508-867-6505
Fax: 508-867-3300
E-mail: admissions@valleyviewschool.org
Web site: http://www.valleyviewschool.org

THE VANGUARD SCHOOL

Lake Wales, Florida

the VANGUARD SCHOOL
Transforming potential. Accelerating achievement.

Type: Coeducational boarding and day college-preparatory and general academic remedial school for students with learning challenges
Grades: 5–PG, ages 10–20
Enrollment: 130
Head of School: Dr. Cathy Wooley-Brown, President

THE SCHOOL

The Vanguard School of Lake Wales, Florida, was founded in 1966 to serve the needs of students with learning disabilities, dyslexia, attention deficit disorder, and other learning challenges. At the time, the School was the residential branch of the Vanguard School of Paoli, Pennsylvania, which was founded in 1959. The Vanguard School of Lake Wales became a separate and independent corporation in 1983.

The mission of the Vanguard School is to provide an individualized program in a nurturing environment that enables students to develop to their fullest: academically, socially, and personally. The School provides a safe and secure but appropriately demanding and structured environment in which students who have been unsuccessful in regular school programs are able to learn and achieve. Believing that a school's most important function is to foster and enhance the total growth of the individual, the Vanguard School focuses on both the academic and social development of its students to prepare them for a full and satisfying adult life. Approximately 95 percent of the School's graduates go on to postsecondary programs, including community colleges, vocational programs, and four-year universities.

Located in the heart of the Sunshine State, the School has a 75-acre campus in the city of Lake Wales. Ideally situated for access to the beaches and cultural and entertainment centers of central Florida, the School is about 70 miles east of Tampa and 45 miles south of Orlando.

A Board of Trustees, made up of prominent representatives of the local business community, oversees the School's operations and establishes its policies. The President and administrative staff make all decisions concerning the program and daily student life. The School is a nonprofit institution, and its plant is conservatively valued at more than $14 million. The annual budget for 2007–08 was approximately $6 million, and the School's endowment funds exceed $5.5 million.

The Vanguard School of Lake Wales is accredited by the Florida Council of Independent Schools and the Southern Association of Colleges and Schools. It is a member of the International Dyslexia Association, the Learning Disabilities Association of America, the Southeastern Association of Boarding Schools, the Association of Boarding Schools, and the Small Boarding School Association.

ACADEMIC PROGRAMS

The Vanguard program is designed to prepare students for the transition from high school to the next stage in the student's progress toward self-sufficiency. The academic classes are individually oriented and based on the needs of each student. Core classes are carefully structured with fewer than 10 students per class to ensure optimal attention to individual needs. The learning activities are explicit and the steps gradual, so that each student may progress in a way that is successful and satisfying.

Additional individualized needs are met through focused educational interventions. Students with communication difficulties receive individualized instruction in language and communication as well as referrals to the speech therapist, as needed. Learning disability specialists provide consultative services to students and staff members. In addition, tutoring is available to all students after school and on Saturday.

Academic classes are held Monday through Friday from 8:40 a.m. to 3:30 p.m. A structured study hall for all students is held daily from 3:35 to 4:30. Students take a core curriculum of reading, language arts, and mathematics that is individually tailored to meet the specific needs of each student. Science, social studies, and elective courses are presented as group-taught subjects with minimal reading requirements. These classes emphasize mastery-based learning through audiovisual presentations, class discussions, hands-on projects, experiments, and field trips. Within this framework, the School offers the basics of a comprehensive high school curriculum; students earn credits and receive a high school diploma upon graduation.

The School offers electives in TV/film production, industrial arts, culinary arts, photography, art, yearbook production, drama, life management, creative writing, and music. Driver's education is available through a local, independent company. Vanguard is a WiFi campus, with wireless access in all buildings.

FACULTY AND ADVISERS

Cathy Wooley-Brown, Ph.D., is the President of the Vanguard School. Dr. Wooley-Brown believes learning is a lifelong journey. She holds a Doctor of Philosophy in curriculum and instruction, an Education Specialist degree in educational leadership, a Master of Arts in special and gifted education, and a Bachelor of Arts in special education, all from the University of South Florida. She has also completed postdoctoral work in school restructuring and school reform at Harvard University. Dr. Wooley-Brown has coauthored several publications on charter schools, special education, and school reform. She has applied her passion for education by serving in virtually every capacity, including positions as professor, teacher, author, and administrator. As a frequent presenter at state and national conferences, Dr. Wooley-Brown recently testified before the Presidential Commission on Special Education and Students with Learning Challenges.

David Lauer is the Principal and holds a B.A. in special education from Bowling Green State University, an M.S. in education from the University of Miami (Florida), and an Education Specialist degree from Florida State University. The academic faculty consists of 20 teachers and specialists. All faculty members hold bachelor's degrees, 5 hold master's degrees, and 1 holds an Education Specialist degree. The School employs 30 residential and recreational staff members who sponsor interscholastic and intramural sports, clubs, activities, weekend trips, and social events and provide structure and support in the dormitories.

Dr. Myron A. "Mike" Harvey is the School psychologist, who supervises admissions evaluations and reevaluations and serves as facilitator and counselor to the students. He also provides group sessions that work on a variety of social skills necessary for success in today's society. Individual psychological counseling may be provided through arrangements with a local, licensed behavioral health counselor. A speech therapist is available to provide direct speech services to students and to provide consultative services to teachers and other staff members.

COLLEGE ADMISSION COUNSELING

The majority of Vanguard students attend some form of postsecondary educational or training program, including two-year and four-year colleges and universities, vocational training programs, and transition programs. The School utilizes the state-of-the-art Envictus "Pathfinder" program to facilitate college planning from the time a student enters high school. In addition, the School psychologist and faculty members counsel students and parents to help them determine the most appropriate placement for each student after Vanguard.

STUDENT BODY AND CONDUCT

The enrollment is 130, with 110 residential students and 20 day students. The residential students come from eighteen states and twenty-three countries. They represent a cross-section of cultural, ethnic, and racial backgrounds.

The School uses an individualized mentoring system to encourage the development of independent, self-responsible behavior among its students. The goal of this program is to provide a student the opportunity to proceed from behavior that requires external control and supervision to behavior that reflects positive, independent decision making; constructive involvement in the student's own development; and contributions to the School community. Each student is assigned a residential hall adviser, who works with the individual student to develop appropriate goals. Privileges received reflect the degree of responsibility and independence the student has achieved. Areas of emphasis in the system focus on the self-care, interpersonal relations, school performance, program participation, individual goals, and general behaviors that are important for the overall development of the School's students.

Within both the academic and residential programs, there are opportunities for student involvement and leadership responsibilities. Peer-to-peer counseling and judicial councils teach self-advocacy skills and help deal with minor differences that arise between students. Student Residential Assistants (RAs) are older students whose primary role is to assist younger students with room care, social skills, and homework. An active Student Government Association, made up of elected representatives, plans social events and addresses School-wide student issues.

ACADEMIC FACILITIES

The three classroom buildings on the Vanguard campus contain twenty-five classrooms (including a spacious, stand-alone art room), a science lab, a computer lab, a woodshop, culinary arts kitchens, a photography darkroom, and seven offices for tutorials and specialists. The Harry E. Nelson Library/Media Center is available to students until 8 p.m. Monday through Friday and from 10 a.m. to 2 p.m. on Saturday. It includes the *Fast ForWord* lab, computer stations with Internet access, and a large conference room.

BOARDING AND GENERAL FACILITIES

A structured but comfortable environment surrounds Vanguard students. The School has undergone complete renovations of its campus over the past two years. In addition to the three dormitories, the campus also has a dining room and administration building. Housed in three spacious dormitories with students of similar ages, Vanguard students are under the supervision of the residential staff. Each of the dormitories is supervised 24 hours per day by staff members who are under the guidance of the Director of Residential Life. A live-in hall adviser is available in each dormitory. This adviser is responsible for creating a cohesive sense of family, which provides a nurturing environment for Vanguard's students. Two nurses monitor the students' health needs and staff the School's infirmary from 7 a.m. to 10 p.m.

Two students share a spacious dormitory room, which they are encouraged to personalize with their own belongings. Television lounges at the center of each hall are available for recreation and relaxation. In addition, a student center/recreation room located on the second floor of the School's gymnasium is available to students during free time.

ATHLETICS

Vanguard provides many opportunities for students to participate in various sports, depending on the student's interests and abilities. The Bartsch Memorial Gymnasium is home to several Panthers sports teams. In addition, the School has an Aquatic Center, which houses a 75-foot by 52-foot NCAA short pool and a bath house. The campus also has three playing fields, a lighted soccer field, lighted tennis courts, a canoe storage facility, and a fishing dock.

The Vanguard School is a member of the Florida High School Activities Association (FHSAA), which sanctions all of the School's interscholastic athletic contests. Boys may participate in football, basketball, cross-country running, golf, soccer, swimming, tennis, track and field, and weight lifting. Girls are offered the opportunity to participate in basketball, cheerleading, cross-country running, swimming, track and field, and volleyball.

Vanguard also offers an opportunity for all students to participate on a less competitive basis through a program of intramural sports. Games and tournaments are scheduled regularly throughout the year in basketball, flag football, indoor hockey, soccer, softball, swimming, tennis, and volleyball.

The health/fitness center houses a complete weight-training room with a Universal weight center, free weights and treadmills, and exercise bicycles. A local personal trainer is available to students for consultation on healthy lifestyle options.

EXTRACURRICULAR OPPORTUNITIES

Students have excellent opportunities to participate in a variety of activities, depending on their interests. Art and photography students participate in local art exhibits, and a variety of specialty clubs offer something for everyone on campus.

In the evenings there is a regularly scheduled period for clubs and activities, during which students can participate in intramural sports, weight lifting, aerobics, and arts and crafts projects. Key Club and the Student Government offer opportunities for leadership and community service. Life Skills classes are also offered through the residential program in the evening.

DAILY LIFE

Breakfast is served from 7:30 to 8:30 a.m., and the School offers a flexible class day. Each student takes eight 45-minute classes per semester, one of which is a required study hour. Dinner is served from 5:30 to 6:30 p.m. Clubs and activities are offered from 7 until 8:55 p.m., seven days a week, depending on the activity. Bedtimes depend on the age of the individual student. Students who wish to achieve additional privileges are required to participate in community service activities.

WEEKEND LIFE

Weekends provide a change of pace and often a change of scenery for Vanguard students. Camping, fishing, shopping, amusement parks, and other off-campus trips are a part of the weekend activities. The School maintains a fleet of vehicles, and it is not uncommon for them to be headed to four or five different destinations on a weekend. Weekend outings offer students the opportunity to visit the beaches and many other attractions of central Florida, including Walt Disney World, Sea World, Cypress Gardens Adventure Park, the Kennedy Space Center, and the metropolitan areas of Tampa and Orlando. A more relaxed atmosphere is offered on Saturday and Sunday mornings, when an extended brunch is served. Students are encouraged to attend religious services at the many places of worship in the area, and transportation is provided.

COSTS AND FINANCIAL AID

The boarding school fee for 2008–09 was $41,500, which covered tuition, room and board, and initial school supplies. The fee for day students was $22,500. An academic activities/materials fee of $600 ($350 for day students) covers extra costs for School photographs, yearbooks, special event tickets, and lab fees. An additional $650 is required for international students to cover medical and miscellaneous expenses. The $4000 enrollment deposit is applied to the current year's tuition.

The Vanguard School Board of Trustees awards annual scholarship aid based on financial need. Following the interview process, families complete and submit a financial aid application and a copy of their current IRS tax return. Thirty-three percent of the 2007–08 enrollment received financial assistance. As a special school, the Internal Revenue Service allows a deduction for the cost of attendance at the Vanguard School. Families should consult their accountant for Schedule A deductions that may be available. In addition, the School is authorized by the state of Florida to accept McKay Scholarships for eligible Florida students.

ADMISSIONS INFORMATION

The Vanguard School's enrollment age is 10 through 20, and it serves students with learning disabilities, dyslexia, and attention deficit disorders who have been unsuccessful in more traditional academic programs. A Thirteenth Year offers recent graduates an opportunity to increase basic skills and further develop social skills. All students must have the ability to speak and understand the English language, as the School does not offer an ESL program. Referrals to the School may originate from physicians, psychologists, educators, educational consultants, child guidance clinics, pediatricians, or other professionals who provide professional services to children, adolescents, and their families. Direct parental inquiries are also welcome.

So that the School may fully consider a student for enrollment, parents are requested to send copies of current academic records, including an official transcript for secondary-level students; a current psychoeducational evaluation (not more than three years old) that includes intelligence testing; and any medical records that would assist the School's professional staff members in determining a student's specific needs. The School also provides teacher and principal/counselor evaluation forms, which should be completed by the student's current school personnel. If, from this material, it appears the Vanguard program would be appropriate for the student, a visit to the campus for a pre-enrollment interview and evaluation is required. Appointments for these interviews are arranged by the admissions office.

Admission to the Vanguard School is open to all applicants regardless of race, creed, color, or national or ethnic origin.

APPLICATION TIMETABLE

Inquiries are welcome at any time. Tours and evaluation interviews are scheduled throughout the year, and admission is offered based on available space. The office is open Monday through Friday from 8 to 4:30. Brochures and additional information about the School are available through the admissions office.

ADMISSIONS CORRESPONDENCE

Melanie Anderson, Director of Admission
The Vanguard School
22000 Highway 27
Lake Wales, Florida 33859-6858
Phone: 863-676-6091
Fax: 863-676-8297
E-mail: vanadmin@vanguardschool.org
Web site: http://www.vanguardschool.org

Junior Boarding Schools

THE AMERICAN BOYCHOIR SCHOOL

19 Lambert Drive
Princeton, New Jersey 08540

Head of School: Robert Rund

General Information Boys' boarding and day college-preparatory, arts, Choral Music, and Music Literacy school. Grades 4–8. Founded: 1937. Setting: small town. Nearest major city is Philadelphia, PA. Students are housed in single-sex dormitories. 17-acre campus. 5 buildings on campus. Approved or accredited by Middle States Association of Colleges and Schools, New Jersey Association of Independent Schools, and The Association of Boarding Schools. Member of Secondary School Admission Test Board. Endowment: $4 million. Total enrollment: 48. Upper school average class size: 11. Upper school faculty-student ratio: 1:3.
Student Profile Grade 6: 17 students (17 boys); Grade 7: 9 students (9 boys); Grade 8: 13 students (13 boys). 63% of students are boarding students. 60% are state residents. 9 states are represented in upper school student body. 8% are international students. International students from France, Republic of Korea, and Taiwan.
Faculty School total: 13. In upper school: 4 men, 8 women; 8 have advanced degrees; 2 reside on campus.
Subjects Offered Computer music, computer skills, English, general science, health, mathematics, music, music performance, music theory, music theory-AP, physical education, social studies, Spanish, Spanish literature.
Secondary School Placement 12 students graduated in 2008; they went to Northfield Mount Hermon School; Peddie School; Portsmouth Abbey School; St. Andrew's School; The Lawrenceville School; Woodberry Forest School.
Student Life Uniform requirement, student council, honor system. Discipline rests primarily with faculty.
Tuition and Aid Day student tuition: $20,650; 5-day tuition and room/board: $26,265; 7-day tuition and room/board: $26,265. Tuition reduction for siblings, need-based scholarship grants available. In 2008–09, 46% of students received aid. Total amount of financial aid awarded in 2008–09: $188,930.
Admissions Achievement/Aptitude/Writing, any standardized test and audition required. Deadline for receipt of application materials: none. No application fee required. On-campus interview required.
Athletics Intramural: basketball, cooperative games, cross-country running, fitness, fitness walking, flag football, football, Frisbee, jogging, outdoor activities, paddle tennis, physical fitness, running, soccer, table tennis, tennis, touch football, ultimate Frisbee, walking. 1 PE instructor.
Computers Computers are regularly used in English, history, mathematics, music, science classes. Computer network features include Internet access, wireless campus network, Internet filtering or blocking technology. Computer access in designated common areas is available to students. The school has a published electronic and media policy.
Contact Sharon Mejias, Assistant Director of Admissions. 609-924-5858 Ext. 34. Fax: 609-924-5812. E-mail: smejias@americanboychoir.org. Web site: www.americanboychoir.org.

THE BEMENT SCHOOL

Main Street
Deerfield, Massachusetts 01342

Head of School: Mrs. Shelley Borror Jackson

General Information Coeducational boarding and day college-preparatory, arts, and bilingual studies school. Boarding grades 3–9, day grades K–9. Founded: 1925. Setting: small town. Nearest major city is Springfield. Students are housed in single-sex dormitories. 12-acre campus. 11 buildings on campus. Approved or accredited by Association of Independent Schools in New England, Junior Boarding Schools Association, and The Association of Boarding Schools. Member of National Association of Independent Schools and Secondary School Admission Test Board. Endowment: $4.2 million. Total enrollment: 240. Upper school average class size: 12. Upper school faculty-student ratio: 1:6.
Student Profile Grade 6: 25 students (16 boys, 9 girls); Grade 7: 33 students (15 boys, 18 girls); Grade 8: 34 students (19 boys, 15 girls); Grade 9: 22 students (7 boys, 15 girls). 27% of students are boarding students. 75% are state residents. 10 states are represented in upper school student body. 15% are international students. International students from China, Japan, Mexico, Nigeria, Republic of Korea, and Singapore.
Faculty School total: 42. In upper school: 10 men, 13 women; 15 have advanced degrees; 11 reside on campus.
Subjects Offered Algebra, American history, art, biology, chemistry, Chinese, community service, creative writing, dance, drama, earth science, English, English literature, fine arts, French, geography, geometry, grammar, health, history, Latin, literature, mathematics, music, photography, physical education, physical science, science, social studies, Spanish, theater, typing, world history, world literature, writing.
Graduation Requirements American history, art history, arts and fine arts (art, music, dance, drama), athletics, biology, drama, English, foreign language, geometry, health, mathematics, music history, science, social studies (includes history). Community service is required.
Special Academic Programs Honors section; study abroad; special instructional classes for deaf students, blind students; ESL (12 students enrolled).
Secondary School Placement 15 students graduated in 2008; they went to Deerfield Academy; Northfield Mount Hermon School; The Williston Northampton School.
Student Life Specified standards of dress. Discipline rests primarily with faculty.
Tuition and Aid Day student tuition: $17,845; 5-day tuition and room/board: $32,560; 7-day tuition and room/board: $39,325. Tuition installment plan (Academic Management Services Plan, monthly payment plans, individually arranged payment plans, 60%/40% payment plan). Need-based scholarship grants available. In 2008–09, 25% of students received aid. Total amount of financial aid awarded in 2008–09: $246,465.
Admissions Traditional entrance grade is 7. For fall 2008, 71 students applied for admission, 33 were accepted, 16 enrolled. Wechsler Intelligence Scale for Children required. Deadline for receipt of application materials: none. Application fee required: $50. On-campus interview required.
Athletics Interscholastic: alpine skiing (boys, girls), baseball (b), basketball (b,g), field hockey (g), lacrosse (b,g), skiing (downhill) (b,g), soccer (b,g), softball (g), swimming and diving (b,g), track and field (b,g); coed interscholastic: cross-country running, ice hockey, squash; coed intramural: aerobics/dance, ballet, dance, fitness walking, golf, indoor soccer, jogging, modern dance, nordic skiing, outdoor activities, physical fitness, running, skiing (cross-country), skiing (downhill), snowboarding, soccer, strength & conditioning, swimming and diving, table tennis, tennis, ultimate Frisbee, walking, weight training.
Computers Computers are regularly used in art, English, foreign language, history, mathematics, science classes. Computer resources include on-campus library services, Internet access.
Contact Ms. Kimberly Caldwell Loughlin, Director of Admission. 413-774-7061 Ext. 104. Fax: 413-774-7863. E-mail: admit@bement.org. Web site: www.bement.org/.

See Close-Up on page 1132.

CARDIGAN MOUNTAIN SCHOOL

62 Alumni Drive
Canaan, New Hampshire 03741-9307

Head of School: Mr. David J. McCusker Jr.

General Information Boys' boarding and day college-preparatory, arts, religious studies, and technology school, affiliated with Christian faith. Grades 6–9. Founded: 1945. Setting: rural. Nearest major city is Manchester. Students are housed in single-sex dormitories. 525-acre campus. 18 buildings on campus. Approved or accredited by Association of Independent Schools in New England, Independent Schools of Northern New England, Junior Boarding Schools Association, New England Association of Schools and Colleges, The Association of Boarding Schools, and New Hampshire Department of Education. Member of National Association of Independent Schools and Secondary School Admission Test Board. Endowment: $14.8 million. Total enrollment: 205. Upper school average class size: 12. Upper school faculty-student ratio: 1:4.
Student Profile Grade 6: 25 students (25 boys); Grade 7: 34 students (34 boys); Grade 8: 74 students (74 boys); Grade 9: 72 students (72 boys). 90% of students are boarding students. 24% are state residents. 21 states are represented in upper school student body. 33% are international students. International students from Canada, China, Japan, Mexico, Republic of Korea, and Taiwan; 6 other countries represented in student body. 80% of students are Christian.
Faculty School total: 53. In upper school: 39 men, 14 women; 23 have advanced degrees; 43 reside on campus.
Subjects Offered Algebra, American history, American literature, art, Bible studies, biology, ceramics, Chinese, computer math, computer programming, computer science, creative writing, drama, earth science, ecology, English, English literature, environmental science, ethics, European history, expository writing, fine arts, French, geography, geology, geometry, grammar, health, history, industrial arts, Latin, life skills, mathematics, music, photography, physical education, physical science, reading, religion, science, social studies, Spanish, speech, study skills, theater, trigonometry, typing, world history, world literature, writing.
Graduation Requirements Arts and fine arts (art, music, dance, drama), computer science, English, foreign language, mathematics, reading, religion (includes Bible studies and theology), science, social studies (includes history), study skills.
Special Academic Programs Honors section; independent study; academic accommodation for the gifted and the artistically talented; remedial reading and/or remedial writing; remedial math; ESL (8 students enrolled).
Secondary School Placement 63 students graduated in 2008; they went to Avon Old Farms School; Berkshire School; Kent School; Phillips Exeter Academy; Pomfret School; Salisbury School.
Student Life Specified standards of dress, student council, honor system. Discipline rests primarily with faculty. Attendance at religious services is required.
Summer Programs Remediation, enrichment, advancement, ESL, sports, art/fine arts programs offered; held on campus; accepts boys and girls; open to students from other schools. 150 students usually enrolled. 2009 schedule: June 27 to August 2. Application deadline: none.
Tuition and Aid Day student tuition: $23,150; 7-day tuition and room/board: $40,185. Tuition installment plan (The Tuition Plan, Insured Tuition Payment Plan, Academic Management Services Plan, Key Tuition Payment Plan, monthly payment plans). Need-based scholarship grants, need-based loans, prepGATE Loans available. In 2008–09, 26% of students received aid. Total amount of financial aid awarded in 2008–09: $860,000.

Admissions Traditional entrance grade is 8. For fall 2008, 218 students applied for admission, 123 were accepted, 108 enrolled. ISEE, SLEP for foreign students, SSAT and Wechsler Intelligence Scale for Children III required. Deadline for receipt of application materials: none. Application fee required: $35. On-campus interview required.
Athletics Interscholastic: alpine skiing, baseball, basketball, cross-country running, football, ice hockey, lacrosse, running, sailing, skiing (cross-country), skiing (downhill), soccer, tennis, track and field, wrestling; intramural: archery, bicycling, bowling, boxing, climbing, equestrian sports, fitness, golf, ice hockey, martial arts, mountain biking, outdoor activities, physical training, riflery, rock climbing, ropes courses, sailing, skiing (downhill), snowboarding, swimming and diving, tennis, trap and skeet, weight lifting, whiffle ball. 1 coach, 1 athletic trainer.
Computers Computers are regularly used in English, history, mathematics, science classes. Computer network features include online commercial services, Internet access, wireless campus network, Internet filtering or blocking technology. Students grades are available online. The school has a published electronic and media policy.
Contact Mrs. Jessica Bayreuther, Admissions Coordinator. 603-523-3548. Fax: 603-523-3565. E-mail: jebayreuther@cardigan.org. Web site: www.cardigan.org.

See Close-Up on page 1134.

EAGLEBROOK SCHOOL

Pine Nook Road
Deerfield, Massachusetts 01342
Head of School: Mr. Andrew C. Chase

General Information Boys' boarding and day college-preparatory, arts, and technology school. Grades 6–9. Founded: 1922. Setting: rural. Nearest major city is Springfield. Students are housed in single-sex dormitories. 750-acre campus. 26 buildings on campus. Approved or accredited by Association of Independent Schools in New England and The Association of Boarding Schools. Member of National Association of Independent Schools and Secondary School Admission Test Board. Endowment: $69 million. Total enrollment: 282. Upper school average class size: 10. Upper school faculty-student ratio: 1:4.
Student Profile Grade 6: 23 students (23 boys); Grade 7: 58 students (58 boys); Grade 8: 111 students (111 boys); Grade 9: 89 students (89 boys). 75% of students are boarding students. 35% are state residents. 28 states are represented in upper school student body. 20% are international students. International students from Bermuda, Hong Kong, Mexico, Republic of Korea, Taiwan, and Venezuela; 18 other countries represented in student body.
Faculty School total: 76. In upper school: 44 men, 24 women; 30 have advanced degrees; 50 reside on campus.
Subjects Offered Acting, African-American history, algebra, American studies, anthropology, architectural drawing, architecture, art, astronomy, band, batik, biology, ceramics, Chinese history, chorus, Civil War, civil war history, community service, computer art, computer keyboarding, computer science, computer-aided design, concert band, CPR, creative writing, current events, desktop publishing, digital music, digital photography, drafting, drama, drawing, drawing and design, earth science, ecology, English, English literature, environmental science, ESL, European history, expository writing, fine arts, first aid, French, general science, geography, geometry, grammar, health, history, industrial arts, instrumental music, journalism, Latin, mathematics, medieval history, music, newspaper, photography, physical education, pottery, pre-algebra, public speaking, publications, Russian history, science, sex education, social science, social studies, Spanish, study skills, swimming, theater, typing, U.S. history, Web site design, woodworking, world history, writing.
Graduation Requirements Arts and fine arts (art, music, dance, drama), English, foreign language, mathematics, physical education (includes health), science, social science, social studies (includes history). Community service is required.
Special Academic Programs Honors section; academic accommodation for the gifted, the musically talented, and the artistically talented; ESL (30 students enrolled).
Secondary School Placement 81 students graduated in 2008; they went to Choate Rosemary Hall; Deerfield Academy; Northfield Mount Hermon School; Phillips Exeter Academy; The Hotchkiss School; The Taft School.
Student Life Specified standards of dress, student council. Discipline rests primarily with faculty.
Summer Programs Enrichment, advancement, ESL, sports, art/fine arts, rigorous outdoor training, computer instruction programs offered; session focuses on enrichment; held on campus; accepts boys and girls; open to students from other schools. 60 students usually enrolled. 2009 schedule: July 6 to August 2. Application deadline: none.
Tuition and Aid Day student tuition: $26,500; 7-day tuition and room/board: $41,500. Tuition installment plan (individually arranged payment plans). Need-based scholarship grants available. In 2008–09, 30% of students received aid. Total amount of financial aid awarded in 2008–09: $1,600,000.
Admissions Wechsler Intelligence Scale for Children required. Deadline for receipt of application materials: none. Application fee required: $50. Interview required.
Athletics Interscholastic: alpine skiing, aquatics, baseball, basketball, cross-country running, diving, football, Frisbee, golf, hiking/backpacking, hockey, ice hockey, ice skating, in-line hockey, indoor hockey, indoor soccer, lacrosse, mountain biking, outdoor activities, outdoor recreation, ski jumping, skiing (downhill), snowboarding, soccer, squash, strength & conditioning, swimming and diving, tennis, track and field, triathlon, ultimate Frisbee, water polo, wrestling; intramural: backpacking, bicycling, broomball, canoeing/kayaking, climbing, fishing, fitness, floor hockey, fly fishing, hiking/backpacking, hockey, ice hockey, ice skating, in-line skating, indoor hockey, indoor soccer, juggling, kayaking, life saving, mountain biking, nordic skiing, outdoor activities, physical training, rafting, riflery, rock climbing, roller blading, roller hockey, roller skating, ropes courses, scuba diving, ski jumping, skiing (cross-country), street hockey, table tennis, volleyball, wallyball, weight lifting, weight training, wilderness survival. 1 athletic trainer.
Computers Computer network features include on-campus library services, Internet access, wireless campus network, Internet filtering or blocking technology. Student e-mail accounts are available to students. The school has a published electronic and media policy.
Contact Mr. Theodore J. Low, Director of Admission. 413-774-9111. Fax: 413-774-9119. E-mail: tlow@eaglebrook.org. Web site: www.eaglebrook.org.

See Close-Up on page 1136.

FAY SCHOOL

48 Main Street
Southborough, Massachusetts 01772-9106
Head of School: Robert J. Gustavson

General Information Coeducational boarding and day college-preparatory, arts, and technology school. Boarding grades 6–9, day grades 1–9. Founded: 1866. Setting: small town. Nearest major city is Boston. Students are housed in single-sex dormitories. 38-acre campus. 16 buildings on campus. Approved or accredited by Association of Independent Schools in New England, The Association of Boarding Schools, and Massachusetts Department of Education. Member of National Association of Independent Schools and Secondary School Admission Test Board. Endowment: $36 million. Total enrollment: 380. Upper school average class size: 12. Upper school faculty-student ratio: 1:6.
Student Profile Grade 6: 44 students (21 boys, 23 girls); Grade 7: 65 students (37 boys, 28 girls); Grade 8: 90 students (46 boys, 44 girls); Grade 9: 62 students (36 boys, 26 girls). 42% of students are boarding students. 65% are state residents. 18 states are represented in upper school student body. 24% are international students. International students from Hong Kong, Japan, Mexico, Republic of Korea, Taiwan, and Thailand; 12 other countries represented in student body.
Faculty School total: 66. In upper school: 31 men, 35 women; 34 have advanced degrees; 32 reside on campus.
Subjects Offered Algebra, American history, American literature, art, astronomy, biology, ceramics, computer science, creative writing, drama, English, English literature, environmental science, ethics, European history, expository writing, fine arts, French, geography, geometry, government/civics, grammar, Latin, mathematics, music, photography, physical education, science, social studies, Spanish, world history, writing.
Graduation Requirements Art, English, history, mathematics, music, science, technology.
Special Academic Programs Honors section; independent study; academic accommodation for the gifted, the musically talented, and the artistically talented; ESL (35 students enrolled).
Secondary School Placement 55 students graduated in 2008; they went to Brooks School; Choate Rosemary Hall; Phillips Exeter Academy; Saint Mark's School; St. George's School; St. Paul's School.
Student Life Specified standards of dress, student council. Discipline rests primarily with faculty.
Summer Programs Enrichment, ESL, sports, computer instruction programs offered; session focuses on ESL; held on campus; accepts boys and girls; open to students from other schools. 67 students usually enrolled. 2009 schedule: June 30 to August 10. Application deadline: February 1.
Tuition and Aid Day student tuition: $16,510–$22,600; 7-day tuition and room/board: $37,780–$43,350. Tuition installment plan (Key Tuition Payment Plan, monthly payment plans, individually arranged payment plans, Key Education Resources—Monthly Payment Plan). Need-based scholarship grants, AchieverLoans (Key Education Resources) available. In 2008–09, 10% of students received aid. Total amount of financial aid awarded in 2008–09: $800,000.
Admissions Traditional entrance grade is 7. For fall 2008, 204 students applied for admission, 102 were accepted, 74 enrolled. Wechsler Intelligence Scale for Children required. Deadline for receipt of application materials: none. Application fee required: $50. Interview required.
Athletics Interscholastic: baseball (boys), basketball (b,g), cross-country running (b,g), field hockey (g), football (b), golf (b,g), hockey (b,g), ice hockey (b,g), independent competitive sports (b,g), lacrosse (b,g), soccer (b,g), softball (g), tennis (b,g), track and field (b,g), volleyball (g), wrestling (b); intramural: basketball (b,g), climbing (b,g), dance (b,g), fitness (b,g), golf (b,g), horseback riding (b,g), physical fitness (b,g), rock climbing (b,g), ropes courses (b,g), skiing (downhill) (b,g), snowboarding (b,g), soccer (b,g), strength & conditioning (b,g), tennis (b,g), trap and skeet (b,g), wall climbing (b,g), weight training (b,g), yoga (b,g); coed interscholastic: basketball, cross-country running, golf, hockey, ice hockey, independent competitive sports, lacrosse, soccer, tennis, track and field, volleyball; coed intramural: aerobics/Nautilus, alpine skiing, basketball, bicycling, climbing, dance, fitness, golf, horseback riding, outdoor activities, outdoors, physical fitness, rock climbing, ropes courses,

skiing (downhill), snowboarding, soccer, squash, strength & conditioning, tennis, trap and skeet, wall climbing, weight training, yoga. 2 PE instructors, 17 coaches, 1 athletic trainer.
Computers Computers are regularly used in art, English, foreign language, history, information technology, mathematics, music, science classes. Computer network features include on-campus library services, Internet access, Internet filtering or blocking technology. Campus intranet, student e-mail accounts, and computer access in designated common areas are available to students. Students grades are available online. The school has a published electronic and media policy.
Contact Mr. James W. Ramsdell, Director of Admission. 508-490-8201. Fax: 508-481-7872. E-mail: fayadmit@fayschool.org. Web site: www.fayschool.org.

See Close-Up on page 1138.

THE FESSENDEN SCHOOL

250 Waltham Street
West Newton, Massachusetts 02465-1750
Head of School: Mr. Peter P. Drake

General Information Boys' boarding and day college-preparatory, general academic, and arts school. Boarding grades 5–9, day grades K–9. Founded: 1903. Setting: suburban. Nearest major city is Boston. Students are housed in single-sex dormitories. 41-acre campus. 25 buildings on campus. Approved or accredited by Association of Independent Schools in New England, The Association of Boarding Schools, and Massachusetts Department of Education. Member of National Association of Independent Schools and Secondary School Admission Test Board. Endowment: $25 million. Total enrollment: 482. Upper school average class size: 12. Upper school faculty-student ratio: 1:7.
Student Profile Grade 7: 74 students (74 boys); Grade 8: 83 students (83 boys); Grade 9: 49 students (49 boys). 50% of students are boarding students. 70% are state residents. 17 states are represented in upper school student body. 19% are international students. International students from Bermuda, Mexico, Republic of Korea, Taiwan, and Thailand; 7 other countries represented in student body.
Faculty School total: 91. In upper school: 40 men, 51 women; 54 have advanced degrees; 43 reside on campus.
Subjects Offered Algebra, American history, American literature, anatomy, art, astronomy, biology, ceramics, chemistry, computer math, computer programming, computer science, creative writing, drama, earth science, English, English literature, European history, expository writing, fine arts, French, geography, geometry, government/civics, grammar, health, history, human sexuality, Latin, library studies, mathematics, music, photography, physical education, physics, science, social science, social studies, Spanish, theater, typing, world history, writing.
Graduation Requirements Arts and fine arts (art, music, dance, drama), computer science, English, foreign language, mathematics, science, social science, social studies (includes history).
Special Academic Programs Honors section; academic accommodation for the gifted, the musically talented, and the artistically talented; remedial reading and/or remedial writing; remedial math; ESL (14 students enrolled).
Secondary School Placement 43 students graduated in 2007; they went to Middlesex School; Milton Academy; Noble and Greenough School; Tabor Academy.
Student Life Specified standards of dress, student council, honor system. Discipline rests primarily with faculty.
Tuition and Aid Day student tuition: $21,150–$27,100; 5-day tuition and room/board: $35,250–$35,950; 7-day tuition and room/board: $40,250–$40,950. Tuition installment plan (Academic Management Services Plan, monthly payment plans). Need-based scholarship grants available. In 2007–08, 63% of students received aid. Total amount of financial aid awarded in 2007–08: $668,120.
Admissions Traditional entrance grade is 7. For fall 2007, 95 students applied for admission, 52 were accepted, 40 enrolled. ISEE, SSAT, TOEFL, Wechsler Intelligence Scale for Children or writing sample required. Deadline for receipt of application materials: February 1. Application fee required: $50. On-campus interview required.
Athletics Interscholastic: baseball (boys), basketball (b), cross-country running (b), football (b), ice hockey (b), lacrosse (b), soccer (b), squash (b), tennis (b), track and field (b), wrestling (b); intramural: alpine skiing (b), baseball (b), basketball (b), canoeing/kayaking (b), fencing (b), football (b), golf (b), ice hockey (b), mountain biking (b), racquetball (b), sailing (b), skiing (cross-country) (b), skiing (downhill) (b), snowboarding (b), soccer (b), strength & conditioning (b), swimming and diving (b), tennis (b), weight training (b). 3 PE instructors, 1 athletic trainer.
Computers Computers are regularly used in English, mathematics, science classes. Computer network features include on-campus library services, Internet access, Internet filtering or blocking technology. Student e-mail accounts are available to students. The school has a published electronic and media policy.
Contact Mr. Caleb Thomson, Director of Admissions. 617-630-2300. Fax: 617-630-2303. E-mail: admissions@fessenden.org. Web site: www.fessenden.org.

ANNOUNCEMENT FROM THE SCHOOL The Wheeler Library, opened in 2004, has been relocated to an expanded space in the heart of the School for convenient access from all academic areas and direct connection to the newly updated computer classrooms. The library features a media classroom and an upgraded 16,000-item collection, including expanded multimedia selections and enlarged professional and language collections. The library also provides a story area and reading benches and other comfortable seating for recreational reading.

See Close-Up on page 1140.

FOX RIVER COUNTRY DAY SCHOOL

1600 Dundee Avenue
Elgin, Illinois 60120
Head of School: Mrs. Karen Morse

General Information Coeducational boarding and day college-preparatory, arts, and Environmental Education school, affiliated with Church of Christ, Scientist. Boarding grades 5–8, day grades PS–8. Founded: 1913. Setting: rural. Nearest major city is Chicago. Students are housed in single-sex by floor dormitories. 53-acre campus. 10 buildings on campus. Approved or accredited by Independent Schools Association of the Central States. Member of National Association of Independent Schools. Total enrollment: 204. Upper school average class size: 13. Upper school faculty-student ratio: 1:13.
Student Profile Grade 6: 12 students (6 boys, 6 girls); Grade 7: 14 students (9 boys, 5 girls); Grade 8: 14 students (5 boys, 9 girls). 26% of students are boarding students. 33% are state residents. 1 state is represented in upper school student body. 67% are international students. International students from Republic of Korea. 5% of students are members of Church of Christ, Scientist.
Faculty School total: 26. In upper school: 5 men, 21 women; 6 have advanced degrees; 3 reside on campus.
Subjects Offered Algebra, American history, American literature, art, creative writing, earth science, English, English literature, environmental education, environmental science, general science, geography, geometry, grammar, history, library studies, mathematics, music, physical education, social studies, Spanish, swimming, world history, world literature, writing.
Graduation Requirements Arts and fine arts (art, music, dance, drama), English, environmental education, foreign language, mathematics, physical education (includes health), science, social studies (includes history).
Special Academic Programs Academic accommodation for the gifted; ESL (5 students enrolled).
Secondary School Placement 10 students graduated in 2008; they went to Conserve School; Elgin Academy; Lake Forest Academy.
Student Life Specified standards of dress, honor system. Discipline rests primarily with faculty.
Summer Programs Remediation, enrichment, ESL, sports, art/fine arts, computer instruction programs offered; session focuses on enrichment, environmental education, swimming, arts, crafts, and field trips; held on campus; accepts boys and girls; open to students from other schools. 80 students usually enrolled. 2009 schedule: June 15 to August 7. Application deadline: none.
Tuition and Aid Day student tuition: $4135–$11,925; 5-day tuition and room/board: $27,350; 7-day tuition and room/board: $32,850. Tuition installment plan (monthly payment plans). Tuition reduction for siblings, need-based scholarship grants available. In 2008–09, 30% of students received aid.
Admissions For fall 2008, 10 students applied for admission, 7 were accepted, 7 enrolled. TOEFL or SLEP or writing sample required. Deadline for receipt of application materials: none. Application fee required: $40. Interview required.
Athletics Interscholastic: basketball (boys, girls), Frisbee (b), soccer (b,g), ultimate Frisbee (b), volleyball (g); intramural: basketball (b,g), wrestling (b); coed interscholastic: cooperative games, cross-country running, swimming and diving, track and field; coed intramural: cooperative games, cross-country running, field hockey, fitness, flag football, floor hockey, Frisbee, gymnastics, jogging, kickball, outdoor activities, outdoor education, outdoor recreation, physical fitness, running, soccer, softball, strength & conditioning, swimming and diving, tennis, track and field, volleyball. 2 PE instructors, 4 coaches.
Computers Computers are regularly used in English, science classes. Computer resources include on-campus library services, Internet access, Internet filtering or blocking technology. Computer access in designated common areas is available to students.
Contact Mr. Chuck Harvuot, Director of Admissions. 847-888-7920 Ext. 167. Fax: 847-888-7878. E-mail: admissions@frcds.org. Web site: www.frcds.org.

THE GREENWOOD SCHOOL

14 Greenwood Lane
Putney, Vermont 05346
Head of School: Mr. Stewart Miller

General Information Boys' boarding arts, drama, and music school; primarily serves underachievers, students with learning disabilities, individuals with Attention Deficit Disorder, and dyslexic students. Ungraded, ages 9–15. Founded: 1978. Setting: rural. Nearest major city is Boston, MA. Students are housed in single-sex dormitories. 100-acre campus. 13 buildings on campus. Approved or accredited by Independent Schools of Northern New England, Junior Boarding Schools Association, New England Association of Schools and Colleges, The Association of Boarding Schools, and Vermont Department of Education. Member of National Association of Inde-

pendent Schools. Endowment: $750,000. Total enrollment: 46. Upper school average class size: 5. Upper school faculty-student ratio: 1:2.
Student Profile 93% of students are boarding students. 20% are state residents. 16 states are represented in upper school student body. 2% are international students. International students from Mozambique; 1 other country represented in student body.
Faculty School total: 25. In upper school: 13 men, 11 women; 14 have advanced degrees; 12 reside on campus.
Subjects Offered American history, American literature, art, biology, crafts, creative writing, drama, earth science, ecology, English, geography, grammar, history, mathematics, music, physical education, pragmatics, speech, theater, woodworking, writing.
Special Academic Programs Academic accommodation for the gifted, the musically talented, and the artistically talented; remedial reading and/or remedial writing; remedial math; programs in English, mathematics, general development for dyslexic students.
Secondary School Placement 10 students graduated in 2008; they went to The Forman School; The Gow School.
Student Life Specified standards of dress, student council, honor system. Discipline rests primarily with faculty.
Tuition and Aid Day student tuition: $43,090; 7-day tuition and room/board: $55,640. Tuition installment plan (monthly payment plans, individually arranged payment plans). Need-based scholarship grants available. In 2008–09, 30% of students received aid. Total amount of financial aid awarded in 2008–09: $235,000.
Admissions Traditional entrance age is 12. For fall 2008, 53 students applied for admission, 18 were accepted, 18 enrolled. Wechsler Intelligence Scale for Children III or Woodcock-Johnson Revised Achievement Test required. Deadline for receipt of application materials: none. Application fee required: $75. On-campus interview required.
Athletics Interscholastic: baseball (boys), basketball (b), wrestling (b); intramural: alpine skiing (b), archery (b), backpacking (b), badminton (b), ball hockey (b), basketball (b), bicycling (b), canoeing/kayaking (b), climbing (b), cooperative games (b), cricket (b), fencing (b), fishing (b), floor hockey (b), in-line skating (b), indoor soccer (b), mountain biking (b), nordic skiing (b), outdoor activities (b), outdoor skills (b), outdoors (b), roller blading (b), skiing (cross-country) (b), skiing (downhill) (b), snowboarding (b). 1 PE instructor, 4 coaches.
Computers Computers are regularly used in English, mathematics, science, social studies, writing classes. Computer network features include on-campus library services, Internet access, wireless campus network, Internet filtering or blocking technology, laptop for each student. Student e-mail accounts are available to students. The school has a published electronic and media policy.
Contact Melanie Miller, Director of Admissions. 802-387-4545 Ext. 199. Fax: 802-387-5396. E-mail: mmiller@greenwood.org. Web site: www.greenwood.org.

HAMPSHIRE COUNTRY SCHOOL

28 Patey Circle
Rindge, New Hampshire 03461
Head of School: William Dickerman

General Information Boys' boarding college-preparatory and general academic school; primarily serves underachievers and non-verbal learning disabilities and Asperger's Syndrome. Grades 3–12. Founded: 1948. Setting: rural. Nearest major city is Boston, MA. Students are housed in single-sex dormitories. 1,700-acre campus. 7 buildings on campus. Approved or accredited by New England Association of Schools and Colleges and New Hampshire Department of Education. Member of National Association of Independent Schools. Total enrollment: 22. Upper school average class size: 4. Upper school faculty-student ratio: 1:4.
Student Profile Grade 6: 2 students (2 boys); Grade 7: 3 students (3 boys); Grade 8: 4 students (4 boys); Grade 9: 6 students (6 boys); Grade 11: 4 students (4 boys). 100% of students are boarding students. 8 states are represented in upper school student body. 10% are international students. International students from China and Saudi Arabia.
Faculty School total: 7. In upper school: 3 men, 3 women; 2 have advanced degrees; all reside on campus.
Subjects Offered Algebra, American history, ancient history, biology, chemistry, earth science, English, environmental science, geography, geometry, history, human anatomy, mathematics, physical science, science, Spanish, world history.
Graduation Requirements English, language arts, mathematics, science, social studies (includes history).
Special Academic Programs Academic accommodation for the gifted; remedial reading and/or remedial writing; remedial math.
Student Life Specified standards of dress. Discipline rests primarily with faculty.
Tuition and Aid 7-day tuition and room/board: $43,500.
Admissions Traditional entrance grade is 7. For fall 2008, 10 students applied for admission, 3 were accepted, 2 enrolled. Any standardized test or Individual IQ required. Deadline for receipt of application materials: none. No application fee required. On-campus interview required.
Athletics Intramural: alpine skiing, backpacking, basketball, bicycling, canoeing/kayaking, cooperative games, croquet, deck hockey, fishing, fitness walking, flag football, floor hockey, hiking/backpacking, ice skating, kickball, outdoor activities, outdoor recreation, skiing (cross-country), skiing (downhill), snowshoeing, soccer, softball, tennis, touch football, volleyball, walking, whiffle ball, winter walking.
Computers Computers are regularly used in writing classes.
Contact William Dickerman, Headmaster. 603-899-3325. Fax: 603-899-6521. E-mail: hampshirecountry@monad.net. Web site: www.hampshirecountryschool.org.

HILLSIDE SCHOOL

Robin Hill Road
Marlborough, Massachusetts 01752
Head of School: David Z. Beecher

General Information Boys' boarding and day college-preparatory and leadership school; primarily serves students with learning disabilities and individuals with Attention Deficit Disorder. Grades 5–9. Founded: 1901. Setting: small town. Nearest major city is Boston. Students are housed in single-sex dormitories. 200-acre campus. 15 buildings on campus. Approved or accredited by Association of Independent Schools in New England, Junior Boarding Schools Association, New England Association of Schools and Colleges, The Association of Boarding Schools, and Massachusetts Department of Education. Member of National Association of Independent Schools and Secondary School Admission Test Board. Endowment: $6 million. Total enrollment: 139. Upper school average class size: 10. Upper school faculty-student ratio: 1:6.
Student Profile Grade 6: 23 students (23 boys); Grade 7: 35 students (35 boys); Grade 8: 38 students (38 boys); Grade 9: 33 students (33 boys). 70% of students are boarding students. 60% are state residents. 15 states are represented in upper school student body. 15% are international students. International students from Ghana, Mexico, Nigeria, Republic of Korea, Uganda, and Ukraine; 3 other countries represented in student body.
Faculty School total: 32. In upper school: 23 men, 9 women; 10 have advanced degrees; 24 reside on campus.
Subjects Offered Algebra, American government, American history, ancient history, art, earth science, economics, English, English literature, environmental science, ESL, French, geography, geometry, international relations, Latin, leadership skills, life science, mathematics, music, physical education, science, social skills, social studies, Spanish, woodworking, writing.
Graduation Requirements English, foreign language, mathematics, science, social studies (includes history).
Special Academic Programs Honors section; academic accommodation for the gifted; remedial reading and/or remedial writing; remedial math; programs in general development for dyslexic students; special instructional classes for students with Attention Deficit Disorder, Attention Deficit Hyperactivity Disorder, and slight dyslexia; ESL (10 students enrolled).
Secondary School Placement 29 students graduated in 2007; they went to Brewster Academy; Dublin School; The Cambridge School of Weston; Vermont Academy; Wilbraham & Monson Academy.
Student Life Specified standards of dress, student council, honor system. Discipline rests primarily with faculty. Attendance at religious services is required.
Tuition and Aid Day student tuition: $25,650; 5-day tuition and room/board: $39,950; 7-day tuition and room/board: $44,400. Tuition installment plan (Insured Tuition Payment Plan, SMART Tuition Payment Plan, monthly payment plans). Need-based scholarship grants available. In 2007–08, 31% of students received aid. Total amount of financial aid awarded in 2007–08: $930,000.
Admissions Traditional entrance grade is 7. For fall 2007, 95 students applied for admission, 72 were accepted, 52 enrolled. Any standardized test or WISC-III and Woodcock-Johnson required. Deadline for receipt of application materials: none. Application fee required: $50. Interview required.
Athletics Interscholastic: baseball, basketball, cross-country running, golf, hockey, ice hockey, lacrosse, running, soccer, track and field, wrestling; intramural: alpine skiing, basketball, bicycling, billiards, canoeing/kayaking, climbing, fishing, fitness, flag football, floor hockey, Frisbee, golf, hiking/backpacking, ice skating, indoor hockey, indoor soccer, juggling, lacrosse, mountain biking, outdoor activities, outdoor adventure, outdoor education, outdoor skills, physical training, rock climbing, ropes courses, running, sailing, skiing (downhill), snowboarding, soccer, swimming and diving, table tennis, tennis, touch football, volleyball, walking, weight training, whiffle ball, yoga.
Computers Computers are regularly used in all academic, art, music classes. Computer network features include on-campus library services, Internet access, Internet filtering or blocking technology. Computer access in designated common areas is available to students.
Contact Kristen J. Naspo, Director of Admissions. 508-485-2824. Fax: 508-485-4420. E-mail: admissions@hillsideschool.net. Web site: www.hillsideschool.net.

ANNOUNCEMENT FROM THE SCHOOL The March 2008 opening of the new Academic and Health Center represents the latest phase in Hillside's multimillion-dollar expansion. The center's features include nine new classrooms, three of which are science labs; flex activity and fitness rooms; and a state-of-the-art health center. In addition, two new dormitories, curricular innovations, and other campus improvements are helping to advance Hillside's reputation as a leading junior boarding school for boys.

See Close-Up on page 1142.

INDIAN MOUNTAIN SCHOOL

211 Indian Mountain Road
Lakeville, Connecticut 06039

Head of School: Mark A. Devey

General Information Coeducational boarding and day college-preparatory, general academic, arts, and ESL school. Boarding grades 6–9, day grades PK–9. Founded: 1922. Setting: rural. Nearest major city is Hartford. Students are housed in single-sex dormitories. 600-acre campus. 12 buildings on campus. Approved or accredited by Connecticut Association of Independent Schools, Junior Boarding Schools Association, The Association of Boarding Schools, and Connecticut Department of Education. Member of National Association of Independent Schools and Secondary School Admission Test Board. Endowment: $6.2 million. Total enrollment: 258. Upper school average class size: 12. Upper school faculty-student ratio: 1:4.
Student Profile Grade 7: 39 students (23 boys, 16 girls); Grade 8: 62 students (38 boys, 24 girls); Grade 9: 44 students (28 boys, 16 girls). 47% of students are boarding students. 21% are state residents. 9 states are represented in upper school student body. 11% are international students. International students from Bahamas, China, France, Japan, Mexico, and Republic of Korea; 3 other countries represented in student body.
Faculty School total: 45. In upper school: 20 men, 25 women; 24 have advanced degrees; 29 reside on campus.
Subjects Offered Algebra, American history, ancient history, art, biology, ceramics, Chinese, computers, earth science, English, film, fine arts, French, general science, geometry, health, history, Latin, mathematics, music, physical science, social studies, Spanish, theater.
Graduation Requirements Arts and fine arts (art, music, dance, drama), English, foreign language, mathematics, music, science, social studies (includes history).
Special Academic Programs ESL (11 students enrolled).
Secondary School Placement 47 students graduated in 2008; they went to Berkshire School; Choate Rosemary Hall; Kent School; Millbrook School; Salisbury School; The Hotchkiss School.
Student Life Specified standards of dress, student council, honor system. Discipline rests primarily with faculty.
Tuition and Aid Day student tuition: $21,300; 7-day tuition and room/board: $39,915. Tuition installment plan (Key Tuition Payment Plan). Need-based scholarship grants available. In 2008–09, 23% of students received aid. Total amount of financial aid awarded in 2008–09: $723,975.
Admissions Traditional entrance grade is 7. For fall 2008, 109 students applied for admission, 71 were accepted, 44 enrolled. WISC or WAIS, WISC-III and Woodcock-Johnson or WISC/Woodcock-Johnson required. Deadline for receipt of application materials: none. Application fee required: $50. Interview required.
Athletics Interscholastic: aerobics/dance (girls), baseball (b), basketball (b,g), football (b), ice hockey (b), lacrosse (b,g), soccer (b,g), softball (g); intramural: dance (g); coed interscholastic: alpine skiing, cross-country running, ice hockey, outdoor adventure, skiing (downhill), squash, tennis, volleyball; coed intramural: alpine skiing, backpacking, skiing (downhill), snowboarding, tennis, ultimate Frisbee.
Computers Computers are regularly used in English, history, mathematics, science, social studies classes. Computer network features include on-campus library services, Internet access, Internet filtering or blocking technology. Student e-mail accounts are available to students. The school has a published electronic and media policy.
Contact Mrs. Mimi L. Babcock, Director of Admission. 860-435-0871. Fax: 860-435-1380. E-mail: admissions@indianmountain.org. Web site: www.indianmountain.org.

LINDEN HILL SCHOOL

154 South Mountain Road
Northfield, Massachusetts 01360-9681

Head of School: Mr. James Allen McDaniel

General Information Boys' boarding and day college-preparatory, general academic, technology, and ESL school; primarily serves underachievers, students with learning disabilities, individuals with Attention Deficit Disorder, dyslexic students, and language-based learning differences. Grades 3–9. Founded: 1961. Setting: rural. Nearest major city is Springfield. Students are housed in single-sex dormitories. 200-acre campus. 15 buildings on campus. Approved or accredited by Association of Independent Schools in New England, Junior Boarding Schools Association, Massachusetts Office of Child Care Services, New England Association of Schools and Colleges, The Association of Boarding Schools, and Massachusetts Department of Education. Member of National Association of Independent Schools. Endowment: $100,000. Total enrollment: 30. Upper school average class size: 4. Upper school faculty-student ratio: 1:3.
Student Profile Grade 9: 5 students (5 boys). 85% of students are boarding students. 28% are state residents. 25% are international students. International students from Republic of Korea; 1 other country represented in student body.
Faculty School total: 13. In upper school: 6 men, 4 women; 6 have advanced degrees; 8 reside on campus.
Subjects Offered Arts, character education, English, ESL, experiential education, freshman seminar, general science, history, industrial arts, instrumental music, lab science, language and composition, language development, leadership and service, life skills, mathematics, outdoor education, strategies for success, woodworking, writing skills.
Special Academic Programs Programs in English, mathematics, general development for dyslexic students; ESL (5 students enrolled).
Secondary School Placement 4 students graduated in 2008.
Student Life Specified standards of dress. Discipline rests primarily with faculty.
Summer Programs Remediation, enrichment, ESL, sports, art/fine arts, computer instruction programs offered; session focuses on remediation and enrichment; held on campus; accepts boys and girls; open to students from other schools. 40 students usually enrolled. 2009 schedule: June 30 to July 30. Application deadline: none.
Tuition and Aid Day student tuition: $31,900; 7-day tuition and room/board: $51,800. Tuition installment plan (FACTS Tuition Payment Plan, individually arranged payment plans). Need-based scholarship grants available. In 2008–09, 28% of students received aid. Total amount of financial aid awarded in 2008–09: $15,000.
Admissions Achievement tests, Wechsler Intelligence Scale for Children III or writing sample required. Deadline for receipt of application materials: none. Application fee required: $60. On-campus interview required.
Athletics Interscholastic: basketball; intramural: alpine skiing, backpacking, basketball, bicycling, blading, bowling, climbing, cooperative games, cross-country running, fishing, golf, ice skating, indoor hockey, indoor soccer, jogging, jump rope, kickball, martial arts, mountain biking, outdoor activities, physical fitness, roller blading, running, skiing (downhill), snowboarding, soccer, softball, swimming and diving, table tennis, tennis, wall climbing, whiffle ball, wrestling. 6 coaches.
Computers Computer network features include Internet access. Campus intranet and student e-mail accounts are available to students. The school has a published electronic and media policy.
Contact Mrs. Patricia K. Sanieski, Academic Dean. 413-498-2906 Ext. 105. Fax: 413-498-2908. E-mail: pksanieski@lindenhs.org. Web site: www.lindenhs.org.

See Close-Up on page 1144.

NORTH COUNTRY SCHOOL

PO Box 187
Cascade Road
Lake Placid, New York 12946

Head of School: David Hochschartner

General Information Coeducational boarding and day college-preparatory, general academic, and arts school. Grades 4–9. Founded: 1938. Setting: rural. Nearest major city is Albany. Students are housed in residential houses. 200-acre campus. 10 buildings on campus. Approved or accredited by New York State Association of Independent Schools and New York Department of Education. Member of National Association of Independent Schools and Secondary School Admission Test Board. Endowment: $7 million. Total enrollment: 88. Upper school average class size: 12. Upper school faculty-student ratio: 1:3.
Student Profile Grade 6: 13 students (7 boys, 6 girls); Grade 7: 19 students (13 boys, 6 girls); Grade 8: 22 students (10 boys, 12 girls); Grade 9: 27 students (15 boys, 12 girls). 95% of students are boarding students. 30% are state residents. 19 states are represented in upper school student body. 18% are international students. International students from Antigua and Barbuda, Bermuda, Canada, Colombia, Japan, and Mexico; 2 other countries represented in student body.
Faculty School total: 33. In upper school: 13 men, 20 women; 9 have advanced degrees; 20 reside on campus.
Subjects Offered Algebra, American history, biology, ceramics, computer science, creative writing, earth science, English, mathematics, music, performing arts, photography, physical education, social studies, Spanish, studio art.
Special Academic Programs Remedial reading and/or remedial writing; remedial math; ESL (10 students enrolled).
Secondary School Placement 20 students graduated in 2007; they went to Dublin School; Gould Academy; Northwood School; Vermont Academy.
Student Life Specified standards of dress, student council. Discipline rests primarily with faculty.
Tuition and Aid Day student tuition: $16,200; 5-day tuition and room/board: $32,800; 7-day tuition and room/board: $43,800. Tuition installment plan (monthly payment plans, individually arranged payment plans, 2-payment plan). Need-based scholarship grants available. In 2007–08, 30% of students received aid. Total amount of financial aid awarded in 2007–08: $450,000.
Admissions Traditional entrance grade is 7. Deadline for receipt of application materials: none. No application fee required. On-campus interview required.
Athletics Coed Interscholastic: aerobics/dance, alpine skiing, artistic gym, bicycling, climbing, curling, drill team, field hockey, fishing, Frisbee, hiking/backpacking, horseback riding, lacrosse, modern dance, mountain biking, mountaineering, nordic skiing, outdoor activities, outdoor adventure, outdoor education, outdoor recreation, outdoor skills, rappelling, rock climbing, skateboarding, ski jumping, skiing (cross-country), skiing (downhill), snowboarding, snowshoeing, swimming and diving, telemark skiing, volleyball, walking, wall climbing, wilderness survival, yoga; coed intramural: basketball, skiing (cross-country), skiing (downhill), soccer.
Computers Computer resources include on-campus library services, Internet access.
Contact Christine LeFevre, Director of Admissions. 518-523-9329. Fax: 518-523-4858. E-mail: admissions@nct.org. Web site: www.nct.org/.

See Close-Up on page 1146.

THE RECTORY SCHOOL

528 Pomfret Street
Pomfret, Connecticut 06258

Head of School: Thomas F. Army

General Information Coeducational boarding and day college-preparatory, general academic, arts, technology, and Music school, affiliated with Episcopal Church; primarily serves underachievers, students with learning disabilities, individuals with Attention Deficit Disorder, and dyslexic students. Boarding grades 5–9, day grades K–9. Founded: 1920. Setting: rural. Nearest major city is Hartford. Students are housed in single-sex dormitories. 138-acre campus. 24 buildings on campus. Approved or accredited by Connecticut Association of Independent Schools, Junior Boarding Schools Association, and The Association of Boarding Schools. Member of National Association of Independent Schools and Secondary School Admission Test Board. Endowment: $10.6 million. Total enrollment: 240. Upper school average class size: 10. Upper school faculty-student ratio: 1:4.

Student Profile Grade 6: 29 students (22 boys, 7 girls); Grade 7: 50 students (35 boys, 15 girls); Grade 8: 68 students (46 boys, 22 girls); Grade 9: 42 students (33 boys, 9 girls). 65% of students are boarding students. 38% are state residents. 19 states are represented in upper school student body. 18% are international students. International students from Bahamas, Bermuda, China, Japan, Mexico, and Republic of Korea; 3 other countries represented in student body. 11% of students are members of Episcopal Church.

Faculty School total: 66. In upper school: 24 men, 42 women; 30 have advanced degrees; 28 reside on campus.

Subjects Offered Algebra, American history, American literature, ancient world history, art, biology, Chinese, chorus, computer science, creative arts, creative writing, drama, earth science, ecology, English, English as a foreign language, English literature, environmental science, European history, expository writing, fine arts, foreign language, general science, geography, geometry, grammar, history, journalism, Latin, life science, mathematics, medieval history, medieval/Renaissance history, music, photography, physical education, physical science, reading, science, social studies, Spanish, study skills, theater, vocal music, world history, world literature, writing.

Graduation Requirements Arts and fine arts (art, music, dance, drama), literature, mathematics, physical education (includes health), science, social studies (includes history).

Special Academic Programs Honors section; academic accommodation for the gifted; remedial reading and/or remedial writing; remedial math; programs in English, mathematics, general development for dyslexic students; special instructional classes for students with learning disabilities, Attention Deficit Disorder, and dyslexia; ESL (5 students enrolled).

Secondary School Placement 48 students graduated in 2008; they went to Brewster Academy; Peddie School; Pomfret School; Suffield Academy; Tabor Academy; The Hotchkiss School.

Student Life Specified standards of dress, student council, honor system. Discipline rests primarily with faculty. Attendance at religious services is required.

Summer Programs Remediation, enrichment, ESL, sports, art/fine arts programs offered; session focuses on study skills, academic enrichment, sports clinics, music; held on campus; accepts boys and girls; open to students from other schools. 80 students usually enrolled. 2009 schedule: June 21 to July 25. Application deadline: none.

Tuition and Aid Day student tuition: $17,800; 7-day tuition and room/board: $37,300. Tuition installment plan (Key Tuition Payment Plan). Need-based scholarship grants available. In 2008–09, 30% of students received aid. Total amount of financial aid awarded in 2008–09: $800,000.

Admissions Traditional entrance grade is 7. For fall 2008, 221 students applied for admission, 142 were accepted, 85 enrolled. Wechsler Intelligence Scale for Children III required. Deadline for receipt of application materials: none. Application fee required: $50. Interview required.

Athletics Interscholastic: baseball (boys), basketball (b,g), cross-country running (b,g), football (b), ice hockey (b), soccer (b,g), softball (g), wrestling (b); intramural: basketball (b,g), football (b), lacrosse (b), rugby (b), soccer (b), softball (b), street hockey (b), strength & conditioning (b), touch football (b), whiffle ball (b), wrestling (b); coed interscholastic: fencing, golf, hockey, ice hockey, lacrosse, outdoor adventure, soccer, tennis, track and field; coed intramural: ball hockey, basketball, bowling, canoeing/kayaking, cross-country running, fishing, fitness, fly fishing, Frisbee, golf, horseback riding, ice hockey, ice skating, lacrosse, life saving, martial arts, mountain biking, Nautilus, outdoor adventure, outdoor recreation, roller blading, ropes courses, running, skateboarding, skiing (cross-country), skiing (downhill), snowboarding, soccer, softball, squash, street hockey, swimming and diving, table tennis, tai chi, tennis, ultimate Frisbee, volleyball, weight training, whiffle ball. 2 athletic trainers.

Computers Computers are regularly used in English, history, mathematics, music, science, writing classes. Computer network features include on-campus library services, online commercial services, Internet access, wireless campus network, Internet filtering or blocking technology. Student e-mail accounts are available to students. The school has a published electronic and media policy.

Contact Vincent Ricci, Assistant Headmaster of Admissions and Marketing. 860-928-1328. Fax: 860-928-4961. E-mail: admissions@rectoryschool.org. Web site: www.rectoryschool.org.

See Close-Up on page 1148.

RUMSEY HALL SCHOOL

201 Romford Road
Washington Depot, Connecticut 06794

Head of School: Thomas W. Farmen

General Information Coeducational boarding and day college-preparatory, general academic, and arts school. Boarding grades 5–9, day grades K–9. Founded: 1900. Setting: rural. Nearest major city is Hartford. Students are housed in single-sex dormitories. 147-acre campus. 29 buildings on campus. Approved or accredited by Connecticut Association of Independent Schools, National Independent Private Schools Association, The Association of Boarding Schools, and Connecticut Department of Education. Member of National Association of Independent Schools and Secondary School Admission Test Board. Endowment: $2.5 million. Total enrollment: 309. Upper school average class size: 13. Upper school faculty-student ratio: 1:8.

Student Profile Grade 6: 24 students (16 boys, 8 girls); Grade 7: 51 students (25 boys, 26 girls); Grade 8: 76 students (51 boys, 25 girls); Grade 9: 75 students (50 boys, 25 girls). 50% of students are boarding students. 50% are state residents. 15 states are represented in upper school student body. 10% are international students. International students from Bermuda, China, Japan, Mexico, Republic of Korea, and Thailand; 6 other countries represented in student body.

Faculty School total: 53. In upper school: 25 men, 26 women; 25 have advanced degrees; 30 reside on campus.

Subjects Offered Algebra, American history, American literature, art, art history, biology, computer science, creative writing, drama, earth science, English, English literature, environmental science, ESL, European history, fine arts, French, geography, geometry, government/civics, grammar, health, history, Japanese history, Latin, mathematics, music, physical education, science, social studies, Spanish, theater, world history, writing.

Graduation Requirements Arts and fine arts (art, music, dance, drama), computer science, English, foreign language, mathematics, physical education (includes health), science, social studies (includes history).

Special Academic Programs Honors section; academic accommodation for the gifted; remedial reading and/or remedial writing; programs in English for dyslexic students; special instructional classes for students with learning disabilities and Attention Deficit Disorder; ESL (25 students enrolled).

Secondary School Placement 66 students graduated in 2008; they went to Choate Rosemary Hall; Kent School; St. George's School; Suffield Academy; The Gunnery; The Taft School.

Student Life Specified standards of dress, student council, honor system. Discipline rests primarily with faculty.

Summer Programs Enrichment, ESL programs offered; session focuses on academic enrichment; held on campus; accepts boys and girls; open to students from other schools. 60 students usually enrolled. 2009 schedule: June 30 to August 2. Application deadline: May 1.

Tuition and Aid Day student tuition: $18,500; 7-day tuition and room/board: $39,000. Tuition installment plan (Insured Tuition Payment Plan, Key Tuition Payment Plan, monthly payment plans, individually arranged payment plans). Need-based scholarship grants available. In 2008–09, 24% of students received aid. Total amount of financial aid awarded in 2008–09: $775,000.

Admissions Traditional entrance grade is 8. For fall 2008, 169 students applied for admission, 96 were accepted, 74 enrolled. Psychoeducational evaluation, SLEP, SSAT, Wechsler Intelligence Scale for Children III or writing sample required. Deadline for receipt of application materials: none. Application fee required: $40. On-campus interview required.

Athletics Interscholastic: baseball (boys), basketball (b,g), field hockey (g), football (b), ice hockey (b,g), lacrosse (b), softball (g), volleyball (g), wrestling (b); coed interscholastic: alpine skiing, crew, cross-country running, equestrian sports, horseback riding, skiing (downhill), soccer, tennis; coed intramural: alpine skiing, backpacking, bicycling, canoeing/kayaking, climbing, fly fishing, Frisbee, golf, hiking/backpacking, ice skating, mountain biking, outdoor activities, physical fitness, physical training, project adventure, roller blading, running, skateboarding, skiing (downhill), snowboarding, street hockey, strength & conditioning, table tennis, tennis, track and field, ultimate Frisbee, weight lifting, weight training, whiffle ball, wilderness, wilderness survival, wildernessways. 1 PE instructor, 28 coaches, 1 athletic trainer.

Computers Computers are regularly used in English, history, mathematics, science classes. Computer network features include online commercial services, Internet access.

Contact Matthew S. Hoeniger, Assistant Headmaster. 860-868-0535. Fax: 860-868-7907. E-mail: admiss@rumseyhall.org. Web site: www.rumseyhall.org.

See Close-Up on page 1150.

ST. CATHERINE'S MILITARY ACADEMY

215 North Harbor Boulevard
Anaheim, California 92805

Head of School: Sr. Johnellen Turner, OP

General Information Boys' boarding and day college-preparatory, general academic, religious studies, Leadership/Military Program, ESL, and military school, affiliated with Roman Catholic Church. Boarding grades 4–8, day grades K–8. Founded: 1889. Setting: suburban. Nearest major city is Los Angeles. Students are housed in single-sex dormitories. 8-acre campus. 8 buildings on campus. Approved or accredited by Military High School and College Association, National Catholic Education Association, The Association of Boarding Schools, Western Association of Schools and Colleges, Western Catholic Education Association, and California Department of Education. Total enrollment: 134. Upper school average class size: 18. Upper school faculty-student ratio: 1:8.

Student Profile Grade 6: 19 students (19 boys); Grade 7: 35 students (35 boys); Grade 8: 46 students (46 boys). 70% of students are Roman Catholic.

Faculty School total: 19. In upper school: 4 men, 15 women; 5 have advanced degrees; 12 reside on campus.

Subjects Offered Art, band, Catholic belief and practice, character education, choir, Civil War, computer applications, computer keyboarding, computer literacy, computer skills, conflict resolution, decision making skills, English, environmental systems, ESL, ethical decision making, ethics and responsibility, fine arts, fitness, grammar, guidance, guitar, health and wellness, health education, healthful living, history, instrumental music, instruments, interpersonal skills, lab/keyboard, leadership, leadership education training, leadership skills, leadership training, life skills, marching band, mathematics, military history, military science, moral and social development, music, music appreciation, music history, music performance, participation in sports, personal development, personal fitness, personal growth, physical education, physical fitness, piano, pre-algebra, reading/study skills, religion, religious education, science, service learning/internship, single survival, social studies, Spanish, sports, survival training, swimming, volleyball, wind instruments, word processing, yearbook.

Graduation Requirements Arts and fine arts (art, music, dance, drama), computer science, English, foreign language, mathematics, physical education (includes health), religion (includes Bible studies and theology), science, social studies (includes history), Spanish.

Special Academic Programs Special instructional classes for Dtudents with Attention Deficit Disorder and learning disabilities; ESL (14 students enrolled).

Secondary School Placement 37 students graduated in 2008; they went to Army and Navy Academy; Mater Dei High School; New Mexico Military Institute; Servite High School.

Student Life Uniform requirement, honor system. Discipline rests equally with students and faculty. Attendance at religious services is required.

Summer Programs Remediation, enrichment, ESL, sports, art/fine arts, computer instruction programs offered; session focuses on academics and athletic activities; held both on and off campus; held at day trips to local attractions, (e.g., beach, aquarium, water park); accepts boys; open to students from other schools. 120 students usually enrolled. 2009 schedule: June 26 to July 22. Application deadline: none.

Tuition and Aid Day student tuition: $9565; 5-day tuition and room/board: $27,115; 7-day tuition and room/board: $36,090. Tuition installment plan (FACTS Tuition Payment Plan, monthly payment plans, individually arranged payment plans, 4 Payments). Need-based scholarship grants available. In 2008–09, 20% of students received aid. Total amount of financial aid awarded in 2008–09: $171,061.

Admissions Any standardized test required. Deadline for receipt of application materials: none. Application fee required: $100. Interview required.

Athletics Interscholastic: basketball, flag football, golf, soccer, touch football, volleyball; intramural: ball hockey, baseball, basketball, bowling, cooperative games, cross-country running, drill team, equestrian sports, field hockey, fitness, flag football, handball, life saving, physical fitness, physical training, soccer, softball, swimming and diving, touch football, track and field, volleyball, water volleyball, weight lifting. 1 PE instructor, 7 coaches.

Computers Computers are regularly used in English, history, science, social studies classes. Computer network features include Internet access, Internet filtering or blocking technology. Student e-mail accounts are available to students.

Contact Graciela Salvador, Director of Admissions. 714-772-1363 Ext. 103. Fax: 714-772-3004. E-mail: admissions@stcatherinesmilitaryacademy.org. Web site: www.StCatherinesMilitaryAcademy.org.

ST. THOMAS CHOIR SCHOOL

202 West 58th Street
New York, New York 10019-1406

Head of School: Rev. Charles Wallace

General Information Boys' boarding college-preparatory, general academic, arts, religious studies, technology, and music school, affiliated with Episcopal Church. Grades 3–8. Founded: 1919. Setting: urban. Students are housed in single-sex dormitories. 1 building on campus. Approved or accredited by National Association of Episcopal Schools, New York State Association of Independent Schools, The Association of Boarding Schools, and New York Department of Education. Member of National Association of Independent Schools and Secondary School Admission Test Board. Endowment: $18 million. Total enrollment: 36. Upper school average class size: 8. Upper school faculty-student ratio: 1:5.

Student Profile Grade 6: 8 students (8 boys); Grade 7: 7 students (7 boys); Grade 8: 6 students (6 boys). 100% of students are boarding students. 10% are state residents. 12 states are represented in upper school student body. 67% of students are members of Episcopal Church.

Faculty School total: 7. In upper school: 5 men, 2 women; 6 have advanced degrees; all reside on campus.

Subjects Offered Algebra, applied music, art, choir, computers, English, French, history, Latin, mathematics, music theory, physical education, science, study skills, theology, visual arts.

Graduation Requirements Arts and fine arts (art, music, dance, drama), English, foreign language, mathematics, physical education (includes health), religion (includes Bible studies and theology), science, social studies (includes history).

Special Academic Programs Academic accommodation for the gifted and the musically talented; remedial reading and/or remedial writing; remedial math; programs in general development for dyslexic students.

Secondary School Placement 5 students graduated in 2008.

Student Life Uniform requirement. Discipline rests primarily with faculty. Attendance at religious services is required.

Tuition and Aid 7-day tuition and room/board: $10,750. Tuition installment plan (individually arranged payment plans). Need-based scholarship grants available. In 2008–09, 70% of students received aid. Total amount of financial aid awarded in 2008–09: $187,950.

Admissions Admissions testing and audition required. Deadline for receipt of application materials: none. No application fee required. On-campus interview required.

Athletics Interscholastic: basketball, soccer, softball; intramural: baseball, basketball, fitness, flag football, floor hockey, independent competitive sports, indoor hockey, indoor soccer, kickball, lacrosse, Newcombe ball, outdoor recreation, physical fitness, running, soccer, softball, strength & conditioning, table tennis, track and field, ultimate Frisbee, volleyball. 1 PE instructor.

Computers Computers are regularly used in art, English, foreign language, history, library, mathematics, music, science classes.

Contact Ms. Ruth S. Cobb, Director of Admissions and Alumni Relations. 212-247-3311 Ext. 304. Fax: 212-247-3393. E-mail: rcobb@choirschool.org. Web site: www.choirschool.org.

Junior Boarding School Close-Ups

THE BEMENT SCHOOL

Deerfield, Massachusetts

Type: Coeducational, day (kindergarten–grade 9) and boarding (grades 3–9), general academic school
Grades: K–9: Lower School, kindergarten–5; Upper School, 6–9
Enrollment: School total: 240; Upper School: 114; Lower School: 126
Head of School: Shelley Borror Jackson

THE SCHOOL

The Bement School began in 1925 when Grace Bement agreed to a request made by Headmaster Frank Boyden of Deerfield Academy to tutor one of his students. The School grew as word spread of her effective teaching. Between 1947 and 1971, Bement was incorporated and further expanded under the direction of Katherine Bartlett and Mary Drexler. Peter Drake led the School from 1985 to 1999, during which time the School expanded its physical plant, doubled the size of its student body, and enhanced its reputation nationally and internationally.

The 12-acre campus is in historic Deerfield, an area steeped in history. Bement's proximity to five area colleges also provides a variety of learning opportunities.

The Bement School offers an education based on proven values. The pervasive atmosphere at Bement is that of a family, learning and living together. Bement actively seeks an academically diverse, international, and multicultural student body. Students and adults at Bement work together to create a climate of acceptance, kindness, stimulation, and challenge in which the academic, creative, physical, and emotional growth of each child is nurtured and realized.

Bement is governed by a board of trustees. Alumni maintain an active role, some serving on the board in support of activities within the Alumni Association.

The Bement School is a member of the National Association of Independent Schools, the Association of Independent Schools of New England, the Junior Boarding Schools Association, the Educational Records Bureau, and the Elementary School Heads Association.

ACADEMIC PROGRAMS

The Upper School (grades 6–9) curriculum is an academic program emphasizing English, mathematics, science, history, fine arts, and world languages. Intermediate and advanced levels of English for English Language Learners (ELL) are also available. Students are exposed to technology in many forms—an introduction to typing and keyboarding skills, word processing, research, the creation of movies and multimedia presentations, and interactive learning programs in several subject areas. Classes typically have from 10 to 15 students. Tutorial help is available from a learning specialist.

Between Thanksgiving vacation and winter break, the entire School participates in a miniterm with a special schedule of courses and electives organized around a theme. The theme changes annually, yet the interdisciplinary format remains the focus of each miniterm.

Teachers evaluate student performance, participation, and effort frequently. The boarding faculty members meet weekly to review the academic and social growth of each boarder. On a triweekly basis, the School sends written comments, which include achievement and effort grades, to parents of both boarding and day students. Students review these reports in private conferences with their advisers. Comprehensive reports are mailed home at the end of each trimester.

Students in grades 7–9 may participate in Bement's cultural exchange program with L'Ermitage School in Maisons-Laffitte, a town 20 kilometers outside of Paris. In alternating years, Bement students travel to France, and their French counterparts spend three weeks at Bement, hosted by day-student families. The exchange is a living study of history, people, culture, architecture, and travel.

The Lower School (kindergarten–grade 5) strives to educate the whole child by challenging each student's intellect, creativity, and physical skills in a nurturing environment. Confidence building is a strong part of the Lower School experience. The program's goal is to instill in each student a respect for nature, mankind, and oneself while developing the skills necessary to become a productive and responsible citizen. Classes range in size from 9 to 12 students.

Teachers evaluate Lower School students' progress in a variety of ways—through conferences with parents in the fall and spring and by written reports twice each trimester. These evaluations review each child's academic progress, effort, personal development, and work habits.

FACULTY AND ADVISERS

The Bement School has 42 faculty members. Eleven live on campus, and 25 hold master's degrees. The average tenure at Bement is about nine years. The student-teacher ratio is 5:1 in the Upper School and 6:1 in the Lower School.

Shelley Borror Jackson was appointed Head of the School in 1999. She earned her Bachelor of Arts degree in English from Wheaton College and holds a Master of Arts degree in English from Ohio State University and a Certificate of Advanced Studies in education and language arts from the University of Maine.

An adviser system, in conjunction with dorm parents, guides the students in both academic and personal areas. Every Friday, Upper School students eat lunch and participate in group activities, community service projects, or a wellness program with their advisers.

SECONDARY SCHOOL PLACEMENT

Bement seeks to place each student in the appropriate secondary school. Students receive preliminary recommendations for their secondary school during the spring of their eighth-grade year. In the fall of the ninth-grade year, each student, along with parents, meets with the Head, the Assistant Head, and the Director of Secondary School Placement to consider appropriate options and to plan school visits. While the student is given the ultimate responsibility for completing admission materials, these administrators provide guidance and encouragement to ensure that all completed applications are submitted in a timely fashion. Once acceptances have been received, the student and family, with assistance from Bement, decide on the appropriate placement. Some of the schools attended in the last five years include Deerfield Academy, Suffield Academy, Northfield Mount Hermon, Emma Willard School, Westminster, Williston-Northampton, and Milton Academy.

STUDENT BODY AND CONDUCT

Of the total 2008–09 enrollment of 240, 208 were day students and 32 were boarders. There were 126 boys and 114 girls. Just over half of the boarding population is composed of international students.

Courtesy and respect for others are practiced in the classroom and throughout the School community, including the athletic fields, where sportsmanship is emphasized. Students learn that personal responsibility, good citizenship, and trust are essential components of their education.

ACADEMIC FACILITIES

The Kittredge Upper School building houses academic classrooms, science laboratories, and locker rooms. The Clagett-McLennan Library provides the School with an all-school library facility, including two multimedia computer laboratories, an ever-expanding collection, the Grace Bement Reading Room, and a dance studio. Lower School classrooms for kindergarten–grade 2 are located in Keith Schoolhouse. The Drake School Building contains classrooms for grades 3–5 and one section of grade 2. Many lower school classrooms have a student computer for typing practice. Older lower school students do word processing and research using these machines. The Drake building is equipped with a work station for students to work on their reading with the Lexia reading program. The Kittredge building has a printing station with three computers for students to use for printing, research, and word processing. Every classroom, as well as the library, is set up for Internet access. The fine arts facility is the home of art classrooms, music/chorus rooms, a darkroom, band performance space, and the Barn, which houses a fully functioning stage, an assembly hall, and meeting space.

BOARDING AND GENERAL FACILITIES

Boarding students live, according to gender and age, in one of four houses. Dorm parents, who are carefully selected and often have families of their own, live with the boarders. Dorm parents commit themselves to guiding each boarder's growth as a person as well as encouraging academic achievement. While each dorm has kitchen facilities where students often gather for an after-school snack or a weekend meal, one of the cornerstones of the Bement community is the kitchen and dining hall in Bement House. Dorm parents and teachers head the tables and serve the meals.

When medical treatment is necessary, students are driven to the Deerfield Academy Health Center, located only a few hundred yards away from Bement. In addition, the Franklin Medical Center in Greenfield is just a short drive away.

ATHLETICS

All students participate daily in some form of sport or physical education throughout the year. The Lower School program develops coordination, game skills, and a general awareness of the importance of physical fitness and sportsmanship. Grades 4 and 5 concentrate on seasonal sports, playing intramural games, and developing sport-specific skills. In the spring, students in kindergarten through grade 5 participate in an instructional swimming program.

Upper School students are involved in a variety of athletic programs suited to their age and interests. In addition to helping each student develop individual talents, coaches emphasize concepts of teamwork and good sportsmanship. During each sports season, both competitive and noncompetitive options are available. In the fall, Bement offers boys' and girls' soccer, field hockey, cross-country, and tennis. In the winter, the School shares nearby Deerfield Academy facilities for swimming, squash, boys' and girls' basketball, and ice hockey. The ski team travels to Berkshire East every day for training and racing events, and cross-country skiers take advantage of the New England countryside. Each Wednesday during the winter trimester, Upper School students participate in Alpine or cross-country skiing or snowboarding and have a half day of school and reduced homework that evening. In the spring, Bement offers baseball, boys' and girls' lacrosse, outdoor skills, softball, and track.

EXTRACURRICULAR OPPORTUNITIES

At Bement, students pursue their interests and develop leadership, not only in academics but also in such areas as drama, art, writing, music, and outdoor skills. Students in grades 7–9 and their advisers participate for one term in an intergenerational community service program. Sixth graders participate in an on-campus community service program and Leadership.

DAILY LIFE

In the Upper School, each day begins with a School meeting and a silent reading period. This is followed by two academic classes, a 20-minute recess, and two more classes. Lunch, which is served family-style, is followed by a class and a study hall, during which time all teachers are available for extra help. Athletic practice and games are after the academic day.

The Lower School day begins with a group meeting. Students and teachers sing, share announcements, and discuss common concerns and current events. After morning meeting, children disperse to self-contained classrooms where academic classes are taught at various times throughout the day. At noon, everyone reconvenes for Lower School lunch, served family-style with a teacher heading a table of 7 or 8 students.

WEEKEND LIFE

Weekends for boarders are carefully planned in advance by the Dean of Boarding. The social curriculum of each boarder is important, and Bement strives to provide opportunities to interact and grow while experiencing exciting and unique trips and events. Typical weekend activities include trips to points of local interest, sporting events, plays, and movies. Weekly outdoor activities include hiking, bicycle trips, and informal sports contests. Skiing and skating are emphasized when the weather permits.

COSTS AND FINANCIAL AID

For 2008–09, tuition and fees were $12,220 for day students in kindergarten, $13,315 for day students in grades 1 and 2, $14,030 for day students in grades 3–5, and $17,845 for day students in grades 6–9. Tuition and fees were $39,325 for all boarding students. Students must have health insurance; if a student is not covered by a family health insurance policy, coverage may be purchased through the School. There is also a one-time refundable security deposit of $500 for boarding students and $100 for day students.

Parents may indicate on the admissions application a desire to be considered for financial assistance. They will be sent a School and Student Service financial aid form to be completed and sent to the School and Student Service. Decisions are based on need and available funds. In 2008–09, 28 percent of the student body received aid.

ADMISSIONS INFORMATION

Bement School accepts day students for kindergarten–grade 9 and boarding students for grades 3–9. The admissions committee looks for students who are likely to benefit from and contribute to the School. Decisions on admission are based on the candidate's school record, the results of the Wechsler Intelligence Scale for Children (grades 3–9), and a personal visit with the Director of Admission. Preference is given to siblings of current students. The kindergarten admissions process follows different guidelines, and those interested should contact the Director of Admission for details.

APPLICATION TIMETABLE

Inquiries and applications are welcome throughout the year. Upon their completion, boarding student folders are reviewed as part of a rolling admission process. Day students should complete application folders by February 6 in order to participate in the first round of admission decisions; notifications of decisions are mailed in early March. Kindergarten screenings take place in March and April.

ADMISSIONS CORRESPONDENCE

Ms. Kimberly Caldwell Loughlin
Director of Admission
The Bement School
Deerfield, Massachusetts 01342
Phone: 413-774-7061
Fax: 413-774-7863
E-mail: admit@bement.org
Web site: http://www.bement.org

CARDIGAN MOUNTAIN SCHOOL

Canaan, New Hampshire

Type: Boys' day and boarding junior high school
Grades: 6–9
Enrollment: 172
Head of School: David J. McCusker Jr. '80, Headmaster

THE SCHOOL

Cardigan Mountain School was founded in 1945 by 2 men whose vision and belief in their goal were unshakable. Harold P. Hinman, a Dartmouth College graduate, and William R. Brewster, then Headmaster of Kimball Union Academy, joined forces with legendary Dartmouth President Ernest M. Hopkins to obtain the land that is now the site of Cardigan Mountain's campus. Cardigan Mountain School opened with 24 boys, and, in 1954, upon merging with the Clark School of Hanover, New Hampshire, the School as it is known today began to emerge. Since that time, the School has grown to its current enrollment of more than 200 boys, while the philosophy and objectives set forth by the founders have remained unchanged.

Cardigan provides boys with a structured, homelike environment within which mastery of the fundamental academic skills, social and physical growth, and spiritual values can be encouraged.

The 525-acre campus, located on Canaan Street Lake, is 18 miles from Dartmouth College. Driving time from Boston is approximately 2½ hours. Some of the finest skiing in New England is only 1 hour away.

The self-perpetuating Board of Trustees and Incorporators is instrumental in guiding the School. The School's endowment is valued at more than $13.4 million. In 2007–08, Annual Giving was just over $895,000.

Cardigan Mountain is accredited by the New England Association of Schools and Colleges. Its memberships include the National Association of Independent Schools (NAIS), the Junior Boarding Schools Association, the Independent Schools Association of Northern New England (ISANNE), the Association of Independent Schools of New England (AISNE), the Secondary School Admission Test Board (SSATB), Boys' Schools, A Better Chance (ABC), the Federation of American Independent Schools, and the Educational Records Bureau (ERB).

ACADEMIC PROGRAMS

Cardigan's curriculum is designed to both support and challenge the student as he prepares for the academic programs characteristic of most independent secondary schools. In all disciplines, emphasis is placed upon the mastery of fundamental skills, content, and study skills.

The curriculum provides each student with instruction in all major courses and exposes him to a number of other subject areas that round out his education. Cardigan requires all students to take yearlong courses in English, mathematics, science, and social studies. In addition, studying a foreign language (Latin, French, or Spanish) is strongly advised.

Beyond these courses, Cardigan also requires each boy to strengthen his program of study through additional course work in reading and study skills, studio art, woodworking/sculpture and design, music history and appreciation, religion, life skills, and keyboarding.

The average class size ranges from 4 to 15 students, and, within each grade, there is ability tracking. There are normally three levels in each subject in grades 7, 8, and 9. The extra help and conference period gives students yet another opportunity to work with faculty members on an individual basis. In addition, a reading and study skills course is required of all students.

Debuting in 2008 is the PEAKS (Personalized Education for the ?Acquisition of Knowledge and Skills) program, which was developed at Cardigan to increase a student's self-awareness regarding his personal development. The PEAKS curriculum revolves around study skills, technology education, and health topics. Similarly, Math Lab is an optional tutorial that provides individualized enrichment or remediation in mathematics. For students for whom English is not the primary language, English as a second language provides instruction in basic English skills. Cardigan uses a trimester system, and grades and teacher comments are sent home at the middle and end of each of the three terms. Grading includes both achievement marks and an effort rating.

FACULTY AND ADVISERS

The faculty consists of 37′ full-time and 5 part-time members, the majority of whom reside on campus. One quarter of the faculty members are women. More than one half of the faculty members have earned advanced academic degrees. All faculty members teach, coach, supervise dormitories, and serve as advisers for the students. Cardigan has a 4:1 student-faculty ratio. Of the greatest importance to Cardigan are the faculty members who, by setting and attaining personal goals, serve as positive role models for the boys. Cardigan faculty members bring with them a love for learning and a variety of skills, experiences, and talents that broaden and enrich the educational experience and inject warmth and enthusiasm into campus life.

SECONDARY SCHOOL PLACEMENT

Cardigan offers extensive assistance to the students and their parents in selecting and then applying to independent secondary schools. The Secondary School Placement Office begins the counseling process in the spring of the eighth grade and continues to guide the student and his family throughout the application experience. The Placement Office offers workshops on interviewing techniques, SSAT preparation, and essay writing.

Over the past few years, a number of Cardigan graduates have matriculated to schools such as Avon Old Farms, Brooks, Deerfield, Holderness, Hotchkiss, Lawrence, Phillips Andover, Phillips Exeter, Pomfret, Salisbury, St. Mark's, St. Paul's, Tabor, Taft, and Westminster.

STUDENT BODY AND CONDUCT

For 2008–09, 172 boys enrolled at Cardigan. There were 58 boys in the ninth grade, 72 in the eighth, 37 in the seventh, and 5 in the sixth. Almost 90 percent of the Cardigan students were boarders. In 2007–08, students came to Cardigan from nineteen states and ten countries.

Cardigan has a two-tiered disciplinary status system in order to inform students, their advisers, and parents when School expectations are not being met. This disciplinary system is used to correct patterns of misbehavior and to discipline those students who commit serious offenses. The Discipline Committee meets to hear cases deemed appropriate by the Headmaster and the Assistant Headmaster. Two student leaders and 3 faculty members are selected by the Assistant Headmaster to join him on the committee. The committee hears cases and makes a recommendation for consequences to the Headmaster.

Cardigan has a clearly stated Honor Code, and all students are expected to abide by the spirit of that code.

ACADEMIC FACILITIES

The numerous buildings that house academic facilities are highlighted by the Bronfman Center. Completed in 1996, Bronfman Center features, among other things, the three Freda R. Caspersen state-of-the-art science laboratories, an art studio, the Bhirombhakdi Computer Center, a School store, and class room for sixth graders. Stoddard Center is the home of both the Kirk Library and the Humann Theatre. Opened in fall 1982, the Kirk Library in Cardigan's Stoddard Center is a three-tiered, well-equipped multimedia resource center that offers students and faculty members computer software, audiotapes, and videocassettes in addition to more than 10,000 volumes and numerous journals and periodicals. Thousands of newspaper and magazine articles are available through the Infoweb NewsBank Reference Service. Computers with Internet access are available in both the Kirk Library and the adjacent writing lab. Affiliation with the New Hampshire State Library's Automated Information Access System enables users at the School to obtain materials through the interlibrary loan process. The library is staffed by 1 full-time librarian and a part-time aid. A flexible access plan allows students and faculty members to work in groups, as well as individually, throughout the day and five evenings each week. Humann, the 250-seat theater, is the site of School meetings, lectures, films, concerts, and drama performances.

Cardigan emphasizes the visual arts. The Williams Woodshop and the new Art Center are focal points for this important aspect of a boy's education. The Hinman Auditorium houses the School's music facilities, where opportunities for vocal and instrumental instruction are available.

All dormitory rooms and many classrooms are wired for access to the Internet.

BOARDING AND GENERAL FACILITIES

Eleven dormitories house from 8 to 16 students each. Each dormitory houses faculty members and their families. Students reside in double rooms, with some singles provided. Two dormitories, referred to as 'houses,' were completed in fall 2000 and house 3 faculty members and their families and 12 students.

The School operates an on-campus health center, where most of the students' medical needs can be met. For extended services, Cardigan students benefit from the Dartmouth-Hitchcock Medical Center Pediatric Clinic in Canaan and the Dartmouth-Hitchcock Medical Center in Lebanon. The Hamilton Health Center on the Cardigan campus has a resident nurse and a visiting physician.

ATHLETICS

The objectives of the activities program at Cardigan are to provide the boys with opportunities to experience success, to offer healthy and enjoyable activities for the boys' free-time periods and weekends, to promote the physical and athletic development of each boy, to teach cooperation with and reliance on teammates, to allow the boys to experience sports and activities that may be new or unfamiliar to them, and to encourage good sportsmanship.

Over the years, Cardigan has been fortunate to acquire extensive athletics facilities, fields, and equipment. These include five fields for soccer, football, and lacrosse; fourteen outdoor tennis courts; two baseball diamonds; a state-of-the-art hockey rink that can be converted to a multipurpose arena in the fall and spring; an on-campus, lighted ski slope; cross-country ski trails; ski team rooms; a wrestling room; an outing club room; a fully equipped weight-training room; an in-line hockey rink; and indoor and outdoor basketball courts.

As the School is situated on the shores of Canaan Street Lake, students and faculty members take full advantage of water-related activities. Sailing is pursued in the School's fleet of Flying Juniors, sailboards, ice boats, and the Hobie catamaran. Motorboats, rowboats, and canoes provide additional opportunities for students to enjoy the water. The waterfront area is well supervised, and instruction is available in all activities.

The Ragged Mountain Ski Area is close to the School and is used on weekdays by the Alpine ski team, recreational skiers, and snowboarders. On Sundays, there are daylong ski trips to major ski areas in New Hampshire and Vermont.

As in the classroom, the focus of interscholastic sports and individual activities is on learning the fundamentals. Teams are fielded on several levels in most sports, and they compete against local independent and public schools. Recreational sports are offered for the student who does not wish to compete interscholastically.

EXTRACURRICULAR OPPORTUNITIES

Many students and faculty members bring to Cardigan skills and interests that, though not included in the usual program of studies, may be pursued and developed in the informal setting of the Club Program. Clubs meet every Thursday afternoon in lieu of athletics, with the opportunity for additional meetings if the members and adviser so desire. Recent clubs have participated in community service, including visits to a local nursing home, hospital volunteer work, recycling, the Big Brother Program, and Red Cross lifeguard training; blues, jazz, and rock bands; a cappella singing groups; technical rock-climbing; horseback riding; mountain-biking; debating; painting; chess; photography; windsurfing; and conversational Chinese, French, German, Hebrew, and Japanese.

A boy may participate in the optional drama program in each of the three seasons. Each year, the drama department presents three major productions. There are extensive stage lighting and sound features, and students interested in the technical aspects of theater enjoy working in this facility.

DAILY LIFE

The typical academic day begins six days per week with a required family-style breakfast. After room inspection in the dormitories, classes begin at 7:45 a.m. Six class periods precede a family-style lunch. On Monday, Tuesday, Thursday, and Friday, lunch is followed by an advisory/conference period. On Wednesday and Saturday, the academic day ends with lunch and is followed by a full slate of athletics and recreational activities. Dinner is a family-style meal every evening except Wednesday and Saturday, when a buffet is scheduled. A study period occurs each school night. Lights-out ranges from 9:30 to 10:15 p.m., depending on the evening and the age of the student.

Cardigan is nondenominational, yet the School seeks to strengthen each boy's spiritual development within his own religious heritage. All boys are required to attend the weekly Thursday afternoon chapel service. Arrangements are made for students of different faiths to attend their own weekly services in the immediate area.

WEEKEND LIFE

In addition to the regularly scheduled vacations, all boys may take weekends away from the campus and parents are invited to the campus to share in their son's experience at any time. The majority of Cardigan students are on campus on weekends, and the School provides an exciting array of options for them. A typical Saturday night's schedule might include a movie, a trip off campus, various other on-campus activities and programs, or an excursion to Dartmouth College to swim in their pool or watch a hockey game.

SUMMER PROGRAMS

The Cardigan Mountain Summer Session, a coeducational experience for 170 girls and boys, was instituted in 1951 to meet the needs of four groups of students: those who may be seeking admission to Cardigan in the fall, those who desire advanced academic work and enrichment, those who require intensive work in basic academic skills, and those who require review. The Summer Session also serves a limited number of international students for whom English is not the first language. Cardigan's outstanding range of sports and activities, along with its academic offerings, makes the Summer Session a special blend of camp and school.

Academic enrichment offerings in the sciences are a focal point for the more able students. Courses in environmental sciences were designed to better prepare youngsters for the changing world. The visual and performing arts, long a part of the Summer Session's afternoon program, achieved curricular status, allowing students to pursue drama, ceramics, and photography as part of their morning academic program of study.

The six-week program is still known for its individualized instruction, close supervision of daily study time, and general emphasis on improving study skills. Academic offerings include English, advanced English composition, computers, prealgebra, algebra I and II, geometry, study skills, French, Spanish, and Latin.

The Summer Session is open to students who have completed third through ninth grade. The cost for the 2008 Summer Session was $7800 for boarding students and $4160 for day students. Need-based aid is available.

COSTS AND FINANCIAL AID

In 2008–09, charges for boarding students were $40,185 and for day students, $23,150. There are additional charges for items such as textbooks, laundry service, and athletic equipment.

Financial aid is available to families of qualified students who complete the School and Student Service for Financial Aid forms and demonstrate need. Information about loans and payment plans is available from the Cardigan Admissions Office. For 2008–09, approximately 34 percent of the student body received more than $1,022,000 in financial assistance.

ADMISSIONS INFORMATION

Cardigan seeks to enroll students of good character and academic promise who will contribute to and benefit from the broad range of academic and extracurricular opportunities available. The Admissions Committee reviews applications on a rolling admissions basis for students wishing to enter the sixth through the ninth grades. Students in grades 3–9 are considered for the Summer Session. Decisions are based upon previous school records, teacher recommendations, aptitude testing, and a campus interview. Cardigan admits students of any race, color, nationality, or ethnic origin to all the rights, privileges, programs, and activities generally accorded or made available to students at the School.

APPLICATION TIMETABLE

Initial inquiries are welcome at any time. Office hours are 8 to 4, Monday through Friday, and 8 to noon on Saturday. School catalogs and applications can be obtained through the Admissions Office. The application fee is $50 for domestic applicants and $125 for international applicants.

ADMISSIONS CORRESPONDENCE

Chip Audett, Director of Admissions
Cardigan Mountain School
62 Alumni Drive
Canaan, New Hampshire 03741
Phone: 603-523-3510
Fax: 603-523-3565
E-mail: caudett@cardigan.org
Web site: http://www.cardigan.org

Marten J. Wennik, Director of Financial Aid
Cardigan Mountain School
62 Alumni Drive
Canaan, New Hampshire 03741
Phone: 603-523-3544
Fax: 603-523-3565
E-mail: mwennik@cardigan.org

Ryan Feeley, Director of the Summer Session
Cardigan Mountain School
62 Alumni Drive
Canaan, New Hampshire 03741
Phone: 603-523-3526
Fax: 603-523-3565
E-mail: rfeely@cardigan.org

EAGLEBROOK SCHOOL

Deerfield, Massachusetts

Type: Boys' day and boarding school
Grades: 6–9
Enrollment: 280
Head of School: Andrew C. Chase, Headmaster

THE SCHOOL

Eaglebrook School was opened in 1922 by its Headmaster and founder, Howard B. Gibbs, a former faculty member of Deerfield Academy. One of the earliest members of his faculty was C. Thurston Chase. When Mr. Gibbs died in 1928, Mr. Chase became Headmaster, a position he held for thirty-eight years. From 1966 to 2002, Stuart and Monie Chase assumed leadership of the School. While continuing to foster the School's traditional commitment to excellence, the Chases have encouraged and developed many components of a vital school: expansion of both academic and recreational facilities, emphasis on the arts, increased endowment and financial aid, student and faculty diversity, and a balanced, healthful diet. Stuart and Monie's son, Andrew C. Chase, now assumes leadership duties as Headmaster. Eaglebrook's goals are simple—to help each boy come into full and confident possession of his innate talents, to improve the skills needed for the challenges of secondary school, and to establish values that will allow him to be a person who acts with thoughtfulness and humanity.

The School owns more than 750 acres on Mt. Pocumtuck, overlooking the Deerfield Valley and the historic town of Deerfield. It is located 100 miles west of Boston and 175 miles north of New York City.

The Allen-Chase Foundation was chartered in 1937 as a charitable, educational trust. It is directed by a 40-member self-perpetuating Board of Trustees, representing alumni, parents, and outside professionals in many fields.

Eaglebrook is a member of the National Association of Independent Schools, the Association of Independent Schools of New England, the Valley Independent School Association, the Junior Boarding School Association, and the Secondary School Admissions Test Board.

ACADEMIC PROGRAMS

Sixth graders are taught primarily in a self-contained setting. Subjects include English, mathematics, reading, Latin, history, science, and trimester-length courses in studio art, computers, music, and woodworking. Required classes for grades 7 through 9 each year include foreign language study in Latin, French, Mandarin Chinese, or Spanish; a full year of mathematics; a full year of Colonial history in seventh grade, followed by a self-selected history the next two years; a full year of English; two trimesters of geography; two trimesters of science in seventh grade, followed by a full-year laboratory course; one trimester of human sexuality in eighth grade; and one trimester of ethics in the ninth grade. The School offers extensive trimester electives, including band and instrumental instruction, computer skills, word processing, current events, conditioning, chess, film classics, drama, public speaking, industrial field trips, music appreciation, first aid, publications, and an extensive variety of studio arts. Drug and alcohol education is required of all students in every grade.

Class enrollment averages 8 to 12 students. Teachers report directly to a student's adviser any time the student's work is noteworthy, either for excellence or deficiency. This allows the adviser to communicate praise or concern effectively and initiate appropriate follow-up. Midway through each trimester, teachers submit brief written evaluations to the advisers of each of their students. Advisers stay in close touch with the parents of their advisees. Grades, along with full academic reports from each of the student's teachers, are given to advisers each trimester and then sent home. The reports are accompanied by a letter from the adviser discussing the student's social adjustment progress, athletic and activity accomplishments, and academic progress and study habits.

FACULTY AND ADVISERS

Andrew C. Chase, the current Headmaster, is a graduate of Deerfield Academy and Williams College. Along with his wife, Rachel Blain, a graduate of Phillips Andover Academy and Amherst College, Andrew succeeded his father as Headmaster in 2002.

Eaglebrook's full- and part-time faculty consists of 72 men and women, 46 of whom live on campus, many with families of their own. Seventy hold undergraduate degrees, and 30 hold graduate degrees. Leaves of absence, sabbaticals, and financial assistance for graduate study are available. The ratio of students to faculty members is 4.9:1.

Teachers endeavor to make learning an adventure and watch over each boy's personal growth. They set the academic tone, coach the teams, serve as dorm parents, and are available for a boy when he needs a friend. They help each individual establish lifelong study habits and set standards for quality. Eaglebrook's teachers have the skill not only to challenge the very able but also to make learning happen for those who need close supervision. Faculty members are chosen primarily for their appreciation of boys this age, their character and integrity as role models, and competence in their subject areas. The fact that many are married and have children of their own helps to create a warm, experienced family atmosphere.

SECONDARY SCHOOL PLACEMENT

The Director of Placement assists families in selecting, visiting, and applying to secondary schools. He meets with parents and students in the spring of a boy's eighth-grade year to discuss which schools might be appropriate based on each boy's aptitude, interests, achievements, and talent. He arranges visits from secondary schools and helps with applications. Parents and the Director of Placement work together until the boy has decided upon his secondary school in April of his ninth-grade year.

Schools frequently attended by Eaglebrook School graduates include Deerfield Academy, Choate Rosemary Hall School, the Hotchkiss School, Loomis Chaffee, Northfield Mount Hermon School, Phillips Andover Academy, Phillips Exeter Academy, Pomfret School, St. George's School, St. Paul's School, Taft School, and Westminster School.

STUDENT BODY AND CONDUCT

In the 2008–09 school year, of the 203 boarding students and 77 day students, 25 were in grade 6, 54 in grade 7, 98 in grade 8, and 103 in grade 9. Twenty-eight states and eighteen countries were represented.

There are specified standards of dress, which are neat and informal most of the time. Discipline is handled on an individual basis by those faculty members who are closely involved with the student.

ACADEMIC FACILITIES

The C. Thurston Chase Learning Center contains classrooms, an audiovisual center, and an assembly area. It also houses the Copley Library, which contains 18,000 volumes and subscriptions to eighty-five publications, books on tape, newspapers, CD-ROMs, and Internet access. The computer room is equipped with state-of-the-art computers, color printers, scanners, digital cameras, and a projection board. The Bartlett Assembly Room is an all-purpose area with seats for the entire School. The Jean Flagler Matthews Science Building houses three laboratories, classrooms, a project room, a library, an online computerized weather station, and teachers' offices. The Bryant Arts Building houses studios for drawing, painting, stained glass, architectural design, computer-aided design, stone carving, ceramics, silk-screening, printmaking, and computer art; a darkroom for photography; a woodworking shop; a band rehearsal room; a publications office; a piano studio; piano practice rooms; and a drama rehearsal room. The campus has a high-speed fiber-optic network with e-mail and access to the World Wide Web for research.

BOARDING AND GENERAL FACILITIES

Dormitories are relatively small; the five dormitories house between 18 and 36 students each, with at least one faculty family to every 8 to 10 boys.

Most students live in double rooms. A limited number of single rooms are available. After the first year, a boy may request a certain dormitory and adviser.

ATHLETICS

The athletics program is suitable for boys of all sizes and abilities. Teams are small enough to allow each boy a chance to play in the games, master skills, and develop a good sense of sportsmanship. The School's Athletic Director arranges a competitive schedule to ensure games with teams of equal ability. Fall sports include cross-country, tennis, hiking, football, water polo, and soccer. Winter sports include ice hockey, basketball, recreational and competitive skiing, swimming and diving, snowboarding, squash, and wrestling. The School maintains the Easton Ski Area, consisting of several ski trails, the Macomber Chair Lift, and snowmaking equipment. Spring sports are baseball, track and field, golf, Ultimate Disc, lacrosse, triathlon, mountain and road biking, and tennis. The School plays host to numerous students throughout the year in seasonal tournaments in ice hockey, soccer, skiing, basketball, Ultimate Disc, swimming, and wrestling. The Schwab Family Pool is a six-lane facility for both competitive and recreational swimming. The McFadden Rink at Alfond Arena features a state-of-the-art NHL-dimensioned 200-foot by 85-foot indoor ice surface. A multisport indoor surface is installed in the arena in the off-season to enable use of the facility for in-line skating, in-line hockey, soccer, lacrosse, and tennis. The Lewis Track and Field was dedicated in 2002.

EXTRACURRICULAR OPPORTUNITIES

Service and leadership opportunities build a sense of pride in the School and camaraderie in the student body. Elected Student Council representatives meet with the Headmaster as an advisory group and discuss School issues. Boys act as admissions guides, help with recycling, organize dances, serve as proctors in the dormitories and the dining room, act as headwaiters, and give the morning assemblies. Boys also assume responsibility, with faculty guidance, for the School newspaper, yearbook, and literary magazine.

Many of the students participate in numerous outdoor activities that are sponsored by the Mountain Club. They maintain an active weekend schedule that includes camping, hiking, backpacking, canoeing, kayaking, white-water rafting, fishing, rock climbing, and snowshoeing.

DAILY LIFE

On weekdays, students rise at 7:20 a.m.; breakfast is at 8. Academic class periods, including assembly, begin at 8:30. Lunch is at noon, and classes resume at 12:33. Study hall and special appointments begin at 2:15, athletics begin at 3:15, and tutorial periods and other activities begin at 5. Dinner is at 6, and evening activities are scheduled between 6:45 and 7:30; study hall is then held until 9:15 p.m. or later, according to the grade.

WEEKEND LIFE

A wide variety of weekend activities are available at Eaglebrook, both on campus and off, including community service, riflery, museum visits, dances, field trips, tournaments, movies, plays, concerts, town trips, Deerfield Academy games, bicycle trips, ski trips, hiking, camping, and mountain climbing. On Sunday, the Coordinator of Religion supervises a nondenominational and nonsectarian meeting for the student body. Attendance is required for boarding students. The aim is to share different beliefs and ways of worship. Transportation is provided for boys who wish to maintain their own religious commitment by attending local places of worship. Students with permission may leave the School for the weekend; 5–10 percent of the student body normally do so on a given weekend.

COSTS AND FINANCIAL AID

Eaglebrook School's tuition for the 2008–09 school year was $41,500 for boarding students and $26,500 for day students. Eaglebrook seeks to enroll boys from different backgrounds from this country and abroad, regardless of their ability to pay. Approximately 30 percent of the students receive financial aid. To apply for tuition assistance, a candidate must complete the School Scholarship Service's Parents' Financial Statement, which is obtainable from the Financial Aid Office.

ADMISSIONS INFORMATION

Most students enter in seventh grade, although students can be admitted to any grade. Information regarding required testing and transcripts can be obtained from the Admissions Office. A School visit and interview are required.

Eaglebrook welcomes boys of any race, color, religion, nation, or creed, and all share the same privileges and duties.

APPLICATION TIMETABLE

The School accepts applications throughout the year, but it is to the candidate's advantage to make application as early as possible. Decisions and notifications are made whenever a boy's file is complete. There is a $50 application fee ($100 for international students).

ADMISSIONS CORRESPONDENCE

Theodore J. Low
Director of Admissions
Eaglebrook School
Pine Nook Road
Deerfield, Massachusetts 01342
Phone: 413-774-9111 (admissions)
413-774-7411 (main)
Fax: 413-774-9119 (admissions)
413-772-2394 (main)
E-mail: admissions@eaglebrook.org
Web site: http://www.eaglebrook.org

FAY SCHOOL

Southborough, Massachusetts

Type: Coeducational high school–preparatory boarding (6–9) and day (1–9) school
Grades: 1–9: Lower School, 1–5; Upper School, 6–9
Enrollment: School total: 380; Upper School: 254; Lower School: 126
Head of School: Robert J. Gustavson Jr., Head of School; Marie Brais, Director of Advancement; Sarah McMillan, Head of Upper School; Anne Bishop, Head of Lower School; Christopher Schoberl, Academic Dean

THE SCHOOL

A dynamic learning environment since 1866, Fay School exemplifies a coeducational tradition of academic excellence coupled with a dedication to maximize the potential of each individual child. With a structured environment that recognizes both effort and achievement, Fay School offers both breadth and depth in academic, artistic, and athletic programs. Multilevel course offerings and the availability of tutorial support ensure each student an appropriate level of academic challenge. In small advisory groups, students receive extensive individualized attention. Relationships between students and teachers mirror those of parent and child. At Fay, faculty members and parents work as partners during the critically important adolescent years. Fay's comprehensive secondary school placement program not only provides guidance in identifying and applying to model secondary schools but also assists students and their parents in selecting the best environment for continuing their education at the next level. Exceptional facilities and a faculty committed to ongoing professional development create an environment where living and learning thrive.

Established in 1866 by two sisters, Eliza Burnett Fay and Harriet Burnett, the School is situated on 42 acres in semirural surroundings 28 miles west of Boston. Fay School's day and boarding students are drawn from twenty states and fifteen countries. The vast majority go on to graduate from independent secondary schools.

At Fay, each child's voice matters. Through its leadership opportunities, cultural program, comprehensive academic program, community service, arts, and sports offerings, the School caters to a wide range of interests and abilities. Students' endeavors are encouraged and supported by a dedicated and highly qualified faculty and monitored by an effort system that measures the level of engagement each student demonstrates in all aspects of campus life. Particular attention is given to the needs of boarding students and to making life in dormitories a "home away from home."

Fay School is a nonprofit institution and is governed by a self-perpetuating board of 27 trustees. Its endowment stands at $34 million and is supplemented by an annual fund of more than $1 million in total gifts, bridging the gap between tuition and the operating budget. Through its development efforts, the School annually receives support from more than 1,000 alumni, parents, and friends.

ACADEMIC PROGRAMS

Fay's program seeks to achieve far more than a sound foundation in course work; the emphasis is on fostering positive attitudes toward learning and living in the world beyond the campus. By limiting class size to an average of 12 Upper School students, Fay provides an environment in which children are active participants in their own education. Each student's specific needs and academic background are carefully considered when scheduling classes. A rotating block schedule and more than 200 class offerings ensure maximum flexibility in designing programs of study.

The School offers different levels in most subject areas. In the Lower School, the program emphasizes individual growth and the development of sound fundamental skills. Courses of study in the Upper School provide sequential programs grounded in strengthening basic practices in grades 6 and 7, a foundation upon which deeper conceptual understanding and application are built in the high school courses offered in grades 8 and 9. At the eighth and ninth grade levels, honors courses are available for students who qualify for this enriched experience. A full complement of courses within the five main disciplines of mathematics, English, history, science, and world languages is offered in the Upper School. Fay also provides leadership training in grades 1–9 through a full-year program that stresses the leadership skills of conflict management, social responsibility, team building, communication, and positive role modeling.

Fay School offers a comprehensive technology education program. Technology is integrated across the curriculum and throughout the grades. The School also offers technology classes to Upper and Lower School students that are designed to help students use technology to enhance their studies and to become safe, ethical, and effective computer users. Technology offerings range from Lower School introductory courses to information literacy, digital video production, and Web site design in the upper grades. All students must complete at least one term of art each year as well as a yearlong course in music.

To facilitate success in a student's academic endeavors, deliberate attention is paid to the development of study skills through a study skills curriculum administered by Learning Center staff members and reinforced in the classroom. In particular, research skills, note-taking, time management, and test-taking strategies are taught at the appropriate grade levels. In the academic and athletics programs, the School also monitors each student's progress by means of biweekly effort evaluations and by trimester reports at the middle and end of terms. Specialized help is available through the Learning Services Department for children who need support in following their regular course of study.

The International Student Program (ISP) offers English courses for students whose native language is not English. Three levels and small classes afford opportunities to tailor ISP courses to individual needs in the areas of speaking, listening, writing, reading, and skill building. As students' proficiency in English increases, they are integrated into mainstream courses. Full participation in art, music, technology classes, and sports activities helps students adapt quickly to life in their new community.

FACULTY AND ADVISERS

Children entering Fay School are welcomed into a family whose heart is the faculty. Faculty members are selected for their empathy and enthusiasm for working with students at the elementary and junior level, as well as for their expertise in a particular discipline. Students and teachers work, learn, play, and have meals together. In the boarding community they also spend weekends together, sharing many vibrant experiences both on and off campus.

Among the 88 faculty members, 3 hold doctoral degrees, 43 hold master's degrees, and 42 hold bachelor's degrees; 32 teachers reside on campus. Twelve dorm parents are directly responsible for the welfare of the boarding students.

Advisers are teachers and administrators who form the nuclei of small groups of 4 to 6 students, both day and boarding. Advisory groups meet at least three times a week. This peer support, combined with the guidance of a concerned and involved adult, makes advisory groups an important source of nurturing for youngsters at Fay. A major responsibility for advisers is communicating with parents.

SECONDARY SCHOOL PLACEMENT

Ensuring a good match between each graduating student and a secondary school is the primary objective in placement. The Director of Secondary School Placement and a second placement counselor work closely with American students, their families, their advisers, coaches, and teachers in identifying the students' needs, strengths, and talents. The Director of the International Student Program provides the same service for Fay's international students. Throughout the application process, the Placement Office provides counsel in selecting and applying to appropriate schools. Schools currently attended by Fay graduates include Berkshire School, Brooks School, Cate School, Choate Rosemary Hall, Concord Academy, Cushing Academy, Deerfield Academy, Emma Willard, Episcopal High School, Governor Dummer Academy, Groton School, Kent School, Lawrence Academy, Lawrenceville School, Loomis Chaffee School, Middlesex School, Milton Academy, Noble and Greenough School, Phillips Andover Academy, Phillips Exeter Academy, Pomfret School, Proctor Academy, Rivers School, St. George's School, St. Mark's School, St. Paul's School, Salisbury School, Suffield Academy, Tabor Academy, Thacher School, Westminster School, and Worcester Academy.

STUDENT BODY AND CONDUCT

Of the 380 students attending Fay, 110 are boarding and 270 are day students. The Upper School numbers 254; the Lower School, 126. Boys make up 55 percent and girls 45 percent of the student population. International students constitute 17 percent of the student body.

At Fay, every effort is made to establish a balance between freedom and responsibility for the young people in its care. Through small advisory groups and the Leadership Program, unstated School rules such as ethical behavior and respect for others are reinforced. Minor misconduct is dealt with by advisers or by the Dean of Students. Where infractions of major School rules are involved, the Discipline Committee, composed of the Dean of Students and 5 faculty members, may convene.

ACADEMIC FACILITIES

The Root Academic Center (1984) houses most of the Upper and Lower School classrooms. The Mars Wing (2001) includes the Learning Center, the media lab, four state-of-the-art science labs, a writing lab, and a multimedia lab. The Reinke Building (1971) contains a large auditorium and houses the Fay Extended Day Program, band room, School Counselor's office, and Summer and Special Programs office. The Picardi Art Center (1987) provides outstanding facilities for art classes, including a darkroom and ceramics studio. The Harris Events Center (1995) is home to Fay's Performing Arts Program and includes five music practice rooms, two music classrooms, a dance studio, and a 400-seat theater.

The School is completely networked and runs almost exclusively on PC technology in each classroom, in the library, the Learning Center, and in three computer labs. In addition, five multimedia carts are outfitted with the equipment necessary to create multimedia presentations, and three mobile laptop labs provide wireless Web connection for full class lessons. The library offers 17,000 volumes and nine computers for student use. The library Web page (http://library.fayschool.org) provides access to a fully automated catalog of Fay holdings, a connection to holdings outside of Fay via the Internet or the CD-ROM Catalogue of Independent Schools in Eastern Massachusetts, a subscription to 10 different databases to support teachers designing lessons and students accomplishing research, and links to many useful Web sites organized by subject and index. The library functions as a key point in the learning experience at Fay, providing students and faculty members with resources for study, research, and pleasure reading. The library program encourages a love of reading and an appreciation of quality literature, equips students with the knowledge and skills to become lifelong learners, and helps ensure that students are effective and responsible users of information and ideas.

BOARDING AND GENERAL FACILITIES

Boarding boys are housed in the Steward Dorm (1978), while girls live on the upper floors of the Dining Room Building (1924), in Webster House (1880), and in East House (circa 1895). Family-style meals are served in the dining room. An infirmary, located in the Dining Room Building, is staffed by registered nurses. Additional campus buildings include Brackett House (1860), home of the admission and development offices; Fay House (1860), the Head of School residence; and the Upjohn Building (1895), currently serving as a multiuse space.

ATHLETICS

Characterized by diversity, spirit, and sportsmanship, Fay's competitive athletics program involves all students and offers a wide range of sports and ability levels each term. Fay's interscholastic teams are noted for the high degree of pride and team spirit they bring with them. Fay's ten athletics fields and eight new tennis courts are in constant use for practices and games during the fall and spring terms, while in warmer weather the pool becomes a popular place to cool off. In snowy weather, the Harlow Gymnasium and the Mars Wrestling Room become the centers of activity, with the ice rinks at the nearby New England Sports Center providing facilities for Fay's hockey teams. Participants in the skiing program enjoy the slopes of SkiWard, a local ski area. Fay hosts annual basketball, wrestling, and tennis tournaments, and many individual athletes and teams participate in tournaments hosted by other schools. The following sports and activities are offered: fall—cross-country, field hockey, football, golf, photography, soccer, and tennis; winter—basketball, dance, drama, fitness, ice hockey, skiing, volleyball, woodworking, and wrestling; and spring—baseball, fitness, golf, lacrosse, softball, squash, tennis, and track.

The School's athletics facilities were greatly enhanced with the completion of the Harlow Gymnasium in 1993. This state-of-the-art facility incorporates four basketball courts, expanded locker room space, team rooms, a wrestling room, a weight room, and a training room.

EXTRACURRICULAR OPPORTUNITIES

Fay's academic program is augmented by a wide choice of extracurricular activities. Dramatic productions and musical groups such as band, bellringers, and chorus offer performance opportunities; aspiring journalists, photographers, and artists work on the yearbook and student newspaper; and activities such as videotaping, woodworking, community service, chess, and computers offer something for everyone. In addition, an 800-square-foot textured rock climbing wall has been added to the state-of-the-art gymnasium. The rock wall, 26 feet in height, provides an ideal setting for climbing, bouldering, and rappelling. Full advantage is taken of the School's proximity to Boston, and visits to museums, sports events, and historic sites take place throughout the year.

DAILY LIFE

Classes are held Monday through Friday in flexible blocks, starting at 8 and ending at 2:30 for all students. Grades 1 and 2 are dismissed at 3. All other students go on to sports, which continue until 3:30 for grades 3 and 4 and 4:30 for grades 5–9. Boarders have free time after sports until a family-style dinner at 6, followed by free time until 7:30 and a study period that ends at 9. Lights-out is between 9:30 and 10, depending on age.

WEEKEND LIFE

Due to the geographic diversity of Fay's boarding community, few boarding students return home on weekends. Boarders look forward to weekends, when the Weekend Coordinator schedules a wide range of activities, including daylong and weekend-long skiing, white-water rafting, and hiking trips; athletics contests; nature trips; attendance at a wide range of cultural events and performances; and visits to amusement and recreational parks, movies, Boston shops, and community service projects.

Families of day students are warmly supportive of the boarders, opening their homes to youngsters for weekends and some holidays. The number of off-campus weekends is not limited, with the exception of a few closed weekends, but permission must be granted by advisers and teachers.

SUMMER PROGRAMS

During the summer months, Fay's campus continues to be active. A six-week summer school offers academic enrichment and review courses in grades 1–9. Students ages 10–15 may live in the school dormitories. The summer school also offers a strong ESL boarding program, which combines English study with opportunities to learn about American culture. Afternoons and weekends are full of fun extracurricular activities such as travel, art, games, computers, and sports options.

In addition to the summer school, an eight-week day camp program is available for local children ages 4–12. The seven-week session combines athletics and the arts in well-supervised activities. A Counselor-in-Training program provides local teenagers with a valuable learning experience.

COSTS AND FINANCIAL AID

Tuition for 2008–09 ranges from $18,150 for day students in grades 1 and 2 to $24,625 for fifth through ninth graders. Tuition for boarding students is $40,300, and tuition for ESL boarding students in the ISP is $47,000. On enrollment, a deposit of $3500 is required for boarding students, $4000 for boarding students in the ISP, and $2000 for day students. Additional fees include $1045 for laundry service (boarders only) and $475 (grades 1–5) or $655 (grades 6–9) for books. The School offers several creative payment plans.

Financial aid is awarded on the basis of need to 10 percent of the student body. Amounts based upon demonstrated need and procedures established by the School and Student Service for Financial Aid range from $1,000 to nearly full tuition. The grants total $925,000 for 2008–09.

ADMISSIONS INFORMATION

Fay School accepts day students for grades 1–9 and boarding students for grades 6–9. The personal requirements for admission include satisfactory evidence of good character, an acceptable record of previous academic work, and the ability and motivation to successfully complete the work at Fay. All applicants must complete the application form and return it to the Director of Admission with the application fee, a transcript, and teacher recommendations. Applicants must visit the School for a personal interview and tour, on weekdays while classes are in session; interested students should call the Admission Office to arrange a time. Candidates for grades 4–9 must take the WISC-IV. Applicants for first grade must be 6 years of age before September 1.

APPLICATION TIMETABLE

Decisions on day student candidates whose folders are complete are announced on March 10. Fay continues to accept qualified candidates after this date until the grades are filled. Wait lists are often established. Decisions on boarding students are made once a candidate's folder is complete, beginning in January. Parents are asked to respond to the acceptance within thirty days. To hold a place for a child, a deposit and enrollment contract must be submitted. Information regarding clothing, course selection, and other pertinent items is sent upon enrollment.

ADMISSIONS CORRESPONDENCE

James Ramsdell '85, Director of Admission
Fay School
Box 9106, 48 Main Street
Southborough, Massachusetts 01772-9106
Phone: 508-485-0100
800-933-2925 (toll-free)
Fax: 508-481-7872
E-mail: fayadmit@fayschool.org
Web site: http://www.fayschool.org

THE FESSENDEN SCHOOL

West Newton, Massachusetts

Type: Boys' boarding and day school
Grades: K–9: Lower School, Kindergarten–4; Middle School, 5–6; Upper School, 7–9
Enrollment: 475
Head of School: Peter P. Drake

THE SCHOOL

The Fessenden School of West Newton, Massachusetts, has enjoyed a long and rich history of providing high-quality education for boys in a supportive yet challenging environment. The School was founded in 1903 by Mr. and Mrs. Frederick J. Fessenden. The founders' original educational philosophy was "to train a boy along the right lines, to teach him how to study and form correct habits of work, and to inculcate principles, which are to regulate his daily conduct and guide his future life." The School adheres to these same principles today. The Fessenden School also recognizes the special requirements of a boy's elementary education experience and focuses on providing that experience in a nurturing environment where a boy can live up to his potential. Intellectual, physical, and emotional development share equal emphasis at Fessenden.

The Fessenden School campus is situated on 41 hilltop acres in a residential community just west of Boston. The School's proximity to the city presents a world of exciting possibilities for year-round activity, including well-known historic sites, first-class music and theater, world-renowned museums, and a multitude of professional and collegiate sports events. The Fessenden campus is convenient to all major highway routes, and Logan International Airport is only a 20-minute drive away.

The Fessenden School is a nonprofit organization. The School's endowment currently stands at $18 million and is supported by alumni and parents, both past and present, through an Annual Fund.

Fessenden's well-established Character Education Program, based on the principles of honesty, compassion, respect, and commitment to academic and athletic excellence, seeks to ensure that every member of the school community is given the support and nurturing he needs to feel secure in his academic, physical, and social ability.

Fessenden holds membership in many academic associations, including the Association of Independent Schools in New England, the National Association of Independent Schools, the Junior Boarding Schools Association, the Secondary School Admission Test Board, and the Massachusetts Association of Nonprofit Schools and Colleges.

ACADEMIC PROGRAMS

The Fessenden School's traditional curriculum is designed to be rigorous yet developmentally appropriate and supportive of each student's learning style, providing him with a foundation of skills that are imperative for the secondary school experience. Each student's needs are carefully considered by his teachers, advisers, and division heads prior to placement in an honors, regular, or moderately paced section. The average class size is 12.

Fessenden's Lower School (K–4) places a heavy emphasis on basic skills in reading, oral and written communication, and mathematics. These areas are complemented with additional work in social studies, FLES (foreign language in elementary school), science, computers, library skills, art, drama, music, sports, and games. A link to Upper School students is maintained through the Big Brother program, peer tutoring, assemblies, and other all-School activities.

In grades 5 and 6, students begin the transition from the self-contained classrooms of the Lower School to the departmentalized structure of the Upper School. Courses in English, math, social studies, geography, science, art, music, and Spanish are required for all Middle School students. Each fifth-grade student is also required to take a reading and study skills course.

The Upper School academic program ensures that each student is properly prepared for the educational programs he will encounter in secondary school. Grades 7–9 focus on the five major academic disciplines of English, history, mathematics, science, and foreign language (Spanish and Latin). Fessenden's commitment to the arts requires each student to choose a class each semester in the fine arts or performing arts. A "help and work" period each day provides additional opportunities for students to consult their teachers on an individual or small-group basis. Students must complete a half-year of computer studies and a course in personal growth and development prior to graduation. In addition, each boy is required to choose from a range of nearly twenty popular electives, including computer studies, student government, theater workshops, art courses at various levels, woodworking, photography, video production, and individual music instruction.

The Fessenden School recognizes that some students may need more specialized help with skill building and therefore offers a Skills Center staffed by professional reading and language specialists. The Skills Center provides individual skills instruction, administers tests, and makes evaluations and recommendations.

Fessenden's English as a second language program (ESL) is offered on both the intermediate and advanced levels, with the goal of mainstreaming students as their English proficiency increases. ESL students are educated using a variety of appropriate teaching resources. Class trips include visits to historic Plymouth, Mystic Seaport, whale watches, Boston's Freedom Trail, Old Sturbridge Village, and the Boston Ballet's production of *The Nutcracker.*

Fessenden's academic year is divided into two semesters. The School acknowledges that a student's effort to learn is as important as standard letter or numerical grades. Teachers give both qualitative and quantitative marks at the middle and end of each semester.

FACULTY AND ADVISERS

The 120 members of Fessenden's dedicated faculty and staff are committed to creating a family-oriented community by serving as teachers, coaches, advisers, dorm parents, and mentors. Seventy-five percent of the faculty and staff members for students in grades 5–9 live on campus, many with families of their own. Fessenden's faculty and staff members hold a combined total of eighty-nine baccalaureate and forty-three advanced degrees. The student-faculty ratio is approximately 6:1.

Each student has his own academic faculty or staff adviser. Advisers foster close relationships with each student, becoming actively involved in all facets of the student's life at school. Each adviser is responsible for communicating to parents all aspects of their sons' experiences at Fessenden.

Peter P. Drake, Headmaster of the Fessenden School, was the Headmaster of the Bement School for fourteen years and then an independent educational consultant for secondary schools and colleges until joining Fessenden. He was educated at Deerfield Academy, University of Virginia, and Boston University.

SECONDARY SCHOOL PLACEMENT

Fessenden seeks to provide each student with the placement guidance needed to ensure a positive secondary school experience. This is achieved by a collaboration between the student and the Director of Placement, advisers, teachers, dorm parents, and coaches. Beginning in the spring of eighth grade, families start selecting an appropriate school based on academic ability, extracurricular activities, and athletic interests. Eighth and ninth grade students are encouraged to take the SSAT preparatory class in English and math. The Placement Director also works with students to teach specific interviewing techniques, including mock interviews. This helps address any placement issues well in advance.

Fessenden graduates have attended a variety of secondary schools, including Avon Old Farms, Belmont Hill, Brooks, Cate School, Choate Rosemary Hall, Cushing, Deerfield, Exeter, Governor's Academy, Holderness, Loomis Chaffee, Middlesex, Noble and Greenough, Phillips Academy, Rivers, Roxbury Latin, Tabor, and Westminster. However, it is ultimately the successful match between student and school that remains essential in the placement process.

STUDENT BODY AND CONDUCT

The Fessenden School seeks boys of solid character who can grow in a supportive environment where a balanced program of academics, athletics, the arts, and social life is vigorously pursued.

Of a total enrollment of 475 students for the academic year 2008–09, 370 are day students and 105 are boarders. Fessenden students come from fifty-eight cities and towns in Massachusetts, seventeen other states, and twelve other countries. International students represent 12 percent of the total student body.

Fessenden's Character Education Program is modeled by its faculty members, who have an extraordinary investment in the boys' care and set guidelines for the students to live by. Rewarding boys for being active and positive contributors within the community in turn places an emphasis on the reinforcement of positive role modeling. Teachers, coaches, and advisers handle disciplinary matters on an individual basis as warranted.

ACADEMIC FACILITIES

Fessenden's state-of-the-art academic building houses twenty-five new classrooms that provide multiple data points, allowing the expanding world of information into each classroom via technology. The campus features a science center, a library, a study hall, two computer centers, a photography lab, a student health center, and a performing arts center that features a theater-size wide-screen projection monitor. The Fessenden School library contains 21,000 volumes, six computers, two digital cameras, a color scanner, and a printer. The School's two computer centers include forty computers, which are networked and have color monitors and an Internet account. Students also have access to more than twenty Power PCs in their math and science classrooms to help integrate the curriculum. There are two art studios with five electric pottery wheels and two kilns, a printmaking machine, and a music center that features two band rehearsal rooms and five individual practice rooms equipped with pianos. The Skills Center contains eight classrooms for one-to-one tutoring.

BOARDING AND GENERAL FACILITIES

Fessenden's boarding students live in homelike dormitories closely supervised by residential faculty members and their families. Dormitories are made up of students in grades 5–8, with proctors who are in grade 9. There are 11 to 19 students per hallway. Students in grade 9 live in two different dormitories. Weekday meals are served family style, with a buffet on weekends.

Students' everyday health-care needs are served at the campus Health Center. Two registered nurses are always available, and a physician makes campus visits several times a week and as needed. Newton-Wellesley Hospital is located only minutes away.

ATHLETICS

The School offers a variety of seasonal athletics for students of every age and ability level. Fessenden's long-standing tradition in sports embodies the philosophy of fair play, sportsmanship, and equal opportunity for all participants. Students may choose from competitive, intramural, or recreational activities each season. Competitive and intramural sports include baseball, basketball, cross-country, football, hockey, lacrosse, soccer, squash, tennis, track and field, and wrestling. Boys may also choose from an exciting range of recreational sports, such as cross-country skiing, fencing, golf, mountain-biking, sailing, and weight lifting and conditioning. The Fessenden School participates in several athletic tournaments each year and also hosts annual soccer, wrestling, and tennis tournaments.

Fessenden completed a state-of-the-art athletic center in spring 2002. The facility houses two basketball courts, a wrestling center with two regulation-size mats, a weight-training suite, and locker rooms for coaches and visiting teams. The facility overlooks Fessenden's six outdoor tennis courts, which are lighted. Rounding out the sports facilities are an indoor hockey rink, thirteen outdoor tennis courts, two outdoor swimming pools, and nine playing fields.

EXTRACURRICULAR OPPORTUNITIES

The Fessenden School provides a variety of opportunities for students to develop leadership skills and exhibit their talents, thus enriching and balancing their academic program. Each year, the theater arts program presents several dramatic and musical productions. Faculty members offer club programs to share specific skills and interests with students, including in-line skating, board games, cooking, floor hockey, billiards, indoor soccer, model building, volleyball, science and aeronautics, and weight lifting.

Fessenden's Student Council is formed by elected officers in grade 9. The Council meets every two weeks for regular business and calls special meetings to discuss important issues. The Student Council has a voice in implementing School rules and planning special events.

DAILY LIFE

Boarding students begin their day with a family-style breakfast. The academic day encompasses eight periods. Athletic activities take place each weekday afternoon. Day students go home after sports; for boarding students, a structured study hall follows. There are also after-dinner study halls and free activities.

WEEKEND LIFE

Fessenden's weekend program is exceptionally full, providing the balance between academic and social life by satisfying the boys' many outside interests. The residential life staff works closely with the residential faculty to offer more than twenty exciting and interesting supervised activities every weekend. A sampling of weekend trips includes college and professional sports events, museum trips, ski outings, movie nights, camping and mountain-biking trips, dances, plays, and concerts. The Fessenden School holds no religious affiliation but can provide transportation to services for all faiths.

An indispensable aspect of Fessenden's boarding life is the host family program. This program connects all new families with a family that currently has a child in the same division. A boarder's evenings, weekends, or holidays can be spent with a host family, creating friendships that can last long after their Fessenden experience is over.

SUMMER PROGRAMS

The Fessenden School's summer ESL program provides five weeks of immersion in the English language and American culture. This program is open to international boys and girls, ages 10 to 16.

The classes are offered at beginning, intermediate, and advanced levels and are designed to develop competent conversational skills and expand English vocabulary. Classes are small to enable every student to participate fully.

Fessenden's summer ESL program also offers films, videos, fun projects, and games, reinforcing classroom work and actively engaging students in the learning process. After-school and weekend trips bring students to such sites as Plymouth Plantation, Martha's Vineyard, Mystic Seaport, and Harvard University.

COSTS AND FINANCIAL AID

Day student tuition ranges from $22,250 to $29,000. Boarding tuition ranges from $37,000 to $42,700. Additional charges may be applicable to all students for supplies and laundry services.

The Fessenden School awards approximately $1 million in financial assistance to more than 13 percent of the student body each academic year. Scholarships are awarded on the basis of need.

ADMISSIONS INFORMATION

Catalogs, applications, and financial aid material may be obtained by contacting Fessenden's Admissions Office.

APPLICATION TIMETABLE

Admissions inquiries are welcome at any time. The application deadline for day students is February 1. Boarding student applications are processed on a rolling admissions basis.

ADMISSIONS CORRESPONDENCE

Caleb W. Thomson '79, Director of Admissions
The Fessenden School
250 Waltham Street
West Newton, Massachusetts 02465-1750

Phone: 617-630-2300
Fax: 617-630-2303
E-mail: admissions@fessenden.org
Web site: http://www.fessenden.org

HILLSIDE SCHOOL

Marlborough, Massachusetts

Type: Boys' boarding and day school
Grades: 5–9
Enrollment: 145
Head of School: Mr. David Z. Beecher

THE SCHOOL

Since 1901, Hillside School has continued its mission of working with boys in their formative years. Students work to develop academic and social skills while building confidence and maturity. Hillside provides small classes instructed by talented educators in a community that emphasizes personal integrity and mutual respect and is dedicated to maintaining diversity.

Hillside is situated on 200 acres of fields, forest, and ponds in Marlborough, Massachusetts. Marlborough is located just 30 miles from Boston, 70 miles from Hartford, 45 miles from Providence, and 3½ hours from New York City. This location is convenient for families, but it is also important to the School's educational and recreational programs. School field trips are bountiful and weekend activity opportunities are endless. The visual arts and athletic programs at Hillside are strong and offer the boys opportunities to succeed and grow. Both boarding and day students take advantage of a high-quality residential life that is supportive, active, and exciting.

Unique to Hillside are the working farm and farmhouse dorm, tutorials available for students who need remediation and organizational skills, a daily and weekly recognition system conveying to students clear expectations regarding social and academic behavior, and excellent programs for students with minor learning disabilities or ADD/ADHD.

Hillside seeks students of average to above-average intelligence who are looking for a supportive, structured school. Family involvement is not only encouraged, it is a critical part of the School's program. Hillside's graduates matriculate at leading independent secondary boarding schools as well as local parochial and public high schools.

Hillside School is a nonprofit institution and is governed by a 23-member Board of Trustees, which includes Hillside alumni, leading citizens of Marlborough and nearby communities, and other individuals with a commitment to the School's educational mission. The School has an endowment of $4 million, with an operating budget of $6 million. Annual Giving for 2007–08 was $524,363. The physical plant is valued at more than $3 million.

Hillside School is a member of the National Association of Independent Schools, the Association of Independent Schools in New England, and the Junior Boarding Schools Association.

ACADEMIC PROGRAMS

Hillside School recognizes the importance of committed faculty members, small classes, and a highly structured program as factors in developing the student's self-confidence, self-esteem, individual thinking, and decision-making ability. Students in grades 5 and 6 learn in self-contained classrooms, with a core curriculum consisting of mathematics, language arts, social studies, and reading and specialized instruction in art, science, and music.

In grades 7–9, the curriculum includes English, history, science, math, studio art, music, farming, and French, Spanish, or Latin.

The new Honors Seminar Program at Hillside School is for eighth and ninth graders. The boys are selected by faculty members to challenge top students and to better prepare them for competitive secondary schools. In 2006, seminars were The Writing of Mathematics and The Myths of the Settling of the American West.

Responding to concerns about global conflict, the Peace Studies course and curriculum are allowing students to review concepts and learn skills for promoting peace within society. Also, starting with the 2007–08 academic year, Hillside incorporated a special health and wellness focus across the entire curriculum to enhance students' well-being and development. For the 2008–09 academic year, the Asian Studies course informs seventh-grade students about a region of the world that is increasingly important to their daily lives.

The leadership program is required of all grades, with the goal of providing a forum for students to learn and discuss leadership skills and teamwork with their peers through hands-on activities.

Other programs were developed in recent years to help meet the needs of students who have been diagnosed with attention deficit hyperactivity disorder and/or mild learning disabilities. These students are in an environment that provides understanding and support so that they may attain a level of academic and personal success.

Hillside establishes an early appreciation for the importance of organizing time and materials. This is accomplished by teaching and reinforcing such study skills as keeping a master organizational notebook in which "two-column" note-taking strategies are utilized as well as test preparation and active reading skills. The curriculum is reinforced by tutorial sessions in which study skills are developed and enhanced in small groups. Each student is provided with instruction in math, science, English, history, skills for life, and writing. French, Spanish, and Latin are offered to seventh-, eighth-, and ninth-grade students. Music and studio art are also taught.

The tutorial program aids students who are having difficulty in a particular subject or need study skills that can be applied to all subjects.

The school year is divided into three trimesters. Students are evaluated midway through each marking period in detail by their teachers and advisers to ensure that each student's academic progress is closely monitored throughout the academic year. Parents receive student report cards three times during the academic year.

FACULTY AND ADVISERS

David Beecher, Head of the School, is a graduate of the Choate School and Lake Forest College. He served as an English and history teacher at Berkshire School as well as a coach, adviser, and dorm parent. Mr. Beecher also served Berkshire as Dean of Students and as an assistant in Admissions and Development. He also served as Director of Admission and Financial Aid at Fay School and at Wilbraham and Monson Academy.

The faculty consists of 45 full-time members; 28 reside on campus. Three counselors are available throughout the week. All 45 faculty members have bachelor's degrees and 10 have master's degrees. Faculty members and students have their meals together, live in the dormitories, and spend recreational time together on the weekends. All faculty members serve as student advisers and meet with their advisees three times per week. The majority of faculty members coach at least one sport. Faculty members use patience, kindness, and empathy as they work alongside students.

SECONDARY SCHOOL PLACEMENT

The Director of Secondary Placement assists students and their families in selecting and applying to schools that best match a student's needs. The needs of each student are identified by the faculty members, advisers, coaches, and families at the beginning of the application process.

Schools recently attended by Hillside graduates include Brewster Academy, Chapel Hill–Chauncey Hall School, Cheshire Academy, Dublin School, Holderness School, Lawrence Academy, the Marvelwood School, Middlesex School, New Hampton School, Pomfret School, St. Andrew's School (Rhode Island), St. Mark's School, Tilton School, Vermont Academy, and Wilbraham and Monson Academy.

STUDENT BODY AND CONDUCT

The 2008–09 student population of 145 students consists of 90 boarding students and 55 day students. These boys are also representative of Hillside's growing diversity, with 30 percent being students of color, 30 percent receiving financial aid, 50 percent participating in the tutorial program, and 20 percent being international students. There is a standard dress code for all students.

Hillside School embraces the five core values of honesty, compassion, respect, determination, and fun as the guiding principles for overseeing student behavior and achievement. Shades of Hillside Blue is a system based on these values that is designed to give students and families comprehensive and timely feedback about a boy's overall performance at school. During a biweekly period, boys are evaluated in all areas of School life using three shades of blue. Royal blue, the School color, signifies that a boy consistently meets established expectations. Sky blue signifies that a boy meets expectations with some assistance, and navy blue indicates that a boy needs frequent guidance in attempting to meet expectations. Each student has an adviser who reviews this feedback with the boy and his family. The adviser works in conjunction with the Dean of Students and other faculty members in helping boys to set and meet appropriate individual goals on an ongoing basis. Parental involvement with the Hillside system is sought and greatly encouraged so that a clear, consistent message is given to students. The Dean of Students is charged with overseeing residential life, counseling, and conduct.

ACADEMIC FACILITIES

The academic hub of the School is centered in the Stevens Wing of the new Academic and Health Center. The Stevens Wing contains fourteen classrooms, WiFi, computer access, and the science laboratory. Linked to the Stevens Wing is the Tracy gymnasium/auditorium. The student center houses the dining room; administrative, admissions, and business offices; and the newly expanded Wick Tutorial Center.

The much-anticipated Academic and Health Center opened its doors in March 2008. This newest campus facility includes fitness rooms; a state-of-the-art health center staffed by a registered nurse; a wrestling/multipurpose room; nine new classrooms, three of which are science labs; and offices for health and wellness and counseling programs.

BOARDING AND GENERAL FACILITIES

The Messman-Saran Library is located in Drinkwater Hall. Students are housed in six dormitories: two new houses—Mack House and Maher House—and Williams, Whittemore, Matthies, and the Farm Dorm. Living in each house are at least 2 faculty members and their respective families. Additional campus buildings include Lowell House, the Headmaster's residence; Tipper House, residence of the Dean of Athletics; Emerson House, residence of the Assistant Headmaster; and the Patten House and other buildings on the farm.

ATHLETICS

Hillside School offers an extensive athletics program and competes with other junior boarding and day schools in the area. The School population is small enough that every student is able to participate. The boys are taught basic skills and participate in a sports program that includes baseball, basketball, cross-country, golf, ice hockey, lacrosse, sailing, skiing, soccer, tennis, track and field, wrestling, and yoga. The School also offers an outdoor program called Eco-Team, which features hiking, canoeing, and working with more than 50 animals on the farm. Fitness activities, weight lifting, Ultimate Frisbee, and volleyball are part of the intramural program.

EXTRACURRICULAR OPPORTUNITIES

The students and the faculty members place great emphasis on service to others. Three times per year, students participate in community service days. In this program, students visit local nursing homes and spend time with the elderly, participate in community social service projects, and assist in a volunteer program for local residents.

Students participate in woodworking, painting, plays, poetry contests, and student government. They can volunteer to be on the yearbook staff. Students help plan and execute a Farm Day harvest festival, Diversity Day, Spring Fling, and a Daughters of the American Revolution Day.

DAILY LIFE

During the school week, students arise at 6:30 a.m. to dress and to clean their rooms before breakfast at 7:15. Classes begin with homeroom at 8 a.m. and end at 3 p.m. Students meet with their adviser three times each week and attend community meetings five times each week. Class periods are 50 minutes long. All students participate in art, music, and the leadership program as part of the academic day. Time is set aside each day from 3 to 5 p.m. for athletics. Dinner is at 5:45, and there is a supervised study hall, located in the main classroom building, from 6:30 to 8. Bedtime varies from 9 to 10 p.m., depending on the age of the student.

WEEKEND LIFE

A wide variety of activities are offered to boarders each weekend. The School takes full advantage of the surrounding area, including Boston and Providence, with day trips to historic sites and museums. There are evening and weekend trips to sports events, live theater, exhibits, movies, and malls. A pond, located on the farm, provides opportunities for fishing, swimming, canoeing, and winter ice-skating. Students can go roller-skating, skiing, and bowling, all within a few miles of the School.

Many families of day students welcome boarders to their homes for weekends, and a day student may spend the night at the School, depending on the activity for that weekend. Weekend permission to go home is granted to seven-day boarders if they have attained minimum standards in academics and if they have no school commitments. Transportation is arranged after permission is given by parents.

COSTS AND FINANCIAL AID

Tuition for 2008–09 is $45,750 for a seven-day boarding student, $41,900 for a five-day boarder, and $26,900 for a day student. Hillside offers tuition payment plans. Every student has a personal account set up in the Business Office from which he receives weekly pocket money. Money can be withdrawn for special needs as long as it is approved by the Dean of Students. Funding for this account varies per year.

Thirty percent of the current student population receives more than $920,000 in financial aid. To apply for tuition assistance, a candidate must complete the Parents' Financial Statement (PFS) from the School and Student Service for Financial Aid (SSS).

ADMISSIONS INFORMATION

The Admissions Office goes to great lengths to admit a diverse group of boys from a broad range of socioeconomic and racial backgrounds. Hillside seeks boys who are in need of a sheltered, structured, and nurturing learning environment. The School can accommodate both traditional learners and those with learning differences and/or attention problems. The boys are generally average to superior in intelligence yet have not reached their full potential. They perform best in an environment that is personalized, supportive, and challenging.

APPLICATION TIMETABLE

Parents interested in Hillside School may write, call, or e-mail the School directly for information. Enrollment is possible throughout the year, provided an opening exists. Decisions and notifications are made once an applicant's file is complete. There is a $50 application fee.

ADMISSIONS CORRESPONDENCE

Kristen Naspo, Director
Admissions and Financial Aid
Hillside School
Robin Hill Road
Marlborough, Massachusetts 01752
Phone: 508-485-2824
Fax: 508-485-4420
E-mail: admissions@hillsideschool.net
Web site: http://www.hillsideschool.net

LINDEN HILL SCHOOL

Northfield, Massachusetts

Type: Boarding and day school for boys with dyslexia or other language-based learning differences
Grades: Ages 9–15 ungraded, along with formal freshman year
Enrollment: 45
Head of School: James A. McDaniel, Headmaster and Summer Program Director

THE SCHOOL

Linden Hill School is an ungraded boarding and day school for boys between the ages of 9 and 15 with language-based learning differences such as dyslexia, ADHD, and others. Located in the town of Northfield (population 3,100), between the Berkshires of Massachusetts and the Green Mountains of Vermont, the School is accessible via Interstate 91. Interstate buses serve the nearby town of Greenfield, Amtrak service is available in Springfield, and major airlines serve Bradley International Airport near Springfield. The 140-acre campus of fields and woods overlooks the Connecticut River. The School's location offers opportunities for skiing and many other outdoor activities.

The School was founded in 1961 to provide a family atmosphere in which the Orton-Gillingham phonics approach could be implemented for the remediation of dyslexic boys. The original dairy farm estate was renovated to provide a country setting.

Today, through a multisensory approach, Linden Hill helps boys of inquisitive mind and good intellect strengthen areas of weakness by establishing a sound language foundation. Each student receives daily remedial language instruction tailored to meet his needs. The School endeavors to awaken creative and athletic talents through extracurricular offerings.

A nonprofit institution, Linden Hill School is governed by a self-perpetuating Board of Trustees, including parents and alumni, which meets three times annually. The School-owned plant is valued at $4 million.

Linden Hill is accredited by the New England Association of Schools and Colleges. It holds memberships in the Association of Independent Schools of New England, the National Association of Schools, the Junior Boarding School Association, the Association of Boarding Schools, and the Pioneer Valley Independent Schools Association.

ACADEMIC PROGRAMS

Linden Hill employs a highly individualized approach to crafting a learning remediation program for each student. The Orton-Gillingham method of language training is at the heart of Linden Hill's curriculum. The Academic Program runs from early September to late May. It includes a Thanksgiving recess, Christmas and spring vacations, and an all-school spring trip. Each year, students study a specific topic and then, with their teachers, take a theme-based trip to further explore that topic. In recent years the school has traveled to Mexico, Florida, and Washington, D.C.

Classes are held five days a week and range in size from a teacher-student ratio of 2:1 in Orton-Gillingham language training sessions to 5:1, on average, in other courses. Each academic day, students participate in language training, literature and composition, science, math, and history. Additional courses include health education, social pragmatics, music, drama, study skills, current events, art, woodshop, and computers. The evening study hall is a time for supervised preparation for classes with faculty members providing individualized assistance.

Narrative reports, grades, and/or standardized test results are sent to parents six times per year. Individual tests are administered at the beginning and end of each year to aid in placement and measure progress. Standardized tests, such as the Woodcock Johnson III, are administered to all students twice yearly.

FACULTY AND ADVISERS

The Headmaster, most of the full-time faculty members and their families, and additional support staff live on campus. All instructors are trained in the Orton-Gillingham method and are experienced in the teaching of students with learning differences. They hold baccalaureate and master's degrees from such institutions as Amherst College, American University, Boston College, Brown, Columbia University, Keene State, Kaplan, Lesley University, Northeastern, Temple, and the Universities of Maryland, Massachusetts, North Carolina, Tampa, and Virginia. Each student has a faculty adviser, who mentors him academically and socially and stays in regular communication with his parents.

The support staff includes a licensed clinical social worker, counselors, an affiliated psychiatrist, a full-time registered nurse, and occupational, speech, and language therapists. Northfield Mount Hermon School Health Services are available, with a 24-hour clinic.

SECONDARY SCHOOL PLACEMENT

At the appropriate time, Linden Hill counsels each boy in the selection of a secondary school. Linden Hill students go on to a variety of schools, including Brewster Academy, Cushing Academy, Dublin School, Eagle Hill, Forman, Gow, The Gunnery, Hoosac, Kents Hill, Kildonan, Landmark, Lawrence Academy, Marvelwood, Proctor Academy, St. Andrew's, South Kent, Trinity Pawling, and Vermont Academy. Some students return to their home schools if the programs are appropriate to their needs.

STUDENT BODY AND CONDUCT

Linden Hill is a national and international school for boys age 9–15 with dyslexia or other language-based learning differences. The School serves boys with average to above-average intelligence who are developmentally delayed academically or socially. Over the years, students have come from most of the fifty states and several other countries, including those in Europe, Asia, and North and South America. The School's values of kindness, helpfulness, and cooperation are instilled in each boy, and each is expected to comport himself as a gentleman. A clear set of age-appropriate rules and a good daily routine provide security in knowing what is expected of them as they grow and learn.

ACADEMIC FACILITIES

The main school building is the former Bennett farmhouse (circa 1835). Its ground floor houses the School's kitchen and food storage area, offices, private meeting rooms, dining rooms, the Reception Room, and the Admission Office.

Haskell Hall contains classrooms, an art room, a library, a greenhouse, and a large room that serves as both study hall and auditorium.

The Duplex extension (2001) has classrooms, science laboratories, a technology center, and a wood shop.

The Hunt Gymnasium (1998), has a full-size hardwood floor basketball court and a climbing wall.

White Cottage (1999) connects with the Headmaster's residence and houses the administrative offices, nurse's office, infirmary, and school store. There is another faculty residence, a maple-sugar shack, and several small buildings on the campus as well.

BOARDING AND GENERAL FACILITIES

There are three dormitories that provide students with a nurturing, "home away from home" environment.

The Bennett Farmhouse extension (2003), the School's latest million-dollar improvement, has three floors. The top floor is a dormitory with three connecting faculty residences. The main dining room, with expansive views of the surrounding valley, is located on the middle floor, and there is a student activity center on the lower level.

The second floor of the Duplex (2001) is a dormitory for 16 students, with three connecting faculty residences.

The Hayes Hillside Dormitory (1971) provides housing for 18 students, with three connecting faculty residences.

ATHLETICS

Linden Hill teams compete with those of other schools in the Pioneer Valley in basketball, golf, soccer, softball, tennis, and wrestling. On weekends, boys choose to participate in a variety of indoor and outdoor activities, including art and woodworking projects, board games, making maple syrup, pool, reading, skating, skiing, snowboarding, table tennis, and various trips. Bicycling, cross-country skiing, flag football, hockey, horseback riding, ice skating, swimming, and track and field are offered on a recreational basis. These programs promote good motor-coordination skills and help build self-confidence.

EXTRACURRICULAR OPPORTUNITIES

Movies and concerts are provided at the School. Other extracurricular activities and events include drama, music lessons, outdoor recreation, wall climbing, and river rafting. Weekend activities include trips to nearby towns for movies, fairs and other community and sporting events, downhill and cross-country skiing, snowboarding, hiking, and rollerblading. The students also attend area cultural events at nearby schools, colleges, towns, and cities. All boys have the opportunity to attend area religious services each week.

DAILY LIFE

The daily schedule, from 6:45 a.m. to lights out at 9:30 p.m., includes seven academic periods, morning jobs, meals, athletics, free time, a 30-minute supervised free-reading session, and an 80-minute evening study hall. Each academic day, students participate in language training, literature and composition, science, math, history, and electives, including health education, art, wood shop, or computers. The structured-reading period fosters independent reading for pleasure or provides an opportunity for extra read-aloud groups. The evening study hall is a time for supervised preparation for classes. Faculty members provide individualized assistance during both of these periods and at other times by arrangement.

SUMMER PROGRAMS

The coeducational Linden Hill Summer Program is a combination of academics and remediation in the mornings and traditional camp activities during afternoons, evenings, and weekends. The 2009 program lasts from July 2 to August 1.

COSTS AND FINANCIAL AID

In 2008–09, tuition, room, and board total $51,800. Day student tuition is $31,900. Extras, including the technology fee, athletic clothing, laundry, haircuts, allowance, and other personal items, amount to approximately $2000.

Under the provisions of Public Law 94-142, boys may be eligible for state funding of the cost of a Linden Hill School education. In addition, the cost of attending the School may qualify as a medical expense.

ADMISSIONS INFORMATION

Linden Hill School enrolls bright, inquisitive, language-disabled or dyslexic boys, ages 9–15, who have become frustrated at their own shortcomings and past failures. Boys are admitted on the basis of previous academic records, teacher references, academic evaluations, and a personal interview. The School has a rolling admission policy, which permits students to enter throughout the academic year, provided there is space available.

Linden Hill does not discriminate on the basis of race, color, religion, or national or ethnic origin in the admission of students, the employment of faculty and staff members, or the administration of its educational programs and policies.

APPLICATION TIMETABLE

Applications are accepted throughout the year, and midyear enrollment is possible if vacancies exist. A $5800 deposit, applicable toward tuition, is due upon acceptance.

ADMISSIONS CORRESPONDENCE

Linden Hill School
154 South Mountain Road
Northfield, Massachusetts 01360
Phone: 413-498-2906
866-498-2906 (toll-free)
Fax: 413-498-2908
E-mail: admissions@lindenhs.org
Web site: http://www.lindenhs.org

NORTH COUNTRY SCHOOL

Lake Placid, New York

Type: Coeducational boarding elementary school
Grades: 4–9
Enrollment: 88
Head of School: David Hochschartner

THE SCHOOL

The student body numbered 6 children when Walter and Leonora Clark started North Country School in 1938. Because construction of their new school building had been delayed, this tiny band of children and adults took temporary shelter on the property in a thin-walled summer-camp building that had neither heat nor electricity. Years later, the Clarks delighted in telling these stories about those early days: borrowing a wood stove from an obliging neighbor, hanging blankets over the windows, and breaking ice in kitchen water buckets. Thus North Country School began with children learning lessons about overcoming unexpected difficulties with energy, cooperation, and good humor.

The 200-acre campus, which is located in the Adirondack High Peaks, includes a working farm, organic gardens, and lakeshore and is abutted by wilderness land. Sharing in the daily chores necessary to the maintenance of the School and farm has always been at the core of a child's experience at North Country. The Clarks believed that real responsibilities fostered feelings of purpose and self-worth in children. The school they envisaged was one in which all the experiences of each day, both in the classroom and out, would have the power to teach. That same belief had informed the founding of Camp Treetops seventeen years earlier on the same site, a project in which the Clarks also participated and which to this day complements the School program, making North Country School–Camp Treetops (NCS-CTT) one of the few truly year-round communities for children in the country.

Today, North Country School–Camp Treetops is overseen by a Board of Trustees, who meet four times a year on the campus so that they may visit classes, talk with students and staff members, and advance the institution's Long Range Plan. Gifts to the institution in 2007–08 totaled approximately $715,000, not including capital campaign contributions.

The institution is accredited by the New York State Association of Independent Schools and the American Camping Association and is a member of the Secondary School Admission Test Board, the Educational Records Bureau, and the National Association of Independent Schools.

ACADEMIC PROGRAMS

North Country School was founded on the dictum of John Dewey that "the educative process is fired and sustained by the impulse that comes from the desires, interests, and purposes of the pupil." The School structures children's study of the traditional school subjects but always encourages children to follow their own interests as they emerge. The School believes that all children are in some way gifted and creates a teaching and learning environment that is designed to find and develop those gifts. Education at North Country is a hands-on as well as a conceptual, social, and aesthetic matter. No summative grades are awarded; instead, teachers write comprehensive reports on each child's work twice a year. Ninth graders do receive course grades for their high school transcripts.

Learning environments are highly enriched with manipulative materials and resources. There is one computer for every 4 students, and students are taught how to use the Internet for information retrieval and global conversation. Some classes are taught by 2 or 3 teachers—1 as lead teacher and the others as coaches.

Science and math classes utilize the farm and mountain environment in their curriculum as well as problem-solving techniques that were recently endorsed by the National Council of Teachers of Mathematics.

FACULTY AND ADVISERS

The Head of North Country School–Camp Treetops is David Hochschartner, a graduate of Union College and the Klingenstein Center at Columbia University Teachers College. Mr. Hochschartner has served as the Director of the Presidio Hill School in San Francisco, California, and as Assistant Director of Burgundy Farm Country Day School in Alexandria, Virginia. He has been an instructor at Colorado Outward Bound School, has served as a coach and blind-racer guide for the U.S. Disabled Ski Team, and has an extensive background in outdoor sports.

The faculty members divide their time among teaching, coaching, tutoring, and the outdoors, where much of the School's program occurs year-round. Though many of the faculty members are experts and hold degrees in a particular subject area, they are primarily generalists who are prepared to work with children in all aspects of North Country School's program. A Faculty Enrichment Fund has been established to support summer study among the faculty, and time is taken before school and during the children's vacation periods for workshops and new-program development.

The staff includes a school nurse and a licensed social counselor. The Adirondack Medical Center is 20 minutes from the School.

SECONDARY SCHOOL PLACEMENT

The ninth-grade curriculum at North Country School includes a directed program in planning for transition. Students examine themselves, their interests and skills, and their aspirations as a basis for thinking about their transition to secondary school. They receive instruction and practice in writing essays as well as in interviewing and evaluating schools.

Parents are brought into the process of school selection at the end of the seventh-grade year and stay in contact with the Secondary School Placement Director from then on.

Schools attended by North Country School graduates include Buxton School, Cushing Academy, Darrow School, Dublin School, Emma Willard School, Gould Academy, High Mowing School, Knox School, Masters School, New Hampton School, Northfield Mount Hermon School, Northwood School, Orme School, Phillips Academy (Andover), Proctor Academy, Putney School, Stony Brook School, Tilton School, and Vermont Academy.

STUDENT BODY AND CONDUCT

Of the 88 children enrolled in 2008–09, 65 were boarders and 23 were day students or faculty children. This student community included 40 girls and 48 boys from nineteen states and eight other countries. The children ranged in age from 9 to 15.

Although North Country School is in many ways a highly structured community, it is also an informal one where everyone is on a first-name basis. Respect for one another is a key prerequisite for the success of the School community and is achieved through conversation and care rather than authority.

Candy, junk food, and television are not allowed except on special occasions. Children who feel the need to test limits do so with candy rather than other substances.

The School believes in the direct arbitration of disputes between children by an adult. Houseparents are regularly in touch with the parents of their charges. When a problem exists academically, socially, or personally, conversation about it begins early and parents are asked to participate in its solution if appropriate.

ACADEMIC FACILITIES

Most classes are held in one building, which was built in 1940 and has since been significantly modernized. Windows are large and rooms sunny; there are slides by three of the staircases. The art, ceramics, weaving, woodworking, and photography studio areas are contiguous and occupy the lower level of the Main Building. A variety of dance, theater, and music classes are held in the spacious, post and beam performing arts building, built in 2001.

The barn, greenhouse, and sugar house are also used for teaching at various times in the year. The library, a bright and many-windowed space, contains 5,000 volumes and is filled with comfortable nooks and crannies for reading as well as state-of-the-art computer retrieval and CD-ROM facilities.

BOARDING AND GENERAL FACILITIES

Students live in one of seven "houses" with resident houseparents. There are no more than 12 boarding students to a house. Genders and ages are mixed much as they would be in a family, and most houseparents have young children of their own who complete the family circle. Two other adults are assigned to each house as well, so that there is always plenty of coverage and the 1:3 adult-child ratio is maintained. Houseparents oversee reading period and homework for the younger students. Eighth and ninth graders attend a supervised study hall in the main building. An evening snack is often prepared by a houseparent and 1–2 children. Younger children are tucked into bed and often read to before going to sleep.

ATHLETICS

Part of North Country School's educational philosophy is to encourage cooperation rather than competition; this is reflected in the School's athletics and recreation program. While some soccer and basketball games are played against local schools and North Country School's ski teams compete throughout the winter, the emphasis is on lifelong sports, free-form games, and play and mastery.

Children may have riding classes once a week in the fall and spring. Children ski on the School's own ski hill and on adjacent cross-country trails. They ski each Tuesday afternoon at Whiteface Mountain and take advantage of Lake Placid's Olympic ski-jumping, bobsled, and luge venues one or two evenings a week throughout the winter. Children sled, toboggan, build snow caves, and wee-bob most afternoons on the hill by the School's lake. Students also enjoy ice skating at the Olympic speed-skating oval in town and on the School's ponds.

A major activity at North Country School is mountain climbing. Many children aim during their years at NCS-CTT to become Adirondack '46ers. There are expeditions nearly every weekend throughout the year, many on snowshoes. There is also a climbing wall in the main building that prepares children for more technical climbs in the out-of-doors. Dave's Crag, North Country's on-site climbing area, is 40-feet high by 250-feet wide and has twenty-five different routes ranging from beginner to advanced.

EXTRACURRICULAR OPPORTUNITIES

The school year is built around a number of all-School special events, many of which date back fifty years. For Halloween, children make their own costumes for an evening of festivities, including a senior-run spook house and a carnival.

The fall harvests are followed by Thanksgiving, which is attended by the children's families and at which the harvest is served. A concert and all-School performance follow.

The winter holiday celebration spans a week of special meals and treats as children go from one house to another and from one faculty residence to another.

Valentine's Day is again a time for creative manufacture and celebration, as are Box Dinners later in the spring. Mountain Cakes, a monthlong escapade of spring mountaineering, is capped off by a big awards dinner, when each house is given a cake whose dimensions reflect the number of miles collectively climbed.

All children study music formally and many informally as well. Sunday dinner may be a special occasion where children dress up and where the meal is followed by a student performance, often of music.

There is a requirement that all children learn to ride, ski, go on at least one overnight a term, and climb Cascade Mountain. A mounted drill team performs in the spring, and there are several horseback expeditions during the fall and spring.

Spring is maple sugar harvest time. The children split wood, gather sap, run the evaporator, and can more than 100 gallons of syrup each year.

A student newspaper and literary journal, a chorus, musical ensembles, and various student-created activities round out the extracurricular program.

DAILY LIFE

Children with barn chores are awakened at 6:30, others at 7 for building chores. All meals are served family-style. Breakfast is at 8, except on weekends, when the day begins a little later. Classes follow at 8:30 Monday through Friday and run through 3 p.m., with a break for lunch at 12:15. There is a 15-minute "council" right after lunch at which announcements are made, afternoon activities planned, recognitions and awards given, and an occasional story told. After lunch, older students choose from a substantial list of elective courses, including photography, wood shop, dance, theater, chorus, and individual music lessons. Sports follow, with various athletic opportunities, depending upon the season. Following sports, children return to their houses to relax and wind down with friends and houseparents before dinner. Occasionally, there are open houses in one living unit or another or at the Head's house. Wednesdays begin with a town meeting and end with an afternoon and evening of house-related activities, including a home-cooked meal.

Dinner is at 6; following that, younger children go to their houses for reading period, study time, and an evening in their houses until bedtime at 8:30. Older children remain in the building for study hall. Bedtime for them is 9:30.

WEEKEND LIFE

Weekends are nonacademic and involve field trips, hikes, sailing, and water activities in the fall and spring as well as games, horseback riding, fort building, off-campus winter competitions, sledding, skating, various homemade entertainments, dances, and free play. Ice cream is served on Saturday nights and followed by a dance or an all-school activity. Children never leave the campus unsupervised but often go 2 or 3 at a time with a faculty member to work on a town-related project, buy fish for the aquarium, get a bicycle fixed, or go in larger groups for an occasional movie.

SUMMER PROGRAMS

North Country School and Camp Treetops are seasonal expressions of the same philosophy. Camp Treetops, which was founded in 1921, provides a seven-week program that, with the exception of the academic component, very much mirrors the School. Children from age 8 to 14 participate in the regular session and children from 14 to 17 in Treetops Expeditions—four- to five-week trips that involve a variety of activities, including hiking, kayaking, cycling, and community service.

COSTS AND FINANCIAL AID

Student tuition for 2008–09 was $46,900. This fee covers such costs as textbooks, art materials, laundry service, field trips, and all ski and recreational passes. ESL is provided at an additional fee.

Financial aid is provided to approximately 35 percent of the students enrolled, the average grant being $18,000. Eligibility for financial aid is based upon the recommendation of the School Scholarship Service and requires submission of a copy of the applicant family's IRS filing for the previous year.

ADMISSIONS INFORMATION

North Country School looks to enroll children who are capable of using the School and the community to their advantage and who are also able to give to others from their own lives. The School is particularly successful with gifted children and children with variant learning styles. A decision to accept is based upon a child's school records, conversations with the child's parents, recommendations from those who have taught the child, the results of Wechsler Intelligence Scale for Children, and an interview with the School administrators. (The interview is occasionally waived for foreign-service families.)

APPLICATION TIMETABLE

Applications to North Country School–Camp Treetops are considered on a rolling admissions basis; midyear enrollment is possible.

ADMISSIONS CORRESPONDENCE

Director of Admissions
North Country School–Camp Treetops
4382 Cascade Road
Lake Placid, New York 12946
Phone: 518-523-9329
Fax: 518-523-4858
E-mail: admissions@nct.org
Web site: http://www.nct.org

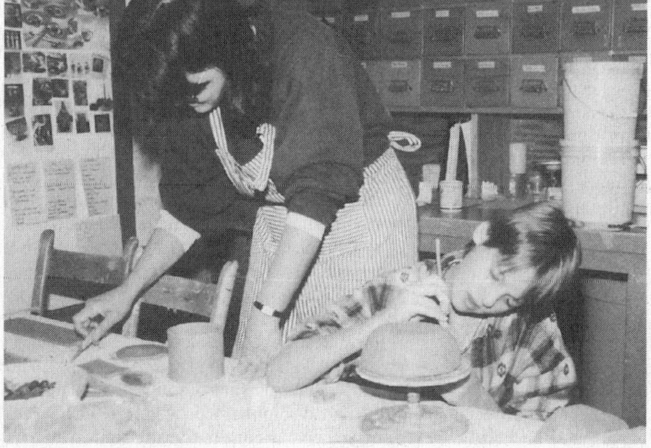

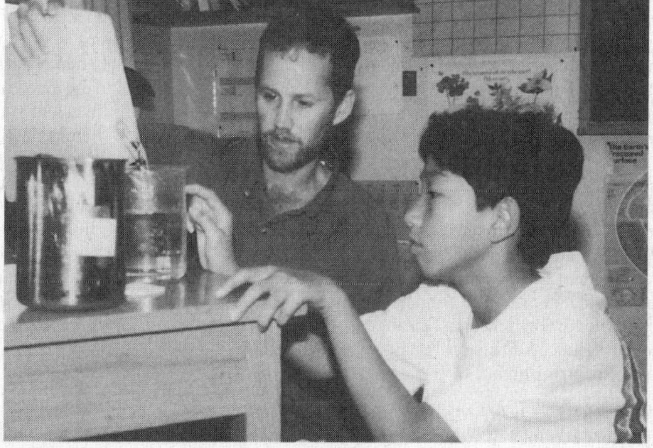

THE RECTORY SCHOOL

Pomfret, Connecticut

Type: Coeducational junior boarding (5–9) and day (K–9) school
Grades: K–9
Enrollment: 236
Head of School: Thomas F. Army Jr., Headmaster

THE SCHOOL

At The Rectory School, students thrive through individualized attention and instruction. The School identifies and understands each student's unique learning style. This focus on developing individual talents also permeates its athletics and extracurricular and arts programs. Rectory's strategy encourages the spark in its students that ignites their desire to excel.

The Rectory School was founded in 1920 by the Rev. Frank H. Bigelow and his wife, Mabel. In its earliest stages, the School was run out of the Bigelows' home, the rectory of Christ Church in Pomfret. The Bigelows instituted the Individualized Instruction Program (IIP), which became the model for many junior boarding schools. Although the School has grown considerably since its birth, its mission has remained constant. The Rectory School seeks to provide for its students an educational and social climate in which individuals, whatever their strengths and weaknesses, can develop their intellectual, ethical, physical, and social being as fully as possible. The School continues to offer an innovative combination of classic academic traditions and one-to-one instruction in a community setting. The U.S. Department of Education bestowed its coveted Blue Ribbon Distinction for Excellence in Education on The Rectory School, specifically citing its individualized instruction, experiential learning program, comprehensive athletic and arts programs, and computer-aided learning.

The School is situated on 138 picturesque acres in rural northeastern Connecticut. With access to three state capitals, the School enjoys a unique location; Hartford is 40 miles to the west, Providence is 30 miles to the east, and Boston is 70 miles to the northeast. The proximity of these major cities affords the opportunity for a variety of educational trips and easy access to airports, yet the School is in a safe, rural setting, only an hour's drive from the mountains and the coast.

Incorporated in 1935 as a nonprofit organization, The Rectory School is directed by a Board of Trustees. The endowment is $10 million. The approximate value of the physical plant is $22.9 million. Over the last several years, the School underwent a $5-million program of capital expansion. This resulted in two new dormitories, a library expansion and renovation, rewiring of the campus to meet technological demands, and the Tang Performing Arts Center, with a 236-seat auditorium. In addition, the School dedicated its new dining hall and the Art Barn, which houses two studios and a darkroom.

The Rectory School is accredited by the Connecticut Association of Independent Schools and approved by the Connecticut State Board of Education. It is a member of the Connecticut Association of Independent Schools, the National Association of Independent Schools, the Association of Boarding Schools, the Junior Boarding School Association, the Secondary School Admission Test Board, and the Educational Records Bureau.

ACADEMIC PROGRAMS

The Rectory School's core curriculum includes major courses in literature, mathematics, history, and science. Minor courses in music, art, and technology are required of each student. World languages may be elected, with English, Spanish, Chinese, and Latin offered. Physics and engineering are also available. Multiple sections in grades 5–9 allow opportunities for achievement to students with varying degrees of ability. The sections range from one with the most rigorous program of study to those with more academic support. Students are grouped by their ability, performance, and need for academic support. The most rigorous section is an honors track that puts students in line for advanced placement in secondary school. Using similar criteria, math sectioning is done separately from the language-based subjects. The guiding principle is that each student should feel challenged by the curriculum without being overwhelmed.

Regardless of the section, every student has an equal opportunity to make the effort and academic honor rolls. The Rectory School commends and recognizes both the gifted scholar and the dogged worker. A daily schedule rotates throughout the week. A 2-hour faculty-assisted study time is held five evenings per week. All students are taught proper study skills and work habits in the small classrooms and through numerous daily contacts with faculty members.

One of the unique and critical elements of The Rectory School's curriculum is the IIP, woven seamlessly into the normal academic day and curriculum. An individualized instructor, provided at additional cost to any student whose parents request one, meets with the student during the academic day five times per week. The IIP is tailored to the specific needs of each student, and it supports the curricular, organizational, time management, and study strategies taught in Rectory's classrooms. Approximately 75 percent of the students take advantage of this program.

Classes average 8–10 students. A student-faculty ratio of 4:1 provides the perfect atmosphere for one-to-one and small-group interaction.

The School's curriculum also includes a mandatory March Experiential Learning Program (MELP). The program, which operates for one week in March, allows students hands-on exploration of an area of interest. Topics have included studying the Battle of Gettysburg, architecture and the history of whaling on Nantucket, mechanical and process engineering by touring factories, and ecology and natural history in Maine and creating a wall-size mosaic for the School's collection. Because of the wide variety of these offerings, expenses for this program cannot be included in the tuition.

MUSH (make-up study hall) is a mechanism to nurture and improve a child's self-esteem and sense of responsibility. Held at the end of the academic day by 2 faculty members, MUSH is an opportunity for classroom teachers and IIP instructors to communicate about unfinished assignments or long-term projects. Through early intervention and this structured program, students are held accountable for their homework and increase their academic performance. With better time management, students grow in confidence, reinforce their understanding of classroom lessons, and enhance their chances for personal success.

FACULTY AND ADVISERS

The full-time faculty consists of 41 women and 26 men. Faculty members hold sixty-seven baccalaureate degrees, twenty-six master's degrees, and one Ph.D. Twelve faculty families and 13 single faculty members live on campus. The Rectory School seeks diversity within its faculty and supports professional growth opportunities during the school year and the summer.

Thomas F. Army Jr. was appointed Headmaster in 1990. A graduate of Wesleyan University (B.A., 1976; M.A.L.S., 1982), he served on The Rectory School's faculty from 1976 to 1978; he also served as Assistant Director of Alumni Relations at Wesleyan University and as a teacher and coach at Kent School.

The faculty members at The Rectory School are involved in all aspects of school life. They may coach, supervise a dormitory and student activities, or act as advisers. Regardless of title or job, all members of the faculty serve as role models for all students.

Every Rectory School student is assigned an adviser, who serves as a mentor, role model, counselor, and advocate for his or her advisee. Further guidance services are provided by the School psychologists, the Director of Student Services, and other administrators.

SECONDARY SCHOOL PLACEMENT

The Rectory School provides placement counseling to all ninth-grade students and their families. The goal is to guide a student to a school where he or she may thrive academically and socially. Several schools are recommended to each student. The academic match is of primary importance, but all interests and talents are taken into consideration. In the past three years, students have matriculated to the following secondary schools: Avon, Berkshire, Blair, Canterbury, Cheshire, Christchurch, Episcopal, Exeter, Forman, Governor's, Gunnery, Hotchkiss, Kent, Lawrence, Loomis Chaffee, Millbrook, Middlesex, Peddie, Pomfret, Portsmouth Abbey, Proctor, St. Andrew's, St. George's, Saint Mark, Salisbury, South Kent, Suffield, Tabor, Taft, Tilton, Trinity-Pawling, Virginia Episcopal, Western Reserve, and Williston Northampton.

STUDENT BODY AND CONDUCT

The Rectory School enrolls 236 students, of whom 190 are in grades 5–9 and 46 are in grades K–4. Typically, in the middle school (5–9), 65 percent are boarders and 35 percent day students. Rectory intends to maintain this ratio to provide students with a strong, viable residential program that is the key focus of the School community. For 2008–09, 25 percent of the students are female, 20 percent are international, and 15 percent are domestic students of color. The School anticipates that total female enrollment at the School will grow toward 40 percent as the new female boarding program gains momentum.

Rectory School students come from twenty U.S. states and territories, including California, Connecticut, Florida, Georgia, Louisiana, Maryland, Massachusetts, Missouri, New Hampshire, New Jersey, New York, Pennsylvania, Rhode Island, Texas, Vermont, Virginia, and Washington. Eight other locations, including the Bahamas, Bermuda, Canada, China, France, Japan, Korea, Mexico, and Taiwan, are represented in the Rectory School student body.

The School creed provides four cornerstone words that form the foundation of conduct at The Rectory School: Responsibility, Respect, Honesty, and Compassion. All students are required to sign a statement of understanding that describes and defines School rules and disciplinary procedures. Each week, students receive a conduct grade that evaluates their behavior over a seven-day period. Conduct grades affect privileges each week, especially weekend activities. The importance of responsibility, accountability, integrity, and concern for others is impressed upon each student throughout the day and during daily assemblies and a weekly nondenominational chapel service. Eighth-grade boarders who have distinguished themselves as leaders are selected by the faculty to serve as proctors, positions of honor and responsibility for ninth graders, in which they act as role models and provide guidance for younger students. The dress code requires jackets and ties for boys and dresses, skirts, or slacks with jackets or sweaters for girls.

ACADEMIC FACILITIES

There are twenty-five buildings on campus, including the John B. Bigelow Academic Center, which houses all classrooms, science labs, a greenhouse, three computer rooms that continue to be upgraded with the latest Mac hardware, and the library, which has undergone an expansion and renovation project. The Tang Performing Arts Center, with music rooms, MIDI labs, and a 236-seat theater, is a hub for student activity. Adjacent to the Academic Center is the Grosvenor House, which contains individualized instruction stations and administrative offices. The Collins Art Barn houses two studios and a darkroom. A new elementary school building is planned in the near future.

BOARDING AND GENERAL FACILITIES

Nonacademic facilities include eight dormitories, faculty residences, the Craig Calhoun Athletic Center, the new Dining Hall, and the Health Center. Since 2007, three on-campus houses have been converted into lovely dormitories for boarding girls. The Deal House, the most recent acquisition on campus, will house the Foundation and Alumni Offices.

ATHLETICS

The Rectory School's athletic facilities include the Craig Calhoun Athletic Center (gym, state-of-the-art weight room, wrestling room, lockers, and training room), six tennis courts, an outdoor basketball court, a street-hockey court, four soccer/lacrosse fields, a new baseball field, a cross-country course, a certified low-ropes course, and hiking trails as well as easy access to an ice rink and golf courses.

Every student must participate in the athletic program. The School offers the opportunity to play on a competitive sports team on many levels for every season. A recreational team sport is available for those students who enjoy athletics without the competition. All students learn the valuable rewards of being part of a team, and they develop a feeling of confidence and self-esteem through their accomplishments. The Rectory School's varsity and junior varsity teams compete with middle and secondary schools in Connecticut, Rhode Island, and Massachusetts. Interscholastic teams compete in baseball, basketball, cross-country, fencing, football, golf, ice hockey, lacrosse, soccer, softball, tennis, track, and wrestling.

EXTRACURRICULAR OPPORTUNITIES

The Rectory School provides extensive opportunities for participation in arts and club programs. Club offerings include bowling, camping, weight lifting, swimming, horseback riding, squash, tennis, fishing, street hockey, hiking, skating, snowboarding, mountain biking, in-line skating, and community service. Arts programs include an extensive music and drama program with groups for voice and band and individual lessons in all the band instruments as well as guitar, piano, and strings. In addition, the Music at Rectory School program, which takes place after school, is a unique opportunity for students to have private lessons with area professional musicians. Fine arts offerings include photography, painting, drawing, and ceramics.

DAILY LIFE

The rising bell rings at 6:45 a.m.; breakfast is at 7:05. The entire community assembles each morning at 8. From 8:30 to 2:45, there are seven class periods, the I-Period, Chapel (Wednesdays), and lunch. On Thursdays, day students meet with their advisers during breakfast. The I-Period is a time for students to participate in activities such as band, chorus, drama, individual music lessons, fine arts, and newspaper. It is also a time when students can get extra help from subject teachers and IIP instructors. Athletic teams practice and play games between 3 and 4:45. Dinner is served at 6, followed by evening study hall from 6:30 to 8:30. Bedtime is 9:30 for grades 5–8 and 10 for ninth graders.

WEEKEND LIFE

There are no Saturday classes. Five times a year, an enrichment program is provided. Otherwise, the club program is run during the morning. Regular athletic practices and games are held in the afternoon. A ski program is run on Saturdays and Sundays during the winter term. Faculty members chaperone these daylong ski trips to nearby mountains. Additional weekend activities include trips to college and professional athletic events, concerts, plays, movies, and other cultural events in nearby Hartford, Boston, Worcester, and Providence. Boarders are sometimes invited to day students' homes for the weekend.

SUMMER PROGRAMS

The Rectory School's five-week summer session, Summer@Rectory, is an innovative, individually designed program that balances academics, sports, art, music, drama, and recreation. Offering a variety of options for academic enrichment or support, Summer@Rectory has enrollment for coeducational day and boarding students who are entering grades 5–9. Day students may enroll in a half-day or a full-day program. While the morning program is five weeks, the afternoon options require a one-week or two-week commitment. Boarding students enroll in the full-day/five-week program.

The morning academic program provides choices for students to explore an interest, challenge their skills, refresh academic knowledge, improve study skills, and increase English language proficiency. Students enroll in four courses for the five-week session. One of these courses may be the one-to-one Individualized Instruction Program. The afternoon sessions include sports clinics such as baseball, lacrosse, golf, and basketball. Music camps promote the performing arts with instrumental ensembles, jazz, stringed instruments, and private lessons. Drama workshops allow students to explore theatrical skills, while recreational activities such as tennis, fishing, canoeing, softball, and soccer create personal enjoyment and team play. Students may elect a different option for each week.

The weekend schedule of field trips and off-campus activities gives Summer@Rectory students more experiences to remember. Area beaches, an overnight trip to Boston, New England excursions, Six Flags, and a professional baseball game all add to the excitement.

Summer@Rectory is being held from June 21 through July 25, 2009. The morning schedule, which runs weekdays from 8:15 a.m. to 12:25 p.m., is divided into four class blocks, with a recess and snack break in the middle of the morning. Afternoon sessions run weekdays from 1 to 4:30. There is a supervised lunch for day children attending both sessions.

COSTS AND FINANCIAL AID

The basic tuition, room, and board for international boarding students in 2008–09 are $38,600 and for domestic boarding students, $37,300. For those students enrolled in the IIP, there is a tutoring fee of $6300. For boarding students, there is an additional required deposit of $2100 ($2500 for international students) to open a bank account, against which students may charge books, School store purchases, taxis for travel, special excursions, and similar items. The unexpended balance in the account at the year's end is refunded. Day student tuition ranges from $16,900 for grades 5 and 6 to $18,900 for grades 7–9. A bank account deposit of $550 is required for day students.

Financial aid is available to qualified applicants according to need. In 2007–08, 30 percent of students received financial assistance.

ADMISSIONS INFORMATION

It is the policy of The Rectory School to admit students regardless of race, color, religion, or national or ethnic origin, provided they are of good character and intelligence and are capable of meeting the School's educational standards for admission. In addition, The Rectory School has day students, both boys and girls, who meet the same criteria. The Rectory School does not discriminate on the basis of race, color, or national or ethnic origin in the administration of its educational policies, admissions policies, scholarship and loan programs, and athletic and other School-administered programs.

New students are accepted in all grades, although new noninternational ninth graders are required to attend Summer@Rectory. In addition, new boarding students are encouraged to attend Summer@Rectory to become acclimated to life on campus. An interview, current transcripts, and testing are required.

APPLICATION TIMETABLE

Admission to The Rectory School is on a rolling basis. There is no application deadline for boarding students. Day students should have their applications in by April 15. Campus interviews may be arranged by calling or writing the Admissions Office. Applications must be accompanied by a nonrefundable fee of $50 ($100 for international students). Students who are accepted are guaranteed a place when the enrollment contract is returned with an advance tuition deposit.

ADMISSIONS CORRESPONDENCE

Vincent Ricci, Assistant Headmaster of Marketing and Admissions
The Rectory School
528 Pomfret Street
P.O. Box 68
Pomfret, Connecticut 06258

Phone: 860-928-1328
Fax: 860-928-4961
E-mail: admissions@rectoryschool.org
Web site: http://www.rectoryschool.org

RUMSEY HALL SCHOOL

Washington Depot, Connecticut

Type: Coeducational boarding (grades 5–9) and day junior prep school
Grades: K–9: Lower School, K–5; Upper School, 6–9
Enrollment: School total: 302
Head of School: Thomas W. Farmen, Headmaster

THE SCHOOL

Rumsey Hall School was founded in 1900 by Mrs. Lillias Rumsey Sanford. Since its inception, Rumsey Hall School has retained its original philosophy: to help each child develop to his or her maximum stature as an individual, as a member of a family, and as a contributing member of society. The curriculum emphasizes basic academic skills, a complete athletic program, fine arts, computer literacy, and numerous extracurricular offerings, which are all designed to encourage individual responsibility for academic achievement, accomplishment in team sports, and service to the School community. The School believes that "effort is the key to success."

The 147-acre campus on the Bantam River provides landscaped and wooded areas in a rural environment located outside of Washington, Connecticut. Rumsey Hall School is 90 miles from New York City and within an hour of the major Connecticut cities of Hartford and New Haven. The School's location enables students to take advantage of major cultural and athletic events in New York City and Boston throughout the school year.

A nonprofit institution, Rumsey Hall School is governed by a 24-member Board of Trustees that meets quarterly. The 2006–07 operating budget totaled $6.1 million. Revenues include tuition and fees and contributions from alumni, parents, corporations, foundations, and friends of the School. The School's endowment is approximately $4.5 million, with the Board of Trustees' long-range planning committee examining ways to increase it. Annual giving was $2.14 million in 2007. Gifts from Dan and Cynthia Lufkin (parents of a current student) and the Peter Jay Sharp Foundation provided a major portion of the financing for an indoor hockey rink, which opened in December 2008.

Rumsey Hall School is a member of the National Association of Independent Schools, the Connecticut Association of Independent Schools, the Junior Boarding Schools Association, the Educational Records Bureau, Western Connecticut Boarding Schools, and the Educational Testing Service, and is a voting member of the Secondary School Admission Test Board.

ACADEMIC PROGRAMS

At Rumsey Hall, effort is as important as academic achievement. Effort as a criterion for success opens a new world to the students. Effort does not start and end with the student. It is a shared responsibility between the student and each faculty member. Just as the faculty members expect maximum effort from each student, they promise in return to give each student their very best effort.

Students in the Upper School (sixth through ninth grades) carry at least five major subjects. There are eight 40-minute periods in each day, including lunch. Extra help is available each day for students who need additional instruction or extra challenges. All classes are departmentalized.

Final examinations are given in all subjects twice a year. Report cards, with numerical grades, are sent home every other week throughout the school year. Anecdotal comments and individualized teacher, adviser, and Headmaster comments are sent home three times each academic year.

A supplementary feature of the academic program is the Language Skills Department, which is directed toward intellectually able students with dyslexia or learning disabilities. Students in this program carry a regular academic course load, with the exception of a foreign language. Eighteen percent of the student body is involved in this program.

The school year, divided into trimesters, begins in September and runs until the first weekend in June. Vacations are scheduled at Thanksgiving and Christmas and in the spring.

Class size averages 13 students. Classes are heterogeneous except for some honors courses offered to exceptional ninth graders.

Students have a study hall built into their daily schedule, and there is an evening study hall for all boarding students. All study halls are supervised by faculty members, and there is ample opportunity for study assistance. The library and computer facilities adjoin the formal study hall and are available at all study times.

FACULTY AND ADVISERS

All 51 full-time faculty members (21 men and 26 women) hold baccalaureate degrees, and half have master's degrees. Most faculty members live on campus with their families. This enables Rumsey to provide the close supervision and warm family atmosphere that is an essential part of the School's culture.

Thomas W. Farmen was appointed Headmaster of Rumsey Hall School in 1985. He holds a Bachelor of Arts degree from New England College and a master's in school administration from Western Connecticut State University. He has served as President of the Association of Boarding Schools for the National Association of Independent Schools, President of the Junior Boarding Schools Association, and a director of the Connecticut Association of Independent Schools.

The Dean of Students supervises and coordinates the advisory program. Each faculty member has 7 or 8 student advisees. Advisers meet with their advisees individually and in a weekly group setting. The adviser is the first link in the line of communication between school and home.

Faculty members at Rumsey Hall are encouraged to continue their professional development by taking postgraduate courses and attending seminars and conferences throughout the year. The School generously funds these programs.

SECONDARY SCHOOL PLACEMENT

The Director of Secondary School Placement supervises all facets of the secondary school search. Beginning in the eighth grade, a process of testing and interviewing with students and parents takes place that enables the placement director to highlight certain schools that seem appropriate. After visits and interviews with the schools, the list is pared down to those to which the student wishes to apply. The class of 2007 wrote applications to fifty-three schools, and 88 percent of the students enrolled in their first-choice schools. Members of the classes of 2006 and 2007 enrolled in the following prep schools: Avon Old Farms, Berkshire, Blair, Canterbury, Cate, Cheshire Academy, Choate Rosemary Hall, Christchurch, Cushing, Deerfield, Emma Willard, George, Governor's Academy, Groton, The Gunnery, Hill, Hotchkiss, Kent, Lawrenceville, Loomis Chaffee, Middlesex, Millbrook, Miss Hall's, Miss Porters, Northfield Mount Hermon, Phillips Exeter, Proctor, Putney, St. Andrew's, St. George's, St. James, St. Mark's, St. Paul's, Salisbury, South Kent, Suffield, Taft, Trinity-Pawling, Vermont Academy, Walnut Hill, Westminster, Westover, and Williston Northampton.

STUDENT BODY AND CONDUCT

In 2008–09, Rumsey Hall enrolled 313 students. The Lower School (grades K–5) enrolled 86 students: 11 in kindergarten, 14 in first grade, 12 in second grade, 14 in third grade, 21 in fourth grade, and 12 in fifth grade. The Upper School enrolled 227 students: 24 in sixth grade, 54 in seventh grade, 75 in eighth grade, and 74 in ninth grade. The Lower School consisted of 84 day students and 2 boarding students while the Upper School had 101 day students and 126 boarders. The School population was 66 percent boys and 34 percent girls.

In 2008–09, Rumsey students came from twenty different states, nine countries, and twenty-nine local communities. Eight percent of the community was composed of international students enrolled in the ESL (English as a second language) program.

The Rumsey dress code requires jackets, collared shirts, and ties for boys and dresses or skirts and collared shirts or blouses for girls. There is a slight change in the winter term, when boys may wear turtlenecks and sweaters and girls may wear slacks.

The School values of honesty, kindness, and respect comprise the yardstick by which Rumsey measures a student's thoughts and actions. Students living outside the spirit of the community are asked to meet with the Disciplinary and Senior Committees. These committees represent a cross section of administrators, faculty members, and students.

ACADEMIC FACILITIES

Situated alongside the Bantam River on a 147-acre campus, the School is housed in twenty-five buildings, most of which have been constructed since 1950. Nine structures house a total of thirty classrooms, including the Dicke Family Math and Science Buildings. Other buildings include the library; the Sanford House, which houses the study and meeting hall; the J. Seward Johnson Sr. Fine Arts Center, with spacious art and music rooms; and the Satyvati Science Center. The centerpiece of the campus is the redbrick School Courtyard.

BOARDING AND GENERAL FACILITIES

The close relationship between teachers and students is a special part of Rumsey Hall School. Students live in dormitories with supportive dorm parents, and students become a part of their dorm parents' families.

Rumsey's boarding students live in one of eight dormitories. Dormitories are assigned by age, and most students have roommates, although single rooms are available in most dorms. Each dormitory has its own common room that is the shared living space for the dorm. A snack bar and store are open every afternoon. Laundry and dry cleaning are sent out on a weekly basis. Four registered nurses staff the School's infirmary, and the School doctor, a local pediatrician, is available on a daily basis. Emergency facilities are available at New Milford Hospital, which is 10 miles away. There are telephones in all dormitories, and every student has an e-mail account.

ATHLETICS

Athletics are a healthy and essential part of the Rumsey experience. On the playing field, lifelong attitudes, values, and habits are born. All students participate at their own level in athletics. Effort is rewarded through athletic letters and certificates at the end of the season.

Rumsey Hall fields twenty-eight interscholastic teams throughout the year. Most sports are offered on different levels so that students are able to compete with children of their own size and skill level. Interscholastic teams are fielded in baseball, basketball, crew, cross-country, field hockey, football, ice hockey, girls' ice hockey, lacrosse, skiing, soccer, softball, tennis, volleyball, and wrestling. Other activities available include horseback riding, Outdoor Club, Lower School games and activities, recreational skiing and snowboarding, biking, and ice-skating.

The Magnoli Gymnasium houses basketball, volleyball, and wrestling facilities. The renovations of the indoor athletic facilities include an indoor climbing wall, boys' and girls' locker rooms and restrooms, updates to the existing gym, and tennis courts. The Cornell Common Room serves as the weight-training room and offers other training machines, as well as housing the athletic director and athletic training staff. The Schereschewsky Center contains three indoor tennis courts. The hockey teams skate at the indoor rinks at neighboring prep schools. In addition, there are seven outdoor playing fields and two skating ponds.

EXTRACURRICULAR OPPORTUNITIES

Throughout the year, students may participate in many activities and clubs. The choices include fishing, computers, chorus, art club, bicycling, fly fishing, School newspaper, yearbook, art, swimming, hiking, rocketry, baking, community service, intramural sports, and participation in School dramatic and musical productions.

Traditional annual events for the School community include fall and spring community work days, a Christmas concert, Parents' Days twice a year, Grandparents' Day in the spring, and a Holiday Carol Sing through the campus. Service to the School and to the greater community is encouraged throughout the year by the community service club and the student government.

The student body is divided into red and blue color teams. These teams enjoy friendly competition throughout the school year in areas of community service, academic achievement, and athletics.

DAILY LIFE

The school day begins at 8 a.m. with an all-School meeting. All administrators, faculty members, and students are in attendance. It is a time to share the news of the School and the world as well as important information and announcements with the whole community. The rest of the academic day consists of eight 40-minute periods and supervised study halls, with a 20-minute recess in the middle of the morning. Extra help is available every day after lunch. Athletic practices or contests take place from 3 to 4:30 p.m. Dinner is served family style at 6 and is followed by study hall from 7 to 8:30. Free time follows, with bedtimes varying depending on the grade of the child.

WEEKEND LIFE

Weekends for boarding students include a variety of activities on and off campus. There are School dances, special theme weekends, off-campus trips, and intramural activities on campus. Rumsey's proximity to four major cities—New York, Boston, Hartford, and New Haven—allows for a wide variety of cultural events, sports events (collegiate and professional), and shopping excursions. All trips are fully supervised, and an appropriate student-teacher ratio is maintained. Day students are encouraged to participate in weekend activities and are also allowed to invite boarding students home with them for the weekend.

SUMMER PROGRAMS

The five-week Rumsey Hall summer session is open to students in the third through ninth grades. The program is designed for students who desire enrichment or need additional work in a subject area in order to move on to the next grade with confidence. There is an emphasis on study skills and a heavy concentration on mathematics and language skills. The morning and evening are set aside for academic work, while the afternoon is purely recreational.

COSTS AND FINANCIAL AID

In 2008–09, tuition was $14,670 for kindergarten, $15,050 for day students in grades 1 and 2, $18,500 for day students in grades 3–9, and $39,000 for boarding students. Additional fees included books, athletic fees, school supplies, and laundry and dry cleaning. A nonrefundable deposit of $2000 serves as the boarding student's drawing account for the year. Two thirds of the tuition is due July 15 and the balance December 15, unless the family chooses to pay in ten monthly installments.

Rumsey Hall is a member of the School and Student Service for Financial Aid and annually awards financial aid to more than a quarter of the students.

ADMISSIONS INFORMATION

Rumsey Hall welcomes students of average to above-average intelligence and achievement. Students must show evidence of good citizenship and the willingness to live in a boarding community. Acceptance is based on past school performance, scores on standardized achievement tests, and a personal interview. Rumsey is able to accept a limited number of students with learning differences if their learning profile is compatible with the School's Orton-Gillingham–based language skills program. Rumsey Hall School admits students of any race, color, religion, or national or ethnic origin.

APPLICATION TIMETABLE

Inquiries are welcome at any time of the year, with most families beginning the admissions process in the fall or winter in anticipation of September enrollment. Admissions interviews and tours are scheduled throughout the year. Boarding student applications are accepted on a rolling basis. A February 15 due date and March 1 notification date apply to day student applicants.

ADMISSIONS CORRESPONDENCE

Matthew S. Hoeniger, Director of Admissions
Rumsey Hall School
201 Romford Road
Washington Depot, Connecticut 06794
Phone: 860-868-0535
Fax: 860-868-7907
E-mail: admiss@rumseyhall.org
Web site: http://www.rumseyhall.org

Specialized Directories

COEDUCATIONAL DAY SCHOOLS

Abington Friends School, PA
Academia Cotopaxi, Ecuador
Academie Sainte Cecile International School, ON, Canada
The Academy at Charlemont, MA
The Academy for Gifted Children (PACE), ON, Canada
Accelerated Schools, CO
ACS Cobham International School, United Kingdom
ACS Egham International School, United Kingdom
ACS Hillingdon International School, United Kingdom
Airdrie Koinonia Christian School, AB, Canada
Alabama Christian Academy, AL
Albert College, ON, Canada
Albuquerque Academy, NM
Alexander Dawson School, CO
The Alexander School, TX
Allen Academy, TX
Allendale Columbia School, NY
Allison Academy, FL
All Saints' Episcopal School of Fort Worth, TX
Alma Heights Christian Academy, CA
The Altamont School, AL
Alternative Learning Program, AB, Canada
American Academy, FL
American Christian Academy, AL
American Community Schools of Athens, Greece
American Heritage School, FL
The American International School, Austria
American International School, Dhaka, Bangladesh
American International School of Bucharest, Romania
American International School Rotterdam, Netherlands
The American School Foundation, Mexico
The American School in London, United Kingdom
The American School of Madrid, Spain
American School of Milan, Italy
American School of Paris, France
The American School of Puerto Vallarta, Mexico
The American School of The Hague, Netherlands
Andrews Osborne Academy, OH
Annie Wright School, WA
Antelope Valley Christian School, CA
Archbishop Edward A. McCarthy High School, FL
Archbishop Hoban High School, OH
Archbishop McNicholas High School, OH
Archbishop Mitty High School, CA
Archbishop Spalding High School, MD
Archmere Academy, DE
Armona Union Academy, CA
Arrowsmith School, ON, Canada
Arthur Morgan School, NC
Ashbury College, ON, Canada
Asheville School, NC
ASSETS School, HI
The Athenian School, CA
Athens Academy, GA
Atlanta International School, GA
Augusta Christian School (I), GA
Augusta Preparatory Day School, GA
Aurora Central High School, IL
Austin Christian Academy, MB, Canada
Austin Preparatory School, MA
The Awty International School, TX
Bakersfield Christian High School, CA
Baldwin School of Puerto Rico, Inc., PR
The Baltimore Actors' Theatre Conservatory, MD
Bancroft School, MA
Baptist High School, NJ
Barnstable Academy, NJ
The Barrie School, MD
The Barstow School, MO
Bass Memorial Academy, MS
Battle Ground Academy, TN
Bavarian International School, Germany
Baylor School, TN
Bearspaw Christian School, AB, Canada
Beaver Country Day School, MA
The Beekman School, NY
Bellarmine-Jefferson High School, CA
Bellevue Christian School, WA
The Bement School, MA
Ben Franklin Academy, GA
Benilde–St. Margaret's School, MN
The Benjamin School, FL
Berkeley Preparatory School, FL
Berkshire School, MA
Berwick Academy, ME
Besant Hill School, CA
Beth Haven Christian School, KY
The Birch Wathen Lenox School, NY
Bishop Alemany High School, CA
Bishop Blanchet High School, WA
Bishop Brady High School, NH
Bishop Carroll High School, PA
Bishop Connolly High School, MA
Bishop Denis J. O'Connell High School, VA
Bishop Eustace Preparatory School, NJ
Bishop Feehan High School, MA
Bishop Fenwick High School, OH
Bishop Garcia Diego High School, CA
Bishop George Ahr High School, NJ
Bishop Gorman High School, NV
Bishop Guertin High School, NH
Bishop Ireton High School, VA
Bishop Kelly High School, ID
Bishop Kenny High School, FL
Bishop Luers High School, IN
Bishop Lynch Catholic High School, TX
Bishop McGuinness Catholic High School, NC
Bishop McGuinness Catholic High School, OK
Bishop McNamara High School, IL
Bishop Montgomery High School, CA
Bishop Stang High School, MA
Bishop Verot High School, FL
Bishop Walsh Middle High School, MD
Blair Academy, NJ
The Blake School, MN
Blanchet School, OR
Blessed Trinity High School, GA
Blue Mountain Academy, PA
Bodwell High School, BC, Canada
The Bolles School, FL
Boston Trinity Academy, MA
Boston University Academy, MA
Boyd-Buchanan School, TN
Boylan Central Catholic High School, IL
The Branson School, CA
Breck School, MN
Brehm Preparatory School, IL

Brentwood College School, BC, Canada
Brentwood School, CA
Brentwood School, GA
Brethren Christian Junior and Senior High Schools, CA
Brewster Academy, NH
Briarwood Christian High School, AL
Bridgemont High School, CA
Bridges Academy, CA
Bridge School, CO
Brimmer and May School, MA
Bronte College of Canada, ON, Canada
Brooks School, MA
Brookstone School, GA
Brownell-Talbot School, NE
Buckingham Browne & Nichols School, MA
The Buckley School, CA
Bulloch Academy, GA
Burke Mountain Academy, VT
Burr and Burton Academy, VT
The Bush School, WA
Butte Central High School, MT
Buxton School, MA
The Byrnes Schools, SC
Calgary Academy, AB, Canada
The Calhoun School, NY
Calvary Christian Academy, KY
The Calverton School, MD
The Cambridge School of Weston, MA
Camelot Academy, NC
Campbell Hall (Episcopal), CA
Canadian Academy, Japan
Cannon School, NC
Canterbury School, CT
Canterbury School, FL
The Canterbury School of Florida, FL
Canyonville Christian Academy, OR
Cape Cod Academy, MA
Cape Fear Academy, NC
Cape Henry Collegiate School, VA
Capistrano Valley Christian Schools, CA
Cardinal Gibbons High School, NC
Cardinal Mooney Catholic College Preparatory High School, MI
Cardinal Mooney High School, FL
Cardinal Newman High School, FL
Cardinal Newman School, SC
The Caribbean School, PR
Carlisle School, VA
Carlucci American International School of Lisbon, Portugal
Carolina Day School, NC
Carrabassett Valley Academy, ME
Cary Academy, NC
Cascadilla School, NY
Cascia Hall Preparatory School, OK
Cate School, CA
Cathedral High School, IN
The Catlin Gabel School, OR
Centennial Academy, QC, Canada
Central Catholic High School, CA
Central Catholic High School, MA
Central Catholic High School, OH
Central Catholic High School, OH
Central Catholic Mid-High School, NE
Central Valley Christian Academy, CA
Century High School, BC, Canada
Chadwick School, CA
Chamberlain-Hunt Academy, MS
Chaminade College Preparatory, CA
Chaminade-Madonna College Preparatory, FL
Chamisa Mesa High School, NM
Chapel Hill–Chauncy Hall School, MA
Chapel School, Brazil
Charlotte Catholic High School, NC
Charlotte Christian School, NC
Charlotte Country Day School, NC
Charlotte Latin School, NC
Chase Collegiate School, CT
Chatham Academy, GA
Chelsea School, MD
Cheshire Academy, CT
Cheverus High School, ME
The Chicago Academy for the Arts, IL
Children's Creative and Performing Arts Academy—Capa Division, CA
Chinese Christian Schools, CA
Choate Rosemary Hall, CT
Christchurch School, VA
Christian Brothers Academy, NY
Christian Central Academy, NY
Christian Heritage School, CT
Christian Home and Bible School, FL
Christian Junior–Senior High School, CA
Christian School of the Desert, CA
Christopher Dock Mennonite High School, PA
Chrysalis School, WA
Cincinnati Country Day School, OH
Coe-Brown Northwood Academy, NH
Colegio Bolivar, Colombia
Colegio Franklin D. Roosevelt, Peru
Colegio Nueva Granada, Colombia
Cole Valley Christian High School, ID
College du Leman International School, Switzerland
The College Preparatory School, CA
The Collegiate School, VA
Colorado Academy, CO
The Colorado Rocky Mountain School, CO
The Colorado Springs School, CO
Columbia Academy, TN
Columbia Grammar and Preparatory School, NY
Columbia International College of Canada, ON, Canada
Columbia International School, Japan
The Columbus Academy, OH
Columbus High School, IA
Commonwealth Parkville School, PR
Commonwealth School, MA
Community Christian Academy, KY
Community High School, NJ
The Community School, ID
Community School, NH
The Community School of Naples, FL
The Concept School, PA
Concord Academy, MA
Concordia Continuing Education High School, AB, Canada
Concordia High School, AB, Canada
Copenhagen International School, Denmark
Cotter Schools, MN
The Country Day School, ON, Canada
Covenant Canadian Reformed School, AB, Canada

The Craig School, NJ
Crawford Adventist Academy, ON, Canada
Crawford Day School, VA
Crestwood Preparatory College, ON, Canada
Cretin-Derham Hall, MN
CrossRoads, OR
Crossroads College Preparatory School, MO
Crossroads School for Arts & Sciences, CA
Crotched Mountain Rehabilitation Center School, NH
Crystal Springs Uplands School, CA
The Culver Academies, IN
Currey Ingram Academy, TN
Cushing Academy, MA
Dallas Academy, TX
Dallas Christian School, TX
The Dalton School, NY
Darlington School, GA
Darrow School, NY
David Lipscomb High School, TN
Deerfield Academy, MA
Deerfield-Windsor School, GA
De La Salle College, ON, Canada
Delaware Valley Friends School, PA
Delphos Saint John's High School, OH
Denver Academy, CO
Denver Christian High School, CO
Denver Lutheran High School, CO
DePaul Catholic High School, NJ
The Derryfield School, NH
Detroit Country Day School, MI
Dickinson Trinity, ND
Doane Stuart School, NY
Donelson Christian Academy, TN
Donna Klein Jewish Academy, FL
Dowling Catholic High School, IA
Drew School, CA
Dubai American Academy, United Arab Emirates
Dublin Christian Academy, NH
Dublin School, NH
Dunn School, CA
Durham Academy, NC
Dwight-Englewood School, NJ
Eagle Hill School, MA
Eagle Hill-Southport, CT
East Catholic High School, CT
Eastern Christian High School, NJ
Eastern Mennonite High School, VA
Eastside Catholic School, WA
Eastside College Preparatory School, CA
Ecole d'Humanité, Switzerland
Ecole Internationale de Boston / International School of Boston, MA
Edison School, AB, Canada
The Education Center, MS
Elgin Academy, IL
Elyria Catholic High School, OH
Emerson Honors High Schools, CA
The Emery Weiner School, TX
Episcopal Collegiate School, AR
Episcopal High School, TX
Episcopal High School of Jacksonville, FL
The Episcopal School of Dallas, TX
Escola Americana de Campinas, Brazil
Escondido Adventist Academy, CA
Evangelical Christian School, TN
Evansville Day School, IN
Excel Academy, Inc., OH
Excel Christian Academy, GA
Explorations Academy, WA
Ezell-Harding Christian School, TN
Fairhill School, TX
Faith Christian High School, CA
Faith Lutheran High School, NV
Falmouth Academy, MA
Father Lopez High School, FL
Father Ryan High School, TN
Fayetteville Academy, NC
Fay School, MA
The Field School, DC
Fieldstone Day School, ON, Canada
The First Academy, FL
First Baptist Academy, TX
First Presbyterian Day School, GA
Flint Hill School, VA
Flint River Academy, GA
Foothills Academy, AB, Canada
The Forman School, CT
Forsyth Country Day School, NC
Fort Lauderdale Preparatory School, FL
Fort Worth Country Day School, TX
Foundation Academy, FL
Fountain Valley School of Colorado, CO
Fowlers Academy, PR
Foxcroft Academy, ME
Fox River Country Day School, IL
Fox Valley Lutheran Academy, IL
Fox Valley Lutheran High School, WI
Franklin Academy, CT
Franklin Road Academy, TN
Fraser Academy, BC, Canada
Freeman Academy, SD
French-American School of New York, NY
Friends' Central School, PA
Front Range Christian High School, CO
The Frostig School, CA
Fryeburg Academy, ME
Fuqua School, VA
Gables Academy, GA
Gabriel Richard High School, MI
Gann Academy (The New Jewish High School of Greater Boston), MA
Garces Memorial High School, CA
Garden School, NY
Gaston Day School, NC
Gateway School, TX
The Geneva School, FL
George School, PA
George Stevens Academy, ME
Georgetown Day School, DC
Georgia Military College High School, GA
Germantown Academy, PA
Germantown Friends School, PA
Gill St. Bernard's School, NJ
Gilmour Academy, OH
Glades Day School, FL
Glen Eden School, BC, Canada
Glenelg Country School, MD
Gordon Technical High School, IL

Gould Academy, ME
The Governor French Academy, IL
The Governor's Academy (formerly Governor Dummer Academy), MA
Grace Baptist Academy, TN
Grace Brethren School, CA
Grace Christian School, AK
The Grauer School, CA
Greater Atlanta Christian Schools, GA
Great Lakes Christian High School, ON, Canada
Greenfield School, NC
Green Fields Country Day School, AZ
Greenhill School, TX
Greenhills School, MI
Greenleaf Academy, ID
Green Meadow Waldorf School, NY
Greensboro Day School, NC
Greens Farms Academy, CT
Greenwood Laboratory School, MO
Griggs University and International Academy, MD
Groton School, MA
Grove School, CT
Guamani Private School, PR
Guerin College Preparatory High School, IL
Guilford Day School, NC
Gulliver Preparatory School, FL
The Gunnery, CT
Gunston Day School, MD
Hackley School, NY
Halstrom High School, CA
Halstrom High School—San Diego, CA
Hamden Hall Country Day School, CT
Hamilton District Christian High, ON, Canada
Hammond School, SC
Hanalani Schools, HI
Hanson Memorial High School, LA
Harding Academy, AR
Harding Academy, TN
The Harker School, CA
The Harley School, NY
Harrells Christian Academy, NC
The Harrisburg Academy, PA
Harvard-Westlake School, CA
Hawaiian Mission Academy, HI
Hawaii Baptist Academy, HI
Hawai'i Preparatory Academy, HI
Hawken School, OH
Hawthorne Christian Academy, NJ
Hayden High School, KS
Head-Royce School, CA
Headwaters Academy, MT
Hebrew Academy-the Five Towns, NY
Hebron Academy, ME
Heritage Christian Academy, MI
Heritage Christian Academy, AB, Canada
Heritage Christian School, ON, Canada
Heritage Hall, OK
The Heritage School, GA
Highland Hall, A Waldorf School, CA
Highland School, VA
High Mowing School, NH
The Hill Center, Durham Academy, NC
Hillcrest Christian School, CA
Hillcrest School, TX
The Hill School, PA
The Hill Top Preparatory School, PA
Hilton Head Preparatory School, SC
Holderness School, NH
Holland Hall, OK
Holy Innocents' Episcopal School, GA
Holy Name High School, PA
Holy Savior Menard Catholic High School, LA
Holy Trinity Diocesan High School, NY
Holy Trinity High School, IL
Hoosac School, NY
Hope Christian School, AB, Canada
Hopkins School, CT
The Horace Mann School, NY
Horizons School, GA
Hosanna Christian School, OR
The Hotchkiss School, CT
Houghton Academy, NY
Howe Military School, IN
The Hudson School, NJ
The Hun School of Princeton, NJ
Huntington-Surrey School, TX
Hyde School, CT
Hyde School, ME
Hyman Brand Hebrew Academy of Greater Kansas City, KS
Idyllwild Arts Academy, CA
Illiana Christian High School, IL
Immaculata High School, KS
Immaculate Conception School, IL
Immaculate High School, CT
Immanuel Christian High School, AB, Canada
Independent School, KS
Indian Mountain School, CT
Indian Springs School, AL
Interlochen Arts Academy, MI
International College Spain, Spain
International High School, CA
International School Bangkok, Thailand
International School Eerde, Netherlands
International School Hamburg, Germany
International School Manila, Philippines
The International School of Aberdeen, United Kingdom
International School of Amsterdam, Netherlands
International School of Aruba, Aruba
International School of Athens, Greece
International School of Berne, Switzerland
The International School of Geneva, Switzerland
International School of Lausanne, Switzerland
The International School of London, United Kingdom
International School of Milan, Italy
The International School of Paris, France
International School of South Africa, South Africa
Iolani School, HI
Isidore Newman School, LA
Island School, HI
Jack M. Barrack Hebrew Academy (formerly Akiba Hebrew Academy), PA
Jackson Academy, MS
Jackson Christian School, TN
Jackson Preparatory School, MS
The Janus School, PA
John Bapst Memorial High School, ME
John Burroughs School, MO
The John Cooper School, TX

John Paul II Catholic High School, FL
Kaplan College Preparatory School, FL
Karachi American School, Pakistan
The Karafin School, NY
Keith Country Day School, IL
Kent Denver School, CO
Kent School, CT
Kents Hill School, ME
Kentucky Country Day School, KY
Kerr-Vance Academy, NC
The Key School, MD
Kildonan School, NY
Kimball Union Academy, NH
Kimberton Waldorf School, PA
King Low Heywood Thomas, CT
The King's Academy, TN
The King's Christian High School, NJ
Kings Christian School, CA
King's-Edgehill School, NS, Canada
King's High School, WA
Kingshill School, VI
King's Ridge Christian School, GA
Kingsway College, ON, Canada
King's West School, WA
Kingswood-Oxford School, CT
The Knox School, NY
Knoxville Catholic High School, TN
Koinonia Christian School, AB, Canada
La Cheim School, CA
Lakefield College School, ON, Canada
Lake Forest Academy, IL
Lakehill Preparatory School, TX
Lakeland Christian Academy, IN
Lake Ridge Academy, OH
Lakeside School, WA
Lakeview Academy, GA
La Lumiere School, IN
Lancaster Country Day School, PA
Lancaster Mennonite High School, PA
Landmark East School, NS, Canada
Landmark School, MA
Lansdale Catholic High School, PA
Lansing Christian School, MI
La Salle Academy, RI
La Salle High School, FL
The Laureate Academy, MB, Canada
Laurel View Academy, ON, Canada
Lausanne Collegiate School, TN
Lawrence Academy, MA
Lawrence School, OH
The Lawrenceville School, NJ
Lee Academy, ME
Lehigh Valley Christian High School, PA
Lehman High School, OH
Le Lycee Francais de Los Angeles, CA
Lester B. Pearson United World College of the Pacific, BC, Canada
Lexington Catholic High School, KY
Lexington Christian Academy, MA
Linfield Christian School, CA
The Linsly School, WV
Little Red School House and Elisabeth Irwin High School, NY
Logos School, MO
The Loomis Chaffee School, CT
Los Angeles Baptist Junior/Senior High School, CA
Los Angeles Lutheran High School, CA
Louisville Collegiate School, KY
Lourdes Catholic High School, AZ
The Lovett School, GA
The Lowell Whiteman School, CO
Loyola School, NY
Lustre Christian High School, MT
Lutheran High North, TX
Lutheran High School, IN
Lutheran High School, MO
Lutheran High School North, MO
Lutheran High School Northwest, MI
Lutheran High School of Hawaii, HI
Lutheran High School of San Diego, CA
Lutheran High School West, OH
Luther College High School, SK, Canada
Luther High School North, IL
Luther High School South, IL
Lycee Claudel, ON, Canada
Lycee Français de New York, NY
The Lycee International, American Section, France
Lydia Patterson Institute, TX
Lyndon Institute, VT
The MacDuffie School, MA
MacLachlan College, ON, Canada
Madison Academy, AL
Madison-Ridgeland Academy, MS
Maharishi School of the Age of Enlightenment, IA
Maine Central Institute, ME
Manlius Pebble Hill School, NY
Maplebrook School, NY
Maret School, DC
Marianapolis Preparatory School, CT
Marian Baker School, Costa Rica
Marian Central Catholic High School, IL
Marian High School, IN
Marin Academy, CA
Marion Academy, AL
Marist High School, IL
Marist High School, NJ
Marist School, GA
Marshall School, MN
Mars Hill Bible School, AL
Martin Luther High School, NY
The Marvelwood School, CT
Maryknoll School, HI
Marymount International School, Italy
Massanutten Military Academy, VA
The Master's School, CT
The Masters School, NY
Mater Dei High School, IN
Matignon High School, MA
Maumee Valley Country Day School, OH
Maur Hill-Mount Academy, KS
McCurdy School, NM
McDonogh School, MD
Meadowridge School, BC, Canada
The Meadows School, NV
Memorial Hall School, TX
Menaul School, NM
Menlo School, CA
Mennonite Collegiate Institute, MB, Canada
Mentor College, ON, Canada

Mercedes College, Australia
Mercersburg Academy, PA
Mercy High School, CA
Mercyhurst Preparatory School, PA
Mercy Vocational High School, PA
Mesa Grande Seventh-Day Academy, CA
Metairie Park Country Day School, LA
Metro-East Lutheran High School, IL
Miami Country Day School, FL
Middlesex School, MA
Midland School, CA
Mid-Pacific Institute, HI
Mid-Peninsula High School, CA
Milken Community High School of Stephen S. Wise Temple, CA
Millbrook School, NY
Miller School, VA
Milton Academy, MA
Minot Bishop Ryan, ND
Mississauga Private School, ON, Canada
MMI Preparatory School, PA
Modesto Christian School, CA
Monmouth Academy, NJ
Monsignor Donovan High School, NJ
Montverde Academy, FL
Moorestown Friends School, NJ
Moravian Academy, PA
Moreau Catholic High School, CA
Morgan Park Academy, IL
Morristown-Beard School, NJ
Moses Brown School, RI
Mounds Park Academy, MN
Mount Saint Charles Academy, RI
Munich International School, Germany
Nancy Campbell Collegiate Institute, ON, Canada
National Sports Academy at Lake Placid, NY
Navajo Preparatory School, Inc., NM
Nazareth Academy, IL
Nebraska Christian Schools, NE
Newark Academy, NJ
Newbury Park Adventist Academy, CA
New Covenant Academy, MO
New Hampton School, NH
New Horizon Youth Ministries, IN
The Newman School, MA
New Summit School, MS
New Tribes Mission Academy, ON, Canada
New Way Learning Academy, AZ
New York Military Academy, NY
Niagara Christian Community of Schools, ON, Canada
The Nichols School, NY
Noah Webster Christian School, WY
Noble and Greenough School, MA
The Nora School, MD
Norfolk Academy, VA
Norfolk Christian School, VA
Norfolk Collegiate School, VA
The North Broward Preparatory Upper School, FL
North Cobb Christian School, GA
North Country School, NY
North Cross School, VA
Northfield Mount Hermon School, MA
North Shore Country Day School, IL
Northside Christian School, FL
The Northwest Academy, OR
Northwest Catholic High School, CT
The Northwest School, WA
Northwest Yeshiva High School, WA
Northwood School, NY
North Yarmouth Academy, ME
The Norwich Free Academy, CT
Notre Dame Academy, VA
Notre Dame- Bishop Gibbons School, NY
Notre Dame-Cathedral Latin School, OH
Notre Dame High School, LA
Notre Dame High School, NJ
Notre Dame High School, TN
Notre Dame Junior/Senior High School, PA
Oak Grove Lutheran School, ND
Oak Grove School, CA
Oak Hill Academy, VA
The Oakland School, PA
Oakland School, VA
Oak Mountain Academy, GA
Oak Ridge Military Academy, NC
The Oakridge School, TX
Oakwood Friends School, NY
Oakwood School, CA
The Oakwood School, NC
Ojai Valley School, CA
Okanagan Adventist Academy, BC, Canada
Oldenburg Academy, IN
Olney Friends School, OH
The O'Neal School, NC
Oneida Baptist Institute, KY
Orangewood Adventist Academy, CA
Oregon Episcopal School, OR
Orinda Academy, CA
The Orme School, AZ
Our Saviour Lutheran School, NY
Out-Of-Door-Academy, FL
The Overlake School, WA
Oxford School, CA
Pace Academy, GA
Pacific Academy, CA
Pacific Crest Community School, OR
Pacific Hills School, CA
The Packer Collegiate Institute, NY
Padua Franciscan High School, OH
The Paideia School, GA
Paradise Adventist Academy, CA
Parish Episcopal School, TX
The Parker School, HI
Parklane Academy, MS
The Park School of Buffalo, NY
Park Tudor School, IN
Peddie School, NJ
The Pennington School, NJ
Pensacola Catholic High School, FL
Peoples Christian Academy, ON, Canada
Perkiomen School, PA
Phillips Academy (Andover), MA
Phillips Exeter Academy, NH
Phoenix Christian Unified Schools, AZ
Phoenix Country Day School, AZ
Pic River Private High School, ON, Canada
Piedmont Academy, GA
Pine Crest School, FL

Pine Ridge School, VT
Pinewood Preparatory School, SC
Pinewood—The International School of Thessaloniki, Greece, Greece
The Pingry School, NJ
Pioneer Valley Christian School, MA
Pius X High School, NE
Poly Prep Country Day School, NY
Polytechnic School, CA
Pomfret School, CT
Pope John XXIII Regional High School, NJ
Porter-Gaud School, SC
Portland Lutheran School, OR
Portledge School, NY
Portsmouth Abbey School, RI
Portsmouth Christian Academy, NH
The Potomac School, VA
Poughkeepsie Day School, NY
Powers Catholic High School, MI
The Prairie School, WI
Prestonwood Christian Academy, TX
Professional Children's School, NY
The Prout School, RI
Providence Country Day School, RI
Providence Day School, NC
Providence High School, CA
Pulaski Academy, AR
Punahou School, HI
The Putney School, VT
Queen Anne School, MD
Queen Margaret's School, BC, Canada
Queensway Christian College, ON, Canada
Quigley Catholic High School, PA
Quinte Christian High School, ON, Canada
Rabbi Alexander S. Gross Hebrew Academy, FL
Rabun Gap-Nacoochee School, GA
Randolph-Macon Academy, VA
Randolph School, AL
Ranney School, NJ
Ransom Everglades School, FL
Ravenscroft School, NC
The Rectory School, CT
Redemption Christian Academy, NY
Redwood Christian Schools, CA
Reitz Memorial High School, IN
Richmond Christian School, BC, Canada
Ridgecroft School, NC
Ridgewood Preparatory School, LA
Ridley College, ON, Canada
Ripon Christian Schools, CA
Riverdale Country School, NY
Rivermont Collegiate, IA
The Rivers School, MA
Riverstone International School, ID
Riverview School, MA
Roanoke Catholic School, VA
Robert Louis Stevenson School, NY
Rockland Country Day School, NY
Rock Point School, VT
Rocky Hill School, RI
Rocky Mount Academy, NC
The Roeper School, MI
Rolling Hills Preparatory School, CA
Roncalli High School, IN
Ron Pettigrew Christian School, BC, Canada
Rosseau Lake College, ON, Canada
Ross School, NY
Rothesay Netherwood School, NB, Canada
Rotterdam International Secondary School, Wolfert van Borselen, Netherlands
Rowland Hall-St. Mark's School, UT
Royal Canadian College, BC, Canada
Roycemore School, IL
Rumsey Hall School, CT
Rundle College, AB, Canada
Rutgers Preparatory School, NJ
Rye Country Day School, NY
Sacramento Adventist Academy, CA
Sacramento Country Day School, CA
Sacramento Waldorf School, CA
Sacred Heart School of Halifax, NS, Canada
Saddle River Day School, NJ
Sage Hill School, CA
Sage Ridge School, NV
St. Andrew's Episcopal School, MD
St. Andrew's Episcopal School, MS
St. Andrew's on the Marsh School, GA
Saint Andrew's School, FL
St. Andrew's School, RI
St. Andrew's–Sewanee School, TN
St. Anne's–Belfield School, VA
St. Anthony Catholic High School, TX
Saint Anthony High School, IL
St. Anthony's Junior-Senior High School, HI
St. Augustine High School, TX
St. Benedict at Auburndale, TN
St. Brendan High School, FL
Saint Cecilia High School, NE
St. Christopher Academy, WA
St. Clement School, ON, Canada
St. Croix Country Day School, VI
St. Croix Lutheran High School, MN
St. David's School, NC
Saint Dominic Regional High School, ME
St. Dominic's International School, Portugal, Portugal
Saint Edmund High School, NY
Saint Edward's School, FL
Saint Elizabeth High School, CA
Saint Francis High School, CA
St. Francis High School, KY
St. Francis School, GA
St. George's Independent School, TN
St. George's School, RI
Saint George's School, WA
St. George's School of Montreal, QC, Canada
St. Gregory College Preparatory School, AZ
St. Gregory's High School, IL
Saint James School, MD
St. Johnsbury Academy, VT
St. John's Catholic Prep, MD
St. John's College High School, DC
St. John's International, BC, Canada
Saint John's Preparatory School, MN
St. John's-Ravenscourt School, MB, Canada
St. Joseph Academy, FL
Saint Joseph Central Catholic High School, OH
St. Joseph High School, CA
St. Joseph High School, CT

Saint Joseph High School, IL
Saint Joseph High School, PA
Saint Joseph High School, WI
St. Joseph's Catholic School, SC
St. Jude's School, ON, Canada
St. Margaret's Episcopal School, CA
Saint Mark's School, MA
St. Martin's Episcopal School, LA
Saint Mary High School, NJ
Saint Mary's College High School, CA
Saint Mary's Hall, TX
St. Mary's Hall–Doane Academy, NJ
Saint Mary's High School, AZ
St. Mary's High School, CO
Saint Mary's High School, MD
St. Mary's School, OR
Saint Maur International School, Japan
Saint Monica's High School, CA
St. Patrick High School, NT, Canada
Saint Patrick—Saint Vincent High School, CA
St. Patrick's Regional Secondary, BC, Canada
Saint Patrick's School, KY
St. Paul Academy and Summit School, MN
Saint Paul Lutheran High School, MO
St. Paul's Episcopal School, AL
St. Pius X Catholic High School, GA
Saints Peter and Paul High School, MD
St. Stephen's & St. Agnes School, VA
Saint Stephen's Episcopal School, FL
St. Stephen's Episcopal School, TX
St. Stephen's School, Rome, Italy
St. Thomas Aquinas High School, FL
Saint Thomas Aquinas High School, KS
St. Thomas Aquinas High School, NH
Saint Viator High School, IL
Salem Baptist Christian School, NC
Salesian High School, CA
Salpointe Catholic High School, AZ
Salt Lake Lutheran High School, UT
Saltus Grammar School, Bermuda
The Samuel Scheck Hillel Community Day School, FL
Sandia Preparatory School, NM
San Diego Academy, CA
San Diego Jewish Academy, CA
San Domenico School, CA
Sandy Spring Friends School, MD
Sanford School, DE
San Francisco University High School, CA
San Francisco Waldorf High School, CA
San Marcos Baptist Academy, TX
Santa Fe Preparatory School, NM
Santa Margarita Catholic High School, CA
Santiam Christian School, OR
Savannah Christian Preparatory School, GA
The Savannah Country Day School, GA
Sayre School, KY
Scarborough Christian School, ON, Canada
Scattergood Friends School, IA
SCECGS Redlands, Australia
Schlarman High School, IL
School for Young Performers, NY
Scotus Central Catholic High School, NE
Seabury Hall, HI
Seattle Academy of Arts and Sciences, WA
Seattle Christian Schools, WA
Seattle Lutheran High School, WA
Second Baptist School, TX
Sedbergh School, QC, Canada
Seoul Foreign School, Republic of Korea
Seton Catholic Central High School, NY
Seton Catholic High School, AZ
The Seven Hills School, OH
Sewickley Academy, PA
Shades Mountain Christian School, AL
Shady Side Academy, PA
Shannon Forest Christian School, SC
Shattuck-St. Mary's School, MN
Sheila Morrison School, ON, Canada
Shelton School and Evaluation Center, TX
Shenandoah Valley Academy, VA
The Shipley School, PA
Shorecrest Preparatory School, FL
Shoreline Christian, WA
Sioux Falls Christian High School, SD
Smith School, NY
Smithville District Christian High School, ON, Canada
Solebury School, PA
Solomon Learning Institute, Ltd., AB, Canada
Soundview Preparatory School, NY
Southfield Christian High School, MI
Southridge School, BC, Canada
Southwestern Academy, AZ
Southwestern Academy, CA
Squaw Valley Academy, CA
Stanbridge Academy, CA
Starkville Academy, MS
Staten Island Academy, NY
Stephen T. Badin High School, OH
Stevenson School, CA
St Leonards School and Sixth Form College, United Kingdom
The Stony Brook School, NY
Storm King School, NY
Stratford Academy, GA
Strathcona-Tweedsmuir School, AB, Canada
Stratton Mountain School, VT
The Sudbury Valley School, MA
Suffield Academy, CT
Summerfield Waldorf School, CA
The Summit Country Day School, OH
Tabor Academy, MA
The Taft School, CT
Tallulah Falls School, GA
Tampa Preparatory School, FL
Tandem Friends School, VA
TASIS The American School in England, United Kingdom
TASIS, The American School in Switzerland, Switzerland
The Tatnall School, DE
Telluride Mountain School, CO
The Tenney School, TX
Teurlings Catholic High School, LA
The Thacher School, CA
Thomas Jefferson School, MO
Thornton Friends School, MD
Tilton School, NH
Timothy Christian High School, IL
TMI—The Episcopal School of Texas, TX
Toronto District Christian High School, ON, Canada
Toronto Waldorf School, ON, Canada

Tower Hill School, DE
Town Centre Private High School, ON, Canada
Tri-City Christian Schools, CA
Trident Academy, SC
Trinity Catholic High School, MA
Trinity Christian Academy, TX
Trinity College School, ON, Canada
Trinity Episcopal School, VA
Trinity High School, NH
Trinity High School, OH
Trinity Preparatory School, FL
Trinity Presbyterian School, AL
Trinity School, NY
Trinity School of Midland, TX
Trinity Valley School, TX
United Mennonite Educational Institute, ON, Canada
United Nations International School, NY
University Christian Preparatory School, LA
University Lake School, WI
University Liggett School, MI
University of Chicago Laboratory Schools, IL
University of Toronto Schools, ON, Canada
University Prep, WA
University School of Jackson, TN
University School of Milwaukee, WI
University School of Nova Southeastern University, FL
The Urban School of San Francisco, CA
Valle Catholic High School, MO
Valley Christian High School, CA
Valley Christian School, CA
Valley Lutheran High School, AZ
Valley Lutheran High School, MI
The Valley School, MI
Valwood School, GA
Vandebilt Catholic High School, LA
Vanguard Preparatory School, TX
Verdala International School, Malta
Verde Valley School, AZ
Victor Valley Christian School, CA
Viewpoint School, CA
Villa Maria Academy, PA
Villanova Preparatory School, CA
Virginia Beach Friends School, VA
Virginia Episcopal School, VA
Wakefield School, VA
Waldorf High School of Massachusetts Bay, MA
The Waldorf School of Garden City, NY
The Walker School, GA
Walnut Hill School, MA
The Wardlaw-Hartridge School, NJ
Waring School, MA
Wasatch Academy, UT
Washington Academy, ME
Washington County Day School, MS
Washington International School, DC
Washington Waldorf School, MD
The Waterford School, UT
Watkinson School, CT
The Waverly School, CA
Wayne Country Day School, NC
Waynflete School, ME
The Webb School, TN
Webb School of Knoxville, TN
The Webb Schools, CA
The Wellington School, OH
Wesleyan Academy, PR
Westbury Christian School, TX
West Catholic High School, MI
Westchester Country Day School, NC
Western Christian Schools, CA
Western Reserve Academy, OH
West Island College, AB, Canada
Westminster Catawba Christian, SC
Westminster Christian Academy, AL
Westminster Christian School, FL
Westminster School, CT
The Westminster Schools, GA
Westminster Schools of Augusta, GA
West Nottingham Academy, MD
Westtown School, PA
Wheaton Academy, IL
The Wheeler School, RI
Whitefield Academy, GA
The White Mountain School, NH
Wichita Collegiate School, KS
William Penn Charter School, PA
The Williams School, CT
The Williston Northampton School, MA
Willow Hill School, MA
Willow Wood School, ON, Canada
Wilmington Friends School, DE
Wilson Hall, SC
The Winchendon School, MA
Winchester Thurston School, PA
Windermere Preparatory School, FL
The Windsor School, NY
Windward School, CA
Winston Preparatory School, NY
The Winston School, TX
The Winston School San Antonio, TX
Wisconsin Academy, WI
Woodside Priory School, CA
Woodstock School, India
Woodward Academy, GA
Wooster School, CT
Worcester Academy, MA
Worcester Preparatory School, MD
Wyoming Seminary, PA
Yokohama International School, Japan
York Country Day School, PA
York Preparatory School, NY
Zurich International School, Switzerland

BOYS' DAY SCHOOLS

Academy of the New Church Boys' School, PA
The American Boychoir School, NJ
Archbishop Curley High School, MD
Archbishop Riordan High School, CA
Archbishop Rummel High School, LA
Army and Navy Academy, CA
Avon Old Farms School, CT
Belmont Hill School, MA
Benedictine High School, OH
Benedictine High School, VA
Benedictine Military School, GA
Bishop Hendricken High School, RI
Bishop Mora Salesian High School, CA

Boston College High School, MA
The Boys' Latin School of Maryland, MD
Brophy College Preparatory, AZ
Brother Martin High School, LA
Brother Rice High School, MI
The Browning School, NY
Brunswick School, CT
Calvert Hall College High School, MD
Cardigan Mountain School, NH
Cardinal Newman High School, CA
Catholic Central High School, MI
Catholic Memorial, MA
Central Catholic High School, PA
CFS, The School at Church Farm, PA
Chaminade College Preparatory School, MO
Chestnut Hill Academy, PA
Christian Brothers Academy, NJ
Christian Brothers Academy, NY
Christ School, NC
Cistercian Preparatory School, TX
Crespi Carmelite High School, CA
De La Salle High School, CA
Delbarton School, NJ
DeMatha Catholic High School, MD
De Smet Jesuit High School, MO
Devon Preparatory School, PA
Eaglebrook School, MA
Fairfield College Preparatory School, CT
Father Judge High School, PA
The Fessenden School, MA
Fishburne Military School, VA
Fordham Preparatory School, NY
Georgetown Preparatory School, MD
Gilman School, MD
Gonzaga College High School, DC
Hargrave Military Academy, VA
The Haverford School, PA
Hillside School, MA
Jesuit College Preparatory School, TX
Jesuit High School, CA
Jesuit High School of Tampa, FL
Junipero Serra High School, CA
Landon School, MD
La Salle Institute, NY
Linden Hill School, MA
Loyola-Blakefield, MD
Loyola High School, Jesuit College Preparatory, CA
Maharishi Academy of Total Knowledge, NH
Marmion Academy, IL
Marquette University High School, WI
The McCallie School, TN
McQuaid Jesuit, NY
Memphis University School, TN
Merchiston Castle School, United Kingdom
Montgomery Bell Academy, TN
Mount Michael Benedictine School, NE
O'Dea High School, WA
Palma High School, CA
The Phelps School, PA
Rambam Mesivta, NY
Regis High School, NY
Rice High School, NY
Riverside Military Academy, GA
The Roxbury Latin School, MA
St. Albans School, DC
St. Andrew's College, ON, Canada
St. Anselm's Abbey School, DC
St. Augustine High School, CA
Saint Augustine Preparatory School, NJ
St. Benedict's Preparatory School, NJ
St. Catherine's Military Academy, CA
St. Christopher's School, VA
St. Francis de Sales High School, OH
St. George's School, BC, Canada
Saint John Bosco High School, CA
St. John's Northwestern Military Academy, WI
St. John's Preparatory School, MA
Saint Joseph Regional High School, NJ
St. Joseph's Preparatory School, PA
St. Mark's School of Texas, TX
St. Mary's International School, Japan
St. Mary's Preparatory School, MI
St. Michael's College School, ON, Canada
Saint Patrick High School, IL
St. Paul's High School, MB, Canada
St. Peter's Preparatory School, NJ
St. Sebastian's School, MA
St. Stanislaus College, MS
Saint Thomas Academy, MN
St. Thomas High School, TX
Saint Xavier High School, KY
Saint Xavier High School, OH
Salesian High School, NY
Salesianum School, DE
Salisbury School, CT
Selwyn House School, QC, Canada
South Kent School, CT
Strake Jesuit College Preparatory, TX
Subiaco Academy, AR
Trinity High School, KY
Trinity-Pawling School, NY
Valley Forge Military Academy & College, PA
Vianney High School, MO
Wediko School and Treatment Program, NH
The Woodhall School, CT
Xaverian Brothers High School, MA

GIRLS' DAY SCHOOLS

Academy of Mount Saint Ursula, NY
Academy of Notre Dame de Namur, PA
Academy of Our Lady of Good Counsel High School, NY
Academy of Our Lady of Mercy, CT
Academy of Our Lady of Peace, CA
Academy of the Holy Angels, NJ
Academy of the Holy Cross, MD
Academy of the New Church Girls' School, PA
Academy of the Sacred Heart, LA
The Agnes Irwin School, PA
Ahliyyah School for Girls, Jordan
The Archer School for Girls, CA
Assumption High School, KY
The Baldwin School, PA
Balmoral Hall School, MB, Canada
The Bermuda High School for Girls, Bermuda
Bishop Conaty-Our Lady of Loretto High School, CA
The Brearley School, NY
Brenau Academy, GA

Buffalo Seminary, NY
Carondelet High School, CA
Carrollton School of the Sacred Heart, FL
Castilleja School, CA
Cathedral High School, NY
The Catholic High School of Baltimore, MD
The Chapin School, NY
Colegio Puertorriqueno de Ninas, PR
Connelly School of the Holy Child, MD
Convent of the Sacred Heart, CT
Convent of the Sacred Heart, NY
Cornelia Connelly School, CA
Country Day School of the Sacred Heart, PA
Crofton House School, BC, Canada
Dana Hall School, MA
The Dominican Academy of the City of New York, NY
Duchesne Academy of the Sacred Heart, TX
Elizabeth Seton High School, MD
The Ellis School, PA
Elmwood School, ON, Canada
Emma Willard School, NY
The Ethel Walker School, CT
Flintridge Sacred Heart Academy, CA
Fontbonne Academy, MA
Fontbonne Hall Academy, NY
Foxcroft School, VA
Garrison Forest School, MD*
Georgetown Visitation Preparatory School, DC
Girls Preparatory School, TN
Greenwich Academy, CT
Gwynedd Mercy Academy, PA
Havergal College, ON, Canada
The Hockaday School, TX
The Holton-Arms School, MD
Holy Names High School, CA
Hutchison School, TN
Immaculate Conception High School, NJ
Immaculate Heart High School, CA
Ladywood High School, MI
La Pietra–Hawaii School for Girls, HI
Linden Hall, PA
The Linden School, ON, Canada
Louisville High School, CA
Ma'ayanot Yeshiva High School for Girls of Bergan County, NJ
Magnificat High School, OH
Marian High School, MI
Marlborough School, CA
Mary Help of Christians Academy, NJ
Marylawn of the Oranges, NJ
The Mary Louis Academy, NY
Marymount High School, CA
Marymount International School, United Kingdom
Maryvale Preparatory School, MD
Mercy High School, CT
Mercy High School, NE
Mercy High School College Preparatory, CA
Miss Edgar's and Miss Cramp's School, QC, Canada
Miss Hall's School, MA
Miss Porter's School, CT
Montrose School, MA
Mother Cabrini High School, NY
Mother McAuley High School, IL
Mt. Saint Dominic Academy, NJ
Mount Saint Joseph Academy, PA
National Cathedral School, DC
Nerinx Hall, MO
Notre Dame Academy, CA
Notre Dame Academy, MA
Notre Dame Academy, MA
Notre Dame High School, CA
Notre Dame Preparatory School, MD
Oldfields School, MD
Our Lady Academy, MS
Our Lady of Mercy Academy, NJ
Our Lady of Mercy High School, NY
Preston High School, NY
Providence High School, TX
Purnell School, NJ
Queen of Peace High School, IL
Regina Dominican High School, IL
Regina High School, OH
Roland Park Country School, MD
St. Agnes Academy, TX
St. Andrew's Priory School, HI
Saint Basil Academy, PA
St. Catherine's School, VA
St. Cecilia Academy, TN
St. Clement's School, ON, Canada
Saint Dominic Academy, NJ
Saint Gertrude High School, VA
Saint Joan Antida High School, WI
St. Joseph's Academy, LA
St. Margaret's School, VA
St. Margaret's School, BC, Canada
St. Mary's Dominican High School, LA
St. Mary's Episcopal School, TN
Saint Mary's School, NC
Saint Matthias High School, CA
St. Paul's School for Girls, MD
Saint Teresa's Academy, MO
St. Timothy's School, MD
Salem Academy, NC
School of the Holy Child, NY
The Spence School, NY
Stella Maris High School, NY
Stoneleigh–Burnham School, MA
The Study School, QC, Canada
Trafalgar Castle School, ON, Canada
Trinity High School, IL
Ursuline Academy, MA
The Ursuline Academy of Dallas, TX
Ursuline High School, CA
The Ursuline School, NY
Villa Joseph Marie High School, PA
Villa Walsh Academy, NJ
Westover School, CT
Westridge School, CA
The Willows Academy, IL
The Winsor School, MA
Woodlands Academy of the Sacred Heart, IL
Xavier College Preparatory, AZ
Xavier University Preparatory School, LA

Coeducational in lower grades

SCHOOLS ACCEPTING BOARDING BOYS AND GIRLS

Academie Sainte Cecile International School, ON, Canada†
The Academy at Charlemont, MA†
Academy at Swift River, MA
Academy for Global Exploration, OR
Accelerated Schools, CO†
ACS Cobham International School, United Kingdom†
Advanced Academy of Georgia, GA
Aiglon College, Switzerland
Albert College, ON, Canada†
Alliance Academy, Ecuador
Andrews Osborne Academy, OH†
Antelope Valley Christian School, CA†
Argo Academy, FL
Arthur Morgan School, NC†
Ashbury College, ON, Canada†
Asheville School, NC†
The Athenian School, CA†
Bass Memorial Academy, MS†
Baylor School, TN†
The Bement School, MA†
Berkshire School, MA†
Besant Hill School, CA†
Blair Academy, NJ†
Blue Mountain Academy, PA†
Bodwell High School, BC, Canada†
The Bolles School, FL†
Brehm Preparatory School, IL†
Brentwood College School, BC, Canada†
Brewster Academy, NH†
Brockwood Park School, United Kingdom
Bronte College of Canada, ON, Canada†
Brooks School, MA†
Burke Mountain Academy, VT†
Burr and Burton Academy, VT†
Buxton School, MA†
The Cambridge School of Weston, MA†
Canadian Academy, Japan†
Canterbury School, CT†
Canyonville Christian Academy, OR†
Carlisle School, VA†
Carrabassett Valley Academy, ME†
Cascadilla School, NY†
Cate School, CA†
Cedar Ridge Academy, UT
Chapel Hill–Chauncy Hall School, MA†
Cheshire Academy, CT†
Children's Creative and Performing Arts Academy—Capa Division, CA†
Choate Rosemary Hall, CT†
College du Leman International School, Switzerland†
The Colorado Rocky Mountain School, CO†
Columbia International College of Canada, ON, Canada†
Columbia International School, Japan†
Concord Academy, MA†
Concordia High School, AB, Canada†
Conserve School, WI
Cotter Schools, MN†
Cross Creek Programs, UT
Crotched Mountain Rehabilitation Center School, NH
The Culver Academies, IN†
Cushing Academy, MA†
Darlington School, GA†
Darrow School, NY†
Deerfield Academy, MA†
Detroit Country Day School, MI†
Dublin Christian Academy, NH†
Dublin School, NH†
Dunn School, CA†
Eagle Hill School, CT
Eagle Hill School, MA†
Eastside College Preparatory School, CA†
Ecole d'Humanité, Switzerland†
Elan School, ME
Emerson Honors High Schools, CA†
Episcopal High School, VA
The Family Foundation School, NY
Fay School, MA†
Forest Lake Academy, FL
The Forman School, CT†
Fountain Valley School of Colorado, CO†
Foxcroft Academy, ME†
Fox River Country Day School, IL†
Franklin Academy, CT†
Freeman Academy, SD†
Fryeburg Academy, ME†
Gables Academy, GA†
George School, PA†
George Stevens Academy, ME†
Gilmour Academy, OH†
Girard College, PA
The Glenholme School, CT
Gould Academy, ME†
The Governor French Academy, IL†
The Governor's Academy (formerly Governor Dummer Academy), MA†
Great Lakes Christian High School, ON, Canada†
Groton School, MA†
Grove School, CT†
The Gunnery, CT†
Hackley School, NY†
Harding Academy, AR†
The Harvey School, NY
Hawaiian Mission Academy, HI†
Hawai'i Preparatory Academy, HI†
Hebron Academy, ME†
Hidden Lake Academy, GA
High Mowing School, NH†
The Hill School, PA†
Hokkaido International School, Japan
Holderness School, NH†
Hoosac School, NY†
Horizons School, GA†
The Hotchkiss School, CT†
Houghton Academy, NY†
Howe Military School, IN†
The Hun School of Princeton, NJ†
Hyde School, CT†
Hyde School, ME†
Idyllwild Arts Academy, CA†
Imperial College of Toronto, ON, Canada
Indian Mountain School, CT†
Indian Springs School, AL†
Interlochen Arts Academy, MI†
International School Eerde, Netherlands†
International School of South Africa, South Africa†
The John Dewey Academy, MA

†Accepts day students

Kent School, CT†
Kents Hill School, ME†
Kildonan School, NY†
Kimball Union Academy, NH†
King George School, VT
The King's Academy, TN†
King's-Edgehill School, NS, Canada†
Kingsway College, ON, Canada†
The Knox School, NY†
Lakefield College School, ON, Canada†
Lake Forest Academy, IL†
La Lumiere School, IN†
Lancaster Mennonite High School, PA†
Landmark East School, NS, Canada†
Landmark School, MA†
Lawrence Academy, MA†
The Lawrenceville School, NJ†
Lee Academy, ME†
Lester B. Pearson United World College of the Pacific, BC, Canada†
The Linsly School, WV†
The Loomis Chaffee School, CT†
The Lowell Whiteman School, CO†
Lustre Christian High School, MT†
Luther College High School, SK, Canada†
Lyndon Institute, VT†
The MacDuffie School, MA†
Maine Central Institute, ME†
Maine School of Science and Mathematics, ME
Maplebrook School, NY
Marianapolis Preparatory School, CT†
The Marvelwood School, CT†
Massanutten Military Academy, VA†
The Masters School, NY†
Maur Hill-Mount Academy, KS†
McDonogh School, MD†
Mennonite Collegiate Institute, MB, Canada†
Mercersburg Academy, PA†
Middlesex School, MA†
Midland School, CA†
Millbrook School, NY†
Miller School, VA†
Milton Academy, MA†
Montana Academy, MT
Montverde Academy, FL†
Mount Bachelor Academy, OR
Nancy Campbell Collegiate Institute, ON, Canada†
National Sports Academy at Lake Placid, NY†
Navajo Preparatory School, Inc., NM†
Nebraska Christian Schools, NE†
Neuchatel Junior College, Switzerland
New Hampton School, NH†
New Horizon Youth Ministries, IN†
New Mexico Military Institute, NM
New York Military Academy, NY†
Niagara Christian Community of Schools, ON, Canada†
Noble and Greenough School, MA†
The North Broward Preparatory Upper School, FL†
North Country School, NY†
Northfield Mount Hermon School, MA†
Northwest Academy, ID
The Northwest School, WA†
Northwood School, NY†
Oak Creek Ranch School, AZ
Oak Grove School, CA†
Oak Hill Academy, VA†
Oakland School, VA†
Oak Ridge Military Academy, NC†
Oakwood Friends School, NY†
Ojai Valley School, CA†
Olney Friends School, OH†
Oneida Baptist Institute, KY†
Oregon Episcopal School, OR†
The Orme School, AZ†
Peddie School, NJ†
The Pennington School, NJ†
Perkiomen School, PA†
Phillips Academy (Andover), MA†
Phillips Exeter Academy, NH†
Pinehurst School, ON, Canada
Pine Ridge School, VT
Pinewood—The International School of Thessaloniki, Greece, Greece†
Pomfret School, CT†
Portland Lutheran School, OR†
Portsmouth Abbey School, RI†
The Putney School, VT†
Rabun Gap-Nacoochee School, GA†
Randolph-Macon Academy, VA†
The Rectory School, CT†
Redemption Christian Academy, NY†
Ridley College, ON, Canada†
Riverview School, MA†
Rock Point School, VT†
Rosseau Lake College, ON, Canada†
Ross School, NY†
Rothesay Netherwood School, NB, Canada†
Rumsey Hall School, CT†
Saint Andrew's School, FL†
St. Andrew's School, RI†
St. Andrew's–Sewanee School, TN†
St. Anne's–Belfield School, VA†
St. Anthony Catholic High School, TX†
St. Croix Lutheran High School, MN†
St. George's School, RI†
Saint James School, MD†
St. Johnsbury Academy, VT†
Saint John's Preparatory School, MN†
St. John's-Ravenscourt School, MB, Canada†
Saint Mark's School, MA†
Saint Paul Lutheran High School, MO†
St. Paul's School, NH
St. Stephen's Episcopal School, TX†
St. Stephen's School, Rome, Italy†
Sandy Spring Friends School, MD†
San Marcos Baptist Academy, TX†
Scattergood Friends School, IA†
Sedbergh School, QC, Canada†
Shady Side Academy, PA†
Shattuck-St. Mary's School, MN†
Sheila Morrison School, ON, Canada†
Shenandoah Valley Academy, VA†
Solebury School, PA†
Sorenson's Ranch School, UT
Southwestern Academy, AZ†
Southwestern Academy, CA†
Squaw Valley Academy, CA†
Stevenson School, CA†

†Accepts day students

Still Creek Christian School, TX
St Leonards School and Sixth Form College, United Kingdom†
The Stony Brook School, NY†
Storm King School, NY†
Stratton Mountain School, VT†
Suffield Academy, CT†
Summit Preparatory School, MT
Tabor Academy, MA†
The Taft School, CT†
Tallulah Falls School, GA†
TASIS The American School in England, United Kingdom†
TASIS, The American School in Switzerland, Switzerland†
The Thacher School, CA†
Thomas Jefferson School, MO†
Tilton School, NH†
TMI—The Episcopal School of Texas, TX†
Trident Academy, SC†
Trinity College School, ON, Canada†
The United World College—USA, NM
The Vanguard School, FL
Verdala International School, Malta†
Verde Valley School, AZ†
Villanova Preparatory School, CA†
Virginia Episcopal School, VA†
Walnut Hill School, MA†
Wasatch Academy, UT†
Washington Academy, ME†
The Webb School, TN†
The Webb Schools, CA†
Western Reserve Academy, OH†
Westminster School, CT†
West Nottingham Academy, MD†
Westtown School, PA†
The White Mountain School, NH†
The Williston Northampton School, MA†
The Winchendon School, MA†
Wisconsin Academy, WI†
Woodside Priory School, CA†
Woodstock School, India†
Worcester Academy, MA†
Wyoming Seminary, PA†

SCHOOLS ACCEPTING BOARDING BOYS

Academy of the New Church Boys' School, PA†
The American Boychoir School, NJ†
Army and Navy Academy, CA†
Avon Old Farms School, CT†
Belmont Hill School, MA†
The Blue Ridge School, VA
Camden Military Academy, SC
Cardigan Mountain School, NH†
Carson Long Military Institute, PA
CFS, The School at Church Farm, PA†
Chamberlain-Hunt Academy, MS†
Chaminade College Preparatory School, MO†
Cherokee Creek Boys School, SC
Cherry Gulch, ID
Christchurch School, VA†
Christ School, NC†
Deck House School, ME
Eaglebrook School, MA†
Elk Mountain Academy, MT
The Fessenden School, MA†
Fishburne Military School, VA†
Georgetown Preparatory School, MD†
The Gow School, NY
The Grand River Academy, OH
The Greenwood School, VT
Hampshire Country School, NH
Hargrave Military Academy, VA†
Hillside School, MA†
Linden Hill School, MA†
Little Keswick School, VA
Lyman Ward Military Academy, AL
Maharishi Academy of Total Knowledge, NH†
The McCallie School, TN†
Merchiston Castle School, United Kingdom
Missouri Military Academy, MO
Mount Michael Benedictine School, NE†
The Oxford Academy, CT
The Penikese Island School, MA
The Phelps School, PA†
Riverside Military Academy, GA†
St. Albans School, DC†
St. Andrew's College, ON, Canada†
St. Catherine's Military Academy, CA†
St. George's School, BC, Canada†
St. John's Northwestern Military Academy, WI†
St. Lawrence Seminary, WI
St. Mary's Preparatory School, MI†
St. Michael's Preparatory School of the Norbertine Fathers, CA
St. Stanislaus College, MS†
St. Thomas Choir School, NY
Saint Thomas More School, CT
Salisbury School, CT†
Sky Ranch for Boys, Inc., SD
South Kent School, CT†
Stone Mountain School, NC
Subiaco Academy, AR†
Timber Ridge School, VA
Trinity-Pawling School, NY†
Valley Forge Military Academy & College, PA†
Valley View School, MA
Wediko School and Treatment Program, NH
The Woodhall School, CT†

SCHOOLS ACCEPTING BOARDING GIRLS

The Academy at Sisters, OR
Academy of the New Church Girls' School, PA†
Alpine Academy, UT
Annie Wright School, WA†
Auldern Academy, NC
Balmoral Hall School, MB, Canada†
The Bishop Strachan School, ON, Canada
Brenau Academy, GA†
Bromley Brook School, VT
Dana Hall School, MA†
Emma Willard School, NY†
The Ethel Walker School, CT†
Flintridge Sacred Heart Academy, CA†
Foxcroft School, VA†
Garrison Forest School, MD†
Havergal College, ON, Canada†
The Hockaday School, TX†
Linden Hall, PA†
Marymount International School, United Kingdom†

†Accepts day students

Miss Hall's School, MA†
Miss Porter's School, CT†
New Haven, UT
Oldfields School, MD†
Purnell School, NJ†
Queen Margaret's School, BC, Canada†
St. Margaret's School, VA†
St. Margaret's School, BC, Canada†
Saint Mary's School, NC†
St. Timothy's School, MD†
Salem Academy, NC†
San Domenico School, CA†
Spring Ridge Academy, AZ
Stoneleigh–Burnham School, MA†
Sunrise Academy, UT
Trafalgar Castle School, ON, Canada†
Westover School, CT†
Woodlands Academy of the Sacred Heart, IL†

MILITARY SCHOOLS

Army and Navy Academy, CA
Benedictine High School, VA
Benedictine Military School, GA
Camden Military Academy, SC
Carson Long Military Institute, PA
Chamberlain-Hunt Academy, MS
Christian Brothers Academy, NY
Fishburne Military School, VA
Georgia Military College High School, GA
Hargrave Military Academy, VA
Howe Military School, IN
La Salle Institute, NY
Lyman Ward Military Academy, AL
Massanutten Military Academy, VA
Missouri Military Academy, MO
New Mexico Military Institute, NM
New York Military Academy, NY
Oak Ridge Military Academy, NC
Randolph-Macon Academy, VA
Riverside Military Academy, GA
St. Catherine's Military Academy, CA
St. John's Northwestern Military Academy, WI
Saint Thomas Academy, MN
Sedbergh School, QC, Canada
Valley Forge Military Academy & College, PA

SCHOOLS WITH A RELIGIOUS AFFILIATION

Advent Christian Church

Saint Francis High School, CA
Scarborough Christian School, ON, Canada

Anglican Church of Canada

Ashbury College, ON, Canada
The Bishop Strachan School, ON, Canada
Rothesay Netherwood School, NB, Canada
St. Clement's School, ON, Canada

Assemblies of God

Antelope Valley Christian School, CA
Valley Christian High School, CA
Victor Valley Christian School, CA

Assembly of God Church

Modesto Christian School, CA

Baha'i

Nancy Campbell Collegiate Institute, ON, Canada

Baptist Bible Fellowship

New Tribes Mission Academy, ON, Canada

Baptist Church

Beth Haven Christian School, KY
Bulloch Academy, GA
Calvary Christian Academy, KY
Dublin Christian Academy, NH
The First Academy, FL
First Baptist Academy, TX
Foundation Academy, FL
Grace Baptist Academy, TN
Los Angeles Baptist Junior/Senior High School, CA
Northside Christian School, FL
Oak Hill Academy, VA
Salem Baptist Christian School, NC
San Marcos Baptist Academy, TX
Second Baptist School, TX

Baptist General Association of Virginia

Hargrave Military Academy, VA

Bible Fellowship Church

Chinese Christian Schools, CA

Brethren Church

Grace Brethren School, CA
New Tribes Mission Academy, ON, Canada

Brethren in Christ Church

Niagara Christian Community of Schools, ON, Canada

Calvinist

Ripon Christian Schools, CA

Christian

Academy of the New Church Boys' School, PA
Academy of the New Church Girls' School, PA
Ahliyyah School for Girls, Jordan
American Christian Academy, AL
Austin Christian Academy, MB, Canada
Brethren Christian Junior and Senior High Schools, CA
Bulloch Academy, GA
Capistrano Valley Christian Schools, CA
Cardigan Mountain School, NH
Cole Valley Christian High School, ID
Faith Christian High School, CA
The Family Foundation School, NY
First Presbyterian Day School, GA
Fowlers Academy, PR
Grace Brethren School, CA
Harrells Christian Academy, NC
Hawthorne Christian Academy, NJ
Heritage Christian Academy, AB, Canada
Marion Academy, AL
Mesa Grande Seventh-Day Academy, CA
New Covenant Academy, MO
New Horizon Youth Ministries, IN

North Cobb Christian School, GA
Peoples Christian Academy, ON, Canada
Porter-Gaud School, SC
Quinte Christian High School, ON, Canada
Riverside Military Academy, GA
St. Croix Lutheran High School, MN
St. David's School, NC
Saint Joseph High School, IL
Scarborough Christian School, ON, Canada
Smithville District Christian High School, ON, Canada
The Stony Brook School, NY
Timothy Christian High School, IL
Toronto District Christian High School, ON, Canada
Trinity Presbyterian School, AL
Valley Christian School, CA
Western Christian Schools, CA
Westminster Christian School, FL
The Westminster Schools, GA
Woodstock School, India

Christian Nondenominational

Airdrie Koinonia Christian School, AB, Canada
Alliance Academy, Ecuador
Alma Heights Christian Academy, CA
Asheville School, NC
Bakersfield Christian High School, CA
Bearspaw Christian School, AB, Canada
Boston Trinity Academy, MA
Bridgemont High School, CA
Canyonville Christian Academy, OR
Charlotte Christian School, NC
Christian Central Academy, NY
Donelson Christian Academy, TN
Dublin Christian Academy, NH
Eastside Christian Academy, AB, Canada
Evangelical Christian School, TN
Franklin Road Academy, TN
Front Range Christian High School, CO
The Geneva School, FL
Grace Christian School, AK
Hamilton District Christian High, ON, Canada
Hanalani Schools, HI
Hawthorne Christian Academy, NJ
Heritage Christian Academy, MI
Hillcrest Christian School, CA
The Hill School, PA
The King's Christian High School, NJ
King's High School, WA
King's Ridge Christian School, GA
King's West School, WA
Koinonia Christian School, AB, Canada
Lakeland Christian Academy, IN
Lansing Christian School, MI
Lexington Christian Academy, MA
Lifegate School, OR
Linfield Christian School, CA
Lyman Ward Military Academy, AL
Massanutten Military Academy, VA
The Master's School, CT
The McCallie School, TN
Merchiston Castle School, United Kingdom
Mid-Pacific Institute, HI
Missouri Military Academy, MO
Norfolk Christian School, VA
Oak Mountain Academy, GA
Parklane Academy, MS
Phoenix Christian Unified Schools, AZ
Portsmouth Christian Academy, NH
Richmond Christian School, BC, Canada
Ron Pettigrew Christian School, BC, Canada
St. Anne's–Belfield School, VA
St. George's Independent School, TN
Santiam Christian School, OR
Savannah Christian Preparatory School, GA
Seattle Christian Schools, WA
Seoul Foreign School, Republic of Korea
Shades Mountain Christian School, AL
Shoreline Christian, WA
Sioux Falls Christian High School, SD
Southfield Christian High School, MI
Still Creek Christian School, TX
Tallulah Falls School, GA
Tri-City Christian Schools, CA
Trinity Christian Academy, TX
University Christian Preparatory School, LA
Wheaton Academy, IL
Whitefield Academy, GA

Christian Reformed Church

Denver Christian High School, CO
Eastern Christian High School, NJ
Illiana Christian High School, IL
Immanuel Christian High School, AB, Canada
Smithville District Christian High School, ON, Canada
Toronto District Christian High School, ON, Canada

Church of Christ

Alabama Christian Academy, AL
Boyd-Buchanan School, TN
Christian Home and Bible School, FL
Columbia Academy, TN
Dallas Christian School, TX
David Lipscomb High School, TN
Ezell-Harding Christian School, TN
Great Lakes Christian High School, ON, Canada
Harding Academy, AR
Jackson Christian School, TN
Madison Academy, AL
Mars Hill Bible School, AL
Westbury Christian School, TX

Church of Christ, Scientist

Fox River Country Day School, IL

Church of England (Anglican)

Havergal College, ON, Canada
King's-Edgehill School, NS, Canada
Lakefield College School, ON, Canada
Ridley College, ON, Canada
Saltus Grammar School, Bermuda
SCECGS Redlands, Australia
Trinity College School, ON, Canada

Church of God
Excel Christian Academy, GA

Church of the New Jerusalem
Academy of the New Church Girls' School, PA

Episcopal Church
All Saints' Episcopal School of Fort Worth, TX
Annie Wright School, WA
Berkeley Preparatory School, FL
The Blue Ridge School, VA
Breck School, MN
Brooks School, MA
Campbell Hall (Episcopal), CA
The Canterbury School of Florida, FL
CFS, The School at Church Farm, PA
Christchurch School, VA
Christ School, NC
Doane Stuart School, NY
Episcopal Collegiate School, AR
Episcopal High School, TX
Episcopal High School, VA
Episcopal High School of Jacksonville, FL
The Episcopal School of Dallas, TX
Groton School, MA
Harvard-Westlake School, CA
Holderness School, NH
Holland Hall, OK
Holy Innocents' Episcopal School, GA
Hoosac School, NY
Howe Military School, IN
Iolani School, HI
Kent School, CT
National Cathedral School, DC
Oregon Episcopal School, OR
Parish Episcopal School, TX
Pomfret School, CT
Porter-Gaud School, SC
Queen Anne School, MD
The Rectory School, CT
Rock Point School, VT
St. Albans School, DC
St. Andrew's Episcopal School, MD
St. Andrew's Episcopal School, MS
St. Andrew's Priory School, HI
Saint Andrew's School, FL
St. Andrew's School, RI
St. Andrew's–Sewanee School, TN
St. Catherine's School, VA
St. Christopher's School, VA
St. David's School, NC
Saint Edward's School, FL
St. George's School, RI
Saint James School, MD
St. John's Northwestern Military Academy, WI
St. Margaret's Episcopal School, CA
St. Margaret's School, VA
Saint Mark's School, MA
St. Martin's Episcopal School, LA
St. Mary's Episcopal School, TN
St. Mary's Hall–Doane Academy, NJ
Saint Mary's School, NC
St. Paul's Episcopal School, AL
St. Paul's School, MD
St. Paul's School, NH
St. Paul's School for Girls, MD
St. Stephen's & St. Agnes School, VA
Saint Stephen's Episcopal School, FL
St. Stephen's Episcopal School, TX
St. Thomas Choir School, NY
St. Timothy's School, MD
Salisbury School, CT
Seabury Hall, HI
Shattuck-St. Mary's School, MN
South Kent School, CT
TMI—The Episcopal School of Texas, TX
Trinity Episcopal School, VA
Trinity-Pawling School, NY
Trinity Preparatory School, FL
Trinity School, NY
Trinity School of Midland, TX
Virginia Episcopal School, VA
The White Mountain School, NH
Wooster School, CT

Evangelical
Heritage Christian Academy, AB, Canada
Hosanna Christian School, OR
New Horizon Youth Ministries, IN
Pioneer Valley Christian School, MA
Southfield Christian High School, MI

Evangelical Free Church of America
Hope Christian School, AB, Canada

Evangelical Friends
Greenleaf Academy, ID

Evangelical/Fundamental
Airdrie Koinonia Christian School, AB, Canada
Chinese Christian Schools, CA
Noah Webster Christian School, WY

Evangelical Lutheran Church in America
Faith Lutheran High School, NV
Luther High School North, IL

General Association of Regular Baptist Churches
Baptist High School, NJ

Jewish
Donna Klein Jewish Academy, FL
The Emery Weiner School, TX
The Family Foundation School, NY
Gann Academy (The New Jewish High School of Greater Boston), MA
Hebrew Academy, CA
Hebrew Academy-the Five Towns, NY
Hyman Brand Hebrew Academy of Greater Kansas City, KS
Jack M. Barrack Hebrew Academy (formerly Akiba Hebrew Academy), PA
Ma'ayanot Yeshiva High School for Girls of Bergan County, NJ
Milken Community High School of Stephen S. Wise Temple, CA
Northwest Yeshiva High School, WA

Rabbi Alexander S. Gross Hebrew Academy, FL
Rambam Mesivta, NY
St. Anne's–Belfield School, VA
The Samuel Scheck Hillel Community Day School, FL
San Diego Jewish Academy, CA

Lutheran Church
Concordia Continuing Education High School, AB, Canada
Concordia High School, AB, Canada
Fox Valley Lutheran Academy, IL
Los Angeles Lutheran High School, CA
Lutheran High School North, MO
Lutheran High School of San Diego, CA
Lutheran High School West, OH
Luther College High School, SK, Canada
Martin Luther High School, NY
Metro-East Lutheran High School, IL
Oak Grove Lutheran School, ND
Portland Lutheran School, OR
Salt Lake Lutheran High School, UT
Seattle Lutheran High School, WA

Lutheran Church–Missouri Synod
Denver Lutheran High School, CO
Faith Lutheran High School, NV
Lutheran High North, TX
Lutheran High School, IN
Lutheran High School, MO
Lutheran High School Northwest, MI
Lutheran High School of Hawaii, HI
Luther High School North, IL
Luther High School South, IL
Our Saviour Lutheran School, NY
Pacific Lutheran High School, CA
Saint Paul Lutheran High School, MO
Valley Lutheran High School, AZ
Valley Lutheran High School, MI

Mennonite Brethren Church
Lustre Christian High School, MT
Mennonite Collegiate Institute, MB, Canada

Mennonite Church
Christopher Dock Mennonite High School, PA
Eastern Mennonite High School, VA
Freeman Academy, SD
Lancaster Mennonite High School, PA
Mennonite Collegiate Institute, MB, Canada

Mennonite Church USA
United Mennonite Educational Institute, ON, Canada

Methodist Church
Kents Hill School, ME
The Pennington School, NJ
Randolph-Macon Academy, VA
Tilton School, NH

Moravian Church
Moravian Academy, PA
Salem Academy, NC

Muslim
Ahliyyah School for Girls, Jordan

Pentecostal Church
Community Christian Academy, KY
Redemption Christian Academy, NY

Presbyterian Church
Blair Academy, NJ
Chamberlain-Hunt Academy, MS
Menaul School, NM
Rabun Gap-Nacoochee School, GA
Shannon Forest Christian School, SC
Westminster Christian Academy, AL

Presbyterian Church in America
Briarwood Christian High School, AL
First Presbyterian Day School, GA
Westminster Catawba Christian, SC
Westminster Schools of Augusta, GA

Protestant
Piedmont Academy, GA
Pioneer Valley Christian School, MA
Queensway Christian College, ON, Canada
Quinte Christian High School, ON, Canada

Protestant Church
Christian Junior–Senior High School, CA

Protestant-Evangelical
Lehigh Valley Christian High School, PA
Nebraska Christian Schools, NE

Reformed Church
Chamberlain-Hunt Academy, MS
Covenant Canadian Reformed School, AB, Canada
Heritage Christian School, ON, Canada
Immanuel Christian High School, AB, Canada

Reformed Church in America
Illiana Christian High School, IL

Roman Catholic Church
Academie Sainte Cecile International School, ON, Canada
Academy of Mount Saint Ursula, NY
Academy of Notre Dame de Namur, PA
Academy of Our Lady of Good Counsel High School, NY
Academy of Our Lady of Mercy, CT
Academy of Our Lady of Peace, CA
Academy of the Holy Angels, NJ
Academy of the Holy Cross, MD
Academy of the Holy Names, FL
Academy of the Sacred Heart, LA
Academy of the Sacred Heart, MI
Archbishop Curley High School, MD
Archbishop Edward A. McCarthy High School, FL
Archbishop Hoban High School, OH
Archbishop McNicholas High School, OH
Archbishop Mitty High School, CA
Archbishop Riordan High School, CA
Archbishop Rummel High School, LA
Archbishop Spalding High School, MD
Archmere Academy, DE
Assumption High School, KY
Aurora Central High School, IL
Austin Preparatory School, MA

Bellarmine-Jefferson High School, CA
Benedictine High School, OH
Benedictine High School, VA
Benedictine Military School, GA
Benilde–St. Margaret's School, MN
Bishop Alemany High School, CA
Bishop Blanchet High School, WA
Bishop Brady High School, NH
Bishop Carroll High School, PA
Bishop Conaty-Our Lady of Loretto High School, CA
Bishop Connolly High School, MA
Bishop Denis J. O'Connell High School, VA
Bishop Eustace Preparatory School, NJ
Bishop Feehan High School, MA
Bishop Fenwick High School, OH
Bishop Garcia Diego High School, CA
Bishop George Ahr High School, NJ
Bishop Gorman High School, NV
Bishop Guertin High School, NH
Bishop Hendricken High School, RI
Bishop Ireton High School, VA
Bishop Kelly High School, ID
Bishop Luers High School, IN
Bishop Lynch Catholic High School, TX
Bishop McGuinness Catholic High School, NC
Bishop McGuinness Catholic High School, OK
Bishop McNamara High School, IL
Bishop Montgomery High School, CA
Bishop Mora Salesian High School, CA
Bishop Stang High School, MA
Bishop Verot High School, FL
Bishop Walsh Middle High School, MD
Blanchet School, OR
Blessed Trinity High School, GA
Boston College High School, MA
Boylan Central Catholic High School, IL
Brother Martin High School, LA
Brother Rice High School, MI
Butte Central High School, MT
Calvert Hall College High School, MD
Canterbury School, CT
Cardinal Gibbons High School, NC
Cardinal Mooney Catholic College Preparatory High School, MI
Cardinal Mooney High School, FL
Cardinal Newman High School, CA
Cardinal Newman High School, FL
Cardinal Newman School, SC
Carondelet High School, CA
Carrollton School of the Sacred Heart, FL
Cascia Hall Preparatory School, OK
Cathedral High School, IN
Cathedral High School, NY
Catholic Central High School, MI
The Catholic High School of Baltimore, MD
Catholic Memorial, MA
Central Catholic High School, CA
Central Catholic High School, MA
Central Catholic High School, OH
Central Catholic High School, OH
Central Catholic High School, PA
Central Catholic Mid-High School, NE
Chaminade College Preparatory, CA
Chaminade College Preparatory School, MO
Chaminade-Madonna College Preparatory, FL
Chapel School, Brazil
Charlotte Catholic High School, NC
Christchurch School, VA
Christian Brothers Academy, NJ
Christian Brothers Academy, NY
Christian Brothers Academy, NY
Cistercian Preparatory School, TX
Columbus High School, IA
Connelly School of the Holy Child, MD
Convent of the Sacred Heart, CT
Convent of the Sacred Heart, NY
Convent of the Visitation School, MN
Cornelia Connelly School, CA
Cotter Schools, MN
Country Day School of the Sacred Heart, PA
Crespi Carmelite High School, CA
Cretin-Derham Hall, MN
De La Salle College, ON, Canada
De La Salle High School, CA
Delbarton School, NJ
Delphos Saint John's High School, OH
DeMatha Catholic High School, MD
DePaul Catholic High School, NJ
De Smet Jesuit High School, MO
Devon Preparatory School, PA
Dickinson Trinity, ND
The Dominican Academy of the City of New York, NY
Dowling Catholic High School, IA
Duchesne Academy of the Sacred Heart, TX
East Catholic High School, CT
Eastside Catholic School, WA
Elizabeth Seton High School, MD
Elyria Catholic High School, OH
Fairfield College Preparatory School, CT
Father Judge High School, PA
Father Lopez High School, FL
Father Ryan High School, TN
Flintridge Sacred Heart Academy, CA
Fontbonne Academy, MA
Fontbonne Hall Academy, NY
Fordham Preparatory School, NY
Gabriel Richard High School, MI
Garces Memorial High School, CA
Georgetown Preparatory School, MD
Georgetown Visitation Preparatory School, DC
Gilmour Academy, OH
Gonzaga College High School, DC
Gordon Technical High School, IL
Guerin College Preparatory High School, IL
Gwynedd Mercy Academy, PA
Hanson Memorial High School, LA
Hayden High School, KS
Holy Name High School, PA
Holy Names High School, CA
Holy Savior Menard Catholic High School, LA
Holy Trinity Diocesan High School, NY
Immaculate Conception High School, NJ

Immaculate Conception School, IL
Immaculate Heart High School, CA
Immaculate High School, CT
Jesuit High School, CA
Jesuit High School of Tampa, FL
John Paul II Catholic High School, FL
Junipero Serra High School, CA
Knoxville Catholic High School, TN
Ladywood High School, MI
Lansdale Catholic High School, PA
La Salle Academy, RI
La Salle High School, FL
La Salle Institute, NY
Lehman High School, OH
Lexington Catholic High School, KY
Loretto Academy, TX
Louisville High School, CA
Lourdes Catholic High School, AZ
Loyola-Blakefield, MD
Loyola High School, Jesuit College Preparatory, CA
Magnificat High School, OH
Marianapolis Preparatory School, CT
Marian Central Catholic High School, IL
Marian High School, IN
Marian High School, MI
Marist High School, IL
Marist High School, NJ
Marist School, GA
Marmion Academy, IL
Marquette University High School, WI
Mary Help of Christians Academy, NJ
Maryknoll School, HI
Marylawn of the Oranges, NJ
The Mary Louis Academy, NY
Marymount High School, CA
Marymount International School, Italy
Marymount International School, United Kingdom
Marymount School, NY
Maryvale Preparatory School, MD
Mater Dei High School, IN
Matignon High School, MA
Maur Hill-Mount Academy, KS
Mercedes College, Australia
Mercy High School, CA
Mercy High School, CT
Mercy High School, NE
Mercy High School College Preparatory, CA
Mercyhurst Preparatory School, PA
Mercy Vocational High School, PA
Minot Bishop Ryan, ND
Monsignor Donovan High School, NJ
Montrose School, MA
Moreau Catholic High School, CA
Mother Cabrini High School, NY
Mother McAuley High School, IL
Mount Michael Benedictine School, NE
Mount Saint Charles Academy, RI
Mt. Saint Dominic Academy, NJ
Mount Saint Joseph Academy, PA
Nazareth Academy, IL
Nerinx Hall, MO
Northwest Catholic High School, CT
Notre Dame Academy, CA
Notre Dame Academy, MA
Notre Dame Academy, MA
Notre Dame Academy, VA
Notre Dame- Bishop Gibbons School, NY
Notre Dame-Cathedral Latin School, OH
Notre Dame High School, CA
Notre Dame High School, LA
Notre Dame High School, NJ
Notre Dame High School, TN
Notre Dame Junior/Senior High School, PA
Notre Dame Preparatory School, MD
Oak Knoll School of the Holy Child, NJ
O'Dea High School, WA
Oldenburg Academy, IN
Our Lady Academy, MS
Our Lady of Mercy Academy, NJ
Our Lady of Mercy High School, NY
Padua Franciscan High School, OH
Palma High School, CA
Pensacola Catholic High School, FL
Pius X High School, NE
Pope John XXIII Regional High School, NJ
Portsmouth Abbey School, RI
Powers Catholic High School, MI
Preston High School, NY
The Prout School, RI
Providence High School, CA
Providence High School, TX
Queen of Peace High School, IL
Quigley Catholic High School, PA
Regina Dominican High School, IL
Regina High School, OH
Regis High School, NY
Reitz Memorial High School, IN
Rice High School, NY
Roanoke Catholic School, VA
Roncalli High School, IN
Sacred Heart School of Halifax, NS, Canada
St. Agnes Academy, TX
St. Anselm's Abbey School, DC
St. Anthony Catholic High School, TX
Saint Anthony High School, IL
St. Anthony's Junior-Senior High School, HI
St. Augustine High School, CA
St. Augustine High School, TX
Saint Augustine Preparatory School, NJ
Saint Basil Academy, PA
St. Benedict at Auburndale, TN
St. Benedict's Preparatory School, NJ
St. Brendan High School, FL
St. Catherine's Military Academy, CA
St. Cecilia Academy, TN
Saint Cecilia High School, NE
St. Clement School, ON, Canada
Saint Dominic Academy, NJ
Saint Dominic Regional High School, ME
Saint Edmund High School, NY
Saint Elizabeth High School, CA
St. Francis de Sales High School, OH

Saint Francis High School, CA
Saint Francis School, HI
Saint Gertrude High School, VA
St. Gregory's High School, IL
Saint Joan Antida High School, WI
Saint John Bosco High School, CA
St. John's Catholic Prep, MD
St. John's College High School, DC
St. John's Preparatory School, MA
Saint John's Preparatory School, MN
St. Joseph Academy, FL
Saint Joseph Central Catholic High School, OH
St. Joseph High School, CA
St. Joseph High School, CT
Saint Joseph High School, PA
Saint Joseph High School, WI
Saint Joseph Regional High School, NJ
St. Joseph's Academy, LA
St. Joseph's Catholic School, SC
St. Joseph's Preparatory School, PA
St. Lawrence Seminary, WI
Saint Mary High School, NJ
St. Mary's Academy, CO
Saint Mary's College High School, CA
St. Mary's Dominican High School, LA
Saint Mary's High School, AZ
St. Mary's High School, CO
Saint Mary's High School, MD
St. Mary's International School, Japan
St. Mary's Preparatory School, MI
St. Mary's School, OR
Saint Matthias High School, CA
Saint Maur International School, Japan
St. Michael's College School, ON, Canada
St. Michael's Preparatory School of the Norbertine Fathers, CA
Saint Monica's High School, CA
Saint Patrick High School, IL
St. Patrick High School, NT, Canada
Saint Patrick—Saint Vincent High School, CA
St. Patrick's Regional Secondary, BC, Canada
Saint Patrick's School, KY
St. Paul's High School, MB, Canada
St. Peter's Preparatory School, NJ
St. Pius X Catholic High School, GA
St. Sebastian's School, MA
Saints Peter and Paul High School, MD
St. Stanislaus College, MS
Saint Teresa's Academy, MO
Saint Thomas Academy, MN
St. Thomas Aquinas High School, FL
Saint Thomas Aquinas High School, KS
St. Thomas Aquinas High School, NH
St. Thomas High School, TX
Saint Thomas More School, CT
Saint Viator High School, IL
Saint Xavier High School, KY
Saint Xavier High School, OH
Salesian High School, CA
Salesian High School, NY
Salesianum School, DE
Salpointe Catholic High School, AZ
San Domenico School, CA
Santa Margarita Catholic High School, CA
Schlarman High School, IL
School of the Holy Child, NY
Scotus Central Catholic High School, NE
Seisen International School, Japan
Seton Catholic Central High School, NY
Seton Catholic High School, AZ
Stella Maris High School, NY
Stephen T. Badin High School, OH
Stuart Country Day School of the Sacred Heart, NJ
Subiaco Academy, AR
The Summit Country Day School, OH
Teurlings Catholic High School, LA
Trinity Catholic High School, MA
Trinity High School, IL
Trinity High School, KY
Trinity High School, NH
Trinity High School, OH
Ursuline Academy, DE
Ursuline Academy, MA
The Ursuline Academy of Dallas, TX
Ursuline High School, CA
The Ursuline School, NY
Valle Catholic High School, MO
Vandebilt Catholic High School, LA
Vianney High School, MO
Villa Duchesne/Oak Hill School, MO
Villa Joseph Marie High School, PA
Villa Maria Academy, PA
Villanova Preparatory School, CA
Villa Walsh Academy, NJ
Visitation Academy of St. Louis County, MO
West Catholic High School, MI
The Willows Academy, IL
Woodlands Academy of the Sacred Heart, IL
Woodside Priory School, CA
Xaverian Brothers High School, MA
Xavier College Preparatory, AZ
Xavier University Preparatory School, LA

Roman Catholic Church (Jesuit Order)

Brophy College Preparatory, AZ
Cheverus High School, ME
Immaculata High School, KS
Jesuit College Preparatory School, TX
Loyola School, NY
McQuaid Jesuit, NY
Strake Jesuit College Preparatory, TX

Schwenkfelder Church

Perkiomen School, PA

Seventh-day Adventist Church

Central Valley Christian Academy, CA
Crawford Adventist Academy, ON, Canada
Escondido Adventist Academy, CA
Griggs University and International Academy, MD
Hawaiian Mission Academy, HI
Newbury Park Adventist Academy, CA
Okanagan Adventist Academy, BC, Canada

Orangewood Adventist Academy, CA
Sacramento Adventist Academy, CA
San Diego Academy, CA
Shenandoah Valley Academy, VA
Wisconsin Academy, WI

Seventh-day Adventists
Armona Union Academy, CA
Bass Memorial Academy, MS
Blue Mountain Academy, PA
Forest Lake Academy, FL
Kingsway College, ON, Canada
Mesa Grande Seventh-Day Academy, CA
Paradise Adventist Academy, CA

Society of Friends
Abington Friends School, PA
Delaware Valley Friends School, PA
Friends' Central School, PA
George School, PA
Germantown Friends School, PA
Lincoln School, RI
Moorestown Friends School, NJ
Moses Brown School, RI
Oakwood Friends School, NY
Olney Friends School, OH
Sandy Spring Friends School, MD
Scattergood Friends School, IA
Tandem Friends School, VA
Thornton Friends School, MD
Virginia Beach Friends School, VA
Westtown School, PA
William Penn Charter School, PA
Wilmington Friends School, DE

Southern Baptist Convention
Hawaii Baptist Academy, HI
The King's Academy, TN
Oneida Baptist Institute, KY
Prestonwood Christian Academy, TX

United Church of Canada
Albert College, ON, Canada

United Methodist Church
Lydia Patterson Institute, TX
McCurdy School, NM
Wyoming Seminary, PA

Wesleyan Church
Houghton Academy, NY
Wesleyan Academy, PR

Wisconsin Evangelical Lutheran Synod
Fox Valley Lutheran High School, WI
St. Croix Lutheran High School, MN

SCHOOLS BEGINNING AT JUNIOR, SENIOR, OR POSTGRADUATE YEAR

Argo Academy, FL 12
Imperial College of Toronto, ON, Canada 11
Lester B. Pearson United World College of the Pacific, BC, Canada 13
Neuchatel Junior College, Switzerland 12
Northwest Academy, ID 11
The United World College—USA, NM 11

SCHOOLS WITH ELEMENTARY DIVISIONS

Abington Friends School, PA
The Academy at Charlemont, MA
Academy of Notre Dame de Namur, PA
The Agnes Irwin School, PA
Albert College, ON, Canada
Albuquerque Academy, NM
Alexander Dawson School, CO
Allendale Columbia School, NY
All Saints' Episcopal School of Fort Worth, TX
The Altamont School, AL
The American International School, Austria
The American School Foundation, Mexico
The American School in London, United Kingdom
The American School of Madrid, Spain
American School of Milan, Italy
American School of Paris, France
Andrews Osborne Academy, OH
Annie Wright School, WA
Army and Navy Academy, CA
Ashbury College, ON, Canada
ASSETS School, HI
The Athenian School, CA
Athens Academy, GA
Atlanta International School, GA
Augusta Preparatory Day School, GA
Austin Preparatory School, MA
The Awty International School, TX
The Baldwin School, PA
Baldwin School of Puerto Rico, Inc., PR
Balmoral Hall School, MB, Canada
Bancroft School, MA
The Barrie School, MD
The Barstow School, MO
Battle Ground Academy, TN
Baylor School, TN
Beaver Country Day School, MA
Belmont Hill School, MA
The Bement School, MA
The Benjamin School, FL
Berkeley Preparatory School, FL
The Bermuda High School for Girls, Bermuda
Berwick Academy, ME
The Birch Wathen Lenox School, NY
The Bishop Strachan School, ON, Canada
The Blake School, MN
The Bolles School, FL
The Boys' Latin School of Maryland, MD
The Brearley School, NY
Breck School, MN
Brehm Preparatory School, IL
Brentwood School, CA
Brimmer and May School, MA
Brookstone School, GA
Brownell-Talbot School, NE
The Browning School, NY
Brunswick School, CT

The Bryn Mawr School for Girls, MD
Buckingham Browne & Nichols School, MA
The Buckley School, CA
Burke Mountain Academy, VT
The Bush School, WA
The Calhoun School, NY
The Calverton School, MD
Camden Military Academy, SC
Campbell Hall (Episcopal), CA
Canterbury School, FL
Cape Cod Academy, MA
Cape Fear Academy, NC
Cape Henry Collegiate School, VA
Cardigan Mountain School, NH
Carlisle School, VA
Carolina Day School, NC
Carson Long Military Institute, PA
Castilleja School, CA
The Catlin Gabel School, OR
CFS, The School at Church Farm, PA
Chadwick School, CA
Chaminade College Preparatory School, MO
The Chapin School, NY
Charlotte Country Day School, NC
Charlotte Latin School, NC
Chase Collegiate School, CT
Cheshire Academy, CT
Chestnut Hill Academy, PA
Christchurch School, VA
Christ School, NC
Cincinnati Country Day School, OH
Cistercian Preparatory School, TX
The Collegiate School, VA
Colorado Academy, CO
The Colorado Springs School, CO
Columbia Grammar and Preparatory School, NY
The Columbus Academy, OH
The Community School, ID
The Community School of Naples, FL
Connelly School of the Holy Child, MD
Convent of the Sacred Heart, CT
Convent of the Sacred Heart, NY
Convent of the Visitation School, MN
Country Day School of the Sacred Heart, PA
Crofton House School, BC, Canada
Crossroads College Preparatory School, MO
Crossroads School for Arts & Sciences, CA
Crystal Springs Uplands School, CA
The Dalton School, NY
Dana Hall School, MA
Darlington School, GA
Delbarton School, NJ
Denver Academy, CO
The Derryfield School, NH
Detroit Country Day School, MI
Doane Stuart School, NY
Dunn School, CA
Durham Academy, NC
Dwight-Englewood School, NJ
Eaglebrook School, MA
Eagle Hill School, MA
Ecole Internationale de Boston / International School of Boston, MA
Elgin Academy, IL
The Ellis School, PA
Episcopal High School of Jacksonville, FL
The Episcopal School of Dallas, TX
The Ethel Walker School, CT
Evansville Day School, IN
Falmouth Academy, MA
Fay School, MA
The Fessenden School, MA
The Field School, DC
Flint Hill School, VA
Forsyth Country Day School, NC
Fort Worth Country Day School, TX
Fox River Country Day School, IL
Franklin Road Academy, TN
Friends' Central School, PA
Garrison Forest School, MD
Gaston Day School, NC
Georgetown Day School, DC
Germantown Academy, PA
Germantown Friends School, PA
Gill St. Bernard's School, NJ
Gilman School, MD
Gilmour Academy, OH
Girard College, PA
Girls Preparatory School, TN
Glenelg Country School, MD
The Glenholme School, CT
The Gow School, NY
Greenfield School, NC
Green Fields Country Day School, AZ
Greenhill School, TX
Greenhills School, MI
Greensboro Day School, NC
Greens Farms Academy, CT
Greenwich Academy, CT
Groton School, MA
Hackley School, NY
Hamden Hall Country Day School, CT
Hammond School, SC
Hampshire Country School, NH
Hargrave Military Academy, VA
The Harker School, CA
The Harley School, NY
The Harrisburg Academy, PA
Harvard-Westlake School, CA
The Harvey School, NY
Hathaway Brown School, OH
The Haverford School, PA
Havergal College, ON, Canada
Hawaii Baptist Academy, HI
Hawai'i Preparatory Academy, HI
Hawken School, OH
Head-Royce School, CA
Hebron Academy, ME
Heritage Hall, OK
The Heritage School, GA
Hidden Lake Academy, GA
Highland School, VA
The Hill Center, Durham Academy, NC
Hillside School, MA
The Hill Top Preparatory School, PA
Hilton Head Preparatory School, SC
The Hockaday School, TX
Holland Hall, OK

The Holton-Arms School, MD
Holy Innocents' Episcopal School, GA
Hoosac School, NY
Hopkins School, CT
The Horace Mann School, NY
Howe Military School, IN
The Hudson School, NJ
The Hun School of Princeton, NJ
Hutchison School, TN
Indian Mountain School, CT
Indian Springs School, AL
International High School, CA
International School Bangkok, Thailand
International School Manila, Philippines
The International School of Paris, France
Iolani School, HI
Isidore Newman School, LA
Jack M. Barrack Hebrew Academy (formerly Akiba Hebrew Academy), PA
Jackson Academy, MS
Jackson Preparatory School, MS
The Janus School, PA
John Burroughs School, MO
The John Cooper School, TX
Keith Country Day School, IL
Kent Denver School, CO
Kent Place School, NJ
Kentucky Country Day School, KY
The Key School, MD
Kildonan School, NY
Kimberton Waldorf School, PA
King Low Heywood Thomas, CT
Kingswood-Oxford School, CT
The Knox School, NY
Lakefield College School, ON, Canada
Lake Ridge Academy, OH
Lakeside School, WA
Lakeview Academy, GA
Lancaster Country Day School, PA
Landmark School, MA
Landon School, MD
La Pietra–Hawaii School for Girls, HI
La Salle Academy, RI
Lausanne Collegiate School, TN
Lexington Christian Academy, MA
Lincoln School, RI
Linden Hall, PA
Linden Hill School, MA
The Linsly School, WV
Little Red School House and Elisabeth Irwin High School, NY
Logos School, MO
Louisville Collegiate School, KY
The Lovett School, GA
The MacDuffie School, MA
Maharishi School of the Age of Enlightenment, IA
Manlius Pebble Hill School, NY
Maret School, DC
Marist School, GA
Marlborough School, CA
Marshall School, MN
Maryknoll School, HI
Marymount School, NY
Maryvale Preparatory School, MD
The Masters School, NY
Maumee Valley Country Day School, OH
The McCallie School, TN
McDonogh School, MD
The Meadows School, NV
Memphis University School, TN
Menlo School, CA
Metairie Park Country Day School, LA
Miami Country Day School, FL
Mid-Pacific Institute, HI
Miller School, VA
Milton Academy, MA
Miss Edgar's and Miss Cramp's School, QC, Canada
Missouri Military Academy, MO
MMI Preparatory School, PA
Montgomery Bell Academy, TN
Montverde Academy, FL
Moorestown Friends School, NJ
Moravian Academy, PA
Morgan Park Academy, IL
Morristown-Beard School, NJ
Moses Brown School, RI
Mounds Park Academy, MN
Munich International School, Germany
National Cathedral School, DC
National Sports Academy at Lake Placid, NY
Newark Academy, NJ
New York Military Academy, NY
The Nichols School, NY
Noble and Greenough School, MA
Norfolk Academy, VA
Norfolk Collegiate School, VA
North Country School, NY
North Cross School, VA
North Shore Country Day School, IL
The Northwest School, WA
North Yarmouth Academy, ME
Notre Dame Preparatory School, MD
Oak Knoll School of the Holy Child, NJ
Oak Ridge Military Academy, NC
The Oakridge School, TX
Oakwood Friends School, NY
Oakwood School, CA
Ojai Valley School, CA
Oldfields School, MD
The O'Neal School, NC
Oregon Episcopal School, OR
The Orme School, AZ
Out-Of-Door-Academy, FL
The Overlake School, WA
Pace Academy, GA
Pacific Hills School, CA
The Packer Collegiate Institute, NY
The Parker School, HI
The Park School of Buffalo, NY
Park Tudor School, IN
The Pennington School, NJ
Perkiomen School, PA
Phoenix Country Day School, AZ
Pine Crest School, FL
The Pingry School, NJ
Poly Prep Country Day School, NY
Polytechnic School, CA
Porter-Gaud School, SC
Portledge School, NY

The Potomac School, VA
Poughkeepsie Day School, NY
The Prairie School, WI
Professional Children's School, NY
Providence Country Day School, RI
Providence Day School, NC
Pulaski Academy, AR
Punahou School, HI
Queen Anne School, MD
Rabun Gap-Nacoochee School, GA
Randolph-Macon Academy, VA
Randolph School, AL
Ranney School, NJ
Ransom Everglades School, FL
Ravenscroft School, NC
The Rectory School, CT
Ridley College, ON, Canada
Riverdale Country School, NY
Rivermont Collegiate, IA
Riverside Military Academy, GA
The Rivers School, MA
Riverview School, MA
Robert Louis Stevenson School, NY
Rockland Country Day School, NY
Rocky Hill School, RI
Rocky Mount Academy, NC
The Roeper School, MI
Roland Park Country School, MD
Rolling Hills Preparatory School, CA
Rowland Hall-St. Mark's School, UT
The Roxbury Latin School, MA
Roycemore School, IL
Rumsey Hall School, CT
Rutgers Preparatory School, NJ
Rye Country Day School, NY
Sacramento Country Day School, CA
Saddle River Day School, NJ
St. Albans School, DC
St. Andrew's College, ON, Canada
St. Andrew's Episcopal School, MD
St. Andrew's Episcopal School, MS
St. Andrew's on the Marsh School, GA
St. Andrew's Priory School, HI
Saint Andrew's School, FL
St. Andrew's School, RI
St. Andrew's–Sewanee School, TN
St. Anne's–Belfield School, VA
St. Anselm's Abbey School, DC
St. Catherine's School, VA
St. Christopher's School, VA
St. Clement's School, ON, Canada
St. Croix Country Day School, VI
Saint Edward's School, FL
Saint George's School, WA
St. George's School, BC, Canada
St. George's School of Montreal, QC, Canada
St. Gregory College Preparatory School, AZ
Saint James School, MD
St. John's Northwestern Military Academy, WI
Saint John's Preparatory School, MN
St. Margaret's Episcopal School, CA
St. Margaret's School, VA
St. Mark's School of Texas, TX
St. Martin's Episcopal School, LA
St. Mary's Academy, CO
St. Mary's Episcopal School, TN
Saint Mary's Hall, TX
St. Mary's Hall–Doane Academy, NJ
St. Mary's School, OR
St. Paul Academy and Summit School, MN
St. Paul's Episcopal School, AL
St. Paul's School, MD
St. Paul's School for Girls, MD
St. Sebastian's School, MA
St. Stephen's & St. Agnes School, VA
Saint Stephen's Episcopal School, FL
St. Stephen's Episcopal School, TX
St. Thomas Choir School, NY
Saint Thomas More School, CT
Saltus Grammar School, Bermuda
Sandia Preparatory School, NM
San Domenico School, CA
Sandy Spring Friends School, MD
Sanford School, DE
San Marcos Baptist Academy, TX
Santa Fe Preparatory School, NM
The Savannah Country Day School, GA
Sayre School, KY
School of the Holy Child, NY
Seabury Hall, HI
Seattle Academy of Arts and Sciences, WA
Selwyn House School, QC, Canada
Seoul Foreign School, Republic of Korea
The Seven Hills School, OH
Sewickley Academy, PA
Shady Side Academy, PA
Shattuck-St. Mary's School, MN
The Shipley School, PA
Shorecrest Preparatory School, FL
Solebury School, PA
The Spence School, NY
Staten Island Academy, NY
Stevenson School, CA
Stoneleigh–Burnham School, MA
The Stony Brook School, NY
Storm King School, NY
Stratford Academy, GA
Strathcona-Tweedsmuir School, AB, Canada
Stratton Mountain School, VT
Stuart Country Day School of the Sacred Heart, NJ
The Study School, QC, Canada
Subiaco Academy, AR
Tampa Preparatory School, FL
Tandem Friends School, VA
TASIS The American School in England, United Kingdom
TASIS, The American School in Switzerland, Switzerland
The Tatnall School, DE
Thomas Jefferson School, MO
Tower Hill School, DE
Trident Academy, SC
Trinity College School, ON, Canada
Trinity Episcopal School, VA
Trinity-Pawling School, NY
Trinity Preparatory School, FL
Trinity School, NY
Trinity School of Midland, TX
Trinity Valley School, TX
United Nations International School, NY

University Lake School, WI
University Liggett School, MI
University of Chicago Laboratory Schools, IL
University Prep, WA
University School of Jackson, TN
University School of Milwaukee, WI
University School of Nova Southeastern University, FL
Ursuline Academy, DE
Ursuline Academy, MA
Valley Forge Military Academy & College, PA
Valwood School, GA
The Vanguard School, FL
Viewpoint School, CA
Visitation Academy of St. Louis County, MO
The Waldorf School of Garden City, NY
The Walker School, GA
The Wardlaw-Hartridge School, NJ
Washington International School, DC
The Waterford School, UT
Watkinson School, CT
Waynflete School, ME
The Webb School, TN
Webb School of Knoxville, TN
The Wellington School, OH
Westchester Country Day School, NC
The Westminster Schools, GA
Westminster Schools of Augusta, GA
Westridge School, CA
Westtown School, PA
The Wheeler School, RI
Wichita Collegiate School, KS
William Penn Charter School, PA
The Williams School, CT
The Williston Northampton School, MA
Willow Hill School, MA
Wilmington Friends School, DE
The Winchendon School, MA
Winchester Thurston School, PA
Windward School, CA
The Winsor School, MA
Winston Preparatory School, NY
The Winston School, TX
Woodside Priory School, CA
Woodward Academy, GA
Wooster School, CT
Worcester Academy, MA
Worcester Preparatory School, MD
Wyoming Seminary, PA
York Country Day School, PA

SCHOOLS REPORTING ACADEMIC ACCOMMODATIONS FOR THE GIFTED AND TALENTED*

Academia Cotopaxi, Ecuador	G,M,A
Academie Sainte Cecile International School, ON, Canada	G,M,A
Academy at Swift River, MA	A
The Academy for Gifted Children (PACE), ON, Canada	G
Academy for Global Exploration, OR	G
Academy of Mount Saint Ursula, NY	M,A
Academy of the Holy Angels, NJ	G,M,A
Academy of the Holy Cross, MD	G,A
Academy of the New Church Boys' School, PA	G,M,A
Academy of the New Church Girls' School, PA	G,M,A
Academy of the Sacred Heart, MI	G,M,A
Accelerated Schools, CO	G
ACS Cobham International School, United Kingdom	G
ACS Egham International School, United Kingdom	G
ACS Hillingdon International School, United Kingdom	G
Advanced Academy of Georgia, GA	G,M,A
The Agnes Irwin School, PA	G
Ahliyyah School for Girls, Jordan	G,A
Aiglon College, Switzerland	G,M,A
Airdrie Koinonia Christian School, AB, Canada	G
Albert College, ON, Canada	G,M,A
Alexander Dawson School, CO	G,M,A
The Alexander School, TX	G
Allison Academy, FL	G,A
Alpine Academy, UT	G
American Academy, FL	G,M,A
American Community Schools of Athens, Greece	G
American Heritage School, FL	G,M,A
American School of Paris, France	G,M,A
The American School of The Hague, Netherlands	G,M,A
Andrews Osborne Academy, OH	G,M,A
Archbishop Hoban High School, OH	G
Archbishop McNicholas High School, OH	G,M,A
Archbishop Spalding High School, MD	G,M,A
Archmere Academy, DE	G,M,A
Asheville School, NC	G
ASSETS School, HI	G
Assumption High School, KY	G
Augusta Preparatory Day School, GA	G
Aurora Central High School, IL	G
Avon Old Farms School, CT	G,A
The Baldwin School, PA	G,M,A
Balmoral Hall School, MB, Canada	G
The Baltimore Actors' Theatre Conservatory, MD	G,M,A
Barnstable Academy, NJ	G,M,A
Bass Memorial Academy, MS	G,M
Baylor School, TN	G,M,A
The Beekman School, NY	G,M,A
Bellevue Christian School, WA	G,M,A
Benedictine High School, VA	G,A
Benedictine Military School, GA	G
The Benjamin School, FL	G,M,A
Berwick Academy, ME	G,M,A
Besant Hill School, CA	M,A
The Birch Wathen Lenox School, NY	G
Bishop Brady High School, NH	G
Bishop Denis J. O'Connell High School, VA	G
Bishop Eustace Preparatory School, NJ	G,M
Bishop Gorman High School, NV	G,M,A
Bishop Guertin High School, NH	G,M,A
Bishop Ireton High School, VA	M
Bishop Luers High School, IN	G,M
Bishop Lynch Catholic High School, TX	G
Bishop McGuinness Catholic High School, OK	G,A
Bishop Mora Salesian High School, CA	M,A
The Bishop Strachan School, ON, Canada	G,M,A
Blue Mountain Academy, PA	M
Blueprint Education, AZ	M,A
Bodwell High School, BC, Canada	G
Boston College High School, MA	G
Boston University Academy, MA	G
Boylan Central Catholic High School, IL	G,M,A

G — gifted; M — musically talented; A — artistically talented

The Boys' Latin School of Maryland, MD	G,M,A
Breck School, MN	G,M,A
Brehm Preparatory School, IL	G
Brenau Academy, GA	G,M,A
Brentwood School, CA	G,A
Brethren Christian Junior and Senior High Schools, CA	G
Briarwood Christian High School, AL	G
Bridges Academy, CA	G
Brockwood Park School, United Kingdom	G,M,A
Brother Martin High School, LA	G,M,A
Brownell-Talbot School, NE	G
The Browning School, NY	G
Brunswick School, CT	G,M,A
The Bryn Mawr School for Girls, MD	G,M,A
Buckingham Browne & Nichols School, MA	G,M,A
Buffalo Seminary, NY	G
Bulloch Academy, GA	G,M,A
Buxton School, MA	G,M,A
The Byrnes Schools, SC	G
The Calhoun School, NY	G
Calvert Hall College High School, MD	G,M,A
Camelot Academy, NC	G
Cape Henry Collegiate School, VA	G,M,A
Cardigan Mountain School, NH	G,A
Cardinal Mooney High School, FL	M,A
Cardinal Newman High School, FL	G
Carlucci American International School of Lisbon, Portugal	G
Carondelet High School, CA	G
Cary Academy, NC	G,M,A
Cascadilla School, NY	G,A
Cascia Hall Preparatory School, OK	G
Castilleja School, CA	G
Cate School, CA	G,M,A
Cathedral High School, IN	G,M,A
Catholic Memorial, MA	M,A
The Catlin Gabel School, OR	G,M,A
Central Catholic High School, CA	G
Central Catholic High School, PA	G
CFS, The School at Church Farm, PA	G,M,A
Chadwick School, CA	G,M,A
Chamberlain-Hunt Academy, MS	G,M,A
Chaminade College Preparatory School, MO	G
Chaminade-Madonna College Preparatory, FL	G,M,A
Charlotte Country Day School, NC	G
Charlotte Latin School, NC	G
Chase Collegiate School, CT	G
Cherry Gulch, ID	G
Cheshire Academy, CT	M,A
Chestnut Hill Academy, PA	G,M,A
The Chicago Academy for the Arts, IL	M,A
Children's Creative and Performing Arts Academy—Capa Division, CA	G,M,A
Chinese Christian Schools, CA	G
Choate Rosemary Hall, CT	G,M,A
Christchurch School, VA	G
Christ School, NC	G
Chrysalis School, WA	G
Colegio Franklin D. Roosevelt, Peru	G,M,A
Colegio Nueva Granada, Colombia	G
College du Leman International School, Switzerland	G,M,A
Colorado Academy, CO	G,M,A
The Colorado Rocky Mountain School, CO	G,M,A
The Colorado Springs School, CO	G
Columbia Grammar and Preparatory School, NY	G
The Columbus Academy, OH	G
Commonwealth School, MA	G,M,A
The Community School, ID	G
Community School, NH	G,A
The Concept School, PA	G,A
Concord Academy, MA	G,M,A
Connelly School of the Holy Child, MD	G,M,A
Conserve School, WI	G
Convent of the Sacred Heart, CT	G
Cotter Schools, MN	G,M,A
Country Day School of the Sacred Heart, PA	M
Cretin-Derham Hall, MN	G
Crossroads School for Arts & Sciences, CA	G,M,A
The Culver Academies, IN	G,M,A
Currey Ingram Academy, TN	G,M,A
Cushing Academy, MA	G,M,A
Darrow School, NY	M,A
Deerfield Academy, MA	G,M,A
Deerfield-Windsor School, GA	G,A
DeMatha Catholic High School, MD	G,M,A
Denver Academy, CO	G
Detroit Country Day School, MI	G,M,A
Dickinson Trinity, ND	G
Doane Stuart School, NY	G,M,A
Donelson Christian Academy, TN	G
Dowling Catholic High School, IA	G,M,A
Dublin Christian Academy, NH	M
Dublin School, NH	A
Duchesne Academy of the Sacred Heart, TX	M,A
Eaglebrook School, MA	G,M,A
Eagle Hill School, MA	G,M,A
Eastern Christian High School, NJ	G,M,A
Eastern Mennonite High School, VA	G
Eastside Christian Academy, AB, Canada	G,M
Ecole d'Humanité, Switzerland	G,M,A
Edison School, AB, Canada	G
The Education Center, MS	G,M,A
Elan School, ME	G
Elizabeth Seton High School, MD	G,M,A
Elmwood School, ON, Canada	G
Emerson Honors High Schools, CA	G,M,A
The Emery Weiner School, TX	G
Emma Willard School, NY	M,A
Episcopal High School, VA	G,M,A
Episcopal High School of Jacksonville, FL	G
The Ethel Walker School, CT	G,M,A
Evangelical Christian School, TN	G,M,A
Evansville Day School, IN	G
Explorations Academy, WA	G
Faith Lutheran High School, NV	M
Father Ryan High School, TN	G,M,A
Fay School, MA	G,M,A
The Fessenden School, MA	G,M,A
The Field School, DC	G,M,A
Fieldstone Day School, ON, Canada	G,M,A
The First Academy, FL	G
Flint River Academy, GA	M,A
Forsyth Country Day School, NC	G
Fort Lauderdale Preparatory School, FL	G
Fort Worth Country Day School, TX	G,M,A
Fountain Valley School of Colorado, CO	G,M,A
Foxcroft Academy, ME	G,M,A
Foxcroft School, VA	G,M,A
Fox River Country Day School, IL	G

G — gifted; M — musically talented; A — artistically talented

Fox Valley Lutheran High School, WI	G
Franklin Academy, CT	G
Franklin Road Academy, TN	G,M,A
Freeman Academy, SD	M,A
Front Range Christian High School, CO	G
Fryeburg Academy, ME	M
Fuqua School, VA	G
Gables Academy, GA	G
Garrison Forest School, MD	G,M,A
Gaston Day School, NC	G
The Geneva School, FL	G,M
George School, PA	G
George Stevens Academy, ME	G,M,A
Georgetown Preparatory School, MD	G
Germantown Friends School, PA	G,M,A
Gill St. Bernard's School, NJ	G
Gilman School, MD	G
Gilmour Academy, OH	G,M,A
Glenelg Country School, MD	G
The Glenholme School, CT	G
Gordon Technical High School, IL	G
Gould Academy, ME	G,M,A
The Governor French Academy, IL	G,M,A
The Gow School, NY	M
The Grauer School, CA	G,M,A
Greater Atlanta Christian Schools, GA	G,M,A
Greenfield School, NC	G
Greenhills School, MI	G
Greensboro Day School, NC	G,A
The Greenwood School, VT	G,M,A
Groton School, MA	G,M,A
Grove School, CT	G,A
Gulliver Preparatory School, FL	G,M,A
The Gunnery, CT	G,M,A
Gunston Day School, MD	G,M,A
Gwynedd Mercy Academy, PA	M,A
Halstrom High School, CA	G,M,A
Halstrom High School—San Diego, CA	G,M,A
Hamilton District Christian High, ON, Canada	M,A
Hammond School, SC	G,M,A
Hampshire Country School, NH	G
Harding Academy, AR	G
The Harker School, CA	G
Harvard-Westlake School, CA	G,M,A
Hathaway Brown School, OH	G,M
The Haverford School, PA	G
Hawken School, OH	G,M
Hayden High School, KS	G,M
Head-Royce School, CA	G,M,A
Headwaters Academy, MT	G,M,A
Hebrew Academy-the Five Towns, NY	A
Hebron Academy, ME	G,M,A
Heritage Hall, OK	G,M,A
Hidden Lake Academy, GA	G,A
High Mowing School, NH	M,A
Hillside School, MA	G
The Hill Top Preparatory School, PA	G,A
Holderness School, NH	G,M,A
The Holton-Arms School, MD	G,A
Holy Names High School, CA	G,M,A
Hoosac School, NY	M,A
The Hotchkiss School, CT	G,M,A
The Hudson School, NJ	G,M,A
Humanex Academy, CO	G

The Hun School of Princeton, NJ	G
Huntington-Surrey School, TX	G
Hutchison School, TN	G
Hyman Brand Hebrew Academy of Greater Kansas City, KS	G
Independent School, KS	G
Indian Springs School, AL	G,M,A
Interlochen Arts Academy, MI	G,M,A
International High School, CA	G,M,A
International School of Amsterdam, Netherlands	G,M,A
The International School of Geneva, Switzerland	M,A
Iolani School, HI	G,M,A
Island School, HI	G
Jack M. Barrack Hebrew Academy (formerly Akiba Hebrew Academy), PA	G
Jackson Preparatory School, MS	G,M,A
The John Dewey Academy, MA	G,A
The Karafin School, NY	G,M,A
Keith Country Day School, IL	G,M,A
Kent School, CT	G,M,A
Kents Hill School, ME	G,A
Kentucky Country Day School, KY	G,M,A
The Key School, MD	G
King George School, VT	G,M,A
King Low Heywood Thomas, CT	G,M,A
King's-Edgehill School, NS, Canada	G
Lakefield College School, ON, Canada	G,M,A
Lake Forest Academy, IL	G,M,A
Lake Ridge Academy, OH	G,M,A
Lakeview Academy, GA	G,M,A
La Lumiere School, IN	G,A
Lancaster Country Day School, PA	G,M,A
Lansing Christian School, MI	G
La Salle Academy, RI	G,M,A
La Salle High School, FL	G
The Laureate Academy, MB, Canada	G
Laurel Springs School, CA	G,M,A
Lausanne Collegiate School, TN	G,M,A
Lawrence Academy, MA	M,A
Lehigh Valley Christian High School, PA	G
Lifegate School, OR	G,A
Linden Hall, PA	G,M,A
The Linden School, ON, Canada	G
The Linsly School, WV	G
Logos School, MO	A
The Loomis Chaffee School, CT	G,M,A
Los Angeles Lutheran High School, CA	G,M,A
The Lovett School, GA	G,M,A
Loyola-Blakefield, MD	G,M,A
Luther College High School, SK, Canada	G
Luther High School North, IL	G,M,A
Lycee Claudel, ON, Canada	M
Lydia Patterson Institute, TX	G
The MacDuffie School, MA	G
Madison-Ridgeland Academy, MS	G
Maharishi School of the Age of Enlightenment, IA	G,M,A
Maine Central Institute, ME	M
Maine School of Science and Mathematics, ME	G
Manlius Pebble Hill School, NY	G
Maret School, DC	G,M,A
Marianapolis Preparatory School, CT	M,A
Marian Baker School, Costa Rica	G
Marin Academy, CA	G,M,A
Marist High School, NJ	G
Marmion Academy, IL	G

G — gifted; M — musically talented; A — artistically talented

Marshall School, MN	G
Marylawn of the Oranges, NJ	G,M,A
The Mary Louis Academy, NY	M,A
Marymount School, NY	G
The Master's School, CT	G,M,A
The Masters School, NY	G,M,A
Maumee Valley Country Day School, OH	G,M,A
The McCallie School, TN	G,M,A
Meadowridge School, BC, Canada	G
The Meadows School, NV	G,M,A
Memorial Hall School, TX	G
Menaul School, NM	G,A
Menlo School, CA	G,M,A
Mennonite Collegiate Institute, MB, Canada	M
Mercedes College, Australia	G
Mercersburg Academy, PA	G
Merchiston Castle School, United Kingdom	G,M,A
Mercyhurst Preparatory School, PA	G,M,A
Metairie Park Country Day School, LA	G,M,A
Middlesex School, MA	G
Mid-Pacific Institute, HI	G,A
Milken Community High School of Stephen S. Wise Temple, CA	G,M,A
Miller School, VA	G,M,A
Milton Academy, MA	G,M,A
Miss Hall's School, MA	G,M,A
Missouri Military Academy, MO	G,M,A
MMI Preparatory School, PA	G,A
Monmouth Academy, NJ	G,A
Monsignor Donovan High School, NJ	G,M,A
Montana Academy, MT	G
Morgan Park Academy, IL	G,M,A
Mount Bachelor Academy, OR	G
Mt. Saint Dominic Academy, NJ	G,M,A
Mount Saint Joseph Academy, PA	G,M,A
Munich International School, Germany	G
National Cathedral School, DC	G
National High School, GA	G,M,A
Newark Academy, NJ	G,M,A
New Hampton School, NH	G,M,A
New Horizon Youth Ministries, IN	G,M,A
New Way Learning Academy, AZ	G
Noble and Greenough School, MA	G,M,A
The Nora School, MD	G,A
Norfolk Academy, VA	G,M,A
Norfolk Christian School, VA	G
Norfolk Collegiate School, VA	G
The North Broward Preparatory Upper School, FL	G,M,A
North Cobb Christian School, GA	M,A
Northfield Mount Hermon School, MA	G,M,A
Northside Christian School, FL	G
Northwest Academy, ID	M
The Northwest Academy, OR	G,M,A
The Northwest School, WA	G,M,A
Northwest Yeshiva High School, WA	G
Notre Dame Academy, MA	M,A
Notre Dame Academy, VA	G,M,A
Notre Dame High School, LA	G
Oak Grove Lutheran School, ND	G,M
The Oakland School, PA	G,A
Oak Ridge Military Academy, NC	G
The Oakridge School, TX	G,M,A
Oakwood School, CA	G
The Oakwood School, NC	G,M
O'Dea High School, WA	G
Ojai Valley School, CA	G,A
Oldfields School, MD	G
Oregon Episcopal School, OR	G
Orinda Academy, CA	G
The Overlake School, WA	G,M,A
The Oxford Academy, CT	G
Pace Academy, GA	G,M,A
Pacific Academy, CA	G
Pacific Lutheran High School, CA	G
The Park School of Buffalo, NY	G
Park Tudor School, IN	G,M,A
The Pennington School, NJ	G
Pensacola Catholic High School, FL	G
Perkiomen School, PA	G,M,A
The Phelps School, PA	G,M,A
Phillips Academy (Andover), MA	G,M,A
Phillips Exeter Academy, NH	G,M,A
The Pingry School, NJ	G
Poly Prep Country Day School, NY	G,A
Pomfret School, CT	G,M,A
Portledge School, NY	G,M,A
Portsmouth Abbey School, RI	G
Portsmouth Christian Academy, NH	G,M
Poughkeepsie Day School, NY	G,M,A
The Prairie School, WI	G,M,A
Prestonwood Christian Academy, TX	G
Providence Country Day School, RI	G,M,A
Providence Day School, NC	G,M,A
Providence High School, CA	M,A
The Putney School, VT	G,M,A
Queen Margaret's School, BC, Canada	G,M,A
Rabbi Alexander S. Gross Hebrew Academy, FL	G
Rambam Mesivta, NY	G
Randolph-Macon Academy, VA	G
Ravenscroft School, NC	G,M,A
The Rectory School, CT	G
Redemption Christian Academy, NY	G
Regina Dominican High School, IL	G,M,A
Regina High School, OH	G,M,A
Richmond Christian School, BC, Canada	G
Ridgewood Preparatory School, LA	G
Ridley College, ON, Canada	M,A
Ripon Christian Schools, CA	M,A
Riverdale Country School, NY	G,M,A
Rivermont Collegiate, IA	G,M
Robert Louis Stevenson School, NY	G
Rockland Country Day School, NY	G,M,A
Rocky Hill School, RI	G,M,A
Rocky Mount Academy, NC	G
The Roeper School, MI	G,M,A
Rolling Hills Preparatory School, CA	G
Roncalli High School, IN	G,M,A
Rosseau Lake College, ON, Canada	G
Rothesay Netherwood School, NB, Canada	G,M,A
The Roxbury Latin School, MA	G,M,A
Rumsey Hall School, CT	G
Rutgers Preparatory School, NJ	G,M,A
Rye Country Day School, NY	G
Saddle River Day School, NJ	G,M,A
Sage Hill School, CA	G,M,A
Sage Ridge School, NV	G
St. Andrew's Episcopal School, MS	G,M,A
St. Andrew's Priory School, HI	M,A

G — gifted; M — musically talented; A — artistically talented

Saint Andrew's School, FL	G
St. Andrew's School, RI	M,A
St. Andrew's–Sewanee School, TN	G,M,A
St. Anselm's Abbey School, DC	G
St. Anthony Catholic High School, TX	G
St. Augustine High School, CA	G
St. Benedict at Auburndale, TN	G,M,A
St. Cecilia Academy, TN	G,M,A
St. Christopher's School, VA	G,M,A
St. Croix Lutheran High School, MN	A
St. Dominic's International School, Portugal, Portugal	G,M,A
Saint Edmund High School, NY	A
Saint Edward's School, FL	G,M,A
St. Francis High School, KY	G,A
St. George's School, RI	G,M,A
St. George's School of Montreal, QC, Canada	G,M,A
St. Gregory College Preparatory School, AZ	G,M,A
St. Johnsbury Academy, VT	G,A
St. John's College High School, DC	G
St. John's Preparatory School, MA	G,M,A
Saint John's Preparatory School, MN	G,M,A
St. Joseph Academy, FL	G,A
St. Joseph High School, CT	G
Saint Joseph High School, IL	G,M,A
St. Joseph's Preparatory School, PA	G,M,A
St. Margaret's Episcopal School, CA	G,M,A
Saint Mark's School, MA	G,M,A
St. Mary's Episcopal School, TN	G,M,A
St. Mary's Hall–Doane Academy, NJ	G,M,A
Saint Mary's High School, MD	G
St. Mary's Preparatory School, MI	M,A
St. Mary's School, OR	G,M,A
Saint Matthias High School, CA	G,M,A
Saint Maur International School, Japan	G,M,A
Saint Patrick—Saint Vincent High School, CA	G
St. Paul's School, MD	G
St. Paul's School, NH	G,M,A
St. Paul's School for Girls, MD	G,M,A
St. Sebastian's School, MA	G,M,A
St. Stephen's & St. Agnes School, VA	G,M,A
Saint Thomas Aquinas High School, KS	G
St. Thomas Choir School, NY	G,M
Saint Xavier High School, KY	G,M,A
Salem Baptist Christian School, NC	G
Salesianum School, DE	G
Salt Lake Lutheran High School, UT	G
The Samuel Scheck Hillel Community Day School, FL	G,A
Sandia Preparatory School, NM	G
San Domenico School, CA	M
San Francisco University High School, CA	G,M,A
San Marcos Baptist Academy, TX	G,M,A
Santa Margarita Catholic High School, CA	G,M,A
Sayre School, KY	G,A
School for Young Performers, NY	G,M,A
Seattle Academy of Arts and Sciences, WA	G,M,A
Seoul Foreign School, Republic of Korea	G,M,A
Seton Catholic Central High School, NY	G
The Seven Hills School, OH	G
Shady Side Academy, PA	G,M,A
Shattuck-St. Mary's School, MN	G,M
Shenandoah Valley Academy, VA	G,M,A
The Shipley School, PA	G
Shorecrest Preparatory School, FL	G
Solebury School, PA	G,M,A
Soundview Preparatory School, NY	G,M,A
Squaw Valley Academy, CA	G,A
Staten Island Academy, NY	G,M,A
Stella Maris High School, NY	G,A
St Leonards School and Sixth Form College, United Kingdom	G,M,A
Stone Mountain School, NC	G
Storm King School, NY	G,M,A
Subiaco Academy, AR	G,M,A
Suffield Academy, CT	G,M,A
The Summit Country Day School, OH	G
Summit Preparatory School, MT	G
Tabor Academy, MA	G,M,A
The Taft School, CT	G,M,A
Tampa Preparatory School, FL	G,M,A
Tandem Friends School, VA	G
TASIS The American School in England, United Kingdom	G
The Tatnall School, DE	G,M,A
The Tenney School, TX	G,M,A
The Thacher School, CA	G,M,A
Thomas Jefferson School, MO	G
Thornton Friends School, MD	G
Tower Hill School, DE	G,M,A
Trinity Episcopal School, VA	G,M,A
Trinity High School, IL	G
Trinity High School, KY	G,M,A
Trinity High School, OH	G,A
Trinity Preparatory School, FL	G,M,A
Trinity School of Midland, TX	M
Trinity Valley School, TX	G,M,A
United Nations International School, NY	G,M,A
The United World College—USA, NM	M,A
University Lake School, WI	G,M,A
University Liggett School, MI	G,M,A
University of Toronto Schools, ON, Canada	G
University School of Jackson, TN	G,M,A
University School of Nova Southeastern University, FL	G,M,A
The Urban School of San Francisco, CA	G,A
The Ursuline Academy of Dallas, TX	G,M,A
The Ursuline School, NY	G,A
Valle Catholic High School, MO	G,A
Valley Christian High School, CA	G
Valley Forge Military Academy & College, PA	M,A
Valley Lutheran High School, AZ	G,M
The Valley School, MI	G,A
Valwood School, GA	G,M
Verde Valley School, AZ	G,M,A
Victor Valley Christian School, CA	G
Villa Joseph Marie High School, PA	G,M,A
Villa Walsh Academy, NJ	G,M,A
Virginia Beach Friends School, VA	G,M,A
The Waldorf School of Garden City, NY	M,A
The Walker School, GA	G,A
Walnut Hill School, MA	G,M,A
The Wardlaw-Hartridge School, NJ	G,M,A
Waring School, MA	G,M,A
Washington Waldorf School, MD	M,A
The Waterford School, UT	G,M,A
Watkinson School, CT	G,M,A
Wayne Country Day School, NC	G
The Webb School, TN	G
The Webb Schools, CA	G
The Wellington School, OH	G,M,A

G — gifted; M — musically talented; A — artistically talented

Western Reserve Academy, OH	G,M,A
West Island College, AB, Canada	G
Westminster Christian Academy, AL	G,M,A
Westminster Christian School, FL	G,M,A
The Westminster Schools, GA	G,M,A
Westminster Schools of Augusta, GA	G
West Nottingham Academy, MD	G,M,A
Westover School, CT	G,M,A
Westtown School, PA	G,M,A
Wheaton Academy, IL	G,M,A
The White Mountain School, NH	G,M,A
Wichita Collegiate School, KS	G
William Penn Charter School, PA	G,M,A
The Williams School, CT	G,M,A
The Williston Northampton School, MA	G,M,A
Willow Hill School, MA	A
Willow Wood School, ON, Canada	G,A
Wilmington Friends School, DE	G,M,A
The Winchendon School, MA	G
Winchester Thurston School, PA	G,M,A
Windermere Preparatory School, FL	M,A
The Windsor School, NY	G,M,A
Woodlands Academy of the Sacred Heart, IL	G
Woodside Priory School, CA	G,M,A
Woodstock School, India	G,M,A
Worcester Preparatory School, MD	G
World Hope Academy, FL	G
Xaverian Brothers High School, MA	G,M,A
Xavier College Preparatory, AZ	G,A
Xavier University Preparatory School, LA	M,A
York Country Day School, PA	G,M,A
York Preparatory School, NY	G,M,A
Zurich International School, Switzerland	G,M,A

SCHOOLS WITH ADVANCED PLACEMENT PREPARATION

Abington Friends School, PA
Academie Sainte Cecile International School, ON, Canada
The Academy for Gifted Children (PACE), ON, Canada
Academy of Mount Saint Ursula, NY
Academy of Our Lady of Peace, CA
Academy of the Holy Angels, NJ
Academy of the Holy Cross, MD
Academy of the Holy Names, FL
Academy of the New Church Boys' School, PA
Academy of the New Church Girls' School, PA
Academy of the Sacred Heart, LA
Academy of the Sacred Heart, MI
Accelerated Schools, CO
ACS Cobham International School, United Kingdom
ACS Hillingdon International School, United Kingdom
The Agnes Irwin School, PA
Alabama Christian Academy, AL
Albert College, ON, Canada
Albuquerque Academy, NM
Alexander Dawson School, CO
The Alexander School, TX
Allen Academy, TX
Allendale Columbia School, NY
Alliance Academy, Ecuador
Allison Academy, FL
All Saints' Episcopal School of Fort Worth, TX
The Altamont School, AL
American Christian Academy, AL
American Community Schools of Athens, Greece
American Heritage School, FL
The American School Foundation, Mexico
The American School in London, United Kingdom
American School of Paris, France
The American School of Puerto Vallarta, Mexico
The American School of The Hague, Netherlands
Andrews Osborne Academy, OH
Antelope Valley Christian School, CA
Archbishop Curley High School, MD
Archbishop McNicholas High School, OH
Archbishop Mitty High School, CA
Archbishop Riordan High School, CA
Archbishop Rummel High School, LA
Archbishop Spalding High School, MD
The Archer School for Girls, CA
Archmere Academy, DE
Army and Navy Academy, CA
Asheville School, NC
Assumption High School, KY
The Athenian School, CA
Athens Academy, GA
Augusta Christian School (I), GA
Auldern Academy, NC
Aurora Central High School, IL
Austin Preparatory School, MA
Avon Old Farms School, CT
Bakersfield Christian High School, CA
The Baldwin School, PA
Baldwin School of Puerto Rico, Inc., PR
Balmoral Hall School, MB, Canada
The Baltimore Actors' Theatre Conservatory, MD
Bancroft School, MA
Baptist High School, NJ
Barnstable Academy, NJ
The Barrie School, MD
The Barstow School, MO
Battle Ground Academy, TN
Baylor School, TN
The Beekman School, NY
Bellarmine-Jefferson High School, CA
Bellevue Christian School, WA
Belmont Hill School, MA
Benedictine High School, OH
Benedictine High School, VA
Benedictine Military School, GA
Ben Franklin Academy, GA
Benilde–St. Margaret's School, MN
The Benjamin School, FL
Berkeley Preparatory School, FL
Berkshire School, MA
Berwick Academy, ME
Besant Hill School, CA
Beth Haven Christian School, KY
The Birch Wathen Lenox School, NY
Bishop Alemany High School, CA
Bishop Blanchet High School, WA
Bishop Brady High School, NH
Bishop Conaty-Our Lady of Loretto High School, CA
Bishop Connolly High School, MA
Bishop Denis J. O'Connell High School, VA
Bishop Eustace Preparatory School, NJ

G — gifted; M — musically talented; A — artistically talented

Bishop Feehan High School, MA
Bishop Fenwick High School, OH
Bishop Garcia Diego High School, CA
Bishop George Ahr High School, NJ
Bishop Gorman High School, NV
Bishop Guertin High School, NH
Bishop Hendricken High School, RI
Bishop Ireton High School, VA
Bishop Kelly High School, ID
Bishop Kenny High School, FL
Bishop Luers High School, IN
Bishop Lynch Catholic High School, TX
Bishop McGuinness Catholic High School, NC
Bishop McGuinness Catholic High School, OK
Bishop McNamara High School, IL
Bishop Montgomery High School, CA
Bishop Mora Salesian High School, CA
Bishop Stang High School, MA
The Bishop Strachan School, ON, Canada
Bishop Verot High School, FL
Bishop Walsh Middle High School, MD
Blair Academy, NJ
The Blake School, MN
Blanchet School, OR
Blue Mountain Academy, PA
Bodwell High School, BC, Canada
The Bolles School, FL
Boston College High School, MA
Boyd-Buchanan School, TN
Boylan Central Catholic High School, IL
The Boys' Latin School of Maryland, MD
The Branson School, CA
The Brearley School, NY
Breck School, MN
Brentwood College School, BC, Canada
Brentwood School, CA
Brentwood School, GA
Brethren Christian Junior and Senior High Schools, CA
Brewster Academy, NH
Briarwood Christian High School, AL
Brimmer and May School, MA
Bronte College of Canada, ON, Canada
Brooks School, MA
Brookstone School, GA
Brophy College Preparatory, AZ
Brother Martin High School, LA
Brother Rice High School, MI
The Browning School, NY
Brunswick School, CT
The Bryn Mawr School for Girls, MD
Buckingham Browne & Nichols School, MA
The Buckley School, CA
Buffalo Seminary, NY
Bulloch Academy, GA
Burke Mountain Academy, VT
Burr and Burton Academy, VT
The Bush School, WA
Butte Central High School, MT
The Byrnes Schools, SC
Calvary Christian Academy, KY
Calvert Hall College High School, MD
The Calverton School, MD
The Cambridge School of Weston, MA
Camden Military Academy, SC
Camelot Academy, NC
Campbell Hall (Episcopal), CA
Canadian Academy, Japan
Cannon School, NC
Canterbury School, CT
Canterbury School, FL
The Canterbury School of Florida, FL
Canyonville Christian Academy, OR
Cape Cod Academy, MA
Cape Fear Academy, NC
Cape Henry Collegiate School, VA
Capistrano Valley Christian Schools, CA
Cardinal Gibbons High School, NC
Cardinal Mooney Catholic College Preparatory High School, MI
Cardinal Mooney High School, FL
Cardinal Newman High School, CA
Cardinal Newman High School, FL
Cardinal Newman School, SC
The Caribbean School, PR
Carlisle School, VA
Carolina Day School, NC
Carondelet High School, CA
Carrollton School of the Sacred Heart, FL
Cary Academy, NC
Cascadilla School, NY
Cascia Hall Preparatory School, OK
Castilleja School, CA
Cate School, CA
Cathedral High School, IN
Cathedral High School, NY
Catholic Central High School, MI
The Catholic High School of Baltimore, MD
Catholic Memorial, MA
Central Catholic High School, CA
Central Catholic High School, OH
Central Catholic High School, PA
Central Catholic Mid-High School, NE
CFS, The School at Church Farm, PA
Chadwick School, CA
Chamberlain-Hunt Academy, MS
Chaminade College Preparatory, CA
Chaminade College Preparatory School, MO
Chaminade-Madonna College Preparatory, FL
Chapel Hill–Chauncy Hall School, MA
The Chapin School, NY
Charlotte Catholic High School, NC
Charlotte Christian School, NC
Charlotte Country Day School, NC
Charlotte Latin School, NC
Chase Collegiate School, CT
Cheshire Academy, CT
Chestnut Hill Academy, PA
Cheverus High School, ME
The Chicago Academy for the Arts, IL
Children's Creative and Performing Arts Academy—Capa Division, CA
Chinese Christian Schools, CA
Choate Rosemary Hall, CT
Christchurch School, VA
Christian Brothers Academy, NJ
Christian Brothers Academy, NY
Christian Brothers Academy, NY
Christian Central Academy, NY

Christian Heritage School, CT
Christian Home and Bible School, FL
Christian Junior–Senior High School, CA
Christian School of the Desert, CA
Christopher Dock Mennonite High School, PA
Christ School, NC
Cincinnati Country Day School, OH
Cistercian Preparatory School, TX
Coe-Brown Northwood Academy, NH
Colegio Bolivar, Colombia
Colegio Nueva Granada, Colombia
Colegio Puertorriqueno de Ninas, PR
Cole Valley Christian High School, ID
College du Leman International School, Switzerland
The College Preparatory School, CA
The Collegiate School, VA
Colorado Academy, CO
The Colorado Rocky Mountain School, CO
The Colorado Springs School, CO
Columbia Academy, TN
Columbia Grammar and Preparatory School, NY
Columbia International College of Canada, ON, Canada
Columbia International School, Japan
The Columbus Academy, OH
Columbus High School, IA
Commonwealth Parkville School, PR
Commonwealth School, MA
The Community School, ID
The Community School of Naples, FL
Connelly School of the Holy Child, MD
Conserve School, WI
Convent of the Sacred Heart, CT
Convent of the Sacred Heart, NY
Convent of the Visitation School, MN
Cornelia Connelly School, CA
The Country Day School, ON, Canada
Country Day School of the Sacred Heart, PA
Crespi Carmelite High School, CA
Crestwood Preparatory College, ON, Canada
Cretin-Derham Hall, MN
Crofton House School, BC, Canada
Crossroads College Preparatory School, MO
Crystal Springs Uplands School, CA
The Culver Academies, IN
Cushing Academy, MA
The Dalton School, NY
Dana Hall School, MA
Darlington School, GA
David Lipscomb High School, TN
Deerfield Academy, MA
Deerfield-Windsor School, GA
De La Salle College, ON, Canada
De La Salle High School, CA
Delbarton School, NJ
DeMatha Catholic High School, MD
Denver Lutheran High School, CO
DePaul Catholic High School, NJ
The Derryfield School, NH
De Smet Jesuit High School, MO
Detroit Country Day School, MI
Devon Preparatory School, PA
Doane Stuart School, NY
The Dominican Academy of the City of New York, NY
Donelson Christian Academy, TN
Donna Klein Jewish Academy, FL
Dowling Catholic High School, IA
Drew School, CA
Dublin Christian Academy, NH
Dublin School, NH
Duchesne Academy of the Sacred Heart, TX
Dunn School, CA
Durham Academy, NC
Dwight-Englewood School, NJ
East Catholic High School, CT
Eastern Christian High School, NJ
Eastern Mennonite High School, VA
Eastside Catholic School, WA
Eastside College Preparatory School, CA
Ecole d'Humanité, Switzerland
Edison School, AB, Canada
The Education Center, MS
Elgin Academy, IL
Elizabeth Seton High School, MD
The Ellis School, PA
Elyria Catholic High School, OH
Emerson Honors High Schools, CA
The Emery Weiner School, TX
Emma Willard School, NY
Episcopal Collegiate School, AR
Episcopal High School, TX
Episcopal High School, VA
Episcopal High School of Jacksonville, FL
The Episcopal School of Dallas, TX
Escola Americana de Campinas, Brazil
Escondido Adventist Academy, CA
The Ethel Walker School, CT
Evangelical Christian School, TN
Evansville Day School, IN
Excel Christian Academy, GA
Explorations Academy, WA
Ezell-Harding Christian School, TN
Fairfield College Preparatory School, CT
Faith Christian High School, CA
Faith Lutheran High School, NV
Falmouth Academy, MA
Father Lopez High School, FL
Father Ryan High School, TN
Fayetteville Academy, NC
The Field School, DC
Fieldstone Day School, ON, Canada
The First Academy, FL
First Baptist Academy, TX
First Presbyterian Day School, GA
Fishburne Military School, VA
Flint Hill School, VA
Flintridge Sacred Heart Academy, CA
Flint River Academy, GA
Fontbonne Academy, MA
Fontbonne Hall Academy, NY
Fordham Preparatory School, NY
The Forman School, CT
Forsyth Country Day School, NC
Fort Lauderdale Preparatory School, FL
Fort Worth Country Day School, TX
Foundation Academy, FL
Fountain Valley School of Colorado, CO
Foxcroft Academy, ME
Foxcroft School, VA

Franklin Road Academy, TN
French-American School of New York, NY
Front Range Christian High School, CO
Fryeburg Academy, ME
Fuqua School, VA
Gabriel Richard High School, MI
Gann Academy (The New Jewish High School of Greater Boston), MA
Garces Memorial High School, CA
Garden School, NY
Garrison Forest School, MD
Gaston Day School, NC
The Geneva School, FL
George School, PA
George Stevens Academy, ME
Georgetown Day School, DC
Georgetown Preparatory School, MD
Georgetown Visitation Preparatory School, DC
Georgia Military College High School, GA
Germantown Academy, PA
Gill St. Bernard's School, NJ
Gilman School, MD
Gilmour Academy, OH
Girard College, PA
Girls Preparatory School, TN
Glades Day School, FL
Glenelg Country School, MD
Gonzaga College High School, DC
Gordon Technical High School, IL
Gould Academy, ME
The Governor French Academy, IL
The Governor's Academy (formerly Governor Dummer Academy), MA
Grace Brethren School, CA
Grace Christian School, AK
The Grand River Academy, OH
The Grauer School, CA
Greater Atlanta Christian Schools, GA
Greenfield School, NC
Green Fields Country Day School, AZ
Greenhill School, TX
Greenhills School, MI
Greensboro Day School, NC
Greens Farms Academy, CT
Greenwich Academy, CT
Greenwood Laboratory School, MO
Groton School, MA
Guamani Private School, PR
Guerin College Preparatory High School, IL
Gulliver Preparatory School, FL
The Gunnery, CT
Gunston Day School, MD
Gwynedd Mercy Academy, PA
Hackley School, NY
Halstrom High School—San Diego, CA
Hamden Hall Country Day School, CT
Hamilton District Christian High, ON, Canada
Hammond School, SC
Hanalani Schools, HI
Harding Academy, AR
Hargrave Military Academy, VA
The Harker School, CA
The Harley School, NY
Harrells Christian Academy, NC
The Harrisburg Academy, PA
Harvard-Westlake School, CA
The Harvey School, NY
Hathaway Brown School, OH
Havergal College, ON, Canada
Hawaii Baptist Academy, HI
Hawai'i Preparatory Academy, HI
Hawken School, OH
Hayden High School, KS
Head-Royce School, CA
Hebrew Academy, CA
Hebrew Academy-the Five Towns, NY
Hebron Academy, ME
Heritage Hall, OK
The Heritage School, GA
Highland School, VA
High Mowing School, NH
Hillcrest Christian School, CA
The Hill School, PA
Hilton Head Preparatory School, SC
The Hockaday School, TX
Hokkaido International School, Japan
Holderness School, NH
Holland Hall, OK
The Holton-Arms School, MD
Holy Innocents' Episcopal School, GA
Holy Name High School, PA
Holy Names High School, CA
Holy Savior Menard Catholic High School, LA
Holy Trinity Diocesan High School, NY
Holy Trinity High School, IL
Hoosac School, NY
Hopkins School, CT
The Horace Mann School, NY
Horizons School, GA
The Hotchkiss School, CT
Howe Military School, IN
The Hudson School, NJ
The Hun School of Princeton, NJ
Hutchison School, TN
Hyde School, CT
Hyman Brand Hebrew Academy of Greater Kansas City, KS
Idyllwild Arts Academy, CA
Illiana Christian High School, IL
Immaculate Conception High School, NJ
Immaculate Conception School, IL
Independent School, KS
Indian Springs School, AL
Interlochen Arts Academy, MI
International School Bangkok, Thailand
International School Manila, Philippines
International School of Aruba, Aruba
Iolani School, HI
Isidore Newman School, LA
Jack M. Barrack Hebrew Academy (formerly Akiba Hebrew Academy), PA
Jackson Academy, MS
Jackson Preparatory School, MS
Jesuit College Preparatory School, TX
Jesuit High School, CA
Jesuit High School of Tampa, FL
John Bapst Memorial High School, ME
John Burroughs School, MO
The John Cooper School, TX

John Paul II Catholic High School, FL
Junipero Serra High School, CA
Kaplan College Preparatory School, FL
Karachi American School, Pakistan
Keith Country Day School, IL
Kent Denver School, CO
Kent Place School, NJ
Kent School, CT
Kents Hill School, ME
Kentucky Country Day School, KY
Kerr-Vance Academy, NC
The Key School, MD
Kimball Union Academy, NH
King Low Heywood Thomas, CT
The King's Academy, TN
The King's Christian High School, NJ
Kings Christian School, CA
King's High School, WA
King's Ridge Christian School, GA
Kingswood-Oxford School, CT
The Knox School, NY
Knoxville Catholic High School, TN
Ladywood High School, MI
Lakefield College School, ON, Canada
Lake Forest Academy, IL
Lakehill Preparatory School, TX
Lake Ridge Academy, OH
Lakeview Academy, GA
La Lumiere School, IN
Lancaster Country Day School, PA
Lancaster Mennonite High School, PA
Landon School, MD
Lansdale Catholic High School, PA
Lansing Christian School, MI
La Pietra–Hawaii School for Girls, HI
La Salle Academy, RI
La Salle High School, FL
La Salle Institute, NY
Lausanne Collegiate School, TN
Lawrence Academy, MA
Lawrence School, OH
Lee Academy, ME
Lehigh Valley Christian High School, PA
Lehman High School, OH
Le Lycee Francais de Los Angeles, CA
Lexington Catholic High School, KY
Lexington Christian Academy, MA
Lifegate School, OR
Lincoln School, RI
Linden Hall, PA
The Linden School, ON, Canada
Linfield Christian School, CA
The Linsly School, WV
The Loomis Chaffee School, CT
Loretto Academy, TX
Los Angeles Baptist Junior/Senior High School, CA
Los Angeles Lutheran High School, CA
Louisville Collegiate School, KY
Louisville High School, CA
The Lovett School, GA
The Lowell Whiteman School, CO
Loyola-Blakefield, MD
Loyola High School, Jesuit College Preparatory, CA
Loyola School, NY
Lutheran High North, TX
Lutheran High School, IN
Lutheran High School North, MO
Lutheran High School Northwest, MI
Lutheran High School of Hawaii, HI
Lutheran High School of San Diego, CA
Lutheran High School West, OH
Luther High School North, IL
Luther High School South, IL
Lycee Claudel, ON, Canada
Lycee Français de New York, NY
The Lycee International, American Section, France
Lydia Patterson Institute, TX
Lyman Ward Military Academy, AL
Lyndon Institute, VT
Ma'ayanot Yeshiva High School for Girls of Bergan County, NJ
The MacDuffie School, MA
MacLachlan College, ON, Canada
Madison-Ridgeland Academy, MS
Magnificat High School, OH
Maine Central Institute, ME
Maine School of Science and Mathematics, ME
Manlius Pebble Hill School, NY
Maret School, DC
Marianapolis Preparatory School, CT
Marian Baker School, Costa Rica
Marian Central Catholic High School, IL
Marian High School, IN
Marian High School, MI
Marin Academy, CA
Marist High School, IL
Marist High School, NJ
Marist School, GA
Marlborough School, CA
Marmion Academy, IL
Marquette University High School, WI
Marshall School, MN
Mars Hill Bible School, AL
Martin Luther High School, NY
The Marvelwood School, CT
Mary Help of Christians Academy, NJ
Maryknoll School, HI
Marylawn of the Oranges, NJ
The Mary Louis Academy, NY
Marymount High School, CA
Marymount International School, Italy
Marymount School, NY
Maryvale Preparatory School, MD
Massanutten Military Academy, VA
The Master's School, CT
The Masters School, NY
Mater Dei High School, IN
Matignon High School, MA
Maumee Valley Country Day School, OH
The McCallie School, TN
McCurdy School, NM
McDonogh School, MD
McQuaid Jesuit, NY
Meadowridge School, BC, Canada
The Meadows School, NV
Memphis University School, TN
Menaul School, NM
Menlo School, CA
Mennonite Collegiate Institute, MB, Canada

Mentor College, ON, Canada
Mercersburg Academy, PA
Mercy High School, CA
Mercy High School, CT
Mercy High School, NE
Mercy High School College Preparatory, CA
Metairie Park Country Day School, LA
Miami Country Day School, FL
Middlesex School, MA
Midland School, CA
Mid-Pacific Institute, HI
Milken Community High School of Stephen S. Wise Temple, CA
Millbrook School, NY
Miller School, VA
Milton Academy, MA
Miss Edgar's and Miss Cramp's School, QC, Canada
Miss Hall's School, MA
Missouri Military Academy, MO
Miss Porter's School, CT
MMI Preparatory School, PA
Modesto Christian School, CA
Monmouth Academy, NJ
Monsignor Donovan High School, NJ
Montana Academy, MT
Montgomery Bell Academy, TN
Montrose School, MA
Montverde Academy, FL
Moorestown Friends School, NJ
Moravian Academy, PA
Moreau Catholic High School, CA
Morgan Park Academy, IL
Morristown-Beard School, NJ
Moses Brown School, RI
Mother Cabrini High School, NY
Mother McAuley High School, IL
Mounds Park Academy, MN
Mount Michael Benedictine School, NE
Mount Saint Charles Academy, RI
Mt. Saint Dominic Academy, NJ
Mount Saint Joseph Academy, PA
Nancy Campbell Collegiate Institute, ON, Canada
National Cathedral School, DC
National High School, GA
National Sports Academy at Lake Placid, NY
Nazareth Academy, IL
Neuchatel Junior College, Switzerland
Newark Academy, NJ
New Hampton School, NH
The Newman School, MA
New York Military Academy, NY
Niagara Christian Community of Schools, ON, Canada
The Nichols School, NY
Noble and Greenough School, MA
Norfolk Academy, VA
Norfolk Christian School, VA
Norfolk Collegiate School, VA
The North Broward Preparatory Upper School, FL
North Cobb Christian School, GA
North Cross School, VA
Northfield Mount Hermon School, MA
North Shore Country Day School, IL
Northside Christian School, FL
Northwest Catholic High School, CT
Northwood School, NY
North Yarmouth Academy, ME
The Norwich Free Academy, CT
Notre Dame Academy, CA
Notre Dame Academy, MA
Notre Dame Academy, MA
Notre Dame Academy, VA
Notre Dame- Bishop Gibbons School, NY
Notre Dame-Cathedral Latin School, OH
Notre Dame High School, CA
Notre Dame High School, NJ
Notre Dame High School, TN
Notre Dame Junior/Senior High School, PA
Notre Dame Preparatory School, MD
Oak Grove Lutheran School, ND
Oak Grove School, CA
Oak Knoll School of the Holy Child, NJ
Oak Mountain Academy, GA
The Oakridge School, TX
Oakwood Friends School, NY
Oakwood School, CA
The Oakwood School, NC
O'Dea High School, WA
Ojai Valley School, CA
Oldenburg Academy, IN
Oldfields School, MD
Olney Friends School, OH
The O'Neal School, NC
Oneida Baptist Institute, KY
Orangewood Adventist Academy, CA
Oregon Episcopal School, OR
Orinda Academy, CA
The Orme School, AZ
Our Lady Academy, MS
Our Lady of Mercy High School, NY
Our Saviour Lutheran School, NY
Out-Of-Door-Academy, FL
The Overlake School, WA
The Oxford Academy, CT
Oxford School, CA
Pace Academy, GA
Pacific Academy, CA
Pacific Hills School, CA
Pacific Lutheran High School, CA
The Packer Collegiate Institute, NY
Padua Franciscan High School, OH
The Paideia School, GA
Palma High School, CA
The Parker School, HI
Parklane Academy, MS
The Park School of Buffalo, NY
Park Tudor School, IN
Peddie School, NJ
The Pennington School, NJ
Pensacola Catholic High School, FL
Perkiomen School, PA
The Phelps School, PA
Phillips Academy (Andover), MA
Phillips Exeter Academy, NH
Phoenix Christian Unified Schools, AZ
Phoenix Country Day School, AZ
Pine Crest School, FL
Pinewood Preparatory School, SC
The Pingry School, NJ

Pioneer Valley Christian School, MA
Pius X High School, NE
Poly Prep Country Day School, NY
Pomfret School, CT
Porter-Gaud School, SC
Portland Lutheran School, OR
Portledge School, NY
Portsmouth Abbey School, RI
Portsmouth Christian Academy, NH
The Potomac School, VA
Poughkeepsie Day School, NY
Powers Catholic High School, MI
The Prairie School, WI
Preston High School, NY
Prestonwood Christian Academy, TX
Providence Country Day School, RI
Providence Day School, NC
Providence High School, CA
Providence High School, TX
Pulaski Academy, AR
Punahou School, HI
The Putney School, VT
Queen Anne School, MD
Quigley Catholic High School, PA
Rabbi Alexander S. Gross Hebrew Academy, FL
Rabun Gap-Nacoochee School, GA
Rambam Mesivta, NY
Randolph-Macon Academy, VA
Randolph School, AL
Ranney School, NJ
Ransom Everglades School, FL
Ravenscroft School, NC
Redwood Christian Schools, CA
Regina Dominican High School, IL
Regina High School, OH
Regis High School, NY
Reitz Memorial High School, IN
Richmond Christian School, BC, Canada
Ridgecroft School, NC
Ridley College, ON, Canada
Ripon Christian Schools, CA
Riverdale Country School, NY
Rivermont Collegiate, IA
Riverside Military Academy, GA
The Rivers School, MA
Roanoke Catholic School, VA
Rockland Country Day School, NY
Rocky Hill School, RI
Rocky Mount Academy, NC
The Roeper School, MI
Roland Park Country School, MD
Rolling Hills Preparatory School, CA
Roncalli High School, IN
Rowland Hall-St. Mark's School, UT
The Roxbury Latin School, MA
Roycemore School, IL
Rutgers Preparatory School, NJ
Rye Country Day School, NY
Sacramento Country Day School, CA
Sacred Heart School of Halifax, NS, Canada
Saddle River Day School, NJ
Sage Hill School, CA
St. Agnes Academy, TX
St. Albans School, DC
St. Andrew's College, ON, Canada
St. Andrew's Episcopal School, MD
St. Andrew's Episcopal School, MS
St. Andrew's on the Marsh School, GA
St. Andrew's Priory School, HI
Saint Andrew's School, FL
St. Andrew's School, RI
St. Anne's–Belfield School, VA
St. Anselm's Abbey School, DC
St. Anthony Catholic High School, TX
Saint Anthony High School, IL
St. Anthony's Junior-Senior High School, HI
St. Augustine High School, CA
St. Augustine High School, TX
Saint Augustine Preparatory School, NJ
Saint Basil Academy, PA
St. Benedict at Auburndale, TN
St. Brendan High School, FL
St. Catherine's School, VA
St. Cecilia Academy, TN
Saint Cecilia High School, NE
St. Christopher's School, VA
St. Clement's School, ON, Canada
St. Croix Country Day School, VI
St. Croix Lutheran High School, MN
St. David's School, NC
Saint Dominic Academy, NJ
Saint Dominic Regional High School, ME
Saint Edmund High School, NY
Saint Edward's School, FL
Saint Elizabeth High School, CA
St. Francis de Sales High School, OH
Saint Francis High School, CA
St. Francis High School, KY
Saint Francis School, HI
St. George's Independent School, TN
St. George's School, RI
Saint George's School, WA
St. George's School, BC, Canada
St. George's School of Montreal, QC, Canada
Saint Gertrude High School, VA
St. Gregory College Preparatory School, AZ
Saint James School, MD
Saint Joan Antida High School, WI
Saint John Bosco High School, CA
St. Johnsbury Academy, VT
St. John's Catholic Prep, MD
St. John's College High School, DC
St. John's Preparatory School, MA
Saint John's Preparatory School, MN
St. John's-Ravenscourt School, MB, Canada
St. Joseph Academy, FL
Saint Joseph Central Catholic High School, OH
St. Joseph High School, CT
Saint Joseph High School, IL
Saint Joseph High School, WI
Saint Joseph Regional High School, NJ
St. Joseph's Academy, LA
St. Joseph's Catholic School, SC
St. Joseph's Preparatory School, PA
St. Margaret's Episcopal School, CA
St. Margaret's School, VA
St. Margaret's School, BC, Canada
Saint Mark's School, MA

St. Mark's School of Texas, TX
St. Martin's Episcopal School, LA
Saint Mary High School, NJ
St. Mary's Academy, CO
Saint Mary's College High School, CA
St. Mary's Dominican High School, LA
St. Mary's Episcopal School, TN
Saint Mary's Hall, TX
St. Mary's Hall–Doane Academy, NJ
Saint Mary's High School, AZ
St. Mary's High School, CO
Saint Mary's High School, MD
St. Mary's Preparatory School, MI
Saint Mary's School, NC
St. Mary's School, OR
Saint Matthias High School, CA
Saint Maur International School, Japan
St. Michael's College School, ON, Canada
St. Michael's Preparatory School of the Norbertine Fathers, CA
Saint Monica's High School, CA
Saint Patrick High School, IL
Saint Patrick—Saint Vincent High School, CA
St. Patrick's Regional Secondary, BC, Canada
St. Paul's Episcopal School, AL
St. Paul's High School, MB, Canada
St. Paul's School, MD
St. Paul's School, NH
St. Paul's School for Girls, MD
St. Peter's Preparatory School, NJ
St. Pius X Catholic High School, GA
St. Sebastian's School, MA
Saints Peter and Paul High School, MD
St. Stanislaus College, MS
St. Stephen's & St. Agnes School, VA
Saint Stephen's Episcopal School, FL
St. Stephen's Episcopal School, TX
St. Stephen's School, Rome, Italy
Saint Thomas Academy, MN
St. Thomas Aquinas High School, FL
Saint Thomas Aquinas High School, KS
St. Thomas Aquinas High School, NH
St. Thomas High School, TX
Saint Xavier High School, KY
Saint Xavier High School, OH
Salem Academy, NC
Salem Baptist Christian School, NC
Salesian High School, CA
Salesian High School, NY
Salesianum School, DE
Salisbury School, CT
Salpointe Catholic High School, AZ
Saltus Grammar School, Bermuda
The Samuel Scheck Hillel Community Day School, FL
San Diego Jewish Academy, CA
San Domenico School, CA
Sandy Spring Friends School, MD
Sanford School, DE
San Francisco University High School, CA
San Marcos Baptist Academy, TX
Santa Fe Preparatory School, NM
Santa Margarita Catholic High School, CA
Santiam Christian School, OR
Savannah Christian Preparatory School, GA
The Savannah Country Day School, GA
Sayre School, KY
Schlarman High School, IL
School for Young Performers, NY
School of the Holy Child, NY
Scotus Central Catholic High School, NE
Seabury Hall, HI
Seattle Christian Schools, WA
Seattle Lutheran High School, WA
Second Baptist School, TX
Seoul Foreign School, Republic of Korea
Seton Catholic Central High School, NY
Seton Catholic High School, AZ
The Seven Hills School, OH
Sewickley Academy, PA
Shades Mountain Christian School, AL
Shady Side Academy, PA
Shannon Forest Christian School, SC
Shattuck-St. Mary's School, MN
Shenandoah Valley Academy, VA
The Shipley School, PA
Shorecrest Preparatory School, FL
Sioux Falls Christian High School, SD
Solebury School, PA
Soundview Preparatory School, NY
Southfield Christian High School, MI
South Kent School, CT
Southridge School, BC, Canada
Southwestern Academy, AZ
Southwestern Academy, CA
The Spence School, NY
Squaw Valley Academy, CA
Starkville Academy, MS
Staten Island Academy, NY
Stella Maris High School, NY
Stephen T. Badin High School, OH
Stevenson School, CA
Stoneleigh–Burnham School, MA
The Stony Brook School, NY
Storm King School, NY
Strake Jesuit College Preparatory, TX
Stratford Academy, GA
Stuart Country Day School of the Sacred Heart, NJ
Subiaco Academy, AR
Suffield Academy, CT
Summerfield Waldorf School, CA
The Summit Country Day School, OH
Tabor Academy, MA
The Taft School, CT
Tallulah Falls School, GA
Tampa Preparatory School, FL
Tandem Friends School, VA
TASIS The American School in England, United Kingdom
TASIS, The American School in Switzerland, Switzerland
The Tatnall School, DE
The Tenney School, TX
Teurlings Catholic High School, LA
The Thacher School, CA
Thomas Jefferson School, MO
Tilton School, NH
Timothy Christian High School, IL
TMI—The Episcopal School of Texas, TX
Tower Hill School, DE
Town Centre Private High School, ON, Canada
Trafalgar Castle School, ON, Canada

Tri-City Christian Schools, CA
Trinity Catholic High School, MA
Trinity Christian Academy, TX
Trinity College School, ON, Canada
Trinity Episcopal School, VA
Trinity High School, KY
Trinity High School, NH
Trinity High School, OH
Trinity-Pawling School, NY
Trinity Preparatory School, FL
Trinity Presbyterian School, AL
Trinity School, NY
Trinity School of Midland, TX
Trinity Valley School, TX
University Lake School, WI
University Liggett School, MI
University of Chicago Laboratory Schools, IL
University of Toronto Schools, ON, Canada
University Prep, WA
University School of Jackson, TN
University School of Milwaukee, WI
University School of Nova Southeastern University, FL
The Urban School of San Francisco, CA
Ursuline Academy, DE
Ursuline Academy, MA
The Ursuline Academy of Dallas, TX
Ursuline High School, CA
The Ursuline School, NY
Valle Catholic High School, MO
Valley Christian School, CA
Valley Forge Military Academy & College, PA
Valley Lutheran High School, MI
Valwood School, GA
Vianney High School, MO
Victor Valley Christian School, CA
Viewpoint School, CA
Villa Duchesne/Oak Hill School, MO
Villa Joseph Marie High School, PA
Villa Maria Academy, PA
Villanova Preparatory School, CA
Villa Walsh Academy, NJ
Virginia Beach Friends School, VA
Virginia Episcopal School, VA
Visitation Academy of St. Louis County, MO
Wakefield School, VA
The Waldorf School of Garden City, NY
The Walker School, GA
Walnut Hill School, MA
The Wardlaw-Hartridge School, NJ
Waring School, MA
Wasatch Academy, UT
Washington Academy, ME
Washington Waldorf School, MD
The Waterford School, UT
The Waverly School, CA
Wayne Country Day School, NC
The Webb School, TN
Webb School of Knoxville, TN
The Webb Schools, CA
The Wellington School, OH
Wesleyan Academy, PR
Westbury Christian School, TX
West Catholic High School, MI
Westchester Country Day School, NC
Western Christian Schools, CA
Western Reserve Academy, OH
West Island College, AB, Canada
Westminster Catawba Christian, SC
Westminster Christian Academy, AL
Westminster Christian School, FL
Westminster School, CT
The Westminster Schools, GA
Westminster Schools of Augusta, GA
West Nottingham Academy, MD
Westover School, CT
Westridge School, CA
Westtown School, PA
Wheaton Academy, IL
The Wheeler School, RI
Whitefield Academy, GA
The White Mountain School, NH
Wichita Collegiate School, KS
William Penn Charter School, PA
The Williams School, CT
The Williston Northampton School, MA
The Willows Academy, IL
Wilmington Friends School, DE
Wilson Hall, SC
The Winchendon School, MA
Winchester Thurston School, PA
Windermere Preparatory School, FL
The Windsor School, NY
Windward School, CA
The Winsor School, MA
The Woodhall School, CT
Woodlands Academy of the Sacred Heart, IL
Woodside Priory School, CA
Woodstock School, India
Woodward Academy, GA
Wooster School, CT
Worcester Academy, MA
Worcester Preparatory School, MD
World Hope Academy, FL
Wyoming Seminary, PA
Xaverian Brothers High School, MA
Xavier College Preparatory, AZ
York Country Day School, PA
York Preparatory School, NY
Zurich International School, Switzerland

SCHOOLS REPORTING A POSTGRADUATE YEAR

The Academy at Charlemont, MA
Aiglon College, Switzerland
Albert College, ON, Canada
Avon Old Farms School, CT
The Beekman School, NY
Berkshire School, MA
Berwick Academy, ME
Blair Academy, NJ
The Bolles School, FL
Brehm Preparatory School, IL
Brenau Academy, GA
Brewster Academy, NH
Burke Mountain Academy, VT
The Cambridge School of Weston, MA
Camden Military Academy, SC
Canterbury School, CT

Carrabassett Valley Academy, ME
Cascadilla School, NY
Chapel Hill–Chauncy Hall School, MA
Cheshire Academy, CT
Choate Rosemary Hall, CT
Christchurch School, VA
The Culver Academies, IN
Cushing Academy, MA
Darlington School, GA
Darrow School, NY
Deerfield Academy, MA
Emma Willard School, NY
Franklin Academy, CT
Fryeburg Academy, ME
Gould Academy, ME
The Gow School, NY
The Grand River Academy, OH
Griggs University and International Academy, MD
Grove School, CT
The Gunnery, CT
Hargrave Military Academy, VA
Hawai'i Preparatory Academy, HI
Hebron Academy, ME
Hidden Lake Academy, GA
The Hill School, PA
Holderness School, NH
Hoosac School, NY
Horizons School, GA
The Hotchkiss School, CT
Houghton Academy, NY
The Hun School of Princeton, NJ
Idyllwild Arts Academy, CA
Interlochen Arts Academy, MI
The John Dewey Academy, MA
Kent School, CT
Kents Hill School, ME
Kildonan School, NY
Kimball Union Academy, NH
La Lumiere School, IN
The Lawrenceville School, NJ
Lee Academy, ME
Lester B. Pearson United World College of the Pacific, BC, Canada
Linden Hall, PA
The Loomis Chaffee School, CT
Maine Central Institute, ME
Manlius Pebble Hill School, NY
Marianapolis Preparatory School, CT
Massanutten Military Academy, VA
Mercersburg Academy, PA
Missouri Military Academy, MO
Montverde Academy, FL
National Sports Academy at Lake Placid, NY
New Hampton School, NH
The Newman School, MA
Northfield Mount Hermon School, MA
Northwood School, NY
Oldfields School, MD
The Orme School, AZ
The Oxford Academy, CT
Peddie School, NJ
Perkiomen School, PA
The Phelps School, PA
Phillips Academy (Andover), MA
Phillips Exeter Academy, NH
Pomfret School, CT
Randolph-Macon Academy, VA
Redemption Christian Academy, NY
Ridley College, ON, Canada
Riverside Military Academy, GA
Robert Louis Stevenson School, NY
St. Gregory College Preparatory School, AZ
St. Johnsbury Academy, VT
Saint John's Preparatory School, MN
St. Stephen's School, Rome, Italy
Saint Thomas More School, CT
Salisbury School, CT
Scattergood Friends School, IA
Soundview Preparatory School, NY
South Kent School, CT
Southwestern Academy, AZ
Southwestern Academy, CA
Stoneleigh–Burnham School, MA
Stratton Mountain School, VT
Suffield Academy, CT
The Taft School, CT
TASIS, The American School in Switzerland, Switzerland
Thomas Jefferson School, MO
Tilton School, NH
Trident Academy, SC
Trinity-Pawling School, NY
Valley Forge Military Academy & College, PA
The Vanguard School, FL
Watkinson School, CT
Western Reserve Academy, OH
Westminster School, CT
West Nottingham Academy, MD
The White Mountain School, NH
The Williston Northampton School, MA
The Winchendon School, MA
The Windsor School, NY
The Woodhall School, CT
Worcester Academy, MA
Wyoming Seminary, PA

SCHOOLS OFFERING THE INTERNATIONAL BACCALAUREATE PROGRAM

Academia Cotopaxi, Ecuador
Academie Sainte Cecile International School, ON, Canada
ACS Cobham International School, United Kingdom
ACS Egham International School, United Kingdom
ACS Hillingdon International School, United Kingdom
Ahliyyah School for Girls, Jordan
American Community Schools of Athens, Greece
The American International School, Austria
American International School, Dhaka, Bangladesh
American International School of Bucharest, Romania
American International School Rotterdam, Netherlands
The American School Foundation, Mexico
The American School of Madrid, Spain
American School of Milan, Italy
American School of Paris, France
The American School of The Hague, Netherlands
Ashbury College, ON, Canada
Atlanta International School, GA
The Awty International School, TX

Bavarian International School, Germany
Bellarmine-Jefferson High School, CA
The Bermuda High School for Girls, Bermuda
Canadian Academy, Japan
Cardinal Newman High School, FL
Carlisle School, VA
Carlucci American International School of Lisbon, Portugal
Carrollton School of the Sacred Heart, FL
Cathedral High School, IN
Chamberlain-Hunt Academy, MS
Chapel School, Brazil
Charlotte Country Day School, NC
Colegio Franklin D. Roosevelt, Peru
Colegio Nueva Granada, Colombia
College du Leman International School, Switzerland
Copenhagen International School, Denmark
Cornelia Connelly School, CA
DePaul Catholic High School, NJ
Detroit Country Day School, MI
Dubai American Academy, United Arab Emirates
Ecole Internationale de Boston / International School of Boston, MA
Elmwood School, ON, Canada
Fort Lauderdale Preparatory School, FL
George School, PA
Gulliver Preparatory School, FL
The Harrisburg Academy, PA
Hebrew Academy, CA
International College Spain, Spain
International High School, CA
International School Bangkok, Thailand
International School Eerde, Netherlands
International School Hamburg, Germany
International School Manila, Philippines
The International School of Aberdeen, United Kingdom
International School of Amsterdam, Netherlands
International School of Athens, Greece
International School of Berne, Switzerland
The International School of Geneva, Switzerland
International School of Lausanne, Switzerland
The International School of London, United Kingdom
International School of Milan, Italy
The International School of Paris, France
King George School, VT
The King's Academy, TN
King's-Edgehill School, NS, Canada
Le Lycee Francais de Los Angeles, CA
Lester B. Pearson United World College of the Pacific, BC, Canada
Luther College High School, SK, Canada
Lycee Claudel, ON, Canada
Lycee Français de New York, NY
Lydia Patterson Institute, TX
Marymount International School, Italy
Marymount International School, United Kingdom
Meadowridge School, BC, Canada
Mercedes College, Australia
Mercyhurst Preparatory School, PA
Mid-Pacific Institute, HI
Munich International School, Germany
Newark Academy, NJ
The North Broward Preparatory Upper School, FL
Pacific Lutheran High School, CA
Pinewood—The International School of Thessaloniki, Greece, Greece
The Prout School, RI
Riverstone International School, ID
Rothesay Netherwood School, NB, Canada
Rotterdam International Secondary School, Wolfert van Borselen, Netherlands
Saint Anthony High School, IL
Saint Dominic Academy, NJ
Saint Dominic Regional High School, ME
St. Dominic's International School, Portugal, Portugal
Saint Edmund High School, NY
Saint Mary High School, NJ
St. Mary's International School, Japan
Saint Maur International School, Japan
Saint Paul Lutheran High School, MO
St. Paul's School, MD
St. Peter's Preparatory School, NJ
St. Stephen's School, Rome, Italy
St. Timothy's School, MD
Santa Margarita Catholic High School, CA
SCECGS Redlands, Australia
Seisen International School, Japan
Seoul Foreign School, Republic of Korea
St Leonards School and Sixth Form College, United Kingdom
Strathcona-Tweedsmuir School, AB, Canada
TASIS The American School in England, United Kingdom
TASIS, The American School in Switzerland, Switzerland
Tri-City Christian Schools, CA
Trinity Episcopal School, VA
Trinity High School, IL
United Nations International School, NY
The United World College—USA, NM
Valle Catholic High School, MO
Verdala International School, Malta
Verde Valley School, AZ
Villa Duchesne/Oak Hill School, MO
Washington International School, DC
Wilmington Friends School, DE
Windermere Preparatory School, FL
World Hope Academy, FL
Xaverian Brothers High School, MA
Yokohama International School, Japan
Zurich International School, Switzerland

SCHOOLS REPORTING THAT THEY AWARD MERIT SCHOLARSHIPS

Academia Cotopaxi, Ecuador
Academie Sainte Cecile International School, ON, Canada
Academy for Global Exploration, OR
Academy of Mount Saint Ursula, NY
Academy of Notre Dame de Namur, PA
Academy of Our Lady of Good Counsel High School, NY
Academy of Our Lady of Mercy, CT
Academy of the Holy Angels, NJ
Academy of the Holy Cross, MD
Academy of the Holy Names, FL
Academy of the Sacred Heart, MI
Advanced Academy of Georgia, GA
Albert College, ON, Canada
Allison Academy, FL
All Saints' Episcopal School of Fort Worth, TX

Alma Heights Christian Academy, CA
The Altamont School, AL
American Heritage School, FL
The American School Foundation, Mexico
Andrews Osborne Academy, OH
Annie Wright School, WA
Archbishop Curley High School, MD
Archbishop Hoban High School, OH
Archbishop McNicholas High School, OH
Archbishop Rummel High School, LA
Archbishop Spalding High School, MD
Archmere Academy, DE
Ashbury College, ON, Canada
Asheville School, NC
Assumption High School, KY
Aurora Central High School, IL
Austin Preparatory School, MA
Avon Old Farms School, CT
Balmoral Hall School, MB, Canada
Bancroft School, MA
Barnstable Academy, NJ
The Barstow School, MO
Bass Memorial Academy, MS
Battle Ground Academy, TN
Baylor School, TN
Bellarmine-Jefferson High School, CA
Benedictine High School, OH
Benedictine High School, VA
Benilde–St. Margaret's School, MN
The Benjamin School, FL
Berkshire School, MA
The Bermuda High School for Girls, Bermuda
The Birch Wathen Lenox School, NY
Bishop Blanchet High School, WA
Bishop Brady High School, NH
Bishop Connolly High School, MA
Bishop Denis J. O'Connell High School, VA
Bishop Eustace Preparatory School, NJ
Bishop Feehan High School, MA
Bishop Fenwick High School, OH
Bishop George Ahr High School, NJ
Bishop Gorman High School, NV
Bishop Guertin High School, NH
Bishop Hendricken High School, RI
Bishop Ireton High School, VA
Bishop Luers High School, IN
Bishop Lynch Catholic High School, TX
Bishop McNamara High School, IL
Bishop Mora Salesian High School, CA
Bishop Stang High School, MA
The Bishop Strachan School, ON, Canada
Bishop Verot High School, FL
Blanchet School, OR
The Blue Ridge School, VA
Bodwell High School, BC, Canada
Boston College High School, MA
Boston University Academy, MA
Bridge School, CO
Brookstone School, GA
Brother Martin High School, LA
Brother Rice High School, MI
Buffalo Seminary, NY
Calvert Hall College High School, MD
Camelot Academy, NC
Canterbury School, FL
Canyonville Christian Academy, OR
Cape Fear Academy, NC
Cape Henry Collegiate School, VA
Cardinal Mooney High School, FL
Cardinal Newman High School, CA
Carlucci American International School of Lisbon, Portugal
Carolina Day School, NC
Carrollton School of the Sacred Heart, FL
Carson Long Military Institute, PA
Cary Academy, NC
Cascadilla School, NY
Cathedral High School, IN
Cathedral High School, NY
Catholic Central High School, MI
The Catholic High School of Baltimore, MD
Catholic Memorial, MA
Centennial Academy, QC, Canada
Central Catholic High School, CA
Central Catholic High School, MA
Central Catholic High School, OH
Chaminade College Preparatory, CA
Chaminade College Preparatory School, MO
Charlotte Latin School, NC
Chase Collegiate School, CT
Cheshire Academy, CT
Cheverus High School, ME
Children's Creative and Performing Arts Academy—
Capa Division, CA
Chinese Christian Schools, CA
Christchurch School, VA
Christian Brothers Academy, NJ
Christian Brothers Academy, NY
Christian Brothers Academy, NY
Christian Central Academy, NY
Christ School, NC
Cincinnati Country Day School, OH
Colegio Puertorriqueno de Ninas, PR
The Colorado Rocky Mountain School, CO
The Colorado Springs School, CO
Columbia International College of Canada, ON, Canada
Columbia International School, Japan
Commonwealth Parkville School, PR
The Community School, ID
Connelly School of the Holy Child, MD
Conserve School, WI
Cornelia Connelly School, CA
Country Day School of the Sacred Heart, PA
Crespi Carmelite High School, CA
Crofton House School, BC, Canada
Crossroads College Preparatory School, MO
Crossroads School for Arts & Sciences, CA
The Culver Academies, IN
Cushing Academy, MA
Dana Hall School, MA
Darlington School, GA
Deerfield-Windsor School, GA
De La Salle College, ON, Canada
DeMatha Catholic High School, MD
Denver Christian High School, CO
DePaul Catholic High School, NJ
De Smet Jesuit High School, MO
Devon Preparatory School, PA
The Dominican Academy of the City of New York, NY

Duchesne Academy of the Sacred Heart, TX
East Catholic High School, CT
Elgin Academy, IL
Elizabeth Seton High School, MD
Elmwood School, ON, Canada
Elyria Catholic High School, OH
Emma Willard School, NY
Episcopal High School, VA
The Ethel Walker School, CT
Evansville Day School, IN
Explorations Academy, WA
Falmouth Academy, MA
First Presbyterian Day School, GA
Fishburne Military School, VA
Flintridge Sacred Heart Academy, CA
Fontbonne Academy, MA
Fontbonne Hall Academy, NY
Fordham Preparatory School, NY
Fort Lauderdale Preparatory School, FL
Fort Worth Country Day School, TX
Fountain Valley School of Colorado, CO
Foxcroft Academy, ME
Foxcroft School, VA
Fox Valley Lutheran Academy, IL
Freeman Academy, SD
Fuqua School, VA
Gabriel Richard High School, MI
Garces Memorial High School, CA
Garden School, NY
Gaston Day School, NC
Gateway School, TX
George School, PA
Georgetown Visitation Preparatory School, DC
Germantown Academy, PA
Gill St. Bernard's School, NJ
Gilmour Academy, OH
Glenelg Country School, MD
Gonzaga College High School, DC
Gordon Technical High School, IL
The Grand River Academy, OH
The Grauer School, CA
Great Lakes Christian High School, ON, Canada
Greenfield School, NC
Green Fields Country Day School, AZ
Guerin College Preparatory High School, IL
The Gunnery, CT
Gunston Day School, MD
Gwynedd Mercy Academy, PA
Hammond School, SC
Hargrave Military Academy, VA
Havergal College, ON, Canada
Hawthorne Christian Academy, NJ
Hayden High School, KS
Headwaters Academy, MT
Hebron Academy, ME
Heritage Hall, OK
Highland School, VA
Holland Hall, OK
Holy Names High School, CA
Holy Savior Menard Catholic High School, LA
Holy Trinity High School, IL
The Hun School of Princeton, NJ
Immaculate Conception High School, NJ
Immaculate Conception School, IL
Immaculate High School, CT
Interlochen Arts Academy, MI
International College Spain, Spain
International School of Milan, Italy
International School of South Africa, South Africa
Jack M. Barrack Hebrew Academy (formerly Akiba Hebrew Academy), PA
Jesuit College Preparatory School, TX
Junipero Serra High School, CA
Keith Country Day School, IL
Kerr-Vance Academy, NC
King Low Heywood Thomas, CT
King's-Edgehill School, NS, Canada
Kingshill School, VI
Kingsway College, ON, Canada
Kingswood-Oxford School, CT
Lake Forest Academy, IL
Lake Ridge Academy, OH
Lakeview Academy, GA
La Lumiere School, IN
Lancaster Mennonite High School, PA
Lansdale Catholic High School, PA
La Salle Academy, RI
La Salle Institute, NY
The Laureate Academy, MB, Canada
Lee Academy, ME
Lehigh Valley Christian High School, PA
Lexington Catholic High School, KY
Lexington Christian Academy, MA
Lincoln School, RI
Linden Hall, PA
The Linden School, ON, Canada
Los Angeles Baptist Junior/Senior High School, CA
Los Angeles Lutheran High School, CA
Louisville Collegiate School, KY
Louisville High School, CA
Lourdes Catholic High School, AZ
The Lowell Whiteman School, CO
Loyola-Blakefield, MD
Loyola High School, Jesuit College Preparatory, CA
Loyola School, NY
Lutheran High North, TX
Lutheran High School, MO
Lutheran High School North, MO
Lutheran High School Northwest, MI
Lutheran High School of Hawaii, HI
Lutheran High School of San Diego, CA
Lutheran High School West, OH
Luther College High School, SK, Canada
Luther High School North, IL
Luther High School South, IL
Lyman Ward Military Academy, AL
The MacDuffie School, MA
Madison-Ridgeland Academy, MS
Maine Central Institute, ME
Manlius Pebble Hill School, NY
Maplebrook School, NY
Marianapolis Preparatory School, CT
Marian High School, MI
Marist High School, IL
Marist High School, NJ
Marmion Academy, IL
Martin Luther High School, NY
Mary Help of Christians Academy, NJ

Maryknoll School, HI
Marylawn of the Oranges, NJ
The Mary Louis Academy, NY
Marymount High School, CA
Massanutten Military Academy, VA
The Master's School, CT
Matignon High School, MA
Maumee Valley Country Day School, OH
Maur Hill-Mount Academy, KS
The McCallie School, TN
McCurdy School, NM
McQuaid Jesuit, NY
Meadowridge School, BC, Canada
Mennonite Collegiate Institute, MB, Canada
Mentor College, ON, Canada
Mercersburg Academy, PA
Merchiston Castle School, United Kingdom
Mercy High School, CT
Mercy High School, NE
Mercyhurst Preparatory School, PA
Mid-Pacific Institute, HI
Miss Edgar's and Miss Cramp's School, QC, Canada
Miss Hall's School, MA
Missouri Military Academy, MO
Miss Porter's School, CT
MMI Preparatory School, PA
Monmouth Academy, NJ
Monsignor Donovan High School, NJ
Montrose School, MA
Moreau Catholic High School, CA
Morgan Park Academy, IL
Morristown-Beard School, NJ
Mother Cabrini High School, NY
Mother McAuley High School, IL
Mount Michael Benedictine School, NE
Mt. Saint Dominic Academy, NJ
Mount Saint Joseph Academy, PA
Nancy Campbell Collegiate Institute, ON, Canada
Nazareth Academy, IL
Nebraska Christian Schools, NE
Nerinx Hall, MO
Neuchatel Junior College, Switzerland
The Newman School, MA
New Mexico Military Institute, NM
New York Military Academy, NY
Niagara Christian Community of Schools, ON, Canada
Norfolk Collegiate School, VA
The North Broward Preparatory Upper School, FL
North Shore Country Day School, IL
Northwest Catholic High School, CT
Notre Dame Academy, CA
Notre Dame Academy, MA
Notre Dame- Bishop Gibbons School, NY
Notre Dame-Cathedral Latin School, OH
Notre Dame High School, CA
Oak Grove Lutheran School, ND
Oak Knoll School of the Holy Child, NJ
The Oakland School, PA
Oak Ridge Military Academy, NC
The Oakwood School, NC
Oldenburg Academy, IN
Oldfields School, MD
The O'Neal School, NC
The Orme School, AZ
Our Lady of Mercy Academy, NJ
Our Lady of Mercy High School, NY
Our Saviour Lutheran School, NY
Pacific Lutheran High School, CA
Padua Franciscan High School, OH
Palma High School, CA
The Parker School, HI
The Park School of Buffalo, NY
Park Tudor School, IN
Peddie School, NJ
The Pennington School, NJ
Poly Prep Country Day School, NY
Portland Lutheran School, OR
Portsmouth Abbey School, RI
Portsmouth Christian Academy, NH
Powers Catholic High School, MI
The Prairie School, WI
Preston High School, NY
Providence High School, CA
Providence High School, TX
Punahou School, HI
Queen Margaret's School, BC, Canada
Quigley Catholic High School, PA
Rabun Gap-Nacoochee School, GA
Rambam Mesivta, NY
Randolph-Macon Academy, VA
Randolph School, AL
Ravenscroft School, NC
Redemption Christian Academy, NY
Regina Dominican High School, IL
Regina High School, OH
Rice High School, NY
Ridley College, ON, Canada
Rivermont Collegiate, IA
Riverside Military Academy, GA
Rocky Mount Academy, NC
Rolling Hills Preparatory School, CA
Roncalli High School, IN
Rosseau Lake College, ON, Canada
Rothesay Netherwood School, NB, Canada
Rowland Hall-St. Mark's School, UT
Royal Canadian College, BC, Canada
Roycemore School, IL
Sacred Heart School of Halifax, NS, Canada
Saddle River Day School, NJ
St. Agnes Academy, TX
St. Andrew's College, ON, Canada
St. Andrew's Episcopal School, MS
St. Andrew's Priory School, HI
St. Andrew's–Sewanee School, TN
St. Anthony's Junior-Senior High School, HI
St. Augustine High School, CA
Saint Augustine Preparatory School, NJ
Saint Basil Academy, PA
St. Benedict at Auburndale, TN
Saint Cecilia High School, NE
St. Christopher's School, VA
St. Clement's School, ON, Canada
St. Croix Country Day School, VI
St. Croix Lutheran High School, MN
Saint Dominic Academy, NJ
St. Dominic's International School, Portugal, Portugal
Saint Edmund High School, NY
Saint Elizabeth High School, CA

St. Francis de Sales High School, OH
St. Francis High School, KY
Saint Francis School, HI
Saint George's School, WA
St. George's School, BC, Canada
Saint Gertrude High School, VA
Saint James School, MD
Saint Joan Antida High School, WI
St. John's Catholic Prep, MD
St. John's College High School, DC
St. John's Northwestern Military Academy, WI
Saint John's Preparatory School, MN
St. John's-Ravenscourt School, MB, Canada
Saint Joseph Central Catholic High School, OH
St. Joseph High School, CA
St. Joseph High School, CT
Saint Joseph High School, IL
Saint Joseph High School, PA
Saint Joseph High School, WI
Saint Joseph Regional High School, NJ
St. Joseph's Catholic School, SC
St. Joseph's Preparatory School, PA
St. Margaret's School, BC, Canada
St. Martin's Episcopal School, LA
Saint Mary High School, NJ
St. Mary's Academy, CO
St. Mary's Dominican High School, LA
Saint Mary's Hall, TX
St. Mary's High School, CO
Saint Mary's High School, MD
St. Mary's Preparatory School, MI
Saint Mary's School, NC
St. Mary's School, OR
Saint Matthias High School, CA
St. Michael's College School, ON, Canada
Saint Monica's High School, CA
St. Paul's School, NH
St. Paul's School for Girls, MD
St. Peter's Preparatory School, NJ
St. Stephen's Episcopal School, TX
Saint Teresa's Academy, MO
Saint Thomas Academy, MN
Saint Thomas More School, CT
St. Timothy's School, MD
Saint Xavier High School, OH
Salem Academy, NC
Salesian High School, CA
Salesian High School, NY
Salesianum School, DE
Salisbury School, CT
Salpointe Catholic High School, AZ
Salt Lake Lutheran High School, UT
Saltus Grammar School, Bermuda
San Diego Jewish Academy, CA
Savannah Christian Preparatory School, GA
The Savannah Country Day School, GA
Sayre School, KY
Scattergood Friends School, IA
SCECGS Redlands, Australia
School of the Holy Child, NY
Seattle Lutheran High School, WA
Second Baptist School, TX
Sedbergh School, QC, Canada
Selwyn House School, QC, Canada
Seton Catholic Central High School, NY
Seton Catholic High School, AZ
Shady Side Academy, PA
Shattuck-St. Mary's School, MN
Shenandoah Valley Academy, VA
Solebury School, PA
South Kent School, CT
Stella Maris High School, NY
Stephen T. Badin High School, OH
Stoneleigh–Burnham School, MA
Storm King School, NY
Stratford Academy, GA
Stuart Country Day School of the Sacred Heart, NJ
The Study School, QC, Canada
Suffield Academy, CT
The Summit Country Day School, OH
Tampa Preparatory School, FL
TASIS The American School in England, United Kingdom
Thomas Jefferson School, MO
Tilton School, NH
TMI—The Episcopal School of Texas, TX
Trafalgar Castle School, ON, Canada
Trident Academy, SC
Trinity Catholic High School, MA
Trinity Episcopal School, VA
Trinity High School, IL
Trinity High School, KY
Trinity Presbyterian School, AL
Trinity School of Midland, TX
The United World College—USA, NM
University Lake School, WI
University Liggett School, MI
University of Toronto Schools, ON, Canada
Ursuline Academy, DE
The Ursuline Academy of Dallas, TX
Ursuline High School, CA
The Ursuline School, NY
Valle Catholic High School, MO
Valley Forge Military Academy & College, PA
Valley Lutheran High School, AZ
The Valley School, MI
Valwood School, GA
Vianney High School, MO
Villa Duchesne/Oak Hill School, MO
Villa Joseph Marie High School, PA
Villa Maria Academy, PA
Villanova Preparatory School, CA
Villa Walsh Academy, NJ
Virginia Beach Friends School, VA
Virginia Episcopal School, VA
Waldorf High School of Massachusetts Bay, MA
The Waldorf School of Garden City, NY
The Wardlaw-Hartridge School, NJ
Wasatch Academy, UT
The Webb School, TN
The Wellington School, OH
Western Reserve Academy, OH
Wheaton Academy, IL
The White Mountain School, NH
Woodlands Academy of the Sacred Heart, IL
Woodside Priory School, CA
Worcester Academy, MA
Wyoming Seminary, PA
Xaverian Brothers High School, MA

Xavier University Preparatory School, LA
York Preparatory School, NY

SCHOOLS REPORTING A GUARANTEED TUITION PLAN

The Academy at Sisters, OR
Academy for Global Exploration, OR
Accelerated Schools, CO
Alabama Christian Academy, AL
Alpine Academy, UT
Armona Union Academy, CA
Auldern Academy, NC
Baldwin School of Puerto Rico, Inc., PR
Bishop Garcia Diego High School, CA
Bishop Kelly High School, ID
Bodwell High School, BC, Canada
Butte Central High School, MT
Cedar Ridge Academy, UT
Central Catholic High School, CA
CFS, The School at Church Farm, PA
Cherry Gulch, ID
Community Christian Academy, KY
Concord Academy, MA
Cross Creek Programs, UT
Deck House School, ME
Ecole d'Humanité, Switzerland
Elk Mountain Academy, MT
Explorations Academy, WA
Foothills Academy, AB, Canada
Foundation Academy, FL
Gateway School, TX
Grace Brethren School, CA
Green Meadow Waldorf School, NY
Hargrave Military Academy, VA
Hawaii Baptist Academy, HI
Hawai'i Preparatory Academy, HI
Hebrew Academy, CA
Hidden Lake Academy, GA
The Hill Center, Durham Academy, NC
Hope Christian School, AB, Canada
Humanex Academy, CO
Imperial College of Toronto, ON, Canada
International School Eerde, Netherlands
Jackson Christian School, TN
John Paul II Catholic High School, FL
Kent School, CT
Koinonia Christian School, AB, Canada
La Pietra–Hawaii School for Girls, HI
Laurel Springs School, CA
Lee Academy, ME
The Loomis Chaffee School, CT
Lourdes Catholic High School, AZ
Marion Academy, AL
Mercy High School College Preparatory, CA
Middlesex School, MA
Montana Academy, MT
National High School, GA
New Covenant Academy, MO
New Horizon Youth Ministries, IN
Notre Dame High School, CA
Oak Creek Ranch School, AZ
Okanagan Adventist Academy, BC, Canada
Parish Episcopal School, TX
Piedmont Academy, GA
Pius X High School, NE
Pomfret School, CT
Pope John XXIII Regional High School, NJ
St. Brendan High School, FL
Saint Cecilia High School, NE
St. Christopher Academy, WA
Saint Francis School, HI
Saint Paul Lutheran High School, MO
San Marcos Baptist Academy, TX
Selwyn House School, QC, Canada
Sorenson's Ranch School, UT
Spring Ridge Academy, AZ
Stanbridge Academy, CA
Sunrise Academy, UT
The Tenney School, TX
Trinity High School, KY
Trinity-Pawling School, NY
The United World College—USA, NM
The Waterford School, UT
Wayne Country Day School, NC
Wesleyan Academy, PR
Westminster Christian Academy, AL
World Hope Academy, FL

SCHOOLS REPORTING A TUITION INSTALLMENT PLAN

Abington Friends School, PA
Academia Cotopaxi, Ecuador
Academie Sainte Cecile International School, ON, Canada
The Academy at Charlemont, MA
The Academy at Sisters, OR
Academy at Swift River, MA
The Academy for Gifted Children (PACE), ON, Canada
Academy for Global Exploration, OR
Academy of Mount Saint Ursula, NY
Academy of Notre Dame de Namur, PA
Academy of Our Lady of Good Counsel High School, NY
Academy of Our Lady of Mercy, CT
Academy of Our Lady of Peace, CA
Academy of the Holy Angels, NJ
Academy of the Holy Cross, MD
Academy of the Holy Names, FL
Academy of the New Church Boys' School, PA
Academy of the New Church Girls' School, PA
Academy of the Sacred Heart, LA
Academy of the Sacred Heart, MI
Accelerated Schools, CO
ACS Cobham International School, United Kingdom
ACS Egham International School, United Kingdom
ACS Hillingdon International School, United Kingdom
The Agnes Irwin School, PA
Ahliyyah School for Girls, Jordan
Airdrie Koinonia Christian School, AB, Canada
Alabama Christian Academy, AL
Albert College, ON, Canada
Albuquerque Academy, NM
Alexander Dawson School, CO
The Alexander School, TX
Allen Academy, TX
Allendale Columbia School, NY

Alliance Academy, Ecuador
Allison Academy, FL
All Saints' Episcopal School of Fort Worth, TX
American Academy, FL
American Christian Academy, AL
American Community Schools of Athens, Greece
American Heritage School, FL
The American International School, Austria
American International School of Bucharest, Romania
American International School Rotterdam, Netherlands
The American School in London, United Kingdom
The American School of Madrid, Spain
American School of Milan, Italy
American School of Paris, France
The American School of Puerto Vallarta, Mexico
The American School of The Hague, Netherlands
Andrews Osborne Academy, OH
Annie Wright School, WA
Archbishop Curley High School, MD
Archbishop Edward A. McCarthy High School, FL
Archbishop Hoban High School, OH
Archbishop McNicholas High School, OH
Archbishop Mitty High School, CA
Archbishop Riordan High School, CA
Archbishop Rummel High School, LA
Archbishop Spalding High School, MD
The Archer School for Girls, CA
Archmere Academy, DE
Armona Union Academy, CA
Army and Navy Academy, CA
Arrowsmith School, ON, Canada
Arthur Morgan School, NC
Ashbury College, ON, Canada
Asheville School, NC
ASSETS School, HI
Assumption High School, KY
The Athenian School, CA
Athens Academy, GA
Atlanta International School, GA
Augusta Christian School (I), GA
Augusta Preparatory Day School, GA
Auldern Academy, NC
Aurora Central High School, IL
Austin Christian Academy, MB, Canada
Austin Preparatory School, MA
Avon Old Farms School, CT
The Awty International School, TX
Bakersfield Christian High School, CA
The Baldwin School, PA
Baldwin School of Puerto Rico, Inc., PR
Balmoral Hall School, MB, Canada
The Baltimore Actors' Theatre Conservatory, MD
Bancroft School, MA
Baptist High School, NJ
Barnstable Academy, NJ
The Barrie School, MD
The Barstow School, MO
Bass Memorial Academy, MS
Battle Ground Academy, TN
Bavarian International School, Germany
Baylor School, TN
Bearspaw Christian School, AB, Canada
Beaver Country Day School, MA
The Beekman School, NY
Bellarmine-Jefferson High School, CA
Bellevue Christian School, WA
Belmont Hill School, MA
The Bement School, MA
Benedictine High School, OH
Benedictine High School, VA
Benedictine Military School, GA
Benilde–St. Margaret's School, MN
The Benjamin School, FL
Berkeley Preparatory School, FL
Berkshire School, MA
The Bermuda High School for Girls, Bermuda
Berwick Academy, ME
Besant Hill School, CA
Beth Haven Christian School, KY
The Birch Wathen Lenox School, NY
Bishop Alemany High School, CA
Bishop Blanchet High School, WA
Bishop Brady High School, NH
Bishop Carroll High School, PA
Bishop Conaty-Our Lady of Loretto High School, CA
Bishop Connolly High School, MA
Bishop Denis J. O'Connell High School, VA
Bishop Eustace Preparatory School, NJ
Bishop Feehan High School, MA
Bishop Fenwick High School, OH
Bishop Garcia Diego High School, CA
Bishop George Ahr High School, NJ
Bishop Gorman High School, NV
Bishop Guertin High School, NH
Bishop Hendricken High School, RI
Bishop Ireton High School, VA
Bishop Kelly High School, ID
Bishop Kenny High School, FL
Bishop Luers High School, IN
Bishop Lynch Catholic High School, TX
Bishop McGuinness Catholic High School, NC
Bishop McGuinness Catholic High School, OK
Bishop McNamara High School, IL
Bishop Montgomery High School, CA
Bishop Mora Salesian High School, CA
Bishop Stang High School, MA
The Bishop Strachan School, ON, Canada
Bishop Verot High School, FL
Bishop Walsh Middle High School, MD
Blair Academy, NJ
The Blake School, MN
Blanchet School, OR
Blessed Trinity High School, GA
The Blue Ridge School, VA
Bodwell High School, BC, Canada
The Bolles School, FL
Boston College High School, MA
Boston Trinity Academy, MA
Boston University Academy, MA
Boyd-Buchanan School, TN
Boylan Central Catholic High School, IL
The Boys' Latin School of Maryland, MD
The Branson School, CA
The Brearley School, NY
Breck School, MN
Brenau Academy, GA
Brentwood School, CA
Brentwood School, GA

Brethren Christian Junior and Senior High Schools, CA
Brewster Academy, NH
Briarwood Christian High School, AL
Bridgemont High School, CA
Bridges Academy, CA
Bridge School, CO
Brimmer and May School, MA
Brockwood Park School, United Kingdom
Bromley Brook School, VT
Bronte College of Canada, ON, Canada
Brooks School, MA
Brookstone School, GA
Brophy College Preparatory, AZ
Brother Martin High School, LA
Brother Rice High School, MI
Brownell-Talbot School, NE
The Browning School, NY
Brunswick School, CT
The Bryn Mawr School for Girls, MD
Buckingham Browne & Nichols School, MA
The Buckley School, CA
Buffalo Seminary, NY
Bulloch Academy, GA
Burke Mountain Academy, VT
Burr and Burton Academy, VT
The Bush School, WA
Butte Central High School, MT
The Byrnes Schools, SC
Calgary Academy, AB, Canada
The Calhoun School, NY
Calvary Christian Academy, KY
Calvert Hall College High School, MD
The Calverton School, MD
The Cambridge School of Weston, MA
Camelot Academy, NC
Campbell Hall (Episcopal), CA
Canadian Academy, Japan
Cannon School, NC
Canterbury School, CT
Canterbury School, FL
The Canterbury School of Florida, FL
Canyonville Christian Academy, OR
Cape Cod Academy, MA
Cape Fear Academy, NC
Cape Henry Collegiate School, VA
Capistrano Valley Christian Schools, CA
Cardigan Mountain School, NH
Cardinal Gibbons High School, NC
Cardinal Mooney Catholic College Preparatory High School, MI
Cardinal Mooney High School, FL
Cardinal Newman High School, CA
Cardinal Newman High School, FL
Cardinal Newman School, SC
Carlisle School, VA
Carlucci American International School of Lisbon, Portugal
Carolina Day School, NC
Carondelet High School, CA
Carrabassett Valley Academy, ME
Carrollton School of the Sacred Heart, FL
Carson Long Military Institute, PA
Cary Academy, NC
Cascadilla School, NY
Cascia Hall Preparatory School, OK
Castilleja School, CA
Cate School, CA
Cathedral High School, IN
Cathedral High School, NY
Catholic Central High School, MI
The Catholic High School of Baltimore, MD
Catholic Memorial, MA
The Catlin Gabel School, OR
Cedar Ridge Academy, UT
Centennial Academy, QC, Canada
Central Catholic High School, CA
Central Catholic High School, MA
Central Catholic High School, OH
Central Catholic High School, PA
Central Catholic Mid-High School, NE
Central Valley Christian Academy, CA
CFS, The School at Church Farm, PA
Chadwick School, CA
Chamberlain-Hunt Academy, MS
Chaminade College Preparatory, CA
Chaminade College Preparatory School, MO
Chaminade-Madonna College Preparatory, FL
Chamisa Mesa High School, NM
Chapel Hill–Chauncy Hall School, MA
Charlotte Catholic High School, NC
Charlotte Christian School, NC
Charlotte Country Day School, NC
Charlotte Latin School, NC
Chase Collegiate School, CT
Chatham Academy, GA
Chelsea School, MD
Cherokee Creek Boys School, SC
Cherry Gulch, ID
Cheshire Academy, CT
Chestnut Hill Academy, PA
Cheverus High School, ME
Children's Creative and Performing Arts Academy—Capa Division, CA
Chinese Christian Schools, CA
Choate Rosemary Hall, CT
Christchurch School, VA
Christian Brothers Academy, NJ
Christian Brothers Academy, NY
Christian Brothers Academy, NY
Christian Central Academy, NY
Christian Heritage School, CT
Christian Home and Bible School, FL
Christian Junior–Senior High School, CA
Christian School of the Desert, CA
Christopher Dock Mennonite High School, PA
Christ School, NC
Chrysalis School, WA
Cincinnati Country Day School, OH
Cistercian Preparatory School, TX
Colegio Bolivar, Colombia
Colegio Franklin D. Roosevelt, Peru
Colegio Nueva Granada, Colombia
Colegio Puertorriqueno de Ninas, PR
Cole Valley Christian High School, ID
College du Leman International School, Switzerland
The College Preparatory School, CA
The Collegiate School, VA
Colorado Academy, CO
The Colorado Rocky Mountain School, CO

The Colorado Springs School, CO
Columbia Academy, TN
Columbia Grammar and Preparatory School, NY
Columbia International School, Japan
The Columbus Academy, OH
Columbus High School, IA
Commonwealth Parkville School, PR
Commonwealth School, MA
Community Christian Academy, KY
The Community School, ID
Community School, NH
The Community School of Naples, FL
The Concept School, PA
Concord Academy, MA
Concordia Continuing Education High School, AB, Canada
Connelly School of the Holy Child, MD
Conserve School, WI
Convent of the Sacred Heart, CT
Convent of the Sacred Heart, NY
Convent of the Visitation School, MN
Copenhagen International School, Denmark
Cornelia Connelly School, CA
Cotter Schools, MN
Country Day School of the Sacred Heart, PA
Covenant Canadian Reformed School, AB, Canada
The Craig School, NJ
Crawford Adventist Academy, ON, Canada
Crespi Carmelite High School, CA
Crestwood Preparatory College, ON, Canada
Cretin-Derham Hall, MN
Crofton House School, BC, Canada
Cross Creek Programs, UT
Crossroads College Preparatory School, MO
Crossroads School for Arts & Sciences, CA
Crystal Springs Uplands School, CA
The Culver Academies, IN
Currey Ingram Academy, TN
Cushing Academy, MA
Dallas Academy, TX
Dallas Christian School, TX
The Dalton School, NY
Dana Hall School, MA
Darlington School, GA
Darrow School, NY
David Lipscomb High School, TN
Deck House School, ME
Deerfield Academy, MA
Deerfield-Windsor School, GA
De La Salle College, ON, Canada
De La Salle High School, CA
Delaware Valley Friends School, PA
Delbarton School, NJ
Delphos Saint John's High School, OH
DeMatha Catholic High School, MD
Denver Academy, CO
Denver Christian High School, CO
DePaul Catholic High School, NJ
The Derryfield School, NH
De Smet Jesuit High School, MO
Devon Preparatory School, PA
Dickinson Trinity, ND
Doane Stuart School, NY
The Dominican Academy of the City of New York, NY
Donelson Christian Academy, TN
Donna Klein Jewish Academy, FL
Dowling Catholic High School, IA
Drew School, CA
Dubai American Academy, United Arab Emirates
Dublin Christian Academy, NH
Dublin School, NH
Duchesne Academy of the Sacred Heart, TX
Dunn School, CA
Durham Academy, NC
Dwight-Englewood School, NJ
Eaglebrook School, MA
Eagle Hill School, CT
Eagle Hill School, MA
Eagle Hill-Southport, CT
East Catholic High School, CT
Eastern Christian High School, NJ
Eastern Mennonite High School, VA
Eastside Catholic School, WA
Eastside Christian Academy, AB, Canada
Ecole d'Humanité, Switzerland
Ecole Internationale de Boston / International School of Boston, MA
Edison School, AB, Canada
The Education Center, MS
Elan School, ME
Elgin Academy, IL
Elizabeth Seton High School, MD
Elk Mountain Academy, MT
The Ellis School, PA
Elmwood School, ON, Canada
Elyria Catholic High School, OH
Emerson Honors High Schools, CA
The Emery Weiner School, TX
Emma Willard School, NY
Episcopal Collegiate School, AR
Episcopal High School, TX
Episcopal High School, VA
Episcopal High School of Jacksonville, FL
The Episcopal School of Dallas, TX
Escola Americana de Campinas, Brazil
Escondido Adventist Academy, CA
The Ethel Walker School, CT
Evangelical Christian School, TN
Evansville Day School, IN
Excel Academy, Inc., OH
Excel Christian Academy, GA
Explorations Academy, WA
Ezell-Harding Christian School, TN
Fairfield College Preparatory School, CT
Faith Christian High School, CA
Faith Lutheran High School, NV
The Family Foundation School, NY
Father Judge High School, PA
Father Lopez High School, FL
Father Ryan High School, TN
Fayetteville Academy, NC
Fay School, MA
The Fessenden School, MA
The Field School, DC
The First Academy, FL
First Baptist Academy, TX
First Presbyterian Day School, GA
Fishburne Military School, VA
Flint Hill School, VA

Flintridge Sacred Heart Academy, CA
Flint River Academy, GA
Fontbonne Academy, MA
Fontbonne Hall Academy, NY
Foothills Academy, AB, Canada
Fordham Preparatory School, NY
Forest Lake Academy, FL
The Forman School, CT
Forsyth Country Day School, NC
Fort Lauderdale Preparatory School, FL
Fort Worth Country Day School, TX
Foundation Academy, FL
Fountain Valley School of Colorado, CO
Fowlers Academy, PR
Foxcroft Academy, ME
Foxcroft School, VA
Fox River Country Day School, IL
Fox Valley Lutheran Academy, IL
Fox Valley Lutheran High School, WI
Franklin Academy, CT
Franklin Road Academy, TN
Fraser Academy, BC, Canada
Freeman Academy, SD
French-American School of New York, NY
Friends' Central School, PA
Front Range Christian High School, CO
The Frostig School, CA
Fryeburg Academy, ME
Fuqua School, VA
Gables Academy, GA
Gabriel Richard High School, MI
Gann Academy (The New Jewish High School of Greater Boston), MA
Garces Memorial High School, CA
Garden School, NY
Garrison Forest School, MD
Gaston Day School, NC
The Geneva School, FL
George School, PA
George Stevens Academy, ME
Georgetown Day School, DC
Georgetown Preparatory School, MD
Georgetown Visitation Preparatory School, DC
Germantown Academy, PA
Germantown Friends School, PA
Gill St. Bernard's School, NJ
Gilman School, MD
Gilmour Academy, OH
Girls Preparatory School, TN
Glades Day School, FL
Glenelg Country School, MD
The Glenholme School, CT
Gonzaga College High School, DC
Gordon Technical High School, IL
Gould Academy, ME
The Governor French Academy, IL
The Governor's Academy (formerly Governor Dummer Academy), MA
The Gow School, NY
Grace Baptist Academy, TN
Grace Brethren School, CA
Grace Christian School, AK
The Grand River Academy, OH
The Grauer School, CA
Greater Atlanta Christian Schools, GA
Great Lakes Christian High School, ON, Canada
Greenfield School, NC
Green Fields Country Day School, AZ
Greenhills School, MI
Greenleaf Academy, ID
Green Meadow Waldorf School, NY
Greensboro Day School, NC
Greens Farms Academy, CT
Greenwich Academy, CT
Greenwood Laboratory School, MO
The Greenwood School, VT
Griggs University and International Academy, MD
Groton School, MA
Grove School, CT
Guerin College Preparatory High School, IL
Guilford Day School, NC
Gulliver Preparatory School, FL
The Gunnery, CT
Gunston Day School, MD
Gwynedd Mercy Academy, PA
Hackley School, NY
Halstrom High School, CA
Halstrom High School—San Diego, CA
Hamden Hall Country Day School, CT
Hamilton District Christian High, ON, Canada
Hammond School, SC
Hanalani Schools, HI
Hanson Memorial High School, LA
Harding Academy, AR
Harding Academy, TN
Hargrave Military Academy, VA
The Harley School, NY
Harrells Christian Academy, NC
The Harrisburg Academy, PA
Harvard-Westlake School, CA
The Harvey School, NY
Hathaway Brown School, OH
The Haverford School, PA
Havergal College, ON, Canada
Hawaiian Mission Academy, HI
Hawaii Baptist Academy, HI
Hawai'i Preparatory Academy, HI
Hawken School, OH
Hawthorne Christian Academy, NJ
Hayden High School, KS
Head-Royce School, CA
Headwaters Academy, MT
Hebrew Academy, CA
Hebrew Academy-the Five Towns, NY
Hebron Academy, ME
Heritage Christian Academy, MI
Heritage Christian Academy, AB, Canada
Heritage Christian School, ON, Canada
Heritage Hall, OK
The Heritage School, GA
Hidden Lake Academy, GA
Highland Hall, A Waldorf School, CA
Highland School, VA
High Mowing School, NH
The Hill Center, Durham Academy, NC
Hillcrest Christian School, CA
The Hill School, PA
Hillside School, MA

The Hill Top Preparatory School, PA
Hilton Head Preparatory School, SC
The Hockaday School, TX
Holderness School, NH
Holland Hall, OK
The Holton-Arms School, MD
Holy Innocents' Episcopal School, GA
Holy Name High School, PA
Holy Names High School, CA
Holy Trinity Diocesan High School, NY
Holy Trinity High School, IL
Hoosac School, NY
Hopkins School, CT
The Horace Mann School, NY
Horizons School, GA
Hosanna Christian School, OR
The Hotchkiss School, CT
Houghton Academy, NY
Howe Military School, IN
The Hudson School, NJ
Humanex Academy, CO
The Hun School of Princeton, NJ
Huntington-Surrey School, TX
Hutchison School, TN
Hyman Brand Hebrew Academy of Greater Kansas City, KS
Idyllwild Arts Academy, CA
Illiana Christian High School, IL
Immaculate Conception High School, NJ
Immaculate Conception School, IL
Immaculate High School, CT
Immanuel Christian High School, AB, Canada
Independent School, KS
Indian Mountain School, CT
Indian Springs School, AL
Interlochen Arts Academy, MI
International College Spain, Spain
International High School, CA
International School Bangkok, Thailand
International School Eerde, Netherlands
International School Hamburg, Germany
International School Manila, Philippines
The International School of Aberdeen, United Kingdom
International School of Amsterdam, Netherlands
International School of Aruba, Aruba
International School of Athens, Greece
International School of Berne, Switzerland
The International School of Geneva, Switzerland
International School of Milan, Italy
The International School of Paris, France
International School of South Africa, South Africa
Iolani School, HI
Isidore Newman School, LA
Island School, HI
Jack M. Barrack Hebrew Academy (formerly Akiba Hebrew Academy), PA
Jackson Academy, MS
Jackson Christian School, TN
Jackson Preparatory School, MS
The Janus School, PA
Jesuit College Preparatory School, TX
Jesuit High School, CA
Jesuit High School of Tampa, FL
John Bapst Memorial High School, ME
John Burroughs School, MO
The John Cooper School, TX
The John Dewey Academy, MA
John Paul II Catholic High School, FL
Junipero Serra High School, CA
Kaplan College Preparatory School, FL
Karachi American School, Pakistan
The Karafin School, NY
Keith Country Day School, IL
Kent Denver School, CO
Kent Place School, NJ
Kent School, CT
Kents Hill School, ME
Kentucky Country Day School, KY
Kerr-Vance Academy, NC
The Key School, MD
Kildonan School, NY
Kimball Union Academy, NH
Kimberton Waldorf School, PA
King George School, VT
King Low Heywood Thomas, CT
The King's Academy, TN
The King's Christian High School, NJ
Kings Christian School, CA
King's High School, WA
Kingshill School, VI
King's Ridge Christian School, GA
Kingsway College, ON, Canada
King's West School, WA
Kingswood-Oxford School, CT
The Knox School, NY
Knoxville Catholic High School, TN
Koinonia Christian School, AB, Canada
La Cheim School, CA
Ladywood High School, MI
Lakefield College School, ON, Canada
Lake Forest Academy, IL
Lakehill Preparatory School, TX
Lakeland Christian Academy, IN
Lake Ridge Academy, OH
Lakeside School, WA
Lakeview Academy, GA
La Lumiere School, IN
Lancaster Country Day School, PA
Lancaster Mennonite High School, PA
Landmark School, MA
Landon School, MD
Lansdale Catholic High School, PA
La Pietra–Hawaii School for Girls, HI
La Salle Academy, RI
La Salle High School, FL
La Salle Institute, NY
The Laureate Academy, MB, Canada
Laurel Springs School, CA
Laurel View Academy, ON, Canada
Lausanne Collegiate School, TN
Lawrence Academy, MA
Lawrence School, OH
The Lawrenceville School, NJ
Lee Academy, ME
Lehigh Valley Christian High School, PA
Lehman High School, OH
Lexington Catholic High School, KY
Lexington Christian Academy, MA
Lifegate School, OR

Lincoln School, RI
Linden Hall, PA
Linden Hill School, MA
The Linden School, ON, Canada
Linfield Christian School, CA
The Linsly School, WV
Little Red School House and Elisabeth Irwin High School, NY
The Loomis Chaffee School, CT
Loretto Academy, TX
Los Angeles Baptist Junior/Senior High School, CA
Los Angeles Lutheran High School, CA
Louisville Collegiate School, KY
Louisville High School, CA
Lourdes Catholic High School, AZ
The Lovett School, GA
The Lowell Whiteman School, CO
Loyola-Blakefield, MD
Loyola High School, Jesuit College Preparatory, CA
Loyola School, NY
Lustre Christian High School, MT
Lutheran High North, TX
Lutheran High School, IN
Lutheran High School, MO
Lutheran High School North, MO
Lutheran High School Northwest, MI
Lutheran High School of Hawaii, HI
Lutheran High School of San Diego, CA
Lutheran High School West, OH
Luther College High School, SK, Canada
Luther High School North, IL
Luther High School South, IL
Lycee Claudel, ON, Canada
Lycee Français de New York, NY
The Lycee International, American Section, France
Lydia Patterson Institute, TX
Lyman Ward Military Academy, AL
Lyndon Institute, VT
The MacDuffie School, MA
MacLachlan College, ON, Canada
Madison Academy, AL
Madison-Ridgeland Academy, MS
Magnificat High School, OH
Maharishi Academy of Total Knowledge, NH
Maharishi School of the Age of Enlightenment, IA
Maine Central Institute, ME
Maine School of Science and Mathematics, ME
Manlius Pebble Hill School, NY
Maplebrook School, NY
Maret School, DC
Marianapolis Preparatory School, CT
Marian Central Catholic High School, IL
Marian High School, IN
Marian High School, MI
Marin Academy, CA
Marist High School, IL
Marist High School, NJ
Marist School, GA
Marlborough School, CA
Marmion Academy, IL
Marquette University High School, WI
Marshall School, MN
Mars Hill Bible School, AL
Martin Luther High School, NY
The Marvelwood School, CT
Mary Help of Christians Academy, NJ
Maryknoll School, HI
Marylawn of the Oranges, NJ
The Mary Louis Academy, NY
Marymount High School, CA
Marymount International School, United Kingdom
Marymount School, NY
Maryvale Preparatory School, MD
Massanutten Military Academy, VA
The Master's School, CT
The Masters School, NY
Matignon High School, MA
Maumee Valley Country Day School, OH
Maur Hill-Mount Academy, KS
The McCallie School, TN
McCurdy School, NM
McDonogh School, MD
McQuaid Jesuit, NY
Meadowridge School, BC, Canada
The Meadows School, NV
Memorial Hall School, TX
Memphis University School, TN
Menaul School, NM
Menlo School, CA
Mennonite Collegiate Institute, MB, Canada
Mercersburg Academy, PA
Mercy High School, CA
Mercy High School, CT
Mercy High School, NE
Mercy High School College Preparatory, CA
Mercyhurst Preparatory School, PA
Mesa Grande Seventh-Day Academy, CA
Metairie Park Country Day School, LA
Miami Country Day School, FL
Middlesex School, MA
Mid-Pacific Institute, HI
Mid-Peninsula High School, CA
Milken Community High School of Stephen S. Wise Temple, CA
Millbrook School, NY
Miller School, VA
Milton Academy, MA
Miss Edgar's and Miss Cramp's School, QC, Canada
Miss Hall's School, MA
Mississauga Private School, ON, Canada
Missouri Military Academy, MO
Miss Porter's School, CT
MMI Preparatory School, PA
Modesto Christian School, CA
Monmouth Academy, NJ
Monsignor Donovan High School, NJ
Montana Academy, MT
Montgomery Bell Academy, TN
Montrose School, MA
Montverde Academy, FL
Moorestown Friends School, NJ
Moravian Academy, PA
Moreau Catholic High School, CA
Morgan Park Academy, IL
Morristown-Beard School, NJ
Moses Brown School, RI
Mother Cabrini High School, NY
Mother McAuley High School, IL
Mounds Park Academy, MN

Mount Bachelor Academy, OR
Mount Michael Benedictine School, NE
Mount Saint Charles Academy, RI
Mt. Saint Dominic Academy, NJ
Mount Saint Joseph Academy, PA
Munich International School, Germany
Nancy Campbell Collegiate Institute, ON, Canada
National Cathedral School, DC
National High School, GA
National Sports Academy at Lake Placid, NY
Nazareth Academy, IL
Nebraska Christian Schools, NE
Nerinx Hall, MO
Newark Academy, NJ
Newbury Park Adventist Academy, CA
New Covenant Academy, MO
New Hampton School, NH
New Horizon Youth Ministries, IN
The Newman School, MA
New Mexico Military Institute, NM
New Summit School, MS
New Tribes Mission Academy, ON, Canada
New Way Learning Academy, AZ
New York Military Academy, NY
Niagara Christian Community of Schools, ON, Canada
The Nichols School, NY
Noble and Greenough School, MA
The Nora School, MD
Norfolk Academy, VA
Norfolk Christian School, VA
Norfolk Collegiate School, VA
The North Broward Preparatory Upper School, FL
North Cobb Christian School, GA
North Country School, NY
North Cross School, VA
Northfield Mount Hermon School, MA
North Shore Country Day School, IL
Northside Christian School, FL
Northwest Academy, ID
The Northwest Academy, OR
Northwest Catholic High School, CT
The Northwest School, WA
Northwest Yeshiva High School, WA
Northwood School, NY
North Yarmouth Academy, ME
Notre Dame Academy, CA
Notre Dame Academy, MA
Notre Dame Academy, MA
Notre Dame Academy, VA
Notre Dame- Bishop Gibbons School, NY
Notre Dame-Cathedral Latin School, OH
Notre Dame High School, CA
Notre Dame High School, LA
Notre Dame High School, NJ
Notre Dame High School, TN
Notre Dame Junior/Senior High School, PA
Notre Dame Preparatory School, MD
Oak Grove Lutheran School, ND
Oak Grove School, CA
Oak Hill Academy, VA
Oak Knoll School of the Holy Child, NJ
The Oakland School, PA
Oakland School, VA
Oak Mountain Academy, GA
Oak Ridge Military Academy, NC
The Oakridge School, TX
Oakwood Friends School, NY
Oakwood School, CA
The Oakwood School, NC
O'Dea High School, WA
Ojai Valley School, CA
Okanagan Adventist Academy, BC, Canada
Oldenburg Academy, IN
Oldfields School, MD
Olney Friends School, OH
The O'Neal School, NC
Oneida Baptist Institute, KY
Orangewood Adventist Academy, CA
Oregon Episcopal School, OR
Orinda Academy, CA
The Orme School, AZ
Our Lady Academy, MS
Our Lady of Mercy Academy, NJ
Our Lady of Mercy High School, NY
Our Saviour Lutheran School, NY
Out-Of-Door-Academy, FL
The Overlake School, WA
The Oxford Academy, CT
Pace Academy, GA
Pacific Academy, CA
Pacific Crest Community School, OR
Pacific Hills School, CA
Pacific Lutheran High School, CA
Padua Franciscan High School, OH
The Paideia School, GA
Palma High School, CA
Paradise Adventist Academy, CA
Parish Episcopal School, TX
The Parker School, HI
Parklane Academy, MS
The Park School of Buffalo, NY
Park Tudor School, IN
Peddie School, NJ
The Penikese Island School, MA
The Pennington School, NJ
Peoples Christian Academy, ON, Canada
Perkiomen School, PA
The Phelps School, PA
Phillips Academy (Andover), MA
Phillips Exeter Academy, NH
Phoenix Christian Unified Schools, AZ
Phoenix Country Day School, AZ
Piedmont Academy, GA
Pine Crest School, FL
Pinehurst School, ON, Canada
Pinewood—The International School of Thessaloniki, Greece, Greece
The Pingry School, NJ
Pioneer Valley Christian School, MA
Pius X High School, NE
Poly Prep Country Day School, NY
Polytechnic School, CA
Pomfret School, CT
Pope John XXIII Regional High School, NJ
Porter-Gaud School, SC
Portland Lutheran School, OR
Portledge School, NY
Portsmouth Abbey School, RI

Portsmouth Christian Academy, NH
The Potomac School, VA
Poughkeepsie Day School, NY
Powers Catholic High School, MI
The Prairie School, WI
Preston High School, NY
Prestonwood Christian Academy, TX
Professional Children's School, NY
The Prout School, RI
Providence Country Day School, RI
Providence Day School, NC
Providence High School, CA
Providence High School, TX
Pulaski Academy, AR
Punahou School, HI
Purnell School, NJ
The Putney School, VT
Queen Anne School, MD
Queen Margaret's School, BC, Canada
Queensway Christian College, ON, Canada
Quigley Catholic High School, PA
Quinte Christian High School, ON, Canada
Rabbi Alexander S. Gross Hebrew Academy, FL
Rabun Gap-Nacoochee School, GA
Rambam Mesivta, NY
Randolph-Macon Academy, VA
Randolph School, AL
Ranney School, NJ
Ransom Everglades School, FL
Ravenscroft School, NC
The Rectory School, CT
Redemption Christian Academy, NY
Redwood Christian Schools, CA
Regina Dominican High School, IL
Regina High School, OH
Reitz Memorial High School, IN
Rice High School, NY
Richmond Christian School, BC, Canada
Ridgecroft School, NC
Ridgewood Preparatory School, LA
Ridley College, ON, Canada
Ripon Christian Schools, CA
Riverdale Country School, NY
Rivermont Collegiate, IA
Riverside Military Academy, GA
The Rivers School, MA
Riverstone International School, ID
Riverview School, MA
Roanoke Catholic School, VA
Robert Louis Stevenson School, NY
Rockland Country Day School, NY
Rock Point School, VT
Rocky Hill School, RI
Rocky Mount Academy, NC
The Roeper School, MI
Roland Park Country School, MD
Rolling Hills Preparatory School, CA
Roncalli High School, IN
Rosseau Lake College, ON, Canada
Ross School, NY
Rothesay Netherwood School, NB, Canada
Rotterdam International Secondary School, Wolfert van Borselen, Netherlands
Rowland Hall-St. Mark's School, UT
The Roxbury Latin School, MA
Roycemore School, IL
Rumsey Hall School, CT
Rundle College, AB, Canada
Rutgers Preparatory School, NJ
Rye Country Day School, NY
Sacramento Adventist Academy, CA
Sacramento Country Day School, CA
Sacramento Waldorf School, CA
Sacred Heart School of Halifax, NS, Canada
Saddle River Day School, NJ
Sage Hill School, CA
Sage Ridge School, NV
St. Agnes Academy, TX
St. Albans School, DC
St. Andrew's College, ON, Canada
St. Andrew's Episcopal School, MD
St. Andrew's Episcopal School, MS
St. Andrew's on the Marsh School, GA
St. Andrew's Priory School, HI
Saint Andrew's School, FL
St. Andrew's School, RI
St. Andrew's–Sewanee School, TN
St. Anne's–Belfield School, VA
St. Anselm's Abbey School, DC
St. Anthony Catholic High School, TX
Saint Anthony High School, IL
St. Anthony's Junior-Senior High School, HI
St. Augustine High School, CA
St. Augustine High School, TX
Saint Augustine Preparatory School, NJ
Saint Basil Academy, PA
St. Benedict at Auburndale, TN
St. Benedict's Preparatory School, NJ
St. Brendan High School, FL
St. Catherine's Military Academy, CA
St. Catherine's School, VA
St. Cecilia Academy, TN
Saint Cecilia High School, NE
St. Christopher's School, VA
St. Clement School, ON, Canada
St. Clement's School, ON, Canada
St. Croix Country Day School, VI
St. Croix Lutheran High School, MN
St. David's School, NC
Saint Dominic Academy, NJ
Saint Dominic Regional High School, ME
Saint Edmund High School, NY
Saint Edward's School, FL
St. Francis de Sales High School, OH
Saint Francis High School, CA
St. Francis High School, KY
St. Francis School, GA
Saint Francis School, HI
St. George's School, RI
Saint George's School, WA
St. George's School, BC, Canada
Saint Gertrude High School, VA
St. Gregory College Preparatory School, AZ
St. Gregory's High School, IL
Saint James School, MD
Saint Joan Antida High School, WI
St. Johnsbury Academy, VT
St. John's Catholic Prep, MD

St. John's College High School, DC
St. John's Northwestern Military Academy, WI
St. John's Preparatory School, MA
Saint John's Preparatory School, MN
St. John's-Ravenscourt School, MB, Canada
St. Joseph Academy, FL
St. Joseph High School, CA
St. Joseph High School, CT
Saint Joseph High School, PA
Saint Joseph High School, WI
Saint Joseph Regional High School, NJ
St. Joseph's Academy, LA
St. Joseph's Catholic School, SC
St. Joseph's Preparatory School, PA
St. Jude's School, ON, Canada
St. Lawrence Seminary, WI
St. Margaret's Episcopal School, CA
St. Margaret's School, VA
St. Margaret's School, BC, Canada
Saint Mark's School, MA
St. Mark's School of Texas, TX
St. Martin's Episcopal School, LA
St. Mary's Academy, CO
Saint Mary's College High School, CA
St. Mary's Episcopal School, TN
Saint Mary's Hall, TX
St. Mary's Hall–Doane Academy, NJ
Saint Mary's High School, AZ
St. Mary's High School, CO
Saint Mary's High School, MD
St. Mary's Preparatory School, MI
Saint Mary's School, NC
St. Mary's School, OR
Saint Matthias High School, CA
St. Michael's College School, ON, Canada
St. Michael's Preparatory School of the Norbertine Fathers, CA
Saint Monica's High School, CA
Saint Patrick High School, IL
Saint Patrick—Saint Vincent High School, CA
Saint Patrick's School, KY
St. Paul Academy and Summit School, MN
Saint Paul Lutheran High School, MO
St. Paul's Episcopal School, AL
St. Paul's High School, MB, Canada
St. Paul's School, MD
St. Paul's School, NH
St. Paul's School for Girls, MD
St. Peter's Preparatory School, NJ
St. Pius X Catholic High School, GA
St. Sebastian's School, MA
Saints Peter and Paul High School, MD
St. Stanislaus College, MS
St. Stephen's & St. Agnes School, VA
Saint Stephen's Episcopal School, FL
St. Stephen's Episcopal School, TX
St. Stephen's School, Rome, Italy
Saint Teresa's Academy, MO
Saint Thomas Academy, MN
Saint Thomas Aquinas High School, KS
St. Thomas Aquinas High School, NH
St. Thomas Choir School, NY
Saint Thomas More School, CT
St. Timothy's School, MD
Salem Academy, NC
Salesian High School, CA
Salesian High School, NY
Salesianum School, DE
Salisbury School, CT
Salpointe Catholic High School, AZ
Salt Lake Lutheran High School, UT
Saltus Grammar School, Bermuda
The Samuel Scheck Hillel Community Day School, FL
Sandia Preparatory School, NM
San Diego Jewish Academy, CA
San Domenico School, CA
Sandy Spring Friends School, MD
Sanford School, DE
San Francisco University High School, CA
San Francisco Waldorf High School, CA
San Marcos Baptist Academy, TX
Santa Fe Preparatory School, NM
Santa Margarita Catholic High School, CA
Santiam Christian School, OR
Savannah Christian Preparatory School, GA
The Savannah Country Day School, GA
Sayre School, KY
Scarborough Christian School, ON, Canada
Scattergood Friends School, IA
Schlarman High School, IL
School for Young Performers, NY
School of the Holy Child, NY
Scotus Central Catholic High School, NE
Seabury Hall, HI
Seattle Academy of Arts and Sciences, WA
Seattle Christian Schools, WA
Seattle Lutheran High School, WA
Second Baptist School, TX
Sedbergh School, QC, Canada
Seisen International School, Japan
Selwyn House School, QC, Canada
Seoul Foreign School, Republic of Korea
Seton Catholic Central High School, NY
Seton Catholic High School, AZ
The Seven Hills School, OH
Sewickley Academy, PA
Shades Mountain Christian School, AL
Shady Side Academy, PA
Shannon Forest Christian School, SC
Shattuck-St. Mary's School, MN
Sheila Morrison School, ON, Canada
Shelton School and Evaluation Center, TX
Shenandoah Valley Academy, VA
The Shipley School, PA
Shorecrest Preparatory School, FL
Shoreline Christian, WA
Smith School, NY
Smithville District Christian High School, ON, Canada
Solebury School, PA
Sorenson's Ranch School, UT
Southfield Christian High School, MI
South Kent School, CT
Southridge School, BC, Canada
Southwestern Academy, AZ
Southwestern Academy, CA
The Spence School, NY
Spring Ridge Academy, AZ
Squaw Valley Academy, CA
Stanbridge Academy, CA

Starkville Academy, MS
Staten Island Academy, NY
Stella Maris High School, NY
Stephen T. Badin High School, OH
Stevenson School, CA
Still Creek Christian School, TX
St Leonards School and Sixth Form College, United Kingdom
Stoneleigh–Burnham School, MA
Stone Mountain School, NC
The Stony Brook School, NY
Storm King School, NY
Stratford Academy, GA
Strathcona-Tweedsmuir School, AB, Canada
Stratton Mountain School, VT
Stuart Country Day School of the Sacred Heart, NJ
The Study School, QC, Canada
Subiaco Academy, AR
Suffield Academy, CT
Summerfield Waldorf School, CA
The Summit Country Day School, OH
Summit Preparatory School, MT
Sunrise Academy, UT
Tabor Academy, MA
The Taft School, CT
Tallulah Falls School, GA
Tampa Preparatory School, FL
Tandem Friends School, VA
TASIS The American School in England, United Kingdom
TASIS, The American School in Switzerland, Switzerland
The Tatnall School, DE
Telluride Mountain School, CO
Teurlings Catholic High School, LA
The Thacher School, CA
Thomas Jefferson School, MO
Thornton Friends School, MD
Tilton School, NH
Timothy Christian High School, IL
TMI—The Episcopal School of Texas, TX
Toronto District Christian High School, ON, Canada
Toronto Waldorf School, ON, Canada
Tower Hill School, DE
Town Centre Private High School, ON, Canada
Trafalgar Castle School, ON, Canada
Tri-City Christian Schools, CA
Trident Academy, SC
Trinity Catholic High School, MA
Trinity Christian Academy, TX
Trinity College School, ON, Canada
Trinity Episcopal School, VA
Trinity High School, IL
Trinity High School, KY
Trinity High School, NH
Trinity High School, OH
Trinity-Pawling School, NY
Trinity Preparatory School, FL
Trinity Presbyterian School, AL
Trinity School of Midland, TX
Trinity Valley School, TX
United Mennonite Educational Institute, ON, Canada
United Nations International School, NY
The United World College—USA, NM
University Christian Preparatory School, LA
University Lake School, WI
University Liggett School, MI
University of Chicago Laboratory Schools, IL
University of Toronto Schools, ON, Canada
University Prep, WA
University School of Jackson, TN
University School of Milwaukee, WI
University School of Nova Southeastern University, FL
The Urban School of San Francisco, CA
Ursuline Academy, DE
Ursuline Academy, MA
The Ursuline Academy of Dallas, TX
Ursuline High School, CA
The Ursuline School, NY
Valle Catholic High School, MO
Valley Christian High School, CA
Valley Christian School, CA
Valley Forge Military Academy & College, PA
Valley Lutheran High School, AZ
Valley Lutheran High School, MI
The Valley School, MI
Valley View School, MA
Valwood School, GA
Vandebilt Catholic High School, LA
Vanguard Preparatory School, TX
The Vanguard School, FL
Verdala International School, Malta
Verde Valley School, AZ
Vianney High School, MO
Victor Valley Christian School, CA
Viewpoint School, CA
Villa Duchesne/Oak Hill School, MO
Villa Joseph Marie High School, PA
Villa Maria Academy, PA
Villanova Preparatory School, CA
Villa Walsh Academy, NJ
Virginia Beach Friends School, VA
Virginia Episcopal School, VA
Visitation Academy of St. Louis County, MO
Wakefield School, VA
Waldorf High School of Massachusetts Bay, MA
The Waldorf School of Garden City, NY
The Walker School, GA
Walnut Hill School, MA
The Wardlaw-Hartridge School, NJ
Waring School, MA
Wasatch Academy, UT
Washington Academy, ME
Washington County Day School, MS
Washington International School, DC
Washington Waldorf School, MD
The Waterford School, UT
Watkinson School, CT
The Waverly School, CA
Waynflete School, ME
The Webb School, TN
Webb School of Knoxville, TN
The Webb Schools, CA
Wediko School and Treatment Program, NH
The Wellington School, OH
Wesleyan Academy, PR
Westbury Christian School, TX
West Catholic High School, MI
Westchester Country Day School, NC
Western Reserve Academy, OH
West Island College, AB, Canada

Westminster Catawba Christian, SC
Westminster Christian Academy, AL
Westminster Christian School, FL
Westminster School, CT
The Westminster Schools, GA
Westminster Schools of Augusta, GA
West Nottingham Academy, MD
Westover School, CT
Westridge School, CA
Westtown School, PA
Wheaton Academy, IL
The Wheeler School, RI
The White Mountain School, NH
Wichita Collegiate School, KS
William Penn Charter School, PA
The Williams School, CT
The Williston Northampton School, MA
Willow Hill School, MA
The Willows Academy, IL
Willow Wood School, ON, Canada
Wilmington Friends School, DE
Wilson Hall, SC
The Winchendon School, MA
Winchester Thurston School, PA
Windermere Preparatory School, FL
The Windsor School, NY
Windward School, CA
The Winsor School, MA
Winston Preparatory School, NY
The Winston School, TX
The Winston School San Antonio, TX
Wisconsin Academy, WI
The Woodhall School, CT
Woodlands Academy of the Sacred Heart, IL
Woodside Priory School, CA
Woodstock School, India
Woodward Academy, GA
Wooster School, CT
Worcester Academy, MA
Worcester Preparatory School, MD
World Hope Academy, FL
Wyoming Seminary, PA
Xaverian Brothers High School, MA
Xavier College Preparatory, AZ
Xavier University Preparatory School, LA
Yokohama International School, Japan
York Country Day School, PA
York Preparatory School, NY
Zurich International School, Switzerland

SCHOOLS REPORTING THAT THEY OFFER LOANS*

Academy at Swift River, MA	M
Academy of the New Church Boys' School, PA	M
Academy of the New Church Girls' School, PA	M,N
Advanced Academy of Georgia, GA	M,N
Alexander Dawson School, CO	N
American Heritage School, FL	N
Archbishop Mitty High School, CA	M
Aurora Central High School, IL	N
Avon Old Farms School, CT	N
The Barstow School, MO	N
Belmont Hill School, MA	M,N
The Benjamin School, FL	N
Berwick Academy, ME	N
Bishop Kenny High School, FL	N
Blair Academy, NJ	N
The Blake School, MN	N
Blue Mountain Academy, PA	M,N
Boston College High School, MA	N
The Brearley School, NY	N
Brookstone School, GA	M,N
The Bryn Mawr School for Girls, MD	M,N
Burke Mountain Academy, VT	N
Canterbury School, CT	M,N
Cardigan Mountain School, NH	N
Cary Academy, NC	N
Chaminade College Preparatory School, MO	N
Cheshire Academy, CT	N
Chestnut Hill Academy, PA	N
Choate Rosemary Hall, CT	N
The Colorado Rocky Mountain School, CO	M
Commonwealth School, MA	N
Concord Academy, MA	N
Connelly School of the Holy Child, MD	M
Convent of the Sacred Heart, NY	N
Cross Creek Programs, UT	M
Crossroads School for Arts & Sciences, CA	N
Dana Hall School, MA	N
Deerfield Academy, MA	N
Detroit Country Day School, MI	N
Dwight-Englewood School, NJ	M,N
Ecole d'Humanité, Switzerland	M,N
Episcopal High School, TX	M
Excel Christian Academy, GA	N
Explorations Academy, WA	N
Falmouth Academy, MA	N
Fontbonne Hall Academy, NY	N
Foxcroft School, VA	M,N
Garden School, NY	N
Garrison Forest School, MD	N
George School, PA	N
Georgetown Preparatory School, MD	M
Germantown Friends School, PA	N
Gilman School, MD	N
Gilmour Academy, OH	N
Gould Academy, ME	N
Great Lakes Christian High School, ON, Canada	M,N
Greenwich Academy, CT	M
Groton School, MA	N
The Gunnery, CT	N
Hackley School, NY	N
Hamden Hall Country Day School, CT	N
Hargrave Military Academy, VA	N
The Harker School, CA	N
The Harrisburg Academy, PA	N
Hawken School, OH	N
Heritage Hall, OK	N
The Hotchkiss School, CT	M,N
Humanex Academy, CO	M
Indian Springs School, AL	M
John Burroughs School, MO	N
The John Cooper School, TX	N
Kent School, CT	N
King George School, VT	M,N
Lakeside School, WA	M,N

M — middle-income loans; N — need-based loans

Lawrence Academy, MA	N
The Loomis Chaffee School, CT	N
Maplebrook School, NY	N
Marian High School, IN	N
Marin Academy, CA	N
Massanutten Military Academy, VA	M,N
The McCallie School, TN	N
McDonogh School, MD	M,N
The Meadows School, NV	N
Mennonite Collegiate Institute, MB, Canada	M,N
Mercersburg Academy, PA	N
Mesa Grande Seventh-Day Academy, CA	N
Middlesex School, MA	N
Midland School, CA	N
Millbrook School, NY	N
Missouri Military Academy, MO	N
Miss Porter's School, CT	N
Moorestown Friends School, NJ	N
Moravian Academy, PA	N
Morristown-Beard School, NJ	N
Mount Michael Benedictine School, NE	N
Noble and Greenough School, MA	N
Norfolk Academy, VA	N
Northfield Mount Hermon School, MA	M,N
North Shore Country Day School, IL	M,N
Ojai Valley School, CA	N
Oldfields School, MD	M
The Orme School, AZ	M,N
Pacific Hills School, CA	N
Pacific Lutheran High School, CA	M
Peddie School, NJ	N
Phillips Academy (Andover), MA	M
Providence High School, CA	M,N
Rambam Mesivta, NY	N
Ravenscroft School, NC	N
Regina High School, OH	N
Reitz Memorial High School, IN	N
Ridley College, ON, Canada	N
Riverview School, MA	M
Robert Louis Stevenson School, NY	N
St. Albans School, DC	N
St. Andrew's School, RI	N
St. George's School, RI	M,N
Saint Joseph Regional High School, NJ	N
St. Joseph's Preparatory School, PA	M,N
Saint Mark's School, MA	N
Saint Mary High School, NJ	M
St. Paul's High School, MB, Canada	N
St. Sebastian's School, MA	N
St. Timothy's School, MD	N
Salisbury School, CT	N
School of the Holy Child, NY	N
South Kent School, CT	M,N
Stone Mountain School, NC	M,N
Suffield Academy, CT	M,N
The Taft School, CT	N
The Tatnall School, DE	N
Tilton School, NH	N
Trinity High School, OH	M
Trinity-Pawling School, NY	N
Trinity Preparatory School, FL	M
Trinity School, NY	M
United Mennonite Educational Institute, ON, Canada	N
Valley Forge Military Academy & College, PA	M
Vandebilt Catholic High School, LA	M
Wasatch Academy, UT	N
The Wellington School, OH	N
Western Reserve Academy, OH	N
Westover School, CT	M,N
Westtown School, PA	N
The Williston Northampton School, MA	N
Windward School, CA	N
Woodlands Academy of the Sacred Heart, IL	N
Wyoming Seminary, PA	N
Xavier University Preparatory School, LA	M

M — middle-income loans; N — need-based loans

TOTAL AMOUNT OF UPPER SCHOOL FINANCIAL AID AWARDED FOR 2008–09

Abington Friends School, PA	$894,900
Academia Cotopaxi, Ecuador	$12,000
Academie Sainte Cecile International School, ON, Canada	CAN$15,000
The Academy at Charlemont, MA	$555,000
Academy of Mount Saint Ursula, NY	$249,220
Academy of Notre Dame de Namur, PA	$467,900
Academy of Our Lady of Good Counsel High School, NY	$242,000
Academy of Our Lady of Mercy, CT	$285,000
Academy of Our Lady of Peace, CA	$990,000
Academy of the Holy Angels, NJ	$162,140
Academy of the Holy Names, FL	$515,525
Academy of the New Church Boys' School, PA	$495,747
Academy of the New Church Girls' School, PA	$375,723
Academy of the Sacred Heart, MI	$669,220
ACS Cobham International School, United Kingdom	£41,320
ACS Egham International School, United Kingdom	£11,426
ACS Hillingdon International School, United Kingdom	£48,000
Advanced Academy of Georgia, GA	$83,700
Ahliyyah School for Girls, Jordan	28,000 Jordanian dinars
Aiglon College, Switzerland	245,000 Swiss francs
Airdrie Koinonia Christian School, AB, Canada	CAN$15,000
Alabama Christian Academy, AL	$60,000
Albert College, ON, Canada	CAN$195,000
Albuquerque Academy, NM	$1,951,829
Alexander Dawson School, CO	$720,000
The Alexander School, TX	$36,000
Allen Academy, TX	$96,000
Allendale Columbia School, NY	$526,475
Alliance Academy, Ecuador	$200,000
Allison Academy, FL	$50,000
All Saints' Episcopal School of Fort Worth, TX	$260,930
Alma Heights Christian Academy, CA	$5500
The Altamont School, AL	$568,684
American Academy, FL	$1,042,945
The American Boychoir School, NJ	$188,930
American Christian Academy, AL	$65,000
American Community Schools of Athens, Greece	€60,000
American Heritage School, FL	$4,800,000
American International School of Bucharest, Romania	$5000
American International School Rotterdam, Netherlands	€15,000
The American School Foundation, Mexico	4,500,000 Mexican pesos
American School of Paris, France	€24,600
Annie Wright School, WA	$300,000
Archbishop Hoban High School, OH	$1,504,618

Archbishop McNicholas High School, OH	$326,450
Archbishop Mitty High School, CA	$1,600,000
Archbishop Riordan High School, CA	$750,000
Archbishop Spalding High School, MD	$792,049
The Archer School for Girls, CA	$1,900,125
Armona Union Academy, CA	$50,000
Army and Navy Academy, CA	$323,475
Arthur Morgan School, NC	$92,469
Ashbury College, ON, Canada	CAN$470,000
Asheville School, NC	$1,803,000
ASSETS School, HI	$164,000
Assumption High School, KY	$360,000
The Athenian School, CA	$1,730,000
Athens Academy, GA	$400,000
Aurora Central High School, IL	$100,000
Austin Preparatory School, MA	$293,004
Avon Old Farms School, CT	$2,970,000
The Awty International School, TX	$271,700
The Baldwin School, PA	$865,226
Baldwin School of Puerto Rico, Inc., PR	$12,000
Balmoral Hall School, MB, Canada	CAN$250,000
The Baltimore Actors' Theatre Conservatory, MD	$12,000
Bancroft School, MA	$80,000
Baptist High School, NJ	$60,000
Barnstable Academy, NJ	$300,000
The Barrie School, MD	$196,860
The Barstow School, MO	$349,386
Battle Ground Academy, TN	$750,000
Baylor School, TN	$2,000,000
Bearspaw Christian School, AB, Canada	CAN$16,725
Beaver Country Day School, MA	$2,200,000
Bellevue Christian School, WA	$900,000
Belmont Hill School, MA	$2,300,000
The Bement School, MA	$246,465
Benedictine High School, VA	$495,000
Benedictine Military School, GA	$380,000
Benilde–St. Margaret's School, MN	$737,600
The Benjamin School, FL	$750,000
Berkshire School, MA	$2,800,000
The Bermuda High School for Girls, Bermuda	332,100 Bermuda dollars
Berwick Academy, ME	$1,450,000
Beth Haven Christian School, KY	$7600
The Birch Wathen Lenox School, NY	$1,200,000
Bishop Alemany High School, CA	$210,000
Bishop Blanchet High School, WA	$1,200,000
Bishop Carroll High School, PA	$462,210
Bishop Conaty-Our Lady of Loretto High School, CA	$581,779
Bishop Denis J. O'Connell High School, VA	$750,000
Bishop Eustace Preparatory School, NJ	$600,000
Bishop Feehan High School, MA	$400,000
Bishop Fenwick High School, OH	$70,000
Bishop Garcia Diego High School, CA	$940,000
Bishop Hendricken High School, RI	$500,000
Bishop Ireton High School, VA	$350,000
Bishop Kelly High School, ID	$879,656
Bishop Lynch Catholic High School, TX	$190,700
Bishop McGuinness Catholic High School, NC	$313,106
Bishop McGuinness Catholic High School, OK	$128,875
Bishop McNamara High School, IL	$200,000
Bishop Montgomery High School, CA	$30,000
Bishop Mora Salesian High School, CA	$2000
Bishop Stang High School, MA	$504,000
The Bishop Strachan School, ON, Canada	CAN$500,000
Bishop Verot High School, FL	$1,057,000
Bishop Walsh Middle High School, MD	$30,000
Blair Academy, NJ	$3,524,500
The Blake School, MN	$1,741,745
Blanchet School, OR	$235,000
Blue Mountain Academy, PA	$265,000
The Blue Ridge School, VA	$1,195,505
The Bolles School, FL	$1,763,724
Boston College High School, MA	$3,100,000
Boston Trinity Academy, MA	$900,000
Boston University Academy, MA	$773,507
Boyd-Buchanan School, TN	$80,000
Boylan Central Catholic High School, IL	$387,263
The Boys' Latin School of Maryland, MD	$1,215,100
The Branson School, CA	$1,400,000
The Brearley School, NY	$1,344,940
Breck School, MN	$1,049,713
Brentwood School, CA	$3,100,000
Brethren Christian Junior and Senior High Schools, CA	$75,000
Brewster Academy, NH	$2,300,000
Bridgemont High School, CA	$107,122
Bridges Academy, CA	$200,000
Bridge School, CO	$120,000
Brimmer and May School, MA	$1,141,575
Brooks School, MA	$2,007,000
Brookstone School, GA	$633,400
Brophy College Preparatory, AZ	$1,953,565
Brother Rice High School, MI	$300,000
Brownell-Talbot School, NE	$206,700
Brunswick School, CT	$1,041,800
The Bryn Mawr School for Girls, MD	$1,008,060
The Buckley School, CA	$551,003
Buffalo Seminary, NY	$400,000
Butte Central High School, MT	$68,000
Buxton School, MA	$1,000,000
The Byrnes Schools, SC	$12,000
Calgary Academy, AB, Canada	CAN$300,000
Calvary Christian Academy, KY	$25,000
Calvert Hall College High School, MD	$1,142,000
The Cambridge School of Weston, MA	$1,700,000
Camelot Academy, NC	$85,000
Campbell Hall (Episcopal), CA	$1,980,955
Canadian Academy, Japan	¥3,966,000
Cannon School, NC	$295,000
Canterbury School, FL	$712,703
The Canterbury School of Florida, FL	$575,000
Canyonville Christian Academy, OR	$80,000
Cape Cod Academy, MA	$1,115,000
Cape Fear Academy, NC	$195,057
Cape Henry Collegiate School, VA	$375,000
Capistrano Valley Christian Schools, CA	$225,000
Cardigan Mountain School, NH	$860,000
Cardinal Mooney High School, FL	$155,650
Cardinal Newman High School, CA	$207,000
Carlisle School, VA	$112,000
Carolina Day School, NC	$537,208
Carrollton School of the Sacred Heart, FL	$920,000
Cary Academy, NC	$647,020
Cascadilla School, NY	$60,000
Cascia Hall Preparatory School, OK	$228,571
Castilleja School, CA	$900,000
Cathedral High School, IN	$2,000,000
Cathedral High School, NY	$310,000

The Catholic High School of Baltimore, MD	$385,000
The Catlin Gabel School, OR	$1,108,088
Cedar Ridge Academy, UT	$45,000
Centennial Academy, QC, Canada	CAN$705,500
Central Catholic High School, CA	$283,480
Central Catholic High School, OH	$125,000
Central Catholic High School, PA	$650,000
CFS, The School at Church Farm, PA	$8,408,700
Chadwick School, CA	$2,400,000
Chamberlain-Hunt Academy, MS	$222,870
Chaminade College Preparatory, CA	$955,760
Chaminade College Preparatory School, MO	$1,400,000
Chaminade-Madonna College Preparatory, FL	$400,000
Chapel Hill–Chauncy Hall School, MA	$825,000
The Chapin School, NY	$1,547,750
Charlotte Christian School, NC	$389,150
Charlotte Country Day School, NC	$1,395,838
Charlotte Latin School, NC	$501,500
Chase Collegiate School, CT	$2,680,000
Chatham Academy, GA	$50,000
Cheshire Academy, CT	$2,000,000
Cheverus High School, ME	$1,549,035
Children's Creative and Performing Arts Academy—Capa Division, CA	$25,000
Chinese Christian Schools, CA	$110,000
Choate Rosemary Hall, CT	$7,500,000
Christchurch School, VA	$1,242,400
Christian Brothers Academy, NJ	$770,650
Christian Brothers Academy, NY	$483,070
Christian Central Academy, NY	$62,500
Christian Heritage School, CT	$500,000
Christian Home and Bible School, FL	$40,000
Christian Junior–Senior High School, CA	$400,000
Christopher Dock Mennonite High School, PA	$400,000
Christ School, NC	$1,300,000
Cincinnati Country Day School, OH	$750,000
Colegio Franklin D. Roosevelt, Peru	$4180
Colegio Nueva Granada, Colombia	68,003,850 Colombian pesos
Colegio Puertorriqueno de Ninas, PR	$172,775
The College Preparatory School, CA	$1,555,285
The Collegiate School, VA	$638,522
Colorado Academy, CO	$2,029,000
The Colorado Springs School, CO	$447,193
Columbia Grammar and Preparatory School, NY	$2,445,655
Columbia International School, Japan	¥3,360,000
The Columbus Academy, OH	$633,830
Commonwealth School, MA	$1,100,000
Community Christian Academy, KY	$5000
The Community School, ID	$497,150
Community School, NH	$108,000
The Community School of Naples, FL	$794,194
Concord Academy, MA	$2,329,142
Connelly School of the Holy Child, MD	$500,000
Conserve School, WI	$2,200,000
Convent of the Sacred Heart, NY	$1,800,000
Convent of the Visitation School, MN	$832,155
Copenhagen International School, Denmark	4,000,000 Danish kroner
Cornelia Connelly School, CA	$162,800
Country Day School of the Sacred Heart, PA	$423,000
Crawford Adventist Academy, ON, Canada	CAN$15,000
Crespi Carmelite High School, CA	$512,600
Cretin-Derham Hall, MN	$1,500,000
Crofton House School, BC, Canada	CAN$154,438
Crossroads School for Arts & Sciences, CA	$1,959,000
Crystal Springs Uplands School, CA	$1,400,000
The Culver Academies, IN	$7,000,000
Currey Ingram Academy, TN	$435,226
Cushing Academy, MA	$2,500,000
Dallas Academy, TX	$60,000
Dallas Christian School, TX	$182,101
The Dalton School, NY	$2,687,955
Dana Hall School, MA	$2,378,827
Darlington School, GA	$1,372,175
Darrow School, NY	$941,850
David Lipscomb High School, TN	$46,840
Deerfield Academy, MA	$6,100,000
Deerfield-Windsor School, GA	$20,000
De La Salle High School, CA	$1,619,300
Delaware Valley Friends School, PA	$490,425
Delbarton School, NJ	$1,200,000
DeMatha Catholic High School, MD	$1,025,467
The Derryfield School, NH	$1,069,506
Detroit Country Day School, MI	$2,500,000
Devon Preparatory School, PA	$725,000
Doane Stuart School, NY	$421,122
The Dominican Academy of the City of New York, NY	$200,000
Donelson Christian Academy, TN	$31,000
Dowling Catholic High School, IA	$1,000,000
Duchesne Academy of the Sacred Heart, TX	$768,490
Dunn School, CA	$625,000
Durham Academy, NC	$433,350
Dwight-Englewood School, NJ	$1,658,500
Eaglebrook School, MA	$1,600,000
Eagle Hill School, CT	$1,500,000
Eagle Hill-Southport, CT	$82,200
Eastern Mennonite High School, VA	$129,736
Eastside Catholic School, WA	$1,540,000
Eastside College Preparatory School, CA	$3,061,000
Ecole d'Humanité, Switzerland	180,000 Swiss francs
Elgin Academy, IL	$1,100,000
Elk Mountain Academy, MT	$100,000
The Ellis School, PA	$616,900
Elmwood School, ON, Canada	CAN$200,000
Elyria Catholic High School, OH	$200,000
Emerson Honors High Schools, CA	$50,000
The Emery Weiner School, TX	$590,000
Emma Willard School, NY	$3,239,800
Episcopal Collegiate School, AR	$525,000
Episcopal High School, TX	$1,700,000
Episcopal High School, VA	$3,300,000
Episcopal High School of Jacksonville, FL	$1,395,000
The Episcopal School of Dallas, TX	$1,700,000
Escola Americana de Campinas, Brazil	$51,000
Escondido Adventist Academy, CA	$30,000
The Ethel Walker School, CT	$2,000,000
Evangelical Christian School, TN	$205,000
Evansville Day School, IN	$183,000
Explorations Academy, WA	$74,000
Fairfield College Preparatory School, CT	$1,500,000
Fairhill School, TX	$50,000
Faith Christian High School, CA	$50,000
Faith Lutheran High School, NV	$220,000
Falmouth Academy, MA	$500,000
The Family Foundation School, NY	$560,000
Father Lopez High School, FL	$100,000

Father Ryan High School, TN	$300,000
Fayetteville Academy, NC	$397,773
Fay School, MA	$800,000
The Field School, DC	$1,250,000
The First Academy, FL	$250,000
First Presbyterian Day School, GA	$140,000
Fishburne Military School, VA	$75,000
Flint Hill School, VA	$1,500,000
Flintridge Sacred Heart Academy, CA	$558,450
Fontbonne Hall Academy, NY	$107,500
Foothills Academy, AB, Canada	CAN$500,000
Fordham Preparatory School, NY	$1,700,000
Forest Lake Academy, FL	$255,000
The Forman School, CT	$849,000
Forsyth Country Day School, NC	$693,755
Fort Lauderdale Preparatory School, FL	$150,000
Fort Worth Country Day School, TX	$820,000
Fountain Valley School of Colorado, CO	$1,650,000
Fowlers Academy, PR	$4650
Foxcroft Academy, ME	$56,000
Foxcroft School, VA	$1,142,075
Fox Valley Lutheran Academy, IL	$12,000
Fox Valley Lutheran High School, WI	$290,000
Franklin Road Academy, TN	$100,000
Freeman Academy, SD	$5000
French-American School of New York, NY	$65,168
Friends' Central School, PA	$1,664,425
Front Range Christian High School, CO	$30,000
The Frostig School, CA	$50,000
Fryeburg Academy, ME	$900,000
Fuqua School, VA	$44,000
Garces Memorial High School, CA	$296,265
Garden School, NY	$306,920
Garrison Forest School, MD	$2,153,805
Gaston Day School, NC	$211,086
George School, PA	$5,387,000
Georgetown Preparatory School, MD	$1,800,000
Georgetown Visitation Preparatory School, DC	$1,250,000
Germantown Academy, PA	$1,700,000
Germantown Friends School, PA	$1,371,796
Gill St. Bernard's School, NJ	$944,000
Gilman School, MD	$140,000
Gilmour Academy, OH	$2,200,000
Girls Preparatory School, TN	$866,383
Glen Eden School, BC, Canada	CAN$30,000
Glenelg Country School, MD	$900,000
Gonzaga College High School, DC	$1,785,000
Gordon Technical High School, IL	$550,000
Gould Academy, ME	$1,355,000
The Governor's Academy (formerly Governor Dummer Academy), MA	$2,200,000
The Gow School, NY	$550,000
Grace Christian School, AK	$170,000
The Grand River Academy, OH	$110,000
The Grauer School, CA	$50,000
Great Lakes Christian High School, ON, Canada	CAN$100,000
Green Fields Country Day School, AZ	$187,987
Greenhill School, TX	$1,036,200
Greenhills School, MI	$642,460
Greenleaf Academy, ID	$55,000
Greens Farms Academy, CT	$877,712
Greenwich Academy, CT	$1,333,870
The Greenwood School, VT	$235,000
Groton School, MA	$4,077,000
Guerin College Preparatory High School, IL	$380,000
Guilford Day School, NC	$31,800
The Gunnery, CT	$2,400,000
Gunston Day School, MD	$500,000
Gwynedd Mercy Academy, PA	$82,000
Hackley School, NY	$3,000,000
Halstrom High School, CA	$10,000
Halstrom High School—San Diego, CA	$6120
Hamilton District Christian High, ON, Canada	CAN$72,000
Hammond School, SC	$1,200,000
Hanalani Schools, HI	$78,363
Hargrave Military Academy, VA	$525,000
Harrells Christian Academy, NC	$21,100
The Harrisburg Academy, PA	$450,811
Harvard-Westlake School, CA	$3,000,850
The Harvey School, NY	$1,150,000
The Haverford School, PA	$1,531,588
Havergal College, ON, Canada	CAN$319,585
Hawaii Baptist Academy, HI	$80,866
Hawai'i Preparatory Academy, HI	$1,600,000
Hawken School, OH	$2,137,466
Hawthorne Christian Academy, NJ	$125,467
Hayden High School, KS	$70,000
Head-Royce School, CA	$1,249,600
Headwaters Academy, MT	$100,000
Hebrew Academy, CA	$30,000
Hebron Academy, ME	$1,700,000
Heritage Hall, OK	$5,110,000
The Heritage School, GA	$154,588
Highland Hall, A Waldorf School, CA	$104,600
Highland School, VA	$465,000
High Mowing School, NH	$500,000
The Hill Center, Durham Academy, NC	$70,100
Hillcrest Christian School, CA	$23,694
Hillcrest School, TX	$21,000
The Hill School, PA	$4,500,000
The Hill Top Preparatory School, PA	$69,400
Hilton Head Preparatory School, SC	$250,000
The Hockaday School, TX	$786,700
Hokkaido International School, Japan	¥2,000,000
Holderness School, NH	$2,200,000
The Holton-Arms School, MD	$2,300,000
Holy Innocents' Episcopal School, GA	$490,725
Holy Name High School, PA	$24,522
Holy Names High School, CA	$324,466
Holy Trinity High School, IL	$1,547,085
Hoosac School, NY	$500,000
Hopkins School, CT	$2,100,000
The Horace Mann School, NY	$3,500,000
Hosanna Christian School, OR	$12,000
The Hotchkiss School, CT	$6,849,356
Houghton Academy, NY	$95,000
Howe Military School, IN	$500,000
The Hudson School, NJ	$200,000
Humanex Academy, CO	$35,000
The Hun School of Princeton, NJ	$2,150,000
Hutchison School, TN	$138,774
Hyde School, CT	$258,000
Hyde School, ME	$820,000
Hyman Brand Hebrew Academy of Greater Kansas City, KS	$800,000
Idyllwild Arts Academy, CA	$397,046
Immaculate Conception High School, NJ	$36,750
Immaculate Conception School, IL	$100,000

Immaculate High School, CT	$80,000
Indian Mountain School, CT	$723,975
Indian Springs School, AL	$987,748
Interlochen Arts Academy, MI	$5,000,000
International College Spain, Spain	€20,445
International High School, CA	$748,000
International School Manila, Philippines	$77,535
International School of Aruba, Aruba	$26,000
International School of Milan, Italy	€30,000
The International School of Paris, France	$200,000
Iolani School, HI	$1,580,000
Isidore Newman School, LA	$492,391
Jack M. Barrack Hebrew Academy (formerly Akiba Hebrew Academy), PA	$980,000
Jackson Academy, MS	$129,070
Jackson Christian School, TN	$15,218
The Janus School, PA	$75,000
Jesuit College Preparatory School, TX	$1,233,850
Jesuit High School, CA	$740,000
Jesuit High School of Tampa, FL	$800,000
John Bapst Memorial High School, ME	$94,240
John Burroughs School, MO	$1,232,650
The John Cooper School, TX	$235,625
John Paul II Catholic High School, FL	$40,000
Junipero Serra High School, CA	$780,150
Keith Country Day School, IL	$358,970
Kent Denver School, CO	$1,600,000
Kent Place School, NJ	$921,243
Kents Hill School, ME	$1,900,000
Kentucky Country Day School, KY	$398,816
Kerr-Vance Academy, NC	$15,000
The Key School, MD	$439,397
Kildonan School, NY	$135,000
Kimball Union Academy, NH	$2,297,435
Kimberton Waldorf School, PA	$164,250
King Low Heywood Thomas, CT	$765,875
The King's Academy, TN	$189,364
The King's Christian High School, NJ	$150,000
Kings Christian School, CA	$150,000
King's-Edgehill School, NS, Canada	CAN$700,000
Kingshill School, VI	$9000
Kingsway College, ON, Canada	CAN$205,365
King's West School, WA	$190,000
Kingswood-Oxford School, CT	$2,658,775
The Knox School, NY	$503,670
Ladywood High School, MI	$75,000
Lakefield College School, ON, Canada	CAN$140,000
Lake Forest Academy, IL	$2,875,100
Lakeland Christian Academy, IN	$75,000
Lake Ridge Academy, OH	$942,676
Lakeside School, WA	$2,562,130
Lakeview Academy, GA	$157,000
La Lumiere School, IN	$500,000
Lancaster Country Day School, PA	$435,250
Lancaster Mennonite High School, PA	$600,000
Landmark East School, NS, Canada	CAN$100,000
Landmark School, MA	$362,041
Landon School, MD	$1,900,000
La Pietra–Hawaii School for Girls, HI	$400,700
La Salle Academy, RI	$1,400,000
La Salle High School, FL	$165,000
La Salle Institute, NY	$372,768
The Laureate Academy, MB, Canada	CAN$35,000
Laurel Springs School, CA	$22,538
Lausanne Collegiate School, TN	$248,208
Lawrence Academy, MA	$2,000,000
Lawrence School, OH	$352,300
The Lawrenceville School, NJ	$8,000,000
Lehigh Valley Christian High School, PA	$54,975
Lehman High School, OH	$271,849
Le Lycee Francais de Los Angeles, CA	$63,000
Lexington Catholic High School, KY	$450,000
Lexington Christian Academy, MA	$739,135
Lincoln School, RI	$1,000,000
Linden Hall, PA	$700,000
Linden Hill School, MA	$15,000
The Linden School, ON, Canada	CAN$150,000
The Linsly School, WV	$900,000
Little Keswick School, VA	$20,000
Logos School, MO	$100,000
The Loomis Chaffee School, CT	$6,000,000
Loretto Academy, TX	$95,000
Los Angeles Baptist Junior/Senior High School, CA	$687,468
Los Angeles Lutheran High School, CA	$25,000
Louisville Collegiate School, KY	$528,150
Louisville High School, CA	$250,000
Lourdes Catholic High School, AZ	$18,840
The Lovett School, GA	$1,870,000
The Lowell Whiteman School, CO	$351,000
Loyola-Blakefield, MD	$1,717,524
Loyola High School, Jesuit College Preparatory, CA	$1,380,000
Loyola School, NY	$725,000
Lustre Christian High School, MT	$2750
Lutheran High North, TX	$175,000
Lutheran High School, IN	$220,000
Lutheran High School, MO	$15,000
Lutheran High School North, MO	$600,000
Lutheran High School Northwest, MI	$2000
Lutheran High School of Hawaii, HI	$50,000
Lutheran High School of San Diego, CA	$28,000
Lutheran High School West, OH	$1,100,000
Luther College High School, SK, Canada	CAN$165,000
Luther High School South, IL	$13,000
The Lycee International, American Section, France	€30,000
Lydia Patterson Institute, TX	$157,950
Lyman Ward Military Academy, AL	$50,000
MacLachlan College, ON, Canada	CAN$9000
Madison Academy, AL	$100,000
Madison-Ridgeland Academy, MS	$123,000
Magnificat High School, OH	$800,000
Maharishi School of the Age of Enlightenment, IA	$535,923
Maine Central Institute, ME	$1,036,339
Maine School of Science and Mathematics, ME	$237,000
Manlius Pebble Hill School, NY	$880,000
Maret School, DC	$995,000
Marian Central Catholic High School, IL	$220,870
Marian High School, IN	$350,000
Marin Academy, CA	$1,781,027
Marist School, GA	$1,082,150
Marmion Academy, IL	$269,812
Marquette University High School, WI	$1,250,000
Marshall School, MN	$680,000
Mars Hill Bible School, AL	$150,000
Martin Luther High School, NY	$103,400
The Marvelwood School, CT	$583,500
Mary Help of Christians Academy, NJ	$378,091
Maryknoll School, HI	$395,000
Marylawn of the Oranges, NJ	$81,200

The Mary Louis Academy, NY	$445,150
Marymount High School, CA	$1,028,517
Marymount School, NY	$2,115,000
Maryvale Preparatory School, MD	$480,000
The Master's School, CT	$194,507
The Masters School, NY	$3,700,000
Matignon High School, MA	$125,000
Maumee Valley Country Day School, OH	$454,900
Maur Hill-Mount Academy, KS	$100,000
The McCallie School, TN	$3,100,000
McCurdy School, NM	$37,664
McDonogh School, MD	$2,013,980
McQuaid Jesuit, NY	$1,225,000
The Meadows School, NV	$555,245
Memphis University School, TN	$843,680
Menaul School, NM	$267,000
Menlo School, CA	$3,500,000
Mennonite Collegiate Institute, MB, Canada	CAN$46,000
Mentor College, ON, Canada	CAN$3002
Mercersburg Academy, PA	$4,500,000
Mercy High School, NE	$500,000
Mercy High School College Preparatory, CA	$1,424,260
Mercyhurst Preparatory School, PA	$492,600
Mesa Grande Seventh-Day Academy, CA	$35,000
Metairie Park Country Day School, LA	$325,000
Metro-East Lutheran High School, IL	$30,000
Miami Country Day School, FL	$550,000
Middlesex School, MA	$3,400,000
Midland School, CA	$848,000
Mid-Pacific Institute, HI	$644,000
Mid-Peninsula High School, CA	$630,000
Milken Community High School of Stephen S. Wise Temple, CA	$1,414,100
Millbrook School, NY	$1,963,750
Miller School, VA	$525,000
Milton Academy, MA	$6,100,000
Minot Bishop Ryan, ND	$5000
Miss Edgar's and Miss Cramp's School, QC, Canada	CAN$103,000
Miss Hall's School, MA	$2,000,000
Missouri Military Academy, MO	$476,000
Miss Porter's School, CT	$3,500,000
MMI Preparatory School, PA	$767,000
Monmouth Academy, NJ	$21,750
Montana Academy, MT	$40,000
Montgomery Bell Academy, TN	$742,225
Montrose School, MA	$90,000
Montverde Academy, FL	$1,000,000
Moorestown Friends School, NJ	$905,350
Moravian Academy, PA	$576,950
Moreau Catholic High School, CA	$775,000
Morgan Park Academy, IL	$137,450
Morristown-Beard School, NJ	$1,000,000
Moses Brown School, RI	$798,040
Mother McAuley High School, IL	$495,100
Mounds Park Academy, MN	$312,705
Mount Michael Benedictine School, NE	$240,000
Mount Saint Charles Academy, RI	$600,000
Mount Saint Joseph Academy, PA	$383,975
Nancy Campbell Collegiate Institute, ON, Canada	CAN$298,600
National Cathedral School, DC	$917,760
Nazareth Academy, IL	$300,000
Nebraska Christian Schools, NE	$90,000
Nerinx Hall, MO	$357,550
Neuchatel Junior College, Switzerland	75,000 Swiss francs
Newark Academy, NJ	$1,400,000
New Horizon Youth Ministries, IN	$710,106
The Newman School, MA	$250,000
New Mexico Military Institute, NM	$750,000
New Way Learning Academy, AZ	$40,000
Niagara Christian Community of Schools, ON, Canada	CAN$250,000
The Nichols School, NY	$1,400,000
Noble and Greenough School, MA	$2,148,500
The Nora School, MD	$115,000
Norfolk Christian School, VA	$379,148
Norfolk Collegiate School, VA	$418,137
The North Broward Preparatory Upper School, FL	$1,000,000
North Cobb Christian School, GA	$100,000
Northfield Mount Hermon School, MA	$5,500,000
North Shore Country Day School, IL	$900,000
Northside Christian School, FL	$20,000
The Northwest Academy, OR	$150,000
The Northwest School, WA	$932,170
Northwest Yeshiva High School, WA	$154,000
Northwood School, NY	$1,150,000
North Yarmouth Academy, ME	$689,404
Notre Dame Academy, MA	$600,000
Notre Dame Academy, VA	$728,502
Notre Dame- Bishop Gibbons School, NY	$90,000
Notre Dame High School, CA	$700,000
Notre Dame High School, NJ	$180,000
Notre Dame High School, TN	$195,000
Notre Dame Preparatory School, MD	$1,131,647
Oak Creek Ranch School, AZ	$36,500
Oak Grove Lutheran School, ND	$250,000
Oak Grove School, CA	$60,000
Oak Hill Academy, VA	$350,000
Oak Knoll School of the Holy Child, NJ	$1,100,000
The Oakland School, PA	$45,000
Oak Mountain Academy, GA	$94,000
The Oakridge School, TX	$456,932
Oakwood Friends School, NY	$747,000
The Oakwood School, NC	$91,500
O'Dea High School, WA	$340,000
Okanagan Adventist Academy, BC, Canada	CAN$55,000
Oldenburg Academy, IN	$50,000
Oldfields School, MD	$1,200,000
The O'Neal School, NC	$274,063
Orangewood Adventist Academy, CA	$75,000
Oregon Episcopal School, OR	$1,131,531
Orinda Academy, CA	$400,000
The Orme School, AZ	$914,450
Our Lady Academy, MS	$10,000
Our Lady of Mercy Academy, NJ	$40,000
Our Lady of Mercy High School, NY	$800,000
Our Saviour Lutheran School, NY	$30,000
Out-Of-Door-Academy, FL	$410,000
The Overlake School, WA	$494,449
Pace Academy, GA	$1,000,000
Pacific Crest Community School, OR	$60,000
Pacific Hills School, CA	$1,895,845
Pacific Lutheran High School, CA	$20,000
Padua Franciscan High School, OH	$777,980
The Paideia School, GA	$1,099,107
Palma High School, CA	$229,000
The Parker School, HI	$117,000

Parklane Academy, MS	$3000
The Park School of Buffalo, NY	$387,150
Park Tudor School, IN	$1,446,312
Peddie School, NJ	$5,000,000
The Pennington School, NJ	$1,265,000
Peoples Christian Academy, ON, Canada	CAN$30,000
Perkiomen School, PA	$1,399,000
The Phelps School, PA	$250,000
Phillips Academy (Andover), MA	$14,600,000
Phoenix Christian Unified Schools, AZ	$83,725
Piedmont Academy, GA	$15,000
Pine Crest School, FL	$1,628,697
Pinewood—The International School of Thessaloniki, Greece, Greece	€3000
The Pingry School, NJ	$1,521,010
Pioneer Valley Christian School, MA	$94,018
Pius X High School, NE	$10,000
Poly Prep Country Day School, NY	$4,600,000
Polytechnic School, CA	$2,800,000
Pomfret School, CT	$2,751,000
Porter-Gaud School, SC	$900,000
Portland Lutheran School, OR	$35,260
Portledge School, NY	$903,500
Portsmouth Abbey School, RI	$2,500,000
Portsmouth Christian Academy, NH	$76,000
The Potomac School, VA	$944,995
Poughkeepsie Day School, NY	$204,295
Powers Catholic High School, MI	$505,838
The Prairie School, WI	$620,000
Prestonwood Christian Academy, TX	$365,693
Professional Children's School, NY	$681,500
The Prout School, RI	$210,000
Providence Country Day School, RI	$1,175,000
Providence Day School, NC	$600,000
Providence High School, CA	$196,750
Providence High School, TX	$200,000
Pulaski Academy, AR	$300,000
Punahou School, HI	$2,180,582
Purnell School, NJ	$500,000
Queen Anne School, MD	$603,819
Queen Margaret's School, BC, Canada	CAN$100,000
Queensway Christian College, ON, Canada	CAN$5000
Quigley Catholic High School, PA	$299,953
Rabbi Alexander S. Gross Hebrew Academy, FL	$300,000
Rabun Gap-Nacoochee School, GA	$2,572,695
Rambam Mesivta, NY	$300,000
Randolph-Macon Academy, VA	$259,341
Randolph School, AL	$88,875
Ransom Everglades School, FL	$2,917,606
Ravenscroft School, NC	$761,005
The Rectory School, CT	$800,000
Redwood Christian Schools, CA	$300,000
Regina High School, OH	$250,000
Rice High School, NY	$600,000
Ridley College, ON, Canada	CAN$1,800,000
Ripon Christian Schools, CA	$20,000
Riverdale Country School, NY	$4,600,000
Rivermont Collegiate, IA	$309,755
Riverside Military Academy, GA	$18,000
The Rivers School, MA	$2,483,400
Riverview School, MA	$156,000
Robert Louis Stevenson School, NY	$12,000
Rockland Country Day School, NY	$409,744
Rocky Hill School, RI	$1,020,500
Rocky Mount Academy, NC	$180,000
The Roeper School, MI	$680,572
Roland Park Country School, MD	$804,325
Rolling Hills Preparatory School, CA	$410,000
Roncalli High School, IN	$725,000
Rosseau Lake College, ON, Canada	CAN$160,000
Ross School, NY	$2,000,000
Rothesay Netherwood School, NB, Canada	CAN$460,000
Rowland Hall-St. Mark's School, UT	$481,088
The Roxbury Latin School, MA	$1,324,550
Roycemore School, IL	$731,056
Rumsey Hall School, CT	$775,000
Rundle College, AB, Canada	CAN$22,250
Rutgers Preparatory School, NJ	$1,011,793
Rye Country Day School, NY	$2,013,540
Sacramento Adventist Academy, CA	$10,000
Sacramento Waldorf School, CA	$126,438
Sacred Heart School of Halifax, NS, Canada	CAN$65,000
Saddle River Day School, NJ	$662,800
Sage Hill School, CA	$1,068,750
Sage Ridge School, NV	$159,290
St. Agnes Academy, TX	$300,000
St. Albans School, DC	$2,849,889
St. Andrew's College, ON, Canada	CAN$1,200,000
St. Andrew's Episcopal School, MD	$1,030,500
St. Andrew's Episcopal School, MS	$167,124
St. Andrew's on the Marsh School, GA	$150,000
St. Andrew's Priory School, HI	$497,989
Saint Andrew's School, FL	$1,960,000
St. Andrew's School, RI	$1,223,225
St. Andrew's–Sewanee School, TN	$1,550,000
St. Anne's–Belfield School, VA	$1,633,575
St. Anselm's Abbey School, DC	$500,000
St. Anthony Catholic High School, TX	$95,000
St. Augustine High School, TX	$46,000
Saint Augustine Preparatory School, NJ	$675,000
Saint Basil Academy, PA	$171,400
St. Benedict at Auburndale, TN	$35,000
St. Benedict's Preparatory School, NJ	$1,186,372
St. Catherine's Military Academy, CA	$171,061
St. Catherine's School, VA	$448,800
St. Cecilia Academy, TN	$430,000
Saint Cecilia High School, NE	$5250
St. Christopher's School, VA	$1,766,800
St. Croix Country Day School, VI	$251,360
St. Croix Lutheran High School, MN	$300,000
Saint Dominic Academy, NJ	$163,900
Saint Edmund High School, NY	$72,000
Saint Edward's School, FL	$845,400
Saint Elizabeth High School, CA	$450,000
St. Francis de Sales High School, OH	$1,051,630
Saint Francis High School, CA	$1,100,000
St. Francis High School, KY	$615,000
St. Francis School, GA	$80,000
Saint Francis School, HI	$80,620
St. George's School, RI	$2,700,000
Saint George's School, WA	$301,781
St. George's School, BC, Canada	CAN$800,000
St. Gregory College Preparatory School, AZ	$383,420
Saint James School, MD	$1,500,000
Saint John Bosco High School, CA	$350,000
St. Johnsbury Academy, VT	$782,900
St. John's Catholic Prep, MD	$250,000
St. John's College High School, DC	$1,700,000

St. John's Northwestern Military Academy, WI	$950,000
St. John's Preparatory School, MA	$2,800,000
Saint John's Preparatory School, MN	$1,100,000
St. John's-Ravenscourt School, MB, Canada	CAN$262,250
St. Joseph Academy, FL	$126,535
Saint Joseph Central Catholic High School, OH	$20,000
St. Joseph High School, CA	$250,000
St. Joseph High School, CT	$235,000
Saint Joseph High School, IL	$500,000
Saint Joseph High School, WI	$100,000
St. Joseph's Academy, LA	$218,295
St. Joseph's Catholic School, SC	$140,500
St. Joseph's Preparatory School, PA	$2,000,000
St. Lawrence Seminary, WI	$778,110
St. Margaret's Episcopal School, CA	$1,431,790
St. Margaret's School, VA	$790,000
St. Margaret's School, BC, Canada	CAN$70,000
Saint Mark's School, MA	$2,700,000
St. Mark's School of Texas, TX	$1,916,667
St. Martin's Episcopal School, LA	$568,210
St. Mary's Academy, CO	$535,289
Saint Mary's College High School, CA	$900,000
St. Mary's Episcopal School, TN	$192,584
Saint Mary's Hall, TX	$509,630
St. Mary's Hall–Doane Academy, NJ	$100,000
Saint Mary's High School, AZ	$2,230,000
St. Mary's High School, CO	$190,000
Saint Mary's High School, MD	$250,000
Saint Mary's School, NC	$1,133,000
St. Mary's School, OR	$580,000
Saint Matthias High School, CA	$250,000
St. Michael's College School, ON, Canada	CAN$1,300,000
St. Michael's Preparatory School of the Norbertine Fathers, CA	$350,000
Saint Patrick High School, IL	$690,000
Saint Patrick—Saint Vincent High School, CA	$205,750
St. Paul Academy and Summit School, MN	$750,000
Saint Paul Lutheran High School, MO	$185,285
St. Paul's Episcopal School, AL	$212,518
St. Paul's High School, MB, Canada	CAN$240,000
St. Paul's School, MD	$741,975
St. Paul's School, NH	$6,056,858
St. Paul's School for Girls, MD	$1,200,000
St. Peter's Preparatory School, NJ	$800,000
St. Pius X Catholic High School, GA	$400,000
St. Sebastian's School, MA	$1,445,000
Saints Peter and Paul High School, MD	$10,350
St. Stephen's & St. Agnes School, VA	$1,728,163
Saint Stephen's Episcopal School, FL	$250,000
St. Stephen's School, Rome, Italy	€336,000
Saint Teresa's Academy, MO	$137,000
Saint Thomas Academy, MN	$1,300,000
St. Thomas Aquinas High School, NH	$270,000
St. Thomas Choir School, NY	$187,950
Saint Thomas More School, CT	$728,900
St. Timothy's School, MD	$1,450,000
Saint Viator High School, IL	$858,000
Saint Xavier High School, OH	$2,300,000
Salem Academy, NC	$1,033,794
Salesian High School, CA	$900,000
Salesian High School, NY	$100,000
Salesianum School, DE	$500,000
Salisbury School, CT	$2,410,000
Salpointe Catholic High School, AZ	$1,000,000
Salt Lake Lutheran High School, UT	$48,000
Saltus Grammar School, Bermuda	300,000 Bermuda dollars
Sandia Preparatory School, NM	$403,500
San Diego Jewish Academy, CA	$553,000
San Domenico School, CA	$1,000,000
Sandy Spring Friends School, MD	$1,089,967
Sanford School, DE	$933,650
San Francisco University High School, CA	$1,680,000
San Marcos Baptist Academy, TX	$325,000
Santa Fe Preparatory School, NM	$631,194
Santa Margarita Catholic High School, CA	$560,000
Santiam Christian School, OR	$130,000
Savannah Christian Preparatory School, GA	$134,000
The Savannah Country Day School, GA	$389,900
Sayre School, KY	$360,550
Scattergood Friends School, IA	$534,000
Schlarman High School, IL	$120,000
Scotus Central Catholic High School, NE	$81,087
Seabury Hall, HI	$664,660
Seattle Christian Schools, WA	$81,058
Seattle Lutheran High School, WA	$92,710
Sedbergh School, QC, Canada	CAN$250,000
Seisen International School, Japan	¥2,910,000
Selwyn House School, QC, Canada	CAN$115,400
Seoul Foreign School, Republic of Korea	$365,000
Seton Catholic High School, AZ	$605,000
The Seven Hills School, OH	$500,000
Sewickley Academy, PA	$600,000
Shades Mountain Christian School, AL	$19,000
Shady Side Academy, PA	$1,364,550
Shannon Forest Christian School, SC	$32,734
Shattuck-St. Mary's School, MN	$3,300,000
Shelton School and Evaluation Center, TX	$485,732
The Shipley School, PA	$1,652,300
Shorecrest Preparatory School, FL	$923,650
Shoreline Christian, WA	$41,869
Sioux Falls Christian High School, SD	$100,000
Solebury School, PA	$1,500,000
Solomon Learning Institute, Ltd., AB, Canada	CAN$5500
Sorenson's Ranch School, UT	$20,000
Soundview Preparatory School, NY	$240,000
Southfield Christian High School, MI	$50,000
Southridge School, BC, Canada	CAN$50,000
The Spence School, NY	$1,416,000
Stanbridge Academy, CA	$80,000
Staten Island Academy, NY	$1,000,000
Stella Maris High School, NY	$85,700
Stephen T. Badin High School, OH	$270,000
Stevenson School, CA	$2,100,000
Stoneleigh–Burnham School, MA	$904,000
Storm King School, NY	$325,000
Strake Jesuit College Preparatory, TX	$1,000,000
Strathcona-Tweedsmuir School, AB, Canada	CAN$37,250
Stratton Mountain School, VT	$689,894
Stuart Country Day School of the Sacred Heart, NJ	$692,800
The Study School, QC, Canada	CAN$169,750
Suffield Academy, CT	$2,605,410
Summit Preparatory School, MT	$100,000
Tabor Academy, MA	$2,100,000
The Taft School, CT	$5,600,000
Tallulah Falls School, GA	$1,000,000
Tampa Preparatory School, FL	$523,787
Tandem Friends School, VA	$205,000

TASIS, The American School in Switzerland, Switzerland	787,000 Swiss francs
The Tatnall School, DE	$971,786
Telluride Mountain School, CO	$56,000
Teurlings Catholic High School, LA	$29,664
The Thacher School, CA	$1,853,000
Thornton Friends School, MD	$230,000
Tilton School, NH	$2,063,364
TMI—The Episcopal School of Texas, TX	$500,000
Tower Hill School, DE	$565,325
Trafalgar Castle School, ON, Canada	CAN$43,000
Tri-City Christian Schools, CA	$50,000
Trident Academy, SC	$32,000
Trinity Catholic High School, MA	$90,000
Trinity Christian Academy, TX	$190,000
Trinity College School, ON, Canada	CAN$1,000,000
Trinity Episcopal School, VA	$781,887
Trinity High School, IL	$427,700
Trinity High School, KY	$1,000,000
Trinity High School, OH	$356,000
Trinity-Pawling School, NY	$2,000,000
Trinity Preparatory School, FL	$1,317,500
Trinity Presbyterian School, AL	$8000
Trinity School, NY	$2,500,000
Trinity School of Midland, TX	$219,785
Trinity Valley School, TX	$423,128
United Mennonite Educational Institute, ON, Canada	CAN$4000
United Nations International School, NY	$476,947
The United World College—USA, NM	$2,700,000
University Lake School, WI	$128,541
University Liggett School, MI	$1,500,000
University of Chicago Laboratory Schools, IL	$866,043
University Prep, WA	$918,780
University School of Jackson, TN	$150,000
University School of Milwaukee, WI	$742,991
University School of Nova Southeastern University, FL	$915,000
Ursuline Academy, DE	$497,000
The Ursuline Academy of Dallas, TX	$732,000
Ursuline High School, CA	$290,000
The Ursuline School, NY	$825,750
Valle Catholic High School, MO	$165,000
Valley Christian High School, CA	$25,000
Valley Christian School, CA	$200,000
Valley Forge Military Academy & College, PA	$2,230,907
Valley Lutheran High School, AZ	$166,770
Valley Lutheran High School, MI	$150,000
The Valley School, MI	$74,992
Valwood School, GA	$139,000
Vandebilt Catholic High School, LA	$90,000
The Vanguard School, FL	$374,700
Verdala International School, Malta	$23,018
Verde Valley School, AZ	$1,403,600
Vianney High School, MO	$528,479
Victor Valley Christian School, CA	$20,000
Viewpoint School, CA	$886,690
Villa Duchesne/Oak Hill School, MO	$800,000
Villa Maria Academy, PA	$330,210
Villanova Preparatory School, CA	$800,000
Villa Walsh Academy, NJ	$80,000
Virginia Beach Friends School, VA	$45,000
Waldorf High School of Massachusetts Bay, MA	$263,200
The Waldorf School of Garden City, NY	$180,000
The Walker School, GA	$1,000,000
Walnut Hill School, MA	$2,800,000
The Wardlaw-Hartridge School, NJ	$522,326
Waring School, MA	$425,000
Wasatch Academy, UT	$600,000
Washington Academy, ME	$515,561
Washington County Day School, MS	$18,000
Washington Waldorf School, MD	$14,950
Watkinson School, CT	$1,374,748
The Waverly School, CA	$17,000
Waynflete School, ME	$787,383
The Webb School, TN	$920,000
Webb School of Knoxville, TN	$799,351
The Webb Schools, CA	$2,600,000
Wesleyan Academy, PR	$5600
Westbury Christian School, TX	$95,000
West Catholic High School, MI	$330,000
Westchester Country Day School, NC	$109,140
Western Reserve Academy, OH	$3,600,000
Westminster Christian Academy, AL	$200,000
Westminster Christian School, FL	$500,000
Westminster School, CT	$3,440,000
The Westminster Schools, GA	$2,800,000
Westminster Schools of Augusta, GA	$152,000
West Nottingham Academy, MD	$721,000
Westover School, CT	$2,194,674
Westridge School, CA	$1,318,800
Westtown School, PA	$3,997,138
Wheaton Academy, IL	$540,000
The Wheeler School, RI	$979,495
Whitefield Academy, GA	$800,000
Wichita Collegiate School, KS	$272,225
William Penn Charter School, PA	$2,259,910
The Williams School, CT	$1,000,000
The Williston Northampton School, MA	$5,197,000
Wilmington Friends School, DE	$640,685
Wilson Hall, SC	$115,000
Winchester Thurston School, PA	$1,085,000
Windermere Preparatory School, FL	$188,900
Windward School, CA	$941,310
The Winsor School, MA	$1,163,898
The Winston School, TX	$233,150
Wisconsin Academy, WI	$190,000
Woodside Priory School, CA	$1,600,000
Woodward Academy, GA	$1,600,000
Wooster School, CT	$945,305
Worcester Academy, MA	$3,000,000
Wyoming Seminary, PA	$5,900,000
Xaverian Brothers High School, MA	$1,200,000
Xavier College Preparatory, AZ	$850,000
Xavier University Preparatory School, LA	$20,000
York Country Day School, PA	$215,000
Zurich International School, Switzerland	97,500 Swiss francs

SCHOOLS REPORTING THAT THEY OFFER ENGLISH AS A SECOND LANGUAGE

Academia Cotopaxi, Ecuador
Academie Sainte Cecile International School, ON, Canada
Academy of the New Church Girls' School, PA
Accelerated Schools, CO
ACS Cobham International School, United Kingdom
ACS Egham International School, United Kingdom
ACS Hillingdon International School, United Kingdom

Aiglon College, Switzerland
Albert College, ON, Canada
Allen Academy, TX
Alliance Academy, Ecuador
Allison Academy, FL
American Academy, FL
American Community Schools of Athens, Greece
American Heritage School, FL
The American International School, Austria
American International School, Dhaka, Bangladesh
American International School of Bucharest, Romania
American International School Rotterdam, Netherlands
The American School Foundation, Mexico
The American School in London, United Kingdom
The American School of Madrid, Spain
American School of Milan, Italy
American School of Paris, France
The American School of The Hague, Netherlands
Andrews Osborne Academy, OH
Antelope Valley Christian School, CA
Army and Navy Academy, CA
Ashbury College, ON, Canada
The Athenian School, CA
Atlanta International School, GA
The Awty International School, TX
Balmoral Hall School, MB, Canada
Baptist High School, NJ
Barnstable Academy, NJ
Bavarian International School, Germany
The Beekman School, NY
Bellevue Christian School, WA
The Bement School, MA
Berkshire School, MA
Besant Hill School, CA
Bishop Brady High School, NH
The Bishop Strachan School, ON, Canada
Blanchet School, OR
The Blue Ridge School, VA
Bodwell High School, BC, Canada
The Bolles School, FL
Boston College High School, MA
Boston Trinity Academy, MA
Brenau Academy, GA
Brewster Academy, NH
Bridge School, CO
Brimmer and May School, MA
Brockwood Park School, United Kingdom
Bronte College of Canada, ON, Canada
Burr and Burton Academy, VT
Buxton School, MA
Canadian Academy, Japan
Canterbury School, CT
Canyonville Christian Academy, OR
Cape Henry Collegiate School, VA
Capistrano Valley Christian Schools, CA
Cardigan Mountain School, NH
Carlisle School, VA
Carlucci American International School of Lisbon, Portugal
Carrabassett Valley Academy, ME
Carson Long Military Institute, PA
Cascadilla School, NY
Century High School, BC, Canada
Chaminade College Preparatory School, MO
Chapel Hill–Chauncy Hall School, MA
Chapel School, Brazil
Charlotte Country Day School, NC
Cheshire Academy, CT
Children's Creative and Performing Arts Academy—Capa Division, CA
Chinese Christian Schools, CA
Christchurch School, VA
Christian Junior–Senior High School, CA
Christ School, NC
Colegio Bolivar, Colombia
Colegio Franklin D. Roosevelt, Peru
Colegio Nueva Granada, Colombia
Colegio Puertorriqueno de Ninas, PR
College du Leman International School, Switzerland
The Colorado Rocky Mountain School, CO
Columbia International College of Canada, ON, Canada
Columbia International School, Japan
Conserve School, WI
Copenhagen International School, Denmark
Cotter Schools, MN
Crawford Adventist Academy, ON, Canada
The Culver Academies, IN
Cushing Academy, MA
Darlington School, GA
Darrow School, NY
Drew School, CA
Dublin School, NH
Eaglebrook School, MA
Eastern Christian High School, NJ
Ecole d'Humanité, Switzerland
Ecole Internationale de Boston / International School of Boston, MA
Elmwood School, ON, Canada
Elves Child Development Centre, AB, Canada
Emerson Honors High Schools, CA
Emma Willard School, NY
Escola Americana de Campinas, Brazil
Fay School, MA
The Fessenden School, MA
Fieldstone Day School, ON, Canada
Flintridge Sacred Heart Academy, CA
The Forman School, CT
Forsyth Country Day School, NC
Fort Lauderdale Preparatory School, FL
Fountain Valley School of Colorado, CO
Foxcroft Academy, ME
Fox River Country Day School, IL
French-American School of New York, NY
Fryeburg Academy, ME
Gables Academy, GA
Garden School, NY
Garrison Forest School, MD
George School, PA
George Stevens Academy, ME
Georgetown Preparatory School, MD
Germantown Friends School, PA
The Glenholme School, CT
Gould Academy, ME
The Governor French Academy, IL
The Governor's Academy (formerly Governor Dummer Academy), MA
The Grand River Academy, OH
The Grauer School, CA
Great Lakes Christian High School, ON, Canada

Green Meadow Waldorf School, NY
Greensboro Day School, NC
Greenwood Laboratory School, MO
Guerin College Preparatory High School, IL
The Gunnery, CT
Gunston Day School, MD
Hamilton District Christian High, ON, Canada
Hargrave Military Academy, VA
Hawaiian Mission Academy, HI
Hawai'i Preparatory Academy, HI
Hebron Academy, ME
Heritage Hall, OK
High Mowing School, NH
Hillcrest Christian School, CA
Hillside School, MA
The Hockaday School, TX
Hokkaido International School, Japan
Hoosac School, NY
Horizons School, GA
Houghton Academy, NY
Howe Military School, IN
The Hudson School, NJ
The Hun School of Princeton, NJ
Idyllwild Arts Academy, CA
Imperial College of Toronto, ON, Canada
Indian Mountain School, CT
Interlochen Arts Academy, MI
International College Spain, Spain
International High School, CA
International School Bangkok, Thailand
International School Eerde, Netherlands
International School Hamburg, Germany
International School Manila, Philippines
The International School of Aberdeen, United Kingdom
International School of Amsterdam, Netherlands
International School of Aruba, Aruba
International School of Athens, Greece
International School of Berne, Switzerland
The International School of Geneva, Switzerland
International School of Lausanne, Switzerland
The International School of London, United Kingdom
International School of Milan, Italy
The International School of Paris, France
Iolani School, HI
Karachi American School, Pakistan
Kent School, CT
Kents Hill School, ME
The King's Academy, TN
The King's Christian High School, NJ
King's-Edgehill School, NS, Canada
Kingsway College, ON, Canada
The Knox School, NY
Knoxville Catholic High School, TN
Koinonia Christian School, AB, Canada
Lake Forest Academy, IL
Lake Ridge Academy, OH
La Lumiere School, IN
Lancaster Mennonite High School, PA
Lansdale Catholic High School, PA
Lansing Christian School, MI
Laurel Springs School, CA
Laurel View Academy, ON, Canada
Lausanne Collegiate School, TN
Lawrence Academy, MA
Lee Academy, ME
Lehigh Valley Christian High School, PA
Le Lycee Francais de Los Angeles, CA
Lexington Christian Academy, MA
Linden Hall, PA
Linden Hill School, MA
The Linden School, ON, Canada
Los Angeles Lutheran High School, CA
Lourdes Catholic High School, AZ
Luther College High School, SK, Canada
Lycee Claudel, ON, Canada
Lycee Français de New York, NY
Lydia Patterson Institute, TX
Lyndon Institute, VT
The MacDuffie School, MA
MacLachlan College, ON, Canada
Maine Central Institute, ME
Manlius Pebble Hill School, NY
Marianapolis Preparatory School, CT
Marian Baker School, Costa Rica
The Marvelwood School, CT
Marylawn of the Oranges, NJ
Marymount International School, Italy
Marymount International School, United Kingdom
Massanutten Military Academy, VA
The Masters School, NY
Maumee Valley Country Day School, OH
Maur Hill-Mount Academy, KS
Memorial Hall School, TX
Menaul School, NM
Mennonite Collegiate Institute, MB, Canada
Mentor College, ON, Canada
Mercedes College, Australia
Merchiston Castle School, United Kingdom
Mid-Pacific Institute, HI
Miller School, VA
Miss Hall's School, MA
Mississauga Private School, ON, Canada
Missouri Military Academy, MO
Miss Porter's School, CT
Monsignor Donovan High School, NJ
Montverde Academy, FL
Munich International School, Germany
Nancy Campbell Collegiate Institute, ON, Canada
National High School, GA
Nebraska Christian Schools, NE
Newbury Park Adventist Academy, CA
New Hampton School, NH
The Newman School, MA
New York Military Academy, NY
Niagara Christian Community of Schools, ON, Canada
The North Broward Preparatory Upper School, FL
North Country School, NY
Northfield Mount Hermon School, MA
The Northwest School, WA
Northwest Yeshiva High School, WA
Northwood School, NY
The Norwich Free Academy, CT
Oak Grove Lutheran School, ND
Oak Grove School, CA
Oak Hill Academy, VA
The Oakland School, PA
Oak Ridge Military Academy, NC
Oakwood Friends School, NY

Ojai Valley School, CA
Olney Friends School, OH
Oneida Baptist Institute, KY
Orangewood Adventist Academy, CA
Oregon Episcopal School, OR
Orinda Academy, CA
The Orme School, AZ
Our Lady Academy, MS
Our Lady of Mercy High School, NY
The Oxford Academy, CT
Oxford School, CA
The Park School of Buffalo, NY
The Pennington School, NJ
Peoples Christian Academy, ON, Canada
Perkiomen School, PA
The Phelps School, PA
Phoenix Christian Unified Schools, AZ
Pinewood—The International School of Thessaloniki, Greece, Greece
Pope John XXIII Regional High School, NJ
Porter-Gaud School, SC
Portland Lutheran School, OR
The Prairie School, WI
Professional Children's School, NY
Purnell School, NJ
The Putney School, VT
Queen Margaret's School, BC, Canada
Queensway Christian College, ON, Canada
Rabbi Alexander S. Gross Hebrew Academy, FL
Rabun Gap-Nacoochee School, GA
Randolph-Macon Academy, VA
Ravenscroft School, NC
The Rectory School, CT
Redemption Christian Academy, NY
Richmond Christian School, BC, Canada
Ridley College, ON, Canada
Riverside Military Academy, GA
Riverstone International School, ID
Rockland Country Day School, NY
Rock Point School, VT
Rocky Hill School, RI
Rolling Hills Preparatory School, CA
Rosseau Lake College, ON, Canada
Ross School, NY
Rothesay Netherwood School, NB, Canada
Rotterdam International Secondary School, Wolfert van Borselen, Netherlands
Royal Canadian College, BC, Canada
Rumsey Hall School, CT
Sacred Heart School of Halifax, NS, Canada
St. Andrew's College, ON, Canada
St. Andrew's Priory School, HI
Saint Andrew's School, FL
St. Andrew's School, RI
St. Andrew's–Sewanee School, TN
St. Anne's–Belfield School, VA
St. Anthony Catholic High School, TX
Saint Augustine Preparatory School, NJ
St. Benedict's Preparatory School, NJ
St. Catherine's Military Academy, CA
Saint Cecilia High School, NE
St. Clement School, ON, Canada
St. Croix Lutheran High School, MN
St. Dominic's International School, Portugal, Portugal
Saint Edward's School, FL
Saint Francis School, HI
St. George's School of Montreal, QC, Canada
St. Johnsbury Academy, VT
St. John's Catholic Prep, MD
St. John's International, BC, Canada
St. John's Northwestern Military Academy, WI
Saint John's Preparatory School, MN
St. John's-Ravenscourt School, MB, Canada
St. Jude's School, ON, Canada
St. Margaret's School, VA
St. Margaret's School, BC, Canada
St. Mary's International School, Japan
St. Mary's Preparatory School, MI
Saint Maur International School, Japan
Saint Patrick High School, IL
St. Patrick's Regional Secondary, BC, Canada
St. Stanislaus College, MS
St. Stephen's Episcopal School, TX
St. Stephen's School, Rome, Italy
Saint Thomas More School, CT
St. Timothy's School, MD
Salem Academy, NC
San Domenico School, CA
Sandy Spring Friends School, MD
San Marcos Baptist Academy, TX
Scarborough Christian School, ON, Canada
Scattergood Friends School, IA
SCECGS Redlands, Australia
School for Young Performers, NY
Seattle Lutheran High School, WA
Sedbergh School, QC, Canada
Seisen International School, Japan
Seoul Foreign School, Republic of Korea
Shattuck-St. Mary's School, MN
Sheila Morrison School, ON, Canada
Shenandoah Valley Academy, VA
Solebury School, PA
Solomon Learning Institute, Ltd., AB, Canada
South Kent School, CT
Southwestern Academy, AZ
Southwestern Academy, CA
Squaw Valley Academy, CA
St Leonards School and Sixth Form College, United Kingdom
Stoneleigh–Burnham School, MA
The Stony Brook School, NY
Storm King School, NY
Stratton Mountain School, VT
Subiaco Academy, AR
Suffield Academy, CT
Tabor Academy, MA
Tallulah Falls School, GA
TASIS The American School in England, United Kingdom
TASIS, The American School in Switzerland, Switzerland
Thomas Jefferson School, MO
Tilton School, NH
Toronto District Christian High School, ON, Canada
Toronto Waldorf School, ON, Canada
Town Centre Private High School, ON, Canada
Trafalgar Castle School, ON, Canada
Trinity College School, ON, Canada
Trinity-Pawling School, NY
United Nations International School, NY
The United World College—USA, NM

University School of Jackson, TN
Valley Christian High School, CA
Verdala International School, Malta
Verde Valley School, AZ
Victor Valley Christian School, CA
Villanova Preparatory School, CA
Walnut Hill School, MA
Wasatch Academy, UT
Washington Academy, ME
Washington International School, DC
Watkinson School, CT
The Webb School, TN
West Nottingham Academy, MD
Westover School, CT
Westtown School, PA
The White Mountain School, NH
The Williston Northampton School, MA
Willow Wood School, ON, Canada
The Winchendon School, MA
The Windsor School, NY
The Woodhall School, CT
Woodlands Academy of the Sacred Heart, IL
Woodstock School, India
Wooster School, CT
Worcester Academy, MA
Wyoming Seminary, PA
York Country Day School, PA
Zurich International School, Switzerland

SCHOOLS REPORTING A COMMUNITY SERVICE REQUIREMENT

Abington Friends School, PA
Academia Cotopaxi, Ecuador
Academy at Swift River, MA
The Academy for Gifted Children (PACE), ON, Canada
Academy of Mount Saint Ursula, NY
Academy of Our Lady of Mercy, CT
Academy of Our Lady of Peace, CA
Academy of the Holy Angels, NJ
Academy of the Holy Names, FL
Academy of the Sacred Heart, LA
Academy of the Sacred Heart, MI
The Agnes Irwin School, PA
Airdrie Koinonia Christian School, AB, Canada
Allison Academy, FL
All Saints' Episcopal School of Fort Worth, TX
American Academy, FL
American Christian Academy, AL
American Heritage School, FL
American International School of Bucharest, Romania
The American School Foundation, Mexico
Andrews Osborne Academy, OH
Archbishop Curley High School, MD
Archbishop McNicholas High School, OH
Archbishop Riordan High School, CA
Archbishop Spalding High School, MD
Armona Union Academy, CA
Ashbury College, ON, Canada
Assumption High School, KY
The Athenian School, CA
Atlanta International School, GA
Aurora Central High School, IL
The Awty International School, TX
Bakersfield Christian High School, CA
Bancroft School, MA
The Barrie School, MD
The Barstow School, MO
Bass Memorial Academy, MS
Battle Ground Academy, TN
Beaver Country Day School, MA
Bellevue Christian School, WA
The Bement School, MA
Benedictine High School, OH
Benedictine Military School, GA
Berkeley Preparatory School, FL
Berkshire School, MA
The Birch Wathen Lenox School, NY
Bishop Brady High School, NH
Bishop Carroll High School, PA
Bishop Conaty-Our Lady of Loretto High School, CA
Bishop Connolly High School, MA
Bishop Eustace Preparatory School, NJ
Bishop Fenwick High School, OH
Bishop Garcia Diego High School, CA
Bishop Gorman High School, NV
Bishop Guertin High School, NH
Bishop Ireton High School, VA
Bishop Kelly High School, ID
Bishop Lynch Catholic High School, TX
Bishop McGuinness Catholic High School, NC
Bishop Stang High School, MA
The Bishop Strachan School, ON, Canada
Blanchet School, OR
Boston College High School, MA
Boston University Academy, MA
The Boys' Latin School of Maryland, MD
The Branson School, CA
Breck School, MN
Brentwood School, CA
Briarwood Christian High School, AL
Brimmer and May School, MA
Brooks School, MA
Brophy College Preparatory, AZ
Brother Martin High School, LA
The Browning School, NY
Brunswick School, CT
The Bryn Mawr School for Girls, MD
Buckingham Browne & Nichols School, MA
The Buckley School, CA
Buffalo Seminary, NY
Burr and Burton Academy, VT
The Bush School, WA
Butte Central High School, MT
The Calhoun School, NY
The Cambridge School of Weston, MA
Campbell Hall (Episcopal), CA
Cannon School, NC
Canterbury School, FL
The Canterbury School of Florida, FL
Cape Cod Academy, MA
Cape Fear Academy, NC
Cape Henry Collegiate School, VA
Cardinal Mooney High School, FL
Cardinal Newman High School, CA
Cardinal Newman High School, FL
Cardinal Newman School, SC

Carrollton School of the Sacred Heart, FL
Cascadilla School, NY
Cascia Hall Preparatory School, OK
Cathedral High School, IN
The Catholic High School of Baltimore, MD
The Catlin Gabel School, OR
Central Catholic High School, CA
Central Valley Christian Academy, CA
CFS, The School at Church Farm, PA
Chaminade College Preparatory, CA
Chaminade College Preparatory School, MO
Chaminade-Madonna College Preparatory, FL
Chapel Hill–Chauncy Hall School, MA
Charlotte Country Day School, NC
Cheshire Academy, CT
Chestnut Hill Academy, PA
Cheverus High School, ME
Children's Creative and Performing Arts Academy—
Capa Division, CA
Choate Rosemary Hall, CT
Christian Brothers Academy, NY
Christian School of the Desert, CA
Cincinnati Country Day School, OH
The Collegiate School, VA
Colorado Academy, CO
The Colorado Rocky Mountain School, CO
The Colorado Springs School, CO
Columbia Grammar and Preparatory School, NY
The Columbus Academy, OH
Commonwealth School, MA
Connelly School of the Holy Child, MD
Convent of the Sacred Heart, CT
Cornelia Connelly School, CA
Cotter Schools, MN
Country Day School of the Sacred Heart, PA
The Craig School, NJ
Crespi Carmelite High School, CA
Crossroads School for Arts & Sciences, CA
The Culver Academies, IN
Currey Ingram Academy, TN
Dallas Academy, TX
The Dalton School, NY
Dana Hall School, MA
David Lipscomb High School, TN
Deerfield-Windsor School, GA
Delaware Valley Friends School, PA
De Smet Jesuit High School, MO
Devon Preparatory School, PA
Dickinson Trinity, ND
Donelson Christian Academy, TN
Dowling Catholic High School, IA
Duchesne Academy of the Sacred Heart, TX
Durham Academy, NC
Dwight-Englewood School, NJ
Eaglebrook School, MA
Eagle Hill School, MA
Eastern Christian High School, NJ
Eastside Catholic School, WA
Ecole d'Humanité, Switzerland
Elizabeth Seton High School, MD
Elyria Catholic High School, OH
Emerson Honors High Schools, CA
The Emery Weiner School, TX
Emma Willard School, NY
Episcopal High School of Jacksonville, FL
The Episcopal School of Dallas, TX
Escola Americana de Campinas, Brazil
The Ethel Walker School, CT
Explorations Academy, WA
Fairfield College Preparatory School, CT
Father Lopez High School, FL
First Baptist Academy, TX
Flint Hill School, VA
Flintridge Sacred Heart Academy, CA
Fontbonne Academy, MA
Forest Lake Academy, FL
Forsyth Country Day School, NC
Fort Worth Country Day School, TX
Foxcroft Academy, ME
Franklin Road Academy, TN
Fryeburg Academy, ME
Fuqua School, VA
Gables Academy, GA
Garces Memorial High School, CA
Gaston Day School, NC
Gateway School, TX
George School, PA
Georgetown Day School, DC
Georgetown Preparatory School, MD
Georgetown Visitation Preparatory School, DC
Gilmour Academy, OH
Girard College, PA
Glenelg Country School, MD
Gonzaga College High School, DC
The Governor's Academy (formerly Governor Dummer
Academy), MA
The Gow School, NY
The Grand River Academy, OH
The Grauer School, CA
Greenfield School, NC
Greenhill School, TX
Greenhills School, MI
Greenleaf Academy, ID
Greenwich Academy, CT
Griggs University and International Academy, MD
Guamani Private School, PR
Gulliver Preparatory School, FL
Gunston Day School, MD
Halstrom High School—San Diego, CA
Hamilton District Christian High, ON, Canada
Hanalani Schools, HI
The Harker School, CA
The Harley School, NY
Harrells Christian Academy, NC
The Harrisburg Academy, PA
Harvard-Westlake School, CA
Havergal College, ON, Canada
Hawaiian Mission Academy, HI
Hawken School, OH
Head-Royce School, CA
Headwaters Academy, MT
Heritage Hall, OK
Highland Hall, A Waldorf School, CA
Highland School, VA
High Mowing School, NH
Hillcrest Christian School, CA
Hilton Head Preparatory School, SC
The Hockaday School, TX

Holderness School, NH
The Holton-Arms School, MD
Hopkins School, CT
The Horace Mann School, NY
Horizons School, GA
The Hudson School, NJ
The Hun School of Princeton, NJ
Hutchison School, TN
Hyman Brand Hebrew Academy of Greater Kansas City, KS
Immaculate Conception High School, NJ
Immaculate High School, CT
Independent School, KS
International College Spain, Spain
International School Bangkok, Thailand
International School of Amsterdam, Netherlands
International School of Aruba, Aruba
International School of Athens, Greece
International School of Lausanne, Switzerland
The International School of London, United Kingdom
Jack M. Barrack Hebrew Academy (formerly Akiba Hebrew Academy), PA
Jesuit College Preparatory School, TX
Jesuit High School, CA
Jesuit High School of Tampa, FL
Junipero Serra High School, CA
Karachi American School, Pakistan
Keith Country Day School, IL
Kent Denver School, CO
Kerr-Vance Academy, NC
Kimberton Waldorf School, PA
Kings Christian School, CA
King's Ridge Christian School, GA
Kingswood-Oxford School, CT
Lake Forest Academy, IL
Lakeside School, WA
Lakeview Academy, GA
La Lumiere School, IN
La Salle Academy, RI
La Salle High School, FL
The Laureate Academy, MB, Canada
Lawrence School, OH
The Lawrenceville School, NJ
Lexington Christian Academy, MA
Lincoln School, RI
Linfield Christian School, CA
Little Red School House and Elisabeth Irwin High School, NY
Logos School, MO
Louisville High School, CA
Loyola High School, Jesuit College Preparatory, CA
Lutheran High School North, MO
Lutheran High School Northwest, MI
MacLachlan College, ON, Canada
Maret School, DC
Marianapolis Preparatory School, CT
Marin Academy, CA
Marist School, GA
Marmion Academy, IL
Marquette University High School, WI
Marshall School, MN
Mars Hill Bible School, AL
The Marvelwood School, CT
Maryknoll School, HI
Marylawn of the Oranges, NJ
Marymount High School, CA
Marymount School, NY
Maryvale Preparatory School, MD
Matignon High School, MA
Maumee Valley Country Day School, OH
McDonogh School, MD
McQuaid Jesuit, NY
The Meadows School, NV
Memorial Hall School, TX
Menaul School, NM
Menlo School, CA
Mercy High School, CA
Mercy High School, CT
Mercy High School College Preparatory, CA
Mesa Grande Seventh-Day Academy, CA
Miami Country Day School, FL
Mid-Peninsula High School, CA
Milken Community High School of Stephen S. Wise Temple, CA
Miller School, VA
Miss Hall's School, MA
Miss Porter's School, CT
Moorestown Friends School, NJ
Moreau Catholic High School, CA
Morristown-Beard School, NJ
Mounds Park Academy, MN
Mount Michael Benedictine School, NE
Mt. Saint Dominic Academy, NJ
Munich International School, Germany
National Cathedral School, DC
National Sports Academy at Lake Placid, NY
Nerinx Hall, MO
Newark Academy, NJ
Newbury Park Adventist Academy, CA
New Hampton School, NH
New York Military Academy, NY
Noble and Greenough School, MA
The Nora School, MD
Norfolk Academy, VA
The North Broward Preparatory Upper School, FL
North Cobb Christian School, GA
North Shore Country Day School, IL
Northside Christian School, FL
The Northwest Academy, OR
Northwest Catholic High School, CT
Northwest Yeshiva High School, WA
Notre Dame Academy, CA
Notre Dame Academy, MA
Notre Dame Academy, VA
Notre Dame-Cathedral Latin School, OH
Notre Dame High School, NJ
Notre Dame Preparatory School, MD
Oak Grove School, CA
Oak Mountain Academy, GA
Oak Ridge Military Academy, NC
The Oakridge School, TX
Oakwood Friends School, NY
O'Dea High School, WA
Oldenburg Academy, IN
Olney Friends School, OH
The O'Neal School, NC
Orinda Academy, CA
The Orme School, AZ
Out-Of-Door-Academy, FL
The Overlake School, WA

The Oxford Academy, CT
Pace Academy, GA
Pacific Academy, CA
Pacific Hills School, CA
The Packer Collegiate Institute, NY
The Paideia School, GA
Palma High School, CA
Paradise Adventist Academy, CA
The Park School of Buffalo, NY
Peddie School, NJ
Perkiomen School, PA
The Phelps School, PA
The Pingry School, NJ
Pioneer Valley Christian School, MA
Poly Prep Country Day School, NY
Pope John XXIII Regional High School, NJ
Portland Lutheran School, OR
Portledge School, NY
Poughkeepsie Day School, NY
Powers Catholic High School, MI
The Prairie School, WI
Pulaski Academy, AR
Queen Margaret's School, BC, Canada
Queensway Christian College, ON, Canada
Rabbi Alexander S. Gross Hebrew Academy, FL
Ravenscroft School, NC
Rice High School, NY
Riverdale Country School, NY
The Rivers School, MA
Rockland Country Day School, NY
Rock Point School, VT
Rocky Hill School, RI
Rocky Mount Academy, NC
Roland Park Country School, MD
Ross School, NY
Rutgers Preparatory School, NJ
Sacramento Adventist Academy, CA
Sacramento Country Day School, CA
Sacramento Waldorf School, CA
Sacred Heart School of Halifax, NS, Canada
Sage Ridge School, NV
St. Agnes Academy, TX
St. Albans School, DC
St. Andrew's College, ON, Canada
St. Andrew's Episcopal School, MD
St. Andrew's Episcopal School, MS
St. Andrew's on the Marsh School, GA
St. Andrew's Priory School, HI
Saint Andrew's School, FL
St. Andrew's–Sewanee School, TN
St. Anne's–Belfield School, VA
St. Anselm's Abbey School, DC
St. Augustine High School, TX
Saint Basil Academy, PA
St. Brendan High School, FL
St. Christopher's School, VA
St. Croix Country Day School, VI
St. David's School, NC
Saint Dominic Academy, NJ
Saint Edward's School, FL
Saint Elizabeth High School, CA
St. Francis de Sales High School, OH
St. Francis High School, KY
St. Francis School, GA
Saint Francis School, HI
Saint George's School, WA
Saint Gertrude High School, VA
St. Gregory College Preparatory School, AZ
Saint James School, MD
St. John's College High School, DC
St. John's Northwestern Military Academy, WI
St. Joseph High School, CT
Saint Joseph High School, IL
St. Joseph's Catholic School, SC
St. Margaret's Episcopal School, CA
St. Margaret's School, VA
St. Mark's School of Texas, TX
St. Martin's Episcopal School, LA
St. Mary's Academy, CO
Saint Mary's High School, AZ
St. Mary's International School, Japan
St. Mary's School, OR
Saint Monica's High School, CA
Saint Patrick High School, IL
Saint Patrick's School, KY
Saint Paul Lutheran High School, MO
St. Paul's Episcopal School, AL
St. Paul's School, MD
St. Paul's School, NH
St. Paul's School for Girls, MD
St. Peter's Preparatory School, NJ
St. Stephen's & St. Agnes School, VA
Saint Stephen's Episcopal School, FL
St. Stephen's Episcopal School, TX
Saint Teresa's Academy, MO
Saint Thomas Academy, MN
St. Thomas Aquinas High School, NH
St. Timothy's School, MD
Salesian High School, NY
Salesianum School, DE
San Domenico School, CA
Sandy Spring Friends School, MD
San Francisco University High School, CA
Santa Fe Preparatory School, NM
Santa Margarita Catholic High School, CA
Sayre School, KY
Scattergood Friends School, IA
School of the Holy Child, NY
Seabury Hall, HI
Seattle Academy of Arts and Sciences, WA
Seattle Lutheran High School, WA
The Seven Hills School, OH
Sewickley Academy, PA
Shannon Forest Christian School, SC
Shattuck-St. Mary's School, MN
The Shipley School, PA
Smith School, NY
Solebury School, PA
Southwestern Academy, AZ
Southwestern Academy, CA
Staten Island Academy, NY
Stephen T. Badin High School, OH
Storm King School, NY
Strake Jesuit College Preparatory, TX
Stratford Academy, GA
Stratton Mountain School, VT
Stuart Country Day School of the Sacred Heart, NJ
The Study School, QC, Canada

Subiaco Academy, AR
Tandem Friends School, VA
TASIS The American School in England, United Kingdom
TASIS, The American School in Switzerland, Switzerland
The Tatnall School, DE
Thomas Jefferson School, MO
Thornton Friends School, MD
Tilton School, NH
Tower Hill School, DE
Tri-City Christian Schools, CA
Trinity Catholic High School, MA
Trinity Christian Academy, TX
Trinity College School, ON, Canada
Trinity Episcopal School, VA
Trinity High School, KY
Trinity Valley School, TX
United Nations International School, NY
The United World College—USA, NM
University Liggett School, MI
University of Chicago Laboratory Schools, IL
University of Toronto Schools, ON, Canada
University Prep, WA
University School of Jackson, TN
University School of Milwaukee, WI
University School of Nova Southeastern University, FL
The Urban School of San Francisco, CA
Ursuline Academy, DE
Ursuline Academy, MA
The Ursuline Academy of Dallas, TX
Valle Catholic High School, MO
Valwood School, GA
Vianney High School, MO
Viewpoint School, CA
Villa Duchesne/Oak Hill School, MO
Villa Maria Academy, PA
Villanova Preparatory School, CA
Virginia Beach Friends School, VA
Visitation Academy of St. Louis County, MO
Waldorf High School of Massachusetts Bay, MA
Wasatch Academy, UT
Washington International School, DC
The Waverly School, CA
Wayne Country Day School, NC
Waynflete School, ME
The Wellington School, OH
Wesleyan Academy, PR
Westbury Christian School, TX
Westminster Catawba Christian, SC
Westminster Christian School, FL
Westover School, CT
Westridge School, CA
Whitefield Academy, GA
The White Mountain School, NH
Willow Wood School, ON, Canada
Wilmington Friends School, DE
Wilson Hall, SC
Windermere Preparatory School, FL
Winston Preparatory School, NY
The Winston School San Antonio, TX
Woodlands Academy of the Sacred Heart, IL
Woodside Priory School, CA
Woodstock School, India
Wooster School, CT
Worcester Academy, MA
Wyoming Seminary, PA
Xavier College Preparatory, AZ
Yokohama International School, Japan
York Country Day School, PA
York Preparatory School, NY
Zurich International School, Switzerland

SCHOOLS REPORTING EXCHANGE PROGRAMS WITH OTHER U.S. SCHOOLS

Academy of the Sacred Heart, MI
Ahliyyah School for Girls, Jordan
Albuquerque Academy, NM
The Athenian School, CA
The Bush School, WA
The Calhoun School, NY
Carrollton School of the Sacred Heart, FL
The Catlin Gabel School, OR
Commonwealth Parkville School, PR
Convent of the Sacred Heart, CT
Convent of the Sacred Heart, NY
Country Day School of the Sacred Heart, PA
Doane Stuart School, NY
Dublin School, NH
Duchesne Academy of the Sacred Heart, TX
Germantown Friends School, PA
Havergal College, ON, Canada
Maumee Valley Country Day School, OH
Ridley College, ON, Canada
Sacred Heart School of Halifax, NS, Canada
St. Benedict's Preparatory School, NJ
St. Paul's School for Girls, MD
St. Stephen's School, Rome, Italy
Salesianum School, DE
San Francisco University High School, CA
School of the Holy Child, NY
The Shipley School, PA
Trafalgar Castle School, ON, Canada
The Urban School of San Francisco, CA
Villa Duchesne/Oak Hill School, MO
Woodlands Academy of the Sacred Heart, IL

SCHOOLS REPORTING PROGRAMS FOR STUDY ABROAD

The Academy at Charlemont, MA
Academy for Global Exploration, OR
Advanced Academy of Georgia, GA
The Agnes Irwin School, PA
Albuquerque Academy, NM
Alexander Dawson School, CO
The Altamont School, AL
American Christian Academy, AL
Annie Wright School, WA
Archmere Academy, DE
Argo Academy, FL
Ashbury College, ON, Canada
The Athenian School, CA
Atlanta International School, GA
Bancroft School, MA
Belmont Hill School, MA
The Bement School, MA
Berkeley Preparatory School, FL

Berkshire School, MA
Berwick Academy, ME
The Birch Wathen Lenox School, NY
Bishop Guertin High School, NH
The Bishop Strachan School, ON, Canada
Blair Academy, NJ
The Blake School, MN
Boston College High School, MA
The Branson School, CA
The Brearley School, NY
Brewster Academy, NH
Brockwood Park School, United Kingdom
Brooks School, MA
Brophy College Preparatory, AZ
The Bryn Mawr School for Girls, MD
Buckingham Browne & Nichols School, MA
The Buckley School, CA
Burke Mountain Academy, VT
Burr and Burton Academy, VT
The Bush School, WA
The Cambridge School of Weston, MA
Canterbury School, FL
The Canterbury School of Florida, FL
Cape Cod Academy, MA
Carrollton School of the Sacred Heart, FL
Cascia Hall Preparatory School, OK
Cate School, CA
The Catlin Gabel School, OR
Chadwick School, CA
The Chapin School, NY
Charlotte Country Day School, NC
Charlotte Latin School, NC
Chase Collegiate School, CT
Chestnut Hill Academy, PA
Choate Rosemary Hall, CT
Cincinnati Country Day School, OH
The Colorado Springs School, CO
Columbia International School, Japan
Commonwealth School, MA
Community School, NH
The Community School of Naples, FL
Concord Academy, MA
Convent of the Sacred Heart, CT
Convent of the Sacred Heart, NY
Cotter Schools, MN
The Country Day School, ON, Canada
Country Day School of the Sacred Heart, PA
Crystal Springs Uplands School, CA
Dana Hall School, MA
Deerfield Academy, MA
Doane Stuart School, NY
Dwight-Englewood School, NJ
Elmwood School, ON, Canada
Emma Willard School, NY
Episcopal High School, VA
Episcopal High School of Jacksonville, FL
Escola Americana de Campinas, Brazil
The Ethel Walker School, CT
Falmouth Academy, MA
Fort Worth Country Day School, TX
Foxcroft School, VA
Franklin Academy, CT
Gann Academy (The New Jewish High School of Greater Boston), MA
Georgetown Preparatory School, MD
Germantown Friends School, PA
Gill St. Bernard's School, NJ
Gould Academy, ME
The Governor's Academy (formerly Governor Dummer Academy), MA
The Grauer School, CA
Greater Atlanta Christian Schools, GA
Green Meadow Waldorf School, NY
Greensboro Day School, NC
Greens Farms Academy, CT
Greenwich Academy, CT
Groton School, MA
The Gunnery, CT
Hammond School, SC
The Harley School, NY
Harvard-Westlake School, CA
Hathaway Brown School, OH
Havergal College, ON, Canada
Hawken School, OH
Hayden High School, KS
Head-Royce School, CA
Hebrew Academy-the Five Towns, NY
Highland Hall, A Waldorf School, CA
High Mowing School, NH
The Hill School, PA
The Hockaday School, TX
Holderness School, NH
Holy Innocents' Episcopal School, GA
Hopkins School, CT
The Hotchkiss School, CT
The Hudson School, NJ
Hutchison School, TN
International High School, CA
Jack M. Barrack Hebrew Academy (formerly Akiba Hebrew Academy), PA
Keith Country Day School, IL
Kents Hill School, ME
Kentucky Country Day School, KY
Kimball Union Academy, NH
Kimberton Waldorf School, PA
King George School, VT
King's-Edgehill School, NS, Canada
Kingswood-Oxford School, CT
The Knox School, NY
Lakefield College School, ON, Canada
Lake Forest Academy, IL
Lakeside School, WA
Landon School, MD
Lawrence Academy, MA
The Lawrenceville School, NJ
Lincoln School, RI
Linden Hall, PA
Little Red School House and Elisabeth Irwin High School, NY
The Loomis Chaffee School, CT
Louisville Collegiate School, KY
The Lovett School, GA
The Lowell Whiteman School, CO
Loyola School, NY
Lutheran High School, MO
Luther College High School, SK, Canada
Lycee Français de New York, NY
Maine Central Institute, ME
Maine School of Science and Mathematics, ME

Manlius Pebble Hill School, NY
Maret School, DC
Marian Baker School, Costa Rica
Marin Academy, CA
Marymount School, NY
The Masters School, NY
Matignon High School, MA
Maumee Valley Country Day School, OH
The McCallie School, TN
Meadowridge School, BC, Canada
Memphis University School, TN
Mercersburg Academy, PA
Merchiston Castle School, United Kingdom
Milken Community High School of Stephen S. Wise Temple, CA
Millbrook School, NY
Milton Academy, MA
Miss Porter's School, CT
Montgomery Bell Academy, TN
Moorestown Friends School, NJ
Morgan Park Academy, IL
Morristown-Beard School, NJ
Mount Bachelor Academy, OR
National Cathedral School, DC
Neuchatel Junior College, Switzerland
Newark Academy, NJ
New Horizon Youth Ministries, IN
The Nichols School, NY
Noble and Greenough School, MA
Norfolk Academy, VA
Northfield Mount Hermon School, MA
North Shore Country Day School, IL
North Yarmouth Academy, ME
Oak Grove Lutheran School, ND
The Oakridge School, TX
Ojai Valley School, CA
Oldfields School, MD
Oregon Episcopal School, OR
The Overlake School, WA
Pace Academy, GA
The Packer Collegiate Institute, NY
Padua Franciscan High School, OH
Park Tudor School, IN
Peddie School, NJ
Phillips Academy (Andover), MA
Phillips Exeter Academy, NH
Phoenix Country Day School, AZ
Polytechnic School, CA
Providence Country Day School, RI
Providence Day School, NC
Pulaski Academy, AR
Punahou School, HI
Purnell School, NJ
Randolph-Macon Academy, VA
Ravenscroft School, NC
Regina High School, OH
Regis High School, NY
Ridley College, ON, Canada
Riverdale Country School, NY
Riverstone International School, ID
Rocky Hill School, RI
Roland Park Country School, MD
Roncalli High School, IN
Rosseau Lake College, ON, Canada
Sacramento Waldorf School, CA
Sacred Heart School of Halifax, NS, Canada
Saddle River Day School, NJ
St. Andrew's College, ON, Canada
St. Andrew's Episcopal School, MS
St. Andrew's on the Marsh School, GA
St. Anthony Catholic High School, TX
Saint Augustine Preparatory School, NJ
St. Catherine's School, VA
Saint Edward's School, FL
St. Francis High School, KY
St. George's School, RI
Saint James School, MD
St. John's Preparatory School, MA
Saint John's Preparatory School, MN
St. Joseph's Preparatory School, PA
St. Margaret's School, VA
Saint Mark's School, MA
Saint Mary's Hall, TX
Saint Mary's High School, MD
St. Paul Academy and Summit School, MN
St. Paul's School, MD
St. Paul's School, NH
St. Paul's School for Girls, MD
St. Peter's Preparatory School, NJ
St. Stephen's & St. Agnes School, VA
St. Stephen's Episcopal School, TX
Salem Academy, NC
Sandia Preparatory School, NM
San Francisco University High School, CA
San Francisco Waldorf High School, CA
Santa Fe Preparatory School, NM
Scattergood Friends School, IA
School for Young Performers, NY
School of the Holy Child, NY
Seattle Academy of Arts and Sciences, WA
Second Baptist School, TX
Sedbergh School, QC, Canada
Sewickley Academy, PA
Shady Side Academy, PA
The Shipley School, PA
Southridge School, BC, Canada
The Spence School, NY
Staten Island Academy, NY
Stephen T. Badin High School, OH
Stevenson School, CA
Stuart Country Day School of the Sacred Heart, NJ
Summerfield Waldorf School, CA
The Summit Country Day School, OH
The Taft School, CT
The Tatnall School, DE
Telluride Mountain School, CO
The Thacher School, CA
Toronto District Christian High School, ON, Canada
Toronto Waldorf School, ON, Canada
Trinity Christian Academy, TX
Trinity College School, ON, Canada
Trinity High School, KY
Trinity School of Midland, TX
University Liggett School, MI
University of Toronto Schools, ON, Canada
University Prep, WA
The Urban School of San Francisco, CA
Valley Forge Military Academy & College, PA

Viewpoint School, CA
Villa Duchesne/Oak Hill School, MO
Virginia Episcopal School, VA
Waldorf High School of Massachusetts Bay, MA
The Waldorf School of Garden City, NY
The Walker School, GA
The Wardlaw-Hartridge School, NJ
Waring School, MA
Washington Waldorf School, MD
Watkinson School, CT
Waynflete School, ME
The Webb School, TN
Webb School of Knoxville, TN
The Wellington School, OH
Western Reserve Academy, OH
West Island College, AB, Canada
Westminster School, CT
The Westminster Schools, GA
Westover School, CT
Westtown School, PA
The Wheeler School, RI
The Williams School, CT
The Williston Northampton School, MA
Willow Wood School, ON, Canada
Wilmington Friends School, DE
Winchester Thurston School, PA
Woodlands Academy of the Sacred Heart, IL
Woodstock School, India
Wooster School, CT
Wyoming Seminary, PA
York Country Day School, PA

SCHOOLS REPORTING SUMMER SESSIONS OPEN TO STUDENTS FROM OTHER SCHOOLS*

Academie Sainte Cecile International School, ON, Canada	A,F
The Academy at Charlemont, MA	F,S
Academy for Global Exploration, OR	A,R,S
Academy of Notre Dame de Namur, PA	A,C,F,S
Academy of Our Lady of Peace, CA	A,C,F,S
Academy of the Holy Cross, MD	A,C,F,S
Academy of the Holy Names, FL	A,F,S
Academy of the New Church Boys' School, PA	A,C,F
Academy of the New Church Girls' School, PA	A,C,F
Academy of the Sacred Heart, MI	A,C,F,S
ACS Cobham International School, United Kingdom	O
ACS Egham International School, United Kingdom	O
ACS Hillingdon International School, United Kingdom	O
Advanced Academy of Georgia, GA	A,F
The Agnes Irwin School, PA	A,C,F,S
Aiglon College, Switzerland	A,S
Albert College, ON, Canada	A
Albuquerque Academy, NM	A,C,F,S
Alexander Dawson School, CO	A,C,F,S
The Alexander School, TX	A,C
Allen Academy, TX	A
Allendale Columbia School, NY	A,F,S
Allison Academy, FL	A
All Saints' Episcopal School of Fort Worth, TX	A,C,F,R,S
The Altamont School, AL	A,C,F,R,S
American Academy, FL	A,C,F
American Community Schools of Athens, Greece	A,C,F,S
American Heritage School, FL	A,C,F
The American School Foundation, Mexico	A,C,F
The American School of Madrid, Spain	A,C,F,S
American School of Paris, France	A,C,F,S
The American School of Puerto Vallarta, Mexico	A,S
Antelope Valley Christian School, CA	A
Archbishop Curley High School, MD	A,F,S
Archbishop Mitty High School, CA	A,C,F,S
Archbishop Rummel High School, LA	A,C,F,R,S
Army and Navy Academy, CA	A,C,F
Ashbury College, ON, Canada	A,C,S
Asheville School, NC	A,C,F,R
Assumption High School, KY	C,F,S
The Athenian School, CA	A,C,F,S
Athens Academy, GA	A,C
Atlanta International School, GA	A,C,F,S
Augusta Christian School (I), GA	A
Augusta Preparatory Day School, GA	A,C,F,S
Aurora Central High School, IL	A,F,S
Baldwin School of Puerto Rico, Inc., PR	A,C
Balmoral Hall School, MB, Canada	A
The Baltimore Actors' Theatre Conservatory, MD	A,F
Bancroft School, MA	A,C,F,S
Baptist High School, NJ	C,S
Barnstable Academy, NJ	A
The Barstow School, MO	A,C,F,S
Battle Ground Academy, TN	A,C,F,S
Bavarian International School, Germany	A,C,F,S
Baylor School, TN	A,C,F,R,S
The Beekman School, NY	A
Belmont Hill School, MA	A,C,F,S
Benedictine High School, OH	A,C,S
Benedictine High School, VA	A
Benilde–St. Margaret's School, MN	F,S
The Benjamin School, FL	A,C,S
Berkeley Preparatory School, FL	A,C,F,S
Berwick Academy, ME	O
Bishop Denis J. O'Connell High School, VA	A,C
Bishop Eustace Preparatory School, NJ	A,S
Bishop Garcia Diego High School, CA	A,C
Bishop Ireton High School, VA	A,C
Bishop Luers High School, IN	A,S
Bishop Lynch Catholic High School, TX	A,F,S
Bishop McNamara High School, IL	A,S
Bishop Montgomery High School, CA	A,C,F,S
Bishop Mora Salesian High School, CA	A,C,F,R,S
The Bishop Strachan School, ON, Canada	A,C,F,R
The Blake School, MN	A,S
Blanchet School, OR	A,S
Blueprint Education, AZ	A
Bodwell High School, BC, Canada	A,C,F,S
The Bolles School, FL	A,C,F
Boston College High School, MA	A,C,F,S
Boston Trinity Academy, MA	A
Boyd-Buchanan School, TN	A,S
Boylan Central Catholic High School, IL	A,F,S
The Boys' Latin School of Maryland, MD	A,S
The Branson School, CA	A,C,F
Brenau Academy, GA	A,F
Brentwood School, CA	A,C,F,S
Brewster Academy, NH	A,C,F,S
Bridgemont High School, CA	S
Bridges Academy, CA	A,C,F
Bronte College of Canada, ON, Canada	A,C
Brooks School, MA	A,C,S

A — academic; C — computer instruction; F — art/fine arts; R — rigorous outdoor training; S — sports; O — other

Brophy College Preparatory, AZ	A,C,F,S
Brother Martin High School, LA	A
Brother Rice High School, MI	A,F
Brownell-Talbot School, NE	A,S
Brunswick School, CT	A
The Bryn Mawr School for Girls, MD	A,F,S
The Buckley School, CA	A,C,F
Bulloch Academy, GA	A,C,F,S
The Byrnes Schools, SC	A
The Calhoun School, NY	F
Calvert Hall College High School, MD	A,C,F,S
The Calverton School, MD	A,C,F,S
The Cambridge School of Weston, MA	F
Camden Military Academy, SC	A,R,S
Camelot Academy, NC	A
Campbell Hall (Episcopal), CA	A,C,F,S
Canadian Academy, Japan	A,S
Canterbury School, FL	A,F,S
The Canterbury School of Florida, FL	A,C,F,S
Cape Fear Academy, NC	A,F,S
Cape Henry Collegiate School, VA	A,C,F,S
Capistrano Valley Christian Schools, CA	A,F,S
Cardigan Mountain School, NH	A,F,S
Cardinal Gibbons High School, NC	S
Cardinal Newman High School, CA	A,C,F
Carlisle School, VA	A,C,F,S
Carolina Day School, NC	A,C,F,S
Carrabassett Valley Academy, ME	A,S
Cary Academy, NC	A,C,F,S
Cascadilla School, NY	A,F
Cascia Hall Preparatory School, OK	F,S
Cathedral High School, NY	A
The Catholic High School of Baltimore, MD	A,F,S
Catholic Memorial, MA	A
The Catlin Gabel School, OR	A,C,F
Central Catholic High School, CA	A
Century High School, BC, Canada	A
Chadwick School, CA	C,F,S
Chamberlain-Hunt Academy, MS	A,R,S
Chaminade College Preparatory, CA	A,C,S
Chaminade College Preparatory School, MO	A,S
Charlotte Christian School, NC	A,C,F,R,S
Charlotte Country Day School, NC	A,C,F,S
Charlotte Latin School, NC	A,C,F,S
Chase Collegiate School, CT	A,C,F,S
Cheshire Academy, CT	S
Cheverus High School, ME	A
Children's Creative and Performing Arts Academy—Capa Division, CA	A,C,F
Chinese Christian Schools, CA	A,S
Choate Rosemary Hall, CT	A,F
Christchurch School, VA	A,S
Christian Brothers Academy, NY	S
Christian Central Academy, NY	S
Christian Junior–Senior High School, CA	A
Cincinnati Country Day School, OH	A,C,F,S
Cistercian Preparatory School, TX	A,C,F,S
Coe-Brown Northwood Academy, NH	A
College du Leman International School, Switzerland	A,C,F,S
The College Preparatory School, CA	A
The Collegiate School, VA	A,C,F,S
Colorado Academy, CO	A,C,F,R,S
The Colorado Springs School, CO	A,F,S
Columbia International College of Canada, ON, Canada	A,F,S
Columbia International School, Japan	A,C,F,S
The Columbus Academy, OH	A,C,F
The Community School, ID	A,C,F,R,S
Concordia Continuing Education High School, AB, Canada	A
Connelly School of the Holy Child, MD	A,F,S
Conserve School, WI	A
Convent of the Sacred Heart, NY	C,F,S
Convent of the Visitation School, MN	A
Copenhagen International School, Denmark	A,C,F,S
Cornelia Connelly School, CA	A
The Country Day School, ON, Canada	A,F
Crawford Day School, VA	A
Crespi Carmelite High School, CA	A,F,S
Cretin-Derham Hall, MN	A,C,F,S
Crossroads College Preparatory School, MO	A,F,S
Crossroads School for Arts & Sciences, CA	A,C,F,S
The Culver Academies, IN	A,C,F,S
Currey Ingram Academy, TN	F
Cushing Academy, MA	A,C,F
Dana Hall School, MA	A,S
Darlington School, GA	A,C,F,S
De La Salle College, ON, Canada	A
Delaware Valley Friends School, PA	A,F
Delbarton School, NJ	A,C,S
DeMatha Catholic High School, MD	A,C,F,S
Denver Academy, CO	A,C,F,R
DePaul Catholic High School, NJ	S
The Derryfield School, NH	F
Detroit Country Day School, MI	A,C,F,S
Duchesne Academy of the Sacred Heart, TX	A,C,F
Dunn School, CA	S
Durham Academy, NC	A,C
Dwight-Englewood School, NJ	A,C,F,S
Eaglebrook School, MA	A,C,F,R,S
Eagle Hill School, MA	A,C,F,S
Eagle Hill-Southport, CT	A
The Education Center, MS	A,C
Elizabeth Seton High School, MD	A,F,S
Elyria Catholic High School, OH	S
Emerson Honors High Schools, CA	A,C,F,S
Episcopal Collegiate School, AR	A,C,F,S
Episcopal High School, TX	A,F
Episcopal High School of Jacksonville, FL	A,C,F,R,S
The Episcopal School of Dallas, TX	A,C,F,R,S
Evansville Day School, IN	A,C,F
Excel Academy, Inc., OH	A,C
Explorations Academy, WA	A,F,R
Fairfield College Preparatory School, CT	A,C,F,S
Fairhill School, TX	A,C
Faith Christian High School, CA	F
Father Ryan High School, TN	A,C,F,S
Fayetteville Academy, NC	A,C,F,S
Fay School, MA	A,C,S
The First Academy, FL	A,F,S
First Presbyterian Day School, GA	A,F,S
Flint Hill School, VA	A,C,F,R,S
Foothills Academy, AB, Canada	A
Forsyth Country Day School, NC	A
Fort Lauderdale Preparatory School, FL	A,C
Fort Worth Country Day School, TX	A,F,S
Foundation Academy, FL	S
Fountain Valley School of Colorado, CO	R,S
Fowlers Academy, PR	A
Foxcroft Academy, ME	F,S

A — academic; C — computer instruction; F — art/fine arts; R — rigorous outdoor training; S — sports; O — other

Fox River Country Day School, IL	A,C,F,S
Franklin Academy, CT	A
Franklin Road Academy, TN	A,C,F,S
Fuqua School, VA	A,S
Gables Academy, GA	A,C,F,S
Garces Memorial High School, CA	A,C,F,S
Garrison Forest School, MD	F,S
Gaston Day School, NC	A,S
The Geneva School, FL	A,F,S
George Stevens Academy, ME	A,F,S
Georgetown Preparatory School, MD	A,S
Germantown Academy, PA	A,C,F,S
Gill St. Bernard's School, NJ	A,F,S
Gilman School, MD	A,S
Gilmour Academy, OH	S
Girls Preparatory School, TN	A,C,F,S
Glenelg Country School, MD	A,S
The Glenholme School, CT	A,C,F,S
Gonzaga College High School, DC	A
The Governor French Academy, IL	A,C,F
The Gow School, NY	A,C,F,R,S
Grace Baptist Academy, TN	A
Grace Christian School, AK	A
The Grand River Academy, OH	A,C,F,S
The Grauer School, CA	A,C,F
Greenfield School, NC	A,C,F,S
Green Fields Country Day School, AZ	S
Greenhill School, TX	A,C,F,S
Greenhills School, MI	A,F,S
Greenleaf Academy, ID	S
Greensboro Day School, NC	A,C,F,S
Greens Farms Academy, CT	A,S
Griggs University and International Academy, MD	A
Guamani Private School, PR	A
Guerin College Preparatory High School, IL	A,C,F,S
Guilford Day School, NC	A,C
Gwynedd Mercy Academy, PA	S
Hackley School, NY	S
Halstrom High School, CA	A,C,F
Halstrom High School—San Diego, CA	A,C,F
Hamden Hall Country Day School, CT	A,C,F,S
Hanalani Schools, HI	A,C,F,S
Hargrave Military Academy, VA	A,C,R,S
The Harker School, CA	A
The Harley School, NY	A,C,F,S
Harvard-Westlake School, CA	A,C,F,R,S
The Harvey School, NY	A
Hawaii Baptist Academy, HI	A,C,F,S
Hawai'i Preparatory Academy, HI	A
Hawken School, OH	A,C
Head-Royce School, CA	A
Heritage Hall, OK	A,C,F,S
Highland School, VA	A,C,F,R,S
The Hill Top Preparatory School, PA	A
Hilton Head Preparatory School, SC	A,C,F,S
The Hockaday School, TX	A,C,F,S
Hokkaido International School, Japan	R
Holy Innocents' Episcopal School, GA	A,F,S
Hopkins School, CT	A,C,F,R,S
The Horace Mann School, NY	A,C,F
The Hotchkiss School, CT	F
Howe Military School, IN	A
The Hun School of Princeton, NJ	A,C,F
Hutchison School, TN	A,C,F,S
Hyde School, CT	A,F,R,S
Hyde School, ME	A,F,S
Idyllwild Arts Academy, CA	A,F
Illiana Christian High School, IL	F,S
Imperial College of Toronto, ON, Canada	A,C
Independent School, KS	A,C,F
Interlochen Arts Academy, MI	F
International College Spain, Spain	A,F
International High School, CA	A,F
International School Bangkok, Thailand	A,F
International School Manila, Philippines	A
International School of Athens, Greece	A,C,F
The International School of Paris, France	A,C,F
Iolani School, HI	A,C,F,S
Isidore Newman School, LA	A,C,F
Island School, HI	A
Jackson Academy, MS	A,C,F,S
The Janus School, PA	A
Jesuit College Preparatory School, TX	A,C,F,S
Jesuit High School, CA	A,C
The John Cooper School, TX	A,C,F,S
Junipero Serra High School, CA	A,C
Kaplan College Preparatory School, FL	A,C,F
Keith Country Day School, IL	A,F,S
Kent Denver School, CO	A,C,F,S
Kentucky Country Day School, KY	A,C,F,R,S
Kerr-Vance Academy, NC	A
The Key School, MD	A,F,R,S
Kildonan School, NY	A,C,F
Kimball Union Academy, NH	A,C,F,S
King George School, VT	A,F
King Low Heywood Thomas, CT	A,F,S
The King's Christian High School, NJ	A,S
King's High School, WA	S
Lake Forest Academy, IL	A
Lakehill Preparatory School, TX	A,C,F,S
Lake Ridge Academy, OH	A,C,F,S
Lakeside School, WA	A,C
Lakeview Academy, GA	A,C,F,S
La Lumiere School, IN	A
Lancaster Mennonite High School, PA	S
Landmark School, MA	A
Landon School, MD	A,F
Lansdale Catholic High School, PA	A,F,S
La Salle High School, FL	A
The Laureate Academy, MB, Canada	A
Laurel Springs School, CA	A,C,F
Lausanne Collegiate School, TN	A,C,F,S
Lawrence School, OH	A,C,F,S
Lee Academy, ME	A,S
Le Lycee Francais de Los Angeles, CA	O
Linden Hall, PA	A,S
Linden Hill School, MA	A,C,F,S
Linfield Christian School, CA	F,S
The Linsly School, WV	A,C
Little Keswick School, VA	A,C,F,R,S
Los Angeles Baptist Junior/Senior High School, CA	A,C,S
Louisville Collegiate School, KY	A,C,F,S
Louisville High School, CA	S
The Lovett School, GA	A
Loyola-Blakefield, MD	A,S
Loyola High School, Jesuit College Preparatory, CA	A,C,F,S
Lutheran High North, TX	A,C,F,S
Luther High School North, IL	A,C,S

A — academic; C — computer instruction; F — art/fine arts; R — rigorous outdoor training; S — sports; O — other

Luther High School South, IL	A,C,S
Lyman Ward Military Academy, AL	A,R
MacLachlan College, ON, Canada	A
Madison-Ridgeland Academy, MS	A,S
Maine School of Science and Mathematics, ME	A
Manlius Pebble Hill School, NY	A,C,F,S
Maret School, DC	A,F,S
Marian Central Catholic High School, IL	S
Marian High School, IN	C,F,S
Marist High School, NJ	A
Marist School, GA	A,F,S
Marshall School, MN	A,C,F,S
Martin Luther High School, NY	A,C
The Marvelwood School, CT	A,C,F
Maryknoll School, HI	A,C,F,S
The Mary Louis Academy, NY	A
Marymount High School, CA	A,C,F,S
Marymount School, NY	A,F
Maryvale Preparatory School, MD	A,C,F,S
The Master's School, CT	A,C,F,S
Matignon High School, MA	A
Maumee Valley Country Day School, OH	A,C,F,S
Maur Hill-Mount Academy, KS	A
The McCallie School, TN	A,R,S
McDonogh School, MD	A,C,F,S
The Meadows School, NV	A
Memorial Hall School, TX	A,C
Memphis University School, TN	A,S
Menaul School, NM	A,C,F
Mentor College, ON, Canada	A,C
Mercersburg Academy, PA	A,F,R,S
Mercy High School College Preparatory, CA	A
Mercyhurst Preparatory School, PA	A,C,F
Mesa Grande Seventh-Day Academy, CA	S
Miami Country Day School, FL	A,C,F
Middlesex School, MA	F
Mid-Pacific Institute, HI	A,C,F
Mid-Peninsula High School, CA	A,F
Milken Community High School of Stephen S. Wise Temple, CA	A,C,F,S
Mississauga Private School, ON, Canada	A,C,F,S
Missouri Military Academy, MO	R,S
Miss Porter's School, CT	A,F,S
MMI Preparatory School, PA	A,C
Montgomery Bell Academy, TN	A,C,S
Montverde Academy, FL	A
Moravian Academy, PA	A,F
Moreau Catholic High School, CA	A,S
Morgan Park Academy, IL	A,C,F
Morristown-Beard School, NJ	A,C,F,S
Moses Brown School, RI	A,C,F
Mother McAuley High School, IL	A,C,F,S
Mounds Park Academy, MN	A,F,S
Mount Saint Charles Academy, RI	F,S
Mt. Saint Dominic Academy, NJ	A,S
Munich International School, Germany	A,R,S
Nancy Campbell Collegiate Institute, ON, Canada	A
National Cathedral School, DC	A,F,S
National High School, GA	A,C,F
National Sports Academy at Lake Placid, NY	S
Newark Academy, NJ	A,C,F,S
New Horizon Youth Ministries, IN	A,R,S
The Newman School, MA	A,C
New Summit School, MS	A
New Way Learning Academy, AZ	A,C
Niagara Christian Community of Schools, ON, Canada	A
The Nichols School, NY	A,F
Norfolk Academy, VA	A,F,S
Norfolk Christian School, VA	A,F,S
Norfolk Collegiate School, VA	A,C,F,R,S
The North Broward Preparatory Upper School, FL	A,C,F,S
North Cobb Christian School, GA	A,C,F,S
North Cross School, VA	A,F,S
Northfield Mount Hermon School, MA	A
North Shore Country Day School, IL	A,C,F,R,S
Northside Christian School, FL	A,C,F,S
The Northwest School, WA	A,C,F,S
The Norwich Free Academy, CT	A,S
Notre Dame Academy, VA	A,F,S
Notre Dame High School, CA	A,C,F,S
Notre Dame High School, NJ	A,F,S
Notre Dame High School, TN	A,S
Oak Creek Ranch School, AZ	A,C
Oak Grove Lutheran School, ND	A,F,S
Oak Hill Academy, VA	A
Oak Knoll School of the Holy Child, NJ	A,S
Oakland School, VA	A,C,F,S
Oak Ridge Military Academy, NC	A
The Oakridge School, TX	A,C,F,S
Oakwood School, CA	A,F,S
The Oakwood School, NC	A,S
Oldfields School, MD	A,F,S
Oneida Baptist Institute, KY	A
Orangewood Adventist Academy, CA	A
Oregon Episcopal School, OR	A,C,F,S
Orinda Academy, CA	A
The Orme School, AZ	A
Our Lady of Mercy High School, NY	A,C,F,S
Our Saviour Lutheran School, NY	A
Out-Of-Door-Academy, FL	A,F,S
The Oxford Academy, CT	A
Oxford School, CA	A
Pace Academy, GA	A,C,F,S
Pacific Academy, CA	A
Pacific Hills School, CA	A
Pacific Lutheran High School, CA	A,S
Padua Franciscan High School, OH	A,C,F,S
Palma High School, CA	A
Parish Episcopal School, TX	A,C,F,S
The Parker School, HI	A
Park Tudor School, IN	A,C,F,R,S
Peddie School, NJ	A
Perkiomen School, PA	A,S
Phillips Academy (Andover), MA	A,C,F
Phoenix Christian Unified Schools, AZ	A
Phoenix Country Day School, AZ	A,C,F,S
Piedmont Academy, GA	F,R,S
Pine Crest School, FL	A,S
The Pingry School, NJ	A
Poly Prep Country Day School, NY	A,C,F,S
Pomfret School, CT	F
Pope John XXIII Regional High School, NJ	A,S
Portledge School, NY	A,C,F,S
Portsmouth Abbey School, RI	A
Portsmouth Christian Academy, NH	A,S
The Potomac School, VA	A,F,S
Poughkeepsie Day School, NY	F
The Prairie School, WI	A,C,F

A — academic; C — computer instruction; F — art/fine arts; R — rigorous outdoor training; S — sports; O — other

Prestonwood Christian Academy, TX	A,C,F,R,S
Providence Day School, NC	A,C,F,S
Providence High School, CA	A,C,F,S
Providence High School, TX	A,F,S
Pulaski Academy, AR	A,C,F
Punahou School, HI	A,F,S
Queen Anne School, MD	A,C,S
Queen Margaret's School, BC, Canada	A,S
Randolph-Macon Academy, VA	A,C,F
Randolph School, AL	A,S
Ransom Everglades School, FL	A,C
Ravenscroft School, NC	A,C,F,S
The Rectory School, CT	A,F,S
Redemption Christian Academy, NY	A,C,S
Regina High School, OH	A,F,S
Reitz Memorial High School, IN	A,S
Richmond Christian School, BC, Canada	A
Ridley College, ON, Canada	A
Rivermont Collegiate, IA	A,S
Riverside Military Academy, GA	A,C,F,R,S
Riverstone International School, ID	A,F,R
Riverview School, MA	A,C,F,S
Robert Louis Stevenson School, NY	A
Rocky Hill School, RI	A,C,F,S
Rocky Mount Academy, NC	A,C,F,S
The Roeper School, MI	F
Roland Park Country School, MD	A,F,S
Rosseau Lake College, ON, Canada	A,C,R,S
Ross School, NY	F,S
The Roxbury Latin School, MA	A,S
Royal Canadian College, BC, Canada	A
Rumsey Hall School, CT	A
Rutgers Preparatory School, NJ	A,C
Rye Country Day School, NY	A,C,F
Sacred Heart School of Halifax, NS, Canada	A
St. Albans School, DC	A,C,F,R,S
St. Andrew's College, ON, Canada	F,S
St. Andrew's Episcopal School, MD	A,F,S
St. Andrew's on the Marsh School, GA	A,F,S
St. Andrew's Priory School, HI	A,C,F,R,S
St. Andrew's School, RI	A,C,F,R,S
St. Anne's–Belfield School, VA	A,S
St. Anselm's Abbey School, DC	A,F,S
St. Anthony Catholic High School, TX	A,S
St. Anthony's Junior-Senior High School, HI	A
St. Augustine High School, CA	A,R,S
Saint Augustine Preparatory School, NJ	A,C,F,R,S
Saint Basil Academy, PA	S
St. Benedict at Auburndale, TN	A
St. Catherine's Military Academy, CA	A,C,F,S
St. Catherine's School, VA	F,S
Saint Cecilia High School, NE	S
St. Christopher's School, VA	A
St. Clement's School, ON, Canada	A,F
St. David's School, NC	A,C,F,S
Saint Dominic Academy, NJ	A,C
Saint Edmund High School, NY	A
Saint Edward's School, FL	A,C,F,S
Saint Francis High School, CA	A,C,F,S
St. Francis High School, KY	A,S
Saint Francis School, HI	A,C
St. George's Independent School, TN	A,C,F,S
St. George's School, BC, Canada	A,C,F,S
St. Gregory College Preparatory School, AZ	A,C,F,S

St. Gregory's High School, IL	A
Saint John Bosco High School, CA	A,C,F,S
St. Johnsbury Academy, VT	A
St. John's Catholic Prep, MD	C,F,S
St. John's International, BC, Canada	A
St. John's Northwestern Military Academy, WI	A,C
St. John's Preparatory School, MA	A
Saint John's Preparatory School, MN	A,F
Saint Joseph High School, IL	A
Saint Joseph High School, PA	A
St. Joseph's Catholic School, SC	F,S
St. Joseph's Preparatory School, PA	A,F
St. Jude's School, ON, Canada	O
St. Margaret's Episcopal School, CA	A,F,S
St. Margaret's School, BC, Canada	A
St. Martin's Episcopal School, LA	A,S
Saint Mary High School, NJ	A
St. Mary's Episcopal School, TN	A,F,S
Saint Mary's Hall, TX	A,C,F,S
St. Mary's Preparatory School, MI	A,S
Saint Mary's School, NC	A,C,F,S
St. Mary's School, OR	A,C,F,S
Saint Matthias High School, CA	A,C,F
Saint Maur International School, Japan	A,C,F,S
Saint Monica's High School, CA	A,C,F,S
Saint Patrick High School, IL	A,C,F,S
St. Paul's Episcopal School, AL	A,C,F,S
St. Paul's High School, MB, Canada	S
St. Paul's School, NH	A
St. Paul's School for Girls, MD	A,S
St. Peter's Preparatory School, NJ	A,F
St. Stephen's & St. Agnes School, VA	A,C,F
Saint Stephen's Episcopal School, FL	A,S
Saint Teresa's Academy, MO	C,F,S
Saint Thomas Aquinas High School, KS	A,S
Saint Thomas More School, CT	A,C,F,S
St. Timothy's School, MD	A
Salesian High School, NY	A,S
Salisbury School, CT	A
Salt Lake Lutheran High School, UT	S
Sandia Preparatory School, NM	A,C,F,S
San Diego Jewish Academy, CA	R,S
Sandy Spring Friends School, MD	A,F,S
Sanford School, DE	A,C,F
Santa Margarita Catholic High School, CA	A,C,F,S
The Savannah Country Day School, GA	A,C,F,S
School for Young Performers, NY	A,F
School of the Holy Child, NY	A,F,S
Seabury Hall, HI	A,F,S
Selwyn House School, QC, Canada	S
Seton Catholic Central High School, NY	A,S
The Seven Hills School, OH	A
Sewickley Academy, PA	A,F,S
Shady Side Academy, PA	A,C,F,S
Shattuck-St. Mary's School, MN	F,S
Shelton School and Evaluation Center, TX	A
Shorecrest Preparatory School, FL	A,F,S
Smith School, NY	A,C
Solebury School, PA	A
Soundview Preparatory School, NY	A
Southridge School, BC, Canada	A,C,F,S
Stella Maris High School, NY	A,S
Stevenson School, CA	A
Stoneleigh–Burnham School, MA	A,F,S

A — academic; C — computer instruction; F — art/fine arts; R — rigorous outdoor training; S — sports; O — other

The Stony Brook School, NY	A
Stuart Country Day School of the Sacred Heart, NJ	A,F
Suffield Academy, CT	A,C,F
The Summit Country Day School, OH	A,C,F,S
The Taft School, CT	A,F,S
Tampa Preparatory School, FL	A,C,S
TASIS The American School in England, United Kingdom	A,C,F,S
TASIS, The American School in Switzerland, Switzerland	A,F,S
The Tatnall School, DE	A,F
The Tenney School, TX	A,C
TMI—The Episcopal School of Texas, TX	A,S
Tri-City Christian Schools, CA	A,S
Trident Academy, SC	A
Trinity Christian Academy, TX	A,C,F,S
Trinity College School, ON, Canada	A,C,F
Trinity High School, OH	A,F,S
Trinity Preparatory School, FL	A,C,F,S
Trinity Valley School, TX	A,F,R,S
United Nations International School, NY	A
University Lake School, WI	A,C,F,S
University Liggett School, MI	A,S
University of Chicago Laboratory Schools, IL	A,S
University School of Jackson, TN	A,C,F,S
University School of Milwaukee, WI	A,C,F,S
University School of Nova Southeastern University, FL	A,F,S
The Ursuline Academy of Dallas, TX	A,C
Valley Christian School, CA	A,F,S
Vianney High School, MO	A,S
Victor Valley Christian School, CA	A
Viewpoint School, CA	A,C,F,S
Villa Duchesne/Oak Hill School, MO	A,C,F,S
Villa Joseph Marie High School, PA	A,S
Visitation Academy of St. Louis County, MO	S
Wakefield School, VA	A,C,F,S
The Waldorf School of Garden City, NY	A
The Walker School, GA	A
Walnut Hill School, MA	F
The Wardlaw-Hartridge School, NJ	A
Waring School, MA	F
Wasatch Academy, UT	A
Washington Academy, ME	A
Washington Waldorf School, MD	S
Watkinson School, CT	A,C,F
The Waverly School, CA	A,F
Waynflete School, ME	A,F,S
Webb School of Knoxville, TN	A,F,S
The Webb Schools, CA	A,C,F
Wediko School and Treatment Program, NH	A,C,F,S
The Wellington School, OH	A,S
Wesleyan Academy, PR	A
Westbury Christian School, TX	S
West Catholic High School, MI	S
Westchester Country Day School, NC	A,C,F,S
Western Christian Schools, CA	A
West Island College, AB, Canada	A,C,S
Westminster Christian School, FL	A,C
Westminster School, CT	S
The Westminster Schools, GA	A,C,F,R,S
Westminster Schools of Augusta, GA	S
Westridge School, CA	A,F,S
Westtown School, PA	A,F,S
Wheaton Academy, IL	A,C,F,S
Whitefield Academy, GA	A,F,S
Wichita Collegiate School, KS	A,C,F,S
William Penn Charter School, PA	A,F,S
The Williams School, CT	S
The Williston Northampton School, MA	F,S
The Willows Academy, IL	A,S
Willow Wood School, ON, Canada	A,C
Winchester Thurston School, PA	A,F,S
Windermere Preparatory School, FL	A,F,S
The Windsor School, NY	A,C,F
Windward School, CA	S
Winston Preparatory School, NY	A,F
The Winston School, TX	A,C,F,S
The Winston School San Antonio, TX	A,C,S
Wooster School, CT	A,C,F,S
Wyoming Seminary, PA	A,C,F,S
Xaverian Brothers High School, MA	A,C,F
Yokohama International School, Japan	A,S

SCHOOLS REPORTING THAT THEY ACCOMMODATE UNDERACHIEVERS

The Academy at Sisters, OR
Accelerated Schools, CO
Alpine Academy, UT
Alternative Learning Program, AB, Canada
American Academy, FL
Arrowsmith School, ON, Canada
Calgary Academy, AB, Canada
Cedar Ridge Academy, UT
Chatham Academy, GA
Cherokee Creek Boys School, SC
Cherry Gulch, ID
The Craig School, NJ
Crawford Day School, VA
Cross Creek Programs, UT
CrossRoads, OR
Crotched Mountain Rehabilitation Center School, NH
Delphos Saint John's High School, OH
Denver Academy, CO
Eagle Hill-Southport, CT
Elan School, ME
Elves Child Development Centre, AB, Canada
Excel Academy, Inc., OH
The Family Foundation School, NY
Foothills Academy, AB, Canada
Fowlers Academy, PR
The Frostig School, CA
Gables Academy, GA
Gateway School, TX
Glen Eden School, BC, Canada
The Glenholme School, CT
The Grand River Academy, OH
The Greenwood School, VT
Halstrom High School—San Diego, CA
Hampshire Country School, NH
The Hill Center, Durham Academy, NC
Humanex Academy, CO
The Janus School, PA
The John Dewey Academy, MA
The Karafin School, NY
King George School, VT
Kingshill School, VI
La Cheim School, CA

A — academic; C — computer instruction; F — art/fine arts; R — rigorous outdoor training; S — sports; O — other

Linden Hill School, MA
Little Keswick School, VA
Logos School, MO
Lyman Ward Military Academy, AL
Maplebrook School, NY
The Marvelwood School, CT
Mid-Peninsula High School, CA
Montana Academy, MT
Mount Bachelor Academy, OR
New Horizon Youth Ministries, IN
New Summit School, MS
Northwest Academy, ID
Oak Creek Ranch School, AZ
Oakland School, VA
The Oxford Academy, CT
Pacific Lutheran High School, CA
The Penikese Island School, MA
The Phelps School, PA
Pine Ridge School, VT
The Rectory School, CT
Riverview School, MA
Robert Louis Stevenson School, NY
St. Christopher Academy, WA
St. John's Northwestern Military Academy, WI
St. Jude's School, ON, Canada
Saint Thomas More School, CT
Sheila Morrison School, ON, Canada
Sky Ranch for Boys, Inc., SD
Sorenson's Ranch School, UT
Stanbridge Academy, CA
Still Creek Christian School, TX
Stone Mountain School, NC
Sunrise Academy, UT
Thornton Friends School, MD
Timber Ridge School, VA
Toronto Waldorf School, ON, Canada
Trident Academy, SC
Valley View School, MA
The Vanguard School, FL
Wediko School and Treatment Program, NH
Willow Hill School, MA
The Winchendon School, MA
Winston Preparatory School, NY
World Hope Academy, FL

SCHOOLS REPORTING PROGRAMS FOR STUDENTS WITH SPECIAL NEEDS

Remedial Reading and/or Writing

Academia Cotopaxi, Ecuador
Academie Sainte Cecile International School, ON, Canada
The Academy at Sisters, OR
Academy for Global Exploration, OR
Academy of Mount Saint Ursula, NY
Academy of the New Church Boys' School, PA
Academy of the New Church Girls' School, PA
Accelerated Schools, CO
Aiglon College, Switzerland
Alliance Academy, Ecuador
Allison Academy, FL
Alpine Academy, UT
American Academy, FL
American Community Schools of Athens, Greece
American International School Rotterdam, Netherlands
The American School Foundation, Mexico
American School of Milan, Italy
American School of Paris, France
The American School of Puerto Vallarta, Mexico
The American School of The Hague, Netherlands
Archbishop Curley High School, MD
Archbishop Hoban High School, OH
Archbishop McNicholas High School, OH
Archbishop Spalding High School, MD
Army and Navy Academy, CA
Arrowsmith School, ON, Canada
ASSETS School, HI
Aurora Central High School, IL
Baptist High School, NJ
Barnstable Academy, NJ
Bass Memorial Academy, MS
Bavarian International School, Germany
The Beekman School, NY
Benedictine High School, OH
The Bermuda High School for Girls, Bermuda
Bishop Alemany High School, CA
Bishop Carroll High School, PA
Bishop Conaty-Our Lady of Loretto High School, CA
Bishop Garcia Diego High School, CA
Bishop Gorman High School, NV
Bishop Kelly High School, ID
Bishop Luers High School, IN
Bishop Lynch Catholic High School, TX
Bishop Mora Salesian High School, CA
Bishop Stang High School, MA
Bishop Walsh Middle High School, MD
Blue Mountain Academy, PA
Blueprint Education, AZ
The Blue Ridge School, VA
Boylan Central Catholic High School, IL
Brehm Preparatory School, IL
Brethren Christian Junior and Senior High Schools, CA
Brockwood Park School, United Kingdom
Brother Rice High School, MI
Burr and Burton Academy, VT
Butte Central High School, MT
Calgary Academy, AB, Canada
Calvert Hall College High School, MD
Camden Military Academy, SC
Camelot Academy, NC
Cardigan Mountain School, NH
Cardinal Newman High School, FL
Carlucci American International School of Lisbon, Portugal
Cascadilla School, NY
Cathedral High School, IN
Cathedral High School, NY
The Catholic High School of Baltimore, MD
Catholic Memorial, MA
Cedar Ridge Academy, UT
Central Catholic High School, CA
Chamberlain-Hunt Academy, MS
Chaminade-Madonna College Preparatory, FL
Chatham Academy, GA
Chelsea School, MD

Cherokee Creek Boys School, SC
Cherry Gulch, ID
Cheshire Academy, CT
Children's Creative and Performing Arts Academy—Capa Division, CA
Chinese Christian Schools, CA
Christopher Dock Mennonite High School, PA
Chrysalis School, WA
Coe-Brown Northwood Academy, NH
Colegio Bolivar, Colombia
Colegio Franklin D. Roosevelt, Peru
College du Leman International School, Switzerland
Columbia Grammar and Preparatory School, NY
Columbia International School, Japan
Community High School, NJ
Community School, NH
The Concept School, PA
Cotter Schools, MN
Covenant Canadian Reformed School, AB, Canada
The Craig School, NJ
Crawford Adventist Academy, ON, Canada
Cretin-Derham Hall, MN
Cross Creek Programs, UT
CrossRoads, OR
Crotched Mountain Rehabilitation Center School, NH
Currey Ingram Academy, TN
Cushing Academy, MA
Dallas Academy, TX
Delaware Valley Friends School, PA
DeMatha Catholic High School, MD
Denver Academy, CO
Denver Lutheran High School, CO
DePaul Catholic High School, NJ
Dickinson Trinity, ND
Dowling Catholic High School, IA
Dublin Christian Academy, NH
Eagle Hill School, CT
Eagle Hill School, MA
Eagle Hill-Southport, CT
Eastern Christian High School, NJ
Eastern Mennonite High School, VA
Eastside Christian Academy, AB, Canada
Ecole d'Humanité, Switzerland
The Education Center, MS
Elan School, ME
Elk Mountain Academy, MT
Elyria Catholic High School, OH
Evangelical Christian School, TN
Excel Academy, Inc., OH
Fairhill School, TX
The Family Foundation School, NY
The Fessenden School, MA
Fishburne Military School, VA
Foothills Academy, AB, Canada
Fort Lauderdale Preparatory School, FL
Foundation Academy, FL
Foxcroft Academy, ME
Fox Valley Lutheran High School, WI
Front Range Christian High School, CO
The Frostig School, CA
Fryeburg Academy, ME
Gables Academy, GA
Gateway School, TX
George Stevens Academy, ME
Girard College, PA
Glen Eden School, BC, Canada
The Glenholme School, CT
Gordon Technical High School, IL
The Gow School, NY
Grace Christian School, AK
The Grand River Academy, OH
Greenfield School, NC
Green Meadow Waldorf School, NY
The Greenwood School, VT
Grove School, CT
Guilford Day School, NC
Halstrom High School, CA
Halstrom High School—San Diego, CA
Hamilton District Christian High, ON, Canada
Hammond School, SC
Hampshire Country School, NH
Hanalani Schools, HI
Hargrave Military Academy, VA
The Haverford School, PA
Hayden High School, KS
Hebrew Academy, CA
Heritage Christian Academy, AB, Canada
Heritage Christian School, ON, Canada
Hidden Lake Academy, GA
The Hill Center, Durham Academy, NC
Hillcrest School, TX
Hillside School, MA
The Hill Top Preparatory School, PA
Hoosac School, NY
Hosanna Christian School, OR
The Hudson School, NJ
Humanex Academy, CO
Hyde School, CT
Hyde School, ME
Illiana Christian High School, IL
International School of Amsterdam, Netherlands
International School of Aruba, Aruba
International School of Athens, Greece
The International School of Geneva, Switzerland
International School of Milan, Italy
Jack M. Barrack Hebrew Academy (formerly Akiba Hebrew Academy), PA
The Janus School, PA
The John Dewey Academy, MA
The Karafin School, NY
Keith Country Day School, IL
Kildonan School, NY
King George School, VT
Kings Christian School, CA
Kingshill School, VI
La Cheim School, CA
Lakeview Academy, GA
Lancaster Mennonite High School, PA
Landmark East School, NS, Canada
Landmark School, MA
Lansdale Catholic High School, PA
La Pietra–Hawaii School for Girls, HI

La Salle Institute, NY
The Laureate Academy, MB, Canada
Laurel Springs School, CA
Lawrence School, OH
Le Lycee Francais de Los Angeles, CA
Logos School, MO
Lourdes Catholic High School, AZ
Lutheran High School, IN
Lutheran High School West, OH
Luther High School North, IL
Luther High School South, IL
Lyman Ward Military Academy, AL
Lyndon Institute, VT
Maharishi School of the Age of Enlightenment, IA
Maine Central Institute, ME
Maplebrook School, NY
Marian Baker School, Costa Rica
Marian Central Catholic High School, IL
Marian High School, IN
Marist High School, IL
Marist High School, NJ
Marshall School, MN
Martin Luther High School, NY
The Marvelwood School, CT
Mary Help of Christians Academy, NJ
Marylawn of the Oranges, NJ
Massanutten Military Academy, VA
Memorial Hall School, TX
Memphis University School, TN
Mennonite Collegiate Institute, MB, Canada
Mercedes College, Australia
Merchiston Castle School, United Kingdom
Mercy High School, NE
Mercyhurst Preparatory School, PA
Mid-Peninsula High School, CA
Modesto Christian School, CA
Monmouth Academy, NJ
Monsignor Donovan High School, NJ
Montana Academy, MT
Moravian Academy, PA
Moses Brown School, RI
Mount Bachelor Academy, OR
National High School, GA
Newbury Park Adventist Academy, CA
New Hampton School, NH
New Summit School, MS
New Way Learning Academy, AZ
The Nora School, MD
Norfolk Christian School, VA
Norfolk Collegiate School, VA
The North Broward Preparatory Upper School, FL
North Country School, NY
Northwest Academy, ID
Northwest Yeshiva High School, WA
Northwood School, NY
The Norwich Free Academy, CT
Notre Dame- Bishop Gibbons School, NY
Notre Dame-Cathedral Latin School, OH
Notre Dame High School, NJ
Oak Creek Ranch School, AZ
Oak Grove Lutheran School, ND
Oak Hill Academy, VA
The Oakland School, PA
Oakland School, VA
O'Dea High School, WA
Ojai Valley School, CA
The O'Neal School, NC
Oneida Baptist Institute, KY
The Orme School, AZ
The Oxford Academy, CT
Pacific Lutheran High School, CA
Padua Franciscan High School, OH
The Penikese Island School, MA
Pensacola Catholic High School, FL
The Phelps School, PA
Pinehurst School, ON, Canada
Pine Ridge School, VT
Pioneer Valley Christian School, MA
Pius X High School, NE
Powers Catholic High School, MI
The Prairie School, WI
The Rectory School, CT
Redemption Christian Academy, NY
Redwood Christian Schools, CA
Regina Dominican High School, IL
Regina High School, OH
Richmond Christian School, BC, Canada
Riverview School, MA
Robert Louis Stevenson School, NY
Rocky Mount Academy, NC
Roncalli High School, IN
Rosseau Lake College, ON, Canada
Rumsey Hall School, CT
St. Andrew's School, RI
St. Andrew's–Sewanee School, TN
St. Augustine High School, CA
St. Benedict at Auburndale, TN
St. Benedict's Preparatory School, NJ
St. Brendan High School, FL
Saint Cecilia High School, NE
St. Croix Lutheran High School, MN
Saint Dominic Academy, NJ
St. Dominic's International School, Portugal, Portugal
Saint Edmund High School, NY
Saint Elizabeth High School, CA
St. Francis School, GA
St. George's School, BC, Canada
St. George's School of Montreal, QC, Canada
Saint Joan Antida High School, WI
St. Johnsbury Academy, VT
Saint Joseph Central Catholic High School, OH
St. Joseph High School, CA
Saint Joseph High School, IL
St. Jude's School, ON, Canada
St. Mary's Hall–Doane Academy, NJ
Saint Mary's High School, AZ
Saint Matthias High School, CA
Saint Monica's High School, CA
Saint Patrick High School, IL
St. Stanislaus College, MS
St. Thomas Aquinas High School, FL
Saint Thomas Aquinas High School, KS

St. Thomas Choir School, NY
Saint Thomas More School, CT
Saint Xavier High School, KY
Salesianum School, DE
Salpointe Catholic High School, AZ
Salt Lake Lutheran High School, UT
The Samuel Scheck Hillel Community Day School, FL
San Marcos Baptist Academy, TX
Santa Margarita Catholic High School, CA
SCECGS Redlands, Australia
School for Young Performers, NY
Seattle Academy of Arts and Sciences, WA
Seattle Christian Schools, WA
Seattle Lutheran High School, WA
Sedbergh School, QC, Canada
Seisen International School, Japan
Seton Catholic Central High School, NY
Shattuck-St. Mary's School, MN
Sheila Morrison School, ON, Canada
Shenandoah Valley Academy, VA
Shoreline Christian, WA
Smith School, NY
Smithville District Christian High School, ON, Canada
Solebury School, PA
Sorenson's Ranch School, UT
Spring Ridge Academy, AZ
Stanbridge Academy, CA
Stephen T. Badin High School, OH
Still Creek Christian School, TX
Stone Mountain School, NC
Storm King School, NY
Tandem Friends School, VA
TASIS The American School in England, United Kingdom
The Tenney School, TX
Timber Ridge School, VA
Toronto District Christian High School, ON, Canada
Trident Academy, SC
Trinity High School, KY
Trinity-Pawling School, NY
University Lake School, WI
University of Chicago Laboratory Schools, IL
University School of Nova Southeastern University, FL
The Ursuline School, NY
Valle Catholic High School, MO
Valley Christian High School, CA
Valley Forge Military Academy & College, PA
Valley View School, MA
The Vanguard School, FL
Washington Academy, ME
Wediko School and Treatment Program, NH
Westminster Christian Academy, AL
West Nottingham Academy, MD
Wheaton Academy, IL
The White Mountain School, NH
Willow Hill School, MA
Willow Wood School, ON, Canada
The Winchendon School, MA
The Windsor School, NY
Winston Preparatory School, NY
The Winston School, TX
World Hope Academy, FL
Xaverian Brothers High School, MA
York Country Day School, PA
Zurich International School, Switzerland

Remedial Math

Academia Cotopaxi, Ecuador
Academie Sainte Cecile International School, ON, Canada
The Academy at Sisters, OR
Academy for Global Exploration, OR
Academy of Mount Saint Ursula, NY
Academy of the New Church Boys' School, PA
Academy of the New Church Girls' School, PA
Accelerated Schools, CO
Airdrie Koinonia Christian School, AB, Canada
Alliance Academy, Ecuador
Allison Academy, FL
Alpine Academy, UT
American Academy, FL
American Community Schools of Athens, Greece
American International School Rotterdam, Netherlands
The American School Foundation, Mexico
American School of Milan, Italy
American School of Paris, France
The American School of Puerto Vallarta, Mexico
Archbishop Curley High School, MD
Archbishop Hoban High School, OH
Archbishop McNicholas High School, OH
Archbishop Spalding High School, MD
Arrowsmith School, ON, Canada
ASSETS School, HI
Aurora Central High School, IL
Baptist High School, NJ
Barnstable Academy, NJ
Bass Memorial Academy, MS
Bavarian International School, Germany
The Beekman School, NY
Benedictine High School, OH
Bishop Alemany High School, CA
Bishop Conaty-Our Lady of Loretto High School, CA
Bishop Denis J. O'Connell High School, VA
Bishop Garcia Diego High School, CA
Bishop Gorman High School, NV
Bishop Luers High School, IN
Bishop Lynch Catholic High School, TX
Bishop Stang High School, MA
Bishop Verot High School, FL
Blue Mountain Academy, PA
Blueprint Education, AZ
Boylan Central Catholic High School, IL
Brehm Preparatory School, IL
Brethren Christian Junior and Senior High Schools, CA
Brockwood Park School, United Kingdom
Brother Rice High School, MI
Burr and Burton Academy, VT
Butte Central High School, MT
Calgary Academy, AB, Canada
Calvert Hall College High School, MD
Camelot Academy, NC
Canyonville Christian Academy, OR
Cardigan Mountain School, NH
Cardinal Newman High School, FL

Carlucci American International School of Lisbon, Portugal
Cascadilla School, NY
Cathedral High School, IN
Cathedral High School, NY
The Catholic High School of Baltimore, MD
Catholic Memorial, MA
Cedar Ridge Academy, UT
Central Catholic High School, CA
Chamberlain-Hunt Academy, MS
Chaminade-Madonna College Preparatory, FL
Chatham Academy, GA
Chelsea School, MD
Cherokee Creek Boys School, SC
Cherry Gulch, ID
Cheshire Academy, CT
Children's Creative and Performing Arts Academy—Capa Division, CA
Chrysalis School, WA
Coe-Brown Northwood Academy, NH
Columbia Grammar and Preparatory School, NY
Columbia International School, Japan
Community High School, NJ
Community School, NH
The Concept School, PA
Cotter Schools, MN
Covenant Canadian Reformed School, AB, Canada
Cretin-Derham Hall, MN
Cross Creek Programs, UT
CrossRoads, OR
Crotched Mountain Rehabilitation Center School, NH
Cushing Academy, MA
Dallas Academy, TX
De La Salle High School, CA
Delaware Valley Friends School, PA
Denver Academy, CO
Denver Lutheran High School, CO
DePaul Catholic High School, NJ
Dickinson Trinity, ND
Dowling Catholic High School, IA
Dublin Christian Academy, NH
Eagle Hill School, CT
Eagle Hill School, MA
Eagle Hill-Southport, CT
Eastern Christian High School, NJ
Eastern Mennonite High School, VA
Eastside Christian Academy, AB, Canada
Ecole d'Humanité, Switzerland
The Education Center, MS
Elan School, ME
Elk Mountain Academy, MT
Elves Child Development Centre, AB, Canada
Elyria Catholic High School, OH
Evangelical Christian School, TN
Excel Academy, Inc., OH
Fairhill School, TX
Faith Lutheran High School, NV
The Fessenden School, MA
The Field School, DC
Fishburne Military School, VA
Flint River Academy, GA
Foothills Academy, AB, Canada
Fort Lauderdale Preparatory School, FL
Foundation Academy, FL
Foxcroft Academy, ME
Fox Valley Lutheran High School, WI
Franklin Academy, CT
Front Range Christian High School, CO
The Frostig School, CA
Fryeburg Academy, ME
Gables Academy, GA
Gateway School, TX
George Stevens Academy, ME
Girard College, PA
Glen Eden School, BC, Canada
The Glenholme School, CT
Gordon Technical High School, IL
The Gow School, NY
Grace Brethren School, CA
The Grauer School, CA
Greenfield School, NC
Green Meadow Waldorf School, NY
The Greenwood School, VT
Grove School, CT
Guilford Day School, NC
Halstrom High School, CA
Halstrom High School—San Diego, CA
Hamilton District Christian High, ON, Canada
Hampshire Country School, NH
Hanalani Schools, HI
Hargrave Military Academy, VA
The Haverford School, PA
Hayden High School, KS
Hebrew Academy, CA
Heritage Christian Academy, AB, Canada
Heritage Christian School, ON, Canada
Hidden Lake Academy, GA
The Hill Center, Durham Academy, NC
Hillcrest School, TX
Hillside School, MA
The Hill Top Preparatory School, PA
Hoosac School, NY
Hosanna Christian School, OR
The Hudson School, NJ
Humanex Academy, CO
Hyde School, CT
Hyde School, ME
Illiana Christian High School, IL
International School of Amsterdam, Netherlands
International School of Athens, Greece
The International School of Geneva, Switzerland
International School of Milan, Italy
Jack M. Barrack Hebrew Academy (formerly Akiba Hebrew Academy), PA
The Janus School, PA
The John Dewey Academy, MA
The Karafin School, NY
King George School, VT
Kings Christian School, CA
Kingshill School, VI
La Cheim School, CA
Lakeview Academy, GA
Lancaster Mennonite High School, PA

Landmark East School, NS, Canada
Landmark School, MA
Lansdale Catholic High School, PA
La Pietra–Hawaii School for Girls, HI
The Laureate Academy, MB, Canada
Laurel Springs School, CA
Lawrence School, OH
Le Lycee Francais de Los Angeles, CA
Lifegate School, OR
Logos School, MO
Lourdes Catholic High School, AZ
Lutheran High School, IN
Lutheran High School West, OH
Luther High School North, IL
Luther High School South, IL
Lyman Ward Military Academy, AL
Lyndon Institute, VT
Maharishi School of the Age of Enlightenment, IA
Maine Central Institute, ME
Maplebrook School, NY
Marian Baker School, Costa Rica
Marian Central Catholic High School, IL
Marian High School, IN
Marist High School, NJ
Marshall School, MN
Martin Luther High School, NY
The Marvelwood School, CT
Mary Help of Christians Academy, NJ
Marylawn of the Oranges, NJ
Massanutten Military Academy, VA
Memorial Hall School, TX
Memphis University School, TN
Mennonite Collegiate Institute, MB, Canada
Merchiston Castle School, United Kingdom
Mercy High School, NE
Mercyhurst Preparatory School, PA
Mid-Peninsula High School, CA
Missouri Military Academy, MO
Modesto Christian School, CA
Monmouth Academy, NJ
Monsignor Donovan High School, NJ
Mount Bachelor Academy, OR
Munich International School, Germany
National High School, GA
Newbury Park Adventist Academy, CA
New Hampton School, NH
New Summit School, MS
New Way Learning Academy, AZ
The Nora School, MD
Norfolk Christian School, VA
Norfolk Collegiate School, VA
The North Broward Preparatory Upper School, FL
North Country School, NY
Northwest Academy, ID
Northwest Yeshiva High School, WA
The Norwich Free Academy, CT
Notre Dame- Bishop Gibbons School, NY
Notre Dame-Cathedral Latin School, OH
Notre Dame High School, NJ
Oak Creek Ranch School, AZ
Oak Grove Lutheran School, ND
The Oakland School, PA
Oakland School, VA
Ojai Valley School, CA
The O'Neal School, NC
Oneida Baptist Institute, KY
The Orme School, AZ
The Oxford Academy, CT
The Penikese Island School, MA
Pensacola Catholic High School, FL
The Phelps School, PA
Pinehurst School, ON, Canada
Pine Ridge School, VT
Pioneer Valley Christian School, MA
Pius X High School, NE
Powers Catholic High School, MI
The Rectory School, CT
Redemption Christian Academy, NY
Redwood Christian Schools, CA
Regina Dominican High School, IL
Regina High School, OH
Richmond Christian School, BC, Canada
Ripon Christian Schools, CA
Riverview School, MA
Robert Louis Stevenson School, NY
Rocky Mount Academy, NC
Roncalli High School, IN
Rosseau Lake College, ON, Canada
Sacramento Adventist Academy, CA
St. Andrew's–Sewanee School, TN
Saint Anthony High School, IL
St. Augustine High School, CA
St. Benedict at Auburndale, TN
St. Benedict's Preparatory School, NJ
Saint Cecilia High School, NE
St. Croix Lutheran High School, MN
Saint Dominic Academy, NJ
St. Dominic's International School, Portugal, Portugal
Saint Edmund High School, NY
Saint Elizabeth High School, CA
St. Francis School, GA
St. George's School of Montreal, QC, Canada
Saint Joan Antida High School, WI
St. Johnsbury Academy, VT
Saint Joseph Central Catholic High School, OH
St. Joseph High School, CA
Saint Joseph High School, IL
St. Jude's School, ON, Canada
St. Mary's Hall–Doane Academy, NJ
Saint Mary's High School, AZ
Saint Matthias High School, CA
Saint Monica's High School, CA
Saint Patrick—Saint Vincent High School, CA
St. Paul's High School, MB, Canada
St. Stanislaus College, MS
St. Thomas Aquinas High School, FL
Saint Thomas Aquinas High School, KS
St. Thomas Choir School, NY
Saint Thomas More School, CT
Saint Xavier High School, KY
Salesianum School, DE
Salpointe Catholic High School, AZ

The Samuel Scheck Hillel Community Day School, FL
San Francisco Waldorf High School, CA
San Marcos Baptist Academy, TX
Santa Margarita Catholic High School, CA
SCECGS Redlands, Australia
School for Young Performers, NY
Seattle Academy of Arts and Sciences, WA
Seattle Lutheran High School, WA
Sedbergh School, QC, Canada
Seisen International School, Japan
Seton Catholic Central High School, NY
Shattuck-St. Mary's School, MN
Sheila Morrison School, ON, Canada
Shenandoah Valley Academy, VA
Smith School, NY
Smithville District Christian High School, ON, Canada
Sorenson's Ranch School, UT
Spring Ridge Academy, AZ
Stanbridge Academy, CA
Stephen T. Badin High School, OH
Still Creek Christian School, TX
Stone Mountain School, NC
Storm King School, NY
Summit Preparatory School, MT
Tandem Friends School, VA
The Tenney School, TX
Teurlings Catholic High School, LA
Timber Ridge School, VA
Toronto District Christian High School, ON, Canada
Trident Academy, SC
Trinity High School, KY
Trinity High School, OH
University Lake School, WI
University of Chicago Laboratory Schools, IL
Valle Catholic High School, MO
Valley Forge Military Academy & College, PA
Valley Lutheran High School, AZ
Valley View School, MA
The Vanguard School, FL
Washington Academy, ME
Wediko School and Treatment Program, NH
Westminster Christian Academy, AL
West Nottingham Academy, MD
Westtown School, PA
Wheaton Academy, IL
The White Mountain School, NH
Willow Hill School, MA
Willow Wood School, ON, Canada
The Winchendon School, MA
The Windsor School, NY
Winston Preparatory School, NY
The Winston School, TX
World Hope Academy, FL
Xaverian Brothers High School, MA
Zurich International School, Switzerland

Deaf Students

Ahliyyah School for Girls, Jordan
Alexander Dawson School, CO
American Christian Academy, AL
American Community Schools of Athens, Greece
Baylor School, TN
The Bement School, MA
Bishop Carroll High School, PA
Blanchet School, OR
Boylan Central Catholic High School, IL
Brethren Christian Junior and Senior High Schools, CA
Brockwood Park School, United Kingdom
Burr and Burton Academy, VT
Calgary Academy, AB, Canada
Cardinal Newman School, SC
Cate School, CA
Cathedral High School, IN
The Chapin School, NY
Coe-Brown Northwood Academy, NH
The Concept School, PA
Crotched Mountain Rehabilitation Center School, NH
Denver Christian High School, CO
DePaul Catholic High School, NJ
The Education Center, MS
Elves Child Development Centre, AB, Canada
Front Range Christian High School, CO
Gables Academy, GA
Grace Brethren School, CA
The Grauer School, CA
Grove School, CT
Halstrom High School, CA
Heritage Christian Academy, AB, Canada
Humanex Academy, CO
Jack M. Barrack Hebrew Academy (formerly Akiba Hebrew Academy), PA
The Karafin School, NY
Lake Ridge Academy, OH
Lancaster Mennonite High School, PA
Landmark School, MA
Lawrence Academy, MA
Loyola High School, Jesuit College Preparatory, CA
Lydia Patterson Institute, TX
Marshall School, MN
Merchiston Castle School, United Kingdom
Mercy High School, NE
Mercyhurst Preparatory School, PA
North Cobb Christian School, GA
Northwest Yeshiva High School, WA
Notre Dame High School, CA
Pensacola Catholic High School, FL
Phillips Academy (Andover), MA
Pioneer Valley Christian School, MA
Rye Country Day School, NY
Saint Anthony High School, IL
Saint Francis School, HI
St. George's School of Montreal, QC, Canada
Saint Matthias High School, CA
Santa Margarita Catholic High School, CA
School for Young Performers, NY
The Tenney School, TX
Trinity High School, KY
University Liggett School, MI
Valley Lutheran High School, AZ
The Webb School, TN
Whitefield Academy, GA

The Williston Northampton School, MA
Xaverian Brothers High School, MA

Blind Students

Alpine Academy, UT
American Community Schools of Athens, Greece
The Bement School, MA
Bishop Carroll High School, PA
Boston College High School, MA
Boylan Central Catholic High School, IL
Brethren Christian Junior and Senior High Schools, CA
Brockwood Park School, United Kingdom
Burr and Burton Academy, VT
Cardinal Newman School, SC
Cathedral High School, IN
Coe-Brown Northwood Academy, NH
The Concept School, PA
Crotched Mountain Rehabilitation Center School, NH
DePaul Catholic High School, NJ
Dowling Catholic High School, IA
Elves Child Development Centre, AB, Canada
Front Range Christian High School, CO
Gables Academy, GA
Greenhills School, MI
Grove School, CT
Halstrom High School, CA
Humanex Academy, CO
Lancaster Mennonite High School, PA
Lawrence Academy, MA
Mennonite Collegiate Institute, MB, Canada
Merchiston Castle School, United Kingdom
Mercy High School, NE
Notre Dame High School, CA
Pensacola Catholic High School, FL
Phillips Academy (Andover), MA
Roncalli High School, IN
Saint Augustine Preparatory School, NJ
Santa Margarita Catholic High School, CA
School for Young Performers, NY
Trinity High School, KY
University Lake School, WI
Whitefield Academy, GA
Xaverian Brothers High School, MA

Index

Alphabetical Listing of Schools

In the index that follows, page numbers for school profiles are shown in regular type, page numbers for profiles accompanied by announcements are shown in *italic* type, and page numbers for Close-Ups are shown in **boldface** type.

NOTES

NOTES

NOTES

NOTES

NOTES

Peterson's
Book Satisfaction Survey

Give Us Your Feedback

Thank you for choosing Peterson's as your source for personalized solutions for your education and career achievement. Please take a few minutes to answer the following questions. Your answers will go a long way in helping us to produce the most user-friendly and comprehensive resources to meet your individual needs.

When completed, please tear out this page and mail it to us at:

Publishing Department
Peterson's, a Nelnet company
2000 Lenox Drive
Lawrenceville, NJ 08648

You can also complete this survey online at **www.petersons.com/booksurvey.**

1. What is the ISBN of the book you have purchased? (The ISBN can be found on the book's back cover in the lower right-hand corner.) ____________________

2. Where did you purchase this book?

❑ Retailer, such as Barnes & Noble
❑ Online reseller, such as Amazon.com
❑ Petersons.com
❑ Other (please specify) ____________________

3. If you purchased this book on Petersons.com, please rate the following aspects of your online purchasing experience on a scale of 4 to 1 (4 = Excellent and 1 = Poor).

	4	3	2	1
Comprehensiveness of Peterson's Online Bookstore page	❑	❑	❑	❑
Overall online customer experience	❑	❑	❑	❑

4. Which category best describes you?

❑ High school student
❑ Parent of high school student
❑ College student
❑ Graduate/professional student
❑ Returning adult student
❑ Teacher
❑ Counselor
❑ Working professional/military
❑ Other (please specify) ____________________

5. Rate your overall satisfaction with this book.

Extremely Satisfied	Satisfied	Not Satisfied
❑	❑	❑

6. Rate each of the following aspects of this book on a scale of 4 to 1 (4 = Excellent and 1 = Poor).

	4	3	2	1
Comprehensiveness of the information	❑	❑	❑	❑
Accuracy of the information	❑	❑	❑	❑
Usability	❑	❑	❑	❑
Cover design	❑	❑	❑	❑
Book layout	❑	❑	❑	❑
Special features *(e.g., CD, flashcards, charts, etc.)*	❑	❑	❑	❑
Value for the money	❑	❑	❑	❑

7. This book was recommended by:

❑ Guidance counselor
❑ Parent/guardian
❑ Family member/relative
❑ Friend
❑ Teacher
❑ Not recommended by anyone—I found the book on my own
❑ Other (please specify) ____________________

8. Would you recommend this book to others?

Yes	Not Sure	No
❑	❑	❑

9. Please provide any additional comments.

____

____

____

____

____

Remember, you can tear out this page and mail it to us at:

Publishing Department
Peterson's, a Nelnet company
2000 Lenox Drive
Lawrenceville, NJ 08648

or you can complete the survey online at **www.petersons.com/booksurvey.**

Your feedback is important to us at Peterson's, and we thank you for your time!

If you would like us to keep in touch with you about new products and services, please include your e-mail address here: ____________________